BARRON'S
PROFILES OF
AMERICAN
COLLEGES

2005 26TH EDITION

Compiled and Edited by the College Division of
Barron's Educational Series

BARRON'S

All inquiries should be addressed to:
Barron's Educational Series, Inc.
250 Wireless Boulevard
Hauppauge, New York 11788
http://www.barronseduc.com

International Standard Book No. 0-7641-2308-4

International Standard Serial No. 1065-5026

PRINTED IN THE UNITED STATES OF AMERICA
9 8 7 6 5 4 3 2 1

CONTENTS

PREFACE

Barron's *Profiles of American Colleges* is the most all-encompassing, easy-to-use guide available. All four-year institutions that offer bachelor's degrees are described if they are fully accredited or are recognized candidates for accreditation. The comprehensive, concise capsule and detailed essay on each school give an easy-to-absorb, complete picture of the colleges that interest the reader. And the attractive graphic design provides added readability.

The capsule of each profile lists important information for quick reference: address and phone and fax numbers; enrollment; calendar; fall application deadline; size and salary level of the faculty; percentage of faculty members who hold doctorates; student/faculty ratio; tuition and fees; room-and-board costs; the number of students who applied to the freshman class, were accepted, and enrolled; the median SAT* I and/or ACT scores; and finally, the College Admissions Selector Rating for the school. The information in the essay portion of each profile ranges from available housing and the financial aid climate to admissions requirements and the success of graduates. There are twenty-one categories of information under eight main headings: Student Life, Programs of Study, Admissions, Financial Aid, International Students, Computers, Graduates, and Admissions Contact. The Admissions Contact section also gives Internet addresses and video availability.

We are confident that the features we have added in recent years, along with those that have appeared in previous editions of Barron's *Profiles*, will make this twenty-sixth edition the most thorough guide available to the college-bound student.

A Word of Thanks

To all the college admissions officers, to participating high school advisers, to the students, parents, and other supporters of Barron's *Profiles of American Colleges*, we offer our sincere thanks.

Grateful acknowledgment is made to the late Gloria M. Barron, who inspired the editors and production personnel to create a book that would offer every possible assistance in selecting the best college.

We acknowledge with thanks the demanding editing tasks performed by Editor Darrell Buono, College Division Coordinator Kathy Ammirati, and Editorial Assistant Alison Carlson, along with the database designers and our hardworking editing and keyboarding staff.

CONTRIBUTORS

Steven R. Antonoff, Ph.D.
Educational Consultant
Antonoff Associates, Inc.
Denver, Colorado

Barbara J. Aronson
Career Center Coordinator
Miramonte High School
Orinda, California

Anthony F. Capraro, III, Ph.D.
President, Teach Inc.
College Counseling
Larchmont, New York

Marguerite J. Dennis
Vice President for
Development and
Enrollment
Suffolk University
Boston, Massachusetts

Benjamin W. Griffith
Former Dean of the
Graduate School
West Georgia College
Carrolton, Georgia

Sheldon Halpern
Former Dean
Enrollment Management
Caldwell College
Caldwell, New Jersey

Ira Wolf, Ph.D.
President
PowerPrep, Inc.
Roslyn Heights, New York

*SAT is a registered trademark owned by the College Entrance Examination Board. No endorsement of this product is implied or given.

AN EXPLANATION OF THE BOOK

You have been thinking about going to college within the next couple of years, and now you're convinced that it's time to get somewhat serious about your plans, and take some steps that will lead to your ultimate college decisions, right?

But how do you go about taking these steps? How much does college cost? How can you and your parents afford it? What about entrance exams? How can you possibly know where you want to go and even if you decide *that*, how do you apply with any degree of assurance that you will be accepted? What if you decide, apply, and then get turned down? How can you ensure that *that* doesn't happen? And if you do get past all those hurdles, how can you determine your college major, when you don't have a clue as to what you want to do *after* college?

But right now—where do you begin? In addition to hundreds of two-year schools, there are more than 1600 accredited four-year colleges in the United States, and your options are almost unlimited. But Barron's *Profiles of American Colleges* can point you in the right direction, and help you through the coming months of decision making.

You will find articles that will guide you in evaluating your own needs and interests, selecting the college, filling out the application, writing the essay, having the interview, finding the money, and surviving the freshman year.

There is advice on selecting a major and a career, and the Index of College Majors—a helpful aid for students who want to know which colleges offer the major they have selected. More than 600 majors are listed, along with the in-state costs and the Admissions Selector Rating in easy-to-read columns.

There is advice for international students, as well as a list of schools' in-state costs from least to most expensive. There is also a geographic chart that gives students quick information about schools on a state-by-state basis.

The College Admissions Selector Ratings give applicants an idea of the competition they will encounter when applying to a particular school. And you will find a key to abbreviations and an explanation of the actual college entries.

The heart of the book, of course, is the detailed descriptions of the colleges, including a special section of religious schools that prepare students for careers in the clergy and related fields. The college Profiles are presented alphabetically by state, and the states are also arranged in alphabetical order. Maps of the states begin each chapter. Actually, Barron's *Profiles of American Colleges* covers more than the fifty states; it also describes colleges in the District of Columbia, Puerto Rico, and selected universities in Canada and abroad (along with advice for international students) as well as state and private systems of higher education, for a total of more than 1700 Profile entries.

This expanded and updated edition of *Profiles of American Colleges* will answer all of your questions as you embark on this most significant experience—college application, acceptance, and enrollment.

KEY TO ABBREVIATIONS

DEGREES

A.A.—Associate of Arts
A.A.S.—Associate of Applied Science
A.B. or B.A.—Bachelor of Arts
A.B.J.—Bachelor of Arts in Journalism
A.S.—Associate of Science

B.A.—Bachelor of Arts
B.A.A.—Bachelor of Applied Arts
B.A.A.S. or B.Applied A.S.—Bachelor of Applied Arts and Sciences
B.Ac. or B.Acc.—Bachelor of Accountancy
B.A.C.—Bachelor of Science in Air Commerce
B.A.C.V.I.—Bachelor of Arts in Computer and Video Imaging
B.A.E. or B.A.Ed.—Bachelor of Arts in Education
B.A.G.E.—Bachelor of Arts in General Education
B.Agri.—Bachelor of Agriculture
B.A.G.S.—Bachelor of Arts in General Studies
B.A.J.S.—Bachelor of Arts in Judaic Studies
B.A.M.—Bachelor of Arts in Music
B.Applied Sc.—Bachelor of Applied Science
B.A.R.—Bachelor of Religion
B.Arch.—Bachelor of Architecture
B.Arch.Hist.—Bachelor of Architectural History
B.Arch.Tech.—Bachelor of Architectural Technology
B.Ar.Sc.—Baccalaurium Artium et Scientiae (honors college degree) (Bachelor of Arts & Sciences)
B.Art.Ed.—Bachelor of Art Education
B.A.S.—Bachelor of Applied Science
B.A.S.—Bachelor of Arts and Sciences
B.A.Sec.Ed.—Bachelor of Arts in Secondary Ed.
B.A.S.W.—B.A. in Social Work
B.A.T.—Bachelor of Arts in Teaching
B.B. or B.Bus.—Bachelor of Business
B.B.A.—Bachelor of Business Administration
B.B.E.—Bachelor of Business Education
B.C. or B.Com. or B.Comm.—Bachelor of Commerce
B.C.A.—Bachelor of Creative Arts
B.C.E.—Bachelor of Civil Engineering
B.C.E.—Bachelor of Computer Engineering
B.Ch. or B.Chem.—Bachelor of Chemistry
B.Ch.E.—Bachelor of Chemical Engineering
B.C.J.—Bachelor of Criminal Justice
B.C.M.—Bachelor of Christian Ministries
B.Church Mus.—Bachelor of Church Music
B.C.S.—Bachelor of College Studies
B.E.—Bachelor of English
B.E. or B.Ed.—Bachelor of Education
B.E.—Bachelor of Engineering
B.E.D.—Bachelor of Environmental Design
B.E.E.—Bachelor of Electrical Engineering
B.En. or B.Eng.—Bachelor of Engineering
B.E.S. or B.Eng.Sc.—Bachelor of Engineering Science
B.E.T.—Bachelor of Engineering Technology
B.F.A.—Bachelor of Fine Arts
B.G.S.—Bachelor of General Studies
B.G.S.—Bachelor of Geological Sciences
B.H.E.—Bachelor of Health Education
B.H.P.E.—Bachelor of Health and Physical Education
B.H.S.—Bachelor of Health Science
B.I.D.—Bachelor of Industrial Design
B.I.M.—Bachelor of Industrial Management
B.Ind.Tech.—Bachelor of Industrial Technology
B.Int.Arch.—Bachelor of Interior Architecture
B.Int.Design—Bachelor of Interior Design
B.I.S.—Bachelor of Industrial Safety
B.I.S.—Bachelor of Interdisciplinary Studies
B.J.—Bachelor of Journalism
B.J.S.—Bachelor of Judaic Studies
B.L.A. or B.Lib.Arts—Bachelor of Liberal Arts
B.L.A. or B.Land.Arch.—Bachelor in Landscape Architecture
B.L.I.—Bachelor of Literary Interpretation
B.L.S.—Bachelor of Liberal Studies
B.M. or B.Mus. or Mus.Bac.—Bachelor of Music
B.M.E.—Bachelor of Mechanical Engineering

B.M.E. or B.M.Ed. or B.Mus.Ed.—Bachelor of Music Education
B.Med.Lab.Sc.—Bachelor of Medical Laboratory Science
B.Min—Bachelor of Ministry
B.M.P. or B.Mu.—Bachelor of Music in Performance
B.Mus.A.—Bachelor of Applied Music
B.M.T.—Bachelor of Music Therapy
B.O.T.—Bachelor of Occupational Therapy
B.P.A.—Bachelor of Public Administration
B.P.E.—Bachelor of Physical Education
B.Perf.Arts—Bachelor of Performing Arts
B.Ph.—Bachelor of Philosophy
B.Pharm.—Bachelor of Pharmacy
B.Phys.Hlth.Ed.—Bachelor of Physical Health Education
B.P.S.—Bachelor of Professional Studies
B.P.T.—Bachelor of Physical Therapy
B.R.E.—Bachelor of Religious Education
B.R.T.—Bachelor of Respiratory Therapy
B.S. or B.Sc. or S.B.—Bachelor of Science
B.S.A. or B.S.Ag. or B.S.Agr.—Bachelor of Science in Agriculture
B.Sacred Mus.—Bachelor of Sacred Music
B.Sacred Theol.—Bachelor of Sacred Theology
B.S.A.E.—Bachelor of Science in Agricultural Engineering
B.S.A.E. or B.S.Art Ed.—Bachelor of Science in Art Education
B.S.Ag.E.—Bachelor of Science in Agricultural Engineering
B.S.A.S.—Bachelor of Science in Administrative Sciences
B.S.A.T.—Bachelor of Science in Athletic Training
B.S.B.—Bachelor of Science (business)
B.S.B.A. or B.S.Bus. Adm.—Bachelor of Science in Business Administration
B.S.Bus.—Bachelor of Science in Business
B.S.Bus.Ed.—Bachelor of Science in Business Education
B.S.C.—Bachelor of Science in Commerce
B.S.C.E. or B.S.C.I.E.—Bachelor of Science in Civil Engineering
B.S.C.E.T—B.S. in Computer Engineering Technology
B.S.Ch. or B.S.Chem. or B.S. in Ch.—Bachelor of Science in Chemistry
B.S.C.H.—Bachelor of Science in Community Health
B.S.Ch.E.—Bachelor of Science in Chemical Engineering
B.S.C.I.S.—Bachelor of Science in Computer Information Sciences
B.S.C.J.—Bachelor of Science in Criminal Justice
B.S.C.L.S.—Bachelor of Science in Clinical Laboratory Science
B.S.Comp.Eng.—Bachelor of Science in Computer Engineering
B.S.Comp.Sci. or B.S.C.S.—Bachelor of Science in Computer Science
B.S.Comp.Soft—Bachelor of Science in Computer Software
B.S.Comp.Tech.—Bachelor of Science in Computer Technology
B.Sc.(P.T.)—Bachelor of Science in Physical Therapy
B.S.C.S.T.—Bachelor of Science in Computer Science Technology
B.S.D.H.—Bachelor of Science in Dental Hygiene
B.S.Die—Bachelor of Science in Dietetics
B.S.E. or B.S.Ed. or B.S.Educ.—Bachelor of Science in Education
B.S.E. or B.S in E. or B.S. in Eng.—Bachelor of Science in Engineering
B.S.E.E.—Bachelor of Science in Electrical Engineering
B.S.E.E.T.—Bachelor of Science in Electrical Engineering Technology
B.S.E.H.—Bachelor of Science in Environmental Health
B.S.Elect.T.—Bachelor of Science in Electronics Technology
B.S.El.Ed. or B.S. in Elem. Ed.—Bachelor of Science in Elementary Education
B.S.E.P.H.—Bachelor of Science in Environmental and Public Health
B.S.E.S.—Bachelor of Science in Engineering Science
B.S.E.S.—Bachelor of Science in Environmental Studies
B.S.E.T.—Bachelor of Science in Engineering Technology
B.S.F.—Bachelor of Science in Forestry
B.S.F.R.—Bachelor of Science in Forestry Resources
B.S.F.W.—Bachelor of Science in Fisheries and Wildlife
B.S.G.—Bachelor of Science in Geology

B.S.G.—Bachelor of Science in Gerontology
B.S.G.E.—Bachelor of Science in Geological Engineering
B.S.G.S.—Bachelor of Science in General Studies
B.S.H.C.A.—Bachelor of Science in Health Care Administration
B.S.H.E.—Bachelor of Science in Home Economics
B.S.H.F.—Bachelor of Science in Health Fitness
B.S.H.M.S.—Bachelor of Science in Health Management Systems
B.S.H.S.—Bachelor of Science in Health Sciences
B.S.H.S.—Bachelor of Science in Human Services
B.S.I.A.—Bachelor of Science in Industrial Arts
B.S.I.E.—Bachelor of Science in Industrial Engineering
B.S.I.M.—Bachelor of Science in Industrial Management
B.S. in Biomed.Eng.—Bachelor of Science in Biomedical Engineering
B.S. in C.D.—Bachelor of Science in Communication Disorders
B.S.Ind.Ed.—Bachelor of Science in Industrial Education
B.S.Ind.Tech.—Bachelor of Science in Industrial Technology
B.S. in Sec.Ed.—Bachelor of Science in Secondary Education
B.S.I.S.—Bachelor of Science in Interdisciplinary Studies
B.S.I.T.—Bachelor of Science in Industrial Technology
B.S.J.—Bachelor of Science in Journalism
B.S.L.E.—Bachelor of Science in Law Enforcement
B.S.M.—Bachelor of Science in Management
B.S.M.—Bachelor of Science in Music
B.S.M.E.—Bachelor of Science in Mechanical Engineering
B.S.Med.Tech. or B.S.M.T.—Bachelor of Science in Medical Technology
B.S.Met.E.—Bachelor of Science in Metallurgical Engineering
B.S.M.R.A.—Bachelor of Science in Medical Records Administration
B.S.M.T.—Bachelor of Science in Medical Technology
B.S.M.T.—Bachelor of Science in Music Therapy
B.S.Mt.E.—Bachelor of Science in Materials Engineering
B.S.Mus.Ed.—Bachelor of Science in Music Education
B.S.N.—Bachelor of Science in Nursing
B.S.Nuc.T.—Bachelor of Science in Nuclear Technology
B.S.O.A.—Bachelor of Science in Office Administration
B.S.O.E.—Bachelor of Science in Occupational Education
B.S.O.T.—Bachelor of Science in Occupational Therapy
B.S.P. or B.S.Pharm—Bachelor of Science in Pharmacy
B.S.P.A.—Bachelor of Science in Public Administration
B.S.Pcs.—Bachelor of Science in Physics
B.S.P.E.—Bachelor of Science in Physical Education
B.S.P.T.—Bachelor of Science in Physical Therapy
B.S.Rad.Tech.—Bachelor of Science in Radiation Technology
B.S.R.C.—Bachelor of Science in Respiratory Care
B.S.R.S.—Bachelor of Science in Radiological Science
B.S.R.T.T.—Bachelor of Science in Radiation Therapy Technology
B.S.S.—Bachelor of Science in Surveying
B.S.S.—Bachelor of Special Studies
B.S.S.A.—Bachelor of Science in Systems Analysis
B.S.Soc. Work or B.S.S.W.—Bachelor of Science in Social Work
B.S.Sp.—Bachelor of Science in Speech
B.S.S.T.—Bachelor of Science in Surveying and Topography
B.S.T. or B.S.Tech.—Bachelor of Science in Technology
B.S.S.W.E.—Bachelor of Science in Software Engineering
B.S.V.T.E.—Bachelor of Science in Vocational Technical Education
B.S.W.—Bachelor of Social Work
B.T. or B.Tech.—Bachelor of Technology
B.Th.—Bachelor of Theology
B.T.S.—Bachelor of Technical Studies
B.U.S.—Bachelor of Urban Studies
B.V.M.—Bachelor of Veterinarian Medicine
B.Voc.Arts or B.V.A.—Bachelor of Vocational Arts
B.V.E.D. or B.Voc.Ed.—Bachelor of Vocational Education

D.D.S.—Doctor of Dental Surgery

Ed.S.—Education Specialist

J.D.—Doctor of Jurisprudence

LL.B.—Bachelor of Laws

M.A.—Master of Arts
M.A.Ed.—Master of Arts in Education
M.A.T.—Master of Arts in Teaching
M.B.A.—Master of Business Administration
M.D.—Doctor of Medicine
M.F.A.—Master of Fine Arts
M.P.A.—Master of Public Administration
M.S.—Master of Science
Mus.B. or Mus.Bac.—Bachelor of Music

Ph.D.—Doctor of Philosophy

R.N.—Registered Nurse

S.B. or B.S. or B.Sc.—Bachelor of Science

OTHER ABBREVIATIONS

AABC—Accrediting Association of Bible Colleges
AACN—American Association of Colleges of Nursing
AACSB—American Assembly of Collegiate Schools of Business
AAFCS—American Association of Family and Consumer Sciences
AALE—American Academy for Liberal Education
AALS—Association of American Law Schools
AAMFT—American Association for Marriage and Family Therapy
ABA—American Bar Association
ABET—Accreditation Board for Engineering and Technology
ABFSE—American Board of Funeral Service Education
ABHES—Accrediting Bureau of Health Education Schools
ACBSP—Association of Collegiate Business Schools and Programs
ACCE—American Council for Construction Education
ACE HSA—Accrediting Commission on Education for Health Services Administration
ACE JMC—American Council on Education in Journalism and Mass Communication
ACOTE—American Council for Occupational Therapy Education
ACPE—Association for Clinical Pastoral Education, Inc.
ACPE—American Council on Pharmaceutical Education
ACS—American Chemical Society
ACT—American College Testing Program
ADA—American Dietetic Association
ADA—American Dental Association
ADDA—American Design Drafting Association
AFSA—Application for Federal Student Aid
AHEA—American Home Economics Association
AHIMA—American Health Information Management Association
ALA—American Library Association
ALIGU—American Language Institute of Georgetown University
AMAC AHEA—American Medical Association Committee on Allied Health Education and Accreditation
AOA—American Osteopathic Association
AOA—American Optometric Association
AOTA—American Occupational Therapy Association
AP—Advanced Placement
APA—American Podiatry Association
APA—American Psychological Association
APET—Asset Placement Evaluation Test
APIEL—Advance Placement International English Language Exam
APTA—American Physical Therapy Association
ASHA—American School Health Association

ASLA—American Society of Landscape Architects
ASLHA—American Speech-Language-Hearing Association
ATSUSC—Association of Theological Schools in the United States and Canada
AUCC—Association of Universities and Colleges of Canada
AVMA—American Veterinary Medical Association

BEOG—Basic Educational Opportunity Grant (now Pell Grant)

CAA—Council on Aviation Accreditation
CAADE—California Association for Alcohol/Drug Educators
CAAHEP—Commission on Accreditation of Allied Health Education Programs
CAAP—College Achievement Admission Program
CACREP—Council for Accreditation of Counseling and Related Educational Programs
CADE—Commission on Accreditation for Dietetics Education
CAPTE—Commission on Accreditation in Physical Therapy Education
CAS—Certificate of Advanced Study
CCE—Council on Chiropractic Education
CCNE—Commission on Collegiate Nursing Education
CCTE—California Commission on Teacher Credentialing
CDN—Canadian
CED—Council for Education of the Deaf
CEEB—College Entrance Examination Board
CELT—Comprehensive English Language Test
CEPH—Council on Education for Public Health
CLAST—College Level Academic Skills Test
CLEP—College-Level Examination Program
COE—Council on Occupational Education
CRDA—Candidates Reply Date Agreement
CRE—Council on Rehabilitation Education
CSAB—Computing Science Accreditation Board
CSS—College Scholarship Service
CSS/Profile—College Scholarship Service Financial Aid Profile
CSWE—Council on Social Work Education
CWS—College Work-Study

EESL—Examination of English as a Second Language
ELPT—English Language Proficiency Test (SAT II)
ELS/ALA—English Language Services/American Language Academy
EMH—Educable Mentally Handicapped
EOP—Equal Opportunity Program
ESL—English as a Second Language
ETS—Educational Testing Service

FAFSA—Free Application for Federal Student Aid
FET—Full-time equivalent
FFS—Family Financial Statement
FIDER—Foundation for Interior Design Education Research
FISL—Federally Insured Student Loan
FTE—Full-Time Equivalent

GED—General Educational Development (high school equivalency examination)
GPA—Grade Point Average
GRE—Graduate Record Examination
GSLP—Guaranteed Student Loan Program
G-STEP—Georgia State Test for English Proficiency

HEOP—Higher Equal Opportunity Program
HPER—Health, Physical Education, and Recreation

IACBE—International Assembly for Collegiate Business Education
IAME—International Association for Management Education
IB—International Baccalaureate
IELTS—International English Language Testing System

JRCERT—Joint Review Committee on Education in Radiologic Technology
JRCNMT—Joint Review Committee on Educational Programs in Nuclear Medicine Technology

LCME—Liaison Committee on Medical Education

MAPS—Multiple Assessment Program/Services
MELAB—Michigan English Language Assessment Battery
MUSIC—Multi User System for Interactive Computing

NAAB—National Architectural Accrediting Board
NAACLS—National Accrediting Agency for Clinical Laboratory Educators
NAIT—National Association of Industrial Technology
NAPNES—National Association for Practical Nurse Education and Service
NASAD—National Association of Schools of Art and Design
NASD—National Associaton of Schools of Dance
NASDTEC—National Association of State Development Teacher Education
NASM—National Association of Schools of Music
NASPAA—National Association of Schools of Public Affairs and Administration
NASPE—National Association of Sport and Physical Education
NAST—National Association of Schools of Theatre
NCATE—National Council for Accreditation of Teacher Education
NCCAA—National Christian College Athletic Association
NCOPE—National Commission on Orthotic and Prosthetic Education
NDEA—National Defense Education Act
NLN—National League for Nursing
NRPA—National Recreation and Park Association

PCS—Parents' Confidential Statement
PAIR—PHEAA Aid Information Request
PEP—Proficiency Examination Program
PHEAA—Pennsylvania Higher Education Assistance Agency
PSAT/NMSQT—Preliminary Scholastic Aptitude Test/National Merit Scholarship Qualifying Test

ROTC—Reserve Officers Training Corps
RSE—Regents Scholarship Examination (New York State)

SAAC—Student Aid Application for California
SACU—Service for Admission to College and University (Canada)
SAF—Society of American Foresters
SAM—Single Application Method
SAR—Student Aid Report
SAT—Scholastic Assessment Testing (formerly ATP–Admissions Testing Program)
SCAT—Scholastic College Aptitude Test
SCS—Students' Confidential Statement
SEOG—Supplementary Educational Opportunity Grant
SOA—Society of Actuaries

TAP—Tuition Assistance Program (New York State)
TDD—Telecommunication Device for the Deaf
TEAC—Teacher Education Accreditation Council
TOEFL—Test of English as a Foreign Language
TTY—Talking Typewriter

UAP—Undergraduate Assessment Program
UP—Undergraduate Program (area tests)

VFAF—Virginia Financial Assistance Form

WPCT—Washington Pre-College Test

PART I

AN INTRODUCTION

TO COLLEGE

You'll soon be on your way to college—but how much thought have you given it so far? Have you started thinking about the career that's in your future?

- Which college will help you make the most of your natural abilities and interests, and get you ready for life?
- Which courses should you take?

This section will help you find answers to these questions. It will also give you advice on:

- how to apply to schools
- how to increase your chances of acceptance
- how to finance your education

And just as important, this introductory section will give you valuable tips on how to get through that critical freshman year.

You have in your hands a book that will give you answers to your questions about the qualities and features of more than 1650 colleges. But before you start reading the descriptions and getting the answers, you need to know what questions to ask about finding the college that is right for you. Although you need to ask questions about "getting in" i.e., exploring colleges in terms of ease of admission for you, most of your questions should focus on the more significant issue of "fitting in." Fitting in means finding a college where you will be comfortable; where you are compatible with your peers, and where the overall atmosphere encourages your growth as a student and as a person.

This article is designed to help you assess some values and attitudes that will help you determine where you will fit in. It will enable you to ask the right questions. Not all colleges are for everyone; careful thinking about your interests, ideals, and values will lead you to find the college that is right *for you*. Colleges are not "good" or "bad" in a generic sense; they are either good or bad matches for you.

The two assessments that follow will be helpful in thinking about yourself as a future college student; they should help you make the right college choice.

THE COLLEGE PLANNING VALUES ASSESSMENT

Students have different reasons for going to college. Eleven reasons or values are found to be most important to students as they think about college. Knowing about your values is the important first step in identifying the colleges where you will fit in and be happy.

To complete the assessment, read through the list of ten values—A through K. Think about the outcomes you hope college will produce for you. Each student will rank them differently; hence, there are no "right" answers. Whereas several, or even most, of these values may be significant for you in one way or another, the goal is to decide which three are the most important. After you read each of the values, go back and circle the THREE most important ones on the basis of the following question:

What do you want college to do for you?
—— A. To provide me with a place to learn and study.
—— B. To provide me with opportunities to interact with teachers inside and outside the classroom.
—— C. To provide me with lots of fun experiences.
—— D. To prepare me to make a lot of money.
—— E. To provide me with recognition for accomplishments.
—— F. To get politically involved and/or to use much of my college years to help those who are disadvantaged.
—— G. To help me prepare for a career.
—— H. To enable me to be more independent.
—— I. To provide opportunities for me to grow religiously or spiritually.
—— J. To provide me with a variety of new experiences.
—— K. To enable me to receive a degree from a prestigious school.
What do your college planning values say about you?

If **A** was among the top three priorities on your list, you will want to explore the academic character of the colleges you are considering. Although all colleges are, by definition, intellectual centers, some put more priority on challenging students and pushing them to their limits. Reading about the academic features of the colleges you are considering will be important. (In the college Profiles, pay attention to the *special* section to learn about these features.) Your high ranking of this value says that you will be able to take advantage of intellectual opportunities at college. You may want to select a college where your SAT scores are similar to or slightly above the ranges of other admitted students—at those colleges you will be able to shine academically. You may desire to take an active part in classroom discussions and will want a college where the student faculty ratio is low.

If **B** was among your top three priorities, you feel challenged and stimulated by academics and classroom learning. You will want to find a college where your mind will be stretched. You will want to choose a college where you can explore a range of new academic subjects. A liberal arts and sciences college may give you an enriching breadth of academic offerings. You will want to look for a college where academic clubs are popular and where you have a good chance of knowing professors and sharing ideas with them. Access to faculty is important to you and you will want to look at the student faculty ratio in colleges you consider. Also note the ratio of undergraduate students to graduate students. Primarily undergraduate institutions will be the colleges that may best be able to meet your needs, because you will be the focus of teachers' attention. Teachers at such colleges place their priority on teaching and are not distracted by the needs of graduate students or by pressure to balance teaching and student time with research and writing.

If **C** was circled, you derive satisfaction from social opportunities. You will want a college where the academic demands will not diminish your ability to socialize. You likely will want a good balance between the social and academic sides of campus life. You will want to explore the percentage of students who get involved in intramural sports, clubs, or fraternities and sororities. (This information is listed in each college profile.) Look at your college choices on the basis of school spirit and sporting events offered. The profiles list popular campus events—see if they sound exciting to you. Also look at the percentage of students who stay on campus over the weekend. You will also want a college where it is easy to make friends. Both small and larger colleges would be appropriate for you. Although a larger college would expose you to more students and a larger quantity of potential friends, studies show that students at smaller colleges become more involved in activities and build deep friendships more quickly. Look for supportiveness and camaraderie in the student body.

If **D** is circled, you will want to consider earning potential, advancement opportunities, and the future market for the careers you consider. You will want to consider this value in your career planning. Remember, however, that there is no sure road to riches! You not only must pick a career direction carefully, but must choose a college where the potential for academic success—good grades—is high. The name of a particular college is less important than good grades or contributions to campus life when securing a good job or being admitted to graduate school. Even if you find that a particular career has tremendous earning potential, those earnings may come to only those who are most successful in the profession. Look at average salaries, but also consider your interests, values, and personality before making your final career choice. Be sure to take advantage of hands-on learning opportunities. Perhaps, for example, there are internships that meet your needs. Also, finding good, career-focused summer jobs can be helpful.

If **E** is high on your list, you take pleasure in being known for your success in an area of interest. For instance, you might feel good about being recognized or known in school as a good student, a top athlete, or a leader in a club. No doubt this type of recognition contributes to your confidence. You might look for colleges where you will be able to acquire or continue to receive this recognition. Often, recognition is easier to achieve at smaller colleges where you would not be competing against large numbers of students hoping to achieve the same recognition. You will also want to choose colleges where it is easy to get involved and where the activities offered are appealing to you. You may want to consider the benefits of being a "big fish in a small pond."

If **F** is important, that value will no doubt guide your vocational or avocational pursuits. You may find yourself choosing a career in which this value can be fulfilled, or you may seek opportunities on a college campus where you can be of service to others. You will want to choose a college where community service is valued. Look at the *activities* section and note whether community service-related involvements are available. Colleges vary a great deal in terms of political awareness. At some colleges, students are attuned to national and international events, often express feelings about current issues and policies, and in general, show interest in political affairs. Students at other colleges show little or no interest in these matters and find other ways to interact with peers.

If **G** was circled, you may know what career you want to pursue or you may be concerned but uncertain about your career decision. If you have tentatively selected a career, you will want to choose a college where you can take courses leading to the attainment of a degree in your chosen field. Explore the *programs of study* section in the profiles to determine whether a college you are considering offers the course work you desire. You will want to make a note of the most popular majors and the strongest majors as they are listed. If you don't yet know what career would suit you, remember, that for most careers, a broad, solid liberal arts foundation is considered good preparation. You will want to look at opportunities for internships and take advantage of the career planning and placement office at your chosen college. Finding a career that will be fulfilling is one of the most important choices you will make in your life. Your selection of a college will be your first step toward achieving your career goal.

If **H** is circled, it suggests that personal autonomy is important to you. College is, in general, a time for independence, and students are often anxious to make their own decisions without parental involvement. If you feel you can handle lots of independence, you will want to look for colleges where there is some freedom in choosing courses and where students are given responsibility for their own lives. Colleges vary in terms of these factors. Note particularly the *required* section under *programs of study*, which tells you the courses that must be fulfilled by all students. Be certain that you will not be stifled by too many rules and regulations. You may also want to look for colleges where the personal development of students receives high priority. A priority on independence also suggests that you will be comfortable being away from home and on your own.

If **I** is one of your top three choices, you will want to look first at the religious affiliation of each of your college options. There are two ways to consider religious life on college campuses. First is the question of how religion affects the day-to-day life of the college. For example, are biblical references made in class? Are religious convocations mandatory? Second is the question of whether there is a religious heritage at the college. Many hundreds of colleges have historical relationships with a religious denomination, but this tie does not affect the rules or the general life of the students. (For example, the college may have a certain number of religion classes required to graduate, but these classes are typically broad-based and not doctrinal.) You may want a college that has a relationship with your particular religious group. Or you may desire a large number of students who belong to the same denomination as you do. The profiles will also give you the percentage of students who are members of the major religious denominations. As you explore colleges, you will also want to see if the college has a commitment to the values and ideals held by you or your family.

If **J** is appealing, you like newness and will likely be stimulated by new experiences and new activities. You are in for a treat at most colleges. New experiences are the "stuff" of which college life is made. You may see college-going as an adventure and will want to pick colleges where you can meet your need for stimulation and excitement. Because you value newness, you should not hesitate to attend college in a different part of the country or to experience an environment or a climate that is quite different from your high school. You will also want to look for evidence of diversity in the student body. As you read the descriptions, look for colleges with lots of new opportunities for growth and for personal expansion.

If **K** is appealing, be cautious. Students who are overly concerned about this value might find college planning traumatic, and even painful, because of the admission

selectivity of "name brand" colleges. Even though it is perfectly acceptable for students to be attuned to the overall excellence of a college, academic quality and prestige are not the same thing. Some colleges are well-known because of, say, a fine football team or because of academic excellence in a subject like psychology or physics. Although it is appropriate to look for a strong faculty and a highly regarded college, you want a college that will give you the greatest chance of academic success. It is success in college, not just academic reputation or prestige, that will lead to admission into graduate school or a broad selection of jobs.

Now that you've read about your top three values, answer the following question on a separate sheet of paper: In your own words, what do your top three values say about what you are looking for in a college? Then, share that information with your college adviser as he or she assists you in finding colleges that are right for you.

SELF-KNOWLEDGE QUESTIONNAIRE

The following seven items—A–G—will help you in thinking about yourself as a college student and the ease with which you will likely proceed through the college selection process. Read each statement and determine whether it is true or not true of you. After each question, you will see numbers ranging from 1 to 5. Circle 1 if the statement is not true of you. Circle 5 if the statement is very true of you. Use 2, 3, or 4 to reflect varying levels of preference. Be realistic and honest.

A. My academic abilities for college (such as reading, writing, and note taking) are good.

Very true of me   1   2   3   4   5   Not true of me

Academic abilities such as reading speed and comprehension, writing, note taking, calculating, speaking, and listening are important for college students. You will be called upon to use such skills in your college classes. If you are confident about your academic skills, you can approach picking a college with the ease of knowing that you will be able to master the academic rigors of college life. If you circled 3, 4, or 5 you will want to work on these skills in your remaining days in high school. You will want to choose colleges where you can work to strengthen these skills. Some colleges provide a learning skills center in which you are able to get help if you are having difficulty writing a paper or understanding the content of a class. If you are less than confident, you might look to colleges where you will not be intimidated by the skills of the other students.

B. My study skills and time management are good.

Very true of me   1   2   3   4   5   Not true of me

Study skills and time management are two of the most important qualities for an efficient and productive college student. Successful college students are average or above in organizing themselves for studying, scheduling, and using study time productively, and differentiating important content of a lecture or a book from supplementary information. In addition, they complete assignments on time and don't get flustered if they have several papers or a couple of tests due on the same day. If you circled 3, 4, or 5, it is important to work on improving these skills during your remaining high school days. You might consider the following:

- Seek help from your parents, a teacher, a counselor, or a learning specialist in becoming more organized.
- Try keeping a calendar. Anticipate each step necessary in preparing for every test and every paper.
- Be responsible for your own appointments.
- Check to see if a study skills course is offered at a local community college or university. Or consider reading a book on study skills.

C. I am motivated to succeed in college.

Very true of me   1   2   3   4   5   Not true of me

Motivation is definitely the most important skill you bring to college. Those students who want to succeed do succeed! Studies show that it is motivation, not your SAT scores, that determines academic success in college. And motivation means knowing not only that you want to go to college, but that you also want to be a student. Some students want to go to college for the fun aspects, but forget that college is primarily an academic experience. So if you circled 1 or 2, great, you're off to a good start. If you circled 3, 4, or 5, it may be an appropriate time to consider your wants and needs in a college. What sort of college would help motivate you? Would a college with a balance between academics and social life be appealing? Would you be more motivated if you were near a large and interesting city? Would nice weather be a distraction rather than an energizer? Is a trade or technical school best for you? Have you considered taking some time off between high school and college? Considering such questions is important, and the time to do that exploration is now.

D. I am a good decision maker.

Very true of me   1   2   3   4   5   Not true of me

Decisions, decisions, decisions. The college selection process is full of decisions! What colleges will I initially consider? To which colleges will I apply for admission? What college will I eventually attend? You will be facing these decisions in the upcoming months. If you circled 1 or 2, you are on your way. If you circled 3, 4, or 5, think about an important decision you made recently. Why didn't it go well? If you can analyze your decision-making weakness in that situation, it may help to avoid any potential pitfalls in your college decision-making. The following suggestions will help you improve your ability to make the right college choice:

- Clearly articulate what you're looking for in a college. Write down those features that will make a college right for you.
- Involve lots of people and resources in your search for a college. Your parents, counselors, and friends can help you.
- List and compare pros and cons of alternative colleges. Every college has both.
- Evaluate each college on the basis of the criteria you set for yourself.

Remember, you're looking for a college where you will get in *and* fit in.

E. I'm a good information gatherer; for example, I am usually able to find books, articles, and so on to help me do a research paper for, say, a history class.

Very true of me   1   2   3   4   5   Not true of me

Finding a college requires you to be a good researcher. There is so much information about colleges to sort through and analyze. If you feel you can do good research, fine, you're on your way. If you circled 3, 4, or 5, the following ideas may be helpful:

- Start with this book and look for colleges that are consistent with what you want. Remember that your primary concern is where you will fit in. Use your college-going values and your responses in this questionnaire to guide your thinking about colleges that will match you.
- Work closely with your college counselor, and seek impressions from students and others with reliable and up-to-date information about colleges of interest. You will make a better decision with credible and extensive input.
- Look for differences in features that are important to you. Is ease of making friends important to you? What about balance between academics and social life? Do you want teachers to know you?

F. I feel I adapt to new situations easily.

Very true of me   1   2   3   4   5   Not true of me

Everyone goes through changes in life. Some move through transition periods with great ease, others find them more difficult. You may have experienced the changes that come after a change of schools (even from middle school to high school), the illness or death of a relative, or the divorce of your parents. If you circled 1 or 2, you are not likely to be intimidated by a college in another part of the country or a college very different from your high school. If you circled 3, 4, or 5, you may want to carefully look at colleges that are a bit closer to home or colleges where the same values, perceptions, and attitudes exist as were true in your high school. Almost everyone has fear and apprehension about leaving for college. But if that fear is significant, you will want to choose a college where you will feel comfortable. Visits to college campuses may be particularly significant in feeling good about potential choices.

G. It is easy for me to meet people and establish friendships.

Very true of me   1   2   3   4   5   Not true of me

Identifying and nurturing friendships is an important skill for college adjustment. If you circled 3, 4, or 5, you will want to look carefully at colleges where there are few cliques, where there is an atmosphere of sharing, and where students report that it is relatively easy to integrate into the campus environment. Your choice of a college is a quest for a good social fit. Your thorough review of the profiles and even visits to college campuses will be helpful in assuring your ability to fit in and be comfortable.

FINAL THOUGHTS

If you took time to carefully consider the issues raised in both the Values Assessment and the Self-Knowledge Questionnaire, you should have gained new insights and perspectives about yourself. You will want to share these results with your parents and with your guidance counselor. Elicit their help in getting more insight as to how they see you as a prospective college student. Finally, two suggestions:

- As you research colleges, consider what you have learned about yourself. You want a college that is a good match with your values and interests.
- Spend time on your college search. It will take many hours of organized planning and investigation. But the time spent will result in a better choice and a greater likelihood that you will spend four productive and exciting years in college.

Good luck. There are lots of colleges out there that want you. Let your knowledge of yourself and your objective analysis of potential college options guide you to college environments where you will be able to shine. Success in college is in your hands. Make the most of the opportunity.

Steven R. Antonoff, Ph.D., Certified Educational Planner
Educational Consultant
Antonoff Associates, Inc.
Denver, Colorado

Start your college search positively. Start with the knowledge that there are many schools out there that want you. Start with the idea that there are many good college choices for every student. Too often these days, articles on college admission make students and their parents apprehensive. You can have choices. You can get financial aid. You can have a happy, successful college career.

When you begin to think about college, you are embarking on a major research project. You have many choices available to you in order to get the best possible education for which you are qualified. This article is intended to help you think of some of the important variables in your college search.

Let us help make the book work for you!

THE CURRENT ADMISSION SCENE

Today there are approximately 1,650 four-year colleges and universities accredited. Most existing institutions have grown larger, and many have expanded their programs, offering master's and doctoral degrees as well as bachelor's.

Total graduate and undergraduate students has also grown, from under 4 million in 1960 to more than 16 million today. In fact, between 2000 and 2013 total enrollment at U.S. colleges and universities is expected to rise 19 percent, to 18.2 million students. Almost 40 percent are part-time students, including many working adults. Part-time enrollments are mostly concentrated in the two-year colleges, which enroll about a third of all students.

What does this all mean to you? There is good news and bad news. The good news is that most of the colleges you will read about in this book are colleges you can get into! In other words, the vast majority of colleges in the U.S. admit more than 70 percent of those who apply. Many hundreds admit all of those who apply. So, on one level, you shouldn't worry that you won't be able to get a college education. The bad news is for the student with extremely high grades who seeks admission to the 50 or so most competitive colleges in the country. These "brand name" colleges have many times more candidates than they admit. Even incredibly qualified students are sometimes denied admission.

The key to good college planning is, as mentioned above, research. Find out about what makes one college different from another. Find out what students say about their experiences. Rely on many sources of information—many people, many books, many web sites, and so on. There are lots of people and materials available to help you. This book is one of them. Let the information be your guide. But also let your instincts and your sense of what's best for you play a part. The higher education opportunities in the U.S. are unlimited. The opportunity to let education help pave the way to achieving your dreams is a worthy goal of your college search.

MAKING A SHORT LIST

You have probably already started a list of colleges you know about from friends or relatives who have attended them, from recommendations by counselors or teachers, or by their academic or social reputations. This list will grow as you read the Profiles, receive college mailings, and attend college fairs. If you are interested in preparing for a very specific career, such as engineering, agriculture, nursing, or architecture, you should add only institutions that offer that program. If you want to study business, teacher education, or the arts and sciences, almost every college can provide a suitable major. Either way, your list will soon include dozens of institutions. Most students apply to between four and seven colleges. To narrow your list, you should keep the following process in mind:

- As you explore, be attuned to the admission requirements. You will want to have colleges on your list that span the admission selectivity continuum—from "reach" colleges (those where your grades, test scores, etc., suggest less chance of admission) to "safety" schools (those where your credentials are a bit better than the average student admitted), eliminating colleges at which you clearly would not qualify for admission.
- You also will want to keep an eye on cost. You want to consider colleges that are generally in line with your family's ability to finance your education. Be very cautious as you do this. Literally millions of dollars are available each year for students. There is both "need-based" aid (aid based on your family's ability to pay) and "merit-based" aid (aid based on such things as grades, test scores, and leadership ability).
- Screen the list according to your preferences, such as size, academic competitiveness, religious focus, and location.
- Make quality judgments, using published information and campus visits, to decide which colleges can give you the best quality and value.

The following sections are organized around the factors most important in researching a college. Discussion of admission competitiveness and cost comes first. After that, a wide range of factors important to consider as you evaluate colleges is examined. These include size, housing, the faculty, academic programs, internships, accreditation, libraries and computer technology, and religious/racial considerations. The final two sections are a discussion of campus visits and, finally, a checklist of 25 important questions to ask about each of the colleges you are exploring.

In the end, you must allow yourself to be a good decision maker. You will have to make some quality judgments. It is not as difficult as you may think. You have to be willing to read the information in this book and the literature that the schools make available, to visit a few campuses, and to ask plenty of questions. Usually you can ask questions of the admissions office by regular mail, e-mail, or in person during a campus visit. Because colleges sincerely are interested in helping you make the right choice, they generally will welcome your questions and answer them politely and honestly. In addition, your high school counselor is a key person who can offer advice and guidance. Finally, there are many resources available, in printed form and on the web, to help you.

SELECTION FACTORS

Admissions Competitiveness

The first question most students ask about a college is, "How hard is it to get in?" It should certainly not be the last question. Admissions competitiveness is not the only, or even the most important, measurement of institutional quality. It makes sense to avoid wasting time, money, and useless disappointment applying to institutions for which you clearly are not qualified. Nevertheless, there are many colleges for which you are qualified, and you can make a good choice from among them. The most prestigious institutions are rarely affected by market conditions. Most of the better known private and public colleges and universities have raised their admission standards in recent years. But there remain hundreds of fine public and private colleges, with good local reputations, that will welcome your application.

Use the College Admissions Selector to compare your qualifications to the admissions competitiveness of the institutions of your list. Make sure you read the descriptions of standards very carefully. Even if you meet the stated qualifications for *Most Competitive* or *Highly Competitive* institutions, you cannot assume that you will be offered admission. These colleges receive applications from many more students than they can enroll and reject far more than they accept. When considering colleges rated *Very Competitive* or *Competitive*, remember that the median test scores identify the middle of the most recent freshman class; half of the admitted students had scores lower than the median, and half were above. Students of average ability are admissible to most of the colleges and universities rated as *Competitive* and to virtually all of those rated as *Less Competitive*.

Cost

The basic cost of the most expensive colleges and universities can exceed $40,000 a year. This is widely publicized and very frightening, especially to your parents. But you don't have to spend that much for a good education. Private colleges charge an average of nearly $30,000 a year for tuition and room and board. Public institutions generally cost an average of $14,000 a year for in-state residents. Because many states have been cutting budgets in recent years, tuition at public institutions is now rising faster than at private ones. If you can commute to school from home, you can save about $6000 to $7000 in room and board, but should add the cost of transportation. The least expensive option is to attend a local community college for two years, at about $1500 a year, and then transfer to a four-year institution to complete your bachelor's degree. Depending on what you may qualify for in financial aid, and what your family is willing to sacrifice, you may have more choices than you think.

Size

Only one-fifth of American colleges and universities have enrollments of 5000 or more, but they account for more than half the ten million plus students who are pursuing bachelor's degrees. The rest are spread out among more than 1000 smaller schools. There are advantages and disadvantages that go with size.

At a college of 5000 or fewer students, you will get to know the campus quickly. You will not have to compete with many other students when registering for courses or for use of the library or other facilities. You can get to know your professors personally and become familiar with most of your fellow students. On the other hand, the school may not have as many majors and it may have less emphasis on spectator sports. Students at small schools are not able to be as "anonymous" as those at larger schools.

As colleges and universities enroll more students, they offer more courses and activities. Within a large campus community, you can probably find others who share your special interests and form a circle of good friends. But you may also find the facilities more crowded, classes closed out, and competition very stiff for athletic teams or musical groups.

Many of the largest institutions are universities offering medical, law, or other doctoral programs as well as bachelor's and master's degrees. Many colleges that do not offer these programs call themselves universities; and a few universities, Dartmouth among them, continue to call themselves colleges. Don't go by the name, but by the academic program. Universities emphasize research. University faculty need specialized laboratory equipment, computers, library material, and technical assistance for their research. Colleges tend to emphasize teaching.

Because research is very expensive, universities usually charge higher tuition than colleges, even to their undergraduate students. In effect, undergraduates at universities subsidize the high cost of graduate programs. Freshmen and sophomores usually receive some instruction from graduate student assistants and fellows, who are paid to be apprentice faculty members.

Of course, many larger private universities, and many public ones, have fine reputations. They have larger and more up-to-date libraries, laboratories, computers, and other special resources than colleges. They attract students from many states and countries and provide a rich social and cultural environment.

Housing

Deciding whether you will stay in a residence hall or at home is more than a matter of finances or how close to the college you live. You should be aware that students who live on campus, especially during the freshman year, are more likely to pass their courses and graduate than students who commute from home. Campus residents spend more time with faculty members, have more opportunity to use the library and laboratories, and are linked to other students who help one another with their studies. Residence hall life usually helps students mature faster as they participate in social and organizational activities.

If you commute to school, you can get maximum benefits from your college experience by spending time on campus between and after classes. If you need a part-time job, get employment in the college library, offices, or dining halls. Use the library to do homework in an environment that may be less distracting than home. If possible, have some dinners on campus, to make friends with other students and participate in evening social and cultural events. Get involved in campus activities, participating in athletics, working on the newspaper, attending a meeting, or rehearsing a play.

You will have a choice of food plans. Most meal plans include a certain number of meals per week. Other plans allow you to prepay a fixed dollar amount and purchase food by the item rather than by the meal. Choose a meal plan that fits your own eating habits. Most colleges today offer a tremendous variety of food and are accommodating to most diets and preferences.

Many students live off campus after their freshman or sophomore year, either by choice or because the school does not have room for them on campus. Schools try to provide listings of available off-campus rooms and apartments that meet good standards for safety and cleanliness. Many colleges also offer health care and food services to students who live off campus.

It is usually more expensive to live in an apartment than in a residence hall, especially if you plan to prepare your own meals. But that option is appealing to some students, particularly those in their junior or senior years.

The Faculty

The most important resources of any college or university are its professors. Admissions brochures usually point out the strengths of the faculty, but provide little detail. You should direct your questions about the faculty and other academic matters to the specific department or to the office that coordinates academic advising. Recruiting brochures also emphasize faculty research, because the prestige of professors depends largely on the books and articles they have published. Good researchers may or may not make good teachers. Ask how often the best researchers teach undergraduate courses, and whether they instruct small as well as large classes. For example, a Nobel prize chemist may lecture to 500 students at a time but never show up in the laboratories where graduate assistants actually teach individual students.

Also ask about class size, because this determines the amount of individual attention students get from professors. Student/faculty ratios, which usually range from 10 to 20 students per professor, don't really tell you much. Every school offers a mixture of large and small classes. Ask admission officers for the average size of a freshman class. You will want to look for such factors as those that follow:

- Science and technology courses should enroll only 25 to 30 students in each laboratory session, but may combine a number of laboratory classes for large weekly lectures.
- Skill development courses such as speech, foreign language, English composition, and fine and performing arts should have classes of 25 or fewer. Mathematics and computer science require considerable graded homework, and classes should be no larger than 35.
- Most other courses in humanities, social sciences, and professional areas are taught by classroom lectures and discussion. Classes should average 35 to 45 in introductory courses such as general psychology or American government. They should be smaller in advanced or specialized courses, such as Shakespeare or tax accounting.
- Many introductory courses, especially at universities, are taught in lecture classes of 100 or more. This is acceptable, if those courses also include small weekly discussion groups for individual instruction. Sometimes these discussion groups are taught by graduate student assistants rather than regular professors. Although graduate assistants lack teaching experience, they are very often highly

capable. You should ask whether the teaching done by graduate assistants is closely supervised by regular faculty members.

Academic Programs

Even colleges and universities that boast fine and well qualified faculties can be short of professors in certain programs. Some schools depend on instruction by part-time faculty members or fill in with available teachers from other specializations. Many international students are enrolled in technical doctoral programs, so you may find yourself being taught mathematics or engineering by a teaching assistant who is not a native English speaker. If you are interested in these subjects, check to see whether full-time faculty members teach the majority of the courses.

Other programs may have sufficient faculty but too few student majors. Majors such as physics and philosophy, for example, often have many students in required introductory courses, but few taking the major. Because of small enrollments, these departments may not be able to offer their advanced and specialized courses on a regular basis.

Academic departments give strength to the program by bringing together faculty members who share a common area of study and make sure their students get the classes they need. Some programs, usually called interdisciplinary, are taught by groups of faculty members from several departments. These programs generally have the word *studies* in their titles; for example, Middle-Eastern Studies, Communication Studies, Women's Studies, or Ethnic Studies. If you are enrolled in one of these programs, be sure to ask about the student advising. (Sometimes, advising suffers if faculty members are primarily loyal to their own department.)

Internships

Internships are available at many colleges. They provide an opportunity to experience work in your major and learn from experienced people in your field. Many students have received job offers after participating in an internship program during the school year or during summer vacation. These internships can make a big difference as you enter the job market.

Accreditation

General standards of academic quality are established by associations of colleges and universities through a process called voluntary accreditation. The criteria include: standards for admission of students; faculty qualifications; content of courses; grading standards; professional success of alumni; adequacy of libraries, laboratories, computers, and other support facilities; administrative systems and policy decision making; and financial support.

Six regional associations (New England, Middle States, Southern, North Central, Northwest, and Western) evaluate and accredit colleges as total institutions. Bible colleges have their own accrediting association. Other organizations evaluate and accredit specific programs, primarily in technical fields, like engineering and architecture; or those that require licensing, such as teaching and health care.

Libraries and Computer Technology

Most people judge libraries by the size of the collection, the bigger the better. Collection size is important, but only in relation to the variety and level of programs offered. A small liberal arts college can support its baccalaureate programs with a collection of 200,000 to 400,000 volumes. A university with many professional schools and doctoral programs may require over 2 million. Many books and journals are available through various methods of information technology, computer storage, and the Internet.

The main stacks should be open to students, with the possible exception of rare books, bound journals, and other special items. Open stacks encourage browsing and save students from waiting on line while a library assistant fetches a few books at a time. Instead, assistants constantly should be picking up unused materials from reading desks or carts and putting them back on the shelves.

Good circulation policies encourage students to check materials out for short periods and to return them promptly. One week or less loans are appropriate for books regularly used in courses, and four week loans should be the maximum for other materials. A recall system should be available to get back borrowed material when it is needed. Journals, reference material, or books placed on reserve for assigned reading should be used within the library while it is open, and circulated overnight only at closing time.

Using a computer is integral to university study. Some institutions require students to have personal computers. Colleges often offer the best price for new computers. You may want to check out the options on campus before you purchase a computer elsewhere. Many residence hall rooms are wired for computers and direct connections are linked to the main campus system. More and more campuses have wireless capability.

Religious/Ethnic Considerations

For some students, the religious life of the campus is important as college choices are reviewed. Religious life can vary from being pervasive to being absent. Most colleges are independent of religious influence. Some are historically affiliated with a religious group, yet religious matters are not part of student life. Other schools exist, in part, to educate students in the doctrine and the practices of their own religious perspective. Information you find on these pages will give you answers to some of your initial questions about religious life at particular schools.

If connecting with and learning from members of your racial/ethnic heritage is important, you will find many colleges and universities from which to choose. Again, this guide provides information about the diversity of the campus and the composition of students who are white, African-American, Hispanic, Asian-American, Latino, and so forth.

GETTING THE MOST FROM YOUR CAMPUS VISIT

It is best not to eliminate any options without at least visiting a few campuses of different types to judge their feeling and style first hand.

To learn everything important about a college, you need more than the standard presentation and tour given to visiting students and parents. Plan your visit for a weekday during the school term. This will let you see how classes are taught and how students live. It also is the best time to meet faculty and staff members. If the college does not schedule group presentations or tours at the time you want, call the office of admissions to arrange for an individual tour and interview. (This is more likely at a small college.) At the same time, ask the admissions office to make appointments with people you want to meet.

To find out about a specific academic program, ask to meet the department chairperson or a professor. If you are interested in athletics, religion, or music, arrange to meet with the coach, the chaplain, or the conductor of the orchestra. Your parents will also want to talk to a financial aid counselor about scholarships, grants, and loans. The office of academic affairs can help with your questions about courses or the faculty. The office of student affairs is in charge of residence halls, health services, and extracurricular activities. Each of these areas has a dean or vice president and a number of assistants, so you should be able to get your questions answered even if you go in without an appointment.

Take advantage of a group presentation and tour if one is scheduled on the day of your visit. Much of what you learn may be familiar, but other students and parents will ask about some of the same things you want to know. Student tour guides are also good sources of information. They love to talk about their own courses, professors, and campus experiences.

Finally, explore the campus on your own. Check the condition of the buildings and the grounds. If they appear well maintained, the college probably has good overall management. If they look run down, the college may have financial problems that also make it scrimp on the book budget or laboratory supplies. Visit a service office, such as the registrar, career planning, or academic advising. Observe whether they treat students courteously and seem genuinely interested in helping them. Look at bulletin boards for signs of campus activities.

And, perhaps most importantly, talk to some of the students who are already enrolled at the college. They will usually speak frankly about weekend activities, whether they find it easy to talk to professors out of class, and how much drinking or drug abuse there is on campus. Most importantly, meeting other students will help you discover how friendly the campus is and whether the college will suit you socially and intellectually.

More than buildings and courses of study, a college is a community of people. Only during a campus visit can you experience the human environment in which you will live and work during four critical years.

25 CRITICAL QUESTIONS

The following questions form a checklist to evaluate each college or university you are considering. Use the profiles, material from the colleges, and your own inquiries and observations to get the answers.

1. Do I have a reasonable chance of being admitted?
2. Can my family manage the costs?
3. Is the overall size of the school right for my personality?
4. Is the location right? (Consider such specifics as region, distance from a major city, distance from home, and weather.)
5. Are class sizes right for my learning style and my need for involvement in class?
6. Will I be comfortable with the setting of the campus?
7. Are the housing and food services suitable?
8. Does the college offer the program I want to study? (Or, often more importantly, does the college offer people and classes that will help me decide what I want to study?)
9. Will the college push me academically, but not shove me?
10. Do the best professors teach undergraduate courses?
11. Can I change majors easily, if I need to?
12. Do students say the majority of classes are taught by fun, stimulating, interesting professors?
13. Is the library collection adequate and accessible?
14. Are computer facilities readily available and are campus networking opportunities up-to-date?
15. Is the connection to the Internet adequate?
16. Are there resources for career development?
17. Do the people in the financial aid, housing, and other service offices seem attentive and genuinely interested in helping students?
18. Will I find activities that meet my interests?
19. Does the campus seem well maintained and managed?
20. Will the college meet my religious and/or ethnic needs?

And, finally, the five most critical questions:

21. Is there a good chance I will be academically successful there?
22. Will I be happy as a student there?
23. Do I seem compatible with the student population? Do they seem to enjoy what I enjoy?
24. Does the student life seem in sync with my personality and my goals? Is the student life what I'm looking for in a college?
25. Does the college "feel" right for me?

Steven R. Antonoff
Sheldon Halpern
Barbara Aronson

SCORING HIGH ON ENTRANCE EXAMINATIONS

COLLEGE ENTRANCE EXAMINATIONS

By providing you with exactly the same information about each of the colleges in which you are interested, the book you are now reading, *Profiles of American Colleges*, will help you narrow down the list of colleges to which you will apply. Of course, your final decision will be influenced by many other factors, many of which are far more important: actual visits to the colleges; virtual visits on the Internet; viewings of videotapes; advice from guidance counselors, parents, teachers, and friends.

In much the same way, by providing college admissions officers with the same information about thousands of applicants, the results of college entrance exams can help them narrow down the list of students they are considering accepting. The results of these exams help admissions officers compare students with widely differing backgrounds. Students from different high schools in different states who earn the same grade in their biology classes, B+ say, have used different textbooks, have performed different labs, have taken different tests, and in general often exhibit great disparity in their level of mastery of the subject; indeed, even within the same school, a grade of B+ from one teacher might not represent the same level of accomplishment as a B+ from another teacher. However, a grade of 650 on the Biology SAT II, or a 4 on the Biology AP test means the same thing whether it was earned by a student from a rural community in Idaho, an inner-city school in New York, or a private prep school in Massachusetts. Because students all across the country take the same standardized test on the same day, colleges can give greater credence to the results, than they can to the results of final exams from different schools.

KINDS OF COLLEGE ENTRANCE EXAMINATIONS

Although some students who go from high school to two-year community colleges do not take any college entrance tests, most do, and virtually all students who are applying to four-year colleges will take some of the following exams:
- PSAT/NMSQT or the Preliminary SAT/National Merit Scholarship Qualifying Test.
- SAT I: Reasoning Tests.
- SAT II: Subject Tests.
- Advanced Placement (AP) Examinations.
- The ACT Assessment.

The PSAT/NMSQT

The PSAT/NMSQT measures verbal and mathematical reasoning necessary for success in college. It is a standardized test taken by students in high schools throughout the country, in October of their junior year. The test consists of five sections: two 25-minute critical reading sections, two 25-minute math sections, and one 25-minute writing section.

This Preliminary SAT is also the qualifying test for the scholarship competition conducted by the National Merit Scholarship Corporation, an independent, nonprofit organization supported by grants from over 600 corporations, private foundations, colleges, and universities. All students whose scores are in the top 5% of students taking the exam that year receive National Merit Letters of Commendation. In addition, students whose scores are in the top 1% of those taking the exam that year become National Merit Semifinalists. Those who advance to finalist standing by meeting additional requirements compete for one-time National Merit $2000 Scholarships and renewable four-year Merit Scholarships, which may be worth as much as $2000 a year or more for four years.

In addition, this test is used by the National Achievement Scholarship Program for outstanding African American students. Top-scoring black students in each of the regional selection units established for the competition continue in the competition for nonrenewable National Achievement $2000 Scholarships and for four-year Achievement Scholarships sponsored by more than 175 organizations.

Test-Taking Strategies for the PSAT/NMSQT

1. Know what to expect. Each critical reading section has sentence completion questions and reading comprehension questions. A few of the reading questions are based on short passages (often a single paragraph), whereas most are based on longer passages (typically four to seven paragraphs). The first math section has 20 multiple-choice questions; the second math section has 10 quantitative comparison questions and 10 questions for which no choices are provided and whose answers must be entered in a special grid. Calculators may be used on any question in the math sections. The writing skills section, which does *not* have an essay, has three types of multiple-choice questions that test your knowledge of standard written English (grammar and usage).

2. On average, wild guessing has no effect on your score. Educated guessing, on the other hand, can improve your score dramatically. On all multiple-choice questions, try to eliminate as many obviously incorrect answer choices as possible, and then guess from among the choices still remaining.

3. Expect easy questions at the beginning of each set of the same question type. Within each set (except for the reading comprehension questions), the questions progress from easy to difficult. In other words, the first sentence completion questions in a set will be easier than the last sentence completion questions in that set; the first grid-in questions will be easier than the last ones.

4. Take advantage of the easy questions to boost your score. Remember: each question is worth the same number of points. Whether it is easy or difficult, whether it takes you ten seconds or two minutes to answer, you get the same number of points for each question you answer correctly. Your job is to answer as many questions as you can without rushing so fast that you make careless errors. Take enough time to get those easy questions right!

The SAT I

The SAT I is a reasoning test consisting of three parts—critical reading, mathematical reasoning, and writing. It is designed to measure your ability to do college work. Part of the test deals with verbal skills with an emphasis on critical reading including a double passage with different points of view. The critical reading sections measure the extent of your vocabulary, your ability to interpret and create ideas, and your ability to reason logically and draw conclusions correctly. The mathematics part measures your ability to reason with numbers and mathematical concepts. It tests your ability to handle general number concepts rather than specific achievement in mathematics. Calculators are permitted on each math section.

The writing part consists of a short essay and multiple-choice questions that test your knowledge of standard written English (grammar and usage).

The SAT I is given on seven Saturdays during the year—once each in January, March (or April), May, June, October, November, and December. Applicants may request, for religious reasons, to take the test on the Sunday following the regularly scheduled date.

You can register by mail by using the registration form available at your school or online at www.collegeboard.org.

On each part of the SAT I—critical reading, math, and writing—you will receive a scaled score between 200 and 800. On each part the national mean is approximately 500.

Test-Taking Strategies for the SAT I

1. Pace yourself properly. It is much better to slow down and avoid careless errors than it is to speed up in an effort to answer all the questions. You can earn an above-average score (over 1000) by correctly answering fewer than half of the questions on the test and omitting the rest. Even scores of 1300 can be achieved by omitting more than 20% of the questions.

2. Read carefully. Make sure you are answering the question asked, not a similar one you once encountered. Underline key words (e.g., NOT and EXCEPT) to make sure you do not answer the opposite of the question asked.

3. Learn the directions for each type of question before taking the test. During the test, do not waste even one second reading the directions or looking at the sample questions.

4. Always answer the easy questions first (the ones at the beginning of each section). Do not panic if you can't answer a question. Do not spend too much time on any one question. If you are truly stuck, make an educated guess if possible (see below), and move on. Remember that each question is worth the same one point, and the next few questions may be much easier for you.

5. On average, wild guessing does not affect your score—it is unlikely to help, but it is equally unlikely to hurt you. The choice is yours. However, educated guessing—when you can eliminate one or more of the answer choices—can significantly increase your score! In particular, don't omit critical reading questions if you have read the passage; you can always eliminate some of the choices. Most math questions contain at least one or two choices that are absurd (for example, negative choices when you know that the answer must be positive); eliminate them and guess.

SAT II: Subject Tests

These tests are one-hour, multiple-choice question tests. You may take one, two, or three tests on any one test date. Some colleges do not require SAT II tests. Of those that do, some colleges require specific subject tests, whereas others allow applicants to choose the ones they wish to present with the admission application. Those colleges that do require these tests may use them to determine acceptance or placement in college courses. The tests in foreign language not only are used for placement, but also for possible exemption from a foreign language requirement. If the college of your choice does not require these tests, but you would like to demonstrate proficiency in a particular field, take the test anyway and have your scores sent. Tests are given in writing, literature, history, mathematics, sciences, and several foreign languages.

Advanced Placement (AP) Examinations

The College Board also conducts Advanced Placement tests, given to high school students who have completed advanced or honors courses and wish to get college credit. Many secondary schools offer college-level courses in calculus, statistics, art, psychology, European history, American history, Latin, Spanish, French, German, biology, chemistry, and physics. As a result of scores obtained on these tests, colleges grant credit or use the results for placement in advanced college courses.

The ACT Assessment

The registration form for the ACT includes a detailed questionnaire that takes about one hour to complete. As a result of the answers to those questions about your high school courses, personal interests, and career plans, plus the scores on your ACT, an ACT Assessment Student Report is produced. This is made available to you, your high school, and to any college or scholarship source that you request. Decisions regarding college acceptance and award of scholarships are the result. This information is kept confidential and is released only according to your written instructions. To obtain an ACT application form, write or call ACT Registration, P.O. Box 414, Iowa City, Iowa 52243, telephone (319) 337-1270.

The ACT measures knowledge, understanding, and skills acquired in the educational process. The test is made up of four distinct sections: English, mathematics, reading, and science reasoning.

On the ACT, you should answer all questions, because your score is based on the number of questions you answer correctly. There is no penalty for wrong answers. For each of the four tests the total number of correct responses yields a raw score. A table is used to convert the raw scores to *scaled scores*. The highest possible scaled score for each test is 36. The average of the four scaled scores yields the *composite score*.

The ACT English Test is a 75-item, 45-minute test that measures punctuation, grammar, usage, sentence structure, spelling, and vocabulary. The test consists of five passages, each accompanied by multiple-choice test items. A total score is reported as well as a subscore for the 40 usage questions and a subscore for the 35 questions dealing with the rhetorical skills.

Test-Taking Strategies for the ACT English Test

1. Pace yourself. You have 45 minutes to complete 75 questions.
2. Read the sentences immediately before and after the one containing an underlined portion.

The ACT Mathematics Test has 60 questions to answer in 60 minutes. The test emphasizes quantitative reasoning rather than memorized formulas. Five content areas are included in the mathematics test. About 12 questions deal with pre-algebra topics, such as operations with whole numbers, decimals, fractions, and integers. About the same number of questions deal with elementary algebra. Usually 18 questions are based on intermediate algebra and coordinate geometry. About 14 questions are based on plane geometry and usually four items are based on right triangle trigonometry and basic trigonometric identities.

Test-Taking Strategies for the ACT Mathematics Test

1. Spend an average of one minute on each question, less on the easy questions, more on the difficult ones.
2. Be sure to answer each question even if you have to guess.
3. Make sure your answers are reasonable.

The ACT Reading Test is a 40-item, 35-minute test that measures reading comprehension. Three scores are reported for this test: a total score, a subscore based on the 20 items in the social studies and natural sciences sections, and a subscore on the 20 items in the prose fiction and humanities sections.

Test-Taking Strategies for the ACT Reading Test

1. Read each passage carefully. Underline important ideas in the passage.
2. Pace yourself. You have 40 questions to answer in 35 minutes.
3. Refer to the passage and in particular to your underlined sections when answering the questions.

The ACT Science Reasoning Test presents seven sets of scientific information in three different formats: graphs, tables, and other schematic forms (38 percent); description of experiments (45 percent); and expression of conflicting viewpoints (17 percent). The 40 items are to be answered in 35 minutes. The content of the test is drawn from biology, chemistry, physics, geology, astronomy, and meteorology. Background knowledge at the level of a high school general science course is all that is needed to answer these questions. The test emphasizes scientific reasoning skills rather than recall of scientific content, skill in mathematics, or reading ability.

Test-Taking Strategies for the ACT Science Reasoning Test

1. Read the scientific material before you begin answering a question. Read tables and text carefully, underlining important ideas.
2. Look for flaws in the experiments and devise ways of improving the experiments.
3. When you are asked to compare viewpoints, make notes in the margin of the printed material summarizing each viewpoint.

A FINAL WORD

Don't take any examination without preparation, even though you will find descriptions of these tests that say they test skills developed over years of study both in and out of school. Don't walk in cold, even though you believe that you meet all the qualities colleges are looking for.

Although the College Board suggests no special preparation, it does distribute to applicants the booklet, "Taking the SAT I Reasoning Test." It also makes available other publications containing former test questions along with advice on how to cope with the questions. Evidently, all candidates need some form of preparation.

The American College Testing Program furnishes the booklet, "Preparing for the ACT Assessment." This gives specific information about the test, test questions, and strategies for taking each of the four parts. It also describes what to expect on the test day and gives practice with typical questions.

Barron's Educational Series publishes books to help you prepare for these tests. They are available at all bookstores and in many libraries. You should be sure to use them before taking any of these tests.

Although no high school student takes all of the college-entrance exams described above, virtually all students planning to attend a four-year college take at least one of them—the SAT I or ACT. Prepare conscientiously for each exam that you take and you will provide the colleges to which you are applying with valuable information about your abilities. Good luck!

Ira K. Wolf
President
PowerPrep, Inc.

The college admission process—getting in—begins the minute you start making your first choices in course selection and in cocurricular activities in junior high school, middle school, and high school. These initial and ongoing decisions are crucial to your future well-being. They lay the groundwork for the curriculum you will follow throughout your high school career: they are not easily reversed. These are the decisions that will allow you to market yourself to the colleges of your choice.

STUDENTS TAKE NOTE!

There is a myth prevalent among college-bound students throughout the country that the best way to gain entrance to the selective colleges is to be well rounded. This term usually refers to students who have earned good grades in high school (B+ or better) and participated in a wide range of cocurricular activities.

However, most admission officers at the selective colleges prefer applications from candidates they term angular—students who have demonstrated solid academic achievement in and out of school and who have developed one or two particularly strong cocurricular skills, interests, and activities. These angular students are very different in character from the well-rounded students who are very good at everything, yet excel at little, if anything.

William Fitzsimmons, Dean of Admission at Harvard, says that Harvard is looking for a well-rounded class, which means Harvard is most interested in admitting angular students—students who have excelled at something. He cautions, though, that "…It is a mistake to denigrate or underestimate that persuasive power of high grades, rank, double 800s on the SAT I, 36 on the ACT, and equally impressive SAT II scores. The selective colleges take many of these academically high profile applicants. But the numbers game alone often won't get you in! It would be fairly simple for Harvard to enroll an entire freshman class with a superior academic profile and little depth of quality in areas that make up the personality of the class. We just would not do that!"

Dean Fitzsimmons is saying that the majority of the successful applicants to selective colleges must have some major commitment(s) combined with excellent academic qualities. A strong impact results from quality involvements rather than a proliferation of joinings and transient interests. Essentially, the angular applicant is a committed individual, while the well-rounded candidate is merely involved.

STUDENTS AND PARENTS TAKE AN EARLY, ACTIVE ROLE

Students and parents must make time to ensure an early, active role in the college admissions process. Each year, starting in the seventh grade, students and parents should take the time to sit down with the student's guidance counselor and talk meaningfully about the following:

- selection and level of courses, projecting through the senior year of high school;
- cocurricular activities available, such as drama, music, athletics, academic clubs, community activities, student government, and other special interest groups; and
- summer study, work, or recreation.

Why is this important to getting in? As sure as taxes and death, there is going to come a time in your senior year when you, the college-bound student, will be asked to choose colleges, complete the college application, write your college essay(s), and have an interview—either on the college campus, or in your hometown.

You must create the personal marketing, which will take place during the application process in your senior year, long before your senior year starts. By the time you reach that long-awaited dream of being a senior, you and you alone have created the person you must market to the colleges of your choice. You must understand that the person you have created is the only person you have to market. There is no Madison Avenue glitz involved in this marketing process! You don't create a pseudo marketing campaign that shows you jumping off a bridge with a bungee cord tied to your sneakers. Admission counselors can tell the difference between a real marketing effort and a pseudo marketing campaign.

THE APPLICATION FORM

Today colleges are offering their application on hard copy, computer disk, E-mail, or through on-line services of the Internet. Each application form differs from college to college, with the exception of those colleges that use the common application. When you start to work, be sure to note all deadlines, follow all directions, be complete, be neat, fill out the geographical data with accurate facts, and type it all (unless you print exceptionally well). Always review the entire application before you start to fill it out, and complete the entire application before you start the next one. Remember the application is you to the admissions committee member reading it. Even though "a book should not be judged by its cover," appearances do influence opinions.

It is best to work through a rough draft of the application before you actually work on the application copy to be submitted. Remember to make a copy of all parts of the finished application in the event that yours gets lost and a replacement must be sent.

You are responsible for giving the Secondary School Report, found in each application, directly to your high school guidance counselor. Your counselor is responsible for sending official copies of grades, rank in class (if any), the school's profile, and a written recommendation regarding you. It also is your responsibility to call or fill out the appropriate forms for either the SAT I and/or SAT II or the ACT, to send the appropriate test information directly to each college to which you have applied, even if your scores are on your high school transcript. Your college file will not be considered complete, and will not be sent to the admission committee for a decision, without these official scores. Additionally, many colleges want recommendations from one or two teachers. Choose wisely and allow each teacher plenty of time. Request letters from teachers who know you best. If English is your interest, be sure to choose an English teacher. If you are fluent in Spanish and have future interest in Spanish at college, ask the Spanish teacher. Remember, though you have many interests and have participated in many activities—you are developing an admissions package as part of your marketing of yourself. Emphasize your strengths and show how they are integrated into your activities and achievements.

Cocurricular activities usually are athletic or nonathletic. If you have won athletic awards, note them. If you have had the starring role in the spring musical for the last two years, say so. If you are an editor on the school newspaper, specify this. Admissions people view your activities with special interest. They realize how very time consuming these activities can be and how they sometimes bring very few accolades. List these activities in the order of importance to you. If you do not believe that the application allows you the opportunity to show your depth of commitment to one or two cocurricular areas, you may add an addendum. Use the KISS (Keep It Short and Simple) method. This is an addendum, not an essay, letter, or dissertation. Be honest!

Some applications have mini essays. When space is provided, be sure you are concise, clear, and grammatically correct. Here, less is more. Your ability to organize your thoughts and present them concisely is being tested. You will receive your chance to impress each college with your prose in the long essay segment of the application. Some colleges have as many as four long essays, whereas some require none. In addition to the short and long essay questions, some colleges ask the student for a graded paper signed by the teacher.

Some colleges encourage you to support your application with additional materials. If you are given this option, consider what will strengthen your application: musical tapes, art and/or photography portfolios, published writings, an exceptional graded term paper, all the additional opportunities for the college to get to know you better and for you to increase your image as an angular candidate. Such additions help the admissions committee to get a better handle on who you are in relation to other applicants. Be sure your presentation is clear and as professional as possible. These additions are not going to be evaluated by the admissions committee. Your material will be directed to the appropriate department for evaluation and an evaluative note will be sent back to the admissions committee. It is this note that will become part of your admissions package, the same way an athletic coach evaluates potential student/athletes.

Proofread all parts of the application. Be sure you, the student, place your signature where it is required. If you are not sending your application on-line, then place everything, including the registration fee check, in a large manila envelope and give it to your college guidance counselor. After adding the completed Secondary School Report to the application, your guidance counselor will mail it. Your job is now finished and the waiting begins!

E-Mail, On-line Services through the College or the Internet

We have joined the 21st century with E-mail and on-line services of the Internet offering college applications. This movement promises to be the wave of the future. Certainly ecologically correct, by producing as close to a paperless process as possible, this method is still in cyberspace. Be sure you know what you are doing when you use any of these methods. It is seriously suggested that you take the time to call the college shortly after sending this type of application, to ensure that your application is on file. If you have an addendum or two, you may want to speak to an admission clerk to make sure each addendum has reached the office of admission in the format you desired. If it were my application and I chose any of these methods, I'd still send my musical tape, the slides for my art portfolio, and such, by certified or registered mail. Clarity is so important to the professionals who will be evaluating these addenda for your college admission process!

PC- and Mac-Based Computer Disk Applications

Since the emergence of on-line applications, fewer colleges have a computer disk application. If you wish to apply this way, make sure that your target college has authorized the disk: there are a number of organizations selling computer disk applications without the consent of the college. Make sure the service to which you have subscribed allows you to print a hard copy of the application, even if they want you to send the disk back to the service or to the college. Do yourself a favor and print an extra copy of the application for your personal college file—it is very easy for the post office or college to lose your information. It is also wise, if you have to send the disk with the application, to write, "DO NOT SCAN" on the envelope. It is highly probable that the information on the disk will be lost if it is passed through a scanning machine.

The Common Application

About 200 colleges in the United States have agreed that students may apply to their colleges by completing one common application. Some of the colleges using the common application also have their own application. Students applying to a college that allows an applicant a choice of using either the college's own application or the common application, obviously face a choice. The use of the common application substantially reduces the time spent composing different essay answers and neatly typing separate application forms. If you are one of those who must make a choice between the common application and the application of the college, you should understand that each college using the common application (either as its only application or as an alternative application) has the right to ask for a supplement. If you choose the common application, be very sure to read the pages surrounding the common application carefully.

Each college has a paragraph in which they discuss their deadlines, requirements for admission, and specify if they require supplemental information. The supplemental information can range from an additional essay or two, to additional information about your cocurricular activities.

All the colleges participating in the common application have each member of their admission staff sign a statement that they will NOT discriminate in the admissions process among students who submit the common application versus students who submit the college's application. However, there are counselors who believe that when there is a choice, the applicant has a better chance of conveying information by using the college's application; there is a vast difference in format between the two applications, even if the college requires a supplement. Check with your guidance counselor if you are unsure regarding your choice of format. To access the common application online, go to:

www.commonapp.org

College Web Sites

Most colleges today have their own web site. Here you will find a wealth of information. Some colleges have even put their viewbook, course curriculum guide, a campus tour, as well as their application, on their site. Visit each college's web page—the addresses are in the Admissions Contact section of the college Profiles in this book. You'll be a much better informed consumer.

THE INTERVIEW

The interview is a contrived situation that few people enjoy, of which many people misunderstand the value, and about which everyone is apprehensive. However, no information from a college catalog, no friend's friend, no high school guidance counselor's comments, and no parental remembrances from bygone days can surpass the value of your college campus visit and interview. This first hand opportunity to assess your future alma mater will confirm or contradict other impressions and help you make a sound college acceptance.

Many colleges will recommend or request a personal interview. It is best to travel to the campus to meet with a member of the admissions staff if you can; however, if you can't, many colleges will arrange to have one of their representatives, usually an alumnus, interview you in your hometown.

Even though the thought of an interview might give you enough butterflies to lift you to the top of your high school's flagpole, here are some tips that might make it a little easier.

1. **Go prepared.** Read the college's catalog and this book's Profile ahead of time so you won't ask "How many books are in your library?" or "How many students do you have?" Ask intelligent questions that introduce a topic of conversation that you want the interviewer to know about you. The key is to distinguish yourself in a positive way from thousands of other applicants. Forge the final steps in the marketing process you have been building since your first choices in the college admission process back in junior high school. The interview is your chance to enhance those decisions.

2. **Nervousness** is absolutely and entirely normal. The best way to handle it is to admit it, out loud, to the interviewer. Richard Shaw, Dean of Admission at Yale University, sometimes relates this true story to his apprehensive applicants. One extremely agitated young applicant sat opposite him for her interview with her legs crossed, wearing loafers on her feet. She swung her top leg back and forth to some inaudible rhythm. The loafer on her top foot flew off her foot, hit him in the head, ricocheted to the desk lamp and broke it. She looked at him in terror, but when their glances met, they both dissolved in

laughter. The moral of the story—the person on the other side of the desk is also a human being and wants to put you at ease. So admit to your anxiety, and don't swing your foot if you're wearing loafers! (And by the way, she was admitted.)

3. **Be yourself.** Nobody's perfect, and everyone knows nobody's perfect, so admit to a flaw or two before the interviewer goes hunting for them. The truly impressive candidate will convey a thorough knowledge of self.

4. **Interview the interviewer.** Don't passively sit there and allow the interviewer to ask all the questions and direct the conversation. Participate in this responsibility by assuming an active role. A thoughtful questioner will accomplish three important tasks in a successful interview:

   demonstrate interest, initiative, and maturity for taking partial responsibility for the content of the conversation;
   guide the conversation to areas where he/she feels most secure and accomplished; and
   obtain answers. Use your genuine feelings to react to the answers you hear. If you are delighted to learn of a certain program or activity, show it. If you are curious, ask more questions. If you are disappointed by something you learn, try to find a path to a positive answer. Then consider yourself lucky that you discovered this particular inadequacy in time.

5. **Parents** do belong in your college decision process as your advisers! Often it is they who spend the megabucks for your next four years. They can provide psychological support and a stabilizing influence for sensible, rational decisions. However, they do NOT belong in your interview session. In essence, the sage senior will find constructive ways to include parents in the decision-making process as catalysts, without letting them take over (as many are apt to do) the interview process. You may want your parents to meet and speak briefly to your interviewer prior to your interview and that is fine, but parents may not accompany you into the interview session! Arrange with your parents to meet somewhere out of the interview building after your interview is over. You do not want the interviewer inviting your parents back to the interview room. As intelligent as parents may be, they do not perceive the answers to questions the same way you do. The worst scenario I can imagine is the interviewer asking your parents some of the same questions that were asked you, and that is highly likely. Parents just answer questions differently than teenagers. At best, the scenario creates a long, long ride home, and when you get home you can't punish your parents by taking the car keys away from them, or grounding them for a week. At worst, the scenario has caused a blight in your admissions file. This is your time! Keep it that way!

6. **Practice makes perfect.** Begin your interviews at colleges that are low on your list of preferred choices, and leave your first-choice colleges until last. If you are shy, you will have a chance to practice vocalizing what your usually silent inner voice tells you. Others will have the opportunity to commit their inevitable first blunders where they won't count as much.

7. **Departing impressions.** There is a remarkable tendency for the student to base final college preferences on the quality of the interview only, or on the personal reaction to the interviewer as the personification of the entire institution. Do not do yourself the disservice of letting it influence an otherwise rational selection, one based on institutional programs, students, services, and environment. After the last good-bye and thank you has been smiled, and you exhale deeply on your way out the door, go ahead and congratulate yourself. If you used the interview properly, you will know whether or not you wish to attend that college and why.

8. **Send a thank-you note** to your interviewer. A short and simple handwritten or typed note will do—and if you forgot to mention something important about yourself at the interview, here's your chance.

WRITING THE COLLEGE ESSAY

Do the colleges read the essays you write on their applications? You bet your diploma they do. Here is your chance to strut your stuff, stand up, be counted, and stylize your way into the hearts of the decision makers.

Write it, edit it, review it. Rewrite it. Try to show why you are unique and how the college will benefit having you in its student body. This is not a routine homework assignment, but a college level essay that will be carefully examined for spelling, grammar, content, and style of a high school senior. As strenuous an effort as it may be, completing the essay gives the admissions committee a chance to know the real you, a three-dimensional human being with passions, preferences, strengths, weaknesses, imagination, energy, and ambition. Your ability to market yourself will help the deans and directors of admission remember your application from among the sea of thousands that flood their offices each year.

First, maximize your strengths—use your essays to say what you want to say. The answer to a specific question on the college's part still provides an opening for you to furnish background information about yourself, your interests, ambitions, and insights. For example, the essay that asks you to name your favorite book and the reason for your selection could be answered with the title of a Dr. Seuss book because you are considering a career as an elementary school teacher. If you are interested in business, read about a famous businessman you admire and then discuss your interest in business.

Whatever the essay questions are, autobiographical or otherwise, select the person or issue that puts you in the position to discuss the subject in which you are the most well versed. In essence, all of your essay responses are autobiographical in the sense that they will illustrate something important about yourself, your values, and the kind of person you are (or hope to become). If personal values are important to you, and they should be, then here is your opportunity to stress their importance.

Because many colleges will ask for more than one essay, make sure that the sum of the essays in any one college application covers your best points. Do not repeat your answers, even if the questions sound alike. Cover the most important academic and cocurricular activities (most important meaning the one in which you excelled and/or in which you spent the most quality time).

If you are fortunate to have a cooperative English teacher, you might request a critique of your first draft, but be sure to allow enough time for a careful evaluation and your revision.

Write the essays yourself—no substitutes or stand-ins. College admission professionals can discern mature adult prose from student prose.

PARTING WORDS

You may wish to ask yourself the following questions to help you decide which is your Paradise College. Most of this information is in the individual college Profiles in this book.

1. **Caliber of School Programs** Is the college known for its English department or chemistry department? What are its strengths?

2. **Selectivity of Admissions** Is the college Most Competitive, Highly Competitive, Very Competitive, Competitive, Less Competitive or Noncompetitive? Check the Selector Ratings.

3. **Chances of Admission** Be realistic. What are your chances of getting in? How far can you reach? Listen when you are given advice!

4. **Location of the School**   Is the school near home, one hour away, 300 miles away, or across the United States?

5. **Rural, Suburban, Urban Campus**   Is the school in the city or in a rural area?

6. **Size of the School**   Can you spend four years at a small liberal arts college of 800 undergraduates? Do you need the larger atmosphere of a university? Do not equate size with social life!

7. **State College vs. Private College**   Is the college a large state university with most of the student population from the state where it's located? Is it one of the public "Ivies"? Will you be a minority in the state school?

8. **Geographical Diversity**   Is the college a regional one attracting students from the same state or region? Or is it a college, regardless of its size, which attracts students from all over the United States, or the world at large?

9. **Cost of College**   What is the tuition? What are the living costs? What travel costs are there from home to campus? Are there hidden costs?

10. **Financial Aid**   With a great percentage of undergraduates at many private colleges on financial aid of some type, where do you fit? What monies are available for the students at the schools of your choice? Is the college need blind in its admission program?

11. **Living Conditions**   Is housing on campus guaranteed for all four years? Are the dorms coed? Are there single-sex dorms? Are alternatives in housing available?

12. **Socialization**   Is it a grind school—all work, work, work? Is it fraternity- and sorority-oriented? What are the on-campus facilities for socialization?

13. **Safety on Campus**   Are the dorms secure and locked? What's the safety system on the campus?

14. **Core Curriculum—Distribution Credits**   Does the college require (for graduation) a specific number of credits in different academic disciplines? For example, does the student have to take six credits in philosophy before graduating? Is a self-designed curriculum possible?

15. **Sophomore Standing**   Does the college accept AP credits? Does it offer advanced standing for an AP course, or just a credit toward graduation?

16. **Junior Year Abroad**   Are there opportunities to study in Italy, Japan, or Australia, for example, while you are an undergraduate?

17. **Internships**   Are there opportunities for hands-on experience while in college? Which departments have formal internship opportunities?

18. **Graduate School After College**   What percentage of its graduates go on to graduate school immediately upon graduation, or within five years? What is the record of those who successfully get into the law, medical, or business school of their choice?

19. **Placement After Graduation**   Is there an office for job placement after college? Is there an alumni network that helps in job placement?

20. **Weekend College**   Do the students remain on campus on weekends, or is it a suitcase college?

21. **Minorities**   What percentage of the students are minorities? Reflect on the racial, ethnic, and religious minority roles in the college you are considering. How would you feel being Jewish at a Roman Catholic college for example—or Catholic at a Jewish college?

22. **Sports Facilities**   Is there a swimming pool? Are there horse stables? Is there an ice hockey rink on campus?

23. **Library Facilities**   How many books are in the library? Is it computerized? Is the campus library tied into a larger network?

24. **Athletic Programs**   Is the ice hockey team a varsity sport? Does the lacrosse team play Division I or III? Is basketball strong? Do they have a women's squash team?

25. **Honors Programs**   Are honors programs available? What are they? Who is eligible?

26. **Student Body**   Are the students politically active? Are they professional in orientation?

27. **Faculty**   Are all classes taught by full professors? Or are TAs (teaching assistants) the norm?

28. **Computer Labs**   Are computers required of incoming freshmen? What are the facilities on campus? Can you have your own PC in your room?

29. **Campus Visits**   If possible, make a visit to the campus. Spend some time talking to students for a feel of the campus.

30. **Special Talents**   Recognize your special talents and discover where they fit best. Often, a special talent becomes a scale-tipper in the admissions process.

31. **Special Family Circumstances**   Talk with your parents about their expectations. Discuss your needs as well as their thoughts.

32. **Legacy**   Does your family have a history at a specific school? Are you interested in continuing the tradition?

33. **Note Well—Final List**   Be sure the final list is a realistic one. It should include "reaches," "targets," and "safeties." No matter which one admits you—it must fit!

Finding and applying to the best colleges for you is not supposed to be easy, but it can be fun. Parents, guidance counselors, and teachers are there to help you, so don't struggle alone. Keep your sense of humor and a smile on your face as you go about researching, exploring, and discovering your ideal college.

Last but not least is The Parent Credo: The right college is the one where your child will fit in scholastically and socially. Be realistic in your aspirations and support the child's choice!

Anthony F. Capraro, III, Ph.D.
President, Teach Inc.
College Counseling
Purchase, New York

Postsecondary education is a major American industry. A greater proportion of students pursue postsecondary education in the United States than in any other industrialized country. Annually, more than 13 million students study at over 8000 institutions of higher learning. The diversity of our system of higher education is admired by educators and students throughout the world. There is no reason to believe that this system will change in the future. However, college costs and the resources available to parents and students to meet those costs have changed.

Unfortunately, many high school students and their parents believe either that there is no financial aid available or that they will not qualify for any type of financial assistance from any source. Neither assumption is correct. College costs have increased and will continue to increase. Federal allocations, for some financial aid programs, have decreased. But this decline has been met with generous increases in financial aid from state and school sources.

American students and their parents should realize that they must assume the primary role in planning to meet their future college costs and that the family financial planning process must begin much earlier than has been the case.

COLLEGE COSTS

- Nearly all parents believe college costs are too expensive.
- Currently, the average cost of education, including tuition, fees, and room and board for one year at a public college would have been about $10,000 and for a private college and university, the total cost could have exceeded $20,000.
- While college costs will increase each year, it is important to remember that currently nearly 3/4 of all college students attend schools with tuition costs below $10,000.

STUDENT FINANCIAL AID

- In 2004, the total amount of financial aid available from federal, state, and institutional sources to postsecondary students is nearly $90 billion.
- A majority of all students enrolled in higher education receive some type of financial assistance.
- Federal student aid remains the largest source of funding at 70 percent of total aid.
- Not long ago the majority of federal financial assistance was grants. Today, a greater amount of financial aid is from loan money.

TIMETABLE FOR APPLYING FOR FINANCIAL AID

Sophomore Year of High School

Most families wait until a child has been accepted into a college or university to begin planning on how the family will meet those college costs. However, a family's college financial planning should begin much earlier.

Students, as early as the sophomore year of high school, should begin a systematic search for colleges that offer courses of study that are of interest. There are many computer programs that can be helpful in this process. These programs can match a student's interest with colleges fitting the profile. Considering that half of all students who enter college either drop out or transfer to another school, this type of early selection analysis can be invaluable.

After selecting certain schools for further consideration, you should write to the school and request a viewbook, catalog, and financial aid brochure. After receiving this information, you and your family should compare the schools. Your comparison should include academic considerations as well as financial. Don't rule out a school because you think you can't afford it. Remember the financial aid programs at that school may be more generous than at a lower-priced school. If possible, visit the college and speak with both an admission and financial aid counselor. If it is not possible to visit all the schools, call the schools and obtain answers to your questions about admission, financial aid, and placement after graduation.

Junior Year of High School

The comparative analysis of colleges and universities that you began in your sophomore year should continue in your junior year. By the completion of your junior year, you and your parents should have some idea of what it will cost to attend and the financial aid policies of each of the schools you are considering.

Some colleges and universities offer prospective applicants an early estimate of their financial aid award. This estimate is based upon information supplied by the family and can provide assistance in planning a family's budget. Remember that for most families, financial aid from federal, state, and school sources will probably not meet the total cost of attendance.

Families should remember that college costs can be met over the course of the academic year. It is not necessary to have all of the money needed to attend school available at the beginning of the academic year. Student and family savings, as well as student employment throughout the year, can be used to meet college costs.

Senior Year of High School

January

By January of your senior year of high school you should know which colleges and universities you want to receive your financial aid application forms. Be certain that you have completed not only the federal financial aid application form, but also any necessary state or school forms. Read carefully all of the instructions. Application methods and deadline dates may differ from one college to another. Submit an application clean of erasures or notations in the margins, and sign all of the application forms.

February

Approximately six weeks after you submit your application for financial aid, you will receive a report from the service agency you selected containing information on your family's expected contribution and your eligibility for financial aid. You and your parents should discuss the results of the financial aid application with regard to family contribution, educational costs, and how those costs can be met.

March

Beginning in March, most colleges begin to make financial aid decisions. If your application is complete, your chances of receiving an award letter early are greater than if additional information is required.

The financial aid award letter you receive from your school serves as your official document indicating the amount of financial aid you will receive for the year. You must sign and return a copy of the award letter to your school if you agree to accept their offer of financial aid.

If your family's financial circumstances change and you need additional funding, you should make an appointment to speak with your school's financial aid director or counselor. College financial aid personnel are permitted to exercise professional judgment and make adjustments to a student's financial need. Your letter of appeal should state explicitly how much money you need and why you need it.

TIPS ON APPLYING FOR FINANCIAL AID

1. Families can no longer wait until a child is accepted into college before deciding how they will finance that education. Earlier college financial planning is necessary.

2. Families should assume a much more active role in locating the resources necessary to fund future college costs.

3. Families should assume that college costs will continue to increase.

4. Families should assume that in the future the federal government will not substantially increase financial aid allocations.

5. Families should obtain information on a wide range of colleges including the many excellent low-cost schools.

6. Families should seek information about all of the funding sources available at each school they are considering.

7. Families should seek the advice and expertise of financial experts for college financing strategies. College financial planning should specify the amount of money a family should invest or save each month in order to meet future college bills.

8. Families should investigate all of the legitimate ways of reducing their income and assets before filing for financial aid.

9. Families should know how financial aid is awarded and the financial aid policies and programs of each school they are considering.

10. Families should realize that although the job of financing a college education rests primarily with them, they probably will not be able to save the entire cost of their child's college education. They probably will be eligible to receive some type of financial aid from some source and they will have to borrow a portion of their child's college education costs.

11. Families should be advised that the federal government frequently changes the rules and regulations governing financial aid eligibility. Check with your high school guidance counselor or college financial aid administrator for the latest program qualifications.

Marguerite J. Dennis
Vice President for Development
and Enrollment
Suffolk University
Boston, Massachusetts

SURVIVING THE FRESHMAN YEAR

COLLEGE: IT'S DIFFERENT

In college you are likely to hear fellow students say, "I don't know what that prof *wants*, and she won't *tell* me." "I wrote about three papers in high school, and now they want one every week." Though these students may be exaggerating a bit, college *is* different, both in the quality and the amount of work expected. Sometimes in high school the basic concepts of a course are reduced to a set of facts on a study sheet, handed to students to be reviewed and learned for a test.

In college, it is the concepts and ideas that are most important. These can only be grasped through a real understanding of the facts as they interrelate and form larger patterns. Writing papers and answering essay questions on tests can demonstrate a genuine understanding of the concepts, and this is why they are so important to college instructors. Learning to deal with ideas in this way can be a long-term asset, developing your independence, intellectual interests, and self-awareness.

Don't be discouraged; you are not alone. Most of your fellow students are having equally difficult times adjusting to a new learning method. Persist, and you will improve, leading to a lifetime habit of critical thinking and problem solving that can benefit you in many important ways.

College is also different outside of classes. Now that you have the freedom to choose how to spend time and what types of relationships to make, you have a bewildering number of possibilities.

MAKING A GOOD IMPRESSION

Here you are, plopped down in a strange place, feeling a bit like Dorothy transported to Oz. Your first goal is to make a good impression, showing your best self to those who will be important in your life for the next four years and even longer.

Impressing Faculty Members Favorably

Faculty members come in all ranks, from the graduate assistant, who teaches part-time while pursuing a degree, to a lofty full professor, who teaches primarily graduate students. Though different in rank and seniority, they respond to their students in roughly the same ways. They are, after all, people, with families and relationships much like your own. To have a good working relationship with them, try the following suggestions:

- **Make up your own mind about your instructors.** Listening to other students talk about teachers can be confusing. If you listen long enough, you will hear arguments for and against each of them. Don't allow hearsay to affect your own personal opinion.
- **Get to know your instructors firsthand.** Set up a meeting, during regular office hours. Don't try to settle important issues in the few moments before and after class.
- **Approach a discussion of grades carefully.** If you honestly believe that you have been graded too low, schedule a conference. Do not attack your instructor's integrity or judgment. Instead, say that you had expected your work to result in a better grade and would like to know ways to improve. Be serious about overcoming faults.
- **Don't make excuses.** Instructors have heard them all and can rarely be fooled. Accept responsibility for your mistakes, and learn from them.
- **Pay attention in class.** Conversing and daydreaming can insult your instructor and inhibit the learning process.
- **Arrive ahead of time for class.** You will be more relaxed, and you can use these moments to review notes or talk with classmates. You also demonstrate to your instructor a commitment to the class.

- **Participate in class discussions.** Ask questions and give answers to the instructor's questions. Nothing pleases an instructor more than an intelligent question that proves you are interested and prepared.
- **Learn from criticism.** It is an instructor's job to correct your errors in thinking. Don't take in-class criticism personally.

Impressing Fellow Students Favorably

Relationships with other students can be complex, but there are some basic suggestions that may make life easier in the residence halls and classrooms:

- **Don't get into the habit of bragging.** Frequent references to your wealth, your outstanding friends, your social status, or your family's successes are offensive to others.
- **Don't pry.** When your fellow students share their feelings and problems, listen carefully and avoid any tendency to intrude or ask embarrassing questions.
- **Don't borrow.** Borrowing a book, a basketball, or a few bucks may seem like a small thing to you, but some people who have trouble saying no may resent your request.
- **Divide chores.** Do your part; agree on a fair division of work in a lab project or a household task.
- **Support others.** Respect your friends' study time and the "Do not disturb" signs on their doors. Helping them to reach their goals will help you as well.
- **Allow others to be upset.** Sometimes, turning someone's anger into a joke, minimizing their difficulties, or belittling their frustration is your worst response. Support them by letting them release their emotions.
- **Don't preach.** Share your opinions when asked for, but don't try to reform the world around you.
- **Tell the truth.** Your reputation is your most important asset. When you make an agreement, keep it.

MANAGING YOUR TIME

Everyone, no matter how prominent or how insignificant, has 168 hours a week to spend. In this one asset we are all equal. There are students on every college campus, however, who seem to accomplish all their goals and still find time for play and socializing. There are others who seem to be alternating between frantic dashes and dull idleness, accomplishing very little. To the first group, college is a happy, fulfilling experience; to the latter, it is maddeningly frustrating. The first group has gained control of time, the second is controlled by that elusive and precious commodity.

- **Know where your time goes.** Unfortunately, we cannot store up time as we do money, to be used when the need is greatest. We use it as it comes, and it is amazing how it sometimes comes slowly (as in the last five minutes of a Friday afternoon class) or quickly (as in the last hour before a final exam). The first step in controlling time is to determine exactly how you use it. For a while, at least, you should carefully record how much time you spend in class, going to and from class, studying, sleeping, eating, listening to music, watching television, and running errands. You need to know what happens to your 168 hours. Only then can you make sensible decisions about managing them.
- **Make a weekly schedule.** You can schedule your routine for the week, using the time plan forms available at most college bookstores or by making your own forms.
- **First schedule the inflexible blocks of time.** Your class periods, transportation time, sleeping, and eating will form relatively routine patterns throughout the week. Trying to shave minutes off these important activities is often a mistake.

- **Plan your study time.** It is preferable, though not always possible, to set your study hours at the same time every weekday. Try to make your study time *prime time*, when your body and mind are ready for a peak performance.

- **Plan time for fun.** No one should plan to spend four years of college as a working robot. Fun and recreation are important, but they can be enjoyed in short periods just as well as long. For example, jogging with friends for 30 minutes can clear the mind, tone up the muscles, and give you those all-important social contacts. Parties and group activities can be scheduled for weekends.

- **Be reasonable in your time allotments.** As you progress through your freshman year, you will learn more precisely how much time is required to write a paper or complete a book report. Until then, schedule some extra minutes for these tasks. You are being unfair to yourself by planning one hour for a job that requires two.

- **Allow flexibility.** The unexpected is to be expected. There will be interruptions to your routine and errands that must be run at certain times. Allow for these unforeseen circumstances.

STUDYING EFFECTIVELY

Your most important activity in college is studying. Efficient study skills separate the inept student (who may spend just as many hours studying as an "A" student) from the excellent student, who thinks while studying and who uses common sense strategies to discover the important core of courses. The following suggested game plan for good study has worked in the past; it can work for you.

- **Make a commitment.** It is universally recommended that you spend two hours studying for every hour in class. At the beginning of your college career, be determined to do just that. It doesn't get easy until you make up your mind to do it.

- **Do the tough jobs first.** If certain courses are boring or particularly difficult, study them first. Don't read the interesting, enjoyable materials first, saving the toughies for the last sleepy twinges of your weary brain.

- **Study in short sessions.** Three two-hour sessions, separated from each other by a different activity, are much better than a long six-hour session.

- **Use your bits of time.** Use those minutes when you're waiting for a bus, a return call, laundry to wash, or a friend to arrive. Some of the best students I know carry 3 × 5 cards filled with definitions, formulas, or equations and learn during brief waiting periods. Most chief executives form the habit early of using bits of time wisely.

Digesting a Textbook

1. **Preview chapters.** Before you read a chapter in your textbook, preview it. Quickly examine the introductory paragraphs, headings, tables, illustrations, and other features of the chapter. The purpose is to discover the major topics. Then you can read with increased comprehension because you know where the author is leading.

2. **Underline the important points as you read.** Underlining should never be overdone; it can leave your textbook almost completely marked and less legible to read. Only the major ideas and concepts should be highlighted.

3. **Seven categories of information are commonly found in textbooks.** Be particularly alert when you see the following; get your marking pen ready:
   Definitions of terms.
   Types or *categories* of items.
   Methods of accomplishing certain tasks.
   Sequences of events or stages in a process.
   Reasons or *causes*.
   Results or *effects*.
   Contrasts or *comparisons* between items.

4. **Repeat information you need to learn.** When the object is to learn information, nothing is so effective as reciting the material, either silently or aloud.

5. **Don't read all material the same way.** Decide what you need to learn from the material and read accordingly. You read a work of fiction to learn the characters and the narrative; a poem, to learn an idea, an emotion, or a theme; a work of history, to learn the interrelationships of events. Do not read every sentence with the same speed and concentration; learn when to skim rapidly along. Remember, your study time is limited and the trick is to discriminate between the most important and the least important. No one can learn *everything* equally well.

6. **The five-minute golden secret.** As soon as possible after class is over—preferably at your desk in the classroom—skim through the chapter that has just been covered, marking the points primarily discussed. Copy what was written on the board. Now you know what the professor thinks is important!

TAKING TESTS SKILLFULLY

Try to predict the test questions. At some college libraries, copies of old examinations are made available to students. If you can legally find out your professor's previous test methods do so.

Ask your professor to describe the format of the upcoming test: multiple-choice? true-false? essay questions? problems? Adjust your study to the format described.

Listen for clues in the professor's lecture. Sometimes the questions posed in class have a way of reappearing on tests. If a statement is repeated several times or recurs in a subsequent lecture, note it as important.

As you review for the test, devise questions based on the material, and answer them. If you are part of a study group, have members ask questions of the others.

Common Sense Tactics

Arrive on the scene early; relax by breathing deeply. If the instructor gives instructions while distributing the test, listen very carefully.

- **Scan the whole test first.** Notice the point value for each section and budget your time accordingly.

- **Read the directions carefully** and then reread them. Don't lose points because you misread the directions.

- **Answer the short, easy questions first.** A bit of early success stimulates the mind and builds your confidence.

- **Leave space between answers.** You may think of a brilliant comment to add later.

- **Your first instinct is often the best** in answering true-false and multiple-choice questions. Look for qualifiers such as *never*, *all*, *often*, or *seldom* in true-false statements. Usually a qualifier that is absolute (*never*, *all*, or *none*) will indicate a false statement. Work fast on short-answer questions: they seldom count many points.

- **Open-book tests are no picnic.** Don't think that less study is required for an open-book test. They are often the most difficult of all examinations. If the material is unfamiliar, you won't have time to locate it and learn it during the test period.

Important Essay Strategies

- **Read the question carefully** and find out exactly what is asked for. If you are asked to contrast the French Revolution with the American Revolution and you spend your time describing each, without any contrasting references, your grade will be lowered.

- **Know the definitions of key words** used in essay questions:
  analyze: discuss the component parts.
  compare: examine for similarities.
  criticize: give a judgment or evaluation.
  define: state precise meaning of terms.

describe: give a detailed picture of qualities and characteristics.

discuss: give the pros and cons: debate them, and come to a conclusion.

enumerate: briefly mention a number of ideas, things, or events.

evaluate: give an opinion, with supporting evidence.

illustrate: give examples (illustrations) relating to a general statement.

interpret: usually means to state in other words, to explain, make clear.

outline: another way of asking for brief listings of principal ideas or characteristics. Normally the sentence or topic outline format is not required.

prove: give evidence and facts to support the premise stated in the test.

summarize: give an abbreviated account, with your conclusions.

- **Write a short outline** before you begin your essay. This organizes your thinking, making you less likely to leave out major topics.
- **Get to the point immediately.** Don't get bogged down in a lengthy introduction.
- **Read your essay over** before you hand it in. Words can be left out or misspelled. Remember that essay answers are graded somewhat subjectively, and papers that are correctly and neatly written make a better impression.
- **Learn from your test paper** when it is returned. Students who look at a test grade and discard the paper are throwing away a valuable tool. Analyze your mistakes honestly; look for clues for improvement in the professor's comments.

WRITING A TERM PAPER

Doing convincing library research and writing a term paper with correct footnotes and bibliography is a complicated procedure. Most first-year English composition courses include this process. Good students will work hard to master this skill because they know that research papers are integral parts of undergraduate and graduate courses.

Many students make the mistake of waiting until near the deadline to begin a term paper. At the busy end of the term, with final exams approaching, they embark on the uncertain time span of research and writing. Begin your term paper early, when the library staff is unhurried and ready to help and when you are under less pressure. It will pay dividends.

REGULATING YOUR RELATIONSHIPS

Find your special friends who believe in your definition of success. In a fast-paced environment like college, it is important to spend most of your time with people who share your ideas toward learning, where you can be yourself, without defensiveness. To find your kind of friends, first ask yourself: What is success? Is it a secure position and a comfortable home? A life of serving others? A position of power with a commodious executive suite? A challenging job that allows you to be creative? When you have answered honestly, you will have a set of long-range personal goals, and you can begin looking for kindred souls to walk with you on the road to success.

There will be, of course, some persons around you who are determined not to succeed, who for some reason program their lives for failure. Many college freshmen never receive a college degree; some may start college with no intention of passing courses. Their goal is to spend one hectic term as a party animal. If you intend to succeed at college, spending time among this type will be a considerable handicap. Consider making friends who will be around longer than the first year.

If possible, steer clear of highly emotional relationships during your first year of college. You don't have time for a broken heart, and relationships that begin with a rush often end that way.

MAINTAINING YOUR HEALTH

Poor health can threaten your success in the first year of college as nothing else can. No matter how busy you are, you must not forget your body and its needs: proper food, sufficient sleep, and healthy exercise. Many students, faced with the stress of college life, find themselves overmunching junk foods and gaining weight. Guard against this. Drugs and alcohol threaten the health and the success of many college students.

A FINAL WORD

So there it is. If you have read this far, you probably have a serious interest in succeeding in your first year of college. You probably have also realized that these suggestions, even if they sound a bit preachy, are practical and workable. They are based on many years of observing college students.

Benjamin W. Griffith
Former Dean, Graduate School
West Georgia College
Carrollton, Georgia

PART II

COLLEGE FACTS

AND FINANCES

Now that you've read through Part I, you'll need specific information on the colleges that best match your needs and aptitudes. Here's where you'll find essential information in a nutshell.

Facts and figures on all schools are listed in chart form to help you make quick and easy comparisons. Thumbnail data include:

- campus environment
- degrees offered
- composition of the student body
- enrollment figures
- test scores of entering freshmen
- fall application deadlines

You'll also see at a glance how much it's going to cost you for tuition, room-and-board, and related expenses. In-state costs are broken down on a state-by-state basis, each range starting with colleges that don't charge tuition and going up the scale to the most expensive schools.

COLLEGES AT A GLANCE

The charts on these pages present some of the basic data that initially concerns many students. All of the four-year accredited schools in the United States are listed here alphabetically by state. The type of college environment (from urban to rural) is given, followed by degrees offered and whether the institution is public or private. Information about whether the student body is coed or primarily men or women, and whether fraternities or sororities are on campus follows. The undergraduate enrollment for the fall of 2003 is given as well as the median test scores for freshmen who took the ACT or the SAT I. Finally, the fall admissions deadline is shown. "Open" usually indicates that admission applications will be accepted until a few weeks before classes begin.

Key: ENVIRONMENT — U-Urban R-Rural SU-Suburban SM-Small Town; DEGREES AWARDED — A-Associate B-Bachelor M-Master D-Doctorate; CONTROL — Pri-Private, Pub-Public; FRATERNITIES AND SORORITIES — F-Fraternities S-Sororities; STUDENTS — C-Coed M-Men W-Women PM-Primarily Men PW-Primarily Women

Name of School	Town	Env	Degrees	Control	Frat/Sor	Students	Enroll. Fall 2003	ACT Median	ACT Below 21	ACT 21-23	ACT 24-26	ACT 27-28	ACT Above 28	SAT V Median	SAT V Below 500	SAT V 500-599	SAT V 600-700	SAT V Above 700	SAT M Median	SAT M Below 500	SAT M 500-599	SAT M 600-700	SAT M Above 700	Deadline
Alabama																								
Alabama Agricultural and Mechanical University	Normal	SU	A,M,D	Pub	F,S	C	4,320																	7/15
Alabama State University	Montgomery	U	B,M	Pub	F,S	C	4,711																	7/30
Auburn University	Auburn	SM	B,M,D	Pub	F,S	C	20,048	24	13	31	29	13	14	550	21	52	23	4	570	16	47	32	5	8/1
Auburn University Montgomery	Montgomery	U	B,M,D	Pub	F,S	C	4,492		65	19	10	2	2											Open
Birmingham-Southern College	Birmingham	U	B,M	Pri	F,S	C	1,303	27						610	9	33	46	12	600	12	36	42	10	1/15
Concordia College	Selma	SM	A,B	Pri	No	C	851	18																Open
Faulkner University	Montgomery	U	A,B,M,D	Pri	F,S	C	2,231	20																Open
Huntingdon College	Montgomery	SU	B,A	Pri	F,S	C	615																	Open
Jacksonville State University	Jacksonville	SM	B,M	Pub	F,S	C	7,289	17	71	29														Open
Judson College	Marion	SM	B	Pri	No	W	369	23	36	30	23	4	7		20		20	60		20	60		20	Open
Miles College	Birmingham	U	A,B	Pri	No	C	1,400																	Open
Oakwood College	Huntsville	SU	A,B	Pri	No	C	1,778																	Open
Samford University	Birmingham	SU	A,B,M,D	Pri	F,S	C	2,836		14	23	30	15	18											3/1
Southern Christian University	Montgomery	U	B,M,D	Pri	No	C	341																	Open
Spring Hill College	Mobile	SU	A,B,M	Pri	F,S	C	1,211	24	26	23	21	17	13	560	27	33	37	3	540	27	44	26	3	7/1
Stillman College	Tuscaloosa	SM	B	Pri	F,S	C	1,460																	Open
Talladega College	Talladega	SM	B	Pri	F,S	C	660																	Open
Troy State University	Troy	SM	A,B,M	Pub	F,S	C	4,607																	Open
Troy State University/Dothan	Dothan	U	A,B,M	Pub	No	C	1,581	22	29	52	19													Open
Troy State University/Montgomery	Montgomery	U	A,B,M	Pub	No	C	3,182																	Open
Tuskegee University	Tuskegee	R	B,M,D	Pri	F,S	C	2,391																	Open
University of Alabama	Tuscaloosa	SU	B,M,D	Pub	F,S	C	15,868	24	23	30	24	12	11	554	26	43	24	8	553	24	46	25	5	8/1
University of Alabama at Birmingham	Birmingham	U	B,M,D	Pub	F,S	C	10,381	22	46	24	15	7	8											7/1
University of Alabama in Huntsville	Huntsville	SU	B,M,D	Pub	F,S	C	5,481	24	14	25	31	15	15	570	17	46	31	5	570	18	45	32	5	8/15
University of Mobile	Mobile	SU	A,B,M	Pri	No	C	1,669	22	49	21	15	7	8											9/10
University of Montevallo	Montevallo	SM	B,M	Pub	F,S	C	2,596																	8/1
University of North Alabama	Florence	U	B,M	Pub	F,S	C	4,995	21	49	22	19	6	4											7/1
University of South Alabama	Mobile	SU	B,M,D	Pub	F,S	C	10,171	22																8/10
University of West Alabama	Livingston	SM	A,B,M	Pub	F,S	C	1,595																	Open
Alaska																								
Alaska Pacific University	Anchorage	SU	A,B,M	Pri	No	C	478	22	40	10	30	10	10	540	50	20	20	10	520	30	50	20		2/1
Sheldon Jackson College	Sitka	SM	A,B	Pri	No	C	240																	Open
University of Alaska Anchorage	Anchorage	U	A,B,M	Pub	No	C	12,600																	Open
University of Alaska Fairbanks	Fairbanks	SM	A,B,M,D	Pub	F,S	C	7,720	21	48	22	17	5	8	510	42	35	18	5	510	43	36	19	3	8/1
University of Alaska Southeast	Juneau	SU	A,B,M	Pub	No	C	1,990																	Open
Arizona																								
American Indian College of the Assemblies of God	Phoenix	U	A,B	Pri	No	C	74	14	100					380					430					Open
Arizona State University-Main	Tempe	U	B,M,D	Pub	F,S	C	38,627	23	27	27	24	11	11	542	30	44	21	5	553	27	41	26	6	Open
DeVry University/Phoenix	Phoenix	SU	A,B,M	Pri	No	C	2,010																	Open
Embry-Riddle Aeronautical University	Prescott	R	B,M	Pri	F,S	C	1,631	24	20	23	26	13	18	540	29	38	28	4	580	20	36	37	7	Open
Grand Canyon University	Phoenix	SU	B,M	Pri	No	C	1,609																	Open
Northern Arizona University	Flagstaff	R	B,M,D	Pub	F,S	C	13,015	22	39	29	20	8	4	524	33	44	20	3	520	37	41	20	2	3/1
Prescott College	Prescott	SM	B,M	Pri	No	C	827																	Open
University of Arizona	Tucson	U	B,M,D	Pub	F,S	C	27,764	24	23	25	28	12	12	552	26	44	24	4	563	23	41	31	5	4/1
Arkansas																								
Arkansas Baptist College	Little Rock	U	A,B	Pri	F,S	C	360																	7/16
Arkansas State University	State University	SM	A,B,M,D	Pub	F,S	C	9,413	21	43	22	23	7	5											Open
Arkansas Tech University	Russellville	SM	A,B,M	Pub	F,S	C	5,889	22	38	23	23	11	5											Open
Harding University	Searcy	SM	B,M	Pri	F,S	C	4,036	24	26	27	20	10	17	550	26	45	24	6	540	35	34	25	6	7/1
Henderson State University	Arkadelphia	SM	A,B,M	Pub	F,S	C	3,052	21	41	22	22		5	539	35	35	30		522	40	40	20		Open
Hendrix College	Conway	SU	B,M	Pri	No	C	1,050	27	6	17	20	21	36	632	7	27	47	19	610	8	31	48	13	Open
John Brown University	Siloam Springs	SM	A,B	Pri	No	C	1,545																	
Lyon College	Batesville	SM	B	Pri	F,S	C	472	24						560					550					8
Ouachita Baptist University	Arkadelphia	SM	A,B	Pri	F,S	C	1,538	25	23	27	26	13	11	560	29	39	24	8	590	26	45	22	7	Open
Philander Smith College	Little Rock	U	B	Pri	No	C	1,000																	Open
Southern Arkansas University	Magnolia	SM	A,B,M	Pub	F,S	C	2,804	21	57	22	15	4	2											Open
University of Arkansas	Fayetteville	U	B,M,D	Pub	F,S	C	13,083	24	17	25	25	13	20	580	16	38	37	9	590	17	34	39	10	8/15
University of Arkansas at Little Rock	Little Rock	U	A,B,M,D	Pub	F,S	C	9,184																	Open
University of Arkansas at Monticello	Monticello	SM	A,B,M	Pub	F,S	C	2,130																	Open
University of Arkansas at Pine Bluff	Pine Bluff	SM	A,B,M	Pub	F,S	C	3,052																	
University of Central Arkansas	Conway	SM	A,B,M,D	Pub	F,S	C	7,650																	8/1

Column key —
- **ENVIRONMENT:** U-Urban, R-Rural, SU-Suburban, SM-Small Town
- **DEGREES AWARDED:** A-Associate, B-Bachelor, M-Master, D-Doctorate
- **CONTROL:** Pri-Private, Pub-Public
- **FRATERNITIES AND SORORITIES:** F-Fraternities, S-Sororities, F,S-Both, No-Neither
- **STUDENTS:** C-Coed, M-Men, PM-Primarily Men, W-Women, PW-Primarily Women

NAME OF SCHOOL	TOWN	ENV	DEGREES	CONTROL	FRAT/SOR	STUDENTS	UNDERGRAD ENROLL FALL 2003	ACT Median	ACT Below 21	ACT 21-23	ACT 24-26	ACT 27-28	ACT Above 28	SAT V Median	SAT V Below 500	SAT V 500-599	SAT V 600-700	SAT V Above 700	SAT M Median	SAT M Below 500	SAT M 500-599	SAT M 600-700	SAT M Above 700	APP DEADLINE
University of the Ozarks	Clarksville	SM	B	Pri	No	C	731	23	34	35	16	8	7	548	6	77	11	6	490	57	33	7	3	4/1
Williams Baptist College	Walnut Ridge	R	A,B	Pri	No	C	653	21	45	23	23	4	5											Open

California

NAME OF SCHOOL	TOWN	ENV	DEGREES	CONTROL	FRAT/SOR	STUDENTS	UNDERGRAD ENROLL FALL 2003	ACT Median	ACT Below 21	ACT 21-23	ACT 24-26	ACT 27-28	ACT Above 28	SAT V Median	SAT V Below 500	SAT V 500-599	SAT V 600-700	SAT V Above 700	SAT M Median	SAT M Below 500	SAT M 500-599	SAT M 600-700	SAT M Above 700	APP DEADLINE
Alliant International University	San Diego	SU	B,M,D	Pri	No	C	419																	Open
Art Center College of Design	Pasadena	SU	B,M	Pri	No	C	1,412																	Open
Art Institute of Southern California	Laguna Beach	SM	B	Pri	No	C	210																	
Azusa Pacific University	Azusa	U	B,M,D	Pri	No	C	4,402		55	37	8				33	43	21	3		33	40	25	3	3/1
Biola University	La Mirada	SU	B,M,D	Pri	No	C	3,012	24	25	21	25	14	15	563	22	42	30	8	555	27	41	26	6	6/1
California Baptist University	Riverside	SU	B,M	Pri	No	C	1,753	20	49	34	11	4	2	508	47	35	17	1	503	44	46	10		Open
California College of the Arts	San Francisco	U	B,M	Pri	No	C	1,269	22	14	50	27	9		547	26	50	19	5	507	45	37	18		2/15
California Institute of Technology	Pasadena	SU	B,M,D	Pri	No	C	891							740	1	5	17	77	790			4	96	1/1
California Institute of the Arts	Valencia	SU	B,M	Pri	No	C	806																	1/5
California Lutheran University	Thousand Oaks	SU	B,M,D	Pri	No	C	1,919																	3/15
California Maritime Academy	Vallejo	SU	B	Pub	No	C	665																	
California Polytechnic State University	San Luis Obispo	SU	B,M	Pub	F,S	C	17,066																	11/30
California State Polytechnic University, Pomona	Pomona	SU	B,M	Pub	F,S	C	17,650	21	50	26	16	6	2	485	54	34	11	1	518	36	39	23	3	11/1
California State University, Bakersfield	Bakersfield	U	B,M	Pub	F,S	C	5,228																	Open
California State University, Chico	Chico	SM	B,M	Pub	F,S	C	14,634																	
California State University, Dominguez Hills	Carson	U	B,M	Pub	F,S	C	7,680																	
California State University, Fresno	Fresno	SU	B,M,D	Pub	F,S	C	18,574	18	68	17	10	3	2	470	62	28	9	1	490	54	34	11	1	5/15
California State University, Fullerton	Fullerton	SU	B,M	Pub	F,S	C	26,896	19	60	23	13	2	3	480	58	33	8		500	48	37	13	1	11/30
California State University, Hayward	Hayward	SU	B,M	Pub	F,S	C	9,387	19	70	17	11	2		450	66	26	7	1	470	61	31	7	1	6/30
California State University, Long Beach	Long Beach	U	B,M,D	Pub	F,S	C	28,067								50	37	12	1		38	43	18	2	11/30
California State University, Los Angeles	Los Angeles	U	B,M,D	Pub	F,S	C	14,421																	6/15
California State University, Monterey Bay	Seaside	SU	B,M	Pub	No	C	3,327	20	62	22	12	2	2	470	54	36	10		460	58	35	7		3/15
California State University, Northridge	Northridge	SU	B,M	Pub	F,S	C	25,480							460	65	27	7	1	470	61	28	11	1	11/30
California State University, Sacramento	Sacramento	SU	B,M,D	Pub	F,S	C	22,562	19	61	23	13	2	1	470	60	31	8	1	490	51	38	10	1	Open
California State University, San Bernardino	San Bernardino	SU	B,M	Pub	F,S	C	12,939	18	71	17	8	2	1	440	76	20	4		450	70	24	6		Open
California State University, San Marcos	San Marcos	SU	B,M	Pub	F,S	C	5,757																	11/30
California State University, Stanislaus	Turlock	R	B,M	Pub	F,S	C	6,154	19	62	18	14	3	3	470	44	46	9	1	490	42	46	11	1	5/1
Chapman University	Orange	SU	B,M,D	Pri	F,S	C	3,443	25						593	6	51	36	7	594	5	50	40	5	1/31
Christian Heritage College	El Cajon	SU	A,B	Pri	No	C	600																	Open
Claremont McKenna College	Claremont	SM	B	Pri	No	C	1,053	30		2	10	19	69	690		7	47	46	700		5	51	44	1/1
Cogswell Polytechnical College	Sunnyvale	SU	B	Pri	No	C	500																	Open
Concordia University	Irvine	SU	A,B,M	Pri	No	C	1,420	22	40	25	20	6	9	530	34	43	21	2	540	32	46	19	3	5/1
DeVry University/Fremont	Fremont	SU	A,B,M	Pri	No	C	1,651																	Open
DeVry University/Long Beach	Long Beach	U	A,B,M	Pri	No	C	1,928																	Open
DeVry University/Pomona	Pomona	U	A,B,M	Pri	No	C	2,377																	Open
DeVry University/West Hills	West Hills	SU	A,B,M	Pri	No	C	1,161																	Open
Dominican University of California	San Rafael	SU	B,M	Pri	No	C	1,146	22						527	36	44	16	4	515	42	40	16	2	3/2
Fresno Pacific University	Fresno	SU	B,M	Pri	No	C	1,055	19	59	24	16	1		510	43	41	15	1	490	51	32	15	2	7/31
Golden Gate University	San Francisco	U	B,M,D	Pri	No	C	686																	6/1
Harvey Mudd College	Claremont	SU	B	Pri	No	C	704							700	1	9	41	49	750		1	17	82	1/15
Holy Names College	Oakland	U	B,M	Pri	No	C	593							490	58	35	7		470	58	35	7		8/1
Hope International University	Fullerton	U	A,B,M	Pri	No	C	840																	5/1
Humboldt State University	Arcata	SM	B,M	Pub	F,S	C	6,682	21	46	26	17	7	4	530	37	39	22	2	520	39	42	17	2	6/1
Humphreys College	Stockton	SU	A,B,D	Pri	No	C	760																	Open
La Sierra University	Riverside	SU	A,B,M,D	Pri	No	C	1,050																	8/15
Loyola Marymount University	Los Angeles	SU	B,M	Pri	F,S	C	5,465							571	13	51	32	4	583	13	46	36	5	2/1
Master's College and Seminary, The	Santa Clarita	R	B,M	Pri	No	C	1,190	25	19	21	31	14	15	580	19	41	34	6	560	20	48	27	5	3/6
Menlo College	Atherton	SU	B	Pri	No	C	630																	Open
Mills College	Oakland	U	B,M,D	Pri	No	W	726							585	14	40	38	8	551	27	40	29	4	2/1
Mount Saint Mary's College	Los Angeles	U	A,B,M	Pri	S	PW	950								43	46	11			43	48	9		2/15
National University	La Jolla	U	A,B,M	Pri	No	C	4,400																	Open
New College of California	San Francisco	U	B,M	Pri	No	C	150																	
Notre Dame de Namur University	Belmont	SU	A,B,M	Pri	No	C	967																	
Occidental College	Los Angeles	U	B,M	Pri	F,S	C	1,840							630					630					1/10
Otis College of Art and Design	Los Angeles	U	B,M	Pri	No	C	1,023	22	48	13	13	13	13	488	53	28	16	3	513	44	40	13	3	Open
Pacific Union College	Angwin	SM	A,B,M	Pri	No	C	1,438	22	38	25	22	7	8	512	38	38	19	5	498	42	35	20	3	Open
Pepperdine University	Malibu	SU	B,M,D	Pri	F,S	C	2,790																	1/15
Pitzer College	Claremont	SU	B	Pri	No	C	942	25	2	32	52		14	615	8	32	46	15	620	10	30	48	12	1/15
Point Loma Nazarene University	San Diego	SU	B,M	Pri	F,S	C	2,353																	3/1
Pomona College	Claremont	SU	B	Pri	F	C	1,570																	1/2
Saint Mary's College of California	Moraga	SU	B,M,D	Pri	No	C	2,494	22	29	28	19	11	13	540	25	53	19	3	550	24	49	25	2	2/1
Samuel Merritt College	Oakland	U	B,M,D	Pri	No	C	285	22		75				515	33	42	25		490	50	42	8		2/1
San Diego State University	San Diego	U	B,M,D	Pub	F,S	C	27,846	22	32	29	26	9	4	530	34	49	16	1	550	25	49	24	2	11/30
San Francisco Art Institute	San Francisco	U	B,M	Pri	No	C	500																	9/1
San Francisco Conservatory of Music	San Francisco	U	B,M	Pri	No	C	141																	2/1
San Francisco State University	San Francisco	U	A,B,M,D	Pub	F,S	C	20,828		33	46	20		2											Open
San Jose State University	San Jose	U	B,M	Pub	F,S	C	21,417																	
Santa Clara University	Santa Clara	SU	B,M,D	Pri	F,S	C	4,363	25	9	22	34	17	18	580	13	44	39	4	610	7	36	49	8	1/15
Scripps College	Claremont	SU	B	Pri	No	W	810	30	1	9	17	26	47	670		13	52	35	650	2	16	58	24	1/15
Simpson College	Redding	SU	A,B,M	Pri	No	C	964	21	42	32	16	6	3	510	43	42	13	2	487	56	33	11	1	Open
Sonoma State University	Rohnert Park	SU	B,M	Pub	F,S	C	6,996	21	39	35	21	3	2	520	39	44	15	2	520	37	47	15	1	11
Stanford University	Stanford	SU	B,M,D	Pri	F,S	C	6,442									8	28	63			5	25	69	12/15
Thomas Aquinas College	Santa Paula	R	B	Pri	No	C	332	28		7	41	11	41	670		12	59	29	610		38	52	9	Open
University of California at Berkeley	Berkeley	U	B,M,D	Pub	F,S	C	23,834							629	10	23	40	27	671	4	15	35	46	11/30

NAME OF SCHOOL	TOWN	ENVIRONMENT U-Urban R-Rural SU-Suburban SM-Small Town	DEGREES AWARDED A-Associate B-Bachelor M-Master D-Doctorate	CONTROL Pri-Private, Pub-Public	FRATERNITIES AND SORORITIES F-Fraternities S-Sororities F, S-Both No-Neither	STUDENTS: C-Coed M-Men W-Women PM-Primarily Men PW-Primarily Women	UNDERGRADUATE ENROLLMENT FALL 2003	TEST SCORES: ACT Median	ACT Below 21	ACT 21-23	ACT 24-26	ACT 27-28	ACT Above 28	SAT I VERBAL REASONING Median	SAT I Verbal Below 500	SAT I Verbal 500-599	SAT I Verbal 600-700	SAT I Verbal Above 700	SAT I MATHEMATICAL REASONING Median	SAT I Math Below 500	SAT I Math 500-599	SAT I Math 600-700	SAT I Math Above 700	APPLICATION DEADLINE Month / Day
University of California at Davis	Davis	SU	B,M,D	Pub	F,S	C		24						568	20	39	33	8	616	8	29	47	16	
University of California at Irvine	Irvine	SU	B,M,D	Pub	F,S	C	19,179							570	13	48	34	5	620	5	32	47	16	11/30
University of California at Los Angeles	Los Angeles	U	B,M,D	Pub	F,S	C	25,715	26	2	26	48		24	630	9	26	43	22	670	5	19	37	39	11/30
University of California at Riverside	Riverside	U	B,M,D	Pub	F,S	C	15,282	21	47	28	17	5	3	510	44	40	14	2	550	28	39	27	6	11/30
University of California at San Diego	La Jolla	SU	B,M,D	Pub	F,S	C	19,872	26	15	15	32	22	26	600	12	33	46	9	650	5	19	52	25	11/30
University of California at Santa Barbara	Santa Barbara	SU	B,M,D	Pub	F,S	C	17,724																	11/30
University of California at Santa Cruz	Santa Cruz	SM	B,M,D	Pub	F,S	C	13,660	23						572	21	40	32	8	577	17	42	36	6	11/30
University of Judaism College of Arts and Sciences	Bel Air	SU	B,M	Pri	No	C	106																	1/31
University of La Verne	La Verne	SU	A,B,M,D	Pri	F,S	C	1,396	20	58	32	6	3		490	50	43	6	1	500	46	45	9		2/1
University of Redlands	Redlands	SM	B,M	Pri	F,S	C	2,223	24	15	29	25	17	14	580	11	50	34	5	570	12	51	32	6	2/1
University of San Diego	San Diego	U	B,M,D	Pri	F,S	C	4,803	26	3	16	34	25	23	600	7	42	44	7	620	4	33	53	10	1/5
University of San Francisco	San Francisco	U	B,M,D	Pri	F,S	C	4,718	23	22	33	25	10	10	550	24	48	25	3	560	21	47	28	4	2/1
University of Southern California	Los Angeles	U	B,M,D	Pri	F,S	C	16,381	29						655	1	18	53	28	680		9	49	42	1/10
University of the Pacific	Stockton	SU	B,M,D	Pri	F,S	C	3,357	24	14	28	29	20	9	570	18	47	33	2	550	10	40	40	10	2/15
Vanguard University of Southern California	Costa Mesa	SU	B,M	Pri	No	C	1,340	22						517	43	35	20	2	497	48	38	13	1	12/1
Westmont College	Santa Barbara	SU	B		No	C	1,343	26	3	20	33	23	21	610	8	35	45	12	600	6	32	41	21	2/15
Whittier College	Whittier	SU	B,M,D	Pri	F,S	C	1,270																	2/1
Woodbury University	Burbank	SU	B,M	Pri	F,S	C	1,020																	Open
Colorado																								
Adams State College	Alamosa	SM	A,B,M	Pub	No	C	2,048																	8/1
Colorado Christian University	Lakewood	SU	A,B,M	Pri	No	C	1,462	24	24	25	28	15	8	550	18	47	25	10	550	31	40	25	4	8/1
Colorado College	Colorado Springs	SU	B,M	Pri	F,S	C	1,929																	1/15
Colorado School of Mines	Golden	SM	B,M,D	Pub	F,S	C	2,667	27	1	11	27	22	39	595	10	38	41	11	650	2	19	54	25	6/1
Colorado State University	Fort Collins	SU	B,M,D	Pub	F,S	C	20,678	24	13	33	31	12	11	550	23	48	26	4	560	19	48	28	5	7/1
Colorado Technical University	Colorado Springs	SU	A,B,M,D	Pri	No	C	1,206																	Open
DeVry University/Colorado Springs	Colorado Springs		A,B,M	Pri	No	C	300																	Open
DeVry University/Westminster	Westminster		A,B	Pri	No	C	670																	Open
Fort Lewis College	Durango	SM	A,B	Pub	No	C	4,182	20	53	28	13	3	3	500	49	36	14		500	46	42	11		8/1
Mesa State College	Grand Junction	SM	A,B,M	Pub	No	C	5,297																	7/31
Metropolitan State College of Denver	Denver	U	B	Pub	No	C	18,445																	8/12
Naropa University	Boulder	U	B,M	Pri	No	C	449	19	66	33				560					555	33	50	17		1/15
Regis University	Denver	SU	B,M	Pri	No	C	1,098																	Open
United States Air Force Academy	USAFA	SU	B	Pub	No	C	4,157							630	2	32	51	15	663	1	20	54	25	1/31
University of Colorado at Boulder	Boulder	SU	B,M,D	Pub	F,S	C	26,186	25	9	24	33	19	16	570	12	48	35	6	600	9	40	42	9	2/15
University of Colorado at Colorado Springs	Colorado Springs	U	B,M,D	Pub	F,S	C	5,875	23	24	21	38	9	8	531	29	47	19	5	540	28	41	29	2	7/1
University of Colorado at Denver	Denver	U	B,M,D	Pub	No	C	8,903								39	43	17	2		37	42	20	1	7/22
University of Denver	Denver	SU	B,M,D	Pri	F,S	C	4,257	24						555					567					2/1
University of Northern Colorado	Greeley	SU	B,M,D	Pub	F,S	C	10,211	22	31	34	24	8	4	520	38	42	18	2	520	37	44	18	1	8/1
University of Southern Colorado	Pueblo	U	B,M	Pub	F,S	C	5,324																	7/28
Western State College of Colorado	Gunnison	R	B	Pub	F,S	C	2,385	21	52	31	14	3	1	510	48	40	12		500	50	38	12		6/1
Connecticut																								
Albertus Magnus College	New Haven	SU	A,B,M	Pri	No	C	1,788							455	69	25	5	1	450	72	21	7	1	Open
Central Connecticut State University	New Britain	SU	B,M,D	Pub	F,S	C	9,399							514	39	49	12	1	515	41	47	11	1	5/1
Charter Oak State College	New Britain	SU	A,B	Pub	No	C	1,578																	Open
Connecticut College	New London	SM	B,M	Pri	No	C	1,837	27						660	2	16	56	26	650	2	10	65	23	1/1
Eastern Connecticut State University	Willimantic	SU	A,B,M	Pub	No	C	5,017																	5/1
Fairfield University	Fairfield	SU	A,B,M	Pri	No	C	4,020	26						590	6	47	41	6	607	4	39	50	7	1/15
Mitchell College	New London	SU	A,B	Pri	No	C	745																	8/30
Quinnipiac University	Hamden	SU	B,M	Pri	F,S	C	5,470	25	10	29	30	25	6	540	23	58	17	1	550	16	57	25	2	2/1
Sacred Heart University	Fairfield	SU	A,B,M	Pri	F,S	C	4,049							520	34	54	11	1	530	14	51	31	1	
Saint Joseph College	West Hartford	SU	B,M	Pri	No	PW	1,193							490	54	34	11	1	470	66	28	6		
Southern Connecticut State University	New Haven	U	A,B,M	Pub	F,S	C	8,316																	Open
Teikyo Post University	Waterbury	U	A,B	Pri	No	C	1,237																	
Trinity College	Hartford	U	B,M	Pri	F	C	2,188	27	5	12	23	25	35	650	3	26	54	15	660	4	22	55	20	1/15
United States Coast Guard Academy	New London	SU	B	Pub	No	C	985	27						620	2	35	51	12	640	1	22	57	20	1/31
University of Bridgeport	Bridgeport	U	A,B,M,D	Pri	F,S	C	1,261							450	69	22	8	1	460	65	25	8	2	4/1
University of Connecticut	Storrs	R	A,B,M,D	Pub	F,S	C	14,757							572	11	52	32	5	593	9	43	40	8	2/1
University of Hartford	West Hartford	SU	A,B,M,D	Pri	F,S	C	5,612	22	35	24	25	9	7	520	32	49	17	1	520	29	52	17	2	Open
University of New Haven	West Haven	SU	A,B,M	Pri	F,S	C	2,627							510	44	40	15	1	510	43	39	16	2	Open
Wesleyan University	Middletown	SU	B,M,D	Pri	F,S	C	2,722	31	1	2	11	15	70	700	1	12	36	51	690		8	48	44	1/1
Western Connecticut State University	Danbury	SU	A,B,M	Pub	F,S	C	5,236							490	54	38	7	1	480	58	33	9	1	Open
Yale University	New Haven	U	B,M,D	Pri	F,S	C	5,354	32						750		3	23	74	750		1	24	74	12/31
Delaware																								
Delaware State University	Dover	SU	B,M	Pub	F,S	C	2,910																	6/1
Goldey-Beacom College	Wilmington	SU	A,B,M	Pri	F,S		1,310																	Open
University of Delaware	Newark	SM	A,B,M,D		F,S	C	15,808								12	46	36	6		9	37	45	9	2/15
Wesley College	Dover	SM	A,B,M	Pri	F,S	C	1,591							495	50	39	10	1	500	50	39	10	1	Open
Wilmington College	New Castle	U	A,B,M,D	Pri	No	C	3,977																	Open
District of Columbia																								
American University	Washington	SU	A,B,M,D	Pri	F,S	C	5,752	27	2	12	34	18	33	620	5	32	46	17	600	5	42	44	9	2/1
Catholic University of America	Washington	U	B,M,D	Pri	No	C	2,759	25	16	18	29	16	21	584	13	41	38	8	577	14	42	40	4	2/15

NAME OF SCHOOL	TOWN	ENVIRONMENT (U-Urban R-Rural SU-Suburban SM-Small Town)	DEGREES AWARDED (A-Associate B-Bachelor M-Master D-Doctorate)	CONTROL (Pri-Private, Pub-Public)	FRATERNITIES AND SORORITIES (F-Fraternities S-Sororities F, S-Both No-Neither)	STUDENTS (C-Coed M-Men W-Women PM-Primarily Men PW-Primarily Women)	UNDERGRADUATE ENROLLMENT FALL 2003	TEST SCORES: ACT Median	ACT Below 21	ACT 21-23	ACT 24-26	ACT 27-28	ACT Above 28	SAT I VERBAL REASONING Median	Below 500	500-599	600-700	Above 700	SAT I MATHEMATICAL REASONING Median	Below 500	500-599	600-700	Above 700	APPLICATION DEADLINE Month / Day
Corcoran School of Art and Design	Washington	U	A,B	Pri	No	C	320																	Open
Gallaudet University	Washington	U	A,B,M,D	Pri	F,S	C	1,250																	Open
George Washington University	Washington	U	A,B,M,D	Pri	F,S	C	9,953	28	2	10	24	26	37	640	3	25	52	20	640	2	25	55	18	1/15
Georgetown University	Washington	U	B,M,D	Pri	No	C	6,550	30	2	3	8	15	72	690	1	11	49	39	690	1	8	48	43	1/10
Howard University	Washington	U	B,M,D	Pri	F,S	C	7,059	22	35	34	18	9	6	544	33	43	20	4	537	36	41	18	5	2/2
Southeastern University	Washington	U	A,B,M	Pri	F		513																	Open
Strayer University	Washington	U	A,B,M	Pri	No	C	11,785																	Open
Trinity College	Washington	U	B,M	Pri	No	W	1,011	16	83	17				430	78	17	5		410	81	18	1		Open
University of the District of Columbia	Washington	SU	A,B,M	Pub	F,S	C	5,006																	Open

Florida

NAME OF SCHOOL	TOWN	ENVIRONMENT	DEGREES AWARDED	CONTROL	FRATERNITIES AND SORORITIES	STUDENTS	UNDERGRADUATE ENROLLMENT FALL 2003	ACT Median	ACT Below 21	ACT 21-23	ACT 24-26	ACT 27-28	ACT Above 28	SAT I Verbal Median	Below 500	500-599	600-700	Above 700	SAT I Math Median	Below 500	500-599	600-700	Above 700	APPLICATION DEADLINE Month / Day
Barry University	Miami Shores	SU	B,M,D	Pri	F,S	C	6,006																	Open
Beacon College	Leesburg	SM	A,B	Pri	S	C	85																	Open
Bethune-Cookman College	Daytona Beach	U	B	Pri	F,S	C	2,794		77	21	2			410	85	12	2	1	410	85	12	2	1	7/30
Carlos Albizu University	Miami	U	B,M,D	Pri	No	C	357																	Open
Clearwater Christian College	Clearwater	SM	A,B	Pri	No	C	640																	
DeVry University/Orlando	Orlando		A,B,M	Pri	No	C	1,346																	Open
Eckerd College	St. Petersburg	SU	B	Pri	No	C	1,631							573	20	37	32	8	570					4/1
Edward Waters College	Jacksonville	U	B	Pri	F,S	C	1,300	16	99					390	98	2			380	98	2			
Embry-Riddle Aeronautical University	Daytona Beach	U	A,B,M	Pri	F,S	C	4,518	24	19	24	31	14	12	550	27	45	25	3	570	17	42	35	5	7/1
Flagler College	St. Augustine	SM	B	Pri	No	C	2,033	23	11	41	30	13	6	570	12	56	30	3	560	13	60	26	2	3/1
Florida Agricultural and Mechanical University	Tallahassee	U	A,B,M,D	Pub	F,S	C	11,801																	5/15
Florida Atlantic University	Boca Raton	SU	A,B,M,D	Pub	F,S	C	21,072	20	57	25	11	5	3	511	44	43	12	1	515	40	44	14	1	6/1
Florida Gulf Coast University	Fort Myers	R	A,B,M	Pub	F,S	C	5,232	21	43	34	16	4	2	520	39	47	12	1	510	41	44	15	1	3/1
Florida Hospital College of Health Sciences	Orlando	U	A,B	Pri	No	C	1,401																	7/13
Florida Institute of Technology	Melbourne	SM	B,M,D	Pri	F,S	C	2,346	25	17	20	32	18	13	560	20	43	33	4	600	10	36	44	10	Open
Florida International University	Miami	U	A,B,M,D	Pub	F,S	C	27,169	25	1	24	50	14	11	570	8	58	30	4	570	6	59	31	4	Open
Florida Memorial College	Miami	U	B	Pri	No	C																		Open
Florida Southern College	Lakeland	SU	B,M	Pri	F,S	C	1,841	21	43	33	18	5	1	508	48	36	15	1	514	42	43	13	2	8/1
Florida State University	Tallahassee	SU	A,B,M,D	Pub	F,S	C	29,630	25	5	28	34	18	14	590	8	50	38	4	600	9	48	40	4	3/1
International College	Naples	SU	A,B,M	Pri	No	C	1,327																	Open
Jacksonville University	Jacksonville	SU	B,M	Pri	F,S	C	2,214	22	28	41	13	13	5	520	38	44	16	2	520	35	41	21	3	Open
Lynn University	Boca Raton	SU	A,B,M,D	Pri	F,S	C	1,903	22	45		55				69	27	4	1		68	26	6	1	Open
New College of Florida	Sarasota	SU	B	Pub	No	C	671	28		6	26	29	39	682	1	7	57	35	630	3	25	60	13	5/1
Northwood University	West Palm Beach	SU	A,B	Pri	No	C	685	19	63	21	12	4		470	66	30	4		480	55	32	13		8/1
Nova Southeastern University	Fort Lauderdale	SU	A,B,M,D	Pri	F,S	C	5,223	20	56	25	11	5	3	480	57	34	8	1	500	46	37	14	3	Open
Palm Beach Atlantic University	West Palm Beach	U	A,B,M,D	Pri	No	C	2,420	23	29	27	27	12	5	550	24	52	21	3	530	30	49	20	1	Open
Ringling School of Art and Design	Sarasota	U	B	Pri	F,S	C	989	23						520	35	47	17	1	510	39	51	10		
Rollins College	Winter Park	SU	B,M	Pri	F,S	C	1,733	24	12	30	31	16	10	570	11	49	35	4	580	10	48	37	6	2/15
Saint Leo University	Saint Leo	R	A,B,M	Pri	F,S	C	1,083	21	44	33	16	2	5	490	51	40	7	1	490	52	41	7		Open
Saint Thomas University	Miami	SU	B,M	Pri	F,S	C	1,171	17						440					445					Open
Southeastern College	Lakeland	SM	B	Pri	No	C	1,363																	8/1
Stetson University	Deland	SM	B,M	Pri	F,S	C	2,161	24	20	24	30	15	12	572	15	50	27	7	564	18	49	29	4	3/1
University of Central Florida	Orlando	U	A,B,M,D	Pub	F,S	C	34,170	25	7	16	42	21	14	583	9	50	37	4	593	7	45	43	5	5/1
University of Florida	Gainesville	SU	B,M,D	Pub	F,S	C	33,982	27	1	10	24	27	38	625	4	30	52	14	642	2	23	56	19	1/13
University of Miami	Coral Gables	SU	B,M,D	Pri	F,S	C	10,003	26						560	9	40	41	11	580	4	33	47	15	2/1
University of North Florida	Jacksonville	U	A,B,M,D	Pub	F,S	C	12,446	22	31	47	17	4	1	576	10	56	31	4	576	9	54	35	2	7/2
University of South Florida	Tampa	U	A,B,M,D	Pub	F,S	C	32,463	22	6	59	32		4	540	29	49	20	2	540	26	48	23	3	5/1
University of Tampa	Tampa	U	A,B,M	Pri	F,S	C	4,125	23	3	48		45	4	545					548	37	48	14	1	Open
University of West Florida	Pensacola	SU	A,B,M,D	Pub	F,S	C	7,500																	6/30
Warner Southern College	Lake Wales	R	A,B,M	Pri	No	C	1,075	19	66	16	13	2	3	470	69	27	21	2	450	69	27	2	2	Open
Webber International University	Babson Park	SM	A,B,M	Pri	No	C	588	18	76	19	4	1		477	81	18			487	79	19	3		8/1

Georgia

NAME OF SCHOOL	TOWN	ENVIRONMENT	DEGREES AWARDED	CONTROL	FRATERNITIES AND SORORITIES	STUDENTS	UNDERGRADUATE ENROLLMENT FALL 2003	ACT Median	ACT Below 21	ACT 21-23	ACT 24-26	ACT 27-28	ACT Above 28	SAT I Verbal Median	Below 500	500-599	600-700	Above 700	SAT I Math Median	Below 500	500-599	600-700	Above 700	APPLICATION DEADLINE Month / Day
Agnes Scott College	Decatur	U	B,M	Pri	No	W	898	26	8	16	30	12	34	620	9	29	46	16	590	17	40	40	4	3/1
Albany State University	Albany	U	A,B,M	Pub	F,S	C	3,015	17	86	9	4	1		450	79	20	1		450	78	19	3		7/1
American InterContinental University	Atlanta	U	A,B	Pri	No	C	990																	Open
Armstrong Atlantic State University	Savannah	U	A,B,M	Pub	F,S	C	5,743	20	52	29	14	4	1	520	36	48	15	1	500	47	41	11	1	7/1
Art Institute of Atlanta	Atlanta	SU	A,B	Pri	No	C	2,699																	Open
Atlanta College of Art	Atlanta	U	B	Pri	No	C	440																	Open
Augusta State University	Augusta	U	A,B,M	Pub	F,S	C	5,276							490	54	35	10	1	480	55	35	9	1	7/21
Berry College	Mount Berry	SU	B,M	Pri	No	C	1,885								11	40	41	8		15	45	33	6	2/1
Brenau University Women's College	Gainesville	SU	B,M	Pri	S	W	586																	Open
Brewton-Parker College	Mt. Vernon	R	A,B	Pri	F,S	C	1,109	18	46	51	2	1		479	55	32	9	4	463	60	32	6	2	Open
Clark Atlanta University	Atlanta	U	B,M,D	Pri	F,S		3,921	20	70	16	12	1	1	460	73	21	5	1	470	68	27	5		6/1
Clayton College and State University	Morrow	SU	A,B	Pub	No	C	5,218	19	65	16	15	3	2	490	53	37	9		480	57	35	8	1	7/1
Columbus State University	Columbus	SU	A,B,M	Pub	F,S	C	6,024	20						493	58	32	9	1	482	60	31	8	1	7/28
Covenant College	Lookout Mountain	SU	A,B,M	Pri	No	C	872	26	18	17	22	21	25	610	14	28	42	16	590	19	32	39	10	5/1
DeVry University/Alpharetta	Alpharetta	SU	A,B,M	Pri	No	C	1,286																	Open
DeVry University/Decatur	Decatur	SU	A,B,M	Pri	No	C	2,561																	Open
Emory University	Atlanta	SU	A,B,M,D	Pri	F,S	C	5,717	29			8	39	54	640		10	50	40	660		5	44	51	1/15
Fort Valley State University	Fort Valley	R	A,B,M		F,S	C	2,291	24						448					448					
Georgia College and State University	Milledgeville	U	B,M	Pub	F,S	C	4,662	22	27	44	19	8	2	540	21	56	20	1	530	24	57	18	1	7/15
Georgia Institute of Technology	Atlanta	U	B,M,D	Pub	F,S	C	11,257	28						644	2	22	54	23	693		5	45	50	1/15
Georgia Southern University	Statesboro	SM	B,M,D	Pub	F,S	C	13,696	21	43	36	14	4	3	520	34	52	13	1	520	35	49	15	1	7/1
Georgia Southwestern State University	Americus	SM	A,B,M	Pub	F,S	C	1,947																	8/1
Georgia State University	Atlanta	U	B,M,D	Pub	F,S	C	20,208	21	40	31	20	8	1	530	32	47	19	2	540	29	49	20	2	3/1
Kennesaw State University	Kennesaw	SU	B,M	Pub	F,S	C	15,589							539	35	48	16	1	535	40	46	13	1	
LaGrange College	LaGrange	SM	A,B,M	Pri	F,S	C	971	22	41	26	17	16		525	38	42	19	1	500	46	38	16		Open

NAME OF SCHOOL	TOWN	ENVIRONMENT U-Urban R-Rural SU-Suburban SM-Small Town	DEGREES AWARDED A-Associate B-Bachelor M-Master D-Doctorate	CONTROL Pri-Private, Pub-Public	FRATERNITIES AND SORORITIES F-Fraternities S-Sororities F,S-Both No-Neither	STUDENTS: C-Coed M-Men W-Women PM-Primarily Men PW-Primarily Women	UNDERGRADUATE ENROLLMENT FALL 2003	TEST SCORES: ACT						SAT I VERBAL REASONING					SAT I MATHEMATICAL REASONING					APPLICATION DEADLINE Month / Day
								Median	Below 21	21-23	24-26	27-28	Above 28	Median	Below 500	500-599	600-700	Above 700	Median	Below 500	500-599	600-700	Above 700	
Mercer University	Macon	SU	B,M,D	Pri	F,S	C	4,580	28																7/1
Morehouse College	Atlanta	U	B	Pri	F	M	2,859	21	48	24	16	6	6	520	39	40	18	3	530	38	42	18	2	2/15
North Georgia College and State University	Dahlonega	SM	A,B,M	Pub	F,S	C	3,946	21	39	36	18	4	3	530	29	54	16	1	520	33	49	17	1	7/1
Oglethorpe University	Atlanta	SU	B,M	Pri	F,S	C	945		5	29	20	33	13		12	34	40	14		21	39	34	6	Open
Paine College	Augusta	U	B	Pri	F,S	C	972	15	95	2	2	1		400	91	8	1		380	87	12	1		8/1
Piedmont College	Demorest	SM	B,M	Pri	No	C	1,010	21	49	31	11	7	2	510	47	31	21	1	510	46	37	16	1	Open
Reinhardt College	Waleska	SM	A,B	Pri	No	C	1,084	19	73	16	10	1		498	52	38	8	1	481	61	32	7	1	Open
Savannah College of Art and Design	Savannah	U	B,M	Pri	No	C	5,318	23	28	28	23	13	8	551	27	38	31	3	532	33	42	24	1	Open
Savannah State University	Savannah	SU	B,M	Pub	F,S	C	2,594	17	95	3	1	1	1	440	85	12	2	1	430	86	12	1	1	6/1
Shorter College	Rome	SM	B	Pri	F,S	C	884	22	36	30	22	5	7	530	36	42	18	4	530	36	44	19	1	Open
South College	Savannah	U	A,B	Pri	No	C	550																	Open
Southern Polytechnic State University	Marietta	SU	A,B,M	Pub	F,S	C	3,015	22						530	26	53	20	1	570	12	53	33	2	8/1
Spelman College	Atlanta	U	B	Pri	S	W	2,081																	2/1
State University of West Georgia	Carrollton	SU	B,M,D	Pub	F,S	C	8,052	21	55	28	11	5	1	512	47	42	10	1	505	49	40	10	1	7/3
Thomas University	Thomasville	R	A,B,M	Pri	No	C	684	17	80	20				490	75	17	8		490	67	25	8		Open
Toccoa Falls College	Toccoa Falls	SM	A,B	Pri	No	C	800	20	53	19	14	11	3	540	33	42	21	4	510	42	43	13	2	8/1
University of Georgia	Athens	SM	A,B,M,D		F,S	C	24,829																	1/15
Valdosta State University	Valdosta	U	A,B,M,D	Pub	F,S	C	10,547	21		16	70	13	1	511	45	45	9	1	504	47	42	10	1	8/1
Wesleyan College	Macon	SU	B,M	Pri	No	W	661		47	15	24	15			27	40	28	5		38	38	18	6	2/1

Hawaii

NAME OF SCHOOL	TOWN	ENVIRONMENT	DEGREES AWARDED	CONTROL	FRATERNITIES AND SORORITIES	STUDENTS	UNDERGRADUATE ENROLLMENT FALL 2003	ACT Median	ACT Below 21	ACT 21-23	ACT 24-26	ACT 27-28	ACT Above 28	SAT I Verbal Median	Verbal Below 500	Verbal 500-599	Verbal 600-700	Verbal Above 700	SAT I Math Median	Math Below 500	Math 500-599	Math 600-700	Math Above 700	APPLICATION DEADLINE Month / Day
Brigham Young University/Hawaii	Laie	SM	A,B	Pri	No	C	2,703		41	31	20	6	2											2/15
Chaminade University of Honolulu	Honolulu	U	A,B,M	Pri	No	C	1,064	21	51	30	9	5	5	470	65	26	9		480	56	33	10	1	Open
Hawaii Pacific University	Honolulu	U	A,B,M	Pri	No	C	6,735	23	36	16	20	11	17	520	38	48	13	1	520	41	37	20	2	Open
University of Hawaii at Hilo	Hilo	SM	B,M	Pub	No	C	2,826																	7/1
University of Hawaii at Manoa	Honolulu	U	B,M,D	Pub	F,S	C	12,810	22						520	36	46	16	2	560	17	50	27	6	6/1

Idaho

NAME OF SCHOOL	TOWN	ENVIRONMENT	DEGREES AWARDED	CONTROL	FRATERNITIES AND SORORITIES	STUDENTS	UNDERGRADUATE ENROLLMENT FALL 2003	ACT Median	ACT Below 21	ACT 21-23	ACT 24-26	ACT 27-28	ACT Above 28	SAT I Verbal Median	Verbal Below 500	Verbal 500-599	Verbal 600-700	Verbal Above 700	SAT I Math Median	Math Below 500	Math 500-599	Math 600-700	Math Above 700	APPLICATION DEADLINE Month / Day
Albertson College of Idaho	Caldwell	SM	B	Pri	F,S	C	803	24							18	49	27	6		21	41	35	4	6/1
Boise State University	Boise	U	A,B,M,D	Pub	F,S	C	16,551	21						508					505					7/14
Idaho State University	Pocatello	SM	A,B,M,D	Pub	F,S	C	11,683	20	52	24	16	5	3	525	37	42	17	4	530	43	30	25	2	8/1
Lewis-Clark State College	Lewiston	U	A,B	Pub	No	C	3,471	19	62	20	13	3	2	490	56	33	10	2	500	50	36	12	3	Open
Northwest Nazarene University	Nampa	SM	A,B,M	Pri	No	C	1,163	23						551	30	41	20	9	545	34	39	17	10	8/8
University of Idaho	Moscow	SM	B,M,D	Pub	F,S	C	9,607	23	31	25	21	12	11	550	28	42	26	4	560	24	41	30	4	8/1

Illinois

NAME OF SCHOOL	TOWN	ENVIRONMENT	DEGREES AWARDED	CONTROL	FRATERNITIES AND SORORITIES	STUDENTS	UNDERGRADUATE ENROLLMENT FALL 2003	ACT Median	ACT Below 21	ACT 21-23	ACT 24-26	ACT 27-28	ACT Above 28	SAT I Verbal Median	Verbal Below 500	Verbal 500-599	Verbal 600-700	Verbal Above 700	SAT I Math Median	Math Below 500	Math 500-599	Math 600-700	Math Above 700	APPLICATION DEADLINE Month / Day
Augustana College	Rock Island	SU	B	Pri	F,S	C	2,309	26	8	20	31	16	25											Open
Aurora University	Aurora	SU	B,M,D	Pri	F,S	C	1,659	20						473	60	40			527	56	45			Open
Benedictine University	Lisle	SU	A,B,M,D	Pri	No	C	2,114	23	28	26	23	12	10											Open
Blackburn College	Carlinville	R	B	Pri	No	C	571																	Open
Bradley University	Peoria	U	B,M	Pri	F,S	C	5,305	25	9	22	32	19	18	550					570	23	37	35	5	Open
Chicago State University	Chicago	U	B,M	Pub	F,S	C	4,904	18	89	8	3													7/15
Columbia College Chicago	Chicago	U	B,M	Pri	No	C	9,265	20																8/15
Concordia University, River Forest	River Forest	SU	B,M,D	Pri	No	C	1,203		37	24	22	8	9											Open
DePaul University	Chicago	U	B,M,D	Pri	F,S	C	14,585	22	22	32	26	12	8	560	22	44	29	5	540	26	47	24	4	2/1
DeVry University/Addison (DuPage County)	Addison	SU	A,B	Pri	No	C	4,827																	Open
DeVry University/Chicago	Chicago	U	A,B	Pri	No	C	2,896																	Open
DeVry University/Tinley Park	Tinley Park		A,B,M	Pri	No	C	1,427																	Open
Dominican University	River Forest	SU	B,M	Pri	No	C	1,211	23	34	27	19	12	8											Open
Eastern Illinois University	Charleston	SM	B,M	Pub	F,S	C	9,845	22	34	37	19	7	3											Open
East-West University	Chicago	U	A,B	Pri	No	C	1,006		70	6	2	1												Open
Elmhurst College	Elmhurst	SU	B,M	Pri	F,S	C	2,396	23	37	17	26	11	9											4/1
Eureka College	Eureka	SM	B	Pri	F,S	C	510																	Open
Greenville College	Greenville	SM	B,M	Pri	No	C	1,160	22	35	21	27	9	8	550	31	44	22	3	510	31	47	22		Open
Illinois College	Jacksonville	SM	B	Pri	No	C	1,016	23	20	31	27	13	9	585	12	42	38	8	595	8	42	38	12	Open
Illinois Institute of Technology	Chicago	U	B,M,D	Pri	F,S	C	1,941	28		6	30	21	43	620	6	28	51	15	670		17	47	35	Open
Illinois State University	Normal	U	B,M,D	Pub	F,S	C	18,097	24	15	36	32	11	6											3/1
Illinois Wesleyan University	Bloomington	SU	B	Pri	F,S	C	2,107	29		5	20	23	52	630	1	30	46	23	640	1	22	54	23	3/1
Judson College	Elgin	SU	B,M	Pri	No	C	1,173																	Open
Kendall College	Evanston	U	A,B	Pri	No	C	628	21	62	20	16		2	490	66		33		410	66		33		Open
Knox College	Galesburg	SM	B	Pri	F,S	C	1,127	27	7	11	28	19	35	620	12	29	40	19	610	12	32	48	8	2/1
Lake Forest College	Lake Forest	SU	B,M	Pri	F,S	C	1,345	25	15	18	29	16	22	578	17	39	36	8	584	14	41	37	8	3/1
Lewis University	Romeoville	SU	A,B,M	Pri	F,S	C	3,216	24	6	65	14	14	4	550	25	50	25		590	25	50	25		Open
Loyola University Chicago	Chicago	U	B,M,D	Pri	F,S	C	7,916	25	7	19	35	17	22	580	15	43	35	7	570	21	38	36	5	4/1
MacMurray College	Jacksonville	SM	A,B	Pri	F,S	C	677	20	63	15	15	4	3	430	75	17	8		500					Open
McKendree College	Lebanon	SU	B,M	Pri	F,S	C	2,115	25	24	27	26	14	10											Open
Millikin University	Decatur	SU	B,M	Pri	F,S	C	2,602	23	27	27	23	13	10	530	33	35	26	6	540	34	38	26	2	Open
Monmouth College	Monmouth	SM	B	Pri	F,S	C	1,162	22	28	32	22	11	7											Open
NAES College	Chicago	U	B	Pri	No	C	80																	Open
National-Louis University	Chicago	SU	B,M,D	Pri	No	PW	2,534																	Open
North Central College	Naperville	SU	B,M	Pri	No	C	2,086	24	16	24	30	16	13	570	18	39	33	10	580	16	37	35	12	Open
North Park University	Chicago	U	B,M,D	Pri	No	C	1,573																	Open
Northeastern Illinois University	Chicago	U	B,M	Pub	S	C	8,324																	7/1
Northern Illinois University	DeKalb	SM	B,M,D	Pub	F,S	C	18,275	22	37	29	21	8	5											8/1
Northwestern University	Evanston	SU	B,M,D	Pri	F,S	C	8,001	31	1	4	7	11	78	695	1	8	40	50	710		6	37	56	1/1
Olivet Nazarene University	Bourbonnais	SM	A,B,M	Pri	No	C	2,432	23	25	25	25	10	15											
Principia College	Elsah	R	B	Pri	No	C	549	26	16	21	25	18	21	580	19	32	36	13	550	13	42	31	14	3/1
Quincy University	Quincy	SM	A,B,M	Pri	F,S	C	1,130	23	19	41	27	9	4											Open

NAME OF SCHOOL	TOWN	ENVIRONMENT (U-Urban R-Rural SU-Suburban SM-Small Town)	DEGREES AWARDED (A-Associate B-Bachelor M-Master D-Doctorate)	CONTROL (Pri-Private, Pub-Public)	FRATERNITIES AND SORORITIES (F-Fraternities S-Sororities F, S-Both No-Neither)	STUDENTS: C-Coed M-Men W-Women PM-Primarily Men PW-Primarily Women	UNDERGRADUATE ENROLLMENT FALL 2003	TEST SCORES: ACT Median	ACT Below 21	ACT 21-23	ACT 24-26	ACT 27-28	ACT Above 28	SAT I VERBAL REASONING Median	SAT I Verbal Below 500	SAT I Verbal 500-599	SAT I Verbal 600-700	SAT I Verbal Above 700	SAT I MATHEMATICAL REASONING Median	SAT I Math Below 500	SAT I Math 500-599	SAT I Math 600-700	SAT I Math Above 700	APPLICATION DEADLINE Month / Day
Rockford College	Rockford	SU	B,M	Pri	No	C	900	23																Open
Roosevelt University	Chicago	U	B,M,D	Pri	F,S	C	4,290	22																Open
Saint Xavier University	Chicago	U	B,M	Pri	No	C	3,062	21	52	25	16	3	3											8/15
School of the Art Institute of Chicago	Chicago	U	B,M	Pri	No	C	1,802																	Open
Shimer College	Waukegan	SU	B	Pri	No	C	123																	3/1
Southern Illinois University Carbondale	Carbondale	R	A,B,M,D	Pub	F,S	C	16,366	22	22	39	23	8	7		42	34	21	4		40	32	21	7	Open
Southern Illinois University Edwardsville	Edwardsville	SU	B,M	Pub	F,S	C	10,014		37	30	21	7	5											5/31
Trinity Christian College	Palos Heights	SU	B	Pri	No	C	1,263	23	30	20	26	13	12											8/15
Trinity College of Nursing and Health Sciences	Rock Island	U	A,B	Pri	No	C																		Open
Trinity International University	Deerfield	SU	B,M,D	Pri	No	C	1,148	23	30	28	24	9	9	584	15	46	29	10	567	24	32	34	10	Open
University of Chicago	Chicago	U	B,M,D	Pri	F,S	C	4,072																	1/1
University of Illinois at Chicago	Chicago	U	B,M,D	Pub	F,S	C	16,012	23	25	30	25	10	10											1/15
University of Illinois at Urbana-Champaign	Urbana	SM	B,M,D	Pub	F,S	C	28,746																	1/1
University of Saint Francis	Joliet	SU	B,M	Pri	No	C	1,143	22																9/1
VanderCook College of Music	Chicago	U	B,M	Pri	F,S	C	83																	6/1
West Suburban College of Nursing	Oak Park	SU	B	Pri	No	C	130																	Open
Western Illinois University	Macomb	R	B,M	Pub	F,S	C	11,027	22	42	33	18	4	3											
Wheaton College	Wheaton	SU	B,M,D	Pri	No	C	2,378																	1/15
Indiana																								
Anderson University	Anderson	SU	A,B,M,D	Pri	No	C	2,005																	Open
Ball State University	Muncie	SU	A,B,M,D	Pub	F,S	C	15,609																	3/1
Bethel College	Mishawaka	SU	A,B,M	Pri	No	C	1,740	22	39	21	18	10	11	530	34	42	23	7	530	32	45	21	1	Open
Butler University	Indianapolis	SU	B,M,D	Pri	F,S	C	3,823	26	6	15	31	21	27	584	13	43	37	7	597	12	36	43	9	Open
Calumet College of St. Joseph	Whiting	U	A,B,M	Pri	No	C	1,156	17											584					Open
DePauw University	Greencastle	SM	B	Pri	F,S	C	2,365	27	4	12	29	22	32	600	5	41	41	13	620	5	33	51	12	2/1
Earlham College	Richmond	SM	B,M	Pri	No	C	1,080	26	18	15	18	17	32	630	10	27	38	25	590	11	44	31	14	2/15
Franklin College	Franklin	SM	B	Pri	F,S	C	1,038	23	18	54	24		4	524	47	39	12	2	530	43	45	10	2	Open
Goshen College	Goshen	SM	B	Pri	No	C	920	25	20	16	26	11	27	590	22	29	31	18	580	17	39	34	10	2/15
Grace College	Winona Lake	U	A,B,M	Pri	No	C	907	23	29	22	23	13	13	532	32	40	26	2	579	32	49	18	1	8/1
Hanover College	Hanover	R	B	Pri	F,S	C	997	23	13	23	32	18	14	570	21	40	34	5	580	14	44	35	7	3/1
Huntington College	Huntington	SM	A,B,M	Pri	No	C	923								22	45	25	8		21	46	27	6	8/15
Indiana Institute of Technology	Fort Wayne	U	A,B,M	Pri	F,S	C	2,868	21						480	52	34	11		510	45	33	18	1	Open
Indiana State University	Terre Haute	U	A,B,M,D	Pub	F,S	C	9,615	19	61	22	11	3	2	475	61	31	7	1	472	61	32	6	1	8/1
Indiana University Bloomington	Bloomington	SM	A,B,M,D	Pub	F,S	C	30,319	24	15	24	31	16	14	550	27	45	25	3	560	24	41	30	5	2/1
Indiana University East	Richmond	SM	A,B	Pub	F,S	C	2,505	19	67	20	12		1	450	70	22	6	1	410	76	22		1	Open
Indiana University Kokomo	Kokomo	SM	A,B,M	Pub	No	C	2,730	19	71	20	9			470	63	32	5		460	66	28	6		8/3
Indiana University Northwest	Gary	U	A,B,M	Pub	F,S	C	3,941	20	64	19	8	4	4	450	66	24	10		440	71	22	6		8/1
Indiana University South Bend	South Bend	SU	A,B,M	Pub	S	C	6,093	20	54	22	11	9	4	480	57	34	9		470	59	34	7		Open
Indiana University Southeast	New Albany	SU	A,B,M	Pub	F,S	C	5,309	19	66	22	9	2	1	470	62	30	7		470			6		7/15
Indiana University-Purdue University Fort Wayne	Fort Wayne	SU	A,B,M	Pub	F,S	C	11,068	20	55	24	15	4	2	479	60	31	8	1	482	58	32	9	1	8/1
Indiana University-Purdue University Indianapolis	Indianapolis	U	A,B,M,D	Pub	F,S	C	21,388	20	52	28	13	4	3	490	52	38	9	1	490	53	35	11	1	Open
Indiana Wesleyan University	Marion	U	A,B,M,D	Pri	No	C	2,505	24	13	18	30	24	15	545	28	43	25	4	540	32	40	25	4	8/1
Manchester College	North Manchester	SM	A,B,M	Pri	No	C	1,114	22	38	23	23	12	4	504	44	38	16	2	511	49	37	13	1	Open
Marian College	Indianapolis	SU	A,B	Pri	No	C	1,179																	Open
Martin University	Indianapolis	U	B,M	Pri	No	C	586																	Open
Oakland City University	Oakland City	SM	A,B,M	Pri	No	C	1,437	21	50	20	20	6	4	450	10	60	20	10	450	10	60	20	10	Open
Purdue University/Calumet	Hammond	U	A,B,M	Pub	F,S	C	8,120																	Open
Purdue University/West Lafayette	West Lafayette	SU	A,B,M,D	Pub	F,S	C	30,851	25	11	21	29	17	22	560	22	47	27	4	590	13	40	36	11	Open
Rose-Hulman Institute of Technology	Terre Haute	SU	B,M	Pri	F,S	C	1,721	29		6	15	21	58	630	2	35	44	19	690		11	43	46	3/1
Saint Joseph's College	Rensselaer	SM	A,B,M	Pri	No	C	998	22	46	17	18	9	10	508	43	48	8	1	510	48	35	14	2	Open
Saint Mary-of-the-Woods College	St. Mary-of-the-Woods	R	A,B,M	Pri	No	W	1,565	22						510					490					7/15
Saint Mary's College	Notre Dame	SU	B	Pri	No	PW	1,523		12															3/1
Taylor University	Upland	R	A,B,M	Pri	No	C	1,834	26	12	19	26	20	24	596	12	36	43	10	586	10	40	34	10	1/15
Tri-State University-Main Campus	Angola	SM	A,B,M	Pri	F,S	C	1,192	23	28	25	26	13	9	530	37	43	18	1	560	24	38	32	6	6/1
University of Evansville	Evansville	U	A,B,M	Pri	F,S	C	2,372	25	13	14	36	16	21	570	23	40	31	6	560	21	42	32	5	
University of Indianapolis	Indianapolis	SU	A,B,M,D	Pri	No	C	2,916	22	14	59	12	13	2	560	48	40	10	2	560	40	44	15	1	Open
University of Notre Dame	Notre Dame	SU	B,M,D	Pri	No	C	8,311	31						667	3	13	44	39	693	1	9	39	51	1/7
University of Saint Francis	Fort Wayne	U	A,B,M	Pri	No	C	1,608	20	64	22	12	2		470	61	29	9		480	55	37	7		Open
University of Southern Indiana	Evansville	SU	A,B,M	Pub	F,S	C	9,154	20	57	24	14	3	2	478	60	30	9	1	474	62	29	8	1	8/15
Valparaiso University	Valparaiso	SM	A,B,M,D	Pri	F,S	C	3,027	26	8	20	28	19	25	570	16	43	33	8	580	16	38	34	11	8/15
Wabash College	Crawfordsville	SM	B	Pri	F	M	863	26	5	19	36	22	18	576	17	44	30	9	604	12	32	42	14	2/1
Iowa																								
Allen College	Waterloo	SU	A,B,M	Pri	No	PW	276	20	42	45	9	3												Open
Briar Cliff University	Sioux City	SU	A,B,M	Pri	No	C	1,063	21	49	28	14	5	4	470	77	23			500	44	56			Open
Buena Vista University	Storm Lake	SM	B,M	Pri	No	C	1,288	22	32	30	24	7	7											Open
Central College	Pella	SU	B	Pri	F,S	C	1,623																	3/1
Clarke College	Dubuque	U	A,B,M	Pri	No	C	995																	Open
Coe College	Cedar Rapids	U	B,M	Pri	F,S	C	1,290	24	20	30	29	11	10	560	19	39	39	3	570	22	37	33	8	3/1
Cornell College	Mount Vernon	SM	B	Pri	F,S	C	1,117	26	6	20	26	18	30	610	6	35	47	12	600	9	37	41	13	2/1
Dordt College	Sioux Center	R	A,B,M	Pri	No	C	1,287	24	12	28	28	18	14	580	15	38	39	8	586	17	38	34	11	
Drake University	Des Moines	SU	B,M,D	Pri	F,S	C	3,434	26	6	20	33	16	23	584	13	41	39	7	594	13	35	40	12	3/1
Franciscan University	Clinton	SM	A,B,M	Pri	No	C	426	19	71	18	7	4	3	445	83	17			435	83	17			8/15
Graceland University	Lamoni	SM	B,M	Pri	No	C	2,033		1						59	30	9	2		44	40	14	2	5/1
Grand View College	Des Moines	U	A,B	Pri	No	C	1,630	20	56	19	17	7	1											Open
Grinnell College	Grinnell	SM	B	Pri	No	C	1,524	30	1	7	8	13	72	680	5	13	40	42	680	3	12	42	43	1/20

NAME OF SCHOOL	TOWN	ENVIRONMENT U-Urban R-Rural SU-Suburban SM-Small Town	DEGREES AWARDED A-Associate B-Bachelor M-Master D-Doctorate	CONTROL Pri-Private, Pub-Public	FRATERNITIES AND SORORITIES F-Fraternities S-Sororities F,S-Both No-Neither	STUDENTS: C-Coed M-Men W-Women PM-Primarily Men PW-Primarily Women	UNDERGRADUATE ENROLLMENT FALL 2003	TEST SCORES: ACT Median	ACT Below 21	ACT 21-23	ACT 24-26	ACT 27-28	ACT Above 28	SAT I VERBAL REASONING Median	SAT I Verbal Below 500	SAT I Verbal 500-599	SAT I Verbal 600-700	SAT I Verbal Above 700	SAT I MATHEMATICAL REASONING Median	SAT I Math Below 500	SAT I Math 500-599	SAT I Math 600-700	SAT I Math Above 700	APPLICATION DEADLINE Month / Day
Iowa State University	Ames	U	B,M,D	Pub	F,S	C	22,230	24	16	25	26	16	17		19	34	34	13		11	29	41	19	8/1
Iowa Wesleyan College	Mount Pleasant	SM	B	Pri	F,S	C	753	19	80	11	9													Open
Loras College	Dubuque	SM	A,B,M	Pri	S	C	1,613	22	33	29	22	9	6	510	27	59	5	9	540	18	64	14	5	Open
Luther College	Decorah	SM	B	Pri	F,S	C	2,565	25	12	22	29	18	19	580	14	42	32	12	620	12	34	44	10	3/1
Maharishi University of Management	Fairfield	SM	B,M,D	Pri	No	C	251	24						575	12	41	35	12	577	15	44	38	3	Open
Mercy College of Health Sciences	Des Moines	U	A,B	Pri	No	C	616																	
Morningside College	Sioux City	SU	B,M	Pri	F,S	C	942	22	40	25	25	7	4											Open
Mount Mercy College	Cedar Rapids	U	B	Pri	No	C	1,473	22	34	33	19	8	5											
Northwestern College of Iowa	Orange City	SM	A,B	Pri	No	C	1,285	24	16	28	34	10	12											Open
Saint Ambrose University	Davenport	U	B,M,D	Pri	No	C	2,483	22	37	27	23	7	6											Open
Simpson College	Indianola	SU	B	Pri	F,S	C	1,937	24	15	28	32	15	9											Open
University of Dubuque	Dubuque	SU	A,B,M,D	Pri	F,S	C	981	23						500	26	64	9	1	500	17	68	15		5/1
University of Iowa	Iowa City	SM	B,M,D	Pub	F,S	C	20,233	24	11	25	33	16	13	590	16	38	36	11	605	12	35	39	14	4/1
University of Northern Iowa	Cedar Falls	SM	B,M,D	Pub	F,S	C	11,774	23	26	33	26	7	8	536	40	29	26	5	542	40	21	33	6	8/15
Upper Iowa University	Fayette	R	A,B,M	Pri	F,S	C	693	19	49	23	21	5	2											Open
Wartburg College	Waverly	SM	B	Pri	No	C	1,649																	8/1
William Penn University	Oskaloosa	R	A,B	Pri	F,S	C	1,547																	Open
Kansas																								
Baker University	Baldwin City	R	B,M	Pri	F,S	C	1,015	24	20	32	25	13	10		39	42	17	2		33	47	20		Open
Benedictine College	Atchison	SM	A,B,M	Pri	No	C	1,271	22						517	34	53	12	3	511					Open
Bethany College	Lindsborg	SM	B	Pri	F,S	C	631	21	45	29	19	4	3	450	68	31	1		480	49	42	9		5/1
Bethel College	North Newton	SU	B	Pri	No	C	470	24	28	20	24	13	15	510	44	33	22		540	33	44		22	Open
Emporia State University	Emporia	SM	B,M,D	Pub	F,S	C	4,434	22																Open
Fort Hays State University	Hays	SM	A,B,M	Pub	F,S	C	5,920		47	24	18	6	5											Open
Friends University	Wichita	U	A,B,M	Pri	F,S	C	1,017																	Open
Kansas State University	Manhattan	SU	A,B,M,D	Pub	F,S	C	19,083		23	26	26	11	13											Open
Kansas Wesleyan University	Salina	U	A,B,M	Pri	F,S	C	768	22																Open
McPherson College	McPherson	SM	A,B	Pri	No	C	412																	Open
MidAmerica Nazarene University	Olathe	SU	A,B,M	Pri	No	C	1,411	22	38	21	22	11	8	519	48	30	19	3	507	41	37	22		8/1
Newman University	Wichita	U	A,B,M	Pri	No	C	1,757																	Open
Ottawa University	Ottawa	SM	B	Pri	No	C	475																	Open
Pittsburg State University	Pittsburg	SM	A,B,M	Pub	F,S	C	5,531	22																Open
Southwestern College	Winfield	SM	B,M	Pri	F,S	C	1,218	21	43	23	24	5	5	470	64	27	7	2	480	54	34	10	2	8/1
Sterling College	Sterling	SM	B	Pri	No	C	495	22	47	14	14	9	16	430	76	24			450	81	14	5		Open
Tabor College	Hillsboro	R	A,B	Pri	No	C	522	22	27	31	14	15	14		38	13	25	25			50	25	25	8/1
University of Kansas	Lawrence	SU	B,M,D	Pub	F,S	C	20,866	24	18	28	27	13	14											4/1
University of Saint Mary	Leavenworth	SM	A,B,M	Pri	No	C	580	21	43	35	16	5	1											Open
Washburn University of Topeka	Topeka	U	A,B,M,D	Pub	F,S	C	5,884	21	44	28	17	7	5											8/4
Wichita State University	Wichita	U	A,B,M,D	Pub	F,S	C	11,692	21	42	26	18	8	6											Open
Kentucky																								
Alice Lloyd College	Pippa Passes	R	B	Pri	No	C	617	20	56	26	14	3	1											7/1
Asbury College	Wilmore	R	B,M	Pri	No	C	1,191	24	19	26	24	16	15	588	14	39	33	14	556	29	34	31	6	Open
Bellarmine University	Louisville	SU	B,M	Pri	F,S	C	2,532	24	14	32	33	11	10	560	21	46	31	2	560	26	46	24	4	2/1
Berea College	Berea	SM	B	Pri	No	C	1,560	23	28	31	21	13	7	545	30	41	24	6	540	28	47	24	1	Open
Brescia University	Owensboro	U	A,B,M	Pri	No	C	802																	Open
Campbellsville University	Campbellsville	SM	A,B,M	Pri	No	C	1,703	21	47	30	17	3	3											7/1
Centre College	Danville	SM	B	Pri	F,S	C	1,062	27	2	13	33	20	32	622	3	35	42	20	606	9	35	44	12	2/1
Cumberland College	Williamsburg	SM	B,M	Pri	No	C	1,601	22	38	33	16	7	6	520	36	47	16	1	510	45	40	14	1	Open
Eastern Kentucky University	Richmond	SM	A,B,M	Pub	F,S	C	13,371	20	59	23	13	4	1	490	94	4	2		480	94	4	2		8/1
Georgetown College	Georgetown	SU	B,M	Pri	F,S	C	1,321	25	13	32	32	10	13											
Kentucky Christian College	Grayson	SM	A,B,M	Pri	No	C	578																	Open
Kentucky State University	Frankfort	SM	A,B,M		F,S	C	2,137	17	86	10	3	1	1	418	87	12	2		426	85	10	5		Open
Kentucky Wesleyan College	Owensboro	U	B	Pri	F,S	C	611	21	41	23	26	5	5	967					500		17	17		Open
Lindsey Wilson College	Columbia	SM	A,B,M	Pri	No	C	1,370																	Open
Midway College	Midway	R	A,B	Pri	No	PW	874																	Open
Morehead State University	Morehead	SM	A,B,M	Pub	F,S	C	7,921	20																Open
Murray State University	Murray	SM	A,B,M	Pub	F,S	C	8,385	23	20	30	30	12	8											8/1
Northern Kentucky University	Highland Heights	SU	A,B,M	Pub	F,S	C	10,838																	8/1
Pikeville College	Pikeville	SM	A,B,D	Pri	No	C	762	19	60	21	12	6	1											8/23
Spalding University	Louisville	U	A,B,M,D	Pri	No	C	841	20																Open
Thomas More College	Crestview Hills	SU	A,B,M	Pri	No	C	1,390	21	43	31	18	5	3	530	37	42	21		520	42	31	24	3	8/15
Transylvania University	Lexington	U	B	Pri	F,S	C	1,134	26	6	15	27	23	29	590	15	35	35	15	590	17	33	39	11	2/1
Union College	Barbourville	SM	A,B,M	Pri	No	C	576																	Open
University of Kentucky	Lexington	SU	B,M,D	Pub	F,S	C	6,845																	2/15
University of Louisville	Louisville	U	A,B,M,D	Pub	F,S	C	14,724	23	25	30	23	11	11											Open
Western Kentucky University	Bowling Green	SU	A,B,M	Pub	F,S	C	14,135																	8/1
Louisiana																								
Centenary College of Louisiana	Shreveport	U	B,M	Pri	F,S	C	845	26	10	20	24	24	22	580	16	38	40	6	570	20	39	36	5	2/15
Dillard University	New Orleans	U	B	Pri	F,S	C	2,312																	7/1
Grambling State University	Grambling	SM	A,B,M,D	Pub	F,S	C		16	90	7	3													Open
Louisiana College	Pineville	SM	B	Pri	F,S	C	1,045	23	24	33	28	2	12	490	55	34	10		490	55	17	24	3	Open
Louisiana State University and Agricultural and Mechanical College	Baton Rouge	U	B,M,D	Pub	F,S	C	26,156	24	11	34	29	15	12											4/15
Louisiana State University in Shreveport	Shreveport	U	B,M	Pub	F,S	C	3,655	20	51	30	14	3	2											8/1
Louisiana Tech University	Ruston	SM	A,B,M,D	Pub	F,S	C	9,739		35	31	20	8	6											8/4
Loyola University New Orleans	New Orleans	U	B,M	Pri	F,S	C	3,649	26						617					603					2/15
McNeese State University	Lake Charles	SU	A,B,M	Pub	F,S	C	6,845																	Open

NAME OF SCHOOL	TOWN	ENVIRON-MENT	DEGREES AWARDED	CONTROL	FRAT/SOR	STUDENTS	UNDERGRAD ENROLL FALL 2003	ACT Median	Below 21	21-23	24-26	27-28	Above 28	SAT I VERBAL Median	Below 500	500-599	600-700	Above 700	SAT I MATH Median	Below 500	500-599	600-700	Above 700	APPLICATION DEADLINE Month/Day
Nicholls State University	Thibodaux	SM	A,B,M	Pub	F,S	C	6,524	20	62	24	10	3	1	482	64	24	12		483	56	41	3		Open
Northwestern State University of Louisiana	Natchitoches	SM	A,B,M	Pub	F,S	C	9,351	19	63	21	11	3	2	510	43	38	18	1	490	52	27	20	1	Open
Our Lady of Holy Cross College	New Orleans	U	A,B,M	Pri	No	C	1,269	19																7/20
Southeastern Louisiana University	Hammond	SM	A,B,M	Pub	F,S	C	13,629	20	60	27	10	2	1											7/15
Southern University and A&M College	Baton Rouge	U	A,B,M,D	Pub	F,S	C	7,571	18	86	11	3			425	80	15	5		415	80	15	5		7/1
Southern University at New Orleans	New Orleans	SU	B	Pub	No	C	450																	7/1
Tulane University	New Orleans	U	A,B,M,D	Pri	F,S	C	7,862							659	3	13	52	32	644	2	19	54	25	1/15
University of Louisiana at Lafayette	Lafayette	U	B,M,D	Pub	F,S	C	14,585	21	50	28	14	5	3											Open
University of Louisiana at Monroe	Monroe	U	A,B,M,D	Pub	F,S	C	8,835																	Open
University of New Orleans	New Orleans	U	B,M,D	Pub	F,S	C	13,338	21	50	28	14	5	4	540	35	35	25	5	520	42	34	20	4	7/1
Xavier University of Louisiana	New Orleans	U	B,M,D	Pri	F,S	C	3,145	21	79		20		1	500	47	42	12		495	48	40	11	1	3/1

Maine

NAME OF SCHOOL	TOWN	ENVIRON-MENT	DEGREES AWARDED	CONTROL	FRAT/SOR	STUDENTS	UNDERGRAD ENROLL FALL 2003	ACT Median	Below 21	21-23	24-26	27-28	Above 28	SAT I VERBAL Median	Below 500	500-599	600-700	Above 700	SAT I MATH Median	Below 500	500-599	600-700	Above 700	APPLICATION DEADLINE Month/Day
Bates College	Lewiston	SM	B	Pri	No	C	1,746							670	1	7	63	29	670		6	59	34	1/15
Bowdoin College	Brunswick	SM	B	Pri	No	C	1,647							690	1	7	45	47	680	1	8	51	40	1/1
Colby College	Waterville	SM	B	Pri	No	C	1,768	28		4	18	28	50	670	2	9	64	26	680	1	11	59	29	1/1
College of the Atlantic	Bar Harbor	SM	B,M	Pri	No	C	278	26			38	25	38	628	7	27	55	11	593	18	34	48		2/15
Husson College	Bangor	U	A,B,M	Pri	F,S	C	1,767	22						459	68	28	4		468	66	27	6	1	Open
Maine College of Art	Portland	U	B,M	Pri	No	C	384	20	67	17	17			540	29	45	22	4	505	49	36	14	1	Open
Maine Maritime Academy	Castine	SM	A,B,M	Pub	F	C	760	21						510					540					7/1
Saint Joseph's College of Maine	Standish	R	A,B,M	Pri	No	C	953							500	50	38	12		490	53	36	11		Open
Thomas College	Waterville	R	A,B,M	Pri	F,S	C	698							439					451					Open
Unity College	Unity	R	A,B	Pri	No	C	512							500										Open
University of Maine	Orono	SM	B,M,D	Pub	F,S	C	8,972	24	28	20	23	15	14	530	31	45	21	3	540	28	44	24	4	Open
University of Maine at Augusta	Augusta	SM	A,B	Pub	No	C	5,943							450					430					6/15
University of Maine at Farmington	Farmington	SM	B	Pub	No	C	2,422							535	35	42	20	3	520	38	46	14	2	Open
University of Maine at Fort Kent	Fort Kent	SM	A,B	Pub	F,S	C	924							440					440					Open
University of Maine at Machias	Machias	R	B	Pub	F,S	C	1,313	21	44	33	11	11		460	65	25	9	1	460	66	29	5		Open
University of Maine at Presque Isle	Presque Isle	R	A,B	Pub	F,S	C	1,546							458	68	25	7		453	70	24	5	1	Open
University of New England	Biddeford	R	A,B,M,D	Pri	No	C	1,541							510	43	42	16		510	43	41	16		Open
University of Southern Maine	Gorham	U	A,B,M,D	Pub	F,S	C	8,613		46	23	26	5		515	38	44	17	1	510	42	46	11	1	2/15

Maryland

NAME OF SCHOOL	TOWN	ENVIRON-MENT	DEGREES AWARDED	CONTROL	FRAT/SOR	STUDENTS	UNDERGRAD ENROLL FALL 2003	ACT Median	Below 21	21-23	24-26	27-28	Above 28	SAT I VERBAL Median	Below 500	500-599	600-700	Above 700	SAT I MATH Median	Below 500	500-599	600-700	Above 700	APPLICATION DEADLINE Month/Day
Baltimore Hebrew University	Baltimore	U	B,M,D	Pri	No	C	78																	8/15
Bowie State University	Bowie	SU	B,M,D	Pub	F,S	C	3,988							448	81	17	3		439	82	15	3		4/1
Capitol College	Laurel	R	B,M,D	Pri	No	C	288							500	5	83	10	2	540	7	75	15	3	Open
College of Notre Dame of Maryland	Baltimore	SU	B,M	Pri	No	PW	1,582	18						530	42	40	14	4	510	46	39	14	1	Open
Columbia Union College	Takoma Park	SU	A,B,M	Pri	No	C	1,159	18						445	7	21	7	1	427					5/1
Coppin State College	Baltimore	U	B,M	Pub	F,S	C	3,273	18						435					415					7/15
Frostburg State University	Frostburg	SM	B,M	Pub	F,S	C	4,588		63	19	17		1	450	45	42	12	1	441	43	14	1		Open
Goucher College	Baltimore	SU	B,M	Pri	No	C	1,310							618	7	33	45	15	594	10	38	44	8	2/1
Hood College	Frederick	SU	B,M	Pri	No	C	864	22	44	26	15	8	8	550	29	40	26	5	543	29	45	24	2	2/15
Johns Hopkins University	Baltimore	SU	B,M,D	Pri	F,S	C	4,177	30						675	1	11	50	38	705		6	35	59	1/1
Loyola College in Maryland	Baltimore	U	B,M,D	Pri	No	C	3,413							606	4	44	44	8	617	3	35	53	9	1/15
Maryland Institute College of Art	Baltimore	U	B,M	Pri	No	C	1,296							600	13	36	41	10	560	20	45	31	4	2/15
McDaniel College	Westminster	SU	B,M	Pri	F,S	C	1,742							550	26	46	23	5	560	22	50	25	2	2/1
Morgan State University	Baltimore	SU	B,M,D	Pub	F,S	C	5,800	21						470					490					4/15
Mount Saint Mary's College	Emmitsburg	R	B,M	Pri	No	C	1,594							540	29	44	23	4	540	30	44	23	3	3/1
Saint John's College	Annapolis	SM	B,M	Pri	No	C	480							700					640					Open
Saint Mary's College of Maryland	St. Marys City	R	B	Pub	No	C	1,922							640	4	23	52	20	630	4	29	51	15	1/15
Salisbury University	Salisbury	SM	B,M	Pub	F,S	C	6,199							556	15	59	23	2	578	10	52	35	4	1/15
Sojourner-Douglass College	Baltimore	U	B	Pri	No	C	240																	Open
Towson University	Towson	SU	B,M,D	Pub	F,S	C	13,982							540	25	54	20	2	550	20	53	24	2	5/2
United States Naval Academy	Annapolis	SM	B		No	C	4,200	29						650					670					Open
University of Maryland/Baltimore County	Baltimore	SU	B,M,D	Pub	F,S	C	9,646	25	13	23	32	12	20	590	9	44	38	9	630	3	32	48	17	2/1
University of Maryland/College Park	College Park	SU	B,M,D	Pub	F,S	C	25,446								7	29	45	49		5	15	51	26	1/20
University of Maryland/Eastern Shore	Princess Anne	R	B,M,D	Pub	F,S	C	3,326	18						450					400					Open
University of Maryland/University College	Adelphi	U	A,B,M	Pub	No	C	16,062																	Open
Villa Julie College	Stevenson	SU	A,B,M	Pri	S	C	2,656							519	41	43	15	1	521	38	41	20	1	Open
Washington College	Chestertown	SM	B,M	Pri	F,S	C	1,399	23						578	10	46	37	7	567	14	53	29	4	3/15

Massachusetts

NAME OF SCHOOL	TOWN	ENVIRON-MENT	DEGREES AWARDED	CONTROL	FRAT/SOR	STUDENTS	UNDERGRAD ENROLL FALL 2003	ACT Median	Below 21	21-23	24-26	27-28	Above 28	SAT I VERBAL Median	Below 500	500-599	600-700	Above 700	SAT I MATH Median	Below 500	500-599	600-700	Above 700	APPLICATION DEADLINE Month/Day
American International College	Springfield	U	A,B,M,D	Pri	No	C	1,188							465	62	35	3		455	65	33	2		Open
Amherst College	Amherst	SM	B	Pri	No	C	1,623	32	4	1	10	10	78	720			7	64	720		7	28	65	12/31
Anna Maria College	Paxton	R	A,B,M	Pri	No	C	731	14	100					460	63	31	6		450	69	23	8		3/1
Art Institute of Boston at Lesley University	Boston	U	B,M	Pri	No	C	516							531	32	47	17	4	512	46	41	13		2/15
Assumption College	Worcester	SU	B,M	Pri	No	C	2,123	21	40	30	21	8	1	580	26	53	20	1	540	26	52	21	1	3/1
Atlantic Union College	South Lancaster	SM	A,B,M	Pri	No	C	443	17						430					400					8/1
Babson College	Babson Park	SU	B,M	Pri	F,S	C	1,717							604	2	43	47	7	648		17	64	19	2/1
Bay Path College	Longmeadow	SU	A,B,M	Pri	No	W	1,242							510	43	46	11		490	55	38	8		Open
Becker College	Worcester	U	A,B	Pri	No	C	1,474		86		14			443	76	22	2		433	81	18	1		Open
Benjamin Franklin Institute of Technology	Boston	U	A,B	Pri	No	C	388																	8/15
Bentley College	Waltham	SU	A,B,M	Pri	F,S	C	4,304							560	13	52	34	1	600	3	35	54	9	2/1
Berklee College of Music	Boston	U	B,M	Pri	No	C	3,799																	Open
Boston Architectural Center	Boston	U	B,M	Pri	No	C	490																	Open
Boston College	Chestnut Hill	SU	B,M,D	Pri	No	C	9,000																	1/2
Boston Conservatory	Boston	U	B	Pri	F,S	C	365																	Open

NAME OF SCHOOL	TOWN	ENVIRONMENT	DEGREES AWARDED	CONTROL	FRATERNITIES AND SORORITIES	STUDENTS	UNDERGRADUATE ENROLLMENT FALL 2003	ACT Median	ACT Below 21	ACT 21-23	ACT 24-26	ACT 27-28	ACT Above 28	SAT I VERBAL Median	SAT I VERBAL Below 500	SAT I VERBAL 500-599	SAT I VERBAL 600-700	SAT I VERBAL Above 700	SAT I MATH Median	SAT I MATH Below 500	SAT I MATH 500-599	SAT I MATH 600-700	SAT I MATH Above 700	APPLICATION DEADLINE Month / Day
Boston University	Boston	U	B,M,D	Pri	F,S	C	17,683	28		3	23	28	46	640		22	62	16	650		15	64	21	1/1
Brandeis University	Waltham	SU	B,M,D	Pri	No	C	3,175							670	1	13	54	33	675	2	15	52	30	1/31
Bridgewater State College	Bridgewater	SU	B,M	Pub	F,S	C	7,597	21	44	38	14		4	520	37	52	10	1	520	36	51	12	1	2/15
Cambridge College	Cambridge	U	B,M	Pri	No	C	893																	2/1
Clark University	Worcester	U	B,M,D	Pri	No	C	2,190	25	20	18	30	15	17	600	10	36	44	10	590	12	39	40	9	2/1
College of Our Lady of the Elms	Chicopee	SU	A,B,M	Pri	No	C	630																	Open
College of the Holy Cross	Worcester	SU	B	Pri	No	C	2,773							633	2	27	52	19	637	2	19	65	14	1/15
Curry College	Milton	SU	B,M	Pri	No	C	2,315																	
Eastern Nazarene College	Quincy	SU	A,B,M	Pri	No	C	640																	
Emerson College	Boston	U	B,M,D	Pri	F,S	C	3,401	26	3	18	31	28	20	621	2	34	51	13	592	6	48	40	6	1/15
Emmanuel College	Boston	U	B,M	Pri	No	C	1,592	24						510	32	46	20	2	490	43	40	16	1	
Endicott College	Beverly	SU	A,B,M	Pri	No	C	1,709							519	37	54	9		527	29	59	12		2/15
Fisher College	Boston	U	A,B	Pri	No	C	534																	Open
Fitchburg State College	Fitchburg	SU	B,M	Pub	F,S	C	3,379							490	48	44	7	1	490	52	38	10		4/1
Framingham State College	Framingham	SU	B,M	Pub	No	C	3,892							533	31	53	15	1	525	33	52	14	1	2/15
Gordon College	Wenham	SM	B,M	Pri	No	C	1,640	27						610	4	36	48	12	600					3/1
Hampshire College	Amherst	R	B	Pri	No	C	1,332	27	2	10	31	24	33	650	2	20	50	28	600	8	36	45	11	2/1
Harvard University/Harvard College	Cambridge	U	B,M,D	Pri	No	C	6,647																	1/1
Hellenic College/Holy Cross Greek Orthodox School of Theology	Brookline	U	B,M	Pri	No		92																	5/1
Lasell College	Newton	SU	B,M	Pri	No	C	1,083	20						480	57	36	7		470	58	35	7		Open
Lesley University	Cambridge	U	A,B,M,D	Pri	No	PW	516							520	29	54	14	3	520	42	47	11		3/1
Massachusetts College of Art	Boston	U	B,M	Pub	No	C	1,473							560	19	50	26	5	530	29	50	19	2	2/15
Massachusetts College of Liberal Arts	North Adams	R	B,M	Pub	F,S	C	1,395																	Open
Massachusetts College of Pharmacy and Health Sciences	Boston	U	A,B,M,D	Pri	F,S	C	1,523	21	10	75	15			496	52	38	10		545	21	55	21	3	2/1
Massachusetts Institute of Technology	Cambridge	U	B,M,D	Pri	F,S	C	4,112	32	1	1	8	8	82	710	1	4	32	63	770			11	89	1/1
Massachusetts Maritime Academy	Buzzards Bay	SM	B,M	Pub	No	C	904							510	48	42	9	1	540	36	47	16	1	Open
Merrimack College	North Andover	SU	A,B,M	Pri	F,S	C	2,389	21	38	34	22	4	2	540	20	64	16		540	10	69	19	2	2/1
Montserrat College of Art	Beverly	SU	B	Pri	No	C	383	19	66		34			530	38	38	21	3	483	54	33	12	1	Open
Mount Holyoke College	South Hadley	SM	B,M	Pri	No	W	2,148	29		5	17	26	52	660	1	13	58	28	630	1	25	60	14	1/15
Mount Ida College	Newton	SU	A,B	Pri	No	C	1,076							450	77	21	4		435	76	20	4		Open
New England Conservatory of Music	Boston	U	B,M,D	Pri	No	C	395																	12/1
Newbury College	Brookline	SU	A,B	Pri	No	C	2,000	20																3/1
Nichols College	Dudley	R	A,B,M	Pri	No	C	1,327							460	76	23	1		450	70	27	3		Open
Northeastern University	Boston	U	A,B,M,D	Pri	F,S	C	14,492							590	9	41	43	6	611	6	31	52	11	2/15
Pine Manor College	Chestnut Hill	SU	A,B	Pri	No	W	487	16	90	5	5			420	80	16	4		400	95	4	1		Open
Regis College	Weston	SU	A,B,M	Pri	No	W	800							500	50	39	10	1	480	55	35	10		
Salem State College	Salem	U	B,M	Pub	No	C	6,508							490	52	38	9	1	480	56	36	7	1	Open
Simmons College	Boston	U	B,M,D	Pri	No	PW	1,555	24						558	21	47	26	5	539	26	55	18	1	2/1
Simon's Rock College of Bard	Great Barrington	SM	A,B	Pri	No	C	399	27		30		50	20	650	5	20	50	25	620	14	30	33	23	
Smith College	Northampton	SM	B,M,D	Pri	No	W	2,665	28	7	9	21	21	41	660					640					1/15
Springfield College	Springfield	SU	B,M,D	Pri	No	C	2,182																	4/1
Stonehill College	Easton	SU	B,M	Pri	No	C	2,567	25						590	6	45	45	3	600	4	42	50	4	1/15
Suffolk University	Boston	U	A,B,M,D	Pri	No	C	4,281	20	51	30	15	4		570	44	42	14	1	500	46	41	12	1	Open
Tufts University	Medford	SU	B,M,D	Pri	F,S	C	4,892	29	1	7	11	24	57	660	2	16	51	31	680	1	11	44	44	1/1
University of Massachusetts Amherst	Amherst	SM	A,B,M,D	Pub	F,S	C	18,718							560	20	47	28	5	570	15	46	32	7	1/15
University of Massachusetts Boston	Boston	U	B,M,D	Pub	No	C	10,071							520	48	35	15	2	520	43	38	16	3	1/1
University of Massachusetts Dartmouth	North Dartmouth	SU	B,M,D	Pub	F,S	C	7,359							530	30	52	17	1	540	27	54	17	2	Open
University of Massachusetts Lowell	Lowell	U	A,B,M,D	Pub	No	C	9,006							537	29	50	18	3	556	18	53	26	3	Open
Wellesley College	Wellesley	SU	B	Pri	No	W		29						678	1	11	43	45	673	1	12	46	41	1/15
Wentworth Institute of Technology	Boston	U	A,B	Pri	No	C	3,235							514	41	44	14	1	553	22	50	25	3	5/1
Western New England College	Springfield	SU	A,B,M	Pri	No	C	3,368							520	36	49	14	1	540	30	46	22	2	Open
Westfield State College	Westfield	R	B,M	Pub	No	C	4,292							520	40	50	9	1	510	42	50	9		3/1
Wheaton College	Norton	SU	B	Pri	No	C	1,565	25		9	44	22	25	620	3	34	52	11	610	3	41	50	6	1/15
Wheelock College	Boston	U	A,B,M	Pri	No	C	587							523	37	45	14	4	483	42	42	15		3/1
Williams College	Williamstown	SM	B,M	Pri	No	C	2,120																	
Worcester Polytechnic Institute	Worcester	SU	B,M,D	Pri	F,S	C	2,773	27	3	13	30	22	32	610	4	35	49	11	660		13	58	28	2/1
Worcester State College	Worcester	U	B,M	Pub		C	4,669																	Open

Michigan

NAME OF SCHOOL	TOWN	ENVIRONMENT	DEGREES AWARDED	CONTROL	FRATERNITIES AND SORORITIES	STUDENTS	UNDERGRADUATE ENROLLMENT FALL 2003	ACT Median	ACT Below 21	ACT 21-23	ACT 24-26	ACT 27-28	ACT Above 28	SAT I VERBAL Median	SAT I VERBAL Below 500	SAT I VERBAL 500-599	SAT I VERBAL 600-700	SAT I VERBAL Above 700	SAT I MATH Median	SAT I MATH Below 500	SAT I MATH 500-599	SAT I MATH 600-700	SAT I MATH Above 700	APPLICATION DEADLINE Month / Day
Adrian College	Adrian	SU	A,B	Pri	F,S	C	1,028	22	46	25	20	7	2											3/15
Albion College	Albion	SM	B	Pri	F,S	C	1,548																	
Alma College	Alma	SM	B	Pri	F,S	C	1,291	25	15	25	29	14	17											
Andrews University	Berrien Springs	R	A,B,M,D	Pri	F,S	C	1,687	23	24	23	23	9	11	530	37	36	20	7	530	48	34	11	7	Open
Aquinas College	Grand Rapids	SU	A,B,M	Pri	No	C	1,828	23	31	23	27	10	9											Open
Baker College of Flint	Flint	U	A,B	Pri	No	C	4,399																	Open
Calvin College	Grand Rapids	SU	B,M	Pri	No	C	4,282	26	6	21	30	18	25	610	8	34	40	18	610	8	38	41	13	8/15
Central Michigan University	Mount Pleasant	SM	B,M,D	Pub	F,S	C	19,642	22	36	31	22	7	4	524	41	34	22	3	525	38	43	21	3	Open
Cleary College	Ann Arbor	SU	A,B	Pri	No	C	655																	Open
College for Creative Studies	Detroit	U	B	Pri	No	C	1,218	21																8/1
Concordia University	Ann Arbor	SU	A,B,M	Pri	No	C	438	22	33	26	4	10	10	550	24	38	38		530	31	54	15		Open
Cornerstone University and Grand Rapids Theological Seminary	Grand Rapids	SU	A,B,M	Pri	No	C	2,071	23	30	29	20	11	10	540	33	44	16	7	520	44	33	16	7	Open
Davenport University	Grand Rapids	U	A,B,M	Pri	No	C	12,716																	9
Eastern Michigan University	Ypsilanti	SU	B,M,D	Pub	F,S	C	19,577	20	52	24	16	4	3	510					510	45	35	16	3	7/31
Ferris State University	Big Rapids	SM	A,B,M	Pub	F,S	C	10,768	21	53	24	15	5	3											8/1
Grace Bible College	Grand Rapids	SU	A,B	Pri	No	C	153	21	43	29	16	4	8	555	25	25	50		522	50		50		Open
Grand Valley State University	Allendale	SM	B,M	Pub	F,S	C	17,807	23	19	34	28	10	9											7/31
Hillsdale College	Hillsdale	SM	B	Pri	F,S	C	1,230	27	4	18	28	19	31	640	3	26	46	25	610	7	31	48	14	6/15
Hope College	Holland	SU	B	Pri	F,S	C	3,068	25		2	31	50	17	588	12	39	35	13	597	11	37	38	13	Open

TEST SCORES

NAME OF SCHOOL	TOWN	ENVIRONMENT	DEGREES AWARDED	CONTROL	FRATERNITIES AND SORORITIES	STUDENTS	UNDERGRADUATE ENROLLMENT FALL 2003	ACT Median	ACT Below 21	ACT 21-23	ACT 24-26	ACT 27-28	ACT Above 28	SAT I VERBAL Median	Below 500	500-599	600-700	Above 700	SAT I MATH Median	Below 500	500-599	600-700	Above 700	APPLICATION DEADLINE Month/Day
Kalamazoo College	Kalamazoo	SU	B	Pri	No	C	1,384																	2/15
Kendall College of Art and Design of Ferris State University	Grand Rapids	U	B	Pub	No	C	906																	Open
Kettering University	Flint	SU	B	Pri	No	C	2,525	26	7	19	30	22	22	590	10	43	39	8	640		22	56	22	Open
Lake Superior State University	Sault Sainte Marie	SM	A,B,M	Pub	F,S	C	3,200																	Open
Lawrence Technological University	Southfield	SU	A,B,M	Pri	No	C	2,953	23	29	23	27	12	9	500	45	27	21	7	580	25	34	25	16	Open
Madonna University	Livonia	SU	A,B,M	Pri	No	C	3,043																	Open
Marygrove College	Detroit	U	A,B,M	Pri	No	C	858	19	95	5														8/15
Michigan State University	East Lansing	SU	B,M,D		F,S	C	34,853	24	14	26	32	14	14	560	24	40	30	6	580	17	37	37	9	7/25
Michigan Technological University	Houghton	SM	A,B,M,D	Pub	F,S	C	5,765	25	11	20	31	18	20	575	16	42	33	9	615	8	30	50	12	Open
Northern Michigan University	Marquette	U	A,B,M	Pub	F,S	C	7,483	23	38	21	19	7	5											Open
Northwood University	Midland	SU	A,B,M	Pri	No	C	1,757	20	55	23	16	4	2	470	81	15	4		480	57	32	11		8/1
Oakland University	Rochester	SU	B,M,D	Pub	F,S	C	12,959	21	44	27	18	7	4											Open
Olivet College	Olivet	SM	B,M	Pri	F,S	C	1,042	19	25	40	15	15	5											Open
Rochester College	Rochester Hills	SU	A,B	Pri	No	C	1,001	21	48	27	14	4	7	500	50	25	25		510	50	33	17		Open
Saginaw Valley State University	University Center	SU	B,M	Pub	F,S	C	7,580	21																Open
Saint Mary's College	Orchard Lake	SU	B	Pri	No	C	345																	
Siena Heights University	Adrian	SM	A,B,M	Pri	F,S	C	966																	Open
Spring Arbor University	Spring Arbor	SM	A,B,M	Pri	No	C	1,453	23	29	28	26	13	4											Open
University of Detroit Mercy	Detroit	U	A,B,M,D	Pri	F,S	C	3,383	21	37	29	18	11	5											
University of Michigan/Ann Arbor	Ann Arbor	SU	B,M,D	Pub	F,S	C	24,517	28	3					630	5	25	50	20	670	3	13	45	39	2/1
University of Michigan/Dearborn	Dearborn	SU	B,M	Pub	No	C	6,359																	Open
University of Michigan/Flint	Flint	U	B,M	Pub	F,S	C	5,578	21	42	29	18	7	4		22	45	33				22	33	45	9/15
Wayne State University	Detroit	U	B,M,D	Pub	F,S	C	20,148	20																8/1
Western Michigan University	Kalamazoo	U	B,M,D	Pub	F,S	C	23,309	22	36	31	21	8	5											Open
William Tyndale College	Farmington Hills	SU	A,B	Pri	No	C	290	23	33	33	17		17											Open

Minnesota

NAME OF SCHOOL	TOWN	ENV	DEGREES	CONTROL	FRAT/SOR	STUDENTS	ENROLL	ACT Median	Below 21	21-23	24-26	27-28	Above 28	SATV Median	Below 500	500-599	600-700	Above 700	SATM Median	Below 500	500-599	600-700	Above 700	DEADLINE
Augsburg College	Minneapolis	U	B,M	Pri	No	C	2,861	23	27	30	24	10	9	541	18	42	35	5	542	15	55	25	5	5/1
Bemidji State University	Bemidji	SM	A,B,M	Pub	F,S	C	4,672	22	27	47	20	6	*											Open
Bethel College	St. Paul	SU	A,B,M	Pri	No	C	2,911	24	18	28	24	15	15	585	20	37	26	17	585	16	35	38	11	12/1
Carleton College	Northfield	SM	B	Pri	No	C	1,946								1	9	39	52			8	48	43	1/15
College of Saint Benedict	St. Joseph	SM	B	Pri	No	W	2,054	25	11	26	35	13	15	560	23	39	34	4	570	20	41	36	3	Open
College of Saint Catherine	St. Paul	U	A,B,M	Pri	S	W	3,681	23	23	30	26	13	8	605	13	28	50	9	590	25	28	25	22	Open
College of Saint Scholastica	Duluth	SU	B,M	Pri	No	C	2,308	24						560	21	46	29	4	560	29	42	25	4	Open
College of Visual Arts	St. Paul	U	B	Pri	No	C	218																	5/1
Concordia College: Moorhead	Moorhead	U	B	Pri	No	C	2,856	24	21	25	28	13	12	580	16	42	36	5	660	19	45	33	4	Open
Concordia University/St.Paul	St. Paul	U	A,B,M	Pri	No	C	1,741	21	47	23	17	6	7											8/1
Gustavus Adolphus College	St. Peter	SM	B	Pri	F,S	C	2,574	25	16	21	26	13	24	610	10	32	41	17	620	6	31	49	14	4/1
Hamline University	St. Paul	U	B,M,D	Pri	S	C	1,980	24						598					589					5/1
Macalester College	St. Paul	U	B	Pri	No	C	1,884	30		1	13	23	62	687		9	40	51	662		13	57	30	1/15
Metropolitan State University	St. Paul	U	B,M	Pub	No	C	5,940																	7/23
Minneapolis College of Art and Design	Minneapolis	U	B,M	Pri	No	C	601	23	20	40	30	7	3	550	20	40	30	10	525	30	35	25	10	2/15
Minnesota State University, Mankato	Mankato	R	A,B,M	Pub	F,S	C	12,388	21	40	36	18	5	2											
Minnesota State University, Moorhead	Moorhead	SU	A,B,M	Pub	F,S	C	5,900																	
North Central University	Minneapolis	U	A,B	Pri	No	C	1,230	22	25	50	10	10	5	500	25	50	25		500	25	50	25		6/1
Northwestern College	St. Paul	SU	A,B	Pri	No	C	1,715	23	23	28	26	13	10	575	26	26	29	19	560	24	38	36	2	8/1
Saint Cloud State University	St. Cloud	SU	A,B,M,D	Pub	F,S	C	14,483	21	43	29	19	6	3											Open
Saint John's University	Collegeville	R	B,M	Pri	No	M	1,940	25	9	27	33	11	20	585	10	45	40	5	605	11	36	43	10	2/15
Saint Mary's University of Minnesota	Winona	SM	B,M,D	Pri	F,S	C	1,357	23	25	29	28	11	7	549	22	49	24	5	557	27	41	29	2	5/1
Saint Olaf College	Northfield	SM	B	Pri	No	C	2,994	27						636	5	25	44	26	635	5	23	51	21	2/1
Southwest Minnesota State University	Marshall	R	A,B,M	Pub	No	C	4,200	22	41	29	18	5	4											8/15
University of Minnesota/Crookston	Crookston	R	B	Pub	No	C	2,170																	Open
University of Minnesota/Duluth	Duluth	SU	B,M	Pub	F,S	C	9,380	23	15	45	24	13	3											8/1
University of Minnesota/Morris	Morris	SM	B	Pub	No	C	1,861	25	10	25	36	15	14	600	15	35	35	15	600	12	35	40	13	2/1
University of Minnesota/Twin Cities	Minneapolis	U	B,M,D	Pub	F,S	C	32,474	25	15	19	29	17	20	596	14	30	44	12	616	12	28	44	19	12/15
University of Saint Thomas	St. Paul	U	B,M,D	Pri	No	C	5,243	24	12	32	32	12	12	570	15	47	27	10	580	11	46	34	9	Open
Winona State University	Winona	SM	A,B,M	Pub	F,S	C	7,536	23																12/1

Mississippi

NAME OF SCHOOL	TOWN	ENV	DEGREES	CONTROL	FRAT/SOR	STUDENTS	ENROLL	ACT Median	Below 21	21-23	24-26	27-28	Above 28	SATV Median	Below 500	500-599	600-700	Above 700	SATM Median	Below 500	500-599	600-700	Above 700	DEADLINE
Alcorn State University	Alcorn State	R	A,B,M	Pub	F,S	C	2,662		79	15	5	1												Open
Belhaven College	Jackson	U	A,B,M	Pri	No	C	1,666																	Open
Blue Mountain College	Blue Mountain	R	B	Pri	No	PW	431	21	58	21	13	2	6											Open
Delta State University	Cleveland	SM	B,M,D	Pub	F,S	C	3,156	20	63	21	8	4	4											8/1
Jackson State University	Jackson	U	B,M,D	Pub	F,S	C	6,292	18	78	14	7	1												Open
Millsaps College	Jackson	U	B,M	Pri	F,S	C	1,123	25	7	25	31	16	23	590	7	45	38	10	570	20	42	28	10	6/1
Mississippi College	Clinton	SU	B,M	Pri	No	C	2,289																	Open
Mississippi State University	Mississippi State	SM	B,M,D	Pub	F,S	C	12,858	22	37	22	17	10	14											8/1
Mississippi University for Women	Columbus	SM	A,B,M	Pub	F,S	C	3,200																	Open
Mississippi Valley State University	Itta Bena	SM	B,M	Pub	F,S	C	3,289	18	88	11	1													8/10
Rust College	Holly Springs	SM	A,B	Pri	F,S	C	988	16	81	18	1													7/15
Tougaloo College	Tougaloo	SU	A,B	Pri	F,S	C	940																	Open
University of Mississippi	University	SM	B,M,D	Pub	F,S	C	9,891																	4/1
University of Southern Mississippi	Hattiesburg	SU	B,M,D	Pub	F,S	C	12,371																	
William Carey College	Hattiesburg	SM	B,M	Pri	F,S	C	1,850																	

Legend:
- **ENVIRONMENT:** U-Urban R-Rural SU-Suburban SM-Small Town
- **DEGREES AWARDED:** A-Associate B-Bachelor M-Master D-Doctorate
- **CONTROL:** Pri-Private Pub-Public
- **FRATERNITIES AND SORORITIES:** F-Fraternities S-Sororities F,S-Both No-Neither
- **STUDENTS:** C-Coed M-Men W-Women PM-Primary Men PW-Primary Women
- **UNDERGRADUATE ENROLLMENT FALL 2003**
- **APPLICATION DEADLINE Month/Day**

NAME OF SCHOOL	TOWN	ENV	DEGREES	CONTROL	FRAT/SOR	STUDENTS	ENROLL. 2003	ACT Median	ACT Below 21	ACT 21-23	ACT 24-26	ACT 27-28	ACT Above 28	SAT V Median	SAT V Below 500	SAT V 500-599	SAT V 600-700	SAT V Above 700	SAT M Median	SAT M Below 500	SAT M 500-599	SAT M 600-700	SAT M Above 700	APP. DEADLINE
Missouri																								
Avila University	Kansas City	SU	B,M	Pri	No	C	1,260	21						530					530					Open
Central Methodist College	Fayette	SM	A,B	Pri	No	C	831																	Open
Central Missouri State University	Warrensburg	SM	A,B,M	Pub	F,S	C	8,707	22	41	31	15	7	6											
College of the Ozarks	Point Lookout	SM	B	Pri	No	C	1,348	22	37	29	19	10	4											2/1
Columbia College	Columbia	SM	A,B,M	Pri	No	C	922	22	37	25	20	10	8											Open
Culver-Stockton College	Canton	R	B	Pri	F,S	C	835	21	44	25	22	4	4											Open
Deaconess College of Nursing	St. Louis	U	A,B	Pri	No	C		21	70	30														Open
DeVry University/Kansas City	Kansas City	U	A,B	Pri	No	C	1,927																	Open
Drury University	Springfield	U	B,M	Pri	F,S	C	1,566	26	9	24	28	13	25	591	12	43	26	19	614	5	29	52	14	8/1
Evangel University	Springfield	U	A,B,M	Pri	No	C	1,689	21	3	51	24	17	5											
Fontbonne University	St. Louis	SU	B,M	Pri	F	C	1,767	21	51	27	14	5	3											8/1
Hannibal-LaGrange College	Hannibal	SM	A,B	Pri	No	C	1,133	22	45	21		5	7											8/29
Harris-Stowe State College	St. Louis	U	B	Pub	F,S	C	1,247	18	76	22			2											Open
Jewish Hospital College of Nursing and Allied Health	St. Louis	U	A,B,M	Pri	No	C	686																	Open
Kansas City Art Institute	Kansas City	U	B	Pri	No	C	572	22	34	34	17	8	7	547	30	38	25	7	516	40	39	18	3	
Lester L. Cox College of Nursing and Health Sciences	Springfield	U	A,B	Pri	No	C	525	22	94	5	1													2/1
Lincoln University	Jefferson City	SM	A,B,M		F,S	C	3,075																	7/15
Lindenwood University	St. Charles	SU	A,B,M	Pri	F,S	C	4,923	23	22	49	15	9	5											Open
Maryville University of Saint Louis	St. Louis	SU	B,M	Pri	No	C	2,705	24	22	28	31	10	9											
Missouri Baptist University	St. Louis	SU	A,B,M	Pri	No	C	2,947	21	46	20	21	8	5											Open
Missouri Southern State University	Joplin	SM	A,B	Pub	F,S	C	5,410	22	50	18	18	7	7											8/21
Missouri Valley College	Marshall	SM	A,B	Pub	F,S	C	1,565	20																Open
Missouri Western State College	St. Joseph	SU	A,B	Pub	F,S	C	4,928	19	65	21	9	4	1											7/25
Northwest Missouri State University	Maryville	R	B,M	Pub	F,S	C	5,650																	Open
Park University	Parkville	SU	A,B,M	Pri	No	C	12,703	20	52	26	12	7	2											8/15
Research College of Nursing	Kansas City	U	B,M	Pri	F,S	C	177	22	23	46	31													6/30
Rockhurst University	Kansas City	U	B,M,D	Pri	F,S	C	1,958	24	21	23	25	15	16	580	20	33	33	14	580	20	42	24	14	6/30
Saint Louis University	St. Louis	U	A,B,M,D	Pri	F,S	C	7,091	26	7	17	29	20	27											12/1
Southeast Missouri State University	Cape Girardeau	SM	A,B,M	Pub	F,S	C	8,483	22	36	29	21	9	6											Open
Southwest Baptist University	Bolivar	R	A,B,M	Pri	No	C	2,746	23	30	20	18	12	20	520	33	50	14	3	540	40	38	17	5	Open
Southwest Missouri State University	Springfield	SU	B,M	Pub	F,S	C	14,550	23	23	31	24	10	13											
Stephens College	Columbia	U	A,B,M	Pri	S	W	577	24	16	31	37	10	6	580	12	54	32	2	530	29	49	22	2	Open
Truman State University	Kirksville	SM	B,M	Pub	F,S	C	5,479	27	4	11	29	19	39	670	5	36	41	18	650	7	34	47	12	3/1
University of Missouri/Columbia	Columbia	SM	B,M,D	Pub	F,S	C	20,441	25	8	25	30	17	21											5/1
University of Missouri/Kansas City	Kansas City	U	B,M,D	Pub	F,S	C	9,167	24	25	22	24	12	16		19	29	40	11		11	38	36	15	Open
University of Missouri/Rolla	Rolla	SM	B,M,D	Pub	F,S	C	4,089	27	5	11	25	20	39											7/1
University of Missouri/St. Louis	St. Louis	U	B,M,D	Pub	F,S	C	12,630		4	52	35	3	6		33	36	26	5		31	40	24	5	7/1
Washington University in St. Louis	St. Louis	SU	B,M,D	Pri	F,S	C	7,188			1	5	11	83			6	47	47			2	38	60	1/15
Webster University	St. Louis	SU	B,M,D	Pri	No	C	5,072	24	21	28	23	15	13	610	11	35	45	9	560	25	40	28	7	3/1
Westminster College	Fulton	SM	B	Pri	F,S	C	823	24	19	32	30	9	10	530	30	34	32	5	530	30	41	23	7	
William Jewell College	Liberty	SU	B	Pri	F,S	C	1,313	25	2	45	43			580	20	33	37	10	580	10	40	35	15	3/15
William Woods University	Fulton	SM	A,B,M	Pri	F,S	C	991	22						508					483					Open
Montana																								
Carroll College	Helena	SM	A,B	Pri	No	C	1,469		2	43	46		9		26	47	20	7		24	53	19	4	6/1
Montana State University-Billings	Billings	U	A,B,M	Pub	No	C	4,139	21	57	20	15	5	3	505	43	42	11	4	514	44	35	15	6	Open
Montana State University-Bozeman	Bozeman	SM	B,M,D	Pub	F,S	C	10,750	23	28	26	26	12	8	544	31	45	22	2	559	24	42	28	6	Open
Montana State University-Northern	Havre	SM	A,B,M	Pub	No	C	1,490																	Open
Montana Tech of The University of Montana	Butte	SM	A,B,M	Pub	No	C	2,142	22	33	30	18	14	4	530	34	46	19	1	549	26	46	23	6	Open
Rocky Mountain College	Billings	SM	A,B,M	Pri	No	C	919	22	36	29	20	9	5	539	27	51	19	4	525	30	55	14	1	8/1
University of Great Falls	Great Falls	U	A,B,M	Pri	No	C	756																	8/1
University of Montana	Missoula	U	A,B,M,D	Pub	F,S	C	10,859																	7/1
University of Montana—Western	Dillon	SM	A,B	Pub	No	C	1,046	19	68	24	6	1	1	470	59	39	2		472	66	32	2		7/1
Nebraska																								
Bellevue University	Bellevue	SU	B,M	Pri	No	C	3,666																	Open
Chadron State College	Chadron	SM	B,M	Pub	No	C	2,294	21	46	25	17	11	1	440	57	14	29		480	57	14	29		Open
Clarkson College	Omaha	U	A,B,M	Pri	No	PW	362																	Open
College of Saint Mary	Omaha	SU	A,B	Pri	No	PW	892	22																Open
Concordia University Nebraska	Seward	SM	B,M	Pri	No	C	1,202	24						543	29	48	14	10	541	36	33	21	10	8/1
Creighton University	Omaha	U	A,B,M,D	Pri	F,S	C	3,736	26	8	22	26	20	24	590	15	38	37	10	600	11	37	42	10	8/1
Dana College	Blair	SM	B	Pri	No	C	581	22	51	25	21	3	2	490	28	41	18	12	505	40	41	18		8/1
Doane College	Crete	SM	A,B	Pri	F,S	C	1,017	23																8/15
Hastings College	Hastings	R	B,M	Pri	F,S	C	1,074	23	13	29	26	18	14		15	40	25	18		19	37	24	20	8/1
Midland Lutheran College	Fremont	SM	A,B	Pri	F,S	C	991																	7/15
Nebraska Methodist College of Nursing and Allied Health	Omaha	U	A,B,M	Pri	No	C	390	20	50	35	10	5												3/1
Nebraska Wesleyan University	Lincoln	SU	B,M	Pri	F,S	C	1,687	24	15	27	32	15	11											5/1
Peru State College	Peru	R	B,M	Pub	No	C	1,450																	Open
Union College	Lincoln	SU	A,B	Pri	No	C	903	21	40	30	17	8	5											Open
University of Nebraska at Kearney	Kearney	SM	B,M	Pub	F,S	C	6,113																	Open
University of Nebraska at Lincoln	Lincoln	U	A,B,M,D	Pub	F,S	C	17,851	24	19	44	25		13	583	18	38	31	13	596	16	33	35	16	6/30
University of Nebraska at Omaha	Omaha	SU	B,M,D	Pub	F,S	C	11,102	23	31	27	24	10	8											8/1
Wayne State College	Wayne	R	B,M	Pub	F,S	C	2,769	21	49	22	20	6	3											Open
York College	York	SM	A,B	Pri	F,S	C	461	22	34	34	19	6	7	509	42	48	5	5	521	26	48	26		Open

Column legend:
- **ENVIRONMENT:** U-Urban R-Rural SU-Suburban SM-Small Town
- **DEGREES AWARDED:** A-Associate B-Bachelor M-Master D-Doctorate
- **CONTROL:** Pri-Private Pub-Public
- **FRATERNITIES AND SORORITIES:** F-Fraternities S-Sororities F,S-Both No-Neither
- **STUDENTS:** C-Coed M-Men PM-Primarily Men W-Women PW-Primarily Women
- **TEST SCORES:** ACT / SAT I Verbal Reasoning / SAT I Mathematical Reasoning
- **APPLICATION DEADLINE:** Month / Day

Name of School	Town	Env.	Degrees	Control	Frat./Sor.	Students	Undergrad Enroll. Fall 2003	ACT Med	ACT <21	ACT 21-23	ACT 24-26	ACT 27-28	ACT >28	SAT V Med	SAT V <500	SAT V 500-599	SAT V 600-700	SAT V >700	SAT M Med	SAT M <500	SAT M 500-599	SAT M 600-700	SAT M >700	App. Deadline
Nevada																								
Sierra Nevada College	Incline Village	R	B	Pri	No	C	293	23						524					518					2/15
University of Nevada/Las Vegas	Las Vegas	U	B,M,D	Pub	F,S	C	20,680	21	47	27	17	6	3	505	45	42	13	1	515	41	40	17	2	4/2
University of Nevada/Reno	Reno	U	B,M,D	Pub	F,S	C	12,118	22	31	30	22	9	3	524	37	44	18	2	531	34	43	20	2	3/1
New Hampshire																								
Colby-Sawyer College	New London	SM	A,B	Pri	No	C	901																	Open
College for Lifelong Learning	Concord	SM	A,B	Pub	No	C	2,200																	Open
Daniel Webster College	Nashua	SU	A,B	Pri	No	C	578																	Open
Dartmouth College	Hanover	R	B,M,D	Pri	F,S	C	4,079							710	1	8	32	59	720	1	5	28	66	1/1
Franklin Pierce College	Rindge	R	B,M	Pri	No	C	1,578							510	45	43	11	1	490	52	37	11		Open
Hesser College	Manchester		A,B	Pri	No	C	819																	
Keene State College	Keene	SU	A,B,M	Pub	F,S	C	4,756	19	66	30	2		3	504	48	41	10	1	499	49	42	9	1	4/1
New England College	Henniker	SM	A,B,M	Pri	F,S	C	878							460	62	30	6	2	450	70	22	7	1	Open
Plymouth State University	Plymouth	SM	B,M	Pub	F,S	C	3,967	18	68	18	14			480	58	36	6	4	480	58	35	7	4	4/1
Rivier College	Nashua	SU	A,B,M	Pri	No	C	1,452							492	50	35	15		478	50	35	15		Open
Saint Anselm College	Manchester	SU	B	Pri	No	C	2,008							560	18	54	26	2	560	17	57	24	2	3/1
Southern New Hampshire University	Manchester	SU	A,B,M,D	Pri	F,S	C	4,227							482	66	30	4		485	59	33	8		3/15
Thomas More College of Liberal Arts	Merrimack	SU	B	Pri	No	C	69																	Open
University of New Hampshire	Durham	R	A,B,M,D		F,S	C	10,937							550	22	52	23	3	560	19	48	29	4	2/1
New Jersey																								
Bloomfield College	Bloomfield	SU	B	Pri	F,S	C	2,075							430	84	13	3		430	82	15	3		3/14
Caldwell College	Caldwell	SU	B,M	Pri	No	C	1,836							440	69	27	4		450	73	23	4	1	Open
Centenary College	Hackettstown	SU	A,B,M	Pri	F,S	C	1,759	20	100					465	70	22	8		462	65	30	4	1	Open
College of New Jersey, The	Ewing	SU	B,M	Pub	F,S	C	5,938							620	7	31	52	10	650	4	18	58	20	2/15
College of Saint Elizabeth	Morristown	SU	B,M	Pri	No	PW	1,276							470	64	30	5	1	470	61	32	5	2	8/15
DeVry College of Technology/North Brunswick	North Brunswick	SM	A,B	Pri	No	C	2,517																	Open
Drew University/College of Liberal Arts	Madison	SM	B,M,D	Pri	No	C	1,606	25	7	28	28	22	15	610	5	38	39	18	600	9	37	44	9	2/15
Fairleigh Dickinson University/College at Florham	Madison	SU	A,B,M	Pri	F,S	C	2,645							510	45	43	11	1	520	41	45	13	1	3/1
Fairleigh Dickinson University/Metropolitan Campus	Teaneck	SU	A,B,M,D	Pri	F,S	C	5,036							480	59	32	8		490	53	36	10	1	3/1
Felician College	Lodi	SU	A,B,M	Pri	No	C	1,416							440	75	21	4		440	71	24	5		Open
Georgian Court College	Lakewood	SU	B,M	Pri	No	PW	1,580																	8/1
Kean University	Union	SU	B,M	Pub	F,S	C	10,179							499	52	42	6		510	50	43	7		6/15
Monmouth University	West Long Branch	SU	A,B,M	Pri	F,S	C	4,381	23	18	35	41		6	533	25	62	11	2	549	18	62	19	1	3/1
Montclair State University	Upper Montclair	SU	B,M	Pub	F,S	C	11,375							524	34	48	16	1	543	23	55	20	2	3/1
New Jersey City University	Jersey City	U	B,M	Pub	F,S	C	6,145							450	79	19	3		440	77	20	3		4/1
New Jersey Institute of Technology	Newark	U	B,M,D	Pub	F,S	C	5,712							540	31	46	21	2	600	4	43	42	12	4/1
Princeton University	Princeton	SM	B,M,D	Pri	No	C	4,675	33						720		4	25	71	730		2	25	73	1/2
Ramapo College of New Jersey	Mahwah	SU	B,M	Pub	F,S	C	5,242							573	7	60	29	4	582	7	53	36	4	3/1
Richard Stockton College of New Jersey	Pomona	SU	B,M	Pub	F,S	C	6,540							550	32	50	16	2	570	30	50	18	2	5/1
Rider University	Lawrenceville	SU	A,B,M	Pri	F,S	C	4,329							520	40	45	14	1	520	36	46	17	2	Open
Rowan University	Glassboro	SU	B,M,D	Pub	F,S	C	7,952							571	9	61	26	3	592	5	53	37	5	3/15
Rutgers, The State University of New Jersey/Camden Campus	Camden	U	B,M	Pub	No	C	3,938							530	26	52	18	4	560	22	45	27	6	Open
Rutgers, The State University of New Jersey/New Brunswick/Piscataway Campus	New Brunswick	SM	B,M,D		F,S	C	26,860							590	8	45	38	9	620	6	32	46	17	Open
Rutgers, The State University of New Jersey/Newark Campus	Newark	U	B,M,D	Pub	No	C	6,276							540	33	49	18	1	570	22	42	31	5	Open
Saint Peter's College	Jersey City	U	A,B,M	Pri	No	C	2,810																	Open
Seton Hall University	South Orange	SU	B,M,D	Pri	F,S	C	5,238							550	24	45	26	5	560	21	46	29	4	3/1
Stevens Institute of Technology	Hoboken	U	B,M,D	Pri	F,S	C	1,707	28	4	18	21	14	43	610	5	39	44	12	670	2	12	54	34	2/15
Thomas Edison State College	Trenton	U	A,B,M	Pub	No	C	10,011																	Open
Westminster Choir College of Rider University	Princeton	SU	B,M	Pri	No	C	320																	Open
William Paterson University of New Jersey	Wayne	SU	B,M	Pub	F,S	C	9,302							520	32	54	13	1	520	29	56	14	1	5/1
New Mexico																								
College of Santa Fe	Santa Fe	SU	A,B,M	Pri	No	C	1,529	22	32	33	20	6	9	580	16	38	38	8	545	32	50	15	3	
College of the Southwest	Hobbs	SM	B,M	Pri	No	C	696	18	70	20	10			436	80	20			455	64	36			Open
Eastern New Mexico University	Portales	SM	A,B,M	Pub	F,S	C	3,024	19	68	19	10	2	2	472	60	29	8	3	461	63	31	6		Open
New Mexico Highlands University	Las Vegas	SM	A,B,M	Pub	No	C	2,103	17	82	16	1		1		77	23				65	34	1		Open
New Mexico Institute of Mining and Technology	Socorro	SM	A,B,M,D	Pub	No	C	1,364	26		1	30	52	17	620	7	27	54	12	630	2	28	53	17	8/1
New Mexico State University	Las Cruces	U	A,B,M,D	Pub	F,S	C	12,797	21	51	25	16	5	3											Open
Saint John's College	Santa Fe	SU	B,M	Pri	No	C	434	29						690	1	13	55	31	600	6	31	50	13	Open
University of New Mexico	Albuquerque	U	A,B,M,D	Pub	F,S	C	17,932	21	43	27	18	7	5	540	30	41	26	3	530	37	39	22	2	6/23
Western New Mexico University	Silver City	SM	A,B,M	Pub	No	C	620																	
New York																								
Adelphi University	Garden City	SU	A,B,M,D	Pri	F,S	C	4,157							530	31	45	21	3	550	23	51	23	4	Open
Albany College of Pharmacy	Albany	U	B,M,D	Pri	F,S	C	703							590					590					2/1
Albert A. List College of Jewish Studies	New York	U	B	Pri	No	C	177																	2/15

TEST SCORES

Column legend:
- ENVIRONMENT: U-Urban, R-Rural, SU-Suburban, SM-Small Town
- DEGREES AWARDED: A-Associate, B-Bachelor, M-Master, D-Doctorate
- CONTROL: Pri-Private, Pub-Public
- FRATERNITIES AND SORORITIES: F-Fraternities, S-Sororities, F,S-Both, N-Neither
- STUDENTS: C-Coed, M-Men, W-Women, PM-Primarily Men, PW-Primarily Women
- APPLICATION DEADLINE: Month/Day

Name of School	Town	Env.	Degrees	Control	Frat./Sor.	Students	Undergrad Enroll. Fall 2003	ACT Median	ACT Below 21	ACT 21-23	ACT 24-26	ACT 27-28	ACT Above 28	SAT V Median	SAT V Below 500	SAT V 500-599	SAT V 600-700	SAT V Above 700	SAT M Median	SAT M Below 500	SAT M 500-599	SAT M 600-700	SAT M Above 700	Application Deadline
Alfred University	Alfred	R	B,M,D	Pri	No	C	2,104							561	20	48	26	6	557	22		25	5	2/1
Bard College	Annandale-on-Hudson	R	A,B,M,D	Pri	No	C	1,377							690		12	57	31	630	1	31	53	15	1/15
Berkeley College	White Plains	SU	A,B	Pri	No	C	690																	Open
Berkeley College of New York City	New York	U	A,B	Pri	No	C	1,720																	Open
Boricua College	New York	U	B	Pri	No	C	1,150																	Open
Canisius College	Buffalo	U	B,M	Pri	F,S	C	3,535	24	27	23	28	11	11	552	23	50	23	4	557	22	46	28	4	Open
Cazenovia College	Cazenovia	SM	A,B	Pri	No	C	984	19	60	33	7			480	57	37	7		480	59	35	6		Open
City University of New York/ Baruch College	New York	U	B,M,D	Pub	F,S	C	13,195																	5/1
City University of New York/ Brooklyn College	Brooklyn	U	B,M	Pub	F,S	C	10,960							515	43	40	14	3	534	33	47	18	2	Open
City University of New York/ City College	New York	U	B,M	Pub	No	C	8,838							460	62	26	10	2	490	50	30	16	4	12/1
City University of New York/ College of Staten Island	Staten Island	U	A,B,M,D	Pub	No	C	11,101							430	48	41	10	2	440	43	43	12	1	Open
City University of New York/ Herbert H. Lehman College	Bronx	U	B,M	Pub	S	C	7,200																	
City University of New York/ Hunter College	New York	U	B,M	Pub	F,S	C	15,905							510	45	38	14	3	520	34	45	18	3	Open
City University of New York/ John Jay College of Criminal Justice	New York	U	A,B,M	Pub	No	C	11,709							480	58	36	5		470	61	33	6		Open
City University of New York/ Medgar Evers College	Brooklyn	U	A,B	Pub	F,S	C	4,722							380	96	3	1		390	92	7	1		Open
City University of New York/ New York City College of Technology	Brooklyn	U	A,B	Pub	No	C	10,982							388	71	26	3		428	66	29	5		Open
City University of New York/ Queens College	Flushing	U	B,M	Pub	F,S	C	12,346							509	47	38	13	2	545	31	45	21	3	
City University of New York/ York College	Jamaica	U	B	Pub	No	C	5,253							570										Open
Clarkson University	Potsdam	R	B,M,D	Pri	F,S	C	2,723												620	2	33	51	14	3/1
Colgate University	Hamilton	R	B,M	Pri	F,S	C	2,796	30	1	5	14	7	74	660	2	16	55	27	680	1	9	55	35	1/15
College of Aeronautics	Flushing	U	A,B	Pri	No	C	1,308							450					490					Open
College of Mount Saint Vincent	Riverdale	U	A,B,M	Pri	No	C	1,282	20						500					500					3/1
College of New Rochelle	New Rochelle	SU	B,M	Pri	No	PW	968	18						490	53	35	10	2	470	67	25	8		8/15
College of New Rochelle - School of New Resources	New Rochelle	U	B	Pri	No	C	4,162																	8/15
College of Saint Rose	Albany	SU	B,M	Pri	No	C	2,898	22	32	30	20	14	4	530	36	48	15	1	530	36	48	14	2	2/1
Columbia University/Barnard College	New York	U	B	Pri	No	W	2,281	29		5	10	22	63	690	2	7	44	47	670	1	10	60	29	1/1
Columbia University/Columbia College	New York	U	B	Pri	F,S	C	4,181	29		4		46	50	710		8	28	64	710		6	34	60	1/2
Columbia University/Fu Foundation School of Engineering and Applied Science	New York	U	B,M,D	Pri	F,S	C	1,360	34			4	8	88	700			4	39	57	760			7	93	1/2
Columbia University/School of General Studies	New York	U	B,M,D	Pri	F,S	C	1,140																	
Concordia College	Bronxville	SU	A,B	Pri	No	C	662	23	19	30	20	15	20	465	41	41	16	2	457	44	45	10		3/15
Cooper Union for the Advancement of Science and Art	New York	U	B,M	Pri	F,S	C	903							680	1	14	55	29	720	2	12	32	53	1/1
Cornell University	Ithaca	R	B,M,D	Pri	F,S	C	13,655	30		5	16	17	62	670	1	13	48	37	710	1	7	33	58	1/1
Daemen College	Amherst	SU	B,M	Pri	F,S	C	1,628	21	43	38	14	4	1	500	46	45	9		510	46	45	9		Open
DeVry Institute of Technology/New York	Long Island City	U	A,B,M	Pri	No	C	1,839																	Open
Dominican College	Orangeburg	SU	A,B,M	Pri	No	C	1,556																	Open
Dowling College	Oakdale	SU	B,M,D	Pri	No	C	3,066							460	66	26	7	1	470	59	32	8	1	Open
D'Youville College	Buffalo	U	B,M,D	Pri	No	C	976	23	16	50	25		8	460	58	32	8	2	480	60	30	7	3	Open
Eastman School of Music	Rochester	U	B,M,D	Pri	F,S	C	487																	12/1
Elmira College	Elmira	SU	B	Pri	No	C	1,533	25	12	22	42	17	7	580	26	49	21	4	560	28	49	19	4	3/15
Eugene Lang College/New School University	New York	U	B	Pri	No	C	733																	2/1
Excelsior College	Albany	SU	A,B,M	Pri	No	C	22,452																	Open
Farmingdale State University of New York	Farmingdale	SU	A,B	Pub	No	C	5,949							471	64	32	4		488	55	39	6		Open
Fashion Institute of Technology/State University of New York	New York	U	A,B,M	Pub	No	C	10,663																	1/1
Five Towns College	Dix Hills	SU	A,B,M,D	Pri	No	C	1,104	19	99	1				484	73	26	1		470	71	28	1		Open
Fordham University	Bronx	U	B,M,D	Pri	No	C	7,403	26						600	10	40	40	9	601	10	41	44	6	2/1
Friends World Program	Southampton	R	B	Pri	No	C	163																	Open
Globe Institute of Technology	New York	U	A,B	Pri	No	C	1,500							500					500					Open
Hamilton College	Clinton	R	B	Pri	F,S	C	1,797							660	3	17	50	30	670	2	10	59	29	
Hartwick College	Oneonta	SM	B	Pri	F,S	C	1,466	24						557	18	53	26	3	564	17	52	28	4	2/15
Hilbert College	Hamburg	U	A,B	Pri	No	C	1,055	19	44	36	8	12		467	68	26	6		465	66	31	3		Open
Hobart and William Smith Colleges	Geneva	SM	B,M	Pri	F		1,873								11	48	36	5		7	48	41	5	2/1
Hofstra University	Hempstead	SU	B,M,D	Pri	F,S	C	9,387	24	9	32	34	16	9	560	17	54	27	2	570	12	53	32	3	12/31
Houghton College	Houghton	R	A,B,M	Pri	No	C	1,424	25	13	26	27	17	20	599	15	36	35	13	579					Open
Iona College	New Rochelle	SU	B,M	Pri	F,S	C	3,395	21						550	26	49	23	2	540	25	50	24	1	3/15
Ithaca College	Ithaca	SM	B,M	Pri	F,S	C	6,260							590	10	44	40	6	594	7	44	44	5	3/1
Juilliard School	New York	U	B,M,D	Pri	No	C	506																	12/1
Keuka College	Keuka Park	R	B,M	Pri	No	C	1,063																	
Laboratory Institute of Merchandising	New York	U	A,B	Pri	No	C	493							480	66	30	4		460	74	24		2	Open
Le Moyne College	Syracuse	SU	B,M	Pri	No	C	2,691	23	23	31	28	10	8	550	22	53	23	2	560	17	54	27	2	2/1
Long Island University/Brooklyn Campus	Brooklyn	U	A,B,M,D	Pri	F,S	C	5,520																	Open
Long Island University/C.W. Post Campus	Brookville	SU	A,B,M,D	Pri	F,S	C	6,619	20	52	33	5	6	4	490					500					Open

NAME OF SCHOOL	TOWN	ENVIRONMENT U-Urban R-Rural SU-Suburban SM-Small Town	DEGREES AWARDED A-Associate B-Bachelor M-Master D-Doctorate	CONTROL Pri-Private Pub-Public	FRATERNITIES AND SORORITIES F-Fraternities S-Sororities F,S-Both No-Neither	STUDENTS C-Coed M-Men W-Women PM-Primarily Men PW-Primarily Women	UNDERGRADUATE ENROLLMENT FALL 2003	ACT						SAT I VERBAL REASONING					SAT I MATHEMATICAL REASONING					APPLICATION DEADLINE Month/Day
								Median	Below 21	21-23	24-26	27-28	Above 28	Median	Below 500	500-599	600-700	Above 700	Median	Below 500	500-599	600-700	Above 700	
Long Island University/Southampton College	Southampton	R	B,M	Pri	No	C	1,196	24	13	24	21	21	21	531	36	43	19	2	521	40	39	19	2	
Manhattan College	Riverdale	U	B,M	Pri	F,S	C	2,886																	3/1
Manhattan School of Music	New York	U	B,M,D	Pri	F,S	C	395																	12/3
Manhattanville College	Purchase	SU	B,M	Pri	No	C	1,671	24						540	35	45	18	2	525	37	48	14	1	12/1
Mannes College of Music	New York	U	B,M	Pri	No	C	130																	12/1
Marist College	Poughkeepsie	SU	B,M	Pri	F,S	C	4,773	25						576	9	54	35	2	586	5	51	41	3	2/15
Marymount College of Fordham University	Tarrytown	SU	B	Pri	No	W	891	21						510	43	43	12	2	470	62	31	6	1	8/1
Marymount Manhattan College	New York	U	B	Pri	S	C	2,183	23	10	45	45			540	30	45	23	3	510	44	39	16		
Medaille College	Buffalo	U	A,B,M	Pri	No	C	1,644							470	70	25	5		450	80	18	2		8/15
Mercy College	Dobbs Ferry	SU	A,B,M	Pri	No	C	6,395							500					500					Open
Metropolitan College of New York	New York	U	A,B,M	Pri	No	C	1,292																	8/1
Molloy College	Rockville Centre	SU	A,B,M	Pri	No	C	2,311							522	38	47	14	1	528	37	46	15	2	Open
Monroe College	Bronx		B		No		5,000																	8/15
Mount Saint Mary College	Newburgh	R	B,M	Pri	No	C	2,130							510	44	43	12	1	500	46	42	11	1	2/15
Nazareth College of Rochester	Rochester	SU	B,M	Pri	No	C	1,997	25	19	30	27	13	11	570	19	44	33	5	570	16	52	29	4	2/1
New York Institute of Technology	Old Westbury	SU	A,B,M,D	Pri	F,S	C	5,376	23	28	24	16	12	20	530	30	45	22	2	580	14	44	34	8	1/15
New York University	New York	U	A,B,M,D	Pri	F,S	C	19,506			1	12	15	71	670			12	52	36	680	1	12	49	39	8/15
Niagara University	Niagara University	SU	A,B,M	Pri	F	C	2,734	21						516	43	44	13	1	525	38	45	16	2	Open
Nyack College	Nyack	SU	A,B,M	Pri	No	C	1,897																	Open
Pace University	New York	U	A,B,M,D	Pri	F,S	C	8,871	22	22	35	25	11	7	540	28	51	19	2	540	25	50	22	3	Open
Parsons School of Design	New York	U	B,M	Pri	No	C	2,311																	Open
Polytechnic University/Brooklyn	Brooklyn	U	B,M,D	Pri	F,S	C	1,559							540	25	50	22	3	640	4	28	52	17	Open
Pratt Institute	Brooklyn	U	A,B,M	Pri	F,S	C	2,994							562					561					2/1
Rensselaer Polytechnic Institute	Troy	SU	B,M,D	Pri	F,S	C	5,210	26	6	15	33	26	20	630	6	25	51	19	680	1	9	46	44	1/1
Roberts Wesleyan College	Rochester	SU	A,B,M	Pri	No	C	1,292	23	30	32	21	4	13	569	29	42	27	2	561	34	39	24	3	2/1
Rochester Institute of Technology	Rochester	SU	A,B,M,D	Pri	F,S	C	12,994	26	7	16	32	20	25	590	10	43	39	8	630	4	32	48	16	
Russell Sage College	Troy	U	B,M	Pri	No	W	811	24	18	29	24	18	12	539	31	49	18	2	516	37	49	14		8/1
Saint Bonaventure University	St. Bonaventure	SM	B,M	Pri	No	C	2,291	22	36	34	19	4	7	530	32	48	16	1	530					4/1
Saint Francis College	Brooklyn	U	A,B	Pri	F,S	C	2,294							470					470					4/1
Saint John Fisher College	Rochester	SU	B,M	Pri	No	C	2,496	22	18	38	31	8	5	520	30	52	15	2	540	25	55	19	1	Open
Saint John's University	Jamaica	SU	A,B,M,D	Pri	F,S	C	14,908							530	34	46	19	1	540	27	46	23	4	Open
Saint Joseph's College, New York	Brooklyn	U	B,M	Pri	F,S	C	1,126							498	45	47	8		502	49	33	18		8/1
Saint Joseph's College, New York	Patchogue	SU	B,M	Pri	F,S	C	2,798	22	37	63				530	30	53	16	1	540	22	53	24	1	
Saint Lawrence University	Canton	R	B,M	Pri	F,S	C	2,160							570	17	45	33	5	570	13	46	36	4	2/15
Saint Thomas Aquinas College	Sparkill	SU	A,B,M	Pri	No	C	2,010																	
Sarah Lawrence College	Bronxville	SU	B,M	Pri	No	C	1,292	27		14	31	20	32	650	4	19	50	27	590	12	41	40	7	1/1
School of Visual Arts	New York	U	B,M	Pri	No	C	2,972	22	32	23	10	33	1	520					520	40	36	21	3	3/15
Siena College	Loudonville	SU	B	Pri	No	C	3,379	24						550	19	55	24	2	570	12	52	33	3	3/1
Skidmore College	Saratoga Springs	SM	B,M	Pri	No	C	2,497	27		9	36	23	32	620	5	28	51	16	630	3	28	57	12	1/15
State University of New York at Oswego	Oswego	SM	B,M	Pub	F,S	C	7,337								24	59	16	1		21	59	19	1	1/15
State University of New York at Potsdam	Potsdam	R	B,M	Pub	F,S	C	3,484	23	38	18	25	11	8	540	35	43	20	2	530	35	41	22	2	Open
State University of New York/College at Brockport	Brockport	SM	B,M	Pub	F,S	C	6,962	22	28	37	27	4	4	540	26	54	18	2	530	32	52	15	1	Open
State University of New York/College at Buffalo	Buffalo	U	B,M	Pub	F,S	C	9,590					1												
State University of New York/College at Cortland	Cortland	SM	B,M	Pub	F,S	C	5,787	24	10	44	33	8	5	530					550					
State University of New York/College at Fredonia	Fredonia	SM	B,M	Pub	F,S	C	4,852	24	4	36	42	10	8	550	13	63	23	1	560	11	65	23	1	
State University of New York/College at Geneseo	Geneseo	SM	B,M	Pub	F,S	C	5,307	27	2	4	37	33	24	621	3	27	58	12	631	1	22	68	9	1/15
State University of New York/College at Old Westbury	Old Westbury	SU	B,M	Pub	F,S	C	3,222							470	73	23	4		480	67	29	4		Open
State University of New York/College at Oneonta	Oneonta	R	B,M	Pub	S	C	5,510	23	9	52	35	4		538	24	60	15	1	548	16	65	18	1	5/1
State University of New York/College at Plattsburgh	Plattsburgh	SU	B,M	Pub	F,S	C	5,403	21	40	34	17	4		510	39	48	12	1	520	35	51	14	1	8/1
State University of New York/College at Purchase	Purchase	SU	B,M	Pub	No	C	3,866																	8/15
State University of New York/College of Agriculture and Technology at Cobleskill	Cobleskill	R	A,B	Pub	No	C	2,450																	Open
State University of New York/College of Environmental Science and Forestry	Syracuse	U	A,B,M,D	Pub	F,S	C	1,549	24	10	40	34	5	11	560	9	55	34	2	570	10	56	32	2	3/1
State University of New York/College of Technology at Alfred	Alfred	R	A,B	Pub	F,S	C	3,471	20						464					488					Open
State University of New York/Empire State College	Saratoga Springs		A,B,M	Pub	No	C	9,355																	
State University of New York/Maritime College	Throggs Neck	SU	A,B,M	Pub	No	C	655																	Open
State University of New York/University at Albany	Albany	SU	B,M,D	Pub	F,S	C	11,796								9	54	34	4		5	50	39	5	3/1
State University of New York/University at Binghamton	Binghamton	SU	B,M,D	Pub	F,S	C	10,563	27	4	10	34	28	25	600	5	42	46	7	630	2	25	56	17	2/15
State University of New York/University at Buffalo	Buffalo	SU	B,M,D	Pub	F,S	C	17,818	26	1	19	37	22	21	570	13	53	30	4	598	5	45	44	6	
State University of New York/University at New Paltz	New Paltz	SM	B,M	Pub	F,S	C	6,292							545	22	49	26	3	550	21	55	22	3	4/1

Column key:
- **ENVIRONMENT:** U-Urban, R-Rural, SU-Suburban, SM-Small Town
- **DEGREES AWARDED:** A-Associate, B-Bachelor, M-Master, D-Doctorate
- **CONTROL:** Pri-Private, Pub-Public
- **FRATERNITIES AND SORORITIES:** F-Fraternities, S-Sororities, F,S-Both, No-Neither
- **STUDENTS:** C-Coed, M-Men, W-Women, PM-Primarily Men, PW-Primarily Women

NAME OF SCHOOL	TOWN	ENV	DEGREES	CONTROL	FRAT	STUDENTS	ENROLL FALL 2003	ACT Med	ACT <21	ACT 21-23	ACT 24-26	ACT 27-28	ACT >28	SAT V Med	SAT V <500	SAT V 500-599	SAT V 600-700	SAT V >700	SAT M Med	SAT M <500	SAT M 500-599	SAT M 600-700	SAT M >700	DEADLINE
State University of New York/University at Stony Brook	Stony Brook	SU	B,M,D	Pub	F,S	C	14,072							580	7	53	35	5	620	1	37	49	13	3/1
Syracuse University	Syracuse	U	B,M,D	Pri	F,S	C	10,840								4	41	46	9		5	32	49	14	1/1
Touro College	New York	U	A,B,M,D	Pri	No	C	9,694	23	8	50	8	17	17	570	22	38	32	8	550	27	40	27	6	Open
Union College	Schenectady	U	B	Pri	F,S	C	2,174	26						610	3	37	48	12	640	1	27	50	22	1/15
United States Merchant Marine Academy	Kings Point	SU	B	Pub	No	C	970	28			37	47	16	629		36	42	22	619		39	53	8	3/1
United States Military Academy	West Point	SM	B	Pub	No	C	4,165																	
University of Rochester	Rochester	SU	B,M,D	Pri	F,S	C	4,665																	1/20
Utica College	Utica	SU	B,M	Pri	F,S	C	2,170																	Open
Vassar College	Poughkeepsie	SU	B,M	Pri	No	C	2,444	30						696		4	47	50	676		8	55	37	1/1
Wagner College	Staten Island	SU	B,M	Pri	F,S	C	1,826	25	7	13	62	15	3	552	18	62	19	1	549	19	60	20	1	2/15
Webb Institute	Glen Cove	SU	B	Pri	No	C	73																	2/15
Wells College	Aurora	SM	B	Pri		W	436	24	16	30	27	16	11	580	16	41	39	4	520	33	41	26	1	3/1
Yeshiva University	New York	U	A,B	Pri	No	C	2,310																	

North Carolina

NAME OF SCHOOL	TOWN	ENV	DEGREES	CONTROL	FRAT	STUDENTS	ENROLL FALL 2003	ACT Med	ACT <21	ACT 21-23	ACT 24-26	ACT 27-28	ACT >28	SAT V Med	SAT V <500	SAT V 500-599	SAT V 600-700	SAT V >700	SAT M Med	SAT M <500	SAT M 500-599	SAT M 600-700	SAT M >700	DEADLINE
Appalachian State University	Boone	R	B,M,D	Pub	F,S	C	12,934							550	26	51	21	3	560	17	51	29	3	Open
Barber-Scotia College	Concord	SU	B	Pri	F,S	C	748		89	6	3		2	375	94	4	2		370	91	7	2		Open
Barton College	Wilson	SU	B	Pri	F,S	C	1,188							480	60	35	2		480	56	35	7	2	Open
Belmont Abbey College	Belmont	SU	B	Pri	F,S	C	1,055							510	50	35	14	1	500	55	35	10		Open
Bennett College	Greensboro	U	A,B	Pri	S	W	520																	Open
Cabarrus College of Health Sciences	Concord	SU	A,B	Pri	No	C	242	21						460					510					3/1
Campbell University	Buies Creek	R	A,B,M,D	Pri	No	C	2,535							544	32	44	21	3	546	24	46	28	2	Open
Catawba College	Salisbury	SM	B,M	Pri	No	C	1,452							510	45	41	12	2	530	33	48	18	1	Open
Davidson College	Davidson	SM	B	Pri	F	C	1,712	29						680	1	12	49	38	680	1	9	52	39	1/2
Duke University	Durham	SU	B,M,D	Pri	F,S	C	6,086	31		2		40	58	700	1	8	35	56	720	1	5	28	66	1/2
East Carolina University	Greenville	U	B,M,D	Pub	F,S	C	16,935	20	58	28	10	2	2	518	40	46	13	1	530	32	52	15	1	3/15
Elizabeth City State University	Elizabeth City	SM	B	Pub	F,S	C	1,965																	Open
Elon University	Elon	SU	B,M,D	Pri	F,S	C	4,431							570	11	52	33	4	580	8	49	38	5	1/10
Fayetteville State University	Fayetteville	U	B,M	Pub	F,S	C	3,807																	Open
Gardner-Webb University	Boiling Springs	SM	A,B,M,D	Pri	No	C	2,682							510					520					Open
Greensboro College	Greensboro	U	B,M	Pri	F,S	C	1,176	20	64	12	16	4	4	480	57	33	8	2	490	55	36	9		
Guilford College	Greensboro	SU	B	Pri	No	C	2,101	24	21	22	33	9	15	580	19	37	32	13	560	21	44	30	5	2/15
High Point University	High Point	SU	B,M	Pri	F,S	C	2,657							510	44	40	14	2	513	41	44	13	2	8/15
Johnson C. Smith University	Charlotte	U	B	Pri	F,S	C	1,474	18						493	89	12	1		481	87	13	1		Open
Lees-McRae College	Banner Elk	R	B	Pri	No	C	792																	Open
Lenoir-Rhyne College	Hickory	SU	B,M	Pri	F,S	C	1,316																	Open
Livingstone College	Salisbury	SM	B	Pri	F,S	C	1,005	14						380					365					
Mars Hill College	Mars Hill	R	B	Pri	F,S	C	1,242																	Open
Meredith College	Raleigh	U	B,M	Pri	No	W	2,000	21	49	24	15	5	7	520	39	42	17	2	520	40	43	16	1	2/15
Methodist College	Fayetteville	SU	A,B,M	Pri	F,S	C	1,845																	Open
Montreat College	Montreat	R	A,B,M	Pri	No	C	944	22	31	35	23	4	8	530	41	34	21	4	500	45	43	10	3	Open
Mount Olive College	Mount Olive	SM	A,B	Pri	No	C	1,775																	Open
North Carolina Agricultural and Technical State University	Greensboro	U	B,M,D	Pub	F,S	C	6,610																	6/1
North Carolina Central University	Durham	U	B,M	Pub	F,S	C	5,362	16	89	7	2	2		415	84	13	2	1	418	85	13	2		7/1
North Carolina School of the Arts	Winston-Salem	U	B,M	Pub	No	C	963	23		1	8	6	7	567	13	27	18	5	547	22	27	13	1	3/1
North Carolina State University	Raleigh	U	A,B,M,D	Pub	F,S	C	22,780	22						580					615					2/1
North Carolina Wesleyan College	Rocky Mount	SU	B	Pri	F,S	C	1,695																	Open
Pfeiffer University	Misenheimer	R	B,M	Pri	No	C	1,185	21	53	33	10	4		490	51	40	8	1	510	43	44	12	1	8/25
Queens University of Charlotte	Charlotte	SU	B,M	Pri	F,S	C	1,411		25	39	28	7	1		31	45	21	3		33	47	20	1	Open
Saint Andrews Presbyterian College	Laurinburg	SM	B	Pri	No	C	693							490	54	31	13	2	485	54	38	8		Open
Saint Augustine's College	Raleigh	U	B	Pri	F,S	C	1,360																	7/1
Salem College	Winston-Salem	U	B,M	Pri	No	PW	910	25	18	14	36	23	9	580	19	41	33	7	540	26	44	29	1	Open
Shaw University	Raleigh	U	A,B,M	Pri	F,S	C	2,446	16	99	1				380	96	4			385	96	3	1		7/30
University of North Carolina at Asheville	Asheville	SU	B,M	Pub	F,S	C	3,410	24	15	27	30	16	12	580	13	43	38	5	590	12	45	41	3	3/12
University of North Carolina at Chapel Hill	Chapel Hill	SU	B,M,D	Pub	F,S	C	15,711	27	6	12	27	23	34	630	4	24	51	21	650	2	20	52	26	1/15
University of North Carolina at Charlotte	Charlotte	SU	B,M,D	Pub	F,S	C	15,694	21	42	33	19	4	2	520	36	49	14	1	540	27	50	21	2	7/1
University of North Carolina at Greensboro	Greensboro	U	B,M,D	Pub	F,S	C	11,106							522	40	42	16	2	523	39	44	16	1	8/1
University of North Carolina at Pembroke	Pembroke	SM	B,M	Pub	F,S	C	4,253							470	67	27	5	1	470	62	31	6	1	7/15
University of North Carolina at Wilmington	Wilmington	SU	B,M	Pub	F,S	C	9,974		6	31	30	31	2	543	29	54	16	1	561	20	54	24	2	2/1
Wake Forest University	Winston-Salem	SU	B,M,D	Pri	F,S	C	4,031								3	14	58	25		2	11	56	31	1/15
Warren Wilson College	Asheville	SM	B	Pri	No	C	769	24						605	9	35	42	15	563	19	44	31	5	3/15
Western Carolina University	Cullowhee	R	B,M,D	Pub	F,S	C	6,087							500	47	40	11	2	510	43	42	14	1	7/15
Wingate University	Wingate	SM	B,M	Pri	F,S	C	1,324	20	38	23	23	10	7	510	41	43	15	1	520	37	43	19	1	
Winston-Salem State University	Winston-Salem	SU	B,M	Pub	F,S	C	3,929							470					470					Open

North Dakota

NAME OF SCHOOL	TOWN	ENV	DEGREES	CONTROL	FRAT	STUDENTS	ENROLL FALL 2003	ACT Med	ACT <21	ACT 21-23	ACT 24-26	ACT 27-28	ACT >28	SAT V Med	SAT V <500	SAT V 500-599	SAT V 600-700	SAT V >700	SAT M Med	SAT M <500	SAT M 500-599	SAT M 600-700	SAT M >700	DEADLINE
Dickinson State University	Dickinson	R	A,B	Pub	No	C	2,351	22	51	25	15	3	3	460	48	45	6		490	51	39	9		8/15
Jamestown College	Jamestown	SM	B	Pri	No	C	1,152	22	34	35	19	7	5											Open
Mayville State University	Mayville	R	A,B	Pub	No	C	817	19	63	26	7	1	2											Open
Minot State University	Minot	SM	A,B,M	Pub	No	C	3,594	22	40	29	21	6	4											Open
North Dakota State University	Fargo	U	B,M,D	Pub	F,S	C	10,148	23		7	49	39	6		24	33	32	11		14	32	42	13	8/15
University of Mary	Bismarck	SU	B,M	Pri	No	C	1,940																	Open
University of North Dakota	Grand Forks	U	B,M,D	Pub	F,S	C	10,711		28	28	25	11	9											7/1
Valley City State University	Valley City	SM	B	Pub	F,S	C	998	21	47	35	13	3	2	475					460					Open

TEST SCORES

Column legend — ENVIRONMENT: U-Urban, R-Rural, SU-Suburban, SM-Small Town · DEGREES AWARDED: A-Associate, B-Bachelor, M-Master, D-Doctorate · CONTROL: Pri-Private, Pub-Public · FRATERNITIES AND SORORITIES: F-Fraternities, S-Sororities, F,S-Both, No-Neither · STUDENTS: C-Coed, M-Men, W-Women, PM-Primarily Men, PW-Primarily Women · ENROLLMENT: Undergraduate Enrollment Fall 2003 · APPLICATION DEADLINE: Month / Day

Name of School	Town	Environ.	Degrees	Control	Frat/Sor	Students	Enroll.	ACT Median	ACT Below 21	ACT 21-23	ACT 24-26	ACT 27-28	ACT Above 28	SAT V Median	SAT V Below 500	SAT V 500-599	SAT V 600-700	SAT V Above 700	SAT M Median	SAT M Below 500	SAT M 500-599	SAT M 600-700	SAT M Above 700	Deadline
Ohio																								
Antioch College	Yellow Springs	SM	B	Pri	No	C	570																	2/1
Art Academy of Cincinnati	Cincinnati	U	A,B,M	Pri	No	C	193	21	52	24	12	4	8	543	33	33	26	8	516	42	50		8	6/30
Ashland University	Ashland	SM	A,B,M,D	Pri	F,S	C	2,782	22	34	28	24	9	6	510	40	39	21	1	512	42	39	17	2	Open
Baldwin-Wallace College	Berea	SU	B,M	Pri	F,S	C	3,862	23	25	28	26	9	11	560	25	42	30	3	550	25	44	26	5	5/1
Bluffton College	Bluffton	SM	B,M	Pri	No	C	1,056	23	24	30	33	10	3	536	37	46	14	3	529	41	32	24	3	5/31
Bowling Green State University	Bowling Green	SM	B,M,D	Pub	F,S	C	15,481	22	43	32	15	5	5	511	46	37	13	3	507	48	36	14	3	7/15
Capital University	Columbus	SU	B,M	Pri	No	C	2,830	23	26	31	24	10	9	541	30	42	24	4	526	28	45	22	5	4/15
Case Western Reserve University	Cleveland	U	B,M,D	Pri	F,S	C	3,587	29	2	8	20	16	54	650	6	21	44	29	680	1	15	40	44	1/15
Cedarville University	Cedarville	SM	A,B,M	Pri	No	C	2,996	25	5	23	30	16	27	590	9	42	37	12	590	13	41	36	8	Open
Central State University	Wilberforce	R	B,M	Pub	F,S	C	1,320																	3/31
Cincinnati College of Mortuary Science	Cincinnati	U	A,B	Pri	No	C	130																	10/1
Cleveland Institute of Art	Cleveland	U	B,M	Pri	F,S	C	618	21	35	27	22	11	5	572	18	39	37	6	509	38	41	21		7/1
Cleveland Institute of Music	Cleveland	U	B,M,D	Pri	No	C	225																	
Cleveland State University	Cleveland	U	B,M,D	Pub	F,S	C	9,173	19	68	19	9	3	1	470	61	30	8	1	470	61	28	9	2	7/15
College of Mount St. Joseph	Cincinnati	SU	A,B,M	Pri	No	C	1,876	21	30	26	25	16	3	500	48	39	12	1	510	45	43	11	1	8/15
College of Wooster	Wooster	SU	B	Pri	F,S	C	1,838	25						600	10	37	39	15	600	9	38	44	9	2/15
Columbus College of Art and Design	Columbus	U	B	Pri	No	C	1,737	21						544					514					Open
David N. Myers College	Cleveland	U	A,B,M	Pri	No	C	1,096																	Open
Defiance College	Defiance	SM	A,B,M	Pri	F,S	C	943	20	38	27	27	6	2	520	47	35	18		470	55	32	10	3	Open
Denison University	Granville	SU	B	Pri	F,S	C	2,142	26	6	13	32	18	31	600	4	40	45	11	610	4	37	48	11	2/1
DeVry University/Columbus	Columbus	U	A,B,M	Pri	No	C	3,145																	Open
Franciscan University of Steubenville	Steubenville	SM	A,B,M	Pri	F,S	C	1,844	24						580	12	41	37	10	560	18	47	31	4	6/30
Franklin University	Columbus	U	A,B,M	Pri	No	C	5,318																	Open
Heidelberg College	Tiffin	SM	B,M	Pri	F,S	C	1,261	22	48	27	13	5	5	515	55	30	15		520	60	33	7		5/1
Hiram College	Hiram	R	B	Pri	No	C	1,110	24	28	22	23	14	13	560	21	37	31	11	560	29	39	29	3	2/1
John Carroll University	University Heights	SU	B,M	Pri	F,S	C	3,449	24	22	25	34	11	8	570	14	51	26	6	580	16	43	34	7	2/1
Kent State University	Kent	SU	A,B,M,D	Pub	F,S	C	19,173	21	43	30	17	6	4	517	42	40	16	2	513	43	40	16	1	5/1
Kenyon College	Gambier	R	B	Pri	F,S	C	1,612	30		2	22	24	51	680	1	15	46	38	650	1	23	54	22	2/2
Lake Erie College	Painesville	SM	B,M	Pri	No	C	803	21	46	27	18	8	1	580	52	28	15	5	510	55	35	10		Open
Lourdes College	Sylvania	SU	A,B,M	Pri	No	C	1,202	20	63	27	8		2	430	100				460	100				Open
Malone College	Canton	SU	B,M	Pri	No	C	1,937	23	27	33	24	8	8	550	27	40	30	3	535	35	41	19	4	7/1
Marietta College	Marietta	SM	A,B,M	Pri	F,S	C	1,227	23	24	30	27	14	5	540					540	33	41	23	3	4/15
Miami University	Oxford	SM	B,M,D	Pub	F,S	C	15,174	27	2	11	35	24	28	610	4	42	47	8	630	3	28	59	11	1/31
Mount Union College	Alliance	SU	B	Pri	F,S	C	2,368																	Open
Mount Vernon Nazarene University	Mt. Vernon	SM	A,B,M	Pri	No	C	2,206	22	32	30	21	9	8	560	30	37	29	4	540	30	43	24	3	5/31
Muskingum College	New Concord	SM	B,M	Pri	F,S	C	1,612	21	47	26	16	6	5	510	45	30	20	5	530	44	30	22	4	6/1
Notre Dame College	South Euclid	SU	A,B,M	Pri	No	C	800																	Open
Oberlin College	Oberlin	SM	B,M	Pri	No	C	2,883	29	3	5	15	27	51	690	2	12	43	43	660	3	18	49	30	1/15
Ohio Dominican University	Columbus	U	A,B,M	Pri	No	C	2,278		52	29	14	4	1											Open
Ohio Northern University	Ada	SM	B,D	Pri	F,S	C	2,296																	8/1
Ohio State University	Columbus	U	B,M,D	Pub	F,S	C	37,605	26	5	19	36	19	21	580	12	44	38	6	610	7	37	46	10	Open
Ohio State University at Lima	Lima	SU	A,B,M	Pub	No	C	2,339																	7/1
Ohio State University at Mansfield	Mansfield	SU	A,B	Pub	No	C	1,230																	Open
Ohio State University at Marion	Marion	R	A,B,M	Pub	No	C																		Open
Ohio State University at Newark	Newark	SU	A,B,M	Pub	No	C	2,069	19	77	15	4	3	1	490					485					7/1
Ohio University	Athens	SM	A,B,M,D	Pub	F,S	C	17,192	23	15	36	28	11	10	550	23	49	25	3	550	23	49	25	3	2/1
Ohio Wesleyan University	Delaware	SM	B	Pri	F,S	C	1,929	27		16	33	24	28	605	12	34	41	14	610	10	37	42	11	Open
Otterbein College	Westerville	SU	B,M	Pri	F,S	C	2,673	23	34	25	25	10	6	533	27	45	25	3	526	32	41	26	1	Open
Shawnee State University	Portsmouth	SM	A,B	Pub	F,S	C	3,693	19	61	24	11	3	1											Open
Tiffin University	Tiffin	SM	A,B,M	Pri	F,S	C	1,026	19	65	22	11	2		465	68	32			465	67	28	3	2	Open
Union Institute and University	Cincinnati	U	B,M,D	Pri	No	C	1,288																	10/1
University of Akron	Akron	U	A,B,M,D	Pub	F,S	C	20,111	20	56	22	13	5	4	500	48	34	16	2	510	46	30	20	4	8/15
University of Cincinnati	Cincinnati	U	A,B,M,D	Pub	F,S	C	19,159	22	37	23	19	10	9	518	36	40	21	3	533	35	36	24	5	7/31
University of Dayton	Dayton	SU	B,M,D	Pri	F,S	C	7,103	25	14	24	28	15	19	560	20	45	30	5	580	18	37	37	8	6/1
University of Findlay	Findlay	SM	A,B,M	Pri	F,S	C	3,381																	Open
University of Rio Grande	Rio Grande	R	A,B,M	Pri	F,S	C	1,855																	Open
University of Toledo	Toledo	SU	A,B,M,D	Pub	F,S	C	17,388	22	42	27	19	6	6	511	44	38	16	2	521	40	35	21	4	Open
Urbana University	Urbana	SM	A,B,M	Pri	No	C	1,441																	Open
Ursuline College	Pepper Pike	SU	B,M	Pri	No	PW	1,095	20	67	19	11	2	1	490	49	39	12		490	51	42	7		8/25
Walsh University	North Canton	SM	A,B,M	Pri	No	C	1,573	22	42	28	18	7	4											Open
Wilberforce University	Wilberforce	R	B	Pri	F,S	C	800																	Open
Wilmington College	Wilmington	SM	B,M	Pri	F,S	C	1,248	21	50	24	20	4	2											Open
Wittenberg University	Springfield	SU	B,M	Pri	F,S	C	2,152	24	24	27	25	12	12	578	13	46	34	7	578	15	45	35	5	3/15
Wright State University	Dayton	SU	B,M,D	Pub	F,S	C	12,220	21	50	25	15	6	4	510	48	37	14	1	510	49	35	14	2	Open
Xavier University	Cincinnati	SU	A,B,M,D	Pri	No	C	3,915	26	10	20	25	19	26	580	12	43	37	8	590	10	46	36	8	2/1
Youngstown State University	Youngstown	U	A,B,M,D	Pub	F,S	C	11,598	20	54	24	14	5	3											8/15
Oklahoma																								
Cameron University	Lawton	SU	A,B,M	Pub	F,S	C	5,205	19																Open
East Central University	Ada	SM	B,M	Pub	F,S	C	3,688	21	53	25	14	5	3											Open
Langston University	Langston	R	A,B,M	Pub	F,S	C	4,020																	Open
Northeastern State University	Tahlequah	SM	B,M,D	Pub	F,S	C	9,297	24																Open
Northwestern Oklahoma State University	Alva	SM	B,M	Pub	F,S	C	1,805	20	56	25	12	5	2											Open
Oklahoma Baptist University	Shawnee	SM	A,B,M	Pri	F,S	C	1,857	25	10	30	25	16	19	590	16	36	36	12	560	21	41	29	9	8/1
Oklahoma Christian University	Oklahoma City	SU	B,M	Pri	No	C	1,526	23	38	14	23	11	14	560	26	40	29	5	560	29	34	31	6	Open
Oklahoma City University	Oklahoma City	U	B,M	Pri	No	C	1,793	24	19	26	26	12	17	570	18	49	35	1	560	28	35	33	4	8/20
Oklahoma Panhandle State University	Goodwell	R	A,B	Pub	No	C	1,145	21																Open
Oklahoma State University	Stillwater	SM	B,M,D	Pub	F,S	C	18,629	24	19	29	25	13	14	550	19	55	22	4	560	17	50	27	6	Open
Oklahoma Wesleyan University	Bartlesville	SU	A,B	Pri	F	C	540																	Open

NAME OF SCHOOL	TOWN	ENVIRONMENT	DEGREES AWARDED	CONTROL	FRATERNITIES AND SORORITIES	STUDENTS	UNDERGRADUATE ENROLLMENT FALL 2003	ACT						SAT I VERBAL REASONING					SAT I MATHEMATICAL REASONING					APPLICATION DEADLINE Month / Day
								Median	Below 21	21-23	24-26	27-28	Above 28	Median	Below 500	500-599	600-700	Above 700	Median	Below 500	500-599	600-700	Above 700	
Oral Roberts University	Tulsa	SU	B,M,D	Pri	No	C	3,087																	Open
Saint Gregory's University	Shawnee	SU	A,B	Pri	F,S	C	757																	Open
Southeastern Oklahoma State University	Durant	R	B,M	Pub	F,S	C	3,738	20	60	23	12	4	1											Open
Southern Nazarene University	Bethany	SU	A,B,M	Pri	No	C	1,705																	8/5
Southwestern Oklahoma State University	Weatherford	SM	A,B,M,D	Pub	F,S	C	3,858																	8/15
University of Central Oklahoma	Edmond	SU	B,M	Pub	F,S	C	13,566	22	41	31	17	7	4	592										8/15
University of Oklahoma	Norman	SU	B,M,D	Pub	F,S	C	20,271	25	9	15	36	17	23	592					598					6/1
University of Science and Arts of Oklahoma	Chickasha	SM	B	Pub	F	C	1,449	20	55	24	14	4	3											9/8
University of Tulsa	Tulsa	U	B,M,D	Pri	F,S	C	2,672	26	14	18	25	15	28	600	17	29	32	22	600	16	33	33	18	Open

Oregon

NAME OF SCHOOL	TOWN	ENVIRONMENT	DEGREES AWARDED	CONTROL	FRATERNITIES AND SORORITIES	STUDENTS	UNDERGRADUATE ENROLLMENT FALL 2003	ACT Median	Below 21	21-23	24-26	27-28	Above 28	SAT I VERBAL Median	Below 500	500-599	600-700	Above 700	SAT I MATH Median	Below 500	500-599	600-700	Above 700	APP DEADLINE
Art Institute of Portland	Portland	U	A,B	Pri	No	C	1,327																	Open
Cascade College	Portland	SU	B	Pri	No	C	280	21	44	21	26	9		485	34	46	20		440	54	37	9		Open
Concordia University	Portland	U	A,B,M	Pri	No	C	905	21	43	24	24	3	5	520	41	45	12	2	510	42	40	17	1	
Eastern Oregon University	La Grande	R	B,M	Pub	No	C	3,041	22						485	49	36	13	2	484	51	35	12	2	Open
George Fox University	Newberg	SM	B,M,D	Pri	No	C	1,663	24	27	21	30	12	10	560	22	45	28	5	550	25	44	26	5	6/1
Lewis and Clark College	Portland	SU	B,M	Pri	No	C	1,792	26	3	12	18	23	44	600	1	21	48	30	570	1	31	51	17	2/1
Linfield College	McMinnville	SM	B	Pri	F,S	C	1,659	24	27	22	28	13	10	550	25	45	24	5	570	19	47	30	5	2/15
Marylhurst University	Marylhurst	SU	B,M	Pri	No	C	701																	Open
Northwest Christian College	Eugene	U	A,B,M	Pri	No	C	392	20	55	13	18	11	3	480	55	32	10	3	520	42	45	13		
Oregon Institute of Technology	Klamath Falls	SM	A,B,M	Pub	F,S	C	3,086							35	42	21	2		29	42	26	3		6/1
Oregon State University	Corvallis	SM	B,M,D	Pub	F,S	C	15,599		31	28	22	9	10	35	42	21	2		29	42	26	3		
Pacific Northwest College of Art	Portland	U	B	Pri	No	C	306		33	67				41	42	17			50	17	33			3/1
Pacific University	Forest Grove	SM	B,M,D	Pri	No	C	1,075																	2/15
Portland State University	Portland	U	B,M,D	Pub	F,S	C	15,917	21	39	30	20	8	3	520	41	39	18	2	520	40	41	18	1	Open
Reed College	Portland	U	B,M	Pri	No	C	1,312	30		1	8	24	67	700	1	6	38	55	660	1	15	53	31	1/15
Southern Oregon University	Ashland	SM	B,M	Pub	No	C	4,964	21	36	34	20	5	5	520	39	39	19	3	510	41	43	15	2	Open
University of Oregon	Eugene	U	B,M,D	Pub	F,S	C	15,983							550	31	41	23	5	550	28	41	26	5	1/15
University of Portland	Portland	SU	B,M	Pri	No	C	2,671	29						588	5	41	42	12	585	5	40	43	12	2/1
Warner Pacific College	Portland	U	A,B,M	Pri	No	C	645																	Open
Western Baptist College	Salem	SU	A,B	Pri	No	C	737	21	7	60	6	7	20	550	24	45	28	3	540	31	44	22	3	8/1
Western Oregon University	Monmouth	R	A,B,M	Pub	No	C	4,470	21	23	50	23	2	2	495	52	37	11		485	55	35	9	1	Open
Willamette University	Salem	U	B,M,D	Pri	F,S	C	1,945	27	4	11	31	23	31	620	6	30	47	17	620	5	31	51	14	2/1

Pennsylvania

NAME OF SCHOOL	TOWN	ENVIRONMENT	DEGREES AWARDED	CONTROL	FRATERNITIES AND SORORITIES	STUDENTS	UNDERGRADUATE ENROLLMENT FALL 2003	ACT Median	Below 21	21-23	24-26	27-28	Above 28	SAT I VERBAL Median	Below 500	500-599	600-700	Above 700	SAT I MATH Median	Below 500	500-599	600-700	Above 700	APP DEADLINE
Albright College	Reading	SU	B,M	Pri	F,S	C	2,050							520		42	18		510	41	40	18	1	Open
Allegheny College	Meadville	SM	B	Pri	F,S	C	1,849	25	11	15	36	22	16	600	11	35	45	9	600	7	41	43	9	2/15
Alvernia College	Reading	SU	A,B,M	Pri	No	C	1,597							470	68	25	7	1	465	67	27	6		Open
Arcadia University	Glenside	SU	B,M,D	Pri	No	C	1,840							540	31	43	25	1	510	35	43	20	2	Open
Bloomsburg University of Pennsylvania	Bloomsburg	SM	A,B,M	Pub	F,S	C	7,521							510	44	46	9		510	40	48	11	1	
Bryn Athyn College of the New Church	Bryn Athyn	SU	A,B,M	Pri	No	C	133							580	24	31	31	13	560	17	52	24	7	2/1
Bryn Mawr College	Bryn Mawr	SU	B,M,D	Pri	No	W	1,334							670	2	16	44	38	630	1	31	53	15	1/15
Bucknell University	Lewisburg	SM	B,M	Pri	F,S	C	3,485							640	1	22	62	15	670		12	59	29	1/1
Cabrini College	Radnor	SU	B,M	Pri	No	C	1,715							490	53	39	7	1	480	59	34	6	1	Open
California University of Pennsylvania	California	SM	A,B,M	Pub	F,S	C	5,076																	Open
Carlow College	Pittsburgh	U	B,M	Pri	No	PW	1,756	20	56	17	17	8	2	490	50	41	8	1	460	62	31	6	1	Open
Carnegie Mellon University	Pittsburgh	SU	B,M,D	Pri	F,S	C	5,135																	Open
Cedar Crest College	Allentown	SU	A,B	Pri	No	W	1,593																	Open
Chatham College	Pittsburgh	U	B,M,D	Pri	No	W	668	24	31	18	38	13		550	26	40	31	3	480	59	28	12	1	Open
Chestnut Hill College	Philadelphia	SU	A,B,M	Pri	No	C	906	18	75	25				480	58	33	8	1	460	66	29	5		Open
Cheyney University of Pennsylvania	Cheyney	SU	B,M	Pub	F,S	C	1,198																	5/30
Clarion University of Pennsylvania	Clarion	SM	A,B,M	Pub	F,S	C	5,812																	Open
College Misericordia	Dallas	SU	B,M	Pri	No	C	1,967	23	29	24	35	6	6	508	47	42	11		510	45	44	11		Open
Curtis Institute of Music	Philadelphia	U	B	Pri	No	C	120																	Open
De Sales University	Center Valley	SU	B,M	Pri	S	C	2,167							530	31	45	21	3	540	29	46	23	2	Open
Delaware Valley College	Doylestown	SU	A,B,M	Pri	F,S	C	1,958	21	42	42	16			497	54	35	10	1	494	52	39	9		Open
DeVry University/Fort Washington	Fort Washington		A,B,M		No	C	663																	Open
Dickinson College	Carlisle	SU	B	Pri	F,S	C	2,276	27	1	3	34	29	32	640		26	59	14	640	2	24	56	18	2/1
Drexel University	Philadelphia	U	B,M,D	Pri	F,S	C	11,011							580	10	47	38	5	620	5	34	50	11	3/1
Duquesne University	Pittsburgh	U	B,M,D	Pri	F,S	C	5,724	24	19	21	30	15	11	560	21	49	27	3	560	21	46	30	3	7/1
East Stroudsburg University of Pennsylvania	East Stroudsburg	SM	B,M	Pub	F,S	C	5,121							490	57	36	6	1	490	53	38	8	1	3/1
Eastern University	St. Davids	SM	A,B,M	Pri	No	C	1,900																	5/1
Edinboro University of Pennsylvania	Edinboro	SM	A,B,M	Pub	F,S	C	7,029	18	69	21	9	1	1	470	61	31	7	1	470	62	31	7		Open
Elizabethtown College	Elizabethtown	SM	A,B,M	Pri	No	C	1,975						6	500	22	49	25	4	510	20	48	28	4	Open
Franklin and Marshall College	Lancaster	SU	B	Pri	F,S	C	1,923	29						620	5	31	48	15	640	3	28	48	21	2/1
Gannon University	Erie	U	A,B,M,D	Pri	F,S	C	2,435	23						520	39	44	15	2	529	34	45	20	1	Open
Geneva College	Beaver Falls	SM	A,B,M	Pri	No	C	1,377	23						540	28	45	23	4	550	40	38	20	2	Open
Gettysburg College	Gettysburg	SU	B	Pri	F,S	C	2,597							630		34	56	9	630		28	63	8	2/15
Grove City College	Grove City	SM	B	Pri	F,S	C	2,276	27	2	10	26	24	38	631	4	25	52	19	637	2	24	51	23	2/1
Gwynedd-Mercy College	Gwynedd Valley	SU	A,B,M	Pri	No	C	2,177							485	55	38	6	1	480	58	35	7		8/1
Haverford College	Haverford	SU	B	Pri	No	C	1,163							690	1	7	46	46	690	1	7	48	44	1/15
Holy Family College	Philadelphia	SU	A,B,M	Pri	No	C	1,849																	Open
Immaculata University	Immaculata	SU	A,B,M,D	Pri	No	W	389							522	38	37	22	3	487	58	30	11	1	5/1
Indiana University of Pennsylvania	Indiana	SM	A,B,M,D	Pub	F,S	C	12,119							522	36	47	15	2	517	42	45	12	1	Open
Juniata College	Huntingdon	SM	B,M	Pri	No	C	1,396							570	12	47	35	7	590	7	47	38	7	3/15
Keystone College	La Plume	R	A,B	Pri	No	C	1,502		87					440	77	16	4		420	82	16	2		Open
King's College	Wilkes Barre	U	A,B,M	Pri	No	C	2,064							520	37	46	15	2	530	35	43	20	2	5/1
Kutztown University of Pennsylvania	Kutztown	SM	B,M	Pub	F,S	C	8,058							495	55				57	37	5			Open
La Roche College	Pittsburgh	SU	A,B,M	Pri	No	C	1,551	21	72	13	5	5	5	470	61	27	12		480	51	38	10	1	Open

Column key

- ENVIRONMENT: U-Urban, R-Rural, SU-Suburban, SM-Small Town
- DEGREES AWARDED: A-Associate, B-Bachelor, M-Master, D-Doctoral
- CONTROL: Pri-Private, Pub-Public
- FRATERNITIES AND SORORITIES: F-Fraternities, S-Sororities, F,S-Both, No-Neither
- STUDENTS: C-Coed, M-Men, W-Women, PM-Primarily Men, PW-Primarily Women
- UNDERGRADUATE ENROLLMENT FALL 2003
- TEST SCORES: ACT / SAT I VERBAL REASONING / SAT I MATHEMATICAL REASONING
- APPLICATION DEADLINE: Month / Day

NAME OF SCHOOL	TOWN	ENV	DEGREES	CONTROL	FRAT	STUD	ENROLL 2003	ACT Median	ACT Below 21	ACT 21-23	ACT 24-26	ACT 27-28	ACT Above 28	SAT V Median	V Below 500	V 500-599	V 600-700	V Above 700	SAT M Median	M Below 500	M 500-599	M 600-700	M Above 700	DEADLINE
La Salle University	Philadelphia	U	A,B,M,D	Pri	F,S	C	4,099							550	24	47	24	4	550	27	47	23	3	4/1
Lafayette College	Easton	SU	B	Pri	F,S	C	2,300	28	1	3	14	66	16	619	3	27	58	12	649	2	22	53	22	1/1
Lebanon Valley College	Annville	SM	A,B,M	Pri	F,S	C	1,765							547	25	48	25	2	563	21	43	32	4	Open
Lehigh University	Bethlehem	SU	B,M,D	Pri	F,S	C	4,679							625	3	26	59	12	670	1	12	52	35	1/1
Lincoln University	Lincoln University	R	B,M	Pub	F,S	C	1,530							440					440					Open
Lock Haven University of Pennsylvania	Lock Haven	R	A,B,M	Pub	F,S	C	4,696	21	49	26	25		1	483	58	34	6	1	489	44	43	11	1	Open
Lycoming College	Williamsport	SM	B	Pri	F,S	C	1,435							565	24	48	24	2	570	28	45	26	1	4/1
Mansfield University	Mansfield	R	A,B,M	Pub	F,S	C	3,168	21	50	30	14	3	3	524	38	48	13	1	518	39	46	13	2	7/1
Marywood University	Scranton	SU	A,B,M,D	Pri	F,S	C	1,751	22	59	18	14		9	515	41	46	12	1	490	52	37	10	1	1/1
MCP Hahnemann University	Philadelphia	U	A,B,M,D	Pri	No	C	672																	6/1
Mercyhurst College	Erie	SU	A,B,M	Pri	No	C	3,200																	Open
Messiah College	Grantham	SM	B	Pri	No	C	2,952	26	4	23	27	15	31	600	7	41	42	11	590	7	45	38	11	
Millersville University of Pennsylvania	Millersville	SM	A,B,M	Pub	F,S	C	6,820	21						530	27	54	17	2	540	26	53	20	2	Open
Moore College of Art and Design	Philadelphia	U	B	Pri	No	W	625	22						530	39	29	25		490	53	25	13	1	Open
Moravian College	Bethlehem	SU	B,M	Pri	F,S	C	1,845							558	21	50	25	4	566	14	52	31	3	3/1
Mount Aloysius College	Cresson	SM	A,B	Pri	No	C	1,447	19	90	2	8			480	77	20	4		450	78	18	4		Open
Muhlenberg College	Allentown	SU	B	Pri	F,S	C	2,452							607	6	38	48	8	619	4	36	51	9	2/15
Neumann College	Aston	SU	A,B,M	Pri	No	C	2,112							440	82	14	3		430	80	17	3		Open
Peirce College	Philadelphia	U	A,B	Pri	No	C	2,176																	Open
Penn State University at Erie/Behrend College	Erie	SU	A,B,M	Pub	F,S	C	3,550																	Open
Penn State University/Altoona	Altoona	SU	A,B		F,S	C	3,813																	Open
Penn State University/University Park Campus	University Park	SU	A,B,M,D		F,S	C	35,002							580	12	44	36	8	620	7	31	47	15	Open
Pennsylvania College of Technology	Williamsport	U	A,B	Pub	No	C	6,255																	Open
Philadelphia Biblical University	Langhorne	SU	B,M	Pri	No	C	1,045	21	46	23	15		15	540	28	45	23	4	510	39	41	19	1	Open
Philadelphia University	Philadelphia	SU	A,B,M	Pri	F,S	C	2,603							520	30	51	18	1	540	28	51	20	1	Open
Point Park University	Pittsburgh	U	A,B,M	Pri	No	C	2,827	22	36	36	17	5	6	527	33	49	18	1	502	45	42	11	1	Open
Robert Morris University	Moon Township	SU	B,M,D	Pri	F,S	C	3,735	19						500	52	40	8		495	46	38	15	1	7/1
Rosemont College	Rosemont	SU	B,M	Pri	No	PW	697	21	100					509	24	44	25	4	493	38	42	15	3	Open
Saint Francis University	Loretto	R	B,M	Pri	F,S	C	1,333		32	21	33	12	2	522	38	48	11	1	517					4/1
Saint Joseph's University	Philadelphia	SU	A,B,M,D	Pri	F,S	C	4,656							600					600					Open
Saint Vincent College	Latrobe	SU	B,M	Pri	No	C	1,440	22	32	20	30	9	9	540	27	50	19	4	540	31	44	22	3	5/1
Seton Hill University	Greensburg	SM	B,M	Pri	No	C	1,240							520	40	51	8	1	510	50	37	13		Open
Shippensburg University of Pennsylvania	Shippensburg	R	B,M	Pub	F,S	C	6,567							531	36	49	14	1	537	32	50	16	1	Open
Slippery Rock University of Pennsylvania	Slippery Rock	SM	B,M,D	Pub	F,S	C	7,054	21	48	31	15	4	1	495	52	40	7	1	495	53	38	8	1	6/1
Susquehanna University	Selinsgrove	SU	A,B	Pri	F,S	C	1,933							570	11	56	30	3	580	10	48	39	3	3/1
Swarthmore College	Swarthmore	SU	B	Pri	F	C	1,500							730	1	6	26	67	720		7	28	65	1/1
Temple University	Philadelphia	U	A,B,M,D	Pub	F,S	C	22,215							540	25	44	26	2	540	24	51	23	2	4/1
Thiel College	Greenville	R	B	Pri	F,S	C	1,261	19	63	18	12	4	3	490	55	35	10	1	480	58	35	6	1	Open
University of Pennsylvania	Philadelphia	U	A,B,M,D	Pri	F,S	C	9,837	30		2	9	16	72	700		7	48	45	720		4	37	60	1/1
University of Pittsburgh at Bradford	Bradford	SM	A,B	Pub	F,S	C	1,417	21	49	33	16		2	500	49	37	13	1	510	47	40	11	2	Open
University of Pittsburgh at Greensburg	Greensburg	SU	B	Pub	No	C	1,916							528	32	53	14	1	532	29	55	15	1	Open
University of Pittsburgh at Johnstown	Johnstown	SU	A,B	Pub	F,S	C	3,146	20	52	36	10	1	1	511	44	48	7	1	521	37	48	14	1	Open
University of Pittsburgh at Pittsburgh	Pittsburgh	U	B,M,D	Pub	F,S	C	17,413							600	7	42	40	11	610	6	33	48	13	Open
University of Scranton	Scranton	U	A,B,M,D	Pri	No	C	4,073							557	20	53	24	3	566	15	53	28	4	3/1
University of the Arts	Philadelphia	U	B,M	Pri	No	C	1,977	23						520	36	42	21	1	510	46	41	12	1	Open
University of the Sciences in Philadelphia	Philadelphia	U	B,M,D	Pri	F,S	C	2,323							540	27	53	19	1	580	9	52	34	5	Open
Ursinus College	Collegeville	SU	B	Pri	F,S	C	1,485							605	7	41	40	12	607	9	34	45	12	2/15
Villanova University	Villanova	SU	A,B,M,D	Pri	F,S	C	7,145							610	4	35	51	10	640	3	20	60	17	1/15
Washington and Jefferson College	Washington	SM	A,B	Pri	F,S	C	1,233	24	11	36	28	13	13	550	16	52	28	4	580	13	48	34	6	3/1
Waynesburg College	Waynesburg	SM	A,B,M	Pri	No	C	1,497	20	60	23	14	3		480	57	35	8		480	55	35	10		Open
West Chester University of Pennsylvania	West Chester	SU	A,B,M	Pub	F,S	C	10,564							530	29	56	14	1	530	29	54	16	1	Open
Westminster College	New Wilmington	R	B,M	Pri	F,S	C	1,473																	
Widener University	Chester	SU	A,B,M,D	Pri	F,S	C	2,327							505	51	37	11	1	510	43	39	16	2	2/15
Wilkes University	Wilkes Barre	U	B,M	Pri	No	C	2,320							533	32	44	21	3	548	29	40	25	6	Open
Wilson College	Chambersburg	SM	A,B	Pri	No	W	330	22	45	18	18	9	9	480	58	32	10		500	47	33	17	2	Open
York College of Pennsylvania	York	SU	A,B,M	Pri	F,S	C	5,286							551	17	55	24	4	542	17	60	21	2	Open

Puerto Rico

NAME OF SCHOOL	TOWN	ENV	DEGREES	CONTROL	FRAT	STUD	ENROLL 2003	ACT Median	ACT Below 21	ACT 21-23	ACT 24-26	ACT 27-28	ACT Above 28	SAT V Median	V Below 500	V 500-599	V 600-700	V Above 700	SAT M Median	M Below 500	M 500-599	M 600-700	M Above 700	DEADLINE
American University of Puerto Rico	Bayamon	U	A,B	Pri	No	C	3,038																	Open
Caribbean University	Bayamon	U	B	Pri	No		3,100																	Open
Central University of Bayamon	Bayamon	U	A,B,M	Pri	No	C	2,885																	
Conservatory of Music of Puerto Rico	San Juan	U	B	Pub	No	C																		
Escuela de Artes Plasticas de Puerto Rico	San Juan	U	B	Pub	No	C	365																	5/16
Inter American University of Puerto Rico/Aguadilla Campus	Aguadilla	SU	A,B,M	Pri	No	C	4,154																	5/1
Inter American University of Puerto Rico/Arecibo Campus	Arecibo	SU	A,B,M	Pri	F,S	C	4,125																	
Inter American University of Puerto Rico/Barranquitas Regional College	Barranquitas	SM	A,B	Pri	No	C	1,700																	
Inter American University of Puerto Rico/Bayamon University College	Bayamon	U	A,B	Pri	No	C	5,021																	5/1
Inter American University of Puerto Rico/Fajardo Campus	Fajardo	U	A,B,M,D	Pri	No	C	2,240																	8/15
Inter American University of Puerto Rico/Metropolitan Campus	San Juan	U	A,B,M,D	Pri	No	C	7,094																	5/1
Inter American University of Puerto Rico/Ponce Regional College	Ponce	U	B	Pri	No	C																		
Inter American University of Puerto Rico/San German	San German	R	A,B,M,D	Pri	No	C	5,086							475	68	27	4		498	63	28	8	1	5/15

Legend: ENVIRONMENT: U-Urban, R-Rural, SU-Suburban, SM-Small Town · DEGREES AWARDED: A-Associate, B-Bachelor, M-Master, D-Doctorate · CONTROL: Pri-Private, Pub-Public · FRATERNITIES/SORORITIES: F-Fraternities, S-Sororities, F,S-Both, No-Neither · STUDENTS: C-Coed, M-Men, W-Women, PM-Primarily Men, PW-Primarily Women

NAME OF SCHOOL	TOWN	ENV	DEGREES	CONTROL	FRAT	STUD	UNDERGRAD ENROLL FALL 2003	ACT Median	ACT Below 21	ACT 21-23	ACT 24-26	ACT 27-28	ACT Above 28	SAT Verbal Median	Verbal Below 500	Verbal 500-599	Verbal 600-700	Verbal Above 700	SAT Math Median	Math Below 500	Math 500-599	Math 600-700	Math Above 700	APP DEADLINE
Pontifical Catholic University of Puerto Rico/Ponce	Ponce	U	A,B,M,D	Pri	F,S	C	7,996								75	19	6			73	19	7	1	7/15
Turabo University	Gurabo	SU	A,B,M	Pri	No																			Open
Universidad Adventista de las Antillas	Mayaguez	SM	A,B,M	Pri	F,S	C	821																	Open
Universidad Metropolitana	Rio Piedras	U	A,B,M	Pri	No	C																		Open
Universidad Politecnica de Puerto Rico	Hato Rey	U	B,M	Pri	No	C	5,168																	7/30
University of Puerto Rico at Humacao	Humacao	SU	A,B	Pub	F	C	4,440							526	39	44	16	1	531	35	43	18	4	11/14
University of Puerto Rico/Arecibo	Arecibo	U	A,B	Pub	F,S	C	4,667																	11/17
University of Puerto Rico/Bayamon University College Campus	Bayamon	SU	A,B	Pub	No	C	5,324																	12/20
University of Puerto Rico/Cayey University College	Cayey	U	A,B	Pub	F	C	3,987																	10/28
University of Puerto Rico/Mayaguez	Mayaguez	U	A,B,M,D	Pub	F,S	C	11,079							550					550					11/15
University of Puerto Rico/Rio Piedras	San Juan	U	B,M,D	Pub	F,S	C	17,845								16	43	37	4		17	33	33	15	2/15
University of the Sacred Heart	Santurce	U	A,B,M	Pri	No	C	4,560																	

Rhode Island

NAME OF SCHOOL	TOWN	ENV	DEGREES	CONTROL	FRAT	STUD	UNDERGRAD ENROLL FALL 2003	ACT Median	ACT Below 21	ACT 21-23	ACT 24-26	ACT 27-28	ACT Above 28	SAT Verbal Median	Verbal Below 500	Verbal 500-599	Verbal 600-700	Verbal Above 700	SAT Math Median	Math Below 500	Math 500-599	Math 600-700	Math Above 700	APP DEADLINE
Brown University	Providence	U	B,M,D	Pri	F,S	C	5,906	29	2	7	16	15	60	700	2	11	36	51	710	1	8	36	55	1/1
Bryant College	Smithfield	SU	B,M	Pri	F,S	C	2,976	24	19	31	23	19	8	530	26	59	14	1	560	14	56	27	3	2/15
Johnson and Wales University	Providence	U	A,B,M,D	Pri	F,S	C	9,220								63	31	6			63	30	7		Open
Providence College	Providence	SU	A,B,M	Pri	No	C	4,342	26	7	18	35	22	18	599	7	40	45	8	607	5	37	50	8	1/15
Rhode Island College	Providence	SU	B,M,D	Pub	No	C	7,305							494	56	33	10	1	491	57	33	10		5/1
Rhode Island School of Design	Providence	U	B,M	Pri	No	C								610	15	29	44	12	610	10	35	43	12	2/15
Roger Williams University	Bristol	SM	B,M	Pri	No	C	3,410							530	32	50	17	1	530	28	51	20	1	
Salve Regina University	Newport	SU	A,B,M,D	Pri	No	C	2,026	22						530	24	60	15	1	520	29	56	15		3/1
University of Rhode Island	Kingston	SM	B,M,D	Pub	F,S	C	11,298							540	21	54	22	3	560	16	52	28	4	3/1

South Carolina

NAME OF SCHOOL	TOWN	ENV	DEGREES	CONTROL	FRAT	STUD	UNDERGRAD ENROLL FALL 2003	ACT Median	ACT Below 21	ACT 21-23	ACT 24-26	ACT 27-28	ACT Above 28	SAT Verbal Median	Verbal Below 500	Verbal 500-599	Verbal 600-700	Verbal Above 700	SAT Math Median	Math Below 500	Math 500-599	Math 600-700	Math Above 700	APP DEADLINE
Allen University	Columbia	SM	A,B	Pri	F,S	C	340																	Open
Benedict College	Columbia	U	B	Pri	F,S	C	2,750																	Open
Charleston Southern University	Charleston	SU	A,B,M	Pri	No	C	2,444																	Open
Citadel, The	Charleston	SU	B,M	Pub	No	C	2,150		29	37	23	7	4		23	51	23	3		20	50	27	3	Open
Claflin University	Orangeburg	SU	B,M	Pri	F,S	C	1,364	19						500	66	26	7	1	425	60	30	9	1	Open
Clemson University	Clemson	SM	B,M,D	Pub	F,S	C	13,813	26	8	15	31	15	31	587	10	43	40	7	617	5	32	50	13	5/1
Coastal Carolina University	Conway	SU	B,M	Pub	F,S	C	5,610	22	43	35	15	5	2	515	44	44	11	1	530	32	50	17	1	8/15
Coker College	Hartsville	SM	B	Pri	No	C	482	19	58	24	12	4	2	490	53	37	12		490	50	40	9	1	Open
College of Charleston	Charleston	U	B,M	Pub	F,S	C	9,824							605	3	42	47	8	601	3	44	48	6	4/1
Columbia College	Columbia	U	B,M	Pri	No	PW	1,187																	Open
Converse College	Spartanburg	U	B,M	Pri	No	W	708	23	31	25	22	13	9	570	20	48	26	6	540	28	45	23	4	8/15
Erskine College	Due West	R	B,M,D	Pri	F,S	C	589	25	27	12	34	5	22	560	23	45	22	10	560	21	46	27	6	Open
Francis Marion University	Florence	R	A,B,M	Pri	F,S	C	3,097	19	78	16	5	1		474	69	25	5	1	480	63	30	6	1	Open
Furman University	Greenville	SU	B,M	Pri	F,S	C	2,773	28	3	8	24	22	44	640	3	21	52	23	640	3	22	56	20	1/15
Lander University	Greenwood	SM	B,M	Pub	F,S	C	2,634	20	56	27	15	1	2	480	56	36	7	1	480	53	38	8	1	Open
Limestone College	Gaffney	SU	A,B	Pri	S	C	552	19	71	15	9	5		468	64	32	4		472	62	29	9		Open
Morris College	Sumter	U	B	Pri	F,S	C	1,007	17	94	6				467	67	33			443	83	17			Open
Newberry College	Newberry	SM	B	Pri	F,S	C	776	18	74	16	8	1		474	61	33	5	1	482	56	35	9		Open
Presbyterian College	Clinton	SM	B	Pri	F,S	C	1,182	23	20	31	31	8	10	556	14	50	32	4	562	16	46	35	3	Open
South Carolina State University	Orangeburg	SM	B,M,D		F,S	C	3,951																	7/31
Southern Wesleyan University	Central	SM	A,B,M	Pri	No	C	1,965	19	62	19	15	2	2	510	42	38		1	510	42	39	16	2	8/2
University of South Carolina at Aiken	Aiken	SU	A,B,M	Pub	No	C	3,139																	Open
University of South Carolina at Columbia	Columbia	U	A,B,M,D	Pub	F,S	C	16,567	24	16	30	30	11	13	550	24	47	23	6	560	17	47	29	7	2/15
University of South Carolina at Spartanburg	Spartanburg	U	A,B,M	Pub	F,S	C	4,397	20						417	54	36	9	1	502	52	39	8	1	Open
Voorhees College	Denmark	R	B	Pri	F,S	C	876																	8/15
Winthrop University	Rock Hill	SM	B,M	Pub	F,S	C	5,161	21	41	28	21	6	4	530	33	45	19	3	520	33	48	17	2	5/1
Wofford College	Spartanburg	U	B	Pri	F,S	C	1,132	25	9	27	37	20	7	600	7	31	53	9	612	2	30	51	17	2/1

South Dakota

NAME OF SCHOOL	TOWN	ENV	DEGREES	CONTROL	FRAT	STUD	UNDERGRAD ENROLL FALL 2003	ACT Median	ACT Below 21	ACT 21-23	ACT 24-26	ACT 27-28	ACT Above 28	SAT Verbal Median	Verbal Below 500	Verbal 500-599	Verbal 600-700	Verbal Above 700	SAT Math Median	Math Below 500	Math 500-599	Math 600-700	Math Above 700	APP DEADLINE
Augustana College	Sioux Falls	SU	B,M	Pri	No	C	1,810	25	16	23	31	14	16	600	12	31	38	19	590	12	42	31	15	Open
Black Hills State University	Spearfish	SM	A,B,M	Pub	F,S	C	3,671	21	54	26	14	4	2											Open
Dakota State University	Madison	SM	A,B,M	Pub	No	C	2,098	22																Open
Dakota Wesleyan University	Mitchell	SM	A,B,M	Pub	No	C	738	20	27	54	16	2	1											8/25
Huron University	Huron	SM	A,B,M	Pri	No	C	544																	8/1
Mount Marty College	Yankton	SM	A,B,M	Pri	No	C	1,069																	Open
National American University	Rapid City	SM	A,B,M	Pri	No	C	852																	Open
Northern State University	Aberdeen	U	A,B,M	Pub	No	C	2,842																	8/15
Oglala Lakota College	Kyle	R	B	Pri	No	C																		Open
Presentation College	Aberdeen	SM	A,B	Pri	No	C	618	21	60	31	6	1	1											Open
Sinte Gleska University	Rosebud	R	A,B,M	Pri	No	C	336																	Open
South Dakota School of Mines and Technology	Rapid City	SU	A,B,M,D	Pub	F,S	C	2,112	24	21	23	28	13	15	550					575					8/15
South Dakota State University	Brookings	SM	A,B,M,D	Pub	F,S	C	9,208	22	35	26	26	8	5											Open
University of Sioux Falls	Sioux Falls	SU	A,B,M	Pri	No	C	1,122																	Open
University of South Dakota	Vermillion	R	A,B,M,D	Pub	F,S	C	5,830	22	36	24	25	8	7	568	15	44	35	6	558	21	48	25	6	Open

Tennessee

NAME OF SCHOOL	TOWN	ENV	DEGREES	CONTROL	FRAT	STUD	UNDERGRAD ENROLL FALL 2003	ACT Median	ACT Below 21	ACT 21-23	ACT 24-26	ACT 27-28	ACT Above 28	SAT Verbal Median	Verbal Below 500	Verbal 500-599	Verbal 600-700	Verbal Above 700	SAT Math Median	Math Below 500	Math 500-599	Math 600-700	Math Above 700	APP DEADLINE
Aquinas College	Nashville	U	A,B	Pri	No	C	520																	Open
Austin Peay State University	Clarksville	U	A,B,M	Pub	F,S	C	6,985																	8/10
Belmont University	Nashville	U	B,M	Pri	F,S	M	2,989	25	11	26	34	13	16	568	15	51	32	2	568	18	46	31	6	8/1

NAME OF SCHOOL	TOWN	ENVIRONMENT U-Urban R-Rural SU-Suburban SM-Small Town	DEGREES AWARDED A-Associate B-Bachelor M-Master D-Doctorate	CONTROL Pri-Private, Pub-Public	FRATERNITIES AND SORORITIES F-Fraternities S-Sororities F,S-Both No-Neither	STUDENTS: C-Coed M-Men W-Women PM-Primarily Men PW-Primarily Women	UNDERGRADUATE ENROLLMENT FALL 2003	TEST SCORES ACT Median	ACT Below 21	ACT 21-23	ACT 24-26	ACT 27-28	ACT Above 28	SAT I VERBAL REASONING Median	SAT I Verbal Below 500	SAT I Verbal 500-599	SAT I Verbal 600-700	SAT I Verbal Above 700	SAT I MATHEMATICAL REASONING Median	SAT I Math Below 500	SAT I Math 500-599	SAT I Math 600-700	SAT I Math Above 700	APPLICATION DEADLINE Month / Day
Bethel College	McKenzie	SM	B,M	Pri	F,S	C	840																	8/30
Bryan College	Dayton	SM	A,B	Pri	No	C	588																	Open
Carson-Newman College	Jefferson City	SM	A,B,M	Pri	F,S	C	1,942	22	38	26	23	8	5											8/15
Christian Brothers University	Memphis	U	B,M	Pri	F,S	C	1,491	23	27	32	24	8	9	539	30	46	20	4	544	29	41	30		7/15
Crichton College	Memphis	U	B	Pri	No	C	870		25	32	21	20	2	540		100			560		100			Open
Cumberland University	Lebanon	SM	A,B,M	Pri	F,S	C	921	20	62	22	13	3		470	60	30	10		470	65	25	10		Open
David Lipscomb University	Nashville	SU	B,M	Pri	No	C	2,394																	Open
East Tennessee State University	Johnson City	SM	A,B,M,D	Pub	F,S	C	9,550	22	40	24	20	9	7	520	41	39	18	2	520	43	39	16	2	Open
Fisk University	Nashville	U	B,M	Pri	F,S	C	850	19	60	28	7	3	2	468	66	28	6		444	71	22	7		Open
Freed-Hardeman University	Henderson	SM	B,M	Pri	No	C	1,447	23	28	32	19	10	10											Open
King College	Bristol	SM	B,M	Pub	No	C	687	25	13	26	31	17	13	580	23	30	37	7	560	33	33	23	9	Open
Knoxville College	Knoxville	U	A,B		No	C																		Open
Lambuth University	Jackson	U	B	Pri	F,S	C	836	22	31	32	22	10	5	550	30	39	25	6	530	30	42	22	6	Open
Lane College	Jackson	SM	B	Pri	F,S	C	952	16	94	6														7/1
Lee University	Cleveland	SU	B,M	Pri	No	C	3,555	22						538	34	38	23	5	517	42	37	18	3	9/1
LeMoyne-Owen College	Memphis	U	B	Pri	F,S	C	782	16	92	7	1			390	100				365	100				4/1
Lincoln Memorial University	Harrogate	R	A,B,M	Pri	F,S	C	1,117																	Open
Maryville College	Maryville	SU	B	Pri	No	C	1,052	24	20	25	22	16	16	560	28	33	35	4	570	32	29	33	7	3/1
Memphis College of Art	Memphis	U	B,M	Pri	No	C	300	21	44	24	19	9	4											Open
Middle Tennessee State University	Murfreesboro	U	A,B,M,D	Pub	F,S	C	19,754	22	34	31	19	7	6	535					518					7/1
Milligan College	Milligan College	SU	B,M	Pri	No	C	736	24	29	17	33	10	11	550	19	50	29	2	550	25	49	23	3	8/15
Rhodes College	Memphis	U	B,M	Pri	F,S	C	1,535																	2/1
Southern Adventist University	Collegedale	SM	A,B,M	Pri	No	C																		Open
Tennessee State University	Nashville	U	A,B,M,D	Pub	F,S	C	7,118	18	77	17	5	1	1	441	76	21	4		440	74	23	3		8/1
Tennessee Technological University	Cookeville	SM	B,M,D	Pub	F,S	C	7,273	23	30	25	23	10	12		24	40	30	6		22	38	34	6	8/1
Tennessee Wesleyan College	Athens	SM	B	Pri	S	C	793	21	50	26	17	5	3											Open
Trevecca Nazarene University	Nashville	U	A,B,M,D	Pri	No	C	1,232	21	42	26	18	4	10	530					510					Open
Tusculum College	Greeneville	SM	B,M	Pri	No	C	1,914	20	60	19	15	4	2	470	61	31	7	1	480	57	31	11	1	Open
Union University	Jackson	SU	A,B,M,D	Pri	F,S	C	2,022	24	20	25	26	12	17	560	17	47	23	12	550	27	43	23	8	Open
University of Memphis	Memphis	U	B,M,D	Pub	F,S	C	15,209	21	44	24	18	9	5	540	34	40	23	4	530	35	39	22	4	8/1
University of Tennessee at Chattanooga	Chattanooga	U	B,M	Pub	F,S	C	7,105																	8/1
University of Tennessee at Knoxville	Knoxville	U	B,M,D	Pub	F,S	C	20,124																	2/1
University of Tennessee at Martin	Martin	R	B,M	Pub	F,S	C	5,375	21	40	29	19	7	5											Open
University of the South	Sewanee	SM	B,M,D	Pri	F,S	C	1,364		1	22	20	43	14		5	40	40	15		7	38	47	8	2/1
Vanderbilt University	Nashville	U	B,M,D	Pri	F,S	C	6,283								2	14	53	31		1	10	50	39	1/7

Texas

NAME OF SCHOOL	TOWN	ENVIRONMENT U-Urban R-Rural SU-Suburban SM-Small Town	DEGREES AWARDED A-Associate B-Bachelor M-Master D-Doctorate	CONTROL Pri-Private, Pub-Public	FRATERNITIES AND SORORITIES F-Fraternities S-Sororities F,S-Both No-Neither	STUDENTS: C-Coed M-Men W-Women PM-Primarily Men PW-Primarily Women	UNDERGRADUATE ENROLLMENT FALL 2003	TEST SCORES ACT Median	ACT Below 21	ACT 21-23	ACT 24-26	ACT 27-28	ACT Above 28	SAT I VERBAL REASONING Median	SAT I Verbal Below 500	SAT I Verbal 500-599	SAT I Verbal 600-700	SAT I Verbal Above 700	SAT I MATHEMATICAL REASONING Median	SAT I Math Below 500	SAT I Math 500-599	SAT I Math 600-700	SAT I Math Above 700	APPLICATION DEADLINE Month / Day
Abilene Christian University	Abilene	U	A,B,M,D	Pri	F,S	C	4,111	24	24	28	27	10	11	547	29	44	22	5	550	28	42	25	5	Open
Angelo State University	San Angelo	U	A,B,M	Pub	F,S	C	5,618	21	37	35	18	7	3	500	43	42	14	1	510	43	42	14	1	8/9
Austin College	Sherman	SU	B,M	Pri	F,S	C	1,294	25	15	15	26	20	24	618	6	31	47	16	613	8	29	53	10	3/1
Baylor University	Waco	U	B,M,D	Pri	F,S	C	11,712	24	14	31	27	17	11	580	12	45	34	9	600	8	41	41	10	Open
Concordia University at Austin	Austin	U	A,B	Pri	No	C	1,031																	
Dallas Baptist University	Dallas	SU	A,B,M	Pri	No	C	3,444	23	27	36	23	4	9	546	25	49	23	3	544	25	51	21	3	Open
DeVry University/Dallas	Irving	SU	A,B,M	Pri	No	C	2,500																	Open
East Texas Baptist University	Marshall	SM	A,B	Pri	F,S	C	1,354	21	49	26	17	4	4											Open
Hardin-Simmons University	Abilene	U	B,M	Pri	F,S	C	1,902																	Open
Houston Baptist University	Houston	U	A,B,M	Pri	F,S	C	1,866	21	48	28	12	7	5	540	30	46	22	2	535	31	42	23	4	Open
Howard Payne University	Brownwood	SM	A,B	Pri	F,S	C	1,385	20	53	24	18	3	2	507	49	32	18	1	505	47	38	14	1	8/1
Huston-Tillotson College	Austin	U	B	Pri	F,S	C	716	16	90	7	2	1		400	89	9	2		400	86	12	2		3/1
Jarvis Christian College	Hawkins	R	B	Pri	F,S	C	654	16	98	2				358	99	1			352	99	2			8/1
Lamar University	Beaumont	U	A,B,M,D	Pub	F,S	C	8,417																	8/10
LeTourneau University	Longview	U	A,B,M	Pri	No	C	3,175																	8/1
Lubbock Christian University	Lubbock	SU	A,B,M	Pri	No	C	1,759	21	48	24	18	6	4	510	42	41	15	2	490	50	37	10	3	Open
McMurry University	Abilene	U	B	Pri	F,S	C	1,376	19	58	25	11	5	1	480	60	30	9	1	490	51	36	12	1	8/8
Midwestern State University	Wichita Falls	U	A,B,M	Pub	F,S	C	5,644	19	60	25	10	3	2	480	57	31	11	1	480	56	33	10	1	8/7
Northwood University	Cedar Hill	SU	A,B	Pri	No	C	653	19	80	17	2	1		460	73	25	2		450	69	25	5	1	8/1
Our Lady of the Lake University of San Antonio	San Antonio	U	B,M,D	Pri	No	C	2,196																	Open
Paul Quinn College	Dallas	U	B	Pri	F,S	C	770																	
Prairie View A&M University	Prairie View	SM	B,M,D		F,S	C	6,042	16	89	8	2	1		410	87	12	1		410	84	14	2		7/1
Rice University	Houston	U	B,M,D	Pri	No	C	2,921								2	7	34	57		1	6	30	64	1/10
Saint Edward's University	Austin	U	B,M	Pri	No	C	3,531	23	23	32	22	14	9	540	23	49	26	2	540	26	46	27	1	7/1
Saint Mary's University of San Antonio	San Antonio	SU	B,M,D	Pri	F,S	C	2,582	22	32	40	18	7	2	540	31	47	21	1	530	28	52	17	3	Open
Sam Houston State University	Huntsville	SM	B,M,D	Pub	F,S	C	11,504	21	57	25	13	3	1	506	54	36	9	1	504	53	37	9	1	Open
Schreiner University	Kerrville	SM	A,B,M	Pri	F,S	C	732	19						490	54	31	13	2	490	55	37	9		8/1
Southern Methodist University	Dallas	SU	B,M,D	Pri	F,S	C	6,299	26	5	15	36	22	23	590	10	43	42	5	600	7	38	47	8	1/15
Southwestern Adventist University	Keene	R	A,B,M	Pri	No	C	1,163	21	46	33	15	1	5	490	52	29	18	1	460	68	26	5	1	9/5
Southwestern University	Georgetown	SU	B	Pri	F,S	C	1,265	26	3	21	28	22	26	621	4	32	47	17	619	3	32	52	12	2/15
Stephen F. Austin State University	Nacogdoches	SM	B,M,D	Pub	F,S	C	9,747	21	52	27	15	5	2	501	48	39	13	1	499	47	42	11		Open
Sul Ross State University	Alpine	R	A,B,M	Pub	No	C	1,488																	Open
Tarleton State University	Stephenville	SM	B,M,D	Pub	F,S	C	7,435	19	65	22	9	2	1	480	61	32	6	1	470	59	34	6	1	8/1
Texas A&M University	College Station	U	B,M,D		F,S	C	36,066	25	10	20	30	15	25	580	18	41	33	8	610	10	35	42	13	2/15
Texas A&M University at Commerce	Commerce	SM	B,M,D	Pub	F,S	C	5,066	20						480					480					8/6
Texas A&M University at Corpus Christi	Corpus Christi	U	B,M,D	Pub			6,283																	7/1
Texas A&M University at Galveston	Galveston	SU	B,M	Pub	No	C	1,366	24	15	24	45	8	8	547	36	43	19	2	567	33	48	18	1	Open
Texas A&M University at Kingsville	Kingsville	SM	B,M,D	Pub	F,S	C	5,550		70	20	7	2	1											Open
Texas Christian University	Fort Worth	SU	B,M,D	Pri	F,S	C	6,933																	2/15
Texas Lutheran University	Seguin	SU	B	Pri	F,S	C	1,410	22											528					6/1
Texas Southern University	Houston	U	B,M,D	Pub	F,S	C	8,909																	8/13
Texas State University	San Marcos	SU	B,M,D	Pub	F,S	C	22,007	22	22	43	24	8	.2	540	26	54	19	1	540	23	55	21	1	6/1
Texas Tech University	Lubbock	U	B,M,D	Pub	F,S	C	23,595	24	19	31	28	12	10	551	22	52	24	2	572	14	49	33	4	Open
Texas Wesleyan University	Fort Worth	U	B,M	Pri	F,S	C	1,669																	Open

NAME OF SCHOOL	TOWN	ENVIRONMENT U-Urban R-Rural SU-Suburban SM-Small Town	DEGREES AWARDED A-Associate B-Bachelor M-Master D-Doctorate	CONTROL Pri-Private, Pub-Public	FRATERNITIES AND SORORITIES F-Fraternities S-Sororities F, S-Both No-Neither	STUDENTS: C-Coed M-Men W-Women PM-Primarily Men PW-Primarily Women	UNDERGRADUATE ENROLLMENT FALL 2003	TEST SCORES: ACT Median	ACT Below 21	ACT 21-23	ACT 24-26	ACT 27-28	ACT Above 28	SAT I VERBAL REASONING Median	SAT I Verbal Below 500	SAT I Verbal 500-599	SAT I Verbal 600-700	SAT I Verbal Above 700	SAT I MATHEMATICAL REASONING Median	SAT I Math Below 500	SAT I Math 500-599	SAT I Math 600-700	SAT I Math Above 700	APPLICATION DEADLINE Month / Day
Texas Woman's University	Denton	U	B,M,D	Pub	S	PW	5,345	19	64	15	10	2	1	460	64	29	7		450	71	24	5		7/15
Trinity University	San Antonio	SU	B,M	Pri	F,S	C	2,406	29			14	35	51	640	1	20	57	21	690		16	63	22	2/1
University of Dallas	Irving	SU	B,M,D	Pri	No	C	1,250	26	16	15	25	23	21	600	11	36	35	18	590	15	38	40	7	1/15
University of Houston	Houston	U	B,M,D	Pub	F,S	C	27,033	21	49	26	16	5	4	510	43	39	15	3	530	33	41	23	3	4/1
University of Houston-Downtown	Houston	U	B,M	Pub	F,S	C	10,862																	
University of Mary Hardin-Baylor	Belton	SM	B,M	Pri	No	C	2,475	23	28	33	22	9	8	532	34	48	16	2	535	31	48	19	2	Open
University of North Texas	Denton	U	B,M,D	Pub	F,S	C	21,675																	6/15
University of Saint Thomas	Houston	U	B,M,D	Pri	No	C	1,907	24	13	31	27	15	15	570	17	44	33	6	570	13	48	34	5	Open
University of Texas at Arlington	Arlington	U	B,M,D	Pub	F,S	C	16,330	21	44	30	19	5	3	520	39	45	16	1	530	34	45	20	1	6/1
University of Texas at Austin	Austin	U	B,M,D	Pub	F,S	C	38,383	25	11	17	27	18	27	600	12	33	40	15	630	8	25	44	24	2/1
University of Texas at Dallas	Richardson	SU	B,M,D	Pub	F,S	C	8,688	26	7	19	30	14	30	602	10	35	41	14	630	3	31	45	21	8/1
University of Texas at El Paso	El Paso	U	B,M,D	Pub	F,S	C	15,085	18	71	20	7	2	1	450	71	24	5		450	68	27	5		7/31
University of Texas at San Antonio	San Antonio	SU	B,M,D	Pub	F,S	C	17,425																	7/1
University of Texas-Pan American	Edinburg	SM	B,M,D	Pub	F,S	C	13,869	18	74	15	8	2	1		71	24	5			69	25	6		7
University of the Incarnate Word	San Antonio	U	B,M,D	Pri	F,S	C	3,665	20	57	20	14	5	4	480	52	34	12	2	470	59	29	11	1	Open
Wayland Baptist University	Plainview	SM	A,B,M	Pri	F,S	C	998	19	57	14	20	5	4	510	45	37	15	2	530	41	42	16	1	Open
West Texas A&M University	Canyon	SM	B,M,D	Pub	F,S	C	5,588	20	52	28	15	3	2	490	52	35	12	2	490					Open
Wiley College	Marshall	SM	B		No																			Open
Utah																								
Brigham Young University	Provo	SU	B,M,D	Pub	No	C	29,932																	2/15
Southern Utah University	Cedar City	SM	A,B,M	Pub	F,S	C	5,840	21						529					522					7/1
University of Utah	Salt Lake City	U	B,M,D	Pub	F,S	C	22,421	23	25	27	25	11	12											4/1
Utah State University	Logan	SM	A,B,M,D	Pub	F,S	C	13,958	23	25	26	24	13	12	550	28	41	24	7	560	25	36	31	8	7/1
Weber State University	Ogden	U	A,B,M	Pub	F,S	C	18,452	22	46	25	19	6	4	506	45	39	13	3	497	48	34	16	2	7/1
Westminster College	Salt Lake City	SU	B,M	Pri	No	C	1,782																	Open
Vermont																								
Bennington College	Bennington	SM	B,M	Pri	No	C	640							645	4	18	48	30	580	16	39	39	6	1/1
Burlington College	Burlington	U	A,B	Pri	No	C	267																	Open
Castleton State College	Castleton	R	A,B,M	Pub	No	C	1,699	19						475	59	32	9		490	60	31	8	1	Open
Champlain College	Burlington	SU	A,B,M	Pri	No	C	2,528	20	59	26	11	4		510	40	50	9	1	520	39	48	12		Open
College of Saint Joseph	Rutland	R	A,B,M	Pri	No	C	309								25	75				25	75			Open
Goddard College	Plainfield	R	B,M	Pri	No	C	319																	Open
Green Mountain College	Poultney	SM	B	Pri	No	C	659	19	64	22		6	8	520	40	39	16	5	505	44	41	15		Open
Johnson State College	Johnson	SM	A,B,M	Pub	No	C	1,532								56	37	7			64	32	4		3/1
Lyndon State College	Lyndonville	SM	A,B,M	Pub	No	C	1,425																	Open
Marlboro College	Marlboro	R	B,M	Pri	No	C	331	26			6	7	85	625	4	26	47	23	580	14	41	35	10	3/1
Middlebury College	Middlebury	SM	B,M,D	Pri	No	C	2,424	32		2	6	52	40	740	1	2	28	69	730	1	4	34	61	12/15
Norwich University	Northfield	R	A,B	Pri	No	C	1,510																	Open
Saint Michael's College	Colchester	SU	B,M	Pri	No	C	1,991							555	18	52	27	3	560	18	53	28	2	2/1
Southern Vermont College	Bennington	SM	A,B	Pri	No	C	464	19	36	57			7			36	5	1	480	70	26	4		Open
Sterling College	Craftsbury Common	R	A,B	Pri	No	C	102	29					100	570	20	30	50		530	30	30	40		Open
University of Vermont	Burlington	SU	A,B,M,D	Pub	F,S	C	9,303	25	14	26	34	17	9	570	13	49	34	4	580	13	44	39	4	1/15
Vermont Technical College	Randolph Center	R	A,B	Pub	No	C	1,218							480					500					Open
Woodbury College	Montpelier	SM	A,B	Pri	No	C	157																	Open
Virginia																								
Averett University	Danville	SM	A,B,M	Pri	F,S	C	2,087	18	81	10	7		2	480	61	29	9	1	470	66	27	7		Open
Bluefield College	Bluefield	SM	B	Pri	F,S	C	731																	Open
Bridgewater College	Bridgewater	SM	B	Pri	No	C	1,403	20	56	26	9	6	4	500	47	39	12	2	510	45	40	15	1	Open
Christendom College	Front Royal	R	A,B,M	Pri	No	C	366	25	6	29	35	16	14	660		20	47	33	570	9	50	29	12	3/1
Christopher Newport University	Newport News	SU	B,M	Pub	F,S	C	5,158																	3/1
College of William and Mary	Williamsburg	SM	B,M,D	Pub	F,S	C	5,748	30		11			89	680	1	11	45	43	670	1	13	51	35	1/5
DeVry University/Crystal City	Arlington		A,B,M	Pri	No	C	607																	Open
Eastern Mennonite University	Harrisonburg	SM	A,B,M	Pri	No	C	917	23	27	24	18	18	12	550	32	35	28	5	530	42	27	19	12	Open
Emory & Henry College	Emory	R	B,M	Pri	F,S	C	886							537	35	36	27	2	530	36	43	18	3	4/15
Ferrum College	Ferrum	R	B	Pri	No	C	954	17	83	14	3			440	74	21	5		450	75	21	5		Open
George Mason University	Fairfax	SU	B,M,D	Pub	F,S	C	17,138							550	25	47	24	3	560	21	49	26	4	2/1
Hampden-Sydney College	Hampden-Sydney	R	B	Pri	F	M	1,039	23	31	28	25	7	10	570	21	46	27	7	570	14	50	32	3	3/1
Hampton University	Hampton	U	A,B,M	Pri	F,S	C	4,953																	3/15
Hollins University	Roanoke	SU	B,M	Pri	No	PW	812	24	4	38	30	18	10	591	19	35	32	14	546	26	42	30	2	2/15
James Madison University	Harrisonburg	SM	B,M,D	Pub	F,S	C	14,683							580	11	54	32	3	590	11	50	36	3	1/15
Liberty University	Lynchburg	SU	A,B,M,D	Pri	No	C	6,326	21	47	23	16	8	6	510	44	37	16	3	490	53	33	12	1	Open
Longwood University	Farmville	SM	B,M	Pub	F,S	C	3,685							547	21	60	18	1	538	25	60	14	1	3/1
Lynchburg College	Lynchburg	SU	B,M	Pri	F,S	C	1,773	20	53	31	9	3	4	510	44	42	13	1	510	42	43	14	1	
Mary Baldwin College	Staunton	SM	B,M	Pri	No	PW	1,427	22						540	30	36	28	6	500	47	35	15	3	4/15
Mary Washington College	Fredericksburg	SM	B,M	Pub	No	C	4,185	27						617	4	33	52	11	606	4	39	49	8	2/1
Marymount University	Arlington	SU	A,B,M	Pri	No	C	2,251	20	65	20	7	5	3	505	44	42	13	1	492	52	38	9	1	Open
Norfolk State University	Norfolk	U	A,B,M,D	Pub	F,S	C	6,039	19	83	11	6			454	79	17	3	1	444	81	16	3		7/15
Old Dominion University	Norfolk	U	B,M,D	Pub	F,S	C	13,229	19	75	18	5	2		520	38	45	15	2	510	40	42	16	2	3/15
Radford University	Radford	SM	B,M	Pub	F,S	C	8,167							500	49	39	11		490	51	39	9	1	
Randolph-Macon College	Ashland	SU	B	Pri	F,S	C	1,118							560	18	52	28	2	540	26	47	26	1	3/1
Randolph-Macon Woman's College	Lynchburg	SU	B	Pri	No	W	737	26	9	25	27	16	23	600	7	39	40	14	560	21	46	29	4	3/1
Roanoke College	Salem	SU	B	Pri	F,S	C	1,899							550	22	48	26	4	550	22	52	23	3	3/1
Saint Paul's College	Lawrenceville	SM	B	Pri	F,S	C	700	15						335					365					Open
Shenandoah University	Winchester	SM	A,B,M,D	Pri	No	C	1,416	19	70	30				506	46	38	14	2	499	50	36	13	1	Open
Sweet Briar College	Sweet Briar	R	B	Pri	No	W	709	23	32	25	18	11	14	560	35	36	23	5	540	43	41	15	2	2/1
University of Richmond	University of Richmond	SU	A,B,M	Pri	F,S	C	2,861		2	6	11	33	47		4	16	59	21		2	11	59	28	1/15
University of Virginia	Charlottesville	SU	B,M,D	Pub	F,S	C	13,829	29						660	3	17	47	31	680	2	13	45	39	1/2

TEST SCORES

Column legend

- ENVIRONMENT: U-Urban, R-Rural, SU-Suburban, SM-Small Town
- DEGREES AWARDED: A-Associate, B-Bachelor, M-Master, D-Doctorate
- CONTROL: Pri-Private, Pub-Public
- FRATERNITIES AND SORORITIES: F-Fraternities, S-Sororities, F,S-Both, No-Neither
- STUDENTS: C-Coed, M-Men, PM-Primarily Men, W-Women, PW-Primarily Women
- ACT / SAT I VERBAL REASONING / SAT I MATHEMATICAL REASONING
- APPLICATION DEADLINE Month/Day

NAME OF SCHOOL	TOWN	Env	Deg	Ctrl	Frat	Stu	Undergrad Enroll Fall 2003	ACT Median	ACT Below 21	ACT 21-23	ACT 24-26	ACT 27-28	ACT Above 28	Verbal Median	Verbal Below 500	Verbal 500-599	Verbal 600-700	Verbal Above 700	Math Median	Math Below 500	Math 500-599	Math 600-700	Math Above 700	App Deadline
University of Virginia's College at Wise	Wise	SM	B	Pub	F,S	C	1,703	21	59	30	9	2		512	53	32	12	3	492	51	39	9	1	8/1
Virginia Commonwealth University	Richmond	U	B,M,D	Pub	F,S	C	17,148																	2/1
Virginia Intermont College	Bristol	U	A,B	Pri	No	C	744	20	63	21	15	1	1	610	60	28	11	1	520	61	28	10	1	Open
Virginia Military Institute	Lexington	SM	B	Pub	No	C	1,311																	4/1
Virginia Polytechnic Institute and State University	Blacksburg	R	B,M,D	Pub	F,S	C	21,344																	1/15
Virginia State University	Petersburg	SU	B,M		F,S	C	3,505	17						460					430					
Virginia Union University	Richmond	U	B,M,D	Pri	F,S	C	1,377																	
Virginia Wesleyan College	Norfolk	SU	B	Pri	F,S	C	1,429	19	67	16	11	3	3	490	54	37	9		490	55	35	9		Open
Washington and Lee University	Lexington	SM	B,D	Pri	F,S	C	1,740	29		1	8	26	65	690		8	48	44	690		4	50	46	1/15
Washington																								
Central Washington University	Ellensburg	R	B,M	Pub	No	C	9,296	20	56	23	12	5	4	490	53	34	12	1	490	51	37	11	1	Open
City University	Renton	SU	A,B,M	Pri	No	C	3,005																	Open
Cornish College of the Arts	Seattle	U	B	Pri	No	C	696																	8/15
DeVry University/Seattle	Federal Way		A,B,M	Pri	No	C	1,071																	Open
Eastern Washington University	Cheney	SM	B,M	Pub	F,S	C	9,067	21						500	50	34	15	1	501	49	35	15	1	3/1
Evergreen State College	Olympia	SM	B,M	Pub	No	C	4,103	24	19	27	24	16	14	600	12	36	40	12	550	27	44	25	4	3/1
Gonzaga University	Spokane	U	B,M,D	Pri	No	C	3,860	26	9	17	35	17	22	588	12	40	39	9	594	11	40	41	8	2/1
Henry Cogswell College	Everett	SU	B	Pri	No	C	230	26		12	25	38	25	540	14	59	18	9	550	27	41	27	5	Open
Heritage College	Toppenish	R	A,B,M	Pri	No	C	743																	Open
Northwest College	Kirkland	SU	A,B,M	Pri	No	C	1,057								33	45	19	3		40	42	15	3	8/1
Pacific Lutheran University	Tacoma	SU	B,M	Pri	No	C	3,185	25	18	21	26	13	22	560	23	39	32	6	560	24	41	32	3	Open
Saint Martin's College	Lacey	SU	B,M	Pri	No	C	1,230	20	63	17	12	2	6	497	46	39	13	2	489	51	30	17	2	8/1
Seattle Pacific University	Seattle	U	B,M,D	Pri	No	C	2,798	25	16	23	29	17	15	584	16	42	33	9	570	20	40	35	5	6/1
Seattle University	Seattle	U	B,M,D	Pri	No	C	3,352																	2/1
University of Puget Sound	Tacoma	SU	B,M	Pri	F,S	C	2,522	27	4	15	29	23	29	620	4	30	50	16	615	5	35	50	10	2/1
University of Washington	Seattle	U	B,M,D	Pub	F,S	C	25,660																	1/15
Walla Walla College	College Place	SM	A,B,M	Pri	No	C	1,667		22	33	24	7	7											Open
Washington State University	Pullman	SM	B,M,D	Pub	F,S	C	19,514							527	41	44	17	2	538	36	42	20	2	3/1
Western Washington University	Bellingham	SM	B,M	Pub	No	C	11,771	24	30	20	29	12	9	560	27	43	26	4	560	26	48	24	2	3/1
Whitman College	Walla Walla	SM	B	Pri	F,S	C	1,454		2	11	16	21	51	670	2	13	45	40	660	1	17	55	28	1/15
Whitworth College	Spokane	SU	B,M	Pri	No	C	2,071	26						573	18	44	31	7	580	15	45	34	6	3/1
West Virginia																								
Alderson-Broaddus College	Philippi	SM	A,B,M	Pri	F,S	C	741																	8/1
Bethany College	Bethany	SM	B	Pri	F,S	C	900	24						605					540					Open
Bluefield State College	Bluefield	SM	A,B	Pub	F,S	C	3,511	18	73	17	8	1	1											Open
Concord College	Athens	SM	A,B	Pub	F,S	C	3,026	20	47	28	15	7	3	500	51	30	15	2	490	53	29	16	2	Open
Davis and Elkins College	Elkins	SM	A,B	Pri	F,S	C	660	21						478					480					Open
Fairmont State	Fairmont	SM	A,B,M	Pub	F,S	C	7,413	20						460					475					8/15
Glenville State College	Glenville	R	A,B	Pub	F,S	C	1,377	19	52	16	6	1		435	70	21	7	2	433	70	23	5	1	Open
Marshall University	Huntington	U	A,B,M,D	Pub	F,S	C	9,558	22	36	32	20	7	5	475	60	30	10		475	60	20	20		9/1
Mountain State University	Beckley	SM	A,B,M	Pri	No	C	3,563	18	78	16	5		1	475	60	30	10		480	45	48	7		Open
Ohio Valley College	Vienna	SU	A,B	Pri	No	C	416	20	57	29	9	3	2	510	59	28	10	3	480	45	48	7		Open
Salem International University	Salem	R	A,B,M	Pri	F,S	C	343	21	51	29	18	2		466	56	35	9		480	56	41	3		Open
Shepherd College	Shepherdstown	SM	A,B,M	Pub	F,S	C	4,804	20	52	26	14	5	3	510	43	44	13	3	500	45	44	9		2/1
University of Charleston	Charleston	U	A,B,M	Pri	F,S	C	981	21	39	38	14	4	1	490	57	33	10		500	45	48	7		Open
West Liberty State College	West Liberty	R	A,B	Pub	F,S	C	2,491	19						452	78	12	10		436	82	14	4		8/1
West Virginia State College	Institute	SU	A,B	Pub	F,S	C	4,823																	8/10
West Virginia University	Morgantown	SM	B,M,D	Pub	F,S	C	17,517	23	26	34	22	10	8	534	37	48	14	1	524	32	47	18	2	8/1
West Virginia University Institute of Technology	Montgomery	SM	A,B,M	Pub	F,S	C	2,353																	8/1
West Virginia Wesleyan College	Buckhannon	SM	B,M	Pri	F,S	C	1,537																	8/1
Wheeling Jesuit University	Wheeling	SU	B,M	Pri	No	C	1,249																	Open
Wisconsin																								
Alverno College	Milwaukee	U	A,B,M	Pri	No	W	1,951	20																Open
Beloit College	Beloit	SM	B	Pri	F,S	C	1,332	27	3	11	24	23	39	640	5	25	48	22	600	10	38	41	11	1/15
Cardinal Stritch University	Milwaukee	SU	A,B,M,D	Pri	No	C	3,123																	4/1
Carroll College	Waukesha	SU	B,M	Pri	F,S	C	2,714	23	29	27	28	10	6											Open
Carthage College	Kenosha	SU	B,M	Pri	F,S	C	2,265																	8/1
Concordia University Wisconsin	Mequon	SU	A,B,M	Pri	No	C	3,845																	8/1
Edgewood College	Madison	SU	A,B,M	Pri	No	C	1,909	21	41	29	23	5	2											8/1
Lakeland College	Sheboygan	R	B,M	Pri	No	C	847																	7/15
Lawrence University	Appleton	U	B	Pri	F,S	C	1,352	27	3	11	24	24	38	630	4	24	54	18	630	4	28	50	18	1/15
Marian College of Fond du Lac	Fond du Lac	SM	B,M	Pri	No	C	1,745	20	59	23	10	6	2											Open
Marquette University	Milwaukee	U	A,B,M,D	Pri	F,S	C	7,775	25	9	24	30	19	19	580	14	44	37	5	586	16	35	41	8	Open
Milwaukee Institute of Art and Design	Milwaukee	U	B	Pri	No	C	650																	4/1
Milwaukee School of Engineering	Milwaukee	U	B,M	Pri	F,S	C	2,101	26	1	24	28	32	15	575	11	46	34	9	600	7	32	45	16	Open
Mount Mary College	Milwaukee	SU	B,M	Pri	No	W	1,371	21	55	25	13	4	2			50	50				50	50		8
Northland College	Ashland	SM	B	Pri	F,S	C	750	23	31	19	27	10	13	576	21	54	20	5	561	22	58	15	5	8/1
Ripon College	Ripon	SM	B	Pri	F,S	C	998	24	18	26	25	13	18	580					588	24	30	21	25	8/1
Saint Norbert College	De Pere	SU	B,M	Pri	F,S	C	2,086																	Open
Silver Lake College of the Holy Family	Manitowoc	R	A,B,M	Pri	No	C	780	18																Open
University of Wisconsin/Eau Claire	Eau Claire	U	A,B,M	Pub	F,S	C	10,059	25	6	33	39	12	10	589	19	30	38	13	584	16	38	38	8	Open
University of Wisconsin/Green Bay	Green Bay	SU	A,B,M	Pub	F,S	C	5,256	23	26	36	24	8	6	510	33	40	25		540	40	35	15	10	2/1
University of Wisconsin/La Crosse	La Crosse	SM	A,B,M	Pub	F,S	C	8,100	24							12	43	39	6		6	33	52	9	Open
University of Wisconsin/Madison	Madison	U	B,M,D	Pub	F,S	C	25,616																	2/1
University of Wisconsin/Milwaukee	Milwaukee	U	B,M,D	Pub	F,S	C	19,785																	8/1

NAME OF SCHOOL	TOWN	ENVIRONMENT (U-Urban R-Rural SU-Suburban SM-Small Town)	DEGREES AWARDED (A-Associate B-Bachelor M-Master D-Doctorate)	CONTROL (Pri-Private Pub-Public)	FRATERNITIES AND SORORITIES (F-Fraternities S-Sororities No-Neither)	STUDENTS (C-Coed M-Men W-Women PM-Primarily Men PW-Primarily Women)	UNDERGRADUATE ENROLLMENT FALL 2003	ACT Median	ACT Below 21	ACT 21-23	ACT 24-26	ACT 27-28	ACT Above 28	SAT I Verbal Median	SAT I Verbal Below 500	SAT I Verbal 500-599	SAT I Verbal 600-700	SAT I Verbal Above 700	SAT I Math Median	SAT I Math Below 500	SAT I Math 500-599	SAT I Math 600-700	SAT I Math Above 700	APPLICATION DEADLINE Month/Day
University of Wisconsin/Oshkosh	Oshkosh	U	A,B,M	Pub	F,S	C	9,216																	8/1
University of Wisconsin/Parkside	Kenosha	SU	B,M	Pub	No	C	4,370																	Open
University of Wisconsin/Platteville	Platteville	R	A,B,M	Pub	F,S	C	5,343		31	32	22	9	6											Open
University of Wisconsin/River Falls	River Falls	SU	B,M	Pub	F,S	C	5,413	22																Open
University of Wisconsin/Stevens Point	Stevens Point	SM	A,B,M	Pub	F,S	C	8,503	22	23	39	24	9	5	560					610	16	24	60	19	Open
University of Wisconsin/Stout	Menomonie	R	B,M	Pub	F,S	C	7,101	22	38	37	19	4	2		33	52	14			29	53	19		Open
University of Wisconsin/Superior	Superior	U	A,B,M	Pub	No	C	2,434																	4/1
University of Wisconsin/Whitewater	Whitewater	SM	A,B,M	Pub	F,S	C	9,350	22	35	33	22	7	3		6									Open
Viterbo University	LaCrosse	SU	B,M	Pri	No	C	1,862	22	38	32	18	7	7		6	14								Open
Wisconsin Lutheran College	Milwaukee	SU	B	Pri	No	C	706	24	14	26	33	12	14											9/1

Wyoming

NAME OF SCHOOL	TOWN	ENVIRONMENT	DEGREES AWARDED	CONTROL	FRATERNITIES AND SORORITIES	STUDENTS	UNDERGRADUATE ENROLLMENT FALL 2003	ACT Median	ACT Below 21	ACT 21-23	ACT 24-26	ACT 27-28	ACT Above 28	SAT I Verbal Median	SAT I Verbal Below 500	SAT I Verbal 500-599	SAT I Verbal 600-700	SAT I Verbal Above 700	SAT I Math Median	SAT I Math Below 500	SAT I Math 500-599	SAT I Math 600-700	SAT I Math Above 700	APPLICATION DEADLINE Month/Day
University of Wyoming	Laramie	SM	B,M,D	Pub	F,S	C	9,385	23	29	27	25	11	10	540	35	42	21	3	550	29	42	25	5	8/10

The breakdown of in-state tuition, room, and board costs for the 2003-2004 academic year is arranged from least expensive to most expensive. Within each range are lists of schools that don't charge for tuition or room and board, and those that do.

Less Than $2000

Colleges without Tuition, Room, and Board

California State University, San Marcos, CA (no R & B)
Charter Oak State College, CT (no R & B)
Conservatory of Music of Puerto Rico, PR (no R & B)
Escuela de Artes Plasticas de Puerto Rico, PR (no R & B)
Excelsior College, NY (no R & B)
Oglala Lakota College, SD (no R & B)
Southern University at New Orleans, LA (no R & B)
United States Military Academy, NY (no R & B)
University of Puerto Rico/Arecibo, PR (no R & B)
University of Puerto Rico/Bayamon University College Campus, PR (no R & B)
University of Puerto Rico/Cayey University College, PR (no R & B)
University of Puerto Rico at Humacao, PR (no R & B)
University of Puerto Rico/Mayaguez, PR (no R & B)

Colleges with Tuition, Room, and Board

Curtis Institute of Music, PA (no R & B)
United States Air Force Academy, CO
United States Coast Guard Academy, CT (no R & B)
United States Naval Academy, MD (no R & B)

$2000-$3999

Colleges without Tuition, Room, and Board

American University of Puerto Rico, PR (no R & B)
Augusta State University, GA (no R & B)
Bluefield State College, WV (no R & B)
Caribbean University, PR (no R & B)
Central University of Bayamon, PR (no R & B)
City University of New York/Baruch College, NY (no R & B)
City University of New York/Herbert H. Lehman College, NY (no R & B)
City University of New York/York College, NY (no R & B)
Clayton College and State University, GA (no R & B)
Harris-Stowe State College, MO (no R & B)
Inter American University of Puerto Rico/Aguadilla Campus, PR (no R & B)
Inter-American University of Puerto Rico/Arecibo Campus, PR (no R & B)
Inter-American University of Puerto Rico/Barranquitas Regional College, PR (no R & B)
Kennesaw State University, GA (no R & B)
Langston University, OK (no R & B)
Louisiana State University in Shreveport, LA (no R & B)
Metropolitan State College of Denver, CO (no R & B)
Metropolitan State University, MN (no R & B)
Northeastern Illinois University, IL (no R & B)
Ohio State University at Mansfield, OH (no R & B)

Sinte Gleska University, SD (no R & B)
Thomas Edison State College, NJ (no R & B)
Troy State University/Dothan, AL (no R & B)
Troy State University/Montgomery, AL (no R & B)
Universidad Metropolitana, PR (no R & B)
University of Colorado at Denver, CO (no R & B)
University of Houston-Downtown, TX (no R & B)
University of the District of Columbia, DC (no R & B)

Colleges with Tuition, Room, and Board

College of the Ozarks, MO
Inter American University of Puerto Rico/Bayamon University College, PR (no R & B)
Inter-American University of Puerto Rico/Ponce Regional College, PR (no R & B)

$4000-$5999

Colleges without Tuition, Room, and Board

Bellevue University, NE (no R & B)
City University of New York/Brooklyn College, NY (no R & B)
City University of New York/City College, NY (no R & B)
City University of New York/College of Staten Island, NY (no R & B)
City University of New York/John Jay College of Criminal Justice, NY (no R & B)
City University of New York/Medgar Evers College, NY (no R & B)
City University of New York/New York City College of Technology, NY (no R & B)
City University of New York/Queens College, NY (no R & B)
College for Lifelong Learning, NH (no R & B)
College of New Rochelle - School of New Resources, NY (no R & B)
Indiana University East, IN (no R & B)
Indiana University Kokomo, IN (no R & B)
Indiana University Northwest, IN (no R & B)
Indiana University-Purdue University Fort Wayne, IN (no R & B)
Indiana University South Bend, IN (no R & B)
Indiana University Southeast, IN (no R & B)
Inter American University of Puerto Rico/Fajardo Campus, PR (no R & B)
Inter American University of Puerto Rico/Metropolitan Campus, PR (no R & B)
NAES College, IL (no R & B)
Ohio State University at Lima, OH (no R & B)
Ohio State University at Marion, OH (no R & B)
Our Lady of Holy Cross College, LA (no R & B)
Sojourner-Douglass College, MD (no R & B)
State University of New York/Empire State College, NY (no R & B)
Trinity College of Nursing and Health Sciences, IL (no R & B)
Universidad Politecnica de Puerto Rico, PR (no R & B)
University of Maine at Augusta, ME (no R & B)

University of Maryland/University College, MD (no R & B)
University of Michigan/Flint, MI (no R & B)
Wilmington College, DE (no R & B)

Colleges with Tuition, Room, and Board

Alabama Agricultural and Mechanical University, AL
Albany State University, GA
Alice Lloyd College, KY
Arkansas Baptist College, AR
Austin Peay State University, TN
Berea College, KY
California State University, Dominguez Hills, CA
California State University, Los Angeles, CA
Cameron University, OK
East Central University, OK
Elizabeth City State University, NC
Fayetteville State University, NC
McNeese State University, LA
Mississippi University for Women, MS
Northeastern State University, OK
Northwestern Oklahoma State University, OK
Oklahoma Panhandle State University, OK
Southwestern Oklahoma State University, OK
Turabo University, PR (no R & B)
Universidad Adventista de las Antillas, PR
University of Arkansas at Little Rock, AR
University of Arkansas at Monticello, AR
University of Louisiana at Lafayette, LA
University of Louisiana at Monroe, LA
University of Puerto Rico/Rio Piedras, PR
University of Science and Arts of Oklahoma, OK
University of Texas at El Paso, TX
University of Texas-Pan American, TX
University of the Sacred Heart, PR
Western New Mexico University, NM

$6000-$7999

Colleges without Tuition, Room, and Board

Boricua College, NY (no R & B)
Boston Architectural Center, MA (no R & B)
Cabarrus College of Health Sciences, NC (no R & B)
City University, WA (no R & B)
Florida Memorial College, FL (no R & B)
Franklin University, OH (no R & B)
Heritage College, WA (no R & B)
Humphreys College, CA (no R & B)
Knoxville College, TN (no R & B)
Union Institute and University, OH (no R & B)
United States Merchant Marine Academy, NY (no R & B)
University of Massachusetts Boston, MA (no R & B)
University of Michigan/Dearborn, MI (no R & B)

Colleges with Tuition, Room, and Board

Adams State College, CO
Alabama State University, AL
Alcorn State University, MS
Angelo State University, TX
Appalachian State University, NC
Arkansas Tech University, AR
Armstrong Atlantic State University, GA
Baker College of Flint, MI
Black Hills State University, SD

Boise State University, ID
Brigham Young University/Hawaii, HI
California State University, Bakersfield, CA
California State University, Fullerton, CA
California State University, Monterey Bay, CA
California State University, Northridge, CA
Chadron State College, NE
City University of New York/Hunter College, NY
Columbus State University, GA
Dakota State University, SD
Delta State University, MS
Dickinson State University, ND
Eastern Kentucky University, KY
Eastern New Mexico University, NM
Emporia State University, KS
Florida Agricultural and Mechanical University, FL
Florida Hospital College of Health Sciences, FL
Fort Hays State University, KS
Fort Valley State University, GA
Georgia Southwestern State University, GA
Glenville State College, WV
Grambling State University, LA
Henderson State University, AR
Inter American University of Puerto Rico/San Germ-n, PR
Jacksonville State University, AL
Lamar University, TX
Lewis-Clark State College, ID
Lincoln University, MO
Louisiana Tech University, LA
Mayville State University, ND
Miles College, AL
Minnesota State University Moorhead, MN
Minot State University, ND
Mississippi Valley State University, MS
Morehead State University, KY
Murray State University, KY
New Mexico Highlands University, NM
New Mexico Institute of Mining and Technology, NM
New Mexico State University, NM
Nicholls State University, LA
North Carolina Agricultural and Technical State University, NC
North Carolina Central University, NC
North Georgia College and State University, GA
Northern Kentucky University, KY
Northern State University, SD
Northwestern State University of Louisiana, LA
Peru State College, NE
Philander Smith College, AR
Pittsburg State University, KS
Pontifical Catholic University of Puerto Rico/Ponce, PR
Purdue University/Calumet, IN (no R & B)
Sam Houston State University, TX
Savannah State University, GA
South Carolina State University, SC
South Dakota School of Mines and Technology, SD
South Dakota State University, SD
Southeastern Louisiana University, LA
Southeastern Oklahoma State University, OK
Southern Arkansas University, AR
Southern Polytechnic State University, GA
Southern University and A&M College, LA
State University of West Georgia, GA
Stephen F. Austin State University, TX
Sul Ross State University, TX
Tarleton State University, TX
Texas A&M University at Kingsville, TX
Texas Woman's University, TX
Troy State University, AL
University of Alaska Southeast, AK
University of Arkansas at Pine Bluff, AR

University of Central Arkansas, AR
University of Hawaii at Hilo, HI
University of Kentucky, KY
University of Mississippi, MS
University of New Orleans, LA
University of North Alabama, AL
University of North Carolina at
  Pembroke, NC
University of North Texas, TX
University of South Alabama, AL
University of South Carolina at Aiken,
  SC
University of South Dakota, SD
University of Southern Colorado, CO
University of Tennessee at
  Chattanooga, TN
University of Tennessee at Martin, TN
University of Texas at Arlington, TX
University of West Alabama, AL
University of Wisconsin/Oshkosh, WI
University of Wisconsin/Parkside, WI
University of Wisconsin/Superior, WI
Utah State University, UT
Valdosta State University, GA
Valley City State University, ND
Wayne State College, NE
Webb Institute, NY
Weber State University, UT
West Liberty State College, WV
West Texas A&M University, TX
West Virginia State College, WV
West Virginia University Institute of
  Technology, WV
Western Carolina University, NC
Western Kentucky University, KY

$8000-$9999

Colleges without Tuition, Room, and Board

Baltimore Hebrew University, MD
  (no R & B)
Calumet College of St. Joseph, IN
  (no R & B)
Colorado Technical University, CO
  (no R & B)
David N. Myers College, OH
  (no R & B)
International College, FL (no R & B)
National University, CA (no R & B)
New College of California, CA
  (no R & B)
South College, GA (no R & B)
Southern Christian University, AL
  (no R & B)
Southeastern University, DC
  (no R & B)
Strayer University, DC (no R & B)

Colleges with Tuition, Room, and Board

American Indian College of the
  Assemblies of God, AZ
Arkansas State University, AR
Auburn University Montgomery, AL
Ball State University, IN
Bemidji State University, MN
Brigham Young University, UT
California Polytechnic State University,
  CA
California State Polytechnic University,
  Pomona, CA
California State University, Chico, CA
California State University, Fresno, CA
California State University, Hayward,
  CA
California State University, Long
  Beach, CA
California State University,
  Sacramento, CA
California State University, Stanislaus,
  CA
Central Missouri State University, MO
Central State University, OH
Central Washington University, WA
Cheyney University of Pennsylvania,
  PA
Christopher Newport University, VA
College of the Southwest, NM
Colorado State University, CO
Concord College, WV
Concordia College, AL
Delaware State University, DE
East Carolina University, NC
East Tennessee State University, TN
Eastern Washington University, WA

Evergreen State College, WA
Fairmont State, WV
Fitchburg State College, MA
Florida Atlantic University, FL
Florida Gulf Coast University, FL
Florida International University, FL
Florida State University, FL
Fort Lewis College, CO
Framingham State College, MA
Francis Marion University, SC
George Mason University, VA
Georgia College and State University,
  GA
Georgia Southern University, GA
Humboldt State University, CA
Idaho State University, ID
Indiana University-Purdue University
  Indianapolis, IN
Jackson State University, MS
Jarvis Christian College, TX
Kansas State University, KS
Kentucky State University, KY
Lake Superior State University, MI
Lester L. Cox College of Nursing and
  Health Sciences, MO
Louisiana State University and
  Agricultural and Mechanical College,
  LA
Marshall University, WV
Massachusetts College of Liberal Arts,
  MA
Mesa State College, CO
Middle Tennessee State University, TN
Midwestern State University, TX
Minnesota State University, Mankato,
  MN
Mississippi State University, MS
Missouri Southern State University,
  MO
Missouri Western State College, MO
Montana State University-Billings, MT
Montana State University-Bozeman,
  MT
Montana State University-Northern,
  MT
Montana Tech of The University of
  Montana, MT
New College of Florida, FL
Norfolk State University, VA
North Carolina School of the Arts, NC
North Carolina State University, NC
North Dakota State University, ND
Northern Arizona University, AZ
Northwest Missouri State University,
  MO
Ohio State University at Newark, OH
Oklahoma State University, OK
Oregon Institute of Technology, OR
Paul Quinn College, TX (no R & B)
Prairie View A&M University, TX
Radford University, VA
Rust College, MS
Saint Cloud State University, MN
Salem State College, MA
San Jose State University, CA
Shepherd College, WV
Southeast Missouri State University,
  MO
Southern Illinois University
  Edwardsville, IL
Southern Utah University, UT
Southwest Minnesota State University,
  MN
Southwest Missouri State University,
  MO
State University of New York/College at
  Buffalo, NY
Tennessee State University, TN
Tennessee Technological University,
  TN
Texas A&M University at Commerce,
  TX
Texas A&M University at Galveston,
  TX
Texas Southern University, TX
Texas State University, TX
Tougaloo College, MS
Truman State University, MO
University of Alabama, AL
University of Alabama in Huntsville, AL
University of Alaska Anchorage, AK
University of Alaska Fairbanks, AK
University of Arkansas, AR
University of Central Oklahoma, OK
University of Florida, FL
University of Georgia, GA
University of Hawaii at Manoa, HI
University of Houston, TX
University of Idaho, ID

University of Kansas, KS
University of Louisville, KY
University of Maine at Fort Kent, ME
University of Maine at Machias, ME
University of Maine at Presque Isle,
  ME
University of Maryland/Eastern Shore,
  MD
University of Memphis, TN
University of Minnesota/Crookston,
  MN
University of Montana, MT
University of Montana—Western, MT
University of Montevallo, AL
University of Nebraska at Kearney, NE
University of Nebraska at Lincoln, NE
University of Nebraska at Omaha, NE
University of Nevada/Reno, NV
University of New Mexico, NM
University of North Carolina at
  Asheville, NC
University of North Carolina at
  Charlotte, NC
University of North Carolina at
  Greensboro, NC
University of North Carolina at
  Wilmington, NC
University of North Dakota, ND
University of North Florida, FL
University of Northern Colorado, CO
University of Northern Iowa, IA
University of Oklahoma, OK
University of Rio Grande, OH
University of South Carolina at
  Spartanburg, SC
University of South Florida, FL
University of Southern Indiana, IN
University of Southern Mississippi, MS
University of Tennessee at Knoxville,
  TN
University of Texas at San Antonio, TX
University of Utah, UT
University of West Florida, FL
University of Wisconsin/Eau Claire, WI
University of Wisconsin/Green Bay, WI
University of Wisconsin/La Crosse, WI
University of Wisconsin/Madison, WI
University of Wisconsin/Milwaukee, WI
University of Wisconsin/Platteville, WI
University of Wisconsin/River Falls, WI
University of Wisconsin/Stevens Point,
  WI
University of Wisconsin/Stout, WI
University of Wisconsin/Whitewater, WI
University of Wyoming, WY
Virginia Commonwealth University, VA
Virginia Military Institute, VA
Virginia Polytechnic Institute and State
  University, VA
Washburn University of Topeka, KS
West Virginia University, WV
Western State College of Colorado,
  CO
Wichita State University, KS
Wiley College, TX (no R & B)
Winona State University, MN
Winston-Salem State University, NC

$10,000-$11,999

Colleges without Tuition, Room, and Board

Aquinas College, TN (no R & B)
Burlington College, VT (no R & B)
Carlos Albizu University, FL
  (no R & B)
Cambridge College, MA (no R & B)
Cincinnati College of Mortuary
  Science, OH (no R & B)
Cleary College, MI (no R & B)
College of Aeronautics, NY
  (no R & B)
DeVry College of Technology/North
  Brunswick, NJ (no R & B)
DeVry Institute of Technology/New
  York, NY (no R & B)
DeVry University/Addison (DuPage
  County), IL (no R & B)
DeVry University/Alpharetta, GA
  (no R & B)
DeVry University/Chicago, IL
  (no R & B)
DeVry University/Colorado Springs,
  CO (no R & B)
DeVry University/Columbus, OH
  (no R & B)

DeVry University/Crystal City, VA
  (no R & B)
DeVry University/Dallas, TX
  (no R & B)
DeVry University/Decatur, GA
  (no R & B)
DeVry University/Fort Washington, PA
  (no R & B)
DeVry University/Fremont, CA
  (no R & B)
DeVry University/Kansas City, MO
  (no R & B)
DeVry University/Long Beach, CA
  (no R & B)
DeVry University/Miramar, FL
  (no R & B)
DeVry University/Orlando, FL
  (no R & B)
DeVry University/Phoenix, AZ
  (no R & B)
DeVry University/Pomona, CA
  (no R & B)
DeVry University/Seattle, WA
  (no R & B)
DeVry University/Tinley Park, IL
  (no R & B)
DeVry University/West Hills, CA
  (no R & B)
DeVry University/Westminster, CO
  (no R & B)
East-West University, IL (no R & B)
Golden Gate University, CA
  (no R & B)
Kendall College of Art and Design of
  Ferris State University, MI
  (no R & B)
Martin University, IN (no R & B)
Mercy College of Health Sciences, IA
  (no R & B)
Ottawa University, KS (no R & B)
Peirce College, PA (no R & B)
Saint Francis College, NY (no R & B)
St. Joseph's College, NY (no R & B)

Colleges with Tuition, Room, and Board

Allen University, SC
Arizona State University-Main, AZ
Auburn University, AL
Bennett College, NC
Bloomsburg University of
  Pennsylvania, PA
Blue Mountain College, MS
Bowie State University, MD
Bridgewater State College, MA
California University of Pennsylvania,
  PA
Castleton State College, VT
Central Michigan University, MI
Chicago State University, IL
Clarion University of Pennsylvania, PA
Clemson University, SC
Coastal Carolina University, SC
College of Charleston, SC
Cooper Union for the Advancement of
  Science and Art, NY
Coppin State College, MD
Davenport University, MI
East Stroudsburg University of
  Pennsylvania, PA
Eastern Connecticut State University,
  CT
Eastern Illinois University, IL
Eastern Michigan University, MI
Eastern Oregon University, OR
Edinboro University of Pennsylvania,
  PA
Fashion Institute of Technology/State
  University of New York, NY
Flagler College, FL
Frostburg State University, MD
Georgia Institute of Technology, GA
Georgia State University, GA
Goldey-Beacom College, DE
Grand Valley State University, MI
Huron University, SD
Illinois State University, IL
Indiana State University, IN
Indiana University of Pennsylvania, PA
Iowa State University, IA
James Madison University, VA
Jewish Hospital College of Nursing
  and Allied Health, MO
Johnson State College, VT
Kutztown University of Pennsylvania,
  PA
Lander University, SC
Lane College, TN

Lock Haven University of
Pennsylvania, PA
Longwood University, VA
Madonna University, MI
Mansfield University, PA
Mary Washington College, VA
Massachusetts Maritime Academy,
MA
Michigan State University, MI
Millersville University of Pennsylvania,
PA
Morgan State University, MD
Morris College, SC
Mountain State University, WV
Nebraska Methodist College of
Nursing and Allied Health, NE
New Jersey City University, NJ
Northern Illinois University, IL
Northern Michigan University, MI
Oakland University, MI
Old Dominion University, VA
Oregon State University, OR
Park University, MO
Rhode Island College, RI
Saginaw Valley State University, MI
San Diego State University, CA
Shawnee State University, OH
Shippensburg University of
Pennsylvania, PA
Slippery Rock University of
Pennsylvania, PA
Sonoma State University, CA
Southeastern University, FL
Southern Connecticut State University,
CT
Southern Illinois University
Carbondale, IL
Southern Oregon University, OR
State University of New York/College at
Fredonia, NY
State University of New York/College at
Geneseo, NY
State University of New York/College at
Oneonta, NY
State University of New York/College at
Plattsburgh, NY
State University of New York/College at
Purchase, NY
State University of New York/College of
Agriculture and Technology at
Cobleskill, NY
State University of New York/Maritime
College, NY
State University of New York/University
at New Paltz, NY
Stillman College, AL
Talladega College, AL
Texas A&M University, TX
Texas A&M University at Corpus
Christi, TX
Texas Tech University, TX
Thomas University, GA
University of Arizona, AZ
University of California at Santa
Barbara, CA
University of Central Florida, FL
University of Colorado at Boulder, CO
University of Colorado at Colorado
Springs, CO
University of Illinois at Urbana-
Champaign, IL
University of Iowa, IA
University of Maine at Farmington, ME
University of Massachusetts Lowell,
MA
University of Missouri/St. Louis, MO
University of Nevada/Las Vegas, NV
University of North Carolina at Chapel
Hill, NC
University of Oregon, OR
University of South Carolina at
Columbia, SC
University of Southern Maine, ME
University of Texas at Austin, TX
University of Texas at Dallas, TX
University of Virginia, VA
University of Virginia's College at Wise,
VA
University of Washington, WA
Virginia State University, VA
Voorhees College, SC
Washington State University, WA
Wayland Baptist University, TX
Wayne State University, MI
West Chester University of
Pennsylvania, PA
Western Connecticut State University,
CT
Western Illinois University, IL

Western Oregon University, OR
Western Washington University, WA
Westfield State College, MA
William Carey College, MS
Williams Baptist College, AR
Winthrop University, SC
Worcester State College, MA
Wright State University, OH
Youngstown State University, OH

$12,000-$13,999

Colleges without Tuition, Room, and Board

American InterContinental University,
GA (no R & B)
Berkeley College of New York City, NY
(no R & B)
Citadel, The, SC (no R & B)
Holy Family College, PA (no R & B)
Prescott College, AZ (no R & B)
Woodbury College, VT (no R & B)

Colleges with Tuition, Room, and Board

Barber-Scotia College, NC
Benedict College, SC
Bethel College, TN
Blackburn College, IL
Bowling Green State University, OH
Bryn Athyn College of the New
Church, PA
Central Connecticut State University,
CT
Clarkson College, NE
Clearwater Christian College, FL
Cleveland State University, OH
College of William and Mary, VA
Colorado School of Mines, CO
East Texas Baptist University, TX
Farmingdale State University of New
York, NY
Ferris State University, MI
Globe Institute of Technology, NY
Hannibal-LaGrange College, MO
Indiana University Bloomington, IN
Jamestown College, ND
Keene State College, NH
Kent State University, OH
Kentucky Christian College, KY
Lee University, TN
LeMoyne-Owen College, TN
Lincoln University, PA
Louisiana College, LA
Lyndon State College, VT
Maine Maritime Academy, ME
Michigan Technological University, MI
Montclair State University, NJ
National American University, SD
Ohio State University, OH
Paine College, GA
Penn State University at Erie/Behrend
College, PA
Penn State University/Altoona, PA
Plymouth State University, NH
Portland State University, OR
Purdue University/West Lafayette, IN
Richard Stockton College of New
Jersey, NJ
Saint Augustine's College, NC
Saint Gregory's University, OK
Saint Mary's College, IN
Salisbury University, MD
San Francisco State University, CA
State University of New York at
Oswego, NY
State University of New York at
Potsdam, NY
State University of New York/College at
Brockport, NY
State University of New York/College at
Cortland, NY
State University of New York/College at
Old Westbury, NY
State University of New York/College of
Technology at Alfred, NY
State University of New York/University
at Albany, NY
State University of New York/University
at Binghamton, NY
State University of New York/University
at Buffalo, NY
State University of New York/University
at Stony Brook, NY
Towson University, MD
University of Akron, OH

University of Alabama at Birmingham,
AL
University of Delaware, DE
University of Illinois at Chicago, IL
University of Maine, ME
University of Mary, ND
University of Massachusetts Amherst,
MA
University of Massachusetts
Dartmouth, MA
University of Michigan/Ann Arbor, MI
University of Minnesota/Duluth, MN
University of Minnesota/Morris, MN
University of Minnesota/Twin Cities,
MN
University of Missouri/Columbia, MO
University of Missouri/Kansas City, MO
University of Missouri/Rolla, MO
University of Mobile, AL
University of Rhode Island, RI
University of Toledo, OH
Vermont Technical College, VT
Western Michigan University, MI
William Tyndale College, MI

$14,000-$15,999

Colleges without Tuition, Room, and Board

Art Institute of Southern California, CA
(no R & B)
Cogswell Polytechnical College, CA
(no R & B)
Henry Cogswell College, WA
(no R & B)
Lourdes College, OH (no R & B)
Metropolitan College of New York, NY
(no R & B)
Molloy College, NY (no R & B)
Pacific Northwest College of Art, OR
(no R & B)

Colleges with Tuition, Room, and Board

Allen College, IA
Bluefield College, VA
Brescia University, KY
Brewton-Parker College, GA
California Maritime Academy, CA
California State University, San
Bernardino, CA
Claflin University, SC
College of New Jersey, The, NJ
Crichton College, TN
Dallas Baptist University, TX
Deaconess College of Nursing, MO
Edward Waters College, FL
Evangel University, MO
Faulkner University, AL
Friends University, KS
Grace Bible College, MI
Grove City College, PA
Harding University, AR
Hardin-Simmons University, TX
Howard Payne University, TX
Huston-Tillotson College, TX
John Brown University, AR
Judson College, AL
Kean University, NJ
Lubbock Christian University, TX
Massachusetts College of Art, MA
Miami University, OH
Midway College, KY
Mississippi College, MS
Monroe College, NY
Mount Marty College, SD
Mount Olive College, NC
North Central University, MN
Oakwood College, AL
Ohio University, OH
Oklahoma Baptist University, OK
Oklahoma Wesleyan University, OK
Penn State University/University Park
Campus, PA
Pennsylvania College of Technology,
PA
Pikeville College, KY
Presentation College, SD
Ramapo College of New Jersey, NJ
Rowan University, NJ
Rutgers, The State University of New
Jersey/Camden Campus, NJ
Rutgers, The State University of New
Jersey/New Brunswick/Piscataway
Campus, NJ

Rutgers, The State University of New
Jersey/Newark Campus, NJ
Saint Mary's College of Maryland, MD
Saint Paul's College, VA
Shaw University, NC
Sheldon Jackson College, AK
Southern Nazarene University, OK
Southwest Baptist University, MO
Southwestern Adventist University, TX
State University of New York/College of
Environmental Science and Forestry,
NY
Temple University, PA
Toccoa Falls College, GA
Touro College, NY
Union College, KY
University of California at Berkeley, CA
University of California at Davis, CA
University of California at Los Angeles,
CA
University of California at Riverside, CA
University of California at San Diego,
CA
University of Cincinnati, OH
University of Connecticut, CT
University of Great Falls, MT
University of Maryland/Baltimore
County, MD
University of Maryland/College Park,
MD
University of New Hampshire, NH
University of Pittsburgh at Bradford, PA
University of Pittsburgh at Greensburg,
PA
University of Pittsburgh at Johnstown,
PA
Virginia Union University, VA
Wilberforce University, OH
William Paterson University of New
Jersey, NJ
York College, NE
York College of Pennsylvania, PA

$16,000-$17,999

Colleges without Tuition, Room, and Board

Art Academy of Cincinnati, OH
(no R & B)
College of Visual Arts, MN
(no R & B)
National-Louis University, IL
(no R & B)

Colleges with Tuition, Room, and Board

Alaska Pacific University, AK
Belhaven College, MS
Bethune-Cookman College, FL
Bryan College, TN
Campbellsville University, KY
Cardinal Stritch University, WI
Carson-Newman College, TN
Cascade College, OR
Central Methodist College, MO
Charleston Southern University, SC
Columbia College, MO
Concordia University Wisconsin, WI
Culver-Stockton College, MO
Cumberland College, KY
Cumberland University, TN
Dakota Wesleyan University, SD
David Lipscomb University, TN
Dillard University, LA
Fisk University, TN
Freed-Hardeman University, TN
Gallaudet University, DC
Hampton University, VA
Hesser College, NH
Hope International University, CA
Houston Baptist University, TX
Howard University, DC
Husson College, ME
Kentucky Wesleyan College, KY
Lakeland College, WI
Lambuth University, TN
Lees-McRae College, NC
Liberty University, VA
Limestone College, SC
Lincoln Memorial University, TN
Lindenwood University, MO
Lindsey Wilson College, KY
Lyon College, AR
Marygrove College, MI
McMurry University, TX
New Jersey Institute of Technology, NJ

North Carolina Wesleyan College, NC
Oakland City University, IN
Ohio Valley College, WV
Oklahoma Christian University, OK
Our Lady of the Lake University of San Antonio, TX
Piedmont College, GA
Rochester College, MI
Shorter College, GA
Siena Heights University, MI
Southern Adventist University, TN
Spalding University, KY
Tennessee Wesleyan College, TN
Texas Wesleyan University, TX
Thomas More College of Liberal Arts, NH
Trevecca Nazarene University, TN
Tuskegee University, AL
Union College, NE
University of California at Santa Cruz, CA
University of Mary Hardin-Baylor, TX
University of Pittsburgh at Pittsburgh, PA
University of Sioux Falls, SD
University of the Ozarks, AR
University of Vermont, VT
Warner Southern College, FL
Webber International University, FL
Wesleyan College, GA
Westminster College, UT
William Penn University, IA
Xavier University of Louisiana, LA

$18,000-$19,999

Colleges without Tuition, Room, and Board

Cornish College of the Arts, WA (no R & B)
San Francisco Art Institute, CA (no R & B)

Colleges with Tuition, Room, and Board

Abilene Christian University, TX
Albert A. List College of Jewish Studies, NY
Albertson College of Idaho, ID
Alderson-Broaddus College, WV
Alverno College, WI
Anderson University, IN
Andrews University, MI
Atlanta College of Art, GA
Atlantic Union College, MA
Baker University, KS
Barton College, NC
Bethany College, KS
Bethany College, WV
Bethel College, IN
Bethel College, KS
Bloomfield College, NJ
California Baptist University, CA
Campbell University, NC
Cedarville University, OH
Christendom College, VA
Christian Heritage College, CA
Clark Atlanta University, GA
College of Saint Joseph, VT
Concordia College, NY
Cornerstone University and Grand Rapids Theological Seminary, MI
Drury University, MO
Eastern Nazarene College, MA
Franciscan University, IA
Gardner-Webb University, NC
Georgian Court College, NJ
Grace College, IN
Graceland University, IA
Grand View College, IA
Hastings College, NE
Hawaii Pacific University, HI
Hilbert College, NY
Huntingdon College, AL
Illinois College, IL
Indiana Wesleyan University, IN
Iowa Wesleyan College, IA
Johnson C. Smith University, NC
Kansas Wesleyan University, KS
La Sierra University, CA
Lenoir-Rhyne College, NC
Livingstone College, NC
Marian College of Fond du Lac, WI
Mars Hill College, NC
Marylhurst University, OR
MCP Hahnemann University, PA

Mercy College, NY
Methodist College, NC
MidAmerica Nazarene University, KS
Midland Lutheran College, NE
Milligan College, TN
Missouri Baptist University, MO
Missouri Valley College, MO
Montreat College, NC
Mount Aloysius College, PA
Mount Vernon Nazarene University, OH
Newman University, KS
Northwest College, WA
Northwestern College of Iowa, IA
Nyack College, NY
Oklahoma City University, OK
Olivet College, MI
Oral Roberts University, OK
Ouachita Baptist University, AR
Pfeiffer University, NC
Philadelphia Biblical University, PA
Rocky Mountain College, MT
Salem International University, WV
Samford University, AL
Shimer College, IL
Silver Lake College of the Holy Family, WI
Southern Vermont College, VT
Southern Wesleyan University, SC
Southwestern College, KS
Spelman College, GA
Sterling College, KS
Tabor College, KS
Thomas College, ME
Tiffin University, OH
Tusculum College, TN
Union University, TN
Unity College, ME
University of California at Irvine, CA
University of Saint Mary, KS
Urbana University, OH
VanderCook College of Music, IL
Villa Julie College, MD
Virginia Intermont College, VA
Waynesburg College, PA
Wesley College, DE
Westminster College, MO

$20,000-$21,999

Colleges without Tuition, Room, and Board

DeVry University/West Hills, CA (no R & B)

Colleges with Tuition, Room, and Board

Adrian College, MI
Aquinas College, MI
Asbury College, KY
Augustana College, SD
Aurora University, IL
Avila University, MO
Belmont University, TN
Benedictine College, KS
Benjamin Franklin Institute of Technology, MA
Berkeley College, NY
Berry College, GA
Brenau University Women's College, GA
Briar Cliff University, IA
Capitol College, MD
Carlow College, PA
Carroll College, MT
Catawba College, NC
Central College, IA
Chaminade University of Honolulu, HI
Coker College, SC
College of New Rochelle, NY
College of Our Lady of the Elms, MA
College of Saint Mary, NE
Colorado Christian University, CO
Columbia Union College, MD
Concordia University at Austin, TX
Concordia University Nebraska, NE
Corcoran School of Art and Design, DC
Dana College, NE
Davis and Elkins College, WV
Doane College, NE
Dordt College, IA
D'Youville College, NY
Edgewood College, WI
Emory & Henry College, VA
Ferrum College, VA

Five Towns College, NY
Fontbonne University, MO
Franciscan University of Steubenville, OH
Geneva College, PA
Goddard College, VT
Greensboro College, NC
Greenville College, IL
Heidelberg College, OH
Hendrix College, AR
Indiana Institute of Technology, IN
Kendall College, IL
Keuka College, NY
Keystone College, PA
LaGrange College, GA
Lawrence Technological University, MI
LeTourneau University, TX
MacMurray College, IL
Malone College, OH
McKendree College, IL
McPherson College, KS
Medaille College, NY
Mercyhurst College, PA
Morningside College, IA
Mount Mary College, WI
Mount Mercy College, IA
Mount Saint Mary College, NY
Mount Union College, OH
Muskingum College, OH
Nebraska Wesleyan University, NE
Northwest Christian College, OR
Northwest Nazarene University, ID
Northwood University, FL
Northwood University, MI
Northwood University, TX
Norwich University, VT
Notre Dame College, OH
Olivet Nazarene University, IL
Palm Beach Atlantic University, FL
Point Loma Nazarene University, CA
Point Park University, PA
Queens University of Charlotte, NC
Reinhardt College, GA
Robert Morris University, PA
Saint Andrews Presbyterian College, NC
Saint Edward's University, TX
Saint Leo University, FL
Saint Mary's University of Minnesota, MN
Saint Thomas Aquinas College, NY
Saint Thomas University, FL
San Francisco Conservatory of Music, CA (no R & B)
Schreiner University, TX
Simpson College, CA
Spring Arbor University, MI
Sterling College, VT
Texas Lutheran University, TX
Thiel College, PA
Thomas More College, KY
Trinity Christian College, IL
University of Dubuque, IA
University of Saint Francis, IN
University of Saint Thomas, TX
University of the Incarnate Word, TX
Upper Iowa University, IA
Viterbo University, WI
Walla Walla College, WA
Walsh University, OH
Warner Pacific College, OR
Warren Wilson College, NC
Wartburg College, IA
Webster University, MO
Wells College, NY
West Suburban College of Nursing, IL
Western Baptist College, OR
Wheaton College, IL
William Jewell College, MO
William Woods University, MO
Wingate University, NC
Wisconsin Lutheran College, WI
Yeshiva University, NY

$22,000-$23,999

Colleges without Tuition, Room, and Board

Art Center College of Design, CA (no R & B)
Otis College of Art and Design, CA (no R & B)

Colleges with Tuition, Room, and Board

Albany College of Pharmacy, NY

Albertus Magnus College, CT
Alliant International University, CA
Alvernia College, PA
Art Institute of Atlanta, GA (no R & B)
Art Institute of Portland, OR
Averett University, VA
Baylor University, TX
Becker College, MA
Belmont Abbey College, NC
Benedictine University, IL
Bluffton College, OH
Bradley University, IL
Calvin College, MI
Carroll College, WI
Cazenovia College, NY
Centenary College of Louisiana, LA
Champlain College, VT
Christian Brothers University, TN
Clarke College, IA
College for Creative Studies, MI
College of Mount St. Joseph, OH
College of Saint Rose, NY
Columbia College, SC
Concordia College: Moorhead, MN
Concordia University, OR
Concordia University, River Forest, IL
Covenant College, GA
Daemen College, NY
Defiance College, OH
Dominican University, IL
Dowling College, NY
Eastern Mennonite University, VA
Elon University, NC
Erskine College, SC
Fisher College, MA
Florida Southern College, FL
Franklin College, IN
Fresno Pacific University, CA
Gannon University, PA
Georgetown College, KY
Goshen College, IN
Hellenic College/Holy Cross Greek Orthodox School of Theology, MA
High Point University, NC
Hillsdale College, MI
Houghton College, NY
Huntington College, IN
Johnson and Wales University, RI
Judson College, IL
King College, TN
La Roche College, PA
Lake Erie College, OH
Lewis University, IL
Manchester College, IN
Marian College, IN
Marymount University, VA
Maryville University of Saint Louis, MO
Master's College and Seminary, The, CA
Memphis College of Art, TN
Meredith College, NC
Monmouth College, IL
Montserrat College of Art, MA
Morehouse College, GA
Naropa University, CO
Neumann College, PA
Newberry College, SC
Newbury College, MA
Northland College, WI
Northwestern College, MN
Nova Southeastern University, FL
Ohio Dominican University, OH
Pacific Union College, CA
Pine Manor College, MA
Quincy University, IL
Research College of Nursing, MO
Roberts Wesleyan College, NY
Rockhurst University, MO
Roosevelt University, IL
Saint Ambrose University, IA
Saint Martin's College, WA
Saint Mary-of-the-Woods College, IN
Saint Mary's University of San Antonio, TX
Saint Peter's College, NJ
Saint Xavier University, IL
Simpson College, IA
Taylor University, IN
Texas Christian University, TX
Thomas Aquinas College, CA
Transylvania University, KY
Trinity International University, IL
Tri-State University-Main Campus, IN
University of Charleston, WV
University of Findlay, OH
University of Indianapolis, IN
University of Saint Francis, IL
University of Tampa, FL

University of Tulsa, OK
Ursuline College, OH
Vanguard University of Southern
  California, CA
Wentworth Institute of Technology, MA
West Virginia Wesleyan College, WV
Westminster College, PA
Wheeling Jesuit University, WV
Wilson College, PA

$24,000-$25,999

Colleges with Tuition, Room, and Board

Albion College, MI
Alma College, MI
American International College, MA
Ashland University, OH
Augsburg College, MN
Austin College, TX
Azusa Pacific University, CA
Baldwin-Wallace College, OH
Barry University, FL
Bay Path College, MA
Beacon College, FL
Bellarmine University, KY
Bethel College, MN
Biola University, CA
Birmingham-Southern College, AL
Bridgewater College, VA
Buena Vista University, IA
Caldwell College, NJ
Carthage College, WI
Cedar Crest College, PA
Centenary College, NJ
Cleveland Institute of Music, OH
College of Saint Catherine, MN
College of Saint Elizabeth, NJ
College of Saint Scholastica, MN
College of Santa Fe, NM
Columbia College Chicago, IL
Columbus College of Art and Design,
  OH
Concordia University, CA
Concordia University, MI
Concordia University/St.Paul, MN
Converse College, SC
Daniel Webster College, NH
De Sales University, PA
Dominican College, NY
Drake University, IA
Eastern University, PA
Elmhurst College, IL
Endicott College, MA
Eureka College, IL
Felician College, NJ
Friends World Program, NY
Gordon College, MA
Green Mountain College, VT
Guilford College, NC
Gwynedd-Mercy College, PA
Hanover College, IN
Hope College, MI
Immaculata University, PA
Jacksonville University, FL
Laboratory Institute of Merchandising,
  NY
Long Island University/Brooklyn
  Campus, NY
Loras College, IA
Luther College, IA
Mary Baldwin College, VA
Maryville College, TN
Menlo College, CA
Messiah College, PA
Millikin University, IL
Millsaps College, MS
Milwaukee Institute of Art and Design,
  WI
Mount Ida College, MA
Nazareth College of Rochester, NY
New York Institute of Technology, NY
Niagara University, NY
North Central College, IL
North Park University, IL
Pacific Lutheran University, WA
Pacific University, OR
Presbyterian College, SC
Principia College, IL
Regis University, CO
Ripon College, WI
Saint Bonaventure University, NY
Saint Francis University, PA
Saint John Fisher College, NY
Saint Joseph's College, IN
Saint Joseph's College of Maine, ME

Saint Mary's College, IN
Saint Norbert College, WI
Saint Vincent College, PA
Salem College, NC
Seattle Pacific University, WA
Seattle University, WA
Seton Hill University, PA
Shenandoah University, VA
Siena College, NY
Southwestern University, TX
Spring Hill College, AL
Springfield College, MA
Stephens College, MO
Teikyo Post University, CT
Trinity College, DC
University of Bridgeport, CT
University of Dallas, TX
University of Dayton, OH
University of Detroit Mercy, MI
University of Evansville, IN
University of Judaism College of Arts
  and Sciences, CA
Virginia Wesleyan College, VA
Westminster Choir College of Rider
  University, NJ
Wilmington College, OH
Woodbury University, CA

$26,000 and over

Colleges without Tuition, Room, and Board

Bates College, ME (no R & B)
Middlebury College, VT (no R & B)

Colleges with Tuition, Room, and Board

Adelphi University, NY
Agnes Scott College, GA
Albright College, PA
Alfred University, NY
Allegheny College, PA
American University, DC
Amherst College, MA
Anna Maria College, MA
Antioch College, OH
Arcadia University, PA
Art Institute of Boston at Lesley
  University, MA
Assumption College, MA
Augustana College, IL
Babson College, MA
Bard College, NY
Beloit College, WI
Bennington College, VT
Bentley College, MA
Berklee College of Music, MA
Boston College, MA
Boston Conservatory, MA
Boston University, MA
Bowdoin College, ME
Brandeis University, MA
Brown University, RI
Bryant College, RI
Bryn Mawr College, PA
Bucknell University, PA
Butler University, IN
Cabrini College, PA
California College of the Arts, CA
California Institute of Technology, CA
California Institute of the Arts, CA
California Lutheran University, CA
Canisius College, NY
Capital University, OH
Carleton College, MN
Carnegie Mellon University, PA
Case Western Reserve University, OH
Catholic University of America, DC
Centre College, KY
Chapman University, CA
Chatham College, PA
Chestnut Hill College, PA
Claremont McKenna College, CA
Clark University, MA
Clarkson University, NY
Cleveland Institute of Art, OH
Coe College, IA
Colby College, ME
Colby-Sawyer College, NH
Colgate University, NY
College Misericordia, PA
College of Mount Saint Vincent, NY
College of Notre Dame of Maryland,
  MD
College of Saint Benedict, MN
College of the Atlantic, ME

College of the Holy Cross, MA
College of Wooster, OH
Colorado College, CO
Columbia University/Barnard College,
  NY
Columbia University/Columbia
  College, NY
Columbia University/Fu Foundation
  School of Engineering and Applied
  Science, NY
Columbia University/School of General
  Studies, NY
Connecticut College, CT
Cornell College, IA
Cornell University, NY
Creighton University, NE
Curry College, MA
Dartmouth College, NH
Davidson College, NC
Delaware Valley College, PA
Denison University, OH
DePaul University, IL
DePauw University, IN
Dickinson College, PA
Dominican University of California, CA
Drew University/College of Liberal
  Arts, NJ
Drexel University, PA
Duke University, NC
Duquesne University, PA
Earlham College, IN
Eastman School of Music, NY
Eckerd College, FL
Elizabethtown College, PA
Elmira College, NY
Embry-Riddle Aeronautical University,
  AZ
Embry-Riddle Aeronautical University,
  FL
Emerson College, MA
Emmanuel College, MA
Emory University, GA
Eugene Lang College/New School
  University, NY
Fairfield University, CT
Fairleigh Dickinson University/College
  at Florham, NJ
Fairleigh Dickinson
  University/Metropolitan Campus, NJ
Florida Institute of Technology, FL
Fordham University, NY
Franklin and Marshall College, PA
Franklin Pierce College, NH
Furman University, SC
George Fox University, OR
George Washington University, DC
Georgetown University, DC
Gettysburg College, PA
Gonzaga University, WA
Goucher College, MD
Grand Canyon University, AZ
Grinnell College, IA
Gustavus Adolphus College, MN
Hamilton College, NY
Hamline University, MN
Hampden-Sydney College, VA
Hampshire College, MA
Hartwick College, NY
Harvard University/Harvard College,
  MA
Harvey Mudd College, CA
Haverford College, PA
Hiram College, OH
Hobart and William Smith Colleges,
  NY
Hofstra University, NY
Hollins University, VA
Holy Names College, CA
Hood College, MD
Illinois Institute of Technology, IL
Illinois Wesleyan University, IL
Iona College, NY
Ithaca College, NY
John Carroll University, OH
Johns Hopkins University, MD
Juilliard School, NY
Juniata College, PA
Kalamazoo College, MI
Kansas City Art Institute, MO
Kenyon College, OH
Kettering University, MI
King's College, PA
Knox College, IL
La Salle University, PA
Lafayette College, PA
Lake Forest College, IL
Lasell College, MA
Lawrence University, WI
Le Moyne College, NY

Lebanon Valley College, PA
Lehigh University, PA
Lesley University, MA
Lewis and Clark College, OR
Linfield College, OR
Long Island University/C.W. Post
  Campus, NY
Long Island University/Southampton
  College, NY
Loyola College in Maryland, MD
Loyola Marymount University, CA
Loyola University Chicago, IL
Loyola University New Orleans, LA
Lycoming College, PA
Lynchburg College, VA
Lynn University, FL
Macalester College, MN
Maharishi University of Management,
  IA
Maine College of Art, ME
Manhattan College, NY
Manhattan School of Music, NY
Manhattanville College, NY
Mannes College of Music, NY
Marietta College, OH
Marist College, NY
Marlboro College, VT
Marquette University, WI
Maryland Institute College of Art, MD
Marymount College of Fordham
  University, NY
Marymount Manhattan College, NY
Marywood University, PA
Massachusetts College of Pharmacy
  and Health Sciences, MA
Massachusetts Institute of Technology,
  MA
McDaniel College, MD
Mercer University, GA
Merrimack College, MA
Mills College, CA
Milwaukee School of Engineering, WI
Minneapolis College of Art and Design,
  MN
Mitchell College, CT
Monmouth University, NJ
Moore College of Art and Design, PA
Moravian College, PA
Mount Holyoke College, MA
Mount Saint Mary's College, CA
Mount Saint Mary's College, MD
Muhlenberg College, PA
New England College, NH
New England Conservatory of Music,
  MA
New York University, NY
Nichols College, MA
Northeastern University, MA
Northwestern University, IL
Notre Dame de Namur University, CA
Oberlin College, OH
Occidental College, CA
Oglethorpe University, GA
Ohio Northern University, OH
Ohio Wesleyan University, OH
Otterbein College, OH
Pace University, NY
Parsons School of Design, NY
Pepperdine University, CA
Philadelphia University, PA
Pitzer College, CA
Polytechnic University/Brooklyn, NY
Pomona College, CA
Pratt Institute, NY
Princeton University, NJ
Providence College, RI
Quinnipiac University, CT
Randolph-Macon College, VA
Randolph-Macon Woman's College,
  VA
Reed College, OR
Regis College, MA
Rensselaer Polytechnic Institute, NY
Rhode Island School of Design, RI
Rhodes College, TN
Rice University, TX
Rider University, NJ
Ringling School of Art and Design, FL
Rivier College, NH
Roanoke College, VA
Rochester Institute of Technology, NY
Rockford College, IL
Roger Williams University, RI
Rollins College, FL
Rose-Hulman Institute of Technology,
  IN
Rosemont College, PA
Russell Sage College, NY
Sacred Heart University, CT

Saint Anselm College, NH
Saint John's College, MD
Saint John's College, NM
Saint John's University, MN
Saint John's University, NY
Saint Joseph College, CT
Saint Joseph's University, PA
Saint Lawrence University, NY
Saint Louis University, MO
Saint Mary's College of California, CA
Saint Michael's College, VT
Saint Olaf College, MN
Salve Regina University, RI
Samuel Merritt College, CA
Santa Clara University, CA
Sarah Lawrence College, NY
Savannah College of Art and Design, GA
School of the Art Institute of Chicago, IL
School of Visual Arts, NY
Scripps College, CA
Seton Hall University, NJ
Sierra Nevada College, NV
Simmons College, MA

Simon's Rock College of Bard, MA
Skidmore College, NY
Smith College, MA
Southern Methodist University, TX
Southern New Hampshire University, NH
Stanford University, CA
Stetson University, FL
Stevens Institute of Technology, NJ
Stonehill College, MA
Suffolk University, MA
Susquehanna University, PA
Swarthmore College, PA
Sweet Briar College, VA
Syracuse University, NY
Trinity College, CT
Trinity University, TX
Tufts University, MA
Tulane University, LA
Union College, NY
University of Chicago, IL
University of Denver, CO
University of Hartford, CT
University of La Verne, CA
University of Miami, FL

University of New England, ME
University of New Haven, CT
University of Notre Dame, IN
University of Pennsylvania, PA
University of Portland, OR
University of Puget Sound, WA
University of Redlands, CA
University of Richmond, VA
University of Rochester, NY
University of Saint Thomas, MN
University of San Diego, CA
University of San Francisco, CA
University of Scranton, PA
University of Southern California, CA
University of the Arts, PA
University of the Pacific, CA
University of the Sciences in Philadelphia, PA
University of the South, TN
Ursinus College, PA
Utica College, NY
Valparaiso University, IN
Vanderbilt University, TN
Vassar College, NY
Villanova University, PA
Wabash College, IN

Wagner College, NY
Wake Forest University, NC
Washington and Jefferson College, PA
Washington and Lee University, VA
Washington College, MD
Washington University in St. Louis, MO
Wellesley College, MA
Wesleyan University, CT
Western New England College, MA
Westmont College, CA
Wheaton College, MA
Wheelock College, MA
Whitman College, WA
Whittier College, CA
Whitworth College, WA
Widener University, PA
Wilkes University, PA
Willamette University, OR
Williams College, MA
Wittenberg University, OH
Wofford College, SC
Worcester Polytechnic Institute, MA
Xavier University, OH
Yale University, CT

PART III

INDEX OF
COLLEGE MAJORS

By now, you either have a clear idea about what your college major will be, or you are worrying about it. This section presents an overview of academic majors as well as information about some of the careers for which each major prepares you.

Majors are listed alphabetically in chart form. This lets you compare the various schools that offer the majors that interest you. You'll also be able to compare each school's Selector Rating and in-state costs.

After you've found a representative sampling of the schools that offer majors in the fields you may want to pursue, go on to the college Profiles that make up this book's main section.

DECIDING ON A COLLEGE MAJOR AND CAREER

What Is a College Major? A major is a field of study in which a student chooses an academic specialty to receive a college degree. A major consists of a concentration of specialized subject matter in a field of study. Most majors occupy about one-quarter to two-thirds of courses in that subject. Most college and university students must complete a required number of courses in their major to earn a Bachelor of Arts (B.A.) or a Bachelor of Science (B.S.) degree. The other twenty-five to fifty percent of courses are occupied by "general education" requirements for graduation, or electives that enhance and broaden a student's academic knowledge. Students' choice of major should be made carefully considering their interests and special talents.

What Is a College Minor? A minor in a field of study usually consists of a number of courses in a field of study other than the major. However, the required units of study are fewer than those required of the major. Many colleges today do not require a formal minor for graduation. The practical reason for a minor is to supplement and strengthen a major. For example, a computer science major may require specified courses in mathematics that, when totaled up, meet the definition of a minor, or perhaps a dual major.

Majors and Careers. Choosing a field of study is one of the most important decisions a student will make in the process of choosing a college major leading to an associate or bachelor's degree. A major with a structured course of study not only provides for intellectual growth, self-improvement, general knowledge, and a search for truth and understanding, but often provides the required technical training to enter and become successful in the world of work. Personal enlightenment is a noble goal, but most students no longer can afford the monetary expenses and the time to pursue courses that do not lead to a major that ties into career goals. Information on majors and careers is presented here to help students to make wise educational and career decisions. Informed educational and career decisions should include interests, academic abilities, and work values.

WHAT ARE SOME DIFFERENT APPROACHES TO CHOOSING A COLLEGE MAJOR?

JOB TRAINING: A student may want to go to college for one main reason: to acquire specific job skills to qualify for direct job entry. Job training course work is usually work-related and technical and it is evident that the skills learned in class can be directly applied to an occupation. For example, students who want to work as engineers in one of the many engineering specialties should pursue a two-year program course work as engineering technicians, or a four- to five-year engineering curriculum to become professional engineers.

Technical preparation: Technical preparation students generally enroll in associate degree programs that provide them with advanced skills through studies and experiences in applied academics, skills, and advanced technology. These students join the workforce after grade 14 or continue their formal preparation by working toward a baccalaureate degree in applied technology. Technical majors can be planned in agriculture, arts and communications, business, engineering and mechanics, health, human service, and natural science.

A general approach: Students may want to pursue a more general major that may not directly tie in to job entry, but will improve their general knowledge and prepare them as generalists with intellectual and problem-solving skills rather than technical training. This kind of major is often referred to as liberal arts, humanities, or general studies. Liberal arts majors can be planned in Social and Behavioral Sciences, The Arts, Communications, Humanities, and Ethnic Studies. A liberal arts major, leading to a baccalaureate degree, may not guarantee direct entry into an occupation associated with the major.

Special talent approach: Students may want to select a major because of a special talent and a strong interest in a certain field of study. Students with a strong interest in writing, drama, music, art, or an academic subject should select a major that helps to further the talent. College life will be more enjoyable if students select majors that will provide personal satisfaction. Designing a career plan that will allow a lifestyle compatible with the special talent will also provide personal satisfaction.

Double major approach: Students often decide to choose two majors in preparation for a career. A double major may be necessary in preparing for occupations in the science field where it is essential to be well-grounded in both the physical and biological sciences.

Independent approach: Students may have highly divergent interests that cut across two or more fields of study. Many colleges allow students to design a major to satisfy their goals. For example, students may have artistic talents and scientific interests. They might combine the two interests and design a scientific illustration major that meets faculty approval.

CONNECTING COLLEGE MAJOR PLANNING AND CAREER PLANNING

All students from the ninth grade through postsecondary school should be following a program of study that will prepare them for specific careers—studies that blend appropriate academics with appropriate skills and knowledge in a particular career area. All students in postsecondary studies should be preparing for life and work after completing their studies. This assertion eliminates a justification for a "general plan" of studies that in theory "leads anywhere," but in fact "leads nowhere." Students should either be in a postsecondary associate, technical, or baccalaureate educational plan that leads to a satisfying career.

The next section presents relevant educational and career information on 14 fields of study from which students may choose a major based on career plans. Each of the 14 fields of study has specific information on majors and careers that students should consider carefully when choosing a college major. Information about employment, growth, and earnings is taken from the Department of Labor figures for 2002, with growth projected to 2012.

1. AGRICULTURAL SCIENCES

Agriculture is a broad and diverse field of study that trains scientists for many rewarding and satisfying careers. These play an important part in maintaining the nation's food supply through ensuring agricultural productivity and the safety of the food supply. Agricultural scientists engage in research, development, and production of farm crops and animals, food sciences, plant sciences, and soil sciences. Others manage marketing or production operations in companies that produce food products or agricultural chemicals, supplies, and machinery. Other agricultural scientists are consultants to business firms, private clients, or governmental agencies.

Interests: Agricultural research, development, and production of farm crops and animals, and development of ways to improve their quantity and quality

Popular majors in this field of study: Agribusiness, Agricultural Education, Agronomy, Animal Science, Entomology, Farm and Ranch Management, Fisheries and Wildlife, Food Sciences, Forestry, Horticultural Science, and Soil Sciences

Employment information/outlook: More than 335,000 people worked in related occupations in this field of study in 2002. The 2002–2012 employment growth is expected to be 12.6%. Median annual earnings are $48,717.

Agribusiness

Agribusiness majors will learn the business aspect of farms, firms, and industries that supply and service the farmer and other farm-related businesses. They will study merchandising, advertising, finance, marketing, and international trade.

Interests: Taking initiative, leadership, decision making, problem solving, analyzing data, global interdependence, working with people

Skills and abilities: Planning, organizing, making business decisions, leadership, teamwork, creative and critical thinking, working with people, written and verbal skills, adapting to change

Occupations related to this major: Agricultural Crop Farm Managers, Farm Products Purchasing Agents and Buyers, Farm and Ranch Managers, Fish Hatchery Managers, Farmers and Ranchers, Agricultural Statisticians, and Farm and Home Management advisers

Agricultural Education

Agricultural Education majors will study those basic courses in agriculture that will prepare them to teach agricultural science in high schools, community colleges, or universities. They will also complete general preparation for a service-type career in agriculture, such as extension services. They will learn to supervise youth and adult groups and to direct programs in both agricultural and human resources.

Interests: Working with people, working with plants, working with animals

Skills and abilities: Communication, science (especially natural sciences and chemistry)

Occupations related to this major: Farm and Home Management Advisers, Park Naturalists, Farmers and Ranchers, Agricultural Science Teachers, and 4-H and Agricultural Extension Agents

Agronomy

Agronomy majors will learn about three basic natural elements—crops, soils, and climates—and their interdependence in producing food, feed, fiber, and fuel. Agronomists study theory and practices for improving crop production while conserving natural resources and maintaining environmental quality.

Interests: Nature and the outdoors, environmental quality (soil, water, and air), conservation of natural resources, biological and physical sciences, problem solving, plant growth and experimentation, weather, climate, geologic formations

Skills and qualities: Oral and written communication skills, group dynamics, leadership, organizational (interpersonal) skills, analytic reasoning, creative thinking

Occupations related to this major: Agricultural Climatologists, Agrochemical Technologists, Environmental Technicians, Food and Drug Inspectors, Farm or Ranch Managers, Plant Breeders, Agricultural Technicians, Soil and Water Conservationists, and Greenhouse Managers

Animal Science

Animal Science majors will learn how to manage livestock and poultry. They will study the role of animals in the economy, how animal products influence eating habits and are part of the global food supply, and how animals help serve people's recreation needs. They will carry out investigations and experiments in the areas of breeding, feeding, management, and disease control in farm and domestic animals.

Interests: Working with plants, working with animals, working with people

Skills and abilities: Speaking and writing effectively

Occupations related to this major: Animal Scientists, Soil and Plant Scientists, Park Naturalists, Biologists, Farm and Ranch Managers, and Soil Conservationists

Entomology

Entomology majors will study the biology, ecology, classification, distribution, physiology, economic importance, and management of insects and their relation to plant and animal life. They will learn to identify species of insects and allied forms, such as mites and spiders. They will study methods of controlling and eliminating agricultural, structural, and forest pests by developing new and improved pesticides and cultural and biological methods, including using natural enemies of pests. They will also study insect distribution and habitat, and methods to prevent importation and spread of injurious species.

Interests: Science, techniques of scientific research, the environment, the health and well-being of people

Skills and abilities: Curiosity, rational thinking, objective thinking, performing laboratory tasks carefully

Occupations related to this major: Entomologists, Environmental Scientists, Soil and Plant Scientists, Biologists, Clinical Laboratory Technologists, and Pest Control Workers

Farm and Ranch Management

Farm and Ranch Management majors will learn to guide and assist farmers and ranchers in maximizing the financial returns to their land by managing the day-to-day activities. Duties and responsibilities may vary widely. For example, the owner of a very large livestock farm may employ a farm manager to oversee a single activity, such as feeding livestock. When managing a small crop farm, on the other hand, a farm manager may assume responsibility for

all functions, from selecting the crop to participating in planting and harvesting.

Interests: Directing and coordinating worker activities, decision making, problem solving, nature and the outdoors, conservation of natural resources, biological and physical science

Skills and abilities: Speaking, motivating people, creative and critical thinking, oral and written expression and comprehension, organizational skills, leadership

Occupations related to this major: Agricultural Crop Farm Managers, Farm and Ranch Managers, Foresters, Dairy Farm Managers, Poultry Farm Managers, and Farm and Home Management Advisers

Fisheries and Wildlife

Fisheries and Wildlife majors will learn about fish eggs, larvae, fish parasites, and diseases. They will learn to operate fish culture facilities, tag and mark fish, detect problems of water pollution, analyze, identify, collect, control, and preserve populations of fur and game animals.

Interests: Nature and the outdoors, science, research

Skills and abilities: Solving problems, communicating effectively, working with others

Occupations related to this major: Fish Culturists, Fish Hatchery Managers, Environmental Scientists, Zoo Workers, Fisheries and Wildlife Biologists, and Park Naturalists

Food Sciences

Food Science majors will learn to use biological, physical, and social sciences to transform raw materials into safe, nutritious, and economical foods. They will learn to apply scientific and engineering principles in research, development, and food production technology. They will also work to improve methods of processing, preserving, packaging, distributing, and preparing food.

Interests: Biological and physical science, public well-being, teamwork, observing details, solving complex problems

Skills and abilities: Good laboratory technique, oral and written expression and comprehension, mathematical reasoning

Occupations related to this major: Food Scientists, Food Science Technicians, Food Chemists, Food Plant Managers, Food Microbiologists, and Biological and Agricultural Technologists

Forestry

Forestry majors will learn to manage, protect, and develop forest lands and other resources for economic and recreational purposes; plan and supervise the cutting and harvesting of timber; carry out forestation and reforestation activities and manage parks and camps.

Interests: Nature and the outdoors, working with people, planning activities, investigative research, solving problems

Skills and abilities: Communicating effectively, working with quantitative and qualitative problems, presenting ideas to others

Occupations related to this major: Foresters, Soil Conservationists, Environmental Scientists, Biologists, Range Managers, Nursery and Greenhouse Managers, Agricultural Engineers, and Forest and Conservation Technicians

Horticultural Science

Horticultural Science majors will study problems of plant production, processing, and disease resistance. They will also study soil and climate to learn the conditions in which different types of plants thrive. They will be concerned with orchards, garden plants, flowers, ornamental plants, and nursery stock.

Interests: Science, working with plants, business, working with people, solving problems, improving the environment

Skills and abilities: Biological and physical sciences, written and oral communication, organization, creativity, quantitative thinking, computer competency, working with people

Occupations related to this major: Horticulturists, Foresters, Conservation Scientists, Landscape Architects, Plant Scientists, Farmers, and Farm Managers

Soil Sciences

Soil Science majors will study the physical, chemical, and geological characteristics and behaviors of soils. They will learn how to investigate soil both in the field and in the lab, and to classify soils in terms of their capability in producing crops, grasses, and trees. They also will learn how to make land appraisals.

Interests: Nature and the outdoors, conservation of natural resources, the environment, science

Skills and abilities: Quantitative reasoning, keen observation of natural phenomena, oral and written communication, applying scientific knowledge to complex systems

Occupations related to this major: Plant Scientists, Conservation Scientists, Botanists, Biochemists, Park Naturalists, and Farm and Range Managers

2. ARCHITECTURE AND DESIGN

Architects learn to plan, design, and supervise the construction of buildings, houses, factories, skyscrapers, schools, and other structures. They learn to make them attractive, usable, energy efficient, and economical. Architects must qualify for a state license after graduation. Most architects work for architectural firms. Others work directly for builders, real estate developers, or large construction projects, as well as governmental agencies responsible for housing and community planning, such as the Department of Defense, Interior, and Housing and Urban Development. Students interested in the field of architecture will do well in such courses as architectural theory design, computer graphics, computer science, general engineering urban planning, mathematics, physics, and economics.

Interests: Architects have an interest in planning, designing, and supervising the construction of buildings, houses, factories, skyscrapers, schools, and other structures.

Popular majors in this field of study: Architectural Engineering, Architecture, City and Regional Planning, Construction Science, Interior Design, Landscape Architecture, Marine Architecture, and Surveying

Employment information/outlook: More than 255,000 people worked in related occupations in this field of study in 2002. The 2002–2012 employment growth is expected to be 15.3%. Median annual earnings are $45,256.

Architectural Engineering

Architectural Engineering majors will learn how different materials interact. They also will learn to calculate loads and stress and study the strength, durability, and safety-factor of materials. They will use artistic, applied physics, and material science skills in the design of buildings.

Interests: Mathematics, physical science, building things, applying mathematics and science to practical use, design, computers

Skills and abilities: Oral and written expression and comprehension, speech clarity, logical thinking, interpersonal skills, teamwork

Occupations related to this major: Architects, Civil Engineers, Marine Architects, Materials Engineers, and Architectural Drafters

Architecture

Architecture majors learn to plan, design, and supervise the construction of buildings, houses, factories, skyscrapers, schools, and other structures. They learn to make them attractive, usable, energy efficient, and economical. They must qualify for a license after graduation. They work in design studios that develop skills and foster creative expression. Architecture students also study the history of the building environment (rooms, buildings, landscapes, cities), the technology required to create it, and related graphic communication.

Interests: The formation of the physical environment; the history of buildings, cities, and landscapes; applied creative expression

Skills and abilities: Communicating by sketching and drafting; solving spatial problems; sensitivity to visual forms, proportions, and colors

Occupations related to this major: Architects, Naval Architects, Landscape Architects, Civil Engineers, Industrial Designers, Interior Designers, and Drafters

City and Regional Planning

City and Regional Planning majors learn to deal with land use and environmental issues created by population movements. They learn how to draw plans for new city environments including streets, sewers, water, and electricity. They also learn to zone areas for residential, commercial, or industrial use. Students commit themselves, through planning, to the future, and to social and environmental improvement.

Interests: Solving problems, working with people, helping groups, communities, and organizations improve people's lives

Skills and abilities: Working with numbers, listening, interpreting and communicating what was observed or heard

Occupations related to this major: Urban and Regional Planners, Architects, Landscape Architects, City Managers, Civil Engineers, and Environmental Engineers

Construction Science

Construction Science majors learn about all areas of construction technology. These areas include contracting, remodeling, cabinet making, building inspection, carpentry, and estimating the costs of building projects.

Interests: Starting and completing projects; leading people and making decisions; risk taking; activities that include practical, hands-on problems and solutions

Skills and abilities: Listening to and understanding information; reading and understanding information; managing one's own time and the time of others; communicating information and ideas in writing

Occupations related to this major: Architects, Property and Real Estate Managers, Real Estate Appraisers, Construction and Building Inspectors, and Industrial Engineers

Interior Design

Interior Design majors learn to arrange the interiors of buildings to fit the functional and aesthetic needs of their owners. They will design everything from lighting and furniture to home decorating accessories. Interior design majors study all aspects of the building environment: scale, proportion, arrangement, light, acoustics, temperature, textures, colors, and materials. They learn how to develop surroundings that are satisfying, creative, and appropriate to human needs.

Interests: Architecture, design (interior, industrial, graphic), building construction, interaction of colors, nature of materials, and textures

Skills and abilities: Design, organization, working with people, drawing, communicating ideas

Occupations related to this major: Interior Designers, Fashion, Furniture, Textile, and Floral Designers, Exhibition Designers, Architects, and Landscape Architects

Landscape Architecture

Landscape Architecture majors learn skills and techniques for planning, designing, and managing the land. They learn about weather, drainage, botany, and construction. They are frequently involved in mapping and consultation. They creatively apply information and principles drawn from both the arts and the sciences to reshape and conserve landscapes.

Interests: Visual arts, ecology, nature, environmental issues

Skills and abilities: Drawing and graphic expression, problem solving, written communication

Occupations related to this major: Landscape Architects, Architects, Surveyors, Civil Engineers, Urban and Regional Planners, Botanists, and Park Naturalists

Marine Architecture

Marine Architecture majors learn to design and oversee construction and repair of marine craft and floating structures, such as ships, barges, tugs, dredges, submarines, torpedoes, floats, and buoys. May confer with marine engineers.

Interests: Design techniques, engineering science and technology, building materials, construction and repair of structures

Skills and abilities: Problem solving, listening and understanding information and ideas, creativity, communicating information and ideas in writing, fluency of ideas

Occupations related to this major: Marine Architects, Aerospace Engineers, Civil Engineers, Materials Engineers, Engineering Technicians, and Drafters

Surveying

Surveying majors learn to make exact measurements and determine property boundaries. They learn to provide data relevant to the shape, contour, gravitation, location, elevation, or dimension of land, or land features on or near the earth's surface, for engineering, mapping, mining, land evaluation, construction, and other purposes.

Interests: Shapes and elevations of geomorphic and topographic features, geography, and methods for describing the features of land, sea, and air masses

Skills and abilities: Communicating effectively in writing; using mathematics to solve problems; understanding written information; using scientific methods to solve problems; motivating, developing, and directing people as they work

Occupations related to this major: Surveyors, Cartographers, Urban Planners, Civil Drafters, Agricultural Engineers, and Landscape Architects

3. THE ARTS

The Arts is a field of study that includes a wider range of subjects than found in other areas of concentration. If students major in one of the arts, they will learn to design products, articles, and materials; they will develop talents as actors; they will study the theory and practice of film production; they will develop talents to draw, paint, or design interpretations of objects, people, and nature, or they will develop talents dealing with the art of sound that express ideas and emotions either by song, dance, or by instrumental musical instruments. This field, in contrast to a liberal arts education, is often thought of as professional training. A major in this field gives information, methods, procedures, and techniques needed in a career. A professional program in this field will offer students good training to make a contribution in the world of art.

Interests: Developing talents to draw, paint, or design interpretations of objects, people, and nature; or developing the art of sound that expresses ideas and emotions either by speech, song, dance, or musical instruments.

Popular majors in this field of study: Art Education, Art History, Arts Management, Dance, Dramatic Arts, Film Arts, Fine Arts, Graphic Design, Music Business Management, Music Education, Music Performance, Music Therapy, Photography, Religious Music, and Studio Art

Employment information/outlook: More than 733,000 people worked in related occupations in this field of study in 2002. The 2002–2012 employment growth is expected to be 17.4%. Median annual earnings are $42,972.

Art Education

Art Education majors learn to develop their artistic talents and gain the knowledge and skills needed to teach art at various education levels. They will explore the value of art both to the individual and to various cultures throughout history.

Interests: Visual arts, creating art, teaching

Skills and abilities: Working with others, solving problems creatively, manipulating materials creatively, responding to other people's art with sensitivity

Occupations related to this major: Art Teachers, Curriculum Specialists, Art Administrators, Manual Arts Therapists, Craft Demonstrators, Curators, Archivists, and Museum Research Workers

Art History

Art History majors study works of art—how they came about and what they mean. They will examine works of art as they appear now and also consider appearance and function in their original contexts. Through their visual analysis and extensive reading and writing, students explore the traditions of appearance and technique that guided the creation of art in different cultures.

Interests: Visual arts, past civilizations, the connections between different aspects of a civilization, artists, art technique

Skills and abilities: Observing carefully, information gathering, reading critically, written expression and comprehension

Occupations related to this major: High School Teachers, College Teachers, Curators, Archivists, Conservators, Museum Directors, and Museum Technicians

Arts Management

Arts Management majors learn to organize and manage art organizations and facilities. They receive instruction in business and financial management and labor relations, event promotion and management, public relations and arts advocacy, and arts law. They will learn to analyze and address the issues concerning the health of theaters, dance companies, museums, and other arts organizations.

Interests: Visual and performance arts, leadership, working with people

Skills and abilities: Oral and written communication, organizational ability, creative thinking, critical thinking

Occupations related to this major: Theater Managers, Symphony Orchestra Managers, Dance Company Managers, Curators, and Museum Technicians and Conservators

Dance

Dance majors learn to interpret an idea or a story through physical expression or rhythm and/or sound. Dance forms vary from ballet and modern interpretative dance to tap and chorus lines. Dance is a demanding discipline. Students learn to develop their bodies as articulate instruments for dance expression: to understand contributions that dance has made to the arts, and to create their own dances.

Interests: Dance, other arts, the physicality of movement

Skills and abilities: Sense of rhythm and musicality, physical stamina, dynamic strength, speed of limb movement, gross body coordination

Occupations related to this major: Dance Teachers, Actors and Performers, Choreographers, Dance Researchers, and Dance Therapists

Dramatic Arts

Dramatic Arts majors learn how to play a part to entertain, inform, or instruct an audience. They learn to be involved in interpreting plays or scripts, selecting plays or scripts, or planning and supervising performances. They gain breadth of knowledge about past and present culture, art, literature, politics, psychology, and philosophy.

Interests: Self-expression, communication of ideas and feelings, literature and language, art and music, human personality and motivation

Skills and abilities: Speech clarity, memorization, originality, oral and written expression and comprehension, emotional openness

Occupations related to this major: Actors, Directors, Designers, Playwrights, Stage Managers, Talent Directors, and Teachers

Film Arts

Film Arts majors study the theory and practice of film production and the techniques used in this medium of communication. They learn to do creative work, as well as learn the rapidly changing technology. They study cinema history, screenwriting, and the aesthetic and technical aspects of cinema production, including directing, cinematography, and editing. They also examine the economic, technical, social, cultural, and ideological aspects of film as a medium for communication and personal expression.

Interests: Film literature, psychology, theater, music, art history, biography, current events

Skills and abilities: Creativity, ability to express oneself verbally and visually, self-discipline, understanding of human psychology, organization, attention to detail, flexibility, working with people

Occupations related to this major: Directors—Stage, Motion Pictures, Television and Radio, Cinematographers, Technical Directors, Programming and Script Editors, Production Assistants

Fine Arts

Fine Arts majors learn to draw or design their interpretations of objects, people, and nature, using a wide variety of materials from watercolors and oils to stone and metal. They learn to create art to satisfy their own need for self-expression. They learn about the creation of art historically, in contemporary society, and through their own efforts in studio classes. They may display their work in museums, art galleries, corporate collections, and private homes.

Interests: Making things with the hands, other cultures, history, paintings, sculpture, film, self-expression

Skills and abilities: Oral and written expression and comprehension, fluency of ideas, originality, visual color discrimination, manual and finger dexterity

Occupations related to this major: Fine Artists, Graphic Artists, Sculptors, Painters, Illustrators, and Cartoonists and Animators

Graphic Design

Graphic Design majors study the principles of design to learn how to create attractive and effective advertisements, flyers, brochures, logos, magazines, or books. They learn how to create images through the use of silkscreen, computers, and printing presses. Students learn to communicate information visually using words and images. They also study how people perceive and interpret information.

Interests: Visual arts, creativity, critical thinking, working with people

Skills and abilities: Drawing, photography, originality, fluency of ideas, oral expression, visual color discrimination

Occupations related to this major: Graphic Designers, Painters, Illustrators, Cartoonists, Animators, Fashion Designers, and Interior Designers

Music Business Management

Music Business Management majors learn to organize and manage music operations, facilities, and personnel. They receive instruction in business and financial management, personnel management and labor relations, event promotion, and music products merchandising. They study the functional area of business as well as music performance, history, and theory.

Interests: Music, leadership, organizing people, business, solving problems, negotiating

Skills and abilities: Oral expression and comprehension, written expression and comprehension, leadership, organization, creative thinking

Occupations related to this major: Music Facilities Managers, Recording Studio Managers, Artists' Representatives, Orchestra Managers, Music Directors, and Concert Booking Agents

Music Education

Music Education majors learn to become music teachers in public and private schools. They learn the basics of music and the fundamentals of teaching to share music with people of all ages and abilities.

Interests: Listening to music, performing, working with young people, leadership

Skills and abilities: Musical ability, a sense of rhythm and pitch, oral and written expression and comprehension, speech clarity, discriminating listening

Occupations related to this major: Music Teachers, Music Therapists, Choir Directors, Conductors, Composers, Arrangers, and Music Librarians

Music Performance

Music Performance majors learn to develop a high level of performance skill and musical understanding. They reach a high level of technical proficiency and musical sensitivity as music performance majors. They become well-rounded musicians through the study of core music theory and history courses.

Interests: Communicating through music performance, the theoretical and historical aspects of musical structure and style, the relation of music to society

Skills and abilities: Natural aptitude for music, technical skill, strong background in piano

Occupations related to this major: Musicians, Singers, Music Directors, Music Composers, Music Teachers, and Positions with Orchestras and Ensembles

Music Therapy

Music Therapy majors learn to design music experiences and activities to the treatment of individuals and groups in all age categories who have psychological, emotional, physical, social, intellectual, or medical disorders.

Interests: Music, the arts, behavioral and life sciences, helping others

Skills and abilities: Competency in music performance and theory, oral and written expression and comprehension, working with people

Occupations related to this major: Music Therapists, Occupational Therapists, Physical Therapists, Musicians, Singers, and Music Directors

Photography

Photography majors learn the use of camera and film to portray people, places, and events. They become involved in everything from creating motion pictures and video/television to still, portrait, aerial, and commercial photography. They learn both the artistic and technical aspects of photography and a broad understanding of the social, political, and interpersonal aspects of society.

Interests: Expressing oneself in a visual medium, creating images from ideas, helping people see and understand subjects to which they might not otherwise have access

Skills and abilities: Visualization, far vision, fluency of ideas, arm-hand steadiness, control precision, color discrimination

Occupations related to this major: Commercial Photographers, Portrait Photographers, Graphic Designers, Photojournalists, Photo Editors, and Technical and Science Photographers

Religious Music

Religious Music majors develop their skills and interests as musicians and learn to use music in religious celebrations while focusing on the role and history of music in worship. They study the history, theory, composition, and performance of music for religious or sacred purposes.

Interests: Music, music history, the fine arts, the place of music in religious celebrations, matters of faith, working with people

Skills and abilities: Ability to listen carefully, hearing sensitivity, auditory attention, oral expression and comprehension, working with people

Occupations related to this major: Music Directors, Music Teachers, Music Conductors, Organists, Cantors, Musicians, and Singers

Studio Art

Studio Art majors learn to create works of art by exploring a variety of techniques and materials. They learn to focus on learning to master new media, discovering unique solutions to visual problems, exploring fresh ways to create satisfying images, and evaluating what is worth doing.

Interests: Visual arts, manipulating materials, observing visual phenomena in nature and works of art, communicating and experimenting with forms, colors, images, and symbols

Skills and abilities: Working independently, creativity, problem solving, oral and written expression and comprehension

Occupations related to this major: Fine Artists, Commercial Artists, Graphic Designers, Art Teachers, Exhibit Designers, and Set Designers

4. BIOLOGICAL AND LIFE SCIENCES

Biological and Life Sciences majors are concerned with the world of living things—people and microbes, wild and domestic animals, plants and insects, birds and fish. Some biological scientists conduct research. Still others apply biological knowledge to the solution of practical problems, such as the development of new drugs and vaccines or new strains of plants. Biological scientists, who may also be called life scientists, study the structure of living organisms, their life processes, and evolutionary development. They may be classified into groups characterized by the type of organism with which they work or the specific activity they perform. Examples of these groups are botanists who study plants, microbiologists who work with microorganisms, and zoologists who work with animals.

Interests: The world of living things—people and microbes, wild and domestic animals, plants and insects, birds and fish—or the evolutionary development of living organisms.

Popular majors in this field of study: Biochemistry, Biology, Biophysics, Biotechnology, Botany, Marine/Aquatic Biology, Microbiology, Molecular and Cell Biology, Science Education, Wildlife Management, and Zoology

Employment information/outlook: More than 94,000 people worked in related occupations in this field of study in 2002. The 2002–2012 employment growth is expected to be 21.9%. Median annual earnings are $54,252.

Biochemistry

Biochemistry majors learn how chemical substances enter into or are created in living things; how drugs, foods, hormones, serums, and other substances can influence organisms. They perform tests to identify, classify, and analyze various chemical reactions. They learn to use the physical and biological sciences to explore the nature of living organisms. They study the structure and behavior of complex molecules and how they interact to form cells, tissues, and entire organisms. They also gain a fundamental grasp of metabolism, energy flow, and the regulation of various life processes.

Interests: Nature, problem solving, investigative research

Skills and abilities: Using information from many areas of science, inductive and deductive reasoning, handling and interpreting data, written expression and comprehension

Occupations related to this major: Microbiologists, Biologists, Toxicologists, Plant Pathologists, Physiologists, Cytologists, and Food Scientists

Biology

Biology majors learn about the structure of living organisms, their life processes and evolutionary development, and the relation between these organisms and their environment. They may specialize in research centering on plants, animals, or human organisms. They study animals, plants, and microorganisms that constitute the living world at the levels of molecule, cell, organism, and population.

Interests: Quality of life, investigative laboratory work, fieldwork

Skills and abilities: Problem solving, deductive and inductive reasoning, information gathering, written expression and comprehension

Occupations related to this major: Biologists, Biochemists, Botanists, Microbiologists, Geneticists, and Zoologists

Biophysics

Biophysics majors learn to apply the laws of physics to biological systems. They study vision, hearing, nerve action, blood flow, and even the behavior of DNA. They also study the effects of radiation and radioactivity on biological systems, and the use of ultrasound scanners to construct images of body interiors. They use biology, physics, chemistry, and mathematics to explore the properties of biological molecules and groups of molecules. They study the inner workings of biological systems with precision to learn how proteins fold, how genes are switched on and off, how organisms respond to light, how cells move, and how the nervous system works.

Interests: Natural history, investigative problem solving

Skills and abilities: Curiosity, deductive and inductive reasoning, written expression and comprehension, information ordering, manual dexterity

Occupations related to this major: Biophysicists, Biologists, Botanists, Geneticists, Microbiologists, and Soil Scientists

Biotechnology

Biotechnology is an interdisciplinary field of study involving the molecular life sciences and engineering fields of study. Students learn techniques for using living matter to develop new products and services in agriculture (plant growth hormones, food additives), health care (vaccines, improved drugs and vitamins), the environment (detoxification of chemicals), and other areas.

Interests: Science, treating and preventing disease, investigative research, and problem solving

Skills and abilities: Creative thinking, oral and written expression and comprehension, deductive and inductive reasoning, problem sensitivity

Occupations related to this major: Biological Technologists, Agricultural Technologists, Environmental Scientists, Food Scientists, Animal Scientists, Botanists, and Microbiologists

Botany

Botany majors focus on all aspects of plant life including taxonomy, genetics, physiology, and plant anatomy. They learn about the economic value of plants in their application to agronomy, forestry, horticulture, and pharmacology. Students study all aspects of plant biology to become familiar with the cellular and molecular functioning of life.

Interests: Nature, investigative problem solving, analytic reasoning

Skills and abilities: Deductive and inductive reasoning, information ordering, written expression and comprehension

Occupations related to this major: Botanists, Agricultural Scientists, Soil Scientists, Ecologists, Microbiologists, Physiologists

Marine/Aquatic Biology

Marine/Aquatic Biology majors learn to research and study marine organisms and their environments. They receive instruction in freshwater and saltwater organisms, physiological and anatomical marine adaptations, ocean and freshwater ecologies, marine micro-

biology, marine mammalogy, ichthyology, marine botany, and biochemical products of marine life used by humans. They learn about the diversity of life in the ocean, how ocean species relate to each other as food and prey, and how different species depend on and use the physical and chemical structures of the ocean.

Interests: Life in the ocean, how organisms use the sea as a habitat

Skills and abilities: Quantitative thinking, deductive and inductive reasoning, information ordering, written expression and comprehension

Occupations related to this major: Marine Biologists, Aquatic Biologists, Biochemists, Botanists, Agricultural Scientists, and Zoologists

Microbiology

Microbiology majors concentrate on microorganisms, bacteria, yeasts, fungi, protozoa, and one-celled algae. They learn about the application of these organisms in the production of food products, antibiotics, and industrial chemicals. They learn to use the basic knowledge acquired from other biological sciences, chemistry/biochemistry, and physics to study microscopic organisms such as bacteria, yeasts, molds, viruses, rickettsia, and protozoa.

Interests: Biological sciences, health and medicine, ecology, food production, investigative research

Skills and abilities: Working with detail, analytic thinking, deductive and inductive reasoning, information ordering

Occupations related to this major: Microbiologists, Botanists, Medical Scientists, Zoologists, Physiologists, and Geneticists

Molecular and Cell Biology

Molecular and Cell Biology majors study the nature of biological phenomena at the molecular level through the study of DNA proteins and other macromolecules relating to genetic information and cell function. They study what cells are, how they are put together, what makes them work, what makes them differ from each other, how they associate and interact, what goes wrong in disease states, and how they can intervene beneficially in these processes. They study how molecular biology underlies many aspects of genetic engineering, protein engineering, and other new approaches to improving upon nature.

Interests: Organisms and their development, how things work, the molecular basis of plant, animal, and human disease, disease prevention

Skills and abilities: Investigative research, laboratory skills, information gathering, deductive and inductive reasoning, oral and written expression and comprehension

Occupations related to this major: Molecular Biologists, Medical Doctors, Toxicologists, Botanists, Plant Pathologists, and Biologists

Science Education

Science Education majors prepare to teach science in grades 7 through 12. Students typically major in one science and take additional course work in two other sciences. They learn techniques for teaching science.

Interests: Working with young people, helping others, the learning process, solving practical problems, understanding complex processes, learning how things work

Skills and abilities: Oral and written expression and comprehension, speech clarity, fluency of ideas, deductive reasoning, working with numbers

Occupations related to this major: Biological Technicians, Health Specialties Teachers, Elementary School Teachers, Dietitians, Nutritionists, Pharmacists, Psychiatrists, Veterinarians, and Medical and Clinical Laboratory Technologists

Wildlife Management

Wildlife Management majors receive a solid background in basic biology. They study natural resources and wildlife management. They study conservation of animal populations and their habitats, paying special attention to species that are hunted regularly and species that are threatened or endangered. They learn to analyze characteristics of animals to identify and classify them; to conduct experimental studies with live animals in controlled or natural surroundings; to study animals in their natural habitats; and to study characteristics of animals such as origin, interrelationships, classification, life histories and diseases, development, genetics, and distribution.

Interests: Nature, conservation of natural resources, hunting, bird-watching

Skills and abilities: Using scientific rules and methods to solve problems, mathematics, deductive and inductive reasoning, problem sensitivity

Occupations related to this major: Wildlife Biologists, Environmental Scientists, Park Naturalists, and Research Wildlife Biologists

Zoology

Zoology majors study the identification, description, and classification of animals. They study life histories, habits, diseases, life processes, and distribution of animal species within the environment. They study living organisms in the animal kingdom, exploring their form and function, chemistry and structure, growth, reproduction, maintenance, and interactions with each other and their world. They study the transmission of characteristics from one generation to the next (genetics and evolution).

Interests: Natural history, wildlife, the outdoors, bird-watching, how things work, living things, fossils, working with animals

Skills and abilities: Deductive and inductive reasoning, synthesizing information, gathering and analyzing information, working with numbers

Occupations related to this major: Zoologists, Ecologists, Agricultural Scientists, Physiologists, Cytologists, Microbiologists, and Botanists

5. BUSINESS AND MANAGEMENT

Business and Management majors are found in every industry. Business executives, administrators, managers, and support staff are found in every organization. They direct and coordinate operations and activities of an organization. Business majors must be comfortable with numbers and the manipulation of data, enjoy working with a computer, and have good communication skills, both written and oral. Business majors deal with large amounts of information to make production, personnel, financial, and marketing decisions.

Interests: Business managers and support workers have an interest in directing and coordinating operations and activities of a business or organization; an interest in making production, personnel, financial, and market decisions of a business.

Popular majors in this field of study: Accounting, Business Administration, Business Education, Finance, Human Resource Management, Insurance and Risk Management, International Business Management, Labor Relations Management, Management, Management Information Systems, Management Science, Marketing, and Real Estate

Employment information/outlook: More than 10,332,000 people worked in related occupations in this field of study in 2002. The 2002–2012 employment growth is expected to be 18.8%. Median annual earnings are $57,196.

Accounting

Accounting majors learn to keep track of expenditures, income, profit and loss, prepare financial reports, and calculate taxes. They may specialize in auditing, taxes, or consulting. Many accountants seek Certified Public Accountant (CPA) certification after graduation. Students will learn to apply this knowledge in all areas of business, government, and nonprofit enterprises.

Interests: Working with numbers, competition, economics, computers, mathematics, entrepreneurship, social and political activism, moral and ethical responsibility

Skills and abilities: Mathematical reasoning, written and oral expression and comprehension, working with people, leadership

Occupations related to this major: Accountants, Auditors, Loan Officers, Loan Counselors, Credit Analysts, Tax Preparers, Budget Analysts, and Marketing Managers

Business Administration

Business Administration majors learn about a variety of managerial opportunities in finance, accounting, marketing, information management, operations and production, general management, retailing, and consulting. They learn the fundamental principles, concepts, and applications of accounting, finance, and management.

Interests: Leadership, organizing people, taking initiative, starting and running a business, working with numbers, solving problems, competing, taking risks, working with people

Skills and abilities: Oral and written expression and comprehension, speech clarity, inductive reasoning, creative and critical thinking

Occupations related to this major: Private Sector Executives, Administrative Services Managers, Human Resources Specialists, Production Managers, Labor Relations Specialists, and Financial Analysts

Business Education

Business Education majors learn to teach vocational business programs at various education levels. They develop instructional methods and training techniques including curriculum design principles, learning theory, group and individual teaching techniques, design of individual development plans, and test design principles.

Interests: Teaching young people, helping people develop their academic interests in business, and helping people develop career plans

Skills and abilities: Working with young people, speech clarity, oral and written expression and comprehension, teaching, learning, understanding human behavior

Occupations related to this major: Business Education Teacher, Education Administrators, Training and Development Managers, and Educational Program Directors

Finance

Finance majors study financial and accounting information, economic models, and analytic techniques that can be applied to financing problems. They learn to determine prices of assets such as stocks, bonds, and businesses, and to manage assets to maximize their economic value.

Interests: Business, the stock market, the economy, budgets

Skills and abilities: Logical thinking, organizational skills, oral and written expression and comprehension, problem sensitivity, mathematical reasoning, working with people, solving problems with computers

Occupations related to this major: Financial Managers, Financial Planners, Treasurers, Controllers, Chief Financial Officers, and Loan Officers and Counselors

Human Resource Management

Human Resource Management majors learn to deal with many personnel activities, including hiring competent workers and dismissing workers when necessary, keeping records, classifying jobs, evaluating and properly placing workers, analyzing and assisting in morale and discipline problems, and promoting and rewarding employees. They learn to deal with issues that affect men and women at work.

Interests: Solving problems, working with numbers, working with people of different ages and backgrounds, leadership

Skills and abilities: Logical and critical thinking, speech clarity, oral and written expression and comprehension, analyzing numerical data, teamwork

Occupations related to this major: Human Resource Specialists, Training and Development Managers, Labor Relations Managers, Employee Assistance Specialists, Employee Benefits Managers, and Career Planning and Placement Counselors

Insurance and Risk Management

Insurance and Risk Management majors learn to analyze and solve problems involving loss of personal and corporate assets. They study programs, integrate knowledge from finance, quantitative analysis, and management, and include study of the legal, social, and institutional environment in which losses may occur.

Interests: Working with numbers, solving problems, competing, leadership, taking initiative

Skills and abilities: Oral and written expression and comprehension, fluency of ideas, problem sensitivity, deductive and inductive reasoning, creative and critical thinking

Occupations related to this major: Insurance Adjusters, Insurance Appraisers, Risk Managers, Insurance Brokers, Insurance Sales Representatives, and Insurance Underwriters

International Business Management

International Business Management majors learn to determine and formulate policies, and provide the overall direction of international companies or private and public sector organizations with international business activities. They learn to conduct management guidelines set up by a board of directors or similar governing body. They learn basic business management techniques and practices and how business is conducted in other countries and between different countries.

Interests: Business operations, other cultures, different people and environments

Skills and abilities: Learning languages, organizing and managing people, oral and written expression and comprehension, deductive and inductive reasoning, fluency of ideas

Occupations related to this major: International Business Managers, International Purchasing Agents and Buyers, International Marketing Managers, International Advertising and Promotions Managers, Compliance Officers and Inspectors, and Investment Bankers

Labor Relations Management

Labor Relations Management majors learn to deal with various aspects of employer-employee relations. They learn to deal with wage and salary negotiations, benefits and welfare, affirmative action, grievances, abuses and demands, labor laws, union organization, and collective bargaining. Particular attention is given to government policies, labor unions, and human resources management.

Interests: The employment relationship, human behavior, problem solving

Skills and abilities: Working with people, oral and written expression and comprehension, problem sensitivity, inductive reasoning

Occupations related to this major: Labor Relations Managers, Human Resource Managers, Training and Development Managers, Employee Assistance Specialists, Employee Benefits Managers, and Union Organizers

Management

Management majors study courses designed for the generalist who wants a broad business background. They take courses in business areas, such as accounting, marketing, finance, and business law, and courses that prepare them to function as managers in any organization.

Interests: Working with people, listening, persuading, leading, starting new systems

Skills and abilities: Thinking analytically, problem sensitivity, oral and written expression and comprehension, speech clarity

Occupations related to this major: General and Operations Managers, Marketing Managers, Public Relations Managers, Corporate Communications Specialists, Human Resource Specialists, and Human Resources Recruiters

Management Information Systems

Management Information Systems majors unite studies in computer science and business knowledge. They learn to act as intermediaries between persons with information needs and the computer programmers who provide the solutions to the problems.

Interests: Computer languages, computer programming, problem solving, logic, taking initiative, organizing groups

Skills and abilities: Oral and written expression and comprehension, deductive and inductive reasoning, information ordering, fluency of ideas, creativity

Occupations related to this major: Management Information Systems Managers, Systems Analysts, Computer Support Specialists, Database Administrators, and Computer Programmers

Management Science

Management Science majors learn to plan, organize, direct, and control the functions and processes of a business firm or organization. They learn about management theory, human resources, management and behavior, accounting and other quantitative methods, purchasing and logistics organization and production, marketing and business decision making. They learn to use mathematics, computers, and statistical and economic analysis to solve managerial and business problems.

Interests: Mathematics, solving business and management problems, computer languages, computer programming

Skills and abilities: Quantitative thinking, computer programming, creativity, oral and written expression and comprehension, speech clarity

Occupations related to this major: Employee Training Specialists, Administrative Service Managers, Purchasing Managers, Association Managers, and Property Managers

Marketing

Marketing majors learn to increase sales of products or services by analyzing and compiling data, and researching and influencing the purchasing power of the public through inventory procedures. They study trend forecasting, product development, management, wholesale selling, and operations. They learn how to display and to buy and sell items through showrooms, department stores, and specialty shops. They learn to make decisions about product design and quality, pricing, advertising, selling, and distribution.

Interests: Running a business, economic issues, social issues, working on new products, problem solving, analyzing data, understanding how people buy, use, and sell products and services

Skills and abilities: Oral and written expression and comprehension, speech clarity, originality, fluency of ideas, mathematical reasoning, persuasion

Occupations related to this major: Marketing Managers, Sales Managers, Public Relations Representatives, Advertising and Promotions Managers, Market Research Analysts, and Advertising Account Executives

Real Estate

Real Estate majors learn to show real estate properties to clients, evaluate and list properties for sale, and advise and arrange financing. They study property management and insurance. They act as independent agents, brokers, or appraisers. They gain an understanding of and proficiency in the business and social principles that affect how real property—buildings and land—is developed, operated, and traded.

Interests: Business, people and social conditions, the economy, public affairs

Skills and abilities: Oral and written expression and comprehension, mathematical reasoning, working independently, critical and analytic thinking

Occupations related to this major: Property Managers, Real Estate Sales Agents, Real Estate Financial Analysts, Real Estate Brokers, Loan Processors, and Real Estate Appraisers

6. COMMUNICATIONS

Communications is the giving or exchanging of information. It is a way to share facts, experiences, or emotions with others. A message can be conveyed through a wide variety of means. These can include writing, speaking, drawing, or using face, hand, and body movements. People receive messages through each of the five senses: taste, touch, sight, smell, and hearing. Communications studies involve the understanding of the role of mass communication in society; broadcast satellites, cable television transmitters, computer networks, and other mass media technology provide a global communication system. The field of communications includes training for those occupations necessary for the system to work efficiently.

Interests: The ways and means of exchanging information; an interest in broadcast satellites, television transmitters, computer networks, and other mass media technology.

Popular majors in this field of study: Advertising, Communications, Creative Writing, Journalism, Public Relations, Radio/Television Broadcasting, and Speech

Employment information/outlook: More than 562,000 people worked in related occupations in this field of study in 2002. The 2002–2012 employment growth is expected to be 18.1%. Median annual earnings are $43,364.

Advertising

Advertising majors learn to plan and prepare advertisements for newspapers, magazines, radio, television, billboards, and brochures. They may specialize in writing copy, layout, or research. They use creative talents to market a product to prospective clients. They learn how advertising campaigns are produced, how advertising is coordinated with marketing, and how advertising strategies develop from research. They learn to write advertising copy for broadcasting and print, and to select media for advertising campaigns.

Interests: Writing, art and design, analysis, knowing something about lots of things, investigative research

Skills and abilities: Oral and written expression and comprehension, originality, fluency of ideas, analytic reasoning, public speaking, art and design

Occupations related to this major: Advertising and Promotions Managers, Advertising Agency Account Executives, Marketing Managers, Sales Managers, Fund-raising Directors, and Advertising Research Specialists

Communications

Communications majors study the role of mass communication in society. They study the nature, function, content, values, and effects of communication on public policy and opinion. They study the nature of language and how it is communicated. They study the history of political and religious oratory; explore the sociology of interpersonal relations, group dynamics, and messages; examine ways of thinking about human symbol systems (semiotics); and examine the ethics of communication.

Interests: Politics, presentations, advertising, television, film, analyzing oral and electronic messages

Skills and abilities: Oral and written expression and comprehension, critical listening, logical analysis, leadership

Occupations related to this major: Communications Managers, Public Relations Specialists, Television Producers and Directors, Press Secretaries, Reporters, and Speech Writers

Creative Writing

Creative Writing majors study the processes and techniques of original composition in various literary forms, such as short stories, novels, biographies, articles, plays, and scripts. They receive instruction in technical and editorial skills, criticism, and the marketing of finished manuscripts.

Interests: Reading, fiction and nonfiction prose, writing, factual information, English language, critical thinking, computers

Skills and abilities: Written and oral expression and comprehension, information ordering, deductive and inductive reasoning, fluency of ideas

Occupations related to this major: Radio and Television Announcers, Broadcast News Analysts, Reporters and Correspondents, Editors, Technical Writers, and Poets and Lyricists

Journalism

Journalism majors learn to write, edit, manage, and produce newspapers and magazines. They learn to interview people, review records, observe events, and conduct journalistic research. They study the liberal arts and sciences to acquire the depth and breadth of knowledge they need to understand the world better and communicate information about it to others. They learn special skills needed by reporters, editors, broadcasters, and photojournalists.

Interests: Human psychology and behavior, reading widely, photography, world events

Skills and abilities: Writing, oral and written expression and comprehension, speech clarity, learning quickly about a wide range of topics

Occupations related to this major: Reporters and Correspondents, Magazine Writers and Editors, Columnists, Critics, Commentators, Creative Writers, Radio and Television Reporters, and Photojournalists

Public Relations

Public Relations majors learn how to manage an organization's or an individual's communication and relationship with others. They develop skills to build trust between an organization and the public. They learn how to write news articles and press releases, give speeches, and create audiovisual presentations designed to build trust. They learn technical and managerial skills, such as writing and producing printed and visual materials, and study strategic planning and problem solving.

Interests: Solving problems, mediating between opposing groups, writing, public speaking, giving advice

Skills and abilities: Communicating clearly, oral and written expression and comprehension, speech clarity, fluency of ideas, creative and critical thinking

Occupations related to this major: Public Relations Specialists, Publicity Writers, Advertising and Promotions Managers, Corporate Video Producers, Staff Writers and Editors, Special Events Planners, and Reporters and Correspondents

Radio/Television Broadcasting

Radio/Television Broadcasting majors learn about the planning, preparation, and production of radio and television programs. They may specialize in announcing, programming, engineering, or sales. They study the relationship between the mass media and society and develop skills in such specialties as reporting, performance, production, sales, and management

Interests: Writing, speaking, editing words, pictures, or sound; operating a camera; sound recording

Skills and abilities: Interviewing people, oral and written expression and comprehension, speech clarity, persuasion, operating technical equipment

Occupations related to this major: Broadcast News Analysts, Reporters and Correspondents, Radio/Television Announcers, Radio/Television Producers, Station Managers, Radio/Television Writers

Speech

Speech majors learn about the human communication process. They learn the principles and practical application of speech communication, and the skills and techniques essential for effective interpersonal communication. They learn to develop listening skills.

Interests: Public speaking, human behavior

Skills and abilities: Working with people, oral and written expression and comprehension, speech clarity

Occupations related to this major: Speech Teachers, Speech Writers, Public Relations Specialists, Journalists, Writers, Editors, and Radio and Television Reporters

7. COMPUTER AND INFORMATION SCIENCES

Computer and Information Sciences field of study prepares students for a wide variety of occupations in most sectors of the economy. This field of study prepares a wide range of professionals who design computers and the software that runs them. Information technology occupations are comprised of computer-related occupations engaged in either managing, storing, transmitting, or generating the information organizations use to make decisions, as well as installing and repairing computer hardware and software used to perform such tasks. Computer science is distinguished by a high level of theoretical expertise and innovation applied to complex problems, as well as the creation or application of new technology. Computer scientists and technicians can be theorists, researchers, or inventors. They may work at an academic institution on theory, hardware, or language design. Others work in industry to apply theory, develop specialized languages, or design programming tools and knowledge-based systems.

Interests: Designing computers and the software that runs them; managing, storing, transmitting, or generating and repairing computer hardware and software used to perform such tasks

Popular majors in this field of study: Computer Software Engineering, Computer Science, Information Sciences and Systems, Computer Programming, Mathematics, Mathematics Education, and Statistics

Employment information/outlook: More than 2,026,000 people worked in related occupations in this field of study in 2002. The 2002–2012 employment growth is expected to be 21.1%. Median annual earnings are $65,988.

Computer Software Engineering

Computer Software Engineering majors study applied mathematical and scientific principles to the design, development, and operational evaluation of computer hardware and software systems and related equipment and facilities. They learn to develop, create, and test applications software and/or operating systems level software. They learn to analyze specific problems in computer applications.

Interests: Computers and electronics, computer programming, problem solving, engineering technology, design

Skills and abilities: Using mathematics to solve problems, computer programming, critical thinking, oral and written expression and comprehension, speech clarity, problem sensitivity

Occupations related to this major: Computer Support Specialists, Mathematical Technicians, Computer Science Teachers, and Numerical Tool and Process Control Programmers

Computer Science

Computer Science majors learn to design new computers, computer languages, and related devices, and research new ways to use computers effectively. They become involved in aspects of artificial intelligence, from pattern recognition to problem solving. They learn how computers work and how to program computers to perform tasks and provide services. They study the physical hardware components of computer systems and software procedures for making computers work.

Interests: Mathematics, electronics, investigative research

Skills and abilities: Oral and written expression and comprehension, mathematical reasoning, problem solving, abstract reasoning, working with people

Occupations related to this major: Computer Scientists, Computer Engineers, Computer Science Teachers, Computer Programmers, Software and Hardware Developers

Information Sciences and Systems

Information Sciences and Systems majors receive broad exposure to computer and programming concepts. They learn to bring people and computers together to solve problems in businesses and other organizations. They learn to plan, direct, and coordinate activities in such fields as electronic data processing, information systems, systems analysis, and computer programming.

Interests: Solving problems, working with details, taking initiative, working with numbers, organizing information, working with people

Skills and abilities: Oral and written expression and comprehension, mathematical reasoning, deductive reasoning, critical and logical thinking, working with changing technology

Occupations related to this major: Computer Programmers, Information Systems Designers, Information Systems Analysts, Computer Security Specialists, Database Administrators

Computer Programming

Computer Programming majors learn to write step-by-step instructions in several computer languages and create video games and software packages. They learn how to write software to handle specific jobs. They learn to convert project specifications and statements of problems and procedures to detailed logical flowcharts for coding into computer language. They learn to develop and write computer programs to store, locate, and retrieve specific documents, data, and information. They learn how to maintain software that controls the operations of entire computer systems.

Interests: Mathematics, electronics, using computers, investigative research, problem solving

Skills and abilities: Programming, critical thinking, active listening, oral and written expression and comprehension, mathematical reasoning, fluency of ideas, problem sensitivity

Occupations related to this major: Computer Programmers, Computer and Information Systems Managers, Computer Support Specialists, Computer Systems Analysts, Numerical Tool and Process Control Programmers, and Computer Science Teachers

Mathematics

Mathematics majors learn to solve both theoretical and practical problems that can be explained in mathematical terms. They study all aspects of algebra, geometry, advanced mathematics, and computer languages. They develop the abilities to explore, conjecture, and reason logically as well as the ability to use various mathematical methods effectively to solve problems.

Interests: Problem solving, working with numbers, games requiring analytic reasoning, investigative research

Skills and abilities: Oral and written comprehension, number facility, mathematical reasoning, deductive reasoning, analytic skills

Occupations related to this major: Mathematicians, Statisticians, Mathematics Teachers, and Financial Analysts

Mathematics Education

Mathematics Education majors learn to teach mathematics at the high school or middle school level. They learn techniques to help students develop skills and knowledge in the field of mathematics; they also take professional education courses.

Interests: Problem solving, analytic reasoning, working with young students, working with computers, leadership, organizing people

Skills and abilities: Oral and written expression and comprehension, speech clarity, organizational skills, creativity, using computers

Occupations related to this major: Middle School Teachers, High School Teachers, Insurance Underwriters, Business Training Specialists, and Education Administrators

Statistics

Statistics majors learn the science of dealing with data. They learn to design efficient data collection systems and to analyze and interpret information derived from the data. They learn to use mathematical theory or apply statistical theory and methods to collect, organize, interpret, and summarize numerical data to provide usable information. They may specialize in fields such as biostatistics, agricultural statistics, business statistics, economic statistics, or other fields.

Interests: Mathematics, working with numbers, problem solving, quantitative problems

Skills and abilities: Mathematical reasoning, computer operations, critical thinking, deductive and inductive reasoning, written expression

Occupations related to this major: Statisticians, Actuaries, Mathematicians, Operations Research Analysts, and Cost Estimators

8. EDUCATION

Education is a people-oriented field of study providing teachers, librarians, and school counselors involved in helping others to learn, acquire information, or gain insight into it. There are many levels on which one can teach. These include preschool and day care facilities, elementary schools, secondary schools, colleges and universities, as well as public and private vocational education institutions, dance, music, and art studios, and many other places. Librarianship and counseling are smaller fields than teaching. Archivists and curators are more involved with things than people. They may also help people learn and gain information, but they do not usually work as closely with people as do teachers, librarians, and counselors. All of these professions usually require a bachelor's degree, although some require a master's or doctoral degree.

Interest: Helping others learn, acquire information; teaching, counseling, or librarianship

Popular majors in this field of study: Early Childhood Education, Elementary School Education, Library Science, Middle School Education, Parks and Recreation Management, Physical Education, Secondary School Education, Special Education, Technology Education, and Vocational and Educational Counseling

Employment information/outlook: More than 7,550,000 people worked in related occupations in this field of study in 2002. The 2002–2012 employment growth is expected to be 21.1%. Median annual earnings are $43,612.

Early Childhood Education

Early Childhood Education majors learn to teach preschool students through art, music, play, poetry, and stories to prepare for learning language, science, numbers, and social studies. They learn to design programs to develop students' mental capacities, learning abilities, and emotional health. They learn a variety of appropriate teaching methods and strategies.

Interests: Childhood development, working with children, communicating with children and their parents

Skills and abilities: Oral expression and comprehension, speech clarity, problem sensitivity, time sharing, creativity, music or artistic ability

Occupations related to this major: Preschool Teachers, Kindergarten Teachers, Elementary School Teachers, Early Childhood Education Program Directors, Child Care Administrators, and Family Service Coordinators

Elementary School Education

Elementary School Education majors learn to teach young students (kindergarten through grade 6) basic academic, social, and manipulative skills. They learn to instill good study and work habits and an appreciation for learning. They learn to prepare lesson plans, tests, records, and reports, and to conduct conferences with parents. They learn a variety of methods for understanding how and why children develop socially and intellectually, and get professional experience that includes research in teaching and learning.

Interests: Communication, creativity, problem solving, flexibility, ability to organize, energy, enthusiasm

Skills and abilities: Oral and written expression and comprehension, speech clarity, problem sensitivity

Occupations related to this major: Elementary School Teachers, Kindergarten Teachers, Middle School Teachers, Secondary School Teachers, Special Education Teachers, and School Counselors

Library Science

Library Science majors learn the science of acquiring and organizing collections of books, pamphlets, manuscripts, clippings, and reports, and assisting readers in their use. They learn how to analyze reader needs, prepare bibliographies, and organize films, tapes, and maps.

Interests: Reading, multimedia communication, working with people, computers

Skills and abilities: Reading comprehension, active listening, oral and written expression and comprehension, speech clarity, fluency of ideas, information ordering

Occupations related to this major: Librarians, Computer and Information Systems Managers, Elementary School Teachers, Secondary School Teachers, and School Administrators

Middle School Education

Middle School Education majors learn to develop a wide array of instructional skills, which include multimedia approaches, classroom management, advisory ability, effective communication, and alternatives to teacher-centered instruction. They learn to build on and extend basic academic skills developed in elementary school students, and introduce them to the world of more abstract thinking and knowledge that they will encounter in high school.

Interests: Helping or providing service to others, communicating with young people, teaching young people, working with ideas

Skills and abilities: Instructing others, active listening, social perceptiveness, oral and written expression and comprehension, speech clarity, problem sensitivity

Occupations related to this major: Middle School Teachers, High School Teachers, Vocational Education Teachers, School Counselors, and Librarians

Parks and Recreation Management

Parks and Recreation Management majors study how individuals and communities pursue leisure and recreation. They explore what recreation is, investigate what motivates people's recreational choices, and develop skills to manage a variety of leisure and recreation enterprises and organizations.

Interests: Working with people; scientific, historic, and natural features of parks, forests, and other attractions

Skills and abilities: Helping others, leadership, solving problems, oral and written expression, speech clarity, problem sensitivity

Occupations related to this major: Community Recreation Planners/Directors, Social Directors, Park Naturalists, Forest Rangers, Amusement and Recreation Establishment Managers, and Camp Directors

Physical Education

Physical Education majors learn to teach and supervise individual and team sports. They learn to demonstrate sports techniques, analyze physical capabilities and needs of students, and administer corrective exercises and physical conditioning. They learn to provide students with activities to maximize physical fitness.

Interests: Physical activity, sports, working with people, health-related issues, biological science

Skills and abilities: Physical stamina, leadership, oral expression, speech clarity, multilimb coordination

Occupations related to this major: Physical Education Teachers, Sports Coaches, Physical Training Instructors, Aerobic Dance Instructors, Athletic Trainers, Fitness Directors, and Athletic Administrators

Secondary School Education

Secondary School Education majors learn to teach one or more high school subjects using various teaching methods. They learn to develop and plan teaching materials and assignments. They learn to construct tests to evaluate learning. They gain depth of knowledge in the subject they intend to teach and develop teaching skills in subject matters such as science, mathematics, social studies, English, music, art, business, physical education, or other subjects.

Interests: Serving others, teaching young people and helping them develop their academic interests and career choices

Skills and abilities: Working with people, teaching, learning, understanding human behavior, oral and written expression and comprehension, speech clarity

Occupations related to this major: Secondary School Teachers, Middle School Teachers, Special Education Teachers, Vocational Education Teachers, and Vocational and Educational School Counselors

Special Education

Special Education majors prepare for a career working with disabled children and adults in a variety of settings. They learn to coordinate the services available to people with disabilities, and provide appropriate educational experiences for people with varying disabilities, including deafness, blindness, aphasia, and mobility impairments.

Interests: Helping others, working with people

Skills and abilities: Accepting differences in people, communicating effectively, teaching, oral and written expression and comprehension, speech clarity, problem sensitivity

Occupations related to this major: Special Education Teachers; Teachers of the Emotionally and Mentally Impaired; Teachers of the Physically, Visually, and Hearing Impaired; Rehabilitation Counselors

Technology Education

Technology Education majors are trained to teach the design, operation, and impact of technological systems to students. They learn technical skills to be used in advanced communication, applied higher mathematics, and science. This major prepares students to teach technical pathway programs found in middle schools, high schools, and colleges. Technical majors can be planned in agriculture, arts, communication, business, engineering, information science, mechanics, and other fields.

Interests: Helping people, design, technological systems, network technology, graphics and multimedia, system designs, programming, teaching

Skills and abilities: Working with people, oral and written expression and comprehension, analyzing and describing technological systems

Occupations related to this major: Agriculture Teachers, Art Teachers, Computer Science Teachers, Business Teachers, Engineering Technology Teachers, and Science Teachers

Vocational and Educational Counseling

Vocational and Educational Counseling majors learn to counsel individuals and provide group educational and vocational guidance services. They learn to promote and enhance student learning through three broad and interrelated areas of student development: academic development, career development, and personal/social development.

Interests: Working with, communicating with, and teaching people; providing service to others

Skills and abilities: Speaking, active listening, oral and written expression and comprehension, problem sensitivity, speech clarity, fluency of ideas

Occupations related to this major: Educational and Vocational School Counselors, Child, Family, and School Social Workers, Health Educators, and Probation Officers

9. ENGINEERING

Engineering field of study involves planning and designing various things. Engineers design machines, processes, systems, and structures. They apply physical laws and mathematical theories and principles to solve practical technical problems. Engineers work in research, development, design, manufacturing and construction, operations, management, technical sales, teaching, and consulting services.

Interests: Designing machines, processes, systems and structures; research, development, design, manufacturing and construction, operations, management, and technical consulting services

Popular majors in this field of study: Aerospace/Aeronautical Engineering, Agricultural Engineering, Chemical Engineering, Civil Engineering, Computer Engineering, Electrical Engineering, Industrial Engineering, Materials Engineering, Mechanical Engineering, and Petroleum Engineering

Employment information/outlook: More than 1,663,000 people worked in related occupations in this field of study in 2002. The 2001–2012 employment growth is expected to be 5.9%. Median annual earnings are $71,437.

Aerospace/Aeronautical Engineering

Aerospace/Aeronautical Engineering majors learn to perform a variety of engineering work in designing, constructing, and testing aircraft, missiles, and spacecraft. They learn to conduct basic and applied research to evaluate adaptability of materials and equipment to aircraft design and manufacture. They learn to make improvements in testing equipment and techniques.

Interests: Model aircraft and rocketry, astronomy, piloting, space exploration, computers, problem solving, working with people

Skills and abilities: Leadership, computer technology, physical science, oral and written expression and comprehension, mathematical reasoning, deductive and inductive reasoning

Occupations related to this major: Aerospace/Aeronautical Engineers, Electronics Engineers, Nuclear Engineers, Ceramic Engineers, Chemical Engineers, and Civil Engineers

Agricultural Engineering

Agricultural Engineering majors learn to apply knowledge of engineering technology and biological science to agricultural problems concerned with power and machinery, electrification, structures, soil and water conservation, and processing of agricultural products.

Interests: Solving problems, improving the quality of life, computers, leadership

Skills and abilities: Problem solving, oral and written expression and comprehension, computer operation, deductive and inductive reasoning, number facility

Occupations related to this major: Soil Conservationists, Landscape Architects, Geoscientists, Foresters, Chemical Engineers, Industrial Engineers, and Mechanical Engineers

Chemical Engineering

Chemical Engineering majors learn to turn chemicals into products through research and development. They learn to devise economical and efficient production processes. They learn to work in a number of fields, such as cosmetics, fertilizers, paints, dyes, pesticides, oil refining, and pollution prevention.

Interests: Science, chemistry, mathematics

Skills and abilities: Applying knowledge of science and mathematics to real-world problems, written expression and comprehension, mathematical reasoning, originality, deductive reasoning

Occupations related to this major: Chemical Engineers, Nuclear Engineers, Civil Engineers, Petroleum Engineers, Agricultural Engineers, and Electrical Engineers

Civil Engineering

Civil Engineering majors learn to solve technical problems involved in providing buildings, bridges, airports, transportation systems, foundations, coastal facilities, environmental control systems, and water supply and purification systems. They become involved in the conception, planning, design, construction, operation, and maintenance of these important public facilities. Studies will include soil mechanics, hydraulics, and structural engineering.

Interests: Mathematics, physical sciences, computers, building things, public service, applying mathematics and science to practical uses

Skills and abilities: Mathematics, physical sciences, logical thinking, interpersonal skills, oral and written expression and comprehension, inductive and deductive reasoning

Occupations related to this major: Civil Engineers, Civil Engineering Technicians, Architectural Engineers, Nuclear Engineers, Electrical Engineers, and Industrial Engineers

Computer Engineering

Computer Engineering majors learn to design and develop computer and computer-related systems. These systems include software systems, hardware systems, and combined hardware/software systems. Students take courses in basic sciences, mathematics, and engineering science and design.

Interests: Mathematics, science, computing, investigative research

Skills and abilities: Mathematics, computer operations, oral and written expression and comprehension, inductive and deductive reasoning

Occupations related to this major: Computer Hardware Engineers, Computer Software Engineers, Electronics Engineers, and Computer Service Technicians

Electrical Engineering

Electrical Engineering majors learn to design, develop, test, or supervise the manufacturing and installation of electrical equipment components or systems for commercial, industrial, military, or scientific use. They learn to design and manufacture a broad array of electrical and electronic devices and systems to meet society's needs.

Interests: Computer languages, computer programming, electronic equipment

Skills and abilities: Mathematics, physical science, oral and written expression and comprehension, deductive reasoning

Occupations related to this major: Electrical Engineers, Electronics Engineers, Mechanical Engineers, Electricians, Nuclear Engineers, and Production Engineers

Industrial Engineering

Industrial Engineering majors learn to plan, design, and implement complex systems for industry that take into account the availability, capabilities, and needs of people, machines, and materials. They learn to plan the layout of factories for efficiency, and engage in time, motion, and incentive studies. They learn about safety studies, cost, and quality control measures, and long-range planning goals.

Interests: Problem solving, leadership

Skills and abilities: Working with people, critical thinking, written and oral expression and comprehension, fluency of ideas, mathematical reasoning

Occupations related to this major: Aerospace Engineers, Materials Engineers, Petroleum Engineers, Industrial Engineers, Mechanical Engineers, and Engineering Technicians

Materials Engineering

Materials Engineering majors learn to evaluate properties of materials used to manufacture products that must meet specialized design and performance criteria. They learn to develop machinery and processes to manufacture materials, such as polymers, plastics, and alloys.

Interests: Nature and the physical sciences, problem solving, computer operations, working with ideas

Skills and abilities: Creative and critical thinking, problem sensitivity, oral and written expression and comprehension, deductive and inductive reasoning

Occupations related to this major: Materials Engineers, Marine Architects, Mechanical Engineers, Electrical Drafters, and Electrical Engineering Technicians

Mechanical Engineering

Mechanical Engineering majors learn to plan and design tools, engines, machines, and other mechanically functioning equipment. They learn to oversee installation, operation, maintenance, and repair of such equipment as centralized heat, gas, water, and steam systems. They learn to create and build machines, devices, and systems that perform useful services.

Interests: Mechanical devices, computers, cars, solving problems, mathematics, physical science

Skills and abilities: Mathematics, critical thinking, complex problem solving, mathematical reasoning, deductive and inductive reasoning, oral and written comprehension

Occupations related to this major: Mechanical Engineers, Marine Architects, Materials Engineers, Petroleum Engineers, Engineering Technicians, and Mechanical Drafters

Petroleum Engineering

Petroleum Engineering majors learn about exploring and drilling for fossil fuel, both on land and under the sea, and how to maximize the recovery of oil and gas through engineering processes. They learn methods of searching for new sources of energy, for example, geothermal energy. They learn to devise methods to improve oil and gas well production and determine the need for new or modified tool designs.

Interests: Solving problems, working with others, using computers, outdoor activities

Skills and abilities: Mathematics, physics, oral and written expression and comprehension, inductive and deductive reasoning, problem sensitivity, fluency of ideas

Occupations related to this major: Petroleum Engineers, Aerospace Engineers, Marine Engineers, Materials Engineers, Mining and Geological Engineers, and Geologists

10. FAMILY AND CONSUMER SCIENCES

Family and Consumer Sciences majors concentrate on issues concerning feeding, clothing, and caring for children, managing resources, and providing housing for individuals and families. Family and Consumer Science majors provide information, gained through research, about families and individuals as consumers and decision makers. These majors provide information about child care, elder care, food, clothing, housing, finance, and other issues of resource management.

Interests: Issues concerning feeding, clothing, and caring for children, managing resources, and providing housing for individuals and families; an interest in families as consumers and decision makers.

Popular majors in this field of study: Day Care Administration, Family and Consumer Education, Fashion Merchandising, Food Science and Nutrition, Hotel and Motel Management, Housing and Human Development, Individual and Family Development, Leisure Studies, Textile Sciences, and Tourism

Employment information/outlook: More than 1,571,000 people worked in related occupations in this field of study in 2002. The 2001–2012 employment growth is expected to be 19.9%. Median annual earnings are $44,137.

Day Care Administration

Day Care Administration majors learn to manage programs that provide education or social services to young children and their families. They gain knowledge of child development and develop skills in teaching young children, in supervising staff, and in business management.

Interests: Leadership, management, supervising people, administering programs, working with children

Skills and abilities: Organizational and managerial skills, program development, oral and written expression and comprehension, speech clarity

Occupations related to this major: Day Care Director, Preschool Director, Head Start Directors, Early Childhood Education Program Directors, and Child Care Workers

Family and Consumer Education

Family and Consumer Education majors learn to use community resources to meet the needs of the individual and the family in the management of time, energy, and money. They learn about parenting skills, communication skills, relationship skills, wellness, foods and nutrition, consumerism, clothing selection, and job skills. They prepare to become family and consumer teachers for preschool through adult education in subjects related to the family. They study various aspects of family life including human development, nutrition, and decision making, in addition to teaching strategies.

Interests: Family life, using current technology, working with people

Skills and abilities: Critical and analytical thinking, oral and written expression and comprehension, speech clarity

Occupations related to this major: Family and Consumer Science Teachers, Consumer Advocates, Education Consultants, Extension Agents, Financial Planners, Housing Administrators

Fashion Merchandising

Fashion Merchandising majors study how to manufacture fashions for consumers and effectively sell those fashions.

Interests: Current trends in apparel, arts, furnishings, travel and leisure, food business trends, fabrics, fashion and fashion designers

Skills and abilities: Motivating people, leadership, organizational ability, originality, fluency of ideas, color discrimination, oral comprehension

Occupations related to this major: Retail Buyers, Manufacturers' Representatives, Product Designer-Pattern Makers, and Fashion Designers

Food Science and Nutrition

Food Science and Nutrition majors study the nature of foods, the causes of their deterioration, and the principles of food processing. They will learn about the selection, preservation, processing, packaging, distribution, and use of safe, nutritious, and wholesome food.

Interests: Social, health, economic, and political issues involved in food production and availability; chemical reactions and what happens to food when it enters the human body; solving problems

Skills and abilities: Organizational abilities, critical thinking, oral and written expression and comprehension, speech clarity, mathematical reasoning

Occupations related to this major: Dietitians, Nutritionists, Nutrition Educators, and Food Scientists and Technicians

Hotel and Motel Management

Hotel Management majors learn the operation of a hotel. They learn the principles of managing lodging facilities efficiently and profitably. They learn about personnel management, services, supplies, business aspects, decision making, accounting, and public relations. They are introduced to the principles of managing these key components of the hospitality industry.

Interests: Working with people, problem solving, attention to detail, leadership

Skills and abilities: Organization ability, creativity, oral and written expression and comprehension, speech clarity, speech recognition

Occupations related to this major: Lodging Managers, Food Service Managers, Retail Store Managers, and Office Managers

Housing and Human Development

Housing and Human Development majors learn to analyze the use of investment in housing and its impact on families, the community, and the larger economy and society.

Interests: Working with people, serving others, real estate, home automation, the family, marketing, management, interior design, environmental design, finance

Skills and abilities: Computer skills, analytical skills, oral and written expression and comprehension, problem sensitivity

Occupations related to this major: Real Estate Managers, Property Managers, Consumer Affairs Specialists, Extension Agents, and Financial/Mortgage Specialists

Individual and Family Development

Individual and Family Development majors study interpersonal relationships and human development from infancy to old age. They study theories of development with an emphasis on techniques to improve quality of life for individuals and families.

Interests: Helping others, family and individual well-being, prevention and elimination of problems facing people in their daily lives

Skills and abilities: Working with people, critical thinking, oral and written expression and comprehension, curiosity about interpersonal and family dynamics, speech clarity

Occupations related to this major: Child Life Specialists, Day Care Teachers, Recreation Activities Directors, Drug and Alcohol Rehabilitation Counselors, and Crisis Center Directors

Leisure Studies

Leisure Studies majors learn to design, manage, and deliver leisure services to a variety of people in diverse settings. They learn about the impact of leisure services upon individual satisfaction and the quality of life.

Interests: Helping people, leadership, organizing individual and group activities

Skills and abilities: Working with people, oral and written expression and comprehension, speech clarity, problem sensitivity, fluency of ideas, memorization

Occupations related to this major: Amusement and Recreation Establishment Managers, Recreation Workers, Tour Guides and Escorts, Social and Community Service Managers, and Meeting and Convention Planners

Textile Sciences

Textile Sciences majors learn how to design fabrics for garments, upholstery, rugs, and other products. They study print, woven, and embroidery styles, and learn how to buy and sell certain fabrics and trims. They learn how to analyze fabric performance in the marketplace.

Interests: Fashion design, garment fashion, art, history of textiles, textile technology, design principles

Skills and abilities: Originality, visualization, visual color discrimination, fluency of ideas, oral expression and comprehension

Occupations related to this major: Textile Designers, Fashion Designers, Quality Control Analysts, Sales Representatives, and Wardrobe Planners

Tourism

Tourism majors study how to manage travel-related enterprises and conventions and tour services. They learn about travel agency management, travel industry operations and procedures, tourism marketing and promotion strategies, and travel industry law.

Interests: Travel, tourism planning, human resource management, travel industry operations, marketing

Skills and abilities: Oral and written expression and comprehension, mathematical reasoning, speech clarity, fluency of ideas

Occupations related to this major: Travel Agents, Travel Guides, Tour Guides and Escorts, Reservation and Transportation Ticket Agents, and Amusement and Recreation Establishment Managers

11. HEALTH SCIENCE

The **Health Science** field of study trains workers in a vast array of occupations. Occupational titles vary, and the training necessary to fill these occupations requires lengthy postgraduate education. Health practitioners diagnose, treat, and prevent illness and disease. While all health practitioners practice the art of healing, they differ in methods of treatment and areas of specialization. Training for this profession is more rigorous than training for most other professional occupations, but practice also offers unusual rewards. Incomes of health practitioners generally are higher than those of other professional workers with similar years of education. Furthermore, most health practitioners derive considerable satisfaction from knowing that their work contributes directly to the well-being of others. Workers in the industry must have the ability and perseverance to complete the years of study required. They should be emotionally stable, able to make decisions in emergencies, and have a strong desire to help the sick and injured. Sincerity and an ability to gain the confidence of patients are important qualities.

Interests: Diagnosing, treating, and preventing illness and disease; an interest in the well-being of others and a desire to help the sick and injured

Popular majors in this field of study: Athletic Training, Clinical Laboratory Science, Dental Hygiene, Health Services Management, Medical Record Administration, Nuclear Medical Technology, Nursing, Occupational Therapy, Pharmacy, and Physical Therapy

Employment information/outlook: More than 2,367,000 people worked in related occupations in this field of study in 2002. The 2002–2012 employment growth is expected to be 25.4%. Median annual earnings are $65,823.

Athletic Training

Athletic Training majors learn to prevent, recognize, refer, and treat injuries and illnesses sustained by athletes. They learn about the administration of athletic training programs in public and private schools, colleges, universities, and with professional teams. They study exercise sciences and the medical aspects of sport. Together with clinical experience, this prepares students for national certification in the field.

Interests: Sports, helping others, health and medicine, physical fitness and exercise, anatomy, nutrition, first aid

Skills and abilities: Manual skills, science, problem solving, interpersonal communication, integrity, oral expression, speech clarity, physical strength

Occupations related to this major: Athletic Trainers, Sports Medicine Clinic Administrators, Exercise Physiologists, Physical and Corrective Therapists, and Occupational Therapists

Clinical Laboratory Science

Clinical Laboratory Science majors learn to perform medical tests to determine the presence and cause of disease. They study sophisticated instrumentation used to perform a variety of laboratory procedures. They study blood and other body fluids that aid in the diagnosis of disease and the maintenance of health.

Interests: Solving problems, working with complex machinery, computer science, laboratory work, helping others, medicine, biological science

Skills and abilities: Computer skills, analytic skills, oral and written expression and comprehension, arm-hand steadiness, visual color discrimination

Occupations related to this major: Laboratory Technologists and Technicians, Research Analysts, Coroners, Clinical Scientists, Environmental Health Officers, and Toxicologists

Dental Hygiene

Dental Hygiene majors learn to work under the supervision of a dentist to clean and polish teeth, massage gums, apply fluoride to prevent decay, and provide dental health education. They obtain the knowledge and clinical skills needed to provide preventive oral health care. They learn skills as an assistant to a dentist performing a number of duties.

Interests: Working with people, helping individuals maintain their health, science

Skills and abilities: Critical thinking, oral expression, arm-hand steadiness, manual dexterity, near vision

Occupations related to this major: Dental Hygienists, Dental Assistants, Dentists, and Medical Assistants

Health Services Management

Health Services Management majors prepare for entry-level positions managing a wide variety of health care organizations such as hospitals, nursing homes, insurance companies, and public agencies. They learn to direct the many activities of health care organizations and coordinate administrative duties with medical services. They learn about space needs, staffing, and supplies. They learn to supervise personnel, prepare budgets, and direct the policies of the organization.

Interests: Working with people, taking initiative, solving problems, working with data

Skills and abilities: Oral and written expression and comprehension, speech clarity, organizational skills, interpersonal skills, critical thinking

Occupations related to this major: Medical and Health Services Managers, Public Health Directors, Educational Program Directors, Nursing Directors, Social Welfare Administrators, and Health Insurance Underwriters

Medical Record Administration

Medical Record Administration majors learn to supervise and manage the preparation, storage, and use of medical records and related information systems. They study the legal and technical aspects of medical records, and the design and management of secure data systems. They learn to merge the study of business and medicine. Students prepare to direct medical record departments in varied health care settings by exploring the health care environment, health care organizations, clinical information systems, medical record department operations, and health care reimbursement systems.

Interests: Leadership, working with people, designing and implementing systems, problem solving, working with detail

Skills and abilities: Writing and speaking effectively, working in a changing environment, oral and written expression and comprehension, near vision, mathematical reasoning

Occupations related to this major: Medical Records Administrators and Directors, Quality Assurance Coordinators, Health Care Administrators, Medical Records Educators, and Research Coordinators

Nuclear Medicine Technology

Nuclear Medicine Technology majors learn how to administer radionuclides to patients and to monitor the characteristics and functions of tissues or organs in which they localize. They learn to operate the cameras that detect the radionuclides and maintain patient records. They learn to prepare and administer radioactive drugs to patients, operate radiation detection equipment, and perform the calculations or computer analysis needed to complete the patient's examination.

Interests: Biological sciences, new technologies, helping others, working in a medical setting, working with people

Skills and abilities: Biological and physical science, working with others, oral and written expression and comprehension, problem sensitivity

Occupations related to this major: Nuclear Medicine Technologists, Radiation Therapists, Radiologic Technologists, Electroneurodiagnostic Technologists, and Medical and Clinical Laboratory Technologists

Nursing

Nursing majors learn to administer nursing care to ill or injured persons. They learn to administer medication and treatments prescribed by medical doctors, observe and record symptoms and behaviors of patients, and promote good health. They learn how to rehabilitate, counsel, and educate patients, and how to work as part of a health care team in many settings. They study humanities, natural sciences, and nursing theory to serve individuals, families, groups, and communities.

Interests: Provide intimate helping services to people, ethical care, chemistry, physics, anatomy, biology

Skills and abilities: Clear thinking, oral and written expression and comprehension, problem sensitivity, speech clarity

Occupations related to this major: Registered Nurses, Doctors of Medicine, Nursing Instructors, Physical Therapists, Medical Assistants, Chiropractors, and Podiatrists

Occupational Therapy

Occupational Therapy majors learn to determine the educational, recreational, and vocational activities needed to hasten a patient's recovery from physical, psychological, social, or developmental problems. They learn to instruct patients in the use of artificial limbs or to regain the use of muscles. They learn to help patients function independently so that they may work, play, take care of themselves, and relate to others in a productive and satisfying manner.

Interests: Solving problems, anatomy, working with people, medicine, health, rehabilitation

Skills and abilities: Logical thinking, working with others, oral and written expression and comprehension, deductive reasoning

Occupations related to this major: Occupational Therapists, Respiratory Therapists, Physical Therapists, Speech-Language Pathologists and Audiologists, Recreational Therapists, and Exercise Physiologists

Pharmacy

Pharmacy majors study the science of drugs, including their chemical and physical properties and composition. They learn to understand the effects of drugs, to test those drugs for purity and strength. They learn to provide drug products and drug information in all areas of patient care. They learn to monitor drug therapy to ensure that the treatment is appropriate, safe, therapeutically effective, and cost-effective.

Interests: Chemistry, biology, mathematics, solving problems, helping others

Skills and abilities: Patience, tact, adapting to change, working carefully, oral and written expression and comprehension, information ordering, mathematical reasoning

Occupations related to this major: Pharmacists, Pharmacy Technicians, Physician Assistants, Opticians, Licensed Practical Nurses, and Dietitians and Nutritionists

Physical Therapy

Physical Therapy majors learn to assist and help persons with injuries, muscle, nerve, and joint problems, burns, and bone diseases. They learn to use exercise, massage, and heat and light to assist in healing. They prepare to take state licensure examinations in this field and qualify for service in the prevention of disabilities and the rehabilitation of the disabled. They learn to test, evaluate, and plan a treatment program for patients who are physically incapacitated as the result of accidents or disease, and for healthy individuals who wish to prevent injuries in work or recreational settings.

Interests: Biological and physical sciences, exercise and fitness, people, analytic reasoning

Skills and abilities: Interpersonal communication, problem solving, visual spatial perception, emotional sensitivity, oral and written expression, speech clarity, problem sensitivity, manual dexterity

Occupations related to this major: Physical Therapists, Occupational Therapists, Respiratory Therapists, Manual Arts Therapists, Corrective Therapists, and Speech-Language Pathologists and Audiologists

Speech Pathology/Audiology

Speech Pathology majors learn to treat people with speech, language, voice, hearing, and communication disorders. These disorders may be the result of hearing loss, brain injury or deterioration, cerebral palsy, stroke, cleft palate, mental retardation, or emotional problems. They receive training in the identification and treatment of human communication disorders. They learn about the normal processes of speech and language development, why problems may occur, and what can be done to minimize their impact.

Interests: Working with children, working with adults, identifying and solving behavioral problems, applying technology to human needs

Skills and abilities: Oral and written expression and comprehension, speech clarity, creativity, working cooperatively in groups

Occupations related to this major: Speech-Language Pathologists and Audiologists, Recreation Therapists, Corrective Therapists, Exercise Physiologists, Occupational Therapists, and Respiratory Therapists

12. HUMANITIES

Humanities students explore thought and expression through aesthetic, historical, philosophical, social, political, psychological, and symbolic contexts. Humanities studies serve as a liberal and broad training for professional careers. Students will enjoy courses in English, literature, history, classics, culture studies, history of art and music, philosophy, foreign language, social and natural sciences. Graduates with a bachelor's degree may qualify for management trainee positions in corporations, banks, and federal and state governmental agencies. Many students use humanities as an undergraduate degree for the teaching or law professions. Other students may become writers or communications specialists in humanistic endeavors.

Interests: Exploring thoughts and expressions through aesthetic, historical, philosophical, social, political, psychological and symbolic contests; literature, history, foreign language, social and natural sciences

Popular majors in this field of study: American Literature, Anthropology, Classics, Comparative Literature, English, English Education, Foreign Language, History, Linguistics, Philosophy, Religion, and Sociology

Employment information/outlook: More than 1,162,000 people worked in related occupations in this field of study in 2002. The 2002–2012 employment growth is expected to be 14.8%. Median annual earnings are $42,552.

American Literature

American Literature majors study the historical development of the culture in which they live. They study the literature and literary development of the United States from the Colonial Era to the present. They learn about the forces—intellectual, economic, geographic, and social—that have shaped their own character. They study periods and genres, authors, literary criticism, and regional and oral traditions.

Interests: Sensitivity to language, the power of ideas, exploring the development of different regional and ethnic traditions that make up American culture

Skills and abilities: Assessing conflicting points of view, oral and written expression and comprehension, speech clarity

Occupations related to this major: English Teachers, Creative Writers, Art, Drama, and Music Teachers, Reporters and Correspondents, and Publicity Writers

Anthropology

Anthropology majors learn to make comparative studies of the distribution, origin, and evolution of man, cultures that man has created, and their social and physical characteristics. Studies include ancient as well as modern man.

Interests: Writing, archeology, sociology, social sciences, investigative research

Skills and abilities: Writing, science, critical thinking, oral and written expression and comprehension, inductive reasoning, fluency of ideas

Occupations related to this major: Anthropologists, Archeologists, Historians, Sociologists, Linguistic Scientists, and Genealogists

Classics

Classics majors immerse themselves in two cultures fundamental to the West—the cultures of ancient Greece and ancient Rome. Students explore the literature, history, art, philosophy, and architecture of those civilizations. Connecting with the past creates a sense of belonging to humanity and participating in human achievement and evokes reflections on the present. Students will explore their poetry, prose, and drama, and consider the relation of literature to other arts and to other fields of study.

Interests: Language, literature, exploring the past, acquiring a broad liberal education

Skills and abilities: Oral and written expression and comprehension, information ordering, skills of analysis and criticism

Occupations related to this major: Classicists, Anthropologists, Art History Teachers, English Teachers, Foreign Language Teachers, and Literature Teachers

Comparative Literature

Comparative Literature majors study the literature of different countries, cultures, and languages. They explore their poetry, prose, and drama, and consider the relation of literature to other arts and to other fields of study.

Interests: Literature, foreign languages, differences between cultures as expressed in their languages and works of art

Skills and abilities: Reading critically, speaking, active listening, oral and written expression and comprehension, speech recognition, information ordering

Occupations related to this major: English Teachers, Foreign Language Teachers, Postsecondary Teachers, Journalists, Lawyers, Reporters and Correspondents, and Writers

English

English majors study the linguistic and literary richness of the English language as well as some of the cultural history of the English-speaking world. They concentrate on specific areas such as creative writing, comparative or American literature, or semantics. They study important works of literature—drama, prose, and poetry—focusing on the point of view, organization, and language of the works. They develop critical and analytical reading skills, and practice language use and composition.

Interests: Reading, talking, writing about literature; music, theater, and film

Skills and abilities: Speaking, writing, oral and written expression and comprehension, speech clarity

Occupations related to this major: English Teachers, Teachers, Journalists, Publishers, Radio and Television Broadcasters, and Social Workers

English Education

English Education majors learn to teach students about English grammar and linguistics. They learn to instruct students in different types of literature such as poetry, short stories, plays, and novels. They learn how to teach students to research and prepare research papers. They learn how to teach public speaking, drama, and English as a second language

Interests: Nature and history of languages, reading, literature, journalism, creative writing, linguistic development of children and teenagers

Skills and abilities: Speaking, working with students, art, guiding discussions

Occupations related to this major: Elementary School Teachers, Secondary School Teachers, Postsecondary School Teachers, Linguistic Scientists, and Speech-Language Pathologists and Audiologists

Foreign Language

Foreign Language majors study foreign languages (French, German, Italian, Japanese, Russian, Spanish, etc.). They study the language, literature, and culture of the country where the language is spoken.

Interests: Literature, history, culture of a language

Skills and abilities: Fluency in speaking and writing, learning languages, oral and written expression and comprehension, speech clarity

Occupations related to this major: Foreign Language Teachers, Translators, Journalists, Foreign Travel Consultants, Diplomats, and Linguists

History

History majors study the social, economic, and political developments of societies. They learn to analyze historical happenings and, as reporters, writers, or teachers, report on their significance. Students expand their knowledge and understanding of the past. Working with written, oral, visual, and art factual evidence they examine the causes, contexts, and chronologies of historical events, thus cultivating a sense of continuity and change in human experiences.

Interests: Curiosity about when, where, and why historical happenings occurred; what it was like to have lived in different times and places

Skills and abilities: Reading carefully, writing clearly, speaking articulately, thinking analytically, oral and written expression and comprehension, expressing ideas with clarity and precision

Occupations related to this major: Historians, Archeologists, Anthropologists, Genealogists, Curators, Archivists, and Teachers

Linguistics

Linguistics majors study the common properties of the world's languages. They study the structure and development of a specific language or language group. They trace the origin and evolution of words through comparative analysis of ancient parent languages and modern language groups. They study word and structural characteristics, such as phonetics and phonology, morphology, syntax, and semantics.

Interests: Language, foreign languages, how people talk and express themselves

Skills and abilities: Learning foreign languages, problem solving, oral and written expression and comprehension, speech recognition

Occupations related to this major: Linguistic Scientists, English as a Second Language Teachers, English Teachers, Foreign Language Teachers, Interpreters, Translators, Public Relations Specialists, and Speech Pathologists

Philosophy

Philosophy majors learn the process of developing a philosophy. They gain insight into how the great minds of the past and present have attempted to answer the most serious questions of the universe. They participate in a tradition of thought as old as civilized life and as new as artificial intelligence and medical ethics. They examine issues of morality, reality, and knowledge. Philosophy is a foundation for teaching, religion, wisdom, and logical thinking.

Interests: Solitary meditation, argument with family and friends, reading, asking the "why" question, seeing the connections between different things

Skills and abilities: Writing, debating, thinking logically, mathematics, oral and written expression and comprehension, speech recognition, information ordering

Occupations related to this major: Philologists, Political Scientists, Anthropologists, Psychologists, Sociologists, and Historians

Religion

Religion majors study and compare the major world religions, as well as many of the lesser-known religions. They study the various branches, sects, and denominations of particular religions. They learn how religion plays an integral part in all societies. They learn to use a range of approaches when examining religion—historical, textual, psychological, philosophical, sociological, and anthropological.

Interests: Different cultures and societies, world religions, human problems and mysteries, such as birth, growth, love, death, grief

Skills and abilities: Reading carefully and critically, foreign languages, oral and written expression and comprehension, problem sensitivity, speech clarity

Occupations related to this major: Clergy, Directors of Religious Activities and Education, Therapists and Counselors, Psychologists, Social Workers, and Teachers

Sociology

Sociology majors study the origin, development, organization, and functions of human society. They trace the origin and growth of human organizations and the behavior and interaction within social groups. They analyze the influence of group activities on individual and group behavior.

Interests: Anthropology, geography, criminology, psychology, investigative research, politics

Skills and abilities: Reading critically, critical thinking, solving problems, oral and written expression and comprehension, deductive reasoning

Occupations related to this major: Sociologists, Anthropologists, Political Scientists, Counseling Psychologists, Historians, and Linguistic Scientists

13. PHYSICAL SCIENCES

Physical Sciences majors in this field of study investigate the structure and composition of the Earth and the universe. Everything in our physical environment, whether naturally occurring or of human design, is composed of chemicals. Chemists search for, and put to practical use, new knowledge about chemicals. Geological scientists play an important role in preserving and cleaning up the environment. Meteorologists forecast the weather. Physicists design and perform experiments with lasers, cyclotrons, telescopes, mass spectrometers, and other equipment. Physical science technicians use the principles and theories of science and mathematics to solve problems in research and development and to help invent and improve products and processes.

Interests: The structure and composition of the Earth and the universe; an interest in our physical environment, whether naturally occurring or of human design

Popular majors in this field of study: Astronomy, Atmospheric Sciences, Chemistry, Environmental Sciences, Geology, Geophysics, and Physics

Employment information/outlook: More than 310,000 people worked in related occupations in this field of study in 2002. The 2002–2012 employment growth is expected to be 8.2%. Median earnings are $68,427.

Astronomy

Astronomy majors study the sizes, shapes, motions, and all other physical properties of the sun, moon, stars, and planets. They may use knowledge of astronomy in space exploration and the development of space technology. Students seek to understand the entire universe—its constituent parts, such as the stars and planets, and the physical and mathematical laws that govern them.

Interests: Nature, the night sky, the expanding universe, physical science, astronomical science

Skills and abilities: Mathematics, science, computers, inductive and deductive reasoning, written comprehension

Occupations related to this major: Astronomers, Geophysicists, Physicists, Geologists, Chemists, and Atmospheric and Space Scientists

Atmospheric Sciences

Atmospheric Sciences majors learn to investigate atmospheric phenomena and interpret meteorological data gathered by surface and air stations, satellites, and radar to prepare reports and weather forecasts for public and other uses. They study the basic principles of atmospheric physics and dynamics and are concerned with understanding and forecasting weather.

Interests: Weather, environment, climate, science, mathematics, computer science, geography, serving the public

Skills and abilities: Analytic reasoning, mechanical reasoning, problem solving, oral and written expression and comprehension, speech clarity, inductive reasoning

Occupations related to this major: Atmospheric Scientists, Space Scientists, Climatologists, Geophysicists, Astronomers, and Meteorologists

Chemistry

Chemistry majors study the sciences of physical substances, atoms, molecules, elements, and compounds. They learn to perform chemical tests, develop new chemical products, and monitor the purity of air, food, and drugs. Because it is an experimental science, students learn to design and perform the experiments that allow a better understanding of the physical world.

Interests: Investigative research, problem solving, curiosity about how things work

Skills and abilities: Analytic and mathematical skills, oral and written expression and comprehension, deductive reasoning, mathematical reasoning

Occupations related to this major: Chemists, Chemical Engineers, Chemical Engineering Technicians, Agricultural Scientists, Biological Scientists, and Physicists

Environmental Sciences

Environmental Sciences majors study the biological and physical aspects of the environment. They learn about the conservation and/or improvement of natural resources, such as air, soil, water, land, fish, and wildlife, as well as methods of controlling environmental pollution. They conduct research or perform investigation for the purpose of identifying, abating, or eliminating sources of pollutants or hazards that affect either the environment or the health of the population.

Interests: Investigative research, solving problems, working with ideas

Skills and abilities: Working with others, oral and written expression and comprehension, problem sensitivity, mathematical reasoning, inductive reasoning

Occupations related to this major: Environmental Scientists, Materials Scientists, Geographers, Geologists, Atmospheric Scientists, and Space Scientists

Geology

Geology majors study the Earth's structure, composition, and history. They examine rocks, minerals, and fossils. They record data, prepare maps, conduct surveys, and advise suitability of sites. They develop skills that are useful for basic research and applied problem solving.

Interests: The outdoors, remote places, problem solving, collecting minerals or fossils

Skills and abilities: Reasoning ability, critical thinking, mathematics, oral and written expression and comprehension, number facility, inductive reasoning

Occupations related to this major: Geologists, Physicists, Geophysicists, Materials Scientists, Geological Data Technicians, and Geographers

Geophysics

Geophysics majors study aspects of the earth, including the atmosphere and hydrosphere. They investigate and measure seismic, gravitational, electrical, thermal, and magnetic forces affecting the Earth, and utilize principles of physics, mathematics, and chemistry. They study the Earth and its atmosphere by physical measurements. Students learn to use mathematics and physics, along with electrical engineering, computer science, geology, and other earth sciences to analyze measurements taken at the surface to infer properties and processes deep within the Earth's complex interior.

Interests: The outdoors, travel, taking measurements, computer languages, graphics, computer programming

Skills and abilities: Natural curiosity, mathematics, physical science, computers, oral and written comprehension, mathematical reasoning, deductive reasoning

Occupations related to this major: Geophysicists, Geologists, Astronomers, Physicists, Atmospheric Scientists, Space Scientists, and Chemists

Physics

Physics majors learn to explore and identify the basic principles of the structure and behavior of matter, the generation and transfer of energy, and the interaction of matter and energy. They learn to use these principles in theoretical areas such as the origin of the universe, or in practical areas to develop advanced materials, electronic devices, or medical equipment.

Interests: Investigative research, mathematics, problem solving, improving the quality of life

Skills and abilities: Computational skills, reasoning logically, solving problems, oral and written expression and comprehension, mathematical reasoning

Occupations related to this major: Physicists, Astronomers, Geologists, Atmospheric Scientists, Space Scientists, Geophysicists, and Environmental Scientists

14. SOCIAL AND BEHAVIORAL SCIENCES

Social and Behavioral Sciences majors learn about the social needs of people. Clinical psychologists help the mentally or emotionally disturbed adjust to life through behavior modification programs and other techniques. Social workers address the needs of individuals, families, groups, and communities. Their work may involve everything from helping an elderly person adjust to life in a nursing home, to organizing fund-raising for community social welfare activities. Other social scientists conduct basic and applied research in the social sciences. They use established methods to assemble a body of fact and theory that contributes to human knowledge. Social scientists investigate all aspects of human society—from anthropologists studying the origins of the human race, or historians studying an ancient civilization—to political scientists analyzing the results of presidential elections.

Interests: Social and emotional needs of people; an interest in all aspects of society—from the origins of the human race, or an ancient civilization, to political results of presidential elections

Popular majors in this field of study: Criminal Justice Studies, Economics, Geography, Gerontology, Political Sciences, Psychology, Public Administration, Social Studies Education, and Social Work

Employment information/outlook: More than 1,731,000 people worked in related occupations in this field of study in 2002. The 2002–2012 employment growth is expected to be 16.1%. Median annual earnings are $49,417.

Criminal Justice Studies

Criminal Justice Studies majors learn about the dimensions and causes of crime and delinquency; the structure of the American criminal justice system; the operation of criminal courts; and the techniques and theories of law enforcement.

Interests: Serving others, court procedures, criminal law, private security, criminal justice

Skills and abilities: Working with others, making decisions, oral and written expression and comprehension, inductive reasoning, speech clarity, problem sensitivity

Occupations related to this major: Criminal Investigators, United States Marshals, Police Detectives, Sheriffs and Deputy Sheriffs, Correction Officers and Jailers, and Child Support and Missing Persons Investigators

Economics

Economics majors learn to plan, design, and conduct research into activities devoted to satisfying human wants. They learn to analyze the relationship between supply and demand. They study the problems of inflation, unemployment, tariffs, taxation, and foreign trade. They learn to analyze such issues as inflation, unemployment, monopoly, and economic growth. They study theory, policy, and trends and explore ways to deal with the economic problems of society and the individual.

Interests: Current issues such as taxes, poverty, health, inflation, the environment, human behavior

Skills and abilities: Solving problems, oral and written expression and comprehension, mathematical reasoning, logical reasoning

Occupations related to this major: Economists, Market Research Analysts, Urban and Regional Planners, Financial Managers, Financial Analysts, and Underwriters

Geography

Geography majors study the activities of people. Students study where people live, why they are located there, and how they earn a living. Students study the physical characteristics of the Earth, such as landforms, vegetation, climate, locale, and mineral and water resources. They study how people relate to and are shaped by their environment. They gain a broad perspective on the world's environments and its peoples while gaining a strong background in the physical and social sciences.

Interests: Analyzing and solving social and environmental problems, doing social and physical scientific research, the relationship between people and their environment

Skills and abilities: Oral and written expression and comprehension, spatial orientation, working individually and in groups, information gathering, working with computers

Occupations related to this major: Geographers, Geophysicists, Geologists, Atmospheric and Space Scientists, Environmental Scientists, and Materials Scientists

Gerontology

Gerontology majors learn about aging and older persons. They study physical, emotional, and intellectual changes in the elderly,

cultural aspects of aging, and governmental policies and programs for the aging.

Interests: Helping people, human development, older people, family relations, improving the quality of life

Skills and abilities: Oral and written expression and comprehension, listening, objectivity, deductive reasoning, determining needs and interests, organizing and managing projects

Occupations related to this major: Gerontologists, Geriatric Nurses, Nursing Home Administrators, Social Welfare Administrators, and Occupational and Physical Therapists

Political Sciences

Political Sciences majors study government and the nature of politics. They analyze the operations of different forms of government, and attempt to find theoretical and practical solutions to political problems. Students learn about the origins, historical development, and social functions of government. They study how electoral, legislative, judicial, and administrative structures and processes vary from one country and one age to another; how and why governments change, fail, and engage in wars. They study the behavior of public officials and other citizens involved in politics.

Interests: Public policy issues such as health care and environmental protection; politicians and public figures, justice, good and bad government, law, criminal justice, the legal system

Skills and abilities: Reading critically, thinking analytically, oral and written expression and comprehension, understanding graphic material

Occupations related to this major: Political Scientists, Legislators, Sociologists, Historians, Anthropologists, and Political Science Teachers

Psychology

Psychology majors learn to collect and interpret scientific data relating to human behavior to understand people and explain their actions. They learn to interview patients, give diagnostic tests, and offer therapy to help people make behavioral adjustments. Students study human and animal behavior and explore the processes involved in normal and abnormal thoughts, feelings, and actions. They increase their understanding of behavior while learning psychological facts, methods, principles, and generalizations about individuals and groups.

Interests: Working with people, scientific method, human and animal behavior

Skills and abilities: Critical thinking, oral and written expression and comprehension, inductive reasoning

Occupations related to this major: Developmental Psychologists, Experimental Psychologists, Educational Psychologists, Social Psychologists, Clinical Psychologists, and Counseling Psychologists

Public Administration

Public Administration majors may study in five areas of specialization: personnel, management, public relations, finance, and planning. They learn to establish government policy, and develop laws, rules and regulations. These studies will prepare students to find positions managing public agencies. Students deal with the operations of all forms and levels of government. Students learn about the many skills and challenges associated with implementing public policy in government and in nonprofit organizations.

Interests: Public and community service, organizing people, leadership, working with people from different backgrounds

Skills and abilities: Leadership, organizational ability, problem solving, oral and written expression and comprehension, inductive reasoning

Occupations related to this major: Government Service Executives, City Managers, Management Analysts, Government Affairs Specialists, and Legislators

Social Studies Education

Social Studies Education majors learn to teach courses pertaining to human society and its characteristic elements. They learn to teach subjects such as psychology, economics, history, political science, and sociology. They learn to teach students in middle school and high school courses in history, citizenship, and other social sciences.

Interests: Serving people, working with people, history, social sciences

Skills and abilities: Speaking, organizing working with people, oral and written expression and comprehension, speech clarity

Occupations related to this major: Middle School Teachers, High School Teachers, Postsecondary School Teachers, Historians, Sociologists, and Psychologists

Social Work

Social Work majors study many types of social issues and needs. They learn to aid families with physical, mental, or social problems, such as poverty, unemployment, illness, broken homes, various disabilities, antisocial behavior, and inadequate housing. Students acquire the knowledge and skills to assist individuals, families, groups, and communities in preventing and alleviating the problems of a modern, rapidly changing society. They learn to help others and to modify harmful social conditions, promote social and economic well being, and increase opportunities for all people to live with dignity and freedom.

Interests: Helping those in need, particularly children, the poor, minorities, the aged, the disabled, and women, enabling others to develop unique, positive responses and solutions to their problems

Skills and abilities: Objectivity, ability to listen, analytic ability, oral and written expression and comprehension, problem sensitivity

Occupations related to this major: Social Workers, Medical and Psychiatric Social Workers, Community Organization Social Workers, Residential Counselors, Probation and Correctional Treatment Specialists, and Human Services Workers

LOCATING OCCUPATIONAL INFORMATION RELATED TO YOUR MAJOR

Students may find occupations in a Field of Study in which they have a work interest. They may wish to conduct research to find specific information about an occupation. Good sources for occupational information are public libraries, high school and college career resource centers, One-Stop Career Centers, America's InfoNet (*www.acinet.org*) and O*Net (*www.online.onetcenter.org*), the occupational information Network.

Recommended books for occupations and college entry research:

Occupational Outlook Handbook, 2004–2005 Edition, U.S. Bureau of Labor Statistics, 2 Massachussetts Avenue, NE, Ste. 2135, Washington, DC 20212 *www.bls.gov*

A Guide to the College Admission Process, National Association for College Admissions Counseling, 1631 Prince Street, Alexandria, VA 22314–2818

College Major Handbook, 3rd Edition, CFKR Career Materials, 11860 Kemper Road, Unit 7, Auburn, CA 95603 *www.cfkr.com*

Federal Student Financial Aid, The Student Guide, Federal Student Aid Information Center, P.O. Box 84, Washington, DC 20044 *www.fafsa.ed.gov*

CHOOSING A COLLEGE

A student's choice of institution may depend on individual needs and talents. A person's career goals, career plans, and choice of college major are very important criteria in choosing a college. A student's choice may be limited by financial or other considerations. However, if at all possible, students should give high priority to their career plans and choice of a college major when choosing a college that best matches their career plans. Students' choice of their college major may influence their final college choice.

Some majors are rare and specialized. Special attention must be given to those majors that are fairly rare and specialized. Students will be limited in the number of colleges from which to choose. There are more than 1800 four-year colleges in the United States; only 78 offer aerospace engineering; 42 offer landscape architecture; 81 offer astronomy; 24 offer petroleum engineering; 8 offer statistics; 8 offer business statistics; 26 offer oceanography; 59 offer pharmacy; and 115 offer occupational therapy majors. This is a partial listing. A student who chooses a specialized major may find it necessary to travel a distance to find a college offering that major. School career centers and public libraries may carry listings of colleges that offer the major of the student's choice.

The most widely offered baccalaureate-level majors are found in four-year colleges. No college, not even the largest university, offers every major; some offer relatively few. Students will want to attend a college that offers several of the majors they are considering. Students can keep their choice of major open by selecting a university or college that offers a wide range of majors. The most common majors are found in the Art, Business, Computer and Information Science, Education, Engineering, Health, Humanities, and the Social and Behavioral Science fields of study.

MAKING THE FINAL DECISION

Making important decisions and setting long-range goals is never an easy task. Making a decision on what to study in college for four or more years, and how this will fit into students' lifestyles and career goals is very important and very personal. With the soaring costs of education and the increasing complexity of the job market, students cannot afford the luxury of trial and error in preparing for a career that requires college training; entering college without a career or major in mind can add time and expense to the entire journey. Good decision-making calls for awareness of one's needs and the matching of those needs with a wide variety of alternate choices. It is to this end that sufficient information has been explored for making a final decision.

In making a final decision, students must take a broad view of the fourteen Fields of Study. They should look carefully at all career and major options within the fourteen fields. Students should not limit themselves to a career or major that has been recommended to them by family or friends. The final decision should be the student's, along with the responsibility to reach their goals. In the final analysis, students will have to look at themselves. As Plato once said, "Know thyself, and to thine own self be true."

- **Assess work interests.** Identify work-related interests. Discover the type of work activities and occupations that match work interests. Identify and learn about the most relevant broad interest areas. Use interest results to explore the world of work.
- **Assess work values.** Pinpoint what is important in a job. Identify occupations that provide satisfaction based on the similarity among work values, conditions of work, and the characteristics of an occupation.
- **Assess work abilities.** Identify user ability strength, parts of work that the user likes to do, parts of work that the user finds important, and training needs of the user.

The more students know about their interests, work values, abilities, and career goals, the better their decisions will be. In the final analysis, good decision-making by students is based on knowing oneself and being flexible enough to sense whether they are on the right track, and to alter decisions when they are not in their best interest. No matter what major is chosen, students must keep in ming that intellectual flexibility is the skill that enables them to work productively when the knowledge they have mastered is challenged or replaced by new ideas.

We wish all students well in their college studies and in the career path that they have chosen.

Robert Kauk and Francis Ferry

Portions of the *College Major Handbook* and *Choosing a Major* have been adapted with the authors' permission. © CFKR Career Materials, *www.cfkr.com*

Occupational information was gathered from *O*Net,* U.S. Department of Labor.

INDEX OF COLLEGE MAJORS

This section of *Profiles of American Colleges* will help you quickly determine which schools offer the major in which you are interested, the in-state tuition, room and board costs, and the Selector Rating. The colleges are listed alphabetically and the first column indicates the state where each is located. These data reflect the 2003-2004 academic year.

You will be able to compare schools offering those majors that interest you the most and see what their in-state costs and Selector Ratings are, before reading the Profiles in the main section of the book (see page 237 for Selector Rating details). You may also discover some new schools or majors that interest you.

ACCOUNTING

School	ST	$IS	SR
Abilene Christian Univ	TX	18,370	VC
Adams State College	CO	7,468	C
Adelphi Univ	NY	26,300	VC
Adrian College	MI	21,950	C
Alabama A&M Univ	AL	5,100	C
Alabama State Univ	AL	6,404	C
Albany State Univ	GA	5,764	C+
Albertus Magnus College	CT	23,130	LC
Albright College	PA	30,579	C
Alcorn State Univ	MS	7,290	C
Alderson-Broaddus College	WV	19,640	C
Alfred Univ	NY	28,290	C
Alvernia College	PA	23,212	LC
American International College	MA	24,690	LC
Anderson Univ	IN	19,430	LC
Andrews Univ	MI	19,550	C
Angelo State Univ	TX	7,576	NC
Appalachian State Univ	NC	7,637	VC
Arcadia Univ	PA	29,890	C
Arizona State Univ-Main	AZ	10,048	C
Arkansas Baptist College	AR	5,530	NC
Arkansas State Univ	AR	8,450	C
Arkansas Tech Univ	AR	7,299	C
Asbury College	KY	20,704	VC
Ashland Univ	OH	24,464	C
Assumption College	MA	29,375	C
Atlantic Union College	MA	18,868	C
Auburn Univ	AL	10,396	VC
Auburn Univ Montgomery	AL	9,020	NC
Augsburg College	MN	25,298	C
Augusta State Univ	GA	2,592	C
Augustana College	IL	26,610	VC+
Augustana College	SD	21,998	VC
Aurora Univ	IL	20,631	C
Austin Peay State Univ	TN	5,814	LC
Averett Univ	VA	23,010	LC
Avila Univ	MO	20,300	C
Azusa Pacific Univ	CA	24,720	VC
Baker College of Flint	MI	7,720	NC
Baker Univ	KS	19,860	VC
Ball State Univ	IN	8,660	C
Barry Univ	FL	24,100	LC
Barton College	NC	19,314	C
Baylor Univ	TX	23,864	VC
Becker College	MA	23,710	LC
Belhaven College	MS	16,040	C+
Bellarmine Univ	KY	24,110	VC
Bellevue Univ	NE	4,440	NC
Belmont Abbey College	NC	23,742	C
Belmont Univ	TN	21,986	VC
Bemidji State Univ	MN	9,103	C
Benedict College	SC	12,662	LC
Benedictine College	KS	20,603	C
Benedictine Univ	IL	23,840	C
Bennett College	NC	11,200	C
Bentley College	MA	33,904	VC
Berkeley College	NY	21,545	LC
Berkeley College of New York City	NY	12,500	LC
Berry College	GA	21,410	VC
Bethany College	WV	19,845	VC
Bethel College	IN	19,670	C
Bethel College	MN	25,180	VC
Bethune-Cookman College	FL	16,480	LC
Biola Univ	CA	25,964	VC
Birmingham-Southern College	AL	25,364	VC+
Black Hills State Univ	SD	7,743	LC
Blackburn College	IL	13,690	C
Bloomfield College	NJ	19,250	LC
Bloomsburg Univ of Pennsylvania	PA	10,844	C
Bluefield State College	WV	2,806	LC
Bluffton College	OH	23,694	C
Boise State Univ	ID	7,657	LC
Boston College	MA	33,284	MC
Boston Univ	MA	38,194	HC+
Bowling Green State Univ	OH	13,036	C
Bradley Univ	IL	22,910	VC
Brenau Univ Women's College	GA	21,800	C
Brescia Univ	KY	14,225	C
Brewton-Parker College	GA	14,200	LC
Briar Cliff Univ	IA	21,660	C
Bridgewater State College	MA	10,482	C
Brigham Young Univ	UT	8,504	HC
Brigham Young Univ/Hawaii	HI	7,240	VC+
Bryant College	RI	31,004	VC
Bucknell Univ	PA	35,262	HC+
Buena Vista Univ	IA	25,406	C
Butler Univ	IN	28,250	VC+
Cabrini College	PA	29,020	C
Caldwell College	NJ	24,060	LC
Calif Lutheran Univ	CA	27,600	LC
Calif State Polytechnic Univ, Pomona	CA	8,793	C+
Cal State, Fullerton	CA	6,648	C
Cal State, Hayward	CA	8,871	LC
Cal State, Long Beach	CA	8,762	C+
Cal State, Northridge	CA	7,757	LC
Cal State, Sacramento	CA	9,543	C
Cal State, San Bernardino	CA	15,238	LC
Cal State, Stanislaus	CA	9,874	C
Calumet College of St. Joseph	IN	9,000	LC
Calvin College	MI	22,615	NC
Cameron Univ	OK	5,692	NC
Campbell Univ	NC	18,268	VC
Campbellsville Univ	KY	17,680	C
Canisius College	NY	28,163	C+
Capital Univ	OH	26,550	C
Cardinal Stritch Univ	WI	17,620	C
Caribbean Univ	PR	3,000	
Carlow College	PA	21,334	C
Carroll College	MT	20,576	VC
Carroll College	WI	22,740	C
Carson-Newman College	TN	16,760	C
Carthage College	WI	25,000	C
Case Western Reserve Univ	OH	32,002	MC
Catawba College	NC	20,500	C
Catholic Univ of America	DC	34,248	VC
Cedar Crest College	PA	25,145	C+
Cedarville Univ	OH	19,954	VC
Centenary College	NJ	25,370	LC
Centenary College of Louisiana	LA	23,100	VC+
Central College	IA	21,206	C
Central Conn State Univ	CT	12,090	C
Central Methodist College	MO	16,460	C
Central Mich Univ	MI	11,142	C
Central Missouri State Univ	MO	9,776	C
Central State Univ	OH	8,922	C+
Central Univ of Bayamon	PR	3,335	
Central Washington Univ	WA	9,768	C
Chaminade Univ of Honolulu	HI	21,430	LC
Champlain College	VT	22,030	C
Chapman Univ	CA	33,118	VC
Chatham College	PA	27,266	C+
Chestnut Hill College	PA	26,450	LC
Chicago State Univ	IL	10,882	C+
Christian Brothers Univ	TN	22,290	VC
Christopher Newport Univ	VA	8,862	VC
City Univ	WA	7,425	NC
CUNY/Baruch College	NY	3,275	VC+
CUNY/Brooklyn College	NY	4,353	C+
CUNY/College of Staten Island	NY	4,308	NC
CUNY/Herbert H. Lehman College	NY	3,320	LC
CUNY/Hunter College	NY	6,729	C+
CUNY/Medgar Evers College	NY	4,232	NC
CUNY/Queens College	NY	4,362	C
CUNY/York College	NY	3,292	NC
Clarion Univ of Pennsylvania	PA	11,272	LC
Clark Atlanta Univ	GA	19,300	C+
Clarke College	IA	23,165	C
Clarkson Univ	NY	32,226	VC
Clayton College and State Univ	GA	2,441	LC
Clearwater Christian College	FL	13,160	LC
Cleary College	MI	10,350	LC
Clemson Univ	SC	11,972	HC
Cleveland State Univ	OH	12,308	LC
Coastal Carolina Univ	SC	11,040	C
Coe College	IA	27,385	VC
College Misericordia	PA	26,350	C
College of Charleston	SC	11,887	HC
College of Mount St. Joseph	OH	22,785	C
College of New Jersey	NJ	15,950	MC
College of Notre Dame of Maryland	MD	27,700	C
College of Our Lady of the Elms	MA	20,644	C
College of St. Benedict	MN	26,672	VC
College of St. Catherine	MN	24,010	VC
College of St. Elizabeth	NJ	25,460	C
College of St. Joseph	VT	19,100	C
College of St. Rose	NY	22,864	C
College of St. Scholastica	MN	24,970	C+
College of Santa Fe	NM	25,293	C+
College of the Ozarks	MO	3,500	VC+
College of the Southwest	NM	9,320	C+
Colo Christian Univ	CO	21,182	VC
Colo State Univ	CO	9,964	VC
Columbia College	MO	16,139	C
Columbia College	SC	22,658	LC
Columbia Union College	MD	20,543	C
Columbus State Univ	GA	7,846	C
Concord College	WV	8,136	C
Concordia College: Moorhead	MN	22,460	VC+
Concordia Univ at Austin	TX	20,450	LC
Concordia Univ Nebr	NE	20,302	C+
Concordia Univ Wisc	WI	16,600	C
Concordia Univ, River Forest	IL	23,600	C
Concordia Univ/St.Paul	MN	24,486	C
Converse College	SC	24,710	VC
Cornerstone Univ and Grand Rapids Theological Seminary	MI	19,846	C
Creighton Univ	NE	26,748	VC+
Culver-Stockton College	MO	17,850	C
Cumberland College	KY	16,384	C
Cumberland Univ	TN	16,910	C
Daemen College	NY	22,120	C
Dakota Wesleyan Univ	SD	17,832	C
Dallas Baptist Univ	TX	15,300	VC
Dana College	NE	20,280	C
Davenport Univ	MI	11,636	NC
David Lipscomb Univ	TN	16,158	VC
David N. Myers College	OH	9,475	C
Davis and Elkins College	WV	20,594	C
De Sales Univ	PA	25,470	C
Defiance College	OH	22,615	C
Delaware State Univ	DE	8,104	LC
Delaware Valley College	PA	26,676	C
Delta State Univ	MS	6,618	C
DePaul Univ	IL	27,580	VC
Dickinson State Univ	ND	6,338	NC
Dillard Univ	LA	17,325	VC
Doane College	NE	20,000	C
Dominican College	NY	24,810	LC
Dominican Univ	IL	23,610	C
Dordt College	IA	20,170	VC
Dowling College	NY	23,870	LC
Drake Univ	IA	25,120	VC+
Drury Univ	MO	18,085	VC+
Duquesne Univ	PA	26,907	VC
D'Youville College	NY	21,080	C
East Carolina Univ	NC	8,671	C
East Central Univ	OK	4,968	C
East Tenn State Univ	TN	8,497	C
East Texas Baptist Univ	TX	13,914	C
Eastern Conn State Univ	CT	10,362	C
Eastern Illinois Univ	IL	11,192	C
Eastern Kentucky Univ	KY	7,708	C
Eastern Mennonite Univ	VA	22,990	C
Eastern Mich Univ	MI	11,478	C
Eastern Nazarene College	MA	19,433	LC
Eastern New Mexico Univ	NM	6,762	LC
Eastern Oregon Univ	OR	10,080	NC
Eastern Univ	PA	24,020	C
Eastern Washington Univ	WA	9,012	C
Edgewood College	WI	20,520	C
Edinboro Univ of Pennsylvania	PA	10,850	LC
Edward Waters College	FL	14,374	LC
Elizabeth City State Univ	NC	5,550	LC
Elizabethtown College	PA	28,800	C
Elmhurst College	IL	24,630	C
Elmira College	NY	33,820	VC
Elon Univ	NC	22,240	VC
Emory Univ	GA	36,872	MC
Emporia State Univ	KS	6,998	C
Eureka College	IL	24,980	LC
Evangel Univ	MO	15,435	C
Excelsior College	NY	975	SP
Fairfield Univ	CT	35,505	HC
Fairleigh Dickinson Univ/College at Florham	NJ	30,130	C
Fairleigh Dickinson Univ/Metropolitan Campus	NJ	28,584	C
Fairmont State	WV	8,280	LC
Fayetteville State Univ	NC	5,590	LC
Ferris State Univ	MI	12,512	C
Ferrum College	VA	21,240	LC
Flagler College	FL	11,860	VC+
Florida A&M Univ	FL	7,564	C
Florida Atlantic Univ	FL	8,543	C
Florida Gulf Coast Univ	FL	9,908	C
Florida Inst of Technology	FL	28,740	VC
Florida International Univ	FL	9,912	VC
Florida Memorial College	FL	6,000	LC
Florida Southern College	FL	23,592	C
Florida State Univ	FL	9,028	HC
Fordham Univ	NY	35,066	HC
Fort Hays State Univ	KS	7,363	C
Fort Lewis College	CO	8,353	C
Fort Valley State Univ	GA	6,960	C
Francis Marion Univ	SC	9,364	C
Franciscan Univ	IA	19,300	C
Franciscan Univ of Steubenville	OH	20,300	VC
Franklin and Marshall College	PA	35,930	HC+
Franklin College	IN		C
Franklin Pierce College	NH	28,980	LC
Franklin Univ	OH	6,720	SP
Freed-Hardeman Univ	TN		NC
Fresno Pacific Univ	CA	22,462	C
Friends Univ	KS	15,962	LC
Frostburg State Univ	MD	11,114	C
Furman Univ	SC	28,976	HC+
Gallaudet Univ	DC	16,554	SP
Gannon Univ	PA	23,260	C
Gardner-Webb Univ	NC	19,300	C
Geneva College	PA	21,850	C
George Mason Univ	VA	9,732	VC
George Washington Univ	DC	41,030	MC
Georgetown College	KY	22,000	VC
Georgetown Univ	DC	38,242	MC
Georgia College and State Univ	GA	9,878	C
Georgia Southern Univ	GA	8,540	C
Georgia Southwestern State Univ	GA	6,013	C
Georgia State Univ	GA	10,658	C
Georgian Court College	NJ	19,040	LC
Glenville State College	WV	7,812	NC
Golden Gate Univ	CA	11,232	NC
Goldey-Beacom College	DE	11,440	C
Gonzaga Univ	WA	26,766	HC
Gordon College	MA	25,982	VC+
Goshen College	IN	22,450	VC
Grace College	IN	19,825	VC
Graceland Univ	IA	19,550	C
Grambling State Univ	LA	6,538	NC
Grand Canyon Univ	AZ	30,000	LC
Grand Valley State Univ	MI	11,022	VC
Grand View College	IA	19,748	LC
Greensboro College	NC	21,750	C
Greenville College	IL	21,342	C
Grove City College	PA	14,228	HC
Guilford College	NC	24,960	VC
Gustavus Adolphus College	MN	27,120	VC+
Gwynedd-Mercy College	PA	24,225	C
Hampton Univ	VA	17,112	C+
Hannibal-LaGrange College	MO	13,940	C
Harding Univ	AR	14,890	VC
Hardin-Simmons Univ	TX	14,165	C
Hartwick College	NY	34,650	C+
Hastings College	NE	19,928	VC
Hawaii Pacific Univ	HI	19,218	C
Heidelberg College	OH	20,266	NC
Henderson State Univ	AR	7,386	C
Hendrix College	AR	20,970	VC+
Hesser College	NH	17,490	LC
High Point Univ	NC	22,480	C
Hilbert College	NY	19,170	LC
Hillsdale College	MI	22,450	HC
Hofstra Univ	NY	27,112	VC
Holy Family College	PA	13,710	LC
Hope College	MI	25,340	VC
Houghton College	NY	23,984	VC
Houston Baptist Univ	TX	16,905	C
Howard Payne Univ	TX	15,176	C
Howard Univ	DC	16,505	C
Humphreys College	CA	7,000	NC
Huntingdon College	AL	18,400	VC
Husson College	ME	16,300	LC
Idaho State Univ	ID	8,128	C
Illinois College	IL	19,100	VC
Illinois State Univ	IL	10,944	C+
Illinois Wesleyan Univ	IL	30,380	HC+
Immaculata Univ	PA	25,200	C
Indiana Inst of Technology	IN	21,620	C
Indiana State Univ	IN	10,719	LC
Indiana Univ Bloomington	IN	12,389	VC
Indiana Univ Kokomo	IN	4,463	LC
Indiana Univ Northwest	IN	4,538	LC

ST = STATE   **$IS** = IN-STATE COSTS   **SR** = SELECTOR RATING

School	ST	$IS	SR
Indiana Univ of Pennsylvania	PA	10,489	C
Indiana Univ South Bend	IN	4,571	LC
Indiana Univ Southeast	IN	4,504	LC
Indiana Univ-Purdue Univ Fort Wayne	IN	5,108	LC
Indiana Univ-Purdue Univ Indianapolis	IN	8,257	LC
Indiana Wesleyan Univ	IN	19,900	C+
Inter American Univ of PR/ Aguadilla Campus	PR	3,544	
Inter American Univ of PR/ Arecibo Campus	PR	3,300	
Inter American Univ of PR/ Barranquitas Regional College	PR	3,300	
Inter American Univ of PR/ Bayamon Univ College	PR	3,522	
Inter American Univ of PR/ Fajardo Campus	PR	4,000	
Inter American Univ of PR/ Metropolitan Campus	PR		
Inter American Univ of PR/ Ponce Regional College	PR	3,700	
Inter American Univ of PR/ San German	PR	6,716	
International College	FL	8,060	LC
Iona College	NY	27,988	VC
Iowa State Univ	IA	10,768	VC
Iowa Wesleyan College	IA	19,990	C
Ithaca College	NY	31,730	HC
Jackson State Univ	MS	8,382	C
Jacksonville State Univ	AL	6,844	LC
Jacksonville Univ	FL	24,040	C
James Madison Univ	VA	10,794	VC
Jamestown College	ND	12,600	NC
John Brown Univ	AR	15,080	VC
John Carroll Univ	OH	27,658	C+
Johnson and Wales Univ	RI	22,965	LC
Johnson State College	VT	11,819	LC
Judson College	IL	22,050	LC
Juniata College	PA	29,080	VC
Kansas State Univ	KS	8,728	VC
Kansas Wesleyan Univ	KS	18,900	VC
Kean Univ	NJ	14,479	C
Kennesaw State Univ	GA	2,724	C
Kent State Univ	OH	12,932	C
Kentucky Wesleyan College	KY	17,250	C
Keuka College	NY	21,170	C
Keystone College	PA	21,405	LC
King's College	PA	26,990	C
Knoxville College	TN	6,200	LC
Kutztown Univ of Pennsylvania	PA	10,786	C
La Roche College	PA	22,094	C
La Salle Univ	PA	31,260	VC
La Sierra Univ	CA	19,260	LC
LaGrange College	GA	20,500	C
Lake Erie College	OH	23,550	C
Lake Superior State Univ	MI	9,034	LC
Lakeland College	WI	17,950	C
Lamar Univ	TX	6,816	LC
Langston Univ	OK	2,308	LC
Lasell College	MA	26,000	C
Le Moyne College	NY	26,400	VC
Lebanon Valley College	PA	28,870	VC
Lee Univ	TN	13,780	NC
Lehigh Univ	PA	37,570	HC+
LeMoyne-Owen College	TN	13,070	LC
Lenoir-Rhyne College	NC	19,186	C
LeTourneau Univ	TX	21,080	C
Lewis Univ	IL	22,950	C+
Liberty Univ	VA	17,220	C
Limestone College	SC	17,700	C
Lincoln Memorial Univ	TN	16,400	LC
Lincoln Univ	MO	7,158	NC
Lincoln Univ	PA	13,320	C+
Lindenwood Univ	MO	17,050	VC
Lindsey Wilson College	KY	16,392	LC
Linfield College	OR	27,090	VC
Livingstone College	NC	18,101	LC
LIU/Brooklyn Campus	NY	24,790	C
LIU/C.W. Post Campus	NY	28,282	C
Loras College	IA	24,233	C
Louisiana State Univ and A&M College	LA	9,126	VC
Louisiana State Univ in Shreveport	LA	2,884	NC
Louisiana Tech Univ	LA	7,361	C
Lourdes College	OH	15,300	LC
Loyola College in Maryland	MD	34,560	HC
Loyola Marymount Univ	CA	32,194	VC
Loyola Univ Chicago	IL	31,164	VC
Loyola Univ New Orleans	LA	31,036	VC+
Lubbock Christian Univ	TX	15,832	C
Luther College	IA	25,700	VC
Lycoming College	PA	27,589	C+
Lynchburg College	VA	26,815	C
Lyndon State College	VT	12,646	LC
Lynn Univ	FL	30,750	C
Lyon College	AR	17,995	VC
MacMurray College	IL	20,005	LC
Madonna Univ	MI	11,504	VC
Malone College	OH	20,995	C
Manchester College	IN	23,390	C
Manhattan College	NY	27,400	VC
Mansfield Univ	PA	11,220	C
Marian College	IN	23,030	C
Marian College of Fond du Lac	WI	19,625	C
Marietta College	OH	27,047	C
Marist College	NY	27,596	VC
Marquette Univ	WI	27,594	VC
Mars Hill College	NC	18,600	LC
Marshall Univ	WV	9,116	C
Martin Univ	IN	10,200	SP
Marymount Manhattan College	NY	27,292	C
Marymount Univ	VA	23,668	C
Maryville Univ of St. Louis	MO	22,090	VC
Marywood Univ	PA	26,050	C
McKendree College	IL	21,120	VC
McMurry Univ	TX	17,846	LC
McNeese State Univ	LA	5,259	LC
McPherson College	KS	20,265	C
Mercer Univ	GA	27,516	VC+
Mercy College	NY	19,200	NC
Mercyhurst College	PA	20,694	C
Meredith College	NC	23,065	C
Merrimack College	MA	29,625	C
Mesa State College	CO	8,051	C
Messiah College	PA	25,890	VC+
Methodist College	NC	19,526	C
Metropolitan State College of Denver	CO	2,338	LC
Metropolitan State Univ	MN	3,852	SP
Miami Univ	OH	15,033	HC
Mich State Univ	MI	11,933	VC
MidAmerica Nazarene Univ	KS	18,688	C
Middle Tenn State Univ	TN	8,534	C
Midland Lutheran College	NE	18,600	C
Midwestern State Univ	TX	8,045	LC
Miles College	AL	7,870	NC
Milligan College	TN	19,860	C+
Millikin Univ	IL	25,555	C
Millsaps College	MS	25,182	VC
Minn State Univ, Mankato	MN	8,803	LC
Minn State Univ, Moorehead	MN	7,000	LC
Minot State Univ	ND	6,602	LC
Miss College	MS	14,574	C
Miss State Univ	MS	9,139	C
Miss Univ for Women	MS	5,446	LC
Miss Valley State Univ	MS	6,765	NC
Missouri Baptist Univ	MO	18,010	C
Missouri Southern State Univ	MO	8,316	C
Missouri Valley College	MO	18,500	C
Missouri Western State College	MO	8,522	NC
Molloy College	NY	15,180	C
Monmouth College	IL	23,600	C
Monmouth Univ	NJ	26,334	C
Montclair State Univ	NJ	13,790	C
Moravian College	PA	28,903	VC
Morehead State Univ	KY	7,464	C
Morehouse College	GA	22,728	C
Morgan State Univ	MD	11,470	C
Morningside College	IA	21,610	C
Mount Aloysius College	PA	19,120	LC
Mount Marty College	SD	15,656	LC
Mount Mary College	WI	20,370	C
Mount Mercy College	IA	21,400	C
Mount Olive College	NC	14,410	LC
Mount St. Mary College	NY	21,270	C
Mount St. Mary's College	MD	28,400	C
Mount Union College	OH	21,120	C
Mount Vernon Nazarene Univ	OH	18,925	C
Mountain State Univ	WV	10,212	NC
Muhlenberg College	PA	31,485	HC
Murray State Univ	KY	7,816	VC
Muskingum College	OH	20,680	C
National American Univ	SD	13,680	NC
National Univ	CA	9,690	SP
National-Louis Univ	IL	16,240	LC
Nazareth College of Rochester	NY	24,936	VC
Nebr Wesleyan Univ	NE	21,197	C+
Neumann College	PA	23,890	LC
New Mexico Highlands Univ	NM	6,182	LC
New Mexico State Univ	NM	7,932	C
New York Inst of Technology	NY	24,205	VC
New York Univ	NY	39,406	MC
Newbury College	MA	23,450	C
Newman Univ	KS	18,018	C
Niagara Univ	NY	25,050	C
Nicholls State Univ	LA	6,395	NC
Nichols College	MA	27,562	LC
Norfolk State Univ	VA	9,722	LC
N Car Agricultural and Technical State Univ	NC	6,659	LC
N Car Central Univ	NC	7,534	LC
N Car State Univ	NC	9,886	VC
N Car Wesleyan College	NC	17,998	C
North Central College	IL	25,656	VC
N Dak State Univ	ND	8,435	C
North Georgia College and State Univ	GA	6,984	C
North Park Univ	IL	24,030	C
Northeastern Illinois Univ	IL	2,898	NC
Northeastern State Univ	OK	4,950	LC
Northeastern Univ	MA	35,650	HC
Northern Arizona Univ	AZ	9,002	C
Northern Illinois Univ	IL	11,472	C
Northern Kentucky Univ	KY	6,352	NC
Northern Mich Univ	MI	10,834	C
Northern State Univ	SD	7,117	LC
Northwest Missouri State Univ	MO	9,334	C
Northwest Nazarene Univ	ID	20,360	VC
Northwestern College	MN	22,820	C+
Northwestern College of Iowa	IA	19,640	C+
Northwestern Okla State Univ	OK	5,433	NC
Northwestern State Univ of Louisiana	LA	6,331	NC
Northwood Univ	FL	21,040	C
Northwood Univ	MI	20,265	LC
Northwood Univ	TX	20,135	LC
Norwich Univ	VT	21,064	LC
Notre Dame College	OH	20,425	C
Notre Dame de Namur Univ	CA	26,932	LC
Nova Southeastern Univ	FL	23,346	C
Nyack College	NY	18,540	LC
Oakland City Univ	IN	16,980	NC
Oakland Univ	MI	10,800	C
Oakwood College	AL	14,904	C
Oglethorpe Univ	GA	26,000	VC
Ohio Dominican Univ	OH	22,700	C
Ohio Northern Univ	OH	27,765	VC
Ohio State Univ	OH	13,080	VC+
Ohio State Univ at Marion	OH	4,801	NC
Ohio Univ	OH	14,448	C
Ohio Valley College	WV	16,036	C+
Ohio Wesleyan Univ	OH	32,550	VC+
Okla Baptist Univ	OK	15,220	VC
Okla Christian Univ	OK	17,690	NC
Okla City Univ	OK	19,580	VC
Okla Panhandle State Univ	OK	5,370	C
Okla State Univ	OK	9,216	VC
Okla Wesleyan Univ	OK	14,100	LC
Old Dominion Univ	VA	10,441	C
Olivet College	MI	19,984	C+
Olivet Nazarene Univ	IL	20,480	C
Oral Roberts Univ	OK	18,490	C
Oregon State Univ	OR	11,055	C
Ottawa Univ	KS	11,800	LC
Otterbein College	OH	26,085	C
Ouachita Baptist Univ	AR	18,900	VC
Our Lady of Holy Cross College	LA	5,900	C
Our Lady of the Lake Univ of San Antonio	TX	17,336	C
Pace Univ	NY	28,652	VC
Park Univ	MO	10,780	C+
Paul Quinn College	TX	8,150	LC
Penn State Univ at Erie/ Behrend College	PA	12,326	C
Penn State Univ/Univ Park Campus	PA	15,646	HC
Pennsylvania College of Technology	PA	15,126	NC
Pepperdine Univ	CA	32,830	VC
Peru State College	NE	6,342	NC
Pfeiffer Univ	NC	18,980	C
Philadelphia Univ	PA	27,354	C
Philander Smith College	AR	7,380	NC
Pittsburg State Univ	KS	7,128	NC
Plymouth State Univ	NH	12,298	LC
Point Loma Nazarene Univ	CA	21,380	VC
Point Park Univ	PA	21,840	C
Pontifical Catholic Univ of PR/Ponce	PR	7,298	
Portland State Univ	OR	12,453	C
Prairie View A&M Univ	TX	9,418	NC
Presbyterian College	SC	25,920	VC
Providence College	RI	30,604	HC
Purdue Univ/Calumet	IN	6,630	NC
Purdue Univ/West Lafayette	IN	12,560	VC
Queens Univ of Charlotte	NC	21,840	C
Quincy Univ	IL	22,330	C
Quinnipiac Univ	CT	30,570	VC
Radford Univ	VA	8,500	C
Ramapo College of New Jersey	NJ	15,203	VC
Randolph-Macon College	VA	27,190	C
Regis Univ	CO	25,740	C+
Rhode Island College	RI	11,565	C
Richard Stockton College of New Jersey	NJ	12,972	VC
Rider Univ	NJ	30,900	C
Robert Morris Univ	PA	20,438	C
Roberts Wesleyan College	NY	23,190	C+
Rochester College	MI	16,718	C
Rochester Inst of Technology	NY	29,217	VC+
Rockford College	IL	28,310	VC
Rockhurst Univ	MO	22,960	C+
Rocky Mountain College	MT	19,015	C
Roger Williams Univ	RI	30,296	C
Roosevelt Univ	IL	22,580	VC
Rosemont College	PA	26,175	C
Rowan Univ	NJ	14,506	VC
Rutgers, The State Univ of New Jersey/Camden Campus	NJ	14,990	VC
Rutgers, The State Univ of New Jersey/New Brunswick/Piscataway Campus	NJ	15,800	HC
Rutgers, The State Univ of New Jersey/Newark Campus	NJ	15,624	VC
Sacred Heart Univ	CT	29,178	C
Saginaw Valley State Univ	MI	11,055	C
St. Ambrose Univ	IA	22,800	C
St. Anselm College	NH	30,250	C
St. Augustine's College	NC	12,990	LC
St. Bonaventure Univ	NY	24,455	LC
St. Cloud State Univ	MN	8,362	C
St. Edward's Univ	TX	20,428	C
St. Francis College	NY	10,880	LC
St. Francis Univ	PA	25,876	LC
St. John Fisher College	NY	24,870	C
St. John's Univ	MN	26,473	VC
St. John's Univ	NY	30,180	C
St. Joseph's, Brooklyn,	NY	10,902	C
St. Joseph's College	IN	24,250	C
St. Joseph's Univ	PA	33,590	VC
St. Leo Univ	FL	20,600	C
St. Louis Univ	MO	29,780	VC+
St. Martin's College	WA	23,245	C
St. Mary-of-the-Woods College	IN	23,280	C
St. Mary's College of Calif	CA	32,850	VC
St. Mary's Univ of Minn	MN	21,535	C
St. Mary's Univ of San Antonio	TX	22,444	C
St. Michael's College	VT	30,100	VC
St. Norbert College	WI	25,810	C
St. Peter's College	NJ	22,292	LC
St. Thomas Aquinas College	NY	20,590	LC
St. Thomas Univ	FL	21,400	LC
St. Vincent College	PA	25,530	VC
St. Xavier Univ	IL	23,144	C
Salem College	NC	24,595	VC
Salem State College	MA	8,592	C
Salisbury Univ	MD	12,664	VC
Salve Regina Univ	RI	29,210	C
Sam Houston State Univ	TX	7,142	C
Samford Univ	AL	18,648	VC
San Diego State Univ	CA	10,321	C
San Francisco State Univ	CA	12,070	C
San Jose State Univ	CA	8,187	C
Santa Clara Univ	CA	34,701	HC
Savannah State Univ	GA	7,328	LC
Schreiner Univ	TX	20,440	C
Seattle Pacific Univ	WA	25,944	VC
Seattle Univ	WA	24,183	VC
Seton Hall Univ	NJ	30,130	VC
Seton Hill Univ	PA	24,930	C
Shaw Univ	NC	14,882	C+
Shepherd College	WV	8,608	C
Shippensburg Univ of Pennsylvania	PA	10,826	C
Shorter College	GA	17,370	C
Siena College	NY	25,310	VC
Siena Heights Univ	MI	16,140	LC
Silver Lake College of the Holy Family	WI	18,450	LC
Simpson College	CA	20,500	C
Simpson College	IA	23,658	C+
Slippery Rock Univ of Pennsylvania	PA	10,343	LC
S Car State Univ	SC	6,586	LC
Southeast Missouri State Univ	MO	9,704	C
Southeastern College	FL	11,648	LC
Southeastern Louisiana Univ	LA	6,791	LC
Southeastern Okla State Univ	OK	6,147	C
Southeastern Univ	DC	8,505	LC
Southern Adventist Univ	TN	17,080	C
Southern Arkansas Univ	AR	6,956	C
Southern Conn State Univ	CT	10,310	C
Southern Illinois Univ Carbondale	IL	10,407	C
Southern Illinois Univ Edwardsville	IL	8,724	C
Southern Methodist Univ	TX	34,210	HC
Southern Nazarene Univ	OK	14,634	NC
Southern New Hampshire Univ	NH	26,242	C
Southern Oregon Univ	OR	10,362	C
Southern Univ and A&M College	LA	7,372	LC
Southern Univ at New Orleans	LA	995	NC
Southern Utah Univ	UT	8,194	C
Southern Wesleyan Univ	SC	19,940	C
Southwest Baptist Univ	MO	15,371	C
Southwest Minn State Univ	MN	9,106	VC
Southwest Missouri State Univ	MO	8,918	C
Southwestern Okla State Univ	OK	4,801	C
Southwestern Univ	TX	25,410	HC

ST = STATE $IS = IN-STATE COSTS SR = SELECTOR RATING

School	ST	$IS	SR
Spalding Univ	KY	17,985	C
Spring Arbor Univ	MI	20,206	C
Spring Hill College	AL	25,868	VC
St. Joseph's Suffolk	NY	11,297	C
SUNY at Oswego	NY	12,650	C
SUNY/College at Brockport	NY	12,111	C
SUNY/College at Fredonia	NY	11,562	VC
SUNY/College at Geneseo	NY	11,330	HC
SUNY/College at Old Westbury	NY	12,784	C
SUNY/College at Oneonta	NY	11,870	VC
SUNY/College at Plattsburgh	NY	11,700	C
SUNY/Univ at Albany	NY	12,951	HC
SUNY/Univ at Binghamton	NY	12,787	HC
SUNY/Univ at New Paltz	NY	11,565	VC
State Univ of West Georgia	GA	7,622	C
Stephen F. Austin State Univ	TX	7,552	C
Stephens College	MO	24,260	C+
Stetson Univ	FL	29,495	VC
Stonehill College	MA	30,752	HC
Strayer Univ	DC	8,789	SP
Suffolk Univ	MA	29,200	C
Sul Ross State Univ	TX	6,582	LC
Susquehanna Univ	PA	29,990	VC
Syracuse Univ	NY	34,720	HC
Tabor College	KS	19,500	NC
Talladega College	AL	10,110	LC
Tarleton State Univ	TX	7,576	C
Taylor Univ	IN	23,820	VC+
Teikyo Post Univ	CT	24,875	C
Temple Univ	PA	15,912	C
Tenn State Univ	TN	9,048	LC
Tenn Tech Univ	TN	8,670	VC
Tenn Wesleyan College	TN	16,540	C
Texas A&M Univ	TX	11,081	HC
Texas A&M Univ at Commerce	TX	8,994	C
Texas A&M Univ at Corpus Christi	TX	10,269	C
Texas A&M Univ at Kingsville	TX	6,740	LC
Texas Christian Univ	TX	23,410	VC
Texas Southern Univ	TX	8,920	NC
Texas State Univ	TX	9,320	VC
Texas Tech Univ	TX	10,768	VC
Texas Wesleyan Univ	TX	16,245	C
Texas Woman's Univ	TX	7,804	LC
Thiel College	PA	20,970	C
Thomas College	ME	19,960	LC
Thomas Edison State College	NJ	3,325	SP
Thomas More College	KY	21,350	C
Tiffin Univ	OH	19,490	LC
Touro College	NY	15,250	VC
Towson Univ	MD	12,694	VC
Transylvania Univ	KY	23,780	VC+
Trevecca Nazarene Univ	TN	17,548	C
Trinity Christian College	IL	21,640	VC
Trinity International Univ	IL	22,980	C+
Tri-State Univ-Main Campus	IN	23,600	C
Troy State Univ	AL	7,696	C
Troy State Univ Dothan	AL	3,842	C
Troy State Univ Montgomery	AL	3,600	NC
Truman State Univ	MO	9,728	HC+
Tulane Univ	LA	37,451	HC+
Turabo Univ	PR	4,110	
Tuskegee Univ	AL	17,250	LC
Union College	KY	15,920	C
Union College	NE	17,130	C
Union Univ	TN	18,800	VC
Universidad Metropolitana	PR	3,324	
Univ of Akron	OH	13,134	NC
Univ of Alabama	AL	9,040	C+
Univ of Alabama at Birmingham	AL	12,901	C
Univ of Alabama in Huntsville	AL	9,126	VC
Univ of Alaska Anchorage	AK	9,100	NC
Univ of Alaska Fairbanks	AK	9,295	C
Univ of Alaska Southeast	AK	7,900	LC
Univ of Arizona	AZ	10,413	VC
Univ of Arkansas	AR	9,855	VC
Univ of Arkansas at Little Rock	AR	5,637	NC
Univ of Arkansas at Monticello	AR	5,940	NC
Univ of Arkansas at Pine Bluff	AR	7,925	C
Univ of Bridgeport	CT	25,924	LC
Univ of Central Arkansas	AR	6,388	C
Univ of Central Florida	FL	10,038	VC
Univ of Central Okla	OK	9,434	C
Univ of Charleston	WV	23,620	C
Univ of Cincinnati	OH	14,736	C
Univ of Colo at Boulder	CO	10,774	VC
Univ of Conn	CT	14,608	VC
Univ of Dayton	OH	24,850	VC
Univ of Delaware	DE	12,616	HC
Univ of Denver	CO	32,148	VC
Univ of Detroit Mercy	MI	25,582	C
Univ of Dubuque	IA	20,950	C
Univ of Evansville	IN	24,190	VC
Univ of Findlay	OH	23,962	NC
Univ of Florida	FL	8,580	MC
Univ of Georgia	GA	8,656	VC
Univ of Great Falls	MT	15,360	C
Univ of Hartford	CT	31,080	C
Univ of Hawaii at Manoa	HI	9,565	VC
Univ of Houston	TX	9,818	C
Univ of Houston-Downtown	TX	2,594	NC
Univ of Idaho	ID	8,216	C
Univ of Illinois at Chicago	IL	13,418	C
Univ of Illinois at Urbana-Champaign	IL	11,316	HC+
Univ of Indianapolis	IN	22,560	VC
Univ of Iowa	IA	10,923	VC
Univ of Kansas	KS	8,923	VC
Univ of Kentucky	KY	7,765	C
Univ of La Verne	CA	28,600	C
Univ of Louisiana at Lafayette	LA	5,826	C
Univ of Louisiana at Monroe	LA	5,207	NC
Univ of Louisville	KY	8,762	VC
Univ of Maine at Augusta	ME	4,065	C
Univ of Maine at Machias	ME	9,271	LC
Univ of Maine at Presque Isle	ME	9,155	LC
Univ of Mary	ND	12,900	C+
Univ of Mary Hardin-Baylor	TX	17,268	C
Univ of Maryland/College Park	MD	14,227	HC
Univ of Maryland/Eastern Shore	MD	9,964	C
Univ of Maryland/Univ College	MD	5,910	SP
Univ of Mass Amherst	MA	13,980	C+
Univ of Mass Dartmouth	MA	12,835	C
Univ of Memphis	TN	8,560	C
Univ of Miami	FL	34,608	HC
Univ of Mich/Flint	MI	5,548	C
Univ of Minn/Crookston	MN	9,626	NC
Univ of Minn/Twin Cities	MN	13,160	VC
Univ of Miss	MS	7,666	C
Univ of Missouri/Columbia	MO	13,782	VC
Univ of Missouri/Kansas City	MO	13,416	VC
Univ of Missouri/St. Louis	MO	11,656	VC
Univ of Mobile	AL	13,620	C
Univ of Montana	MT	9,395	C
Univ of Montevallo	AL	8,478	C
Univ of Nebr at Kearney	NE	8,286	NC
Univ of Nebr at Lincoln	NE	9,975	C+
Univ of Nebr at Omaha	NE	8,080	C
Univ of Nevada/Las Vegas	NV	11,566	C
Univ of Nevada/Reno	NV	9,792	C
Univ of New Haven	CT	28,650	C
Univ of New Mexico	NM	9,223	C
Univ of New Orleans	LA	7,356	C
Univ of North Alabama	AL	7,972	NC
Univ of N Car at Asheville	NC	8,079	VC
Univ of N Car at Chapel Hill	NC	10,117	MC
Univ of N Car at Charlotte	NC	8,185	C
Univ of N Car at Greensboro	NC	8,248	C
Univ of N Car at Pembroke	NC	6,929	LC
Univ of N Car at Wilmington	NC	8,940	VC
Univ of N Dak	ND	8,390	C
Univ of North Florida	FL	8,769	VC
Univ of North Texas	TX	7,629	C
Univ of Northern Colo	CO	8,987	C
Univ of Northern Iowa	IA	9,834	C
Univ of Notre Dame	IN	34,442	MC
Univ of Okla	OK	9,226	VC
Univ of Oregon	OR	11,479	VC
Univ of Pennsylvania	PA	37,960	MC
Univ of Pittsburgh at Greensburg	PA	15,984	C
Univ of Pittsburgh at Johnstown	PA	15,216	LC
Univ of Pittsburgh at Pittsburgh	PA	16,074	HC
Univ of Portland	OR	28,500	VC
Univ of PR at Humacao	PR	1,245	
Univ of PR/Bayamon Univ College Campus	PR	1,600	
Univ of PR/Cayey Univ College	PR	1,245	
Univ of PR/Mayaguez	PR		
Univ of PR/Rio Piedras	PR	5,730	
Univ of Redlands	CA	32,576	VC
Univ of Rhode Island	RI	13,720	VC
Univ of Richmond	VA	30,100	MC
Univ of Rio Grande	OH	8,728	NC
Univ of St. Francis	IL	22,850	C
Univ of St. Francis	IN	20,964	C
Univ of St. Mary	KS	18,868	C
Univ of St. Thomas	MN	26,918	VC
Univ of St. Thomas	TX	21,952	VC
Univ of San Diego	CA	33,156	HC
Univ of San Francisco	CA	34,700	VC
Univ of Scranton	PA	30,836	VC
Univ of Sioux Falls	SD	16,390	C
Univ of South Alabama	AL	7,760	LC
Univ of S Car at Columbia	SC	10,048	VC
Univ of S Car at Spartanburg	SC	9,936	C+
Univ of S Dak	SD	7,710	C+
Univ of South Florida	FL	9,454	C
Univ of Southern Calif	CA	37,459	MC
Univ of Southern Colo	CO	7,821	LC
Univ of Southern Indiana	IN	9,025	LC
Univ of Southern Maine	ME	11,212	C
Univ of Southern Miss	MS	8,324	LC
Univ of Tampa	FL	23,982	VC
Univ of Tenn at Knoxville	TN	8,214	C
Univ of Tenn at Martin	TN	7,748	C
Univ of Texas at Arlington	TX	7,192	LC
Univ of Texas at Austin	TX	10,630	HC
Univ of Texas at Dallas	TX	10,234	HC
Univ of Texas at El Paso	TX	5,799	NC
Univ of Texas at San Antonio	TX	9,088	NC
Univ of Texas-Pan American	TX	5,954	LC
Univ of the District of Columbia	DC	2,070	LC
Univ of the Incarnate Word	TX	21,772	LC
Univ of the Ozarks	AR	16,574	C
Univ of the Sacred Heart	PR	5,590	
Univ of Toledo	OH	12,479	NC
Univ of Tulsa	OK	22,090	VC+
Univ of Utah	UT	9,205	C
Univ of Virginia's College at Wise	VA	10,116	C
Univ of Washington	WA	10,361	VC
Univ of West Alabama	AL	6,048	C
Univ of West Florida	FL	8,470	C
Univ of Wisc/Eau Claire	WI	8,463	VC
Univ of Wisc/Green Bay	WI	8,154	C
Univ of Wisc/La Crosse	WI	8,991	VC
Univ of Wisc/Madison	WI	8,262	VC
Univ of Wisc/Milwaukee	WI	9,427	LC
Univ of Wisc/Oshkosh	WI	6,130	LC
Univ of Wisc/Platteville	WI	8,450	C
Univ of Wisc/River Falls	WI	8,358	LC
Univ of Wisc/Stevens Point	WI	8,116	VC
Univ of Wisc/Superior	WI	7,051	C+
Univ of Wisc/Whitewater	WI	8,626	C
Univ of Wyoming	WY	8,636	C
Upper Iowa Univ	IA	20,076	C
Ursuline College	OH	22,728	LC
Utah State Univ	UT	7,371	C
Utica College	NY	28,340	C
Valdosta State Univ	GA	7,798	C
Valparaiso Univ	IN	26,118	VC+
Vanguard Univ of Southern Calif	CA	22,208	C
Villanova Univ	PA	35,050	HC
Virginia Commonwealth Univ	VA	9,030	C
Virginia Polytechnic Inst and State Univ	VA	9,179	C
Virginia State Univ	VA	10,358	C
Virginia Union Univ	VA	15,358	LC
Viterbo Univ	WI	20,430	C
Voorhees College	SC	11,678	LC
Wagner College	NY	29,900	VC
Wake Forest Univ	NC	34,090	MC
Walsh Univ	OH	20,890	C
Warner Southern College	FL	16,738	LC
Wartburg College	IA	21,165	VC
Washburn Univ of Topeka	KS	8,984	NC
Washington and Jefferson College	PA	29,570	VC
Washington and Lee Univ	VA	29,663	MC
Washington State Univ	WA	11,334	C
Washington Univ in St. Louis	MO	38,293	MC
Wayne State Univ	MI	11,774	C
Waynesburg College	PA	19,370	C
Webber International Univ	FL	16,510	C
Weber State Univ	UT	7,945	NC
Webster Univ	MO	21,848	VC
Wesley College	DE	19,905	C
West Chester Univ of Pennsylvania	PA	11,164	C
West Liberty State College	WV	7,868	LC
West Texas A&M Univ	TX	7,533	C
West Virginia State College	WV	6,264	NC
West Virginia Univ	WV	9,370	C
West Virginia Univ Inst of Technology	WV	7,518	NC
West Virginia Wesleyan College	WV	22,920	C
Western Baptist College	OR	21,808	C
Western Carolina Univ	NC	6,742	C
Western Conn State Univ	CT	11,625	C
Western Illinois Univ	IL	10,363	C
Western Kentucky Univ	KY	6,834	C
Western Mich Univ	MI	12,031	C
Western New England College	MA	28,924	C
Western New Mexico Univ	NM	5,950	LC
Western State College of Colo	CO	9,014	C
Western Washington Univ	WA	10,119	VC
Westminster College	MO	18,150	C+
Westminster College	PA	22,960	C
Westminster College	UT	17,226	C
Wheeling Jesuit Univ	WV	22,660	C
Whitworth College	WA	26,428	VC+
Wichita State Univ	KS	8,092	C
Widener Univ	PA	27,020	C
Wilberforce Univ	OH	14,937	LC
Wilkes Univ	PA	28,060	C
William Jewell College	MO	21,320	VC
William Paterson Univ of New Jersey	NJ	14,450	C
William Penn Univ	IA	17,575	LC
William Woods Univ	MO	20,120	C
Wilmington College	DE	5,594	NC
Wilmington College	OH	24,172	LC
Wilson College	PA	23,912	C
Wingate Univ	NC	21,200	C
Winona State Univ	MN		C
Winston-Salem State Univ	NC	8,926	LC
Wofford College	SC	26,710	HC
Woodbury Univ	CA	25,344	LC
Wright State Univ	OH	11,490	LC
Xavier Univ	OH	26,850	VC+
Xavier Univ of Louisiana	LA	17,600	C
Yeshiva Univ	NY	21,400	C
York College	NE	14,975	C
York College of Pennsylvania	PA	14,500	VC
Youngstown State Univ	OH	11,148	NC

ACTUARIAL SCIENCE

School	ST	$IS	SR
Ball State Univ	IN	8,660	C
Bellarmine Univ	KY	24,110	VC
Bradley Univ	IL	22,910	VC
Brigham Young Univ	UT	8,504	HC
Bryant College	RI	31,004	VC
Butler Univ	IN	28,250	VC+
Carroll College	WI	22,740	C
Central Conn State Univ	CT	12,090	C
Central Mich Univ	MI	11,142	C
Central Missouri State Univ	MO	9,776	C
Central Washington Univ	WA	9,768	C
CUNY/Baruch College	NY	3,275	VC+
Drake Univ	IA	25,120	VC+
Eastern Mich Univ	MI	11,478	C
Florida A&M Univ	FL	7,564	C
Florida State Univ	FL	9,028	HC
Frostburg State Univ	MD	11,114	C
Georgia State Univ	GA	10,658	C
Hofstra Univ	NY	27,112	VC
Indiana Univ Northwest	IN	4,538	LC
Indiana Univ South Bend	IN	4,571	LC
Lebanon Valley College	PA	28,870	VC
Lincoln Univ	PA	13,320	C+
Maryville Univ of St. Louis	MO	22,090	VC
Missouri Valley College	MO	18,500	C
New York Univ	NY	39,406	MC
North Central College	IL	25,656	VC
N Dak State Univ	ND	8,435	C
Northwestern College of Iowa	IA	19,640	C+
Ohio State Univ	OH	13,080	VC+
Ohio Univ	OH	14,448	C
Penn State Univ/Univ Park Campus	PA	15,646	HC
Purdue Univ/West Lafayette	IN	12,560	VC
Rider Univ	NJ	30,900	C
Robert Morris Univ	PA	20,438	C
Roosevelt Univ	IL	22,580	VC
Seton Hill Univ	PA	24,930	C
Southern Adventist Univ	TN	17,080	C
SUNY/College at Brockport	NY	12,111	C
SUNY/Univ at Albany	NY	12,951	HC
SUNY/Univ at Binghamton	NY	12,787	HC
Temple Univ	PA	15,912	C
Thiel College	PA	20,970	C
Univ of Central Okla	OK	9,434	C
Univ of Illinois at Urbana-Champaign	IL	11,316	HC+
Univ of Iowa	IA	10,923	VC
Univ of Minn/Twin Cities	MN	13,160	VC
Univ of Nebr at Lincoln	NE	9,975	C+
Univ of Northern Colo	CO	8,987	C
Univ of Pennsylvania	PA	37,960	MC
Univ of St. Thomas	MN	26,918	VC
Univ of Wisc/Madison	WI	8,262	VC
Utica College	NY	28,340	C
Valparaiso Univ	IN	26,118	VC+

ADDICTION STUDIES

School	ST	$IS	SR
Alvernia College	PA	23,212	LC
Cal State, Stanislaus	CA	9,874	C
Graceland Univ	IA	19,550	C
Kansas Wesleyan Univ	KS	18,900	VC
Metropolitan State Univ	MN	3,852	SP
Minot State Univ	ND	6,602	LC
Missouri Valley College	MO	18,500	C
Southern Univ at New Orleans	LA	995	NC
Univ of Central Okla	OK	9,434	C
Univ of Detroit Mercy	MI	25,582	C
Univ of Mary	ND	12,900	C+
Univ of S Dak	SD	7,710	C+

ADVERTISING

School	ST	$IS	SR
Abilene Christian Univ	TX	18,370	VC
Adams State College	CO	7,468	C
American International College	MA	24,690	LC

ST = STATE **$IS** = IN-STATE COSTS **SR** = SELECTOR RATING

School	ST	$IS	SR
Appalachian State Univ	NC	7,637	VC
Art Center College of Design	CA	23,450	SP
Art Inst of Atlanta	GA	23,205	SP
Art Inst of Portland	OR	23,040	SP
Atlanta College of Art	GA	18,600	SP
Barry Univ	FL	24,100	LC
Brigham Young Univ	UT	8,504	HC
Cal State, Fullerton	CA	6,648	C
Cal State, Hayward	CA	8,871	LC
Cal State, San Bernardino	CA	15,238	LC
Campbell Univ	NC	18,268	VC
Central State Univ	OH	8,922	C+
CUNY/Baruch College	NY	3,275	VC+
Clarke College	IA	23,165	C
Cleveland Inst of Art	OH	30,371	SP
College for Creative Studies	MI	23,298	SP
Columbia College Chicago	IL	25,108	LC
Columbus College of Art and Design	OH	24,180	SP
Concordia College: Moorhead	MN	22,460	VC+
Davenport Univ	MI	11,636	NC
Drake Univ	IA	25,120	VC+
Drury Univ	MO	18,085	VC+
East Central Univ	OK	4,968	C
Eastern Mich Univ	MI	11,478	C
Eastern Nazarene College	MA	19,433	LC
Edinboro Univ of Pennsylvania	PA	10,850	LC
Emerson College	MA	32,205	HC
Fashion Inst of Technology/ SUNY	NY	11,169	C+
Ferris State Univ	MI	12,512	C
Florida Southern College	FL	23,592	C
Florida State Univ	FL	9,028	HC
Fontbonne Univ	MO	21,508	C
Franklin Pierce College	NH	28,980	LC
Gannon Univ	PA	23,260	C
Grand Valley State Univ	MI	11,022	VC
Harding Univ	AR	14,890	VC
Hawaii Pacific Univ	HI	19,218	C
Indiana Univ South Bend	IN	4,571	LC
Iona College	NY	27,988	VC
Iowa State Univ	IA	10,768	VC
Johnson and Wales Univ	RI	22,965	LC
Kent State Univ	OH	12,932	C
Lamar Univ	TX	6,816	LC
Marietta College	OH	27,047	C
Marquette Univ	WI	27,594	VC
Marywood Univ	PA	26,050	C
Mercyhurst College	PA	20,694	C
Metropolitan State Univ	MN	3,852	SP
Mich State Univ	MI	11,933	VC
Midland Lutheran College	NE	18,600	C
Minneapolis College of Art and Design	MN	28,950	SP
Minn State Univ, Moorehead	MN	7,000	LC
Murray State Univ	KY	7,816	VC
New York Inst of Technology	NY	24,205	VC
Northeastern State Univ	OK	4,950	LC
Northeastern Univ	MA	35,650	HC
Northern Arizona Univ	AZ	9,002	C
Northwest Missouri State Univ	MO	9,334	C
Northwood Univ	FL	21,040	C
Northwood Univ	MI	20,265	LC
Northwood Univ	TX	20,135	LC
Okla Christian Univ	OK	17,690	NC
Okla City Univ	OK	19,580	VC
Otis College of Art and Design	CA	23,420	SP
Parsons School of Design	NY	32,242	SP
Penn State Univ/Univ Park Campus	PA	15,646	HC
Pepperdine Univ	CA	32,830	VC
Point Park Univ	PA	21,840	C
Portland State Univ	OR	12,453	C
Quinnipiac Univ	CT	30,570	VC
Rider Univ	NJ	30,900	C
Roosevelt Univ	IL	22,580	VC
St. Cloud State Univ	MN	8,362	C
Salem State College	MA	8,592	C
San Jose State Univ	CA	8,187	C
School of Visual Arts	NY	30,200	SP
Simmons College	MA	33,000	VC
Southeast Missouri State Univ	MO	9,704	C
Southern Methodist Univ	TX	34,210	HC
Syracuse Univ	NY	34,720	HC
Texas A&M Univ at Commerce	TX	8,994	C
Texas Christian Univ	TX	23,410	VC
Texas State Univ	TX	9,320	VC
Texas Tech Univ	TX	10,768	VC
Thomas Edison State College	NJ	3,325	SP
Union Univ	TN	18,800	VC
Univ of Akron	OH	13,134	NC
Univ of Alabama	AL	9,040	C+
Univ of Arkansas at Little Rock	AR	5,637	NC
Univ of Central Florida	FL	10,038	VC
Univ of Central Okla	OK	9,434	C
Univ of Colo at Boulder	CO	10,774	VC
Univ of Florida	FL	8,580	MC
Univ of Georgia	GA	8,656	VC
Univ of Illinois at Urbana-Champaign	IL	11,316	HC+
Univ of Kentucky	KY	7,765	C
Univ of Louisiana at Lafayette	LA	5,826	C
Univ of Miami	FL	34,608	HC
Univ of Miss	MS	7,666	C
Univ of Missouri/Columbia	MO	13,782	VC
Univ of Nebr at Kearney	NE	8,286	NC
Univ of Nebr at Lincoln	NE	9,975	C+
Univ of Northern Colo	CO	8,987	C
Univ of Okla	OK	9,226	VC
Univ of S Car at Columbia	SC	10,048	VC
Univ of Southern Miss	MS	8,324	LC
Univ of Tenn at Knoxville	TN	8,214	C
Univ of Texas at Austin	TX	10,630	HC
Univ of the Sacred Heart	PR	5,590	
Univ of Wisc/Eau Claire	WI	8,463	VC
Washington State Univ	WA	11,334	C
Washington Univ in St. Louis	MO	38,293	MC
Waynesburg College	PA	19,370	C
Webster Univ	MO	21,848	VC
Wesleyan College	GA	17,870	VC
West Virginia Univ	WV	9,370	C
Western Kentucky Univ	KY	6,834	C
Western Mich Univ	MI	12,031	C
Western New England College	MA	28,924	C
Winona State Univ	MN		C
Xavier Univ	OH	26,850	VC+
Youngstown State Univ	OH	11,148	NC

AERONAUTICAL ENGINEERING

School	ST	$IS	SR
Arizona State Univ-Main	AZ	10,048	C
Auburn Univ	AL	10,396	VC
Bethel College	IN	19,670	C
Boston Univ	MA	38,194	HC+
Calif Inst of Technology	CA	31,677	MC
Calif Polytechnic State Univ	CA	8,747	VC
Calif State Polytechnic Univ, Pomona	CA	8,793	C+
Case Western Reserve Univ	OH	32,002	MC
Clarkson Univ	NY	32,226	VC
Embry-Riddle Aeronautical Univ	AZ	27,710	C+
Embry-Riddle Aeronautical Univ	FL	27,730	C+
Florida Inst of Technology	FL	28,740	VC
Georgia Inst of Technology	GA	10,340	HC+
Illinois Inst of Technology	IL	26,456	HC+
Iowa State Univ	IA	10,768	VC
Mass Inst of Technology	MA	38,310	MC
New York Inst of Technology	NY	24,205	VC
N Car State Univ	NC	9,886	VC
Ohio State Univ	OH	13,080	VC+
Okla State Univ	OK	9,216	VC
Penn State Univ/Univ Park Campus	PA	15,646	HC
Princeton Univ	NJ	36,649	MC
Purdue Univ/West Lafayette	IN	12,560	VC
Rensselaer Polytechnic Inst	NY	37,579	HC+
St. Louis Univ	MO	29,780	VC+
San Diego State Univ	CA	10,321	C
San Jose State Univ	CA	8,187	C
SUNY/Univ at Buffalo	NY	12,563	VC
Syracuse Univ	NY	34,720	HC
Texas A&M Univ	TX	11,081	HC
United States Air Force Academy	CO		HC+
United States Naval Academy	MD		MC
Univ of Arizona	AZ	10,413	VC
Univ of Calif at Davis	CA	14,995	VC
Univ of Calif at Irvine	CA	19,808	HC
Univ of Calif at Los Angeles	CA	15,330	MC
Univ of Central Florida	FL	10,038	VC
Univ of Cincinnati	OH	14,736	C
Univ of Colo at Boulder	CO	10,774	VC
Univ of Florida	FL	8,580	MC
Univ of Illinois at Urbana-Champaign	IL	11,316	HC+
Univ of Kansas	KS	8,923	VC
Univ of Maryland/College Park	MD	14,227	HC
Univ of Miami	FL	34,608	HC
Univ of Mich/Ann Arbor	MI	13,864	HC+
Univ of Minn/Twin Cities	MN	13,160	VC
Univ of Missouri/Rolla	MO	12,292	HC
Univ of Notre Dame	IN	34,442	MC
Univ of Okla	OK	9,226	VC
Univ of Southern Calif	CA	37,459	MC
Univ of Washington	WA	10,361	VC
West Virginia Univ	WV	9,370	C
Western Mich Univ	MI	12,031	C
Wichita State Univ	KS	8,092	C

AERONAUTICAL SCIENCE

School	ST	$IS	SR
Averett Univ	VA	23,010	LC
Dowling College	NY	23,870	LC
Embry-Riddle Aeronautical Univ	AZ	27,710	C+
Embry-Riddle Aeronautical Univ	FL	27,730	C+
Farmingdale SUNY	NY	12,891	C
Florida Inst of Technology	FL	28,740	VC
Inter American Univ of PR/ Bayamon Univ College	PR	3,522	
Kent State Univ	OH	12,932	C
LeTourneau Univ	TX	21,080	C
Rocky Mountain College	MT	19,015	C
Stanford Univ	CA	37,612	MC
Univ of Maryland/Eastern Shore	MD	9,964	C
Western Mich Univ	MI	12,031	C
Wilmington College	DE	5,594	NC

AERONAUTICAL TECHNOLOGY

School	ST	$IS	SR
Andrews Univ	MI	19,550	C
Central Washington Univ	WA	9,768	C
Dowling College	NY	23,870	LC
Embry-Riddle Aeronautical Univ	FL	27,730	C+
Indiana State Univ	IN	10,719	LC
Inter American Univ of PR/ Bayamon Univ College	PR	3,522	
Kansas State Univ	KS	8,728	VC
LeTourneau Univ	TX	21,080	C
Purdue Univ/West Lafayette	IN	12,560	VC
St. Louis Univ	MO	29,780	VC+
Tenn State Univ	TN	9,048	LC
Univ of Alaska Anchorage	AK	9,100	NC

AEROSPACE STUDIES

School	ST	$IS	SR
Averett Univ	VA	23,010	LC
Cal State, Long Beach	CA	8,762	C+
Cornell Univ	NY	38,253	MC
Embry-Riddle Aeronautical Univ	AZ	27,710	C+
Embry-Riddle Aeronautical Univ	FL	27,730	C+
Indiana Univ Bloomington	IN	12,389	VC
Mass Inst of Technology	MA	38,310	MC
Miss State Univ	MS	9,139	C
Rochester Inst of Technology	NY	29,217	VC+
United States Air Force Academy	CO		HC+
Univ of Alabama	AL	9,040	C+
Univ of Arizona	AZ	10,413	VC
Univ of Calif at San Diego	CA	14,127	HC
Univ of Central Florida	FL	10,038	VC
Univ of N Dak	ND	8,390	C
Univ of Southern Calif	CA	37,459	MC
Univ of Tenn at Knoxville	TN	8,214	C
Univ of Texas at Austin	TX	10,630	HC
Univ of Virginia	VA	11,740	MC
Washington Univ in St. Louis	MO	38,293	MC
West Virginia Univ	WV	9,370	C

AFRICAN AMERICAN STUDIES

School	ST	$IS	SR
Amherst College	MA	37,470	MC
Arizona State Univ-Main	AZ	10,048	C
Bates College	ME	37,500	MC
Brandeis Univ	MA	38,198	MC
Brown Univ	RI	38,174	MC
Cal State, Fresno	CA	8,414	LC
Cal State, Fullerton	CA	6,648	C
Cal State, Long Beach	CA	8,762	C+
Cal State, Los Angeles	CA	5,778	C
Cal State, Northridge	CA	7,757	LC
Carleton College	MN	34,395	MC
Chicago State Univ	IL	10,882	C+
CUNY/College of Staten Island	NY	4,308	NC
CUNY/Herbert H. Lehman College	NY	3,320	LC
CUNY/Hunter College	NY	6,729	C+
CUNY/York College	NY	3,292	NC
Claflin Univ	SC	14,838	C+
Claremont McKenna College	CA	36,880	MC
Coe College	IA	27,385	VC
College of Wooster	OH	31,300	HC
Columbia Univ/Columbia College	NY	38,590	MC
Columbia Univ/School of General Studies	NY	35,000	C
Dartmouth College	NH	37,770	MC
Denison Univ	OH	33,050	HC
DePauw Univ	IN	31,500	HC
Duke Univ	NC	37,555	MC
Earlham College	IN	29,976	VC+
Eastern Illinois Univ	IL	11,192	C
Eastern Mich Univ	MI	11,478	C
Fordham Univ	NY	35,066	HC
Guilford College	NC	24,960	VC
Hampshire College	MA	37,037	HC
Harvard Univ/Harvard College	MA	37,928	MC
Howard Univ	DC	16,505	C
Indiana State Univ	IN	10,719	LC
Indiana Univ Bloomington	IN	12,389	VC
Indiana Univ Northwest	IN	4,538	LC
Knox College	IL	30,294	VC+
Lincoln Univ	PA	13,320	C+
Loyola Marymount Univ	CA	32,194	VC
Luther College	IA	25,700	VC
Martin Univ	IN	10,200	SP
Metropolitan State College of Denver	CO	2,338	LC
Miami Univ	OH	15,033	HC
Morehouse College	GA	22,728	C
Morgan State Univ	MD	11,470	C
Mount Holyoke College	MA	37,918	HC+
Northeastern Univ	MA	35,650	HC
Northwestern Univ	IL	37,491	MC
Oakland Univ	MI	10,800	C
Oberlin College	OH	36,938	MC
Ohio State Univ	OH	13,080	VC+
Ohio Univ	OH	14,448	C
Ohio Wesleyan Univ	OH	32,550	VC+
Penn State Univ/Univ Park Campus	PA	15,646	HC
Pitzer College	CA	37,590	HC
Pomona College	CA	33,960	MC
Purdue Univ/West Lafayette	IN	12,560	VC
Rhode Island College	RI	11,565	C
Roosevelt Univ	IL	22,580	VC
Rutgers, The State Univ of New Jersey/Camden Campus	NJ	14,990	VC
Rutgers, The State Univ of New Jersey/New Brunswick/Piscataway Campus	NJ	15,800	HC
Rutgers, The State Univ of New Jersey/Newark Campus	NJ	15,624	VC
St. Augustine's College	NC	12,990	LC
San Francisco State Univ	CA	12,070	C
Scripps College	CA	35,700	HC+
Seton Hall Univ	NJ	30,130	VC
Simmons College	MA	33,000	VC
Simon's Rock College of Bard	MA	36,580	HC
Smith College	MA	37,034	HC+
Sonoma State Univ	CA	10,421	C
Southern Methodist Univ	TX	34,210	HC
Stanford Univ	CA	37,612	MC
SUNY/College at Brockport	NY	12,111	C
SUNY/College at Cortland	NY	12,095	C
SUNY/College at Geneseo	NY	11,330	HC
SUNY/Univ at Albany	NY	12,951	HC
SUNY/Univ at Binghamton	NY	12,787	HC
SUNY/Univ at Buffalo	NY	12,563	VC
Syracuse Univ	NY	34,720	HC
Temple Univ	PA	15,912	C
Univ of Alabama at Birmingham	AL	12,901	C
Univ of Calif at Berkeley	CA	15,563	MC
Univ of Calif at Los Angeles	CA	15,330	MC
Univ of Calif at Riverside	CA	15,300	C
Univ of Calif at Santa Barbara	CA	11,732	VC
Univ of Chicago	IL	35,087	MC
Univ of Cincinnati	OH	14,736	C
Univ of Illinois at Chicago	IL	13,418	C
Univ of Iowa	IA	10,923	VC
Univ of Kansas	KS	8,923	VC
Univ of Maryland/Baltimore County	MD	14,668	VC+
Univ of Maryland/College Park	MD	14,227	HC
Univ of Mass Amherst	MA	13,980	C+
Univ of Mass Boston	MA	6,227	C
Univ of Memphis	TN	8,560	C
Univ of Miami	FL	34,608	HC
Univ of Mich/Ann Arbor	MI	13,864	HC+
Univ of Minn/Twin Cities	MN	13,160	VC
Univ of New Mexico	NM	9,223	C
Univ of N Car at Chapel Hill	NC	10,117	MC
Univ of N Car at Charlotte	NC	8,185	C
Univ of N Car at Greensboro	NC	8,248	C
Univ of Northern Colo	CO	8,987	C
Univ of Okla	OK	9,226	VC
Univ of Pennsylvania	PA	37,960	MC
Univ of Pittsburgh at Pittsburgh	PA	16,074	HC
Univ of Puget Sound	WA	31,760	HC
Univ of S Car at Columbia	SC	10,048	VC
Univ of South Florida	FL	9,454	C
Univ of Southern Calif	CA	37,459	MC
Univ of Tenn at Knoxville	TN	8,214	C
Univ of Virginia	VA	11,740	MC
Univ of Washington	WA	10,361	VC
Univ of Wisc/Madison	WI	8,262	VC
Univ of Wisc/Milwaukee	WI	9,427	LC
Vanderbilt Univ	TN	37,897	MC
Washington Univ in St. Louis	MO	38,293	MC

ST = STATE $IS = IN-STATE COSTS SR = SELECTOR RATING

School	ST	$IS	SR
Wellesley College	MA	36,516	MC
Wesleyan Univ	CT	35,139	MC
William Paterson Univ of New Jersey	NJ	14,450	C
Yale Univ	CT	37,000	MC

AFRICAN LANGUAGES

School	ST	$IS	SR
Duke Univ	NC	37,555	MC
Univ of Calif at Los Angeles	CA	15,330	MC
Univ of Wisc/Madison	WI	8,262	VC

AFRICAN STUDIES

School	ST	$IS	SR
Bard College	NY	37,352	HC+
Bowdoin College	ME	37,790	MC
Bowling Green State Univ	OH	13,036	C
Brandeis Univ	MA	38,198	MC
Brown Univ	RI	38,174	MC
Cal State, Dominguez Hills	CA	5,840	LC
Carleton College	MN	34,395	MC
CUNY/Brooklyn College	NY	4,353	C+
CUNY/Queens College	NY	4,362	C
Colgate Univ	NY	37,095	MC
College of the Holy Cross	MA	36,451	MC
Conn College	CT	37,900	MC
Cornell Univ	NY	38,253	MC
Dartmouth College	NH	37,770	MC
Dillard Univ	LA	17,325	VC
Duke Univ	NC	37,555	MC
Emory Univ	GA	36,872	MC
Fordham Univ	NY	35,066	HC
Franklin and Marshall College	PA	35,930	HC+
Hamilton College	NY	37,560	MC
Hampshire College	MA	37,037	HC
Hobart and William Smith Colleges	NY	36,536	HC
Hofstra Univ	NY	27,112	VC
Howard Univ	DC	16,505	C
Kent State Univ	OH	12,932	C
Lafayette College	PA	35,746	MC
Lehigh Univ	PA	37,570	HC+
New York Univ	NY	39,406	MC
Ohio Univ	OH	14,448	C
St. Lawrence Univ	NY	35,945	VC
San Diego State Univ	CA	10,321	C
Shaw Univ	NC	14,882	C+
SUNY/College at Brockport	NY	12,111	C
SUNY/College at Oneonta	NY	11,870	VC
SUNY/Univ at Stony Brook	NY	12,763	HC
Tenn State Univ	TN	9,048	LC
Texas State Univ	TX	9,320	VC
Tulane Univ	LA	37,451	HC+
Union College	NY	36,005	HC
Univ of Calif at Davis	CA	14,995	VC
Univ of Kansas	KS	8,923	VC
Univ of Louisville	KY	8,762	VC
Univ of Mich/Ann Arbor	MI	13,864	HC+
Univ of Minn/Twin Cities	MN	13,160	VC
Univ of N Car at Chapel Hill	NC	10,117	MC
Univ of Pennsylvania	PA	37,960	MC
Vassar College	NY	37,030	MC
Washington Univ in St. Louis	MO	38,293	MC
Wayne State Univ	MI	11,774	C
Western Mich Univ	MI	12,031	C
Youngstown State Univ	OH	11,148	NC

AGRICULTURAL BUSINESS MANAGEMENT

School	ST	$IS	SR
Alabama A&M Univ	AL	5,100	LC
Arkansas State Univ	AR	8,450	C
Arkansas Tech Univ	AR	7,299	C
Auburn Univ	AL	10,396	VC
Brigham Young Univ	UT	8,504	HC
Calif Polytechnic State Univ	CA	8,747	VC
Calif State Polytechnic Univ, Pomona	CA	8,793	C+
Cal State, Chico	CA	8,598	LC
Cal State, Fresno	CA	8,414	LC
Central Missouri State Univ	MO	9,776	C
College of the Ozarks	MO	3,500	VC+
Colo State Univ	CO	9,964	VC
Cornell Univ	NY	38,253	MC
Delaware State Univ	DE	8,104	LC
Dickinson State Univ	ND	6,338	NC
Eastern New Mexico Univ	NM	6,762	LC
Eastern Oregon Univ	OR	10,080	NC
Fort Hays State Univ	KS	7,363	C
Freed-Hardeman Univ	TN		NC
Iowa State Univ	IA	10,768	VC
Kansas State Univ	KS	8,728	VC
Lindenwood Univ	MO	17,050	VC
Louisiana State Univ and A&M College	LA	9,126	VC
Louisiana Tech Univ	LA	7,361	C
Lubbock Christian Univ	TX	15,832	C
McNeese State Univ	LA	5,259	LC
Middle Tenn State Univ	TN	8,534	C
Miss State Univ	MS	9,139	C
Missouri Valley College	MO	18,500	C
Montana State Univ-Bozeman	MT	9,515	C
New Mexico State Univ	NM	7,932	C
Nicholls State Univ	LA	6,395	NC
N Car Agricultural and Technical State Univ	NC	6,659	LC
N Car State Univ	NC	9,886	VC
N Dak State Univ	ND	8,435	C
Northwest Missouri State Univ	MO	9,334	C
Northwestern College of Iowa	IA	19,640	C+
Northwestern Okla State Univ	OK	5,433	NC
Okla Panhandle State Univ	OK	5,370	C
Okla State Univ	OK	9,216	VC
Oregon State Univ	OR	11,055	C
Penn State Univ/Univ Park Campus	PA	15,646	HC
Prairie View A&M Univ	TX	9,418	NC
Purdue Univ/West Lafayette	IN	12,560	VC
S Car State Univ	SC	6,586	LC
S Dak State Univ	SD	7,782	C
Southeast Missouri State Univ	MO	9,704	C
Southern Arkansas Univ	AR	6,956	C
Southwest Minn State Univ	MN	9,106	VC
SUNY/College of Agriculture and Technology at Cobleskill	NY	11,200	C+
Stephen F. Austin State Univ	TX	7,552	C
Sul Ross State Univ	TX	6,582	LC
Tarleton State Univ	TX	7,576	C
Texas A&M Univ	TX	11,081	HC
Texas A&M Univ at Kingsville	TX	6,740	LC
Texas State Univ	TX	9,320	VC
Texas Tech Univ	TX	10,768	VC
Univ of Arkansas	AR	9,855	VC
Univ of Calif at Davis	CA	14,995	VC
Univ of Delaware	DE	12,616	HC
Univ of Florida	FL	8,580	MC
Univ of Idaho	ID	8,216	C
Univ of Louisiana at Monroe	LA	5,207	NC
Univ of Maryland/College Park	MD	14,227	HC
Univ of Minn/Crookston	MN	9,626	NC
Univ of Minn/Twin Cities	MN	13,160	VC
Univ of Missouri/Columbia	MO	13,782	VC
Univ of Nebr at Lincoln	NE	9,975	C+
Univ of Tenn at Martin	TN	7,748	C
Univ of Wisc/Madison	WI	8,262	VC
Univ of Wisc/Platteville	WI	8,450	C
Univ of Wisc/River Falls	WI	8,358	LC
Univ of Wyoming	WY	8,636	C
Utah State Univ	UT	7,371	C
Washington State Univ	WA	11,334	C
West Texas A&M Univ	TX	7,533	C
West Virginia Univ	WV	9,370	C

AGRICULTURAL COMMUNICATIONS

School	ST	$IS	SR
Univ of Wyoming	WY	8,636	C

AGRICULTURAL ECONOMICS

School	ST	$IS	SR
Alabama A&M Univ	AL	5,100	LC
Alcorn State Univ	MS	7,290	C
Central Missouri State Univ	MO	9,776	C
Colo State Univ	CO	9,964	VC
Cornell Univ	NY	38,253	MC
Eastern Oregon Univ	OR	10,080	NC
Fort Valley State Univ	GA	6,960	C
Kansas State Univ	KS	8,728	VC
Langston Univ	OK	2,308	LC
McPherson College	KS	20,265	C
Miss State Univ	MS	9,139	C
N Car Agricultural and Technical State Univ	NC	6,659	LC
N Car State Univ	NC	9,886	VC
N Dak State Univ	ND	8,435	C
Ohio State Univ	OH	13,080	VC+
Okla State Univ	OK	9,216	VC
Oregon State Univ	OR	11,055	C
Prairie View A&M Univ	TX	9,418	NC
Purdue Univ/West Lafayette	IN	12,560	VC
S Dak State Univ	SD	7,782	C
Southern Illinois Univ Carbondale	IL	10,407	C
Southern Univ and A&M College	LA	7,372	LC
Tarleton State Univ	TX	7,576	C
Tenn Tech Univ	TN	8,670	VC
Texas A&M Univ	TX	11,081	HC
Texas A&M Univ at Commerce	TX	8,994	C
Truman State Univ	MO	9,728	HC+
Univ of Arizona	AZ	10,413	VC
Univ of Arkansas	AR	9,855	VC
Univ of Calif at Davis	CA	14,995	VC
Univ of Conn	CT	14,608	VC
Univ of Delaware	DE	12,616	HC
Univ of Georgia	GA	8,656	VC
Univ of Hawaii at Manoa	HI	9,565	VC
Univ of Idaho	ID	8,216	C
Univ of Illinois at Urbana-Champaign	IL	11,316	HC+
Univ of Kentucky	KY	7,765	C
Univ of Maryland/College Park	MD	14,227	HC
Univ of Minn/Twin Cities	MN	13,160	VC
Univ of Missouri/Columbia	MO	13,782	VC
Univ of Nebr at Lincoln	NE	9,975	C+
Univ of Nevada/Reno	NV	9,792	C
Univ of Tenn at Knoxville	TN	8,214	C
Univ of Wisc/Madison	WI	8,262	VC
Univ of Wisc/Platteville	WI	8,450	C
Utah State Univ	UT	7,371	C
Virginia Polytechnic Inst and State Univ	VA	9,179	C
Washington State Univ	WA	11,334	C
West Texas A&M Univ	TX	7,533	C

AGRICULTURAL EDUCATION

School	ST	$IS	SR
Alabama A&M Univ	AL	5,100	LC
Arkansas State Univ	AR	8,450	C
Cal State, Fresno	CA	8,414	LC
Central Missouri State Univ	MO	9,776	C
Clemson Univ	SC	11,972	HC
College of the Ozarks	MO	3,500	VC+
Colo State Univ	CO	9,964	VC
Delaware State Univ	DE	8,104	LC
Eastern New Mexico Univ	NM	6,762	LC
Fort Valley State Univ	GA	6,960	C
Iowa State Univ	IA	10,768	VC
Kansas State Univ	KS	8,728	VC
Mich State Univ	MI	11,933	VC
Miss State Univ	MS	9,139	C
Montana State Univ-Bozeman	MT	9,515	C
Morehead State Univ	KY	7,464	C
Murray State Univ	KY	7,816	VC
New Mexico State Univ	NM	7,932	C
N Car Agricultural and Technical State Univ	NC	6,659	LC
N Car State Univ	NC	9,886	VC
N Dak State Univ	ND	8,435	C
Northwest Missouri State Univ	MO	9,334	C
Ohio State Univ	OH	13,080	VC+
Okla Panhandle State Univ	OK	5,370	C
Okla State Univ	OK	9,216	VC
Penn State Univ/Univ Park Campus	PA	15,646	HC
Purdue Univ/West Lafayette	IN	12,560	VC
S Dak State Univ	SD	7,782	C
Southern Arkansas Univ	AR	6,956	C
Southwest Missouri State Univ	MO	8,918	C
Stephen F. Austin State Univ	TX	7,552	C
Tarleton State Univ	TX	7,576	C
Tenn Tech Univ	TN	8,670	VC
Texas A&M Univ at Commerce	TX	8,994	C
Texas A&M Univ at Kingsville	TX	6,740	LC
Univ of Arizona	AZ	10,413	VC
Univ of Arkansas	AR	9,855	VC
Univ of Arkansas at Pine Bluff	AR	7,925	C
Univ of Conn	CT	14,608	VC
Univ of Delaware	DE	12,616	HC
Univ of Florida	FL	8,580	MC
Univ of Georgia	GA	8,656	VC
Univ of Idaho	ID	8,216	C
Univ of Illinois at Urbana-Champaign	IL	11,316	HC+
Univ of Kentucky	KY	7,765	C
Univ of Louisiana at Lafayette	LA	5,826	C
Univ of Maryland/Eastern Shore	MD	9,964	C
Univ of Minn/Twin Cities	MN	13,160	VC
Univ of Nebr at Lincoln	NE	9,975	C+
Univ of Tenn at Knoxville	TN	8,214	C
Univ of Wisc/Madison	WI	8,262	VC
Univ of Wisc/Platteville	WI	8,450	C
Univ of Wisc/River Falls	WI	8,358	LC
Utah State Univ	UT	7,371	C
Virginia Polytechnic Inst and State Univ	VA	9,179	C
Washington State Univ	WA	11,334	C
West Virginia Univ	WV	9,370	C

AGRICULTURAL ENGINEERING

School	ST	$IS	SR
Auburn Univ	AL	10,396	VC
Calif Polytechnic State Univ	CA	8,747	VC
Clemson Univ	SC	11,972	HC
Colo State Univ	CO	9,964	VC
Cornell Univ	NY	38,253	MC
Iowa State Univ	IA	10,768	VC
Kansas State Univ	KS	8,728	VC
N Car State Univ	NC	9,886	VC
N Dak State Univ	ND	8,435	C
Penn State Univ/Univ Park Campus	PA	15,646	HC
Purdue Univ/West Lafayette	IN	12,560	VC
S Dak State Univ	SD	7,782	C
Texas A&M Univ	TX	11,081	HC
Univ of Arkansas	AR	9,855	VC
Univ of Calif at Davis	CA	14,995	VC
Univ of Florida	FL	8,580	MC
Univ of Georgia	GA	8,656	VC
Univ of Idaho	ID	8,216	C
Univ of Illinois at Urbana-Champaign	IL	11,316	HC+
Univ of Minn/Twin Cities	MN	13,160	VC
Univ of Nebr at Lincoln	NE	9,975	C+
Univ of Tenn at Knoxville	TN	8,214	C
Univ of Wisc/Madison	WI	8,262	VC
Univ of Wisc/River Falls	WI	8,358	LC
Utah State Univ	UT	7,371	C
Virginia Polytechnic Inst and State Univ	VA	9,179	C
Washington State Univ	WA	11,334	C

AGRICULTURAL ENGINEERING TECHNOLOGY

School	ST	$IS	SR
Central Missouri State Univ	MO	9,776	C
College of the Ozarks	MO	3,500	VC+
Fort Valley State Univ	GA	6,960	C
Kansas State Univ	KS	8,728	VC
Miss State Univ	MS	9,139	C
Montana State Univ-Bozeman	MT	9,515	C
S Dak State Univ	SD	7,782	C
Univ of Arizona	AZ	10,413	VC
Univ of Wisc/Platteville	WI	8,450	C

AGRICULTURAL MECHANICS

School	ST	$IS	SR
Montana State Univ-Northern	MT	8,600	NC
Murray State Univ	KY	7,816	VC
N Dak State Univ	ND	8,435	C
Northwest Missouri State Univ	MO	9,334	C
Purdue Univ/West Lafayette	IN	12,560	VC
SUNY/College of Agriculture and Technology at Cobleskill	NY	11,200	C+
Stephen F. Austin State Univ	TX	7,552	C
Tarleton State Univ	TX	7,576	C
Univ of Idaho	ID	8,216	C
Univ of Illinois at Urbana-Champaign	IL	11,316	HC+
Univ of Nebr at Lincoln	NE	9,975	C+
Univ of Wisc/Madison	WI	8,262	VC
Washington State Univ	WA	11,334	C

AGRICULTURE

School	ST	$IS	SR
Alcorn State Univ	MS	7,290	C
Andrews Univ	MI	19,550	C
Arkansas State Univ	AR	8,450	C
Auburn Univ	AL	10,396	VC
Austin Peay State Univ	TN	5,814	LC
Berea College	KY	5,030	VC+
Calif Polytechnic State Univ	CA	8,747	VC
Calif State Polytechnic Univ, Pomona	CA	8,793	C+
Cal State, Chico	CA	8,598	LC
Cal State, Stanislaus	CA	9,874	C
Cameron Univ	OK	5,692	NC
Clemson Univ	SC	11,972	HC
College of the Ozarks	MO	3,500	VC+
Cornell Univ	NY	38,253	MC
Delaware Valley College	PA	26,676	C
Eastern Kentucky Univ	KY	7,708	C
Eastern New Mexico Univ	NM	6,762	LC
Ferrum College	VA	21,240	LC
Fort Hays State Univ	KS	7,363	C
Hampshire College	MA	37,037	HC
Illinois State Univ	IL	10,944	C+
Iowa State Univ	IA	10,768	VC
Lincoln Univ	MO	7,158	NC
McNeese State Univ	LA	5,259	LC
Mich State Univ	MI	11,933	VC
Miss State Univ	MS	9,139	C
Morehead State Univ	KY	7,464	C
Murray State Univ	KY	7,816	VC
New Mexico State Univ	NM	7,932	C
N Car State Univ	NC	9,886	VC
N Dak State Univ	ND	8,435	C
Northwest Missouri State Univ	MO	9,334	C
Northwestern Okla State Univ	OK	5,433	NC
Oregon State Univ	OR	11,055	C
Penn State Univ/Univ Park Campus	PA	15,646	HC
Purdue Univ/West Lafayette	IN	12,560	VC
Rutgers, The State Univ of New Jersey/New Brunswick/Piscataway Campus	NJ	15,800	HC
Sam Houston State Univ	TX	7,142	C
S Dak State Univ	SD	7,782	C

ST = STATE $IS = IN-STATE COSTS SR = SELECTOR RATING

School	ST	$IS	SR
Southeast Missouri State Univ	MO	9,704	C
Southern Arkansas Univ	AR	6,956	C
Southern Illinois Univ Carbondale	IL	10,407	C
Southern Nazarene Univ	OK	14,634	NC
Southern Univ and A&M College	LA	7,372	LC
Southern Utah Univ	UT	8,194	C
Southwest Missouri State Univ	MO	8,918	C
Stephen F. Austin State Univ	TX	7,552	C
Tarleton State Univ	TX	7,576	C
Tenn State Univ	TN	9,048	LC
Tenn Tech Univ	TN	8,670	VC
Texas A&M Univ at Commerce	TX	8,994	C
Texas State Univ	TX	9,320	VC
Truman State Univ	MO	9,728	HC+
Univ of Arkansas at Monticello	AR	5,940	NC
Univ of Arkansas at Pine Bluff	AR	7,925	C
Univ of Conn	CT	14,608	VC
Univ of Delaware	DE	12,616	HC
Univ of Georgia	GA	8,656	VC
Univ of Hawaii at Hilo	HI	6,497	C
Univ of Hawaii at Manoa	HI	9,565	VC
Univ of Idaho	ID	8,216	C
Univ of Kentucky	KY	7,765	C
Univ of Maine	ME	12,080	C+
Univ of Maryland/College Park	MD	14,227	HC
Univ of Maryland/Eastern Shore	MD	9,964	C
Univ of Missouri/Columbia	MO	13,782	VC
Univ of Nebr at Lincoln	NE	9,975	C+
Univ of Tenn at Knoxville	TN	8,214	C
Univ of Tenn at Martin	TN	7,748	C
Univ of Vermont	VT	16,316	VC
Univ of Wyoming	WY	8,636	C
Virginia State Univ	VA	10,358	C
Washington State Univ	WA	11,334	C
West Texas A&M Univ	TX	7,533	C
West Virginia Univ	WV	9,370	C
Western Illinois Univ	IL	10,363	C
Western Kentucky Univ	KY	6,834	C
Wilmington College	OH	24,172	LC

AGRONOMY

School	ST	$IS	SR
Alabama A&M Univ	AL	5,100	LC
Brigham Young Univ	UT	8,504	HC
Calif State Polytechnic Univ, Pomona	CA	8,793	C+
College of the Ozarks	MO	3,500	VC+
Colo State Univ	CO	9,964	VC
Cornell Univ	NY	38,253	MC
Iowa State Univ	IA	10,768	VC
Kansas State Univ	KS	8,728	VC
McPherson College	KS	20,265	C
Miss State Univ	MS	9,139	C
New Mexico State Univ	NM	7,932	C
N Car State Univ	NC	9,886	VC
Northwest Missouri State Univ	MO	9,334	C
Okla Panhandle State Univ	OK	5,370	C
Penn State Univ/Univ Park Campus	PA	15,646	HC
Prairie View A&M Univ	TX	9,418	NC
Purdue Univ/West Lafayette	IN	12,560	VC
S Dak State Univ	SD	7,782	C
Southeast Missouri State Univ	MO	9,704	C
Southwest Missouri State Univ	MO	8,918	C
Stephen F. Austin State Univ	TX	7,552	C
Tarleton State Univ	TX	7,576	C
Texas Tech Univ	TX	10,768	VC
Truman State Univ	MO	9,728	HC+
Univ of Conn	CT	14,608	VC
Univ of Florida	FL	8,580	MC
Univ of Illinois at Urbana-Champaign	IL	11,316	HC+
Univ of Maryland/College Park	MD	14,227	HC
Univ of Nebr at Lincoln	NE	9,975	C+
Univ of Wisc/River Falls	WI	8,358	LC
Washington State Univ	WA	11,334	C
West Virginia Univ	WV	9,370	C

AIR TRAFFIC CONTROL

School	ST	$IS	SR
Daniel Webster College	NH	24,870	C
Embry-Riddle Aeronautical Univ	FL	27,730	C+
Florida Memorial College	FL	6,000	LC
Thomas Edison State College	NJ	3,325	SP
Univ of N Dak	ND	8,390	C

AIRCRAFT MECHANICS

School	ST	$IS	SR
Andrews Univ	MI	19,550	C
Averett Univ	VA	23,010	LC
College of Aeronautics	NY	10,790	SP
Kent State Univ	OH	12,932	C
Lewis Univ	IL	22,950	C+
Pennsylvania College of Technology	PA	15,126	NC
St. John's Univ	NY	30,180	C
St. Louis Univ	MO	29,780	VC+
Western Mich Univ	MI	12,031	C

AIRLINE PILOTING AND NAVIGATION

School	ST	$IS	SR
Baylor Univ	TX	23,864	VC
College of Aeronautics	NY	10,790	SP
Daniel Webster College	NH	24,870	C
Eastern Kentucky Univ	KY	7,708	C
Indiana State Univ	IN	10,719	LC
Kansas State Univ	KS	8,728	VC
Lewis Univ	IL	22,950	C+
Louisiana Tech Univ	LA	7,361	C
Metropolitan State College of Denver	CO	2,338	LC
Ohio Univ	OH	14,448	C
Pacific Union College	CA	22,065	C+
St. Louis Univ	MO	29,780	VC+
Univ of Illinois at Urbana-Champaign	IL	11,316	HC+
Univ of Louisville	KY	8,762	VC
Univ of N Dak	ND	8,390	C
Western Mich Univ	MI	12,031	C

ALLIED HEALTH

School	ST	$IS	SR
Adams State College	CO	7,468	C
Albany State Univ	GA	5,764	C+
Andrews Univ	MI	19,550	C
Bloomfield College	NJ	19,250	LC
Bridgewater College	VA	25,150	C
Champlain College	VT	22,030	C
Clark Atlanta Univ	GA	19,300	C+
Clayton College and State Univ	GA	2,441	LC
College of Mount St. Vincent	NY	26,800	C
East Stroudsburg Univ of Pennsylvania	PA	10,336	C
East Tenn State Univ	TN	8,497	C
Eastern Mich Univ	MI	11,478	C
Fairleigh Dickinson Univ/College at Florham	NJ	30,130	C
Fairleigh Dickinson Univ/Metropolitan Campus	NJ	28,584	C
Hofstra Univ	NY	27,112	VC
Indiana Univ South Bend	IN	4,571	LC
Ithaca College	NY	31,730	HC
Johnson State College	VT	11,819	LC
Madonna Univ	MI	11,504	VC
Mars Hill College	NC	18,600	LC
Mass College of Pharmacy and Health Sciences	MA	28,770	SP
Merrimack College	MA	29,625	C
Montclair State Univ	NJ	13,790	C
National American Univ	SD	13,680	NC
Ramapo College of New Jersey	NJ	15,203	VC
Rochester Inst of Technology	NY	29,217	VC+
Roosevelt Univ	IL	22,580	VC
Rutgers, The State Univ of New Jersey/Newark Campus	NJ	15,624	VC
Saginaw Valley State Univ	MI	11,055	C
San Francisco State Univ	CA	12,070	C
Univ of Florida	FL	8,580	MC
Univ of Northern Colo	CO	8,987	C
Univ of St. Francis	IL	22,850	C
Univ of Texas at El Paso	TX	5,799	NC
Ursuline College	OH	22,728	LC
West Texas A&M Univ	TX	7,533	C
Youngstown State Univ	OH	11,148	NC

AMERICAN INDIAN STUDIES

School	ST	$IS	SR
Arizona State Univ-Main	AZ	10,048	C
Black Hills State Univ	SD	7,743	LC
Sonoma State Univ	CA	10,421	C
Univ of Minn/Twin Cities	MN	13,160	VC
Univ of N Car at Pembroke	NC	6,929	LC
Univ of Science and Arts of Okla	OK	5,982	C
Univ of S Dak	SD	7,710	C+
Univ of Wisc/Eau Claire	WI	8,463	VC

AMERICAN LITERATURE

School	ST	$IS	SR
Bard College	NY	37,352	HC+
Blackburn College	IL	13,690	C
Brandeis Univ	MA	38,198	MC
Brown Univ	RI	38,174	MC
Eastern Mich Univ	MI	11,478	C
Florida State Univ	FL	9,028	HC
Hofstra Univ	NY	27,112	VC
Middlebury College	VT	38,100	MC
New York Univ	NY	39,406	MC
Washington Univ in St. Louis	MO	38,293	MC

AMERICAN SIGN LANGUAGE

School	ST	$IS	SR
College of St. Catherine	MN	24,010	VC
East Central Univ	OK	4,968	C
Gardner-Webb Univ	NC	19,300	C
Goshen College	IN	22,450	VC
Indiana Univ-Purdue Univ Indianapolis	IN	8,257	LC
Kent State Univ	OH	12,932	C
Keuka College	NY	21,170	C
Maryville College	TN	25,960	VC
Univ of Rochester	NY	32,979	HC
Western Oregon Univ	OR	10,281	C

AMERICAN STUDIES

School	ST	$IS	SR
Albion College	MI	25,224	VC
Albright College	PA	30,579	C
American Univ	DC	34,585	VC+
Amherst College	MA	37,470	MC
Ashland Univ	OH	24,464	C
Austin College	TX	24,747	HC
Bard College	NY	37,352	HC+
Bates College	ME	37,500	MC
Baylor Univ	TX	23,864	VC
Boston Univ	MA	38,194	HC+
Bowling Green State Univ	OH	13,036	C
Brandeis Univ	MA	38,198	MC
Brigham Young Univ	UT	8,504	HC
Brown Univ	RI	38,174	MC
Cabrini College	PA	29,020	C
Cal State, Chico	CA	8,598	LC
Cal State, Fullerton	CA	6,648	C
Cal State, San Bernardino	CA	15,238	LC
Calvin College	MI	22,615	NC
Carleton College	MN	34,395	MC
Case Western Reserve Univ	OH	32,002	MC
Cedarville Univ	OH	19,954	VC
CUNY/Brooklyn College	NY	4,353	C+
CUNY/City College	NY	4,230	C+
CUNY/College of Staten Island	NY	4,308	NC
CUNY/Herbert H. Lehman College	NY	3,320	LC
CUNY/Queens College	NY	4,362	C
Claflin Univ	SC	14,838	C+
Claremont McKenna College	CA	36,880	MC
Coe College	IA	27,385	VC
Colby College	ME	37,570	MC
College of Our Lady of the Elms	MA	20,644	C
College of St. Elizabeth	NJ	25,460	C
College of St. Rose	NY	22,864	C
College of William and Mary	VA	12,224	MC
Columbia Univ/Barnard College	NY	36,990	MC
Columbia Univ/Columbia College	NY	38,590	MC
Conn College	CT	37,900	MC
Cornell Univ	NY	38,253	MC
Creighton Univ	NE	26,748	VC+
Cumberland Univ	TN	16,910	C
David Lipscomb Univ	TN	16,158	VC
DePaul Univ	IL	27,580	VC
Dickinson College	PA	35,825	HC
Dominican College	NY	24,810	LC
Dominican Univ	IL	23,610	C
Drew Univ/College of Liberal Arts	NJ	35,550	VC
Eastern Conn State Univ	CT	10,362	C
Eckerd College	FL	28,744	C+
Elmhurst College	IL	24,630	C
Elmira College	NY	33,820	VC
Erskine College	SC	23,166	VC
Fairfield Univ	CT	35,505	HC
Florida State Univ	FL	9,028	HC
Fordham Univ	NY	35,066	HC
Franklin and Marshall College	PA	35,930	HC+
Franklin College	IN		C
Franklin Pierce College	NH	28,980	LC
George Washington Univ	DC	41,030	MC
Georgetown College	KY	22,000	VC
Georgetown Univ	DC	38,242	MC
Goucher College	MD	32,650	HC
Hamilton College	NY	37,560	MC
Hampshire College	MA	37,037	HC
Harding Univ	AR	14,890	VC
Harvard Univ/Harvard College	MA	37,928	MC
High Point Univ	NC	22,480	C
Hillsdale College	MI	22,450	HC
Hobart and William Smith Colleges	NY	36,536	HC
Hofstra Univ	NY	27,112	VC
Huntingdon College	AL	18,400	VC
Idaho State Univ	ID	8,128	C
Illinois Wesleyan Univ	IL	30,380	HC+
Johns Hopkins Univ	MD	38,372	MC
Keene State College	NH	12,212	C
Kent State Univ	OH	12,932	C
King College	TN	22,500	VC
Knox College	IL	30,294	VC+
Lafayette College	PA	35,746	MC
Lake Forest College	IL	30,270	VC
Lebanon Valley College	PA	28,870	VC
Lehigh Univ	PA	37,570	HC+
Lenoir-Rhyne College	NC	19,186	C
Lindsey Wilson College	KY	16,392	LC
Macalester College	MN	31,944	MC
Manhattanville College	NY	32,420	C+
Marist College	NY	27,596	VC
Mary Washington College	VA	10,166	HC
Marymount College of Fordham Univ	NY	27,686	C
Mass Inst of Technology	MA	38,310	MC
Meredith College	NC	23,065	C
Miami Univ	OH	15,033	HC
Mich State Univ	MI	11,933	VC
Middlebury College	VT	38,100	MC
Millikin Univ	IL	25,555	C
Mills College	CA	33,371	VC
Minn State Univ, Moorehead	MN	7,000	LC
Miss College	MS	14,574	C
Montreat College	NC	18,762	C
Mount Holyoke College	MA	37,918	HC+
Mount St. Mary's College	CA	28,307	VC
Mount Union College	OH	21,120	C
Muhlenberg College	PA	31,485	HC
Muskingum College	OH	20,680	C
Nazareth College of Rochester	NY	24,936	VC
Northwestern Univ	IL	37,491	MC
Oberlin College	OH	36,938	MC
Occidental College	CA	35,922	HC
Oglethorpe Univ	GA	26,000	VC
Okla State Univ	OK	9,216	VC
Oregon State Univ	OR	11,055	C
Our Lady of the Lake Univ of San Antonio	TX	17,336	C
Penn State Univ/Univ Park Campus	PA	15,646	HC
Pfeiffer Univ	NC	18,980	C
Pitzer College	CA	37,590	HC
Pomona College	CA	33,960	MC
Providence College	RI	30,604	HC
Purdue Univ/West Lafayette	IN	12,560	VC
Queens Univ of Charlotte	NC	21,840	C
Ramapo College of New Jersey	NJ	15,203	VC
Randolph-Macon Woman's College	VA	28,430	VC+
Rider Univ	NJ	30,900	C
Roger Williams Univ	RI	30,296	C
Roosevelt Univ	IL	22,580	VC
Rutgers, The State Univ of New Jersey/New Brunswick/Piscataway Campus	NJ	15,800	HC
Rutgers, The State Univ of New Jersey/Newark Campus	NJ	15,624	VC
St. John Fisher College	NY	24,870	C
St. John's Univ	NY	30,180	C
St. Joseph College	CT	29,685	C
St. Louis Univ	MO	29,780	VC+
St. Michael's College	VT	30,100	VC
St. Olaf College	MN	28,500	HC
St. Peter's College	NJ	22,292	LC
St. Thomas Univ	FL	21,400	LC
Salem College	NC	24,595	VC
Salve Regina Univ	RI	29,210	C
San Diego State Univ	CA	10,321	C
San Francisco State Univ	CA	12,070	C
Scripps College	CA	35,700	HC+
Shenandoah Univ	VA	25,190	NC
Siena College	NY	25,310	VC
Siena Heights Univ	MI	16,140	LC
Simon's Rock College of Bard	MA	36,580	HC
Skidmore College	NY	37,930	HC
Smith College	MA	37,034	HC+
Southwestern Univ	TX	25,410	HC
Stanford Univ	CA	37,612	MC
SUNY at Oswego	NY	12,650	C
SUNY/College at Geneseo	NY	11,330	HC
SUNY/College at Old Westbury	NY	12,784	C
SUNY/Univ at Buffalo	NY	12,563	VC
SUNY/Univ at Stony Brook	NY	12,763	HC
Stetson Univ	FL	29,495	VC
Stonehill College	MA	30,752	HC
Syracuse Univ	NY	34,720	HC
Temple Univ	PA	15,912	C
Texas State Univ	TX	9,320	VC
Trinity College	CT	38,040	HC+
Tufts Univ	MA	38,233	MC
Tulane Univ	LA	37,451	HC+
Union College	NY	36,005	HC
Univ of Alabama	AL	9,040	C+
Univ of Arkansas	AR	9,855	VC
Univ of Calif at Berkeley	CA	15,563	MC

ST = STATE $IS = IN-STATE COSTS SR = SELECTOR RATING

School	ST	$IS	SR
National-Louis Univ	IL	16,240	LC
Nazareth College of Rochester	NY	24,936	VC
Nebr Wesleyan Univ	NE	21,197	C+
New College of Calif	CA	8,900	NC
New College of Florida	FL	8,906	HC+
New Mexico Highlands Univ	NM	6,182	LC
New Mexico State Univ	NM	7,932	C
New York Univ	NY	39,406	MC
North Central College	IL	25,656	VC
N Dak State Univ	ND	8,435	C
North Park Univ	IL	24,030	C
Northeastern Illinois Univ	IL	2,898	NC
Northeastern Univ	MA	35,650	HC
Northern Arizona Univ	AZ	9,002	C
Northern Illinois Univ	IL	11,472	C
Northern Kentucky Univ	KY	6,352	NC
Northwestern State Univ of Louisiana	LA	6,331	NC
Northwestern Univ	IL	37,491	MC
Oakland Univ	MI	10,800	C
Oberlin College	OH	36,938	MC
Occidental College	CA	35,922	HC
Ohio State Univ	OH	13,080	VC+
Ohio Univ	OH	14,448	C
Ohio Wesleyan Univ	OH	32,550	VC+
Old Dominion Univ	VA	10,441	C
Olivet College	MI	19,984	C+
Oregon State Univ	OR	11,055	C
Pacific Lutheran Univ	WA	25,715	VC
Penn State Univ/Univ Park Campus	PA	15,646	HC
Pitzer College	CA	37,590	HC
Plymouth State Univ	NH	12,298	LC
Pomona College	CA	33,960	MC
Portland State Univ	OR	12,453	C
Prescott College	AZ	13,430	C
Princeton Univ	NJ	36,649	MC
Purdue Univ/West Lafayette	IN	12,560	VC
Radford Univ	VA	8,500	C
Reed College	OR	36,950	MC
Rhode Island College	RI	11,565	C
Rhodes College	TN	26,466	HC+
Rice Univ	TX	27,550	MC
Richard Stockton College of New Jersey	NJ	12,972	VC
Ripon College	WI	24,995	VC
Rockford College	IL	28,310	VC
Rocky Mountain College	MT	19,015	C
Rollins College	FL	34,300	VC
Rutgers, The State Univ of New Jersey/New Brunswick/Piscataway Campus	NJ	15,800	HC
Rutgers, The State Univ of New Jersey/Newark Campus	NJ	15,624	VC
St. Cloud State Univ	MN	8,362	C
St. John Fisher College	NY	24,870	C
St. John's Univ	NY	30,180	C
St. Lawrence Univ	NY	35,945	VC
St. Mary's College of Calif	CA	32,850	VC
St. Mary's College of Maryland	MD	15,908	VC+
St. Michael's College	VT	30,100	VC
St. Vincent College	PA	25,530	VC
Salve Regina Univ	RI	29,210	C
San Diego State Univ	CA	10,321	C
San Francisco State Univ	CA	12,070	C
San Jose State Univ	CA	8,187	C
Santa Clara Univ	CA	34,701	HC
Sarah Lawrence College	NY	41,218	HC
Scripps College	CA	35,700	HC+
Seton Hall Univ	NJ	30,130	VC
Skidmore College	NY	37,930	HC
Slippery Rock Univ of Pennsylvania	PA	10,343	LC
Smith College	MA	37,034	HC+
Sonoma State Univ	CA	10,421	C
Southeast Missouri State Univ	MO	9,704	C
Southern Illinois Univ Carbondale	IL	10,407	C
Southern Illinois Univ Edwardsville	IL	8,724	C
Southern Methodist Univ	TX	34,210	HC
Southern Oregon Univ	OR	10,362	C
Southwest Missouri State Univ	MO	8,918	C
Spelman College	GA	19,215	C+
Stanford Univ	CA	37,612	MC
SUNY at Oswego	NY	12,650	C
SUNY at Potsdam	NY	12,160	C
SUNY/College at Brockport	NY	12,111	C
SUNY/College at Buffalo	NY	8,025	C
SUNY/College at Cortland	NY	12,095	C
SUNY/College at Geneseo	NY	11,330	HC
SUNY/College at Oneonta	NY	11,870	VC
SUNY/College at Plattsburgh	NY	11,700	C
SUNY/College at Purchase	NY	10,587	VC
SUNY/Univ at Albany	NY	12,951	HC
SUNY/Univ at Binghamton	NY	12,787	HC
SUNY/Univ at Buffalo	NY	12,563	VC
SUNY/Univ at New Paltz	NY	11,565	VC
SUNY/Univ at Stony Brook	NY	12,763	HC
State Univ of West Georgia	GA	7,622	C
Swarthmore College	PA	37,716	MC
Sweet Briar College	VA	27,940	C
Syracuse Univ	NY	34,720	HC
Temple Univ	PA	15,912	C
Texas A&M Univ	TX	11,081	HC
Texas A&M Univ at Commerce	TX	8,994	C
Texas A&M Univ at Kingsville	TX	6,740	LC
Texas State Univ	TX	9,320	VC
Texas Tech Univ	TX	10,768	VC
Thomas Edison State College	NJ	3,325	SP
Towson Univ	MD	12,694	VC
Transylvania Univ	KY	23,780	VC+
Trinity College	CT	38,040	HC+
Trinity Univ	TX	26,466	HC+
Tufts Univ	MA	38,233	MC
Tulane Univ	LA	37,451	HC+
Union College	NY	36,005	HC
Univ of Akron	OH	13,134	NC
Univ of Alabama	AL	9,040	C+
Univ of Alabama at Birmingham	AL	12,901	C
Univ of Alaska Anchorage	AK	9,100	NC
Univ of Alaska Fairbanks	AK	9,295	C
Univ of Arizona	AZ	10,413	VC
Univ of Arkansas	AR	9,855	VC
Univ of Calif at Berkeley	CA	15,563	MC
Univ of Calif at Davis	CA	14,995	VC
Univ of Calif at Irvine	CA	19,808	HC
Univ of Calif at Los Angeles	CA	15,330	MC
Univ of Calif at Riverside	CA	15,300	C
Univ of Calif at San Diego	CA	14,127	HC
Univ of Calif at Santa Barbara	CA	11,732	VC
Univ of Calif at Santa Cruz	CA	16,505	VC
Univ of Central Florida	FL	10,038	VC
Univ of Chicago	IL	35,087	MC
Univ of Cincinnati	OH	14,736	C
Univ of Colo at Boulder	CO	10,774	VC
Univ of Colo at Colo Springs	CO	10,667	C
Univ of Colo at Denver	CO	3,302	C
Univ of Conn	CT	14,608	VC
Univ of Delaware	DE	12,616	HC
Univ of Denver	CO	32,148	VC
Univ of Evansville	IN	24,190	VC
Univ of Florida	FL	8,580	MC
Univ of Georgia	GA	8,656	VC
Univ of Hawaii at Hilo	HI	6,497	C
Univ of Hawaii at Manoa	HI	9,565	VC
Univ of Houston	TX	9,818	C
Univ of Idaho	ID	8,216	C
Univ of Illinois at Chicago	IL	13,418	C
Univ of Illinois at Urbana-Champaign	IL	11,316	HC+
Univ of Indianapolis	IN	22,560	VC
Univ of Iowa	IA	10,923	VC
Univ of Kansas	KS	8,923	VC
Univ of Kentucky	KY	7,765	C
Univ of La Verne	CA	28,600	C
Univ of Louisiana at Lafayette	LA	5,826	C
Univ of Louisville	KY	8,762	VC
Univ of Maine	ME	12,080	C+
Univ of Maryland/Baltimore County	MD	14,668	VC+
Univ of Maryland/College Park	MD	14,227	HC
Univ of Mass Amherst	MA	13,980	C+
Univ of Mass Boston	MA	6,227	C
Univ of Mass Dartmouth	MA	12,835	C
Univ of Memphis	TN	8,560	C
Univ of Miami	FL	34,608	HC
Univ of Mich/Ann Arbor	MI	13,864	HC+
Univ of Mich/Dearborn	MI	6,843	VC
Univ of Mich/Flint	MI	5,548	C
Univ of Minn/Duluth	MN	12,470	C
Univ of Minn/Morris	MN	12,896	VC
Univ of Minn/Twin Cities	MN	13,160	VC
Univ of Miss	MS	7,666	C
Univ of Missouri/Columbia	MO	13,782	VC
Univ of Missouri/St. Louis	MO	11,656	VC
Univ of Montana	MT	9,395	C
Univ of Nebr at Lincoln	NE	9,975	C+
Univ of Nevada/Las Vegas	NV	11,566	C
Univ of Nevada/Reno	NV	9,792	C
Univ of New Hampshire	NH	14,828	VC
Univ of New Mexico	NM	9,223	C
Univ of New Orleans	LA	7,356	C
Univ of N Car at Chapel Hill	NC	10,117	MC
Univ of N Car at Charlotte	NC	8,185	C
Univ of N Car at Greensboro	NC	8,248	C
Univ of N Car at Wilmington	NC	8,940	VC
Univ of N Dak	ND	8,390	C
Univ of North Florida	FL	8,769	VC
Univ of North Texas	TX	7,629	C
Univ of Northern Iowa	IA	9,834	C
Univ of Notre Dame	IN	34,442	MC
Univ of Okla	OK	9,226	VC
Univ of Oregon	OR	11,479	VC
Univ of Pennsylvania	PA	37,960	MC
Univ of Pittsburgh at Greensburg	PA	15,984	C
Univ of Pittsburgh at Pittsburgh	PA	16,074	HC
Univ of PR/Rio Piedras	PR	5,730	
Univ of Redlands	CA	32,576	VC
Univ of Rhode Island	RI	13,720	VC
Univ of Rochester	NY	32,979	HC
Univ of San Diego	CA	33,156	HC
Univ of South Alabama	AL	7,760	LC
Univ of S Car at Columbia	SC	10,048	VC
Univ of S Dak	SD	7,710	C+
Univ of South Florida	FL	9,454	C
Univ of Southern Calif	CA	37,459	MC
Univ of Southern Maine	ME	11,212	C
Univ of Southern Miss	MS	8,324	LC
Univ of Tenn at Knoxville	TN	8,214	C
Univ of Texas at Arlington	TX	7,192	LC
Univ of Texas at Austin	TX	10,630	HC
Univ of Texas at El Paso	TX	5,799	NC
Univ of Texas at San Antonio	TX	9,088	NC
Univ of Texas-Pan American	TX	5,954	LC
Univ of the South	TN	30,855	HC
Univ of Toledo	OH	12,479	NC
Univ of Tulsa	OK	22,090	VC+
Univ of Utah	UT	9,205	C
Univ of Vermont	VT	16,316	VC
Univ of Virginia	VA	11,740	MC
Univ of Washington	WA	10,361	VC
Univ of Wisc/Madison	WI	8,262	VC
Univ of Wisc/Milwaukee	WI	9,427	LC
Univ of Wisc/Oshkosh	WI	6,130	LC
Univ of Wyoming	WY	8,636	C
Ursinus College	PA	34,400	VC
Valdosta State Univ	GA	7,798	C
Vanderbilt Univ	TN	37,897	MC
Vanguard Univ of Southern Calif	CA	22,208	C
Vassar College	NY	37,030	MC
Wagner College	NY	29,900	VC
Wake Forest Univ	NC	34,090	MC
Warren Wilson College	NC	21,794	VC
Washburn Univ of Topeka	KS	8,984	NC
Washington College	MD	30,540	VC
Washington State Univ	WA	11,334	C
Washington Univ in St. Louis	MO	38,293	MC
Wayne State Univ	MI	11,774	C
Webster Univ	MO	21,848	VC
Wellesley College	MA	36,516	MC
Wells College	NY	21,122	VC
Wesleyan Univ	CT	35,139	MC
West Chester Univ of Pennsylvania	PA	11,164	C
West Virginia Univ	WV	9,370	C
Western Carolina Univ	NC	6,742	C
Western Conn State Univ	CT	11,625	C
Western Kentucky Univ	KY	6,834	C
Western Mich Univ	MI	12,031	C
Western Oregon Univ	OR	10,281	C
Western State College of Colo	CO	9,014	C
Western Washington Univ	WA	10,119	VC
Westminster College	MO	18,150	C+
Wheaton College	IL	21,934	HC
Wheaton College	MA	36,330	HC
Whitman College	WA	32,526	HC+
Wichita State Univ	KS	8,092	C
Widener Univ	PA	27,020	C
Willamette Univ	OR	32,032	VC+
William Paterson Univ of New Jersey	NJ	14,450	C
Williams College	MA	32,270	MC
Wright State Univ	OH	11,490	LC
Yale Univ	CT	37,000	MC
Youngstown State Univ	OH	11,148	NC

APPAREL AND ACCESSORIES MARKETING

School	ST	$IS	SR
Bluffton College	OH	23,694	C
Bowling Green State Univ	OH	13,036	C
Calif State Polytechnic Univ, Pomona	CA	8,793	C+
Colo State Univ	CO	9,964	VC
Fashion Inst of Technology/SUNY	NY	11,169	C+
Indiana Univ Bloomington	IN	12,389	VC
Kansas State Univ	KS	8,728	VC
Kentucky State Univ	KY	9,062	NC
Northwood Univ	TX	20,135	LC
S Dak State Univ	SD	7,782	C
Univ of Arkansas	AR	9,855	VC
Youngstown State Univ	OH	11,148	NC

APPAREL DESIGN

School	ST	$IS	SR
Art Inst of Portland	OR	23,040	SP
Boston Univ	MA	38,194	HC+
Concordia College: Moorhead	MN	22,460	VC+
Florida State Univ	FL	9,028	HC
Gallaudet Univ	DC	16,554	SP
Kansas State Univ	KS	8,728	VC
Oregon State Univ	OR	11,055	C
Purdue Univ/West Lafayette	IN	12,560	VC
Rhode Island School of Design	RI	33,569	SP
Univ of Hawaii at Manoa	HI	9,565	VC
Univ of Wisc/Stout	WI	9,718	C

APPLIED ART

School	ST	$IS	SR
Calif Baptist Univ	CA	19,924	C
Centenary College	NJ	25,370	LC
Cleveland Inst of Art	OH	30,371	SP
Daemen College	NY	22,120	C
Edinboro Univ of Pennsylvania	PA	10,850	LC
Minn State Univ, Mankato	MN	8,803	LC
Oral Roberts Univ	OK	18,490	C
Point Park Univ	PA	21,840	C
Rochester Inst of Technology	NY	29,217	VC+
Tabor College	KS	19,500	NC
Texas State Univ	TX	9,320	VC
Univ of North Texas	TX	7,629	C
West Texas A&M Univ	TX	7,533	C

APPLIED MATHEMATICS

School	ST	$IS	SR
American Univ	DC	34,585	VC+
Andrews Univ	MI	19,550	C
Asbury College	KY	20,704	VC
Auburn Univ	AL	10,396	VC
Baylor Univ	TX	23,864	VC
Biola Univ	CA	25,964	VC
Bloomfield College	NJ	19,250	LC
Brown Univ	RI	38,174	MC
Cal State, Long Beach	CA	8,762	C+
Carroll College	WI	22,740	C
Case Western Reserve Univ	OH	32,002	MC
Clarkson Univ	NY	32,226	VC
Colby College	ME	37,570	MC
Columbia Univ/Fu Foundation School of Engineering and Applied Science	NY	38,590	MC
Columbia Univ/School of General Studies	NY	35,000	C
Dowling College	NY	23,870	LC
East Central Univ	OK	4,968	C
Eastern Mich Univ	MI	11,478	C
Ferris State Univ	MI	12,512	C
Florida Inst of Technology	FL	28,740	VC
Florida International Univ	FL	9,912	VC
Florida State Univ	FL	9,028	HC
Geneva College	PA	21,850	C
George Washington Univ	DC	41,030	MC
Georgia Inst of Technology	GA	10,340	HC+
Grand View College	IA	19,748	LC
Hampden-Sydney College	VA	28,407	VC
Harvard Univ/Harvard College	MA	37,928	MC
Hawaii Pacific Univ	HI	19,218	C
Hofstra Univ	NY	27,112	VC
Illinois Inst of Technology	IL	26,456	HC+
Indiana Univ of Pennsylvania	PA	10,489	C
Indiana Univ South Bend	IN	4,571	LC
Johns Hopkins Univ	MD	38,372	MC
Johnson C. Smith Univ	NC	18,187	LC
Kent State Univ	OH	12,932	C
Kentucky State Univ	KY	9,062	NC
Kettering Univ	MI	26,478	HC
King College	TN	22,500	VC
Le Moyne College	NY	26,400	VC
Mary Baldwin College	VA	24,939	C
Metropolitan State Univ	MN	3,852	SP
Montclair State Univ	NJ	13,790	C
New Jersey Inst of Technology	NJ	16,396	VC
North Central College	IL	25,656	VC
Northwestern Univ	IL	37,491	MC
Ohio Univ	OH	14,448	C
Pacific Union College	CA	22,065	C+
Purdue Univ/West Lafayette	IN	12,560	VC
Rice Univ	TX	27,550	MC
Rochester Inst of Technology	NY	29,217	VC+
Rutgers, The State Univ of New Jersey/Newark Campus	NJ	15,624	VC
St. Augustine's College	NC	12,990	LC
San Francisco State Univ	CA	12,070	C
Simon's Rock College of Bard	MA	36,580	HC
SUNY at Oswego	NY	12,650	C
SUNY/Univ at Albany	NY	12,951	HC
SUNY/Univ at Stony Brook	NY	12,763	HC
Univ of Arkansas at Pine Bluff	AR	7,925	C
Univ of Calif at Berkeley	CA	15,563	MC
Univ of Calif at Los Angeles	CA	15,330	MC
Univ of Calif at San Diego	CA	14,127	HC
Univ of Colo at Boulder	CO	10,774	VC
Univ of Colo at Denver	CO	3,302	C
Univ of Houston-Downtown	TX	2,594	NC

ST = STATE $IS = IN-STATE COSTS SR = SELECTOR RATING

School	ST	$IS	SR
Univ of Idaho	ID	8,216	C
Univ of Mass Boston	MA	6,227	C
Univ of Mass Lowell	MA	11,937	VC
Univ of Miami	FL	34,608	HC
Univ of Mich/Ann Arbor	MI	13,864	HC+
Univ of Missouri/Rolla	MO	12,292	HC
Univ of Missouri/St. Louis	MO	11,656	VC
Univ of New Haven	CT	28,650	C
Univ of Pittsburgh at Greensburg	PA	15,984	C
Univ of PR/Rio Piedras	PR	5,730	
Univ of Rochester	NY	32,979	HC
Univ of S Car at Aiken	SC	7,828	LC
Univ of Tenn at Chattanooga	TN	7,783	C
Univ of Texas at Dallas	TX	10,234	HC
Univ of Texas at El Paso	TX	5,799	NC
Univ of the Pacific	CA	31,090	VC
Univ of Virginia	VA	11,740	MC
Univ of Wisc/Madison	WI	8,262	VC
Univ of Wisc/Milwaukee	WI	9,427	LC
Univ of Wisc/Stout	WI	9,718	C
Valdosta State Univ	GA	7,798	C
Washington Univ in St. Louis	MO	38,293	MC
West Virginia State College	WV	6,264	NC
Wingate Univ	NC	21,200	C
Yale Univ	CT	37,000	MC

APPLIED MUSIC

School	ST	$IS	SR
Baylor Univ	TX	23,864	VC
Concordia College	NY	19,200	VC
Covenant College	GA	23,830	VC+
Dallas Baptist Univ	TX	15,300	VC
DePaul Univ	IL	27,580	VC
Eastern Mich Univ	MI	11,478	C
Geneva College	PA	21,850	C
Grand Canyon Univ	AZ	30,000	LC
Hardin-Simmons Univ	TX	14,165	C
Inter American Univ of PR/ Fajardo Campus	PR	4,000	
Inter American Univ of PR/ Ponce Regional College	PR	3,700	
Judson College	AL	14,650	C
Kansas State Univ	KS	8,728	VC
Lenoir-Rhyne College	NC	19,186	C
Meredith College	NC	23,065	C
Miss College	MS	14,574	C
Nebr Wesleyan Univ	NE	21,197	C+
New England Conservatory of Music	MA	35,000	SP
Newberry College	SC	22,871	LC
Sul Ross State Univ	TX	6,582	LC
Trinity Christian College	IL	21,640	VC
Univ of Houston	TX	9,818	C
Univ of Idaho	ID	8,216	C
Univ of Memphis	TN	8,560	C
Univ of Mich/Ann Arbor	MI	13,864	HC+
Univ of Nevada/Reno	NV	9,792	C
Univ of Texas at Austin	TX	10,630	HC
Viterbo Univ	WI	20,430	C
Wartburg College	IA	21,165	VC

APPLIED PHYSICS

School	ST	$IS	SR
Angelo State Univ	TX	7,576	NC
Armstrong Atlantic State Univ	GA	7,102	C
Beloit College	WI	29,864	HC
Bethel College	IN	19,670	C
Bridgewater College	VA	25,150	C
Cal State, San Bernardino	CA	15,238	LC
Cal State, Stanislaus	CA	9,874	C
Columbia Univ/Fu Foundation School of Engineering and Applied Science	NY	38,590	MC
East Carolina Univ	NC	8,671	C
Goucher College	MD	32,650	HC
Hiram College	OH	28,234	VC
Hofstra Univ	NY	27,112	VC
Indiana Univ of Pennsylvania	PA	10,489	C
Kettering Univ	MI	26,478	HC
Linfield College	OR	27,090	VC
New Jersey Inst of Technology	NJ	16,396	VC
Northeastern Univ	MA	35,650	HC
Pacific Lutheran Univ	WA	25,715	VC
Providence College	RI	30,604	HC
Purdue Univ/West Lafayette	IN	12,560	VC
Rutgers, The State Univ of New Jersey/Newark Campus	NJ	15,624	VC
Saginaw Valley State Univ	MI	11,055	C
Shippensburg Univ of Pennsylvania	PA	10,826	C
SUNY/College at Geneseo	NY	11,330	HC
Texas Tech Univ	TX	10,768	VC
Tufts Univ	MA	38,233	MC
Univ of Alaska Fairbanks	AK	9,295	C
Univ of Calif at Los Angeles	CA	15,330	MC
Univ of Calif at San Diego	CA	14,127	HC
Univ of Nevada/Las Vegas	NV	11,566	C
Univ of N Dak	ND	8,390	C
Univ of Notre Dame	IN	34,442	MC
Whitworth College	WA	26,428	VC+
Xavier Univ	OH	26,850	VC+

APPLIED PSYCHOLOGY

School	ST	$IS	SR
Christian Brothers Univ	TN	22,290	VC
College of Santa Fe	NM	25,293	C+
Indiana Univ South Bend	IN	4,571	LC
New York Univ	NY	39,406	MC
Russell Sage College	NY	26,811	C
Univ of St. Mary	KS	18,868	C

APPLIED SCIENCE

School	ST	$IS	SR
Univ of Arizona	AZ	10,413	VC
Univ of N Car at Chapel Hill	NC	10,117	MC
Univ of Wisc/Stout	WI	9,718	C

ARABIC

School	ST	$IS	SR
Brigham Young Univ	UT	8,504	HC
Dartmouth College	NH	37,770	MC
Georgetown Univ	DC	38,242	MC
Middlebury College	VT	38,100	MC
Ohio State Univ	OH	13,080	VC+
SUNY/Univ at Binghamton	NY	12,787	HC
Univ of Calif at Los Angeles	CA	15,330	MC
Univ of Mich/Ann Arbor	MI	13,864	HC+
Univ of Texas at Austin	TX	10,630	HC
Washington Univ in St. Louis	MO	38,293	MC
Wayne State Univ	MI	11,774	C

ARCHEOLOGY

School	ST	$IS	SR
Bard College	NY	37,352	HC+
Baylor Univ	TX	23,864	VC
Boston Univ	MA	38,194	HC+
Bowdoin College	ME	37,790	MC
Brown Univ	RI	38,174	MC
Bryn Mawr College	PA	36,890	HC+
Cal State, Stanislaus	CA	9,874	C
CUNY/Brooklyn College	NY	4,353	C+
CUNY/Hunter College	NY	6,729	C+
College of Wooster	OH	31,300	HC
Columbia Univ/Columbia College	NY	38,590	MC
Columbia Univ/School of General Studies	NY	35,000	C
Cornell Univ	NY	38,253	MC
Dickinson College	PA	35,825	HC
George Washington Univ	DC	41,030	MC
Hamilton College	NY	37,560	MC
Haverford College	PA	37,900	MC
Mass Inst of Technology	MA	38,310	MC
Mercyhurst College	PA	20,694	C
Oberlin College	OH	36,938	MC
Princeton Univ	NJ	36,649	MC
Stanford Univ	CA	37,612	MC
SUNY at Potsdam	NY	12,160	C
Texas A&M Univ at Galveston	TX	9,948	C+
Tufts Univ	MA	38,233	MC
Univ of Evansville	IN	24,190	VC
Univ of Indianapolis	IN	22,560	VC
Univ of Kansas	KS	8,923	VC
Univ of Mich/Ann Arbor	MI	13,864	HC+
Univ of Missouri/Columbia	MO	13,782	VC
Univ of Texas at Austin	TX	10,630	HC
Univ of Wisc/La Crosse	WI	8,991	VC
Washington and Lee Univ	VA	29,663	MC
Washington Univ in St. Louis	MO	38,293	MC
Wellesley College	MA	36,516	MC
Wesleyan Univ	CT	35,139	MC
Wheaton College	IL	21,934	HC
Yale Univ	CT	37,000	MC

ARCHITECTURAL ENGINEERING

School	ST	$IS	SR
Calif Polytechnic State Univ	CA	8,747	VC
Drexel Univ	PA	27,655	VC
Illinois Inst of Technology	IL	26,456	HC+
Kansas State Univ	KS	8,728	VC
Milwaukee School of Engineering	WI	28,479	VC+
N Car Agricultural and Technical State Univ	NC	6,659	LC
Okla State Univ	OK	9,216	VC
Parsons School of Design	NY	32,242	SP
Penn State Univ/Univ Park Campus	PA	15,646	HC
Princeton Univ	NJ	36,649	MC
Purdue Univ/West Lafayette	IN	12,560	VC
Rice Univ	TX	27,550	MC
Tenn State Univ	TN	9,048	LC
Univ of Cincinnati	OH	14,736	C
Univ of Colo at Boulder	CO	10,774	VC
Univ of Hartford	CT	31,080	C
Univ of Houston	TX	9,818	C
Univ of Idaho	ID	8,216	C
Univ of Kansas	KS	8,923	VC
Univ of Miami	FL	34,608	HC
Univ of Missouri/Rolla	MO	12,292	HC
Univ of Nebr at Lincoln	NE	9,975	C+
Univ of Nevada/Las Vegas	NV	11,566	C
Univ of Texas at Austin	TX	10,630	HC
Univ of Wyoming	WY	8,636	C
Vermont Technical College	VT	13,684	C

ARCHITECTURAL TECHNOLOGY

School	ST	$IS	SR
Brown Univ	RI	38,174	MC
Fairmont State	WV	8,280	LC
Florida International Univ	FL	9,912	VC
SUNY/College of Technology at Alfred	NY	12,416	C
SUNY/Univ at Buffalo	NY	12,563	VC
Univ of Cincinnati	OH	14,736	C
Univ of Memphis	TN	8,560	C
Univ of Southern Miss	MS	8,324	LC
Washington Univ in St. Louis	MO	38,293	MC
Wentworth Inst of Technology	MA	23,000	C

ARCHITECTURE

School	ST	$IS	SR
Andrews Univ	MI	19,550	C
Arizona State Univ-Main	AZ	10,048	C
Auburn Univ	AL	10,396	VC
Ball State Univ	IN	8,660	C
Baylor Univ	TX	23,864	VC
Bennington College	VT	35,910	HC
Boston Architectural Center	MA	6,405	SP
Brown Univ	RI	38,174	MC
Calif College of the Arts	CA	31,530	SP
Calif Polytechnic State Univ	CA	8,747	VC
Calif State Polytechnic Univ, Pomona	CA	8,793	C+
Catholic Univ of America	DC	34,248	VC
CUNY/City College	NY	4,230	C+
Columbia Univ/Barnard College	NY	36,990	MC
Columbia Univ/Columbia College	NY	38,590	MC
Columbia Univ/School of General Studies	NY	35,000	C
Conn College	CT	37,900	MC
Cooper Union for the Advancement of Science and Art	NY	10,400	MC
Cornell Univ	NY	38,253	MC
Drexel Univ	PA	27,655	VC
Drury Univ	MO	18,085	VC+
Florida Atlantic Univ	FL	8,543	C
Georgia Inst of Technology	GA	10,340	HC+
Hampshire College	MA	37,037	HC
Hampton Univ	VA	17,112	C+
Hobart and William Smith Colleges	NY	36,536	HC
Howard Univ	DC	16,505	C
Illinois Inst of Technology	IL	26,456	HC+
Iowa State Univ	IA	10,768	VC
Kansas State Univ	KS	8,728	VC
Kent State Univ	OH	12,932	C
Lawrence Tech Univ	MI	20,487	C
Lehigh Univ	PA	37,570	HC+
Louisiana State Univ and A&M College	LA	9,126	VC
Louisiana Tech Univ	LA	7,361	C
Mass College of Art	MA	15,568	SP
Miami Univ	OH	15,033	HC
Miss State Univ	MS	9,139	C
New Jersey Inst of Technology	NJ	16,396	VC
New York Inst of Technology	NY	24,205	VC
N Car State Univ	NC	9,886	VC
N Dak State Univ	ND	8,435	C
Northeastern Univ	MA	35,650	HC
Norwich Univ	VT	21,064	LC
Ohio State Univ	OH	13,080	VC+
Okla State Univ	OK	9,216	VC
Penn State Univ/Univ Park Campus	PA	15,646	HC
Philadelphia Univ	PA	27,354	C
Portland State Univ	OR	12,453	C
Prairie View A&M Univ	TX	9,418	NC
Pratt Inst	NY	34,350	SP
Princeton Univ	NJ	36,649	MC
Rensselaer Polytechnic Inst	NY	37,579	HC+
Rhode Island School of Design	RI	33,569	SP
Rice Univ	TX	27,550	MC
Roger Williams Univ	RI	30,296	C
Savannah College of Art and Design	GA	27,560	SP
Smith College	MA	37,034	HC+
Southern Illinois Univ Carbondale	IL	10,407	C
Southern Polytechnic State Univ	GA	7,620	VC
Southern Univ and A&M College	LA	7,372	LC
SUNY/Univ at Buffalo	NY	12,563	VC
Syracuse Univ	NY	34,720	HC
Temple Univ	PA	15,912	C
Texas Tech Univ	TX	10,768	VC
Thomas Edison State College	NJ	3,325	SP
Tufts Univ	MA	38,233	MC
Tulane Univ	LA	37,451	HC+
Univ of Arizona	AZ	10,413	VC
Univ of Arkansas	AR	9,855	VC
Univ of Calif at Berkeley	CA	15,563	MC
Univ of Detroit Mercy	MI	25,582	C
Univ of Florida	FL	8,580	MC
Univ of Hawaii at Manoa	HI	9,565	VC
Univ of Houston	TX	9,818	C
Univ of Illinois at Chicago	IL	13,418	C
Univ of Illinois at Urbana-Champaign	IL	11,316	HC+
Univ of Kansas	KS	8,923	VC
Univ of Maryland/College Park	MD	14,227	HC
Univ of Memphis	TN	8,560	C
Univ of Miami	FL	34,608	HC
Univ of Mich/Ann Arbor	MI	13,864	HC+
Univ of Minn/Twin Cities	MN	13,160	VC
Univ of Nebr at Lincoln	NE	9,975	C+
Univ of New Mexico	NM	9,223	C
Univ of N Car at Charlotte	NC	8,185	C
Univ of Notre Dame	IN	34,442	MC
Univ of Okla	OK	9,226	VC
Univ of Oregon	OR	11,479	VC
Univ of Pennsylvania	PA	37,960	MC
Univ of San Francisco	CA	34,700	VC
Univ of Southern Calif	CA	37,459	MC
Univ of Tenn at Knoxville	TN	8,214	C
Univ of Texas at Arlington	TX	7,192	LC
Univ of Texas at Austin	TX	10,630	HC
Univ of Texas at San Antonio	TX	9,088	NC
Univ of the District of Columbia	DC	2,070	LC
Univ of Utah	UT	9,205	C
Univ of Virginia	VA	11,740	MC
Univ of Wisc/Milwaukee	WI	9,427	LC
Virginia Polytechnic Inst and State Univ	VA	9,179	C
Washington State Univ	WA	11,334	C
Washington Univ in St. Louis	MO	38,293	MC
Wellesley College	MA	36,516	MC
Wentworth Inst of Technology	MA	23,000	C
Woodbury Univ	CA	25,344	LC
Yale Univ	CT	37,000	MC

AREA STUDIES

School	ST	$IS	SR
American Univ	DC	34,585	VC+
Bard College	NY	37,352	HC+
CUNY/City College	NY	4,230	C+
College of Wooster	OH	31,300	HC
Columbia Univ/Columbia College	NY	38,590	MC
Duke Univ	NC	37,555	MC
Eastern Mich Univ	MI	11,478	C
Lake Forest College	IL	30,270	VC
Univ of Alaska Fairbanks	AK	9,295	C
Univ of Miss	MS	7,666	C
Univ of Okla	OK	9,226	VC
Univ of Virginia	VA	11,740	MC
Washington State Univ	WA	11,334	C
Washington Univ in St. Louis	MO	38,293	MC

ART

School	ST	$IS	SR
Abilene Christian Univ	TX	18,370	VC
Adams State College	CO	7,468	C
Adrian College	MI	21,950	C
Alabama A&M Univ	AL	5,100	LC
Albany State Univ	GA	5,764	C+
Albertson College of Idaho	ID	19,415	VC
Albion College	MI	25,224	VC
Albright College	PA	30,579	C
Allegheny College	PA	30,280	VC
Alma College	MI	25,566	VC
Alverno College	WI	18,898	C
Andrews Univ	MI	19,550	C
Angelo State Univ	TX	7,576	NC
Anna Maria College	MA	26,140	LC
Appalachian State Univ	NC	7,637	VC
Aquinas College	MI	21,894	C
Arizona State Univ-Main	AZ	10,048	C
Arkansas Tech Univ	AR	7,299	C
Armstrong Atlantic State Univ	GA	7,102	C
Asbury College	KY	20,704	VC
Ashland Univ	OH	24,464	C
Atlantic Union College	MA	18,868	C
Augusta State Univ	GA	2,592	C
Augustana College	IL	26,610	VC+
Augustana College	SD	21,998	VC
Austin College	TX	24,747	HC
Austin Peay State Univ	TN	5,814	LC
Averett Univ	VA	23,010	LC
Avila Univ	MO	20,300	C
Ball State Univ	IN	8,660	C
Barry Univ	FL	24,100	LC

ST = STATE $IS = IN-STATE COSTS SR = SELECTOR RATING

School	ST	$IS	SR
Bates College	ME	37,500	MC
Baylor Univ	TX	23,864	VC
Belhaven College	MS	16,040	C+
Bellarmine Univ	KY	24,110	VC
Bennington College	VT	35,910	HC
Berea College	KY	5,030	VC+
Berry College	GA	21,410	VC
Bethany College	KS	18,675	LC
Bethel College	IN	19,670	C
Bethel College	KS	19,800	C+
Biola Univ	CA	25,964	VC
Black Hills State Univ	SD	7,743	LC
Blackburn College	IL	13,690	C
Bluffton College	OH	23,694	C
Boise State Univ	ID	7,657	LC
Bowling Green State Univ	OH	13,036	C
Brescia Univ	KY	14,225	C
Briar Cliff Univ	IA	21,660	C
Bridgewater College	VA	25,150	C
Bridgewater State College	MA	10,482	C
Brigham Young Univ	UT	8,504	HC
Brigham Young Univ/Hawaii	HI	7,240	VC+
Brown Univ	RI	38,174	MC
Bucknell Univ	PA	35,262	HC+
Buena Vista Univ	IA	25,406	C
Caldwell College	NJ	24,060	LC
Calif Lutheran Univ	CA	27,600	LC
Calif State Polytechnic Univ, Pomona	CA	8,793	C+
Cal State, Bakersfield	CA	6,090	LC
Cal State, Chico	CA	8,598	LC
Cal State, Dominguez Hills	CA	5,840	LC
Cal State, Fresno	CA	8,414	LC
Cal State, Hayward	CA	8,871	LC
Cal State, Long Beach	CA	8,762	C+
Cal State, Northridge	CA	7,757	LC
Cal State, San Bernardino	CA	15,238	LC
Cal State, Stanislaus	CA	9,874	C
Calif Univ of Pennsylvania	PA	10,388	C
Cameron Univ	OK	5,692	NC
Campbell Univ	NC	18,268	VC
Campbellsville Univ	KY	17,680	C
Cardinal Stritch Univ	WI	17,620	C
Carlow College	PA	21,334	C
Carroll College	WI	22,740	C
Carthage College	WI	25,000	C
Castleton State College	VT	11,820	C
Catholic Univ of America	DC	34,248	VC
Cedar Crest College	PA	25,145	C+
Centenary College of Louisiana	LA	23,100	VC+
Central Conn State Univ	CT	12,090	C
Central Washington Univ	WA	9,768	C
Chadron State College	NE	6,286	NC
Chapman Univ	CA	33,118	VC
Chicago State Univ	IL	10,882	C+
CUNY/Brooklyn College	NY	4,353	C+
CUNY/City College	NY	4,230	C+
CUNY/College of Staten Island	NY	4,308	NC
CUNY/Queens College	NY	4,362	C
Claflin Univ	SC	14,838	C+
Clarion Univ of Pennsylvania	PA	11,272	LC
Clark Atlanta Univ	GA	19,300	C+
Clarke College	IA	23,165	C
Cleveland State Univ	OH	12,308	LC
Coe College	IA	27,385	VC
Coker College	SC	21,491	C
Colby College	ME	37,570	MC
Colby-Sawyer College	NH	27,850	LC
College of Mount St. Joseph	OH	22,785	C
College of St. Benedict	MN	26,672	VC
College of St. Catherine	MN	24,010	VC
College of St. Elizabeth	NJ	25,460	C
College of St. Mary	NE	21,510	C
College of the Ozarks	MO	3,500	VC+
Colo Christian Univ	CO	21,182	VC
Colo State Univ	CO	9,964	VC
Columbia College	MO	16,139	C
Columbia College Chicago	IL	25,108	LC
Columbus State Univ	GA	7,846	C
Concordia Univ	CA	24,420	C
Concordia Univ	MI	24,095	C
Concordia Univ Wisc	WI	16,600	C
Concordia Univ, River Forest	IL	23,600	C
Concordia Univ/St.Paul	MN	24,486	C
Conn College	CT	37,900	MC
Creighton Univ	NE	26,748	VC+
Culver-Stockton College	MO	17,850	C
Cumberland College	KY	16,384	C
Daemen College	NY	22,120	C
Dakota Wesleyan Univ	SD	17,832	C
Dana College	NE	20,280	C
Davidson College	NC	33,274	MC
Davis and Elkins College	WV	20,594	C
Defiance College	OH	22,615	C
Delta State Univ	MS	6,618	C
DePaul Univ	IL	27,580	VC
Dillard Univ	LA	17,325	VC
Doane College	NE	20,000	C
Dominican Univ	IL	23,610	C
Dominican Univ of Calif	CA	31,670	C
Drew Univ/College of Liberal Arts	NJ	35,550	VC
Earlham College	IN	29,976	VC+
East Carolina Univ	NC	8,671	C
East Central Univ	OK	4,968	C
East Stroudsburg Univ of Pennsylvania	PA	10,336	C
East Tenn State Univ	TN	8,497	C
Eastern Illinois Univ	IL	11,192	C
Eastern Kentucky Univ	KY	7,708	C
Eastern Mennonite Univ	VA	22,990	C
Eastern Mich Univ	MI	11,478	C
Eastern New Mexico Univ	NM	6,762	LC
Eastern Oregon Univ	OR	10,080	NC
Eastern Washington Univ	WA	9,012	C
Edgewood College	WI	20,520	C
Edinboro Univ of Pennsylvania	PA	10,850	LC
Elizabeth City State Univ	NC	5,550	LC
Elizabethtown College	PA	28,800	C
Elmhurst College	IL	24,630	C
Elmira College	NY	33,820	VC
Elon Univ	NC	22,240	VC
Emory & Henry College	VA	21,950	C
Emporia State Univ	KS	6,998	C
Erskine College	SC	23,166	VC
Evangel Univ	MO	15,435	C
Felician College	NJ	24,300	C
Ferrum College	VA	21,240	LC
Flagler College	FL	11,860	VC+
Florida Atlantic Univ	FL	8,543	C
Florida International Univ	FL	9,912	VC
Fontbonne Univ	MO	21,508	C
Fort Hays State Univ	KS	7,363	C
Fort Lewis College	CO	8,353	C
Freed-Hardeman Univ	TN		NC
Friends Univ	KS	15,962	LC
Furman Univ	SC	28,976	HC+
Gardner-Webb Univ	NC	19,300	C
George Fox Univ	OR	26,110	VC
Georgetown College	KY	22,000	VC
Georgia College and State Univ	GA	9,878	C
Georgia Southern Univ	GA	8,540	C
Georgia State Univ	GA	10,658	C
Georgian Court College	NJ	19,040	LC
Gonzaga Univ	WA	26,766	HC
Gordon College	MA	25,982	VC+
Grace College	IN	19,825	VC
Grambling State Univ	LA	6,538	NC
Green Mountain College	VT	24,130	C
Greensboro College	NC	21,750	C
Greenville College	IL	21,342	C
Grinnell College	IA	31,060	HC+
Guilford College	NC	24,960	VC
Hamilton College	NY	37,560	MC
Hamline Univ	MN	27,052	VC
Hampton Univ	VA	17,112	C+
Hannibal-LaGrange College	MO	13,940	C
Hanover College	IN	25,200	VC
Harding Univ	AR	14,890	VC
Hartwick College	NY	34,650	C+
Hendrix College	AR	20,970	VC+
High Point Univ	NC	22,480	C
Hiram College	OH	28,234	VC
Holy Family College	PA	13,710	LC
Hood College	MD	27,795	VC
Houghton College	NY	23,984	VC
Howard Payne Univ	TX	15,176	C
Humboldt State Univ	CA	9,400	C
Huntingdon College	AL	18,400	VC
Huntington College	IN	23,590	C
Idaho State Univ	ID	8,128	C
Illinois State Univ	IL	10,944	C+
Indiana Univ of Pennsylvania	PA	10,489	C
Indiana Wesleyan Univ	IN	19,900	C+
Ithaca College	NY	31,730	HC
Jackson State Univ	MS	8,382	C
James Madison Univ	VA	10,794	VC
John Brown Univ	AR	15,080	VC
Johnson State College	VT	11,819	LC
Judson College	AL	14,650	C
Kalamazoo College	MI	26,955	HC+
Kansas State Univ	KS	8,728	VC
Keene State College	NH	12,212	C
Kennesaw State Univ	GA	2,724	C
Kentucky State Univ	KY	9,062	NC
Kentucky Wesleyan College	KY	17,250	C
La Sierra Univ	CA	19,260	LC
Lafayette College	PA	35,746	MC
LaGrange College	GA	20,500	C
Lake Forest College	IL	30,270	VC
Lakeland College	WI	17,950	C
Lebanon Valley College	PA	28,870	VC
Lehigh Univ	PA	37,570	HC+
LeMoyne-Owen College	TN	13,070	LC
Lincoln Univ	MO	7,158	NC
Lindsey Wilson College	KY	16,392	LC
Linfield College	OR	27,090	VC
Longwood Univ	VA	11,175	C
Lourdes College	OH	15,300	LC
Luther College	IA	25,700	VC
Lynchburg College	VA	26,815	C
Lyon College	AR	17,995	VC
Macalester College	MN	31,944	MC
MacMurray College	IL	20,005	LC
Madonna Univ	MI	11,504	VC
Malone College	OH	20,995	C
Manchester College	IN	23,390	C
Manhattanville College	NY	32,420	C+
Marian College of Fond du Lac	WI	19,625	C
Mary Baldwin College	VA	24,939	C
Marygrove College	MI	17,550	C
Marylhurst Univ	OR	18,465	NC
Maryville College	TN	25,960	VC
McKendree College	IL	21,120	VC
McMurry Univ	TX	17,846	LC
McPherson College	KS	20,265	C
Meredith College	NC	23,065	C
Methodist College	NC	19,526	C
Metropolitan State College of Denver	CO	2,338	LC
Miami Univ	OH	15,033	HC
Millersville Univ of Pennsylvania	PA	11,269	C
Millikin Univ	IL	25,555	C
Millsaps College	MS	25,182	VC
Minn State Univ, Mankato	MN	8,803	LC
Minot State Univ	ND	6,602	LC
Miss College	MS	14,574	C
Miss State Univ	MS	9,139	C
Miss Valley State Univ	MS	6,765	NC
Missouri Southern State Univ	MO	8,316	C
Missouri Valley College	MO	18,500	C
Molloy College	NY	15,180	C
Monmouth College	IL	23,600	C
Monmouth Univ	NJ	26,334	C
Montana State Univ-Billings	MT	9,550	C
Montana State Univ-Bozeman	MT	9,515	C
Montclair State Univ	NJ	13,790	C
Morehouse College	GA	22,728	C
Morningside College	IA	21,610	C
Mount Mercy College	IA	21,400	C
Mount Olive College	NC	14,410	LC
Mount St. Mary's College	CA	28,307	VC
Mount Union College	OH	21,120	C
Mount Vernon Nazarene Univ	OH	18,925	C
Muhlenberg College	PA	31,485	HC
Muskingum College	OH	20,680	C
Nazareth College of Rochester	NY	24,936	VC
Nebr Wesleyan Univ	NE	21,197	C+
New Mexico Highlands Univ	NM	6,182	LC
New Mexico State Univ	NM	7,932	C
Newberry College	SC	22,871	LC
Newman Univ	KS	18,018	C
Nicholls State Univ	LA	6,395	NC
N Car Central Univ	NC	7,534	LC
N Dak State Univ	ND	8,435	C
North Georgia College and State Univ	GA	6,984	C
Northeastern Univ	MA	35,650	HC
Northern Illinois Univ	IL	11,472	C
Northern Kentucky Univ	KY	6,352	NC
Northwest Missouri State Univ	MO	9,334	C
Northwest Nazarene Univ	ID	20,360	VC
Northwestern Univ	IL	37,491	MC
Notre Dame College	OH	20,425	C
Notre Dame de Namur Univ	CA	26,932	LC
Oberlin College	OH	36,938	MC
Oglethorpe Univ	GA	26,000	VC
Ohio Dominican Univ	OH	22,700	C
Ohio State Univ	OH	13,080	VC+
Ohio Univ	OH	14,448	C
Okla Christian Univ	OK	17,690	NC
Okla City Univ	OK	19,580	VC
Okla State Univ	OK	9,216	VC
Olivet Nazarene Univ	IL	20,480	C
Oregon State Univ	OR	11,055	C
Ottawa Univ	KS	11,800	LC
Otterbein College	OH	26,085	C
Our Lady of the Lake Univ of San Antonio	TX	17,336	C
Pacific Lutheran Univ	WA	25,715	VC
Palm Beach Atlantic Univ	FL	20,690	C
Penn State Univ/Univ Park Campus	PA	15,646	HC
Pepperdine Univ	CA	32,830	VC
Piedmont College	GA	16,900	C
Pikeville College	KY	14,900	NC
Pine Manor College	MA	22,138	LC
Pittsburg State Univ	KS	7,128	NC
Pitzer College	CA	37,590	HC
Plymouth State Univ	NH	12,298	LC
Point Loma Nazarene Univ	CA	21,380	VC
Prairie View A&M Univ	TX	9,418	NC
Quincy Univ	IL	22,330	C
Radford Univ	VA	8,500	C
Ramapo College of New Jersey	NJ	15,203	VC
Randolph-Macon Woman's College	VA	28,430	VC+
Reed College	OR	36,950	MC
Regis College	MA	29,000	C
Rhodes College	TN	26,466	HC+
Rider Univ	NJ	30,900	C
Roanoke College	VA	27,393	C
Rockford College	IL	28,310	VC
Rocky Mountain College	MT	19,015	C
Rowan Univ	NJ	14,506	VC
Rutgers, The State Univ of New Jersey/Camden Campus	NJ	14,990	VC
Rutgers, The State Univ of New Jersey/New Brunswick/Piscataway Campus	NJ	15,800	HC
Rutgers, The State Univ of New Jersey/Newark Campus	NJ	15,624	VC
Sacred Heart Univ	CT	29,178	C
Saginaw Valley State Univ	MI	11,055	C
St. Edward's Univ	TX	20,428	C
St. John's Univ	MN	26,473	VC
St. John's Univ	NY	30,180	C
St. Joseph's College	IN	24,250	C
St. Mary's College	IN	24,474	VC
St. Mary's College of Calif	CA	32,850	VC
St. Norbert College	WI	25,810	C
St. Olaf College	MN	28,500	HC
St. Vincent College	PA	25,530	VC
Salisbury Univ	MD	12,664	VC
Sam Houston State Univ	TX	7,142	C
Savannah College of Art and Design	GA	27,560	SP
Schreiner Univ	TX	20,440	C
Seattle Pacific Univ	WA	25,944	VC
Seton Hall Univ	NJ	30,130	VC
Shepherd College	WV	8,608	C
Shippensburg Univ of Pennsylvania	PA	10,826	C
Shorter College	GA	17,370	C
Simmons College	MA	33,000	VC
Simon's Rock College of Bard	MA	36,580	HC
Simpson College	IA	23,658	C+
Sinte Gleska Univ	SD	2,268	NC
Skidmore College	NY	37,930	HC
Sonoma State Univ	CA	10,421	C
S Dak State Univ	SD	7,782	C
Southeast Missouri State Univ	MO	9,704	C
Southeastern Louisiana Univ	LA	6,791	LC
Southeastern Okla State Univ	OK	6,147	C
Southern Adventist Univ	TN	17,080	C
Southern Arkansas Univ	AR	6,956	C
Southern Illinois Univ Carbondale	IL	10,407	C
Southern Illinois Univ Edwardsville	IL	8,724	C
Southern Oregon Univ	OR	10,362	C
Southern Utah Univ	UT	8,194	C
Southwest Baptist Univ	MO	15,371	C
Southwest Minn State Univ	MN	9,106	VC
Southwest Missouri State Univ	MO	8,918	C
Southwestern Univ	TX	25,410	HC
Spelman College	GA	19,215	C+
Spring Arbor Univ	MI	20,206	C
Stanford Univ	CA	37,612	MC
SUNY at Oswego	NY	12,650	C
SUNY/College at Buffalo	NY	8,025	C
SUNY/College at Cortland	NY	12,095	C
SUNY/College at Oneonta	NY	11,870	VC
SUNY/Univ at Binghamton	NY	12,787	HC
State Univ of West Georgia	GA	7,622	C
Stephen F. Austin State Univ	TX	7,552	C
Sterling College	KS	18,763	C
Stetson Univ	FL	29,495	VC
Stillman College	AL	11,370	LC
Susquehanna Univ	PA	29,990	VC
Swarthmore College	PA	37,716	MC
Syracuse Univ	NY	34,720	HC
Tarleton State Univ	TX	7,576	C
Taylor Univ	IN	23,820	VC+
Temple Univ	PA	15,912	C
Tenn State Univ	TN	9,048	LC
Texas A&M Univ at Corpus Christi	TX	10,269	C
Texas Lutheran Univ	TX	20,370	C
Texas Southern Univ	TX	8,920	NC
Texas State Univ	TX	9,320	VC
Texas Tech Univ	TX	10,768	VC
Texas Wesleyan Univ	TX	16,245	C
Texas Woman's Univ	TX	7,804	LC
Thiel College	PA	20,970	C
Thomas Edison State College	NJ	3,325	SP
Thomas More College	KY	21,350	C
Tougaloo College	MS	9,200	NC
Towson Univ	MD	12,694	VC
Trinity Christian College	IL	21,640	VC
Truman State Univ	MO	9,728	HC+
Union Univ	TN	18,800	VC
Univ of Akron	OH	13,134	NC
Univ of Alabama at Birmingham	AL	12,901	C
Univ of Alaska Anchorage	AK	9,100	NC
Univ of Alaska Fairbanks	AK	9,295	C

ST = STATE **$IS** = IN-STATE COSTS **SR** = SELECTOR RATING

School	ST	$IS	SR
Univ of Alaska Southeast	AK	7,900	LC
Univ of Arkansas	AR	9,855	VC
Univ of Arkansas at Little Rock	AR	5,637	NC
Univ of Arkansas at Monticello	AR	5,940	NC
Univ of Arkansas at Pine Bluff	AR	7,925	C
Univ of Calif at Los Angeles	CA	15,330	MC
Univ of Calif at Riverside	CA	15,300	C
Univ of Calif at Santa Barbara	CA	11,732	VC
Univ of Calif at Santa Cruz	CA	16,505	VC
Univ of Central Florida	FL	10,038	VC
Univ of Charleston	WV	23,620	C
Univ of Conn	CT	14,608	VC
Univ of Delaware	DE	12,616	HC
Univ of Denver	CO	32,148	VC
Univ of Evansville	IN	24,190	VC
Univ of Florida	FL	8,580	MC
Univ of Georgia	GA	8,656	VC
Univ of Great Falls	MT	15,360	C
Univ of Hawaii at Hilo	HI	6,497	C
Univ of Hawaii at Manoa	HI	9,565	VC
Univ of Houston	TX	9,818	C
Univ of Idaho	ID	8,216	C
Univ of Indianapolis	IN	22,560	VC
Univ of Iowa	IA	10,923	VC
Univ of Kansas	KS	8,923	VC
Univ of La Verne	CA	28,600	C
Univ of Louisiana at Monroe	LA	5,207	NC
Univ of Louisville	KY	8,762	VC
Univ of Maine	ME	12,080	C+
Univ of Maine at Augusta	ME	4,065	C
Univ of Maine at Farmington	ME	10,108	C
Univ of Maine at Presque Isle	ME	9,155	LC
Univ of Mass Boston	MA	6,227	C
Univ of Memphis	TN	8,560	C
Univ of Miami	FL	34,608	HC
Univ of Minn/Duluth	MN	12,470	C
Univ of Miss	MS	7,666	C
Univ of Missouri/Kansas City	MO	13,416	VC
Univ of Montana--Western	MT	8,073	NC
Univ of Montevallo	AL	8,478	C
Univ of Nebr at Lincoln	NE	9,975	C+
Univ of Nevada/Reno	NV	9,792	C
Univ of New Haven	CT	28,650	C
Univ of New Orleans	LA	7,356	C
Univ of North Alabama	AL	7,972	NC
Univ of N Car at Asheville	NC	8,079	VC
Univ of N Car at Charlotte	NC	8,185	C
Univ of N Car at Greensboro	NC	8,248	C
Univ of N Car at Pembroke	NC	6,929	LC
Univ of North Florida	FL	8,769	VC
Univ of North Texas	TX	7,629	C
Univ of Northern Colo	CO	8,987	C
Univ of Okla	OK	9,226	VC
Univ of Puget Sound	WA	31,760	HC
Univ of Redlands	CA	32,576	VC
Univ of Rhode Island	RI	13,720	VC
Univ of Rio Grande	OH	8,728	NC
Univ of St. Mary	KS	18,868	C
Univ of Science and Arts of Okla	OK	5,982	C
Univ of S Dak	SD	7,710	C+
Univ of South Florida	FL	9,454	C
Univ of Southern Colo	CO	7,821	LC
Univ of Tampa	FL	23,982	VC
Univ of Texas at El Paso	TX	5,799	NC
Univ of Texas at San Antonio	TX	9,088	NC
Univ of Texas-Pan American	TX	5,954	LC
Univ of the Incarnate Word	TX	21,772	LC
Univ of the Ozarks	AR	16,574	C
Univ of the Pacific	CA	31,090	VC
Univ of the South	TN	30,855	HC
Univ of Tulsa	OK	22,090	VC+
Univ of Utah	UT	9,205	C
Univ of Vermont	VT	16,316	VC
Univ of Virginia	VA	11,740	MC
Univ of Virginia's College at Wise	VA	10,116	C
Univ of Wisc/Eau Claire	WI	8,463	VC
Univ of Wisc/La Crosse	WI	8,991	VC
Univ of Wisc/Oshkosh	WI	6,130	LC
Univ of Wisc/River Falls	WI	8,358	LC
Univ of Wisc/Stout	WI	9,718	C
Univ of Wyoming	WY	8,636	C
Upper Iowa Univ	IA	20,076	C
Ursinus College	PA	34,400	VC
Ursuline College	OH	22,728	LC
Valdosta State Univ	GA	7,798	C
Valley City State Univ	ND	7,281	LC
Valparaiso Univ	IN	26,118	VC+
Vassar College	NY	37,030	MC
Virginia Intermont College	VA	19,800	C
Virginia Wesleyan College	VA	25,350	C
Wabash College	IN	27,932	VC
Wake Forest Univ	NC	34,090	MC
Walla Walla College	WA	21,600	NC
Warren Wilson College	NC	21,794	VC
Wartburg College	IA	21,165	VC
Washburn Univ of Topeka	KS	8,984	NC
Washington and Jefferson College	PA	29,570	VC
Washington College	MD	30,540	VC
Wayland Baptist Univ	TX	11,919	NC
Wayne State College	NE	7,352	NC
Wayne State Univ	MI	11,774	C
Waynesburg College	PA	19,370	C
Webster Univ	MO	21,848	VC
West Chester Univ of Pennsylvania	PA	11,164	C
West Texas A&M Univ	TX	7,533	C
West Virginia Univ	WV	9,370	C
Western Carolina Univ	NC	6,742	C
Western Conn State Univ	CT	11,625	C
Western Illinois Univ	IL	10,363	C
Western Mich Univ	MI	12,031	C
Western Oregon Univ	OR	10,281	C
Western State College of Colo	CO	9,014	C
Western Washington Univ	WA	10,119	VC
Westminster College	PA	22,960	C
Westmont College	CA	33,062	VC+
Wheaton College	IL	21,934	HC
Whittier College	CA	29,108	C
Whitworth College	WA	26,428	VC+
Wichita State Univ	KS	8,092	C
William Carey College	MS	10,150	LC
William Jewell College	MO	21,320	VC
William Woods Univ	MO	20,120	C
Williams Baptist College	AR	11,950	C
Williams College	MA	32,270	MC
Wilmington College	OH	24,172	LC
Wingate Univ	NC	21,200	C
Winston-Salem State Univ	NC	8,926	LC
Winthrop Univ	SC	11,302	C
Wisc Lutheran College	WI	21,430	VC
Xavier Univ	OH	26,850	VC+
Yale Univ	CT	37,000	MC
Youngstown State Univ	OH	11,148	NC

ART EDUCATION

School	ST	$IS	SR
Abilene Christian Univ	TX	18,370	VC
Adams State College	CO	7,468	C
Adelphi Univ	NY	26,300	VC
Alabama A&M Univ	AL	5,100	LC
Alabama State Univ	AL	6,404	C
Alfred Univ	NY	28,290	C
Alverno College	WI	18,898	C
Anderson Univ	IN	19,430	LC
Andrews Univ	MI	19,550	C
Anna Maria College	MA	26,140	LC
Appalachian State Univ	NC	7,637	VC
Arcadia Univ	PA	29,890	C
Arkansas State Univ	AR	8,450	C
Arkansas Tech Univ	AR	7,299	C
Armstrong Atlantic State Univ	GA	7,102	C
Asbury College	KY	20,704	VC
Ashland Univ	OH	24,464	C
Augustana College	IL	26,610	VC+
Averett Univ	VA	23,010	LC
Azusa Pacific Univ	CA	24,720	VC
Baker Univ	KS	19,860	VC
Baldwin-Wallace College	OH	24,678	C
Ball State Univ	IN	8,660	C
Barton College	NC	19,314	C
Baylor Univ	TX	23,864	VC
Beloit College	WI	29,864	HC
Bemidji State Univ	MN	9,103	C
Berea College	KY	5,030	VC+
Berry College	GA	21,410	VC
Bethany College	KS	18,675	LC
Bethel College	MN	25,180	VC
Birmingham-Southern College	AL	25,364	VC+
Black Hills State Univ	SD	7,743	LC
Blackburn College	IL	13,690	LC
Boise State Univ	ID	7,657	LC
Boston Univ	MA	38,194	HC+
Bowling Green State Univ	OH	13,036	C
Bradley Univ	IL	22,910	VC
Brenau Univ Women's College	GA	21,800	C
Brescia Univ	KY	14,225	C
Brigham Young Univ	UT	8,504	HC
Brigham Young Univ/Hawaii	HI	7,240	VC+
Buena Vista Univ	IA	25,406	C
Cal State, Fullerton	CA	6,648	C
Calvin College	MI	22,615	NC
Carlow College	PA	21,334	C
Carroll College	WI	22,740	C
Carson-Newman College	TN	16,760	C
Case Western Reserve Univ	OH	32,002	MC
Catholic Univ of America	DC	34,248	VC
Central Conn State Univ	CT	12,090	C
Central Mich Univ	MI	11,142	C
Central Missouri State Univ	MO	9,776	C
Central State Univ	OH	8,922	C+
Central Washington Univ	WA	9,768	C
Chicago State Univ	IL	10,882	C+
CUNY/Brooklyn College	NY	4,353	C+
CUNY/City College	NY	4,230	C+
CUNY/Herbert H. Lehman College	NY	3,320	LC
CUNY/Hunter College	NY	6,729	C+
CUNY/Queens College	NY	4,362	C
Claflin Univ	SC	14,838	C+
Clarke College	IA	23,165	C
Coker College	SC	21,491	C
Colby-Sawyer College	NH	27,850	LC
College for Creative Studies	MI	23,298	SP
College of Mount St. Joseph	OH	22,785	C
College of New Jersey	NJ	15,950	MC
College of New Rochelle	NY	21,800	C
College of Notre Dame of Maryland	MD	27,700	C
College of St. Catherine	MN	24,010	VC
College of St. Rose	NY	22,864	C
College of the Ozarks	MO	3,500	VC+
Columbus State Univ	GA	7,846	C
Concord College	WV	8,136	C
Concordia College: Moorhead	MN	22,460	VC+
Converse College	SC	24,710	VC
Cornell College	IA	27,825	VC+
Culver-Stockton College	MO	17,850	C
Cumberland College	KY	16,384	C
Daemen College	NY	22,120	C
Dakota State Univ	SD	7,466	C
Dana College	NE	20,280	C
David Lipscomb Univ	TN	16,158	VC
Defiance College	OH	22,615	C
Delaware State Univ	DE	8,104	LC
Dickinson State Univ	ND	6,338	NC
Dordt College	IA	20,170	VC
Dowling College	NY	23,870	LC
East Carolina Univ	NC	8,671	C
East Central Univ	OK	4,968	C
Eastern Kentucky Univ	KY	7,708	C
Eastern Mich Univ	MI	11,478	C
Eastern Washington Univ	WA	9,012	C
Edinboro Univ of Pennsylvania	PA	10,850	LC
Elmhurst College	IL	24,630	C
Elmira College	NY	33,820	VC
Emmanuel College	MA	27,600	C+
Emporia State Univ	KS	6,998	C
Escuela de Artes Plasticas de PR	PR		
Fairmont State	WV	8,280	LC
Fisk Univ	TN	17,305	LC
Flagler College	FL	11,860	VC+
Florida A&M Univ	FL	7,564	C
Florida International Univ	FL	9,912	VC
Florida Southern College	FL	23,592	C
Florida State Univ	FL	9,028	HC
Fontbonne Univ	MO	21,508	C
Fort Hays State Univ	KS	7,363	C
Francis Marion Univ	SC	9,364	C
Freed-Hardeman Univ	TN		NC
Friends Univ	KS	15,962	LC
Gallaudet Univ	DC	16,554	SP
Georgia Southern Univ	GA	8,540	C
Georgia Southwestern State Univ	GA	6,013	C
Georgia State Univ	GA	10,658	C
Goshen College	IN	22,450	VC
Grace College	IN	19,825	VC
Grambling State Univ	LA	6,538	NC
Grand Canyon Univ	AZ	30,000	LC
Grand Valley State Univ	MI	11,022	VC
Green Mountain College	VT	24,130	C
Greensboro College	NC	21,750	C
Gustavus Adolphus College	MN	27,120	VC+
Hardin-Simmons Univ	TX	14,165	C
Hastings College	NE	19,928	VC
High Point Univ	NC	22,480	C
Hillsdale College	MI	22,450	HC
Hofstra Univ	NY	27,112	VC
Hope College	MI	25,340	VC
Houston Baptist Univ	TX	16,905	C
Howard Univ	DC	16,505	C
Huntingdon College	AL	18,400	VC
Huntington College	IN	23,590	C
Indiana State Univ	IN	10,719	LC
Indiana Univ of Pennsylvania	PA	10,489	C
Indiana Univ-Purdue Univ Fort Wayne	IN	5,108	LC
Indiana Univ-Purdue Univ Indianapolis	IN	8,257	LC
Indiana Wesleyan Univ	IN	19,900	C+
Inter American Univ of PR/ San German	PR	6,716	
Iowa Wesleyan College	IA	19,990	C
Ithaca College	NY	31,730	HC
Jacksonville Univ	FL	24,040	C
Johnson State College	VT	11,819	LC
Kansas State Univ	KS	8,728	VC
Kansas Wesleyan Univ	KS	18,900	VC
Kendall College of Art and Design of Ferris State Univ	MI	10,784	SP
Kennesaw State Univ	GA	2,724	C
Kent State Univ	OH	12,932	C
Kentucky State Univ	KY	9,062	NC
Kentucky Wesleyan College	KY	17,250	C
Keystone College	PA	21,405	LC
Kutztown Univ of Pennsylvania	PA	10,786	C
Lamar Univ	TX	6,816	LC
Lawrence Univ	WI	30,900	HC
Lenoir-Rhyne College	NC	19,186	C
Limestone College	SC	17,700	C
Lincoln Univ	MO	7,158	NC
Lindenwood Univ	MO	17,050	VC
LIU/Brooklyn Campus	NY	24,790	C
LIU/C.W. Post Campus	NY	28,282	C
LIU/Southampton College	NY	29,370	C+
Longwood Univ	VA	11,175	C
Loras College	IA	24,233	C
Louisiana College	LA	13,450	C
Louisiana State Univ in Shreveport	LA	2,884	NC
Louisiana Tech Univ	LA	7,361	C
Lubbock Christian Univ	TX	15,832	C
Malone College	OH	20,995	C
Manchester College	IN	23,390	C
Mansfield Univ	PA	11,220	C
Marian College of Fond du Lac	WI	19,625	C
Mars Hill College	NC	18,600	LC
Mary Baldwin College	VA	24,939	C
Marymount College of Fordham Univ	NY	27,686	C
Maryville Univ of St. Louis	MO	22,090	VC
Marywood Univ	PA	26,050	C
Mass College of Art	MA	15,568	SP
McKendree College	IL	21,120	VC
McMurry Univ	TX	17,846	LC
Mercyhurst College	PA	20,694	C
Messiah College	PA	25,890	VC+
Methodist College	NC	19,526	C
Miami Univ	OH	15,033	HC
Mich State Univ	MI	11,933	VC
Middle Tenn State Univ	TN	8,534	C
Midland Lutheran College	NE	18,600	C
Millersville Univ of Pennsylvania	PA	11,269	C
Millikin Univ	IL	25,555	C
Minn State Univ, Mankato	MN	8,803	LC
Minn State Univ, Moorehead	MN	7,000	LC
Miss College	MS	14,574	C
Miss Univ for Women	MS	5,446	LC
Missouri Southern State Univ	MO	8,316	C
Missouri Western State College	MO	8,522	NC
Monmouth Univ	NJ	26,334	C
Montana State Univ-Billings	MT	9,550	C
Montclair State Univ	NJ	13,790	C
Montserrat College of Art	MA	22,790	SP
Moore College of Art and Design	PA	27,096	SP
Moravian College	PA	28,903	VC
Morningside College	IA	21,610	C
Mount Mary College	WI	20,370	C
Mount Vernon Nazarene Univ	OH	18,925	C
Murray State Univ	KY	7,816	VC
Nazareth College of Rochester	NY	24,936	VC
New Jersey City Univ	NJ	11,850	LC
New York Inst of Technology	NY	24,205	VC
N Car Agricultural and Technical State Univ	NC	6,659	LC
North Georgia College and State Univ	GA	6,984	C
Northeastern State Univ	OK	4,950	LC
Northern Arizona Univ	AZ	9,002	C
Northern Illinois Univ	IL	11,472	C
Northern Kentucky Univ	KY	6,352	NC
Northern Mich Univ	MI	10,834	C
Northern State Univ	SD	7,117	LC
Northwest Missouri State Univ	MO	9,334	C
Northwest Nazarene Univ	ID	20,360	VC
Northwestern College	MN	22,820	C+
Northwestern College of Iowa	IA	19,640	C+
Oakland City Univ	IN	16,980	NC
Ohio State Univ	OH	13,080	VC+
Ohio Univ	OH	14,448	C
Ohio Wesleyan Univ	OH	32,550	VC+
Okla Baptist Univ	OK	15,220	VC
Okla Christian Univ	OK	17,690	NC
Okla Wesleyan Univ	OK	14,100	LC
Old Dominion Univ	VA	10,441	C
Oral Roberts Univ	OK	18,490	C
Ouachita Baptist Univ	AR	18,900	VC
Our Lady of the Lake Univ of San Antonio	TX	17,336	C
Palm Beach Atlantic Univ	FL	20,690	C
Penn State Univ/Univ Park Campus	PA	15,646	HC
Peru State College	NE	6,342	NC
Pittsburg State Univ	KS	7,128	NC
Plymouth State Univ	NH	12,298	LC
Pontifical Catholic Univ of PR/Ponce	PR	7,298	
Pratt Inst	NY	34,350	SP

School	ST	$IS	SR
Prescott College	AZ	13,430	C
Purdue Univ/West Lafayette	IN	12,560	VC
Radford Univ	VA	8,500	C
Rhode Island College	RI	11,565	C
Rivier College	NH	26,217	C
Roberts Wesleyan College	NY	23,190	C+
Rocky Mountain College	MT	19,015	C
Rosemont College	PA	26,175	C
Saginaw Valley State Univ	MI	11,055	C
St. Ambrose Univ	IA	22,800	C
St. Cloud State Univ	MN	8,362	C
St. Edward's Univ	TX	20,428	C
St. John's Univ	NY	30,180	C
St. Joseph's College	IN	24,250	C
St. Mary-of-the-Woods College	IN	23,280	C
St. Michael's College	VT	30,100	VC
St. Thomas Aquinas College	NY	20,590	LC
St. Vincent College	PA	25,530	VC
St. Xavier Univ	IL	23,144	C
Salem State College	MA	8,592	C
School of the Art Inst of Chicago	IL	27,800	SP
Schreiner Univ	TX	20,440	C
Seattle Pacific Univ	WA	25,944	VC
Seton Hill Univ	PA	24,930	C
Shepherd College	WV	8,608	C
Silver Lake College of the Holy Family	WI	18,450	LC
S Car State Univ	SC	6,586	LC
S Dak State Univ	SD	7,782	C
Southeast Missouri State Univ	MO	9,704	C
Southeastern Louisiana Univ	LA	6,791	LC
Southeastern Okla State Univ	OK	6,147	C
Southern Arkansas Univ	AR	6,956	C
Southern Conn State Univ	CT	10,310	C
Southern Univ at New Orleans	LA	995	NC
Southern Utah Univ	UT	8,194	C
Southwest Baptist Univ	MO	15,371	C
Southwest Minn State Univ	MN	9,106	VC
Southwest Missouri State Univ	MO	8,918	C
Southwestern Okla State Univ	OK	4,801	C
Spelman College	GA	19,215	C+
SUNY/College at Buffalo	NY	8,025	C
SUNY/Univ at New Paltz	NY	11,565	VC
State Univ of West Georgia	GA	7,622	C
Sul Ross State Univ	TX	6,582	LC
Syracuse Univ	NY	34,720	HC
Tarleton State Univ	TX	7,576	C
Taylor Univ	IN	23,820	VC+
Temple Univ	PA	15,912	C
Tenn Tech Univ	TN	8,670	VC
Texas Christian Univ	TX	23,410	VC
Texas State Univ	TX	9,320	VC
Texas Tech Univ	TX	10,768	VC
Towson Univ	MD	12,694	VC
Trinity Christian College	IL	21,640	VC
Trinity Univ	TX	26,466	HC+
Troy State Univ	AL	7,696	C
Union College	NE	17,130	C
Univ of Akron	OH	13,134	NC
Univ of Arizona	AZ	10,413	VC
Univ of Arkansas at Pine Bluff	AR	7,925	C
Univ of Central Arkansas	AR	6,388	C
Univ of Central Florida	FL	10,038	VC
Univ of Central Okla	OK	9,434	C
Univ of Cincinnati	OH	14,736	C
Univ of Dallas	TX	25,898	VC+
Univ of Dayton	OH	24,850	VC
Univ of Evansville	IN	24,190	VC
Univ of Findlay	OH	23,962	NC
Univ of Florida	FL	8,580	MC
Univ of Georgia	GA	8,656	VC
Univ of Idaho	ID	8,216	C
Univ of Illinois at Chicago	IL	13,418	C
Univ of Illinois at Urbana-Champaign	IL	11,316	HC+
Univ of Indianapolis	IN	22,560	VC
Univ of Iowa	IA	10,923	VC
Univ of Kansas	KS	8,923	VC
Univ of Kentucky	KY	7,765	C
Univ of Louisiana at Lafayette	LA	5,826	C
Univ of Louisiana at Monroe	LA	5,207	NC
Univ of Louisville	KY	8,762	VC
Univ of Maine	ME	12,080	C+
Univ of Mary Hardin-Baylor	TX	17,268	C
Univ of Maryland/College Park	MD	14,227	HC
Univ of Maryland/Eastern Shore	MD	9,964	C
Univ of Mass Dartmouth	MA	12,835	C
Univ of Mich/Ann Arbor	MI	13,864	HC+
Univ of Minn/Duluth	MN	12,470	C
Univ of Minn/Twin Cities	MN	13,160	VC
Univ of Missouri/Columbia	MO	13,782	VC
Univ of Montana--Western	MT	8,073	NC
Univ of Montevallo	AL	8,478	C
Univ of Nebr at Kearney	NE	8,286	NC
Univ of Nebr at Lincoln	NE	9,975	C+
Univ of New Mexico	NM	9,223	C
Univ of North Alabama	AL	7,972	NC
Univ of N Car at Charlotte	NC	8,185	C
Univ of N Car at Greensboro	NC	8,248	C
Univ of N Car at Pembroke	NC	6,929	LC
Univ of North Florida	FL	8,769	VC
Univ of Northern Iowa	IA	9,834	C
Univ of Rio Grande	OH	8,728	NC
Univ of St. Francis	IN	20,964	C
Univ of Sioux Falls	SD	16,390	C
Univ of S Car at Columbia	SC	10,048	VC
Univ of S Dak	SD	7,710	C+
Univ of South Florida	FL	9,454	C
Univ of Southern Indiana	IN	9,025	LC
Univ of Southern Miss	MS	8,324	LC
Univ of Tenn at Chattanooga	TN	7,783	C
Univ of Tenn at Knoxville	TN	8,214	C
Univ of Toledo	OH	12,479	NC
Univ of Vermont	VT	16,316	VC
Univ of West Florida	FL	8,470	C
Univ of Wisc/Eau Claire	WI	8,463	VC
Univ of Wisc/Madison	WI	8,262	VC
Univ of Wisc/Milwaukee	WI	9,427	LC
Univ of Wisc/Oshkosh	WI	6,130	LC
Univ of Wisc/Platteville	WI	8,450	C
Univ of Wisc/River Falls	WI	8,358	LC
Univ of Wisc/Stout	WI	9,718	C
Univ of Wisc/Superior	WI	7,051	C+
Univ of Wisc/Whitewater	WI	8,626	C
Utah State Univ	UT	7,371	C
Valdosta State Univ	GA	7,798	C
Virginia Commonwealth Univ	VA	9,030	C
Virginia Union Univ	VA	15,358	LC
Virginia Wesleyan College	VA	25,350	C
Viterbo Univ	WI	20,430	C
Wartburg College	IA	21,165	VC
Washburn Univ of Topeka	KS	8,984	NC
Washington and Jefferson College	PA	29,570	VC
Washington Univ in St. Louis	MO	38,293	MC
Wayne State Univ	MI	11,774	C
Weber State Univ	UT	7,945	NC
West Liberty State College	WV	7,868	LC
West Texas A&M Univ	TX	7,533	C
West Virginia State College	WV	6,264	NC
West Virginia Wesleyan College	WV	22,920	C
Western Carolina Univ	NC	6,742	C
Western Kentucky Univ	KY	6,834	C
Western Mich Univ	MI	12,031	C
Western New Mexico Univ	NM	5,950	LC
Western State College of Colo	CO	9,014	C
Western Washington Univ	WA	10,119	VC
Westfield State College	MA	10,147	C
Westmont College	CA	33,062	VC+
Wichita State Univ	KS	8,092	C
Wingate Univ	NC	21,200	C
Winona State Univ	MN		C
Wright State Univ	OH	11,490	LC
Xavier Univ of Louisiana	LA	17,600	C
Youngstown State Univ	OH	11,148	NC

ART HISTORY AND APPRECIATION

School	ST	$IS	SR
Adelphi Univ	NY	26,300	VC
Albion College	MI	25,224	VC
Allegheny College	PA	30,280	VC
American Univ	DC	34,585	VC+
Aquinas College	MI	21,894	C
Arizona State Univ-Main	AZ	10,048	C
Art Academy of Cincinnati	OH	17,300	SP
Augsburg College	MN	25,298	C
Augustana College	IL	26,610	VC+
Baker Univ	KS	19,860	VC
Baldwin-Wallace College	OH	24,678	C
Bard College	NY	37,352	HC+
Baylor Univ	TX	23,864	VC
Beloit College	WI	29,864	HC
Birmingham-Southern College	AL	25,364	VC+
Bloomsburg Univ of Pennsylvania	PA	10,844	C
Boston College	MA	33,284	MC
Bowdoin College	ME	37,790	MC
Bowling Green State Univ	OH	13,036	C
Bradley Univ	IL	22,910	VC
Brandeis Univ	MA	38,198	MC
Brigham Young Univ	UT	8,504	HC
Brown Univ	RI	38,174	MC
Bryn Mawr College	PA	36,890	HC+
Bucknell Univ	PA	35,262	HC+
Cal State, Fullerton	CA	6,648	C
Cal State, San Bernardino	CA	15,238	LC
Cal State, Stanislaus	CA	9,874	C
Calvin College	MI	22,615	NC
Canisius College	NY	28,163	C+
Carleton College	MN	34,395	MC
Carlow College	PA	21,334	C
Case Western Reserve Univ	OH	32,002	MC
Catholic Univ of America	DC	34,248	VC
Chapman Univ	CA	33,118	VC
Chatham College	PA	27,266	C+
Chestnut Hill College	PA	26,450	LC
CUNY/Brooklyn College	NY	4,353	C+
CUNY/Queens College	NY	4,362	C
CUNY/York College	NY	3,292	NC
Clark Univ	MA	32,115	VC
Clarke College	IA	23,165	C
Colgate Univ	NY	37,095	MC
College of Charleston	SC	11,887	HC
College of New Rochelle	NY	21,800	C
College of Notre Dame of Maryland	MD	27,700	C
College of Santa Fe	NM	25,293	C+
College of the Holy Cross	MA	36,451	MC
Colo College	CO	36,860	HC
Columbia Univ/Barnard College	NY	36,990	MC
Columbia Univ/Columbia College	NY	38,590	MC
Columbia Univ/School of General Studies	NY	35,000	C
Concordia College: Moorhead	MN	22,460	VC+
Conn College	CT	37,900	MC
Cornell Univ	NY	38,253	MC
Dartmouth College	NH	37,770	MC
Denison Univ	OH	33,050	HC
DePauw Univ	IN	31,500	HC
Dominican Univ of Calif	CA	31,670	C
Drake Univ	IA	25,120	VC+
Drury Univ	MO	18,085	VC+
Duke Univ	NC	37,555	MC
Duquesne Univ	PA	26,907	VC
East Carolina Univ	NC	8,671	C
Eastern Univ	PA	24,020	C
Eastern Washington Univ	WA	9,012	C
Edinboro Univ of Pennsylvania	PA	10,850	LC
Emmanuel College	MA	27,600	C+
Emory Univ	GA	36,872	MC
Florida International Univ	FL	9,912	VC
Florida State Univ	FL	9,028	HC
Fordham Univ	NY	35,066	HC
Framingham State College	MA	9,381	C
Franklin and Marshall College	PA	35,930	HC+
Gallaudet Univ	DC	16,554	SP
George Mason Univ	VA	9,732	VC
George Washington Univ	DC	41,030	MC
Georgian Court College	NJ	19,040	LC
Gettysburg College	PA	35,646	HC
Goucher College	MD	32,650	HC
Hamilton College	NY	37,560	MC
Hamline Univ	MN	27,052	VC
Hampshire College	MA	37,037	HC
Hanover College	IN	25,200	VC
Hartwick College	NY	34,650	C+
Harvard Univ/Harvard College	MA	37,928	MC
Haverford College	PA	37,900	MC
Hiram College	OH	28,234	VC
Hobart and William Smith Colleges	NY	36,536	HC
Hofstra Univ	NY	27,112	VC
Hollins Univ	VA	27,965	VC
Howard Univ	DC	16,505	C
Indiana State Univ	IN	10,719	LC
Indiana Univ Bloomington	IN	12,389	VC
Indiana Univ-Purdue Univ Indianapolis	IN	8,257	LC
Ithaca College	NY	31,730	HC
Jacksonville Univ	FL	24,040	C
James Madison Univ	VA	10,794	VC
John Carroll Univ	OH	27,658	C+
Johns Hopkins Univ	MD	38,372	MC
Juniata College	PA	29,080	VC
Kalamazoo College	MI	26,955	HC+
Kansas City Art Inst	MO	26,850	SP
Kean Univ	NJ	14,479	C
Kendall College of Art and Design of Ferris State Univ	MI	10,784	SP
Kent State Univ	OH	12,932	C
Kenyon College	OH	35,370	HC+
Knox College	IL	30,294	VC+
Lawrence Univ	WI	30,900	HC
Lewis and Clark College	OR	30,620	VC
Lindenwood Univ	MO	17,050	VC
Lourdes College	OH	15,300	LC
Loyola Marymount Univ	CA	32,194	VC
Lycoming College	PA	27,589	C+
Manhattanville College	NY	32,420	C+
Mansfield Univ	PA	11,220	C
Marian College	IN	23,030	C
Mars Hill College	NC	18,600	LC
Mary Washington College	VA	10,166	HC
Marymount College of Fordham Univ	NY	27,686	C
Mass College of Art	MA	15,568	SP
McDaniel College	MD	28,440	VC
Messiah College	PA	25,890	VC+
Miami Univ	OH	15,033	HC
Mich State Univ	MI	11,933	VC
Middlebury College	VT	38,100	MC
Mills College	CA	33,371	VC
Monmouth Univ	NJ	26,334	C
Montclair State Univ	NJ	13,790	C
Moravian College	PA	28,903	VC
Mount Holyoke College	MA	37,918	HC+
Nazareth College of Rochester	NY	24,936	VC
New College of Florida	FL	8,906	HC+
New England College	NH	28,860	LC
New York Univ	NY	39,406	MC
Northern Arizona Univ	AZ	9,002	C
Northern Illinois Univ	IL	11,472	C
Northwestern Univ	IL	37,491	MC
Oakland Univ	MI	10,800	C
Occidental College	CA	35,922	HC
Ohio Univ	OH	14,448	C
Old Dominion Univ	VA	10,441	C
Penn State Univ/Univ Park Campus	PA	15,646	HC
Pomona College	CA	33,960	MC
Portland State Univ	OR	12,453	C
Pratt Inst	NY	34,350	SP
Providence College	RI	30,604	HC
Purdue Univ/West Lafayette	IN	12,560	VC
Randolph-Macon College	VA	27,190	C
Rice Univ	TX	27,550	MC
Ripon College	WI	24,995	VC
Rockford College	IL	28,310	VC
Roger Williams Univ	RI	30,296	C
Rollins College	FL	34,300	VC
Roosevelt Univ	IL	22,580	VC
Rutgers, The State Univ of New Jersey/Camden Campus	NJ	14,990	VC
Rutgers, The State Univ of New Jersey/New Brunswick/Piscataway Campus	NJ	15,800	HC
St. Joseph College	CT	29,685	C
St. Louis Univ	MO	29,780	VC+
St. Olaf College	MN	28,500	HC
St. Peter's College	NJ	22,292	LC
St. Vincent College	PA	25,530	VC
Salem College	NC	24,595	VC
Salve Regina Univ	RI	29,210	C
Santa Clara Univ	CA	34,701	HC
Sarah Lawrence College	NY	41,218	HC
Savannah College of Art and Design	GA	27,560	SP
School of the Art Inst of Chicago	IL	27,800	SP
Scripps College	CA	35,700	HC+
Seton Hill Univ	PA	24,930	C
Siena Heights Univ	MI	16,140	LC
Simon's Rock College of Bard	MA	36,580	HC
Skidmore College	NY	37,930	HC
Smith College	MA	37,034	HC+
Southern Conn State Univ	CT	10,310	C
Southern Methodist Univ	TX	34,210	HC
SUNY at Potsdam	NY	12,160	C
SUNY/College at Buffalo	NY	8,025	C
SUNY/College at Geneseo	NY	11,330	HC
SUNY/College at Purchase	NY	10,587	VC
SUNY/Univ at Albany	NY	12,951	HC
SUNY/Univ at Binghamton	NY	12,787	HC
SUNY/Univ at Buffalo	NY	12,563	VC
SUNY/Univ at New Paltz	NY	11,565	VC
SUNY/Univ at Stony Brook	NY	12,763	HC
Susquehanna Univ	PA	29,990	VC
Swarthmore College	PA	37,716	MC
Sweet Briar College	VA	27,940	C
Syracuse Univ	NY	34,720	HC
Temple Univ	PA	15,912	C
Texas Christian Univ	TX	23,410	VC
Texas Tech Univ	TX	10,768	VC
Trinity College	CT	38,040	HC+
Troy State Univ	AL	7,696	C
Truman State Univ	MO	9,728	HC+
Tufts Univ	MA	38,233	MC
Tulane Univ	LA	37,451	HC+
Univ of Alabama	AL	9,040	C+
Univ of Arizona	AZ	10,413	VC
Univ of Arkansas at Little Rock	AR	5,637	NC
Univ of Calif at Berkeley	CA	15,563	MC
Univ of Calif at Davis	CA	14,995	VC
Univ of Calif at Irvine	CA	19,808	HC
Univ of Calif at Los Angeles	CA	15,330	MC
Univ of Calif at Riverside	CA	15,300	C
Univ of Calif at San Diego	CA	14,127	HC
Univ of Calif at Santa Barbara	CA	11,732	VC
Univ of Calif at Santa Cruz	CA	16,505	VC
Univ of Chicago	IL	35,087	MC
Univ of Colo at Boulder	CO	10,774	VC
Univ of Conn	CT	14,608	VC
Univ of Dallas	TX	25,898	VC+
Univ of Dayton	OH	24,850	VC
Univ of Delaware	DE	12,616	HC
Univ of Denver	CO	32,148	VC
Univ of Evansville	IN	24,190	VC
Univ of Florida	FL	8,580	MC
Univ of Hartford	CT	31,080	C

ST = STATE $IS = IN-STATE COSTS SR = SELECTOR RATING

School	ST	$IS	SR
Univ of Houston	TX	9,818	C
Univ of Illinois at Chicago	IL	13,418	C
Univ of Illinois at Urbana-Champaign	IL	11,316	HC+
Univ of Iowa	IA	10,923	VC
Univ of Kansas	KS	8,923	VC
Univ of Kentucky	KY	7,765	C
Univ of La Verne	CA	28,600	C
Univ of Louisville	KY	8,762	VC
Univ of Maryland/College Park	MD	14,227	HC
Univ of Mass Amherst	MA	13,980	C+
Univ of Mass Dartmouth	MA	12,835	C
Univ of Memphis	TN	8,560	C
Univ of Miami	FL	34,608	HC
Univ of Mich/Ann Arbor	MI	13,864	HC+
Univ of Mich/Dearborn	MI	6,843	VC
Univ of Minn/Morris	MN	12,896	VC
Univ of Minn/Twin Cities	MN	13,160	VC
Univ of Miss	MS	7,666	C
Univ of Missouri/Columbia	MO	13,782	VC
Univ of Missouri/Kansas City	MO	13,416	VC
Univ of Missouri/St. Louis	MO	11,656	VC
Univ of Nebr at Lincoln	NE	9,975	C+
Univ of Nevada/Las Vegas	NV	11,566	C
Univ of New Hampshire	NH	14,828	VC
Univ of New Mexico	NM	9,223	C
Univ of N Car at Chapel Hill	NC	10,117	MC
Univ of N Car at Wilmington	NC	8,940	VC
Univ of North Texas	TX	7,629	C
Univ of Northern Iowa	IA	9,834	C
Univ of Notre Dame	IN	34,442	MC
Univ of Okla	OK	9,226	VC
Univ of Oregon	OR	11,479	VC
Univ of Pennsylvania	PA	37,960	MC
Univ of Richmond	VA	30,100	MC
Univ of Rochester	NY	32,979	HC
Univ of St. Thomas	MN	26,918	VC
Univ of San Francisco	CA	34,700	VC
Univ of S Car at Columbia	SC	10,048	VC
Univ of Southern Calif	CA	37,459	MC
Univ of Tenn at Knoxville	TN	8,214	C
Univ of Texas at Arlington	TX	7,192	LC
Univ of Texas at Austin	TX	10,630	HC
Univ of the Pacific	CA	31,090	VC
Univ of the South	TN	30,855	HC
Univ of Toledo	OH	12,479	NC
Univ of Utah	UT	9,205	C
Univ of Vermont	VT	16,316	VC
Univ of Washington	WA	10,361	VC
Univ of Wisc/Madison	WI	8,262	VC
Univ of Wisc/Milwaukee	WI	9,427	LC
Univ of Wisc/Superior	WI	7,051	C+
Univ of Wisc/Whitewater	WI	8,626	C
Villanova Univ	PA	35,050	HC
Washburn Univ of Topeka	KS	8,984	NC
Washington and Lee Univ	VA	29,663	MC
Washington Univ in St. Louis	MO	38,293	MC
Wayne State Univ	MI	11,774	C
Wellesley College	MA	36,516	MC
Wesleyan College	GA	17,870	VC
Wesleyan Univ	CT	35,139	MC
Western Mich Univ	MI	12,031	C
Wheaton College	MA	36,330	HC
Whitman College	WA	32,526	HC+
Wichita State Univ	KS	8,092	C
Willamette Univ	OR	32,032	VC+
William Paterson Univ of New Jersey	NJ	14,450	C
Williams College	MA	32,270	MC
Winthrop Univ	SC	11,302	C
Wofford College	SC	26,710	HC
Wright State Univ	OH	11,490	LC
Yale Univ	CT	37,000	MC
Youngstown State Univ	OH	11,148	NC

ART THERAPY

School	ST	$IS	SR
Albertus Magnus College	CT	23,130	LC
Alverno College	WI	18,898	C
Andrews Univ	MI	19,550	C
Anna Maria College	MA	26,140	LC
Arcadia Univ	PA	29,890	C
Bowling Green State Univ	OH	13,036	C
Brescia Univ	KY	14,225	C
Capital Univ	OH	26,550	C
Carlow College	PA	21,334	C
College of New Rochelle	NY	21,800	C
Converse College	SC	24,710	VC
Edgewood College	WI	20,520	C
Emmanuel College	MA	27,600	C+
LIU/C.W. Post Campus	NY	28,282	C
Marygrove College	MI	17,550	C
Marywood Univ	PA	26,050	C
Mercyhurst College	PA	20,694	C
Millikin Univ	IL	25,555	C
Mount Mary College	WI	20,370	C
Russell Sage College	NY	26,811	C
Seton Hill Univ	PA	24,930	C
Spring Hill College	AL	25,868	VC
Springfield College	MA	24,520	C
Univ of Indianapolis	IN	22,560	VC
Univ of Wisc/Superior	WI	7,051	C+

ARTS ADMINISTRATION/MANAGEMENT

School	ST	$IS	SR
Adrian College	MI	21,950	C
Appalachian State Univ	NC	7,637	VC
Bellarmine Univ	KY	24,110	VC
Benedictine Univ	IL	23,840	C
Bennett College	NC	11,200	C
Brenau Univ Women's College	GA	21,800	C
Buena Vista Univ	IA	25,406	C
Butler Univ	IN	28,250	VC+
Cal State, Hayward	CA	8,871	LC
Chatham College	PA	27,266	C+
College of Santa Fe	NM	25,293	C+
Concordia College	NY	19,200	VC
Culver-Stockton College	MO	17,850	C
Drury Univ	MO	18,085	VC+
Eastern Mich Univ	MI	11,478	C
Franklin Pierce College	NH	28,980	LC
Goucher College	MD	32,650	HC
Green Mountain College	VT	24,130	C
Huntingdon College	AL	18,400	VC
Lees-McRae College	NC	17,106	LC
LIU/C.W. Post Campus	NY	28,282	C
Mary Baldwin College	VA	24,939	C
Marywood Univ	PA	26,050	C
Millikin Univ	IL	25,555	C
North Georgia College and State Univ	GA	6,984	C
Northern Arizona Univ	AZ	9,002	C
Pfeiffer Univ	NC	18,980	C
Point Park Univ	PA	21,840	C
Randolph-Macon College	VA	27,190	C
Salem College	NC	24,595	VC
Seton Hill Univ	PA	24,930	C
Shenandoah Univ	VA	25,190	NC
Simmons College	MA	33,000	VC
Southeastern Louisiana Univ	LA	6,791	LC
Spring Hill College	AL	25,868	VC
Univ of Findlay	OH	23,962	NC
Univ of Kentucky	KY	7,765	C
Univ of Mich/Dearborn	MI	6,843	VC
Univ of San Francisco	CA	34,700	VC
Univ of Tulsa	OK	22,090	VC+
Univ of Wisc/Stevens Point	WI	8,116	VC
Upper Iowa Univ	IA	20,076	C
Viterbo Univ	WI	20,430	C
Wagner College	NY	29,900	VC
Wartburg College	IA	21,165	VC
Waynesburg College	PA	19,370	C
Wright State Univ	OH	11,490	LC

ASIAN/AMERICAN STUDIES

School	ST	$IS	SR
Cal State, Fullerton	CA	6,648	C
Cal State, Northridge	CA	7,757	LC
Columbia Univ/Columbia College	NY	38,590	MC
Pitzer College	CA	37,590	HC
St. Olaf College	MN	28,500	HC
Scripps College	CA	35,700	HC+
SUNY/Univ at Binghamton	NY	12,787	HC
Univ of Calif at Berkeley	CA	15,563	MC
Univ of Calif at Los Angeles	CA	15,330	MC
Univ of Calif at Santa Barbara	CA	11,732	VC
Univ of Southern Calif	CA	37,459	MC
Univ of Washington	WA	10,361	VC

ASIAN/ORIENTAL STUDIES

School	ST	$IS	SR
Amherst College	MA	37,470	MC
Augustana College	IL	26,610	VC+
Bard College	NY	37,352	HC+
Baylor Univ	TX	23,864	VC
Birmingham-Southern College	AL	25,364	VC+
Boston Univ	MA	38,194	HC+
Bowdoin College	ME	37,790	MC
Bowling Green State Univ	OH	13,036	C
Brigham Young Univ	UT	8,504	HC
Cal State, Chico	CA	8,598	LC
Cal State, Long Beach	CA	8,762	C+
Carleton College	MN	34,395	MC
Case Western Reserve Univ	OH	32,002	MC
Central Washington Univ	WA	9,768	C
CUNY/City College	NY	4,230	C+
Claremont McKenna College	CA	36,880	MC
Coe College	IA	27,385	VC
Colgate Univ	NY	37,095	MC
College of the Holy Cross	MA	36,451	MC
Colo College	CO	36,860	HC
Columbia Univ/Columbia College	NY	38,590	MC
Cornell Univ	NY	38,253	MC
Dartmouth College	NH	37,770	MC
Duke Univ	NC	37,555	MC
Emory Univ	GA	36,872	MC
Florida International Univ	FL	9,912	VC
Florida State Univ	FL	9,028	HC
Furman Univ	SC	28,976	HC+
Hamilton College	NY	37,560	MC
Hampshire College	MA	37,037	HC
Harvard Univ/Harvard College	MA	37,928	MC
Hobart and William Smith Colleges	NY	36,536	HC
Hofstra Univ	NY	27,112	VC
Lake Forest College	IL	30,270	VC
Lehigh Univ	PA	37,570	HC+
Loyola Marymount Univ	CA	32,194	VC
Macalester College	MN	31,944	MC
Manhattanville College	NY	32,420	C+
Mary Baldwin College	VA	24,939	C
Mount Holyoke College	MA	37,918	HC+
Oakland Univ	MI	10,800	C
Occidental College	CA	35,922	HC
Pacific Lutheran Univ	WA	25,715	VC
Pitzer College	CA	37,590	HC
Pomona College	CA	33,960	MC
Rice Univ	TX	27,550	MC
Rutgers, The State Univ of New Jersey/New Brunswick/Piscataway Campus	NJ	15,800	HC
St. Andrews Presbyterian College	NC	20,525	C
St. John's Univ	NY	30,180	C
St. Lawrence Univ	NY	35,945	VC
Samford Univ	AL	18,648	VC
San Diego State Univ	CA	10,321	C
Sarah Lawrence College	NY	41,218	HC
Scripps College	CA	35,700	HC+
Seton Hall Univ	NJ	30,130	VC
Simon's Rock College of Bard	MA	36,580	HC
Skidmore College	NY	37,930	HC
SUNY/Univ at Albany	NY	12,951	HC
SUNY/Univ at Buffalo	NY	12,563	VC
SUNY/Univ at New Paltz	NY	11,565	VC
Swarthmore College	PA	37,716	MC
Temple Univ	PA	15,912	C
Texas State Univ	TX	9,320	VC
Tufts Univ	MA	38,233	MC
Tulane Univ	LA	37,451	HC+
Univ of Calif at Berkeley	CA	15,563	MC
Univ of Calif at Riverside	CA	15,300	C
Univ of Calif at Santa Barbara	CA	11,732	VC
Univ of Chicago	IL	35,087	MC
Univ of Cincinnati	OH	14,736	C
Univ of Colo at Boulder	CO	10,774	VC
Univ of Denver	CO	32,148	VC
Univ of Florida	FL	8,580	MC
Univ of Hawaii at Manoa	HI	9,565	VC
Univ of Iowa	IA	10,923	VC
Univ of Mich/Ann Arbor	MI	13,864	HC+
Univ of New Mexico	NM	9,223	C
Univ of N Car at Chapel Hill	NC	10,117	MC
Univ of Northern Iowa	IA	9,834	C
Univ of Okla	OK	9,226	VC
Univ of Oregon	OR	11,479	VC
Univ of Pennsylvania	PA	37,960	MC
Univ of Puget Sound	WA	31,760	HC
Univ of Redlands	CA	32,576	VC
Univ of Tenn at Knoxville	TN	8,214	C
Univ of Texas at Austin	TX	10,630	HC
Univ of the South	TN	30,855	HC
Univ of Utah	UT	9,205	C
Univ of Vermont	VT	16,316	VC
Univ of Washington	WA	10,361	VC
Univ of Wisc/Madison	WI	8,262	VC
Valparaiso Univ	IN	26,118	VC+
Vassar College	NY	37,030	MC
Washington State Univ	WA	11,334	C
Washington Univ in St. Louis	MO	38,293	MC
Wellesley College	MA	36,516	MC
Wesleyan Univ	CT	35,139	MC
Wheaton College	MA	36,330	HC
Whitman College	WA	32,526	HC+
Williams College	MA	32,270	MC

ASTRONOMY

School	ST	$IS	SR
Amherst College	MA	37,470	MC
Benedictine College	KS	20,603	C
Boston Univ	MA	38,194	HC+
Bryn Mawr College	PA	36,890	HC+
Calif Inst of Technology	CA	31,677	MC
Case Western Reserve Univ	OH	32,002	MC
Colgate Univ	NY	37,095	MC
Columbia Univ/Barnard College	NY	36,990	MC
Columbia Univ/Columbia College	NY	38,590	MC
Columbia Univ/School of General Studies	NY	35,000	C
Cornell Univ	NY	38,253	MC
Earlham College	IN	29,976	VC+
Eastern Mich Univ	MI	11,478	C
Eastern Univ	PA	24,020	C
Franklin and Marshall College	PA	35,930	HC+
George Mason Univ	VA	9,732	VC
Harvard Univ/Harvard College	MA	37,928	MC
Haverford College	PA	37,900	MC
Indiana Univ Bloomington	IN	12,389	VC
Lycoming College	PA	27,589	C+
Minn State Univ, Mankato	MN	8,803	LC
Mount Holyoke College	MA	37,918	HC+
Mount Union College	OH	21,120	C
Northwestern Univ	IL	37,491	MC
Oberlin College	OH	36,938	MC
Ohio State Univ	OH	13,080	VC+
Penn State Univ/Univ Park Campus	PA	15,646	HC
San Diego State Univ	CA	10,321	C
Smith College	MA	37,034	HC+
SUNY/Univ at Stony Brook	NY	12,763	HC
Swarthmore College	PA	37,716	MC
Univ of Arizona	AZ	10,413	VC
Univ of Colo at Boulder	CO	10,774	VC
Univ of Delaware	DE	12,616	HC
Univ of Denver	CO	32,148	VC
Univ of Florida	FL	8,580	MC
Univ of Georgia	GA	8,656	VC
Univ of Hawaii at Hilo	HI	6,497	C
Univ of Illinois at Urbana-Champaign	IL	11,316	HC+
Univ of Iowa	IA	10,923	VC
Univ of Kansas	KS	8,923	VC
Univ of Maryland/College Park	MD	14,227	HC
Univ of Mass Amherst	MA	13,980	C+
Univ of Mich/Ann Arbor	MI	13,864	HC+
Univ of Minn/Twin Cities	MN	13,160	VC
Univ of Okla	OK	9,226	VC
Univ of Pittsburgh at Pittsburgh	PA	16,074	HC
Univ of Southern Calif	CA	37,459	MC
Univ of Texas at Austin	TX	10,630	HC
Univ of Virginia	VA	11,740	MC
Univ of Washington	WA	10,361	VC
Univ of Wisc/Madison	WI	8,262	VC
Univ of Wyoming	WY	8,636	C
Valdosta State Univ	GA	7,798	C
Vassar College	NY	37,030	MC
Villanova Univ	PA	35,050	HC
Wellesley College	MA	36,516	MC
Wesleyan Univ	CT	35,139	MC
Wheaton College	MA	36,330	HC
Williams College	MA	32,270	MC
Yale Univ	CT	37,000	MC
Youngstown State Univ	OH	11,148	NC

ASTROPHYSICS

School	ST	$IS	SR
Agnes Scott College	GA	28,230	HC
Boston Univ	MA	38,194	HC+
Cal State, Northridge	CA	7,757	LC
Colgate Univ	NY	37,095	MC
Columbia Univ/Columbia College	NY	38,590	MC
Conn College	CT	37,900	MC
Florida Inst of Technology	FL	28,740	VC
Franklin and Marshall College	PA	35,930	HC+
Indiana Univ Bloomington	IN	12,389	VC
Mich State Univ	MI	11,933	VC
Princeton Univ	NJ	36,649	MC
Rutgers, The State Univ of New Jersey/New Brunswick/Piscataway Campus	NJ	15,800	HC
Swarthmore College	PA	37,716	MC
Texas Christian Univ	TX	23,410	VC
Tufts Univ	MA	38,233	MC
Univ of Calif at Berkeley	CA	15,563	MC
Univ of Calif at Los Angeles	CA	15,330	MC
Univ of Mich/Ann Arbor	MI	13,864	HC+
Univ of Minn/Twin Cities	MN	13,160	VC
Univ of New Mexico	NM	9,223	C
Univ of Okla	OK	9,226	VC
Villanova Univ	PA	35,050	HC
Wellesley College	MA	36,516	MC
Williams College	MA	32,270	MC

ATHLETIC TRAINING

School	ST	$IS	SR
Adams State College	CO	7,468	C
Alderson-Broaddus College	WV	19,640	C
Alfred Univ	NY	28,290	C
Alvernia College	PA	23,212	LC
Arkansas State Univ	AR	8,450	C
Ashland Univ	OH	24,464	C
Augustana College	SD	21,998	VC
Averett Univ	VA	23,010	LC
Barton College	NC	19,314	C
Belhaven College	MS	16,040	C+
Benedictine College	KS	20,603	C
Bethany College	KS	18,675	LC
Bethel College	KS	19,800	C+
Bethel College	MN	25,180	VC
Boston Univ	MA	38,194	HC+
Bridgewater College	VA	25,150	C
Bryan College	TN	17,900	VC
Calif Univ of Pennsylvania	PA	10,388	C
Campbell Univ	NC	18,268	VC
Campbellsville Univ	KY	17,680	C

School	ST	$IS	SR
Canisius College	NY	28,163	C+
Carroll College	WI	22,740	C
Catawba College	NC	20,500	C
Cedarville Univ	OH	19,954	VC
Central Conn State Univ	CT	12,090	C
Central Methodist College	MO	16,460	C
Chapman Univ	CA	33,118	VC
Coe College	IA	27,385	VC
Colby-Sawyer College	NH	27,850	LC
College of Charleston	SC	11,887	HC
College of Mount St. Joseph	OH	22,785	C
Concordia Univ Wisc	WI	16,600	C
Culver-Stockton College	MO	17,850	C
Dakota Wesleyan Univ	SD	17,832	C
Delta State Univ	MS	6,618	C
Dominican College	NY	24,810	LC
Duquesne Univ	PA	26,907	VC
East Carolina Univ	NC	8,671	C
East Central Univ	OK	4,968	C
East Texas Baptist Univ	TX	13,914	C
Eastern Nazarene College	MA	19,433	LC
Elmhurst College	IL	24,630	C
Emporia State Univ	KS	6,998	C
Endicott College	MA	25,266	C+
Erskine College	SC	23,166	VC
Eureka College	IL	24,980	LC
Florida Southern College	FL	23,592	C
Florida State Univ	FL	9,028	HC
Franklin College	IN		C
Gardner-Webb Univ	NC	19,300	C
George Mason Univ	VA	9,732	VC
Graceland Univ	IA	19,550	C
Greensboro College	NC	21,750	C
Guilford College	NC	24,960	VC
Hamline Univ	MN	27,052	VC
Heidelberg College	OH	20,266	NC
Henderson State Univ	AR	7,386	C
High Point Univ	NC	22,480	C
Hofstra Univ	NY	27,112	VC
Howard Payne Univ	TX	15,176	C
Huntingdon College	AL	18,400	VC
Indiana Univ Bloomington	IN	12,389	VC
Ithaca College	NY	31,730	HC
Johnson State College	VT	11,819	LC
Kansas State Univ	KS	8,728	VC
Kent State Univ	OH	12,932	C
Lake Superior State Univ	MI	9,034	LC
Lambuth Univ	TN	16,520	C
Lasell College	MA	26,000	C
Lewis Univ	IL	22,950	C+
Liberty Univ	VA	17,220	C
Limestone College	SC	17,700	C
Lincoln Memorial Univ	TN	16,400	LC
Lindenwood Univ	MO	17,050	VC
Linfield College	OR	27,090	VC
Louisiana College	LA	13,450	C
Lynchburg College	VA	26,815	C
Marist College	NY	27,596	VC
Mars Hill College	NC	18,600	LC
Marywood Univ	PA	26,050	C
McKendree College	IL	21,120	VC
McMurry Univ	TX	17,846	LC
Mercyhurst College	PA	20,694	C
Meredith College	NC	23,065	C
Messiah College	PA	25,890	VC+
Methodist College	NC	19,526	C
Miami Univ	OH	15,033	HC
MidAmerica Nazarene Univ	KS	18,688	C
Middle Tenn State Univ	TN	8,534	C
Minn State Univ, Mankato	MN	8,803	LC
Missouri Baptist Univ	MO	18,010	C
Montclair State Univ	NJ	13,790	C
Mount Marty College	SD	15,656	LC
Mount Union College	OH	21,120	C
National American Univ	SD	13,680	NC
Nebr Wesleyan Univ	NE	21,197	C+
Neumann College	PA	23,890	LC
New Mexico State Univ	NM	7,932	C
N Dak State Univ	ND	8,435	C
Northeastern Univ	MA	35,650	HC
Northwestern College of Iowa	IA	19,640	C+
Nova Southeastern Univ	FL	23,346	C
Ohio Northern Univ	OH	27,765	VC
Ohio Univ	OH	14,448	C
Okla Wesleyan Univ	OK	14,100	LC
Olivet College	MI	19,984	C+
Otterbein College	OH	26,085	C
Palm Beach Atlantic Univ	FL	20,690	C
Park Univ	MO	10,780	C+
Pfeiffer Univ	NC	18,980	C
Plymouth State Univ	NH	12,298	LC
Purdue Univ/West Lafayette	IN	12,560	VC
Roanoke College	VA	27,393	C
Rockford College	IL	28,310	VC
Russell Sage College	NY	26,811	C
Salem International Univ	WV	19,770	C
Salisbury Univ	MD	12,664	VC
Samford Univ	AL	18,648	VC
Shaw Univ	NC	14,882	C+
Simpson College	IA	23,658	C+
S Dak State Univ	SD	7,782	C
Southeast Missouri State Univ	MO	9,704	C
Southern Nazarene Univ	OK	14,634	NC
Southern Utah Univ	UT	8,194	C
Southwest Baptist Univ	MO	15,371	C
Southwest Missouri State Univ	MO	8,918	C
Southwestern Okla State Univ	OK	4,801	C
SUNY/College at Cortland	NY	12,095	C
SUNY/Univ at Stony Brook	NY	12,763	HC
Sterling College	KS	18,763	C
Tabor College	KS	19,500	NC
Taylor Univ	IN	23,820	VC+
Texas State Univ	TX	9,320	VC
Towson Univ	MD	12,694	VC
Trinity International Univ	IL	22,980	C+
Univ of Akron	OH	13,134	NC
Univ of Alabama	AL	9,040	C+
Univ of Central Arkansas	AR	6,388	C
Univ of Conn	CT	14,608	VC
Univ of Delaware	DE	12,616	HC
Univ of Evansville	IN	24,190	VC
Univ of Findlay	OH	23,962	NC
Univ of Hawaii at Manoa	HI	9,565	VC
Univ of Indianapolis	IN	22,560	VC
Univ of Kansas	KS	8,923	VC
Univ of La Verne	CA	28,600	C
Univ of Mary	ND	12,900	C+
Univ of Mary Hardin-Baylor	TX	17,268	C
Univ of Miami	FL	34,608	HC
Univ of Minn/Duluth	MN	12,470	C
Univ of Nebr at Lincoln	NE	9,975	C+
Univ of New Hampshire	NH	14,828	VC
Univ of New Mexico	NM	9,223	C
Univ of N Car at Charlotte	NC	8,185	C
Univ of N Car at Wilmington	NC	8,940	VC
Univ of N Dak	ND	8,390	C
Univ of North Florida	FL	8,769	VC
Univ of Northern Iowa	IA	9,834	C
Univ of Pittsburgh at Bradford	PA	15,294	C
Univ of San Francisco	CA	34,700	VC
Univ of Tulsa	OK	22,090	VC+
Univ of West Alabama	AL	6,048	C
Univ of Wisc/Eau Claire	WI	8,463	VC
Univ of Wisc/La Crosse	WI	8,991	VC
Univ of Wisc/Stevens Point	WI	8,116	VC
Upper Iowa Univ	IA	20,076	C
Valparaiso Univ	IN	26,118	VC+
Virginia State Univ	VA	10,358	C
Washington State Univ	WA	11,334	C
Waynesburg College	PA	19,370	C
Weber State Univ	UT	7,945	NC
West Chester Univ of Pennsylvania	PA	11,164	C
West Virginia Univ	WV	9,370	C
Western Mich Univ	MI	12,031	C
Whitworth College	WA	26,428	VC+
William Woods Univ	MO	20,120	C
Wilmington College	OH	24,172	LC
Wingate Univ	NC	21,200	C
Xavier Univ	OH	26,850	VC+

ATMOSPHERIC SCIENCES AND METEOROLOGY

School	ST	$IS	SR
CUNY/City College	NY	4,230	C+
Cornell Univ	NY	38,253	MC
Creighton Univ	NE	26,748	VC+
Embry-Riddle Aeronautical Univ	AZ	27,710	C+
Embry-Riddle Aeronautical Univ	FL	27,730	C+
Florida Inst of Technology	FL	28,740	VC
Florida State Univ	FL	9,028	HC
Indiana Univ Bloomington	IN	12,389	VC
Iowa State Univ	IA	10,768	VC
Jackson State Univ	MS	8,382	C
Lewis Univ	IL	22,950	C+
Lyndon State College	VT	12,646	LC
Metropolitan State College of Denver	CO	2,338	LC
Millersville Univ of Pennsylvania	PA	11,269	C
N Car State Univ	NC	9,886	VC
Northern Illinois Univ	IL	11,472	C
Northland College	WI	22,170	C+
Penn State Univ/Univ Park Campus	PA	15,646	HC
Plymouth State Univ	NH	12,298	LC
Purdue Univ/West Lafayette	IN	12,560	VC
St. Cloud State Univ	MN	8,362	C
St. Louis Univ	MO	29,780	VC+
SUNY at Oswego	NY	12,650	C
SUNY/College at Brockport	NY	12,111	C
SUNY/College at Oneonta	NY	11,870	VC
SUNY/Maritime College	NY	10,025	LC
SUNY/Univ at Albany	NY	12,951	HC
SUNY/Univ at Stony Brook	NY	12,763	HC
Texas A&M Univ	TX	11,081	HC
United States Air Force Academy	CO		HC+
Univ of Arizona	AZ	10,413	VC
Univ of Calif at Davis	CA	14,995	VC
Univ of Calif at Los Angeles	CA	15,330	MC
Univ of Hawaii at Manoa	HI	9,565	VC
Univ of Kansas	KS	8,923	VC
Univ of Louisiana at Monroe	LA	5,207	NC
Univ of Mich/Ann Arbor	MI	13,864	HC+
Univ of Missouri/Columbia	MO	13,782	VC
Univ of Nebr at Lincoln	NE	9,975	C+
Univ of N Car at Asheville	NC	8,079	VC
Univ of N Dak	ND	8,390	C
Univ of Northern Colo	CO	8,987	C
Univ of Okla	OK	9,226	VC
Univ of South Alabama	AL	7,760	LC
Univ of Utah	UT	9,205	C
Univ of Washington	WA	10,361	VC
Univ of Wisc/Madison	WI	8,262	VC
Valparaiso Univ	IN	26,118	VC+
Western Conn State Univ	CT	11,625	C

AUDIO TECHNOLOGY

School	ST	$IS	SR
American Univ	DC	34,585	VC+
Berklee College of Music	MA	32,447	SP
Cogswell Polytechnical College	CA	14,400	LC
Columbia College Chicago	IL	25,108	LC
Five Towns College	NY	21,050	SP
Hofstra Univ	NY	27,112	VC
Indiana Univ Bloomington	IN	12,389	VC
Ithaca College	NY	31,730	HC
Lebanon Valley College	PA	28,870	VC
School of the Art Inst of Chicago	IL	27,800	SP
SUNY/College at Fredonia	NY	11,562	VC
Texas State Univ	TX	9,320	VC
Univ of Hartford	CT	31,080	C
Univ of Miami	FL	34,608	HC
Univ of New Haven	CT	28,650	C
Webster Univ	MO	21,848	VC

AUTOMOTIVE TECHNOLOGY

School	ST	$IS	SR
Andrews Univ	MI	19,550	C
Benjamin Franklin Inst of Technology	MA	21,839	SP
Central Missouri State Univ	MO	9,776	C
Farmingdale SUNY	NY	12,891	C
Minn State Univ, Mankato	MN	8,803	LC
Montana State Univ-Northern	MT	8,600	NC
Pennsylvania College of Technology	PA	15,126	NC
Southern Illinois Univ Carbondale	IL	10,407	C
Univ of Southern Colo	CO	7,821	LC
Walla Walla College	WA	21,600	NC
Weber State Univ	UT	7,945	NC

AVIAN SCIENCES

School	ST	$IS	SR
Bowling Green State Univ	OH	13,036	C
Minn State Univ, Mankato	MN	8,803	LC
Southern Illinois Univ Carbondale	IL	10,407	C
Univ of Calif at Davis	CA	14,995	VC

AVIATION ADMINISTRATION/MANAGEMENT

School	ST	$IS	SR
Andrews Univ	MI	19,550	C
Auburn Univ	AL	10,396	VC
Averett Univ	VA	23,010	LC
Baker College of Flint	MI	7,720	NC
Bridgewater State College	MA	10,482	C
Central Washington Univ	WA	9,768	C
Christian Heritage College	CA	19,990	C
College of Aeronautics	NY	10,790	SP
Daniel Webster College	NH	24,870	C
Delta State Univ	MS	6,618	C
Dowling College	NY	23,870	LC
Eastern Mich Univ	MI	11,478	C
Embry-Riddle Aeronautical Univ	AZ	27,710	C+
Farmingdale SUNY	NY	12,891	C
Florida Inst of Technology	FL	28,740	VC
Florida Memorial College	FL	6,000	LC
Geneva College	PA	21,850	C
Henderson State Univ	AR	7,386	C
Inter American Univ of PR/Bayamon Univ College	PR	3,522	
Jacksonville Univ	FL	24,040	C
Lewis Univ	IL	22,950	C+
Louisiana Tech Univ	LA	7,361	C
Lynn Univ	FL	30,750	C
Marywood Univ	PA	26,050	C
Metropolitan State College of Denver	CO	2,338	LC
Minn State Univ, Mankato	MN	8,803	LC
Mountain State Univ	WV	10,212	NC
Ohio Univ	OH	14,448	C
Park Univ	MO	10,780	C+
Quincy Univ	IL	22,330	C
Robert Morris Univ	PA	20,438	C
Rocky Mountain College	MT	19,015	C
St. Cloud State Univ	MN	8,362	C
St. Francis College	NY	10,880	LC
St. Louis Univ	MO	29,780	VC+
Salem International Univ	WV	19,770	C
Southeastern Okla State Univ	OK	6,147	C
Southern Illinois Univ Carbondale	IL	10,407	C
Southern Nazarene Univ	OK	14,634	NC
Texas Southern Univ	TX	8,920	NC
Univ of Dubuque	IA	20,950	C
Univ of Louisiana at Monroe	LA	5,207	NC
Univ of New Haven	CT	28,650	C
Univ of N Dak	ND	8,390	C
Univ of Okla	OK	9,226	VC
Univ of the District of Columbia	DC	2,070	LC
Western Mich Univ	MI	12,031	C
Westminster College	UT	17,226	C
Wilmington College	DE	5,594	NC

AVIATION COMPUTER TECHNOLOGY

School	ST	$IS	SR
Andrews Univ	MI	19,550	C
Central Missouri State Univ	MO	9,776	C
College of the Ozarks	MO	3,500	VC+
Florida Inst of Technology	FL	28,740	VC
Florida Memorial College	FL	6,000	LC
Inter American Univ of PR/Bayamon Univ College	PR	3,522	
Kent State Univ	OH	12,932	C
Metropolitan State College of Denver	CO	2,338	LC
Okla State Univ	OK	9,216	VC
Southern Illinois Univ Carbondale	IL	10,407	C
Univ of N Dak	ND	8,390	C
Walla Walla College	WA	21,600	NC

AVIATION MAINTENANCE MANAGEMENT

School	ST	$IS	SR
Central Washington Univ	WA	9,768	C
Embry-Riddle Aeronautical Univ	AZ	27,710	C+
Embry-Riddle Aeronautical Univ	FL	27,730	C+
Thomas Edison State College	NJ	3,325	SP

BACTERIOLOGY

School	ST	$IS	SR
Univ of Calif at Davis	CA	14,995	VC
Univ of Wisc/Madison	WI	8,262	VC

BALLET

School	ST	$IS	SR
Belhaven College	MS	16,040	C+
Friends Univ	KS	15,962	LC
Indiana Univ Bloomington	IN	12,389	VC
N Car School of the Arts	NC	8,565	SP
Texas Christian Univ	TX	23,410	VC

BANKING AND FINANCE

School	ST	$IS	SR
Abilene Christian Univ	TX	18,370	VC
Adams State College	CO	7,468	C
Adelphi Univ	NY	26,300	VC
Alabama A&M Univ	AL	5,100	LC
Alabama State Univ	AL	6,404	C
Alfred Univ	NY	28,290	C
American Univ	DC	34,585	VC+
Anderson Univ	IN	19,430	LC
Andrews Univ	MI	19,550	C
Angelo State Univ	TX	7,576	NC
Appalachian State Univ	NC	7,637	VC
Arcadia Univ	PA	29,890	C
Arizona State Univ-Main	AZ	10,048	C
Arkansas State Univ	AR	8,450	C
Ashland Univ	OH	24,464	C
Auburn Univ	AL	10,396	VC
Auburn Univ Montgomery	AL	9,020	NC
Augusta State Univ	GA	2,592	C
Austin Peay State Univ	TN	5,814	LC
Averett Univ	VA	23,010	LC
Avila Univ	MO	20,300	C
Baker Univ	KS	19,860	VC
Ball State Univ	IN	8,660	C
Baylor Univ	TX	23,864	VC
Becker College	MA	23,710	LC
Benedictine Univ	IL	23,840	C
Bentley College	MA	33,904	VC
Berry College	GA	21,410	VC
Bethel College	MN	25,180	VC
Boise State Univ	ID	7,657	LC
Boston College	MA	33,284	MC
Boston Univ	MA	38,194	HC+
Bowling Green State Univ	OH	13,036	C
Bradley Univ	IL	22,910	VC
Brescia Univ	KY	14,225	C
Bryant College	RI	31,004	VC
Buena Vista Univ	IA	25,406	C
Butler Univ	IN	28,250	VC+
Cabrini College	PA	29,020	C
Calif State Polytechnic Univ, Pomona	CA	8,793	C+
Cal State, Fullerton	CA	6,648	C
Cal State, Long Beach	CA	8,762	C+
Cal State, Northridge	CA	7,757	LC
Cal State, Sacramento	CA	9,543	C

ST = STATE $IS = IN-STATE COSTS SR = SELECTOR RATING

School	ST	$IS	SR
Cal State, San Bernardino	CA	15,238	LC
Cal State, Stanislaus	CA	9,874	C
Canisius College	NY	28,163	C+
Caribbean Univ	PR	3,000	
Catholic Univ of America	DC	34,248	VC
Cedarville Univ	OH	19,954	VC
Central Conn State Univ	CT	12,090	C
Central Mich Univ	MI	11,142	C
Central Missouri State Univ	MO	9,776	C
Central State Univ	OH	8,922	C+
Central Washington Univ	WA	9,768	C
Chestnut Hill College	PA	26,450	LC
Chicago State Univ	IL	10,882	C+
Christopher Newport Univ	VA	8,862	VC
CUNY/Brooklyn College	NY	4,353	C+
Clarion Univ of Pennsylvania	PA	11,272	LC
Clarkson Univ	NY	32,226	VC
Cleary College	MI	10,350	LC
Clemson Univ	SC	11,972	HC
Cleveland State Univ	OH	12,308	LC
Coastal Carolina Univ	SC	11,040	C
College of Notre Dame of Maryland	MD	27,700	C
Colo State Univ	CO	9,964	VC
Columbia College	MO	16,139	C
Columbus State Univ	GA	7,846	C
Concord College	WV	8,136	C
Concordia Univ Wisc	WI	16,600	C
Concordia Univ/St.Paul	MN	24,486	C
Creighton Univ	NE	26,748	VC+
Culver-Stockton College	MO	17,850	C
Dallas Baptist Univ	TX	15,300	VC
Davenport Univ	MI	11,636	NC
David Lipscomb Univ	TN	16,158	VC
De Sales Univ	PA	25,470	LC
Defiance College	OH	22,615	C
DePaul Univ	IL	27,580	VC
Dominican College	NY	24,810	LC
Dowling College	NY	23,870	LC
Drake Univ	IA	25,120	VC+
Duquesne Univ	PA	26,907	VC
East Carolina Univ	NC	8,671	C
East Central Univ	OK	4,968	C
East Texas Baptist Univ	TX	13,914	C
Eastern Illinois Univ	IL	11,192	C
Eastern Kentucky Univ	KY	7,708	C
Eastern Mich Univ	MI	11,478	C
Eastern New Mexico Univ	NM	6,762	LC
Eastern Washington Univ	WA	9,012	C
Edinboro Univ of Pennsylvania	PA	10,850	LC
Elmhurst College	IL	24,630	C
Emory Univ	GA	36,872	MC
Excelsior College	NY	975	SP
Fairfield Univ	CT	35,505	HC
Fairmont State	WV	8,280	LC
Fayetteville State Univ	NC	5,590	LC
Ferris State Univ	MI	12,512	C
Florida A&M Univ	FL	7,564	C
Florida Atlantic Univ	FL	8,543	C
Florida Gulf Coast Univ	FL	9,908	C
Florida International Univ	FL	9,912	VC
Florida Southern College	FL	23,592	C
Florida State Univ	FL	9,028	HC
Fort Hays State Univ	KS	7,363	C
Francis Marion Univ	SC	9,364	C
Franklin and Marshall College	PA	35,930	HC+
Franklin Pierce College	NH	28,980	LC
Franklin Univ	OH	6,720	SP
Freed-Hardeman Univ	TN		NC
Gannon Univ	PA	23,260	C
George Mason Univ	VA	9,732	VC
George Washington Univ	DC	41,030	MC
Georgetown College	KY	22,000	VC
Georgetown Univ	DC	38,242	MC
Georgia Southern Univ	GA	8,540	C
Georgia State Univ	GA	10,658	C
Glenville State College	WV	7,812	NC
Golden Gate Univ	CA	11,232	NC
Goldey-Beacom College	DE	11,440	C
Gordon College	MA	25,982	VC+
Grand Canyon Univ	AZ	30,000	LC
Grand Valley State Univ	MI	11,022	VC
Grove City College	PA	14,228	HC
Gwynedd-Mercy College	PA	24,225	C
Hampton Univ	VA	17,112	C+
Hardin-Simmons Univ	TX	14,165	C
Hawaii Pacific Univ	HI	19,218	C
Hillsdale College	MI	22,450	HC
Hofstra Univ	NY	27,112	VC
Houston Baptist Univ	TX	16,905	C
Howard Univ	DC	16,505	C
Huron Univ	SD	10,450	C
Husson College	ME	16,300	LC
Idaho State Univ	ID	8,128	C
Illinois State Univ	IL	10,944	C+
Immaculata Univ	PA	25,200	C
Indiana State Univ	IN	10,719	LC
Indiana Univ Bloomington	IN	12,389	VC
Indiana Univ of Pennsylvania	PA	10,489	C
Indiana Univ South Bend	IN	4,571	LC
Indiana Univ Southeast	IN	4,504	LC
Indiana Univ-Purdue Univ Fort Wayne	IN	5,108	LC
Indiana Univ-Purdue Univ Indianapolis	IN	8,257	LC
Inter American Univ of PR/ Bayamon Univ College	PR	3,522	
Inter American Univ of PR/ Fajardo Campus	PR	4,000	
Inter American Univ of PR/ Metropolitan Campus	PR		
Inter American Univ of PR/ Ponce Regional College	PR	3,700	
Inter American Univ of PR/ San German	PR	6,716	
Iona College	NY	27,988	VC
Iowa State Univ	IA	10,768	VC
Ithaca College	NY	31,730	HC
Jackson State Univ	MS	8,382	C
Jacksonville State Univ	AL	6,844	LC
Jacksonville Univ	FL	24,040	C
James Madison Univ	VA	10,794	VC
John Carroll Univ	OH	27,658	C+
Johns Hopkins Univ	MD	38,372	MC
Juniata College	PA	29,080	VC
Kansas State Univ	KS	8,728	VC
Kean Univ	NJ	14,479	C
Kennesaw State Univ	GA	2,724	C
Kent State Univ	OH	12,932	C
King's College	PA	26,990	C
Knox College	IL	30,294	VC+
Kutztown Univ of Pennsylvania	PA	10,786	C
La Roche College	PA	22,094	C
La Salle Univ	PA	31,260	VC
La Sierra Univ	CA	19,260	LC
Lasell College	MA	26,000	C
Lehigh Univ	PA	37,570	HC+
Lewis Univ	IL	22,950	C+
Lincoln Univ	PA	13,320	C+
Lindenwood Univ	MO	17,050	VC
Linfield College	OR	27,090	VC
LIU/Brooklyn Campus	NY	24,790	C
LIU/C.W. Post Campus	NY	28,282	C
Loras College	IA	24,233	C
Louisiana State Univ and A&M College	LA	9,126	VC
Louisiana State Univ in Shreveport	LA	2,884	NC
Louisiana Tech Univ	LA	7,361	C
Loyola Univ Chicago	IL	31,164	VC
Loyola Univ New Orleans	LA	31,036	VC+
Lubbock Christian Univ	TX	15,832	C
Manchester College	IN	23,390	C
Manhattan College	NY	27,400	VC
Manhattanville College	NY	32,420	C+
Marian College	IN	23,030	C
Marquette Univ	WI	27,594	VC
Marshall Univ	WV	9,116	C
Marymount Univ	VA	23,668	C
Marywood Univ	PA	26,050	C
McKendree College	IL	21,120	VC
McMurry Univ	TX	17,846	LC
McNeese State Univ	LA	5,259	LC
Medaille College	NY	20,060	C
Mercer Univ	GA	27,516	VC+
Mercyhurst College	PA	20,694	C
Metropolitan State College of Denver	CO	2,338	LC
Metropolitan State Univ	MN	3,852	SP
Miami Univ	OH	15,033	HC
Mich State Univ	MI	11,933	VC
Middle Tenn State Univ	TN	8,534	C
Midwestern State Univ	TX	8,045	LC
Millikin Univ	IL	25,555	C
Minn State Univ, Mankato	MN	8,803	LC
Minn State Univ, Moorehead	MN	7,000	LC
Minot State Univ	ND	6,602	LC
Miss State Univ	MS	9,139	C
Missouri Southern State Univ	MO	8,316	C
Monmouth Univ	NJ	26,334	C
Montclair State Univ	NJ	13,790	C
Morehead State Univ	KY	7,464	C
Morehouse College	GA	22,728	C
Mountain State Univ	WV	10,212	NC
Murray State Univ	KY	7,816	VC
National Univ	CA	9,690	SP
New Mexico Highlands Univ	NM	6,182	LC
New Mexico State Univ	NM	7,932	C
New York Inst of Technology	NY	24,205	VC
New York Univ	NY	39,406	MC
Nicholls State Univ	LA	6,395	NC
Nichols College	MA	27,562	LC
Norfolk State Univ	VA	9,722	LC
North Central College	IL	25,656	VC
North Georgia College and State Univ	GA	6,984	C
North Park Univ	IL	24,030	C
Northeastern State Univ	OK	4,950	LC
Northern Arizona Univ	AZ	9,002	C
Northern Illinois Univ	IL	11,472	C
Northern Mich Univ	MI	10,834	C
Northern State Univ	SD	7,117	LC
Northwest Missouri State Univ	MO	9,334	C
Northwestern College	MN	22,820	C+
Northwood Univ	FL	21,040	C
Northwood Univ	MI	20,265	LC
Northwood Univ	TX	20,135	LC
Notre Dame de Namur Univ	CA	26,932	LC
Nova Southeastern Univ	FL	23,346	C
Oakland Univ	MI	10,800	C
Ohio Dominican Univ	OH	22,700	C
Ohio State Univ	OH	13,080	VC+
Ohio Univ	OH	14,448	C
Okla Baptist Univ	OK	15,220	VC
Okla City Univ	OK	19,580	VC
Okla State Univ	OK	9,216	VC
Old Dominion Univ	VA	10,441	C
Oral Roberts Univ	OK	18,490	C
Pace Univ	NY	28,652	VC
Palm Beach Atlantic Univ	FL	20,690	C
Penn State Univ at Erie/ Behrend College	PA	12,326	C
Penn State Univ/Univ Park Campus	PA	15,646	HC
Pennsylvania College of Technology	PA	15,126	NC
Philadelphia Univ	PA	27,354	C
Pittsburg State Univ	KS	7,128	NC
Pontifical Catholic Univ of PR/Ponce	PR	7,298	
Prairie View A&M Univ	TX	9,418	NC
Providence College	RI	30,604	HC
Purdue Univ/Calumet	IN	6,630	NC
Quincy Univ	IL	22,330	C
Quinnipiac Univ	CT	30,570	VC
Radford Univ	VA	8,500	C
Richard Stockton College of New Jersey	NJ	12,972	VC
Rider Univ	NJ	30,900	C
Robert Morris Univ	PA	20,438	C
Rochester Inst of Technology	NY	29,217	VC+
Rockhurst Univ	MO	22,960	C+
Roger Williams Univ	RI	30,296	C
Roosevelt Univ	IL	22,580	VC
Rutgers, The State Univ of New Jersey/Camden Campus	NJ	14,990	VC
Rutgers, The State Univ of New Jersey/New Brunswick/Piscataway Campus	NJ	15,800	HC
Rutgers, The State Univ of New Jersey/Newark Campus	NJ	15,624	VC
Sacred Heart Univ	CT	29,178	C
Saginaw Valley State Univ	MI	11,055	C
St. Anselm College	NH	30,250	C
St. Bonaventure Univ	NY	24,455	LC
St. Cloud State Univ	MN	8,362	C
St. Edward's Univ	TX	20,428	C
St. John's Univ	NY	30,180	C
St. Joseph's Univ	PA	33,590	VC
St. Louis Univ	MO	29,780	VC+
St. Martin's College	WA	23,245	C
St. Mary's Univ of San Antonio	TX	22,444	C
St. Thomas Aquinas College	NY	20,590	LC
St. Thomas Univ	FL	21,400	LC
St. Vincent College	PA	25,530	VC
St. Xavier Univ	IL	23,144	C
Salem State College	MA	8,592	C
Salisbury Univ	MD	12,664	VC
Sam Houston State Univ	TX	7,142	C
San Diego State Univ	CA	10,321	C
San Francisco State Univ	CA	12,070	C
San Jose State Univ	CA	8,187	C
Santa Clara Univ	CA	34,701	HC
Seattle Univ	WA	24,183	VC
Seton Hall Univ	NJ	30,130	VC
Seton Hill Univ	PA	24,930	C
Shippensburg Univ of Pennsylvania	PA	10,826	C
Siena College	NY	25,310	VC
Simmons College	MA	33,000	VC
Southeast Missouri State Univ	MO	9,704	C
Southeastern Louisiana Univ	LA	6,791	LC
Southeastern Univ	DC	8,505	LC
Southern Conn State Univ	CT	10,310	C
Southern Illinois Univ Carbondale	IL	10,407	C
Southern Methodist Univ	TX	34,210	HC
Southern Nazarene Univ	OK	14,634	NC
Southern Univ and A&M College	LA	7,372	LC
Southern Utah Univ	UT	8,194	C
Southwest Missouri State Univ	MO	8,918	C
Southwestern Okla State Univ	OK	4,801	C
Spring Hill College	AL	25,868	VC
SUNY at Oswego	NY	12,650	C
SUNY/College at Old Westbury	NY	12,784	C
SUNY/Univ at New Paltz	NY	11,565	VC
State Univ of West Georgia	GA	7,622	C
Stephen F. Austin State Univ	TX	7,552	C
Stetson Univ	FL	29,495	VC
Stonehill College	MA	30,752	HC
Suffolk Univ	MA	29,200	C
Syracuse Univ	NY	34,720	HC
Talladega College	AL	10,110	LC
Tarleton State Univ	TX	7,576	C
Taylor Univ	IN	23,018	VC+
Teikyo Post Univ	CT	24,875	C
Temple Univ	PA	15,912	C
Tenn Tech Univ	TN	8,670	VC
Texas A&M Univ	TX	11,081	HC
Texas A&M Univ at Commerce	TX	8,994	C
Texas A&M Univ at Corpus Christi	TX	10,269	C
Texas A&M Univ at Kingsville	TX	6,740	LC
Texas Christian Univ	TX	23,410	VC
Texas Southern Univ	TX	8,920	NC
Texas State Univ	TX	9,320	VC
Texas Tech Univ	TX	10,768	VC
Thomas Edison State College	NJ	3,325	SP
Tiffin Univ	OH	19,490	LC
Touro College	NY	15,250	VC
Tri-State Univ-Main Campus	IN	23,600	C
Troy State Univ	AL	7,696	C
Troy State Univ Dothan	AL	3,842	C
Troy State Univ Montgomery	AL	3,600	NC
Tuskegee Univ	AL	17,250	LC
Union College	NE	17,130	C
Union Univ	TN	18,800	VC
Univ of Akron	OH	13,134	NC
Univ of Alabama	AL	9,040	C+
Univ of Alabama at Birmingham	AL	12,901	C
Univ of Alabama in Huntsville	AL	9,126	VC
Univ of Alaska Anchorage	AK	9,100	NC
Univ of Arizona	AZ	10,413	VC
Univ of Arkansas	AR	9,855	VC
Univ of Arkansas at Little Rock	AR	5,637	NC
Univ of Bridgeport	CT	25,924	LC
Univ of Central Arkansas	AR	6,388	C
Univ of Central Florida	FL	10,038	VC
Univ of Central Okla	OK	9,434	C
Univ of Charleston	WV	23,620	C
Univ of Cincinnati	OH	14,736	C
Univ of Colo at Boulder	CO	10,774	VC
Univ of Conn	CT	14,608	VC
Univ of Dayton	OH	24,850	VC
Univ of Delaware	DE	12,616	HC
Univ of Denver	CO	32,148	VC
Univ of Evansville	IN	24,190	VC
Univ of Findlay	OH	23,962	NC
Univ of Florida	FL	8,580	MC
Univ of Hartford	CT	31,080	C
Univ of Hawaii at Manoa	HI	9,565	VC
Univ of Houston	TX	9,818	C
Univ of Houston-Downtown	TX	2,594	NC
Univ of Idaho	ID	8,216	C
Univ of Illinois at Chicago	IL	13,418	C
Univ of Illinois at Urbana-Champaign	IL	11,316	HC+
Univ of Indianapolis	IN	22,560	VC
Univ of Iowa	IA	10,923	VC
Univ of Kentucky	KY	7,765	C
Univ of Louisiana at Lafayette	LA	5,826	C
Univ of Louisiana at Monroe	LA	5,207	NC
Univ of Louisville	KY	8,762	VC
Univ of Mary Hardin-Baylor	TX	17,268	C
Univ of Maryland/College Park	MD	14,227	HC
Univ of Mass Amherst	MA	13,980	C+
Univ of Mass Dartmouth	MA	12,835	C
Univ of Memphis	TN	8,560	C
Univ of Miami	FL	34,608	HC
Univ of Mich/Flint	MI	5,548	C
Univ of Miss	MS	7,666	C
Univ of Missouri/Columbia	MO	13,782	VC
Univ of Montana	MT	9,395	C
Univ of Montevallo	AL	8,478	C
Univ of Nebr at Kearney	NE	8,286	NC
Univ of Nebr at Lincoln	NE	9,975	C+
Univ of Nebr at Omaha	NE	8,080	C
Univ of Nevada/Las Vegas	NV	11,566	C
Univ of Nevada/Reno	NV	9,792	C
Univ of New Haven	CT	28,650	C
Univ of New Mexico	NM	9,223	C
Univ of New Orleans	LA	7,356	C
Univ of North Alabama	AL	7,972	NC
Univ of N Car at Charlotte	NC	8,185	C
Univ of N Car at Greensboro	NC	8,248	C
Univ of N Car at Wilmington	NC	8,940	VC
Univ of N Dak	ND	8,390	C
Univ of North Florida	FL	8,769	VC
Univ of North Texas	TX	7,629	C

ST = STATE $IS = IN-STATE COSTS SR = SELECTOR RATING

School	ST	$IS	SR
Univ of Northern Iowa	IA	9,834	C
Univ of Notre Dame	IN	34,442	MC
Univ of Okla	OK	9,226	VC
Univ of Pennsylvania	PA	37,960	MC
Univ of Pittsburgh at Johnstown	PA	15,216	LC
Univ of Pittsburgh at Pittsburgh	PA	16,074	HC
Univ of Portland	OR	28,500	VC
Univ of PR/Bayamon Univ College Campus	PR	1,600	
Univ of PR/Mayaguez	PR		
Univ of PR/Rio Piedras	PR	5,730	
Univ of Rhode Island	RI	13,720	VC
Univ of St. Francis	IL	22,850	C
Univ of St. Thomas	MN	26,918	VC
Univ of St. Thomas	TX	21,952	VC
Univ of San Francisco	CA	34,700	VC
Univ of Scranton	PA	30,836	VC
Univ of South Alabama	AL	7,760	LC
Univ of S Car at Columbia	SC	10,048	VC
Univ of South Florida	FL	9,454	C
Univ of Southern Indiana	IN	9,025	LC
Univ of Southern Miss	MS	8,324	LC
Univ of Tampa	FL	23,982	VC
Univ of Tenn at Knoxville	TN	8,214	C
Univ of Texas at Arlington	TX	7,192	LC
Univ of Texas at Austin	TX	10,630	HC
Univ of Texas at El Paso	TX	5,799	NC
Univ of Texas at San Antonio	TX	9,088	NC
Univ of Texas-Pan American	TX	5,954	LC
Univ of the District of Columbia	DC	2,070	LC
Univ of the Incarnate Word	TX	21,772	LC
Univ of Toledo	OH	12,479	NC
Univ of Tulsa	OK	22,090	VC+
Univ of Utah	UT	9,205	C
Univ of Washington	WA	10,361	VC
Univ of West Florida	FL	8,470	C
Univ of Wisc/Eau Claire	WI	8,463	VC
Univ of Wisc/La Crosse	WI	8,991	VC
Univ of Wisc/Madison	WI	8,262	VC
Univ of Wisc/Milwaukee	WI	9,427	LC
Univ of Wisc/Oshkosh	WI	6,130	LC
Univ of Wisc/Whitewater	WI	8,626	C
Univ of Wyoming	WY	8,636	C
Upper Iowa Univ	IA	20,076	C
Utah State Univ	UT	7,371	C
Valdosta State Univ	GA	7,798	C
Valparaiso Univ	IN	26,118	VC+
Vanguard Univ of Southern Calif	CA	22,208	C
Villanova Univ	PA	35,050	HC
Virginia Polytechnic Inst and State Univ	VA	9,179	C
Virginia Union Univ	VA	15,358	LC
Wake Forest Univ	NC	34,090	MC
Walsh Univ	OH	20,890	C
Warner Southern College	FL	16,738	LC
Wartburg College	IA	21,165	VC
Washburn Univ of Topeka	KS	8,984	NC
Washington State Univ	WA	11,334	C
Washington Univ in St. Louis	MO	38,293	MC
Wayne State Univ	MI	11,774	C
Waynesburg College	PA	19,370	C
Webber International Univ	FL	16,510	C
Weber State Univ	UT	7,945	NC
West Liberty State College	WV	7,868	LC
West Texas A&M Univ	TX	7,533	C
West Virginia State College	WV	6,264	NC
West Virginia Univ	WV	9,370	C
Western Carolina Univ	NC	6,742	C
Western Conn State Univ	CT	11,625	C
Western Illinois Univ	IL	10,363	C
Western Kentucky Univ	KY	6,834	C
Western Mich Univ	MI	12,031	C
Western New England College	MA	28,924	C
Westminster College	PA	22,960	C
Wichita State Univ	KS	8,092	C
Wilberforce Univ	OH	14,937	LC
William Paterson Univ of New Jersey	NJ	14,450	C
Wilmington College	DE	5,594	NC
Wingate Univ	NC	21,200	C
Winona State Univ	MN		C
Wofford College	SC	26,710	HC
Woodbury Univ	CA	25,344	LC
Wright State Univ	OH	11,490	LC
Xavier Univ	OH	26,850	VC+
Xavier Univ of Louisiana	LA	17,600	C
York College of Pennsylvania	PA	14,500	VC
Youngstown State Univ	OH	11,148	NC

BEHAVIORAL SCIENCE

School	ST	$IS	SR
Andrews Univ	MI	19,550	C
Calif Baptist Univ	CA	19,924	C
Calif State Polytechnic Univ, Pomona	CA	8,793	C+
Cal State, Dominguez Hills	CA	5,840	LC
Cal State, Monterey Bay	CA	6,683	LC
Capital Univ	OH	26,550	C
Chaminade Univ of Honolulu	HI	21,430	LC
College for Lifelong Learning	NH	4,100	SP
College of St. Scholastica	MN	24,970	C+
Concordia College	NY	19,200	VC
Concordia Univ	CA	24,420	C
Concordia Univ at Austin	TX	20,450	LC
Concordia Univ Nebr	NE	20,302	C+
Dakota Wesleyan Univ	SD	17,832	C
Drew Univ/College of Liberal Arts	NJ	35,550	VC
East-West Univ	IL	10,365	LC
Erskine College	SC	23,166	VC
Glenville State College	WV	7,812	NC
Green Mountain College	VT	24,130	C
Indiana Univ East	IN	4,433	LC
Indiana Univ Kokomo	IN	4,463	LC
Iona College	NY	27,988	VC
Johnson State College	VT	11,819	LC
King College	TN	22,500	VC
Lakeland College	WI	17,950	C
Lehigh Univ	PA	37,570	HC+
Mercy College	NY	19,200	NC
Metropolitan State College of Denver	CO	2,338	LC
Missouri Baptist Univ	MO	18,010	C
Mount Marty College	SD	15,656	LC
Mount Mary College	WI	20,370	C
National Univ	CA	9,690	SP
New York Inst of Technology	NY	24,205	VC
North Central Univ	MN	14,904	C
Northwest College	WA	18,854	C
Oglethorpe Univ	GA	26,000	VC
Okla Wesleyan Univ	OK	14,100	LC
Our Lady of Holy Cross College	LA	5,900	C
Our Lady of the Lake Univ of San Antonio	TX	17,336	C
Pacific Union College	CA	22,065	C+
Point Park Univ	PA	21,840	C
Rochester College	MI	16,718	C
Southern Adventist Univ	TN	17,080	C
Sterling College	KS	18,763	C
Tenn Wesleyan College	TN	16,540	C
Trevecca Nazarene Univ	TN	17,548	C
United States Air Force Academy	CO		HC+
United States Military Academy	NY		MC
Univ of Calif at Davis	CA	14,995	VC
Univ of Evansville	IN	24,190	VC
Univ of Kansas	KS	8,923	VC
Univ of La Verne	CA	28,600	C
Univ of Maine at Fort Kent	ME	9,770	LC
Univ of Maine at Machias	ME	9,271	LC
Univ of Maine at Presque Isle	ME	9,155	LC
Univ of Mary	ND	12,900	C+
Univ of Mich/Dearborn	MI	6,843	VC
Univ of Rio Grande	OH	8,728	NC
Univ of Utah	UT	9,205	C
Univ of Wisc/Madison	WI	8,262	VC
Warren Wilson College	NC	21,794	VC
Widener Univ	PA	27,020	C
Wilmington College	DE	5,594	NC
Wilson College	PA	23,912	C
York College of Pennsylvania	PA	14,500	VC

BIBLICAL LANGUAGES

School	ST	$IS	SR
Abilene Christian Univ	TX	18,370	VC
Asbury College	KY	20,704	VC
Baylor Univ	TX	23,864	VC
Concordia Univ	MI	24,095	C
Concordia Univ Wisc	WI	16,600	C
Cornerstone Univ and Grand Rapids Theological Seminary	MI	19,846	C
David Lipscomb Univ	TN	16,158	VC
Luther College	IA	25,700	VC
North Central Univ	MN	14,904	C
Southern Nazarene Univ	OK	14,634	NC
Toccoa Falls College	GA	15,600	C
Union Univ	TN	18,800	VC
Univ of Mich/Ann Arbor	MI	13,864	HC+
Walla Walla College	WA	21,600	NC

BIBLICAL STUDIES

School	ST	$IS	SR
Abilene Christian Univ	TX	18,370	VC
Albert A. List College of Jewish Studies	NY	18,500	HC+
Asbury College	KY	20,704	VC
Azusa Pacific Univ	CA	24,720	VC
Belhaven College	MS	16,040	C+
Bethel College	IN	19,670	C
Biola Univ	CA	25,964	VC
Blue Mountain College	MS	10,226	C
Cascade College	OR	16,700	NC
Cedarville Univ	OH	19,954	VC
Christian Heritage College	CA	19,990	C
Clearwater Christian College	FL	13,160	LC
Colo Christian Univ	CO	21,182	VC
Cornerstone Univ and Grand Rapids Theological Seminary	MI	19,846	C
Covenant College	GA	23,830	VC+
Crichton College	TN	15,215	C
Dallas Baptist Univ	TX	15,300	VC
Eastern Mennonite Univ	VA	22,990	C
Eastern Univ	PA	24,020	C
Evangel Univ	MO	15,435	C
Faulkner Univ	AL	14,500	C
Freed-Hardeman Univ	TN		NC
Geneva College	PA	21,850	C
George Fox Univ	OR	26,110	VC
Gordon College	MA	25,982	VC+
Goshen College	IN	22,450	VC
Grace College	IN	19,825	VC
Hannibal-LaGrange College	MO	13,940	C
Hope International Univ	CA	16,940	NC
Houghton College	NY	23,984	VC
Huntington College	IN	23,590	C
Indiana Wesleyan Univ	IN	19,900	C+
John Brown Univ	AR	15,080	VC
Kentucky Christian College	KY	13,472	C
King College	TN	22,500	VC
LeTourneau Univ	TX	21,080	C
Lubbock Christian Univ	TX	15,832	C
Malone College	OH	20,995	C
Master's College and Seminary	CA	23,250	VC
Messiah College	PA	25,890	VC+
Milligan College	TN	19,860	C+
Montreat College	NC	18,762	C
Northwest College	WA	18,854	C
Northwestern College	MN	22,820	C+
Nyack College	NY	18,540	C
Ohio Valley College	WV	16,036	C+
Okla Christian Univ	OK	17,690	NC
Oral Roberts Univ	OK	18,490	C
Ouachita Baptist Univ	AR	18,900	VC
Palm Beach Atlantic Univ	FL	20,690	C
Philadelphia Biblical Univ	PA	18,395	C
Rochester College	MI	16,718	C
Samford Univ	AL	18,648	VC
Simpson College	CA	20,500	C
Southeastern College	FL	11,648	LC
Southern Christian Univ	AL	9,440	LC
Southwest Baptist Univ	MO	15,371	C
Tabor College	KS	19,500	NC
Taylor Univ	IN	23,820	VC+
Toccoa Falls College	GA	15,600	C
Trinity Bible College	ND		
Trinity Christian College	IL	21,640	VC
Trinity International Univ	IL	22,980	C+
Union Univ	TN	18,800	VC
Univ of Evansville	IN	24,190	VC
Univ of Mich/Ann Arbor	MI	13,864	HC+
Vanguard Univ of Southern Calif	CA	22,208	C
Warner Southern College	FL	16,738	LC
Western Baptist College	OR	21,808	C
Wheaton College	IL	21,934	HC
William Tyndale College	MI	12,170	NC
York College	NE	14,975	C

BILINGUAL/BICULTURAL EDUCATION

School	ST	$IS	SR
Boston Univ	MA	38,194	HC+
Cal State, San Bernardino	CA	15,238	LC
Cal State, Stanislaus	CA	9,874	C
Central Mich Univ	MI	11,142	C
Chicago State Univ	IL	10,882	C+
CUNY/Brooklyn College	NY	4,353	C+
CUNY/City College	NY	4,230	C+
College of Our Lady of the Elms	MA	20,644	C
Eastern Mich Univ	MI	11,478	C
Hofstra Univ	NY	27,112	VC
McMurry Univ	TX	17,846	LC
Mount Mary College	WI	20,370	C
Northeastern Illinois Univ	IL	2,898	NC
St. John's Univ	NY	30,180	C
St. Thomas Aquinas College	NY	20,590	LC
SUNY/College at Old Westbury	NY	12,784	C
Texas Christian Univ	TX	23,410	VC
Texas Southern Univ	TX	8,920	NC
Texas State Univ	TX	9,320	VC
Univ of Findlay	OH	23,962	NC
Univ of Houston-Downtown	TX	2,594	NC
Univ of Minn/Twin Cities	MN	13,160	VC
Univ of New Mexico	NM	9,223	C
Western Illinois Univ	IL	10,363	C

BIOCHEMISTRY

School	ST	$IS	SR
Abilene Christian Univ	TX	18,370	VC
Adelphi Univ	NY	26,300	VC
Agnes Scott College	GA	28,230	HC
Albright College	PA	30,579	C
Allegheny College	PA	30,280	VC
Alma College	MI	25,566	VC
Alvernia College	PA	23,212	LC
American International College	MA	24,690	LC
American Univ	DC	34,585	VC+
Andrews Univ	MI	19,550	C
Angelo State Univ	TX	7,576	NC
Arizona State Univ-Main	AZ	10,048	C
Asbury College	KY	20,704	VC
Auburn Univ	AL	10,396	VC
Austin College	TX	24,747	HC
Averett Univ	VA	23,010	LC
Azusa Pacific Univ	CA	24,720	VC
Bard College	NY	37,352	HC+
Bates College	ME	37,500	MC
Baylor Univ	TX	23,864	VC
Beloit College	WI	29,864	HC
Benedictine College	KS	20,603	C
Benedictine Univ	IL	23,840	C
Bennington College	VT	35,910	HC
Bethany College	WV	19,845	VC
Bethel College	MN	25,180	VC
Biola Univ	CA	25,964	VC
Boston College	MA	33,284	MC
Boston Univ	MA	38,194	HC+
Bowdoin College	ME	37,790	MC
Bowling Green State Univ	OH	13,036	C
Bradley Univ	IL	22,910	VC
Brandeis Univ	MA	38,198	MC
Brigham Young Univ	UT	8,504	HC
Brown Univ	RI	38,174	MC
Bucknell Univ	PA	35,262	HC+
Calif Lutheran Univ	CA	27,600	LC
Calif Polytechnic State Univ	CA	8,747	VC
Cal State, Fullerton	CA	6,648	C
Cal State, Hayward	CA	8,871	LC
Cal State, Long Beach	CA	8,762	C+
Cal State, Los Angeles	CA	5,778	C
Cal State, Northridge	CA	7,757	LC
Cal State, San Bernardino	CA	15,238	LC
Calvin College	MI	22,615	NC
Campbell Univ	NC	18,268	VC
Canisius College	NY	28,163	C+
Capital Univ	OH	26,550	C
Carroll College	WI	22,740	C
Case Western Reserve Univ	OH	32,002	MC
Catholic Univ of America	DC	34,248	VC
Cedar Crest College	PA	25,145	C+
Centenary College of Louisiana	LA	23,100	VC+
Centre College	KY	27,300	HC
Charleston Southern Univ	SC	17,122	C
Chatham College	PA	27,266	C+
Chestnut Hill College	PA	26,450	LC
Chicago State Univ	IL	10,882	C+
CUNY/College of Staten Island	NY	4,308	NC
CUNY/Queens College	NY	4,362	C
Claflin Univ	SC	14,838	C+
Claremont McKenna College	CA	36,880	MC
Clark Univ	MA	32,115	VC
Clemson Univ	SC	11,972	HC
Coe College	IA	27,385	VC
Colgate Univ	NY	37,095	MC
College Misericordia	PA	26,350	C
College of Charleston	SC	11,887	HC
College of Mount St. Vincent	NY	26,800	C
College of St. Benedict	MN	26,672	VC
College of St. Catherine	MN	24,010	VC
College of St. Elizabeth	NJ	25,460	C
College of St. Rose	NY	22,864	C
College of St. Scholastica	MN	24,970	C+
College of Wooster	OH	31,300	HC
Colo College	CO	36,860	HC
Colo State Univ	CO	9,964	VC
Columbia Union College	MD	20,543	C
Columbia Univ/Barnard College	NY	36,990	MC
Columbia Univ/Columbia College	NY	38,590	MC
Conn College	CT	37,900	MC
Daemen College	NY	22,120	C
Dartmouth College	NH	37,770	MC
David Lipscomb Univ	TN	16,158	VC
Denison Univ	OH	33,050	HC
DePauw Univ	IN	31,500	HC
Dickinson College	PA	35,825	HC
Dominican Univ	IL	23,610	C
Duquesne Univ	PA	26,907	VC
Earlham College	IN	29,976	VC+
East Carolina Univ	NC	8,671	C
East Stroudsburg Univ of Pennsylvania	PA	10,336	C
Eastern Mennonite Univ	VA	22,990	C
Eastern Mich Univ	MI	11,478	C
Eastern Univ	PA	24,020	C
Eastern Washington Univ	WA	9,012	C
Edinboro Univ of Pennsylvania	PA	10,850	LC
Elizabethtown College	PA	28,800	C
Elmira College	NY	33,820	VC
Emmanuel College	MA	27,600	C+

ST = STATE **$IS** = IN-STATE COSTS **SR** = SELECTOR RATING

School	ST	$IS	SR
Fairleigh Dickinson Univ/Metropolitan Campus	NJ	28,584	C
Florida Inst of Technology	FL	28,740	VC
Florida State Univ	FL	9,028	HC
Franklin and Marshall College	PA	35,930	HC+
Georgetown Univ	DC	38,242	MC
Georgian Court College	NJ	19,040	LC
Gettysburg College	PA	35,646	HC
Grinnell College	IA	31,060	HC+
Grove City College	PA	14,228	HC
Gustavus Adolphus College	MN	27,120	VC+
Hamilton College	NY	37,560	MC
Harding Univ	AR	14,890	VC
Hartwick College	NY	34,650	C+
Harvard Univ/Harvard College	MA	37,928	MC
Hofstra Univ	NY	27,112	VC
Holy Family College	PA	13,710	LC
Hood College	MD	27,795	VC
Hope College	MI	25,340	VC
Idaho State Univ	ID	8,128	C
Illinois Inst of Technology	IL	26,456	HC+
Illinois State Univ	IL	10,944	C+
Immaculata Univ	PA	25,200	C
Indiana Univ Bloomington	IN	12,389	VC
Indiana Univ of Pennsylvania	PA	10,489	C
Iona College	NY	27,988	VC
Iowa State Univ	IA	10,768	VC
Ithaca College	NY	31,730	HC
Jamestown College	ND	12,600	NC
John Brown Univ	AR	15,080	VC
Juniata College	PA	29,080	VC
Kansas State Univ	KS	8,728	VC
Kennesaw State Univ	GA	2,724	C
Kenyon College	OH	35,370	HC+
Keuka College	NY	21,170	C
King College	TN	22,500	VC
Knox College	IL	30,294	VC+
La Salle Univ	PA	31,260	VC
La Sierra Univ	CA	19,260	LC
Lafayette College	PA	35,746	MC
LaGrange College	GA	20,500	C
Le Moyne College	NY	26,400	VC
Lebanon Valley College	PA	28,870	VC
Lehigh Univ	PA	37,570	HC+
Lewis and Clark College	OR	30,620	VC
Lewis Univ	IL	22,950	C+
Loras College	IA	24,233	C
Louisiana State Univ and A&M College	LA	9,126	VC
Louisiana State Univ in Shreveport	LA	2,884	NC
Loyola Marymount Univ	CA	32,194	VC
Madonna Univ	MI	11,504	VC
Manchester College	IN	23,390	C
Manhattan College	NY	27,400	VC
Manhattanville College	NY	32,420	C+
Mansfield Univ	PA	11,220	C
Marietta College	OH	27,047	C
Marlboro College	VT	29,055	VC+
Marquette Univ	WI	27,594	VC
Mary Baldwin College	VA	24,939	C
Maryville College	TN	25,960	VC
McMurry Univ	TX	17,846	LC
Mercyhurst College	PA	20,694	C
Merrimack College	MA	29,625	C
Messiah College	PA	25,890	VC+
Miami Univ	OH	15,033	HC
Mich State Univ	MI	11,933	VC
Middlebury College	VT	38,100	MC
Mills College	CA	33,371	VC
Minn State Univ, Mankato	MN	8,803	LC
Miss College	MS	14,574	C
Miss State Univ	MS	9,139	C
Monmouth College	IL	23,600	C
Montclair State Univ	NJ	13,790	C
Mount Holyoke College	MA	37,918	HC+
Mount St. Mary's College	CA	28,307	VC
Mount St. Mary's College	MD	28,400	C
Muhlenberg College	PA	31,485	HC
Murray State Univ	KY	7,816	VC
Nazareth College of Rochester	NY	24,936	VC
Nebr Wesleyan Univ	NE	21,197	C+
New Mexico State Univ	NM	7,932	C
New York Univ	NY	39,406	MC
Newman Univ	KS	18,018	C
Niagara Univ	NY	25,050	C
N Car State Univ	NC	9,886	VC
North Central College	IL	25,656	VC
Northeastern Univ	MA	35,650	HC
Northern Mich Univ	MI	10,834	C
Northwest Nazarene Univ	ID	20,360	VC
Norwich Univ	VT	21,064	LC
Notre Dame de Namur Univ	CA	26,932	LC
Oakland Univ	MI	10,800	C
Oakwood College	AL	14,904	C
Oberlin College	OH	36,938	MC
Occidental College	CA	35,922	HC
Ohio Northern Univ	OH	27,765	VC
Ohio State Univ	OH	13,080	VC+
Ohio Univ	OH	14,448	C
Ohio Wesleyan Univ	OH	32,550	VC+
Okla Christian Univ	OK	17,690	NC
Okla City Univ	OK	19,580	VC
Okla State Univ	OK	9,216	VC
Old Dominion Univ	VA	10,441	C
Olivet College	MI	19,984	C+
Oregon State Univ	OR	11,055	C
Otterbein College	OH	26,085	C
Penn State Univ/Univ Park Campus	PA	15,646	HC
Philadelphia Univ	PA	27,354	C
Pitzer College	CA	37,590	HC
Portland State Univ	OR	12,453	C
Providence College	RI	30,604	HC
Purdue Univ/West Lafayette	IN	12,560	VC
Queens Univ of Charlotte	NC	21,840	C
Quinnipiac Univ	CT	30,570	VC
Ramapo College of New Jersey	NJ	15,203	VC
Regis College	MA	29,000	C
Regis Univ	CO	25,740	C+
Rensselaer Polytechnic Inst	NY	37,579	HC+
Richard Stockton College of New Jersey	NJ	12,972	VC
Rider Univ	NJ	30,900	C
Ripon College	WI	24,995	VC
Roanoke College	VA	27,393	C
Roberts Wesleyan College	NY	23,190	C+
Rochester Inst of Technology	NY	29,217	VC+
Rosemont College	PA	26,175	C
Russell Sage College	NY	26,811	C
Rutgers, The State Univ of New Jersey/Camden Campus	NJ	14,990	VC
Rutgers, The State Univ of New Jersey/New Brunswick/Piscataway Campus	NJ	15,800	HC
Saginaw Valley State Univ	MI	11,055	C
St. Anselm College	NH	30,250	C
St. Bonaventure Univ	NY	24,455	LC
St. Edward's Univ	TX	20,428	C
St. John's Univ	MN	26,473	VC
St. Lawrence Univ	NY	35,945	VC
St. Mary's College of Maryland	MD	15,908	VC+
St. Mary's Univ of San Antonio	TX	22,444	C
St. Michael's College	VT	30,100	VC
St. Peter's College	NJ	22,292	LC
St. Vincent College	PA	25,530	VC
Samford Univ	AL	18,648	VC
San Francisco State Univ	CA	12,070	C
San Jose State Univ	CA	8,187	C
Schreiner Univ	TX	20,440	C
Seattle Pacific Univ	WA	25,944	VC
Seattle Univ	WA	24,183	VC
Seton Hall Univ	NJ	30,130	VC
Seton Hill Univ	PA	24,930	C
Siena College	NY	25,310	VC
Simmons College	MA	33,000	VC
Simpson College	IA	23,658	C+
Skidmore College	NY	37,930	HC
Smith College	MA	37,034	HC+
S Dak State Univ	SD	7,782	C
Southern Conn State Univ	CT	10,310	C
Southern Methodist Univ	TX	34,210	HC
Southwestern College	KS	19,560	C
Spelman College	GA	19,215	C+
Spring Arbor Univ	MI	20,206	C
Spring Hill College	AL	25,868	VC
Springfield College	MA	24,520	C
SUNY at Potsdam	NY	12,160	C
SUNY/College at Fredonia	NY	11,562	VC
SUNY/College at Geneseo	NY	11,330	HC
SUNY/College at Old Westbury	NY	12,784	C
SUNY/College at Plattsburgh	NY	11,700	C
SUNY/Univ at Albany	NY	12,951	HC
SUNY/Univ at Binghamton	NY	12,787	HC
SUNY/Univ at Buffalo	NY	12,563	VC
SUNY/Univ at Stony Brook	NY	12,763	HC
Stetson Univ	FL	29,495	VC
Stevens Inst of Technology	NJ	35,300	HC+
Stonehill College	MA	30,752	HC
Suffolk Univ	MA	29,200	C
Susquehanna Univ	PA	29,990	VC
Swarthmore College	PA	37,716	MC
Sweet Briar College	VA	27,940	C
Temple Univ	PA	15,912	C
Tenn Tech Univ	TN	8,670	VC
Texas A&M Univ	TX	11,081	HC
Texas State Univ	TX	9,320	VC
Texas Tech Univ	TX	10,768	VC
Texas Wesleyan Univ	TX	16,245	C
Trinity College	CT	38,040	HC+
Trinity College	DC	24,150	LC
Trinity Univ	TX	26,466	HC+
Tufts Univ	MA	38,233	MC
Tulane Univ	LA	37,451	HC+
Union College	NY	36,005	HC
Univ of Arizona	AZ	10,413	VC
Univ of Calif at Davis	CA	14,995	VC
Univ of Calif at Los Angeles	CA	15,330	MC
Univ of Calif at Riverside	CA	15,300	C
Univ of Calif at San Diego	CA	14,127	HC
Univ of Calif at Santa Barbara	CA	11,732	VC
Univ of Calif at Santa Cruz	CA	16,505	VC
Univ of Chicago	IL	35,087	MC
Univ of Cincinnati	OH	14,736	C
Univ of Colo at Boulder	CO	10,774	VC
Univ of Dallas	TX	25,898	VC+
Univ of Dayton	OH	24,850	VC
Univ of Delaware	DE	12,616	HC
Univ of Denver	CO	32,148	VC
Univ of Detroit Mercy	MI	25,582	C
Univ of Georgia	GA	8,656	VC
Univ of Houston	TX	9,818	C
Univ of Illinois at Chicago	IL	13,418	C
Univ of Illinois at Urbana-Champaign	IL	11,316	HC+
Univ of Iowa	IA	10,923	VC
Univ of Kansas	KS	8,923	VC
Univ of Maine	ME	12,080	C+
Univ of Maryland/Baltimore County	MD	14,668	VC+
Univ of Maryland/College Park	MD	14,227	HC
Univ of Mass Amherst	MA	13,980	C+
Univ of Mass Boston	MA	6,227	C
Univ of Mass Dartmouth	MA	12,835	C
Univ of Miami	FL	34,608	HC
Univ of Mich/Ann Arbor	MI	13,864	HC+
Univ of Mich/Dearborn	MI	6,843	VC
Univ of Minn/Twin Cities	MN	13,160	VC
Univ of Missouri/Columbia	MO	13,782	VC
Univ of Nebr at Lincoln	NE	9,975	C+
Univ of Nevada/Reno	NV	9,792	C
Univ of New Mexico	NM	9,223	C
Univ of N Car at Greensboro	NC	8,248	C
Univ of North Texas	TX	7,629	C
Univ of Northern Colo	CO	8,987	C
Univ of Notre Dame	IN	34,442	MC
Univ of Oregon	OR	11,479	VC
Univ of Pennsylvania	PA	37,960	MC
Univ of PR/Mayaguez	PR		
Univ of Redlands	CA	32,576	VC
Univ of Richmond	VA	30,100	MC
Univ of Rochester	NY	32,979	HC
Univ of St. Thomas	MN	26,918	VC
Univ of Scranton	PA	30,836	VC
Univ of Southern Colo	CO	7,821	LC
Univ of Tampa	FL	23,982	VC
Univ of Tenn at Knoxville	TN	8,214	C
Univ of Texas at Arlington	TX	7,192	LC
Univ of Texas at Austin	TX	10,630	HC
Univ of Texas at Dallas	TX	10,234	HC
Univ of the Pacific	CA	31,090	VC
Univ of the Sciences in Philadelphia	PA	29,310	VC
Univ of Tulsa	OK	22,090	VC+
Univ of Vermont	VT	16,316	VC
Univ of Washington	WA	10,361	VC
Univ of Wisc/Eau Claire	WI	8,463	VC
Univ of Wisc/Madison	WI	8,262	VC
Univ of Wisc/Milwaukee	WI	9,427	LC
Ursinus College	PA	34,400	VC
Utah State Univ	UT	7,371	C
Vassar College	NY	37,030	MC
Virginia Polytechnic Inst and State Univ	VA	9,179	C
Walla Walla College	WA	21,600	NC
Wartburg College	IA	21,165	VC
Washington and Jefferson College	PA	29,570	VC
Washington and Lee Univ	VA	29,663	MC
Washington State Univ	WA	11,334	C
Washington Univ in St. Louis	MO	38,293	MC
Wellesley College	MA	36,516	MC
Wells College	NY	21,122	VC
Wesleyan Univ	CT	35,139	MC
West Chester Univ of Pennsylvania	PA	11,164	C
Western Kentucky Univ	KY	6,834	C
Western Mich Univ	MI	12,031	C
Western Washington Univ	WA	10,119	VC
Wheaton College	MA	36,330	HC
Whittier College	CA	29,108	C
Widener Univ	PA	27,020	C
Wilkes Univ	PA	28,060	C
William Jewell College	MO	21,320	VC
Worcester Polytechnic Inst	MA	37,404	HC
Xavier Univ of Louisiana	LA	17,600	C
Yale Univ	CT	37,000	MC

BIOENGINEERING

School	ST	$IS	SR
Arizona State Univ-Main	AZ	10,048	C
Florida State Univ	FL	9,028	HC
Louisiana State Univ and A&M College	LA	9,126	VC
Miss State Univ	MS	9,139	C
Okla State Univ	OK	9,216	VC
Oral Roberts Univ	OK	18,490	C
Rice Univ	TX	27,550	MC
SUNY/Univ at Binghamton	NY	12,787	HC
Syracuse Univ	NY	34,720	HC
Texas A&M Univ	TX	11,081	HC
Univ of Arizona	AZ	10,413	VC
Univ of Arkansas	AR	9,855	VC
Univ of Calif at Berkeley	CA	15,563	MC
Univ of Calif at Davis	CA	14,995	VC
Univ of Calif at San Diego	CA	14,127	HC
Univ of Delaware	DE	12,616	HC
Univ of Georgia	GA	8,656	VC
Univ of Hawaii at Manoa	HI	9,565	VC
Univ of Idaho	ID	8,216	C
Univ of Illinois at Chicago	IL	13,418	C
Univ of Illinois at Urbana-Champaign	IL	11,316	HC+
Univ of Maine	ME	12,080	C+
Univ of Maryland/College Park	MD	14,227	HC
Univ of Nebr at Lincoln	NE	9,975	C+
Univ of Pennsylvania	PA	37,960	MC
Univ of Pittsburgh at Pittsburgh	PA	16,074	HC
Univ of Toledo	OH	12,479	NC
Univ of Utah	UT	9,205	C
Vanderbilt Univ	TN	37,897	MC
Walla Walla College	WA	21,600	NC
Washington Univ in St. Louis	MO	38,293	MC
Western New England College	MA	28,924	C

BIOINFORMATICS

School	ST	$IS	SR
Canisius College	NY	28,163	C+
Chatham College	PA	27,266	C+
DeVry Univ/Alpharetta	GA	10,670	LC
DeVry Univ/Dallas	TX	10,640	LC
DeVry Univ/Decatur	GA	10,670	LC
DeVry Univ/Fremont	CA	11,860	LC
DeVry Univ/Kansas City	MO	10,670	LC
DeVry Univ/Long Beach	CA	11,310	LC
DeVry Univ/Phoenix	AZ	10,670	LC
DeVry Univ/Westminster	CO	11,310	LC
Inter American Univ of PR/Bayamon Univ College	PR	3,522	
Mich State Univ	MI	11,933	VC
Rochester Inst of Technology	NY	29,217	VC+
St. Edward's Univ	TX	20,428	C
Univ of Calif at San Diego	CA	14,127	HC
Univ of Calif at Santa Cruz	CA	16,505	VC
Univ of the Sciences in Philadelphia	PA	29,310	VC

BIOLOGY/BIOLOGICAL SCIENCE

School	ST	$IS	SR
Abilene Christian Univ	TX	18,370	VC
Adams State College	CO	7,468	C
Adelphi Univ	NY	26,300	VC
Adrian College	MI	21,950	C
Agnes Scott College	GA	28,230	HC
Alabama A&M Univ	AL	5,100	LC
Alabama State Univ	AL	6,404	C
Albany State Univ	GA	5,764	C+
Albertson College of Idaho	ID	19,415	VC
Albertus Magnus College	CT	23,130	LC
Albion College	MI	25,224	VC
Albright College	PA	30,579	C
Alcorn State Univ	MS	7,290	C
Alderson-Broaddus College	WV	19,640	C
Alfred Univ	NY	28,290	C
Alice Lloyd College	KY	4,040	C
Allegheny College	PA	30,280	VC
Allen Univ	SC	10,300	NC
Alma College	MI	25,566	VC
Alvernia College	PA	23,212	LC
Alverno College	WI	18,898	C
American International College	MA	24,690	LC
American Univ	DC	34,585	VC+
Amherst College	MA	37,470	MC
Anderson Univ	IN	19,430	LC
Andrews Univ	MI	19,550	C
Angelo State Univ	TX	7,576	NC
Anna Maria College	MA	26,140	LC
Appalachian State Univ	NC	7,637	VC
Aquinas College	MI	21,894	C
Arcadia Univ	PA	29,890	C
Arizona State Univ-Main	AZ	10,048	C
Arkansas State Univ	AR	8,450	C
Arkansas Tech Univ	AR	7,299	C
Armstrong Atlantic State Univ	GA	7,102	C
Asbury College	KY	20,704	VC
Ashland Univ	OH	24,464	C
Assumption College	MA	29,375	C
Atlantic Union College	MA	18,868	C
Auburn Univ	AL	10,396	VC
Auburn Univ Montgomery	AL	9,020	NC
Augsburg College	MN	25,298	C
Augusta State Univ	GA	2,592	C
Augustana College	IL	26,610	VC+
Augustana College	SD	21,998	VC
Aurora Univ	IL	20,631	C
Austin College	TX	24,747	HC
Austin Peay State Univ	TN	5,814	LC
Averett Univ	VA	23,010	LC
Avila Univ	MO	20,300	C

ST = STATE $IS = IN-STATE COSTS SR = SELECTOR RATING

School	ST	$IS	SR
Azusa Pacific Univ	CA	24,720	VC
Baker Univ	KS	19,860	VC
Baldwin-Wallace College	OH	24,678	C
Ball State Univ	IN	8,660	C
Barber-Scotia College	NC	13,900	LC
Bard College	NY	37,352	HC+
Barry Univ	FL	24,100	LC
Barton College	NC	19,314	C
Bates College	ME	37,500	MC
Bay Path College	MA	24,910	C
Baylor Univ	TX	23,864	VC
Belhaven College	MS	16,040	C+
Bellarmine Univ	KY	24,110	VC
Belmont Abbey College	NC	23,742	C
Belmont Univ	TN	21,986	VC
Beloit College	WI	29,864	HC
Bemidji State Univ	MN	9,103	C
Benedict College	SC	12,662	LC
Benedictine College	KS	20,603	C
Benedictine Univ	IL	23,840	C
Bennett College	NC	11,200	C
Bennington College	VT	35,910	HC
Berea College	KY	5,030	VC+
Berry College	GA	21,410	VC
Bethany College	KS	18,675	LC
Bethany College	WV	19,845	VC
Bethel College	IN	19,670	C
Bethel College	KS	19,800	C+
Bethel College	MN	25,180	VC
Bethel College	TN	12,980	C
Bethune-Cookman College	FL	16,480	LC
Biola Univ	CA	25,964	VC
Birmingham-Southern College	AL	25,364	VC+
Black Hills State Univ	SD	7,743	LC
Blackburn College	IL	13,690	C
Bloomfield College	NJ	19,250	LC
Bloomsburg Univ of Pennsylvania	PA	10,844	C
Blue Mountain College	MS	10,226	C
Bluefield College	VA	15,575	C
Bluefield State College	WV	2,806	LC
Bluffton College	OH	23,694	C
Boise State Univ	ID	7,657	LC
Boston College	MA	33,284	MC
Boston Univ	MA	38,194	HC+
Bowdoin College	ME	37,790	MC
Bowie State Univ	MD	10,873	C+
Bowling Green State Univ	OH	13,036	C
Bradley Univ	IL	22,910	VC
Brandeis Univ	MA	38,198	MC
Brenau Univ Women's College	GA	21,800	C
Brescia Univ	KY	14,225	C
Brewton-Parker College	GA	14,200	LC
Briar Cliff Univ	IA	21,660	C
Bridgewater College	VA	25,150	C
Bridgewater State College	MA	10,482	C
Brigham Young Univ	UT	8,504	HC
Brigham Young Univ/Hawaii	HI	7,240	VC+
Brown Univ	RI	38,174	MC
Bryan College	TN	17,900	VC
Bryn Athyn College of the New Church	PA	12,612	NC
Bryn Mawr College	PA	36,890	HC+
Bucknell Univ	PA	35,262	HC+
Buena Vista Univ	IA	25,406	C
Butler Univ	IN	28,250	VC+
Cabrini College	PA	29,020	C
Caldwell College	NJ	24,060	LC
Calif Baptist Univ	CA	19,924	C
Calif Inst of Technology	CA	31,677	MC
Calif Lutheran Univ	CA	27,600	LC
Calif Polytechnic State Univ	CA	8,747	VC
Calif State Polytechnic Univ, Pomona	CA	8,793	C+
Cal State, Bakersfield	CA	6,090	LC
Cal State, Chico	CA	8,598	LC
Cal State, Dominguez Hills	CA	5,840	LC
Cal State, Fresno	CA	8,414	LC
Cal State, Fullerton	CA	6,648	C
Cal State, Hayward	CA	8,871	LC
Cal State, Long Beach	CA	8,762	C+
Cal State, Los Angeles	CA	5,778	C
Cal State, Northridge	CA	7,757	LC
Cal State, Sacramento	CA	9,543	C
Cal State, San Bernardino	CA	15,238	LC
Cal State, San Marcos	CA	1,736	LC
Cal State, Stanislaus	CA	9,874	C
Calif Univ of Pennsylvania	PA	10,388	C
Calvin College	MI	22,615	NC
Cameron Univ	OK	5,692	NC
Campbell Univ	NC	18,268	VC
Campbellsville Univ	KY	17,680	C
Canisius College	NY	28,163	C+
Capital Univ	OH	26,550	C
Cardinal Stritch Univ	WI	17,620	C
Caribbean Univ	PR	3,000	
Carleton College	MN	34,395	MC
Carlow College	PA	21,334	C
Carnegie Mellon Univ	PA	32,682	MC
Carroll College	MT	20,576	VC
Carroll College	WI	22,740	C
Carson-Newman College	TN	16,760	C
Carthage College	WI	25,000	C
Case Western Reserve Univ	OH	32,002	MC
Castleton State College	VT	11,820	C
Catawba College	NC	20,500	C
Catholic Univ of America	DC	34,248	VC
Cedar Crest College	PA	25,145	C+
Cedarville Univ	OH	19,954	VC
Centenary College	NJ	25,370	LC
Centenary College of Louisiana	LA	23,100	VC+
Central College	IA	21,206	C
Central Conn State Univ	CT	12,090	C
Central Methodist College	MO	16,460	C
Central Mich Univ	MI	11,142	C
Central Missouri State Univ	MO	9,776	C
Central State Univ	OH	8,922	C+
Central Univ of Bayamon	PR	3,335	
Central Washington Univ	WA	9,768	C
Centre College	KY	27,300	HC
Chadron State College	NE	6,286	NC
Chaminade Univ of Honolulu	HI	21,430	LC
Chapman Univ	CA	33,118	VC
Charleston Southern Univ	SC	17,122	C
Chatham College	PA	27,266	C+
Chestnut Hill College	PA	26,450	LC
Cheyney Univ of Pennsylvania	PA	9,993	C
Chicago State Univ	IL	10,882	C+
Christian Brothers Univ	TN	22,290	VC
Christian Heritage College	CA	19,990	C
Christopher Newport Univ	VA	8,862	VC
Citadel, The	SC	12,295	C+
CUNY/Brooklyn College	NY	4,353	C+
CUNY/City College	NY	4,230	C+
CUNY/College of Staten Island	NY	4,308	NC
CUNY/Herbert H. Lehman College	NY	3,320	LC
CUNY/Hunter College	NY	6,729	C+
CUNY/Medgar Evers College	NY	4,232	NC
CUNY/Queens College	NY	4,362	C
CUNY/York College	NY	3,292	NC
Claflin Univ	SC	14,838	C+
Claremont McKenna College	CA	36,880	MC
Clarion Univ of Pennsylvania	PA	11,272	LC
Clark Atlanta Univ	GA	19,300	C+
Clark Univ	MA	32,115	VC
Clarke College	IA	23,165	C
Clarkson Univ	NY	32,226	VC
Clearwater Christian College	FL	13,160	LC
Clemson Univ	SC	11,972	HC
Cleveland State Univ	OH	12,308	LC
Coastal Carolina Univ	SC	11,040	C
Coe College	IA	27,385	VC
Coker College	SC	21,491	C
Colby College	ME	37,570	MC
Colby-Sawyer College	NH	27,850	LC
Colgate Univ	NY	37,095	MC
College Misericordia	PA	26,350	C
College of Charleston	SC	11,887	HC
College of Mount St. Vincent	NY	26,800	C
College of Mount St. Joseph	OH	22,785	C
College of New Jersey	NJ	15,950	MC
College of New Rochelle	NY	21,800	C
College of Notre Dame of Maryland	MD	27,700	C
College of Our Lady of the Elms	MA	20,644	C
College of St. Benedict	MN	26,672	VC
College of St. Catherine	MN	24,010	VC
College of St. Elizabeth	NJ	25,460	C
College of St. Mary	NE	21,510	C
College of St. Rose	NY	22,864	C
College of St. Scholastica	MN	24,970	C+
College of the Holy Cross	MA	36,451	MC
College of the Ozarks	MO	3,500	VC+
College of the Southwest	NM	9,320	C+
College of William and Mary	VA	12,224	MC
College of Wooster	OH	31,300	HC
Colo Christian Univ	CO	21,182	VC
Colo College	CO	36,860	HC
Colo State Univ	CO	9,964	VC
Columbia College	MO	16,139	C
Columbia College	SC	22,658	LC
Columbia Univ/Barnard College	NY	36,990	MC
Columbia Univ/Columbia College	NY	38,590	MC
Columbia Univ/School of General Studies	NY	35,000	C
Columbus State Univ	GA	7,846	C
Concord College	WV	8,136	C
Concordia College	NY	19,200	VC
Concordia College: Moorhead	MN	22,460	VC+
Concordia Univ	CA	24,420	C
Concordia Univ	MI	24,095	C
Concordia Univ	OR	22,450	C
Concordia Univ Nebr	NE	20,302	C+
Concordia Univ Wisc	WI	16,600	C
Concordia Univ, River Forest	IL	23,600	C
Concordia Univ/St.Paul	MN	24,486	C
Conn College	CT	37,900	MC
Converse College	SC	24,710	VC
Coppin State College	MD	10,191	LC
Cornell College	IA	27,825	VC+
Cornell Univ	NY	38,253	MC
Cornerstone Univ and Grand Rapids Theological Seminary	MI	19,846	C
Covenant College	GA	23,830	VC+
Creighton Univ	NE	26,748	VC+
Crichton College	TN	15,215	C
Culver-Stockton College	MO	17,850	C
Cumberland College	KY	16,384	C
Cumberland Univ	TN	16,910	C
Curry College	MA	26,025	LC
Daemen College	NY	22,120	C
Dakota State Univ	SD	7,466	C
Dakota Wesleyan Univ	SD	17,832	C
Dallas Baptist Univ	TX	15,300	VC
Dana College	NE	20,280	C
Dartmouth College	NH	37,770	MC
David Lipscomb Univ	TN	16,158	VC
Davidson College	NC	33,274	MC
Davis and Elkins College	WV	20,594	C
De Sales Univ	PA	25,470	C
Defiance College	OH	22,615	C
Delaware State Univ	DE	8,104	LC
Delaware Valley College	PA	26,676	C
Delta State Univ	MS	6,618	C
Denison Univ	OH	33,050	HC
DePaul Univ	IL	27,580	VC
DePauw Univ	IN	31,500	HC
Dickinson College	PA	35,825	HC
Dickinson State Univ	ND	6,338	NC
Dillard Univ	LA	17,325	VC
Doane College	NE	20,000	C
Dominican College	NY	24,810	LC
Dominican Univ	IL	23,610	C
Dominican Univ of Calif	CA	31,670	C
Dordt College	IA	20,170	VC
Dowling College	NY	23,870	LC
Drake Univ	IA	25,120	VC+
Drew Univ/College of Liberal Arts	NJ	35,550	VC
Drexel Univ	PA	27,655	VC
Drury Univ	MO	18,085	VC+
Duke Univ	NC	37,555	MC
Duquesne Univ	PA	26,907	VC
D'Youville College	NY	21,080	C
Earlham College	IN	29,976	VC+
East Carolina Univ	NC	8,671	C
East Central Univ	OK	4,968	C
East Stroudsburg Univ of Pennsylvania	PA	10,336	C
East Tenn State Univ	TN	8,497	C
East Texas Baptist Univ	TX	13,914	C
Eastern Conn State Univ	CT	10,362	C
Eastern Illinois Univ	IL	11,192	C
Eastern Kentucky Univ	KY	7,708	C
Eastern Mennonite Univ	VA	22,990	C
Eastern Mich Univ	MI	11,478	C
Eastern Nazarene College	MA	19,433	LC
Eastern New Mexico Univ	NM	6,762	LC
Eastern Oregon Univ	OR	10,080	NC
Eastern Univ	PA	24,020	C
Eastern Washington Univ	WA	9,012	C
Eckerd College	FL	28,744	C+
Edgewood College	WI	20,520	C
Edinboro Univ of Pennsylvania	PA	10,850	LC
Edward Waters College	FL	14,374	LC
Elizabeth City State Univ	NC	5,550	LC
Elizabethtown College	PA	28,800	C
Elmhurst College	IL	24,630	C
Elmira College	NY	33,820	VC
Elon Univ	NC	22,240	VC
Emmanuel College	MA	27,600	C+
Emory & Henry College	VA	21,950	C
Emory Univ	GA	36,872	MC
Emporia State Univ	KS	6,998	C
Erskine College	SC	23,166	VC
Eureka College	IL	24,980	LC
Evangel Univ	MO	15,435	C
Fairfield Univ	CT	35,505	HC
Fairleigh Dickinson Univ/College at Florham	NJ	30,130	C
Fairleigh Dickinson Univ/Metropolitan Campus	NJ	28,584	C
Fairmont State	WV	8,280	LC
Farmingdale SUNY	NY	12,891	C
Faulkner Univ	AL	14,500	C
Fayetteville State Univ	NC	5,590	LC
Felician College	NJ	24,300	C
Ferris State Univ	MI	12,512	C
Ferrum College	VA	21,240	LC
Fisk Univ	TN	17,305	LC
Fitchburg State College	MA	9,622	C
Florida A&M Univ	FL	7,564	C
Florida Atlantic Univ	FL	8,543	C
Florida Inst of Technology	FL	28,740	VC
Florida International Univ	FL	9,912	VC
Florida Memorial College	FL	6,000	LC
Florida Southern College	FL	23,592	C
Florida State Univ	FL	9,028	HC
Fontbonne Univ	MO	21,508	C
Fordham Univ	NY	35,066	HC
Fort Hays State Univ	KS	7,363	C
Fort Lewis College	CO	8,353	C
Fort Valley State Univ	GA	6,960	C
Framingham State College	MA	9,381	C
Francis Marion Univ	SC	9,364	C
Franciscan Univ	IA	19,300	C
Franciscan Univ of Steubenville	OH	20,300	VC
Franklin and Marshall College	PA	35,930	HC+
Franklin College	IN		C
Franklin Pierce College	NH	28,980	LC
Freed-Hardeman Univ	TN		NC
Fresno Pacific Univ	CA	22,462	C
Friends Univ	KS	15,962	LC
Frostburg State Univ	MD	11,114	C
Furman Univ	SC	28,976	HC+
Gallaudet Univ	DC	16,554	SP
Gannon Univ	PA	23,260	C
Gardner-Webb Univ	NC	19,300	C
Geneva College	PA	21,850	C
George Fox Univ	OR	26,110	VC
George Mason Univ	VA	9,732	VC
George Washington Univ	DC	41,030	MC
Georgetown College	KY	22,000	VC
Georgetown Univ	DC	38,242	MC
Georgia College and State Univ	GA	9,878	C
Georgia Inst of Technology	GA	10,340	HC+
Georgia Southern Univ	GA	8,540	C
Georgia Southwestern State Univ	GA	6,013	C
Georgia State Univ	GA	10,658	C
Georgian Court College	NJ	19,040	LC
Gettysburg College	PA	35,646	HC
Glenville State College	WV	7,812	NC
Gonzaga Univ	WA	26,766	HC
Gordon College	MA	25,982	VC+
Goshen College	IN	22,450	VC
Goucher College	MD	32,650	HC
Grace College	IN	19,825	VC
Graceland Univ	IA	19,550	C
Grambling State Univ	LA	6,538	NC
Grand Canyon Univ	AZ	30,000	LC
Grand Valley State Univ	MI	11,022	VC
Grand View College	IA	19,748	LC
Green Mountain College	VT	24,130	C
Greensboro College	NC	21,750	C
Greenville College	IL	21,342	C
Grinnell College	IA	31,060	HC+
Grove City College	PA	14,228	HC
Guilford College	NC	24,960	VC
Gustavus Adolphus College	MN	27,120	VC+
Gwynedd-Mercy College	PA	24,225	C
Hamilton College	NY	37,560	MC
Hamline Univ	MN	27,052	VC
Hampden-Sydney College	VA	28,407	VC
Hampshire College	MA	37,037	HC
Hampton Univ	VA	17,112	C+
Hannibal-LaGrange College	MO	13,940	C
Hanover College	IN	25,200	VC
Harding Univ	AR	14,890	VC
Hardin-Simmons Univ	TX	14,165	C
Hartwick College	NY	34,650	C+
Harvard Univ/Harvard College	MA	37,928	MC
Harvey Mudd College	CA	38,080	MC
Hastings College	NE	19,928	VC
Haverford College	PA	37,900	MC
Hawaii Pacific Univ	HI	19,218	C
Heidelberg College	OH	20,266	NC
Henderson State Univ	AR	7,386	C
Hendrix College	AR	20,970	VC+
High Point Univ	NC	22,480	C
Hillsdale College	MI	22,450	HC
Hiram College	OH	28,234	VC
Hobart and William Smith Colleges	NY	36,536	HC
Hofstra Univ	NY	27,112	VC
Hollins Univ	VA	27,965	VC
Holy Family College	PA	13,710	LC
Holy Names College	CA	27,980	NC
Hood College	MD	27,795	VC
Hope College	MI	25,340	VC
Houghton College	NY	23,984	VC
Houston Baptist Univ	TX	16,905	C
Howard Payne Univ	TX	15,176	C
Howard Univ	DC	16,505	C
Humboldt State Univ	CA	9,400	C
Huntingdon College	AL	18,400	VC
Huntington College	IN	23,590	C
Husson College	ME	16,300	LC
Huston-Tillotson College	TX	14,232	NC
Idaho State Univ	ID	8,128	C
Illinois College	IL	19,100	VC
Illinois Inst of Technology	IL	26,456	HC+
Illinois State Univ	IL	10,944	C+
Illinois Wesleyan Univ	IL	30,380	HC+
Immaculata Univ	PA	25,200	C
Indiana State Univ	IN	10,719	LC
Indiana Univ Bloomington	IN	12,389	VC
Indiana Univ East	IN	4,433	LC

ST = STATE **$IS** = IN-STATE COSTS **SR** = SELECTOR RATING

School	ST	$IS	SR
Indiana Univ Kokomo	IN	4,463	LC
Indiana Univ Northwest	IN	4,538	LC
Indiana Univ of Pennsylvania	PA	10,489	C
Indiana Univ South Bend	IN	4,571	LC
Indiana Univ Southeast	IN	4,504	LC
Indiana Univ-Purdue Univ Fort Wayne	IN	5,108	LC
Indiana Univ-Purdue Univ Indianapolis	IN	8,257	LC
Indiana Wesleyan Univ	IN	19,900	C+
Inter American Univ of PR/ Aguadilla Campus	PR	3,544	
Inter American Univ of PR/ Arecibo Campus	PR	3,300	
Inter American Univ of PR/ Bayamon Univ College	PR	3,522	
Inter American Univ of PR/ Fajardo Campus	PR	4,000	
Inter American Univ of PR/ Metropolitan Campus	PR		
Inter American Univ of PR/ Ponce Regional College	PR	3,700	
Inter American Univ of PR/ San German	PR	6,716	
Iona College	NY	27,988	VC
Iowa State Univ	IA	10,768	VC
Iowa Wesleyan College	IA	19,990	C
Ithaca College	NY	31,730	HC
Jackson State Univ	MS	8,382	C
Jacksonville State Univ	AL	6,844	LC
Jacksonville Univ	FL	24,040	C
James Madison Univ	VA	10,794	VC
Jamestown College	ND	12,600	NC
Jarvis Christian College	TX	9,035	NC
John Brown Univ	AR	15,080	VC
John Carroll Univ	OH	27,658	C+
Johns Hopkins Univ	MD	38,372	MC
Johnson C. Smith Univ	NC	18,108	C
Johnson State College	VT	11,819	LC
Judson College	AL	14,650	C
Judson College	IL	22,050	LC
Juniata College	PA	29,080	VC
Kalamazoo College	MI	26,955	HC+
Kansas State Univ	KS	8,728	VC
Kansas Wesleyan Univ	KS	18,900	VC
Kean Univ	NJ	14,479	C
Keene State College	NH	12,212	C
Kennesaw State Univ	GA	2,724	C
Kent State Univ	OH	12,932	C
Kentucky State Univ	KY	9,062	NC
Kentucky Wesleyan College	KY	17,250	C
Kenyon College	OH	35,370	HC+
Keuka College	NY	21,170	C
King College	TN	22,500	VC
King's College	PA	26,990	C
Knox College	IL	30,294	VC+
Knoxville College	TN	6,200	LC
Kutztown Univ of Pennsylvania	PA	10,786	C
La Roche College	PA	22,094	C
La Salle Univ	PA	31,260	VC
La Sierra Univ	CA	19,260	LC
Lafayette College	PA	35,746	MC
LaGrange College	GA	20,500	C
Lake Erie College	OH	23,550	C
Lake Forest College	IL	30,270	VC
Lake Superior State Univ	MI	9,034	LC
Lakeland College	WI	17,950	C
Lamar Univ	TX	6,816	LC
Lambuth Univ	TN	16,520	C
Lander Univ	SC	10,496	C
Lane College	TN	11,178	C+
Langston Univ	OK	2,308	LC
Lawrence Univ	WI	30,900	HC
Le Moyne College	NY	26,400	VC
Lebanon Valley College	PA	28,870	VC
Lee Univ	TN	13,780	NC
Lees-McRae College	NC	17,106	LC
Lehigh Univ	PA	37,570	HC+
LeMoyne-Owen College	TN	13,070	LC
Lenoir-Rhyne College	NC	19,186	C
LeTourneau Univ	TX	21,080	C
Lewis and Clark College	OR	30,620	VC
Lewis Univ	IL	22,950	C+
Lewis-Clark State College	ID	6,981	C
Liberty Univ	VA	17,220	C
Limestone College	SC	17,700	C
Lincoln Memorial Univ	TN	16,400	LC
Lincoln Univ	MO	7,158	NC
Lincoln Univ	PA	13,320	C+
Lindenwood Univ	MO	17,050	VC
Lindsey Wilson College	KY	16,392	LC
Linfield College	OR	27,090	VC
Livingstone College	NC	18,101	LC
Lock Haven Univ of Pennsylvania	PA	11,098	LC
LIU/Brooklyn Campus	NY	24,790	C
LIU/C.W. Post Campus	NY	28,282	C
LIU/Southampton College	NY	29,370	C+
Longwood Univ	VA	11,175	C
Loras College	IA	24,233	C
Louisiana College	LA	13,450	C
Louisiana State Univ and A&M College	LA	9,126	VC
Louisiana State Univ in Shreveport	LA	2,884	NC
Louisiana Tech Univ	LA	7,361	C
Lourdes College	OH	15,300	LC
Loyola College in Maryland	MD	34,560	HC
Loyola Marymount Univ	CA	32,194	VC
Loyola Univ Chicago	IL	31,164	VC
Loyola Univ New Orleans	LA	31,036	VC+
Lubbock Christian Univ	TX	15,832	C
Luther College	IA	25,700	VC
Lycoming College	PA	27,589	C+
Lynchburg College	VA	26,815	C
Lyon College	AR	17,995	VC
Macalester College	MN	31,944	MC
MacMurray College	IL	20,005	LC
Madonna Univ	MI	11,504	VC
Malone College	OH	20,995	C
Manchester College	IN	23,390	C
Manhattan College	NY	27,400	VC
Manhattanville College	NY	32,420	C+
Mansfield Univ	PA	11,220	C
Marian College	IN	23,030	C
Marian College of Fond du Lac	WI	19,625	C
Marietta College	OH	27,047	C
Marist College	NY	27,596	VC
Marlboro College	VT	29,055	VC+
Marquette Univ	WI	27,594	VC
Mars Hill College	NC	18,600	LC
Marshall Univ	WV	9,116	C
Martin Univ	IN	10,200	SP
Mary Baldwin College	VA	24,939	C
Mary Washington College	VA	10,166	HC
Marygrove College	MI	17,550	C
Marymount College of Fordham Univ	NY	27,686	C
Marymount Manhattan College	NY	27,292	C
Marymount Univ	VA	23,668	C
Maryville College	TN	25,960	VC
Maryville Univ of St. Louis	MO	22,090	VC
Marywood Univ	PA	26,050	C
Mass College of Liberal Arts	MA	8,717	LC
Mass Inst of Technology	MA	38,310	MC
Master's College and Seminary	CA	23,250	VC
Mayville State Univ	ND	7,325	NC
McDaniel College	MD	28,440	VC
McKendree College	IL	21,120	VC
McMurry Univ	TX	17,846	LC
McNeese State Univ	LA	5,259	LC
McPherson College	KS	20,265	C
Medaille College	NY	20,060	C
Mercer Univ	GA	27,516	VC+
Mercy College	NY	19,200	NC
Mercyhurst College	PA	20,694	C
Meredith College	NC	23,065	C
Merrimack College	MA	29,625	C
Mesa State College	CO	8,051	C
Messiah College	PA	25,890	VC+
Methodist College	NC	19,526	C
Metropolitan State College of Denver	CO	2,338	LC
Metropolitan State Univ	MN	3,852	SP
Miami Univ	OH	15,033	HC
Mich State Univ	MI	11,933	VC
Mich Tech Univ	MI	13,235	VC
MidAmerica Nazarene Univ	KS	18,688	C
Middle Tenn State Univ	TN	8,534	C
Middlebury College	VT	38,100	MC
Midland Lutheran College	NE	18,600	C
Midway College	KY	15,815	C
Midwestern State Univ	TX	8,045	LC
Miles College	AL	7,870	NC
Millersville Univ of Pennsylvania	PA	11,269	C
Milligan College	TN	19,860	C+
Millikin Univ	IL	25,555	C
Mills College	CA	33,371	VC
Millsaps College	MS	25,182	VC
Minn State Univ, Mankato	MN	8,803	LC
Minn State Univ, Moorehead	MN	7,000	LC
Minot State Univ	ND	6,602	LC
Miss College	MS	14,574	C
Miss State Univ	MS	9,139	C
Miss Univ for Women	MS	5,446	LC
Miss Valley State Univ	MS	6,765	NC
Missouri Baptist Univ	MO	18,010	C
Missouri Southern State Univ	MO	8,316	C
Missouri Valley College	MO	18,500	C
Missouri Western State College	MO	8,522	NC
Molloy College	NY	15,180	C
Monmouth College	IL	23,600	C
Monmouth Univ	NJ	26,334	C
Montana State Univ-Billings	MT	9,550	C
Montana State Univ-Bozeman	MT	9,515	C
Montana State Univ-Northern	MT	8,600	NC
Montana Tech of The Univ of Montana	MT	9,314	NC
Montclair State Univ	NJ	13,790	C
Moravian College	PA	28,903	VC
Morehead State Univ	KY	7,464	C
Morehouse College	GA	22,728	C
Morgan State Univ	MD	11,470	C
Morningside College	IA	21,610	C
Morris College	SC	10,974	LC
Mount Holyoke College	MA	37,918	HC+
Mount Marty College	SD	15,656	LC
Mount Mary College	WI	20,370	C
Mount Mercy College	IA	21,400	C
Mount Olive College	NC	14,410	LC
Mount St. Mary College	NY	21,270	C
Mount St. Mary's College	CA	28,307	VC
Mount St. Mary's College	MD	28,400	C
Mount Union College	OH	21,120	C
Mount Vernon Nazarene Univ	OH	18,925	C
Mountain State Univ	WV	10,212	NC
Muhlenberg College	PA	31,485	HC
Murray State Univ	KY	7,816	VC
Muskingum College	OH	20,680	C
National-Louis Univ	IL	16,240	LC
Nazareth College of Rochester	NY	24,936	VC
Nebr Wesleyan Univ	NE	21,197	C+
Neumann College	PA	23,890	LC
New College of Florida	FL	8,906	HC+
New England College	NH	28,860	LC
New Jersey City Univ	NJ	11,850	LC
New Jersey Inst of Technology	NJ	16,396	VC
New Mexico Highlands Univ	NM	6,182	LC
New Mexico Inst of Mining and Technology	NM	7,580	NC
New Mexico State Univ	NM	7,932	C
New York Inst of Technology	NY	24,205	VC
New York Univ	NY	39,406	MC
Newberry College	SC	22,871	LC
Newman Univ	KS	18,018	C
Niagara Univ	NY	25,050	C
Nicholls State Univ	LA	6,395	NC
Norfolk State Univ	VA	9,722	LC
N Car Agricultural and Technical State Univ	NC	6,659	LC
N Car Central Univ	NC	7,534	LC
N Car State Univ	NC	9,886	VC
N Car Wesleyan College	NC	17,998	C
North Central College	IL	25,656	VC
N Dak State Univ	ND	8,435	C
North Georgia College and State Univ	GA	6,984	C
North Park Univ	IL	24,030	C
Northeastern Illinois Univ	IL	2,898	NC
Northeastern State Univ	OK	4,950	LC
Northeastern Univ	MA	35,650	HC
Northern Arizona Univ	AZ	9,002	C
Northern Illinois Univ	IL	11,472	C
Northern Kentucky Univ	KY	6,352	NC
Northern Mich Univ	MI	10,834	C
Northern State Univ	SD	7,117	LC
Northland College	WI	22,170	C+
Northwest Missouri State Univ	MO	9,334	C
Northwest Nazarene Univ	ID	20,360	VC
Northwestern College	MN	22,820	C+
Northwestern College of Iowa	IA	19,640	C+
Northwestern Okla State Univ	OK	5,433	NC
Northwestern State Univ of Louisiana	LA	6,331	NC
Northwestern Univ	IL	37,491	MC
Norwich Univ	VT	21,064	LC
Notre Dame College	OH	20,425	C
Notre Dame de Namur Univ	CA	26,932	LC
Nova Southeastern Univ	FL	23,346	C
Oakland City Univ	IN	16,980	NC
Oakland Univ	MI	10,800	C
Oakwood College	AL	14,904	C
Oberlin College	OH	36,938	MC
Occidental College	CA	35,922	HC
Oglethorpe Univ	GA	26,000	VC
Ohio Dominican Univ	OH	22,700	C
Ohio Northern Univ	OH	27,765	VC
Ohio State Univ	OH	13,080	VC+
Ohio Univ	OH	14,448	C
Ohio Wesleyan Univ	OH	32,550	VC+
Okla Baptist Univ	OK	15,220	VC
Okla Christian Univ	OK	17,690	NC
Okla City Univ	OK	19,580	VC
Okla Panhandle State Univ	OK	5,370	C
Okla State Univ	OK	9,216	VC
Okla Wesleyan Univ	OK	14,100	LC
Old Dominion Univ	VA	10,441	C
Olivet College	MI	19,984	C+
Olivet Nazarene Univ	IL	20,480	C
Oral Roberts Univ	OK	18,490	C
Oregon State Univ	OR	11,065	C
Ottawa Univ	KS	11,800	LC
Ouachita Baptist Univ	AR	18,900	VC
Our Lady of Holy Cross College	LA	5,900	C
Our Lady of the Lake Univ of San Antonio	TX	17,336	C
Pace Univ	NY	28,652	VC
Pacific Lutheran Univ	WA	25,715	VC
Pacific Union College	CA	22,065	C+
Pacific Univ	OR	24,250	C
Paine College	GA	13,022	LC
Palm Beach Atlantic Univ	FL	20,690	C
Park Univ	MO	10,780	C+
Paul Quinn College	TX	8,150	LC
Penn State Univ at Erie/ Behrend College	PA	12,326	C
Penn State Univ/Univ Park Campus	PA	15,646	HC
Pepperdine Univ	CA	32,830	VC
Peru State College	NE	6,342	NC
Pfeiffer Univ	NC	18,980	C
Philadelphia Univ	PA	27,354	C
Philander Smith College	AR	7,380	NC
Piedmont College	GA	16,900	C
Pikeville College	KY	14,900	NC
Pine Manor College	MA	22,138	LC
Pittsburg State Univ	KS	7,128	NC
Pitzer College	CA	37,590	HC
Plymouth State Univ	NH	12,298	LC
Point Loma Nazarene Univ	CA	21,380	VC
Point Park Univ	PA	21,840	C
Pomona College	CA	33,960	MC
Pontifical Catholic Univ of PR/Ponce	PR	7,298	
Portland State Univ	OR	12,453	C
Prairie View A&M Univ	TX	9,418	NC
Presbyterian College	SC	25,920	VC
Prescott College	AZ	13,430	C
Presentation College	SD	14,700	LC
Princeton Univ	NJ	36,649	MC
Principia College	IL	25,044	C+
Providence College	RI	30,604	HC
Purdue Univ/Calumet	IN	6,630	NC
Purdue Univ/West Lafayette	IN	12,560	VC
Queens Univ of Charlotte	NC	21,840	C
Quincy Univ	IL	22,330	C
Quinnipiac Univ	CT	30,570	VC
Radford Univ	VA	8,500	C
Ramapo College of New Jersey	NJ	15,203	VC
Randolph-Macon College	VA	27,190	C
Randolph-Macon Woman's College	VA	28,430	VC+
Reed College	OR	36,950	MC
Regis College	MA	29,000	C
Regis Univ	CO	25,740	C+
Reinhardt College	GA	20,750	C
Rensselaer Polytechnic Inst	NY	37,579	HC+
Rhode Island College	RI	11,565	C
Rhodes College	TN	26,466	HC+
Rice Univ	TX	27,550	MC
Richard Stockton College of New Jersey	NJ	12,972	VC
Rider Univ	NJ	30,900	C
Ripon College	WI	24,995	VC
Rivier College	NH	26,217	C
Roanoke College	VA	27,393	C
Roberts Wesleyan College	NY	23,190	C+
Rochester Inst of Technology	NY	29,217	VC+
Rockford College	IL	28,310	VC
Rockhurst Univ	MO	22,960	C+
Rocky Mountain College	MT	19,015	C
Roger Williams Univ	RI	30,296	C
Rollins College	FL	34,300	VC
Roosevelt Univ	IL	22,580	VC
Rose-Hulman Inst of Technology	IN	31,425	HC+
Rosemont College	PA	26,175	C
Rowan Univ	NJ	14,506	VC
Russell Sage College	NY	26,811	C
Rust College	MS	8,200	C+
Rutgers, The State Univ of New Jersey/Camden Campus	NJ	14,990	VC
Rutgers, The State Univ of New Jersey/New Brunswick/Piscataway Campus	NJ	15,800	HC
Rutgers, The State Univ of New Jersey/Newark Campus	NJ	15,624	VC
Sacred Heart Univ	CT	29,178	C
Saginaw Valley State Univ	MI	11,055	C
St. Ambrose Univ	IA	22,800	C
St. Andrews Presbyterian College	NC	20,525	C
St. Anselm College	NH	30,250	C
St. Augustine's College	NC	12,990	LC
St. Bonaventure Univ	NY	24,455	LC
St. Cloud State Univ	MN	8,362	C
St. Edward's Univ	TX	20,428	C
St. Francis College	NY	10,880	LC
St. Francis Univ	PA	25,876	LC
St. John Fisher College	NY	24,870	C
St. John's Univ	MN	26,473	VC
St. John's Univ	NY	30,180	C
St. Joseph College	CT	29,685	C
St. Joseph's, Brooklyn,	NY	10,902	C
St. Joseph's College	IN	24,250	C
St. Joseph's College of Maine	ME	25,600	C
St. Joseph's Univ	PA	33,590	VC

ST = STATE **$IS** = IN-STATE COSTS **SR** = SELECTOR RATING

School	ST	$IS	SR
St. Lawrence Univ	NY	35,945	VC
St. Leo Univ	FL	20,600	C
St. Louis Univ	MO	29,780	VC+
St. Martin's College	WA	23,245	C
St. Mary-of-the-Woods College	IN	23,280	C
St. Mary's College	IN	24,474	VC
St. Mary's College	MI	13,314	LC
St. Mary's College of Calif	CA	32,850	VC
St. Mary's College of Maryland	MD	15,908	VC+
St. Mary's Univ of Minn	MN	21,535	C
St. Mary's Univ of San Antonio	TX	22,444	C
St. Michael's College	VT	30,100	VC
St. Norbert College	WI	25,810	C
St. Olaf College	MN	28,500	HC
St. Paul's College	VA	14,344	NC
St. Peter's College	NJ	22,292	LC
St. Thomas Univ	FL	21,400	LC
St. Vincent College	PA	25,530	VC
St. Xavier Univ	IL	23,144	C
Salem College	NC	24,595	VC
Salem International Univ	WV	19,770	C
Salem State College	MA	8,592	C
Salisbury Univ	MD	12,664	VC
Salve Regina Univ	RI	29,210	C
Sam Houston State Univ	TX	7,142	C
Samford Univ	AL	18,648	VC
San Diego State Univ	CA	10,321	C
San Francisco State Univ	CA	12,070	C
San Jose State Univ	CA	8,187	C
Santa Clara Univ	CA	34,701	HC
Sarah Lawrence College	NY	41,218	HC
Savannah State Univ	GA	7,328	LC
Schreiner Univ	TX	20,440	C
Scripps College	CA	35,700	HC+
Seattle Pacific Univ	WA	25,944	VC
Seattle Univ	WA	24,183	VC
Seton Hall Univ	NJ	30,130	VC
Seton Hill Univ	PA	24,930	C
Shaw Univ	NC	14,882	C+
Shawnee State Univ	OH	11,031	NC
Shenandoah Univ	VA	25,190	NC
Shepherd College	WV	8,608	C
Shippensburg Univ of Pennsylvania	PA	10,826	C
Shorter College	GA	17,370	C
Siena College	NY	25,310	VC
Siena Heights Univ	MI	16,140	LC
Silver Lake College of the Holy Family	WI	18,450	LC
Simmons College	MA	33,000	VC
Simon's Rock College of Bard	MA	36,580	HC
Simpson College	IA	23,658	C+
Skidmore College	NY	37,930	HC
Slippery Rock Univ of Pennsylvania	PA	10,343	LC
Smith College	MA	37,034	HC+
Sonoma State Univ	CA	10,421	C
S Car State Univ	SC	6,586	LC
S Dak State Univ	SD	7,782	C
Southeast Missouri State Univ	MO	9,704	C
Southeastern College	FL	11,648	LC
Southeastern Louisiana Univ	LA	6,791	LC
Southeastern Okla State Univ	OK	6,147	C
Southern Adventist Univ	TN	17,080	C
Southern Arkansas Univ	AR	6,956	C
Southern Conn State Univ	CT	10,310	C
Southern Illinois Univ Carbondale	IL	10,407	C
Southern Illinois Univ Edwardsville	IL	8,724	C
Southern Methodist Univ	TX	34,210	HC
Southern Nazarene Univ	OK	14,634	NC
Southern Oregon Univ	OR	10,362	C
Southern Polytechnic State Univ	GA	7,620	VC
Southern Univ and A&M College	LA	7,372	LC
Southern Univ at New Orleans	LA	995	NC
Southern Utah Univ	UT	8,194	C
Southern Wesleyan Univ	SC	19,940	C
Southwest Baptist Univ	MO	15,371	C
Southwest Minn State Univ	MN	9,106	VC
Southwest Missouri State Univ	MO	8,918	C
Southwestern Adventist Univ	TX	14,798	C
Southwestern College	KS	19,560	C
Southwestern Okla State Univ	OK	4,801	C
Southwestern Univ	TX	25,410	HC
Spelman College	GA	19,215	C+
Spring Arbor Univ	MI	20,206	C
Spring Hill College	AL	25,868	VC
Springfield College	MA	24,520	C
St. Joseph's, Suffolk	NY	11,297	C
Stanford Univ	CA	37,612	MC
SUNY at Oswego	NY	12,650	C
SUNY at Potsdam	NY	12,160	C
SUNY/College at Brockport	NY	12,111	C
SUNY/College at Buffalo	NY	8,025	C
SUNY/College at Cortland	NY	12,095	C
SUNY/College at Fredonia	NY	11,562	VC
SUNY/College at Geneseo	NY	11,330	HC
SUNY/College at Old Westbury	NY	12,784	C
SUNY/College at Oneonta	NY	11,870	VC
SUNY/College at Plattsburgh	NY	11,700	C
SUNY/College at Purchase	NY	10,587	VC
SUNY/College of Environmental Science and Forestry	NY	14,167	VC
SUNY/Univ at Albany	NY	12,951	HC
SUNY/Univ at Binghamton	NY	12,787	HC
SUNY/Univ at Buffalo	NY	12,563	VC
SUNY/Univ at New Paltz	NY	11,565	VC
SUNY/Univ at Stony Brook	NY	12,763	HC
State Univ of West Georgia	GA	7,622	C
Stephen F. Austin State Univ	TX	7,552	C
Stephens College	MO	24,260	C+
Sterling College	KS	18,763	C
Stetson Univ	FL	29,495	VC
Stillman College	AL	11,370	LC
Stonehill College	MA	30,752	HC
Suffolk Univ	MA	29,200	C
Sul Ross State Univ	TX	6,582	LC
Susquehanna Univ	PA	29,990	VC
Swarthmore College	PA	37,716	MC
Sweet Briar College	VA	27,940	C
Syracuse Univ	NY	34,720	HC
Tabor College	KS	19,500	NC
Talladega College	AL	10,110	LC
Tarleton State Univ	TX	7,576	C
Taylor Univ	IN	23,820	VC+
Temple Univ	PA	15,912	C
Tenn State Univ	TN	9,048	LC
Tenn Tech Univ	TN	8,670	VC
Tenn Wesleyan College	TN	16,540	C
Texas A&M Univ	TX	11,081	HC
Texas A&M Univ at Commerce	TX	8,994	C
Texas A&M Univ at Corpus Christi	TX	10,269	C
Texas A&M Univ at Galveston	TX	9,948	C+
Texas A&M Univ at Kingsville	TX	6,740	LC
Texas Christian Univ	TX	23,410	VC
Texas Lutheran Univ	TX	20,370	C
Texas Southern Univ	TX	8,920	NC
Texas State Univ	TX	9,320	VC
Texas Tech Univ	TX	10,768	VC
Texas Wesleyan Univ	TX	16,245	C
Texas Woman's Univ	TX	7,804	LC
Thiel College	PA	20,970	C
Thomas Edison State College	NJ	3,325	SP
Thomas More College	KY	21,350	C
Thomas More College of Liberal Arts	NH	17,700	C
Thomas Univ	GA	11,490	NC
Tougaloo College	MS	9,200	NC
Touro College	NY	15,250	VC
Towson Univ	MD	12,694	VC
Transylvania Univ	KY	23,780	VC+
Trevecca Nazarene Univ	TN	17,548	C
Trinity Christian College	IL	21,640	VC
Trinity College	CT	38,040	HC+
Trinity College	DC	24,150	LC
Trinity International Univ	IL	22,980	C+
Trinity Univ	TX	26,466	HC+
Tri-State Univ-Main Campus	IN	23,600	C
Troy State Univ	AL	7,696	C
Troy State Univ Dothan	AL	3,842	C
Truman State Univ	MO	9,728	HC+
Tufts Univ	MA	38,233	MC
Turabo Univ	PR	4,110	
Tusculum College	TN	19,990	C
Tuskegee Univ	AL	17,250	LC
Union College	KY	15,920	C
Union College	NE	17,130	C
Union College	NY	36,005	HC
Union Univ	TN	18,800	VC
United States Air Force Academy	CO		HC+
Universidad Adventista de las Antillas	PR	5,460	
Univ of Akron	OH	13,134	NC
Univ of Alabama	AL	9,040	C+
Univ of Alabama at Birmingham	AL	12,901	C
Univ of Alabama in Huntsville	AL	9,126	VC
Univ of Alaska Anchorage	AK	9,100	NC
Univ of Alaska Fairbanks	AK	9,295	C
Univ of Alaska Southeast	AK	7,900	LC
Univ of Arizona	AZ	10,413	VC
Univ of Arkansas	AR	9,855	VC
Univ of Arkansas at Little Rock	AR	5,637	NC
Univ of Arkansas at Monticello	AR	5,940	NC
Univ of Arkansas at Pine Bluff	AR	7,925	C
Univ of Bridgeport	CT	25,924	LC
Univ of Calif at Berkeley	CA	15,563	MC
Univ of Calif at Davis	CA	14,995	VC
Univ of Calif at Irvine	CA	19,808	HC
Univ of Calif at Los Angeles	CA	15,330	MC
Univ of Calif at Riverside	CA	15,300	C
Univ of Calif at San Diego	CA	14,127	HC
Univ of Calif at Santa Barbara	CA	11,732	VC
Univ of Calif at Santa Cruz	CA	16,505	VC
Univ of Central Arkansas	AR	6,388	C
Univ of Central Florida	FL	10,038	VC
Univ of Central Okla	OK	9,434	C
Univ of Charleston	WV	23,620	C
Univ of Chicago	IL	35,087	MC
Univ of Cincinnati	OH	14,736	C
Univ of Colo at Colo Springs	CO	10,667	C
Univ of Colo at Denver	CO	3,302	C
Univ of Conn	CT	14,608	VC
Univ of Dallas	TX	25,898	VC+
Univ of Dayton	OH	24,850	VC
Univ of Delaware	DE	12,616	HC
Univ of Denver	CO	32,148	VC
Univ of Detroit Mercy	MI	25,582	C
Univ of Dubuque	IA	20,950	C
Univ of Evansville	IN	24,190	VC
Univ of Findlay	OH	23,962	NC
Univ of Georgia	GA	8,656	VC
Univ of Great Falls	MT	15,360	C
Univ of Hartford	CT	31,080	C
Univ of Hawaii at Hilo	HI	6,497	C
Univ of Hawaii at Manoa	HI	9,565	VC
Univ of Houston	TX	9,818	C
Univ of Idaho	ID	8,216	C
Univ of Illinois at Chicago	IL	13,418	C
Univ of Illinois at Urbana-Champaign	IL	11,316	HC+
Univ of Indianapolis	IN	22,560	VC
Univ of Iowa	IA	10,923	VC
Univ of Kansas	KS	8,923	VC
Univ of Kentucky	KY	7,765	C
Univ of La Verne	CA	28,600	C
Univ of Louisiana at Monroe	LA	5,207	NC
Univ of Louisville	KY	8,762	VC
Univ of Maine	ME	12,080	C+
Univ of Maine at Augusta	ME	4,065	C
Univ of Maine at Farmington	ME	10,108	C
Univ of Maine at Fort Kent	ME	9,770	LC
Univ of Maine at Machias	ME	9,271	LC
Univ of Maine at Presque Isle	ME	9,155	LC
Univ of Mary	ND	12,900	C+
Univ of Mary Hardin-Baylor	TX	17,268	C
Univ of Maryland/Baltimore County	MD	14,668	VC+
Univ of Maryland/College Park	MD	14,227	HC
Univ of Maryland/Eastern Shore	MD	9,964	C
Univ of Mass Amherst	MA	13,980	C+
Univ of Mass Boston	MA	6,227	C
Univ of Mass Dartmouth	MA	12,835	C
Univ of Mass Lowell	MA	11,937	VC
Univ of Memphis	TN	8,560	C
Univ of Miami	FL	34,608	HC
Univ of Mich/Ann Arbor	MI	13,864	HC+
Univ of Mich/Dearborn	MI	6,843	VC
Univ of Mich/Flint	MI	5,548	C
Univ of Minn/Duluth	MN	12,470	C
Univ of Minn/Morris	MN	12,896	VC
Univ of Minn/Twin Cities	MN	13,160	VC
Univ of Miss	MS	7,666	C
Univ of Missouri/Columbia	MO	13,782	VC
Univ of Missouri/Kansas City	MO	13,416	VC
Univ of Missouri/Rolla	MO	12,292	HC
Univ of Missouri/St. Louis	MO	11,656	VC
Univ of Mobile	AL	13,620	C
Univ of Montana	MT	9,395	C
Univ of Montevallo	AL	8,478	C
Univ of Nebr at Kearney	NE	8,286	NC
Univ of Nebr at Lincoln	NE	9,975	C+
Univ of Nebr at Omaha	NE	8,080	C
Univ of Nevada/Las Vegas	NV	11,566	C
Univ of Nevada/Reno	NV	9,792	C
Univ of New England	ME	27,200	LC
Univ of New Hampshire	NH	14,828	VC
Univ of New Haven	CT	28,650	C
Univ of New Mexico	NM	9,223	C
Univ of New Orleans	LA	7,356	C
Univ of North Alabama	AL	7,972	NC
Univ of N Car at Asheville	NC	8,079	VC
Univ of N Car at Chapel Hill	NC	10,117	MC
Univ of N Car at Charlotte	NC	8,185	C
Univ of N Car at Greensboro	NC	8,248	C
Univ of N Car at Pembroke	NC	6,929	LC
Univ of N Car at Wilmington	NC	8,940	VC
Univ of N Dak	ND	8,390	C
Univ of North Florida	FL	8,769	VC
Univ of North Texas	TX	7,629	C
Univ of Northern Colo	CO	8,987	C
Univ of Northern Iowa	IA	9,834	C
Univ of Notre Dame	IN	34,442	MC
Univ of Oregon	OR	11,479	VC
Univ of Pennsylvania	PA	37,960	MC
Univ of Pittsburgh at Bradford	PA	15,294	C
Univ of Pittsburgh at Greensburg	PA	15,984	C
Univ of Pittsburgh at Johnstown	PA	15,216	LC
Univ of Pittsburgh at Pittsburgh	PA	16,074	HC
Univ of Portland	OR	28,500	VC
Univ of PR at Humacao	PR	1,245	
Univ of PR/Cayey Univ College	PR	1,245	
Univ of PR/Mayaguez	PR		
Univ of PR/Rio Piedras	PR	5,730	
Univ of Puget Sound	WA	31,760	HC
Univ of Redlands	CA	32,576	VC
Univ of Rhode Island	RI	13,720	VC
Univ of Richmond	VA	30,100	MC
Univ of Rio Grande	OH	8,728	NC
Univ of Rochester	NY	32,979	HC
Univ of St. Francis	IL	22,850	C
Univ of St. Francis	IN	20,964	C
Univ of St. Mary	KS	18,868	C
Univ of St. Thomas	MN	26,918	VC
Univ of St. Thomas	TX	21,952	VC
Univ of San Diego	CA	33,156	HC
Univ of San Francisco	CA	34,700	VC
Univ of Science and Arts of Okla	OK	5,982	C
Univ of Scranton	PA	30,836	VC
Univ of Sioux Falls	SD	16,390	C
Univ of South Alabama	AL	7,760	LC
Univ of S Car at Aiken	SC	7,828	LC
Univ of S Car at Columbia	SC	10,048	VC
Univ of S Car at Spartanburg	SC	9,936	C+
Univ of S Dak	SD	7,710	C+
Univ of South Florida	FL	9,454	C
Univ of Southern Calif	CA	37,459	MC
Univ of Southern Colo	CO	7,821	LC
Univ of Southern Indiana	IN	9,025	LC
Univ of Southern Maine	ME	11,212	C
Univ of Southern Miss	MS	8,324	LC
Univ of Tampa	FL	23,982	VC
Univ of Tenn at Chattanooga	TN	7,783	C
Univ of Tenn at Knoxville	TN	8,214	C
Univ of Tenn at Martin	TN	7,748	C
Univ of Texas at Arlington	TX	7,192	LC
Univ of Texas at Austin	TX	10,630	HC
Univ of Texas at Dallas	TX	10,234	HC
Univ of Texas at El Paso	TX	5,799	NC
Univ of Texas at San Antonio	TX	9,088	NC
Univ of Texas-Pan American	TX	5,954	LC
Univ of the District of Columbia	DC	2,070	LC
Univ of the Incarnate Word	TX	21,772	LC
Univ of the Ozarks	AR	16,574	C
Univ of the Pacific	CA	31,090	VC
Univ of the Sacred Heart	PR	5,590	
Univ of the Sciences in Philadelphia	PA	29,310	VC
Univ of the South	TN	30,855	HC
Univ of Toledo	OH	12,479	NC
Univ of Tulsa	OK	22,090	VC+
Univ of Utah	UT	9,205	C
Univ of Vermont	VT	16,316	VC
Univ of Virginia	VA	11,740	MC
Univ of Virginia's College at Wise	VA	10,116	C
Univ of Washington	WA	10,361	VC
Univ of West Alabama	AL	6,048	C
Univ of West Florida	FL	8,470	C
Univ of Wisc/Eau Claire	WI	8,463	VC
Univ of Wisc/Green Bay	WI	8,154	C
Univ of Wisc/La Crosse	WI	8,991	VC
Univ of Wisc/Milwaukee	WI	9,427	LC
Univ of Wisc/Oshkosh	WI	6,130	LC
Univ of Wisc/Parkside	WI	6,160	LC
Univ of Wisc/Platteville	WI	8,450	C
Univ of Wisc/River Falls	WI	8,358	LC
Univ of Wisc/Stevens Point	WI	8,116	VC
Univ of Wisc/Superior	WI	7,051	C+
Univ of Wisc/Whitewater	WI	8,626	C
Univ of Wyoming	WY	8,636	C
Upper Iowa Univ	IA	20,076	C
Ursinus College	PA	34,400	VC
Ursuline College	OH	22,728	LC
Utah State Univ	UT	7,371	C
Utica College	NY	28,340	C
Valdosta State Univ	GA	7,798	C
Valley City State Univ	ND	7,281	LC
Valparaiso Univ	IN	26,118	VC+
Vanderbilt Univ	TN	37,897	MC
Vanguard Univ of Southern Calif	CA	22,208	C
Vassar College	NY	37,030	MC
Villa Julie College	MD	18,393	C
Villanova Univ	PA	35,050	HC

ST = STATE $IS = IN-STATE COSTS SR = SELECTOR RATING

School	ST	$IS	SR
Virginia Commonwealth Univ	VA	9,030	C
Virginia Intermont College	VA	19,800	C
Virginia Military Inst	VA	9,968	C+
Virginia Polytechnic Inst and State Univ	VA	9,179	C
Virginia State Univ	VA	10,358	C
Virginia Union Univ	VA	15,358	LC
Virginia Wesleyan College	VA	25,350	C
Viterbo Univ	WI	20,430	C
Voorhees College	SC	11,678	LC
Wabash College	IN	27,932	VC
Wagner College	NY	29,900	VC
Wake Forest Univ	NC	34,090	MC
Walla Walla College	WA	21,600	NC
Walsh Univ	OH	20,890	C
Warner Pacific College	OR	21,900	C
Warner Southern College	FL	16,738	LC
Warren Wilson College	NC	21,794	VC
Wartburg College	IA	21,165	VC
Washburn Univ of Topeka	KS	8,984	NC
Washington and Jefferson College	PA	29,570	VC
Washington and Lee Univ	VA	29,663	MC
Washington College	MD	30,540	VC
Washington State Univ	WA	11,334	C
Washington Univ in St. Louis	MO	38,293	MC
Wayland Baptist Univ	TX	11,919	NC
Wayne State College	NE	7,352	NC
Wayne State Univ	MI	11,774	C
Waynesburg College	PA	19,370	C
Weber State Univ	UT	7,945	NC
Webster Univ	MO	21,848	VC
Wellesley College	MA	36,516	MC
Wells College	NY	21,122	VC
Wesley College	DE	19,905	C
Wesleyan College	GA	17,870	VC
Wesleyan Univ	CT	35,139	MC
West Chester Univ of Pennsylvania	PA	11,164	C
West Liberty State College	WV	7,868	LC
West Texas A&M Univ	TX	7,533	C
West Virginia State College	WV	6,264	NC
West Virginia Univ	WV	9,370	C
West Virginia Univ Inst of Technology	WV	7,518	NC
West Virginia Wesleyan College	WV	22,920	C
Western Carolina Univ	NC	6,742	C
Western Conn State Univ	CT	11,625	C
Western Illinois Univ	IL	10,363	C
Western Kentucky Univ	KY	6,834	C
Western Mich Univ	MI	12,031	C
Western New England College	MA	28,924	C
Western New Mexico Univ	NM	5,950	LC
Western Oregon Univ	OR	10,281	C
Western State College of Colo	CO	9,014	C
Western Washington Univ	WA	10,119	VC
Westfield State College	MA	10,147	C
Westminster College	MO	18,150	C+
Westminster College	PA	22,960	C
Westminster College	UT	17,226	C
Westmont College	CA	33,062	VC+
Wheaton College	IL	21,934	HC
Wheaton College	MA	36,330	HC
Wheeling Jesuit Univ	WV	22,660	C
Whitman College	WA	32,526	HC+
Whittier College	CA	29,108	C
Whitworth College	WA	26,428	VC+
Wichita State Univ	KS	8,092	C
Widener Univ	PA	27,020	C
Wilberforce Univ	OH	14,937	LC
Wiley College	TX	8,100	LC
Wilkes Univ	PA	28,060	C
Willamette Univ	OR	32,032	VC+
William Carey College	MS	10,150	LC
William Jewell College	MO	21,320	VC
William Paterson Univ of New Jersey	NJ	14,450	C
William Penn Univ	IA	17,575	LC
William Woods Univ	MO	20,120	C
Williams Baptist College	AR	11,950	C
Williams College	MA	32,270	MC
Wilmington College	OH	24,172	LC
Wilson College	PA	23,912	C
Wingate Univ	NC	21,200	C
Winona State Univ	MN		C
Winston-Salem State Univ	NC	8,926	LC
Winthrop Univ	SC	11,302	C
Wisc Lutheran College	WI	21,430	VC
Wittenberg Univ	OH	31,316	VC
Wofford College	SC	26,710	HC
Worcester Polytechnic Inst	MA	37,404	HC
Worcester State College	MA	10,005	C
Wright State Univ	OH	11,490	LC
Xavier Univ	OH	26,850	VC+
Xavier Univ of Louisiana	LA	17,600	C
Yale Univ	CT	37,000	MC
Yeshiva Univ	NY	21,400	C
York College	NE	14,975	C
York College of Pennsylvania	PA	14,500	VC
Youngstown State Univ	OH	11,148	NC

BIOMATHEMATICS

School	ST	$IS	SR
Rutgers, The State Univ of New Jersey/New Brunswick/Piscataway Campus	NJ	15,800	HC

BIOMEDICAL ENGINEERING

School	ST	$IS	SR
Boston Univ	MA	38,194	HC+
Bucknell Univ	PA	35,262	HC+
Case Western Reserve Univ	OH	32,002	MC
Catholic Univ of America	DC	34,248	VC
CUNY/City College	NY	4,230	C+
Columbia Univ/Fu Foundation School of Engineering and Applied Science	NY	38,590	MC
DeVry Univ/Dallas	TX	10,640	LC
DeVry Univ/Decatur	GA	10,670	LC
DeVry Univ/Fremont	CA	11,860	LC
DeVry Univ/Kansas City	MO	10,670	LC
DeVry Univ/Phoenix	AZ	10,670	LC
DeVry Univ/Pomona	CA	11,310	LC
DeVry Univ/West Hills	CA	11,310	LC
DeVry Univ/Westminster	CO	11,310	LC
Drexel Univ	PA	27,655	VC
Duke Univ	NC	37,555	MC
Florida International Univ	FL	9,912	VC
Florida State Univ	FL	9,028	HC
Hofstra Univ	NY	27,112	VC
Indiana Inst of Technology	IN	21,620	C
Indiana Univ-Purdue Univ Indianapolis	IN	8,257	LC
Johns Hopkins Univ	MD	38,372	MC
Louisiana Tech Univ	LA	7,361	C
Marquette Univ	WI	27,594	VC
Mercer Univ	GA	27,516	VC+
Mich Tech Univ	MI	13,235	VC
Milwaukee School of Engineering	WI	28,479	VC+
New Jersey Inst of Technology	NJ	16,396	VC
New York Inst of Technology	NY	24,205	VC
Northwestern Univ	IL	37,491	MC
Purdue Univ/West Lafayette	IN	12,560	VC
Rensselaer Polytechnic Inst	NY	37,579	HC+
Rochester Inst of Technology	NY	29,217	VC+
Rose-Hulman Inst of Technology	IN	31,425	HC+
St. Louis Univ	MO	29,780	VC+
SUNY/Univ at Stony Brook	NY	12,763	HC
Stevens Inst of Technology	NJ	35,300	HC+
Tufts Univ	MA	38,233	MC
Tulane Univ	LA	37,451	HC+
Univ of Akron	OH	13,134	NC
Univ of Alabama at Birmingham	AL	12,901	C
Univ of Conn	CT	14,608	VC
Univ of Hartford	CT	31,080	C
Univ of Iowa	IA	10,923	VC
Univ of Miami	FL	34,608	HC
Univ of Missouri/Columbia	MO	13,782	VC
Univ of Rhode Island	RI	13,720	VC
Univ of Rochester	NY	32,979	HC
Univ of Southern Calif	CA	37,459	MC
Univ of Texas at Austin	TX	10,630	HC
Univ of Utah	UT	9,205	C
Univ of Virginia	VA	11,740	MC
Univ of Wisc/Madison	WI	8,262	VC
Washington Univ in St. Louis	MO	38,293	MC
Western New England College	MA	28,924	C
Worcester Polytechnic Inst	MA	37,404	HC
Wright State Univ	OH	11,490	LC
Yale Univ	CT	37,000	MC

BIOMEDICAL EQUIPMENT TECHNOLOGY

School	ST	$IS	SR
Andrews Univ	MI	19,550	C
Thomas Edison State College	NJ	3,325	SP
Univ of Houston	TX	9,818	C

BIOMEDICAL SCIENCE

School	ST	$IS	SR
Andrews Univ	MI	19,550	C
Averett Univ	VA	23,010	LC
Brown Univ	RI	38,174	MC
Cal State, Northridge	CA	7,757	LC
CUNY/City College	NY	4,230	C+
LIU/C.W. Post Campus	NY	28,282	C
Lynchburg College	VA	26,815	C
Marquette Univ	WI	27,594	VC
MCP Hahnemann Univ	PA	18,510	SP
Okla State Univ	OK	9,216	VC
Oral Roberts Univ	OK	18,490	C
Rutgers, The State Univ of New Jersey/New Brunswick/Piscataway Campus	NJ	15,800	HC
Texas A&M Univ	TX	11,081	HC
Univ of Mich/Ann Arbor	MI	13,864	HC+
Univ of Miss	MS	7,666	C
Univ of New England	ME	27,200	LC
Univ of Pennsylvania	PA	37,960	MC
Univ of South Alabama	AL	7,760	LC
Univ of Vermont	VT	16,316	VC
Western Mich Univ	MI	12,031	C

BIOMETRICS AND BIOSTATISTICS

School	ST	$IS	SR
Brigham Young Univ	UT	8,504	HC
Cornell Univ	NY	38,253	MC
La Sierra Univ	CA	19,260	LC
Southwestern Adventist Univ	TX	14,798	C
Univ of N Car at Chapel Hill	NC	10,117	MC
Univ of Pennsylvania	PA	37,960	MC

BIOPHYSICS

School	ST	$IS	SR
Andrews Univ	MI	19,550	C
Brigham Young Univ	UT	8,504	HC
Brown Univ	RI	38,174	MC
Centenary College of Louisiana	LA	23,100	VC+
Columbia Univ/Columbia College	NY	38,590	MC
Harvard Univ/Harvard College	MA	37,928	MC
Illinois Inst of Technology	IL	26,456	HC+
Iowa State Univ	IA	10,768	VC
Johns Hopkins Univ	MD	38,372	MC
La Sierra Univ	CA	19,260	LC
Okla City Univ	OK	19,580	VC
Oregon State Univ	OR	11,055	C
Pacific Union College	CA	22,065	C+
Rensselaer Polytechnic Inst	NY	37,579	HC+
St. Bonaventure Univ	NY	24,455	LC
St. Mary's Univ of Minn	MN	21,535	C
Southwestern Okla State Univ	OK	4,801	C
SUNY/College at Geneseo	NY	11,330	HC
SUNY/Univ at Buffalo	NY	12,563	VC
Temple Univ	PA	15,912	C
Univ of Calif at San Diego	CA	14,127	HC
Univ of Conn	CT	14,608	VC
Univ of Houston	TX	9,818	C
Univ of Illinois at Urbana-Champaign	IL	11,316	HC+
Univ of Mich/Ann Arbor	MI	13,864	HC+
Univ of Pennsylvania	PA	37,960	MC
Univ of Scranton	PA	30,836	VC
Univ of Southern Calif	CA	37,459	MC
Univ of Southern Indiana	IN	9,025	LC
Walla Walla College	WA	21,600	NC
Washington Univ in St. Louis	MO	38,293	MC
Yale Univ	CT	37,000	MC

BIOPSYCHOLOGY

School	ST	$IS	SR
Columbia Univ/Barnard College	NY	36,990	MC
Mills College	CA	33,371	VC
Monmouth College	IL	23,600	C
Nebr Wesleyan Univ	NE	21,197	C+
Philadelphia Univ	PA	27,354	C
Rider Univ	NJ	30,900	C
Russell Sage College	NY	26,811	C
Tufts Univ	MA	38,233	MC
Univ of Calif at Santa Barbara	CA	11,732	VC
Univ of Mich/Ann Arbor	MI	13,864	HC+
Vassar College	NY	37,030	MC
Washington Univ in St. Louis	MO	38,293	MC

BIORESOURCE ENGINEERING

School	ST	$IS	SR
Rutgers, The State Univ of New Jersey/New Brunswick/Piscataway Campus	NJ	15,800	HC

BIOTECHNOLOGY

School	ST	$IS	SR
Albany College of Pharmacy	NY	22,320	SP
Averett Univ	VA	23,010	LC
Brigham Young Univ	UT	8,504	HC
Cabrini College	PA	29,020	C
Calif State Polytechnic Univ, Pomona	CA	8,793	C+
Calvin College	MI	22,615	NC
CUNY/York College	NY	3,292	NC
Elizabethtown College	PA	28,800	C
Fontbonne Univ	MO	21,508	C
Inter American Univ of PR/Bayamon Univ College	PR	3,522	
Kennesaw State Univ	GA	2,724	C
Kent State Univ	OH	12,932	C
Marywood Univ	PA	26,050	C
Mich State Univ	MI	11,933	VC
Minn State Univ, Mankato	MN	8,803	LC
Missouri Southern State Univ	MO	8,316	C
Montana State Univ-Bozeman	MT	9,515	C
N Dak State Univ	ND	8,435	C
Plymouth State Univ	NH	12,298	LC
Point Park Univ	PA	21,840	C
Purdue Univ/Calumet	IN	6,630	NC
Quinnipiac Univ	CT	30,570	VC
Ramapo College of New Jersey	NJ	15,203	VC
Rochester Inst of Technology	NY	29,217	VC+
Rutgers, The State Univ of New Jersey/New Brunswick/Piscataway Campus	NJ	15,800	HC
Southeastern Okla State Univ	OK	6,147	C
Springfield College	MA	24,520	C
SUNY/Univ at Buffalo	NY	12,563	VC
Tufts Univ	MA	38,233	MC
Univ of Calif at San Diego	CA	14,127	HC
Univ of Delaware	DE	12,616	HC
Univ of Maine	ME	12,080	C+
Univ of New Hampshire	NH	14,828	VC
Univ of New Haven	CT	28,650	C
Univ of Northern Iowa	IA	9,834	C
Univ of PR/Mayaguez	PR		
Univ of Southern Colo	CO	7,821	LC
Univ of Wisc/River Falls	WI	8,358	LC
Ursuline College	OH	22,728	LC
Villa Julie College	MD	18,393	C
William Paterson Univ of New Jersey	NJ	14,450	C
William Penn Univ	IA	17,575	LC
Worcester Polytechnic Inst	MA	37,404	HC
Worcester State College	MA	10,005	C

BOTANY

School	ST	$IS	SR
Andrews Univ	MI	19,550	C
Auburn Univ	AL	10,396	VC
Ball State Univ	IN	8,660	C
Brigham Young Univ	UT	8,504	HC
Calif State Polytechnic Univ, Pomona	CA	8,793	C+
Cal State, Long Beach	CA	8,762	C+
Cal State, Stanislaus	CA	9,874	C
Colo State Univ	CO	9,964	VC
Conn College	CT	37,900	MC
Cornell Univ	NY	38,253	MC
Delaware State Univ	DE	8,104	LC
Eastern Mich Univ	MI	11,478	C
Eastern Washington Univ	WA	9,012	C
Hampshire College	MA	37,037	HC
Humboldt State Univ	CA	9,400	C
Idaho State Univ	ID	8,128	C
Iowa State Univ	IA	10,768	VC
Juniata College	PA	29,080	VC
Kent State Univ	OH	12,932	C
Marlboro College	VT	29,055	VC+
Mars Hill College	NC	18,600	LC
Miami Univ	OH	15,033	HC
Mich State Univ	MI	11,933	VC
N Car State Univ	NC	9,886	VC
N Dak State Univ	ND	8,435	C
Northern Arizona Univ	AZ	9,002	C
Northern Mich Univ	MI	10,834	C
Northwest Missouri State Univ	MO	9,334	C
Ohio Wesleyan Univ	OH	32,550	VC+
Okla State Univ	OK	9,216	VC
Oregon State Univ	OR	11,055	C
Rutgers, The State Univ of New Jersey/New Brunswick/Piscataway Campus	NJ	15,800	HC
Rutgers, The State Univ of New Jersey/Newark Campus	NJ	15,624	VC
San Francisco State Univ	CA	12,070	C
San Jose State Univ	CA	8,187	C
Southern Illinois Univ Carbondale	IL	10,407	C
SUNY/College of Environmental Science and Forestry	NY	14,167	VC
Texas A&M Univ	TX	11,081	HC
Texas A&M Univ at Commerce	TX	8,994	C
Texas State Univ	TX	9,320	VC
Univ of Akron	OH	13,134	NC
Univ of Arkansas	AR	9,855	VC
Univ of Calif at Davis	CA	14,995	VC
Univ of Calif at Los Angeles	CA	15,330	MC
Univ of Calif at Riverside	CA	15,170	C
Univ of Florida	FL	8,580	MC
Univ of Georgia	GA	8,656	VC
Univ of Great Falls	MT	15,360	C
Univ of Hawaii at Manoa	HI	9,565	VC

ST = STATE $IS = IN-STATE COSTS SR = SELECTOR RATING

School	ST	$IS	SR
Univ of Idaho	ID	8,216	C
Univ of Kentucky	KY	7,765	C
Univ of Maine	ME	12,080	C+
Univ of Mich/Ann Arbor	MI	13,864	HC+
Univ of Minn/Twin Cities	MN	13,160	VC
Univ of Montana	MT	9,395	C
Univ of Okla	OK	9,226	VC
Univ of Tenn at Knoxville	TN	8,214	C
Univ of Texas at Austin	TX	10,630	HC
Univ of Vermont	VT	16,316	VC
Univ of Washington	WA	10,361	VC
Univ of Wisc/Madison	WI	8,262	VC
Univ of Wisc/Milwaukee	WI	9,427	LC
Univ of Wyoming	WY	8,636	C
Weber State Univ	UT	7,945	NC
Western New Mexico Univ	NM	5,950	LC

BRITISH STUDIES

School	ST	$IS	SR
Bard College	NY	37,352	HC+

BROADCASTING

School	ST	$IS	SR
Abilene Christian Univ	TX	18,370	VC
Alabama State Univ	AL	6,404	C
Arizona State Univ-Main	AZ	10,048	C
Asbury College	KY	20,704	VC
Ashland Univ	OH	24,464	C
Baldwin-Wallace College	OH	24,678	C
Ball State Univ	IN	8,660	C
Barry Univ	FL	24,100	LC
Baylor Univ	TX	23,864	VC
Bemidji State Univ	MN	9,103	C
Biola Univ	CA	25,964	VC
Black Hills State Univ	SD	7,743	LC
Bowie State Univ	MD	10,873	C+
Bowling Green State Univ	OH	13,036	C
Cal State, Fullerton	CA	6,648	C
Cal State, Hayward	CA	8,871	LC
Campbell Univ	NC	18,268	VC
Central Methodist College	MO	16,460	C
Central Mich Univ	MI	11,142	C
Central Missouri State Univ	MO	9,776	C
Central State Univ	OH	8,922	C+
Central Washington Univ	WA	9,768	C
Chicago State Univ	IL	10,882	C+
CUNY/Brooklyn College	NY	4,353	C+
College of the Ozarks	MO	3,500	VC+
Concord College	WV	8,136	C
Dordt College	IA	20,170	VC
Drake Univ	IA	25,120	VC+
Drury Univ	MO	18,085	VC+
Eastern Kentucky Univ	KY	7,708	C
Eastern Nazarene College	MA	19,433	LC
Eastern Washington Univ	WA	9,012	C
Edinboro Univ of Pennsylvania	PA	10,850	LC
Elon Univ	NC	22,240	VC
Emerson College	MA	32,205	HC
Evangel Univ	MO	15,435	C
Florida State Univ	FL	9,028	HC
Fontbonne Univ	MO	21,508	C
Fordham Univ	NY	35,066	HC
Freed-Hardeman Univ	TN		NC
Geneva College	PA	21,850	C
George Washington Univ	DC	41,030	MC
Georgia Southern Univ	GA	8,540	C
Gonzaga Univ	WA	26,766	HC
Grand Valley State Univ	MI	11,022	VC
Grand View College	IA	19,748	LC
Harding Univ	AR	14,890	VC
Hastings College	NE	19,928	VC
Indiana State Univ	IN	10,719	LC
Indiana Univ-Purdue Univ Fort Wayne	IN	5,108	LC
Ithaca College	NY	31,730	HC
John Brown Univ	AR	15,080	VC
Kent State Univ	OH	12,932	C
Lewis Univ	IL	22,950	C+
Lincoln Memorial Univ	TN	16,400	LC
LIU/Brooklyn Campus	NY	24,790	C
LIU/C.W. Post Campus	NY	28,282	C
Loras College	IA	24,233	C
Mansfield Univ	PA	11,220	C
Marietta College	OH	27,047	C
Marquette Univ	WI	27,594	VC
McNeese State Univ	LA	5,259	LC
Mercyhurst College	PA	20,694	C
Messiah College	PA	25,890	VC+
Miami Univ	OH	15,033	HC
Minn State Univ, Moorehead	MN	7,000	LC
Minot State Univ	ND	6,602	LC
Montclair State Univ	NJ	13,790	C
Morris College	SC	10,974	LC
Murray State Univ	KY	7,816	VC
North Central College	IL	25,656	VC
Northern Arizona Univ	AZ	9,002	C
Northern Mich Univ	MI	10,834	C
Northwest Missouri State Univ	MO	9,334	C
Northwestern College	MN	22,820	C+
Northwestern Okla State Univ	OK	5,433	NC
Ohio Northern Univ	OH	27,765	VC
Ohio Univ	OH	14,448	C
Ohio Wesleyan Univ	OH	32,550	VC+
Okla Baptist Univ	OK	15,220	VC
Okla Christian Univ	OK	17,690	NC
Okla City Univ	OK	19,580	VC
Oral Roberts Univ	OK	18,490	C
Otterbein College	OH	26,085	C
Penn State Univ/Univ Park Campus	PA	15,646	HC
Point Park Univ	PA	21,840	C
Prairie View A&M Univ	TX	9,418	NC
Purdue Univ/Calumet	IN	6,630	NC
Radford Univ	VA	8,500	C
Rider Univ	NJ	30,900	C
Roosevelt Univ	IL	22,580	VC
Rowan Univ	NJ	14,506	VC
St. Cloud State Univ	MN	8,362	C
San Diego State Univ	CA	10,321	C
San Francisco State Univ	CA	12,070	C
San Jose State Univ	CA	8,187	C
Savannah State Univ	GA	7,328	LC
Shaw Univ	NC	14,882	C+
Sojourner-Douglass College	MD	4,170	LC
Southern Adventist Univ	TN	17,080	C
Southern Arkansas Univ	AR	6,956	C
Southern Illinois Univ Carbondale	IL	10,407	C
Southern Methodist Univ	TX	34,210	HC
Southwest Missouri State Univ	MO	8,918	C
Southwestern Adventist Univ	TX	14,798	C
SUNY at Oswego	NY	12,650	C
SUNY/College at Buffalo	NY	8,025	C
SUNY/Univ at New Paltz	NY	11,565	VC
Stephen F. Austin State Univ	TX	7,552	C
Suffolk Univ	MA	29,200	C
Syracuse Univ	NY	34,720	HC
Temple Univ	PA	15,912	C
Texas A&M Univ at Commerce	TX	8,994	C
Texas Christian Univ	TX	23,410	VC
Texas State Univ	TX	9,320	VC
Texas Tech Univ	TX	10,768	VC
Toccoa Falls College	GA	15,600	C
Trevecca Nazarene Univ	TN	17,548	C
Troy State Univ	AL	7,696	C
Union Univ	TN	18,800	VC
Univ of Akron	OH	13,134	NC
Univ of Central Florida	FL	10,038	VC
Univ of Central Okla	OK	9,434	C
Univ of Cincinnati	OH	14,736	C
Univ of Colo at Boulder	CO	10,774	VC
Univ of Dayton	OH	24,850	VC
Univ of Findlay	OH	23,962	NC
Univ of Georgia	GA	8,656	VC
Univ of Illinois at Urbana-Champaign	IL	11,316	HC+
Univ of Indianapolis	IN	22,560	VC
Univ of Iowa	IA	10,923	VC
Univ of La Verne	CA	28,600	C
Univ of Louisiana at Lafayette	LA	5,826	C
Univ of Miami	FL	34,608	HC
Univ of Miss	MS	7,666	C
Univ of Missouri/Columbia	MO	13,782	VC
Univ of Nebr at Kearney	NE	8,286	NC
Univ of Nebr at Lincoln	NE	9,975	C+
Univ of Nebr at Omaha	NE	8,080	C
Univ of N Car at Pembroke	NC	6,929	LC
Univ of Northern Iowa	IA	9,834	C
Univ of Okla	OK	9,226	VC
Univ of S Car at Columbia	SC	10,048	VC
Univ of Southern Calif	CA	37,459	MC
Univ of Southern Colo	CO	7,821	LC
Univ of Southern Indiana	IN	9,025	LC
Univ of Tenn at Knoxville	TN	8,214	C
Univ of Texas at Arlington	TX	7,192	LC
Univ of Wisc/Eau Claire	WI	8,463	VC
Valparaiso Univ	IN	26,118	VC+
Wartburg College	IA	21,165	VC
Washington State Univ	WA	11,334	C
Wayne State Univ	MI	11,774	C
Waynesburg College	PA	19,370	C
Webster Univ	MO	21,848	VC
West Texas A&M Univ	TX	7,533	C
West Virginia Univ	WV	9,370	C
Western Kentucky Univ	KY	6,834	C
Western Mich Univ	MI	12,031	C
Westminster College	PA	22,960	C
Winona State Univ	MN		C
York College of Pennsylvania	PA	14,500	VC
Youngstown State Univ	OH	11,148	NC

BUSINESS ADMINISTRATION AND MANAGEMENT

School	ST	$IS	SR
Adams State College	CO	7,468	C
Adelphi Univ	NY	26,300	VC
Adrian College	MI	21,950	C
Alabama A&M Univ	AL	5,100	LC
Alabama State Univ	AL	6,404	C
Alaska Pacific Univ	AK	17,910	C
Albertson College of Idaho	ID	19,415	VC
Albertus Magnus College	CT	23,130	LC
Albright College	PA	30,579	C
Alcorn State Univ	MS	7,290	C
Alderson-Broaddus College	WV	19,640	C
Alfred Univ	NY	28,290	C
Alice Lloyd College	KY	4,040	C
Allen Univ	SC	10,300	NC
Alliant International Univ	CA	23,640	C
Alma College	MI	25,566	VC
Alvernia College	PA	23,212	LC
Alverno College	WI	18,898	C
American InterContinental Univ	GA	12,000	NC
American International College	MA	24,690	LC
American Univ	DC	34,585	VC+
Anderson Univ	IN	19,430	LC
Andrews Univ	MI	19,550	C
Angelo State Univ	TX	7,576	NC
Anna Maria College	MA	26,140	LC
Aquinas College	MI	21,894	C
Aquinas College	TN	10,660	LC
Arcadia Univ	PA	29,890	C
Arkansas Baptist College	AR	5,530	NC
Arkansas State Univ	AR	8,450	C
Arkansas Tech Univ	AR	7,299	C
Asbury College	KY	20,704	VC
Ashland Univ	OH	24,464	C
Assumption College	MA	29,375	C
Atlantic Union College	MA	18,868	C
Auburn Univ	AL	10,396	VC
Auburn Univ Montgomery	AL	9,020	NC
Augsburg College	MN	25,298	C
Augusta State Univ	GA	2,592	C
Augustana College	IL	26,610	VC+
Augustana College	SD	21,998	VC
Aurora Univ	IL	20,631	C
Austin College	TX	24,747	HC
Austin Peay State Univ	TN	5,814	LC
Avila Univ	MO	20,300	C
Azusa Pacific Univ	CA	24,720	VC
Babson College	MA	37,226	HC
Baker College of Flint	MI	7,720	NC
Baker Univ	KS	19,860	VC
Baldwin-Wallace College	OH	24,678	C
Ball State Univ	IN	8,660	C
Barber-Scotia College	NC	13,900	LC
Barton College	NC	19,314	C
Bay Path College	MA	24,910	C
Baylor Univ	TX	23,864	VC
Becker College	MA	23,710	LC
Belhaven College	MS	16,040	C+
Bellarmine Univ	KY	24,110	VC
Bellevue Univ	NE	4,440	NC
Belmont Abbey College	NC	23,742	C
Belmont Univ	TN	21,986	VC
Beloit College	WI	29,864	HC
Bemidji State Univ	MN	9,103	C
Benedict College	SC	12,662	LC
Benedictine College	KS	20,603	C
Benedictine Univ	IL	23,840	C
Bennett College	NC	11,200	C
Bentley College	MA	33,904	VC
Berea College	KY	5,030	VC+
Berkeley College	NY	21,545	LC
Berkeley College of New York City	NY	12,500	LC
Berry College	GA	21,410	VC
Bethany College	KS	18,675	LC
Bethel College	IN	19,670	C
Bethel College	KS	19,800	C+
Bethel College	MN	25,180	VC
Bethel College	TN	12,980	C
Bethune-Cookman College	FL	16,480	LC
Biola Univ	CA	25,964	VC
Birmingham-Southern College	AL	25,364	VC+
Black Hills State Univ	SD	7,743	LC
Blackburn College	IL	13,690	C
Bloomfield College	NJ	19,250	LC
Bloomsburg Univ of Pennsylvania	PA	10,844	C
Blue Mountain College	MS	10,226	C
Bluefield College	VA	15,575	C
Bluefield State College	WV	2,806	LC
Bluffton College	OH	23,694	C
Boise State Univ	ID	7,657	LC
Boricua College	NY	7,375	C
Boston College	MA	33,284	MC
Boston Univ	MA	38,194	HC+
Bowie State Univ	MD	10,873	C+
Bowling Green State Univ	OH	13,036	C
Bradley Univ	IL	22,910	VC
Brenau Univ Women's College	GA	21,800	C
Brescia Univ	KY	14,225	C
Brewton-Parker College	GA	14,200	LC
Briar Cliff Univ	IA	21,660	C
Bridgewater College	VA	25,150	C
Brigham Young Univ	UT	8,504	HC
Bryan College	TN	17,900	VC
Bryant College	RI	31,004	VC
Bucknell Univ	PA	35,262	HC+
Buena Vista Univ	IA	25,406	C
Cabrini College	PA	29,020	C
Caldwell College	NJ	24,060	LC
Calif Baptist Univ	CA	19,924	C
Calif Lutheran Univ	CA	27,600	LC
Calif Maritime Academy	CA	14,296	C
Calif Polytechnic State Univ	CA	8,747	VC
Calif State Polytechnic Univ, Pomona	CA	8,793	C+
Cal State, Bakersfield	CA	6,090	LC
Cal State, Chico	CA	8,598	LC
Cal State, Dominguez Hills	CA	5,840	LC
Cal State, Fresno	CA	8,414	LC
Cal State, Fullerton	CA	6,648	C
Cal State, Hayward	CA	8,871	LC
Cal State, Long Beach	CA	8,762	C+
Cal State, Los Angeles	CA	5,778	C
Cal State, Northridge	CA	7,757	LC
Cal State, Sacramento	CA	9,543	C
Cal State, San Bernardino	CA	15,238	LC
Cal State, San Marcos	CA	1,736	LC
Cal State, Stanislaus	CA	9,874	C
Calif Univ of Pennsylvania	PA	10,388	C
Calumet College of St. Joseph	IN	9,000	LC
Calvin College	MI	22,615	NC
Cameron Univ	OK	5,692	NC
Campbell Univ	NC	18,268	VC
Campbellsville Univ	KY	17,680	C
Canisius College	NY	28,163	C+
Capital Univ	OH	26,550	C
Cardinal Stritch Univ	WI	17,620	C
Caribbean Univ	PR	3,000	
Carlos Albizu Univ	FL	10,569	C
Carlow College	PA	21,334	C
Carnegie Mellon Univ	PA	32,682	MC
Carroll College	MT	20,576	VC
Carroll College	WI	22,740	C
Carson-Newman College	TN	16,760	C
Carthage College	WI	25,000	C
Cascade College	OR	16,700	NC
Case Western Reserve Univ	OH	32,002	MC
Castleton State College	VT	11,820	C
Catawba College	NC	20,500	C
Catholic Univ of America	DC	34,248	VC
Cedar Crest College	PA	25,145	C+
Cedarville Univ	OH	19,954	VC
Centenary College	NJ	25,370	LC
Centenary College of Louisiana	LA	23,100	VC+
Central College	IA	21,206	C
Central Conn State Univ	CT	12,090	C
Central Methodist College	MO	16,460	C
Central Mich Univ	MI	11,142	C
Central Missouri State Univ	MO	9,776	C
Central State Univ	OH	8,922	C+
Central Univ of Bayamon	PR	3,335	
Central Washington Univ	WA	9,768	C
Chadron State College	NE	6,286	NC
Champlain College	VT	22,030	C
Chapman Univ	CA	33,118	VC
Charleston Southern Univ	SC	17,122	C
Chatham College	PA	27,266	C+
Chestnut Hill College	PA	26,450	LC
Cheyney Univ of Pennsylvania	PA	9,993	C
Chicago State Univ	IL	10,882	C+
Christian Brothers Univ	TN	22,290	VC
Christian Heritage College	CA	19,990	C
Christopher Newport Univ	VA	8,862	VC
Citadel, The	SC	12,295	C+
City Univ	WA	7,425	NC
CUNY/Brooklyn College	NY	4,353	C+
CUNY/City College	NY	4,230	C+
CUNY/College of Staten Island	NY	4,308	NC
CUNY/Herbert H. Lehman College	NY	3,320	LC
CUNY/Medgar Evers College	NY	4,232	NC
CUNY/Queens College	NY	4,362	C
CUNY/York College	NY	3,292	NC
Claflin Univ	SC	14,838	C+
Clarion Univ of Pennsylvania	PA	11,272	LC
Clark Atlanta Univ	GA	19,300	C+
Clark Univ	MA	32,115	VC
Clarke College	IA	23,165	C
Clarkson College	NE	12,178	C
Clarkson Univ	NY	32,226	VC
Clayton College and State Univ	GA	2,441	LC
Clearwater Christian College	FL	13,160	LC
Cleary College	MI	10,350	LC
Clemson Univ	SC	11,972	HC
Coastal Carolina Univ	SC	11,040	C
Coe College	IA	27,385	VC
Coker College	SC	21,491	C
Colby-Sawyer College	NH	27,850	LC
College Misericordia	PA	26,350	C
College of Charleston	SC	11,887	HC
College of Mount St. Vincent	NY	26,800	C
College of Mount St. Joseph	OH	22,785	C
College of New Jersey	NJ	15,950	MC
College of New Rochelle	NY	21,800	C

ST = STATE $IS = IN-STATE COSTS SR = SELECTOR RATING

School	ST	$IS	SR
College of Notre Dame of Maryland	MD	27,700	C
College of Our Lady of the Elms	MA	20,644	C
College of St. Catherine	MN	24,010	VC
College of St. Elizabeth	NJ	25,460	C
College of St. Joseph	VT	19,100	C
College of St. Mary	NE	21,510	C
College of St. Rose	NY	22,864	C
College of St. Scholastica	MN	24,970	C+
College of Santa Fe	NM	25,293	C+
College of the Ozarks	MO	3,500	VC+
College of the Southwest	NM	9,320	C+
College of William and Mary	VA	12,224	MC
Colo Christian Univ	CO	21,182	VC
Colo State Univ	CO	9,964	VC
Colo Technical Univ	CO	9,500	LC
Columbia College	MO	16,139	C
Columbia College	SC	22,658	LC
Columbia Union College	MD	20,543	C
Columbus State Univ	GA	7,846	C
Concord College	WV	8,136	C
Concordia College	AL	9,774	NC
Concordia College	NY	19,200	VC
Concordia College: Moorhead	MN	22,460	VC+
Concordia Univ	CA	24,420	C
Concordia Univ	MI	24,095	C
Concordia Univ	OR	22,450	C
Concordia Univ at Austin	TX	20,450	LC
Concordia Univ Nebr	NE	20,302	C+
Concordia Univ Wisc	WI	16,600	C
Concordia Univ, River Forest	IL	23,600	C
Concordia Univ/St.Paul	MN	24,486	C
Converse College	SC	24,710	VC
Coppin State College	MD	10,191	LC
Cornerstone Univ and Grand Rapids Theological Seminary	MI	19,846	C
Covenant College	GA	23,830	VC+
Creighton Univ	NE	26,748	VC+
Crichton College	TN	15,215	C
Culver-Stockton College	MO	17,850	C
Cumberland College	KY	16,384	C
Cumberland Univ	TN	16,910	C
Curry College	MA	26,025	LC
Daemen College	NY	22,120	C
Dakota State Univ	SD	7,466	C
Dakota Wesleyan Univ	SD	17,832	C
Dallas Baptist Univ	TX	15,300	VC
Dana College	NE	20,280	C
Daniel Webster College	NH	24,870	C
David Lipscomb Univ	TN	16,158	VC
David N. Myers College	OH	9,475	C
Davis and Elkins College	WV	20,594	C
De Sales Univ	PA	25,470	C
Defiance College	OH	22,615	C
Delaware State Univ	DE	8,104	LC
Delaware Valley College	PA	26,676	C
Delta State Univ	MS	6,618	C
DePaul Univ	IL	27,580	VC
DeVry/New York	NY	11,860	LC
DeVry Univ/Addison (DuPage County)	IL	10,790	LC
DeVry Univ/Alpharetta	GA	10,670	LC
DeVry Univ/Chicago	IL	10,790	LC
DeVry Univ/Colo Springs	CO	11,310	LC
DeVry Univ/Columbus	OH	10,670	LC
DeVry Univ/Crystal City	VA	11,860	C
DeVry Univ/Dallas	TX	10,640	LC
DeVry Univ/Decatur	GA	10,670	LC
DeVry Univ/Fort Washington	PA	11,860	LC
DeVry Univ/Fremont	CA	11,860	LC
DeVry Univ/Kansas City	MO	10,670	LC
DeVry Univ/Long Beach	CA	11,310	LC
DeVry Univ/Miramar	FL	11,310	LC
DeVry Univ/Orlando	FL	11,310	LC
DeVry Univ/Phoenix	AZ	10,670	LC
DeVry Univ/Pomona	CA	11,310	LC
DeVry Univ/Seattle	WA	11,860	LC
DeVry Univ/Tinley Park	IL	10,790	LC
DeVry Univ/West Hills	CA	11,310	LC
DeVry Univ/Westminster	CO	11,310	LC
Dickinson State Univ	ND	6,338	NC
Dillard Univ	LA	17,325	VC
Doane College	NE	20,000	C
Dominican College	NY	24,810	LC
Dominican Univ	IL	23,610	C
Dordt College	IA	20,170	VC
Dowling College	NY	23,870	LC
Drake Univ	IA	25,120	VC+
Drexel Univ	PA	27,655	VC
Drury Univ	MO	18,085	VC+
Duquesne Univ	PA	26,907	VC
D'Youville College	NY	21,080	C
Earlham College	IN	29,976	VC+
East Carolina Univ	NC	8,671	C
East Central Univ	OK	4,968	C
East Stroudsburg Univ of Pennsylvania	PA	10,336	C
East Texas Baptist Univ	TX	13,914	C
Eastern Conn State Univ	CT	10,362	C
Eastern Illinois Univ	IL	11,192	C
Eastern Kentucky Univ	KY	7,708	C
Eastern Mennonite Univ	VA	22,990	C
Eastern Mich Univ	MI	11,478	C
Eastern Nazarene College	MA	19,433	LC
Eastern New Mexico Univ	NM	6,762	LC
Eastern Oregon Univ	OR	10,080	NC
Eastern Univ	PA	24,020	C
Eastern Washington Univ	WA	9,012	C
East-West Univ	IL	10,365	LC
Eckerd College	FL	28,744	C+
Edgewood College	WI	20,520	C
Edinboro Univ of Pennsylvania	PA	10,850	LC
Edward Waters College	FL	14,374	LC
Elizabeth City State Univ	NC	5,550	LC
Elizabethtown College	PA	28,800	C
Elmhurst College	IL	24,630	C
Elmira College	NY	33,820	VC
Elon Univ	NC	22,240	VC
Embry-Riddle Aeronautical Univ	FL	27,730	C+
Emmanuel College	MA	27,600	C+
Emory & Henry College	VA	21,950	C
Emory Univ	GA	36,872	MC
Emporia State Univ	KS	6,998	C
Endicott College	MA	25,266	C+
Erskine College	SC	23,166	VC
Eureka College	IL	24,980	LC
Excelsior College	NY	975	SP
Fairfield Univ	CT	35,505	HC
Fairleigh Dickinson Univ/College at Florham	NJ	30,130	C
Fairleigh Dickinson Univ/Metropolitan Campus	NJ	28,584	C
Fairmont State	WV	8,280	LC
Faulkner Univ	AL	14,500	C
Fayetteville State Univ	NC	5,590	LC
Felician College	NJ	24,300	C
Ferris State Univ	MI	12,512	C
Ferrum College	VA	21,240	LC
Fisher College	MA	23,100	C
Fisk Univ	TN	17,305	LC
Fitchburg State College	MA	9,622	C
Flagler College	FL	11,860	VC+
Florida A&M Univ	FL	7,564	C
Florida Atlantic Univ	FL	8,543	C
Florida Inst of Technology	FL	28,740	VC
Florida International Univ	FL	9,912	VC
Florida Memorial College	FL	6,000	LC
Florida Southern College	FL	23,592	C
Florida State Univ	FL	9,028	HC
Fontbonne Univ	MO	21,508	C
Fordham Univ	NY	35,066	HC
Fort Hays State Univ	KS	7,363	C
Fort Lewis College	CO	8,353	C
Fort Valley State Univ	GA	6,960	C
Framingham State College	MA	9,381	C
Francis Marion Univ	SC	9,364	C
Franciscan Univ	IA	19,300	C
Franciscan Univ of Steubenville	OH	20,300	VC
Franklin and Marshall College	PA	35,930	HC+
Franklin College	IN		C
Franklin Pierce College	NH	28,980	LC
Franklin Univ	OH	6,720	SP
Freed-Hardeman Univ	TN		NC
Fresno Pacific Univ	CA	22,462	C
Friends Univ	KS	15,962	LC
Frostburg State Univ	MD	11,114	C
Furman Univ	SC	28,976	HC+
Gallaudet Univ	DC	16,554	SP
Gannon Univ	PA	23,260	C
Gardner-Webb Univ	NC	19,300	C
Geneva College	PA	21,850	C
George Mason Univ	VA	9,732	VC
George Washington Univ	DC	41,030	MC
Georgetown Univ	DC	38,242	MC
Georgia College and State Univ	GA	9,878	C
Georgia Inst of Technology	GA	10,340	HC+
Georgia Southwestern State Univ	GA	6,013	C
Georgia State Univ	GA	10,658	C
Georgian Court College	NJ	19,040	LC
Gettysburg College	PA	35,646	HC
Glenville State College	WV	7,812	NC
Gonzaga Univ	WA	26,766	HC
Gordon College	MA	25,982	VC+
Goshen College	IN	22,450	VC
Grace Bible College	MI	15,890	C
Grace College	IN	19,825	VC
Graceland Univ	IA	19,550	C
Grambling State Univ	LA	6,538	NC
Grand Canyon Univ	AZ	30,000	LC
Grand Valley State Univ	MI	11,022	VC
Grand View College	IA	19,748	LC
Green Mountain College	VT	24,130	C
Greensboro College	NC	21,750	C
Greenville College	IL	21,342	C
Grove City College	PA	14,228	HC
Guilford College	NC	24,960	VC
Gustavus Adolphus College	MN	27,120	VC+
Gwynedd-Mercy College	PA	24,225	C
Hamline Univ	MN	27,052	VC
Hampton Univ	VA	17,112	C+
Hannibal-LaGrange College	MO	13,940	C
Hanover College	IN	25,200	VC
Harding Univ	AR	14,890	VC
Hardin-Simmons Univ	TX	14,165	C
Harris-Stowe State College	MO	3,200	SP
Hartwick College	NY	34,650	C+
Hastings College	NE	19,928	VC
Hawaii Pacific Univ	HI	19,218	C
Heidelberg College	OH	20,266	NC
Henderson State Univ	AR	7,386	C
Henry Cogswell College	WA	14,400	SP
Heritage College	WA	6,720	NC
Hesser College	NH	17,490	LC
High Point Univ	NC	22,480	C
Hilbert College	NY	19,170	LC
Hillsdale College	MI	22,450	HC
Hofstra Univ	NY	27,112	VC
Hollins Univ	VA	27,965	VC
Holy Family College	PA	13,710	LC
Holy Names College	CA	27,980	NC
Hood College	MD	27,795	VC
Hope College	MI	25,340	VC
Hope International Univ	CA	16,940	NC
Houghton College	NY	23,984	VC
Houston Baptist Univ	TX	16,905	C
Howard Payne Univ	TX	15,176	C
Howard Univ	DC	16,505	C
Humboldt State Univ	CA	9,400	C
Humphreys College	CA	7,000	NC
Huntingdon College	AL	18,400	VC
Huntington College	IN	23,590	C
Huron Univ	SD	10,450	C
Husson College	ME	16,300	LC
Huston-Tillotson College	TX	14,232	NC
Idaho State Univ	ID	8,128	C
Illinois College	IL	19,100	VC
Illinois State Univ	IL	10,944	C+
Illinois Wesleyan Univ	IL	30,380	HC+
Immaculata Univ	PA	25,200	C
Indiana Inst of Technology	IN	21,620	C
Indiana State Univ	IN	10,719	LC
Indiana Univ Bloomington	IN	12,389	VC
Indiana Univ East	IN	4,433	LC
Indiana Univ Kokomo	IN	4,463	LC
Indiana Univ Northwest	IN	4,538	LC
Indiana Univ of Pennsylvania	PA	10,489	C
Indiana Univ South Bend	IN	4,571	LC
Indiana Univ Southeast	IN	4,504	LC
Indiana Univ-Purdue Univ Indianapolis	IN	8,257	LC
Indiana Wesleyan Univ	IN	19,900	C+
Inter American Univ of PR/Aguadilla Campus	PR	3,544	
Inter American Univ of PR/Arecibo Campus	PR	3,300	
Inter American Univ of PR/Barranquitas Regional College	PR	3,300	
Inter American Univ of PR/Bayamon Univ College	PR	3,522	
Inter American Univ of PR/Fajardo Campus	PR	4,000	
Inter American Univ of PR/Metropolitan Campus	PR		
Inter American Univ of PR/Ponce Regional College	PR	3,700	
Inter American Univ of PR/San German	PR	6,716	
International College	FL	8,060	LC
Iona College	NY	27,988	VC
Iowa State Univ	IA	10,768	VC
Iowa Wesleyan College	IA	19,990	C
Ithaca College	NY	31,730	HC
Jackson State Univ	MS	8,382	C
Jacksonville Univ	FL	24,040	C
James Madison Univ	VA	10,794	VC
Jamestown College	ND	12,600	NC
John Brown Univ	AR	15,080	VC
John Carroll Univ	OH	27,658	C+
Johns Hopkins Univ	MD	38,372	MC
Johnson and Wales Univ	RI	22,965	LC
Johnson C. Smith Univ	NC	18,108	C
Johnson State College	VT	11,819	LC
Judson College	AL	14,650	C
Judson College	IL	22,050	LC
Juniata College	PA	29,080	VC
Kansas State Univ	KS	8,728	VC
Kean Univ	NJ	14,479	C
Kendall College	IL	21,350	NC
Kent State Univ	OH	12,932	C
Kentucky Christian College	KY	13,472	C
Kentucky State Univ	KY	9,062	NC
Kentucky Wesleyan College	KY	17,250	C
Kettering Univ	MI	26,478	HC
Keuka College	NY	21,170	C
Keystone College	PA	21,405	LC
King College	TN	22,500	VC
King's College	PA	26,990	C
Knoxville College	TN	6,200	LC
Kutztown Univ of Pennsylvania	PA	10,786	C
La Roche College	PA	22,094	C
La Salle Univ	PA	31,260	VC
La Sierra Univ	CA	19,260	LC
LaGrange College	GA	20,500	C
Lake Erie College	OH	23,550	C
Lake Superior State Univ	MI	9,034	LC
Lakeland College	WI	17,950	C
Lamar Univ	TX	6,816	LC
Lambuth Univ	TN	16,520	C
Lander Univ	SC	10,496	C
Lane College	TN	11,178	C+
Langston Univ	OK	2,308	LC
Lasell College	MA	26,000	C
Lawrence Tech Univ	MI	20,487	C
Le Moyne College	NY	26,400	VC
Lee Univ	TN	13,780	NC
Lees-McRae College	NC	17,106	LC
Lehigh Univ	PA	37,570	HC+
LeMoyne-Owen College	TN	13,070	LC
Lenoir-Rhyne College	NC	19,186	C
LeTourneau Univ	TX	21,080	C
Lewis Univ	IL	22,950	C+
Lewis-Clark State College	ID	6,981	C
Liberty Univ	VA	17,220	C
Limestone College	SC	17,700	C
Lincoln Memorial Univ	TN	16,400	LC
Lincoln Univ	MO	7,158	NC
Lincoln Univ	PA	13,320	C+
Lindenwood Univ	MO	17,050	VC
Lindsey Wilson College	KY	16,392	LC
Linfield College	OR	27,090	VC
Livingstone College	NC	18,101	LC
Lock Haven Univ of Pennsylvania	PA	11,098	LC
LIU/Brooklyn Campus	NY	24,790	C
LIU/C.W. Post Campus	NY	28,282	C
Longwood Univ	VA	11,175	C
Loras College	IA	24,233	C
Louisiana College	LA	13,450	C
Louisiana State Univ and A&M College	LA	9,126	VC
Louisiana State Univ in Shreveport	LA	2,884	NC
Louisiana Tech Univ	LA	7,361	C
Lourdes College	OH	15,300	LC
Loyola College in Maryland	MD	34,560	HC
Loyola Marymount Univ	CA	32,194	VC
Loyola Univ Chicago	IL	31,164	VC
Loyola Univ New Orleans	LA	31,036	VC+
Lubbock Christian Univ	TX	15,832	C
Lycoming College	PA	27,589	C+
Lynchburg College	VA	26,815	C
Lyndon State College	VT	12,646	LC
Lynn Univ	FL	30,750	C
Lyon College	AR	17,995	VC
MacMurray College	IL	20,005	LC
Madonna Univ	MI	11,504	VC
Malone College	OH	20,995	C
Manchester College	IN	23,390	C
Mansfield Univ	PA	11,220	C
Marian College	IN	23,030	C
Marian College of Fond du Lac	WI	19,625	C
Marist College	NY	27,596	VC
Marquette Univ	WI	27,594	VC
Mars Hill College	NC	18,600	LC
Martin Univ	IN	10,200	SP
Mary Baldwin College	VA	24,939	C
Mary Washington College	VA	10,166	HC
Marygrove College	MI	17,550	C
Marymount College of Fordham Univ	NY	27,686	C
Marymount Manhattan College	NY	27,292	C
Marymount Univ	VA	23,668	C
Maryville College	TN	25,960	VC
Maryville Univ of St. Louis	MO	22,090	VC
Marywood Univ	PA	26,050	C
Mass College of Liberal Arts	MA	8,717	LC
Master's College and Seminary	CA	23,250	VC
Mayville State Univ	ND	7,325	NC
McDaniel College	MD	28,440	VC
McKendree College	IL	21,120	VC
McMurry Univ	TX	17,846	LC
McNeese State Univ	LA	5,259	LC
McPherson College	KS	20,265	C
Medaille College	NY	20,060	C
Menlo College	CA	24,000	LC
Mercer Univ	GA	27,516	VC+
Mercy College	NY	19,200	NC
Mercyhurst College	PA	20,694	C
Meredith College	NC	23,065	C
Merrimack College	MA	29,625	C
Mesa State College	CO	8,051	C
Messiah College	PA	25,890	VC+
Methodist College	NC	19,526	C
Metropolitan College of New York	NY	15,771	C
Metropolitan State Univ	MN	3,852	SP
Miami Univ	OH	15,033	HC
Mich State Univ	MI	11,933	VC
Mich Tech Univ	MI	13,235	VC
MidAmerica Nazarene Univ	KS	18,688	C
Middle Tenn State Univ	TN	8,534	C
Midland Lutheran College	NE	18,600	C
Midway College	KY	15,815	C
Midwestern State Univ	TX	8,045	LC
Miles College	AL	7,870	NC

ST = STATE **$IS** = IN-STATE COSTS **SR** = SELECTOR RATING

School	ST	$IS	SR
Millersville Univ of Pennsylvania	PA	11,269	C
Milligan College	TN	19,860	C+
Millikin Univ	IL	25,555	C
Millsaps College	MS	25,182	VC
Milwaukee School of Engineering	WI	28,479	VC+
Minn State Univ, Mankato	MN	8,803	LC
Minn State Univ, Moorehead	MN	7,000	LC
Miss College	MS	14,574	C
Miss State Univ	MS	9,139	C
Miss Univ for Women	MS	5,446	LC
Miss Valley State Univ	MS	6,765	NC
Missouri Baptist Univ	MO	18,010	C
Missouri Southern State Univ	MO	8,316	C
Missouri Valley College	MO	18,500	C
Missouri Western State College	MO	8,522	NC
Mitchell College	CT	26,396	C
Molloy College	NY	15,180	C
Monmouth College	IL	23,600	C
Monmouth Univ	NJ	26,334	C
Montana State Univ-Billings	MT	9,550	C
Montana State Univ-Bozeman	MT	9,515	C
Montclair State Univ	NJ	13,790	C
Montreat College	NC	18,762	C
Moravian College	PA	28,903	VC
Morehouse College	GA	22,728	C
Morgan State Univ	MD	11,470	C
Morningside College	IA	21,610	C
Morris College	SC	10,974	LC
Mount Aloysius College	PA	19,120	LC
Mount Ida College	MA	25,596	LC
Mount Marty College	SD	15,656	LC
Mount Mary College	WI	20,370	C
Mount Mercy College	IA	21,400	C
Mount Olive College	NC	14,410	LC
Mount St. Mary College	NY	21,270	C
Mount St. Mary's College	CA	28,307	VC
Mount St. Mary's College	MD	28,400	C
Mount Union College	OH	21,120	C
Mount Vernon Nazarene Univ	OH	18,925	C
Mountain State Univ	WV	10,212	NC
Muhlenberg College	PA	31,485	HC
Murray State Univ	KY	7,816	VC
Muskingum College	OH	20,680	C
National American Univ	SD	13,680	NC
National Univ	CA	9,690	SP
National-Louis Univ	IL	16,240	LC
Nazareth College of Rochester	NY	24,936	VC
Nebr Wesleyan Univ	NE	21,197	C+
Neumann College	PA	23,890	LC
New England College	NH	28,860	LC
New Jersey City Univ	NJ	11,850	LC
New Mexico Highlands Univ	NM	6,182	LC
New Mexico Inst of Mining and Technology	NM	7,580	NC
New Mexico State Univ	NM	7,932	C
New York Inst of Technology	NY	24,205	VC
New York Univ	NY	39,406	MC
Newberry College	SC	22,871	LC
Newbury College	MA	23,450	C
Newman Univ	KS	18,018	C
Niagara Univ	NY	25,050	C
Nicholls State Univ	LA	6,395	NC
Nichols College	MA	27,562	LC
N Car Agricultural and Technical State Univ	NC	6,659	LC
N Car Central Univ	NC	7,534	LC
N Car State Univ	NC	9,886	VC
N Car Wesleyan College	NC	17,998	C
North Central College	IL	25,656	VC
N Dak State Univ	ND	8,435	C
North Georgia College and State Univ	GA	6,984	C
North Park Univ	IL	24,030	C
Northeastern Illinois Univ	IL	2,898	NC
Northeastern State Univ	OK	4,950	LC
Northeastern Univ	MA	35,650	HC
Northern Arizona Univ	AZ	9,002	C
Northern Illinois Univ	IL	11,472	C
Northern Mich Univ	MI	10,834	C
Northern State Univ	SD	7,117	LC
Northland College	WI	22,170	C+
Northwest Christian College	OR	21,860	C
Northwest College	WA	18,854	C
Northwest Missouri State Univ	MO	9,334	C
Northwest Nazarene Univ	ID	20,360	VC
Northwestern College	MN	22,820	C+
Northwestern College of Iowa	IA	19,640	C+
Northwestern Okla State Univ	OK	5,433	NC
Northwestern State Univ of Louisiana	LA	6,331	NC
Northwood Univ	FL	21,040	C
Northwood Univ	MI	20,265	LC
Northwood Univ	TX	20,135	LC
Norwich Univ	VT	21,064	LC
Notre Dame de Namur Univ	CA	26,932	LC
Nova Southeastern Univ	FL	23,346	C
Nyack College	NY	18,540	C
Oakland City Univ	IN	16,980	NC
Oakland Univ	MI	10,800	C
Oakwood College	AL	14,904	C
Oglala Lakota College	SD	1,950	NC
Oglethorpe Univ	GA	26,000	VC
Ohio Dominican Univ	OH	22,700	C
Ohio Northern Univ	OH	27,765	VC
Ohio State Univ at Lima	OH	4,416	NC
Ohio State Univ at Newark	OH	9,881	NC
Ohio Univ	OH	14,448	C
Ohio Valley College	WV	16,036	C+
Ohio Wesleyan Univ	OH	32,550	VC+
Okla Baptist Univ	OK	15,220	VC
Okla Christian Univ	OK	17,690	NC
Okla City Univ	OK	19,580	VC
Okla Panhandle State Univ	OK	5,370	C
Okla State Univ	OK	9,216	VC
Okla Wesleyan Univ	OK	14,100	LC
Old Dominion Univ	VA	10,441	C
Olivet College	MI	19,984	C+
Olivet Nazarene Univ	IL	20,480	C
Oral Roberts Univ	OK	18,490	C
Oregon State Univ	OR	11,055	C
Ottawa Univ	KS	11,800	LC
Otterbein College	OH	26,085	C
Ouachita Baptist Univ	AR	18,900	VC
Our Lady of Holy Cross College	LA	5,900	C
Our Lady of the Lake Univ of San Antonio	TX	17,336	C
Pacific Lutheran Univ	WA	25,715	VC
Pacific Union College	CA	22,065	C+
Pacific Univ	OR	24,250	C
Paine College	GA	13,022	LC
Palm Beach Atlantic Univ	FL	20,690	C
Park Univ	MO	10,780	C+
Paul Quinn College	TX	8,150	LC
Peirce College	PA	11,800	NC
Penn State Univ at Erie/Behrend College	PA	12,326	C
Penn State Univ/Altoona	PA	12,578	C
Penn State Univ/Univ Park Campus	PA	15,646	HC
Pennsylvania College of Technology	PA	15,126	NC
Pepperdine Univ	CA	32,830	VC
Peru State College	NE	6,342	NC
Pfeiffer Univ	NC	18,980	C
Philadelphia Biblical Univ	PA	18,395	C
Philander Smith College	AR	7,380	NC
Piedmont College	GA	16,900	C
Pikeville College	KY	14,900	NC
Pine Manor College	MA	22,138	LC
Pittsburg State Univ	KS	7,128	NC
Plymouth State Univ	NH	12,298	LC
Point Loma Nazarene Univ	CA	21,380	VC
Point Park Univ	PA	21,840	C
Pontifical Catholic Univ of PR/Ponce	PR	7,298	
Portland State Univ	OR	12,453	C
Prairie View A&M Univ	TX	9,418	NC
Presbyterian College	SC	25,920	VC
Presentation College	SD	14,700	LC
Principia College	IL	25,044	C+
Providence College	RI	30,604	HC
Queens Univ of Charlotte	NC	21,840	C
Quincy Univ	IL	22,330	C
Quinnipiac Univ	CT	30,570	VC
Radford Univ	VA	8,500	C
Ramapo College of New Jersey	NJ	15,203	VC
Regis Univ	CO	25,740	C+
Reinhardt College	GA	20,750	C
Rhode Island College	RI	11,565	C
Rhodes College	TN	26,466	HC+
Richard Stockton College of New Jersey	NJ	12,972	VC
Rider Univ	NJ	30,900	C
Ripon College	WI	24,995	VC
Rivier College	NH	26,217	C
Roanoke College	VA	27,393	C
Robert Morris Univ	PA	20,438	C
Roberts Wesleyan College	NY	23,190	C+
Rochester College	MI	16,718	C
Rochester Inst of Technology	NY	29,217	VC+
Rockford College	IL	28,310	VC
Rockhurst Univ	MO	22,960	C+
Rocky Mountain College	MT	19,015	C
Roger Williams Univ	RI	30,296	C
Roosevelt Univ	IL	22,580	VC
Rosemont College	PA	26,175	C
Rowan Univ	NJ	14,506	VC
Russell Sage College	NY	26,811	C
Rust College	MS	8,200	C+
Rutgers, The State Univ of New Jersey/New Brunswick/Piscataway Campus	NJ	15,800	HC
Rutgers, The State Univ of New Jersey/Newark Campus	NJ	15,624	VC
Sacred Heart Univ	CT	29,178	C
Saginaw Valley State Univ	MI	11,055	C
St. Ambrose Univ	IA	22,800	C
St. Andrews Presbyterian College	NC	20,525	C
St. Anselm College	NH	30,250	C
St. Augustine's College	NC	12,990	LC
St. Cloud State Univ	MN	8,362	C
St. Edward's Univ	TX	20,428	C
St. John's Univ	NY	30,180	C
St. Joseph's, Brooklyn,	NY	10,902	C
St. Joseph's College	IN	24,250	C
St. Joseph's College of Maine	ME	25,600	C
St. Joseph's Univ	PA	33,590	VC
St. Leo Univ	FL	20,600	C
St. Louis Univ	MO	29,780	VC+
St. Mary-of-the-Woods College	IN	23,280	C
St. Mary's College	IN	24,474	VC
St. Mary's College	MI	13,314	LC
St. Mary's College of Calif	CA	32,850	VC
St. Mary's Univ of Minn	MN	21,535	C
St. Mary's Univ of San Antonio	TX	22,444	C
St. Michael's College	VT	30,100	VC
St. Norbert College	WI	25,810	C
St. Paul's College	VA	14,344	NC
St. Peter's College	NJ	22,292	LC
St. Thomas Aquinas College	NY	20,590	LC
St. Thomas Univ	FL	21,400	LC
St. Vincent College	PA	25,530	VC
St. Xavier Univ	IL	23,144	C
Salem College	NC	24,595	VC
Salem International Univ	WV	19,770	C
Salem State College	MA	8,592	C
Salisbury Univ	MD	12,664	VC
Salve Regina Univ	RI	29,210	C
Sam Houston State Univ	TX	7,142	C
Samford Univ	AL	18,648	VC
San Diego State Univ	CA	10,321	C
San Francisco State Univ	CA	12,070	C
San Jose State Univ	CA	8,187	C
Santa Clara Univ	CA	34,701	HC
Schreiner Univ	TX	20,440	C
Seattle Pacific Univ	WA	25,944	VC
Seattle Univ	WA	24,183	VC
Seton Hall Univ	NJ	30,130	VC
Seton Hill Univ	PA	24,930	C
Shaw Univ	NC	14,882	C+
Shawnee State Univ	OH	11,031	NC
Shenandoah Univ	VA	25,190	NC
Shepherd College	WV	8,608	C
Shippensburg Univ of Pennsylvania	PA	10,826	C
Shorter College	GA	17,370	C
Siena Heights Univ	MI	16,140	LC
Sierra Nevada College	NV	26,136	C
Silver Lake College of the Holy Family	WI	18,450	LC
Simpson College	CA	20,500	C
Skidmore College	NY	37,930	HC
Slippery Rock Univ of Pennsylvania	PA	10,343	LC
Sojourner-Douglass College	MD	4,170	LC
Sonoma State Univ	CA	10,421	C
S Car State Univ	SC	6,586	LC
South College	GA	8,720	LC
Southeastern College	FL	11,648	LC
Southeastern Louisiana Univ	LA	6,791	LC
Southeastern Okla State Univ	OK	6,147	C
Southeastern Univ	DC	8,505	LC
Southern Adventist Univ	TN	17,080	C
Southern Arkansas Univ	AR	6,956	C
Southern Conn State Univ	CT	10,310	C
Southern Illinois Univ Carbondale	IL	10,407	C
Southern Illinois Univ Edwardsville	IL	8,724	C
Southern Methodist Univ	TX	34,210	HC
Southern Nazarene Univ	OK	14,634	NC
Southern New Hampshire Univ	NH	26,242	C
Southern Oregon Univ	OR	10,362	C
Southern Polytechnic State Univ	GA	7,620	VC
Southern Univ and A&M College	LA	7,372	LC
Southern Univ at New Orleans	LA	995	NC
Southern Utah Univ	UT	8,194	C
Southern Vermont College	VT	18,226	LC
Southern Wesleyan Univ	SC	19,940	C
Southwest Baptist Univ	MO	15,371	C
Southwest Minn State Univ	MN	9,106	VC
Southwest Missouri State Univ	MO	8,918	C
Southwestern Adventist Univ	TX	14,798	C
Southwestern College	KS	19,560	C
Southwestern Okla State Univ	OK	4,801	C
Southwestern Univ	TX	25,410	HC
Spalding Univ	KY	17,985	C
Spring Arbor Univ	MI	20,206	C
Spring Hill College	AL	25,868	VC
Springfield College	MA	24,520	C
St. Joseph's, Suffolk	NY	11,297	C
SUNY at Oswego	NY	12,650	C
SUNY at Potsdam	NY	12,160	C
SUNY/College at Brockport	NY	12,111	C
SUNY/College at Buffalo	NY	8,025	C
SUNY/College at Fredonia	NY	11,562	VC
SUNY/College at Geneseo	NY	11,330	HC
SUNY/College at Old Westbury	NY	12,784	C
SUNY/College at Plattsburgh	NY	11,700	C
SUNY/Empire State College	NY	4,505	SP
SUNY/Maritime College	NY	10,025	LC
SUNY/Univ at Albany	NY	12,951	HC
SUNY/Univ at Binghamton	NY	12,787	HC
SUNY/Univ at Buffalo	NY	12,563	VC
SUNY/Univ at New Paltz	NY	11,565	VC
SUNY/Univ at Stony Brook	NY	12,763	HC
Stephen F. Austin State Univ	TX	7,552	C
Stephens College	MO	24,260	C+
Sterling College	KS	18,763	C
Stetson Univ	FL	29,495	VC
Stillman College	AL	11,370	LC
Stonehill College	MA	30,752	HC
Strayer Univ	DC	8,789	SP
Sul Ross State Univ	TX	6,582	LC
Susquehanna Univ	PA	29,990	VC
Sweet Briar College	VA	27,940	C
Syracuse Univ	NY	34,720	HC
Tabor College	KS	19,500	NC
Talladega College	AL	10,110	LC
Tarleton State Univ	TX	7,576	C
Teikyo Post Univ	CT	24,875	C
Temple Univ	PA	15,912	C
Tenn State Univ	TN	9,048	LC
Tenn Tech Univ	TN	8,670	VC
Tenn Wesleyan College	TN	16,540	C
Texas A&M Univ at Commerce	TX	8,994	C
Texas A&M Univ at Corpus Christi	TX	10,269	C
Texas A&M Univ at Kingsville	TX	6,740	LC
Texas Christian Univ	TX	23,410	VC
Texas Lutheran Univ	TX	20,370	C
Texas Southern Univ	TX	8,920	NC
Texas State Univ	TX	9,320	VC
Texas Tech Univ	TX	10,768	VC
Texas Wesleyan Univ	TX	16,245	C
Texas Woman's Univ	TX	7,804	LC
Thiel College	PA	20,970	C
Thomas College	ME	19,960	LC
Thomas More College	KY	21,350	C
Thomas Univ	GA	11,490	NC
Tiffin Univ	OH	19,490	LC
Toccoa Falls College	GA	15,600	C
Touro College	NY	15,250	VC
Towson Univ	MD	12,694	VC
Transylvania Univ	KY	23,780	VC+
Trevecca Nazarene Univ	TN	17,548	C
Trinity Christian College	IL	21,640	VC
Trinity College	DC	24,150	LC
Trinity International Univ	IL	22,980	C+
Trinity Univ	TX	26,466	HC+
Tri-State Univ-Main Campus	IN	23,600	C
Troy State Univ	AL	7,696	C
Troy State Univ Dothan	AL	3,842	C
Troy State Univ Montgomery	AL	3,600	NC
Truman State Univ	MO	9,728	HC+
Tulane Univ	LA	37,451	HC+
Turabo Univ	PR	4,110	
Tuskegee Univ	AL	17,250	LC
Union College	KY	15,920	C
Union College	NE	17,130	C
Union Inst and Univ	OH	7,848	SP
Union Univ	TN	18,800	VC
Universidad Adventista de las Antillas	PR	5,460	
Universidad Metropolitana	PR	3,324	
Universidad Politecnica de PR	PR	5,370	
Univ of Akron	OH	13,134	NC
Univ of Alabama at Birmingham	AL	12,901	C
Univ of Alabama in Huntsville	AL	9,126	VC
Univ of Alaska Anchorage	AK	9,100	NC
Univ of Alaska Fairbanks	AK	9,295	C
Univ of Alaska Southeast	AK	7,900	LC
Univ of Arizona	AZ	10,413	VC
Univ of Arkansas	AR	9,855	VC
Univ of Arkansas at Little Rock	AR	5,637	NC
Univ of Arkansas at Monticello	AR	5,940	NC
Univ of Arkansas at Pine Bluff	AR	7,925	C
Univ of Bridgeport	CT	25,924	LC
Univ of Calif at Berkeley	CA	15,563	MC
Univ of Calif at Riverside	CA	15,300	C

ST = STATE **$IS** = IN-STATE COSTS **SR** = SELECTOR RATING

School	ST	$IS	SR
Univ of Central Arkansas	AR	6,388	C
Univ of Central Florida	FL	10,038	VC
Univ of Central Okla	OK	9,434	C
Univ of Charleston	WV	23,620	C
Univ of Cincinnati	OH	14,736	C
Univ of Colo at Boulder	CO	10,774	VC
Univ of Colo at Colo Springs	CO	10,667	C
Univ of Colo at Denver	CO	3,302	C
Univ of Conn	CT	14,608	VC
Univ of Dallas	TX	25,898	VC+
Univ of Delaware	DE	12,616	HC
Univ of Denver	CO	32,148	VC
Univ of Detroit Mercy	MI	25,582	C
Univ of Dubuque	IA	20,950	C
Univ of Evansville	IN	24,190	VC
Univ of Findlay	OH	23,962	NC
Univ of Florida	FL	8,580	MC
Univ of Georgia	GA	8,656	VC
Univ of Great Falls	MT	15,360	C
Univ of Hartford	CT	31,080	C
Univ of Hawaii at Hilo	HI	6,497	C
Univ of Hawaii at Manoa	HI	9,565	VC
Univ of Houston	TX	9,818	C
Univ of Houston-Downtown	TX	2,594	NC
Univ of Illinois at Chicago	IL	13,418	C
Univ of Illinois at Urbana-Champaign	IL	11,316	HC+
Univ of Indianapolis	IN	22,560	VC
Univ of Iowa	IA	10,923	VC
Univ of Judaism College of A&S	CA	24,230	C
Univ of Kansas	KS	8,923	VC
Univ of La Verne	CA	28,600	C
Univ of Louisiana at Lafayette	LA	5,826	C
Univ of Louisiana at Monroe	LA	5,207	NC
Univ of Louisville	KY	8,762	VC
Univ of Maine	ME	12,080	C+
Univ of Maine at Augusta	ME	4,065	C
Univ of Maine at Fort Kent	ME	9,770	LC
Univ of Maine at Machias	ME	9,271	LC
Univ of Maine at Presque Isle	ME	9,155	LC
Univ of Mary	ND	12,900	C+
Univ of Mary Hardin-Baylor	TX	17,268	C
Univ of Maryland/College Park	MD	14,227	HC
Univ of Maryland/Eastern Shore	MD	9,964	C
Univ of Maryland/Univ College	MD	5,910	SP
Univ of Mass Amherst	MA	13,980	C+
Univ of Mass Dartmouth	MA	12,835	C
Univ of Mass Lowell	MA	11,937	VC
Univ of Memphis	TN	8,560	C
Univ of Miami	FL	34,608	HC
Univ of Mich/Ann Arbor	MI	13,864	HC+
Univ of Mich/Dearborn	MI	6,843	VC
Univ of Mich/Flint	MI	5,548	C
Univ of Minn/Crookston	MN	9,626	NC
Univ of Minn/Duluth	MN	12,470	C
Univ of Minn/Twin Cities	MN	13,160	VC
Univ of Miss	MS	7,666	C
Univ of Missouri/Columbia	MO	13,782	VC
Univ of Missouri/Kansas City	MO	13,416	VC
Univ of Missouri/Rolla	MO	12,292	HC
Univ of Missouri/St. Louis	MO	11,656	VC
Univ of Mobile	AL	13,620	C
Univ of Montana	MT	9,395	C
Univ of Montevallo	AL	8,478	C
Univ of Nebr at Kearney	NE	8,286	NC
Univ of Nebr at Lincoln	NE	9,975	C+
Univ of Nebr at Omaha	NE	8,080	C
Univ of New England	ME	27,200	LC
Univ of New Hampshire	NH	14,828	VC
Univ of New Haven	CT	28,650	C
Univ of New Mexico	NM	9,223	C
Univ of New Orleans	LA	7,356	C
Univ of N Car at Asheville	NC	8,079	VC
Univ of N Car at Chapel Hill	NC	10,117	MC
Univ of N Car at Charlotte	NC	8,185	C
Univ of N Car at Greensboro	NC	8,248	C
Univ of N Car at Pembroke	NC	6,929	LC
Univ of N Car at Wilmington	NC	8,940	VC
Univ of North Florida	FL	8,769	VC
Univ of North Texas	TX	7,629	C
Univ of Northern Colo	CO	8,987	C
Univ of Okla	OK	9,226	VC
Univ of Oregon	OR	11,479	VC
Univ of Pennsylvania	PA	37,960	MC
Univ of Pittsburgh at Bradford	PA	15,294	C
Univ of Pittsburgh at Johnstown	PA	15,216	LC
Univ of Pittsburgh at Pittsburgh	PA	16,074	HC
Univ of PR at Humacao	PR	1,245	
Univ of PR/Arecibo	PR	1,095	
Univ of PR/Bayamon Univ College Campus	PR	1,600	
Univ of PR/Cayey Univ College	PR	1,245	
Univ of PR/Mayaguez	PR		
Univ of PR/Rio Piedras	PR	5,730	
Univ of Puget Sound	WA	31,760	HC
Univ of Redlands	CA	32,576	VC
Univ of Rhode Island	RI	13,720	VC
Univ of Richmond	VA	30,100	MC
Univ of Rio Grande	OH	8,728	NC
Univ of St. Francis	IL	22,850	C
Univ of St. Francis	IN	20,964	C
Univ of St. Mary	KS	18,868	C
Univ of St. Thomas	MN	26,918	VC
Univ of St. Thomas	TX	21,952	VC
Univ of San Diego	CA	33,156	HC
Univ of San Francisco	CA	34,700	VC
Univ of Science and Arts of Okla	OK	5,982	C
Univ of Scranton	PA	30,836	VC
Univ of Sioux Falls	SD	16,390	C
Univ of South Alabama	AL	7,760	LC
Univ of S Car at Aiken	SC	7,828	LC
Univ of S Car at Columbia	SC	10,048	VC
Univ of S Car at Spartanburg	SC	9,936	C+
Univ of South Florida	FL	9,454	C
Univ of Southern Calif	CA	37,459	MC
Univ of Southern Colo	CO	7,821	LC
Univ of Southern Indiana	IN	9,025	LC
Univ of Southern Maine	ME	11,212	C
Univ of Southern Miss	MS	8,324	LC
Univ of Tampa	FL	23,982	VC
Univ of Tenn at Chattanooga	TN	7,783	C
Univ of Tenn at Knoxville	TN	8,214	C
Univ of Tenn at Martin	TN	7,748	C
Univ of Texas at Arlington	TX	7,192	LC
Univ of Texas at Austin	TX	10,630	HC
Univ of Texas at Dallas	TX	10,234	HC
Univ of Texas at San Antonio	TX	9,088	NC
Univ of the District of Columbia	DC	2,070	LC
Univ of the Incarnate Word	TX	21,772	LC
Univ of the Ozarks	AR	16,574	C
Univ of the Pacific	CA	31,090	VC
Univ of the Sacred Heart	PR	5,590	
Univ of Toledo	OH	12,479	NC
Univ of Utah	UT	9,205	C
Univ of Vermont	VT	16,316	VC
Univ of Virginia's College at Wise	VA	10,116	C
Univ of Washington	WA	10,361	VC
Univ of West Alabama	AL	6,048	C
Univ of West Florida	FL	8,470	C
Univ of Wisc/Eau Claire	WI	8,463	VC
Univ of Wisc/Green Bay	WI	8,154	C
Univ of Wisc/La Crosse	WI	8,991	VC
Univ of Wisc/Madison	WI	8,262	VC
Univ of Wisc/Milwaukee	WI	9,427	LC
Univ of Wisc/Oshkosh	WI	6,130	LC
Univ of Wisc/Parkside	WI	6,160	LC
Univ of Wisc/Platteville	WI	8,450	C
Univ of Wisc/River Falls	WI	8,358	LC
Univ of Wisc/Stevens Point	WI	8,116	VC
Univ of Wisc/Stout	WI	9,718	C
Univ of Wisc/Superior	WI	7,051	C+
Univ of Wisc/Whitewater	WI	8,626	C
Univ of Wyoming	WY	8,636	C
Upper Iowa Univ	IA	20,076	C
Urbana Univ	OH	19,115	C
Ursinus College	PA	34,400	VC
Ursuline College	OH	22,728	LC
Utah State Univ	UT	7,371	C
Utica College	NY	28,340	C
Valdosta State Univ	GA	7,798	C
Valley City State Univ	ND	7,281	LC
Valparaiso Univ	IN	26,118	VC+
Vanguard Univ of Southern Calif	CA	22,208	C
Villa Julie College	MD	18,393	C
Villanova Univ	PA	35,050	HC
Virginia Commonwealth Univ	VA	9,030	C
Virginia Intermont College	VA	19,800	C
Virginia State Univ	VA	10,358	C
Virginia Union Univ	VA	15,358	LC
Virginia Wesleyan College	VA	25,350	C
Viterbo Univ	WI	20,430	C
Voorhees College	SC	11,678	LC
Wagner College	NY	29,900	VC
Wake Forest Univ	NC	34,090	MC
Walla Walla College	WA	21,600	NC
Walsh Univ	OH	20,890	C
Warner Pacific College	OR	21,900	C
Warner Southern College	FL	16,738	LC
Wartburg College	IA	21,165	VC
Washburn Univ of Topeka	KS	8,984	NC
Washington and Jefferson College	PA	29,570	VC
Washington and Lee Univ	VA	29,663	MC
Washington College	MD	30,540	VC
Washington State Univ	WA	11,334	C
Washington Univ in St. Louis	MO	38,293	MC
Wayland Baptist Univ	TX	11,919	NC
Wayne State College	NE	7,352	NC
Webber International Univ	FL	16,510	C
Weber State Univ	UT	7,945	NC
Webster Univ	MO	21,848	VC
Wells College	NY	21,122	VC
Wesley College	DE	19,905	C
Wesleyan College	GA	17,870	VC
West Chester Univ of Pennsylvania	PA	11,164	C
West Liberty State College	WV	7,868	LC
West Texas A&M Univ	TX	7,533	C
West Virginia State College	WV	6,264	NC
West Virginia Univ	WV	9,370	C
West Virginia Univ Inst of Technology	WV	7,518	NC
West Virginia Wesleyan College	WV	22,920	C
Western Baptist College	OR	21,808	C
Western Conn State Univ	CT	11,625	C
Western Illinois Univ	IL	10,363	C
Western Kentucky Univ	KY	6,834	C
Western Mich Univ	MI	12,031	C
Western New England College	MA	28,924	C
Western New Mexico Univ	NM	5,950	LC
Western Oregon Univ	OR	10,281	C
Western State College of Colo	CO	9,014	C
Western Washington Univ	WA	10,119	VC
Westfield State College	MA	10,147	C
Westminster College	MO	18,150	C+
Westminster College	PA	22,960	C
Westminster College	UT	17,226	C
Whittier College	CA	29,108	C
Whitworth College	WA	26,428	VC+
Wichita State Univ	KS	8,092	C
Widener Univ	PA	27,020	C
Wilberforce Univ	OH	14,937	LC
Wiley College	TX	8,100	LC
Wilkes Univ	PA	28,060	C
William Carey College	MS	10,150	LC
William Jewell College	MO	21,320	VC
William Paterson Univ of New Jersey	NJ	14,450	C
William Penn Univ	IA	17,575	LC
William Tyndale College	MI	12,170	NC
William Woods Univ	MO	20,120	C
Williams Baptist College	AR	11,950	C
Wilmington College	DE	5,594	NC
Wilmington College	OH	24,172	LC
Wingate Univ	NC	21,200	C
Winona State Univ	MN		C
Winston-Salem State Univ	NC	8,926	LC
Winthrop Univ	SC	11,302	C
Wittenberg Univ	OH	31,316	VC
Woodbury Univ	CA	25,344	LC
Worcester State College	MA	10,005	C
Xavier Univ	OH	26,850	VC+
Xavier Univ of Louisiana	LA	17,600	C
Yeshiva Univ	NY	21,400	C
York College	NE	14,975	C
York College of Pennsylvania	PA	14,500	VC
Youngstown State Univ	OH	11,148	NC

BUSINESS COMMUNICATIONS

School	ST	$IS	SR
Chestnut Hill College	PA	26,450	LC
Univ of Indianapolis	IN	22,560	VC
Western Mich Univ	MI	12,031	C

BUSINESS DATA PROCESSING

School	ST	$IS	SR
Eastern Mich Univ	MI	11,478	C
Faulkner Univ	AL	14,500	C

BUSINESS ECONOMICS

School	ST	$IS	SR
Adams State College	CO	7,468	C
Alabama State Univ	AL	6,404	C
Alfred Univ	NY	28,290	C
American International College	MA	24,690	LC
Andrews Univ	MI	19,550	C
Aquinas College	MI	21,894	C
Arkansas State Univ	AR	8,450	C
Ashland Univ	OH	24,464	C
Auburn Univ	AL	10,396	VC
Auburn Univ Montgomery	AL	9,020	NC
Aurora Univ	IL	20,631	C
Baker Univ	KS	19,860	VC
Ball State Univ	IN	8,660	C
Baylor Univ	TX	23,864	VC
Benedictine Univ	IL	23,840	C
Bentley College	MA	33,904	VC
Bethany College	KS	18,675	LC
Bethany College	WV	19,845	VC
Bloomsburg Univ of Pennsylvania	PA	10,844	C
Boston College	MA	33,284	MC
Bowling Green State Univ	OH	13,036	C
Brescia Univ	KY	14,225	C
Buena Vista Univ	IA	25,406	C
Cal State, Fullerton	CA	6,648	C
Cal State, San Bernardino	CA	15,238	LC
Campbell Univ	NC	18,268	VC
Carnegie Mellon Univ	PA	32,682	MC
Carson-Newman College	TN	16,760	C
Centenary College of Louisiana	LA	23,100	VC+
Central Washington Univ	WA	9,768	C
Christian Brothers Univ	TN	22,290	VC
Christopher Newport Univ	VA	8,862	VC
Claremont McKenna College	CA	36,880	MC
Clarion Univ of Pennsylvania	PA	11,272	LC
Cleveland State Univ	OH	12,308	LC
College of the Ozarks	MO	3,500	VC+
College of Wooster	OH	31,300	HC
DePaul Univ	IL	27,580	VC
Dominican College	NY	24,810	LC
Eastern Mich Univ	MI	11,478	C
Eastern New Mexico Univ	NM	6,762	LC
Elmira College	NY	33,820	VC
Emory Univ	GA	36,872	MC
Eureka College	IL	24,980	LC
Fairmont State	WV	8,280	LC
Fayetteville State Univ	NC	5,590	LC
Florida A&M Univ	FL	7,564	C
Florida Southern College	FL	23,592	C
Fordham Univ	NY	35,066	HC
Francis Marion Univ	SC	9,364	C
Franklin Pierce College	NH	28,980	LC
George Fox Univ	OR	26,110	VC
George Washington Univ	DC	41,030	MC
Georgetown College	KY	22,000	VC
Georgia State Univ	GA	10,658	C
Gonzaga Univ	WA	26,766	HC
Grambling State Univ	LA	6,538	NC
Grand Valley State Univ	MI	11,022	VC
Gustavus Adolphus College	MN	27,120	VC+
Hampden-Sydney College	VA	28,407	VC
Harding Univ	AR	14,890	VC
Hawaii Pacific Univ	HI	19,218	C
Heidelberg College	OH	20,266	NC
Hendrix College	AR	20,970	VC+
Houston Baptist Univ	TX	16,905	C
Humboldt State Univ	CA	9,400	C
Indiana Univ Bloomington	IN	12,389	VC
Indiana Univ Kokomo	IN	4,463	LC
Indiana Univ Southeast	IN	4,504	LC
Indiana Univ-Purdue Univ Fort Wayne	IN	5,108	LC
Indiana Univ-Purdue Univ Indianapolis	IN	8,257	LC
Inter American Univ of PR/ Bayamon Univ College	PR	3,522	
Ithaca College	NY	31,730	HC
James Madison Univ	VA	10,794	VC
Johnson C. Smith Univ	NC	18,108	C
Kalamazoo College	MI	26,955	HC+
Kansas Wesleyan Univ	KS	18,900	VC
Kennesaw State Univ	GA	2,724	C
Kent State Univ	OH	12,932	C
Kentucky Wesleyan College	KY	17,250	C
King College	TN	22,500	VC
Kutztown Univ of Pennsylvania	PA	10,786	C
Lafayette College	PA	35,746	MC
Lake Forest College	IL	30,270	VC
Lakeland College	WI	17,950	C
Lamar Univ	TX	6,816	LC
Lehigh Univ	PA	37,570	HC+
Limestone College	SC	17,700	C
Louisiana State Univ and A&M College	LA	9,126	VC
Louisiana State Univ in Shreveport	LA	2,884	NC
Louisiana Tech Univ	LA	7,361	C
Loyola Univ Chicago	IL	31,164	VC
Manhattan College	NY	27,400	VC
Mansfield Univ	PA	11,220	C
Marquette Univ	WI	27,594	VC
Marshall Univ	WV	9,116	C
Mary Baldwin College	VA	24,939	C
Marymount Univ	VA	23,668	C
McMurry Univ	TX	17,846	LC
Merrimack College	MA	29,625	C
Messiah College	PA	25,890	VC+
Miami Univ	OH	15,033	HC
Mich Tech Univ	MI	13,235	VC
Midland Lutheran College	NE	18,600	C
Midwestern State Univ	TX	8,045	LC
Mills College	CA	33,371	VC
Missouri Southern State Univ	MO	8,316	C
Monmouth College	IL	23,600	C
Monmouth Univ	NJ	26,334	C
Montclair State Univ	NJ	13,790	C
Moravian College	PA	28,903	VC
Morehead State Univ	KY	7,464	C
Murray State Univ	KY	7,816	VC
New Mexico State Univ	NM	7,932	C
New York Univ	NY	39,406	MC
Niagara Univ	NY	25,050	C
N Car State Univ	NC	9,886	VC
North Georgia College and State Univ	GA	6,984	C
Northern Arizona Univ	AZ	9,002	C
Northern State Univ	SD	7,117	LC
Northland College	WI	22,170	C+

School	ST	$IS	SR
Northwest Missouri State Univ	MO	9,334	C
Northwestern College of Iowa	IA	19,640	C+
Northwood Univ	MI	20,265	LC
Norwich Univ	VT	21,064	LC
Notre Dame College	OH	20,425	C
Notre Dame de Namur Univ	CA	26,932	LC
Ohio Northern Univ	OH	27,765	VC
Ohio State Univ	OH	13,080	VC+
Ohio Univ	OH	14,448	C
Ohio Wesleyan Univ	OH	32,550	VC+
Okla State Univ	OK	9,216	VC
Ouachita Baptist Univ	AR	18,900	VC
Pace Univ	NY	28,652	VC
Park Univ	MO	10,780	C+
Penn State Univ at Erie/Behrend College	PA	12,326	C
Pontifical Catholic Univ of PR/Ponce	PR	7,298	
Purdue Univ/Calumet	IN	6,630	NC
Quinnipiac Univ	CT	30,570	VC
Randolph-Macon College	VA	27,190	C
Regis Univ	CO	25,740	C+
Rhode Island College	RI	11,565	C
Rider Univ	NJ	30,900	C
Rockhurst Univ	MO	22,960	C+
Rocky Mountain College	MT	19,015	C
Saginaw Valley State Univ	MI	11,055	C
St. Ambrose Univ	IA	22,800	C
St. Cloud State Univ	MN	8,362	C
St. John's Univ	NY	30,180	C
St. Joseph College	CT	29,685	C
Santa Clara Univ	CA	34,701	HC
Seattle Univ	WA	24,183	VC
Seton Hall Univ	NJ	30,130	VC
Seton Hill Univ	PA	24,930	C
Siena College	NY	25,310	VC
Skidmore College	NY	37,930	HC
S Car State Univ	SC	6,586	LC
Southeast Missouri State Univ	MO	9,704	C
Southern Conn State Univ	CT	10,310	C
Southern Illinois Univ Carbondale	IL	10,407	C
Southern Illinois Univ Edwardsville	IL	8,724	C
Southern Nazarene Univ	OK	14,634	NC
Southern Univ and A&M College	LA	7,372	LC
SUNY at Potsdam	NY	12,160	C
SUNY/College at Fredonia	NY	11,562	VC
SUNY/College at Oneonta	NY	11,870	VC
SUNY/College at Plattsburgh	NY	11,700	C
State Univ of West Georgia	GA	7,622	C
Stetson Univ	FL	29,495	VC
Stonehill College	MA	30,752	HC
Temple Univ	PA	15,912	C
Tenn State Univ	TN	9,048	LC
Texas A&M Univ at Kingsville	TX	6,740	LC
Texas State Univ	TX	9,320	VC
Texas Tech Univ	TX	10,768	VC
Texas Wesleyan Univ	TX	16,245	C
Thomas College	ME	19,960	LC
Trinity College	DC	24,150	LC
Troy State Univ Dothan	AL	3,842	C
Tuskegee Univ	AL	17,250	LC
Union College	NY	36,005	HC
Univ of Akron	OH	13,134	NC
Univ of Alaska Fairbanks	AK	9,295	C
Univ of Arizona	AZ	10,413	VC
Univ of Arkansas	AR	9,855	VC
Univ of Calif at Los Angeles	CA	15,330	MC
Univ of Calif at Riverside	CA	15,300	C
Univ of Calif at Santa Barbara	CA	11,732	VC
Univ of Calif at Santa Cruz	CA	16,505	VC
Univ of Central Arkansas	AR	6,388	C
Univ of Central Okla	OK	9,434	C
Univ of Dayton	OH	24,850	VC
Univ of Denver	CO	32,148	VC
Univ of Findlay	OH	23,962	NC
Univ of Hawaii at Manoa	HI	9,565	VC
Univ of Indianapolis	IN	22,560	VC
Univ of Iowa	IA	10,923	VC
Univ of Kentucky	KY	7,765	C
Univ of La Verne	CA	28,600	C
Univ of Louisville	KY	8,762	VC
Univ of Maine	ME	12,080	C+
Univ of Maine at Farmington	ME	10,108	C
Univ of Mary Hardin-Baylor	TX	17,268	C
Univ of Memphis	TN	8,560	C
Univ of Miss	MS	7,666	C
Univ of Missouri/Columbia	MO	13,782	VC
Univ of Nebr at Kearney	NE	8,286	NC
Univ of Nebr at Lincoln	NE	9,975	C+
Univ of Nevada/Reno	NV	9,792	C
Univ of New Haven	CT	28,650	C
Univ of New Orleans	LA	7,356	C
Univ of North Alabama	AL	7,972	NC
Univ of N Car at Charlotte	NC	8,185	C
Univ of N Car at Greensboro	NC	8,248	C
Univ of N Car at Pembroke	NC	6,929	LC
Univ of N Car at Wilmington	NC	8,940	VC
Univ of N Dak	ND	8,390	C
Univ of North Florida	FL	8,769	VC
Univ of North Texas	TX	7,629	C
Univ of Okla	OK	9,226	VC
Univ of Pittsburgh at Johnstown	PA	15,216	LC
Univ of PR/Mayaguez	PR		
Univ of PR/Rio Piedras	PR	5,730	
Univ of Richmond	VA	30,100	MC
Univ of Rio Grande	OH	8,728	NC
Univ of San Diego	CA	33,156	HC
Univ of Scranton	PA	30,836	VC
Univ of Sioux Falls	SD	16,390	C
Univ of South Alabama	AL	7,760	LC
Univ of S Car at Columbia	SC	10,048	VC
Univ of South Florida	FL	9,454	C
Univ of Southern Indiana	IN	9,025	LC
Univ of Southern Miss	MS	8,324	LC
Univ of Tampa	FL	23,982	VC
Univ of Tenn at Knoxville	TN	8,214	C
Univ of Tenn at Martin	TN	7,748	C
Univ of Texas at Arlington	TX	7,192	LC
Univ of Texas at El Paso	TX	5,799	NC
Univ of Texas at San Antonio	TX	9,088	NC
Univ of Virginia	VA	11,740	MC
Univ of Washington	WA	10,361	VC
Univ of West Florida	FL	8,470	C
Univ of Wisc/Eau Claire	WI	8,463	VC
Univ of Wisc/Platteville	WI	8,450	C
Univ of Wisc/Whitewater	WI	8,626	C
Univ of Wyoming	WY	8,636	C
Ursinus College	PA	34,400	VC
Utah State Univ	UT	7,371	C
Utica College	NY	28,340	C
Valdosta State Univ	GA	7,798	C
Villanova Univ	PA	35,050	HC
Virginia Commonwealth Univ	VA	9,030	C
Virginia Military Inst	VA	9,968	C+
Virginia Polytechnic Inst and State Univ	VA	9,179	C
Warren Wilson College	NC	21,794	VC
Washburn Univ of Topeka	KS	8,984	NC
Washington State Univ	WA	11,334	C
Washington Univ in St. Louis	MO	38,293	MC
Wayne State Univ	MI	11,774	C
Weber State Univ	UT	7,945	NC
West Chester Univ of Pennsylvania	PA	11,164	C
West Liberty State College	WV	7,868	LC
West Texas A&M Univ	TX	7,533	C
Western Kentucky Univ	KY	6,834	C
Western Mich Univ	MI	12,031	C
Westmont College	CA	33,062	VC+
Wheaton College	IL	21,934	HC
Widener Univ	PA	27,020	C
Wilberforce Univ	OH	14,937	LC
William Jewell College	MO	21,320	VC
Wilson College	PA	23,912	C
Wingate Univ	NC	21,200	C
Winona State Univ	MN		C
Wisc Lutheran College	WI	21,430	VC
Wofford College	SC	26,710	HC
Wright State Univ	OH	11,490	LC
Xavier Univ	OH	26,850	VC+
Xavier Univ of Louisiana	LA	17,600	C
Youngstown State Univ	OH	11,148	NC

BUSINESS EDUCATION

School	ST	$IS	SR
Abilene Christian Univ	TX	18,370	VC
Adams State College	CO	7,468	C
Alabama State Univ	AL	6,404	C
Alfred Univ	NY	28,290	C
Appalachian State Univ	NC	7,637	VC
Arkansas State Univ	AR	8,450	C
Arkansas Tech Univ	AR	7,299	C
Armstrong Atlantic State Univ	GA	7,102	C
Auburn Univ	AL	10,396	VC
Avila Univ	MO	20,300	C
Baker Univ	KS	19,860	VC
Baldwin-Wallace College	OH	24,678	C
Ball State Univ	IN	8,660	C
Baylor Univ	TX	23,864	VC
Bethany College	KS	18,675	LC
Bethel College	IN	19,670	C
Bethel College	MN	25,180	VC
Bethune-Cookman College	FL	16,480	LC
Black Hills State Univ	SD	7,743	LC
Bloomsburg Univ of Pennsylvania	PA	10,844	C
Blue Mountain College	MS	10,226	C
Bowling Green State Univ	OH	13,036	C
Brigham Young Univ	UT	8,504	HC
Brigham Young Univ/Hawaii	HI	7,240	VC+
Buena Vista Univ	IA	25,406	C
Cal State, Northridge	CA	7,757	LC
Cal State, Sacramento	CA	9,543	C
Canisius College	NY	28,163	C+
Caribbean Univ	PR	3,000	
Central Mich Univ	MI	11,142	C
Central Missouri State Univ	MO	9,776	C
Central Washington Univ	WA	9,768	C
Chicago State Univ	IL	10,882	C+
CUNY/Herbert H. Lehman College	NY	3,320	LC
Clark Atlanta Univ	GA	19,300	C+
College of Santa Fe	NM	25,293	C+
College of the Ozarks	MO	3,500	VC+
Concord College	WV	8,136	C
Concordia College	NY	19,200	VC
Concordia College: Moorhead	MN	22,460	VC+
Concordia Univ Nebr	NE	20,302	C+
Cumberland College	KY	16,384	C
Daemen College	NY	22,120	C
Dakota State Univ	SD	7,466	C
Dana College	NE	20,280	C
Delaware State Univ	DE	8,104	LC
Delta State Univ	MS	6,618	C
Dickinson State Univ	ND	6,338	NC
Doane College	NE	20,000	C
Dordt College	IA	20,170	VC
D'Youville College	NY	21,080	C
East Carolina Univ	NC	8,671	C
East Central Univ	OK	4,968	C
Eastern Kentucky Univ	KY	7,708	C
Eastern Mich Univ	MI	11,478	C
Eastern New Mexico Univ	NM	6,762	LC
Elizabeth City State Univ	NC	5,550	LC
Emporia State Univ	KS	6,998	C
Evangel Univ	MO	15,435	C
Fairmont State	WV	8,280	LC
Fayetteville State Univ	NC	5,590	LC
Ferris State Univ	MI	12,512	C
Florida A&M Univ	FL	7,564	C
Franciscan Univ	IA	19,300	C
Friends Univ	KS	15,962	LC
Frostburg State Univ	MD	11,114	C
Georgia Southern Univ	GA	8,540	C
Georgia Southwestern State Univ	GA	6,013	C
Glenville State College	WV	7,812	NC
Goshen College	IN	22,450	VC
Grace College	IN	19,825	VC
Grambling State Univ	LA	6,538	NC
Grand Canyon Univ	AZ	30,000	LC
Gustavus Adolphus College	MN	27,120	VC+
Gwynedd-Mercy College	PA	24,225	C
Hardin-Simmons Univ	TX	14,165	C
Hastings College	NE	19,928	VC
Henderson State Univ	AR	7,386	C
Hofstra Univ	NY	27,112	VC
Hope College	MI	25,340	VC
Humboldt State Univ	CA	9,400	C
Illinois State Univ	IL	10,944	C+
Indiana State Univ	IN	10,719	LC
Indiana Univ of Pennsylvania	PA	10,489	C
Jackson State Univ	MS	8,382	C
James Madison Univ	VA	10,794	VC
John Brown Univ	AR	15,080	VC
Kent State Univ	OH	12,932	C
Knoxville College	TN	6,200	LC
Lakeland College	WI	17,950	C
Langston Univ	OK	2,308	LC
Lenoir-Rhyne College	NC	19,186	C
LeTourneau Univ	TX	21,080	C
Lincoln Memorial Univ	TN	16,400	LC
Lincoln Univ	MO	7,158	NC
Lindenwood Univ	MO	17,050	VC
LIU/Brooklyn Campus	NY	24,790	C
Louisiana College	LA	13,450	C
Lubbock Christian Univ	TX	15,832	C
Mayville State Univ	ND	7,325	NC
McKendree College	IL	21,120	VC
McNeese State Univ	LA	5,259	LC
Mercyhurst College	PA	20,694	C
MidAmerica Nazarene Univ	KS	18,688	C
Middle Tenn State Univ	TN	8,534	C
Midland Lutheran College	NE	18,600	C
Minot State Univ	ND	6,602	LC
Miss College	MS	14,574	C
Miss State Univ	MS	9,139	C
Missouri Southern State Univ	MO	8,316	C
Montana State Univ-Northern	MT	8,600	NC
Montclair State Univ	NJ	13,790	C
Morehead State Univ	KY	7,464	C
Morningside College	IA	21,610	C
Mount Mary College	WI	20,370	C
Mount Vernon Nazarene Univ	OH	18,925	C
Murray State Univ	KY	7,816	VC
Nazareth College of Rochester	NY	24,936	VC
New York Inst of Technology	NY	24,205	VC
Nicholls State Univ	LA	6,395	NC
Norfolk State Univ	VA	9,722	LC
N Car Agricultural and Technical State Univ	NC	6,659	LC
Northern Arizona Univ	AZ	9,002	C
Northern Kentucky Univ	KY	6,352	NC
Northern Mich Univ	MI	10,834	C
Northern State Univ	SD	7,117	LC
Northwest Missouri State Univ	MO	9,334	C
Northwestern College of Iowa	IA	19,640	C+
Northwestern Okla State Univ	OK	5,433	NC
Oakland City Univ	IN	16,980	NC
Oakwood College	AL	14,904	C
Oglala Lakota College	SD	1,950	NC
Ohio Univ	OH	14,448	C
Okla Panhandle State Univ	OK	5,370	C
Okla Wesleyan Univ	OK	14,100	LC
Oral Roberts Univ	OK	18,490	C
Ouachita Baptist Univ	AR	18,900	VC
Pace Univ	NY	28,652	VC
Philander Smith College	AR	7,380	NC
Pontifical Catholic Univ of PR/Ponce	PR	7,298	
Robert Morris Univ	PA	20,438	C
Rust College	MS	8,200	C+
St. Augustine's College	NC	12,990	LC
St. Mary's Univ of San Antonio	TX	22,444	C
St. Paul's College	VA	14,344	NC
St. Vincent College	PA	25,530	VC
Salem State College	MA	8,592	C
Shippensburg Univ of Pennsylvania	PA	10,826	C
Siena Heights Univ	MI	16,140	LC
Simpson College	IA	23,658	C+
S Car State Univ	SC	6,586	LC
Southeast Missouri State Univ	MO	9,704	C
Southeastern Okla State Univ	OK	6,147	C
Southern Arkansas Univ	AR	6,956	C
Southern Illinois Univ Carbondale	IL	10,407	C
Southern Nazarene Univ	OK	14,634	NC
Southern New Hampshire Univ	NH	26,242	C
Southern Univ at New Orleans	LA	995	NC
Southern Utah Univ	UT	8,194	C
Southwest Minn State Univ	MN	9,106	VC
Southwest Missouri State Univ	MO	8,918	C
Southwestern Adventist Univ	TX	14,798	C
SUNY at Oswego	NY	12,650	C
SUNY/College at Buffalo	NY	8,025	C
SUNY/College at Oneonta	NY	11,870	VC
State Univ of West Georgia	GA	7,622	C
Suffolk Univ	MA	29,200	C
Tabor College	KS	19,500	NC
Tarleton State Univ	TX	7,576	C
Temple Univ	PA	15,912	C
Texas A&M Univ at Commerce	TX	8,994	C
Texas Wesleyan Univ	TX	16,245	C
Thomas College	ME	19,960	LC
Union College	KY	15,920	C
Union College	NE	17,130	C
Univ of Akron	OH	13,134	NC
Univ of Arkansas at Monticello	AR	5,940	NC
Univ of Arkansas at Pine Bluff	AR	7,925	C
Univ of Central Florida	FL	10,038	VC
Univ of Central Okla	OK	9,434	C
Univ of Cincinnati	OH	14,736	C
Univ of Findlay	OH	23,962	NC
Univ of Georgia	GA	8,656	VC
Univ of Idaho	ID	8,216	C
Univ of Indianapolis	IN	22,560	VC
Univ of Kentucky	KY	7,765	C
Univ of Louisville	KY	8,762	VC
Univ of Maine at Machias	ME	9,271	LC
Univ of Mary Hardin-Baylor	TX	17,268	C
Univ of Maryland/Eastern Shore	MD	9,964	C
Univ of Minn/Twin Cities	MN	13,160	VC
Univ of Montana--Western	MT	8,073	NC
Univ of Nebr at Kearney	NE	8,286	NC
Univ of Nebr at Lincoln	NE	9,975	C+
Univ of New Mexico	NM	9,223	C
Univ of New Orleans	LA	7,356	C
Univ of North Alabama	AL	7,972	NC
Univ of N Dak	ND	8,390	C
Univ of North Texas	TX	7,629	C
Univ of Northern Iowa	IA	9,834	C
Univ of Rio Grande	OH	8,728	NC
Univ of St. Francis	IN	20,964	C
Univ of South Florida	FL	9,454	C
Univ of Southern Indiana	IN	9,025	LC
Univ of Southern Miss	MS	8,324	LC
Univ of the Incarnate Word	TX	21,772	LC
Univ of the Ozarks	AR	16,574	C
Univ of Toledo	OH	12,479	NC
Univ of Wisc/Eau Claire	WI	8,463	VC
Univ of Wisc/Whitewater	WI	8,626	C
Utah State Univ	UT	7,371	C
Valdosta State Univ	GA	7,798	C
Valley City State Univ	ND	7,281	LC
Virginia Polytechnic Inst and State Univ	VA	9,179	C

ST = STATE $IS = IN-STATE COSTS SR = SELECTOR RATING

School	ST	$IS	SR
Virginia State Univ	VA	10,358	C
Virginia Union Univ	VA	15,358	LC
Viterbo Univ	WI	20,430	C
Walla Walla College	WA	21,600	NC
Warner Southern College	FL	16,738	LC
Washburn Univ of Topeka	KS	8,984	NC
Wayne State Univ	MI	11,774	C
Weber State Univ	UT	7,945	NC
West Texas A&M Univ	TX	7,533	C
Western Kentucky Univ	KY	6,834	C
Western Mich Univ	MI	12,031	C
Western New Mexico Univ	NM	5,950	LC
Westfield State College	MA	10,147	C
Wiley College	TX	8,100	LC
Winona State Univ	MN		C
Wright State Univ	OH	11,490	LC
York College of Pennsylvania	PA	14,500	VC
Youngstown State Univ	OH	11,148	NC

BUSINESS LAW

School	ST	$IS	SR
Bowling Green State Univ	OH	13,036	C
Hofstra Univ	NY	27,112	VC
Lamar Univ	TX	6,816	LC
Marymount Univ	VA	23,668	C
Ohio Univ	OH	14,448	C
Saginaw Valley State Univ	MI	11,055	C
Temple Univ	PA	15,912	C
Univ of Pennsylvania	PA	37,960	MC
Warner Southern College	FL	16,738	LC
Washington State Univ	WA	11,334	C
Western Carolina Univ	NC	6,742	C

BUSINESS STATISTICS

School	ST	$IS	SR
Baylor Univ	TX	23,864	VC
Univ of PR/Rio Piedras	PR	5,730	
Washington State Univ	WA	11,334	C

BUSINESS SYSTEMS ANALYSIS

School	ST	$IS	SR
Arkansas State Univ	AR	8,450	C
Baylor Univ	TX	23,864	VC
Eastern Mich Univ	MI	11,478	C
Husson College	ME	16,300	LC
Johnson State College	VT	11,819	LC
Louisiana Tech Univ	LA	7,361	C
Messiah College	PA	25,890	VC+
Montana Tech of The Univ of Montana	MT	9,314	NC
Rochester Inst of Technology	NY	29,217	VC+
Southern Illinois Univ Carbondale	IL	10,407	C
Texas A&M Univ	TX	11,081	HC
Univ of Findlay	OH	23,962	NC
Univ of N Car at Wilmington	NC	8,940	VC
Univ of St. Mary	KS	18,868	C
Villa Julie College	MD	18,393	C

CANADIAN STUDIES

School	ST	$IS	SR
Brigham Young Univ	UT	8,504	HC
Duke Univ	NC	37,555	MC
Franklin College	IN		C
St. Lawrence Univ	NY	35,945	VC
SUNY/College at Plattsburgh	NY	11,700	C
Univ of Vermont	VT	16,316	VC
Univ of Washington	WA	10,361	VC
Western Washington Univ	WA	10,119	VC

CARIBBEAN STUDIES

School	ST	$IS	SR
CUNY/Brooklyn College	NY	4,353	C+
Florida State Univ	FL	9,028	HC
Hofstra Univ	NY	27,112	VC
Pitzer College	CA	37,590	HC
SUNY/Univ at Albany	NY	12,951	HC
SUNY/Univ at Binghamton	NY	12,787	HC

CARTOGRAPHY

School	ST	$IS	SR
East Central Univ	OK	4,968	C
Ohio Univ	OH	14,448	C
Salem State College	MA	8,592	C
Southwest Missouri State Univ	MO	8,918	C
Texas State Univ	TX	9,320	VC
Univ of Idaho	ID	8,216	C
Univ of Wisc/Madison	WI	8,262	VC

CELL BIOLOGY

School	ST	$IS	SR
Ball State Univ	IN	8,660	C
Bard College	NY	37,352	HC+
Beloit College	WI	29,864	HC
Bucknell Univ	PA	35,262	HC+
Cal State, Long Beach	CA	8,762	C+
Florida State Univ	FL	9,028	HC
Johns Hopkins Univ	MD	38,372	MC
Johnson State College	VT	11,819	LC
Mansfield Univ	PA	11,220	C
Montana State Univ-Bozeman	MT	9,515	C
Ohio Univ	OH	14,448	C
Okla State Univ	OK	9,216	VC
Rutgers, The State Univ of New Jersey/New Brunswick/Piscataway Campus	NJ	15,800	HC
San Francisco State Univ	CA	12,070	C
Southwest Missouri State Univ	MO	8,918	C
SUNY/College at Plattsburgh	NY	11,700	C
Texas Tech Univ	TX	10,768	VC
Tulane Univ	LA	37,451	HC+
Univ of Calif at Santa Barbara	CA	11,732	VC
Univ of Colo at Boulder	CO	10,774	VC
Univ of Maine	ME	12,080	C+
Univ of Mich/Ann Arbor	MI	13,864	HC+
Univ of Minn/Twin Cities	MN	13,160	VC
Univ of Rochester	NY	32,979	HC
Washington State Univ	WA	11,334	C

CELTIC STUDIES

School	ST	$IS	SR
Bard College	NY	37,352	HC+
Univ of Calif at Berkeley	CA	15,563	MC

CERAMIC ART AND DESIGN

School	ST	$IS	SR
Alfred Univ	NY	28,290	C
Andrews Univ	MI	19,550	C
Arizona State Univ-Main	AZ	10,048	C
Calif College of the Arts	CA	31,530	SP
Cal State, Fullerton	CA	6,648	C
Cal State, San Bernardino	CA	15,238	LC
College for Creative Studies	MI	23,298	SP
Edinboro Univ of Pennsylvania	PA	10,850	LC
Hofstra Univ	NY	27,112	VC
Indiana Univ Bloomington	IN	12,389	VC
Indiana Univ-Purdue Univ Indianapolis	IN	8,257	LC
Kansas City Art Inst	MO	26,850	SP
Maryland Inst College of Art	MD	30,890	SP
Mass College of Art	MA	15,568	SP
McMurry Univ	TX	17,846	LC
Northwest Nazarene Univ	ID	20,360	VC
Ohio Northern Univ	OH	27,765	VC
Ohio Univ	OH	14,448	C
Rhode Island School of Design	RI	33,569	SP
Rochester Inst of Technology	NY	29,217	VC+
School of the Art Inst of Chicago	IL	27,800	SP
SUNY at Potsdam	NY	12,160	C
Syracuse Univ	NY	34,720	HC
Univ of Dallas	TX	25,898	VC+
Univ of Hartford	CT	31,080	C
Univ of Mass Dartmouth	MA	12,835	C
Univ of Miami	FL	34,608	HC
Univ of Mich/Ann Arbor	MI	13,864	HC+
Univ of North Texas	TX	7,629	C
Univ of Oregon	OR	11,479	VC
Washington Univ in St. Louis	MO	38,293	MC

CERAMIC ENGINEERING

School	ST	$IS	SR
Alfred Univ	NY	28,290	C
Clemson Univ	SC	11,972	HC
Ohio State Univ	OH	13,080	VC+
Rutgers, The State Univ of New Jersey/New Brunswick/Piscataway Campus	NJ	15,800	HC
Univ of Illinois at Urbana-Champaign	IL	11,316	HC+
Univ of Missouri/Rolla	MO	12,292	HC
Univ of Washington	WA	10,361	VC

CERAMIC SCIENCE

School	ST	$IS	SR
Maine College of Art	ME	28,812	SP

CHEMICAL ENGINEERING

School	ST	$IS	SR
Arizona State Univ-Main	AZ	10,048	C
Auburn Univ	AL	10,396	VC
Bethel College	IN	19,670	C
Brigham Young Univ	UT	8,504	HC
Bucknell Univ	PA	35,262	HC+
Calif Inst of Technology	CA	31,677	MC
Calif State Polytechnic Univ, Pomona	CA	8,793	C+
Cal State, Long Beach	CA	8,762	C+
Calvin College	MI	22,615	NC
Carnegie Mellon Univ	PA	32,682	MC
Case Western Reserve Univ	OH	32,002	MC
Christian Brothers Univ	TN	22,290	VC
CUNY/City College	NY	4,230	C+
Clarkson Univ	NY	32,226	VC
Clemson Univ	SC	11,972	HC
Cleveland State Univ	OH	12,308	LC
Colo School of Mines	CO	12,533	HC
Colo State Univ	CO	9,964	VC
Columbia Univ/Fu Foundation School of Engineering and Applied Science	NY	38,590	MC
Cooper Union for the Advancement of Science and Art	NY	10,400	MC
Cornell Univ	NY	38,253	MC
Delaware State Univ	DE	8,104	LC
Dordt College	IA	20,170	VC
Drexel Univ	PA	27,655	VC
Florida A&M Univ	FL	7,564	C
Florida Inst of Technology	FL	28,740	VC
Florida International Univ	FL	9,912	VC
Florida State Univ	FL	9,028	HC
Geneva College	PA	21,850	C
Georgia Inst of Technology	GA	10,340	HC+
Hampton Univ	VA	17,112	C+
Howard Univ	DC	16,505	C
Illinois Inst of Technology	IL	26,456	HC+
Iowa State Univ	IA	10,768	VC
Johns Hopkins Univ	MD	38,372	MC
Kansas State Univ	KS	8,728	VC
Lafayette College	PA	35,746	MC
Lamar Univ	TX	6,816	LC
Lehigh Univ	PA	37,570	HC+
Louisiana State Univ and A&M College	LA	9,126	VC
Louisiana Tech Univ	LA	7,361	C
Manhattan College	NY	27,400	VC
Mass Inst of Technology	MA	38,310	MC
McNeese State Univ	LA	5,259	LC
Mich State Univ	MI	11,933	VC
Mich Tech Univ	MI	13,235	VC
Miss State Univ	MS	9,139	C
Montana State Univ-Bozeman	MT	9,515	C
New Jersey Inst of Technology	NJ	16,396	VC
New Mexico Inst of Mining and Technology	NM	7,580	NC
New Mexico State Univ	NM	7,932	C
N Car Agricultural and Technical State Univ	NC	6,659	LC
N Car State Univ	NC	9,886	VC
Northeastern Univ	MA	35,650	HC
Northwestern Univ	IL	37,491	MC
Oakland Univ	MI	10,800	C
Ohio State Univ	OH	13,080	VC+
Ohio Univ	OH	14,448	C
Okla State Univ	OK	9,216	VC
Oregon State Univ	OR	11,055	C
Penn State Univ/Univ Park Campus	PA	15,646	HC
Polytechnic Univ/Brooklyn	NY	33,770	VC
Prairie View A&M Univ	TX	9,418	NC
Princeton Univ	NJ	36,649	MC
Purdue Univ/West Lafayette	IN	12,560	VC
Rensselaer Polytechnic Inst	NY	37,579	HC+
Rice Univ	TX	27,550	MC
Rose-Hulman Inst of Technology	IN	31,425	HC+
Rutgers, The State Univ of New Jersey/New Brunswick/Piscataway Campus	NJ	15,800	HC
San Jose State Univ	CA	8,187	C
Savannah State Univ	GA	7,328	LC
S Dak School of Mines and Technology	SD	7,854	C+
Stanford Univ	CA	37,612	MC
SUNY/College of Environmental Science and Forestry	NY	14,167	VC
SUNY/Univ at Buffalo	NY	12,563	VC
SUNY/Univ at Stony Brook	NY	12,763	HC
Stevens Inst of Technology	NJ	35,300	HC+
Syracuse Univ	NY	34,720	HC
Tenn Tech Univ	TN	8,670	VC
Texas A&M Univ	TX	11,081	HC
Texas A&M Univ at Kingsville	TX	6,740	LC
Texas Tech Univ	TX	10,768	VC
Tri-State Univ-Main Campus	IN	23,600	C
Tufts Univ	MA	38,233	MC
Tulane Univ	LA	37,451	HC+
Tuskegee Univ	AL	17,250	LC
Universidad Politecnica de PR	PR	5,370	
Univ of Akron	OH	13,134	NC
Univ of Alabama	AL	9,040	C+
Univ of Alabama in Huntsville	AL	9,126	VC
Univ of Arizona	AZ	10,413	VC
Univ of Arkansas	AR	9,855	VC
Univ of Calif at Berkeley	CA	15,563	MC
Univ of Calif at Davis	CA	14,995	VC
Univ of Calif at Irvine	CA	19,808	HC
Univ of Calif at Los Angeles	CA	15,330	MC
Univ of Calif at Riverside	CA	15,300	C
Univ of Calif at San Diego	CA	14,127	HC
Univ of Calif at Santa Barbara	CA	11,732	VC
Univ of Cincinnati	OH	14,736	C
Univ of Colo at Boulder	CO	10,774	VC
Univ of Conn	CT	14,608	VC
Univ of Dayton	OH	24,850	VC
Univ of Delaware	DE	12,616	HC
Univ of Florida	FL	8,580	MC
Univ of Houston	TX	9,818	C
Univ of Idaho	ID	8,216	C
Univ of Illinois at Chicago	IL	13,418	C
Univ of Illinois at Urbana-Champaign	IL	11,316	HC+
Univ of Iowa	IA	10,923	VC
Univ of Kansas	KS	8,923	VC
Univ of Kentucky	KY	7,765	C
Univ of Louisiana at Lafayette	LA	5,826	C
Univ of Louisville	KY	8,762	VC
Univ of Maine	ME	12,080	C+
Univ of Maryland/Baltimore County	MD	14,668	VC+
Univ of Maryland/College Park	MD	14,227	HC
Univ of Mass Amherst	MA	13,980	C+
Univ of Mass Lowell	MA	11,937	VC
Univ of Mich/Ann Arbor	MI	13,864	HC+
Univ of Minn/Duluth	MN	12,470	C
Univ of Minn/Twin Cities	MN	13,160	VC
Univ of Miss	MS	7,666	C
Univ of Missouri/Columbia	MO	13,782	VC
Univ of Missouri/Rolla	MO	12,292	HC
Univ of Nebr at Lincoln	NE	9,975	C+
Univ of Nevada/Reno	NV	9,792	C
Univ of New Hampshire	NH	14,828	VC
Univ of New Haven	CT	28,650	C
Univ of New Mexico	NM	9,223	C
Univ of N Dak	ND	8,390	C
Univ of Notre Dame	IN	34,442	MC
Univ of Okla	OK	9,226	VC
Univ of Pennsylvania	PA	37,960	MC
Univ of Pittsburgh at Pittsburgh	PA	16,074	HC
Univ of PR/Mayaguez	PR		
Univ of Rhode Island	RI	13,720	VC
Univ of Rochester	NY	32,979	HC
Univ of South Alabama	AL	7,760	LC
Univ of S Car at Columbia	SC	10,048	VC
Univ of South Florida	FL	9,454	C
Univ of Southern Calif	CA	37,459	MC
Univ of Tenn at Knoxville	TN	8,214	C
Univ of Texas at Austin	TX	10,630	HC
Univ of Toledo	OH	12,479	NC
Univ of Tulsa	OK	22,090	VC+
Univ of Utah	UT	9,205	C
Univ of Virginia	VA	11,740	MC
Univ of Washington	WA	10,361	VC
Univ of Wisc/Madison	WI	8,262	VC
Univ of Wyoming	WY	8,636	C
Vanderbilt Univ	TN	37,897	MC
Villanova Univ	PA	35,050	HC
Virginia Commonwealth Univ	VA	9,030	C
Virginia Polytechnic Inst and State Univ	VA	9,179	C
Washington and Lee Univ	VA	29,663	MC
Washington State Univ	WA	11,334	C
Washington Univ in St. Louis	MO	38,293	MC
Wayne State Univ	MI	11,774	C
West Virginia Univ	WV	9,370	C
West Virginia Univ Inst of Technology	WV	7,518	NC
Western Mich Univ	MI	12,031	C
Widener Univ	PA	27,020	C
Worcester Polytechnic Inst	MA	37,404	HC
Xavier Univ	OH	26,850	VC+
Yale Univ	CT	37,000	MC
Youngstown State Univ	OH	11,148	NC

CHEMICAL ENGINEERING TECHNOLOGY

School	ST	$IS	SR
Univ of Hartford	CT	31,080	C
Univ of PR/Arecibo	PR	1,095	

CHEMICAL PHYSICS

School	ST	$IS	SR
Bowdoin College	ME	37,790	MC
Brown Univ	RI	38,174	MC
Maryville College	TN	25,960	VC
Mich State Univ	MI	11,933	VC

CHEMICAL TECHNOLOGY

School	ST	$IS	SR
Florida State Univ	FL	9,028	HC
Gallaudet Univ	DC	16,554	SP
Inter American Univ of PR/Arecibo Campus	PR	3,300	
Inter American Univ of PR/Bayamon Univ College	PR	3,522	
Inter American Univ of PR/Fajardo Campus	PR	4,000	

ST = STATE $IS = IN-STATE COSTS SR = SELECTOR RATING

School	ST	$IS	SR
Inter American Univ of PR/ Ponce Regional College	PR	3,700	
Midwestern State Univ	TX	8,045	LC
Univ of Cincinnati	OH	14,736	C

CHEMISTRY

School	ST	$IS	SR
Abilene Christian Univ	TX	18,370	VC
Adams State College	CO	7,468	C
Adelphi Univ	NY	26,300	VC
Adrian College	MI	21,950	C
Agnes Scott College	GA	28,230	HC
Alabama A&M Univ	AL	5,100	LC
Alabama State Univ	AL	6,404	C
Albany State Univ	GA	5,764	C+
Albertson College of Idaho	ID	19,415	VC
Albion College	MI	25,224	VC
Albright College	PA	30,579	C
Alcorn State Univ	MS	7,290	C
Alderson-Broaddus College	WV	19,640	C
Alfred Univ	NY	28,290	C
Allegheny College	PA	30,280	VC
Alma College	MI	25,566	VC
Alvernia College	PA	23,212	LC
Alverno College	WI	18,898	C
American International College	MA	24,690	LC
American Univ	DC	34,585	VC+
Amherst College	MA	37,470	MC
Anderson Univ	IN	19,430	LC
Andrews Univ	MI	19,550	C
Angelo State Univ	TX	7,576	NC
Appalachian State Univ	NC	7,637	VC
Aquinas College	MI	21,894	C
Arcadia Univ	PA	29,890	C
Arizona State Univ-Main	AZ	10,048	C
Arkansas State Univ	AR	8,450	C
Arkansas Tech Univ	AR	7,299	C
Armstrong Atlantic State Univ	GA	7,102	C
Asbury College	KY	20,704	VC
Ashland Univ	OH	24,464	C
Assumption College	MA	29,375	C
Auburn Univ	AL	10,396	VC
Augsburg College	MN	25,298	C
Augusta State Univ	GA	2,592	C
Augustana College	IL	26,610	VC+
Augustana College	SD	21,998	VC
Austin College	TX	24,747	HC
Austin Peay State Univ	TN	5,814	LC
Averett Univ	VA	23,010	LC
Avila Univ	MO	20,300	C
Azusa Pacific Univ	CA	24,720	VC
Baker Univ	KS	19,860	VC
Baldwin-Wallace College	OH	24,678	C
Ball State Univ	IN	8,660	C
Bard College	NY	37,352	HC+
Barry Univ	FL	24,100	LC
Barton College	NC	19,314	C
Bates College	ME	37,500	MC
Baylor Univ	TX	23,864	VC
Belhaven College	MS	16,040	C+
Bellarmine Univ	KY	24,110	VC
Belmont Univ	TN	21,986	VC
Beloit College	WI	29,864	HC
Bemidji State Univ	MN	9,103	C
Benedict College	SC	12,662	LC
Benedictine College	KS	20,603	C
Benedictine Univ	IL	23,840	C
Bennett College	NC	11,200	C
Bennington College	VT	35,910	HC
Berea College	KY	5,030	VC+
Berry College	GA	21,410	VC
Bethany College	KS	18,675	LC
Bethany College	WV	19,845	VC
Bethel College	IN	19,670	C
Bethel College	KS	19,800	C+
Bethel College	MN	25,180	VC
Bethel College	TN	12,980	C
Bethune-Cookman College	FL	16,480	LC
Birmingham-Southern College	AL	25,364	VC+
Black Hills State Univ	SD	7,743	LC
Blackburn College	IL	13,690	C
Bloomfield College	NJ	19,250	LC
Bloomsburg Univ of Pennsylvania	PA	10,844	C
Blue Mountain College	MS	10,226	C
Bluefield College	VA	15,575	C
Bluffton College	OH	23,694	C
Boise State Univ	ID	7,657	LC
Boston College	MA	33,284	MC
Boston Univ	MA	38,194	HC+
Bowdoin College	ME	37,790	MC
Bowling Green State Univ	OH	13,036	C
Bradley Univ	IL	22,910	VC
Brandeis Univ	MA	38,198	MC
Brescia Univ	KY	14,225	C
Briar Cliff Univ	IA	21,660	C
Bridgewater College	VA	25,150	C
Bridgewater State College	MA	10,482	C
Brigham Young Univ	UT	8,504	HC
Brown Univ	RI	38,174	MC
Bryn Mawr College	PA	36,890	HC+
Bucknell Univ	PA	35,262	HC+
Buena Vista Univ	IA	25,406	C
Butler Univ	IN	28,250	VC+
Cabrini College	PA	29,020	C
Caldwell College	NJ	24,060	LC
Calif Inst of Technology	CA	31,677	MC
Calif Lutheran Univ	CA	27,600	LC
Calif Polytechnic State Univ	CA	8,747	VC
Calif State Polytechnic Univ, Pomona	CA	8,793	C+
Cal State, Bakersfield	CA	6,090	LC
Cal State, Chico	CA	8,598	LC
Cal State, Dominguez Hills	CA	5,840	LC
Cal State, Fresno	CA	8,414	LC
Cal State, Fullerton	CA	6,648	C
Cal State, Hayward	CA	8,871	LC
Cal State, Long Beach	CA	8,762	C+
Cal State, Los Angeles	CA	5,778	C
Cal State, Northridge	CA	7,757	LC
Cal State, Sacramento	CA	9,543	C
Cal State, San Bernardino	CA	15,238	LC
Cal State, San Marcos	CA	1,736	LC
Cal State, Stanislaus	CA	9,874	C
Calif Univ of Pennsylvania	PA	10,388	C
Calvin College	MI	22,615	NC
Cameron Univ	OK	5,692	NC
Campbell Univ	NC	18,268	VC
Campbellsville Univ	KY	17,680	C
Canisius College	NY	28,163	C+
Capital Univ	OH	26,550	C
Cardinal Stritch Univ	WI	17,620	C
Carleton College	MN	34,395	MC
Carlow College	PA	21,334	C
Carnegie Mellon Univ	PA	32,682	MC
Carroll College	MT	20,576	VC
Carroll College	WI	22,740	C
Carthage College	WI	25,000	C
Case Western Reserve Univ	OH	32,002	MC
Catawba College	NC	20,500	C
Catholic Univ of America	DC	34,248	VC
Cedar Crest College	PA	25,145	C+
Cedarville Univ	OH	19,954	VC
Centenary College of Louisiana	LA	23,100	VC+
Central College	IA	21,206	C
Central Conn State Univ	CT	12,090	C
Central Methodist College	MO	16,460	C
Central Mich Univ	MI	11,142	C
Central Missouri State Univ	MO	9,776	C
Central State Univ	OH	8,922	C+
Central Univ of Bayamon	PR	3,335	
Central Washington Univ	WA	9,768	C
Centre College	KY	27,300	HC
Chadron State College	NE	6,286	NC
Chapman Univ	CA	33,118	VC
Charleston Southern Univ	SC	17,122	C
Chatham College	PA	27,266	C+
Chestnut Hill College	PA	26,450	LC
Cheyney Univ of Pennsylvania	PA	9,993	C
Chicago State Univ	IL	10,882	C+
Christian Brothers Univ	TN	22,290	VC
Citadel, The	SC	12,295	C+
CUNY/Brooklyn College	NY	4,353	C+
CUNY/City College	NY	4,230	C+
CUNY/College of Staten Island	NY	4,308	NC
CUNY/Herbert H. Lehman College	NY	3,320	LC
CUNY/Hunter College	NY	6,729	C+
CUNY/Queens College	NY	4,362	C
CUNY/York College	NY	3,292	NC
Claflin Univ	SC	14,838	C+
Claremont McKenna College	CA	36,880	MC
Clarion Univ of Pennsylvania	PA	11,272	LC
Clark Atlanta Univ	GA	19,300	C+
Clark Univ	MA	32,115	VC
Clarke College	IA	23,165	C
Clarkson Univ	NY	32,226	VC
Clemson Univ	SC	11,972	HC
Cleveland State Univ	OH	12,308	LC
Coastal Carolina Univ	SC	11,040	C
Coe College	IA	27,385	VC
Coker College	SC	21,491	C
Colby College	ME	37,570	MC
Colgate Univ	NY	37,095	MC
College Misericordia	PA	26,350	C
College of Charleston	SC	11,887	HC
College of Mount St. Vincent	NY	26,800	C
College of Mount St. Joseph	OH	22,785	C
College of New Jersey	NJ	15,950	MC
College of New Rochelle	NY	21,800	C
College of Notre Dame of Maryland	MD	27,700	C
College of Our Lady of the Elms	MA	20,644	C
College of St. Benedict	MN	26,672	VC
College of St. Catherine	MN	24,010	VC
College of St. Elizabeth	NJ	25,460	C
College of St. Mary	NE	21,510	C
College of St. Rose	NY	22,864	C
College of St. Scholastica	MN	24,970	C+
College of the Holy Cross	MA	36,451	MC
College of the Ozarks	MO	3,500	VC+
College of William and Mary	VA	12,224	MC
College of Wooster	OH	31,300	HC
Colo College	CO	36,860	HC
Colo School of Mines	CO	12,533	HC
Colo State Univ	CO	9,964	VC
Columbia College	MO	16,139	C
Columbia College	SC	22,658	LC
Columbia Union College	MD	20,543	C
Columbia Univ/Barnard College	NY	36,990	MC
Columbia Univ/Columbia College	NY	38,590	MC
Columbia Univ/School of General Studies	NY	35,000	C
Columbus State Univ	GA	7,846	C
Concord College	WV	8,136	C
Concordia College: Moorhead	MN	22,460	VC+
Concordia Univ	OR	22,450	C
Concordia Univ Nebr	NE	20,302	C+
Concordia Univ, River Forest	IL	23,600	C
Conn College	CT	37,900	MC
Converse College	SC	24,710	VC
Coppin State College	MD	10,191	LC
Cornell College	IA	27,825	VC+
Cornell Univ	NY	38,253	MC
Covenant College	GA	23,830	VC+
Creighton Univ	NE	26,748	VC+
Crichton College	TN	15,215	C
Culver-Stockton College	MO	17,850	C
Cumberland College	KY	16,384	C
Curry College	MA	26,025	LC
Dakota State Univ	SD	7,466	C
Dana College	NE	20,280	C
Dartmouth College	NH	37,770	MC
David Lipscomb Univ	TN	16,158	VC
Davidson College	NC	33,274	MC
Davis and Elkins College	WV	20,594	C
De Sales Univ	PA	25,470	C
Delaware State Univ	DE	8,104	LC
Delaware Valley College	PA	26,676	C
Delta State Univ	MS	6,618	C
Denison Univ	OH	33,050	HC
DePaul Univ	IL	27,580	VC
DePauw Univ	IN	31,500	HC
Dickinson College	PA	35,825	HC
Dickinson State Univ	ND	6,338	NC
Dillard Univ	LA	17,325	VC
Doane College	NE	20,000	C
Dominican Univ	IL	23,610	C
Dordt College	IA	20,170	VC
Drake Univ	IA	25,120	VC+
Drew Univ/College of Liberal Arts	NJ	35,550	VC
Drexel Univ	PA	27,655	VC
Drury Univ	MO	18,085	VC+
Duke Univ	NC	37,555	MC
Duquesne Univ	PA	26,907	VC
Earlham College	IN	29,976	VC+
East Carolina Univ	NC	8,671	C
East Central Univ	OK	4,968	C
East Stroudsburg Univ of Pennsylvania	PA	10,336	C
East Tenn State Univ	TN	8,497	C
East Texas Baptist Univ	TX	13,914	C
Eastern Illinois Univ	IL	11,192	C
Eastern Kentucky Univ	KY	7,708	C
Eastern Mennonite Univ	VA	22,990	C
Eastern Mich Univ	MI	11,478	C
Eastern Nazarene College	MA	19,433	LC
Eastern New Mexico Univ	NM	6,762	LC
Eastern Oregon Univ	OR	10,080	NC
Eastern Univ	PA	24,020	C
Eastern Washington Univ	WA	9,012	C
Eckerd College	FL	28,744	C+
Edgewood College	WI	20,520	C
Edinboro Univ of Pennsylvania	PA	10,850	LC
Elizabeth City State Univ	NC	5,550	LC
Elizabethtown College	PA	28,800	C
Elmhurst College	IL	24,630	C
Elmira College	NY	33,820	VC
Elon Univ	NC	22,240	VC
Emmanuel College	MA	27,600	C+
Emory & Henry College	VA	21,950	C
Emory Univ	GA	36,872	MC
Emporia State Univ	KS	6,998	C
Erskine College	SC	23,166	VC
Eureka College	IL	24,980	LC
Evangel Univ	MO	15,435	C
Fairfield Univ	CT	35,505	HC
Fairleigh Dickinson Univ/ College at Florham	NJ	30,130	C
Fairleigh Dickinson Univ/ Metropolitan Campus	NJ	28,584	C
Fairmont State	WV	8,280	LC
Fayetteville State Univ	NC	5,590	LC
Ferrum College	VA	21,240	LC
Fisk Univ	TN	17,305	LC
Florida A&M Univ	FL	7,564	C
Florida Atlantic Univ	FL	8,543	C
Florida Inst of Technology	FL	28,740	VC
Florida International Univ	FL	9,912	VC
Florida Memorial College	FL	6,000	LC
Florida Southern College	FL	23,592	C
Florida State Univ	FL	9,028	HC
Fordham Univ	NY	35,066	HC
Fort Hays State Univ	KS	7,363	C
Fort Lewis College	CO	8,353	C
Fort Valley State Univ	GA	6,960	C
Framingham State College	MA	9,381	C
Francis Marion Univ	SC	9,364	C
Franciscan Univ of Steubenville	OH	20,300	VC
Franklin and Marshall College	PA	35,930	HC+
Franklin College	IN		C
Freed-Hardeman Univ	TN		NC
Fresno Pacific Univ	CA	22,462	C
Friends Univ	KS	15,962	LC
Frostburg State Univ	MD	11,114	C
Furman Univ	SC	28,976	HC+
Gallaudet Univ	DC	16,554	SP
Gannon Univ	PA	23,260	C
Gardner-Webb Univ	NC	19,300	C
Geneva College	PA	21,850	C
George Fox Univ	OR	26,110	VC
George Mason Univ	VA	9,732	VC
George Washington Univ	DC	41,030	MC
Georgetown College	KY	22,000	VC
Georgetown Univ	DC	38,242	MC
Georgia College and State Univ	GA	9,878	C
Georgia Inst of Technology	GA	10,340	HC+
Georgia Southern Univ	GA	8,540	C
Georgia Southwestern State Univ	GA	6,013	C
Georgia State Univ	GA	10,658	C
Georgian Court College	NJ	19,040	LC
Gettysburg College	PA	35,646	HC
Glenville State College	WV	7,812	NC
Gonzaga Univ	WA	26,766	HC
Gordon College	MA	25,982	VC+
Goshen College	IN	22,450	VC
Goucher College	MD	32,650	HC
Graceland Univ	IA	19,550	C
Grambling State Univ	LA	6,538	NC
Grand Canyon Univ	AZ	30,000	LC
Grand Valley State Univ	MI	11,022	VC
Greensboro College	NC	21,750	C
Greenville College	IL	21,342	C
Grinnell College	IA	31,060	HC+
Grove City College	PA	14,228	HC
Guilford College	NC	24,960	VC
Gustavus Adolphus College	MN	27,120	VC+
Hamilton College	NY	37,560	MC
Hamline Univ	MN	27,052	VC
Hampden-Sydney College	VA	28,407	VC
Hampshire College	MA	37,037	HC
Hampton Univ	VA	17,112	C+
Hanover College	IN	25,200	VC
Harding Univ	AR	14,890	VC
Hardin-Simmons Univ	TX	14,165	C
Hartwick College	NY	34,650	C+
Harvard Univ/Harvard College	MA	37,928	MC
Harvey Mudd College	CA	38,080	MC
Hastings College	NE	19,928	VC
Haverford College	PA	37,900	MC
Heidelberg College	OH	20,266	NC
Henderson State Univ	AR	7,386	C
Hendrix College	AR	20,970	VC+
High Point Univ	NC	22,480	C
Hillsdale College	MI	22,450	HC
Hiram College	OH	28,234	VC
Hobart and William Smith Colleges	NY	36,536	HC
Hofstra Univ	NY	27,112	VC
Hollins Univ	VA	27,965	VC
Holy Family College	PA	13,710	LC
Hood College	MD	27,795	VC
Hope College	MI	25,340	VC
Houghton College	NY	23,984	VC
Houston Baptist Univ	TX	16,905	C
Howard Payne Univ	TX	15,176	C
Howard Univ	DC	16,505	C
Humboldt State Univ	CA	9,400	C
Huntingdon College	AL	18,400	VC
Huntington College	IN	23,590	C
Huston-Tillotson College	TX	14,232	NC
Idaho State Univ	ID	8,128	C
Illinois College	IL	19,100	VC
Illinois Inst of Technology	IL	26,456	HC+
Illinois State Univ	IL	10,944	C+
Illinois Wesleyan Univ	IL	30,380	HC+
Indiana State Univ	IN	10,719	LC
Indiana Univ Bloomington	IN	12,389	VC
Indiana Univ Kokomo	IN	4,463	LC
Indiana Univ Northwest	IN	4,538	LC
Indiana Univ of Pennsylvania	PA	10,489	C
Indiana Univ South Bend	IN	4,571	LC
Indiana Univ Southeast	IN	4,504	LC
Indiana Univ-Purdue Univ Fort Wayne	IN	5,108	LC
Indiana Univ-Purdue Univ Indianapolis	IN	8,257	LC
Indiana Wesleyan Univ	IN	19,900	C+
Inter American Univ of PR/ Arecibo Campus	PR	3,300	

ST = STATE **$IS** = IN-STATE COSTS **SR** = SELECTOR RATING

ST = STATE $IS = IN-STATE COSTS   SR = SELECTOR RATING

School	ST	$IS	SR
S Dak School of Mines and Technology	SD	7,854	C+
S Dak State Univ	SD	7,782	C
Southeast Missouri State Univ	MO	9,704	C
Southeastern Louisiana Univ	LA	6,791	LC
Southeastern Okla State Univ	OK	6,147	C
Southern Adventist Univ	TN	17,080	C
Southern Arkansas Univ	AR	6,956	C
Southern Conn State Univ	CT	10,310	C
Southern Illinois Univ Carbondale	IL	10,407	C
Southern Illinois Univ Edwardsville	IL	8,724	C
Southern Methodist Univ	TX	34,210	HC
Southern Nazarene Univ	OK	14,634	NC
Southern Oregon Univ	OR	10,362	C
Southern Univ and A&M College	LA	7,372	LC
Southern Univ at New Orleans	LA	995	NC
Southern Utah Univ	UT	8,194	C
Southern Wesleyan Univ	SC	19,940	C
Southwest Baptist Univ	MO	15,371	C
Southwest Minn State Univ	MN	9,106	VC
Southwest Missouri State Univ	MO	8,918	C
Southwestern Adventist Univ	TX	14,798	C
Southwestern College	KS	19,560	C
Southwestern Okla State Univ	OK	4,801	C
Southwestern Univ	TX	25,410	HC
Spelman College	GA	19,215	C+
Spring Arbor Univ	MI	20,206	C
Spring Hill College	AL	25,868	VC
Springfield College	MA	24,520	C
Stanford Univ	CA	37,612	MC
SUNY at Oswego	NY	12,650	C
SUNY at Potsdam	NY	12,160	C
SUNY/College at Brockport	NY	12,111	C
SUNY/College at Buffalo	NY	8,025	C
SUNY/College at Cortland	NY	12,095	C
SUNY/College at Fredonia	NY	11,562	VC
SUNY/College at Geneseo	NY	11,330	HC
SUNY/College at Old Westbury	NY	12,784	C
SUNY/College at Oneonta	NY	11,870	VC
SUNY/College at Plattsburgh	NY	11,700	C
SUNY/College at Purchase	NY	10,587	VC
SUNY/College of Environmental Science and Forestry	NY	14,167	VC
SUNY/Univ at Albany	NY	12,951	HC
SUNY/Univ at Binghamton	NY	12,787	HC
SUNY/Univ at Buffalo	NY	12,563	VC
SUNY/Univ at New Paltz	NY	11,565	VC
SUNY/Univ at Stony Brook	NY	12,763	HC
State Univ of West Georgia	GA	7,622	C
Stephen F. Austin State Univ	TX	7,552	C
Stetson Univ	FL	29,495	VC
Stevens Inst of Technology	NJ	35,300	HC+
Stonehill College	MA	30,752	HC
Suffolk Univ	MA	29,200	C
Sul Ross State Univ	TX	6,582	LC
Susquehanna Univ	PA	29,990	VC
Swarthmore College	PA	37,716	MC
Sweet Briar College	VA	27,940	C
Syracuse Univ	NY	34,720	HC
Tabor College	KS	19,500	NC
Talladega College	AL	10,110	LC
Tarleton State Univ	TX	7,576	C
Taylor Univ	IN	23,820	VC+
Temple Univ	PA	15,912	C
Tenn State Univ	TN	9,048	LC
Tenn Tech Univ	TN	8,670	VC
Tenn Wesleyan College	TN	16,540	C
Texas A&M Univ	TX	11,081	HC
Texas A&M Univ at Commerce	TX	8,994	C
Texas A&M Univ at Corpus Christi	TX	10,269	C
Texas A&M Univ at Kingsville	TX	6,740	LC
Texas Christian Univ	TX	23,410	VC
Texas Lutheran Univ	TX	20,370	C
Texas Southern Univ	TX	8,920	NC
Texas State Univ	TX	9,320	VC
Texas Tech Univ	TX	10,768	VC
Texas Wesleyan Univ	TX	16,245	C
Texas Woman's Univ	TX	7,804	LC
Thiel College	PA	20,970	C
Thomas More College	KY	21,350	C
Tougaloo College	MS	9,200	NC
Touro College	NY	15,250	VC
Towson Univ	MD	12,694	VC
Transylvania Univ	KY	23,780	VC+
Trevecca Nazarene Univ	TN	17,548	C
Trinity Christian College	IL	21,640	VC
Trinity College	CT	38,040	HC+
Trinity College	DC	24,150	LC
Trinity International Univ	IL	22,980	C+
Trinity Univ	TX	26,466	HC+
Tri-State Univ-Main Campus	IN	23,600	C
Troy State Univ	AL	7,696	C
Troy State Univ Dothan	AL	3,842	C
Truman State Univ	MO	9,728	HC+
Tufts Univ	MA	38,233	MC
Tulane Univ	LA	37,451	HC+
Turabo Univ	PR	4,110	
Tuskegee Univ	AL	17,250	LC
Union College	NE	17,130	C
Union College	NY	36,005	HC
Union Univ	TN	18,800	VC
United States Air Force Academy	CO		HC+
United States Military Academy	NY		MC
United States Naval Academy	MD		MC
Univ of Akron	OH	13,134	NC
Univ of Alabama	AL	9,040	C+
Univ of Alabama at Birmingham	AL	12,901	C
Univ of Alabama in Huntsville	AL	9,126	VC
Univ of Alaska Anchorage	AK	9,100	NC
Univ of Alaska Fairbanks	AK	9,295	C
Univ of Arizona	AZ	10,413	VC
Univ of Arkansas	AR	9,855	VC
Univ of Arkansas at Little Rock	AR	5,637	NC
Univ of Arkansas at Monticello	AR	5,940	NC
Univ of Arkansas at Pine Bluff	AR	7,925	C
Univ of Calif at Berkeley	CA	15,563	MC
Univ of Calif at Davis	CA	14,995	VC
Univ of Calif at Irvine	CA	19,808	HC
Univ of Calif at Los Angeles	CA	15,330	MC
Univ of Calif at Riverside	CA	15,300	C
Univ of Calif at San Diego	CA	14,127	HC
Univ of Calif at Santa Barbara	CA	11,732	VC
Univ of Calif at Santa Cruz	CA	16,505	VC
Univ of Central Arkansas	AR	6,388	C
Univ of Central Florida	FL	10,038	VC
Univ of Central Okla	OK	9,434	C
Univ of Charleston	WV	23,620	C
Univ of Chicago	IL	35,087	MC
Univ of Cincinnati	OH	14,736	C
Univ of Colo at Boulder	CO	10,774	VC
Univ of Colo at Colo Springs	CO	10,667	C
Univ of Colo at Denver	CO	3,302	C
Univ of Conn	CT	14,608	VC
Univ of Dallas	TX	25,898	VC+
Univ of Dayton	OH	24,850	VC
Univ of Delaware	DE	12,616	HC
Univ of Denver	CO	32,348	VC
Univ of Detroit Mercy	MI	25,582	C
Univ of Evansville	IN	24,190	VC
Univ of Florida	FL	8,580	MC
Univ of Georgia	GA	8,656	VC
Univ of Hartford	CT	31,080	C
Univ of Hawaii at Hilo	HI	6,497	C
Univ of Hawaii at Manoa	HI	9,565	VC
Univ of Houston	TX	9,818	C
Univ of Idaho	ID	8,216	C
Univ of Illinois at Chicago	IL	13,418	C
Univ of Illinois at Urbana-Champaign	IL	11,316	HC+
Univ of Indianapolis	IN	22,560	VC
Univ of Iowa	IA	10,923	VC
Univ of Kansas	KS	8,923	VC
Univ of Kentucky	KY	7,765	C
Univ of La Verne	CA	28,600	C
Univ of Louisiana at Lafayette	LA	5,826	C
Univ of Louisiana at Monroe	LA	5,207	NC
Univ of Louisville	KY	8,762	VC
Univ of Maine	ME	12,080	C+
Univ of Mary Hardin-Baylor	TX	17,268	C
Univ of Maryland/Baltimore County	MD	14,668	VC+
Univ of Maryland/College Park	MD	14,227	HC
Univ of Maryland/Eastern Shore	MD	9,964	C
Univ of Mass Amherst	MA	13,980	C+
Univ of Mass Boston	MA	6,227	C
Univ of Mass Dartmouth	MA	12,835	C
Univ of Mass Lowell	MA	11,937	VC
Univ of Memphis	TN	8,560	C
Univ of Miami	FL	34,608	HC
Univ of Mich/Ann Arbor	MI	13,864	HC+
Univ of Mich/Dearborn	MI	6,843	VC
Univ of Mich/Flint	MI	5,548	C
Univ of Minn/Duluth	MN	12,470	C
Univ of Minn/Morris	MN	12,896	VC
Univ of Minn/Twin Cities	MN	13,160	VC
Univ of Miss	MS	7,666	C
Univ of Missouri/Columbia	MO	13,782	VC
Univ of Missouri/Kansas City	MO	13,416	VC
Univ of Missouri/Rolla	MO	12,292	HC
Univ of Missouri/St. Louis	MO	11,656	VC
Univ of Mobile	AL	13,620	C
Univ of Montana	MT	9,395	C
Univ of Montevallo	AL	8,478	C
Univ of Nebr at Kearney	NE	8,286	NC
Univ of Nebr at Lincoln	NE	9,975	C+
Univ of Nebr at Omaha	NE	8,080	C
Univ of Nevada/Las Vegas	NV	11,566	C
Univ of Nevada/Reno	NV	9,792	C
Univ of New Hampshire	NH	14,828	VC
Univ of New Haven	CT	28,650	C
Univ of New Mexico	NM	9,223	C
Univ of New Orleans	LA	7,356	C
Univ of North Alabama	AL	7,972	NC
Univ of N Car at Asheville	NC	8,079	VC
Univ of N Car at Chapel Hill	NC	10,117	MC
Univ of N Car at Charlotte	NC	8,185	C
Univ of N Car at Greensboro	NC	8,248	C
Univ of N Car at Pembroke	NC	6,929	LC
Univ of N Car at Wilmington	NC	8,940	VC
Univ of N Dak	ND	8,390	C
Univ of North Florida	FL	8,769	VC
Univ of North Texas	TX	7,629	C
Univ of Northern Colo	CO	8,987	C
Univ of Northern Iowa	IA	9,834	C
Univ of Notre Dame	IN	34,442	MC
Univ of Okla	OK	9,226	VC
Univ of Oregon	OR	11,479	VC
Univ of Pennsylvania	PA	37,960	MC
Univ of Pittsburgh at Bradford	PA	15,294	C
Univ of Pittsburgh at Johnstown	PA	15,216	LC
Univ of Pittsburgh at Pittsburgh	PA	16,074	HC
Univ of Portland	OR	28,500	VC
Univ of PR at Humacao	PR	1,245	
Univ of PR/Cayey Univ College	PR	1,245	
Univ of PR/Mayaguez	PR		
Univ of PR/Rio Piedras	PR	5,730	
Univ of Puget Sound	WA	31,760	HC
Univ of Redlands	CA	32,576	VC
Univ of Rhode Island	RI	13,720	VC
Univ of Richmond	VA	30,100	MC
Univ of Rio Grande	OH	8,728	NC
Univ of Rochester	NY	32,979	HC
Univ of St. Francis	IN	20,964	C
Univ of St. Mary	KS	18,868	C
Univ of St. Thomas	MN	26,918	VC
Univ of St. Thomas	TX	21,952	VC
Univ of San Diego	CA	33,156	HC
Univ of San Francisco	CA	34,700	VC
Univ of Science and Arts of Okla	OK	5,982	C
Univ of Scranton	PA	30,836	VC
Univ of Sioux Falls	SD	16,390	C
Univ of South Alabama	AL	7,760	LC
Univ of S Car at Aiken	SC	7,828	LC
Univ of S Car at Columbia	SC	10,048	VC
Univ of S Car at Spartanburg	SC	9,936	C+
Univ of S Dak	SD	7,710	C+
Univ of South Florida	FL	9,454	C
Univ of Southern Calif	CA	37,459	MC
Univ of Southern Colo	CO	7,821	LC
Univ of Southern Indiana	IN	9,025	LC
Univ of Southern Maine	ME	11,212	C
Univ of Southern Miss	MS	8,324	LC
Univ of Tampa	FL	23,982	VC
Univ of Tenn at Chattanooga	TN	7,783	C
Univ of Tenn at Knoxville	TN	8,214	C
Univ of Tenn at Martin	TN	7,748	C
Univ of Texas at Arlington	TX	7,192	LC
Univ of Texas at Austin	TX	10,630	HC
Univ of Texas at Dallas	TX	10,234	HC
Univ of Texas at El Paso	TX	5,799	NC
Univ of Texas at San Antonio	TX	9,088	NC
Univ of Texas-Pan American	TX	5,954	LC
Univ of the District of Columbia	DC	2,070	LC
Univ of the Incarnate Word	TX	21,772	LC
Univ of the Ozarks	AR	16,574	C
Univ of the Pacific	CA	31,090	VC
Univ of the Sacred Heart	PR	5,590	
Univ of the Sciences in Philadelphia	PA	29,310	VC
Univ of the South	TN	30,855	HC
Univ of Toledo	OH	12,479	NC
Univ of Tulsa	OK	22,090	VC+
Univ of Utah	UT	9,205	C
Univ of Vermont	VT	16,316	VC
Univ of Virginia	VA	11,740	MC
Univ of Virginia's College at Wise	VA	10,116	C
Univ of West Alabama	AL	6,048	C
Univ of West Florida	FL	8,470	C
Univ of Wisc/Eau Claire	WI	8,463	VC
Univ of Wisc/Green Bay	WI	8,154	C
Univ of Wisc/La Crosse	WI	8,991	VC
Univ of Wisc/Madison	WI	8,262	VC
Univ of Wisc/Milwaukee	WI	9,427	LC
Univ of Wisc/Oshkosh	WI	6,130	LC
Univ of Wisc/Parkside	WI	6,160	LC
Univ of Wisc/Platteville	WI	8,450	C
Univ of Wisc/River Falls	WI	8,358	LC
Univ of Wisc/Stevens Point	WI	8,116	VC
Univ of Wisc/Superior	WI	7,051	C+
Univ of Wisc/Whitewater	WI	8,626	C
Univ of Wyoming	WY	8,636	C
Upper Iowa Univ	IA	20,076	C
Ursinus College	PA	34,400	VC
Utah State Univ	UT	7,371	C
Utica College	NY	28,340	C
Valdosta State Univ	GA	7,798	C
Valley City State Univ	ND	7,281	LC
Valparaiso Univ	IN	26,118	VC+
Vanderbilt Univ	TN	37,897	MC
Vanguard Univ of Southern Calif	CA	22,208	C
Vassar College	NY	37,030	MC
Villa Julie College	MD	18,393	C
Villanova Univ	PA	35,050	HC
Virginia Commonwealth Univ	VA	9,030	C
Virginia Military Inst	VA	9,968	C+
Virginia Polytechnic Inst and State Univ	VA	9,179	C
Virginia State Univ	VA	10,358	C
Virginia Union Univ	VA	15,358	LC
Virginia Wesleyan College	VA	25,350	C
Viterbo Univ	WI	20,430	C
Wabash College	IN	27,932	VC
Wagner College	NY	29,900	VC
Wake Forest Univ	NC	34,090	MC
Walla Walla College	WA	21,600	NC
Walsh Univ	OH	20,890	C
Warren Wilson College	NC	21,794	VC
Wartburg College	IA	21,165	VC
Washburn Univ of Topeka	KS	8,984	NC
Washington and Jefferson College	PA	29,570	VC
Washington and Lee Univ	VA	29,663	MC
Washington College	MD	30,540	VC
Washington State Univ	WA	11,334	C
Washington Univ in St. Louis	MO	38,293	MC
Wayland Baptist Univ	TX	11,919	NC
Wayne State College	NE	7,352	NC
Wayne State Univ	MI	11,774	C
Waynesburg College	PA	19,370	C
Weber State Univ	UT	7,945	NC
Wellesley College	MA	36,516	MC
Wells College	NY	21,122	VC
Wesleyan College	GA	17,870	VC
Wesleyan Univ	CT	35,139	MC
West Chester Univ of Pennsylvania	PA	11,164	C
West Liberty State College	WV	7,868	LC
West Texas A&M Univ	TX	7,533	C
West Virginia State College	WV	6,264	NC
West Virginia Univ	WV	9,370	C
West Virginia Univ Inst of Technology	WV	7,518	NC
West Virginia Wesleyan College	WV	22,920	C
Western Carolina Univ	NC	6,742	C
Western Conn State Univ	CT	11,625	C
Western Illinois Univ	IL	10,363	C
Western Kentucky Univ	KY	6,834	C
Western Mich Univ	MI	12,031	C
Western New England College	MA	28,924	C
Western New Mexico Univ	NM	5,950	LC
Western Oregon Univ	OR	10,281	C
Western State College of Colo	CO	9,014	C
Western Washington Univ	WA	10,119	VC
Westminster College	MO	18,150	C+
Westminster College	PA	22,960	C
Westminster College	UT	17,226	C
Westmont College	CA	33,062	VC+
Wheaton College	IL	21,934	HC
Wheaton College	MA	36,330	HC
Wheeling Jesuit Univ	WV	22,660	C
Whitman College	WA	32,526	HC+
Whittier College	CA	29,108	C
Whitworth College	WA	26,428	VC+
Wichita State Univ	KS	8,092	C
Widener Univ	PA	27,020	C
Wilberforce Univ	OH	14,937	LC
Wiley College	TX	8,100	LC
Wilkes Univ	PA	28,060	C
Willamette Univ	OR	32,032	VC+
William Carey College	MS	10,150	LC
William Jewell College	MO	21,320	VC
William Paterson Univ of New Jersey	NJ	14,450	C
Williams College	MA	32,270	MC
Wilmington College	OH	24,172	LC
Wilson College	PA	23,912	C
Wingate Univ	NC	21,200	C
Winona State Univ	MN		C
Winston-Salem State Univ	NC	8,926	LC
Winthrop Univ	SC	11,302	C
Wisc Lutheran College	WI	21,430	VC
Wittenberg Univ	OH	31,316	VC
Wofford College	SC	26,710	HC
Worcester Polytechnic Inst	MA	37,404	HC

ST = STATE $IS = IN-STATE COSTS SR = SELECTOR RATING

School ST $IS SR

Worcester State College MA 10,005 C
Wright State Univ OH 11,490 LC
Xavier Univ OH 26,850 VC+
Xavier Univ of Louisiana LA 17,600 C
Yale Univ CT 37,000 MC
Yeshiva Univ NY 21,400 C
York College of
  Pennsylvania PA 14,500 VC
Youngstown State Univ OH 11,148 NC

CHILD CARE/CHILD AND FAMILY STUDIES

Albright College PA 30,579 C
Alcorn State Univ MS 7,290 C
Ashland Univ OH 24,464 C
Baylor Univ TX 23,864 VC
Bennington College VT 35,910 HC
Berea College KY 5,030 VC+
Bowling Green State Univ OH 13,036 C
Central Missouri State Univ MO 9,776 C
Chestnut Hill College PA 26,450 LC
Concordia Univ/St.Paul MN 24,486 C
East Carolina Univ NC 8,671 C
Eastern Kentucky Univ KY 7,708 C
Edgewood College WI 20,520 C
Eureka College IL 24,980 LC
Florida State Univ FL 9,028 HC
Freed-Hardeman Univ TN NC
Gallaudet Univ DC 16,554 SP
Georgetown College KY 22,000 VC
Georgia Southern Univ GA 8,540 C
Indiana State Univ IN 10,719 LC
Indiana Univ of
  Pennsylvania PA 10,489 LC
Iowa State Univ IA 10,768 VC
Jackson State Univ MS 8,382 C
Lasell College MA 26,000 C
Medaille College NY 20,060 C
Metropolitan College of
  New York NY 15,771 C
N Car Central Univ NC 7,534 LC
N Dak State Univ ND 8,435 C
Northern Illinois Univ IL 11,472 C
Northwest Missouri State
  Univ MO 9,334 C
Ohio Univ OH 14,448 C
Okla Christian Univ OK 17,690 NC
Okla State Univ OK 9,216 VC
Park Univ MO 10,780 C+
Plymouth State Univ NH 12,298 LC
Portland State Univ OR 12,453 C
Purdue Univ/West Lafayette IN 12,560 VC
Seton Hill Univ PA 24,930 C
Southwest Missouri State
  Univ MO 8,918 C
St. Joseph's, Suffolk NY 11,297 C
SUNY/College at Oneonta NY 11,870 VC
SUNY/College at
  Plattsburgh NY 11,700 C
Syracuse Univ NY 34,720 VC
Tenn Tech Univ TN 8,670 VC
Texas A&M Univ at
  Kingsville TX 6,740 LC
Texas State Univ TX 9,320 VC
Univ of Arizona AZ 10,413 VC
Univ of Georgia GA 8,656 VC
Univ of Louisiana at Monroe LA 5,207 NC
Univ of Maine ME 12,080 C+
Univ of Nevada/Reno NV 9,792 C
Univ of New Mexico NM 9,223 C
Univ of N Car at Chapel Hill NC 10,117 MC
Univ of N Car at Charlotte NC 8,185 C
Univ of N Car at
  Greensboro NC 8,248 C
Univ of Tenn at Knoxville TN 8,214 C
Univ of Tenn at Martin TN 7,748 C
Univ of Texas at Austin TX 10,630 HC
Univ of Wisc/Madison WI 8,262 VC
Univ of Wisc/Stout WI 9,718 C
Ursuline College OH 22,728 LC
Utah State Univ UT 7,371 C
Virginia Polytechnic Inst
  and State Univ VA 9,179 C
West Virginia Univ WV 9,370 C
Wheelock College MA 29,000 C
Youngstown State Univ OH 11,148 NC

CHILD PSYCHOLOGY/ DEVELOPMENT

Alverno College WI 18,898 C
Appalachian State Univ NC 7,637 VC
Bay Path College MA 24,910 C
Bethel Univ TN 12,980 C
Bluffton College OH 23,694 C
Cal State, Bakersfield CA 6,090 LC
Cal State, Chico CA 8,598 LC
Cal State, Fresno CA 8,414 LC
Cal State, Fullerton CA 6,648 C
Cal State, Los Angeles CA 5,778 C
Cal State, Northridge CA 7,757 LC
Cal State, San Bernardino CA 15,238 LC
Cal State, Stanislaus CA 9,874 C
Claflin Univ SC 14,838 C+

Colby-Sawyer College NH 27,850 LC
College of the Ozarks MO 3,500 VC+
East Tenn State Univ TN 8,497 C
Eastern Nazarene College MA 19,433 LC
Fort Valley State Univ GA 6,960 C
Hope International Univ CA 16,940 NC
Humboldt State Univ CA 9,400 C
Iowa State Univ IA 10,768 VC
Kansas State Univ KS 8,728 VC
Madonna Univ MI 11,504 VC
Marygrove College MI 17,550 C
Meredith College NC 23,065 C
Mich State Univ MI 11,933 VC
Mills College CA 33,371 VC
Missouri Baptist Univ MO 18,010 C
Mount Ida College MA 25,596 LC
Mount St. Mary's College CA 28,307 VC
New Mexico State Univ NM 7,932 C
N Car Agricultural and
  Technical State Univ NC 6,659 LC
N Car Central Univ NC 7,534 LC
Point Loma Nazarene Univ CA 21,380 VC
St. Joseph College CT 29,685 C
San Diego State Univ CA 10,321 C
Siena Heights Univ MI 16,140 LC
Spelman College GA 19,215 C+
Stephen F. Austin State
  Univ TX 7,552 C
Texas Woman's Univ TX 7,804 LC
Thomas Edison State
  College NJ 3,325 SP
Tufts Univ MA 38,233 MC
Univ of La Verne CA 28,600 C
Univ of Minn/Twin Cities MN 13,160 VC
Univ of North Texas TX 7,629 C
Univ of Pittsburgh at
  Pittsburgh PA 16,074 HC
Univ of St. Mary KS 18,868 C
Utica College NY 28,340 C
Vanderbilt Univ TN 37,897 MC
Whittier College CA 29,108 C

CHINESE

Arizona State Univ-Main AZ 10,048 C
Bard College NY 37,352 HC+
Bates College ME 37,500 MC
Bennington College VT 35,910 HC
Brigham Young Univ UT 8,504 NC
Central Washington Univ WA 9,768 C
CUNY/Hunter College NY 6,729 C+
Colgate Univ NY 37,095 MC
Conn College CT 37,900 MC
Dartmouth College NH 37,770 MC
George Washington Univ DC 41,030 MC
Georgetown Univ DC 38,242 MC
Grinnell College IA 31,060 HC+
Harvard Univ/Harvard
  College MA 37,928 MC
Lincoln Univ PA 13,320 C+
Middlebury College VT 38,100 MC
Oakland Univ MI 10,800 C
Ohio State Univ OH 13,080 VC+
Pomona College CA 33,960 MC
Portland State Univ OR 12,453 C
Reed College OR 36,950 MC
Rutgers, The State Univ of
  New Jersey/New
  Brunswick/Piscataway
  Campus NJ 15,800 HC
San Francisco State Univ CA 12,070 C
Stanford Univ CA 37,612 MC
SUNY/Univ at Albany NY 12,951 VC
Tufts Univ MA 38,233 MC
Univ of Calif at Berkeley CA 15,563 MC
Univ of Calif at Davis CA 14,995 VC
Univ of Calif at Irvine CA 19,808 VC
Univ of Calif at Los Angeles CA 15,330 MC
Univ of Calif at Riverside CA 15,300 C
Univ of Calif at San Diego CA 14,127 HC
Univ of Calif at Santa
  Barbara CA 11,732 VC
Univ of Colo at Boulder CO 10,774 VC
Univ of Hawaii at Manoa HI 9,565 VC
Univ of Maryland/College
  Park MD 14,227 HC
Univ of Mass Amherst MA 13,980 C+
Univ of Mich/Ann Arbor MI 13,864 HC+
Univ of Minn/Twin Cities MN 13,160 VC
Univ of Notre Dame IN 34,442 MC
Univ of Oregon OR 11,479 VC
Univ of Pittsburgh at
  Pittsburgh PA 16,074 HC
Univ of Utah UT 9,205 C
Univ of Wisc/Madison WI 8,262 VC
Washington Univ in St.
  Louis MO 38,293 MC
Wellesley College MA 36,516 MC
Yale Univ CT 37,000 MC

CHIROPRACTIC

Juniata College PA 29,080 VC
Univ of Hartford CT 31,080 C
Univ of Southern Colo CO 7,821 LC

CHRISTIAN EDUCATION

Anderson Univ IN 19,430 LC
Bethany College KS 18,675 LC
Biola Univ CA 25,964 VC
Catawba College NC 20,500 C
Cedarville Univ OH 19,954 VC
Columbia College SC 22,658 LC
Concordia Univ CA 24,420 C
Concordia Univ Nebr NE 20,302 C+
Defiance College OH 22,615 C
Erskine College SC 23,166 VC
Hannibal-LaGrange College MO 13,940 C
Malone College OH 20,995 C
MidAmerica Nazarene Univ KS 18,688 C
Mount Vernon Nazarene
  Univ OH 18,925 C
Muskingum College OH 20,680 C
Northwestern College MN 22,820 C+
Northwestern College of
  Iowa IA 19,640 C+
Olivet Nazarene Univ IL 20,480 C
Pfeiffer Univ NC 18,980 C
Seattle Pacific Univ WA 25,944 VC
Southeastern College FL 11,648 LC
Spring Arbor Univ MI 20,206 C
Taylor Univ IN 23,820 VC+
Toccoa Falls College GA 15,600 C
Westminster College PA 22,960 C

CHRISTIAN STUDIES

Alderson-Broaddus College WV 19,640 C
Bluefield College VA 15,575 C
Brewton-Parker College GA 14,200 LC
Bryan College TN 17,900 VC
Calif Baptist Univ CA 19,924 C
Campbellsville Univ KY 17,680 C
Eastern Nazarene College MA 19,433 LC
Grand Canyon Univ AZ 30,000 LC
Hillsdale College MI 22,450 HC
Houston Baptist Univ TX 16,905 C
Howard Payne Univ TX 15,176 C
Lewis Univ IL 22,950 C+
Miss College MS 14,574 C
Rochester College MI 16,718 C
Seton Hall Univ NJ 30,130 VC
Shorter College GA 17,370 C
Texas Wesleyan Univ TX 16,245 C
Trinity International Univ IL 22,980 C
Union Univ TN 18,800 VC
Univ of Chicago IL 35,087 MC
Univ of St. Thomas MN 26,918 VC
William Tyndale College MI 12,170 NC

CITY/COMMUNITY/REGIONAL PLANNING

Alabama A&M Univ AL 5,100 LC
Calif Polytechnic State Univ CA 8,747 VC
Cornell Univ NY 38,253 MC
East Carolina Univ NC 8,671 C
Eastern Mich Univ MI 11,478 C
Eastern Univ PA 24,020 C
Indiana Univ of
  Pennsylvania PA 10,489 C
Iowa State Univ IA 10,768 VC
Mansfield Univ PA 11,220 C
Mich State Univ MI 11,933 VC
New Mexico State Univ NM 7,932 C
Plymouth State Univ NH 12,298 LC
Texas State Univ TX 9,320 VC
Univ of Arizona AZ 10,413 VC
Univ of Cincinnati OH 14,736 C
Univ of Illinois at Urbana-
  Champaign IL 11,316 HC+
Univ of New Hampshire NH 14,828 VC
Univ of Virginia VA 11,740 MC

CIVIL ENGINEERING

Alabama A&M Univ AL 5,100 LC
Arizona State Univ-Main AZ 10,048 C
Auburn Univ AL 10,396 VC
Bethel College IN 19,670 C
Bradley Univ IL 22,910 VC
Brigham Young Univ UT 8,504 NC
Bucknell Univ PA 35,262 HC+
Calif Inst of Technology CA 31,677 MC
Calif Polytechnic State Univ CA 8,747 VC
Calif State Polytechnic
  Univ, Pomona CA 8,793 C+
Cal State, Chico CA 8,598 LC
Cal State, Fresno CA 8,414 LC
Cal State, Fullerton CA 6,648 C
Cal State, Long Beach CA 8,762 C+
Cal State, Los Angeles CA 5,778 C
Cal State, Sacramento CA 9,543 C
Calvin College MI 22,615 NC
Caribbean Univ PR 3,000 C
Carnegie Mellon Univ PA 32,682 MC
Carroll College MT 20,576 VC
Case Western Reserve
  Univ OH 32,002 MC
Catholic Univ of America DC 34,248 VC

Christian Brothers Univ TN 22,290 VC
Citadel, The SC 12,295 C+
CUNY/City College NY 4,230 C+
Clarkson Univ NY 32,226 VC
Clemson Univ SC 11,972 HC
Cleveland State Univ OH 12,308 LC
Colo State Univ CO 9,964 VC
Columbia Univ/Fu
  Foundation School of
  Engineering and Applied
  Science NY 38,590 MC
Cooper Union for the
  Advancement of Science
  and Art NY 10,400 MC
Cornell Univ NY 38,253 MC
Delaware State Univ DE 8,104 LC
Drexel Univ PA 27,655 VC
Duke Univ NC 37,555 MC
Embry-Riddle Aeronautical
  Univ AZ 27,710 C+
Embry-Riddle Aeronautical
  Univ FL 27,730 C+
Florida A&M Univ FL 7,564 C
Florida Inst of Technology FL 28,740 VC
Florida International Univ FL 9,912 VC
Florida State Univ FL 9,028 HC
George Mason Univ VA 9,732 VC
George Washington Univ DC 41,030 MC
Georgia Inst of Technology GA 10,340 HC+
Gonzaga Univ WA 26,766 HC
Hofstra Univ NY 27,112 VC
Howard Univ DC 16,505 C
Illinois Inst of Technology IL 26,456 HC+
Indiana Inst of Technology IN 21,620 C
Iowa State Univ IA 10,768 VC
Johns Hopkins Univ MD 38,372 MC
Kansas State Univ KS 8,728 VC
Lafayette College PA 35,746 MC
Lamar Univ TX 6,816 LC
Lawrence Tech Univ MI 20,487 C
Lehigh Univ PA 37,570 HC+
Louisiana State Univ and
  A&M College LA 9,126 VC
Louisiana Tech Univ LA 7,361 C
Loyola Marymount Univ CA 32,194 VC
Manhattan College NY 27,400 VC
Marquette Univ WI 27,594 VC
Mass Inst of Technology MA 38,310 MC
McNeese State Univ LA 5,259 LC
Merrimack College MA 29,625 C
Mich State Univ MI 11,933 VC
Mich Tech Univ MI 13,235 VC
Miss State Univ MS 9,139 C
Montana State Univ-
  Bozeman MT 9,515 C
Morgan State Univ MD 11,470 C
New Jersey Inst of
  Technology NJ 16,396 VC
New Mexico State Univ NM 7,932 C
N Car Agricultural and
  Technical State Univ NC 6,659 LC
N Car State Univ NC 9,886 VC
N Dak State Univ ND 8,435 C
Northeastern Univ MA 35,650 HC
Northern Arizona Univ AZ 9,002 C
Northwestern Univ IL 37,491 MC
Norwich Univ VT 21,064 LC
Ohio Northern Univ OH 27,765 VC
Ohio State Univ OH 13,080 VC+
Ohio Univ OH 14,448 C
Okla State Univ OK 9,216 VC
Old Dominion Univ VA 10,441 C
Oregon Inst of Technology OR 8,718 C
Oregon State Univ OR 11,055 C
Penn State Univ/Univ Park
  Campus PA 15,646 HC
Pennsylvania College of
  Technology PA 15,126 NC
Polytechnic Univ/Brooklyn NY 33,770 VC
Portland State Univ OR 12,453 C
Prairie View A&M Univ TX 9,418 NC
Princeton Univ NJ 36,649 MC
Purdue Univ/West Lafayette IN 12,560 VC
Rensselaer Polytechnic Inst NY 37,579 HC+
Rice Univ TX 27,550 MC
Rose-Hulman Inst of
  Technology IN 31,425 HC+
Rowan Univ NJ 14,506 V
Rutgers, The State Univ of
  New Jersey/New
  Brunswick/Piscataway
  Campus NJ 15,800 HC
St. Martin's College WA 23,245 C
San Diego State Univ CA 10,321 C
San Francisco State Univ CA 12,070 C
San Jose State Univ CA 8,187 C
Santa Clara Univ CA 34,701 HC
Savannah State Univ GA 7,328 LC
Seattle Univ WA 24,183 VC
S Dak School of Mines and
  Technology SD 7,854 C+
S Dak State Univ SD 7,782 C
Southern Illinois Univ
  Carbondale IL 10,407 C
Southern Illinois Univ
  Edwardsville IL 8,724 C

ST = STATE $IS = IN-STATE COSTS   SR = SELECTOR RATING

School	ST	$IS	SR
Southern Univ and A&M College	LA	7,372	LC
Stanford Univ	CA	37,612	MC
SUNY/Univ at Buffalo	NY	12,563	VC
Stevens Inst of Technology	NJ	35,300	HC+
Syracuse Univ	NY	34,720	HC
Temple Univ	PA	15,912	C
Tenn State Univ	TN	9,048	LC
Tenn Tech Univ	TN	8,670	VC
Texas A&M Univ	TX	11,081	HC
Texas A&M Univ at Galveston	TX	9,948	C+
Texas A&M Univ at Kingsville	TX	6,740	LC
Texas Tech Univ	TX	10,768	VC
Tri-State Univ-Main Campus	IN	23,600	C
Tufts Univ	MA	38,233	MC
Tulane Univ	LA	37,451	HC+
United States Air Force Academy	CO		HC+
United States Coast Guard Academy	CT		MC
United States Military Academy	NY		MC
Universidad Politecnica de PR	PR	5,370	
Univ of Akron	OH	13,134	NC
Univ of Alabama	AL	9,040	C+
Univ of Alabama at Birmingham	AL	12,901	C
Univ of Alabama in Huntsville	AL	9,126	VC
Univ of Alaska Anchorage	AK	9,100	NC
Univ of Alaska Fairbanks	AK	9,295	C
Univ of Arizona	AZ	10,413	VC
Univ of Arkansas	AR	9,855	VC
Univ of Calif at Berkeley	CA	15,563	MC
Univ of Calif at Davis	CA	14,995	VC
Univ of Calif at Irvine	CA	19,808	HC
Univ of Calif at Los Angeles	CA	15,330	MC
Univ of Central Florida	FL	10,038	VC
Univ of Cincinnati	OH	14,736	C
Univ of Colo at Boulder	CO	10,774	VC
Univ of Colo at Denver	CO	3,302	C
Univ of Conn	CT	14,608	VC
Univ of Dayton	OH	24,850	VC
Univ of Delaware	DE	12,616	HC
Univ of Detroit Mercy	MI	25,582	C
Univ of Evansville	IN	24,190	VC
Univ of Florida	FL	8,580	MC
Univ of Hartford	CT	31,080	C
Univ of Hawaii at Manoa	HI	9,565	VC
Univ of Houston	TX	9,818	C
Univ of Idaho	ID	8,216	C
Univ of Illinois at Chicago	IL	13,418	C
Univ of Illinois at Urbana-Champaign	IL	11,316	HC+
Univ of Iowa	IA	10,923	VC
Univ of Kansas	KS	8,923	VC
Univ of Kentucky	KY	7,765	C
Univ of Louisiana at Lafayette	LA	5,826	C
Univ of Louisville	KY	8,762	VC
Univ of Maine	ME	12,080	C+
Univ of Maryland/College Park	MD	14,227	HC
Univ of Mass Amherst	MA	13,980	C+
Univ of Mass Dartmouth	MA	12,835	C
Univ of Mass Lowell	MA	11,937	VC
Univ of Memphis	TN	8,560	C
Univ of Miami	FL	34,608	HC
Univ of Mich/Ann Arbor	MI	13,864	HC+
Univ of Minn/Twin Cities	MN	13,160	VC
Univ of Miss	MS	7,666	C
Univ of Missouri/Columbia	MO	13,782	VC
Univ of Missouri/Kansas City	MO	13,416	VC
Univ of Missouri/Rolla	MO	12,292	HC
Univ of Missouri/St. Louis	MO	11,656	VC
Univ of Nebr at Lincoln	NE	9,975	C+
Univ of Nevada/Las Vegas	NV	11,566	C
Univ of Nevada/Reno	NV	9,792	C
Univ of New Hampshire	NH	14,828	VC
Univ of New Haven	CT	28,650	C
Univ of New Mexico	NM	9,223	C
Univ of New Orleans	LA	7,356	C
Univ of N Car at Charlotte	NC	8,185	C
Univ of N Dak	ND	8,390	C
Univ of North Florida	FL	8,769	VC
Univ of Notre Dame	IN	34,442	MC
Univ of Okla	OK	9,226	VC
Univ of Pennsylvania	PA	37,960	MC
Univ of Pittsburgh at Pittsburgh	PA	16,074	HC
Univ of Portland	OR	28,500	VC
Univ of PR/Mayaguez	PR		
Univ of Rhode Island	RI	13,720	VC
Univ of South Alabama	AL	7,760	LC
Univ of S Car at Columbia	SC	10,048	VC
Univ of South Florida	FL	9,454	C
Univ of Southern Calif	CA	37,459	MC
Univ of Tenn at Knoxville	TN	8,214	C
Univ of Texas at Arlington	TX	7,192	LC
Univ of Texas at Austin	TX	10,630	HC
Univ of Texas at El Paso	TX	5,799	NC
Univ of Texas at San Antonio	TX	9,088	NC
Univ of the District of Columbia	DC	2,070	LC
Univ of the Pacific	CA	31,090	VC
Univ of Toledo	OH	12,479	NC
Univ of Utah	UT	9,205	C
Univ of Vermont	VT	16,316	VC
Univ of Virginia	VA	11,740	MC
Univ of Washington	WA	10,361	VC
Univ of Wisc/Madison	WI	8,262	VC
Univ of Wisc/Milwaukee	WI	9,427	LC
Univ of Wisc/Platteville	WI	8,450	C
Univ of Wyoming	WY	8,636	C
Utah State Univ	UT	7,371	C
Valparaiso Univ	IN	26,118	VC+
Vanderbilt Univ	TN	37,897	MC
Villanova Univ	PA	35,050	HC
Virginia Military Inst	VA	9,968	C+
Virginia Polytechnic Inst and State Univ	VA	9,179	C
Washington State Univ	WA	11,334	C
Washington Univ in St. Louis	MO	38,293	MC
Wayne State Univ	MI	11,774	C
West Virginia Univ	WV	9,370	C
West Virginia Univ Inst of Technology	WV	7,518	NC
Western Kentucky Univ	KY	6,834	C
Western Mich Univ	MI	12,031	C
Widener Univ	PA	27,020	C
Worcester Polytechnic Inst	MA	37,404	HC
Youngstown State Univ	OH	11,148	NC

CIVIL ENGINEERING TECHNOLOGY

School	ST	$IS	SR
Alabama A&M Univ	AL	5,100	LC
Central Conn State Univ	CT	12,090	C
Fairleigh Dickinson Univ/Metropolitan Campus	NJ	28,584	C
Fairmont State	WV	8,280	LC
Georgia Southern Univ	GA	8,540	C
Lincoln Univ	MO	7,158	NC
Metropolitan State College of Denver	CO	2,338	LC
Montana State Univ-Northern	MT	8,600	NC
Murray State Univ	KY	7,816	VC
Old Dominion Univ	VA	10,441	C
Pennsylvania College of Technology	PA	15,126	NC
Point Park Univ	PA	21,840	C
Rochester Inst of Technology	NY	29,217	VC+
S Car State Univ	SC	6,586	LC
Southern Polytechnic State Univ	GA	7,620	VC
Texas Southern Univ	TX	8,920	NC
Thomas Edison State College	NJ	3,325	SP
Univ of Houston	TX	9,818	C
Univ of N Car at Charlotte	NC	8,185	C
Univ of Pittsburgh at Johnstown	PA	15,216	LC
Univ of Southern Colo	CO	7,821	LC
Wentworth Inst of Technology	MA	23,000	C
Western Kentucky Univ	KY	6,834	C
Youngstown State Univ	OH	11,148	NC

CLASSICAL LANGUAGES

School	ST	$IS	SR
Agnes Scott College	GA	28,230	HC
Asbury College	KY	20,704	VC
Ball State Univ	IN	8,660	C
Bard College	NY	37,352	HC+
Beloit College	WI	29,864	HC
Berea College	KY	5,030	VC+
Bryn Mawr College	PA	36,890	HC+
Calvin College	MI	22,615	NC
Carroll College	MT	20,576	VC
Concordia College: Moorhead	MN	22,460	VC+
DePauw Univ	IN	31,500	HC
Dickinson College	PA	35,825	HC
Duke Univ	NC	37,555	MC
Duquesne Univ	PA	26,907	VC
Eastern Mich Univ	MI	11,478	C
Fordham Univ	NY	35,066	HC
La Salle Univ	PA	31,260	VC
Luther College	IA	25,700	VC
Marquette Univ	WI	27,594	VC
Ohio Univ	OH	14,448	C
Rockford College	IL	28,310	VC
St. Bonaventure Univ	NY	24,455	LC
St. Mary's College of Calif	CA	32,850	VC
St. Peter's College	NJ	22,292	LC
Santa Clara Univ	CA	34,701	HC
Scripps College	CA	35,700	HC+
Siena College	NY	25,310	VC
Texas Tech Univ	TX	10,768	VC
Univ of Calif at Berkeley	CA	15,563	MC
Univ of Calif at Santa Cruz	CA	16,505	VC
Univ of Houston	TX	9,818	C
Univ of Kansas	KS	8,923	VC
Univ of Mass Boston	MA	6,227	C
Univ of Mich/Ann Arbor	MI	13,864	HC+
Univ of Minn/Twin Cities	MN	13,160	VC
Univ of St. Thomas	MN	26,918	VC
Vanderbilt Univ	TN	37,897	MC
Washington Univ in St. Louis	MO	38,293	MC
Wright State Univ	OH	11,490	LC
Yeshiva Univ	NY	21,400	C

CLASSICAL/ANCIENT CIVILIZATION

School	ST	$IS	SR
Agnes Scott College	GA	28,230	HC
Bates College	ME	37,500	MC
Beloit College	WI	29,864	HC
Boston College	MA	33,284	MC
Boston Univ	MA	38,194	HC+
Bowdoin College	ME	37,790	MC
Bowling Green State Univ	OH	13,036	C
Brown Univ	RI	38,174	MC
Carleton College	MN	34,395	MC
Centre College	KY	27,300	HC
Christendom College	VA	18,410	VC+
CUNY/Queens College	NY	4,362	C
Clark Univ	MA	32,115	VC
Cleveland State Univ	OH	12,308	LC
Coe College	IA	27,385	VC
Colby College	ME	37,570	MC
Columbia Univ/Barnard College	NY	36,990	MC
Columbia Univ/Columbia College	NY	38,590	MC
Columbia Univ/School of General Studies	NY	35,000	C
Cornell College	IA	27,825	VC+
Cornell Univ	NY	38,253	MC
Creighton Univ	NE	26,748	VC+
Dartmouth College	NH	37,770	MC
Denison Univ	OH	33,050	HC
DePauw Univ	IN	31,500	HC
Dickinson College	PA	35,825	HC
Duke Univ	NC	37,555	MC
Duquesne Univ	PA	26,907	VC
Earlham College	IN	29,976	VC+
Emory Univ	GA	36,872	MC
Florida State Univ	FL	9,028	HC
Fordham Univ	NY	35,066	HC
Gonzaga Univ	WA	26,766	HC
Hamilton College	NY	37,560	MC
Hawaii Pacific Univ	HI	19,218	C
Hollins Univ	VA	27,965	VC
Indiana Univ Bloomington	IN	12,389	VC
Kalamazoo College	MI	26,955	HC+
Lehigh Univ	PA	37,570	HC+
Loras College	IA	24,233	C
Loyola College in Maryland	MD	34,560	HC
Loyola Marymount Univ	CA	32,194	VC
Loyola Univ Chicago	IL	31,164	VC
Loyola Univ New Orleans	LA	31,036	VC+
Miami Univ	OH	15,033	HC
Mich State Univ	MI	11,933	VC
Mount Holyoke College	MA	37,918	HC+
New York Univ	NY	39,406	MC
North Central College	IL	25,656	VC
Rhodes College	TN	26,466	HC+
Rice Univ	TX	27,550	MC
Rollins College	FL	34,300	VC
St. Louis Univ	MO	29,780	VC+
St. Olaf College	MN	28,500	HC
St. Peter's College	NJ	22,292	LC
Santa Clara Univ	CA	34,701	HC
Scripps College	CA	35,700	HC+
Seton Hall Univ	NJ	30,130	VC
Smith College	MA	37,034	HC+
SUNY/Univ at Albany	NY	12,951	HC
SUNY/Univ at Binghamton	NY	12,787	HC
Swarthmore College	PA	37,716	MC
Sweet Briar College	VA	27,940	C
Syracuse Univ	NY	34,720	HC
Trinity College	CT	38,040	HC+
Univ of Calif at Berkeley	CA	15,563	MC
Univ of Calif at Davis	CA	14,995	VC
Univ of Calif at Irvine	CA	19,808	HC
Univ of Calif at Los Angeles	CA	15,330	MC
Univ of Calif at Riverside	CA	15,300	C
Univ of Chicago	IL	35,087	MC
Univ of Cincinnati	OH	14,736	C
Univ of Evansville	IN	24,190	VC
Univ of Florida	FL	8,580	MC
Univ of Georgia	GA	8,656	VC
Univ of Idaho	ID	8,216	C
Univ of Illinois at Chicago	IL	13,418	C
Univ of Iowa	IA	10,923	VC
Univ of Maryland/Baltimore County	MD	14,668	VC+
Univ of Mich/Ann Arbor	MI	13,864	HC+
Univ of Miss	MS	7,666	C
Univ of N Dak	ND	8,390	C
Univ of Notre Dame	IN	34,442	MC
Univ of Oregon	OR	11,479	VC
Univ of Richmond	VA	30,100	MC
Univ of St. Thomas	MN	26,918	VC
Univ of Tenn at Knoxville	TN	8,214	C
Univ of Texas at Arlington	TX	7,192	LC
Univ of Texas at Austin	TX	10,630	HC
Vassar College	NY	37,030	MC
Wellesley College	MA	36,516	MC
Wesleyan Univ	CT	35,139	MC
Wheaton College	MA	36,330	HC
Willamette Univ	OR	32,032	VC+
Yale Univ	CT	37,000	MC

CLASSICS

School	ST	$IS	SR
Agnes Scott College	GA	28,230	HC
Amherst College	MA	37,470	MC
Assumption College	MA	29,375	C
Augustana College	IL	26,610	VC+
Austin College	TX	24,747	HC
Ball State Univ	IN	8,660	C
Bard College	NY	37,352	HC+
Baylor Univ	TX	23,864	VC
Boston College	MA	33,284	MC
Boston Univ	MA	38,194	HC+
Bowdoin College	ME	37,790	MC
Brandeis Univ	MA	38,198	MC
Brigham Young Univ	UT	8,504	HC
Brown Univ	RI	38,174	MC
Bryn Mawr College	PA	36,890	HC+
Bucknell Univ	PA	35,262	HC+
Calvin College	MI	22,615	NC
Carleton College	MN	34,395	MC
Case Western Reserve Univ	OH	32,002	MC
Catholic Univ of America	DC	34,248	VC
CUNY/Brooklyn College	NY	4,353	C+
CUNY/Hunter College	NY	6,729	C+
Colby College	ME	37,570	MC
Colgate Univ	NY	37,095	MC
College of Charleston	SC	11,887	HC
College of New Rochelle	NY	21,800	C
College of Notre Dame of Maryland	MD	27,700	C
College of St. Benedict	MN	26,972	VC
College of the Holy Cross	MA	36,451	MC
College of William and Mary	VA	12,224	MC
Colo College	CO	36,860	HC
Columbia Univ/Barnard College	NY	36,990	MC
Columbia Univ/Columbia College	NY	38,590	MC
Columbia Univ/School of General Studies	NY	35,000	C
Conn College	CT	37,900	MC
Cornell Univ	NY	38,253	MC
Dartmouth College	NH	37,770	MC
Davidson College	NC	33,274	MC
Drew Univ/College of Liberal Arts	NJ	35,550	VC
Duquesne Univ	PA	26,907	VC
Elmira College	NY	33,820	VC
Emory Univ	GA	36,872	MC
Florida State Univ	FL	9,028	HC
Franciscan Univ of Steubenville	OH	20,300	VC
Franklin and Marshall College	PA	35,930	HC+
George Washington Univ	DC	41,030	MC
Georgetown Univ	DC	38,242	MC
Georgia State Univ	GA	10,658	C
Gettysburg College	PA	35,646	HC
Grinnell College	IA	31,060	HC+
Gustavus Adolphus College	MN	27,120	VC+
Hamilton College	NY	37,560	MC
Hampden-Sydney College	VA	28,407	VC
Hanover College	IN	25,200	VC
Harvard Univ/Harvard College	MA	37,928	MC
Haverford College	PA	37,900	MC
Hellenic College/Holy Cross Greek Orthodox School of Theology	MA	22,815	C
Hillsdale College	MI	22,450	HC
Hiram College	OH	28,234	VC
Hobart and William Smith Colleges	NY	36,536	HC
Hofstra Univ	NY	27,112	VC
Howard Univ	DC	16,505	C
Indiana Univ Bloomington	IN	12,389	VC
Johns Hopkins Univ	MD	38,372	MC
Kent State Univ	OH	12,932	C
Kenyon College	OH	35,370	HC+
Knox College	IL	30,294	VC+
Lawrence Univ	WI	30,900	HC
Lehigh Univ	PA	37,570	HC+
Lenoir-Rhyne College	NC	19,186	C
Loyola Marymount Univ	CA	32,194	VC
Macalester College	MN	31,944	MC
Manhattanville College	NY	32,420	C+
Marquette Univ	WI	27,594	VC
Mary Washington College	VA	10,166	HC
Middlebury College	VT	38,100	MC
Millsaps College	MS	25,182	VC
Monmouth College	IL	23,600	C
Montclair State Univ	NJ	13,790	C
Moravian College	PA	28,903	VC
Mount Holyoke College	MA	37,918	HC+
New College of Florida	FL	8,906	HC+
New York Univ	NY	39,406	MC
Northwestern Univ	IL	37,491	MC

School	ST	$IS	SR
Oberlin College	OH	36,938	MC
Ohio State Univ	OH	13,080	VC+
Pacific Lutheran Univ	WA	25,715	VC
Penn State Univ/Univ Park Campus	PA	15,646	HC
Pitzer College	CA	37,590	HC
Pomona College	CA	33,960	MC
Princeton Univ	NJ	36,649	MC
Purdue Univ/West Lafayette	IN	12,560	VC
Randolph-Macon College	VA	27,190	C
Randolph-Macon Woman's College	VA	28,430	VC+
Reed College	OR	36,950	MC
Rice Univ	TX	27,550	MC
Rutgers, The State Univ of New Jersey/New Brunswick/Piscataway Campus	NJ	15,800	HC
St. Anselm College	NH	30,250	C
St. John's Univ	MN	26,473	VC
St. Olaf College	MN	28,500	HC
St. Peter's College	NJ	22,292	LC
Samford Univ	AL	18,648	VC
San Diego State Univ	CA	10,321	C
San Francisco State Univ	CA	12,070	C
Santa Clara Univ	CA	34,701	HC
Sarah Lawrence College	NY	41,218	HC
Seattle Pacific Univ	WA	25,944	VC
Skidmore College	NY	37,930	HC
Smith College	MA	37,034	HC+
Southern Illinois Univ Carbondale	IL	10,407	C
Southwestern Univ	TX	25,410	HC
Stanford Univ	CA	37,612	MC
SUNY/Univ at Binghamton	NY	12,787	HC
SUNY/Univ at Buffalo	NY	12,563	VC
Swarthmore College	PA	37,716	MC
Syracuse Univ	NY	34,720	HC
Temple Univ	PA	15,912	C
Trinity College	CT	38,040	HC+
Truman State Univ	MO	9,728	HC+
Tufts Univ	MA	38,233	MC
Tulane Univ	LA	37,451	HC+
Union College	NY	36,005	HC
Univ of Akron	OH	13,134	NC
Univ of Alabama	AL	9,040	C+
Univ of Arizona	AZ	10,413	VC
Univ of Arkansas	AR	9,855	VC
Univ of Calif at Irvine	CA	19,808	HC
Univ of Calif at Riverside	CA	15,300	C
Univ of Calif at San Diego	CA	14,127	HC
Univ of Calif at Santa Barbara	CA	11,732	VC
Univ of Chicago	IL	35,087	MC
Univ of Colo at Boulder	CO	10,774	VC
Univ of Conn	CT	14,608	VC
Univ of Dallas	TX	25,898	VC+
Univ of Hawaii at Manoa	HI	9,565	VC
Univ of Houston	TX	9,818	C
Univ of Illinois at Chicago	IL	13,418	C
Univ of Illinois at Urbana-Champaign	IL	11,316	HC+
Univ of Iowa	IA	10,923	VC
Univ of Maryland/College Park	MD	14,227	HC
Univ of Mass Amherst	MA	13,980	C+
Univ of Mass Boston	MA	6,227	C
Univ of Missouri/Columbia	MO	13,782	VC
Univ of Montana	MT	9,395	C
Univ of Nebr at Lincoln	NE	9,975	C+
Univ of New Hampshire	NH	14,828	VC
Univ of New Mexico	NM	9,223	C
Univ of N Car at Asheville	NC	8,079	VC
Univ of N Car at Chapel Hill	NC	10,117	MC
Univ of N Car at Greensboro	NC	8,248	C
Univ of Okla	OK	9,226	VC
Univ of Oregon	OR	11,479	VC
Univ of Pennsylvania	PA	37,960	MC
Univ of Pittsburgh at Pittsburgh	PA	16,074	HC
Univ of Puget Sound	WA	31,760	HC
Univ of Rhode Island	RI	13,720	VC
Univ of Rochester	NY	32,979	HC
Univ of S Car at Columbia	SC	10,048	VC
Univ of South Florida	FL	9,454	C
Univ of Southern Calif	CA	37,459	MC
Univ of Tenn at Knoxville	TN	8,214	C
Univ of Texas at Austin	TX	10,630	HC
Univ of Texas at San Antonio	TX	9,088	NC
Univ of the Pacific	CA	31,090	VC
Univ of Utah	UT	9,205	C
Univ of Vermont	VT	16,316	VC
Univ of Virginia	VA	11,740	MC
Univ of Washington	WA	10,361	VC
Univ of Wisc/Madison	WI	8,262	VC
Univ of Wisc/Milwaukee	WI	9,427	LC
Ursinus College	PA	34,400	VC
Valparaiso Univ	IN	26,118	VC+
Vanderbilt Univ	TN	37,897	MC
Villanova Univ	PA	35,050	HC
Wabash College	IN	27,932	VC
Wake Forest Univ	NC	34,090	MC
Washington and Lee Univ	VA	29,663	MC
Washington State Univ	WA	11,334	C
Washington Univ in St. Louis	MO	38,293	MC
Wayne State Univ	MI	11,774	C
Wesleyan Univ	CT	35,139	MC
Wheaton College	MA	36,330	HC
Whitman College	WA	32,526	HC+
Williams College	MA	32,270	MC
Xavier Univ	OH	26,850	VC+
Yale Univ	CT	37,000	MC

CLINICAL PSYCHOLOGY

School	ST	$IS	SR
Averett Univ	VA	23,010	LC
Bard College	NY	37,352	HC+
Crichton College	TN	15,215	C
Drake Univ	IA	25,120	VC+
Eastern Nazarene College	MA	19,433	LC
Marywood Univ	PA	26,050	C
Tufts Univ	MA	38,233	MC
Univ of New Haven	CT	28,650	C

CLINICAL SCIENCE

School	ST	$IS	SR
Appalachian State Univ	NC	7,637	VC
Arizona State Univ-Main	AZ	10,048	C
Benedictine Univ	IL	23,840	C
Bethune-Cookman College	FL	16,480	LC
Bloomfield College	NJ	19,250	LC
Brigham Young Univ	UT	8,504	HC
Cal State, Bakersfield	CA	6,090	LC
Cal State, Dominguez Hills	CA	5,840	LC
Cal State, Stanislaus	CA	9,874	C
Campbell Univ	NC	18,268	VC
Carroll College	MT	20,576	VC
Carroll College	WI	22,740	C
Elizabethtown College	PA	28,800	C
Fairleigh Dickinson Univ/College at Florham	NJ	30,130	C
Fairleigh Dickinson Univ/Metropolitan Campus	NJ	28,584	C
Felician College	NJ	24,300	C
Franciscan Univ	IA	19,300	C
George Washington Univ	DC	41,030	MC
Gwynedd-Mercy College	PA	24,225	C
Indiana Univ Southeast	IN	4,504	LC
Indiana Univ-Purdue Univ Indianapolis	IN	8,257	LC
Ithaca College	NY	31,730	HC
Jamestown College	ND	12,600	NC
Jewish Hospital College of Nursing and Allied Health	MO	11,200	SP
Maryville Univ of St. Louis	MO	22,090	VC
MCP Hahnemann Univ	PA	18,510	SP
Mich State Univ	MI	11,933	VC
Monmouth Univ	NJ	26,334	C
New York Inst of Technology	NY	24,205	VC
N Dak State Univ	ND	8,435	C
Northern Illinois Univ	IL	11,472	C
Northern Mich Univ	MI	10,834	C
Olivet Nazarene Univ	IL	20,480	C
Ramapo College of New Jersey	NJ	15,203	VC
Rockhurst Univ	MO	22,960	C+
Rutgers, The State Univ of New Jersey/Newark Campus	NJ	15,624	VC
St. Louis Univ	MO	29,780	VC+
San Francisco State Univ	CA	12,070	C
S Dak State Univ	SD	7,782	C
SUNY/Univ at Stony Brook	NY	12,763	HC
Texas A&M Univ at Corpus Christi	TX	10,269	C
Texas State Univ	TX	9,320	VC
Thomas Edison State College	NJ	3,325	SP
Univ of Kansas	KS	8,923	VC
Univ of Louisiana at Monroe	LA	5,207	NC
Univ of Maine	ME	12,080	C+
Univ of Mass Lowell	MA	11,937	VC
Univ of Nevada/Las Vegas	NV	11,566	C
Univ of N Car at Chapel Hill	NC	10,117	MC
Univ of N Dak	ND	8,390	C
Univ of Rhode Island	RI	13,720	VC
Univ of South Alabama	AL	7,760	LC
Univ of Texas at El Paso	TX	5,799	NC
Univ of Texas at San Antonio	TX	9,088	NC
Univ of Wisc/Milwaukee	WI	9,427	LC
Univ of Wisc/Stevens Point	WI	8,116	VC
Walsh Univ	OH	20,890	C
Weber State Univ	UT	7,945	NC
West Liberty State College	WV	7,868	LC
Western Carolina Univ	NC	6,742	C

CLOTHING AND TEXTILES MANAGEMENT/ PRODUCTION/SERVICES

School	ST	$IS	SR
Appalachian State Univ	NC	7,637	VC
Cheyney Univ of Pennsylvania	PA	9,993	C
College of the Ozarks	MO	3,500	VC+
East Carolina Univ	NC	8,671	C
Eastern Mich Univ	MI	11,478	C
Florida State Univ	FL	9,028	HC
Johnson and Wales Univ	RI	22,965	LC
Louisiana State Univ and A&M College	LA	9,126	VC
Miss Univ for Women	MS	5,446	LC
N Car Agricultural and Technical State Univ	NC	6,659	LC
N Car State Univ	NC	9,886	VC
Northwest Missouri State Univ	MO	9,334	C
Ohio State Univ	OH	13,080	VC+
San Francisco State Univ	CA	12,070	C
Seattle Pacific Univ	WA	25,944	VC
Southern Illinois Univ Carbondale	IL	10,407	C
Southwest Missouri State Univ	MO	8,918	C
Texas Southern Univ	TX	8,920	NC
Texas Tech Univ	TX	10,768	VC
Univ of Alabama	AL	9,040	C+
Univ of Georgia	GA	8,656	VC
Univ of North Texas	TX	7,629	C
Univ of Northern Iowa	IA	9,834	C

COGNITIVE SCIENCE

School	ST	$IS	SR
Averett Univ	VA	23,010	LC
Brown Univ	RI	38,174	MC
Cal State, Stanislaus	CA	9,874	C
Dartmouth College	NH	37,770	MC
George Fox Univ	OR	26,110	VC
Hampshire College	MA	37,037	HC
Indiana Univ Bloomington	IN	12,389	VC
Johns Hopkins Univ	MD	38,372	MC
Lehigh Univ	PA	37,570	HC+
Mass Inst of Technology	MA	38,310	MC
Northwestern Univ	IL	37,491	MC
Occidental College	CA	35,922	HC
Rice Univ	TX	27,550	MC
SUNY at Oswego	NY	12,650	C
Tulane Univ	LA	37,451	HC+
Univ of Calif at Berkeley	CA	15,563	MC
Univ of Calif at Los Angeles	CA	15,330	MC
Univ of Calif at San Diego	CA	14,127	HC
Univ of Denver	CO	32,148	VC
Univ of Georgia	GA	8,656	VC
Univ of Pennsylvania	PA	37,960	MC
Univ of Rochester	NY	32,979	HC
Univ of Texas at Dallas	TX	10,234	HC
Vanderbilt Univ	TN	37,897	MC
Vassar College	NY	37,030	MC
Villanova Univ	PA	35,050	HC
Wellesley College	MA	36,516	MC

COMMERCIAL ART

School	ST	$IS	SR
American InterContinental Univ	GA	12,000	NC
Ashland Univ	OH	24,464	C
Brenau Univ Women's College	GA	21,800	C
Cazenovia College	NY	23,940	C
Central Missouri State Univ	MO	9,776	C
Fort Valley State Univ	GA	6,960	C
Graceland Univ	IA	19,550	C
Madonna Univ	MI	11,504	VC
Millikin Univ	IL	25,555	C
Oral Roberts Univ	OK	18,490	C
St. Thomas Aquinas College	NY	20,590	LC
Southwest Baptist Univ	MO	15,371	C
Univ of Indianapolis	IN	22,560	VC
Univ of North Texas	TX	7,629	C
Washington Univ in St. Louis	MO	38,293	MC

COMMUNICATIONS

School	ST	$IS	SR
Abilene Christian Univ	TX	18,370	VC
Adelphi Univ	NY	26,300	VC
Adrian College	MI	21,950	C
Alabama State Univ	AL	6,404	C
Albertus Magnus College	CT	23,130	LC
Albright College	PA	30,579	C
Alcorn State Univ	MS	7,290	C
Alderson-Broaddus College	WV	19,640	C
Alfred Univ	NY	28,290	C
Allegheny College	PA	30,280	VC
Alma College	MI	25,566	VC
Alvernia College	PA	23,212	LC
Alverno College	WI	18,898	C
American International College	MA	24,690	LC
American Univ	DC	34,585	VC+
Anderson Univ	IN	19,430	LC
Andrews Univ	MI	19,550	C
Angelo State Univ	TX	7,576	NC
Antioch College	OH	29,269	C
Appalachian State Univ	NC	7,637	VC
Aquinas College	MI	21,894	C
Arcadia Univ	PA	29,890	C
Arizona State Univ-Main	AZ	10,048	C
Asbury College	KY	20,704	VC
Ashland Univ	OH	24,464	C
Auburn Univ	AL	10,396	VC
Auburn Univ Montgomery	AL	9,020	NC
Augsburg College	MN	25,298	C
Augusta State Univ	GA	2,592	C
Augustana College	SD	21,998	VC
Aurora Univ	IL	20,631	C
Austin College	TX	24,747	HC
Austin Peay State Univ	TN	5,814	LC
Avila Univ	MO	20,300	C
Azusa Pacific Univ	CA	24,720	VC
Baker Univ	KS	19,860	VC
Baldwin-Wallace College	OH	24,678	C
Ball State Univ	IN	8,660	C
Barber-Scotia College	NC	13,900	LC
Barry Univ	FL	24,100	LC
Barton College	NC	19,314	C
Bay Path College	MA	24,910	C
Baylor Univ	TX	23,864	VC
Becker College	MA	23,710	LC
Belhaven College	MS	16,040	C+
Bellarmine Univ	KY	24,110	VC
Bellevue Univ	NE	4,440	NC
Belmont Univ	TN	21,986	VC
Bemidji State Univ	MN	9,103	C
Benedictine Univ	IL	23,840	C
Bennett College	NC	11,200	C
Bentley College	MA	33,904	VC
Berry College	GA	21,410	VC
Bethany College	KS	18,675	LC
Bethany College	WV	19,845	VC
Bethel College	IN	19,670	C
Bethel College	KS	19,800	C+
Bethel College	MN	25,180	VC
Bethune-Cookman College	FL	16,480	LC
Biola Univ	CA	25,964	VC
Black Hills State Univ	SD	7,743	LC
Bloomsburg Univ of Pennsylvania	PA	10,844	C
Bluefield College	VA	15,575	C
Bluffton College	OH	23,694	C
Boise State Univ	ID	7,657	LC
Boston College	MA	33,284	MC
Boston Univ	MA	38,194	HC+
Bowling Green State Univ	OH	13,036	C
Bradley Univ	IL	22,910	VC
Brenau Univ Women's College	GA	21,800	C
Briar Cliff Univ	IA	21,660	C
Bridgewater College	VA	25,150	C
Bridgewater State College	MA	10,482	C
Brigham Young Univ	UT	8,504	HC
Bryan College	TN	17,900	VC
Bryant College	RI	31,004	VC
Buena Vista Univ	IA	25,406	C
Butler Univ	IN	28,250	VC+
Cabrini College	PA	29,020	C
Caldwell College	NJ	24,060	LC
Calif Baptist Univ	CA	19,924	C
Calif Lutheran Univ	CA	27,600	LC
Calif State Polytechnic Univ, Pomona	CA	8,793	C+
Cal State, Bakersfield	CA	6,090	LC
Cal State, Chico	CA	8,598	LC
Cal State, Dominguez Hills	CA	5,840	LC
Cal State, Fresno	CA	8,414	LC
Cal State, Fullerton	CA	6,648	C
Cal State, Hayward	CA	8,871	LC
Cal State, Long Beach	CA	8,762	C+
Cal State, Sacramento	CA	9,543	C
Cal State, San Bernardino	CA	15,238	LC
Cal State, San Marcos	CA	1,736	LC
Cal State, Stanislaus	CA	9,874	C
Calif Univ of Pennsylvania	PA	10,388	C
Calvin College	MI	22,615	NC
Cameron Univ	OK	5,692	NC
Campbell Univ	NC	18,268	VC
Campbellsville Univ	KY	17,680	C
Canisius College	NY	28,163	C+
Capital Univ	OH	26,550	C
Cardinal Stritch Univ	WI	17,620	C
Carlow College	PA	21,334	C
Carnegie Mellon Univ	PA	32,682	MC
Carroll College	MT	20,576	VC
Carroll College	WI	22,740	C
Carson-Newman College	TN	16,760	C
Castleton State College	VT	11,820	C
Catawba College	NC	20,500	C
Catholic Univ of America	DC	34,248	VC
Cedar Crest College	PA	25,145	C+
Cedarville Univ	OH	19,954	VC
Centenary College	NJ	25,370	LC
Centenary College of Louisiana	LA	23,100	VC+
Central College	IA	21,206	C
Central Conn State Univ	CT	12,090	C
Central Methodist College	MO	16,460	C
Central Mich Univ	MI	11,142	C
Central Missouri State Univ	MO	9,776	C
Central Washington Univ	WA	9,768	C
Chaminade Univ of Honolulu	HI	21,430	LC
Champlain College	VT	22,030	C
Chapman Univ	CA	33,118	VC
Chatham College	PA	27,266	C+
Cheyney Univ of Pennsylvania	PA	9,993	C
Christian Heritage College	CA	19,990	C

ST = STATE $IS = IN-STATE COSTS SR = SELECTOR RATING

School	ST	$IS	SR
Christopher Newport Univ	VA	8,862	VC
CUNY/Baruch College	NY	3,275	VC+
CUNY/City College	NY	4,230	C+
CUNY/College of Staten Island	NY	4,308	NC
CUNY/Herbert H. Lehman College	NY	3,320	LC
CUNY/Queens College	NY	4,362	C
Claflin Univ	SC	14,838	C+
Clarion Univ of Pennsylvania	PA	11,272	LC
Clark Atlanta Univ	GA	19,300	C+
Clark Univ	MA	32,115	VC
Clarke College	IA	23,165	C
Clearwater Christian College	FL	13,160	LC
Clemson Univ	SC	11,972	HC
Cleveland State Univ	OH	12,308	LC
Coker College	SC	21,491	C
Colby-Sawyer College	NH	27,850	LC
College Misericordia	PA	26,350	C
College of Charleston	SC	11,887	HC
College of Mount St. Vincent	NY	26,800	C
College of Mount St. Joseph	OH	22,785	C
College of New Jersey	NJ	15,950	MC
College of New Rochelle	NY	21,800	C
College of Notre Dame of Maryland	MD	27,700	C
College of St. Benedict	MN	26,672	VC
College of St. Catherine	MN	24,010	VC
College of St. Elizabeth	NJ	25,460	C
College of St. Joseph	VT	19,100	C
College of St. Rose	NY	22,864	C
College of St. Scholastica	MN	24,970	C+
College of Santa Fe	NM	25,293	C+
College of the Ozarks	MO	3,500	VC+
College of Wooster	OH	31,300	HC
Colo Christian Univ	CO	21,182	VC
Columbia College	SC	22,658	LC
Columbia Union College	MD	20,543	C
Columbus State Univ	GA	7,846	C
Concord College	WV	8,136	C
Concordia College: Moorhead	MN	22,460	VC+
Concordia Univ	CA	24,420	C
Concordia Univ	MI	24,095	C
Concordia Univ at Austin	TX	20,450	LC
Concordia Univ Nebr	NE	20,302	C+
Concordia Univ Wisc	WI	16,600	C
Concordia Univ, River Forest	IL	23,600	C
Concordia Univ/St.Paul	MN	24,486	C
Cornell Univ	NY	38,253	MC
Cornerstone Univ and Grand Rapids Theological Seminary	MI	19,846	C
Creighton Univ	NE	26,748	VC+
Culver-Stockton College	MO	17,850	C
Cumberland College	KY	16,384	C
Curry College	MA	26,025	LC
Dakota Wesleyan Univ	SD	17,832	C
Dallas Baptist Univ	TX	15,300	VC
Dana College	NE	20,280	C
David Lipscomb Univ	TN	16,158	VC
Davis and Elkins College	WV	20,594	C
De Sales Univ	PA	25,470	C
Defiance College	OH	22,615	C
Denison Univ	OH	33,050	HC
DePaul Univ	IL	27,580	VC
DePauw Univ	IN	31,500	HC
Dickinson State Univ	ND	6,338	NC
Dillard Univ	LA	17,325	VC
Doane College	NE	20,000	C
Dominican Univ	IL	23,610	C
Dominican Univ of Calif	CA	31,670	C
Dordt College	IA	20,170	VC
Dowling College	NY	23,870	LC
Drake Univ	IA	25,120	VC+
Drexel Univ	PA	27,655	VC
Drury Univ	MO	18,085	VC+
Duquesne Univ	PA	26,907	VC
East Carolina Univ	NC	8,671	C
East Central Univ	OK	4,968	C
East Stroudsburg Univ of Pennsylvania	PA	10,336	C
East Tenn State Univ	TN	8,497	C
Eastern Conn State Univ	CT	10,362	C
Eastern Illinois Univ	IL	11,192	C
Eastern Mennonite Univ	VA	22,990	C
Eastern Mich Univ	MI	11,478	C
Eastern Nazarene College	MA	19,433	LC
Eastern New Mexico Univ	NM	6,762	LC
Eastern Univ	PA	24,020	C
Eastern Washington Univ	WA	9,012	C
East-West Univ	IL	10,365	LC
Eckerd College	FL	28,744	C+
Edward Waters College	FL	14,374	LC
Elizabethtown College	PA	28,800	C
Elmhurst College	IL	24,630	C
Elon Univ	NC	22,240	VC
Embry-Riddle Aeronautical Univ	AZ	27,710	C+
Embry-Riddle Aeronautical Univ	FL	27,730	C+
Emerson College	MA	32,205	HC
Emmanuel College	MA	27,600	C+
Emory & Henry College	VA	21,950	C
Emporia State Univ	KS	6,998	C
Endicott College	MA	25,266	C+
Eureka College	IL	24,980	LC
Evangel Univ	MO	15,435	C
Fairfield Univ	CT	35,505	HC
Fairleigh Dickinson Univ/College at Florham	NJ	30,130	C
Fairleigh Dickinson Univ/Metropolitan Campus	NJ	28,584	C
Fairmont State	WV	8,280	LC
Fitchburg State College	MA	9,622	C
Five Towns College	NY	21,050	SP
Flagler College	FL	11,860	VC+
Florida Atlantic Univ	FL	8,543	C
Florida Inst of Technology	FL	28,740	VC
Florida International Univ	FL	9,912	VC
Florida Southern College	FL	23,592	C
Florida State Univ	FL	9,028	HC
Fontbonne Univ	MO	21,508	C
Fordham Univ	NY	35,066	HC
Fort Hays State Univ	KS	7,363	C
Fort Valley State Univ	GA	6,960	C
Framingham State College	MA	9,381	C
Francis Marion Univ	SC	9,364	C
Franciscan Univ of Steubenville	OH	20,300	VC
Franklin Pierce College	NH	28,980	LC
Freed-Hardeman Univ	TN		NC
Frostburg State Univ	MD	11,114	C
Furman Univ	SC	28,976	HC+
Gallaudet Univ	DC	16,554	SP
Gannon Univ	PA	23,260	C
Gardner-Webb Univ	NC	19,300	C
Geneva College	PA	21,850	C
George Fox Univ	OR	26,110	VC
George Mason Univ	VA	9,732	VC
George Washington Univ	DC	41,030	MC
Georgetown College	KY	22,000	VC
Georgia Southern Univ	GA	8,540	C
Gordon College	MA	25,982	VC+
Goshen College	IN	22,450	VC
Goucher College	MD	32,650	HC
Grace College	IN	19,825	VC
Graceland Univ	IA	19,550	C
Grambling State Univ	LA	6,538	NC
Grand Canyon Univ	AZ	30,000	LC
Grand Valley State Univ	MI	11,022	VC
Grand View College	IA	19,748	LC
Green Mountain College	VT	24,130	C
Greenville College	IL	21,342	C
Grove City College	PA	14,228	HC
Gustavus Adolphus College	MN	27,120	VC+
Gwynedd-Mercy College	PA	24,225	C
Hamilton College	NY	37,560	MC
Hamline Univ	MN	27,052	VC
Hampshire College	MA	37,037	HC
Hampton Univ	VA	17,112	C+
Hannibal-LaGrange College	MO	13,940	C
Hanover College	IN	25,200	VC
Harding Univ	AR	14,890	VC
Hardin-Simmons Univ	TX	14,165	C
Hastings College	NE	19,928	VC
Hawaii Pacific Univ	HI	19,218	C
Heidelberg College	OH	20,266	NC
Henderson State Univ	AR	7,386	C
Hiram College	OH	28,234	VC
Hollins Univ	VA	27,965	VC
Holy Names College	CA	27,980	NC
Hood College	MD	27,795	VC
Hope College	MI	25,340	VC
Houghton College	NY	23,984	VC
Houston Baptist Univ	TX	16,905	C
Howard Payne Univ	TX	15,176	C
Howard Univ	DC	16,505	C
Humboldt State Univ	CA	9,400	C
Huntingdon College	AL	18,400	VC
Huntington College	IN	23,590	C
Huston-Tillotson College	TX	14,232	NC
Idaho State Univ	ID	8,128	C
Illinois College	IL	19,100	VC
Illinois State Univ	IL	10,944	C+
Indiana State Univ	IN	10,719	LC
Indiana Univ Bloomington	IN	12,389	VC
Indiana Univ East	IN	4,433	LC
Indiana Univ Kokomo	IN	4,463	LC
Indiana Univ Northwest	IN	4,538	LC
Indiana Univ of Pennsylvania	PA	10,489	C
Indiana Univ South Bend	IN	4,571	LC
Indiana Univ Southeast	IN	4,504	LC
Indiana Univ-Purdue Univ Fort Wayne	IN	5,108	LC
Indiana Univ-Purdue Univ Indianapolis	IN	8,257	LC
Indiana Wesleyan Univ	IN	19,900	C+
Iona College	NY	27,988	VC
Iowa State Univ	IA	10,768	VC
Iowa Wesleyan College	IA	19,990	C
Ithaca College	NY	31,730	HC
Jackson State Univ	MS	8,382	C
Jacksonville State Univ	AL	6,844	LC
Jacksonville Univ	FL	24,040	C
James Madison Univ	VA	10,794	VC
Jamestown College	ND	12,600	NC
John Carroll Univ	OH	27,658	C+
Johnson C. Smith Univ	NC	18,108	C
Judson College	IL	22,050	LC
Juniata College	PA	29,080	VC
Kansas State Univ	KS	8,728	VC
Kansas Wesleyan Univ	KS	18,900	VC
Kean Univ	NJ	14,479	C
Keene State College	NH	12,212	C
Kennesaw State Univ	GA	2,724	C
Kent State Univ	OH	12,932	C
Kentucky Wesleyan College	KY	17,250	C
Keuka College	NY	21,170	C
Keystone College	PA	21,405	LC
King's College	PA	26,990	C
La Roche College	PA	22,094	C
La Salle Univ	PA	31,260	VC
La Sierra Univ	CA	19,260	LC
Lake Erie College	OH	23,550	C
Lake Forest College	IL	30,270	VC
Lamar Univ	TX	6,816	LC
Lambuth Univ	TN	16,520	C
Lander Univ	SC	10,496	C
Lane College	TN	11,178	C+
Le Moyne College	NY	26,400	VC
Lee Univ	TN	13,780	NC
Lees-McRae College	NC	17,106	LC
Lenoir-Rhyne College	NC	19,186	C
Lewis and Clark College	OR	30,620	VC
Lewis Univ	IL	22,950	C+
Lewis-Clark State College	ID	6,981	C
Liberty Univ	VA	17,220	C
Lincoln Memorial Univ	TN	16,400	LC
Lincoln Univ	PA	13,320	C+
Lindenwood Univ	MO	17,050	VC
Lindsey Wilson College	KY	16,392	LC
Linfield College	OR	27,090	VC
Lock Haven Univ of Pennsylvania	PA	11,098	LC
LIU/Brooklyn Campus	NY	24,790	C
LIU/C.W. Post Campus	NY	28,282	C
LIU/Southampton College	NY	29,370	C+
Longwood Univ	VA	11,175	C
Louisiana College	LA	13,450	C
Louisiana State Univ and A&M College	LA	9,126	VC
Louisiana State Univ in Shreveport	LA	2,884	NC
Loyola College in Maryland	MD	34,560	HC
Loyola Marymount Univ	CA	32,194	VC
Loyola Univ Chicago	IL	31,164	VC
Loyola Univ New Orleans	LA	31,036	VC+
Lubbock Christian Univ	TX	15,832	C
Luther College	IA	25,700	VC
Lycoming College	PA	27,589	C+
Lynchburg College	VA	26,815	C
Lyndon State College	VT	12,646	LC
Lynn Univ	FL	30,750	C
Malone College	OH	20,995	C
Manchester College	IN	23,390	C
Manhattan College	NY	27,400	VC
Marian College	IN	23,030	C
Marian College of Fond du Lac	WI	19,625	C
Marietta College	OH	27,047	C
Marist College	NY	27,596	VC
Marquette Univ	WI	27,594	VC
Mars Hill College	NC	18,600	LC
Marshall Univ	WV	9,116	C
Martin Univ	IN	10,200	SP
Mary Baldwin College	VA	24,939	C
Marylhurst Univ	OR	18,465	NC
Marymount Manhattan College	NY	27,292	C
Marymount Univ	VA	23,668	C
Maryville Univ of St. Louis	MO	22,090	VC
Marywood Univ	PA	26,050	C
Master's College and Seminary	CA	23,250	VC
McDaniel College	MD	28,440	VC
McMurry Univ	TX	17,846	LC
McNeese State Univ	LA	5,259	LC
Medaille College	NY	20,060	C
Menlo College	CA	24,000	LC
Mercyhurst College	PA	20,694	C
Meredith College	NC	23,065	C
Merrimack College	MA	29,625	C
Mesa State College	CO	8,051	C
Messiah College	PA	25,890	VC+
Methodist College	NC	19,526	C
Metropolitan State College of Denver	CO	2,338	LC
Miami Univ	OH	15,033	HC
Mich State Univ	MI	11,933	VC
MidAmerica Nazarene Univ	KS	18,688	C
Middle Tenn State Univ	TN	8,534	C
Midland Lutheran College	NE	18,600	C
Midwestern State Univ	TX	8,045	LC
Miles College	AL	7,870	NC
Millersville Univ of Pennsylvania	PA	11,269	C
Milligan College	TN	19,860	C+
Millikin Univ	IL	25,555	C
Minn State Univ, Mankato	MN	8,803	LC
Minn State Univ, Moorehead	MN	7,000	LC
Minot State Univ	ND	6,602	LC
Miss College	MS	14,574	C
Miss State Univ	MS	9,139	C
Miss Univ for Women	MS	5,446	LC
Miss Valley State Univ	MS	6,765	NC
Missouri Baptist Univ	MO	18,010	C
Missouri Southern State Univ	MO	8,316	C
Missouri Valley College	MO	18,500	C
Missouri Western State College	MO	8,522	NC
Molloy College	NY	15,180	C
Monmouth College	IL	23,600	C
Monmouth Univ	NJ	26,334	C
Montana State Univ-Billings	MT	9,550	C
Montana State Univ-Northern	MT	8,600	NC
Montana Tech of The Univ of Montana	MT	9,314	NC
Montclair State Univ	NJ	13,790	C
Morehead State Univ	KY	7,464	C
Morningside College	IA	21,610	C
Mount Ida College	MA	25,596	LC
Mount Mary College	WI	20,370	C
Mount Mercy College	IA	21,400	C
Mount Olive College	NC	14,410	LC
Mount St. Mary College	NY	21,270	C
Mount St. Mary's College	MD	28,400	C
Mount Union College	OH	21,120	C
Mount Vernon Nazarene Univ	OH	18,925	C
Mountain State Univ	WV	10,212	NC
Muhlenberg College	PA	31,485	HC
Murray State Univ	KY	7,816	VC
Muskingum College	OH	20,680	C
National Univ	CA	9,690	SP
Nebr Wesleyan Univ	NE	21,197	C+
Neumann College	PA	23,890	LC
New England College	NH	28,860	LC
New Jersey Inst of Technology	NJ	16,396	VC
New Mexico Highlands Univ	NM	6,182	LC
New Mexico State Univ	NM	7,932	C
New York Inst of Technology	NY	24,205	VC
New York Univ	NY	39,406	MC
Newberry College	SC	22,871	LC
Newbury College	MA	23,450	C
Newman Univ	KS	18,018	C
Niagara Univ	NY	25,050	C
Nicholls State Univ	LA	6,395	NC
Norfolk State Univ	VA	9,722	LC
N Car Agricultural and Technical State Univ	NC	6,659	LC
N Car State Univ	NC	9,886	VC
North Central College	IL	25,656	VC
North Central Univ	MN	14,904	C
N Dak State Univ	ND	8,435	C
North Park Univ	IL	24,030	C
Northeastern State Univ	OK	4,950	LC
Northeastern Univ	MA	35,650	HC
Northern Arizona Univ	AZ	9,002	C
Northern Illinois Univ	IL	11,472	C
Northern Mich Univ	MI	10,834	C
Northwest Christian College	OR	21,860	C
Northwest College	WA	18,854	C
Northwest Missouri State Univ	MO	9,334	C
Northwest Nazarene Univ	ID	20,360	VC
Northwestern College	MN	22,820	C+
Northwestern College of Iowa	IA	19,640	C+
Northwestern Okla State Univ	OK	5,433	NC
Northwestern Univ	IL	37,491	MC
Norwich Univ	VT	21,064	LC
Notre Dame College	OH	20,425	C
Notre Dame de Namur Univ	CA	26,932	LC
Nyack College	NY	18,540	C
Oakland Univ	MI	10,800	C
Oakwood College	AL	14,904	C
Oglethorpe Univ	GA	26,000	VC
Ohio Dominican Univ	OH	22,700	C
Ohio Northern Univ	OH	27,765	VC
Ohio State Univ	OH	13,080	VC+
Ohio Univ	OH	14,448	C
Okla Baptist Univ	OK	15,220	VC
Okla Christian Univ	OK	17,690	NC
Okla City Univ	OK	19,580	VC
Okla State Univ	OK	9,216	VC
Okla Wesleyan Univ	OK	14,100	LC
Old Dominion Univ	VA	10,441	C
Olivet College	MI	19,984	C+
Oral Roberts Univ	OK	18,490	C
Ottawa Univ	KS	11,800	LC
Otterbein College	OH	26,085	C
Ouachita Baptist Univ	AR	18,900	VC
Our Lady of the Lake Univ of San Antonio	TX	17,336	C
Pace Univ	NY	28,652	VC
Pacific Lutheran Univ	WA	25,715	VC
Pacific Union College	CA	22,065	C+
Paine College	GA	13,022	LC
Palm Beach Atlantic Univ	FL	20,690	C
Park Univ	MO	10,780	C+

ST = STATE $IS = IN-STATE COSTS   SR = SELECTOR RATING

ST = STATE   **$IS** = IN-STATE COSTS   **SR** = SELECTOR RATING

School	ST	$IS	SR
Winthrop Univ	SC	11,302	C
Wisc Lutheran College	WI	21,430	VC
Wittenberg Univ	OH	31,316	VC
Worcester State College	MA	10,005	C
Wright State Univ	OH	11,490	LC
Xavier Univ	OH	26,850	VC+
Xavier Univ of Louisiana	LA	17,600	C
Yeshiva Univ	NY	21,400	C
York College	NE	14,975	C
York College of Pennsylvania	PA	14,500	VC
Youngstown State Univ	OH	11,148	NC

COMMUNICATIONS TECHNOLOGY

School	ST	$IS	SR
Alverno College	WI	18,898	C
Cal State, Monterey Bay	CA	6,683	LC
Champlain College	VT	22,030	C
Chestnut Hill College	PA	26,450	LC
Eastern Mich Univ	MI	11,478	C
Inter American Univ of PR/ Bayamon Univ College	PR	3,522	
James Madison Univ	VA	10,794	VC
Lebanon Valley College	PA	28,870	VC
Lewis Univ	IL	22,950	C+
Loyola Univ New Orleans	LA	31,036	VC+
Montana Tech of The Univ of Montana	MT	9,314	NC
Montclair State Univ	NJ	13,790	C
New York Univ	NY	39,406	MC
Northwestern Univ	IL	37,491	MC
Rochester Inst of Technology	NY	29,217	VC+
Salve Regina Univ	RI	29,210	C
Trevecca Nazarene Univ	TN	17,548	C
Univ of S Dak	SD	7,710	C+
Wilmington College	DE	5,594	NC

COMMUNITY HEALTH WORK

School	ST	$IS	SR
Baylor Univ	TX	23,864	VC
Brown Univ	RI	38,174	MC
Central Washington Univ	WA	9,768	C
CUNY/York College	NY	3,292	NC
Delaware State Univ	DE	8,104	LC
Florida State Univ	FL	9,028	HC
Georgia Southern Univ	GA	8,540	C
Hofstra Univ	NY	27,112	VC
Ithaca College	NY	31,730	HC
John Brown Univ	AR	15,080	VC
Kent State Univ	OH	12,932	C
Lewis Univ	IL	22,950	C+
Liberty Univ	VA	17,220	C
Longwood Univ	VA	11,175	C
Malone College	OH	20,995	C
Montclair State Univ	NJ	13,790	C
Morris College	SC	10,974	LC
New Mexico State Univ	NM	7,932	C
Northern Illinois Univ	IL	11,472	C
Ohio Univ	OH	14,448	C
Purdue Univ/West Lafayette	IN	12,560	VC
St. Joseph's, Brooklyn,	NY	10,902	C
Slippery Rock Univ of Pennsylvania	PA	10,343	LC
SUNY at Potsdam	NY	12,160	C
SUNY/College at Old Westbury	NY	12,784	C
Texas State Univ	TX	9,320	VC
Univ of Calif at Davis	CA	14,995	VC
Univ of Central Okla	OK	9,434	C
Univ of Kansas	KS	8,923	VC
Univ of Maine at Farmington	ME	10,108	C
Univ of Mass Lowell	MA	11,937	VC
Univ of N Car at Greensboro	NC	8,248	C
Univ of N Car at Pembroke	NC	6,929	LC
Univ of N Dak	ND	8,390	C
Univ of Northern Colo	CO	8,987	C
Univ of St. Thomas	MN	26,918	VC
Univ of Tenn at Knoxville	TN	8,214	C
Univ of Wisc/La Crosse	WI	8,991	VC
Univ of Wisc/Superior	WI	7,051	C+
Western Conn State Univ	CT	11,625	C
Western Mich Univ	MI	12,031	C
William Paterson Univ of New Jersey	NJ	14,450	C
Youngstown State Univ	OH	11,148	NC

COMMUNITY PSYCHOLOGY

School	ST	$IS	SR
East Texas Baptist Univ	TX	13,914	C
Southwestern Okla State Univ	OK	4,801	C
Univ of Mich/Flint	MI	5,548	C
Univ of New Haven	CT	28,650	C

COMMUNITY SERVICES

School	ST	$IS	SR
Alverno College	WI	18,898	C
Aquinas College	MI	21,894	C
Arkansas State Univ	AR	8,450	C
Bemidji State Univ	MN	9,103	C
Bethel College	KS	19,800	C+
Emory & Henry College	VA	21,950	C
Guilford College	NC	24,960	VC
Humphreys College	CA	7,000	NC
Martin Univ	IN	10,200	SP
Metropolitan College of New York	NY	15,771	C
Midland Lutheran College	NE	18,600	C
NAES College	IL	5,140	SP
Northern State Univ	SD	7,117	LC
Ohio Univ	OH	14,448	C
Portland State Univ	OR	12,453	C
Prescott College	AZ	13,430	C
Providence College	RI	30,604	HC
St. Martin's College	WA	23,245	C
St. Mary's College	MI	13,314	LC
Samford Univ	AL	18,648	VC
Southern Arkansas Univ	AR	6,956	C
SUNY/College at Plattsburgh	NY	11,700	C
SUNY/Empire State College	NY	4,505	SP
Thomas Edison State College	NJ	3,325	SP
Univ of Calif at Riverside	CA	15,300	C
Univ of Calif at Santa Cruz	CA	16,505	VC
Univ of Delaware	DE	12,616	HC
Univ of Mass Boston	MA	6,227	C
Univ of Toledo	OH	12,479	NC
Winona State Univ	MN		C
Woodbury College	VT	12,060	LC

COMPARATIVE LITERATURE

School	ST	$IS	SR
Beloit College	WI	29,864	HC
Bennington College	VT	35,910	HC
Brandeis Univ	MA	38,198	MC
Brigham Young Univ	UT	8,504	HC
Brown Univ	RI	38,174	MC
Bryn Mawr College	PA	36,890	HC+
Cal State, Fullerton	CA	6,648	C
Cal State, Long Beach	CA	8,762	C+
Case Western Reserve Univ	OH	32,002	MC
Cedar Crest College	PA	25,145	C+
CUNY/Brooklyn College	NY	4,353	C+
CUNY/City College	NY	4,230	C+
CUNY/Herbert H. Lehman College	NY	3,320	LC
CUNY/Hunter College	NY	6,729	C+
CUNY/Queens College	NY	4,362	C
Clark Univ	MA	32,115	VC
College of Wooster	OH	31,300	HC
Colo College	CO	36,860	HC
Columbia Univ/Barnard College	NY	36,990	MC
Columbia Univ/Columbia College	NY	38,590	MC
Columbia Univ/School of General Studies	NY	35,000	C
Conn College	CT	37,900	MC
Cornell Univ	NY	38,253	MC
Dartmouth College	NH	37,770	MC
DePaul Univ	IL	27,580	VC
Eckerd College	FL	28,744	C+
Emory Univ	GA	36,872	MC
Fordham Univ	NY	35,066	HC
Georgetown Univ	DC	38,242	MC
Hamilton College	NY	37,560	MC
Hampshire College	MA	37,037	HC
Haverford College	PA	37,900	MC
Hillsdale College	MI	22,450	HC
Hobart and William Smith Colleges	NY	36,536	HC
Hofstra Univ	NY	27,112	VC
Indiana Univ Bloomington	IN	12,389	VC
Mills College	CA	33,371	VC
New England College	NH	28,860	LC
New York Univ	NY	39,406	MC
Northwestern Univ	IL	37,491	MC
Oberlin College	OH	36,938	MC
Occidental College	CA	35,922	HC
Penn State Univ/Univ Park Campus	PA	15,646	HC
Princeton Univ	NJ	36,649	MC
Purdue Univ/West Lafayette	IN	12,560	VC
Rutgers, The State Univ of New Jersey/New Brunswick/Piscataway Campus	NJ	15,800	HC
San Diego State Univ	CA	10,321	C
San Francisco State Univ	CA	12,070	C
Smith College	MA	37,034	HC+
Stanford Univ	CA	37,612	MC
SUNY/College at Geneseo	NY	11,330	HC
SUNY/Univ at Binghamton	NY	12,787	HC
SUNY/Univ at Stony Brook	NY	12,763	HC
Swarthmore College	PA	37,716	MC
Syracuse Univ	NY	34,720	HC
Trinity College	CT	38,040	HC+
Univ of Calif at Berkeley	CA	15,563	MC
Univ of Calif at Davis	CA	14,995	VC
Univ of Calif at Irvine	CA	19,808	HC
Univ of Calif at Los Angeles	CA	15,330	MC
Univ of Calif at Riverside	CA	15,300	C
Univ of Calif at Santa Barbara	CA	11,732	VC
Univ of Chicago	IL	35,087	MC
Univ of Cincinnati	OH	14,736	C
Univ of Delaware	DE	12,616	HC
Univ of Georgia	GA	8,656	VC
Univ of Illinois at Urbana-Champaign	IL	11,316	HC+
Univ of Iowa	IA	10,923	VC
Univ of La Verne	CA	28,600	C
Univ of Mass Amherst	MA	13,980	C+
Univ of Mich/Ann Arbor	MI	13,864	HC+
Univ of New Mexico	NM	9,223	C
Univ of N Car at Chapel Hill	NC	10,117	MC
Univ of Oregon	OR	11,479	VC
Univ of Pennsylvania	PA	37,960	MC
Univ of PR/Rio Piedras	PR	5,730	
Univ of Rhode Island	RI	13,720	VC
Univ of Rochester	NY	32,979	HC
Univ of Southern Calif	CA	37,459	MC
Univ of Tenn at Knoxville	TN	8,214	C
Univ of Virginia	VA	11,740	MC
Univ of Washington	WA	10,361	VC
Univ of Wisc/Madison	WI	8,262	VC
Univ of Wisc/Milwaukee	WI	9,427	LC
Washington Univ in St. Louis	MO	38,293	MC
Wellesley College	MA	36,516	MC
West Chester Univ of Pennsylvania	PA	11,164	C
Willamette Univ	OR	32,032	VC+

COMPUTATIONAL SCIENCES

School	ST	$IS	SR
Brown Univ	RI	38,174	MC
Mich State Univ	MI	11,933	VC
Park Univ	MO	10,780	C+
SUNY/College at Brockport	NY	12,111	C
Stevens Inst of Technology	NJ	35,300	HC+

COMPUTER EDUCATION

School	ST	$IS	SR
Averett Univ	VA	23,010	LC
Baylor Univ	TX	23,864	VC
College of St. Joseph	VT	19,100	C
Concordia Univ, River Forest	IL	23,600	C
Eastern Mich Univ	MI	11,478	C
Eastern Washington Univ	WA	9,012	C
Florida Inst of Technology	FL	28,740	VC
Illinois State Univ	IL	10,944	C+
Northern Mich Univ	MI	10,834	C
St. Martin's College	WA	23,245	C
Union College	NE	17,130	C
Univ of Illinois at Urbana-Champaign	IL	11,316	HC+
Viterbo Univ	WI	20,430	C
Youngstown State Univ	OH	11,148	NC

COMPUTER ENGINEERING

School	ST	$IS	SR
Arizona State Univ-Main	AZ	10,048	C
Auburn Univ	AL	10,396	VC
Baylor Univ	TX	23,864	VC
Bellarmine Univ	KY	24,110	VC
Bethune-Cookman College	FL	16,480	LC
Boston Univ	MA	38,194	HC+
Brigham Young Univ	UT	8,504	HC
Bucknell Univ	PA	35,262	HC+
Calif Polytechnic State Univ	CA	8,747	VC
Cal State, Chico	CA	8,598	LC
Cal State, Fresno	CA	8,414	LC
Cal State, Long Beach	CA	8,762	C+
Cal State, Sacramento	CA	9,543	C
Capitol College	MD	21,250	C
Carnegie Mellon Univ	PA	32,682	MC
Case Western Reserve Univ	OH	32,002	MC
Cedarville Univ	OH	19,954	VC
Christopher Newport Univ	VA	8,862	VC
CUNY/City College	NY	4,230	C+
Clarkson Univ	NY	32,226	VC
Clemson Univ	SC	11,972	HC
Cogswell Polytechnical College	CA	14,400	LC
Colo Technical Univ	CO	9,500	LC
Columbia Univ/Fu Foundation School of Engineering and Applied Science	NY	38,590	MC
Cornell Univ	NY	38,253	MC
DeVry Univ/Addison (DuPage County)	IL	10,790	LC
DeVry Univ/Alpharetta	GA	10,670	LC
DeVry Univ/Chicago	IL	10,790	LC
DeVry Univ/Columbus	OH	10,670	LC
DeVry Univ/Crystal City	VA	11,860	C
DeVry Univ/Dallas	TX	10,640	LC
DeVry Univ/Decatur	GA	10,670	LC
DeVry Univ/Fort Washington	PA	11,860	LC
DeVry Univ/Fremont	CA	11,860	LC
DeVry Univ/Kansas City	MO	10,670	LC
DeVry Univ/Long Beach	CA	11,310	LC
DeVry Univ/Miramar	FL	11,310	LC
DeVry Univ/Orlando	FL	11,310	LC
DeVry Univ/Phoenix	AZ	10,670	LC
DeVry Univ/Pomona	CA	11,310	LC
DeVry Univ/Seattle	WA	11,860	LC
DeVry Univ/Tinley Park	IL	10,790	LC
DeVry Univ/West Hills	CA	11,310	LC
DeVry Univ/Westminster	CO	11,310	LC
Drexel Univ	PA	27,655	VC
Eastern Nazarene College	MA	19,433	LC
Elizabethtown College	PA	28,800	C
Embry-Riddle Aeronautical Univ	AZ	27,710	C+
Embry-Riddle Aeronautical Univ	FL	27,730	C+
Fairfield Univ	CT	35,505	HC
Florida Atlantic Univ	FL	8,543	C
Florida Inst of Technology	FL	28,740	VC
Florida International Univ	FL	9,912	VC
Florida State Univ	FL	9,028	HC
George Mason Univ	VA	9,732	VC
George Washington Univ	DC	41,030	MC
Georgia Inst of Technology	GA	10,340	HC+
Gonzaga Univ	WA	26,766	HC
Hofstra Univ	NY	27,112	VC
Illinois Inst of Technology	IL	26,456	HC+
Indiana Inst of Technology	IN	21,620	C
Indiana Univ-Purdue Univ Indianapolis	IN	8,257	LC
Iowa State Univ	IA	10,768	VC
Johns Hopkins Univ	MD	38,372	MC
Johnson C. Smith Univ	NC	18,108	C
Kansas State Univ	KS	8,728	VC
Kettering Univ	MI	26,478	HC
Lawrence Tech Univ	MI	20,487	C
Lehigh Univ	PA	37,570	HC+
LeTourneau Univ	TX	21,080	C
Louisiana State Univ and A&M College	LA	9,126	VC
Marquette Univ	WI	27,594	VC
Mass Inst of Technology	MA	38,310	MC
Mich State Univ	MI	11,933	VC
Mich Tech Univ	MI	13,235	VC
Milwaukee School of Engineering	WI	28,479	VC+
Miss State Univ	MS	9,139	C
Montana State Univ-Bozeman	MT	9,515	C
Montana Tech of The Univ of Montana	MT	9,314	NC
New Jersey Inst of Technology	NJ	16,396	VC
New York Inst of Technology	NY	24,205	VC
New York Univ	NY	39,406	MC
N Car State Univ	NC	9,886	VC
N Dak State Univ	ND	8,435	C
Northeastern Univ	MA	35,650	HC
Northern Arizona Univ	AZ	9,002	C
Northwestern Univ	IL	37,491	MC
Oakland Univ	MI	10,800	C
Ohio Northern Univ	OH	27,765	VC
Ohio State Univ	OH	13,080	VC+
Ohio Univ	OH	14,448	C
Okla Christian Univ	OK	17,690	NC
Old Dominion Univ	VA	10,491	C
Oral Roberts Univ	OK	18,490	C
Oregon State Univ	OR	11,055	C
Pacific Lutheran Univ	WA	25,715	VC
Penn State Univ at Erie/ Behrend College	PA	12,326	C
Penn State Univ/Univ Park Campus	PA	15,646	HC
Pennsylvania College of Technology	PA	15,126	NC
Polytechnic Univ/Brooklyn	NY	33,770	VC
Portland State Univ	OR	12,453	C
Prairie View A&M Univ	TX	9,418	NC
Purdue Univ/Calumet	IN	6,630	NC
Purdue Univ/West Lafayette	IN	12,560	VC
Rensselaer Polytechnic Inst	NY	37,579	HC+
Rochester Inst of Technology	NY	29,217	VC+
Roger Williams Univ	RI	30,296	C
Rose-Hulman Inst of Technology	IN	31,425	HC+
St. Mary's Univ of San Antonio	TX	22,444	C
San Diego State Univ	CA	10,321	C
San Jose State Univ	CA	8,187	C
Santa Clara Univ	CA	34,701	HC
S Dak School of Mines and Technology	SD	7,854	C+
Southern Illinois Univ Carbondale	IL	10,407	C
Southern Illinois Univ Edwardsville	IL	8,724	C
Southern Methodist Univ	TX	34,210	HC
Southern Polytechnic State Univ	GA	7,620	VC
Southwestern Okla State Univ	OK	4,801	C
SUNY/Univ at Binghamton	NY	12,787	HC
SUNY/Univ at Buffalo	NY	12,563	VC
SUNY/Univ at New Paltz	NY	11,565	VC
SUNY/Univ at Stony Brook	NY	12,763	HC
Stevens Inst of Technology	NJ	35,300	HC+
Stonehill College	MA	30,752	HC
Suffolk Univ	MA	29,200	C
Syracuse Univ	NY	34,720	HC

ST = STATE $IS = IN-STATE COSTS   SR = SELECTOR RATING

ST = STATE   **$IS** = IN-STATE COSTS   **SR** = SELECTOR RATING

School	ST	$IS	SR
Montana Tech of The Univ of Montana	MT	9,314	NC
Montclair State Univ	NJ	13,790	C
Moravian College	PA	28,903	VC
Morehouse College	GA	22,728	C
Morgan State Univ	MD	11,470	C
Morningside College	IA	21,610	C
Mount Holyoke College	MA	37,918	HC+
Mount Marty College	SD	15,656	LC
Mount Mary College	WI	20,370	C
Mount Mercy College	IA	21,400	C
Mount St. Mary College	NY	21,270	C
Mount St. Mary's College	MD	28,400	C
Mount Union College	OH	21,120	C
Mount Vernon Nazarene Univ	OH	18,925	C
Mountain State Univ	WV	10,212	NC
Muhlenberg College	PA	31,485	HC
Murray State Univ	KY	7,816	VC
Muskingum College	OH	20,680	C
National Univ	CA	9,690	SP
Nebr Wesleyan Univ	NE	21,197	C+
Neumann College	PA	23,890	LC
New Jersey City Univ	NJ	11,850	LC
New Jersey Inst of Technology	NJ	16,396	VC
New Mexico Highlands Univ	NM	6,182	LC
New Mexico Inst of Mining and Technology	NM	7,580	NC
New Mexico State Univ	NM	7,932	C
New York Inst of Technology	NY	24,205	VC
New York Univ	NY	39,406	MC
Newberry College	SC	22,871	LC
Newbury College	MA	23,450	C
Niagara Univ	NY	25,050	C
Nicholls State Univ	LA	6,395	NC
Norfolk State Univ	VA	9,722	LC
N Car Agricultural and Technical State Univ	NC	6,659	LC
N Car Central Univ	NC	7,534	LC
N Car State Univ	NC	9,886	VC
North Central College	IL	25,656	VC
N Dak State Univ	ND	8,435	C
North Georgia College and State Univ	GA	6,984	C
Northeastern Illinois Univ	IL	2,898	NC
Northeastern State Univ	OK	4,950	LC
Northeastern Univ	MA	35,650	HC
Northern Arizona Univ	AZ	9,002	C
Northern Illinois Univ	IL	11,472	C
Northern Kentucky Univ	KY	6,352	NC
Northern Mich Univ	MI	10,834	C
Northwest Missouri State Univ	MO	9,334	C
Northwest Nazarene Univ	ID	20,360	VC
Northwestern College of Iowa	IA	19,640	C+
Northwestern Okla State Univ	OK	5,433	NC
Northwestern Univ	IL	37,491	MC
Norwich Univ	VT	21,064	LC
Notre Dame de Namur Univ	CA	26,932	LC
Nova Southeastern Univ	FL	23,346	C
Nyack College	NY	18,540	C
Oakland City Univ	IN	16,980	NC
Oakland Univ	MI	10,800	C
Oakwood College	AL	14,904	C
Oberlin College	OH	36,938	MC
Oglethorpe Univ	GA	26,000	VC
Ohio Dominican Univ	OH	22,700	C
Ohio Northern Univ	OH	27,765	VC
Ohio State Univ	OH	13,080	VC+
Ohio Univ	OH	14,448	C
Ohio Wesleyan Univ	OH	32,550	VC+
Okla Baptist Univ	OK	15,220	VC
Okla Christian Univ	OK	17,690	NC
Okla City Univ	OK	19,580	VC
Okla State Univ	OK	9,216	VC
Okla Wesleyan Univ	OK	14,100	LC
Old Dominion Univ	VA	10,441	C
Olivet College	MI	19,984	C+
Olivet Nazarene Univ	IL	20,480	C
Oral Roberts Univ	OK	18,490	C
Oregon State Univ	OR	11,055	C
Otterbein College	OH	26,085	C
Ouachita Baptist Univ	AR	18,900	VC
Pace Univ	NY	28,652	VC
Pacific Lutheran Univ	WA	25,715	VC
Pacific Union College	CA	22,065	C+
Pacific Univ	OR	24,250	C
Palm Beach Atlantic Univ	FL	20,690	C
Park Univ	MO	10,780	C+
Paul Quinn College	TX	8,150	LC
Penn State Univ at Erie/ Behrend College	PA	12,326	C
Penn State Univ/Univ Park Campus	PA	15,646	HC
Pepperdine Univ	CA	32,830	VC
Peru State College	NE	6,342	NC
Philadelphia Univ	PA	27,354	C
Philander Smith College	AR	7,380	NC
Pikeville College	KY	14,900	NC
Pittsburg State Univ	KS	7,128	NC
Plymouth State Univ	NH	12,298	LC
Point Loma Nazarene Univ	CA	21,380	VC

School	ST	$IS	SR
Point Park Univ	PA	21,840	C
Polytechnic Univ/Brooklyn	NY	33,770	VC
Pomona College	CA	33,960	MC
Portland State Univ	OR	12,453	C
Prairie View A&M Univ	TX	9,418	NC
Princeton Univ	NJ	36,649	MC
Principia College	IL	25,044	C+
Providence College	RI	30,604	HC
Purdue Univ/Calumet	IN	6,630	NC
Purdue Univ/West Lafayette	IN	12,560	VC
Quincy Univ	IL	22,330	C
Quinnipiac Univ	CT	30,570	VC
Radford Univ	VA	8,500	C
Ramapo College of New Jersey	NJ	15,203	VC
Randolph-Macon College	VA	27,190	C
Regis College	MA	29,000	C
Regis Univ	CO	25,740	C+
Rensselaer Polytechnic Inst	NY	37,579	HC+
Rhode Island College	RI	11,565	C
Rhodes College	TN	26,466	HC+
Rice Univ	TX	27,550	MC
Richard Stockton College of New Jersey	NJ	12,972	VC
Ripon College	WI	24,995	VC
Rivier College	NH	26,217	C
Roanoke College	VA	27,393	C
Roberts Wesleyan College	NY	23,190	C+
Rochester Inst of Technology	NY	29,217	VC+
Rockford College	IL	28,310	VC
Rockhurst Univ	MO	22,960	C+
Rocky Mountain College	MT	19,015	C
Roger Williams Univ	RI	30,296	C
Rollins College	FL	34,300	VC
Roosevelt Univ	IL	22,580	VC
Rose-Hulman Inst of Technology	IN	31,425	HC+
Rowan Univ	NJ	14,506	VC
Russell Sage College	NY	26,811	C
Rust College	MS	8,200	C+
Rutgers, The State Univ of New Jersey/Camden Campus	NJ	14,990	VC
Rutgers, The State Univ of New Jersey/New Brunswick/Piscataway Campus	NJ	15,800	HC
Rutgers, The State Univ of New Jersey/Newark Campus	NJ	15,624	VC
Sacred Heart Univ	CT	29,178	C
Saginaw Valley State Univ	MI	11,055	C
St. Ambrose Univ	IA	22,800	C
St. Anselm College	NH	30,250	C
St. Augustine's College	NC	12,990	LC
St. Bonaventure Univ	NY	24,455	LC
St. Cloud State Univ	MN	8,362	C
St. Edward's Univ	TX	20,428	C
St. Francis Univ	PA	25,876	LC
St. John Fisher College	NY	24,870	C
St. John's Univ	MN	26,473	VC
St. John's Univ	NY	30,180	C
St. Joseph's College	IN	24,250	C
St. Joseph's Univ	PA	33,590	VC
St. Lawrence Univ	NY	35,945	VC
St. Louis Univ	MO	29,780	VC+
St. Martin's College	WA	23,245	C
St. Mary-of-the-Woods College	IN	23,280	C
St. Mary's College	MI	13,314	LC
St. Mary's College of Maryland	MD	15,908	VC+
St. Mary's Univ of Minn	MN	21,535	C
St. Mary's Univ of San Antonio	TX	22,444	C
St. Michael's College	VT	30,100	VC
St. Norbert College	WI	25,810	C
St. Olaf College	MN	28,500	HC
St. Peter's College	NJ	22,292	LC
St. Thomas Univ	FL	21,400	LC
St. Vincent College	PA	25,530	VC
St. Xavier Univ	IL	23,144	C
Salisbury Univ	MD	12,664	VC
Sam Houston State Univ	TX	7,142	C
Samford Univ	AL	18,648	VC
San Diego State Univ	CA	10,321	C
San Francisco State Univ	CA	12,070	C
San Jose State Univ	CA	8,187	C
Santa Clara Univ	CA	34,701	HC
Savannah State Univ	GA	7,328	LC
Seattle Pacific Univ	WA	25,944	VC
Seattle Univ	WA	24,183	VC
Seton Hall Univ	NJ	30,130	VC
Seton Hill Univ	PA	24,930	C
Shaw Univ	NC	14,882	C+
Shepherd College	WV	8,608	C
Shippensburg Univ of Pennsylvania	PA	10,826	C
Siena College	NY	25,310	VC
Silver Lake College of the Holy Family	WI	18,450	LC
Simmons College	MA	33,000	VC
Simpson College	IA	23,658	C+
Skidmore College	NY	37,930	HC

School	ST	$IS	SR
Slippery Rock Univ of Pennsylvania	PA	10,343	LC
Smith College	MA	37,034	HC+
Sonoma State Univ	CA	10,421	C
S Car State Univ	SC	6,586	LC
S Dak School of Mines and Technology	SD	7,854	C+
S Dak State Univ	SD	7,782	C
Southeast Missouri State Univ	MO	9,704	C
Southeastern Louisiana Univ	LA	6,791	LC
Southeastern Okla State Univ	OK	6,147	C
Southern Adventist Univ	TN	17,080	C
Southern Arkansas Univ	AR	6,956	C
Southern Conn State Univ	CT	10,310	C
Southern Illinois Univ Carbondale	IL	10,407	C
Southern Illinois Univ Edwardsville	IL	8,724	C
Southern Methodist Univ	TX	34,210	HC
Southern Nazarene Univ	OK	14,634	NC
Southern Oregon Univ	OR	10,362	C
Southern Polytechnic State Univ	GA	7,620	VC
Southern Univ and A&M College	LA	7,372	LC
Southern Univ at New Orleans	LA	995	NC
Southern Utah Univ	UT	8,194	C
Southwest Baptist Univ	MO	15,371	C
Southwest Minn State Univ	MN	9,106	VC
Southwest Missouri State Univ	MO	8,918	C
Southwestern Adventist Univ	TX	14,798	C
Southwestern College	KS	19,560	C
Southwestern Okla State Univ	OK	4,801	C
Southwestern Univ	TX	25,410	HC
Spelman College	GA	19,215	C+
Spring Arbor Univ	MI	20,206	C
Spring Hill College	AL	25,868	VC
Stanford Univ	CA	37,612	MC
SUNY at Oswego	NY	12,650	C
SUNY at Potsdam	NY	12,160	C
SUNY/College at Brockport	NY	12,111	C
SUNY/College at Fredonia	NY	11,562	VC
SUNY/College at Geneseo	NY	11,330	HC
SUNY/College at Old Westbury	NY	12,784	C
SUNY/College at Oneonta	NY	11,870	VC
SUNY/College at Plattsburgh	NY	11,700	C
SUNY/Univ at Albany	NY	12,951	HC
SUNY/Univ at Binghamton	NY	12,787	HC
SUNY/Univ at Buffalo	NY	12,563	VC
SUNY/Univ at New Paltz	NY	11,565	VC
SUNY/Univ at Stony Brook	NY	12,763	HC
State Univ of West Georgia	GA	7,622	C
Stephen F. Austin State Univ	TX	7,552	C
Sterling College	KS	18,763	C
Stetson Univ	FL	29,495	VC
Stevens Inst of Technology	NJ	35,300	HC+
Stillman College	AL	11,370	LC
Stonehill College	MA	30,752	HC
Suffolk Univ	MA	29,200	C
Sul Ross State Univ	TX	6,582	LC
Susquehanna Univ	PA	29,990	VC
Swarthmore College	PA	37,716	MC
Sweet Briar College	VA	27,940	C
Syracuse Univ	NY	34,720	HC
Tabor College	KS	19,500	NC
Talladega College	AL	10,110	LC
Tarleton State Univ	TX	7,576	C
Taylor Univ	IN	23,820	VC+
Temple Univ	PA	15,912	C
Tenn State Univ	TN	9,048	LC
Tenn Tech Univ	TN	8,670	VC
Texas A&M Univ	TX	11,081	HC
Texas A&M Univ at Commerce	TX	8,994	C
Texas A&M Univ at Corpus Christi	TX	10,269	C
Texas A&M Univ at Kingsville	TX	6,740	LC
Texas Christian Univ	TX	23,410	VC
Texas Lutheran Univ	TX	20,370	C
Texas Southern Univ	TX	8,920	NC
Texas State Univ	TX	9,320	VC
Texas Tech Univ	TX	10,768	VC
Texas Wesleyan Univ	TX	16,245	C
Texas Woman's Univ	TX	7,804	LC
Thiel College	PA	20,970	C
Thomas Edison State College	NJ	3,325	SP
Thomas More College	KY	21,350	C
Touro College	NY	15,250	VC
Towson Univ	MD	12,694	VC
Transylvania Univ	KY	23,780	VC+
Trinity Christian College	IL	21,640	VC
Trinity College	CT	38,040	HC+
Trinity College	DC	24,150	LC
Trinity Univ	TX	26,466	HC+

School	ST	$IS	SR
Tri-State Univ-Main Campus	IN	23,600	C
Troy State Univ	AL	7,696	C
Troy State Univ Dothan	AL	3,842	C
Troy State Univ Montgomery	AL	3,600	NC
Truman State Univ	MO	9,728	HC+
Tufts Univ	MA	38,233	MC
Tulane Univ	LA	37,451	HC+
Tusculum College	TN	19,990	C
Tuskegee Univ	AL	17,250	LC
Union College	NE	17,130	C
Union College	NY	36,005	HC
Union Inst and Univ	OH	7,848	SP
Union Univ	TN	18,800	VC
United States Air Force Academy	CO		HC+
United States Military Academy	NY		MC
United States Naval Academy	MD		MC
Universidad Adventista de las Antillas	PR	5,460	
Univ of Akron	OH	13,134	NC
Univ of Alabama	AL	9,040	C+
Univ of Alabama at Birmingham	AL	12,901	C
Univ of Alabama in Huntsville	AL	9,126	VC
Univ of Alaska Anchorage	AK	9,100	NC
Univ of Alaska Fairbanks	AK	9,295	C
Univ of Arizona	AZ	10,413	VC
Univ of Arkansas	AR	9,855	VC
Univ of Arkansas at Little Rock	AR	5,637	NC
Univ of Arkansas at Pine Bluff	AR	7,925	C
Univ of Bridgeport	CT	25,924	LC
Univ of Calif at Berkeley	CA	15,563	MC
Univ of Calif at Davis	CA	14,995	VC
Univ of Calif at Los Angeles	CA	15,330	MC
Univ of Calif at Riverside	CA	15,300	C
Univ of Calif at San Diego	CA	14,127	HC
Univ of Calif at Santa Barbara	CA	11,732	VC
Univ of Calif at Santa Cruz	CA	16,505	VC
Univ of Central Arkansas	AR	6,388	C
Univ of Central Florida	FL	10,038	VC
Univ of Central Okla	OK	9,434	C
Univ of Chicago	IL	35,087	MC
Univ of Cincinnati	OH	14,736	C
Univ of Colo at Boulder	CO	10,774	VC
Univ of Colo at Colo Springs	CO	10,667	C
Univ of Colo at Denver	CO	3,302	C
Univ of Conn	CT	14,608	VC
Univ of Dallas	TX	25,898	VC+
Univ of Dayton	OH	24,850	VC
Univ of Delaware	DE	12,616	HC
Univ of Denver	CO	32,148	VC
Univ of Detroit Mercy	MI	25,582	C
Univ of Dubuque	IA	20,950	C
Univ of Evansville	IN	24,190	VC
Univ of Findlay	OH	23,962	NC
Univ of Florida	FL	8,580	MC
Univ of Georgia	GA	8,656	VC
Univ of Great Falls	MT	15,360	C
Univ of Hartford	CT	31,080	C
Univ of Hawaii at Hilo	HI	6,497	C
Univ of Hawaii at Manoa	HI	9,565	VC
Univ of Houston	TX	9,818	C
Univ of Houston-Downtown	TX	2,594	NC
Univ of Idaho	ID	8,216	C
Univ of Illinois at Chicago	IL	13,418	C
Univ of Illinois at Urbana-Champaign	IL	11,316	HC+
Univ of Indianapolis	IN	22,560	VC
Univ of Iowa	IA	10,923	VC
Univ of Kansas	KS	8,923	VC
Univ of Kentucky	KY	7,765	C
Univ of La Verne	CA	28,600	C
Univ of Louisiana at Lafayette	LA	5,826	C
Univ of Louisiana at Monroe	LA	5,207	NC
Univ of Louisville	KY	8,762	VC
Univ of Maine	ME	12,080	C+
Univ of Maine at Farmington	ME	10,108	C
Univ of Maine at Fort Kent	ME	9,770	LC
Univ of Mary Hardin-Baylor	TX	17,268	C
Univ of Maryland/Baltimore County	MD	14,668	VC+
Univ of Maryland/College Park	MD	14,227	HC
Univ of Maryland/Eastern Shore	MD	9,964	C
Univ of Maryland/Univ College	MD	5,910	SP
Univ of Mass Amherst	MA	13,980	C+
Univ of Mass Boston	MA	6,227	C
Univ of Mass Dartmouth	MA	12,835	C
Univ of Mass Lowell	MA	11,937	VC
Univ of Memphis	TN	8,560	C
Univ of Miami	FL	34,608	HC
Univ of Mich/Ann Arbor	MI	13,864	HC+
Univ of Mich/Dearborn	MI	6,843	VC

ST = STATE **$IS** = IN-STATE COSTS **SR** = SELECTOR RATING

School	ST	$IS	SR
Univ of Mich/Flint	MI	5,548	C
Univ of Minn/Duluth	MN	12,470	C
Univ of Minn/Morris	MN	12,896	VC
Univ of Minn/Twin Cities	MN	13,160	VC
Univ of Miss	MS	7,666	C
Univ of Missouri/Columbia	MO	13,782	VC
Univ of Missouri/Kansas City	MO	13,416	VC
Univ of Missouri/Rolla	MO	12,292	HC
Univ of Missouri/St. Louis	MO	11,656	VC
Univ of Mobile	AL	13,620	C
Univ of Montana	MT	9,395	C
Univ of Nebr at Kearney	NE	8,286	NC
Univ of Nebr at Lincoln	NE	9,975	C+
Univ of Nebr at Omaha	NE	8,080	C
Univ of Nevada/Las Vegas	NV	11,566	C
Univ of Nevada/Reno	NV	9,792	C
Univ of New Hampshire	NH	14,828	VC
Univ of New Haven	CT	28,650	C
Univ of New Mexico	NM	9,223	C
Univ of New Orleans	LA	7,356	C
Univ of North Alabama	AL	7,972	NC
Univ of N Car at Asheville	NC	8,079	VC
Univ of N Car at Chapel Hill	NC	10,117	MC
Univ of N Car at Charlotte	NC	8,185	C
Univ of N Car at Greensboro	NC	8,248	C
Univ of N Car at Pembroke	NC	6,929	LC
Univ of N Car at Wilmington	NC	8,940	VC
Univ of N Dak	ND	8,390	C
Univ of North Florida	FL	8,769	VC
Univ of North Texas	TX	7,629	C
Univ of Northern Colo	CO	8,987	C
Univ of Northern Iowa	IA	9,834	C
Univ of Notre Dame	IN	34,442	MC
Univ of Okla	OK	9,226	VC
Univ of Oregon	OR	11,479	VC
Univ of Pennsylvania	PA	37,960	MC
Univ of Pittsburgh at Bradford	PA	15,294	C
Univ of Pittsburgh at Johnstown	PA	15,216	LC
Univ of Pittsburgh at Pittsburgh	PA	16,074	HC
Univ of Portland	OR	28,500	VC
Univ of PR/Arecibo	PR	1,095	
Univ of PR/Bayamon Univ College Campus	PR	1,600	
Univ of PR/Mayaguez	PR		
Univ of PR/Rio Piedras	PR	5,730	
Univ of Puget Sound	WA	31,760	HC
Univ of Redlands	CA	32,576	VC
Univ of Rhode Island	RI	13,720	VC
Univ of Richmond	VA	30,100	MC
Univ of Rio Grande	OH	8,728	NC
Univ of Rochester	NY	32,979	HC
Univ of St. Francis	IL	22,850	C
Univ of St. Thomas	MN	26,918	VC
Univ of San Diego	CA	33,156	HC
Univ of San Francisco	CA	34,700	VC
Univ of Science and Arts of Okla	OK	5,982	C
Univ of Scranton	PA	30,836	VC
Univ of Sioux Falls	SD	16,390	C
Univ of South Alabama	AL	7,760	LC
Univ of S Car at Columbia	SC	10,048	VC
Univ of S Car at Spartanburg	SC	9,936	C+
Univ of S Dak	SD	7,710	C+
Univ of Southern Calif	CA	37,459	MC
Univ of Southern Maine	ME	11,212	C
Univ of Southern Miss	MS	8,324	LC
Univ of Tenn at Chattanooga	TN	7,783	C
Univ of Tenn at Knoxville	TN	8,214	C
Univ of Tenn at Martin	TN	7,748	C
Univ of Texas at Arlington	TX	7,192	LC
Univ of Texas at Austin	TX	10,630	HC
Univ of Texas at Dallas	TX	10,234	HC
Univ of Texas at El Paso	TX	5,799	NC
Univ of Texas at San Antonio	TX	9,088	NC
Univ of Texas-Pan American	TX	5,954	LC
Univ of the District of Columbia	DC	2,070	LC
Univ of the Pacific	CA	31,090	VC
Univ of the Sacred Heart	PR	5,590	
Univ of the Sciences in Philadelphia	PA	29,310	VC
Univ of the South	TN	30,855	HC
Univ of Toledo	OH	12,479	NC
Univ of Tulsa	OK	22,090	VC+
Univ of Utah	UT	9,205	C
Univ of Vermont	VT	16,316	VC
Univ of Virginia	VA	11,740	MC
Univ of Washington	WA	10,361	VC
Univ of West Alabama	AL	6,048	C
Univ of West Florida	FL	8,470	C
Univ of Wisc/Eau Claire	WI	8,463	VC
Univ of Wisc/Green Bay	WI	8,154	C
Univ of Wisc/La Crosse	WI	8,991	VC
Univ of Wisc/Madison	WI	8,262	VC
Univ of Wisc/Milwaukee	WI	9,427	LC
Univ of Wisc/Oshkosh	WI	6,130	LC
Univ of Wisc/Parkside	WI	6,160	LC
Univ of Wisc/Platteville	WI	8,450	C
Univ of Wisc/Superior	WI	7,051	C+
Univ of Wyoming	WY	8,636	C
Ursinus College	PA	34,400	VC
Utah State Univ	UT	7,371	C
Utica College	NY	28,340	C
Valdosta State Univ	GA	7,798	C
Valparaiso Univ	IN	26,118	VC+
Vassar College	NY	37,030	MC
Villanova Univ	PA	35,050	HC
Virginia Commonwealth Univ	VA	9,030	C
Virginia Military Inst	VA	9,968	C+
Virginia Polytechnic Inst and State Univ	VA	9,179	C
Virginia Wesleyan College	VA	25,350	C
Voorhees College	SC	11,678	LC
Wagner College	NY	29,900	VC
Wake Forest Univ	NC	34,090	MC
Walla Walla College	WA	21,600	NC
Walsh Univ	OH	20,890	C
Wartburg College	IA	21,165	VC
Washburn Univ of Topeka	KS	8,984	NC
Washington and Lee Univ	VA	29,663	MC
Washington College	MD	30,540	VC
Washington State Univ	WA	11,334	C
Washington Univ in St. Louis	MO	38,293	MC
Wayne State College	NE	7,352	NC
Wayne State Univ	MI	11,774	C
Waynesburg College	PA	19,370	C
Weber State Univ	UT	7,945	NC
Webster Univ	MO	21,848	VC
Wellesley College	MA	36,516	MC
Wells College	NY	21,122	VC
Wentworth Inst of Technology	MA	23,000	C
Wesleyan Univ	CT	35,139	MC
West Chester Univ of Pennsylvania	PA	11,164	C
West Texas A&M Univ	TX	7,533	C
West Virginia Univ	WV	9,370	C
West Virginia Univ Inst of Technology	WV	7,518	NC
West Virginia Wesleyan College	WV	22,920	C
Western Baptist College	OR	21,808	C
Western Carolina Univ	NC	6,742	C
Western Conn State Univ	CT	11,625	C
Western Illinois Univ	IL	10,363	C
Western Kentucky Univ	KY	6,834	C
Western Mich Univ	MI	12,031	C
Western New England College	MA	28,924	C
Western New Mexico Univ	NM	5,950	LC
Western Oregon Univ	OR	10,281	C
Western State College of Colo	CO	9,014	C
Western Washington Univ	WA	10,119	VC
Westfield State College	MA	10,147	C
Westminster College	MO	18,150	C+
Westminster College	PA	22,960	C
Westminster College	UT	17,226	C
Westmont College	CA	33,062	VC+
Wheaton College	IL	21,934	HC
Wheaton College	MA	36,330	HC
Wheeling Jesuit Univ	WV	22,660	C
Whitworth College	WA	26,428	VC+
Wichita State Univ	KS	8,092	C
Widener Univ	PA	27,020	C
Wilberforce Univ	OH	14,937	LC
Wiley College	TX	8,100	LC
Wilkes Univ	PA	28,060	C
Willamette Univ	OR	32,032	VC+
William Jewell College	MO	21,320	VC
William Paterson Univ of New Jersey	NJ	14,450	C
William Penn Univ	IA	17,575	LC
William Woods Univ	MO	20,120	C
Williams Baptist College	AR	11,950	C
Williams College	MA	32,270	MC
Wilmington College	OH	24,172	LC
Wingate Univ	NC	21,200	C
Winona State Univ	MN		C
Winston-Salem State Univ	NC	8,926	LC
Winthrop Univ	SC	11,302	C
Wittenberg Univ	OH	31,316	VC
Wofford College	SC	26,710	HC
Worcester Polytechnic Inst	MA	37,404	HC
Worcester State College	MA	10,005	C
Wright State Univ	OH	11,490	LC
Xavier Univ	OH	26,850	VC+
Xavier Univ of Louisiana	LA	17,600	C
Yale Univ	CT	37,000	MC
Yeshiva Univ	NY	21,400	C
Youngstown State Univ	OH	11,148	NC

COMPUTER TECHNOLOGY

School	ST	$IS	SR
Andrews Univ	MI	19,550	C
Bowie State Univ	MD	10,873	C+
Bowling Green State Univ	OH	13,036	C
Calif State Polytechnic Univ, Pomona	CA	8,793	C+
Daniel Webster College	NH	24,870	C
DeVry/New York	NY	11,860	LC
Eastern Mich Univ	MI	11,478	C
Eastern Washington Univ	WA	9,012	C
Endicott College	MA	25,266	C+
Excelsior College	NY	975	SP
Farmingdale SUNY	NY	12,891	C
Georgia Southwestern State Univ	GA	6,013	C
Guilford College	NC	24,960	VC
Idaho State Univ	ID	8,128	C
Indiana State Univ	IN	10,719	LC
Indiana Univ-Purdue Univ Indianapolis	IN	8,257	LC
Inter American Univ of PR/Bayamon Univ College	PR	3,522	
International College	FL	8,060	LC
LeTourneau Univ	TX	21,080	C
Martin Univ	IN	10,200	SP
Methodist College	NC	19,526	C
Missouri Southern State Univ	MO	8,316	C
Mountain State Univ	WV	10,212	NC
Murray State Univ	KY	7,816	VC
New Jersey Inst of Technology	NJ	16,396	VC
Norfolk State Univ	VA	9,722	LC
Northeastern Univ	MA	35,650	HC
Oregon Inst of Technology	OR	8,718	C
Pennsylvania College of Technology	PA	15,126	NC
Purdue Univ/Calumet	IN	6,630	NC
Purdue Univ/West Lafayette	IN	12,560	VC
Rochester Inst of Technology	NY	29,217	VC+
Rockhurst Univ	MO	22,960	C+
St. John's Univ	NY	30,180	C
St. Louis Univ	MO	29,780	VC+
Shawnee State Univ	OH	11,031	NC
Southwestern College	KS	19,560	C
SUNY/College of Technology at Alfred	NY	12,416	C
Thomas Edison State College	NJ	3,325	SP
Univ of Arkansas at Little Rock	AR	5,637	NC
Univ of Dayton	OH	24,850	VC
Univ of Houston	TX	9,818	C
Univ of Maryland/Univ College	MD	5,910	SP
Univ of Memphis	TN	8,560	C
Univ of Rio Grande	OH	8,728	NC
Univ of St. Francis	IL	22,850	C
Univ of Southern Miss	MS	8,324	LC
Wayne State Univ	MI	11,774	C
Wentworth Inst of Technology	MA	23,000	C
Youngstown State Univ	OH	11,148	NC

CONSERVATION AND REGULATION

School	ST	$IS	SR
Austin Peay State Univ	TN	5,814	LC
Brigham Young Univ	UT	8,504	HC
Central Missouri State Univ	MO	9,776	C
College of Santa Fe	NM	25,293	C+
College of the Ozarks	MO	3,500	VC+
Kent State Univ	OH	12,932	C
LIU/C.W. Post Campus	NY	28,282	C
Muskingum College	OH	20,680	C
N Car State Univ	NC	9,886	VC
Northwest Missouri State Univ	MO	9,334	C
Northwestern Okla State Univ	OK	5,433	NC
Purdue Univ/West Lafayette	IN	12,560	VC
Southeastern Okla State Univ	OK	6,147	C
Southwest Missouri State Univ	MO	8,918	C
Sterling College	VT	21,114	C+
Unity College	ME	19,845	LC
Univ of Arkansas at Pine Bluff	AR	7,925	C
Univ of Calif at Berkeley	CA	15,563	MC
Univ of Wisc/Madison	WI	8,262	VC
Univ of Wisc/Milwaukee	WI	9,427	LC
Univ of Wisc/River Falls	WI	8,358	LC
Upper Iowa Univ	IA	20,076	C

CONSTRUCTION ENGINEERING

School	ST	$IS	SR
Arizona State Univ-Main	AZ	10,048	C
Bradley Univ	IL	22,910	VC
Fairleigh Dickinson Univ/Metropolitan Campus	NJ	28,584	C
Iowa State Univ	IA	10,768	VC
Louisiana Tech Univ	LA	7,361	C
Minn State Univ, Moorehead	MN	7,000	LC
Montana State Univ-Bozeman	MT	9,515	C
N Dak State Univ	ND	8,435	C
Purdue Univ/West Lafayette	IN	12,560	VC
Rensselaer Polytechnic Inst	NY	37,579	HC+
Southern Illinois Univ Edwardsville	IL	8,724	C
Southern Polytechnic State Univ	GA	7,620	VC
Texas A&M Univ	TX	11,081	HC
Thomas Edison State College	NJ	3,325	SP
Univ of Florida	FL	8,580	MC
Univ of Louisiana at Monroe	LA	5,207	NC
Univ of New Mexico	NM	9,223	C
Univ of the District of Columbia	DC	2,070	LC
Univ of Washington	WA	10,361	VC
Virginia Polytechnic Inst and State Univ	VA	9,179	C
Western Mich Univ	MI	12,031	C

CONSTRUCTION MANAGEMENT

School	ST	$IS	SR
Andrews Univ	MI	19,550	C
Auburn Univ	AL	10,396	VC
Boise State Univ	ID	7,657	LC
Brigham Young Univ	UT	8,504	HC
Calif Polytechnic State Univ	CA	8,747	VC
Cal State, Chico	CA	8,598	LC
Cal State, Fresno	CA	8,414	LC
Central Missouri State Univ	MO	9,776	C
Central Washington Univ	WA	9,768	C
Clemson Univ	SC	11,972	HC
Colo State Univ	CO	9,964	VC
Drexel Univ	PA	27,655	VC
East Carolina Univ	NC	8,671	C
Eastern Mich Univ	MI	11,478	C
Farmingdale SUNY	NY	12,891	C
Ferris State Univ	MI	12,512	C
Florida International Univ	FL	9,912	VC
Georgia Inst of Technology	GA	10,340	HC+
Georgia Southern Univ	GA	8,540	C
John Brown Univ	AR	15,080	VC
Kansas State Univ	KS	8,728	VC
Lawrence Tech Univ	MI	20,487	C
Louisiana State Univ and A&M College	LA	9,126	VC
Mich State Univ	MI	11,933	VC
Milwaukee School of Engineering	WI	28,479	VC+
Minn State Univ, Mankato	MN	8,803	LC
N Car State Univ	NC	9,886	VC
N Dak State Univ	ND	8,435	C
Northern Mich Univ	MI	10,834	C
Okla State Univ	OK	9,216	VC
Oregon State Univ	OR	11,055	C
Pennsylvania College of Technology	PA	15,126	NC
Pratt Inst	NY	34,350	SP
Roger Williams Univ	RI	30,296	C
S Dak State Univ	SD	7,782	C
Southern Utah Univ	UT	8,194	C
Southwest Missouri State Univ	MO	8,918	C
SUNY/College of Environmental Science and Forestry	NY	14,167	VC
SUNY/College of Technology at Alfred	NY	12,416	C
Tuskegee Univ	AL	17,250	LC
Univ of Cincinnati	OH	14,736	C
Univ of Denver	CO	32,148	VC
Univ of Houston	TX	9,818	C
Univ of Nebr at Lincoln	NE	9,975	C+
Univ of Nevada/Las Vegas	NV	11,566	C
Univ of North Florida	FL	8,769	VC
Univ of Northern Iowa	IA	9,834	C
Univ of Okla	OK	9,226	VC
Univ of Texas at San Antonio	TX	9,088	NC
Utica College	NY	28,340	C
Virginia Polytechnic Inst and State Univ	VA	9,179	C
Washington State Univ	WA	11,334	C
Wentworth Inst of Technology	MA	23,000	C
Western Carolina Univ	NC	6,742	C

CONSTRUCTION TECHNOLOGY

School	ST	$IS	SR
Appalachian State Univ	NC	7,637	VC
Bowling Green State Univ	OH	13,036	C
Calif State Polytechnic Univ, Pomona	CA	8,793	C+
Central Conn State Univ	CT	12,090	C
Eastern Kentucky Univ	KY	7,708	C
Indiana State Univ	IN	10,719	LC
Indiana Univ-Purdue Univ Indianapolis	IN	8,257	LC
Montana State Univ-Northern	MT	8,600	NC
Murray State Univ	KY	7,816	VC
Norfolk State Univ	VA	9,722	LC
Northern Kentucky Univ	KY	6,352	NC
Pennsylvania College of Technology	PA	15,126	NC
Purdue Univ/Calumet	IN	6,630	NC

ST = STATE $IS = IN-STATE COSTS SR = SELECTOR RATING

School	ST	$IS	SR
Purdue Univ/West Lafayette	IN	12,560	VC
Texas Southern Univ	TX	8,920	NC
Texas State Univ	TX	9,320	VC
Texas Tech Univ	TX	10,768	VC
Univ of Akron	OH	13,134	NC
Univ of Arkansas at Little Rock	AR	5,637	NC
Univ of Houston	TX	9,818	C
Univ of Maine	ME	12,080	C+
Univ of Maryland/Eastern Shore	MD	9,964	C
Univ of Mass Amherst	MA	13,980	C+
Univ of Nebr at Lincoln	NE	9,975	C+
Univ of Southern Miss	MS	8,324	LC
Univ of Wisc/Stout	WI	9,718	C
Wentworth Inst of Technology	MA	23,000	C

CONSUMER SERVICES

School	ST	$IS	SR
Framingham State College	MA	9,381	C
Indiana Univ of Pennsylvania	PA	10,489	C
Purdue Univ/West Lafayette	IN	12,560	VC
S Dak State Univ	SD	7,782	C
Syracuse Univ	NY	34,720	HC
Texas Woman's Univ	TX	7,804	LC
Univ of Delaware	DE	12,616	HC
Univ of Memphis	TN	8,560	C
Univ of Wisc/Madison	WI	8,262	VC

CORRECTIONS

School	ST	$IS	SR
Cal State, Stanislaus	CA	9,874	C
CUNY/John Jay College of Criminal Justice	NY	4,259	C
College of the Ozarks	MO	3,500	VC+
Eastern Kentucky Univ	KY	7,708	C
Jackson State Univ	MS	8,382	C
Limestone College	SC	17,700	C
Minn State Univ, Mankato	MN	8,803	LC
Southeast Missouri State Univ	MO	9,704	C
Stephen F. Austin State Univ	TX	7,552	C
Texas State Univ	TX	9,320	VC
Tiffin Univ	OH	19,490	LC
Univ of Indianapolis	IN	22,560	VC
Univ of New Haven	CT	28,650	C
Univ of Texas-Pan American	TX	5,954	LC
Washburn Univ of Topeka	KS	8,984	NC
Western Oregon Univ	OR	10,281	C
Youngstown State Univ	OH	11,148	NC

COUNSELING/PSYCHOLOGY

School	ST	$IS	SR
Averett Univ	VA	23,010	LC
College of Santa Fe	NM	25,293	C+
Crichton College	TN	15,215	C
Dallas Baptist Univ	TX	15,300	VC
Eastern Mich Univ	MI	11,478	C
Geneva College	PA	21,850	C
Goddard College	VT	21,056	C+
Grace College	IN	19,825	VC
Indiana Univ South Bend	IN	4,571	LC
Kentucky Christian College	KY	13,472	C
Limestone College	SC	17,700	C
Martin Univ	IN	10,200	SP
Moravian College	PA	28,903	VC
Newman Univ	KS	18,018	C
Northwest College	WA	18,854	C
Samford Univ	AL	18,648	VC
Toccoa Falls College	GA	15,600	C
Univ of Great Falls	MT	15,360	C
Univ of North Texas	TX	7,629	C
Wayne State College	NE	7,352	NC
Williams Baptist College	AR	11,950	C

COURT REPORTING

School	ST	$IS	SR
Central Mich Univ	MI	11,142	C
Humphreys College	CA	7,000	NC
Northwood Univ	TX	20,135	LC
Univ of Miss	MS	7,666	C

CRAFTS

School	ST	$IS	SR
Cal State, Fullerton	CA	6,648	C
Kent State Univ	OH	12,932	C
Kutztown Univ of Pennsylvania	PA	10,786	C
Purdue Univ/West Lafayette	IN	12,560	VC
Rochester Inst of Technology	NY	29,217	VC+
Univ of Illinois at Urbana-Champaign	IL	11,316	HC+

CREATIVE WRITING

School	ST	$IS	SR
Agnes Scott College	GA	28,230	HC
Albertson College of Idaho	ID	19,415	VC
Alderson-Broaddus College	WV	19,640	C
Andrews Univ	MI	19,550	C
Arkansas Tech Univ	AR	7,299	C
Ashland Univ	OH	24,464	C
Bard College	NY	37,352	HC+
Baylor Univ	TX	23,864	VC
Beloit College	WI	29,864	HC
Bennington College	VT	35,910	HC
Bluffton College	OH	23,694	C
Bowling Green State Univ	OH	13,036	C
Calif College of the Arts	CA	31,530	SP
Cal State, San Marcos	CA	1,736	LC
Cardinal Stritch Univ	WI	17,620	C
Carlow College	PA	21,334	C
Carroll College	MT	20,576	VC
Chapman Univ	CA	33,118	VC
Christopher Newport Univ	VA	8,862	VC
CUNY/Brooklyn College	NY	4,353	C+
CUNY/Hunter College	NY	6,729	C+
Colby College	ME	37,570	MC
College of Santa Fe	NM	25,293	C+
Colo College	CO	36,860	HC
Columbia College Chicago	IL	25,108	LC
Concordia College: Moorhead	MN	22,460	VC+
Dartmouth College	NH	37,770	MC
Dominican Univ of Calif	CA	31,670	C
Drexel Univ	PA	27,655	VC
Eastern Washington Univ	WA	9,012	C
Eckerd College	FL	28,744	C+
Edinboro Univ of Pennsylvania	PA	10,850	LC
Emerson College	MA	32,205	HC
Emory & Henry College	VA	21,950	C
Emory Univ	GA	36,872	MC
Eugene Lang College/New School Univ	NY	34,940	C
Fairleigh Dickinson Univ/ College at Florham	NJ	30,130	C
Florida State Univ	FL	9,028	HC
Geneva College	PA	21,850	C
Goddard College	VT	21,056	C+
Green Mountain College	VT	24,130	C
Hamilton College	NY	37,560	MC
Hampshire College	MA	37,037	HC
Harvard Univ/Harvard College	MA	37,928	MC
Hofstra Univ	NY	27,112	VC
Hollins Univ	VA	27,965	VC
Houghton College	NY	23,984	VC
Indiana Univ Bloomington	IN	12,389	VC
Indiana Wesleyan Univ	IN	19,900	C+
Ithaca College	NY	31,730	HC
Johnson State College	VT	11,819	LC
Kansas City Art Inst	MO	26,850	SP
Knox College	IL	30,294	VC+
La Roche College	PA	22,094	C
Lakeland College	WI	17,950	C
Le Moyne College	NY	26,400	VC
Lindenwood Univ	MO	17,050	VC
Linfield College	OR	27,090	VC
Loras College	IA	24,233	C
Loyola College in Maryland	MD	34,560	HC
Loyola Univ New Orleans	LA	31,036	VC+
Marlboro College	VT	29,055	VC+
Maryville College	TN	25,960	VC
Mass Inst of Technology	MA	38,310	MC
Methodist College	NC	19,526	C
Millikin Univ	IL	25,555	C
Mills College	CA	33,371	VC
Montclair State Univ	NJ	13,790	C
Mount Union College	OH	21,120	C
Naropa Univ	CO	23,364	SP
New England College	NH	28,860	LC
New York Univ	NY	39,406	MC
Northland College	WI	22,170	C+
Oberlin College	OH	36,938	MC
Ohio Northern Univ	OH	27,765	VC
Ohio Univ	OH	14,448	C
Okla Christian Univ	OK	17,690	NC
Pacific Univ	OR	24,250	C
Pratt Inst	NY	34,350	SP
Purdue Univ/West Lafayette	IN	12,560	VC
Roger Williams Univ	RI	30,296	C
St. Andrews Presbyterian College	NC	20,525	C
St. Joseph's College	IN	24,250	C
St. Mary's Univ of Minn	MN	21,535	C
Sarah Lawrence College	NY	41,218	HC
Seattle Univ	WA	24,183	VC
Seton Hill Univ	PA	24,930	C
Simon's Rock College of Bard	MA	36,580	HC
Southern Methodist Univ	TX	34,210	HC
Southern Nazarene Univ	OK	14,634	NC
Southern Vermont College	VT	18,226	LC
Southwest Minn State Univ	MN	9,106	VC
Spring Hill College	AL	25,868	VC
SUNY/College at Purchase	NY	10,587	VC
Stephens College	MO	24,260	C+
Susquehanna Univ	PA	29,990	VC
Sweet Briar College	VA	27,940	C
Univ of Arizona	AZ	10,413	VC
Univ of Calif at Riverside	CA	15,300	C
Univ of Central Okla	OK	9,434	C
Univ of Colo at Denver	CO	3,302	C
Univ of Evansville	IN	24,190	VC
Univ of Houston	TX	9,818	C
Univ of Maine at Farmington	ME	10,108	C
Univ of Miami	FL	34,608	HC
Univ of Mich/Ann Arbor	MI	13,864	HC+
Univ of Montana--Western	MT	8,073	NC
Univ of New Haven	CT	28,650	C
Univ of New Mexico	NM	9,223	C
Univ of N Car at Wilmington	NC	8,940	VC
Univ of Pittsburgh at Greensburg	PA	15,984	C
Univ of Pittsburgh at Johnstown	PA	15,216	LC
Univ of Pittsburgh at Pittsburgh	PA	16,074	HC
Univ of Tampa	FL	23,982	VC
Warren Wilson College	NC	21,794	VC
Wartburg College	IA	21,165	VC
Washington Univ in St. Louis	MO	38,293	MC
Wheaton College	MA	36,330	HC

CRIMINAL JUSTICE

School	ST	$IS	SR
Abilene Christian Univ	TX	18,370	VC
Adrian College	MI	21,950	C
Alabama State Univ	AL	6,404	C
Albany State Univ	GA	5,764	C+
Albright College	PA	30,579	C
Alcorn State Univ	MS	7,290	C
Alfred Univ	NY	28,290	C
Alvernia College	PA	23,212	LC
American International College	MA	24,690	LC
American Univ	DC	34,585	VC+
Anderson Univ	IN	19,430	LC
Angelo State Univ	TX	7,576	NC
Anna Maria College	MA	26,140	LC
Appalachian State Univ	NC	7,637	VC
Arizona State Univ-Main	AZ	10,048	C
Armstrong Atlantic State Univ	GA	7,102	C
Ashland Univ	OH	24,464	C
Auburn Univ Montgomery	AL	9,020	NC
Augusta State Univ	GA	2,592	C
Aurora Univ	IL	20,631	C
Averett Univ	VA	23,010	LC
Baldwin-Wallace College	OH	24,678	C
Ball State Univ	IN	8,660	C
Barton College	NC	19,314	C
Bay Path College	MA	24,910	C
Becker College	MA	23,710	LC
Bellarmine Univ	KY	24,110	VC
Bellevue Univ	NE	4,440	NC
Bemidji State Univ	MN	9,103	C
Benedict College	SC	12,662	LC
Bethany College	KS	18,675	LC
Bethel College	IN	19,670	C
Bethune-Cookman College	FL	16,480	LC
Bloomsburg Univ of Pennsylvania	PA	10,844	C
Bluefield College	VA	15,575	C
Bluefield State College	WV	2,806	LC
Bluffton College	OH	23,694	C
Boise State Univ	ID	7,657	LC
Bowie State Univ	MD	10,873	C+
Bowling Green State Univ	OH	13,036	C
Bradley Univ	IL	22,910	VC
Briar Cliff Univ	IA	21,660	C
Bridgewater State College	MA	10,482	C
Buena Vista Univ	IA	25,406	C
Butler Univ	IN	28,250	VC+
Cabrini College	PA	29,020	C
Caldwell College	NJ	24,060	LC
Calif Baptist Univ	CA	19,924	C
Calif Lutheran Univ	CA	27,600	LC
Cal State, Bakersfield	CA	6,090	LC
Cal State, Fullerton	CA	6,648	C
Cal State, Hayward	CA	8,871	LC
Cal State, Los Angeles	CA	5,778	C
Cal State, Sacramento	CA	9,543	C
Cal State, San Bernardino	CA	15,238	LC
Cal State, Stanislaus	CA	9,874	C
Calumet College of St. Joseph	IN	9,000	LC
Calvin College	MI	22,615	NC
Cameron Univ	OK	5,692	NC
Campbell Univ	NC	18,268	VC
Canisius College	NY	28,163	C+
Capital Univ	OH	26,550	C
Caribbean Univ	PR	3,000	
Carlow College	PA	21,334	C
Carroll College	WI	22,740	C
Carthage College	WI	25,000	C
Castleton State College	VT	11,820	C
Cedarville Univ	OH	19,954	VC
Centenary College	NJ	25,370	LC
Central Methodist College	MO	16,460	C
Central Missouri State Univ	MO	9,776	C
Central Washington Univ	WA	9,768	C
Chadron State College	NE	6,286	NC
Chaminade Univ of Honolulu	HI	21,430	LC
Champlain College	VT	22,030	C
Charleston Southern Univ	SC	17,122	C
Chestnut Hill College	PA	26,450	LC
Chicago State Univ	IL	10,882	C+
Christopher Newport Univ	VA	8,862	VC
Citadel, The	SC	12,295	C+
CUNY/John Jay College of Criminal Justice	NY	4,259	C
College of New Jersey	NJ	15,950	MC
College of St. Rose	NY	22,864	C
College of Santa Fe	NM	25,293	C+
College of the Ozarks	MO	3,500	VC+
College of the Southwest	NM	9,320	C+
Colo Technical Univ	CO	9,500	LC
Columbia College	MO	16,139	C
Columbus State Univ	GA	7,846	C
Concordia Univ	MI	24,095	C
Concordia Univ Wisc	WI	16,600	C
Concordia Univ/St.Paul	MN	24,486	C
Coppin State College	MD	10,191	LC
Culver-Stockton College	MO	17,850	C
Cumberland Univ	TN	16,910	C
Curry College	MA	26,025	LC
Dakota Wesleyan Univ	SD	17,832	C
Dallas Baptist Univ	TX	15,300	VC
De Sales Univ	PA	25,470	C
Defiance College	OH	22,615	C
Delaware Valley College	PA	26,676	C
Delta State Univ	MS	6,618	C
Dordt College	IA	20,170	VC
East Carolina Univ	NC	8,671	C
East Central Univ	OK	4,968	C
East Tenn State Univ	TN	8,497	C
Eastern Mich Univ	MI	11,478	C
Eastern New Mexico Univ	NM	6,762	LC
Eastern Washington Univ	WA	9,012	C
Edgewood College	WI	20,520	C
Edinboro Univ of Pennsylvania	PA	10,850	LC
Edward Waters College	FL	14,374	LC
Elizabeth City State Univ	NC	5,550	LC
Elmira College	NY	33,820	VC
Endicott College	MA	25,266	C+
Evangel Univ	MO	15,435	C
Fairleigh Dickinson Univ/ Metropolitan Campus	NJ	28,584	C
Fairmont State	WV	8,280	LC
Fayetteville State Univ	NC	5,590	LC
Ferris State Univ	MI	12,512	C
Ferrum College	VA	21,240	LC
Fitchburg State College	MA	9,622	C
Florida A&M Univ	FL	7,564	C
Florida Atlantic Univ	FL	8,543	C
Florida Gulf Coast Univ	FL	9,908	C
Florida International Univ	FL	9,912	VC
Florida Memorial College	FL	6,000	LC
Florida Southern College	FL	23,592	C
Fort Hays State Univ	KS	7,363	C
Fort Valley State Univ	GA	6,960	C
Franciscan Univ	IA	19,300	C
Franklin Pierce College	NH	28,980	LC
Frostburg State Univ	MD	11,114	C
Gannon Univ	PA	23,260	C
George Mason Univ	VA	9,732	VC
George Washington Univ	DC	41,030	MC
Georgia College and State Univ	GA	9,878	C
Georgia Southern Univ	GA	8,540	C
Georgia State Univ	GA	10,658	C
Gonzaga Univ	WA	26,766	HC
Grace College	IN	19,825	VC
Graceland Univ	IA	19,550	C
Grambling State Univ	LA	6,538	NC
Grand Canyon Univ	AZ	30,000	LC
Grand Valley State Univ	MI	11,022	VC
Grand View College	IA	19,748	LC
Guilford College	NC	24,960	VC
Gustavus Adolphus College	MN	27,120	VC+
Gwynedd-Mercy College	PA	24,225	C
Hamline Univ	MN	27,052	VC
Hannibal-LaGrange College	MO	13,940	C
Hardin-Simmons Univ	TX	14,165	C
Hawaii Pacific Univ	HI	19,218	C
Hesser College	NH	17,490	LC
High Point Univ	NC	22,480	C
Hilbert College	NY	19,170	LC
Holy Family College	PA	13,710	LC
Howard Univ	DC	16,505	C
Huron Univ	SD	10,450	C
Husson College	ME	16,300	LC
Illinois State Univ	IL	10,944	C+
Indiana Univ Bloomington	IN	12,389	VC
Indiana Univ East	IN	4,433	LC
Indiana Univ Kokomo	IN	4,463	LC
Indiana Univ Northwest	IN	4,538	LC
Indiana Univ South Bend	IN	4,571	LC
Indiana Univ Southeast	IN	4,504	LC
Indiana Univ-Purdue Univ Fort Wayne	IN	5,108	LC
Indiana Univ-Purdue Univ Indianapolis	IN	8,257	LC
Indiana Wesleyan Univ	IN	19,900	C+
Inter American Univ of PR/ Aguadilla Campus	PR	3,544	
Inter American Univ of PR/ Arecibo Campus	PR	3,300	
Inter American Univ of PR/ Barranquitas Regional College	PR	3,300	

ST = STATE $IS = IN-STATE COSTS SR = SELECTOR RATING

CRIMINOLOGY

ST = STATE   **$IS** = IN-STATE COSTS   **SR** = SELECTOR RATING

School	ST	$IS	SR
Arkansas State Univ	AR	8,450	C
Auburn Univ	AL	10,396	VC
Barry Univ	FL	24,100	LC
Cal State, Fresno	CA	8,414	LC
Cal State, Northridge	CA	7,757	LC
Cal State, Stanislaus	CA	9,874	C
Central Conn State Univ	CT	12,090	C
Christopher Newport Univ	VA	8,862	VC
CUNY/John Jay College of Criminal Justice	NY	4,259	C
Coker College	SC	21,491	C
College of the Ozarks	MO	3,500	VC+
Dominican Univ	IL	23,610	C
Drury Univ	MO	18,085	VC+
Florida State Univ	FL	9,028	HC
Hilbert College	NY	19,170	LC
Indiana State Univ	IN	10,719	LC
Indiana Univ of Pennsylvania	PA	10,489	C
Le Moyne College	NY	26,400	VC
Limestone College	SC	17,700	C
Longwood Univ	VA	11,175	C
Marquette Univ	WI	27,594	VC
Maryville Univ of St. Louis	MO	22,090	VC
Mount Aloysius College	PA	19,120	LC
Ohio State Univ	OH	13,080	VC+
Pontifical Catholic Univ of PR/Ponce	PR	7,298	
St. Ambrose Univ	IA	22,800	C
Southern Oregon Univ	OR	10,362	C
SUNY/College at Old Westbury	NY	12,784	C
State Univ of West Georgia	GA	7,622	C
Texas State Univ	TX	9,320	VC
Tiffin Univ	OH	19,490	LC
Turabo Univ	PR	4,110	
Univ of Calif at Irvine	CA	19,808	HC
Univ of Florida	FL	8,580	MC
Univ of La Verne	CA	28,600	C
Univ of Maryland/College Park	MD	14,227	HC
Univ of Memphis	TN	8,560	C
Univ of Miami	FL	34,608	HC
Univ of Minn/Duluth	MN	12,470	C
Univ of Northern Iowa	IA	9,834	C
Univ of South Florida	FL	9,454	C
Univ of Southern Colo	CO	7,821	LC
Univ of Tampa	FL	23,982	VC
Univ of Texas at Dallas	TX	10,234	HC
Upper Iowa Univ	IA	20,076	C
Valparaiso Univ	IN	26,118	VC+
Virginia Union Univ	VA	15,358	LC
Wilkes Univ	PA	28,060	C
William Penn Univ	IA	17,575	LC

CROSSCULTURAL STUDIES

School	ST	$IS	SR
Alfred Univ	NY	28,290	C
Andrews Univ	MI	19,550	C
Antioch College	OH	29,269	C
Biola Univ	CA	25,964	VC
Chatham College	PA	27,266	C+
Columbia College Chicago	IL	25,108	LC
Eugene Lang College/New School Univ	NY	34,940	C
Goddard College	VT	21,056	C+
Hampshire College	MA	37,037	HC
Hope International Univ	CA	16,940	NC
Houghton College	NY	23,984	VC
John Brown Univ	AR	15,080	VC
Johns Hopkins Univ	MD	38,372	MC
Lee Univ	TN	13,780	NC
Murray State Univ	KY	7,816	VC
National-Louis Univ	IL	16,240	LC
Nyack College	NY	18,540	C
Simon's Rock College of Bard	MA	36,580	HC
Stanford Univ	CA	37,612	MC
Towson Univ	MD	12,694	VC
Univ of Calif at Irvine	CA	19,808	HC
Univ of Calif at Los Angeles	CA	15,330	MC
Waynesburg College	PA	19,370	C
Western Baptist College	OR	21,808	C
Whitworth College	WA	26,428	VC+
Wofford College	SC	26,710	HC

CULINARY ARTS

School	ST	$IS	SR
Art Inst of Atlanta	GA	23,205	SP
Metropolitan State Univ	MN	3,852	SP
Pennsylvania College of Technology	PA	15,126	NC
Virginia Intermont College	VA	19,800	C

CYBERNETICS

School	ST	$IS	SR
Univ of Calif at Los Angeles	CA	15,330	MC

CYTOTECHNOLOGY

School	ST	$IS	SR
Alderson-Broaddus College	WV	19,640	C
Barry Univ	FL	24,100	LC
Bellarmine Univ	KY	24,140	VC
College of St. Elizabeth	NJ	25,460	C
College of St. Rose	NY	22,864	C
Edgewood College	WI	20,520	C
Franciscan Univ	IA	19,300	C
Indiana Univ Kokomo	IN	4,463	LC
Indiana Univ-Purdue Univ Indianapolis	IN	8,257	LC
Jewish Hospital College of Nursing and Allied Health	MO	11,200	SP
Kent State Univ	OH	12,932	C
Marian College of Fond du Lac	WI	19,625	C
Marshall Univ	WV	9,116	C
Northern Mich Univ	MI	10,834	C
St. John's Univ	NY	30,180	C
St. Mary's Univ of Minn	MN	21,535	C
Salve Regina Univ	RI	29,210	C
SUNY/Univ at Stony Brook	NY	12,763	HC
Suffolk Univ	MA	29,200	C
Thiel College	PA	20,970	C
Thomas Edison State College	NJ	3,325	SP
Univ of Alabama at Birmingham	AL	12,901	C
Univ of Conn	CT	14,608	VC
Univ of Kansas	KS	8,923	VC
Univ of N Dak	ND	8,390	C
Univ of North Texas	TX	7,629	C
Winona State Univ	MN		C

DAIRY SCIENCE

School	ST	$IS	SR
Calif Polytechnic State Univ	CA	8,747	VC
Delaware Valley College	PA	26,676	C
Iowa State Univ	IA	10,768	VC
Louisiana State Univ and A&M College	LA	9,126	VC
Penn State Univ/Univ Park Campus	PA	15,646	HC
S Dak State Univ	SD	7,782	C
Texas A&M Univ	TX	11,081	HC
Univ of Florida	FL	8,580	MC
Univ of Georgia	GA	8,656	VC
Univ of New Hampshire	NH	14,828	VC
Univ of Wisc/Madison	WI	8,262	VC
Utah State Univ	UT	7,371	C
Virginia Polytechnic Inst and State Univ	VA	9,179	C

DANCE

School	ST	$IS	SR
Adelphi Univ	NY	26,300	VC
Amherst College	MA	37,470	MC
Arizona State Univ-Main	AZ	10,048	C
Baldwin-Wallace College	OH	24,678	C
Ball State Univ	IN	8,660	C
Bard College	NY	37,352	HC+
Belhaven College	MS	16,040	C+
Bennington College	VT	35,910	HC
Birmingham-Southern College	AL	25,364	VC+
Boston Conservatory	MA	26,900	SP
Bowling Green State Univ	OH	13,036	C
Brenau Univ Women's College	GA	21,800	C
Brigham Young Univ	UT	8,504	HC
Butler Univ	IN	28,250	VC+
Calif Inst of the Arts	CA	30,690	SP
Cal State, Fullerton	CA	6,648	C
Cal State, Long Beach	CA	8,762	C+
Cal State, Northridge	CA	7,757	LC
Cal State, San Bernardino	CA	15,238	LC
Cedar Crest College	PA	25,145	C+
Centenary College of Louisiana	LA	23,100	VC+
Chapman Univ	CA	33,118	VC
CUNY/Herbert H. Lehman College	NY	3,320	LC
CUNY/Hunter College	NY	6,729	C+
CUNY/Queens College	NY	4,362	C
Coker College	SC	21,491	C
Colo College	CO	36,860	HC
Columbia College	SC	22,658	LC
Columbia College Chicago	IL	25,108	LC
Columbia Univ/Barnard College	NY	36,990	MC
Columbia Univ/Columbia College	NY	38,590	MC
Columbia Univ/School of General Studies	NY	35,000	C
Conn College	CT	37,900	MC
Cornell Univ	NY	38,253	MC
Cornish College of the Arts	WA	19,900	SP
De Sales Univ	PA	25,470	C
Denison Univ	OH	33,050	HC
Dickinson College	PA	35,825	HC
East Carolina Univ	NC	8,671	C
Eastern Mich Univ	MI	11,478	C
Eastern Univ	PA	24,020	C
Eastern Washington Univ	WA	9,012	C
Elon Univ	NC	22,240	VC
Emory Univ	GA	36,872	MC
Florida International Univ	FL	9,912	VC
Florida State Univ	FL	9,028	HC
Fordham Univ	NY	35,066	HC
Franklin Pierce College	NH	28,980	LC
George Mason Univ	VA	9,732	VC
George Washington Univ	DC	41,030	MC
Georgia State Univ	GA	10,658	C
Goucher College	MD	32,650	HC
Gustavus Adolphus College	MN	27,120	VC+
Hamilton College	NY	37,560	MC
Hampshire College	MA	37,037	HC
Hobart and William Smith Colleges	NY	36,536	HC
Hofstra Univ	NY	27,112	VC
Hollins Univ	VA	27,965	VC
Hope College	MI	25,340	VC
Howard Univ	DC	16,505	C
Huntingdon College	AL	18,400	VC
Jacksonville Univ	FL	24,040	C
James Madison Univ	VA	10,794	VC
Juilliard School	NY	30,385	SP
Kent State Univ	OH	12,932	C
Kenyon College	OH	35,370	HC+
La Roche College	PA	22,094	C
Lake Erie College	OH	23,550	C
Lindenwood Univ	MO	17,050	VC
LIU/C.W. Post Campus	NY	28,282	C
Loyola Marymount Univ	CA	32,194	VC
Luther College	IA	25,700	VC
Manhattanville College	NY	32,420	C+
Marlboro College	VT	29,055	VC+
Marygrove College	MI	17,550	C
Marymount Manhattan College	NY	27,292	C
Mercyhurst College	PA	20,694	C
Meredith College	NC	23,065	C
Middlebury College	VT	38,100	MC
Mills College	CA	33,371	VC
Minn State Univ, Mankato	MN	8,803	LC
Montclair State Univ	NJ	13,790	C
Mount Holyoke College	MA	37,918	HC+
Muhlenberg College	PA	31,485	HC
New Mexico State Univ	NM	7,932	C
New York Univ	NY	39,406	MC
N Car School of the Arts	NC	8,565	SP
Northwestern Univ	IL	37,491	MC
Oberlin College	OH	36,938	MC
Ohio State Univ	OH	13,080	VC+
Ohio Univ	OH	14,448	C
Okla City Univ	OK	19,580	VC
Old Dominion Univ	VA	10,441	C
Palm Beach Atlantic Univ	FL	20,690	C
Pitzer College	CA	37,590	HC
Point Park Univ	PA	21,840	C
Radford Univ	VA	8,500	C
Randolph-Macon Woman's College	VA	28,430	VC+
Richard Stockton College of New Jersey	NJ	12,972	VC
Rider Univ	NJ	30,900	C
Roger Williams Univ	RI	30,296	C
Rutgers, The State Univ of New Jersey/New Brunswick/Piscataway Campus	NJ	15,800	HC
St. Olaf College	MN	28,500	HC
Sam Houston State Univ	TX	7,142	C
San Diego State Univ	CA	10,321	C
San Francisco State Univ	CA	12,070	C
San Jose State Univ	CA	8,187	C
Sarah Lawrence College	NY	41,218	HC
Scripps College	CA	35,700	HC+
Shenandoah Univ	VA	25,190	NC
Simon's Rock College of Bard	MA	36,580	HC
Skidmore College	NY	37,930	HC
Slippery Rock Univ of Pennsylvania	PA	10,343	LC
Smith College	MA	37,034	HC+
Southern Illinois Univ Edwardsville	IL	8,724	C
Southern Methodist Univ	TX	34,210	HC
Southern Utah Univ	UT	8,194	C
Southwest Missouri State Univ	MO	8,918	C
SUNY at Potsdam	NY	12,160	C
SUNY/College at Brockport	NY	12,111	C
SUNY/College at Purchase	NY	10,587	VC
SUNY/Univ at Buffalo	NY	12,563	VC
Stephen F. Austin State Univ	TX	7,552	C
Stephens College	MO	24,260	C+
Swarthmore College	PA	37,716	MC
Sweet Briar College	VA	27,940	C
Temple Univ	PA	15,912	C
Texas Christian Univ	TX	23,410	VC
Texas State Univ	TX	9,320	VC
Texas Tech Univ	TX	10,768	VC
Texas Woman's Univ	TX	7,804	LC
Towson Univ	MD	12,694	VC
Trinity College	CT	38,040	HC+
Tulane Univ	LA	37,451	HC+
Univ of Akron	OH	13,134	NC
Univ of Alabama	AL	9,040	C+
Univ of Arizona	AZ	10,413	VC
Univ of Calif at Berkeley	CA	15,563	MC
Univ of Calif at Irvine	CA	19,808	HC
Univ of Calif at Riverside	CA	15,300	C
Univ of Calif at San Diego	CA	14,127	HC
Univ of Calif at Santa Barbara	CA	11,732	VC
Univ of Cincinnati	OH	14,736	C
Univ of Colo at Boulder	CO	10,774	VC
Univ of Florida	FL	8,580	MC
Univ of Hartford	CT	31,080	C
Univ of Hawaii at Manoa	HI	9,565	VC
Univ of Idaho	ID	8,216	C
Univ of Illinois at Urbana-Champaign	IL	11,316	HC+
Univ of Iowa	IA	10,923	VC
Univ of Kansas	KS	8,923	VC
Univ of Louisiana at Lafayette	LA	5,826	C
Univ of Maryland/Baltimore County	MD	14,668	VC+
Univ of Maryland/College Park	MD	14,227	HC
Univ of Mass Amherst	MA	13,980	C+
Univ of Mich/Ann Arbor	MI	13,864	HC+
Univ of Minn/Twin Cities	MN	13,160	VC
Univ of Missouri/Kansas City	MO	13,416	VC
Univ of Nebr at Lincoln	NE	9,975	C+
Univ of Nevada/Las Vegas	NV	11,566	C
Univ of New Mexico	NM	9,223	C
Univ of N Car at Charlotte	NC	8,185	C
Univ of N Car at Greensboro	NC	8,248	C
Univ of North Texas	TX	7,629	C
Univ of Northern Colo	CO	8,987	C
Univ of Okla	OK	9,226	VC
Univ of Oregon	OR	11,479	VC
Univ of South Florida	FL	9,454	C
Univ of Southern Miss	MS	8,324	LC
Univ of Texas at Austin	TX	10,630	HC
Univ of the Arts	PA	29,510	SP
Univ of Utah	UT	9,205	C
Univ of Washington	WA	10,361	VC
Univ of Wisc/Milwaukee	WI	9,427	LC
Univ of Wisc/Stevens Point	WI	8,116	VC
Utah State Univ	UT	7,371	C
Virginia Commonwealth Univ	VA	9,030	C
Virginia Intermont College	VA	19,800	C
Washington Univ in St. Louis	MO	38,293	MC
Wayne State Univ	MI	11,774	C
Weber State Univ	UT	7,945	NC
Webster Univ	MO	21,848	VC
Wells College	NY	21,122	VC
Wesleyan Univ	CT	35,139	MC
West Texas A&M Univ	TX	7,533	C
Western Mich Univ	MI	12,031	C
Western Oregon Univ	OR	10,281	C
Winthrop Univ	SC	11,302	C
Wright State Univ	OH	11,490	LC

DANCE EDUCATION

School	ST	$IS	SR
Birmingham-Southern College	AL	25,364	VC+
Brenau Univ Women's College	GA	21,800	C
Brigham Young Univ	UT	8,504	HC
Columbia College	SC	22,658	LC
East Carolina Univ	NC	8,671	C
Huntingdon College	AL	18,400	VC
Jacksonville Univ	FL	24,040	C
Ohio State Univ	OH	13,080	VC+
Point Park Univ	PA	21,840	C
Shenandoah Univ	VA	25,190	NC
Southern Utah Univ	UT	8,194	C
Towson Univ	MD	12,694	VC
Univ of Central Okla	OK	9,434	C
Univ of N Car at Charlotte	NC	8,185	C
Univ of N Car at Greensboro	NC	8,248	C
Univ of the Arts	PA	29,510	SP

DATA PROCESSING

School	ST	$IS	SR
St. John's Univ	NY	30,180	C
Youngstown State Univ	OH	11,148	NC

DENTAL HYGIENE

School	ST	$IS	SR
Armstrong Atlantic State Univ	GA	7,102	C
Clayton College and State Univ	GA	2,441	LC
East Tenn State Univ	TN	8,497	C
Eastern Washington Univ	WA	9,012	C
Idaho State Univ	ID	8,128	C
Indiana Univ-Purdue Univ Indianapolis	IN	8,257	LC
Mass College of Pharmacy and Health Sciences	MA	28,770	SP
Midwestern State Univ	TX	8,045	LC
Minn State Univ, Mankato	MN	8,803	LC
New York Univ	NY	39,406	MC
Ohio State Univ	OH	13,080	VC+
Old Dominion Univ	VA	10,441	C
Oregon Inst of Technology	OR	8,718	C
Pennsylvania College of Technology	PA	15,126	NC
Southern Illinois Univ Carbondale	IL	10,407	C

ST = STATE $IS = IN-STATE COSTS SR = SELECTOR RATING

School	ST	$IS	SR
Tenn State Univ	TN	9,048	LC
Texas Woman's Univ	TX	7,804	LC
Thomas Edison State College	NJ	3,325	SP
Univ of Bridgeport	CT	25,924	LC
Univ of Detroit Mercy	MI	25,582	C
Univ of Hawaii at Manoa	HI	9,565	VC
Univ of Louisiana at Monroe	LA	5,207	NC
Univ of Maine at Augusta	ME	4,065	C
Univ of Mich/Ann Arbor	MI	13,864	HC+
Univ of Minn/Twin Cities	MN	13,160	VC
Univ of Missouri/Kansas City	MO	13,416	VC
Univ of Nebr at Lincoln	NE	9,975	C+
Univ of New England	ME	27,200	LC
Univ of New Haven	CT	28,650	C
Univ of New Mexico	NM	9,223	C
Univ of N Car at Chapel Hill	NC	10,117	MC
Univ of Rhode Island	RI	13,720	VC
Univ of S Dak	SD	7,710	C+
Univ of Washington	WA	10,361	VC
Univ of Wyoming	WY	8,636	C
Weber State Univ	UT	7,945	NC
West Liberty State College	WV	7,868	LC
West Virginia Univ	WV	9,370	C
Western Kentucky Univ	KY	6,834	C
Youngstown State Univ	OH	11,148	NC

DENTAL LABORATORY TECHNOLOGY

School	ST	$IS	SR
Minot State Univ	ND	6,602	LC
Southern Illinois Univ Carbondale	IL	10,407	C

DESIGN

School	ST	$IS	SR
Abilene Christian Univ	TX	18,370	VC
Adelphi Univ	NY	26,300	VC
Alma College	MI	25,566	VC
Andrews Univ	MI	19,550	C
Art Center College of Design	CA	23,450	SP
Art Inst of Boston at Lesley Univ	MA	28,080	SP
Atlanta College of Art	GA	18,600	SP
Auburn Univ	AL	10,396	VC
Becker College	MA	23,710	LC
Bowling Green State Univ	OH	13,036	C
Cal State, Long Beach	CA	8,762	C+
Carnegie Mellon Univ	PA	32,682	MC
Clemson Univ	SC	11,972	HC
Cleveland Inst of Art	OH	30,371	SP
Colby-Sawyer College	NH	27,850	LC
Cornell Univ	NY	38,253	MC
Cornish College of the Arts	WA	19,900	SP
Drexel Univ	PA	27,655	VC
East Carolina Univ	NC	8,671	C
Eastern Mich Univ	MI	11,478	C
Evangel Univ	MO	15,435	C
Fashion Inst of Technology/SUNY	NY	11,169	C+
Frostburg State Univ	MD	11,114	C
Grand Valley State Univ	MI	11,022	VC
Harding Univ	AR	14,890	VC
Hofstra Univ	NY	27,112	VC
Howard Univ	DC	16,505	C
Iowa State Univ	IA	10,768	VC
John Brown Univ	AR	15,080	VC
Kansas City Art Inst	MO	26,850	SP
Kent State Univ	OH	12,932	C
Lamar Univ	TX	6,816	LC
Lynn Univ	FL	30,750	C
Marywood Univ	PA	26,050	C
Memphis College of Art	TN	23,360	SP
Minneapolis College of Art and Design	MN	28,950	SP
New Jersey City Univ	NJ	11,850	LC
New York Univ	NY	39,406	MC
N Car State Univ	NC	9,886	VC
Northern Arizona Univ	AZ	9,002	C
Northern Mich Univ	MI	10,834	C
Okla Christian Univ	OK	17,690	NC
Okla State Univ	OK	9,216	VC
Olivet College	MI	19,984	C+
Otis College of Art and Design	CA	23,420	SP
Parsons School of Design	NY	32,242	SP
Purdue Univ/West Lafayette	IN	12,560	VC
Radford Univ	VA	8,500	C
Rochester Inst of Technology	NY	29,217	VC+
Saginaw Valley State Univ	MI	11,055	C
Salem State College	MA	8,592	C
San Jose State Univ	CA	8,187	C
School of the Art Inst of Chicago	IL	27,800	SP
Southern Illinois Univ Carbondale	IL	10,407	C
Southern Illinois Univ Edwardsville	IL	8,724	C
Southwest Missouri State Univ	MO	8,918	C
SUNY/College at Buffalo	NY	8,025	C
SUNY/Univ at New Paltz	NY	11,565	VC
Syracuse Univ	NY	34,720	HC
Texas Tech Univ	TX	10,768	VC
Univ of Akron	OH	13,134	NC
Univ of Calif at Davis	CA	14,995	VC
Univ of Calif at Los Angeles	CA	15,330	MC
Univ of Cincinnati	OH	14,736	C
Univ of Dayton	OH	24,850	VC
Univ of Georgia	GA	8,656	VC
Univ of Hartford	CT	31,080	C
Univ of Idaho	ID	8,216	C
Univ of Illinois at Chicago	IL	13,418	C
Univ of Kansas	KS	8,923	VC
Univ of Mass Amherst	MA	13,980	C+
Univ of Mass Dartmouth	MA	12,835	C
Univ of Mich/Ann Arbor	MI	13,864	HC+
Univ of Miss	MS	7,666	C
Univ of Missouri/Columbia	MO	13,782	VC
Univ of Nebr at Lincoln	NE	9,975	C+
Univ of Southern Miss	MS	8,324	LC
Univ of Texas at Austin	TX	10,630	HC
Villa Julie College	MD	18,393	C
Virginia Commonwealth Univ	VA	9,030	C
Washington Univ in St. Louis	MO	38,293	MC
Wayne State Univ	MI	11,774	C

DEVELOPMENT ECONOMICS

School	ST	$IS	SR
Eastern Mennonite Univ	VA	22,990	C

DEVELOPMENTAL PSYCHOLOGY

School	ST	$IS	SR
Bard College	NY	37,352	HC+
Bennington College	VT	35,910	HC
Cal State, Stanislaus	CA	9,874	C
Moravian College	PA	28,903	VC

DIETETICS

School	ST	$IS	SR
Abilene Christian Univ	TX	18,370	VC
Andrews Univ	MI	19,550	C
Ball State Univ	IN	8,660	C
Baylor Univ	TX	23,864	VC
Bennett College	NC	11,200	C
Berea College	KY	5,030	VC+
Bowling Green State Univ	OH	13,036	C
Bradley Univ	IL	22,910	VC
Brigham Young Univ	UT	8,504	HC
Cal State, Los Angeles	CA	5,778	C
Central Missouri State Univ	MO	9,776	C
CUNY/Herbert H. Lehman College	NY	3,320	LC
College of St. Benedict	MN	26,672	VC
College of St. Catherine	MN	24,010	VC
College of the Ozarks	MO	3,500	VC+
Concordia College: Moorhead	MN	22,460	VC+
David Lipscomb Univ	TN	16,158	VC
Dominican Univ	IL	23,610	C
D'Youville College	NY	21,080	C
East Carolina Univ	NC	8,671	C
Eastern Kentucky Univ	KY	7,708	C
Eastern Mich Univ	MI	11,478	C
Florida International Univ	FL	9,912	VC
Florida State Univ	FL	9,028	HC
Fontbonne Univ	MO	21,508	C
Gannon Univ	PA	23,260	C
Harding Univ	AR	14,890	VC
Howard Univ	DC	16,505	C
Idaho State Univ	ID	8,128	C
Immaculata Univ	PA	25,200	C
Indiana State Univ	IN	10,719	LC
Indiana Univ Bloomington	IN	12,389	VC
Indiana Univ of Pennsylvania	PA	10,489	C
Iowa State Univ	IA	10,768	VC
James Madison Univ	VA	10,794	VC
Kansas State Univ	KS	8,728	VC
Keene State College	NH	12,212	C
Louisiana Tech Univ	LA	7,361	C
Madonna Univ	MI	11,504	VC
Mansfield Univ	PA	11,220	C
Marshall Univ	WV	9,116	C
Marywood Univ	PA	26,050	C
Mercyhurst College	PA	20,694	C
Messiah College	PA	25,890	VC+
Miami Univ	OH	15,033	HC
Mich State Univ	MI	11,933	VC
Minn State Univ, Mankato	MN	8,803	LC
Mount Mary College	WI	20,370	C
Murray State Univ	KY	7,816	VC
Nicholls State Univ	LA	6,395	NC
Northern Illinois Univ	IL	11,472	C
Oakwood College	AL	14,904	C
Ohio Univ	OH	14,448	C
Olivet Nazarene Univ	IL	20,480	C
Ouachita Baptist Univ	AR	18,900	VC
Point Loma Nazarene Univ	CA	21,380	VC
Prairie View A&M Univ	TX	9,418	NC
Purdue Univ/West Lafayette	IN	12,560	VC
Rochester Inst of Technology	NY	29,217	VC+
St. John's Univ	MN	26,473	VC
St. Joseph College	CT	29,685	C
San Francisco State Univ	CA	12,070	C
Seton Hill Univ	PA	24,930	C
Simmons College	MA	33,000	VC
Southern Illinois Univ Carbondale	IL	10,407	C
Southwest Missouri State Univ	MO	8,918	C
SUNY/College at Buffalo	NY	8,025	C
SUNY/College at Oneonta	NY	11,870	VC
SUNY/College at Plattsburgh	NY	11,700	C
Stephen F. Austin State Univ	TX	7,552	C
Syracuse Univ	NY	34,720	HC
Tarleton State Univ	TX	7,576	C
Texas Christian Univ	TX	23,410	VC
Texas Southern Univ	TX	8,920	NC
Texas Tech Univ	TX	10,768	VC
Texas Woman's Univ	TX	7,804	LC
Tuskegee Univ	AL	17,250	LC
Univ of Akron	OH	13,134	NC
Univ of Calif at Davis	CA	14,995	VC
Univ of Central Arkansas	AR	6,388	C
Univ of Conn	CT	14,608	VC
Univ of Dayton	OH	24,850	VC
Univ of Delaware	DE	12,616	HC
Univ of Georgia	GA	8,656	VC
Univ of Idaho	ID	8,216	C
Univ of Louisiana at Lafayette	LA	5,826	C
Univ of Maryland/College Park	MD	14,227	HC
Univ of Nebr at Lincoln	NE	9,975	C+
Univ of New Haven	CT	28,650	C
Univ of New Mexico	NM	9,223	C
Univ of N Dak	ND	8,390	C
Univ of Northern Colo	CO	8,987	C
Univ of Northern Iowa	IA	9,834	C
Univ of Rhode Island	RI	13,720	VC
Univ of Texas at Austin	TX	10,630	HC
Univ of Texas-Pan American	TX	5,954	LC
Univ of the Incarnate Word	TX	21,772	LC
Univ of Vermont	VT	16,316	VC
Univ of Wisc/Madison	WI	8,262	VC
Univ of Wisc/Stevens Point	WI	8,116	VC
Univ of Wisc/Stout	WI	9,718	C
Viterbo Univ	WI	20,430	C
Wayne State Univ	MI	11,774	C
Western Carolina Univ	NC	6,742	C
Western Kentucky Univ	KY	6,834	C
Western Mich Univ	MI	12,031	C
Youngstown State Univ	OH	11,148	NC

DIGITAL ARTS/TECHNOLOGY

School	ST	$IS	SR
Bethel College	IN	19,670	C
Cal State, Dominguez Hills	CA	5,840	LC
Calvin College	MI	22,615	NC
Canisius College	NY	28,163	C+
Cogswell Polytechnical College	CA	14,400	LC
College for Creative Studies	MI	23,298	SP
Dominican Univ of Calif	CA	31,670	C
Drexel Univ	PA	27,655	VC
Grace Bible College	MI	15,890	C
Henry Cogswell College	WA	14,400	SP
Huntingdon College	AL	18,400	VC
Illinois State Univ	IL	10,944	C+
Indiana Univ Bloomington	IN	12,389	VC
Indiana Univ South Bend	IN	4,571	LC
Kendall College of Art and Design of Ferris State Univ	MI	10,784	SP
Marist College	NY	27,596	VC
Minneapolis College of Art and Design	MN	28,950	SP
Otis College of Art and Design	CA	23,420	SP
Pacific Union College	CA	22,065	C+
Point Park Univ	PA	21,840	C
Quinnipiac Univ	CT	30,570	VC
School of the Art Inst of Chicago	IL	27,800	SP
Stetson Univ	FL	29,495	VC
Stevens Inst of Technology	NJ	35,300	HC+
Texas State Univ	TX	9,320	VC
Univ of Central Florida	FL	10,038	VC
Univ of Denver	CO	32,148	VC
Univ of Pennsylvania	PA	37,960	MC
Viterbo Univ	WI	20,430	C
Walla Walla College	WA	21,600	NC
Western Mich Univ	MI	12,031	C

DRAFTING AND DESIGN

School	ST	$IS	SR
Appalachian State Univ	NC	7,637	VC
Pennsylvania College of Technology	PA	15,126	NC
Southwest Missouri State Univ	MO	8,918	C
Thomas Edison State College	NJ	3,325	SP
Youngstown State Univ	OH	11,148	NC

DRAFTING AND DESIGN TECHNOLOGY

School	ST	$IS	SR
Alabama A&M Univ	AL	5,100	LC
Baker College of Flint	MI	7,720	NC
Central Missouri State Univ	MO	9,776	C
Montana State Univ-Northern	MT	8,600	NC
Norfolk State Univ	VA	9,722	LC
School of the Art Inst of Chicago	IL	27,800	SP
Texas Southern Univ	TX	8,920	NC
Tri-State Univ-Main Campus	IN	23,600	C
Univ of Houston	TX	9,818	C
Univ of Nebr at Lincoln	NE	9,975	C+
Univ of Rio Grande	OH	8,728	NC
Western Mich Univ	MI	12,031	C
Youngstown State Univ	OH	11,148	NC

DRAMA EDUCATION

School	ST	$IS	SR
Appalachian State Univ	NC	7,637	VC
Augustana College	SD	21,998	VC
Averett Univ	VA	23,010	LC
Baylor Univ	TX	23,864	VC
Boston Univ	MA	38,194	HC+
Bradley Univ	IL	22,910	VC
Brigham Young Univ	UT	8,504	HC
Catholic Univ of America	DC	34,248	VC
Columbus State Univ	GA	7,846	C
Culver-Stockton College	MO	17,850	C
Dana College	NE	20,280	C
East Carolina Univ	NC	8,671	C
East Central Univ	OK	4,968	C
East Texas Baptist Univ	TX	13,914	C
Eastern Mich Univ	MI	11,478	C
Elmhurst College	IL	24,630	C
Grambling State Univ	LA	6,538	NC
Greensboro College	NC	21,750	C
Indiana Univ-Purdue Univ Indianapolis	IN	8,257	LC
Kean Univ	NJ	14,479	C
Mars Hill College	NC	18,600	LC
Minot State Univ	ND	6,602	LC
Missouri Southern State Univ	MO	8,316	C
Oral Roberts Univ	OK	18,490	C
Palm Beach Atlantic Univ	FL	20,690	C
Point Park Univ	PA	21,840	C
St. Edward's Univ	TX	20,428	C
Simpson College	IA	23,658	C+
Southern Utah Univ	UT	8,194	C
Southwestern College	KS	19,560	C
Univ of Arizona	AZ	10,413	VC
Univ of Indianapolis	IN	22,560	VC
Univ of Maryland/College Park	MD	14,227	HC
Univ of N Car at Charlotte	NC	8,185	C
Univ of N Car at Greensboro	NC	8,248	C
Viterbo Univ	WI	20,430	C
West Texas A&M Univ	TX	7,533	C
Youngstown State Univ	OH	11,148	NC

DRAMATIC ARTS

School	ST	$IS	SR
Abilene Christian Univ	TX	18,370	VC
Adams State College	CO	7,468	C
Adelphi Univ	NY	26,300	VC
Adrian College	MI	21,950	C
Agnes Scott College	GA	28,230	HC
Alabama A&M Univ	AL	5,100	LC
Albany State Univ	GA	5,764	C+
Albertson College of Idaho	ID	19,415	VC
Albertus Magnus College	CT	23,130	LC
Albright College	PA	30,579	C
Alfred Univ	NY	28,290	C
Allegheny College	PA	30,280	VC
Alma College	MI	25,566	VC
American Univ	DC	34,585	VC+
Amherst College	MA	37,470	MC
Anderson Univ	IN	19,430	LC
Angelo State Univ	TX	7,576	NC
Appalachian State Univ	NC	7,637	VC
Arcadia Univ	PA	29,890	C
Arizona State Univ-Main	AZ	10,048	C
Arkansas State Univ	AR	8,450	C
Armstrong Atlantic State Univ	GA	7,102	C
Ashland Univ	OH	24,464	C
Auburn Univ	AL	10,396	VC
Augsburg College	MN	25,298	C
Augustana College	IL	26,610	VC+
Augustana College	SD	21,998	VC
Averett Univ	VA	23,010	LC
Avila Univ	MO	20,300	C
Baker Univ	KS	19,860	VC
Baldwin-Wallace College	OH	24,678	C
Ball State Univ	IN	8,660	C
Bard College	NY	37,352	HC+
Barry Univ	FL	24,100	LC
Barton College	NC	19,314	C
Bates College	ME	37,500	MC
Baylor Univ	TX	23,864	VC

School	ST	$IS	SR
Belhaven College	MS	16,040	C+
Beloit College	WI	29,864	HC
Benedictine College	KS	20,603	C
Bennington College	VT	35,910	HC
Berea College	KY	5,030	VC+
Berry College	GA	21,410	VC
Bethel College	IN	19,670	C
Bethel College	KS	19,800	C+
Bethel College	MN	25,180	VC
Bethune-Cookman College	FL	16,480	LC
Birmingham-Southern College	AL	25,364	VC+
Bloomsburg Univ of Pennsylvania	PA	10,844	C
Blue Mountain College	MS	10,226	C
Boise State Univ	ID	7,657	LC
Boston College	MA	33,284	MC
Boston Univ	MA	38,194	HC+
Bowdoin College	ME	37,790	MC
Bowling Green State Univ	OH	13,036	C
Bradley Univ	IL	22,910	VC
Brandeis Univ	MA	38,198	MC
Brenau Univ Women's College	GA	21,800	C
Briar Cliff Univ	IA	21,660	C
Brigham Young Univ	UT	8,504	HC
Bucknell Univ	PA	35,262	HC+
Butler Univ	IN	28,250	VC+
Calif Inst of the Arts	CA	30,690	SP
Calif Lutheran Univ	CA	27,600	LC
Calif State Polytechnic Univ, Pomona	CA	8,793	C+
Cal State, Bakersfield	CA	6,090	LC
Cal State, Chico	CA	8,598	LC
Cal State, Dominguez Hills	CA	5,840	LC
Cal State, Fresno	CA	8,414	LC
Cal State, Fullerton	CA	6,648	C
Cal State, Hayward	CA	8,871	LC
Cal State, Long Beach	CA	8,762	C+
Cal State, Los Angeles	CA	5,778	C
Cal State, Northridge	CA	7,757	LC
Cal State, Sacramento	CA	9,543	C
Cal State, San Bernardino	CA	15,238	LC
Cal State, Stanislaus	CA	9,874	C
Calif Univ of Pennsylvania	PA	10,388	C
Calvin College	MI	22,615	NC
Campbell Univ	NC	18,268	VC
Capital Univ	OH	26,550	C
Cardinal Stritch Univ	WI	17,620	C
Carnegie Mellon Univ	PA	32,682	MC
Carroll College	MT	20,576	VC
Carroll College	WI	22,740	C
Case Western Reserve Univ	OH	32,002	MC
Castleton State College	VT	11,820	C
Catawba College	NC	20,500	C
Catholic Univ of America	DC	34,248	VC
Cedar Crest College	PA	25,145	C+
Cedarville Univ	OH	19,954	VC
Centenary College	NJ	25,370	LC
Central College	IA	21,206	C
Central Conn State Univ	CT	12,090	C
Central Methodist College	MO	16,460	C
Central Mich Univ	MI	11,142	C
Central Washington Univ	WA	9,768	C
Centre College	KY	27,300	HC
Chadron State College	NE	6,286	NC
Chapman Univ	CA	33,118	VC
Charleston Southern Univ	SC	17,122	C
Chatham College	PA	27,266	C+
Cheyney Univ of Pennsylvania	PA	9,993	C
Christopher Newport Univ	VA	8,862	VC
CUNY/City College	NY	4,230	C+
CUNY/College of Staten Island	NY	4,308	NC
CUNY/Hunter College	NY	6,729	C+
CUNY/Queens College	NY	4,362	C
CUNY/York College	NY	3,292	NC
Claremont McKenna College	CA	36,880	MC
Clarion Univ of Pennsylvania	PA	11,272	LC
Clark Univ	MA	32,115	VC
Clarke College	IA	23,165	C
Cleveland State Univ	OH	12,308	LC
Coastal Carolina Univ	SC	11,040	C
Coe College	IA	27,385	VC
Coker College	SC	21,491	C
Colgate Univ	NY	37,095	MC
College of Charleston	SC	11,887	HC
College of St. Benedict	MN	26,672	VC
College of St. Catherine	MN	24,010	VC
College of Santa Fe	NM	25,293	C+
College of the Holy Cross	MA	36,451	MC
College of the Ozarks	MO	3,500	VC+
College of Wooster	OH	31,300	HC
Colo College	CO	36,860	HC
Columbia College Chicago	IL	25,108	LC
Columbia Univ/Barnard College	NY	36,990	MC
Columbia Univ/Columbia College	NY	38,590	MC
Columbia Univ/School of General Studies	NY	35,000	C
Columbus State Univ	GA	7,846	C
Concordia College: Moorhead	MN	22,460	VC+
Concordia Univ	CA	24,420	C
Concordia Univ Nebr	NE	20,302	C+
Concordia Univ/St.Paul	MN	24,486	C
Conn College	CT	37,900	MC
Cornell College	IA	27,825	VC+
Cornell Univ	NY	38,253	MC
Cornish College of the Arts	WA	19,900	SP
Creighton Univ	NE	26,748	VC+
Culver-Stockton College	MO	17,850	C
Cumberland College	KY	16,384	C
Dakota Wesleyan Univ	SD	17,832	C
Dartmouth College	NH	37,770	MC
Davidson College	NC	33,274	MC
Davis and Elkins College	WV	20,594	C
De Sales Univ	PA	25,470	C
Denison Univ	OH	33,050	HC
DePaul Univ	IL	27,580	VC
Dickinson College	PA	35,825	HC
Doane College	NE	20,000	C
Dominican Univ	IL	23,610	C
Dordt College	IA	20,170	VC
Drake Univ	IA	25,120	VC+
Drew Univ/College of Liberal Arts	NJ	35,550	VC
Drury Univ	MO	18,085	VC+
Duke Univ	NC	37,555	MC
Duquesne Univ	PA	26,907	VC
Earlham College	IN	29,976	VC+
East Carolina Univ	NC	8,671	C
East Central Univ	OK	4,968	C
East Stroudsburg Univ of Pennsylvania	PA	10,336	C
East Texas Baptist Univ	TX	13,914	C
Eastern Illinois Univ	IL	11,192	C
Eastern Kentucky Univ	KY	7,708	C
Eastern Mennonite Univ	VA	22,990	C
Eastern Mich Univ	MI	11,478	C
Eastern Nazarene College	MA	19,433	LC
Eastern New Mexico Univ	NM	6,762	LC
Eastern Oregon Univ	OR	10,080	NC
Eastern Washington Univ	WA	9,012	C
Eckerd College	FL	28,744	C+
Edinboro Univ of Pennsylvania	PA	10,850	LC
Elmhurst College	IL	24,630	C
Elmira College	NY	33,820	VC
Elon Univ	NC	22,240	VC
Emerson College	MA	32,205	HC
Emory & Henry College	VA	21,950	C
Emory Univ	GA	36,872	MC
Emporia State Univ	KS	6,998	C
Eugene Lang College/New School Univ	NY	34,940	C
Eureka College	IL	24,980	LC
Evangel Univ	MO	15,435	C
Fairleigh Dickinson Univ/ College at Florham	NJ	30,130	C
Fairleigh Dickinson Univ/ Metropolitan Campus	NJ	28,584	C
Fayetteville State Univ	NC	5,590	LC
Ferrum College	VA	21,240	LC
Fisk Univ	TN	17,305	LC
Five Towns College	NY	21,050	SP
Flagler College	FL	11,860	VC+
Florida A&M Univ	FL	7,564	C
Florida Atlantic Univ	FL	8,543	C
Florida International Univ	FL	9,912	VC
Florida Southern College	FL	23,592	C
Florida State Univ	FL	9,028	HC
Fordham Univ	NY	35,066	HC
Fort Lewis College	CO	8,353	C
Francis Marion Univ	SC	9,364	C
Franklin and Marshall College	PA	35,930	HC+
Franklin College	IN		C
Franklin Pierce College	NH	28,980	LC
Freed-Hardeman Univ	TN		NC
Frostburg State Univ	MD	11,114	C
Furman Univ	SC	28,976	HC+
Gallaudet Univ	DC	16,554	SP
Gannon Univ	PA	23,260	C
George Mason Univ	VA	9,732	VC
George Washington Univ	DC	41,030	MC
Georgia College and State Univ	GA	9,878	C
Georgia Southern Univ	GA	8,540	C
Georgia State Univ	GA	10,658	C
Gettysburg College	PA	35,646	HC
Gonzaga Univ	WA	26,766	HC
Gordon College	MA	25,982	VC+
Goshen College	IN	22,450	VC
Goucher College	MD	32,650	HC
Graceland Univ	IA	19,550	C
Grambling State Univ	LA	6,538	NC
Grand Canyon Univ	AZ	30,000	LC
Grand Valley State Univ	MI	11,022	VC
Greensboro College	NC	21,750	C
Greenville College	IL	21,342	C
Grinnell College	IA	31,060	HC+
Guilford College	NC	24,960	VC
Gustavus Adolphus College	MN	27,120	VC+
Hamilton College	NY	37,560	MC
Hamline Univ	MN	27,052	VC
Hampshire College	MA	37,037	HC
Hampton Univ	VA	17,112	C+
Hannibal-LaGrange College	MO	13,940	C
Hanover College	IN	25,200	VC
Harding Univ	AR	14,890	VC
Hartwick College	NY	34,650	C+
Hastings College	NE	19,928	VC
Heidelberg College	OH	20,266	NC
Henderson State Univ	AR	7,386	C
Hendrix College	AR	20,970	VC+
High Point Univ	NC	22,480	C
Hillsdale College	MI	22,450	HC
Hiram College	OH	28,234	VC
Hofstra Univ	NY	27,112	VC
Hollins Univ	VA	27,965	VC
Hope College	MI	25,340	VC
Howard Payne Univ	TX	15,176	C
Howard Univ	DC	16,505	C
Humboldt State Univ	CA	9,400	C
Huntingdon College	AL	18,400	VC
Idaho State Univ	ID	8,128	C
Illinois College	IL	19,100	VC
Illinois State Univ	IL	10,944	C+
Illinois Wesleyan Univ	IL	30,380	HC+
Indiana State Univ	IN	10,719	LC
Indiana Univ Bloomington	IN	12,389	VC
Indiana Univ Northwest	IN	4,538	LC
Indiana Univ of Pennsylvania	PA	10,489	C
Indiana Univ South Bend	IN	4,571	LC
Indiana Univ-Purdue Univ Fort Wayne	IN	5,108	LC
Iona College	NY	27,988	VC
Ithaca College	NY	31,730	HC
Jacksonville State Univ	AL	6,844	LC
Jacksonville Univ	FL	24,040	C
James Madison Univ	VA	10,794	VC
Judson College	IL	22,050	LC
Juilliard School	NY	30,385	SP
Kalamazoo College	MI	26,955	HC+
Kansas State Univ	KS	8,728	VC
Kansas Wesleyan Univ	KS	18,900	VC
Kean Univ	NJ	14,479	C
Kennesaw State Univ	GA	2,724	C
Kent State Univ	OH	12,932	C
Kentucky Wesleyan College	KY	17,250	C
Kenyon College	OH	35,370	HC+
King's College	PA	26,990	C
Knox College	IL	30,294	VC+
Kutztown Univ of Pennsylvania	PA	10,786	C
LaGrange College	GA	20,500	C
Lakeland College	WI	17,950	C
Lamar Univ	TX	6,816	LC
Lambuth Univ	TN	16,520	C
Lander Univ	SC	10,496	C
Langston Univ	OK	2,308	LC
Lawrence Univ	WI	30,900	HC
Le Moyne College	NY	26,400	VC
Lees-McRae College	NC	17,106	LC
Lehigh Univ	PA	37,570	HC+
Lenoir-Rhyne College	NC	19,186	C
Lewis and Clark College	OR	30,620	VC
Lewis Univ	IL	22,950	C+
Limestone College	SC	17,700	C
Lindenwood Univ	MO	17,050	VC
Linfield College	OR	27,090	VC
LIU/C.W. Post Campus	NY	28,282	C
Louisiana College	LA	13,450	C
Louisiana State Univ and A&M College	LA	9,126	VC
Loyola Marymount Univ	CA	32,194	VC
Loyola Univ Chicago	IL	31,164	VC
Loyola Univ New Orleans	LA	31,036	VC+
Lycoming College	PA	27,589	C+
Lynchburg College	VA	26,815	C
Lyon College	AR	17,995	VC
Macalester College	MN	31,944	MC
MacMurray College	IL	20,005	LC
Maharishi Univ of Management	IA	29,230	VC
Mansfield Univ	PA	11,220	C
Marian College	IN	23,030	C
Marietta College	OH	27,047	C
Marlboro College	VT	29,055	VC+
Marquette Univ	WI	27,594	VC
Mars Hill College	NC	18,600	LC
Mary Baldwin College	VA	24,939	C
Mary Washington College	VA	10,166	HC
Marymount College of Fordham Univ	NY	27,686	C
Marymount Manhattan College	NY	27,292	C
Maryville College	TN	25,960	VC
Marywood Univ	PA	26,050	C
Mass Inst of Technology	MA	38,310	MC
McDaniel College	MD	28,440	VC
McMurry Univ	TX	17,846	LC
McNeese State Univ	LA	5,259	LC
Meredith College	NC	23,065	C
Messiah College	PA	25,890	VC+
Methodist College	NC	19,526	C
Metropolitan State Univ	MN	3,852	SP
Miami Univ	OH	15,033	HC
Mich State Univ	MI	11,933	VC
MidAmerica Nazarene Univ	KS	18,688	C
Middlebury College	VT	38,100	MC
Midwestern State Univ	TX	8,045	LC
Millikin Univ	IL	25,555	C
Millsaps College	MS	25,182	VC
Minn State Univ, Mankato	MN	8,803	LC
Minn State Univ, Moorehead	MN	7,000	LC
Missouri Southern State Univ	MO	8,316	C
Missouri Valley College	MO	18,500	C
Monmouth College	IL	23,600	C
Montana State Univ-Billings	MT	9,550	C
Montana State Univ-Northern	MT	8,600	NC
Montclair State Univ	NJ	13,790	C
Moravian College	PA	28,903	VC
Morehead State Univ	KY	7,464	C
Morgan State Univ	MD	11,470	C
Morningside College	IA	21,610	C
Mount Holyoke College	MA	37,918	HC+
Mount Mercy College	IA	21,400	C
Mount Union College	OH	21,120	C
Muhlenberg College	PA	31,485	HC
Murray State Univ	KY	7,816	VC
Muskingum College	OH	20,680	C
Nazareth College of Rochester	NY	24,936	VC
Nebr Wesleyan Univ	NE	21,197	C+
New College of Calif	CA	8,900	NC
New College of Florida	FL	8,906	HC+
New England College	NH	28,860	LC
New Mexico State Univ	NM	7,932	C
New York Univ	NY	39,406	MC
Newberry College	SC	22,871	LC
Niagara Univ	NY	25,050	C
N Car Agricultural and Technical State Univ	NC	6,659	LC
N Car Central Univ	NC	7,534	LC
N Car School of the Arts	NC	8,565	SP
N Car Wesleyan College	NC	17,998	C
N Dak State Univ	ND	8,435	C
Northeastern Univ	MA	35,650	HC
Northern Arizona Univ	AZ	9,002	C
Northern Illinois Univ	IL	11,472	C
Northern Kentucky Univ	KY	6,352	NC
Northern Mich Univ	MI	10,834	C
Northwest Missouri State Univ	MO	9,334	C
Northwestern College	MN	22,820	C+
Northwestern College of Iowa	IA	19,640	C+
Northwestern Okla State Univ	OK	5,433	NC
Northwestern State Univ of Louisiana	LA	6,331	NC
Northwestern Univ	IL	37,491	MC
Notre Dame de Namur Univ	CA	26,932	LC
Oberlin College	OH	36,938	MC
Occidental College	CA	35,922	HC
Ohio Northern Univ	OH	27,765	VC
Ohio Univ	OH	14,448	C
Ohio Wesleyan Univ	OH	32,550	VC+
Okla Baptist Univ	OK	15,220	VC
Okla City Univ	OK	19,580	VC
Okla State Univ	OK	9,216	VC
Old Dominion Univ	VA	10,441	C
Oral Roberts Univ	OK	18,490	C
Oregon State Univ	OR	11,055	C
Ottawa Univ	KS	11,800	LC
Otterbein College	OH	26,085	C
Ouachita Baptist Univ	AR	18,900	VC
Our Lady of the Lake Univ of San Antonio	TX	17,336	C
Pacific Univ	OR	24,250	C
Palm Beach Atlantic Univ	FL	20,690	C
Penn State Univ/Univ Park Campus	PA	15,646	HC
Pepperdine Univ	CA	32,830	VC
Pfeiffer Univ	NC	18,980	C
Piedmont College	GA	16,900	C
Pitzer College	CA	37,590	HC
Point Loma Nazarene Univ	CA	21,380	VC
Point Park Univ	PA	21,840	C
Pomona College	CA	33,960	MC
Portland State Univ	OR	12,453	C
Prairie View A&M Univ	TX	9,418	NC
Principia College	IL	25,044	C+
Providence College	RI	30,604	HC
Purdue Univ/West Lafayette	IN	12,560	VC
Queens Univ of Charlotte	NC	21,840	C
Radford Univ	VA	8,500	C
Ramapo College of New Jersey	NJ	15,203	VC
Randolph-Macon College	VA	27,190	C
Randolph-Macon Woman's College	VA	28,430	VC+
Reed College	OR	36,950	MC
Regis College	MA	29,000	C
Rhode Island College	RI	11,565	C
Rhodes College	TN	26,466	HC+
Richard Stockton College of New Jersey	NJ	12,972	VC
Rider Univ	NJ	30,900	C
Ripon College	WI	24,995	VC
Roanoke College	VA	27,393	C
Rockford College	IL	28,310	VC
Rockhurst Univ	MO	22,960	C+

ST = STATE **$IS** = IN-STATE COSTS **SR** = SELECTOR RATING

School	ST	$IS	SR
Rocky Mountain College	MT	19,015	C
Roger Williams Univ	RI	30,296	C
Rollins College	FL	34,300	VC
Roosevelt Univ	IL	22,580	VC
Rowan Univ	NJ	14,506	VC
Rutgers, The State Univ of New Jersey/Camden Campus	NJ	14,990	VC
Rutgers, The State Univ of New Jersey/New Brunswick/Piscataway Campus	NJ	15,800	HC
Rutgers, The State Univ of New Jersey/Newark Campus	NJ	15,624	VC
Saginaw Valley State Univ	MI	11,055	C
St. Cloud State Univ	MN	8,362	C
St. Edward's Univ	TX	20,428	C
St. John's Univ	MN	26,473	VC
St. Lawrence Univ	NY	35,945	VC
St. Louis Univ	MO	29,780	VC+
St. Mary's College	IN	24,474	VC
St. Mary's College of Maryland	MD	15,908	VC+
St. Mary's Univ of Minn	MN	21,535	C
St. Michael's College	VT	30,100	VC
St. Olaf College	MN	28,500	HC
Salem State College	MA	8,592	C
Salve Regina Univ	RI	29,210	C
Sam Houston State Univ	TX	7,142	C
Samford Univ	AL	18,648	VC
San Diego State Univ	CA	10,321	C
San Francisco State Univ	CA	12,070	C
San Jose State Univ	CA	8,187	C
Santa Clara Univ	CA	34,701	HC
Sarah Lawrence College	NY	41,218	HC
Schreiner Univ	TX	20,440	C
Scripps College	CA	35,700	HC+
Seattle Pacific Univ	WA	25,944	VC
Seattle Univ	WA	24,183	VC
Seton Hill Univ	PA	24,930	C
Shenandoah Univ	VA	25,190	NC
Shorter College	GA	17,370	C
Simon's Rock College of Bard	MA	36,580	HC
Simpson College	IA	23,658	C+
Skidmore College	NY	37,930	HC
Smith College	MA	37,034	HC+
S Car State Univ	SC	6,586	LC
S Dak State Univ	SD	7,782	C
Southeast Missouri State Univ	MO	9,704	C
Southeastern Okla State Univ	OK	6,147	C
Southern Conn State Univ	CT	10,310	C
Southern Illinois Univ Carbondale	IL	10,407	C
Southern Illinois Univ Edwardsville	IL	8,724	C
Southern Methodist Univ	TX	34,210	HC
Southern Oregon Univ	OR	10,362	C
Southern Univ and A&M College	LA	7,372	LC
Southern Utah Univ	UT	8,194	C
Southwest Baptist Univ	MO	15,371	C
Southwest Missouri State Univ	MO	8,918	C
Southwestern College	KS	19,560	C
Southwestern Univ	TX	25,410	HC
Spelman College	GA	19,215	C+
Spring Hill College	AL	25,868	VC
Stanford Univ	CA	37,612	MC
SUNY at Oswego	NY	12,650	C
SUNY at Potsdam	NY	12,160	C
SUNY/College at Brockport	NY	12,111	C
SUNY/College at Buffalo	NY	8,025	C
SUNY/College at Fredonia	NY	11,562	VC
SUNY/College at Geneseo	NY	11,330	HC
SUNY/College at Oneonta	NY	11,870	VC
SUNY/College at Plattsburgh	NY	11,700	C
SUNY/College at Purchase	NY	10,587	VC
SUNY/Univ at Albany	NY	12,951	HC
SUNY/Univ at Binghamton	NY	12,787	HC
SUNY/Univ at Buffalo	NY	12,563	VC
SUNY/Univ at New Paltz	NY	11,565	VC
SUNY/Univ at Stony Brook	NY	12,763	HC
Stephen F. Austin State Univ	TX	7,552	C
Stephens College	MO	24,260	C+
Sterling College	KS	18,763	C
Stetson Univ	FL	29,495	VC
Suffolk Univ	MA	29,200	C
Sul Ross State Univ	TX	6,582	LC
Susquehanna Univ	PA	29,990	VC
Swarthmore College	PA	37,716	MC
Sweet Briar College	VA	27,940	C
Syracuse Univ	NY	34,720	HC
Tarleton State Univ	TX	7,576	C
Taylor Univ	IN	23,820	VC+
Temple Univ	PA	15,912	C
Tenn State Univ	TN	9,048	LC
Texas A&M Univ at Commerce	TX	8,994	C
Texas A&M Univ at Corpus Christi	TX	10,269	C
Texas A&M Univ at Kingsville	TX	6,740	LC
Texas Christian Univ	TX	23,410	VC
Texas Lutheran Univ	TX	20,370	C
Texas Southern Univ	TX	8,920	NC
Texas State Univ	TX	9,320	VC
Texas Tech Univ	TX	10,768	VC
Texas Wesleyan Univ	TX	16,245	C
Texas Woman's Univ	TX	7,804	LC
Thomas Edison State College	NJ	3,325	SP
Thomas More College	KY	21,350	C
Transylvania Univ	KY	23,780	VC+
Trevecca Nazarene Univ	TN	17,548	C
Trinity College	CT	38,040	HC+
Trinity Univ	TX	26,466	HC+
Troy State Univ	AL	7,696	C
Truman State Univ	MO	9,728	HC+
Tufts Univ	MA	38,233	MC
Union College	KY	15,920	C
Union Univ	TN	18,800	VC
Univ of Akron	OH	13,134	NC
Univ of Alabama at Birmingham	AL	12,901	C
Univ of Alaska Anchorage	AK	9,100	NC
Univ of Alaska Fairbanks	AK	9,295	C
Univ of Arizona	AZ	10,413	VC
Univ of Arkansas	AR	9,855	VC
Univ of Arkansas at Little Rock	AR	5,637	NC
Univ of Calif at Berkeley	CA	15,563	MC
Univ of Calif at Davis	CA	14,995	VC
Univ of Calif at Irvine	CA	19,808	HC
Univ of Calif at Los Angeles	CA	15,330	MC
Univ of Calif at Riverside	CA	15,300	C
Univ of Calif at San Diego	CA	14,127	HC
Univ of Calif at Santa Barbara	CA	11,732	VC
Univ of Calif at Santa Cruz	CA	16,505	VC
Univ of Central Florida	FL	10,038	VC
Univ of Central Okla	OK	9,434	C
Univ of Cincinnati	OH	14,736	C
Univ of Colo at Boulder	CO	10,774	VC
Univ of Colo at Denver	CO	3,302	C
Univ of Conn	CT	14,608	VC
Univ of Dallas	TX	25,898	VC+
Univ of Dayton	OH	24,850	VC
Univ of Denver	CO	32,148	VC
Univ of Detroit Mercy	MI	25,582	C
Univ of Evansville	IN	24,190	VC
Univ of Findlay	OH	23,962	NC
Univ of Georgia	GA	8,656	VC
Univ of Hartford	CT	31,080	C
Univ of Hawaii at Manoa	HI	9,565	VC
Univ of Houston	TX	9,818	C
Univ of Idaho	ID	8,216	C
Univ of Illinois at Chicago	IL	13,418	C
Univ of Illinois at Urbana-Champaign	IL	11,316	HC+
Univ of Indianapolis	IN	22,560	VC
Univ of Iowa	IA	10,923	VC
Univ of Kansas	KS	8,923	VC
Univ of Kentucky	KY	7,765	C
Univ of La Verne	CA	28,600	C
Univ of Louisiana at Lafayette	LA	5,826	C
Univ of Louisville	KY	8,762	VC
Univ of Maine	ME	12,080	C+
Univ of Maryland/Baltimore County	MD	14,668	VC+
Univ of Maryland/College Park	MD	14,227	HC
Univ of Mass Amherst	MA	13,980	C+
Univ of Mass Boston	MA	6,227	C
Univ of Memphis	TN	8,560	C
Univ of Miami	FL	34,608	HC
Univ of Mich/Ann Arbor	MI	13,864	HC+
Univ of Mich/Flint	MI	5,548	C
Univ of Minn/Duluth	MN	12,470	C
Univ of Minn/Morris	MN	12,896	VC
Univ of Miss	MS	7,666	C
Univ of Missouri/Columbia	MO	13,782	VC
Univ of Missouri/Kansas City	MO	13,416	VC
Univ of Montana	MT	9,395	C
Univ of Montevallo	AL	8,478	C
Univ of Nebr at Kearney	NE	8,286	NC
Univ of Nebr at Lincoln	NE	9,975	C+
Univ of Nebr at Omaha	NE	8,080	C
Univ of Nevada/Las Vegas	NV	11,566	C
Univ of Nevada/Reno	NV	9,792	C
Univ of New Hampshire	NH	14,828	VC
Univ of New Mexico	NM	9,223	C
Univ of New Orleans	LA	7,356	C
Univ of North Alabama	AL	7,972	NC
Univ of N Car at Asheville	NC	8,079	VC
Univ of N Car at Chapel Hill	NC	10,117	MC
Univ of N Car at Charlotte	NC	8,185	C
Univ of N Car at Greensboro	NC	8,248	C
Univ of N Car at Wilmington	NC	8,940	VC
Univ of N Dak	ND	8,390	C
Univ of North Texas	TX	7,629	C
Univ of Northern Colo	CO	8,987	C
Univ of Northern Iowa	IA	9,834	C
Univ of Okla	OK	9,226	VC
Univ of Oregon	OR	11,479	VC
Univ of Pennsylvania	PA	37,960	MC
Univ of Pittsburgh at Johnstown	PA	15,216	LC
Univ of Pittsburgh at Pittsburgh	PA	16,074	HC
Univ of Portland	OR	28,500	VC
Univ of PR/Rio Piedras	PR	5,730	
Univ of Puget Sound	WA	31,760	HC
Univ of Rhode Island	RI	13,720	VC
Univ of Richmond	VA	30,100	MC
Univ of St. Mary	KS	18,868	C
Univ of St. Thomas	MN	26,918	VC
Univ of St. Thomas	TX	21,952	VC
Univ of Science and Arts of Okla	OK	5,982	C
Univ of Scranton	PA	30,836	VC
Univ of South Alabama	AL	7,760	LC
Univ of S Car at Columbia	SC	10,048	VC
Univ of S Dak	SD	7,710	C+
Univ of South Florida	FL	9,454	C
Univ of Southern Calif	CA	37,459	MC
Univ of Southern Indiana	IN	9,025	LC
Univ of Southern Maine	ME	11,212	C
Univ of Southern Miss	MS	8,324	LC
Univ of Tenn at Chattanooga	TN	7,783	C
Univ of Tenn at Knoxville	TN	8,214	C
Univ of Texas at Arlington	TX	7,192	LC
Univ of Texas at Austin	TX	10,630	HC
Univ of Texas at El Paso	TX	5,799	NC
Univ of Texas-Pan American	TX	5,954	LC
Univ of the District of Columbia	DC	2,070	LC
Univ of the Incarnate Word	TX	21,772	LC
Univ of the Ozarks	AR	16,574	C
Univ of the Pacific	CA	31,090	VC
Univ of the South	TN	30,855	HC
Univ of Toledo	OH	12,479	NC
Univ of Utah	UT	9,205	C
Univ of Vermont	VT	16,316	VC
Univ of Virginia	VA	11,740	MC
Univ of Virginia's College at Wise	VA	10,116	C
Univ of Washington	WA	10,361	VC
Univ of Wisc/Eau Claire	WI	8,463	VC
Univ of Wisc/Green Bay	WI	8,154	C
Univ of Wisc/La Crosse	WI	8,991	VC
Univ of Wisc/Madison	WI	8,262	VC
Univ of Wisc/Milwaukee	WI	9,427	LC
Univ of Wisc/Parkside	WI	6,160	LC
Univ of Wisc/Stevens Point	WI	8,116	VC
Univ of Wisc/Superior	WI	7,051	C+
Univ of Wisc/Whitewater	WI	8,626	C
Univ of Wyoming	WY	8,636	C
Utah State Univ	UT	7,371	C
Valdosta State Univ	GA	7,798	C
Valparaiso Univ	IN	26,118	VC+
Vanguard Univ of Southern Calif	CA	22,208	C
Vassar College	NY	37,030	MC
Virginia Commonwealth Univ	VA	9,030	C
Virginia Intermont College	VA	19,800	C
Virginia Polytechnic Inst and State Univ	VA	9,179	C
Virginia Wesleyan College	VA	25,350	C
Viterbo Univ	WI	20,430	C
Wabash College	IN	27,932	VC
Wagner College	NY	29,900	VC
Wake Forest Univ	NC	34,090	MC
Wartburg College	IA	21,165	VC
Washburn Univ of Topeka	KS	8,984	NC
Washington and Jefferson College	PA	29,570	VC
Washington and Lee Univ	VA	29,663	MC
Washington College	MD	30,540	VC
Washington Univ in St. Louis	MO	38,293	MC
Wayland Baptist Univ	TX	11,919	NC
Wayne State College	NE	7,352	NC
Wayne State Univ	MI	11,774	C
Weber State Univ	UT	7,945	NC
Webster Univ	MO	21,848	VC
Wellesley College	MA	36,516	MC
Wells College	NY	21,122	VC
Wesleyan Univ	CT	35,139	MC
West Chester Univ of Pennsylvania	PA	11,164	C
West Texas A&M Univ	TX	7,533	C
West Virginia Univ	WV	9,370	C
West Virginia Wesleyan College	WV	22,920	C
Western Carolina Univ	NC	6,742	C
Western Conn State Univ	CT	11,625	C
Western Illinois Univ	IL	10,363	C
Western Kentucky Univ	KY	6,834	C
Western Mich Univ	MI	12,031	C
Western Oregon Univ	OR	10,281	C
Western State College of Colo	CO	9,014	C
Western Washington Univ	WA	10,119	VC
Westfield State College	MA	10,147	C
Westminster College	PA	22,960	C
Westmont College	CA	33,062	VC+
Wheaton College	MA	36,330	HC
Whitman College	WA	32,526	HC+
Whittier College	CA	29,108	C
Whitworth College	WA	26,428	VC+
Wilkes Univ	PA	28,060	C
Willamette Univ	OR	32,032	VC+
William Carey College	MS	10,150	LC
William Jewell College	MO	21,320	VC
William Paterson Univ of New Jersey	NJ	14,450	C
William Woods Univ	MO	20,120	C
Williams College	MA	32,270	MC
Wilmington College	OH	24,172	LC
Winona State Univ	MN		C
Winthrop Univ	SC	11,302	C
Wisc Lutheran College	WI	21,430	VC
Wittenberg Univ	OH	31,316	VC
Wofford College	SC	26,710	HC
Wright State Univ	OH	11,490	LC
Yale Univ	CT	37,000	MC
Youngstown State Univ	OH	11,148	NC

DRAWING

School	ST	$IS	SR
Aquinas College	MI	21,894	C
Arizona State Univ-Main	AZ	10,048	C
Art Inst of Southern Calif	CA	14,500	SP
Atlanta College of Art	GA	18,600	SP
Bard College	NY	37,352	HC+
Cal State, Fullerton	CA	6,648	C
College of Visual Arts	MN		SP
Edinboro Univ of Pennsylvania	PA	10,850	LC
Kendall College of Art and Design of Ferris State Univ	MI	10,784	SP
Lewis Univ	IL	22,950	C+
Maryland Inst College of Art	MD	30,890	SP
Milwaukee Inst of Art and Design	WI	24,388	SP
Minneapolis College of Art and Design	MN	28,950	SP
School of the Art Inst of Chicago	IL	27,800	SP
Simon's Rock College of Bard	MA	36,580	HC
Univ of Hartford	CT	31,080	C
Univ of North Texas	TX	7,629	C
Univ of San Francisco	CA	34,700	VC
Washington Univ in St. Louis	MO	38,293	MC
Youngstown State Univ	OH	11,148	NC

DUTCH

School	ST	$IS	SR
Calvin College	MI	22,615	NC
Dordt College	IA	20,170	VC
Indiana Univ Bloomington	IN	12,389	VC
Univ of Calif at Berkeley	CA	15,563	MC

EARLY CHILDHOOD EDUCATION

School	ST	$IS	SR
Abilene Christian Univ	TX	18,370	VC
Alabama A&M Univ	AL	5,100	LC
Alabama State Univ	AL	6,404	C
Albany State Univ	GA	5,764	C+
American International College	MA	24,690	LC
Angelo State Univ	TX	7,576	NC
Anna Maria College	MA	26,140	LC
Appalachian State Univ	NC	7,637	VC
Arcadia Univ	PA	29,890	C
Arizona State Univ-Main	AZ	10,048	C
Arkansas State Univ	AR	8,450	C
Ashland Univ	OH	24,464	C
Atlantic Union College	MA	18,868	C
Auburn Univ	AL	10,396	VC
Augusta State Univ	GA	2,592	C
Baldwin-Wallace College	OH	24,678	C
Ball State Univ	IN	8,660	C
Barber-Scotia College	NC	13,900	LC
Barry Univ	FL	24,100	LC
Bay Path College	MA	24,910	C
Becker College	MA	23,710	LC
Bemidji State Univ	MN	9,103	C
Benedict College	SC	12,662	LC
Bennett College	NC	11,200	C
Bennington College	VT	35,910	HC
Berea College	KY	5,030	VC+
Berry College	GA	21,410	VC
Bethany College	WV	19,845	VC
Bethel College	MN	25,180	VC
Bethel College	TN	12,980	C
Bloomsburg Univ of Pennsylvania	PA	10,844	C
Bluffton College	OH	23,694	C
Boston College	MA	33,284	MC
Boston Univ	MA	38,194	HC+
Bowie State Univ	MD	10,873	C+
Bowling Green State Univ	OH	13,036	C
Bradley Univ	IL	22,910	VC
Brenau Univ Women's College	GA	21,800	C
Brewton-Parker College	GA	14,200	LC

ST = STATE $IS = IN-STATE COSTS SR = SELECTOR RATING

School	ST	$IS	SR
Univ of Sioux Falls	SD	16,390	C
Univ of South Alabama	AL	7,760	LC
Univ of S Car at Aiken	SC	7,828	LC
Univ of S Car at Columbia	SC	10,048	VC
Univ of S Car at Spartanburg	SC	9,936	C+
Univ of Southern Miss	MS	8,324	LC
Univ of Tenn at Martin	TN	7,748	C
Univ of the District of Columbia	DC	2,070	LC
Univ of the Incarnate Word	TX	21,772	LC
Univ of the Ozarks	AR	16,574	C
Univ of Toledo	OH	12,479	NC
Univ of Vermont	VT	16,316	VC
Univ of West Alabama	AL	6,048	C
Univ of West Florida	FL	8,470	C
Univ of Wisc/Stevens Point	WI	8,116	VC
Univ of Wisc/Stout	WI	9,718	C
Univ of Wisc/Whitewater	WI	8,626	C
Ursuline College	OH	22,728	LC
Utah State Univ	UT	7,371	C
Valdosta State Univ	GA	7,798	C
Vanderbilt Univ	TN	37,897	MC
Virginia Polytechnic Inst and State Univ	VA	9,179	C
Virginia Union Univ	VA	15,358	LC
Walsh Univ	OH	20,890	C
Washburn Univ of Topeka	KS	8,984	NC
Washington and Jefferson College	PA	29,570	VC
Weber State Univ	UT	7,945	NC
Wesleyan College	GA	17,870	VC
West Chester Univ of Pennsylvania	PA	11,164	C
West Liberty State College	WV	7,868	LC
West Virginia State College	WV	6,264	NC
Western Carolina Univ	NC	6,742	C
Western Washington Univ	WA	10,119	VC
Westfield State College	MA	10,147	C
Westminster College	UT	17,226	C
Wheelock College	MA	29,000	C
Widener Univ	PA	27,020	C
William Woods Univ	MO	20,120	C
Wilmington College	DE	5,594	NC
Wilmington College	OH	24,172	LC
Winona State Univ	MN		C
Winthrop Univ	SC	11,302	C
Worcester State College	MA	10,005	C
Xavier Univ	OH	26,850	VC+
Xavier Univ of Louisiana	LA	17,600	C
Youngstown State Univ	OH	11,148	NC

EARLY CHILDHOOD STUDIES

School	ST	$IS	SR
Claflin Univ	SC	14,838	C+
Grace Bible College	MI	15,890	C
Kentucky Wesleyan College	KY	17,250	C
Langston Univ	OK	2,308	LC
Louisiana State Univ and A&M College	LA	9,126	VC
Metropolitan State Univ	MN	3,852	SP
Northern Illinois Univ	IL	11,472	C
Plymouth State Univ	NH	12,298	LC
Southwestern Univ	TX	25,410	HC
Univ of Minn/Duluth	MN	12,470	C
Wayne State College	NE	7,352	NC
Weber State Univ	UT	7,945	NC
Youngstown State Univ	OH	11,148	NC

EARTH SCIENCE

School	ST	$IS	SR
Adams State College	CO	7,468	C
Adelphi Univ	NY	26,300	VC
Adrian College	MI	21,950	C
Albion College	MI	25,224	VC
Augustana College	IL	26,610	VC+
Baylor Univ	TX	23,864	VC
Bemidji State Univ	MN	9,103	C
Bloomsburg Univ of Pennsylvania	PA	10,844	C
Boston Univ	MA	38,194	HC+
Bridgewater State College	MA	10,482	C
Cal State, Long Beach	CA	8,762	C+
Cal State, Monterey Bay	CA	6,683	LC
Cal State, Northridge	CA	7,757	LC
Cal State, Stanislaus	CA	9,874	C
Calif Univ of Pennsylvania	PA	10,388	C
Central Conn State Univ	CT	12,090	C
Central Mich Univ	MI	11,142	C
Central Missouri State Univ	MO	9,776	C
Central Washington Univ	WA	9,768	C
CUNY/City College	NY	4,230	C+
Clarion Univ of Pennsylvania	PA	11,272	LC
Columbia Univ/Columbia College	NY	38,590	MC
Cornell Univ	NY	38,253	MC
Dartmouth College	NH	37,770	MC
DePauw Univ	IN	31,500	HC
Dickinson State Univ	ND	6,338	NC
East Stroudsburg Univ of Pennsylvania	PA	10,336	C
Eastern Mich Univ	MI	11,478	C
Edinboro Univ of Pennsylvania	PA	10,850	LC
Emporia State Univ	KS	6,998	C
Fitchburg State College	MA	9,622	C
George Mason Univ	VA	9,732	VC
Georgia Inst of Technology	GA	10,340	HC+
Guilford College	NC	24,960	VC
Indiana Univ-Purdue Univ Fort Wayne	IN	5,108	LC
Iowa State Univ	IA	10,768	VC
Johns Hopkins Univ	MD	38,372	MC
Juniata College	PA	29,080	VC
Kean Univ	NJ	14,479	C
Kent State Univ	OH	12,932	C
Lock Haven Univ of Pennsylvania	PA	11,098	LC
Mass Inst of Technology	MA	38,310	MC
Mercyhurst College	PA	20,694	C
Mich State Univ	MI	11,933	VC
Millersville Univ of Pennsylvania	PA	11,269	C
Minn State Univ, Mankato	MN	8,803	LC
Minot State Univ	ND	6,602	LC
Montana State Univ-Bozeman	MT	9,515	C
Morehead State Univ	KY	7,464	C
Murray State Univ	KY	7,816	VC
Muskingum College	OH	20,680	C
National Univ	CA	9,690	SP
N Car State Univ	NC	9,886	VC
N Dak State Univ	ND	8,435	C
Northeastern Illinois Univ	IL	2,898	NC
Northern Mich Univ	MI	10,834	C
Northland College	WI	22,170	C+
Northwest Missouri State Univ	MO	9,334	C
Ohio Univ	OH	14,448	C
Ohio Wesleyan Univ	OH	32,550	VC+
Old Dominion Univ	VA	10,441	C
Penn State Univ/Univ Park Campus	PA	15,646	HC
Prescott College	AZ	13,430	C
Purdue Univ/West Lafayette	IN	12,560	VC
Rice Univ	TX	27,550	MC
Rocky Mountain College	MT	19,015	C
St. Cloud State Univ	MN	8,362	C
St. Louis Univ	MO	29,780	VC+
St. Mary's Univ of San Antonio	TX	22,444	C
Salem State College	MA	8,592	C
Shippensburg Univ of Pennsylvania	PA	10,826	C
Slippery Rock Univ of Pennsylvania	PA	10,343	LC
Southeast Missouri State Univ	MO	9,704	C
Southern Conn State Univ	CT	10,310	C
Southwest Missouri State Univ	MO	8,918	C
Stanford Univ	CA	37,612	MC
SUNY/College at Brockport	NY	12,111	C
SUNY/College at Buffalo	NY	8,025	C
SUNY/College at Fredonia	NY	11,562	VC
SUNY/College at Oneonta	NY	11,870	VC
SUNY/Univ at Albany	NY	12,951	HC
SUNY/Univ at Stony Brook	NY	12,763	HC
State Univ of West Georgia	GA	7,622	C
Tarleton State Univ	TX	7,576	C
Temple Univ	PA	15,912	C
Texas A&M Univ at Commerce	TX	8,994	C
Texas A&M Univ at Galveston	TX	9,948	C+
Texas Wesleyan Univ	TX	16,245	C
Towson Univ	MD	12,694	VC
Tulane Univ	LA	37,451	HC+
Univ of Akron	OH	13,134	NC
Univ of Alaska Fairbanks	AK	9,295	C
Univ of Arizona	AZ	10,413	VC
Univ of Arkansas	AR	9,855	VC
Univ of Calif at Berkeley	CA	15,563	MC
Univ of Calif at Los Angeles	CA	15,330	MC
Univ of Calif at San Diego	CA	14,127	HC
Univ of Calif at Santa Cruz	CA	16,505	VC
Univ of Florida	FL	8,580	MC
Univ of Houston	TX	9,818	C
Univ of Indianapolis	IN	22,560	VC
Univ of Mass Amherst	MA	13,980	C+
Univ of Mass Boston	MA	6,227	C
Univ of Minn/Duluth	MN	12,470	C
Univ of Nevada/Las Vegas	NV	11,566	C
Univ of New Hampshire	NH	14,828	VC
Univ of New Mexico	NM	9,223	C
Univ of N Car at Charlotte	NC	8,185	C
Univ of Northern Colo	CO	8,987	C
Univ of Northern Iowa	IA	9,834	C
Univ of S Dak	SD	7,710	C+
Univ of Texas at El Paso	TX	5,799	NC
Univ of Wisc/Green Bay	WI	8,154	C
Univ of Wyoming	WY	8,636	C
Utah State Univ	UT	7,371	C
Virginia Wesleyan College	VA	25,350	C
Washington Univ in St. Louis	MO	38,293	MC
Weber State Univ	UT	7,945	NC
Wesleyan Univ	CT	35,139	MC
West Chester Univ of Pennsylvania	PA	11,164	C
Western Conn State Univ	CT	11,625	C
Western Mich Univ	MI	12,031	C
Western Oregon Univ	OR	10,281	C
Whittier College	CA	29,108	C
Wilkes Univ	PA	28,060	C
Winona State Univ	MN		C
Youngstown State Univ	OH	11,148	NC

EAST ASIAN LANGUAGES AND LITERATURE

School	ST	$IS	SR
Bates College	ME	37,500	MC
Beloit College	WI	29,864	HC
Boston Univ	MA	38,194	HC+
Indiana Univ Bloomington	IN	12,389	VC
Mich State Univ	MI	11,933	VC
Rutgers, The State Univ of New Jersey/New Brunswick/Piscataway Campus	NJ	15,800	HC
Smith College	MA	37,034	HC+
Univ of Florida	FL	8,580	MC
Univ of Kansas	KS	8,923	VC
Washington Univ in St. Louis	MO	38,293	MC

EAST ASIAN STUDIES

School	ST	$IS	SR
Augsburg College	MN	25,298	C
Boston Univ	MA	38,194	HC+
Brigham Young Univ	UT	8,504	HC
Brown Univ	RI	38,174	MC
Bryn Mawr College	PA	36,890	HC+
Bucknell Univ	PA	35,262	HC+
CUNY/Queens College	NY	4,362	C
Colby College	ME	37,570	MC
Columbia Univ/Barnard College	NY	36,990	MC
Columbia Univ/Columbia College	NY	38,590	MC
Columbia Univ/School of General Studies	NY	35,000	C
Conn College	CT	37,900	MC
Denison Univ	OH	33,050	HC
DePauw Univ	IN	31,500	HC
Dickinson College	PA	35,825	HC
Emory & Henry College	VA	21,950	C
George Washington Univ	DC	41,030	MC
Hamline Univ	MN	27,052	VC
Haverford College	PA	37,900	MC
Indiana Univ Bloomington	IN	12,389	VC
Johns Hopkins Univ	MD	38,372	MC
Lawrence Univ	WI	30,900	HC
Lewis and Clark College	OR	30,620	VC
Mass Inst of Technology	MA	38,310	MC
Middlebury College	VT	38,100	MC
New York Univ	NY	39,406	MC
Oakland Univ	MI	10,800	C
Oberlin College	OH	36,938	MC
Penn State Univ/Univ Park Campus	PA	15,646	HC
Princeton Univ	NJ	36,649	MC
Simmons College	MA	33,000	VC
Simon's Rock College of Bard	MA	36,580	HC
Stanford Univ	CA	37,612	MC
Union College	NY	36,005	HC
Univ of Arizona	AZ	10,413	VC
Univ of Calif at Davis	CA	14,995	VC
Univ of Calif at Irvine	CA	19,808	HC
Univ of Calif at Los Angeles	CA	15,330	MC
Univ of Illinois at Urbana-Champaign	IL	11,316	HC+
Univ of Minn/Twin Cities	MN	13,160	VC
Univ of St. Thomas	MN	26,918	VC
Ursinus College	PA	34,400	VC
Vanderbilt Univ	TN	37,897	MC
Washington and Lee Univ	VA	29,663	MC
Washington Univ in St. Louis	MO	38,293	MC
Western Washington Univ	WA	10,119	VC
Wittenberg Univ	OH	31,316	VC
Yale Univ	CT	37,000	MC

EASTERN EUROPEAN STUDIES

School	ST	$IS	SR
Bard College	NY	37,352	HC+
Boston Univ	MA	38,194	HC+
Florida State Univ	FL	9,028	HC
Kent State Univ	OH	12,932	C
Rutgers, The State Univ of New Jersey/Newark Campus	NJ	15,624	VC
Simon's Rock College of Bard	MA	36,580	HC
SUNY/Univ at Albany	NY	12,951	HC
Univ of Conn	CT	14,608	VC
Univ of Texas at Austin	TX	10,630	HC
Washington Univ in St. Louis	MO	38,293	MC
Yale Univ	CT	37,000	MC

ECOLOGY

School	ST	$IS	SR
Adams State College	CO	7,468	C
Appalachian State Univ	NC	7,637	VC
Bard College	NY	37,352	HC+
Beloit College	WI	29,864	HC
Bennington College	VT	35,910	HC
Boston Univ	MA	38,194	HC+
Calif Polytechnic State Univ	CA	8,747	VC
Cal State, Long Beach	CA	8,762	C+
Cal State, Stanislaus	CA	9,874	C
Defiance College	OH	22,615	C
Florida Inst of Technology	FL	28,740	VC
Florida State Univ	FL	9,028	HC
Hampshire College	MA	37,037	HC
Idaho State Univ	ID	8,128	C
Indiana Univ Bloomington	IN	12,389	VC
Iona College	NY	27,988	VC
Johns Hopkins Univ	MD	38,372	MC
Juniata College	PA	29,080	VC
Mich Tech Univ	MI	13,235	VC
Missouri Southern State Univ	MO	8,316	C
Montana State Univ-Northern	MT	8,600	NC
Morehead State Univ	KY	7,464	C
Mountain State Univ	WV	10,212	NC
Northern Mich Univ	MI	10,834	C
Northwestern Univ	IL	37,491	MC
Penn State Univ/Univ Park Campus	PA	15,646	HC
Purdue Univ/West Lafayette	IN	12,560	VC
Rutgers, The State Univ of New Jersey/New Brunswick/Piscataway Campus	NJ	15,800	HC
St. John's Univ	NY	30,180	C
San Francisco State Univ	CA	12,070	C
Seattle Univ	WA	24,183	VC
Simon's Rock College of Bard	MA	36,580	HC
SUNY/College of Environmental Science and Forestry	NY	14,167	VC
Tulane Univ	LA	37,451	HC+
Unity College	ME	19,845	LC
Univ of Arizona	AZ	10,413	VC
Univ of Calif at Davis	CA	14,995	VC
Univ of Calif at Irvine	CA	19,808	HC
Univ of Calif at San Diego	CA	14,127	HC
Univ of Georgia	GA	8,656	VC
Univ of Mich/Ann Arbor	MI	13,864	HC+
Univ of Mich/Flint	MI	5,548	C
Univ of Minn/Twin Cities	MN	13,160	VC
Univ of New Hampshire	NH	14,828	VC
Univ of Pittsburgh at Pittsburgh	PA	16,074	HC
Univ of Rochester	NY	32,979	HC
Univ of Vermont	VT	16,316	VC

ECONOMICS

School	ST	$IS	SR
Adelphi Univ	NY	26,300	VC
Adrian College	MI	21,950	C
Agnes Scott College	GA	28,230	HC
Alabama A&M Univ	AL	5,100	LC
Albertson College of Idaho	ID	19,415	VC
Albion College	MI	25,224	VC
Albright College	PA	30,579	C
Alcorn State Univ	MS	7,290	C
Alfred Univ	NY	28,290	C
Allegheny College	PA	30,280	VC
Alma College	MI	25,566	VC
American International College	MA	24,690	LC
American Univ	DC	34,585	VC+
Amherst College	MA	37,470	MC
Anderson Univ	IN	19,430	LC
Andrews Univ	MI	19,550	C
Appalachian State Univ	NC	7,637	VC
Aquinas College	MI	21,894	C
Arizona State Univ-Main	AZ	10,048	C
Arkansas State Univ	AR	8,450	C
Arkansas Tech Univ	AR	7,299	C
Armstrong Atlantic State Univ	GA	7,102	C
Ashland Univ	OH	24,464	C
Assumption College	MA	29,375	C
Auburn Univ	AL	10,396	VC
Augsburg College	MN	25,298	C
Augustana College	IL	26,610	VC+
Augustana College	SD	21,998	VC
Austin College	TX	24,747	HC
Austin Peay State Univ	TN	5,814	LC
Baker Univ	KS	19,860	VC
Baldwin-Wallace College	OH	24,678	C
Ball State Univ	IN	8,660	C
Bard College	NY	37,352	HC+
Barry Univ	FL	24,100	LC
Barton College	NC	19,314	C
Bates College	ME	37,500	MC
Baylor Univ	TX	23,864	VC
Bellarmine Univ	KY	24,110	VC
Belmont Abbey College	NC	23,742	C
Belmont Univ	TN	21,986	VC
Beloit College	WI	29,864	HC
Bemidji State Univ	MN	9,103	C
Benedictine College	KS	20,653	C
Benedictine Univ	IL	23,840	C

ST = STATE $IS = IN-STATE COSTS SR = SELECTOR RATING

School	ST	$IS	SR
Berea College	KY	5,030	VC+
Berry College	GA	21,410	VC
Bethany College	KS	18,675	LC
Bethany College	WV	19,845	VC
Bethel College	MN	25,180	VC
Birmingham-Southern College	AL	25,364	VC+
Bloomsburg Univ of Pennsylvania	PA	10,844	C
Bluffton College	OH	23,694	C
Boise State Univ	ID	7,657	LC
Boston College	MA	33,284	MC
Boston Univ	MA	38,194	HC+
Bowdoin College	ME	37,790	MC
Bowling Green State Univ	OH	13,036	C
Bradley Univ	IL	22,910	VC
Brandeis Univ	MA	38,198	MC
Bridgewater College	VA	25,150	C
Bridgewater State College	MA	10,482	C
Brigham Young Univ	UT	8,504	HC
Brown Univ	RI	38,174	MC
Bryant College	RI	31,004	VC
Bryn Mawr College	PA	36,890	HC+
Bucknell Univ	PA	35,262	HC+
Buena Vista Univ	IA	25,406	C
Butler Univ	IN	28,250	VC+
Calif Inst of Technology	CA	31,677	MC
Calif Lutheran Univ	CA	27,600	LC
Calif Polytechnic State Univ	CA	8,747	VC
Calif State Polytechnic Univ, Pomona	CA	8,793	C+
Cal State, Bakersfield	CA	6,090	LC
Cal State, Chico	CA	8,598	LC
Cal State, Dominguez Hills	CA	5,840	LC
Cal State, Fresno	CA	8,414	LC
Cal State, Fullerton	CA	6,648	C
Cal State, Hayward	CA	8,871	LC
Cal State, Long Beach	CA	8,762	C+
Cal State, Los Angeles	CA	5,778	C
Cal State, Northridge	CA	7,757	LC
Cal State, Sacramento	CA	9,543	C
Cal State, San Bernardino	CA	15,238	LC
Cal State, San Marcos	CA	1,736	LC
Cal State, Stanislaus	CA	9,874	C
Calif Univ of Pennsylvania	PA	10,388	C
Calvin College	MI	22,615	NC
Campbell Univ	NC	18,268	VC
Campbellsville Univ	KY	17,680	C
Canisius College	NY	28,163	C+
Capital Univ	OH	26,550	C
Carleton College	MN	34,395	MC
Carnegie Mellon Univ	PA	32,682	MC
Carson-Newman College	TN	16,760	C
Carthage College	WI	25,000	C
Case Western Reserve Univ	OH	32,002	MC
Catholic Univ of America	DC	34,248	VC
Centenary College of Louisiana	LA	23,100	VC+
Central College	IA	21,206	C
Central Conn State Univ	CT	12,090	C
Central Methodist College	MO	16,460	C
Central Mich Univ	MI	11,142	C
Central Missouri State Univ	MO	9,776	C
Central State Univ	OH	8,922	C+
Central Washington Univ	WA	9,768	C
Centre College	KY	27,300	HC
Chapman Univ	CA	33,118	VC
Charleston Southern Univ	SC	17,122	C
Chatham College	PA	27,266	C+
Cheyney Univ of Pennsylvania	PA	9,993	C
Chicago State Univ	IL	10,882	C+
Christopher Newport Univ	VA	8,862	VC
CUNY/Baruch College	NY	3,275	VC+
CUNY/Brooklyn College	NY	4,353	C+
CUNY/City College	NY	4,230	C+
CUNY/College of Staten Island	NY	4,308	NC
CUNY/Herbert H. Lehman College	NY	3,320	LC
CUNY/Hunter College	NY	6,729	C+
CUNY/Queens College	NY	4,362	C
CUNY/York College	NY	3,292	NC
Claremont McKenna College	CA	36,880	MC
Clarion Univ of Pennsylvania	PA	11,272	LC
Clark Atlanta Univ	GA	19,300	C+
Clark Univ	MA	32,115	VC
Clarkson Univ	NY	32,226	VC
Clemson Univ	SC	11,972	HC
Cleveland State Univ	OH	12,308	LC
Coe College	IA	27,385	VC
Colby College	ME	37,570	MC
Colgate Univ	NY	37,095	MC
College of Charleston	SC	11,887	HC
College of Mount St. Vincent	NY	26,800	C
College of New Jersey	NJ	15,950	MC
College of New Rochelle	NY	21,800	C
College of Notre Dame of Maryland	MD	27,700	C
College of St. Benedict	MN	26,672	VC
College of St. Catherine	MN	24,010	VC
College of St. Elizabeth	NJ	25,460	C
College of St. Scholastica	MN	24,970	C+
College of the Holy Cross	MA	36,451	MC
College of William and Mary	VA	12,224	MC
College of Wooster	OH	31,300	HC
Colo College	CO	36,860	HC
Colo School of Mines	CO	12,533	HC
Colo State Univ	CO	9,964	VC
Columbia Univ/Barnard College	NY	36,990	MC
Columbia Univ/Columbia College	NY	38,590	MC
Columbia Univ/School of General Studies	NY	35,000	C
Concordia College: Moorhead	MN	22,460	VC+
Conn College	CT	37,900	MC
Converse College	SC	24,710	VC
Cornell College	IA	27,825	VC+
Cornell Univ	NY	38,253	MC
Covenant College	GA	23,830	VC+
Creighton Univ	NE	26,748	VC+
Dartmouth College	NH	37,770	MC
David N. Myers College	OH	9,475	C
Davidson College	NC	33,274	MC
Davis and Elkins College	WV	20,594	C
Delaware State Univ	DE	8,104	LC
Denison Univ	OH	33,050	HC
DePaul Univ	IL	27,580	VC
DePauw Univ	IN	31,500	HC
Dickinson College	PA	35,825	HC
Dillard Univ	LA	17,325	VC
Doane College	NE	20,000	C
Dowling College	NY	23,870	LC
Drake Univ	IA	25,120	VC+
Drew Univ/College of Liberal Arts	NJ	35,550	VC
Drury Univ	MO	18,085	VC+
Duke Univ	NC	37,555	MC
Duquesne Univ	PA	26,907	VC
Earlham College	IN	29,976	VC+
East Carolina Univ	NC	8,671	C
East Stroudsburg Univ of Pennsylvania	PA	10,336	C
East Tenn State Univ	TN	8,497	C
Eastern Conn State Univ	CT	10,362	C
Eastern Illinois Univ	IL	11,192	C
Eastern Kentucky Univ	KY	7,708	C
Eastern Mennonite Univ	VA	22,990	C
Eastern Mich Univ	MI	11,478	C
Eastern New Mexico Univ	NM	6,762	LC
Eastern Washington Univ	WA	9,012	C
Eckerd College	FL	28,744	C+
Edgewood College	WI	20,520	C
Edinboro Univ of Pennsylvania	PA	10,850	LC
Elizabethtown College	PA	28,800	C
Elmhurst College	IL	24,630	C
Elon Univ	NC	22,240	VC
Emory & Henry College	VA	21,950	C
Emory Univ	GA	36,872	MC
Emporia State Univ	KS	6,998	C
Eugene Lang College/New School Univ	NY	34,940	C
Fairfield Univ	CT	35,505	HC
Fairleigh Dickinson Univ/College at Florham	NJ	30,130	C
Fairleigh Dickinson Univ/Metropolitan Campus	NJ	28,584	C
Fayetteville State Univ	NC	5,590	LC
Fisk Univ	TN	17,305	LC
Fitchburg State College	MA	9,622	C
Florida A&M Univ	FL	7,564	C
Florida Atlantic Univ	FL	8,543	C
Florida International Univ	FL	9,912	VC
Florida Southern College	FL	23,592	C
Florida State Univ	FL	9,028	HC
Fordham Univ	NY	35,066	HC
Fort Hays State Univ	KS	7,363	C
Fort Lewis College	CO	8,353	C
Fort Valley State Univ	GA	6,960	C
Framingham State College	MA	9,381	C
Francis Marion Univ	SC	9,364	C
Franciscan Univ of Steubenville	OH	20,300	VC
Franklin and Marshall College	PA	35,930	HC+
Franklin College	IN		C
Frostburg State Univ	MD	11,114	C
Furman Univ	SC	28,976	HC+
Gallaudet Univ	DC	16,554	SP
George Fox Univ	OR	26,110	VC
George Mason Univ	VA	9,732	VC
George Washington Univ	DC	41,030	MC
Georgetown Univ	DC	38,242	MC
Georgia College and State Univ	GA	9,878	C
Georgia Inst of Technology	GA	10,340	HC+
Georgia Southern Univ	GA	8,540	C
Georgia State Univ	GA	10,658	C
Gettysburg College	PA	35,646	HC
Gonzaga Univ	WA	26,766	HC
Gordon College	MA	25,982	VC+
Goucher College	MD	32,650	HC
Graceland Univ	IA	19,550	C
Grand Canyon Univ	AZ	30,000	LC
Grand Valley State Univ	MI	11,022	VC
Grinnell College	IA	31,060	HC+
Grove City College	PA	14,228	HC
Guilford College	NC	24,960	VC
Gustavus Adolphus College	MN	27,120	VC+
Hamilton College	NY	37,560	MC
Hamline Univ	MN	27,052	VC
Hampden-Sydney College	VA	28,407	VC
Hampshire College	MA	37,037	HC
Hampton Univ	VA	17,112	C+
Hanover College	IN	25,200	VC
Harding Univ	AR	14,890	VC
Hartwick College	NY	34,650	C+
Harvard Univ/Harvard College	MA	37,928	MC
Hastings College	NE	19,928	VC
Haverford College	PA	37,900	MC
Hawaii Pacific Univ	HI	19,218	C
Heidelberg College	OH	20,266	NC
Hillsdale College	MI	22,450	HC
Hiram College	OH	28,234	VC
Hobart and William Smith Colleges	NY	36,536	HC
Hofstra Univ	NY	27,112	VC
Hollins Univ	VA	27,965	VC
Holy Family College	PA	13,710	LC
Hood College	MD	27,795	VC
Hope College	MI	25,340	VC
Howard Univ	DC	16,505	C
Idaho State Univ	ID	8,128	C
Illinois College	IL	19,100	VC
Illinois State Univ	IL	10,944	C+
Illinois Wesleyan Univ	IL	30,380	HC+
Immaculata Univ	PA	25,200	C
Indiana State Univ	IN	10,719	LC
Indiana Univ Bloomington	IN	12,389	VC
Indiana Univ Northwest	IN	4,538	LC
Indiana Univ of Pennsylvania	PA	10,489	C
Indiana Univ South Bend	IN	4,571	LC
Indiana Univ Southeast	IN	4,504	LC
Indiana Univ-Purdue Univ Fort Wayne	IN	5,108	LC
Indiana Univ-Purdue Univ Indianapolis	IN	8,257	LC
Indiana Wesleyan Univ	IN	19,900	C+
Inter American Univ of PR/San German	PR	6,716	
Iona College	NY	27,988	VC
Iowa State Univ	IA	10,768	VC
Ithaca College	NY	31,730	HC
Jackson State Univ	MS	8,382	C
Jacksonville State Univ	AL	6,844	LC
Jacksonville Univ	FL	24,040	C
James Madison Univ	VA	10,794	VC
John Carroll Univ	OH	27,658	C+
Johns Hopkins Univ	MD	38,372	MC
Johnson C. Smith Univ	NC	18,108	C
Juniata College	PA	29,080	VC
Kansas State Univ	KS	8,728	VC
Kean Univ	NJ	14,479	C
Keene State College	NH	12,212	C
Kent State Univ	OH	12,932	C
Kenyon College	OH	35,370	HC+
King's College	PA	26,990	C
Knox College	IL	30,294	VC+
La Salle Univ	PA	31,260	VC
Lafayette College	PA	35,746	MC
Lake Forest College	IL	30,270	VC
Lake Superior State Univ	MI	9,034	LC
Lakeland College	WI	17,950	C
Lamar Univ	TX	6,816	LC
Langston Univ	OK	2,308	LC
Lawrence Univ	WI	30,900	HC
Le Moyne College	NY	26,400	VC
Lebanon Valley College	PA	28,870	VC
Lehigh Univ	PA	37,570	HC+
Lenoir-Rhyne College	NC	19,186	C
Lewis and Clark College	OR	30,620	VC
Lewis Univ	IL	22,950	C+
Lincoln Univ	MO	7,158	NC
Lincoln Univ	PA	13,320	C+
Linfield College	OR	27,090	VC
Lock Haven Univ of Pennsylvania	PA	11,098	LC
LIU/Brooklyn Campus	NY	24,790	C
LIU/C.W. Post Campus	NY	28,282	C
Longwood Univ	VA	11,175	C
Loras College	IA	24,233	C
Louisiana College	LA	13,450	C
Louisiana State Univ and A&M College	LA	9,126	VC
Louisiana State Univ in Shreveport	LA	2,884	NC
Loyola College in Maryland	MD	34,560	HC
Loyola Marymount Univ	CA	32,194	VC
Loyola Univ Chicago	IL	31,164	VC
Loyola Univ New Orleans	LA	31,036	VC+
Luther College	IA	25,700	VC
Lycoming College	PA	27,589	C+
Lynchburg College	VA	26,815	C
Lyon College	AR	17,995	VC
Macalester College	MN	31,944	MC
Manchester College	IN	23,390	C
Manhattan College	NY	27,400	VC
Manhattanville College	NY	32,420	C+
Mansfield Univ	PA	11,220	C
Marian College	IN	23,030	C
Marian College of Fond du Lac	WI	19,625	C
Marietta College	OH	27,047	C
Marist College	NY	27,596	VC
Marlboro College	VT	29,055	VC+
Marquette Univ	WI	27,594	VC
Marshall Univ	WV	9,116	C
Mary Baldwin College	VA	24,939	C
Mary Washington College	VA	10,166	HC
Marymount College of Fordham Univ	NY	27,686	C
Marymount Univ	VA	23,668	C
Maryville College	TN	25,960	VC
Mass Inst of Technology	MA	38,310	MC
McDaniel College	MD	28,440	VC
McKendree College	IL	21,120	VC
McMurry Univ	TX	17,846	LC
McNeese State Univ	LA	5,259	LC
Mercer Univ	GA	27,516	VC+
Meredith College	NC	23,065	C
Merrimack College	MA	29,625	C
Messiah College	PA	25,890	VC+
Methodist College	NC	19,526	C
Metropolitan State College of Denver	CO	2,338	LC
Metropolitan State Univ	MN	3,852	SP
Miami Univ	OH	15,033	HC
Mich State Univ	MI	11,933	VC
Middle Tenn State Univ	TN	8,534	C
Middlebury College	VT	38,100	MC
Midland Lutheran College	NE	18,600	C
Midwestern State Univ	TX	8,045	LC
Millersville Univ of Pennsylvania	PA	11,269	C
Millikin Univ	IL	25,555	C
Mills College	CA	33,371	VC
Millsaps College	MS	25,182	VC
Minn State Univ, Mankato	MN	8,803	LC
Minn State Univ, Moorhead	MN	7,000	LC
Minot State Univ	ND	6,602	LC
Miss State Univ	MS	9,139	C
Missouri Southern State Univ	MO	8,316	C
Missouri Valley College	MO	18,500	C
Missouri Western State College	MO	8,522	NC
Montana State Univ-Bozeman	MT	9,515	C
Montclair State Univ	NJ	13,790	C
Moravian College	PA	28,903	VC
Morehouse College	GA	22,728	C
Morgan State Univ	MD	11,470	C
Mount Holyoke College	MA	37,918	HC+
Mount St. Mary's College	MD	28,400	C
Mount Union College	OH	21,120	C
Muhlenberg College	PA	31,485	HC
Murray State Univ	KY	7,816	VC
Muskingum College	OH	20,680	C
Nazareth College of Rochester	NY	24,936	VC
Nebr Wesleyan Univ	NE	21,197	C+
New College of Florida	FL	8,906	HC+
New Jersey City Univ	NJ	11,850	LC
New Mexico State Univ	NM	7,932	C
New York Univ	NY	39,406	MC
Nichols College	MA	27,562	LC
N Car Agricultural and Technical State Univ	NC	6,659	LC
N Car State Univ	NC	9,886	VC
North Central College	IL	25,656	VC
N Dak State Univ	ND	8,435	C
North Park Univ	IL	24,030	C
Northeastern Illinois Univ	IL	2,898	NC
Northeastern Univ	MA	35,650	HC
Northern Arizona Univ	AZ	9,002	C
Northern Illinois Univ	IL	11,472	C
Northern Kentucky Univ	KY	6,352	NC
Northern Mich Univ	MI	10,834	C
Northern State Univ	SD	7,117	LC
Northwest Missouri State Univ	MO	9,334	C
Northwest Nazarene Univ	ID	20,360	VC
Northwestern College of Iowa	IA	19,640	C+
Northwestern Okla State Univ	OK	5,433	NC
Northwestern Univ	IL	37,491	MC
Notre Dame College	OH	20,425	C
Oakland Univ	MI	10,800	C
Oberlin College	OH	36,938	MC
Occidental College	CA	35,922	HC
Oglethorpe Univ	GA	26,000	VC
Ohio Dominican Univ	OH	22,700	C
Ohio State Univ	OH	13,080	VC+
Ohio Univ	OH	14,448	C
Ohio Wesleyan Univ	OH	32,550	VC+
Okla City Univ	OK	19,580	VC
Okla State Univ	OK	9,216	VC
Old Dominion Univ	VA	10,441	C
Olivet College	MI	19,984	C+
Olivet Nazarene Univ	IL	20,480	C
Oregon State Univ	OR	11,055	C
Otterbein College	OH	26,085	C
Ouachita Baptist Univ	AR	18,900	VC

ST = STATE **$IS** = IN-STATE COSTS **SR** = SELECTOR RATING

School	ST	$IS	SR
Pace Univ	NY	28,652	VC
Pacific Lutheran Univ	WA	25,715	VC
Pacific Univ	OR	24,250	C
Park Univ	MO	10,780	C+
Penn State Univ at Erie/Behrend College	PA	12,326	C
Penn State Univ/Univ Park Campus	PA	15,646	HC
Pepperdine Univ	CA	32,830	VC
Pfeiffer Univ	NC	18,980	C
Pittsburg State Univ	KS	7,128	NC
Pitzer College	CA	37,590	HC
Plymouth State Univ	NH	12,298	LC
Point Loma Nazarene Univ	CA	21,380	VC
Pomona College	CA	33,960	MC
Portland State Univ	OR	12,453	C
Presbyterian College	SC	25,920	VC
Prescott College	AZ	13,430	C
Princeton Univ	NJ	36,649	MC
Principia College	IL	25,044	C+
Providence College	RI	30,604	HC
Purdue Univ/West Lafayette	IN	12,560	VC
Quinnipiac Univ	CT	30,570	VC
Radford Univ	VA	8,500	C
Ramapo College of New Jersey	NJ	15,203	VC
Randolph-Macon College	VA	27,190	C
Randolph-Macon Woman's College	VA	28,430	VC+
Reed College	OR	36,950	MC
Regis Univ	CO	25,740	C+
Rensselaer Polytechnic Inst	NY	37,579	HC+
Rhode Island College	RI	11,565	C
Rhodes College	TN	26,466	HC+
Rice Univ	TX	27,550	MC
Richard Stockton College of New Jersey	NJ	12,972	VC
Rider Univ	NJ	30,900	C
Ripon College	WI	24,995	VC
Roanoke College	VA	27,393	C
Robert Morris Univ	PA	20,438	C
Rochester Inst of Technology	NY	29,217	VC+
Rockford College	IL	28,310	VC
Rockhurst Univ	MO	22,960	C+
Rocky Mountain College	MT	19,015	C
Rollins College	FL	34,300	VC
Roosevelt Univ	IL	22,580	VC
Rose-Hulman Inst of Technology	IN	31,425	HC+
Rosemont College	PA	26,175	C
Rowan Univ	NJ	14,506	VC
Rutgers, The State Univ of New Jersey/Camden Campus	NJ	14,990	VC
Rutgers, The State Univ of New Jersey/New Brunswick/Piscataway Campus	NJ	15,800	HC
Rutgers, The State Univ of New Jersey/Newark Campus	NJ	15,624	VC
Sacred Heart Univ	CT	29,178	C
Saginaw Valley State Univ	MI	11,055	C
St. Ambrose Univ	IA	22,800	C
St. Anselm College	NH	30,250	C
St. Cloud State Univ	MN	8,362	C
St. Edward's Univ	TX	20,428	C
St. Francis College	NY	10,880	LC
St. Francis Univ	PA	25,876	LC
St. John Fisher College	NY	24,870	C
St. John's Univ	MN	26,473	VC
St. John's Univ	NY	30,180	C
St. Joseph's College	IN	24,250	C
St. Joseph's Univ	PA	33,590	VC
St. Lawrence Univ	NY	35,945	VC
St. Louis Univ	MO	29,780	VC+
St. Martin's College	WA	23,245	C
St. Mary's College	IN	24,474	VC
St. Mary's College of Calif	CA	32,850	VC
St. Mary's College of Maryland	MD	15,908	VC+
St. Mary's Univ of San Antonio	TX	22,444	C
St. Michael's College	VT	30,100	VC
St. Norbert College	WI	25,810	C
St. Olaf College	MN	28,500	HC
St. Peter's College	NJ	22,292	LC
St. Thomas Univ	FL	21,400	LC
St. Vincent College	PA	25,530	VC
Salem College	NC	24,595	VC
Salem State College	MA	8,592	C
Salisbury Univ	MD	12,664	VC
Salve Regina Univ	RI	29,210	C
Sam Houston State Univ	TX	7,142	C
San Diego State Univ	CA	10,321	C
San Francisco State Univ	CA	12,070	C
San Jose State Univ	CA	8,187	C
Santa Clara Univ	CA	34,701	HC
Sarah Lawrence College	NY	41,218	HC
Scripps College	CA	35,700	HC+
Seattle Pacific Univ	WA	25,944	VC
Seattle Univ	WA	24,183	VC
Seton Hall Univ	NJ	30,130	VC
Seton Hill Univ	PA	24,930	C
Shepherd College	WV	8,608	C
Shippensburg Univ of Pennsylvania	PA	10,826	C
Shorter College	GA	17,370	C
Siena College	NY	25,310	VC
Simmons College	MA	33,000	VC
Simpson College	IA	23,658	C+
Skidmore College	NY	37,930	HC
Slippery Rock Univ of Pennsylvania	PA	10,343	LC
Smith College	MA	37,034	HC+
Sonoma State Univ	CA	10,421	C
S Dak State Univ	SD	7,782	C
Southeast Missouri State Univ	MO	9,704	C
Southeastern Okla State Univ	OK	6,147	C
Southern Conn State Univ	CT	10,310	C
Southern Illinois Univ Carbondale	IL	10,407	C
Southern Illinois Univ Edwardsville	IL	8,724	C
Southern Methodist Univ	TX	34,210	HC
Southern New Hampshire Univ	NH	26,242	C
Southern Oregon Univ	OR	10,362	C
Southern Univ at New Orleans	LA	995	NC
Southern Utah Univ	UT	8,194	C
Southwest Missouri State Univ	MO	8,918	C
Southwestern Univ	TX	25,410	HC
Spelman College	GA	19,215	C+
Spring Hill College	AL	25,868	VC
Stanford Univ	CA	37,612	MC
SUNY at Oswego	NY	12,650	C
SUNY at Potsdam	NY	12,160	C
SUNY/College at Buffalo	NY	8,025	C
SUNY/College at Cortland	NY	12,095	C
SUNY/College at Geneseo	NY	11,330	HC
SUNY/College at Old Westbury	NY	12,784	C
SUNY/College at Oneonta	NY	11,870	VC
SUNY/College at Plattsburgh	NY	11,700	C
SUNY/College at Purchase	NY	10,587	VC
SUNY/Empire State College	NY	4,505	SP
SUNY/Univ at Albany	NY	12,951	HC
SUNY/Univ at Binghamton	NY	12,787	HC
SUNY/Univ at Buffalo	NY	12,563	VC
SUNY/Univ at New Paltz	NY	11,565	VC
SUNY/Univ at Stony Brook	NY	12,763	HC
State Univ of West Georgia	GA	7,622	C
Stephen F. Austin State Univ	TX	7,552	C
Stetson Univ	FL	29,495	VC
Stonehill College	MA	30,752	HC
Strayer Univ	DC	8,789	SP
Suffolk Univ	MA	29,200	C
Susquehanna Univ	PA	29,990	VC
Swarthmore College	PA	37,716	MC
Sweet Briar College	VA	27,940	C
Syracuse Univ	NY	34,720	HC
Talladega College	AL	10,110	LC
Tarleton State Univ	TX	7,576	C
Taylor Univ	IN	23,820	VC+
Temple Univ	PA	15,912	C
Tenn Tech Univ	TN	8,670	VC
Texas A&M Univ	TX	11,081	HC
Texas A&M Univ at Commerce	TX	8,994	C
Texas Christian Univ	TX	23,410	VC
Texas Lutheran Univ	TX	20,370	C
Texas Southern Univ	TX	8,920	NC
Texas State Univ	TX	9,320	VC
Texas Tech Univ	TX	10,768	VC
Texas Wesleyan Univ	TX	16,245	C
Thomas Edison State College	NJ	3,325	SP
Thomas More College	KY	21,350	C
Tougaloo College	MS	9,200	NC
Touro College	NY	15,250	VC
Towson Univ	MD	12,694	VC
Transylvania Univ	KY	23,780	VC+
Trinity College	CT	38,040	HC+
Trinity College	DC	24,150	LC
Trinity Univ	TX	26,466	HC+
Truman State Univ	MO	9,728	HC+
Tufts Univ	MA	38,233	MC
Tulane Univ	LA	37,451	HC+
Turabo Univ	PR	4,110	
Union College	NY	36,005	HC
Union Univ	TN	18,800	VC
United States Air Force Academy	CO		HC+
United States Military Academy	NY		MC
United States Naval Academy	MD		MC
Univ of Akron	OH	13,134	NC
Univ of Alabama	AL	9,040	C+
Univ of Alabama at Birmingham	AL	12,901	C
Univ of Alaska Anchorage	AK	9,100	NC
Univ of Arizona	AZ	10,413	VC
Univ of Arkansas	AR	9,855	VC
Univ of Arkansas at Little Rock	AR	5,637	NC
Univ of Bridgeport	CT	25,924	LC
Univ of Calif at Berkeley	CA	15,563	MC
Univ of Calif at Davis	CA	14,995	VC
Univ of Calif at Irvine	CA	19,808	HC
Univ of Calif at Los Angeles	CA	15,330	MC
Univ of Calif at Riverside	CA	15,300	C
Univ of Calif at San Diego	CA	14,127	HC
Univ of Calif at Santa Barbara	CA	11,732	VC
Univ of Calif at Santa Cruz	CA	16,505	VC
Univ of Central Arkansas	AR	6,388	C
Univ of Central Florida	FL	10,038	VC
Univ of Central Okla	OK	9,434	C
Univ of Chicago	IL	35,087	MC
Univ of Cincinnati	OH	14,736	C
Univ of Colo at Boulder	CO	10,774	VC
Univ of Colo at Colo Springs	CO	10,667	C
Univ of Colo at Denver	CO	3,302	C
Univ of Conn	CT	14,608	VC
Univ of Dallas	TX	25,898	VC+
Univ of Dayton	OH	24,850	VC
Univ of Delaware	DE	12,616	HC
Univ of Denver	CO	32,148	VC
Univ of Detroit Mercy	MI	25,582	C
Univ of Evansville	IN	24,190	VC
Univ of Findlay	OH	23,962	NC
Univ of Florida	FL	8,580	MC
Univ of Georgia	GA	8,656	VC
Univ of Hartford	CT	31,080	C
Univ of Hawaii at Hilo	HI	6,497	C
Univ of Hawaii at Manoa	HI	9,565	VC
Univ of Houston	TX	9,818	C
Univ of Idaho	ID	8,216	C
Univ of Illinois at Chicago	IL	13,418	C
Univ of Illinois at Urbana-Champaign	IL	11,316	HC+
Univ of Indianapolis	IN	22,560	VC
Univ of Iowa	IA	10,923	VC
Univ of Kansas	KS	8,923	VC
Univ of Kentucky	KY	7,765	C
Univ of Louisiana at Lafayette	LA	5,826	C
Univ of Louisiana at Monroe	LA	5,207	NC
Univ of Maine	ME	12,080	C+
Univ of Mary Hardin-Baylor	TX	17,268	C
Univ of Maryland/Baltimore County	MD	14,668	VC+
Univ of Maryland/College Park	MD	14,227	HC
Univ of Mass Amherst	MA	13,980	C+
Univ of Mass Boston	MA	6,227	C
Univ of Mass Dartmouth	MA	12,835	C
Univ of Mass Lowell	MA	11,937	VC
Univ of Memphis	TN	8,560	C
Univ of Miami	FL	34,608	HC
Univ of Mich/Ann Arbor	MI	13,864	HC+
Univ of Mich/Dearborn	MI	6,843	VC
Univ of Mich/Flint	MI	5,548	C
Univ of Minn/Duluth	MN	12,470	C
Univ of Minn/Morris	MN	12,896	VC
Univ of Minn/Twin Cities	MN	13,160	VC
Univ of Miss	MS	7,666	C
Univ of Missouri/Columbia	MO	13,782	VC
Univ of Missouri/Kansas City	MO	13,416	VC
Univ of Missouri/Rolla	MO	12,292	HC
Univ of Missouri/St. Louis	MO	11,656	VC
Univ of Mobile	AL	13,620	C
Univ of Montana	MT	9,395	C
Univ of Nebr at Kearney	NE	8,286	NC
Univ of Nebr at Lincoln	NE	9,975	C+
Univ of Nebr at Omaha	NE	8,080	C
Univ of Nevada/Las Vegas	NV	11,566	C
Univ of New Hampshire	NH	14,828	VC
Univ of New Mexico	NM	9,223	C
Univ of New Orleans	LA	7,356	C
Univ of N Car at Asheville	NC	8,079	VC
Univ of N Car at Chapel Hill	NC	10,117	MC
Univ of N Car at Charlotte	NC	8,185	C
Univ of N Car at Greensboro	NC	8,248	C
Univ of N Car at Wilmington	NC	8,940	VC
Univ of N Dak	ND	8,390	C
Univ of North Florida	FL	8,769	VC
Univ of North Texas	TX	7,629	C
Univ of Northern Colo	CO	8,987	C
Univ of Northern Iowa	IA	9,834	C
Univ of Notre Dame	IN	34,442	MC
Univ of Okla	OK	9,226	VC
Univ of Oregon	OR	11,479	VC
Univ of Pennsylvania	PA	37,960	MC
Univ of Pittsburgh at Bradford	PA	15,294	C
Univ of Pittsburgh at Johnstown	PA	15,216	LC
Univ of Pittsburgh at Pittsburgh	PA	16,074	HC
Univ of PR/Cayey Univ College	PR	1,245	
Univ of PR/Mayaguez	PR		
Univ of PR/Rio Piedras	PR	5,730	
Univ of Puget Sound	WA	31,760	HC
Univ of Redlands	CA	32,576	VC
Univ of Rhode Island	RI	13,720	VC
Univ of Richmond	VA	30,100	MC
Univ of Rio Grande	OH	8,728	NC
Univ of Rochester	NY	32,979	HC
Univ of St. Thomas	MN	26,918	VC
Univ of St. Thomas	TX	21,952	VC
Univ of San Diego	CA	33,156	HC
Univ of San Francisco	CA	34,700	VC
Univ of Science and Arts of Okla	OK	5,982	C
Univ of Scranton	PA	30,836	VC
Univ of S Car at Columbia	SC	10,048	VC
Univ of S Car at Spartanburg	SC	9,936	C+
Univ of S Dak	SD	7,710	C+
Univ of South Florida	FL	9,454	C
Univ of Southern Calif	CA	37,459	MC
Univ of Southern Colo	CO	7,821	LC
Univ of Southern Indiana	IN	9,025	LC
Univ of Southern Maine	ME	11,212	C
Univ of Southern Miss	MS	8,324	LC
Univ of Tampa	FL	23,982	VC
Univ of Tenn at Chattanooga	TN	7,783	C
Univ of Tenn at Knoxville	TN	8,214	C
Univ of Tenn at Martin	TN	7,748	C
Univ of Texas at Arlington	TX	7,192	LC
Univ of Texas at Austin	TX	10,630	HC
Univ of Texas at Dallas	TX	10,234	HC
Univ of Texas at El Paso	TX	5,799	NC
Univ of Texas at San Antonio	TX	9,088	NC
Univ of Texas-Pan American	TX	5,954	LC
Univ of the District of Columbia	DC	2,070	LC
Univ of the Ozarks	AR	16,574	C
Univ of the Pacific	CA	31,090	VC
Univ of the South	TN	30,855	HC
Univ of Toledo	OH	12,479	NC
Univ of Tulsa	OK	22,090	VC+
Univ of Utah	UT	9,205	C
Univ of Vermont	VT	16,316	VC
Univ of Virginia	VA	11,740	MC
Univ of Virginia's College at Wise	VA	10,116	C
Univ of Washington	WA	10,361	VC
Univ of Wisc/Eau Claire	WI	8,463	VC
Univ of Wisc/Green Bay	WI	8,154	C
Univ of Wisc/La Crosse	WI	8,991	VC
Univ of Wisc/Madison	WI	8,262	VC
Univ of Wisc/Milwaukee	WI	9,427	LC
Univ of Wisc/Oshkosh	WI	6,130	LC
Univ of Wisc/Parkside	WI	6,160	LC
Univ of Wisc/Platteville	WI	8,450	C
Univ of Wisc/River Falls	WI	8,358	LC
Univ of Wisc/Stevens Point	WI	8,116	VC
Univ of Wisc/Whitewater	WI	8,626	C
Univ of Wyoming	WY	8,636	C
Ursinus College	PA	34,400	VC
Utah State Univ	UT	7,371	C
Utica College	NY	28,340	C
Valparaiso Univ	IN	26,118	VC+
Vanderbilt Univ	TN	37,897	MC
Vassar College	NY	37,030	MC
Villanova Univ	PA	35,050	HC
Virginia Commonwealth Univ	VA	9,030	C
Virginia Polytechnic Inst and State Univ	VA	9,179	C
Virginia State Univ	VA	10,358	C
Wabash College	IN	27,932	VC
Wake Forest Univ	NC	34,090	MC
Wartburg College	IA	21,165	VC
Washburn Univ of Topeka	KS	8,984	NC
Washington and Jefferson College	PA	29,570	VC
Washington and Lee Univ	VA	29,663	MC
Washington College	MD	30,540	VC
Washington State Univ	WA	11,334	C
Washington Univ in St. Louis	MO	38,293	MC
Wayne State Univ	MI	11,774	C
Weber State Univ	UT	7,945	NC
Webster Univ	MO	21,848	VC
Wellesley College	MA	36,516	MC
Wells College	NY	21,122	VC
Wesleyan College	GA	17,870	VC
Wesleyan Univ	CT	35,139	MC
West Chester Univ of Pennsylvania	PA	11,164	C
West Liberty State College	WV	7,868	LC
West Texas A&M Univ	TX	7,533	C
West Virginia State College	WV	6,264	NC
West Virginia Univ	WV	9,370	C
West Virginia Wesleyan College	WV	22,920	C
Western Conn State Univ	CT	11,625	C
Western Illinois Univ	IL	10,363	C
Western Kentucky Univ	KY	6,834	C
Western Mich Univ	MI	12,031	C
Western New England College	MA	28,924	C
Western Oregon Univ	OR	10,281	C
Western State College of Colo	CO	9,014	C

ST = STATE **$IS** = IN-STATE COSTS **SR** = SELECTOR RATING

School	ST	$IS	SR
Western Washington Univ	WA	10,119	VC
Westfield State College	MA	10,147	C
Westminster College	MO	18,150	C+
Westminster College	PA	22,960	C
Westminster College	UT	17,226	C
Wheaton College	IL	21,934	HC
Wheaton College	MA	36,330	HC
Whitman College	WA	32,526	HC+
Whittier College	CA	29,108	C
Whitworth College	WA	26,428	VC+
Wichita State Univ	KS	8,092	C
Widener Univ	PA	27,020	C
Wilberforce Univ	OH	14,937	LC
Willamette Univ	OR	32,032	VC+
William Paterson Univ of New Jersey	NJ	14,450	C
Williams College	MA	32,270	MC
Winona State Univ	MN		
Winston-Salem State Univ	NC	8,926	LC
Wittenberg Univ	OH	31,316	VC
Wofford College	SC	26,710	HC
Worcester Polytechnic Inst	MA	37,404	HC
Worcester State College	MA	10,005	C
Wright State Univ	OH	11,490	LC
Xavier Univ	OH	26,850	VC+
Yale Univ	CT	37,000	MC
Yeshiva Univ	NY	21,400	C
York College of Pennsylvania	PA	14,500	VC
Youngstown State Univ	OH	11,148	NC

EDUCATION

School	ST	$IS	SR
Aquinas College	MI	21,894	C
Baldwin-Wallace College	OH	24,678	C
Belmont Abbey College	NC	23,742	C
Beloit College	WI	29,864	HC
Bennington College	VT	35,910	HC
Bloomfield College	NJ	19,250	LC
Boise State Univ	ID	7,657	LC
Boston Univ	MA	38,194	HC+
Brewton-Parker College	GA	14,200	LC
Brown Univ	RI	38,174	MC
Bryn Athyn College of the New Church	PA	12,612	NC
Bucknell Univ	PA	35,262	HC+
Cabrini College	PA	29,020	C
Calif Lutheran Univ	CA	27,600	LC
Cal State, Monterey Bay	CA	6,683	LC
Catawba College	NC	20,500	C
Catholic Univ of America	DC	34,248	VC
Central Mich Univ	MI	11,142	C
Chatham College	PA	27,266	C+
Christian Heritage College	CA	19,990	C
CUNY/College of Staten Island	NY	4,308	NC
Coker College	SC	21,491	C
Colgate Univ	NY	37,095	MC
College of St. Mary	NE	21,510	C
College of St. Scholastica	MN	24,970	C+
Columbia Univ/Columbia College	NY	38,590	MC
Concordia College	NY	19,200	VC
Cornell Univ	NY	38,253	MC
Denison Univ	OH	33,050	HC
Drexel Univ	PA	27,655	VC
Duquesne Univ	PA	26,907	VC
Earlham College	IN	29,976	VC+
East Texas Baptist Univ	TX	13,914	C
Eastern Mich Univ	MI	11,478	C
Eastern Nazarene College	MA	19,433	LC
Eastern Oregon Univ	OR	10,080	NC
Endicott College	MA	25,266	C+
Eugene Lang College/New School Univ	NY	34,940	C
Eureka College	IL	24,980	LC
Franklin Pierce College	NH	28,980	LC
Furman Univ	SC	28,976	HC+
Goddard College	VT	21,056	C+
Guilford College	NC	24,960	VC
Hampshire College	MA	37,037	HC
Harris-Stowe State College	MO	3,200	SP
Hope International Univ	CA	16,940	NC
Huntington College	IN	23,590	C
Huston-Tillotson College	TX	14,232	NC
Ithaca College	NY	31,730	HC
Johnson State College	VT	11,819	LC
Keene State College	NH	12,212	C
Kent State Univ	OH	12,932	C
Lake Forest College	IL	30,270	VC
Lourdes College	OH	15,300	LC
Lynchburg College	VA	26,815	C
Lynn Univ	FL	30,750	C
Maharishi Univ of Management	IA	29,230	VC
Manhattanville College	NY	32,420	C+
Martin Univ	IN	10,200	SP
Mary Baldwin College	VA	24,939	C
Mass College of Liberal Arts	MA	8,717	LC
Mich State Univ	MI	11,933	VC
Midway College	KY	15,815	C
Miss State Univ	MS	9,139	C
Montana State Univ-Billings	MT	9,550	C
New York Inst of Technology	NY	24,205	VC
N Car State Univ	NC	9,886	VC
Northwest College	WA	18,854	C
Northwestern Univ	IL	37,491	MC
Ohio State Univ at Lima	OH	4,416	NC
Pacific Lutheran Univ	WA	25,715	VC
Philadelphia Biblical Univ	PA	18,395	C
Prescott College	AZ	13,430	C
Rocky Mountain College	MT	19,015	C
St. Louis Univ	MO	29,780	VC+
St. Mary's College	MI	13,314	LC
Salem State College	MA	8,592	C
Schreiner Univ	TX	20,440	C
Shawnee State Univ	OH	11,031	NC
Smith College	MA	37,034	HC+
Spalding Univ	KY	17,985	C
SUNY/Empire State College	NY	4,505	SP
Stonehill College	MA	30,752	HC
Susquehanna Univ	PA	29,990	VC
Swarthmore College	PA	37,716	MC
Temple Univ	PA	15,912	C
Tenn Wesleyan College	TN	16,540	C
Texas A&M Univ at Corpus Christi	TX	10,269	C
Texas Lutheran Univ	TX	20,370	C
Texas Tech Univ	TX	10,768	VC
Towson Univ	MD	12,694	VC
Trevecca Nazarene Univ	TN	17,548	C
Trinity Christian College	IL	21,640	VC
Trinity College	CT	38,040	HC+
Tusculum College	TN	19,990	C
Union Inst and Univ	OH	7,848	SP
Union Univ	TN	18,800	VC
Univ of Alabama in Huntsville	AL	9,126	VC
Univ of Conn	CT	14,608	VC
Univ of Delaware	DE	12,616	HC
Univ of Dubuque	IA	20,950	C
Univ of Illinois at Chicago	IL	13,418	C
Univ of La Verne	CA	28,600	C
Univ of Missouri/Columbia	MO	13,782	VC
Univ of Nebr at Lincoln	NE	9,975	C+
Univ of N Car at Chapel Hill	NC	10,117	MC
Univ of Oregon	OR	11,479	VC
Univ of Pennsylvania	PA	37,960	MC
Univ of PR/Rio Piedras	PR	5,730	
Univ of Puget Sound	WA	31,760	HC
Univ of St. Thomas	TX	21,952	VC
Univ of South Alabama	AL	7,760	LC
Univ of South Florida	FL	9,454	C
Univ of Tenn at Chattanooga	TN	7,783	C
Univ of Texas at Austin	TX	10,630	HC
Univ of the Pacific	CA	31,090	VC
Univ of Tulsa	OK	22,090	VC+
Univ of Vermont	VT	16,316	VC
Univ of Wisc/Green Bay	WI	8,154	C
Univ of Wisc/Milwaukee	WI	9,427	LC
Univ of Wisc/Parkside	WI	6,160	LC
Vanderbilt Univ	TN	37,897	MC
Virginia Intermont College	VA	19,800	C
Wake Forest Univ	NC	34,090	MC
Washburn Univ of Topeka	KS	8,984	NC
Washington State Univ	WA	11,334	C
Washington Univ in St. Louis	MO	38,293	MC
Webster Univ	MO	21,848	VC
Western Baptist College	OR	21,808	C
Western Oregon Univ	OR	10,281	C
Xavier Univ	OH	26,850	VC+
York College	NE	14,975	C
Youngstown State Univ	OH	11,148	NC

EDUCATION ADMINISTRATION

School	ST	$IS	SR
Ashland Univ	OH	24,464	C
Philander Smith College	AR	7,380	NC
Southwestern Okla State Univ	OK	4,801	C
Washburn Univ of Topeka	KS	8,984	NC

EDUCATION OF THE DEAF AND HEARING IMPAIRED

School	ST	$IS	SR
Adelphi Univ	NY	26,300	VC
Augustana College	SD	21,998	VC
Ball State Univ	IN	8,660	C
Barton College	NC	19,314	C
Boston Univ	MA	38,194	HC+
Cal State, Northridge	CA	7,757	LC
CUNY/Brooklyn College	NY	4,353	C+
College of New Jersey	NJ	15,950	MC
Eastern Kentucky Univ	KY	7,708	C
Eastern Mich Univ	MI	11,478	C
Flagler College	FL	11,860	VC+
Fontbonne Univ	MO	21,508	C
Indiana Univ of Pennsylvania	PA	10,489	C
Ithaca College	NY	31,730	HC
Lenoir-Rhyne College	NC	19,186	C
MacMurray College	IL	20,005	LC
Mercy College	NY	19,200	NC
Minot State Univ	ND	6,602	LC
Rochester Inst of Technology	NY	29,217	VC+
St. John's Univ	NY	30,180	C
Southern Univ at New Orleans	LA	995	NC
SUNY/College at Plattsburgh	NY	11,700	C
Texas Christian Univ	TX	23,410	VC
Towson Univ	MD	12,694	VC
Univ of Arkansas at Little Rock	AR	5,637	NC
Univ of Montevallo	AL	8,478	C
Univ of N Car at Greensboro	NC	8,248	C
Univ of Science and Arts of Okla	OK	5,982	C
Univ of Tulsa	OK	22,090	VC+

EDUCATION OF THE EMOTIONALLY HANDICAPPED

School	ST	$IS	SR
CUNY/City College	NY	4,230	C+
East Carolina Univ	NC	8,671	C
Eastern Mich Univ	MI	11,478	C
Florida International Univ	FL	9,912	VC
Florida State Univ	FL	9,028	HC
Univ of South Florida	FL	9,454	C
Youngstown State Univ	OH	11,148	NC

EDUCATION OF THE EXCEPTIONAL CHILD

School	ST	$IS	SR
Ashland Univ	OH	24,464	C
Bethel College	TN	12,980	C
Bethune-Cookman College	FL	16,480	LC
Edgewood College	WI	20,520	C
Jacksonville Univ	FL	24,040	C
Mansfield Univ	PA	11,220	C
Minot State Univ	ND	6,602	LC
Nova Southeastern Univ	FL	23,346	C
St. Augustine's College	NC	12,990	LC
Southeastern College	FL	11,648	LC
Texas Christian Univ	TX	23,410	VC
Univ of Central Arkansas	AR	6,388	C
Univ of Central Florida	FL	10,038	VC
Univ of Great Falls	MT	15,360	C
Univ of Wisc/Stevens Point	WI	8,116	VC
Warner Southern College	FL	16,738	LC

EDUCATION OF THE MENTALLY HANDICAPPED

School	ST	$IS	SR
Augusta State Univ	GA	2,592	C
Calif Univ of Pennsylvania	PA	10,388	C
CUNY/City College	NY	4,230	C+
East Carolina Univ	NC	8,671	C
Eastern Mich Univ	MI	11,478	C
Florida International Univ	FL	9,912	VC
Florida State Univ	FL	9,028	HC
Indiana Univ of Pennsylvania	PA	10,489	C
Minot State Univ	ND	6,602	LC
Northern Mich Univ	MI	10,834	C
Northwest Missouri State Univ	MO	9,334	C
Southeastern Okla State Univ	OK	6,147	C
Univ of N Car at Charlotte	NC	8,185	C
Univ of Rio Grande	OH	8,728	NC
Univ of South Florida	FL	9,454	C
Youngstown State Univ	OH	11,148	NC

EDUCATION OF THE MULTIPLY HANDICAPPED

School	ST	$IS	SR
Eastern Mich Univ	MI	11,478	C
Ohio Univ	OH	14,448	C
Univ of Alabama	AL	9,040	C+
Youngstown State Univ	OH	11,148	NC

EDUCATION OF THE PHYSICALLY HANDICAPPED

School	ST	$IS	SR
Calif Univ of Pennsylvania	PA	10,388	C
Eastern Mich Univ	MI	11,478	C
Indiana Univ of Pennsylvania	PA	10,489	C
Ohio Univ	OH	14,448	C

EDUCATION OF THE VISUALLY HANDICAPPED

School	ST	$IS	SR
Dominican College	NY	24,810	LC
Eastern Mich Univ	MI	11,478	C
Florida State Univ	FL	9,028	HC

EDUCATIONAL MEDIA

School	ST	$IS	SR
Ball State Univ	IN	8,660	C
College of St. Scholastica	MN	24,970	C+
Duquesne Univ	PA	26,907	VC
Eastern Mich Univ	MI	11,478	C
Indiana State Univ	IN	10,719	LC
Indiana Univ Bloomington	IN	12,389	VC
Ithaca College	NY	31,730	HC
Purdue Univ/West Lafayette	IN	12,560	VC

EDUCATIONAL STATISTICS AND RESEARCH

School	ST	$IS	SR
Bucknell Univ	PA	35,262	HC+
Emory Univ	GA	36,872	MC

ELECTRICAL/ELECTRONICS ENGINEERING

School	ST	$IS	SR
Alabama A&M Univ	AL	5,100	LC
Alfred Univ	NY	28,290	C
Andrews Univ	MI	19,550	C
Arizona State Univ-Main	AZ	10,048	C
Auburn Univ	AL	10,396	VC
Baylor Univ	TX	23,864	VC
Bethel College	IN	19,670	C
Bloomsburg Univ of Pennsylvania	PA	10,844	C
Boston Univ	MA	38,194	HC+
Bradley Univ	IL	22,910	VC
Brigham Young Univ	UT	8,504	HC
Bucknell Univ	PA	35,262	HC+
Calif Inst of Technology	CA	31,677	MC
Calif Polytechnic State Univ	CA	8,747	VC
Calif State Polytechnic Univ, Pomona	CA	8,793	C+
Cal State, Chico	CA	8,598	LC
Cal State, Fresno	CA	8,414	LC
Cal State, Fullerton	CA	6,648	C
Cal State, Long Beach	CA	8,762	C+
Cal State, Los Angeles	CA	5,778	C
Cal State, Sacramento	CA	9,543	C
Calvin College	MI	22,615	NC
Capitol College	MD	21,250	C
Carnegie Mellon Univ	PA	32,682	MC
Case Western Reserve Univ	OH	32,002	MC
Catholic Univ of America	DC	34,248	VC
Cedarville Univ	OH	19,954	VC
Central Missouri State Univ	MO	9,776	C
Central Washington Univ	WA	9,768	C
Christian Brothers Univ	TN	22,290	VC
Citadel, The	SC	12,295	C+
CUNY/City College	NY	4,230	C+
Clarkson Univ	NY	32,226	VC
Clemson Univ	SC	11,972	HC
Cleveland State Univ	OH	12,308	LC
Cogswell Polytechnical College	CA	14,400	LC
Colo State Univ	CO	9,964	VC
Colo Technical Univ	CO	9,500	LC
Columbia Univ/Fu Foundation School of Engineering and Applied Science	NY	38,590	MC
Cooper Union for the Advancement of Science and Art	NY	10,400	MC
Cornell Univ	NY	38,253	MC
Delaware State Univ	DE	8,104	LC
Dordt College	IA	20,170	VC
Drexel Univ	PA	27,655	VC
Duke Univ	NC	37,555	MC
Embry-Riddle Aeronautical Univ	AZ	27,710	C+
Embry-Riddle Aeronautical Univ	FL	27,730	C+
Fairfield Univ	CT	35,505	HC
Fairleigh Dickinson Univ/Metropolitan Campus	NJ	28,584	C
Florida A&M Univ	FL	7,564	C
Florida Atlantic Univ	FL	8,543	C
Florida Inst of Technology	FL	28,740	VC
Florida International Univ	FL	9,912	VC
Florida State Univ	FL	9,028	HC
Gannon Univ	PA	23,260	C
George Mason Univ	VA	9,732	VC
George Washington Univ	DC	41,030	MC
Georgia Inst of Technology	GA	10,340	HC+
Gonzaga Univ	WA	26,766	HC
Grove City College	PA	14,228	HC
Hampton Univ	VA	17,112	C+
Henry Cogswell College	WA	14,400	SP
Hofstra Univ	NY	27,112	VC
Howard Univ	DC	16,505	C
Illinois Inst of Technology	IL	26,456	HC+
Indiana Inst of Technology	IN	21,620	C
Indiana Univ-Purdue Univ Fort Wayne	IN	5,108	LC
Indiana Univ-Purdue Univ Indianapolis	IN	8,257	LC
Inter American Univ of PR/Bayamon Univ College	PR	3,522	
Iowa State Univ	IA	10,768	VC
Jacksonville Univ	FL	24,040	C
John Brown Univ	AR	15,080	VC
Johns Hopkins Univ	MD	38,372	MC
Johnson and Wales Univ	RI	22,965	LC
Kansas State Univ	KS	8,728	VC
Kettering Univ	MI	26,478	HC
Lafayette College	PA	35,746	MC
Lake Superior State Univ	MI	9,034	LC
Lamar Univ	TX	6,816	LC
Lawrence Tech Univ	MI	20,487	C
Lehigh Univ	PA	37,570	HC+

School	ST	$IS	SR
LeTourneau Univ	TX	21,080	C
Loras College	IA	24,233	C
Louisiana State Univ and A&M College	LA	9,126	VC
Loyola College in Maryland	MD	34,560	HC
Loyola Marymount Univ	CA	32,194	VC
Manhattan College	NY	27,400	VC
Marquette Univ	WI	27,594	VC
Mass Inst of Technology	MA	38,310	MC
McNeese State Univ	LA	5,259	LC
Mercer Univ	GA	27,516	VC+
Merrimack College	MA	29,625	C
Miami Univ	OH	15,033	HC
Mich State Univ	MI	11,933	VC
Mich Tech Univ	MI	13,235	VC
Milwaukee School of Engineering	WI	28,479	VC+
Minn State Univ, Mankato	MN	8,803	LC
Miss State Univ	MS	9,139	C
Montana State Univ-Bozeman	MT	9,515	C
Morgan State Univ	MD	11,470	C
New Jersey Inst of Technology	NJ	16,396	VC
New Mexico Inst of Mining and Technology	NM	7,580	NC
New Mexico State Univ	NM	7,932	C
New York Inst of Technology	NY	24,205	VC
N Car Agricultural and Technical State Univ	NC	6,659	LC
N Car State Univ	NC	9,886	VC
N Dak State Univ	ND	8,435	C
Northeastern Univ	MA	35,650	HC
Northern Arizona Univ	AZ	9,002	C
Northern Illinois Univ	IL	11,472	C
Northwestern Univ	IL	37,491	MC
Norwich Univ	VT	21,064	LC
Oakland Univ	MI	10,800	C
Ohio Northern Univ	OH	27,765	VC
Ohio State Univ	OH	13,080	VC+
Ohio Univ	OH	14,448	C
Okla Christian Univ	OK	17,690	NC
Okla State Univ	OK	9,216	VC
Old Dominion Univ	VA	10,441	C
Oral Roberts Univ	OK	18,490	C
Penn State Univ/Univ Park Campus	PA	15,646	HC
Polytechnic Univ/Brooklyn	NY	33,770	VC
Portland State Univ	OR	12,453	C
Prairie View A&M Univ	TX	9,418	NC
Princeton Univ	NJ	36,649	MC
Purdue Univ/Calumet	IN	6,630	NC
Purdue Univ/West Lafayette	IN	12,560	VC
Rensselaer Polytechnic Inst	NY	37,579	HC+
Rice Univ	TX	27,550	MC
Rochester Inst of Technology	NY	29,217	VC+
Rose-Hulman Inst of Technology	IN	31,425	HC+
Rutgers, The State Univ of New Jersey/New Brunswick/Piscataway Campus	NJ	15,800	HC
Saginaw Valley State Univ	MI	11,055	C
St. Cloud State Univ	MN	8,362	C
St. Louis Univ	MO	29,780	VC+
St. Mary's Univ of San Antonio	TX	22,444	C
San Diego State Univ	CA	10,321	C
San Francisco State Univ	CA	12,070	C
San Jose State Univ	CA	8,187	C
Santa Clara Univ	CA	34,701	HC
Seattle Pacific Univ	WA	25,944	VC
Seattle Univ	WA	24,183	VC
S Dak School of Mines and Technology	SD	7,854	C+
S Dak State Univ	SD	7,782	C
Southern Illinois Univ Carbondale	IL	10,407	C
Southern Illinois Univ Edwardsville	IL	8,724	C
Southern Methodist Univ	TX	34,210	HC
Southern Univ and A&M College	LA	7,372	LC
Stanford Univ	CA	37,612	MC
SUNY/Maritime College	NY	10,025	LC
SUNY/Univ at Binghamton	NY	12,787	HC
SUNY/Univ at Buffalo	NY	12,563	VC
SUNY/Univ at New Paltz	NY	11,565	VC
SUNY/Univ at Stony Brook	NY	12,763	HC
Stevens Inst of Technology	NJ	35,300	HC+
Suffolk Univ	MA	29,200	C
Syracuse Univ	NY	34,720	HC
Temple Univ	PA	15,912	C
Tenn State Univ	TN	9,048	LC
Tenn Tech Univ	TN	8,670	VC
Texas A&M Univ	TX	11,081	HC
Texas A&M Univ at Kingsville	TX	6,740	LC
Texas Tech Univ	TX	10,768	VC
Tri-State Univ-Main Campus	IN	23,600	C
Tufts Univ	MA	38,233	MC
Tulane Univ	LA	37,451	HC+
Tuskegee Univ	AL	17,250	LC
Union College	NY	36,005	HC
United States Air Force Academy	CO		HC+
United States Coast Guard Academy	CT		MC
United States Military Academy	NY		MC
United States Naval Academy	MD		MC
Universidad Politecnica de PR	PR	5,370	
Univ of Akron	OH	13,134	NC
Univ of Alabama	AL	9,040	C+
Univ of Alabama at Birmingham	AL	12,901	C
Univ of Alabama in Huntsville	AL	9,126	VC
Univ of Alaska Fairbanks	AK	9,295	C
Univ of Arizona	AZ	10,413	VC
Univ of Arkansas	AR	9,855	VC
Univ of Calif at Berkeley	CA	15,563	MC
Univ of Calif at Davis	CA	14,995	VC
Univ of Calif at Irvine	CA	19,808	HC
Univ of Calif at Los Angeles	CA	15,330	MC
Univ of Calif at Riverside	CA	15,300	C
Univ of Calif at San Diego	CA	14,127	HC
Univ of Calif at Santa Barbara	CA	11,732	VC
Univ of Central Florida	FL	10,038	VC
Univ of Cincinnati	OH	14,736	C
Univ of Colo at Boulder	CO	10,774	VC
Univ of Colo at Colo Springs	CO	10,667	C
Univ of Colo at Denver	CO	3,302	C
Univ of Conn	CT	14,608	VC
Univ of Dayton	OH	24,850	VC
Univ of Delaware	DE	12,616	HC
Univ of Denver	CO	32,148	VC
Univ of Detroit Mercy	MI	25,582	C
Univ of Evansville	IN	24,190	VC
Univ of Florida	FL	8,580	MC
Univ of Hartford	CT	31,080	C
Univ of Hawaii at Manoa	HI	9,565	VC
Univ of Houston	TX	9,818	C
Univ of Idaho	ID	8,216	C
Univ of Illinois at Chicago	IL	13,418	C
Univ of Illinois at Urbana-Champaign	IL	11,316	HC+
Univ of Indianapolis	IN	22,560	VC
Univ of Iowa	IA	10,923	VC
Univ of Kansas	KS	8,923	VC
Univ of Kentucky	KY	7,765	C
Univ of Louisiana at Lafayette	LA	5,826	C
Univ of Louisville	KY	8,762	VC
Univ of Maine	ME	12,080	C+
Univ of Maryland/College Park	MD	14,227	HC
Univ of Mass Amherst	MA	13,980	C+
Univ of Mass Dartmouth	MA	12,835	C
Univ of Mass Lowell	MA	11,937	VC
Univ of Memphis	TN	8,560	C
Univ of Miami	FL	34,608	HC
Univ of Mich/Ann Arbor	MI	13,864	HC+
Univ of Mich/Dearborn	MI	6,843	VC
Univ of Minn/Duluth	MN	12,470	C
Univ of Minn/Twin Cities	MN	13,160	VC
Univ of Miss	MS	7,666	C
Univ of Missouri/Columbia	MO	13,782	VC
Univ of Missouri/Kansas City	MO	13,416	VC
Univ of Missouri/Rolla	MO	12,292	HC
Univ of Missouri/St. Louis	MO	11,656	VC
Univ of Nebr at Lincoln	NE	9,975	C+
Univ of Nevada/Las Vegas	NV	11,566	C
Univ of Nevada/Reno	NV	9,792	C
Univ of New Hampshire	NH	14,828	VC
Univ of New Haven	CT	28,650	C
Univ of New Mexico	NM	9,223	C
Univ of New Orleans	LA	7,356	C
Univ of N Car at Charlotte	NC	8,185	C
Univ of N Dak	ND	8,390	C
Univ of North Florida	FL	8,769	VC
Univ of Notre Dame	IN	34,442	MC
Univ of Okla	OK	9,226	VC
Univ of Pennsylvania	PA	37,960	MC
Univ of Pittsburgh at Pittsburgh	PA	16,074	HC
Univ of Portland	OR	28,500	VC
Univ of PR/Mayaguez	PR		
Univ of Rhode Island	RI	13,720	VC
Univ of Rochester	NY	32,979	HC
Univ of St. Thomas	MN	26,918	VC
Univ of San Diego	CA	33,156	HC
Univ of Scranton	PA	30,836	VC
Univ of South Alabama	AL	7,760	LC
Univ of S Car at Columbia	SC	10,048	VC
Univ of South Florida	FL	9,454	C
Univ of Southern Calif	CA	37,459	MC
Univ of Southern Maine	ME	11,212	C
Univ of Tenn at Knoxville	TN	8,214	C
Univ of Texas at Arlington	TX	7,192	LC
Univ of Texas at Austin	TX	10,630	HC
Univ of Texas at Dallas	TX	10,234	HC
Univ of Texas at El Paso	TX	5,799	NC
Univ of Texas at San Antonio	TX	9,088	NC
Univ of Texas-Pan American	TX	5,954	LC
Univ of the District of Columbia	DC	2,070	LC
Univ of the Pacific	CA	31,090	VC
Univ of Toledo	OH	12,479	NC
Univ of Tulsa	OK	22,090	VC+
Univ of Utah	UT	9,205	C
Univ of Vermont	VT	16,316	VC
Univ of Virginia	VA	11,740	MC
Univ of Washington	WA	10,361	VC
Univ of West Florida	FL	8,470	C
Univ of Wisc/Madison	WI	8,262	VC
Univ of Wisc/Milwaukee	WI	9,427	LC
Univ of Wisc/Platteville	WI	8,450	C
Univ of Wyoming	WY	8,636	C
Utah State Univ	UT	7,371	C
Valparaiso Univ	IN	26,118	VC+
Vanderbilt Univ	TN	37,897	MC
Villanova Univ	PA	35,050	HC
Virginia Commonwealth Univ	VA	9,030	C
Virginia Military Inst	VA	9,968	C+
Virginia Polytechnic Inst and State Univ	VA	9,179	C
Washington State Univ	WA	11,334	C
Washington Univ in St. Louis	MO	38,293	MC
Wayne State Univ	MI	11,774	C
West Virginia Univ	WV	9,370	C
West Virginia Univ Inst of Technology	WV	7,518	NC
Western Kentucky Univ	KY	6,834	C
Western Mich Univ	MI	12,031	C
Western New England College	MA	28,924	C
Wichita State Univ	KS	8,092	C
Widener Univ	PA	27,020	C
Wilkes Univ	PA	28,060	C
Worcester Polytechnic Inst	MA	37,404	HC
Wright State Univ	OH	11,490	LC
Yale Univ	CT	37,000	MC
Youngstown State Univ	OH	11,148	NC

ELECTRICAL/ELECTRONICS ENGINEERING TECHNOLOGY

School	ST	$IS	SR
Alabama A&M Univ	AL	5,100	LC
Andrews Univ	MI	19,550	C
Appalachian State Univ	NC	7,637	VC
Baker College of Flint	MI	7,720	NC
Brigham Young Univ	UT	8,504	HC
Calif Univ of Pennsylvania	PA	10,388	C
Central Conn State Univ	CT	12,090	C
Central Missouri State Univ	MO	9,776	C
Colo Technical Univ	CO	9,500	LC
DeVry College of Technology/North Brunswick	NJ	10,100	LC
DeVry/New York	NY	11,860	LC
DeVry Univ/Addison (DuPage County)	IL	10,790	LC
DeVry Univ/Alpharetta	GA	10,670	LC
DeVry Univ/Chicago	IL	10,790	LC
DeVry Univ/Columbus	OH	10,670	LC
DeVry Univ/Crystal City	VA	11,860	C
DeVry Univ/Dallas	TX	10,640	LC
DeVry Univ/Decatur	GA	10,670	LC
DeVry Univ/Fort Washington	PA	11,860	LC
DeVry Univ/Fremont	CA	11,860	LC
DeVry Univ/Kansas City	MO	10,670	LC
DeVry Univ/Long Beach	CA	11,310	LC
DeVry Univ/Miramar	FL	11,310	LC
DeVry Univ/Orlando	FL	11,310	LC
DeVry Univ/Phoenix	AZ	10,670	LC
DeVry Univ/Pomona	CA	11,310	LC
DeVry Univ/Seattle	WA	11,860	LC
DeVry Univ/Tinley Park	IL	10,790	LC
DeVry Univ/West Hills	CA	11,310	LC
DeVry Univ/Westminster	CO	11,310	LC
East Carolina Univ	NC	8,671	C
Eastern New Mexico Univ	NM	6,762	LC
East-West Univ	IL	10,365	LC
Excelsior College	NY	975	SP
Fairleigh Dickinson Univ/Metropolitan Campus	NJ	28,584	C
Fairmont State	WV	8,280	LC
Farmingdale SUNY	NY	12,891	C
Fort Valley State Univ	GA	6,960	C
Georgia Southern Univ	GA	8,540	C
Indiana State Univ	IN	10,719	LC
Indiana Univ-Purdue Univ Indianapolis	IN	8,257	LC
Inter American Univ of PR/Aguadilla Campus	PR	3,544	
Inter American Univ of PR/Bayamon Univ College	PR	3,522	
Inter American Univ of PR/Fajardo Campus	PR	4,000	
Inter American Univ of PR/Ponce Regional College	PR	3,700	
Kansas State Univ	KS	8,728	VC
Louisiana Tech Univ	LA	7,361	C
Metropolitan State College of Denver	CO	2,338	LC
Minn State Univ, Mankato	MN	8,803	LC
Montana State Univ-Northern	MT	8,600	NC
Murray State Univ	KY	7,816	VC
New York Inst of Technology	NY	24,205	VC
Norfolk State Univ	VA	9,722	LC
Northeastern Univ	MA	35,650	HC
Northern Mich Univ	MI	10,834	C
Northwestern State Univ of Louisiana	LA	6,331	NC
Okla State Univ	OK	9,216	VC
Old Dominion Univ	VA	10,441	C
Oregon Inst of Technology	OR	8,718	C
Pacific Union College	CA	22,065	C+
Pennsylvania College of Technology	PA	15,126	NC
Point Park Univ	PA	21,840	C
Purdue Univ/Calumet	IN	6,630	NC
Purdue Univ/West Lafayette	IN	12,560	VC
Rochester Inst of Technology	NY	29,217	VC+
Roosevelt Univ	IL	22,580	VC
Savannah State Univ	GA	7,328	LC
S Car State Univ	SC	6,586	LC
S Dak State Univ	SD	7,782	C
Southern Illinois Univ Carbondale	IL	10,407	C
Southern Polytechnic State Univ	GA	7,620	VC
Southwest Missouri State Univ	MO	8,918	C
Southwestern Okla State Univ	OK	4,801	C
SUNY/College at Buffalo	NY	8,025	C
SUNY/College of Technology at Alfred	NY	12,416	C
Temple Univ	PA	15,912	C
Texas A&M Univ at Galveston	TX	9,948	C+
Texas Southern Univ	TX	8,920	NC
Texas Tech Univ	TX	10,768	VC
Thomas Edison State College	NJ	3,325	SP
Univ of Arkansas at Little Rock	AR	5,637	NC
Univ of Central Florida	FL	10,038	VC
Univ of Cincinnati	OH	14,736	C
Univ of Dayton	OH	24,850	VC
Univ of Hartford	CT	31,080	C
Univ of Houston	TX	9,818	C
Univ of Maine	ME	12,080	C+
Univ of Memphis	TN	8,560	C
Univ of Nebr at Lincoln	NE	9,975	C+
Univ of N Car at Charlotte	NC	8,185	C
Univ of Pittsburgh at Johnstown	PA	15,216	LC
Univ of PR/Bayamon Univ College Campus	PR	1,600	
Univ of Rio Grande	OH	8,728	NC
Univ of Southern Colo	CO	7,821	LC
Univ of Southern Miss	MS	8,324	LC
Weber State Univ	UT	7,945	NC
Wentworth Inst of Technology	MA	23,000	C
West Virginia Univ Inst of Technology	WV	7,518	NC
Western Carolina Univ	NC	6,742	C
Western Kentucky Univ	KY	6,834	C
Western Washington Univ	WA	10,119	VC
Youngstown State Univ	OH	11,148	NC

ELECTROMECHANICAL TECHNOLOGY

School	ST	$IS	SR
CUNY/New York City College of Technology	NY	4,269	NC
Cleveland State Univ	OH	12,308	LC
Penn State Univ/Altoona	PA	12,578	C
SUNY/College of Technology at Alfred	NY	12,416	C
Texas A&M Univ at Galveston	TX	9,948	C+
Univ of Houston	TX	9,818	C
Univ of Northern Iowa	IA	9,834	C
Univ of the District of Columbia	DC	2,070	LC
Univ of Toledo	OH	12,479	NC
Vermont Technical College	VT	13,684	C
Wentworth Inst of Technology	MA	23,000	C
Western Kentucky Univ	KY	6,834	C

ELECTRONIC BUSINESS

School	ST	$IS	SR
Averett Univ	VA	23,010	LC
Clarkson Univ	NY	32,226	VC
Dakota State Univ	SD	7,466	C
Davenport Univ	MI	11,636	NC
De Sales Univ	PA	25,470	C
Dominican Univ of Calif	CA	31,670	C
Indiana Univ Kokomo	IN	4,463	LC

ST = STATE $IS = IN-STATE COSTS SR = SELECTOR RATING

School	ST	$IS	SR
Ithaca College	NY	31,730	HC
King College	TN	22,500	VC
La Sierra Univ	CA	19,260	LC
Maryville Univ of St. Louis	MO	22,090	VC
Messiah College	PA	25,890	VC+
Mountain State Univ	WV	10,212	NC
Old Dominion Univ	VA	10,441	C
St. Mary-of-the-Woods College	IN	23,280	C
Spring Hill College	AL	25,868	VC
Stetson Univ	FL	29,495	VC
Temple Univ	PA	15,912	C
Texas Christian Univ	TX	23,410	VC
Univ of La Verne	CA	28,600	C
Univ of Missouri/Rolla	MO	12,292	HC
Univ of Scranton	PA	30,836	VC
Univ of South Alabama	AL	7,760	LC
Univ of Southern Indiana	IN	9,025	LC
Wilkes Univ	PA	28,060	C

ELEMENTARY EDUCATION

School	ST	$IS	SR
Abilene Christian Univ	TX	18,370	VC
Adams State College	CO	7,468	C
Adelphi Univ	NY	26,300	VC
Adrian College	MI	21,950	C
Alabama A&M Univ	AL	5,100	LC
Alabama State Univ	AL	6,404	C
Alaska Pacific Univ	AK	17,910	C
Albright College	PA	30,579	C
Alcorn State Univ	MS	7,290	C
Alderson-Broaddus College	WV	19,640	C
Alfred Univ	NY	28,290	C
Alice Lloyd College	KY	4,040	C
Alma College	MI	25,566	VC
Alvernia College	PA	23,212	LC
Alverno College	WI	18,898	C
American Indian College of the Assemblies of God	AZ	9,275	LC
American International College	MA	24,690	LC
American Univ	DC	34,585	VC+
Anderson Univ	IN	19,430	LC
Andrews Univ	MI	19,550	C
Anna Maria College	MA	26,140	LC
Appalachian State Univ	NC	7,637	VC
Aquinas College	TN	10,660	LC
Arcadia Univ	PA	29,890	C
Arizona State Univ-Main	AZ	10,048	C
Arkansas Baptist College	AR	5,530	NC
Arkansas State Univ	AR	8,450	C
Arkansas Tech Univ	AR	7,299	C
Armstrong Atlantic State Univ	GA	7,102	C
Asbury College	KY	20,704	VC
Ashland Univ	OH	24,464	C
Atlantic Union College	MA	18,868	C
Auburn Univ	AL	10,396	VC
Auburn Univ Montgomery	AL	9,020	NC
Augsburg College	MN	25,298	C
Augusta State Univ	GA	2,592	C
Augustana College	IL	26,610	VC+
Augustana College	SD	21,998	VC
Aurora Univ	IL	20,631	C
Austin Peay State Univ	TN	5,814	LC
Averett Univ	VA	23,010	LC
Avila Univ	MO	20,300	C
Baker Univ	KS	19,860	VC
Baldwin-Wallace College	OH	24,678	C
Ball State Univ	IN	8,660	C
Barton College	NC	19,314	C
Bay Path College	MA	24,910	C
Baylor Univ	TX	23,864	VC
Becker College	MA	23,710	LC
Belhaven College	MS	16,040	C+
Bellarmine Univ	KY	24,110	VC
Belmont Abbey College	NC	23,742	C
Belmont Univ	TN	21,986	VC
Bemidji State Univ	MN	9,103	C
Benedict College	SC	12,662	LC
Benedictine College	KS	20,603	C
Benedictine Univ	IL	23,840	C
Bennett College	NC	11,200	C
Berea College	KY	5,030	VC+
Bethany College	KS	18,675	LC
Bethany College	WV	19,845	VC
Bethel College	IN	19,670	C
Bethel College	KS	19,800	C+
Bethel College	MN	25,180	VC
Bethune-Cookman College	FL	16,480	LC
Birmingham-Southern College	AL	25,364	VC+
Black Hills State Univ	SD	7,743	LC
Blackburn College	IL	13,690	C
Bloomsburg Univ of Pennsylvania	PA	10,844	C
Blue Mountain College	MS	10,226	C
Bluefield State College	WV	2,806	LC
Boise State Univ	ID	7,657	LC
Boricua College	NY	7,375	C
Boston College	MA	33,284	MC
Boston Univ	MA	38,194	HC+
Bowie State Univ	MD	10,873	C+
Bowling Green State Univ	OH	13,036	C
Bradley Univ	IL	22,910	VC
Brescia Univ	KY	14,225	C
Briar Cliff Univ	IA	21,660	C
Bridgewater State College	MA	10,482	C
Brigham Young Univ	UT	8,504	HC
Brigham Young Univ/Hawaii	HI	7,240	VC+
Bryan College	TN	17,900	VC
Bucknell Univ	PA	35,262	HC+
Buena Vista Univ	IA	25,406	C
Butler Univ	IN	28,250	VC+
Cabrini College	PA	29,020	C
Caldwell College	NJ	24,060	LC
Cal State, Long Beach	CA	8,762	C+
Calif Univ of Pennsylvania	PA	10,388	C
Calumet College of St. Joseph	IN	9,000	LC
Calvin College	MI	22,615	NC
Cameron Univ	OK	5,692	NC
Campbell Univ	NC	18,268	VC
Campbellsville Univ	KY	17,680	C
Canisius College	NY	28,163	C+
Capital Univ	OH	26,550	C
Cardinal Stritch Univ	WI	17,620	C
Caribbean Univ	PR	3,000	
Carlos Albizu Univ	FL	10,569	C
Carlow College	PA	21,334	C
Carroll College	MT	20,576	VC
Carroll College	WI	22,740	C
Carson-Newman College	TN	16,760	C
Carthage College	WI	25,000	C
Catawba College	NC	20,500	C
Catholic Univ of America	DC	34,248	VC
Cazenovia College	NY	23,940	C
Cedar Crest College	PA	25,145	C+
Centenary College	NJ	25,370	LC
Centenary College of Louisiana	LA	23,100	VC+
Central College	IA	21,206	C
Central Conn State Univ	CT	12,090	C
Central Methodist College	MO	16,460	C
Central Mich Univ	MI	11,142	C
Central Missouri State Univ	MO	9,776	C
Central State Univ	OH	8,922	C+
Central Univ of Bayamon	PR	3,335	
Central Washington Univ	WA	9,768	C
Centre College	KY	27,300	HC
Chadron State College	NE	6,286	NC
Chaminade Univ of Honolulu	HI	21,430	LC
Champlain College	VT	22,030	C
Charleston Southern Univ	SC	17,122	C
Chestnut Hill College	PA	26,450	LC
Cheyney Univ of Pennsylvania	PA	9,993	C
Chicago State Univ	IL	10,882	C+
City Univ	WA	7,425	NC
CUNY/Brooklyn College	NY	4,353	C+
CUNY/City College	NY	4,230	C+
CUNY/Herbert H. Lehman College	NY	3,320	LC
CUNY/Hunter College	NY	6,729	C+
CUNY/Medgar Evers College	NY	4,232	NC
CUNY/Queens College	NY	4,362	C
Claflin Univ	SC	14,838	C+
Clarion Univ of Pennsylvania	PA	11,272	LC
Clarke College	IA	23,165	C
Clearwater Christian College	FL	13,160	LC
Clemson Univ	SC	11,972	HC
Cleveland State Univ	OH	12,308	LC
Coastal Carolina Univ	SC	11,040	C
Coe College	IA	27,385	VC
Coker College	SC	21,491	C
College Misericordia	PA	26,350	C
College of Charleston	SC	11,887	HC
College of Mount St. Joseph	OH	22,785	C
College of New Jersey	NJ	15,950	MC
College of Notre Dame of Maryland	MD	27,700	C
College of Our Lady of the Elms	MA	20,644	C
College of St. Benedict	MN	26,762	VC
College of St. Catherine	MN	24,010	VC
College of St. Elizabeth	NJ	25,460	C
College of St. Joseph	VT	19,100	C
College of St. Mary	NE	21,510	C
College of St. Rose	NY	22,864	C
College of St. Scholastica	MN	24,970	C+
College of Santa Fe	NM	25,293	C+
College of the Ozarks	MO	3,500	VC+
College of the Southwest	NM	9,320	C+
Colo Christian Univ	CO	21,182	VC
Columbia College	MO	16,139	C
Columbia College	SC	22,658	LC
Columbia Union College	MD	20,543	C
Concord College	WV	8,136	C
Concordia College	AL	9,774	NC
Concordia College	NY	19,200	VC
Concordia College: Moorhead	MN	22,460	VC+
Concordia Univ	MI	24,095	C
Concordia Univ	OR	22,450	C
Concordia Univ at Austin	TX	20,450	LC
Concordia Univ Nebr	NE	20,302	C+
Concordia Univ Wisc	WI	16,600	C
Concordia Univ, River Forest	IL	23,600	C
Concordia Univ/St.Paul	MN	24,486	C
Converse College	SC	24,710	VC
Coppin State College	MD	10,191	LC
Cornell College	IA	27,825	VC+
Cornerstone Univ and Grand Rapids Theological Seminary	MI	19,846	C
Covenant College	GA	23,830	VC+
Creighton Univ	NE	26,748	VC+
Crichton College	TN	15,215	C
Culver-Stockton College	MO	17,850	C
Cumberland College	KY	16,384	C
Cumberland Univ	TN	16,910	C
Curry College	MA	26,025	LC
Daemen College	NY	22,120	C
Dakota State Univ	SD	7,466	C
Dakota Wesleyan Univ	SD	17,832	C
Dallas Baptist Univ	TX	15,300	VC
Dana College	NE	20,280	C
David Lipscomb Univ	TN	16,158	VC
Davis and Elkins College	WV	20,594	C
De Sales Univ	PA	25,470	C
Defiance College	OH	22,615	C
Delaware State Univ	DE	8,104	LC
Delta State Univ	MS	6,618	C
DePaul Univ	IL	27,580	VC
DePauw Univ	IN	31,500	HC
Dickinson State Univ	ND	6,338	NC
Dillard Univ	LA	17,325	VC
Doane College	NE	20,000	C
Dominican College	NY	24,810	LC
Dordt College	IA	20,170	VC
Dowling College	NY	23,870	LC
Drake Univ	IA	25,120	VC+
Drury Univ	MO	18,085	VC+
Duquesne Univ	PA	26,907	VC
D'Youville College	NY	21,080	C
East Carolina Univ	NC	8,671	C
East Central Univ	OK	4,968	C
East Stroudsburg Univ of Pennsylvania	PA	10,336	C
East Texas Baptist Univ	TX	13,914	C
Eastern Illinois Univ	IL	11,192	C
Eastern Kentucky Univ	KY	7,708	C
Eastern Mennonite Univ	VA	22,990	C
Eastern Mich Univ	MI	11,478	C
Eastern Nazarene College	MA	19,433	LC
Eastern New Mexico Univ	NM	6,762	LC
Eastern Univ	PA	24,020	C
Eastern Washington Univ	WA	9,012	C
Edgewood College	WI	20,520	C
Edinboro Univ of Pennsylvania	PA	10,850	LC
Edward Waters College	FL	14,374	LC
Elizabeth City State Univ	NC	5,550	LC
Elizabethtown College	PA	28,800	C
Elmhurst College	IL	24,630	C
Elmira College	NY	33,820	VC
Elon Univ	NC	22,240	VC
Emmanuel College	MA	27,600	C+
Emporia State Univ	KS	6,998	C
Erskine College	SC	23,166	VC
Eureka College	IL	24,980	LC
Evangel Univ	MO	15,435	C
Fairmont State	WV	8,280	LC
Faulkner Univ	AL	14,500	C
Fayetteville State Univ	NC	5,590	LC
Felician College	NJ	24,300	C
Fitchburg State College	MA	9,622	C
Five Towns College	NY	21,050	SP
Flagler College	FL	11,860	VC+
Florida A&M Univ	FL	7,564	C
Florida Atlantic Univ	FL	8,543	C
Florida Gulf Coast Univ	FL	9,908	C
Florida International Univ	FL	9,912	VC
Florida Memorial College	FL	6,000	LC
Florida Southern College	FL	23,592	C
Florida State Univ	FL	9,028	HC
Fontbonne Univ	MO	21,508	C
Fort Hays State Univ	KS	7,363	C
Framingham State College	MA	9,381	C
Francis Marion Univ	SC	9,364	C
Franciscan Univ	IA	19,300	C
Franciscan Univ of Steubenville	OH	20,300	VC
Franklin College	IN		C
Franklin Pierce College	NH	28,980	LC
Freed-Hardeman Univ	TN		NC
Friends Univ	KS	15,962	LC
Frostburg State Univ	MD	11,114	C
Furman Univ	SC	28,976	HC+
Gallaudet Univ	DC	16,554	SP
Gannon Univ	PA	23,260	C
Gardner-Webb Univ	NC	19,300	C
Geneva College	PA	21,850	C
George Fox Univ	OR	26,110	VC
Georgetown College	KY	22,000	VC
Georgia Southwestern State Univ	GA	6,013	C
Georgian Court College	NJ	19,040	LC
Gettysburg College	PA	35,646	HC
Glenville State College	WV	7,812	NC
Gordon College	MA	25,982	VC+
Goshen College	IN	22,450	VC
Goucher College	MD	32,650	HC
Grace Bible College	MI	15,890	C
Grace College	IN	19,825	VC
Graceland Univ	IA	19,550	C
Grambling State Univ	LA	6,538	NC
Grand Canyon Univ	AZ	30,000	LC
Grand Valley State Univ	MI	11,022	VC
Grand View College	IA	19,748	LC
Green Mountain College	VT	24,130	C
Greensboro College	NC	21,750	C
Greenville College	IL	21,342	C
Grove City College	PA	14,228	HC
Gustavus Adolphus College	MN	27,120	VC+
Gwynedd-Mercy College	PA	24,225	C
Hamline Univ	MN	27,052	VC
Hannibal-LaGrange College	MO	13,940	C
Harding Univ	AR	14,890	VC
Hardin-Simmons Univ	TX	14,165	C
Harris-Stowe State College	MO	3,200	SP
Hastings College	NE	19,928	VC
Heidelberg College	OH	20,266	NC
Hellenic College/Holy Cross Greek Orthodox School of Theology	MA	22,815	C
Henderson State Univ	AR	7,386	C
Hendrix College	AR	20,970	VC+
Heritage College	WA	6,720	NC
High Point Univ	NC	22,480	C
Hillsdale College	MI	22,450	HC
Hiram College	OH	28,234	VC
Hofstra Univ	NY	27,112	VC
Holy Family College	PA	13,710	LC
Hope College	MI	25,340	VC
Houghton College	NY	23,984	VC
Houston Baptist Univ	TX	16,905	C
Howard Payne Univ	TX	15,176	C
Howard Univ	DC	16,505	C
Humboldt State Univ	CA	9,400	C
Huntington College	IN	23,590	C
Huron Univ	SD	10,450	C
Huston-Tillotson College	TX	14,232	NC
Idaho State Univ	ID	8,128	C
Illinois College	IL	19,100	VC
Illinois State Univ	IL	10,944	C+
Illinois Wesleyan Univ	IL	30,380	HC+
Immaculata Univ	PA	25,200	C
Indiana State Univ	IN	10,719	LC
Indiana Univ Bloomington	IN	12,389	VC
Indiana Univ East	IN	4,433	LC
Indiana Univ Kokomo	IN	4,463	LC
Indiana Univ Northwest	IN	4,538	LC
Indiana Univ of Pennsylvania	PA	10,489	C
Indiana Univ South Bend	IN	4,571	LC
Indiana Univ Southeast	IN	4,504	LC
Indiana Univ-Purdue Univ Fort Wayne	IN	5,108	LC
Indiana Univ-Purdue Univ Indianapolis	IN	8,257	LC
Indiana Wesleyan Univ	IN	19,900	C+
Inter American Univ of PR/ Aguadilla Campus	PR	3,544	
Inter American Univ of PR/ Arecibo Campus	PR	3,300	
Inter American Univ of PR/ Barranquitas Regional College	PR	3,300	
Inter American Univ of PR/ Fajardo Campus	PR	4,000	
Inter American Univ of PR/ Metropolitan Campus	PR		
Inter American Univ of PR/ Ponce Regional College	PR	3,700	
Inter American Univ of PR/ San German	PR	6,716	
Iona College	NY	27,988	VC
Iowa State Univ	IA	10,768	VC
Iowa Wesleyan College	IA	19,990	C
Jackson State Univ	MS	8,382	C
Jacksonville State Univ	AL	6,844	LC
Jacksonville Univ	FL	24,040	C
Jamestown College	ND	12,600	NC
Jarvis Christian College	TX	9,035	NC
John Brown Univ	AR	15,080	VC
John Carroll Univ	OH	27,658	C+
Johnson C. Smith Univ	NC	18,108	C
Johnson State College	VT	11,819	LC
Judson College	AL	14,650	C
Judson College	IL	22,050	LC
Juniata College	PA	29,080	VC
Kansas State Univ	KS	8,728	VC
Kean Univ	NJ	14,479	C
Keene State College	NH	12,212	C
Kennesaw State Univ	GA	2,724	C
Kent State Univ	OH	12,932	C
Kentucky Christian College	KY	13,472	C
Kentucky State Univ	KY	9,062	NC
Kentucky Wesleyan College	KY	17,250	C
Keuka College	NY	21,170	C
Keystone College	PA	21,405	LC
King College	TN	22,500	VC
King's College	PA	26,990	C
Knox College	IL	30,294	VC+
Knoxville College	TN	6,200	LC
Kutztown Univ of Pennsylvania	PA	10,786	C

ST = STATE $IS = IN-STATE COSTS SR = SELECTOR RATING

School	ST	$IS	SR
La Roche College	PA	22,094	C
La Salle Univ	PA	31,260	VC
La Sierra Univ	CA	19,260	LC
Lake Erie College	OH	23,550	C
Lake Superior State Univ	MI	9,034	LC
Lakeland College	WI	17,950	C
Lamar Univ	TX	6,816	LC
Lambuth Univ	TN	16,520	C
Lander Univ	SC	10,496	C
Langston Univ	OK	2,308	LC
Lasell College	MA	26,000	C
Le Moyne College	NY	26,400	VC
Lebanon Valley College	PA	28,870	VC
Lee Univ	TN	13,780	NC
Lees-McRae College	NC	17,106	LC
Lenoir-Rhyne College	NC	19,186	C
Lesley Univ	MA	30,695	C
LeTourneau Univ	TX	21,080	C
Lewis Univ	IL	22,950	C+
Lewis-Clark State College	ID	6,981	C
Liberty Univ	VA	17,220	C
Limestone College	SC	17,700	C
Lincoln Memorial Univ	TN	16,400	LC
Lincoln Univ	MO	7,158	NC
Lincoln Univ	PA	13,320	C+
Lindenwood Univ	MO	17,050	VC
Lindsey Wilson College	KY	16,392	LC
Linfield College	OR	27,090	VC
Livingstone College	NC	18,101	LC
Lock Haven Univ of Pennsylvania	PA	11,098	LC
LIU/Brooklyn Campus	NY	24,790	C
LIU/C.W. Post Campus	NY	28,282	C
LIU/Southampton College	NY	29,370	C+
Longwood Univ	VA	11,175	C
Loras College	IA	24,233	C
Louisiana College	LA	13,450	C
Louisiana State Univ and A&M College	LA	9,126	VC
Louisiana State Univ in Shreveport	LA	2,884	NC
Louisiana Tech Univ	LA	7,361	C
Loyola College in Maryland	MD	34,560	HC
Loyola Univ Chicago	IL	31,164	VC
Loyola Univ New Orleans	LA	31,036	VC+
Lubbock Christian Univ	TX	15,832	C
Luther College	IA	25,700	VC
Lyndon State College	VT	12,646	LC
Lynn Univ	FL	30,750	C
MacMurray College	IL	20,005	LC
Malone College	OH	20,995	C
Manchester College	IN	23,390	C
Manhattan College	NY	27,400	VC
Mansfield Univ	PA	11,220	C
Marian College	IN	23,030	C
Marian College of Fond du Lac	WI	19,625	C
Marietta College	OH	27,047	C
Mars Hill College	NC	18,600	LC
Marshall Univ	WV	9,116	C
Marymount College of Fordham Univ	NY	27,686	C
Marymount Manhattan College	NY	27,292	C
Maryville College	TN	25,960	VC
Maryville Univ of St. Louis	MO	22,090	VC
Marywood Univ	PA	26,050	C
Master's College and Seminary	CA	23,250	VC
Mayville State Univ	ND	7,325	NC
McKendree College	IL	21,120	VC
McMurry Univ	TX	17,846	LC
McNeese State Univ	LA	5,259	LC
McPherson College	KS	20,265	C
Medaille College	NY	20,060	C
Mercer Univ	GA	27,516	VC+
Mercy College	NY	19,200	NC
Mercyhurst College	PA	20,694	C
Merrimack College	MA	29,625	C
Messiah College	PA	25,890	VC+
Methodist College	NC	19,526	C
Miami Univ	OH	15,033	HC
MidAmerica Nazarene Univ	KS	18,688	C
Midland Lutheran College	NE	18,600	C
Miles College	AL	7,870	NC
Millersville Univ of Pennsylvania	PA	11,269	C
Millikin Univ	IL	25,555	C
Millsaps College	MS	25,182	VC
Minn State Univ, Mankato	MN	8,803	LC
Minn State Univ, Moorehead	MN	7,000	LC
Minot State Univ	ND	6,602	LC
Miss College	MS	14,574	C
Miss State Univ	MS	9,139	C
Miss Univ for Women	MS	5,446	LC
Miss Valley State Univ	MS	6,765	NC
Missouri Baptist Univ	MO	18,010	C
Missouri Southern State Univ	MO	8,316	C
Missouri Valley College	MO	18,500	C
Missouri Western State College	MO	8,522	NC
Molloy College	NY	15,180	C
Monmouth College	IL	23,600	C
Montana State Univ-Billings	MT	9,550	C
Montana State Univ-Bozeman	MT	9,515	C
Montana State Univ-Northern	MT	8,600	NC
Montreat College	NC	18,762	C
Moravian College	PA	28,903	VC
Morehead State Univ	KY	7,464	C
Morgan State Univ	MD	11,470	C
Morningside College	IA	21,610	C
Morris College	SC	10,974	LC
Mount Aloysius College	PA	19,120	LC
Mount Holyoke College	MA	37,918	HC+
Mount Marty College	SD	15,656	LC
Mount Mary College	WI	20,370	C
Mount Mercy College	IA	21,400	C
Mount St. Mary College	NY	21,270	C
Mount St. Mary's College	CA	28,307	VC
Mount St. Mary's College	MD	28,400	C
Mount Union College	OH	21,120	C
Mount Vernon Nazarene Univ	OH	18,925	C
Murray State Univ	KY	7,816	VC
Muskingum College	OH	20,680	C
National-Louis Univ	IL	16,240	LC
Nazareth College of Rochester	NY	24,936	VC
Nebr Wesleyan Univ	NE	21,197	C+
Neumann College	PA	23,890	LC
New England College	NH	28,860	LC
New Jersey City Univ	NJ	11,850	LC
New Mexico Highlands Univ	NM	6,182	LC
New Mexico State Univ	NM	7,932	C
New York Inst of Technology	NY	24,205	VC
Newberry College	SC	22,871	LC
Newman Univ	KS	18,018	C
Niagara Univ	NY	25,050	C
Nicholls State Univ	LA	6,395	NC
N Car Central Univ	NC	7,534	LC
N Car Wesleyan College	NC	17,998	C
North Central College	IL	25,656	VC
North Central Univ	MN	14,904	C
N Dak State Univ	ND	8,435	C
North Georgia College and State Univ	GA	6,984	C
North Park Univ	IL	24,030	C
Northeastern Illinois Univ	IL	2,898	NC
Northeastern State Univ	OK	4,950	LC
Northeastern Univ	MA	35,650	HC
Northern Arizona Univ	AZ	9,002	C
Northern Illinois Univ	IL	11,472	C
Northern Kentucky Univ	KY	6,352	NC
Northern Mich Univ	MI	10,834	C
Northern State Univ	SD	7,117	LC
Northland College	WI	22,170	C+
Northwest Christian College	OR	21,860	C
Northwest College	WA	18,854	C
Northwest Missouri State Univ	MO	9,334	C
Northwest Nazarene Univ	ID	20,360	VC
Northwestern College	MN	22,820	C+
Northwestern College of Iowa	IA	19,640	C+
Northwestern Okla State Univ	OK	5,433	NC
Northwestern State Univ of Louisiana	LA	6,331	NC
Notre Dame College	OH	20,425	C
Nova Southeastern Univ	FL	23,346	C
Nyack College	NY	18,540	C
Oakland City Univ	IN	16,980	NC
Oakland Univ	MI	10,800	C
Oakwood College	AL	14,904	C
Oglala Lakota College	SD	1,950	NC
Ohio State Univ at Mansfield	OH	3,606	NC
Ohio State Univ at Marion	OH	4,801	NC
Ohio State Univ at Newark	OH	9,881	NC
Ohio Univ	OH	14,448	C
Ohio Valley College	WV	16,036	C+
Ohio Wesleyan Univ	OH	32,550	VC+
Okla Baptist Univ	OK	15,220	VC
Okla Christian Univ	OK	17,690	NC
Okla City Univ	OK	19,580	VC
Okla Panhandle State Univ	OK	5,370	C
Okla State Univ	OK	9,216	VC
Okla Wesleyan Univ	OK	14,100	LC
Old Dominion Univ	VA	10,441	C
Olivet College	MI	19,984	C+
Olivet Nazarene Univ	IL	20,480	C
Oral Roberts Univ	OK	18,490	C
Ottawa Univ	KS	11,800	LC
Otterbein College	OH	26,085	C
Ouachita Baptist Univ	AR	18,900	VC
Our Lady of Holy Cross College	LA	5,900	C
Pace Univ	NY	28,652	VC
Palm Beach Atlantic Univ	FL	20,690	C
Park Univ	MO	10,780	C+
Penn State Univ/Univ Park Campus	PA	15,646	HC
Pepperdine Univ	CA	32,830	VC
Peru State College	NE	6,342	NC
Pfeiffer Univ	NC	18,980	C
Pikeville College	KY	14,900	NC
Pittsburg State Univ	KS	7,128	NC
Point Park Univ	PA	21,840	C
Pontifical Catholic Univ of PR/Ponce	PR	7,298	
Presbyterian College	SC	25,920	VC
Prescott College	AZ	13,430	C
Principia College	IL	25,044	C+
Providence College	RI	30,604	HC
Purdue Univ/Calumet	IN	6,630	NC
Purdue Univ/West Lafayette	IN	12,560	VC
Queens Univ of Charlotte	NC	21,840	C
Quincy Univ	IL	22,330	C
Rhode Island College	RI	11,565	C
Rider Univ	NJ	30,900	C
Ripon College	WI	24,995	VC
Rivier College	NH	26,217	C
Robert Morris Univ	PA	20,438	C
Roberts Wesleyan College	NY	23,190	C+
Rockford College	IL	28,310	VC
Rockhurst Univ	MO	22,960	C+
Rocky Mountain College	MT	19,015	C
Roger Williams Univ	RI	30,296	C
Rollins College	FL	34,300	VC
Roosevelt Univ	IL	22,580	VC
Rowan Univ	NJ	14,506	VC
Russell Sage College	NY	26,811	C
Rust College	MS	8,200	C+
Saginaw Valley State Univ	MI	11,055	C
St. Ambrose Univ	IA	22,800	C
St. Andrews Presbyterian College	NC	20,525	C
St. Augustine's College	NC	12,990	LC
St. Bonaventure Univ	NY	24,455	LC
St. Cloud State Univ	MN	8,362	C
St. Francis College	NY	10,880	LC
St. Francis Univ	PA	25,876	LC
St. John's Univ	MN	26,473	VC
St. John's Univ	NY	30,180	C
St. Joseph's, Brooklyn,	NY	10,902	C
St. Joseph's College	IN	24,250	C
St. Joseph's College of Maine	ME	25,600	C
St. Joseph's Univ	PA	33,590	VC
St. Leo Univ	FL	20,600	C
St. Martin's College	WA	23,245	C
St. Mary-of-the-Woods College	IN	23,280	C
St. Mary's College	IN	24,474	VC
St. Mary's Univ of Minn	MN	21,535	C
St. Mary's Univ of San Antonio	TX	22,444	C
St. Michael's College	VT	30,100	VC
St. Norbert College	WI	25,810	C
St. Paul's College	VA	14,344	NC
St. Peter's College	NJ	22,292	LC
St. Thomas Aquinas College	NY	20,590	LC
St. Thomas Univ	FL	21,400	LC
St. Xavier Univ	IL	23,144	C
Salem International Univ	WV	19,770	C
Salisbury Univ	MD	12,664	VC
Salve Regina Univ	RI	29,210	C
Samford Univ	AL	18,648	VC
San Francisco State Univ	CA	12,070	C
Schreiner Univ	TX	20,440	C
Seton Hall Univ	NJ	30,130	VC
Seton Hill Univ	PA	24,930	C
Shaw Univ	NC	14,882	C+
Shawnee State Univ	OH	11,031	NC
Sheldon Jackson College	AK	14,940	LC
Shepherd College	WV	8,608	C
Shippensburg Univ of Pennsylvania	PA	10,826	C
Siena Heights Univ	MI	16,140	LC
Silver Lake College of the Holy Family	WI	18,450	LC
Simmons College	MA	33,000	VC
Simpson College	CA	20,500	C
Simpson College	IA	23,658	C+
Sinte Gleska Univ	SD	2,268	NC
Skidmore College	NY	37,930	HC
Slippery Rock Univ of Pennsylvania	PA	10,343	LC
Smith College	MA	37,034	HC+
S Car State Univ	SC	6,586	LC
Southeast Missouri State Univ	MO	9,704	C
Southeastern College	FL	11,648	LC
Southeastern Louisiana Univ	LA	6,791	LC
Southeastern Okla State Univ	OK	6,147	C
Southern Adventist Univ	TN	17,080	C
Southern Arkansas Univ	AR	6,956	C
Southern Conn State Univ	CT	10,310	C
Southern Illinois Univ Carbondale	IL	10,407	C
Southern Illinois Univ Edwardsville	IL	8,724	C
Southern Nazarene Univ	OK	14,634	NC
Southern Univ and A&M College	LA	7,372	LC
Southern Univ at New Orleans	LA	995	NC
Southern Utah Univ	UT	8,194	C
Southern Wesleyan Univ	SC	19,940	C
Southwest Baptist Univ	MO	15,371	C
Southwest Minn State Univ	MN	9,106	VC
Southwest Missouri State Univ	MO	8,918	C
Southwestern Adventist Univ	TX	14,798	C
Southwestern College	KS	19,560	C
Southwestern Okla State Univ	OK	4,801	C
Spalding Univ	KY	17,985	C
Spring Hill College	AL	25,868	VC
Springfield College	MA	24,520	C
SUNY at Oswego	NY	12,650	C
SUNY at Potsdam	NY	12,160	C
SUNY/College at Buffalo	NY	8,025	C
SUNY/College at Fredonia	NY	11,562	VC
SUNY/College at Geneseo	NY	11,330	HC
SUNY/College at Old Westbury	NY	12,784	C
SUNY/College at Oneonta	NY	11,870	VC
SUNY/College at Plattsburgh	NY	11,700	C
SUNY/Univ at New Paltz	NY	11,565	VC
Stephens College	MO	24,260	C+
Sterling College	KS	18,763	C
Stetson Univ	FL	29,495	VC
Stillman College	AL	11,370	LC
Suffolk Univ	MA	29,200	C
Sul Ross State Univ	TX	6,582	LC
Susquehanna Univ	PA	29,990	VC
Syracuse Univ	NY	34,720	HC
Tabor College	KS	19,500	NC
Taylor Univ	IN	23,820	VC+
Temple Univ	PA	15,912	C
Texas A&M Univ	TX	11,081	HC
Texas A&M Univ at Commerce	TX	8,994	C
Texas A&M Univ at Kingsville	TX	6,740	LC
Texas Christian Univ	TX	23,410	VC
Texas State Univ	TX	9,320	VC
Texas Tech Univ	TX	10,768	VC
Texas Wesleyan Univ	TX	16,245	C
Thiel College	PA	20,970	C
Thomas College	ME	19,960	LC
Thomas More College	KY	21,350	C
Tougaloo College	MS	9,200	NC
Touro College	NY	15,250	VC
Towson Univ	MD	12,694	VC
Transylvania Univ	KY	23,780	VC+
Trinity Bible College	ND		
Trinity Christian College	IL	21,640	VC
Trinity College	DC	24,150	LC
Trinity International Univ	IL	22,980	C+
Tri-State Univ-Main Campus	IN	23,600	C
Troy State Univ	AL	7,696	C
Troy State Univ Dothan	AL	3,842	C
Turabo Univ	PR	4,110	
Tusculum College	TN	19,990	C
Tuskegee Univ	AL	17,250	LC
Union College	KY	15,920	C
Union College	NE	17,130	C
Union Univ	TN	18,800	VC
Universidad Adventista de las Antillas	PR	5,460	
Universidad Metropolitana	PR	3,324	
Univ of Akron	OH	13,134	NC
Univ of Alabama	AL	9,040	C+
Univ of Alabama at Birmingham	AL	12,901	C
Univ of Alaska Anchorage	AK	9,100	NC
Univ of Alaska Fairbanks	AK	9,295	C
Univ of Alaska Southeast	AK	7,900	LC
Univ of Arizona	AZ	10,413	VC
Univ of Arkansas	AR	9,855	VC
Univ of Arkansas at Little Rock	AR	5,637	NC
Univ of Arkansas at Monticello	AR	5,940	NC
Univ of Central Arkansas	AR	6,388	C
Univ of Central Florida	FL	10,038	VC
Univ of Central Okla	OK	9,434	C
Univ of Charleston	WV	23,620	C
Univ of Cincinnati	OH	14,736	C
Univ of Conn	CT	14,608	VC
Univ of Dallas	TX	25,898	VC+
Univ of Dayton	OH	24,850	VC
Univ of Delaware	DE	12,616	NC
Univ of Detroit Mercy	MI	25,582	C
Univ of Evansville	IN	24,190	VC
Univ of Findlay	OH	23,962	NC
Univ of Florida	FL	8,580	MC
Univ of Georgia	GA	8,656	VC
Univ of Great Falls	MT	15,360	C
Univ of Hartford	CT	31,080	C
Univ of Hawaii at Manoa	HI	9,565	VC
Univ of Houston-Downtown	TX	2,594	NC
Univ of Idaho	ID	8,216	C
Univ of Illinois at Chicago	IL	13,418	C
Univ of Illinois at Urbana-Champaign	IL	11,316	HC+
Univ of Indianapolis	IN	22,560	VC
Univ of Iowa	IA	10,923	VC
Univ of Kansas	KS	8,923	VC
Univ of Kentucky	KY	7,765	C

School	ST	$IS	SR
Univ of Louisiana at Lafayette	LA	5,826	C
Univ of Louisiana at Monroe	LA	5,207	NC
Univ of Louisville	KY	8,762	VC
Univ of Maine	ME	12,080	C+
Univ of Maine at Farmington	ME	10,108	C
Univ of Maine at Fort Kent	ME	9,770	LC
Univ of Maine at Machias	ME	9,271	LC
Univ of Maine at Presque Isle	ME	9,155	LC
Univ of Mary	ND	12,900	C+
Univ of Mary Hardin-Baylor	TX	17,268	C
Univ of Maryland/College Park	MD	14,227	HC
Univ of Maryland/Eastern Shore	MD	9,964	C
Univ of Mass Amherst	MA	13,980	C+
Univ of Memphis	TN	8,560	C
Univ of Miami	FL	34,608	HC
Univ of Mich/Ann Arbor	MI	13,864	HC+
Univ of Mich/Dearborn	MI	6,843	VC
Univ of Mich/Flint	MI	5,548	C
Univ of Minn/Duluth	MN	12,470	C
Univ of Minn/Morris	MN	12,896	VC
Univ of Minn/Twin Cities	MN	13,160	VC
Univ of Miss	MS	7,666	C
Univ of Missouri/Columbia	MO	13,782	VC
Univ of Missouri/Kansas City	MO	13,416	VC
Univ of Missouri/St. Louis	MO	11,656	VC
Univ of Mobile	AL	13,620	C
Univ of Montana	MT	9,395	C
Univ of Montana--Western	MT	8,073	NC
Univ of Montevallo	AL	8,478	C
Univ of Nebr at Kearney	NE	8,286	NC
Univ of Nebr at Lincoln	NE	9,975	C+
Univ of Nebr at Omaha	NE	8,080	C
Univ of Nevada/Las Vegas	NV	11,566	C
Univ of Nevada/Reno	NV	9,792	C
Univ of New England	ME	27,200	LC
Univ of New Mexico	NM	9,223	C
Univ of New Orleans	LA	7,356	C
Univ of North Alabama	AL	7,972	NC
Univ of N Car at Chapel Hill	NC	10,117	MC
Univ of N Car at Charlotte	NC	8,185	C
Univ of N Car at Greensboro	NC	8,248	C
Univ of N Car at Pembroke	NC	6,929	LC
Univ of N Car at Wilmington	NC	8,940	VC
Univ of N Dak	ND	8,390	C
Univ of North Florida	FL	8,769	VC
Univ of North Texas	TX	7,629	C
Univ of Northern Iowa	IA	9,834	C
Univ of Okla	OK	9,226	VC
Univ of Pennsylvania	PA	37,960	MC
Univ of Pittsburgh at Johnstown	PA	15,216	LC
Univ of Portland	OR	28,500	VC
Univ of PR at Humacao	PR	1,245	
Univ of PR/Arecibo	PR	1,095	
Univ of PR/Bayamon Univ College Campus	PR	1,600	
Univ of PR/Cayey Univ College	PR	1,245	
Univ of PR/Rio Piedras	PR	5,730	
Univ of Rhode Island	RI	13,720	VC
Univ of Rio Grande	OH	8,728	NC
Univ of St. Francis	IL	22,850	C
Univ of St. Francis	IN	20,964	C
Univ of St. Mary	KS	18,868	C
Univ of St. Thomas	MN	26,918	VC
Univ of San Diego	CA	33,156	HC
Univ of San Francisco	CA	34,700	VC
Univ of Science and Arts of Okla	OK	5,982	C
Univ of Scranton	PA	30,836	VC
Univ of Sioux Falls	SD	16,390	C
Univ of South Alabama	AL	7,760	LC
Univ of S Car at Aiken	SC	7,828	LC
Univ of S Car at Columbia	SC	10,048	VC
Univ of S Car at Spartanburg	SC	9,936	C+
Univ of S Dak	SD	7,710	C+
Univ of South Florida	FL	9,454	C
Univ of Southern Indiana	IN	9,025	LC
Univ of Southern Miss	MS	8,324	LC
Univ of Tampa	FL	23,982	VC
Univ of Tenn at Knoxville	TN	8,214	C
Univ of Tenn at Martin	TN	7,748	C
Univ of the District of Columbia	DC	2,070	LC
Univ of the Incarnate Word	TX	21,772	LC
Univ of the Sacred Heart	PR	5,590	
Univ of Toledo	OH	12,479	NC
Univ of Tulsa	OK	22,090	VC+
Univ of Utah	UT	9,205	C
Univ of Vermont	VT	16,316	VC
Univ of West Alabama	AL	6,048	C
Univ of West Florida	FL	8,470	C
Univ of Wisc/Eau Claire	WI	8,463	VC
Univ of Wisc/La Crosse	WI	8,991	VC
Univ of Wisc/Madison	WI	8,262	VC
Univ of Wisc/Oshkosh	WI	6,130	LC
Univ of Wisc/Platteville	WI	8,450	C
Univ of Wisc/River Falls	WI	8,358	LC

School	ST	$IS	SR
Univ of Wisc/Stevens Point	WI	8,116	VC
Univ of Wisc/Superior	WI	7,051	C+
Univ of Wisc/Whitewater	WI	8,626	C
Univ of Wyoming	WY	8,636	C
Upper Iowa Univ	IA	20,076	C
Urbana Univ	OH	19,115	C
Ursuline College	OH	22,728	LC
Utah State Univ	UT	7,371	C
Valley City State Univ	ND	7,281	LC
Valparaiso Univ	IN	26,118	VC+
Vanderbilt Univ	TN	37,897	MC
Vanguard Univ of Southern Calif	CA	22,208	C
Villanova Univ	PA	35,050	HC
Virginia Commonwealth Univ	VA	9,030	C
Virginia Union Univ	VA	15,358	LC
Viterbo Univ	WI	20,430	C
Wagner College	NY	29,900	VC
Walla Walla College	WA	21,600	NC
Walsh Univ	OH	20,890	C
Warner Southern College	FL	16,738	LC
Warren Wilson College	NC	21,794	VC
Wartburg College	IA	21,165	VC
Washburn Univ of Topeka	KS	8,984	NC
Washington Univ in St. Louis	MO	38,293	MC
Wayne State College	NE	7,352	NC
Wayne State Univ	MI	11,774	C
Waynesburg College	PA	19,370	C
Weber State Univ	UT	7,945	NC
Wells College	NY	21,122	VC
Wesley College	DE	19,905	C
West Chester Univ of Pennsylvania	PA	11,164	C
West Liberty State College	WV	7,868	LC
West Virginia State College	WV	6,264	NC
West Virginia Wesleyan College	WV	22,920	C
Western Carolina Univ	NC	6,742	C
Western Conn State Univ	CT	11,625	C
Western Illinois Univ	IL	10,363	C
Western Kentucky Univ	KY	6,834	C
Western Mich Univ	MI	12,031	C
Western New England College	MA	28,924	C
Western New Mexico Univ	NM	5,950	LC
Western State College of Colo	CO	9,014	C
Western Washington Univ	WA	10,119	VC
Westfield State College	MA	10,147	C
Westminster College	MO	18,150	C+
Westminster College	PA	22,960	C
Westminster College	UT	17,226	C
Wheaton College	IL	21,934	HC
Wheelock College	MA	29,000	C
Whitworth College	WA	26,428	VC+
Wichita State Univ	KS	8,092	C
Widener Univ	PA	27,020	C
Wiley College	TX	8,100	LC
Wilkes Univ	PA	28,060	C
William Carey College	MS	10,150	LC
William Jewell College	MO	21,320	VC
William Penn Univ	IA	17,575	LC
William Woods Univ	MO	20,120	C
Williams Baptist College	AR	11,950	C
Wilmington College	DE	5,594	NC
Wilmington College	OH	24,172	LC
Wilson College	PA	23,912	C
Wingate Univ	NC	21,200	C
Winona State Univ	MN		C
Winston-Salem State Univ	NC	8,926	LC
Winthrop Univ	SC	11,302	C
Wisc Lutheran College	WI	21,430	VC
Wittenberg Univ	OH	31,316	VC
Worcester State College	MA	10,005	C
Wright State Univ	OH	11,490	LC
Xavier Univ of Louisiana	LA	17,600	C
York College of Pennsylvania	PA	14,500	VC
Youngstown State Univ	OH	11,148	NC

ELEMENTARY PARTICLE PHYSICS

School	ST	$IS	SR
Catholic Univ of America	DC	34,248	VC

EMERGENCY MEDICAL TECHNOLOGIES

School	ST	$IS	SR
Central Washington Univ	WA	9,768	C
Creighton Univ	NE	26,748	VC+
George Washington Univ	DC	41,030	MC
MCP Hahnemann Univ	PA	18,510	SP
Springfield College	MA	24,520	C
Univ of Akron	OH	13,134	NC
Univ of Maryland/Baltimore County	MD	14,668	VC+
Univ of New Mexico	NM	9,223	C
Univ of Pittsburgh at Pittsburgh	PA	16,074	HC
Western Carolina Univ	NC	6,742	C

EMERGENCY/DISASTER SCIENCE

School	ST	$IS	SR
Arkansas Tech Univ	AR	7,299	C
Thomas Edison State College	NJ	3,325	SP
Univ of Akron	OH	13,134	NC
Univ of Florida	FL	8,580	MC
Univ of North Texas	TX	7,629	C
West Texas A&M Univ	TX	7,533	C
Western Carolina Univ	NC	6,742	C

ENERGY MANAGEMENT TECHNOLOGY

School	ST	$IS	SR
CUNY/Hunter College	NY	6,729	C+
Penn State Univ/Univ Park Campus	PA	15,646	HC
Univ of Northern Iowa	IA	9,834	C

ENGINEERING

School	ST	$IS	SR
Alabama State Univ	AL	6,404	C
Andrews Univ	MI	19,550	C
Arcadia Univ	PA	29,890	C
Arizona State Univ-Main	AZ	10,048	C
Arkansas State Univ	AR	8,450	C
Arkansas Tech Univ	AR	7,299	C
Baylor Univ	TX	23,864	VC
Boston Univ	MA	38,194	HC+
Brown Univ	RI	38,174	MC
Bucknell Univ	PA	35,262	HC+
Calif Inst of Technology	CA	31,677	MC
Calif Polytechnic State Univ	CA	8,747	VC
Cal State, Hayward	CA	8,871	LC
Cal State, Los Angeles	CA	5,778	C
Cal State, Northridge	CA	7,757	LC
Calvin College	MI	22,615	NC
Carnegie Mellon Univ	PA	32,682	MC
Case Western Reserve Univ	OH	32,002	MC
Catholic Univ of America	DC	34,248	VC
Central Missouri State Univ	MO	9,776	C
Clark Atlanta Univ	GA	19,300	C+
Colo School of Mines	CO	12,533	HC
Cooper Union for the Advancement of Science and Art	NY	10,400	MC
Dominican Univ	IL	23,610	C
Dordt College	IA	20,170	VC
Elizabethtown College	PA	28,800	C
Elon Univ	NC	22,240	VC
Geneva College	PA	21,850	C
George Fox Univ	OR	26,110	VC
George Washington Univ	DC	41,030	MC
Grand Valley State Univ	MI	11,022	VC
Harvard Univ/Harvard College	MA	37,928	MC
Harvey Mudd College	CA	38,080	MC
Hope College	MI	25,340	VC
Idaho State Univ	ID	8,128	C
Indiana Univ-Purdue Univ Fort Wayne	IN	5,108	LC
Indiana Univ-Purdue Univ Indianapolis	IN	8,257	LC
Iowa State Univ	IA	10,768	VC
John Brown Univ	AR	15,080	VC
Johns Hopkins Univ	MD	38,372	MC
Johnson C. Smith Univ	NC	18,108	C
Lafayette College	PA	35,746	MC
Lake Superior State Univ	MI	9,034	LC
Lebanon Valley College	PA	28,870	VC
LeTourneau Univ	TX	21,080	C
Lincoln Univ	MO	7,158	NC
Lindenwood Univ	MO	17,050	VC
Loyola College in Maryland	MD	34,560	HC
Lubbock Christian Univ	TX	15,832	C
Lynchburg College	VA	26,815	C
Maine Maritime Academy	ME	12,380	C
Manchester College	IN	23,390	C
Marquette Univ	WI	27,594	VC
Maryville College	TN	25,960	VC
Messiah College	PA	25,890	VC+
Miami Univ	OH	15,033	HC
Mich State Univ	MI	11,933	VC
Mich Tech Univ	MI	13,235	VC
Montana Tech of The Univ of Montana	MT	9,314	NC
Mount Holyoke College	MA	37,918	HC+
New Mexico Highlands Univ	NM	6,182	LC
New Mexico Inst of Mining and Technology	NM	7,580	NC
N Car State Univ	NC	9,886	VC
Northeastern Univ	MA	35,650	HC
Northern Arizona Univ	AZ	9,002	C
Northwestern Univ	IL	37,491	MC
Okla State Univ	OK	9,216	VC
Olivet Nazarene Univ	IL	20,480	C
Oral Roberts Univ	OK	18,490	C
Penn State Univ at Erie/Behrend College	PA	12,326	C
Penn State Univ/Univ Park Campus	PA	15,646	HC
Pennsylvania College of Technology	PA	15,126	NC
Pepperdine Univ	CA	32,830	VC
Purdue Univ/Calumet	IN	6,630	NC
Purdue Univ/West Lafayette	IN	12,560	VC
Regis Univ	CO	25,740	C+
Rensselaer Polytechnic Inst	NY	37,579	HC+
Robert Morris Univ	PA	20,438	C
Rochester Inst of Technology	NY	29,217	VC+
Roger Williams Univ	RI	30,296	C
Rowan Univ	NJ	14,506	VC
St. Anselm College	NH	30,250	C
St. Mary's Univ of San Antonio	TX	22,444	C
San Francisco State Univ	CA	12,070	C
San Jose State Univ	CA	8,187	C
Santa Clara Univ	CA	34,701	HC
Scripps College	CA	35,700	HC+
Seton Hill Univ	PA	24,930	C
Smith College	MA	37,034	HC+
Spelman College	GA	19,215	C+
Spring Hill College	AL	25,868	VC
Stanford Univ	CA	37,612	MC
SUNY/Maritime College	NY	10,025	LC
Stevens Inst of Technology	NJ	35,300	HC+
Swarthmore College	PA	37,716	MC
Temple Univ	PA	15,912	C
Tenn Tech Univ	TN	8,670	VC
Texas Christian Univ	TX	23,410	VC
Texas Tech Univ	TX	10,768	VC
Trinity College	CT	38,040	HC+
Trinity College	DC	24,150	LC
Tufts Univ	MA	38,233	MC
Tulane Univ	LA	37,451	HC+
United States Air Force Academy	CO		HC+
United States Merchant Marine Academy	NY	6,250	HC+
United States Naval Academy	MD		MC
Univ of Arizona	AZ	10,413	VC
Univ of Calif at Irvine	CA	19,808	HC
Univ of Calif at San Diego	CA	14,127	HC
Univ of Cincinnati	OH	14,736	C
Univ of Colo at Boulder	CO	10,774	VC
Univ of Detroit Mercy	MI	25,582	C
Univ of Hartford	CT	31,080	C
Univ of Illinois at Chicago	IL	13,418	C
Univ of Illinois at Urbana-Champaign	IL	11,316	HC+
Univ of Iowa	IA	10,923	VC
Univ of Louisville	KY	8,762	VC
Univ of Maryland/College Park	MD	14,227	HC
Univ of Mass Boston	MA	6,227	C
Univ of Memphis	TN	8,560	C
Univ of Miami	FL	34,608	HC
Univ of Mich/Ann Arbor	MI	13,864	HC+
Univ of Mich/Flint	MI	5,548	C
Univ of Miss	MS	7,666	C
Univ of Missouri/Rolla	MO	12,292	HC
Univ of Missouri/St. Louis	MO	11,656	VC
Univ of New Haven	CT	28,650	C
Univ of Okla	OK	9,226	VC
Univ of Pennsylvania	PA	37,960	MC
Univ of Portland	OR	28,500	VC
Univ of PR/Mayaguez	PR		
Univ of South Florida	FL	9,454	C
Univ of Southern Indiana	IN	9,025	LC
Univ of Tenn at Chattanooga	TN	7,783	C
Univ of Tenn at Knoxville	TN	8,214	C
Univ of Tenn at Martin	TN	7,748	C
Univ of Toledo	OH	12,479	NC
Univ of Washington	WA	10,361	VC
Univ of Wisc/Milwaukee	WI	9,427	LC
Univ of Wisc/Platteville	WI	8,450	C
Utah State Univ	UT	7,371	C
Walla Walla College	WA	21,600	NC
Washington Univ in St. Louis	MO	38,293	MC
Waynesburg College	PA	19,370	C
West Virginia Univ	WV	9,370	C
Yale Univ	CT	37,000	MC
Youngstown State Univ	OH	11,148	NC

ENGINEERING AND APPLIED SCIENCE

School	ST	$IS	SR
Abilene Christian Univ	TX	18,370	VC
Benedictine Univ	IL	23,840	C
Bethel College	MN	25,180	VC
Calif Inst of Technology	CA	31,677	MC
Cal State, Fullerton	CA	6,648	C
CUNY/College of Staten Island	NY	4,308	NC
College of New Jersey	NJ	15,950	MC
Colo State Univ	CO	9,964	C
Dartmouth College	NH	37,770	MC
Franciscan Univ of Steubenville	OH	20,300	VC
New Jersey Inst of Technology	NJ	16,396	VC
Pacific Lutheran Univ	WA	25,715	VC

School	ST	$IS	SR
Rutgers, The State Univ of New Jersey/New Brunswick/Piscataway Campus	NJ	15,800	HC
Seattle Pacific Univ	WA	25,944	VC
Southern Polytechnic State Univ	GA	7,620	VC
SUNY/Univ at Stony Brook	NY	12,763	HC
Trinity Univ	TX	26,466	HC+
Tufts Univ	MA	38,233	MC
United States Air Force Academy	CO		HC+
Univ of Calif at Berkeley	CA	15,563	MC
Univ of Florida	FL	8,580	MC
Univ of Mich/Ann Arbor	MI	13,864	HC+
Univ of Rochester	NY	32,979	HC
Univ of Southern Calif	CA	37,459	MC
Univ of Tenn at Knoxville	TN	8,214	C
Univ of Virginia	VA	11,740	MC
Vanderbilt Univ	TN	37,897	MC
Wartburg College	IA	21,165	VC
Wilkes Univ	PA	28,060	C
Yale Univ	CT	37,000	MC

ENGINEERING CHEMISTRY

School	ST	$IS	SR
Oakland Univ	MI	10,800	C
SUNY/Univ at Stony Brook	NY	12,763	HC

ENGINEERING MANAGEMENT

School	ST	$IS	SR
Clarkson Univ	NY	32,226	VC
Columbia Univ/Fu Foundation School of Engineering and Applied Science	NY	38,590	MC
Idaho State Univ	ID	8,128	C
Kansas State Univ	KS	8,728	VC
Lake Superior State Univ	MI	9,034	LC
Miami Univ	OH	15,033	HC
N Dak State Univ	ND	8,435	C
Oral Roberts Univ	OK	18,490	C
Park Univ	MO	10,780	C+
Point Park Univ	PA	21,840	C
St. Louis Univ	MO	29,780	VC+
Southern Illinois Univ Carbondale	IL	10,407	C
Stevens Inst of Technology	NJ	35,300	HC+
Texas A&M Univ at Kingsville	TX	6,740	LC
Tri-State Univ-Main Campus	IN	23,600	C
United States Military Academy	NY		MC
Univ of Evansville	IN	24,190	VC
Univ of Illinois at Chicago	IL	13,418	C
Univ of Louisville	KY	8,762	VC
Univ of Missouri/Rolla	MO	12,292	HC
Univ of Portland	OR	28,500	VC
Univ of Tenn at Chattanooga	TN	7,783	C
Univ of the Pacific	CA	31,090	VC
Univ of Vermont	VT	16,316	VC
Western Mich Univ	MI	12,031	C
Wilkes Univ	PA	28,060	C
York College of Pennsylvania	PA	14,500	VC

ENGINEERING MECHANICS

School	ST	$IS	SR
Columbia Univ/Fu Foundation School of Engineering and Applied Science	NY	38,590	MC
Johns Hopkins Univ	MD	38,372	MC
Lehigh Univ	PA	37,570	HC+
Mich State Univ	MI	11,933	VC
New Mexico Inst of Mining and Technology	NM	7,580	NC
United States Air Force Academy	CO		HC+
Univ of Cincinnati	OH	14,736	C
Univ of Illinois at Urbana-Champaign	IL	11,316	HC+
Univ of Missouri/Rolla	MO	12,292	HC
Univ of Wisc/Madison	WI	8,262	VC
Washington Univ in St. Louis	MO	38,293	MC

ENGINEERING PHYSICS

School	ST	$IS	SR
Abilene Christian Univ	TX	18,370	VC
Augustana College	IL	26,610	VC+
Augustana College	SD	21,998	VC
Bradley Univ	IL	22,910	VC
Case Western Reserve Univ	OH	32,002	MC
Christian Brothers Univ	TN	22,290	VC
Conn College	CT	37,900	MC
Cornell Univ	NY	38,253	MC
Dartmouth College	NH	37,770	MC
Eastern Nazarene College	MA	19,433	LC
Edinboro Univ of Pennsylvania	PA	10,850	LC
Elizabethtown College	PA	28,800	C
Embry-Riddle Aeronautical Univ	AZ	27,710	C+
Embry-Riddle Aeronautical Univ	FL	27,730	C+
Jacksonville Univ	FL	24,040	C
John Carroll Univ	OH	27,658	C+
Juniata College	PA	29,080	VC
Lehigh Univ	PA	37,570	HC+
Loyola Marymount Univ	CA	32,194	VC
Miami Univ	OH	15,033	HC
Miss College	MS	14,574	C
Morgan State Univ	MD	11,470	C
N Car Agricultural and Technical State Univ	NC	6,659	LC
Northwest Nazarene Univ	ID	20,360	VC
Oakland Univ	MI	10,800	C
Ohio State Univ	OH	13,080	VC+
Okla Christian Univ	OK	17,690	NC
Point Loma Nazarene Univ	CA	21,380	VC
Rensselaer Polytechnic Inst	NY	37,579	HC+
Rose-Hulman Inst of Technology	IN	31,425	HC+
St. Ambrose Univ	IA	22,800	C
St. Bonaventure Univ	NY	24,455	LC
Samford Univ	AL	18,648	VC
Santa Clara Univ	CA	34,701	HC
S Dak State Univ	SD	7,782	C
Southwest Missouri State Univ	MO	8,918	C
Southwestern Okla State Univ	OK	4,801	C
SUNY/Univ at Buffalo	NY	12,563	VC
Stevens Inst of Technology	NJ	35,300	HC+
Syracuse Univ	NY	34,720	HC
Taylor Univ	IN	23,820	VC+
Texas Tech Univ	TX	10,768	VC
Tufts Univ	MA	38,233	MC
United States Military Academy	NY		MC
Univ of Arizona	AZ	10,413	VC
Univ of Calif at Berkeley	CA	15,563	MC
Univ of Calif at San Diego	CA	14,127	HC
Univ of Central Okla	OK	9,434	C
Univ of Colo at Boulder	CO	10,774	VC
Univ of Illinois at Chicago	IL	13,418	C
Univ of Illinois at Urbana-Champaign	IL	11,316	HC+
Univ of Kansas	KS	8,923	VC
Univ of Maine	ME	12,080	C+
Univ of Mass Boston	MA	6,227	C
Univ of Mich/Ann Arbor	MI	13,864	HC+
Univ of Nebr at Omaha	NE	8,080	C
Univ of Nevada/Reno	NV	9,792	C
Univ of Okla	OK	9,226	VC
Univ of Pittsburgh at Pittsburgh	PA	16,074	HC
Univ of Tenn at Knoxville	TN	8,214	C
Univ of the Pacific	CA	31,090	VC
Univ of Tulsa	OK	22,090	VC+
Univ of Wisc/Madison	WI	8,262	VC
Washington and Lee Univ	VA	29,663	MC
Washington Univ in St. Louis	MO	38,293	MC
West Virginia Wesleyan College	WV	22,920	C
Westmont College	CA	33,062	VC+
Worcester Polytechnic Inst	MA	37,404	HC
Wright State Univ	OH	11,490	LC

ENGINEERING TECHNOLOGY

School	ST	$IS	SR
Austin Peay State Univ	TN	5,814	LC
Bluefield State College	WV	2,806	LC
Calif Maritime Academy	CA	14,296	C
Calif State Polytechnic Univ, Pomona	CA	8,793	C+
Cal State, Long Beach	CA	8,762	C+
Cal State, Sacramento	CA	9,543	C
Capitol College	MD	21,250	C
Central Conn State Univ	CT	12,090	C
Central Mich Univ	MI	11,142	C
Central Missouri State Univ	MO	9,776	C
Central Washington Univ	WA	9,768	C
East Tenn State Univ	TN	8,497	C
Embry-Riddle Aeronautical Univ	FL	27,730	C+
Fairmont State	WV	8,280	LC
Ferris State Univ	MI	12,512	C
Florida A&M Univ	FL	7,564	C
Francis Marion Univ	SC	9,364	C
Gallaudet Univ	DC	16,554	SP
Georgia Southern Univ	GA	8,540	C
Grambling State Univ	LA	6,538	NC
Indiana Univ Northwest	IN	4,538	LC
Indiana Univ-Purdue Univ Fort Wayne	IN	5,108	LC
Iowa State Univ	IA	10,768	VC
Kent State Univ	OH	12,932	C
Lake Superior State Univ	MI	9,034	LC
Lawrence Tech Univ	MI	20,487	C
LeTourneau Univ	TX	21,080	C
Maine Maritime Academy	ME	12,380	C
Miami Univ	OH	15,033	HC
Mich Tech Univ	MI	13,235	VC
Middle Tenn State Univ	TN	8,534	C
Midwestern State Univ	TX	8,045	LC
Milwaukee School of Engineering	WI	28,479	VC+
Minn State Univ, Mankato	MN	8,803	LC
Missouri Western State College	MO	8,522	NC
Montana State Univ-Northern	MT	8,600	NC
Murray State Univ	KY	7,816	VC
New Jersey Inst of Technology	NJ	16,396	VC
New York Inst of Technology	NY	24,205	VC
Northeastern Univ	MA	35,650	HC
Old Dominion Univ	VA	10,441	C
Oregon Inst of Technology	OR	8,718	C
Pacific Union College	CA	22,065	C+
Penn State Univ at Erie/Behrend College	PA	12,326	C
Pittsburg State Univ	KS	7,128	NC
Prairie View A&M Univ	TX	9,418	NC
Purdue Univ/Calumet	IN	6,630	NC
Rochester Inst of Technology	NY	29,217	VC+
St. Cloud State Univ	MN	8,362	C
Savannah State Univ	GA	7,328	LC
S Car State Univ	SC	6,586	LC
S Dak State Univ	SD	7,782	C
Southeast Missouri State Univ	MO	9,704	C
Southern Illinois Univ Carbondale	IL	10,407	C
Southern Univ and A&M College	LA	7,372	LC
Southern Utah Univ	UT	8,194	C
Southwestern Okla State Univ	OK	4,801	C
Temple Univ	PA	15,912	C
Texas A&M Univ	TX	11,081	HC
Texas A&M Univ at Commerce	TX	8,994	C
Texas A&M Univ at Corpus Christi	TX	10,269	C
Texas Southern Univ	TX	8,920	NC
Texas State Univ	TX	9,320	VC
Univ of Central Florida	FL	10,038	VC
Univ of Cincinnati	OH	14,736	C
Univ of Dayton	OH	24,850	VC
Univ of Delaware	DE	12,616	HC
Univ of Hartford	CT	31,080	C
Univ of Houston-Downtown	TX	2,594	NC
Univ of Maryland/Eastern Shore	MD	9,964	C
Univ of Mass Lowell	MA	11,937	VC
Univ of New Hampshire	NH	14,828	VC
Univ of North Texas	TX	7,629	C
Univ of Southern Miss	MS	8,324	LC
Univ of Toledo	OH	12,479	NC
Univ of Wisc/Stout	WI	9,718	C
Virginia State Univ	VA	10,358	C
West Texas A&M Univ	TX	7,533	C
West Virginia Univ Inst of Technology	WV	7,518	NC
Western Carolina Univ	NC	6,742	C
Western Washington Univ	WA	10,119	VC
Youngstown State Univ	OH	11,148	NC

ENGLISH

School	ST	$IS	SR
Abilene Christian Univ	TX	18,370	VC
Adams State College	CO	7,468	C
Adelphi Univ	NY	26,300	VC
Adrian College	MI	21,950	C
Agnes Scott College	GA	28,230	HC
Alabama A&M Univ	AL	5,100	LC
Alabama State Univ	AL	6,404	C
Albany State Univ	GA	5,764	C+
Albertson College of Idaho	ID	19,415	VC
Albertus Magnus College	CT	23,130	LC
Albion College	MI	25,224	VC
Albright College	PA	30,579	C
Alcorn State Univ	MS	7,290	C
Alfred Univ	NY	28,290	C
Alice Lloyd College	KY	4,040	C
Allegheny College	PA	30,280	VC
Allen Univ	SC	10,300	NC
Alma College	MI	25,566	VC
Alvernia College	PA	23,212	LC
Alverno College	WI	18,898	C
American International College	MA	24,690	LC
Amherst College	MA	37,470	MC
Anderson Univ	IN	19,430	LC
Andrews Univ	MI	19,550	C
Angelo State Univ	TX	7,576	NC
Anna Maria College	MA	26,140	LC
Appalachian State Univ	NC	7,637	VC
Aquinas College	MI	21,894	C
Arcadia Univ	PA	29,890	C
Arizona State Univ-Main	AZ	10,048	C
Arkansas State Univ	AR	8,450	C
Arkansas Tech Univ	AR	7,299	C
Armstrong Atlantic State Univ	GA	7,102	C
Asbury College	KY	20,704	VC
Ashland Univ	OH	24,464	C
Assumption College	MA	29,375	C
Atlantic Union College	MA	18,868	C
Auburn Univ	AL	10,396	VC
Auburn Univ Montgomery	AL	9,020	NC
Augsburg College	MN	25,298	C
Augusta State Univ	GA	2,592	C
Augustana College	IL	26,610	VC+
Augustana College	SD	21,998	VC
Aurora Univ	IL	20,631	C
Austin College	TX	24,747	HC
Austin Peay State Univ	TN	5,814	LC
Averett Univ	VA	23,010	LC
Avila Univ	MO	20,300	C
Azusa Pacific Univ	CA	24,720	VC
Baker Univ	KS	19,860	VC
Baldwin-Wallace College	OH	24,678	C
Ball State Univ	IN	8,660	C
Barber-Scotia College	NC	13,900	LC
Bard College	NY	37,352	HC+
Barry Univ	FL	24,100	LC
Barton College	NC	19,314	C
Bates College	ME	37,500	MC
Baylor Univ	TX	23,864	VC
Belhaven College	MS	16,040	C+
Bellarmine Univ	KY	24,110	VC
Bellevue Univ	NE	4,440	NC
Belmont Abbey College	NC	23,742	C
Belmont Univ	TN	21,986	VC
Beloit College	WI	29,864	HC
Bemidji State Univ	MN	9,103	C
Benedict College	SC	12,662	LC
Benedictine College	KS	20,603	C
Bennett College	NC	11,200	C
Bennington College	VT	35,910	HC
Bentley College	MA	33,904	VC
Berea College	KY	5,030	VC+
Berry College	GA	21,410	VC
Bethany College	KS	18,675	LC
Bethany College	WV	19,845	VC
Bethel College	IN	19,670	C
Bethel College	KS	19,800	C+
Bethel College	MN	25,180	VC
Bethel College	TN	12,980	C
Bethune-Cookman College	FL	16,480	LC
Biola Univ	CA	25,964	VC
Birmingham-Southern College	AL	25,364	VC+
Black Hills State Univ	SD	7,743	LC
Bloomfield College	NJ	19,250	LC
Bloomsburg Univ of Pennsylvania	PA	10,844	C
Blue Mountain College	MS	10,226	C
Bluefield College	VA	15,575	C
Bluffton College	OH	23,694	C
Boise State Univ	ID	7,657	LC
Boston College	MA	33,284	MC
Boston Univ	MA	38,194	HC+
Bowdoin College	ME	37,790	MC
Bowie State Univ	MD	10,873	C+
Bowling Green State Univ	OH	13,036	C
Bradley Univ	IL	22,910	VC
Brandeis Univ	MA	38,198	MC
Brenau Univ Women's College	GA	21,800	C
Brescia Univ	KY	14,225	C
Brewton-Parker College	GA	14,200	LC
Briar Cliff Univ	IA	21,660	C
Bridgewater College	VA	25,150	C
Bridgewater State College	MA	10,482	C
Brigham Young Univ	UT	8,504	HC
Brigham Young Univ/Hawaii	HI	7,240	VC+
Brown Univ	RI	38,174	MC
Bryan College	TN	17,900	VC
Bryant College	RI	31,004	VC
Bryn Athyn College of the New Church	PA	12,612	NC
Bryn Mawr College	PA	36,890	HC+
Bucknell Univ	PA	35,262	HC+
Buena Vista Univ	IA	25,406	C
Butler Univ	IN	28,250	VC+
Cabrini College	PA	29,020	C
Caldwell College	NJ	24,060	LC
Calif Baptist Univ	CA	19,924	C
Calif Lutheran Univ	CA	27,600	LC
Calif Polytechnic State Univ	CA	8,747	VC
Calif State Polytechnic Univ, Pomona	CA	8,793	C+
Cal State, Bakersfield	CA	6,090	LC
Cal State, Chico	CA	8,598	LC
Cal State, Dominguez Hills	CA	5,840	LC
Cal State, Fresno	CA	8,414	LC
Cal State, Fullerton	CA	6,648	C
Cal State, Hayward	CA	8,871	LC
Cal State, Long Beach	CA	8,762	C+
Cal State, Los Angeles	CA	5,778	C
Cal State, Northridge	CA	7,757	LC
Cal State, Sacramento	CA	9,543	C
Cal State, San Bernardino	CA	15,238	LC
Cal State, Stanislaus	CA	9,874	C
Calif Univ of Pennsylvania	PA	10,388	C
Calumet College of St. Joseph	IN	9,000	LC
Calvin College	MI	22,615	NC
Cameron Univ	OK	5,692	NC
Campbell Univ	NC	18,268	VC
Campbellsville Univ	KY	17,680	C
Canisius College	NY	28,163	C+

School	ST	$IS	SR
Capital Univ	OH	26,550	C
Cardinal Stritch Univ	WI	17,620	C
Carleton College	MN	34,395	MC
Carlow College	PA	21,334	C
Carnegie Mellon Univ	PA	32,682	MC
Carroll College	MT	20,576	VC
Carroll College	WI	22,740	C
Carson-Newman College	TN	16,760	C
Carthage College	WI	25,000	C
Cascade College	OR	16,700	NC
Case Western Reserve Univ	OH	32,002	MC
Catawba College	NC	20,500	C
Catholic Univ of America	DC	34,248	VC
Cazenovia College	NY	23,940	C
Cedar Crest College	PA	25,145	C+
Cedarville Univ	OH	19,954	VC
Centenary College	NJ	25,370	LC
Centenary College of Louisiana	LA	23,100	VC+
Central College	IA	21,206	C
Central Conn State Univ	CT	12,090	C
Central Methodist College	MO	16,460	C
Central Mich Univ	MI	11,142	C
Central Missouri State Univ	MO	9,776	C
Central State Univ	OH	8,922	C+
Central Washington Univ	WA	9,768	C
Centre College	KY	27,300	HC
Chadron State College	NE	6,286	NC
Chaminade Univ of Honolulu	HI	21,430	LC
Chapman Univ	CA	33,118	VC
Charleston Southern Univ	SC	17,122	C
Chatham College	PA	27,266	C+
Chestnut Hill College	PA	26,450	LC
Cheyney Univ of Pennsylvania	PA	9,993	C
Chicago State Univ	IL	10,882	C+
Christendom College	VA	18,410	VC+
Christian Brothers Univ	TN	22,290	VC
Christian Heritage College	CA	19,990	C
Christopher Newport Univ	VA	8,862	VC
Citadel, The	SC	12,295	C+
CUNY/Baruch College	NY	3,275	VC+
CUNY/Brooklyn College	NY	4,353	C+
CUNY/City College	NY	4,230	C+
CUNY/College of Staten Island	NY	4,308	NC
CUNY/Herbert H. Lehman College	NY	3,320	LC
CUNY/Hunter College	NY	6,729	C+
CUNY/Medgar Evers College	NY	4,232	NC
CUNY/Queens College	NY	4,362	C
CUNY/York College	NY	3,292	NC
Claflin Univ	SC	14,838	C+
Clarion Univ of Pennsylvania	PA	11,272	LC
Clark Atlanta Univ	GA	19,300	C+
Clark Univ	MA	32,115	VC
Clarke College	IA	23,165	C
Clearwater Christian College	FL	13,160	LC
Clemson Univ	SC	11,972	HC
Cleveland State Univ	OH	12,308	LC
Coastal Carolina Univ	SC	11,040	C
Coe College	IA	27,385	VC
Coker College	SC	21,491	C
Colby College	ME	37,570	MC
Colby-Sawyer College	NH	27,850	LC
Colgate Univ	NY	37,095	MC
College Misericordia	PA	26,350	C
College of Charleston	SC	11,887	HC
College of Mount St. Vincent	NY	26,800	C
College of Mount St. Joseph	OH	22,785	C
College of New Jersey	NJ	15,950	MC
College of New Rochelle	NY	21,800	C
College of Notre Dame of Maryland	MD	27,700	C
College of Our Lady of the Elms	MA	20,644	C
College of St. Benedict	MN	26,672	VC
College of St. Catherine	MN	24,010	VC
College of St. Elizabeth	NJ	25,460	C
College of St. Joseph	VT	19,100	C
College of St. Mary	NE	21,510	C
College of St. Rose	NY	22,864	C
College of St. Scholastica	MN	24,970	C+
College of Santa Fe	NM	25,293	C+
College of the Holy Cross	MA	36,451	MC
College of the Ozarks	MO	3,500	VC+
College of the Southwest	NM	9,320	C+
College of William and Mary	VA	12,224	MC
College of Wooster	OH	31,300	HC
Colo Christian Univ	CO	21,182	VC
Colo College	CO	36,860	HC
Colo State Univ	CO	9,964	VC
Columbia College	MO	16,139	C
Columbia College	SC	22,658	LC
Columbia Union College	MD	20,543	C
Columbia Univ/Barnard College	NY	36,990	MC
Columbia Univ/Columbia College	NY	38,590	MC
Columbus State Univ	GA	7,846	C
Concord College	WV	8,136	C
Concordia College	NY	19,200	VC
Concordia College: Moorhead	MN	22,460	VC+
Concordia Univ	CA	24,420	C
Concordia Univ	MI	24,095	C
Concordia Univ	OR	22,450	C
Concordia Univ at Austin	TX	20,450	LC
Concordia Univ Nebr	NE	20,302	C+
Concordia Univ Wisc	WI	16,600	C
Concordia Univ, River Forest	IL	23,600	C
Concordia Univ/St.Paul	MN	24,486	C
Conn College	CT	37,900	MC
Converse College	SC	24,710	VC
Coppin State College	MD	10,191	LC
Cornell College	IA	27,825	VC+
Cornell Univ	NY	38,253	MC
Cornerstone Univ and Grand Rapids Theological Seminary	MI	19,846	C
Covenant College	GA	23,830	VC+
Creighton Univ	NE	26,748	VC+
Crichton College	TN	15,215	C
Culver-Stockton College	MO	17,850	C
Cumberland College	KY	16,384	C
Cumberland Univ	TN	16,910	C
Curry College	MA	26,025	LC
Daemen College	NY	22,120	C
Dakota State Univ	SD	7,466	C
Dakota Wesleyan Univ	SD	17,832	C
Dallas Baptist Univ	TX	15,300	VC
Dana College	NE	20,280	C
Dartmouth College	NH	37,770	MC
David Lipscomb Univ	TN	16,158	VC
Davidson College	NC	33,274	MC
Davis and Elkins College	WV	20,594	C
De Sales Univ	PA	25,470	C
Delaware State Univ	DE	8,104	LC
Delaware Valley College	PA	26,676	C
Delta State Univ	MS	6,618	C
Denison Univ	OH	33,050	HC
DePaul Univ	IL	27,580	VC
DePauw Univ	IN	31,500	HC
Dickinson College	PA	35,825	HC
Dickinson State Univ	ND	6,338	NC
Dillard Univ	LA	17,325	VC
Doane College	NE	20,000	C
Dominican College	NY	24,810	LC
Dominican Univ	IL	23,610	C
Dordt College	IA	20,170	VC
Dowling College	NY	23,870	LC
Drake Univ	IA	25,120	VC+
Drew Univ/College of Liberal Arts	NJ	35,550	VC
Drury Univ	MO	18,085	VC+
Duke Univ	NC	37,555	MC
Duquesne Univ	PA	26,907	VC
D'Youville College	NY	21,080	C
Earlham College	IN	29,976	VC+
East Carolina Univ	NC	8,671	C
East Central Univ	OK	4,968	C
East Stroudsburg Univ of Pennsylvania	PA	10,336	C
East Tenn State Univ	TN	8,497	C
East Texas Baptist Univ	TX	13,914	C
Eastern Conn State Univ	CT	10,362	C
Eastern Illinois Univ	IL	11,192	C
Eastern Kentucky Univ	KY	7,708	C
Eastern Mennonite Univ	VA	22,990	C
Eastern Mich Univ	MI	11,478	C
Eastern Nazarene College	MA	19,433	LC
Eastern New Mexico Univ	NM	6,762	LC
Eastern Oregon Univ	OR	10,080	NC
Eastern Washington Univ	WA	9,012	C
East-West Univ	IL	10,365	LC
Eckerd College	FL	28,744	C+
Edgewood College	WI	20,520	C
Edinboro Univ of Pennsylvania	PA	10,850	LC
Edward Waters College	FL	14,374	LC
Elizabeth City State Univ	NC	5,550	LC
Elizabethtown College	PA	28,800	C
Elmhurst College	IL	24,630	C
Elon Univ	NC	22,240	VC
Emmanuel College	MA	27,600	C+
Emory Univ	GA	36,872	MC
Emporia State Univ	KS	6,998	C
Endicott College	MA	25,266	C+
Erskine College	SC	23,166	VC
Eugene Lang College/New School Univ	NY	34,940	C
Eureka College	IL	24,980	LC
Evangel Univ	MO	15,435	C
Fairfield Univ	CT	35,505	HC
Fairmont State	WV	8,280	LC
Faulkner Univ	AL	14,500	C
Fayetteville State Univ	NC	5,590	LC
Felician College	NJ	24,300	C
Ferrum College	VA	21,240	LC
Fisk Univ	TN	17,305	LC
Fitchburg State College	MA	9,622	C
Flagler College	FL	11,860	VC+
Florida A&M Univ	FL	7,564	C
Florida Atlantic Univ	FL	8,543	C
Florida International Univ	FL	9,912	VC
Florida Memorial College	FL	6,000	LC
Florida Southern College	FL	23,592	C
Florida State Univ	FL	9,028	HC
Fontbonne Univ	MO	21,508	C
Fordham Univ	NY	35,066	HC
Fort Hays State Univ	KS	7,363	C
Fort Lewis College	CO	8,353	C
Fort Valley State Univ	GA	6,960	C
Framingham State College	MA	9,381	C
Francis Marion Univ	SC	9,364	C
Franciscan Univ	IA	19,300	C
Franciscan Univ of Steubenville	OH	20,300	VC
Franklin and Marshall College	PA	35,930	HC+
Franklin College	IN		C
Franklin Pierce College	NH	28,980	LC
Freed-Hardeman Univ	TN		NC
Fresno Pacific Univ	CA	22,462	C
Friends Univ	KS	15,962	LC
Frostburg State Univ	MD	11,114	C
Furman Univ	SC	28,976	HC+
Gallaudet Univ	DC	16,554	SP
Gannon Univ	PA	23,260	C
Gardner-Webb Univ	NC	19,300	C
Geneva College	PA	21,850	C
George Mason Univ	VA	9,732	VC
George Washington Univ	DC	41,030	MC
Georgetown College	KY	22,000	VC
Georgetown Univ	DC	38,242	MC
Georgia College and State Univ	GA	9,878	C
Georgia Southern Univ	GA	8,540	C
Georgia Southwestern State Univ	GA	6,013	C
Georgia State Univ	GA	10,658	C
Georgian Court College	NJ	19,040	LC
Gettysburg College	PA	35,646	HC
Glenville State College	WV	7,812	NC
Gonzaga Univ	WA	26,766	HC
Gordon College	MA	25,982	VC+
Goshen College	IN	22,450	VC
Goucher College	MD	32,650	HC
Grace College	IN	19,825	VC
Graceland Univ	IA	19,550	C
Grambling State Univ	LA	6,538	NC
Grand Canyon Univ	AZ	30,000	LC
Grand Valley State Univ	MI	11,022	VC
Grand View College	IA	19,748	LC
Green Mountain College	VT	24,130	C
Greensboro College	NC	21,750	C
Greenville College	IL	21,342	C
Grinnell College	IA	31,060	HC+
Grove City College	PA	14,228	HC
Guilford College	NC	24,960	VC
Gustavus Adolphus College	MN	27,120	VC+
Gwynedd-Mercy College	PA	24,225	C
Hamilton College	NY	37,560	MC
Hamline Univ	MN	27,052	VC
Hampden-Sydney College	VA	28,407	VC
Hampton Univ	VA	17,112	C+
Hannibal-LaGrange College	MO	13,940	C
Hanover College	IN	25,200	VC
Harding Univ	AR	14,890	VC
Hardin-Simmons Univ	TX	14,165	C
Hartwick College	NY	34,650	C+
Harvard Univ/Harvard College	MA	37,928	MC
Hastings College	NE	19,928	VC
Haverford College	PA	37,900	MC
Hawaii Pacific Univ	HI	19,218	C
Heidelberg College	OH	20,266	NC
Henderson State Univ	AR	7,386	C
Hendrix College	AR	20,970	VC+
Heritage College	WA	6,720	NC
High Point Univ	NC	22,480	C
Hilbert College	NY	19,170	LC
Hillsdale College	MI	22,450	HC
Hiram College	OH	28,234	VC
Hobart and William Smith Colleges	NY	36,536	HC
Hollins Univ	VA	27,965	VC
Holy Family College	PA	13,710	LC
Holy Names College	CA	27,980	NC
Hood College	MD	27,795	VC
Hope College	MI	25,340	VC
Houghton College	NY	23,984	VC
Houston Baptist Univ	TX	16,905	C
Howard Payne Univ	TX	15,176	C
Howard Univ	DC	16,505	C
Humboldt State Univ	CA	9,400	C
Huntingdon College	AL	18,400	VC
Huntington College	IN	23,590	C
Huston-Tillotson College	TX	14,232	NC
Idaho State Univ	ID	8,128	C
Illinois College	IL	19,100	VC
Illinois State Univ	IL	10,944	C+
Illinois Wesleyan Univ	IL	30,380	HC+
Immaculata Univ	PA	25,200	C
Indiana State Univ	IN	10,719	LC
Indiana Univ Bloomington	IN	12,389	VC
Indiana Univ East	IN	4,433	LC
Indiana Univ Kokomo	IN	4,463	LC
Indiana Univ Northwest	IN	4,538	LC
Indiana Univ of Pennsylvania	PA	10,489	C
Indiana Univ South Bend	IN	4,571	LC
Indiana Univ Southeast	IN	4,504	LC
Indiana Univ-Purdue Univ Fort Wayne	IN	5,108	LC
Indiana Univ-Purdue Univ Indianapolis	IN	8,257	LC
Indiana Wesleyan Univ	IN	19,900	C+
Inter American Univ of PR/San German	PR	6,716	
Iona College	NY	27,988	VC
Iowa State Univ	IA	10,768	VC
Iowa Wesleyan College	IA	19,990	C
Ithaca College	NY	31,730	HC
Jackson State Univ	MS	8,382	C
Jacksonville State Univ	AL	6,844	LC
Jacksonville Univ	FL	24,040	C
James Madison Univ	VA	10,794	VC
Jamestown College	ND	12,600	NC
Jarvis Christian College	TX	9,035	NC
John Brown Univ	AR	15,080	VC
John Carroll Univ	OH	27,658	C+
Johns Hopkins Univ	MD	38,372	MC
Johnson C. Smith Univ	NC	18,108	C
Johnson State College	VT	11,819	LC
Judson College	AL	14,650	C
Judson College	IL	22,050	LC
Juniata College	PA	29,080	VC
Kalamazoo College	MI	26,955	HC+
Kansas State Univ	KS	8,728	VC
Kansas Wesleyan Univ	KS	18,900	VC
Kean Univ	NJ	14,479	C
Keene State College	NH	12,212	C
Kennesaw State Univ	GA	2,724	C
Kent State Univ	OH	12,932	C
Kentucky State Univ	KY	9,062	NC
Kentucky Wesleyan College	KY	17,250	C
Kenyon College	OH	35,370	HC+
Keuka College	NY	21,170	C
King College	TN	22,500	VC
King's College	PA	26,990	C
Knoxville College	TN	6,200	LC
Kutztown Univ of Pennsylvania	PA	10,786	C
La Roche College	PA	22,094	C
La Salle Univ	PA	31,260	VC
La Sierra Univ	CA	19,260	LC
Lafayette College	PA	35,746	MC
LaGrange College	GA	20,500	C
Lake Erie College	OH	23,550	C
Lake Forest College	IL	30,270	VC
Lake Superior State Univ	MI	9,034	LC
Lakeland College	WI	17,950	C
Lamar Univ	TX	6,816	LC
Lambuth Univ	TN	16,520	C
Lander Univ	SC	10,496	C
Lane College	TN	11,178	C+
Langston Univ	OK	2,308	LC
Lawrence Univ	WI	30,900	HC
Le Moyne College	NY	26,400	VC
Lebanon Valley College	PA	28,870	VC
Lee Univ	TN	13,780	NC
Lees-McRae College	NC	17,106	LC
Lehigh Univ	PA	37,570	HC+
LeMoyne-Owen College	TN	13,070	LC
Lenoir-Rhyne College	NC	19,186	C
LeTourneau Univ	TX	21,080	C
Lewis and Clark College	OR	30,620	VC
Lewis Univ	IL	22,950	C+
Lewis-Clark State College	ID	6,981	C
Liberty Univ	VA	17,220	C
Limestone College	SC	17,700	C
Lincoln Memorial Univ	TN	16,400	LC
Lincoln Univ	MO	7,158	NC
Lincoln Univ	PA	13,320	C+
Lindenwood Univ	MO	17,050	VC
Lindsey Wilson College	KY	16,392	LC
Linfield College	OR	27,090	VC
Livingstone College	NC	18,101	LC
Lock Haven Univ of Pennsylvania	PA	11,098	LC
LIU/Brooklyn Campus	NY	24,790	C
LIU/C.W. Post Campus	NY	28,282	C
LIU/Southampton College	NY	29,370	C+
Longwood Univ	VA	11,175	C
Louisiana College	LA	13,450	C
Louisiana State Univ and A&M College	LA	9,126	VC
Louisiana State Univ in Shreveport	LA	2,884	NC
Louisiana Tech Univ	LA	7,361	C
Lourdes College	OH	15,300	LC
Loyola College in Maryland	MD	34,560	HC
Loyola Marymount Univ	CA	32,194	VC
Loyola Univ Chicago	IL	31,164	VC
Loyola Univ New Orleans	LA	31,036	VC+
Luther College	IA	25,700	VC
Lycoming College	PA	27,589	C+
Lynchburg College	VA	26,815	C
Lyndon State College	VT	12,646	LC
Lyon College	AR	17,995	VC
Macalester College	MN	31,944	MC
MacMurray College	IL	20,005	LC
Madonna Univ	MI	11,504	VC
Malone College	OH	20,995	C

ST = STATE **$IS** = IN-STATE COSTS **SR** = SELECTOR RATING

INDEX OF COLLEGE MAJORS

School	ST	$IS	SR
Manchester College	IN	23,390	C
Manhattan College	NY	27,400	VC
Manhattanville College	NY	32,420	C+
Mansfield Univ	PA	11,220	C
Marian College	IN	23,030	C
Marian College of Fond du Lac	WI	19,625	C
Marietta College	OH	27,047	C
Marist College	NY	27,596	VC
Marlboro College	VT	29,055	VC+
Marquette Univ	WI	27,594	VC
Mars Hill College	NC	18,600	LC
Marshall Univ	WV	9,116	C
Mary Baldwin College	VA	24,939	C
Mary Washington College	VA	10,166	HC
Marygrove College	MI	17,550	C
Marymount College of Fordham Univ	NY	27,686	C
Marymount Manhattan College	NY	27,292	C
Marymount Univ	VA	23,668	C
Maryville College	TN	25,960	VC
Maryville Univ of St. Louis	MO	22,090	VC
Marywood Univ	PA	26,050	C
Mass College of Liberal Arts	MA	8,717	LC
Master's College and Seminary	CA	23,250	VC
Mayville State Univ	ND	7,325	NC
McDaniel College	MD	28,440	VC
McKendree College	IL	21,120	VC
McMurry Univ	TX	17,846	LC
McNeese State Univ	LA	5,259	LC
McPherson College	KS	20,265	C
Mercer Univ	GA	27,516	VC+
Mercy College	NY	19,200	NC
Mercyhurst College	PA	20,694	C
Meredith College	NC	23,065	C
Merrimack College	MA	29,625	C
Mesa State College	CO	8,051	C
Messiah College	PA	25,890	VC+
Methodist College	NC	19,526	C
Metropolitan State College of Denver	CO	2,338	LC
Metropolitan State Univ	MN	3,852	SP
Miami Univ	OH	15,033	HC
Mich State Univ	MI	11,933	VC
MidAmerica Nazarene Univ	KS	18,688	C
Middle Tenn State Univ	TN	8,534	C
Middlebury College	VT	38,100	MC
Midland Lutheran College	NE	18,600	C
Midway College	KY	15,815	C
Midwestern State Univ	TX	8,045	LC
Miles College	AL	7,870	NC
Millersville Univ of Pennsylvania	PA	11,269	C
Milligan College	TN	19,860	C+
Millikin Univ	IL	25,555	C
Mills College	CA	33,371	VC
Millsaps College	MS	25,182	VC
Minn State Univ, Mankato	MN	8,803	LC
Minn State Univ, Moorehead	MN	7,000	LC
Minot State Univ	ND	6,602	LC
Miss College	MS	14,574	C
Miss State Univ	MS	9,139	C
Miss Univ for Women	MS	5,446	LC
Miss Valley State Univ	MS	6,765	NC
Missouri Baptist Univ	MO	18,010	C
Missouri Southern State Univ	MO	8,316	C
Missouri Valley College	MO	18,500	C
Missouri Western State College	MO	8,522	NC
Molloy College	NY	15,180	C
Monmouth College	IL	23,600	C
Monmouth Univ	NJ	26,334	C
Montana State Univ-Billings	MT	9,550	C
Montana State Univ-Bozeman	MT	9,515	C
Montana State Univ-Northern	MT	8,600	NC
Montclair State Univ	NJ	13,790	C
Montreat College	NC	18,762	C
Moravian College	PA	28,903	VC
Morehead State Univ	KY	7,464	C
Morehouse College	GA	22,728	C
Morgan State Univ	MD	11,470	C
Morningside College	IA	21,610	C
Morris College	SC	10,974	LC
Mount Aloysius College	PA	19,120	LC
Mount Holyoke College	MA	37,918	HC+
Mount Marty College	SD	15,656	LC
Mount Mary College	WI	20,370	C
Mount Mercy College	IA	21,400	C
Mount Olive College	NC	14,410	LC
Mount St. Mary College	NY	21,270	C
Mount St. Mary's College	CA	28,307	VC
Mount St. Mary's College	MD	28,400	C
Mount Union College	OH	21,120	C
Mount Vernon Nazarene Univ	OH	18,925	C
Muhlenberg College	PA	31,485	HC
Murray State Univ	KY	7,816	VC
Muskingum College	OH	20,680	C
National Univ	CA	9,690	SP
National-Louis Univ	IL	16,240	LC
Nazareth College of Rochester	NY	24,936	VC
Nebr Wesleyan Univ	NE	21,197	C+
Neumann College	PA	23,890	LC
New College of Calif	CA	8,900	NC
New College of Florida	FL	8,906	HC+
New Jersey City Univ	NJ	11,850	LC
New Mexico Highlands Univ	NM	6,182	LC
New Mexico State Univ	NM	7,932	C
New York Inst of Technology	NY	24,205	VC
New York Univ	NY	39,406	MC
Newberry College	SC	22,871	LC
Newman Univ	KS	18,018	C
Niagara Univ	NY	25,050	C
Nicholls State Univ	LA	6,395	NC
Nichols College	MA	27,562	LC
Norfolk State Univ	VA	9,722	LC
N Car Agricultural and Technical State Univ	NC	6,659	LC
N Car Central Univ	NC	7,534	LC
N Car State Univ	NC	9,886	VC
N Car Wesleyan College	NC	17,998	C
North Central College	IL	25,656	VC
N Dak State Univ	ND	8,435	C
North Georgia College and State Univ	GA	6,984	C
North Park Univ	IL	24,030	C
Northeastern Illinois Univ	IL	2,898	NC
Northeastern State Univ	OK	4,950	LC
Northeastern Univ	MA	35,650	HC
Northern Arizona Univ	AZ	9,002	C
Northern Illinois Univ	IL	11,472	C
Northern Kentucky Univ	KY	6,352	NC
Northern Mich Univ	MI	10,834	C
Northern State Univ	SD	7,117	LC
Northland College	WI	22,170	C+
Northwest College	WA	18,854	C
Northwest Missouri State Univ	MO	9,334	C
Northwest Nazarene Univ	ID	20,360	VC
Northwestern College	MN	22,820	C+
Northwestern College of Iowa	IA	19,640	C+
Northwestern Okla State Univ	OK	5,433	NC
Northwestern State Univ of Louisiana	LA	6,331	NC
Northwestern Univ	IL	37,491	MC
Norwich Univ	VT	21,064	LC
Notre Dame College	OH	20,425	C
Notre Dame de Namur Univ	CA	26,932	LC
Nova Southeastern Univ	FL	23,346	C
Nyack College	NY	18,540	C
Oakland City Univ	IN	16,980	NC
Oakland Univ	MI	10,800	C
Oakwood College	AL	14,904	C
Oberlin College	OH	36,938	MC
Oglethorpe Univ	GA	26,000	VC
Ohio Dominican Univ	OH	22,700	C
Ohio Northern Univ	OH	27,765	VC
Ohio State Univ	OH	13,080	VC+
Ohio State Univ at Lima	OH	4,416	NC
Ohio State Univ at Marion	OH	4,801	NC
Ohio State Univ at Newark	OH	9,881	NC
Ohio Univ	OH	14,448	C
Ohio Wesleyan Univ	OH	32,550	VC+
Okla Baptist Univ	OK	15,220	VC
Okla Christian Univ	OK	17,690	NC
Okla City Univ	OK	19,580	VC
Okla Panhandle State Univ	OK	5,370	C
Okla State Univ	OK	9,216	VC
Okla Wesleyan Univ	OK	14,100	LC
Old Dominion Univ	VA	10,441	C
Olivet College	MI	19,984	C+
Olivet Nazarene Univ	IL	20,480	C
Oral Roberts Univ	OK	18,490	C
Oregon State Univ	OR	11,055	C
Ottawa Univ	KS	11,800	LC
Otterbein College	OH	26,085	C
Ouachita Baptist Univ	AR	18,900	VC
Our Lady of Holy Cross College	LA	5,900	C
Our Lady of the Lake Univ of San Antonio	TX	17,336	C
Pace Univ	NY	28,652	VC
Pacific Lutheran Univ	WA	25,715	VC
Pacific Union College	CA	22,065	C+
Paine College	GA	13,022	LC
Palm Beach Atlantic Univ	FL	20,690	C
Park Univ	MO	10,780	C+
Paul Quinn College	TX	8,150	LC
Penn State Univ at Erie/Behrend College	PA	12,326	C
Penn State Univ/Altoona	PA	12,578	C
Penn State Univ/Univ Park Campus	PA	15,646	HC
Pepperdine Univ	CA	32,830	VC
Peru State College	NE	6,342	NC
Piedmont College	GA	16,900	C
Pikeville College	KY	14,900	NC
Pine Manor College	MA	22,138	LC
Pittsburg State Univ	KS	7,128	NC
Pitzer College	CA	37,590	HC
Plymouth State Univ	NH	12,298	LC
Point Park Univ	PA	21,840	C
Pomona College	CA	33,960	MC
Pontifical Catholic Univ of PR/Ponce	PR	7,298	
Portland State Univ	OR	12,453	C
Prairie View A&M Univ	TX	9,418	NC
Presbyterian College	SC	25,920	VC
Prescott College	AZ	13,430	C
Princeton Univ	NJ	36,649	MC
Principia College	IL	25,044	C+
Providence College	RI	30,604	HC
Purdue Univ/Calumet	IN	6,630	NC
Purdue Univ/West Lafayette	IN	12,560	VC
Queens Univ of Charlotte	NC	21,840	C
Quincy Univ	IL	22,330	C
Quinnipiac Univ	CT	30,570	VC
Radford Univ	VA	8,500	C
Randolph-Macon College	VA	27,190	C
Randolph-Macon Woman's College	VA	28,430	VC+
Regis College	MA	29,000	C
Regis Univ	CO	25,740	C+
Rhode Island College	RI	11,565	C
Rhodes College	TN	26,466	HC+
Rice Univ	TX	27,550	MC
Rider Univ	NJ	30,900	C
Ripon College	WI	24,995	VC
Rivier College	NH	26,217	C
Roanoke College	VA	27,393	C
Robert Morris Univ	PA	20,438	C
Roberts Wesleyan College	NY	23,190	C+
Rochester College	MI	16,718	C
Rockford College	IL	28,310	VC
Rockhurst Univ	MO	22,960	C+
Roger Williams Univ	RI	30,296	C
Rollins College	FL	34,300	VC
Roosevelt Univ	IL	22,580	VC
Rosemont College	PA	26,175	C
Rowan Univ	NJ	14,506	VC
Russell Sage College	NY	26,811	C
Rust College	MS	8,200	C+
Rutgers, The State Univ of New Jersey/Camden Campus	NJ	14,990	VC
Rutgers, The State Univ of New Jersey/New Brunswick/Piscataway Campus	NJ	15,800	HC
Rutgers, The State Univ of New Jersey/Newark Campus	NJ	15,624	VC
Sacred Heart Univ	CT	29,178	C
Saginaw Valley State Univ	MI	11,055	C
St. Ambrose Univ	IA	22,800	C
St. Andrews Presbyterian College	NC	20,525	C
St. Anselm College	NH	30,250	C
St. Augustine's College	NC	12,990	LC
St. Bonaventure Univ	NY	24,455	LC
St. Cloud State Univ	MN	8,362	C
St. Francis College	NY	10,880	LC
St. Francis Univ	PA	25,876	LC
St. John Fisher College	NY	24,870	C
St. John's Univ	MN	26,473	VC
St. John's Univ	NY	30,180	C
St. Joseph College	CT	29,685	C
St. Joseph's, Brooklyn,	NY	10,902	C
St. Joseph's College	IN	24,250	C
St. Joseph's College of Maine	ME	25,600	C
St. Joseph's Univ	PA	33,590	VC
St. Lawrence Univ	NY	35,945	VC
St. Leo Univ	FL	20,600	C
St. Louis Univ	MO	29,780	VC+
St. Martin's College	WA	23,245	C
St. Mary-of-the-Woods College	IN	23,280	C
St. Mary's College	IN	24,474	VC
St. Mary's College	MI	13,314	LC
St. Mary's College of Calif	CA	32,850	VC
St. Mary's College of Maryland	MD	15,908	VC+
St. Mary's Univ of San Antonio	TX	22,444	C
St. Michael's College	VT	30,100	VC
St. Norbert College	WI	25,810	C
St. Olaf College	MN	28,500	HC
St. Paul's College	VA	14,344	NC
St. Peter's College	NJ	22,292	LC
St. Thomas Aquinas College	NY	20,590	LC
St. Thomas Univ	FL	21,400	LC
St. Vincent College	PA	25,530	VC
St. Xavier Univ	IL	23,144	C
Salem College	NC	24,595	VC
Salem State College	MA	8,592	C
Salisbury Univ	MD	12,664	VC
Salve Regina Univ	RI	29,210	C
Sam Houston State Univ	TX	7,142	C
Samford Univ	AL	18,648	VC
San Diego State Univ	CA	10,321	C
San Francisco State Univ	CA	12,070	C
San Jose State Univ	CA	8,187	C
Santa Clara Univ	CA	34,701	HC
Sarah Lawrence College	NY	41,218	HC
Savannah State Univ	GA	7,328	LC
Schreiner Univ	TX	20,440	C
Scripps College	CA	35,700	HC+
Seattle Pacific Univ	WA	25,944	VC
Seattle Univ	WA	24,183	VC
Seton Hall Univ	NJ	30,130	VC
Seton Hill Univ	PA	24,930	C
Shaw Univ	NC	14,882	C+
Shawnee State Univ	OH	11,031	NC
Shenandoah Univ	VA	25,190	NC
Shepherd College	WV	8,608	C
Shippensburg Univ of Pennsylvania	PA	10,826	C
Shorter College	GA	17,370	C
Siena College	NY	25,310	VC
Siena Heights Univ	MI	16,140	LC
Silver Lake College of the Holy Family	WI	18,450	LC
Simmons College	MA	33,000	VC
Simpson College	CA	20,500	C
Simpson College	IA	23,658	C+
Skidmore College	NY	37,930	HC
Slippery Rock Univ of Pennsylvania	PA	10,343	LC
Smith College	MA	37,034	HC+
Sonoma State Univ	CA	10,421	C
S Car State Univ	SC	6,586	LC
S Dak State Univ	SD	7,782	C
Southeast Missouri State Univ	MO	9,704	C
Southeastern College	FL	11,648	LC
Southeastern Louisiana Univ	LA	6,791	LC
Southeastern Okla State Univ	OK	6,147	C
Southern Adventist Univ	TN	17,080	C
Southern Arkansas Univ	AR	6,956	C
Southern Conn State Univ	CT	10,310	C
Southern Illinois Univ Carbondale	IL	10,407	C
Southern Illinois Univ Edwardsville	IL	8,724	C
Southern Methodist Univ	TX	34,210	HC
Southern Nazarene Univ	OK	14,634	NC
Southern New Hampshire Univ	NH	26,242	C
Southern Oregon Univ	OR	10,362	C
Southern Univ and A&M College	LA	7,372	LC
Southern Univ at New Orleans	LA	995	NC
Southern Utah Univ	UT	8,194	C
Southern Vermont College	VT	18,226	LC
Southern Wesleyan Univ	SC	19,940	C
Southwest Baptist Univ	MO	15,371	C
Southwest Missouri State Univ	MO	8,918	C
Southwestern Adventist Univ	TX	14,798	C
Southwestern College	KS	19,560	C
Southwestern Okla State Univ	OK	4,801	C
Southwestern Univ	TX	25,410	HC
Spelman College	GA	19,215	C+
Spring Arbor Univ	MI	20,206	C
Spring Hill College	AL	25,868	VC
Springfield College	MA	24,520	C
St. Joseph's, Suffolk	NY	11,297	C
Stanford Univ	CA	37,612	MC
SUNY at Oswego	NY	12,650	C
SUNY at Potsdam	NY	12,160	C
SUNY/College at Brockport	NY	12,111	C
SUNY/College at Buffalo	NY	8,025	C
SUNY/College at Cortland	NY	12,095	C
SUNY/College at Fredonia	NY	11,562	VC
SUNY/College at Geneseo	NY	11,330	HC
SUNY/College at Oneonta	NY	11,870	VC
SUNY/College at Plattsburgh	NY	11,700	C
SUNY/Univ at Albany	NY	12,951	HC
SUNY/Univ at Binghamton	NY	12,787	HC
SUNY/Univ at Buffalo	NY	12,563	VC
SUNY/Univ at New Paltz	NY	11,565	VC
SUNY/Univ at Stony Brook	NY	12,763	HC
State Univ of West Georgia	GA	7,622	C
Stephen F. Austin State Univ	TX	7,552	C
Stephens College	MO	24,260	C+
Sterling College	KS	18,763	C
Stetson Univ	FL	29,495	VC
Stillman College	AL	11,370	LC
Stonehill College	MA	30,752	HC
Suffolk Univ	MA	29,200	C
Sul Ross State Univ	TX	6,582	LC
Susquehanna Univ	PA	29,990	VC
Sweet Briar College	VA	27,940	C
Syracuse Univ	NY	34,720	HC
Tabor College	KS	19,500	NC
Talladega College	AL	10,110	LC
Tarleton State Univ	TX	7,576	C
Taylor Univ	IN	23,820	VC+
Teikyo Post Univ	CT	24,875	C
Temple Univ	PA	15,912	C
Tenn State Univ	TN	9,048	LC
Tenn Tech Univ	TN	8,670	VC
Tenn Wesleyan College	TN	16,540	C
Texas A&M Univ	TX	11,081	HC

ST = STATE **$IS** = IN-STATE COSTS **SR** = SELECTOR RATING

School	ST	$IS	SR
Texas A&M Univ at Commerce	TX	8,994	C
Texas A&M Univ at Corpus Christi	TX	10,269	C
Texas A&M Univ at Kingsville	TX	6,740	LC
Texas Christian Univ	TX	23,410	VC
Texas Lutheran Univ	TX	20,370	C
Texas Southern Univ	TX	8,920	NC
Texas State Univ	TX	9,320	C
Texas Tech Univ	TX	10,768	VC
Texas Wesleyan Univ	TX	16,245	C
Texas Woman's Univ	TX	7,804	LC
Thiel College	PA	20,970	C
Thomas Edison State College	NJ	3,325	SP
Thomas More College	KY	21,350	C
Thomas Univ	GA	11,490	NC
Toccoa Falls College	GA	15,600	C
Tougaloo College	MS	9,200	NC
Touro College	NY	15,250	NC
Towson Univ	MD	12,694	VC
Transylvania Univ	KY	23,780	VC+
Trevecca Nazarene Univ	TN	17,548	C
Trinity Christian College	IL	21,640	VC
Trinity College	CT	38,040	HC+
Trinity College	DC	24,150	LC
Trinity International Univ	IL	22,980	C+
Trinity Univ	TX	26,466	VC
Troy State Univ	AL	7,696	C
Troy State Univ Dothan	AL	3,842	C
Troy State Univ Montgomery	AL	3,600	NC
Truman State Univ	MO	9,728	HC+
Tufts Univ	MA	38,233	MC
Tulane Univ	LA	37,451	HC+
Turabo Univ	PR	4,110	
Tusculum College	TN	19,990	C
Tuskegee Univ	AL	17,250	LC
Union College	KY	15,920	C
Union College	NE	17,130	C
Union College	NY	36,005	C
Union Univ	TN	18,800	VC
United States Air Force Academy	CO		HC+
United States Naval Academy	MD		MC
Univ of Akron	OH	13,134	NC
Univ of Alabama	AL	9,040	C+
Univ of Alabama at Birmingham	AL	12,901	C
Univ of Alabama in Huntsville	AL	9,126	VC
Univ of Alaska Anchorage	AK	9,100	NC
Univ of Alaska Fairbanks	AK	9,295	C
Univ of Arizona	AZ	10,413	VC
Univ of Arkansas	AR	9,855	VC
Univ of Arkansas at Little Rock	AR	5,637	NC
Univ of Arkansas at Monticello	AR	5,940	NC
Univ of Arkansas at Pine Bluff	AR	7,925	C
Univ of Bridgeport	CT	25,924	LC
Univ of Calif at Berkeley	CA	15,563	MC
Univ of Calif at Davis	CA	14,995	VC
Univ of Calif at Irvine	CA	19,808	VC
Univ of Calif at Los Angeles	CA	15,330	MC
Univ of Calif at Riverside	CA	15,300	C
Univ of Calif at Santa Barbara	CA	11,732	VC
Univ of Central Arkansas	AR	6,388	C
Univ of Central Florida	FL	10,038	VC
Univ of Central Okla	OK	9,434	C
Univ of Charleston	WV	23,620	C
Univ of Chicago	IL	35,087	MC
Univ of Cincinnati	OH	14,736	C
Univ of Colo at Boulder	CO	10,774	VC
Univ of Colo at Colo Springs	CO	10,667	C
Univ of Colo at Denver	CO	3,302	C
Univ of Conn	CT	14,608	VC
Univ of Dallas	TX	25,898	VC+
Univ of Dayton	OH	24,850	VC
Univ of Delaware	DE	12,616	HC
Univ of Denver	CO	32,148	VC
Univ of Detroit Mercy	MI	25,582	C
Univ of Dubuque	IA	20,950	C
Univ of Evansville	IN	24,190	VC
Univ of Findlay	OH	23,962	NC
Univ of Florida	FL	8,580	MC
Univ of Georgia	GA	8,656	VC
Univ of Great Falls	MT	15,360	C
Univ of Hartford	CT	31,080	C
Univ of Hawaii at Hilo	HI	6,497	C
Univ of Hawaii at Manoa	HI	9,565	VC
Univ of Houston	TX	9,818	VC
Univ of Houston-Downtown	TX	2,594	NC
Univ of Idaho	ID	8,216	C
Univ of Illinois at Urbana-Champaign	IL	11,316	HC+
Univ of Indianapolis	IN	22,560	VC
Univ of Iowa	IA	10,923	VC
Univ of Kansas	KS	8,923	VC
Univ of Kentucky	KY	7,765	VC
Univ of La Verne	CA	28,600	C
Univ of Louisiana at Lafayette	LA	5,826	C
Univ of Louisiana at Monroe	LA	5,207	NC
Univ of Louisville	KY	8,762	VC
Univ of Maine	ME	12,080	C+
Univ of Maine at Augusta	ME	4,065	C
Univ of Maine at Farmington	ME	10,108	C
Univ of Maine at Fort Kent	ME	9,770	LC
Univ of Maine at Machias	ME	9,271	LC
Univ of Maine at Presque Isle	ME	9,155	LC
Univ of Mary	ND	12,900	C+
Univ of Mary Hardin-Baylor	TX	17,268	C
Univ of Maryland/Baltimore County	MD	14,668	VC+
Univ of Maryland/College Park	MD	14,227	HC
Univ of Maryland/Eastern Shore	MD	9,964	C
Univ of Maryland/Univ College	MD	5,910	SP
Univ of Mass Amherst	MA	13,980	C+
Univ of Mass Boston	MA	6,227	C
Univ of Mass Dartmouth	MA	12,835	C
Univ of Mass Lowell	MA	11,937	VC
Univ of Memphis	TN	8,560	C
Univ of Miami	FL	34,608	NC
Univ of Mich/Ann Arbor	MI	13,864	HC+
Univ of Mich/Dearborn	MI	6,843	VC
Univ of Mich/Flint	MI	5,548	C
Univ of Minn/Duluth	MN	12,470	C
Univ of Minn/Morris	MN	12,896	VC
Univ of Minn/Twin Cities	MN	13,160	VC
Univ of Miss	MS	7,666	C
Univ of Missouri/Columbia	MO	13,782	VC
Univ of Missouri/Kansas City	MO	13,416	VC
Univ of Missouri/Rolla	MO	12,292	HC
Univ of Missouri/St. Louis	MO	11,656	VC
Univ of Mobile	AL	13,620	C
Univ of Montana	MT	9,395	C
Univ of Montevallo	AL	8,478	C
Univ of Nebr at Kearney	NE	8,286	NC
Univ of Nebr at Lincoln	NE	9,975	C+
Univ of Nebr at Omaha	NE	8,080	C
Univ of Nevada/Las Vegas	NV	11,566	C
Univ of Nevada/Reno	NV	9,792	C
Univ of New England	ME	27,200	LC
Univ of New Hampshire	NH	14,828	VC
Univ of New Haven	CT	28,650	C
Univ of New Mexico	NM	9,223	C
Univ of New Orleans	LA	7,356	C
Univ of North Alabama	AL	7,972	NC
Univ of N Car at Chapel Hill	NC	10,117	MC
Univ of N Car at Charlotte	NC	8,185	C
Univ of N Car at Greensboro	NC	8,248	C
Univ of N Car at Pembroke	NC	6,929	LC
Univ of N Car at Wilmington	NC	8,940	VC
Univ of N Dak	ND	8,390	C
Univ of North Florida	FL	8,769	VC
Univ of North Texas	TX	7,629	C
Univ of Northern Colo	CO	8,987	C
Univ of Northern Iowa	IA	9,834	C
Univ of Notre Dame	IN	34,442	MC
Univ of Okla	OK	9,226	VC
Univ of Oregon	OR	11,479	VC
Univ of Pennsylvania	PA	37,960	MC
Univ of Pittsburgh at Bradford	PA	15,294	C
Univ of Pittsburgh at Johnstown	PA	15,216	LC
Univ of Portland	OR	28,500	VC
Univ of PR at Humacao	PR	1,245	
Univ of PR/Cayey Univ College	PR	1,245	
Univ of PR/Mayaguez	PR		
Univ of PR/Rio Piedras	PR	5,730	
Univ of Puget Sound	WA	31,760	HC
Univ of Redlands	CA	32,576	VC
Univ of Rhode Island	RI	13,720	VC
Univ of Richmond	VA	30,100	MC
Univ of Rio Grande	OH	8,728	NC
Univ of Rochester	NY	32,979	HC
Univ of St. Francis	IL	22,850	C
Univ of St. Francis	IN	20,964	C
Univ of St. Mary	KS	18,868	C
Univ of St. Thomas	MN	26,918	VC
Univ of St. Thomas	TX	21,952	VC
Univ of San Diego	CA	33,156	HC
Univ of San Francisco	CA	34,700	VC
Univ of Science and Arts of Okla	OK	5,982	C
Univ of Scranton	PA	30,836	VC
Univ of Sioux Falls	SD	16,390	C
Univ of South Alabama	AL	7,760	LC
Univ of S Car at Aiken	SC	7,828	LC
Univ of S Car at Columbia	SC	10,048	NC
Univ of S Car at Spartanburg	SC	9,936	C+
Univ of S Dak	SD	7,710	C+
Univ of Southern Calif	CA	37,459	MC
Univ of Southern Colo	CO	7,821	LC
Univ of Southern Indiana	IN	9,025	LC
Univ of Southern Maine	ME	11,212	C
Univ of Southern Miss	MS	8,324	C
Univ of Tampa	FL	23,982	VC
Univ of Tenn at Chattanooga	TN	7,783	C
Univ of Tenn at Knoxville	TN	8,214	C
Univ of Tenn at Martin	TN	7,748	C
Univ of Texas at Arlington	TX	7,192	LC
Univ of Texas at Austin	TX	10,630	HC
Univ of Texas at El Paso	TX	5,799	NC
Univ of Texas at San Antonio	TX	9,088	NC
Univ of Texas-Pan American	TX	5,954	C
Univ of the District of Columbia	DC	2,070	LC
Univ of the Incarnate Word	TX	21,772	C
Univ of the Ozarks	AR	16,574	C
Univ of the Pacific	CA	31,090	VC
Univ of the South	TN	30,855	HC
Univ of Toledo	OH	12,479	NC
Univ of Tulsa	OK	22,090	VC+
Univ of Utah	UT	9,205	C
Univ of Vermont	VT	16,316	VC
Univ of Virginia	VA	11,740	MC
Univ of Virginia's College at Wise	VA	10,116	C
Univ of Washington	WA	10,361	VC
Univ of West Alabama	AL	6,048	C
Univ of West Florida	FL	8,470	C
Univ of Wisc/Eau Claire	WI	8,463	VC
Univ of Wisc/Green Bay	WI	8,154	C
Univ of Wisc/La Crosse	WI	8,991	VC
Univ of Wisc/Madison	WI	8,262	VC
Univ of Wisc/Milwaukee	WI	9,427	LC
Univ of Wisc/Oshkosh	WI	6,130	C
Univ of Wisc/Parkside	WI	6,160	LC
Univ of Wisc/Platteville	WI	8,450	C
Univ of Wisc/River Falls	WI	8,358	LC
Univ of Wisc/Stevens Point	WI	8,116	VC
Univ of Wisc/Superior	WI	7,051	C+
Univ of Wisc/Whitewater	WI	8,626	C
Univ of Wyoming	WY	8,636	C
Upper Iowa Univ	IA	20,076	C
Urbana Univ	OH	19,115	C
Ursinus College	PA	34,400	VC
Ursuline College	OH	22,728	LC
Utah State Univ	UT	7,371	C
Utica College	NY	28,340	C
Valdosta State Univ	GA	7,798	C
Valley City State Univ	ND	7,281	LC
Valparaiso Univ	IN	26,118	VC+
Vanderbilt Univ	TN	37,897	MC
Vanguard Univ of Southern Calif	CA	22,208	C
Vassar College	NY	37,030	MC
Villa Julie College	MD	18,393	C
Villanova Univ	PA	35,050	HC
Virginia Commonwealth Univ	VA	9,030	C
Virginia Intermont College	VA	19,800	C
Virginia Military Inst	VA	9,968	C+
Virginia Polytechnic Inst and State Univ	VA	9,179	C
Virginia Union Univ	VA	15,358	LC
Virginia Wesleyan College	VA	25,350	C
Viterbo Univ	WI	20,430	C
Voorhees College	SC	11,678	LC
Wabash College	IN	27,932	VC
Wagner College	NY	29,900	VC
Wake Forest Univ	NC	34,090	MC
Walla Walla College	WA	21,600	NC
Walsh Univ	OH	20,890	C
Warner Pacific College	OR	21,900	C
Warner Southern College	FL	16,738	LC
Warren Wilson College	NC	21,794	VC
Wartburg College	IA	21,165	VC
Washburn Univ of Topeka	KS	8,984	NC
Washington and Jefferson College	PA	29,570	VC
Washington and Lee Univ	VA	29,663	MC
Washington College	MD	30,540	VC
Washington State Univ	WA	11,334	C
Washington Univ in St. Louis	MO	38,293	MC
Wayland Baptist Univ	TX	11,919	NC
Wayne State College	NE	7,352	NC
Wayne State Univ	MI	11,774	C
Waynesburg College	PA	19,370	C
Weber State Univ	UT	7,945	NC
Webster Univ	MO	21,848	VC
Wellesley College	MA	36,516	MC
Wells College	NY	21,122	VC
Wesley College	DE	19,905	C
Wesleyan College	GA	17,870	VC
Wesleyan Univ	CT	35,139	MC
West Chester Univ of Pennsylvania	PA	11,164	C
West Liberty State College	WV	7,868	LC
West Texas A&M Univ	TX	7,533	C
West Virginia State College	WV	6,264	NC
West Virginia Univ	WV	9,370	C
West Virginia Wesleyan College	WV	22,920	C
Western Baptist College	OR	21,808	C
Western Carolina Univ	NC	6,742	C
Western Conn State Univ	CT	11,625	C
Western Illinois Univ	IL	10,363	C
Western Kentucky Univ	KY	6,834	C
Western Mich Univ	MI	12,031	C
Western New England College	MA	28,924	C
Western New Mexico Univ	NM	5,950	LC
Western Oregon Univ	OR	10,281	C
Western State College of Colo	CO	9,014	C
Western Washington Univ	WA	10,119	VC
Westfield State College	MA	10,147	C
Westminster College	MO	18,150	C+
Westminster College	PA	22,960	C
Westminster College	UT	17,226	C
Westmont College	CA	33,062	VC+
Wheaton College	IL	21,934	HC
Wheaton College	MA	36,330	HC
Wheeling Jesuit Univ	WV	22,660	C
Whitman College	WA	32,526	HC+
Whittier College	CA	29,108	C
Whitworth College	WA	26,428	VC+
Wichita State Univ	KS	8,092	C
Widener Univ	PA	27,020	C
Wiley College	TX	8,100	C
Wilkes Univ	PA	28,060	C
Willamette Univ	OR	32,032	VC+
William Carey College	MS	10,150	LC
William Jewell College	MO	21,320	VC
William Paterson Univ of New Jersey	NJ	14,450	C
William Penn Univ	IA	17,575	LC
William Tyndale College	MI	12,170	NC
William Woods Univ	MO	20,120	C
Williams Baptist College	AR	11,950	C
Williams College	MA	32,270	MC
Wilmington College	OH	24,172	LC
Wilson College	PA	23,912	C
Wingate Univ	NC	21,200	C
Winona State Univ	MN		C
Winston-Salem State Univ	NC	8,926	LC
Winthrop Univ	SC	11,302	C
Wisc Lutheran College	WI	21,430	VC
Wittenberg Univ	OH	31,316	VC
Wofford College	SC	26,710	HC
Worcester State College	MA	10,005	C
Wright State Univ	OH	11,490	LC
Xavier Univ	OH	26,850	VC+
Xavier Univ of Louisiana	LA	17,600	C
Yale Univ	CT	37,000	MC
Yeshiva Univ	NY	21,400	C
York College	NE	14,975	C
York College of Pennsylvania	PA	14,500	VC
Youngstown State Univ	OH	11,148	NC

ENGLISH AS A SECOND/FOREIGN LANGUAGE

School	ST	$IS	SR
Doane College	NE	20,000	C
Eastern Mich Univ	MI	11,478	C
Holy Names College	CA	27,980	NC
La Sierra Univ	CA	19,260	LC
Liberty Univ	VA	17,220	C
Maryville College	TN	25,960	VC
Salem International Univ	WV	19,770	C
Simmons College	MA	33,000	VC
Union Univ	TN	18,800	VC
Univ of Findlay	OH	23,962	NC
Univ of Hawaii at Manoa	HI	9,565	VC
Univ of Nebr at Lincoln	NE	9,975	C+

ENGLISH EDUCATION

School	ST	$IS	SR
Adams State College	CO	7,468	C
Adelphi Univ	NY	26,300	VC
Alabama State Univ	AL	6,404	C
Alfred Univ	NY	28,290	C
Andrews Univ	MI	19,550	C
Arkansas State Univ	AR	8,450	C
Asbury College	KY	20,704	VC
Ashland Univ	OH	24,464	C
Auburn Univ	AL	10,396	VC
Averett Univ	VA	23,010	LC
Baylor Univ	TX	23,864	VC
Bennett College	NC	11,200	C
Bethany College	KS	18,675	LC
Bethany College	WV	19,845	VC
Bethel College	IN	19,670	C
Bethune-Cookman College	FL	16,480	VC
Blackburn College	IL	13,690	C
Blue Mountain College	MS	10,226	C
Boise State Univ	ID	7,657	LC
Boston Univ	MA	38,194	HC+
Bowie State Univ	MD	10,873	C+
Brigham Young Univ	UT	8,504	HC
Brigham Young Univ/Hawaii	HI	7,240	VC+
Calif Univ of Pennsylvania	PA	10,388	C
Canisius College	NY	28,163	C+
Carthage College	WI	25,000	C
Catholic Univ of America	DC	34,248	VC
Central Missouri State Univ	MO	9,776	C
Central Univ of Bayamon	PR	3,335	
Central Washington Univ	WA	9,768	C
CUNY/Brooklyn College	NY	4,353	C+
CUNY/City College	NY	4,230	C+

School	ST	$IS	SR
Claflin Univ	SC	14,838	C+
Coker College	SC	21,491	C
Colby-Sawyer College	NH	27,850	LC
College of New Jersey	NJ	15,950	MC
College of St. Rose	NY	22,864	C
College of Santa Fe	NM	25,293	C+
College of the Ozarks	MO	3,500	VC+
Columbia Union College	MD	20,543	C
Concordia Univ/St.Paul	MN	24,486	C
Cumberland College	KY	16,384	C
Daemen College	NY	22,120	C
Dakota State Univ	SD	7,466	C
Dana College	NE	20,280	C
Delta State Univ	MS	6,618	C
Duquesne Univ	PA	26,907	VC
East Carolina Univ	NC	8,671	C
East Central Univ	OK	4,968	C
East Texas Baptist Univ	TX	13,914	C
Eastern Mich Univ	MI	11,478	C
Eastern Univ	PA	24,020	C
Edinboro Univ of Pennsylvania	PA	10,850	LC
Emory & Henry College	VA	21,950	C
Florida Atlantic Univ	FL	8,543	C
Florida International Univ	FL	9,912	VC
Florida State Univ	FL	9,028	HC
Franklin College	IN		C
Fresno Pacific Univ	CA	22,462	C
Friends Univ	KS	15,962	LC
Georgia Southwestern State Univ	GA	6,013	C
Grace College	IN	19,825	VC
Grambling State Univ	LA	6,538	NC
Green Mountain College	VT	24,130	C
Greensboro College	NC	21,750	C
Greenville College	IL	21,342	C
Hofstra Univ	NY	27,112	VC
Hood College	MD	27,795	VC
Humboldt State Univ	CA	9,400	C
Huntington College	IN	23,590	C
Indiana Univ of Pennsylvania	PA	10,489	C
Indiana Univ South Bend	IN	4,571	LC
Indiana Univ Southeast	IN	4,504	LC
Indiana Univ-Purdue Univ Indianapolis	IN	8,257	LC
Indiana Wesleyan Univ	IN	19,900	C+
Ithaca College	NY	31,730	HC
Johnson C. Smith Univ	NC	18,108	C
Johnson State College	VT	11,819	LC
Judson College	AL	14,650	C
Judson College	IL	22,050	LC
Juniata College	PA	29,080	VC
Kennesaw State Univ	GA	2,724	C
Kent State Univ	OH	12,932	C
La Roche College	PA	22,094	C
Le Moyne College	NY	26,400	VC
Limestone College	SC	17,700	C
Lincoln Univ	PA	13,320	C+
LIU/C.W. Post Campus	NY	28,282	C
Louisiana College	LA	13,450	C
Lyndon State College	VT	12,646	LC
Mansfield Univ	PA	11,220	C
Mary Baldwin College	VA	24,939	C
Messiah College	PA	25,890	VC+
MidAmerica Nazarene Univ	KS	18,688	C
Minot State Univ	ND	6,602	LC
Miss Valley State Univ	MS	6,765	NC
Missouri Southern State Univ	MO	8,316	C
Monmouth Univ	NJ	26,334	C
Morningside College	IA	21,610	C
Morris College	SC	10,974	LC
Mount Vernon Nazarene Univ	OH	18,925	C
Nazareth College of Rochester	NY	24,936	VC
Nebr Wesleyan Univ	NE	21,197	C+
New York Univ	NY	39,406	MC
Niagara Univ	NY	25,050	C
N Car Agricultural and Technical State Univ	NC	6,659	LC
Northwest Nazarene Univ	ID	20,360	VC
Northwestern College	MN	22,820	C+
Northwestern Okla State Univ	OK	5,433	NC
Oakwood College	AL	14,904	C
Okla Christian Univ	OK	17,690	NC
Okla Panhandle State Univ	OK	5,370	C
Okla Wesleyan Univ	OK	14,100	LC
Old Dominion Univ	VA	10,441	C
Oral Roberts Univ	OK	18,490	C
Palm Beach Atlantic Univ	FL	20,690	C
Philander Smith College	AR	7,380	NC
Providence College	RI	30,604	HC
Purdue Univ/West Lafayette	IN	12,560	VC
Rider Univ	NJ	30,900	C
Rivier College	NH	26,217	C
Rocky Mountain College	MT	19,015	C
Rust College	MS	8,200	C+
Saginaw Valley State Univ	MI	11,055	C
St. Augustine's College	NC	12,990	LC
St. Edward's Univ	TX	20,428	C
St. John Fisher College	NY	24,870	C
St. John's Univ	NY	30,180	C
St. Mary's Univ of Minn	MN	21,535	C
Schreiner Univ	TX	20,440	C
Seattle Pacific Univ	WA	25,944	VC
Seton Hill Univ	PA	24,930	C
Shaw Univ	NC	14,882	C+
Shepherd College	WV	8,608	C
Southeast Missouri State Univ	MO	9,704	C
Southeastern Louisiana Univ	LA	6,791	LC
Southern New Hampshire Univ	NH	26,242	C
Southern Univ at New Orleans	LA	995	NC
Southern Utah Univ	UT	8,194	C
Southwestern College	KS	19,560	C
Southwestern Okla State Univ	OK	4,801	C
SUNY at Potsdam	NY	12,160	C
SUNY/College at Oneonta	NY	11,870	VC
SUNY/College at Plattsburgh	NY	11,700	C
SUNY/Univ at Albany	NY	12,951	HC
Syracuse Univ	NY	34,720	HC
Taylor Univ	IN	23,820	VC+
Temple Univ	PA	15,912	C
Texas Christian Univ	TX	23,410	VC
Texas Southern Univ	TX	8,920	NC
Toccoa Falls College	GA	15,600	C
Trevecca Nazarene Univ	TN	17,548	C
Tri-State Univ-Main Campus	IN	23,600	C
Troy State Univ	AL	7,696	C
Troy State Univ Dothan	AL	3,842	C
Turabo Univ	PR	4,110	
Union College	NE	17,130	C
Univ of Arkansas at Pine Bluff	AR	7,925	C
Univ of Central Florida	FL	10,038	VC
Univ of Central Okla	OK	9,434	C
Univ of Charleston	WV	23,620	C
Univ of Conn	CT	14,608	VC
Univ of Delaware	DE	12,616	HC
Univ of Evansville	IN	24,190	VC
Univ of Georgia	GA	8,656	VC
Univ of Illinois at Chicago	IL	13,418	C
Univ of Indianapolis	IN	22,560	VC
Univ of Louisiana at Lafayette	LA	5,826	C
Univ of Louisiana at Monroe	LA	5,207	NC
Univ of Mary	ND	12,900	C+
Univ of Maryland/College Park	MD	14,227	HC
Univ of Minn/Duluth	MN	12,470	C
Univ of Minn/Twin Cities	MN	13,160	VC
Univ of Miss	MS	7,666	C
Univ of New Hampshire	NH	14,828	VC
Univ of New Orleans	LA	7,356	C
Univ of N Car at Chapel Hill	NC	10,117	MC
Univ of N Car at Charlotte	NC	8,185	C
Univ of N Car at Greensboro	NC	8,248	C
Univ of N Car at Pembroke	NC	6,929	LC
Univ of Pittsburgh at Johnstown	PA	15,216	LC
Univ of Rio Grande	OH	8,728	NC
Univ of St. Francis	IN	20,964	C
Univ of S Car at Spartanburg	SC	9,936	C+
Univ of South Florida	FL	9,454	C
Univ of Vermont	VT	16,316	VC
Warner Southern College	FL	16,738	LC
Warren Wilson College	NC	21,794	VC
Wartburg College	IA	21,165	VC
Wesley College	DE	19,905	C
West Texas A&M Univ	TX	7,533	C
West Virginia Univ	WV	9,370	C
Western Carolina Univ	NC	6,742	C
Westmont College	CA	33,062	VC+
Whitworth College	WA	26,428	VC+
Wiley College	TX	8,100	LC
Wingate Univ	NC	21,200	C
Xavier Univ of Louisiana	LA	17,600	C
Youngstown State Univ	OH	11,148	NC

ENGLISH LITERATURE

School	ST	$IS	SR
Bard College	NY	37,352	HC+
Blackburn College	IL	13,690	C
Brandeis Univ	MA	38,198	MC
Chatham College	PA	27,266	C+
Christopher Newport Univ	VA	8,862	VC
CUNY/Hunter College	NY	6,729	C+
Claremont McKenna College	CA	36,880	MC
Columbia Univ/School of General Studies	NY	35,000	C
Dartmouth College	NH	37,770	MC
DePauw Univ	IN	31,500	HC
Dominican Univ of Calif	CA	31,670	C
Eastern Mich Univ	MI	11,478	C
Eastern Univ	PA	24,020	C
Edinboro Univ of Pennsylvania	PA	10,850	LC
Elmira College	NY	33,820	VC
Emory & Henry College	VA	21,950	C
Fairleigh Dickinson Univ/Metropolitan Campus	NJ	28,584	C
Hofstra Univ	NY	27,112	VC
Knox College	IL	30,294	VC+
Loras College	IA	24,233	C
Middlebury College	VT	38,100	MC
Mountain State Univ	WV	10,212	NC
New England College	NH	28,860	LC
New York Univ	NY	39,406	MC
Oral Roberts Univ	OK	18,490	C
Pfeiffer Univ	NC	18,980	C
Reed College	OR	36,950	MC
Rider Univ	NJ	30,900	C
St. Edward's Univ	TX	20,428	C
Simon's Rock College of Bard	MA	36,580	HC
Southern Illinois Univ Carbondale	IL	10,407	C
Southern New Hampshire Univ	NH	26,242	C
Swarthmore College	PA	37,716	MC
Syracuse Univ	NY	34,720	HC
Union Univ	TN	18,800	VC
Univ of Calif at San Diego	CA	14,127	HC
Univ of Montana--Western	MT	8,073	NC
Univ of New Hampshire	NH	14,828	VC
Univ of Pittsburgh at Greensburg	PA	15,984	C
Univ of Pittsburgh at Pittsburgh	PA	16,074	HC
Univ of South Florida	FL	9,454	C
Virginia State Univ	VA	10,358	C
Washington Univ in St. Louis	MO	38,293	MC

ENTOMOLOGY

School	ST	$IS	SR
Auburn Univ	AL	10,396	VC
Cal State, Stanislaus	CA	9,874	C
Cornell Univ	NY	38,253	MC
Iowa State Univ	IA	10,768	VC
Kansas State Univ	KS	8,728	VC
Mich State Univ	MI	11,933	VC
Ohio State Univ	OH	13,080	VC+
Okla State Univ	OK	9,216	VC
Oregon State Univ	OR	11,055	C
Purdue Univ/West Lafayette	IN	12,560	VC
SUNY/College of Environmental Science and Forestry	NY	14,167	VC
Texas A&M Univ	TX	11,081	HC
Univ of Calif at Davis	CA	14,995	VC
Univ of Calif at Riverside	CA	15,300	C
Univ of Delaware	DE	12,616	HC
Univ of Florida	FL	8,580	MC
Univ of Georgia	GA	8,656	VC
Univ of Idaho	ID	8,216	C
Univ of Wisc/Madison	WI	8,262	VC
Washington State Univ	WA	11,334	C

ENTREPRENEURIAL STUDIES

School	ST	$IS	SR
American International College	MA	24,690	LC
Antioch College	OH	29,269	C
Baylor Univ	TX	23,864	VC
Boston Univ	MA	38,194	HC+
Central Conn State Univ	CT	12,090	C
Davenport Univ	MI	11,636	NC
Duquesne Univ	PA	26,907	VC
Fairleigh Dickinson Univ/College at Florham	NJ	30,130	C
Fairleigh Dickinson Univ/Metropolitan Campus	NJ	28,584	C
Florida State Univ	FL	9,028	HC
Gallaudet Univ	DC	16,554	SP
Gannon Univ	PA	23,260	C
Hawaii Pacific Univ	HI	19,218	C
Hofstra Univ	NY	27,112	VC
Indiana Univ Bloomington	IN	12,389	VC
Johnson and Wales Univ	RI	22,965	LC
Messiah College	PA	25,890	VC+
Middle Tenn State Univ	TN	8,534	C
Mountain State Univ	WV	10,212	NC
Northern Mich Univ	MI	10,834	C
Northwood Univ	TX	20,135	LC
Palm Beach Atlantic Univ	FL	20,690	C
Quinnipiac Univ	CT	30,570	VC
St. Edward's Univ	TX	20,428	C
Seton Hill Univ	PA	24,930	C
Southern Adventist Univ	TN	17,080	C
Suffolk Univ	MA	29,200	C
Syracuse Univ	NY	34,720	HC
Temple Univ	PA	15,912	C
Texas Christian Univ	TX	23,410	VC
Univ of Arizona	AZ	10,413	VC
Univ of Charleston	WV	23,620	C
Univ of Hartford	CT	31,080	C
Univ of Illinois at Chicago	IL	13,418	C
Univ of Indianapolis	IN	22,560	VC
Univ of Miami	FL	34,608	HC
Univ of New Mexico	NM	9,223	C
Univ of N Dak	ND	8,390	C
Univ of North Texas	TX	7,629	C
Univ of Pennsylvania	PA	37,960	MC
Univ of St. Thomas	MN	26,918	VC
Univ of Texas at San Antonio	TX	9,088	NC
Univ of Vermont	VT	16,316	VC
Washington State Univ	WA	11,334	C
Washington Univ in St. Louis	MO	38,293	MC
Western Carolina Univ	NC	6,742	C
Wichita State Univ	KS	8,092	C
Xavier Univ	OH	26,850	VC+

ENVIRONMENTAL BIOLOGY

School	ST	$IS	SR
Arizona State Univ-Main	AZ	10,048	C
Averett Univ	VA	23,010	LC
Beloit College	WI	29,864	HC
Bennington College	VT	35,910	HC
Bethel College	IN	19,670	C
Boston Univ	MA	38,194	HC+
Brigham Young Univ	UT	8,504	HC
Cal State, Northridge	CA	7,757	LC
Columbia Univ/Columbia College	NY	38,590	MC
East Texas Baptist Univ	TX	13,914	C
Grand Canyon Univ	AZ	30,000	LC
Greenville College	IL	21,342	C
Heidelberg College	OH	20,266	NC
Lock Haven Univ of Pennsylvania	PA	11,098	LC
Mich State Univ	MI	11,933	VC
Montclair State Univ	NJ	13,790	C
Mount Union College	OH	21,120	C
Norfolk State Univ	VA	9,722	LC
Ohio Univ	OH	14,448	C
Plymouth State Univ	NH	12,298	LC
St. Mary's Univ of Minn	MN	21,535	C
SUNY at Potsdam	NY	12,160	C
SUNY/College of Environmental Science and Forestry	NY	14,167	VC
Taylor Univ	IN	23,820	VC+
Texas A&M Univ at Galveston	TX	9,948	C+
Unity College	ME	19,845	LC
Univ of Calif at Davis	CA	14,995	VC
Univ of Colo at Boulder	CO	10,774	VC
Univ of Dayton	OH	24,850	VC
Univ of La Verne	CA	28,600	C
Univ of Missouri/Rolla	MO	12,292	HC
Univ of New England	ME	27,200	LC
Univ of North Alabama	AL	7,972	NC
Western Carolina Univ	NC	6,742	C

ENVIRONMENTAL DESIGN

School	ST	$IS	SR
Art Center College of Design	CA	23,450	SP
Ball State Univ	IN	8,660	C
Bowling Green State Univ	OH	13,036	C
Brigham Young Univ	UT	8,504	HC
Hampshire College	MA	37,037	HC
Harvard Univ/Harvard College	MA	37,928	MC
Maryland Inst College of Art	MD	30,890	SP
Miami Univ	OH	15,033	HC
Montana State Univ-Bozeman	MT	9,515	C
New York Inst of Technology	NY	24,205	VC
N Car State Univ	NC	9,886	VC
N Dak State Univ	ND	8,435	C
Olivet Nazarene Univ	IL	20,480	C
Otis College of Art and Design	CA	23,420	SP
SUNY/College of Environmental Science and Forestry	NY	14,167	VC
SUNY/Univ at Buffalo	NY	12,563	VC
Syracuse Univ	NY	34,720	HC
Texas A&M Univ	TX	11,081	HC
Univ of Calif at Davis	CA	14,995	VC
Univ of Calif at Irvine	CA	19,808	HC
Univ of Colo at Boulder	CO	10,774	VC
Univ of Houston	TX	9,818	C
Univ of Mass Amherst	MA	13,980	C+
Univ of Minn/Twin Cities	MN	13,160	VC
Univ of New Mexico	NM	9,223	C
Univ of Okla	OK	9,226	VC
Univ of Pennsylvania	PA	37,960	MC
Univ of PR/Rio Piedras	PR	5,730	

ENVIRONMENTAL EDUCATION

School	ST	$IS	SR
Johnson State College	VT	11,819	LC
Messiah College	PA	25,890	VC+
Ohio State Univ	OH	13,080	VC+
Prescott College	AZ	13,430	C
SUNY/College of Environmental Science and Forestry	NY	14,167	VC
Unity College	ME	19,845	LC
West Virginia Univ	WV	9,370	C

ST = STATE $IS = IN-STATE COSTS SR = SELECTOR RATING

ENVIRONMENTAL ENGINEERING

School	ST	$IS	SR
Calif Polytechnic State Univ	CA	8,747	VC
Drexel Univ	PA	27,655	VC
Florida State Univ	FL	9,028	HC
Hofstra Univ	NY	27,112	VC
Humboldt State Univ	CA	9,400	C
Johns Hopkins Univ	MD	38,372	MC
Louisiana State Univ and A&M College	LA	9,126	VC
Manhattan College	NY	27,400	VC
Marietta College	OH	27,047	C
Marquette Univ	WI	27,594	VC
Mass Inst of Technology	MA	38,310	MC
Mass Maritime Academy	MA	10,472	C
Mercer Univ	GA	27,516	VC+
Mich Tech Univ	MI	13,235	VC
Montana Tech of The Univ of Montana	MT	9,314	NC
New Jersey Inst of Technology	NJ	16,396	VC
New Mexico Inst of Mining and Technology	NM	7,580	NC
New Mexico State Univ	NM	7,932	C
N Car State Univ	NC	9,886	VC
Northern Arizona Univ	AZ	9,002	C
Northwestern Univ	IL	37,491	MC
Old Dominion Univ	VA	10,441	C
Penn State Univ/Univ Park Campus	PA	15,646	HC
Rensselaer Polytechnic Inst	NY	37,579	HC+
Rice Univ	TX	27,550	MC
Roger Williams Univ	RI	30,296	C
San Diego State Univ	CA	10,321	C
Seattle Univ	WA	24,183	VC
S Dak State Univ	SD	7,782	C
Southern Methodist Univ	TX	34,210	HC
SUNY/College of Environmental Science and Forestry	NY	14,167	VC
SUNY/Univ at Buffalo	NY	12,563	VC
Stevens Inst of Technology	NJ	35,300	HC+
Suffolk Univ	MA	29,200	C
Syracuse Univ	NY	34,720	HC
Taylor Univ	IN	23,820	VC+
Tenn Tech Univ	TN	8,670	VC
Texas Tech Univ	TX	10,768	VC
Tulane Univ	LA	37,451	HC+
United States Air Force Academy	CO		HC+
United States Military Academy	NY		MC
Universidad Politecnica de PR	PR	5,370	
Univ of Calif at Berkeley	CA	15,563	MC
Univ of Calif at Irvine	CA	19,808	HC
Univ of Calif at Riverside	CA	15,300	C
Univ of Calif at San Diego	CA	14,127	HC
Univ of Central Florida	FL	10,038	VC
Univ of Colo at Boulder	CO	10,774	VC
Univ of Conn	CT	14,608	VC
Univ of Delaware	DE	12,616	HC
Univ of Florida	FL	8,580	MC
Univ of Miami	FL	34,608	HC
Univ of Mich/Ann Arbor	MI	13,864	HC+
Univ of Missouri/Rolla	MO	12,292	HC
Univ of New Hampshire	NH	14,828	VC
Univ of N Car at Chapel Hill	NC	10,117	MC
Univ of Notre Dame	IN	34,442	MC
Univ of Okla	OK	9,226	VC
Univ of Southern Calif	CA	37,459	MC
Univ of Utah	UT	9,205	C
Univ of Vermont	VT	16,316	VC
Wentworth Inst of Technology	MA	23,000	C
Wilkes Univ	PA	28,060	C

ENVIRONMENTAL ENGINEERING TECHNOLOGY

School	ST	$IS	SR
Cornell Univ	NY	38,253	MC
East Carolina Univ	NC	8,671	C
Inter American Univ of PR/Bayamon Univ College	PR	3,522	
Lake Superior State Univ	MI	9,034	LC
Mesa State College	CO	8,051	C
New York Inst of Technology	NY	24,205	VC
Rochester Inst of Technology	NY	29,217	VC+
Shawnee State Univ	OH	11,031	NC
Southwestern Okla State Univ	OK	4,801	C
Suffolk Univ	MA	29,200	C
Temple Univ	PA	15,912	C
Texas Southern Univ	TX	8,920	NC
Univ of Minn/Crookston	MN	9,626	NC
Univ of N Dak	ND	8,390	C

ENVIRONMENTAL GEOLOGY

School	ST	$IS	SR
Univ of Wyoming	WY	8,636	C

ENVIRONMENTAL HEALTH SCIENCE

School	ST	$IS	SR
Benedict College	SC	12,662	LC
Boise State Univ	ID	7,657	LC
Bowling Green State Univ	OH	13,036	C
Cal State, Sacramento	CA	9,543	C
Cal State, San Bernardino	CA	15,238	LC
CUNY/York College	NY	3,292	NC
Colo State Univ	CO	9,964	VC
Delaware State Univ	DE	8,104	LC
Dickinson College	PA	35,825	HC
East Carolina Univ	NC	8,671	C
East Central Univ	OK	4,968	C
East Tenn State Univ	TN	8,497	C
Eastern Kentucky Univ	KY	7,708	C
Illinois State Univ	IL	10,944	C+
Indiana State Univ	IN	10,719	LC
Indiana Univ of Pennsylvania	PA	10,489	C
Iowa Wesleyan College	IA	19,990	C
Miss Valley State Univ	MS	6,765	NC
Missouri Southern State Univ	MO	8,316	C
Oakland Univ	MI	10,800	C
Old Dominion Univ	VA	10,441	C
Oregon State Univ	OR	11,055	C
Purdue Univ/West Lafayette	IN	12,560	VC
Salisbury Univ	MD	12,664	VC
Springfield College	MA	24,520	C
Texas Southern Univ	TX	8,920	NC
Unity College	ME	19,845	LC
Univ of Arkansas at Little Rock	AR	5,637	NC
Univ of Calif at Davis	CA	14,995	VC
Univ of Georgia	GA	8,656	VC
Univ of Mich/Flint	MI	5,548	C
Univ of Missouri/Rolla	MO	12,292	HC
Univ of Southern Colo	CO	7,821	LC
Univ of Southern Maine	ME	11,212	C
Univ of Washington	WA	10,361	VC
Western Carolina Univ	NC	6,742	C
Wright State Univ	OH	11,490	LC

ENVIRONMENTAL SCIENCE

School	ST	$IS	SR
Abilene Christian Univ	TX	18,370	VC
Adrian College	MI	21,950	C
Alabama A&M Univ	AL	5,100	LC
Alaska Pacific Univ	AK	17,910	C
Albright College	PA	30,579	C
Alfred Univ	NY	28,290	C
Allegheny College	PA	30,280	VC
Alverno College	WI	18,898	C
American Univ	DC	34,585	VC+
Andrews Univ	MI	19,550	C
Antioch College	OH	29,269	C
Appalachian State Univ	NC	7,637	VC
Aquinas College	MI	21,894	C
Arcadia Univ	PA	29,890	C
Ashland Univ	OH	24,464	C
Assumption College	MA	29,375	C
Auburn Univ	AL	10,396	VC
Aurora Univ	IL	20,631	C
Austin Peay State Univ	TN	5,814	LC
Averett Univ	VA	23,010	LC
Bard College	NY	37,352	HC+
Barton College	NC	19,314	C
Bates College	ME	37,500	MC
Baylor Univ	TX	23,864	VC
Beloit College	WI	29,864	HC
Benedictine Univ	IL	23,840	C
Bennington College	VT	35,910	HC
Berry College	GA	21,410	VC
Bethel College	MN	25,180	VC
Boston College	MA	33,284	MC
Boston Univ	MA	38,194	HC+
Bowdoin College	ME	37,790	MC
Bowling Green State Univ	OH	13,036	C
Bradley Univ	IL	22,910	VC
Brenau Univ Women's College	GA	21,800	C
Briar Cliff Univ	IA	21,660	C
Bridgewater College	VA	25,150	C
Brown Univ	RI	38,174	MC
Bucknell Univ	PA	35,262	HC+
Cal State, Chico	CA	8,598	LC
Cal State, Hayward	CA	8,871	LC
Calif Univ of Pennsylvania	PA	10,388	C
Calvin College	MI	22,615	NC
Canisius College	NY	28,163	C+
Capital Univ	OH	26,550	C
Carroll College	MT	20,576	VC
Carroll College	WI	22,740	C
Case Western Reserve Univ	OH	32,002	MC
Castleton State College	VT	11,820	C
Catawba College	NC	20,500	C
Catholic Univ of America	DC	34,248	VC
Cedar Crest College	PA	25,145	C+
Centenary College of Louisiana	LA	23,100	VC+
Central College	IA	21,206	C
Central Methodist College	MO	16,460	C
Chapman Univ	CA	33,118	VC
Charleston Southern Univ	SC	17,122	C
Chatham College	PA	27,266	C+
Chestnut Hill College	PA	26,450	LC
Christopher Newport Univ	VA	8,862	VC
CUNY/Hunter College	NY	6,729	C+
CUNY/Medgar Evers College	NY	4,232	NC
CUNY/Queens College	NY	4,362	C
Claremont McKenna College	CA	36,880	MC
Clarion Univ of Pennsylvania	PA	11,272	LC
Clark Univ	MA	32,115	VC
Clarkson Univ	NY	32,226	VC
Cleveland State Univ	OH	12,308	LC
Coe College	IA	27,385	VC
Colby College	ME	37,570	MC
Colgate Univ	NY	37,095	MC
College of St. Rose	NY	22,864	C
College of Santa Fe	NM	25,293	C+
Colo College	CO	36,860	HC
Columbia Univ/Barnard College	NY	36,990	MC
Columbia Univ/Columbia College	NY	38,590	MC
Columbia Univ/School of General Studies	NY	35,000	C
Concordia College	NY	19,200	VC
Concordia College: Moorhead	MN	22,460	VC+
Concordia Univ	OR	22,450	C
Concordia Univ at Austin	TX	20,450	LC
Concordia Univ/St.Paul	MN	24,486	C
Conn College	CT	37,900	MC
Cornell College	IA	27,825	VC+
Creighton Univ	NE	26,748	VC+
Curry College	MA	26,025	LC
Dana College	NE	20,280	C
Dartmouth College	NH	37,770	MC
Davis and Elkins College	WV	20,594	C
De Sales Univ	PA	25,470	C
Defiance College	OH	22,615	C
Delta State Univ	MS	6,618	C
DePaul Univ	IL	27,580	VC
DePauw Univ	IN	31,500	HC
Dickinson College	PA	35,825	HC
Doane College	NE	20,000	C
Dominican Univ	IL	23,610	C
Dordt College	IA	20,170	VC
Drake Univ	IA	25,120	VC+
Drexel Univ	PA	27,655	VC
Drury Univ	MO	18,085	VC+
Duke Univ	NC	37,555	MC
Duquesne Univ	PA	26,907	VC
Earlham College	IN	29,976	VC+
East Stroudsburg Univ of Pennsylvania	PA	10,336	C
Eastern Conn State Univ	CT	10,362	C
Eastern Kentucky Univ	KY	7,708	C
Eastern Mennonite Univ	VA	22,990	C
Eastern Nazarene College	MA	19,433	LC
Edinboro Univ of Pennsylvania	PA	10,850	LC
Elizabethtown College	PA	28,800	C
Elmhurst College	IL	24,630	C
Elmira College	NY	33,820	VC
Elon Univ	NC	22,240	VC
Emory & Henry College	VA	21,950	C
Fairleigh Dickinson Univ/Metropolitan Campus	NJ	28,584	C
Ferrum College	VA	21,240	LC
Florida Inst of Technology	FL	28,740	VC
Florida International Univ	FL	9,912	VC
Florida Southern College	FL	23,592	C
Florida State Univ	FL	9,028	HC
Franklin and Marshall College	PA	35,930	HC+
Franklin Pierce College	NH	28,980	LC
Fresno Pacific Univ	CA	22,462	C
Friends Univ	KS	15,962	LC
Frostburg State Univ	MD	11,114	C
Furman Univ	SC	28,976	HC+
Gannon Univ	PA	23,260	C
George Washington Univ	DC	41,030	MC
Georgetown College	KY	22,000	VC
Georgia College and State Univ	GA	9,878	C
Gettysburg College	PA	35,646	HC
Goddard College	VT	21,056	C+
Goshen College	IN	22,450	VC
Hamline Univ	MN	27,052	VC
Hampshire College	MA	37,037	HC
Harvard Univ/Harvard College	MA	37,928	MC
Hawaii Pacific Univ	HI	19,218	C
Heritage College	WA	6,720	NC
Hiram College	OH	28,234	VC
Hobart and William Smith Colleges	NY	36,536	HC
Hood College	MD	27,795	VC
Houghton College	NY	23,984	VC
Humboldt State Univ	CA	9,400	C
Illinois College	IL	19,100	VC
Indiana Univ Bloomington	IN	12,389	VC
Iowa State Univ	IA	10,768	VC
Ithaca College	NY	31,730	HC
Jacksonville Univ	FL	24,040	C
Johns Hopkins Univ	MD	38,372	MC
Johnson State College	VT	11,819	LC
Juniata College	PA	29,080	VC
Keene State College	NH	12,212	C
Kettering Univ	MI	26,478	HC
Keuka College	NY	21,170	C
Keystone College	PA	21,405	LC
Knox College	IL	30,294	VC+
Kutztown Univ of Pennsylvania	PA	10,786	C
La Salle Univ	PA	31,260	VC
Lake Erie College	OH	23,550	C
Lake Forest College	IL	30,270	VC
Lake Superior State Univ	MI	9,034	LC
Lander Univ	SC	10,496	C
Lawrence Tech Univ	MI	20,487	C
Lawrence Univ	WI	30,900	HC
Lehigh Univ	PA	37,570	HC+
Lewis Univ	IL	22,950	C+
Lincoln Memorial Univ	TN	16,400	LC
Linfield College	OR	27,090	VC
Louisiana State Univ and A&M College	LA	9,126	VC
Louisiana State Univ in Shreveport	LA	2,884	NC
Louisiana Tech Univ	LA	7,361	C
Lourdes College	OH	15,300	LC
Loyola Marymount Univ	CA	32,194	VC
Lubbock Christian Univ	TX	15,832	C
Lynchburg College	VA	26,815	C
Macalester College	MN	31,944	MC
Mansfield Univ	PA	11,220	C
Marian College	IN	23,030	C
Marietta College	OH	27,047	C
Marist College	NY	27,596	VC
Marshall Univ	WV	9,116	C
Martin Univ	IN	10,200	SP
Mary Washington College	VA	10,166	HC
Marygrove College	MI	17,550	C
Marymount Univ	VA	23,668	C
Maryville Univ of St. Louis	MO	22,090	VC
Marywood Univ	PA	26,050	C
McMurry Univ	TX	17,846	LC
McNeese State Univ	LA	5,259	LC
Mercyhurst College	PA	20,694	C
Merrimack College	MA	29,625	C
Messiah College	PA	25,890	VC+
Metropolitan State College of Denver	CO	2,338	LC
Miami Univ	OH	15,033	HC
Middle Tenn State Univ	TN	8,534	C
Middlebury College	VT	38,100	MC
Midway College	KY	15,815	C
Midwestern State Univ	TX	8,045	LC
Miles College	AL	7,870	NC
Mills College	CA	33,371	VC
Minn State Univ, Mankato	MN	8,803	LC
Molloy College	NY	15,180	C
Monmouth College	IL	23,600	C
Montana State Univ-Billings	MT	9,550	C
Montana State Univ-Bozeman	MT	9,515	C
Montana State Univ-Northern	MT	8,600	NC
Montreat College	NC	18,762	C
Mount Marty College	SD	15,656	LC
Mount Olive College	NC	14,410	LC
Muhlenberg College	PA	31,485	HC
Muskingum College	OH	20,680	C
Naropa Univ	CO	23,364	SP
Nazareth College of Rochester	NY	24,936	VC
New College of Florida	FL	8,906	HC+
New England College	NH	28,860	LC
New Jersey Inst of Technology	NJ	16,396	VC
New Mexico Highlands Univ	NM	6,182	LC
New Mexico Inst of Mining and Technology	NM	7,580	NC
New Mexico State Univ	NM	7,932	C
N Car Central Univ	NC	7,534	LC
N Car State Univ	NC	9,886	VC
N Car Wesleyan College	NC	17,998	C
Northern State Univ	SD	7,117	LC
Northland College	WI	22,170	C+
Northwest College	WA	18,854	C
Northwestern Univ	IL	37,491	MC
Norwich Univ	VT	21,064	LC
Notre Dame College	OH	20,425	C
Oberlin College	OH	36,938	MC
Occidental College	CA	35,922	HC
Ohio State Univ	OH	13,080	VC+
Ohio Wesleyan Univ	OH	32,550	VC+
Okla State Univ	OK	9,216	VC
Olivet College	MI	19,984	C+
Olivet Nazarene Univ	IL	20,480	C
Oregon Inst of Technology	OR	8,718	C
Oregon State Univ	OR	11,055	C
Pacific Lutheran Univ	WA	25,715	VC
Pfeiffer Univ	NC	18,980	C
Philadelphia Univ	PA	27,354	C
Piedmont College	GA	16,900	C
Pitzer College	CA	37,590	HC
Point Park Univ	PA	21,840	C
Portland State Univ	OR	12,453	C

ST = STATE $IS = IN-STATE COSTS SR = SELECTOR RATING

School	ST	$IS	SR
Prescott College	AZ	13,430	C
Principia College	IL	25,044	C+
Ramapo College of New Jersey	NJ	15,203	VC
Richard Stockton College of New Jersey	NJ	12,972	VC
Rider Univ	NJ	30,900	C
Ripon College	WI	24,995	VC
Roanoke College	VA	27,393	C
Rochester Inst of Technology	NY	29,217	VC+
Roger Williams Univ	RI	30,296	C
Rollins College	FL	34,300	VC
Roosevelt Univ	IL	22,580	VC
Rosemont College	PA	26,175	C
Russell Sage College	NY	26,811	C
Rutgers, The State Univ of New Jersey/New Brunswick/Piscataway Campus	NJ	15,800	HC
Rutgers, The State Univ of New Jersey/Newark Campus	NJ	15,624	VC
Sacred Heart Univ	CT	29,178	C
Saginaw Valley State Univ	MI	11,055	C
St. Anselm College	NH	30,250	C
St. Bonaventure Univ	NY	24,455	LC
St. John's Univ	NY	30,180	C
St. Joseph College	CT	29,685	C
St. Joseph's College	IN	24,250	C
St. Joseph's College of Maine	ME	25,600	C
St. Joseph's Univ	PA	33,590	VC
St. Lawrence Univ	NY	35,945	VC
St. Leo Univ	FL	20,600	C
St. Louis Univ	MO	29,780	VC+
St. Michael's College	VT	30,100	VC
St. Norbert College	WI	25,810	VC
St. Paul's College	VA	14,344	NC
St. Vincent College	PA	25,530	VC
Salem International Univ	WV	19,770	C
Sam Houston State Univ	TX	7,142	C
Samford Univ	AL	18,648	VC
Santa Clara Univ	CA	34,701	HC
Savannah State Univ	GA	7,328	LC
Scripps College	CA	35,700	HC+
Shaw Univ	NC	14,882	C+
Shenandoah Univ	VA	25,190	NC
Shepherd College	WV	8,608	C
Shippensburg Univ of Pennsylvania	PA	10,826	C
Siena College	NY	25,310	VC
Sierra Nevada College	NV	26,136	C
Simmons College	MA	33,000	VC
Simpson College	IA	23,658	C+
Skidmore College	NY	37,930	HC
Sonoma State Univ	CA	10,421	C
Southeast Missouri State Univ	MO	9,704	C
Southern Vermont College	VT	18,226	LC
Spring Hill College	AL	25,868	VC
SUNY/College at Brockport	NY	12,111	C
SUNY/College at Cortland	NY	12,095	C
SUNY/College at Oneonta	NY	11,870	VC
SUNY/College at Plattsburgh	NY	11,700	C
SUNY/College at Purchase	NY	10,587	VC
SUNY/Maritime College	NY	10,025	LC
SUNY/Univ at Binghamton	NY	12,787	HC
State Univ of West Georgia	GA	7,622	C
Stephen F. Austin State Univ	TX	7,552	C
Stephens College	MO	24,260	C+
Stetson Univ	FL	29,495	VC
Suffolk Univ	MA	29,200	C
Sul Ross State Univ	TX	6,582	LC
Susquehanna Univ	PA	29,990	VC
Sweet Briar College	VA	27,940	C
Syracuse Univ	NY	34,720	HC
Taylor Univ	IN	23,820	VC+
Temple Univ	PA	15,912	C
Texas A&M Univ	TX	11,081	HC
Texas A&M Univ at Corpus Christi	TX	10,269	C
Texas A&M Univ at Galveston	TX	9,948	C+
Texas Christian Univ	TX	23,410	VC
Texas State Univ	TX	9,320	VC
Thiel College	PA	20,970	C
Thomas Edison State College	NJ	3,325	SP
Towson Univ	MD	12,694	VC
Trinity College	CT	38,040	HC+
Trinity College	DC	24,150	LC
Tri-State Univ-Main Campus	IN	23,600	C
Tufts Univ	MA	38,233	MC
Tulane Univ	LA	37,451	HC+
Tusculum College	TN	19,990	C
Unity College	ME	19,845	LC
Univ of Alabama	AL	9,040	C+
Univ of Alaska Fairbanks	AK	9,295	C
Univ of Alaska Southeast	AK	7,900	LC
Univ of Arizona	AZ	10,413	VC
Univ of Arkansas	AR	9,855	VC
Univ of Calif at Berkeley	CA	15,563	MC
Univ of Calif at Davis	CA	14,995	VC
Univ of Calif at Riverside	CA	15,300	C
Univ of Calif at San Diego	CA	14,127	HC
Univ of Calif at Santa Barbara	CA	11,732	VC
Univ of Central Arkansas	AR	6,388	C
Univ of Charleston	WV	23,620	C
Univ of Chicago	IL	35,087	MC
Univ of Colo at Boulder	CO	10,774	VC
Univ of Conn	CT	14,608	VC
Univ of Delaware	DE	12,616	HC
Univ of Denver	CO	32,148	VC
Univ of Dubuque	IA	20,950	C
Univ of Evansville	IN	24,190	VC
Univ of Findlay	OH	23,962	NC
Univ of Georgia	GA	8,656	VC
Univ of Hawaii at Manoa	HI	9,565	VC
Univ of Illinois at Urbana-Champaign	IL	11,316	HC+
Univ of Indianapolis	IN	22,560	VC
Univ of Iowa	IA	10,923	VC
Univ of La Verne	CA	28,600	C
Univ of Maine	ME	12,080	C+
Univ of Maine at Farmington	ME	10,108	C
Univ of Maine at Fort Kent	ME	9,770	LC
Univ of Maine at Machias	ME	9,271	LC
Univ of Maine at Presque Isle	ME	9,155	LC
Univ of Maryland/Baltimore County	MD	14,668	VC+
Univ of Maryland/College Park	MD	14,227	HC
Univ of Maryland/Eastern Shore	MD	9,964	C
Univ of Maryland/Univ College	MD	5,910	SP
Univ of Mass Amherst	MA	13,980	C+
Univ of Mass Lowell	MA	11,937	VC
Univ of Miami	FL	34,608	HC
Univ of Mich/Ann Arbor	MI	13,864	HC+
Univ of Mich/Dearborn	MI	6,843	VC
Univ of Minn/Duluth	MN	12,470	C
Univ of Missouri/Kansas City	MO	13,416	VC
Univ of Montana--Western	MT	8,073	NC
Univ of Nebr at Lincoln	NE	9,975	C+
Univ of Nevada/Las Vegas	NV	11,566	C
Univ of Nevada/Reno	NV	9,792	C
Univ of New England	ME	27,200	LC
Univ of New Hampshire	NH	14,828	VC
Univ of New Haven	CT	28,650	C
Univ of N Car at Asheville	NC	8,079	VC
Univ of N Car at Chapel Hill	NC	10,117	MC
Univ of N Car at Wilmington	NC	8,940	VC
Univ of Notre Dame	IN	34,442	MC
Univ of Okla	OK	9,226	VC
Univ of Oregon	OR	11,479	VC
Univ of Pennsylvania	PA	37,960	MC
Univ of Pittsburgh at Bradford	PA	15,294	C
Univ of Pittsburgh at Pittsburgh	PA	16,074	HC
Univ of Portland	OR	28,500	VC
Univ of Redlands	CA	32,576	VC
Univ of Rhode Island	RI	13,720	VC
Univ of Rio Grande	OH	8,728	NC
Univ of Rochester	NY	32,979	HC
Univ of St. Francis	IL	22,850	C
Univ of St. Francis	IN	20,964	C
Univ of St. Thomas	MN	26,918	VC
Univ of St. Thomas	TX	21,952	VC
Univ of San Francisco	CA	34,700	VC
Univ of Scranton	PA	30,836	VC
Univ of South Florida	FL	9,454	C
Univ of Southern Calif	CA	37,459	MC
Univ of Southern Maine	ME	11,212	C
Univ of Tampa	FL	23,982	VC
Univ of Tenn at Chattanooga	TN	7,783	C
Univ of Tenn at Knoxville	TN	8,214	C
Univ of the District of Columbia	DC	2,070	LC
Univ of the Incarnate Word	TX	21,772	LC
Univ of the Ozarks	AR	16,574	C
Univ of the Pacific	CA	31,090	VC
Univ of the Sciences in Philadelphia	PA	29,310	VC
Univ of Toledo	OH	12,479	NC
Univ of Vermont	VT	16,316	VC
Univ of Virginia	VA	11,740	MC
Univ of Virginia's College at Wise	VA	10,116	C
Univ of West Alabama	AL	6,048	C
Univ of Wisc/Green Bay	WI	8,154	C
Ursinus College	PA	34,400	VC
Utah State Univ	UT	7,371	C
Valdosta State Univ	GA	7,798	C
Valparaiso Univ	IN	26,118	VC+
Virginia Polytechnic Inst and State Univ	VA	9,179	C
Walla Walla College	WA	21,600	NC
Washington and Lee Univ	VA	29,663	MC
Washington College	MD	30,540	VC
Washington State Univ	WA	11,334	C
Washington Univ in St. Louis	MO	38,293	MC
Waynesburg College	PA	19,370	C
Weber State Univ	UT	7,945	NC
Webster Univ	MO	21,848	VC
Wesley College	DE	19,905	C
West Texas A&M Univ	TX	7,533	C
West Virginia Univ	WV	9,370	C
Western Conn State Univ	CT	11,625	C
Western Kentucky Univ	KY	6,834	C
Western Washington Univ	WA	10,119	VC
Westfield State College	MA	10,147	C
Westminster College	MO	18,150	C+
Wheaton College	IL	21,934	HC
Wheaton College	MA	36,330	HC
Wheeling Jesuit Univ	WV	22,660	C
Whitman College	WA	32,526	HC+
Whitworth College	WA	26,428	VC+
Widener Univ	PA	27,020	C
Willamette Univ	OR	32,032	VC+
William Paterson Univ of New Jersey	NJ	14,450	C
William Penn Univ	IA	17,575	LC
Wilson College	PA	23,912	C
Youngstown State Univ	OH	11,148	NC

ENVIRONMENTAL STUDIES

School	ST	$IS	SR
Adelphi Univ	NY	26,300	VC
Albertson College of Idaho	ID	19,415	VC
Allegheny College	PA	30,280	VC
Boston Univ	MA	38,194	HC+
Brenau Univ Women's College	GA	21,800	C
Brigham Young Univ	UT	8,504	HC
Cal State, Hayward	CA	8,871	LC
Cal State, San Bernardino	CA	15,238	LC
Catawba College	NC	20,500	C
Chaminade Univ of Honolulu	HI	21,430	LC
Chatham College	PA	27,266	C+
CUNY/Queens College	NY	4,362	C
Claremont McKenna College	CA	36,880	MC
Colby-Sawyer College	NH	27,850	LC
College of New Rochelle	NY	21,800	C
College of St. Benedict	MN	26,672	VC
College of Santa Fe	NM	25,293	C+
College of the Holy Cross	MA	36,451	MC
Columbia College	MO	16,139	C
Denison Univ	OH	33,050	HC
Dominican Univ of Calif	CA	31,670	C
Eastern Univ	PA	24,020	C
Eckerd College	FL	28,744	C+
Endicott College	MA	25,266	C+
Florida State Univ	FL	9,028	HC
Franklin and Marshall College	PA	35,930	HC+
Green Mountain College	VT	24,130	C
Guilford College	NC	24,960	VC
Gustavus Adolphus College	MN	27,120	VC+
Hendrix College	AR	20,970	VC+
Hofstra Univ	NY	27,112	VC
Indiana Univ Bloomington	IN	12,389	VC
Indiana Univ South Bend	IN	4,571	LC
Juniata College	PA	29,080	VC
King's College	PA	26,990	C
Lewis and Clark College	OR	30,620	VC
Lyon College	AR	17,995	VC
Maharishi Univ of Management	IA	29,230	VC
Marietta College	OH	27,047	C
Maryville College	TN	25,960	VC
Maryville Univ of St. Louis	MO	22,090	VC
Meredith College	NC	23,065	C
Mich State Univ	MI	11,933	VC
Mills College	CA	33,371	VC
Mount Holyoke College	MA	37,918	HC+
Mountain State Univ	WV	10,212	NC
Neumann College	PA	23,890	LC
Northeastern Illinois Univ	IL	2,898	NC
Ohio Northern Univ	OH	27,765	VC
Penn State Univ/Altoona	PA	12,578	C
Pennsylvania College of Technology	PA	15,126	NC
Piedmont College	GA	16,900	C
Prescott College	AZ	13,430	C
Ramapo College of New Jersey	NJ	15,203	VC
Randolph-Macon College	VA	27,190	C
Randolph-Macon Woman's College	VA	28,430	VC+
Roanoke College	VA	27,393	C
St. John's Univ	MN	26,473	VC
St. Olaf College	MN	28,500	HC
Salisbury Univ	MD	12,664	VC
Santa Clara Univ	CA	34,701	HC
Southeastern Okla State Univ	OK	6,147	C
Southwestern Univ	TX	25,410	HC
SUNY/College at Brockport	NY	12,111	C
SUNY/College of Environmental Science and Forestry	NY	14,167	VC
SUNY/Univ at Stony Brook	NY	12,763	HC
State Univ of West Georgia	GA	7,622	C
Sweet Briar College	VA	27,940	C
Temple Univ	PA	15,912	C
Texas A&M Univ at Galveston	TX	9,948	C+
Thomas Edison State College	NJ	3,325	SP
Union College	NY	36,005	HC
Univ of Calif at San Diego	CA	14,127	HC
Univ of Calif at Santa Cruz	CA	16,505	VC
Univ of Kansas	KS	8,923	VC
Univ of Maryland/Baltimore County	MD	14,668	VC+
Univ of Montana	MT	9,395	C
Univ of Nebr at Lincoln	NE	9,975	C+
Univ of N Car at Chapel Hill	NC	10,117	MC
Univ of Pennsylvania	PA	37,960	MC
Univ of Pittsburgh at Johnstown	PA	15,216	LC
Univ of Puget Sound	WA	31,760	HC
Univ of Rochester	NY	32,979	HC
Univ of St. Thomas	MN	26,918	VC
Univ of the South	TN	30,855	HC
Univ of Tulsa	OK	22,090	VC+
Univ of Vermont	VT	16,316	VC
Vassar College	NY	37,030	MC
Warren Wilson College	NC	21,794	VC
Washington Univ in St. Louis	MO	38,293	MC
Wellesley College	MA	36,516	MC
Wells College	NY	21,122	VC
Western Mich Univ	MI	12,031	C

EQUINE SCIENCE

School	ST	$IS	SR
Averett Univ	VA	23,010	LC
Centenary College	NJ	25,370	LC
Colo State Univ	CO	9,964	VC
Johnson and Wales Univ	RI	22,965	LC
Lake Erie College	OH	23,550	C
Midway College	KY	15,815	C
Mount Ida College	MA	25,596	LC
N Dak State Univ	ND	8,435	C
Otterbein College	OH	26,085	C
Rocky Mountain College	MT	19,015	C
St. Mary-of-the-Woods College	IN	23,280	C
Salem International Univ	WV	19,770	C
Stephens College	MO	24,260	C+
Sul Ross State Univ	TX	6,582	LC
Truman State Univ	MO	9,728	HC+
Univ of Findlay	OH	23,962	NC
Univ of Louisville	KY	8,762	VC
Univ of New Hampshire	NH	14,828	VC
Virginia Intermont College	VA	19,800	C
William Woods Univ	MO	20,120	C
Wilson College	PA	23,912	C

ESKIMO

School	ST	$IS	SR
Univ of Alaska Fairbanks	AK	9,295	C

ETHICS, POLITICS, AND SOCIAL POLICY

School	ST	$IS	SR
Bloomsburg Univ of Pennsylvania	PA	10,844	C
Drake Univ	IA	25,120	VC+
Indiana Univ Bloomington	IN	12,389	VC
Mount Holyoke College	MA	37,918	HC+
Northwestern Univ	IL	37,491	MC
Pine Manor College	MA	22,138	LC
Simon's Rock College of Bard	MA	36,580	HC
Syracuse Univ	NY	34,720	HC
Univ of Judaism College of A&S	CA	24,230	C
Univ of Mass Amherst	MA	13,980	C+
Univ of Mass Boston	MA	6,227	C
Wells College	NY	21,122	VC
Wheeling Jesuit Univ	WV	22,660	C
Yale Univ	CT	37,000	MC

ETHNIC STUDIES

School	ST	$IS	SR
Bethel College	MN	25,180	VC
Bowling Green State Univ	OH	13,036	C
Brown Univ	RI	38,174	MC
Cal State, Chico	CA	8,598	LC
Cal State, Hayward	CA	8,871	LC
Cal State, San Bernardino	CA	15,238	LC
Cal State, Stanislaus	CA	9,874	C
CUNY/City College	NY	4,230	C+
College of St. Catherine	MN	24,010	VC
Drew Univ/College of Liberal Arts	NJ	35,550	VC
Kent State Univ	OH	12,932	C
Metropolitan State Univ	MN	3,852	SP
Mills College	CA	33,371	VC
Minn State Univ, Mankato	MN	8,803	LC
St. Olaf College	MN	28,500	HC
Sonoma State Univ	CA	10,421	C
SUNY/College at Purchase	NY	10,587	VC
SUNY/Univ at Stony Brook	NY	12,763	HC
Univ of Alaska Fairbanks	AK	9,295	C
Univ of Arizona	AZ	10,413	VC

ST = STATE $IS = IN-STATE COSTS SR = SELECTOR RATING

School	ST	$IS	SR
Univ of Calif at Berkeley	CA	15,563	MC
Univ of Calif at Riverside	CA	15,300	C
Univ of Calif at San Diego	CA	14,127	HC
Univ of Colo at Boulder	CO	10,774	VC
Univ of Hawaii at Manoa	HI	9,565	VC
Univ of Oregon	OR	11,479	VC
Univ of Texas at Austin	TX	10,630	HC
Univ of Washington	WA	10,361	VC
Washington Univ in St. Louis	MO	38,293	MC
Wichita State Univ	KS	8,092	C
Yale Univ	CT	37,000	MC

EUROPEAN STUDIES

School	ST	$IS	SR
Amherst College	MA	37,470	MC
Bard College	NY	37,352	HC+
Bennington College	VT	35,910	HC
Bowdoin College	ME	37,790	MC
Brandeis Univ	MA	38,198	MC
Brigham Young Univ	UT	8,504	HC
Calvin College	MI	22,615	NC
Canisius College	NY	28,163	C+
Columbia Univ/Barnard College	NY	36,990	MC
Emory & Henry College	VA	21,950	C
Emory Univ	GA	36,872	MC
George Washington Univ	DC	41,030	MC
Georgetown College	KY	22,000	VC
Hamline Univ	MN	27,052	VC
Harvard Univ/Harvard College	MA	37,928	MC
Hillsdale College	MI	22,450	HC
Hobart and William Smith Colleges	NY	36,536	HC
Huntingdon College	AL	18,400	VC
Loyola Marymount Univ	CA	32,194	VC
Middlebury College	VT	38,100	MC
Millsaps College	MS	25,182	VC
Mount Holyoke College	MA	37,918	HC+
New York Univ	NY	39,406	MC
Northwestern Univ	IL	37,491	MC
Pitzer College	CA	37,590	HC
Rollins College	FL	34,300	VC
St. Joseph's Univ	PA	33,590	VC
San Diego State Univ	CA	10,321	C
Scripps College	CA	35,700	HC+
Seattle Pacific Univ	WA	25,944	VC
Simon's Rock College of Bard	MA	36,580	HC
Syracuse Univ	NY	34,720	HC
Texas State Univ	TX	9,320	VC
Univ of Calif at Los Angeles	CA	15,330	MC
Univ of Hawaii at Manoa	HI	9,565	VC
Univ of Kansas	KS	8,923	VC
Univ of Minn/Morris	MN	12,896	VC
Univ of New Mexico	NM	9,223	C
Univ of Northern Iowa	IA	9,834	C
Univ of S Car at Columbia	SC	10,048	VC
Univ of Vermont	VT	16,316	VC
Valparaiso Univ	IN	26,118	VC+
Vanderbilt Univ	TN	37,897	MC
Washington Univ in St. Louis	MO	38,293	MC
Westmont College	CA	33,062	VC+

EVOLUTIONARY BIOLOGY

School	ST	$IS	SR
Case Western Reserve Univ	OH	32,002	MC
Cornell Univ	NY	38,253	MC
Dartmouth College	NH	37,770	MC
Florida State Univ	FL	9,028	HC
Ohio State Univ	OH	13,080	VC+
Rutgers, The State Univ of New Jersey/New Brunswick/Piscataway Campus	NJ	15,800	HC
Tulane Univ	LA	37,451	HC+
Univ of Arizona	AZ	10,413	VC
Univ of Calif at Santa Barbara	CA	11,732	VC
Univ of Conn	CT	14,608	VC
Univ of Minn/Twin Cities	MN	13,160	VC
Univ of Pittsburgh at Pittsburgh	PA	16,074	HC

EXERCISE SCIENCE

School	ST	$IS	SR
Albertson College of Idaho	ID	19,415	VC
Andrews Univ	MI	19,550	C
Angelo State Univ	TX	7,576	NC
Appalachian State Univ	NC	7,637	VC
Arkansas State Univ	AR	8,450	C
Asbury College	KY	20,704	VC
Augustana College	SD	21,998	VC
Baldwin-Wallace College	OH	24,678	C
Barton College	NC	19,314	C
Becker College	MA	23,710	LC
Belhaven College	MS	16,040	C+
Bethel College	IN	19,670	C
Bluefield College	VA	15,575	C
Boston Univ	MA	38,194	HC+
Bowling Green State Univ	OH	13,036	C
Bryan College	TN	17,900	VC
Calif Baptist Univ	CA	19,924	C
Cal State, Chico	CA	8,598	LC
Cal State, Northridge	CA	7,757	LC
Cal State, San Bernardino	CA	15,238	LC
Carroll College	WI	22,740	C
Cedarville Univ	OH	19,954	VC
Central College	IA	21,206	C
Central Washington Univ	WA	9,768	C
Chatham College	PA	27,266	C+
CUNY/York College	NY	3,292	NC
Colby-Sawyer College	NH	27,850	LC
College of St. Scholastica	MN	24,970	C+
Columbus State Univ	GA	7,846	C
Concordia Univ	CA	24,420	C
Concordia Univ Nebr	NE	20,302	C+
Drury Univ	MO	18,085	VC+
D'Youville College	NY	21,080	C
East Carolina Univ	NC	8,671	C
East Central Univ	OK	4,968	C
Fort Lewis College	CO	8,353	C
George Mason Univ	VA	9,732	VC
Georgia Southern Univ	GA	8,540	C
Gonzaga Univ	WA	26,766	HC
Greensboro College	NC	21,750	C
Guilford College	NC	24,960	VC
Hendrix College	AR	20,970	VC+
High Point Univ	NC	22,480	C
Hofstra Univ	NY	27,112	VC
Howard Payne Univ	TX	15,176	C
Huntingdon College	AL	18,400	VC
Indiana Univ Bloomington	IN	12,389	VC
Ithaca College	NY	31,730	HC
La Sierra Univ	CA	19,260	LC
Lake Superior State Univ	MI	9,034	LC
Lander Univ	SC	10,496	C
Lasell College	MA	26,000	C
Liberty Univ	VA	17,220	C
Linfield College	OR	27,090	VC
Loras College	IA	24,233	C
Louisiana College	LA	13,450	C
Lubbock Christian Univ	TX	15,832	C
Lynchburg College	VA	26,815	C
Malone College	OH	20,995	C
Marquette Univ	WI	27,594	VC
Meredith College	NC	23,065	C
Messiah College	PA	25,890	VC+
Miami Univ	OH	15,033	HC
Milligan College	TN	19,860	C+
Missouri Valley College	MO	18,500	C
Mount Vernon Nazarene Univ	OH	18,925	C
Murray State Univ	KY	7,816	VC
Nebr Wesleyan Univ	NE	21,197	C+
Norfolk State Univ	VA	9,722	LC
N Car Wesleyan College	NC	17,998	C
Palm Beach Atlantic Univ	FL	20,690	C
Purdue Univ/West Lafayette	IN	12,560	VC
Rice Univ	TX	27,550	MC
Ripon College	WI	24,995	VC
Rutgers, The State Univ of New Jersey/New Brunswick/Piscataway Campus	NJ	15,800	HC
St. Louis Univ	MO	29,780	VC+
St. Olaf College	MN	28,500	HC
Salisbury Univ	MD	12,664	VC
Samford Univ	AL	18,648	VC
San Diego State Univ	CA	10,321	C
Schreiner Univ	TX	20,440	C
Seattle Pacific Univ	WA	25,944	VC
Skidmore College	NY	37,930	HC
Southern Illinois Univ Edwardsville	IL	8,724	C
Southern Nazarene Univ	OK	14,634	NC
Southwestern Adventist Univ	TX	14,798	C
Spring Arbor Univ	MI	20,206	C
SUNY/Univ at Buffalo	NY	12,563	VC
Sterling College	KS	18,763	C
Syracuse Univ	NY	34,720	HC
Texas State Univ	TX	9,320	VC
Texas Tech Univ	TX	10,768	VC
Towson Univ	MD	12,694	VC
Transylvania Univ	KY	23,780	VC+
Tulane Univ	LA	37,451	HC+
Univ of Arkansas	AR	9,855	VC
Univ of Central Arkansas	AR	6,388	C
Univ of Colo at Boulder	CO	10,774	VC
Univ of Conn	CT	14,608	VC
Univ of Dayton	OH	24,850	VC
Univ of Evansville	IN	24,190	VC
Univ of Florida	FL	8,580	MC
Univ of Indianapolis	IN	22,560	VC
Univ of Mary Hardin-Baylor	TX	17,268	C
Univ of Mass Amherst	MA	13,980	C+
Univ of Mass Lowell	MA	11,937	VC
Univ of Memphis	TN	8,560	C
Univ of Miss	MS	7,666	C
Univ of Nebr at Lincoln	NE	9,975	C+
Univ of Nevada/Las Vegas	NV	11,566	C
Univ of New Mexico	NM	9,223	C
Univ of N Car at Chapel Hill	NC	10,117	MC
Univ of N Car at Greensboro	NC	8,248	C
Univ of Oregon	OR	11,479	VC
Univ of Pittsburgh at Pittsburgh	PA	16,074	HC
Univ of Puget Sound	WA	31,760	HC
Univ of San Francisco	CA	34,700	VC
Univ of Scranton	PA	30,836	VC
Univ of S Car at Columbia	SC	10,048	VC
Univ of Southern Colo	CO	7,821	LC
Univ of Tampa	FL	23,982	VC
Univ of Tulsa	OK	22,090	VC+
Univ of Utah	UT	9,205	C
Univ of Wisc/La Crosse	WI	8,991	VC
Univ of Wyoming	WY	8,636	C
Ursinus College	PA	34,400	VC
Valdosta State Univ	GA	7,798	C
Valparaiso Univ	IN	26,118	VC+
Wake Forest Univ	NC	34,090	MC
Warner Southern College	FL	16,738	LC
Washington State Univ	WA	11,334	C
Waynesburg College	PA	19,370	C
West Texas A&M Univ	TX	7,533	C
Western Mich Univ	MI	12,031	C
Westmont College	CA	33,062	VC+
Willamette Univ	OR	32,032	VC+
Wilson College	PA	23,912	C
Winona State Univ	MN		C

EXPERIMENTAL PSYCHOLOGY

School	ST	$IS	SR
Cal State, Stanislaus	CA	9,874	C
Immaculata Univ	PA	25,200	C
Millikin Univ	IL	25,555	C
Moravian College	PA	28,903	VC
Rochester Inst of Technology	NY	29,217	VC+
Tufts Univ	MA	38,233	MC

FAMILY AND COMMUNITY SERVICES

School	ST	$IS	SR
Central Washington Univ	WA	9,768	C
East Carolina Univ	NC	8,671	C
John Brown Univ	AR	15,080	VC
Kansas State Univ	KS	8,728	VC
Mich State Univ	MI	11,933	VC
Point Loma Nazarene Univ	CA	21,380	VC
Prairie View A&M Univ	TX	9,418	NC
Purdue Univ/West Lafayette	IN	12,560	VC
Union Univ	TN	18,800	VC
Univ of Delaware	DE	12,616	HC
Univ of Northern Iowa	IA	9,834	C
Univ of Oregon	OR	11,479	VC
Youngstown State Univ	OH	11,148	NC

FAMILY/CONSUMER RESOURCE MANAGEMENT

School	ST	$IS	SR
Arizona State Univ-Main	AZ	10,048	C
Bowling Green State Univ	OH	13,036	C
East Central Univ	OK	4,968	C
Iowa State Univ	IA	10,768	VC
Mich State Univ	MI	11,933	VC
Northwest Missouri State Univ	MO	9,334	C
Ohio State Univ at Lima	OH	4,416	NC
Ohio Univ	OH	14,448	C
Seton Hill Univ	PA	24,930	C
Southern Illinois Univ Carbondale	IL	10,407	C
Texas Tech Univ	TX	10,768	VC
Univ of Alabama	AL	9,040	C+
Univ of Arizona	AZ	10,413	VC
Univ of Hawaii at Manoa	HI	9,565	VC
Univ of Missouri/Columbia	MO	13,782	VC
West Virginia Univ	WV	9,370	C

FAMILY/CONSUMER STUDIES

School	ST	$IS	SR
Alabama A&M Univ	AL	5,100	LC
Alcorn State Univ	MS	7,290	C
Anderson Univ	IN	19,430	LC
Andrews Univ	MI	19,550	C
Appalachian State Univ	NC	7,637	VC
Baldwin-Wallace College	OH	24,678	C
Baylor Univ	TX	23,864	VC
Bluffton College	OH	23,694	C
Bradley Univ	IL	22,910	VC
Bridgewater College	VA	25,150	C
Brigham Young Univ	UT	8,504	HC
Cal State, Fresno	CA	8,414	LC
Cal State, Northridge	CA	7,757	LC
Campbell Univ	NC	18,268	VC
Central Washington Univ	WA	9,768	C
CUNY/Queens College	NY	4,362	C
College of St. Catherine	MN	24,010	VC
College of the Ozarks	MO	3,500	VC+
Concordia College: Moorhead	MN	22,460	VC+
Concordia Univ	MI	24,095	C
Cornell Univ	NY	38,253	MC
Cornerstone Univ and Grand Rapids Theological Seminary	MI	19,846	C
De Sales Univ	PA	25,470	C
Delta State Univ	MS	6,618	C
Eastern Mich Univ	MI	11,478	C
Fairmont State	WV	8,280	LC
Florida State Univ	FL	9,028	HC
Fontbonne Univ	MO	21,508	C
Framingham State College	MA	9,381	C
Freed-Hardeman Univ	TN		NC
Gallaudet Univ	DC	16,554	SP
Georgia Southern Univ	GA	8,540	C
Hampshire College	MA	37,037	HC
Henderson State Univ	AR	7,386	C
Indiana Univ Bloomington	IN	12,389	VC
Indiana Univ of Pennsylvania	PA	10,489	C
Iowa State Univ	IA	10,768	VC
Kansas State Univ	KS	8,728	VC
Kent State Univ	OH	12,932	C
Lamar Univ	TX	6,816	LC
Lambuth Univ	TN	16,520	C
Liberty Univ	VA	17,220	C
Louisiana State Univ and A&M College	LA	9,126	VC
Madonna Univ	MI	11,504	VC
McNeese State Univ	LA	5,259	LC
Mercyhurst College	PA	20,694	C
Meredith College	NC	23,065	C
Miami Univ	OH	15,033	HC
Mich State Univ	MI	11,933	VC
Middle Tenn State Univ	TN	8,534	C
Minn State Univ, Mankato	MN	8,803	LC
Miss College	MS	14,574	C
Mount Vernon Nazarene Univ	OH	18,925	C
New Mexico State Univ	NM	7,932	C
Nicholls State Univ	LA	6,395	NC
Northwestern State Univ of Louisiana	LA	6,331	NC
Oakwood College	AL	14,904	C
Olivet Nazarene Univ	IL	20,480	C
Oregon State Univ	OR	11,055	C
Pittsburg State Univ	KS	7,128	NC
St. Joseph College	CT	29,685	C
St. Olaf College	MN	28,500	HC
Samford Univ	AL	18,648	VC
Seattle Pacific Univ	WA	25,944	VC
Seton Hill Univ	PA	24,930	C
Shepherd College	WV	8,608	C
S Dak State Univ	SD	7,782	C
Southeast Missouri State Univ	MO	9,704	C
Southeastern Louisiana Univ	LA	6,791	LC
Southern Univ and A&M College	LA	7,372	LC
Southern Utah Univ	UT	8,194	C
Syracuse Univ	NY	34,720	HC
Tenn State Univ	TN	9,048	LC
Texas State Univ	TX	9,320	VC
Texas Tech Univ	TX	10,768	VC
Texas Woman's Univ	TX	7,804	LC
Towson Univ	MD	12,694	VC
Univ of Akron	OH	13,134	NC
Univ of Arizona	AZ	10,413	VC
Univ of Arkansas at Pine Bluff	AR	7,925	C
Univ of Central Arkansas	AR	6,388	C
Univ of Central Okla	OK	9,434	C
Univ of Georgia	GA	8,656	VC
Univ of Houston	TX	9,818	C
Univ of Illinois at Urbana-Champaign	IL	11,316	HC+
Univ of Louisiana at Monroe	LA	5,207	NC
Univ of Maryland/College Park	MD	14,227	HC
Univ of Miss	MS	7,666	C
Univ of Nebr at Kearney	NE	8,286	NC
Univ of Nebr at Lincoln	NE	9,975	C+
Univ of New Hampshire	NH	14,828	VC
Univ of New Mexico	NM	9,223	C
Univ of PR/Rio Piedras	PR	5,730	
Univ of Rhode Island	RI	13,720	VC
Univ of Utah	UT	9,205	C
Univ of Vermont	VT	16,316	VC
Univ of Wisc/Madison	WI	8,262	VC
Univ of Wisc/Stevens Point	WI	8,116	VC
Univ of Wisc/Stout	WI	9,718	C
Univ of Wyoming	WY	8,636	C
Villa Julie College	MD	18,393	C
Wayne State College	NE	7,352	NC
Weber State Univ	UT	7,945	NC
Western Illinois Univ	IL	10,363	C
Western Mich Univ	MI	12,031	C
Youngstown State Univ	OH	11,148	NC

FAMILY/JUVENILE JUSTICE

School	ST	$IS	SR
Thiel College	PA	20,970	C
William Woods Univ	MO	20,120	C

FASHION DESIGN AND TECHNOLOGY

School	ST	$IS	SR
American InterContinental Univ	GA	12,000	NC
Baylor Univ	TX	23,864	VC
Calif College of the Arts	CA	31,530	SP

ST = STATE $IS = IN-STATE COSTS SR = SELECTOR RATING

School	ST	$IS	SR
Centenary College	NJ	25,370	LC
College of St. Catherine	MN	24,010	VC
Columbus College of Art and Design	OH	24,180	SP
Dominican Univ	IL	23,610	C
Drexel Univ	PA	27,655	VC
Fashion Inst of Technology/ SUNY	NY	11,169	C+
Florida State Univ	FL	9,028	HC
Framingham State College	MA	9,381	C
Illinois State Univ	IL	10,944	C+
Iowa State Univ	IA	10,768	VC
Kent State Univ	OH	12,932	C
Lasell College	MA	26,000	C
Lindenwood Univ	MO	17,050	VC
Marist College	NY	27,596	VC
Marymount College of Fordham Univ	NY	27,686	C
Marymount Univ	VA	23,668	C
Mass College of Art	MA	15,568	SP
Moore College of Art and Design	PA	27,096	SP
Mount Ida College	MA	25,596	LC
Mount Mary College	WI	20,370	C
Oregon State Univ	OR	11,055	C
Otis College of Art and Design	CA	23,420	SP
Parsons School of Design	NY	32,242	SP
Philadelphia Univ	PA	27,354	C
Pratt Inst	NY	34,350	SP
Savannah College of Art and Design	GA	27,560	SP
School of the Art Inst of Chicago	IL	27,800	SP
Stephens College	MO	24,260	C+
Syracuse Univ	NY	34,720	HC
Texas Tech Univ	TX	10,768	VC
Texas Woman's Univ	TX	7,804	LC
Univ of Delaware	DE	12,616	HC
Univ of North Texas	TX	7,629	C
Univ of the Incarnate Word	TX	21,772	LC
Ursuline College	OH	22,728	LC
Washington Univ in St. Louis	MO	38,293	MC
Woodbury Univ	CA	25,344	LC
Youngstown State Univ	OH	11,148	NC

FASHION MERCHANDISING

School	ST	$IS	SR
Albright College	PA	30,579	C
American InterContinental Univ	GA	12,000	NC
Ashland Univ	OH	24,464	C
Auburn Univ	AL	10,396	VC
Baylor Univ	TX	23,864	VC
Bennett College	NC	11,200	C
Bowling Green State Univ	OH	13,036	C
Brenau Univ Women's College	GA	21,800	C
Central Washington Univ	WA	9,768	C
College of St. Catherine	MN	24,010	VC
David Lipscomb Univ	TN	16,158	VC
Delaware State Univ	DE	8,104	LC
Delta State Univ	MS	6,618	C
Dominican Univ	IL	23,610	C
Drexel Univ	PA	27,655	VC
East Central Univ	OK	4,968	C
Eastern Mich Univ	MI	11,478	C
Fashion Inst of Technology/ SUNY	NY	11,169	C+
Florida State Univ	FL	9,028	HC
Fontbonne Univ	MO	21,508	C
Framingham State College	MA	9,381	C
Georgia Southern Univ	GA	8,540	C
Immaculata Univ	PA	25,200	C
Indiana Univ of Pennsylvania	PA	10,489	C
Iowa State Univ	IA	10,768	VC
Johnson and Wales Univ	RI	22,965	LC
Kent State Univ	OH	12,932	C
Laboratory Inst of Merchandising	NY	25,150	SP
Lasell College	MA	26,000	C
Lynn Univ	FL	30,750	C
Marist College	NY	27,596	VC
Mars Hill College	NC	18,600	LC
Marymount College of Fordham Univ	NY	27,686	C
Marymount Univ	VA	23,668	C
Mercyhurst College	PA	20,694	C
Meredith College	NC	23,065	C
Miss Univ for Women	MS	5,446	LC
Mount Ida College	MA	25,596	LC
Mount Mary College	WI	20,370	C
New Mexico State Univ	NM	7,932	C
Northwood Univ	MI	20,265	LC
Old Dominion Univ	VA	10,441	C
Olivet Nazarene Univ	IL	20,480	C
Philadelphia Univ	PA	27,354	C
Southeast Missouri State Univ	MO	9,704	C
Southern Illinois Univ Carbondale	IL	10,407	C
SUNY/College at Oneonta	NY	11,870	VC
Stephen F. Austin State Univ	TX	7,552	C
Stephens College	MO	24,260	C+
Tarleton State Univ	TX	7,576	C
Texas A&M Univ at Kingsville	TX	6,740	LC
Texas Christian Univ	TX	23,410	VC
Texas State Univ	TX	9,320	VC
Texas Woman's Univ	TX	7,804	LC
Univ of Bridgeport	CT	25,924	LC
Univ of Central Okla	OK	9,434	C
Univ of Georgia	GA	8,656	VC
Univ of Louisiana at Lafayette	LA	5,826	C
Univ of Rhode Island	RI	13,720	VC
Univ of the Incarnate Word	TX	21,772	LC
Ursuline College	OH	22,728	LC
Utah State Univ	UT	7,371	C
West Virginia Univ	WV	9,370	C
Woodbury Univ	CA	25,344	LC
Youngstown State Univ	OH	11,148	NC

FIBER/TEXTILES/WEAVING

School	ST	$IS	SR
Edinboro Univ of Pennsylvania	PA	10,850	LC
Fashion Inst of Technology/ SUNY	NY	11,169	C+
Florida State Univ	FL	9,028	HC
Kansas City Art Inst	MO	26,850	SP
Maryland Inst College of Art	MD	30,890	SP
Mass College of Art	MA	15,568	SP
Ohio Univ	OH	14,448	C
Savannah College of Art and Design	GA	27,560	SP
School of the Art Inst of Chicago	IL	27,800	SP
Syracuse Univ	NY	34,720	HC
Univ of Mass Dartmouth	MA	12,835	C
Univ of Mich/Ann Arbor	MI	13,864	HC+
Univ of North Texas	TX	7,629	C
Univ of Oregon	OR	11,479	VC
Univ of Washington	WA	10,361	VC

FILM ARTS

School	ST	$IS	SR
American Univ	DC	34,585	VC+
Art Center College of Design	CA	23,450	SP
Ball State Univ	IN	8,660	C
Bard College	NY	37,352	HC+
Bennington College	VT	35,910	HC
Boston College	MA	33,284	MC
Boston Univ	MA	38,194	HC+
Bowling Green State Univ	OH	13,036	C
Burlington College	VT	10,640	SP
Calif College of the Arts	CA	31,530	SP
Calif Inst of the Arts	CA	30,690	SP
Cal State, Fullerton	CA	6,648	C
Cal State, Long Beach	CA	8,762	C+
Cal State, Northridge	CA	7,757	LC
Calvin College	MI	22,615	NC
Chapman Univ	CA	33,118	VC
CUNY/Brooklyn College	NY	4,353	C+
CUNY/City College	NY	4,230	C+
CUNY/College of Staten Island	NY	4,308	NC
CUNY/Hunter College	NY	6,729	C+
CUNY/Queens College	NY	4,362	C
Clark Univ	MA	32,115	VC
College of Santa Fe	NM	25,293	C+
College of the Holy Cross	MA	36,451	MC
Colo College	CO	36,860	HC
Columbia College Chicago	IL	25,108	LC
Columbia Univ/Barnard College	NY	36,990	MC
Columbia Univ/Columbia College	NY	38,590	MC
Columbia Univ/School of General Studies	NY	35,000	C
Cornell Univ	NY	38,253	MC
Dartmouth College	NH	37,770	MC
De Sales Univ	PA	25,470	C
Denison Univ	OH	33,050	HC
Drexel Univ	PA	27,655	VC
Eastern Mich Univ	MI	11,478	C
Edinboro Univ of Pennsylvania	PA	10,850	LC
Elon Univ	NC	22,240	VC
Emerson College	MA	32,205	HC
Emory Univ	GA	36,872	MC
Florida State Univ	FL	9,028	HC
Fordham Univ	NY	35,066	HC
Georgia State Univ	GA	10,658	C
Grand Valley State Univ	MI	11,022	VC
Hampshire College	MA	37,037	HC
Hofstra Univ	NY	27,112	VC
Indiana State Univ	IN	10,719	LC
Ithaca College	NY	31,730	HC
Keene State College	NH	12,212	C
Kent State Univ	OH	12,932	C
LIU/C.W. Post Campus	NY	28,282	C
Mass College of Art	MA	15,568	SP
Minneapolis College of Art and Design	MN	28,950	SP
Mount Holyoke College	MA	37,918	HC+
New College of Calif	CA	8,900	NC
New York Univ	NY	39,406	MC
N Car School of the Arts	NC	8,565	SP
Oberlin College	OH	36,938	MC
Oral Roberts Univ	OK	18,490	C
Penn State Univ/Univ Park Campus	PA	15,646	HC
Pitzer College	CA	37,590	HC
Point Park Univ	PA	21,840	C
Pratt Inst	NY	34,350	SP
Purdue Univ/West Lafayette	IN	12,560	VC
Rhode Island College	RI	11,565	C
Rhode Island School of Design	RI	33,569	SP
Rochester Inst of Technology	NY	29,217	VC+
St. John's Univ	NY	30,180	C
San Francisco Art Inst	CA	19,300	SP
San Francisco State Univ	CA	12,070	C
San Jose State Univ	CA	8,187	C
Sarah Lawrence College	NY	41,218	HC
School of the Art Inst of Chicago	IL	27,800	SP
School of Visual Arts	NY	30,200	SP
Southern Adventist Univ	TN	17,080	C
Southern Illinois Univ Carbondale	IL	10,407	C
Southern Methodist Univ	TX	34,210	HC
Southwest Missouri State Univ	MO	8,918	C
Spring Arbor Univ	MI	20,206	C
SUNY/College at Cortland	NY	12,095	C
SUNY/College at Purchase	NY	10,587	VC
SUNY/Univ at Binghamton	NY	12,787	HC
SUNY/Univ at Stony Brook	NY	12,763	HC
Syracuse Univ	NY	34,720	HC
Temple Univ	PA	15,912	C
Texas Christian Univ	TX	23,410	VC
Univ of Calif at Berkeley	CA	15,563	MC
Univ of Calif at Irvine	CA	19,808	HC
Univ of Calif at Los Angeles	CA	15,330	MC
Univ of Calif at Santa Barbara	CA	11,732	VC
Univ of Calif at Santa Cruz	CA	16,505	VC
Univ of Central Florida	FL	10,038	VC
Univ of Chicago	IL	35,087	MC
Univ of Colo at Boulder	CO	10,774	VC
Univ of Hartford	CT	31,080	C
Univ of Iowa	IA	10,923	VC
Univ of Louisiana at Monroe	LA	5,207	NC
Univ of Miami	FL	34,608	HC
Univ of Mich/Ann Arbor	MI	13,864	HC+
Univ of Minn/Twin Cities	MN	13,160	VC
Univ of Nebr at Lincoln	NE	9,975	C+
Univ of Nevada/Las Vegas	NV	11,566	C
Univ of N Car at Wilmington	NC	8,940	VC
Univ of North Texas	TX	7,629	C
Univ of Notre Dame	IN	34,442	MC
Univ of Okla	OK	9,226	VC
Univ of Pittsburgh at Pittsburgh	PA	16,074	HC
Univ of Rochester	NY	32,979	HC
Univ of Southern Calif	CA	37,459	MC
Univ of Tenn at Knoxville	TN	8,214	C
Univ of Texas at Austin	TX	10,630	HC
Univ of the Arts	PA	29,510	SP
Univ of Toledo	OH	12,479	NC
Univ of Tulsa	OK	22,090	VC+
Univ of Utah	UT	9,205	C
Univ of Wisc/Milwaukee	WI	9,427	LC
Vassar College	NY	37,030	MC
Washington Univ in St. Louis	MO	38,293	MC
Wayne State Univ	MI	11,774	C
Webster Univ	MO	21,848	VC
Wellesley College	MA	36,516	MC
Wesleyan Univ	CT	35,139	MC
Whitman College	WA	32,526	HC+
Wright State Univ	OH	11,490	LC
Yale Univ	CT	37,000	MC

FINE ARTS

School	ST	$IS	SR
Abilene Christian Univ	TX	18,370	VC
Adelphi Univ	NY	26,300	VC
Agnes Scott College	GA	28,230	HC
Alabama State Univ	AL	6,404	C
Albany State Univ	GA	5,764	C+
Albertus Magnus College	CT	23,130	LC
Alfred Univ	NY	28,290	C
American Univ	DC	34,585	VC+
Amherst College	MA	37,470	MC
Anderson Univ	IN	19,430	LC
Aquinas College	MI	21,894	C
Arcadia Univ	PA	29,890	C
Arkansas State Univ	AR	8,450	C
Art Academy of Cincinnati	OH	17,300	SP
Art Center College of Design	CA	23,450	SP
Art Inst of Boston at Lesley Univ	MA	28,080	SP
Ashland Univ	OH	24,464	C
Atlanta College of Art	GA	18,600	SP
Auburn Univ Montgomery	AL	9,020	NC
Baker Univ	KS	19,860	VC
Ball State Univ	IN	8,660	C
Bellevue Univ	NE	4,440	NC
Bemidji State Univ	MN	9,103	C
Bennington College	VT	35,910	HC
Bethany College	KS	18,675	LC
Bethany College	WV	19,845	VC
Bethel College	KS	19,800	C+
Bethel College	MN	25,180	VC
Black Hills State Univ	SD	7,743	LC
Bloomfield College	NJ	19,250	LC
Bluefield College	VA	15,575	C
Boise State Univ	ID	7,657	LC
Bowie State Univ	MD	10,873	C+
Bowling Green State Univ	OH	13,036	C
Brandeis Univ	MA	38,198	MC
Brenau Univ Women's College	GA	21,800	C
Briar Cliff Univ	IA	21,660	C
Brigham Young Univ/Hawaii	HI	7,240	VC+
Bryn Mawr College	PA	36,890	HC+
Bucknell Univ	PA	35,262	HC+
Burlington College	VT	10,640	SP
Caldwell College	NJ	24,060	LC
Calif Inst of the Arts	CA	30,690	SP
Cal State, Chico	CA	8,598	LC
Cal State, Fullerton	CA	6,648	C
Cal State, Stanislaus	CA	9,874	C
Capital Univ	OH	26,550	C
Cardinal Stritch Univ	WI	17,620	C
Carnegie Mellon Univ	PA	32,682	MC
Carson-Newman College	TN	16,760	C
Carthage College	WI	25,000	C
Cedar Crest College	PA	25,145	C+
Central College	IA	21,206	C
Central Mich Univ	MI	11,142	C
Central Washington Univ	WA	9,768	C
Centre College	KY	27,300	HC
Charleston Southern Univ	SC	17,122	C
Christopher Newport Univ	VA	8,862	VC
CUNY/City College	NY	4,230	C+
CUNY/Herbert H. Lehman College	NY	3,320	LC
CUNY/Hunter College	NY	6,729	C+
Clark Univ	MA	32,115	VC
Clemson Univ	SC	11,972	HC
Coastal Carolina Univ	SC	11,040	C
College for Creative Studies	MI	23,298	SP
College of Mount St. Joseph	OH	22,785	C
College of New Jersey	NJ	15,950	MC
College of Our Lady of the Elms	MA	20,644	C
College of St. Benedict	MN	26,672	VC
College of St. Catherine	MN	24,010	VC
College of St. Elizabeth	NJ	25,460	C
College of Visual Arts	MN		SP
College of William and Mary	VA	12,224	MC
College of Wooster	OH	31,300	HC
Columbia College	MO	16,139	C
Columbus College of Art and Design	OH	24,180	SP
Concordia Univ Nebr	NE	20,302	C+
Converse College	SC	24,710	VC
Cooper Union for the Advancement of Science and Art	NY	10,400	MC
Corcoran School of Art and Design	DC	21,035	SP
Cornell College	IA	27,825	VC+
Cornell Univ	NY	38,253	MC
Cornerstone Univ and Grand Rapids Theological Seminary	MI	19,846	C
Cornish College of the Arts	WA	19,900	SP
Creighton Univ	NE	26,748	VC+
Cumberland Univ	TN	16,910	C
Daemen College	NY	22,120	C
Dakota State Univ	SD	7,466	C
Dallas Baptist Univ	TX	15,300	VC
Denison Univ	OH	33,050	HC
DePaul Univ	IL	27,580	VC
Dickinson College	PA	35,825	HC
Dickinson State Univ	ND	6,338	NC
Dominican Univ	IL	23,610	C
Dordt College	IA	20,170	VC
Dowling College	NY	23,870	LC
Drury Univ	MO	18,085	VC+
East Stroudsburg Univ of Pennsylvania	PA	10,336	C
East Tenn State Univ	TN	8,497	C
Eastern Conn State Univ	CT	10,362	C
Eastern Mich Univ	MI	11,478	C
Eastern New Mexico Univ	NM	6,762	LC
Edinboro Univ of Pennsylvania	PA	10,850	LC
Elmira College	NY	33,820	VC
Emmanuel College	MA	27,600	C+
Endicott College	MA	25,266	C+
Eureka College	IL	24,980	LC
Fairfield Univ	CT	35,505	HC
Fairleigh Dickinson Univ/ College at Florham	NJ	30,130	C
Fairleigh Dickinson Univ/ Metropolitan Campus	NJ	28,584	C
Fisk Univ	TN	17,305	C
Flagler College	FL	11,860	VC+
Florida A&M Univ	FL	7,564	C
Florida Atlantic Univ	FL	8,543	C
Florida Memorial College	FL	6,000	LC

ST = STATE $IS = IN-STATE COSTS SR = SELECTOR RATING

School	ST	$IS	SR
Fontbonne Univ	MO	21,508	C
Fordham Univ	NY	35,066	HC
Fort Hays State Univ	KS	7,363	C
Franklin and Marshall College	PA	35,930	HC+
Franklin Pierce College	NH	28,980	LC
Freed-Hardeman Univ	TN		NC
Friends Univ	KS	15,962	LC
George Washington Univ	DC	41,030	MC
Georgetown Univ	DC	38,242	MC
Georgia Southwestern State Univ	GA	6,013	C
Georgia State Univ	GA	10,658	C
Grand Canyon Univ	AZ	30,000	LC
Grand Valley State Univ	MI	11,022	VC
Green Mountain College	VT	24,130	C
Gustavus Adolphus College	MN	27,120	VC+
Hamline Univ	MN	27,052	VC
Hampden-Sydney College	VA	28,407	VC
Hampshire College	MA	37,037	HC
Harding Univ	AR	14,890	VC
Harvard Univ/Harvard College	MA	37,928	MC
Hastings College	NE	19,928	VC
Haverford College	PA	37,900	MC
High Point Univ	NC	22,480	C
Hillsdale College	MI	22,450	HC
Hobart and William Smith Colleges	NY	36,536	HC
Hofstra Univ	NY	27,112	VC
Hope College	MI	25,340	VC
Humboldt State Univ	CA	9,400	C
Idaho State Univ	ID	8,128	C
Illinois College	IL	19,100	VC
Indiana State Univ	IN	10,719	LC
Indiana Univ Bloomington	IN	12,389	VC
Indiana Univ East	IN	4,433	LC
Indiana Univ Northwest	IN	4,538	LC
Indiana Univ of Pennsylvania	PA	10,489	C
Indiana Univ South Bend	IN	4,571	LC
Indiana Univ Southeast	IN	4,504	LC
Indiana Univ-Purdue Univ Fort Wayne	IN	5,108	LC
Indiana Univ-Purdue Univ Indianapolis	IN	8,257	LC
Inter American Univ of PR/San German	PR	6,716	
Iowa State Univ	IA	10,768	VC
Iowa Wesleyan College	IA	19,990	C
Ithaca College	NY	31,730	HC
James Madison Univ	VA	10,794	VC
Jamestown College	ND	12,600	NC
Johnson State College	VT	11,819	LC
Judson College	IL	22,050	LC
Kean Univ	NJ	14,479	C
Keene State College	NH	12,212	C
Kent State Univ	OH	12,932	C
Kentucky State Univ	KY	9,062	NC
Kentucky Wesleyan College	KY	17,250	C
Kutztown Univ of Pennsylvania	PA	10,786	C
La Salle Univ	PA	31,260	VC
La Sierra Univ	CA	19,260	LC
LaGrange College	GA	20,500	C
Lake Erie College	OH	23,550	C
Lake Superior State Univ	MI	9,034	LC
Lamar Univ	TX	6,816	LC
Lambuth Univ	TN	16,520	C
Lewis and Clark College	OR	30,620	VC
Lincoln Memorial Univ	TN	16,400	LC
Lock Haven Univ of Pennsylvania	PA	11,098	LC
LIU/Brooklyn Campus	NY	24,790	C
LIU/C.W. Post Campus	NY	28,282	C
LIU/Southampton College	NY	29,370	C+
Louisiana State Univ and A&M College	LA	9,126	VC
Louisiana State Univ in Shreveport	LA	2,884	NC
Louisiana Tech Univ	LA	7,361	C
Lourdes College	OH	15,300	LC
Loyola College in Maryland	MD	34,560	HC
Loyola Univ Chicago	IL	31,164	VC
Loyola Univ New Orleans	LA	31,036	VC+
Lynn Univ	FL	30,750	C
Madonna Univ	MI	11,504	VC
Maharishi Univ of Management	IA	29,230	VC
Marietta College	OH	27,047	C
Marist College	NY	27,596	VC
Marlboro College	VT	29,055	VC+
Marshall Univ	WV	9,116	C
Martin Univ	IN	10,200	SP
Mary Baldwin College	VA	24,939	C
Maryland Inst College of Art	MD	30,890	SP
Marylhurst Univ	OR	18,465	NC
Marymount College of Fordham Univ	NY	27,686	C
Marymount Manhattan College	NY	27,292	C
Mass College of Art	MA	15,568	SP
Mass College of Liberal Arts	MA	8,717	LC
McDaniel College	MD	28,440	VC
McNeese State Univ	LA	5,259	LC
Memphis College of Art	TN	23,360	SP
Meredith College	NC	23,065	C
Mesa State College	CO	8,051	C
Metropolitan State College of Denver	CO	2,338	LC
Miami Univ	OH	15,033	HC
Midland Lutheran College	NE	18,600	C
Midwestern State Univ	TX	8,045	LC
Milligan College	TN	19,860	C+
Milwaukee Inst of Art and Design	WI	24,388	SP
Minn State Univ, Moorehead	MN	7,000	LC
Miss Univ for Women	MS	5,446	LC
Miss Valley State Univ	MS	6,765	NC
Missouri Southern State Univ	MO	8,316	C
Missouri Western State College	MO	8,522	NC
Montana State Univ-Bozeman	MT	9,515	C
Montana State Univ-Northern	MT	8,600	NC
Montclair State Univ	NJ	13,790	C
Montserrat College of Art	MA	22,790	SP
Moore College of Art and Design	PA	27,096	SP
Morgan State Univ	MD	11,470	C
Mount Mary College	WI	20,370	C
Mount Olive College	NC	14,410	LC
Mount St. Mary's College	MD	28,400	C
Muhlenberg College	PA	31,485	HC
Murray State Univ	KY	7,816	VC
National-Louis Univ	IL	16,240	LC
Nazareth College of Rochester	NY	24,936	VC
New College of Calif	CA	8,900	NC
New College of Florida	FL	8,906	HC+
New England College	NH	28,860	LC
New Jersey City Univ	NJ	11,850	LC
New Mexico State Univ	NM	7,932	C
New York Inst of Technology	NY	24,205	VC
New York Univ	NY	39,406	MC
Norfolk State Univ	VA	9,722	LC
North Central College	IL	25,656	VC
Northeastern Illinois Univ	IL	2,898	NC
Northeastern State Univ	OK	4,950	LC
Northern Arizona Univ	AZ	9,002	C
Northern Mich Univ	MI	10,834	C
Northern State Univ	SD	7,117	LC
Northland College	WI	22,170	C+
Northwest Missouri State Univ	MO	9,334	C
Northwestern College of Iowa	IA	19,640	C+
Northwestern State Univ of Louisiana	LA	6,331	NC
Northwestern Univ	IL	37,491	MC
Notre Dame de Namur Univ	CA	26,932	LC
Oakland City Univ	IN	16,980	NC
Oakland Univ	MI	10,800	C
Oberlin College	OH	36,938	MC
Ohio Northern Univ	OH	27,765	VC
Ohio Univ	OH	14,448	C
Ohio Wesleyan Univ	OH	32,550	VC+
Okla Baptist Univ	OK	15,220	VC
Old Dominion Univ	VA	10,441	C
Olivet College	MI	19,984	C+
Our Lady of the Lake Univ of San Antonio	TX	17,336	C
Pacific Lutheran Univ	WA	25,715	VC
Pacific Northwest College of Art	OR	14,890	SP
Pacific Union College	CA	22,065	C+
Park Univ	MO	10,780	C+
Parsons School of Design	NY	32,242	SP
Penn State Univ/Univ Park Campus	PA	15,646	HC
Pomona College	CA	33,960	MC
Pontifical Catholic Univ of PR/Ponce	PR	7,298	
Portland State Univ	OR	12,453	C
Pratt Inst	NY	34,350	SP
Presbyterian College	SC	25,920	VC
Prescott College	AZ	13,430	C
Principia College	IL	25,044	C+
Purdue Univ/West Lafayette	IN	12,560	VC
Queens Univ of Charlotte	NC	21,840	C
Radford Univ	VA	8,500	C
Rhode Island College	RI	11,565	C
Richard Stockton College of New Jersey	NJ	12,972	VC
Rider Univ	NJ	30,900	C
Ringling School of Art and Design	FL	27,530	SP
Roberts Wesleyan College	NY	23,190	C+
Rochester Inst of Technology	NY	29,217	VC+
Rockford College	IL	28,310	VC
Rosemont College	PA	26,175	C
Rowan Univ	NJ	14,506	VC
Saginaw Valley State Univ	MI	11,055	C
St. Ambrose Univ	IA	22,800	C
St. Anselm College	NH	30,250	C
St. Augustine's College	NC	12,990	LC
St. Cloud State Univ	MN	8,362	C
St. John's Univ	MN	26,473	VC
St. John's Univ	NY	30,180	C
St. Joseph's Univ	PA	33,590	VC
St. Lawrence Univ	NY	35,945	VC
St. Mary-of-the-Woods College	IN	23,280	C
St. Mary's College	IN	24,474	VC
St. Mary's College of Maryland	MD	15,908	VC+
St. Michael's College	VT	30,100	VC
St. Norbert College	WI	25,810	C
St. Peter's College	NJ	22,292	LC
St. Thomas Aquinas College	NY	20,590	LC
St. Vincent College	PA	25,530	VC
Salem State College	MA	8,592	C
Salisbury Univ	MD	12,664	VC
Samford Univ	AL	18,648	VC
San Diego State Univ	CA	10,321	C
San Francisco Art Inst	CA	19,300	SP
San Francisco State Univ	CA	12,070	C
San Jose State Univ	CA	8,187	C
Sarah Lawrence College	NY	41,218	HC
School of Visual Arts	NY	30,200	SP
Seattle Univ	WA	24,183	VC
Seton Hill Univ	PA	24,930	C
Shawnee State Univ	OH	11,031	NC
Siena Heights Univ	MI	16,140	LC
Sierra Nevada College	NV	26,136	C
Silver Lake College of the Holy Family	WI	18,450	LC
Simon's Rock College of Bard	MA	36,580	HC
Skidmore College	NY	37,930	HC
Slippery Rock Univ of Pennsylvania	PA	10,343	LC
Sonoma State Univ	CA	10,421	C
S Car State Univ	SC	6,586	LC
Southeastern Okla State Univ	OK	6,147	C
Southern Adventist Univ	TN	17,080	C
Southern Conn State Univ	CT	10,310	C
Southern Illinois Univ Carbondale	IL	10,407	C
Southern Nazarene Univ	OK	14,634	NC
Southern Univ and A&M College	LA	7,372	LC
Southern Univ at New Orleans	LA	995	NC
Spelman College	GA	19,215	C+
Springfield College	MA	24,520	C
Stanford Univ	CA	37,612	MC
SUNY/College at Buffalo	NY	8,025	C
SUNY/College at Fredonia	NY	11,562	VC
SUNY/College at Oneonta	NY	11,870	VC
SUNY/Univ at Albany	NY	12,951	HC
SUNY/Univ at Binghamton	NY	12,787	HC
SUNY/Univ at Buffalo	NY	12,563	VC
SUNY/Univ at New Paltz	NY	11,565	VC
State Univ of West Georgia	GA	7,622	C
Stephen F. Austin State Univ	TX	7,552	C
Sterling College	KS	18,763	C
Stonehill College	MA	30,752	HC
Suffolk Univ	MA	29,200	C
Sul Ross State Univ	TX	6,582	LC
Syracuse Univ	NY	34,720	HC
Tarleton State Univ	TX	7,576	C
Temple Univ	PA	15,912	C
Tenn Tech Univ	TN	8,670	VC
Texas A&M Univ at Commerce	TX	8,994	C
Texas A&M Univ at Kingsville	TX	6,740	LC
Texas State Univ	TX	9,320	VC
Texas Wesleyan Univ	TX	16,245	C
Texas Woman's Univ	TX	7,804	LC
Thomas More College	KY	21,350	C
Trinity College	CT	38,040	HC+
Truman State Univ	MO	9,728	HC+
Tusculum College	TN	19,990	C
Union College	NY	36,005	HC
Univ of Akron	OH	13,134	NC
Univ of Alabama in Huntsville	AL	9,126	VC
Univ of Alaska Anchorage	AK	9,100	NC
Univ of Arizona	AZ	10,413	VC
Univ of Calif at Davis	CA	14,995	VC
Univ of Central Florida	FL	10,038	VC
Univ of Central Okla	OK	9,434	C
Univ of Chicago	IL	35,087	MC
Univ of Cincinnati	OH	14,736	C
Univ of Colo at Boulder	CO	10,774	VC
Univ of Colo at Colo Springs	CO	10,667	C
Univ of Colo at Denver	CO	3,302	C
Univ of Dayton	OH	24,850	VC
Univ of Delaware	DE	12,616	HC
Univ of Great Falls	MT	15,360	C
Univ of Hartford	CT	31,080	C
Univ of Houston	TX	9,818	C
Univ of Idaho	ID	8,216	C
Univ of Iowa	IA	10,923	VC
Univ of Louisiana at Lafayette	LA	5,826	C
Univ of Maine at Machias	ME	9,271	LC
Univ of Mary Hardin-Baylor	TX	17,268	C
Univ of Maryland/Baltimore County	MD	14,668	VC+
Univ of Mass Lowell	MA	11,937	VC
Univ of Miami	FL	34,608	HC
Univ of Missouri/Kansas City	MO	13,416	VC
Univ of Missouri/St. Louis	MO	11,656	VC
Univ of Montana	MT	9,395	C
Univ of Nebr at Kearney	NE	8,286	NC
Univ of Nebr at Lincoln	NE	9,975	C+
Univ of Nebr at Omaha	NE	8,080	C
Univ of Nevada/Las Vegas	NV	11,566	C
Univ of New Hampshire	NH	14,828	VC
Univ of New Mexico	NM	9,223	C
Univ of New Orleans	LA	7,356	C
Univ of N Car at Charlotte	NC	8,185	C
Univ of North Florida	FL	8,769	VC
Univ of Northern Colo	CO	8,987	C
Univ of Northern Iowa	IA	9,834	C
Univ of Okla	OK	9,226	VC
Univ of Oregon	OR	11,479	VC
Univ of Pennsylvania	PA	37,960	MC
Univ of Pittsburgh at Pittsburgh	PA	16,074	HC
Univ of PR/Mayaguez	PR		
Univ of PR/Rio Piedras	PR	5,730	
Univ of Puget Sound	WA	31,760	HC
Univ of Rhode Island	RI	13,720	VC
Univ of Rio Grande	OH	8,728	NC
Univ of Rochester	NY	32,979	HC
Univ of St. Francis	IL	22,850	C
Univ of St. Francis	IN	20,964	C
Univ of St. Thomas	TX	21,952	VC
Univ of San Diego	CA	33,156	HC
Univ of San Francisco	CA	34,700	VC
Univ of Science and Arts of Okla	OK	5,982	C
Univ of South Alabama	AL	7,760	LC
Univ of S Car at Aiken	SC	7,828	LC
Univ of S Car at Columbia	SC	10,048	VC
Univ of Southern Calif	CA	37,459	MC
Univ of Southern Maine	ME	11,212	C
Univ of Southern Miss	MS	8,324	LC
Univ of Tampa	FL	23,982	VC
Univ of Tenn at Chattanooga	TN	7,783	C
Univ of Tenn at Knoxville	TN	8,214	C
Univ of Tenn at Martin	TN	7,748	C
Univ of Texas at San Antonio	TX	9,088	NC
Univ of Texas-Pan American	TX	5,954	LC
Univ of the District of Columbia	DC	2,070	LC
Univ of Toledo	OH	12,479	NC
Univ of Wisc/Eau Claire	WI	8,463	VC
Univ of Wisc/Green Bay	WI	8,154	C
Univ of Wisc/La Crosse	WI	8,991	VC
Univ of Wisc/Milwaukee	WI	9,427	LC
Univ of Wisc/Oshkosh	WI	6,130	LC
Univ of Wisc/Parkside	WI	6,160	LC
Univ of Wisc/Platteville	WI	8,450	C
Univ of Wisc/River Falls	WI	8,358	LC
Univ of Wisc/Stevens Point	WI	8,116	VC
Univ of Wisc/Stout	WI	9,718	C
Univ of Wisc/Superior	WI	7,051	C+
Upper Iowa Univ	IA	20,076	C
Utah State Univ	UT	7,371	C
Utica College	NY	28,340	C
Vanderbilt Univ	TN	37,897	MC
Virginia Commonwealth Univ	VA	9,030	C
Virginia Intermont College	VA	19,800	C
Viterbo Univ	WI	20,430	C
Wagner College	NY	29,900	VC
Washington College	MD	30,540	VC
Washington State Univ	WA	11,334	C
Washington Univ in St. Louis	MO	38,293	MC
Wayne State Univ	MI	11,774	C
Weber State Univ	UT	7,945	NC
Wells College	NY	21,122	VC
West Liberty State College	WV	7,868	LC
West Virginia State College	WV	6,264	NC
Western Kentucky Univ	KY	6,834	C
Western New Mexico Univ	NM	5,950	LC
Western State College of Colo	CO	9,014	C
Western Washington Univ	WA	10,119	VC
Westfield State College	MA	10,147	C
Westminster College	PA	22,960	C
Westminster College	UT	17,226	C
Wheaton College	MA	36,330	HC
Whitman College	WA	32,526	HC+
Wilberforce Univ	OH	14,937	LC
William Paterson Univ of New Jersey	NJ	14,450	C
William Penn Univ	IA	17,575	LC
Williams College	MA	32,270	MC
Wilson College	PA	23,912	C
Wingate Univ	NC	21,200	C
Winona State Univ	MN		C
Winthrop Univ	SC	11,302	C
Wittenberg Univ	OH	31,316	VC

ST = STATE **$IS** = IN-STATE COSTS **SR** = SELECTOR RATING

School	ST	$IS	SR
Wright State Univ	OH	11,490	LC
Xavier Univ	OH	26,850	VC+
Xavier Univ of Louisiana	LA	17,600	C
York College of Pennsylvania	PA	14,500	VC

FIRE CONTROL AND SAFETY TECHNOLOGY

School	ST	$IS	SR
Cogswell Polytechnical College	CA	14,400	LC
Okla State Univ	OK	9,216	VC
Univ of New Haven	CT	28,650	C
Univ of N Car at Charlotte	NC	8,185	C

FIRE PROTECTION

School	ST	$IS	SR
Cal State, Los Angeles	CA	5,778	C
Cogswell Polytechnical College	CA	14,400	LC
Eastern Kentucky Univ	KY	7,708	C
Okla Panhandle State Univ	OK	5,370	C
Park Univ	MO	10,780	C+
Southern Illinois Univ Carbondale	IL	10,407	C
Thomas Edison State College	NJ	3,325	SP
Western Oregon Univ	OR	10,281	C

FIRE PROTECTION ENGINEERING

School	ST	$IS	SR
Univ of Maryland/College Park	MD	14,227	HC
Univ of Nebr at Lincoln	NE	9,975	C+
Univ of New Haven	CT	28,650	C

FIRE SCIENCE

School	ST	$IS	SR
Anna Maria College	MA	26,140	LC
CUNY/John Jay College of Criminal Justice	NY	4,259	C
Lake Superior State Univ	MI	9,034	LC
Madonna Univ	MI	11,504	VC
Univ of Maryland/Univ College	MD	5,910	SP
Univ of New Haven	CT	28,650	C
Univ of the District of Columbia	DC	2,070	LC

FIRE SERVICES ADMINISTRATION

School	ST	$IS	SR
Park Univ	MO	10,780	C+

FISH AND GAME MANAGEMENT

School	ST	$IS	SR
Delaware State Univ	DE	8,104	LC
Frostburg State Univ	MD	11,114	C
Kansas State Univ	KS	8,728	VC
Lake Superior State Univ	MI	9,034	LC
Louisiana State Univ and A&M College	LA	9,126	VC
Okla State Univ	OK	9,216	VC
S Dak State Univ	SD	7,782	C
Stephen F. Austin State Univ	TX	7,552	C
Tenn Tech Univ	TN	8,670	VC
Texas A&M Univ	TX	11,081	HC
Univ of Nebr at Lincoln	NE	9,975	C+
Univ of N Dak	ND	8,390	C
West Virginia Univ	WV	9,370	C

FISHING AND FISHERIES

School	ST	$IS	SR
Auburn Univ	AL	10,396	VC
Ball State Univ	IN	8,660	C
Colo State Univ	CO	9,964	VC
Humboldt State Univ	CA	9,400	C
Mansfield Univ	PA	11,220	C
Mich State Univ	MI	11,933	VC
Miss State Univ	MS	9,139	C
Murray State Univ	KY	7,816	VC
N Car State Univ	NC	9,886	VC
Ohio State Univ	OH	13,080	VC+
Oregon State Univ	OR	11,055	C
Penn State Univ/Univ Park Campus	PA	15,646	HC
Texas A&M Univ	TX	11,081	HC
Texas A&M Univ at Galveston	TX	9,948	C+
Unity College	ME	19,845	LC
Univ of Alaska Fairbanks	AK	9,295	C
Univ of Arkansas at Pine Bluff	AR	7,925	C
Univ of Georgia	GA	8,656	VC
Univ of Idaho	ID	8,216	C
Univ of Maine	ME	12,080	C+
Univ of Minn/Twin Cities	MN	13,160	VC
Univ of Rhode Island	RI	13,720	VC
Univ of Tenn at Knoxville	TN	8,214	C
Univ of Vermont	VT	16,316	VC
Univ of Washington	WA	10,361	VC
West Virginia Univ	WV	9,370	C

FLUID AND THERMAL SCIENCE

School	ST	$IS	SR
Case Western Reserve Univ	OH	32,002	MC

FOLKLORE AND MYTHOLOGY

School	ST	$IS	SR
Harvard Univ/Harvard College	MA	37,928	MC
Indiana Univ Bloomington	IN	12,389	VC
Univ of Pennsylvania	PA	37,960	MC

FOOD PRODUCTION/ MANAGEMENT/SERVICES

School	ST	$IS	SR
Ball State Univ	IN	8,660	C
Cornell Univ	NY	38,253	MC
David Lipscomb Univ	TN	16,158	VC
Delaware Valley College	PA	26,676	C
Dominican Univ	IL	23,610	C
Drexel Univ	PA	27,655	VC
Georgia Southern Univ	GA	8,540	C
Grambling State Univ	LA	6,538	NC
Indiana Univ of Pennsylvania	PA	10,489	C
Johnson and Wales Univ	RI	22,965	LC
Kendall College	IL	21,350	NC
Metropolitan State Univ	MN	3,852	SP
Mich State Univ	MI	11,933	VC
Miss Univ for Women	MS	5,446	LC
Montclair State Univ	NJ	13,790	C
Mount Marty College	SD	15,656	LC
Newbury College	MA	23,450	C
Nicholls State Univ	LA	6,395	NC
Ohio Univ	OH	14,448	C
Rochester Inst of Technology	NY	29,217	VC+
Seton Hill Univ	PA	24,930	C
S Dak State Univ	SD	7,782	C
Stephen F. Austin State Univ	TX	7,552	C
Syracuse Univ	NY	34,720	HC
Texas A&M Univ at Kingsville	TX	6,740	LC
Texas Christian Univ	TX	23,410	VC
Texas Tech Univ	TX	10,768	VC
Univ of Alabama	AL	9,040	C+
Univ of Minn/Crookston	MN	9,626	NC
Univ of Nevada/Las Vegas	NV	11,566	C
Univ of N Car at Greensboro	NC	8,248	C
Univ of Wisc/Stout	WI	9,718	C
Wayne State College	NE	7,352	NC
Western Mich Univ	MI	12,031	C

FOOD SCIENCE

School	ST	$IS	SR
Alabama A&M Univ	AL	5,100	LC
Ashland Univ	OH	24,464	C
Auburn Univ	AL	10,396	VC
Bluffton College	OH	23,694	C
Bowling Green State Univ	OH	13,036	C
Brigham Young Univ	UT	8,504	HC
Calif Polytechnic State Univ	CA	8,747	VC
Calif State Polytechnic Univ, Pomona	CA	8,793	C+
Cal State, Fresno	CA	8,414	LC
Cal State, San Bernardino	CA	15,238	LC
Case Western Reserve Univ	OH	32,002	MC
Central Washington Univ	WA	9,768	C
Chapman Univ	CA	33,118	VC
Clemson Univ	SC	11,972	HC
College of the Ozarks	MO	3,500	VC+
Cornell Univ	NY	38,253	MC
Delaware Valley College	PA	26,676	C
Dominican Univ	IL	23,610	C
Florida State Univ	FL	9,028	HC
Framingham State College	MA	9,381	C
Georgia Southern Univ	GA	8,540	C
Immaculata Univ	PA	25,200	C
Indiana State Univ	IN	10,719	LC
Indiana Univ of Pennsylvania	PA	10,489	C
Iowa State Univ	IA	10,768	VC
Kansas State Univ	KS	8,728	VC
Louisiana State Univ and A&M College	LA	9,126	VC
Madonna Univ	MI	11,504	VC
Marymount College of Fordham Univ	NY	27,686	C
Meredith College	NC	23,065	C
Mich State Univ	MI	11,933	VC
Minn State Univ, Mankato	MN	8,803	LC
Miss State Univ	MS	9,139	C
N Car State Univ	NC	9,886	VC
N Dak State Univ	ND	8,435	C
Northwest Missouri State Univ	MO	9,334	C
Oregon State Univ	OR	11,055	C
Penn State Univ/Univ Park Campus	PA	15,646	HC
Purdue Univ/West Lafayette	IN	12,560	VC
Radford Univ	VA	8,500	C
Rutgers, The State Univ of New Jersey/New Brunswick/Piscataway Campus	NJ	15,800	HC
San Jose State Univ	CA	8,187	C
Seattle Pacific Univ	WA	25,944	VC
Simmons College	MA	33,000	VC
S Car State Univ	SC	6,586	LC
S Dak State Univ	SD	7,782	C
Southeast Missouri State Univ	MO	9,704	C
Southern Illinois Univ Carbondale	IL	10,407	C
Stephen F. Austin State Univ	TX	7,552	C
Texas A&M Univ at Kingsville	TX	6,740	LC
Texas State Univ	TX	9,320	VC
Texas Tech Univ	TX	10,768	VC
Tuskegee Univ	AL	17,250	LC
Univ of Alabama	AL	9,040	C+
Univ of Arkansas	AR	9,855	VC
Univ of Calif at Davis	CA	14,995	VC
Univ of Delaware	DE	12,616	HC
Univ of Florida	FL	8,580	MC
Univ of Georgia	GA	8,656	VC
Univ of Hawaii at Manoa	HI	9,565	VC
Univ of Idaho	ID	8,216	C
Univ of Illinois at Urbana-Champaign	IL	11,316	HC+
Univ of Kentucky	KY	7,765	C
Univ of Maine	ME	12,080	C+
Univ of Maryland/College Park	MD	14,227	HC
Univ of Mass Amherst	MA	13,980	C+
Univ of Minn/Twin Cities	MN	13,160	VC
Univ of Missouri/Columbia	MO	13,782	VC
Univ of Nebr at Lincoln	NE	9,975	C+
Univ of Rhode Island	RI	13,720	VC
Univ of Tenn at Knoxville	TN	8,214	C
Univ of the District of Columbia	DC	2,070	LC
Univ of Vermont	VT	16,316	VC
Univ of Washington	WA	10,361	VC
Univ of Wisc/Madison	WI	8,262	VC
Univ of Wisc/River Falls	WI	8,358	LC
Utah State Univ	UT	7,371	C
Virginia Polytechnic Inst and State Univ	VA	9,179	C
Washington State Univ	WA	11,334	C
Wayne State Univ	MI	11,774	C
Winthrop Univ	SC	11,302	C

FOOD SERVICES TECHNOLOGY

School	ST	$IS	SR
Brigham Young Univ	UT	8,504	HC
Delaware Valley College	PA	26,676	C
Inter American Univ of PR/Bayamon Univ College	PR	3,522	
Johnson and Wales Univ	RI	22,965	LC
Kent State Univ	OH	12,932	C
Mount Mary College	WI	20,370	C
Pennsylvania College of Technology	PA	15,126	NC
Univ of Tenn at Knoxville	TN	8,214	C

FOREIGN LANGUAGES EDUCATION

School	ST	$IS	SR
Abilene Christian Univ	TX	18,370	VC
Adams State College	CO	7,468	C
Adelphi Univ	NY	26,300	VC
Alabama State Univ	AL	6,404	C
Alfred Univ	NY	28,290	C
American International College	MA	24,690	LC
Anderson Univ	IN	19,430	LC
Appalachian State Univ	NC	7,637	VC
Arkansas State Univ	AR	8,450	C
Asbury College	KY	20,704	VC
Ashland Univ	OH	24,464	C
Auburn Univ	AL	10,396	VC
Averett Univ	VA	23,010	LC
Ball State Univ	IN	8,660	C
Baylor Univ	TX	23,864	VC
Bemidji State Univ	MN	9,103	C
Berea College	KY	5,030	VC+
Bethany College	WV	19,845	VC
Bethel College	MN	25,180	VC
Blue Mountain College	MS	10,226	C
Boston Univ	MA	38,194	HC+
Bowling Green State Univ	OH	13,036	C
Calif Univ of Pennsylvania	PA	10,388	C
Canisius College	NY	28,163	C+
Carroll College	MT	20,576	VC
Carroll College	WI	22,740	C
Carson-Newman College	TN	16,760	C
Carthage College	WI	25,000	C
Cedarville Univ	OH	19,954	VC
Centenary College of Louisiana	LA	23,100	VC+
Central Methodist College	MO	16,460	C
Central Mich Univ	MI	11,142	C
Central Missouri State Univ	MO	9,776	C
Central Washington Univ	WA	9,768	C
Christopher Newport Univ	VA	8,862	VC
CUNY/Brooklyn College	NY	4,353	C+
CUNY/City College	NY	4,230	C+
CUNY/Herbert H. Lehman College	NY	3,320	LC
CUNY/Hunter College	NY	6,729	C+
Clarion Univ of Pennsylvania	PA	11,272	LC
College of New Jersey	NJ	15,950	MC
College of Notre Dame of Maryland	MD	27,700	C
College of Our Lady of the Elms	MA	20,644	C
College of St. Rose	NY	22,864	C
College of the Ozarks	MO	3,500	VC+
Columbus State Univ	GA	7,846	C
Concordia College: Moorhead	MN	22,460	VC+
Conn College	CT	37,900	MC
Converse College	SC	24,710	VC
Cornell College	IA	27,825	VC+
Daemen College	NY	22,120	C
Dana College	NE	20,280	C
David Lipscomb Univ	TN	16,158	VC
Delta State Univ	MS	6,618	C
DePaul Univ	IL	27,580	VC
Dordt College	IA	20,170	VC
Duquesne Univ	PA	26,907	VC
East Carolina Univ	NC	8,671	C
East Stroudsburg Univ of Pennsylvania	PA	10,336	C
East Tenn State Univ	TN	8,497	C
Eastern Kentucky Univ	KY	7,708	C
Eastern Mich Univ	MI	11,478	C
Eastern Washington Univ	WA	9,012	C
Edinboro Univ of Pennsylvania	PA	10,850	LC
Elmira College	NY	33,820	VC
Elon Univ	NC	22,240	VC
Emporia State Univ	KS	6,998	C
Erskine College	SC	23,166	VC
Evangel Univ	MO	15,435	C
Fairmont State	WV	8,280	LC
Florida Atlantic Univ	FL	8,543	C
Florida International Univ	FL	9,912	VC
Florida Southern College	FL	23,592	C
Florida State Univ	FL	9,028	HC
Friends Univ	KS	15,962	LC
Gannon Univ	PA	23,260	C
Gardner-Webb Univ	NC	19,300	C
George Mason Univ	VA	9,732	VC
Georgetown College	KY	22,000	VC
Georgia Southwestern State Univ	GA	6,013	C
Gettysburg College	PA	35,646	HC
Goshen College	IN	22,450	VC
Grace College	IN	19,825	VC
Grambling State Univ	LA	6,538	NC
Grand Valley State Univ	MI	11,022	VC
Greensboro College	NC	21,750	C
Greenville College	IL	21,342	C
Gustavus Adolphus College	MN	27,120	VC+
Hamline Univ	MN	27,052	VC
Harding Univ	AR	14,890	VC
Hardin-Simmons Univ	TX	14,165	C
Hastings College	NE	19,928	VC
Heidelberg College	OH	20,266	NC
Hillsdale College	MI	22,450	HC
Hofstra Univ	NY	27,112	VC
Holy Family College	PA	13,710	LC
Hood College	MD	27,795	VC
Hope College	MI	25,340	VC
Houston Baptist Univ	TX	16,905	C
Illinois College	IL	19,100	VC
Immaculata Univ	PA	25,200	C
Indiana State Univ	IN	10,719	LC
Indiana Univ of Pennsylvania	PA	10,489	C
Indiana Univ-Purdue Univ Fort Wayne	IN	5,108	LC
Indiana Univ-Purdue Univ Indianapolis	IN	8,257	LC
Iona College	NY	27,988	VC
Ithaca College	NY	31,730	HC
Juniata College	PA	29,080	VC
Keene State College	NH	12,212	C
Kennesaw State Univ	GA	2,724	C
Kent State Univ	OH	12,932	C
King's College	PA	26,990	C
La Roche College	PA	22,094	C
La Salle Univ	PA	31,260	VC
Lamar Univ	TX	6,816	LC
Le Moyne College	NY	26,400	VC
Lenoir-Rhyne College	NC	19,186	C
Lock Haven Univ of Pennsylvania	PA	11,098	LC
LIU/C.W. Post Campus	NY	28,282	C
Loras College	IA	24,233	C
Louisiana Tech Univ	LA	7,361	C
Malone College	OH	20,995	C
Manhattan College	NY	27,400	VC
Mansfield Univ	PA	11,220	C
Marshall Univ	WV	9,116	C

ST = STATE $IS = IN-STATE COSTS SR = SELECTOR RATING

School	ST	$IS	SR
Mary Baldwin College	VA	24,939	C
Marymount College of Fordham Univ	NY	27,686	C
McNeese State Univ	LA	5,259	LC
Messiah College	PA	25,890	VC+
Miami Univ	OH	15,033	HC
Millikin Univ	IL	25,555	C
Minn State Univ, Mankato	MN	8,803	LC
Minn State Univ, Moorehead	MN	7,000	LC
Minot State Univ	ND	6,602	LC
Missouri Southern State Univ	MO	8,316	C
Missouri Western State College	MO	8,522	NC
Monmouth Univ	NJ	26,334	C
Mount Mary College	WI	20,370	C
Mount Vernon Nazarene Univ	OH	18,925	C
Murray State Univ	KY	7,816	VC
Muskingum College	OH	20,680	C
Nazareth College of Rochester	NY	24,936	VC
New York Univ	NY	39,406	MC
Niagara Univ	NY	25,050	C
N Car State Univ	NC	9,886	VC
North Georgia College and State Univ	GA	6,984	C
Northern Arizona Univ	AZ	9,002	C
Northern State Univ	SD	7,117	LC
Northwest Nazarene Univ	ID	20,360	VC
Northwestern College of Iowa	IA	19,640	C+
Ohio Wesleyan Univ	OH	32,550	VC+
Okla Baptist Univ	OK	15,220	VC
Okla City Univ	OK	19,580	VC
Old Dominion Univ	VA	10,441	C
Oral Roberts Univ	OK	18,490	C
Ouachita Baptist Univ	AR	18,900	VC
Pittsburg State Univ	KS	7,128	NC
Prescott College	AZ	13,430	C
Providence College	RI	30,604	HC
Purdue Univ/Calumet	IN	6,630	NC
Purdue Univ/West Lafayette	IN	12,560	VC
Radford Univ	VA	8,500	C
Rhode Island College	RI	11,565	C
Rider Univ	NJ	30,900	C
Rockhurst Univ	MO	22,960	C+
Rosemont College	PA	26,175	C
Rowan Univ	NJ	14,506	VC
Saginaw Valley State Univ	MI	11,055	C
St. Cloud State Univ	MN	8,362	C
St. Edward's Univ	TX	20,428	C
St. John's Univ	NY	30,180	C
St. Mary-of-the-Woods College	IN	23,280	C
St. Mary's Univ of Minn	MN	21,535	C
St. Michael's College	VT	30,100	VC
St. Thomas Aquinas College	NY	20,590	LC
St. Xavier Univ	IL	23,144	C
Seton Hill Univ	PA	24,930	C
Slippery Rock Univ of Pennsylvania	PA	10,343	LC
Southeast Missouri State Univ	MO	9,704	C
Southeastern Louisiana Univ	LA	6,791	LC
Southern Conn State Univ	CT	10,310	C
Southern Nazarene Univ	OK	14,634	NC
Southern Univ at New Orleans	LA	995	NC
Southern Utah Univ	UT	8,194	C
Southwest Missouri State Univ	MO	8,918	C
Southwestern College	KS	19,560	C
SUNY at Oswego	NY	12,650	C
SUNY at Potsdam	NY	12,160	C
SUNY/College at Buffalo	NY	8,025	C
SUNY/College at Cortland	NY	12,095	C
SUNY/College at Fredonia	NY	11,562	VC
SUNY/College at Old Westbury	NY	12,784	C
SUNY/College at Oneonta	NY	11,870	VC
SUNY/Univ at Albany	NY	12,951	HC
SUNY/Univ at New Paltz	NY	11,565	VC
Taylor Univ	IN	23,820	VC+
Temple Univ	PA	15,912	C
Texas Southern Univ	TX	8,920	NC
Texas State Univ	TX	9,320	VC
Thomas Edison State College	NJ	3,325	SP
Trinity Univ	TX	26,466	HC+
Troy State Univ	AL	7,696	C
Turabo Univ	PR	4,110	
Univ of Akron	OH	13,134	NC
Univ of Central Arkansas	AR	6,388	C
Univ of Central Florida	FL	10,038	VC
Univ of Central Okla	OK	9,434	C
Univ of Cincinnati	OH	14,736	C
Univ of Conn	CT	14,608	VC
Univ of Delaware	DE	12,616	HC
Univ of Evansville	IN	24,190	VC
Univ of Findlay	OH	23,962	NC
Univ of Georgia	GA	8,656	VC
Univ of Idaho	ID	8,216	C
Univ of Illinois at Chicago	IL	13,418	C
Univ of Illinois at Urbana-Champaign	IL	11,316	HC+
Univ of Indianapolis	IN	22,560	VC
Univ of Iowa	IA	10,923	VC
Univ of Kentucky	KY	7,765	C
Univ of Louisiana at Lafayette	LA	5,826	C
Univ of Louisiana at Monroe	LA	5,207	NC
Univ of Louisville	KY	8,762	VC
Univ of Mary Hardin-Baylor	TX	17,268	C
Univ of Mich/Flint	MI	5,548	C
Univ of Minn/Duluth	MN	12,470	C
Univ of Miss	MS	7,666	C
Univ of Nebr at Kearney	NE	8,286	NC
Univ of Nebr at Lincoln	NE	9,975	C+
Univ of New Orleans	LA	7,356	C
Univ of North Alabama	AL	7,972	NC
Univ of N Car at Chapel Hill	NC	10,117	MC
Univ of N Car at Charlotte	NC	8,185	C
Univ of N Car at Greensboro	NC	8,248	C
Univ of Northern Iowa	IA	9,834	C
Univ of Okla	OK	9,226	VC
Univ of PR/Mayaguez	PR		
Univ of South Florida	FL	9,454	C
Univ of Southern Miss	MS	8,324	LC
Univ of Toledo	OH	12,479	NC
Univ of Vermont	VT	16,316	VC
Univ of Wisc/Eau Claire	WI	8,463	VC
Univ of Wisc/River Falls	WI	8,358	LC
Univ of Wisc/Whitewater	WI	8,626	C
Utah State Univ	UT	7,371	C
Vassar College	NY	37,030	MC
Wartburg College	IA	21,165	VC
Washington Univ in St. Louis	MO	38,293	MC
Wayne State College	NE	7,352	NC
Weber State Univ	UT	7,945	NC
West Chester Univ of Pennsylvania	PA	11,164	C
West Texas A&M Univ	TX	7,533	C
West Virginia Univ	WV	9,370	C
Western Carolina Univ	NC	6,742	C
Western State College of Colo	CO	9,014	C
Western Washington Univ	WA	10,119	VC
Whitworth College	WA	26,428	VC+
Winona State Univ	MN		C
Wittenberg Univ	OH	31,316	VC
Wright State Univ	OH	11,490	LC
Youngstown State Univ	OH	11,148	NC

FORENSIC STUDIES

School	ST	$IS	SR
Albany State Univ	GA	5,764	C+
Alvernia College	PA	23,212	LC
Bay Path College	MA	24,910	C
Baylor Univ	TX	23,864	VC
Cal State, Stanislaus	CA	9,874	C
Chaminade Univ of Honolulu	HI	21,430	LC
Champlain College	VT	22,030	C
Chatham College	PA	27,266	C+
CUNY/John Jay College of Criminal Justice	NY	4,259	C
College of the Ozarks	MO	3,500	VC+
Columbia College	MO	16,139	C
Defiance College	OH	22,615	C
Eastern Kentucky Univ	KY	7,708	C
Edinboro Univ of Pennsylvania	PA	10,850	LC
Florida Inst of Technology	FL	28,740	VC
Guilford College	NC	24,960	VC
Inter American Univ of PR/Bayamon Univ College	PR	3,522	
Loyola Univ New Orleans	LA	31,036	VC+
Mercyhurst College	PA	20,694	C
Mountain State Univ	WV	10,212	NC
Russell Sage College	NY	26,811	C
St. Andrews Presbyterian College	NC	20,525	C
St. Edward's Univ	TX	20,428	C
Tri-State Univ-Main Campus	IN	23,600	C
Univ of Central Florida	FL	10,038	VC
Univ of Central Okla	OK	9,434	C
Univ of Miss	MS	7,666	C
Univ of New Haven	CT	28,650	C
Univ of N Dak	ND	8,390	C
Waynesburg College	PA	19,370	C
Youngstown State Univ	OH	11,148	NC

FOREST ENGINEERING

School	ST	$IS	SR
Auburn Univ	AL	10,396	VC
Oregon State Univ	OR	11,055	C
SUNY/College of Environmental Science and Forestry	NY	14,167	VC
Univ of Maine	ME	12,080	C+
Univ of Washington	WA	10,361	VC

FORESTRY AND RELATED SCIENCES

School	ST	$IS	SR
Alabama A&M Univ	AL	5,100	LC
Baylor Univ	TX	23,864	VC
Clemson Univ	SC	11,972	HC
College of St. Benedict	MN	26,672	VC
Colo State Univ	CO	9,964	VC
Eastern Mich Univ	MI	11,478	C
Eastern Oregon Univ	OR	10,080	NC
Elizabethtown College	PA	28,800	C
High Point Univ	NC	22,480	C
Humboldt State Univ	CA	9,400	C
Iowa State Univ	IA	10,768	VC
Louisiana State Univ and A&M College	LA	9,126	VC
Louisiana Tech Univ	LA	7,361	C
Mich State Univ	MI	11,933	VC
Mich Tech Univ	MI	13,235	VC
N Car State Univ	NC	9,886	VC
Northern Arizona Univ	AZ	9,002	C
Northwest Missouri State Univ	MO	9,334	C
Ohio State Univ	OH	13,080	VC+
Okla State Univ	OK	9,216	VC
Oregon State Univ	OR	11,055	C
Penn State Univ/Univ Park Campus	PA	15,646	HC
Purdue Univ/West Lafayette	IN	12,560	VC
St. John's Univ	MN	26,473	VC
Southern Illinois Univ Carbondale	IL	10,407	C
Southern Univ and A&M College	LA	7,372	LC
SUNY/College of Environmental Science and Forestry	NY	14,167	VC
Stephen F. Austin State Univ	TX	7,552	C
Texas A&M Univ	TX	11,081	HC
Thomas Edison State College	NJ	3,325	SP
Univ of Arkansas at Monticello	AR	5,940	NC
Univ of Calif at Berkeley	CA	15,563	MC
Univ of Florida	FL	8,580	MC
Univ of Georgia	GA	8,656	VC
Univ of Illinois at Urbana-Champaign	IL	11,316	HC+
Univ of Kentucky	KY	7,765	C
Univ of Maine	ME	12,080	C+
Univ of Mass Amherst	MA	13,980	C+
Univ of Minn/Twin Cities	MN	13,160	VC
Univ of Montana	MT	9,395	C
Univ of New Hampshire	NH	14,828	VC
Univ of Tenn at Knoxville	TN	8,214	C
Univ of the South	TN	30,855	HC
Univ of Vermont	VT	16,316	VC
Univ of Wisc/Madison	WI	8,262	VC
Univ of Wisc/Stevens Point	WI	8,116	VC
Utah State Univ	UT	7,371	C
Virginia Polytechnic Inst and State Univ	VA	9,179	C
Washington State Univ	WA	11,334	C
West Virginia Univ	WV	9,370	C
Western New Mexico Univ	NM	5,950	LC

FORESTRY PRODUCTION AND PROCESSING

School	ST	$IS	SR
Auburn Univ	AL	10,396	VC
Clemson Univ	SC	11,972	HC
Louisiana State Univ and A&M College	LA	9,126	VC
Miss State Univ	MS	9,139	C
Oregon State Univ	OR	11,055	C
Penn State Univ/Univ Park Campus	PA	15,646	HC
Stephen F. Austin State Univ	TX	7,552	C
Univ of Idaho	ID	8,216	C
Univ of Minn/Twin Cities	MN	13,160	VC
Univ of Washington	WA	10,361	VC

FRENCH

School	ST	$IS	SR
Adrian College	MI	21,950	C
Agnes Scott College	GA	28,230	HC
Alabama A&M Univ	AL	5,100	LC
Alabama State Univ	AL	6,404	C
Albany State Univ	GA	5,764	C+
Albion College	MI	25,224	VC
Albright College	PA	30,579	C
Alfred Univ	NY	28,290	C
Allegheny College	PA	30,280	VC
Alma College	MI	25,566	VC
Amherst College	MA	37,470	MC
Anderson Univ	IN	19,430	LC
Andrews Univ	MI	19,550	C
Angelo State Univ	TX	7,576	NC
Appalachian State Univ	NC	7,637	VC
Aquinas College	MI	21,894	C
Arizona State Univ-Main	AZ	10,048	C
Arkansas State Univ	AR	8,450	C
Asbury College	KY	20,704	VC
Ashland Univ	OH	24,464	C
Assumption College	MA	29,375	C
Auburn Univ	AL	10,396	VC
Augsburg College	MN	25,298	C
Augusta State Univ	GA	2,592	C
Augustana College	IL	26,610	VC+
Augustana College	SD	21,998	VC
Austin College	TX	24,747	HC
Austin Peay State Univ	TN	5,814	LC
Baker Univ	KS	19,860	VC
Baldwin-Wallace College	OH	24,678	C
Ball State Univ	IN	8,660	C
Bard College	NY	37,352	HC+
Barry Univ	FL	24,100	LC
Bates College	ME	37,500	MC
Baylor Univ	TX	23,864	VC
Belmont Univ	TN	21,986	VC
Beloit College	WI	29,864	HC
Benedictine College	KS	20,603	C
Bennington College	VT	35,910	HC
Berea College	KY	5,030	VC+
Berry College	GA	21,410	VC
Bethany College	WV	19,845	VC
Birmingham-Southern College	AL	25,364	VC+
Bloomsburg Univ of Pennsylvania	PA	10,844	C
Boston College	MA	33,284	MC
Boston Univ	MA	38,194	HC+
Bowdoin College	ME	37,790	MC
Bowling Green State Univ	OH	13,036	C
Bradley Univ	IL	22,910	VC
Brandeis Univ	MA	38,198	MC
Bridgewater College	VA	25,150	C
Brigham Young Univ	UT	8,504	HC
Bryn Mawr College	PA	36,890	HC+
Bucknell Univ	PA	35,262	HC+
Butler Univ	IN	28,250	VC+
Cabrini College	PA	29,020	C
Caldwell College	NJ	24,060	LC
Calif Lutheran Univ	CA	27,600	LC
Cal State, Chico	CA	8,598	LC
Cal State, Fresno	CA	8,414	LC
Cal State, Fullerton	CA	6,648	C
Cal State, Hayward	CA	8,871	LC
Cal State, Long Beach	CA	8,762	C+
Cal State, Los Angeles	CA	5,778	C
Cal State, Northridge	CA	7,757	LC
Cal State, Sacramento	CA	9,543	C
Cal State, San Bernardino	CA	15,238	LC
Cal State, Stanislaus	CA	9,874	C
Calif Univ of Pennsylvania	PA	10,388	C
Calvin College	MI	22,615	NC
Campbell Univ	NC	18,268	VC
Canisius College	NY	28,163	C+
Capital Univ	OH	26,550	C
Cardinal Stritch Univ	WI	17,620	C
Carleton College	MN	34,395	MC
Carnegie Mellon Univ	PA	32,682	MC
Carroll College	MT	20,576	VC
Carson-Newman College	TN	16,760	C
Carthage College	WI	25,000	C
Case Western Reserve Univ	OH	32,002	MC
Catawba College	NC	20,500	C
Catholic Univ of America	DC	34,248	VC
Cedar Crest College	PA	25,145	C+
Centenary College of Louisiana	LA	23,100	VC+
Central College	IA	21,206	C
Central Conn State Univ	CT	12,090	C
Central Methodist College	MO	16,460	C
Central Mich Univ	MI	11,142	C
Central Missouri State Univ	MO	9,776	C
Central Washington Univ	WA	9,768	C
Centre College	KY	27,300	HC
Chapman Univ	CA	33,118	VC
Chatham College	PA	27,266	C+
Chestnut Hill College	PA	26,450	LC
Christendom College	VA	18,410	VC+
Christopher Newport Univ	VA	8,862	VC
Citadel, The	SC	12,295	C+
CUNY/Brooklyn College	NY	4,353	C+
CUNY/City College	NY	4,230	C+
CUNY/Herbert H. Lehman College	NY	3,320	LC
CUNY/Hunter College	NY	6,729	C+
CUNY/Queens College	NY	4,362	C
CUNY/York College	NY	3,292	NC
Claremont McKenna College	CA	36,880	MC
Clarion Univ of Pennsylvania	PA	11,272	LC
Clark Univ	MA	32,115	VC
Clemson Univ	SC	11,972	HC
Cleveland State Univ	OH	12,308	LC
Coe College	IA	27,385	VC
Coker College	SC	21,491	VC
Colgate Univ	NY	37,095	MC
College of Charleston	SC	11,887	HC
College of Mount St. Vincent	NY	26,800	C
College of New Rochelle	NY	21,800	C
College of St. Benedict	MN	26,672	VC
College of St. Catherine	MN	24,010	VC
College of the Holy Cross	MA	36,451	MC

ST = STATE $IS = IN-STATE COSTS SR = SELECTOR RATING

ST = STATE   **$IS** = IN-STATE COSTS   **SR** = SELECTOR RATING

School	ST	$IS	SR
Tulane Univ	LA	37,451	HC+
Union College	NE	17,130	C
Union Univ	TN	18,800	VC
Univ of Akron	OH	13,134	NC
Univ of Alabama	AL	9,040	C+
Univ of Alabama at Birmingham	AL	12,901	C
Univ of Arizona	AZ	10,413	VC
Univ of Arkansas	AR	9,855	VC
Univ of Arkansas at Little Rock	AR	5,637	NC
Univ of Calif at Berkeley	CA	15,563	MC
Univ of Calif at Davis	CA	14,995	VC
Univ of Calif at Irvine	CA	19,808	HC
Univ of Calif at Los Angeles	CA	15,330	MC
Univ of Calif at Riverside	CA	15,300	C
Univ of Calif at Santa Barbara	CA	11,732	VC
Univ of Calif at Santa Cruz	CA	16,505	VC
Univ of Central Arkansas	AR	6,388	C
Univ of Central Florida	FL	10,038	VC
Univ of Central Okla	OK	9,434	C
Univ of Cincinnati	OH	14,736	C
Univ of Colo at Boulder	CO	10,774	VC
Univ of Colo at Denver	CO	3,302	C
Univ of Conn	CT	14,608	VC
Univ of Dallas	TX	25,898	VC+
Univ of Dayton	OH	24,850	VC
Univ of Denver	CO	32,148	VC
Univ of Evansville	IN	24,190	VC
Univ of Florida	FL	8,580	MC
Univ of Georgia	GA	8,656	VC
Univ of Hawaii at Manoa	HI	9,565	VC
Univ of Houston	TX	9,818	C
Univ of Idaho	ID	8,216	C
Univ of Illinois at Chicago	IL	13,418	C
Univ of Illinois at Urbana-Champaign	IL	11,316	HC+
Univ of Indianapolis	IN	22,560	VC
Univ of Iowa	IA	10,923	VC
Univ of Kansas	KS	8,923	VC
Univ of Kentucky	KY	7,765	C
Univ of La Verne	CA	28,600	C
Univ of Louisiana at Lafayette	LA	5,826	C
Univ of Louisiana at Monroe	LA	5,207	NC
Univ of Louisville	KY	8,762	VC
Univ of Maine	ME	12,080	C+
Univ of Maine at Fort Kent	ME	9,770	LC
Univ of Maryland/Baltimore County	MD	14,668	VC+
Univ of Maryland/College Park	MD	14,227	HC
Univ of Mass Amherst	MA	13,980	C+
Univ of Mass Boston	MA	6,227	C
Univ of Mass Dartmouth	MA	12,835	C
Univ of Miami	FL	34,608	HC
Univ of Mich/Ann Arbor	MI	13,864	HC+
Univ of Mich/Flint	MI	5,548	C
Univ of Minn/Morris	MN	12,896	VC
Univ of Minn/Twin Cities	MN	13,160	VC
Univ of Miss	MS	7,666	C
Univ of Missouri/Columbia	MO	13,782	VC
Univ of Missouri/Kansas City	MO	13,416	VC
Univ of Missouri/St. Louis	MO	11,656	VC
Univ of Montana	MT	9,395	C
Univ of Montevallo	AL	8,478	C
Univ of Nebr at Kearney	NE	8,286	NC
Univ of Nebr at Lincoln	NE	9,975	C+
Univ of Nebr at Omaha	NE	8,080	C
Univ of Nevada/Las Vegas	NV	11,566	C
Univ of Nevada/Reno	NV	9,792	C
Univ of New Hampshire	NH	14,828	VC
Univ of New Mexico	NM	9,223	C
Univ of New Orleans	LA	7,356	C
Univ of North Alabama	AL	7,972	NC
Univ of N Car at Asheville	NC	8,079	VC
Univ of N Car at Charlotte	NC	8,185	C
Univ of N Car at Greensboro	NC	8,248	C
Univ of N Car at Wilmington	NC	8,940	VC
Univ of N Dak	ND	8,390	C
Univ of North Texas	TX	7,629	C
Univ of Northern Colo	CO	8,987	C
Univ of Northern Iowa	IA	9,834	C
Univ of Notre Dame	IN	34,442	MC
Univ of Okla	OK	9,226	VC
Univ of Oregon	OR	11,479	VC
Univ of Pennsylvania	PA	37,960	MC
Univ of Pittsburgh at Pittsburgh	PA	16,074	HC
Univ of PR/Mayaguez	PR		
Univ of Puget Sound	WA	31,760	HC
Univ of Redlands	CA	32,576	VC
Univ of Rhode Island	RI	13,720	VC
Univ of Richmond	VA	30,100	MC
Univ of Rochester	NY	32,979	HC
Univ of St. Thomas	MN	26,918	VC
Univ of St. Thomas	TX	21,952	VC
Univ of San Diego	CA	33,156	HC
Univ of San Francisco	CA	34,700	VC
Univ of Scranton	PA	30,836	VC
Univ of S Car at Columbia	SC	10,048	VC
Univ of S Car at Spartanburg	SC	9,936	C+
Univ of South Florida	FL	9,454	C
Univ of Southern Calif	CA	37,459	MC
Univ of Southern Maine	ME	11,212	C
Univ of Tenn at Chattanooga	TN	7,783	C
Univ of Tenn at Knoxville	TN	8,214	C
Univ of Tenn at Martin	TN	7,748	C
Univ of Texas at Arlington	TX	7,192	LC
Univ of Texas at Austin	TX	10,630	HC
Univ of Texas at El Paso	TX	5,799	NC
Univ of Texas at San Antonio	TX	9,088	NC
Univ of the District of Columbia	DC	2,070	LC
Univ of the Pacific	CA	31,090	VC
Univ of the South	TN	30,855	HC
Univ of Toledo	OH	12,479	NC
Univ of Tulsa	OK	22,090	VC+
Univ of Utah	UT	9,205	C
Univ of Vermont	VT	16,316	VC
Univ of Virginia	VA	11,740	MC
Univ of Virginia's College at Wise	VA	10,116	C
Univ of Washington	WA	10,361	VC
Univ of Wisc/Eau Claire	WI	8,463	VC
Univ of Wisc/Green Bay	WI	8,154	C
Univ of Wisc/La Crosse	WI	8,991	VC
Univ of Wisc/Madison	WI	8,262	VC
Univ of Wisc/Milwaukee	WI	9,427	LC
Univ of Wisc/Oshkosh	WI	6,130	LC
Univ of Wisc/Parkside	WI	6,160	LC
Univ of Wisc/Platteville	WI	8,450	C
Univ of Wisc/Stevens Point	WI	8,116	VC
Univ of Wisc/Whitewater	WI	8,626	C
Univ of Wyoming	WY	8,636	C
Ursinus College	PA	34,400	VC
Utah State Univ	UT	7,371	C
Valdosta State Univ	GA	7,798	C
Valparaiso Univ	IN	26,118	VC+
Vanderbilt Univ	TN	37,897	MC
Villanova Univ	PA	35,050	HC
Virginia Polytechnic Inst and State Univ	VA	9,179	C
Virginia Wesleyan College	VA	25,350	C
Wabash College	IN	27,932	VC
Wake Forest Univ	NC	34,090	MC
Walla Walla College	WA	21,600	NC
Walsh Univ	OH	20,890	C
Wartburg College	IA	21,165	VC
Washburn Univ of Topeka	KS	8,984	NC
Washington and Jefferson College	PA	29,570	VC
Washington and Lee Univ	VA	29,663	MC
Washington College	MD	30,540	VC
Washington State Univ	WA	11,334	C
Washington Univ in St. Louis	MO	38,293	MC
Weber State Univ	UT	7,945	NC
Webster Univ	MO	21,848	VC
Wellesley College	MA	36,516	MC
Wells College	NY	21,122	VC
Wesleyan College	GA	17,870	VC
Wesleyan Univ	CT	35,139	MC
West Chester Univ of Pennsylvania	PA	11,164	C
Western Carolina Univ	NC	6,742	C
Western Illinois Univ	IL	10,363	C
Western Kentucky Univ	KY	6,834	C
Western Mich Univ	MI	12,031	C
Western Washington Univ	WA	10,119	VC
Westminster College	MO	18,150	C+
Westminster College	PA	22,960	C
Westmont College	CA	33,062	VC+
Wheaton College	IL	21,934	HC
Wheaton College	MA	36,330	HC
Wheeling Jesuit Univ	WV	22,660	C
Whitman College	WA	32,526	HC+
Whittier College	CA	29,108	C
Whitworth College	WA	26,428	VC+
Wichita State Univ	KS	8,092	C
Wilkes Univ	PA	28,060	C
Willamette Univ	OR	32,032	VC+
William Jewell College	MO	21,320	VC
Williams College	MA	32,270	MC
Wilson College	PA	23,912	C
Winona State Univ	MN		C
Winthrop Univ	SC	11,302	C
Wittenberg Univ	OH	31,316	VC
Wofford College	SC	26,710	HC
Wright State Univ	OH	11,490	LC
Xavier Univ	OH	26,850	VC+
Xavier Univ of Louisiana	LA	17,600	C
Yale Univ	CT	37,000	MC
Yeshiva Univ	NY	21,400	C
Youngstown State Univ	OH	11,148	NC

FRENCH STUDIES

School	ST	$IS	SR
American Univ	DC	34,585	VC+
Assumption College	MA	29,375	C
Bard College	NY	37,352	HC+
Boston Univ	MA	38,194	HC+
Brown Univ	RI	38,174	MC
Case Western Reserve Univ	OH	32,002	MC
Colby College	ME	37,570	MC
Columbia Univ/School of General Studies	NY	35,000	C
Duke Univ	NC	37,555	MC
Emory Univ	GA	36,872	MC
Fairleigh Dickinson Univ/College at Florham	NJ	30,130	C
Fairleigh Dickinson Univ/Metropolitan Campus	NJ	28,584	C
Fordham Univ	NY	35,066	HC
Lewis and Clark College	OR	30,620	VC
New College of Florida	FL	8,906	HC+
Reed College	OR	36,950	MC
Rice Univ	TX	27,550	MC
St. Joseph's Univ	PA	33,590	VC
Scripps College	CA	35,700	HC+
Simon's Rock College of Bard	MA	36,580	HC
Skidmore College	NY	37,930	HC
Smith College	MA	37,034	HC+
S Dak State Univ	SD	7,782	C
SUNY/Univ at Stony Brook	NY	12,763	HC
Univ of Calif at San Diego	CA	14,127	HC
Univ of New Hampshire	NH	14,828	VC
Univ of S Dak	SD	7,710	C+
Univ of the South	TN	30,855	HC
Wartburg College	IA	21,165	VC
Wayne State Univ	MI	11,774	C
Wellesley College	MA	36,516	MC
Wesleyan Univ	CT	35,139	MC

FUNERAL HOME SERVICES

School	ST	$IS	SR
Cincinnati College of Mortuary Science	OH	11,865	SP
Mount Ida College	MA	25,596	LC
Point Park Univ	PA	21,840	C
St. John's Univ	NY	30,180	C
Southern Illinois Univ Carbondale	IL	10,407	C
Univ of Central Okla	OK	9,434	C
Wayne State Univ	MI	11,774	C

FURNITURE DESIGN

School	ST	$IS	SR
Calif College of the Arts	CA	31,530	SP
Cal State, San Bernardino	CA	15,238	LC
Indiana Univ-Purdue Univ Indianapolis	IN	8,257	LC
Kendall College of Art and Design of Ferris State Univ	MI	10,784	SP
Minneapolis College of Art and Design	MN	28,950	SP
N Car State Univ	NC	9,886	VC
Rhode Island School of Design	RI	33,569	SP
Rochester Inst of Technology	NY	29,217	VC+
Savannah College of Art and Design	GA	27,560	SP

GENDER STUDIES

School	ST	$IS	SR
Brown Univ	RI	38,174	MC
Conn College	CT	37,900	MC
Indiana Univ Bloomington	IN	12,389	VC
Lawrence Univ	WI	30,900	HC
Louisiana State Univ and A&M College	LA	9,126	VC
New York Univ	NY	39,406	MC
Northwestern Univ	IL	37,491	MC
Sonoma State Univ	CA	10,421	C
Univ of Calif at San Diego	CA	14,127	HC
Univ of Chicago	IL	35,087	MC
Univ of Texas at Dallas	TX	10,234	HC

GENETICS

School	ST	$IS	SR
Ball State Univ	IN	8,660	C
Cal State, Stanislaus	CA	9,874	C
Cedar Crest College	PA	25,145	C+
Cornell Univ	NY	38,253	MC
Dartmouth College	NH	37,770	MC
Florida State Univ	FL	9,028	HC
Iowa State Univ	IA	10,768	VC
Missouri Southern State Univ	MO	8,316	C
Ohio Wesleyan Univ	OH	32,550	VC+
Rutgers, The State Univ of New Jersey/New Brunswick/Piscataway Campus	NJ	15,800	HC
Texas A&M Univ	TX	11,081	HC
Univ of Calif at Davis	CA	14,995	VC
Univ of Conn	CT	14,608	VC
Univ of Georgia	GA	8,656	VC
Univ of Minn/Twin Cities	MN	13,160	VC
Univ of Rochester	NY	32,979	HC
Univ of Vermont	VT	16,316	VC
Univ of Wisc/Madison	WI	8,262	VC
Washington State Univ	WA	11,334	C
Western Kentucky Univ	KY	6,834	C

GEOCHEMISTRY

School	ST	$IS	SR
Calif Inst of Technology	CA	31,677	MC
Columbia Univ/Columbia College	NY	38,590	MC
Occidental College	CA	35,922	HC
SUNY at Oswego	NY	12,650	C
SUNY/College at Cortland	NY	12,095	C
SUNY/College at Geneseo	NY	11,330	HC
Univ of Maine at Farmington	ME	10,108	C
Western Mich Univ	MI	12,031	C

GEODETIC SCIENCE

School	ST	$IS	SR
Univ of Arkansas at Monticello	AR	5,940	NC

GEOGRAPHY

School	ST	$IS	SR
Appalachian State Univ	NC	7,637	VC
Aquinas College	MI	21,894	C
Arizona State Univ-Main	AZ	10,048	C
Arkansas State Univ	AR	8,450	C
Auburn Univ	AL	10,396	VC
Augustana College	IL	26,610	VC+
Austin Peay State Univ	TN	5,814	LC
Ball State Univ	IN	8,660	C
Baylor Univ	TX	23,864	VC
Bellevue Univ	NE	4,440	NC
Bemidji State Univ	MN	9,103	C
Bloomsburg Univ of Pennsylvania	PA	10,844	C
Boston Univ	MA	38,194	HC+
Bowling Green State Univ	OH	13,036	C
Bridgewater State College	MA	10,482	C
Brigham Young Univ	UT	8,504	HC
Bucknell Univ	PA	35,262	HC+
Calif State Polytechnic Univ, Pomona	CA	8,793	C+
Cal State, Chico	CA	8,598	LC
Cal State, Dominguez Hills	CA	5,840	LC
Cal State, Fresno	CA	8,414	LC
Cal State, Fullerton	CA	6,648	C
Cal State, Hayward	CA	8,871	LC
Cal State, Long Beach	CA	8,762	C+
Cal State, Los Angeles	CA	5,778	C
Cal State, Northridge	CA	7,757	LC
Cal State, Sacramento	CA	9,543	C
Cal State, San Bernardino	CA	15,238	LC
Cal State, Stanislaus	CA	9,874	C
Calif Univ of Pennsylvania	PA	10,388	C
Calvin College	MI	22,615	NC
Carroll College	WI	22,740	C
Carthage College	WI	25,000	C
Central Conn State Univ	CT	12,090	C
Central Mich Univ	MI	11,142	C
Central Missouri State Univ	MO	9,776	C
Central Washington Univ	WA	9,768	C
Charleston Southern Univ	SC	17,122	C
Cheyney Univ of Pennsylvania	PA	9,993	C
Chicago State Univ	IL	10,882	C+
CUNY/Herbert H. Lehman College	NY	3,320	LC
CUNY/Hunter College	NY	6,729	C+
Clarion Univ of Pennsylvania	PA	11,272	LC
Clark Univ	MA	32,115	VC
Colgate Univ	NY	37,095	MC
Concord College	WV	8,136	C
Concordia Univ Nebr	NE	20,302	C+
Concordia Univ, River Forest	IL	23,600	C
Dartmouth College	NH	37,770	MC
DePaul Univ	IL	27,580	VC
DePauw Univ	IN	31,500	HC
Dickinson State Univ	ND	6,338	NC
East Carolina Univ	NC	8,671	C
East Stroudsburg Univ of Pennsylvania	PA	10,336	C
East Tenn State Univ	TN	8,497	C
Eastern Illinois Univ	IL	11,192	C
Eastern Kentucky Univ	KY	7,708	C
Eastern Mich Univ	MI	11,478	C
Eastern Washington Univ	WA	9,012	C
Edinboro Univ of Pennsylvania	PA	10,850	LC
Elmhurst College	IL	24,630	C
Emory & Henry College	VA	21,950	C
Fayetteville State Univ	NC	5,590	LC
Fitchburg State College	MA	9,622	C
Florida Atlantic Univ	FL	8,543	C
Florida International Univ	FL	9,912	VC
Florida State Univ	FL	9,028	HC
Framingham State College	MA	9,381	C
Francis Marion Univ	SC	9,364	C
Frostburg State Univ	MD	11,114	C
George Mason Univ	VA	9,732	VC
George Washington Univ	DC	41,030	MC
Georgia Southern Univ	GA	8,540	C
Georgia State Univ	GA	10,658	C
Grand Valley State Univ	MI	11,022	VC
Gustavus Adolphus College	MN	27,120	VC+
Hampshire College	MA	37,037	HC

School	ST	$IS	SR
James Madison Univ	VA	10,794	VC
Johns Hopkins Univ	MD	38,372	MC
Juniata College	PA	29,080	VC
Kansas State Univ	KS	8,728	VC
Keene State College	NH	12,212	C
Kent State Univ	OH	12,932	C
Kutztown Univ of Pennsylvania	PA	10,786	C
La Salle Univ	PA	31,260	VC
Lafayette College	PA	35,746	MC
Lake Superior State Univ	MI	9,034	LC
Lamar Univ	TX	6,816	LC
Lawrence Univ	WI	30,900	HC
Lock Haven Univ of Pennsylvania	PA	11,098	LC
LIU/C.W. Post Campus	NY	28,282	C
Louisiana State Univ and A&M College	LA	9,126	VC
Louisiana Tech Univ	LA	7,361	C
Macalester College	MN	31,944	MC
Marietta College	OH	27,047	C
Marshall Univ	WV	9,116	C
Mary Washington College	VA	10,166	HC
McNeese State Univ	LA	5,259	LC
Mercyhurst College	PA	20,694	C
Miami Univ	OH	15,033	HC
Mich State Univ	MI	11,933	VC
Mich Tech Univ	MI	13,235	VC
Middlebury College	VT	38,100	MC
Midwestern State Univ	TX	8,045	LC
Millersville Univ of Pennsylvania	PA	11,269	C
Millsaps College	MS	25,182	VC
Minot State Univ	ND	6,602	LC
Morehead State Univ	KY	7,464	C
Mount Holyoke College	MA	37,918	HC+
Mount Union College	OH	21,120	C
Murray State Univ	KY	7,816	VC
Muskingum College	OH	20,680	C
New Jersey City Univ	NJ	11,850	LC
New Mexico Inst of Mining and Technology	NM	7,580	NC
New Mexico State Univ	NM	7,932	C
N Car State Univ	NC	9,886	VC
N Dak State Univ	ND	8,435	C
Northeastern Univ	MA	35,650	HC
Northern Arizona Univ	AZ	9,002	C
Northern Illinois Univ	IL	11,472	C
Northern Kentucky Univ	KY	6,352	NC
Northwest Missouri State Univ	MO	9,334	C
Northwestern Univ	IL	37,491	MC
Norwich Univ	VT	21,064	LC
Oberlin College	OH	36,938	MC
Occidental College	CA	35,922	HC
Ohio State Univ	OH	13,080	VC+
Ohio Univ	OH	14,448	C
Ohio Wesleyan Univ	OH	32,550	VC+
Okla State Univ	OK	9,216	VC
Old Dominion Univ	VA	10,441	C
Olivet Nazarene Univ	IL	20,480	C
Oregon State Univ	OR	11,055	C
Pomona College	CA	33,960	MC
Portland State Univ	OR	12,453	C
Prescott College	AZ	13,430	C
Princeton Univ	NJ	36,649	MC
Purdue Univ/West Lafayette	IN	12,560	VC
Radford Univ	VA	8,500	C
Rensselaer Polytechnic Inst	NY	37,579	HC+
Rice Univ	TX	27,550	MC
Rutgers, The State Univ of New Jersey/New Brunswick/Piscataway Campus	NJ	15,800	HC
Rutgers, The State Univ of New Jersey/Newark Campus	NJ	15,624	VC
St. Cloud State Univ	MN	8,362	C
St. Lawrence Univ	NY	35,945	VC
St. Louis Univ	MO	29,780	VC+
St. Norbert College	WI	25,810	C
Salem State College	MA	8,592	C
Sam Houston State Univ	TX	7,142	C
San Diego State Univ	CA	10,321	C
San Francisco State Univ	CA	12,070	C
San Jose State Univ	CA	8,187	C
Skidmore College	NY	37,930	HC
Slippery Rock Univ of Pennsylvania	PA	10,343	LC
Smith College	MA	37,034	HC+
Sonoma State Univ	CA	10,421	C
S Dak School of Mines and Technology	SD	7,854	C+
Southern Illinois Univ Carbondale	IL	10,407	C
Southern Methodist Univ	TX	34,210	HC
Southern Oregon Univ	OR	10,362	C
Southern Utah Univ	UT	8,194	C
Southwest Missouri State Univ	MO	8,918	C
Stanford Univ	CA	37,612	MC
SUNY at Oswego	NY	12,650	C
SUNY at Potsdam	NY	12,160	C
SUNY/College at Brockport	NY	12,111	C
SUNY/College at Buffalo	NY	8,025	C
SUNY/College at Cortland	NY	12,095	C
SUNY/College at Fredonia	NY	11,562	VC
SUNY/College at Geneseo	NY	11,330	HC
SUNY/College at Oneonta	NY	11,870	VC
SUNY/College at Plattsburgh	NY	11,700	C
SUNY/Univ at Albany	NY	12,951	HC
SUNY/Univ at Binghamton	NY	12,787	HC
SUNY/Univ at Buffalo	NY	12,563	VC
SUNY/Univ at New Paltz	NY	11,565	VC
SUNY/Univ at Stony Brook	NY	12,763	HC
State Univ of West Georgia	GA	7,622	C
Stephen F. Austin State Univ	TX	7,552	C
Sul Ross State Univ	TX	6,582	LC
Syracuse Univ	NY	34,720	HC
Tarleton State Univ	TX	7,576	C
Temple Univ	PA	15,912	C
Tenn Tech Univ	TN	8,670	VC
Texas A&M Univ	TX	11,081	HC
Texas A&M Univ at Commerce	TX	8,994	C
Texas A&M Univ at Corpus Christi	TX	10,269	C
Texas A&M Univ at Kingsville	TX	6,740	LC
Texas Christian Univ	TX	23,410	VC
Texas Tech Univ	TX	10,768	VC
Towson Univ	MD	12,694	VC
Tufts Univ	MA	38,233	MC
Tulane Univ	LA	37,451	HC+
Union College	NY	36,005	HC
Univ of Akron	OH	13,134	NC
Univ of Alabama	AL	9,040	C+
Univ of Alaska Fairbanks	AK	9,295	C
Univ of Arizona	AZ	10,413	VC
Univ of Arkansas	AR	9,855	VC
Univ of Arkansas at Little Rock	AR	5,637	NC
Univ of Calif at Davis	CA	14,995	VC
Univ of Calif at Los Angeles	CA	15,330	MC
Univ of Calif at Riverside	CA	15,300	C
Univ of Calif at Santa Barbara	CA	11,732	VC
Univ of Calif at Santa Cruz	CA	16,505	VC
Univ of Cincinnati	OH	14,736	C
Univ of Colo at Boulder	CO	10,774	VC
Univ of Conn	CT	14,608	VC
Univ of Dayton	OH	24,850	VC
Univ of Delaware	DE	12,616	HC
Univ of Florida	FL	8,580	MC
Univ of Georgia	GA	8,656	VC
Univ of Hawaii at Hilo	HI	6,497	C
Univ of Hawaii at Manoa	HI	9,565	VC
Univ of Houston	TX	9,818	C
Univ of Idaho	ID	8,216	C
Univ of Illinois at Chicago	IL	13,418	C
Univ of Illinois at Urbana-Champaign	IL	11,316	HC+
Univ of Iowa	IA	10,923	VC
Univ of Kansas	KS	8,923	VC
Univ of Kentucky	KY	7,765	C
Univ of Louisiana at Lafayette	LA	5,826	C
Univ of Louisiana at Monroe	LA	5,207	NC
Univ of Maine	ME	12,080	C+
Univ of Maine at Farmington	ME	10,108	C
Univ of Maryland/College Park	MD	14,227	HC
Univ of Mass Amherst	MA	13,980	C+
Univ of Memphis	TN	8,560	C
Univ of Miami	FL	34,608	HC
Univ of Minn/Duluth	MN	12,470	C
Univ of Minn/Morris	MN	12,896	VC
Univ of Minn/Twin Cities	MN	13,160	VC
Univ of Miss	MS	7,666	C
Univ of Missouri/Columbia	MO	13,782	VC
Univ of Missouri/Kansas City	MO	13,416	VC
Univ of Missouri/Rolla	MO	12,292	HC
Univ of Montana	MT	9,395	C
Univ of Nebr at Lincoln	NE	9,975	C+
Univ of Nebr at Omaha	NE	8,080	C
Univ of Nevada/Las Vegas	NV	11,566	C
Univ of Nevada/Reno	NV	9,792	C
Univ of New Hampshire	NH	14,828	VC
Univ of New Orleans	LA	7,356	C
Univ of North Alabama	AL	7,972	NC
Univ of N Car at Chapel Hill	NC	10,117	MC
Univ of N Car at Charlotte	NC	8,185	C
Univ of N Car at Wilmington	NC	8,940	VC
Univ of N Dak	ND	8,390	C
Univ of Northern Colo	CO	8,987	C
Univ of Northern Iowa	IA	9,834	C
Univ of Okla	OK	9,226	VC
Univ of Oregon	OR	11,479	VC
Univ of Pennsylvania	PA	37,960	MC
Univ of Pittsburgh at Bradford	PA	15,294	C
Univ of Pittsburgh at Johnstown	PA	15,216	LC
Univ of Pittsburgh at Pittsburgh	PA	16,074	HC
Univ of PR/Mayaguez	PR		
Univ of Puget Sound	WA	31,760	HC
Univ of Rhode Island	RI	13,720	VC
Univ of Rochester	NY	32,979	HC
Univ of St. Thomas	MN	26,918	VC
Univ of South Alabama	AL	7,760	LC
Univ of S Car at Columbia	SC	10,048	VC
Univ of South Florida	FL	9,454	C
Univ of Southern Calif	CA	37,459	MC
Univ of Southern Maine	ME	11,212	C
Univ of Southern Miss	MS	8,324	LC
Univ of Tenn at Chattanooga	TN	7,783	C
Univ of Tenn at Knoxville	TN	8,214	C
Univ of Tenn at Martin	TN	7,748	C
Univ of Texas at Arlington	TX	7,192	LC
Univ of Texas at Austin	TX	10,630	HC
Univ of Texas at El Paso	TX	5,799	NC
Univ of Texas at San Antonio	TX	9,088	NC
Univ of the Pacific	CA	31,090	VC
Univ of the South	TN	30,855	HC
Univ of Toledo	OH	12,479	NC
Univ of Tulsa	OK	22,090	VC+
Univ of Utah	UT	9,205	C
Univ of Vermont	VT	16,316	VC
Univ of Washington	WA	10,361	VC
Univ of Wisc/Eau Claire	WI	8,463	VC
Univ of Wisc/Madison	WI	8,262	VC
Univ of Wisc/Milwaukee	WI	9,427	LC
Univ of Wisc/Oshkosh	WI	6,130	LC
Univ of Wisc/Parkside	WI	6,160	LC
Univ of Wisc/River Falls	WI	8,358	LC
Univ of Wyoming	WY	8,636	C
Utah State Univ	UT	7,371	C
Valparaiso Univ	IN	26,118	VC+
Vanderbilt Univ	TN	37,897	MC
Vassar College	NY	37,030	MC
Virginia Polytechnic Inst and State Univ	VA	9,179	C
Washington and Lee Univ	VA	29,663	MC
Washington State Univ	WA	11,334	C
Washington Univ in St. Louis	MO	38,293	MC
Wayne State Univ	MI	11,774	C
Weber State Univ	UT	7,945	NC
Wellesley College	MA	36,516	MC
West Texas A&M Univ	TX	7,533	C
West Virginia Univ	WV	9,370	C
Western Carolina Univ	NC	6,742	C
Western Illinois Univ	IL	10,363	C
Western Kentucky Univ	KY	6,834	C
Western Mich Univ	MI	12,031	C
Western State College of Colo	CO	9,014	C
Western Washington Univ	WA	10,119	VC
Wheaton College	IL	21,934	HC
Whitman College	WA	32,526	HC+
Wichita State Univ	KS	8,092	C
Williams College	MA	32,270	MC
Winona State Univ	MN		C
Wittenberg Univ	OH	31,316	VC
Wright State Univ	OH	11,490	LC
Yale Univ	CT	37,000	MC
Youngstown State Univ	OH	11,148	NC

GEOPHYSICAL ENGINEERING

School	ST	$IS	SR
Colo School of Mines	CO	12,533	HC
Montana Tech of The Univ of Montana	MT	9,314	NC
New Jersey Inst of Technology	NJ	16,396	VC
Univ of Calif at Los Angeles	CA	15,330	MC
Univ of Texas at Austin	TX	10,630	HC

GEOPHYSICS AND SEISMOLOGY

School	ST	$IS	SR
Baylor Univ	TX	23,864	VC
Boise State Univ	ID	7,657	LC
Boston College	MA	33,284	MC
Boston Univ	MA	38,194	HC+
Calif Inst of Technology	CA	31,677	MC
Colgate Univ	NY	37,095	MC
Columbia Univ/Columbia College	NY	38,590	MC
Harvard Univ/Harvard College	MA	37,928	MC
Johns Hopkins Univ	MD	38,372	MC
Kansas State Univ	KS	8,728	VC
Mich State Univ	MI	11,933	VC
Mich Tech Univ	MI	13,235	VC
New Mexico Inst of Mining and Technology	NM	7,580	NC
Occidental College	CA	35,922	HC
Rice Univ	TX	27,550	MC
St. Louis Univ	MO	29,780	VC+
Southern Methodist Univ	TX	34,210	HC
Stanford Univ	CA	37,612	MC
SUNY/College at Cortland	NY	12,095	C
SUNY/College at Geneseo	NY	11,330	HC
Texas A&M Univ	TX	11,081	HC
Texas Tech Univ	TX	10,768	VC
Univ of Calif at Los Angeles	CA	15,330	MC
Univ of Calif at Riverside	CA	15,300	C
Univ of Calif at Santa Barbara	CA	11,732	VC
Univ of Delaware	DE	12,616	HC
Univ of Hawaii at Manoa	HI	9,565	VC
Univ of Houston	TX	9,818	C
Univ of Minn/Twin Cities	MN	13,160	VC
Univ of Missouri/Rolla	MO	12,292	HC
Univ of Nevada/Reno	NV	9,792	C
Univ of New Orleans	LA	7,356	C
Univ of Okla	OK	9,226	VC
Univ of S Car at Columbia	SC	10,048	VC
Univ of Texas at Austin	TX	10,630	HC
Univ of Texas at El Paso	TX	5,799	NC
Univ of the Pacific	CA	31,090	VC
Univ of Utah	UT	9,205	C
Western Mich Univ	MI	12,031	C
Wright State Univ	OH	11,490	LC

GEOSCIENCE

School	ST	$IS	SR
Albion College	MI	25,224	VC
Bradley Univ	IL	22,910	VC
Cal State, Chico	CA	8,598	LC
Columbia Univ/School of General Studies	NY	35,000	C
Earlham College	IN	29,976	VC+
Hobart and William Smith Colleges	NY	36,536	HC
Indiana Univ of Pennsylvania	PA	10,489	C
Lewis-Clark State College	ID	6,981	C
Mich State Univ	MI	11,933	VC
Miss State Univ	MS	9,139	C
Montclair State Univ	NJ	13,790	C
Northern Illinois Univ	IL	11,472	C
Pacific Lutheran Univ	WA	25,715	VC
Penn State Univ/Univ Park Campus	PA	15,646	HC
Rider Univ	NJ	30,900	C
Rutgers, The State Univ of New Jersey/Newark Campus	NJ	15,624	VC
Southeast Missouri State Univ	MO	9,704	C
Stanford Univ	CA	37,612	MC
Texas A&M Univ at Galveston	TX	9,948	C+
Texas Tech Univ	TX	10,768	VC
Towson Univ	MD	12,694	VC
Trinity Univ	TX	26,466	HC+
Univ of Arizona	AZ	10,413	VC
Univ of Chicago	IL	35,087	MC
Univ of Mich/Ann Arbor	MI	13,864	HC+
Univ of Okla	OK	9,226	VC
Univ of Southern Maine	ME	11,212	C
Univ of Texas at Dallas	TX	10,234	HC
Univ of Tulsa	OK	22,090	VC+
Univ of Wisc/Milwaukee	WI	9,427	LC
West Chester Univ of Pennsylvania	PA	11,164	C
West Virginia Univ	WV	9,370	C

GERMAN

School	ST	$IS	SR
Adrian College	MI	21,950	C
Agnes Scott College	GA	28,230	HC
Albion College	MI	25,224	VC
Alfred Univ	NY	28,290	C
Allegheny College	PA	30,280	VC
Alma College	MI	25,566	VC
Amherst College	MA	37,470	MC
Anderson Univ	IN	19,430	LC
Angelo State Univ	TX	7,576	NC
Aquinas College	MI	21,894	C
Arizona State Univ-Main	AZ	10,048	C
Auburn Univ	AL	10,396	VC
Augsburg College	MN	25,298	C
Augustana College	IL	26,610	VC+
Augustana College	SD	21,998	VC
Austin College	TX	24,747	HC
Austin Peay State Univ	TN	5,814	LC
Baker Univ	KS	19,860	VC
Baldwin-Wallace College	OH	24,678	C
Ball State Univ	IN	8,660	C
Bard College	NY	37,352	HC+
Bates College	ME	37,500	MC
Baylor Univ	TX	23,864	VC
Beloit College	WI	29,864	HC
Bemidji State Univ	MN	9,103	C
Bennington College	VT	35,910	HC
Berea College	KY	5,030	VC+
Berry College	GA	21,410	VC
Bethany College	WV	19,845	VC
Bethel College	KS	19,800	C+
Birmingham-Southern College	AL	25,364	VC+
Bloomsburg Univ of Pennsylvania	PA	10,844	C
Boston Univ	MA	38,194	HC+
Bowdoin College	ME	37,790	MC
Bowling Green State Univ	OH	13,036	C
Bradley Univ	IL	22,910	VC
Brandeis Univ	MA	38,198	MC
Brigham Young Univ	UT	8,504	HC
Bryn Mawr College	PA	36,890	HC+
Bucknell Univ	PA	35,262	HC+
Butler Univ	IN	28,250	VC+
Calif Lutheran Univ	CA	27,600	LC

ST = STATE $IS = IN-STATE COSTS SR = SELECTOR RATING

School	ST	$IS	SR
Cal State, Chico	CA	8,598	LC
Cal State, Fullerton	CA	6,648	C
Cal State, Long Beach	CA	8,762	C+
Cal State, Northridge	CA	7,757	LC
Cal State, Sacramento	CA	9,543	C
Calif Univ of Pennsylvania	PA	10,388	C
Calvin College	MI	22,615	NC
Canisius College	NY	28,163	C+
Carleton College	MN	34,395	MC
Carnegie Mellon Univ	PA	32,682	MC
Carthage College	WI	25,000	C
Case Western Reserve Univ	OH	32,002	MC
Catholic Univ of America	DC	34,248	VC
Centenary College of Louisiana	LA	23,100	VC+
Central College	IA	21,206	C
Central Conn State Univ	CT	12,090	C
Central Mich Univ	MI	11,142	C
Central Missouri State Univ	MO	9,776	C
Central Washington Univ	WA	9,768	C
Centre College	KY	27,300	HC
Christopher Newport Univ	VA	8,862	VC
Citadel, The	SC	12,295	C+
CUNY/Brooklyn College	NY	4,353	C+
CUNY/Herbert H. Lehman College	NY	3,320	LC
CUNY/Hunter College	NY	6,729	C+
CUNY/Queens College	NY	4,362	C
Claremont McKenna College	CA	36,880	MC
Clemson Univ	SC	11,972	HC
Cleveland State Univ	OH	12,308	LC
Coe College	IA	27,385	VC
Colby College	ME	37,570	MC
Colgate Univ	NY	37,095	MC
College of Charleston	SC	11,887	HC
College of St. Benedict	MN	26,672	VC
College of the Holy Cross	MA	36,451	MC
College of the Ozarks	MO	3,500	VC+
College of William and Mary	VA	12,224	MC
College of Wooster	OH	31,300	HC
Colo College	CO	36,860	HC
Colo State Univ	CO	9,964	VC
Columbia Univ/Barnard College	NY	36,990	MC
Columbia Univ/Columbia College	NY	38,590	MC
Columbia Univ/School of General Studies	NY	35,000	C
Concordia College: Moorhead	MN	22,460	VC+
Conn College	CT	37,900	MC
Cornell College	IA	27,825	VC+
Cornell Univ	NY	38,253	MC
Creighton Univ	NE	26,748	VC+
Dana College	NE	20,280	C
Dartmouth College	NH	37,770	MC
David Lipscomb Univ	TN	16,158	VC
Davidson College	NC	33,274	MC
Denison Univ	OH	33,050	HC
DePaul Univ	IL	27,580	VC
DePauw Univ	IN	31,500	HC
Dickinson College	PA	35,825	HC
Doane College	NE	20,000	C
Dordt College	IA	20,170	VC
Drew Univ/College of Liberal Arts	NJ	35,550	VC
Drury Univ	MO	18,085	VC+
Earlham College	IN	29,976	VC+
East Carolina Univ	NC	8,671	C
Eastern Mennonite Univ	VA	22,990	C
Eastern Mich Univ	MI	11,478	C
Eastern Washington Univ	WA	9,012	C
Eckerd College	FL	28,744	C+
Edinboro Univ of Pennsylvania	PA	10,850	LC
Elizabethtown College	PA	28,800	C
Elmhurst College	IL	24,630	C
Fairfield Univ	CT	35,505	HC
Florida Atlantic Univ	FL	8,543	C
Florida International Univ	FL	9,912	VC
Florida State Univ	FL	9,028	HC
Fordham Univ	NY	35,066	HC
Fort Hays State Univ	KS	7,363	C
Francis Marion Univ	SC	9,364	C
Franciscan Univ of Steubenville	OH	20,300	VC
Franklin and Marshall College	PA	35,930	HC+
Furman Univ	SC	28,976	HC+
Gallaudet Univ	DC	16,554	SP
George Washington Univ	DC	41,030	MC
Georgetown College	KY	22,000	VC
Georgetown Univ	DC	38,242	MC
Georgia Southern Univ	GA	8,540	C
Georgia State Univ	GA	10,658	C
Gettysburg College	PA	35,646	HC
Gonzaga Univ	WA	26,766	HC
Gordon College	MA	25,982	VC+
Grace College	IN	19,825	VC
Graceland Univ	IA	19,550	C
Grinnell College	IA	31,060	HC+
Guilford College	NC	24,960	VC
Gustavus Adolphus College	MN	27,120	VC+
Hamilton College	NY	37,560	MC
Hamline Univ	MN	27,052	VC
Hampden-Sydney College	VA	28,407	VC
Hanover College	IN	25,200	VC
Hardin-Simmons Univ	TX	14,165	C
Hartwick College	NY	34,650	C+
Harvard Univ/Harvard College	MA	37,928	MC
Hastings College	NE	19,928	VC
Haverford College	PA	37,900	MC
Heidelberg College	OH	20,266	NC
Hendrix College	AR	20,970	VC+
Hillsdale College	MI	22,450	HC
Hiram College	OH	28,234	VC
Hofstra Univ	NY	27,112	VC
Hollins Univ	VA	27,965	VC
Hood College	MD	27,795	VC
Hope College	MI	25,340	VC
Howard Univ	DC	16,505	C
Humboldt State Univ	CA	9,400	C
Idaho State Univ	ID	8,128	C
Illinois College	IL	19,100	VC
Illinois State Univ	IL	10,944	C+
Illinois Wesleyan Univ	IL	30,380	HC+
Indiana State Univ	IN	10,719	LC
Indiana Univ Bloomington	IN	12,389	VC
Indiana Univ of Pennsylvania	PA	10,489	C
Indiana Univ South Bend	IN	4,571	LC
Indiana Univ Southeast	IN	4,504	LC
Indiana Univ-Purdue Univ Fort Wayne	IN	5,108	LC
Indiana Univ-Purdue Univ Indianapolis	IN	8,257	LC
Iowa State Univ	IA	10,768	VC
Ithaca College	NY	31,730	HC
John Carroll Univ	OH	27,658	C+
Johns Hopkins Univ	MD	38,372	MC
Juniata College	PA	29,080	VC
Kalamazoo College	MI	26,955	HC+
Kent State Univ	OH	12,932	C
Kenyon College	OH	35,370	HC+
Knox College	IL	30,294	VC+
La Salle Univ	PA	31,260	VC
Lafayette College	PA	35,746	MC
Lake Erie College	OH	23,550	C
Lakeland College	WI	17,950	C
Lambuth Univ	TN	16,520	C
Lawrence Univ	WI	30,900	HC
Lebanon Valley College	PA	28,870	VC
Lee Univ	TN	13,780	NC
Lehigh Univ	PA	37,570	HC+
Lenoir-Rhyne College	NC	19,186	C
Linfield College	OR	27,090	VC
Lock Haven Univ of Pennsylvania	PA	11,098	LC
LIU/C.W. Post Campus	NY	28,282	C
Louisiana State Univ and A&M College	LA	9,126	VC
Loyola College in Maryland	MD	34,560	HC
Loyola Univ Chicago	IL	31,164	VC
Loyola Univ New Orleans	LA	31,036	VC+
Luther College	IA	25,700	VC
Lycoming College	PA	27,589	C+
Manchester College	IN	23,390	C
Manhattanville College	NY	32,420	C+
Mansfield Univ	PA	11,220	C
Marlboro College	VT	29,055	VC+
Marquette Univ	WI	27,594	VC
Mary Baldwin College	VA	24,939	C
Mary Washington College	VA	10,166	HC
Mass Inst of Technology	MA	38,310	MC
McDaniel College	MD	28,440	VC
McMurry Univ	TX	17,846	LC
Mercer Univ	GA	27,516	VC+
Messiah College	PA	25,890	VC+
Miami Univ	OH	15,033	HC
Mich State Univ	MI	11,933	VC
Middle Tenn State Univ	TN	8,534	C
Middlebury College	VT	38,100	MC
Millersville Univ of Pennsylvania	PA	11,269	C
Millikin Univ	IL	25,555	C
Millsaps College	MS	25,182	VC
Minn State Univ, Mankato	MN	8,803	LC
Minn State Univ, Moorehead	MN	7,000	LC
Minot State Univ	ND	6,602	LC
Missouri Southern State Univ	MO	8,316	C
Moravian College	PA	28,903	VC
Morehouse College	GA	22,728	C
Mount St. Mary's College	MD	28,400	C
Mount Union College	OH	21,120	C
Muhlenberg College	PA	31,485	HC
Murray State Univ	KY	7,816	VC
Muskingum College	OH	20,680	C
Nazareth College of Rochester	NY	24,936	VC
Nebr Wesleyan Univ	NE	21,197	C+
New York Univ	NY	39,406	MC
Newberry College	SC	22,871	LC
North Central College	IL	25,656	VC
Northern Arizona Univ	AZ	9,002	C
Northern Illinois Univ	IL	11,472	C
Northern State Univ	SD	7,117	LC
Northwestern Univ	IL	37,491	MC
Oakland Univ	MI	10,800	C
Oberlin College	OH	36,938	MC
Occidental College	CA	35,922	HC
Ohio State Univ	OH	13,080	VC+
Ohio Univ	OH	14,448	C
Ohio Wesleyan Univ	OH	32,550	VC+
Okla Baptist Univ	OK	15,220	VC
Okla City Univ	OK	19,580	VC
Okla State Univ	OK	9,216	VC
Old Dominion Univ	VA	10,441	C
Oral Roberts Univ	OK	18,490	C
Oregon State Univ	OR	11,055	C
Pacific Lutheran Univ	WA	25,715	VC
Penn State Univ/Univ Park Campus	PA	15,646	HC
Pepperdine Univ	CA	32,830	VC
Pomona College	CA	33,960	MC
Portland State Univ	OR	12,453	C
Presbyterian College	SC	25,920	VC
Purdue Univ/Calumet	IN	6,630	NC
Purdue Univ/West Lafayette	IN	12,560	VC
Randolph-Macon College	VA	27,190	C
Randolph-Macon Woman's College	VA	28,430	VC+
Rhodes College	TN	26,466	HC+
Rider Univ	NJ	30,900	C
Ripon College	WI	24,995	VC
Rockford College	IL	28,310	VC
Rosemont College	PA	26,175	C
Rutgers, The State Univ of New Jersey/Camden Campus	NJ	14,990	VC
Rutgers, The State Univ of New Jersey/New Brunswick/Piscataway Campus	NJ	15,800	HC
Rutgers, The State Univ of New Jersey/Newark Campus	NJ	15,624	VC
St. Ambrose Univ	IA	22,800	C
St. John's Univ	MN	26,473	VC
St. John's Univ	NY	30,180	C
St. Joseph's Univ	PA	33,590	VC
St. Lawrence Univ	NY	35,945	VC
St. Louis Univ	MO	29,780	VC+
St. Mary's Univ of San Antonio	TX	22,444	C
St. Norbert College	WI	25,810	C
St. Olaf College	MN	28,500	HC
Salem College	NC	24,595	VC
Sam Houston State Univ	TX	7,142	C
Samford Univ	AL	18,648	VC
San Diego State Univ	CA	10,321	C
San Francisco State Univ	CA	12,070	C
San Jose State Univ	CA	8,187	C
Santa Clara Univ	CA	34,701	HC
Sarah Lawrence College	NY	41,218	HC
Seattle Pacific Univ	WA	25,944	VC
Seattle Univ	WA	24,183	VC
Simon's Rock College of Bard	MA	36,580	HC
Simpson College	IA	23,658	C+
Skidmore College	NY	37,930	HC
Slippery Rock Univ of Pennsylvania	PA	10,343	LC
S Dak State Univ	SD	7,782	C
Southeast Missouri State Univ	MO	9,704	C
Southern Conn State Univ	CT	10,310	C
Southern Illinois Univ Carbondale	IL	10,407	C
Southern Methodist Univ	TX	34,210	HC
Southern Utah Univ	UT	8,194	C
Southwest Missouri State Univ	MO	8,918	C
Southwestern Univ	TX	25,410	HC
SUNY at Oswego	NY	12,650	C
SUNY/Univ at Binghamton	NY	12,787	HC
SUNY/Univ at Buffalo	NY	12,563	VC
SUNY/Univ at New Paltz	NY	11,565	VC
Stetson Univ	FL	29,495	VC
Susquehanna Univ	PA	29,990	VC
Swarthmore College	PA	37,716	MC
Sweet Briar College	VA	27,940	C
Temple Univ	PA	15,912	C
Tenn Tech Univ	TN	8,670	VC
Texas A&M Univ	TX	11,081	HC
Texas A&M Univ at Commerce	TX	8,994	C
Texas State Univ	TX	9,320	VC
Texas Tech Univ	TX	10,768	VC
Towson Univ	MD	12,694	VC
Trinity College	CT	38,040	HC+
Trinity Univ	TX	26,466	HC+
Truman State Univ	MO	9,728	HC+
Tufts Univ	MA	38,233	MC
Tulane Univ	LA	37,451	HC+
Union College	NE	17,130	C
Univ of Akron	OH	13,134	NC
Univ of Alabama	AL	9,040	C+
Univ of Arizona	AZ	10,413	VC
Univ of Arkansas	AR	9,855	VC
Univ of Calif at Berkeley	CA	15,563	MC
Univ of Calif at Davis	CA	14,995	VC
Univ of Calif at Irvine	CA	19,808	HC
Univ of Calif at Los Angeles	CA	15,330	MC
Univ of Calif at Riverside	CA	15,300	C
Univ of Calif at Santa Barbara	CA	11,732	VC
Univ of Central Okla	OK	9,434	C
Univ of Chicago	IL	35,087	MC
Univ of Cincinnati	OH	14,736	C
Univ of Conn	CT	14,608	VC
Univ of Dallas	TX	25,898	VC+
Univ of Dayton	OH	24,850	VC
Univ of Denver	CO	32,148	VC
Univ of Evansville	IN	24,190	VC
Univ of Florida	FL	8,580	MC
Univ of Georgia	GA	8,656	VC
Univ of Hawaii at Manoa	HI	9,565	VC
Univ of Houston	TX	9,818	C
Univ of Idaho	ID	8,216	C
Univ of Indianapolis	IN	22,560	VC
Univ of Iowa	IA	10,923	VC
Univ of Kansas	KS	8,923	VC
Univ of Kentucky	KY	7,765	C
Univ of La Verne	CA	28,600	C
Univ of Maine	ME	12,080	C+
Univ of Maryland/Baltimore County	MD	14,668	VC+
Univ of Mass Amherst	MA	13,980	C+
Univ of Miami	FL	34,608	HC
Univ of Mich/Ann Arbor	MI	13,864	HC+
Univ of Minn/Morris	MN	12,896	VC
Univ of Minn/Twin Cities	MN	13,160	VC
Univ of Miss	MS	7,666	C
Univ of Missouri/Columbia	MO	13,782	VC
Univ of Missouri/Kansas City	MO	13,416	VC
Univ of Montana	MT	9,395	C
Univ of Nebr at Kearney	NE	8,286	NC
Univ of Nebr at Lincoln	NE	9,975	C+
Univ of Nebr at Omaha	NE	8,080	C
Univ of Nevada/Las Vegas	NV	11,566	C
Univ of Nevada/Reno	NV	9,792	C
Univ of New Hampshire	NH	14,828	VC
Univ of New Mexico	NM	9,223	C
Univ of North Alabama	AL	7,972	NC
Univ of N Car at Asheville	NC	8,079	VC
Univ of N Car at Chapel Hill	NC	10,117	MC
Univ of N Car at Charlotte	NC	8,185	C
Univ of N Car at Greensboro	NC	8,248	C
Univ of N Dak	ND	8,390	C
Univ of North Texas	TX	7,629	C
Univ of Northern Colo	CO	8,987	C
Univ of Northern Iowa	IA	9,834	C
Univ of Notre Dame	IN	34,442	MC
Univ of Okla	OK	9,226	VC
Univ of Oregon	OR	11,479	VC
Univ of Pennsylvania	PA	37,960	MC
Univ of Pittsburgh at Pittsburgh	PA	16,074	HC
Univ of Puget Sound	WA	31,760	HC
Univ of Redlands	CA	32,576	VC
Univ of Rhode Island	RI	13,720	VC
Univ of Richmond	VA	30,100	MC
Univ of Rochester	NY	32,979	HC
Univ of St. Thomas	MN	26,918	VC
Univ of Scranton	PA	30,836	VC
Univ of S Car at Columbia	SC	10,048	VC
Univ of S Dak	SD	7,710	C+
Univ of South Florida	FL	9,454	C
Univ of Southern Calif	CA	37,459	MC
Univ of Southern Indiana	IN	9,025	LC
Univ of Tenn at Knoxville	TN	8,214	C
Univ of Texas at Arlington	TX	7,192	LC
Univ of Texas at Austin	TX	10,630	HC
Univ of Texas at El Paso	TX	5,799	NC
Univ of Texas at San Antonio	TX	9,088	NC
Univ of the Pacific	CA	31,090	VC
Univ of the South	TN	30,855	HC
Univ of Toledo	OH	12,479	NC
Univ of Tulsa	OK	22,090	VC+
Univ of Utah	UT	9,205	C
Univ of Vermont	VT	16,316	VC
Univ of Virginia	VA	11,740	MC
Univ of Wisc/Eau Claire	WI	8,463	VC
Univ of Wisc/Green Bay	WI	8,154	C
Univ of Wisc/Madison	WI	8,262	VC
Univ of Wisc/Milwaukee	WI	9,427	LC
Univ of Wisc/Oshkosh	WI	6,130	LC
Univ of Wisc/Parkside	WI	6,160	LC
Univ of Wisc/Platteville	WI	8,450	C
Univ of Wisc/Stevens Point	WI	8,116	VC
Univ of Wisc/Whitewater	WI	8,626	C
Univ of Wyoming	WY	8,636	C
Ursinus College	PA	34,400	VC
Utah State Univ	UT	7,371	C
Valparaiso Univ	IN	26,118	VC+
Vanderbilt Univ	TN	37,897	MC
Villanova Univ	PA	35,050	HC
Virginia Polytechnic Inst and State Univ	VA	9,179	C
Virginia Wesleyan College	VA	25,350	C
Wabash College	IN	27,932	VC
Wake Forest Univ	NC	34,090	MC
Walla Walla College	WA	21,600	NC
Wartburg College	IA	21,165	VC
Washburn Univ of Topeka	KS	8,984	NC

ST = STATE **$IS** = IN-STATE COSTS **SR** = SELECTOR RATING

School	ST	$IS	SR
Washington and Jefferson College	PA	29,570	VC
Washington and Lee Univ	VA	29,663	MC
Washington College	MD	30,540	VC
Washington State Univ	WA	11,334	C
Washington Univ in St. Louis	MO	38,293	MC
Wayne State Univ	MI	11,774	C
Weber State Univ	UT	7,945	NC
Webster Univ	MO	21,848	VC
Wellesley College	MA	36,516	MC
Wells College	NY	21,122	VC
Wesleyan Univ	CT	35,139	MC
West Chester Univ of Pennsylvania	PA	11,164	C
Western Carolina Univ	NC	6,742	C
Western Kentucky Univ	KY	6,834	C
Western Mich Univ	MI	12,031	C
Western Washington Univ	WA	10,119	VC
Westminster College	PA	22,960	C
Wheaton College	IL	21,934	HC
Wheaton College	MA	36,330	HC
Whitman College	WA	32,526	HC+
Willamette Univ	OR	32,032	VC+
Williams College	MA	32,270	MC
Winona State Univ	MN		C
Wittenberg Univ	OH	31,316	VC
Wofford College	SC	26,710	HC
Wright State Univ	OH	11,490	LC
Xavier Univ	OH	26,850	VC+
Yale Univ	CT	37,000	MC

GERMAN AREA STUDIES

School	ST	$IS	SR
American Univ	DC	34,585	VC+
Boston College	MA	33,284	MC
Brown Univ	RI	38,174	MC
Case Western Reserve Univ	OH	32,002	MC
College of the Holy Cross	MA	36,451	MC
Columbia Univ/School of General Studies	NY	35,000	C
Cornell Univ	NY	38,253	MC
Dartmouth College	NH	37,770	MC
Emory Univ	GA	36,872	MC
Fordham Univ	NY	35,066	HC
Guilford College	NC	24,960	VC
Knox College	IL	30,294	VC+
Lewis and Clark College	OR	30,620	VC
Macalester College	MN	31,944	MC
Mount Holyoke College	MA	37,918	HC+
Muhlenberg College	PA	31,485	HC
Pomona College	CA	33,960	MC
Principia College	IL	25,044	C+
Rice Univ	TX	27,550	MC
Scripps College	CA	35,700	HC+
Simon's Rock College of Bard	MA	36,580	HC
Southern Illinois Univ Carbondale	IL	10,407	C
Southern Methodist Univ	TX	34,210	HC
Stanford Univ	CA	37,612	MC
Swarthmore College	PA	37,716	MC
Sweet Briar College	VA	27,940	C
Tufts Univ	MA	38,233	MC
Univ of Arizona	AZ	10,413	VC
Univ of Calif at Santa Cruz	CA	16,505	VC
Univ of Colo at Boulder	CO	10,774	VC
Univ of Houston	TX	9,818	C
Univ of Illinois at Chicago	IL	13,418	C
Univ of Mass Boston	MA	6,227	C
Univ of the South	TN	30,855	HC
Univ of Wisc/La Crosse	WI	8,991	VC
Wartburg College	IA	21,165	VC
Wellesley College	MA	36,516	MC
Wheaton College	MA	36,330	HC
Yale Univ	CT	37,000	MC

GERMANIC LANGUAGES AND LITERATURE

School	ST	$IS	SR
Bard College	NY	37,352	HC+
Boston Univ	MA	38,194	HC+
Colby College	ME	37,570	MC
Columbia Univ/Columbia College	NY	38,590	MC
Duke Univ	NC	37,555	MC
New College of Florida	FL	8,906	HC+
New York Univ	NY	39,406	MC
Princeton Univ	NJ	36,649	MC
Reed College	OR	36,950	MC
Scripps College	CA	35,700	HC+
Simon's Rock College of Bard	MA	36,580	HC
Smith College	MA	37,034	HC+
SUNY/Univ at Stony Brook	NY	12,763	HC
Syracuse Univ	NY	34,720	HC
Temple Univ	PA	15,912	C
Univ of Calif at San Diego	CA	14,127	HC
Univ of Calif at Santa Barbara	CA	11,732	VC
Univ of Colo at Boulder	CO	10,774	VC
Univ of Georgia	GA	8,656	VC
Univ of Illinois at Urbana-Champaign	IL	11,316	HC+
Univ of Kansas	KS	8,923	VC
Univ of Maryland/College Park	MD	14,227	HC
Univ of Washington	WA	10,361	VC
Washington and Lee Univ	VA	29,663	MC
Washington Univ in St. Louis	MO	38,293	MC

GERONTOLOGY

School	ST	$IS	SR
Alfred Univ	NY	28,290	C
Barton College	NC	19,314	C
Bethune-Cookman College	FL	16,480	LC
Bowling Green State Univ	OH	13,036	C
Cal State, San Bernardino	CA	15,238	LC
Calif Univ of Pennsylvania	PA	10,388	C
Case Western Reserve Univ	OH	32,002	MC
Central Washington Univ	WA	9,768	C
Chestnut Hill College	PA	26,450	LC
CUNY/York College	NY	3,292	NC
College of Mount St. Joseph	OH	22,785	C
College of the Ozarks	MO	3,500	VC+
East Central Univ	OK	4,968	C
Eastern Mich Univ	MI	11,478	C
Indiana Univ Kokomo	IN	4,463	LC
Ithaca College	NY	31,730	HC
Kent State Univ	OH	12,932	C
King's College	PA	26,990	C
Langston Univ	OK	2,308	LC
Madonna Univ	MI	11,504	VC
McKendree College	IL	21,120	VC
Metropolitan College of New York	NY	15,771	C
Molloy College	NY	15,180	C
Mount St. Mary's College	CA	28,307	VC
Pontifical Catholic Univ of PR/Ponce	PR	7,298	
Quinnipiac Univ	CT	30,570	VC
St. Mary-of-the-Woods College	IN	23,280	C
San Diego State Univ	CA	10,321	C
Shaw Univ	NC	14,882	C+
Sojourner-Douglass College	MD	4,170	LC
Southeastern Okla State Univ	OK	6,147	C
Southwest Missouri State Univ	MO	8,918	C
Springfield College	MA	24,520	C
SUNY/College at Oneonta	NY	11,870	VC
Stephen F. Austin State Univ	TX	7,552	C
Thomas Edison State College	NJ	3,325	SP
Towson Univ	MD	12,694	VC
Univ of Arkansas at Pine Bluff	AR	7,925	C
Univ of Central Arkansas	AR	6,388	C
Univ of Evansville	IN	24,190	VC
Univ of Mass Boston	MA	6,227	C
Univ of Northern Colo	CO	8,987	C
Univ of Scranton	PA	30,836	VC
Univ of South Florida	FL	9,454	C
Univ of Southern Calif	CA	37,459	MC
Wagner College	NY	29,900	VC
Weber State Univ	UT	7,945	NC
Western Mich Univ	MI	12,031	C
Wichita State Univ	KS	8,092	C

GLASS

School	ST	$IS	SR
Alfred Univ	NY	28,290	C
Calif College of the Arts	CA	31,530	SP
College for Creative Studies	MI	23,298	SP
Mass College of Art	MA	15,568	SP
Rhode Island School of Design	RI	33,569	SP
Rochester Inst of Technology	NY	29,217	VC+

GRAPHIC AND PRINTING PRODUCTION

School	ST	$IS	SR
Brenau Univ Women's College	GA	21,800	C
CUNY/New York City College of Technology	NY	4,269	NC
Rochester Inst of Technology	NY	29,217	VC+
Texas State Univ	TX	9,320	VC
Univ of Wisc/Stout	WI	9,718	C

GRAPHIC ARTS TECHNOLOGY

School	ST	$IS	SR
Andrews Univ	MI	19,550	C
Appalachian State Univ	NC	7,637	VC
Ball State Univ	IN	8,660	C
Bloomfield College	NJ	19,250	LC
Calif Univ of Pennsylvania	PA	10,388	C
Carroll College	WI	22,740	C
Central Missouri State Univ	MO	9,776	C
Central State Univ	OH	8,922	C+
Clemson Univ	SC	11,972	HC
College of the Ozarks	MO	3,500	VC+
Colo Technical Univ	CO	9,500	LC
Farmingdale SUNY	NY	12,891	C
Florida State Univ	FL	9,028	HC
Kean Univ	NJ	14,479	C
New York Univ	NY	39,406	MC
Pacific Union College	CA	22,065	C+
Pennsylvania College of Technology	PA	15,126	NC
Purdue Univ/West Lafayette	IN	12,560	VC
Rochester Inst of Technology	NY	29,217	VC+
Texas Southern Univ	TX	8,920	NC
Univ of Houston	TX	9,818	C
Univ of Wisc/Stout	WI	9,718	C
Western Mich Univ	MI	12,031	C

GRAPHIC DESIGN

School	ST	$IS	SR
American Univ	DC	34,585	VC+
Anderson Univ	IN	19,430	LC
Andrews Univ	MI	19,550	C
Appalachian State Univ	NC	7,637	VC
Arcadia Univ	PA	29,890	C
Arizona State Univ-Main	AZ	10,048	C
Arkansas State Univ	AR	8,450	C
Art Academy of Cincinnati	OH	17,300	SP
Art Center College of Design	CA	23,450	SP
Art Inst of Atlanta	GA	23,205	SP
Art Inst of Portland	OR	23,040	SP
Art Inst of Southern Calif	CA	14,500	SP
Atlanta College of Art	GA	18,600	SP
Ball State Univ	IN	8,660	C
Barton College	NC	19,314	C
Bay Path College	MA	24,910	C
Becker College	MA	23,710	LC
Bethel College	IN	19,670	C
Boston Univ	MA	38,194	HC+
Bradley Univ	IL	22,910	VC
Brescia Univ	KY	14,225	C
Briar Cliff Univ	IA	21,660	C
Brigham Young Univ	UT	8,504	HC
Buena Vista Univ	IA	25,406	C
Cabrini College	PA	29,020	C
Calif College of the Arts	CA	31,530	SP
Calif Polytechnic State Univ	CA	8,747	VC
Cal State, Fresno	CA	8,414	LC
Cal State, Fullerton	CA	6,648	C
Cal State, Los Angeles	CA	5,778	C
Cal State, San Bernardino	CA	15,238	LC
Carthage College	WI	25,000	C
Cedarville Univ	OH	19,954	VC
Central Conn State Univ	CT	12,090	C
Champlain College	VT	22,030	C
Chapman Univ	CA	33,118	VC
Cleveland Inst of Art	OH	30,371	SP
Coker College	SC	21,491	C
Colby-Sawyer College	NH	27,850	LC
College for Creative Studies	MI	23,298	SP
College of Mount St. Joseph	OH	22,785	C
College of New Jersey	NJ	15,950	MC
College of Notre Dame of Maryland	MD	27,700	C
College of St. Rose	NY	22,864	C
College of Visual Arts	MN		SP
Columbus College of Art and Design	OH	24,180	SP
Concordia Univ Wisc	WI	16,600	C
Cooper Union for the Advancement of Science and Art	NY	10,400	MC
Corcoran School of Art and Design	DC	21,035	SP
Daemen College	NY	22,120	C
Defiance College	OH	22,615	C
Dominican Univ	IL	23,610	C
Dordt College	IA	20,170	VC
Drake Univ	IA	25,120	VC+
Drexel Univ	PA	27,655	VC
Eastern Mich Univ	MI	11,478	C
Eastern Washington Univ	WA	9,012	C
Edgewood College	WI	20,520	C
Edinboro Univ of Pennsylvania	PA	10,850	LC
Escuela de Artes Plasticas de PR	PR		
Fashion Inst of Technology/SUNY	NY	11,169	C+
Flagler College	FL	11,860	VC+
Florida Atlantic Univ	FL	8,543	C
Franklin Pierce College	NH	28,980	LC
Gallaudet Univ	DC	16,554	SP
Grace College	IN	19,825	VC
Graceland Univ	IA	19,550	C
Grand Canyon Univ	AZ	30,000	LC
Grand View College	IA	19,748	LC
Harding Univ	AR	14,890	VC
Indiana Univ Bloomington	IN	12,389	VC
Iowa State Univ	IA	10,768	VC
Kean Univ	NJ	14,479	C
Kendall College of Art and Design of Ferris State Univ	MI	10,784	SP
Kent State Univ	OH	12,932	C
Kutztown Univ of Pennsylvania	PA	10,786	C
La Roche College	PA	22,094	C
La Sierra Univ	CA	19,260	LC
Limestone College	SC	17,700	C
LIU/Southampton College	NY	29,370	C+
Louisiana College	LA	13,450	C
Loyola Univ New Orleans	LA	31,036	VC+
Lyndon State College	VT	12,646	LC
Lynn Univ	FL	30,750	C
Madonna Univ	MI	11,504	VC
Maine College of Art	ME	28,812	SP
Marian College	IN	23,030	C
Marietta College	OH	27,047	C
Maryland Inst College of Art	MD	30,890	SP
Marymount Univ	VA	23,668	C
Maryville Univ of St. Louis	MO	22,090	VC
Mass College of Art	MA	15,568	SP
McMurry Univ	TX	17,846	LC
Mercyhurst College	PA	20,694	C
Miami Univ	OH	15,033	HC
Middle Tenn State Univ	TN	8,534	C
Milwaukee Inst of Art and Design	WI	24,388	SP
Minneapolis College of Art and Design	MN	28,950	SP
Miss College	MS	14,574	C
Missouri Southern State Univ	MO	8,316	C
Missouri Western State College	MO	8,522	NC
Montserrat College of Art	MA	22,790	SP
Moore College of Art and Design	PA	27,096	SP
Moravian College	PA	28,903	VC
Morningside College	IA	21,610	C
Mount Ida College	MA	25,596	LC
Mount Mary College	WI	20,370	C
Mount Vernon Nazarene Univ	OH	18,925	C
New Mexico Highlands Univ	NM	6,182	LC
New York Inst of Technology	NY	24,205	VC
Newbury College	MA	23,450	C
Norfolk State Univ	VA	9,722	LC
N Car State Univ	NC	9,886	VC
Northern Kentucky Univ	KY	6,352	NC
Northwest Nazarene Univ	ID	20,360	VC
Northwestern College	MN	22,820	C+
Notre Dame College	OH	20,425	C
Notre Dame de Namur Univ	CA	26,932	LC
Ohio Dominican Univ	OH	22,700	C
Ohio Northern Univ	OH	27,765	VC
Okla City Univ	OK	19,580	VC
Old Dominion Univ	VA	10,441	C
Otis College of Art and Design	CA	23,420	SP
Pacific Northwest College of Art	OR	14,890	SP
Pacific Union College	CA	22,065	C+
Park Univ	MO	10,780	C+
Parsons School of Design	NY	32,242	SP
Pennsylvania College of Technology	PA	15,126	NC
Philadelphia Univ	PA	27,354	C
Plymouth State Univ	NH	12,298	LC
Rhode Island School of Design	RI	33,569	SP
Ringling School of Art and Design	FL	27,530	SP
Rivier College	NH	26,217	C
Rochester Inst of Technology	NY	29,217	VC+
St. Ambrose Univ	IA	22,800	C
St. Edward's Univ	TX	20,428	C
St. John's Univ	NY	30,180	C
St. Mary-of-the-Woods College	IN	23,280	C
St. Mary's Univ of Minn	MN	21,535	C
St. Norbert College	WI	25,810	C
Sam Houston State Univ	TX	7,142	C
Samford Univ	AL	18,648	VC
Savannah College of Art and Design	GA	27,560	SP
School of Visual Arts	NY	30,200	SP
Schreiner Univ	TX	20,440	C
Seton Hill Univ	PA	24,930	C
Shepherd College	WV	8,608	C
S Dak State Univ	SD	7,782	C
Southern Adventist Univ	TN	17,080	C
Southwestern Okla State Univ	OK	4,801	C
Spring Hill College	AL	25,868	VC
SUNY/College at Fredonia	NY	11,562	VC
Stephens College	MO	24,260	C+
Suffolk Univ	MA	29,200	C
Susquehanna Univ	PA	29,990	VC
Syracuse Univ	NY	34,720	HC
Tabor College	KS	19,500	NC
Texas Christian Univ	TX	23,410	VC
Texas State Univ	TX	9,320	VC
Union College	NE	17,130	C
Union Univ	TN	18,800	VC
Univ of Bridgeport	CT	25,924	LC
Univ of Central Okla	OK	9,434	C
Univ of Evansville	IN	24,190	VC

School	ST	$IS	SR
Univ of Florida	FL	8,580	MC
Univ of Illinois at Chicago	IL	13,418	C
Univ of Illinois at Urbana-Champaign	IL	11,316	HC+
Univ of Mass Dartmouth	MA	12,835	C
Univ of Miami	FL	34,608	HC
Univ of Mich/Ann Arbor	MI	13,864	HC+
Univ of Minn/Duluth	MN	12,470	C
Univ of New Haven	CT	28,650	C
Univ of Northern Colo	CO	8,987	C
Univ of Northern Iowa	IA	9,834	C
Univ of Oregon	OR	11,479	VC
Univ of San Francisco	CA	34,700	VC
Univ of S Car at Spartanburg	SC	9,936	C+
Univ of Tampa	FL	23,982	VC
Univ of Tenn at Knoxville	TN	8,214	C
Univ of the Arts	PA	29,510	SP
Univ of the Pacific	CA	31,090	VC
Univ of Washington	WA	10,361	VC
Upper Iowa Univ	IA	20,076	C
Ursuline College	OH	22,728	LC
Viterbo Univ	WI	20,430	C
Walla Walla College	WA	21,600	NC
Wartburg College	IA	21,165	VC
Washington Univ in St. Louis	MO	38,293	MC
Wayne State College	NE	7,352	NC
Waynesburg College	PA	19,370	C
Weber State Univ	UT	7,945	NC
West Liberty State College	WV	7,868	LC
West Texas A&M Univ	TX	7,533	C
Western Conn State Univ	CT	11,625	C
Western Mich Univ	MI	12,031	C
Wichita State Univ	KS	8,092	C
William Woods Univ	MO	20,120	C
Winona State Univ	MN		C
York College of Pennsylvania	PA	14,500	VC
Youngstown State Univ	OH	11,148	NC

GREEK

School	ST	$IS	SR
Amherst College	MA	37,470	MC
Asbury College	KY	20,704	VC
Brigham Young Univ	UT	8,504	HC
Bryn Mawr College	PA	36,890	HC+
Butler Univ	IN	28,250	VC+
Calvin College	MI	22,615	NC
Carleton College	MN	34,395	MC
CUNY/Brooklyn College	NY	4,353	C+
CUNY/Herbert H. Lehman College	NY	3,320	LC
CUNY/Hunter College	NY	6,729	C+
CUNY/Queens College	NY	4,362	C+
Colgate Univ	NY	37,095	MC
Columbia Univ/Barnard College	NY	36,990	MC
Columbia Univ/Columbia College	NY	38,590	MC
Cornell Univ	NY	38,253	MC
Creighton Univ	NE	26,748	VC+
DePauw Univ	IN	31,500	HC
Dickinson College	PA	35,825	HC
Florida State Univ	FL	9,028	HC
Franklin and Marshall College	PA	35,930	HC+
Furman Univ	SC	28,976	HC+
Gettysburg College	PA	35,646	HC
Hampden-Sydney College	VA	28,407	VC
Harvard Univ/Harvard College	MA	37,928	MC
Howard Univ	DC	16,505	C
Indiana Univ Bloomington	IN	12,389	VC
John Carroll Univ	OH	27,658	C+
Loyola Univ Chicago	IL	31,164	VC
Luther College	IA	25,700	VC
Marlboro College	VT	29,055	VC+
Mercer Univ	GA	27,516	VC+
Miami Univ	OH	15,033	HC
Monmouth College	IL	23,600	C
Mount Holyoke College	MA	37,918	HC+
New York Univ	NY	39,406	MC
Ohio State Univ	OH	13,080	VC+
Randolph-Macon College	VA	27,190	C
St. Louis Univ	MO	29,780	VC+
St. Olaf College	MN	28,500	HC
Samford Univ	AL	18,648	VC
Santa Clara Univ	CA	34,701	HC
Sarah Lawrence College	NY	41,218	HC
Smith College	MA	37,034	HC+
Swarthmore College	PA	37,716	MC
Sweet Briar College	VA	27,940	C
Temple Univ	PA	15,912	C
Tufts Univ	MA	38,233	MC
Union Univ	TN	18,800	VC
Univ of Calif at Berkeley	CA	15,563	MC
Univ of Calif at Davis	CA	14,995	VC
Univ of Calif at Los Angeles	CA	15,330	MC
Univ of Georgia	GA	8,656	VC
Univ of Iowa	IA	10,923	VC
Univ of Mich/Ann Arbor	MI	13,864	HC+
Univ of Minn/Twin Cities	MN	13,160	VC
Univ of Nebr at Lincoln	NE	9,975	C+
Univ of New Hampshire	NH	14,828	VC
Univ of Notre Dame	IN	34,442	MC
Univ of Oregon	OR	11,479	VC
Univ of Richmond	VA	30,100	MC
Univ of Scranton	PA	30,836	VC
Univ of S Car at Columbia	SC	10,048	VC
Univ of Tenn at Chattanooga	TN	7,783	C
Univ of Texas at Austin	TX	10,630	HC
Univ of the South	TN	30,855	HC
Univ of Vermont	VT	16,316	VC
Univ of Wisc/Madison	WI	8,262	VC
Wabash College	IN	27,932	VC
Wake Forest Univ	NC	34,090	MC
Wellesley College	MA	36,516	MC
Wheaton College	MA	36,330	HC

GREEK (CLASSICAL)

School	ST	$IS	SR
Baylor Univ	TX	23,864	VC
Boston Univ	MA	38,194	HC+
College of Wooster	OH	31,300	HC
Duquesne Univ	PA	26,907	VC
Kenyon College	OH	35,370	HC+
New York Univ	NY	39,406	MC
Ohio Univ	OH	14,448	C
Univ of Mass Boston	MA	6,227	C
Washington Univ in St. Louis	MO	38,293	MC

GREEK (MODERN)

School	ST	$IS	SR
Boston Univ	MA	38,194	HC+

GUIDANCE EDUCATION

School	ST	$IS	SR
Central Mich Univ	MI	11,142	C
Eastern Washington Univ	WA	9,012	C
McNeese State Univ	LA	5,259	LC
Prescott College	AZ	13,430	C
St. Cloud State Univ	MN	8,362	C
S Car State Univ	SC	6,586	LC
Texas A&M Univ at Commerce	TX	8,994	C
Univ of Akron	OH	13,134	NC
Univ of Central Arkansas	AR	6,388	C
Univ of Cincinnati	OH	14,736	C
Univ of Nebr at Lincoln	NE	9,975	C+
Univ of Southern Miss	MS	8,324	LC
Westminster College	PA	22,960	C

GUITAR

School	ST	$IS	SR
Ball State Univ	IN	8,660	C
Boston Conservatory	MA	26,900	SP
Central Washington Univ	WA	9,768	C
Indiana Univ Bloomington	IN	12,389	VC
Roosevelt Univ	IL	22,580	VC
Stetson Univ	FL	29,495	VC
Temple Univ	PA	15,912	C
Univ of Miami	FL	34,608	HC

HAWAIIAN

School	ST	$IS	SR
Univ of Hawaii at Manoa	HI	9,565	VC

HAWAIIAN STUDIES

School	ST	$IS	SR
Brigham Young Univ/Hawaii	HI	7,240	VC+
Univ of Hawaii at Hilo	HI	6,497	C
Univ of Hawaii at Manoa	HI	9,565	VC

HEALTH

School	ST	$IS	SR
Aquinas College	MI	21,894	C
Becker College	MA	23,710	LC
Bloomsburg Univ of Pennsylvania	PA	10,844	C
Boston Univ	MA	38,194	HC+
Cal State, Northridge	CA	7,757	LC
Cameron Univ	OK	5,692	NC
Chicago State Univ	IL	10,882	C+
Coastal Carolina Univ	SC	11,040	C
College of Mount St. Joseph	OH	22,785	C
College of the Ozarks	MO	3,500	VC+
Concordia College: Moorhead	MN	22,460	VC+
Concordia Univ Nebr	NE	20,302	C+
Cumberland College	KY	16,384	C
Eastern Oregon Univ	OR	10,080	NC
Georgetown Univ	DC	38,242	MC
Georgia Southern Univ	GA	8,540	C
Graceland Univ	IA	19,550	C
International College	FL	8,060	LC
Ithaca College	NY	31,730	HC
LeTourneau Univ	TX	21,080	C
Luther College	IA	25,700	VC
Mass College of Pharmacy and Health Sciences	MA	28,770	SP
Miami Univ	OH	15,033	HC
Montana State Univ-Bozeman	MT	9,515	C
Nebr Wesleyan Univ	NE	21,197	C+
New Mexico Highlands Univ	NM	6,182	LC
Ohio Northern Univ	OH	27,765	VC
Olivet College	MI	19,984	C+
Oregon State Univ	OR	11,055	C
Prairie View A&M Univ	TX	9,418	NC
Rowan Univ	NJ	14,506	VC
Rust College	MS	8,200	C+
Sam Houston State Univ	TX	7,142	C
Samford Univ	AL	18,648	VC
Southern Oregon Univ	OR	10,362	C
Southwestern Adventist Univ	TX	14,798	C
SUNY/College at Buffalo	NY	8,025	C
SUNY/College at Old Westbury	NY	12,784	C
Tenn Wesleyan College	TN	16,540	C
Texas Christian Univ	TX	23,410	VC
Texas Southern Univ	TX	8,920	NC
Texas State Univ	TX	9,320	VC
Texas Tech Univ	TX	10,768	VC
Thomas Edison State College	NJ	3,325	SP
Union Inst and Univ	OH	7,848	SP
Univ of Houston	TX	9,818	C
Univ of Louisiana at Monroe	LA	5,207	NC
Univ of Louisville	KY	8,762	VC
Univ of Pennsylvania	PA	37,960	MC
Univ of Rochester	NY	32,979	HC
Univ of St. Francis	IL	22,850	C
Univ of Texas at San Antonio	TX	9,088	NC
Univ of Texas-Pan American	TX	5,954	LC
Upper Iowa Univ	IA	20,076	C
Voorhees College	SC	11,678	LC
Walla Walla College	WA	21,600	NC
West Chester Univ of Pennsylvania	PA	11,164	C
Western Mich Univ	MI	12,031	C
Worcester State College	MA	10,005	C
Youngstown State Univ	OH	11,148	NC

HEALTH CARE ADMINISTRATION

School	ST	$IS	SR
Alfred Univ	NY	28,290	C
Appalachian State Univ	NC	7,637	VC
Arcadia Univ	PA	29,890	C
Auburn Univ	AL	10,396	VC
Austin Peay State Univ	TN	5,814	LC
Baker College of Flint	MI	7,720	NC
Benedictine Univ	IL	23,840	C
Black Hills State Univ	SD	7,743	LC
Bowling Green State Univ	OH	13,036	C
Cabarrus College of Health Sciences	NC	7,000	SP
Cal State, Long Beach	CA	8,762	C+
Cal State, Northridge	CA	7,757	LC
Cal State, San Bernardino	CA	15,238	LC
Calumet College of St. Joseph	IN	9,000	LC
Carroll College	MT	20,576	VC
Chestnut Hill College	PA	26,450	LC
Chicago State Univ	IL	10,882	C+
CUNY/Herbert H. Lehman College	NY	3,320	LC
Clayton College and State Univ	GA	2,441	LC
Cleary College	MI	10,350	LC
College of Mount St. Joseph	OH	22,785	C
College of St. Catherine	MN	24,010	VC
College of St. Scholastica	MN	24,970	C+
Columbia Union College	MD	20,543	C
Concordia College: Moorhead	MN	22,460	VC+
Concordia Univ	OR	22,450	C
Daemen College	NY	22,120	C
David N. Myers College	OH	9,475	C
Dominican College	NY	24,810	LC
Duquesne Univ	PA	26,907	VC
Eastern Kentucky Univ	KY	7,708	C
Eastern Mich Univ	MI	11,478	C
Eastern Univ	PA	24,020	C
Eastern Washington Univ	WA	9,012	C
Emmanuel College	MA	27,600	C+
Ferris State Univ	MI	12,512	C
Florida Atlantic Univ	FL	8,543	C
Florida International Univ	FL	9,912	VC
Franklin Univ	OH	6,720	SP
Gwynedd-Mercy College	PA	24,225	C
Hastings College	NE	19,928	VC
Huron Univ	SD	10,450	C
Idaho State Univ	ID	8,128	C
Illinois State Univ	IL	10,944	C+
Indiana Univ Bloomington	IN	12,389	VC
Indiana Univ Kokomo	IN	4,463	LC
Indiana Univ Northwest	IN	4,538	LC
Indiana Univ South Bend	IN	4,571	LC
Indiana Univ-Purdue Univ Fort Wayne	IN	5,108	LC
Indiana Univ-Purdue Univ Indianapolis	IN	8,257	LC
International College	FL	8,060	LC
Iona College	NY	27,988	VC
Ithaca College	NY	31,730	HC
Kean Univ	NJ	14,479	C
Knoxville College	TN	6,200	LC
Langston Univ	OK	2,308	LC
Lasell College	MA	26,000	C
Lewis Univ	IL	22,950	C+
LIU/C.W. Post Campus	NY	28,282	C
Lourdes College	OH	15,300	LC
Lynn Univ	FL	30,750	C
Mary Baldwin College	VA	24,939	C
Maryville Univ of St. Louis	MO	22,090	VC
Marywood Univ	PA	26,050	C
Mercy College of Health Sciences	IA	10,500	SP
Metropolitan State College of Denver	CO	2,338	LC
Midwestern State Univ	TX	8,045	LC
Montana State Univ-Billings	MT	9,550	C
Mount Marty College	SD	15,656	LC
Mount Mercy College	IA	21,400	C
Mountain State Univ	WV	10,212	NC
National-Louis Univ	IL	16,240	LC
New York Univ	NY	39,406	MC
Newbury College	MA	23,450	C
Norfolk State Univ	VA	9,722	LC
Ohio Univ	OH	14,448	C
Oregon State Univ	OR	11,055	C
Park Univ	MO	10,780	C+
Penn State Univ/Univ Park Campus	PA	15,646	HC
Pennsylvania College of Technology	PA	15,126	NC
Point Park Univ	PA	21,840	C
Presentation College	SD	14,700	LC
Providence College	RI	30,604	HC
Quinnipiac Univ	CT	30,570	VC
Robert Morris Univ	PA	20,438	C
St. Francis College	NY	10,880	LC
St. John's Univ	NY	30,180	C
St. Joseph's, Brooklyn,	NY	10,902	C
St. Joseph's Univ	PA	33,590	VC
St. Leo Univ	FL	20,600	C
St. Louis Univ	MO	29,780	VC+
St. Peter's College	NJ	22,292	LC
Sojourner-Douglass College	MD	4,170	LC
Southern Adventist Univ	TN	17,080	C
Southern Illinois Univ Carbondale	IL	10,407	C
Southern Univ at New Orleans	LA	995	NC
Southwestern Okla State Univ	OK	4,801	C
Spring Arbor Univ	MI	20,206	C
Springfield College	MA	24,520	C
SUNY/College at Fredonia	NY	11,562	VC
Stonehill College	MA	30,752	HC
Tenn State Univ	TN	9,048	LC
Texas Southern Univ	TX	8,920	NC
Texas State Univ	TX	9,320	VC
Thomas Edison State College	NJ	3,325	SP
Towson Univ	MD	12,694	VC
Univ of Alabama	AL	9,040	C+
Univ of Arizona	AZ	10,413	VC
Univ of Central Arkansas	AR	6,388	C
Univ of Central Florida	FL	10,038	VC
Univ of Colo at Colo Springs	CO	10,667	C
Univ of Conn	CT	14,608	VC
Univ of Detroit Mercy	MI	25,582	C
Univ of Evansville	IN	24,190	VC
Univ of Great Falls	MT	15,360	C
Univ of La Verne	CA	28,600	C
Univ of Mich/Flint	MI	5,548	C
Univ of Minn/Crookston	MN	9,626	NC
Univ of Nevada/Las Vegas	NV	11,566	C
Univ of New England	ME	27,200	LC
Univ of New Hampshire	NH	14,828	VC
Univ of N Car at Chapel Hill	NC	10,117	MC
Univ of Pennsylvania	PA	37,960	MC
Univ of Rhode Island	RI	13,720	VC
Univ of Scranton	PA	30,836	VC
Univ of S Dak	SD	7,710	C+
Univ of Washington	WA	10,361	VC
Univ of Wisc/Eau Claire	WI	8,463	VC
Univ of Wisc/Milwaukee	WI	9,427	LC
Upper Iowa Univ	IA	20,076	C
Ursuline College	OH	22,728	LC
Viterbo Univ	WI	20,430	C
Weber State Univ	UT	7,945	NC
West Virginia Univ Inst of Technology	WV	7,518	NC
Western Kentucky Univ	KY	6,834	C
Wichita State Univ	KS	8,092	C
Wilberforce Univ	OH	14,937	LC

HEALTH EDUCATION

School	ST	$IS	SR
Albany State Univ	GA	5,764	C+
Anderson Univ	IN	19,430	LC
Appalachian State Univ	NC	7,637	VC
Arkansas State Univ	AR	8,450	C
Arkansas Tech Univ	AR	7,299	C
Ashland Univ	OH	24,464	C
Auburn Univ	AL	10,396	VC
Augsburg College	MN	25,298	C
Augusta State Univ	GA	2,592	C
Austin Peay State Univ	TN	5,814	LC
Averett Univ	VA	23,010	LC

School	ST	$IS	SR
Baldwin-Wallace College	OH	24,678	C
Ball State Univ	IN	8,660	C
Baylor Univ	TX	23,864	VC
Bemidji State Univ	MN	9,103	C
Bethel College	MN	25,180	VC
Bethel College	TN	12,980	C
Black Hills State Univ	SD	7,743	LC
Bowling Green State Univ	OH	13,036	C
Brewton-Parker College	GA	14,200	LC
Briar Cliff Univ	IA	21,660	C
Bridgewater State College	MA	10,482	C
Cal State, Sacramento	CA	9,543	C
Cal State, San Bernardino	CA	15,238	LC
Cal State, Stanislaus	CA	9,874	C
Carson-Newman College	TN	16,760	C
Central Mich Univ	MI	11,142	C
Central State Univ	OH	8,922	C+
Central Washington Univ	WA	9,768	C
Chadron State College	NE	6,286	NC
Citadel, The	SC	12,295	C+
CUNY/Brooklyn College	NY	4,353	C+
CUNY/Herbert H. Lehman College	NY	3,320	LC
CUNY/Hunter College	NY	6,729	C+
College of Mount St. Vincent	NY	26,800	C
College of New Jersey	NJ	15,950	MC
Columbus State Univ	GA	7,846	C
Concordia College: Moorhead	MN	22,460	VC+
Cumberland College	KY	16,384	C
Curry College	MA	26,025	LC
Daemen College	NY	22,120	C
Dakota State Univ	SD	7,466	C
Defiance College	OH	22,615	C
Delaware State Univ	DE	8,104	LC
Delta State Univ	MS	6,618	C
East Carolina Univ	NC	8,671	C
East Central Univ	OK	4,968	C
East Stroudsburg Univ of Pennsylvania	PA	10,336	C
Eastern Kentucky Univ	KY	7,708	C
Eastern Mich Univ	MI	11,478	C
Eastern Washington Univ	WA	9,012	C
Edinboro Univ of Pennsylvania	PA	10,850	LC
Elon Univ	NC	22,240	VC
Emporia State Univ	KS	6,998	C
Fairmont State	WV	8,280	LC
Fayetteville State Univ	NC	5,590	LC
Florida International Univ	FL	9,912	VC
Florida State Univ	FL	9,028	HC
Franklin College	IN		C
Freed-Hardeman Univ	TN		NC
Friends Univ	KS	15,962	LC
Gardner-Webb Univ	NC	19,300	C
George Fox Univ	OR	26,110	VC
Georgia College and State Univ	GA	9,878	C
Georgia Southern Univ	GA	8,540	C
Georgia State Univ	GA	10,658	C
Gustavus Adolphus College	MN	27,120	VC+
Hardin-Simmons Univ	TX	14,165	C
Hofstra Univ	NY	27,112	VC
Howard Univ	DC	16,505	C
Idaho State Univ	ID	8,128	C
Illinois State Univ	IL	10,944	C+
Indiana State Univ	IN	10,719	LC
Indiana Univ Bloomington	IN	12,389	VC
Indiana Univ-Purdue Univ Indianapolis	IN	8,257	LC
Inter American Univ of PR/ San German	PR	6,716	
Iowa State Univ	IA	10,768	VC
Ithaca College	NY	31,730	HC
Jackson State Univ	MS	8,382	C
Jacksonville State Univ	AL	6,844	LC
Johnson C. Smith Univ	NC	18,108	C
Juniata College	PA	29,080	VC
Kennesaw State Univ	GA	2,724	C
Kent State Univ	OH	12,932	C
Knoxville College	TN	6,200	LC
Lamar Univ	TX	6,816	LC
Lenoir-Rhyne College	NC	19,186	C
Lincoln Memorial Univ	TN	16,400	LC
Linfield College	OR	27,090	VC
LIU/C.W. Post Campus	NY	28,282	C
Louisiana College	LA	13,450	C
Malone College	OH	20,995	C
Manchester College	IN	23,390	C
Manhattan College	NY	27,400	VC
Mayville State Univ	ND	7,325	NC
McNeese State Univ	LA	5,259	LC
Miami Univ	OH	15,033	HC
MidAmerica Nazarene Univ	KS	18,688	C
Middle Tenn State Univ	TN	8,534	C
Minn State Univ, Mankato	MN	8,803	LC
Minn State Univ, Moorehead	MN	7,000	LC
Missouri Southern State Univ	MO	8,316	C
Montana State Univ-Billings	MT	9,550	C
Montclair State Univ	NJ	13,790	C
Morehead State Univ	KY	7,464	C
Morgan State Univ	MD	11,470	C
Mountain State Univ	WV	10,212	NC
Murray State Univ	KY	7,816	VC
New Jersey City Univ	NJ	11,850	LC
New York Inst of Technology	NY	24,205	VC
N Car Central Univ	NC	7,534	LC
N Dak State Univ	ND	8,435	C
Northeastern State Univ	OK	4,950	LC
Northern Arizona Univ	AZ	9,002	C
Northern Illinois Univ	IL	11,472	C
Northern Mich Univ	MI	10,834	C
Northern State Univ	SD	7,117	LC
Northwestern State Univ of Louisiana	LA	6,331	NC
Ohio Northern Univ	OH	27,765	VC
Okla Panhandle State Univ	OK	5,370	C
Okla State Univ	OK	9,216	VC
Oral Roberts Univ	OK	18,490	C
Oregon State Univ	OR	11,055	C
Otterbein College	OH	26,085	C
Ouachita Baptist Univ	AR	18,900	VC
Penn State Univ/Univ Park Campus	PA	15,646	HC
Plymouth State Univ	NH	12,298	LC
Portland State Univ	OR	12,453	C
Purdue Univ/West Lafayette	IN	12,560	VC
Rhode Island College	RI	11,565	C
St. Cloud State Univ	MN	8,362	C
St. Mary's College of Calif	CA	32,850	VC
Salisbury Univ	MD	12,664	VC
Shepherd College	WV	8,608	C
Slippery Rock Univ of Pennsylvania	PA	10,343	LC
S Car State Univ	SC	6,586	LC
S Dak State Univ	SD	7,782	C
Southern Arkansas Univ	AR	6,956	C
Southern Conn State Univ	CT	10,310	C
Southern Illinois Univ Carbondale	IL	10,407	C
Southern Illinois Univ Edwardsville	IL	8,724	C
Southwest Minn State Univ	MN	9,106	VC
Southwest Missouri State Univ	MO	8,918	C
Southwestern Okla State Univ	OK	4,801	C
Springfield College	MA	24,520	C
SUNY/College at Cortland	NY	12,095	C
Tabor College	KS	19,500	NC
Tenn State Univ	TN	9,048	LC
Texas A&M Univ	TX	11,081	HC
Texas A&M Univ at Commerce	TX	8,994	C
Texas A&M Univ at Kingsville	TX	6,740	LC
Texas State Univ	TX	9,320	VC
Thomas Edison State College	NJ	3,325	SP
Tougaloo College	MS	9,200	NC
Troy State Univ	AL	7,696	C
Univ of Akron	OH	13,134	NC
Univ of Alabama	AL	9,040	C+
Univ of Alabama at Birmingham	AL	12,901	C
Univ of Arizona	AZ	10,413	VC
Univ of Arkansas at Little Rock	AR	5,637	NC
Univ of Arkansas at Monticello	AR	5,940	NC
Univ of Cincinnati	OH	14,736	C
Univ of Florida	FL	8,580	MC
Univ of Georgia	GA	8,656	VC
Univ of Great Falls	MT	15,360	C
Univ of Iowa	IA	10,923	VC
Univ of Kansas	KS	8,923	VC
Univ of Kentucky	KY	7,765	C
Univ of Louisiana at Lafayette	LA	5,826	C
Univ of Maine	ME	12,080	C+
Univ of Maine at Farmington	ME	10,108	C
Univ of Maine at Presque Isle	ME	9,155	LC
Univ of Maryland/Eastern Shore	MD	9,964	C
Univ of Minn/Duluth	MN	12,470	C
Univ of Missouri/Kansas City	MO	13,416	VC
Univ of Nebr at Kearney	NE	8,286	NC
Univ of Nebr at Lincoln	NE	9,975	C+
Univ of Nevada/Las Vegas	NV	11,566	C
Univ of New Mexico	NM	9,223	C
Univ of N Car at Chapel Hill	NC	10,117	MC
Univ of N Car at Greensboro	NC	8,248	C
Univ of North Texas	TX	7,629	C
Univ of Northern Iowa	IA	9,834	C
Univ of Rio Grande	OH	8,728	NC
Univ of St. Francis	IN	20,964	C
Univ of St. Thomas	MN	26,918	VC
Univ of South Alabama	AL	7,760	LC
Univ of Southern Miss	MS	8,324	LC
Univ of Tenn at Knoxville	TN	8,214	C
Univ of the District of Columbia	DC	2,070	LC
Univ of Toledo	OH	12,479	NC
Univ of Utah	UT	9,205	C
Univ of Vermont	VT	16,316	VC
Univ of Virginia	VA	11,740	MC
Univ of West Florida	FL	8,470	C
Univ of Wisc/La Crosse	WI	8,991	VC
Univ of Wisc/Stevens Point	WI	8,116	VC
Univ of Wyoming	WY	8,636	C
Utah State Univ	UT	7,371	C
Valdosta State Univ	GA	7,798	C
Valley City State Univ	ND	7,281	LC
Virginia Commonwealth Univ	VA	9,030	C
Virginia Polytechnic Inst and State Univ	VA	9,179	C
Wayne State College	NE	7,352	NC
Weber State Univ	UT	7,945	NC
West Chester Univ of Pennsylvania	PA	11,164	C
West Liberty State College	WV	7,868	LC
Western Conn State Univ	CT	11,625	C
Western Kentucky Univ	KY	6,834	C
Western Mich Univ	MI	12,031	C
Western Oregon Univ	OR	10,281	C
Western Washington Univ	WA	10,119	VC
William Paterson Univ of New Jersey	NJ	14,450	C
William Penn Univ	IA	17,575	LC
Winona State Univ	MN		C
Youngstown State Univ	OH	11,148	NC

HEALTH SCIENCE

School	ST	$IS	SR
Alcorn State Univ	MS	7,290	C
Alma College	MI	25,566	VC
American Univ	DC	34,585	VC+
Appalachian State Univ	NC	7,637	VC
Armstrong Atlantic State Univ	GA	7,102	C
Ball State Univ	IN	8,660	C
Baylor Univ	TX	23,864	VC
Benedictine Univ	IL	23,840	C
Bethel College	KS	19,800	C+
Boise State Univ	ID	7,657	LC
Boston Univ	MA	38,194	HC+
Bowling Green State Univ	OH	13,036	C
Bradley Univ	IL	22,910	VC
Bridgewater College	VA	25,150	C
Brigham Young Univ	UT	8,504	HC
Cal State, Chico	CA	8,598	LC
Cal State, Dominguez Hills	CA	5,840	LC
Cal State, Fresno	CA	8,414	LC
Cal State, Fullerton	CA	6,648	C
Cal State, Hayward	CA	8,871	LC
Cal State, Long Beach	CA	8,762	C+
Cal State, Los Angeles	CA	5,778	C
Cal State, San Bernardino	CA	15,238	LC
Carlow College	PA	21,334	C
Castleton State College	VT	11,820	C
Centenary College of Louisiana	LA	23,100	VC+
Chapman Univ	CA	33,118	VC
Chicago State Univ	IL	10,882	C+
CUNY/Brooklyn College	NY	4,353	C+
CUNY/Queens College	NY	4,362	C
College of Our Lady of the Elms	MA	20,644	C
College of St. Scholastica	MN	24,970	C+
Columbus State Univ	GA	7,846	C
Dordt College	IA	20,170	VC
Duquesne Univ	PA	26,907	VC
East Tenn State Univ	TN	8,497	C
Eastern Univ	PA	24,020	C
Erskine College	SC	23,166	VC
Florida Atlantic Univ	FL	8,543	C
Florida Gulf Coast Univ	FL	9,908	C
Florida Hospital College of Health Sciences	FL	6,900	SP
Florida International Univ	FL	9,912	VC
Furman Univ	SC	28,976	HC+
George Mason Univ	VA	9,732	VC
Gettysburg College	PA	35,646	HC
Grand Valley State Univ	MI	11,022	VC
Guilford College	NC	24,960	VC
Hampshire College	MA	37,037	HC
Hope International Univ	CA	16,940	NC
Ithaca College	NY	31,730	HC
James Madison Univ	VA	10,794	VC
Johnson State College	VT	11,819	LC
Kalamazoo College	MI	26,955	HC+
Keene State College	NH	12,212	C
Kent State Univ	OH	12,932	C
La Sierra Univ	CA	19,260	LC
Lincoln Univ	PA	13,320	C+
Lock Haven Univ of Pennsylvania	PA	11,098	LC
Marymount Univ	VA	23,668	C
Maryville Univ of St. Louis	MO	22,090	VC
Marywood Univ	PA	26,050	C
MCP Hahnemann Univ	PA	18,510	SP
Middle Tenn State Univ	TN	8,534	C
Midwestern State Univ	TX	8,045	LC
Minn State Univ, Mankato	MN	8,803	LC
Missouri Baptist Univ	MO	18,010	C
New England College	NH	28,860	LC
Nicholls State Univ	LA	6,395	NC
Norfolk State Univ	VA	9,722	LC
Northeastern Univ	MA	35,650	HC
Northern Illinois Univ	IL	11,472	C
Nova Southeastern Univ	FL	23,346	C
Oakland Univ	MI	10,800	C
Old Dominion Univ	VA	10,441	C
Oral Roberts Univ	OK	18,490	C
Oregon Inst of Technology	OR	8,718	C
Our Lady of Holy Cross College	LA	5,900	C
Pennsylvania College of Technology	PA	15,126	NC
Purdue Univ/West Lafayette	IN	12,560	VC
Quinnipiac Univ	CT	30,570	VC
Randolph-Macon Woman's College	VA	28,430	VC+
St. Ambrose Univ	IA	22,800	C
St. Francis College	NY	10,880	LC
St. Mary's College	MI	13,314	LC
St. Mary's College of Calif	CA	32,850	VC
San Diego State Univ	CA	10,321	C
San Francisco State Univ	CA	12,070	C
Southern Adventist Univ	TN	17,080	C
Southwestern Okla State Univ	OK	4,801	C
SUNY/College at Brockport	NY	12,111	C
SUNY/College at Cortland	NY	12,095	C
SUNY/Univ at Stony Brook	NY	12,763	HC
Stephen F. Austin State Univ	TX	7,552	C
Stetson Univ	FL	29,495	VC
Syracuse Univ	NY	34,720	HC
Taylor Univ	IN	23,820	VC+
Temple Univ	PA	15,912	C
Texas A&M Univ at Corpus Christi	TX	10,269	C
Texas Woman's Univ	TX	7,804	LC
Towson Univ	MD	12,694	VC
Truman State Univ	MO	9,728	HC+
Universidad Adventista de las Antillas	PR	5,460	
Univ of Alabama at Birmingham	AL	12,901	C
Univ of Arkansas	AR	9,855	VC
Univ of Arkansas at Little Rock	AR	5,637	NC
Univ of Calif at Santa Cruz	CA	16,505	VC
Univ of Central Arkansas	AR	6,388	C
Univ of Central Florida	FL	10,038	VC
Univ of Findlay	OH	23,962	NC
Univ of Florida	FL	8,580	MC
Univ of Hartford	CT	31,080	C
Univ of Maryland/Baltimore County	MD	14,668	VC+
Univ of Miami	FL	34,608	HC
Univ of Mich/Flint	MI	5,548	C
Univ of Missouri/St. Louis	MO	11,656	VC
Univ of N Dak	ND	8,390	C
Univ of North Florida	FL	8,769	VC
Univ of Okla	OK	9,226	VC
Univ of Southern Maine	ME	11,212	C
Univ of Tenn at Knoxville	TN	8,214	C
Univ of Texas at El Paso	TX	5,799	NC
Univ of the Sciences in Philadelphia	PA	29,310	VC
Univ of Wisc/Milwaukee	WI	9,427	LC
Univ of Wyoming	WY	8,636	C
West Chester Univ of Pennsylvania	PA	11,164	C
Western Baptist College	OR	21,808	C
Western Illinois Univ	IL	10,363	C
William Paterson Univ of New Jersey	NJ	14,450	C
Worcester State College	MA	10,005	C
Yeshiva Univ	NY	21,400	C
Youngstown State Univ	OH	11,148	NC

HEBREW

School	ST	$IS	SR
CUNY/Brooklyn College	NY	4,353	C+
CUNY/Herbert H. Lehman College	NY	3,320	LC
CUNY/Hunter College	NY	6,729	C+
CUNY/Queens College	NY	4,362	C
Harvard Univ/Harvard College	MA	37,928	MC
Hofstra Univ	NY	27,112	VC
New York Univ	NY	39,406	MC
Ohio State Univ	OH	13,080	VC+
SUNY/Univ at Albany	NY	12,951	HC
SUNY/Univ at Binghamton	NY	12,787	HC
Temple Univ	PA	15,912	C
Touro College	NY	15,250	VC
Univ of Calif at Los Angeles	CA	15,330	MC
Univ of Mich/Ann Arbor	MI	13,864	HC+
Univ of Minn/Twin Cities	MN	13,160	VC
Univ of Texas at Austin	TX	10,630	HC
Univ of Wisc/Madison	WI	8,262	VC
Univ of Wisc/Milwaukee	WI	9,427	LC
Washington Univ in St. Louis	MO	38,293	MC
Yeshiva Univ	NY	21,400	C

HISPANIC AMERICAN STUDIES

School	ST	$IS	SR
Arizona State Univ-Main	AZ	10,048	C

School	ST	$IS	SR
Boston College	MA	33,284	MC
Boston Univ	MA	38,194	HC+
Brown Univ	RI	38,174	MC
Cal State, Long Beach	CA	8,762	C+
CUNY/Brooklyn College	NY	4,353	C+
CUNY/Hunter College	NY	6,729	C+
Columbia Univ/Columbia College	NY	38,590	MC
Columbia Univ/School of General Studies	NY	35,000	C
Conn College	CT	37,900	MC
Earlham College	IN	29,976	VC+
East Carolina Univ	NC	8,671	C
Hofstra Univ	NY	27,112	VC
Illinois Wesleyan Univ	IL	30,380	HC+
Lewis and Clark College	OR	30,620	VC
Mills College	CA	33,371	VC
Mount St. Mary College	NY	21,270	C
Rice Univ	TX	27,550	MC
Rutgers, The State Univ of New Jersey/New Brunswick/Piscataway Campus	NJ	15,800	HC
St. Olaf College	MN	28,500	HC
Scripps College	CA	35,700	HC+
SUNY/College at Oneonta	NY	11,870	VC
SUNY/Univ at Albany	NY	12,951	HC
Univ of Calif at Berkeley	CA	15,563	MC
Univ of Calif at Los Angeles	CA	15,330	MC
Univ of Mass Boston	MA	6,227	C
Univ of Mich/Ann Arbor	MI	13,864	HC+
Univ of PR/Cayey Univ College	PR	1,245	
Western New Mexico Univ	NM	5,950	LC
Wheaton College	MA	36,330	HC

HISTORIC PRESERVATION

School	ST	$IS	SR
Eastern Mich Univ	MI	11,478	C
Goucher College	MD	32,650	HC
Mary Washington College	VA	10,166	HC
Roger Williams Univ	RI	30,296	C
Salve Regina Univ	RI	29,210	C
Savannah College of Art and Design	GA	27,560	SP
Univ of Delaware	DE	12,616	HC
Ursuline College	OH	22,728	LC

HISTORY

School	ST	$IS	SR
Abilene Christian Univ	TX	18,370	VC
Adams State College	CO	7,468	C
Adelphi Univ	NY	26,300	VC
Adrian College	MI	21,950	C
Agnes Scott College	GA	28,230	HC
Alabama A&M Univ	AL	5,100	LC
Alabama State Univ	AL	6,404	C
Albany State Univ	GA	5,764	C+
Albertson College of Idaho	ID	19,415	VC
Albertus Magnus College	CT	23,130	LC
Albion College	MI	25,224	VC
Albright College	PA	30,579	C
Alcorn State Univ	MS	7,290	C
Alderson-Broaddus College	WV	19,640	C
Alfred Univ	NY	28,290	C
Alice Lloyd College	KY	4,040	C
Allegheny College	PA	30,280	VC
Allen Univ	SC	10,300	NC
Alma College	MI	25,566	VC
Alvernia College	PA	23,212	LC
Alverno College	WI	18,898	C
American International College	MA	24,690	LC
American Univ	DC	34,585	VC+
Amherst College	MA	37,470	MC
Anderson Univ	IN	19,430	LC
Andrews Univ	MI	19,550	C
Angelo State Univ	TX	7,576	NC
Anna Maria College	MA	26,140	LC
Appalachian State Univ	NC	7,637	VC
Aquinas College	MI	21,894	C
Arcadia Univ	PA	29,890	C
Arizona State Univ-Main	AZ	10,048	C
Arkansas State Univ	AR	8,450	C
Arkansas Tech Univ	AR	7,299	C
Armstrong Atlantic State Univ	GA	7,102	C
Asbury College	KY	20,704	VC
Ashland Univ	OH	24,464	C
Assumption College	MA	29,375	C
Atlantic Union College	MA	18,868	C
Auburn Univ	AL	10,396	VC
Auburn Univ Montgomery	AL	9,020	NC
Augsburg College	MN	25,298	C
Augusta State Univ	GA	2,592	C
Augustana College	IL	26,610	VC+
Augustana College	SD	21,998	VC
Aurora Univ	IL	20,631	C
Austin College	TX	24,747	HC
Austin Peay State Univ	TN	5,814	LC
Averett Univ	VA	23,010	LC
Avila Univ	MO	20,300	C
Azusa Pacific Univ	CA	24,720	VC
Baker Univ	KS	19,860	VC
Baldwin-Wallace College	OH	24,678	C
Ball State Univ	IN	8,660	C
Bard College	NY	37,352	HC+
Barry Univ	FL	24,100	LC
Barton College	NC	19,314	C
Bates College	ME	37,500	MC
Baylor Univ	TX	23,864	VC
Belhaven College	MS	16,040	C+
Bellarmine Univ	KY	24,110	VC
Bellevue Univ	NE	4,440	NC
Belmont Abbey College	NC	23,742	C
Belmont Univ	TN	21,986	VC
Beloit College	WI	29,864	HC
Bemidji State Univ	MN	9,103	C
Benedictine College	KS	20,603	C
Benedictine Univ	IL	23,840	C
Bennington College	VT	35,910	HC
Bentley College	MA	33,904	VC
Berea College	KY	5,030	VC+
Berry College	GA	21,410	VC
Bethany College	KS	18,675	LC
Bethany College	WV	19,845	VC
Bethel College	IN	19,670	C
Bethel College	KS	19,800	C+
Bethel College	MN	25,180	VC
Bethel College	TN	12,980	C
Bethune-Cookman College	FL	16,480	LC
Biola Univ	CA	25,964	VC
Birmingham-Southern College	AL	25,364	VC+
Black Hills State Univ	SD	7,743	LC
Blackburn College	IL	13,690	C
Bloomfield College	NJ	19,250	LC
Bloomsburg Univ of Pennsylvania	PA	10,844	C
Blue Mountain College	MS	10,226	C
Bluefield College	VA	15,575	C
Bluffton College	OH	23,694	C
Boise State Univ	ID	7,657	LC
Boston College	MA	33,284	MC
Boston Univ	MA	38,194	HC+
Bowdoin College	ME	37,790	MC
Bowie State Univ	MD	10,873	C+
Bowling Green State Univ	OH	13,036	C
Bradley Univ	IL	22,910	VC
Brandeis Univ	MA	38,198	MC
Brenau Univ Women's College	GA	21,800	C
Brescia Univ	KY	14,225	C
Brewton-Parker College	GA	14,200	LC
Briar Cliff Univ	IA	21,660	C
Bridgewater College	VA	25,150	C
Bridgewater State College	MA	10,482	C
Brigham Young Univ	UT	8,504	HC
Brigham Young Univ/Hawaii	HI	7,240	VC+
Brown Univ	RI	38,174	MC
Bryan College	TN	17,900	VC
Bryant College	RI	31,004	VC
Bryn Athyn College of the New Church	PA	12,612	NC
Bryn Mawr College	PA	36,890	HC+
Bucknell Univ	PA	35,262	HC+
Buena Vista Univ	IA	25,406	C
Butler Univ	IN	28,250	VC+
Cabrini College	PA	29,020	C
Caldwell College	NJ	24,060	LC
Calif Baptist Univ	CA	19,924	C
Calif Inst of Technology	CA	31,677	MC
Calif Lutheran Univ	CA	27,600	LC
Calif Polytechnic State Univ	CA	8,747	VC
Calif State Polytechnic Univ, Pomona	CA	8,793	C+
Cal State, Bakersfield	CA	6,090	LC
Cal State, Chico	CA	8,598	LC
Cal State, Dominguez Hills	CA	5,840	LC
Cal State, Fresno	CA	8,414	LC
Cal State, Fullerton	CA	6,648	C
Cal State, Hayward	CA	8,871	LC
Cal State, Long Beach	CA	8,762	C+
Cal State, Los Angeles	CA	5,778	C
Cal State, Northridge	CA	7,757	LC
Cal State, Sacramento	CA	9,543	C
Cal State, San Bernardino	CA	15,238	LC
Cal State, San Marcos	CA	1,736	LC
Cal State, Stanislaus	CA	9,874	C
Calif Univ of Pennsylvania	PA	10,388	C
Calvin College	MI	22,615	NC
Cameron Univ	OK	5,692	NC
Campbell Univ	NC	18,268	VC
Campbellsville Univ	KY	17,680	C
Canisius College	NY	28,163	C+
Capital Univ	OH	26,550	C
Cardinal Stritch Univ	WI	17,620	C
Carleton College	MN	34,395	MC
Carlow College	PA	21,334	C
Carnegie Mellon Univ	PA	32,682	MC
Carroll College	MT	20,576	VC
Carroll College	WI	22,740	C
Carson-Newman College	TN	16,760	C
Carthage College	WI	25,000	C
Case Western Reserve Univ	OH	32,002	MC
Castleton State College	VT	11,820	C
Catawba College	NC	20,500	C
Catholic Univ of America	DC	34,248	VC
Cedar Crest College	PA	25,145	C+
Cedarville Univ	OH	19,954	VC
Centenary College	NJ	25,370	LC
Centenary College of Louisiana	LA	23,100	VC+
Central College	IA	21,206	C
Central Conn State Univ	CT	12,090	C
Central Methodist College	MO	16,460	C
Central Mich Univ	MI	11,142	C
Central Missouri State Univ	MO	9,776	C
Central State Univ	OH	8,922	C+
Central Washington Univ	WA	9,768	C
Centre College	KY	27,300	HC
Chadron State College	NE	6,286	NC
Chaminade Univ of Honolulu	HI	21,430	LC
Chapman Univ	CA	33,118	VC
Charleston Southern Univ	SC	17,122	C
Chatham College	PA	27,266	C+
Chestnut Hill College	PA	26,450	LC
Chicago State Univ	IL	10,882	C+
Christendom College	VA	18,410	VC+
Christian Brothers Univ	TN	22,290	VC
Christian Heritage College	CA	19,990	C
Christopher Newport Univ	VA	8,862	VC
Citadel, The	SC	12,295	C+
CUNY/Baruch College	NY	3,275	VC+
CUNY/Brooklyn College	NY	4,353	C+
CUNY/City College	NY	4,230	C+
CUNY/College of Staten Island	NY	4,308	NC
CUNY/Herbert H. Lehman College	NY	3,320	LC
CUNY/Hunter College	NY	6,729	C+
CUNY/Queens College	NY	4,362	C
CUNY/York College	NY	3,292	NC
Claflin Univ	SC	14,838	C+
Claremont McKenna College	CA	36,880	MC
Clarion Univ of Pennsylvania	PA	11,272	LC
Clark Atlanta Univ	GA	19,300	C+
Clark Univ	MA	32,115	VC
Clarke College	IA	23,165	C
Clarkson Univ	NY	32,226	VC
Clayton College and State Univ	GA	2,441	LC
Clearwater Christian College	FL	13,160	LC
Clemson Univ	SC	11,972	HC
Cleveland State Univ	OH	12,308	LC
Coastal Carolina Univ	SC	11,040	C
Coe College	IA	27,385	VC
Coker College	SC	21,491	C
Colby College	ME	37,570	MC
Colby-Sawyer College	NH	27,850	LC
Colgate Univ	NY	37,095	MC
College Misericordia	PA	26,350	C
College of Charleston	SC	11,887	HC
College of Mount St. Vincent	NY	26,800	C
College of Mount St. Joseph	OH	22,785	C
College of New Jersey	NJ	15,950	MC
College of New Rochelle	NY	21,800	C
College of Notre Dame of Maryland	MD	27,700	C
College of St. Benedict	MN	26,672	VC
College of St. Catherine	MN	24,010	VC
College of St. Elizabeth	NJ	25,460	C
College of St. Joseph	VT	19,100	C
College of St. Rose	NY	22,864	C
College of St. Scholastica	MN	24,970	C+
College of the Holy Cross	MA	36,451	MC
College of the Ozarks	MO	3,500	VC+
College of the Southwest	NM	9,320	C+
College of William and Mary	VA	12,224	MC
College of Wooster	OH	31,300	HC
Colo Christian Univ	CO	21,182	VC
Colo College	CO	36,860	HC
Colo State Univ	CO	9,964	VC
Columbia College	MO	16,139	C
Columbia College	SC	22,658	LC
Columbia Union College	MD	20,543	C
Columbia Univ/Barnard College	NY	36,990	MC
Columbia Univ/Columbia College	NY	38,590	MC
Columbia Univ/School of General Studies	NY	35,000	C
Columbus State Univ	GA	7,846	C
Concord College	WV	8,136	C
Concordia College	NY	19,200	VC
Concordia College: Moorhead	MN	22,460	VC+
Concordia Univ	CA	24,420	C
Concordia Univ	MI	24,095	C
Concordia Univ at Austin	TX	20,450	LC
Concordia Univ Nebr	NE	20,302	C+
Concordia Univ Wisc	WI	16,600	C
Concordia Univ, River Forest	IL	23,600	C
Concordia Univ/St.Paul	MN	24,486	C
Conn College	CT	37,900	MC
Converse College	SC	24,710	VC
Coppin State College	MD	10,191	LC
Cornell College	IA	27,825	VC+
Cornell Univ	NY	38,253	MC
Cornerstone Univ and Grand Rapids Theological Seminary	MI	19,846	C
Covenant College	GA	23,830	VC+
Creighton Univ	NE	26,748	VC+
Crichton College	TN	15,215	C
Culver-Stockton College	MO	17,850	C
Cumberland College	KY	16,384	C
Cumberland Univ	TN	16,910	C
Curry College	MA	26,025	LC
Daemen College	NY	22,120	C
Dakota Wesleyan Univ	SD	17,832	C
Dallas Baptist Univ	TX	15,300	VC
Dana College	NE	20,280	C
Dartmouth College	NH	37,770	MC
David Lipscomb Univ	TN	16,158	VC
Davidson College	NC	33,274	MC
Davis and Elkins College	WV	20,594	C
De Sales Univ	PA	25,470	C
Defiance College	OH	22,615	C
Delaware State Univ	DE	8,104	LC
Delta State Univ	MS	6,618	C
Denison Univ	OH	33,050	HC
DePaul Univ	IL	27,580	VC
DePauw Univ	IN	31,500	HC
Dickinson College	PA	35,825	HC
Dickinson State Univ	ND	6,338	NC
Dillard Univ	LA	17,325	VC
Doane College	NE	20,000	C
Dominican College	NY	24,810	LC
Dominican Univ	IL	23,610	C
Dominican Univ of Calif	CA	31,670	C
Dordt College	IA	20,170	VC
Dowling College	NY	23,870	LC
Drake Univ	IA	25,120	VC+
Drew Univ/College of Liberal Arts	NJ	35,550	VC
Drexel Univ	PA	27,655	VC
Drury Univ	MO	18,085	VC+
Duke Univ	NC	37,555	MC
Duquesne Univ	PA	26,907	VC
D'Youville College	NY	21,080	C
Earlham College	IN	29,976	VC+
East Carolina Univ	NC	8,671	C
East Central Univ	OK	4,968	C
East Stroudsburg Univ of Pennsylvania	PA	10,336	C
East Tenn State Univ	TN	8,497	C
East Texas Baptist Univ	TX	13,914	C
Eastern Conn State Univ	CT	10,362	C
Eastern Illinois Univ	IL	11,192	C
Eastern Kentucky Univ	KY	7,708	C
Eastern Mennonite Univ	VA	22,990	C
Eastern Mich Univ	MI	11,478	C
Eastern Nazarene College	MA	19,433	LC
Eastern New Mexico Univ	NM	6,762	LC
Eastern Oregon Univ	OR	10,080	NC
Eastern Univ	PA	24,020	C
Eastern Washington Univ	WA	9,012	C
Eckerd College	FL	28,744	C+
Edgewood College	WI	20,520	C
Edinboro Univ of Pennsylvania	PA	10,850	LC
Edward Waters College	FL	14,374	LC
Elizabeth City State Univ	NC	5,550	LC
Elizabethtown College	PA	28,800	C
Elmhurst College	IL	24,630	C
Elmira College	NY	33,820	VC
Elon Univ	NC	22,240	VC
Emory & Henry College	VA	21,950	C
Emory Univ	GA	36,872	MC
Emporia State Univ	KS	6,998	C
Erskine College	SC	23,166	VC
Eugene Lang College/New School Univ	NY	34,940	C
Eureka College	IL	24,980	LC
Evangel Univ	MO	15,435	C
Fairfield Univ	CT	35,505	HC
Fairleigh Dickinson Univ/College at Florham	NJ	30,130	C
Fairleigh Dickinson Univ/Metropolitan Campus	NJ	28,584	C
Fairmont State	WV	8,280	LC
Fayetteville State Univ	NC	5,590	LC
Felician College	NJ	24,300	C
Ferrum College	VA	21,240	LC
Fisk Univ	TN	17,305	LC
Fitchburg State College	MA	9,622	C
Flagler College	FL	11,860	VC+
Florida A&M Univ	FL	7,564	C
Florida Atlantic Univ	FL	8,543	C
Florida International Univ	FL	9,912	VC
Florida Southern College	FL	23,592	C
Florida State Univ	FL	9,028	HC
Fontbonne Univ	MO	21,508	C
Fordham Univ	NY	35,066	HC
Fort Hays State Univ	KS	7,363	C
Fort Lewis College	CO	8,353	C
Framingham State College	MA	9,381	C
Francis Marion Univ	SC	9,364	C
Franciscan Univ of Steubenville	OH	20,300	VC
Franklin and Marshall College	PA	35,930	HC+
Franklin College	IN		C
Franklin Pierce College	NH	28,980	LC

ST = STATE $IS = IN-STATE COSTS SR = SELECTOR RATING

School	ST	$IS	SR
Freed-Hardeman Univ	TN		NC
Fresno Pacific Univ	CA	22,462	C
Friends Univ	KS	15,962	LC
Frostburg State Univ	MD	11,114	C
Furman Univ	SC	28,976	HC+
Gallaudet Univ	DC	16,554	SP
Gannon Univ	PA	23,260	C
Gardner-Webb Univ	NC	19,300	C
Geneva College	PA	21,850	C
George Fox Univ	OR	26,110	VC
George Mason Univ	VA	9,732	VC
George Washington Univ	DC	41,030	MC
Georgetown College	KY	22,000	VC
Georgetown Univ	DC	38,242	MC
Georgia College and State Univ	GA	9,878	C
Georgia Inst of Technology	GA	10,340	HC+
Georgia Southern Univ	GA	8,540	C
Georgia Southwestern State Univ	GA	6,013	C
Georgia State Univ	GA	10,658	C
Georgian Court College	NJ	19,040	LC
Gettysburg College	PA	35,646	HC
Glenville State College	WV	7,812	NC
Gonzaga Univ	WA	26,766	HC
Gordon College	MA	25,982	VC+
Goshen College	IN	22,450	VC
Goucher College	MD	32,650	HC
Graceland Univ	IA	19,550	C
Grambling State Univ	LA	6,538	NC
Grand Canyon Univ	AZ	30,000	LC
Grand Valley State Univ	MI	11,022	VC
Green Mountain College	VT	24,130	C
Greensboro College	NC	21,750	C
Greenville College	IL	21,342	C
Grinnell College	IA	31,060	HC+
Grove City College	PA	14,228	HC
Guilford College	NC	24,960	VC
Gustavus Adolphus College	MN	27,120	VC+
Gwynedd-Mercy College	PA	24,225	C
Hamilton College	NY	37,560	MC
Hamline Univ	MN	27,052	VC
Hampden-Sydney College	VA	28,407	VC
Hampshire College	MA	37,037	HC
Hampton Univ	VA	17,112	C+
Hannibal-LaGrange College	MO	13,940	C
Hanover College	IN	25,200	VC
Harding Univ	AR	14,890	VC
Hardin-Simmons Univ	TX	14,165	C
Hartwick College	NY	34,650	C
Harvard Univ/Harvard College	MA	37,928	MC
Hastings College	NE	19,928	VC
Haverford College	PA	37,900	MC
Hawaii Pacific Univ	HI	19,218	C
Heidelberg College	OH	20,266	NC
Henderson State Univ	AR	7,386	C
Hendrix College	AR	20,970	VC+
High Point Univ	NC	22,480	C
Hillsdale College	MI	22,450	HC
Hiram College	OH	28,234	VC
Hobart and William Smith Colleges	NY	36,536	HC
Hofstra Univ	NY	27,112	VC
Hollins Univ	VA	27,965	VC
Holy Family College	PA	13,710	LC
Holy Names College	CA	27,980	NC
Hood College	MD	27,795	VC
Hope College	MI	25,340	VC
Houghton College	NY	23,984	VC
Houston Baptist Univ	TX	16,905	C
Howard Payne Univ	TX	15,176	C
Howard Univ	DC	16,505	C
Humboldt State Univ	CA	9,400	C
Huntingdon College	AL	18,400	VC
Huntington College	IN	23,590	C
Idaho State Univ	ID	8,128	C
Illinois College	IL	19,100	VC
Illinois State Univ	IL	10,944	C+
Illinois Wesleyan Univ	IL	30,380	HC+
Immaculata Univ	PA	25,200	C
Indiana State Univ	IN	10,719	LC
Indiana Univ Bloomington	IN	12,389	VC
Indiana Univ Northwest	IN	4,538	LC
Indiana Univ of Pennsylvania	PA	10,489	C
Indiana Univ South Bend	IN	4,571	LC
Indiana Univ Southeast	IN	4,504	LC
Indiana Univ-Purdue Univ Fort Wayne	IN	5,108	LC
Indiana Univ-Purdue Univ Indianapolis	IN	8,257	LC
Indiana Wesleyan Univ	IN	19,900	C+
Inter American Univ of PR/ Fajardo Campus	PR	4,000	
Inter American Univ of PR/ Metropolitan Campus	PR		
Inter American Univ of PR/ Ponce Regional Campus	PR	3,700	
Inter American Univ of PR/ San German	PR	6,716	
Iona College	NY	27,988	VC
Iowa State Univ	IA	10,768	VC
Iowa Wesleyan College	IA	19,990	C
Ithaca College	NY	31,730	HC
Jackson State Univ	MS	8,382	C
Jacksonville State Univ	AL	6,844	LC
Jacksonville Univ	FL	24,040	C
James Madison Univ	VA	10,794	VC
Jamestown College	ND	12,600	NC
Jarvis Christian College	TX	9,035	NC
John Brown Univ	AR	15,080	VC
John Carroll Univ	OH	27,658	C+
Johns Hopkins Univ	MD	38,372	MC
Johnson C. Smith Univ	NC	18,108	C
Johnson State Univ	VT	11,819	LC
Judson College	AL	14,650	C
Judson College	IL	22,050	LC
Juniata College	PA	29,080	VC
Kalamazoo College	MI	26,955	HC+
Kansas State Univ	KS	8,728	C
Kansas Wesleyan Univ	KS	18,900	VC
Kean Univ	NJ	14,479	C
Keene State College	NH	12,212	C
Kennesaw State Univ	GA	2,724	C
Kent State Univ	OH	12,932	C
Kentucky Christian College	KY	13,472	C
Kentucky State Univ	KY	9,062	NC
Kentucky Wesleyan College	KY	17,250	C
Kenyon College	OH	35,370	HC+
King College	TN	22,500	VC
King's College	PA	26,990	C
Knox College	IL	30,294	VC+
Kutztown Univ of Pennsylvania	PA	10,786	C
La Roche College	PA	22,094	C
La Salle Univ	PA	31,260	VC
La Sierra Univ	CA	19,260	LC
Lafayette College	PA	35,746	MC
LaGrange College	GA	20,500	C
Lake Forest College	IL	30,270	VC
Lake Superior State Univ	MI	9,034	LC
Lakeland College	WI	17,950	C
Lamar Univ	TX	6,816	LC
Lambuth Univ	TN	16,520	C
Lander Univ	SC	10,496	C
Lane College	TN	11,178	C+
Langston Univ	OK	2,308	LC
Lawrence Univ	WI	30,900	HC
Le Moyne College	NY	26,400	VC
Lebanon Valley College	PA	28,870	VC
Lee Univ	TN	13,780	NC
Lees-McRae College	NC	17,106	C
Lehigh Univ	PA	37,570	HC+
LeMoyne-Owen College	TN	13,070	LC
Lenoir-Rhyne College	NC	19,186	C
LeTourneau Univ	TX	21,080	C
Lewis and Clark College	OR	30,620	VC
Lewis Univ	IL	22,950	C+
Lewis-Clark State College	ID	6,981	C
Liberty Univ	VA	17,220	C
Limestone College	SC	17,700	C
Lincoln Memorial Univ	TN	16,400	LC
Lincoln Univ	MO	7,158	NC
Lincoln Univ	PA	13,320	C+
Lindenwood Univ	MO	17,050	C
Lindsey Wilson College	KY	16,392	LC
Linfield College	OR	27,090	VC
LIU/Brooklyn Campus	NY	24,790	C
LIU/C.W. Post Campus	NY	28,282	C
LIU/Southampton College	NY	29,370	C+
Livingstone College	NC	18,101	C
Lock Haven Univ of Pennsylvania	PA	11,098	LC
Longwood Univ	VA	11,175	C
Loras College	IA	24,233	C
Louisiana College	LA	13,450	C
Louisiana State Univ and A&M College	LA	9,126	VC
Louisiana State Univ in Shreveport	LA	2,884	NC
Louisiana Tech Univ	LA	7,361	C
Lourdes College	OH	15,300	C
Loyola College in Maryland	MD	34,560	HC
Loyola Marymount Univ	CA	32,194	VC
Loyola Univ Chicago	IL	31,164	VC
Loyola Univ New Orleans	LA	31,036	VC+
Luther College	IA	25,700	VC
Lycoming College	PA	27,589	C+
Lynchburg College	VA	26,815	C
Lynn Univ	FL	30,750	C
Lyon College	AR	17,995	VC
Macalester College	MN	31,944	MC
MacMurray College	IL	20,005	LC
Madonna Univ	MI	11,504	C
Malone College	OH	20,995	C
Manchester College	IN	23,390	C
Manhattan College	NY	27,400	VC
Manhattanville College	NY	32,420	C+
Mansfield Univ	PA	11,220	C
Marian College	IN	23,030	C
Marian College of Fond du Lac	WI	19,625	C
Marietta College	OH	27,047	C
Marist College	NY	27,596	VC
Marlboro College	VT	29,055	VC+
Marquette Univ	WI	27,594	VC
Mars Hill College	NC	18,600	LC
Marshall Univ	WV	9,116	C
Martin Univ	IN	10,200	SP
Mary Baldwin College	VA	24,939	C
Mary Washington College	VA	10,166	HC
Marygrove College	MI	17,550	C
Marymount College of Fordham Univ	NY	27,686	C
Marymount Manhattan College	NY	27,292	C
Marymount Univ	VA	23,668	C
Maryville College	TN	25,960	VC
Maryville Univ of St. Louis	MO	22,090	VC
Marywood Univ	PA	26,050	C
Mass College of Liberal Arts	MA	8,717	LC
Mass Inst of Technology	MA	38,310	MC
Master's College and Seminary	CA	23,250	VC
McDaniel College	MD	28,440	VC
McKendree College	IL	21,120	VC
McMurry Univ	TX	17,846	LC
McNeese State Univ	LA	5,259	LC
McPherson College	KS	20,265	C
Mercer Univ	GA	27,516	VC+
Mercy College	NY	19,200	NC
Mercyhurst College	PA	20,694	C
Meredith College	NC	23,065	C
Merrimack College	MA	29,625	C
Mesa State College	CO	8,051	C
Messiah College	PA	25,890	VC+
Methodist College	NC	19,526	C
Metropolitan State College of Denver	CO	2,338	LC
Metropolitan State Univ	MN	3,852	SP
Miami Univ	OH	15,033	HC
Mich State Univ	MI	11,933	VC
MidAmerica Nazarene Univ	KS	18,688	C
Middle Tenn State Univ	TN	8,534	C
Middlebury College	VT	38,100	MC
Midland Lutheran College	NE	18,600	C
Midwestern State Univ	TX	8,045	LC
Millersville Univ of Pennsylvania	PA	11,269	C
Milligan College	TN	19,860	C+
Millikin Univ	IL	25,555	C
Mills College	CA	33,371	VC
Millsaps College	MS	25,182	VC
Minn State Univ, Mankato	MN	8,803	LC
Minn State Univ, Moorehead	MN	7,000	LC
Minot State Univ	ND	6,602	LC
Miss College	MS	14,574	C
Miss State Univ	MS	9,139	C
Miss Univ for Women	MS	5,446	LC
Miss Valley State Univ	MS	6,765	NC
Missouri Baptist Univ	MO	18,010	C
Missouri Southern State Univ	MO	8,316	C
Missouri Valley College	MO	18,500	C
Missouri Western State College	MO	8,522	NC
Molloy College	NY	15,180	C
Monmouth College	IL	23,600	C
Monmouth Univ	NJ	26,334	C
Montana State Univ-Billings	MT	9,550	C
Montana State Univ-Bozeman	MT	9,515	C
Montana State Univ-Northern	MT	8,600	NC
Montclair State Univ	NJ	13,790	C
Montreat College	NC	18,762	C
Moravian College	PA	28,903	VC
Morehead State Univ	KY	7,464	C
Morehouse College	GA	22,728	C
Morgan State Univ	MD	11,470	C
Morningside College	IA	21,610	C
Morris College	SC	10,974	LC
Mount Holyoke College	MA	37,918	HC+
Mount Marty College	SD	15,656	LC
Mount Mary College	WI	20,370	C
Mount Mercy College	IA	21,400	C
Mount Olive College	NC	14,410	LC
Mount St. Mary College	NY	21,270	C
Mount St. Mary's College	CA	28,307	VC
Mount St. Mary's College	MD	28,400	C
Mount Union College	OH	21,120	C
Mount Vernon Nazarene Univ	OH	18,925	C
Muhlenberg College	PA	31,485	HC
Murray State Univ	KY	7,816	VC
Muskingum College	OH	20,680	C
Nazareth College of Rochester	NY	24,936	VC
Nebr Wesleyan Univ	NE	21,197	C+
New College of Florida	FL	8,906	HC+
New Jersey City Univ	NJ	11,850	VC
New Jersey Inst of Technology	NJ	16,396	VC
New Mexico Highlands Univ	NM	6,182	LC
New Mexico State Univ	NM	7,932	C
New York Univ	NY	39,406	MC
Newberry College	SC	22,871	LC
Newman Univ	KS	18,018	C
Niagara Univ	NY	25,050	C
Nicholls State Univ	LA	6,395	NC
Nichols College	MA	27,562	LC
Norfolk State Univ	VA	9,722	LC
N Car Agricultural and Technical State Univ	NC	6,659	LC
N Car Central Univ	NC	7,534	LC
N Car State Univ	NC	9,886	VC
N Car Wesleyan College	NC	17,998	C
North Central College	IL	25,656	VC
N Dak State Univ	ND	8,435	C
North Georgia College and State Univ	GA	6,984	C
North Park Univ	IL	24,030	C
Northeastern Illinois Univ	IL	2,898	NC
Northeastern State Univ	OK	4,950	LC
Northeastern Univ	MA	35,650	HC
Northern Arizona Univ	AZ	9,002	C
Northern Illinois Univ	IL	11,472	C
Northern Kentucky Univ	KY	6,352	NC
Northern Mich Univ	MI	10,834	C
Northern State Univ	SD	7,117	LC
Northland College	WI	22,170	C+
Northwest College	WA	18,854	C
Northwest Missouri State Univ	MO	9,334	C
Northwest Nazarene Univ	ID	20,360	VC
Northwestern College	MN	22,820	C+
Northwestern College of Iowa	IA	19,640	C+
Northwestern Okla State Univ	OK	5,433	NC
Northwestern State Univ of Louisiana	LA	6,331	NC
Northwestern Univ	IL	37,491	MC
Norwich Univ	VT	21,064	LC
Notre Dame College	OH	20,425	C
Notre Dame de Namur Univ	CA	26,932	LC
Nova Southeastern Univ	FL	23,346	C
Nyack College	NY	18,540	C
Oakland Univ	MI	10,800	C
Oakwood College	AL	14,904	C
Oberlin College	OH	36,938	MC
Occidental College	CA	35,922	HC
Oglala Lakota College	SD	1,950	NC
Oglethorpe Univ	GA	26,000	VC
Ohio Dominican Univ	OH	22,700	C
Ohio Northern Univ	OH	27,765	VC
Ohio State Univ	OH	13,080	VC+
Ohio State Univ at Lima	OH	4,416	NC
Ohio State Univ at Newark	OH	9,881	NC
Ohio Univ	OH	14,448	C
Ohio Wesleyan Univ	OH	32,550	VC+
Okla Baptist Univ	OK	15,220	VC
Okla Christian Univ	OK	17,690	NC
Okla City Univ	OK	19,580	VC
Okla Panhandle State Univ	OK	5,370	C
Okla State Univ	OK	9,216	VC
Okla Wesleyan Univ	OK	14,100	LC
Old Dominion Univ	VA	10,441	C
Olivet College	MI	19,984	C+
Olivet Nazarene Univ	IL	20,480	C
Oral Roberts Univ	OK	18,490	C
Oregon State Univ	OR	11,055	C
Ottawa Univ	KS	11,800	LC
Otterbein College	OH	26,085	C
Ouachita Baptist Univ	AR	18,900	C
Our Lady of Holy Cross College	LA	5,900	C
Our Lady of the Lake Univ of San Antonio	TX	17,336	C
Pace Univ	NY	28,652	VC
Pacific Lutheran Univ	WA	25,715	VC
Pacific Union College	CA	22,065	C+
Pacific Univ	OR	24,250	C
Paine College	GA	13,022	LC
Palm Beach Atlantic Univ	FL	20,690	C
Park Univ	MO	10,780	C+
Paul Quinn College	TX	8,150	LC
Penn State Univ at Erie/ Behrend College	PA	12,326	C
Penn State Univ/Univ Park Campus	PA	15,646	HC
Pepperdine Univ	CA	32,830	VC
Peru State College	NE	6,342	NC
Pfeiffer Univ	NC	18,980	C
Piedmont College	GA	16,900	C
Pikeville College	KY	14,900	NC
Pine Manor College	MA	22,138	LC
Pittsburg State Univ	KS	7,128	NC
Pitzer College	CA	37,590	HC
Plymouth State Univ	NH	12,298	LC
Point Loma Nazarene Univ	CA	21,380	VC
Point Park Univ	PA	21,840	C
Pomona College	CA	33,960	MC
Pontifical Catholic Univ of PR/Ponce	PR	7,298	
Portland State Univ	OR	12,453	C
Prairie View A&M Univ	TX	9,418	NC
Presbyterian College	SC	25,920	VC
Princeton Univ	NJ	36,649	MC
Principia College	IL	25,044	C+
Providence College	RI	30,604	HC
Purdue Univ/Calumet	IN	6,630	NC
Purdue Univ/West Lafayette	IN	12,560	VC
Queens Univ of Charlotte	NC	21,840	C
Quincy Univ	IL	22,330	C
Quinnipiac Univ	CT	30,570	VC
Radford Univ	VA	8,500	C
Ramapo College of New Jersey	NJ	15,203	VC
Randolph-Macon College	VA	27,190	C

ST = STATE   **$IS** = IN-STATE COSTS   **SR** = SELECTOR RATING

INDEX OF COLLEGE MAJORS

School	ST	$IS	SR
Randolph-Macon Woman's College	VA	28,430	VC+
Reed College	OR	36,950	MC
Regis College	MA	29,000	C
Regis Univ	CO	25,740	C
Rhode Island College	RI	11,565	C
Rhodes College	TN	26,466	HC+
Rice Univ	TX	27,550	MC
Richard Stockton College of New Jersey	NJ	12,972	VC
Rider Univ	NJ	30,900	C
Ripon College	WI	24,995	VC
Rivier College	NH	26,217	C
Roanoke College	VA	27,393	C
Roberts Wesleyan College	NY	23,190	C+
Rochester College	MI	16,718	C
Rockford College	IL	28,310	VC
Rocky Mountain College	MT	19,015	C
Roger Williams Univ	RI	30,296	C
Rollins College	FL	34,300	VC
Roosevelt Univ	IL	22,580	VC
Rosemont College	PA	26,175	C
Rowan Univ	NJ	14,506	VC
Russell Sage College	NY	26,811	C
Rutgers, The State Univ of New Jersey/Camden Campus	NJ	14,990	VC
Rutgers, The State Univ of New Jersey/New Brunswick/Piscataway Campus	NJ	15,800	HC
Rutgers, The State Univ of New Jersey/Newark Campus	NJ	15,624	VC
Sacred Heart Univ	CT	29,178	C
Saginaw Valley State Univ	MI	11,055	C
St. Ambrose Univ	IA	22,800	C
St. Andrews Presbyterian College	NC	20,525	C
St. Anselm College	NH	30,250	C
St. Augustine's College	NC	12,990	LC
St. Bonaventure Univ	NY	24,455	LC
St. Cloud State Univ	MN	8,362	C
St. Edward's Univ	TX	20,428	C
St. Francis College	NY	10,880	LC
St. Francis Univ	PA	25,876	LC
St. John Fisher College	NY	24,870	C
St. John's Univ	MN	26,473	VC
St. John's Univ	NY	30,180	C
St. Joseph College	CT	29,685	C
St. Joseph's, Brooklyn,	NY	10,902	C
St. Joseph's College	IN	24,250	C
St. Joseph's College of Maine	ME	25,600	C
St. Joseph's Univ	PA	33,590	VC
St. Lawrence Univ	NY	35,945	VC
St. Leo Univ	FL	20,600	C
St. Louis Univ	MO	29,780	VC+
St. Martin's College	WA	23,245	C
St. Mary-of-the-Woods College	IN	23,280	C
St. Mary's College	IN	24,474	VC
St. Mary's College of Calif	CA	32,850	VC
St. Mary's College of Maryland	MD	15,908	VC+
St. Mary's Univ of Minn	MN	21,535	C
St. Mary's Univ of San Antonio	TX	22,444	C
St. Michael's College	VT	30,100	VC
St. Norbert College	WI	25,810	C
St. Olaf College	MN	28,500	HC
St. Peter's College	NJ	22,292	LC
St. Thomas Aquinas College	NY	20,590	LC
St. Thomas Univ	FL	21,400	C
St. Vincent College	PA	25,530	VC
St. Xavier Univ	IL	23,144	C
Salem College	NC	24,595	VC
Salem State College	MA	8,592	C
Salisbury Univ	MD	12,664	VC
Salve Regina Univ	RI	29,210	C
Sam Houston State Univ	TX	7,142	C
Samford Univ	AL	18,648	VC
San Diego State Univ	CA	10,321	C
San Francisco State Univ	CA	12,070	C
San Jose State Univ	CA	8,187	C
Santa Clara Univ	CA	34,701	NC
Sarah Lawrence College	NY	41,218	HC
Savannah State Univ	GA	7,328	LC
Schreiner Univ	TX	20,440	C
Scripps College	CA	35,700	HC+
Seattle Pacific Univ	WA	25,944	VC
Seattle Univ	WA	24,183	VC
Seton Hall Univ	NJ	30,130	C
Seton Hill Univ	PA	24,930	C
Shawnee State Univ	OH	11,031	NC
Shenandoah Univ	VA	25,190	NC
Shepherd College	WV	8,608	C
Shippensburg Univ of Pennsylvania	PA	10,826	C
Shorter College	GA	17,370	C
Siena College	NY	25,310	VC
Siena Heights Univ	MI	16,140	LC
Silver Lake College of the Holy Family	WI	18,450	LC
Simmons College	MA	33,000	VC
Simpson College	CA	20,500	C
Simpson College	IA	23,658	C+
Skidmore College	NY	37,930	HC
Slippery Rock Univ of Pennsylvania	PA	10,343	LC
Smith College	MA	37,034	HC+
Sonoma State Univ	CA	10,421	C
S Car State Univ	SC	6,586	LC
S Dak State Univ	SD	7,782	C
Southeast Missouri State Univ	MO	9,704	C
Southeastern Louisiana Univ	LA	6,791	LC
Southeastern Okla State Univ	OK	6,147	C
Southern Adventist Univ	TN	17,080	C
Southern Arkansas Univ	AR	6,956	C
Southern Conn State Univ	CT	10,310	C
Southern Illinois Univ Carbondale	IL	10,407	C
Southern Illinois Univ Edwardsville	IL	8,724	C
Southern Methodist Univ	TX	34,210	HC
Southern Nazarene Univ	OK	14,634	NC
Southern Oregon Univ	OR	10,362	C
Southern Univ and A&M College	LA	7,372	LC
Southern Univ at New Orleans	LA	995	NC
Southern Utah Univ	UT	8,194	C
Southern Wesleyan Univ	SC	19,940	C
Southwest Baptist Univ	MO	15,371	C
Southwest Minn State Univ	MN	9,106	VC
Southwest Missouri State Univ	MO	8,918	C
Southwestern Adventist Univ	TX	14,798	C
Southwestern College	KS	19,560	C
Southwestern Okla State Univ	OK	4,801	C
Southwestern Univ	TX	25,410	HC
Spelman College	GA	19,215	C+
Spring Arbor Univ	MI	20,206	C
Spring Hill College	AL	25,868	VC
Springfield College	MA	24,520	C
St. Joseph's, Suffolk	NY	11,297	C
Stanford Univ	CA	37,612	MC
SUNY at Oswego	NY	12,650	C
SUNY at Potsdam	NY	12,160	C
SUNY/College at Brockport	NY	12,111	C
SUNY/College at Buffalo	NY	8,025	C
SUNY/College at Cortland	NY	12,095	C
SUNY/College at Fredonia	NY	11,562	NC
SUNY/College at Geneseo	NY	11,330	HC
SUNY/College at Oneonta	NY	11,870	VC
SUNY/College at Plattsburgh	NY	11,700	C
SUNY/College at Purchase	NY	10,587	VC
SUNY/Empire State College	NY	4,505	SP
SUNY/Univ at Albany	NY	12,951	HC
SUNY/Univ at Binghamton	NY	12,787	HC
SUNY/Univ at Buffalo	NY	12,563	VC
SUNY/Univ at New Paltz	NY	11,565	VC
SUNY/Univ at Stony Brook	NY	12,763	HC
State Univ of West Georgia	GA	7,622	C
Stephen F. Austin State Univ	TX	7,552	C
Sterling College	KS	18,763	C
Stetson Univ	FL	29,495	VC
Stevens Inst of Technology	NJ	35,300	HC+
Stillman College	AL	11,370	LC
Stonehill College	MA	30,752	HC
Suffolk Univ	MA	29,200	C
Sul Ross State Univ	TX	6,582	LC
Susquehanna Univ	PA	29,990	C
Swarthmore College	PA	37,716	MC
Sweet Briar College	VA	27,940	C
Syracuse Univ	NY	34,720	HC
Tabor College	KS	19,500	NC
Talladega College	AL	10,110	LC
Tarleton State Univ	TX	7,576	C
Taylor Univ	IN	23,820	VC+
Teikyo Post Univ	CT	24,875	C
Temple Univ	PA	15,912	C
Tenn State Univ	TN	9,048	LC
Tenn Tech Univ	TN	8,670	C
Tenn Wesleyan College	TN	16,540	C
Texas A&M Univ	TX	11,081	HC
Texas A&M Univ at Commerce	TX	8,994	C
Texas A&M Univ at Corpus Christi	TX	10,269	C
Texas A&M Univ at Kingsville	TX	6,740	LC
Texas Christian Univ	TX	23,410	VC
Texas Lutheran Univ	TX	20,370	C
Texas Southern Univ	TX	8,920	NC
Texas State Univ	TX	9,320	VC
Texas Tech Univ	TX	10,768	VC
Texas Wesleyan Univ	TX	16,245	C
Texas Woman's Univ	TX	7,804	LC
Thiel College	PA	20,970	C
Thomas Edison State College	NJ	3,325	SP
Thomas More College	KY	21,350	C
Tougaloo College	MS	9,200	NC
Touro College	NY	15,250	VC
Towson Univ	MD	12,694	VC
Transylvania Univ	KY	23,780	VC+
Trevecca Nazarene Univ	TN	17,548	C
Trinity Christian College	IL	21,640	VC
Trinity College	CT	38,040	HC+
Trinity College	DC	24,150	LC
Trinity International Univ	IL	22,980	C+
Trinity Univ	TX	26,466	HC+
Troy State Univ	AL	7,696	C
Troy State Univ Montgomery	AL	3,600	NC
Truman State Univ	MO	9,728	HC+
Tufts Univ	MA	38,233	MC
Tulane Univ	LA	37,451	HC+
Turabo Univ	PR	4,110	
Tusculum College	TN	19,990	C
Tuskegee Univ	AL	17,250	LC
Union College	KY	15,920	C
Union College	NE	17,130	C
Union College	NY	36,005	HC
Union Univ	TN	18,800	VC
United States Air Force Academy	CO		HC+
United States Military Academy	NY		MC
United States Naval Academy	MD		MC
Universidad Adventista de las Antillas	PR	5,460	
Univ of Akron	OH	13,134	NC
Univ of Alabama	AL	9,040	C+
Univ of Alabama at Birmingham	AL	12,901	C
Univ of Alabama in Huntsville	AL	9,126	VC
Univ of Alaska Anchorage	AK	9,100	NC
Univ of Alaska Fairbanks	AK	9,295	C
Univ of Arizona	AZ	10,413	VC
Univ of Arkansas	AR	9,855	VC
Univ of Arkansas at Little Rock	AR	5,637	NC
Univ of Arkansas at Monticello	AR	5,940	NC
Univ of Arkansas at Pine Bluff	AR	7,925	C
Univ of Calif at Berkeley	CA	15,563	MC
Univ of Calif at Davis	CA	14,995	VC
Univ of Calif at Irvine	CA	19,808	HC
Univ of Calif at Los Angeles	CA	15,330	MC
Univ of Calif at Riverside	CA	15,300	C
Univ of Calif at San Diego	CA	14,127	HC
Univ of Calif at Santa Barbara	CA	11,732	VC
Univ of Calif at Santa Cruz	CA	16,505	VC
Univ of Central Arkansas	AR	6,388	C
Univ of Central Florida	FL	10,038	VC
Univ of Central Okla	OK	9,434	C
Univ of Charleston	WV	23,620	C
Univ of Chicago	IL	35,087	MC
Univ of Cincinnati	OH	14,736	C
Univ of Colo at Boulder	CO	10,774	VC
Univ of Colo at Colo Springs	CO	10,667	C
Univ of Colo at Denver	CO	3,302	C
Univ of Conn	CT	14,608	VC
Univ of Dallas	TX	25,898	VC+
Univ of Dayton	OH	24,850	VC
Univ of Delaware	DE	12,616	HC
Univ of Denver	CO	32,148	VC
Univ of Detroit Mercy	MI	25,582	C
Univ of Evansville	IN	24,190	VC
Univ of Findlay	OH	23,962	NC
Univ of Florida	FL	8,580	MC
Univ of Georgia	GA	8,656	VC
Univ of Great Falls	MT	15,360	C
Univ of Hartford	CT	31,080	C
Univ of Hawaii at Hilo	HI	6,497	C
Univ of Hawaii at Manoa	HI	9,565	VC
Univ of Houston	TX	9,818	C
Univ of Idaho	ID	8,216	C
Univ of Illinois at Chicago	IL	13,418	C
Univ of Illinois at Urbana-Champaign	IL	11,316	HC+
Univ of Indianapolis	IN	22,560	C
Univ of Iowa	IA	10,923	VC
Univ of Kansas	KS	8,923	VC
Univ of Kentucky	KY	7,765	C
Univ of La Verne	CA	28,600	C
Univ of Louisiana at Lafayette	LA	5,826	C
Univ of Louisiana at Monroe	LA	5,207	NC
Univ of Louisville	KY	8,762	VC
Univ of Maine	ME	12,080	C+
Univ of Maine at Farmington	ME	10,108	C
Univ of Maine at Machias	ME	9,211	C
Univ of Mary Hardin-Baylor	TX	17,268	C
Univ of Maryland/Baltimore County	MD	14,668	VC+
Univ of Maryland/College Park	MD	14,227	HC
Univ of Maryland/Eastern Shore	MD	9,964	C
Univ of Maryland/Univ College	MD	5,910	SP
Univ of Mass Amherst	MA	13,980	C+
Univ of Mass Boston	MA	6,227	C
Univ of Mass Dartmouth	MA	12,835	C
Univ of Mass Lowell	MA	11,937	C
Univ of Memphis	TN	8,560	C
Univ of Miami	FL	34,608	HC
Univ of Mich/Ann Arbor	MI	13,864	HC+
Univ of Mich/Dearborn	MI	6,843	VC
Univ of Mich/Flint	MI	5,548	C
Univ of Minn/Duluth	MN	12,470	C
Univ of Minn/Morris	MN	12,896	VC
Univ of Minn/Twin Cities	MN	13,160	VC
Univ of Miss	MS	7,666	C
Univ of Missouri/Columbia	MO	13,782	VC
Univ of Missouri/Kansas City	MO	13,416	VC
Univ of Missouri/Rolla	MO	12,292	HC
Univ of Missouri/St. Louis	MO	11,656	VC
Univ of Mobile	AL	13,620	C
Univ of Montana	MT	9,395	C
Univ of Montevallo	AL	8,478	C
Univ of Nebr at Kearney	NE	8,286	NC
Univ of Nebr at Lincoln	NE	9,975	C+
Univ of Nebr at Omaha	NE	8,080	C
Univ of Nevada/Las Vegas	NV	11,566	C
Univ of Nevada/Reno	NV	9,792	C
Univ of New Hampshire	NH	14,828	VC
Univ of New Haven	CT	28,650	C
Univ of New Mexico	NM	9,223	C
Univ of New Orleans	LA	7,356	C
Univ of North Alabama	AL	7,972	NC
Univ of N Car at Asheville	NC	8,079	VC
Univ of N Car at Chapel Hill	NC	10,117	MC
Univ of N Car at Charlotte	NC	8,185	C
Univ of N Car at Greensboro	NC	8,248	C
Univ of N Car at Pembroke	NC	6,929	LC
Univ of N Car at Wilmington	NC	8,940	VC
Univ of N Dak	ND	8,390	C
Univ of North Florida	FL	8,769	VC
Univ of North Texas	TX	7,629	C
Univ of Northern Colo	CO	8,987	C
Univ of Northern Iowa	IA	9,834	C
Univ of Notre Dame	IN	34,442	MC
Univ of Okla	OK	9,226	VC
Univ of Oregon	OR	11,479	VC
Univ of Pennsylvania	PA	37,960	MC
Univ of Pittsburgh at Bradford	PA	15,294	C
Univ of Pittsburgh at Johnstown	PA	15,216	LC
Univ of Pittsburgh at Pittsburgh	PA	16,074	HC
Univ of Portland	OR	28,500	VC
Univ of PR/Cayey Univ College	PR	1,245	
Univ of PR/Mayaguez	PR		
Univ of PR/Rio Piedras	PR	5,730	
Univ of Puget Sound	WA	31,760	HC
Univ of Redlands	CA	32,576	VC
Univ of Rhode Island	RI	13,720	VC
Univ of Richmond	VA	30,100	MC
Univ of Rio Grande	OH	8,728	NC
Univ of Rochester	NY	32,979	HC
Univ of St. Francis	IL	22,850	C
Univ of St. Francis	IN	20,964	C
Univ of St. Mary	KS	18,868	C
Univ of St. Thomas	MN	26,918	VC
Univ of St. Thomas	TX	21,952	VC
Univ of San Diego	CA	33,156	HC
Univ of San Francisco	CA	34,700	VC
Univ of Science and Arts of Okla	OK	5,982	C
Univ of Scranton	PA	30,836	VC
Univ of Sioux Falls	SD	16,390	C
Univ of South Alabama	AL	7,760	LC
Univ of S Car at Aiken	SC	7,828	LC
Univ of S Car at Columbia	SC	10,048	VC
Univ of S Car at Spartanburg	SC	9,936	C+
Univ of S Dak	SD	7,710	C+
Univ of South Florida	FL	9,454	C
Univ of Southern Calif	CA	37,459	MC
Univ of Southern Colo	CO	7,821	LC
Univ of Southern Indiana	IN	9,025	C
Univ of Southern Maine	ME	11,212	C
Univ of Southern Miss	MS	8,324	C
Univ of Tampa	FL	23,982	VC
Univ of Tenn at Chattanooga	TN	7,783	C
Univ of Tenn at Knoxville	TN	8,214	C
Univ of Tenn at Martin	TN	7,748	C
Univ of Texas at Arlington	TX	7,192	LC
Univ of Texas at Austin	TX	10,630	HC
Univ of Texas at Dallas	TX	10,234	HC
Univ of Texas at El Paso	TX	5,799	NC
Univ of Texas at San Antonio	TX	9,088	NC
Univ of Texas-Pan American	TX	5,954	LC
Univ of the District of Columbia	DC	2,070	LC
Univ of the Incarnate Word	TX	21,772	C
Univ of the Ozarks	AR	16,574	C

ST = STATE   **$IS** = IN-STATE COSTS   **SR** = SELECTOR RATING

HISTORY OF PHILOSOPHY

HISTORY OF SCIENCE

HOME ECONOMICS

HOME ECONOMICS EDUCATION

HOME FURNISHINGS AND EQUIPMENT MANAGEMENT/ PRODUCTION/SERVICES

HORTICULTURE

HOSPICE CARE

HOSPITAL ADMINISTRATION

HOSPITALITY MANAGEMENT SERVICES

ST = STATE　　$IS = IN-STATE COSTS　　SR = SELECTOR RATING

School	ST	$IS	SR
Eastern Mich Univ	MI	11,478	C
Ferris State Univ	MI	12,512	C
Florida International Univ	FL	9,912	VC
Georgia State Univ'	GA	10,658	C
Howard Univ	DC	16,505	C
Husson College	ME	16,300	LC
Indiana Univ-Purdue Univ Fort Wayne	IN	5,108	LC
James Madison Univ	VA	10,794	VC
Johnson and Wales Univ	RI	22,965	LC
Johnson State College	VT	11,819	LC
Kendall College	IL	21,350	NC
Lakeland College	WI	17,950	C
Lasell College	MA	26,000	C
Madonna Univ	MI	11,504	VC
Marywood Univ	PA	26,050	C
Metropolitan State College of Denver	CO	2,338	LC
Metropolitan State Univ	MN	3,852	SP
Mich State Univ	MI	11,933	VC
Montclair State Univ	NJ	13,790	C
Morgan State Univ	MD	11,470	C
Mount Ida College	MA	25,596	LC
New York Inst of Technology	NY	24,205	VC
Norfolk State Univ	VA	9,722	LC
Northwestern State Univ of Louisiana	LA	6,331	NC
Ohio State Univ	OH	13,080	VC+
Ohio State Univ at Lima	OH	4,416	NC
Philander Smith College	AR	7,380	NC
Robert Morris Univ	PA	20,438	C
Rutgers, The State Univ of New Jersey/Camden Campus	NJ	14,990	VC
St. John's Univ	NY	30,180	C
St. Leo Univ	FL	20,600	C
St. Thomas Univ	FL	21,400	LC
Shepherd College	WV	8,608	C
Southern New Hampshire Univ	NH	26,242	C
SUNY/College at Buffalo	NY	8,025	C
Stephen F. Austin State Univ	TX	7,552	C
Syracuse Univ	NY	34,720	HC
Tuskegee Univ	AL	17,250	LC
Univ of Akron	OH	13,134	NC
Univ of Central Florida	FL	10,038	VC
Univ of Denver	CO	32,148	VC
Univ of Findlay	OH	23,962	NC
Univ of Memphis	TN	8,560	C
Univ of N Car at Greensboro	NC	8,248	C
Univ of San Francisco	CA	34,700	VC
Univ of Wisc/Stout	WI	9,718	C
Western Carolina Univ	NC	6,742	C
Widener Univ	PA	27,020	C
Youngstown State Univ	OH	11,148	NC

HOTEL/MOTEL AND RESTAURANT MANAGEMENT

School	ST	$IS	SR
Alliant International Univ	CA	23,640	C
Arkansas Tech Univ	AR	7,299	C
Ashland Univ	OH	24,464	C
Auburn Univ	AL	10,396	VC
Belmont Univ	TN	21,986	VC
Bethune-Cookman College	FL	16,480	LC
Black Hills State Univ	SD	7,743	LC
Boston Univ	MA	38,194	HC+
Bowling Green State Univ	OH	13,036	C
Brigham Young Univ	UT	8,504	HC
Calif State Polytechnic Univ, Pomona	CA	8,793	C+
Central Missouri State Univ	MO	9,776	C
Champlain College	VT	22,030	C
Cheyney Univ of Pennsylvania	PA	9,993	C
CUNY/New York City College of Technology	NY	4,269	NC
College of the Ozarks	MO	3,500	VC+
Colo State Univ	CO	9,964	VC
Concord College	WV	8,136	C
Cornell Univ	NY	38,253	MC
Delaware State Univ	DE	8,104	LC
Drexel Univ	PA	27,655	VC
East Stroudsburg Univ of Pennsylvania	PA	10,336	C
Endicott College	MA	25,266	C+
Fairleigh Dickinson Univ/College at Florham	NJ	30,130	C
Fairleigh Dickinson Univ/Metropolitan Campus	NJ	28,584	C
Florida Southern College	FL	23,592	C
Florida State Univ	FL	9,028	HC
Georgia Southern Univ	GA	8,540	C
Grambling State Univ	LA	6,538	NC
Grand Valley State Univ	MI	11,022	VC
Indiana State Univ	IN	10,719	LC
Indiana Univ of Pennsylvania	PA	10,489	C
Iowa State Univ	IA	10,768	VC
Johnson and Wales Univ	RI	22,965	LC
Kansas State Univ	KS	8,728	VC
Kendall College	IL	21,350	NC
Keuka College	NY	21,170	C
Lasell College	MA	26,000	C
Lynn Univ	FL	30,750	C
Mercyhurst College	PA	20,694	C
Minn State Univ, Moorehead	MN	7,000	LC
Mountain State Univ	WV	10,212	NC
New Mexico State Univ	NM	7,932	C
New York Univ	NY	39,406	MC
Newbury College	MA	23,450	C
Niagara Univ	NY	25,050	C
N Car Wesleyan College	NC	17,998	C
N Dak State Univ	ND	8,435	C
Northern Arizona Univ	AZ	9,002	C
Northwood Univ	FL	21,040	C
Northwood Univ	MI	20,265	LC
Northwood Univ	TX	20,135	LC
Okla State Univ	OK	9,216	VC
Oregon State Univ	OR	11,055	C
Penn State Univ/Univ Park Campus	PA	15,646	HC
Purdue Univ/Calumet	IN	6,630	NC
Purdue Univ/West Lafayette	IN	12,560	VC
Rochester Inst of Technology	NY	29,217	VC+
Roosevelt Univ	IL	22,580	VC
St. Thomas Univ	FL	21,400	LC
Siena Heights Univ	MI	16,140	LC
S Dak State Univ	SD	7,782	C
Southern New Hampshire Univ	NH	26,242	C
Southwest Missouri State Univ	MO	8,918	C
SUNY/College at Plattsburgh	NY	11,700	C
Tenn State Univ	TN	9,048	LC
Texas Tech Univ	TX	10,768	VC
Thomas Edison State College	NJ	3,325	SP
Tiffin Univ	OH	19,490	LC
Univ of Alaska Anchorage	AK	9,100	NC
Univ of Central Okla	OK	9,434	C
Univ of Delaware	DE	12,616	HC
Univ of Houston	TX	9,818	C
Univ of Kentucky	KY	7,765	C
Univ of Louisiana at Lafayette	LA	5,826	C
Univ of Maryland/Eastern Shore	MD	9,964	C
Univ of Mass Amherst	MA	13,980	C+
Univ of Minn/Crookston	MN	9,626	NC
Univ of Missouri/Columbia	MO	13,782	VC
Univ of Nevada/Las Vegas	NV	11,566	C
Univ of New Hampshire	NH	14,828	VC
Univ of New Haven	CT	28,650	C
Univ of New Orleans	LA	7,356	C
Univ of North Texas	TX	7,629	C
Univ of San Francisco	CA	34,700	VC
Univ of S Car at Columbia	SC	10,048	VC
Univ of Southern Miss	MS	8,324	LC
Univ of Tenn at Knoxville	TN	8,214	C
Univ of the Incarnate Word	TX	21,772	LC
Virginia Polytechnic Inst and State Univ	VA	9,179	C
Virginia State Univ	VA	10,358	C
Washington State Univ	WA	11,334	C
Webber International Univ	FL	16,510	C
Western Kentucky Univ	KY	6,834	C
Wiley College	TX	8,100	LC
Youngstown State Univ	OH	11,148	NC

HUMAN DEVELOPMENT

School	ST	$IS	SR
Alabama A&M Univ	AL	5,100	LC
Andrews Univ	MI	19,550	C
Anna Maria College	MA	26,140	LC
Auburn Univ	AL	10,396	VC
Bard College	NY	37,352	HC+
Becker College	MA	23,710	LC
Boston College	MA	33,284	MC
Brescia Univ	KY	14,225	C
Brigham Young Univ	UT	8,504	HC
Calif Polytechnic State Univ	CA	8,747	VC
Cal State, Hayward	CA	8,871	LC
Cal State, Long Beach	CA	8,762	C+
Cal State, San Bernardino	CA	15,238	LC
Cal State, San Marcos	CA	1,736	LC
Christian Brothers Univ	TN	22,290	VC
Christian Heritage College	CA	19,990	C
Colo State Univ	CO	9,964	VC
Conn College	CT	37,900	MC
Cornell Univ	NY	38,253	MC
Earlham College	IN	29,976	VC+
East Tenn State Univ	TN	8,497	C
Eckerd College	FL	28,744	C+
Hellenic College/Holy Cross Greek Orthodox School of Theology	MA	22,815	C
Indiana Univ Bloomington	IN	12,389	VC
Kalamazoo College	MI	26,955	HC+
Kansas State Univ	KS	8,728	VC
Kent State Univ	OH	12,932	C
Lee Univ	TN	13,780	NC
Lynchburg College	VA	26,815	C
Marylhurst Univ	OR	18,465	NC
Messiah College	PA	25,890	VC+
Miss Univ for Women	MS	5,446	LC
Mitchell College	CT	26,396	C
Montana State Univ-Bozeman	MT	9,515	C
National-Louis Univ	IL	16,240	LC
Northwestern Univ	IL	37,491	MC
Oakwood College	AL	14,904	C
Ohio State Univ	OH	13,080	VC+
Oregon State Univ	OR	11,055	C
Penn State Univ/Altoona	PA	12,578	C
Penn State Univ/Univ Park Campus	PA	15,646	HC
Radford Univ	VA	8,500	C
Rivier College	NH	26,217	C
St. Mary's College of Maryland	MD	15,908	VC+
Sonoma State Univ	CA	10,421	C
S Dak State Univ	SD	7,782	C
Southern Christian Univ	AL	9,440	LC
SUNY at Oswego	NY	12,650	C
SUNY/Empire State College	NY	4,505	SP
SUNY/Univ at Binghamton	NY	12,787	HC
Suffolk Univ	MA	29,200	C
Tarleton State Univ	TX	7,576	C
Tenn Wesleyan College	TN	16,540	C
Texas Tech Univ	TX	10,768	VC
Texas Wesleyan Univ	TX	16,245	C
Univ of Alabama	AL	9,040	C+
Univ of Arkansas	AR	9,855	VC
Univ of Calif at Davis	CA	14,995	VC
Univ of Calif at Riverside	CA	15,300	C
Univ of Calif at San Diego	CA	14,127	HC
Univ of Conn	CT	14,608	VC
Univ of Delaware	DE	12,616	HC
Univ of Houston	TX	9,818	C
Univ of Illinois at Urbana-Champaign	IL	11,316	HC+
Univ of Memphis	TN	8,560	C
Univ of Missouri/Columbia	MO	13,782	VC
Univ of Nebr at Kearney	NE	8,286	NC
Univ of Nebr at Lincoln	NE	9,975	C+
Univ of N Car at Greensboro	NC	8,248	C
Univ of Rhode Island	RI	13,720	VC
Univ of Vermont	VT	16,316	VC
Univ of Wisc/Green Bay	WI	8,154	C
Utah State Univ	UT	7,371	C
Vanderbilt Univ	TN	37,897	MC
Warner Pacific College	OR	21,900	C
Washington State Univ	WA	11,334	C
Westminster College	UT	17,226	C
Wheelock College	MA	29,000	C

HUMAN ECOLOGY

School	ST	$IS	SR
Cameron Univ	OK	5,692	NC
College of the Atlantic	ME	30,504	VC+
Goddard College	VT	21,056	C+
Montclair State Univ	NJ	13,790	C
Ohio State Univ	OH	13,080	VC+
Tenn Tech Univ	TN	8,670	VC
Unity College	ME	19,845	LC
Univ of Calif at Davis	CA	14,995	VC
Univ of Calif at Irvine	CA	19,808	HC
Univ of Calif at Los Angeles	CA	15,330	MC
Univ of Nevada/Reno	NV	9,792	C
Univ of Texas at Austin	TX	10,630	HC
Virginia Wesleyan College	VA	25,350	C
Youngstown State Univ	OH	11,148	NC

HUMAN RESOURCES

School	ST	$IS	SR
American International College	MA	24,690	LC
Barton College	NC	19,314	C
Baylor Univ	TX	23,864	VC
Becker College	MA	23,710	LC
Black Hills State Univ	SD	7,743	LC
Boston College	MA	33,284	MC
Brescia Univ	KY	14,225	C
Briar Cliff Univ	IA	21,660	C
Cabrini College	PA	29,020	C
Calif State Polytechnic Univ, Pomona	CA	8,793	C+
Cal State, San Bernardino	CA	15,238	LC
Carlow College	PA	21,334	C
Catholic Univ of America	DC	34,248	VC
Central Missouri State Univ	MO	9,776	C
Chestnut Hill College	PA	26,450	LC
Cleary College	MI	10,350	LC
Colo Christian Univ	CO	21,182	VC
Crichton College	TN	15,215	C
Davenport Univ	MI	11,636	NC
De Sales Univ	PA	25,470	C
Defiance College	OH	22,615	C
Dominican College	NY	24,810	LC
Dominican Univ of Calif	CA	31,670	C
Excelsior College	NY	975	SP
Ferris State Univ	MI	12,512	C
Franklin Univ	OH	6,720	SP
George Fox Univ	OR	26,110	VC
George Washington Univ	DC	41,030	MC
Georgia Southern Univ	GA	8,540	C
Georgia State Univ	GA	10,658	C
Golden Gate Univ	CA	11,232	NC
Grand Canyon Univ	AZ	30,000	LC
Gwynedd-Mercy College	PA	24,225	C
Harding Univ	AR	14,890	VC
Hawaii Pacific Univ	HI	19,218	C
Holy Names College	CA	27,980	NC
Huron Univ	SD	10,450	C
Idaho State Univ	ID	8,128	C
Indiana Univ of Pennsylvania	PA	10,489	C
Indiana Univ South Bend	IN	4,571	LC
Indiana Univ-Purdue Univ Indianapolis	IN	8,257	LC
Inter American Univ of PR/Bayamon Univ College	PR	3,522	
Ithaca College	NY	31,730	HC
Johns Hopkins Univ	MD	38,372	MC
Juniata College	PA	29,080	VC
Kentucky Wesleyan College	KY	17,250	C
Keystone College	PA	21,405	LC
Le Moyne College	NY	26,400	VC
Lewis Univ	IL	22,950	C+
Limestone College	SC	17,700	C
Lindenwood Univ	MO	17,050	VC
Lourdes College	OH	15,300	LC
Marietta College	OH	27,047	C
Marquette Univ	WI	27,594	VC
Marymount Univ	VA	23,668	C
Medaille College	NY	20,060	C
Metropolitan State Univ	MN	3,852	SP
Miami Univ	OH	15,033	HC
Mich State Univ	MI	11,933	VC
Mount Olive College	NC	14,410	LC
Niagara Univ	NY	25,050	C
Northeastern Univ	MA	35,650	HC
Notre Dame College	OH	20,425	C
Oakland Univ	MI	10,800	C
Ohio State Univ	OH	13,080	VC+
Ohio Valley College	WV	16,036	C+
Okla Wesleyan Univ	OK	14,100	LC
Our Lady of the Lake Univ of San Antonio	TX	17,336	C
Park Univ	MO	10,780	C+
Point Park Univ	PA	21,840	C
Rider Univ	NJ	30,900	C
Robert Morris Univ	PA	20,438	C
Rockhurst Univ	MO	22,960	C+
St. Leo Univ	FL	20,600	C
St. Louis Univ	MO	29,780	VC+
St. Mary-of-the-Woods College	IN	23,280	C
St. Mary's Univ of San Antonio	TX	22,444	C
St. Thomas Univ	FL	21,400	LC
Samford Univ	AL	18,648	VC
Seton Hill Univ	PA	24,930	C
Silver Lake College of the Holy Family	WI	18,450	LC
Simpson College	CA	20,500	C
Southern Christian Univ	AL	9,440	LC
Southwestern College	KS	19,560	C
SUNY at Oswego	NY	12,650	C
Tarleton State Univ	TX	7,576	C
Temple Univ	PA	15,912	C
Thomas Edison State College	NJ	3,325	SP
Trinity International Univ	IL	22,980	C+
Univ of Arizona	AZ	10,413	VC
Univ of Central Okla	OK	9,434	C
Univ of Findlay	OH	23,962	NC
Univ of Florida	FL	8,580	MC
Univ of Hawaii at Manoa	HI	9,565	VC
Univ of Maryland/College Park	MD	14,227	HC
Univ of Maryland/Univ College	MD	5,910	SP
Univ of Miami	FL	34,608	HC
Univ of Mich/Flint	MI	5,548	C
Univ of Nevada/Las Vegas	NV	11,566	C
Univ of North Texas	TX	7,629	C
Univ of PR at Humacao	PR	1,245	
Univ of Scranton	PA	30,836	VC
Univ of Texas at San Antonio	TX	9,088	NC
Univ of Wisc/Oshkosh	WI	6,130	LC
Ursuline College	OH	22,728	LC
Valley City State Univ	ND	7,281	LC
Washington Univ in St. Louis	MO	38,293	MC
Western Mich Univ	MI	12,031	C
Wichita State Univ	KS	8,092	C
Winona State Univ	MN		C
Xavier Univ	OH	26,850	VC+
York College	NE	14,975	C

HUMAN SERVICES

School	ST	$IS	SR
Adrian College	MI	21,950	C
Alaska Pacific Univ	AK	17,910	C
Albertus Magnus College	CT	23,130	LC
Arkansas Baptist College	AR	5,530	NC
Beacon College	FL	25,900	LC
Bethel College	IN	19,670	C
Bethel College	TN	12,980	C
Black Hills State Univ	SD	7,743	LC
Boricua College	NY	7,375	C
Burlington College	VT	10,640	SP
Cal State, Dominguez Hills	CA	5,840	LC

ST = STATE $IS = IN-STATE COSTS SR = SELECTOR RATING

School	ST	$IS	SR
Cal State, Fullerton	CA	6,648	C
Cal State, San Bernardino	CA	15,238	LC
Cal State, Stanislaus	CA	9,874	C
Calumet College of St. Joseph	IN	9,000	LC
Cambridge College	MA	10,800	SP
Cazenovia College	NY	23,940	C
Chestnut Hill College	PA	26,450	LC
CUNY/New York City College of Technology	NY	4,269	NC
Coe College	IA	27,385	VC
College of Mount St. Joseph	OH	22,785	C
College of St. Joseph	VT	19,100	C
College of St. Mary	NE	21,510	C
Dakota Wesleyan Univ	SD	17,832	C
East Central Univ	OK	4,968	C
Eastern New Mexico Univ	NM	6,762	LC
Elmira College	NY	33,820	VC
Elon Univ	NC	22,240	VC
Fitchburg State College	MA	9,622	C
Florida Gulf Coast Univ	FL	9,908	C
Fontbonne Univ	MO	21,508	C
Friends Univ	KS	15,962	LC
Geneva College	PA	21,850	C
George Washington Univ	DC	41,030	MC
Georgetown College	KY	22,000	VC
Grace Bible College	MI	15,890	C
Graceland Univ	IA	19,550	C
Grand View College	IA	19,748	LC
Hannibal-LaGrange College	MO	13,940	C
Hastings College	NE	19,928	VC
Hawaii Pacific Univ	HI	19,218	C
Henderson State Univ	AR	7,386	C
High Point Univ	NC	22,480	C
Hilbert College	NY	19,170	LC
Holy Names College	CA	27,980	NC
Hope International Univ	CA	16,940	NC
Indiana Inst of Technology	IN	21,620	C
Indiana Univ South Bend	IN	4,571	LC
Indiana Univ-Purdue Univ Fort Wayne	IN	5,108	LC
Kendall College	IL	21,350	NC
Kennesaw State Univ	GA	2,724	C
La Roche College	PA	22,094	C
LaGrange College	GA	20,500	C
Lake Superior State Univ	MI	9,034	LC
Lasell College	MA	26,000	C
Lenoir-Rhyne College	NC	19,186	C
Lesley Univ	MA	30,695	C
Limestone College	SC	17,700	C
Lincoln Univ	PA	13,320	C+
Lindenwood Univ	MO	17,050	VC
Lindsey Wilson College	KY	16,392	LC
Lyndon State College	VT	12,646	LC
Lynn Univ	FL	30,750	C
Marian College of Fond du Lac	WI	19,625	C
Marymount Univ	VA	23,668	C
Medaille College	NY	20,060	C
Metropolitan College of New York	NY	15,771	C
Metropolitan State College of Denver	CO	2,338	LC
Metropolitan State Univ	MN	3,852	SP
Millikin Univ	IL	25,555	C
Missouri Baptist Univ	MO	18,010	C
Missouri Valley College	MO	18,500	C
Montreat College	NC	18,762	C
Mount Olive College	NC	14,410	LC
Mount St. Mary College	NY	21,270	C
National-Louis Univ	IL	16,240	LC
N Car Central Univ	NC	7,534	LC
Northeastern Univ	MA	35,650	HC
Northern State Univ	SD	7,117	LC
Northwest Christian College	OR	21,860	C
Notre Dame de Namur Univ	CA	26,932	LC
Oglala Lakota College	SD	1,950	NC
Old Dominion Univ	VA	10,441	C
Ottawa Univ	KS	11,800	LC
Park Univ	MO	10,780	C+
Pennsylvania College of Technology	PA	15,126	NC
Pfeiffer Univ	NC	18,980	C
Pikeville College	KY	14,900	NC
Quincy Univ	IL	22,330	C
Rockford College	IL	28,310	VC
St. John's Univ	NY	30,180	C
St. Leo Univ	FL	20,600	C
St. Mary-of-the-Woods College	IN	23,280	C
St. Mary's College	MI	13,314	LC
St. Mary's Univ of Minn	MN	21,535	C
St. Thomas Univ	FL	21,400	LC
Salem International Univ	WV	19,770	C
Seton Hill Univ	PA	24,930	C
Siena Heights Univ	MI	16,140	LC
Simmons College	MA	33,000	VC
Sinte Gleska Univ	SD	2,268	NC
S Car State Univ	SC	6,586	LC
Southern Vermont College	VT	18,226	LC
Southwest Baptist Univ	MO	15,371	C
Springfield College	MA	24,520	C
SUNY/College at Cortland	NY	12,095	C
Suffolk Univ	MA	29,200	C
Tenn Wesleyan College	TN	16,540	C
Texas Southern Univ	TX	8,920	NC
Touro College	NY	15,250	VC
Trinity College	DC	24,150	LC
Troy State Univ	AL	7,696	C
Univ of Alaska Anchorage	AK	9,100	NC
Univ of Bridgeport	CT	25,924	LC
Univ of Detroit Mercy	MI	25,582	C
Univ of Great Falls	MT	15,360	C
Univ of Hartford	CT	31,080	C
Univ of Maine at Machias	ME	9,271	LC
Univ of Mass Boston	MA	6,227	C
Univ of Rhode Island	RI	13,720	VC
Univ of Scranton	PA	30,836	VC
Univ of Tenn at Chattanooga	TN	7,783	C
Univ of Tenn at Knoxville	TN	8,214	C
Univ of Wisc/Oshkosh	WI	6,130	LC
Upper Iowa Univ	IA	20,076	C
Villanova Univ	PA	35,050	HC
Washburn Univ of Topeka	KS	8,984	NC
Wayland Baptist Univ	TX	11,919	NC
Waynesburg College	PA	19,370	C
Western New Mexico Univ	NM	5,950	LC
Western Washington Univ	WA	10,119	VC
William Penn Univ	IA	17,575	LC
Wingate Univ	NC	21,200	C
Woodbury College	VT	12,060	LC
York College	NE	14,975	C

HUMANITIES

School	ST	$IS	SR
Albertus Magnus College	CT	23,130	LC
Arizona State Univ-Main	AZ	10,048	C
Aurora Univ	IL	20,631	C
Belhaven College	MS	16,040	C+
Bennington College	VT	35,910	HC
Biola Univ	CA	25,964	VC
Bloomsburg Univ of Pennsylvania	PA	10,844	C
Bluefield State College	WV	2,806	LC
Brigham Young Univ	UT	8,504	HC
Bucknell Univ	PA	35,262	HC+
Burlington College	VT	10,640	SP
Cal State, Chico	CA	8,598	LC
Cal State, Northridge	CA	7,757	LC
Cal State, San Bernardino	CA	15,238	LC
Calif Univ of Pennsylvania	PA	10,388	C
Canisius College	NY	28,163	C+
Chaminade Univ of Honolulu	HI	21,430	LC
Charleston Southern Univ	SC	17,122	C
Clarion Univ of Pennsylvania	PA	11,272	LC
Clarkson Univ	NY	32,226	VC
Clearwater Christian College	FL	13,160	LC
Colgate Univ	NY	37,095	MC
College of Mount St. Joseph	OH	22,785	C
College of St. Benedict	MN	26,672	VC
College of St. Mary	NE	21,510	C
College of St. Scholastica	MN	24,970	C+
College of Santa Fe	NM	25,293	C+
Concordia College: Moorhead	MN	22,460	VC+
Concordia Univ	CA	24,420	C
Concordia Univ	OR	22,450	C
Concordia Univ Wisc	WI	16,600	C
Daemen College	NY	22,120	C
Defiance College	OH	22,615	C
Dominican College	NY	24,810	LC
Dominican Univ of Calif	CA	31,670	C
Dowling College	NY	23,870	LC
Eastern Washington Univ	WA	9,012	C
Eckerd College	FL	28,744	C+
Edinboro Univ of Pennsylvania	PA	10,850	LC
Fairleigh Dickinson Univ/College at Florham	NJ	30,130	C
Fairleigh Dickinson Univ/Metropolitan Campus	NJ	28,584	C
Felician College	NJ	24,300	C
Florida Inst of Technology	FL	28,740	VC
Florida International Univ	FL	9,912	VC
Florida Southern College	FL	23,592	C
Florida State Univ	FL	9,028	HC
Fort Lewis College	CO	8,353	C
George Washington Univ	DC	41,030	MC
Georgian Court College	NJ	19,040	LC
Hampden-Sydney College	VA	28,407	VC
Hampshire College	MA	37,037	HC
Harvard Univ/Harvard College	MA	37,928	MC
Hawaii Pacific Univ	HI	19,218	C
Hofstra Univ	NY	27,112	VC
Holy Family College	PA	13,710	LC
Holy Names College	CA	27,980	NC
Houghton College	NY	23,984	VC
Indiana Univ East	IN	4,433	LC
Indiana Univ Kokomo	IN	4,463	LC
Iona College	NY	27,988	VC
Jacksonville Univ	FL	24,040	C
John Carroll Univ	OH	27,658	C+
Johns Hopkins Univ	MD	38,372	MC
Johnson State College	VT	11,819	LC
Juniata College	PA	29,080	VC
Kansas State Univ	KS	8,728	VC
Lawrence Tech Univ	MI	20,487	C
Lees-McRae College	NC	17,106	LC
LeMoyne-Owen College	TN	13,070	LC
Lesley Univ	MA	30,695	C
Loyola Marymount Univ	CA	32,194	VC
Lubbock Christian Univ	TX	15,832	C
Lynn Univ	FL	30,750	C
Marshall Univ	WV	9,116	C
Martin Univ	IN	10,200	SP
MCP Hahnemann Univ	PA	18,510	SP
Medaille College	NY	20,060	C
Messiah College	PA	25,890	VC+
Mich State Univ	MI	11,933	VC
Midwestern State Univ	TX	8,045	LC
Milligan College	TN	19,860	C+
Minn State Univ, Mankato	MN	8,803	LC
Montana State Univ-Northern	MT	8,600	NC
Montclair State Univ	NJ	13,790	C
Mountain State Univ	WV	10,212	NC
New College of Florida	FL	8,906	HC+
New York Univ	NY	39,406	MC
N Dak State Univ	ND	8,435	C
Northwest Christian College	OR	21,860	C
Northwest Missouri State Univ	MO	9,334	C
Notre Dame de Namur Univ	CA	26,932	LC
Nova Southeastern Univ	FL	23,346	C
Oberlin College	OH	36,938	MC
Okla City Univ	OK	19,580	VC
Okla Panhandle State Univ	OK	5,370	C
Pacific Univ	OR	24,250	C
Pepperdine Univ	CA	32,830	VC
Plymouth State Univ	NH	12,298	LC
Polytechnic Univ/Brooklyn	NY	33,770	VC
Providence College	RI	30,604	HC
Quincy Univ	IL	22,330	C
Rockford College	IL	28,310	VC
Rosemont College	PA	26,175	C
Rutgers, The State Univ of New Jersey/New Brunswick/Piscataway Campus	NJ	15,800	HC
St. John's Univ	MN	26,473	VC
St. Joseph's Univ	PA	33,590	VC
St. Louis Univ	MO	29,780	VC+
St. Martin's College	WA	23,245	C
St. Mary-of-the-Woods College	IN	23,280	C
St. Mary's College	IN	24,474	VC
St. Norbert College	WI	25,810	C
St. Peter's College	NJ	22,292	LC
San Diego State Univ	CA	10,321	C
San Francisco State Univ	CA	12,070	C
Schreiner Univ	TX	20,440	C
Scripps College	CA	35,700	HC+
Seattle Univ	WA	24,183	VC
Shawnee State Univ	OH	11,031	NC
Shimer College	IL	19,655	LC
Siena Heights Univ	MI	16,140	LC
Sierra Nevada College	NV	26,136	C
Southern Methodist Univ	TX	34,210	HC
Spalding Univ	KY	17,985	C
Spring Hill College	AL	25,868	VC
SUNY/College at Buffalo	NY	8,025	C
SUNY/College at Old Westbury	NY	12,784	C
SUNY/Maritime College	NY	10,025	LC
SUNY/Univ at Stony Brook	NY	12,763	HC
Stephen F. Austin State Univ	TX	7,552	C
Stetson Univ	FL	29,495	VC
Suffolk Univ	MA	29,200	C
Tabor College	KS	19,500	NC
Texas Wesleyan Univ	TX	16,245	C
Thomas Edison State College	NJ	3,325	SP
Thomas Univ	GA	11,490	NC
Trinity International Univ	IL	22,980	C+
Turabo Univ	PR	4,110	
Union College	NY	36,005	HC
United States Air Force Academy	CO		HC+
Universidad Metropolitana	PR	3,324	
Univ of Akron	OH	13,134	NC
Univ of Arizona	AZ	10,413	VC
Univ of Calif at Irvine	CA	19,808	HC
Univ of Calif at Riverside	CA	15,300	C
Univ of Central Florida	FL	10,038	VC
Univ of Chicago	IL	35,087	MC
Univ of Colo at Boulder	CO	10,774	VC
Univ of Houston-Downtown	TX	2,594	NC
Univ of Illinois at Urbana-Champaign	IL	11,316	HC+
Univ of Kansas	KS	8,923	VC
Univ of Louisville	KY	8,762	VC
Univ of Maryland/Univ College	MD	5,910	SP
Univ of Mich/Ann Arbor	MI	13,864	HC+
Univ of Mich/Dearborn	MI	6,843	VC
Univ of Minn/Twin Cities	MN	13,160	VC
Univ of New Hampshire	NH	14,828	VC
Univ of Northern Iowa	IA	9,834	C
Univ of Oregon	OR	11,479	VC
Univ of Pennsylvania	PA	37,960	MC
Univ of Pittsburgh at Greensburg	PA	15,984	C
Univ of Pittsburgh at Johnstown	PA	15,216	LC
Univ of Pittsburgh at Pittsburgh	PA	16,074	HC
Univ of PR/Cayey Univ College	PR	1,245	
Univ of Rio Grande	OH	8,728	NC
Univ of San Diego	CA	33,156	HC
Univ of South Florida	FL	9,454	C
Univ of Tenn at Chattanooga	TN	7,783	C
Univ of Texas at Austin	TX	10,630	HC
Univ of Texas at Dallas	TX	10,234	HC
Univ of Texas at San Antonio	TX	9,088	NC
Univ of Toledo	OH	12,479	NC
Univ of Wisc/Green Bay	WI	8,154	C
Univ of Wisc/Madison	WI	8,262	VC
Univ of Wisc/Parkside	WI	6,160	LC
Univ of Wyoming	WY	8,636	C
Ursuline College	OH	22,728	LC
Virginia Wesleyan College	VA	25,350	C
Walla Walla College	WA	21,600	NC
Warren Wilson College	NC	21,794	VC
Washington College	MD	30,540	VC
Washington State Univ	WA	11,334	C
Washington Univ in St. Louis	MO	38,293	MC
Wesleyan College	GA	17,870	VC
Western Baptist College	OR	21,808	C
Western New Mexico Univ	NM	5,950	LC
Western Oregon Univ	OR	10,281	C
Widener Univ	PA	27,020	C
Willamette Univ	OR	32,032	VC+
Wofford College	SC	26,710	HC
Woodbury Univ	CA	25,344	LC
Worcester Polytechnic Inst	MA	37,404	HC
Wright State Univ	OH	11,490	LC
Xavier Univ	OH	26,850	VC+
Yale Univ	CT	37,000	MC
York College of Pennsylvania	PA	14,500	VC

HUMANITIES AND SOCIAL SCIENCE

School	ST	$IS	SR
Antioch College	OH	29,269	C
Conn College	CT	37,900	MC
Franciscan Univ of Steubenville	OH	20,300	VC
Lock Haven Univ of Pennsylvania	PA	11,098	LC
Montana Tech of The Univ of Montana	MT	9,314	NC
SUNY/Empire State College	NY	4,505	SP
Texas A&M Univ at Galveston	TX	9,948	C+
Univ of Mass Dartmouth	MA	12,835	C

HYDROLOGY

School	ST	$IS	SR
Indiana Univ Bloomington	IN	12,389	VC
Texas A&M Univ at Galveston	TX	9,948	C+
Univ of Arizona	AZ	10,413	VC
Univ of Calif at Davis	CA	14,995	VC
Univ of Calif at Santa Barbara	CA	11,732	VC
Univ of Nevada/Reno	NV	9,792	C
Univ of New Hampshire	NH	14,828	VC
Western Mich Univ	MI	12,031	C

ILLUSTRATION

School	ST	$IS	SR
Arcadia Univ	PA	29,890	C
Art Academy of Cincinnati	OH	17,300	SP
Art Center College of Design	CA	23,450	SP
Art Inst of Boston at Lesley Univ	MA	28,080	SP
Art Inst of Southern Calif	CA	14,500	SP
Atlanta College of Art	GA	18,600	SP
Brigham Young Univ	UT	8,504	HC
Calif College of the Arts	CA	31,530	SP
Cal State, Fullerton	CA	6,648	C
College for Creative Studies	MI	23,298	SP
College of Visual Arts	MN		SP
Columbus College of Art and Design	OH	24,180	SP
Fashion Inst of Technology/SUNY	NY	11,169	C+
Kansas City Art Inst	MO	26,850	SP
Kendall College of Art and Design of Ferris State Univ	MI	10,784	SP
Kent State Univ	OH	12,932	C
Lawrence Tech Univ	MI	20,487	C
Lewis Univ	IL	22,950	C+
Maryland Inst College of Art	MD	30,890	SP
Mass College of Art	MA	15,568	SP
Milwaukee Inst of Art and Design	WI	24,388	SP

ST = STATE $IS = IN-STATE COSTS SR = SELECTOR RATING

School	ST	$IS	SR
Minneapolis College of Art and Design	MN	28,950	SP
Montserrat College of Art	MA	22,790	SP
Moore College of Art and Design	PA	27,096	SP
Olivet College	MI	19,984	C+
Otis College of Art and Design	CA	23,420	SP
Pacific Northwest College of Art	OR	14,890	SP
Parsons School of Design	NY	32,242	SP
Rhode Island School of Design	RI	33,569	SP
Ringling School of Art and Design	FL	27,530	SP
Rivier College	NH	26,217	C
Rochester Inst of Technology	NY	29,217	VC+
St. John's Univ	NY	30,180	C
Savannah College of Art and Design	GA	27,560	SP
School of Visual Arts	NY	30,200	SP
Syracuse Univ	NY	34,720	HC
Univ of Bridgeport	CT	25,924	LC
Univ of Findlay	OH	23,962	NC
Univ of Hartford	CT	31,080	C
Univ of Mass Dartmouth	MA	12,835	C
Univ of San Francisco	CA	34,700	VC
Univ of the Arts	PA	29,510	SP
Washington Univ in St. Louis	MO	38,293	MC
Western Conn State Univ	CT	11,625	C

INDUSTRIAL ADMINISTRATION/ MANAGEMENT

School	ST	$IS	SR
Alcorn State Univ	MS	7,290	C
Aurora Univ	IL	20,631	C
Brigham Young Univ	UT	8,504	HC
Calif Univ of Pennsylvania	PA	10,388	C
Central Mich Univ	MI	11,142	C
Clarion Univ of Pennsylvania	PA	11,272	LC
Clarkson Univ	NY	32,226	VC
Clemson Univ	SC	11,972	HC
David N. Myers College	OH	9,475	C
Farmingdale SUNY	NY	12,891	C
Gardner-Webb Univ	NC	19,300	C
Georgia Southern Univ	GA	8,540	C
Grove City College	PA	14,228	HC
Indiana Univ South Bend	IN	4,571	LC
Inter American Univ of PR/ Bayamon Univ College	PR	3,522	
Kent State Univ	OH	12,932	C
Lawrence Tech Univ	MI	20,487	C
LeTourneau Univ	TX	21,080	C
Limestone College	SC	17,700	C
Metropolitan State College of Denver	CO	2,338	LC
Millikin Univ	IL	25,555	C
Northern State Univ	SD	7,117	LC
Oregon Inst of Technology	OR	8,718	C
Penn State Univ/Univ Park Campus	PA	15,646	HC
Purdue Univ/West Lafayette	IN	12,560	VC
Rockhurst Univ	MO	22,960	C+
Saginaw Valley State Univ	MI	11,055	C
St. Augustine's College	NC	12,990	LC
San Francisco State Univ	CA	12,070	C
S Dak State Univ	SD	7,782	C
Southwest Missouri State Univ	MO	8,918	C
Southwestern Okla State Univ	OK	4,801	C
Tri-State Univ-Main Campus	IN	23,600	C
Universidad Politecnica de PR	PR	5,370	
Univ of Alabama	AL	9,040	C+
Univ of Alabama at Birmingham	AL	12,901	C
Univ of Arkansas at Little Rock	AR	5,637	NC
Univ of Cincinnati	OH	14,736	C
Univ of Houston	TX	9,818	C
Univ of Iowa	IA	10,923	VC
Univ of Mass Lowell	MA	11,937	VC
Univ of Memphis	TN	8,560	C
Univ of N Car at Asheville	NC	8,079	VC
Univ of N Car at Chapel Hill	NC	10,117	MC
Univ of N Car at Charlotte	NC	8,185	C
Univ of North Texas	TX	7,629	C
Univ of Southern Colo	CO	7,821	LC
Univ of Wisc/Milwaukee	WI	9,427	LC
Univ of Wisc/Parkside	WI	6,160	LC
Univ of Wisc/Stout	WI	9,718	C
Washington and Jefferson College	PA	29,570	VC
Wentworth Inst of Technology	MA	23,000	C
West Virginia Univ Inst of Technology	WV	7,518	NC
William Penn Univ	IA	17,575	LC
Youngstown State Univ	OH	11,148	NC

INDUSTRIAL AND ORGANIZATIONAL PSYCHOLOGY

School	ST	$IS	SR
Albertus Magnus College	CT	23,130	LC
Averett Univ	VA	23,010	LC
Calif Univ of Pennsylvania	PA	10,388	C
CUNY/Baruch College	NY	3,275	VC+
High Point Univ	NC	22,480	C
Ithaca College	NY	31,730	HC
Lincoln Univ	PA	13,320	C+
Marywood Univ	PA	26,050	C
Moravian College	PA	28,903	VC
Northwest Missouri State Univ	MO	9,334	C
Ohio State Univ	OH	13,080	VC+
Oregon Inst of Technology	OR	8,718	C
Point Loma Nazarene Univ	CA	21,380	VC
St. Joseph's Univ	PA	33,590	VC
Suffolk Univ	MA	29,200	C
Washington Univ in St. Louis	MO	38,293	MC

INDUSTRIAL ARTS EDUCATION

School	ST	$IS	SR
Alabama A&M Univ	AL	5,100	LC
Alcorn State Univ	MS	7,290	C
Appalachian State Univ	NC	7,637	VC
Auburn Univ	AL	10,396	VC
Ball State Univ	IN	8,660	C
Bemidji State Univ	MN	9,103	C
Calif Polytechnic State Univ	CA	8,747	VC
Cal State, Los Angeles	CA	5,778	C
Calif Univ of Pennsylvania	PA	10,388	C
Central Mich Univ	MI	11,142	C
Central Missouri State Univ.	MO	9,776	C
Central Washington Univ	WA	9,768	C
Chicago State Univ	IL	10,882	C+
Clemson Univ	SC	11,972	HC
College of the Ozarks	MO	3,500	VC+
Concordia Univ Nebr	NE	20,302	C+
Eastern Kentucky Univ	KY	7,708	C
Eastern Mich Univ	MI	11,478	C
Elizabeth City State Univ	NC	5,550	LC
Fitchburg State College	MA	9,622	C
Florida A&M Univ	FL	7,564	C
Grambling State Univ	LA	6,538	NC
Humboldt State Univ	CA	9,400	C
Indiana State Univ	IN	10,719	LC
Iowa State Univ	IA	10,768	VC
Jackson State Univ	MS	8,382	C
Kean Univ	NJ	14,479	C
Langston Univ	OK	2,308	LC
Minn State Univ, Mankato	MN	8,803	LC
Minn State Univ, Moorehead	MN	7,000	LC
Montana State Univ-Northern	MT	8,600	NC
Morehead State Univ	KY	7,464	C
Murray State Univ	KY	7,816	VC
N Car Agricultural and Technical State Univ	NC	6,659	LC
N Car State Univ	NC	9,886	VC
Northeastern State Univ	OK	4,950	LC
Northern Arizona Univ	AZ	9,002	C
Northern Kentucky Univ	KY	6,352	NC
Northern Mich Univ	MI	10,834	C
Northern State Univ	SD	7,117	LC
Old Dominion Univ	VA	10,441	C
Penn State Univ/Univ Park Campus	PA	15,646	HC
Purdue Univ/West Lafayette	IN	12,560	VC
Rhode Island College	RI	11,565	C
St. Cloud State Univ	MN	8,362	C
San Francisco State Univ	CA	12,070	C
S Car State Univ	SC	6,586	LC
Southeast Missouri State Univ	MO	9,704	C
Southwest Missouri State Univ	MO	8,918	C
Southwestern Okla State Univ	OK	4,801	C
SUNY/College at Buffalo	NY	8,025	C
Tarleton State Univ	TX	7,576	C
Temple Univ	PA	15,912	C
Texas A&M Univ at Commerce	TX	8,994	C
Univ of Arkansas at Pine Bluff	AR	7,925	C
Univ of Central Okla	OK	9,434	C
Univ of Cincinnati	OH	14,736	C
Univ of Idaho	ID	8,216	C
Univ of Louisiana at Lafayette	LA	5,826	C
Univ of Maryland/Eastern Shore	MD	9,964	C
Univ of Minn/Twin Cities	MN	13,160	VC
Univ of Montana--Western	MT	8,073	NC
Univ of Nebr at Lincoln	NE	9,975	C+
Univ of Southern Miss	MS	8,324	LC
Univ of Wyoming	WY	8,636	C
Utah State Univ	UT	7,371	C
Wayne State College	NE	7,352	NC
Western Illinois Univ	IL	10,363	C

INDUSTRIAL DESIGN

School	ST	$IS	SR
Arizona State Univ-Main	AZ	10,048	C
Art Center College of Design	CA	23,450	SP
Auburn Univ	AL	10,396	VC
Berea College	KY	5,030	VC+
Brigham Young Univ	UT	8,504	HC
Calif College of the Arts	CA	31,530	SP
Cleveland Inst of Art	OH	30,371	SP
College for Creative Studies	MI	23,298	SP
Columbus College of Art and Design	OH	24,180	SP
Georgia Inst of Technology	GA	10,340	HC+
Kean Univ	NJ	14,479	C
Kendall College of Art and Design of Ferris State Univ	MI	10,784	SP
Kent State Univ	OH	12,932	C
Mass College of Art	MA	15,568	SP
Metropolitan State College of Denver	CO	2,338	LC
Milwaukee Inst of Art and Design	WI	24,388	SP
N Car State Univ	NC	9,886	VC
Ohio State Univ	OH	13,080	VC+
Philadelphia Univ	PA	27,354	C
Pratt Inst	NY	34,350	SP
Purdue Univ/West Lafayette	IN	12,560	VC
Rhode Island School of Design	RI	33,569	SP
Rochester Inst of Technology	NY	29,217	VC+
Savannah College of Art and Design	GA	27,560	SP
Syracuse Univ	NY	34,720	HC
Univ of Bridgeport	CT	25,924	LC
Univ of Illinois at Chicago	IL	13,418	C
Univ of Illinois at Urbana-Champaign	IL	11,316	HC+
Univ of Mich/Ann Arbor	MI	13,864	HC+
Univ of the Arts	PA	29,510	SP
Wentworth Inst of Technology	MA	23,000	C
Western Mich Univ	MI	12,031	C

INDUSTRIAL ENGINEERING

School	ST	$IS	SR
Andrews Univ	MI	19,550	C
Arizona State Univ-Main	AZ	10,048	C
Bradley Univ	IL	22,910	VC
Calif Polytechnic State Univ	CA	8,747	VC
Calif State Polytechnic Univ, Pomona	CA	8,793	C+
Cal State, Fresno	CA	8,414	LC
Cal State, Hayward	CA	8,871	LC
Clemson Univ	SC	11,972	HC
Cleveland State Univ	OH	12,308	LC
Elizabethtown College	PA	28,800	C
Florida A&M Univ	FL	7,564	C
Florida International Univ	FL	9,912	VC
Florida State Univ	FL	9,028	HC
Georgia Inst of Technology	GA	10,340	HC+
Hofstra Univ	NY	27,112	VC
Indiana Inst of Technology	IN	21,620	C
Inter American Univ of PR/ Bayamon Univ College	PR	3,522	
Johns Hopkins Univ	MD	38,372	MC
Kansas State Univ	KS	8,728	VC
Kettering Univ	MI	26,478	HC
Lamar Univ	TX	6,816	LC
Lehigh Univ	PA	37,570	HC+
Louisiana State Univ and A&M College	LA	9,126	VC
Louisiana Tech Univ	LA	7,361	C
Mass Maritime Academy	MA	10,472	C
Mercer Univ	GA	27,516	VC+
Milwaukee School of Engineering	WI	28,479	VC+
Miss State Univ	MS	9,139	C
Montana State Univ-Bozeman	MT	9,515	C
New Jersey Inst of Technology	NJ	16,396	VC
New Mexico State Univ	NM	7,932	C
New York Inst of Technology	NY	24,205	VC
N Car Agricultural and Technical State Univ	NC	6,659	LC
N Car State Univ	NC	9,886	VC
N Dak State Univ	ND	8,435	C
Northeastern Univ	MA	35,650	HC
Northern Illinois Univ	IL	11,472	C
Northwestern Univ	IL	37,491	MC
Ohio State Univ	OH	13,080	VC+
Ohio Univ	OH	14,448	C
Okla State Univ	OK	9,216	VC
Penn State Univ/Univ Park Campus	PA	15,646	HC
Purdue Univ/West Lafayette	IN	12,560	VC
Rensselaer Polytechnic Inst	NY	37,579	HC+
Rochester Inst of Technology	NY	29,217	VC+
Rutgers, The State Univ of New Jersey/New Brunswick/Piscataway Campus	NJ	15,800	HC
St. Ambrose Univ	IA	22,800	C
St. Augustine's College	NC	12,990	LC
St. Mary's Univ of San Antonio	TX	22,444	C
San Jose State Univ	CA	8,187	C
S Dak School of Mines and Technology	SD	7,854	C+
Southern Illinois Univ Edwardsville	IL	8,724	C
Stanford Univ	CA	37,612	MC
SUNY/Univ at Binghamton	NY	12,787	HC
SUNY/Univ at Buffalo	NY	12,563	VC
Tenn Tech Univ	TN	8,670	VC
Universidad Politecnica de PR	PR	5,370	
Univ of Alabama	AL	9,040	C+
Univ of Alabama in Huntsville	AL	9,126	VC
Univ of Arizona	AZ	10,413	VC
Univ of Arkansas	AR	9,855	VC
Univ of Calif at Berkeley	CA	15,563	MC
Univ of Houston	TX	9,818	C
Univ of Illinois at Urbana-Champaign	IL	11,316	HC+
Univ of Iowa	IA	10,923	VC
Univ of Louisiana at Lafayette	LA	5,826	C
Univ of Louisville	KY	8,762	VC
Univ of Mass Amherst	MA	13,980	C+
Univ of Memphis	TN	8,560	C
Univ of Miami	FL	34,608	HC
Univ of Mich/Ann Arbor	MI	13,864	HC+
Univ of Mich/Dearborn	MI	6,843	VC
Univ of Minn/Duluth	MN	12,470	C
Univ of Minn/Twin Cities	MN	13,160	VC
Univ of Missouri/Columbia	MO	13,782	VC
Univ of Missouri/Rolla	MO	12,292	HC
Univ of Nebr at Lincoln	NE	9,975	C+
Univ of New Haven	CT	28,650	C
Univ of Okla	OK	9,226	VC
Univ of Pittsburgh at Pittsburgh	PA	16,074	HC
Univ of PR/Mayaguez	PR		
Univ of Rhode Island	RI	13,720	VC
Univ of San Diego	CA	33,156	HC
Univ of South Florida	FL	9,454	C
Univ of Southern Colo	CO	7,821	LC
Univ of Tenn at Knoxville	TN	8,214	C
Univ of Toledo	OH	12,479	NC
Univ of Wisc/Madison	WI	8,262	VC
Univ of Wisc/Milwaukee	WI	9,427	LC
Univ of Wisc/Platteville	WI	8,450	C
Utah State Univ	UT	7,371	C
Western Mich Univ	MI	12,031	C
Western New England College	MA	28,924	C
Wichita State Univ	KS	8,092	C
Worcester Polytechnic Inst	MA	37,404	HC
Youngstown State Univ	OH	11,148	NC

INDUSTRIAL ENGINEERING TECHNOLOGY

School	ST	$IS	SR
Alabama A&M Univ	AL	5,100	LC
Appalachian State Univ	NC	7,637	VC
Bemidji State Univ	MN	9,103	C
Berea College	KY	5,030	VC+
Bowling Green State Univ	OH	13,036	C
Cal State, Chico	CA	8,598	LC
Cal State, Fresno	CA	8,414	LC
Cal State, Los Angeles	CA	5,778	C
Caribbean Univ	PR	3,000	
Central Conn State Univ	CT	12,090	C
Central Missouri State Univ	MO	9,776	C
Central Washington Univ	WA	9,768	C
Chadron State College	NE	6,286	NC
College of the Ozarks	MO	3,500	VC+
Colo State Univ	CO	9,964	VC
Columbia Univ/Fu Foundation School of Engineering and Applied Science	NY	38,590	MC
East Carolina Univ	NC	8,671	C
Eastern Illinois Univ	IL	11,192	C
Elizabeth City State Univ	NC	5,550	LC
Farmingdale SUNY	NY	12,891	C
Fitchburg State College	MA	9,622	C
Grand Valley State Univ	MI	11,022	VC
Humboldt State Univ	CA	9,400	C
Illinois State Univ	IL	10,944	C+
Indiana State Univ	IN	10,719	LC
Indiana Univ-Purdue Univ Fort Wayne	IN	5,108	LC
Iowa State Univ	IA	10,768	VC
Kean Univ	NJ	14,479	C
Kent State Univ	OH	12,932	C
Lamar Univ	TX	6,816	LC
Langston Univ	OK	2,308	LC
Marquette Univ	WI	27,594	VC
McPherson College	KS	20,265	C
Metropolitan State College of Denver	CO	2,338	LC

ST = STATE $IS = IN-STATE COSTS SR = SELECTOR RATING

School	ST	$IS	SR
Middle Tenn State Univ	TN	8,534	C
Millersville Univ of Pennsylvania	PA	11,269	C
Miss State Univ	MS	9,139	C
Miss Valley State Univ	MS	6,765	NC
Morehead State Univ	KY	7,464	C
Morgan State Univ	MD	11,470	C
Northern Kentucky Univ	KY	6,352	NC
Northern Mich Univ	MI	10,834	C
Northern State Univ	SD	7,117	LC
Northwestern State Univ of Louisiana	LA	6,331	NC
Okla Panhandle State Univ	OK	5,370	C
Oregon State Univ	OR	11,055	C
Prairie View A&M Univ	TX	9,418	NC
Purdue Univ/Calumet	IN	6,630	NC
Purdue Univ/West Lafayette	IN	12,560	VC
Southeast Missouri State Univ	MO	9,704	C
Southeastern Louisiana Univ	LA	6,791	LC
Southern Illinois Univ Carbondale	IL	10,407	C
Southern Polytechnic State Univ	GA	7,620	VC
Southwestern Okla State Univ	OK	4,801	C
SUNY/College at Buffalo	NY	8,025	C
Sul Ross State Univ	TX	6,582	LC
Tarleton State Univ	TX	7,576	C
Tenn Tech Univ	TN	8,670	VC
Texas A&M Univ	TX	11,081	HC
Texas A&M Univ at Kingsville	TX	6,740	LC
Texas Southern Univ	TX	8,920	NC
Texas State Univ	TX	9,320	VC
Texas Tech Univ	TX	10,768	VC
Univ of Arkansas at Pine Bluff	AR	7,925	C
Univ of Central Florida	FL	10,038	VC
Univ of Cincinnati	OH	14,736	C
Univ of Dayton	OH	24,850	VC
Univ of Florida	FL	8,580	MC
Univ of Houston	TX	9,818	C
Univ of Illinois at Chicago	IL	13,418	C
Univ of Mass Lowell	MA	11,937	VC
Univ of Nebr at Lincoln	NE	9,975	C+
Univ of New Haven	CT	28,650	C
Univ of N Dak	ND	8,390	C
Univ of Northern Iowa	IA	9,834	C
Univ of Rio Grande	OH	8,728	NC
Univ of Southern Maine	ME	11,212	C
Univ of Texas at Arlington	TX	7,192	LC
Univ of Texas at El Paso	TX	5,799	NC
Univ of West Alabama	AL	6,048	C
Univ of Wisc/Platteville	WI	8,450	C
Univ of Wisc/Stout	WI	9,718	C
Utah State Univ	UT	7,371	C
Wayne State Univ	MI	11,774	C
West Virginia Univ Inst of Technology	WV	7,518	NC
Western Carolina Univ	NC	6,742	C
Western Illinois Univ	IL	10,363	C
Western Kentucky Univ	KY	6,834	C
Western Mich Univ	MI	12,031	C
William Penn Univ	IA	17,575	LC

INDUSTRIAL HYGIENE

School	ST	$IS	SR
Clarkson Univ	NY	32,226	VC
Doane College	NE	20,000	C
Oakland Univ	MI	10,800	C
St. Augustine's College	NC	12,990	LC
Univ of Central Okla	OK	9,434	C
Univ of Memphis	TN	8,560	C
Univ of North Alabama	AL	7,972	NC

INFORMATION SCIENCES AND SYSTEMS

School	ST	$IS	SR
Abilene Christian Univ	TX	18,370	VC
Alabama State Univ	AL	6,404	C
Albany State Univ	GA	5,764	C+
Albright College	PA	30,579	C
Alvernia College	PA	23,212	LC
Alverno College	WI	18,898	C
American InterContinental Univ	GA	12,000	NC
American Univ	DC	34,585	VC+
Andrews Univ	MI	19,550	C
Appalachian State Univ	NC	7,637	VC
Aquinas College	MI	21,894	C
Arizona State Univ-Main	AZ	10,048	C
Armstrong Atlantic State Univ	GA	7,102	C
Asbury College	KY	20,704	VC
Atlantic Union College	MA	18,868	C
Auburn Univ Montgomery	AL	9,020	NC
Averett Univ	VA	23,010	LC
Avila Univ	MO	20,300	C
Azusa Pacific Univ	CA	24,720	VC
Baker Univ	KS	19,860	VC
Baldwin-Wallace College	OH	24,678	C
Barton College	NC	19,314	C
Bay Path College	MA	24,910	C
Baylor Univ	TX	23,864	VC
Belhaven College	MS	16,040	C+
Bellarmine Univ	KY	24,110	VC
Bellevue Univ	NE	4,440	NC
Belmont Abbey College	NC	23,742	C
Bethel College	KS	19,800	C+
Bethune-Cookman College	FL	16,480	LC
Biola Univ	CA	25,964	VC
Bloomfield College	NJ	19,250	LC
Bluffton College	OH	23,694	C
Boise State Univ	ID	7,657	LC
Boston College	MA	33,284	MC
Bowling Green State Univ	OH	13,036	C
Bradley Univ	IL	22,910	VC
Briar Cliff Univ	IA	21,660	C
Bridgewater College	VA	25,150	C
Brigham Young Univ	UT	8,504	HC
Brigham Young Univ/Hawaii	HI	7,240	VC+
Bryant College	RI	31,004	VC
Cabrini College	PA	29,020	C
Caldwell College	NJ	24,060	LC
Calif Baptist Univ	CA	19,924	C
Calif Lutheran Univ	CA	27,600	LC
Calif State Polytechnic Univ, Pomona	CA	8,793	C+
Cal State, Chico	CA	8,598	LC
Cal State, Los Angeles	CA	5,778	C
Cal State, Stanislaus	CA	9,874	C
Calumet College of St. Joseph	IN	9,000	LC
Calvin College	MI	22,615	NC
Campbell Univ	NC	18,268	VC
Campbellsville Univ	KY	17,680	C
Carlow College	PA	21,334	C
Carnegie Mellon Univ	PA	32,682	MC
Carroll College	WI	22,740	C
Catawba College	NC	20,500	C
Cedar Crest College	PA	25,145	C+
Cedarville Univ	OH	19,954	VC
Central Missouri State Univ	MO	9,776	C
Central Washington Univ	WA	9,768	C
Chaminade Univ of Honolulu	HI	21,430	LC
Champlain College	VT	22,030	C
Chapman Univ	CA	33,118	VC
Chicago State Univ	IL	10,882	C+
Christian Brothers Univ	TN	22,290	VC
Christopher Newport Univ	VA	8,862	VC
CUNY/Baruch College	NY	3,275	VC+
CUNY/Brooklyn College	NY	4,353	C+
CUNY/College of Staten Island	NY	4,308	NC
CUNY/John Jay College of Criminal Justice	NY	4,259	C
CUNY/York College	NY	3,292	NC
Clarion Univ of Pennsylvania	PA	11,272	LC
Clarke College	IA	23,165	C
Clarkson Univ	NY	32,226	VC
Clayton College and State Univ	GA	2,441	LC
Cleary College	MI	10,350	LC
Clemson Univ	SC	11,972	HC
Cleveland State Univ	OH	12,308	LC
College Misericordia	PA	26,350	C
College of Charleston	SC	11,887	HC
College of Notre Dame of Maryland	MD	27,700	C
College of St. Catherine	MN	24,010	VC
College of St. Rose	NY	22,864	C
College of St. Scholastica	MN	24,970	C+
College of the Ozarks	MO	3,500	VC+
Colo State Univ	CO	9,964	VC
Colo Technical Univ	CO	9,500	LC
Columbia College	MO	16,139	C
Columbia College	SC	22,658	LC
Columbia Union College	MD	20,543	C
Concord College	WV	8,136	C
Concordia Univ	MI	24,095	C
Covenant College	GA	23,830	VC+
Culver-Stockton College	MO	17,850	C
Cumberland College	KY	16,384	C
Dakota State Univ	SD	7,466	C
Daniel Webster College	NH	24,870	C
Davenport Univ	MI	11,636	NC
David N. Myers College	OH	9,475	C
Delta State Univ	MS	6,618	C
DePaul Univ	IL	27,580	VC
DeVry College of Technology/North Brunswick	NJ	10,100	LC
DeVry/New York	NY	11,860	LC
DeVry Univ/Addison (DuPage County)	IL	10,790	LC
DeVry Univ/Alpharetta	GA	10,670	LC
DeVry Univ/Chicago	IL	10,790	LC
DeVry Univ/Colo Springs	CO	11,310	LC
DeVry Univ/Columbus	OH	10,670	LC
DeVry Univ/Crystal City	VA	11,860	C
DeVry Univ/Dallas	TX	10,640	LC
DeVry Univ/Decatur	GA	10,670	LC
DeVry Univ/Fort Washington	PA	11,860	LC
DeVry Univ/Fremont	CA	11,860	LC
DeVry Univ/Kansas City	MO	10,670	LC
DeVry Univ/Long Beach	CA	11,310	LC
DeVry Univ/Miramar	FL	11,310	LC
DeVry Univ/Orlando	FL	11,310	LC
DeVry Univ/Phoenix	AZ	10,670	LC
DeVry Univ/Pomona	CA	11,310	LC
DeVry Univ/Seattle	WA	11,860	LC
DeVry Univ/Tinley Park	IL	10,790	LC
DeVry Univ/West Hills	CA	11,310	LC
DeVry Univ/Westminster	CO	11,310	LC
Dominican College	NY	24,810	LC
Dominican Univ	IL	23,610	C
Dordt College	IA	20,170	VC
Dowling College	NY	23,870	LC
Drake Univ	IA	25,120	VC+
Drexel Univ	PA	27,655	VC
Drury Univ	MO	18,085	VC+
D'Youville College	NY	21,080	C
East Tenn State Univ	TN	8,497	C
East Texas Baptist Univ	TX	13,914	C
Eastern Mich Univ	MI	11,478	C
Eastern New Mexico Univ	NM	6,762	LC
Eastern Washington Univ	WA	9,012	C
Edgewood College	WI	20,520	C
Elmhurst College	IL	24,630	C
Elon Univ	NC	22,240	VC
Emporia State Univ	KS	6,998	C
Excelsior College	NY	975	SP
Fairfield Univ	CT	35,505	HC
Fairleigh Dickinson Univ/Metropolitan Campus	NJ	28,584	C
Ferrum College	VA	21,240	LC
Florida Atlantic Univ	FL	8,543	C
Florida Gulf Coast Univ	FL	9,908	C
Florida Inst of Technology	FL	28,740	VC
Florida International Univ	FL	9,912	VC
Florida Southern College	FL	23,592	C
Florida State Univ	FL	9,028	HC
Fontbonne Univ	MO	21,508	C
Fordham Univ	NY	35,066	HC
Fort Hays State Univ	KS	7,363	C
Fort Lewis College	CO	8,353	C
Fort Valley State Univ	GA	6,960	C
Francis Marion Univ	SC	9,364	C
Franciscan Univ of Steubenville	OH	20,300	VC
Franklin College	IN		C
Franklin Pierce College	NH	28,980	LC
Freed-Hardeman Univ	TN		NC
Friends Univ	KS	15,962	LC
Gardner-Webb Univ	NC	19,300	C
George Fox Univ	OR	26,110	VC
George Mason Univ	VA	9,732	VC
George Washington Univ	DC	41,030	MC
Georgia College and State Univ	GA	9,878	C
Georgia Southern Univ	GA	8,540	C
Glenville State College	WV	7,812	NC
Goshen College	IN	22,450	VC
Graceland Univ	IA	19,550	C
Grambling State Univ	LA	6,538	NC
Grand View College	IA	19,748	LC
Guilford College	NC	24,960	VC
Gwynedd-Mercy College	PA	24,225	C
Hampton Univ	VA	17,112	C+
Hannibal-LaGrange College	MO	13,940	C
Hartwick College	NY	34,650	C+
Haverford College	PA	37,900	MC
Heidelberg College	OH	20,266	NC
High Point Univ	NC	22,480	C
Holy Family College	PA	13,710	LC
Hood College	MD	27,795	VC
Houston Baptist Univ	TX	16,905	C
Howard Univ	DC	16,505	C
Humboldt State Univ	CA	9,400	C
Huntington College	IN	23,590	C
Idaho State Univ	ID	8,128	C
Illinois College	IL	19,100	VC
Illinois Inst of Technology	IL	26,456	HC+
Illinois State Univ	IL	10,944	C+
Immaculata Univ	PA	25,200	C
Indiana Inst of Technology	IN	21,620	C
Indiana Univ Bloomington	IN	12,389	VC
Indiana Univ East	IN	4,433	LC
Indiana Univ Kokomo	IN	4,463	LC
Indiana Univ Northwest	IN	4,538	LC
Indiana Univ South Bend	IN	4,571	LC
Indiana Univ-Purdue Univ Fort Wayne	IN	5,108	LC
Indiana Univ-Purdue Univ Indianapolis	IN	8,257	LC
International College	FL	8,060	LC
Ithaca College	NY	31,730	HC
Jacksonville Univ	FL	24,040	C
James Madison Univ	VA	10,794	VC
Jamestown College	ND	12,600	NC
Johns Hopkins Univ	MD	38,372	MC
Johnson and Wales Univ	RI	22,965	LC
Johnson State College	VT	11,819	LC
Juniata College	PA	29,080	VC
Kansas State Univ	KS	8,728	VC
Kennesaw State Univ	GA	2,724	C
Kent State Univ	OH	12,932	C
Keystone College	PA	21,405	LC
King's College	PA	26,990	C
La Roche College	PA	22,094	C
La Salle Univ	PA	31,260	VC
La Sierra Univ	CA	19,260	LC
Lamar Univ	TX	6,816	LC
Lawrence Tech Univ	MI	20,487	C
Le Moyne College	NY	26,400	VC
Lehigh Univ	PA	37,570	HC+
Limestone College	SC	17,700	C
Lincoln Memorial Univ	TN	16,400	LC
Lincoln Univ	MO	7,158	NC
Lock Haven Univ of Pennsylvania	PA	11,098	LC
LIU/Brooklyn Campus	NY	24,790	C
LIU/C.W. Post Campus	NY	28,282	C
Louisiana State Univ and A&M College	LA	9,126	VC
Loyola Univ New Orleans	LA	31,036	VC+
Lubbock Christian Univ	TX	15,832	C
Madonna Univ	MI	11,504	VC
Manhattan College	NY	27,400	VC
Mansfield Univ	PA	11,220	C
Marian College of Fond du Lac	WI	19,625	C
Marietta College	OH	27,047	C
Marist College	NY	27,596	VC
Marquette Univ	WI	27,594	VC
Marshall Univ	WV	9,116	C
Marygrove College	MI	17,550	C
Marymount College of Fordham Univ	NY	27,686	C
Marymount Manhattan College	NY	27,292	C
Marymount Univ	VA	23,668	C
Maryville Univ of St. Louis	MO	22,090	VC
Marywood Univ	PA	26,050	C
Master's College and Seminary	CA	23,250	VC
McKendree College	IL	21,120	VC
McMurry Univ	TX	17,846	LC
McNeese State Univ	LA	5,259	LC
Medaille College	NY	20,060	C
Mercy College	NY	19,200	NC
Meredith College	NC	23,065	C
Metropolitan State College of Denver	CO	2,338	LC
Metropolitan State Univ	MN	3,852	SP
Mich State Univ	MI	11,933	VC
Middle Tenn State Univ	TN	8,534	C
Midwestern State Univ	TX	8,045	LC
Milligan College	TN	19,860	C+
Minn State Univ, Mankato	MN	8,803	LC
Miss State Univ	MS	9,139	C
Missouri Baptist Univ	MO	18,010	C
Missouri Southern State Univ	MO	8,316	C
Missouri Valley College	MO	18,500	C
Missouri Western State College	MO	8,522	NC
Molloy College	NY	15,180	C
Montana State Univ-Billings	MT	9,550	C
Montclair State Univ	NJ	13,790	C
Morgan State Univ	MD	11,470	C
Mount Mercy College	IA	21,400	C
Mount Olive College	NC	14,410	LC
Mount St. Mary College	NY	21,270	C
Mount St. Mary's College	MD	28,400	C
Mount Union College	OH	21,120	C
Murray State Univ	KY	7,816	VC
National American Univ	SD	13,680	NC
National Univ	CA	9,690	SP
National-Louis Univ	IL	16,240	LC
Nazareth College of Rochester	NY	24,936	VC
Nebr Wesleyan Univ	NE	21,197	C+
New Jersey Inst of Technology	NJ	16,396	VC
New York Univ	NY	39,406	MC
Newman Univ	KS	18,018	C
Niagara Univ	NY	25,050	C
Nicholls State Univ	LA	6,395	NC
N Car Wesleyan College	NC	17,998	C
Northeastern State Univ	OK	4,950	LC
Northeastern Univ	MA	35,650	HC
Northern Arizona Univ	AZ	9,002	C
Northern Illinois Univ	IL	11,472	C
Northern Kentucky Univ	KY	6,352	NC
Northern Mich Univ	MI	10,834	C
Northland College	WI	22,170	C+
Northwest Christian College	OR	21,860	C
Northwest Missouri State Univ	MO	9,334	C
Northwestern State Univ of Louisiana	LA	6,331	NC
Northwestern Univ	IL	37,491	MC
Norwich Univ	VT	21,064	LC
Notre Dame College	OH	20,425	C
Notre Dame de Namur Univ	CA	26,932	LC
Nova Southeastern Univ	FL	23,346	C
Oakland Univ	MI	10,800	C
Oakwood College	AL	14,904	C
Ohio Dominican Univ	OH	22,700	C
Ohio State Univ	OH	13,080	VC+
Okla Baptist Univ	OK	15,220	VC
Okla Christian Univ	OK	17,690	NC
Okla Panhandle State Univ	OK	5,370	C
Okla Wesleyan Univ	OK	14,100	LC
Old Dominion Univ	VA	10,441	C
Ottawa Univ	KS	11,800	LC

ST = STATE **$IS** = IN-STATE COSTS **SR** = SELECTOR RATING

School	ST	$IS	SR
Our Lady of the Lake Univ of San Antonio	TX	17,336	C
Pace Univ	NY	28,652	VC
Park Univ	MO	10,780	C+
Peirce College	PA	11,800	NC
Pfeiffer Univ	NC	18,980	C
Pittsburg State Univ	KS	7,128	NC
Plymouth State Univ	NH	12,298	LC
Point Park Univ	PA	21,840	C
Polytechnic Univ/Brooklyn	NY	33,770	VC
Portland State Univ	OR	12,453	C
Purdue Univ/Calumet	IN	6,630	NC
Purdue Univ/West Lafayette	IN	12,560	VC
Quincy Univ	IL	22,330	C
Radford Univ	VA	8,500	C
Ramapo College of New Jersey	NJ	15,203	VC
Rhode Island College	RI	11,565	C
Richard Stockton College of New Jersey	NJ	12,972	VC
Rider Univ	NJ	30,900	C
Roanoke College	VA	27,393	C
Robert Morris Univ	PA	20,438	C
Rochester Inst of Technology	NY	29,217	VC+
Rockhurst Univ	MO	22,960	C+
Rocky Mountain College	MT	19,015	C
Roger Williams Univ	RI	30,296	C
Roosevelt Univ	IL	22,580	VC
Rutgers, The State Univ of New Jersey/New Brunswick/Piscataway Campus	NJ	15,800	HC
Rutgers, The State Univ of New Jersey/Newark Campus	NJ	15,624	VC
St. Augustine's College	NC	12,990	LC
St. Edward's Univ	TX	20,428	C
St. Joseph's, Brooklyn,	NY	10,902	C
St. Joseph's Univ	PA	33,590	VC
St. Leo Univ	FL	20,600	C
St. Louis Univ	MO	29,780	VC+
St. Mary-of-the-Woods College	IN	23,280	C
St. Michael's College	VT	30,100	VC
St. Norbert College	WI	25,810	C
St. Vincent College	PA	25,530	VC
Salem International Univ	WV	19,770	C
Salve Regina Univ	RI	29,210	C
San Diego State Univ	CA	10,321	C
San Francisco State Univ	CA	12,070	C
Santa Clara Univ	CA	34,701	HC
Shepherd College	WV	8,608	C
Shippensburg Univ of Pennsylvania	PA	10,826	C
Siena Heights Univ	MI	16,140	LC
Silver Lake College of the Holy Family	WI	18,450	LC
Simpson College	IA	23,658	C+
Slippery Rock Univ of Pennsylvania	PA	10,343	LC
Southeastern Okla State Univ	OK	6,147	C
Southeastern Univ	DC	8,505	LC
Southern Adventist Univ	TN	17,080	C
Southern Illinois Univ Carbondale	IL	10,407	C
Southern New Hampshire Univ	NH	26,242	C
Southern Polytechnic State Univ	GA	7,620	VC
Southern Utah Univ	UT	8,194	C
Southern Wesleyan Univ	SC	19,940	C
Southwest Baptist Univ	MO	15,371	C
Southwest Missouri State Univ	MO	8,918	C
Southwestern Adventist Univ	TX	14,798	C
Southwestern Okla State Univ	OK	4,801	C
Springfield College	MA	24,520	C
St. Joseph's, Suffolk	NY	11,297	C
SUNY at Oswego	NY	12,650	C
SUNY/College at Brockport	NY	12,111	C
SUNY/College at Buffalo	NY	8,025	C
SUNY/College at Old Westbury	NY	12,784	C
SUNY/College of Technology at Alfred	NY	12,416	C
SUNY/Univ at Albany	NY	12,951	HC
SUNY/Univ at Stony Brook	NY	12,763	HC
Stephen F. Austin State Univ	TX	7,552	C
Strayer Univ	DC	8,789	SP
Suffolk Univ	MA	29,200	C
Susquehanna Univ	PA	29,990	VC
Syracuse Univ	NY	34,720	HC
Tarleton State Univ	TX	7,576	C
Temple Univ	PA	15,912	C
Texas Christian Univ	TX	23,410	VC
Texas State Univ	TX	9,320	VC
Texas Wesleyan Univ	TX	16,245	C
Thomas College	ME	19,960	LC
Thomas Edison State College	NJ	3,325	SP
Tiffin Univ	OH	19,490	LC
Towson Univ	MD	12,694	VC
Trevecca Nazarene Univ	TN	17,548	C
Trinity Christian College	IL	21,640	VC
Tri-State Univ-Main Campus	IN	23,600	C
Tulane Univ	LA	37,451	HC+
Tusculum College	TN	19,990	C
Univ of Alabama at Birmingham	AL	12,901	C
Univ of Arkansas at Little Rock	AR	5,637	NC
Univ of Calif at Irvine	CA	19,808	HC
Univ of Calif at Riverside	CA	15,300	C
Univ of Calif at San Diego	CA	14,127	HC
Univ of Calif at Santa Cruz	CA	16,505	VC
Univ of Central Arkansas	AR	6,388	C
Univ of Charleston	WV	23,620	C
Univ of Cincinnati	OH	14,736	C
Univ of Colo at Boulder	CO	10,774	VC
Univ of Dayton	OH	24,850	VC
Univ of Delaware	DE	12,616	HC
Univ of Detroit Mercy	MI	25,582	C
Univ of Florida	FL	8,580	MC
Univ of Hartford	CT	31,080	C
Univ of Hawaii at Manoa	HI	9,565	VC
Univ of Houston	TX	9,818	C
Univ of Houston-Downtown	TX	2,594	NC
Univ of Idaho	ID	8,216	C
Univ of Illinois at Chicago	IL	13,418	C
Univ of Iowa	IA	10,923	VC
Univ of Kansas	KS	8,923	VC
Univ of Louisville	KY	8,762	VC
Univ of Maine	ME	12,080	C+
Univ of Maine at Augusta	ME	4,065	C
Univ of Mary Hardin-Baylor	TX	17,268	C
Univ of Maryland/Baltimore County	MD	14,668	VC+
Univ of Maryland/College Park	MD	14,227	HC
Univ of Maryland/Univ College	MD	5,910	SP
Univ of Mass Lowell	MA	11,937	VC
Univ of Memphis	TN	8,560	C
Univ of Minn/Crookston	MN	9,626	NC
Univ of Missouri/Kansas City	MO	13,416	VC
Univ of Missouri/Rolla	MO	12,292	HC
Univ of Nebr at Kearney	NE	8,286	NC
Univ of Nevada/Reno	NV	9,792	C
Univ of North Alabama	AL	7,972	NC
Univ of N Car at Chapel Hill	NC	10,117	MC
Univ of N Car at Charlotte	NC	8,185	C
Univ of N Dak	ND	8,390	C
Univ of North Florida	FL	8,769	VC
Univ of North Texas	TX	7,629	C
Univ of Northern Colo	CO	8,987	C
Univ of Northern Iowa	IA	9,834	C
Univ of Okla	OK	9,226	VC
Univ of Pittsburgh at Pittsburgh	PA	16,074	HC
Univ of PR/Bayamon Univ College Campus	PR	1,600	
Univ of PR/Mayaguez	PR		
Univ of PR/Rio Piedras	PR	5,730	
Univ of St. Francis	IL	22,850	C
Univ of St. Mary	KS	18,868	C
Univ of San Francisco	CA	34,700	VC
Univ of Scranton	PA	30,836	VC
Univ of S Car at Spartanburg	SC	9,936	C+
Univ of Southern Colo	CO	7,821	LC
Univ of Southern Miss	MS	8,324	LC
Univ of Tampa	FL	23,982	VC
Univ of Texas at Arlington	TX	7,192	LC
Univ of Texas at San Antonio	TX	9,088	NC
Univ of Texas-Pan American	TX	5,954	LC
Univ of the Incarnate Word	TX	21,772	LC
Univ of the Pacific	CA	31,090	VC
Univ of Toledo	OH	12,479	NC
Univ of Tulsa	OK	22,090	VC+
Univ of Vermont	VT	16,316	VC
Univ of Virginia's College at Wise	VA	10,116	C
Univ of Washington	WA	10,361	VC
Univ of Wisc/Eau Claire	WI	8,463	VC
Univ of Wisc/Green Bay	WI	8,154	C
Univ of Wisc/La Crosse	WI	8,991	VC
Univ of Wisc/Madison	WI	8,262	VC
Univ of Wisc/Stevens Point	WI	8,116	VC
Univ of Wisc/Superior	WI	7,051	C+
Utah State Univ	UT	7,371	C
Valdosta State Univ	GA	7,798	C
Valley City State Univ	ND	7,281	LC
Valparaiso Univ	IN	26,118	VC+
Villa Julie College	MD	18,393	C
Villanova Univ	PA	35,050	HC
Virginia Commonwealth Univ	VA	9,030	C
Virginia Intermont College	VA	19,800	C
Viterbo Univ	WI	20,430	C
Walla Walla College	WA	21,600	NC
Warner Southern College	FL	16,738	LC
Wartburg College	IA	21,165	VC
Washburn Univ of Topeka	KS	8,984	NC
Washington Univ in St. Louis	MO	38,293	MC
Wayne State Univ	MI	11,774	C
Waynesburg College	PA	19,370	C
Weber State Univ	UT	7,945	NC
Webster Univ	MO	21,848	VC
Wentworth Inst of Technology	MA	23,000	C
West Liberty State College	WV	7,868	LC
West Texas A&M Univ	TX	7,533	C
Western Carolina Univ	NC	6,742	C
Western Kentucky Univ	KY	6,834	C
Western Mich Univ	MI	12,031	C
Western New England College	MA	28,924	C
Western Oregon Univ	OR	10,281	C
Westfield State College	MA	10,147	C
Widener Univ	PA	27,020	C
Wilberforce Univ	OH	14,937	LC
Wilkes Univ	PA	28,060	C
William Jewell College	MO	21,320	VC
William Woods Univ	MO	20,120	C
Woodbury Univ	CA	25,344	LC
Xavier Univ	OH	26,850	VC+
York College of Pennsylvania	PA	14,500	VC
Youngstown State Univ	OH	11,148	NC

INSTITUTIONAL MANAGEMENT

School	ST	$IS	SR
Assumption College	MA	29,375	C
Baldwin-Wallace College	OH	24,678	C
Bowling Green State Univ	OH	13,036	C
Calumet College of St. Joseph	IN	9,000	LC
Felician College	NJ	24,300	C
Goshen College	IN	22,450	VC
Kent State Univ	OH	12,932	C
La Roche College	PA	22,094	C
N Dak State Univ	ND	8,435	C
Rockhurst Univ	MO	22,960	C+
Simpson College	CA	20,500	C
Southwest Missouri State Univ	MO	8,918	C
Spring Arbor Univ	MI	20,206	C
Thomas Edison State College	NJ	3,325	SP
Univ of La Verne	CA	28,600	C
Viterbo Univ	WI	20,430	C
Warner Southern College	FL	16,738	LC

INSURANCE

School	ST	$IS	SR
Ball State Univ	IN	8,660	C
Baylor Univ	TX	23,864	VC
Cal State, Sacramento	CA	9,543	C
Delta State Univ	MS	6,618	C
Ferris State Univ	MI	12,512	C
Howard Univ	DC	16,505	C
Illinois State Univ	IL	10,944	C+
Indiana State Univ	IN	10,719	LC
Inter American Univ of PR/Fajardo Campus	PR	4,000	
Inter American Univ of PR/Ponce Regional College	PR	3,700	
Martin Univ	IN	10,200	SP
Miss State Univ	MS	9,139	C
Olivet College	MI	19,984	C+
Penn State Univ/Univ Park Campus	PA	15,646	HC
Roosevelt Univ	IL	22,580	VC
Southwest Missouri State Univ	MO	8,918	C
Texas Southern Univ	TX	8,920	NC
Thomas Edison State College	NJ	3,325	SP
Univ of Central Okla	OK	9,434	C
Univ of Florida	FL	8,580	MC
Univ of Hartford	CT	31,080	C
Univ of Louisiana at Monroe	LA	5,207	NC
Univ of Miss	MS	7,666	C
Univ of North Texas	TX	7,629	C
Univ of S Car at Columbia	SC	10,048	VC

INSURANCE AND RISK MANAGEMENT

School	ST	$IS	SR
Appalachian State Univ	NC	7,637	VC
Bradley Univ	IL	22,910	VC
Drake Univ	IA	25,120	VC+
Eastern Mich Univ	MI	11,478	C
Excelsior College	NY	975	SP
Florida State Univ	FL	9,028	HC
Georgia State Univ	GA	10,658	C
Illinois Wesleyan Univ	IL	30,380	HC+
Mercyhurst College	PA	20,694	C
Ohio State Univ	OH	13,080	VC+
Roosevelt Univ	IL	22,580	VC
St. John's Univ	NY	30,180	C
Southwestern Adventist Univ	TX	14,798	C
Univ of Central Arkansas	AR	6,388	C
Univ of Conn	CT	14,608	VC
Univ of Memphis	TN	8,560	C
Univ of Pennsylvania	PA	37,960	MC
Univ of Wisc/Madison	WI	8,262	VC
Washington State Univ	WA	11,334	C

INTERDISCIPLINARY STUDIES

School	ST	$IS	SR
Adams State College	CO	7,468	C
Alfred Univ	NY	28,290	C
American Univ	DC	34,585	VC+
Amherst College	MA	37,470	MC
Andrews Univ	MI	19,550	C
Angelo State Univ	TX	7,576	NC
Antioch College	OH	29,269	C
Appalachian State Univ	NC	7,637	VC
Aquinas College	MI	21,894	C
Arizona State Univ-Main	AZ	10,048	C
Austin College	TX	24,747	HC
Austin Peay State Univ	TN	5,814	LC
Averett Univ	VA	23,010	LC
Bard College	NY	37,352	HC+
Baylor Univ	TX	23,864	VC
Beloit College	WI	29,864	HC
Bennett College	NC	11,200	C
Bennington College	VT	35,910	HC
Bentley College	MA	33,904	VC
Berry College	GA	21,410	VC
Bluefield College	VA	15,575	C
Boise State Univ	ID	7,657	LC
Boston Univ	MA	38,194	HC+
Bowie State Univ	MD	10,873	C+
Brigham Young Univ/Hawaii	HI	7,240	VC+
Bryn Athyn College of the New Church	PA	12,612	NC
Bucknell Univ	PA	35,262	HC+
Calif Lutheran Univ	CA	27,600	LC
Cal State, Dominguez Hills	CA	5,840	LC
Cal State, Long Beach	CA	8,762	C+
Cal State, Los Angeles	CA	5,778	C
Cal State, Stanislaus	CA	9,874	C
Cambridge College	MA	10,800	SP
Cameron Univ	OK	5,692	NC
Cascade College	OR	16,700	NC
Centenary College	NJ	25,370	LC
Central Methodist College	MO	16,460	C
Chatham College	PA	27,266	C+
Christian Heritage College	CA	19,990	C
Christopher Newport Univ	VA	8,862	VC
CUNY/Queens College	NY	4,362	C
Claremont McKenna College	CA	36,880	MC
Clayton College and State Univ	GA	2,441	LC
Coastal Carolina Univ	SC	11,040	C
Coe College	IA	27,385	VC
College Misericordia	PA	26,350	C
College of Notre Dame of Maryland	MD	27,700	C
College of St. Rose	NY	22,864	C
College of Santa Fe	NM	25,293	C+
College of the Ozarks	MO	3,500	VC+
College of William and Mary	VA	12,224	MC
College of Wooster	OH	31,300	HC
Columbia College	MO	16,139	C
Concordia College	NY	19,200	VC
Cornerstone Univ and Grand Rapids Theological Seminary	MI	19,846	C
Covenant College	GA	23,830	VC+
Crichton College	TN	15,215	C
Dallas Baptist Univ	TX	15,300	VC
Dana College	NE	20,280	C
Davidson College	NC	33,274	MC
DePauw Univ	IN	31,500	HC
East Tenn State Univ	TN	8,497	C
Eastern Mich Univ	MI	11,478	C
Emerson College	MA	32,205	HC
Emmanuel College	MA	27,600	C+
Emory & Henry College	VA	21,950	C
Fairleigh Dickinson Univ/Metropolitan Campus	NJ	28,584	C
Florida Atlantic Univ	FL	8,543	C
Florida Inst of Technology	FL	28,740	VC
Framingham State College	MA	9,381	C
Franciscan Univ	IA	19,300	C
Franklin and Marshall College	PA	35,930	HC+
Friends World Program	NY	24,800	C
Geneva College	PA	21,850	C
George Mason Univ	VA	9,732	VC
George Washington Univ	DC	41,030	MC
Georgetown Univ	DC	38,242	MC
Georgia State Univ	GA	10,658	C
Goddard College	VT	21,056	C+
Gonzaga Univ	WA	26,766	HC
Goucher College	MD	32,650	HC
Grace Bible College	MI	15,890	C
Haverford College	PA	37,900	MC
Hendrix College	AR	20,970	VC+
Heritage College	WA	6,720	NC
Hofstra Univ	NY	27,112	VC
Hollins Univ	VA	27,965	VC
Hope International Univ	CA	16,940	NC
Illinois Wesleyan Univ	IL	30,380	HC+
Indiana State Univ	IN	10,719	LC
International College	FL	8,060	LC
Ithaca College	NY	31,730	HC

ST = STATE $IS = IN-STATE COSTS SR = SELECTOR RATING

School	ST	$IS	SR
John Brown Univ	AR	15,080	VC
Johns Hopkins Univ	MD	38,372	MC
Judson College	AL	14,650	C
Kalamazoo College	MI	26,955	HC+
Lafayette College	PA	35,746	MC
Lambuth Univ	TN	16,520	C
Lander Univ	SC	10,496	C
Lane College	TN	11,178	C+
Lees-McRae College	NC	17,106	LC
LeTourneau Univ	TX	21,080	C
Lewis and Clark College	OR	30,620	VC
Liberty Univ	VA	17,220	C
Lyndon State College	VT	12,646	LC
Manchester College	IN	23,390	C
Marian College of Fond du Lac	WI	19,625	C
Marist College	NY	27,596	VC
Marlboro College	VT	29,055	VC+
Marquette Univ	WI	27,594	VC
Marylhurst Univ	OR	18,465	NC
Marymount College of Fordham Univ	NY	27,686	C
Mass College of Liberal Arts	MA	8,717	LC
McMurry Univ	TX	17,846	LC
Mercy College	NY	19,200	NC
Miami Univ	OH	15,033	HC
Mich State Univ	MI	11,933	VC
Middle Tenn State Univ	TN	8,534	C
Midwestern State Univ	TX	8,045	LC
Miss State Univ	MS	9,139	C
Molloy College	NY	15,180	C
Monmouth Univ	NJ	26,334	C
Montana State Univ-Northern	MT	8,600	NC
Mount St. Mary College	NY	21,270	C
Mount St. Mary's College	MD	28,400	C
Mountain State Univ	WV	10,212	NC
Naropa Univ	CO	23,364	SP
National Univ	CA	9,690	SP
New York Inst of Technology	NY	24,205	VC
Norfolk State Univ	VA	9,722	LC
N Car State Univ	NC	9,886	VC
Northeastern Univ	MA	35,650	HC
Northwest Christian College	OR	21,860	C
Northwest College	WA	18,854	C
Nyack College	NY	18,540	C
Ohio Dominican Univ	OH	22,700	C
Old Dominion Univ	VA	10,441	C
Piedmont College	GA	16,900	C
Plymouth State Univ	NH	12,298	LC
Prairie View A&M Univ	TX	9,418	NC
Radford Univ	VA	8,500	C
Rensselaer Polytechnic Inst	NY	37,579	HC+
Rhodes College	TN	26,466	HC+
Rochester College	MI	16,718	C
Russell Sage College	NY	26,811	C
Saginaw Valley State Univ	MI	11,055	C
St. Edward's Univ	TX	20,428	C
St. John Fisher College	NY	24,870	C
St. Lawrence Univ	NY	35,945	VC
St. Olaf College	MN	28,500	HC
Salisbury Univ	MD	12,664	VC
San Francisco State Univ	CA	12,070	C
Santa Clara Univ	CA	34,701	HC
Shawnee State Univ	OH	11,031	NC
Sheldon Jackson College	AK	14,940	LC
Shippensburg Univ of Pennsylvania	PA	10,826	C
Simon's Rock College of Bard	MA	36,580	HC
Sonoma State Univ	CA	10,421	C
S Dak School of Mines and Technology	SD	7,854	C+
Southeastern College	FL	11,648	LC
Southern Utah Univ	UT	8,194	C
Southwest Minn State Univ	MN	9,106	VC
SUNY at Potsdam	NY	12,160	C
SUNY/College at Brockport	NY	12,111	C
SUNY/College at Fredonia	NY	11,562	VC
SUNY/College at Oneonta	NY	11,870	VC
SUNY/College at Plattsburgh	NY	11,700	C
SUNY/Empire State College	NY	4,505	SP
SUNY/Univ at Binghamton	NY	12,787	HC
SUNY/Univ at Stony Brook	NY	12,763	HC
Stephen F. Austin State Univ	TX	7,552	C
Stonehill College	MA	30,752	HC
Tarleton State Univ	TX	7,576	C
Temple Univ	PA	15,912	C
Tenn State Univ	TN	9,048	LC
Tenn Wesleyan College	TN	16,540	C
Texas Southern Univ	TX	8,920	NC
Texas State Univ	TX	9,320	VC
Texas Wesleyan Univ	TX	16,245	C
Texas Woman's Univ	TX	7,804	LC
Touro College	NY	15,250	VC
Towson Univ	MD	12,694	VC
Trinity College	CT	38,040	HC+
Union College	NY	36,005	HC
Unity College	ME	19,845	LC
Univ of Alabama	AL	9,040	C+
Univ of Alaska Anchorage	AK	9,100	NC
Univ of Alaska Fairbanks	AK	9,295	C
Univ of Arizona	AZ	10,413	VC
Univ of Bridgeport	CT	25,924	LC
Univ of Calif at Berkeley	CA	15,563	MC
Univ of Calif at Los Angeles	CA	15,330	MC
Univ of Calif at Santa Barbara	CA	11,732	VC
Univ of Colo at Denver	CO	3,302	C
Univ of Delaware	DE	12,616	HC
Univ of Florida	FL	8,580	MC
Univ of Georgia	GA	8,656	VC
Univ of Hartford	CT	31,080	C
Univ of Houston	TX	9,818	C
Univ of Houston-Downtown	TX	2,594	NC
Univ of Idaho	ID	8,216	C
Univ of Maine	ME	12,080	C+
Univ of Maine at Augusta	ME	4,065	C
Univ of Maine at Farmington	ME	10,108	C
Univ of Maryland/Baltimore County	MD	14,668	VC+
Univ of Mass Amherst	MA	13,980	C+
Univ of Mass Dartmouth	MA	12,835	C
Univ of Memphis	TN	8,560	C
Univ of Minn/Duluth	MN	12,470	C
Univ of Nebr at Omaha	NE	8,080	C
Univ of Nevada/Las Vegas	NV	11,566	C
Univ of N Car at Asheville	NC	8,079	VC
Univ of N Car at Chapel Hill	NC	10,117	MC
Univ of N Dak	ND	8,390	C
Univ of North Texas	TX	7,629	C
Univ of Northern Colo	CO	8,987	C
Univ of Portland	OR	28,500	VC
Univ of PR/Rio Piedras	PR	5,730	
Univ of Richmond	VA	30,100	MC
Univ of St. Mary	KS	18,868	C
Univ of S Car at Aiken	SC	7,828	LC
Univ of S Car at Columbia	SC	10,048	VC
Univ of S Car at Spartanburg	SC	9,936	C+
Univ of Texas at Arlington	TX	7,192	LC
Univ of Texas at Dallas	TX	10,234	HC
Univ of Texas at El Paso	TX	5,799	NC
Univ of Texas at San Antonio	TX	9,088	NC
Univ of Texas-Pan American	TX	5,954	LC
Univ of Virginia	VA	11,740	MC
Vanderbilt Univ	TN	37,897	MC
Villa Julie College	MD	18,393	C
Virginia Intermont College	VA	19,800	C
Virginia State Univ	VA	10,358	C
Virginia Wesleyan College	VA	25,350	C
Washington and Lee Univ	VA	29,663	MC
Washington Univ in St. Louis	MO	38,293	MC
Wayland Baptist Univ	TX	11,919	NC
Wayne State College	NE	7,352	NC
Weber State Univ	UT	7,945	NC
Wesleyan College	GA	17,870	VC
West Liberty State College	WV	7,868	LC
West Texas A&M Univ	TX	7,533	C
West Virginia Univ	WV	9,370	C
Western Mich Univ	MI	12,031	C
Western Oregon Univ	OR	10,281	C
Westfield State College	MA	10,147	C
Wheaton College	IL	21,934	HC
William Woods Univ	MO	20,120	C
Wisc Lutheran College	WI	21,430	VC
Woodbury College	VT	12,060	LC
Worcester Polytechnic Inst	MA	37,404	HC

INTERIOR DESIGN

School	ST	$IS	SR
Adrian College	MI	21,950	C
American InterContinental Univ	GA	12,000	NC
Appalachian State Univ	NC	7,637	VC
Arcadia Univ	PA	29,890	C
Arizona State Univ-Main	AZ	10,048	C
Art Inst of Atlanta	GA	23,205	SP
Art Inst of Portland	OR	23,040	SP
Atlanta College of Art	GA	18,600	SP
Auburn Univ	AL	10,396	VC
Baker College of Flint	MI	7,720	NC
Bay Path College	MA	24,910	C
Baylor Univ	TX	23,864	VC
Becker College	MA	23,710	LC
Bethel College	IN	19,670	C
Boston Architectural Center	MA	6,405	SP
Bowling Green State Univ	OH	13,036	C
Brenau Univ Women's College	GA	21,800	C
Calif College of the Arts	CA	31,530	SP
Cal State, Fresno	CA	8,414	LC
Cazenovia College	NY	23,940	C
Central Missouri State Univ	MO	9,776	C
Chaminade Univ of Honolulu	HI	21,430	LC
College for Creative Studies	MI	23,298	SP
College of Mount St. Joseph	OH	22,785	C
Colo State Univ	CO	9,964	VC
Columbus College of Art and Design	OH	24,180	SP
Concordia Univ Wisc	WI	16,600	C
Converse College	SC	24,710	VC
Drexel Univ	PA	27,655	VC
East Carolina Univ	NC	8,671	C
Eastern Kentucky Univ	KY	7,708	C
Eastern Mich Univ	MI	11,478	C
Endicott College	MA	25,266	C+
Fashion Inst of Technology/SUNY	NY	11,169	C+
Florida International Univ	FL	9,912	VC
Florida State Univ	FL	9,028	HC
Georgia Southern Univ	GA	8,540	C
Harding Univ	AR	14,890	VC
High Point Univ	NC	22,480	C
Indiana State Univ	IN	10,719	LC
Indiana Univ Bloomington	IN	12,389	VC
Indiana Univ of Pennsylvania	PA	10,489	C
Iowa State Univ	IA	10,768	VC
Kansas State Univ	KS	8,728	VC
Kean Univ	NJ	14,479	C
Kendall College of Art and Design of Ferris State Univ	MI	10,784	SP
Kent State Univ	OH	12,932	C
La Roche College	PA	22,094	C
Lambuth Univ	TN	16,520	C
Lawrence Tech Univ	MI	20,487	C
Louisiana State Univ and A&M College	LA	9,126	VC
Maryland Inst College of Art	MD	30,890	SP
Marymount College of Fordham Univ	NY	27,686	C
Marymount Univ	VA	23,668	C
Maryville Univ of St. Louis	MO	22,090	VC
Mercyhurst College	PA	20,694	C
Meredith College	NC	23,065	C
Miami Univ	OH	15,033	HC
Mich State Univ	MI	11,933	VC
Middle Tenn State Univ	TN	8,534	C
Milwaukee Inst of Art and Design	WI	24,388	SP
Minn State Univ, Mankato	MN	8,803	LC
Miss College	MS	14,574	C
Moore College of Art and Design	PA	27,096	SP
Mount Ida College	MA	25,596	LC
Mount Mary College	WI	20,370	C
New York Inst of Technology	NY	24,205	VC
Newbury College	MA	23,450	C
N Dak State Univ	ND	8,435	C
Ohio State Univ	OH	13,080	VC+
Okla Christian Univ	OK	17,690	NC
Park Univ	MO	10,780	C+
Parsons School of Design	NY	32,242	SP
Philadelphia Univ	PA	27,354	C
Pratt Inst	NY	34,350	SP
Purdue Univ/West Lafayette	IN	12,560	VC
Rhode Island School of Design	RI	33,569	SP
Ringling School of Art and Design	FL	27,530	SP
Rochester Inst of Technology	NY	29,217	VC+
Salem College	NC	24,595	VC
Samford Univ	AL	18,648	VC
San Francisco State Univ	CA	12,070	C
San Jose State Univ	CA	8,187	C
Savannah College of Art and Design	GA	27,560	SP
School of the Art Inst of Chicago	IL	27,800	SP
School of Visual Arts	NY	30,200	SP
S Dak State Univ	SD	7,782	C
Southeast Missouri State Univ	MO	9,704	C
Southern Illinois Univ Carbondale	IL	10,407	C
Southwest Missouri State Univ	MO	8,918	C
Stephen F. Austin State Univ	TX	7,552	C
Suffolk Univ	MA	29,200	C
Syracuse Univ	NY	34,720	HC
Texas A&M Univ at Kingsville	TX	6,740	LC
Texas Christian Univ	TX	23,410	VC
Texas State Univ	TX	9,320	VC
Texas Tech Univ	TX	10,768	VC
Univ of Alabama	AL	9,040	C+
Univ of Arkansas	AR	9,855	VC
Univ of Bridgeport	CT	25,924	LC
Univ of Central Arkansas	AR	6,388	C
Univ of Central Okla	OK	9,434	C
Univ of Charleston	WV	23,620	C
Univ of Florida	FL	8,580	MC
Univ of Georgia	GA	8,656	VC
Univ of Houston	TX	9,818	C
Univ of Idaho	ID	8,216	C
Univ of Louisiana at Lafayette	LA	5,826	C
Univ of Mich/Ann Arbor	MI	13,864	HC+
Univ of Minn/Twin Cities	MN	13,160	VC
Univ of Nevada/Las Vegas	NV	11,566	C
Univ of Nevada/Reno	NV	9,792	C
Univ of New Haven	CT	28,650	C
Univ of North Alabama	AL	7,972	NC
Univ of N Car at Greensboro	NC	8,248	C
Univ of North Texas	TX	7,629	C
Univ of Okla	OK	9,226	VC
Univ of Oregon	OR	11,479	VC
Univ of Tenn at Knoxville	TN	8,214	C
Univ of Texas at Arlington	TX	7,192	LC
Univ of Texas at Austin	TX	10,630	HC
Univ of Texas at San Antonio	TX	9,088	NC
Univ of the Incarnate Word	TX	21,772	LC
Univ of Wisc/Madison	WI	8,262	VC
Univ of Wisc/Stevens Point	WI	8,116	VC
Utah State Univ	UT	7,371	C
Valdosta State Univ	GA	7,798	C
Virginia Polytechnic Inst and State Univ	VA	9,179	C
Washington State Univ	WA	11,334	C
Wentworth Inst of Technology	MA	23,000	C
West Virginia Univ	WV	9,370	C
Western Carolina Univ	NC	6,742	C
Western Kentucky Univ	KY	6,834	C
Western Mich Univ	MI	12,031	C
Woodbury Univ	CA	25,344	LC

INTERNATIONAL AGRICULTURE

School	ST	$IS	SR
Cornell Univ	NY	38,253	MC
Eastern Mennonite Univ	VA	22,990	C
Iowa State Univ	IA	10,768	VC
MidAmerica Nazarene Univ	KS	18,688	C
Tarleton State Univ	TX	7,576	C
Univ of Calif at Davis	CA	14,995	VC
Utah State Univ	UT	7,371	C

INTERNATIONAL BUSINESS MANAGEMENT

School	ST	$IS	SR
Adams State College	CO	7,468	C
Adrian College	MI	21,950	C
Albertson College of Idaho	ID	19,415	VC
Alliant International Univ	CA	23,640	C
Alma College	MI	25,566	VC
Alverno College	WI	18,898	C
American International College	MA	24,690	LC
American Univ	DC	34,585	VC+
Aquinas College	MI	21,894	C
Arkansas State Univ	AR	8,450	C
Assumption College	MA	29,375	C
Auburn Univ	AL	10,396	VC
Augsburg College	MN	25,298	C
Averett Univ	VA	23,010	LC
Avila Univ	MO	20,300	C
Baker Univ	KS	19,860	VC
Barry Univ	FL	24,100	LC
Bay Path College	MA	24,910	C
Baylor Univ	TX	23,864	VC
Bellarmine Univ	KY	24,110	VC
Belmont Abbey College	NC	23,742	C
Benedictine Univ	IL	23,840	C
Berkeley College	NY	21,545	LC
Berkeley College of New York City	NY	12,500	LC
Bethune-Cookman College	FL	16,480	LC
Blackburn College	IL	13,690	C
Boston Univ	MA	38,194	HC+
Bowling Green State Univ	OH	13,036	C
Bradley Univ	IL	22,910	VC
Brigham Young Univ/Hawaii	HI	7,240	VC+
Buena Vista Univ	IA	25,406	C
Butler Univ	IN	28,250	VC+
Caldwell College	NJ	24,060	LC
Calif State Polytechnic Univ, Pomona	CA	8,793	C+
Cal State, Fullerton	CA	6,648	C
Cal State, Long Beach	CA	8,476	C+
Cal State, Sacramento	CA	9,543	C
Cal State, San Bernardino	CA	15,238	LC
Campbell Univ	NC	18,268	VC
Canisius College	NY	28,163	C+
Cardinal Stritch Univ	WI	17,620	C
Carlow College	PA	21,334	C
Catawba College	NC	20,500	C
Central College	IA	21,206	C
Central Conn State Univ	CT	12,090	C
Central Washington Univ	WA	9,768	C
Champlain College	VT	22,030	C
Chatham College	PA	27,266	C+
Christopher Newport Univ	VA	8,862	VC
Clarion Univ of Pennsylvania	PA	11,272	LC
College of Charleston	SC	11,887	HC
College of New Jersey	NJ	15,950	MC
College of Notre Dame of Maryland	MD	27,700	C
College of Our Lady of the Elms	MA	20,644	C
College of Santa Fe	NM	25,293	C+
College of the Ozarks	MO	3,500	VC+
Concordia College: Moorhead	MN	22,460	VC+
Cornell College	IA	27,825	VC+

School	ST	$IS	SR
Cornerstone Univ and Grand Rapids Theological Seminary	MI	19,846	C
Creighton Univ	NE	26,748	VC+
Davenport Univ	MI	11,636	NC
Dickinson College	PA	35,825	HC
Dominican College	NY	24,810	LC
Dominican Univ	IL	23,610	C
Dominican Univ of Calif	CA	31,670	C
Dowling College	NY	23,870	LC
Drake Univ	IA	25,120	VC+
Drury Univ	MO	18,085	VC+
Duquesne Univ	PA	26,907	VC
D'Youville College	NY	21,080	C
Eastern Mennonite Univ	VA	22,990	C
Eastern Mich Univ	MI	11,478	C
Eckerd College	FL	28,744	C+
Elizabethtown College	PA	28,800	C
Elmhurst College	IL	24,630	C
Elmira College	NY	33,820	VC
Excelsior College	NY	975	SP
Fairfield Univ	CT	35,505	HC
Ferris State Univ	MI	12,512	C
Florida Atlantic Univ	FL	8,543	C
Florida International Univ	FL	9,912	VC
Florida Southern College	FL	23,592	C
Florida State Univ	FL	9,028	HC
Fordham Univ	NY	35,066	HC
Friends Univ	KS	15,962	LC
Gannon Univ	PA	23,260	C
Gardner-Webb Univ	NC	19,300	C
George Washington Univ	DC	41,030	MC
Georgetown College	KY	22,000	VC
Georgetown Univ	DC	38,242	MC
Georgia College and State Univ	GA	9,878	C
Golden Gate Univ	CA	11,232	NC
Goldey-Beacom College	DE	11,440	C
Graceland Univ	IA	19,550	C
Grand Canyon Univ	AZ	30,000	LC
Grand Valley State Univ	MI	11,022	VC
Grove City College	PA	14,228	HC
Gustavus Adolphus College	MN	27,120	VC+
Gwynedd-Mercy College	PA	24,225	C
Hamline Univ	MN	27,052	VC
Harding Univ	AR	14,890	VC
Hawaii Pacific Univ	HI	19,218	C
High Point Univ	NC	22,480	C
Hillsdale College	MI	22,450	HC
Hofstra Univ	NY	27,112	VC
Howard Univ	DC	16,505	C
Illinois State Univ	IL	10,944	C+
Illinois Wesleyan Univ	IL	30,380	HC+
Indiana Univ Bloomington	IN	12,389	VC
Indiana Univ of Pennsylvania	PA	10,489	C
Iona College	NY	27,988	VC
Iowa State Univ	IA	10,768	VC
Ithaca College	NY	31,730	HC
Jacksonville Univ	FL	24,040	C
James Madison Univ	VA	10,794	VC
Johnson and Wales Univ	RI	22,965	LC
Judson College	IL	22,050	LC
Juniata College	PA	29,080	VC
King's College	PA	26,990	C
Kutztown Univ of Pennsylvania	PA	10,786	C
La Roche College	PA	22,094	C
La Sierra Univ	CA	19,260	LC
Lake Erie College	OH	23,550	C
Lakeland College	WI	17,950	C
Lasell College	MA	26,000	C
Lenoir-Rhyne College	NC	19,186	C
Linfield College	OR	27,090	VC
Loras College	IA	24,233	C
Loyola Univ New Orleans	LA	31,036	VC+
Madonna Univ	MI	11,504	VC
Maine Maritime Academy	ME	12,380	C
Manhattan College	NY	27,400	VC
Mansfield Univ	PA	11,220	C
Marietta College	OH	27,047	C
Marquette Univ	WI	27,594	VC
Marymount College of Fordham Univ	NY	27,686	C
Marywood Univ	PA	26,050	C
Mass Maritime Academy	MA	10,472	C
Menlo College	CA	24,000	LC
Meredith College	NC	23,065	C
Merrimack College	MA	29,625	C
Messiah College	PA	25,890	VC+
Metropolitan State Univ	MN	3,852	SP
Millikin Univ	IL	25,555	C
Milwaukee School of Engineering	WI	28,479	VC+
Minn State Univ, Mankato	MN	8,803	LC
Minn State Univ, Moorehead	MN	7,000	LC
Minot State Univ	ND	6,602	LC
Missouri Southern State Univ	MO	8,316	C
Monmouth College	IL	23,600	C
Montclair State Univ	NJ	13,790	C
Moravian College	PA	28,903	VC
Mount Union College	OH	21,120	C
Muskingum College	OH	20,680	C
Nebr Wesleyan Univ	NE	21,197	C+
Neumann College	PA	23,890	LC
New Mexico State Univ	NM	7,932	C
New York Univ	NY	39,406	MC
Newbury College	MA	23,450	C
North Central College	IL	25,656	VC
North Park Univ	IL	24,030	C
Northeastern Univ	MA	35,650	HC
Northern State Univ	SD	7,117	LC
Northwest Missouri State Univ	MO	9,334	C
Northwest Nazarene Univ	ID	20,360	VC
Northwestern College	MN	22,820	C+
Northwood Univ	FL	21,040	C
Northwood Univ	MI	20,265	LC
Northwood Univ	TX	20,135	LC
Notre Dame de Namur Univ	CA	26,932	LC
Ohio Dominican Univ	OH	22,700	C
Ohio Northern Univ	OH	27,765	VC
Ohio State Univ	OH	13,080	VC+
Ohio Univ	OH	14,448	C
Ohio Wesleyan Univ	OH	32,550	VC+
Okla State Univ	OK	9,216	VC
Old Dominion Univ	VA	10,441	C
Olivet College	MI	19,984	C+
Oral Roberts Univ	OK	18,490	C
Pace Univ	NY	28,652	VC
Palm Beach Atlantic Univ	FL	20,690	C
Penn State Univ/Univ Park Campus	PA	15,646	HC
Pepperdine Univ	CA	32,830	VC
Philadelphia Univ	PA	27,354	C
Quinnipiac Univ	CT	30,570	VC
Ramapo College of New Jersey	NJ	15,203	VC
Regis Univ	CO	25,740	C+
Rider Univ	NJ	30,900	C
Rochester Inst of Technology	NY	29,217	VC+
Roger Williams Univ	RI	30,296	C
Rollins College	FL	34,300	VC
Sacred Heart Univ	CT	29,178	C
St. Ambrose Univ	IA	22,800	C
St. Augustine's College	NC	12,990	LC
St. Cloud State Univ	MN	8,362	C
St. Edward's Univ	TX	20,428	C
St. Joseph's Univ	PA	33,590	VC
St. Louis Univ	MO	29,780	VC+
St. Mary's Univ of Minn	MN	21,535	C
St. Mary's Univ of San Antonio	TX	22,444	C
St. Norbert College	WI	25,810	C
St. Peter's College	NJ	22,292	LC
St. Thomas Univ	FL	21,400	LC
St. Vincent College	PA	25,530	VC
St. Xavier Univ	IL	23,144	C
Salem College	NC	24,595	VC
San Diego State Univ	CA	10,321	C
San Francisco State Univ	CA	12,070	C
San Jose State Univ	CA	8,187	C
Seattle Univ	WA	24,183	VC
Seton Hill Univ	PA	24,930	C
Simpson College	IA	23,658	C+
Slippery Rock Univ of Pennsylvania	PA	10,343	LC
Southern Adventist Univ	TN	17,080	C
Southern New Hampshire Univ	NH	26,242	C
Spring Hill College	AL	25,868	VC
SUNY/College at Brockport	NY	12,111	C
Stephen F. Austin State Univ	TX	7,552	C
Stetson Univ	FL	29,495	VC
Strayer Univ	DC	8,789	SP
Suffolk Univ	MA	29,200	C
Taylor Univ	IN	23,820	VC+
Temple Univ	PA	15,912	C
Texas A&M Univ at Galveston	TX	9,948	C+
Texas Christian Univ	TX	23,410	VC
Texas Tech Univ	TX	10,768	VC
Texas Wesleyan Univ	TX	16,245	C
Thiel College	PA	20,970	C
Thomas Edison State College	NJ	3,325	SP
Trinity International Univ	IL	22,980	C+
Univ of Akron	OH	13,134	NC
Univ of Arkansas	AR	9,855	VC
Univ of Bridgeport	CT	25,924	LC
Univ of Colo at Boulder	CO	10,774	VC
Univ of Dayton	OH	24,850	VC
Univ of Denver	CO	32,148	VC
Univ of Evansville	IN	24,190	VC
Univ of Findlay	OH	23,962	NC
Univ of Georgia	GA	8,656	VC
Univ of Hawaii at Manoa	HI	9,565	VC
Univ of Indianapolis	IN	22,560	VC
Univ of La Verne	CA	28,600	C
Univ of Memphis	TN	8,560	C
Univ of Miami	FL	34,608	HC
Univ of Miss	MS	7,666	C
Univ of Nebr at Lincoln	NE	9,975	C+
Univ of Nevada/Las Vegas	NV	11,566	C
Univ of New Haven	CT	28,650	C
Univ of New Mexico	NM	9,223	C
Univ of N Car at Charlotte	NC	8,185	C
Univ of N Car at Greensboro	NC	8,248	C
Univ of Okla	OK	9,226	VC
Univ of Portland	OR	28,500	VC
Univ of Rio Grande	OH	8,728	NC
Univ of St. Thomas	MN	26,918	VC
Univ of San Francisco	CA	34,700	VC
Univ of Scranton	PA	30,836	VC
Univ of Southern Miss	MS	8,324	LC
Univ of Tampa	FL	23,982	VC
Univ of Texas at San Antonio	TX	9,088	NC
Univ of Texas-Pan American	TX	5,954	LC
Univ of the Incarnate Word	TX	21,772	LC
Univ of Tulsa	OK	22,090	VC+
Univ of Washington	WA	10,361	VC
Univ of Wisc/La Crosse	WI	8,991	VC
Utah State Univ	UT	7,371	C
Valparaiso Univ	IN	26,118	VC+
Vanguard Univ of Southern Calif	CA	22,208	C
Wartburg College	IA	21,165	VC
Washington and Jefferson College	PA	29,570	VC
Washington State Univ	WA	11,334	C
Washington Univ in St. Louis	MO	38,293	MC
Waynesburg College	PA	19,370	C
Webber International Univ	FL	16,510	C
Wesleyan College	GA	17,870	VC
Western Carolina Univ	NC	6,742	C
Western New Mexico Univ	NM	5,950	LC
Western Washington Univ	WA	10,119	VC
Westminster College	MO	18,150	C+
Westminster College	PA	22,960	C
Wheeling Jesuit Univ	WV	22,660	C
Whitworth College	WA	26,428	VC+
Wichita State Univ	KS	8,092	C
Widener Univ	PA	27,020	C
William Jewell College	MO	21,320	VC
Woodbury Univ	CA	25,344	LC
Xavier Univ	OH	26,850	VC+
York College of Pennsylvania	PA	14,500	VC

INTERNATIONAL ECONOMICS

School	ST	$IS	SR
Albertson College of Idaho	ID	19,415	VC
Assumption College	MA	29,375	C
Austin College	TX	24,747	HC
Blackburn College	IL	13,690	C
Carthage College	WI	25,000	C
Catholic Univ of America	DC	34,248	VC
College of St. Catherine	MN	24,010	VC
Colo College	CO	36,860	HC
Franklin Pierce College	NH	28,980	LC
Georgia Southern Univ	GA	8,540	C
Hiram College	OH	28,234	VC
Kent State Univ	OH	12,932	C
La Salle Univ	PA	31,260	VC
Lafayette College	PA	35,746	MC
Louisiana State Univ and A&M College	LA	9,126	VC
Middlebury College	VT	38,100	MC
Midwestern State Univ	TX	8,045	LC
Pontifical Catholic Univ of PR/Ponce	PR	7,298	
St. Norbert College	WI	25,810	C
Southwestern Adventist Univ	TX	14,798	C
SUNY at Oswego	NY	12,650	C
State Univ of West Georgia	GA	7,622	C
Suffolk Univ	MA	29,200	C
Texas Christian Univ	TX	23,410	VC
Texas Tech Univ	TX	10,768	VC
Univ of Bridgeport	CT	25,924	LC
Univ of Calif at Los Angeles	CA	15,330	MC
Univ of Calif at Santa Cruz	CA	16,505	VC
Univ of Puget Sound	WA	31,760	HC
Valparaiso Univ	IN	26,118	VC+
Washington Univ in St. Louis	MO	38,293	MC
Youngstown State Univ	OH	11,148	NC

INTERNATIONAL PUBLIC SERVICE

School	ST	$IS	SR
Baylor Univ	TX	23,864	VC
Christopher Newport Univ	VA	8,862	VC
Lehigh Univ	PA	37,570	HC+
Valparaiso Univ	IN	26,118	VC+

INTERNATIONAL RELATIONS

School	ST	$IS	SR
Abilene Christian Univ	TX	18,370	VC
Agnes Scott College	GA	28,230	HC
Alliant International Univ	CA	23,640	C
Alverno College	WI	18,898	C
American International College	MA	24,690	LC
Augsburg College	MN	25,298	C
Augustana College	SD	21,998	VC
Baldwin-Wallace College	OH	24,678	C
Beloit College	WI	29,864	HC
Bennington College	VT	35,910	HC
Bethel College	MN	25,180	VC
Birmingham-Southern College	AL	25,364	VC+
Boston Univ	MA	38,194	HC+
Brigham Young Univ	UT	8,504	HC
Brown Univ	RI	38,174	MC
Bucknell Univ	PA	35,262	HC+
Cal State, Chico	CA	8,598	LC
Cal State, Sacramento	CA	9,543	C
Canisius College	NY	28,163	C+
Capital Univ	OH	26,550	C
Carleton College	MN	34,395	MC
Carroll College	MT	20,576	VC
Carroll College	WI	22,740	C
Centre College	KY	27,300	HC
Chaminade Univ of Honolulu	HI	21,430	LC
Chatham College	PA	27,266	C+
Christopher Newport Univ	VA	8,862	VC
CUNY/Herbert H. Lehman College	NY	3,320	LC
CUNY/Hunter College	NY	6,729	C+
Claremont McKenna College	CA	36,880	MC
Clark Univ	MA	32,115	VC
Cleveland State Univ	OH	12,308	LC
Colgate Univ	NY	37,095	MC
College of Notre Dame of Maryland	MD	27,700	C
College of St. Catherine	MN	24,010	VC
College of William and Mary	VA	12,224	MC
College of Wooster	OH	31,300	HC
Concordia College: Moorhead	MN	22,460	VC+
Conn College	CT	37,900	MC
Cornell College	IA	27,825	VC+
Dana College	NE	20,280	C
Dominican Univ	IL	23,610	C
Drake Univ	IA	25,120	VC+
Duquesne Univ	PA	26,907	VC
Eastern Mich Univ	MI	11,478	C
Eastern Washington Univ	WA	9,012	C
Eckerd College	FL	28,744	C+
Edgewood College	WI	20,520	C
Florida International Univ	FL	9,912	VC
Florida State Univ	FL	9,028	HC
George Washington Univ	DC	41,030	MC
Georgetown Univ	DC	38,242	MC
Georgia Inst of Technology	GA	10,340	HC+
Gettysburg College	PA	35,646	HC
Goucher College	MD	32,650	HC
Grand Valley State Univ	MI	11,022	VC
Hamilton College	NY	37,560	MC
Hamline Univ	MN	27,052	VC
Hampshire College	MA	37,037	HC
Hawaii Pacific Univ	HI	19,218	C
Hendrix College	AR	20,970	VC+
Hobart and William Smith Colleges	NY	36,536	HC
Hope College	MI	25,340	VC
Houghton College	NY	23,984	VC
Illinois College	IL	19,100	VC
Immaculata Univ	PA	25,200	C
Iowa State Univ	IA	10,768	VC
Juniata College	PA	29,080	VC
Kalamazoo College	MI	26,955	HC+
Kent State Univ	OH	12,932	C
Knox College	IL	30,294	VC+
Lafayette College	PA	35,746	MC
Lake Forest College	IL	30,270	VC
Lambuth Univ	TN	16,520	C
Lawrence Univ	WI	30,900	HC
Lehigh Univ	PA	37,570	HC+
Lewis and Clark College	OR	30,620	VC+
Lincoln Univ	PA	13,320	C+
Lynchburg College	VA	26,815	C
Macalester College	MN	31,944	MC
Marquette Univ	WI	27,594	VC
Marshall Univ	WV	9,116	C
Mary Baldwin College	VA	24,939	C
Mary Washington College	VA	10,166	HC
Maryville College	TN	25,960	VC
McKendree College	IL	21,120	VC
Miami Univ	OH	15,033	HC
Middle Tenn State Univ	TN	8,534	C
Middlebury College	VT	38,100	MC
Mills College	CA	33,371	VC
Morehouse College	GA	22,728	C
Mount Holyoke College	MA	37,918	HC+
Muskingum College	OH	20,680	C
New York Univ	NY	39,406	MC
North Park Univ	IL	24,030	C
Northeastern Univ	MA	35,650	HC
Northern Arizona Univ	AZ	9,002	C
Occidental College	CA	35,922	HC
Ohio Wesleyan Univ	OH	32,550	VC+
Oral Roberts Univ	OK	18,490	C
Penn State Univ/Univ Park Campus	PA	15,646	HC
Pitzer College	CA	37,590	HC
Pomona College	CA	33,960	MC
Princeton Univ	NJ	36,649	MC
Principia College	IL	25,044	C+
Purdue Univ/Calumet	IN	6,630	NC
Randolph-Macon College	VA	27,190	C

ST = STATE $IS = IN-STATE COSTS SR = SELECTOR RATING

School	ST	$IS	SR
Randolph-Macon Woman's College	VA	28,430	VC+
Roanoke College	VA	27,393	C
Rockhurst Univ	MO	22,960	C+
Rollins College	FL	34,300	VC
St. Cloud State Univ	MN	8,362	C
St. Edward's Univ	TX	20,428	C
St. Joseph's Univ	PA	33,590	VC
St. Mary's Univ of San Antonio	TX	22,444	C
St. Thomas Univ	FL	21,400	LC
Salem College	NC	24,595	VC
Samford Univ	AL	18,648	VC
San Francisco State Univ	CA	12,070	C
Seton Hall Univ	NJ	30,130	VC
Shaw Univ	NC	14,882	C+
Shawnee State Univ	OH	11,031	NC
Simmons College	MA	33,000	VC
Simpson College	IA	23,658	C+
Southern Illinois Univ Carbondale	IL	10,407	C
Southwestern Adventist Univ	TX	14,798	C
Stanford Univ	CA	37,612	MC
SUNY/College at Geneseo	NY	11,330	HC
SUNY/Univ at New Paltz	NY	11,565	VC
Sweet Briar College	VA	27,940	C
Syracuse Univ	NY	34,720	HC
Texas State Univ	TX	9,320	VC
Trinity Univ	TX	26,466	HC+
Troy State Univ	AL	7,696	C
Tufts Univ	MA	38,233	MC
Univ of Arkansas	AR	9,855	VC
Univ of Calif at Davis	CA	14,995	VC
Univ of Colo at Boulder	CO	10,774	VC
Univ of Delaware	DE	12,616	HC
Univ of Idaho	ID	8,216	C
Univ of Indianapolis	IN	22,560	VC
Univ of Minn/Twin Cities	MN	13,160	VC
Univ of Nebr at Lincoln	NE	9,975	C+
Univ of Nevada/Reno	NV	9,792	C
Univ of Northern Colo	CO	8,987	C
Univ of Pennsylvania	PA	37,960	MC
Univ of Redlands	CA	32,576	VC
Univ of San Diego	CA	33,156	HC
Univ of Scranton	PA	30,836	VC
Univ of S Car at Columbia	SC	10,048	VC
Univ of South Florida	FL	9,454	C
Univ of Southern Calif	CA	37,459	MC
Univ of the Pacific	CA	31,090	VC
Univ of Toledo	OH	12,479	NC
Univ of Virginia	VA	11,740	MC
Univ of Washington	WA	10,361	VC
Univ of Wisc/Madison	WI	8,262	VC
Ursinus College	PA	34,400	VC
Utah State Univ	UT	7,371	C
Virginia Wesleyan College	VA	25,350	C
Wartburg College	IA	21,165	VC
Washington Univ in St. Louis	MO	38,293	MC
Webster Univ	MO	21,848	VC
Wellesley College	MA	36,516	MC
Wesleyan College	GA	17,870	VC
Westminster College	PA	22,960	C
Wheaton College	MA	36,330	HC
Widener Univ	PA	27,020	C
William Jewell College	MO	21,320	VC
Winona State Univ	MN		C
Wittenberg Univ	OH	31,316	VC
Wright State Univ	OH	11,490	LC
Xavier Univ	OH	26,850	VC+

INTERNATIONAL STUDIES

School	ST	$IS	SR
Adrian College	MI	21,950	C
Albion College	MI	25,224	VC
Allegheny College	PA	30,280	VC
American Univ	DC	34,585	VC+
Aquinas College	MI	21,894	C
Arkansas Tech Univ	AR	7,299	C
Ashland Univ	OH	24,464	C
Assumption College	MA	29,375	C
Auburn Univ Montgomery	AL	9,020	NC
Augustana College	SD	21,998	VC
Austin College	TX	24,747	HC
Azusa Pacific Univ	CA	24,720	VC
Baldwin-Wallace College	OH	24,678	C
Barry Univ	FL	24,100	LC
Bellarmine Univ	KY	24,110	VC
Benedictine Univ	IL	23,840	C
Bentley College	MA	33,904	VC
Berry College	GA	21,410	VC
Bethany College	WV	19,845	VC
Bethel College	IN	19,670	C
Bethune-Cookman College	FL	16,480	LC
Bowling Green State Univ	OH	13,036	C
Bradley Univ	IL	22,910	VC
Brenau Univ Women's College	GA	21,800	C
Bridgewater College	VA	25,150	C
Brigham Young Univ/Hawaii	HI	7,240	VC+
Bryant College	RI	31,004	VC
Butler Univ	IN	28,250	VC+
Calif Lutheran Univ	CA	27,600	LC
Cal State, Hayward	CA	8,871	LC
Cal State, Long Beach	CA	8,762	C+
Cal State, Monterey Bay	CA	6,683	LC
Cal State, Stanislaus	CA	9,874	C
Calif Univ of Pennsylvania	PA	10,388	C
Calvin College	MI	22,615	NC
Case Western Reserve Univ	OH	32,002	MC
Cedarville Univ	OH	19,954	VC
Centenary College	NJ	25,370	LC
Central College	IA	21,206	C
Central Conn State Univ	CT	12,090	C
CUNY/City College	NY	4,230	C+
CUNY/College of Staten Island	NY	4,308	NC
Clark Univ	MA	32,115	VC
Colby College	ME	37,570	MC
College of New Jersey	NJ	15,950	MC
College of New Rochelle	NY	21,800	C
College of Our Lady of the Elms	MA	20,644	C
College of St. Elizabeth	NJ	25,460	C
College of William and Mary	VA	12,224	MC
Columbia Univ/Barnard College	NY	36,990	MC
Concordia College	NY	19,200	VC
Denison Univ	OH	33,050	HC
DePaul Univ	IL	27,580	VC
Dickinson College	PA	35,825	HC
Doane College	NE	20,000	C
Dominican Univ of Calif	CA	31,670	C
Drexel Univ	PA	27,655	VC
Drury Univ	MO	18,085	VC+
Earlham College	IN	29,976	VC+
Elmira College	NY	33,820	VC
Elon Univ	NC	22,240	VC
Emmanuel College	MA	27,600	C+
Emory & Henry College	VA	21,950	C
Emory Univ	GA	36,872	MC
Endicott College	MA	25,266	C+
Evangel Univ	MO	15,435	C
Fairfield Univ	CT	35,505	HC
Fairleigh Dickinson Univ/ Metropolitan Campus	NJ	28,584	C
Ferrum College	VA	21,240	LC
Fordham Univ	NY	35,066	HC
Francis Marion Univ	SC	9,364	C
Frostburg State Univ	MD	11,114	C
Gannon Univ	PA	23,260	C
George Fox Univ	OR	26,110	VC
Georgia Southern Univ	GA	8,540	C
Gonzaga Univ	WA	26,766	HC
Gordon College	MA	25,982	VC+
Goucher College	MD	32,650	HC
Graceland Univ	IA	19,550	C
Guilford College	NC	24,960	VC
Hampshire College	MA	37,037	HC
Hanover College	IN	25,200	VC
Harding Univ	AR	14,890	VC
Hawaii Pacific Univ	HI	19,218	C
Heidelberg College	OH	20,266	NC
High Point Univ	NC	22,480	C
Hollins Univ	VA	27,965	VC
Huntingdon College	AL	18,400	VC
Idaho State Univ	ID	8,128	C
Illinois Wesleyan Univ	IL	30,380	HC+
Indiana Univ Bloomington	IN	12,389	VC
Indiana Univ of Pennsylvania	PA	10,489	C
Indiana Univ-Purdue Univ Indianapolis	IN	8,257	LC
Iona College	NY	27,988	VC
Jacksonville Univ	FL	24,040	C
James Madison Univ	VA	10,794	VC
John Brown Univ	AR	15,080	VC
Johns Hopkins Univ	MD	38,372	MC
Juniata College	PA	29,080	VC
Kalamazoo College	MI	26,955	HC+
Kennesaw State Univ	GA	2,724	C
Kenyon College	OH	35,370	HC+
La Roche College	PA	22,094	C
Le Moyne College	NY	26,400	VC
Lees-McRae College	NC	17,106	LC
Liberty Univ	VA	17,220	C
Lindenwood Univ	MO	17,050	VC
Lock Haven Univ of Pennsylvania	PA	11,098	LC
LIU/C.W. Post Campus	NY	28,282	C
Loras College	IA	24,233	C
Louisiana State Univ and A&M College	LA	9,126	VC
Lycoming College	PA	27,589	C+
Manhattanville College	NY	32,420	C+
Mansfield Univ	PA	11,220	C
Marietta College	OH	27,047	C
Marlboro College	VT	29,055	VC+
Mars Hill College	NC	18,600	LC
Marymount College of Fordham Univ	NY	27,686	C
Marymount Manhattan College	NY	27,292	C
Meredith College	NC	23,065	C
Methodist College	NC	19,526	C
Miami Univ	OH	15,033	HC
Middlebury College	VT	38,100	MC
Millersville Univ of Pennsylvania	PA	11,269	C
Millikin Univ	IL	25,555	C
Missouri Southern State Univ	MO	8,316	C
Monmouth College	IL	23,600	C
Mount Mary College	WI	20,370	C
Mount Mercy College	IA	21,400	C
Mount St. Mary College	NY	21,270	C
Mount St. Mary's College	MD	28,400	C
Mount Union College	OH	21,120	C
Muhlenberg College	PA	31,485	HC
Murray State Univ	KY	7,816	VC
National Univ	CA	9,690	SP
Nazareth College of Rochester	NY	24,936	VC
Nebr Wesleyan Univ	NE	21,197	C+
New College of Florida	FL	8,906	HC+
Niagara Univ	NY	25,050	C
N Dak State Univ	ND	8,435	C
Northern Kentucky Univ	KY	6,352	NC
Northern Mich Univ	MI	10,834	C
Northwest Christian College	OR	21,860	C
Northwest Nazarene Univ	ID	20,360	VC
Northwestern Univ	IL	37,491	MC
Norwich Univ	VT	21,064	LC
Oakwood College	AL	14,904	C
Oglethorpe Univ	GA	26,000	VC
Ohio Northern Univ	OH	27,765	VC
Ohio State Univ	OH	13,080	VC+
Ohio Univ	OH	14,448	C
Old Dominion Univ	VA	10,441	C
Oral Roberts Univ	OK	18,490	C
Otterbein College	OH	26,085	C
Pacific Lutheran Univ	WA	25,715	VC
Pepperdine Univ	CA	32,830	VC
Point Park Univ	PA	21,840	C
Portland State Univ	OR	12,453	C
Queens Univ of Charlotte	NC	21,840	C
Ramapo College of New Jersey	NJ	15,203	VC
Randolph-Macon College	VA	27,190	C
Rhodes College	TN	26,466	HC+
Ripon College	WI	24,995	VC
Roosevelt Univ	IL	22,580	VC
Russell Sage College	NY	26,811	C
Sacred Heart Univ	CT	29,178	C
Saginaw Valley State Univ	MI	11,055	C
St. Francis Univ	PA	25,876	LC
St. John Fisher College	NY	24,870	C
St. Joseph College	CT	29,685	C
St. Joseph's College	IN	24,250	C
St. Lawrence Univ	NY	35,945	VC
St. Leo Univ	FL	20,600	C
St. Louis Univ	MO	29,780	VC+
St. Mary-of-the-Woods College	IN	23,280	C
St. Mary's Univ of San Antonio	TX	22,444	C
St. Norbert College	WI	25,810	C
Salisbury Univ	MD	12,664	VC
Seattle Univ	WA	24,183	VC
Seton Hill Univ	PA	24,930	C
Shaw Univ	NC	14,882	C+
Sonoma State Univ	CA	10,421	C
Southern Adventist Univ	TN	17,080	C
Southern Methodist Univ	TX	34,210	HC
Southern Nazarene Univ	OK	14,634	NC
Southern Oregon Univ	OR	10,362	C
Southern Polytechnic State Univ	GA	7,620	VC
Southwestern Univ	TX	25,410	HC
Spring Hill College	AL	25,868	VC
SUNY at Oswego	NY	12,650	C
SUNY/College at Brockport	NY	12,111	C
SUNY/College at Cortland	NY	12,095	C
SUNY/College at Old Westbury	NY	12,784	C
SUNY/College at Oneonta	NY	11,870	VC
State Univ of West Georgia	GA	7,622	C
Stephens College	MO	24,260	C+
Stetson Univ	FL	29,495	VC
Stonehill College	MA	30,752	HC
Susquehanna Univ	PA	29,990	VC
Tabor College	KS	19,500	NC
Taylor Univ	IN	23,820	VC+
Texas A&M Univ	TX	11,081	HC
Texas State Univ	TX	9,320	VC
Texas Wesleyan Univ	TX	16,245	C
Thomas College	ME	19,960	LC
Thomas More College	KY	21,350	C
Tiffin Univ	OH	19,490	LC
Towson Univ	MD	12,694	VC
Trinity College	CT	38,040	HC+
Trinity College	DC	24,150	LC
Union College	NE	17,130	C
United States Air Force Academy	CO		HC+
United States Military Academy	NY		MC
Univ of Alabama	AL	9,040	C+
Univ of Alabama at Birmingham	AL	12,901	C
Univ of Arkansas at Little Rock	AR	5,637	NC
Univ of Bridgeport	CT	25,924	LC
Univ of Calif at Irvine	CA	19,808	HC
Univ of Calif at Los Angeles	CA	15,330	MC
Univ of Calif at San Diego	CA	14,127	HC
Univ of Chicago	IL	35,087	MC
Univ of Cincinnati	OH	14,736	C
Univ of Dayton	OH	24,850	VC
Univ of Denver	CO	32,148	VC
Univ of Evansville	IN	24,190	VC
Univ of Findlay	OH	23,962	NC
Univ of Hartford	CT	31,080	C
Univ of Illinois at Urbana-Champaign	IL	11,316	HC+
Univ of Kansas	KS	8,923	VC
Univ of La Verne	CA	28,600	C
Univ of Maine	ME	12,080	C+
Univ of Maine at Farmington	ME	10,108	C
Univ of Maine at Presque Isle	ME	9,155	LC
Univ of Memphis	TN	8,560	C
Univ of Miami	FL	34,608	HC
Univ of Mich/Dearborn	MI	6,843	VC
Univ of Minn/Duluth	MN	12,470	C
Univ of Miss	MS	7,666	C
Univ of Missouri/Columbia	MO	13,782	VC
Univ of Nebr at Kearney	NE	8,286	NC
Univ of New Hampshire	NH	14,828	VC
Univ of N Car at Chapel Hill	NC	10,117	MC
Univ of N Car at Charlotte	NC	8,185	C
Univ of N Dak	ND	8,390	C
Univ of Okla	OK	9,226	VC
Univ of Oregon	OR	11,479	VC
Univ of Richmond	VA	30,100	MC
Univ of St. Mary	KS	18,868	C
Univ of St. Thomas	MN	26,918	VC
Univ of St. Thomas	TX	21,952	VC
Univ of South Alabama	AL	7,760	LC
Univ of S Dak	SD	7,710	C+
Univ of Southern Miss	MS	8,324	LC
Univ of Tampa	FL	23,982	VC
Univ of Tenn at Martin	TN	7,748	C
Univ of the Pacific	CA	31,090	VC
Univ of Virginia's College at Wise	VA	10,116	C
Univ of Wisc/Oshkosh	WI	6,130	LC
Univ of Wisc/Parkside	WI	6,160	LC
Univ of Wisc/Platteville	WI	8,450	C
Univ of Wisc/Stevens Point	WI	8,116	VC
Univ of Wisc/Superior	WI	7,051	C+
Univ of Wisc/Whitewater	WI	8,626	C
Univ of Wyoming	WY	8,636	C
Utica College	NY	28,340	C
Vassar College	NY	37,030	MC
Villanova Univ	PA	35,050	HC
Virginia Military Inst	VA	9,968	C+
Virginia Polytechnic Inst and State Univ	VA	9,179	C
Walsh Univ	OH	20,890	C
Warren Wilson College	NC	21,794	VC
Washington College	MD	30,540	VC
Washington Univ in St. Louis	MO	38,293	MC
Wayne State Univ	MI	11,774	C
Webster Univ	MO	21,848	VC
Wells College	NY	21,122	VC
West Virginia Univ	WV	9,370	C
West Virginia Wesleyan College	WV	22,920	C
Western Mich Univ	MI	12,031	C
Western New England College	MA	28,924	C
Western Oregon Univ	OR	10,281	C
Westminster College	MO	18,150	C+
Wheeling Jesuit Univ	WV	22,660	C
Whittier College	CA	29,108	C
Whitworth College	WA	26,428	VC+
Wilkes Univ	PA	28,060	C
Willamette Univ	OR	32,032	VC+
William Woods Univ	MO	20,120	C
Wilson College	PA	23,912	C

INTERPRETER FOR THE DEAF

School	ST	$IS	SR
Bethel College	IN	19,670	C
Bloomsburg Univ of Pennsylvania	PA	10,844	C
Columbia College Chicago	IL	25,108	LC
Gallaudet Univ	DC	16,554	SP
Gardner-Webb Univ	NC	19,300	C
MacMurray College	IL	20,005	LC
Madonna Univ	MI	11,504	VC
Maryville College	TN	25,960	VC
Mount Aloysius College	PA	19,120	LC
Northeastern Univ	MA	35,650	HC
Rochester Inst of Technology	NY	29,217	VC+
Univ of Arkansas at Little Rock	AR	5,637	NC
Univ of New Mexico	NM	9,223	C
Univ of Rochester	NY	32,979	HC
Western Oregon Univ	OR	10,281	C
William Woods Univ	MO	20,120	C

INVESTMENTS AND SECURITIES

School	ST	$IS	SR
Campbell Univ	NC	18,268	VC
CUNY/Baruch College	NY	3,275	VC+

ST = STATE $IS = IN-STATE COSTS   SR = SELECTOR RATING

School	ST	$IS	SR
Duquesne Univ	PA	26,907	VC
Univ of Miss	MS	7,666	C

ISLAMIC STUDIES

School	ST	$IS	SR
Brandeis Univ	MA	38,198	MC
Ohio State Univ	OH	13,080	VC+
Univ of Calif at Santa Barbara	CA	11,732	VC
Univ of Mich/Ann Arbor	MI	13,864	HC+
Univ of Texas at Austin	TX	10,630	HC
Washington Univ in St. Louis	MO	38,293	MC

ITALIAN

School	ST	$IS	SR
Arizona State Univ-Main	AZ	10,048	C
Bard College	NY	37,352	HC+
Bennington College	VT	35,910	HC
Boston College	MA	33,284	MC
Boston Univ	MA	38,194	HC+
Brigham Young Univ	UT	8,504	HC
Bryn Mawr College	PA	36,890	HC+
Central Conn State Univ	CT	12,090	C
CUNY/Brooklyn College	NY	4,353	C+
CUNY/Herbert H. Lehman College	NY	3,320	LC
CUNY/Hunter College	NY	6,729	C+
CUNY/Queens College	NY	4,362	C
College of the Holy Cross	MA	36,451	MC
Columbia Univ/Barnard College	NY	36,990	MC
Columbia Univ/School of General Studies	NY	35,000	C
Conn College	CT	37,900	MC
Cornell Univ	NY	38,253	MC
Dartmouth College	NH	37,770	MC
DePaul Univ	IL	27,580	VC
Dominican Univ	IL	23,610	C
Fairfield Univ	CT	35,505	HC
Florida Atlantic Univ	FL	8,543	C
Florida State Univ	FL	9,028	HC
Fordham Univ	NY	35,066	HC
Georgetown Univ	DC	38,242	MC
Harvard Univ/Harvard College	MA	37,928	MC
Haverford College	PA	37,900	MC
Hofstra Univ	NY	27,112	VC
Indiana Univ Bloomington	IN	12,389	VC
Iona College	NY	27,988	VC
Johns Hopkins Univ	MD	38,372	MC
La Salle Univ	PA	31,260	VC
Lake Erie College	OH	23,550	C
LIU/C.W. Post Campus	NY	28,282	C
Loyola Univ Chicago	IL	31,164	VC
Marlboro College	VT	29,055	VC+
Middlebury College	VT	38,100	MC
Montclair State Univ	NJ	13,790	C
Mount Holyoke College	MA	37,918	HC+
Nazareth College of Rochester	NY	24,936	VC
New York Univ	NY	39,406	MC
Northwestern Univ	IL	37,491	MC
Ohio State Univ	OH	13,080	VC+
Penn State Univ/Univ Park Campus	PA	15,646	HC
Providence College	RI	30,604	HC
Rutgers, The State Univ of New Jersey/New Brunswick/Piscataway Campus	NJ	15,800	HC
St. John's Univ	NY	30,180	C
San Francisco State Univ	CA	12,070	C
Santa Clara Univ	CA	34,701	HC
Sarah Lawrence College	NY	41,218	HC
Scripps College	CA	35,700	HC+
Seton Hall Univ	NJ	30,130	VC
Smith College	MA	37,034	HC+
Southern Conn State Univ	CT	10,310	C
Stanford Univ	CA	37,612	MC
SUNY/College at Buffalo	NY	8,025	C
SUNY/Univ at Albany	NY	12,951	HC
SUNY/Univ at Binghamton	NY	12,787	HC
SUNY/Univ at Buffalo	NY	12,563	VC
Temple Univ	PA	15,912	C
Trinity College	CT	38,040	HC+
Tulane Univ	LA	37,451	HC+
Univ of Arizona	AZ	10,413	VC
Univ of Calif at Berkeley	CA	15,563	MC
Univ of Calif at Davis	CA	14,995	VC
Univ of Calif at Los Angeles	CA	15,330	MC
Univ of Colo at Boulder	CO	10,774	VC
Univ of Delaware	DE	12,616	HC
Univ of Denver	CO	32,148	VC
Univ of Georgia	GA	8,656	VC
Univ of Illinois at Chicago	IL	13,418	C
Univ of Illinois at Urbana-Champaign	IL	11,316	HC+
Univ of Iowa	IA	10,923	VC
Univ of Kentucky	KY	7,765	C
Univ of Mass Boston	MA	6,227	C
Univ of Miami	FL	34,608	HC
Univ of Mich/Ann Arbor	MI	13,864	HC+
Univ of Minn/Twin Cities	MN	13,160	VC
Univ of Notre Dame	IN	34,442	MC
Univ of Oregon	OR	11,479	VC
Univ of Pennsylvania	PA	37,960	MC
Univ of Pittsburgh at Pittsburgh	PA	16,074	HC
Univ of Rhode Island	RI	13,720	VC
Univ of S Car at Columbia	SC	10,048	VC
Univ of South Florida	FL	9,454	C
Univ of Tenn at Knoxville	TN	8,214	C
Univ of Texas at Austin	TX	10,630	HC
Univ of Virginia	VA	11,740	MC
Univ of Washington	WA	10,361	VC
Univ of Wisc/Madison	WI	8,262	VC
Univ of Wisc/Milwaukee	WI	9,427	LC
Washington Univ in St. Louis	MO	38,293	MC
Wayne State Univ	MI	11,774	C
Wesleyan Univ	CT	35,139	MC
Yale Univ	CT	37,000	MC
Youngstown State Univ	OH	11,148	NC

ITALIAN STUDIES

School	ST	$IS	SR
Bard College	NY	37,352	HC+
Boston Univ	MA	38,194	HC+
Brown Univ	RI	38,174	MC
Columbia Univ/Columbia College	NY	38,590	MC
Columbia Univ/School of General Studies	NY	35,000	C
Conn College	CT	37,900	MC
Dickinson College	PA	35,825	HC
Duke Univ	NC	37,555	MC
Florida International Univ	FL	9,912	VC
Fordham Univ	NY	35,066	HC
Gonzaga Univ	WA	26,766	HC
Purdue Univ/West Lafayette	IN	12,560	VC
Rosemont College	PA	26,175	C
Scripps College	CA	35,700	HC+
Southern Methodist Univ	TX	34,210	HC
SUNY/Univ at Stony Brook	NY	12,763	HC
Sweet Briar College	VA	27,940	C
Syracuse Univ	NY	34,720	HC
Univ of Calif at Los Angeles	CA	15,330	MC
Univ of Calif at San Diego	CA	14,127	HC
Univ of Calif at Santa Barbara	CA	11,732	VC
Univ of Calif at Santa Cruz	CA	16,505	VC
Univ of Conn	CT	14,608	VC
Univ of Houston	TX	9,818	C
Univ of Maryland/College Park	MD	14,227	HC
Univ of Mass Amherst	MA	13,980	C+
Univ of Pennsylvania	PA	37,960	MC
Wellesley College	MA	36,516	MC
Wheaton College	MA	36,330	HC

JAPANESE

School	ST	$IS	SR
Arizona State Univ-Main	AZ	10,048	C
Bates College	ME	37,500	MC
Brigham Young Univ	UT	8,504	HC
Cal State, Fullerton	CA	6,648	C
Cal State, Long Beach	CA	8,762	C+
Cal State, Los Angeles	CA	5,778	C
Central Washington Univ	WA	9,768	C
Colgate Univ	NY	37,095	MC
Conn College	CT	37,900	MC
Earlham College	IN	29,976	VC+
Eastern Mich Univ	MI	11,478	C
George Washington Univ	DC	41,030	MC
Georgetown Univ	DC	38,242	MC
Harvard Univ/Harvard College	MA	37,928	MC
Macalester College	MN	31,944	MC
Middlebury College	VT	38,100	MC
Mount Union College	OH	21,120	C
North Central College	IL	25,656	VC
Oakland Univ	MI	10,800	C
Ohio State Univ	OH	13,080	VC+
Pacific Univ	OR	24,250	C
Pomona College	CA	33,960	MC
Portland State Univ	OR	12,453	C
Purdue Univ/West Lafayette	IN	12,560	VC
San Diego State Univ	CA	10,321	C
San Francisco State Univ	CA	12,070	C
Stanford Univ	CA	37,612	MC
Tufts Univ	MA	38,233	MC
Univ of Calif at Berkeley	CA	15,563	MC
Univ of Calif at Davis	CA	14,995	VC
Univ of Calif at Irvine	CA	19,808	HC
Univ of Calif at Los Angeles	CA	15,330	MC
Univ of Calif at Santa Barbara	CA	11,732	VC
Univ of Chicago	IL	35,087	MC
Univ of Colo at Boulder	CO	10,774	VC
Univ of Findlay	OH	23,962	NC
Univ of Hawaii at Manoa	HI	9,565	VC
Univ of Maryland/College Park	MD	14,227	HC
Univ of Mass Amherst	MA	13,980	C+
Univ of Mich/Ann Arbor	MI	13,864	HC+
Univ of Minn/Twin Cities	MN	13,160	VC
Univ of Montana	MT	9,395	C
Univ of Notre Dame	IN	34,442	MC
Univ of Oregon	OR	11,479	VC
Univ of Pittsburgh at Pittsburgh	PA	16,074	HC
Univ of Rochester	NY	32,979	HC
Univ of the Pacific	CA	31,090	VC
Univ of Utah	UT	9,205	C
Univ of Washington	WA	10,361	VC
Univ of Wisc/Madison	WI	8,262	VC
Washington Univ in St. Louis	MO	38,293	MC
Wellesley College	MA	36,516	MC
Yale Univ	CT	37,000	MC

JAPANESE STUDIES

School	ST	$IS	SR
Boston Univ	MA	38,194	HC+
Case Western Reserve Univ	OH	32,002	MC
Dillard Univ	LA	17,325	VC
Earlham College	IN	29,976	VC+
Gettysburg College	PA	35,646	HC
Salem International Univ	WV	19,770	C
Univ of Alaska Fairbanks	AK	9,295	C
Univ of Calif at San Diego	CA	14,127	HC
Univ of Georgia	GA	8,656	VC
Univ of Hawaii at Hilo	HI	6,497	C
Wellesley College	MA	36,516	MC
Willamette Univ	OR	32,032	VC+
William Jewell College	MO	21,320	VC

JAZZ

School	ST	$IS	SR
Berklee College of Music	MA	32,447	SP
Bowling Green State Univ	OH	13,036	C
Brigham Young Univ	UT	8,504	HC
DePaul Univ	IL	27,580	VC
Eastman School of Music	NY	33,741	SP
Five Towns College	NY	21,050	SP
Florida State Univ	FL	9,028	HC
Hofstra Univ	NY	27,112	VC
Howard Univ	DC	16,505	C
Indiana Univ Bloomington	IN	12,389	VC
Ithaca College	NY	31,730	HC
Johnson State College	VT	11,819	LC
Limestone College	SC	17,700	C
Loyola Univ New Orleans	LA	31,036	VC+
Manhattan School of Music	NY	31,500	SP
Mich State Univ	MI	11,933	VC
New England Conservatory of Music	MA	35,000	SP
N Car Central Univ	NC	7,534	LC
Northwestern Univ	IL	37,491	MC
Ohio State Univ	OH	13,080	VC+
Roosevelt Univ	IL	22,580	VC
Shenandoah Univ	VA	25,190	NC
Temple Univ	PA	15,912	C
Texas State Univ	TX	9,320	VC
Univ of Cincinnati	OH	14,736	C
Univ of Denver	CO	32,148	VC
Univ of Hartford	CT	31,080	C
Univ of Maine at Augusta	ME	4,065	C
Univ of Miami	FL	34,608	HC
Univ of Mich/Ann Arbor	MI	13,864	HC+
Univ of Minn/Duluth	MN	12,470	C
Univ of N Car at Greensboro	NC	8,248	C
Univ of North Florida	FL	8,769	VC
Univ of North Texas	TX	7,629	C
Univ of Oregon	OR	11,479	VC
Univ of Rochester	NY	32,979	HC
Univ of Southern Calif	CA	37,459	MC
Univ of Washington	WA	10,361	VC
Western Mich Univ	MI	12,031	C

JOURNALISM

School	ST	$IS	SR
Abilene Christian Univ	TX	18,370	VC
Adams State College	CO	7,468	C
American Univ	DC	34,585	VC+
Andrews Univ	MI	19,550	C
Angelo State Univ	TX	7,576	NC
Appalachian State Univ	NC	7,637	VC
Arizona State Univ-Main	AZ	10,048	C
Arkansas State Univ	AR	8,450	C
Arkansas Tech Univ	AR	7,299	C
Asbury College	KY	20,704	VC
Ashland Univ	OH	24,464	C
Auburn Univ	AL	10,396	VC
Augustana College	SD	21,998	VC
Averett Univ	VA	23,010	LC
Ball State Univ	IN	8,660	C
Baylor Univ	TX	23,864	VC
Bemidji State Univ	MN	9,103	C
Benedict College	SC	12,662	LC
Benedictine College	KS	20,603	C
Bethany College	WV	19,845	VC
Biola Univ	CA	25,964	VC
Boston Univ	MA	38,194	HC+
Bowling Green State Univ	OH	13,036	C
Butler Univ	IN	28,250	VC+
Calif Polytechnic State Univ	CA	8,747	VC
Cal State, Chico	CA	8,598	LC
Cal State, Fresno	CA	8,414	LC
Cal State, Fullerton	CA	6,648	C
Cal State, Hayward	CA	8,871	LC
Cal State, Long Beach	CA	8,762	C+
Cal State, Northridge	CA	7,757	LC
Cal State, Sacramento	CA	9,543	C
Campbell Univ	NC	18,268	VC
Carnegie Mellon Univ	PA	32,682	MC
Central Mich Univ	MI	11,142	C
Central Missouri State Univ	MO	9,776	C
Central State Univ	OH	8,922	C+
Central Univ of Bayamon	PR	3,335	
Central Washington Univ	WA	9,768	C
Champlain College	VT	22,030	C
Christopher Newport Univ	VA	8,862	VC
CUNY/Baruch College	NY	3,275	VC+
CUNY/Brooklyn College	NY	4,353	C+
College of New Jersey	NJ	15,950	MC
College of St. Joseph	VT	19,100	C
College of the Ozarks	MO	3,500	VC+
Colo State Univ	CO	9,964	VC
Columbia College Chicago	IL	25,108	LC
Columbia Union College	MD	20,543	C
Concordia College: Moorhead	MN	22,460	VC+
Creighton Univ	NE	26,748	VC+
Delaware State Univ	DE	8,104	LC
Delta State Univ	MS	6,618	C
Dickinson State Univ	ND	6,338	NC
Dominican Univ	IL	23,610	C
Dordt College	IA	20,170	VC
Drake Univ	IA	25,120	VC+
Drury Univ	MO	18,085	VC+
Duquesne Univ	PA	26,907	VC
Earlham College	IN	29,976	VC+
East Central Univ	OK	4,968	C
Eastern Illinois Univ	IL	11,192	C
Eastern Kentucky Univ	KY	7,708	C
Eastern Mich Univ	MI	11,478	C
Eastern Nazarene College	MA	19,433	LC
Eastern New Mexico Univ	NM	6,762	LC
Eastern Washington Univ	WA	9,012	C
Elon Univ	NC	22,240	VC
Emerson College	MA	32,205	HC
Emory & Henry College	VA	21,950	C
Evangel Univ	MO	15,435	C
Florida A&M Univ	FL	7,564	C
Florida Atlantic Univ	FL	8,543	C
Florida Southern College	FL	23,592	C
Fordham Univ	NY	35,066	HC
Franklin College	IN		C
George Washington Univ	DC	41,030	MC
Georgia Southern Univ	GA	8,540	C
Georgia State Univ	GA	10,658	C
Gonzaga Univ	WA	26,766	HC
Grace College	IN	19,825	VC
Grand Valley State Univ	MI	11,022	VC
Grand View College	IA	19,748	LC
Hampshire College	MA	37,037	HC
Hawaii Pacific Univ	HI	19,218	C
Hofstra Univ	NY	27,112	VC
Howard Univ	DC	16,505	C
Humboldt State Univ	CA	9,400	C
Indiana State Univ	IN	10,719	LC
Indiana Univ Bloomington	IN	12,389	VC
Indiana Univ of Pennsylvania	PA	10,489	C
Indiana Univ South Bend	IN	4,571	LC
Indiana Univ Southeast	IN	4,504	LC
Indiana Univ-Purdue Univ Indianapolis	IN	8,257	LC
Iona College	NY	27,988	VC
Iowa State Univ	IA	10,768	VC
Ithaca College	NY	31,730	HC
John Brown Univ	AR	15,080	VC
Johnson State College	VT	11,819	LC
Kansas State Univ	KS	8,728	VC
Keene State College	NH	12,212	C
Kent State Univ	OH	12,932	C
Lehigh Univ	PA	37,570	HC+
Lewis Univ	IL	22,950	C+
Lincoln Univ	MO	7,158	NC
Lincoln Univ	PA	13,320	C+
Lock Haven Univ of Pennsylvania	PA	11,098	LC
LIU/Brooklyn Campus	NY	24,790	C
LIU/C.W. Post Campus	NY	28,282	C
Loras College	IA	24,233	C
Louisiana College	LA	13,450	C
Louisiana State Univ in Shreveport	LA	2,884	NC
Louisiana Tech Univ	LA	7,361	C
Lyndon State College	VT	12,646	LC
MacMurray College	IL	20,005	LC
Madonna Univ	MI	11,504	VC
Mansfield Univ	PA	11,220	C
Marietta College	OH	27,047	C
Marquette Univ	WI	27,594	VC
Marshall Univ	WV	9,116	C
Mercy College	NY	19,200	NC
Mercyhurst College	PA	20,694	C
Messiah College	PA	25,890	VC+
Metropolitan State College of Denver	CO	2,338	LC
Mich State Univ	MI	11,933	VC
Midland Lutheran College	NE	18,600	C
Minn State Univ, Mankato	MN	8,803	C
Minn State Univ, Moorehead	MN	7,000	LC
Morris College	SC	10,974	LC
Mount Ida College	MA	25,596	LC
Mount Marty College	SD	15,656	LC

School	ST	$IS	SR
Mount Vernon Nazarene Univ	OH	18,925	C
Murray State Univ	KY	7,816	VC
Muskingum College	OH	20,680	C
New Mexico State Univ	NM	7,932	C
New York Univ	NY	39,406	MC
Nicholls State Univ	LA	6,395	NC
Norfolk State Univ	VA	9,722	LC
Northeastern State Univ	OK	4,950	LC
Northeastern Univ	MA	35,650	HC
Northern Arizona Univ	AZ	9,002	C
Northern Illinois Univ	IL	11,472	C
Northern Kentucky Univ	KY	6,352	NC
Northwest College	WA	18,854	C
Northwest Missouri State Univ	MO	9,334	C
Northwestern College	MN	22,820	C+
Northwestern State Univ of Louisiana	LA	6,331	NC
Northwestern Univ	IL	37,491	MC
Oakland Univ	MI	10,800	C
Ohio Northern Univ	OH	27,765	VC
Ohio State Univ	OH	13,080	VC+
Ohio Univ	OH	14,448	C
Ohio Wesleyan Univ	OH	32,550	VC+
Okla Baptist Univ	OK	15,220	VC
Okla Christian Univ	OK	17,690	NC
Okla City Univ	OK	19,580	VC
Okla State Univ	OK	9,216	VC
Old Dominion Univ	VA	10,441	C
Olivet College	MI	19,984	C+
Otterbein College	OH	26,085	C
Pacific Union College	CA	22,065	C+
Penn State Univ/Univ Park Campus	PA	15,646	HC
Pepperdine Univ	CA	32,830	VC
Point Loma Nazarene Univ	CA	21,380	VC
Point Park Univ	PA	21,840	C
Prairie View A&M Univ	TX	9,418	NC
Prescott College	AZ	13,430	C
Purdue Univ/West Lafayette	IN	12,560	VC
Quinnipiac Univ	CT	30,570	VC
Rider Univ	NJ	30,900	C
Roosevelt Univ	IL	22,580	VC
Rowan Univ	NJ	14,506	VC
Rust College	MS	8,200	C+
Rutgers, The State Univ of New Jersey/New Brunswick/Piscataway Campus	NJ	15,800	HC
Rutgers, The State Univ of New Jersey/Newark Campus	NJ	15,624	VC
St. Bonaventure Univ	NY	24,455	LC
St. Cloud State Univ	MN	8,362	C
St. John's Univ	NY	30,180	C
St. Mary-of-the-Woods College	IN	23,280	C
St. Michael's College	VT	30,100	VC
Sam Houston State Univ	TX	7,142	C
Samford Univ	AL	18,648	VC
San Diego State Univ	CA	10,321	C
San Francisco State Univ	CA	12,070	C
San Jose State Univ	CA	8,187	C
Seattle Univ	WA	24,183	VC
Seton Hill Univ	PA	24,930	C
Simpson College	IA	23,658	C+
S Dak State Univ	SD	7,782	C
Southeast Missouri State Univ	MO	9,704	C
Southern Adventist Univ	TN	17,080	C
Southern Arkansas Univ	AR	6,956	C
Southern Conn State Univ	CT	10,310	C
Southern Illinois Univ Carbondale	IL	10,407	C
Southern Methodist Univ	TX	34,210	HC
Southern Nazarene Univ	OK	14,634	NC
Southern Univ at New Orleans	LA	995	NC
Southwestern Adventist Univ	TX	14,798	C
Spring Hill College	AL	25,868	VC
SUNY at Oswego	NY	12,650	C
SUNY/College at Brockport	NY	12,111	C
SUNY/College at Buffalo	NY	8,025	C
SUNY/College at Plattsburgh	NY	11,700	C
SUNY/College at Purchase	NY	10,587	VC
SUNY/Univ at New Paltz	NY	11,565	VC
Stephen F. Austin State Univ	TX	7,552	C
Suffolk Univ	MA	29,200	C
Syracuse Univ	NY	34,720	HC
Taylor Univ	IN	23,820	VC+
Temple Univ	PA	15,912	C
Tenn Tech Univ	TN	8,670	VC
Texas A&M Univ	TX	11,081	HC
Texas A&M Univ at Commerce	TX	8,994	C
Texas Christian Univ	TX	23,410	VC
Texas Southern Univ	TX	8,920	NC
Texas State Univ	TX	9,320	VC
Texas Tech Univ	TX	10,768	VC
Thomas Edison State College	NJ	3,325	SP
Toccoa Falls College	GA	15,600	C
Troy State Univ	AL	7,696	C
Truman State Univ	MO	9,728	HC+
Union College	NE	17,130	C
Union Univ	TN	18,800	VC
Univ of Alabama	AL	9,040	C+
Univ of Alaska Anchorage	AK	9,100	NC
Univ of Alaska Fairbanks	AK	9,295	C
Univ of Arizona	AZ	10,413	VC
Univ of Arkansas	AR	9,855	VC
Univ of Arkansas at Little Rock	AR	5,637	NC
Univ of Arkansas at Pine Bluff	AR	7,925	C
Univ of Bridgeport	CT	25,924	LC
Univ of Central Arkansas	AR	6,388	C
Univ of Central Florida	FL	10,038	VC
Univ of Central Okla	OK	9,434	C
Univ of Colo at Boulder	CO	10,774	VC
Univ of Conn	CT	14,608	VC
Univ of Dayton	OH	24,850	VC
Univ of Delaware	DE	12,616	HC
Univ of Denver	CO	32,148	VC
Univ of Florida	FL	8,580	MC
Univ of Georgia	GA	8,656	VC
Univ of Hawaii at Manoa	HI	9,565	VC
Univ of Houston	TX	9,818	C
Univ of Idaho	ID	8,216	C
Univ of Illinois at Urbana-Champaign	IL	11,316	HC+
Univ of Indianapolis	IN	22,560	VC
Univ of Iowa	IA	10,923	VC
Univ of Judaism College of A&S	CA	24,230	C
Univ of Kansas	KS	8,923	VC
Univ of Kentucky	KY	7,765	C
Univ of La Verne	CA	28,600	C
Univ of Louisiana at Monroe	LA	5,207	NC
Univ of Maine	ME	12,080	C+
Univ of Mary Hardin-Baylor	TX	17,268	C
Univ of Maryland/College Park	MD	14,227	HC
Univ of Mass Amherst	MA	13,980	C+
Univ of Memphis	TN	8,560	C
Univ of Miami	FL	34,608	HC
Univ of Mich/Ann Arbor	MI	13,864	HC+
Univ of Miss	MS	7,666	C
Univ of Missouri/Columbia	MO	13,782	VC
Univ of Montana	MT	9,395	C
Univ of Montevallo	AL	8,478	C
Univ of Nebr at Kearney	NE	8,286	NC
Univ of Nebr at Lincoln	NE	9,975	C+
Univ of Nebr at Omaha	NE	8,080	C
Univ of Nevada/Reno	NV	9,792	C
Univ of New Hampshire	NH	14,828	VC
Univ of New Mexico	NM	9,223	C
Univ of North Alabama	AL	7,972	NC
Univ of N Car at Chapel Hill	NC	10,117	MC
Univ of N Car at Pembroke	NC	6,929	LC
Univ of North Texas	TX	7,629	C
Univ of Northern Colo	CO	8,987	C
Univ of Okla	OK	9,226	VC
Univ of Oregon	OR	11,479	VC
Univ of Pittsburgh at Johnstown	PA	15,216	LC
Univ of PR/Rio Piedras	PR	5,730	
Univ of Rhode Island	RI	13,720	VC
Univ of Richmond	VA	30,100	MC
Univ of St. Francis	IL	22,850	C
Univ of St. Thomas	MN	26,918	VC
Univ of S Car at Columbia	SC	10,048	VC
Univ of S Dak	SD	7,710	C+
Univ of Southern Calif	CA	37,459	MC
Univ of Southern Colo	CO	7,821	LC
Univ of Southern Indiana	IN	9,025	LC
Univ of Southern Miss	MS	8,324	LC
Univ of Tenn at Knoxville	TN	8,214	C
Univ of Texas at Arlington	TX	7,192	LC
Univ of Texas at Austin	TX	10,630	HC
Univ of Texas at El Paso	TX	5,799	NC
Univ of Texas-Pan American	TX	5,954	LC
Univ of Wisc/Eau Claire	WI	8,463	VC
Univ of Wisc/Madison	WI	8,262	VC
Univ of Wisc/Oshkosh	WI	6,130	LC
Univ of Wisc/River Falls	WI	8,358	LC
Univ of Wisc/Whitewater	WI	8,626	C
Univ of Wyoming	WY	8,636	C
Utah State Univ	UT	7,371	C
Utica College	NY	28,340	C
Valparaiso Univ	IN	26,118	VC+
Virginia Union Univ	VA	15,358	LC
Virginia Wesleyan College	VA	25,350	C
Wartburg College	IA	21,165	VC
Washington and Lee Univ	VA	29,663	MC
Washington State Univ	WA	11,334	C
Washington Univ in St. Louis	MO	38,293	MC
Wayne State Univ	MI	11,774	C
Weber State Univ	UT	7,945	NC
Webster Univ	MO	21,848	VC
West Virginia Univ	WV	9,370	C
Western Illinois Univ	IL	10,363	C
Western Kentucky Univ	KY	6,834	C
Western Mich Univ	MI	12,031	C
Western Washington Univ	WA	10,119	VC
Whitworth College	WA	26,428	VC+
William Penn Univ	IA	17,575	LC
William Woods Univ	MO	20,120	C
Winona State Univ	MN		C
Youngstown State Univ	OH	11,148	NC

JOURNALISM EDUCATION

School	ST	$IS	SR
Averett Univ	VA	23,010	LC
Ball State Univ	IN	8,660	C
Baylor Univ	TX	23,864	VC
Franklin College	IN		C
Grace College	IN	19,825	VC
Wartburg College	IA	21,165	VC

JUDAIC STUDIES

School	ST	$IS	SR
Albert A. List College of Jewish Studies	NY	18,500	HC+
American Univ	DC	34,585	VC+
Baltimore Hebrew Univ	MD	8,900	SP
Bard College	NY	37,352	HC+
Brandeis Univ	MA	38,198	MC
Brown Univ	RI	38,174	MC
CUNY/Brooklyn College	NY	4,353	C+
CUNY/Hunter College	NY	6,729	C+
CUNY/Queens College	NY	4,362	C
DePaul Univ	IL	27,580	VC
Dickinson College	PA	35,825	HC
Earlham College	IN	29,976	VC+
Emory Univ	GA	36,872	MC
Florida Atlantic Univ	FL	8,543	C
George Washington Univ	DC	41,030	MC
Hampshire College	MA	37,037	HC
Hofstra Univ	NY	27,112	VC
Indiana Univ Bloomington	IN	12,389	VC
Mount Holyoke College	MA	37,918	HC+
New York Univ	NY	39,406	MC
Oberlin College	OH	36,938	MC
Ohio State Univ	OH	13,080	VC+
Purdue Univ/West Lafayette	IN	12,560	VC
Rutgers, The State Univ of New Jersey/New Brunswick/Piscataway Campus	NJ	15,800	HC
Scripps College	CA	35,700	HC+
SUNY/Univ at Binghamton	NY	12,787	HC
Touro College	NY	15,250	VC
Trinity College	CT	38,040	HC+
Tufts Univ	MA	38,233	MC
Tulane Univ	LA	37,451	HC+
Univ of Arizona	AZ	10,413	VC
Univ of Calif at Los Angeles	CA	15,330	MC
Univ of Calif at San Diego	CA	14,127	HC
Univ of Chicago	IL	35,087	MC
Univ of Cincinnati	OH	14,736	C
Univ of Florida	FL	8,580	MC
Univ of Hartford	CT	31,080	C
Univ of Judaism College of A&S	CA	24,230	C
Univ of Maryland/College Park	MD	14,227	HC
Univ of Mass Amherst	MA	13,980	C+
Univ of Miami	FL	34,608	HC
Univ of Mich/Ann Arbor	MI	13,864	HC+
Univ of Missouri/Kansas City	MO	13,416	VC
Univ of Oregon	OR	11,479	VC
Univ of Pennsylvania	PA	37,960	MC
Univ of Texas at Austin	TX	10,630	HC
Univ of Washington	WA	10,361	VC
Univ of Wisc/Madison	WI	8,262	VC
Vassar College	NY	37,030	MC
Washington Univ in St. Louis	MO	38,293	MC
Wellesley College	MA	36,516	MC
Yale Univ	CT	37,000	MC

KOREAN

School	ST	$IS	SR
Brigham Young Univ	UT	8,504	HC
Univ of Calif at Los Angeles	CA	15,330	MC
Univ of Chicago	IL	35,087	MC
Univ of Hawaii at Manoa	HI	9,565	VC

LABOR STUDIES

School	ST	$IS	SR
Bowling Green State Univ	OH	13,036	C
Cal State, Dominguez Hills	CA	5,840	LC
CUNY/Queens College	NY	4,362	C
Cleveland State Univ	OH	12,308	LC
Cornell Univ	NY	38,253	MC
Eastern Mich Univ	MI	11,478	C
Hofstra Univ	NY	27,112	VC
Indiana Univ Bloomington	IN	12,389	VC
Indiana Univ Kokomo	IN	4,463	LC
Indiana Univ Northwest	IN	4,538	LC
Indiana Univ South Bend	IN	4,571	LC
Indiana Univ-Purdue Univ Indianapolis	IN	8,257	LC
Le Moyne College	NY	26,400	VC
Northern Kentucky Univ	KY	6,352	NC
Penn State Univ/Univ Park Campus	PA	15,646	HC
Rhode Island College	RI	11,565	C
Rutgers, The State Univ of New Jersey/New Brunswick/Piscataway Campus	NJ	15,800	HC
San Francisco State Univ	CA	12,070	C
SUNY/College at Old Westbury	NY	12,784	C
SUNY/Empire State College	NY	4,505	SP
Thomas Edison State College	NJ	3,325	SP
Univ of Mass Boston	MA	6,227	C
Univ of PR/Rio Piedras	PR	5,730	
Wayne State Univ	MI	11,774	C
Youngstown State Univ	OH	11,148	NC

LAND USE MANAGEMENT AND RECLAMATION

School	ST	$IS	SR
Alverno College	WI	18,898	C
Cal State, Bakersfield	CA	6,090	LC
Eastern Mich Univ	MI	11,478	C
Humboldt State Univ	CA	9,400	C
Metropolitan State College of Denver	CO	2,338	LC
Montana State Univ-Bozeman	MT	9,515	C
Texas A&M Univ at Galveston	TX	9,948	C+
Univ of Louisiana at Lafayette	LA	5,826	C
Univ of Okla	OK	9,226	VC
Univ of Wisc/Platteville	WI	8,450	C
Univ of Wisc/River Falls	WI	8,358	LC

LANDSCAPE ARCHITECTURE/DESIGN

School	ST	$IS	SR
Andrews Univ	MI	19,550	C
Arizona State Univ-Main	AZ	10,048	C
Auburn Univ	AL	10,396	VC
Augustana College	IL	26,610	VC+
Ball State Univ	IN	8,660	C
Brigham Young Univ	UT	8,504	HC
Calif Polytechnic State Univ	CA	8,747	VC
Calif State Polytechnic Univ, Pomona	CA	8,473	C+
CUNY/City College	NY	4,230	C+
Clemson Univ	SC	11,972	HC
Colo State Univ	CO	9,964	VC
Cornell Univ	NY	38,253	MC
Iowa State Univ	IA	10,768	VC
Kansas State Univ	KS	8,728	VC
Louisiana State Univ and A&M College	LA	9,126	VC
Mich State Univ	MI	11,933	VC
Miss State Univ	MS	9,139	C
N Car Agricultural and Technical State Univ	NC	6,659	LC
N Car State Univ	NC	9,886	VC
N Dak State Univ	ND	8,435	C
Ohio State Univ	OH	13,080	VC+
Okla State Univ	OK	9,216	VC
Oregon State Univ	OR	11,055	C
Penn State Univ/Univ Park Campus	PA	15,646	HC
Purdue Univ/West Lafayette	IN	12,560	VC
S Dak State Univ	SD	7,782	C
SUNY/College of Environmental Science and Forestry	NY	14,167	VC
Temple Univ	PA	15,912	C
Texas A&M Univ	TX	11,081	HC
Texas Tech Univ	TX	10,768	VC
Univ of Arizona	AZ	10,413	VC
Univ of Arkansas	AR	9,855	VC
Univ of Calif at Berkeley	CA	15,563	MC
Univ of Calif at Davis	CA	14,995	VC
Univ of Conn	CT	14,608	VC
Univ of Delaware	DE	12,616	HC
Univ of Florida	FL	8,580	MC
Univ of Georgia	GA	8,656	VC
Univ of Idaho	ID	8,216	C
Univ of Illinois at Urbana-Champaign	IL	11,316	HC+
Univ of Kentucky	KY	7,765	C
Univ of Maryland/College Park	MD	14,227	HC
Univ of Mass Amherst	MA	13,980	C+
Univ of Mich/Ann Arbor	MI	13,864	HC+
Univ of Minn/Twin Cities	MN	13,160	VC
Univ of Nevada/Las Vegas	NV	11,566	C
Univ of Oregon	OR	11,479	VC
Univ of Rhode Island	RI	13,720	VC
Univ of Tenn at Knoxville	TN	8,214	C
Univ of Texas at Arlington	TX	7,192	LC
Univ of Texas at Austin	TX	10,630	HC
Univ of Vermont	VT	16,316	VC
Univ of Washington	WA	10,361	VC
Univ of Wisc/Madison	WI	8,262	VC
Utah State Univ	UT	7,371	C
Virginia Polytechnic Inst and State Univ	VA	9,179	C
Washington State Univ	WA	11,334	C
West Virginia Univ	WV	9,370	C

LANGUAGE ARTS

School	ST	$IS	SR
Aquinas College	MI	21,894	C
Catawba College	NC	20,500	C
Central Washington Univ	WA	9,768	C
Christian Brothers Univ	TN	22,290	VC
Doane College	NE	20,000	C
Hiram College	OH	28,234	VC
Kent State Univ	OH	12,932	C
LeMoyne-Owen College	TN	13,070	LC
Malone College	OH	20,995	C
Marygrove College	MI	17,550	C
Miles College	AL	7,870	NC
Nebr Wesleyan Univ	NE	21,197	C+
Ohio Northern Univ	OH	27,765	VC
Samford Univ	AL	18,648	VC
Spring Arbor Univ	MI	20,206	C
Univ of Arizona	AZ	10,413	VC
Univ of Maine at Farmington	ME	10,108	C
Wells College	NY	21,122	VC

LANGUAGES

School	ST	$IS	SR
Adelphi Univ	NY	26,300	VC
Antioch College	OH	29,269	C
Arkansas Tech Univ	AR	7,299	C
Assumption College	MA	29,375	C
Auburn Univ	AL	10,396	VC
Austin Peay State Univ	TN	5,814	LC
Baylor Univ	TX	23,864	VC
Bemidji State Univ	MN	9,103	C
Bennington College	VT	35,910	HC
Bethany College	WV	19,845	VC
Canisius College	NY	28,163	C+
Carnegie Mellon Univ	PA	32,682	MC
Carson-Newman College	TN	16,760	C
Carthage College	WI	25,000	C
Central College	IA	21,206	C
Central Mich Univ	MI	11,142	C
CUNY/Brooklyn College	NY	4,353	C+
CUNY/Herbert H. Lehman College	NY	3,320	LC
CUNY/Hunter College	NY	6,729	C+
Clark Atlanta Univ	GA	19,300	C+
Clark Univ	MA	32,115	VC
College of St. Scholastica	MN	24,970	C+
Columbia College	SC	22,658	LC
Converse College	SC	24,710	VC
Cornell College	IA	27,825	VC+
Cornell Univ	NY	38,253	MC
David Lipscomb Univ	TN	16,158	VC
Davis and Elkins College	WV	20,594	C
Denison Univ	OH	33,050	HC
Dillard Univ	LA	17,325	VC
Dordt College	IA	20,170	VC
Dowling College	NY	23,870	LC
Earlham College	IN	29,976	VC+
Eastern Illinois Univ	IL	11,192	C
Elmira College	NY	33,820	VC
Frostburg State Univ	MD	11,114	C
Gannon Univ	PA	23,260	C
Gordon College	MA	25,982	VC+
Grand Valley State Univ	MI	11,022	VC
Hamilton College	NY	37,560	MC
Hartwick College	NY	34,650	C+
Ithaca College	NY	31,730	HC
Jackson State Univ	MS	8,382	C
Judson College	AL	14,650	C
King's College	PA	26,990	C
Lewis and Clark College	OR	30,620	VC
LIU/Brooklyn Campus	NY	24,790	C
Louisiana College	LA	13,450	C
Mary Washington College	VA	10,166	HC
McNeese State Univ	LA	5,259	LC
Mercyhurst College	PA	20,694	C
Miss College	MS	14,574	C
Miss State Univ	MS	9,139	C
Murray State Univ	KY	7,816	VC
New College of Florida	FL	8,906	HC+
New Mexico State Univ	NM	7,932	C
Newberry College	SC	22,871	LC
Northeastern Univ	MA	35,650	HC
Occidental College	CA	35,922	HC
Pomona College	CA	33,960	MC
Portland State Univ	OR	12,453	C
Principia College	IL	25,044	C+
Purdue Univ/West Lafayette	IN	12,560	VC
Roger Williams Univ	RI	30,296	C
Roosevelt Univ	IL	22,580	VC
St. Cloud State Univ	MN	8,362	C
St. John's Univ	NY	30,180	C
St. Mary-of-the-Woods College	IN	23,280	C
St. Mary's College of Maryland	MD	15,908	VC+
Scripps College	CA	35,700	HC+
Southern Illinois Univ Edwardsville	IL	8,724	C
Southern Methodist Univ	TX	34,210	HC
Southern Oregon Univ	OR	10,362	C
Stonehill College	MA	30,752	HC
Syracuse Univ	NY	34,720	HC
Tenn State Univ	TN	9,048	LC
Texas A&M Univ at Commerce	TX	8,994	C
Trinity College	DC	24,150	LC
United States Military Academy	NY		MC
Univ of Alabama in Huntsville	AL	9,126	VC
Univ of Alaska Anchorage	AK	9,100	NC
Univ of Calif at Riverside	CA	15,300	C
Univ of Central Florida	FL	10,038	VC
Univ of Delaware	DE	12,616	HC
Univ of Denver	CO	32,148	VC
Univ of Hartford	CT	31,080	C
Univ of Memphis	TN	8,560	C
Univ of Mich/Dearborn	MI	6,843	VC
Univ of Minn/Twin Cities	MN	13,160	VC
Univ of Nebr at Lincoln	NE	9,975	C+
Univ of New Mexico	NM	9,223	C
Univ of Okla	OK	9,226	VC
Univ of PR/Rio Piedras	PR	5,730	
Univ of South Alabama	AL	7,760	LC
Univ of South Florida	FL	9,454	C
Univ of Southern Miss	MS	8,324	LC
Univ of Tenn at Knoxville	TN	8,214	C
Univ of Texas at El Paso	TX	5,799	NC
Vassar College	NY	37,030	MC
Virginia Commonwealth Univ	VA	9,030	C
Virginia Wesleyan College	VA	25,350	C
Washington Univ in St. Louis	MO	38,293	MC
Wilson College	PA	23,912	C
Youngstown State Univ	OH	11,148	NC

LASER ELECTRO-OPTICS TECHNOLOGY

School	ST	$IS	SR
Oregon Inst of Technology	OR	8,718	C

LATIN

School	ST	$IS	SR
Amherst College	MA	37,470	MC
Asbury College	KY	20,704	VC
Austin College	TX	24,747	HC
Baylor Univ	TX	23,864	VC
Boston Univ	MA	38,194	HC+
Bowling Green State Univ	OH	13,036	C
Bryn Mawr College	PA	36,890	HC+
Butler Univ	IN	28,250	VC+
Calvin College	MI	22,615	NC
Carleton College	MN	34,395	MC
Catholic Univ of America	DC	34,248	VC
Centenary College of Louisiana	LA	23,100	VC+
CUNY/Brooklyn College	NY	4,353	C+
CUNY/Herbert H. Lehman College	NY	3,320	LC
CUNY/Hunter College	NY	6,729	C+
CUNY/Queens College	NY	4,362	C
Colgate Univ	NY	37,095	MC
College of Wooster	OH	31,300	HC
Columbia Univ/Barnard College	NY	36,990	MC
Columbia Univ/Columbia College	NY	38,590	MC
Concordia College: Moorhead	MN	22,460	VC+
Cornell Univ	NY	38,253	MC
Creighton Univ	NE	26,748	VC+
Denison Univ	OH	33,050	HC
DePauw Univ	IN	31,500	HC
Dickinson College	PA	35,825	HC
Duquesne Univ	PA	26,907	VC
Emory Univ	GA	36,872	MC
Florida State Univ	FL	9,028	HC
Franklin and Marshall College	PA	35,930	HC+
Furman Univ	SC	28,976	HC+
Gettysburg College	PA	35,646	HC
Hampden-Sydney College	VA	28,407	VC
Harvard Univ/Harvard College	MA	37,928	MC
Hope College	MI	25,340	VC
Indiana State Univ	IN	10,719	LC
Indiana Univ Bloomington	IN	12,389	VC
John Carroll Univ	OH	27,658	C+
Kent State Univ	OH	12,932	C
Kenyon College	OH	35,370	HC+
Louisiana State Univ and A&M College	LA	9,126	VC
Loyola College in Maryland	MD	34,560	HC
Loyola Univ Chicago	IL	31,164	VC
Luther College	IA	25,700	VC
Marlboro College	VT	29,055	VC+
Mary Washington College	VA	10,166	HC
Mercer Univ	GA	27,516	VC+
Miami Univ	OH	15,033	HC
Mich State Univ	MI	11,933	VC
Monmouth College	IL	23,600	C
Montclair State Univ	NJ	13,790	C
Mount Holyoke College	MA	37,918	HC+
New York Univ	NY	39,406	MC
Purdue Univ/West Lafayette	IN	12,560	VC
Randolph-Macon College	VA	27,190	C
Rutgers, The State Univ of New Jersey/New Brunswick/Piscataway Campus	NJ	15,800	HC
St. Joseph's Univ	PA	33,590	VC
St. Louis Univ	MO	29,780	VC+
St. Olaf College	MN	28,500	HC
Samford Univ	AL	18,648	VC
Sarah Lawrence College	NY	41,218	HC
Seattle Pacific Univ	WA	25,944	VC
Smith College	MA	37,034	HC+
Southwest Missouri State Univ	MO	8,918	C
Southwestern Univ	TX	25,410	HC
SUNY/Univ at Albany	NY	12,951	HC
SUNY/Univ at Binghamton	NY	12,787	HC
Swarthmore College	PA	37,716	MC
Sweet Briar College	VA	27,940	C
Texas Tech Univ	TX	10,768	VC
Tufts Univ	MA	38,233	MC
Univ of Akron	OH	13,134	NC
Univ of Arizona	AZ	10,413	VC
Univ of Calif at Berkeley	CA	15,563	MC
Univ of Calif at Davis	CA	14,995	VC
Univ of Calif at Los Angeles	CA	15,330	MC
Univ of Georgia	GA	8,656	VC
Univ of Idaho	ID	8,216	C
Univ of Iowa	IA	10,923	VC
Univ of Maine	ME	12,080	C+
Univ of Mass Boston	MA	6,227	C
Univ of Mich/Ann Arbor	MI	13,864	HC+
Univ of Minn/Twin Cities	MN	13,160	VC
Univ of Nebr at Lincoln	NE	9,975	C+
Univ of New Hampshire	NH	14,828	VC
Univ of Notre Dame	IN	34,442	MC
Univ of Oregon	OR	11,479	VC
Univ of Richmond	VA	30,100	MC
Univ of St. Thomas	MN	26,918	VC
Univ of Scranton	PA	30,836	VC
Univ of S Car at Columbia	SC	10,048	VC
Univ of Tenn at Chattanooga	TN	7,783	C
Univ of Texas at Austin	TX	10,630	HC
Univ of the South	TN	30,855	HC
Univ of Vermont	VT	16,316	VC
Univ of Wisc/Madison	WI	8,262	VC
Wabash College	IN	27,932	VC
Wake Forest Univ	NC	34,090	MC
Washington Univ in St. Louis	MO	38,293	MC
Wellesley College	MA	36,516	MC
West Chester Univ of Pennsylvania	PA	11,164	C
Western Mich Univ	MI	12,031	C
Westminster College	PA	22,960	C
Wheaton College	MA	36,330	HC
Wichita State Univ	KS	8,092	C

LATIN AMERICAN STUDIES

School	ST	$IS	SR
Adelphi Univ	NY	26,300	VC
Albright College	PA	30,579	C
American Univ	DC	34,585	VC+
Assumption College	MA	29,375	C
Austin College	TX	24,747	HC
Ball State Univ	IN	8,660	C
Bard College	NY	37,352	HC+
Baylor Univ	TX	23,864	VC
Boston Univ	MA	38,194	HC+
Bowdoin College	ME	37,790	MC
Brandeis Univ	MA	38,198	MC
Brigham Young Univ	UT	8,504	HC
Brown Univ	RI	38,174	MC
Bucknell Univ	PA	35,262	HC+
Cal State, Chico	CA	8,598	LC
Cal State, Fullerton	CA	6,648	C
Cal State, Hayward	CA	8,871	LC
Cal State, Los Angeles	CA	5,778	C
Carleton College	MN	34,395	MC
CUNY/Brooklyn College	NY	4,353	C+
CUNY/City College	NY	4,230	C+
CUNY/Hunter College	NY	6,729	C+
CUNY/Queens College	NY	4,362	C
Claremont McKenna College	CA	36,880	MC
Colby College	ME	37,570	MC
Colgate Univ	NY	37,095	MC
Columbia Univ/Columbia College	NY	38,590	MC
Columbia Univ/School of General Studies	NY	35,000	C
Conn College	CT	37,900	MC
Cornell College	IA	27,825	VC+
Dartmouth College	NH	37,770	MC
Denison Univ	OH	33,050	HC
DePaul Univ	IL	27,580	VC
Earlham College	IN	29,976	VC+
Emory Univ	GA	36,872	MC
Flagler College	FL	11,860	VC+
Florida State Univ	FL	9,028	HC
Fordham Univ	NY	35,066	HC
George Washington Univ	DC	41,030	MC
Hamline Univ	MN	27,052	VC
Hampshire College	MA	37,037	HC
Hanover College	IN	25,200	VC
Hobart and William Smith Colleges	NY	36,536	HC
Hofstra Univ	NY	27,112	VC
Hood College	MD	27,795	VC
Johns Hopkins Univ	MD	38,372	MC
Kent State Univ	OH	12,932	C
Lake Forest College	IL	30,270	VC
Lock Haven Univ of Pennsylvania	PA	11,098	LC
Macalester College	MN	31,944	MC
Mass Inst of Technology	MA	38,310	MC
Middlebury College	VT	38,100	MC
Mount Holyoke College	MA	37,918	HC+
New York Univ	NY	39,406	MC
Notre Dame de Namur Univ	CA	26,932	LC
Oakland Univ	MI	10,800	C
Oberlin College	OH	36,938	MC
Ohio Univ	OH	14,448	C
Penn State Univ/Univ Park Campus	PA	15,646	HC
Pitzer College	CA	37,590	HC
Pomona College	CA	33,960	MC
Rhodes College	TN	26,466	HC+
Ripon College	WI	24,995	VC
Rollins College	FL	34,300	VC
Rutgers, The State Univ of New Jersey/New Brunswick/Piscataway Campus	NJ	15,800	HC
St. Edward's Univ	TX	20,428	C
St. Mary's Univ of San Antonio	TX	22,444	C
Samford Univ	AL	18,648	VC
San Diego State Univ	CA	10,321	C
Scripps College	CA	35,700	HC+
Seattle Pacific Univ	WA	25,944	VC
Simon's Rock College of Bard	MA	36,580	HC
Smith College	MA	37,034	HC+
Sonoma State Univ	CA	10,421	C
Southern Methodist Univ	TX	34,210	HC
SUNY/College at Plattsburgh	NY	11,700	C
SUNY/Univ at Albany	NY	12,951	HC
SUNY/Univ at Binghamton	NY	12,787	HC
SUNY/Univ at New Paltz	NY	11,565	VC
Stetson Univ	FL	29,495	VC
Syracuse Univ	NY	34,720	HC
Temple Univ	PA	15,912	C
Texas Christian Univ	TX	23,410	VC
Texas Tech Univ	TX	10,768	VC
Tulane Univ	LA	37,451	HC+
Union College	NY	36,005	HC
Univ of Arizona	AZ	10,413	VC
Univ of Calif at Berkeley	CA	15,563	MC
Univ of Calif at Los Angeles	CA	15,330	MC
Univ of Calif at Riverside	CA	15,300	C
Univ of Calif at San Diego	CA	14,127	HC
Univ of Calif at Santa Barbara	CA	11,732	VC
Univ of Calif at Santa Cruz	CA	16,505	VC
Univ of Chicago	IL	35,087	MC
Univ of Cincinnati	OH	14,736	C
Univ of Conn	CT	14,608	VC
Univ of Delaware	DE	12,616	HC
Univ of Idaho	ID	8,216	C
Univ of Illinois at Chicago	IL	13,418	C
Univ of Illinois at Urbana-Champaign	IL	11,316	HC+
Univ of Kansas	KS	8,923	VC
Univ of Kentucky	KY	7,765	C
Univ of Miami	FL	34,608	HC
Univ of Mich/Ann Arbor	MI	13,864	HC+
Univ of Minn/Morris	MN	12,896	VC
Univ of Nebr at Lincoln	NE	9,975	C+
Univ of New Mexico	NM	9,223	C
Univ of N Car at Chapel Hill	NC	10,117	MC
Univ of Northern Iowa	IA	9,834	C
Univ of Pennsylvania	PA	37,960	MC
Univ of Puget Sound	WA	31,760	HC
Univ of Rhode Island	RI	13,720	VC
Univ of San Francisco	CA	34,700	VC
Univ of S Car at Columbia	SC	10,048	VC
Univ of Tenn at Knoxville	TN	8,214	C
Univ of Texas at Austin	TX	10,630	HC
Univ of Texas at El Paso	TX	5,799	NC
Univ of Texas-Pan American	TX	5,954	LC
Univ of Vermont	VT	16,316	VC
Univ of Wisc/Eau Claire	WI	8,463	VC
Univ of Wisc/Madison	WI	8,262	VC
Vanderbilt Univ	TN	37,897	MC
Vassar College	NY	37,030	MC
Villanova Univ	PA	35,050	HC
Washington Univ in St. Louis	MO	38,293	MC
Wellesley College	MA	36,516	MC
Wesleyan Univ	CT	35,139	MC
Willamette Univ	OR	32,032	VC+
Yale Univ	CT	37,000	MC

LAW

School	ST	$IS	SR
American Univ	DC	34,585	VC+
Amherst College	MA	37,470	MC
Bay Path College	MA	24,910	C

ST = STATE $IS = IN-STATE COSTS SR = SELECTOR RATING

School	ST	$IS	SR
Baylor Univ	TX	23,864	VC
Becker College	MA	23,710	LC
Brigham Young Univ	UT	8,504	HC
Chapman Univ	CA	33,118	VC
Christopher Newport Univ	VA	8,862	VC
Claremont McKenna College	CA	36,880	MC
Drake Univ	IA	25,120	VC+
Earlham College	IN	29,976	VC+
Hampshire College	MA	37,037	HC
Hood College	MD	27,795	VC
Indiana Univ Bloomington	IN	12,389	VC
Lasell College	MA	26,000	C
Mount Ida College	MA	25,596	LC
Mountain State Univ	WV	10,212	NC
National Univ	CA	9,690	SP
Oberlin College	OH	36,938	MC
Park Univ	MO	10,780	C+
Purdue Univ/West Lafayette	IN	12,560	VC
Ramapo College of New Jersey	NJ	15,203	VC
St. Joseph's Univ	PA	33,590	VC
Southeastern Univ	DC	8,505	LC
Southern Illinois Univ Carbondale	IL	10,407	C
Texas Wesleyan Univ	TX	16,245	C
Towson Univ	MD	12,694	VC
United States Air Force Academy	CO		HC+
United States Military Academy	NY		MC
Univ of Calif at Berkeley	CA	15,563	MC
Univ of Calif at Santa Barbara	CA	11,732	VC
Univ of Calif at Santa Cruz	CA	16,505	VC
Univ of Central Florida	FL	10,038	VC
Univ of Mass Amherst	MA	13,980	C+
Univ of Nebr at Lincoln	NE	9,975	C+
Univ of Pittsburgh at Pittsburgh	PA	16,074	HC
Univ of Wisc/Milwaukee	WI	9,427	LC
Univ of Wisc/Superior	WI	7,051	C+
Ursuline College	OH	22,728	LC
Webster Univ	MO	21,848	VC
Wilson College	PA	23,912	C
Wingate Univ	NC	21,200	C
Woodbury College	VT	12,060	LC

LAW ENFORCEMENT AND CORRECTIONS

School	ST	$IS	SR
Averett Univ	VA	23,010	LC
Cal State, Stanislaus	CA	9,874	C
Calumet College of St. Joseph	IN	9,000	LC
CUNY/John Jay College of Criminal Justice	NY	4,259	C
College of the Ozarks	MO	3,500	VC+
Frostburg State Univ	MD	11,114	C
Hardin-Simmons Univ	TX	14,165	C
Metropolitan State Univ	MN	3,852	SP
Minn State Univ, Mankato	MN	8,803	LC
Point Park Univ	PA	21,840	C
Portland State Univ	OR	12,453	C
St. Paul's College	VA	14,344	NC
Sam Houston State Univ	TX	7,142	C
Shenandoah Univ	VA	25,190	NC
Southeast Missouri State Univ	MO	9,704	C
Southern Christian Univ	AL	9,440	LC
Stephen F. Austin State Univ	TX	7,552	C
Tarleton State Univ	TX	7,576	C
Texas State Univ	TX	9,320	VC
Tiffin Univ	OH	19,490	LC
Univ of Great Falls	MT	15,360	C
Univ of Indianapolis	IN	22,560	VC
Univ of Maine at Augusta	ME	4,065	C
Univ of New Haven	CT	28,650	C
Univ of Pittsburgh at Pittsburgh	PA	16,074	HC
Univ of San Francisco	CA	34,700	VC
Univ of Virginia's College at Wise	VA	10,116	C
Washburn Univ of Topeka	KS	8,984	NC
Western Conn State Univ	CT	11,625	C
Western Illinois Univ	IL	10,363	C
Western New England College	MA	28,924	C
Western New Mexico Univ	NM	5,950	LC
Western Oregon Univ	OR	10,281	C
Youngstown State Univ	OH	11,148	NC

LIBERAL ARTS/GENERAL STUDIES

School	ST	$IS	SR
Adelphi Univ	NY	26,300	VC
Alaska Pacific Univ	AK	17,910	C
Albertus Magnus College	CT	23,130	LC
Alcorn State Univ	MS	7,290	C
Alderson-Broaddus College	WV	19,640	C
Alvernia College	PA	23,212	LC
American International College	MA	24,690	LC
Angelo State Univ	TX	7,576	NC
Anna Maria College	MA	26,140	LC
Aquinas College	TN	10,660	LC
Arcadia Univ	PA	29,890	C
Arkansas State Univ	AR	8,450	C
Armstrong Atlantic State Univ	GA	7,102	C
Atlantic Union College	MA	18,868	C
Auburn Univ Montgomery	AL	9,020	NC
Averett Univ	VA	23,010	LC
Avila Univ	MO	20,300	C
Azusa Pacific Univ	CA	24,720	VC
Ball State Univ	IN	8,660	C
Barry Univ	FL	24,100	LC
Bay Path College	MA	24,910	C
Beacon College	FL	25,900	LC
Bellarmine Univ	KY	24,110	VC
Belmont Abbey College	NC	23,742	C
Belmont Univ	TN	21,986	VC
Benedictine College	KS	20,063	VC
Bennington College	VT	35,910	HC
Bentley College	MA	33,904	VC
Bethel College	IN	19,670	C
Bethel College	TN	12,980	C
Bethune-Cookman College	FL	16,480	LC
Biola Univ	CA	25,964	VC
Boricua College	NY	7,375	C
Bowling Green State Univ	OH	13,036	C
Brenau Univ Women's College	GA	21,800	C
Brescia Univ	KY	14,225	C
Brewton-Parker College	GA	14,200	LC
Bridgewater College	VA	25,150	C
Bryan College	TN	17,900	VC
Cabrini College	PA	29,020	C
Calif Baptist Univ	CA	19,924	C
Calif Lutheran Univ	CA	27,600	LC
Calif State Polytechnic Univ, Pomona	CA	8,793	C+
Cal State, Bakersfield	CA	6,090	LC
Cal State, Chico	CA	8,598	LC
Cal State, Dominguez Hills	CA	5,840	LC
Cal State, Fresno	CA	8,414	LC
Cal State, Fullerton	CA	6,648	C
Cal State, Hayward	CA	8,871	LC
Cal State, Los Angeles	CA	5,778	C
Cal State, Monterey Bay	CA	6,683	LC
Cal State, Northridge	CA	7,757	LC
Cal State, San Bernardino	CA	15,238	LC
Cal State, San Marcos	CA	1,736	LC
Cal State, Stanislaus	CA	9,874	C
Calumet College of St. Joseph	IN	9,000	LC
Cameron Univ	OK	5,692	NC
Carlow College	PA	21,334	C
Catholic Univ of America	DC	34,248	VC
Cazenovia College	NY	23,940	C
Cedar Crest College	PA	25,145	C+
Centenary College of Louisiana	LA	23,100	VC+
Central Washington Univ	WA	9,768	C
Champlain College	VT	22,030	C
Chapman Univ	CA	33,118	VC
Charter Oak State College	CT		SP
Christian Brothers Univ	TN	22,290	VC
Christian Heritage College	CA	19,990	C
City Univ	WA	7,425	NC
CUNY/Medgar Evers College	NY	4,232	NC
CUNY/York College	NY	3,292	NC
Clarion Univ of Pennsylvania	PA	11,272	LC
Clarke College	IA	23,165	C
Cleveland State Univ	OH	12,308	LC
College for Lifelong Learning	NH	4,100	SP
College Misericordia	PA	26,350	C
College of Mount St. Vincent	NY	26,800	C
College of Mount St. Joseph	OH	22,785	C
College of New Rochelle - School of New Resources	NY	5,450	SP
College of Notre Dame of Maryland	MD	27,700	C
College of St. Benedict	MN	26,672	VC
College of St. Joseph	VT	19,100	C
College of St. Mary	NE	21,510	C
Colo Christian Univ	CO	21,182	VC
Colo College	CO	36,860	HC
Colo State Univ	CO	9,964	VC
Columbia Union College	MD	20,543	C
Concordia Univ	CA	24,420	C
Concordia Univ at Austin	TX	20,450	LC
Coppin State College	MD	10,191	LC
Crichton College	TN	15,215	C
Dallas Baptist Univ	TX	15,300	VC
Dana College	NE	20,280	C
De Sales Univ	PA	25,470	C
Dominican Univ of Calif	CA	31,670	C
Dowling College	NY	23,870	LC
Duquesne Univ	PA	26,907	VC
East Carolina Univ	NC	8,671	C
East Central Univ	OK	4,968	C
East Tenn State Univ	TN	8,497	C
Eastern Conn State Univ	CT	10,362	C
Eastern Mennonite Univ	VA	22,990	C
Eastern Mich Univ	MI	11,478	C
Eastern Oregon Univ	OR	10,080	NC
Edinboro Univ of Pennsylvania	PA	10,850	LC
Elmhurst College	IL	24,630	C
Emmanuel College	MA	27,600	C+
Emporia State Univ	KS	6,998	C
Endicott College	MA	25,266	C+
Eureka College	IL	24,980	LC
Evergreen State College	WA	9,576	C+
Excelsior College	NY	975	SP
Fairleigh Dickinson Univ/College at Florham	NJ	30,130	C
Fairleigh Dickinson Univ/Metropolitan Campus	NJ	28,584	C
Faulkner Univ	AL	14,500	C
Ferrum College	VA	21,240	LC
Fitchburg State College	MA	9,622	C
Florida Atlantic Univ	FL	8,543	C
Florida Gulf Coast Univ	FL	9,908	C
Florida International Univ	FL	9,912	VC
Fontbonne Univ	MO	21,508	C
Fort Hays State Univ	KS	7,363	C
Francis Marion Univ	SC	9,364	C
Franciscan Univ	IA	19,300	C
Frostburg State Univ	MD	11,114	C
Gannon Univ	PA	23,260	C
George Washington Univ	DC	41,030	MC
Georgia College and State Univ	GA	9,878	C
Glenville State College	WV	7,812	NC
Gonzaga Univ	WA	26,766	HC
Graceland Univ	IA	19,550	C
Green Mountain College	VT	24,130	C
Greenville College	IL	21,342	C
Guilford College	NC	24,960	VC
Hannibal-LaGrange College	MO	13,940	C
Harding Univ	AR	14,890	VC
Haverford College	PA	37,900	MC
Hilbert College	NY	19,170	LC
Hofstra Univ	NY	27,112	VC
Holy Names College	CA	27,980	NC
Hope International Univ	CA	16,940	NC
Howard Payne Univ	TX	15,176	C
Humboldt State Univ	CA	9,400	C
Idaho State Univ	ID	8,128	C
Indiana State Univ	IN	10,719	LC
Indiana Univ Bloomington	IN	12,389	VC
Indiana Univ East	IN	4,433	LC
Indiana Univ Kokomo	IN	4,463	LC
Indiana Univ Northwest	IN	4,538	LC
Indiana Univ South Bend	IN	4,571	LC
Indiana Univ Southeast	IN	4,504	LC
Indiana Univ-Purdue Univ Fort Wayne	IN	5,108	LC
Indiana Univ-Purdue Univ Indianapolis	IN	8,257	LC
Iowa State Univ	IA	10,768	VC
Ithaca College	NY	31,730	HC
James Madison Univ	VA	10,794	VC
Johnson C. Smith Univ	NC	18,108	C
Johnson State College	VT	11,819	LC
Juniata College	PA	29,080	VC
Kent State Univ	OH	12,932	C
Kentucky State Univ	KY	9,062	NC
Kutztown Univ of Pennsylvania	PA	10,786	C
La Roche College	PA	22,094	C
La Sierra Univ	CA	19,260	LC
Lasell College	MA	26,000	C
Lewis Univ	IL	22,950	C+
Lewis-Clark State College	ID	6,981	C
Liberty Univ	VA	17,220	C
Limestone College	SC	17,700	C
Lincoln Univ	MO	7,158	NC
Lincoln Univ	PA	13,320	C+
Lindenwood Univ	MO	17,050	VC
Lindsey Wilson College	KY	16,392	LC
Lock Haven Univ of Pennsylvania	PA	11,098	LC
LIU/Southampton College	NY	29,370	C+
Longwood Univ	VA	11,175	C
Louisiana State Univ and A&M College	LA	9,126	VC
Louisiana State Univ in Shreveport	LA	2,884	NC
Louisiana Tech Univ	LA	7,361	C
MacMurray College	IL	20,005	LC
Madonna Univ	MI	11,504	VC
Malone College	OH	20,995	C
Mansfield Univ	PA	11,220	C
Marymount College of Fordham Univ	NY	27,686	C
Marymount Manhattan College	NY	27,292	C
Marymount Univ	VA	23,668	C
Maryville Univ of St. Louis	MO	22,090	VC
Master's College and Seminary	CA	23,250	VC
Mayville State Univ	ND	7,325	NC
McNeese State Univ	LA	5,259	LC
Medaille College	NY	20,060	C
Menlo College	CA	24,000	LC
Mesa State College	CO	8,051	C
Metropolitan State Univ	MN	3,852	SP
Mich Tech Univ	MI	13,235	VC
Middlebury College	VT	38,100	MC
Midway College	KY	15,815	C
Mills College	CA	33,371	VC
Minot State Univ	ND	6,602	LC
Miss State Univ	MS	9,139	C
Missouri Southern State Univ	MO	8,316	C
Missouri Valley College	MO	18,500	C
Mitchell College	CT	26,396	C
Montana State Univ-Billings	MT	9,550	C
Montana Tech of The Univ of Montana	MT	9,314	NC
Montreat College	NC	18,762	C
Morehead State Univ	KY	7,464	C
Morris College	SC	10,974	LC
Mount Ida College	MA	25,596	LC
Mount Olive College	NC	14,410	LC
Mount St. Mary's College	CA	28,307	VC
Murray State Univ	KY	7,816	VC
National Univ	CA	9,690	SP
Neumann College	PA	23,890	LC
New Mexico Inst of Mining and Technology	NM	7,580	NC
Newman Univ	KS	18,018	C
Northern Illinois Univ	IL	11,472	C
Northwest College	WA	18,854	C
Northwest Nazarene Univ	ID	20,360	VC
Northwestern State Univ of Louisiana	LA	6,331	NC
Norwich Univ	VT	21,064	LC
Notre Dame de Namur Univ	CA	26,932	LC
Oakland Univ	MI	10,800	C
Ohio Dominican Univ	OH	22,700	C
Ohio Valley College	WV	16,036	C+
Okla Christian Univ	OK	17,690	NC
Okla State Univ	OK	9,216	VC
Okla Wesleyan Univ	OK	14,100	LC
Olivet Nazarene Univ	IL	20,480	C
Oral Roberts Univ	OK	18,490	C
Oregon State Univ	OR	11,055	C
Otterbein College	OH	26,085	C
Our Lady of Holy Cross College	LA	5,900	C
Our Lady of the Lake Univ of San Antonio	TX	17,336	C
Palm Beach Atlantic Univ	FL	20,690	C
Park Univ	MO	10,780	C+
Penn State Univ/Altoona	PA	12,578	C
Penn State Univ/Univ Park Campus	PA	15,646	HC
Pepperdine Univ	CA	32,830	VC
Pine Manor College	MA	22,138	LC
Point Loma Nazarene Univ	CA	21,380	VC
Point Park Univ	PA	21,840	C
Polytechnic Univ/Brooklyn	NY	33,770	VC
Pontifical Catholic Univ of PR/Ponce	PR	7,298	
Portland State Univ	OR	12,453	C
Purdue Univ/West Lafayette	IN	12,560	VC
Quinnipiac Univ	CT	30,570	VC
Radford Univ	VA	8,500	C
Reinhardt College	GA	20,750	C
Richard Stockton College of New Jersey	NJ	12,972	VC
Rider Univ	NJ	30,900	C
Rivier College	NH	26,217	C
Roosevelt Univ	IL	22,580	VC
Rosemont College	PA	26,175	C
Rowan Univ	NJ	14,506	VC
Rutgers, The State Univ of New Jersey/Camden Campus	NJ	14,990	VC
Sacred Heart Univ	CT	29,178	C
St. Andrews Presbyterian College	NC	20,525	C
St. Anselm College	NH	30,250	C
St. Edward's Univ	TX	20,428	C
St. John's College	MD	36,360	HC+
St. John's College	NM	36,360	VC+
St. John's Univ	MN	26,473	VC
St. John's Univ	NY	30,180	C
St. Joseph College	CT	29,685	C
St. Mary-of-the-Woods College	IN	23,280	C
St. Mary's College of Calif	CA	32,850	VC
St. Thomas Univ	FL	21,400	LC
St. Vincent College	PA	25,530	VC
Salem International Univ	WV	19,770	C
Samford Univ	AL	18,648	VC
San Francisco State Univ	CA	12,070	C
Santa Clara Univ	CA	34,701	HC
Sarah Lawrence College	NY	41,218	HC
Schreiner Univ	TX	20,440	C
Seattle Pacific Univ	WA	25,944	VC
Seattle Univ	WA	24,183	VC
Seton Hall Univ	NJ	30,130	VC
Seton Hill Univ	PA	24,930	C
Shaw Univ	NC	14,882	C+
Sheldon Jackson College	AK	14,940	LC
Shenandoah Univ	VA	25,190	NC
Siena Heights Univ	MI	16,140	LC
Simpson College	CA	20,500	C
Skidmore College	NY	37,930	HC
Sonoma State Univ	CA	10,421	C
Southeast Missouri State Univ	MO	9,704	C

ST = STATE $IS = IN-STATE COSTS SR = SELECTOR RATING

School	ST	$IS	SR
Southeastern Louisiana Univ	LA	6,791	LC
Southeastern Univ	DC	8,505	LC
Southern Christian Univ	AL	9,440	LC
Southern Illinois Univ Carbondale	IL	10,407	C
Southern Illinois Univ Edwardsville	IL	8,724	C
Southern Methodist Univ	TX	34,210	HC
Southern Oregon Univ	OR	10,362	C
Southern Vermont College	VT	18,226	LC
Southwestern College	KS	19,560	C
Spring Hill College	AL	25,868	VC
SUNY/College at Purchase	NY	10,587	VC
SUNY/Empire State College	NY	4,505	SP
Stephens College	MO	24,260	C+
Sweet Briar College	VA	27,940	C
Teikyo Post Univ	CT	24,875	C
Texas A&M Univ at Galveston	TX	9,948	C+
Texas Christian Univ	TX	23,410	VC
Texas Tech Univ	TX	10,768	VC
Thomas Aquinas College	CA	22,000	VC+
Thomas Edison State College	NJ	3,325	SP
Thomas More College	KY	21,350	C
Thomas Univ	GA	11,490	NC
Tiffin Univ	OH	19,490	LC
Touro College	NY	15,250	VC
Trinity International Univ	IL	22,980	C+
Union Inst and Univ	OH	7,848	SP
Univ of Alaska Southeast	AK	7,900	LC
Univ of Arizona	AZ	10,413	VC
Univ of Arkansas at Little Rock	AR	5,637	NC
Univ of Arkansas at Pine Bluff	AR	7,925	C
Univ of Calif at Riverside	CA	15,300	C
Univ of Central Florida	FL	10,038	VC
Univ of Central Okla	OK	9,434	C
Univ of Charleston	WV	23,620	C
Univ of Detroit Mercy	MI	25,582	C
Univ of Evansville	IN	24,190	VC
Univ of Hawaii at Hilo	HI	6,497	C
Univ of Hawaii at Manoa	HI	9,565	VC
Univ of Illinois at Urbana-Champaign	IL	11,316	HC+
Univ of Iowa	IA	10,923	VC
Univ of Judaism College of A&S	CA	24,230	C
Univ of La Verne	CA	28,600	C
Univ of Louisiana at Monroe	LA	5,207	NC
Univ of Louisville	KY	8,762	VC
Univ of Maine at Farmington	ME	10,108	C
Univ of Maine at Fort Kent	ME	9,770	LC
Univ of Maine at Machias	ME	9,271	LC
Univ of Maine at Presque Isle	ME	9,155	LC
Univ of Maryland/Eastern Shore	MD	9,964	C
Univ of Maryland/Univ College	MD	5,910	SP
Univ of Mass Amherst	MA	13,980	C+
Univ of Mass Lowell	MA	11,937	VC
Univ of Mich/Ann Arbor	MI	13,864	HC+
Univ of Mich/Dearborn	MI	6,843	VC
Univ of Minn/Morris	MN	12,896	VC
Univ of Miss	MS	7,666	C
Univ of Missouri/Columbia	MO	13,782	VC
Univ of Missouri/Kansas City	MO	13,416	VC
Univ of Mobile	AL	13,620	C
Univ of Montana	MT	9,395	C
Univ of Montana--Western	MT	8,073	NC
Univ of Nevada/Reno	NV	9,792	C
Univ of New Haven	CT	28,650	C
Univ of N Car at Greensboro	NC	8,248	C
Univ of N Dak	ND	8,390	C
Univ of North Texas	TX	7,629	C
Univ of Northern Iowa	IA	9,834	C
Univ of Notre Dame	IN	34,442	MC
Univ of Okla	OK	9,226	VC
Univ of Pennsylvania	PA	37,960	MC
Univ of Pittsburgh at Bradford	PA	15,294	C
Univ of Pittsburgh at Pittsburgh	PA	16,074	HC
Univ of PR/Rio Piedras	PR	5,730	
Univ of Redlands	CA	32,576	VC
Univ of St. Francis	IL	22,850	C
Univ of St. Francis	IN	20,964	C
Univ of St. Mary	KS	18,868	C
Univ of St. Thomas	TX	21,952	VC
Univ of San Diego	CA	33,156	HC
Univ of S Dak	SD	7,710	C+
Univ of South Florida	FL	9,454	C
Univ of Tampa	FL	23,982	VC
Univ of Texas at Austin	TX	10,630	HC
Univ of Texas-Pan American	TX	5,954	LC
Univ of the Ozarks	AR	16,574	C
Univ of the Pacific	CA	31,090	VC
Univ of Virginia's College at Wise	VA	10,116	C
Univ of Washington	WA	10,361	VC
Univ of Wisc/Green Bay	WI	8,154	C
Univ of Wisc/Oshkosh	WI	6,130	LC
Univ of Wisc/Stevens Point	WI	8,116	VC
Urbana Univ	OH	19,115	C
Utah State Univ	UT	7,371	C
Valdosta State Univ	GA	7,798	C
Villa Julie College	MD	18,393	C
Villanova Univ	PA	35,050	HC
Virginia Intermont College	VA	19,800	C
Virginia Polytechnic Inst and State Univ	VA	9,179	C
Virginia Wesleyan College	VA	25,350	C
Viterbo Univ	WI	20,430	C
Warner Pacific College	OR	21,900	C
Washburn Univ of Topeka	KS	8,984	NC
Washington State Univ	WA	11,334	C
Wayne State Univ	MI	11,774	C
Wesley College	DE	19,905	C
West Chester Univ of Pennsylvania	PA	11,164	C
West Texas A&M Univ	TX	7,533	C
West Virginia Univ	WV	9,370	C
Western Carolina Univ	NC	6,742	C
Western New England College	MA	28,924	C
Westmont College	CA	33,062	VC+
Wichita State Univ	KS	8,092	C
Wilberforce Univ	OH	14,937	LC
Wiley College	TX	8,100	LC
Wilkes Univ	PA	28,060	C
William Carey College	MS	10,150	LC
Wilmington College	OH	24,172	LC
Wingate Univ	NC	21,200	C
Winona State Univ	MN		C
Xavier Univ	OH	26,850	VC+
York College	NE	14,975	C

LIBRARY SCIENCE

School	ST	$IS	SR
Clarion Univ of Pennsylvania	PA	11,272	LC
Eastern Conn State Univ	CT	10,362	C
Kutztown Univ of Pennsylvania	PA	10,786	C
Northwestern Okla State Univ	OK	5,433	NC
Southern Conn State Univ	CT	10,310	C
Univ of Central Arkansas	AR	6,388	C
Univ of Maine at Augusta	ME	4,065	C
Western Kentucky Univ	KY	6,834	C

LIFE SCIENCE

School	ST	$IS	SR
Atlantic Union College	MA	18,868	C
Baylor Univ	TX	23,864	VC
Bowling Green State Univ	OH	13,036	C
Guilford College	NC	24,960	VC
Iowa Wesleyan College	IA	19,990	C
Johns Hopkins Univ	MD	38,372	MC
Kansas State Univ	KS	8,728	VC
Kent State Univ	OH	12,932	C
Malone College	OH	20,995	C
Morehead State Univ	KY	7,464	C
National Univ	CA	9,690	SP
New York Inst of Technology	NY	24,205	VC
Niagara Univ	NY	25,050	C
Northwest College	WA	18,854	C
Otterbein College	OH	26,085	C
United States Military Academy	NY		MC
Univ of Missouri/Rolla	MO	12,292	HC
Univ of New Mexico	NM	9,223	C
Wayne State College	NE	7,352	NC

LINGUISTICS

School	ST	$IS	SR
Alabama A&M Univ	AL	5,100	LC
Boston College	MA	33,284	MC
Boston Univ	MA	38,194	HC+
Brandeis Univ	MA	38,198	MC
Brigham Young Univ	UT	8,504	HC
Brown Univ	RI	38,174	MC
Cal State, Fresno	CA	8,414	LC
Cal State, Fullerton	CA	6,648	C
Cal State, Northridge	CA	7,757	LC
Central College	IA	21,206	C
CUNY/Brooklyn College	NY	4,353	C+
CUNY/Herbert H. Lehman College	NY	3,320	LC
CUNY/Queens College	NY	4,362	C
Cleveland State Univ	OH	12,308	LC
Columbia Univ/Barnard College	NY	36,990	MC
Columbia Univ/Columbia College	NY	38,590	MC
Cornell Univ	NY	38,253	MC
Dartmouth College	NH	37,770	MC
Duke Univ	NC	37,555	MC
Eastern Mich Univ	MI	11,478	C
Florida Atlantic Univ	FL	8,543	C
Florida State Univ	FL	9,028	HC
Georgetown Univ	DC	38,242	MC
Hampshire College	MA	37,037	HC
Harvard Univ/Harvard College	MA	37,928	MC
Haverford College	PA	37,900	MC
Indiana Univ Bloomington	IN	12,389	VC
Iowa State Univ	IA	10,768	VC
Lawrence Univ	WI	30,900	HC
Macalester College	MN	31,944	MC
Marlboro College	VT	29,055	VC+
Miami Univ	OH	15,033	HC
Mich State Univ	MI	11,933	VC
Montclair State Univ	NJ	13,790	C
New York Univ	NY	39,406	MC
Northeastern Univ	MA	35,650	HC
Northwestern Univ	IL	37,491	MC
Oakland Univ	MI	10,800	C
Ohio State Univ	OH	13,080	VC+
Ohio Univ	OH	14,448	C
Pitzer College	CA	37,590	HC
Pomona College	CA	33,960	MC
Purdue Univ/West Lafayette	IN	12,560	VC
Reed College	OR	36,950	MC
Rice Univ	TX	27,550	MC
Rutgers, The State Univ of New Jersey/New Brunswick/Piscataway Campus	NJ	15,800	HC
San Diego State Univ	CA	10,321	C
Southern Illinois Univ Carbondale	IL	10,407	C
Stanford Univ	CA	37,612	MC
SUNY at Oswego	NY	12,650	C
SUNY/Univ at Albany	NY	12,951	HC
SUNY/Univ at Binghamton	NY	12,787	HC
SUNY/Univ at Buffalo	NY	12,563	VC
SUNY/Univ at Stony Brook	NY	12,763	HC
Swarthmore College	PA	37,716	MC
Syracuse Univ	NY	34,720	HC
Temple Univ	PA	15,912	C
Tulane Univ	LA	37,451	HC+
Univ of Alaska Fairbanks	AK	9,295	C
Univ of Arizona	AZ	10,413	VC
Univ of Calif at Berkeley	CA	15,563	MC
Univ of Calif at Davis	CA	14,995	VC
Univ of Calif at Irvine	CA	19,808	HC
Univ of Calif at Los Angeles	CA	15,330	MC
Univ of Calif at Riverside	CA	15,300	C
Univ of Calif at San Diego	CA	14,127	HC
Univ of Calif at Santa Barbara	CA	11,732	VC
Univ of Calif at Santa Cruz	CA	16,505	VC
Univ of Chicago	IL	35,087	MC
Univ of Cincinnati	OH	14,736	C
Univ of Colo at Boulder	CO	10,774	VC
Univ of Conn	CT	14,608	VC
Univ of Florida	FL	8,580	MC
Univ of Georgia	GA	8,656	VC
Univ of Hawaii at Hilo	HI	6,497	C
Univ of Hawaii at Manoa	HI	9,565	VC
Univ of Illinois at Urbana-Champaign	IL	11,316	HC+
Univ of Iowa	IA	10,923	VC
Univ of Kansas	KS	8,923	VC
Univ of Kentucky	KY	7,765	C
Univ of Louisville	KY	8,762	VC
Univ of Maryland/Baltimore County	MD	14,668	VC+
Univ of Maryland/College Park	MD	14,227	HC
Univ of Mass Amherst	MA	13,980	C+
Univ of Mich/Ann Arbor	MI	13,864	HC+
Univ of Minn/Twin Cities	MN	13,160	VC
Univ of Miss	MS	7,666	C
Univ of Missouri/Columbia	MO	13,782	VC
Univ of New Hampshire	NH	14,828	VC
Univ of New Mexico	NM	9,223	C
Univ of N Car at Chapel Hill	NC	10,117	MC
Univ of Okla	OK	9,226	VC
Univ of Oregon	OR	11,479	VC
Univ of Pennsylvania	PA	37,960	MC
Univ of Pittsburgh at Pittsburgh	PA	16,074	HC
Univ of Rochester	NY	32,979	HC
Univ of Southern Calif	CA	37,459	MC
Univ of Tenn at Knoxville	TN	8,214	C
Univ of Texas at Austin	TX	10,630	HC
Univ of Texas at El Paso	TX	5,799	NC
Univ of Toledo	OH	12,479	NC
Univ of Utah	UT	9,205	C
Univ of Wisc/Madison	WI	8,262	VC
Univ of Wisc/Milwaukee	WI	9,427	LC
Washington State Univ	WA	11,334	C
Wayne State Univ	MI	11,774	C
Western Washington Univ	WA	10,119	VC
Yale Univ	CT	37,000	MC

LITERATURE

School	ST	$IS	SR
Alderson-Broaddus College	WV	19,640	C
American Univ	DC	34,585	VC+
Andrews Univ	MI	19,550	C
Aurora Univ	IL	20,631	C
Austin Peay State Univ	TN	5,814	LC
Beloit College	WI	29,864	HC
Benedictine Univ	IL	23,840	C
Bennington College	VT	35,910	HC
Burlington College	VT	10,640	SP
Calif Inst of Technology	CA	31,677	MC
Cal State, San Marcos	CA	1,736	LC
Castleton State College	VT	11,820	C
Claremont McKenna College	CA	36,880	MC
Coe College	IA	27,385	VC
College of the Holy Cross	MA	36,451	MC
Columbia Univ/School of General Studies	NY	35,000	C
Concordia College: Moorhead	MN	22,460	VC+
Drexel Univ	PA	27,655	VC
Duke Univ	NC	37,555	MC
Duquesne Univ	PA	26,907	VC
Eastern Mich Univ	MI	11,478	C
Eastern Nazarene College	MA	19,433	LC
Eastern Washington Univ	WA	9,012	C
Emory & Henry College	VA	21,950	C
Fairleigh Dickinson Univ/College at Florham	NJ	30,130	C
George Fox Univ	OR	26,110	VC
George Washington Univ	DC	41,030	MC
Gonzaga Univ	WA	26,766	HC
Graceland Univ	IA	19,550	C
Hampshire College	MA	37,037	HC
Harvard Univ/Harvard College	MA	37,928	MC
Hawaii Pacific Univ	HI	19,218	C
John Carroll Univ	OH	27,658	C+
Kentucky Christian College	KY	13,472	C
Maharishi Univ of Management	IA	29,230	VC
Mass Inst of Technology	MA	38,310	MC
Naropa Univ	CO	23,364	SP
New College of Florida	FL	8,906	HC+
Ohio Northern Univ	OH	27,765	VC
Oral Roberts Univ	OK	18,490	C
Pacific Univ	OR	24,250	C
Point Loma Nazarene Univ	CA	21,380	VC
Pomona College	CA	33,960	MC
Ramapo College of New Jersey	NJ	15,203	VC
Rocky Mountain College	MT	19,015	C
Roosevelt Univ	IL	22,580	VC
St. John's Univ	NY	30,180	C
St. Mary's Univ of Minn	MN	21,535	C
Sarah Lawrence College	NY	41,218	HC
Simon's Rock College of Bard	MA	36,580	HC
Southwest Minn State Univ	MN	9,106	VC
SUNY/College at Purchase	NY	10,587	VC
Stevens Inst of Technology	NJ	35,300	HC+
Swarthmore College	PA	37,716	MC
Sweet Briar College	VA	27,940	C
Thomas More College of Liberal Arts	NH	17,700	C
Touro College	NY	15,250	VC
Union College	NE	17,130	C
United States Military Academy	NY		MC
Univ of Alaska Southeast	AK	7,900	LC
Univ of Bridgeport	CT	25,924	LC
Univ of Calif at San Diego	CA	14,127	HC
Univ of Calif at Santa Barbara	CA	11,732	VC
Univ of Calif at Santa Cruz	CA	16,505	VC
Univ of Evansville	IN	24,190	VC
Univ of Illinois at Chicago	IL	13,418	C
Univ of Judaism College of A&S	CA	24,230	C
Univ of Mich/Ann Arbor	MI	13,864	HC+
Univ of New Haven	CT	28,650	C
Univ of N Car at Asheville	NC	8,079	VC
Univ of Rhode Island	RI	13,720	VC
Univ of St. Thomas	MN	26,918	VC
Univ of Texas at Dallas	TX	10,234	HC
Washington Univ in St. Louis	MO	38,293	MC
Waynesburg College	PA	19,370	C
Webster Univ	MO	21,848	VC
West Chester Univ of Pennsylvania	PA	11,164	C
Wheaton College	MA	36,330	HC
Wilberforce Univ	OH	14,937	LC
Williams College	MA	32,270	MC
Yale Univ	CT	37,000	MC

LOGISTICS

School	ST	$IS	SR
Duquesne Univ	PA	26,907	VC
Georgia Southern Univ	GA	8,540	C
Inter American Univ of PR/Bayamon Univ College	PR	3,522	
Thomas Edison State College	NJ	3,325	SP
United States Merchant Marine Academy	NY	6,250	HC+
Univ of Memphis	TN	8,560	C
Western Mich Univ	MI	12,031	C

LUSO-BRAZILIAN STUDIES

School	ST	$IS	SR
New York Univ	NY	39,406	MC
Smith College	MA	37,034	HC+

ST = STATE $IS = IN-STATE COSTS SR = SELECTOR RATING

MANAGEMENT ENGINEERING

School	ST	$IS	SR
Claremont McKenna College	CA	36,880	MC
Pitzer College	CA	37,590	HC
Univ of PR/Bayamon Univ College Campus	PR	1,600	
Worcester Polytechnic Inst	MA	37,404	HC

MANAGEMENT INFORMATION SYSTEMS

School	ST	$IS	SR
Adams State College	CO	7,468	C
Adelphi Univ	NY	26,300	VC
Albertus Magnus College	CT	23,130	LC
Alderson-Broaddus College	WV	19,640	C
American Univ	DC	34,585	VC+
Andrews Univ	MI	19,550	C
Arkansas State Univ	AR	8,450	C
Ashland Univ	OH	24,464	C
Augsburg College	MN	25,298	C
Augustana College	SD	21,998	VC
Aurora Univ	IL	20,631	C
Barry Univ	FL	24,100	LC
Bay Path College	MA	24,910	C
Baylor Univ	TX	23,864	VC
Benedictine Univ	IL	23,840	C
Bentley College	MA	33,904	VC
Boston Univ	MA	38,194	HC+
Bowling Green State Univ	OH	13,036	C
Bradley Univ	IL	22,910	VC
Brigham Young Univ	UT	8,504	HC
Cal State, Fullerton	CA	6,648	C
Cal State, Long Beach	CA	8,762	C+
Cal State, Northridge	CA	7,757	LC
Cal State, Sacramento	CA	9,543	C
Cal State, San Bernardino	CA	15,238	LC
Canisius College	NY	28,163	C+
Cedarville Univ	OH	19,954	VC
Central Conn State Univ	CT	12,090	C
Champlain College	VT	22,030	C
Chatham College	PA	27,266	C+
CUNY/Medgar Evers College	NY	4,232	NC
Clarkson Univ	NY	32,226	VC
Cleveland State Univ	OH	12,308	LC
College of St. Catherine	MN	24,010	VC
College of Santa Fe	NM	25,293	C+
Colo Christian Univ	CO	21,182	VC
Colo Technical Univ	CO	9,500	LC
Columbus State Univ	GA	7,846	C
Concordia Univ/St.Paul	MN	24,486	C
Creighton Univ	NE	26,748	VC+
Crichton College	TN	15,215	C
Dallas Baptist Univ	TX	15,300	VC
Daniel Webster College	NH	24,870	C
De Sales Univ	PA	25,470	C
Duquesne Univ	PA	26,907	VC
East Carolina Univ	NC	8,671	C
East Central Univ	OK	4,968	C
Eastern Mich Univ	MI	11,478	C
Eastern Univ	PA	24,020	C
Emporia State Univ	KS	6,998	C
Eureka College	IL	24,980	LC
Excelsior College	NY	975	SP
Florida Inst of Technology	FL	28,740	VC
Florida International Univ	FL	9,912	VC
Florida State Univ	FL	9,028	HC
Fort Hays State Univ	KS	7,363	C
Franciscan Univ	IA	19,300	C
Friends Univ	KS	15,962	LC
Gannon Univ	PA	23,260	C
George Mason Univ	VA	9,732	VC
Georgetown College	KY	22,000	VC
Georgia State Univ	GA	10,658	C
Goshen College	IN	22,450	VC
Grace College	IN	19,825	VC
Greenville College	IL	21,342	C
Grove City College	PA	14,228	HC
Hellenic College/Holy Cross Greek Orthodox School of Theology	MA	22,815	C
Hofstra Univ	NY	27,112	VC
Humphreys College	CA	7,000	NC
Huron Univ	SD	10,450	C
Indiana State Univ	IN	10,719	LC
Indiana Univ Bloomington	IN	12,389	VC
Indiana Univ of Pennsylvania	PA	10,489	C
Inter American Univ of PR/ Aguadilla Campus	PR	3,544	
Inter American Univ of PR/ Bayamon Univ College	PR	3,522	
Inter American Univ of PR/ Fajardo Campus	PR	4,000	
Inter American Univ of PR/ Metropolitan Campus	PR		
Inter American Univ of PR/ Ponce Regional College	PR	3,700	
Iona College	NY	27,988	VC
Johnson and Wales Univ	RI	22,965	LC
Johnson State College	VT	11,819	LC
Juniata College	PA	29,080	VC
Kansas State Univ	KS	8,728	VC
La Salle Univ	PA	31,260	VC
Lasell College	MA	26,000	C
Le Moyne College	NY	26,400	VC
LeTourneau Univ	TX	21,080	C
Lewis Univ	IL	22,950	C+
Liberty Univ	VA	17,220	C
Lindenwood Univ	MO	17,050	VC
Loras College	IA	24,233	C
Luther College	IA	25,700	VC
MacMurray College	IL	20,005	LC
Marietta College	OH	27,047	C
Marquette Univ	WI	27,594	VC
McMurry Univ	TX	17,846	LC
Menlo College	CA	24,000	LC
Mercyhurst College	PA	20,694	C
Metropolitan State Univ	MN	3,852	SP
Miami Univ	OH	15,033	HC
Midland Lutheran College	NE	18,600	C
Millikin Univ	IL	25,555	C
Milwaukee School of Engineering	WI	28,479	VC+
Minot State Univ	ND	6,602	LC
Missouri Southern State Univ	MO	8,316	C
Monmouth College	IL	23,600	C
Montclair State Univ	NJ	13,790	C
National Univ	CA	9,690	SP
New Mexico Highlands Univ	NM	6,182	LC
New Mexico State Univ	NM	7,932	C
Newman Univ	KS	18,018	C
Nichols College	MA	27,562	LC
N Dak State Univ	ND	8,435	C
Northeastern Univ	MA	35,650	HC
Northwestern College	MN	22,820	C+
Northwood Univ	FL	21,040	C
Northwood Univ	MI	20,265	LC
Northwood Univ	TX	20,135	LC
Oakland Univ	MI	10,800	C
Ohio Dominican Univ	OH	22,700	C
Ohio State Univ	OH	13,080	VC+
Okla State Univ	OK	9,216	VC
Old Dominion Univ	VA	10,441	C
Oral Roberts Univ	OK	18,490	C
Oregon Inst of Technology	OR	8,718	C
Ottawa Univ	KS	11,800	LC
Our Lady of the Lake Univ of San Antonio	TX	17,336	C
Park Univ	MO	10,780	C+
Penn State Univ at Erie/ Behrend College	PA	12,326	C
Penn State Univ/Univ Park Campus	PA	15,646	HC
Pennsylvania College of Technology	PA	15,126	NC
Philadelphia Univ	PA	27,354	C
Point Loma Nazarene Univ	CA	21,380	VC
Rensselaer Polytechnic Inst	NY	37,579	HC+
Rivier College	NH	26,217	C
Rochester Inst of Technology	NY	29,217	VC+
Rockhurst Univ	MO	22,960	C+
Rutgers, The State Univ of New Jersey/New Brunswick/Piscataway Campus	NJ	15,800	HC
St. Francis Univ	PA	25,876	LC
St. Joseph's College	IN	24,250	C
St. Joseph's Univ	PA	33,590	VC
Salisbury Univ	MD	12,664	VC
Santa Clara Univ	CA	34,701	HC
Savannah State Univ	GA	7,328	LC
Schreiner Univ	TX	20,440	C
Seton Hall Univ	NJ	30,130	VC
Seton Hill Univ	PA	24,930	C
Shippensburg Univ of Pennsylvania	PA	10,826	C
Simmons College	MA	33,000	VC
Southern Christian Univ	AL	9,440	LC
Southern Illinois Univ Edwardsville	IL	8,724	C
Southern Methodist Univ	TX	34,210	HC
Southern Nazarene Univ	OK	14,634	NC
Southwestern College	KS	19,560	C
Southwestern Okla State Univ	OK	4,801	C
Spring Arbor Univ	MI	20,206	C
SUNY/College at Old Westbury	NY	12,784	C
State Univ of West Georgia	GA	7,622	C
Stephen F. Austin State Univ	TX	7,552	C
Syracuse Univ	NY	34,720	HC
Temple Univ	PA	15,912	C
Texas A&M Univ at Corpus Christi	TX	10,269	C
Texas Lutheran Univ	TX	20,370	C
Texas Tech Univ	TX	10,768	VC
Texas Wesleyan Univ	TX	16,245	C
Thiel College	PA	20,970	C
Thomas College	ME	19,960	LC
Tri-State Univ-Main Campus	IN	23,600	C
Tusculum College	TN	19,990	C
Univ of Alabama	AL	9,040	C+
Univ of Alabama in Huntsville	AL	9,126	VC
Univ of Alaska Anchorage	AK	9,100	NC
Univ of Arizona	AZ	10,413	VC
Univ of Arkansas at Monticello	AR	5,940	NC
Univ of Bridgeport	CT	25,924	LC
Univ of Central Florida	FL	10,038	VC
Univ of Central Okla	OK	9,434	C
Univ of Conn	CT	14,608	VC
Univ of Dayton	OH	24,850	VC
Univ of Georgia	GA	8,656	VC
Univ of Hartford	CT	31,080	C
Univ of Hawaii at Manoa	HI	9,565	VC
Univ of Houston	TX	9,818	C
Univ of Idaho	ID	8,216	C
Univ of Indianapolis	IN	22,560	VC
Univ of Louisiana at Monroe	LA	5,207	NC
Univ of Mary	ND	12,900	C+
Univ of Maryland/College Park	MD	14,227	HC
Univ of Mass Dartmouth	MA	12,835	C
Univ of Memphis	TN	8,560	C
Univ of Miami	FL	34,608	HC
Univ of Miss	MS	7,666	C
Univ of Missouri/Rolla	MO	12,292	HC
Univ of Missouri/St. Louis	MO	11,656	VC
Univ of Nebr at Omaha	NE	8,080	C
Univ of Nevada/Las Vegas	NV	11,566	C
Univ of N Car at Charlotte	NC	8,185	C
Univ of N Car at Greensboro	NC	8,248	C
Univ of N Dak	ND	8,390	C
Univ of North Texas	TX	7,629	C
Univ of Northern Iowa	IA	9,834	C
Univ of Notre Dame	IN	34,442	MC
Univ of Okla	OK	9,226	VC
Univ of Pennsylvania	PA	37,960	MC
Univ of Rhode Island	RI	13,720	VC
Univ of St. Thomas	TX	21,952	VC
Univ of San Francisco	CA	34,700	VC
Univ of South Florida	FL	9,454	C
Univ of Texas at Austin	TX	10,630	HC
Univ of Texas at El Paso	TX	5,799	NC
Univ of Texas at San Antonio	TX	9,088	NC
Univ of the Sacred Heart	PR	5,590	
Univ of Tulsa	OK	22,090	VC+
Univ of Wisc/Milwaukee	WI	9,427	LC
Univ of Wisc/Oshkosh	WI	6,130	LC
Univ of Wyoming	WY	8,636	C
Upper Iowa Univ	IA	20,076	C
Ursuline College	OH	22,728	LC
Utah State Univ	UT	7,371	C
Villanova Univ	PA	35,050	HC
Virginia State Univ	VA	10,358	C
Viterbo Univ	WI	20,430	C
Wake Forest Univ	NC	34,090	MC
Washington and Jefferson College	PA	29,570	VC
Washington State Univ	WA	11,334	C
Wayne State Univ	MI	11,774	C
Weber State Univ	UT	7,945	NC
Western Conn State Univ	CT	11,625	C
Western Illinois Univ	IL	10,363	C
Western Mich Univ	MI	12,031	C
Western New Mexico Univ	NM	5,950	LC
Westminster College	MO	18,150	C+
Wingate Univ	NC	21,200	C
Winona State Univ	MN		C
Winston-Salem State Univ	NC	8,926	LC
Worcester Polytechnic Inst	MA	37,404	HC
Wright State Univ	OH	11,490	LC
Youngstown State Univ	OH	11,148	NC

MANAGEMENT SCIENCE

School	ST	$IS	SR
Abilene Christian Univ	TX	18,370	VC
Alfred Univ	NY	28,290	C
Anderson Univ	IN	19,430	LC
Arizona State Univ-Main	AZ	10,048	C
Aurora Univ	IL	20,631	C
Austin Peay State Univ	TN	5,814	LC
Avila Univ	MO	20,300	C
Ball State Univ	IN	8,660	C
Barry Univ	FL	24,100	LC
Belmont Univ	TN	21,986	VC
Bethel College	TN	12,980	C
Biola Univ	CA	25,964	VC
Boston College	MA	33,284	MC
Boston Univ	MA	38,194	HC+
Bridgewater State College	MA	10,482	C
Brigham Young Univ	UT	8,504	HC
Caldwell College	NJ	24,060	LC
Calif Baptist Univ	CA	19,924	C
Cal State, Fullerton	CA	6,648	C
Cal State, Monterey Bay	CA	6,683	LC
Cal State, San Bernardino	CA	15,238	LC
Cal State, Stanislaus	CA	9,874	C
Cambridge College	MA	10,800	SP
Catholic Univ of America	DC	34,248	VC
Cazenovia College	NY	23,940	C
Central Mich Univ	MI	11,142	C
Central Missouri State Univ	MO	9,776	C
Chaminade Univ of Honolulu	HI	21,430	LC
Champlain College	VT	22,030	C
Chestnut Hill College	PA	26,450	LC
Chicago State Univ	IL	10,882	C+
Christian Brothers Univ	TN	22,290	VC
CUNY/Baruch College	NY	3,275	VC+
CUNY/Herbert H. Lehman College	NY	3,320	LC
Clemson Univ	SC	11,972	HC
Cleveland State Univ	OH	12,308	LC
College for Lifelong Learning	NH	4,100	SP
College of New Jersey	NJ	15,950	MC
College of St. Benedict	MN	26,672	VC
Colo Christian Univ	CO	21,182	VC
Colo Technical Univ	CO	9,500	LC
Columbia Union College	MD	20,543	C
Concordia Univ Wisc	WI	16,600	C
Covenant College	GA	23,830	VC+
Culver-Stockton College	MO	17,850	C
Cumberland Univ	TN	16,910	C
Davenport Univ	MI	11,636	NC
Davis and Elkins College	WV	20,594	C
Defiance College	OH	22,615	C
Delta State Univ	MS	6,618	C
Drake Univ	IA	25,120	VC+
Duquesne Univ	PA	26,907	VC
East Central Univ	OK	4,968	C
East Tenn State Univ	TN	8,497	C
Eastern Mich Univ	MI	11,478	C
Eastern Washington Univ	WA	9,012	C
Eckerd College	FL	28,744	C+
Emporia State Univ	KS	6,998	C
Evangel Univ	MO	15,435	C
Florida Gulf Coast Univ	FL	9,908	C
Florida International Univ	FL	9,912	VC
Florida State Univ	FL	9,028	HC
Franklin Pierce College	NH	28,980	LC
Franklin Univ	OH	6,720	SP
Gallaudet Univ	DC	16,554	SP
George Fox Univ	OR	26,110	VC
Georgetown College	KY	22,000	VC
Georgia College and State Univ	GA	9,878	C
Georgia Inst of Technology	GA	10,340	HC+
Georgia Southern Univ	GA	8,540	C
Goucher College	MD	32,650	HC
Grand Valley State Univ	MI	11,022	VC
Gwynedd-Mercy College	PA	24,225	C
Hawaii Pacific Univ	HI	19,218	C
Heidelberg College	OH	20,266	NC
Hiram College	OH	28,234	VC
Hofstra Univ	NY	27,112	VC
Hood College	MD	27,795	VC
Huron Univ	SD	10,450	C
Idaho State Univ	ID	8,128	C
Illinois State Univ	IL	10,944	C+
Indiana Univ Bloomington	IN	12,389	VC
Indiana Univ Southeast	IN	4,504	LC
Indiana Univ-Purdue Univ Fort Wayne	IN	5,108	LC
Iona College	NY	27,988	VC
Iowa State Univ	IA	10,768	VC
Ithaca College	NY	31,730	HC
Johns Hopkins Univ	MD	38,372	MC
Keene State College	NH	12,212	C
Kennesaw State Univ	GA	2,724	C
Kent State Univ	OH	12,932	C
Langston Univ	OK	2,308	LC
Lesley Univ	MA	30,695	C
Louisiana State Univ in Shreveport	LA	2,884	NC
Louisiana Tech Univ	LA	7,361	C
Loyola Univ New Orleans	LA	31,036	VC+
Luther College	IA	25,700	VC
Lynchburg College	VA	26,815	C
Madonna Univ	MI	11,504	VC
Maharishi Univ of Management	IA	29,230	VC
Manhattanville College	NY	32,420	C+
Marian College of Fond du Lac	WI	19,625	C
Marietta College	OH	27,047	C
Marshall Univ	WV	9,116	C
Marylhurst Univ	OR	18,465	NC
Marymount Univ	VA	23,668	C
Mass Inst of Technology	MA	38,310	MC
McMurry Univ	TX	17,846	LC
Metropolitan State College of Denver	CO	2,338	LC
Miami Univ	OH	15,033	HC
Midwestern State Univ	TX	8,045	LC
Milwaukee School of Engineering	WI	28,479	VC+
Minn State Univ, Mankato	MN	8,803	LC
Minot State Univ	ND	6,602	LC
Missouri Baptist Univ	MO	18,010	C
Missouri Southern State Univ	MO	8,316	C
Morehead State Univ	KY	7,464	C
National-Louis Univ	IL	16,240	LC
New Jersey Inst of Technology	NJ	16,396	VC
New York Univ	NY	39,406	MC
Newman Univ	KS	18,018	C
Northern Kentucky Univ	KY	6,352	NC
Notre Dame College	OH	20,425	C
Ohio Northern Univ	OH	27,765	VC
Okla State Univ	OK	9,216	VC
Oral Roberts Univ	OK	18,490	C

School	ST	$IS	SR
Palm Beach Atlantic Univ	FL	20,690	C
Penn State Univ/Univ Park Campus	PA	15,646	HC
Philadelphia Univ	PA	27,354	C
Point Park Univ	PA	21,840	C
Portland State Univ	OR	12,453	C
Purdue Univ/West Lafayette	IN	12,560	VC
Quinnipiac Univ	CT	30,570	VC
Regis College	MA	29,000	C
Rensselaer Polytechnic Inst	NY	37,579	HC+
Rice Univ	TX	27,550	MC
Richard Stockton College of New Jersey	NJ	12,972	VC
Rider Univ	NJ	30,900	C
Rivier College	NH	26,217	C
Robert Morris Univ	PA	20,438	C
Rochester Inst of Technology	NY	29,217	VC+
Rockhurst Univ	MO	22,960	C+
Roosevelt Univ	IL	22,580	VC
Rutgers, The State Univ of New Jersey/Camden Campus	NJ	14,990	VC
Rutgers, The State Univ of New Jersey/New Brunswick/Piscataway Campus	NJ	15,800	HC
Rutgers, The State Univ of New Jersey/Newark Campus	NJ	15,624	VC
Sacred Heart Univ	CT	29,178	C
St. Ambrose Univ	IA	22,800	C
St. Bonaventure Univ	NY	24,455	LC
St. Francis Univ	PA	25,876	LC
St. John Fisher College	NY	24,870	C
St. John's Univ	MN	26,473	VC
St. John's Univ	NY	30,180	C
St. Joseph College	CT	29,685	C
St. Louis Univ	MO	29,780	VC+
St. Martin's College	WA	23,245	C
Salve Regina Univ	RI	29,210	C
San Francisco State Univ	CA	12,070	C
Southern Illinois Univ Carbondale	IL	10,407	C
Southern Methodist Univ	TX	34,210	HC
Southwestern Adventist Univ	TX	14,798	C
Southwestern College	KS	19,560	C
Southwestern Okla State Univ	OK	4,801	C
SUNY at Oswego	NY	12,650	C
SUNY/College at Cortland	NY	12,095	C
SUNY/Empire State College	NY	4,505	SP
State Univ of West Georgia	GA	7,622	C
Stephen F. Austin State Univ	TX	7,552	C
Stetson Univ	FL	29,495	VC
Suffolk Univ	MA	29,200	C
Tarleton State Univ	TX	7,576	C
Taylor Univ	IN	23,820	VC+
Teikyo Post Univ	CT	24,875	C
Tenn Tech Univ	TN	8,670	VC
Texas A&M Univ	TX	11,081	HC
Texas A&M Univ at Kingsville	TX	6,740	LC
Texas Christian Univ	TX	23,410	VC
Thomas College	ME	19,960	LC
Thomas Edison State College	NJ	3,325	SP
Touro College	NY	15,250	VC
Tri-State Univ-Main Campus	IN	23,600	C
Troy State Univ Montgomery	AL	3,600	NC
Tulane Univ	LA	37,451	HC+
Turabo Univ	PR	4,110	
Tusculum College	TN	19,990	C
Tuskegee Univ	AL	17,250	LC
Union College	NE	17,130	C
Union Univ	TN	18,800	VC
United States Air Force Academy	CO		HC+
United States Coast Guard Academy	CT		MC
United States Military Academy	NY		MC
Universidad Metropolitana	PR	3,324	
Univ of Arizona	AZ	10,413	VC
Univ of Arkansas at Little Rock	AR	5,637	NC
Univ of Bridgeport	CT	25,924	LC
Univ of Calif at San Diego	CA	14,127	HC
Univ of Central Florida	FL	10,038	VC
Univ of Cincinnati	OH	14,736	C
Univ of Colo at Boulder	CO	10,774	VC
Univ of Dayton	OH	24,850	VC
Univ of Delaware	DE	12,616	HC
Univ of Florida	FL	8,580	MC
Univ of Georgia	GA	8,656	VC
Univ of Great Falls	MT	15,360	C
Univ of Hartford	CT	31,080	C
Univ of Illinois at Chicago	IL	13,418	C
Univ of Iowa	IA	10,923	VC
Univ of Louisiana at Lafayette	LA	5,826	C
Univ of Louisiana at Monroe	LA	5,207	NC
Univ of Louisville	KY	8,762	VC
Univ of Maryland/Univ College	MD	5,910	SP
Univ of Mass Boston	MA	6,227	C
Univ of Minn/Crookston	MN	9,626	NC
Univ of Minn/Morris	MN	12,896	VC
Univ of Minn/Twin Cities	MN	13,160	VC
Univ of Miss	MS	7,666	C
Univ of Montevallo	AL	8,478	C
Univ of Nebr at Lincoln	NE	9,975	C+
Univ of Nebr at Omaha	NE	8,080	C
Univ of Nevada/Las Vegas	NV	11,566	C
Univ of Nevada/Reno	NV	9,792	C
Univ of New Mexico	NM	9,223	C
Univ of N Dak	ND	8,390	C
Univ of North Texas	TX	7,629	C
Univ of Northern Colo	CO	8,987	C
Univ of Northern Iowa	IA	9,834	C
Univ of Notre Dame	IN	34,442	MC
Univ of Pittsburgh at Greensburg	PA	15,984	C
Univ of Pittsburgh at Pittsburgh	PA	16,074	HC
Univ of PR/Cayey Univ College	PR	1,245	
Univ of PR/Rio Piedras	PR	5,730	
Univ of S Car at Columbia	SC	10,048	VC
Univ of S Dak	SD	7,710	C+
Univ of South Florida	FL	9,454	C
Univ of Tenn at Knoxville	TN	8,214	C
Univ of Tenn at Martin	TN	7,748	C
Univ of Texas at Arlington	TX	7,192	LC
Univ of Texas at Austin	TX	10,630	HC
Univ of Texas at El Paso	TX	5,799	NC
Univ of Texas at San Antonio	TX	9,088	NC
Univ of Texas-Pan American	TX	5,954	LC
Univ of the Incarnate Word	TX	21,772	LC
Univ of Tulsa	OK	22,090	VC+
Univ of Wisc/Platteville	WI	8,450	C
Univ of Wisc/Stevens Point	WI	8,116	VC
Univ of Wisc/Stout	WI	9,718	C
Upper Iowa Univ	IA	20,076	C
Virginia Polytechnic Inst and State Univ	VA	9,179	C
Viterbo Univ	WI	20,430	C
Washington State Univ	WA	11,334	C
Wayne State Univ	MI	11,774	C
Waynesburg College	PA	19,370	C
Webster Univ	MO	21,848	VC
Wesley College	DE	19,905	C
West Liberty State College	WV	7,868	LC
West Texas A&M Univ	TX	7,533	C
Western Carolina Univ	NC	6,742	C
Western Mich Univ	MI	12,031	C
Western New England College	MA	28,924	C
Western Washington Univ	WA	10,119	VC
Wheeling Jesuit Univ	WV	22,660	C
Wichita State Univ	KS	8,092	C
Wilberforce Univ	OH	14,937	LC
Woodbury Univ	CA	25,344	LC
Worcester Polytechnic Inst	MA	37,404	HC
Wright State Univ	OH	11,490	LC
Xavier Univ	OH	26,850	VC+
York College of Pennsylvania	PA	14,500	VC

MANUFACTURING ENGINEERING

School	ST	$IS	SR
Boston Univ	MA	38,194	HC+
Bradley Univ	IL	22,910	VC
Brigham Young Univ	UT	8,504	HC
Calif Polytechnic State Univ	CA	8,747	VC
Calif State Polytechnic Univ, Pomona	CA	8,793	C+
Central State Univ	OH	8,922	C+
Hofstra Univ	NY	27,112	VC
Indiana Inst of Technology	IN	21,620	C
Kansas State Univ	KS	8,728	VC
Miami Univ	OH	15,033	HC
Mich State Univ	MI	11,933	VC
Midwestern State Univ	TX	8,045	LC
New Jersey Inst of Technology	NJ	16,396	VC
New York Inst of Technology	NY	24,205	VC
N Dak State Univ	ND	8,435	C
Northern Kentucky Univ	KY	6,352	NC
Northwestern Univ	IL	37,491	MC
Pennsylvania College of Technology	PA	15,126	NC
Rochester Inst of Technology	NY	29,217	VC+
St. Cloud State Univ	MN	8,362	C
Seattle Univ	WA	24,183	VC
Southern Illinois Univ Edwardsville	IL	8,724	C
Southern Polytechnic State Univ	GA	7,620	VC
Southwestern Okla State Univ	OK	4,801	C
Tenn Tech Univ	TN	8,670	VC
Texas State Univ	TX	9,320	VC
Univ of Arkansas at Little Rock	AR	5,637	NC
Univ of Calif at Berkeley	CA	15,563	MC
Univ of Conn	CT	14,608	VC
Univ of Detroit Mercy	MI	25,582	C
Univ of Hartford	CT	31,080	C
Univ of Miami	FL	34,608	HC
Univ of Mich/Dearborn	MI	6,843	VC
Univ of Missouri/Rolla	MO	12,292	HC
Univ of New Mexico	NM	9,223	C
Univ of N Car at Charlotte	NC	8,185	C
Univ of Texas-Pan American	TX	5,954	LC
Univ of Wisc/Stout	WI	9,718	C
Washington State Univ	WA	11,334	C
Western Mich Univ	MI	12,031	C
Wichita State Univ	KS	8,092	C
Worcester Polytechnic Inst	MA	37,404	HC

MANUFACTURING TECHNOLOGY

School	ST	$IS	SR
Arkansas State Univ	AR	8,450	C
Bowling Green State Univ	OH	13,036	C
Bradley Univ	IL	22,910	VC
Brigham Young Univ	UT	8,504	HC
Calif Univ of Pennsylvania	PA	10,388	C
Central Conn State Univ	CT	12,090	C
Central Missouri State Univ	MO	9,776	C
East Carolina Univ	NC	8,671	C
Eastern Kentucky Univ	KY	7,708	C
Eastern Mich Univ	MI	11,478	C
Fairmont State	WV	8,280	LC
Farmingdale SUNY	NY	12,891	C
Illinois Inst of Technology	IL	26,456	HC+
Indiana State Univ	IN	10,719	LC
Indiana Univ-Purdue Univ Indianapolis	IN	8,257	LC
Lake Superior State Univ	MI	9,034	LC
Minn State Univ, Mankato	MN	8,803	LC
Missouri Southern State Univ	MO	8,316	C
Montana State Univ-Northern	MT	8,600	NC
Nicholls State Univ	LA	6,395	NC
Northern Kentucky Univ	KY	6,352	NC
Northern Mich Univ	MI	10,834	C
Oregon Inst of Technology	OR	8,718	C
Rochester Inst of Technology	NY	29,217	VC+
S Dak State Univ	SD	7,782	C
Southern Arkansas Univ	AR	6,956	C
Southwest Missouri State Univ	MO	8,918	C
Southwestern College	KS	19,560	C
Southwestern Okla State Univ	OK	4,801	C
Texas State Univ	TX	9,320	VC
Thomas Edison State College	NJ	3,325	SP
Univ of Akron	OH	13,134	NC
Univ of Dayton	OH	24,850	VC
Univ of Houston	TX	9,818	C
Univ of Memphis	TN	8,560	C
Univ of Nebr at Lincoln	NE	9,975	C+
Univ of N Car at Charlotte	NC	8,185	C
Univ of Northern Iowa	IA	9,834	C
Univ of Rio Grande	OH	8,728	NC
Wayne State Univ	MI	11,774	C
Weber State Univ	UT	7,945	NC
Western Carolina Univ	NC	6,742	C
Western Illinois Univ	IL	10,363	C
Western Mich Univ	MI	12,031	C
Western Washington Univ	WA	10,119	VC

MARINE BIOLOGY

School	ST	$IS	SR
Alaska Pacific Univ	AK	17,910	C
Auburn Univ	AL	10,396	VC
Barry Univ	FL	24,100	LC
Brown Univ	RI	38,174	MC
Cal State, Stanislaus	CA	9,874	C
Carroll College	WI	22,740	C
College of Charleston	SC	11,887	HC
Dowling College	NY	23,870	LC
Eastern Nazarene College	MA	19,433	LC
Fairleigh Dickinson Univ/College at Florham	NJ	30,130	C
Fairleigh Dickinson Univ/Metropolitan Campus	NJ	28,584	C
Florida Atlantic Univ	FL	8,543	C
Florida Inst of Technology	FL	28,740	VC
Florida International Univ	FL	9,912	VC
Florida State Univ	FL	9,028	HC
Hampshire College	MA	37,037	HC
Missouri Southern State Univ	MO	8,316	C
Nova Southeastern Univ	FL	23,346	C
Roger Williams Univ	RI	30,296	C
St. Paul's College	VA	14,344	NC
San Francisco State Univ	CA	12,070	C
Savannah State Univ	GA	7,328	LC
Southwestern College	KS	19,560	C
Spring Hill College	AL	25,868	VC
Stetson Univ	FL	29,495	VC
Texas A&M Univ at Galveston	TX	9,948	C+
Texas State Univ	TX	9,320	VC
Troy State Univ	AL	7,696	C
Univ of Alaska Southeast	AK	7,900	LC
Univ of Calif at Los Angeles	CA	15,330	MC
Univ of Calif at Santa Barbara	CA	11,732	VC
Univ of Calif at Santa Cruz	CA	16,505	VC
Univ of Maine	ME	12,080	C+
Univ of Maine at Machias	ME	9,271	LC
Univ of Maryland/College Park	MD	14,227	HC
Univ of Mass Dartmouth	MA	12,835	C
Univ of New England	ME	27,200	LC
Univ of New Hampshire	NH	14,828	VC
Univ of New Haven	CT	28,650	C
Univ of N Car at Wilmington	NC	8,940	VC
Univ of PR at Humacao	PR	1,245	
Univ of West Alabama	AL	6,048	C
Univ of West Florida	FL	8,470	C
Waynesburg College	PA	19,370	C

MARINE ENGINEERING

School	ST	$IS	SR
Calif Maritime Academy	CA	14,296	C
Maine Maritime Academy	ME	12,380	C
Mass Maritime Academy	MA	10,472	C
SUNY/Maritime College	NY	10,025	LC
Texas A&M Univ at Galveston	TX	9,948	C+
Thomas Edison State College	NJ	3,325	SP
United States Merchant Marine Academy	NY	6,250	HC+
United States Naval Academy	MD		MC
Univ of New Orleans	LA	7,356	C

MARINE SCIENCE

School	ST	$IS	SR
American Univ	DC	34,585	VC+
Coastal Carolina Univ	SC	11,040	C
East Stroudsburg Univ of Pennsylvania	PA	10,336	C
Eckerd College	FL	28,744	C+
Hawaii Pacific Univ	HI	19,218	C
Jacksonville Univ	FL	24,040	C
Juniata College	PA	29,080	VC
Kutztown Univ of Pennsylvania	PA	10,786	C
LIU/Southampton College	NY	29,370	C+
Old Dominion Univ	VA	10,441	C
Richard Stockton College of New Jersey	NJ	12,972	VC
Rider Univ	NJ	30,900	C
Rutgers, The State Univ of New Jersey/New Brunswick/Piscataway Campus	NJ	15,800	HC
St. Paul's College	VA	14,344	NC
Samford Univ	AL	18,648	VC
SUNY/Maritime College	NY	10,025	LC
Suffolk Univ	MA	29,200	C
Texas A&M Univ at Galveston	TX	9,948	C+
United States Coast Guard Academy	CT		MC
Univ of Alabama	AL	9,040	C+
Univ of Conn	CT	14,608	VC
Univ of Hawaii at Hilo	HI	6,497	C
Univ of Maine	ME	12,080	C+
Univ of Miami	FL	34,608	HC
Univ of N Car at Wilmington	NC	8,940	VC
Univ of Rhode Island	RI	13,720	VC
Univ of San Diego	CA	33,156	HC
Univ of S Car at Columbia	SC	10,048	VC
Univ of Tampa	FL	23,982	VC

MARITIME SCIENCE

School	ST	$IS	SR
Calif Maritime Academy	CA	14,296	C
Maine Maritime Academy	ME	12,380	C
SUNY/Maritime College	NY	10,025	LC
Texas A&M Univ at Galveston	TX	9,948	C+
United States Merchant Marine Academy	NY	6,250	HC+

MARKETING AND DISTRIBUTION

School	ST	$IS	SR
Alvernia College	PA	23,212	LC
Becker College	MA	23,710	LC
Caldwell College	NJ	24,060	LC
Cal State, Stanislaus	CA	9,874	C
Clayton College and State Univ	GA	2,441	LC
Duquesne Univ	PA	26,907	VC
Florida Gulf Coast Univ	FL	9,908	C
Franklin Univ	OH	6,720	SP
Georgia College and State Univ	GA	9,878	C
Georgia Southern Univ	GA	8,540	C
Gwynedd-Mercy College	PA	24,225	C

ST = STATE $IS = IN-STATE COSTS SR = SELECTOR RATING

School	ST	$IS	SR
Indiana State Univ	IN	10,719	LC
Indiana Univ-Purdue Univ Indianapolis	IN	8,257	LC
Inter American Univ of PR/ Arecibo Campus	PR	3,300	
Johnson and Wales Univ	RI	22,965	LC
Mountain State Univ	WV	10,212	NC
Neumann College	PA	23,890	LC
New York Inst of Technology	NY	24,205	VC
Newman Univ	KS	18,018	C
Northwest Nazarene Univ	ID	20,360	VC
Ohio State Univ	OH	13,080	VC+
Our Lady of Holy Cross College	LA	5,900	C
Pennsylvania College of Technology	PA	15,126	NC
St. John's Univ	NY	30,180	C
Tarleton State Univ	TX	7,576	C
Taylor Univ	IN	23,820	VC+
Thomas Edison State College	NJ	3,325	SP
Union College	NE	17,130	C
Univ of Houston	TX	9,818	C
Univ of La Verne	CA	28,600	C
Univ of Memphis	TN	8,560	C
West Virginia Univ	WV	9,370	C
Western Carolina Univ	NC	6,742	C
Youngstown State Univ	OH	11,148	NC

MARKETING AND DISTRIBUTION EDUCATION

School	ST	$IS	SR
Bowling Green State Univ	OH	13,036	C
Central Washington Univ	WA	9,768	C
Dakota State Univ	SD	7,466	C
East Carolina Univ	NC	8,671	C
Eastern Washington Univ	WA	9,012	C
Fayetteville State Univ	NC	5,590	LC
Johnson and Wales Univ	RI	22,965	LC
Kent State Univ	OH	12,932	C
N Car State Univ	NC	9,886	VC
Rider Univ	NJ	30,900	C
Southern New Hampshire Univ	NH	26,242	C
Temple Univ	PA	15,912	C
Univ of Central Okla	OK	9,434	C
Univ of Georgia	GA	8,656	VC
Univ of Idaho	ID	8,216	C
Univ of Tenn at Knoxville	TN	8,214	C
Univ of Wisc/Stout	WI	9,718	C
Virginia Polytechnic Inst and State Univ	VA	9,179	C
Western Mich Univ	MI	12,031	C

MARKETING MANAGEMENT

School	ST	$IS	SR
American Univ	DC	34,585	VC+
Assumption College	MA	29,375	C
Averett Univ	VA	23,010	LC
Baker College of Flint	MI	7,720	NC
Benedictine Univ	IL	23,840	C
Bentley College	MA	33,904	VC
Berry College	GA	21,410	VC
Biola Univ	CA	25,964	VC
Carthage College	WI	25,000	C
Catawba College	NC	20,500	C
Champlain College	VT	22,030	C
Chatham College	PA	27,266	C+
Christopher Newport Univ	VA	8,862	VC
CUNY/Baruch College	NY	3,275	VC+
Clarke College	IA	23,165	C
Cleary College	MI	10,350	LC
College of St. Elizabeth	NJ	25,460	C
College of St. Joseph	VT	19,100	C
College of St. Scholastica	MN	24,970	C+
College of the Ozarks	MO	3,500	VC+
Columbia College Chicago	IL	25,108	LC
Concordia Univ/St.Paul	MN	24,486	C
Coppin State College	MD	10,191	LC
Cumberland Univ	TN	16,910	C
Davenport Univ	MI	11,636	NC
Drake Univ	IA	25,120	VC+
East Carolina Univ	NC	8,671	C
East Texas Baptist Univ	TX	13,914	C
Edinboro Univ of Pennsylvania	PA	10,850	LC
Emerson College	MA	32,205	HC
Fordham Univ	NY	35,066	HC
Franciscan Univ	IA	19,300	C
George Washington Univ	DC	41,030	MC
Hawaii Pacific Univ	HI	19,218	C
Hofstra Univ	NY	27,112	VC
Indiana Univ Kokomo	IN	4,463	LC
Iona College	NY	27,988	VC
Ithaca College	NY	31,730	HC
Johns Hopkins Univ	MD	38,372	MC
Johnson and Wales Univ	RI	22,965	LC
La Roche College	PA	22,094	C
La Sierra Univ	CA	19,260	LC
Lakeland College	WI	17,950	C
LeTourneau Univ	TX	21,080	C
Limestone College	SC	17,700	C
Lourdes College	OH	15,300	LC
Metropolitan State Univ	MN	3,852	SP
Mich State Univ	MI	11,933	VC
Montclair State Univ	NJ	13,790	C
Morehead State Univ	KY	7,464	C
Northwestern College	MN	22,820	C+
Northwood Univ	FL	21,040	C
Northwood Univ	MI	20,265	LC
Northwood Univ	TX	20,135	LC
Ohio Univ	OH	14,448	C
Old Dominion Univ	VA	10,441	C
Olivet College	MI	19,984	C+
Oregon State Univ	OR	11,055	C
Our Lady of the Lake Univ of San Antonio	TX	17,336	C
Palm Beach Atlantic Univ	FL	20,690	C
Park Univ	MO	10,780	C+
Penn State Univ at Erie/ Behrend College	PA	12,326	C
Pennsylvania College of Technology	PA	15,126	NC
Plymouth State Univ	NH	12,298	LC
Purdue Univ/West Lafayette	IN	12,560	VC
Rochester College	MI	16,718	C
Rochester Inst of Technology	NY	29,217	VC+
Saginaw Valley State Univ	MI	11,055	C
St. Edward's Univ	TX	20,428	C
Siena College	NY	25,310	VC
Southern Utah Univ	UT	8,194	C
Spring Hill College	AL	25,868	VC
Stephen F. Austin State Univ	TX	7,552	C
Syracuse Univ	NY	34,720	HC
Thomas College	ME	19,960	LC
Troy State Univ Dothan	AL	3,842	C
Troy State Univ Montgomery	AL	3,600	NC
Tulane Univ	LA	37,451	HC+
Union Univ	TN	18,800	VC
Univ of Arkansas	AR	9,855	VC
Univ of Colo at Boulder	CO	10,774	VC
Univ of Maryland/College Park	MD	14,227	HC
Univ of Maryland/Univ College	MD	5,910	SP
Univ of Mass Amherst	MA	13,980	C+
Univ of Memphis	TN	8,560	C
Univ of Miami	FL	34,608	HC
Univ of North Florida	FL	8,769	VC
Univ of PR/Rio Piedras	PR	5,730	
Univ of Rio Grande	OH	8,728	NC
Univ of St. Thomas	MN	26,918	VC
Univ of S Car at Spartanburg	SC	9,936	C+
Univ of Texas at Austin	TX	10,630	HC
Univ of the Sciences in Philadelphia	PA	29,310	VC
Ursuline College	OH	22,728	LC
Virginia State Univ	VA	10,358	C
Warner Southern College	FL	16,738	LC
Washington State Univ	WA	11,334	C
Washington Univ in St. Louis	MO	38,293	MC
Weber State Univ	UT	7,945	NC
Western Carolina Univ	NC	6,742	C
Western Conn State Univ	CT	11,625	C
Youngstown State Univ	OH	11,148	NC

MARKETING/RETAILING/ MERCHANDISING

School	ST	$IS	SR
Abilene Christian Univ	TX	18,370	VC
Adams State College	CO	7,468	C
Alabama A&M Univ	AL	5,100	LC
Alabama State Univ	AL	6,404	C
Albany State Univ	GA	5,764	C+
Alfred Univ	NY	28,290	C
American International College	MA	24,690	LC
Anderson Univ	IN	19,430	LC
Andrews Univ	MI	19,550	C
Angelo State Univ	TX	7,576	NC
Appalachian State Univ	NC	7,637	VC
Arcadia Univ	PA	29,890	C
Arizona State Univ-Main	AZ	10,048	C
Arkansas State Univ	AR	8,450	C
Ashland Univ	OH	24,464	C
Auburn Univ	AL	10,396	VC
Auburn Univ Montgomery	AL	9,020	NC
Augsburg College	MN	25,298	C
Augusta State Univ	GA	2,592	C
Aurora Univ	IL	20,631	C
Austin Peay State Univ	TN	5,814	LC
Avila Univ	MO	20,300	C
Azusa Pacific Univ	CA	24,720	VC
Ball State Univ	IN	8,660	C
Barry Univ	FL	24,100	LC
Bay Path College	MA	24,910	C
Baylor Univ	TX	23,864	VC
Belmont Univ	TN	21,986	VC
Benedictine Univ	IL	23,840	C
Berkeley College	NY	21,545	LC
Berkeley College of New York City	NY	12,500	LC
Bethel College	MN	25,180	VC
Black Hills State Univ	SD	7,743	LC
Boise State Univ	ID	7,657	LC
Boston College	MA	33,284	MC
Boston Univ	MA	38,194	HC+
Bowling Green State Univ	OH	13,036	C
Bradley Univ	IL	22,910	VC
Brenau Univ Women's College	GA	21,800	C
Bryant College	RI	31,004	VC
Buena Vista Univ	IA	25,406	C
Butler Univ	IN	28,250	VC+
Cabrini College	PA	29,020	C
Calif Lutheran Univ	CA	27,600	LC
Calif State Polytechnic Univ, Pomona	CA	8,793	C+
Cal State, Fullerton	CA	6,648	C
Cal State, Hayward	CA	8,871	LC
Cal State, Long Beach	CA	8,762	C+
Cal State, Northridge	CA	7,757	LC
Cal State, Sacramento	CA	9,543	C
Canisius College	NY	28,163	C+
Caribbean Univ	PR	3,000	
Carnegie Mellon Univ	PA	32,682	MC
Cedarville Univ	OH	19,954	VC
Central Conn State Univ	CT	12,090	C
Central Mich Univ	MI	11,142	C
Central Missouri State Univ	MO	9,776	C
Central State Univ	OH	8,922	C+
Central Univ of Bayamon	PR	3,335	
Central Washington Univ	WA	9,768	C
Chaminade Univ of Honolulu	HI	21,430	LC
Chestnut Hill College	PA	26,450	LC
Chicago State Univ	IL	10,882	C+
Christian Brothers Univ	TN	22,290	VC
Christopher Newport Univ	VA	8,862	VC
City Univ	WA	7,425	NC
CUNY/Baruch College	NY	3,275	VC+
CUNY/York College	NY	3,292	NC
Clarion Univ of Pennsylvania	PA	11,272	LC
Clarkson Univ	NY	32,226	VC
Clemson Univ	SC	11,972	HC
Cleveland State Univ	OH	12,308	LC
Coastal Carolina Univ	SC	11,040	C
College Misericordia	PA	26,350	C
College of New Jersey	NJ	15,950	MC
College of Notre Dame of Maryland	MD	27,700	C
College of Our Lady of the Elms	MA	20,644	C
College of St. Catherine	MN	24,010	VC
College of the Southwest	NM	9,320	C+
Colo State Univ	CO	9,964	VC
Columbia College	MO	16,139	C
Columbus State Univ	GA	7,846	C
Concord College	WV	8,136	C
Concordia Univ Wisc	WI	16,600	C
Cornerstone Univ and Grand Rapids Theological Seminary	MI	19,846	C
Creighton Univ	NE	26,748	VC+
Dallas Baptist Univ	TX	15,300	VC
David Lipscomb Univ	TN	16,158	VC
David N. Myers College	OH	9,475	C
Davis and Elkins College	WV	20,594	C
De Sales Univ	PA	25,470	C
Defiance College	OH	22,615	C
Delaware State Univ	DE	8,104	LC
Delaware Valley College	PA	26,676	C
Delta State Univ	MS	6,618	C
DePaul Univ	IL	27,580	VC
Dominican College	NY	24,810	LC
Dowling College	NY	23,870	LC
Drake Univ	IA	25,120	VC+
Drexel Univ	PA	27,655	VC
Duquesne Univ	PA	26,907	VC
East Central Univ	OK	4,968	C
East Tenn State Univ	TN	8,497	C
Eastern Illinois Univ	IL	11,192	C
Eastern Kentucky Univ	KY	7,708	C
Eastern Mich Univ	MI	11,478	C
Eastern New Mexico Univ	NM	6,762	LC
Eastern Univ	PA	24,020	C
Eastern Washington Univ	WA	9,012	C
Elmhurst College	IL	24,630	C
Elmira College	NY	33,820	VC
Emory Univ	GA	36,872	MC
Emporia State Univ	KS	6,998	C
Evangel Univ	MO	15,435	C
Excelsior College	NY	975	SP
Fairfield Univ	CT	35,505	HC
Fairleigh Dickinson Univ/ College at Florham	NJ	30,130	C
Fairleigh Dickinson Univ/ Metropolitan Campus	NJ	28,584	C
Fairmont State	WV	8,280	LC
Fashion Inst of Technology/ SUNY	NY	11,169	C+
Ferris State Univ	MI	12,512	C
Florida Atlantic Univ	FL	8,543	C
Florida International Univ	FL	9,912	VC
Florida Southern College	FL	23,592	C
Florida State Univ	FL	9,028	HC
Fort Hays State Univ	KS	7,363	C
Fort Valley State Univ	GA	6,960	C
Francis Marion Univ	SC	9,364	C
Franklin Pierce College	NH	28,980	LC
Freed-Hardeman Univ	TN		NC
Gannon Univ	PA	23,260	C
George Mason Univ	VA	9,732	VC
Georgetown College	KY	22,000	VC
Georgetown Univ	DC	38,242	MC
Georgia Southern Univ	GA	8,540	C
Georgia Southwestern State Univ	GA	6,013	C
Georgia State Univ	GA	10,658	C
Glenville State College	WV	7,812	NC
Goldey-Beacom College	DE	11,440	C
Grambling State Univ	LA	6,538	NC
Grand Canyon Univ	AZ	30,000	LC
Grand Valley State Univ	MI	11,022	VC
Greenville College	IL	21,342	C
Grove City College	PA	14,228	HC
Hampton Univ	VA	17,112	C+
Harding Univ	AR	14,890	VC
Hardin-Simmons Univ	TX	14,165	C
High Point Univ	NC	22,480	C
Hillsdale College	MI	22,450	HC
Holy Family College	PA	13,710	LC
Houston Baptist Univ	TX	16,905	C
Howard Univ	DC	16,505	C
Huron Univ	SD	10,450	C
Husson College	ME	16,300	LC
Huston-Tillotson College	TX	14,232	NC
Idaho State Univ	ID	8,128	C
Illinois State Univ	IL	10,944	C+
Indiana State Univ	IN	10,719	LC
Indiana Univ Bloomington	IN	12,389	VC
Indiana Univ of Pennsylvania	PA	10,489	C
Indiana Univ South Bend	IN	4,571	LC
Indiana Univ Southeast	IN	4,504	LC
Indiana Univ-Purdue Univ Fort Wayne	IN	5,108	LC
Indiana Univ-Purdue Univ Indianapolis	IN	8,257	LC
Indiana Wesleyan Univ	IN	19,900	C+
Inter American Univ of PR/ Aguadilla Campus	PR	3,544	
Inter American Univ of PR/ Bayamon Univ College	PR	3,522	
Inter American Univ of PR/ Fajardo Campus	PR	4,000	
Inter American Univ of PR/ Metropolitan Campus	PR		
Inter American Univ of PR/ Ponce Regional College	PR	3,700	
Inter American Univ of PR/ San German	PR	6,716	
Iowa State Univ	IA	10,768	VC
Ithaca College	NY	31,730	HC
Jackson State Univ	MS	8,382	C
Jacksonville State Univ	AL	6,844	LC
Jacksonville Univ	FL	24,040	C
James Madison Univ	VA	10,794	VC
John Carroll Univ	OH	27,658	C+
Johnson and Wales Univ	RI	22,965	LC
Juniata College	PA	29,080	VC
Kansas State Univ	KS	8,728	VC
Kean Univ	NJ	14,479	C
Kennesaw State Univ	GA	2,724	C
Kent State Univ	OH	12,932	C
Keuka College	NY	21,170	C
King's College	PA	26,990	C
Kutztown Univ of Pennsylvania	PA	10,786	C
La Salle Univ	PA	31,260	VC
Laboratory Inst of Merchandising	NY	25,150	SP
Lake Superior State Univ	MI	9,034	LC
Lamar Univ	TX	6,816	LC
Lasell College	MA	26,000	C
Lehigh Univ	PA	37,570	HC+
LeTourneau Univ	TX	21,080	C
Lewis Univ	IL	22,950	C+
Lincoln Univ	MO	7,158	NC
Lindenwood Univ	MO	17,050	VC
LIU/Brooklyn Campus	NY	24,790	C
LIU/C.W. Post Campus	NY	28,282	C
Loras College	IA	24,233	C
Louisiana State Univ and A&M College	LA	9,126	VC
Louisiana State Univ in Shreveport	LA	2,884	NC
Louisiana Tech Univ	LA	7,361	C
Loyola Univ Chicago	IL	31,164	VC
Loyola Univ New Orleans	LA	31,036	VC+
Lynchburg College	VA	26,815	C
Lynn Univ	FL	30,750	C
MacMurray College	IL	20,005	LC
Madonna Univ	MI	11,504	VC
Manhattan College	NY	27,400	VC
Mansfield Univ	PA	11,220	C
Marian College of Fond du Lac	WI	19,625	C
Marietta College	OH	27,047	C
Marquette Univ	WI	27,594	VC
Marshall Univ	WV	9,116	C
Martin Univ	IN	10,200	SP
Marymount Univ	VA	23,668	C
Maryville Univ of St. Louis	MO	22,090	VC
Marywood Univ	PA	26,050	C
McKendree College	IL	21,120	VC

School	ST	$IS	SR
McMurry Univ	TX	17,846	LC
McNeese State Univ	LA	5,259	LC
Mercer Univ	GA	27,516	VC+
Mercyhurst College	PA	20,694	C
Merrimack College	MA	29,625	C
Messiah College	PA	25,890	VC+
Methodist College	NC	19,526	C
Metropolitan State College of Denver	CO	2,338	LC
Miami Univ	OH	15,033	HC
Mich State Univ	MI	11,933	VC
Middle Tenn State Univ	TN	8,534	C
Midland Lutheran College	NE	18,600	C
Midwestern State Univ	TX	8,045	LC
Millikin Univ	IL	25,555	C
Minn State Univ, Mankato	MN	8,803	LC
Minn State Univ, Moorehead	MN	7,000	LC
Minot State Univ	ND	6,602	LC
Miss College	MS	14,574	C
Miss State Univ	MS	9,139	C
Missouri Southern State Univ	MO	8,316	C
Missouri Western State College	MO	8,522	NC
Monmouth Univ	NJ	26,334	C
Morehouse College	GA	22,728	C
Morgan State Univ	MD	11,470	C
Mount Ida College	MA	25,596	LC
Mount Mercy College	IA	21,400	C
Murray State Univ	KY	7,816	VC
New Mexico Highlands Univ	NM	6,182	LC
New Mexico State Univ	NM	7,932	C
New York Inst of Technology	NY	24,205	VC
New York Univ	NY	39,406	MC
Niagara Univ	NY	25,050	C
Nicholls State Univ	LA	6,395	NC
Nichols College	MA	27,562	LC
North Central College	IL	25,656	VC
North Georgia College and State Univ	GA	6,984	C
North Park Univ	IL	24,030	C
Northeastern Illinois Univ	IL	2,898	NC
Northeastern State Univ	OK	4,950	LC
Northeastern Univ	MA	35,650	HC
Northern Arizona Univ	AZ	9,002	C
Northern Illinois Univ	IL	11,472	C
Northern Kentucky Univ	KY	6,352	NC
Northern Mich Univ	MI	10,834	C
Northern State Univ	SD	7,117	LC
Northwest Missouri State Univ	MO	9,334	C
Notre Dame College	OH	20,425	C
Notre Dame de Namur Univ	CA	26,932	LC
Oakland Univ	MI	10,800	C
Okla Baptist Univ	OK	15,220	VC
Okla Christian Univ	OK	17,690	NC
Okla State Univ	OK	9,216	VC
Oral Roberts Univ	OK	18,490	C
Oregon State Univ	OR	11,055	C
Pace Univ	NY	28,652	VC
Parsons School of Design	NY	32,242	SP
Penn State Univ/Univ Park Campus	PA	15,646	HC
Peru State College	NE	6,342	NC
Philadelphia Univ	PA	27,354	C
Pittsburg State Univ	KS	7,128	NC
Pontifical Catholic Univ of PR/Ponce	PR	7,298	
Portland State Univ	OR	12,453	C
Prairie View A&M Univ	TX	9,418	NC
Providence College	RI	30,604	HC
Purdue Univ/Calumet	IN	6,630	NC
Quincy Univ	IL	22,330	C
Quinnipiac Univ	CT	30,570	VC
Radford Univ	VA	8,500	C
Regis Univ	CO	25,740	C+
Rhode Island College	RI	11,565	C
Rider Univ	NJ	30,900	C
Robert Morris Univ	PA	20,438	C
Rockhurst Univ	MO	22,960	C+
Roger Williams Univ	RI	30,296	C
Roosevelt Univ	IL	22,580	VC
Rowan Univ	NJ	14,506	VC
Rutgers, The State Univ of New Jersey/Camden Campus	NJ	14,990	VC
Rutgers, The State Univ of New Jersey/New Brunswick/Piscataway Campus	NJ	15,800	HC
Rutgers, The State Univ of New Jersey/Newark Campus	NJ	15,624	VC
St. Ambrose Univ	IA	22,800	C
St. Bonaventure Univ	NY	24,455	LC
St. Cloud State Univ	MN	8,362	C
St. Joseph's Univ	PA	33,590	VC
St. Louis Univ	MO	29,780	VC+
St. Martin's College	WA	23,245	C
St. Mary-of-the-Woods College	IN	23,280	C
St. Mary's Univ of Minn	MN	21,535	C
St. Mary's Univ of San Antonio	TX	22,444	C

School	ST	$IS	SR
St. Peter's College	NJ	22,292	LC
St. Thomas Aquinas College	NY	20,590	LC
St. Thomas Univ	FL	21,400	LC
St. Vincent College	PA	25,530	VC
St. Xavier Univ	IL	23,144	C
Salem State College	MA	8,592	C
Salisbury Univ	MD	12,664	VC
Sam Houston State Univ	TX	7,142	C
San Diego State Univ	CA	10,321	C
San Francisco State Univ	CA	12,070	C
San Jose State Univ	CA	8,187	C
Santa Clara Univ	CA	34,701	HC
Savannah State Univ	GA	7,328	LC
Seattle Univ	WA	24,183	VC
Seton Hall Univ	NJ	30,130	VC
Seton Hill Univ	PA	24,930	C
Shippensburg Univ of Pennsylvania	PA	10,826	C
Simmons College	MA	33,000	VC
Simpson College	IA	23,658	C+
Slippery Rock Univ of Pennsylvania	PA	10,343	LC
S Car State Univ	SC	6,586	LC
Southeast Missouri State Univ	MO	9,704	C
Southeastern College	FL	11,648	LC
Southeastern Louisiana Univ	LA	6,791	LC
Southeastern Univ	DC	8,505	LC
Southern Adventist Univ	TN	17,080	C
Southern Conn State Univ	CT	10,310	C
Southern Illinois Univ Carbondale	IL	10,407	C
Southern Methodist Univ	TX	34,210	HC
Southern Nazarene Univ	OK	14,634	NC
Southern New Hampshire Univ	NH	26,242	C
Southern Oregon Univ	OR	10,362	C
Southern Univ and A&M College	LA	7,372	LC
Southern Utah Univ	UT	8,194	C
Southwest Minn State Univ	MN	9,106	VC
Southwest Missouri State Univ	MO	8,918	C
Southwestern Okla State Univ	OK	4,801	C
SUNY at Oswego	NY	12,650	C
SUNY/College at Old Westbury	NY	12,784	C
SUNY/Univ at New Paltz	NY	11,565	VC
State Univ of West Georgia	GA	7,622	C
Stephen F. Austin State Univ	TX	7,552	C
Stetson Univ	FL	29,495	VC
Stonehill College	MA	30,752	HC
Suffolk Univ	MA	29,200	C
Syracuse Univ	NY	34,720	HC
Tabor College	KS	19,500	NC
Tarleton State Univ	TX	7,576	C
Teikyo Post Univ	CT	24,875	C
Temple Univ	PA	15,912	C
Tenn Tech Univ	TN	8,670	VC
Texas A&M Univ	TX	11,081	HC
Texas A&M Univ at Commerce	TX	8,994	C
Texas A&M Univ at Corpus Christi	TX	10,269	C
Texas A&M Univ at Kingsville	TX	6,740	LC
Texas Christian Univ	TX	23,410	VC
Texas Southern Univ	TX	8,920	NC
Texas State Univ	TX	9,320	VC
Texas Tech Univ	TX	10,768	VC
Texas Wesleyan Univ	TX	16,245	C
Texas Woman's Univ	TX	7,804	LC
Tiffin Univ	OH	19,490	LC
Touro College	NY	15,250	VC
Trevecca Nazarene Univ	TN	17,548	C
Trinity International Univ	IL	22,980	C+
Tri-State Univ-Main Campus	IN	23,600	C
Troy State Univ	AL	7,696	C
Turabo Univ	PR	4,110	
Tuskegee Univ	AL	17,250	LC
Union Univ	TN	18,800	VC
Univ of Akron	OH	13,134	NC
Univ of Alabama at Birmingham	AL	12,901	C
Univ of Alabama in Huntsville	AL	9,126	VC
Univ of Alaska Anchorage	AK	9,100	NC
Univ of Arizona	AZ	10,413	VC
Univ of Arkansas	AR	9,855	VC
Univ of Arkansas at Little Rock	AR	5,637	NC
Univ of Bridgeport	CT	25,924	LC
Univ of Central Arkansas	AR	6,388	C
Univ of Central Florida	FL	10,038	VC
Univ of Central Okla	OK	9,434	C
Univ of Cincinnati	OH	14,736	C
Univ of Conn	CT	14,608	VC
Univ of Dayton	OH	24,850	VC
Univ of Delaware	DE	12,616	HC
Univ of Denver	CO	32,148	VC
Univ of Evansville	IN	24,190	VC

School	ST	$IS	SR
Univ of Findlay	OH	23,962	NC
Univ of Florida	FL	8,580	MC
Univ of Georgia	GA	8,656	VC
Univ of Great Falls	MT	15,360	C
Univ of Hartford	CT	31,080	C
Univ of Hawaii at Manoa	HI	9,565	VC
Univ of Houston	TX	9,818	C
Univ of Houston-Downtown	TX	2,594	NC
Univ of Idaho	ID	8,216	C
Univ of Illinois at Chicago	IL	13,418	C
Univ of Illinois at Urbana-Champaign	IL	11,316	HC+
Univ of Indianapolis	IN	22,560	VC
Univ of Iowa	IA	10,923	VC
Univ of Kentucky	KY	7,765	C
Univ of Louisiana at Lafayette	LA	5,826	C
Univ of Louisiana at Monroe	LA	5,207	NC
Univ of Louisville	KY	8,762	VC
Univ of Maine at Machias	ME	9,271	LC
Univ of Mary Hardin-Baylor	TX	17,268	C
Univ of Mass Dartmouth	MA	12,835	C
Univ of Memphis	TN	8,560	C
Univ of Mich/Flint	MI	5,548	C
Univ of Minn/Twin Cities	MN	13,160	VC
Univ of Miss	MS	7,666	C
Univ of Missouri/Columbia	MO	13,782	VC
Univ of Mobile	AL	13,620	C
Univ of Montana	MT	9,395	C
Univ of Montevallo	AL	8,478	C
Univ of Nebr at Kearney	NE	8,286	NC
Univ of Nebr at Lincoln	NE	9,975	C+
Univ of Nebr at Omaha	NE	8,080	C
Univ of Nevada/Las Vegas	NV	11,566	C
Univ of Nevada/Reno	NV	9,792	C
Univ of New Haven	CT	28,650	C
Univ of New Mexico	NM	9,223	C
Univ of New Orleans	LA	7,356	C
Univ of North Alabama	AL	7,972	NC
Univ of N Car at Charlotte	NC	8,185	C
Univ of N Car at Wilmington	NC	8,940	VC
Univ of N Dak	ND	8,390	C
Univ of North Texas	TX	7,629	C
Univ of Northern Colo	CO	8,987	C
Univ of Northern Iowa	IA	9,834	C
Univ of Notre Dame	IN	34,442	MC
Univ of Okla	OK	9,226	VC
Univ of Pennsylvania	PA	37,960	MC
Univ of Pittsburgh at Pittsburgh	PA	16,074	HC
Univ of Portland	OR	28,500	VC
Univ of PR/Bayamon Univ College Campus	PR	1,600	
Univ of PR/Mayaguez	PR		
Univ of Rhode Island	RI	13,720	VC
Univ of St. Francis	IL	22,850	C
Univ of St. Thomas	TX	21,952	VC
Univ of San Francisco	CA	34,700	VC
Univ of Scranton	PA	30,836	VC
Univ of Sioux Falls	SD	16,390	C
Univ of South Alabama	AL	7,760	LC
Univ of S Car at Columbia	SC	10,048	VC
Univ of South Florida	FL	9,454	C
Univ of Southern Indiana	IN	9,025	LC
Univ of Southern Miss	MS	8,324	LC
Univ of Tampa	FL	23,982	VC
Univ of Tenn at Knoxville	TN	8,214	C
Univ of Tenn at Martin	TN	7,748	C
Univ of Texas at Arlington	TX	7,192	LC
Univ of Texas at El Paso	TX	5,799	NC
Univ of Texas at San Antonio	TX	9,088	NC
Univ of Texas-Pan American	TX	5,954	LC
Univ of the District of Columbia	DC	2,070	LC
Univ of the Incarnate Word	TX	21,772	LC
Univ of the Ozarks	AR	16,574	C
Univ of the Sacred Heart	PR	5,590	
Univ of Toledo	OH	12,479	NC
Univ of Tulsa	OK	22,090	VC+
Univ of Utah	UT	9,205	C
Univ of Washington	WA	10,361	VC
Univ of West Florida	FL	8,470	C
Univ of Wisc/Eau Claire	WI	8,463	VC
Univ of Wisc/La Crosse	WI	8,991	VC
Univ of Wisc/Madison	WI	8,262	VC
Univ of Wisc/Milwaukee	WI	9,427	LC
Univ of Wisc/Oshkosh	WI	6,130	LC
Univ of Wisc/Stout	WI	9,718	C
Univ of Wisc/Whitewater	WI	8,626	C
Univ of Wyoming	WY	8,636	C
Upper Iowa Univ	IA	20,076	C
Utah State Univ	UT	7,371	C
Valdosta State Univ	GA	7,798	C
Valparaiso Univ	IN	26,118	VC+
Vanguard Univ of Southern Calif	CA	22,208	C
Villanova Univ	PA	35,050	HC
Virginia Commonwealth Univ	VA	9,030	C
Virginia Polytechnic Inst and State Univ	VA	9,179	C
Viterbo Univ	WI	20,430	C
Walsh Univ	OH	20,890	C
Wartburg College	IA	21,165	VC

School	ST	$IS	SR
Washburn Univ of Topeka	KS	8,984	NC
Washington Univ in St. Louis	MO	38,293	MC
Wayne State Univ	MI	11,774	C
Waynesburg College	PA	19,370	C
Webber International Univ	FL	16,510	C
Wesley College	DE	19,905	C
West Chester Univ of Pennsylvania	PA	11,164	C
West Liberty State College	WV	7,868	LC
West Texas A&M Univ	TX	7,533	C
West Virginia State College	WV	6,264	NC
West Virginia Wesleyan College	WV	22,920	C
Western Illinois Univ	IL	10,363	C
Western Kentucky Univ	KY	6,834	C
Western Mich Univ	MI	12,031	C
Western New England College	MA	28,924	C
Western New Mexico Univ	NM	5,950	LC
Western Washington Univ	WA	10,119	VC
Westminster College	PA	22,960	C
Westminster College	UT	17,226	C
Wheeling Jesuit Univ	WV	22,660	C
Wichita State Univ	KS	8,092	C
Wilberforce Univ	OH	14,937	LC
Wingate Univ	NC	21,200	C
Winona State Univ	MN		C
Woodbury Univ	CA	25,344	LC
Wright State Univ	OH	11,490	LC
Xavier Univ	OH	26,850	VC+
Xavier Univ of Louisiana	LA	17,600	C
Yeshiva Univ	NY	21,400	C
York College of Pennsylvania	PA	14,500	VC
Youngstown State Univ	OH	11,148	NC

MATERIALS ENGINEERING

School	ST	$IS	SR
Alfred Univ	NY	28,290	C
Calif Polytechnic State Univ	CA	8,747	VC
Calif State Polytechnic Univ, Pomona	CA	8,793	C+
Drexel Univ	PA	27,655	VC
Florida State Univ	FL	9,028	HC
Georgia Inst of Technology	GA	10,340	HC+
Iowa State Univ	IA	10,768	VC
Johns Hopkins Univ	MD	38,372	MC
Lehigh Univ	PA	37,570	HC+
Mass Inst of Technology	MA	38,310	MC
Mich State Univ	MI	11,933	VC
New Mexico Inst of Mining and Technology	NM	7,580	NC
Northwestern Univ	IL	37,491	MC
Ohio State Univ	OH	13,080	VC+
Purdue Univ/West Lafayette	IN	12,560	VC
Rensselaer Polytechnic Inst	NY	37,579	HC+
San Jose State Univ	CA	8,187	C
Univ of Alabama at Birmingham	AL	12,901	C
Univ of Arizona	AZ	10,413	VC
Univ of Calif at Berkeley	CA	15,563	MC
Univ of Calif at Davis	CA	14,995	VC
Univ of Calif at Los Angeles	CA	15,330	MC
Univ of Cincinnati	OH	14,736	C
Univ of Conn	CT	14,608	VC
Univ of Florida	FL	8,580	MC
Univ of Kentucky	KY	7,765	C
Univ of Maryland/College Park	MD	14,227	HC
Univ of Mich/Ann Arbor	MI	13,864	HC+
Univ of Minn/Twin Cities	MN	13,160	VC
Univ of Missouri/Rolla	MO	12,292	HC
Univ of Pennsylvania	PA	37,960	MC
Univ of Pittsburgh at Pittsburgh	PA	16,074	HC
Univ of Tenn at Knoxville	TN	8,214	C
Univ of Utah	UT	9,205	C
Univ of Wisc/Milwaukee	WI	9,427	LC
Virginia Polytechnic Inst and State Univ	VA	9,179	C
Washington State Univ	WA	11,334	C
Winona State Univ	MN		C
Wright State Univ	OH	11,490	LC
Youngstown State Univ	OH	11,148	NC

MATERIALS SCIENCE

School	ST	$IS	SR
Arizona State Univ-Main	AZ	10,048	C
Case Western Reserve Univ	OH	32,002	MC
Columbia Univ/Fu Foundation School of Engineering and Applied Science	NY	38,590	MC
Cornell Univ	NY	38,253	MC
Duke Univ	NC	37,555	MC
Georgia Inst of Technology	GA	10,340	HC+
Johns Hopkins Univ	MD	38,372	MC
Mass Inst of Technology	MA	38,310	MC
N Car State Univ	NC	9,886	VC
Northwestern Univ	IL	37,491	MC
Ohio State Univ	OH	13,080	VC+
Penn State Univ/Univ Park Campus	PA	15,646	HC

School	ST	$IS	SR
Rochester Inst of Technology	NY	29,217	VC+
Stanford Univ	CA	37,612	MC
Temple Univ	PA	15,912	C
Univ of Calif at Berkeley	CA	15,563	MC
Univ of Illinois at Urbana-Champaign	IL	11,316	HC+
Univ of Mass Dartmouth	MA	12,835	C
Univ of Mich/Ann Arbor	MI	13,864	HC+
Univ of Minn/Twin Cities	MN	13,160	VC
Univ of New Haven	CT	28,650	C
Univ of Pittsburgh at Pittsburgh	PA	16,074	HC
Univ of Tenn at Knoxville	TN	8,214	C
Univ of the Ozarks	AR	16,574	C
Univ of Washington	WA	10,361	VC
Univ of Wisc/Madison	WI	8,262	VC

MATHEMATICS

School	ST	$IS	SR
Abilene Christian Univ	TX	18,370	VC
Adams State College	CO	7,468	C
Adelphi Univ	NY	26,300	VC
Adrian College	MI	21,950	C
Agnes Scott College	GA	28,230	HC
Alabama A&M Univ	AL	5,100	LC
Alabama State Univ	AL	6,404	C
Albany State Univ	GA	5,764	C+
Albertson College of Idaho	ID	19,415	VC
Albertus Magnus College	CT	23,130	LC
Albion College	MI	25,224	VC
Albright College	PA	30,579	C
Alcorn State Univ	MS	7,290	C
Alderson-Broaddus College	WV	19,640	C
Alfred Univ	NY	28,290	C
Allegheny College	PA	30,280	VC
Allen Univ	SC	10,300	NC
Alma College	MI	25,566	VC
Alvernia College	PA	23,212	LC
Alverno College	WI	18,898	C
American International College	MA	24,690	LC
American Univ	DC	34,585	VC+
Amherst College	MA	37,470	MC
Anderson Univ	IN	19,430	LC
Andrews Univ	MI	19,550	C
Angelo State Univ	TX	7,576	NC
Appalachian State Univ	NC	7,637	VC
Aquinas College	MI	21,894	C
Arcadia Univ	PA	29,890	C
Arizona State Univ-Main	AZ	10,048	C
Arkansas State Univ	AR	8,450	C
Arkansas Tech Univ	AR	7,299	C
Armstrong Atlantic State Univ	GA	7,102	C
Asbury College	KY	20,704	VC
Ashland Univ	OH	24,464	C
Assumption College	MA	29,375	C
Atlantic Union College	MA	18,868	C
Auburn Univ	AL	10,396	VC
Auburn Univ Montgomery	AL	9,020	NC
Augsburg College	MN	25,298	C
Augusta State Univ	GA	2,592	C
Augustana College	IL	26,610	VC+
Augustana College	SD	21,998	VC
Aurora Univ	IL	20,631	C
Austin College	TX	24,747	HC
Austin Peay State Univ	TN	5,814	LC
Averett Univ	VA	23,010	LC
Avila Univ	MO	20,300	C
Azusa Pacific Univ	CA	24,720	VC
Baker Univ	KS	19,860	VC
Baldwin-Wallace College	OH	24,678	C
Ball State Univ	IN	8,660	C
Barber-Scotia College	NC	13,900	LC
Bard College	NY	37,352	HC+
Barry Univ	FL	24,100	LC
Barton College	NC	19,314	C
Bates College	ME	37,500	MC
Baylor Univ	TX	23,864	VC
Belhaven College	MS	16,040	C+
Bellarmine Univ	KY	24,110	VC
Belmont Univ	TN	21,986	VC
Beloit College	WI	29,864	HC
Bemidji State Univ	MN	9,103	C
Benedict College	SC	12,662	LC
Benedictine College	KS	20,603	C
Benedictine Univ	IL	23,840	C
Bennett College	NC	11,200	C
Bennington College	VT	35,910	HC
Bentley College	MA	33,904	VC
Berea College	KY	5,030	VC+
Berry College	GA	21,410	VC
Bethany College	KS	18,675	LC
Bethany College	WV	19,845	VC
Bethel College	IN	19,670	C
Bethel College	KS	19,800	C+
Bethel College	MN	25,180	VC
Bethel College	TN	12,980	C
Bethune-Cookman College	FL	16,480	LC
Biola Univ	CA	25,964	VC
Birmingham-Southern College	AL	25,364	VC+
Black Hills State Univ	SD	7,743	LC
Blackburn College	IL	13,690	C
Bloomsburg Univ of Pennsylvania	PA	10,844	C
Blue Mountain College	MS	10,226	C
Bluefield College	VA	15,575	C
Bluffton College	OH	23,694	C
Boise State Univ	ID	7,657	LC
Boston College	MA	33,284	MC
Boston Univ	MA	38,194	HC+
Bowdoin College	ME	37,790	MC
Bowie State Univ	MD	10,873	C+
Bowling Green State Univ	OH	13,036	C
Bradley Univ	IL	22,910	VC
Brandeis Univ	MA	38,198	MC
Brescia Univ	KY	14,225	C
Brewton-Parker College	GA	14,200	LC
Briar Cliff Univ	IA	21,660	C
Bridgewater College	VA	25,150	C
Bridgewater State College	MA	10,482	C
Brigham Young Univ	UT	8,504	HC
Brigham Young Univ/Hawaii	HI	7,240	VC+
Brown Univ	RI	38,174	MC
Bryan College	TN	17,900	VC
Bryn Mawr College	PA	36,890	HC+
Bucknell Univ	PA	35,262	HC+
Buena Vista Univ	IA	25,406	C
Butler Univ	IN	28,250	VC+
Cabrini College	PA	29,020	C
Caldwell College	NJ	24,060	LC
Calif Baptist Univ	CA	19,924	C
Calif Inst of Technology	CA	31,677	MC
Calif Lutheran Univ	CA	27,600	LC
Calif Polytechnic State Univ	CA	8,747	VC
Calif State Polytechnic Univ, Pomona	CA	8,793	C+
Cal State, Bakersfield	CA	6,090	LC
Cal State, Chico	CA	8,598	LC
Cal State, Dominguez Hills	CA	5,840	LC
Cal State, Fresno	CA	8,414	LC
Cal State, Fullerton	CA	6,648	C
Cal State, Hayward	CA	8,871	LC
Cal State, Long Beach	CA	8,762	C+
Cal State, Los Angeles	CA	5,778	C
Cal State, Northridge	CA	7,757	LC
Cal State, Sacramento	CA	9,543	C
Cal State, San Bernardino	CA	15,238	LC
Cal State, San Marcos	CA	1,736	LC
Cal State, Stanislaus	CA	9,874	C
Calif Univ of Pennsylvania	PA	10,388	C
Calvin College	MI	22,615	NC
Cameron Univ	OK	5,692	NC
Campbell Univ	NC	18,268	VC
Campbellsville Univ	KY	17,680	C
Canisius College	NY	28,163	C+
Capital Univ	OH	26,550	C
Cardinal Stritch Univ	WI	17,620	C
Caribbean Univ	PR	3,000	
Carleton College	MN	34,395	MC
Carlow College	PA	21,334	C
Carnegie Mellon Univ	PA	32,682	MC
Carroll College	MT	20,576	VC
Carroll College	WI	22,740	C
Carthage College	WI	25,000	C
Case Western Reserve Univ	OH	32,002	MC
Castleton State College	VT	11,820	C
Catawba College	NC	20,500	C
Catholic Univ of America	DC	34,248	VC
Cedar Crest College	PA	25,145	C+
Cedarville Univ	OH	19,954	VC
Centenary College	NJ	25,370	LC
Centenary College of Louisiana	LA	23,100	VC+
Central College	IA	21,206	C
Central Conn State Univ	CT	12,090	C
Central Methodist College	MO	16,460	C
Central Mich Univ	MI	11,142	C
Central Missouri State Univ	MO	9,776	C
Central State Univ	OH	8,922	C+
Central Washington Univ	WA	9,768	C
Centre College	KY	27,300	HC
Chadron State College	NE	6,286	NC
Chapman Univ	CA	33,118	VC
Charleston Southern Univ	SC	17,122	C
Chatham College	PA	27,266	C+
Chestnut Hill College	PA	26,450	LC
Cheyney Univ of Pennsylvania	PA	9,993	C
Chicago State Univ	IL	10,882	C+
Christian Brothers Univ	TN	22,290	VC
Christian Heritage College	CA	19,990	C
Christopher Newport Univ	VA	8,862	VC
Citadel, The	SC	12,295	C+
CUNY/Baruch College	NY	3,275	VC+
CUNY/Brooklyn College	NY	4,353	C+
CUNY/City College	NY	4,230	C+
CUNY/College of Staten Island	NY	4,308	NC
CUNY/Herbert H. Lehman College	NY	3,320	LC
CUNY/Hunter College	NY	6,729	C+
CUNY/Medgar Evers College	NY	4,232	NC
CUNY/Queens College	NY	4,362	C
CUNY/York College	NY	3,292	NC
Claflin Univ	SC	14,838	C+
Claremont McKenna College	CA	36,880	MC
Clarion Univ of Pennsylvania	PA	11,272	LC
Clark Atlanta Univ	GA	19,300	C+
Clark Univ	MA	32,115	VC
Clarke College	IA	23,165	C
Clarkson Univ	NY	32,226	VC
Clearwater Christian College	FL	13,160	LC
Clemson Univ	SC	11,972	HC
Cleveland State Univ	OH	12,308	LC
Coastal Carolina Univ	SC	11,040	C
Coe College	IA	27,385	VC
Coker College	SC	21,491	C
Colby College	ME	37,570	MC
Colgate Univ	NY	37,095	MC
College Misericordia	PA	26,350	C
College of Charleston	SC	11,887	HC
College of Mount St. Vincent	NY	26,800	C
College of Mount St. Joseph	OH	22,785	C
College of New Jersey	NJ	15,950	MC
College of New Rochelle	NY	21,800	C
College of Notre Dame of Maryland	MD	27,700	C
College of Our Lady of the Elms	MA	20,644	C
College of St. Benedict	MN	26,672	VC
College of St. Catherine	MN	24,010	VC
College of St. Elizabeth	NJ	25,460	C
College of St. Mary	NE	21,510	C
College of St. Rose	NY	22,864	C
College of St. Scholastica	MN	24,970	C+
College of the Holy Cross	MA	36,451	MC
College of the Ozarks	MO	3,500	VC+
College of the Southwest	NM	9,320	C+
College of William and Mary	VA	12,224	MC
College of Wooster	OH	31,300	HC
Colo College	CO	36,860	HC
Colo School of Mines	CO	12,533	HC
Colo State Univ	CO	9,964	VC
Columbia College	SC	22,658	LC
Columbia Union College	MD	20,543	C
Columbia Univ/Barnard College	NY	36,990	MC
Columbia Univ/Columbia College	NY	38,590	MC
Columbia Univ/School of General Studies	NY	35,000	C
Columbus State Univ	GA	7,846	C
Concord College	WV	8,136	C
Concordia College	NY	19,200	VC
Concordia College: Moorhead	MN	22,460	VC+
Concordia Univ	CA	24,420	C
Concordia Univ	MI	24,095	C
Concordia Univ Nebr	NE	20,302	C+
Concordia Univ Wisc	WI	16,600	C
Concordia Univ, River Forest	IL	23,600	C
Conn College	CT	37,900	MC
Converse College	SC	24,710	VC
Coppin State College	MD	10,191	LC
Cornell College	IA	27,825	VC+
Cornell Univ	NY	38,253	MC
Covenant College	GA	23,830	VC+
Creighton Univ	NE	26,748	VC+
Culver-Stockton College	MO	17,850	C
Cumberland College	KY	16,384	C
Cumberland Univ	TN	16,910	C
Daemen College	NY	22,120	C
Dakota State Univ	SD	7,466	C
Dakota Wesleyan Univ	SD	17,832	C
Dallas Baptist Univ	TX	15,300	VC
Dana College	NE	20,280	C
Dartmouth College	NH	37,770	MC
David Lipscomb Univ	TN	16,158	VC
Davidson College	NC	33,274	MC
Davis and Elkins College	WV	20,594	C
De Sales Univ	PA	25,470	C
Defiance College	OH	22,615	C
Delaware State Univ	DE	8,104	LC
Delaware Valley College	PA	26,676	C
Delta State Univ	MS	6,618	C
Denison Univ	OH	33,050	HC
DePaul Univ	IL	27,580	VC
DePauw Univ	IN	31,500	HC
Dickinson College	PA	35,825	HC
Dickinson State Univ	ND	6,338	NC
Dillard Univ	LA	17,325	VC
Doane College	NE	20,000	C
Dominican College	NY	24,810	LC
Dominican Univ	IL	23,610	C
Dordt College	IA	20,170	VC
Dowling College	NY	23,870	LC
Drake Univ	IA	25,120	VC+
Drew Univ/College of Liberal Arts	NJ	35,550	VC
Drexel Univ	PA	27,655	VC
Drury Univ	MO	18,085	VC+
Duke Univ	NC	37,555	MC
Duquesne Univ	PA	26,907	VC
Earlham College	IN	29,976	VC+
East Carolina Univ	NC	8,671	C
East Central Univ	OK	4,968	C
East Stroudsburg Univ of Pennsylvania	PA	10,336	C
East Tenn State Univ	TN	8,497	C
East Texas Baptist Univ	TX	13,914	C
Eastern Conn State Univ	CT	10,362	C
Eastern Illinois Univ	IL	11,192	C
Eastern Kentucky Univ	KY	7,708	C
Eastern Mennonite Univ	VA	22,990	C
Eastern Mich Univ	MI	11,478	C
Eastern Nazarene College	MA	19,433	LC
Eastern New Mexico Univ	NM	6,762	LC
Eastern Oregon Univ	OR	10,080	NC
Eastern Univ	PA	24,020	C
Eastern Washington Univ	WA	9,012	C
Eckerd College	FL	28,744	C+
Edgewood College	WI	20,520	C
Edinboro Univ of Pennsylvania	PA	10,850	LC
Edward Waters College	FL	14,374	LC
Elizabeth City State Univ	NC	5,550	LC
Elizabethtown College	PA	28,800	C
Elmhurst College	IL	24,630	C
Elmira College	NY	33,820	VC
Elon Univ	NC	22,240	VC
Emmanuel College	MA	27,600	C+
Emory & Henry College	VA	21,950	C
Emory Univ	GA	36,872	MC
Emporia State Univ	KS	6,998	C
Erskine College	SC	23,166	VC
Eureka College	IL	24,980	LC
Evangel Univ	MO	15,435	C
Fairfield Univ	CT	35,505	HC
Fairleigh Dickinson Univ/College at Florham	NJ	30,130	C
Fairleigh Dickinson Univ/Metropolitan Campus	NJ	28,584	C
Fairmont State	WV	8,280	LC
Fayetteville State Univ	NC	5,590	LC
Felician College	NJ	24,300	C
Ferrum College	VA	21,240	LC
Fisk Univ	TN	17,305	LC
Fitchburg State College	MA	9,622	C
Florida A&M Univ	FL	7,564	C
Florida Atlantic Univ	FL	8,543	C
Florida International Univ	FL	9,912	VC
Florida Memorial College	FL	6,000	LC
Florida Southern College	FL	23,592	C
Florida State Univ	FL	9,028	HC
Fontbonne Univ	MO	21,508	C
Fordham Univ	NY	35,066	HC
Fort Hays State Univ	KS	7,363	C
Fort Lewis College	CO	8,353	C
Fort Valley State Univ	GA	6,960	C
Framingham State College	MA	9,381	C
Francis Marion Univ	SC	9,364	C
Franciscan Univ of Steubenville	OH	20,300	VC
Franklin and Marshall College	PA	35,930	HC+
Franklin College	IN		C
Franklin Pierce College	NH	28,980	LC
Freed-Hardeman Univ	TN		NC
Fresno Pacific Univ	CA	22,462	C
Friends Univ	KS	15,962	LC
Frostburg State Univ	MD	11,114	C
Furman Univ	SC	28,976	HC+
Gallaudet Univ	DC	16,554	SP
Gannon Univ	PA	23,260	C
Gardner-Webb Univ	NC	19,300	C
George Fox Univ	OR	26,110	VC
George Mason Univ	VA	9,732	VC
George Washington Univ	DC	41,030	MC
Georgetown College	KY	22,000	VC
Georgetown Univ	DC	38,242	MC
Georgia College and State Univ	GA	9,878	C
Georgia Inst of Technology	GA	10,340	HC+
Georgia Southern Univ	GA	8,540	C
Georgia Southwestern State Univ	GA	6,013	C
Georgia State Univ	GA	10,658	C
Georgian Court College	NJ	19,040	LC
Gettysburg College	PA	35,646	HC
Gonzaga Univ	WA	26,766	HC
Gordon College	MA	25,982	VC+
Goshen College	IN	22,450	VC
Goucher College	MD	32,650	HC
Grace College	IN	19,825	VC
Graceland Univ	IA	19,550	C
Grambling State Univ	LA	6,538	NC
Grand Canyon Univ	AZ	30,000	LC
Grand Valley State Univ	MI	11,022	VC
Greensboro College	NC	21,750	C
Greenville College	IL	21,342	C
Grinnell College	IA	31,060	HC+
Grove City College	PA	14,228	HC
Guilford College	NC	24,960	VC
Gustavus Adolphus College	MN	27,120	VC+
Gwynedd-Mercy College	PA	24,225	C
Hamilton College	NY	37,560	MC
Hamline Univ	MN	27,052	VC
Hampden-Sydney College	VA	28,407	VC
Hampshire College	MA	37,037	HC
Hampton Univ	VA	17,112	C+
Hannibal-LaGrange College	MO	13,940	C

ST = STATE $IS = IN-STATE COSTS SR = SELECTOR RATING

School	ST	$IS	SR
Hanover College	IN	25,200	VC
Harding Univ	AR	14,890	VC
Hardin-Simmons Univ	TX	14,165	C
Hartwick College	NY	34,650	C+
Harvard Univ/Harvard College	MA	37,928	MC
Harvey Mudd College	CA	38,080	MC
Hastings College	NE	19,928	VC
Haverford College	PA	37,900	MC
Heidelberg College	OH	20,266	NC
Henderson State Univ	AR	7,386	C
Hendrix College	AR	20,970	VC+
Heritage College	WA	6,720	NC
High Point Univ	NC	22,480	C
Hillsdale College	MI	22,450	HC
Hiram College	OH	28,234	VC
Hobart and William Smith Colleges	NY	36,536	HC
Hofstra Univ	NY	27,112	VC
Hollins Univ	VA	27,965	VC
Holy Family College	PA	13,710	LC
Hood College	MD	27,795	VC
Hope College	MI	25,340	VC
Houghton College	NY	23,984	VC
Houston Baptist Univ	TX	16,905	C
Howard Payne Univ	TX	15,176	C
Howard Univ	DC	16,505	C
Humboldt State Univ	CA	9,400	C
Huntingdon College	AL	18,400	VC
Huntington College	IN	23,590	C
Huston-Tillotson College	TX	14,232	NC
Idaho State Univ	ID	8,128	C
Illinois College	IL	19,100	VC
Illinois State Univ	IL	10,944	C+
Illinois Wesleyan Univ	IL	30,380	HC+
Immaculata Univ	PA	25,200	C
Indiana State Univ	IN	10,719	LC
Indiana Univ Bloomington	IN	12,389	VC
Indiana Univ East	IN	4,433	LC
Indiana Univ Kokomo	IN	4,463	LC
Indiana Univ Northwest	IN	4,538	LC
Indiana Univ of Pennsylvania	PA	10,489	C
Indiana Univ South Bend	IN	4,571	LC
Indiana Univ Southeast	IN	4,504	LC
Indiana Univ-Purdue Univ Fort Wayne	IN	5,108	LC
Indiana Univ-Purdue Univ Indianapolis	IN	8,257	LC
Indiana Wesleyan Univ	IN	19,900	C+
Inter American Univ of PR/ Bayamon Univ College	PR	3,522	
Inter American Univ of PR/ Fajardo Campus	PR	4,000	
Inter American Univ of PR/ Metropolitan Campus	PR		
Inter American Univ of PR/ Ponce Regional College	PR	3,700	
Inter American Univ of PR/ San German	PR	6,716	
Iona College	NY	27,988	VC
Iowa State Univ	IA	10,768	VC
Iowa Wesleyan College	IA	19,990	C
Ithaca College	NY	31,730	VC
Jackson State Univ	MS	8,382	C
Jacksonville State Univ	AL	6,844	LC
Jacksonville Univ	FL	24,040	C
James Madison Univ	VA	10,794	VC
Jamestown College	ND	12,600	NC
Jarvis Christian College	TX	9,035	NC
John Brown Univ	AR	15,690	VC
John Carroll Univ	OH	27,658	C+
Johns Hopkins Univ	MD	38,372	MC
Johnson C. Smith Univ	NC	18,108	C
Johnson State College	VT	11,819	LC
Judson College	AL	14,650	C
Judson College	IL	22,050	LC
Juniata College	PA	29,080	VC
Kalamazoo College	MI	26,955	HC+
Kansas State Univ	KS	8,728	VC
Kansas Wesleyan Univ	KS	18,900	VC
Kean Univ	NJ	14,479	C
Keene State College	NH	12,212	C
Kennesaw State Univ	GA	2,724	C
Kent State Univ	OH	12,932	C
Kentucky Christian College	KY	13,472	C
Kentucky State Univ	KY	9,062	NC
Kenyon College	OH	35,370	HC+
King College	TN	22,500	VC
King's College	PA	26,990	C
Knox College	IL	30,294	VC+
Kutztown Univ of Pennsylvania	PA	10,786	C
La Roche College	PA	22,094	C
La Salle Univ	PA	31,260	VC
La Sierra Univ	CA	19,260	LC
Lafayette College	PA	35,746	MC
LaGrange College	GA	20,500	C
Lake Erie College	OH	23,550	C
Lake Forest College	IL	30,270	VC
Lake Superior State Univ	MI	9,034	LC
Lakeland College	WI	17,950	C
Lamar Univ	TX	6,816	LC
Lambuth Univ	TN	16,520	C
Lander Univ	SC	10,496	C
Lane College	TN	11,178	C+
Langston Univ	OK	2,308	LC
Lawrence Tech Univ	MI	20,487	C
Lawrence Univ	WI	30,900	HC
Le Moyne College	NY	26,400	VC
Lebanon Valley College	PA	28,870	VC
Lee Univ	TN	13,780	NC
Lees-McRae College	NC	17,106	LC
Lehigh Univ	PA	37,570	HC+
LeMoyne-Owen College	TN	13,070	LC
Lenoir-Rhyne College	NC	19,186	C
LeTourneau Univ	TX	21,080	C
Lewis and Clark College	OR	30,620	VC
Lewis Univ	IL	22,950	C+
Lewis-Clark State College	ID	6,981	C
Liberty Univ	VA	17,220	C
Limestone College	SC	17,700	C
Lincoln Memorial Univ	TN	16,400	LC
Lincoln Univ	MO	7,158	NC
Lincoln Univ	PA	13,320	C
Lindenwood Univ	MO	17,050	VC
Linfield College	OR	27,090	VC
Livingstone College	NC	18,101	LC
Lock Haven Univ of Pennsylvania	PA	11,098	LC
LIU/Brooklyn Campus	NY	24,790	C
LIU/C.W. Post Campus	NY	28,282	C
Longwood Univ	VA	11,175	C
Loras College	IA	24,233	C
Louisiana College	LA	13,450	C
Louisiana State Univ and A&M College	LA	9,126	VC
Louisiana State Univ in Shreveport	LA	2,884	NC
Louisiana Tech Univ	LA	7,361	C
Loyola College in Maryland	MD	34,560	VC
Loyola Marymount Univ	CA	32,194	VC
Loyola Univ Chicago	IL	31,164	VC
Loyola Univ New Orleans	LA	31,036	VC+
Lubbock Christian Univ	TX	15,832	C
Luther College	IA	25,700	VC
Lycoming College	PA	27,589	C+
Lynchburg College	VA	26,815	C
Lyndon State College	VT	12,646	LC
Lyon College	AR	17,995	VC
Macalester College	MN	31,944	MC
MacMurray College	IL	20,005	LC
Madonna Univ	MI	11,504	VC
Maharishi Univ of Management	IA	29,230	VC
Malone College	OH	20,995	C
Manchester College	IN	23,390	C
Manhattan College	NY	27,400	VC
Manhattanville College	NY	32,420	C+
Mansfield Univ	PA	11,220	C
Marian College	IN	23,030	C
Marian College of Fond du Lac	WI	19,625	C
Marietta College	OH	27,047	C
Marist College	NY	27,596	VC
Marlboro College	VT	29,055	VC+
Marquette Univ	WI	27,594	VC
Mars Hill College	NC	18,600	LC
Marshall Univ	WV	9,116	C
Martin Univ	IN	10,200	SP
Mary Baldwin College	VA	24,939	C
Mary Washington College	VA	10,166	HC
Marygrove College	MI	17,550	C
Marymount College of Fordham Univ	NY	27,686	C
Marymount Univ	VA	23,668	C
Maryville College	TN	25,960	VC
Maryville Univ of St. Louis	MO	22,090	VC
Marywood Univ	PA	26,050	C
Mass College of Liberal Arts	MA	8,717	LC
Mass Inst of Technology	MA	38,310	MC
Master's College and Seminary	CA	23,250	VC
Mayville State Univ	ND	7,325	NC
McDaniel College	MD	28,440	VC
McKendree College	IL	21,120	VC
McMurry Univ	TX	17,846	LC
McNeese State Univ	LA	5,259	LC
McPherson College	KS	20,265	C
Mercer Univ	GA	27,516	VC+
Mercy College	NY	19,200	NC
Mercyhurst College	PA	20,694	C
Meredith College	NC	23,065	C
Merrimack College	MA	29,625	C
Mesa State College	CO	8,051	C
Messiah College	PA	25,890	VC+
Methodist College	NC	19,526	C
Metropolitan State College of Denver	CO	2,338	LC
Miami Univ	OH	15,033	HC
Mich State Univ	MI	11,933	VC
Mich Tech Univ	MI	13,235	VC
MidAmerica Nazarene Univ	KS	18,688	C
Middle Tenn State Univ	TN	8,534	C
Middlebury College	VT	38,100	MC
Midland Lutheran College	NE	18,600	C
Midway College	KY	15,915	C
Midwestern State Univ	TX	8,045	LC
Miles College	AL	7,870	NC
Milligan College	TN	19,860	C+
Millikin Univ	IL	25,555	C
Mills College	CA	33,371	VC
Millsaps College	MS	25,182	VC
Minn State Univ, Mankato	MN	8,803	LC
Minn State Univ, Moorehead	MN	7,000	LC
Minot State Univ	ND	6,602	LC
Miss College	MS	14,574	C
Miss State Univ	MS	9,139	C
Miss Univ for Women	MS	5,446	LC
Miss Valley State Univ	MS	6,765	NC
Missouri Baptist Univ	MO	18,010	C
Missouri Southern State Univ	MO	8,316	C
Missouri Valley College	MO	18,500	C
Missouri Western State College	MO	8,522	NC
Molloy College	NY	15,180	C
Monmouth College	IL	23,600	C
Monmouth Univ	NJ	26,334	C
Montana State Univ-Billings	MT	9,550	C
Montana State Univ-Bozeman	MT	9,515	C
Montana Tech of The Univ of Montana	MT	9,314	NC
Montclair State Univ	NJ	13,790	C
Montreat College	NC	18,762	C
Moravian College	PA	28,903	VC
Morehead State Univ	KY	7,464	C
Morehouse College	GA	22,728	C
Morgan State Univ	MD	11,470	C
Morningside College	IA	21,610	C
Morris College	SC	10,974	LC
Mount Holyoke College	MA	37,918	HC+
Mount Marty College	SD	15,656	LC
Mount Mary College	WI	20,370	C
Mount Mercy College	IA	21,400	C
Mount Olive College	NC	14,410	LC
Mount St. Mary College	NY	21,270	C
Mount St. Mary's College	CA	28,307	VC
Mount St. Mary's College	MD	28,400	C
Mount Union College	OH	21,120	C
Mount Vernon Nazarene Univ	OH	18,925	C
Muhlenberg College	PA	31,485	HC
Murray State Univ	KY	7,816	VC
Muskingum College	OH	20,680	C
National Univ	CA	9,690	SP
National-Louis Univ	IL	16,240	LC
Nazareth College of Rochester	NY	24,936	VC
Nebr Wesleyan Univ	NE	21,197	C+
New College of Florida	FL	8,906	HC+
New England College	NH	28,860	LC
New Jersey City Univ	NJ	11,850	LC
New Jersey Inst of Technology	NJ	16,396	C
New Mexico Highlands Univ	NM	6,182	LC
New Mexico Inst of Mining and Technology	NM	7,580	NC
New Mexico State Univ	NM	7,932	C
New York Inst of Technology	NY	24,205	VC
New York Univ	NY	39,406	MC
Newberry College	SC	22,871	LC
Newman Univ	KS	18,018	C
Niagara Univ	NY	25,050	C
Nicholls State Univ	LA	6,395	NC
Nichols College	MA	27,562	LC
Norfolk State Univ	VA	9,722	LC
N Car Agricultural and Technical State Univ	NC	6,659	LC
N Car Central Univ	NC	7,534	LC
N Car State Univ	NC	9,896	NC
N Car Wesleyan College	NC	17,998	C
North Central College	IL	25,656	VC
N Dak State Univ	ND	8,435	C
North Georgia College and State Univ	GA	6,984	C
North Park Univ	IL	24,030	C
Northeastern Illinois Univ	IL	2,898	NC
Northeastern State Univ	OK	4,950	LC
Northeastern Univ	MA	35,650	HC
Northern Arizona Univ	AZ	9,002	C
Northern Illinois Univ	IL	11,472	C
Northern Kentucky Univ	KY	6,352	NC
Northern Mich Univ	MI	10,834	C
Northern State Univ	SD	7,117	LC
Northland College	WI	22,170	C+
Northwest Missouri State Univ	MO	9,334	C
Northwest Nazarene Univ	ID	20,360	VC
Northwestern College	MN	22,820	C+
Northwestern College of Iowa	IA	19,640	C+
Northwestern Okla State Univ	OK	5,433	NC
Northwestern State Univ of Louisiana	LA	6,331	NC
Northwestern Univ	IL	37,491	MC
Norwich Univ	VT	21,064	LC
Notre Dame College	OH	20,425	C
Notre Dame de Namur Univ	CA	26,932	LC
Nyack College	NY	18,540	C
Oakland City Univ	IN	16,980	NC
Oakland Univ	MI	10,800	C
Oakwood College	AL	14,904	N
Oberlin College	OH	36,938	MC
Occidental College	CA	35,922	HC
Oglethorpe Univ	GA	26,000	VC
Ohio Dominican Univ	OH	22,700	C
Ohio Northern Univ	OH	27,765	VC
Ohio State Univ	OH	13,080	VC+
Ohio Univ	OH	14,448	C
Ohio Wesleyan Univ	OH	32,550	VC+
Okla Baptist Univ	OK	15,220	C
Okla Christian Univ	OK	17,690	NC
Okla City Univ	OK	19,580	VC
Okla Panhandle State Univ	OK	5,370	C
Okla State Univ	OK	9,216	VC
Okla Wesleyan Univ	OK	14,100	LC
Old Dominion Univ	VA	10,441	C
Olivet College	MI	19,984	C+
Olivet Nazarene Univ	IL	20,480	C
Oral Roberts Univ	OK	18,490	C
Oregon State Univ	OR	11,055	C
Ottawa Univ	KS	11,800	LC
Otterbein College	OH	26,085	C
Ouachita Baptist Univ	AR	18,900	VC
Our Lady of the Lake Univ of San Antonio	TX	17,336	C
Pace Univ	NY	28,652	VC
Pacific Lutheran Univ	WA	25,715	VC
Pacific Union College	CA	22,065	C+
Pacific Univ	OR	24,250	C
Paine College	GA	13,022	LC
Palm Beach Atlantic Univ	FL	20,690	C
Park Univ	MO	10,780	C+
Paul Quinn College	TX	8,150	LC
Penn State Univ at Erie/ Behrend College	PA	12,326	C
Penn State Univ/Univ Park Campus	PA	15,646	HC
Pepperdine Univ	CA	32,830	VC
Peru State College	NE	6,342	NC
Pfeiffer Univ	NC	18,980	C
Piedmont College	GA	16,900	C
Pikeville College	KY	14,900	NC
Pittsburg State Univ	KS	7,128	NC
Pitzer College	CA	37,590	HC
Plymouth State Univ	NH	12,298	LC
Point Loma Nazarene Univ	CA	21,380	VC
Polytechnic Univ/Brooklyn	NY	33,770	VC
Pomona College	CA	33,960	MC
Pontifical Catholic Univ of PR/Ponce	PR	7,298	
Portland State Univ	OR	12,453	C
Prairie View A&M Univ	TX	9,418	NC
Presbyterian College	SC	25,920	VC
Princeton Univ	NJ	36,936	MC
Principia College	IL	25,044	C+
Providence College	RI	30,604	HC
Purdue Univ/Calumet	IN	6,630	NC
Purdue Univ/West Lafayette	IN	12,560	VC
Queens Univ of Charlotte	NC	21,840	C
Quinnipiac Univ	CT	30,570	VC
Radford Univ	VA	8,500	C
Ramapo College of New Jersey	NJ	15,203	VC
Randolph-Macon College	VA	27,190	C
Randolph-Macon Woman's College	VA	28,430	VC+
Reed College	OR	36,950	MC
Regis Univ	CO	25,740	C+
Rensselaer Polytechnic Inst	NY	37,579	HC+
Rhode Island College	RI	11,565	C
Rhodes College	TN	26,466	HC+
Rice Univ	TX	27,550	MC
Richard Stockton College of New Jersey	NJ	12,972	VC
Rider Univ	NJ	30,900	C
Ripon College	WI	24,995	VC
Rivier College	NH	26,217	C
Roanoke College	VA	27,393	C
Robert Morris Univ	PA	20,438	C
Roberts Wesleyan College	NY	23,190	C+
Rochester Inst of Technology	NY	29,217	VC+
Rockford College	IL	28,310	VC
Rockhurst Univ	MO	22,960	C+
Rocky Mountain College	MT	19,015	C
Roger Williams Univ	RI	30,296	C
Rollins College	FL	34,300	VC
Roosevelt Univ	IL	22,580	VC
Rose-Hulman Inst of Technology	IN	31,425	HC+
Rosemont College	PA	26,175	C
Rowan Univ	NJ	14,506	VC
Russell Sage College	NY	26,811	C
Rust College	MS	8,200	C+
Rutgers, The State Univ of New Jersey/Camden Campus	NJ	14,990	VC
Rutgers, The State Univ of New Jersey/New Brunswick/Piscataway Campus	NJ	15,800	HC
Rutgers, The State Univ of New Jersey/Newark Campus	NJ	15,624	VC
Sacred Heart Univ	CT	29,178	C
Saginaw Valley State Univ	MI	11,055	C
St. Ambrose Univ	IA	22,800	C

ST = STATE $IS = IN-STATE COSTS   SR = SELECTOR RATING

School	ST	$IS	SR
St. Andrews Presbyterian College	NC	20,525	C
St. Anselm College	NH	30,250	C
St. Augustine's College	NC	12,990	LC
St. Bonaventure Univ	NY	24,455	LC
St. Cloud State Univ	MN	8,362	C
St. Edward's Univ	TX	20,428	C
St. Francis College	NY	10,880	LC
St. Francis Univ	PA	25,876	LC
St. John Fisher College	NY	24,870	C
St. John's Univ	MN	26,473	VC
St. John's Univ	NY	30,180	C
St. Joseph College	CT	29,685	C
St. Joseph's, Brooklyn,	NY	10,902	C
St. Joseph's College	IN	24,250	C
St. Joseph's College of Maine	ME	25,600	C
St. Joseph's Univ	PA	33,590	VC
St. Lawrence Univ	NY	35,945	VC
St. Louis Univ	MO	29,780	VC+
St. Martin's College	WA	23,245	C
St. Mary-of-the-Woods College	IN	23,280	C
St. Mary's College	IN	24,474	VC
St. Mary's College of Calif	CA	32,850	VC
St. Mary's College of Maryland	MD	15,908	VC+
St. Mary's Univ of Minn	MN	21,535	C
St. Mary's Univ of San Antonio	TX	22,444	C
St. Michael's College	VT	30,100	VC
St. Norbert College	WI	25,810	C
St. Olaf College	MN	28,500	HC
St. Paul's College	VA	14,344	NC
St. Peter's College	NJ	22,292	LC
St. Vincent College	PA	25,530	VC
St. Xavier Univ	IL	23,144	C
Salem College	NC	24,595	VC
Salem State College	MA	8,592	C
Salisbury Univ	MD	12,664	VC
Salve Regina Univ	RI	29,210	C
Sam Houston State Univ	TX	7,142	C
Samford Univ	AL	18,648	VC
San Diego State Univ	CA	10,321	C
San Francisco State Univ	CA	12,070	C
San Jose State Univ	CA	8,187	C
Santa Clara Univ	CA	34,701	HC
Sarah Lawrence College	NY	41,218	HC
Savannah State Univ	GA	7,328	LC
Schreiner Univ	TX	20,440	C
Scripps College	CA	35,700	HC+
Seattle Pacific Univ	WA	25,944	VC
Seattle Univ	WA	24,183	VC
Seton Hall Univ	NJ	30,130	VC
Seton Hill Univ	PA	24,930	C
Shaw Univ	NC	14,882	C+
Shawnee State Univ	OH	11,031	NC
Shenandoah Univ	VA	25,190	NC
Shepherd College	WV	8,608	C
Shippensburg Univ of Pennsylvania	PA	10,826	C
Shorter College	GA	17,370	C
Siena College	NY	25,310	VC
Siena Heights Univ	MI	16,140	LC
Silver Lake College of the Holy Family	WI	18,450	LC
Simmons College	MA	33,000	VC
Simon's Rock College of Bard	MA	36,580	HC
Simpson College	CA	20,500	C
Simpson College	IA	23,658	C+
Skidmore College	NY	37,930	HC
Slippery Rock Univ of Pennsylvania	PA	10,343	LC
Smith College	MA	37,034	HC+
Sonoma State Univ	CA	10,421	C
S Car State Univ	SC	6,586	LC
S Dak School of Mines and Technology	SD	7,854	C+
S Dak State Univ	SD	7,782	C
Southeast Missouri State Univ	MO	9,704	C
Southeastern Louisiana Univ	LA	6,791	LC
Southeastern Okla State Univ	OK	6,147	C
Southern Adventist Univ	TN	17,080	C
Southern Arkansas Univ	AR	6,956	C
Southern Conn State Univ	CT	10,310	C
Southern Illinois Univ Carbondale	IL	10,407	C
Southern Illinois Univ Edwardsville	IL	8,724	C
Southern Methodist Univ	TX	34,210	HC
Southern Nazarene Univ	OK	14,634	NC
Southern Oregon Univ	OR	10,362	C
Southern Polytechnic State Univ	GA	7,620	VC
Southern Univ and A&M College	LA	7,372	LC
Southern Univ at New Orleans	LA	995	NC
Southern Utah Univ	UT	8,194	C
Southern Wesleyan Univ	SC	19,940	C
Southwest Baptist Univ	MO	15,371	C
Southwest Minn State Univ	MN	9,106	VC

School	ST	$IS	SR
Southwest Missouri State Univ	MO	8,918	C
Southwestern Adventist Univ	TX	14,798	C
Southwestern College	KS	19,560	C
Southwestern Okla State Univ	OK	4,801	C
Southwestern Univ	TX	25,410	HC
Spelman College	GA	19,215	C+
Spring Arbor Univ	MI	20,206	C
Spring Hill College	AL	25,868	VC
Springfield College	MA	24,520	C
St. Joseph's, Suffolk	NY	11,297	C
Stanford Univ	CA	37,612	MC
SUNY at Oswego	NY	12,650	C
SUNY at Potsdam	NY	12,160	C
SUNY/College at Brockport	NY	12,111	C
SUNY/College at Buffalo	NY	8,025	C
SUNY/College at Cortland	NY	12,095	C
SUNY/College at Fredonia	NY	11,562	VC
SUNY/College at Geneseo	NY	11,330	HC
SUNY/College at Old Westbury	NY	12,784	C
SUNY/College at Oneonta	NY	11,870	VC
SUNY/College at Plattsburgh	NY	11,700	C
SUNY/College at Purchase	NY	10,587	VC
SUNY/Empire State College	NY	4,505	SP
SUNY/Univ at Albany	NY	12,951	HC
SUNY/Univ at Binghamton	NY	12,787	HC
SUNY/Univ at Buffalo	NY	12,563	VC
SUNY/Univ at New Paltz	NY	11,565	VC
SUNY/Univ at Stony Brook	NY	12,763	HC
State Univ of West Georgia	GA	7,622	C
Stephen F. Austin State Univ	TX	7,552	C
Stephens College	MO	24,260	C+
Sterling College	KS	18,763	C
Stetson Univ	FL	29,495	VC
Stevens Inst of Technology	NJ	35,300	HC+
Stillman College	AL	11,370	LC
Stonehill College	MA	30,752	HC
Suffolk Univ	MA	29,200	C
Sul Ross State Univ	TX	6,582	LC
Susquehanna Univ	PA	29,990	VC
Swarthmore College	PA	37,716	MC
Sweet Briar College	VA	27,940	C
Syracuse Univ	NY	34,720	HC
Tabor College	KS	19,500	NC
Talladega College	AL	10,110	LC
Tarleton State Univ	TX	7,576	C
Taylor Univ	IN	23,820	VC+
Temple Univ	PA	15,912	C
Tenn State Univ	TN	9,048	LC
Tenn Tech Univ	TN	8,670	VC
Tenn Wesleyan College	TN	16,540	C
Texas A&M Univ	TX	11,081	HC
Texas A&M Univ at Commerce	TX	8,994	C
Texas A&M Univ at Corpus Christi	TX	10,269	C
Texas A&M Univ at Kingsville	TX	6,740	LC
Texas Christian Univ	TX	23,410	VC
Texas Lutheran Univ	TX	20,370	C
Texas Southern Univ	TX	8,920	NC
Texas State Univ	TX	9,320	VC
Texas Tech Univ	TX	10,768	VC
Texas Wesleyan Univ	TX	16,245	C
Texas Woman's Univ	TX	7,804	LC
Thiel College	PA	20,970	C
Thomas Edison State College	NJ	3,325	SP
Thomas More College	KY	21,350	C
Tougaloo College	MS	9,200	NC
Touro College	NY	15,250	VC
Towson Univ	MD	12,694	VC
Transylvania Univ	KY	23,780	VC+
Trevecca Nazarene Univ	TN	17,548	C
Trinity Christian College	IL	21,640	VC
Trinity College	CT	38,040	HC+
Trinity College	DC	24,150	LC
Trinity International Univ	IL	22,980	C+
Trinity Univ	TX	26,466	HC+
Tri-State Univ-Main Campus	IN	23,600	C
Troy State Univ	AL	7,696	C
Troy State Univ Dothan	AL	3,842	C
Troy State Univ Montgomery	AL	3,600	NC
Truman State Univ	MO	9,728	HC+
Tufts Univ	MA	38,233	MC
Tulane Univ	LA	37,451	HC+
Turabo Univ	PR	4,110	
Tuskegee Univ	AL	17,250	LC
Union College	NE	17,130	C
Union College	NY	36,005	HC
Union Univ	TN	18,800	VC
United States Air Force Academy	CO		HC+
United States Military Academy	NY		MC
United States Naval Academy	MD		MC
Univ of Akron	OH	13,134	NC
Univ of Alabama	AL	9,040	C+

School	ST	$IS	SR
Univ of Alabama at Birmingham	AL	12,901	C
Univ of Alabama in Huntsville	AL	9,126	VC
Univ of Alaska Anchorage	AK	9,100	NC
Univ of Alaska Fairbanks	AK	9,295	C
Univ of Alaska Southeast	AK	7,900	LC
Univ of Arizona	AZ	10,413	VC
Univ of Arkansas	AR	9,855	VC
Univ of Arkansas at Little Rock	AR	5,637	NC
Univ of Arkansas at Monticello	AR	5,940	NC
Univ of Arkansas at Pine Bluff	AR	7,925	C
Univ of Bridgeport	CT	25,924	LC
Univ of Calif at Berkeley	CA	15,563	MC
Univ of Calif at Davis	CA	14,995	VC
Univ of Calif at Irvine	CA	19,808	HC
Univ of Calif at Los Angeles	CA	15,330	MC
Univ of Calif at Riverside	CA	15,300	C
Univ of Calif at San Diego	CA	14,127	HC
Univ of Calif at Santa Barbara	CA	11,732	VC
Univ of Calif at Santa Cruz	CA	16,505	VC
Univ of Central Arkansas	AR	6,388	C
Univ of Central Florida	FL	10,038	VC
Univ of Central Okla	OK	9,434	C
Univ of Chicago	IL	35,087	MC
Univ of Cincinnati	OH	14,736	C
Univ of Colo at Boulder	CO	10,774	VC
Univ of Colo at Colo Springs	CO	10,667	C
Univ of Colo at Denver	CO	3,302	C
Univ of Conn	CT	14,608	VC
Univ of Dallas	TX	25,898	VC+
Univ of Dayton	OH	24,850	VC
Univ of Delaware	DE	12,616	HC
Univ of Denver	CO	32,148	VC
Univ of Detroit Mercy	MI	25,582	C
Univ of Evansville	IN	24,190	VC
Univ of Findlay	OH	23,962	NC
Univ of Florida	FL	8,580	MC
Univ of Georgia	GA	8,656	VC
Univ of Great Falls	MT	15,360	C
Univ of Hartford	CT	31,080	C
Univ of Hawaii at Hilo	HI	6,497	C
Univ of Hawaii at Manoa	HI	9,565	VC
Univ of Houston	TX	9,818	C
Univ of Idaho	ID	8,216	C
Univ of Illinois at Chicago	IL	13,418	C
Univ of Illinois at Urbana-Champaign	IL	11,316	HC+
Univ of Indianapolis	IN	22,560	VC
Univ of Iowa	IA	10,923	VC
Univ of Kansas	KS	8,923	VC
Univ of Kentucky	KY	7,765	C
Univ of La Verne	CA	28,600	C
Univ of Louisiana at Lafayette	LA	5,826	C
Univ of Louisiana at Monroe	LA	5,207	NC
Univ of Louisville	KY	8,762	VC
Univ of Maine	ME	12,080	C+
Univ of Maine at Farmington	ME	10,108	C
Univ of Mary	ND	12,900	C+
Univ of Mary Hardin-Baylor	TX	17,268	C
Univ of Maryland/Baltimore County	MD	14,668	VC+
Univ of Maryland/College Park	MD	14,227	HC
Univ of Maryland/Eastern Shore	MD	9,964	C
Univ of Mass Amherst	MA	13,980	C+
Univ of Mass Boston	MA	6,227	C
Univ of Mass Dartmouth	MA	12,835	C
Univ of Mass Lowell	MA	11,937	VC
Univ of Memphis	TN	8,560	C
Univ of Miami	FL	34,608	HC
Univ of Mich/Ann Arbor	MI	13,864	HC+
Univ of Mich/Dearborn	MI	6,843	VC
Univ of Mich/Flint	MI	5,548	C
Univ of Minn/Duluth	MN	12,470	C
Univ of Minn/Morris	MN	12,896	VC
Univ of Minn/Twin Cities	MN	13,160	VC
Univ of Missouri/Columbia	MO	13,782	VC
Univ of Missouri/Kansas City	MO	13,416	VC
Univ of Missouri/Rolla	MO	12,292	HC
Univ of Missouri/St. Louis	MO	11,656	VC
Univ of Mobile	AL	13,620	C
Univ of Montana	MT	9,395	C
Univ of Montevallo	AL	8,478	C
Univ of Nebr at Kearney	NE	8,286	NC
Univ of Nebr at Lincoln	NE	9,975	C+
Univ of Nebr at Omaha	NE	8,080	C
Univ of Nevada/Las Vegas	NV	11,566	C
Univ of Nevada/Reno	NV	9,792	C
Univ of New Hampshire	NH	14,828	VC
Univ of New Haven	CT	28,650	C
Univ of New Mexico	NM	9,223	C
Univ of New Orleans	LA	7,356	C
Univ of North Alabama	AL	7,972	NC
Univ of N Car at Asheville	NC	8,079	VC
Univ of N Car at Chapel Hill	NC	10,117	MC
Univ of N Car at Charlotte	NC	8,185	C

School	ST	$IS	SR
Univ of N Car at Greensboro	NC	8,248	C
Univ of N Car at Pembroke	NC	6,929	LC
Univ of N Car at Wilmington	NC	8,940	VC
Univ of N Dak	ND	8,390	C
Univ of North Florida	FL	8,769	VC
Univ of North Texas	TX	7,629	C
Univ of Northern Colo	CO	8,987	C
Univ of Northern Iowa	IA	9,834	C
Univ of Notre Dame	IN	34,442	MC
Univ of Okla	OK	9,226	VC
Univ of Oregon	OR	11,479	VC
Univ of Pennsylvania	PA	37,960	MC
Univ of Pittsburgh at Bradford	PA	15,294	C
Univ of Pittsburgh at Johnstown	PA	15,216	LC
Univ of Pittsburgh at Pittsburgh	PA	16,074	HC
Univ of Portland	OR	28,500	VC
Univ of PR at Humacao	PR	1,245	
Univ of PR/Cayey Univ College	PR	1,245	
Univ of PR/Mayaguez	PR		
Univ of Puget Sound	WA	31,760	HC
Univ of Redlands	CA	32,576	VC
Univ of Rhode Island	RI	13,720	VC
Univ of Richmond	VA	30,100	MC
Univ of Rio Grande	OH	8,728	NC
Univ of Rochester	NY	32,979	HC
Univ of St. Francis	IL	22,850	C
Univ of St. Mary	KS	18,868	C
Univ of St. Thomas	MN	26,918	VC
Univ of St. Thomas	TX	21,952	VC
Univ of San Diego	CA	33,156	HC
Univ of San Francisco	CA	34,700	VC
Univ of Science and Arts of Okla	OK	5,982	C
Univ of Scranton	PA	30,836	VC
Univ of Sioux Falls	SD	16,390	C
Univ of South Alabama	AL	7,760	LC
Univ of S Car at Columbia	SC	10,048	VC
Univ of S Car at Spartanburg	SC	9,936	C+
Univ of S Dak	SD	7,710	C+
Univ of South Florida	FL	9,454	C
Univ of Southern Calif	CA	37,459	MC
Univ of Southern Colo	CO	7,821	LC
Univ of Southern Indiana	IN	9,025	LC
Univ of Southern Maine	ME	11,212	C
Univ of Southern Miss	MS	8,324	LC
Univ of Tampa	FL	23,982	VC
Univ of Tenn at Chattanooga	TN	7,783	C
Univ of Tenn at Knoxville	TN	8,214	C
Univ of Tenn at Martin	TN	7,748	C
Univ of Texas at Arlington	TX	7,192	LC
Univ of Texas at Austin	TX	10,630	HC
Univ of Texas at Dallas	TX	10,234	HC
Univ of Texas at El Paso	TX	5,799	NC
Univ of Texas at San Antonio	TX	9,088	NC
Univ of Texas-Pan American	TX	5,954	LC
Univ of the District of Columbia	DC	2,070	LC
Univ of the Incarnate Word	TX	21,772	LC
Univ of the Ozarks	AR	16,574	C
Univ of the Pacific	CA	31,090	VC
Univ of the Sacred Heart	PR	5,590	
Univ of the South	TN	30,855	HC
Univ of Toledo	OH	12,479	NC
Univ of Tulsa	OK	22,090	VC+
Univ of Utah	UT	9,205	C
Univ of Vermont	VT	16,316	VC
Univ of Virginia	VA	11,740	MC
Univ of Virginia's College at Wise	VA	10,116	C
Univ of Washington	WA	10,361	VC
Univ of West Alabama	AL	6,048	C
Univ of West Florida	FL	8,470	C
Univ of Wisc/Eau Claire	WI	8,463	VC
Univ of Wisc/Green Bay	WI	8,154	C
Univ of Wisc/La Crosse	WI	8,991	VC
Univ of Wisc/Madison	WI	8,262	VC
Univ of Wisc/Milwaukee	WI	9,427	LC
Univ of Wisc/Oshkosh	WI	6,130	LC
Univ of Wisc/Parkside	WI	6,160	LC
Univ of Wisc/Platteville	WI	8,450	C
Univ of Wisc/River Falls	WI	8,358	LC
Univ of Wisc/Stevens Point	WI	8,116	VC
Univ of Wisc/Superior	WI	7,051	C+
Univ of Wisc/Whitewater	WI	8,626	C
Univ of Wyoming	WY	8,636	C
Upper Iowa Univ	IA	20,500	VC
Ursinus College	PA	34,400	VC
Ursuline College	OH	22,728	LC
Utah State Univ	UT	7,371	C
Utica College	NY	28,340	C
Valdosta State Univ	GA	7,798	C
Valley City State Univ	ND	7,281	LC
Valparaiso Univ	IN	26,118	VC+
Vanderbilt Univ	TN	37,897	MC
Vanguard Univ of Southern Calif	CA	22,208	C
Vassar College	NY	37,030	MC

ST = STATE $IS = IN-STATE COSTS SR = SELECTOR RATING

School	ST	$IS	SR
Villanova Univ	PA	35,050	HC
Virginia Commonwealth Univ	VA	9,030	C
Virginia Military Inst	VA	9,968	C+
Virginia Polytechnic Inst and State Univ	VA	9,179	C
Virginia State Univ	VA	10,358	C
Virginia Union Univ	VA	15,358	LC
Virginia Wesleyan College	VA	25,350	C
Viterbo Univ	WI	20,430	C
Voorhees College	SC	11,678	LC
Wabash College	IN	27,932	VC
Wagner College	NY	29,900	VC
Wake Forest Univ	NC	34,090	MC
Walla Walla College	WA	21,600	NC
Walsh Univ	OH	20,890	C
Warren Wilson College	NC	21,794	VC
Wartburg College	IA	21,165	VC
Washburn Univ of Topeka	KS	8,984	NC
Washington and Jefferson College	PA	29,570	VC
Washington and Lee Univ	VA	29,663	MC
Washington College	MD	30,540	VC
Washington State Univ	WA	11,334	C
Washington Univ in St. Louis	MO	38,293	MC
Wayland Baptist Univ	TX	11,919	NC
Wayne State College	NE	7,352	NC
Wayne State Univ	MI	11,774	C
Waynesburg College	PA	19,370	C
Weber State Univ	UT	7,945	NC
Webster Univ	MO	21,848	VC
Wellesley College	MA	36,516	MC
Wells College	NY	21,122	VC
Wesleyan College	GA	17,870	VC
Wesleyan Univ	CT	35,139	MC
West Chester Univ of Pennsylvania	PA	11,164	C
West Liberty State College	WV	7,868	LC
West Texas A&M Univ	TX	7,533	C
West Virginia State College	WV	6,264	NC
West Virginia Univ	WV	9,370	C
West Virginia Wesleyan College	WV	22,920	C
Western Baptist College	OR	21,808	C
Western Carolina Univ	NC	6,742	C
Western Conn State Univ	CT	11,625	C
Western Illinois Univ	IL	10,363	C
Western Kentucky Univ	KY	6,834	C
Western Mich Univ	MI	12,031	C
Western New England College	MA	28,924	C
Western New Mexico Univ	NM	5,950	LC
Western Oregon Univ	OR	10,281	C
Western State College of Colo	CO	9,014	C
Western Washington Univ	WA	10,119	VC
Westfield State College	MA	10,147	C
Westminster College	MO	18,150	C+
Westminster College	PA	22,960	C
Westminster College	UT	17,226	C
Westmont College	CA	33,062	VC+
Wheaton College	IL	21,934	HC
Wheaton College	MA	36,330	HC
Wheeling Jesuit Univ	WV	22,660	C
Whitman College	WA	32,526	HC+
Whittier College	CA	29,108	C
Whitworth College	WA	26,428	VC+
Wichita State Univ	KS	8,092	C
Widener Univ	PA	27,020	C
Wilberforce Univ	OH	14,937	LC
Wiley College	TX	8,100	LC
Wilkes Univ	PA	28,060	C
Willamette Univ	OR	32,032	VC+
William Carey College	MS	10,150	LC
William Jewell College	MO	21,320	VC
William Paterson Univ of New Jersey	NJ	14,450	C
William Woods Univ	MO	20,120	C
Williams College	MA	32,270	MC
Wilmington College	OH	24,172	LC
Wilson College	PA	23,912	C
Wingate Univ	NC	21,200	C
Winona State Univ	MN		C
Winston-Salem State Univ	NC	8,926	LC
Winthrop Univ	SC	11,302	C
Wisc Lutheran College	WI	21,430	VC
Wittenberg Univ	OH	31,316	VC
Wofford College	SC	26,710	HC
Worcester Polytechnic Inst	MA	37,404	HC
Worcester State College	MA	10,005	C
Wright State Univ	OH	11,490	LC
Xavier Univ	OH	26,850	VC+
Xavier Univ of Louisiana	LA	17,600	C
Yale Univ	CT	37,000	MC
Yeshiva Univ	NY	21,400	C
York College of Pennsylvania	PA	14,500	VC
Youngstown State Univ	OH	11,148	NC

MATHEMATICS EDUCATION

School	ST	$IS	SR
Adams State College	CO	7,468	C
Adelphi Univ	NY	26,300	VC
Alfred Univ	NY	28,290	C
Andrews Univ	MI	19,550	C
Arkansas State Univ	AR	8,450	C
Asbury College	KY	20,704	VC
Auburn Univ	AL	10,396	VC
Averett Univ	VA	23,010	LC
Baylor Univ	TX	23,864	VC
Bennett College	NC	11,200	C
Berry College	GA	21,410	VC
Bethany College	KS	18,675	LC
Bethel College	IN	19,670	C
Bethel College	MN	25,180	VC
Bethune-Cookman College	FL	16,480	LC
Biola Univ	CA	25,964	VC
Blue Mountain College	MS	10,226	C
Boston Univ	MA	38,194	HC+
Brewton-Parker College	GA	14,200	LC
Brigham Young Univ	UT	8,504	HC
Brigham Young Univ/Hawaii	HI	7,240	VC+
Cal State, Long Beach	CA	8,762	C+
Calif Univ of Pennsylvania	PA	10,388	C
Canisius College	NY	28,163	C+
Carthage College	WI	25,000	C
Catawba College	NC	20,500	C
Catholic Univ of America	DC	34,248	VC
Cedarville Univ	OH	19,954	VC
Central Missouri State Univ	MO	9,776	C
Central Washington Univ	WA	9,768	C
CUNY/Brooklyn College	NY	4,353	C+
CUNY/City College	NY	4,230	C+
Claflin Univ	SC	14,838	C+
Coker College	SC	21,491	C
College of New Jersey	NJ	15,950	MC
College of St. Rose	NY	22,864	C
College of the Ozarks	MO	3,500	VC+
Columbia Union College	MD	20,543	C
Concordia Univ/St.Paul	MN	24,486	C
Cumberland College	KY	16,384	C
Daemen College	NY	22,120	C
Dana College	NE	20,280	C
Defiance College	OH	22,615	C
Delta State Univ	MS	6,618	C
Dominican College	NY	24,810	LC
Drake Univ	IA	25,120	VC+
Duquesne Univ	PA	26,907	VC
East Carolina Univ	NC	8,671	C
East Central Univ	OK	4,968	C
East Texas Baptist Univ	TX	13,914	C
Eastern Mich Univ	MI	11,478	C
Eastern Washington Univ	WA	9,012	C
Edinboro Univ of Pennsylvania	PA	10,850	LC
Elmhurst College	IL	24,630	C
Elon Univ	NC	22,240	VC
Emory & Henry College	VA	21,950	C
Ferris State Univ	MI	12,512	C
Florida Inst of Technology	FL	28,740	VC
Florida International Univ	FL	9,912	VC
Florida State Univ	FL	9,028	HC
Fort Valley State Univ	GA	6,960	C
Franklin College	IN		C
Fresno Pacific Univ	CA	22,462	C
Geneva College	PA	21,850	C
George Fox Univ	OR	26,110	VC
Georgia Southwestern State Univ	GA	6,013	C
Grace College	IN	19,825	VC
Grambling State Univ	LA	6,538	NC
Greensboro College	NC	21,750	C
Greenville College	IL	21,342	C
Gwynedd-Mercy College	PA	24,225	C
Hofstra Univ	NY	27,112	VC
Hood College	MD	27,795	VC
Humboldt State Univ	CA	9,400	C
Huntington College	IN	23,590	C
Indiana Univ of Pennsylvania	PA	10,489	C
Indiana Univ South Bend	IN	4,571	LC
Indiana Univ Southeast	IN	4,504	LC
Indiana Univ-Purdue Univ Indianapolis	IN	8,257	LC
Ithaca College	NY	31,730	HC
Jackson State Univ	MS	8,382	C
John Carroll Univ	OH	27,658	C+
Johnson C. Smith Univ	NC	18,108	C
Johnson State College	VT	11,819	LC
Judson College	AL	14,650	C
Judson College	IL	22,050	LC
Juniata College	PA	29,080	VC
Keene State College	NH	12,212	C
Kennesaw State Univ	GA	2,724	C
Kent State Univ	OH	12,932	C
Kentucky State Univ	KY	9,062	NC
Knoxville College	TN	6,200	LC
Langston Univ	OK	2,308	LC
Le Moyne College	NY	26,400	VC
Limestone College	SC	17,700	C
Lincoln Univ	PA	13,320	C+
Louisiana College	LA	13,450	C
Mansfield Univ	PA	11,220	C
Mars Hill College	NC	18,600	LC
Mary Baldwin College	VA	24,939	C
Marymount College of Fordham Univ	NY	27,686	C
Mercyhurst College	PA	20,694	C
Messiah College	PA	25,890	VC+
MidAmerica Nazarene Univ	KS	18,688	C
Minot State Univ	ND	6,602	LC
Miss Valley State Univ	MS	6,765	NC
Missouri Southern State Univ	MO	8,316	C
Monmouth Univ	NJ	26,334	C
Montana State Univ-Billings	MT	9,550	C
Morningside College	IA	21,610	C
Morris College	SC	10,974	LC
Mount Holyoke College	MA	37,918	HC+
Mount Vernon Nazarene Univ	OH	18,925	C
Nazareth College of Rochester	NY	24,936	VC
New York Univ	NY	39,406	MC
Niagara Univ	NY	25,050	C
N Car Agricultural and Technical State Univ	NC	6,659	LC
N Car State Univ	NC	9,886	VC
North Georgia College and State Univ	GA	6,984	C
Northwest Missouri State Univ	MO	9,334	C
Northwest Nazarene Univ	ID	20,360	VC
Northwestern College	MN	22,820	C+
Northwestern Okla State Univ	OK	5,433	NC
Northwestern Univ	IL	37,491	MC
Oakwood College	AL	14,904	C
Okla Christian Univ	OK	17,690	NC
Okla Panhandle State Univ	OK	5,370	C
Okla Wesleyan Univ	OK	14,100	LC
Old Dominion Univ	VA	10,441	C
Oral Roberts Univ	OK	18,490	C
Palm Beach Atlantic Univ	FL	20,690	C
Philander Smith College	AR	7,380	NC
Pontifical Catholic Univ of PR/Ponce	PR	7,298	
Providence College	RI	30,604	HC
Purdue Univ/West Lafayette	IN	12,560	VC
Rider Univ	NJ	30,900	C
Rivier College	NH	26,217	C
Rocky Mountain College	MT	19,015	C
Rust College	MS	8,200	C+
Saginaw Valley State Univ	MI	11,055	C
St. Augustine's College	NC	12,990	LC
St. Edward's Univ	TX	20,428	C
St. John Fisher College	NY	24,870	C
St. John's Univ	NY	30,180	C
Schreiner Univ	TX	20,440	C
Seattle Pacific Univ	WA	25,944	VC
Seton Hill Univ	PA	24,930	C
Shaw Univ	NC	14,882	C+
Sheldon Jackson College	AK	14,940	LC
Shepherd College	WV	8,608	C
Shorter College	GA	17,370	C
Southeast Missouri State Univ	MO	9,704	C
Southeastern Louisiana Univ	LA	6,791	LC
Southeastern Okla State Univ	OK	6,147	C
Southern Univ at New Orleans	LA	995	NC
Southern Utah Univ	UT	8,194	C
Southwest Minn State Univ	MN	9,106	VC
Southwestern College	KS	19,560	C
Southwestern Okla State Univ	OK	4,801	C
SUNY at Potsdam	NY	12,160	C
SUNY/College at Old Westbury	NY	12,784	C
SUNY/College at Oneonta	NY	11,870	VC
SUNY/College at Plattsburgh	NY	11,700	C
SUNY/Univ at Albany	NY	12,951	HC
Syracuse Univ	NY	34,720	HC
Taylor Univ	IN	23,820	VC+
Temple Univ	PA	15,912	C
Texas Southern Univ	TX	8,920	NC
Trevecca Nazarene Univ	TN	17,548	C
Tri-State Univ-Main Campus	IN	23,600	C
Troy State Univ	AL	7,696	C
Troy State Univ Dothan	AL	3,842	C
Turabo Univ	PR	4,110	
Union College	NE	17,130	C
Univ of Arkansas at Pine Bluff	AR	7,925	C
Univ of Calif at San Diego	CA	14,127	HC
Univ of Central Florida	FL	10,038	VC
Univ of Central Okla	OK	9,434	C
Univ of Conn	CT	14,608	VC
Univ of Delaware	DE	12,616	HC
Univ of Evansville	IN	24,190	VC
Univ of Georgia	GA	8,656	VC
Univ of Great Falls	MT	15,360	C
Univ of Illinois at Chicago	IL	13,418	C
Univ of Indianapolis	IN	22,560	VC
Univ of Kentucky	KY	7,765	C
Univ of Louisiana at Lafayette	LA	5,826	C
Univ of Louisiana at Monroe	LA	5,207	NC
Univ of Mary	ND	12,900	C+
Univ of Maryland/College Park	MD	14,227	HC
Univ of Maryland/Eastern Shore	MD	9,964	C
Univ of Minn/Duluth	MN	12,470	C
Univ of Minn/Twin Cities	MN	13,160	VC
Univ of Miss	MS	7,666	C
Univ of New Hampshire	NH	14,828	VC
Univ of New Orleans	LA	7,356	C
Univ of N Car at Chapel Hill	NC	10,117	MC
Univ of N Car at Charlotte	NC	8,185	C
Univ of N Car at Greensboro	NC	8,248	C
Univ of N Car at Pembroke	NC	6,929	LC
Univ of North Florida	FL	8,769	VC
Univ of Okla	OK	9,226	VC
Univ of Pittsburgh at Johnstown	PA	15,216	LC
Univ of Rio Grande	OH	8,728	NC
Univ of S Car at Spartanburg	SC	9,936	C+
Univ of South Florida	FL	9,454	C
Univ of Vermont	VT	16,316	VC
Univ of Wisc/Superior	WI	7,051	C+
Utah State Univ	UT	7,371	C
Wartburg College	IA	21,165	VC
Washington Univ in St. Louis	MO	38,293	MC
Wayne State Univ	MI	11,774	C
West Texas A&M Univ	TX	7,533	C
West Virginia Univ	WV	9,370	C
Western Carolina Univ	NC	6,742	C
Westmont College	CA	33,062	VC+
Whitworth College	WA	26,428	VC+
Wiley College	TX	8,100	LC
Wingate Univ	NC	21,200	C
Xavier Univ of Louisiana	LA	17,600	C
Youngstown State Univ	OH	11,148	NC

MECHANICAL DESIGN TECHNOLOGY

School	ST	$IS	SR
Bowling Green State Univ	OH	13,036	C
Lincoln Univ	MO	7,158	NC
Pennsylvania College of Technology	PA	15,126	NC
Southwest Missouri State Univ	MO	8,918	C

MECHANICAL ENGINEERING

School	ST	$IS	SR
Alabama A&M Univ	AL	5,100	LC
Alfred Univ	NY	28,290	C
Arizona State Univ-Main	AZ	10,048	C
Auburn Univ	AL	10,396	VC
Baylor Univ	TX	23,864	VC
Bethel College	IN	19,670	C
Boston Univ	MA	38,194	HC+
Bradley Univ	IL	22,910	VC
Brigham Young Univ	UT	8,504	HC
Bucknell Univ	PA	35,262	HC+
Calif Inst of Technology	CA	31,677	MC
Calif Maritime Academy	CA	14,296	C
Calif Polytechnic State Univ	CA	8,747	VC
Calif State Polytechnic Univ, Pomona	CA	8,793	C+
Cal State, Chico	CA	8,598	LC
Cal State, Fresno	CA	8,414	LC
Cal State, Fullerton	CA	6,648	C
Cal State, Long Beach	CA	8,762	C+
Cal State, Los Angeles	CA	5,778	C
Cal State, Sacramento	CA	9,543	C
Calvin College	MI	22,615	NC
Carnegie Mellon Univ	PA	32,682	MC
Case Western Reserve Univ	OH	32,002	MC
Catholic Univ of America	DC	34,248	VC
Cedarville Univ	OH	19,954	VC
Central Washington Univ	WA	9,768	C
Christian Brothers Univ	TN	22,290	VC
CUNY/City College	NY	4,230	C+
Clarkson Univ	NY	32,226	VC
Clemson Univ	SC	11,972	HC
Cleveland State Univ	OH	12,308	LC
Colo State Univ	CO	9,964	VC
Columbia Univ/Fu Foundation School of Engineering and Applied Science	NY	38,590	MC
Cooper Union for the Advancement of Science and Art	NY	10,400	MC
Cornell Univ	NY	38,253	MC
Delaware State Univ	DE	8,104	LC
Dordt College	IA	20,170	VC
Drexel Univ	PA	27,655	VC
Duke Univ	NC	37,555	MC
Fairfield Univ	CT	35,505	HC
Florida A&M Univ	FL	7,564	C
Florida Atlantic Univ	FL	8,543	C
Florida Inst of Technology	FL	28,740	VC
Florida International Univ	FL	9,912	VC
Florida State Univ	FL	9,028	HC
Gannon Univ	PA	23,260	C
George Washington Univ	DC	41,030	MC
Georgia Inst of Technology	GA	10,340	HC+
Gonzaga Univ	WA	26,766	HC
Grove City College	PA	14,228	HC
Henry Cogswell College	WA	14,400	SP

ST = STATE $IS = IN-STATE COSTS SR = SELECTOR RATING

School	ST	$IS	SR
Hofstra Univ	NY	27,112	VC
Howard Univ	DC	16,505	C
Illinois Inst of Technology	IL	26,456	HC+
Indiana Inst of Technology	IN	21,620	C
Indiana Univ-Purdue Univ Fort Wayne	IN	5,108	LC
Indiana Univ-Purdue Univ Indianapolis	IN	8,257	LC
Inter American Univ of PR/ Bayamon Univ College	PR	3,522	
Iowa State Univ	IA	10,768	VC
Jacksonville Univ	FL	24,040	C
Johns Hopkins Univ	MD	38,372	MC
Kansas State Univ	KS	8,728	VC
Kettering Univ	MI	26,478	HC
Lafayette College	PA	35,746	MC
Lake Superior State Univ	MI	9,034	LC
Lamar Univ	TX	6,816	LC
Lawrence Tech Univ	MI	20,487	C
Lehigh Univ	PA	37,570	HC+
LeTourneau Univ	TX	21,080	C
Louisiana State Univ and A&M College	LA	9,126	VC
Louisiana Tech Univ	LA	7,361	C
Loyola Marymount Univ	CA	32,194	VC
Manhattan College	NY	27,400	VC
Marquette Univ	WI	27,594	VC
Mass Inst of Technology	MA	38,310	MC
McNeese State Univ	LA	5,259	LC
Mercer Univ	GA	27,516	VC+
Miami Univ	OH	15,033	HC
Mich State Univ	MI	11,933	VC
Mich Tech Univ	MI	13,235	VC
Milwaukee School of Engineering	WI	28,479	VC+
Minn State Univ, Mankato	MN	8,803	LC
Miss State Univ	MS	9,139	C
Montana State Univ- Bozeman	MT	9,515	C
New Jersey Inst of Technology	NJ	16,396	VC
New Mexico State Univ	NM	7,932	C
New York Inst of Technology	NY	24,205	VC
N Car Agricultural and Technical State Univ	NC	6,659	LC
N Car State Univ	NC	9,886	VC
N Dak State Univ	ND	8,435	C
Northeastern Univ	MA	35,650	HC
Northern Arizona Univ	AZ	9,002	C
Northern Illinois Univ	IL	11,472	C
Northwestern Univ	IL	37,491	MC
Norwich Univ	VT	21,064	LC
Oakland Univ	MI	10,800	C
Ohio Northern Univ	OH	27,765	VC
Ohio State Univ	OH	13,080	VC+
Okla Christian Univ	OK	17,690	NC
Okla State Univ	OK	9,216	VC
Old Dominion Univ	VA	10,441	VC
Oral Roberts Univ	OK	18,490	C
Oregon State Univ	OR	11,055	C
Penn State Univ/Univ Park Campus	PA	15,646	HC
Polytechnic Univ/Brooklyn	NY	33,770	VC
Prairie View A&M Univ	TX	9,418	NC
Princeton Univ	NJ	36,649	MC
Purdue Univ/Calumet	IN	6,630	NC
Purdue Univ/West Lafayette	IN	12,560	VC
Rensselaer Polytechnic Inst	NY	37,579	HC+
Rice Univ	TX	27,550	MC
Rochester Inst of Technology	NY	29,217	VC+
Rose-Hulman Inst of Technology	IN	31,425	HC+
Rutgers, The State Univ of New Jersey/New Brunswick/Piscataway Campus	NJ	15,800	HC
Saginaw Valley State Univ	MI	11,055	C
St. Louis Univ	MO	29,780	VC+
St. Martin's College	WA	23,245	C
San Diego State Univ	CA	10,321	C
San Francisco State Univ	CA	12,070	C
San Jose State Univ	CA	8,187	C
Santa Clara Univ	CA	34,701	HC
Savannah State Univ	GA	7,328	LC
Seattle Univ	WA	24,183	VC
S Dak School of Mines and Technology	SD	7,854	C+
S Dak State Univ	SD	7,782	C
Southern Illinois Univ Carbondale	IL	10,407	C
Southern Illinois Univ Edwardsville	IL	8,724	C
Southern Methodist Univ	TX	34,210	HC
Southern Univ and A&M College	LA	7,372	LC
Stanford Univ	CA	37,612	MC
SUNY/Univ at Binghamton	NY	12,787	HC
SUNY/Univ at Buffalo	NY	12,563	VC
SUNY/Univ at Stony Brook	NY	12,763	HC
Stevens Inst of Technology	NJ	35,300	HC+
Syracuse Univ	NY	34,720	HC
Temple Univ	PA	15,912	C
Tenn State Univ	TN	9,048	LC
Tenn Tech Univ	TN	8,670	VC

School	ST	$IS	SR
Texas A&M Univ	TX	11,081	HC
Texas A&M Univ at Kingsville	TX	6,740	LC
Texas Tech Univ	TX	10,768	LC
Tri-State Univ-Main Campus	IN	23,600	C
Tufts Univ	MA	38,233	MC
Tulane Univ	LA	37,451	HC+
Tuskegee Univ	AL	17,250	LC
Union College	NY	36,005	HC
United States Air Force Academy	CO		HC+
United States Coast Guard Academy	CT		MC
United States Military Academy	NY		MC
United States Naval Academy	MD		MC
Universidad Politecnica de PR	PR	5,370	
Univ of Akron	OH	13,134	NC
Univ of Alabama	AL	9,040	C+
Univ of Alabama at Birmingham	AL	12,901	C
Univ of Alabama in Huntsville	AL	9,126	VC
Univ of Alaska Fairbanks	AK	9,295	C
Univ of Arizona	AZ	10,413	VC
Univ of Arkansas	AR	9,855	VC
Univ of Calif at Berkeley	CA	15,563	MC
Univ of Calif at Davis	CA	14,995	VC
Univ of Calif at Irvine	CA	19,808	HC
Univ of Calif at Los Angeles	CA	15,330	MC
Univ of Calif at Riverside	CA	15,300	C
Univ of Calif at San Diego	CA	14,127	HC
Univ of Calif at Santa Barbara	CA	11,732	VC
Univ of Central Florida	FL	10,038	VC
Univ of Cincinnati	OH	14,736	C
Univ of Colo at Boulder	CO	10,774	VC
Univ of Colo at Denver	CO	3,302	C
Univ of Conn	CT	14,608	VC
Univ of Dayton	OH	24,850	VC
Univ of Delaware	DE	12,616	HC
Univ of Denver	CO	32,148	VC
Univ of Detroit Mercy	MI	25,582	C
Univ of Evansville	IN	24,190	VC
Univ of Florida	FL	8,580	MC
Univ of Hartford	CT	31,080	C
Univ of Hawaii at Manoa	HI	9,565	VC
Univ of Houston	TX	9,818	C
Univ of Idaho	ID	8,216	C
Univ of Illinois at Chicago	IL	13,418	C
Univ of Illinois at Urbana- Champaign	IL	11,316	HC+
Univ of Indianapolis	IN	22,560	VC
Univ of Iowa	IA	10,923	VC
Univ of Kansas	KS	8,923	VC
Univ of Kentucky	KY	7,765	C
Univ of Louisiana at Lafayette	LA	5,826	C
Univ of Louisville	KY	8,762	VC
Univ of Maine	ME	12,080	C+
Univ of Maryland/Baltimore County	MD	14,668	VC+
Univ of Maryland/College Park	MD	14,227	HC
Univ of Mass Amherst	MA	13,980	C+
Univ of Mass Dartmouth	MA	12,835	C
Univ of Mass Lowell	MA	11,937	VC
Univ of Memphis	TN	8,560	C
Univ of Miami	FL	34,608	HC
Univ of Mich/Ann Arbor	MI	13,864	HC+
Univ of Mich/Dearborn	MI	6,843	VC
Univ of Minn/Twin Cities	MN	13,160	VC
Univ of Miss	MS	7,666	C
Univ of Missouri/Columbia	MO	13,782	VC
Univ of Missouri/Kansas City	MO	13,416	VC
Univ of Missouri/Rolla	MO	12,292	HC
Univ of Missouri/St. Louis	MO	11,656	VC
Univ of Nebr at Lincoln	NE	9,975	C+
Univ of Nevada/Las Vegas	NV	11,566	C
Univ of Nevada/Reno	NV	9,792	VC
Univ of New Hampshire	NH	14,828	VC
Univ of New Haven	CT	28,650	C
Univ of New Mexico	NM	9,223	C
Univ of New Orleans	LA	7,356	C
Univ of N Car at Charlotte	NC	8,185	C
Univ of N Dak	ND	8,390	C
Univ of North Florida	FL	8,769	VC
Univ of Notre Dame	IN	34,442	MC
Univ of Okla	OK	9,226	VC
Univ of Pennsylvania	PA	37,960	MC
Univ of Pittsburgh at Pittsburgh	PA	16,074	HC
Univ of Portland	OR	28,500	VC
Univ of PR/Mayaguez	PR		
Univ of Rhode Island	RI	13,720	VC
Univ of Rochester	NY	32,979	HC
Univ of St. Thomas	MN	26,918	VC
Univ of South Alabama	AL	7,760	LC
Univ of S Car at Columbia	SC	10,048	VC
Univ of South Florida	FL	9,454	C
Univ of Southern Calif	CA	37,459	MC
Univ of Tenn at Knoxville	TN	8,214	C

School	ST	$IS	SR
Univ of Texas at Arlington	TX	7,192	LC
Univ of Texas at Austin	TX	10,630	HC
Univ of Texas at El Paso	TX	5,799	NC
Univ of Texas at San Antonio	TX	9,088	NC
Univ of Texas-Pan American	TX	5,954	LC
Univ of the District of Columbia	DC	2,070	LC
Univ of the Pacific	CA	31,090	VC
Univ of Toledo	OH	12,479	NC
Univ of Tulsa	OK	22,090	VC+
Univ of Utah	UT	9,205	C
Univ of Vermont	VT	16,316	VC
Univ of Virginia	VA	11,740	MC
Univ of Wisc/Madison	WI	8,262	VC
Univ of Wisc/Milwaukee	WI	9,427	LC
Univ of Wisc/Platteville	WI	8,450	C
Univ of Wyoming	WY	8,636	C
Utah State Univ	UT	7,371	C
Valparaiso Univ	IN	26,118	VC+
Vanderbilt Univ	TN	37,897	MC
Villanova Univ	PA	35,050	HC
Virginia Commonwealth Univ	VA	9,030	C
Virginia Military Inst	VA	9,968	C+
Virginia Polytechnic Inst and State Univ	VA	9,179	C
Washington Univ in St. Louis	MO	38,293	MC
Wayne State Univ	MI	11,774	C
West Virginia Univ	WV	9,370	C
West Virginia Univ Inst of Technology	WV	7,518	NC
Western Kentucky Univ	KY	6,834	C
Western Mich Univ	MI	12,031	C
Western New England College	MA	28,924	C
Wichita State Univ	KS	8,092	C
Widener Univ	PA	27,020	C
Wilkes Univ	PA	28,060	C
Worcester Polytechnic Inst	MA	37,404	HC
Wright State Univ	OH	11,490	LC
Yale Univ	CT	37,000	MC
York College of Pennsylvania	PA	14,500	VC
Youngstown State Univ	OH	11,148	NC

MECHANICAL ENGINEERING TECHNOLOGY

School	ST	$IS	SR
Alabama A&M Univ	AL	5,100	LC
Andrews Univ	MI	19,550	C
Central Conn State Univ	CT	12,090	C
Cleveland State Univ	OH	12,308	LC
Eastern Washington Univ	WA	9,012	C
Fairleigh Dickinson Univ/ Metropolitan Campus	NJ	28,584	C
Fairmont State	WV	8,280	LC
Georgia Southern Univ	GA	8,540	C
Henry Cogswell College	WA	14,400	SP
Indiana State Univ	IN	10,719	VC
Indiana Univ-Purdue Univ Indianapolis	IN	8,257	LC
Kansas State Univ	KS	8,728	VC
Metropolitan State College of Denver	CO	2,338	LC
Montana State Univ- Bozeman	MT	9,515	C
Northeastern Univ	MA	35,650	HC
Okla State Univ	OK	9,216	VC
Old Dominion Univ	VA	10,441	VC
Oregon Inst of Technology	OR	8,718	C
Penn State Univ at Erie/ Behrend College	PA	12,326	C
Pennsylvania College of Technology	PA	15,126	NC
Point Park Univ	PA	21,840	C
Purdue Univ/Calumet	IN	6,630	NC
Purdue Univ/West Lafayette	IN	12,560	VC
Rochester Inst of Technology	NY	29,217	VC+
S Car State Univ	SC	6,586	LC
Southern Polytechnic State Univ	GA	7,620	VC
SUNY/College at Buffalo	NY	8,025	C
SUNY/College of Technology at Alfred	NY	12,416	C
Temple Univ	PA	15,912	C
Texas A&M Univ at Corpus Christi	TX	10,269	C
Texas A&M Univ at Galveston	TX	9,948	C+
Texas Tech Univ	TX	10,768	LC
Thomas Edison State College	NJ	3,325	SP
Univ of Akron	OH	13,134	NC
Univ of Arkansas at Little Rock	AR	5,637	NC
Univ of Cincinnati	OH	14,736	C
Univ of Dayton	OH	24,850	VC
Univ of Hartford	CT	31,080	C
Univ of Houston	TX	9,818	C
Univ of Maine	ME	12,080	C+
Univ of New Hampshire	NH	14,828	VC
Univ of N Car at Charlotte	NC	8,185	C

School	ST	$IS	SR
Univ of Pittsburgh at Johnstown	PA	15,216	LC
Univ of Southern Colo	CO	7,821	LC
Univ of Southern Miss	MS	8,324	LC
Wayne State Univ	MI	11,774	C
Weber State Univ	UT	7,945	NC
Wentworth Inst of Technology	MA	23,000	C
Western Kentucky Univ	KY	6,834	C
Youngstown State Univ	OH	11,148	NC

MEDIA ARTS

School	ST	$IS	SR
Arizona State Univ-Main	AZ	10,048	C
Arkansas State Univ	AR	8,450	C
Art Inst of Portland	OR	23,040	SP
Ashland Univ	OH	24,464	C
Brigham Young Univ	UT	8,504	HC
Brown Univ	RI	38,174	MC
Cal State, Los Angeles	CA	5,778	C
Cal State, Stanislaus	CA	9,874	C
Calumet College of St. Joseph	IN	9,000	LC
Calvin College	MI	22,615	NC
Champlain College	VT	22,030	C
Chatham College	PA	27,266	C+
CUNY/Hunter College	NY	6,729	C+
CUNY/Queens College	NY	4,362	C
College of St. Catherine	MN	24,010	VC
College of the Ozarks	MO	3,500	VC+
Columbus College of Art and Design	OH	24,180	SP
Denison Univ	OH	33,050	HC
East Stroudsburg Univ of Pennsylvania	PA	10,336	C
Edinboro Univ of Pennsylvania	PA	10,850	LC
Emerson College	MA	32,205	HC
Gallaudet Univ	DC	16,554	SP
Goddard College	VT	21,056	C+
Hampshire College	MA	37,037	HC
Hofstra Univ	NY	27,112	VC
Hollins Univ	VA	27,965	VC
Indiana Univ Bloomington	IN	12,389	VC
Indiana Univ of Pennsylvania	PA	10,489	C
Ithaca College	NY	31,730	HC
James Madison Univ	VA	10,794	VC
Johns Hopkins Univ	MD	38,372	MC
Judson College	IL	22,050	C
Kendall College of Art and Design of Ferris State Univ	MI	10,784	SP
Loyola Marymount Univ	CA	32,194	VC
Maine College of Art	ME	28,812	SP
Maryland Inst College of Art	MD	30,890	SP
Mass College of Art	MA	15,568	SP
Mass Inst of Technology	MA	38,310	MC
Mills College	CA	33,371	VC
Montana State Univ- Bozeman	MT	9,515	C
Mount Ida College	MA	25,596	LC
Mount St. Mary College	NY	21,270	C
Mount Union College	OH	21,120	C
National Univ	CA	9,690	SP
New Jersey City Univ	NJ	11,850	LC
New York Univ	NY	39,406	MC
Pitzer College	CA	37,590	HC
Point Park Univ	PA	21,840	C
Pomona College	CA	33,960	MC
Purdue Univ/West Lafayette	IN	12,560	VC
Rensselaer Polytechnic Inst	NY	37,579	HC+
Robert Morris Univ	PA	20,438	C
Roosevelt Univ	IL	22,580	VC
Sacred Heart Univ	CT	29,178	C
Salve Regina Univ	RI	29,210	C
Savannah College of Art and Design	GA	27,560	SP
Southern Methodist Univ	TX	34,210	HC
SUNY/College at Fredonia	NY	11,562	VC
SUNY/College at Old Westbury	NY	12,784	C
SUNY/Univ at Buffalo	NY	12,563	VC
Syracuse Univ	NY	34,720	HC
Towson Univ	MD	12,694	VC
Tulane Univ	LA	37,451	HC+
Univ of Arizona	AZ	10,413	VC
Univ of Hartford	CT	31,080	C
Univ of Illinois at Urbana- Champaign	IL	11,316	HC+
Univ of Maine	ME	12,080	C+
Univ of Mich/Ann Arbor	MI	13,864	HC+
Univ of New Mexico	NM	9,223	C
Univ of N Car at Asheville	NC	8,079	VC
Univ of N Car at Greensboro	NC	8,248	C
Univ of San Francisco	CA	34,700	VC
Univ of S Car at Columbia	SC	10,048	VC
Univ of the District of Columbia	DC	2,070	LC
Valdosta State Univ	GA	7,798	C
Washburn Univ of Topeka	KS	8,984	NC
Weber State Univ	UT	7,945	NC
Webster Univ	MO	21,848	VC

School	ST	$IS	SR
Western Illinois Univ	IL	10,363	C
Western Mich Univ	MI	12,031	C
Wilmington College	DE	5,594	NC

MEDICAL LABORATORY SCIENCE

School	ST	$IS	SR
Culver-Stockton College	MO	17,850	C
Eastern Illinois Univ	IL	11,192	C
Marquette Univ	WI	27,594	VC
Northeastern Univ	MA	35,650	HC
Oakland Univ	MI	10,800	C
Shawnee State Univ	OH	11,031	NC
Univ of Illinois at Chicago	IL	13,418	C
Univ of Mary	ND	12,900	C+
Univ of Mass Dartmouth	MA	12,835	C
Univ of New Hampshire	NH	14,828	VC
Univ of Utah	UT	9,205	C
Univ of Vermont	VT	16,316	VC

MEDICAL LABORATORY TECHNOLOGY

School	ST	$IS	SR
Alabama A&M Univ	AL	5,100	LC
American International College	MA	24,690	LC
Anderson Univ	IN	19,430	LC
Andrews Univ	MI	19,550	C
Angelo State Univ	TX	7,576	NC
Arkansas State Univ	AR	8,450	C
Arkansas Tech Univ	AR	7,299	C
Asbury College	KY	20,704	VC
Auburn Univ	AL	10,396	VC
Austin Peay State Univ	TN	5,814	LC
Avila Univ	MO	20,300	C
Baldwin-Wallace College	OH	24,678	C
Ball State Univ	IN	8,660	C
Baylor Univ	TX	23,864	VC
Belmont Abbey College	NC	23,742	C
Bemidji State Univ	MN	9,103	C
Blackburn College	IL	13,690	C
Bloomsburg Univ of Pennsylvania	PA	10,844	C
Boise State Univ	ID	7,657	LC
Bowling Green State Univ	OH	13,036	C
Cabrini College	PA	29,020	C
Caldwell College	NJ	24,060	LC
Cal State, Northridge	CA	7,757	LC
Cal State, Sacramento	CA	9,543	C
Calif Univ of Pennsylvania	PA	10,388	C
Campbellsville Univ	KY	17,680	C
Canisius College	NY	28,163	C+
Catholic Univ of America	DC	34,248	VC
Cedar Crest College	PA	25,145	C+
Central Missouri State Univ	MO	9,776	C
Cheyney Univ of Pennsylvania	PA	9,993	C
CUNY/Hunter College	NY	6,729	C+
CUNY/York College	NY	3,292	NC
Clemson Univ	SC	11,972	HC
Coe College	IA	27,385	VC
Coker College	SC	21,491	C
College Misericordia	PA	26,350	C
College of Mount St. Joseph	OH	22,785	C
College of Our Lady of the Elms	MA	20,644	C
College of St. Mary	NE	21,510	C
Columbia College	SC	22,658	LC
Concord College	WV	8,136	C
Concordia College: Moorhead	MN	22,460	VC+
Concordia Univ Nebr	NE	20,302	C+
Cumberland College	KY	16,384	C
Dakota State Univ	SD	7,466	C
Defiance College	OH	22,615	C
DePaul Univ	IL	27,580	VC
Dordt College	IA	20,170	VC
East Central Univ	OK	4,968	C
East Stroudsburg Univ of Pennsylvania	PA	10,336	C
Eastern Mennonite Univ	VA	22,990	C
Eastern Mich Univ	MI	11,478	C
Eastern New Mexico Univ	NM	6,762	LC
Eastern Washington Univ	WA	9,012	C
Edinboro Univ of Pennsylvania	PA	10,850	LC
Elmira College	NY	33,820	VC
Emmanuel College	MA	27,600	C+
Erskine College	SC	23,166	VC
Eureka College	IL	24,980	LC
Evangel Univ	MO	15,435	C
Fairleigh Dickinson Univ/ College at Florham	NJ	30,130	C
Fairleigh Dickinson Univ/ Metropolitan Campus	NJ	28,584	C
Fayetteville State Univ	NC	5,590	LC
Ferrum College	VA	21,240	LC
Florida Atlantic Univ	FL	8,543	C
Gannon Univ	PA	23,260	C
George Washington Univ	DC	41,030	MC
Georgetown College	KY	22,000	VC
Graceland Univ	IA	19,550	C
Grand Valley State Univ	MI	11,022	VC
Gwynedd-Mercy College	PA	24,225	C
High Point Univ	NC	22,480	C
Holy Family College	PA	13,710	LC
Howard Univ	DC	16,505	C
Huntington College	IN	23,590	C
Idaho State Univ	ID	8,128	C
Illinois College	IL	19,100	VC
Illinois State Univ	IL	10,944	C+
Indiana State Univ	IN	10,719	LC
Indiana Univ Kokomo	IN	4,463	LC
Indiana Univ-Purdue Univ Indianapolis	IN	8,257	LC
Indiana Wesleyan Univ	IN	19,900	C+
Inter American Univ of PR/ San German	PR	6,716	
Iona College	NY	27,988	VC
John Brown Univ	AR	15,080	VC
Judson College	IL	22,050	LC
Keuka College	NY	21,170	C
King's College	PA	26,990	C
Knoxville College	TN	6,200	LC
Kutztown Univ of Pennsylvania	PA	10,786	C
Lake Superior State Univ	MI	9,034	LC
Lamar Univ	TX	6,816	LC
Langston Univ	OK	2,308	LC
Lebanon Valley College	PA	28,870	VC
Lee Univ	TN	13,780	NC
Lenoir-Rhyne College	NC	19,186	C
Lincoln Memorial Univ	TN	16,400	LC
Lock Haven Univ of Pennsylvania	PA	11,098	LC
LIU/C.W. Post Campus	NY	28,282	C
Louisiana College	LA	13,450	C
Louisiana Tech Univ	LA	7,361	C
Madonna Univ	MI	11,504	VC
Malone College	OH	20,995	C
Manchester College	IN	23,390	C
Marian College of Fond du Lac	WI	19,625	C
Marshall Univ	WV	9,116	C
Mary Baldwin College	VA	24,939	C
Marywood Univ	PA	26,050	C
McKendree College	IL	21,120	VC
McNeese State Univ	LA	5,259	LC
Mercy College	NY	19,200	NC
Mercyhurst College	PA	20,694	C
Mich State Univ	MI	11,933	VC
Mich Tech Univ	MI	13,235	VC
Midwestern State Univ	TX	8,045	LC
Minn State Univ, Mankato	MN	8,803	LC
Minn State Univ, Moorehead	MN	7,000	LC
Missouri Southern State Univ	MO	8,316	C
Missouri Western State College	MO	8,522	NC
Monmouth Univ	NJ	26,334	C
Morehead State Univ	KY	7,464	C
Morgan State Univ	MD	11,470	C
Mount Mercy College	IA	21,400	C
Mount St. Mary College	NY	21,270	C
National-Louis Univ	IL	16,240	LC
New Jersey City Univ	NJ	11,850	LC
N Car State Univ	NC	9,886	VC
North Park Univ	IL	24,030	C
Northeastern State Univ	OK	4,950	LC
Northern Mich Univ	MI	10,834	C
Northern State Univ	SD	7,117	LC
Northwestern College of Iowa	IA	19,640	C+
Northwestern Okla State Univ	OK	5,433	NC
Norwich Univ	VT	21,064	LC
Okla Christian Univ	OK	17,690	NC
Oral Roberts Univ	OK	18,490	C
Ouachita Baptist Univ	AR	18,900	VC
Pace Univ	NY	28,652	VC
Pacific Union College	CA	22,065	C+
Pontifical Catholic Univ of PR/Ponce	PR	7,298	
Purdue Univ/Calumet	IN	6,630	NC
Quincy Univ	IL	22,330	C
Rhode Island College	RI	11,565	C
Rutgers, The State Univ of New Jersey/Camden Campus	NJ	14,990	VC
St. Augustine's College	NC	12,990	LC
St. Bonaventure Univ	NY	24,455	LC
St. Francis College	NY	10,880	LC
St. Francis Univ	PA	25,876	LC
St. Mary's Univ of Minn	MN	21,535	C
St. Peter's College	NJ	22,292	LC
St. Thomas Aquinas College	NY	20,590	LC
Salem College	NC	24,595	VC
Salem State College	MA	8,592	C
Salve Regina Univ	RI	29,210	C
San Francisco State Univ	CA	12,070	C
Seton Hill Univ	PA	24,930	C
Shorter College	GA	17,370	C
Slippery Rock Univ of Pennsylvania	PA	10,343	LC
Southeastern Okla State Univ	OK	6,147	C
Southern Arkansas Univ	AR	6,956	C
Southern Wesleyan Univ	SC	19,940	C
Southwest Missouri State Univ	MO	8,918	C
SUNY/College at Fredonia	NY	11,562	VC
SUNY/College at Plattsburgh	NY	11,700	C
SUNY/Univ at Albany	NY	12,951	HC
Suffolk Univ	MA	29,200	C
Tarleton State Univ	TX	7,576	C
Texas A&M Univ at Kingsville	TX	6,740	LC
Texas State Univ	TX	9,320	VC
Thiel College	PA	20,970	C
Thomas More College	KY	21,350	C
Towson Univ	MD	12,694	VC
Trevecca Nazarene Univ	TN	17,548	C
Union College	NE	17,130	C
Union Univ	TN	18,800	VC
Univ of Akron	OH	13,134	NC
Univ of Central Florida	FL	10,038	VC
Univ of Central Okla	OK	9,434	C
Univ of Cincinnati	OH	14,736	C
Univ of Conn	CT	14,608	VC
Univ of Delaware	DE	12,616	HC
Univ of Hartford	CT	31,080	C
Univ of Hawaii at Manoa	HI	9,565	VC
Univ of Idaho	ID	8,216	C
Univ of Indianapolis	IN	22,560	VC
Univ of Iowa	IA	10,923	VC
Univ of Louisville	KY	8,762	VC
Univ of Maine	ME	12,080	C+
Univ of Mass Amherst	MA	13,980	C+
Univ of Mich/Flint	MI	5,548	C
Univ of Minn/Twin Cities	MN	13,160	VC
Univ of Miss	MS	7,666	C
Univ of Nebr at Lincoln	NE	9,975	C+
Univ of New Mexico	NM	9,223	C
Univ of N Car at Chapel Hill	NC	10,117	MC
Univ of N Car at Greensboro	NC	8,248	C
Univ of N Car at Wilmington	NC	8,940	VC
Univ of North Texas	TX	7,629	C
Univ of Okla	OK	9,226	VC
Univ of Pittsburgh at Johnstown	PA	15,216	LC
Univ of Pittsburgh at Pittsburgh	PA	16,074	HC
Univ of Rhode Island	RI	13,720	VC
Univ of St. Francis	IN	20,964	C
Univ of Scranton	PA	30,836	VC
Univ of Sioux Falls	SD	16,390	C
Univ of S Car at Columbia	SC	10,048	VC
Univ of Southern Miss	MS	8,324	LC
Univ of Tenn at Chattanooga	TN	7,783	C
Univ of Texas at El Paso	TX	5,799	NC
Univ of the Incarnate Word	TX	21,772	LC
Univ of Vermont	VT	16,316	VC
Univ of Virginia's College at Wise	VA	10,116	C
Univ of Washington	WA	10,361	VC
Univ of West Florida	FL	8,470	C
Univ of Wisc/La Crosse	WI	8,991	VC
Univ of Wisc/Madison	WI	8,262	VC
Univ of Wisc/Oshkosh	WI	6,130	LC
Utah State Univ	UT	7,371	C
Wagner College	NY	29,900	VC
Wartburg College	IA	21,165	VC
Washburn Univ of Topeka	KS	8,984	NC
Waynesburg College	PA	19,370	C
Wesley College	DE	19,905	C
Western Conn State Univ	CT	11,625	C
Western New Mexico Univ	NM	5,950	LC
Wichita State Univ	KS	8,092	C
William Carey College	MS	10,150	LC
William Jewell College	MO	21,320	VC
Winona State Univ	MN		C
Winthrop Univ	SC	11,302	C
Wright State Univ	OH	11,490	LC
Xavier Univ	OH	26,850	VC+
York College of Pennsylvania	PA	14,500	VC
Youngstown State Univ	OH	11,148	NC

MEDICAL PHYSICS

School	ST	$IS	SR
Oakland Univ	MI	10,800	C

MEDICAL RECORDS ADMINISTRATION/SERVICES

School	ST	$IS	SR
College of St. Catherine	MN	24,010	VC
Dakota State Univ	SD	7,466	C
Davenport Univ	MI	11,636	NC
East Carolina Univ	NC	8,671	C
East Central Univ	OK	4,968	C
LIU/C.W. Post Campus	NY	28,282	C
Louisiana Tech Univ	LA	7,361	C
Norfolk State Univ	VA	9,722	LC
Regis Univ	CO	25,740	C+
Southwestern Okla State Univ	OK	4,801	C
Tenn State Univ	TN	9,048	LC
Texas State Univ	TX	9,320	VC
Univ of Alabama at Birmingham	AL	12,901	C
Univ of Pittsburgh at Pittsburgh	PA	16,074	HC
Western Carolina Univ	NC	6,742	C

MEDICAL SCIENCE

School	ST	$IS	SR
Alderson-Broaddus College	WV	19,640	C
Suffolk Univ	MA	29,200	C
Univ of Arkansas	AR	9,855	VC
Univ of Louisville	KY	8,762	VC
Univ of Wisc/Madison	WI	8,262	VC
Univ of Wisc/Milwaukee	WI	9,427	LC

MEDICAL TECHNOLOGY

School	ST	$IS	SR
Alderson-Broaddus College	WV	19,640	C
Aquinas College	MI	21,894	C
Armstrong Atlantic State Univ	GA	7,102	C
Augustana College	SD	21,998	VC
Averett Univ	VA	23,010	LC
Barry Univ	FL	24,100	LC
Bellarmine Univ	KY	24,110	VC
Blue Mountain College	MS	10,226	C
Bradley Univ	IL	22,910	VC
Brescia Univ	KY	14,225	C
Briar Cliff Univ	IA	21,660	C
Bridgewater College	VA	25,150	C
Catawba College	NC	20,500	C
CUNY/College of Staten Island	NY	4,308	NC
Clarion Univ of Pennsylvania	PA	11,272	LC
Cleveland State Univ	OH	12,308	LC
College of St. Elizabeth	NJ	25,460	C
College of St. Rose	NY	22,864	C
College of the Ozarks	MO	3,500	VC+
East Carolina Univ	NC	8,671	C
East Texas Baptist Univ	TX	13,914	C
Edgewood College	WI	20,520	C
Elon Univ	NC	22,240	VC
Gardner-Webb Univ	NC	19,300	C
George Mason Univ	VA	9,732	VC
Georgia State Univ	GA	10,658	C
Harding Univ	AR	14,890	VC
Hartwick College	NY	34,650	C+
Houghton College	NY	23,984	VC
Indiana Univ of Pennsylvania	PA	10,489	C
Indiana Univ Southeast	IN	4,504	LC
Inter American Univ of PR/ Fajardo Campus	PR	4,000	
Inter American Univ of PR/ Metropolitan Campus	PR		
Inter American Univ of PR/ Ponce Regional College	PR	3,700	
Kansas State Univ	KS	8,728	VC
Kean Univ	NJ	14,479	C
Kent State Univ	OH	12,932	C
King College	TN	22,500	VC
Lincoln Univ	MO	7,158	NC
Lindenwood Univ	MO	17,050	VC
Lubbock Christian Univ	TX	15,832	C
Mansfield Univ	PA	11,220	C
Marist College	NY	27,596	VC
Miami Univ	OH	15,033	HC
Miss State Univ	MS	9,139	C
Mount Marty College	SD	15,656	LC
Mount Vernon Nazarene Univ	OH	18,925	C
Norfolk State Univ	VA	9,722	LC
Northwestern State Univ of Louisiana	LA	6,331	NC
Oakwood College	AL	14,904	C
Ohio Northern Univ	OH	27,765	VC
Ohio State Univ	OH	13,080	VC+
Okla Panhandle State Univ	OK	5,370	C
Okla State Univ	OK	9,216	VC
Old Dominion Univ	VA	10,441	C
Oregon State Univ	OR	11,055	C
Pittsburg State Univ	KS	7,128	NC
Prairie View A&M Univ	TX	9,418	NC
Purdue Univ/West Lafayette	IN	12,560	VC
Radford Univ	VA	8,500	C
Roanoke College	VA	27,393	C
Roosevelt Univ	IL	22,580	VC
Rutgers, The State Univ of New Jersey/New Brunswick/Piscataway Campus	NJ	15,800	HC
Sacred Heart Univ	CT	29,178	C
St. John's Univ	NY	30,180	C
St. Joseph's College	IN	24,250	C
St. Leo Univ	FL	20,600	C
St. Mary-of-the-Woods College	IN	23,280	C
Salisbury Univ	MD	12,664	VC
Sam Houston State Univ	TX	7,142	C
Seattle Univ	WA	24,183	VC
Southern Adventist Univ	TN	17,080	C
Southwest Baptist Univ	MO	15,371	C
Southwest Minn State Univ	MN	9,106	VC
Southwestern Adventist Univ	TX	14,798	C
Southwestern Okla State Univ	OK	4,801	C

School	ST	$IS	SR
SUNY/College at Brockport	NY	12,111	C
SUNY/Univ at Buffalo	NY	12,563	VC
Stetson Univ	FL	29,495	VC
Stonehill College	MA	30,752	HC
Tenn State Univ	TN	9,048	LC
Texas Southern Univ	TX	8,920	NC
Texas Woman's Univ	TX	7,804	LC
Troy State Univ	AL	7,696	C
Truman State Univ	MO	9,728	HC+
Tusculum College	TN	19,990	C
Univ of Alabama at Birmingham	AL	12,901	C
Univ of Arizona	AZ	10,413	VC
Univ of Central Arkansas	AR	6,388	C
Univ of Mary Hardin-Baylor	TX	17,268	C
Univ of Mass Boston	MA	6,227	C
Univ of Mich/Ann Arbor	MI	13,864	HC+
Univ of Miss	MS	7,666	C
Univ of Missouri/Kansas City	MO	13,416	VC
Univ of Montana	MT	9,395	C
Univ of New Orleans	LA	7,356	C
Univ of N Car at Charlotte	NC	8,185	C
Univ of Rio Grande	OH	8,728	NC
Univ of St. Francis	IL	22,850	C
Univ of St. Mary	KS	18,868	C
Univ of S Dak	SD	7,710	C+
Univ of South Florida	FL	9,454	C
Univ of Southern Colo	CO	7,821	LC
Univ of Texas at Arlington	TX	7,192	LC
Univ of Texas at Austin	TX	10,630	HC
Univ of Texas-Pan American	TX	5,954	LC
Univ of the Sacred Heart	PR	5,590	
Univ of the Sciences in Philadelphia	PA	29,310	VC
West Texas A&M Univ	TX	7,533	C
West Virginia Univ	WV	9,370	C
Western Illinois Univ	IL	10,363	C
Western Kentucky Univ	KY	6,834	C
Wilkes Univ	PA	28,060	C
Winston-Salem State Univ	NC	8,926	LC
Youngstown State Univ	OH	11,148	NC

MEDIEVAL STUDIES

School	ST	$IS	SR
Bard College	NY	37,352	HC+
Brown Univ	RI	38,174	MC
Catholic Univ of America	DC	34,248	VC
College of the Holy Cross	MA	36,451	MC
Columbia Univ/Barnard College	NY	36,990	MC
Columbia Univ/Columbia College	NY	38,590	MC
Conn College	CT	37,900	MC
Cornell College	IA	27,825	VC+
Dickinson College	PA	35,825	HC
Duke Univ	NC	37,555	MC
Emory Univ	GA	36,872	MC
Fordham Univ	NY	35,066	HC
Hanover College	IN	25,200	VC
Mass Inst of Technology	MA	38,310	MC
Mount Holyoke College	MA	37,918	HC+
New College of Florida	FL	8,906	HC+
New York Univ	NY	39,406	MC
Ohio State Univ	OH	13,080	VC+
Penn State Univ/Univ Park Campus	PA	15,646	HC
Plymouth State Univ	NH	12,298	LC
Purdue Univ/West Lafayette	IN	12,560	VC
Rice Univ	TX	27,550	MC
Rutgers, The State Univ of New Jersey/New Brunswick/Piscataway Campus	NJ	15,800	HC
Rutgers, The State Univ of New Jersey/Newark Campus	NJ	15,624	VC
St. Olaf College	MN	28,500	HC
Smith College	MA	37,034	HC+
Southern Methodist Univ	TX	34,210	HC
SUNY/Univ at Albany	NY	12,951	HC
SUNY/Univ at Binghamton	NY	12,787	HC
Swarthmore College	PA	37,716	MC
Syracuse Univ	NY	34,720	HC
Tulane Univ	LA	37,451	HC+
Univ of Calif at Davis	CA	14,995	VC
Univ of Calif at Santa Barbara	CA	11,732	VC
Univ of Chicago	IL	35,087	MC
Univ of Mich/Ann Arbor	MI	13,864	HC+
Univ of Nebr at Lincoln	NE	9,975	C+
Univ of Notre Dame	IN	34,442	MC
Univ of Tenn at Knoxville	TN	8,214	C
Univ of the South	TN	30,855	HC
Vassar College	NY	37,030	MC
Washington and Lee Univ	VA	29,663	MC
Washington Univ in St. Louis	MO	38,293	MC
Wellesley College	MA	36,516	MC
Wesleyan Univ	CT	35,139	MC

MENTAL HEALTH/HUMAN SERVICES

School	ST	$IS	SR
Baldwin-Wallace College	OH	24,678	C
Franciscan Univ of Steubenville	OH	20,300	VC
Inter American Univ of PR/Aguadilla Campus	PR	3,544	
Iona College	NY	27,988	VC
MCP Hahnemann Univ	PA	18,510	SP
Metropolitan College of New York	NY	15,771	C
Morgan State Univ	MD	11,470	C
Northern Kentucky Univ	KY	6,352	NC
Pennsylvania College of Technology	PA	15,126	NC
Sinte Gleska Univ	SD	2,268	NC
Thomas Edison State College	NJ	3,325	SP
Univ of Maine at Augusta	ME	4,065	C
Univ of the Sciences in Philadelphia	PA	29,310	VC

METAL/JEWELRY

School	ST	$IS	SR
Arizona State Univ-Main	AZ	10,048	C
Calif College of the Arts	CA	31,530	SP
College for Creative Studies	MI	23,298	SP
Edinboro Univ of Pennsylvania	PA	10,850	LC
Hofstra Univ	NY	27,112	VC
Indiana Univ Bloomington	IN	12,389	VC
Kendall College of Art and Design of Ferris State Univ	MI	10,784	SP
Maine College of Art	ME	28,812	SP
Mass College of Art	MA	15,568	SP
Rhode Island School of Design	RI	33,569	SP
Rochester Inst of Technology	NY	29,217	VC+
Savannah College of Art and Design	GA	27,560	SP
Syracuse Univ	NY	34,720	HC
Univ of Mass Dartmouth	MA	12,835	C
Univ of Mich/Ann Arbor	MI	13,864	HC+
Univ of North Texas	TX	7,629	C
Univ of Oregon	OR	11,479	VC
Univ of Washington	WA	10,361	VC

METALLURGICAL ENGINEERING

School	ST	$IS	SR
Calif Polytechnic State Univ	CA	8,747	VC
Colo School of Mines	CO	12,533	HC
Columbia Univ/Fu Foundation School of Engineering and Applied Science	NY	38,590	MC
Illinois Inst of Technology	IL	26,456	HC+
Montana Tech of The Univ of Montana	MT	9,314	NC
New Mexico Inst of Mining and Technology	NM	7,580	NC
Ohio State Univ	OH	13,080	VC+
S Dak School of Mines and Technology	SD	7,854	C+
Univ of Alabama	AL	9,040	C+
Univ of Cincinnati	OH	14,736	C
Univ of Idaho	ID	8,216	C
Univ of Illinois at Urbana-Champaign	IL	11,316	HC+
Univ of Minn/Twin Cities	MN	13,160	VC
Univ of Missouri/Rolla	MO	12,292	HC
Univ of Nevada/Reno	NV	9,792	C
Univ of Pittsburgh at Pittsburgh	PA	16,074	HC
Univ of Texas at El Paso	TX	5,799	NC
Univ of Utah	UT	9,205	C
Univ of Wisc/Madison	WI	8,262	VC

MEXICAN-AMERICAN/CHICANO STUDIES

School	ST	$IS	SR
Cal State, Dominguez Hills	CA	5,840	LC
Cal State, Fresno	CA	8,414	LC
Cal State, Fullerton	CA	6,648	C
Cal State, Los Angeles	CA	5,778	C
Cal State, Northridge	CA	7,757	LC
Claremont McKenna College	CA	36,880	MC
Concordia Univ at Austin	TX	20,450	LC
Metropolitan State College of Denver	CO	2,338	LC
Pitzer College	CA	37,590	HC
San Diego State Univ	CA	10,321	C
Scripps College	CA	35,700	HC+
Sonoma State Univ	CA	10,421	C
Southern Methodist Univ	TX	34,210	HC
Sul Ross State Univ	TX	6,582	LC
Univ of Arizona	AZ	10,413	VC
Univ of Calif at Davis	CA	14,995	VC
Univ of Calif at Riverside	CA	15,300	C
Univ of Calif at Santa Barbara	CA	11,732	VC
Univ of Minn/Twin Cities	MN	13,160	VC
Univ of Northern Colo	CO	8,987	C
Univ of Texas at El Paso	TX	5,799	NC
Univ of Texas at San Antonio	TX	9,088	NC
Univ of Texas-Pan American	TX	5,954	LC
Wayne State Univ	MI	11,774	C

MICROBIOLOGY

School	ST	$IS	SR
Arizona State Univ-Main	AZ	10,048	C
Auburn Univ	AL	10,396	VC
Ball State Univ	IN	8,660	C
Bard College	NY	37,352	HC+
Bowling Green State Univ	OH	13,036	C
Brigham Young Univ	UT	8,504	HC
Calif Polytechnic State Univ	CA	8,747	VC
Calif State Polytechnic Univ, Pomona	CA	8,793	C+
Cal State, Chico	CA	8,598	LC
Cal State, Los Angeles	CA	5,778	C
Cal State, Northridge	CA	7,757	LC
Cal State, Sacramento	CA	9,543	C
Cal State, Stanislaus	CA	9,874	C
Clemson Univ	SC	11,972	HC
Colo State Univ	CO	9,964	VC
Duquesne Univ	PA	26,907	VC
Eastern Kentucky Univ	KY	7,708	C
Eastern Mich Univ	MI	11,478	C
Eastern Washington Univ	WA	9,012	C
Howard Univ	DC	16,505	C
Idaho State Univ	ID	8,128	C
Indiana Univ Bloomington	IN	12,389	VC
Inter American Univ of PR/Aguadilla Campus	PR	3,544	
Inter American Univ of PR/Arecibo Campus	PR	3,300	
Iowa State Univ	IA	10,768	VC
Juniata College	PA	29,080	VC
Kansas State Univ	KS	8,728	VC
Marlboro College	VT	29,055	VC+
Miami Univ	OH	15,033	HC
Mich State Univ	MI	11,933	VC
Miss State Univ	MS	9,139	C
Miss Univ for Women	MS	5,446	LC
Missouri Southern State Univ	MO	8,316	C
Montana State Univ-Bozeman	MT	9,515	C
New Mexico State Univ	NM	7,932	C
N Car State Univ	NC	9,886	VC
N Dak State Univ	ND	8,435	C
Northern Arizona Univ	AZ	9,002	C
Northern Mich Univ	MI	10,834	C
Ohio State Univ	OH	13,080	VC+
Ohio Univ	OH	14,448	C
Ohio Wesleyan Univ	OH	32,550	VC+
Okla State Univ	OK	9,216	VC
Oregon State Univ	OR	11,055	C
Penn State Univ/Univ Park Campus	PA	15,646	HC
Purdue Univ/Calumet	IN	6,630	NC
Quinnipiac Univ	CT	30,570	VC
Rutgers, The State Univ of New Jersey/New Brunswick/Piscataway Campus	NJ	15,800	HC
San Diego State Univ	CA	10,321	C
San Francisco State Univ	CA	12,070	C
San Jose State Univ	CA	8,187	C
S Dak State Univ	SD	7,782	C
Southern Illinois Univ Carbondale	IL	10,407	C
SUNY/College of Environmental Science and Forestry	NY	14,167	VC
Texas A&M Univ	TX	11,081	HC
Texas State Univ	TX	9,320	VC
Texas Tech Univ	TX	10,768	VC
Univ of Akron	OH	13,134	NC
Univ of Alabama	AL	9,040	C+
Univ of Arizona	AZ	10,413	VC
Univ of Arkansas	AR	9,855	VC
Univ of Calif at Berkeley	CA	15,563	MC
Univ of Calif at Davis	CA	14,995	VC
Univ of Calif at Los Angeles	CA	15,330	MC
Univ of Calif at San Diego	CA	14,127	HC
Univ of Calif at Santa Barbara	CA	11,732	VC
Univ of Central Florida	FL	10,038	VC
Univ of Florida	FL	8,580	MC
Univ of Georgia	GA	8,656	VC
Univ of Great Falls	MT	15,360	C
Univ of Hawaii at Manoa	HI	9,565	VC
Univ of Houston-Downtown	TX	2,594	NC
Univ of Idaho	ID	8,216	C
Univ of Illinois at Urbana-Champaign	IL	11,316	HC+
Univ of Iowa	IA	10,923	VC
Univ of Kansas	KS	8,923	VC
Univ of Maine	ME	12,080	C+
Univ of Maryland/College Park	MD	14,227	HC
Univ of Mass Amherst	MA	13,980	C+
Univ of Memphis	TN	8,560	C
Univ of Miami	FL	34,608	HC
Univ of Mich/Ann Arbor	MI	13,864	HC+
Univ of Mich/Dearborn	MI	6,843	VC
Univ of Minn/Twin Cities	MN	13,160	VC
Univ of Missouri/Columbia	MO	13,782	VC
Univ of Montana	MT	9,395	C
Univ of New Hampshire	NH	14,828	VC
Univ of Northern Iowa	IA	9,834	C
Univ of Okla	OK	9,226	VC
Univ of Pittsburgh at Pittsburgh	PA	16,074	HC
Univ of PR at Humacao	PR	1,245	
Univ of PR/Arecibo	PR	1,095	
Univ of PR/Mayaguez	PR		
Univ of Rhode Island	RI	13,720	VC
Univ of Rochester	NY	32,979	HC
Univ of South Florida	FL	9,454	C
Univ of Tenn at Knoxville	TN	8,214	C
Univ of Texas at Arlington	TX	7,192	LC
Univ of Texas at Austin	TX	10,630	HC
Univ of Texas at El Paso	TX	5,799	NC
Univ of the Sciences in Philadelphia	PA	29,310	VC
Univ of Vermont	VT	16,316	VC
Univ of Washington	WA	10,361	VC
Univ of Wisc/La Crosse	WI	8,991	C
Univ of Wisc/Madison	WI	8,262	VC
Univ of Wisc/Milwaukee	WI	9,427	LC
Univ of Wisc/Oshkosh	WI	6,130	LC
Univ of Wyoming	WY	8,636	C
Utah State Univ	UT	7,371	C
Wagner College	NY	29,900	VC
Washington State Univ	WA	11,334	C
Weber State Univ	UT	7,945	NC
Xavier Univ of Louisiana	LA	17,600	C

MIDDLE EASTERN STUDIES

School	ST	$IS	SR
Brandeis Univ	MA	38,198	MC
Brigham Young Univ	UT	8,504	HC
Brown Univ	RI	38,174	MC
College of the Holy Cross	MA	36,451	MC
Columbia Univ/Barnard College	NY	36,990	MC
Columbia Univ/Columbia College	NY	38,590	MC
Columbia Univ/School of General Studies	NY	35,000	C
Dartmouth College	NH	37,770	MC
Emory & Henry College	VA	21,950	C
Emory Univ	GA	36,872	MC
Fordham Univ	NY	35,066	HC
George Washington Univ	DC	41,030	MC
Hampshire College	MA	37,037	HC
Harvard Univ/Harvard College	MA	37,928	MC
New York Univ	NY	39,406	MC
Rutgers, The State Univ of New Jersey/New Brunswick/Piscataway Campus	NJ	15,800	HC
Texas State Univ	TX	9,320	VC
Tufts Univ	MA	38,233	MC
Univ of Arkansas	AR	9,855	VC
Univ of Calif at Berkeley	CA	15,563	MC
Univ of Conn	CT	14,608	VC
Univ of Mass Amherst	MA	13,980	C+
Univ of Mich/Ann Arbor	MI	13,864	HC+
Univ of Minn/Twin Cities	MN	13,160	VC
Univ of Texas at Austin	TX	10,630	HC
Univ of Utah	UT	9,205	C
Washington Univ in St. Louis	MO	38,293	MC
Wellesley College	MA	36,516	MC

MIDDLE SCHOOL EDUCATION

School	ST	$IS	SR
Abilene Christian Univ	TX	18,370	VC
Alabama A&M Univ	AL	5,100	LC
Albany State Univ	GA	5,764	C+
Alice Lloyd College	KY	4,040	C
Alverno College	WI	18,898	C
American International College	MA	24,690	LC
Appalachian State Univ	NC	7,637	VC
Arkansas State Univ	AR	8,450	C
Arkansas Tech Univ	AR	7,299	C
Armstrong Atlantic State Univ	GA	7,102	C
Asbury College	KY	20,704	VC
Auburn Univ	AL	10,396	VC
Augusta State Univ	GA	2,592	C
Averett Univ	VA	23,010	LC
Avila Univ	MO	20,300	C
Baldwin-Wallace College	OH	24,678	C
Ball State Univ	IN	8,660	C
Barton College	NC	19,314	C
Bellarmine Univ	KY	24,110	VC
Bemidji State Univ	MN	9,103	C
Bennett College	NC	11,200	C
Berea College	KY	5,030	VC+
Berry College	GA	21,410	VC
Bethany College	KS	18,675	LC
Bluefield College	VA	15,575	C

School	ST	$IS	SR
Bluefield State College	WV	2,806	LC
Bluffton College	OH	23,694	C
Brenau Univ Women's College	GA	21,800	C
Brewton-Parker College	GA	14,200	LC
Buena Vista Univ	IA	25,406	C
Campbell Univ	NC	18,268	VC
Campbellsville Univ	KY	17,680	C
Capital Univ	OH	26,550	C
Cardinal Stritch Univ	WI	17,620	C
Caribbean Univ	PR	3,000	
Carson-Newman College	TN	16,760	C
Carthage College	WI	25,000	C
Catawba College	NC	20,500	C
Cedarville Univ	OH	19,954	VC
Central Mich Univ	MI	11,142	C
Central Missouri State Univ	MO	9,776	C
Central Washington Univ	WA	9,768	C
Christopher Newport Univ	VA	8,862	VC
City Univ	WA	7,425	NC
CUNY/Hunter College	NY	6,729	C+
Clark Atlanta Univ	GA	19,300	C+
Clayton College and State Univ	GA	2,441	LC
Coastal Carolina Univ	SC	11,040	C
College of Mount St. Joseph	OH	22,785	C
College of Our Lady of the Elms	MA	20,644	C
College of the Ozarks	MO	3,500	VC+
Columbus State Univ	GA	7,846	C
Concord College	WV	8,136	C
Concordia College: Moorhead	MN	22,460	VC+
Concordia Univ Nebr	NE	20,302	C+
Concordia Univ, River Forest	IL	23,600	C
Concordia Univ/St.Paul	MN	24,486	C
Cornerstone Univ and Grand Rapids Theological Seminary	MI	19,846	C
Cumberland College	KY	16,384	C
Cumberland Univ	TN	16,910	C
Dickinson State Univ	ND	6,338	NC
East Carolina Univ	NC	8,671	C
Eastern Conn State Univ	CT	10,362	C
Eastern Illinois Univ	IL	11,192	C
Eastern Kentucky Univ	KY	7,708	C
Eastern Mich Univ	MI	11,478	C
Eastern Washington Univ	WA	9,012	C
Elizabeth City State Univ	NC	5,550	LC
Elon Univ	NC	22,240	VC
Fairmont State	WV	8,280	LC
Fayetteville State Univ	NC	5,590	LC
Fitchburg State College	MA	9,622	C
Florida Southern College	FL	23,592	C
Fontbonne Univ	MO	21,508	C
Fort Valley State Univ	GA	6,960	C
Freed-Hardeman Univ	TN		NC
Frostburg State Univ	MD	11,114	C
Gardner-Webb Univ	NC	19,300	C
George Fox Univ	OR	26,110	VC
Georgia College and State Univ	GA	9,878	C
Georgia Southern Univ	GA	8,540	C
Georgia Southwestern State Univ	GA	6,013	C
Georgia State Univ	GA	10,658	C
Glenville State College	WV	7,812	NC
Gordon College	MA	25,982	VC+
Goshen College	IN	22,450	VC
Grand Valley State Univ	MI	11,022	VC
Greensboro College	NC	21,750	C
Gustavus Adolphus College	MN	27,120	VC+
Harris-Stowe State College	MO	3,200	SP
Heidelberg College	OH	20,266	NC
High Point Univ	NC	22,480	C
Hillsdale College	MI	22,450	HC
Humboldt State Univ	CA	9,400	C
Illinois State Univ	IL	10,944	C+
Immaculata Univ	PA	25,200	C
Indiana State Univ	IN	10,719	LC
Iona College	NY	27,988	VC
Ithaca College	NY	31,730	HC
Johnson C. Smith Univ	NC	18,108	C
Johnson State College	VT	11,819	LC
Judson College	AL	14,650	C
Kennesaw State Univ	GA	2,724	C
Kent State Univ	OH	12,932	C
Kentucky Christian College	KY	13,472	C
Kentucky Wesleyan College	KY	17,250	C
King's College	PA	26,990	C
LaGrange College	GA	20,500	C
Lake Erie College	OH	23,550	C
Lenoir-Rhyne College	NC	19,186	C
Lesley Univ	MA	30,695	C
Lincoln Memorial Univ	TN	16,400	LC
Lubbock Christian Univ	TX	15,832	C
Malone College	OH	20,995	C
Manchester College	IN	23,390	C
Manhattan College	NY	27,400	VC
Marian College of Fond du Lac	WI	19,625	C
Mars Hill College	NC	18,600	LC
Marshall Univ	WV	9,116	C
Mary Baldwin College	VA	24,939	C
Maryville Univ of St. Louis	MO	22,090	VC
McMurry Univ	TX	17,846	LC
Methodist College	NC	19,526	C
Miami Univ	OH	15,033	HC
Midland Lutheran College	NE	18,600	C
Millikin Univ	IL	25,555	C
Missouri Baptist Univ	MO	18,010	C
Missouri Southern State Univ	MO	8,316	C
Missouri Western State College	MO	8,522	NC
Montana State Univ-Billings	MT	9,550	C
Morehead State Univ	KY	7,464	C
Mount Olive College	NC	14,410	LC
Mount Union College	OH	21,120	C
Mount Vernon Nazarene Univ	OH	18,925	C
Murray State Univ	KY	7,816	VC
Nazareth College of Rochester	NY	24,936	VC
Nebr Wesleyan Univ	NE	21,197	C+
New York Inst of Technology	NY	24,205	VC
N Car Central Univ	NC	7,534	LC
N Car State Univ	NC	9,886	VC
N Car Wesleyan College	NC	17,998	C
North Georgia College and State Univ	GA	6,984	C
Northern Kentucky Univ	KY	6,352	NC
Northern State Univ	SD	7,117	LC
Northland College	WI	22,170	C+
Northwest College	WA	18,854	C
Northwest Missouri State Univ	MO	9,334	C
Northwestern College of Iowa	IA	19,640	C+
Northwestern State Univ of Louisiana	LA	6,331	NC
Notre Dame College	OH	20,425	C
Oakland City Univ	IN	16,980	NC
Oglethorpe Univ	GA	26,000	VC
Ohio Dominican Univ	OH	22,700	C
Ohio Northern Univ	OH	27,765	VC
Ohio Wesleyan Univ	OH	32,550	VC+
Okla Christian Univ	OK	17,690	NC
Okla Wesleyan Univ	OK	14,100	LC
Ouachita Baptist Univ	AR	18,900	VC
Paine College	GA	13,022	LC
Piedmont College	GA	16,900	C
Pikeville College	KY	14,900	NC
Prescott College	AZ	13,430	C
Rhode Island College	RI	11,565	C
Ripon College	WI	24,995	VC
St. Francis College	NY	10,880	LC
St. John's Univ	NY	30,180	C
St. Joseph's College	IN	24,250	C
St. Mary-of-the-Woods College	IN	23,280	C
St. Mary's Univ of Minn	MN	21,535	C
St. Xavier Univ	IL	23,144	C
Schreiner Univ	TX	20,440	C
Shorter College	GA	17,370	C
Southeastern College	FL	11,648	LC
Southern Arkansas Univ	AR	6,956	C
Southern Univ and A&M College	LA	7,372	LC
Southwest Baptist Univ	MO	15,371	C
Southwest Missouri State Univ	MO	8,918	C
Spalding Univ	KY	17,985	C
Springfield College	MA	24,520	C
SUNY at Potsdam	NY	12,160	C
SUNY/College at Cortland	NY	12,095	C
SUNY/College at Fredonia	NY	11,562	VC
SUNY/College at Old Westbury	NY	12,784	C
SUNY/Univ at New Paltz	NY	11,565	VC
State Univ of West Georgia	GA	7,622	C
Syracuse Univ	NY	34,720	HC
Tabor College	KS	19,500	NC
Temple Univ	PA	15,912	C
Texas Christian Univ	TX	23,410	VC
Texas Wesleyan Univ	TX	16,245	C
Thomas More College	KY	21,350	C
Thomas Univ	GA	11,490	NC
Toccoa Falls College	GA	15,600	C
Transylvania Univ	KY	23,780	VC+
Tusculum College	TN	19,990	C
Union College	KY	15,920	C
Union Univ	TN	18,800	VC
Univ of Arkansas	AR	9,855	VC
Univ of Arkansas at Pine Bluff	AR	7,925	C
Univ of Central Arkansas	AR	6,388	C
Univ of Cincinnati	OH	14,736	C
Univ of Detroit Mercy	MI	25,582	C
Univ of Evansville	IN	24,190	VC
Univ of Findlay	OH	23,962	NC
Univ of Georgia	GA	8,656	VC
Univ of Great Falls	MT	15,360	C
Univ of Indianapolis	IN	22,560	VC
Univ of Iowa	IA	10,923	VC
Univ of Kansas	KS	8,923	VC
Univ of Kentucky	KY	7,765	C
Univ of Louisville	KY	8,762	VC
Univ of Mary Hardin-Baylor	TX	17,268	C
Univ of Missouri/Columbia	MO	13,782	VC
Univ of Montana--Western	MT	8,073	NC
Univ of Nebr at Kearney	NE	8,286	NC
Univ of Nebr at Lincoln	NE	9,975	C+
Univ of N Car at Chapel Hill	NC	10,117	MC
Univ of N Car at Charlotte	NC	8,185	C
Univ of N Car at Greensboro	NC	8,248	C
Univ of N Car at Pembroke	NC	6,929	LC
Univ of N Car at Wilmington	NC	8,940	VC
Univ of N Dak	ND	8,390	C
Univ of North Florida	FL	8,769	VC
Univ of Northern Iowa	IA	9,834	C
Univ of San Francisco	CA	34,700	VC
Univ of Sioux Falls	SD	16,390	C
Univ of Southern Indiana	IN	9,025	LC
Univ of Southern Miss	MS	8,324	LC
Univ of the Incarnate Word	TX	21,772	LC
Univ of the Ozarks	AR	16,574	C
Univ of Vermont	VT	16,316	VC
Univ of West Alabama	AL	6,048	C
Univ of West Florida	FL	8,470	C
Univ of Wisc/Platteville	WI	8,450	C
Univ of Wisc/Whitewater	WI	8,626	C
Urbana Univ	OH	19,115	C
Ursuline College	OH	22,728	LC
Valdosta State Univ	GA	7,798	C
Valparaiso Univ	IN	26,118	VC+
Wagner College	NY	29,900	VC
Walsh Univ	OH	20,890	C
Warren Wilson College	NC	21,794	VC
Washington Univ in St. Louis	MO	38,293	MC
Wesleyan College	GA	17,870	VC
West Liberty State College	WV	7,868	LC
Western Carolina Univ	NC	6,742	C
Western Kentucky Univ	KY	6,834	C
Westfield State College	MA	10,147	C
Westminster College	MO	18,150	C+
William Woods Univ	MO	20,120	C
Wingate Univ	NC	21,200	C
Wittenberg Univ	OH	31,316	VC
Xavier Univ	OH	26,850	VC+
Youngstown State Univ	OH	11,148	NC

MILITARY SCIENCE

School	ST	$IS	SR
Austin Peay State Univ	TN	5,814	LC
Campbell Univ	NC	18,268	VC
Eastern Mich Univ	MI	11,478	C
Eastern Washington Univ	WA	9,012	C
Elon Univ	NC	22,240	VC
Florida Inst of Technology	FL	28,740	VC
Hawaii Pacific Univ	HI	19,218	C
Norfolk State Univ	VA	9,722	LC
Norwich Univ	VT	21,064	LC
Rochester Inst of Technology	NY	29,217	VC+
Rockford College	IL	28,310	VC
United States Air Force Academy	CO		HC+
United States Military Academy	NY		MC

MINING AND MINERAL ENGINEERING

School	ST	$IS	SR
Colo School of Mines	CO	12,533	HC
Columbia Univ/Fu Foundation School of Engineering and Applied Science	NY	38,590	MC
Mich Tech Univ	MI	13,235	VC
Montana Tech of The Univ of Montana	MT	9,314	NC
New Mexico Inst of Mining and Technology	NM	7,580	NC
Penn State Univ/Univ Park Campus	PA	15,646	HC
S Dak School of Mines and Technology	SD	7,854	C+
Southern Illinois Univ Carbondale	IL	10,407	C
Univ of Alaska Fairbanks	AK	9,295	C
Univ of Arizona	AZ	10,413	VC
Univ of Idaho	ID	8,216	C
Univ of Kentucky	KY	7,765	C
Univ of Missouri/Rolla	MO	12,292	HC
Univ of Nevada/Reno	NV	9,792	C
Univ of Utah	UT	9,205	C
Virginia Polytechnic Inst and State Univ	VA	9,179	C
West Virginia Univ	WV	9,370	C

MINISTRIES

School	ST	$IS	SR
Abilene Christian Univ	TX	18,370	VC
American Indian College of the Assemblies of God	AZ	9,275	LC
Asbury College	KY	20,704	VC
Atlantic Union College	MA	18,868	C
Azusa Pacific Univ	CA	24,720	VC
Bethany College	KS	18,675	LC
Bethel College	IN	19,670	C
Clearwater Christian College	FL	13,160	LC
College of St. Benedict	MN	26,672	VC
Concordia College	NY	19,200	VC
Concordia College: Moorhead	MN	22,460	VC+
Concordia Univ Wisc	WI	16,600	C
Creighton Univ	NE	26,748	VC+
Crichton College	TN	15,215	C
Dakota Wesleyan Univ	SD	17,832	C
East Texas Baptist Univ	TX	13,914	C
Eastern Mennonite Univ	VA	22,990	C
Eastern Nazarene College	MA	19,433	LC
Freed-Hardeman Univ	TN		NC
Fresno Pacific Univ	CA	22,462	C
Geneva College	PA	21,850	C
George Fox Univ	OR	26,110	VC
Greenville College	IL	21,342	C
Harding Univ	AR	14,890	VC
Hardin-Simmons Univ	TX	14,165	C
Hope International Univ	CA	16,940	NC
Houghton College	NY	23,984	VC
Huntington College	IN	23,590	C
Indiana Wesleyan Univ	IN	19,900	C+
John Brown Univ	AR	15,080	VC
Juniata College	PA	29,080	VC
Kentucky Christian College	KY	13,472	C
Lindenwood Univ	MO	17,050	VC
Lubbock Christian Univ	TX	15,832	C
Malone College	OH	20,995	C
Marylhurst Univ	OR	18,465	NC
Messiah College	PA	25,890	VC+
MidAmerica Nazarene Univ	KS	18,688	C
Missouri Baptist Univ	MO	18,010	C
Mount Olive College	NC	14,410	LC
North Central Univ	MN	14,904	C
Northwest Christian College	OR	21,860	C
Northwest College	WA	18,854	C
Northwest Nazarene Univ	ID	20,360	VC
Northwestern College	MN	22,820	C+
Notre Dame College	OH	20,425	C
Oakwood College	AL	14,904	C
Okla Christian Univ	OK	17,690	NC
Oral Roberts Univ	OK	18,490	C
Ouachita Baptist Univ	AR	18,900	VC
Palm Beach Atlantic Univ	FL	20,690	C
Rochester College	MI	16,718	C
St. Joseph's College	IN	24,250	C
Simpson College	CA	20,500	C
Southeastern College	FL	11,648	LC
Southern Christian Univ	AL	9,440	LC
Southwest Baptist Univ	MO	15,371	C
Spring Arbor Univ	MI	20,206	C
Tabor College	KS	19,500	NC
Tenn Wesleyan College	TN	16,540	C
Toccoa Falls College	GA	15,600	C
Trinity Bible College	ND		
Union Univ	TN	18,800	VC
Univ of Mary	ND	12,900	C+
Univ of St. Francis	IN	20,964	C
Valparaiso Univ	IN	26,118	VC+
Vanguard Univ of Southern Calif	CA	22,208	C
Viterbo Univ	WI	20,430	C
Warner Pacific College	OR	21,900	C
Waynesburg College	PA	19,370	C
Western Baptist College	OR	21,808	C

MISSIONS

School	ST	$IS	SR
Abilene Christian Univ	TX	18,370	VC
Asbury College	KY	20,704	VC
Bethel College	IN	19,670	C
Cascade College	OR	16,700	NC
Cedarville Univ	OH	19,954	VC
Covenant College	GA	23,830	VC+
Eastern Univ	PA	24,020	C
Evangel Univ	MO	15,435	C
Fresno Pacific Univ	CA	22,462	C
Grace Bible College	MI	15,890	C
King College	TN	22,500	VC
Northwest College	WA	18,854	C
Northwestern College	MN	22,820	C+
Nyack College	NY	18,540	C
Okla Christian Univ	OK	17,690	NC
Simpson College	CA	20,500	C
Southern Nazarene Univ	OK	14,634	NC
Toccoa Falls College	GA	15,600	C
Trinity Bible College	ND		
Union Univ	TN	18,800	VC

MODERN LANGUAGE

School	ST	$IS	SR
Augustana College	SD	21,998	VC
Beloit College	WI	29,864	HC
Bethune-Cookman College	FL	16,480	LC
Clemson Univ	SC	11,972	HC
College of Mount St. Vincent	NY	26,800	C
College of Notre Dame of Maryland	MD	27,700	C
Converse College	SC	24,710	VC
Emory & Henry College	VA	21,950	C
Emory Univ	GA	36,872	MC
Fort Hays State Univ	KS	7,363	C
Graceland Univ	IA	19,550	C

School	ST	$IS	SR
Greenville College	IL	21,342	C
High Point Univ	NC	22,480	C
Hobart and William Smith Colleges	NY	36,536	HC
Ithaca College	NY	31,730	HC
James Madison Univ	VA	10,794	VC
Kansas State Univ	KS	8,728	VC
Kenyon College	OH	35,370	HC+
King College	TN	22,500	VC
Knox College	IL	30,294	VC+
Longwood Univ	VA	11,175	C
Merrimack College	MA	29,625	C
Metropolitan State College of Denver	CO	2,338	LC
MidAmerica Nazarene Univ	KS	18,688	C
Millikin Univ	IL	25,555	C
Mills College	CA	33,371	VC
Miss College	MS	14,574	C
Monmouth Univ	NJ	26,334	C
Montana State Univ-Bozeman	MT	9,515	C
St. Francis Univ	PA	25,876	LC
St. Mary's College	MI	13,314	LC
Seton Hall Univ	NJ	30,130	VC
Simon's Rock College of Bard	MA	36,580	HC
Sweet Briar College	VA	27,940	C
Syracuse Univ	NY	34,720	HC
Trinity College	CT	38,040	HC+
Union College	NY	36,005	HC
Univ of Alaska Fairbanks	AK	9,295	C
Univ of Maine	ME	12,080	C+
Univ of Maryland/Baltimore County	MD	14,668	VC+
Univ of Mass Lowell	MA	11,937	VC
Univ of Wisc/River Falls	WI	8,358	LC
Wayne State College	NE	7,352	NC
Westmont College	CA	33,062	VC+
Widener Univ	PA	27,020	C
Wright State Univ	OH	11,490	LC

MOLECULAR BIOLOGY

School	ST	$IS	SR
Alverno College	WI	18,898	C
Andrews Univ	MI	19,550	C
Arizona State Univ-Main	AZ	10,048	C
Auburn Univ	AL	10,396	VC
Ball State Univ	IN	8,660	C
Bard College	NY	37,352	HC+
Benedictine Univ	IL	23,840	C
Bradley Univ	IL	22,910	VC
Brigham Young Univ	UT	8,504	HC
Centre College	KY	27,300	HC
Chestnut Hill College	PA	26,450	LC
Clarion Univ of Pennsylvania	PA	11,272	LC
Clarkson Univ	NY	32,226	VC
Coe College	IA	27,385	VC
Colgate Univ	NY	37,095	MC
Florida Inst of Technology	FL	28,740	VC
Florida State Univ	FL	9,028	HC
Goshen College	IN	22,450	VC
Illinois Inst of Technology	IL	26,456	HC+
Johns Hopkins Univ	MD	38,372	MC
Juniata College	PA	29,080	VC
Kenyon College	OH	35,370	HC+
Lehigh Univ	PA	37,570	HC+
LIU/C.W. Post Campus	NY	28,282	C
Mansfield Univ	PA	11,220	C
Marquette Univ	WI	27,594	VC
Middlebury College	VT	38,100	MC
Montclair State Univ	NJ	13,790	C
Muskingum College	OH	20,680	C
Nebr Wesleyan Univ	NE	21,197	C+
Northwestern Univ	IL	37,491	MC
Ohio Northern Univ	OH	27,765	VC
Okla State Univ	OK	9,216	VC
Otterbein College	OH	26,085	C
Penn State Univ/Univ Park Campus	PA	15,646	HC
Pomona College	CA	33,960	MC
Rutgers, The State Univ of New Jersey/New Brunswick/Piscataway Campus	NJ	15,800	HC
Salem International Univ	WV	19,770	C
SUNY/College of Environmental Science and Forestry	NY	14,167	VC
SUNY/Univ at Albany	NY	12,951	HC
Stetson Univ	FL	29,495	VC
Sweet Briar College	VA	27,940	C
Texas Tech Univ	TX	10,768	VC
Towson Univ	MD	12,694	VC
Univ of Arizona	AZ	10,413	VC
Univ of Calif at Berkeley	CA	15,563	MC
Univ of Calif at Los Angeles	CA	15,330	MC
Univ of Calif at San Diego	CA	14,127	HC
Univ of Colo at Boulder	CO	10,774	VC
Univ of Conn	CT	14,608	VC
Univ of Great Falls	MT	15,360	C
Univ of Idaho	ID	8,216	C
Univ of Illinois at Urbana-Champaign	IL	11,316	HC+
Univ of Kansas	KS	8,923	VC
Univ of Maine	ME	12,080	C+
Univ of New Hampshire	NH	14,828	VC
Univ of Pittsburgh at Pittsburgh	PA	16,074	HC
Univ of Redlands	CA	32,576	VC
Univ of Richmond	VA	30,100	MC
Univ of Texas at Austin	TX	10,630	HC
Univ of Texas at Dallas	TX	10,234	HC
Univ of Wisc/Madison	WI	8,262	VC
Univ of Wyoming	WY	8,636	C
Vanderbilt Univ	TN	37,897	MC
Wells College	NY	21,122	VC
Wesleyan Univ	CT	35,139	MC
Westminster College	PA	22,960	C

MULTIMEDIA

School	ST	$IS	SR
Appalachian State Univ	NC	7,637	VC
Art Inst of Atlanta	GA	23,205	SP
Art Inst of Portland	OR	23,040	SP
Bethel College	MN	25,180	VC
Bradley Univ	IL	22,910	VC
Calif Lutheran Univ	CA	27,600	LC
Cameron Univ	OK	5,692	NC
Cedarville Univ	OH	19,954	VC
Champlain College	VT	22,030	C
CUNY/City College	NY	4,230	C+
College of Santa Fe	NM	25,293	C+
Columbia College Chicago	IL	25,108	LC
Dakota Wesleyan Univ	SD	17,832	C
George Washington Univ	DC	41,030	MC
Howard Payne Univ	TX	15,176	C
Kean Univ	NJ	14,479	C
Kendall College of Art and Design of Ferris State Univ	MI	10,784	SP
La Salle Univ	PA	31,260	VC
Lewis Univ	IL	22,950	C+
Louisiana College	LA	13,450	C
Lyndon State College	VT	12,646	LC
McMurry Univ	TX	17,846	LC
Minot State Univ	ND	6,602	LC
Rider Univ	NJ	30,900	C
St. John's Univ	NY	30,180	C
Univ of N Car at Asheville	NC	8,079	VC
Univ of Oregon	OR	11,479	VC
Univ of the Arts	PA	29,510	SP
Waynesburg College	PA	19,370	C
Wilmington College	DE	5,594	NC

MUSEUM STUDIES

School	ST	$IS	SR
Baylor Univ	TX	23,864	VC
Earlham College	IN	29,976	VC+
Juniata College	PA	29,080	VC
Regis College	MA	29,000	C
Tusculum College	TN	19,990	C
Univ of Central Okla	OK	9,434	C

MUSIC

School	ST	$IS	SR
Abilene Christian Univ	TX	18,370	VC
Adams State College	CO	7,468	C
Adelphi Univ	NY	26,300	VC
Adrian College	MI	21,950	C
Agnes Scott College	GA	28,230	HC
Alabama State Univ	AL	6,404	C
Albany State Univ	GA	5,764	C+
Albertson College of Idaho	ID	19,415	VC
Albion College	MI	25,224	VC
Alderson-Broaddus College	WV	19,640	C
Allegheny College	PA	30,280	VC
Allen Univ	SC	10,300	NC
Alma College	MI	25,566	VC
Alverno College	WI	18,898	C
American Univ	DC	34,585	VC+
Amherst College	MA	37,470	MC
Andrews Univ	MI	19,550	C
Angelo State Univ	TX	7,576	NC
Anna Maria College	MA	26,140	LC
Aquinas College	MI	21,894	C
Arizona State Univ-Main	AZ	10,048	C
Arkansas State Univ	AR	8,450	C
Arkansas Tech Univ	AR	7,299	C
Armstrong Atlantic State Univ	GA	7,102	C
Asbury College	KY	20,704	VC
Ashland Univ	OH	24,464	C
Atlantic Union College	MA	18,868	C
Augsburg College	MN	25,298	C
Augusta State Univ	GA	2,592	C
Augustana College	IL	26,610	VC+
Augustana College	SD	21,998	VC
Austin College	TX	24,747	HC
Austin Peay State Univ	TN	5,814	LC
Averett Univ	VA	23,010	LC
Avila Univ	MO	20,300	C
Azusa Pacific Univ	CA	24,720	VC
Baker Univ	KS	19,860	VC
Baldwin-Wallace College	OH	24,678	C
Ball State Univ	IN	8,660	C
Bates College	ME	37,500	MC
Baylor Univ	TX	23,864	VC
Belhaven College	MS	16,040	C+
Bellarmine Univ	KY	24,110	VC
Belmont Univ	TN	21,986	VC
Beloit College	WI	29,864	HC
Bemidji State Univ	MN	9,103	C
Benedict College	SC	12,662	LC
Benedictine College	KS	20,603	C
Benedictine Univ	IL	23,840	C
Bennett College	NC	11,200	C
Bennington College	VT	35,910	HC
Berea College	KY	5,030	VC+
Berklee College of Music	MA	32,447	SP
Berry College	GA	21,410	VC
Bethany College	KS	18,675	LC
Bethel College	IN	19,670	C
Bethel College	KS	19,800	C+
Bethel College	MN	25,180	VC
Bethune-Cookman College	FL	16,480	LC
Biola Univ	CA	25,964	VC
Birmingham-Southern College	AL	25,364	VC+
Black Hills State Univ	SD	7,743	LC
Bloomsburg Univ of Pennsylvania	PA	10,844	C
Blue Mountain College	MS	10,226	C
Bluefield College	VA	15,575	C
Bluffton College	OH	23,694	C
Boise State Univ	ID	7,657	LC
Boston College	MA	33,284	MC
Boston Conservatory	MA	26,900	SP
Boston Univ	MA	38,194	HC+
Bowdoin College	ME	37,790	MC
Bradley Univ	IL	22,910	VC
Brandeis Univ	MA	38,198	MC
Brewton-Parker College	GA	14,200	LC
Briar Cliff Univ	IA	21,660	C
Bridgewater College	VA	25,150	C
Bridgewater State College	MA	10,482	C
Brigham Young Univ	UT	8,504	HC
Brigham Young Univ/Hawaii	HI	7,240	VC+
Brown Univ	RI	38,174	MC
Bryan College	TN	17,900	VC
Bryn Mawr College	PA	36,890	HC+
Bucknell Univ	PA	35,262	HC+
Buena Vista Univ	IA	25,406	C
Butler Univ	IN	28,250	VC+
Caldwell College	NJ	24,060	LC
Calif Baptist Univ	CA	19,924	C
Calif Inst of the Arts	CA	30,690	SP
Calif Lutheran Univ	CA	27,600	LC
Calif State Polytechnic Univ, Pomona	CA	8,793	C+
Cal State, Bakersfield	CA	6,090	LC
Cal State, Chico	CA	8,598	LC
Cal State, Dominguez Hills	CA	5,840	LC
Cal State, Fresno	CA	8,414	LC
Cal State, Fullerton	CA	6,648	C
Cal State, Hayward	CA	8,871	LC
Cal State, Long Beach	CA	8,762	C+
Cal State, Los Angeles	CA	5,778	C
Cal State, Northridge	CA	7,757	LC
Cal State, Sacramento	CA	9,543	C
Cal State, San Bernardino	CA	15,238	LC
Cal State, Stanislaus	CA	9,874	C
Calvin College	MI	22,615	NC
Cameron Univ	OK	5,692	NC
Campbell Univ	NC	18,268	VC
Campbellsville Univ	KY	17,680	C
Canisius College	NY	28,163	C+
Capital Univ	OH	26,550	C
Cardinal Stritch Univ	WI	17,620	C
Carleton College	MN	34,395	MC
Carnegie Mellon Univ	PA	32,682	MC
Carroll College	WI	22,740	C
Carson-Newman College	TN	16,760	C
Carthage College	WI	25,000	C
Case Western Reserve Univ	OH	32,002	MC
Castleton State College	VT	11,820	C
Catawba College	NC	20,500	C
Catholic Univ of America	DC	34,248	VC
Cedar Crest College	PA	25,145	C+
Cedarville Univ	OH	19,954	VC
Centenary College of Louisiana	LA	23,100	VC+
Central College	IA	21,206	C
Central Conn State Univ	CT	12,090	C
Central Methodist College	MO	16,460	C
Central Mich Univ	MI	11,142	C
Central Missouri State Univ	MO	9,776	C
Central State Univ	OH	8,922	C+
Central Washington Univ	WA	9,768	C
Centre College	KY	27,300	HC
Chadron State College	NE	6,286	NC
Chapman Univ	CA	33,118	VC
Charleston Southern Univ	SC	17,122	C
Chatham College	PA	27,266	C+
Cheyney Univ of Pennsylvania	PA	9,993	C
Chicago State Univ	IL	10,882	C+
Christian Heritage College	CA	19,990	C
Christopher Newport Univ	VA	8,862	VC
CUNY/Baruch College	NY	3,275	VC+
CUNY/Brooklyn College	NY	4,353	C+
CUNY/City College	NY	4,230	C+
CUNY/College of Staten Island	NY	4,308	NC
CUNY/Herbert H. Lehman College	NY	3,320	LC
CUNY/Hunter College	NY	6,729	C+
CUNY/Queens College	NY	4,362	C
CUNY/York College	NY	3,292	NC
Claflin Univ	SC	14,838	C+
Clarion Univ of Pennsylvania	PA	11,272	LC
Clark Atlanta Univ	GA	19,300	C+
Clark Univ	MA	32,115	VC
Clarke College	IA	23,165	C
Clayton College and State Univ	GA	2,441	LC
Clearwater Christian College	FL	13,160	LC
Cleveland Inst of Music	OH	25,880	SP
Cleveland State Univ	OH	12,308	LC
Coastal Carolina Univ	SC	11,040	C
Coe College	IA	27,385	VC
Coker College	SC	21,491	C
Colby College	ME	37,570	MC
Colgate Univ	NY	37,095	MC
College of Charleston	SC	11,887	HC
College of Mount St. Joseph	OH	22,785	C
College of New Jersey	NJ	15,950	MC
College of Notre Dame of Maryland	MD	27,700	C
College of St. Benedict	MN	26,672	VC
College of St. Catherine	MN	24,010	VC
College of St. Elizabeth	NJ	25,460	C
College of St. Rose	NY	22,864	C
College of St. Scholastica	MN	24,970	C+
College of Santa Fe	NM	25,293	C+
College of the Holy Cross	MA	36,451	MC
College of the Ozarks	MO	3,500	VC+
College of William and Mary	VA	12,224	MC
College of Wooster	OH	31,300	HC
Colo Christian Univ	CO	21,182	VC
Colo College	CO	36,860	HC
Colo State Univ	CO	9,964	VC
Columbia College	SC	22,658	LC
Columbia College Chicago	IL	25,108	LC
Columbia Union College	MD	20,543	C
Columbia Univ/Barnard College	NY	36,990	MC
Columbia Univ/Columbia College	NY	38,590	MC
Columbia Univ/School of General Studies	NY	35,000	C
Columbus State Univ	GA	7,846	C
Concordia College	NY	19,200	VC
Concordia College: Moorhead	MN	22,460	VC+
Concordia Univ	CA	24,420	C
Concordia Univ	MI	24,095	C
Concordia Univ at Austin	TX	20,450	LC
Concordia Univ Nebr	NE	20,302	C+
Concordia Univ Wisc	WI	16,600	C
Concordia Univ, River Forest	IL	23,600	C
Concordia Univ/St.Paul	MN	24,486	C
Conn College	CT	37,900	MC
Converse College	SC	24,710	VC
Cornell College	IA	27,825	VC+
Cornell Univ	NY	38,253	MC
Cornerstone Univ and Grand Rapids Theological Seminary	MI	19,846	C
Cornish College of the Arts	WA	19,900	SP
Covenant College	GA	23,830	VC+
Creighton Univ	NE	26,748	VC+
Culver-Stockton College	MO	17,850	C
Cumberland College	KY	16,384	C
Cumberland Univ	TN	16,910	C
Curtis Inst of Music	PA		SP
Dakota State Univ	SD	7,466	C
Dallas Baptist Univ	TX	15,300	VC
Dana College	NE	20,280	C
Dartmouth College	NH	37,770	MC
David Lipscomb Univ	TN	16,158	VC
Davidson College	NC	33,274	MC
Davis and Elkins College	WV	20,594	C
Delaware State Univ	DE	8,104	LC
Delta State Univ	MS	6,618	C
Denison Univ	OH	33,050	HC
DePaul Univ	IL	27,580	VC
DePauw Univ	IN	31,500	HC
Dickinson College	PA	35,825	HC
Dickinson State Univ	ND	6,338	NC
Dillard Univ	LA	17,325	VC
Doane College	NE	20,000	C
Dominican Univ	IL	23,610	C
Dominican Univ of Calif	CA	31,670	C
Dordt College	IA	20,170	VC
Dowling College	NY	23,870	LC
Drake Univ	IA	25,120	VC+
Drew Univ/College of Liberal Arts	NJ	35,550	VC
Drexel Univ	PA	27,655	VC
Drury Univ	MO	18,085	VC+
Duke Univ	NC	37,555	MC
Duquesne Univ	PA	26,907	VC
Earlham College	IN	29,976	VC+
East Central Univ	OK	4,968	C
East Stroudsburg Univ of Pennsylvania	PA	10,336	C
East Tenn State Univ	TN	8,497	C

School	ST	$IS	SR	School	ST	$IS	SR	School	ST	$IS	SR	School	ST	$IS	SR
East Texas Baptist Univ	TX	13,914	C	Illinois State Univ	IL	10,944	C+	McMurry Univ	TX	17,846	LC	Oakwood College	AL	14,904	C
Eastern Illinois Univ	IL	11,192	C	Illinois Wesleyan Univ	IL	30,380	HC+	McNeese State Univ	LA	5,259	LC	Oberlin College	OH	36,938	MC
Eastern Kentucky Univ	KY	7,708	C	Immaculata Univ	PA	25,200	C	McPherson College	KS	20,265	C	Occidental College	CA	35,922	HC
Eastern Mennonite Univ	VA	22,990	C	Indiana State Univ	IN	10,719	LC	Mercer Univ	GA	27,516	VC+	Ohio Northern Univ	OH	27,765	VC
Eastern Mich Univ	MI	11,478	C	Indiana Univ Bloomington	IN	12,389	VC	Mercy College	NY	19,200	NC	Ohio State Univ	OH	13,080	VC+
Eastern Nazarene College	MA	19,433	LC	Indiana Univ of				Mercyhurst College	PA	20,694	C	Ohio Univ	OH	14,448	C
Eastern New Mexico Univ	NM	6,762	LC	Pennsylvania	PA	10,489	C	Meredith College	NC	23,065	C	Ohio Wesleyan Univ	OH	32,550	VC+
Eastern Oregon Univ	OR	10,080	NC	Indiana Univ South Bend	IN	4,571	LC	Messiah College	PA	25,890	VC+	Okla Baptist Univ	OK	15,220	VC
Eastern Univ	PA	24,020	C	Indiana Univ Southeast	IN	4,504	LC	Methodist College	NC	19,526	C	Okla Christian Univ	OK	17,690	NC
Eastern Washington Univ	WA	9,012	C	Indiana Wesleyan Univ	IN	19,900	C	Miami Univ	OH	15,033	HC	Okla City Univ	OK	19,580	VC
Eastman School of Music	NY	33,741	SP	Inter American Univ of PR/				Mich State Univ	MI	11,933	VC	Okla Panhandle State Univ	OK	5,370	C
Eckerd College	FL	28,744	C+	San German	PR	6,716		MidAmerica Nazarene Univ	KS	18,688	C	Okla State Univ	OK	9,216	VC
Edgewood College	WI	20,520	C	Iowa State Univ	IA	10,768	VC	Middle Tenn State Univ	TN	8,534	C	Okla Wesleyan Univ	OK	14,100	LC
Edinboro Univ of				Iowa Wesleyan College	IA	19,990	C	Middlebury College	VT	38,100	MC	Old Dominion Univ	VA	10,441	C
Pennsylvania	PA	10,850	LC	Ithaca College	NY	31,730	HC	Midland Lutheran College	NE	18,600	C	Olivet Nazarene Univ	IL	20,480	C
Elizabeth City State Univ	NC	5,550	LC	Jacksonville State Univ	AL	6,844	LC	Midwestern State Univ	TX	8,045	LC	Oral Roberts Univ	OK	18,490	C
Elizabethtown College	PA	28,800	C	Jacksonville Univ	FL	24,040	C	Millersville Univ of				Oregon State Univ	OR	11,055	C
Elmhurst College	IL	24,630	C	James Madison Univ	VA	10,794	VC	Pennsylvania	PA	11,269	C	Ottawa Univ	KS	11,800	LC
Elmira College	NY	33,820	VC	Jamestown College	ND	12,600	NC	Milligan College	TN	19,860	C+	Otterbein College	OH	26,085	C
Elon Univ	NC	22,240	VC	John Brown Univ	AR	15,080	VC	Millikin Univ	IL	25,555	C	Ouachita Baptist Univ	AR	18,900	VC
Emory Univ	GA	36,872	MC	Johns Hopkins Univ	MD	38,372	MC	Mills College	CA	33,371	VC	Our Lady of the Lake Univ			
Emporia State Univ	KS	6,998	C	Johnson State College	VT	11,819	LC	Millsaps College	MS	25,182	VC	of San Antonio	TX	17,336	C
Erskine College	SC	23,166	VC	Judson College	AL	14,650	C	Minn State Univ, Mankato	MN	8,803	LC	Pacific Lutheran Univ	WA	25,715	VC
Eureka College	IL	24,980	LC	Judson College	IL	22,050	LC	Minn State Univ,				Pacific Union College	CA	22,065	C+
Evangel Univ	MO	15,435	C	Kalamazoo College	MI	26,955	HC+	Moorehead	MN	7,000	LC	Pacific Univ	OR	24,250	C
Fisk Univ	TN	17,305	LC	Kansas State Univ	KS	8,728	VC	Minot State Univ	ND	6,602	LC	Palm Beach Atlantic Univ	FL	20,690	C
Florida A&M Univ	FL	7,564	C	Kansas Wesleyan Univ	KS	18,900	VC	Miss College	MS	14,574	C	Paul Quinn College	TX	8,150	LC
Florida Atlantic Univ	FL	8,543	C	Kean Univ	NJ	14,479	C	Miss Univ for Women	MS	5,446	LC	Penn State Univ/Univ Park			
Florida International Univ	FL	9,912	VC	Keene State College	NH	12,212	C	Missouri Southern State				Campus	PA	15,646	HC
Florida Memorial College	FL	6,000	LC	Kennesaw State Univ	GA	2,724	C	Univ	MO	8,316	C	Pepperdine Univ	CA	32,830	VC
Florida Southern College	FL	23,592	VC	Kent State Univ	OH	12,932	C	Missouri Western State				Peru State College	NE	6,342	NC
Florida State Univ	FL	9,028	LC	Kentucky Christian College	KY	13,472	C	College	MO	8,522	NC	Pfeiffer Univ	NC	18,980	C
Fordham Univ	NY	35,066	HC	Kenyon College	OH	35,370	HC+	Molloy College	NY	15,180	C	Philadelphia Biblical Univ	PA	18,395	C
Fort Hays State Univ	KS	7,363	C	Knox College	IL	30,294	VC+	Monmouth College	IL	23,600	C	Philander Smith College	AR	7,380	NC
Fort Lewis College	CO	8,353	C	Knoxville College	TN	6,200	LC	Monmouth Univ	NJ	26,334	C	Piedmont College	GA	16,900	C
Franklin and Marshall				Kutztown Univ of				Montana State Univ-Billings	MT	9,550	C	Pittsburg State Univ	KS	7,128	NC
College	PA	35,930	HC+	Pennsylvania	PA	10,786	C	Montana State Univ-				Pitzer College	CA	37,590	HC
Franklin Pierce College	NH	28,980	LC	La Salle Univ	PA	31,260	VC	Bozeman	MT	9,515	C	Plymouth State Univ	NH	12,298	C
Fresno Pacific Univ	CA	22,462	C	La Sierra Univ	CA	19,260	LC	Montana State Univ-				Point Loma Nazarene Univ	CA	21,380	VC
Friends Univ	KS	15,962	LC	Lafayette College	PA	35,746	MC	Northern	MT	8,600	NC	Pomona College	CA	33,960	MC
Frostburg State Univ	MD	11,114	C	LaGrange College	GA	20,500	C	Montclair State Univ	NJ	13,790	C	Portland State Univ	OR	12,453	C
Furman Univ	SC	28,976	HC+	Lake Erie College	OH	23,550	C	Moravian College	PA	28,903	VC	Prairie View A&M Univ	TX	9,418	NC
Gardner-Webb Univ	NC	19,300	C	Lake Forest College	IL	30,270	VC	Morehead State Univ	KY	7,464	C	Presbyterian College	SC	25,920	VC
Geneva College	PA	21,850	C	Lakeland College	WI	17,950	C	Morehouse College	GA	22,728	C	Princeton Univ	NJ	36,649	MC
George Fox Univ	OR	26,110	VC	Lamar Univ	TX	6,816	LC	Morgan State Univ	MD	11,470	C	Principia College	IL	25,044	C+
George Mason Univ	VA	9,732	VC	Lambuth Univ	TN	16,520	C	Morningside College	IA	21,610	C	Providence College	RI	30,604	HC
George Washington Univ	DC	41,030	MC	Lander Univ	SC	10,496	C	Mount Holyoke College	MA	37,918	HC+	Queens Univ of Charlotte	NC	21,840	C
Georgetown College	KY	22,000	VC	Lane College	TN	11,178	C+	Mount Marty College	SD	15,656	LC	Quincy Univ	IL	22,330	C
Georgia College and State				Langston Univ	OK	2,308	LC	Mount Mary College	WI	20,370	C	Radford Univ	VA	8,500	C
Univ	GA	9,878	C	Lebanon Valley College	PA	28,870	VC	Mount Mercy College	IA	21,400	C	Ramapo College of New			
Georgia Southern Univ	GA	8,540	C	Lee Univ	TN	13,780	NC	Mount Olive College	NC	14,410	LC	Jersey	NJ	15,203	VC
Georgia Southwestern State				Lehigh Univ	PA	37,570	HC+	Mount St. Mary's College	CA	28,307	VC	Randolph-Macon College	VA	27,190	C
Univ	GA	6,013	C	LeMoyne-Owen College	TN	13,070	LC	Mount Union College	OH	21,120	C	Randolph-Macon Woman's			
Georgia State Univ	GA	10,658	C	Lenoir-Rhyne College	NC	19,186	C	Mount Vernon Nazarene				College	VA	28,430	VC+
Georgian Court College	NJ	19,040	LC	Lewis and Clark College	OR	30,620	VC	Univ	OH	18,925	C	Reed College	OR	36,950	MC
Gettysburg College	PA	35,646	HC	Lewis Univ	IL	22,950	C+	Muhlenberg College	PA	31,485	HC	Rhode Island College	RI	11,565	C
Gonzaga Univ	WA	26,766	HC	Liberty Univ	VA	17,220	C	Murray State Univ	KY	7,816	VC	Rhodes College	TN	26,466	VC+
Gordon College	MA	25,982	VC+	Limestone College	SC	17,700	C	Muskingum College	OH	20,680	C	Rice Univ	TX	27,550	MC
Goshen College	IN	22,450	VC	Lincoln Univ	PA	13,320	C+	Nazareth College of				Richard Stockton College of			
Goucher College	MD	32,650	HC	Lindenwood Univ	MO	17,050	VC	Rochester	NY	24,936	VC	New Jersey	NJ	12,972	VC
Grace Bible College	MI	15,890	C	Linfield College	OR	27,090	VC	Nebr Wesleyan Univ	NE	21,197	C+	Rider Univ	NJ	30,900	C
Grace College	IN	19,825	VC	Livingstone College	NC	18,101	LC	New College of Calif	CA	8,900	NC	Ripon College	WI	24,995	VC
Graceland Univ	IA	19,550	C	Lock Haven Univ of				New College of Florida	FL	8,906	HC+	Roanoke College	VA	27,393	C
Grambling State Univ	LA	6,538	NC	Pennsylvania	PA	11,098	LC	New England Conservatory				Roberts Wesleyan College	NY	23,190	C+
Grand Canyon Univ	AZ	30,000	LC	LIU/Brooklyn Campus	NY	24,790	C	of Music	MA	35,000	SP	Rochester College	MI	16,718	C
Grand Valley State Univ	MI	11,022	VC	LIU/C.W. Post Campus	NY	28,282	C	New Jersey City Univ	NJ	11,850	C	Rockford College	IL	28,310	VC
Greensboro College	NC	21,750	C	Longwood Univ	VA	11,175	C	New Mexico Highlands Univ	NM	6,182	LC	Roosevelt Univ	IL	22,580	VC
Greenville College	IL	21,342	C	Loras College	IA	24,233	C	New Mexico State Univ	NM	7,932	C	Rowan Univ	NJ	14,506	VC
Grinnell College	IA	31,060	HC+	Louisiana College	LA	13,450	C	New York Univ	NY	39,406	MC	Rust College	MS	8,200	C+
Grove City College	PA	14,228	HC	Louisiana State Univ and				Newberry College	SC	22,871	LC	Rutgers, The State Univ of			
Guilford College	NC	24,960	VC	A&M College	LA	9,126	VC	Newman Univ	KS	18,018	C	New Jersey/Camden			
Gustavus Adolphus College	MN	27,120	VC+	Louisiana Tech Univ	LA	7,361	C	Nicholls State Univ	LA	6,395	NC	Campus	NJ	14,990	VC
Hamilton College	NY	37,560	MC	Loyola Marymount Univ	CA	32,194	VC	N Car Agricultural and				Rutgers, The State Univ of			
Hamline Univ	MN	27,052	VC	Lubbock Christian Univ	TX	15,832	C	Technical State Univ	NC	6,659	LC	New Brunswick/Piscataway			
Hampshire College	MA	37,037	HC	Luther College	IA	25,700	VC	N Car Central Univ	NC	7,534	LC	Campus	NJ	15,800	HC
Hampton Univ	VA	17,112	C+	Lycoming College	PA	27,589	C+	N Car School of the Arts	NC	8,565	SP	Rutgers, The State Univ of			
Hannibal-LaGrange College	MO	13,940	C	Lynchburg College	VA	26,815	C	North Central College	IL	25,656	VC	New Jersey/Newark			
Hanover College	IN	25,200	VC	Lyon College	AR	17,995	VC	N Dak State Univ	ND	8,435	C	Campus	NJ	15,624	VC
Harding Univ	AR	14,890	VC	Macalester College	MN	31,944	MC	North Georgia College and				Saginaw Valley State Univ	MI	11,055	C
Hardin-Simmons Univ	TX	14,165	C	MacMurray College	IL	20,005	LC	State Univ	GA	6,984	C	St. Ambrose Univ	IA	22,800	C
Hartwick College	NY	34,650	C+	Madonna Univ	MI	11,504	VC	North Park Univ	IL	24,300	C	St. Augustine's College	NC	12,990	LC
Harvard Univ/Harvard				Malone College	OH	20,995	C	Northeastern Illinois Univ	IL	2,898	NC	St. Cloud State Univ	MN	8,362	C
College	MA	37,928	MC	Manchester College	IN	23,390	C	Northeastern State Univ	OK	4,950	LC	St. John's Univ	MN	26,473	VC
Hastings College	NE	19,928	VC	Manhattan School of Music	NY	31,500	SP	Northeastern Univ	MA	35,650	HC	St. Joseph's College	IN	24,250	C
Haverford College	PA	37,900	MC	Manhattanville College	NY	32,420	C+	Northern Arizona Univ	AZ	9,002	C	St. Lawrence Univ	NY	35,945	VC
Heidelberg College	OH	20,266	NC	Mannes College of Music	NY	31,930	SP	Northern Illinois Univ	IL	11,472	C	St. Louis Univ	MO	29,780	VC+
Henderson State Univ	AR	7,386	C	Mansfield Univ	PA	11,220	C	Northern Kentucky Univ	KY	6,352	NC	St. Martin's College	WA	23,245	C
Hendrix College	AR	20,970	VC+	Marian College	IN	23,030	C	Northern Mich Univ	MI	10,834	C	St. Mary-of-the-Woods			
Hillsdale College	MI	22,450	HC	Marian College of Fond du				Northern State Univ	SD	7,117	LC	College	IN	23,280	C
Hiram College	OH	28,234	VC	Lac	WI	19,625	C	Northwest Christian College	OR	21,860	C	St. Mary's College	IN	24,474	VC
Hobart and William Smith				Marietta College	OH	27,047	C	Northwest College	WA	18,854	C	St. Mary's College of			
Colleges	NY	36,536	HC	Marlboro College	VT	29,055	VC+	Northwest Missouri State				Maryland	MD	15,908	VC+
Hofstra Univ	NY	27,112	VC	Mars Hill College	NC	18,600	LC	Univ	MO	9,334	C	St. Mary's Univ of San			
Hollins Univ	VA	27,965	VC	Marshall Univ	WV	9,116	C	Northwest Nazarene Univ	ID	20,360	VC	Antonio	TX	22,444	C
Holy Names College	CA	27,980	NC	Martin Univ	IN	10,200	SP	Northwestern College	MN	22,820	C+	St. Michael's College	VT	30,100	VC
Hood College	MD	27,795	VC	Mary Baldwin College	VA	24,939	C	Northwestern College of				St. Norbert College	WI	25,810	C
Hope College	MI	25,340	VC	Mary Washington College	VA	10,166	HC	Iowa	IA	19,640	C+	St. Olaf College	MN	28,500	HC
Hope International Univ	CA	16,940	NC	Marygrove College	MI	17,550	C	Northwestern Okla State				St. Vincent College	PA	25,530	VC
Houston Baptist Univ	TX	16,905	C	Marylhurst Univ	OR	18,465	NC	Univ	OK	5,433	NC	St. Xavier Univ	IL	23,144	C
Howard Payne Univ	TX	15,176	C	Maryville College	TN	25,960	VC	Northwestern State Univ of				Salem College	NC	24,595	VC
Howard Univ	DC	16,505	C	Marywood Univ	PA	26,050	C	Louisiana	LA	6,331	NC	Salisbury Univ	MD	12,664	VC
Humboldt State Univ	CA	9,400	C	Mass Inst of Technology	MA	38,310	MC	Northwestern Univ	IL	37,491	MC	Salve Regina Univ	RI	29,210	C
Huntingdon College	AL	18,400	VC	Master's College and				Notre Dame de Namur Univ	CA	26,932	LC	Sam Houston State Univ	TX	7,142	C
Huston-Tillotson College	TX	14,232	NC	Seminary	CA	23,250	VC	Nyack College	NY	18,540	C	Samford Univ	AL	18,648	VC
Idaho State Univ	ID	8,128	C	McDaniel College	MD	28,440	VC	Oakland City Univ	IN	16,980	NC	San Diego State Univ	CA	10,321	C
Illinois College	IL	19,100	VC	McKendree College	IL	21,120	VC	Oakland Univ	MI	10,800	C				

ST = STATE $IS = IN-STATE COSTS   SR = SELECTOR RATING

School	ST	$IS	SR
San Francisco Conservatory of Music	CA	20,780	SP
San Francisco State Univ	CA	12,070	C
San Jose State Univ	CA	8,187	C
Santa Clara Univ	CA	34,701	C
Sarah Lawrence College	NY	41,218	HC
Savannah State Univ	GA	7,328	LC
Schreiner Univ	TX	20,440	C
Scripps College	CA	35,700	HC+
Seattle Pacific Univ	WA	25,944	VC
Seton Hall Univ	NJ	30,130	VC
Seton Hill Univ	PA	24,930	C
Shenandoah Univ	VA	25,190	NC
Shepherd College	WV	8,608	C
Shorter College	GA	17,370	C
Siena Heights Univ	MI	16,140	LC
Sierra Nevada College	NV	26,136	C
Silver Lake College of the Holy Family	WI	18,450	LC
Simmons College	MA	33,000	VC
Simpson College	CA	20,500	C
Simpson College	IA	23,658	C+
Skidmore College	NY	37,930	HC
Slippery Rock Univ of Pennsylvania	PA	10,343	LC
Smith College	MA	37,034	HC+
Sonoma State Univ	CA	10,421	C
S Dak State Univ	SD	7,782	C
Southeast Missouri State Univ	MO	9,704	C
Southeastern College	FL	11,648	LC
Southeastern Louisiana Univ	LA	6,791	LC
Southeastern Okla State Univ	OK	6,147	C
Southern Adventist Univ	TN	17,080	C
Southern Illinois Univ Carbondale	IL	10,407	C
Southern Illinois Univ Edwardsville	IL	8,724	C
Southern Nazarene Univ	OK	14,634	NC
Southern Oregon Univ	OR	10,362	C
Southern Univ and A&M College	LA	7,372	LC
Southern Utah Univ	UT	8,194	C
Southern Wesleyan Univ	SC	19,940	C
Southwest Baptist Univ	MO	15,371	C
Southwest Minn State Univ	MN	9,106	VC
Southwest Missouri State Univ	MO	8,918	C
Southwestern Adventist Univ	TX	14,798	C
Southwestern College	KS	19,560	C
Southwestern Univ	TX	25,410	HC
Spelman College	GA	19,215	C+
Spring Arbor Univ	MI	20,206	C
Stanford Univ	CA	37,612	MC
SUNY at Oswego	NY	12,650	C
SUNY at Potsdam	NY	12,160	C
SUNY/College at Buffalo	NY	8,025	C
SUNY/College at Fredonia	NY	11,562	NC
SUNY/College at Geneseo	NY	11,330	C
SUNY/College at Oneonta	NY	11,870	VC
SUNY/College at Plattsburgh	NY	11,700	C
SUNY/College at Purchase	NY	10,587	VC
SUNY/Univ at Albany	NY	12,951	HC
SUNY/Univ at Binghamton	NY	12,787	HC
SUNY/Univ at Buffalo	NY	12,563	VC
SUNY/Univ at New Paltz	NY	11,565	VC
SUNY/Univ at Stony Brook	NY	12,763	HC
State Univ of West Georgia	GA	7,622	C
Stephen F. Austin State Univ	TX	7,552	C
Sterling College	KS	18,763	C
Stetson Univ	FL	29,495	VC
Stillman College	AL	11,370	LC
Susquehanna Univ	PA	29,990	VC
Swarthmore College	PA	37,716	MC
Sweet Briar College	VA	27,940	C
Syracuse Univ	NY	34,720	HC
Tabor College	KS	19,500	NC
Tarleton State Univ	TX	7,576	C
Taylor Univ	IN	23,820	VC+
Temple Univ	PA	15,912	C
Tenn State Univ	TN	9,048	C
Tenn Wesleyan College	TN	16,540	C
Texas A&M Univ at Commerce	TX	8,994	C
Texas A&M Univ at Corpus Christi	TX	10,269	C
Texas A&M Univ at Kingsville	TX	6,740	LC
Texas Christian Univ	TX	23,410	VC
Texas Lutheran Univ	TX	20,370	C
Texas Southern Univ	TX	8,920	NC
Texas State Univ	TX	9,320	VC
Texas Tech Univ	TX	10,768	VC
Texas Wesleyan Univ	TX	16,245	C
Texas Woman's Univ	TX	7,804	LC
Thomas Edison State College	NJ	3,325	SP
Toccoa Falls College	GA	15,600	C
Tougaloo College	MS	9,200	NC
Towson Univ	MD	12,694	VC
Transylvania Univ	KY	23,780	VC+
Trevecca Nazarene Univ	TN	17,548	C
Trinity Christian College	IL	21,640	VC
Trinity College	CT	38,040	HC+
Trinity International Univ	IL	22,980	C+
Trinity Univ	TX	26,466	HC+
Truman State Univ	MO	9,728	HC
Tufts Univ	MA	38,233	MC
Tulane Univ	LA	37,451	HC+
Union College	KY	15,920	C
Union College	NE	17,130	C
Union Univ	TN	18,800	C
Universidad Adventista de las Antillas	PR	5,460	
Univ of Akron	OH	13,134	NC
Univ of Alabama	AL	9,040	C+
Univ of Alabama at Birmingham	AL	12,901	C
Univ of Alabama in Huntsville	AL	9,126	VC
Univ of Alaska Anchorage	AK	9,100	NC
Univ of Alaska Fairbanks	AK	9,295	C
Univ of Arizona	AZ	10,413	VC
Univ of Arkansas	AR	9,855	VC
Univ of Arkansas at Little Rock	AR	5,637	NC
Univ of Arkansas at Monticello	AR	5,940	NC
Univ of Arkansas at Pine Bluff	AR	7,925	C
Univ of Bridgeport	CT	25,924	C
Univ of Calif at Berkeley	CA	15,563	MC
Univ of Calif at Davis	CA	14,995	VC
Univ of Calif at Irvine	CA	19,808	VC
Univ of Calif at Los Angeles	CA	15,330	MC
Univ of Calif at Riverside	CA	15,300	C
Univ of Calif at San Diego	CA	14,127	VC
Univ of Calif at Santa Barbara	CA	11,732	VC
Univ of Calif at Santa Cruz	CA	16,505	VC
Univ of Central Arkansas	AR	6,388	C
Univ of Central Florida	FL	10,038	VC
Univ of Central Okla	OK	9,434	C
Univ of Charleston	WV	23,620	C
Univ of Chicago	IL	35,087	MC
Univ of Cincinnati	OH	14,736	C
Univ of Colo at Boulder	CO	10,774	VC
Univ of Colo at Denver	CO	3,302	C
Univ of Conn	CT	14,608	VC
Univ of Dayton	OH	24,850	VC
Univ of Delaware	DE	12,616	HC
Univ of Denver	CO	32,148	VC
Univ of Evansville	IN	24,190	C
Univ of Florida	FL	8,580	MC
Univ of Georgia	GA	8,656	VC
Univ of Hartford	CT	31,080	C
Univ of Hawaii at Hilo	HI	6,497	C
Univ of Hawaii at Manoa	HI	9,565	VC
Univ of Houston	TX	9,818	C
Univ of Idaho	ID	8,216	C
Univ of Illinois at Chicago	IL	13,418	C
Univ of Illinois at Urbana-Champaign	IL	11,316	HC+
Univ of Indianapolis	IN	22,560	VC
Univ of Iowa	IA	10,923	VC
Univ of Kentucky	KY	7,765	C
Univ of La Verne	CA	28,600	C
Univ of Louisiana at Lafayette	LA	5,826	C
Univ of Louisiana at Monroe	LA	5,207	NC
Univ of Louisville	KY	8,762	C
Univ of Maine	ME	12,080	C+
Univ of Maine at Farmington	ME	10,108	C
Univ of Mary	ND	12,900	C+
Univ of Mary Hardin-Baylor	TX	17,268	C
Univ of Maryland/Baltimore County	MD	14,668	VC+
Univ of Maryland/College Park	MD	14,227	HC
Univ of Mass Amherst	MA	13,980	C+
Univ of Mass Boston	MA	6,227	C
Univ of Mass Dartmouth	MA	12,835	C
Univ of Memphis	TN	8,560	C
Univ of Miami	FL	34,608	HC
Univ of Mich/Ann Arbor	MI	13,864	HC+
Univ of Mich/Flint	MI	5,548	C
Univ of Minn/Duluth	MN	12,470	C
Univ of Minn/Morris	MN	12,896	VC
Univ of Minn/Twin Cities	MN	13,160	VC
Univ of Miss	MS	7,666	C
Univ of Missouri/Columbia	MO	13,782	VC
Univ of Missouri/Kansas City	MO	13,416	VC
Univ of Missouri/St. Louis	MO	11,656	VC
Univ of Mobile	AL	13,620	C
Univ of Montana	MT	9,395	C
Univ of Montevallo	AL	8,478	C
Univ of Nebr at Kearney	NE	8,286	NC
Univ of Nebr at Lincoln	NE	9,975	C+
Univ of Nebr at Omaha	NE	8,080	C
Univ of Nevada/Las Vegas	NV	11,566	C
Univ of Nevada/Reno	NV	9,792	C
Univ of New Hampshire	NH	14,828	VC
Univ of New Haven	CT	28,650	C
Univ of New Mexico	NM	9,223	C
Univ of New Orleans	LA	7,356	C
Univ of North Alabama	AL	7,972	NC
Univ of N Car at Asheville	NC	8,079	VC
Univ of N Car at Chapel Hill	NC	10,117	MC
Univ of N Car at Charlotte	NC	8,185	C
Univ of N Car at Greensboro	NC	8,248	C
Univ of N Car at Pembroke	NC	6,929	LC
Univ of N Car at Wilmington	NC	8,940	VC
Univ of N Dak	ND	8,390	C
Univ of North Florida	FL	8,769	VC
Univ of North Texas	TX	7,629	C
Univ of Northern Colo	CO	8,987	C
Univ of Northern Iowa	IA	9,834	C
Univ of Notre Dame	IN	34,442	MC
Univ of Okla	OK	9,226	VC
Univ of Oregon	OR	11,479	VC
Univ of Pennsylvania	PA	37,960	MC
Univ of Pittsburgh at Pittsburgh	PA	16,074	HC
Univ of Portland	OR	28,500	VC
Univ of PR/Rio Piedras	PR	5,730	
Univ of Puget Sound	WA	31,760	HC
Univ of Redlands	CA	32,576	VC
Univ of Rhode Island	RI	13,720	VC
Univ of Richmond	VA	30,100	MC
Univ of Rio Grande	OH	8,728	NC
Univ of Rochester	NY	32,979	HC
Univ of St. Thomas	MN	26,918	VC
Univ of St. Thomas	TX	21,952	VC
Univ of San Diego	CA	33,156	HC
Univ of Science and Arts of Okla	OK	5,982	C
Univ of Sioux Falls	SD	16,390	C
Univ of South Alabama	AL	7,760	LC
Univ of S Car at Columbia	SC	10,048	VC
Univ of S Dak	SD	7,710	C+
Univ of South Florida	FL	9,454	C
Univ of Southern Calif	CA	37,459	MC
Univ of Southern Maine	ME	11,212	C
Univ of Southern Miss	MS	8,324	C
Univ of Tampa	FL	23,982	VC
Univ of Tenn at Chattanooga	TN	7,783	C
Univ of Tenn at Knoxville	TN	8,214	C
Univ of Tenn at Martin	TN	7,748	C
Univ of Texas at Arlington	TX	7,192	C
Univ of Texas at Austin	TX	10,630	HC
Univ of Texas at El Paso	TX	5,799	NC
Univ of Texas at San Antonio	TX	9,088	NC
Univ of Texas-Pan American	TX	5,954	LC
Univ of the District of Columbia	DC	2,070	LC
Univ of the Incarnate Word	TX	21,772	LC
Univ of the Ozarks	AR	16,574	C
Univ of the Pacific	CA	31,090	VC
Univ of the South	TN	30,855	HC
Univ of Toledo	OH	12,479	NC
Univ of Tulsa	OK	22,090	VC+
Univ of Utah	UT	9,205	C
Univ of Vermont	VT	16,316	VC
Univ of Virginia	VA	11,740	MC
Univ of West Florida	FL	8,470	C
Univ of Wisc/Eau Claire	WI	8,463	VC
Univ of Wisc/Green Bay	WI	8,154	C
Univ of Wisc/La Crosse	WI	8,991	VC
Univ of Wisc/Madison	WI	8,262	VC
Univ of Wisc/Milwaukee	WI	9,427	LC
Univ of Wisc/Oshkosh	WI	6,130	LC
Univ of Wisc/Parkside	WI	6,160	LC
Univ of Wisc/Platteville	WI	8,450	C
Univ of Wisc/River Falls	WI	8,358	LC
Univ of Wisc/Stevens Point	WI	8,116	VC
Univ of Wisc/Superior	WI	7,051	C+
Univ of Wisc/Whitewater	WI	8,626	C
Univ of Wyoming	WY	8,636	C
Ursinus College	PA	34,400	VC
Utah State Univ	UT	7,371	C
Valdosta State Univ	GA	7,798	C
Valley City State Univ	ND	7,281	C
Valparaiso Univ	IN	26,118	VC+
Vanguard Univ of Southern Calif	CA	22,208	C
Vassar College	NY	37,030	MC
Virginia Commonwealth Univ	VA	9,030	C
Virginia Polytechnic Inst and State Univ	VA	9,179	C
Virginia Union Univ	VA	15,358	LC
Virginia Wesleyan College	VA	25,350	C
Viterbo Univ	WI	20,430	C
Wabash College	IN	27,932	VC
Wagner College	NY	29,900	C
Wake Forest Univ	NC	34,090	MC
Walla Walla College	WA	21,600	NC
Warner Pacific College	OR	21,900	C
Wartburg College	IA	21,165	VC
Washburn Univ of Topeka	KS	8,984	NC
Washington and Jefferson College	PA	29,570	VC
Washington and Lee Univ	VA	29,663	MC
Washington College	MD	30,540	VC
Washington State Univ	WA	11,334	C
Washington Univ in St. Louis	MO	38,293	MC
Wayland Baptist Univ	TX	11,919	NC
Wayne State College	NE	7,352	NC
Wayne State Univ	MI	11,774	C
Weber State Univ	UT	7,945	NC
Webster Univ	MO	21,848	VC
Wellesley College	MA	36,516	MC
Wells College	NY	21,122	VC
Wesleyan College	GA	17,870	VC
Wesleyan Univ	CT	35,139	MC
West Chester Univ of Pennsylvania	PA	11,164	C
West Liberty State College	WV	7,868	LC
West Texas A&M Univ	TX	7,533	C
West Virginia Univ	WV	9,370	C
West Virginia Wesleyan College	WV	22,920	C
Western Baptist College	OR	21,808	C
Western Carolina Univ	NC	6,742	C
Western Conn State Univ	CT	11,625	C
Western Illinois Univ	IL	10,363	C
Western Kentucky Univ	KY	6,834	C
Western Mich Univ	MI	12,031	C
Western New Mexico Univ	NM	5,950	C
Western Oregon Univ	OR	10,281	C
Western State College of Colo	CO	9,014	C
Western Washington Univ	WA	10,119	VC
Westfield State College	MA	10,147	C
Westminster Choir College of Rider Univ	NJ	25,400	SP
Westminster College	PA	22,960	C
Westmont College	CA	33,062	VC+
Wheaton College	IL	21,934	HC
Wheaton College	MA	36,330	HC
Whitman College	WA	32,526	HC+
Whittier College	CA	29,108	C
Whitworth College	WA	26,428	VC+
Wichita State Univ	KS	8,092	C
Wilberforce Univ	OH	14,937	LC
Wiley College	TX	8,100	LC
Wilkes Univ	PA	28,060	C
Willamette Univ	OR	32,032	VC+
William Carey College	MS	10,150	LC
William Jewell College	MO	21,320	VC
William Paterson Univ of New Jersey	NJ	14,450	C
William Tyndale College	MI	12,170	NC
Williams Baptist College	AR	11,950	C
Williams College	MA	32,270	MC
Wingate Univ	NC	21,200	C
Winona State Univ	MN		C
Winthrop Univ	SC	11,302	C
Wisc Lutheran College	WI	21,430	VC
Wittenberg Univ	OH	31,316	VC
Wright State Univ	OH	11,490	LC
Xavier Univ	OH	26,850	VC+
Xavier Univ of Louisiana	LA	17,600	C
Yale Univ	CT	37,000	MC
Yeshiva Univ	NY	21,400	C
York College	NE	14,975	C
York College of Pennsylvania	PA	14,500	C
Youngstown State Univ	OH	11,148	NC

MUSIC BUSINESS MANAGEMENT

School	ST	$IS	SR
Anderson Univ	IN	19,430	LC
Appalachian State Univ	NC	7,637	VC
Baldwin-Wallace College	OH	24,678	C
Belmont Univ	TN	21,986	VC
Berklee College of Music	MA	32,447	SP
Blackburn College	IL	13,690	C
Bradley Univ	IL	22,910	VC
Butler Univ	IN	28,250	VC+
Central Washington Univ	WA	9,768	C
College of the Ozarks	MO	3,500	VC+
Columbia College Chicago	IL	25,108	LC
DePaul Univ	IL	27,580	VC
DePauw Univ	IN	31,500	HC
Dillard Univ	LA	17,325	VC
Drake Univ	IA	25,120	VC+
Elmhurst College	IL	24,630	C
Five Towns College	NY	21,050	SP
Geneva College	PA	21,850	C
Grove City College	PA	14,228	HC
Hofstra Univ	NY	27,112	VC
Howard Univ	DC	16,505	C
Johnson C. Smith Univ	NC	18,108	C
Johnson State College	VT	11,819	LC
Lewis Univ	IL	22,950	C+
Loyola Univ New Orleans	LA	31,036	VC+
Mansfield Univ	PA	11,220	C
Marian College of Fond du Lac	WI	19,625	C
Middle Tenn State Univ	TN	8,534	C
Minn State Univ, Mankato	MN	8,803	LC
Monmouth Univ	NJ	26,334	C
Montreat College	NC	18,762	C
New York Univ	NY	39,406	MC
Northwest College	WA	18,854	C
Oakwood College	AL	14,904	C
Ohio Northern Univ	OH	27,765	VC
Peru State College	NE	6,342	NC
Point Loma Nazarene Univ	CA	21,380	VC
Quincy Univ	IL	22,330	C

School	ST	$IS	SR
St. Augustine's College	NC	12,990	LC
St. Joseph's College	IN	24,250	C
St. Mary's Univ of Minn	MN	21,535	C
S Car State Univ	SC	6,586	LC
S Dak State Univ	SD	7,782	C
Southern Nazarene Univ	OK	14,634	NC
Southern Oregon Univ	OR	10,362	C
SUNY at Potsdam	NY	12,160	C
SUNY/College at Oneonta	NY	11,870	VC
Syracuse Univ	NY	34,720	HC
Trevecca Nazarene Univ	TN	17,548	C
Univ of Charleston	WV	23,620	C
Univ of Evansville	IN	24,190	VC
Univ of Hartford	CT	31,080	C
Univ of Memphis	TN	8,560	C
Univ of New Haven	CT	28,650	C
Univ of St. Thomas	MN	26,918	VC
Univ of Southern Calif	CA	37,459	MC
Univ of the Incarnate Word	TX	21,772	LC
Univ of the Pacific	CA	31,090	VC
Valparaiso Univ	IN	26,118	VC+
Wingate Univ	NC	21,200	C
Winston-Salem State Univ	NC	8,926	LC

MUSIC EDUCATION

School	ST	$IS	SR
Abilene Christian Univ	TX	18,370	VC
Adams State College	CO	7,468	C
Adelphi Univ	NY	26,300	VC
Alabama A&M Univ	AL	5,100	LC
Alabama State Univ	AL	6,404	C
Albany State Univ	GA	5,764	C+
Alcorn State Univ	MS	7,290	C
Alderson-Broaddus College	WV	19,640	C
Alverno College	WI	18,898	C
Anderson Univ	IN	19,430	LC
Andrews Univ	MI	19,550	C
Anna Maria College	MA	26,140	LC
Appalachian State Univ	NC	7,637	VC
Arizona State Univ-Main	AZ	10,048	C
Arkansas State Univ	AR	8,450	C
Arkansas Tech Univ	AR	7,299	C
Armstrong Atlantic State Univ	GA	7,102	C
Asbury College	KY	20,704	VC
Ashland Univ	OH	24,464	C
Atlantic Union College	MA	18,868	C
Augsburg College	MN	25,298	C
Augusta State Univ	GA	2,592	C
Augustana College	IL	26,610	VC+
Augustana College	SD	21,998	VC
Azusa Pacific Univ	CA	24,720	VC
Baker Univ	KS	19,860	VC
Baldwin-Wallace College	OH	24,678	C
Ball State Univ	IN	8,660	C
Baylor Univ	TX	23,864	VC
Benedictine College	KS	20,603	C
Bennett College	NC	11,200	C
Berea College	KY	5,030	VC+
Berklee College of Music	MA	32,447	SP
Berry College	GA	21,410	VC
Bethany College	KS	18,675	LC
Bethel College	IN	19,670	C
Bethel College	MN	25,180	VC
Bethune-Cookman College	FL	16,480	LC
Biola Univ	CA	25,964	VC
Birmingham-Southern College	AL	25,364	VC+
Black Hills State Univ	SD	7,743	LC
Blackburn College	IL	13,690	C
Blue Mountain College	MS	10,226	C
Bluffton College	OH	23,694	C
Boise State Univ	ID	7,657	LC
Boston Conservatory	MA	26,900	SP
Boston Univ	MA	38,194	HC+
Bowling Green State Univ	OH	13,036	C
Bradley Univ	IL	22,910	VC
Brenau Univ Women's College	GA	21,800	C
Brewton-Parker College	GA	14,200	LC
Brigham Young Univ	UT	8,504	HC
Bucknell Univ	PA	35,262	HC+
Buena Vista Univ	IA	25,406	C
Butler Univ	IN	28,250	VC+
Cal State, Fullerton	CA	6,648	C
Cal State, San Bernardino	CA	15,238	LC
Cal State, Stanislaus	CA	9,874	C
Carnegie Mellon Univ	PA	32,682	MC
Carroll College	WI	22,740	C
Carson-Newman College	TN	16,760	C
Carthage College	WI	25,000	C
Case Western Reserve Univ	OH	32,002	MC
Catawba College	NC	20,500	C
Catholic Univ of America	DC	34,248	VC
Cedarville Univ	OH	19,954	VC
Centenary College of Louisiana	LA	23,100	VC+
Central College	IA	21,206	C
Central Conn State Univ	CT	12,090	C
Central Methodist College	MO	16,460	C
Central Mich Univ	MI	11,142	C
Central Missouri State Univ	MO	9,776	C
Central State Univ	OH	8,922	C+
Central Washington Univ	WA	9,768	C
Chapman Univ	CA	33,118	VC
Charleston Southern Univ	SC	17,122	C
Chicago State Univ	IL	10,882	C+
Christopher Newport Univ	VA	8,862	VC
CUNY/Brooklyn College	NY	4,353	C+
CUNY/Hunter College	NY	6,729	C+
CUNY/Queens College	NY	4,362	C
Claflin Univ	SC	14,838	C+
Clarion Univ of Pennsylvania	PA	11,272	LC
Clarke College	IA	23,165	C
Clearwater Christian College	FL	13,160	LC
Cleveland Inst of Music	OH	25,880	SP
Coe College	IA	27,385	VC
Coker College	SC	21,491	C
College of Mount St. Joseph	OH	22,785	C
College of New Jersey	NJ	15,950	MC
College of Notre Dame of Maryland	MD	27,700	C
College of St. Catherine	MN	24,010	VC
College of St. Rose	NY	22,864	C
College of the Ozarks	MO	3,500	VC+
Colo Christian Univ	CO	21,182	VC
Columbia College	SC	22,658	LC
Columbus State Univ	GA	7,846	C
Concord College	WV	8,136	C
Concordia College	NY	19,200	VC
Concordia College: Moorhead	MN	22,460	VC+
Concordia Univ Nebr	NE	20,302	C+
Concordia Univ, River Forest	IL	23,600	C
Concordia Univ/St.Paul	MN	24,486	C
Conn College	CT	37,900	MC
Converse College	SC	24,710	VC
Cornell College	IA	27,825	VC+
Cornerstone Univ and Grand Rapids Theological Seminary	MI	19,846	C
Culver-Stockton College	MO	17,850	C
Cumberland College	KY	16,384	C
Cumberland Univ	TN	16,910	C
Dakota State Univ	SD	7,466	C
Dana College	NE	20,280	C
David Lipscomb Univ	TN	16,158	VC
Delaware State Univ	DE	8,104	LC
Delta State Univ	MS	6,618	C
DePaul Univ	IL	27,580	VC
DePauw Univ	IN	31,500	HC
Dickinson State Univ	ND	6,338	NC
Dordt College	IA	20,170	VC
Dowling College	NY	23,870	LC
Drake Univ	IA	25,120	VC+
Drury Univ	MO	18,085	VC+
Duquesne Univ	PA	26,907	VC
East Carolina Univ	NC	8,671	C
East Central Univ	OK	4,968	C
East Texas Baptist Univ	TX	13,914	C
Eastern Kentucky Univ	KY	7,708	C
Eastern Mich Univ	MI	11,478	C
Eastern Nazarene College	MA	19,433	LC
Eastern New Mexico Univ	NM	6,762	LC
Eastern Washington Univ	WA	9,012	C
Eastman School of Music	NY	33,741	SP
Edinboro Univ of Pennsylvania	PA	10,850	LC
Elizabethtown College	PA	28,800	C
Elmhurst College	IL	24,630	C
Elon Univ	NC	22,240	VC
Emporia State Univ	KS	6,998	C
Erskine College	SC	23,136	VC
Eureka College	IL	24,980	LC
Evangel Univ	MO	15,435	C
Fairmont State	WV	8,280	LC
Fayetteville State Univ	NC	5,590	LC
Five Towns College	NY	21,050	SP
Florida A&M Univ	FL	7,564	C
Florida International Univ	FL	9,912	VC
Florida Southern College	FL	23,592	C
Florida State Univ	FL	9,028	HC
Fort Hays State Univ	KS	7,363	C
Freed-Hardeman Univ	TN		NC
Fresno Pacific Univ	CA	22,462	C
Friends Univ	KS	15,962	LC
Furman Univ	SC	28,976	HC+
Gardner-Webb Univ	NC	19,300	C
Geneva College	PA	21,850	C
George Fox Univ	OR	26,110	VC
Georgetown College	KY	22,000	VC
Georgia College and State Univ	GA	9,878	C
Georgia Southern Univ	GA	8,540	C
Georgia Southwestern State Univ	GA	6,013	C
Gettysburg College	PA	35,646	HC
Glenville State College	WV	7,812	NC
Gonzaga Univ	WA	26,766	HC
Gordon College	MA	25,982	VC+
Goshen College	IN	22,450	VC
Grace College	IN	19,825	VC
Graceland Univ	IA	19,550	C
Grambling State Univ	LA	6,538	NC
Grand Canyon Univ	AZ	30,000	LC
Grand Valley State Univ	MI	11,022	VC
Greensboro College	NC	21,750	C
Greenville College	IL	21,342	C
Grove City College	PA	14,228	HC
Gustavus Adolphus College	MN	27,120	VC+
Hannibal-LaGrange College	MO	13,940	C
Harding Univ	AR	14,890	VC
Hardin-Simmons Univ	TX	14,165	C
Hartwick College	NY	34,650	C+
Hastings College	NE	19,928	VC
Heidelberg College	OH	20,266	NC
Henderson State Univ	AR	7,386	C
Hillsdale College	MI	22,450	HC
Hofstra Univ	NY	27,112	VC
Hope College	MI	25,340	VC
Hope International Univ	CA	16,940	NC
Houghton College	NY	23,984	VC
Houston Baptist Univ	TX	16,905	C
Howard Univ	DC	16,505	C
Humboldt State Univ	CA	9,400	C
Huntingdon College	AL	18,400	VC
Huntington College	IN	23,590	C
Idaho State Univ	ID	8,128	C
Illinois State Univ	IL	10,944	C+
Immaculata Univ	PA	25,200	C
Indiana State Univ	IN	10,719	LC
Indiana Univ Bloomington	IN	12,389	VC
Indiana Univ of Pennsylvania	PA	10,489	C
Indiana Univ South Bend	IN	4,571	LC
Indiana Univ-Purdue Univ Fort Wayne	IN	5,108	LC
Indiana Wesleyan Univ	IN	19,900	C+
Inter American Univ of PR/ Fajardo Campus	PR	4,000	
Inter American Univ of PR/ Ponce Regional College	PR	3,700	
Inter American Univ of PR/ San German	PR	6,716	
Iowa State Univ	IA	10,768	VC
Iowa Wesleyan College	IA	19,990	C
Ithaca College	NY	31,730	HC
Jackson State Univ	MS	8,382	C
Jacksonville State Univ	AL	6,844	LC
Jacksonville Univ	FL	24,040	C
Jarvis Christian College	TX	9,035	NC
John Brown Univ	AR	15,080	VC
Johns Hopkins Univ	MD	38,372	MC
Johnson State College	VT	11,819	LC
Judson College	AL	14,650	C
Judson College	IL	22,050	LC
Kansas State Univ	KS	8,728	VC
Kansas Wesleyan Univ	KS	18,900	VC
Kean Univ	NJ	14,479	C
Keene State College	NH	12,212	C
Kennesaw State Univ	GA	2,724	C
Kent State Univ	OH	12,932	C
Kentucky Christian College	KY	13,472	C
Kentucky State Univ	KY	9,062	NC
Kentucky Wesleyan College	KY	17,250	C
Knoxville College	TN	6,200	LC
La Sierra Univ	CA	19,260	LC
Lakeland College	WI	17,950	C
Lamar Univ	TX	6,816	LC
Lambuth Univ	TN	16,520	C
Lander Univ	SC	10,496	C
Lawrence Univ	WI	30,900	HC
Lebanon Valley College	PA	28,870	VC
Lee Univ	TN	13,780	NC
Lenoir-Rhyne College	NC	19,186	C
Limestone College	SC	17,700	C
Lincoln Univ	MO	7,158	NC
Lincoln Univ	PA	13,320	C+
Lindenwood Univ	MO	17,050	VC
Livingstone College	NC	18,101	LC
LIU/Brooklyn Campus	NY	24,790	C
LIU/C.W. Post Campus	NY	28,282	C
Longwood Univ	VA	11,175	C
Loras College	IA	24,233	C
Louisiana College	LA	13,450	C
Louisiana State Univ and A&M College	LA	9,126	VC
Louisiana Tech Univ	LA	7,361	C
Loyola Univ New Orleans	LA	31,036	VC+
Lubbock Christian Univ	TX	15,832	C
MacMurray College	IL	20,005	LC
Madonna Univ	MI	11,504	VC
Malone College	OH	20,995	C
Mansfield Univ	PA	11,220	C
Marian College of Fond du Lac	WI	19,625	C
Mars Hill College	NC	18,600	LC
Maryville College	TN	25,960	VC
Marywood Univ	PA	26,050	C
McMurry Univ	TX	17,846	LC
Mercer Univ	GA	27,516	VC+
Mercyhurst College	PA	20,694	C
Meredith College	NC	23,065	C
Messiah College	PA	25,890	VC+
Methodist College	NC	19,526	C
Metropolitan State College of Denver	CO	2,338	LC
Miami Univ	OH	15,033	HC
Mich State Univ	MI	11,933	VC
MidAmerica Nazarene Univ	KS	18,688	C
Midland Lutheran College	NE	18,600	C
Midwestern State Univ	TX	8,045	LC
Millersville Univ of Pennsylvania	PA	11,269	C
Milligan College	TN	19,860	C+
Millikin Univ	IL	25,555	C
Minn State Univ, Mankato	MN	8,803	LC
Minn State Univ, Moorehead	MN	7,000	LC
Minot State Univ	ND	6,602	LC
Miss College	MS	14,574	C
Miss State Univ	MS	9,139	C
Miss Univ for Women	MS	5,446	LC
Miss Valley State Univ	MS	6,765	NC
Missouri Baptist Univ	MO	18,010	C
Missouri Southern State Univ	MO	8,316	C
Missouri Western State College	MO	8,522	NC
Monmouth Univ	NJ	26,334	C
Montana State Univ-Billings	MT	9,550	C
Montana State Univ-Bozeman	MT	9,515	C
Montclair State Univ	NJ	13,790	C
Moravian College	PA	28,903	VC
Morehead State Univ	KY	7,464	C
Morningside College	IA	21,610	C
Mount Mary College	WI	20,370	C
Mount Mercy College	IA	21,400	C
Mount Union College	OH	21,120	C
Mount Vernon Nazarene Univ	OH	18,925	C
Murray State Univ	KY	7,816	VC
Muskingum College	OH	20,680	C
Nazareth College of Rochester	NY	24,936	VC
Nebr Wesleyan Univ	NE	21,197	C+
New Jersey City Univ	NJ	11,850	LC
New Mexico State Univ	NM	7,932	C
New York Univ	NY	39,406	MC
Newberry College	SC	22,871	LC
Nicholls State Univ	LA	6,395	NC
Norfolk State Univ	VA	9,722	LC
N Car Agricultural and Technical State Univ	NC	6,659	LC
N Dak State Univ	ND	8,435	C
North Georgia College and State Univ	GA	6,984	C
Northeastern State Univ	OK	4,950	LC
Northern Arizona Univ	AZ	9,002	C
Northern Illinois Univ	IL	11,472	C
Northern Mich Univ	MI	10,834	C
Northern State Univ	SD	7,117	LC
Northland College	WI	22,170	C+
Northwest Missouri State Univ	MO	9,334	C
Northwest Nazarene Univ	ID	20,360	VC
Northwestern College	MN	22,820	C+
Northwestern College of Iowa	IA	19,640	C+
Northwestern Okla State Univ	OK	5,433	NC
Northwestern State Univ of Louisiana	LA	6,331	NC
Northwestern Univ	IL	37,491	MC
Nyack College	NY	18,540	C
Oakland City Univ	IN	16,980	NC
Oakland Univ	MI	10,800	C
Oakwood College	AL	14,904	C
Oberlin College	OH	36,938	MC
Ohio Northern Univ	OH	27,765	VC
Ohio State Univ	OH	13,080	VC+
Ohio Univ	OH	14,448	C
Ohio Wesleyan Univ	OH	32,550	VC+
Okla Baptist Univ	OK	15,220	VC
Okla Christian Univ	OK	17,690	NC
Okla City Univ	OK	19,580	VC
Okla Panhandle State Univ	OK	5,370	C
Okla State Univ	OK	9,216	VC
Okla Wesleyan Univ	OK	14,100	LC
Old Dominion Univ	VA	10,441	C
Oral Roberts Univ	OK	18,490	C
Otterbein College	OH	26,085	C
Ouachita Baptist Univ	AR	18,900	VC
Pacific Lutheran Univ	WA	25,715	VC
Palm Beach Atlantic Univ	FL	20,690	C
Penn State Univ/Univ Park Campus	PA	15,646	HC
Peru State College	NE	6,342	NC
Pfeiffer Univ	NC	18,980	C
Pittsburg State Univ	KS	7,128	NC
Plymouth State Univ	NH	12,298	LC
Pontifical Catholic Univ of PR/Ponce	PR	7,298	
Presbyterian College	SC	25,920	VC
Providence College	RI	30,604	HC
Quincy Univ	IL	22,330	C
Rhode Island College	RI	11,565	C
Roberts Wesleyan College	NY	23,190	C+
Rocky Mountain College	MT	19,015	C
Roosevelt Univ	IL	22,580	VC
Rowan Univ	NJ	14,506	VC
Saginaw Valley State Univ	MI	11,055	C
St. Ambrose Univ	IA	22,800	C
St. Augustine's College	NC	12,990	LC
St. Cloud State Univ	MN	8,362	C
St. Joseph's College	IN	24,250	C

ST = STATE **$IS** = IN-STATE COSTS **SR** = SELECTOR RATING

School	ST	$IS	SR
St. Mary-of-the-Woods College	IN	23,280	C
St. Mary's Univ of Minn	MN	21,535	C
St. Norbert College	WI	25,810	C
St. Olaf College	MN	28,500	HC
St. Vincent College	PA	25,530	VC
St. Xavier Univ	IL	23,144	C
Samford Univ	AL	18,648	VC
Schreiner Univ	TX	20,440	C
Seattle Pacific Univ	WA	25,944	VC
Seton Hill Univ	PA	24,930	C
Shenandoah Univ	VA	25,190	NC
Shepherd College	WV	8,608	C
Shorter College	GA	17,370	C
Siena Heights Univ	MI	16,140	LC
Silver Lake College of the Holy Family	WI	18,450	LC
Simpson College	IA	23,658	C+
Slippery Rock Univ of Pennsylvania	PA	10,343	LC
S Car State Univ	SC	6,586	LC
S Dak State Univ	SD	7,782	C
Southeast Missouri State Univ	MO	9,704	C
Southeastern College	FL	11,648	LC
Southeastern Louisiana Univ	LA	6,791	LC
Southeastern Okla State Univ	OK	6,147	C
Southern Adventist Univ	TN	17,080	C
Southern Arkansas Univ	AR	6,956	C
Southern Methodist Univ	TX	34,210	HC
Southern Nazarene Univ	OK	14,634	NC
Southern Univ and A&M College	LA	7,372	LC
Southern Univ at New Orleans	LA	995	NC
Southern Utah Univ	UT	8,194	C
Southern Wesleyan Univ	SC	19,940	C
Southwest Baptist Univ	MO	15,371	C
Southwest Minn State Univ	MN	9,106	VC
Southwest Missouri State Univ	MO	8,918	C
Southwestern College	KS	19,560	C
Southwestern Okla State Univ	OK	4,801	C
Spring Arbor Univ	MI	20,206	C
SUNY at Potsdam	NY	12,160	C
SUNY/College at Fredonia	NY	11,562	VC
State Univ of West Georgia	GA	7,622	C
Sterling College	KS	18,763	C
Stetson Univ	FL	29,495	VC
Susquehanna Univ	PA	29,990	VC
Syracuse Univ	NY	34,720	HC
Tabor College	KS	19,500	NC
Talladega College	AL	10,110	LC
Taylor Univ	IN	23,820	VC+
Temple Univ	PA	15,912	C
Tenn Tech Univ	TN	8,670	VC
Tenn Wesleyan College	TN	16,540	C
Texas A&M Univ at Commerce	TX	8,994	C
Texas A&M Univ at Kingsville	TX	6,740	LC
Texas Christian Univ	TX	23,410	VC
Texas State Univ	TX	9,320	VC
Texas Tech Univ	TX	10,768	VC
Texas Wesleyan Univ	TX	16,245	C
Toccoa Falls College	GA	15,600	C
Towson Univ	MD	12,694	VC
Trevecca Nazarene Univ	TN	17,548	C
Trinity Christian College	IL	21,640	VC
Troy State Univ	AL	7,696	C
Union College	KY	15,920	C
Union College	NE	17,130	C
Union Univ	TN	18,800	VC
Universidad Adventista de las Antillas	PR	5,460	
Univ of Akron	OH	13,134	NC
Univ of Alabama	AL	9,040	C+
Univ of Alaska Anchorage	AK	9,100	NC
Univ of Alaska Fairbanks	AK	9,295	C
Univ of Arizona	AZ	10,413	VC
Univ of Arkansas	AR	9,855	VC
Univ of Arkansas at Monticello	AR	5,940	NC
Univ of Arkansas at Pine Bluff	AR	7,925	C
Univ of Central Arkansas	AR	6,388	C
Univ of Central Florida	FL	10,038	VC
Univ of Central Okla	OK	9,434	C
Univ of Charleston	WV	23,620	C
Univ of Cincinnati	OH	14,736	C
Univ of Colo at Boulder	CO	10,774	VC
Univ of Conn	CT	14,608	VC
Univ of Dayton	OH	24,850	VC
Univ of Delaware	DE	12,616	HC
Univ of Evansville	IN	24,190	VC
Univ of Florida	FL	8,580	MC
Univ of Georgia	GA	8,656	VC
Univ of Hartford	CT	31,080	C
Univ of Idaho	ID	8,216	C
Univ of Illinois at Urbana-Champaign	IL	11,316	HC+
Univ of Indianapolis	IN	22,560	VC
Univ of Iowa	IA	10,923	VC
Univ of Kansas	KS	8,923	VC
Univ of Kentucky	KY	7,765	C
Univ of Louisiana at Lafayette	LA	5,826	C
Univ of Louisiana at Monroe	LA	5,207	NC
Univ of Louisville	KY	8,762	VC
Univ of Maine	ME	12,080	C+
Univ of Mary	ND	12,900	C+
Univ of Mary Hardin-Baylor	TX	17,268	C
Univ of Maryland/College Park	MD	14,227	HC
Univ of Maryland/Eastern Shore	MD	9,964	C
Univ of Miami	FL	34,608	HC
Univ of Mich/Ann Arbor	MI	13,864	HC+
Univ of Mich/Flint	MI	5,548	C
Univ of Minn/Duluth	MN	12,470	C
Univ of Minn/Twin Cities	MN	13,160	VC
Univ of Missouri/Columbia	MO	13,782	VC
Univ of Missouri/Kansas City	MO	13,416	VC
Univ of Missouri/St. Louis	MO	11,656	VC
Univ of Montana	MT	9,395	C
Univ of Montana--Western	MT	8,073	NC
Univ of Montevallo	AL	8,478	C
Univ of Nebr at Kearney	NE	8,286	NC
Univ of Nebr at Lincoln	NE	9,975	C+
Univ of Nevada/Reno	NV	9,792	C
Univ of New Hampshire	NH	14,828	VC
Univ of New Mexico	NM	9,223	C
Univ of New Orleans	LA	7,356	C
Univ of North Alabama	AL	7,972	NC
Univ of N Car at Chapel Hill	NC	10,117	MC
Univ of N Car at Charlotte	NC	8,185	C
Univ of N Car at Greensboro	NC	8,248	C
Univ of N Car at Pembroke	NC	6,929	LC
Univ of N Car at Wilmington	NC	8,940	VC
Univ of N Dak	ND	8,390	C
Univ of North Florida	FL	8,769	VC
Univ of Northern Iowa	IA	9,834	C
Univ of Okla	OK	9,226	VC
Univ of Oregon	OR	11,479	VC
Univ of Portland	OR	28,500	VC
Univ of Puget Sound	WA	31,760	HC
Univ of Rhode Island	RI	13,720	VC
Univ of Rio Grande	OH	8,728	NC
Univ of Rochester	NY	32,979	HC
Univ of St. Thomas	MN	26,918	VC
Univ of St. Thomas	TX	21,952	VC
Univ of Sioux Falls	SD	16,390	C
Univ of S Car at Columbia	SC	10,048	VC
Univ of S Dak	SD	7,710	C+
Univ of South Florida	FL	9,454	C
Univ of Southern Calif	CA	37,459	MC
Univ of Southern Colo	CO	7,821	LC
Univ of Southern Maine	ME	11,212	C
Univ of Southern Miss	MS	8,324	LC
Univ of Tenn at Chattanooga	TN	7,783	C
Univ of Tenn at Knoxville	TN	8,214	C
Univ of the Incarnate Word	TX	21,772	LC
Univ of the Pacific	CA	31,090	VC
Univ of Toledo	OH	12,479	NC
Univ of Tulsa	OK	22,090	VC+
Univ of Vermont	VT	16,316	VC
Univ of Washington	WA	10,361	VC
Univ of West Florida	FL	8,470	C
Univ of Wisc/Eau Claire	WI	8,463	VC
Univ of Wisc/Milwaukee	WI	9,427	LC
Univ of Wisc/Oshkosh	WI	6,130	LC
Univ of Wisc/Platteville	WI	8,450	C
Univ of Wisc/River Falls	WI	8,358	LC
Univ of Wisc/Stevens Point	WI	8,116	VC
Univ of Wisc/Superior	WI	7,051	C+
Univ of Wisc/Whitewater	WI	8,626	C
Univ of Wyoming	WY	8,636	C
Utah State Univ	UT	7,371	C
Valdosta State Univ	GA	7,798	C
Valparaiso Univ	IN	26,118	VC+
VanderCook College of Music	IL	19,410	SP
Virginia Union Univ	VA	15,358	LC
Viterbo Univ	WI	20,430	C
Walla Walla College	WA	21,600	NC
Warner Pacific College	OR	21,900	C
Warner Southern College	FL	16,738	LC
Wartburg College	IA	21,165	VC
Washburn Univ of Topeka	KS	8,984	NC
Wayland Baptist Univ	TX	11,919	NC
Wayne State College	NE	7,352	NC
Weber State Univ	UT	7,945	NC
Webster Univ	MO	21,848	VC
West Chester Univ of Pennsylvania	PA	11,164	C
West Liberty State College	WV	7,868	LC
West Texas A&M Univ	TX	7,533	C
West Virginia Wesleyan College	WV	22,920	C
Western Carolina Univ	NC	6,742	C
Western Conn State Univ	CT	11,625	C
Western Mich Univ	MI	12,031	C
Western State College of Colo	CO	9,014	C
Western Washington Univ	WA	10,119	VC
Westfield State College	MA	10,147	C
Westminster Choir College of Rider Univ	NJ	25,400	SP
Westminster College	PA	22,960	C
Westmont College	CA	33,062	VC+
Wheaton College	IL	21,934	HC
Whitworth College	WA	26,428	VC+
Wichita State Univ	KS	8,092	C
Wiley College	TX	8,100	LC
Wilkes Univ	PA	28,060	C
Willamette Univ	OR	32,032	VC+
William Carey College	MS	10,150	LC
William Jewell College	MO	21,320	VC
William Paterson Univ of New Jersey	NJ	14,450	C
Wingate Univ	NC	21,200	C
Winona State Univ	MN		C
Winston-Salem State Univ	NC	8,926	LC
Winthrop Univ	SC	11,302	C
Wittenberg Univ	OH	31,316	VC
Wright State Univ	OH	11,490	LC
Xavier Univ	OH	26,850	VC+
Xavier Univ of Louisiana	LA	17,600	C
York College	NE	14,975	C
Youngstown State Univ	OH	11,148	NC

MUSIC HISTORY AND APPRECIATION

School	ST	$IS	SR
Baldwin-Wallace College	OH	24,678	C
Bard College	NY	37,352	HC+
Baylor Univ	TX	23,864	VC
Boston Univ	MA	38,194	HC+
Bucknell Univ	PA	35,262	HC+
Cal State, San Bernardino	CA	15,238	LC
Catholic Univ of America	DC	34,248	VC
Florida State Univ	FL	9,028	HC
Hofstra Univ	NY	27,112	VC
Howard Univ	DC	16,505	C
Johnson State College	VT	11,819	LC
McKendree College	IL	21,120	VC
Nazareth College of Rochester	NY	24,936	VC
New England Conservatory of Music	MA	35,000	SP
Oberlin College	OH	36,938	MC
Ohio State Univ	OH	13,080	VC+
Ohio Univ	OH	14,448	C
Rice Univ	TX	27,550	MC
Rollins College	FL	34,300	VC
Roosevelt Univ	IL	22,580	VC
Simon's Rock College of Bard	MA	36,580	HC
Temple Univ	PA	15,912	C
Texas Tech Univ	TX	10,768	VC
Univ of Calif at Los Angeles	CA	15,330	MC
Univ of Calif at San Diego	CA	14,127	HC
Univ of Cincinnati	OH	14,736	C
Univ of Hartford	CT	31,080	C
Univ of Idaho	ID	8,216	C
Univ of Illinois at Urbana-Champaign	IL	11,316	HC+
Univ of Kansas	KS	8,923	VC
Univ of Mich/Ann Arbor	MI	13,864	HC+
Univ of Mich/Dearborn	MI	6,843	VC
Univ of New Hampshire	NH	14,828	VC
Univ of North Texas	TX	7,629	C
Univ of the Pacific	CA	31,090	VC
Univ of Washington	WA	10,361	VC
Vanderbilt Univ	TN	37,897	MC
Western Mich Univ	MI	12,031	C
Wright State Univ	OH	11,490	LC
Youngstown State Univ	OH	11,148	NC

MUSIC PERFORMANCE

School	ST	$IS	SR
Adams State College	CO	7,468	C
Anderson Univ	IN	19,430	LC
Andrews Univ	MI	19,550	C
Anna Maria College	MA	26,140	LC
Appalachian State Univ	NC	7,637	VC
Arizona State Univ-Main	AZ	10,048	C
Arkansas State Univ	AR	8,450	C
Augustana College	IL	26,610	VC+
Baldwin-Wallace College	OH	24,678	C
Ball State Univ	IN	8,660	C
Bard College	NY	37,352	HC+
Barry Univ	FL	24,100	LC
Baylor Univ	TX	23,864	VC
Belmont Univ	TN	21,986	VC
Berklee College of Music	MA	32,447	SP
Berry College	GA	21,410	VC
Bethel College	IN	19,670	C
Biola Univ	CA	25,964	VC
Blackburn College	IL	13,690	C
Boston Conservatory	MA	26,900	SP
Boston Univ	MA	38,194	HC+
Bowling Green State Univ	OH	13,036	C
Bradley Univ	IL	22,910	VC
Brenau Univ Women's College	GA	21,800	C
Brewton-Parker College	GA	14,200	LC
Bucknell Univ	PA	35,262	HC+
Butler Univ	IN	28,250	VC+
Cal State, Los Angeles	CA	5,778	C
Cal State, San Bernardino	CA	15,238	LC
Cal State, Stanislaus	CA	9,874	C
Catholic Univ of America	DC	34,248	VC
Centenary College of Louisiana	LA	23,100	VC+
Chapman Univ	CA	33,118	VC
Christopher Newport Univ	VA	8,862	VC
CUNY/Brooklyn College	NY	4,353	C+
Clayton College and State Univ	GA	2,441	LC
Columbia College	SC	22,658	LC
Columbus State Univ	GA	7,846	C
Concordia College: Moorhead	MN	22,460	VC+
Cornerstone Univ and Grand Rapids Theological Seminary	MI	19,846	C
Dallas Baptist Univ	TX	15,300	VC
Delta State Univ	MS	6,618	C
DePauw Univ	IN	31,500	HC
Dillard Univ	LA	17,325	VC
Drake Univ	IA	25,120	VC+
Duquesne Univ	PA	26,907	VC
East Carolina Univ	NC	8,671	C
East Texas Baptist Univ	TX	13,914	C
Eastern Mich Univ	MI	11,478	C
Eastern Nazarene College	MA	19,433	LC
Eastern New Mexico Univ	NM	6,762	LC
Eastern Washington Univ	WA	9,012	C
Eastman School of Music	NY	33,741	SP
Elon Univ	NC	22,240	VC
Emory & Henry College	VA	21,950	C
Evangel Univ	MO	15,435	C
Five Towns College	NY	21,050	SP
Florida State Univ	FL	9,028	HC
Fort Hays State Univ	KS	7,363	C
Furman Univ	SC	28,976	HC+
George Washington Univ	DC	41,030	MC
Gordon College	MA	25,982	VC+
Grace Bible College	MI	15,890	C
Grove City College	PA	14,228	HC
Hannibal-LaGrange College	MO	13,940	C
Hofstra Univ	NY	27,112	VC
Houghton College	NY	23,984	VC
Houston Baptist Univ	TX	16,905	C
Huntington College	IN	23,590	C
Idaho State Univ	ID	8,128	C
Illinois State Univ	IL	10,944	C+
Indiana Univ Bloomington	IN	12,389	VC
Indiana Univ of Pennsylvania	PA	10,489	C
Inter American Univ of PR/ Metropolitan Campus	PR		
Ithaca College	NY	31,730	HC
Jacksonville Univ	FL	24,040	C
Johns Hopkins Univ	MD	38,372	MC
Johnson State College	VT	11,819	LC
Keene State College	NH	12,212	C
Kennesaw State Univ	GA	2,724	C
Kentucky Christian College	KY	13,472	C
Kentucky State Univ	KY	9,062	NC
La Sierra Univ	CA	19,260	LC
LaGrange College	GA	20,500	C
Lawrence Univ	WI	30,900	HC
Louisiana Tech Univ	LA	7,361	C
Loyola Univ New Orleans	LA	31,036	VC+
Manhattan School of Music	NY	31,500	SP
Mannes College of Music	NY	31,930	SP
Mansfield Univ	PA	11,220	C
Mars Hill College	NC	18,600	LC
Maryville College	TN	25,960	VC
Marywood Univ	PA	26,050	C
McMurry Univ	TX	17,846	LC
Meredith College	NC	23,065	C
Methodist College	NC	19,526	C
Metropolitan State College of Denver	CO	2,338	LC
Miami Univ	OH	15,033	HC
Mich State Univ	MI	11,933	VC
Millikin Univ	IL	25,555	C
Missouri Baptist Univ	MO	18,010	C
Montana State Univ-Billings	MT	9,550	C
Montclair State Univ	NJ	13,790	C
Montreat College	NC	18,762	C
Mount Union College	OH	21,120	C
Mount Vernon Nazarene Univ	OH	18,925	C
Nazareth College of Rochester	NY	24,936	VC
New England Conservatory of Music	MA	35,000	SP
New York Univ	NY	39,406	MC
Newberry College	SC	22,871	LC
Northwestern College	MN	22,820	C+
Northwestern Univ	IL	37,491	MC
Nyack College	NY	18,540	C
Oakwood College	AL	14,904	C
Oberlin College	OH	36,938	MC
Ohio Northern Univ	OH	27,765	VC
Ohio State Univ	OH	13,080	VC+
Old Dominion Univ	VA	10,441	C
Oral Roberts Univ	OK	18,490	C
Otterbein College	OH	26,085	C
Pacific Lutheran Univ	WA	25,715	VC
Palm Beach Atlantic Univ	FL	20,690	C
Rice Univ	TX	27,550	MC
Rocky Mountain College	MT	19,015	C

ST = STATE $IS = IN-STATE COSTS SR = SELECTOR RATING

School	ST	$IS	SR
Rollins College	FL	34,300	VC
Roosevelt Univ	IL	22,580	VC
St. Mary's Univ of Minn	MN	21,535	C
St. Olaf College	MN	28,500	HC
St. Vincent College	PA	25,530	VC
Sam Houston State Univ	TX	7,142	C
Samford Univ	AL	18,648	VC
Shenandoah Univ	VA	25,190	NC
Shepherd College	WV	8,608	C
Simon's Rock College of Bard	MA	36,580	HC
Simpson College	IA	23,658	C+
Southeast Missouri State Univ	MO	9,704	C
Southern Methodist Univ	TX	34,210	HC
Southern Nazarene Univ	OK	14,634	NC
Southwest Missouri State Univ	MO	8,918	C
SUNY at Potsdam	NY	12,160	C
SUNY/Univ at Binghamton	NY	12,787	HC
SUNY/Univ at Buffalo	NY	12,563	VC
Stetson Univ	FL	29,495	VC
Susquehanna Univ	PA	29,990	VC
Syracuse Univ	NY	34,720	HC
Talladega College	AL	10,110	LC
Temple Univ	PA	15,912	C
Texas Christian Univ	TX	23,410	VC
Texas State Univ	TX	9,320	VC
Texas Tech Univ	TX	10,768	VC
Toccoa Falls College	GA	15,600	C
Trinity Christian College	IL	21,640	VC
Truman State Univ	MO	9,728	HC+
Union College	NE	17,130	C
Union Univ	TN	18,800	VC
Univ of Alaska Fairbanks	AK	9,295	C
Univ of Arizona	AZ	10,413	VC
Univ of Calif at Santa Barbara	CA	11,732	VC
Univ of Dayton	OH	24,850	VC
Univ of Denver	CO	32,148	VC
Univ of Evansville	IN	24,190	VC
Univ of Georgia	GA	8,656	VC
Univ of Hartford	CT	31,080	C
Univ of Idaho	ID	8,216	C
Univ of Indianapolis	IN	22,560	VC
Univ of Kansas	KS	8,923	VC
Univ of Kentucky	KY	7,765	C
Univ of Maine	ME	12,080	C+
Univ of Mary Hardin-Baylor	TX	17,268	C
Univ of Maryland/College Park	MD	14,227	HC
Univ of Mass Lowell	MA	11,937	VC
Univ of Miami	FL	34,608	HC
Univ of Mich/Ann Arbor	MI	13,864	HC+
Univ of Minn/Duluth	MN	12,470	C
Univ of Missouri/Kansas City	MO	13,416	VC
Univ of Montana	MT	9,395	C
Univ of New Hampshire	NH	14,828	VC
Univ of N Car at Chapel Hill	NC	10,117	MC
Univ of N Car at Charlotte	NC	8,185	C
Univ of N Car at Greensboro	NC	8,248	C
Univ of N Car at Wilmington	NC	8,940	VC
Univ of N Dak	ND	8,390	C
Univ of North Florida	FL	8,769	VC
Univ of North Texas	TX	7,629	C
Univ of Northern Iowa	IA	9,834	C
Univ of Oregon	OR	11,479	VC
Univ of Puget Sound	WA	31,760	HC
Univ of S Car at Columbia	SC	10,048	VC
Univ of S Dak	SD	7,710	C+
Univ of Southern Calif	CA	37,459	MC
Univ of Southern Colo	CO	7,821	LC
Univ of Southern Maine	ME	11,212	C
Univ of the Arts	PA	29,510	SP
Univ of the Pacific	CA	31,090	VC
Univ of Tulsa	OK	22,090	VC+
Univ of Washington	WA	10,361	VC
Univ of Wisc/Superior	WI	7,051	C+
Univ of Wyoming	WY	8,636	C
Valdosta State Univ	GA	7,798	C
Vanderbilt Univ	TN	37,897	MC
Virginia State Univ	VA	10,358	C
Viterbo Univ	WI	20,430	C
Walla Walla College	WA	21,600	NC
Wartburg College	IA	21,165	VC
Washburn Univ of Topeka	KS	8,984	NC
Washington State Univ	WA	11,334	C
Weber State Univ	UT	7,945	NC
West Chester Univ of Pennsylvania	PA	11,164	C
Western Conn State Univ	CT	11,625	C
Western Kentucky Univ	KY	6,834	C
Western Mich Univ	MI	12,031	C
Westminster Choir College of Rider Univ	NJ	25,400	SP
Westminster College	PA	22,960	C
Wiley College	TX	8,100	LC
Willamette Univ	OR	32,032	VC+
William Carey College	MS	10,150	LC
William Tyndale College	MI	12,170	NC
York College	NE	14,975	C
Youngstown State Univ	OH	11,148	NC

MUSIC TECHNOLOGY

School	ST	$IS	SR
Bloomfield College	NJ	19,250	LC
Brigham Young Univ	UT	8,504	HC
Cal State, San Bernardino	CA	15,238	LC
Cal State, Stanislaus	CA	9,874	C
Cogswell Polytechnical College	CA	14,400	LC
Conn College	CT	37,900	MC
LaGrange College	GA	20,500	C
Malone College	OH	20,995	C
New York Univ	NY	39,406	MC
Northwestern Univ	IL	37,491	MC
Stevens Inst of Technology	NJ	35,300	HC+
Univ of Calif at San Diego	CA	14,127	HC
Univ of Hartford	CT	31,080	C
Univ of N Car at Asheville	NC	8,079	VC

MUSIC THEORY AND COMPOSITION

School	ST	$IS	SR
Arizona State Univ-Main	AZ	10,048	C
Baldwin-Wallace College	OH	24,678	C
Bard College	NY	37,352	HC+
Baylor Univ	TX	23,864	VC
Berklee College of Music	MA	32,447	SP
Biola Univ	CA	25,964	VC
Boston Conservatory	MA	26,900	SP
Boston Univ	MA	38,194	HC+
Bowling Green State Univ	OH	13,036	C
Bradley Univ	IL	22,910	VC
Brigham Young Univ	UT	8,504	HC
Bucknell Univ	PA	35,262	HC+
Butler Univ	IN	28,250	VC+
Cal State, Stanislaus	CA	9,874	C
Catholic Univ of America	DC	34,248	VC
Central Washington Univ	WA	9,768	C
Christopher Newport Univ	VA	8,862	VC
CUNY/Brooklyn College	NY	4,353	C+
Clayton College and State Univ	GA	2,441	LC
Cornerstone Univ and Grand Rapids Theological Seminary	MI	19,846	C
DePauw Univ	IN	31,500	HC
East Carolina Univ	NC	8,671	C
Eastman School of Music	NY	33,741	SP
Emory & Henry College	VA	21,950	C
Five Towns College	NY	21,050	SP
Florida State Univ	FL	9,028	HC
Fort Hays State Univ	KS	7,363	C
Furman Univ	SC	28,976	HC+
Hofstra Univ	NY	27,112	VC
Houghton College	NY	23,984	VC
Houston Baptist Univ	TX	16,905	C
Illinois Wesleyan Univ	IL	30,380	HC+
Indiana Univ Bloomington	IN	12,389	VC
Indiana Univ South Bend	IN	4,571	LC
Ithaca College	NY	31,730	HC
Jacksonville Univ	FL	24,040	C
Johns Hopkins Univ	MD	38,372	MC
Juilliard School	NY	30,385	SP
Lawrence Univ	WI	30,900	HC
Loyola Univ New Orleans	LA	31,036	VC+
Manhattan School of Music	NY	31,500	SP
Mannes College of Music	NY	31,930	SP
Mich State Univ	MI	11,933	VC
Miss College	MS	14,574	C
Montclair State Univ	NJ	13,790	C
New England Conservatory of Music	MA	35,000	SP
New York Univ	NY	39,406	MC
Newberry College	SC	22,871	LC
Northwestern Univ	IL	37,491	MC
Nyack College	NY	18,540	C
Oberlin College	OH	36,938	MC
Ohio Northern Univ	OH	27,765	VC
Ohio State Univ	OH	13,080	VC+
Ohio Univ	OH	14,448	C
Old Dominion Univ	VA	10,441	C
Oral Roberts Univ	OK	18,490	C
Pacific Lutheran Univ	WA	25,715	VC
Palm Beach Atlantic Univ	FL	20,690	C
Rice Univ	TX	27,550	MC
Roosevelt Univ	IL	22,580	VC
St. Olaf College	MN	28,500	HC
Sam Houston State Univ	TX	7,142	C
Samford Univ	AL	18,648	VC
Shenandoah Univ	VA	25,190	NC
Shepherd College	WV	8,608	C
Simon's Rock College of Bard	MA	36,580	HC
Southeast Missouri State Univ	MO	9,704	C
Southern Methodist Univ	TX	34,210	HC
SUNY at Potsdam	NY	12,160	C
Stetson Univ	FL	29,495	VC
Syracuse Univ	NY	34,720	HC
Temple Univ	PA	15,912	C
Texas Christian Univ	TX	23,410	VC
Texas Tech Univ	TX	10,768	VC
Union Univ	TN	18,800	VC
Univ of Arizona	AZ	10,413	VC
Univ of Calif at Santa Barbara	CA	11,732	VC
Univ of Cincinnati	OH	14,736	C
Univ of Dayton	OH	24,850	VC
Univ of Delaware	DE	12,616	HC
Univ of Georgia	GA	8,656	VC
Univ of Hartford	CT	31,080	C
Univ of Houston	TX	9,818	C
Univ of Idaho	ID	8,216	C
Univ of Illinois at Urbana-Champaign	IL	11,316	HC+
Univ of Kansas	KS	8,923	VC
Univ of Miami	FL	34,608	HC
Univ of Mich/Ann Arbor	MI	13,864	HC+
Univ of Missouri/Kansas City	MO	13,416	VC
Univ of New Hampshire	NH	14,828	VC
Univ of N Car at Greensboro	NC	8,248	C
Univ of North Texas	TX	7,629	C
Univ of Northern Iowa	IA	9,834	C
Univ of Oregon	OR	11,479	VC
Univ of Rochester	NY	32,979	HC
Univ of Southern Calif	CA	37,459	MC
Univ of Southern Colo	CO	7,821	LC
Univ of Texas at Austin	TX	10,630	HC
Univ of the Arts	PA	29,510	SP
Univ of the Pacific	CA	31,090	VC
Univ of Wyoming	WY	8,636	C
Vanderbilt Univ	TN	37,897	MC
Wartburg College	IA	21,165	VC
Washington State Univ	WA	11,334	C
Washington Univ in St. Louis	MO	38,293	MC
West Chester Univ of Pennsylvania	PA	11,164	C
West Texas A&M Univ	TX	7,533	C
Western Mich Univ	MI	12,031	C
Westminster Choir College of Rider Univ	NJ	25,400	SP
Westminster College	PA	22,960	C
Willamette Univ	OR	32,032	VC+
Wright State Univ	OH	11,490	LC
Youngstown State Univ	OH	11,148	NC

MUSIC THERAPY

School	ST	$IS	SR
Alverno College	WI	18,898	C
Anna Maria College	MA	26,140	LC
Appalachian State Univ	NC	7,637	VC
Arizona State Univ-Main	AZ	10,048	C
Augsburg College	MN	25,298	C
Baldwin-Wallace College	OH	24,678	C
Berklee College of Music	MA	32,447	SP
Chapman Univ	CA	33,118	VC
Charleston Southern Univ	SC	17,122	C
Duquesne Univ	PA	26,907	VC
East Carolina Univ	NC	8,671	C
Eastern Mich Univ	MI	11,478	C
Elizabethtown College	PA	28,800	C
Florida State Univ	FL	9,028	HC
Georgia College and State Univ	GA	9,878	C
Howard Univ	DC	16,505	C
Immaculata Univ	PA	25,200	C
Indiana Univ-Purdue Univ Fort Wayne	IN	5,108	LC
Louisiana College	LA	13,450	C
Loyola Univ New Orleans	LA	31,036	VC+
Mansfield Univ	PA	11,220	C
Maryville Univ of St. Louis	MO	22,090	VC
Marywood Univ	PA	26,050	C
Mich State Univ	MI	11,933	VC
Molloy College	NY	15,180	C
Montclair State Univ	NJ	13,790	C
Nazareth College of Rochester	NY	24,936	VC
Queens Univ of Charlotte	NC	21,840	C
St. Mary-of-the-Woods College	IN	23,280	C
Sam Houston State Univ	TX	7,142	C
Seton Hill Univ	PA	24,930	C
Shenandoah Univ	VA	25,190	NC
Southern Methodist Univ	TX	34,210	HC
Southwestern Okla State Univ	OK	4,801	C
Temple Univ	PA	15,912	C
Texas Woman's Univ	TX	7,804	LC
Univ of Alabama	AL	9,040	C+
Univ of Dayton	OH	24,850	VC
Univ of Evansville	IN	24,190	VC
Univ of Georgia	GA	8,656	VC
Univ of Kansas	KS	8,923	VC
Univ of Miami	FL	34,608	HC
Univ of Minn/Twin Cities	MN	13,160	VC
Univ of Missouri/Kansas City	MO	13,416	VC
Univ of N Dak	ND	8,390	C
Univ of the Incarnate Word	TX	21,772	LC
Univ of the Pacific	CA	31,090	VC
Univ of Wisc/Eau Claire	WI	8,463	VC
Univ of Wisc/Oshkosh	WI	6,130	LC
Utah State Univ	UT	7,371	C
Wartburg College	IA	21,165	VC
West Texas A&M Univ	TX	7,533	C
Western Mich Univ	MI	12,031	C
William Carey College	MS	10,150	LC

MUSICAL THEATER

School	ST	$IS	SR
Adrian College	MI	21,950	C
Ashland Univ	OH	24,464	C
Baldwin-Wallace College	OH	24,678	C
Birmingham-Southern College	AL	25,364	VC+
Boston Conservatory	MA	26,900	SP
Brenau Univ Women's College	GA	21,800	C
Brigham Young Univ	UT	8,504	HC
Cal State, Chico	CA	8,598	LC
Catawba College	NC	20,500	C
Catholic Univ of America	DC	34,248	VC
Coastal Carolina Univ	SC	11,040	C
Coker College	SC	21,491	C
College of Santa Fe	NM	25,293	C+
College of the Ozarks	MO	3,500	VC+
Elon Univ	NC	22,240	VC
Emerson College	MA	32,205	HC
Florida State Univ	FL	9,028	HC
Friends Univ	KS	15,962	LC
Howard Univ	DC	16,505	C
Huntingdon College	AL	18,400	VC
Illinois Wesleyan Univ	IL	30,380	HC+
Ithaca College	NY	31,730	HC
Lees-McRae College	NC	17,106	LC
Marietta College	OH	27,047	C
Mars Hill College	NC	18,600	LC
Mercyhurst College	PA	20,694	C
Meredith College	NC	23,065	C
Millikin Univ	IL	25,555	C
Otterbein College	OH	26,085	C
Ouachita Baptist Univ	AR	18,900	VC
Palm Beach Atlantic Univ	FL	20,690	C
Roosevelt Univ	IL	22,580	VC
Russell Sage College	NY	26,811	C
Sam Houston State Univ	TX	7,142	C
Samford Univ	AL	18,648	VC
Seton Hill Univ	PA	24,930	C
Shenandoah Univ	VA	25,190	NC
Shorter College	GA	17,370	C
SUNY/Univ at Buffalo	NY	12,563	VC
Syracuse Univ	NY	34,720	HC
Univ of Arizona	AZ	10,413	VC
Univ of Hartford	CT	31,080	C
Univ of Indianapolis	IN	22,560	VC
Univ of Miami	FL	34,608	HC
Univ of Mich/Ann Arbor	MI	13,864	HC+
Univ of the Arts	PA	29,510	SP
Univ of Tulsa	OK	22,090	VC+
Viterbo Univ	WI	20,430	C
Weber State Univ	UT	7,945	NC
Webster Univ	MO	21,848	VC
West Texas A&M Univ	TX	7,533	C
Western Mich Univ	MI	12,031	C
Wilkes Univ	PA	28,060	C
Youngstown State Univ	OH	11,148	NC

MUSICOLOGY/ ETHNOMUSICOLOGY

School	ST	$IS	SR
Cal State, San Bernardino	CA	15,238	LC

NATIVE AMERICAN STUDIES

School	ST	$IS	SR
Colgate Univ	NY	37,095	MC
College of St. Scholastica	MN	24,970	C+
Dartmouth College	NH	37,770	MC
Humboldt State Univ	CA	9,400	C
Montana State Univ-Northern	MT	8,600	NC
Univ of Alaska Fairbanks	AK	9,295	C
Univ of Calif at Berkeley	CA	15,563	MC
Univ of Calif at Davis	CA	14,995	VC
Univ of Calif at Riverside	CA	15,300	C
Univ of Minn/Duluth	MN	12,470	C
Univ of Montana	MT	9,395	C
Univ of N Dak	ND	8,390	C
Univ of Okla	OK	9,226	VC
Univ of the Incarnate Word	TX	21,772	LC

NATURAL RESOURCE MANAGEMENT

School	ST	$IS	SR
Alaska Pacific Univ	AK	17,910	C
Ball State Univ	IN	8,660	C
Calif Polytechnic State Univ	CA	8,747	VC
Colo State Univ	CO	9,964	VC
Cornell Univ	NY	38,253	MC
Delaware State Univ	DE	8,104	LC
Dominican Univ	IL	23,610	C
Humboldt State Univ	CA	9,400	C
Johnson State College	VT	11,819	LC
Keystone College	PA	21,405	LC
Mich State Univ	MI	11,933	VC
Montana State Univ-Bozeman	MT	9,515	C
New Mexico Highlands Univ	NM	6,182	LC
N Car State Univ	NC	9,886	VC
N Dak State Univ	ND	8,435	C
Northland College	WI	22,170	C+
Ohio State Univ	OH	13,080	VC+
Penn State Univ/Univ Park Campus	PA	15,646	HC

ST = STATE $IS = IN-STATE COSTS SR = SELECTOR RATING

School	ST	$IS	SR
Purdue Univ/West Lafayette	IN	12,560	VC
Rutgers, The State Univ of New Jersey/New Brunswick/Piscataway Campus	NJ	15,800	HC
SUNY/College of Environmental Science and Forestry	NY	14,167	VC
Sterling College	VT	21,114	C+
Sul Ross State Univ	TX	6,582	LC
Texas A&M Univ at Galveston	TX	9,948	C+
Univ of Alaska Fairbanks	AK	9,295	C
Univ of Arizona	AZ	10,413	VC
Univ of Conn	CT	14,608	VC
Univ of Delaware	DE	12,616	HC
Univ of Florida	FL	8,580	MC
Univ of Maine	ME	12,080	C+
Univ of Maryland/College Park	MD	14,227	HC
Univ of Mass Amherst	MA	13,980	C+
Univ of Mich/Ann Arbor	MI	13,864	HC+
Univ of Minn/Crookston	MN	9,626	NC
Univ of Minn/Twin Cities	MN	13,160	VC
Univ of Nebr at Lincoln	NE	9,975	C+
Univ of Nevada/Reno	NV	9,792	C
Univ of New Hampshire	NH	14,828	VC
Univ of Northern Colo	CO	8,987	C
Univ of PR/Rio Piedras	PR	5,730	
Univ of Rhode Island	RI	13,720	VC
Univ of Tenn at Martin	TN	7,748	C
Univ of the South	TN	30,855	HC
Univ of Vermont	VT	16,316	VC
Univ of Wisc/Stevens Point	WI	8,116	VC
Univ of Wyoming	WY	8,636	C
Utah State Univ	UT	7,371	C
Washington State Univ	WA	11,334	C
West Virginia Univ	WV	9,370	C
Western Carolina Univ	NC	6,742	C

NATURAL SCIENCES

School	ST	$IS	SR
Adelphi Univ	NY	26,300	VC
Arkansas Tech Univ	AR	7,299	C
Avila Univ	MO	20,300	C
Bard College	NY	37,352	HC+
Benedictine College	KS	20,603	C
Bennington College	VT	35,910	HC
Bethel College	KS	19,800	C+
Bloomsburg Univ of Pennsylvania	PA	10,844	C
Cal State, Fresno	CA	8,414	LC
Cal State, Los Angeles	CA	5,778	C
Cameron Univ	OK	5,692	NC
Carthage College	WI	25,000	C
Case Western Reserve Univ	OH	32,002	MC
Castleton State College	VT	11,820	C
Charleston Southern Univ	SC	17,122	C
Christian Brothers Univ	TN	22,290	VC
Clarion Univ of Pennsylvania	PA	11,272	LC
Colgate Univ	NY	37,095	MC
College of Mount St. Joseph	OH	22,785	C
College of Our Lady of the Elms	MA	20,644	C
College of St. Benedict	MN	26,672	VC
College of St. Mary	NE	21,510	C
College of St. Scholastica	MN	24,970	C+
Columbia College	MO	16,139	C
Concordia Univ Nebr	NE	20,302	C+
Concordia Univ, River Forest	IL	23,600	C
Concordia Univ/St.Paul	MN	24,486	C
Covenant College	GA	23,830	VC+
Daemen College	NY	22,120	C
Dowling College	NY	23,870	LC
Edgewood College	WI	20,520	C
Edinboro Univ of Pennsylvania	PA	10,850	LC
Erskine College	SC	23,166	VC
Fresno Pacific Univ	CA	22,462	C
Gwynedd-Mercy College	PA	24,225	C
Hofstra Univ	NY	27,112	VC
Indiana Univ East	IN	4,433	LC
Indiana Univ of Pennsylvania	PA	10,489	C
Johns Hopkins Univ	MD	38,372	MC
Juniata College	PA	29,080	VC
Keystone College	PA	21,405	LC
Lehigh Univ	PA	37,570	HC+
LeMoyne-Owen College	TN	13,070	LC
Lesley Univ	MA	30,695	C
Lewis-Clark State College	ID	6,981	C
Loyola Marymount Univ	CA	32,194	VC
Lyndon State College	VT	12,646	LC
Madonna Univ	MI	11,504	VC
Master's College and Seminary	CA	23,250	VC
McMurry Univ	TX	17,846	LC
Mercer Univ	GA	27,516	VC+
Missouri Western State College	MO	8,522	NC
Muhlenberg College	PA	31,485	HC
New College of Florida	FL	8,906	HC+
Northwest Nazarene Univ	ID	20,360	VC
Oakwood College	AL	14,904	C
Our Lady of the Lake Univ of San Antonio	TX	17,336	C
Pacific Union College	CA	22,065	C+
Park Univ	MO	10,780	C+
Pepperdine Univ	CA	32,830	VC
Rocky Mountain College	MT	19,015	C
St. Anselm College	NH	30,250	C
St. John's Univ	MN	26,473	VC
St. Mary's College of Maryland	MD	15,908	VC+
St. Norbert College	WI	25,810	C
St. Peter's College	NJ	22,292	LC
Shawnee State Univ	OH	11,031	NC
Shimer College	IL	19,655	LC
Shorter College	GA	17,370	C
Siena Heights Univ	MI	16,140	LC
Simon's Rock College of Bard	MA	36,580	HC
Southwestern Okla State Univ	OK	4,801	C
Spalding Univ	KY	17,985	C
Spelman College	GA	19,215	C+
SUNY/College at Geneseo	NY	11,330	HC
Tabor College	KS	19,500	NC
Taylor Univ	IN	23,820	VC+
Texas A&M Univ at Galveston	TX	9,948	C+
Thomas Edison State College	NJ	3,325	SP
Turabo Univ	PR	4,110	
Universidad Metropolitana	PR	3,324	
Univ of Akron	OH	13,134	NC
Univ of Alabama at Birmingham	AL	12,901	C
Univ of Alaska Anchorage	AK	9,100	NC
Univ of Arizona	AZ	10,413	VC
Univ of Hawaii at Hilo	HI	6,497	C
Univ of Houston-Downtown	TX	2,594	NC
Univ of La Verne	CA	28,600	C
Univ of New Haven	CT	28,650	C
Univ of Pittsburgh at Greensburg	PA	15,984	C
Univ of Pittsburgh at Pittsburgh	PA	16,074	HC
Univ of PR/Cayey Univ College	PR	1,245	
Univ of Puget Sound	WA	31,760	HC
Univ of Science and Arts of Okla	OK	5,982	C
Univ of Wisc/Stevens Point	WI	8,116	VC
Virginia Wesleyan College	VA	25,350	C
Washington and Lee Univ	VA	29,663	MC
Western Oregon Univ	OR	10,281	C
Worcester State College	MA	10,005	C
Xavier Univ	OH	26,850	VC+
York College	NE	14,975	C

NAVAL ARCHITECTURE AND MARINE ENGINEERING

School	ST	$IS	SR
SUNY/Maritime College	NY	10,025	LC
Texas A&M Univ at Galveston	TX	9,948	C+
United States Coast Guard Academy	CT		MC
United States Merchant Marine Academy	NY	6,250	HC+
United States Naval Academy	MD		MC
Univ of Mich/Ann Arbor	MI	13,864	HC+
Univ of New Orleans	LA	7,356	C
Webb Inst	NY	6,250	MC

NEAR EASTERN STUDIES

School	ST	$IS	SR
Brandeis Univ	MA	38,198	MC
Brigham Young Univ	UT	8,504	HC
Cornell Univ	NY	38,253	MC
Indiana Univ Bloomington	IN	12,389	VC
Johns Hopkins Univ	MD	38,372	MC
Mount Union College	OH	21,120	C
Oberlin College	OH	36,938	MC
Princeton Univ	NJ	36,649	MC
Univ of Arizona	AZ	10,413	VC
Univ of Calif at Berkeley	CA	15,563	MC
Univ of Calif at Los Angeles	CA	15,330	MC
Univ of Chicago	IL	35,087	MC
Univ of Mich/Ann Arbor	MI	13,864	HC+
Univ of Washington	WA	10,361	VC
Washington Univ in St. Louis	MO	38,293	MC
Wayne State Univ	MI	11,774	C
Yale Univ	CT	37,000	MC

NEUROSCIENCES

School	ST	$IS	SR
Allegheny College	PA	30,280	VC
Amherst College	MA	37,470	MC
Baldwin-Wallace College	OH	24,678	C
Bates College	ME	37,500	MC
Baylor Univ	TX	23,864	VC
Boston Univ	MA	38,194	HC+
Bowdoin College	ME	37,790	MC
Bowling Green State Univ	OH	13,036	C
Brandeis Univ	MA	38,198	MC
Brown Univ	RI	38,174	MC
Cedar Crest College	PA	25,145	C+
Centenary College of Louisiana	LA	23,100	VC+
Claremont McKenna College	CA	36,880	MC
Colgate Univ	NY	37,095	MC
Colo College	CO	36,860	HC
Columbia Univ/Columbia College	NY	38,590	MC
Conn College	CT	37,900	MC
Drake Univ	IA	25,120	VC+
Emory Univ	GA	36,872	MC
Fairfield Univ	CT	35,505	HC
Franklin and Marshall College	PA	35,930	HC+
Hamilton College	NY	37,560	MC
Johns Hopkins Univ	MD	38,372	MC
Kenyon College	OH	35,370	HC+
King's College	PA	26,990	C
Lafayette College	PA	35,746	MC
Lawrence Univ	WI	30,900	HC
Macalester College	MN	31,944	MC
Middlebury College	VT	38,100	MC
Montana State Univ-Bozeman	MT	9,515	C
Mount Holyoke College	MA	37,918	HC+
Muskingum College	OH	20,680	C
New York Univ	NY	39,406	MC
Northeastern Univ	MA	35,650	HC
Northwestern Univ	IL	37,491	MC
Oberlin College	OH	36,938	MC
Pitzer College	CA	37,590	HC
Pomona College	CA	33,960	MC
Regis Univ	CO	25,740	C+
St. Andrews Presbyterian College	NC	20,525	C
St. Lawrence Univ	NY	35,945	VC
Scripps College	CA	35,700	HC+
Skidmore College	NY	37,930	HC
Smith College	MA	37,034	HC+
Texas Christian Univ	TX	23,410	VC
Trinity College	CT	38,040	HC+
Univ of Calif at Los Angeles	CA	15,330	MC
Univ of Calif at Riverside	CA	15,300	C
Univ of Pittsburgh at Pittsburgh	PA	16,074	HC
Univ of Rochester	NY	32,979	HC
Univ of St. Thomas	MN	26,918	VC
Univ of Scranton	PA	30,836	VC
Univ of Texas at Dallas	TX	10,234	HC
Univ of Washington	WA	10,361	VC
Ursinus College	PA	34,400	VC
Washington and Lee Univ	VA	29,663	MC
Washington State Univ	WA	11,334	C
Washington Univ in St. Louis	MO	38,293	MC
Wellesley College	MA	36,516	MC
Wesleyan Univ	CT	35,139	MC
Westmont College	CA	33,062	VC+

NUCLEAR ENGINEERING

School	ST	$IS	SR
Georgia Inst of Technology	GA	10,340	HC+
Mass Inst of Technology	MA	38,310	MC
N Car State Univ	NC	9,886	VC
Oregon State Univ	OR	11,055	C
Penn State Univ/Univ Park Campus	PA	15,646	HC
Purdue Univ/West Lafayette	IN	12,560	VC
Rensselaer Polytechnic Inst	NY	37,579	HC+
Texas A&M Univ	TX	11,081	HC
United States Military Academy	NY		MC
Univ of Arizona	AZ	10,413	VC
Univ of Calif at Berkeley	CA	15,563	MC
Univ of Cincinnati	OH	14,736	C
Univ of Florida	FL	8,580	MC
Univ of Illinois at Urbana-Champaign	IL	11,316	HC+
Univ of Maryland/College Park	MD	14,227	HC
Univ of Mich/Ann Arbor	MI	13,864	HC+
Univ of Missouri/Rolla	MO	12,292	HC
Univ of New Mexico	NM	9,223	C
Univ of Tenn at Knoxville	TN	8,214	C
Univ of Wisc/Madison	WI	8,262	VC

NUCLEAR ENGINEERING TECHNOLOGY

School	ST	$IS	SR
Old Dominion Univ	VA	10,441	C
Thomas Edison State College	NJ	3,325	SP
Univ of Florida	FL	8,580	MC

NUCLEAR MEDICAL TECHNOLOGY

School	ST	$IS	SR
Aquinas College	MI	21,894	C
Barry Univ	FL	24,100	LC
Benedictine Univ	IL	23,840	C
Cedar Crest College	PA	25,145	C+
Edinboro Univ of Pennsylvania	PA	10,850	LC
Ferris State Univ	MI	12,512	C
Franciscan Univ	IA	19,300	C
George Washington Univ	DC	41,030	MC
Indiana Univ Kokomo	IN	4,463	LC
Indiana Univ of Pennsylvania	PA	10,489	C
Indiana Univ-Purdue Univ Indianapolis	IN	8,257	LC
Mass College of Pharmacy and Health Sciences	MA	28,770	SP
New Jersey City Univ	NJ	11,850	LC
Old Dominion Univ	VA	10,441	C
Roosevelt Univ	IL	22,580	VC
St. Louis Univ	MO	29,780	VC+
St. Mary's Univ of Minn	MN	21,535	C
SUNY/Univ at Buffalo	NY	12,563	VC
Thomas Edison State College	NJ	3,325	SP
Univ of Alabama at Birmingham	AL	12,901	C
Univ of Central Arkansas	AR	6,388	C
Univ of Cincinnati	OH	14,736	C
Univ of Findlay	OH	23,962	NC
Univ of Iowa	IA	10,923	VC
Univ of Nevada/Las Vegas	NV	11,566	C
Univ of St. Francis	IL	22,850	C
Univ of the Incarnate Word	TX	21,772	LC
Univ of Vermont	VT	16,316	VC
Univ of Wisc/La Crosse	WI	8,991	VC
Wheeling Jesuit Univ	WV	22,660	C
York College of Pennsylvania	PA	14,500	VC

NUCLEAR TECHNOLOGY

School	ST	$IS	SR
Excelsior College	NY	975	SP
Peru State College	NE	6,342	NC

NURSING

School	ST	$IS	SR
Abilene Christian Univ	TX	18,370	VC
Adelphi Univ	NY	26,300	VC
Albany State Univ	GA	5,764	C+
Alcorn State Univ	MS	7,290	C
Alderson-Broaddus College	WV	19,640	C
Allen College	IA	14,521	SP
Alvernia College	PA	23,212	LC
Alverno College	WI	18,898	C
American International College	MA	24,690	LC
Anderson Univ	IN	19,430	LC
Andrews Univ	MI	19,550	C
Angelo State Univ	TX	7,576	NC
Anna Maria College	MA	26,140	LC
Aquinas College	TN	10,660	LC
Arizona State Univ-Main	AZ	10,048	C
Arkansas State Univ	AR	8,450	C
Arkansas Tech Univ	AR	7,299	C
Armstrong Atlantic State Univ	GA	7,102	C
Atlantic Union College	MA	18,868	C
Auburn Univ	AL	10,396	VC
Auburn Univ Montgomery	AL	9,020	NC
Augustana College	SD	21,998	VC
Aurora Univ	IL	20,631	C
Austin Peay State Univ	TN	5,814	LC
Avila Univ	MO	20,300	C
Azusa Pacific Univ	CA	24,720	VC
Baker Univ	KS	19,860	VC
Ball State Univ	IN	8,660	C
Barry Univ	FL	24,100	LC
Barton College	NC	19,314	C
Baylor Univ	TX	23,864	VC
Bellarmine Univ	KY	24,110	VC
Belmont Univ	TN	21,986	VC
Bemidji State Univ	MN	9,103	C
Benedictine Univ	IL	23,840	C
Berea College	KY	5,030	VC+
Bethel College	IN	19,670	C
Bethel College	KS	19,800	C+
Bethel College	MN	25,180	VC
Bethune-Cookman College	FL	16,480	LC
Biola Univ	CA	25,964	VC
Bloomfield College	NJ	19,250	LC
Bloomsburg Univ of Pennsylvania	PA	10,844	C
Bluefield State College	WV	2,806	LC
Boise State Univ	ID	7,657	LC
Boston College	MA	33,284	MC
Bowie State Univ	MD	10,873	C+
Bowling Green State Univ	OH	13,036	C
Bradley Univ	IL	22,910	VC
Brenau Univ Women's College	GA	21,800	C
Briar Cliff Univ	IA	21,660	C
Brigham Young Univ	UT	8,504	HC
Cabarrus College of Health Sciences	NC	7,000	SP
Cal State, Bakersfield	CA	6,090	LC
Cal State, Chico	CA	8,598	LC
Cal State, Dominguez Hills	CA	5,840	LC
Cal State, Fresno	CA	8,414	LC
Cal State, Fullerton	CA	6,648	C
Cal State, Hayward	CA	8,871	LC

School	ST	$IS	SR
Cal State, Los Angeles	CA	5,778	C
Cal State, Northridge	CA	7,757	LC
Cal State, Sacramento	CA	9,543	C
Cal State, San Bernardino	CA	15,238	LC
Cal State, Stanislaus	CA	9,874	C
Calif Univ of Pennsylvania	PA	10,388	C
Calvin College	MI	22,615	NC
Capital Univ	OH	26,550	C
Cardinal Stritch Univ	WI	17,620	C
Caribbean Univ	PR	3,000	
Carlow College	PA	21,334	C
Carroll College	MT	20,576	VC
Carroll College	WI	22,740	C
Carson-Newman College	TN	16,760	C
Case Western Reserve Univ	OH	32,002	MC
Catholic Univ of America	DC	34,248	VC
Cedar Crest College	PA	25,145	C+
Cedarville Univ	OH	19,954	VC
Central Conn State Univ	CT	12,090	C
Central Methodist College	MO	16,460	C
Central Missouri State Univ	MO	9,776	C
Central Univ of Bayamon	PR	3,335	
Charleston Southern Univ	SC	17,122	C
Chicago State Univ	IL	10,882	C+
Christopher Newport Univ	VA	8,862	VC
CUNY/College of Staten Island	NY	4,308	NC
CUNY/Herbert H. Lehman College	NY	3,320	LC
CUNY/Hunter College	NY	6,729	C+
CUNY/Medgar Evers College	NY	4,232	NC
CUNY/York College	NY	3,292	NC
Clarion Univ of Pennsylvania	PA	11,272	LC
Clarke College	IA	23,165	C
Clarkson College	NE	12,178	C
Clayton College and State Univ	GA	2,441	LC
Clemson Univ	SC	11,972	HC
Cleveland State Univ	OH	12,308	LC
Coe College	IA	27,385	VC
Colby-Sawyer College	NH	27,850	LC
College Misericordia	PA	26,350	C
College of Mount St. Vincent	NY	26,800	C
College of Mount St. Joseph	OH	22,785	C
College of New Jersey	NJ	15,950	MC
College of New Rochelle	NY	21,800	C
College of Notre Dame of Maryland	MD	27,700	C
College of Our Lady of the Elms	MA	20,644	C
College of St. Benedict	MN	26,672	VC
College of St. Catherine	MN	24,010	VC
College of St. Elizabeth	NJ	25,460	C
College of St. Mary	NE	21,510	C
College of St. Scholastica	MN	24,970	C+
Columbia Union College	MD	20,543	C
Columbus State Univ	GA	7,846	C
Concordia College: Moorhead	MN	22,460	VC+
Concordia Univ Wisc	WI	16,600	C
Coppin State College	MD	10,191	LC
Creighton Univ	NE	26,748	VC+
Crichton College	TN	15,215	C
Culver-Stockton College	MO	17,850	C
Cumberland Univ	TN	16,910	C
Curry College	MA	26,025	LC
Daemen College	NY	22,120	C
Davenport Univ	MI	11,636	NC
De Sales Univ	PA	25,470	C
Deaconess College of Nursing	MO	15,941	SP
Delaware State Univ	DE	8,104	LC
Delta State Univ	MS	6,618	C
Dickinson State Univ	ND	6,338	NC
Dillard Univ	LA	17,325	VC
Dominican College	NY	24,810	LC
Dominican Univ of Calif	CA	31,670	C
Dordt College	IA	20,170	VC
Duquesne Univ	PA	26,907	VC
D'Youville College	NY	21,080	C
East Carolina Univ	NC	8,671	C
East Central Univ	OK	4,968	C
East Stroudsburg Univ of Pennsylvania	PA	10,336	C
East Tenn State Univ	TN	8,497	C
East Texas Baptist Univ	TX	13,914	C
Eastern Kentucky Univ	KY	7,708	C
Eastern Mennonite Univ	VA	22,990	C
Eastern Mich Univ	MI	11,478	C
Eastern New Mexico Univ	NM	6,762	LC
Eastern Oregon Univ	OR	10,080	NC
Eastern Washington Univ	WA	9,012	C
Edgewood College	WI	20,520	C
Edinboro Univ of Pennsylvania	PA	10,850	LC
Elmhurst College	IL	24,630	C
Elmira College	NY	33,820	VC
Emmanuel College	MA	27,600	C+
Emory Univ	GA	36,872	MC
Emporia State Univ	KS	6,998	C
Endicott College	MA	25,266	C+
Excelsior College	NY	975	SP
Fairfield Univ	CT	35,505	HC
Fairleigh Dickinson Univ/ Metropolitan Campus	NJ	28,584	C
Fayetteville State Univ	NC	5,590	LC
Felician College	NJ	24,300	C
Ferris State Univ	MI	12,512	C
Fitchburg State College	MA	9,622	C
Florida A&M Univ	FL	7,564	C
Florida Atlantic Univ	FL	8,543	C
Florida Gulf Coast Univ	FL	9,908	C
Florida Hospital College of Health Sciences	FL	6,900	SP
Florida International Univ	FL	9,912	VC
Florida State Univ	FL	9,028	HC
Fort Hays State Univ	KS	7,363	C
Framingham State College	MA	9,381	C
Franciscan Univ of Steubenville	OH	20,300	VC
Gannon Univ	PA	23,260	C
Gardner-Webb Univ	NC	19,300	C
George Mason Univ	VA	9,732	VC
Georgetown College	KY	22,000	VC
Georgetown Univ	DC	38,242	MC
Georgia College and State Univ	GA	9,878	C
Georgia Southern Univ	GA	8,540	C
Georgia Southwestern State Univ	GA	6,013	C
Georgia State Univ	GA	10,658	C
Glenville State College	WV	7,812	NC
Gonzaga Univ	WA	26,766	HC
Goshen College	IN	22,450	VC
Graceland Univ	IA	19,550	C
Grambling State Univ	LA	6,538	NC
Grand Canyon Univ	AZ	30,000	LC
Grand Valley State Univ	MI	11,022	VC
Grand View College	IA	19,748	LC
Gustavus Adolphus College	MN	27,120	VC+
Gwynedd-Mercy College	PA	24,225	C
Hampton Univ	VA	17,112	C+
Hannibal-LaGrange College	MO	13,940	C
Harding Univ	AR	14,890	VC
Hardin-Simmons Univ	TX	14,165	C
Hartwick College	NY	34,650	C+
Hawaii Pacific Univ	HI	19,218	C
Henderson State Univ	AR	7,386	C
Holy Family College	PA	13,710	LC
Holy Names College	CA	27,980	NC
Hope College	MI	25,340	VC
Houston Baptist Univ	TX	16,905	C
Howard Univ	DC	16,505	C
Humboldt State Univ	CA	9,400	C
Huron Univ	SD	10,450	C
Husson College	ME	16,300	LC
Idaho State Univ	ID	8,128	C
Illinois State Univ	IL	10,944	C+
Illinois Wesleyan Univ	IL	30,380	HC+
Immaculata Univ	PA	25,200	C
Indiana State Univ	IN	10,719	LC
Indiana Univ Bloomington	IN	12,389	VC
Indiana Univ East	IN	4,433	LC
Indiana Univ Kokomo	IN	4,463	LC
Indiana Univ Northwest	IN	4,538	LC
Indiana Univ of Pennsylvania	PA	10,489	C
Indiana Univ South Bend	IN	4,571	LC
Indiana Univ Southeast	IN	4,504	LC
Indiana Univ-Purdue Univ Fort Wayne	IN	5,108	LC
Indiana Univ-Purdue Univ Indianapolis	IN	8,257	LC
Inter American Univ of PR/ Aguadilla Campus	PR	3,544	
Inter American Univ of PR/ Arecibo Campus	PR	3,300	
Inter American Univ of PR/ Fajardo Campus	PR	4,000	
Inter American Univ of PR/ Metropolitan Campus	PR		
Inter American Univ of PR/ Ponce Regional College	PR	3,700	
Inter American Univ of PR/ San German	PR	6,716	
Iowa Wesleyan College	IA	19,990	C
Jacksonville State Univ	AL	6,844	LC
Jacksonville Univ	FL	24,040	C
James Madison Univ	VA	10,794	VC
Jamestown College	ND	12,600	NC
Jewish Hospital College of Nursing and Allied Health	MO	11,200	SP
Johns Hopkins Univ	MD	38,372	MC
Johnson C. Smith Univ	NC	18,108	C
Judson College	IL	22,050	LC
Kansas Wesleyan Univ	KS	18,900	VC
Kean Univ	NJ	14,479	C
Kennesaw State Univ	GA	2,724	C
Kent State Univ	OH	12,932	C
Kentucky Wesleyan College	KY	17,250	C
Keuka College	NY	21,170	C
King College	TN	22,500	VC
Kutztown Univ of Pennsylvania	PA	10,786	C
La Roche College	PA	22,094	C
La Salle Univ	PA	31,260	VC
LaGrange College	GA	20,500	C
Lake Superior State Univ	MI	9,034	LC
Lamar Univ	TX	6,816	LC
Lander Univ	SC	10,496	C
Langston Univ	OK	2,308	LC
Lenoir-Rhyne College	NC	19,186	C
Lester L. Cox College of Nursing and Health Sciences	MO	9,292	SP
Lewis Univ	IL	22,950	C+
Lewis-Clark State College	ID	6,981	C
Liberty Univ	VA	17,220	C
Lincoln Memorial Univ	TN	16,400	LC
Lincoln Univ	MO	7,158	NC
LIU/Brooklyn Campus	NY	24,790	C
LIU/C.W. Post Campus	NY	28,282	C
Louisiana College	LA	13,450	C
Lourdes College	OH	15,300	LC
Loyola Univ Chicago	IL	31,164	VC
Loyola Univ New Orleans	LA	31,036	VC+
Lubbock Christian Univ	TX	15,832	C
Luther College	IA	25,700	VC
Lynchburg College	VA	26,815	C
MacMurray College	IL	20,005	LC
Madonna Univ	MI	11,504	VC
Malone College	OH	20,995	C
Mansfield Univ	PA	11,220	C
Marian College	IN	23,030	C
Marian College of Fond du Lac	WI	19,625	C
Marquette Univ	WI	27,594	VC
Marshall Univ	WV	9,116	C
Marymount Univ	VA	23,668	C
Maryville College	TN	25,960	VC
Maryville Univ of St. Louis	MO	22,090	VC
Marywood Univ	PA	26,050	C
McKendree College	IL	21,120	VC
McMurry Univ	TX	17,846	LC
McNeese State Univ	LA	5,259	LC
MCP Hahnemann Univ	PA	18,510	SP
Mercy College	NY	19,200	NC
Mercy College of Health Sciences	IA	10,500	SP
Mesa State College	CO	8,051	C
Messiah College	PA	25,890	VC+
Metropolitan State College of Denver	CO	2,338	LC
Metropolitan State Univ	MN	3,852	SP
Miami Univ	OH	15,033	HC
Mich State Univ	MI	11,933	VC
MidAmerica Nazarene Univ	KS	18,688	C
Middle Tenn State Univ	TN	8,534	C
Midland Lutheran College	NE	18,600	C
Midway College	KY	15,815	C
Midwestern State Univ	TX	8,045	LC
Millersville Univ of Pennsylvania	PA	11,269	C
Milligan College	TN	19,860	C+
Millikin Univ	IL	25,555	C
Milwaukee School of Engineering	WI	28,479	VC+
Minn State Univ, Mankato	MN	8,803	LC
Minn State Univ, Moorehead	MN	7,000	LC
Minot State Univ	ND	6,602	LC
Miss College	MS	14,574	C
Miss Univ for Women	MS	5,446	LC
Missouri Baptist Univ	MO	18,010	C
Missouri Southern State Univ	MO	8,316	C
Missouri Western State College	MO	8,522	NC
Molloy College	NY	15,180	C
Monmouth Univ	NJ	26,334	C
Montana State Univ-Bozeman	MT	9,515	C
Montana State Univ-Northern	MT	8,600	NC
Moravian College	PA	28,903	VC
Morehead State Univ	KY	7,464	C
Morningside College	IA	21,610	C
Mount Aloysius College	PA	19,120	LC
Mount Marty College	SD	15,656	LC
Mount Mary College	WI	20,370	C
Mount Mercy College	IA	21,400	C
Mount St. Mary College	NY	21,270	C
Mount St. Mary's College	CA	28,307	VC
Mountain State Univ	WV	10,212	NC
Murray State Univ	KY	7,816	VC
National Univ	CA	9,690	SP
Nazareth College of Rochester	NY	24,936	VC
Nebr Methodist College of Nursing and Allied Health	NE	11,900	SP
Nebr Wesleyan Univ	NE	21,197	C+
Neumann College	PA	23,890	LC
New Jersey City Univ	NJ	11,850	LC
New Mexico State Univ	NM	7,932	C
New York Inst of Technology	NY	24,205	VC
New York Univ	NY	39,406	MC
Newman Univ	KS	18,018	C
Niagara Univ	NY	25,050	C
Nicholls State Univ	LA	6,395	NC
Norfolk State Univ	VA	9,722	LC
N Car Agricultural and Technical State Univ	NC	6,659	LC
N Car Central Univ	NC	7,534	LC
N Dak State Univ	ND	8,435	C
North Georgia College and State Univ	GA	6,984	C
North Park Univ	IL	24,030	C
Northeastern State Univ	OK	4,950	LC
Northeastern Univ	MA	35,650	HC
Northern Arizona Univ	AZ	9,002	C
Northern Illinois Univ	IL	11,472	C
Northern Kentucky Univ	KY	6,352	NC
Northern Mich Univ	MI	10,834	C
Northwest College	WA	18,854	C
Northwest Nazarene Univ	ID	20,360	VC
Northwestern Okla State Univ	OK	5,433	NC
Northwestern State Univ of Louisiana	LA	6,331	NC
Norwich Univ	VT	21,064	LC
Nova Southeastern Univ	FL	23,346	C
Oakland Univ	MI	10,800	C
Oakwood College	AL	14,904	C
Ohio State Univ	OH	13,080	VC+
Ohio Univ	OH	14,448	C
Okla Baptist Univ	OK	15,220	VC
Okla City Univ	OK	19,580	VC
Okla Panhandle State Univ	OK	5,370	C
Old Dominion Univ	VA	10,441	C
Olivet Nazarene Univ	IL	20,480	C
Oral Roberts Univ	OK	18,490	C
Oregon State Univ	OR	11,055	C
Otterbein College	OH	26,085	C
Our Lady of Holy Cross College	LA	5,900	C
Pace Univ	NY	28,652	VC
Pacific Lutheran Univ	WA	25,715	VC
Pacific Union College	CA	22,065	C+
Penn State Univ/Altoona	PA	12,578	C
Penn State Univ/Univ Park Campus	PA	15,646	HC
Pennsylvania College of Technology	PA	15,126	NC
Piedmont College	GA	16,900	C
Pittsburg State Univ	KS	7,128	NC
Point Loma Nazarene Univ	CA	21,380	VC
Pontifical Catholic Univ of PR/Ponce	PR	7,298	
Prairie View A&M Univ	TX	9,418	NC
Presentation College	SD	14,700	LC
Purdue Univ/Calumet	IN	6,630	NC
Purdue Univ/West Lafayette	IN	12,560	VC
Queens Univ of Charlotte	NC	21,840	C
Quincy Univ	IL	22,330	C
Quinnipiac Univ	CT	30,570	VC
Radford Univ	VA	8,500	C
Ramapo College of New Jersey	NJ	15,203	VC
Regis College	MA	29,000	C
Regis Univ	CO	25,740	C+
Research College of Nursing	MO	22,960	SP
Rhode Island College	RI	11,565	C
Richard Stockton College of New Jersey	NJ	12,972	VC
Rivier College	NH	26,217	C
Robert Morris Univ	PA	20,438	C
Roberts Wesleyan College	NY	23,190	C+
Rockford College	IL	28,310	VC
Rockhurst Univ	MO	22,960	C+
Russell Sage College	NY	26,811	C
Rutgers, The State Univ of New Jersey/Camden Campus	NJ	14,990	VC
Rutgers, The State Univ of New Jersey/Newark Campus	NJ	15,624	VC
Sacred Heart Univ	CT	29,178	C
Saginaw Valley State Univ	MI	11,055	C
St. Anselm College	NH	30,250	C
St. Francis Univ	PA	25,876	LC
St. John Fisher College	NY	24,870	C
St. John's Univ	MN	26,473	VC
St. John's Univ	NY	30,198	C
St. Joseph College	CT	29,685	C
St. Joseph's, Brooklyn,	NY	10,902	C
St. Joseph's College	IN	24,250	C
St. Joseph's College of Maine	ME	25,600	C
St. Louis Univ	MO	29,780	VC+
St. Mary's College	IN	24,474	VC
St. Mary's College of Calif	CA	32,850	VC
St. Olaf College	MN	28,500	HC
St. Peter's College	NJ	22,292	LC
St. Xavier Univ	IL	23,144	C
Salem State College	MA	8,592	C
Salisbury Univ	MD	12,664	VC
Salve Regina Univ	RI	29,210	C
Samford Univ	AL	18,648	VC
Samuel Merritt College	CA	30,619	SP
San Diego State Univ	CA	10,321	C
San Francisco State Univ	CA	12,070	C
San Jose State Univ	CA	8,187	C
Seattle Pacific Univ	WA	25,944	VC
Seattle Univ	WA	24,183	VC
Seton Hall Univ	NJ	30,130	VC
Seton Hill Univ	PA	24,930	C
Shawnee State Univ	OH	11,031	NC

ST = STATE **$IS** = IN-STATE COSTS **SR** = SELECTOR RATING

School	ST	$IS	SR
Cal State, Dominguez Hills	CA	5,840	LC
CUNY/York College	NY	3,292	NC
Cleveland State Univ	OH	12,308	LC
College Misericordia	PA	26,350	LC
College of St. Benedict	MN	26,672	VC
College of St. Catherine	MN	24,010	VC
College of St. Mary	NE	21,510	C
Colo State Univ	CO	9,964	VC
Concordia Univ Wisc	WI	16,600	C
Dominican College	NY	24,810	LC
Dominican Univ of Calif	CA	31,670	C
Duquesne Univ	PA	26,907	VC
D'Youville College	NY	21,080	C
East Carolina Univ	NC	8,671	C
Eastern Kentucky Univ	KY	7,708	C
Eastern Mich Univ	MI	11,478	C
Elizabethtown College	PA	28,800	C
Florida A&M Univ	FL	7,564	C
Florida International Univ	FL	9,912	VC
Howard Univ	DC	16,505	C
Indiana Univ Kokomo	IN	4,463	LC
Ithaca College	NY	31,730	HC
Kean Univ	NJ	14,479	C
Keuka College	NY	21,170	C
Lamar Univ	TX	6,816	LC
Lebanon Valley College	PA	28,870	VC
Lenoir-Rhyne College	NC	19,186	C
LIU/Brooklyn Campus	NY	24,790	C
Mount Aloysius College	PA	19,120	LC
Mount Mary College	WI	20,370	C
New York Inst of Technology	NY	24,205	VC
Newman Univ	KS	18,018	C
North Park Univ	IL	24,030	C
Ohio State Univ	OH	13,080	VC+
Pennsylvania College of Technology	PA	15,126	NC
Quinnipiac Univ	CT	30,570	VC
Russell Sage College	NY	26,811	C
Saginaw Valley State Univ	MI	11,055	C
St. Francis Univ	PA	25,876	LC
St. John's Univ	MN	26,473	VC
St. Louis Univ	MO	29,780	VC+
St. Vincent College	PA	25,530	VC
San Jose State Univ	CA	8,187	C
Shawnee State Univ	OH	11,031	NC
Spalding Univ	KY	17,985	C
SUNY/Univ at Buffalo	NY	12,563	VC
Temple Univ	PA	15,912	C
Tenn State Univ	TN	9,048	LC
Touro College	NY	15,250	VC
Towson Univ	MD	12,694	VC
Tuskegee Univ	AL	17,250	LC
Univ of Central Arkansas	AR	6,388	C
Univ of Findlay	OH	23,962	NC
Univ of Florida	FL	8,580	MC
Univ of Hartford	CT	31,080	C
Univ of Louisiana at Monroe	LA	5,207	NC
Univ of Mary	ND	12,900	C+
Univ of Minn/Twin Cities	MN	13,160	VC
Univ of Missouri/Columbia	MO	13,782	VC
Univ of New Hampshire	NH	14,828	VC
Univ of New Mexico	NM	9,223	C
Univ of Pittsburgh at Pittsburgh	PA	16,074	HC
Univ of PR at Humacao	PR	1,245	
Univ of Puget Sound	WA	31,760	HC
Univ of Scranton	PA	30,836	VC
Univ of Southern Calif	CA	37,459	MC
Univ of Southern Colo	CO	7,821	LC
Univ of Southern Indiana	IN	9,025	LC
Univ of Tenn at Chattanooga	TN	7,783	C
Univ of Texas at San Antonio	TX	9,088	NC
Univ of Texas-Pan American	TX	5,954	LC
Univ of the Sciences in Philadelphia	PA	29,310	VC
Univ of Utah	UT	9,205	C
Univ of Wisc/La Crosse	WI	8,991	VC
Univ of Wisc/Madison	WI	8,262	VC
Univ of Wisc/Milwaukee	WI	9,427	LC
Utica College	NY	28,340	C
Virginia Commonwealth Univ	VA	9,030	C
Wartburg College	IA	21,165	VC
Wayne State Univ	MI	11,774	C
West Virginia Univ	WV	9,370	C
Western Mich Univ	MI	12,031	C
Worcester State College	MA	10,005	C
Xavier Univ	OH	26,850	VC+

OCEAN ENGINEERING

School	ST	$IS	SR
Florida Atlantic Univ	FL	8,543	C
Florida Inst of Technology	FL	28,740	VC
Mass Inst of Technology	MA	38,310	MC
Purdue Univ/West Lafayette	IN	12,560	VC
Texas A&M Univ at Galveston	TX	9,948	C+
United States Naval Academy	MD		MC
Univ of Rhode Island	RI	13,720	VC
Univ of Washington	WA	10,361	VC
Virginia Polytechnic Inst and State Univ	VA	9,179	C

OCEANOGRAPHY

School	ST	$IS	SR
Florida Inst of Technology	FL	28,740	VC
Hawaii Pacific Univ	HI	19,218	C
Humboldt State Univ	CA	9,400	C
Johns Hopkins Univ	MD	38,372	MC
Maine Maritime Academy	ME	12,380	C
Millersville Univ of Pennsylvania	PA	11,269	C
Texas A&M Univ at Galveston	TX	9,948	C+
United States Naval Academy	MD		MC
Univ of Mich/Ann Arbor	MI	13,864	HC+
Univ of San Diego	CA	33,156	HC
Univ of Washington	WA	10,361	VC

OFFICE SUPERVISION AND MANAGEMENT

School	ST	$IS	SR
Adams State College	CO	7,468	C
Alabama A&M Univ	AL	5,100	LC
Albany State Univ	GA	5,764	C+
Alcorn State Univ	MS	7,290	C
Arkansas Tech Univ	AR	7,299	C
Baker College of Flint	MI	7,720	NC
Campbellsville Univ	KY	17,680	C
Central Conn State Univ	CT	12,090	C
College of St. Elizabeth	NJ	25,460	C
Concord College	WV	8,136	C
Concordia College: Moorhead	MN	22,460	VC+
Cumberland College	KY	16,384	C
David N. Myers College	OH	9,475	C
East Central Univ	OK	4,968	C
Eastern Mich Univ	MI	11,478	C
Fayetteville State Univ	NC	5,590	LC
Fort Hays State Univ	KS	7,363	C
Fort Valley State Univ	GA	6,960	C
Georgia College and State Univ	GA	9,878	C
Gwynedd-Mercy College	PA	24,225	C
Indiana State Univ	IN	10,719	LC
Indiana Univ-Purdue Univ Indianapolis	IN	8,257	LC
Inter American Univ of PR/ Bayamon Univ College	PR	3,522	
Jackson State Univ	MS	8,382	C
John Brown Univ	AR	15,080	VC
Johnson and Wales Univ	RI	22,965	LC
Lincoln Univ	MO	7,158	NC
Mayville State Univ	ND	7,325	NC
Middle Tenn State Univ	TN	8,534	C
Miss Valley State Univ	MS	6,765	NC
Mount Vernon Nazarene Univ	OH	18,925	C
Northwestern Okla State Univ	OK	5,433	NC
Philander Smith College	AR	7,380	NC
Purdue Univ/West Lafayette	IN	12,560	VC
St. John's Univ	NY	30,180	C
S Car State Univ	SC	6,586	LC
Southeast Missouri State Univ	MO	9,704	C
Southern Nazarene Univ	OK	14,634	NC
Southwest Minn State Univ	MN	9,106	VC
Southwestern Adventist Univ	TX	14,798	C
Stephen F. Austin State Univ	TX	7,552	C
Sul Ross State Univ	TX	6,582	LC
Tabor College	KS	19,500	NC
Tarleton State Univ	TX	7,576	C
Thomas Edison State College	NJ	3,325	SP
Universidad Adventista de las Antillas	PR	5,460	
Univ of Houston-Downtown	TX	2,594	NC
Univ of Idaho	ID	8,216	C
Univ of S Car at Columbia	SC	10,048	VC
Univ of the District of Columbia	DC	2,070	LC
Univ of Wisc/Whitewater	WI	8,626	C
Valley City State Univ	ND	7,281	LC
Wiley College	TX	8,100	LC
Youngstown State Univ	OH	11,148	NC

OPERA

School	ST	$IS	SR
Boston Conservatory	MA	26,900	SP
Indiana Univ Bloomington	IN	12,389	VC

OPERATIONS RESEARCH

School	ST	$IS	SR
Boston College	MA	33,284	MC
Boston Univ	MA	38,194	HC+
Calif State Polytechnic Univ, Pomona	CA	8,793	C+
CUNY/Baruch College	NY	3,275	VC+
Columbia Univ/Fu Foundation School of Engineering and Applied Science	NY	38,590	MC
Cornell Univ	NY	38,253	MC
Indiana Univ Bloomington	IN	12,389	VC
Miami Univ	OH	15,033	HC
New York Univ	NY	39,406	MC
Seattle Univ	WA	24,183	VC
United States Air Force Academy	CO		HC+
United States Coast Guard Academy	CT		MC
United States Military Academy	NY		MC
Univ of Dayton	OH	24,850	VC
Univ of Houston	TX	9,818	C
Univ of North Texas	TX	7,629	C
Univ of Pennsylvania	PA	37,960	MC
Univ of Scranton	PA	30,836	VC

OPHTHALMIC TECHNOLOGY

School	ST	$IS	SR
Alderson-Broaddus College	WV	19,640	C

OPTICAL ENGINEERING

School	ST	$IS	SR
Rose-Hulman Inst of Technology	IN	31,425	HC+
Univ of Alabama in Huntsville	AL	9,126	VC
Univ of Arizona	AZ	10,413	VC

OPTICS

School	ST	$IS	SR
Capitol College	MD	21,250	C
Saginaw Valley State Univ	MI	11,055	C
Univ of Rochester	NY	32,979	HC

OPTOMETRY

School	ST	$IS	SR
Baylor Univ	TX	23,864	VC
Ferris State Univ	MI	12,512	C
Oral Roberts Univ	OK	18,490	C
Purdue Univ/Calumet	IN	6,630	NC
Univ of Calif at Berkeley	CA	15,563	MC
Univ of Houston	TX	9,818	C

ORGANIZATIONAL BEHAVIOR

School	ST	$IS	SR
Averett Univ	VA	23,010	LC
Benedictine Univ	IL	23,840	C
Bluffton College	OH	23,694	C
Boston Univ	MA	38,194	HC+
Carroll College	WI	22,740	C
Central Missouri State Univ	MO	9,776	C
Chapman Univ	CA	33,118	VC
College of St. Scholastica	MN	24,970	C+
College of Santa Fe	NM	25,293	C+
Concordia Univ/St.Paul	MN	24,486	C
Franklin Univ	OH	6,720	SP
Hannibal-LaGrange College	MO	13,940	C
Huntington College	IN	23,590	C
Huron Univ	SD	10,450	C
Indiana Univ South Bend	IN	4,571	LC
Indiana Univ Southeast	IN	4,504	LC
Ithaca College	NY	31,730	HC
La Salle Univ	PA	31,260	VC
Loyola Univ New Orleans	LA	31,036	VC+
Maryville Univ of St. Louis	MO	22,090	VC
Methodist College	NC	19,526	C
Miami Univ	OH	15,033	HC
Mountain State Univ	WV	10,212	NC
National Univ	CA	9,690	SP
New York Univ	NY	39,406	MC
Northern Kentucky Univ	KY	6,352	NC
Northwestern Univ	IL	37,491	MC
Oral Roberts Univ	OK	18,490	C
Pitzer College	CA	37,590	HC
Robert Morris Univ	PA	20,438	C
St. Joseph's, Brooklyn,	NY	10,902	C
St. Louis Univ	MO	29,780	VC+
Southern Methodist Univ	TX	34,210	HC
Spring Hill College	AL	25,868	VC
Univ of Calif at Davis	CA	14,995	VC
Univ of Memphis	TN	8,560	C
Univ of North Texas	TX	7,629	C
Univ of San Francisco	CA	34,700	VC
Viterbo Univ	WI	20,430	C
Wilmington College	OH	24,172	LC

PACIFIC AREA STUDIES

School	ST	$IS	SR
Brigham Young Univ/Hawaii	HI	7,240	VC+
Hawaii Pacific Univ	HI	19,218	C
Univ of Hawaii at Manoa	HI	9,565	VC

PAINTING

School	ST	$IS	SR
Andrews Univ	MI	19,550	C
Aquinas College	MI	21,894	C
Arizona State Univ-Main	AZ	10,048	C
Art Inst of Southern Calif	CA	14,500	SP
Atlanta College of Art	GA	18,600	SP
Bard College	NY	37,352	HC+
Barton College	NC	19,314	C
Birmingham-Southern College	AL	25,364	VC+
Boston Univ	MA	38,194	HC+
Calif College of the Arts	CA	31,530	SP
Cal State, San Bernardino	CA	15,238	LC
Cal State, Stanislaus	CA	9,874	C
Catholic Univ of America	DC	34,248	VC
Cleveland Inst of Art	OH	30,371	SP
College for Creative Studies	MI	23,298	SP
College of Santa Fe	NM	25,293	C+
College of Visual Arts	MN		SP
Edinboro Univ of Pennsylvania	PA	10,850	LC
Escuela de Artes Plasticas de PR	PR		
Harding Univ	AR	14,890	VC
Hofstra Univ	NY	27,112	VC
Indiana Univ Bloomington	IN	12,389	VC
Indiana Univ-Purdue Univ Indianapolis	IN	8,257	LC
Kansas City Art Inst	MO	26,850	SP
Lewis Univ	IL	22,950	C+
Maine College of Art	ME	28,812	SP
Maryland Inst College of Art	MD	30,890	SP
Mass College of Art	MA	15,568	SP
McMurry Univ	TX	17,846	LC
Milwaukee Inst of Art and Design	WI	24,388	SP
Minneapolis College of Art and Design	MN	28,950	SP
Montserrat College of Art	MA	22,790	SP
Moore College of Art and Design	PA	27,096	SP
Northwest Nazarene Univ	ID	20,360	VC
Ohio Univ	OH	14,448	C
Otis College of Art and Design	CA	23,420	SP
Pacific Northwest College of Art	OR	14,890	SP
Rhode Island School of Design	RI	33,569	SP
Rochester Inst of Technology	NY	29,217	VC+
San Francisco Art Inst	CA	19,300	SP
Savannah College of Art and Design	GA	27,560	SP
School of the Art Inst of Chicago	IL	27,800	SP
Shepherd College	WV	8,608	C
Simon's Rock College of Bard	MA	36,580	HC
SUNY at Potsdam	NY	12,160	C
SUNY/College at Buffalo	NY	8,025	C
Syracuse Univ	NY	34,720	HC
Univ of Dallas	TX	25,898	VC+
Univ of Hartford	CT	31,080	C
Univ of Houston	TX	9,818	C
Univ of Illinois at Urbana-Champaign	IL	11,316	HC+
Univ of Kansas	KS	8,923	VC
Univ of Mass Dartmouth	MA	12,835	C
Univ of Miami	FL	34,608	HC
Univ of Mich/Ann Arbor	MI	13,864	HC+
Univ of North Texas	TX	7,629	C
Univ of Oregon	OR	11,479	VC
Univ of San Francisco	CA	34,700	VC
Univ of the Arts	PA	29,510	SP
Univ of Washington	WA	10,361	VC
Washington Univ in St. Louis	MO	38,293	MC
Youngstown State Univ	OH	11,148	NC

PALEONTOLOGY

School	ST	$IS	SR
Univ of Calif at Los Angeles	CA	15,330	MC

PAPER AND PULP SCIENCE

School	ST	$IS	SR
Miami Univ	OH	15,033	HC
N Car State Univ	NC	9,886	VC
SUNY/College of Environmental Science and Forestry	NY	14,167	VC
Univ of Maine	ME	12,080	C+
Univ of Washington	WA	10,361	VC
Univ of Wisc/Stevens Point	WI	8,116	VC
Western Mich Univ	MI	12,031	C

PAPER ENGINEERING

School	ST	$IS	SR
SUNY/College of Environmental Science and Forestry	NY	14,167	VC
Western Mich Univ	MI	12,031	C

PARALEGAL STUDIES

School	ST	$IS	SR
Anna Maria College	MA	26,140	LC
Avila Univ	MO	20,300	C
Ball State Univ	IN	8,660	C
Bentley College	MA	33,904	VC
Brenau Univ Women's College	GA	21,800	C

School	ST	$IS	SR
Cal State, San Bernardino	CA	15,238	LC
Calumet College of St. Joseph	IN	9,000	LC
Central Washington Univ	WA	9,768	C
Champlain College	VT	22,030	C
College of Mount St. Joseph	OH	22,785	C
College of Our Lady of the Elms	MA	20,644	C
College of St. Mary	NE	21,510	C
Concordia Univ Wisc	WI	16,600	C
Davenport Univ	MI	11,636	NC
David N. Myers College	OH	9,475	C
East Central Univ	OK	4,968	C
Eastern Kentucky Univ	KY	7,708	C
Eastern Mich Univ	MI	11,478	C
Florida Gulf Coast Univ	FL	9,908	C
Franciscan Univ of Steubenville	OH	20,300	VC
Gannon Univ	PA	23,260	C
Hamline Univ	MN	27,052	VC
Hilbert College	NY	19,170	LC
Humphreys College	CA	7,000	NC
Husson College	ME	16,300	LC
International College	FL	8,060	LC
Johnson and Wales Univ	RI	22,965	LC
Kent State Univ	OH	12,932	C
Lake Erie College	OH	23,550	C
Lake Superior State Univ	MI	9,034	LC
Lasell College	MA	26,000	C
Lock Haven Univ of Pennsylvania	PA	11,098	LC
Marymount Univ	VA	23,668	C
Maryville Univ of St. Louis	MO	22,090	VC
Marywood Univ	PA	26,050	C
Mercy College	NY	19,200	NC
Minn State Univ, Moorehead	MN	7,000	LC
Miss College	MS	14,574	C
Miss Univ for Women	MS	5,446	LC
Montclair State Univ	NJ	13,790	C
Morehead State Univ	KY	7,464	C
National American Univ	SD	13,680	NC
Nebr Wesleyan Univ	NE	21,197	C+
Newbury College	MA	23,450	C
Nova Southeastern Univ	FL	23,346	C
Peirce College	PA	11,800	NC
Pennsylvania College of Technology	PA	15,126	NC
Point Park Univ	PA	21,840	C
Quinnipiac Univ	CT	30,570	VC
Roger Williams Univ	RI	30,296	C
St. John's Univ	NY	30,180	C
St. Mary-of-the-Woods College	IN	23,280	C
Southern Illinois Univ Carbondale	IL	10,407	C
Suffolk Univ	MA	29,200	C
Texas Wesleyan Univ	TX	16,245	C
Univ of Detroit Mercy	MI	25,582	C
Univ of Evansville	IN	24,190	VC
Univ of Great Falls	MT	15,360	C
Univ of La Verne	CA	28,600	C
Univ of Louisville	KY	8,762	VC
Univ of Maryland/Univ College	MD	5,910	SP
Univ of Mass Boston	MA	6,227	C
Univ of Memphis	TN	8,560	C
Univ of Tenn at Chattanooga	TN	7,783	C
Valdosta State Univ	GA	7,798	C
Villa Julie College	MD	18,393	C
Virginia Intermont College	VA	19,800	C
Wesley College	DE	19,905	C
Western Conn State Univ	CT	11,625	C
William Woods Univ	MO	20,120	C
Winona State Univ	MN		C
Woodbury College	VT	12,060	LC

PARKS AND RECREATION MANAGEMENT

School	ST	$IS	SR
Arkansas Tech Univ	AR	7,299	C
Auburn Univ	AL	10,396	VC
Aurora Univ	IL	20,631	C
Ball State Univ	IN	8,660	C
Bemidji State Univ	MN	9,103	C
Bethany College	KS	18,675	LC
Bowling Green State Univ	OH	13,036	C
Cal State, Chico	CA	8,598	LC
Cal State, Sacramento	CA	9,543	C
Calif Univ of Pennsylvania	PA	10,388	C
Central Mich Univ	MI	11,142	C
Central Washington Univ	WA	9,768	C
Cheyney Univ of Pennsylvania	PA	9,993	C
Christopher Newport Univ	VA	8,862	VC
Clemson Univ	SC	11,972	HC
Concord College	WV	8,136	C
Delaware State Univ	DE	8,104	LC
East Carolina Univ	NC	8,671	C
East Stroudsburg Univ of Pennsylvania	PA	10,336	C
Eastern Mich Univ	MI	11,478	C
Eastern Washington Univ	WA	9,012	C
Evangel Univ	MO	15,435	C
Florida International Univ	FL	9,912	VC
Gallaudet Univ	DC	16,554	SP
Humboldt State Univ	CA	9,400	C
Huntington College	IN	23,590	C
Illinois State Univ	IL	10,944	C+
Indiana Inst of Technology	IN	21,620	C
Indiana State Univ	IN	10,719	LC
Indiana Univ Bloomington	IN	12,389	VC
Johnson and Wales Univ	RI	22,965	LC
Kansas State Univ	KS	8,728	VC
Lake Superior State Univ	MI	9,034	LC
Marshall Univ	WV	9,116	C
Mich State Univ	MI	11,933	VC
Midland Lutheran College	NE	18,600	C
Minn State Univ, Mankato	MN	8,803	LC
Missouri Western State College	MO	8,522	NC
Montclair State Univ	NJ	13,790	C
Murray State Univ	KY	7,816	VC
N Car State Univ	NC	9,886	VC
Northern Arizona Univ	AZ	9,002	C
Northern Mich Univ	MI	10,834	C
Northland College	WI	22,170	C+
Ohio Univ	OH	14,448	C
Penn State Univ/Univ Park Campus	PA	15,646	HC
San Diego State Univ	CA	10,321	C
Shorter College	GA	17,370	C
Slippery Rock Univ of Pennsylvania	PA	10,343	LC
S Dak State Univ	SD	7,782	C
Southern Illinois Univ Carbondale	IL	10,407	C
Southwest Missouri State Univ	MO	8,918	C
Springfield College	MA	24,520	C
State Univ of West Georgia	GA	7,622	C
Stephen F. Austin State Univ	TX	7,552	C
Temple Univ	PA	15,912	C
Texas A&M Univ	TX	11,081	HC
Texas Tech Univ	TX	10,768	VC
Unity College	ME	19,845	LC
Univ of Arkansas at Pine Bluff	AR	7,925	C
Univ of Delaware	DE	12,616	HC
Univ of Idaho	ID	8,216	C
Univ of Iowa	IA	10,923	VC
Univ of Maine	ME	12,080	C+
Univ of Mary Hardin-Baylor	TX	17,268	C
Univ of Memphis	TN	8,560	C
Univ of Missouri/Columbia	MO	13,782	VC
Univ of Nebr at Lincoln	NE	9,975	C+
Univ of New Mexico	NM	9,223	C
Univ of N Car at Pembroke	NC	6,929	LC
Univ of N Car at Wilmington	NC	8,940	VC
Univ of Southern Miss	MS	8,324	LC
Univ of Tenn at Martin	TN	7,748	C
Univ of Utah	UT	9,205	C
Univ of Vermont	VT	16,316	VC
Univ of Wisc/La Crosse	WI	8,991	VC
Univ of Wyoming	WY	8,636	C
Utah State Univ	UT	7,371	C
Virginia Wesleyan College	VA	25,350	C
Wayne State College	NE	7,352	NC
Wayne State Univ	MI	11,774	C
West Virginia Univ	WV	9,370	C
Western Carolina Univ	NC	6,742	C
Western Illinois Univ	IL	10,363	C
Western Kentucky Univ	KY	6,834	C
Western Washington Univ	WA	10,119	VC
Wingate Univ	NC	21,200	C
Winona State Univ	MN		C
York College of Pennsylvania	PA	14,500	VC

PASTORAL STUDIES

School	ST	$IS	SR
Andrews Univ	MI	19,550	C
Brescia Univ	KY	14,225	C
Cedarville Univ	OH	19,954	VC
Clearwater Christian College	FL	13,160	LC
College of Mount St. Joseph	OH	22,785	C
College of St. Benedict	MN	26,672	VC
College of Santa Fe	NM	25,293	C+
Concordia Univ Wisc	WI	16,600	C
Dallas Baptist Univ	TX	15,300	VC
Grace Bible College	MI	15,890	C
Greenville College	IL	21,342	C
John Brown Univ	AR	15,080	VC
Madonna Univ	MI	11,504	VC
Marian College	IN	23,030	C
Morris College	SC	10,974	LC
Newman Univ	KS	18,018	C
North Central Univ	MN	14,904	C
Northwest College	WA	18,854	C
Northwestern College	MN	22,820	C+
Nyack College	NY	18,540	C
Okla Wesleyan Univ	OK	14,100	LC
St. John's Univ	MN	26,473	VC
Simpson College	CA	20,500	C
Southeastern College	FL	11,648	LC
Southwestern College	KS	19,560	C
Spalding Univ	KY	17,985	C
Tenn Wesleyan College	TN	16,540	C
Toccoa Falls College	GA	15,600	C
Union College	NE	17,130	C
Union Univ	TN	18,800	VC
Universidad Adventista de las Antillas	PR	5,460	
Univ of St. Mary	KS	18,868	C
Univ of St. Thomas	TX	21,952	VC
Walsh Univ	OH	20,890	C
Warner Southern College	FL	16,738	LC
William Tyndale College	MI	12,170	NC

PEACE STUDIES

School	ST	$IS	SR
Bethel College	KS	19,800	C+
Chapman Univ	CA	33,118	VC
Colgate Univ	NY	37,095	MC
College of St. Benedict	MN	26,672	VC
College of St. Elizabeth	NJ	25,460	C
DePauw Univ	IN	31,500	HC
Earlham College	IN	29,976	VC+
Eastern Mennonite Univ	VA	22,990	C
Goshen College	IN	22,450	VC
Guilford College	NC	24,960	VC
Hamline Univ	MN	27,052	VC
Hampshire College	MA	37,037	HC
Juniata College	PA	29,080	VC
Kent State Univ	OH	12,932	C
Manchester College	IN	23,390	C
Manhattan College	NY	27,400	VC
Molloy College	NY	15,180	C
Northland College	WI	22,170	C+
Norwich Univ	VT	21,064	LC
Prescott College	AZ	13,430	C
St. John's Univ	MN	26,473	VC
Salisbury Univ	MD	12,664	VC
San Diego State Univ	CA	10,321	C
Syracuse Univ	NY	34,720	HC
Tufts Univ	MA	38,233	MC
Univ of Calif at Berkeley	CA	15,563	MC
Univ of Hawaii at Manoa	HI	9,565	VC
Univ of N Car at Chapel Hill	NC	10,117	MC
Univ of St. Thomas	MN	26,918	VC
Univ of Washington	WA	10,361	VC
Villanova Univ	PA	35,050	HC
Wayne State Univ	MI	11,774	C
Wellesley College	MA	36,516	MC
Whitworth College	WA	26,428	VC+

PERCUSSION

School	ST	$IS	SR
Central Washington Univ	WA	9,768	C
Juilliard School	NY	30,385	SP
Northwestern Univ	IL	37,491	MC
Roosevelt Univ	IL	22,580	VC
Temple Univ	PA	15,912	C
Univ of Miami	FL	34,608	HC
Univ of Mich/Ann Arbor	MI	13,864	HC+
Youngstown State Univ	OH	11,148	NC

PERFORMING ARTS

School	ST	$IS	SR
Adelphi Univ	NY	26,300	VC
Alfred Univ	NY	28,290	C
American Univ	DC	34,585	VC+
Averett Univ	VA	23,010	LC
Baylor Univ	TX	23,864	VC
Boston Univ	MA	38,194	HC+
Brandeis Univ	MA	38,198	MC
Brigham Young Univ	UT	8,504	HC
Brown Univ	RI	38,174	MC
Butler Univ	IN	28,250	VC+
Carroll College	MT	20,576	VC
Carthage College	WI	25,000	C
Christopher Newport Univ	VA	8,862	VC
CUNY/City College	NY	4,230	C+
Colby College	ME	37,570	MC
College of Santa Fe	NM	25,293	C+
College of the Ozarks	MO	3,500	VC+
Colo State Univ	CO	9,964	VC
Columbia College	SC	22,658	LC
De Sales Univ	PA	25,470	C
Dominican Univ	IL	23,610	C
Eastern Kentucky Univ	KY	7,708	C
Eastern Mich Univ	MI	11,478	C
Edgewood College	WI	20,520	C
Emerson College	MA	32,205	HC
Ferrum College	VA	21,240	LC
Fontbonne Univ	MO	21,508	C
Fordham Univ	NY	35,066	HC
Franklin Pierce College	NH	28,980	LC
Georgia Southern Univ	GA	8,540	C
Hampshire College	MA	37,037	HC
Indiana Univ South Bend	IN	4,571	LC
Ithaca College	NY	31,730	HC
Johns Hopkins Univ	MD	38,372	MC
Johnson State College	VT	11,819	LC
Lindenwood Univ	MO	17,050	VC
Mars Hill College	NC	18,600	LC
Marywood Univ	PA	26,050	C
Naropa Univ	CO	23,364	SP
N Car School of the Arts	NC	8,565	SP
N Dak State Univ	ND	8,435	C
Northeastern Univ	MA	35,650	HC
Northern Kentucky Univ	KY	6,352	NC
Northwestern Univ	IL	37,491	MC
Oakland Univ	MI	10,800	C
Old Dominion Univ	VA	10,441	C
Plymouth State Univ	NH	12,298	LC
Roosevelt Univ	IL	22,580	VC
St. Mary's College of Calif	CA	32,850	VC
Savannah College of Art and Design	GA	27,560	SP
Seton Hill Univ	PA	24,930	C
Shenandoah Univ	VA	25,190	NC
Simon's Rock College of Bard	MA	36,580	HC
SUNY/College at Geneseo	NY	11,330	HC
Suffolk Univ	MA	29,200	C
Temple Univ	PA	15,912	C
Univ of Arizona	AZ	10,413	VC
Univ of Florida	FL	8,580	MC
Univ of Mary Hardin-Baylor	TX	17,268	C
Univ of Mich/Ann Arbor	MI	13,864	HC+
Univ of Missouri/Kansas City	MO	13,416	VC
Univ of New Hampshire	NH	14,828	VC
Univ of San Francisco	CA	34,700	VC
Univ of Tampa	FL	23,982	VC
Virginia Intermont College	VA	19,800	C
Washington Univ in St. Louis	MO	38,293	MC
West Texas A&M Univ	TX	7,533	C
Western Kentucky Univ	KY	6,834	C
Youngstown State Univ	OH	11,148	NC

PERSONNEL MANAGEMENT

School	ST	$IS	SR
Arcadia Univ	PA	29,890	C
Auburn Univ	AL	10,396	VC
Auburn Univ Montgomery	AL	9,020	NC
Ball State Univ	IN	8,660	C
Baylor Univ	TX	23,864	VC
Bellevue Univ	NE	4,440	NC
Bowling Green State Univ	OH	13,036	C
Cal State, Long Beach	CA	8,762	C+
CUNY/Baruch College	NY	3,275	VC+
Columbia Union College	MD	20,543	C
Dickinson State Univ	ND	6,338	NC
Eastern Mich Univ	MI	11,478	C
Eastern New Mexico Univ	NM	6,762	LC
Eastern Washington Univ	WA	9,012	C
Faulkner Univ	AL	14,500	C
Florida International Univ	FL	9,912	VC
Florida Southern College	FL	23,592	C
Florida State Univ	FL	9,028	HC
Grand Canyon Univ	AZ	30,000	LC
Grand Valley State Univ	MI	11,022	VC
Hawaii Pacific Univ	HI	19,218	C
Ithaca College	NY	31,730	HC
Kent State Univ	OH	12,932	C
King's College	PA	26,990	C
Lamar Univ	TX	6,816	LC
Loras College	IA	24,233	C
Louisiana Tech Univ	LA	7,361	C
Loyola Univ Chicago	IL	31,164	VC
Mansfield Univ	PA	11,220	C
Messiah College	PA	25,890	VC+
Miami Univ	OH	15,033	HC
Mich State Univ	MI	11,933	VC
Murray State Univ	KY	7,816	VC
Nicholls State Univ	LA	6,395	NC
Nichols College	MA	27,562	LC
Northern State Univ	SD	7,117	LC
Northwest Missouri State Univ	MO	9,334	C
Oakland Univ	MI	10,800	C
Ohio Univ	OH	14,448	C
Our Lady of the Lake Univ of San Antonio	TX	17,336	C
Portland State Univ	OR	12,453	C
Rhode Island College	RI	11,565	C
Rockhurst Univ	MO	22,960	C+
Roosevelt Univ	IL	22,580	VC
Rowan Univ	NJ	14,506	VC
St. Cloud State Univ	MN	8,362	C
San Francisco State Univ	CA	12,070	C
Seton Hill Univ	PA	24,930	C
Silver Lake College of the Holy Family	WI	18,450	LC
Southern Nazarene Univ	OK	14,634	NC
Southern Wesleyan Univ	SC	19,940	C
Spring Arbor Univ	MI	20,206	C
Tarleton State Univ	TX	7,576	C
Temple Univ	PA	15,912	C
Texas A&M Univ	TX	11,081	HC
Tiffin Univ	OH	19,490	LC
Troy State Univ Dothan	AL	3,842	C
Univ of Akron	OH	13,134	NC
Univ of Houston	TX	9,818	C
Univ of Idaho	ID	8,216	C
Univ of Louisiana at Lafayette	LA	5,826	C
Univ of Mary Hardin-Baylor	TX	17,268	C
Univ of Montana	MT	9,395	C
Univ of Nebr at Kearney	NE	8,286	NC
Univ of New Mexico	NM	9,223	C
Univ of North Texas	TX	7,629	C
Univ of PR/Rio Piedras	PR	5,730	
Univ of St. Thomas	MN	26,918	VC
Univ of Southern Miss	MS	8,324	LC

ST = STATE $IS = IN-STATE COSTS SR = SELECTOR RATING

School	ST	$IS	SR
Univ of Texas at San Antonio	TX	9,088	NC
Univ of the Sacred Heart	PR	5,590	
Univ of Washington	WA	10,361	VC
Univ of Wisc/Whitewater	WI	8,626	C
Utah State Univ	UT	7,371	C
Vanguard Univ of Southern Calif	CA	22,208	C
Washington State Univ	WA	11,334	C
Weber State Univ	UT	7,945	NC
Western Illinois Univ	IL	10,363	C
Wilmington College	DE	5,594	NC
Winona State Univ	MN		C
Xavier Univ of Louisiana	LA	17,600	C
Youngstown State Univ	OH	11,148	NC

PETROLEUM/NATURAL GAS ENGINEERING

School	ST	$IS	SR
Colo School of Mines	CO	12,533	HC
Louisiana State Univ and A&M College	LA	9,126	VC
Marietta College	OH	27,047	C
Montana Tech of The Univ of Montana	MT	9,314	NC
New Mexico Inst of Mining and Technology	NM	7,580	NC
Nicholls State Univ	LA	6,395	NC
Penn State Univ/Univ Park Campus	PA	15,646	HC
Savannah State Univ	GA	7,328	LC
Stanford Univ	CA	37,612	MC
Texas A&M Univ	TX	11,081	HC
Texas A&M Univ at Kingsville	TX	6,740	LC
Texas Tech Univ	TX	10,768	VC
Univ of Alaska Fairbanks	AK	9,295	C
Univ of Kansas	KS	8,923	VC
Univ of Louisiana at Lafayette	LA	5,826	C
Univ of Missouri/Rolla	MO	12,292	HC
Univ of Okla	OK	9,226	VC
Univ of Texas at Austin	TX	10,630	HC
Univ of Tulsa	OK	22,090	VC+
West Virginia Univ	WV	9,370	C

PHARMACOLOGY

School	ST	$IS	SR
SUNY/Univ at Stony Brook	NY	12,763	HC
Univ of the Sciences in Philadelphia	PA	29,310	VC

PHARMACY

School	ST	$IS	SR
Albany College of Pharmacy	NY	22,320	SP
Butler Univ	IN	28,250	VC+
Drake Univ	IA	25,120	VC+
Duquesne Univ	PA	26,907	VC
Ferris State Univ	MI	12,512	C
Florida A&M Univ	FL	7,564	C
Howard Univ	DC	16,505	C
Johnson C. Smith Univ	NC	18,108	C
Lamar Univ	TX	6,816	LC
LIU/Brooklyn Campus	NY	24,790	C
Mass College of Pharmacy and Health Sciences	MA	28,770	SP
N Dak State Univ	ND	8,435	C
Northeastern Univ	MA	35,650	HC
Ohio Northern Univ	OH	27,765	VC
Purdue Univ/West Lafayette	IN	12,560	VC
Rutgers, The State Univ of New Jersey/New Brunswick/Piscataway Campus	NJ	15,800	HC
St. John's Univ	NY	30,180	C
S Dak State Univ	SD	7,782	C
Southern Illinois Univ Edwardsville	IL	8,724	C
SUNY/Univ at Buffalo	NY	12,563	VC
Temple Univ	PA	15,912	C
Texas Southern Univ	TX	8,920	NC
Univ of Arizona	AZ	10,413	VC
Univ of Calif at Santa Barbara	CA	11,732	VC
Univ of Cincinnati	OH	14,736	C
Univ of Conn	CT	14,608	VC
Univ of Georgia	GA	8,656	VC
Univ of Houston	TX	9,818	C
Univ of Iowa	IA	10,923	VC
Univ of Kansas	KS	8,923	VC
Univ of Louisiana at Monroe	LA	5,207	NC
Univ of Mich/Ann Arbor	MI	13,864	HC+
Univ of Minn/Twin Cities	MN	13,160	VC
Univ of Miss	MS	7,666	C
Univ of Montana	MT	9,395	C
Univ of New Mexico	NM	9,223	C
Univ of Rhode Island	RI	13,720	VC
Univ of Texas at Austin	TX	10,630	HC
Univ of the Sciences in Philadelphia	PA	29,310	VC
Univ of Toledo	OH	12,479	NC
Univ of Wisc/Madison	WI	8,262	VC
Washington Univ in St. Louis	MO	38,293	MC
Wayne State Univ	MI	11,774	C
West Virginia Univ	WV	9,370	C

PHILOSOPHY

School	ST	$IS	SR
Adelphi Univ	NY	26,300	VC
Adrian College	MI	21,950	C
Agnes Scott College	GA	28,230	HC
Albertson College of Idaho	ID	19,415	VC
Albertus Magnus College	CT	23,130	LC
Albion College	MI	25,224	VC
Albright College	PA	30,579	C
Alfred Univ	NY	28,290	C
Allegheny College	PA	30,280	VC
Alma College	MI	25,566	VC
Alvernia College	PA	23,212	LC
Alverno College	WI	18,898	C
American International College	MA	24,690	LC
American Univ	DC	34,585	VC+
Amherst College	MA	37,470	MC
Anderson Univ	IN	19,430	LC
Appalachian State Univ	NC	7,637	VC
Aquinas College	MI	21,894	C
Arcadia Univ	PA	29,890	C
Arizona State Univ-Main	AZ	10,048	C
Arkansas State Univ	AR	8,450	C
Asbury College	KY	20,704	VC
Ashland Univ	OH	24,464	C
Assumption College	MA	29,375	C
Auburn Univ	AL	10,396	VC
Augsburg College	MN	25,298	C
Augustana College	IL	26,610	VC+
Augustana College	SD	21,998	VC
Aurora Univ	IL	20,631	C
Austin College	TX	24,747	HC
Austin Peay State Univ	TN	5,814	LC
Azusa Pacific Univ	CA	24,720	VC
Baker Univ	KS	19,860	VC
Baldwin-Wallace College	OH	24,678	C
Ball State Univ	IN	8,660	C
Bard College	NY	37,352	HC+
Barry Univ	FL	24,100	LC
Bates College	ME	37,500	MC
Baylor Univ	TX	23,864	VC
Belhaven College	MS	16,040	C+
Bellarmine Univ	KY	24,110	VC
Bellevue Univ	NE	4,440	NC
Belmont Abbey College	NC	23,742	C
Belmont Univ	TN	21,986	VC
Beloit College	WI	29,864	HC
Bemidji State Univ	MN	9,103	C
Benedict College	SC	12,662	LC
Benedictine College	KS	20,603	C
Benedictine Univ	IL	23,840	C
Bennington College	VT	35,910	HC
Bentley College	MA	33,904	VC
Berea College	KY	5,030	VC+
Berry College	GA	21,410	VC
Bethany College	WV	19,845	VC
Bethel College	IN	19,670	C
Bethel College	MN	25,180	VC
Biola Univ	CA	25,964	VC
Birmingham-Southern College	AL	25,364	VC+
Bloomfield College	NJ	19,250	LC
Bloomsburg Univ of Pennsylvania	PA	10,844	C
Boise State Univ	ID	7,657	LC
Boston College	MA	33,284	MC
Boston Univ	MA	38,194	HC+
Bowdoin College	ME	37,790	MC
Bowling Green State Univ	OH	13,036	C
Bradley Univ	IL	22,910	VC
Brandeis Univ	MA	38,198	MC
Bridgewater College	VA	25,150	C
Bridgewater State College	MA	10,482	C
Brigham Young Univ	UT	8,504	HC
Brown Univ	RI	38,174	MC
Bryn Mawr College	PA	36,890	HC+
Bucknell Univ	PA	35,262	HC+
Buena Vista Univ	IA	25,406	C
Butler Univ	IN	28,250	VC+
Cabrini College	PA	29,020	C
Calif Baptist Univ	CA	19,924	C
Calif Lutheran Univ	CA	27,600	LC
Calif Polytechnic State Univ	CA	8,747	VC
Calif State Polytechnic Univ, Pomona	CA	8,793	C+
Cal State, Bakersfield	CA	6,090	LC
Cal State, Chico	CA	8,598	LC
Cal State, Dominguez Hills	CA	5,840	LC
Cal State, Fresno	CA	8,414	LC
Cal State, Fullerton	CA	6,648	C
Cal State, Hayward	CA	8,871	LC
Cal State, Long Beach	CA	8,762	C+
Cal State, Los Angeles	CA	5,778	C
Cal State, Northridge	CA	7,757	LC
Cal State, Sacramento	CA	9,543	C
Cal State, San Bernardino	CA	15,238	LC
Cal State, Stanislaus	CA	9,874	C
Calif Univ of Pennsylvania	PA	10,388	C
Calvin College	MI	22,615	NC
Canisius College	NY	28,163	C+
Capital Univ	OH	26,550	C
Carleton College	MN	34,395	MC
Carlow College	PA	21,334	C
Carnegie Mellon Univ	PA	32,682	MC
Carroll College	MT	20,576	VC
Carson-Newman College	TN	16,760	C
Carthage College	WI	25,000	C
Case Western Reserve Univ	OH	32,002	MC
Catawba College	NC	20,500	C
Catholic Univ of America	DC	34,248	VC
Cedar Crest College	PA	25,145	C+
Cedarville Univ	OH	19,954	VC
Centenary College of Louisiana	LA	23,100	VC+
Central College	IA	21,206	C
Central Conn State Univ	CT	12,090	C
Central Methodist College	MO	16,460	C
Central Mich Univ	MI	11,142	C
Central Univ of Bayamon	PR	3,335	
Central Washington Univ	WA	9,768	C
Centre College	KY	27,300	HC
Chapman Univ	CA	33,118	VC
Christendom College	VA	18,410	VC+
Christopher Newport Univ	VA	8,862	VC
CUNY/Baruch College	NY	3,275	VC+
CUNY/Brooklyn College	NY	4,353	C+
CUNY/City College	NY	4,230	C+
CUNY/College of Staten Island	NY	4,308	NC
CUNY/Herbert H. Lehman College	NY	3,320	LC
CUNY/Hunter College	NY	6,729	C+
CUNY/Queens College	NY	4,362	C
CUNY/York College	NY	3,292	NC
Claremont McKenna College	CA	36,880	MC
Clarion Univ of Pennsylvania	PA	11,272	LC
Clark Atlanta Univ	GA	19,300	C+
Clark Univ	MA	32,115	VC
Clarke College	IA	23,165	C
Clemson Univ	SC	11,972	HC
Cleveland State Univ	OH	12,308	LC
Coastal Carolina Univ	SC	11,040	C
Coe College	IA	27,385	VC
Colby College	ME	37,570	MC
Colgate Univ	NY	37,095	MC
College Misericordia	PA	26,350	C
College of Charleston	SC	11,887	HC
College of Mount St. Vincent	NY	26,800	C
College of New Jersey	NJ	15,950	MC
College of New Rochelle	NY	21,800	C
College of St. Benedict	MN	26,672	VC
College of St. Catherine	MN	24,010	VC
College of St. Elizabeth	NJ	25,460	C
College of the Holy Cross	MA	36,451	MC
College of the Ozarks	MO	3,500	VC+
College of William and Mary	VA	12,224	MC
College of Wooster	OH	31,300	HC
Colo College	CO	36,860	HC
Colo State Univ	CO	9,964	VC
Columbia College	MO	16,139	C
Columbia Univ/Barnard College	NY	36,990	MC
Columbia Univ/Columbia College	NY	38,590	MC
Columbia Univ/School of General Studies	NY	35,000	C
Concordia College: Moorhead	MN	22,460	VC+
Conn College	CT	37,900	MC
Cornell College	IA	27,825	VC+
Cornell Univ	NY	38,253	MC
Cornerstone Univ and Grand Rapids Theological Seminary	MI	19,846	C
Covenant College	GA	23,830	VC+
Creighton Univ	NE	26,748	VC+
Curry College	MA	26,025	LC
Dakota Wesleyan Univ	SD	17,832	C
Dallas Baptist Univ	TX	15,300	VC
Dartmouth College	NH	37,770	MC
Davidson College	NC	33,274	MC
De Sales Univ	PA	25,470	C
Denison Univ	OH	33,050	HC
DePaul Univ	IL	27,580	VC
DePauw Univ	IN	31,500	HC
Dickinson College	PA	35,825	HC
Doane College	NE	20,000	C
Dominican Univ	IL	23,610	C
Dordt College	IA	20,170	VC
Dowling College	NY	23,870	LC
Drake Univ	IA	25,120	VC+
Drew Univ/College of Liberal Arts	NJ	35,550	VC
Drury Univ	MO	18,085	VC+
Duke Univ	NC	37,555	MC
Duquesne Univ	PA	26,907	VC
D'Youville College	NY	21,080	C
Earlham College	IN	29,976	VC+
East Carolina Univ	NC	8,671	C
East Stroudsburg Univ of Pennsylvania	PA	10,336	C
East Tenn State Univ	TN	8,497	C
Eastern Illinois Univ	IL	11,192	C
Eastern Kentucky Univ	KY	7,708	C
Eastern Mennonite Univ	VA	22,990	C
Eastern Mich Univ	MI	11,478	C
Eastern Washington Univ	WA	9,012	C
Eckerd College	FL	28,744	C+
Edinboro Univ of Pennsylvania	PA	10,850	LC
Edward Waters College	FL	14,374	LC
Elizabethtown College	PA	28,800	C
Elmhurst College	IL	24,630	C
Elmira College	NY	33,820	VC
Elon Univ	NC	22,240	VC
Emory & Henry College	VA	21,950	C
Emory Univ	GA	36,872	MC
Erskine College	SC	23,166	VC
Eureka College	IL	24,980	LC
Fairfield Univ	CT	35,505	HC
Fairleigh Dickinson Univ/College at Florham	NJ	30,130	C
Fairleigh Dickinson Univ/Metropolitan Campus	NJ	28,584	C
Felician College	NJ	24,300	C
Ferrum College	VA	21,240	LC
Fisk Univ	TN	17,305	LC
Flagler College	FL	11,860	VC+
Florida Atlantic Univ	FL	8,543	C
Florida International Univ	FL	9,912	VC
Florida Memorial College	FL	6,000	LC
Florida State Univ	FL	9,028	HC
Fordham Univ	NY	35,066	HC
Fort Hays State Univ	KS	7,363	C
Fort Lewis College	CO	8,353	C
Franciscan Univ of Steubenville	OH	20,300	VC
Franklin and Marshall College	PA	35,930	HC+
Franklin College	IN		C
Fresno Pacific Univ	CA	22,462	C
Frostburg State Univ	MD	11,114	C
Furman Univ	SC	28,976	HC+
Gallaudet Univ	DC	16,554	SP
Gannon Univ	PA	23,260	C
Geneva College	PA	21,850	C
George Mason Univ	VA	9,732	VC
George Washington Univ	DC	41,030	MC
Georgetown College	KY	22,000	VC
Georgetown Univ	DC	38,242	MC
Georgia Southern Univ	GA	8,540	C
Georgia State Univ	GA	10,658	C
Gettysburg College	PA	35,646	HC
Gonzaga Univ	WA	26,766	HC
Gordon College	MA	25,982	VC+
Goucher College	MD	32,650	HC
Graceland Univ	IA	19,550	C
Grand Valley State Univ	MI	11,022	VC
Green Mountain College	VT	24,130	C
Greenville College	IL	21,342	C
Grinnell College	IA	31,060	HC+
Grove City College	PA	14,228	HC
Guilford College	NC	24,960	VC
Gustavus Adolphus College	MN	27,120	VC+
Hamilton College	NY	37,560	MC
Hamline Univ	MN	27,052	VC
Hampden-Sydney College	VA	28,407	VC
Hampshire College	MA	37,037	HC
Hanover College	IN	25,200	VC
Hardin-Simmons Univ	TX	14,165	C
Hartwick College	NY	34,650	C+
Harvard Univ/Harvard College	MA	37,928	MC
Hastings College	NE	19,928	VC
Haverford College	PA	37,900	MC
Heidelberg College	OH	20,266	NC
Hendrix College	AR	20,970	VC+
High Point Univ	NC	22,480	C
Hiram College	OH	28,234	VC
Hobart and William Smith Colleges	NY	36,536	HC
Hofstra Univ	NY	27,112	VC
Hollins Univ	VA	27,965	VC
Holy Names College	CA	27,980	NC
Hood College	MD	27,795	VC
Hope College	MI	25,340	VC
Houghton College	NY	23,984	VC
Howard Univ	DC	16,505	C
Humboldt State Univ	CA	9,400	C
Huntington College	IN	23,590	C
Idaho State Univ	ID	8,128	C
Illinois College	IL	19,100	VC
Illinois State Univ	IL	10,944	C+
Illinois Wesleyan Univ	IL	30,380	HC+
Indiana State Univ	IN	10,719	LC
Indiana Univ Bloomington	IN	12,389	VC
Indiana Univ Northwest	IN	4,538	LC
Indiana Univ of Pennsylvania	PA	10,489	C
Indiana Univ South Bend	IN	4,571	LC
Indiana Univ Southeast	IN	4,504	LC
Indiana Univ-Purdue Univ Fort Wayne	IN	5,108	LC
Indiana Univ-Purdue Univ Indianapolis	IN	8,257	LC
Iona College	NY	27,998	VC
Iowa State Univ	IA	10,768	VC
Ithaca College	NY	31,730	HC
Jacksonville Univ	FL	24,040	C
James Madison Univ	VA	10,794	VC

School	ST	$IS	SR
Jamestown College	ND	12,600	NC
John Carroll Univ	OH	27,658	C+
Johns Hopkins Univ	MD	38,372	MC
Juniata College	PA	29,080	VC
Kalamazoo College	MI	26,955	HC+
Kansas State Univ	KS	8,728	VC
Kean Univ	NJ	14,479	C
Kent State Univ	OH	12,932	C
Kentucky Christian College	KY	13,472	C
Kenyon College	OH	35,370	HC+
King's College	PA	26,990	C
Knox College	IL	30,294	VC+
Kutztown Univ of Pennsylvania	PA	10,786	C
La Salle Univ	PA	31,260	VC
Lafayette College	PA	35,746	MC
Lake Forest College	IL	30,270	VC
Lakeland College	WI	17,950	C
Lawrence Univ	WI	30,900	HC
Le Moyne College	NY	26,400	VC
Lebanon Valley College	PA	28,870	VC
Lehigh Univ	PA	37,570	HC+
Lenoir-Rhyne College	NC	19,186	C
Lewis and Clark College	OR	30,620	VC
Lewis Univ	IL	22,950	C+
Lincoln Univ	MO	7,158	NC
Lincoln Univ	PA	13,320	C+
Linfield College	OR	27,090	VC
Lock Haven Univ of Pennsylvania	PA	11,098	LC
LIU/Brooklyn Campus	NY	24,790	C
LIU/C.W. Post Campus	NY	28,282	C
Loras College	IA	24,233	C
Louisiana College	LA	13,450	C
Louisiana State Univ and A&M College	LA	9,126	VC
Loyola College in Maryland	MD	34,560	HC
Loyola Marymount Univ	CA	32,194	VC
Loyola Univ Chicago	IL	31,164	VC
Loyola Univ New Orleans	LA	31,036	VC+
Luther College	IA	25,700	VC
Lycoming College	PA	27,589	C+
Lynchburg College	VA	26,815	C
Macalester College	MN	31,944	MC
MacMurray College	IL	20,005	LC
Manchester College	IN	23,390	C
Manhattan College	NY	27,400	VC
Manhattanville College	NY	32,420	C+
Mansfield Univ	PA	11,220	C
Marian College	IN	23,030	C
Marist College	NY	27,596	VC
Marlboro College	VT	29,055	VC+
Marquette Univ	WI	27,594	VC
Mary Baldwin College	VA	24,939	C
Mary Washington College	VA	10,166	HC
Marymount Univ	VA	23,668	C
Mass College of Liberal Arts	MA	8,717	LC
Mass Inst of Technology	MA	38,310	MC
McDaniel College	MD	28,440	VC
McKendree College	IL	21,120	VC
McMurry Univ	TX	17,846	LC
McPherson College	KS	20,265	C
Mercer Univ	GA	27,516	VC+
Mercyhurst College	PA	20,694	C
Merrimack College	MA	29,625	C
Messiah College	PA	25,890	VC+
Metropolitan State College of Denver	CO	2,338	LC
Metropolitan State Univ	MN	3,852	SP
Miami Univ	OH	15,033	HC
Mich State Univ	MI	11,933	VC
Middle Tenn State Univ	TN	8,534	C
Middlebury College	VT	38,100	MC
Millersville Univ of Pennsylvania	PA	11,269	C
Millikin Univ	IL	25,555	C
Mills College	CA	33,371	VC
Millsaps College	MS	25,182	VC
Minn State Univ, Mankato	MN	8,803	LC
Minn State Univ, Moorehead	MN	7,000	LC
Miss State Univ	MS	9,139	C
Missouri Valley College	MO	18,500	C
Molloy College	NY	15,180	C
Monmouth College	IL	23,600	C
Montana State Univ-Bozeman	MT	9,515	C
Montclair State Univ	NJ	13,790	C
Moravian College	PA	28,903	VC
Morehead State Univ	KY	7,464	C
Morehouse College	GA	22,728	C
Morgan State Univ	MD	11,470	C
Morningside College	IA	21,610	C
Mount Holyoke College	MA	37,918	HC+
Mount Mary College	WI	20,370	C
Mount St. Mary's College	CA	28,307	VC
Mount St. Mary's College	MD	28,400	C
Mount Union College	OH	21,120	C
Mount Vernon Nazarene Univ	OH	18,925	C
Muhlenberg College	PA	31,485	HC
Murray State Univ	KY	7,816	VC
Muskingum College	OH	20,680	C
Nazareth College of Rochester	NY	24,936	VC
Nebr Wesleyan Univ	NE	21,197	C+
New College of Florida	FL	8,906	HC+
New England College	NH	28,860	LC
New Jersey City Univ	NJ	11,850	LC
New Mexico State Univ	NM	7,932	C
New York Univ	NY	39,406	MC
Newberry College	SC	22,871	LC
Niagara Univ	NY	25,050	C
N Car State Univ	NC	9,886	VC
North Central College	IL	25,656	VC
North Park Univ	IL	24,030	C
Northeastern Illinois Univ	IL	2,898	NC
Northeastern Univ	MA	35,650	HC
Northern Arizona Univ	AZ	9,002	C
Northern Illinois Univ	IL	11,472	C
Northern Kentucky Univ	KY	6,352	NC
Northern Mich Univ	MI	10,834	C
Northwest College	WA	18,854	C
Northwest Missouri State Univ	MO	9,334	C
Northwest Nazarene Univ	ID	20,360	VC
Northwestern College of Iowa	IA	19,640	C+
Northwestern Univ	IL	37,491	MC
Notre Dame de Namur Univ	CA	26,932	LC
Nyack College	NY	18,540	C
Oakland Univ	MI	10,800	C
Oberlin College	OH	36,938	MC
Occidental College	CA	35,922	HC
Oglethorpe Univ	GA	26,000	VC
Ohio Dominican Univ	OH	22,700	C
Ohio Northern Univ	OH	27,765	VC
Ohio State Univ	OH	13,080	VC+
Ohio Univ	OH	14,448	C
Ohio Wesleyan Univ	OH	32,550	VC+
Okla City Univ	OK	19,580	VC
Okla State Univ	OK	9,216	VC
Old Dominion Univ	VA	10,441	C
Olivet Nazarene Univ	IL	20,480	C
Oral Roberts Univ	OK	18,490	C
Oregon State Univ	OR	11,055	C
Otterbein College	OH	26,085	C
Ouachita Baptist Univ	AR	18,900	VC
Our Lady of the Lake Univ of San Antonio	TX	17,336	C
Pacific Lutheran Univ	WA	25,715	VC
Pacific Univ	OR	24,250	C
Paine College	GA	13,022	LC
Palm Beach Atlantic Univ	FL	20,690	C
Penn State Univ/Univ Park Campus	PA	15,646	HC
Pepperdine Univ	CA	32,830	VC
Piedmont College	GA	16,900	C
Pitzer College	CA	37,590	HC
Plymouth State Univ	NH	12,298	LC
Point Loma Nazarene Univ	CA	21,380	VC
Pomona College	CA	33,960	MC
Pontifical Catholic Univ of PR/Ponce	PR	7,298	
Portland State Univ	OR	12,453	C
Princeton Univ	NJ	36,649	MC
Principia College	IL	25,044	C+
Providence College	RI	30,604	HC
Purdue Univ/Calumet	IN	6,630	NC
Purdue Univ/West Lafayette	IN	12,560	VC
Queens Univ of Charlotte	NC	21,840	C
Radford Univ	VA	8,500	C
Randolph-Macon College	VA	27,190	C
Randolph-Macon Woman's College	VA	28,430	VC+
Reed College	OR	36,950	MC
Regis Univ	CO	25,740	C+
Rensselaer Polytechnic Inst	NY	37,579	HC+
Rhode Island College	RI	11,565	C
Rhodes College	TN	26,466	HC+
Rice Univ	TX	27,550	MC
Richard Stockton College of New Jersey	NJ	12,972	VC
Rider Univ	NJ	30,900	C
Ripon College	WI	24,995	VC
Roanoke College	VA	27,393	C
Rockford College	IL	28,310	VC
Rockhurst Univ	MO	22,960	C+
Rocky Mountain College	MT	19,015	C
Roger Williams Univ	RI	30,296	C
Rollins College	FL	34,300	VC
Roosevelt Univ	IL	22,580	VC
Rosemont College	PA	26,175	C
Rutgers, The State Univ of New Jersey/Camden Campus	NJ	14,990	VC
Rutgers, The State Univ of New Jersey/New Brunswick/Piscataway Campus	NJ	15,800	HC
Rutgers, The State Univ of New Jersey/Newark Campus	NJ	15,624	VC
Sacred Heart Univ	CT	29,178	C
St. Ambrose Univ	IA	22,800	C
St. Andrews Presbyterian College	NC	20,525	C
St. Anselm College	NH	30,250	C
St. Bonaventure Univ	NY	24,455	LC
St. Cloud State Univ	MN	8,362	C
St. Edward's Univ	TX	20,428	C
St. Francis College	NY	10,880	LC
St. Francis Univ	PA	25,876	LC
St. John Fisher College	NY	24,870	C
St. John's Univ	MN	26,473	VC
St. John's Univ	NY	30,180	C
St. Joseph College	CT	29,685	C
St. Joseph's College	IN	24,250	C
St. Joseph's College of Maine	ME	25,600	C
St. Joseph's Univ	PA	33,590	VC
St. Lawrence Univ	NY	35,945	VC
St. Louis Univ	MO	29,780	VC+
St. Mary's College	IN	24,474	VC
St. Mary's College	MI	13,314	LC
St. Mary's College of Calif	CA	32,850	VC
St. Mary's College of Maryland	MD	15,908	VC+
St. Mary's Univ of Minn	MN	21,535	C
St. Mary's Univ of San Antonio	TX	22,444	C
St. Michael's College	VT	30,100	VC
St. Norbert College	WI	25,810	C
St. Olaf College	MN	28,500	HC
St. Peter's College	NJ	22,292	LC
St. Thomas Aquinas College	NY	20,590	LC
St. Vincent College	PA	25,530	VC
St. Xavier Univ	IL	23,144	C
Salem College	NC	24,595	VC
Salisbury Univ	MD	12,664	VC
Salve Regina Univ	RI	29,210	C
Sam Houston State Univ	TX	7,142	C
Samford Univ	AL	18,648	VC
San Diego State Univ	CA	10,321	C
San Francisco State Univ	CA	12,070	C
San Jose State Univ	CA	8,187	C
Santa Clara Univ	CA	34,701	HC
Sarah Lawrence College	NY	41,218	HC
Schreiner Univ	TX	20,440	C
Scripps College	CA	35,700	HC+
Seattle Pacific Univ	WA	25,944	VC
Seattle Univ	WA	24,183	VC
Seton Hall Univ	NJ	30,130	VC
Siena College	NY	25,310	VC
Siena Heights Univ	MI	16,140	LC
Simmons College	MA	33,000	VC
Simon's Rock College of Bard	MA	36,580	HC
Simpson College	IA	23,658	C+
Skidmore College	NY	37,930	HC
Slippery Rock Univ of Pennsylvania	PA	10,343	LC
Smith College	MA	37,034	HC+
Sonoma State Univ	CA	10,421	C
Southeast Missouri State Univ	MO	9,704	C
Southern Conn State Univ	CT	10,310	C
Southern Illinois Univ Carbondale	IL	10,407	C
Southern Illinois Univ Edwardsville	IL	8,724	C
Southern Methodist Univ	TX	34,210	HC
Southern Nazarene Univ	OK	14,634	NC
Southwest Missouri State Univ	MO	8,918	C
Southwestern Univ	TX	25,410	HC
Spelman College	GA	19,215	C+
Spring Arbor Univ	MI	20,206	C
Spring Hill College	AL	25,868	VC
Stanford Univ	CA	37,612	MC
SUNY at Oswego	NY	12,650	C
SUNY at Potsdam	NY	12,160	C
SUNY/College at Brockport	NY	12,111	C
SUNY/College at Buffalo	NY	8,025	C
SUNY/College at Cortland	NY	12,095	C
SUNY/College at Fredonia	NY	11,562	VC
SUNY/College at Geneseo	NY	11,330	HC
SUNY/College at Old Westbury	NY	12,784	C
SUNY/College at Oneonta	NY	11,870	VC
SUNY/College at Plattsburgh	NY	11,700	C
SUNY/College at Purchase	NY	10,587	VC
SUNY/Univ at Albany	NY	12,951	HC
SUNY/Univ at Binghamton	NY	12,787	HC
SUNY/Univ at Buffalo	NY	12,563	VC
SUNY/Univ at New Paltz	NY	11,565	VC
SUNY/Univ at Stony Brook	NY	12,763	HC
State Univ of West Georgia	GA	7,622	C
Stephens College	MO	24,260	C+
Stetson Univ	FL	29,495	VC
Stevens Inst of Technology	NJ	35,300	HC+
Stonehill College	MA	30,752	HC
Suffolk Univ	MA	29,200	C
Susquehanna Univ	PA	29,990	VC
Swarthmore College	PA	37,716	MC
Sweet Briar College	VA	27,940	C
Syracuse Univ	NY	34,720	HC
Tabor College	KS	19,500	NC
Taylor Univ	IN	23,820	VC+
Temple Univ	PA	15,912	C
Texas A&M Univ	TX	11,081	HC
Texas Christian Univ	TX	23,410	VC
Texas Lutheran Univ	TX	20,370	C
Texas State Univ	TX	9,320	VC
Texas Tech Univ	TX	10,768	VC
Thiel College	PA	20,970	C
Thomas Edison State College	NJ	3,325	SP
Thomas More College	KY	21,350	C
Thomas More College of Liberal Arts	NH	17,700	C
Toccoa Falls College	GA	15,600	C
Touro College	NY	15,250	VC
Towson Univ	MD	12,694	VC
Transylvania Univ	KY	23,780	VC+
Trinity Christian College	IL	21,640	VC
Trinity College	CT	38,040	HC+
Trinity International Univ	IL	22,980	C+
Trinity Univ	TX	26,466	HC+
Truman State Univ	MO	9,728	HC+
Tufts Univ	MA	38,233	MC
Tulane Univ	LA	37,451	HC+
Union College	NY	36,005	HC
Union Univ	TN	18,800	VC
United States Military Academy	NY		MC
Univ of Akron	OH	13,134	NC
Univ of Alabama	AL	9,040	C+
Univ of Alabama at Birmingham	AL	12,901	C
Univ of Alabama in Huntsville	AL	9,126	VC
Univ of Alaska Fairbanks	AK	9,295	C
Univ of Arizona	AZ	10,413	VC
Univ of Arkansas	AR	9,855	VC
Univ of Arkansas at Little Rock	AR	5,637	NC
Univ of Calif at Berkeley	CA	15,563	MC
Univ of Calif at Davis	CA	14,995	VC
Univ of Calif at Irvine	CA	19,808	HC
Univ of Calif at Los Angeles	CA	15,330	MC
Univ of Calif at Riverside	CA	15,300	C
Univ of Calif at San Diego	CA	14,127	HC
Univ of Calif at Santa Barbara	CA	11,732	VC
Univ of Calif at Santa Cruz	CA	16,505	VC
Univ of Central Arkansas	AR	6,388	C
Univ of Central Florida	FL	10,038	VC
Univ of Central Okla	OK	9,434	C
Univ of Chicago	IL	35,087	MC
Univ of Cincinnati	OH	14,736	C
Univ of Colo at Boulder	CO	10,774	VC
Univ of Colo at Colo Springs	CO	10,667	C
Univ of Colo at Denver	CO	3,302	C
Univ of Conn	CT	14,608	VC
Univ of Dallas	TX	25,898	VC+
Univ of Dayton	OH	24,850	VC
Univ of Delaware	DE	12,616	HC
Univ of Denver	CO	32,148	VC
Univ of Detroit Mercy	MI	25,582	C
Univ of Dubuque	IA	20,950	C
Univ of Evansville	IN	24,190	VC
Univ of Findlay	OH	23,962	NC
Univ of Florida	FL	8,580	MC
Univ of Georgia	GA	8,656	VC
Univ of Hartford	CT	31,080	C
Univ of Hawaii at Hilo	HI	6,497	C
Univ of Hawaii at Manoa	HI	9,565	VC
Univ of Houston	TX	9,818	C
Univ of Idaho	ID	8,216	C
Univ of Illinois at Chicago	IL	13,418	C
Univ of Illinois at Urbana-Champaign	IL	11,316	HC+
Univ of Indianapolis	IN	22,560	VC
Univ of Iowa	IA	10,923	VC
Univ of Kansas	KS	8,923	VC
Univ of Kentucky	KY	7,765	C
Univ of La Verne	CA	28,600	C
Univ of Louisiana at Lafayette	LA	5,826	C
Univ of Louisville	KY	8,762	VC
Univ of Maine	ME	12,080	C+
Univ of Maine at Farmington	ME	10,108	C
Univ of Maryland/Baltimore County	MD	14,668	VC+
Univ of Maryland/College Park	MD	14,227	HC
Univ of Mass Amherst	MA	13,980	C+
Univ of Mass Boston	MA	6,227	C
Univ of Mass Dartmouth	MA	12,835	C
Univ of Mass Lowell	MA	11,937	VC
Univ of Memphis	TN	8,560	C
Univ of Miami	FL	34,608	HC
Univ of Mich/Ann Arbor	MI	13,864	HC+
Univ of Mich/Dearborn	MI	6,843	VC
Univ of Mich/Flint	MI	5,548	C
Univ of Minn/Duluth	MN	12,470	C
Univ of Minn/Morris	MN	12,896	VC
Univ of Minn/Twin Cities	MN	13,160	VC
Univ of Miss	MS	7,666	C
Univ of Missouri/Columbia	MO	13,782	VC
Univ of Missouri/Kansas City	MO	13,416	VC
Univ of Missouri/Rolla	MO	12,292	HC
Univ of Missouri/St. Louis	MO	11,656	VC
Univ of Montana	MT	9,395	C
Univ of Nebr at Lincoln	NE	9,975	C+
Univ of Nebr at Omaha	NE	8,080	C
Univ of Nevada/Las Vegas	NV	11,566	C

ST = STATE **$IS** = IN-STATE COSTS **SR** = SELECTOR RATING

School	ST	$IS	SR
Univ of Nevada/Reno	NV	9,792	C
Univ of New Hampshire	NH	14,828	VC
Univ of New Mexico	NM	9,223	C
Univ of New Orleans	LA	7,356	C
Univ of N Car at Asheville	NC	8,079	VC
Univ of N Car at Chapel Hill	NC	10,117	MC
Univ of N Car at Charlotte	NC	8,185	C
Univ of N Car at Greensboro	NC	8,248	C
Univ of N Car at Pembroke	NC	6,929	LC
Univ of N Car at Wilmington	NC	8,940	VC
Univ of N Dak	ND	8,390	C
Univ of North Florida	FL	8,769	VC
Univ of North Texas	TX	7,629	C
Univ of Northern Colo	CO	8,987	C
Univ of Northern Iowa	IA	9,834	C
Univ of Notre Dame	IN	34,442	MC
Univ of Okla	OK	9,226	VC
Univ of Oregon	OR	11,479	VC
Univ of Pennsylvania	PA	37,960	MC
Univ of Pittsburgh at Pittsburgh	PA	16,074	HC
Univ of Portland	OR	28,500	VC
Univ of PR/Mayaguez	PR		
Univ of PR/Rio Piedras	PR	5,730	
Univ of Puget Sound	WA	31,760	HC
Univ of Redlands	CA	32,576	VC
Univ of Rhode Island	RI	13,720	VC
Univ of Richmond	VA	30,100	MC
Univ of Rochester	NY	32,979	HC
Univ of St. Thomas	MN	26,918	VC
Univ of St. Thomas	TX	21,952	VC
Univ of San Diego	CA	33,156	HC
Univ of San Francisco	CA	34,700	VC
Univ of Scranton	PA	30,836	VC
Univ of Sioux Falls	SD	16,390	C
Univ of South Alabama	AL	7,760	LC
Univ of S Car at Columbia	SC	10,048	VC
Univ of S Dak	SD	7,710	C+
Univ of South Florida	FL	9,454	C
Univ of Southern Calif	CA	37,459	MC
Univ of Southern Indiana	IN	9,025	LC
Univ of Southern Maine	ME	11,212	C
Univ of Southern Miss	MS	8,324	LC
Univ of Tenn at Chattanooga	TN	7,783	C
Univ of Tenn at Knoxville	TN	8,214	C
Univ of Tenn at Martin	TN	7,748	C
Univ of Texas at Arlington	TX	7,192	LC
Univ of Texas at Austin	TX	10,630	HC
Univ of Texas at El Paso	TX	5,799	NC
Univ of Texas at San Antonio	TX	9,088	NC
Univ of Texas-Pan American	TX	5,954	LC
Univ of the District of Columbia	DC	2,070	LC
Univ of the Incarnate Word	TX	21,772	LC
Univ of the Pacific	CA	31,090	VC
Univ of the South	TN	30,855	HC
Univ of Toledo	OH	12,479	NC
Univ of Tulsa	OK	22,090	VC+
Univ of Utah	UT	9,205	C
Univ of Vermont	VT	16,316	VC
Univ of Virginia	VA	11,740	MC
Univ of Washington	WA	10,361	VC
Univ of West Florida	FL	8,470	C
Univ of Wisc/Eau Claire	WI	8,463	VC
Univ of Wisc/Green Bay	WI	8,154	C
Univ of Wisc/La Crosse	WI	8,991	VC
Univ of Wisc/Madison	WI	8,262	VC
Univ of Wisc/Milwaukee	WI	9,427	LC
Univ of Wisc/Oshkosh	WI	6,130	LC
Univ of Wisc/Parkside	WI	6,160	LC
Univ of Wisc/Platteville	WI	8,450	C
Univ of Wisc/Stevens Point	WI	8,116	VC
Univ of Wyoming	WY	8,636	C
Urbana Univ	OH	19,115	C
Ursinus College	PA	34,400	VC
Ursuline College	OH	22,728	LC
Utah State Univ	UT	7,371	C
Utica College	NY	28,340	C
Valdosta State Univ	GA	7,798	C
Valparaiso Univ	IN	26,118	VC+
Vanderbilt Univ	TN	37,897	MC
Vassar College	NY	37,030	MC
Villanova Univ	PA	35,050	HC
Virginia Polytechnic Inst and State Univ	VA	9,179	C
Virginia Wesleyan College	VA	25,350	C
Wabash College	IN	27,932	VC
Wake Forest Univ	NC	34,090	MC
Walsh Univ	OH	20,890	C
Warren Wilson College	NC	21,794	VC
Wartburg College	IA	21,165	VC
Washburn Univ of Topeka	KS	8,984	NC
Washington and Jefferson College	PA	29,570	VC
Washington and Lee Univ	VA	29,663	MC
Washington College	MD	30,540	VC
Washington State Univ	WA	11,334	C
Washington Univ in St. Louis	MO	38,293	MC
Wayne State Univ	MI	11,774	C
Webster Univ	MO	21,848	VC
Wellesley College	MA	36,516	MC
Wells College	NY	21,122	VC
Wesleyan College	GA	17,870	VC
Wesleyan Univ	CT	35,139	MC
West Chester Univ of Pennsylvania	PA	11,164	C
West Virginia Univ	WV	9,370	C
West Virginia Wesleyan College	WV	22,920	C
Western Carolina Univ	NC	6,742	C
Western Illinois Univ	IL	10,363	C
Western Kentucky Univ	KY	6,834	C
Western Mich Univ	MI	12,031	C
Western Oregon Univ	OR	10,281	C
Western Washington Univ	WA	10,119	VC
Westminster College	MO	18,150	C+
Westminster College	PA	22,960	C
Westminster College	UT	17,226	C
Westmont College	CA	33,062	VC+
Wheaton College	IL	21,934	HC
Wheaton College	MA	36,330	HC
Wheeling Jesuit Univ	WV	22,660	C
Whitman College	WA	32,526	HC+
Whittier College	CA	29,108	C
Whitworth College	WA	26,428	VC+
Wichita State Univ	KS	8,092	C
Wiley College	TX	8,100	LC
Wilkes Univ	PA	28,060	C
Willamette Univ	OR	32,032	VC+
William Jewell College	MO	21,320	VC
William Paterson Univ of New Jersey	NJ	14,450	C
Williams College	MA	32,270	MC
Wilson College	PA	23,912	C
Wingate Univ	NC	21,200	C
Winthrop Univ	SC	11,302	C
Wittenberg Univ	OH	31,316	VC
Wofford College	SC	26,710	HC
Wright State Univ	OH	11,490	LC
Xavier Univ	OH	26,850	VC+
Xavier Univ of Louisiana	LA	17,600	C
Yale Univ	CT	37,000	MC
Yeshiva Univ	NY	21,400	C
York College of Pennsylvania	PA	14,500	VC
Youngstown State Univ	OH	11,148	NC

PHOTOGRAPHY

School	ST	$IS	SR
Andrews Univ	MI	19,550	C
Aquinas College	MI	21,894	C
Arcadia Univ	PA	29,890	C
Arizona State Univ-Main	AZ	10,048	C
Art Center College of Design	CA	23,450	SP
Art Inst of Atlanta	GA	23,205	SP
Art Inst of Boston at Lesley Univ	MA	28,080	SP
Atlanta College of Art	GA	18,600	SP
Ball State Univ	IN	8,660	C
Bard College	NY	37,352	HC+
Barry Univ	FL	24,100	LC
Bellevue Univ	NE	4,440	NC
Bennington College	VT	35,910	HC
Bethel College	IN	19,670	C
Birmingham-Southern College	AL	25,364	VC+
Bradley Univ	IL	22,910	VC
Brigham Young Univ	UT	8,504	HC
Calif College of the Arts	CA	31,530	SP
Cal State, Fullerton	CA	6,648	C
Cal State, San Bernardino	CA	15,238	LC
Central Missouri State Univ	MO	9,776	C
Cleveland Inst of Art	OH	30,371	SP
Coker College	SC	21,491	C
College for Creative Studies	MI	23,298	SP
College of Notre Dame of Maryland	MD	27,700	C
College of Santa Fe	NM	25,293	C+
College of Visual Arts	MN		SP
Columbia College Chicago	IL	25,108	LC
Corcoran School of Art and Design	DC	21,035	SP
Dominican Univ	IL	23,610	C
Drexel Univ	PA	27,655	VC
Edinboro Univ of Pennsylvania	PA	10,850	LC
Grand Valley State Univ	MI	11,022	VC
Hampshire College	MA	37,037	HC
Hofstra Univ	NY	27,112	VC
Howard Univ	DC	16,505	C
Indiana Univ Bloomington	IN	12,389	VC
Indiana Univ-Purdue Univ Indianapolis	IN	8,257	LC
Ithaca College	NY	31,730	HC
Kansas City Art Inst	MO	26,850	SP
Kendall College of Art and Design of Ferris State Univ	MI	10,784	SP
LIU/C.W. Post Campus	NY	28,282	C
Maine College of Art	ME	28,812	SP
Marlboro College	VT	29,055	VC+
Maryland Inst College of Art	MD	30,890	SP
Mass College of Art	MA	15,568	SP
Milwaukee Inst of Art and Design	WI	24,388	SP
Minneapolis College of Art and Design	MN	28,950	SP
Montserrat College of Art	MA	22,790	SP
Morningside College	IA	21,610	C
New Jersey City Univ	NJ	11,850	LC
New York Univ	NY	39,406	MC
Otis College of Art and Design	CA	23,420	SP
Pacific Northwest College of Art	OR	14,890	SP
Parsons School of Design	NY	32,242	SP
Point Park Univ	PA	21,840	C
Pratt Inst	NY	34,350	SP
Prescott College	AZ	13,430	C
Purdue Univ/West Lafayette	IN	12,560	VC
Rhode Island College	RI	11,565	C
Rhode Island School of Design	RI	33,569	SP
Ringling School of Art and Design	FL	27,530	SP
Rochester Inst of Technology	NY	29,217	VC+
St. Edward's Univ	TX	20,428	C
St. John's Univ	NY	30,180	C
St. Mary-of-the-Woods College	IN	23,280	C
Salem State College	MA	8,592	C
Sam Houston State Univ	TX	7,142	C
San Francisco Art Inst	CA	19,300	SP
Savannah College of Art and Design	GA	27,560	SP
School of the Art Inst of Chicago	IL	27,800	SP
School of Visual Arts	NY	30,200	SP
Shepherd College	WV	8,608	C
Simon's Rock College of Bard	MA	36,580	HC
Southern Illinois Univ Carbondale	IL	10,407	C
SUNY at Potsdam	NY	12,160	C
SUNY/College at Buffalo	NY	8,025	C
SUNY/Univ at New Paltz	NY	11,565	VC
Syracuse Univ	NY	34,720	HC
Temple Univ	PA	15,912	C
Texas A&M Univ at Commerce	TX	8,994	C
Texas Tech Univ	TX	10,768	VC
Thomas Edison State College	NJ	3,325	SP
Univ of Akron	OH	13,134	NC
Univ of Central Okla	OK	9,434	C
Univ of Dayton	OH	24,850	VC
Univ of Florida	FL	8,580	MC
Univ of Hartford	CT	31,080	C
Univ of Houston	TX	9,818	C
Univ of Idaho	ID	8,216	C
Univ of Illinois at Chicago	IL	13,418	C
Univ of Illinois at Urbana-Champaign	IL	11,316	HC+
Univ of Louisiana at Monroe	LA	5,207	NC
Univ of Mass Dartmouth	MA	12,835	C
Univ of Miami	FL	34,608	HC
Univ of Mich/Ann Arbor	MI	13,864	HC+
Univ of North Texas	TX	7,629	C
Univ of Okla	OK	9,226	VC
Univ of Oregon	OR	11,479	VC
Univ of the Arts	PA	29,510	SP
Univ of Washington	WA	10,361	VC
Univ of Wisc/Eau Claire	WI	8,463	VC
Virginia Intermont College	VA	19,800	C
Washington Univ in St. Louis	MO	38,293	MC
Weber State Univ	UT	7,945	NC
Webster Univ	MO	21,848	VC
Western Conn State Univ	CT	11,625	C
Youngstown State Univ	OH	11,148	NC

PHYSICAL CHEMISTRY

School	ST	$IS	SR
Averett Univ	VA	23,010	LC
Centre College	KY	27,300	HC
St. Mary's Univ of Minn	MN	21,535	C
Union Univ	TN	18,800	VC
Univ of Calif at San Diego	CA	14,127	HC

PHYSICAL EDUCATION

School	ST	$IS	SR
Abilene Christian Univ	TX	18,370	VC
Adams State College	CO	7,468	C
Adelphi Univ	NY	26,300	VC
Adrian College	MI	21,950	C
Alabama A&M Univ	AL	5,100	LC
Albany State Univ	GA	5,764	C+
Albertson College of Idaho	ID	19,415	VC
Albion College	MI	25,224	VC
Alcorn State Univ	MS	7,290	C
Alice Lloyd College	KY	4,040	C
Anderson Univ	IN	19,430	LC
Andrews Univ	MI	19,550	C
Appalachian State Univ	NC	7,637	VC
Aquinas College	MI	21,894	C
Arkansas State Univ	AR	8,450	C
Armstrong Atlantic State Univ	GA	7,102	C
Asbury College	KY	20,704	VC
Ashland Univ	OH	24,464	C
Auburn Univ	AL	10,396	VC
Augsburg College	MN	25,298	C
Augustana College	IL	26,610	VC+
Augustana College	SD	21,998	VC
Aurora Univ	IL	20,631	C
Averett Univ	VA	23,010	LC
Azusa Pacific Univ	CA	24,720	VC
Baldwin-Wallace College	OH	24,678	C
Barry Univ	FL	24,100	LC
Barton College	NC	19,314	C
Baylor Univ	TX	23,864	VC
Bellevue Univ	NE	4,440	NC
Belmont Univ	TN	21,986	VC
Benedictine College	KS	20,603	C
Berea College	KY	5,030	VC+
Berry College	GA	21,410	VC
Bethany College	KS	18,675	LC
Bethany College	WV	19,845	VC
Bethel College	IN	19,670	C
Bethel College	MN	25,180	VC
Bethel College	TN	12,980	C
Bethune-Cookman College	FL	16,480	LC
Biola Univ	CA	25,964	VC
Black Hills State Univ	SD	7,743	LC
Blackburn College	IL	13,690	C
Blue Mountain College	MS	10,226	C
Bluffton College	OH	23,694	C
Boise State Univ	ID	7,657	LC
Boston Univ	MA	38,194	HC+
Bowling Green State Univ	OH	13,036	C
Brewton-Parker College	GA	14,200	LC
Bridgewater State College	MA	10,482	C
Brigham Young Univ	UT	8,504	HC
Bryan College	TN	17,900	VC
Calif Baptist Univ	CA	19,924	C
Calif Lutheran Univ	CA	27,600	LC
Calif Polytechnic State Univ	CA	8,747	VC
Cal State, Chico	CA	8,598	LC
Cal State, Dominguez Hills	CA	5,840	LC
Cal State, Fullerton	CA	6,648	C
Cal State, Los Angeles	CA	5,778	C
Cal State, Northridge	CA	7,757	LC
Cal State, Stanislaus	CA	9,874	C
Calvin College	MI	22,615	NC
Cameron Univ	OK	5,692	NC
Campbellsville Univ	KY	17,680	C
Canisius College	NY	28,163	C+
Capital Univ	OH	26,550	C
Carroll College	MT	20,576	VC
Carroll College	WI	22,740	C
Carthage College	WI	25,000	C
Castleton State College	VT	11,820	C
Catawba College	NC	20,500	C
Cedarville Univ	OH	19,954	VC
Central Conn State Univ	CT	12,090	C
Central Methodist College	MO	16,460	C
Central Missouri State Univ	MO	9,776	C
Central State Univ	OH	8,922	C+
Central Washington Univ	WA	9,768	C
Charleston Southern Univ	SC	17,122	C
Chicago State Univ	IL	10,882	C+
Citadel, The	SC	12,295	C+
CUNY/Brooklyn College	NY	4,353	C+
CUNY/Queens College	NY	4,362	C
CUNY/York College	NY	3,292	NC
Claflin Univ	SC	14,838	C+
Clark Atlanta Univ	GA	19,300	C+
Clearwater Christian College	FL	13,160	LC
Cleveland State Univ	OH	12,308	LC
Coastal Carolina Univ	SC	11,040	C
Coe College	IA	27,385	VC
Coker College	SC	21,491	C
College of Charleston	SC	11,887	HC
College of Mount St. Vincent	NY	26,800	C
College of Mount St. Joseph	OH	22,785	C
College of New Jersey	NJ	15,950	MC
College of St. Catherine	MN	24,010	VC
College of the Ozarks	MO	3,500	VC+
Colo State Univ	CO	9,964	VC
Concordia College: Moorhead	MN	22,460	VC+
Concordia Univ	MI	24,095	C
Concordia Univ Nebr	NE	20,302	C+
Concordia Univ Wisc	WI	16,600	C
Concordia Univ, River Forest	IL	23,600	C
Concordia Univ/St.Paul	MN	24,486	C
Cornerstone Univ and Grand Rapids Theological Seminary	MI	19,846	C
Culver-Stockton College	MO	17,850	C
Cumberland College	KY	16,384	C
Cumberland Univ	TN	16,910	C
Dakota Wesleyan Univ	SD	17,832	C
Dallas Baptist Univ	TX	15,300	VC
Dana College	NE	20,280	C
David Lipscomb Univ	TN	16,158	VC
Davis and Elkins College	WV	20,594	C
Defiance College	OH	22,615	C
Delaware State Univ	DE	8,104	LC
Denison Univ	OH	33,050	HC
DePaul Univ	IL	27,580	VC
Doane College	NE	20,000	C

School	ST	$IS	SR
Drury Univ	MO	18,085	VC+
East Carolina Univ	NC	8,671	C
East Central Univ	OK	4,968	C
East Tenn State Univ	TN	8,497	C
East Texas Baptist Univ	TX	13,914	C
Eastern Conn State Univ	CT	10,362	C
Eastern Illinois Univ	IL	11,192	C
Eastern Kentucky Univ	KY	7,708	C
Eastern Mennonite Univ	VA	22,990	C
Eastern Mich Univ	MI	11,478	C
Eastern New Mexico Univ	NM	6,762	LC
Eastern Oregon Univ	OR	10,080	NC
Eastern Washington Univ	WA	9,012	C
Edinboro Univ of Pennsylvania	PA	10,850	LC
Edward Waters College	FL	14,374	LC
Elizabeth City State Univ	NC	5,550	LC
Elmhurst College	IL	24,630	C
Elon Univ	NC	22,240	VC
Emory & Henry College	VA	21,950	C
Emporia State Univ	KS	6,998	C
Endicott College	MA	25,266	C+
Erskine College	SC	23,166	VC
Eureka College	IL	24,980	LC
Evangel Univ	MO	15,435	C
Faulkner Univ	AL	14,500	C
Ferrum College	VA	21,240	LC
Florida Atlantic Univ	FL	8,543	C
Florida International Univ	FL	9,912	VC
Florida Memorial College	FL	6,000	LC
Florida State Univ	FL	9,028	HC
Fort Hays State Univ	KS	7,363	C
Fort Valley State Univ	GA	6,960	C
Franklin College	IN		C
Freed-Hardeman Univ	TN		NC
Fresno Pacific Univ	CA	22,462	C
Frostburg State Univ	MD	11,114	C
Gallaudet Univ	DC	16,554	SP
Gardner-Webb Univ	NC	19,300	C
George Fox Univ	OR	26,110	VC
George Mason Univ	VA	9,732	VC
Georgetown College	KY	22,000	VC
Georgia College and State Univ	GA	9,878	C
Glenville State College	WV	7,812	NC
Gonzaga Univ	WA	26,766	HC
Goshen College	IN	22,450	VC
Grace College	IN	19,825	VC
Graceland Univ	IA	19,550	C
Grambling State Univ	LA	6,538	NC
Grand Canyon Univ	AZ	30,000	LC
Greensboro College	NC	21,750	C
Greenville College	IL	21,342	C
Hamline Univ	MN	27,052	VC
Hampton Univ	VA	17,112	C+
Hanover College	IN	25,200	VC
Hardin-Simmons Univ	TX	14,165	C
Heidelberg College	OH	20,266	NC
Henderson State Univ	AR	7,386	C
High Point Univ	NC	22,480	C
Hillsdale College	MI	22,450	HC
Hofstra Univ	NY	27,112	VC
Houghton College	NY	23,984	VC
Howard Univ	DC	16,505	C
Humboldt State Univ	CA	9,400	C
Huntingdon College	AL	18,400	VC
Huntington College	IN	23,590	C
Huron Univ	SD	10,450	C
Husson College	ME	16,300	LC
Huston-Tillotson College	TX	14,232	NC
Idaho State Univ	ID	8,128	C
Illinois College	IL	19,100	VC
Illinois State Univ	IL	10,944	C+
Indiana State Univ	IN	10,719	LC
Indiana Univ Bloomington	IN	12,389	VC
Indiana Univ of Pennsylvania	PA	10,489	C
Indiana Univ-Purdue Univ Indianapolis	IN	8,257	LC
Indiana Wesleyan Univ	IN	19,900	C+
Iowa State Univ	IA	10,768	VC
Iowa Wesleyan College	IA	19,990	C
Ithaca College	NY	31,730	HC
Jacksonville Univ	FL	24,040	C
Jamestown College	ND	12,600	NC
John Brown Univ	AR	15,080	VC
John Carroll Univ	OH	27,658	C+
Johnson C. Smith Univ	NC	18,108	C
Johnson State College	VT	11,819	LC
Judson College	IL	22,050	LC
Kansas Wesleyan Univ	KS	18,900	VC
Kean Univ	NJ	14,479	C
Keene State College	NH	12,212	C
Kennesaw State Univ	GA	2,724	C
Kent State Univ	OH	12,932	C
Kentucky State Univ	KY	9,062	NC
Kentucky Wesleyan College	KY	17,250	C
Knoxville College	TN	6,200	LC
La Sierra Univ	CA	19,260	LC
Lambuth Univ	TN	16,520	C
Lander Univ	SC	10,496	C
Lane College	TN	11,178	C+
Langston Univ	OK	2,308	LC
Lee Univ	TN	13,780	NC
Lees-McRae College	NC	17,106	LC
LeTourneau Univ	TX	21,080	C
Liberty Univ	VA	17,220	C
Limestone College	SC	17,700	C
Lincoln Univ	MO	7,158	NC
Lincoln Univ	PA	13,320	C+
Lindenwood Univ	MO	17,050	VC
Linfield College	OR	27,090	VC
Lock Haven Univ of Pennsylvania	PA	11,098	LC
Longwood Univ	VA	11,175	C
Loras College	IA	24,233	C
Louisiana Tech Univ	LA	7,361	C
Lubbock Christian Univ	TX	15,832	C
Luther College	IA	25,700	VC
Lyndon State College	VT	12,646	LC
MacMurray College	IL	20,005	LC
Malone College	OH	20,995	C
Manhattan College	NY	27,400	VC
Marian College	IN	23,030	C
Mars Hill College	NC	18,600	LC
Maryville College	TN	25,960	VC
Marywood Univ	PA	26,050	C
Master's College and Seminary	CA	23,250	VC
Mayville State Univ	ND	7,325	NC
McDaniel College	MD	28,440	VC
McKendree College	IL	21,120	VC
McMurry Univ	TX	17,846	LC
McPherson College	KS	20,265	C
Messiah College	PA	25,890	VC+
Methodist College	NC	19,526	C
Metropolitan State College of Denver	CO	2,338	LC
Miami Univ	OH	15,033	HC
Mich State Univ	MI	11,933	VC
MidAmerica Nazarene Univ	KS	18,688	C
Middle Tenn State Univ	TN	8,534	C
Midwestern State Univ	TX	8,045	LC
Millikin Univ	IL	25,555	C
Minn State Univ, Mankato	MN	8,803	LC
Minot State Univ	ND	6,602	LC
Miss State Univ	MS	9,139	C
Miss Valley State Univ	MS	6,765	NC
Missouri Southern State Univ	MO	8,316	C
Missouri Valley College	MO	18,500	C
Monmouth College	IL	23,600	C
Montana State Univ-Billings	MT	9,550	C
Montana State Univ-Northern	MT	8,600	NC
Montclair State Univ	NJ	13,790	C
Morehead State Univ	KY	7,464	C
Morehouse College	GA	22,728	C
Morgan State Univ	MD	11,470	C
Mount Marty College	SD	15,656	LC
Mount Union College	OH	21,120	C
Mount Vernon Nazarene Univ	OH	18,925	C
Muskingum College	OH	20,680	C
Nebr Wesleyan Univ	NE	21,197	C+
New England College	NH	28,860	LC
New Mexico State Univ	NM	7,932	C
Newberry College	SC	22,871	LC
N Car Agricultural and Technical State Univ	NC	6,659	LC
N Car Central Univ	NC	7,534	LC
N Dak State Univ	ND	8,435	C
North Georgia College and State Univ	GA	6,984	C
Northeastern Illinois Univ	IL	2,898	NC
Northern Illinois Univ	IL	11,472	C
Northern Kentucky Univ	KY	6,352	NC
Northern Mich Univ	MI	10,834	C
Northern State Univ	SD	7,117	LC
Northwest College	WA	18,854	C
Northwest Missouri State Univ	MO	9,334	C
Northwest Nazarene Univ	ID	20,360	VC
Northwestern College	MN	22,820	C+
Northwestern College of Iowa	IA	19,640	C+
Northwestern Okla State Univ	OK	5,433	NC
Norwich Univ	VT	21,064	LC
Oakwood College	AL	14,904	C
Ohio Northern Univ	OH	27,765	VC
Ohio Wesleyan Univ	OH	32,550	VC+
Okla Baptist Univ	OK	15,220	VC
Okla Christian Univ	OK	17,690	NC
Okla City Univ	OK	19,580	VC
Okla Panhandle State Univ	OK	5,370	C
Okla State Univ	OK	9,216	VC
Okla Wesleyan Univ	OK	14,100	LC
Old Dominion Univ	VA	10,441	C
Olivet College	MI	19,984	C+
Olivet Nazarene Univ	IL	20,480	C
Oral Roberts Univ	OK	18,490	C
Ottawa Univ	KS	11,800	LC
Otterbein College	OH	26,085	C
Pacific Lutheran Univ	WA	25,715	VC
Pacific Union College	CA	22,065	C+
Palm Beach Atlantic Univ	FL	20,690	C
Paul Quinn College	TX	8,150	LC
Pepperdine Univ	CA	32,830	VC
Peru State College	NE	6,342	NC
Pfeiffer Univ	NC	18,980	C
Philander Smith College	AR	7,380	NC
Plymouth State Univ	NH	12,298	LC
Point Loma Nazarene Univ	CA	21,380	VC
Pontifical Catholic Univ of PR/Ponce	PR	7,298	
Prairie View A&M Univ	TX	9,418	NC
Purdue Univ/West Lafayette	IN	12,560	VC
Quincy Univ	IL	22,330	C
Radford Univ	VA	8,500	C
Rhode Island College	RI	11,565	C
Roanoke College	VA	27,393	C
Rockford College	IL	28,310	VC
Rocky Mountain College	MT	19,015	C
Saginaw Valley State Univ	MI	11,055	C
St. Ambrose Univ	IA	22,800	C
St. Andrews Presbyterian College	NC	20,525	C
St. Augustine's College	NC	12,990	LC
St. Bonaventure Univ	NY	24,455	LC
St. Edward's Univ	TX	20,428	C
St. Francis College	NY	10,880	LC
St. Joseph's College	IN	24,250	C
St. Joseph's College of Maine	ME	25,600	C
St. Mary's College of Calif	CA	32,850	VC
Salisbury Univ	MD	12,664	VC
Sam Houston State Univ	TX	7,142	C
Samford Univ	AL	18,648	VC
San Francisco State Univ	CA	12,070	C
Schreiner Univ	TX	20,440	C
Shaw Univ	NC	14,882	C+
Shepherd College	WV	8,608	C
Simpson College	IA	23,658	C+
S Car State Univ	SC	6,586	LC
S Dak State Univ	SD	7,782	C
Southeast Missouri State Univ	MO	9,704	C
Southeastern Okla State Univ	OK	6,147	C
Southern Adventist Univ	TN	17,080	C
Southern Conn State Univ	CT	10,310	C
Southern Illinois Univ Carbondale	IL	10,407	C
Southern Nazarene Univ	OK	14,634	NC
Southern Oregon Univ	OR	10,362	C
Southern Univ at New Orleans	LA	995	NC
Southern Utah Univ	UT	8,194	C
Southern Wesleyan Univ	SC	19,940	C
Southwest Baptist Univ	MO	15,371	C
Southwest Minn State Univ	MN	9,106	VC
Southwest Missouri State Univ	MO	8,918	C
Southwestern Adventist Univ	TX	14,798	C
Southwestern College	KS	19,560	C
Southwestern Okla State Univ	OK	4,801	C
Springfield College	MA	24,520	C
SUNY/College at Brockport	NY	12,111	C
SUNY/College at Cortland	NY	12,095	C
State Univ of West Georgia	GA	7,622	C
Stillman College	AL	11,370	LC
Syracuse Univ	NY	34,720	HC
Tabor College	KS	19,500	NC
Tarleton State Univ	TX	7,576	C
Taylor Univ	IN	23,820	VC+
Temple Univ	PA	15,912	C
Tenn Tech Univ	TN	8,670	VC
Tenn Wesleyan College	TN	16,540	C
Texas A&M Univ	TX	11,081	HC
Texas A&M Univ at Kingsville	TX	6,740	LC
Texas Christian Univ	TX	23,410	VC
Texas Southern Univ	TX	8,920	NC
Texas State Univ	TX	9,320	VC
Texas Wesleyan Univ	TX	16,245	C
Tougaloo College	MS	9,200	NC
Towson Univ	MD	12,694	VC
Trevecca Nazarene Univ	TN	17,548	C
Trinity International Univ	IL	22,980	C+
Tri-State Univ-Main Campus	IN	23,600	C
Troy State Univ	AL	7,696	C
Turabo Univ	PR	4,110	
Tusculum College	TN	19,990	C
Tuskegee Univ	AL	17,250	LC
Union College	NE	17,130	C
Union Univ	TN	18,800	VC
Univ of Akron	OH	13,134	NC
Univ of Alabama	AL	9,040	C+
Univ of Alabama at Birmingham	AL	12,901	C
Univ of Alaska Anchorage	AK	9,100	NC
Univ of Arizona	AZ	10,413	VC
Univ of Arkansas at Monticello	AR	5,940	NC
Univ of Arkansas at Pine Bluff	AR	7,925	C
Univ of Calif at Davis	CA	14,995	VC
Univ of Central Arkansas	AR	6,388	C
Univ of Central Florida	FL	10,038	VC
Univ of Central Okla	OK	9,434	C
Univ of Charleston	WV	23,620	C
Univ of Dayton	OH	24,850	VC
Univ of Delaware	DE	12,616	HC
Univ of Dubuque	IA	20,950	C
Univ of Evansville	IN	24,190	VC
Univ of Findlay	OH	23,962	NC
Univ of Great Falls	MT	15,360	C
Univ of Hawaii at Manoa	HI	9,565	VC
Univ of Idaho	ID	8,216	C
Univ of Illinois at Chicago	IL	13,418	C
Univ of Illinois at Urbana-Champaign	IL	11,316	HC+
Univ of Indianapolis	IN	22,560	VC
Univ of Kansas	KS	8,923	VC
Univ of Kentucky	KY	7,765	C
Univ of Louisiana at Monroe	LA	5,207	NC
Univ of Louisville	KY	8,762	VC
Univ of Maine	ME	12,080	C+
Univ of Maine at Presque Isle	ME	9,155	LC
Univ of Mary	ND	12,900	C+
Univ of Maryland/College Park	MD	14,227	HC
Univ of Maryland/Eastern Shore	MD	9,964	C
Univ of Mass Boston	MA	6,227	C
Univ of Memphis	TN	8,560	C
Univ of Mich/Ann Arbor	MI	13,864	HC+
Univ of Minn/Duluth	MN	12,470	C
Univ of Minn/Twin Cities	MN	13,160	VC
Univ of Missouri/Kansas City	MO	13,416	VC
Univ of Missouri/St. Louis	MO	11,656	VC
Univ of Mobile	AL	13,620	C
Univ of Montana	MT	9,395	C
Univ of Montevallo	AL	8,478	C
Univ of Nebr at Kearney	NE	8,286	NC
Univ of Nebr at Omaha	NE	8,080	C
Univ of Nevada/Las Vegas	NV	11,566	C
Univ of New Hampshire	NH	14,828	VC
Univ of New Mexico	NM	9,223	C
Univ of New Orleans	LA	7,356	C
Univ of North Alabama	AL	7,972	NC
Univ of N Car at Chapel Hill	NC	10,117	MC
Univ of N Car at Greensboro	NC	8,248	C
Univ of N Car at Pembroke	NC	6,929	LC
Univ of N Car at Wilmington	NC	8,940	VC
Univ of N Dak	ND	8,390	C
Univ of North Florida	FL	8,769	VC
Univ of North Texas	TX	7,629	C
Univ of Northern Colo	CO	8,987	C
Univ of Northern Iowa	IA	9,834	C
Univ of Rhode Island	RI	13,720	VC
Univ of Rio Grande	OH	8,728	NC
Univ of St. Thomas	MN	26,918	VC
Univ of Science and Arts of Okla	OK	5,982	C
Univ of South Alabama	AL	7,760	LC
Univ of S Car at Columbia	SC	10,048	VC
Univ of S Car at Spartanburg	SC	9,936	C+
Univ of S Dak	SD	7,710	C+
Univ of South Florida	FL	9,454	C
Univ of Tenn at Knoxville	TN	8,214	C
Univ of Texas at Arlington	TX	7,192	LC
Univ of the District of Columbia	DC	2,070	LC
Univ of the Incarnate Word	TX	21,772	LC
Univ of the Ozarks	AR	16,574	C
Univ of the Pacific	CA	31,090	VC
Univ of the Sacred Heart	PR	5,590	
Univ of Toledo	OH	12,479	NC
Univ of Vermont	VT	16,316	VC
Univ of Virginia	VA	11,740	MC
Univ of West Alabama	AL	6,048	C
Univ of Wisc/La Crosse	WI	8,991	VC
Univ of Wisc/Madison	WI	8,262	VC
Univ of Wisc/Oshkosh	WI	6,130	LC
Univ of Wisc/Platteville	WI	8,450	C
Univ of Wisc/River Falls	WI	8,358	LC
Univ of Wisc/Stevens Point	WI	8,116	VC
Univ of Wisc/Superior	WI	7,051	C+
Univ of Wisc/Whitewater	WI	8,626	C
Univ of Wyoming	WY	8,636	C
Upper Iowa Univ	IA	20,076	C
Utah State Univ	UT	7,371	C
Valdosta State Univ	GA	7,798	C
Valley City State Univ	ND	7,281	LC
Valparaiso Univ	IN	26,118	VC+
Vanguard Univ of Southern Calif	CA	22,208	C
Virginia Polytechnic Inst and State Univ	VA	9,179	C
Virginia State Univ	VA	10,358	C
Walla Walla College	WA	21,600	NC
Walsh Univ	OH	20,890	C
Warner Pacific College	OR	21,900	C
Warner Southern College	FL	16,736	LC
Wartburg College	IA	21,165	VC
Washburn Univ of Topeka	KS	8,984	NC
Washington State Univ	WA	11,334	C
Wayland Baptist Univ	TX	11,919	NC
Wayne State Univ	MI	11,774	C
Weber State Univ	UT	7,945	NC
Wesley College	DE	19,905	C
West Chester Univ of Pennsylvania	PA	11,164	C
West Liberty State College	WV	7,868	LC
West Texas A&M Univ	TX	7,533	C

ST = STATE $IS = IN-STATE COSTS SR = SELECTOR RATING

School	ST	$IS	SR
West Virginia Univ	WV	9,370	C
West Virginia Wesleyan College	WV	22,920	C
Western Baptist College	OR	21,808	C
Western Carolina Univ	NC	6,742	C
Western Illinois Univ	IL	10,363	C
Western Kentucky Univ	KY	6,834	C
Western Mich Univ	MI	12,031	C
Western New Mexico Univ	NM	5,950	LC
Westminster College	MO	18,150	C+
Westmont College	CA	33,062	VC+
Whittier College	CA	29,108	C
Wichita State Univ	KS	8,092	C
Wiley College	TX	8,100	LC
William Carey College	MS	10,150	LC
William Paterson Univ of New Jersey	NJ	14,450	C
William Penn Univ	IA	17,575	LC
William Woods Univ	MO	20,120	C
Williams Baptist College	AR	11,950	C
Wilmington College	OH	24,172	LC
Wingate Univ	NC	21,200	C
Winona State Univ	MN		C
Winston-Salem State Univ	NC	8,926	LC
Winthrop Univ	SC	11,302	C
Wright State Univ	OH	11,490	LC
Xavier Univ of Louisiana	LA	17,600	C
Youngstown State Univ	OH	11,148	NC

PHYSICAL FITNESS/ MOVEMENT

School	ST	$IS	SR
Adelphi Univ	NY	26,300	VC
Arizona State Univ-Main	AZ	10,048	C
Ashland Univ	OH	24,464	C
Auburn Univ	AL	10,396	VC
Augustana College	SD	21,998	VC
Baldwin-Wallace College	OH	24,678	C
Ball State Univ	IN	8,660	C
Baylor Univ	TX	23,864	VC
Bethel College	TN	12,980	C
Bloomsburg Univ of Pennsylvania	PA	10,844	C
Boston Univ	MA	38,194	HC+
Bowling Green State Univ	OH	13,036	C
Brigham Young Univ/Hawaii	HI	7,240	VC+
Buena Vista Univ	IA	25,406	C
Calif State Polytechnic Univ, Pomona	CA	8,793	C+
Cal State, Fresno	CA	8,414	LC
Cal State, Hayward	CA	8,871	LC
Campbell Univ	NC	18,268	VC
Capital Univ	OH	26,550	C
Chapman Univ	CA	33,118	VC
Christian Heritage College	CA	19,990	C
Clarke College	IA	23,165	C
College of St. Catherine	MN	24,010	VC
Concordia Univ Nebr	NE	20,302	C+
Concordia Univ, River Forest	IL	23,600	C
Dallas Baptist Univ	TX	15,300	VC
Defiance College	OH	22,615	C
DePauw Univ	IN	31,500	HC
Earlham College	IN	29,976	VC+
East Carolina Univ	NC	8,671	C
East Stroudsburg Univ of Pennsylvania	PA	10,336	C
East Texas Baptist Univ	TX	13,914	C
Eastern Nazarene College	MA	19,433	LC
Eureka College	IL	24,980	LC
George Washington Univ	DC	41,030	MC
Georgia State Univ	GA	10,658	C
Gordon College	MA	25,982	VC+
Grand Canyon Univ	AZ	30,000	LC
Hardin-Simmons Univ	TX	14,165	C
High Point Univ	NC	22,480	C
Hope College	MI	25,340	VC
Houston Baptist Univ	TX	16,905	C
Humboldt State Univ	CA	9,400	C
Indiana Univ Bloomington	IN	12,389	VC
Ithaca College	NY	31,730	HC
James Madison Univ	VA	10,794	VC
Johnson State College	VT	11,819	LC
Kansas State Univ	KS	8,728	VC
Lakeland College	WI	17,950	C
Lasell College	MA	26,000	C
Lewis-Clark State College	ID	6,981	C
Louisiana State Univ and A&M College	LA	9,126	VC
Lubbock Christian Univ	TX	15,832	C
Lynchburg College	VA	26,815	C
Malone College	OH	20,995	C
Marshall Univ	WV	9,116	C
Marymount Univ	VA	23,668	C
Mesa State College	CO	8,051	C
Metropolitan State College of Denver	CO	2,338	LC
Miami Univ	OH	15,033	HC
Minot State Univ	ND	6,602	LC
Miss Univ for Women	MS	5,446	LC
Missouri Baptist Univ	MO	18,010	C
Mount Union College	OH	21,120	C
New England College	NH	28,860	LC
New Mexico Highlands Univ	NM	6,182	LC
New Mexico State Univ	NM	7,932	C
N Dak State Univ	ND	8,435	C
Northeastern Univ	MA	35,650	HC
Northern Illinois Univ	IL	11,472	C
Northern Kentucky Univ	KY	6,352	NC
Northern Mich Univ	MI	10,834	C
Northern State Univ	SD	7,117	LC
Northwestern College of Iowa	IA	19,640	C+
Oakwood College	AL	14,904	C
Occidental College	CA	35,922	HC
Penn State Univ/Univ Park Campus	PA	15,646	HC
Sacred Heart Univ	CT	29,178	C
St. Augustine's College	NC	12,990	LC
St. Edward's Univ	TX	20,428	C
Sam Houston State Univ	TX	7,142	C
Seattle Pacific Univ	WA	25,944	VC
Shenandoah Univ	VA	25,190	NC
Shepherd College	WV	8,608	C
Sonoma State Univ	CA	10,421	C
Southwestern Univ	TX	25,410	HC
Spring Arbor Univ	MI	20,206	C
Springfield College	MA	24,520	C
Stephen F. Austin State Univ	TX	7,552	C
Sul Ross State Univ	TX	6,582	LC
Tarleton State Univ	TX	7,576	C
Temple Univ	PA	15,912	C
Texas Christian Univ	TX	23,410	VC
Texas Lutheran Univ	TX	20,370	C
Texas Southern Univ	TX	8,920	NC
Texas Woman's Univ	TX	7,804	LC
Truman State Univ	MO	9,728	HC+
Union College	NE	17,130	C
Univ of Alabama	AL	9,040	C+
Univ of Central Okla	OK	9,434	C
Univ of Delaware	DE	12,616	HC
Univ of Evansville	IN	24,190	VC
Univ of Florida	FL	8,580	MC
Univ of Houston	TX	9,818	C
Univ of La Verne	CA	28,600	C
Univ of Mich/Ann Arbor	MI	13,864	HC+
Univ of Nevada/Las Vegas	NV	11,566	C
Univ of New Hampshire	NH	14,828	VC
Univ of New Mexico	NM	9,223	C
Univ of N Car at Charlotte	NC	8,185	C
Univ of North Texas	TX	7,629	C
Univ of Northern Colo	CO	8,987	C
Univ of Pittsburgh at Pittsburgh	PA	16,074	HC
Univ of Puget Sound	WA	31,760	HC
Univ of Rio Grande	OH	8,728	NC
Univ of S Car at Aiken	SC	7,828	LC
Univ of Texas at Austin	TX	10,630	HC
Univ of Texas at El Paso	TX	5,799	NC
Univ of Texas at San Antonio	TX	9,088	NC
Univ of Texas-Pan American	TX	5,954	LC
Univ of Toledo	OH	12,479	NC
Univ of Wisc/Eau Claire	WI	8,463	VC
Univ of Wisc/Stevens Point	WI	8,116	VC
Upper Iowa Univ	IA	20,076	C
Urbana Univ	OH	19,115	C
West Liberty State College	WV	7,868	LC
Western State College of Colo	CO	9,014	C
Westfield State College	MA	10,147	C
Wheaton College	IL	21,934	HC
Winona State Univ	MN		C
Youngstown State Univ	OH	11,148	NC

PHYSICAL SCIENCES

School	ST	$IS	SR
Alverno College	WI	18,898	C
Antioch College	OH	29,269	C
Arkansas Tech Univ	AR	7,299	C
Asbury College	KY	20,704	VC
Auburn Univ Montgomery	AL	9,020	NC
Biola Univ	CA	25,964	VC
Black Hills State Univ	SD	7,743	LC
Bluffton College	OH	23,694	C
Bowling Green State Univ	OH	13,036	C
Brescia Univ	KY	14,225	C
Calif Polytechnic State Univ	CA	8,747	VC
Cal State, Chico	CA	8,598	LC
Cal State, Hayward	CA	8,871	LC
Cal State, Sacramento	CA	9,543	C
Cal State, Stanislaus	CA	9,874	C
Central Conn State Univ	CT	12,090	C
Central Mich Univ	MI	11,142	C
Colgate Univ	NY	37,095	MC
Colo State Univ	CO	9,964	VC
Concordia Univ Nebr	NE	20,302	C+
Concordia Univ, River Forest	IL	23,600	C
Doane College	NE	20,000	C
East Stroudsburg Univ of Pennsylvania	PA	10,336	C
Emporia State Univ	KS	6,998	C
Eureka College	IL	24,980	LC
Fort Hays State Univ	KS	7,363	C
Freed-Hardeman Univ	TN		NC
Harvard Univ/Harvard College	MA	37,928	MC
Indiana Univ Kokomo	IN	4,463	LC
Kansas State Univ	KS	8,728	VC
Keene State College	NH	12,212	C
Kent State Univ	OH	12,932	C
Le Moyne College	NY	26,400	VC
Lynchburg College	VA	26,815	C
Malone College	OH	20,995	C
Mayville State Univ	ND	7,325	NC
Mesa State College	CO	8,051	C
Mich State Univ	MI	11,933	VC
Minot State Univ	ND	6,602	LC
Miss Univ for Women	MS	5,446	LC
Muhlenberg College	PA	31,485	HC
Okla Panhandle State Univ	OK	5,370	C
Olivet Nazarene Univ	IL	20,480	C
Peru State College	NE	6,342	NC
Radford Univ	VA	8,500	C
Ripon College	WI	24,995	VC
St. John's Univ	NY	30,180	C
St. Michael's College	VT	30,100	VC
San Diego State Univ	CA	10,321	C
Shawnee State Univ	OH	11,031	NC
Texas Wesleyan Univ	TX	16,245	C
Trinity College	DC	24,150	LC
Tri-State Univ-Main Campus	IN	23,600	C
Union Univ	TN	18,800	VC
Univ of Arkansas at Monticello	AR	5,940	NC
Univ of Calif at Berkeley	CA	15,563	MC
Univ of Calif at Riverside	CA	15,300	C
Univ of Dayton	OH	24,850	VC
Univ of Great Falls	MT	15,360	C
Univ of Maryland/College Park	MD	14,227	HC
Univ of Mich/Flint	MI	5,548	C
Univ of Pittsburgh at Bradford	PA	15,294	C
Univ of Rio Grande	OH	8,728	NC
Univ of South Florida	FL	9,454	C
Univ of Southern Calif	CA	37,459	MC
Univ of Wisc/Eau Claire	WI	8,463	VC
Univ of Wisc/Platteville	WI	8,450	C
Washington State Univ	WA	11,334	C
Washington Univ in St. Louis	MO	38,293	MC
Wayland Baptist Univ	TX	11,919	NC
Weber State Univ	UT	7,945	NC
Wesleyan College	GA	17,870	VC
Wheaton College	IL	21,934	HC
York College of Pennsylvania	PA	14,500	VC

PHYSICAL THERAPY

School	ST	$IS	SR
American International College	MA	24,690	LC
Armstrong Atlantic State Univ	GA	7,102	C
Bellarmine Univ	KY	24,110	VC
Boston Univ	MA	38,194	HC+
Bowling Green State Univ	OH	13,036	C
Bradley Univ	IL	22,910	VC
Cal State, Northridge	CA	7,757	LC
Cal State, Sacramento	CA	9,543	C
Carson-Newman College	TN	16,760	C
CUNY/College of Staten Island	NY	4,308	NC
CUNY/Hunter College	NY	6,729	C+
Clarke College	IA	23,165	C
Cleveland State Univ	OH	12,308	LC
Coe College	IA	27,385	VC
College Misericordia	PA	26,350	C
College of St. Benedict	MN	26,672	VC
Concordia College	NY	19,200	VC
Daemen College	NY	22,120	C
Duquesne Univ	PA	26,907	VC
D'Youville College	NY	21,080	C
Florida A&M Univ	FL	7,564	C
Florida Gulf Coast Univ	FL	9,908	C
Grand Valley State Univ	MI	11,022	VC
Gustavus Adolphus College	MN	27,120	VC+
Howard Univ	DC	16,505	C
Indiana Univ-Purdue Univ Indianapolis	IN	8,257	LC
Ithaca College	NY	31,730	HC
Lamar Univ	TX	6,816	LC
Langston Univ	OK	2,308	LC
Lebanon Valley College	PA	28,870	VC
Lewis Univ	IL	22,950	C+
LIU/Brooklyn Campus	NY	24,790	C
Missouri Southern State Univ	MO	8,316	C
Nazareth College of Rochester	NY	24,936	VC
New York Inst of Technology	NY	24,205	VC
Newman Univ	KS	18,018	C
North Park Univ	IL	24,030	C
Northeastern Univ	MA	35,650	HC
Oakland Univ	MI	10,800	C
Ohio State Univ	OH	13,080	VC+
Okla Baptist Univ	OK	15,220	VC
Purdue Univ/Calumet	IN	6,630	NC
Richard Stockton College of New Jersey	NJ	12,972	VC
Russell Sage College	NY	26,811	C
St. Francis Univ	PA	25,876	LC
St. John's Univ	MN	26,473	VC
St. Mary's Univ of Minn	MN	21,535	C
St. Vincent College	PA	25,530	VC
San Francisco State Univ	CA	12,070	C
Simmons College	MA	33,000	VC
Southern Nazarene Univ	OK	14,634	NC
SUNY/Univ at Buffalo	NY	12,563	VC
Tarleton State Univ	TX	7,576	C
Tenn State Univ	TN	9,048	LC
Thiel College	PA	20,970	C
Touro College	NY	15,250	VC
Trinity International Univ	IL	22,980	C+
Truman State Univ	MO	9,728	HC+
Univ of Central Arkansas	AR	6,388	C
Univ of Conn	CT	14,608	VC
Univ of Evansville	IN	24,190	VC
Univ of Florida	FL	8,580	MC
Univ of Hartford	CT	31,080	C
Univ of Kentucky	KY	7,765	C
Univ of Mary	ND	12,900	C+
Univ of Maryland/Eastern Shore	MD	9,964	C
Univ of Mich/Flint	MI	5,548	C
Univ of Minn/Twin Cities	MN	13,160	VC
Univ of Missouri/Columbia	MO	13,782	VC
Univ of New Mexico	NM	9,223	C
Univ of N Dak	ND	8,390	C
Univ of Scranton	PA	30,836	VC
Univ of the Sciences in Philadelphia	PA	29,310	VC
Univ of Toledo	OH	12,479	NC
Univ of Utah	UT	9,205	C
Utica College	NY	28,340	C
Virginia Commonwealth Univ	VA	9,030	C
Walsh Univ	OH	20,890	C
Waynesburg College	PA	19,370	C
West Virginia Univ	WV	9,370	C
Western State College of Colo	CO	9,014	C
Winona State Univ	MN		C
Winston-Salem State Univ	NC	8,926	LC
Youngstown State Univ	OH	11,148	NC

PHYSICIAN'S ASSISTANT

School	ST	$IS	SR
Butler Univ	IN	28,250	VC+
CUNY/City College	NY	4,230	C+
CUNY/College of Staten Island	NY	4,308	NC
Daemen College	NY	22,120	C
De Sales Univ	PA	25,470	C
Duquesne Univ	PA	26,907	VC
D'Youville College	NY	21,080	C
East Carolina Univ	NC	8,671	C
Gannon Univ	PA	23,260	C
Gardner-Webb Univ	NC	19,300	C
George Washington Univ	DC	41,030	MC
Grand Valley State Univ	MI	11,022	VC
Hofstra Univ	NY	27,112	VC
Howard Univ	DC	16,505	C
Idaho State Univ	ID	8,128	C
Juniata College	PA	29,080	VC
Le Moyne College	NY	26,400	VC
Lenoir-Rhyne College	NC	19,186	C
LIU/Brooklyn Campus	NY	24,790	C
Mars Hill College	NC	18,600	LC
Marywood Univ	PA	26,050	C
MCP Hahnemann Univ	PA	18,510	SP
Methodist College	NC	19,526	C
Mountain State Univ	WV	10,212	NC
New York Inst of Technology	NY	24,205	VC
Nova Southeastern Univ	FL	23,346	C
Pace Univ	NY	28,652	VC
Pennsylvania College of Technology	PA	15,126	NC
Philadelphia Univ	PA	27,354	C
Rochester Inst of Technology	NY	29,217	VC+
St. Francis College	NY	10,880	LC
St. Francis Univ	PA	25,876	LC
St. John's Univ	NY	30,180	C
St. Vincent College	PA	25,530	VC
Seton Hill Univ	PA	24,930	C
South College	GA	8,720	LC
Southern Illinois Univ Carbondale	IL	10,407	C
SUNY/Univ at Stony Brook	NY	12,763	HC
Union College	NE	17,130	C
Univ of Alabama at Birmingham	AL	12,901	C
Univ of Findlay	OH	23,962	NC
Univ of Kentucky	KY	7,765	C
Univ of New Mexico	NM	9,223	C
Univ of S Dak	SD	7,710	C+
Univ of Southern Colo	CO	7,821	LC
Univ of Texas-Pan American	TX	5,954	LC
Univ of the Sciences in Philadelphia	PA	29,310	VC
Univ of Wisc/La Crosse	WI	8,991	VC
Univ of Wisc/Madison	WI	8,262	VC
Wagner College	NY	29,900	VC
Wichita State Univ	KS	8,092	C

ST = STATE $IS = IN-STATE COSTS SR = SELECTOR RATING

PHYSICS

School	ST	$IS	SR
Abilene Christian Univ	TX	18,370	VC
Adelphi Univ	NY	26,300	VC
Adrian College	MI	21,950	C
Agnes Scott College	GA	28,230	HC
Alabama A&M Univ	AL	5,100	LC
Alabama State Univ	AL	6,404	C
Albion College	MI	25,224	VC
Albright College	PA	30,579	C
Alfred Univ	NY	28,290	C
Allegheny College	PA	30,280	VC
Alma College	MI	25,566	VC
American Univ	DC	34,585	VC+
Amherst College	MA	37,470	MC
Anderson Univ	IN	19,430	LC
Andrews Univ	MI	19,550	C
Angelo State Univ	TX	7,576	NC
Appalachian State Univ	NC	7,637	VC
Arizona State Univ-Main	AZ	10,048	C
Arkansas State Univ	AR	8,450	C
Ashland Univ	OH	24,464	C
Auburn Univ	AL	10,396	VC
Augsburg College	MN	25,298	C
Augusta State Univ	GA	2,592	C
Augustana College	IL	26,610	VC+
Augustana College	SD	21,998	VC
Austin College	TX	24,747	HC
Austin Peay State Univ	TN	5,814	LC
Azusa Pacific Univ	CA	24,720	VC
Baker Univ	KS	19,860	VC
Baldwin-Wallace College	OH	24,678	C
Ball State Univ	IN	8,660	C
Bard College	NY	37,352	HC+
Bates College	ME	37,500	MC
Baylor Univ	TX	23,864	VC
Belmont Univ	TN	21,986	VC
Beloit College	WI	29,864	HC
Bemidji State Univ	MN	9,103	C
Benedict College	SC	12,662	LC
Benedictine College	KS	20,603	C
Benedictine Univ	IL	23,840	C
Bennington College	VT	35,910	HC
Berea College	KY	5,030	VC+
Berry College	GA	21,410	VC
Bethany College	WV	19,845	VC
Bethel College	IN	19,670	C
Bethel College	KS	19,800	C+
Bethel College	MN	25,180	VC
Bethune-Cookman College	FL	16,480	LC
Birmingham-Southern College	AL	25,364	VC+
Bloomsburg Univ of Pennsylvania	PA	10,844	C
Boise State Univ	ID	7,657	LC
Boston College	MA	33,284	MC
Boston Univ	MA	38,194	HC+
Bowdoin College	ME	37,790	MC
Bowling Green State Univ	OH	13,036	C
Bradley Univ	IL	22,910	VC
Brandeis Univ	MA	38,198	MC
Bridgewater State College	MA	10,482	C
Brigham Young Univ	UT	8,504	HC
Brown Univ	RI	38,174	MC
Bryn Mawr College	PA	36,890	HC+
Bucknell Univ	PA	35,262	HC+
Buena Vista Univ	IA	25,406	C
Butler Univ	IN	28,250	VC+
Calif Inst of Technology	CA	31,677	MC
Calif Lutheran Univ	CA	27,600	LC
Calif Polytechnic State Univ	CA	8,747	VC
Calif State Polytechnic Univ, Pomona	CA	8,793	C+
Cal State, Bakersfield	CA	6,090	LC
Cal State, Chico	CA	8,598	LC
Cal State, Dominguez Hills	CA	5,840	LC
Cal State, Fresno	CA	8,414	LC
Cal State, Fullerton	CA	6,648	C
Cal State, Hayward	CA	8,871	LC
Cal State, Long Beach	CA	8,762	C+
Cal State, Los Angeles	CA	5,778	C
Cal State, Northridge	CA	7,757	LC
Cal State, Sacramento	CA	9,543	C
Cal State, San Bernardino	CA	15,238	LC
Cal State, Stanislaus	CA	9,874	C
Calif Univ of Pennsylvania	PA	10,388	C
Calvin College	MI	22,615	NC
Cameron Univ	OK	5,692	NC
Canisius College	NY	28,163	C+
Carleton College	MN	34,395	MC
Carnegie Mellon Univ	PA	32,682	MC
Carthage College	WI	25,000	C
Case Western Reserve Univ	OH	32,002	MC
Catholic Univ of America	DC	34,248	VC
Cedarville Univ	OH	19,954	VC
Centenary College of Louisiana	LA	23,100	VC+
Central College	IA	21,206	C
Central Conn State Univ	CT	12,090	C
Central Methodist College	MO	16,460	C
Central Mich Univ	MI	11,142	C
Central Missouri State Univ	MO	9,776	C
Central Washington Univ	WA	9,768	C
Centre College	KY	27,300	HC
Chadron State College	NE	6,286	NC
Chatham College	PA	27,266	C+
Chicago State Univ	IL	10,882	C+
Christian Brothers Univ	TN	22,290	VC
Christopher Newport Univ	VA	8,862	VC
Citadel, The	SC	12,295	C+
CUNY/Brooklyn College	NY	4,353	C+
CUNY/City College	NY	4,230	C+
CUNY/College of Staten Island	NY	4,308	NC
CUNY/Herbert H. Lehman College	NY	3,320	LC
CUNY/Hunter College	NY	6,729	C+
CUNY/Queens College	NY	4,362	C
CUNY/York College	NY	3,292	NC
Claremont McKenna College	CA	36,880	MC
Clarion Univ of Pennsylvania	PA	11,272	LC
Clark Atlanta Univ	GA	19,300	C+
Clark Univ	MA	32,115	VC
Clarkson Univ	NY	32,226	VC
Clemson Univ	SC	11,972	HC
Cleveland State Univ	OH	12,308	LC
Coe College	IA	27,385	VC
Colby College	ME	37,580	MC
Colgate Univ	NY	37,095	MC
College of Charleston	SC	11,887	HC
College of Mount St. Vincent	NY	26,800	C
College of New Jersey	NJ	15,950	MC
College of Notre Dame of Maryland	MD	27,700	C
College of St. Benedict	MN	26,672	VC
College of the Holy Cross	MA	36,451	MC
College of William and Mary	VA	12,224	MC
College of Wooster	OH	31,300	HC
Colo College	CO	36,860	HC
Colo School of Mines	CO	12,533	HC
Colo State Univ	CO	9,964	VC
Columbia Univ/Barnard College	NY	36,990	MC
Columbia Univ/Columbia College	NY	38,590	MC
Columbia Univ/School of General Studies	NY	35,000	C
Concordia College: Moorhead	MN	22,460	VC+
Conn College	CT	37,900	MC
Cornell College	IA	27,825	VC+
Cornell Univ	NY	38,253	MC
Covenant College	GA	23,830	VC+
Creighton Univ	NE	26,748	VC+
Cumberland College	KY	16,384	C
Curry College	MA	26,025	LC
Dakota State Univ	SD	7,466	C
Dartmouth College	NH	37,770	MC
David Lipscomb Univ	TN	16,158	VC
Davidson College	NC	33,274	MC
Delaware State Univ	DE	8,104	LC
Denison Univ	OH	33,050	HC
DePaul Univ	IL	27,580	VC
DePauw Univ	IN	31,500	HC
Dickinson College	PA	35,825	HC
Dillard Univ	LA	17,325	VC
Doane College	NE	20,000	C
Dordt College	IA	20,170	VC
Drake Univ	IA	25,120	VC+
Drew Univ/College of Liberal Arts	NJ	35,550	VC
Drexel Univ	PA	27,655	VC
Drury Univ	MO	18,085	VC+
Duke Univ	NC	37,555	MC
Duquesne Univ	PA	26,907	VC
Earlham College	IN	29,976	VC+
East Carolina Univ	NC	8,671	C
East Central Univ	OK	4,968	C
East Tenn State Univ	TN	8,497	C
Eastern Illinois Univ	IL	11,192	C
Eastern Mich Univ	MI	11,478	C
Eastern Nazarene College	MA	19,433	LC
Eastern New Mexico Univ	NM	6,762	LC
Eastern Oregon Univ	OR	10,080	NC
Eastern Washington Univ	WA	9,012	C
Eckerd College	FL	28,744	C+
Edinboro Univ of Pennsylvania	PA	10,850	LC
Elizabeth City State Univ	NC	5,550	LC
Elizabethtown College	PA	28,800	C
Elmhurst College	IL	24,630	C
Elon Univ	NC	22,240	VC
Emory & Henry College	VA	21,950	C
Emory Univ	GA	36,872	MC
Emporia State Univ	KS	6,998	C
Erskine College	SC	23,166	VC
Fairfield Univ	CT	35,505	HC
Fisk Univ	TN	17,305	LC
Florida A&M Univ	FL	7,564	C
Florida Atlantic Univ	FL	8,543	C
Florida Inst of Technology	FL	28,740	VC
Florida International Univ	FL	9,912	VC
Florida State Univ	FL	9,028	HC
Fordham Univ	NY	35,066	HC
Fort Hays State Univ	KS	7,363	C
Fort Lewis College	CO	8,353	C
Francis Marion Univ	SC	9,364	C
Franklin and Marshall College	PA	35,930	HC+
Frostburg State Univ	MD	11,114	C
Furman Univ	SC	28,976	HC+
Gallaudet Univ	DC	16,554	SP
Geneva College	PA	21,850	C
George Mason Univ	VA	9,732	VC
George Washington Univ	DC	41,030	MC
Georgetown College	KY	22,000	VC
Georgetown Univ	DC	38,242	MC
Georgia Inst of Technology	GA	10,340	HC+
Georgia Southern Univ	GA	8,540	C
Georgia State Univ	GA	10,658	C
Georgian Court College	NJ	19,040	LC
Gettysburg College	PA	35,646	HC
Gonzaga Univ	WA	26,766	HC
Gordon College	MA	25,982	VC+
Goshen College	IN	22,450	VC
Goucher College	MD	32,650	HC
Grambling State Univ	LA	6,538	NC
Grand Valley State Univ	MI	11,022	VC
Greenville College	IL	21,342	C
Grinnell College	IA	31,060	HC+
Grove City College	PA	14,228	HC
Guilford College	NC	24,960	VC
Gustavus Adolphus College	MN	27,120	VC+
Hamilton College	NY	37,560	MC
Hamline Univ	MN	27,052	VC
Hampden-Sydney College	VA	28,407	VC
Hampshire College	MA	37,037	HC
Hampton Univ	VA	17,112	C+
Hanover College	IN	25,200	VC
Harding Univ	AR	14,890	VC
Hardin-Simmons Univ	TX	14,165	C
Hartwick College	NY	34,650	C+
Harvard Univ/Harvard College	MA	37,928	MC
Harvey Mudd College	CA	38,080	MC
Hastings College	NE	19,928	VC
Haverford College	PA	37,900	MC
Heidelberg College	OH	20,266	NC
Henderson State Univ	AR	7,386	C
Hendrix College	AR	20,970	VC+
Hillsdale College	MI	22,450	HC
Hobart and William Smith Colleges	NY	36,536	HC
Hofstra Univ	NY	27,112	VC
Hollins Univ	VA	27,965	VC
Hope College	MI	25,340	VC
Houghton College	NY	23,984	VC
Houston Baptist Univ	TX	16,905	C
Howard Univ	DC	16,505	C
Humboldt State Univ	CA	9,400	C
Idaho State Univ	ID	8,128	C
Illinois College	IL	19,100	VC
Illinois Inst of Technology	IL	26,456	HC+
Illinois State Univ	IL	10,944	C+
Illinois Wesleyan Univ	IL	30,380	HC+
Indiana State Univ	IN	10,719	LC
Indiana Univ Bloomington	IN	12,389	VC
Indiana Univ of Pennsylvania	PA	10,489	C
Indiana Univ South Bend	IN	4,571	LC
Indiana Univ-Purdue Univ Fort Wayne	IN	5,108	LC
Indiana Univ-Purdue Univ Indianapolis	IN	8,257	LC
Iona College	NY	27,988	VC
Iowa State Univ	IA	10,768	VC
Ithaca College	NY	31,730	HC
Jackson State Univ	MS	8,382	C
Jacksonville State Univ	AL	6,844	LC
Jacksonville Univ	FL	24,040	C
James Madison Univ	VA	10,794	VC
John Carroll Univ	OH	27,658	C+
Johns Hopkins Univ	MD	38,372	MC
Johnson C. Smith Univ	NC	18,108	C
Juniata College	PA	29,080	VC
Kalamazoo College	MI	26,955	HC+
Kansas State Univ	KS	8,728	VC
Kansas Wesleyan Univ	KS	18,900	VC
Kent State Univ	OH	12,932	C
Kentucky Wesleyan College	KY	17,250	C
Kenyon College	OH	35,370	HC+
King College	TN	22,500	VC
Knox College	IL	30,294	VC+
Kutztown Univ of Pennsylvania	PA	10,786	C
La Sierra Univ	CA	19,260	LC
Lafayette College	PA	35,746	MC
Lake Forest College	IL	30,270	VC
Lamar Univ	TX	6,816	LC
Lane College	TN	11,178	C+
Lawrence Tech Univ	MI	20,487	C
Lawrence Univ	WI	30,900	HC
Le Moyne College	NY	26,400	VC
Lebanon Valley College	PA	28,870	VC
Lehigh Univ	PA	37,570	HC+
Lenoir-Rhyne College	NC	19,186	C
Lewis and Clark College	OR	30,620	VC
Lewis Univ	IL	22,950	C+
Lincoln Univ	MO	7,158	NC
Lincoln Univ	PA	13,320	C+
Linfield College	OR	27,090	VC
Lock Haven Univ of Pennsylvania	PA	11,098	LC
LIU/C.W. Post Campus	NY	28,282	C
Longwood Univ	VA	11,175	C
Louisiana State Univ and A&M College	LA	9,126	VC
Louisiana State Univ in Shreveport	LA	2,884	NC
Louisiana Tech Univ	LA	7,361	C
Loyola College in Maryland	MD	34,560	HC
Loyola Marymount Univ	CA	32,194	VC
Loyola Univ Chicago	IL	31,164	VC
Loyola Univ New Orleans	LA	31,036	VC+
Luther College	IA	25,700	VC
Lycoming College	PA	27,589	C+
Macalester College	MN	31,944	MC
MacMurray College	IL	20,005	LC
Manchester College	IN	23,390	C
Manhattan College	NY	27,400	VC
Manhattanville College	NY	32,420	C+
Mansfield Univ	PA	11,220	C
Marietta College	OH	27,047	C
Marlboro College	VT	29,055	VC+
Marquette Univ	WI	27,594	VC
Marshall Univ	WV	9,116	C
Mary Baldwin College	VA	24,939	C
Mary Washington College	VA	10,166	HC
Mass College of Liberal Arts	MA	8,717	LC
Mass Inst of Technology	MA	38,310	MC
McDaniel College	MD	28,440	VC
McMurry Univ	TX	17,846	LC
McNeese State Univ	LA	5,259	LC
McPherson College	KS	20,265	C
Mercer Univ	GA	27,516	VC+
Merrimack College	MA	29,625	C
Messiah College	PA	25,890	VC+
Metropolitan State College of Denver	CO	2,338	LC
Miami Univ	OH	15,033	HC
Mich State Univ	MI	11,933	VC
Mich Tech Univ	MI	13,235	VC
MidAmerica Nazarene Univ	KS	18,688	C
Middle Tenn State Univ	TN	8,534	C
Middlebury College	VT	38,100	MC
Millersville Univ of Pennsylvania	PA	11,269	C
Millikin Univ	IL	25,555	C
Millsaps College	MS	25,182	VC
Minn State Univ, Mankato	MN	8,803	LC
Minn State Univ, Moorehead	MN	7,000	LC
Minot State Univ	ND	6,602	LC
Miss College	MS	14,574	C
Miss State Univ	MS	9,139	C
Missouri Southern State Univ	MO	8,316	C
Monmouth College	IL	23,600	C
Montana State Univ-Bozeman	MT	9,515	C
Montclair State Univ	NJ	13,790	C
Moravian College	PA	28,903	VC
Morehead State Univ	KY	7,464	C
Morehouse College	GA	22,728	C
Morgan State Univ	MD	11,470	C
Morningside College	IA	21,610	C
Mount Holyoke College	MA	37,918	HC+
Mount Union College	OH	21,120	C
Muhlenberg College	PA	31,485	HC
Murray State Univ	KY	7,816	VC
Muskingum College	OH	20,680	C
Nebr Wesleyan Univ	NE	21,197	C+
New College of Florida	FL	8,906	HC+
New Jersey City Univ	NJ	11,850	LC
New Mexico Highlands Univ	NM	6,182	LC
New Mexico Inst of Mining and Technology	NM	7,580	NC
New Mexico State Univ	NM	7,932	C
New York Inst of Technology	NY	24,205	VC
New York Univ	NY	39,406	MC
Norfolk State Univ	VA	9,722	LC
N Car Agricultural and Technical State Univ	NC	6,659	LC
N Car Central Univ	NC	7,534	LC
N Car State Univ	NC	9,886	VC
North Central College	IL	25,656	VC
N Dak State Univ	ND	8,435	C
North Georgia College and State Univ	GA	6,984	C
North Park Univ	IL	24,030	C
Northeastern Illinois Univ	IL	2,898	NC
Northeastern State Univ	OK	4,950	LC
Northeastern Univ	MA	35,650	HC
Northern Arizona Univ	AZ	9,002	C
Northern Illinois Univ	IL	11,472	C
Northern Kentucky Univ	KY	6,352	NC
Northern Mich Univ	MI	10,834	C
Northwest Missouri State Univ	MO	9,334	C
Northwest Nazarene Univ	ID	20,360	VC
Northwestern Okla State Univ	OK	5,433	NC
Northwestern State Univ of Louisiana	LA	6,331	NC
Northwestern Univ	IL	37,491	MC
Norwich Univ	VT	21,064	LC
Oakland Univ	MI	10,800	C

ST = STATE $IS = IN-STATE COSTS SR = SELECTOR RATING

INDEX OF COLLEGE MAJORS

School	ST	$IS	SR
Oberlin College	OH	36,938	MC
Occidental College	CA	35,922	HC
Oglethorpe Univ	GA	26,000	VC
Ohio Northern Univ	OH	27,765	VC
Ohio State Univ	OH	13,080	VC+
Ohio Univ	OH	14,448	C
Ohio Wesleyan Univ	OH	32,550	VC+
Okla Baptist Univ	OK	15,220	VC
Okla City Univ	OK	19,580	VC
Okla State Univ	OK	9,216	VC
Old Dominion Univ	VA	10,441	C
Oral Roberts Univ	OK	18,490	C
Oregon State Univ	OR	11,055	C
Otterbein College	OH	26,085	C
Ouachita Baptist Univ	AR	18,900	VC
Pace Univ	NY	28,652	VC
Pacific Lutheran Univ	WA	25,715	VC
Pacific Union College	CA	22,065	C+
Pacific Univ	OR	24,250	C
Penn State Univ at Erie/ Behrend College	PA	12,326	C
Penn State Univ/Univ Park Campus	PA	15,646	HC
Pittsburg State Univ	KS	7,128	NC
Pitzer College	CA	37,590	HC
Point Loma Nazarene Univ	CA	21,380	VC
Polytechnic Univ/Brooklyn	NY	33,770	VC
Pomona College	CA	33,960	MC
Pontifical Catholic Univ of PR/Ponce	PR	7,298	
Portland State Univ	OR	12,453	C
Prairie View A&M Univ	TX	9,418	NC
Presbyterian College	SC	25,920	VC
Princeton Univ	NJ	36,649	MC
Principia College	IL	25,044	C+
Purdue Univ/Calumet	IN	6,630	NC
Purdue Univ/West Lafayette	IN	12,560	VC
Ramapo College of New Jersey	NJ	15,203	VC
Randolph-Macon College	VA	27,190	C
Randolph-Macon Woman's College	VA	28,430	VC+
Reed College	OR	36,950	MC
Rensselaer Polytechnic Inst	NY	37,579	HC+
Rhode Island College	RI	11,565	C
Rhodes College	TN	26,466	HC+
Rice Univ	TX	27,550	MC
Richard Stockton College of New Jersey	NJ	12,972	VC
Rider Univ	NJ	30,900	C
Roanoke College	VA	27,393	C
Roberts Wesleyan College	NY	23,190	C+
Rochester Inst of Technology	NY	29,217	VC+
Rockhurst Univ	MO	22,960	C+
Rollins College	FL	34,300	VC
Rose-Hulman Inst of Technology	IN	31,425	HC+
Rowan Univ	NJ	14,506	VC
Rutgers, The State Univ of New Jersey/Camden Campus	NJ	14,990	VC
Rutgers, The State Univ of New Jersey/New Brunswick/Piscataway Campus	NJ	15,800	HC
Rutgers, The State Univ of New Jersey/Newark Campus	NJ	15,624	VC
Saginaw Valley State Univ	MI	11,055	C
St. Ambrose Univ	IA	22,800	C
St. Bonaventure Univ	NY	24,455	LC
St. Cloud State Univ	MN	8,362	C
St. John Fisher College	NY	24,870	C
St. John's Univ	MN	26,473	VC
St. John's Univ	NY	30,180	C
St. Joseph's Univ	PA	33,590	VC
St. Lawrence Univ	NY	35,945	VC
St. Louis Univ	MO	29,780	VC+
St. Mary's College of Calif	CA	32,850	VC
St. Mary's College of Maryland	MD	15,908	VC+
St. Mary's Univ of Minn	MN	21,535	C
St. Mary's Univ of San Antonio	TX	22,444	C
St. Michael's College	VT	30,100	VC
St. Norbert College	WI	25,810	C
St. Olaf College	MN	28,500	HC
St. Peter's College	NJ	22,292	LC
St. Vincent College	PA	25,530	VC
Salisbury Univ	MD	12,664	VC
Sam Houston State Univ	TX	7,142	C
Samford Univ	AL	18,648	VC
San Diego State Univ	CA	10,321	C
San Francisco State Univ	CA	12,070	C
San Jose State Univ	CA	8,187	C
Santa Clara Univ	CA	34,701	HC
Savannah State Univ	GA	7,328	LC
Scripps College	CA	35,700	HC+
Seattle Pacific Univ	WA	25,944	VC
Seattle Univ	WA	24,183	VC
Seton Hall Univ	NJ	30,130	VC
Seton Hill Univ	PA	24,930	C
Shaw Univ	NC	14,882	C+
Shippensburg Univ of Pennsylvania	PA	10,826	C
Siena College	NY	25,310	VC
Simon's Rock College of Bard	MA	36,580	HC
Simpson College	IA	23,658	C+
Skidmore College	NY	37,930	HC
Slippery Rock Univ of Pennsylvania	PA	10,343	LC
Smith College	MA	37,034	HC+
Sonoma State Univ	CA	10,421	C
S Car State Univ	SC	6,586	LC
S Dak School of Mines and Technology	SD	7,854	C+
S Dak State Univ	SD	7,782	C
Southeast Missouri State Univ	MO	9,704	C
Southeastern Louisiana Univ	LA	6,791	LC
Southeastern Okla State Univ	OK	6,147	C
Southern Adventist Univ	TN	17,080	C
Southern Conn State Univ	CT	10,310	C
Southern Illinois Univ Carbondale	IL	10,407	C
Southern Illinois Univ Edwardsville	IL	8,724	C
Southern Methodist Univ	TX	34,210	HC
Southern Nazarene Univ	OK	14,634	NC
Southern Oregon Univ	OR	10,362	C
Southern Polytechnic State Univ	GA	7,620	VC
Southern Univ and A&M College	LA	7,372	LC
Southern Univ at New Orleans	LA	995	NC
Southwest Missouri State Univ	MO	8,918	C
Southwestern Adventist Univ	TX	14,798	C
Southwestern College	KS	19,560	C
Southwestern Okla State Univ	OK	4,801	C
Southwestern Univ	TX	25,410	HC
Spelman College	GA	19,215	C+
Spring Arbor Univ	MI	20,206	C
Stanford Univ	CA	37,612	MC
SUNY at Oswego	NY	12,650	C
SUNY at Potsdam	NY	12,160	C
SUNY/College at Brockport	NY	12,111	C
SUNY/College at Buffalo	NY	8,025	C
SUNY/College at Cortland	NY	12,095	C
SUNY/College at Fredonia	NY	11,562	VC
SUNY/College at Geneseo	NY	11,330	HC
SUNY/College at Oneonta	NY	11,870	VC
SUNY/College at Plattsburgh	NY	11,700	C
SUNY/Univ at Albany	NY	12,951	HC
SUNY/Univ at Binghamton	NY	12,787	HC
SUNY/Univ at Buffalo	NY	12,563	VC
SUNY/Univ at New Paltz	NY	11,565	VC
SUNY/Univ at Stony Brook	NY	12,763	HC
State Univ of West Georgia	GA	7,622	C
Stephen F. Austin State Univ	TX	7,552	C
Stetson Univ	FL	29,495	VC
Stevens Inst of Technology	NJ	35,300	HC+
Suffolk Univ	MA	29,200	C
Susquehanna Univ	PA	29,990	VC
Swarthmore College	PA	37,716	MC
Sweet Briar College	VA	27,940	C
Syracuse Univ	NY	34,720	HC
Talladega College	AL	10,110	LC
Tarleton State Univ	TX	7,576	C
Taylor Univ	IN	23,820	VC+
Temple Univ	PA	15,912	C
Tenn State Univ	TN	9,048	LC
Tenn Tech Univ	TN	8,670	VC
Texas A&M Univ	TX	11,081	HC
Texas A&M Univ at Commerce	TX	8,994	C
Texas A&M Univ at Kingsville	TX	6,740	LC
Texas Christian Univ	TX	23,410	VC
Texas Lutheran Univ	TX	20,370	C
Texas Southern Univ	TX	8,920	NC
Texas State Univ	TX	9,320	VC
Texas Tech Univ	TX	10,768	VC
Thiel College	PA	20,970	C
Thomas More College	KY	21,350	C
Tougaloo College	MS	9,200	NC
Touro College	NY	15,250	VC
Towson Univ	MD	12,694	VC
Transylvania Univ	KY	23,780	VC+
Trevecca Nazarene Univ	TN	17,548	C
Trinity College	CT	38,040	HC+
Trinity Univ	TX	26,466	HC+
Truman State Univ	MO	9,728	HC+
Tufts Univ	MA	38,233	MC
Tulane Univ	LA	37,451	HC+
Tuskegee Univ	AL	17,250	LC
Union College	KY	15,920	C
Union College	NE	17,130	C
Union College	NY	36,005	HC
Union Univ	TN	18,800	VC
United States Air Force Academy	CO		HC+
United States Military Academy	NY		MC
United States Naval Academy	MD		MC
Univ of Akron	OH	13,134	NC
Univ of Alabama	AL	9,040	C+
Univ of Alabama at Birmingham	AL	12,901	C
Univ of Alabama in Huntsville	AL	9,126	VC
Univ of Alaska Fairbanks	AK	9,295	C
Univ of Arizona	AZ	10,413	VC
Univ of Arkansas	AR	9,855	VC
Univ of Arkansas at Little Rock	AR	5,637	NC
Univ of Arkansas at Pine Bluff	AR	7,925	C
Univ of Calif at Berkeley	CA	15,563	MC
Univ of Calif at Davis	CA	14,995	VC
Univ of Calif at Irvine	CA	19,808	HC
Univ of Calif at Los Angeles	CA	15,330	MC
Univ of Calif at Riverside	CA	15,300	C
Univ of Calif at San Diego	CA	14,127	HC
Univ of Calif at Santa Barbara	CA	11,732	VC
Univ of Calif at Santa Cruz	CA	16,505	VC
Univ of Central Arkansas	AR	6,388	C
Univ of Central Florida	FL	10,038	VC
Univ of Chicago	IL	35,087	MC
Univ of Cincinnati	OH	14,736	C
Univ of Colo at Boulder	CO	10,774	VC
Univ of Colo at Colo Springs	CO	10,667	C
Univ of Colo at Denver	CO	3,302	C
Univ of Conn	CT	14,608	VC
Univ of Dallas	TX	25,898	VC+
Univ of Dayton	OH	24,850	VC
Univ of Delaware	DE	12,616	HC
Univ of Denver	CO	32,148	VC
Univ of Evansville	IN	24,190	VC
Univ of Florida	FL	8,580	MC
Univ of Georgia	GA	8,656	VC
Univ of Hartford	CT	31,080	C
Univ of Hawaii at Hilo	HI	6,497	C
Univ of Hawaii at Manoa	HI	9,565	VC
Univ of Houston	TX	9,818	C
Univ of Houston-Downtown	TX	2,594	NC
Univ of Idaho	ID	8,216	C
Univ of Illinois at Chicago	IL	13,418	C
Univ of Illinois at Urbana-Champaign	IL	11,316	HC+
Univ of Indianapolis	IN	22,560	VC
Univ of Iowa	IA	10,923	VC
Univ of Kansas	KS	8,923	VC
Univ of Kentucky	KY	7,765	C
Univ of La Verne	CA	28,600	C
Univ of Louisiana at Lafayette	LA	5,826	C
Univ of Louisiana at Monroe	LA	5,207	NC
Univ of Louisville	KY	8,762	VC
Univ of Maine	ME	12,080	C+
Univ of Maryland/Baltimore County	MD	14,668	VC+
Univ of Maryland/College Park	MD	14,227	HC
Univ of Mass Amherst	MA	13,980	C+
Univ of Mass Boston	MA	6,227	C
Univ of Mass Dartmouth	MA	12,835	C
Univ of Mass Lowell	MA	11,937	VC
Univ of Memphis	TN	8,560	C
Univ of Miami	FL	34,608	HC
Univ of Mich/Ann Arbor	MI	13,864	HC+
Univ of Mich/Dearborn	MI	6,843	VC
Univ of Mich/Flint	MI	5,548	C
Univ of Minn/Duluth	MN	12,470	C
Univ of Minn/Morris	MN	12,896	VC
Univ of Minn/Twin Cities	MN	13,160	VC
Univ of Miss	MS	7,666	C
Univ of Missouri/Columbia	MO	13,782	VC
Univ of Missouri/Kansas City	MO	13,416	VC
Univ of Missouri/Rolla	MO	12,292	HC
Univ of Missouri/St. Louis	MO	11,656	VC
Univ of Montana	MT	9,395	C
Univ of Nebr at Kearney	NE	8,286	NC
Univ of Nebr at Lincoln	NE	9,975	C+
Univ of Nebr at Omaha	NE	8,080	C
Univ of Nevada/Las Vegas	NV	11,566	C
Univ of Nevada/Reno	NV	9,792	C
Univ of New Hampshire	NH	14,828	VC
Univ of New Mexico	NM	9,223	C
Univ of New Orleans	LA	7,356	C
Univ of North Alabama	AL	7,972	NC
Univ of N Car at Asheville	NC	8,079	VC
Univ of N Car at Chapel Hill	NC	10,117	MC
Univ of N Car at Charlotte	NC	8,185	C
Univ of N Car at Greensboro	NC	8,248	C
Univ of N Car at Wilmington	NC	8,940	VC
Univ of N Dak	ND	8,390	C
Univ of North Florida	FL	8,769	VC
Univ of North Texas	TX	7,629	C
Univ of Northern Colo	CO	8,987	C
Univ of Northern Iowa	IA	9,834	C
Univ of Notre Dame	IN	34,442	MC
Univ of Okla	OK	9,226	VC
Univ of Oregon	OR	11,479	VC
Univ of Pennsylvania	PA	37,960	MC
Univ of Pittsburgh at Pittsburgh	PA	16,074	HC
Univ of Portland	OR	28,500	VC
Univ of PR at Humacao	PR	1,245	
Univ of PR/Mayaguez	PR		
Univ of Puget Sound	WA	31,760	HC
Univ of Redlands	CA	32,576	VC
Univ of Rhode Island	RI	13,720	VC
Univ of Richmond	VA	30,100	MC
Univ of Rochester	NY	32,979	HC
Univ of St. Thomas	MN	26,918	VC
Univ of San Diego	CA	33,156	HC
Univ of San Francisco	CA	34,700	VC
Univ of Science and Arts of Okla	OK	5,982	C
Univ of Scranton	PA	30,836	VC
Univ of South Alabama	AL	7,760	LC
Univ of S Car at Columbia	SC	10,048	VC
Univ of S Dak	SD	7,710	C+
Univ of South Florida	FL	9,454	C
Univ of Southern Calif	CA	37,459	MC
Univ of Southern Colo	CO	7,821	LC
Univ of Southern Maine	ME	11,212	C
Univ of Southern Miss	MS	8,324	LC
Univ of Tenn at Chattanooga	TN	7,783	C
Univ of Tenn at Knoxville	TN	8,214	C
Univ of Texas at Arlington	TX	7,192	LC
Univ of Texas at Austin	TX	10,630	HC
Univ of Texas at Dallas	TX	10,234	HC
Univ of Texas at El Paso	TX	5,799	NC
Univ of Texas at San Antonio	TX	9,088	NC
Univ of Texas-Pan American	TX	5,954	LC
Univ of the District of Columbia	DC	2,070	LC
Univ of the Pacific	CA	31,090	VC
Univ of the South	TN	30,855	HC
Univ of Toledo	OH	12,479	NC
Univ of Tulsa	OK	22,090	VC+
Univ of Utah	UT	9,205	C
Univ of Vermont	VT	16,316	VC
Univ of Virginia	VA	11,740	MC
Univ of Washington	WA	10,361	VC
Univ of West Alabama	AL	6,048	C
Univ of West Florida	FL	8,470	C
Univ of Wisc/Eau Claire	WI	8,463	VC
Univ of Wisc/La Crosse	WI	8,991	VC
Univ of Wisc/Madison	WI	8,262	VC
Univ of Wisc/Milwaukee	WI	9,427	LC
Univ of Wisc/Oshkosh	WI	6,130	LC
Univ of Wisc/Parkside	WI	6,160	LC
Univ of Wisc/Platteville	WI	8,450	C
Univ of Wisc/River Falls	WI	8,358	LC
Univ of Wisc/Stevens Point	WI	8,116	VC
Univ of Wisc/Whitewater	WI	8,626	C
Univ of Wyoming	WY	8,636	C
Ursinus College	PA	34,400	VC
Utah State Univ	UT	7,371	C
Utica College	NY	28,340	C
Valdosta State Univ	GA	7,798	C
Valparaiso Univ	IN	26,118	VC+
Vanderbilt Univ	TN	37,897	MC
Vassar College	NY	37,030	MC
Villanova Univ	PA	35,050	HC
Virginia Commonwealth Univ	VA	9,030	C
Virginia Military Inst	VA	9,968	C+
Virginia Polytechnic Inst and State Univ	VA	9,179	C
Virginia State Univ	VA	10,358	C
Wabash College	IN	27,932	VC
Wagner College	NY	29,900	VC
Wake Forest Univ	NC	34,090	MC
Walla Walla College	WA	21,600	NC
Wartburg College	IA	21,165	VC
Washburn Univ of Topeka	KS	8,984	NC
Washington and Jefferson College	PA	29,570	VC
Washington and Lee Univ	VA	29,663	MC
Washington College	MD	30,540	VC
Washington State Univ	WA	11,334	C
Washington Univ in St. Louis	MO	38,293	MC
Wayne State Univ	MI	11,774	C
Weber State Univ	UT	7,945	NC
Wellesley College	MA	36,516	MC
Wells College	NY	21,122	VC
Wesleyan College	GA	17,870	VC
Wesleyan Univ	CT	35,139	MC
West Chester Univ of Pennsylvania	PA	11,164	C
West Texas A&M Univ	TX	7,533	C
West Virginia Univ	WV	9,370	C
West Virginia Univ Inst of Technology	WV	7,518	NC
West Virginia Wesleyan College	WV	22,920	C
Western Illinois Univ	IL	10,363	C
Western Kentucky Univ	KY	6,834	C
Western Mich Univ	MI	12,031	C
Western Washington Univ	WA	10,119	VC
Westminster College	MO	18,150	C+

ST = STATE **$IS** = IN-STATE COSTS **SR** = SELECTOR RATING

School	ST	$IS	SR
Westminster College	PA	22,960	C
Westminster College	UT	17,226	C
Westmont College	CA	33,062	VC+
Wheaton College	IL	21,934	HC
Wheaton College	MA	36,330	HC
Wheeling Jesuit Univ	WV	22,660	C
Whitman College	WA	32,526	HC+
Whittier College	CA	29,108	C
Whitworth College	WA	26,428	VC+
Wichita State Univ	KS	8,092	C
Widener Univ	PA	27,020	C
Wiley College	TX	8,100	LC
Willamette Univ	OR	32,032	VC+
William Jewell College	MO	21,320	VC
Williams College	MA	32,270	MC
Winona State Univ	MN		C
Wittenberg Univ	OH	31,316	VC
Wofford College	SC	26,710	HC
Worcester Polytechnic Inst	MA	37,404	HC
Wright State Univ	OH	11,490	LC
Xavier Univ	OH	26,850	VC+
Xavier Univ of Louisiana	LA	17,600	C
Yale Univ	CT	37,000	MC
Youngstown State Univ	OH	11,148	NC

PHYSIOLOGY

School	ST	$IS	SR
Andrews Univ	MI	19,550	C
Boston Univ	MA	38,194	HC+
Brigham Young Univ	UT	8,504	HC
Cal State, Long Beach	CA	8,762	C+
Florida State Univ	FL	9,028	HC
Hampshire College	MA	37,037	HC
Marquette Univ	WI	27,594	VC
Mich State Univ	MI	11,933	VC
Northern Mich Univ	MI	10,834	C
Okla State Univ	OK	9,216	VC
Rutgers, The State Univ of New Jersey/New Brunswick/Piscataway Campus	NJ	15,800	HC
San Francisco State Univ	CA	12,070	C
Southern Illinois Univ Carbondale	IL	10,407	C
Texas State Univ	TX	9,320	VC
Univ of Arizona	AZ	10,413	VC
Univ of Calif at Davis	CA	14,995	VC
Univ of Calif at Los Angeles	CA	15,330	MC
Univ of Calif at San Diego	CA	14,127	HC
Univ of Calif at Santa Barbara	CA	11,732	VC
Univ of Conn	CT	14,608	VC
Univ of Great Falls	MT	15,360	C
Univ of Hawaii at Manoa	HI	9,565	VC
Univ of Illinois at Urbana-Champaign	IL	11,316	HC+
Univ of Minn/Twin Cities	MN	13,160	VC

PIANO/ORGAN

School	ST	$IS	SR
Ball State Univ	IN	8,660	C
Blue Mountain College	MS	10,226	C
Boston Conservatory	MA	26,900	SP
Catholic Univ of America	DC	34,248	VC
Central Washington Univ	WA	9,768	C
Columbia College	SC	22,658	LC
East Central Univ	OK	4,968	C
East Texas Baptist Univ	TX	13,914	C
Eastern Mich Univ	MI	11,478	C
Florida State Univ	FL	9,028	HC
Furman Univ	SC	28,976	HC+
Grand Canyon Univ	AZ	30,000	LC
Hannibal-LaGrange College	MO	13,940	C
Illinois Wesleyan Univ	IL	30,380	HC+
Indiana Univ Bloomington	IN	12,389	VC
Indiana Univ South Bend	IN	4,571	LC
Jackson State Univ	MS	8,382	C
Juilliard School	NY	30,385	SP
Loyola Univ New Orleans	LA	31,036	VC+
Manhattan School of Music	NY	31,500	SP
McMurry Univ	TX	17,846	LC
Miss College	MS	14,574	C
Northwestern Univ	IL	37,491	MC
Nyack College	NY	18,540	C
Okla City Univ	OK	19,580	VC
Pacific Lutheran Univ	WA	25,715	VC
Roosevelt Univ	IL	22,580	VC
Samford Univ	AL	18,648	VC
Shenandoah Univ	VA	25,190	NC
Shorter College	GA	17,370	C
Southern Methodist Univ	TX	34,210	HC
Southern Nazarene Univ	OK	14,634	NC
Stetson Univ	FL	29,495	VC
Temple Univ	PA	15,912	C
Texas Christian Univ	TX	23,410	VC
Union Univ	TN	18,800	VC
Univ of Cincinnati	OH	14,736	C
Univ of Miami	FL	34,608	HC
Univ of Mich/Ann Arbor	MI	13,864	HC+
Univ of Tulsa	OK	22,090	VC+
Weber State Univ	UT	7,945	NC
Westminster Choir College of Rider Univ	NJ	25,400	SP
Youngstown State Univ	OH	11,148	NC

PLANETARY AND SPACE SCIENCE

School	ST	$IS	SR
Boston Univ	MA	38,194	HC+
Brigham Young Univ	UT	8,504	HC
Calif Inst of Technology	CA	31,677	MC
Florida Inst of Technology	FL	28,740	VC
Juniata College	PA	29,080	VC
Univ of New Mexico	NM	9,223	C

PLANT GENETICS

School	ST	$IS	SR
SUNY/College of Environmental Science and Forestry	NY	14,167	VC
Univ of Calif at Berkeley	CA	15,563	MC
Washington State Univ	WA	11,334	C

PLANT PATHOLOGY

School	ST	$IS	SR
Iowa State Univ	IA	10,768	VC
Kansas State Univ	KS	8,728	VC
Mich State Univ	MI	11,933	VC
Oregon State Univ	OR	11,055	C
Univ of Delaware	DE	12,616	HC
Univ of Wisc/Madison	WI	8,262	VC
Washington State Univ	WA	11,334	C

PLANT PHYSIOLOGY

School	ST	$IS	SR
Calif State Polytechnic Univ, Pomona	CA	8,793	C+
Ohio State Univ	OH	13,080	VC+
SUNY/College of Environmental Science and Forestry	NY	14,167	VC

PLANT PROTECTION (PEST MANAGEMENT)

School	ST	$IS	SR
Iowa State Univ	IA	10,768	VC
Miss State Univ	MS	9,139	C
N Dak State Univ	ND	8,435	C
Purdue Univ/West Lafayette	IN	12,560	VC
Univ of Arkansas	AR	9,855	VC
Univ of Georgia	GA	8,656	VC
Univ of Hawaii at Manoa	HI	9,565	VC
Univ of Nebr at Lincoln	NE	9,975	C+
Washington State Univ	WA	11,334	C
West Texas A&M Univ	TX	7,533	C

PLANT SCIENCE

School	ST	$IS	SR
Alcorn State Univ	MS	7,290	C
Arizona State Univ-Main	AZ	10,048	C
Arkansas State Univ	AR	8,450	C
Brigham Young Univ	UT	8,504	HC
Cal State, Fresno	CA	8,414	LC
Cornell Univ	NY	38,253	MC
Florida State Univ	FL	9,028	HC
Fort Valley State Univ	GA	6,960	C
Iowa State Univ	IA	10,768	VC
Louisiana State Univ and A&M College	LA	9,126	VC
Middle Tenn State Univ	TN	8,534	C
Montana State Univ-Bozeman	MT	9,515	C
N Dak State Univ	ND	8,435	C
Ohio State Univ	OH	13,080	VC+
Ohio Univ	OH	14,448	C
Okla State Univ	OK	9,216	VC
Penn State Univ/Univ Park Campus	PA	15,646	HC
Rutgers, The State Univ of New Jersey/New Brunswick/Piscataway Campus	NJ	15,800	HC
Southern Illinois Univ Carbondale	IL	10,407	C
SUNY/College of Agriculture and Technology at Cobleskill	NY	11,200	C+
SUNY/College of Environmental Science and Forestry	NY	14,167	VC
Tarleton State Univ	TX	7,576	C
Tenn Tech Univ	TN	8,670	VC
Texas A&M Univ at Kingsville	TX	6,740	LC
Univ of Arizona	AZ	10,413	VC
Univ of Calif at Davis	CA	14,995	VC
Univ of Delaware	DE	12,616	HC
Univ of Florida	FL	8,580	MC
Univ of Hawaii at Manoa	HI	9,565	VC
Univ of Maryland/College Park	MD	14,227	HC
Univ of Mass Amherst	MA	13,980	C+
Univ of Missouri/Columbia	MO	13,782	VC
Univ of New Hampshire	NH	14,828	VC
Univ of Tenn at Knoxville	TN	8,214	C
Univ of Tenn at Martin	TN	7,748	C
Univ of Vermont	VT	16,316	VC
Utah State Univ	UT	7,371	C
Washington Univ in St. Louis	MO	38,293	MC
West Texas A&M Univ	TX	7,533	C
West Virginia Univ	WV	9,370	C

PLASTICS ENGINEERING

School	ST	$IS	SR
Ferris State Univ	MI	12,512	C
Pennsylvania College of Technology	PA	15,126	NC
Univ of Mass Lowell	MA	11,937	VC
Univ of Missouri/Rolla	MO	12,292	HC

PLASTICS TECHNOLOGY

School	ST	$IS	SR
Eastern Mich Univ	MI	11,478	C
Penn State Univ at Erie/Behrend College	PA	12,326	C
Pennsylvania College of Technology	PA	15,126	NC
Shawnee State Univ	OH	11,031	NC

PLAYWRITING/SCREENWRITING

School	ST	$IS	SR
Metropolitan State Univ	MN	3,852	SP

POLISH

School	ST	$IS	SR
Univ of Illinois at Chicago	IL	13,418	C
Univ of Pittsburgh at Pittsburgh	PA	16,074	HC
Univ of Wisc/Madison	WI	8,262	VC

POLITICAL SCIENCE/GOVERNMENT

School	ST	$IS	SR
Abilene Christian Univ	TX	18,370	VC
Adams State College	CO	7,468	C
Adelphi Univ	NY	26,300	VC
Adrian College	MI	21,950	C
Agnes Scott College	GA	28,230	HC
Alabama A&M Univ	AL	5,100	LC
Alabama State Univ	AL	6,404	C
Albany State Univ	GA	5,764	C+
Albertson College of Idaho	ID	19,415	VC
Albertus Magnus College	CT	23,130	LC
Albion College	MI	25,224	VC
Albright College	PA	30,579	C
Alcorn State Univ	MS	7,290	C
Alderson-Broaddus College	WV	19,640	C
Alfred Univ	NY	28,290	C
Allegheny College	PA	30,280	VC
Allen Univ	SC	10,300	NC
Alma College	MI	25,566	VC
Alvernia College	PA	23,212	LC
American International College	MA	24,690	LC
American Univ	DC	34,585	VC+
Amherst College	MA	37,470	MC
Anderson Univ	IN	19,430	LC
Andrews Univ	MI	19,550	C
Angelo State Univ	TX	7,576	NC
Anna Maria College	MA	26,140	LC
Appalachian State Univ	NC	7,637	VC
Aquinas College	MI	21,894	C
Arcadia Univ	PA	29,890	C
Arizona State Univ-Main	AZ	10,048	C
Arkansas State Univ	AR	8,450	C
Armstrong Atlantic State Univ	GA	7,102	C
Ashland Univ	OH	24,464	C
Assumption College	MA	29,375	C
Auburn Univ	AL	10,396	VC
Auburn Univ Montgomery	AL	9,020	NC
Augsburg College	MN	25,298	C
Augusta State Univ	GA	2,592	C
Augustana College	IL	26,610	VC+
Augustana College	SD	21,998	VC
Aurora Univ	IL	20,631	C
Austin College	TX	24,747	HC
Austin Peay State Univ	TN	5,814	LC
Averett Univ	VA	23,010	LC
Avila Univ	MO	20,300	C
Azusa Pacific Univ	CA	24,720	VC
Baker Univ	KS	19,860	VC
Baldwin-Wallace College	OH	24,678	C
Ball State Univ	IN	8,660	C
Barber-Scotia College	NC	13,900	LC
Bard College	NY	37,352	HC+
Barry Univ	FL	24,100	LC
Barton College	NC	19,314	C
Bates College	ME	37,500	MC
Baylor Univ	TX	23,864	VC
Belhaven College	MS	16,040	C+
Bellarmine Univ	KY	24,110	VC
Bellevue Univ	NE	4,440	NC
Belmont Abbey College	NC	23,742	C
Belmont Univ	TN	21,986	VC
Beloit College	WI	29,864	HC
Bemidji State Univ	MN	9,103	C
Benedictine College	KS	20,603	C
Benedictine Univ	IL	23,840	C
Bennett College	NC	11,200	C
Berea College	KY	5,030	VC+
Berry College	GA	21,410	VC
Bethany College	WV	19,845	VC
Bethel College	MN	25,180	VC
Bethune-Cookman College	FL	16,480	LC
Birmingham-Southern College	AL	25,364	VC+
Black Hills State Univ	SD	7,743	LC
Blackburn College	IL	13,690	C
Bloomfield College	NJ	19,250	LC
Bloomsburg Univ of Pennsylvania	PA	10,844	C
Boise State Univ	ID	7,657	LC
Boston College	MA	33,284	MC
Boston Univ	MA	38,194	HC+
Bowdoin College	ME	37,790	MC
Bowie State Univ	MD	10,873	C+
Bowling Green State Univ	OH	13,036	C
Bradley Univ	IL	22,910	VC
Brandeis Univ	MA	38,198	MC
Brenau Univ Women's College	GA	21,800	C
Brewton-Parker College	GA	14,200	LC
Briar Cliff Univ	IA	21,660	C
Bridgewater College	VA	25,150	C
Bridgewater State College	MA	10,482	C
Brigham Young Univ	UT	8,504	HC
Brigham Young Univ/Hawaii	HI	7,240	VC+
Brown Univ	RI	38,174	MC
Bryn Mawr College	PA	36,890	HC+
Bucknell Univ	PA	35,262	HC+
Buena Vista Univ	IA	25,406	C
Butler Univ	IN	28,250	VC+
Cabrini College	PA	29,020	C
Caldwell College	NJ	24,060	LC
Calif Baptist Univ	CA	19,924	C
Calif Inst of Technology	CA	31,677	MC
Calif Lutheran Univ	CA	27,600	LC
Calif Polytechnic State Univ	CA	8,747	VC
Calif State Polytechnic Univ, Pomona	CA	8,793	C+
Cal State, Bakersfield	CA	6,090	LC
Cal State, Chico	CA	8,598	LC
Cal State, Dominguez Hills	CA	5,840	LC
Cal State, Fresno	CA	8,414	LC
Cal State, Fullerton	CA	6,648	C
Cal State, Hayward	CA	8,871	LC
Cal State, Long Beach	CA	8,762	C+
Cal State, Los Angeles	CA	5,778	C
Cal State, Northridge	CA	7,757	LC
Cal State, San Bernardino	CA	15,238	LC
Cal State, San Marcos	CA	1,736	LC
Cal State, Stanislaus	CA	9,874	C
Calif Univ of Pennsylvania	PA	10,388	C
Calvin College	MI	22,615	NC
Cameron Univ	OK	5,692	NC
Campbell Univ	NC	18,268	VC
Campbellsville Univ	KY	17,680	C
Canisius College	NY	28,163	C+
Capital Univ	OH	26,550	C
Carleton College	MN	34,395	MC
Carnegie Mellon Univ	PA	32,682	MC
Carroll College	MT	20,576	VC
Carroll College	WI	22,740	C
Carthage College	WI	25,000	C
Case Western Reserve Univ	OH	32,002	MC
Catawba College	NC	20,500	C
Catholic Univ of America	DC	34,248	VC
Cedar Crest College	PA	25,145	C+
Cedarville Univ	OH	19,954	VC
Centenary College	NJ	25,370	LC
Centenary College of Louisiana	LA	23,100	VC+
Central College	IA	21,206	C
Central Conn State Univ	CT	12,090	C
Central Methodist College	MO	16,460	C
Central Mich Univ	MI	11,142	C
Central Missouri State Univ	MO	9,776	C
Central State Univ	OH	8,922	C+
Central Washington Univ	WA	9,768	C
Centre College	KY	27,300	HC
Chadron State College	NE	6,286	NC
Chapman Univ	CA	33,118	VC
Charleston Southern Univ	SC	17,122	C
Chatham College	PA	27,266	C+
Chestnut Hill College	PA	26,450	LC
Cheyney Univ of Pennsylvania	PA	9,993	C
Chicago State Univ	IL	10,882	C+
Christendom College	VA	18,410	VC+
Christopher Newport Univ	VA	8,862	VC
Citadel, The	SC	12,295	C+
CUNY/Baruch College	NY	3,275	VC+
CUNY/Brooklyn College	NY	4,353	C+
CUNY/City College	NY	4,230	C+
CUNY/College of Staten Island	NY	4,308	NC
CUNY/Herbert H. Lehman College	NY	3,320	LC
CUNY/Hunter College	NY	6,729	C+
CUNY/John Jay College of Criminal Justice	NY	4,259	C
CUNY/Queens College	NY	4,362	C
CUNY/York College	NY	3,292	NC
Claremont McKenna College	CA	36,880	MC

ST = STATE $IS = IN-STATE COSTS SR = SELECTOR RATING

School	ST	$IS	SR
Clarion Univ of Pennsylvania	PA	11,272	LC
Clark Atlanta Univ	GA	19,300	C+
Clark Univ	MA	32,115	VC
Clarke College	IA	23,165	C
Clarkson Univ	NY	32,226	VC
Clemson Univ	SC	11,972	HC
Cleveland State Univ	OH	12,308	LC
Coastal Carolina Univ	SC	11,040	C
Coe College	IA	27,385	VC
Coker College	SC	21,491	C
Colby College	ME	37,570	MC
Colgate Univ	NY	37,095	MC
College of Charleston	SC	11,887	HC
College of New Jersey	NJ	15,950	MC
College of New Rochelle	NY	21,800	C
College of Notre Dame of Maryland	MD	27,700	C
College of St. Benedict	MN	26,672	VC
College of St. Catherine	MN	24,010	VC
College of St. Rose	NY	22,864	C
College of Santa Fe	NM	25,293	C+
College of the Holy Cross	MA	36,451	MC
College of the Ozarks	MO	3,500	VC+
College of William and Mary	VA	12,224	MC
College of Wooster	OH	31,300	HC
Colo College	CO	36,860	HC
Colo State Univ	CO	9,964	VC
Columbia College	MO	16,139	C
Columbia College	SC	22,658	LC
Columbia Univ/Barnard College	NY	36,990	MC
Columbia Univ/Columbia College	NY	38,590	MC
Columbia Univ/School of General Studies	NY	35,000	C
Columbus State Univ	GA	7,846	C
Concord College	WV	8,136	C
Concordia College: Moorhead	MN	22,460	VC+
Concordia Univ, River Forest	IL	23,600	C
Conn College	CT	37,900	MC
Converse College	SC	24,710	VC
Cornell College	IA	27,825	VC+
Cornell Univ	NY	38,253	MC
Cornerstone Univ and Grand Rapids Theological Seminary	MI	19,846	C
Creighton Univ	NE	26,748	VC+
Cumberland College	KY	16,384	C
Cumberland Univ	TN	16,910	C
Daemen College	NY	22,120	C
Dartmouth College	NH	37,770	MC
David Lipscomb Univ	TN	16,158	VC
Davidson College	NC	33,274	MC
Davis and Elkins College	WV	20,594	C
De Sales Univ	PA	25,470	C
Delaware State Univ	DE	8,104	LC
Delta State Univ	MS	6,618	C
Denison Univ	OH	33,050	HC
DePaul Univ	IL	27,580	VC
DePauw Univ	IN	31,500	HC
Dickinson College	PA	35,825	HC
Dickinson State Univ	ND	6,338	NC
Dillard Univ	LA	17,325	VC
Doane College	NE	20,000	C
Dominican Univ	IL	23,610	C
Dominican Univ of Calif	CA	31,670	C
Dordt College	IA	20,170	VC
Dowling College	NY	23,870	LC
Drake Univ	IA	25,120	VC+
Drew Univ/College of Liberal Arts	NJ	35,550	VC
Drexel Univ	PA	27,655	VC
Drury Univ	MO	18,085	VC+
Duke Univ	NC	37,555	MC
Duquesne Univ	PA	26,907	VC
Earlham College	IN	29,976	VC+
East Carolina Univ	NC	8,671	C
East Central Univ	OK	4,968	C
East Stroudsburg Univ of Pennsylvania	PA	10,336	C
East Tenn State Univ	TN	8,497	C
Eastern Conn State Univ	CT	10,362	C
Eastern Illinois Univ	IL	11,192	C
Eastern Kentucky Univ	KY	7,708	C
Eastern Mich Univ	MI	11,478	C
Eastern New Mexico Univ	NM	6,762	LC
Eastern Univ	PA	24,020	C
Eastern Washington Univ	WA	9,012	C
Eckerd College	FL	28,744	C+
Edgewood College	WI	20,520	C
Edinboro Univ of Pennsylvania	PA	10,850	LC
Edward Waters College	FL	14,374	LC
Elizabeth City State Univ	NC	5,550	LC
Elizabethtown College	PA	28,800	C
Elmhurst College	IL	24,630	C
Elmira College	NY	33,820	VC
Elon Univ	NC	22,240	VC
Emmanuel College	MA	27,600	C+
Emory & Henry College	VA	21,950	C
Emory Univ	GA	36,872	MC
Emporia State Univ	KS	6,998	C

School	ST	$IS	SR
Eugene Lang College/New School Univ	NY	34,940	C
Eureka College	IL	24,980	LC
Evangel Univ	MO	15,435	C
Fairfield Univ	CT	35,505	HC
Fairleigh Dickinson Univ/College at Florham	NJ	30,130	C
Fairleigh Dickinson Univ/Metropolitan Campus	NJ	28,584	C
Fairmont State	WV	8,280	LC
Fayetteville State Univ	NC	5,590	LC
Ferrum College	VA	21,240	LC
Fisk Univ	TN	17,305	LC
Fitchburg State College	MA	9,622	C
Flagler College	FL	11,860	VC+
Florida A&M Univ	FL	7,564	C
Florida Atlantic Univ	FL	8,543	C
Florida Gulf Coast Univ	FL	9,908	C
Florida International Univ	FL	9,912	VC
Florida Memorial College	FL	6,000	LC
Florida Southern College	FL	23,592	C
Florida State Univ	FL	9,028	HC
Fordham Univ	NY	35,066	HC
Fort Hays State Univ	KS	7,363	C
Fort Lewis College	CO	8,353	C
Fort Valley State Univ	GA	6,960	C
Framingham State College	MA	9,381	C
Francis Marion Univ	SC	9,364	C
Franciscan Univ of Steubenville	OH	20,300	VC
Franklin and Marshall College	PA	35,930	HC+
Franklin College	IN		C
Franklin Pierce College	NH	28,980	LC
Friends Univ	KS	15,962	LC
Frostburg State Univ	MD	11,114	C
Furman Univ	SC	28,976	HC+
Gallaudet Univ	DC	16,554	SP
Gannon Univ	PA	23,260	C
Geneva College	PA	21,850	C
George Fox Univ	OR	26,110	VC
George Mason Univ	VA	9,732	VC
George Washington Univ	DC	41,030	MC
Georgetown College	KY	22,000	VC
Georgetown Univ	DC	38,242	MC
Georgia College and State Univ	GA	9,878	C
Georgia Southern Univ	GA	8,540	C
Georgia Southwestern State Univ	GA	6,013	C
Georgia State Univ	GA	10,658	C
Gettysburg College	PA	35,646	HC
Gonzaga Univ	WA	26,766	HC
Gordon College	MA	25,982	VC+
Goucher College	MD	32,650	HC
Grambling State Univ	LA	6,538	NC
Grand Valley State Univ	MI	11,022	VC
Grand View College	IA	19,748	LC
Greensboro College	NC	21,750	C
Greenville College	IL	21,342	C
Grinnell College	IA	31,060	HC+
Grove City College	PA	14,228	HC
Guilford College	NC	24,960	VC
Gustavus Adolphus College	MN	27,120	VC+
Hamilton College	NY	37,560	MC
Hamline Univ	MN	27,052	VC
Hampden-Sydney College	VA	28,407	VC
Hampshire College	MA	37,037	HC
Hampton Univ	VA	17,112	C+
Hanover College	IN	25,200	VC
Harding Univ	AR	14,890	VC
Hardin-Simmons Univ	TX	14,165	C
Hartwick College	NY	34,650	C+
Harvard Univ/Harvard College	MA	37,928	MC
Hastings College	NE	19,928	VC
Haverford College	PA	37,900	MC
Hawaii Pacific Univ	HI	19,218	C
Heidelberg College	OH	20,266	NC
Henderson State Univ	AR	7,386	C
Hendrix College	AR	20,970	VC+
High Point Univ	NC	22,480	C
Hillsdale College	MI	22,450	HC
Hiram College	OH	28,234	VC
Hobart and William Smith Colleges	NY	36,536	HC
Hofstra Univ	NY	27,112	VC
Hollins Univ	VA	27,965	VC
Hood College	MD	27,795	VC
Hope College	MI	25,340	VC
Houghton College	NY	23,984	VC
Houston Baptist Univ	TX	16,905	C
Howard Payne Univ	TX	15,176	C
Howard Univ	DC	16,505	C
Humboldt State Univ	CA	9,400	C
Huntingdon College	AL	18,400	VC
Huston-Tillotson College	TX	14,232	NC
Idaho State Univ	ID	8,128	C
Illinois College	IL	19,100	VC
Illinois Inst of Technology	IL	26,456	HC+
Illinois State Univ	IL	10,944	C+
Illinois Wesleyan Univ	IL	30,380	HC+
Indiana State Univ	IN	10,719	LC
Indiana Univ Bloomington	IN	12,389	VC
Indiana Univ Northwest	IN	4,538	LC

School	ST	$IS	SR
Indiana Univ of Pennsylvania	PA	10,489	C
Indiana Univ South Bend	IN	4,571	LC
Indiana Univ Southeast	IN	4,504	LC
Indiana Univ-Purdue Univ Fort Wayne	IN	5,108	LC
Indiana Univ-Purdue Univ Indianapolis	IN	8,257	LC
Indiana Wesleyan Univ	IN	19,900	C+
Inter American Univ of PR/Fajardo Campus	PR	4,000	
Inter American Univ of PR/Metropolitan Campus	PR		
Inter American Univ of PR/Ponce Regional College	PR	3,700	
Inter American Univ of PR/San German	PR	6,716	
Iona College	NY	27,988	VC
Iowa State Univ	IA	10,768	VC
Ithaca College	NY	31,730	HC
Jackson State Univ	MS	8,382	C
Jacksonville State Univ	AL	6,844	LC
Jacksonville Univ	FL	24,040	C
James Madison Univ	VA	10,794	VC
Jamestown College	ND	12,600	NC
John Carroll Univ	OH	27,658	C+
Johns Hopkins Univ	MD	38,372	MC
Johnson C. Smith Univ	NC	18,108	C
Johnson State College	VT	11,819	LC
Judson College	IL	22,050	LC
Juniata College	PA	29,080	VC
Kalamazoo College	MI	26,955	HC+
Kansas State Univ	KS	8,728	VC
Kean Univ	NJ	14,479	C
Kennesaw State Univ	GA	2,724	C
Kent State Univ	OH	12,932	C
Kentucky State Univ	KY	9,062	NC
Kentucky Wesleyan College	KY	17,250	C
Kenyon College	OH	35,370	HC+
Keuka College	NY	21,170	C
King College	TN	22,500	VC
King's College	PA	26,990	C
Knox College	IL	30,294	VC+
Knoxville College	TN	6,200	LC
Kutztown Univ of Pennsylvania	PA	10,786	C
La Salle Univ	PA	31,260	VC
La Sierra Univ	CA	19,260	LC
Lafayette College	PA	35,746	MC
LaGrange College	GA	20,500	C
Lake Forest College	IL	30,270	VC
Lake Superior State Univ	MI	9,034	LC
Lamar Univ	TX	6,816	LC
Lambuth Univ	TN	16,520	C
Lander Univ	SC	10,496	C
Lawrence Univ	WI	30,900	HC
Le Moyne College	NY	26,400	VC
Lebanon Valley College	PA	28,870	VC
Lehigh Univ	PA	37,570	HC+
LeMoyne-Owen College	TN	13,070	LC
Lenoir-Rhyne College	NC	19,186	C
Lewis and Clark College	OR	30,620	VC
Lewis Univ	IL	22,950	C+
Liberty Univ	VA	17,220	C
Lincoln Univ	MO	7,158	NC
Lincoln Univ	PA	13,320	C+
Lindenwood Univ	MO	17,050	VC
Linfield College	OR	27,090	VC
Livingstone College	NC	18,101	LC
Lock Haven Univ of Pennsylvania	PA	11,098	LC
LIU/Brooklyn Campus	NY	24,790	C
LIU/C.W. Post Campus	NY	28,282	C
LIU/Southampton College	NY	29,370	C+
Longwood Univ	VA	11,175	C
Loras College	IA	24,233	C
Louisiana State Univ and A&M College	LA	9,126	VC
Louisiana State Univ in Shreveport	LA	2,884	NC
Louisiana Tech Univ	LA	7,361	C
Loyola College in Maryland	MD	34,560	HC
Loyola Marymount Univ	CA	32,194	VC
Loyola Univ Chicago	IL	31,164	VC
Loyola Univ New Orleans	LA	31,036	VC+
Luther College	IA	25,700	VC
Lycoming College	PA	27,589	C+
Lynchburg College	VA	26,815	C
Lynn Univ	FL	30,750	C
Lyon College	AR	17,995	VC
Macalester College	MN	31,944	MC
MacMurray College	IL	20,005	LC
Malone College	OH	20,995	C
Manchester College	IN	23,390	C
Manhattan College	NY	27,400	VC
Manhattanville College	NY	32,420	C+
Mansfield Univ	PA	11,220	C
Marian College	IN	23,030	C
Marietta College	OH	27,047	C
Marist College	NY	27,596	VC
Marlboro College	VT	29,055	VC+
Marquette Univ	WI	27,594	VC
Mars Hill College	NC	18,600	LC
Marshall Univ	WV	9,116	C
Martin Univ	IN	10,200	SP
Mary Baldwin College	VA	24,939	C

School	ST	$IS	SR
Mary Washington College	VA	10,166	HC
Marygrove College	MI	17,550	C
Marymount College of Fordham Univ	NY	27,686	C
Marymount Manhattan College	NY	27,292	C
Marymount Univ	VA	23,668	C
Maryville College	TN	25,960	VC
Mass Inst of Technology	MA	38,310	MC
Master's College and Seminary	CA	23,250	VC
McDaniel College	MD	28,440	VC
McKendree College	IL	21,120	VC
McMurry Univ	TX	17,846	LC
Medaille College	NY	20,060	C
Mercer Univ	GA	27,516	VC+
Mercy College	NY	19,200	NC
Mercyhurst College	PA	20,694	C
Meredith College	NC	23,065	C
Merrimack College	MA	29,625	C
Mesa State College	CO	8,051	C
Messiah College	PA	25,890	VC+
Methodist College	NC	19,526	C
Metropolitan State College of Denver	CO	2,338	LC
Miami Univ	OH	15,033	HC
Mich State Univ	MI	11,933	VC
Middle Tenn State Univ	TN	8,534	C
Middlebury College	VT	38,100	MC
Midwestern State Univ	TX	8,045	LC
Miles College	AL	7,870	NC
Millersville Univ of Pennsylvania	PA	11,269	C
Millikin Univ	IL	25,555	C
Mills College	CA	33,371	VC
Millsaps College	MS	25,182	VC
Minn State Univ, Mankato	MN	8,803	LC
Minn State Univ, Moorehead	MN	7,000	LC
Miss College	MS	14,574	C
Miss State Univ	MS	9,139	C
Miss Univ for Women	MS	5,446	LC
Miss Valley State Univ	MS	6,765	NC
Missouri Southern State Univ	MO	8,316	C
Missouri Valley College	MO	18,500	C
Missouri Western State College	MO	8,522	NC
Molloy College	NY	15,180	C
Monmouth College	IL	23,600	C
Monmouth Univ	NJ	26,334	C
Montana State Univ-Bozeman	MT	9,515	C
Montclair State Univ	NJ	13,790	C
Moravian College	PA	28,903	VC
Morehead State Univ	KY	7,464	C
Morehouse College	GA	22,728	C
Morgan State Univ	MD	11,470	C
Morningside College	IA	21,610	C
Morris College	SC	10,974	LC
Mount Holyoke College	MA	37,918	HC+
Mount Mercy College	IA	21,400	C
Mount St. Mary College	NY	21,270	C
Mount St. Mary's College	CA	28,307	VC
Mount St. Mary's College	MD	28,400	C
Mount Union College	OH	21,120	C
Muhlenberg College	PA	31,485	HC
Murray State Univ	KY	7,816	VC
Muskingum College	OH	20,680	C
Nazareth College of Rochester	NY	24,936	VC
Nebr Wesleyan Univ	NE	21,197	C+
Neumann College	PA	23,890	LC
New College of Calif	CA	8,900	NC
New College of Florida	FL	8,906	HC+
New England College	NH	28,860	LC
New Jersey City Univ	NJ	11,850	LC
New Mexico Highlands Univ	NM	6,182	LC
New Mexico State Univ	NM	7,932	C
New York Inst of Technology	NY	24,205	VC
New York Univ	NY	39,406	MC
Newberry College	SC	22,871	LC
Niagara Univ	NY	25,050	C
Nicholls State Univ	LA	6,395	NC
Norfolk State Univ	VA	9,722	LC
N Car Agricultural and Technical State Univ	NC	6,659	LC
N Car Central Univ	NC	7,534	LC
N Car State Univ	NC	9,886	VC
N Car Wesleyan College	NC	17,998	C
North Central College	IL	25,656	VC
N Dak State Univ	ND	8,435	C
North Georgia College and State Univ	GA	6,984	C
North Park Univ	IL	24,030	C
Northeastern Illinois Univ	IL	2,898	NC
Northeastern State Univ	OK	4,950	LC
Northeastern Univ	MA	35,650	HC
Northern Arizona Univ	AZ	9,002	C
Northern Illinois Univ	IL	11,472	C
Northern Kentucky Univ	KY	6,352	NC
Northern Mich Univ	MI	10,834	C
Northern State Univ	SD	7,117	LC
Northwest Missouri State Univ	MO	9,334	C

ST = STATE $IS = IN-STATE COSTS SR = SELECTOR RATING

School	ST	$IS	SR
Northwest Nazarene Univ	ID	20,360	VC
Northwestern College of Iowa	IA	19,640	C+
Northwestern Okla State Univ	OK	5,433	NC
Northwestern State Univ of Louisiana	LA	6,331	NC
Northwestern Univ	IL	37,491	MC
Norwich Univ	VT	21,064	LC
Notre Dame College	OH	20,425	C
Notre Dame de Namur Univ	CA	26,932	LC
Oakland Univ	MI	10,800	C
Oberlin College	OH	36,938	MC
Occidental College	CA	35,922	HC
Oglethorpe Univ	GA	26,000	VC
Ohio Dominican Univ	OH	22,700	C
Ohio Northern Univ	OH	27,765	VC
Ohio State Univ	OH	13,080	VC+
Ohio Univ	OH	14,448	C
Ohio Wesleyan Univ	OH	32,550	VC+
Okla Baptist Univ	OK	15,220	VC
Okla City Univ	OK	19,580	VC
Okla State Univ	OK	9,216	VC
Okla Wesleyan Univ	OK	14,100	LC
Old Dominion Univ	VA	10,441	C
Olivet Nazarene Univ	IL	20,480	C
Oral Roberts Univ	OK	18,490	C
Oregon State Univ	OR	11,055	C
Ottawa Univ	KS	11,800	LC
Otterbein College	OH	26,085	C
Ouachita Baptist Univ	AR	18,900	VC
Our Lady of the Lake Univ of San Antonio	TX	17,336	C
Pace Univ	NY	28,652	VC
Pacific Lutheran Univ	WA	25,715	VC
Pacific Univ	OR	24,250	C
Palm Beach Atlantic Univ	FL	20,690	C
Park Univ	MO	10,780	C+
Penn State Univ at Erie/Behrend College	PA	12,326	C
Penn State Univ/Univ Park Campus	PA	15,646	HC
Pepperdine Univ	CA	32,830	VC
Pfeiffer Univ	NC	18,980	C
Philander Smith College	AR	7,380	NC
Piedmont College	GA	16,900	C
Pittsburg State Univ	KS	7,128	NC
Pitzer College	CA	37,590	HC
Plymouth State Univ	NH	12,298	LC
Point Loma Nazarene Univ	CA	21,380	VC
Point Park Univ	PA	21,840	C
Pomona College	CA	33,960	MC
Pontifical Catholic Univ of PR/Ponce	PR	7,298	
Portland State Univ	OR	12,453	C
Prairie View A&M Univ	TX	9,418	NC
Presbyterian College	SC	25,920	VC
Princeton Univ	NJ	36,649	MC
Principia College	IL	25,044	C+
Providence College	RI	30,604	HC
Purdue Univ/Calumet	IN	6,630	NC
Purdue Univ/West Lafayette	IN	12,560	VC
Queens Univ of Charlotte	NC	21,840	C
Quincy Univ	IL	22,330	C
Quinnipiac Univ	CT	30,570	VC
Radford Univ	VA	8,500	C
Ramapo College of New Jersey	NJ	15,203	VC
Randolph-Macon College	VA	27,190	C
Randolph-Macon Woman's College	VA	28,430	VC+
Reed College	OR	36,950	MC
Regis College	MA	29,000	C
Regis Univ	CO	25,740	C+
Rhode Island College	RI	11,565	C
Rhodes College	TN	26,466	HC+
Rice Univ	TX	27,550	MC
Richard Stockton College of New Jersey	NJ	12,972	VC
Rider Univ	NJ	30,900	C
Ripon College	WI	24,995	VC
Rivier College	NH	26,217	C
Roanoke College	VA	27,393	C
Rockford College	IL	28,310	VC
Rockhurst Univ	MO	22,960	C+
Rocky Mountain College	MT	19,015	C
Roger Williams Univ	RI	30,296	C
Rollins College	FL	34,300	VC
Roosevelt Univ	IL	22,580	VC
Rosemont College	PA	26,175	C
Rowan Univ	NJ	14,506	VC
Russell Sage College	NY	26,811	C
Rust College	MS	8,200	C+
Rutgers, The State Univ of New Jersey/Camden Campus	NJ	14,990	VC
Rutgers, The State Univ of New Jersey/New Brunswick/Piscataway Campus	NJ	15,800	HC
Rutgers, The State Univ of New Jersey/Newark Campus	NJ	15,624	VC
Sacred Heart Univ	CT	29,178	C
Saginaw Valley State Univ	MI	11,055	C
St. Ambrose Univ	IA	22,800	C

School	ST	$IS	SR
St. Andrews Presbyterian College	NC	20,525	C
St. Anselm College	NH	30,250	C
St. Augustine's College	NC	12,990	LC
St. Bonaventure Univ	NY	24,455	LC
St. Cloud State Univ	MN	8,362	C
St. Edward's Univ	TX	20,428	C
St. Francis College	NY	10,880	LC
St. Francis Univ	PA	25,876	LC
St. John Fisher College	NY	24,870	C
St. John's Univ	MN	26,473	VC
St. John's Univ	NY	30,180	C
St. Joseph's College	IN	24,250	C
St. Joseph's Univ	PA	33,590	VC
St. Lawrence Univ	NY	35,945	VC
St. Leo Univ	FL	20,600	C
St. Louis Univ	MO	29,780	VC+
St. Martin's College	WA	23,245	C
St. Mary-of-the-Woods College	IN	23,280	C
St. Mary's College	IN	24,474	VC
St. Mary's College of Calif	CA	32,850	VC
St. Mary's College of Maryland	MD	15,908	VC+
St. Mary's Univ of Minn	MN	21,535	C
St. Mary's Univ of San Antonio	TX	22,444	C
St. Michael's College	VT	30,100	VC
St. Norbert College	WI	25,810	C
St. Olaf College	MN	28,500	HC
St. Paul's College	VA	14,344	NC
St. Peter's College	NJ	22,292	LC
St. Thomas Univ	FL	21,400	LC
St. Vincent College	PA	25,530	VC
St. Xavier Univ	IL	23,144	C
Salisbury Univ	MD	12,664	VC
Salve Regina Univ	RI	29,210	C
Sam Houston State Univ	TX	7,142	C
Samford Univ	AL	18,648	VC
San Diego State Univ	CA	10,321	C
San Francisco State Univ	CA	12,070	C
San Jose State Univ	CA	8,187	C
Santa Clara Univ	CA	34,701	HC
Sarah Lawrence College	NY	41,218	HC
Savannah State Univ	GA	7,328	LC
Schreiner Univ	TX	20,400	C
Scripps College	CA	35,700	HC+
Seattle Pacific Univ	WA	25,944	VC
Seattle Univ	WA	24,183	VC
Seton Hall Univ	NJ	30,130	VC
Seton Hill Univ	PA	24,930	C
Shaw Univ	NC	14,882	C+
Shepherd College	WV	8,608	C
Shippensburg Univ of Pennsylvania	PA	10,826	C
Siena College	NY	25,310	VC
Simmons College	MA	33,000	VC
Simon's Rock College of Bard	MA	36,580	HC
Simpson College	IA	23,658	C+
Skidmore College	NY	37,930	HC
Slippery Rock Univ of Pennsylvania	PA	10,343	LC
Smith College	MA	37,034	HC+
Sonoma State Univ	CA	10,421	C
S Car State Univ	SC	6,586	LC
S Dak State Univ	SD	7,782	C
Southeast Missouri State Univ	MO	9,704	C
Southeastern Louisiana Univ	LA	6,791	LC
Southeastern Okla State Univ	OK	6,147	C
Southern Arkansas Univ	AR	6,956	C
Southern Conn State Univ	CT	10,310	C
Southern Illinois Univ Carbondale	IL	10,407	C
Southern Illinois Univ Edwardsville	IL	8,724	C
Southern Methodist Univ	TX	34,210	HC
Southern Nazarene Univ	OK	14,634	NC
Southern Oregon Univ	OR	10,362	C
Southern Univ and A&M College	LA	7,372	LC
Southern Univ at New Orleans	LA	995	NC
Southern Utah Univ	UT	8,194	C
Southwest Baptist Univ	MO	15,371	C
Southwest Minn State Univ	MN	9,106	VC
Southwest Missouri State Univ	MO	8,918	C
Southwestern Okla State Univ	OK	4,801	C
Southwestern Univ	TX	25,410	HC
Spelman College	GA	19,215	C+
Spring Hill College	AL	25,868	VC
Springfield College	MA	24,520	C
Stanford Univ	CA	37,612	MC
SUNY at Oswego	NY	12,650	C
SUNY at Potsdam	NY	12,160	C
SUNY/College at Brockport	NY	12,111	C
SUNY/College at Buffalo	NY	8,025	C
SUNY/College at Cortland	NY	12,095	C
SUNY/College at Fredonia	NY	11,562	VC
SUNY/College at Geneseo	NY	11,330	HC

School	ST	$IS	SR
SUNY/College at Old Westbury	NY	12,784	C
SUNY/College at Oneonta	NY	11,870	VC
SUNY/College at Plattsburgh	NY	11,700	C
SUNY/College at Purchase	NY	10,587	VC
SUNY/Univ at Albany	NY	12,951	HC
SUNY/Univ at Binghamton	NY	12,787	HC
SUNY/Univ at Buffalo	NY	12,563	VC
SUNY/Univ at New Paltz	NY	11,565	VC
SUNY/Univ at Stony Brook	NY	12,763	HC
State Univ of West Georgia	GA	7,622	C
Stephen F. Austin State Univ	TX	7,552	C
Stephens College	MO	24,260	C+
Stetson Univ	FL	29,495	VC
Stonehill College	MA	30,752	HC
Suffolk Univ	MA	29,200	C
Sul Ross State Univ	TX	6,582	LC
Susquehanna Univ	PA	29,990	VC
Swarthmore College	PA	37,716	MC
Sweet Briar College	VA	27,940	C
Syracuse Univ	NY	34,720	HC
Tarleton State Univ	TX	7,576	C
Taylor Univ	IN	23,820	VC+
Temple Univ	PA	15,912	C
Tenn State Univ	TN	9,048	LC
Tenn Tech Univ	TN	8,670	VC
Texas A&M Univ	TX	11,081	HC
Texas A&M Univ at Commerce	TX	8,994	C
Texas A&M Univ at Corpus Christi	TX	10,269	C
Texas A&M Univ at Kingsville	TX	6,740	LC
Texas Christian Univ	TX	23,410	VC
Texas Lutheran Univ	TX	20,370	C
Texas Southern Univ	TX	8,920	NC
Texas State Univ	TX	9,320	VC
Texas Tech Univ	TX	10,768	VC
Texas Wesleyan Univ	TX	16,245	C
Texas Woman's Univ	TX	7,804	LC
Thiel College	PA	20,970	C
Thomas Edison State College	NJ	3,325	SP
Thomas More College of Liberal Arts	NH	17,700	C
Tougaloo College	MS	9,200	NC
Touro College	NY	15,250	VC
Towson Univ	MD	12,694	VC
Transylvania Univ	KY	23,780	VC+
Trevecca Nazarene Univ	TN	17,548	C
Trinity College	CT	38,040	HC+
Trinity College	DC	24,150	LC
Trinity Univ	TX	26,466	HC+
Troy State Univ	AL	7,696	C
Troy State Univ Montgomery	AL	3,600	NC
Truman State Univ	MO	9,728	HC+
Tufts Univ	MA	38,233	MC
Tulane Univ	LA	37,451	HC+
Tuskegee Univ	AL	17,250	LC
Union College	NY	36,005	HC
Union Univ	TN	18,800	VC
United States Air Force Academy	CO		HC+
United States Coast Guard Academy	CT		MC
United States Military Academy	NY		MC
United States Naval Academy	MD		MC
Univ of Akron	OH	13,134	NC
Univ of Alabama	AL	9,040	C+
Univ of Alabama at Birmingham	AL	12,901	C
Univ of Alabama in Huntsville	AL	9,126	VC
Univ of Alaska Anchorage	AK	9,100	NC
Univ of Alaska Fairbanks	AK	9,295	C
Univ of Alaska Southeast	AK	7,900	LC
Univ of Arizona	AZ	10,413	VC
Univ of Arkansas	AR	9,855	VC
Univ of Arkansas at Little Rock	AR	5,637	NC
Univ of Arkansas at Monticello	AR	5,940	NC
Univ of Arkansas at Pine Bluff	AR	7,925	C
Univ of Calif at Berkeley	CA	15,563	MC
Univ of Calif at Davis	CA	14,995	VC
Univ of Calif at Irvine	CA	19,808	HC
Univ of Calif at Los Angeles	CA	15,330	MC
Univ of Calif at Riverside	CA	15,300	C
Univ of Calif at San Diego	CA	14,127	HC
Univ of Calif at Santa Barbara	CA	11,732	VC
Univ of Calif at Santa Cruz	CA	16,505	VC
Univ of Central Arkansas	AR	6,388	C
Univ of Central Florida	FL	10,038	VC
Univ of Central Okla	OK	9,434	C
Univ of Charleston	WV	23,620	C
Univ of Chicago	IL	35,087	MC
Univ of Cincinnati	OH	14,736	C
Univ of Colo at Boulder	CO	10,774	VC

School	ST	$IS	SR
Univ of Colo at Colo Springs	CO	10,667	C
Univ of Colo at Denver	CO	3,302	C
Univ of Conn	CT	14,608	VC
Univ of Dallas	TX	25,898	VC+
Univ of Dayton	OH	24,850	VC
Univ of Delaware	DE	12,616	HC
Univ of Denver	CO	32,148	VC
Univ of Detroit Mercy	MI	25,582	C
Univ of Evansville	IN	24,190	VC
Univ of Findlay	OH	23,962	NC
Univ of Florida	FL	8,580	MC
Univ of Georgia	GA	8,656	VC
Univ of Great Falls	MT	15,360	C
Univ of Hartford	CT	31,080	C
Univ of Hawaii at Hilo	HI	6,497	C
Univ of Hawaii at Manoa	HI	9,565	VC
Univ of Houston	TX	9,818	C
Univ of Idaho	ID	8,216	C
Univ of Illinois at Chicago	IL	13,418	C
Univ of Illinois at Urbana-Champaign	IL	11,316	HC+
Univ of Indianapolis	IN	22,560	VC
Univ of Iowa	IA	10,923	VC
Univ of Judaism College of A&S	CA	24,230	C
Univ of Kansas	KS	8,923	VC
Univ of Kentucky	KY	7,765	C
Univ of La Verne	CA	28,600	C
Univ of Louisiana at Lafayette	LA	5,826	C
Univ of Louisiana at Monroe	LA	5,207	NC
Univ of Louisville	KY	8,762	VC
Univ of Maine	ME	12,080	C+
Univ of Maine at Farmington	ME	10,108	C
Univ of Mary Hardin-Baylor	TX	17,268	C
Univ of Maryland/Baltimore County	MD	14,668	VC+
Univ of Maryland/College Park	MD	14,227	HC
Univ of Mass Amherst	MA	13,980	C+
Univ of Mass Boston	MA	6,227	C
Univ of Mass Dartmouth	MA	12,835	C
Univ of Mass Lowell	MA	11,937	VC
Univ of Memphis	TN	8,560	C
Univ of Miami	FL	34,608	HC
Univ of Mich/Ann Arbor	MI	13,864	HC+
Univ of Mich/Dearborn	MI	6,843	VC
Univ of Mich/Flint	MI	5,548	C
Univ of Minn/Duluth	MN	12,470	C
Univ of Minn/Morris	MN	12,896	VC
Univ of Minn/Twin Cities	MN	13,160	VC
Univ of Miss	MS	7,666	C
Univ of Missouri/Columbia	MO	13,782	VC
Univ of Missouri/Kansas City	MO	13,416	VC
Univ of Missouri/St. Louis	MO	11,656	VC
Univ of Montana	MT	9,395	C
Univ of Montevallo	AL	8,478	C
Univ of Nebr at Kearney	NE	8,286	NC
Univ of Nebr at Lincoln	NE	9,975	C+
Univ of Nebr at Omaha	NE	8,080	C
Univ of Nevada/Las Vegas	NV	11,566	C
Univ of Nevada/Reno	NV	9,792	C
Univ of New Hampshire	NH	14,828	VC
Univ of New Haven	CT	28,650	C
Univ of New Mexico	NM	9,223	C
Univ of New Orleans	LA	7,356	C
Univ of North Alabama	AL	7,972	NC
Univ of N Car at Asheville	NC	8,079	VC
Univ of N Car at Chapel Hill	NC	10,117	MC
Univ of N Car at Charlotte	NC	8,185	C
Univ of N Car at Greensboro	NC	8,248	C
Univ of N Car at Pembroke	NC	6,929	LC
Univ of N Car at Wilmington	NC	8,490	VC
Univ of N Dak	ND	8,390	C
Univ of North Florida	FL	8,769	VC
Univ of North Texas	TX	7,629	C
Univ of Northern Colo	CO	8,987	C
Univ of Northern Iowa	IA	9,834	C
Univ of Notre Dame	IN	34,442	MC
Univ of Okla	OK	9,226	VC
Univ of Oregon	OR	11,479	VC
Univ of Pennsylvania	PA	37,960	MC
Univ of Pittsburgh at Bradford	PA	15,294	C
Univ of Pittsburgh at Greensburg	PA	15,984	C
Univ of Pittsburgh at Johnstown	PA	15,216	LC
Univ of Pittsburgh at Pittsburgh	PA	16,074	HC
Univ of Portland	OR	28,500	VC
Univ of PR/Mayaguez	PR		
Univ of PR/Rio Piedras	PR	5,730	
Univ of Puget Sound	WA	31,760	HC
Univ of Redlands	CA	32,576	VC
Univ of Rhode Island	RI	13,720	VC
Univ of Richmond	VA	30,100	MC
Univ of Rio Grande	OH	8,728	NC
Univ of Rochester	NY	32,979	HC
Univ of St. Francis	IL	22,850	C
Univ of St. Mary	KS	18,868	C
Univ of St. Thomas	MN	26,918	VC

ST = STATE **$IS** = IN-STATE COSTS **SR** = SELECTOR RATING

School	ST	$IS	SR
Univ of St. Thomas	TX	21,952	VC
Univ of San Diego	CA	33,156	HC
Univ of San Francisco	CA	34,700	VC
Univ of Science and Arts of Okla	OK	5,982	C
Univ of Scranton	PA	30,836	VC
Univ of Sioux Falls	SD	16,390	C
Univ of South Alabama	AL	7,760	LC
Univ of S Car at Aiken	SC	7,828	LC
Univ of S Car at Columbia	SC	10,048	VC
Univ of S Car at Spartanburg	SC	9,936	C+
Univ of S Dak	SD	7,710	C+
Univ of South Florida	FL	9,454	C
Univ of Southern Calif	CA	37,459	MC
Univ of Southern Colo	CO	7,821	LC
Univ of Southern Indiana	IN	9,025	LC
Univ of Southern Maine	ME	11,212	C
Univ of Southern Miss	MS	8,324	LC
Univ of Tampa	FL	23,982	VC
Univ of Tenn at Chattanooga	TN	7,783	C
Univ of Tenn at Knoxville	TN	8,214	C
Univ of Tenn at Martin	TN	7,748	C
Univ of Texas at Arlington	TX	7,192	LC
Univ of Texas at Austin	TX	10,630	HC
Univ of Texas at Dallas	TX	10,234	HC
Univ of Texas at El Paso	TX	5,799	NC
Univ of Texas at San Antonio	TX	9,088	NC
Univ of Texas-Pan American	TX	5,954	LC
Univ of the District of Columbia	DC	2,070	LC
Univ of the Incarnate Word	TX	21,772	LC
Univ of the Ozarks	AR	16,574	C
Univ of the Pacific	CA	31,090	VC
Univ of the South	TN	30,855	HC
Univ of Toledo	OH	12,479	NC
Univ of Tulsa	OK	22,090	VC+
Univ of Utah	UT	9,205	C
Univ of Vermont	VT	16,316	VC
Univ of Virginia	VA	11,740	MC
Univ of Virginia's College at Wise	VA	10,116	C
Univ of Washington	WA	10,361	VC
Univ of West Florida	FL	8,470	C
Univ of Wisc/Eau Claire	WI	8,463	VC
Univ of Wisc/Green Bay	WI	8,154	C
Univ of Wisc/La Crosse	WI	8,991	VC
Univ of Wisc/Madison	WI	8,262	VC
Univ of Wisc/Milwaukee	WI	9,427	LC
Univ of Wisc/Oshkosh	WI	6,130	LC
Univ of Wisc/Parkside	WI	6,160	LC
Univ of Wisc/Platteville	WI	8,450	C
Univ of Wisc/River Falls	WI	8,358	LC
Univ of Wisc/Stevens Point	WI	8,116	VC
Univ of Wisc/Superior	WI	7,051	C+
Univ of Wisc/Whitewater	WI	8,626	C
Univ of Wyoming	WY	8,636	C
Ursinus College	PA	34,400	VC
Utah State Univ	UT	7,371	C
Utica College	NY	28,340	C
Valdosta State Univ	GA	7,798	C
Valparaiso Univ	IN	26,118	VC+
Vanderbilt Univ	TN	37,897	MC
Vanguard Univ of Southern Calif	CA	22,208	C
Vassar College	NY	37,030	MC
Villanova Univ	PA	35,050	HC
Virginia Commonwealth Univ	VA	9,030	C
Virginia Intermont College	VA	19,800	C
Virginia Polytechnic Inst and State Univ	VA	9,179	C
Virginia State Univ	VA	10,358	C
Virginia Union Univ	VA	15,358	LC
Virginia Wesleyan College	VA	25,350	C
Wabash College	IN	27,932	VC
Wagner College	NY	29,900	VC
Wake Forest Univ	NC	34,090	MC
Walsh Univ	OH	20,890	C
Wartburg College	IA	21,165	VC
Washburn Univ of Topeka	KS	8,984	NC
Washington and Jefferson College	PA	29,570	VC
Washington and Lee Univ	VA	29,663	MC
Washington College	MD	30,540	VC
Washington State Univ	WA	11,334	C
Washington Univ in St. Louis	MO	38,293	MC
Wayland Baptist Univ	TX	11,919	NC
Wayne State College	NE	7,352	NC
Wayne State Univ	MI	11,774	C
Waynesburg College	PA	19,370	C
Weber State Univ	UT	7,945	NC
Webster Univ	MO	21,848	VC
Wellesley College	MA	36,516	MC
Wells College	NY	21,122	VC
Wesley College	DE	19,905	C
Wesleyan College	GA	17,870	VC
Wesleyan Univ	CT	35,139	MC
West Chester Univ of Pennsylvania	PA	11,164	C
West Liberty State College	WV	7,868	LC
West Texas A&M Univ	TX	7,533	C
West Virginia State College	WV	6,264	NC
West Virginia Univ	WV	9,370	C
West Virginia Wesleyan College	WV	22,920	C
Western Carolina Univ	NC	6,742	C
Western Conn State Univ	CT	11,625	C
Western Illinois Univ	IL	10,363	C
Western Kentucky Univ	KY	6,834	C
Western Mich Univ	MI	12,031	C
Western New England College	MA	28,924	C
Western Oregon Univ	OR	10,281	C
Western State College of Colo	CO	9,014	C
Western Washington Univ	WA	10,119	VC
Westfield State College	MA	10,147	C
Westminster College	MO	18,150	C+
Westminster College	PA	22,960	C
Westmont College	CA	33,062	VC+
Wheaton College	IL	21,934	HC
Wheaton College	MA	36,330	HC
Wheeling Jesuit Univ	WV	22,660	C
Whitman College	WA	32,526	HC+
Whittier College	CA	29,108	C
Whitworth College	WA	26,428	VC+
Wichita State Univ	KS	8,092	C
Widener Univ	PA	27,020	C
Wilberforce Univ	OH	14,937	LC
Wilkes Univ	PA	28,060	C
Willamette Univ	OR	32,032	VC+
William Jewell College	MO	21,320	VC
William Paterson Univ of New Jersey	NJ	14,450	C
William Penn Univ	IA	17,575	LC
William Woods Univ	MO	20,120	C
Williams College	MA	32,270	MC
Wilson College	PA	23,912	C
Winona State Univ	MN		C
Winston-Salem State Univ	NC	8,926	LC
Winthrop Univ	SC	11,302	C
Wisc Lutheran College	WI	21,430	VC
Wittenberg Univ	OH	31,316	VC
Wofford College	SC	26,710	HC
Woodbury Univ	CA	25,344	LC
Wright State Univ	OH	11,490	LC
Xavier Univ	OH	26,850	VC+
Xavier Univ of Louisiana	LA	17,600	C
Yale Univ	CT	37,000	MC
Yeshiva Univ	NY	21,400	C
York College of Pennsylvania	PA	14,500	VC
Youngstown State Univ	OH	11,148	NC

POLYMER SCIENCE

School	ST	$IS	SR
Case Western Reserve Univ	OH	32,002	MC
Eastern Mich Univ	MI	11,478	C
Georgia Inst of Technology	GA	10,340	HC+
Pennsylvania College of Technology	PA	15,126	NC
Rochester Inst of Technology	NY	29,217	VC+
SUNY/College of Environmental Science and Forestry	NY	14,167	VC
Univ of Calif at Davis	CA	14,995	VC
Univ of Missouri/Rolla	MO	12,292	HC
Univ of Southern Calif	CA	37,459	MC
Univ of Southern Miss	MS	8,324	LC

PORTUGUESE

School	ST	$IS	SR
Brigham Young Univ	UT	8,504	HC
Brown Univ	RI	38,174	MC
Florida International Univ	FL	9,912	VC
Georgetown Univ	DC	38,242	MC
Harvard Univ/Harvard College	MA	37,928	MC
Indiana Univ Bloomington	IN	12,389	VC
New York Univ	NY	39,406	MC
Ohio State Univ	OH	13,080	VC+
Rutgers, The State Univ of New Jersey/New Brunswick/Piscataway Campus	NJ	15,800	HC
Rutgers, The State Univ of New Jersey/Newark Campus	NJ	15,624	VC
Tulane Univ	LA	37,451	HC+
Univ of Arizona	AZ	10,413	VC
Univ of Calif at Los Angeles	CA	15,330	MC
Univ of Calif at Santa Barbara	CA	11,732	VC
Univ of Conn	CT	14,608	VC
Univ of Florida	FL	8,580	MC
Univ of Illinois at Urbana-Champaign	IL	11,316	HC+
Univ of Iowa	IA	10,923	VC
Univ of Mass Amherst	MA	13,980	C+
Univ of Mass Dartmouth	MA	12,835	C
Univ of New Mexico	NM	9,223	C
Univ of Texas at Austin	TX	10,630	HC
Univ of Wisc/Madison	WI	8,262	VC
Yale Univ	CT	37,000	MC

POULTRY SCIENCE

School	ST	$IS	SR
Auburn Univ	AL	10,396	VC
College of the Ozarks	MO	3,500	VC+
Louisiana State Univ and A&M College	LA	9,126	VC
Miss State Univ	MS	9,139	C
N Car State Univ	NC	9,886	VC
Oregon State Univ	OR	11,055	C
Penn State Univ/Univ Park Campus	PA	15,646	HC
Stephen F. Austin State Univ	TX	7,552	C
Texas A&M Univ	TX	11,081	HC
Univ of Arkansas	AR	9,855	VC
Univ of Georgia	GA	8,656	VC
Univ of Maryland/Eastern Shore	MD	9,964	C
Univ of Wisc/Madison	WI	8,262	VC
Virginia Polytechnic Inst and State Univ	VA	9,179	C

PREALLIED HEALTH

School	ST	$IS	SR
Juniata College	PA	29,080	VC
La Salle Univ	PA	31,260	VC

PREDENTISTRY

School	ST	$IS	SR
Abilene Christian Univ	TX	18,370	VC
Adams State College	CO	7,468	C
Albertus Magnus College	CT	23,130	LC
Albion College	MI	25,224	VC
American International College	MA	24,690	LC
Arcadia Univ	PA	29,890	C
Ashland Univ	OH	24,464	C
Auburn Univ	AL	10,396	VC
Austin Peay State Univ	TN	5,814	LC
Averett Univ	VA	23,010	LC
Baldwin-Wallace College	OH	24,678	C
Ball State Univ	IN	8,660	C
Bard College	NY	37,352	HC+
Barry Univ	FL	24,100	LC
Baylor Univ	TX	23,864	VC
Bellarmine Univ	KY	24,110	VC
Belmont Abbey College	NC	23,742	C
Beloit College	WI	29,864	HC
Bemidji State Univ	MN	9,103	C
Berry College	GA	21,410	VC
Bethany College	KS	18,675	LC
Bethany College	WV	19,845	VC
Bethel College	IN	19,670	C
Boise State Univ	ID	7,657	LC
Briar Cliff Univ	IA	21,660	C
Brigham Young Univ/Hawaii	HI	7,240	VC+
Calif Lutheran Univ	CA	27,600	LC
Calif Univ of Pennsylvania	PA	10,388	C
Calvin College	MI	22,615	NC
Capital Univ	OH	26,550	C
Cardinal Stritch Univ	WI	17,620	C
Carroll College	MT	20,576	VC
Central Missouri State Univ	MO	9,776	C
Chadron State College	NE	6,286	NC
Chicago State Univ	IL	10,882	C+
Christopher Newport Univ	VA	8,862	VC
Citadel, The	SC	12,295	C+
CUNY/City College	NY	4,230	C+
CUNY/Herbert H. Lehman College	NY	3,320	LC
CUNY/Hunter College	NY	6,729	C+
CUNY/Queens College	NY	4,362	C
Clark Univ	MA	32,115	VC
Clemson Univ	SC	11,972	HC
Coastal Carolina Univ	SC	11,040	C
Coe College	IA	27,385	VC
College Misericordia	PA	26,350	C
College of Charleston	SC	11,887	HC
College of Notre Dame of Maryland	MD	27,700	C
College of Our Lady of the Elms	MA	20,644	C
College of St. Benedict	MN	26,672	VC
College of St. Elizabeth	NJ	25,460	C
Columbia Union College	MD	20,543	C
Concord College	WV	8,136	C
Concordia College: Moorhead	MN	22,460	VC+
Concordia Univ Nebr	NE	20,302	C+
Converse College	SC	24,710	VC
Coppin State College	MD	10,191	LC
Cornerstone Univ and Grand Rapids Theological Seminary	MI	19,846	C
Dakota Wesleyan Univ	SD	17,832	C
David Lipscomb Univ	TN	16,158	VC
Davis and Elkins College	WV	20,594	C
Delta State Univ	MS	6,618	C
Dordt College	IA	20,170	VC
Drexel Univ	PA	27,655	VC
Drury Univ	MO	18,085	VC+
Eastern Mich Univ	MI	11,478	C
Eastern Washington Univ	WA	9,012	C
Eckerd College	FL	28,744	C+
Edinboro Univ of Pennsylvania	PA	10,850	LC
Elmira College	NY	33,820	VC
Emmanuel College	MA	27,600	C+
Florida A&M Univ	FL	7,564	C
Florida State Univ	FL	9,028	HC
Freed-Hardeman Univ	TN		NC
Gannon Univ	PA	23,260	C
George Fox Univ	OR	26,110	VC
Gettysburg College	PA	35,646	HC
Goshen College	IN	22,450	VC
Grace College	IN	19,825	VC
Graceland Univ	IA	19,550	C
Grand Valley State Univ	MI	11,022	VC
Grove City College	PA	14,228	HC
Gustavus Adolphus College	MN	27,120	VC+
Hamline Univ	MN	27,052	VC
Harding Univ	AR	14,890	VC
Heidelberg College	OH	20,266	NC
Hillsdale College	MI	22,450	HC
Hofstra Univ	NY	27,112	VC
Hope College	MI	25,340	VC
Howard Univ	DC	16,505	C
Humboldt State Univ	CA	9,400	C
Indiana State Univ	IN	10,719	LC
Indiana Univ South Bend	IN	4,571	LC
Indiana Univ-Purdue Univ Fort Wayne	IN	5,108	LC
Indiana Univ-Purdue Univ Indianapolis	IN	8,257	LC
Iona College	NY	27,988	VC
Iowa Wesleyan College	IA	19,990	C
Ithaca College	NY	31,730	HC
Johnson C. Smith Univ	NC	18,108	C
Judson College	IL	22,050	LC
Juniata College	PA	29,080	VC
Kent State Univ	OH	12,932	C
Kentucky Wesleyan College	KY	17,250	C
Keuka College	NY	21,170	C
King's College	PA	26,990	C
La Salle Univ	PA	31,260	VC
LaGrange College	GA	20,500	C
Lake Superior State Univ	MI	9,034	LC
Lamar Univ	TX	6,816	LC
Le Moyne College	NY	26,400	VC
Lebanon Valley College	PA	28,870	VC
Lehigh Univ	PA	37,570	HC+
Lewis Univ	IL	22,950	C+
Lincoln Memorial Univ	TN	16,400	LC
Livingstone College	NC	18,101	LC
LIU/Brooklyn Campus	NY	24,790	C
LIU/C.W. Post Campus	NY	28,282	C
Louisiana College	LA	13,450	C
Loyola Univ Chicago	IL	31,164	VC
MacMurray College	IL	20,005	LC
Manhattan College	NY	27,400	VC
Mars Hill College	NC	18,600	LC
Mary Washington College	VA	10,166	HC
Maryville College	TN	25,960	VC
Mercer Univ	GA	27,516	VC+
Mercyhurst College	PA	20,694	C
Merrimack College	MA	29,625	C
Methodist College	NC	19,526	C
Midland Lutheran College	NE	18,600	C
Midwestern State Univ	TX	8,045	LC
Miles College	AL	7,870	NC
Minn State Univ, Mankato	MN	8,803	LC
Minn State Univ, Moorehead	MN	7,000	LC
Missouri Southern State Univ	MO	8,316	C
Montclair State Univ	NJ	13,790	C
Mount Mary College	WI	20,370	C
Murray State Univ	KY	7,816	LC
New York Univ	NY	39,406	MC
Newman Univ	KS	18,018	C
Niagara Univ	NY	25,050	C
N Car State Univ	NC	9,886	VC
North Central College	IL	25,656	VC
North Georgia College and State Univ	GA	6,984	C
North Park Univ	IL	24,030	C
Northeastern State Univ	OK	4,950	LC
Northern Arizona Univ	AZ	9,002	C
Northern Kentucky Univ	KY	6,352	NC
Northern Mich Univ	MI	10,834	C
Northern State Univ	SD	7,117	LC
Northwest Missouri State Univ	MO	9,334	C
Northwestern College of Iowa	IA	19,640	C+
Notre Dame de Namur Univ	CA	26,932	LC
Ohio Univ	OH	14,448	C
Ohio Wesleyan Univ	OH	32,550	VC+
Okla Baptist Univ	OK	15,220	VC
Okla Wesleyan Univ	OK	14,100	LC
Olivet College	MI	19,984	C+
Oral Roberts Univ	OK	18,490	C
Ouachita Baptist Univ	AR	18,900	VC
Purdue Univ/Calumet	IN	6,630	NC
Purdue Univ/West Lafayette	IN	12,560	VC
Quinnipiac Univ	CT	30,570	VC
Rensselaer Polytechnic Inst	NY	37,579	HC+
Rivier College	NH	26,217	C
Rochester Inst of Technology	NY	29,217	VC+

ST = STATE $IS = IN-STATE COSTS SR = SELECTOR RATING

School	ST	$IS	SR
Rockford College	IL	28,310	VC
Roosevelt Univ	IL	22,580	VC
Rosemont College	PA	26,175	C
St. Anselm College	NH	30,250	C
St. Cloud State Univ	MN	8,362	C
St. Edward's Univ	TX	20,428	C
St. John's Univ	MN	26,473	VC
St. John's Univ	NY	30,180	C
St. Joseph's College	IN	24,250	C
St. Martin's College	WA	23,245	C
St. Mary-of-the-Woods College	IN	23,280	C
St. Mary's Univ of Minn	MN	21,535	C
St. Mary's Univ of San Antonio	TX	22,444	C
St. Michael's College	VT	30,100	VC
St. Peter's College	NJ	22,292	LC
St. Thomas Univ	FL	21,400	LC
St. Vincent College	PA	25,530	VC
St. Xavier Univ	IL	23,144	C
Savannah State Univ	GA	7,328	LC
Seton Hill Univ	PA	24,930	C
Southern Nazarene Univ	OK	14,634	NC
Southwest Missouri State Univ	MO	8,918	C
Spring Hill College	AL	25,868	VC
Springfield College	MA	24,520	C
SUNY/College at Fredonia	NY	11,562	VC
SUNY/College at Oneonta	NY	11,870	VC
SUNY/College of Environmental Science and Forestry	NY	14,167	VC
SUNY/Univ at Albany	NY	12,951	HC
Stevens Inst of Technology	NJ	35,300	HC+
Syracuse Univ	NY	34,720	HC
Tarleton State Univ	TX	7,576	C
Temple Univ	PA	15,912	C
Texas A&M Univ at Commerce	TX	8,994	C
Texas A&M Univ at Kingsville	TX	6,740	LC
Texas Tech Univ	TX	10,768	VC
Thiel College	PA	20,970	C
Touro College	NY	15,250	VC
Trinity Christian College	IL	21,640	VC
Truman State Univ	MO	9,728	HC+
Union Univ	TN	18,800	VC
Univ of Akron	OH	13,134	NC
Univ of Arkansas	AR	9,855	VC
Univ of Arkansas at Pine Bluff	AR	7,925	C
Univ of Bridgeport	CT	25,924	LC
Univ of Central Arkansas	AR	6,388	C
Univ of Cincinnati	OH	14,736	C
Univ of Dayton	OH	24,850	VC
Univ of Detroit Mercy	MI	25,582	C
Univ of Evansville	IN	24,190	VC
Univ of Georgia	GA	8,656	VC
Univ of Great Falls	MT	15,360	C
Univ of Hartford	CT	31,080	C
Univ of Iowa	IA	10,923	VC
Univ of Mass Amherst	MA	13,980	C+
Univ of Miami	FL	34,608	HC
Univ of Minn/Twin Cities	MN	13,160	VC
Univ of Missouri/Rolla	MO	12,292	HC
Univ of Nebr at Kearney	NE	8,286	NC
Univ of Nebr at Lincoln	NE	9,975	C+
Univ of New Haven	CT	28,650	C
Univ of New Mexico	NM	9,223	C
Univ of North Florida	FL	8,769	VC
Univ of Notre Dame	IN	34,442	MC
Univ of Rio Grande	OH	8,728	NC
Univ of St. Francis	IL	22,850	C
Univ of St. Francis	IN	20,964	C
Univ of Southern Colo	CO	7,821	LC
Univ of Southern Indiana	IN	9,025	LC
Univ of Southern Miss	MS	8,324	LC
Univ of Tenn at Knoxville	TN	8,214	C
Univ of Tenn at Martin	TN	7,748	C
Univ of the Incarnate Word	TX	21,772	LC
Univ of West Alabama	AL	6,048	C
Univ of West Florida	FL	8,470	C
Univ of Wisc/Milwaukee	WI	9,427	LC
Utah State Univ	UT	7,371	C
Walsh Univ	OH	20,890	C
Washington State Univ	WA	11,334	C
Washington Univ in St. Louis	MO	38,293	MC
Waynesburg College	PA	19,370	C
West Chester Univ of Pennsylvania	PA	11,164	C
West Liberty State College	WV	7,868	LC
West Texas A&M Univ	TX	7,533	C
Western Carolina Univ	NC	6,742	C
Western Mich Univ	MI	12,031	C
Western New Mexico Univ	NM	5,950	LC
Western State College of Colo	CO	9,014	C
Westminster College	PA	22,960	C
Whitworth College	WA	26,428	VC+
Widener Univ	PA	27,020	C
Wilkes Univ	PA	28,060	C
Wilmington College	OH	24,172	LC
Wingate Univ	NC	21,200	C
Winona State Univ	MN		C
Wittenberg Univ	OH	31,316	VC
Wright State Univ	OH	11,490	LC
Xavier Univ of Louisiana	LA	17,600	C
Youngstown State Univ	OH	11,148	NC

PREENGINEERING

School	ST	$IS	SR
Adams State College	CO	7,468	C
Alice Lloyd College	KY	4,040	C
Augustana College	IL	26,610	VC+
Baldwin-Wallace College	OH	24,678	C
Barry Univ	FL	24,100	LC
Bellarmine Univ	KY	24,110	VC
Belmont Abbey College	NC	23,742	C
Berry College	GA	21,410	VC
Bethel College	TN	12,980	C
Campbell Univ	NC	18,268	VC
CUNY/Hunter College	NY	6,729	C+
Coe College	IA	27,385	VC
College of Notre Dame of Maryland	MD	27,700	C
College of St. Benedict	MN	26,672	VC
College of the Ozarks	MO	3,500	VC+
Concordia College: Moorhead	MN	22,460	VC+
Coppin State College	MD	10,191	LC
David Lipscomb Univ	TN	16,158	VC
DePauw Univ	IN	31,500	HC
Eastern Mich Univ	MI	11,478	C
Edgewood College	WI	20,520	C
Freed-Hardeman Univ	TN		NC
Furman Univ	SC	28,976	HC+
Goshen College	IN	22,450	VC
Harvard Univ/Harvard College	MA	37,928	MC
Heidelberg College	OH	20,266	NC
Indiana State Univ	IN	10,719	LC
Indiana Univ South Bend	IN	4,571	LC
Iowa Wesleyan College	IA	19,990	C
Johnson C. Smith Univ	NC	18,108	C
Judson College	IL	22,050	LC
Juniata College	PA	29,080	VC
Kentucky Wesleyan College	KY	17,250	C
Lewis Univ	IL	22,950	C+
Lincoln Univ	PA	13,320	C+
LIU/C.W. Post Campus	NY	28,282	C
MacMurray College	IL	20,005	LC
Mansfield Univ	PA	11,220	C
Maryville College	TN	25,960	VC
Midwestern State Univ	TX	8,045	LC
Miles College	AL	7,870	NC
Minn State Univ, Mankato	MN	8,803	LC
Newman Univ	KS	18,018	C
Niagara Univ	NY	25,050	C
North Central College	IL	25,656	VC
North Georgia College and State Univ	GA	6,984	C
Northern Kentucky Univ	KY	6,352	NC
Northwest Missouri State Univ	MO	9,334	C
Oral Roberts Univ	OK	18,490	C
Peru State College	NE	6,342	NC
Pfeiffer Univ	NC	18,980	C
Providence College	RI	30,604	HC
Purdue Univ/West Lafayette	IN	12,560	VC
Richard Stockton College of New Jersey	NJ	12,972	VC
Rockford College	IL	28,310	VC
St. Edward's Univ	TX	20,428	C
St. John's Univ	MN	26,473	VC
St. John's Univ	NY	30,180	C
St. Mary's College of Calif	CA	32,850	VC
St. Michael's College	VT	30,100	VC
Scripps College	CA	35,700	HC+
Shaw Univ	NC	14,882	C+
Southern Nazarene Univ	OK	14,634	NC
Stephen F. Austin State Univ	TX	7,552	C
Texas A&M Univ at Commerce	TX	8,994	C
Thiel College	PA	20,970	C
Truman State Univ	MO	9,728	HC+
Union Univ	TN	18,800	VC
Univ of Arkansas at Pine Bluff	AR	7,925	C
Univ of Central Arkansas	AR	6,388	C
Univ of Findlay	OH	23,962	NC
Univ of Georgia	GA	8,656	VC
Univ of Rio Grande	OH	8,728	NC
Univ of Southern Colo	CO	7,821	LC
West Liberty State College	WV	7,868	LC
West Texas A&M Univ	TX	7,533	C
Western Carolina Univ	NC	6,742	C
Western State College of Colo	CO	9,014	C
Wilberforce Univ	OH	14,937	LC
Wingate Univ	NC	21,200	C
Yeshiva Univ	NY	21,400	C
Youngstown State Univ	OH	11,148	NC

PRELAW

School	ST	$IS	SR
Abilene Christian Univ	TX	18,370	VC
Adams State College	CO	7,468	C
Albertus Magnus College	CT	23,130	LC
American International College	MA	24,690	LC
Arcadia Univ	PA	29,890	C
Ashland Univ	OH	24,464	C
Austin Peay State Univ	TN	5,814	LC
Averett Univ	VA	23,010	LC
Baldwin-Wallace College	OH	24,678	C
Ball State Univ	IN	8,660	C
Bard College	NY	37,352	HC+
Barry Univ	FL	24,100	LC
Baylor Univ	TX	23,864	VC
Bellarmine Univ	KY	24,110	VC
Belmont Abbey College	NC	23,742	C
Beloit College	WI	29,864	HC
Bemidji State Univ	MN	9,103	C
Berry College	GA	21,410	VC
Bethany College	KS	18,675	LC
Bethany College	WV	19,845	VC
Bethel College	IN	19,670	C
Black Hills State Univ	SD	7,743	LC
Calif Lutheran Univ	CA	27,600	LC
Calvin College	MI	22,615	NC
Campbell Univ	NC	18,268	VC
Capital Univ	OH	26,550	C
Cardinal Stritch Univ	WI	17,620	C
Carroll College	MT	20,576	VC
Catawba College	NC	20,500	C
Cedar Crest College	PA	25,145	C+
Cedarville Univ	OH	19,954	VC
Central Missouri State Univ	MO	9,776	C
Central Washington Univ	WA	9,768	C
Chadron State College	NE	6,286	NC
Champlain College	VT	22,030	C
Chicago State Univ	IL	10,882	C+
Christopher Newport Univ	VA	8,862	VC
CUNY/City College	NY	4,230	C+
CUNY/Herbert H. Lehman College	NY	3,320	LC
CUNY/Hunter College	NY	6,729	C+
Clark Univ	MA	32,115	VC
Clearwater Christian College	FL	13,160	LC
Clemson Univ	SC	11,972	HC
Coastal Carolina Univ	SC	11,040	C
Coe College	IA	27,385	VC
College Misericordia	PA	26,350	C
College of Notre Dame of Maryland	MD	27,700	C
College of Our Lady of the Elms	MA	20,644	C
College of St. Benedict	MN	26,672	VC
College of St. Elizabeth	NJ	25,460	C
College of the Ozarks	MO	3,500	VC+
College of the Southwest	NM	9,320	C+
Columbia Union College	MD	20,543	C
Concord College	WV	8,136	C
Concordia College: Moorhead	MN	22,460	VC+
Concordia Univ Nebr	NE	20,302	C+
Concordia Univ, River Forest	IL	23,600	C
Converse College	SC	24,710	VC
Cornerstone Univ and Grand Rapids Theological Seminary	MI	19,846	C
Creighton Univ	NE	26,748	VC+
David Lipscomb Univ	TN	16,158	VC
Davis and Elkins College	WV	20,594	C
Dordt College	IA	20,170	VC
Drexel Univ	PA	27,655	VC
Drury Univ	MO	18,085	VC+
East Central Univ	OK	4,968	C
Eastern Mich Univ	MI	11,478	C
Eastern Washington Univ	WA	9,012	C
Eckerd College	FL	28,744	C+
Edgewood College	WI	20,520	C
Edinboro Univ of Pennsylvania	PA	10,850	LC
Elmira College	NY	33,820	VC
Emmanuel College	MA	27,600	C+
Eugene Lang College/New School Univ	NY	34,940	C
Faulkner Univ	AL	14,500	C
Florida State Univ	FL	9,028	HC
Fontbonne Univ	MO	21,508	C
Fresno Pacific Univ	CA	22,462	C
Gannon Univ	PA	23,260	C
George Fox Univ	OR	26,110	VC
Gettysburg College	PA	35,646	HC
Grace College	IN	19,825	VC
Grambling State Univ	LA	6,538	NC
Grand Valley State Univ	MI	11,022	VC
Grove City College	PA	14,228	HC
Gustavus Adolphus College	MN	27,120	VC+
Hamline Univ	MN	27,052	VC
Heidelberg College	OH	20,266	NC
Hillsdale College	MI	22,450	HC
Holy Family College	PA	13,710	LC
Hope College	MI	25,340	VC
Humboldt State Univ	CA	9,400	C
Huntington College	IN	23,590	C
Illinois College	IL	19,100	VC
Immaculata Univ	PA	25,200	C
Indiana State Univ	IN	10,719	LC
Indiana Univ of Pennsylvania	PA	10,489	C
Indiana Univ South Bend	IN	4,571	LC
Indiana Univ-Purdue Univ Fort Wayne	IN	5,108	LC
Indiana Univ-Purdue Univ Indianapolis	IN	8,257	LC
Iowa Wesleyan College	IA	19,990	C
Ithaca College	NY	31,730	HC
John Brown Univ	AR	15,080	VC
Johns Hopkins Univ	MD	38,372	MC
Johnson C. Smith Univ	NC	18,108	C
Johnson State College	VT	11,819	LC
Judson College	IL	22,050	LC
Juniata College	PA	29,080	VC
Kansas Wesleyan Univ	KS	18,900	VC
Kent State Univ	OH	12,932	C
Kentucky Wesleyan College	KY	17,250	C
Keuka College	NY	21,170	C
King's College	PA	26,990	C
La Salle Univ	PA	31,260	VC
Lafayette College	PA	35,746	MC
LaGrange College	GA	20,500	C
Lake Superior State Univ	MI	9,034	LC
Lamar Univ	TX	6,816	LC
Le Moyne College	NY	26,400	VC
Lebanon Valley College	PA	28,870	VC
Lenoir-Rhyne College	NC	19,186	C
LeTourneau Univ	TX	21,080	C
Lewis Univ	IL	22,950	C+
Limestone College	SC	17,700	C
Lincoln Memorial Univ	TN	16,400	LC
Lindenwood Univ	MO	17,050	VC
Livingstone College	NC	18,101	LC
LIU/Brooklyn Campus	NY	24,790	C
LIU/C.W. Post Campus	NY	28,282	C
LIU/Southampton College	NY	29,370	C+
Louisiana College	LA	13,450	C
Lynn Univ	FL	30,750	C
MacMurray College	IL	20,005	LC
Manchester College	IN	23,390	C
Manhattan College	NY	27,400	VC
Mansfield Univ	PA	11,220	C
Marlboro College	VT	29,055	VC+
Mars Hill College	NC	18,600	LC
Mary Washington College	VA	10,166	HC
Maryville College	TN	25,960	VC
Mercer Univ	GA	27,516	VC+
Mercyhurst College	PA	20,694	C
Merrimack College	MA	29,625	C
Methodist College	NC	19,526	C
Metropolitan College of New York	NY	15,771	C
Miami Univ	OH	15,033	HC
Mich State Univ	MI	11,933	VC
Middle Tenn State Univ	TN	8,534	C
Midland Lutheran College	NE	18,600	C
Midwestern State Univ	TX	8,045	LC
Minn State Univ, Mankato	MN	8,803	LC
Minn State Univ, Moorhead	MN	7,000	LC
Monmouth Univ	NJ	26,334	C
Mount Aloysius College	PA	19,120	LC
Mount Mary College	WI	20,370	C
Mount St. Mary College	NY	21,270	C
Murray State Univ	KY	7,816	VC
New Mexico Highlands Univ	NM	6,182	LC
New York Inst of Technology	NY	24,205	VC
Newbury College	MA	23,450	C
Newman Univ	KS	18,018	C
Niagara Univ	NY	25,050	C
N Car State Univ	NC	9,886	VC
North Central College	IL	25,656	VC
North Georgia College and State Univ	GA	6,984	C
North Park Univ	IL	24,030	C
Northeastern State Univ	OK	4,950	LC
Northern Arizona Univ	AZ	9,002	C
Northern Kentucky Univ	KY	6,352	NC
Northern Mich Univ	MI	10,834	C
Northern State Univ	SD	7,117	LC
Northwest Missouri State Univ	MO	9,334	C
Northwestern College of Iowa	IA	19,640	C+
Notre Dame de Namur Univ	CA	26,932	LC
Nova Southeastern Univ	FL	23,346	C
Oakland City Univ	IN	16,980	NC
Ohio Univ	OH	14,448	C
Ohio Wesleyan Univ	OH	32,550	VC+
Okla Baptist Univ	OK	15,220	VC
Okla Christian Univ	OK	17,690	NC
Okla City Univ	OK	19,580	VC
Okla State Univ	OK	9,216	VC
Okla Wesleyan Univ	OK	14,100	LC
Olivet College	MI	19,984	C+
Oral Roberts Univ	OK	18,490	C
Ouachita Baptist Univ	AR	18,900	VC
Palm Beach Atlantic Univ	FL	20,690	C
Penn State Univ/Univ Park Campus	PA	15,646	HC
Peru State College	NE	6,342	NC
Pfeiffer Univ	NC	18,980	C
Purdue Univ/Calumet	IN	6,630	NC
Purdue Univ/West Lafayette	IN	12,560	VC
Quinnipiac Univ	CT	30,570	VC
Regis Univ	CO	25,740	C+
Rensselaer Polytechnic Inst	NY	37,579	HC+

School	ST	$IS	SR
Rhode Island College	RI	11,565	C
Rider Univ	NJ	30,900	C
Rivier College	NH	26,217	C
Roberts Wesleyan College	NY	23,190	C+
Rochester Inst of Technology	NY	29,217	VC+
Rockford College	IL	28,310	C
Roger Williams Univ	RI	30,296	C
Roosevelt Univ	IL	22,580	VC
Rosemont College	PA	26,175	C
St. Anselm College	NH	30,250	C
St. Augustine's College	NC	12,990	C
St. Bonaventure Univ	NY	24,455	LC
St. Cloud State Univ	MN	8,362	C
St. Edward's Univ	TX	20,428	C
St. John's Univ	MN	26,473	VC
St. John's Univ	NY	30,180	C
St. Joseph's College	IN	24,250	C
St. Martin's College	WA	23,245	C
St. Mary-of-the-Woods College	IN	23,280	C
St. Mary's College	MI	13,314	LC
St. Mary's Univ of Minn	MN	21,535	C
St. Mary's Univ of San Antonio	TX	22,444	C
St. Michael's College	VT	30,100	VC
St. Peter's College	NJ	22,292	LC
St. Thomas Aquinas College	NY	20,590	LC
St. Thomas Univ	FL	21,400	LC
St. Vincent College	PA	25,530	VC
St. Xavier Univ	IL	23,144	C
Schreiner Univ	TX	20,440	C
Scripps College	CA	35,700	HC+
Seton Hill Univ	PA	24,930	C
Shawnee State Univ	OH	11,031	NC
Simmons College	MA	33,000	VC
Southern Nazarene Univ	OK	14,634	NC
Southern Oregon Univ	OR	10,362	C
Springfield College	MA	24,520	C
SUNY/College at Oneonta	NY	11,870	VC
SUNY/College of Environmental Science and Forestry	NY	14,167	VC
SUNY/Univ at Albany	NY	12,951	HC
Stephen F. Austin State Univ	TX	7,552	C
Stephens College	MO	24,260	C+
Stetson Univ	FL	29,495	VC
Stevens Inst of Technology	NJ	35,300	HC+
Stillman College	AL	11,370	LC
Syracuse Univ	NY	34,720	HC
Tarleton State Univ	TX	7,576	C
Temple Univ	PA	15,912	C
Texas A&M Univ at Commerce	TX	8,994	C
Texas A&M Univ at Kingsville	TX	6,740	LC
Texas Tech Univ	TX	10,768	LC
Thiel College	PA	20,970	C
Touro College	NY	15,250	VC
Trinity Christian College	IL	21,640	VC
Trinity College	DC	24,150	LC
Truman State Univ	MO	9,728	HC+
Union Univ	TN	18,800	VC
Univ of Akron	OH	13,134	NC
Univ of Arkansas	AR	9,855	VC
Univ of Bridgeport	CT	25,924	LC
Univ of Cincinnati	OH	14,736	C
Univ of Dayton	OH	24,850	VC
Univ of Detroit Mercy	MI	25,582	C
Univ of Evansville	IN	24,190	VC
Univ of Findlay	OH	23,962	NC
Univ of Great Falls	MT	15,360	C
Univ of Iowa	IA	10,923	VC
Univ of Louisiana at Monroe	LA	5,207	NC
Univ of Mary	ND	12,900	C+
Univ of Mass Amherst	MA	13,980	C+
Univ of Miami	FL	34,608	HC
Univ of Minn/Morris	MN	12,896	VC
Univ of Minn/Twin Cities	MN	13,160	VC
Univ of Missouri/Rolla	MO	12,292	HC
Univ of Nebr at Kearney	NE	8,286	NC
Univ of New Mexico	NM	9,223	C
Univ of N Car at Pembroke	NC	6,929	LC
Univ of North Florida	FL	8,769	VC
Univ of Rio Grande	OH	8,728	NC
Univ of St. Francis	IL	22,850	C
Univ of Sioux Falls	SD	16,390	C
Univ of Southern Colo	CO	7,821	LC
Univ of Southern Indiana	IN	9,025	LC
Univ of Southern Miss	MS	8,324	LC
Univ of Tenn at Martin	TN	7,748	C
Univ of the Incarnate Word	TX	21,772	LC
Univ of Tulsa	OK	22,090	VC+
Univ of West Alabama	AL	6,048	LC
Univ of West Florida	FL	8,470	C
Univ of Wisc/Milwaukee	WI	9,427	LC
Univ of Wisc/River Falls	WI	8,358	LC
Univ of Wisc/Whitewater	WI	8,626	C
Urbana Univ	OH	19,115	C
Ursinus College	PA	34,400	C
Ursuline College	OH	22,728	LC
Utah State Univ	UT	7,371	C
Vanguard Univ of Southern Calif	CA	22,208	C

School	ST	$IS	SR
Vassar College	NY	37,030	MC
Walsh Univ	OH	20,890	C
Waynesburg College	PA	19,370	C
Webber International Univ	FL	16,510	C
West Chester Univ of Pennsylvania	PA	11,164	C
West Liberty State College	WV	7,868	LC
West Texas A&M Univ	TX	7,533	C
Western Carolina Univ	NC	6,742	C
Western Mich Univ	MI	12,031	C
Western State College of Colo	CO	9,014	C
Westminster College	PA	22,960	C
Whitworth College	WA	26,428	VC+
Widener Univ	PA	27,020	C
Wilberforce Univ	OH	14,937	LC
Wilkes Univ	PA	28,060	C
Wilmington College	OH	24,172	LC
Wingate Univ	NC	21,200	C
Winona State Univ	MN		C
Wittenberg Univ	OH	31,316	VC
Wright State Univ	OH	11,490	LC
Xavier Univ of Louisiana	LA	17,600	C
York College of Pennsylvania	PA	14,500	VC
Youngstown State Univ	OH	11,148	NC

PREMEDICINE

School	ST	$IS	SR
Abilene Christian Univ	TX	18,370	VC
Adams State College	CO	7,468	C
Albertus Magnus College	CT	23,130	LC
Albion College	MI	25,224	VC
American International College	MA	24,690	LC
Arcadia Univ	PA	29,890	C
Ashland Univ	OH	24,464	C
Auburn Univ	AL	10,396	VC
Augustana College	IL	26,610	VC+
Austin Peay State Univ	TN	5,814	LC
Averett Univ	VA	23,010	LC
Avila Univ	MO	20,300	C
Azusa Pacific Univ	CA	24,720	VC
Baldwin-Wallace College	OH	24,678	C
Ball State Univ	IN	8,660	C
Bard College	NY	37,352	HC+
Barry Univ	FL	24,100	LC
Baylor Univ	TX	23,864	VC
Bellarmine Univ	KY	24,110	VC
Belmont Abbey College	NC	23,742	C
Beloit College	WI	29,864	HC
Bemidji State Univ	MN	9,103	C
Bennington College	VT	35,910	HC
Berry College	GA	21,410	VC
Bethany College	KS	18,675	LC
Bethany College	WV	19,845	VC
Bethel College	IN	19,670	C
Bluffton College	OH	23,694	C
Boise State Univ	ID	7,657	LC
Bowling Green State Univ	OH	13,036	C
Briar Cliff Univ	IA	21,660	C
Brigham Young Univ/Hawaii	HI	7,240	VC+
Calif Lutheran Univ	CA	27,600	LC
Cal State, San Bernardino	CA	15,238	LC
Calif Univ of Pennsylvania	PA	10,388	C
Capital Univ	OH	26,550	C
Cardinal Stritch Univ	WI	17,620	C
Carroll College	MT	20,576	VC
Central Missouri State Univ	MO	9,776	C
Central Univ of Bayamon	PR	3,335	
Chadron State College	NE	6,286	NC
Chicago State Univ	IL	10,882	C+
Christopher Newport Univ	VA	8,862	VC
Citadel, The	SC	12,295	C+
CUNY/City College	NY	4,230	C+
CUNY/Herbert H. Lehman College	NY	3,320	LC
CUNY/Hunter College	NY	6,729	C+
CUNY/Queens College	NY	4,362	C
Clark Univ	MA	32,115	VC
Clearwater Christian College	FL	13,160	LC
Clemson Univ	SC	11,972	HC
Cleveland State Univ	OH	12,308	LC
Coastal Carolina Univ	SC	11,040	C
Coe College	IA	27,385	VC
College Misericordia	PA	26,350	C
College of Charleston	SC	11,887	HC
College of Mount St. Joseph	OH	22,785	C
College of Notre Dame of Maryland	MD	27,700	C
College of Our Lady of the Elms	MA	20,644	C
College of St. Benedict	MN	26,672	VC
College of St. Elizabeth	NJ	25,460	C
College of the Ozarks	MO	3,500	VC+
Columbia Union College	MD	20,543	C
Concord College	WV	8,136	C
Concordia College: Moorhead	MN	22,460	VC+
Concordia Univ	OR	22,450	C
Concordia Univ Nebr	NE	20,302	C+
Concordia Univ, River Forest	IL	23,600	C
Converse College	SC	24,710	VC

School	ST	$IS	SR
Cornerstone Univ and Grand Rapids Theological Seminary	MI	19,846	C
Dakota State Univ	SD	7,466	C
Dakota Wesleyan Univ	SD	17,832	C
David Lipscomb Univ	TN	16,158	VC
Davis and Elkins College	WV	20,594	C
Delta State Univ	MS	6,618	C
Dominican Univ of Calif	CA	31,670	C
Dordt College	IA	20,170	VC
Drexel Univ	PA	27,655	VC
Drury Univ	MO	18,085	VC+
East Stroudsburg Univ of Pennsylvania	PA	10,336	C
Eastern Mich Univ	MI	11,478	C
Eastern Washington Univ	WA	9,012	C
Eckerd College	FL	28,744	C+
Edgewood College	WI	20,520	C
Edinboro Univ of Pennsylvania	PA	10,850	LC
Elmira College	NY	33,820	VC
Emmanuel College	MA	27,600	C+
Florida A&M Univ	FL	7,564	C
Florida Inst of Technology	FL	28,740	VC
Florida State Univ	FL	9,028	HC
Freed-Hardeman Univ	TN		NC
Fresno Pacific Univ	CA	22,462	C
Friends Univ	KS	15,962	LC
Gannon Univ	PA	23,260	C
George Fox Univ	OR	26,110	VC
George Washington Univ	DC	41,030	MC
Gettysburg College	PA	35,646	HC
Goshen College	IN	22,450	VC
Grace College	IN	19,825	VC
Graceland Univ	IA	19,550	C
Grambling State Univ	LA	6,538	NC
Grand Valley State Univ	MI	11,022	VC
Grove City College	PA	14,228	HC
Gustavus Adolphus College	MN	27,120	VC+
Hamline Univ	MN	27,052	VC
Hampshire College	MA	37,037	HC
Harding Univ	AR	14,890	VC
Hawaii Pacific Univ	HI	19,218	C
Heidelberg College	OH	20,266	NC
Hillsdale College	MI	22,450	HC
Hofstra Univ	NY	27,112	VC
Holy Family College	PA	13,710	LC
Hope College	MI	25,340	VC
Howard Univ	DC	16,505	C
Humboldt State Univ	CA	9,400	C
Huntington College	IN	23,590	C
Immaculata Univ	PA	25,200	C
Indiana State Univ	IN	10,719	LC
Indiana Univ of Pennsylvania	PA	10,489	C
Indiana Univ South Bend	IN	4,571	LC
Indiana Univ-Purdue Univ Fort Wayne	IN	5,108	LC
Indiana Univ-Purdue Univ Indianapolis	IN	8,257	LC
Indiana Wesleyan Univ	IN	19,900	C+
Inter American Univ of PR/San German	PR	6,716	
Iona College	NY	27,988	VC
Iowa Wesleyan College	IA	19,990	C
Ithaca College	NY	31,730	HC
Jackson State Univ	MS	8,382	C
Jarvis Christian College	TX	9,035	NC
Johns Hopkins Univ	MD	38,372	MC
Johnson C. Smith Univ	NC	18,108	C
Johnson State College	VT	11,819	C
Judson College	IL	22,050	C
Juniata College	PA	29,080	VC
Kent State Univ	OH	12,932	C
Kentucky Wesleyan College	KY	17,250	C
Keuka College	NY	21,170	C
King's College	PA	26,990	C
La Salle Univ	PA	31,260	VC
LaGrange College	GA	20,500	C
Lake Superior State Univ	MI	9,034	LC
Lamar Univ	TX	6,816	LC
Le Moyne College	NY	26,400	VC
Lebanon Valley College	PA	28,870	VC
Lehigh Univ	PA	37,570	HC+
Lenoir-Rhyne College	NC	19,186	C
LeTourneau Univ	TX	21,080	C
Lewis Univ	IL	22,950	C+
Lincoln Memorial Univ	TN	16,400	LC
Livingstone College	NC	18,101	LC
LIU/Brooklyn Campus	NY	24,790	C
LIU/C.W. Post Campus	NY	28,282	C
Louisiana College	LA	13,450	C
Loyola Univ Chicago	IL	31,164	VC
MacMurray College	IL	20,005	C
Manhattan College	NY	27,400	VC
Mansfield Univ	PA	11,220	C
Marlboro College	VT	29,055	VC+
Marquette Univ	WI	27,594	VC
Mars Hill College	NC	18,600	LC
Mary Washington College	VA	10,166	HC
Marymount Manhattan College	NY	27,292	C
Maryville College	TN	25,960	VC
Mass College of Pharmacy and Health Sciences	MA	28,770	SP
Mercer Univ	GA	27,516	VC+

School	ST	$IS	SR
Mercyhurst College	PA	20,694	C
Merrimack College	MA	29,625	C
Miami Univ	OH	15,033	HC
Midland Lutheran College	NE	18,600	C
Midwestern State Univ	TX	8,045	LC
Miles College	AL	7,870	NC
Milligan College	TN	19,860	C+
Minn State Univ, Mankato	MN	8,803	LC
Minn State Univ, Moorehead	MN	7,000	LC
Missouri Southern State Univ	MO	8,316	C
Monmouth Univ	NJ	26,334	C
Montclair State Univ	NJ	13,790	C
Mount Mary College	WI	20,370	C
Mount St. Mary College	NY	21,270	C
Murray State Univ	KY	7,816	VC
New Mexico Highlands Univ	NM	6,182	LC
New York Univ	NY	39,406	MC
Newman Univ	KS	18,018	C
Niagara Univ	NY	25,050	C
N Car State Univ	NC	9,886	VC
N Car Wesleyan College	NC	17,998	C
North Central College	IL	25,656	VC
North Georgia College and State Univ	GA	6,984	C
North Park Univ	IL	24,030	C
Northeastern State Univ	OK	4,950	LC
Northern Arizona Univ	AZ	9,002	C
Northern Kentucky Univ	KY	6,362	NC
Northern Mich Univ	MI	10,834	C
Northern State Univ	SD	7,117	LC
Northwest Missouri State Univ	MO	9,334	C
Northwest Nazarene Univ	ID	20,360	VC
Northwestern College of Iowa	IA	19,640	C+
Northwestern Univ	IL	37,491	MC
Notre Dame de Namur Univ	CA	26,932	LC
Oakland City Univ	IN	16,980	NC
Ohio Univ	OH	14,448	C
Ohio Wesleyan Univ	OH	32,550	VC+
Okla Baptist Univ	OK	15,220	VC
Okla Christian Univ	OK	17,690	NC
Okla City Univ	OK	19,580	VC
Okla State Univ	OK	9,216	VC
Okla Wesleyan Univ	OK	14,100	LC
Olivet College	MI	19,984	C+
Oral Roberts Univ	OK	18,490	C
Ouachita Baptist Univ	AR	18,900	VC
Penn State Univ/Univ Park Campus	PA	15,646	HC
Peru State College	NE	6,342	NC
Pfeiffer Univ	NC	18,980	C
Philadelphia Univ	PA	27,354	C
Purdue Univ/Calumet	IN	6,630	NC
Purdue Univ/West Lafayette	IN	12,560	VC
Quinnipiac Univ	CT	30,570	VC
Rensselaer Polytechnic Inst	NY	37,579	HC+
Rider Univ	NJ	30,900	C
Rivier College	NH	26,217	C
Roberts Wesleyan College	NY	23,190	C+
Rochester Inst of Technology	NY	29,217	VC+
Rockford College	IL	28,310	C
Roger Williams Univ	RI	30,296	C
Roosevelt Univ	IL	22,580	VC
Rosemont College	PA	26,175	C
St. Anselm College	NH	30,250	C
St. Augustine's College	NC	12,990	C
St. Bonaventure Univ	NY	24,455	LC
St. Cloud State Univ	MN	8,362	C
St. Edward's Univ	TX	20,428	C
St. John's Univ	MN	26,473	VC
St. John's Univ	NY	30,180	C
St. Joseph's College	IN	24,250	C
St. Martin's College	WA	23,245	C
St. Mary-of-the-Woods College	IN	23,280	C
St. Mary's College	MI	13,314	LC
St. Mary's Univ of Minn	MN	21,535	C
St. Mary's Univ of San Antonio	TX	22,444	C
St. Peter's College	NJ	22,292	LC
St. Thomas Aquinas College	NY	20,590	LC
St. Thomas Univ	FL	21,400	LC
St. Vincent College	PA	25,530	VC
St. Xavier Univ	IL	23,144	C
Sarah Lawrence College	NY	41,218	HC
Seton Hill Univ	PA	24,930	C
Shawnee State Univ	OH	11,031	NC
Siena Heights Univ	MI	16,140	LC
Simmons College	MA	33,000	VC
Simon's Rock College of Bard	MA	36,580	HC
Southern Nazarene Univ	OK	14,634	NC
Southern Oregon Univ	OR	10,362	C
Spring Hill College	AL	25,868	VC
Springfield College	MA	24,520	C
SUNY/College at Fredonia	NY	11,562	VC
SUNY/College at Oneonta	NY	11,870	VC
SUNY/College of Environmental Science and Forestry	NY	14,167	VC
SUNY/Univ at Albany	NY	12,951	HC

ST = STATE $IS = IN-STATE COSTS   SR = SELECTOR RATING

School	ST	$IS	SR
SUNY/Univ at New Paltz	NY	11,565	VC
Stephen F. Austin State Univ	TX	7,552	C
Stevens Inst of Technology	NJ	35,300	HC+
Stillman College	AL	11,370	LC
Syracuse Univ	NY	34,720	HC
Tarleton State Univ	TX	7,576	C
Temple Univ	PA	15,912	C
Texas A&M Univ at Commerce	TX	8,994	C
Texas A&M Univ at Kingsville	TX	6,740	LC
Texas Tech Univ	TX	10,768	VC
Thiel College	PA	20,970	C
Touro College	NY	15,250	VC
Trinity Christian College	IL	21,640	VC
Trinity College	DC	24,150	LC
Trinity International Univ	IL	22,980	C+
Tri-State Univ-Main Campus	IN	23,600	C
Truman State Univ	MO	9,728	HC+
Tusculum College	TN	19,990	C
Union Univ	TN	18,800	VC
Univ of Akron	OH	13,134	NC
Univ of Arkansas	AR	9,855	VC
Univ of Arkansas at Pine Bluff	AR	7,925	C
Univ of Bridgeport	CT	25,924	LC
Univ of Calif at Riverside	CA	15,300	C
Univ of Central Arkansas	AR	6,388	C
Univ of Cincinnati	OH	14,736	C
Univ of Dayton	OH	24,850	VC
Univ of Detroit Mercy	MI	25,582	C
Univ of Evansville	IN	24,190	VC
Univ of Findlay	OH	23,962	NC
Univ of Georgia	GA	8,656	VC
Univ of Great Falls	MT	15,360	C
Univ of Hartford	CT	31,080	C
Univ of Iowa	IA	10,923	VC
Univ of Judaism College of A&S	CA	24,230	C
Univ of Louisiana at Monroe	LA	5,207	NC
Univ of Mary	ND	12,900	C+
Univ of Mass Amherst	MA	13,980	C+
Univ of Miami	FL	34,608	HC
Univ of Minn/Morris	MN	12,896	VC
Univ of Minn/Twin Cities	MN	13,160	VC
Univ of Missouri/Rolla	MO	12,292	HC
Univ of Nebr at Kearney	NE	8,286	NC
Univ of Nebr at Lincoln	NE	9,975	C+
Univ of New Haven	CT	28,650	C
Univ of New Mexico	NM	9,223	C
Univ of New Orleans	LA	7,356	C
Univ of N Car at Pembroke	NC	6,929	LC
Univ of Notre Dame	IN	34,442	MC
Univ of PR/Mayaguez	PR		
Univ of Rio Grande	OH	8,728	NC
Univ of St. Francis	IL	22,850	C
Univ of St. Francis	IN	20,964	C
Univ of Sioux Falls	SD	16,390	C
Univ of Southern Colo	CO	7,821	LC
Univ of Southern Indiana	IN	9,025	LC
Univ of Southern Miss	MS	8,324	LC
Univ of Tenn at Knoxville	TN	8,214	C
Univ of Tenn at Martin	TN	7,748	C
Univ of the Incarnate Word	TX	21,772	LC
Univ of the Sciences in Philadelphia	PA	29,310	VC
Univ of Tulsa	OK	22,090	VC+
Univ of West Alabama	AL	6,048	C
Univ of West Florida	FL	8,470	C
Univ of Wisc/Milwaukee	WI	9,427	LC
Univ of Wisc/River Falls	WI	8,358	LC
Urbana Univ	OH	19,115	C
Ursinus College	PA	34,400	VC
Ursuline College	OH	22,728	LC
Utah State Univ	UT	7,371	C
Vanguard Univ of Southern Calif	CA	22,208	C
Vassar College	NY	37,030	MC
Virginia Intermont College	VA	19,800	C
Walsh Univ	OH	20,890	C
Washington State Univ	WA	11,334	C
Washington Univ in St. Louis	MO	38,293	MC
Waynesburg College	PA	19,370	C
West Chester Univ of Pennsylvania	PA	11,164	C
West Liberty State College	WV	7,868	LC
West Texas A&M Univ	TX	7,533	C
Western Carolina Univ	NC	6,742	C
Western Mich Univ	MI	12,031	C
Western New Mexico Univ	NM	5,950	LC
Westminster College	PA	22,960	C
Whitworth College	WA	26,428	VC+
Widener Univ	PA	27,020	C
Wilkes Univ	PA	28,060	C
Wilmington College	OH	24,172	LC
Wingate Univ	NC	21,200	C
Winona State Univ	MN		C
Wittenberg Univ	OH	31,316	VC
Wright State Univ	OH	11,490	LC
Xavier Univ of Louisiana	LA	17,600	C
York College of Pennsylvania	PA	14,500	VC
Youngstown State Univ	OH	11,148	NC

PREOPTOMETRY

School	ST	$IS	SR
Adams State College	CO	7,468	C
Arcadia Univ	PA	29,890	C
Ashland Univ	OH	24,464	C
Auburn Univ	AL	10,396	VC
Berry College	GA	21,410	VC
Cardinal Stritch Univ	WI	17,620	C
Carroll College	MT	20,576	VC
Eastern Mich Univ	MI	11,478	C
Florida State Univ	FL	9,028	HC
Freed-Hardeman Univ	TN		NC
Gannon Univ	PA	23,260	C
Hofstra Univ	NY	27,112	VC
Indiana Univ South Bend	IN	4,571	LC
Indiana Univ-Purdue Univ Indianapolis	IN	8,257	LC
Iowa Wesleyan College	IA	19,990	C
Juniata College	PA	29,080	VC
Le Moyne College	NY	26,400	VC
Lehigh Univ	PA	37,570	HC+
Lewis Univ	IL	22,950	C+
Louisiana College	LA	13,450	C
Missouri Southern State Univ	MO	8,316	C
Newman Univ	KS	18,018	C
Stephen F. Austin State Univ	TX	7,552	C
Trinity Christian College	IL	21,640	VC
Truman State Univ	MO	9,728	HC+
Univ of Arkansas	AR	9,855	VC
Univ of Central Arkansas	AR	6,388	C
Univ of Hartford	CT	31,080	C
Univ of Southern Colo	CO	7,821	LC
Univ of Tenn at Martin	TN	7,748	C
Western Carolina Univ	NC	6,742	C
Youngstown State Univ	OH	11,148	NC

PREOSTEOPATHY

School	ST	$IS	SR
Gannon Univ	PA	23,260	C
Hofstra Univ	NY	27,112	VC
Indiana Univ-Purdue Univ Indianapolis	IN	8,257	LC
Mercyhurst College	PA	20,694	C
Minn State Univ, Mankato	MN	8,803	LC
New York Inst of Technology	NY	24,205	VC
Univ of Southern Colo	CO	7,821	LC
Youngstown State Univ	OH	11,148	NC

PREPHARMACY

School	ST	$IS	SR
Adams State College	CO	7,468	C
Alice Lloyd College	KY	4,040	C
Austin Peay State Univ	TN	5,814	LC
Ball State Univ	IN	8,660	C
Barry Univ	FL	24,100	LC
Bellarmine Univ	KY	24,110	VC
Belmont Abbey College	NC	23,742	C
Berry College	GA	21,410	VC
Briar Cliff Univ	IA	21,660	C
Campbell Univ	NC	18,268	VC
Carroll College	MT	20,576	VC
Clemson Univ	SC	11,972	HC
College of Notre Dame of Maryland	MD	27,700	C
College of St. Benedict	MN	26,672	VC
College of the Ozarks	MO	3,500	VC+
Concord College	WV	8,136	C
Coppin State College	MD	10,191	LC
David Lipscomb Univ	TN	16,158	VC
Eastern Mich Univ	MI	11,478	C
Edgewood College	WI	20,520	C
Florida State Univ	FL	9,028	HC
Freed-Hardeman Univ	TN		NC
Gannon Univ	PA	23,260	C
Goshen College	IN	22,450	VC
Huntingdon College	AL	18,400	VC
Indiana State Univ	IN	10,719	LC
Indiana Univ South Bend	IN	4,571	LC
Indiana Univ-Purdue Univ Indianapolis	IN	8,257	LC
Iona College	NY	27,988	VC
Juniata College	PA	29,080	VC
Le Moyne College	NY	26,400	VC
Lebanon Valley College	PA	28,870	VC
Lewis Univ	IL	22,950	C+
LIU/C.W. Post Campus	NY	28,282	C
Mars Hill College	NC	18,600	LC
Mercer Univ	GA	27,516	VC+
Mercyhurst College	PA	20,694	C
Midwestern State Univ	TX	8,045	LC
Minn State Univ, Mankato	MN	8,803	LC
Minn State Univ, Moorehead	MN	7,000	LC
Missouri Southern State Univ	MO	8,316	C
Montclair State Univ	NJ	13,790	C
Newman Univ	KS	18,018	C
North Georgia College and State Univ	GA	6,984	C
Northern Kentucky Univ	KY	6,352	NC
Northwest Missouri State Univ	MO	9,334	C
Notre Dame de Namur Univ	CA	26,932	LC
Ohio Univ	OH	14,448	C
Peru State College	NE	6,342	NC
Purdue Univ/Calumet	IN	6,630	NC
Purdue Univ/West Lafayette	IN	12,560	VC
Roberts Wesleyan College	NY	23,190	C+
Rockford College	IL	28,310	VC
Roosevelt Univ	IL	22,580	VC
St. John's Univ	MN	26,473	VC
St. Joseph's College of Maine	ME	25,600	C
St. Martin's College	WA	23,245	C
St. Vincent College	PA	25,530	VC
St. Xavier Univ	IL	23,144	C
Southern Nazarene Univ	OK	14,634	NC
SUNY/College of Environmental Science and Forestry	NY	14,167	VC
Stephen F. Austin State Univ	TX	7,552	C
Tarleton State Univ	TX	7,576	C
Texas A&M Univ at Commerce	TX	8,994	C
Texas A&M Univ at Kingsville	TX	6,740	LC
Texas Tech Univ	TX	10,768	VC
Thiel College	PA	20,970	C
Truman State Univ	MO	9,728	HC+
Union Univ	TN	18,800	VC
Univ of Akron	OH	13,134	NC
Univ of Arkansas	AR	9,855	VC
Univ of Arkansas at Pine Bluff	AR	7,925	C
Univ of Central Arkansas	AR	6,388	C
Univ of Evansville	IN	24,190	VC
Univ of Florida	FL	8,580	MC
Univ of Houston	TX	9,818	C
Univ of Miami	FL	34,608	HC
Univ of Minn/Twin Cities	MN	13,160	VC
Univ of Nebr at Lincoln	NE	9,975	C+
Univ of Southern Colo	CO	7,821	LC
Univ of Tenn at Martin	TN	7,748	C
Univ of the Pacific	CA	31,090	VC
Univ of Wisc/River Falls	WI	8,358	LC
Washington Univ in St. Louis	MO	38,293	MC
West Liberty State College	WV	7,868	LC
West Texas A&M Univ	TX	7,533	C
Western Carolina Univ	NC	6,742	C
Western New Mexico Univ	NM	5,950	LC
Wilkes Univ	PA	28,060	C
Wingate Univ	NC	21,200	C
Xavier Univ	OH	26,850	VC+
Youngstown State Univ	OH	11,148	NC

PREPODIATRY

School	ST	$IS	SR
Gannon Univ	PA	23,260	C
Hofstra Univ	NY	27,112	VC
Juniata College	PA	29,080	VC
Le Moyne College	NY	26,400	VC
Minn State Univ, Mankato	MN	8,803	LC
Univ of Arkansas	AR	9,855	VC
Univ of Southern Colo	CO	7,821	LC
Wilkes Univ	PA	28,060	C

PREVENTIVE/WELLNESS HEALTH CARE

School	ST	$IS	SR
Oakland Univ	MI	10,800	C

PREVETERINARY SCIENCE

School	ST	$IS	SR
Adams State College	CO	7,468	C
Alabama A&M Univ	AL	5,100	LC
Albertus Magnus College	CT	23,130	LC
Andrews Univ	MI	19,550	C
Arcadia Univ	PA	29,890	C
Ashland Univ	OH	24,464	C
Auburn Univ	AL	10,396	VC
Bellarmine Univ	KY	24,110	VC
Beloit College	WI	29,864	HC
Bennington College	VT	35,910	HC
Berry College	GA	21,410	VC
Cardinal Stritch Univ	WI	17,620	C
Carroll College	MT	20,576	VC
Clemson Univ	SC	11,972	HC
College of St. Benedict	MN	26,672	VC
College of the Ozarks	MO	3,500	VC+
Concordia College: Moorhead	MN	22,460	VC+
Cornerstone Univ and Grand Rapids Theological Seminary	MI	19,846	C
Drury Univ	MO	18,085	VC+
Eastern Washington Univ	WA	9,012	C
Edgewood College	WI	20,520	C
Edinboro Univ of Pennsylvania	PA	10,850	LC
Emmanuel College	MA	27,600	C+
Florida State Univ	FL	9,028	HC
Freed-Hardeman Univ	TN		NC
Gannon Univ	PA	23,260	C
George Fox Univ	OR	26,110	VC
Goshen College	IN	22,450	VC
Graceland Univ	IA	19,550	C
Hillsdale College	MI	22,450	HC
Hofstra Univ	NY	27,112	VC
Indiana State Univ	IN	10,719	LC
Indiana Univ South Bend	IN	4,571	LC
Indiana Univ-Purdue Univ Indianapolis	IN	8,257	LC
Iona College	NY	27,988	VC
Iowa Wesleyan College	IA	19,990	C
Juniata College	PA	29,080	VC
Kent State Univ	OH	12,932	C
Keuka College	NY	21,170	C
Le Moyne College	NY	26,400	VC
Lebanon Valley College	PA	28,870	VC
LeTourneau Univ	TX	21,080	C
Lewis Univ	IL	22,950	C+
Louisiana College	LA	13,450	C
Loyola Univ Chicago	IL	31,164	VC
MacMurray College	IL	20,005	LC
Mars Hill College	NC	18,600	LC
Mary Washington College	VA	10,166	HC
Mercyhurst College	PA	20,694	C
Midwestern State Univ	TX	8,045	LC
Miles College	AL	7,870	NC
Minn State Univ, Mankato	MN	8,803	LC
Minn State Univ, Moorehead	MN	7,000	LC
Missouri Southern State Univ	MO	8,316	C
Mount St. Mary College	NY	21,270	C
New Mexico Highlands Univ	NM	6,182	LC
Newman Univ	KS	18,018	C
N Car State Univ	NC	9,886	VC
North Central College	IL	25,656	VC
N Dak State Univ	ND	8,435	C
North Georgia College and State Univ	GA	6,984	C
Northern Kentucky Univ	KY	6,352	NC
Northern Mich Univ	MI	10,834	C
Northwest Missouri State Univ	MO	9,334	C
Notre Dame de Namur Univ	CA	26,932	LC
Ohio Wesleyan Univ	OH	32,550	VC+
Okla State Univ	OK	9,216	VC
Olivet College	MI	19,984	C+
Peru State College	NE	6,342	NC
Purdue Univ/Calumet	IN	6,630	NC
Rivier College	NH	26,217	C
Roberts Wesleyan College	NY	23,190	C+
Rochester Inst of Technology	NY	29,217	VC+
Rockford College	IL	28,310	VC
Roger Williams Univ	RI	30,296	C
Roosevelt Univ	IL	22,580	VC
St. John's Univ	MN	26,473	VC
St. Martin's College	WA	23,245	C
St. Mary-of-the-Woods College	IN	23,280	C
St. Mary's Univ of Minn	MN	21,535	C
St. Vincent College	PA	25,530	VC
Seton Hill Univ	PA	24,930	C
Spring Hill College	AL	25,868	VC
Stephen F. Austin State Univ	TX	7,552	C
Syracuse Univ	NY	34,720	HC
Tarleton State Univ	TX	7,576	C
Texas A&M Univ at Kingsville	TX	6,740	LC
Thiel College	PA	20,970	C
Truman State Univ	MO	9,728	HC+
Univ of Akron	OH	13,134	NC
Univ of Central Arkansas	AR	6,388	C
Univ of Findlay	OH	23,962	NC
Univ of Georgia	GA	8,656	VC
Univ of Mass Amherst	MA	13,980	C+
Univ of Miami	FL	34,608	HC
Univ of Minn/Twin Cities	MN	13,160	VC
Univ of New Hampshire	NH	14,828	VC
Univ of New Haven	CT	28,650	C
Univ of New Orleans	LA	7,356	C
Univ of Rio Grande	OH	8,728	NC
Univ of St. Francis	IL	22,850	C
Univ of Southern Colo	CO	7,821	LC
Univ of Tenn at Knoxville	TN	8,214	C
Virginia Intermont College	VA	19,800	C
Walsh Univ	OH	20,890	C
Washington Univ in St. Louis	MO	38,293	MC
Waynesburg College	PA	19,370	C
West Texas A&M Univ	TX	7,533	C
Western Carolina Univ	NC	6,742	C
Wilkes Univ	PA	28,060	C
Wilmington College	OH	24,172	LC
Wingate Univ	NC	21,200	C
Winona State Univ	MN		C
Youngstown State Univ	OH	11,148	NC

PRINTING TECHNOLOGY

School	ST	$IS	SR
Arkansas State Univ	AR	8,450	C
Georgia Southern Univ	GA	8,540	C
Pennsylvania College of Technology	PA	15,126	NC
Pittsburg State Univ	KS	7,128	NC
Rochester Inst of Technology	NY	29,217	VC+

ST = STATE $IS = IN-STATE COSTS SR = SELECTOR RATING

School	ST	$IS	SR
Southwest Missouri State Univ	MO	8,918	C

PRINTMAKING

School	ST	$IS	SR
Aquinas College	MI	21,894	C
Arizona State Univ-Main	AZ	10,048	C
Atlanta College of Art	GA	18,600	SP
Birmingham-Southern College	AL	25,364	VC+
Bradley Univ	IL	22,910	VC
Calif College of the Arts	CA	31,530	SP
Cal State, Fullerton	CA	6,648	C
Cal State, San Bernardino	CA	15,238	LC
Cal State, Stanislaus	CA	9,874	C
College for Creative Studies	MI	23,298	SP
College of Santa Fe	NM	25,293	C+
College of Visual Arts	MN		SP
Drake Univ	IA	25,120	VC+
Edinboro Univ of Pennsylvania	PA	10,850	LC
Howard Univ	DC	16,505	C
Indiana Univ Bloomington	IN	12,389	VC
Indiana Univ-Purdue Univ Indianapolis	IN	8,257	LC
Kansas City Art Inst	MO	26,850	SP
Kendall College of Art and Design of Ferris State Univ	MI	10,784	SP
Maine College of Art	ME	28,812	SP
Maryland Inst College of Art	MD	30,890	SP
Mass College of Art	MA	15,568	SP
Milwaukee Inst of Art and Design	WI	24,388	SP
Minneapolis College of Art and Design	MN	28,950	SP
Montserrat College of Art	MA	22,790	SP
Ohio Univ	OH	14,448	C
Pacific Northwest College of Art	OR	14,890	SP
Rhode Island School of Design	RI	33,569	SP
San Francisco Art Inst	CA	19,300	SP
School of the Art Inst of Chicago	IL	27,800	SP
Shepherd College	WV	8,608	C
SUNY at Potsdam	NY	12,160	C
SUNY/College at Buffalo	NY	8,025	C
Syracuse Univ	NY	34,720	HC
Texas A&M Univ at Commerce	TX	8,994	C
Univ of Dallas	TX	25,898	VC+
Univ of Hartford	CT	31,080	C
Univ of Houston	TX	9,818	C
Univ of Kansas	KS	8,923	VC
Univ of Miami	FL	34,608	HC
Univ of Mich/Ann Arbor	MI	13,864	HC+
Univ of North Texas	TX	7,629	C
Univ of Oregon	OR	11,479	VC
Univ of the Arts	PA	29,510	SP
Univ of Washington	WA	10,361	VC
Washington Univ in St. Louis	MO	38,293	MC
Youngstown State Univ	OH	11,148	NC

PSYCHOBIOLOGY

School	ST	$IS	SR
Albright College	PA	30,579	C
Arcadia Univ	PA	29,890	C
Averett Univ	VA	23,010	LC
Centre College	KY	27,300	HC
Drew Univ/College of Liberal Arts	NJ	35,550	VC
Earlham College	IN	29,976	VC+
Florida Atlantic Univ	FL	8,543	C
Hamilton College	NY	37,560	MC
Hiram College	OH	28,234	VC
La Sierra Univ	CA	19,260	LC
Lebanon Valley College	PA	28,870	VC
Lincoln Univ	PA	13,320	C+
Luther College	IA	25,700	VC
Mount Holyoke College	MA	37,918	HC+
Occidental College	CA	35,922	HC
Quinnipiac Univ	CT	30,570	VC
Ripon College	WI	24,995	VC
Simmons College	MA	33,000	VC
SUNY/Univ at Binghamton	NY	12,787	HC
Swarthmore College	PA	37,716	MC
Univ of Calif at Los Angeles	CA	15,330	MC
Univ of Calif at Riverside	CA	15,300	C
Univ of Calif at Santa Cruz	CA	16,505	VC
Univ of Evansville	IN	24,190	VC
Univ of Miami	FL	34,608	HC
Univ of Pennsylvania	PA	37,960	MC
Wheaton College	MA	36,330	HC
Wilson College	PA	23,912	C

PSYCHOLOGY

School	ST	$IS	SR
Abilene Christian Univ	TX	18,370	VC
Adams State College	CO	7,468	C
Adelphi Univ	NY	26,300	VC
Adrian College	MI	21,950	C
Agnes Scott College	GA	28,230	HC
Alabama A&M Univ	AL	5,100	LC
Alabama State Univ	AL	6,404	C
Alaska Pacific Univ	AK	17,910	C
Albany State Univ	GA	5,764	C+
Albertson College of Idaho	ID	19,415	VC
Albertus Magnus College	CT	23,130	LC
Albion College	MI	25,224	VC
Albright College	PA	30,579	C
Alcorn State Univ	MS	7,290	C
Alderson-Broaddus College	WV	19,640	C
Alfred Univ	NY	28,290	C
Allegheny College	PA	30,280	VC
Alliant International Univ	CA	23,640	C
Alma College	MI	25,566	VC
Alvernia College	PA	23,212	LC
Alverno College	WI	18,898	C
American International College	MA	24,690	LC
American Univ	DC	34,585	VC+
Amherst College	MA	37,470	MC
Anderson Univ	IN	19,430	LC
Andrews Univ	MI	19,550	C
Angelo State Univ	TX	7,576	NC
Anna Maria College	MA	26,140	LC
Appalachian State Univ	NC	7,637	VC
Aquinas College	MI	21,894	C
Arcadia Univ	PA	29,890	C
Arizona State Univ-Main	AZ	10,048	C
Arkansas State Univ	AR	8,450	C
Arkansas Tech Univ	AR	7,299	C
Armstrong Atlantic State Univ	GA	7,102	C
Asbury College	KY	20,704	VC
Ashland Univ	OH	24,464	C
Assumption College	MA	29,375	C
Atlantic Union College	MA	18,868	C
Auburn Univ	AL	10,396	VC
Auburn Univ Montgomery	AL	9,020	NC
Augsburg College	MN	25,298	C
Augusta State Univ	GA	2,592	C
Augustana College	IL	26,610	VC+
Augustana College	SD	21,998	VC
Aurora Univ	IL	20,631	C
Austin College	TX	24,747	HC
Austin Peay State Univ	TN	5,814	LC
Averett Univ	VA	23,010	LC
Avila Univ	MO	20,300	C
Azusa Pacific Univ	CA	24,720	VC
Baker Univ	KS	19,860	VC
Baldwin-Wallace College	OH	24,678	C
Ball State Univ	IN	8,660	C
Barry Univ	FL	24,100	LC
Barton College	NC	19,314	C
Bates College	ME	37,500	MC
Bay Path College	MA	24,910	C
Baylor Univ	TX	23,864	VC
Becker College	MA	23,710	LC
Belhaven College	MS	16,040	C+
Bellarmine Univ	KY	24,110	VC
Bellevue Univ	NE	4,440	NC
Belmont Abbey College	NC	23,742	C
Belmont Univ	TN	21,986	VC
Beloit College	WI	29,864	HC
Bemidji State Univ	MN	9,103	C
Benedictine College	KS	20,603	C
Benedictine Univ	IL	23,840	C
Bennett College	NC	11,200	C
Bennington College	VT	35,910	HC
Berea College	KY	5,030	VC+
Berry College	GA	21,410	VC
Bethany College	KS	18,675	LC
Bethany College	WV	19,845	VC
Bethel College	IN	19,670	C
Bethel College	KS	19,800	C+
Bethel College	MN	25,180	VC
Bethel College	TN	12,980	C
Bethune-Cookman College	FL	16,480	LC
Biola Univ	CA	25,964	VC
Birmingham-Southern College	AL	25,364	VC+
Black Hills State Univ	SD	7,743	LC
Blackburn College	IL	13,690	C
Bloomfield College	NJ	19,250	LC
Bloomsburg Univ of Pennsylvania	PA	10,844	C
Blue Mountain College	MS	10,226	C
Bluefield College	VA	15,575	C
Bluffton College	OH	23,694	C
Boise State Univ	ID	7,657	LC
Boston College	MA	33,284	MC
Boston Univ	MA	38,194	HC+
Bowdoin College	ME	37,790	MC
Bowie State Univ	MD	10,873	C+
Bowling Green State Univ	OH	13,036	C
Bradley Univ	IL	22,910	VC
Brandeis Univ	MA	38,198	MC
Brenau Univ Women's College	GA	21,800	C
Brescia Univ	KY	14,225	C
Brewton-Parker College	GA	14,200	LC
Briar Cliff Univ	IA	21,660	C
Bridgewater College	VA	25,150	C
Bridgewater State College	MA	10,482	C
Brigham Young Univ	UT	8,504	HC
Brigham Young Univ/Hawaii	HI	7,240	VC+
Brown Univ	RI	38,174	MC
Bryan College	TN	17,900	VC
Bryant College	RI	31,004	VC
Bryn Mawr College	PA	36,890	HC+
Bucknell Univ	PA	35,262	HC+
Buena Vista Univ	IA	25,406	C
Burlington College	VT	10,640	SP
Butler Univ	IN	28,250	VC+
Cabrini College	PA	29,020	C
Caldwell College	NJ	24,060	LC
Calif Baptist Univ	CA	19,924	C
Calif Lutheran Univ	CA	27,600	LC
Calif Polytechnic State Univ	CA	8,747	VC
Calif State Polytechnic Univ, Pomona	CA	8,793	C+
Cal State, Bakersfield	CA	6,090	LC
Cal State, Chico	CA	8,598	LC
Cal State, Dominguez Hills	CA	5,840	LC
Cal State, Fresno	CA	8,414	LC
Cal State, Fullerton	CA	6,648	C
Cal State, Hayward	CA	8,871	LC
Cal State, Long Beach	CA	8,762	C+
Cal State, Los Angeles	CA	5,778	C
Cal State, Northridge	CA	7,757	LC
Cal State, Sacramento	CA	9,543	C
Cal State, San Bernardino	CA	15,238	LC
Cal State, San Marcos	CA	1,736	LC
Cal State, Stanislaus	CA	9,874	C
Calif Univ of Pennsylvania	PA	10,388	C
Calumet College of St. Joseph	IN	9,000	LC
Calvin College	MI	22,615	NC
Cambridge College	MA	10,800	SP
Cameron Univ	OK	5,692	NC
Campbell Univ	NC	18,268	VC
Campbellsville Univ	KY	17,680	C
Canisius College	NY	28,163	C+
Capital Univ	OH	26,550	C
Cardinal Stritch Univ	WI	17,620	C
Carleton College	MN	34,395	MC
Carlos Albizu Univ	FL	10,569	C
Carlow College	PA	21,334	C
Carnegie Mellon Univ	PA	32,682	MC
Carroll College	MT	20,576	VC
Carroll College	WI	22,740	C
Carson-Newman College	TN	16,760	C
Carthage College	WI	25,000	C
Cascade College	OR	16,700	NC
Case Western Reserve Univ	OH	32,002	MC
Castleton State College	VT	11,820	C
Catawba College	NC	20,500	C
Catholic Univ of America	DC	34,248	VC
Cazenovia College	NY	23,940	C
Cedar Crest College	PA	25,145	C+
Cedarville Univ	OH	19,954	VC
Centenary College	NJ	25,370	LC
Centenary College of Louisiana	LA	23,100	VC+
Central College	IA	21,206	C
Central Conn State Univ	CT	12,090	C
Central Methodist College	MO	16,460	C
Central Mich Univ	MI	11,142	C
Central Missouri State Univ	MO	9,776	C
Central State Univ	OH	8,922	C+
Central Univ of Bayamon	PR	3,335	
Central Washington Univ	WA	9,768	C
Centre College	KY	27,300	HC
Chadron State College	NE	6,286	NC
Chaminade Univ of Honolulu	HI	21,430	LC
Champlain College	VT	22,030	C
Chapman Univ	CA	33,118	VC
Charleston Southern Univ	SC	17,122	C
Chatham College	PA	27,266	C+
Chestnut Hill College	PA	26,450	LC
Cheyney Univ of Pennsylvania	PA	9,993	C
Chicago State Univ	IL	10,882	C+
Christian Brothers Univ	TN	22,290	VC
Christian Heritage College	CA	19,990	C
Christopher Newport Univ	VA	8,862	VC
Citadel, The	SC	12,295	C+
CUNY/Baruch College	NY	3,275	VC+
CUNY/Brooklyn College	NY	4,353	C+
CUNY/City College	NY	4,230	C+
CUNY/College of Staten Island	NY	4,308	NC
CUNY/Herbert H. Lehman College	NY	3,320	LC
CUNY/Hunter College	NY	6,729	C+
CUNY/Medgar Evers College	NY	4,232	NC
CUNY/Queens College	NY	4,362	C
CUNY/York College	NY	3,292	NC
Claremont McKenna College	CA	36,880	MC
Clarion Univ of Pennsylvania	PA	11,272	LC
Clark Atlanta Univ	GA	19,300	C+
Clark Univ	MA	32,115	VC
Clarke College	IA	23,165	C
Clarkson Univ	NY	32,226	VC
Clearwater Christian College	FL	13,160	LC
Clemson Univ	SC	11,972	HC
Cleveland State Univ	OH	12,308	LC
Coastal Carolina Univ	SC	11,040	C
Coe College	IA	27,385	VC
Coker College	SC	21,491	C
Colby College	ME	37,570	MC
Colby-Sawyer College	NH	27,850	LC
Colgate Univ	NY	37,095	MC
College Misericordia	PA	26,350	C
College of Charleston	SC	11,887	HC
College of Mount St. Vincent	NY	26,800	C
College of Mount St. Joseph	OH	22,785	C
College of New Jersey	NJ	15,950	MC
College of New Rochelle	NY	21,800	C
College of Notre Dame of Maryland	MD	27,700	C
College of Our Lady of the Elms	MA	20,644	C
College of St. Benedict	MN	26,672	VC
College of St. Catherine	MN	24,010	VC
College of St. Elizabeth	NJ	25,460	C
College of St. Joseph	VT	19,100	C
College of St. Mary	NE	21,510	C
College of St. Rose	NY	22,846	C
College of St. Scholastica	MN	24,970	C+
College of Santa Fe	NM	25,293	C+
College of the Holy Cross	MA	36,451	MC
College of the Ozarks	MO	3,500	VC+
College of the Southwest	NM	9,320	C+
College of William and Mary	VA	12,224	MC
College of Wooster	OH	31,300	HC
Colo Christian Univ	CO	21,182	VC
Colo College	CO	36,860	HC
Colo State Univ	CO	9,964	VC
Columbia College	MO	16,139	C
Columbia College	SC	22,658	LC
Columbia Union College	MD	20,543	C
Columbia Univ/Barnard College	NY	36,990	MC
Columbia Univ/Columbia College	NY	38,590	MC
Columbia Univ/School of General Studies	NY	35,000	C
Columbus State Univ	GA	7,846	C
Concord College	WV	8,136	C
Concordia College: Moorhead	MN	22,460	VC+
Concordia Univ	CA	24,420	C
Concordia Univ	MI	24,095	C
Concordia Univ	OR	22,450	C
Concordia Univ Nebr	NE	20,302	C+
Concordia Univ Wisc	WI	16,600	C
Concordia Univ, River Forest	IL	23,600	C
Concordia Univ/St.Paul	MN	24,486	C
Conn College	CT	37,900	MC
Converse College	SC	24,710	VC
Coppin State College	MD	10,191	LC
Cornell College	IA	27,825	VC+
Cornell Univ	NY	38,253	MC
Cornerstone Univ and Grand Rapids Theological Seminary	MI	19,846	C
Covenant College	GA	23,830	VC+
Creighton Univ	NE	26,748	VC+
Crichton College	TN	15,215	C
Culver-Stockton College	MO	17,850	C
Cumberland College	KY	16,384	C
Cumberland Univ	TN	16,910	C
Curry College	MA	26,025	LC
Daemen College	NY	22,120	C
Dakota Wesleyan Univ	SD	17,832	C
Dallas Baptist Univ	TX	15,300	VC
Dana College	NE	20,280	C
Dartmouth College	NH	37,770	MC
David Lipscomb Univ	TN	16,158	VC
Davidson College	NC	33,274	MC
Davis and Elkins College	WV	20,594	C
De Sales Univ	PA	25,470	C
Defiance College	OH	22,615	C
Delaware State Univ	DE	8,104	LC
Delta State Univ	MS	6,618	C
Denison Univ	OH	33,050	HC
DePaul Univ	IL	27,580	VC
DePauw Univ	IN	31,500	HC
Dickinson College	PA	35,825	HC
Dillard Univ	LA	17,325	VC
Doane College	NE	20,000	C
Dominican College	NY	24,810	LC
Dominican Univ	IL	23,610	C
Dominican Univ of Calif	CA	31,670	C
Dordt College	IA	20,170	VC
Dowling College	NY	23,870	LC
Drake Univ	IA	25,120	VC+
Drew Univ/College of Liberal Arts	NJ	35,550	VC
Drexel Univ	PA	27,655	VC
Drury Univ	MO	18,085	VC+
Duke Univ	NC	37,555	MC
Duquesne Univ	PA	26,907	VC
D'Youville College	NY	21,080	C
Earlham College	IN	29,976	VC+
East Carolina Univ	NC	8,671	C
East Central Univ	OK	4,968	C
East Stroudsburg Univ of Pennsylvania	PA	10,336	C
East Tenn State Univ	TN	8,497	C

ST = STATE $IS = IN-STATE COSTS SR = SELECTOR RATING

School	ST	$IS	SR
East Texas Baptist Univ	TX	13,914	C
Eastern Conn State Univ	CT	10,362	C
Eastern Illinois Univ	IL	11,192	C
Eastern Kentucky Univ	KY	7,708	C
Eastern Mennonite Univ	VA	22,990	C
Eastern Mich Univ	MI	11,478	C
Eastern Nazarene College	MA	19,433	LC
Eastern New Mexico Univ	NM	6,762	LC
Eastern Oregon Univ	OR	10,080	NC
Eastern Univ	PA	24,020	C
Eastern Washington Univ	WA	9,012	C
Eckerd College	FL	28,744	C+
Edgewood College	WI	20,520	C
Edinboro Univ of Pennsylvania	PA	10,850	LC
Edward Waters College	FL	14,374	LC
Elizabeth City State Univ	NC	5,550	LC
Elizabethtown College	PA	28,800	C
Elmhurst College	IL	24,630	C
Elmira College	NY	33,820	VC
Elon Univ	NC	22,240	VC
Emmanuel College	MA	27,600	C+
Emory & Henry College	VA	21,950	C
Emory Univ	GA	36,872	MC
Emporia State Univ	KS	6,998	C
Endicott College	MA	25,266	C+
Erskine College	SC	23,166	VC
Eugene Lang College/New School Univ	NY	34,940	C
Eureka College	IL	24,980	LC
Evangel Univ	MO	15,435	C
Fairfield Univ	CT	35,505	HC
Fairleigh Dickinson Univ/ College at Florham	NJ	30,130	C
Fairleigh Dickinson Univ/ Metropolitan Campus	NJ	28,584	C
Fairmont State	WV	8,280	LC
Fayetteville State Univ	NC	5,590	LC
Felician College	NJ	24,300	C
Ferrum College	VA	21,240	LC
Fisk Univ	TN	17,305	LC
Fitchburg State College	MA	9,622	C
Flagler College	FL	11,860	VC+
Florida A&M Univ	FL	7,564	C
Florida Atlantic Univ	FL	8,543	C
Florida Inst of Technology	FL	28,740	VC
Florida International Univ	FL	9,912	VC
Florida Memorial College	FL	6,000	LC
Florida Southern College	FL	23,592	C
Florida State Univ	FL	9,028	HC
Fordham Univ	NY	35,066	HC
Fort Hays State Univ	KS	7,363	C
Fort Lewis College	CO	8,353	C
Fort Valley State Univ	GA	6,960	C
Framingham State College	MA	9,381	C
Francis Marion Univ	SC	9,364	C
Franciscan Univ	IA	19,300	C
Franciscan Univ of Steubenville	OH	20,300	VC
Franklin and Marshall College	PA	35,930	HC+
Franklin College	IN		C
Franklin Pierce College	NH	28,980	LC
Freed-Hardeman Univ	TN		NC
Fresno Pacific Univ	CA	22,462	C
Friends Univ	KS	15,962	LC
Frostburg State Univ	MD	11,114	C
Furman Univ	SC	28,976	HC+
Gallaudet Univ	DC	16,554	SP
Gannon Univ	PA	23,260	C
Gardner-Webb Univ	NC	19,300	C
Geneva College	PA	21,850	C
George Fox Univ	OR	26,110	VC
George Mason Univ	VA	9,732	VC
George Washington Univ	DC	41,030	MC
Georgetown College	KY	22,000	VC
Georgetown Univ	DC	38,242	MC
Georgia College and State Univ	GA	9,878	C
Georgia Inst of Technology	GA	10,340	HC+
Georgia Southern Univ	GA	8,540	C
Georgia Southwestern State Univ	GA	6,013	C
Georgia State Univ	GA	10,658	C
Georgian Court College	NJ	19,040	LC
Gettysburg College	PA	35,646	HC
Gonzaga Univ	WA	26,766	HC
Gordon College	MA	25,982	VC+
Goshen College	IN	22,450	VC
Goucher College	MD	32,650	HC
Grace College	IN	19,825	VC
Graceland Univ	IA	19,550	C
Grambling State Univ	LA	6,538	NC
Grand Canyon Univ	AZ	30,000	LC
Grand Valley State Univ	MI	11,022	VC
Grand View College	IA	19,748	LC
Green Mountain College	VT	24,130	C
Greensboro College	NC	21,750	C
Greenville College	IL	21,342	C
Grinnell College	IA	31,060	HC+
Grove City College	PA	14,228	HC
Guilford College	NC	24,960	VC
Gustavus Adolphus College	MN	27,120	VC+
Gwynedd-Mercy College	PA	24,225	C
Hamilton College	NY	37,560	MC
Hamline Univ	MN	27,052	VC

School	ST	$IS	SR
Hampden-Sydney College	VA	28,407	VC
Hampshire College	MA	37,037	HC
Hampton Univ	VA	17,112	C+
Hannibal-LaGrange College	MO	13,940	C
Hanover College	IN	25,200	VC
Harding Univ	AR	14,890	VC
Hardin-Simmons Univ	TX	14,165	C
Hartwick College	NY	34,650	C+
Harvard Univ/Harvard College	MA	37,928	MC
Hastings College	NE	19,928	VC
Haverford College	PA	37,900	MC
Hawaii Pacific Univ	HI	19,218	C
Heidelberg College	OH	20,266	NC
Henderson State Univ	AR	7,386	C
Hendrix College	AR	20,970	VC+
Heritage College	WA	6,720	NC
High Point Univ	NC	22,480	C
Hilbert College	NY	19,170	LC
Hillsdale College	MI	22,450	HC
Hiram College	OH	28,234	VC
Hobart and William Smith Colleges	NY	36,536	HC
Hofstra Univ	NY	27,112	VC
Hollins Univ	VA	27,965	VC
Holy Family College	PA	13,710	LC
Holy Names College	CA	27,980	NC
Hood College	MD	27,795	VC
Hope College	MI	25,340	VC
Hope International Univ	CA	16,940	NC
Houghton College	NY	23,984	VC
Houston Baptist Univ	TX	16,905	C
Howard Payne Univ	TX	15,176	C
Howard Univ	DC	16,505	C
Humboldt State Univ	CA	9,400	C
Huntingdon College	AL	18,400	VC
Huntington College	IN	23,590	C
Husson College	ME	16,300	LC
Idaho State Univ	ID	8,128	C
Illinois College	IL	19,100	VC
Illinois Inst of Technology	IL	26,456	HC+
Illinois State Univ	IL	10,944	C+
Illinois Wesleyan Univ	IL	30,380	HC+
Immaculata Univ	PA	25,200	C
Indiana Inst of Technology	IN	21,620	C
Indiana State Univ	IN	10,719	LC
Indiana Univ Bloomington	IN	12,389	VC
Indiana Univ Kokomo	IN	4,463	LC
Indiana Univ Northwest	IN	4,538	LC
Indiana Univ of Pennsylvania	PA	10,489	C
Indiana Univ South Bend	IN	4,571	LC
Indiana Univ Southeast	IN	4,504	LC
Indiana Univ-Purdue Univ Fort Wayne	IN	5,108	LC
Indiana Univ-Purdue Univ Indianapolis	IN	8,257	LC
Indiana Wesleyan Univ	IN	19,900	C+
Inter American Univ of PR/ Fajardo Campus	PR	4,000	
Inter American Univ of PR/ Metropolitan Campus	PR		
Inter American Univ of PR/ Ponce Regional College	PR	3,700	
Inter American Univ of PR/ San German	PR	6,716	
Iona College	NY	27,988	VC
Iowa State Univ	IA	10,768	VC
Iowa Wesleyan College	IA	19,990	C
Ithaca College	NY	31,730	HC
Jackson State Univ	MS	8,382	C
Jacksonville State Univ	AL	6,844	LC
Jacksonville Univ	FL	24,040	C
James Madison Univ	VA	10,794	VC
Jamestown College	ND	12,600	NC
John Brown Univ	AR	15,080	VC
John Carroll Univ	OH	27,658	C+
Johns Hopkins Univ	MD	38,372	MC
Johnson C. Smith Univ	NC	18,108	C
Johnson State College	VT	11,819	LC
Judson College	AL	14,650	C
Judson College	IL	22,050	LC
Juniata College	PA	29,080	VC
Kalamazoo College	MI	26,955	HC+
Kansas State Univ	KS	8,728	VC
Kansas Wesleyan Univ	KS	18,900	VC
Kean Univ	NJ	14,479	C
Keene State College	NH	12,212	C
Kennesaw State Univ	GA	2,724	C
Kent State Univ	OH	12,932	C
Kentucky Christian College	KY	13,472	C
Kentucky State Univ	KY	9,062	NC
Kentucky Wesleyan College	KY	17,250	C
Kenyon College	OH	35,370	HC+
Keuka College	NY	21,170	C
King College	TN	22,500	VC
King's College	PA	26,990	C
Knox College	IL	30,294	VC+
Knoxville College	TN	6,200	LC
Kutztown Univ of Pennsylvania	PA	10,786	C
La Roche College	PA	22,094	C
La Salle Univ	PA	31,260	VC
La Sierra Univ	CA	19,260	LC
Lafayette College	PA	35,746	MC
LaGrange College	GA	20,500	C

School	ST	$IS	SR
Lake Erie College	OH	23,550	C
Lake Forest College	IL	30,270	VC
Lake Superior State Univ	MI	9,034	LC
Lakeland College	WI	17,950	C
Lamar Univ	TX	6,816	LC
Lambuth Univ	TN	16,520	C
Lander Univ	SC	10,496	C
Langston Univ	OK	2,308	LC
Lasell College	MA	26,000	C
Lawrence Tech Univ	MI	20,487	C
Lawrence Univ	WI	30,900	HC
Le Moyne College	NY	26,400	VC
Lebanon Valley College	PA	28,870	VC
Lee Univ	TN	13,780	NC
Lees-McRae College	NC	17,106	LC
Lehigh Univ	PA	37,570	HC+
Lenoir-Rhyne College	NC	19,186	C
LeTourneau Univ	TX	21,080	C
Lewis and Clark College	OR	30,620	VC
Lewis Univ	IL	22,950	C+
Lewis-Clark State College	ID	6,981	C
Liberty Univ	VA	17,220	C
Limestone College	SC	17,700	C
Lincoln Memorial Univ	TN	16,400	LC
Lincoln Univ	MO	7,158	NC
Lincoln Univ	PA	13,320	C+
Lindenwood Univ	MO	17,050	VC
Linfield College	OR	27,090	VC
Livingstone College	NC	18,101	LC
Lock Haven Univ of Pennsylvania	PA	11,098	LC
LIU/Brooklyn Campus	NY	24,790	C
LIU/C.W. Post Campus	NY	28,282	C
LIU/Southampton College	NY	29,370	C+
Longwood Univ	VA	11,175	C
Loras College	IA	24,233	C
Louisiana College	LA	13,450	C
Louisiana State Univ and A&M College	LA	9,126	VC
Louisiana State Univ in Shreveport	LA	2,884	NC
Louisiana Tech Univ	LA	7,361	C
Lourdes College	OH	15,300	LC
Loyola College in Maryland	MD	34,560	HC
Loyola Marymount Univ	CA	32,194	VC
Loyola Univ Chicago	IL	31,164	VC
Loyola Univ New Orleans	LA	31,036	VC+
Lubbock Christian Univ	TX	15,832	C
Luther College	IA	25,700	VC
Lycoming College	PA	27,589	C+
Lynchburg College	VA	26,815	C
Lyndon State College	VT	12,646	LC
Lynn Univ	FL	30,750	C
Lyon College	AR	17,995	VC
Macalester College	MN	31,944	MC
MacMurray College	IL	20,005	LC
Madonna Univ	MI	11,504	VC
Malone College	OH	20,995	C
Manchester College	IN	23,390	C
Manhattan College	NY	27,400	VC
Manhattanville College	NY	32,420	C+
Mansfield Univ	PA	11,220	C
Marian College	IN	23,030	C
Marian College of Fond du Lac	WI	19,625	C
Marietta College	OH	27,047	C
Marist College	NY	27,596	VC
Marlboro College	VT	29,055	VC+
Marquette Univ	WI	27,594	VC
Mars Hill College	NC	18,600	LC
Marshall Univ	WV	9,116	C
Martin Univ	IN	10,200	SP
Mary Baldwin College	VA	24,939	C
Mary Washington College	VA	10,166	HC
Marygrove College	MI	17,550	C
Marymount College of Fordham Univ	NY	27,686	C
Marymount Manhattan College	NY	27,292	C
Marymount Univ	VA	23,668	C
Maryville College	TN	25,960	VC
Maryville Univ of St. Louis	MO	22,090	VC
Marywood Univ	PA	26,050	C
Mass College of Liberal Arts	MA	8,717	LC
Mass College of Pharmacy and Health Sciences	MA	28,770	SP
Mass Inst of Technology	MA	38,310	MC
McDaniel College	MD	28,440	VC
McKendree College	IL	21,120	VC
McMurry Univ	TX	17,846	LC
McNeese State Univ	LA	5,259	LC
McPherson College	KS	20,265	C
Medaille College	NY	20,060	C
Menlo College	CA	24,000	LC
Mercer Univ	GA	27,516	VC+
Mercy College	NY	19,200	NC
Mercyhurst College	PA	20,694	C
Meredith College	NC	23,065	C
Merrimack College	MA	29,625	C
Mesa State College	CO	8,051	C
Messiah College	PA	25,890	VC+
Methodist College	NC	19,526	C
Metropolitan College of New York	NY	15,771	C

School	ST	$IS	SR
Metropolitan State College of Denver	CO	2,338	LC
Metropolitan State Univ	MN	3,852	SP
Miami Univ	OH	15,033	HC
Mich State Univ	MI	11,933	VC
MidAmerica Nazarene Univ	KS	18,688	C
Middle Tenn State Univ	TN	8,534	C
Middlebury College	VT	38,100	MC
Midland Lutheran College	NE	18,600	C
Midway College	KY	15,815	C
Midwestern State Univ	TX	8,045	LC
Millersville Univ of Pennsylvania	PA	11,269	C
Milligan College	TN	19,860	C+
Millikin Univ	IL	25,555	C
Mills College	CA	33,371	VC
Millsaps College	MS	25,182	VC
Minn State Univ, Mankato	MN	8,803	LC
Minn State Univ, Moorehead	MN	7,000	LC
Minot State Univ	ND	6,602	LC
Miss College	MS	14,574	C
Miss State Univ	MS	9,139	C
Miss Univ for Women	MS	5,446	LC
Missouri Baptist Univ	MO	18,010	C
Missouri Southern State Univ	MO	8,316	C
Missouri Valley College	MO	18,500	C
Missouri Western State College	MO	8,522	NC
Mitchell College	CT	26,396	C
Molloy College	NY	15,180	C
Monmouth College	IL	23,600	C
Monmouth Univ	NJ	26,334	C
Montana State Univ-Billings	MT	9,550	C
Montana State Univ-Bozeman	MT	9,515	C
Montclair State Univ	NJ	13,790	C
Moravian College	PA	28,903	VC
Morehead State Univ	KY	7,464	C
Morehouse College	GA	22,728	C
Morgan State Univ	MD	11,470	C
Morningside College	IA	21,610	C
Mount Aloysius College	PA	19,120	LC
Mount Mary College	WI	20,370	C
Mount Mercy College	IA	21,400	C
Mount Olive College	NC	14,410	LC
Mount St. Mary College	NY	21,270	C
Mount St. Mary's College	CA	28,307	VC
Mount St. Mary's College	MD	28,400	C
Mount Union College	OH	21,120	C
Mount Vernon Nazarene Univ	OH	18,925	C
Mountain State Univ	WV	10,212	NC
Muhlenberg College	PA	31,485	HC
Murray State Univ	KY	7,816	VC
Muskingum College	OH	20,680	C
Naropa Univ	CO	23,364	SP
National Univ	CA	9,690	SP
National-Louis Univ	IL	16,240	LC
Nazareth College of Rochester	NY	24,936	VC
Nebr Wesleyan Univ	NE	21,197	C+
Neumann College	PA	23,890	LC
New College of Calif	CA	8,900	NC
New College of Florida	FL	8,906	HC+
New England College	NH	28,860	LC
New Jersey City Univ	NJ	11,850	LC
New Mexico Highlands Univ	NM	6,182	LC
New Mexico Inst of Mining and Technology	NM	7,580	NC
New Mexico State Univ	NM	7,932	C
New York Univ	NY	39,406	MC
Newberry College	SC	22,871	LC
Newbury College	MA	23,450	C
Newman Univ	KS	18,018	C
Niagara Univ	NY	25,050	C
Nicholls State Univ	LA	6,395	NC
Nichols College	MA	27,562	LC
Norfolk State Univ	VA	9,722	LC
N Car Agricultural and Technical State Univ	NC	6,659	LC
N Car Central Univ	NC	7,534	LC
N Car State Univ	NC	9,886	VC
N Car Wesleyan College	NC	17,998	C
North Central College	IL	25,656	VC
N Dak State Univ	ND	8,435	C
North Georgia College and State Univ	GA	6,984	C
North Park Univ	IL	24,030	C
Northeastern Illinois Univ	IL	2,898	NC
Northeastern State Univ	OK	4,950	LC
Northeastern Univ	MA	35,650	HC
Northern Arizona Univ	AZ	9,002	C
Northern Illinois Univ	IL	11,472	C
Northern Kentucky Univ	KY	6,352	NC
Northern Mich Univ	MI	10,834	C
Northern State Univ	SD	7,117	LC
Northland College	WI	22,170	C+
Northwest Christian College	OR	21,860	C
Northwest College	WA	18,854	C
Northwest Missouri State Univ	MO	9,334	C
Northwest Nazarene Univ	ID	20,360	VC
Northwestern College	MN	22,820	C+

ST = STATE $IS = IN-STATE COSTS SR = SELECTOR RATING

School	ST	$IS	SR
Northwestern College of Iowa	IA	19,640	C+
Northwestern Okla State Univ	OK	5,433	NC
Northwestern State Univ of Louisiana	LA	6,331	NC
Northwestern Univ	IL	37,491	MC
Norwich Univ	VT	21,064	LC
Notre Dame College	OH	20,425	C
Notre Dame de Namur Univ	CA	26,932	LC
Nova Southeastern Univ	FL	23,346	C
Nyack College	NY	18,540	C
Oakland Univ	MI	10,800	C
Oakwood College	AL	14,904	C
Oberlin College	OH	36,938	MC
Occidental College	CA	35,922	HC
Oglethorpe Univ	GA	26,000	VC
Ohio Dominican Univ	OH	22,700	C
Ohio Northern Univ	OH	27,765	VC
Ohio State Univ	OH	13,080	VC+
Ohio State Univ at Lima	OH	4,416	NC
Ohio State Univ at Marion	OH	4,801	NC
Ohio State Univ at Newark	OH	9,881	NC
Ohio Univ	OH	14,448	C
Ohio Valley College	WV	16,036	C+
Ohio Wesleyan Univ	OH	32,550	VC+
Okla Baptist Univ	OK	15,220	VC
Okla Christian Univ	OK	17,690	NC
Okla City Univ	OK	19,580	VC
Okla Panhandle State Univ	OK	5,370	C
Okla State Univ	OK	9,216	VC
Old Dominion Univ	VA	10,441	C
Olivet College	MI	19,984	C+
Olivet Nazarene Univ	IL	20,480	C
Oral Roberts Univ	OK	18,490	C
Oregon State Univ	OR	11,055	C
Ottawa Univ	KS	11,800	LC
Otterbein College	OH	26,085	C
Ouachita Baptist Univ	AR	18,900	VC
Our Lady of the Lake Univ of San Antonio	TX	17,336	C
Pace Univ	NY	28,652	VC
Pacific Lutheran Univ	WA	25,715	VC
Pacific Union College	CA	22,065	C+
Pacific Univ	OR	24,250	C
Paine College	GA	13,022	LC
Palm Beach Atlantic Univ	FL	20,690	C
Park Univ	MO	10,780	C+
Penn State Univ at Erie/ Behrend College	PA	12,326	C
Penn State Univ/Univ Park Campus	PA	15,646	HC
Pepperdine Univ	CA	32,830	VC
Peru State College	NE	6,342	NC
Pfeiffer Univ	NC	18,980	C
Philadelphia Univ	PA	27,354	C
Philander Smith College	AR	7,380	NC
Piedmont College	GA	16,900	C
Pikeville College	KY	14,900	NC
Pine Manor College	MA	22,138	LC
Pittsburg State Univ	KS	7,128	NC
Pitzer College	CA	37,590	HC
Plymouth State Univ	NH	12,298	LC
Point Loma Nazarene Univ	CA	21,380	VC
Point Park Univ	PA	21,840	C
Pomona College	CA	33,960	MC
Pontifical Catholic Univ of PR/Ponce	PR	7,298	
Portland State Univ	OR	12,453	C
Prairie View A&M Univ	TX	9,418	NC
Presbyterian College	SC	25,920	VC
Prescott College	AZ	13,430	C
Princeton Univ	NJ	36,649	MC
Providence College	RI	30,604	HC
Purdue Univ/Calumet	IN	6,630	NC
Purdue Univ/West Lafayette	IN	12,560	VC
Queens Univ of Charlotte	NC	21,840	C
Quincy Univ	IL	22,330	C
Quinnipiac Univ	CT	30,570	VC
Radford Univ	VA	8,500	C
Ramapo College of New Jersey	NJ	15,203	VC
Randolph-Macon College	VA	27,190	C
Randolph-Macon Woman's College	VA	28,430	VC+
Reed College	OR	36,950	MC
Regis College	MA	29,000	C
Regis Univ	CO	25,740	C+
Rensselaer Polytechnic Inst	NY	37,579	HC+
Rhode Island College	RI	11,565	C
Rhodes College	TN	26,466	HC+
Rice Univ	TX	27,550	MC
Richard Stockton College of New Jersey	NJ	12,972	VC
Rider Univ	NJ	30,900	C
Ripon College	WI	24,995	VC
Rivier College	NH	26,217	C
Roanoke College	VA	27,393	C
Roberts Wesleyan College	NY	23,190	C+
Rochester College	MI	16,718	C
Rochester Inst of Technology	NY	29,217	VC+
Rockford College	IL	28,310	C
Rockhurst Univ	MO	22,960	C+
Rocky Mountain College	MT	19,015	C
Roger Williams Univ	RI	30,296	C
Rollins College	FL	34,300	VC
Roosevelt Univ	IL	22,580	VC
Rosemont College	PA	26,175	C
Rowan Univ	NJ	14,506	VC
Russell Sage College	NY	26,811	C
Rutgers, The State Univ of New Jersey/Camden Campus	NJ	14,990	VC
Rutgers, The State Univ of New Jersey/New Brunswick/Piscataway Campus	NJ	15,800	HC
Rutgers, The State Univ of New Jersey/Newark Campus	NJ	15,624	VC
Sacred Heart Univ	CT	29,178	C
Saginaw Valley State Univ	MI	11,055	C
St. Ambrose Univ	IA	22,800	C
St. Andrews Presbyterian College	NC	20,525	C
St. Anselm College	NH	30,250	C
St. Augustine's College	NC	12,990	LC
St. Bonaventure Univ	NY	24,455	LC
St. Cloud State Univ	MN	8,362	C
St. Edward's Univ	TX	20,428	C
St. Francis College	NY	10,880	LC
St. Francis Univ	PA	25,876	LC
St. John Fisher College	NY	24,870	C
St. John's Univ	MN	26,473	VC
St. John's Univ	NY	30,180	C
St. Joseph College	CT	29,685	C
St. Joseph's, Brooklyn,	NY	10,902	C
St. Joseph's College	IN	24,250	C
St. Joseph's College of Maine	ME	25,600	C
St. Joseph's Univ	PA	33,590	VC
St. Lawrence Univ	NY	35,945	VC
St. Leo Univ	FL	20,600	C
St. Louis Univ	MO	29,780	VC+
St. Martin's College	WA	23,245	C
St. Mary-of-the-Woods College	IN	23,280	C
St. Mary's College	IN	24,474	VC
St. Mary's College	MI	13,314	LC
St. Mary's College of Calif	CA	32,850	VC
St. Mary's College of Maryland	MD	15,908	VC+
St. Mary's Univ of Minn	MN	21,535	C
St. Mary's Univ of San Antonio	TX	22,444	C
St. Michael's College	VT	30,100	VC
St. Norbert College	WI	25,810	C
St. Olaf College	MN	28,500	HC
St. Peter's College	NJ	22,292	LC
St. Thomas Aquinas College	NY	20,590	LC
St. Thomas Univ	FL	21,400	LC
St. Vincent College	PA	25,530	VC
St. Xavier Univ	IL	23,144	C
Salem College	NC	24,595	VC
Salem State College	MA	8,592	C
Salisbury Univ	MD	12,664	VC
Salve Regina Univ	RI	29,210	C
Sam Houston State Univ	TX	7,142	C
Samford Univ	AL	18,648	VC
San Diego State Univ	CA	10,321	C
San Francisco State Univ	CA	12,070	C
San Jose State Univ	CA	8,187	C
Santa Clara Univ	CA	34,701	HC
Sarah Lawrence College	NY	41,218	HC
Schreiner Univ	TX	20,440	C
Scripps College	CA	35,700	HC+
Seattle Pacific Univ	WA	25,944	VC
Seattle Univ	WA	24,183	VC
Seton Hall Univ	NJ	30,130	VC
Seton Hill Univ	PA	24,930	C
Shaw Univ	NC	14,882	C+
Shawnee State Univ	OH	11,031	NC
Shenandoah Univ	VA	25,190	NC
Shepherd College	WV	8,608	C
Shippensburg Univ of Pennsylvania	PA	10,826	C
Shorter College	GA	17,370	C
Siena College	NY	25,310	VC
Siena Heights Univ	MI	16,140	LC
Silver Lake College of the Holy Family	WI	18,450	LC
Simmons College	MA	33,000	VC
Simon's Rock College of Bard	MA	36,580	HC
Simpson College	CA	20,500	C
Simpson College	IA	23,658	C+
Skidmore College	NY	37,930	HC
Slippery Rock Univ of Pennsylvania	PA	10,343	LC
Smith College	MA	37,034	HC+
Sojourner-Douglass College	MD	4,170	LC
Sonoma State Univ	CA	10,421	C
S Car State Univ	SC	6,586	LC
S Dak State Univ	SD	7,782	C
Southeast Missouri State Univ	MO	9,704	C
Southeastern College	FL	11,648	LC
Southeastern Louisiana Univ	LA	6,791	LC
Southeastern Okla State Univ	OK	6,147	C
Southern Adventist Univ	TN	17,080	C
Southern Arkansas Univ	AR	6,956	C
Southern Conn State Univ	CT	10,310	C
Southern Illinois Univ Carbondale	IL	10,407	C
Southern Illinois Univ Edwardsville	IL	8,724	C
Southern Methodist Univ	TX	34,210	HC
Southern Nazarene Univ	OK	14,634	NC
Southern New Hampshire Univ	NH	26,242	C
Southern Oregon Univ	OR	10,362	C
Southern Univ and A&M College	LA	7,372	LC
Southern Univ at New Orleans	LA	995	NC
Southern Utah Univ	UT	8,194	C
Southern Vermont College	VT	18,226	LC
Southern Wesleyan Univ	SC	19,940	C
Southwest Baptist Univ	MO	15,371	C
Southwest Minn State Univ	MN	9,106	VC
Southwest Missouri State Univ	MO	8,918	C
Southwestern Adventist Univ	TX	14,798	C
Southwestern College	KS	19,560	C
Southwestern Okla State Univ	OK	4,801	C
Southwestern Univ	TX	25,410	HC
Spalding Univ	KY	17,985	C
Spelman College	GA	19,215	C+
Spring Arbor Univ	MI	20,206	C
Spring Hill College	AL	25,868	VC
Springfield College	MA	24,520	C
St. Joseph's, Suffolk	NY	11,297	C
Stanford Univ	CA	37,612	MC
SUNY at Oswego	NY	12,650	C
SUNY at Potsdam	NY	12,160	C
SUNY/College at Brockport	NY	12,111	C
SUNY/College at Buffalo	NY	8,025	C
SUNY/College at Cortland	NY	12,095	C
SUNY/College at Fredonia	NY	11,562	VC
SUNY/College at Geneseo	NY	11,330	HC
SUNY/College at Old Westbury	NY	12,784	C
SUNY/College at Oneonta	NY	11,870	VC
SUNY/College at Purchase	NY	10,587	VC
SUNY/Univ at Albany	NY	12,951	HC
SUNY/Univ at Binghamton	NY	12,787	HC
SUNY/Univ at Buffalo	NY	12,563	VC
SUNY/Univ at New Paltz	NY	11,565	VC
SUNY/Univ at Stony Brook	NY	12,763	HC
State Univ of West Georgia	GA	7,622	C
Stephen F. Austin State Univ	TX	7,552	C
Stetson Univ	FL	29,495	VC
Stonehill College	MA	30,752	HC
Suffolk Univ	MA	29,200	C
Sul Ross State Univ	TX	6,582	LC
Susquehanna Univ	PA	29,990	VC
Swarthmore College	PA	37,716	MC
Sweet Briar College	VA	27,940	C
Syracuse Univ	NY	34,720	HC
Tabor College	KS	19,500	NC
Talladega College	AL	10,110	LC
Taylor Univ	IN	23,820	VC+
Teikyo Post Univ	CT	24,875	C
Temple Univ	PA	15,912	C
Tenn State Univ	TN	9,048	LC
Tenn Tech Univ	TN	8,670	VC
Tenn Wesleyan College	TN	16,540	C
Texas A&M Univ	TX	11,081	HC
Texas A&M Univ at Commerce	TX	8,994	C
Texas A&M Univ at Corpus Christi	TX	10,269	C
Texas A&M Univ at Kingsville	TX	6,740	LC
Texas Christian Univ	TX	23,410	VC
Texas Lutheran Univ	TX	20,370	C
Texas Southern Univ	TX	8,920	NC
Texas State Univ	TX	9,320	VC
Texas Tech Univ	TX	10,768	VC
Texas Wesleyan Univ	TX	16,245	C
Texas Woman's Univ	TX	7,804	LC
Thiel College	PA	20,970	C
Thomas College	ME	19,960	LC
Thomas Edison State College	NJ	3,325	SP
Thomas More College	KY	21,350	C
Thomas Univ	GA	11,490	NC
Tougaloo College	MS	9,200	NC
Touro College	NY	15,250	VC
Towson Univ	MD	12,694	VC
Transylvania Univ	KY	23,780	VC+
Trevecca Nazarene Univ	TN	17,548	C
Trinity Christian College	IL	21,640	VC
Trinity College	CT	38,040	HC+
Trinity College	DC	24,150	LC
Trinity International Univ	IL	22,980	C+
Trinity Univ	TX	26,466	HC+
Tri-State Univ-Main Campus	IN	23,600	C
Troy State Univ	AL	7,696	C
Troy State Univ Dothan	AL	3,842	C
Troy State Univ Montgomery	AL	3,600	NC
Truman State Univ	MO	9,728	HC+
Tufts Univ	MA	38,233	MC
Tulane Univ	LA	37,451	HC+
Turabo Univ	PR	4,110	
Tusculum College	TN	19,990	C
Tuskegee Univ	AL	17,250	LC
Union College	KY	15,920	C
Union College	NE	17,130	C
Union College	NY	36,005	HC
Union Inst and Univ	OH	7,848	SP
Union Univ	TN	18,800	VC
United States Air Force Academy	CO		HC+
Universidad Metropolitana	PR	3,324	
Univ of Akron	OH	13,134	NC
Univ of Alabama	AL	9,040	C+
Univ of Alabama at Birmingham	AL	12,901	C
Univ of Alabama in Huntsville	AL	9,126	VC
Univ of Alaska Anchorage	AK	9,100	NC
Univ of Alaska Fairbanks	AK	9,295	C
Univ of Arizona	AZ	10,413	VC
Univ of Arkansas	AR	9,855	VC
Univ of Arkansas at Little Rock	AR	5,637	NC
Univ of Arkansas at Monticello	AR	5,940	NC
Univ of Arkansas at Pine Bluff	AR	7,925	C
Univ of Bridgeport	CT	25,924	LC
Univ of Calif at Berkeley	CA	15,563	MC
Univ of Calif at Davis	CA	14,995	VC
Univ of Calif at Irvine	CA	19,808	HC
Univ of Calif at Los Angeles	CA	15,330	MC
Univ of Calif at Riverside	CA	15,300	C
Univ of Calif at San Diego	CA	14,127	HC
Univ of Calif at Santa Barbara	CA	11,732	VC
Univ of Calif at Santa Cruz	CA	16,505	VC
Univ of Central Arkansas	AR	6,388	C
Univ of Central Florida	FL	10,038	VC
Univ of Central Okla	OK	9,434	C
Univ of Charleston	WV	23,620	C
Univ of Chicago	IL	35,087	MC
Univ of Cincinnati	OH	14,736	C
Univ of Colo at Boulder	CO	10,774	VC
Univ of Colo at Colo Springs	CO	10,667	C
Univ of Colo at Denver	CO	3,302	C
Univ of Conn	CT	14,608	VC
Univ of Dallas	TX	25,898	VC+
Univ of Dayton	OH	24,850	VC
Univ of Delaware	DE	12,616	HC
Univ of Denver	CO	32,148	VC
Univ of Detroit Mercy	MI	25,582	C
Univ of Dubuque	IA	20,950	C
Univ of Evansville	IN	24,390	VC
Univ of Findlay	OH	23,962	NC
Univ of Florida	FL	8,580	MC
Univ of Georgia	GA	8,656	VC
Univ of Great Falls	MT	15,360	C
Univ of Hartford	CT	31,080	C
Univ of Hawaii at Hilo	HI	6,497	C
Univ of Hawaii at Manoa	HI	9,565	VC
Univ of Houston	TX	9,818	C
Univ of Idaho	ID	8,216	C
Univ of Illinois at Chicago	IL	13,418	C
Univ of Illinois at Urbana-Champaign	IL	11,316	HC+
Univ of Indianapolis	IN	22,560	VC
Univ of Iowa	IA	10,923	VC
Univ of Judaism College of A&S	CA	24,230	C
Univ of Kansas	KS	8,923	VC
Univ of Kentucky	KY	7,765	C
Univ of La Verne	CA	28,600	C
Univ of Louisiana at Lafayette	LA	5,826	C
Univ of Louisiana at Monroe	LA	5,207	NC
Univ of Louisville	KY	8,762	VC
Univ of Maine	ME	12,080	C+
Univ of Maine at Farmington	ME	10,108	C
Univ of Mary	ND	12,900	C+
Univ of Mary Hardin-Baylor	TX	17,268	C
Univ of Maryland/Baltimore County	MD	14,668	VC+
Univ of Maryland/College Park	MD	14,227	HC
Univ of Maryland/Univ College	MD	5,910	SP
Univ of Mass Amherst	MA	13,980	C+
Univ of Mass Boston	MA	6,227	C
Univ of Mass Dartmouth	MA	12,835	C
Univ of Mass Lowell	MA	11,937	VC
Univ of Memphis	TN	8,560	C
Univ of Miami	FL	34,608	HC
Univ of Mich/Ann Arbor	MI	13,864	HC+
Univ of Mich/Dearborn	MI	6,843	VC
Univ of Mich/Flint	MI	5,548	C
Univ of Minn/Duluth	MN	12,470	C
Univ of Minn/Morris	MN	12,896	VC

ST = STATE $IS = IN-STATE COSTS SR = SELECTOR RATING

School	ST	$IS	SR
Univ of Minn/Twin Cities	MN	13,160	VC
Univ of Miss	MS	7,666	C
Univ of Missouri/Columbia	MO	13,782	VC
Univ of Missouri/Kansas City	MO	13,416	VC
Univ of Missouri/Rolla	MO	12,292	HC
Univ of Missouri/St. Louis	MO	11,656	VC
Univ of Mobile	AL	13,620	C
Univ of Montana	MT	9,395	C
Univ of Montevallo	AL	8,478	C
Univ of Nebr at Kearney	NE	8,286	NC
Univ of Nebr at Lincoln	NE	9,975	C+
Univ of Nebr at Omaha	NE	8,080	C
Univ of Nevada/Las Vegas	NV	11,566	C
Univ of Nevada/Reno	NV	9,792	C
Univ of New England	ME	27,200	LC
Univ of New Hampshire	NH	14,828	VC
Univ of New Haven	CT	28,650	C
Univ of New Mexico	NM	9,223	C
Univ of New Orleans	LA	7,356	C
Univ of North Alabama	AL	7,972	NC
Univ of N Car at Asheville	NC	8,079	VC
Univ of N Car at Chapel Hill	NC	10,117	MC
Univ of N Car at Charlotte	NC	8,185	C
Univ of N Car at Greensboro	NC	8,248	C
Univ of N Car at Pembroke	NC	6,929	LC
Univ of N Car at Wilmington	NC	8,940	VC
Univ of N Dak	ND	8,390	C
Univ of North Florida	FL	8,769	VC
Univ of North Texas	TX	7,629	C
Univ of Northern Colo	CO	8,987	C
Univ of Northern Iowa	IA	9,834	C
Univ of Notre Dame	IN	34,442	MC
Univ of Okla	OK	9,226	VC
Univ of Oregon	OR	11,479	VC
Univ of Pennsylvania	PA	37,960	MC
Univ of Pittsburgh at Bradford	PA	15,294	C
Univ of Pittsburgh at Greensburg	PA	15,984	C
Univ of Pittsburgh at Johnstown	PA	15,216	LC
Univ of Pittsburgh at Pittsburgh	PA	16,074	HC
Univ of Portland	OR	28,500	VC
Univ of PR/Cayey Univ College	PR	1,245	
Univ of PR/Mayaguez	PR		
Univ of PR/Rio Piedras	PR	5,730	
Univ of Puget Sound	WA	31,760	HC
Univ of Redlands	CA	32,576	VC
Univ of Rhode Island	RI	13,720	VC
Univ of Richmond	VA	30,100	MC
Univ of Rio Grande	OH	8,728	NC
Univ of Rochester	NY	32,979	HC
Univ of St. Francis	IL	22,850	C
Univ of St. Francis	IN	20,964	C
Univ of St. Mary	KS	18,868	C
Univ of St. Thomas	MN	26,918	VC
Univ of St. Thomas	TX	21,952	VC
Univ of San Diego	CA	33,156	HC
Univ of San Francisco	CA	34,700	VC
Univ of Science and Arts of Okla	OK	5,982	C
Univ of Scranton	PA	30,836	VC
Univ of Sioux Falls	SD	16,390	C
Univ of South Alabama	AL	7,760	LC
Univ of S Car at Aiken	SC	7,828	LC
Univ of S Car at Columbia	SC	10,048	VC
Univ of S Car at Spartanburg	SC	9,936	C+
Univ of S Dak	SD	7,710	C+
Univ of South Florida	FL	9,454	C
Univ of Southern Calif	CA	37,459	MC
Univ of Southern Colo	CO	7,821	LC
Univ of Southern Indiana	IN	9,025	LC
Univ of Southern Maine	ME	11,212	C
Univ of Southern Miss	MS	8,324	LC
Univ of Tampa	FL	23,982	VC
Univ of Tenn at Chattanooga	TN	7,783	C
Univ of Tenn at Knoxville	TN	8,214	C
Univ of Tenn at Martin	TN	7,748	C
Univ of Texas at Arlington	TX	7,192	LC
Univ of Texas at Austin	TX	10,630	HC
Univ of Texas at Dallas	TX	10,234	HC
Univ of Texas at El Paso	TX	5,799	NC
Univ of Texas at San Antonio	TX	9,088	NC
Univ of Texas-Pan American	TX	5,954	LC
Univ of the District of Columbia	DC	2,070	LC
Univ of the Incarnate Word	TX	21,772	LC
Univ of the Ozarks	AR	16,574	C
Univ of the Pacific	CA	31,090	VC
Univ of the Sacred Heart	PR	5,590	
Univ of the Sciences in Philadelphia	PA	29,310	VC
Univ of the South	TN	30,855	HC
Univ of Toledo	OH	12,479	NC
Univ of Tulsa	OK	22,090	VC+
Univ of Utah	UT	9,205	C
Univ of Vermont	VT	16,316	VC
Univ of Virginia	VA	11,740	MC
Univ of Virginia's College at Wise	VA	10,116	C
Univ of Washington	WA	10,361	VC
Univ of West Alabama	AL	6,048	C
Univ of West Florida	FL	8,470	C
Univ of Wisc/Eau Claire	WI	8,463	VC
Univ of Wisc/Green Bay	WI	8,154	C
Univ of Wisc/La Crosse	WI	8,991	VC
Univ of Wisc/Madison	WI	8,262	VC
Univ of Wisc/Milwaukee	WI	9,427	LC
Univ of Wisc/Oshkosh	WI	6,130	LC
Univ of Wisc/Parkside	WI	6,160	LC
Univ of Wisc/Platteville	WI	8,450	C
Univ of Wisc/River Falls	WI	8,358	LC
Univ of Wisc/Stevens Point	WI	8,116	VC
Univ of Wisc/Stout	WI	9,718	C
Univ of Wisc/Superior	WI	7,051	C+
Univ of Wisc/Whitewater	WI	8,626	C
Univ of Wyoming	WY	8,636	C
Upper Iowa Univ	IA	20,076	C
Urbana Univ	OH	19,115	C
Ursinus College	PA	34,400	VC
Ursuline College	OH	22,728	LC
Utah State Univ	UT	7,371	C
Utica College	NY	28,340	C
Valdosta State Univ	GA	7,798	C
Valparaiso Univ	IN	26,118	VC+
Vanderbilt Univ	TN	37,897	MC
Vanguard Univ of Southern Calif	CA	22,208	C
Vassar College	NY	37,030	MC
Villa Julie College	MD	18,393	C
Villanova Univ	PA	35,050	HC
Virginia Commonwealth Univ	VA	9,030	C
Virginia Intermont College	VA	19,800	C
Virginia Military Inst	VA	9,968	C+
Virginia Polytechnic Inst and State Univ	VA	9,179	C
Virginia State Univ	VA	10,358	C
Virginia Union Univ	VA	15,358	LC
Virginia Wesleyan College	VA	25,350	C
Viterbo Univ	WI	20,430	C
Wabash College	IN	27,932	VC
Wagner College	NY	29,900	VC
Wake Forest Univ	NC	34,090	MC
Walla Walla College	WA	21,600	NC
Walsh Univ	OH	20,890	C
Warner Southern College	FL	16,738	LC
Warren Wilson College	NC	21,794	VC
Wartburg College	IA	21,165	VC
Washburn Univ of Topeka	KS	8,984	NC
Washington and Jefferson College	PA	29,570	VC
Washington and Lee Univ	VA	29,663	MC
Washington College	MD	30,540	VC
Washington State Univ	WA	11,334	C
Washington Univ in St. Louis	MO	38,293	MC
Wayland Baptist Univ	TX	11,919	NC
Wayne State College	NE	7,352	NC
Wayne State Univ	MI	11,774	C
Waynesburg College	PA	19,370	C
Weber State Univ	UT	7,945	NC
Webster Univ	MO	21,848	VC
Wellesley College	MA	36,516	MC
Wells College	NY	21,122	VC
Wesley College	DE	19,905	C
Wesleyan College	GA	17,870	VC
Wesleyan Univ	CT	35,139	MC
West Chester Univ of Pennsylvania	PA	11,164	C
West Liberty State College	WV	7,868	LC
West Texas A&M Univ	TX	7,533	C
West Virginia State College	WV	6,264	NC
West Virginia Univ	WV	9,370	C
West Virginia Wesleyan College	WV	22,920	C
Western Baptist College	OR	21,808	C
Western Carolina Univ	NC	6,742	C
Western Conn State Univ	CT	11,625	C
Western Illinois Univ	IL	10,363	C
Western Kentucky Univ	KY	6,834	C
Western Mich Univ	MI	12,031	C
Western New England College	MA	28,924	C
Western New Mexico Univ	NM	5,950	LC
Western Oregon Univ	OR	10,281	C
Western State College of Colo	CO	9,014	C
Western Washington Univ	WA	10,119	VC
Westfield State College	MA	10,147	C
Westminster College	MO	18,150	C+
Westminster College	PA	22,960	C
Westminster College	UT	17,226	C
Westmont College	CA	33,062	VC+
Wheaton College	IL	21,934	HC
Wheaton College	MA	36,330	HC
Wheeling Jesuit Univ	WV	22,660	C
Whitman College	WA	32,526	HC+
Whittier College	CA	29,108	C
Whitworth College	WA	26,428	VC+
Wichita State Univ	KS	8,092	C
Widener Univ	PA	27,020	C
Wilberforce Univ	OH	14,937	LC
Wilkes Univ	PA	28,060	C
Willamette Univ	OR	32,032	VC+
William Carey College	MS	10,150	LC
William Jewell College	MO	21,320	VC
William Paterson Univ of New Jersey	NJ	14,450	C
William Penn Univ	IA	17,575	LC
William Tyndale College	MI	12,170	NC
William Woods Univ	MO	20,120	C
Williams Baptist College	AR	11,950	C
Williams College	MA	32,270	MC
Wilmington College	OH	24,172	LC
Wingate Univ	NC	21,200	C
Winona State Univ	MN		C
Winston-Salem State Univ	NC	8,926	LC
Winthrop Univ	SC	11,302	C
Wisc Lutheran College	WI	21,430	VC
Wittenberg Univ	OH	31,316	VC
Wofford College	SC	26,710	HC
Woodbury Univ	CA	25,344	LC
Worcester State College	MA	10,005	C
Wright State Univ	OH	11,490	LC
Xavier Univ	OH	26,850	VC+
Xavier Univ of Louisiana	LA	17,600	C
Yale Univ	CT	37,000	MC
Yeshiva Univ	NY	21,400	C
York College	NE	14,975	C
York College of Pennsylvania	PA	14,500	VC
Youngstown State Univ	OH	11,148	NC

PSYCHOLOGY EDUCATION

School	ST	$IS	SR
Eastern Mich Univ	MI	11,478	C
Mount Holyoke College	MA	37,918	HC+
Rocky Mountain College	MT	19,015	C
St. Vincent College	PA	25,530	VC
Shenandoah Univ	VA	25,190	NC
Univ of Delaware	DE	12,616	HC
Univ of Rio Grande	OH	8,728	NC

PUBLIC ADMINISTRATION

School	ST	$IS	SR
Abilene Christian Univ	TX	18,370	VC
Alfred Univ	NY	28,290	C
American International College	MA	24,690	LC
Auburn Univ	AL	10,396	VC
Augustana College	IL	26,610	VC+
Austin Peay State Univ	TN	5,814	LC
Baylor Univ	TX	23,864	VC
Blackburn College	IL	13,690	C
Bowling Green State Univ	OH	13,036	C
Brown Univ	RI	38,174	MC
Buena Vista Univ	IA	25,406	C
Cal State, Bakersfield	CA	6,090	LC
Cal State, Chico	CA	8,598	LC
Cal State, Dominguez Hills	CA	5,840	LC
Cal State, Fresno	CA	8,414	LC
Cal State, Fullerton	CA	6,648	C
Cal State, Sacramento	CA	9,543	C
Cal State, San Bernardino	CA	15,238	LC
Cal State, Stanislaus	CA	9,874	C
Carnegie Mellon Univ	PA	32,682	MC
Carroll College	MT	20,576	VC
Catawba College	NC	20,500	C
Cedarville Univ	OH	19,954	VC
Central Methodist College	MO	16,460	C
Central State Univ	OH	8,922	C+
Central Washington Univ	WA	9,768	C
Christopher Newport Univ	VA	8,862	VC
CUNY/John Jay College of Criminal Justice	NY	4,259	C
CUNY/Medgar Evers College	NY	4,232	NC
College of Santa Fe	NM	25,293	C+
David N. Myers College	OH	9,475	C
Doane College	NE	20,000	C
Eastern Mich Univ	MI	11,478	C
Edgewood College	WI	20,520	C
Elon Univ	NC	22,240	VC
Evangel Univ	MO	15,435	C
Fayetteville State Univ	NC	5,590	LC
Florida A&M Univ	FL	7,564	C
Florida Atlantic Univ	FL	8,543	C
Florida International Univ	FL	9,912	VC
Florida Memorial College	FL	6,000	LC
George Mason Univ	VA	9,732	VC
Grambling State Univ	LA	6,538	NC
Grand Valley State Univ	MI	11,022	VC
Harding Univ	AR	14,890	VC
Hawaii Pacific Univ	HI	19,218	C
Heidelberg College	OH	20,266	NC
Henderson State Univ	AR	7,386	C
Heritage College	WA	6,720	NC
Huntingdon College	AL	18,400	VC
Indiana Univ Bloomington	IN	12,389	VC
Indiana Univ Northwest	IN	4,538	LC
Indiana Univ South Bend	IN	4,571	LC
Indiana Univ-Purdue Univ Fort Wayne	IN	5,108	LC
Inter American Univ of PR/ Fajardo Campus	PR	4,000	
Inter American Univ of PR/ Ponce Regional College	PR	3,700	
Inter American Univ of PR/ San German	PR	6,716	
James Madison Univ	VA	10,794	VC
John Carroll Univ	OH	27,658	C+
Juniata College	PA	29,080	VC
Kean Univ	NJ	14,479	C
Kentucky State Univ	KY	9,062	NC
Kutztown Univ of Pennsylvania	PA	10,786	C
La Salle Univ	PA	31,260	VC
Lakeland College	WI	17,950	C
Lamar Univ	TX	6,816	LC
LeTourneau Univ	TX	21,080	C
Lewis Univ	IL	22,950	C+
Lincoln Univ	MO	7,158	NC
Lindenwood Univ	MO	17,050	VC
LIU/C.W. Post Campus	NY	28,282	C
Louisiana College	LA	13,450	C
Metropolitan State Univ	MN	3,852	SP
Miami Univ	OH	15,033	HC
Mich State Univ	MI	11,933	VC
Middle Tenn State Univ	TN	8,534	C
Mills College	CA	33,371	VC
Miss Valley State Univ	MS	6,765	NC
Missouri Valley College	MO	18,500	C
Mountain State Univ	WV	10,212	NC
New College of Florida	FL	8,906	HC+
Norfolk State Univ	VA	9,722	LC
Northern Arizona Univ	AZ	9,002	C
Northern Kentucky Univ	KY	6,352	NC
Northern Mich Univ	MI	10,834	C
Northland College	WI	22,170	C+
Northwest Missouri State Univ	MO	9,334	C
Oakland Univ	MI	10,800	C
Park Univ	MO	10,780	C+
Penn State Univ/Univ Park Campus	PA	15,646	HC
Plymouth State Univ	NH	12,298	LC
Point Park Univ	PA	21,840	C
Pontifical Catholic Univ of PR/Ponce	PR	7,298	
Rhode Island College	RI	11,565	C
Roosevelt Univ	IL	22,580	VC
Saginaw Valley State Univ	MI	11,055	C
St. Ambrose Univ	IA	22,800	C
St. Cloud State Univ	MN	8,362	C
St. Francis Univ	PA	25,876	LC
St. John's Univ	NY	30,180	C
St. Joseph's Univ	PA	33,590	VC
St. Mary's Univ of Minn	MN	21,535	C
St. Thomas Univ	FL	21,400	LC
Samford Univ	AL	18,648	VC
San Diego State Univ	CA	10,321	C
Seattle Univ	WA	24,183	VC
Shaw Univ	NC	14,882	C+
Shenandoah Univ	VA	25,190	NC
Shippensburg Univ of Pennsylvania	PA	10,826	C
Siena Heights Univ	MI	16,140	LC
Silver Lake College of the Holy Family	WI	18,450	LC
Slippery Rock Univ of Pennsylvania	PA	10,343	LC
Sojourner-Douglass College	MD	4,170	LC
Southeastern Univ	DC	8,505	LC
Southern Adventist Univ	TN	17,080	C
Southwest Missouri State Univ	MO	8,918	C
Stephen F. Austin State Univ	TX	7,552	C
Stonehill College	MA	30,752	HC
Suffolk Univ	MA	29,200	C
Talladega College	AL	10,110	LC
Texas A&M Univ at Kingsville	TX	6,740	LC
Texas State Univ	TX	9,320	VC
Thomas Edison State College	NJ	3,325	SP
Turabo Univ	PR	4,110	
Union Inst and Univ	OH	7,848	SP
Univ of Akron	OH	13,134	NC
Univ of Alaska Southeast	AK	7,900	LC
Univ of Arizona	AZ	10,413	VC
Univ of Arkansas	AR	9,855	VC
Univ of Central Arkansas	AR	6,388	C
Univ of Central Florida	FL	10,038	VC
Univ of Central Okla	OK	9,434	C
Univ of La Verne	CA	28,600	C
Univ of Maine	ME	12,080	C+
Univ of Maine at Augusta	ME	4,065	C
Univ of Mich/Flint	MI	5,548	C
Univ of Miss	MS	7,666	C
Univ of Nebr at Omaha	NE	8,080	C
Univ of Nevada/Las Vegas	NV	11,566	C
Univ of N Car at Pembroke	NC	6,929	LC
Univ of N Dak	ND	8,390	C
Univ of Northern Iowa	IA	9,834	C
Univ of Oregon	OR	11,479	VC
Univ of Pennsylvania	PA	37,960	MC
Univ of Pittsburgh at Pittsburgh	PA	16,074	HC
Univ of San Francisco	CA	34,700	VC
Univ of Southern Calif	CA	37,459	MC
Univ of Tenn at Knoxville	TN	8,214	C
Univ of Tenn at Martin	TN	7,748	C
Univ of Texas at Dallas	TX	10,234	HC

ST = STATE $IS = IN-STATE COSTS   SR = SELECTOR RATING

School	ST	$IS	SR
Univ of the District of Columbia	DC	2,070	LC
Univ of Wisc/Green Bay	WI	8,154	C
Univ of Wisc/La Crosse	WI	8,991	VC
Univ of Wisc/Stevens Point	WI	8,116	VC
Univ of Wisc/Superior	WI	7,051	C+
Univ of Wisc/Whitewater	WI	8,626	C
Virginia Intermont College	VA	19,800	C
Virginia Polytechnic Inst and State Univ	VA	9,179	C
Virginia State Univ	VA	10,358	C
Wagner College	NY	29,900	VC
Washburn Univ of Topeka	KS	8,984	NC
West Chester Univ of Pennsylvania	PA	11,164	C
West Texas A&M Univ	TX	7,533	C
West Virginia Univ Inst of Technology	WV	7,518	NC
Western Mich Univ	MI	12,031	C
Western New Mexico Univ	NM	5,950	LC
Western Oregon Univ	OR	10,281	C
Winona State Univ	MN		C
Winston-Salem State Univ	NC	8,926	LC
Youngstown State Univ	OH	11,148	NC

PUBLIC AFFAIRS

School	ST	$IS	SR
Albion College	MI	25,224	VC
Bentley College	MA	33,904	VC
Chatham College	PA	27,266	C+
CUNY/Baruch College	NY	3,275	VC+
Columbia College	SC	22,658	LC
Cornell Univ	NY	38,253	MC
Dickinson College	PA	35,825	HC
Duke Univ	NC	37,555	MC
Emory & Henry College	VA	21,950	C
Georgia Inst of Technology	GA	10,340	HC+
Hamilton College	NY	37,560	MC
Huntingdon College	AL	18,400	VC
Indiana Univ Bloomington	IN	12,389	VC
Indiana Univ Kokomo	IN	4,463	LC
Indiana Univ South Bend	IN	4,571	LC
Indiana Univ-Purdue Univ Indianapolis	IN	8,257	LC
Johns Hopkins Univ	MD	38,372	MC
Marymount College of Fordham Univ	NY	27,686	C
Meredith College	NC	23,065	C
Mills College	CA	33,371	VC
Muskingum College	OH	20,680	C
Olivet Nazarene Univ	IL	20,480	C
Pomona College	CA	33,960	MC
Rice Univ	TX	27,550	MC
Rochester Inst of Technology	NY	29,217	VC+
St. Mary's College of Maryland	MD	15,908	VC+
St. Vincent College	PA	25,530	VC
Southern Methodist Univ	TX	34,210	HC
Syracuse Univ	NY	34,720	HC
Texas Lutheran Univ	TX	20,370	C
Texas Southern Univ	TX	8,920	NC
Trinity College	CT	38,040	HC+
Univ of Calif at Santa Barbara	CA	11,732	VC
Univ of Chicago	IL	35,087	MC
Univ of Denver	CO	32,148	VC
Univ of N Car at Chapel Hill	NC	10,117	MC
Univ of Okla	OK	9,226	VC
Vanderbilt Univ	TN	37,897	MC
Washington and Lee Univ	VA	29,663	MC
Washington State Univ	WA	11,334	C
Wayne State Univ	MI	11,774	C
Wells College	NY	21,122	VC

PUBLIC HEALTH

School	ST	$IS	SR
Andrews Univ	MI	19,550	C
Arkansas State Univ	AR	8,450	C
Central Washington Univ	WA	9,768	C
CUNY/Hunter College	NY	6,729	C+
Cumberland College	KY	16,384	C
Dillard Univ	LA	17,325	VC
East Tenn State Univ	TN	8,497	C
Edinboro Univ of Pennsylvania	PA	10,850	LC
Indiana Univ Bloomington	IN	12,389	VC
Indiana Univ-Purdue Univ Indianapolis	IN	8,257	LC
Ithaca College	NY	31,730	HC
Johns Hopkins Univ	MD	38,372	MC
Minn State Univ, Mankato	MN	8,803	LC
New Jersey City Univ	NJ	11,850	LC
Penn State Univ/Univ Park Campus	PA	15,646	HC
Richard Stockton College of New Jersey	NJ	12,972	VC
Russell Sage College	NY	26,811	C
Rutgers, The State Univ of New Jersey/New Brunswick/Piscataway Campus	NJ	15,800	HC
St. Cloud State Univ	MN	8,362	C
San Francisco State Univ	CA	12,070	C
Southern Conn State Univ	CT	10,310	C
Univ of Calif at Berkeley	CA	15,563	MC
Univ of Illinois at Urbana-Champaign	IL	11,316	HC+
Univ of Nebr at Lincoln	NE	9,975	C+
Univ of N Car at Chapel Hill	NC	10,117	MC
Univ of Rochester	NY	32,979	HC
Univ of Wisc/Eau Claire	WI	8,463	VC
Utah State Univ	UT	7,371	C
West Chester Univ of Pennsylvania	PA	11,164	C
Western Kentucky Univ	KY	6,834	C
Western New Mexico Univ	NM	5,950	LC
Winona State Univ	MN		C

PUBLIC HISTORY/ARCHIVES

School	ST	$IS	SR
St. Andrews Presbyterian College	NC	20,525	C

PUBLIC RELATIONS

School	ST	$IS	SR
American Univ	DC	34,585	VC+
Andrews Univ	MI	19,550	C
Appalachian State Univ	NC	7,637	VC
Auburn Univ	AL	10,396	VC
Barry Univ	FL	24,100	LC
Boston Univ	MA	38,194	HC+
Brigham Young Univ	UT	8,504	HC
Cal State, Fullerton	CA	6,648	C
Capital Univ	OH	26,550	C
Cardinal Stritch Univ	WI	17,620	C
Carroll College	MT	20,576	VC
Central Missouri State Univ	MO	9,776	C
Central Washington Univ	WA	9,768	C
Champlain College	VT	22,030	C
Chapman Univ	CA	33,118	VC
Coe College	IA	27,385	VC
College of the Ozarks	MO	3,500	VC+
Concordia College: Moorhead	MN	22,460	VC+
David Lipscomb Univ	TN	16,158	VC
Drake Univ	IA	25,120	VC+
Drury Univ	MO	18,085	VC+
East Central Univ	OK	4,968	C
Eastern Kentucky Univ	KY	7,708	C
Emerson College	MA	32,205	HC
Ferris State Univ	MI	12,512	C
Florida Southern College	FL	23,592	C
Florida State Univ	FL	9,028	HC
Freed-Hardeman Univ	TN		NC
George Washington Univ	DC	41,030	MC
Georgia Southern Univ	GA	8,540	C
Gonzaga Univ	WA	26,766	HC
Greenville College	IL	21,342	C
Gwynedd-Mercy College	PA	24,225	C
Hawaii Pacific Univ	HI	19,218	C
Heidelberg College	OH	20,266	NC
Hofstra Univ	NY	27,112	VC
Illinois State Univ	IL	10,944	C+
Indiana Univ South Bend	IN	4,571	LC
Iona College	NY	27,988	VC
Ithaca College	NY	31,730	HC
John Brown Univ	AR	15,080	VC
Kent State Univ	OH	12,932	C
Lewis Univ	IL	22,950	C+
LIU/C.W. Post Campus	NY	28,282	C
Loras College	IA	24,233	C
Mansfield Univ	PA	11,220	C
Marietta College	OH	27,047	C
Marquette Univ	WI	27,594	VC
Mary Baldwin College	VA	24,939	C
McKendree College	IL	21,120	VC
Mercyhurst College	PA	20,694	C
Middle Tenn State Univ	TN	8,534	C
Minn State Univ, Moorehead	MN	7,000	LC
Montana State Univ-Billings	MT	9,550	C
Montclair State Univ	NJ	13,790	C
Mount Mary College	WI	20,370	C
Mount St. Mary College	NY	21,270	C
Murray State Univ	KY	7,816	VC
Northeastern Univ	MA	35,650	HC
Northern Mich Univ	MI	10,834	C
Northwest Missouri State Univ	MO	9,334	C
Northwestern Okla State Univ	OK	5,433	NC
Ohio Dominican Univ	OH	22,700	C
Ohio Northern Univ	OH	27,765	VC
Otterbein College	OH	26,085	C
Pacific Union College	CA	22,065	C+
Park Univ	MO	10,780	C+
Pepperdine Univ	CA	32,830	VC
Pontifical Catholic Univ of PR/Ponce	PR	7,298	
Purdue Univ/West Lafayette	IN	12,560	VC
Quinnipiac Univ	CT	30,570	VC
Rider Univ	NJ	30,900	C
Roosevelt Univ	IL	22,580	VC
St. Mary's Univ of Minn	MN	21,535	C
Shorter College	GA	17,370	C
Southeast Missouri State Univ	MO	9,704	C
Southern Adventist Univ	TN	17,080	C
Southern Methodist Univ	TX	34,210	HC
SUNY at Oswego	NY	12,650	C
Stephens College	MO	24,260	C+
Suffolk Univ	MA	29,200	C
Syracuse Univ	NY	34,720	HC
Texas State Univ	TX	9,320	VC
Texas Tech Univ	TX	10,768	VC
Toccoa Falls College	GA	15,600	C
Union College	NE	17,130	C
Union Univ	TN	18,800	VC
Univ of Alabama	AL	9,040	C+
Univ of Central Florida	FL	10,038	VC
Univ of Central Okla	OK	9,434	C
Univ of Dayton	OH	24,850	VC
Univ of Florida	FL	8,580	MC
Univ of Georgia	GA	8,656	VC
Univ of Indianapolis	IN	22,560	VC
Univ of Louisiana at Lafayette	LA	5,826	C
Univ of Miami	FL	34,608	HC
Univ of North Alabama	AL	7,972	NC
Univ of Northern Colo	CO	8,987	C
Univ of Northern Iowa	IA	9,834	C
Univ of Okla	OK	9,226	VC
Univ of Pittsburgh at Bradford	PA	15,294	C
Univ of Rio Grande	OH	8,728	NC
Univ of S Car at Columbia	SC	10,048	VC
Univ of Southern Calif	CA	37,459	MC
Univ of Texas at Austin	TX	10,630	HC
Univ of Wisc/Whitewater	WI	8,626	C
Ursuline College	OH	22,728	LC
Utica College	NY	28,340	C
Valparaiso Univ	IN	26,118	VC+
Wartburg College	IA	21,165	VC
Washington State Univ	WA	11,334	C
Wayne State Univ	MI	11,774	C
Weber State Univ	UT	7,945	NC
Webster Univ	MO	21,848	VC
West Texas A&M Univ	TX	7,533	C
West Virginia Univ	WV	9,370	C
West Virginia Wesleyan College	WV	22,920	C
Western Kentucky Univ	KY	6,834	C
Western Mich Univ	MI	12,031	C
Westminster College	PA	22,960	C
William Penn Univ	IA	17,575	LC
Winthrop Univ	SC	11,302	C
Xavier Univ	OH	26,850	VC+
Youngstown State Univ	OH	11,148	NC

PUBLISHING

School	ST	$IS	SR
Benedictine Univ	IL	23,840	C
Emerson College	MA	32,205	HC
Hofstra Univ	NY	27,112	VC
Rochester Inst of Technology	NY	29,217	VC+
St. Mary's Univ of Minn	MN	21,535	C
Syracuse Univ	NY	34,720	HC
West Texas A&M Univ	TX	7,533	C

PUERTO RICAN STUDIES

School	ST	$IS	SR
Rutgers, The State Univ of New Jersey/Newark Campus	NJ	15,624	VC

PURCHASING/INVENTORY MANAGEMENT

School	ST	$IS	SR
Arizona State Univ-Main	AZ	10,048	C
Bowling Green State Univ	OH	13,036	C
College of Mount St. Joseph	OH	22,785	C
Duquesne Univ	PA	26,907	VC
Kennesaw State Univ	GA	2,724	C
Miami Univ	OH	15,033	HC
St. Joseph's Univ	PA	33,590	VC
Southwestern College	KS	19,560	C
Syracuse Univ	NY	34,720	HC
Thomas Edison State College	NJ	3,325	SP
Univ of Houston-Downtown	TX	2,594	NC
Weber State Univ	UT	7,945	NC

QUANTITATIVE METHODS

School	ST	$IS	SR
CUNY/City College	NY	4,230	C+
Johns Hopkins Univ	MD	38,372	MC
Simon's Rock College of Bard	MA	36,580	HC
Univ of Cincinnati	OH	14,736	C
Univ of Houston	TX	9,818	C
Univ of Houston-Downtown	TX	2,594	NC
Univ of Washington	WA	10,361	VC
Univ of Wisc/Madison	WI	8,262	VC
Whitworth College	WA	26,428	VC+

RADIATION THERAPY

School	ST	$IS	SR
Gwynedd-Mercy College	PA	24,225	C
Indiana Univ Kokomo	IN	4,463	LC
Indiana Univ-Purdue Univ Indianapolis	IN	8,257	LC
National-Louis Univ	IL	16,240	LC
Texas State Univ	TX	9,320	VC
Thomas Edison State College	NJ	3,325	SP
Univ of Mich/Flint	MI	5,548	C
Univ of St. Francis	IL	22,850	C
Univ of Vermont	VT	16,316	VC
Univ of Wisc/La Crosse	WI	8,991	VC
Wayne State Univ	MI	11,774	C

RADIO/TELEVISION TECHNOLOGY

School	ST	$IS	SR
Arkansas State Univ	AR	8,450	C
CUNY/Brooklyn College	NY	4,353	C+
Columbia College Chicago	IL	25,108	LC
De Sales Univ	PA	25,470	C
Emerson College	MA	32,205	HC
Hofstra Univ	NY	27,112	VC
Kent State Univ	OH	12,932	C
Lewis Univ	IL	22,950	C+
Lyndon State College	VT	12,646	LC
Mount Ida College	MA	25,596	LC
New York Univ	NY	39,406	MC
Northern Kentucky Univ	KY	6,352	NC
Northwestern Univ	IL	37,491	MC
Southeast Missouri State Univ	MO	9,704	C
Southern Illinois Univ Carbondale	IL	10,407	C
Texas Christian Univ	TX	23,410	VC
Univ of Arkansas at Little Rock	AR	5,637	NC
Univ of Houston	TX	9,818	C
Univ of Louisiana at Monroe	LA	5,207	NC
Univ of Miss	MS	7,666	C
Univ of Montana	MT	9,395	C
Univ of North Texas	TX	7,629	C
Univ of Southern Miss	MS	8,324	LC

RADIOGRAPH MEDICAL TECHNOLOGY

School	ST	$IS	SR
Alderson-Broaddus College	WV	19,640	C
Averett Univ	VA	23,010	LC
Champlain College	VT	22,030	C
Clarkson College	NE	12,178	C
College Misericordia	PA	26,350	C
Howard Univ	DC	16,505	C
Indiana Univ Kokomo	IN	4,463	LC
La Roche College	PA	22,094	C
Ohio State Univ	OH	13,080	VC+
Oregon Inst of Technology	OR	8,718	C
Pennsylvania College of Technology	PA	15,126	NC
Southwest Missouri State Univ	MO	8,918	C
Univ of St. Francis	IL	22,850	C
Weber State Univ	UT	7,945	NC

RADIOLOGICAL SCIENCE

School	ST	$IS	SR
Arkansas State Univ	AR	8,450	C
Armstrong Atlantic State Univ	GA	7,102	C
Florida Hospital College of Health Sciences	FL	6,900	SP
Gannon Univ	PA	23,260	C
George Washington Univ	DC	41,030	MC
Idaho State Univ	ID	8,128	C
Indiana Univ Kokomo	IN	4,463	LC
Indiana Univ Northwest	IN	4,538	LC
Jewish Hospital College of Nursing and Allied Health	MO	11,200	SP
Kent State Univ	OH	12,932	C
Manhattan College	NY	27,400	VC
Midwestern State Univ	TX	8,045	LC
Northwestern State Univ of Louisiana	LA	6,331	NC
Pennsylvania College of Technology	PA	15,126	NC
Quinnipiac Univ	CT	30,570	VC
St. Francis College	NY	10,880	LC
Suffolk Univ	MA	29,200	C
Univ of Alabama at Birmingham	AL	12,901	C
Univ of Central Arkansas	AR	6,388	C
Univ of Central Florida	FL	10,038	VC
Univ of Charleston	WV	23,620	C
Univ of Missouri/Columbia	MO	13,782	VC
Univ of New Mexico	NM	9,223	C
Univ of N Car at Chapel Hill	NC	10,117	MC
Univ of Pittsburgh at Bradford	PA	15,294	C
Univ of South Alabama	AL	7,760	LC

RADIOLOGICAL TECHNOLOGY

School	ST	$IS	SR
Austin Peay State Univ	TN	5,814	LC
Averett Univ	VA	23,010	LC
Avila Univ	MO	20,300	C
Bloomsburg Univ of Pennsylvania	PA	10,844	C
Boise State Univ	ID	7,657	LC
Briar Cliff Univ	IA	21,660	C
Cal State, Northridge	CA	7,757	LC

ST = STATE $IS = IN-STATE COSTS SR = SELECTOR RATING

School	ST	$IS	SR
Clarion Univ of Pennsylvania	PA	11,272	LC
Clarkson College	NE	12,178	C
Concordia Univ Wisc	WI	16,600	C
Fairleigh Dickinson Univ/ College at Florham	NJ	30,130	C
Fairleigh Dickinson Univ/ Metropolitan Campus	NJ	28,584	C
Fort Hays State Univ	KS	7,363	C
Friends Univ	KS	15,962	LC
Jamestown College	ND	12,600	NC
LIU/C.W. Post Campus	NY	28,282	C
Marian College of Fond du Lac	WI	19,625	C
Mass College of Pharmacy and Health Sciences	MA	28,770	SP
McNeese State Univ	LA	5,259	LC
Minot State Univ	ND	6,602	LC
Mount Marty College	SD	15,656	LC
N Dak State Univ	ND	8,435	C
Presentation College	SD	14,700	LC
Rhode Island College	RI	11,565	C
St. Mary's College	MI	13,314	LC
Southern Illinois Univ Carbondale	IL	10,407	C
Univ of Hartford	CT	31,080	C
Univ of Louisiana at Monroe	LA	5,207	NC
Univ of Mary	ND	12,900	C+
Univ of Nevada/Las Vegas	NV	11,566	C
William Carey College	MS	10,150	LC

RANGE/FARM MANAGEMENT

School	ST	$IS	SR
Brigham Young Univ	UT	8,504	HC
Colo State Univ	CO	9,964	VC
Eastern Oregon Univ	OR	10,080	NC
Montana State Univ-Bozeman	MT	9,515	C
New Mexico State Univ	NM	7,932	C
N Dak State Univ	ND	8,435	C
Oregon State Univ	OR	11,055	C
S Dak State Univ	SD	7,782	C
Stephen F. Austin State Univ	TX	7,552	C
Tarleton State Univ	TX	7,576	C
Texas A&M Univ	TX	11,081	HC
Texas A&M Univ at Kingsville	TX	6,740	LC
Texas Tech Univ	TX	10,768	VC
Univ of Arizona	AZ	10,413	VC
Univ of Calif at Davis	CA	14,995	VC
Univ of Idaho	ID	8,216	C
Univ of Nebr at Lincoln	NE	9,975	C+
Univ of Wyoming	WY	8,636	C
Utah State Univ	UT	7,371	C
Washington State Univ	WA	11,334	C

READING EDUCATION

School	ST	$IS	SR
Baylor Univ	TX	23,864	VC
Defiance College	OH	22,615	C
Eastern Mich Univ	MI	11,478	C
Florida State Univ	FL	9,028	HC
Hardin-Simmons Univ	TX	14,165	C
Houston Baptist Univ	TX	16,905	C
Jarvis Christian College	TX	9,035	NC
Missouri Southern State Univ	MO	8,316	C
Muskingum College	OH	20,680	C
S Car State Univ	SC	6,586	LC
Texas Southern Univ	TX	8,920	NC
Texas State Univ	TX	9,320	VC
Texas Wesleyan Univ	TX	16,245	C
Univ of Great Falls	MT	15,360	C
Univ of North Texas	TX	7,629	C
Univ of Rio Grande	OH	8,728	NC
Washburn Univ of Topeka	KS	8,984	NC
West Texas A&M Univ	TX	7,533	C
Wingate Univ	NC	21,200	C

REAL ESTATE

School	ST	$IS	SR
Arizona State Univ-Main	AZ	10,048	C
Ball State Univ	IN	8,660	C
Baylor Univ	TX	23,864	VC
Calif State Polytechnic Univ, Pomona	CA	8,793	C+
Cal State, Sacramento	CA	9,543	C
Christopher Newport Univ	VA	8,862	VC
CUNY/Baruch College	NY	3,275	VC+
Clarion Univ of Pennsylvania	PA	11,272	LC
David N. Myers College	OH	9,475	C
Eastern Mich Univ	MI	11,478	C
Florida Atlantic Univ	FL	8,543	C
Florida International Univ	FL	9,912	VC
Georgia State Univ	GA	10,658	C
Indiana Univ Bloomington	IN	12,389	VC
Kent State Univ	OH	12,932	C
La Roche College	PA	22,094	C
Miss State Univ	MS	9,139	C
Morehead State Univ	KY	7,464	C
New York Univ	NY	39,406	MC
Ohio State Univ	OH	13,080	VC+

School	ST	$IS	SR
Penn State Univ/Univ Park Campus	PA	15,646	HC
St. John's Univ	NY	30,180	C
San Diego State Univ	CA	10,321	C
San Francisco State Univ	CA	12,070	C
Southern Methodist Univ	TX	34,210	HC
State Univ of West Georgia	GA	7,622	C
Temple Univ	PA	15,912	C
Texas A&M Univ at Kingsville	TX	6,740	LC
Thomas Edison State College	NJ	3,325	SP
Univ of Cincinnati	OH	14,736	C
Univ of Conn	CT	14,608	VC
Univ of Denver	CO	32,148	VC
Univ of Georgia	GA	8,656	VC
Univ of Hawaii at Manoa	HI	9,565	VC
Univ of Memphis	TN	8,560	C
Univ of Miss	MS	7,666	C
Univ of Missouri/Columbia	MO	13,782	VC
Univ of Nevada/Las Vegas	NV	11,566	C
Univ of North Texas	TX	7,629	C
Univ of Okla	OK	9,226	VC
Univ of Pennsylvania	PA	37,960	MC
Univ of St. Thomas	MN	26,918	VC
Univ of S Car at Columbia	SC	10,048	VC
Univ of Texas at Arlington	TX	7,192	LC
Univ of Wisc/Madison	WI	8,262	VC
Univ of Wisc/Milwaukee	WI	9,427	LC
Washington State Univ	WA	11,334	C

RECREATION AND LEISURE SERVICES

School	ST	$IS	SR
Arizona State Univ-Main	AZ	10,048	C
Arkansas Tech Univ	AR	7,299	C
Asbury College	KY	20,704	VC
Austin Peay State Univ	TN	5,814	LC
Belmont Abbey College	NC	23,742	C
Bowling Green State Univ	OH	13,036	C
Brigham Young Univ	UT	8,504	HC
Calif Polytechnic State Univ	CA	8,747	VC
Cal State, Dominguez Hills	CA	5,840	LC
Cal State, Hayward	CA	8,871	LC
Cal State, Northridge	CA	7,757	LC
Calvin College	MI	22,615	NC
Catawba College	NC	20,500	C
Central Missouri State Univ	MO	9,776	C
Central Washington Univ	WA	9,768	C
Chicago State Univ	IL	10,882	C+
Christopher Newport Univ	VA	8,862	VC
Cumberland Univ	TN	16,910	C
East Central Univ	OK	4,968	C
Eastern Conn State Univ	CT	10,362	C
Eastern Mich Univ	MI	11,478	C
Eastern Washington Univ	WA	9,012	C
Emporia State Univ	KS	6,998	C
Ferrum College	VA	21,240	LC
Florida State Univ	FL	9,028	HC
Franklin College	IN		C
Frostburg State Univ	MD	11,114	C
Gallaudet Univ	DC	16,554	SP
Georgetown College	KY	22,000	VC
Georgia Southern Univ	GA	8,540	C
Georgia State Univ	GA	10,658	C
Gordon College	MA	25,982	VC+
Graceland Univ	IA	19,550	C
Grambling State Univ	LA	6,538	NC
Green Mountain College	VT	24,130	C
Greenville College	IL	21,342	C
Hannibal-LaGrange College	MO	13,940	C
Henderson State Univ	AR	7,386	C
High Point Univ	NC	22,480	C
Houghton College	NY	23,984	VC
Indiana State Univ	IN	10,719	LC
Indiana Univ Bloomington	IN	12,389	VC
Ithaca College	NY	31,730	HC
James Madison Univ	VA	10,794	VC
Johnson and Wales Univ	RI	22,965	LC
Kean Univ	NJ	14,479	C
Kent State Univ	OH	12,932	C
Lyndon State College	VT	12,646	LC
Mars Hill College	NC	18,600	LC
Maryville College	TN	25,960	VC
Metropolitan State College of Denver	CO	2,338	LC
Middle Tenn State Univ	TN	8,534	C
Montclair State Univ	NJ	13,790	C
Morris College	SC	10,974	LC
Mount Olive College	NC	14,410	LC
Mountain State Univ	WV	10,212	NC
Murray State Univ	KY	7,816	VC
New Mexico Highlands Univ	NM	6,182	LC
New York Univ	NY	39,406	MC
N Car State Univ	NC	9,886	VC
N Dak State Univ	ND	8,435	C
North Georgia College and State Univ	GA	6,984	C
Northwest Missouri State Univ	MO	9,334	C
Northwest Nazarene Univ	ID	20,360	VC
Ohio Univ	OH	14,448	C
Okla State Univ	OK	9,216	VC
Old Dominion Univ	VA	10,441	C
Oral Roberts Univ	OK	18,490	C
Pacific Lutheran Univ	WA	25,715	VC
Pacific Union College	CA	22,065	C+
Plymouth State Univ	NH	12,298	LC
Purdue Univ/West Lafayette	IN	12,560	VC
Radford Univ	VA	8,500	C
St. Thomas Aquinas College	NY	20,590	LC
Shaw Univ	NC	14,882	C+
Shepherd College	WV	8,608	C
Southeastern Okla State Univ	OK	6,147	C
Southern Conn State Univ	CT	10,310	C
Southern Illinois Univ Carbondale	IL	10,407	C
Southern Wesleyan Univ	SC	19,940	C
Southwest Baptist Univ	MO	15,371	C
Southwest Missouri State Univ	MO	8,918	C
St. Joseph's, Suffolk	NY	11,297	C
SUNY/College at Brockport	NY	12,111	C
Taylor Univ	IN	23,820	VC+
Tenn Wesleyan College	TN	16,540	C
Texas A&M Univ at Galveston	TX	9,948	C+
Texas Tech Univ	TX	10,768	VC
Thomas Edison State College	NJ	3,325	SP
Tougaloo College	MS	9,200	NC
Tri-State Univ-Main Campus	IN	23,600	C
Univ of Delaware	DE	12,616	HC
Univ of Florida	FL	8,580	MC
Univ of Georgia	GA	8,656	VC
Univ of Hawaii at Manoa	HI	9,565	VC
Univ of Illinois at Urbana-Champaign	IL	11,316	HC+
Univ of Iowa	IA	10,923	VC
Univ of Maine at Machias	ME	9,271	LC
Univ of Maine at Presque Isle	ME	9,155	LC
Univ of Memphis	TN	8,560	C
Univ of Mich/Ann Arbor	MI	13,864	HC+
Univ of Minn/Twin Cities	MN	13,160	VC
Univ of Miss	MS	7,666	C
Univ of New Hampshire	NH	14,828	VC
Univ of N Car at Greensboro	NC	8,248	C
Univ of N Dak	ND	8,390	C
Univ of North Texas	TX	7,629	C
Univ of Northern Iowa	IA	9,834	C
Univ of South Alabama	AL	7,760	LC
Univ of S Dak	SD	7,710	C+
Univ of Southern Colo	CO	7,821	LC
Univ of Tenn at Chattanooga	TN	7,783	C
Univ of Toledo	OH	12,479	NC
Univ of Wisc/Madison	WI	8,262	VC
Univ of Wisc/Milwaukee	WI	9,427	LC
Upper Iowa Univ	IA	20,076	C
Voorhees College	SC	11,678	LC
Wartburg College	IA	21,165	VC
West Virginia Univ	WV	9,370	C
Western Kentucky Univ	KY	6,834	C
Western Mich Univ	MI	12,031	C
Western State College of Colo	CO	9,014	C
William Penn Univ	IA	17,575	LC
Winona State Univ	MN		C

RECREATION EDUCATION

School	ST	$IS	SR
Alcorn State Univ	MS	7,290	C
Alderson-Broaddus College	WV	19,640	C
Baylor Univ	TX	23,864	VC
Campbellsville Univ	KY	17,680	C
College of the Ozarks	MO	3,500	VC+
Eastern Washington Univ	WA	9,012	C
Georgia College and State Univ	GA	9,878	C
Georgia Southwestern State Univ	GA	6,013	C
Howard Univ	DC	16,505	C
Johnson State College	VT	11,819	LC
Knoxville College	TN	6,200	LC
Lyndon State College	VT	12,646	LC
Northwest Missouri State Univ	MO	9,334	C
Oral Roberts Univ	OK	18,490	C
Plymouth State Univ	NH	12,298	LC
Prescott College	AZ	13,430	C
St. Mary's College of Calif	CA	32,850	VC
San Francisco State Univ	CA	12,070	C
Southern Univ at New Orleans	LA	995	NC
SUNY/College at Cortland	NY	12,095	C
Sterling College	VT	21,114	C+
Univ of Arkansas	AR	9,855	VC
Univ of Conn	CT	14,608	VC
Univ of Hawaii at Manoa	HI	9,565	VC
Univ of Idaho	ID	8,216	C
Univ of Maine	ME	12,080	C+
Univ of Minn/Duluth	MN	12,470	C
Univ of Nevada/Las Vegas	NV	11,566	C
Univ of New Hampshire	NH	14,828	VC
Univ of Tenn at Knoxville	TN	8,214	C
Warren Wilson College	NC	21,794	VC
Washington State Univ	WA	11,334	C

RECREATION THERAPY

School	ST	$IS	SR
Ashland Univ	OH	24,464	C
Cal State, Northridge	CA	7,757	LC
Catawba College	NC	20,500	C
College of Mount St. Joseph	OH	22,785	C
East Carolina Univ	NC	8,671	C
Eastern Mich Univ	MI	11,478	C
Eastern Washington Univ	WA	9,012	C
Gallaudet Univ	DC	16,554	SP
Georgia Southern Univ	GA	8,540	C
Green Mountain College	VT	24,130	C
Hampton Univ	VA	17,112	C+
Indiana Inst of Technology	IN	21,620	C
Ithaca College	NY	31,730	HC
Lake Superior State Univ	MI	9,034	LC
Lincoln Univ	PA	13,320	C+
Longwood Univ	VA	11,175	C
Mercy College	NY	19,200	NC
Messiah College	PA	25,890	VC+
Shaw Univ	NC	14,882	C+
Shepherd College	WV	8,608	C
Southern Univ and A&M College	LA	7,372	LC
Springfield College	MA	24,520	C
Univ of N Car at Wilmington	NC	8,940	VC
Univ of Southern Maine	ME	11,212	C
Univ of Wisc/La Crosse	WI	8,991	VC
Utica College	NY	28,340	C
West Virginia State College	WV	6,264	NC
Western Carolina Univ	NC	6,742	C
Winston-Salem State Univ	NC	8,926	LC

RECREATIONAL FACILITIES MANAGEMENT

School	ST	$IS	SR
Alaska Pacific Univ	AK	17,910	C
Appalachian State Univ	NC	7,637	VC
Ashland Univ	OH	24,464	C
Barber-Scotia College	NC	13,900	LC
Bluffton College	OH	23,694	C
Cal State, Fresno	CA	8,414	LC
Central Methodist College	MO	16,460	C
College of St. Joseph	VT	19,100	C
Colo State Univ	CO	9,964	VC
Culver-Stockton College	MO	17,850	C
East Carolina Univ	NC	8,671	C
East Texas Baptist Univ	TX	13,914	C
Eastern Mennonite Univ	VA	22,990	C
Elmhurst College	IL	24,630	C
Florida State Univ	FL	9,028	HC
Georgia Southern Univ	GA	8,540	C
Graceland Univ	IA	19,550	C
Green Mountain College	VT	24,130	C
Indiana Wesleyan Univ	IN	19,900	C+
Inter American Univ of PR/ Aguadilla Campus	PR	3,544	
Johnson and Wales Univ	RI	22,965	LC
Johnson State College	VT	11,819	LC
Keystone College	PA	21,405	LC
Lynn Univ	FL	30,750	C
Malone College	OH	20,995	C
Missouri Valley College	MO	18,500	C
New Mexico State Univ	NM	7,932	C
Savannah State Univ	GA	7,328	LC
Shorter College	GA	17,370	C
Sierra Nevada College	NV	26,136	C
Southwestern Okla State Univ	OK	4,801	C
Texas State Univ	TX	9,320	VC
Tri-State Univ-Main Campus	IN	23,600	C
Univ of Central Okla	OK	9,434	C
Univ of Minn/Twin Cities	MN	13,160	VC
Univ of Miss	MS	7,666	C
Univ of Nevada/Las Vegas	NV	11,566	C
Univ of N Car at Chapel Hill	NC	10,117	MC
Univ of St. Francis	IL	22,850	C
Webber International Univ	FL	16,510	C

REHABILITATION THERAPY

School	ST	$IS	SR
Arkansas Tech Univ	AR	7,299	C
Assumption College	MA	29,375	C
Boston Univ	MA	38,194	HC+
Cal State, Los Angeles	CA	5,778	C
Clarion Univ of Pennsylvania	PA	11,272	LC
College of St. Catherine	MN	24,010	VC
East Carolina Univ	NC	8,671	C
East Central Univ	OK	4,968	C
Emporia State Univ	KS	6,998	C
Florida International Univ	FL	9,912	VC
Florida State Univ	FL	9,028	HC
Indiana Univ of Pennsylvania	PA	10,489	C
Ithaca College	NY	31,730	HC
Kean Univ	NJ	14,479	C
Montana State Univ-Billings	MT	9,550	C
Northeastern Univ	MA	35,650	HC
Penn State Univ/Univ Park Campus	PA	15,646	HC
Shaw Univ	NC	14,882	C+

School	ST	$IS	SR
Southern Illinois Univ Carbondale	IL	10,407	C
Southern Univ and A&M College	LA	7,372	LC
Springfield College	MA	24,520	C
Stephen F. Austin State Univ	TX	7,552	C
Stetson Univ	FL	29,495	VC
Thomas Univ	GA	11,490	NC
Univ of Arkansas at Pine Bluff	AR	7,925	C
Univ of Florida	FL	8,580	MC
Univ of Maine at Farmington	ME	10,108	C
Univ of Maryland/Eastern Shore	MD	9,964	C
Univ of Memphis	TN	8,560	C
Univ of N Dak	ND	8,390	C
Univ of North Texas	TX	7,629	C
Univ of Northern Colo	CO	8,987	C
Univ of Tenn at Chattanooga	TN	7,783	C
Univ of Texas-Pan American	TX	5,954	LC
Univ of Wisc/Stout	WI	9,718	C
Wilberforce Univ	OH	14,937	LC
Wright State Univ	OH	11,490	LC

RELIGION

School	ST	$IS	SR
Abilene Christian Univ	TX	18,370	VC
Adrian College	MI	21,950	C
Agnes Scott College	GA	28,230	HC
Albertson College of Idaho	ID	19,415	VC
Albertus Magnus College	CT	23,130	LC
Albion College	MI	25,224	VC
Albright College	PA	30,579	C
Allegheny College	PA	30,280	VC
Alma College	MI	25,566	VC
Alverno College	WI	18,898	C
American Univ	DC	34,585	VC+
Amherst College	MA	37,470	MC
Anderson Univ	IN	19,430	LC
Andrews Univ	MI	19,550	C
Appalachian State Univ	NC	7,637	VC
Arizona State Univ-Main	AZ	10,048	C
Arkansas Baptist College	AR	5,530	NC
Ashland Univ	OH	24,464	C
Atlantic Union College	MA	18,868	C
Augsburg College	MN	25,298	C
Augustana College	IL	26,610	VC+
Augustana College	SD	21,998	VC
Aurora Univ	IL	20,631	C
Austin College	TX	24,747	HC
Averett Univ	VA	23,010	LC
Azusa Pacific Univ	CA	24,720	VC
Baker Univ	KS	19,860	VC
Baldwin-Wallace College	OH	24,678	C
Ball State Univ	IN	8,660	C
Bard College	NY	37,352	HC+
Barton College	NC	19,314	C
Bates College	ME	37,500	MC
Baylor Univ	TX	23,864	VC
Belmont Univ	TN	21,986	VC
Beloit College	WI	29,864	HC
Benedict College	SC	12,662	LC
Benedictine College	KS	20,603	C
Berea College	KY	5,030	VC+
Berry College	GA	21,410	VC
Bethany College	WV	19,845	VC
Bethel College	IN	19,670	C
Bethel College	KS	19,800	C+
Bethel College	MN	25,180	VC
Bethune-Cookman College	FL	16,480	LC
Birmingham-Southern College	AL	25,364	VC+
Bloomfield College	NJ	19,250	LC
Bluefield College	VA	15,575	C
Bluffton College	OH	23,694	C
Boston Univ	MA	38,194	HC+
Bowdoin College	ME	37,790	MC
Bradley Univ	IL	22,910	VC
Brescia Univ	KY	14,225	C
Brewton-Parker College	GA	14,200	LC
Bridgewater College	VA	25,150	C
Bryan College	TN	17,900	VC
Bryn Athyn College of the New Church	PA	12,612	NC
Bryn Mawr College	PA	36,890	HC+
Bucknell Univ	PA	35,262	HC+
Buena Vista Univ	IA	25,406	C
Butler Univ	IN	28,250	VC+
Cabrini College	PA	29,020	C
Calif Lutheran Univ	CA	27,600	LC
Cal State, Bakersfield	CA	6,090	LC
Cal State, Chico	CA	8,598	LC
Cal State, Fullerton	CA	6,648	C
Cal State, Long Beach	CA	8,762	C+
Calumet College of St. Joseph	IN	9,000	LC
Calvin College	MI	22,615	NC
Campbell Univ	NC	18,268	VC
Canisius College	NY	28,163	C+
Capital Univ	OH	26,550	C
Cardinal Stritch Univ	WI	17,620	C
Carleton College	MN	34,395	MC
Carroll College	MT	20,576	VC
Carroll College	WI	22,740	C
Carson-Newman College	TN	16,760	C
Carthage College	WI	25,000	C
Case Western Reserve Univ	OH	32,002	MC
Catawba College	NC	20,500	C
Catholic Univ of America	DC	34,248	VC
Centenary College of Louisiana	LA	23,100	VC+
Central College	IA	21,206	C
Central Methodist College	MO	16,460	C
Central Mich Univ	MI	11,142	C
Central Univ of Bayamon	PR	3,335	
Centre College	KY	27,300	HC
Chaminade Univ of Honolulu	HI	21,430	LC
Chapman Univ	CA	33,118	VC
Charleston Southern Univ	SC	17,122	C
Christian Brothers Univ	TN	22,290	VC
Christopher Newport Univ	VA	8,862	VC
CUNY/Brooklyn College	NY	4,353	C+
CUNY/Hunter College	NY	6,729	C+
CUNY/Queens College	NY	4,362	C
Claflin Univ	SC	14,838	C+
Claremont McKenna College	CA	36,880	MC
Clark Atlanta Univ	GA	19,300	C+
Clarke College	IA	23,165	C
Cleveland State Univ	OH	12,308	LC
Coe College	IA	27,385	VC
Colby College	ME	37,570	MC
Colgate Univ	NY	37,095	MC
College of Charleston	SC	11,887	HC
College of Mount St. Vincent	NY	26,800	C
College of Mount St. Joseph	OH	22,785	C
College of New Rochelle	NY	21,800	C
College of Notre Dame of Maryland	MD	27,700	C
College of Our Lady of the Elms	MA	20,644	C
College of St. Rose	NY	22,864	C
College of St. Scholastica	MN	24,970	C+
College of Santa Fe	NM	25,293	C+
College of the Holy Cross	MA	36,451	MC
College of the Ozarks	MO	3,500	VC+
College of William and Mary	VA	12,224	MC
College of Wooster	OH	31,300	HC
Colo College	CO	36,860	HC
Columbia College	SC	22,658	LC
Columbia Union College	MD	20,543	C
Columbia Univ/Barnard College	NY	36,990	MC
Columbia Univ/Columbia College	NY	38,590	MC
Columbia Univ/School of General Studies	NY	35,000	C
Concordia College	NY	19,200	VC
Concordia College: Moorhead	MN	22,460	VC+
Concordia Univ	CA	24,420	C
Concordia Univ	MI	24,095	C
Concordia Univ Wisc	WI	16,600	C
Concordia Univ, River Forest	IL	23,600	C
Concordia Univ/St.Paul	MN	24,486	C
Conn College	CT	37,900	MC
Converse College	SC	24,710	VC
Cornell College	IA	27,825	VC+
Cornell Univ	NY	38,253	MC
Cornerstone Univ and Grand Rapids Theological Seminary	MI	19,846	C
Covenant College	GA	23,830	VC+
Culver-Stockton College	MO	17,850	C
Cumberland College	KY	16,384	C
Daemen College	NY	22,120	C
Dakota Wesleyan Univ	SD	17,832	C
Dana College	NE	20,280	C
Dartmouth College	NH	37,770	MC
David Lipscomb Univ	TN	16,158	VC
Davidson College	NC	33,274	MC
Davis and Elkins College	WV	20,594	C
Defiance College	OH	22,615	C
Denison Univ	OH	33,050	HC
DePaul Univ	IL	27,580	VC
DePauw Univ	IN	31,500	HC
Dickinson College	PA	35,825	HC
Doane College	NE	20,000	C
Dominican Univ	IL	23,610	C
Dominican Univ of Calif	CA	31,670	C
Dordt College	IA	20,170	VC
Drake Univ	IA	25,120	VC+
Drew Univ/College of Liberal Arts	NJ	35,550	VC
Duke Univ	NC	37,555	MC
Earlham College	IN	29,976	VC+
East Texas Baptist Univ	TX	13,914	C
Eastern Mennonite Univ	VA	22,990	C
Eastern Nazarene College	MA	19,433	LC
Eastern New Mexico Univ	NM	6,762	LC
Eckerd College	FL	28,744	C+
Edgewood College	WI	20,520	C
Edward Waters College	FL	14,374	LC
Elizabethtown College	PA	28,800	C
Elmhurst College	IL	24,630	C
Elon Univ	NC	22,240	VC
Emory & Henry College	VA	21,950	C
Emory Univ	GA	36,872	MC
Erskine College	SC	23,166	VC
Eureka College	IL	24,980	LC
Evangel Univ	MO	15,435	C
Fairfield Univ	CT	35,505	HC
Felician College	NJ	24,300	C
Ferrum College	VA	21,240	LC
Fisk Univ	TN	17,305	LC
Flagler College	FL	11,860	VC+
Florida International Univ	FL	9,912	VC
Florida Memorial College	FL	6,000	LC
Florida Southern College	FL	23,592	C
Florida State Univ	FL	9,028	HC
Fordham Univ	NY	35,066	HC
Franciscan Univ	IA	19,300	C
Franciscan Univ of Steubenville	OH	20,300	VC
Franklin and Marshall College	PA	35,930	HC+
Franklin College	IN		C
Fresno Pacific Univ	CA	22,462	C
Friends Univ	KS	15,962	LC
Furman Univ	SC	28,976	HC+
Gallaudet Univ	DC	16,554	SP
Gardner-Webb Univ	NC	19,300	C
George Fox Univ	OR	26,110	VC
George Mason Univ	VA	9,732	VC
George Washington Univ	DC	41,030	MC
Georgetown College	KY	22,000	VC
Georgetown Univ	DC	38,242	MC
Georgia State Univ	GA	10,658	C
Georgian Court College	NJ	19,040	LC
Gettysburg College	PA	35,646	HC
Gonzaga Univ	WA	26,766	HC
Goshen College	IN	22,450	VC
Grace Bible College	MI	15,890	C
Grace College	IN	19,825	VC
Graceland Univ	IA	19,550	C
Greensboro College	NC	21,750	C
Greenville College	IL	21,342	C
Grinnell College	IA	31,060	HC+
Grove City College	PA	14,228	HC
Guilford College	NC	24,960	VC
Gustavus Adolphus College	MN	27,120	VC+
Hamilton College	NY	37,560	MC
Hamline Univ	MN	27,052	VC
Hampden-Sydney College	VA	28,407	VC
Hampshire College	MA	37,037	HC
Harding Univ	AR	14,890	VC
Hardin-Simmons Univ	TX	14,165	C
Hartwick College	NY	34,650	C+
Harvard Univ/Harvard College	MA	37,928	MC
Hastings College	NE	19,928	VC
Haverford College	PA	37,900	MC
Heidelberg College	OH	20,266	NC
Hellenic College/Holy Cross Greek Orthodox School of Theology	MA	22,815	C
Hendrix College	AR	20,970	VC+
High Point Univ	NC	22,480	C
Hillsdale College	MI	22,450	HC
Hiram College	OH	28,234	VC
Hobart and William Smith Colleges	NY	36,536	HC
Hollins Univ	VA	27,965	VC
Holy Family College	PA	13,710	LC
Holy Names College	CA	27,980	NC
Hood College	MD	27,795	VC
Hope College	MI	25,340	VC
Houghton College	NY	23,984	VC
Humboldt State Univ	CA	9,400	C
Huntingdon College	AL	18,400	VC
Illinois College	IL	19,100	VC
Illinois Wesleyan Univ	IL	30,380	HC+
Indiana State Univ	IN	10,719	LC
Indiana Univ Bloomington	IN	12,389	VC
Indiana Univ of Pennsylvania	PA	10,489	C
Indiana Univ-Purdue Univ Indianapolis	IN	8,257	LC
Indiana Wesleyan Univ	IN	19,900	C+
Iona College	NY	27,988	VC
Iowa State Univ	IA	10,768	VC
James Madison Univ	VA	10,794	VC
Jamestown College	ND	12,600	NC
Jarvis Christian College	TX	9,035	NC
John Carroll Univ	OH	27,658	C+
Judson College	AL	14,650	C
Kalamazoo College	MI	26,955	HC+
Kansas Wesleyan Univ	KS	18,900	VC
Kenyon College	OH	35,370	HC+
La Roche College	PA	22,094	C
La Salle Univ	PA	31,260	VC
La Sierra Univ	CA	19,260	LC
Lafayette College	PA	35,746	MC
LaGrange College	GA	20,500	C
Lakeland College	WI	17,950	C
Lambuth Univ	TN	16,520	C
Lane College	TN	11,178	C+
Lawrence Univ	WI	30,900	HC
Le Moyne College	NY	26,400	VC
Lebanon Valley College	PA	28,870	VC
Lees-McRae College	NC	17,106	LC
Lehigh Univ	PA	37,570	HC+
Lewis and Clark College	OR	30,620	VC
Lewis Univ	IL	22,950	C+
Liberty Univ	VA	17,220	C
Lincoln Univ	PA	13,320	C+
Lindenwood Univ	MO	17,050	VC
Linfield College	OR	27,090	VC
Loras College	IA	24,233	C
Louisiana College	LA	13,450	C
Lourdes College	OH	15,300	LC
Loyola Univ Chicago	IL	31,164	VC
Loyola Univ New Orleans	LA	31,036	VC+
Luther College	IA	25,700	VC
Lycoming College	PA	27,589	C+
Lynchburg College	VA	26,815	C
Lyon College	AR	17,995	VC
Macalester College	MN	31,944	MC
MacMurray College	IL	20,005	LC
Madonna Univ	MI	11,504	VC
Manchester College	IN	23,390	C
Manhattan College	NY	27,400	VC
Manhattanville College	NY	32,420	C+
Mars Hill College	NC	18,600	LC
Martin Univ	IN	10,200	SP
Mary Washington College	VA	10,166	HC
Marygrove College	MI	17,550	C
Maryville College	TN	25,960	VC
Marywood Univ	PA	26,050	C
McDaniel College	MD	28,440	VC
McKendree College	IL	21,120	VC
McMurry Univ	TX	17,846	LC
McPherson College	KS	20,265	C
Mercer Univ	GA	27,516	VC+
Mercyhurst College	PA	20,694	C
Meredith College	NC	23,065	C
Merrimack College	MA	29,625	C
Messiah College	PA	25,890	VC+
Methodist College	NC	19,526	C
Miami Univ	OH	15,033	HC
Mich State Univ	MI	11,933	VC
Middlebury College	VT	38,100	MC
Midland Lutheran College	NE	18,600	C
Millikin Univ	IL	25,555	C
Millsaps College	MS	25,182	VC
Missouri Baptist Univ	MO	18,010	C
Missouri Valley College	MO	18,500	C
Monmouth College	IL	23,600	C
Montclair State Univ	NJ	13,790	C
Montreat College	NC	18,762	C
Moravian College	PA	28,903	VC
Morehouse College	GA	22,728	C
Morgan State Univ	MD	11,470	C
Morningside College	IA	21,610	C
Mount Holyoke College	MA	37,918	HC+
Mount Marty College	SD	15,656	LC
Mount Mercy College	IA	21,400	C
Mount Olive College	NC	14,410	LC
Mount St. Mary's College	CA	28,307	VC
Mount Union College	OH	21,120	C
Mount Vernon Nazarene Univ	OH	18,925	C
Muhlenberg College	PA	31,485	HC
Muskingum College	OH	20,680	C
Naropa Univ	CO	23,364	SP
Nazareth College of Rochester	NY	24,936	VC
Nebr Wesleyan Univ	NE	21,197	C+
New College of Florida	FL	8,906	HC+
New York Univ	NY	39,406	MC
Newberry College	SC	22,871	LC
Niagara Univ	NY	25,050	C
N Car State Univ	NC	9,886	VC
N Car Wesleyan College	NC	17,998	C
North Central College	IL	25,656	VC
North Central Univ	MN	14,904	C
North Park Univ	IL	24,030	C
Northern Arizona Univ	AZ	9,002	C
Northland College	WI	22,170	C+
Northwest College	WA	18,854	C
Northwest Nazarene Univ	ID	20,360	VC
Northwestern College of Iowa	IA	19,640	C+
Northwestern Univ	IL	37,491	MC
Notre Dame de Namur Univ	CA	26,932	LC
Nyack College	NY	18,540	C
Oakland City Univ	IN	16,980	NC
Oakwood College	AL	14,904	C
Oberlin College	OH	36,938	MC
Occidental College	CA	35,922	HC
Ohio Northern Univ	OH	27,765	VC
Ohio Valley College	WV	16,036	C+
Ohio Wesleyan Univ	OH	32,550	VC+
Okla Baptist Univ	OK	15,220	VC
Okla City Univ	OK	19,580	VC
Okla Wesleyan Univ	OK	14,100	LC
Olivet Nazarene Univ	IL	20,480	C
Oral Roberts Univ	OK	18,490	C
Ottawa Univ	KS	11,800	LC
Otterbein College	OH	26,085	C
Ouachita Baptist Univ	AR	18,900	VC
Our Lady of the Lake Univ of San Antonio	TX	17,336	C
Pacific Lutheran Univ	WA	25,715	VC
Pacific Union College	CA	22,065	C+

ST = STATE $IS = IN-STATE COSTS SR = SELECTOR RATING

School	ST	$IS	SR
Palm Beach Atlantic Univ	FL	20,690	C
Paul Quinn College	TX	8,150	LC
Penn State Univ/Univ Park Campus	PA	15,646	HC
Pepperdine Univ	CA	32,830	VC
Pfeiffer Univ	NC	18,980	C
Piedmont College	GA	16,900	C
Pikeville College	KY	14,900	NC
Point Loma Nazarene Univ	CA	21,380	VC
Pomona College	CA	33,960	MC
Pontifical Catholic Univ of PR/Ponce	PR	7,298	
Presbyterian College	SC	25,920	VC
Princeton Univ	NJ	36,649	MC
Principia College	IL	25,044	C+
Purdue Univ/West Lafayette	IN	12,560	VC
Queens Univ of Charlotte	NC	21,840	C
Radford Univ	VA	8,500	C
Randolph-Macon College	VA	27,190	C
Randolph-Macon Woman's College	VA	28,430	VC+
Reed College	OR	36,950	MC
Regis Univ	CO	25,740	C+
Rhodes College	TN	26,466	HC+
Rice Univ	TX	27,550	MC
Richard Stockton College of New Jersey	NJ	12,972	VC
Ripon College	WI	24,995	VC
Roanoke College	VA	27,393	C
Rockford College	IL	28,310	VC
Rocky Mountain College	MT	19,015	C
Rollins College	FL	34,300	VC
Rosemont College	PA	26,175	C
Rutgers, The State Univ of New Jersey/Camden Campus	NJ	14,990	VC
Rutgers, The State Univ of New Jersey/New Brunswick/Piscataway Campus	NJ	15,800	HC
Sacred Heart Univ	CT	29,178	C
St. Andrews Presbyterian College	NC	20,525	C
St. Edward's Univ	TX	20,428	C
St. Francis Univ	PA	25,876	LC
St. John Fisher College	NY	24,870	C
St. Joseph College	CT	29,685	C
St. Joseph's College	IN	24,250	C
St. Joseph's Univ	PA	33,590	VC
St. Lawrence Univ	NY	35,945	VC
St. Leo Univ	FL	20,600	C
St. Martin's College	WA	23,245	C
St. Mary's College	IN	24,474	VC
St. Mary's College of Calif	CA	32,850	VC
St. Mary's College of Maryland	MD	15,908	VC+
St. Michael's College	VT	30,100	VC
St. Norbert College	WI	25,810	C
St. Olaf College	MN	28,500	HC
St. Thomas Aquinas College	NY	20,590	LC
St. Thomas Univ	FL	21,400	LC
St. Xavier Univ	IL	23,144	C
Salem College	NC	24,595	VC
Salve Regina Univ	RI	29,210	C
Samford Univ	AL	18,648	VC
San Diego State Univ	CA	10,321	C
San Jose State Univ	CA	8,187	C
Santa Clara Univ	CA	34,701	HC
Sarah Lawrence College	NY	41,218	HC
Schreiner Univ	TX	20,440	C
Scripps College	CA	35,700	HC+
Seattle Pacific Univ	WA	25,944	VC
Seattle Univ	WA	24,183	VC
Seton Hall Univ	NJ	30,130	VC
Seton Hill Univ	PA	24,930	C
Shaw Univ	NC	14,882	C+
Shenandoah Univ	VA	25,190	NC
Shorter College	GA	17,370	C
Siena College	NY	25,310	VC
Siena Heights Univ	MI	16,140	LC
Silver Lake College of the Holy Family	WI	18,450	LC
Simpson College	CA	20,500	C
Simpson College	IA	23,658	C+
Skidmore College	NY	37,930	HC
Smith College	MA	37,034	HC+
Southeastern College	FL	11,648	LC
Southern Methodist Univ	TX	34,210	HC
Southern Nazarene Univ	OK	14,634	NC
Southern Wesleyan Univ	SC	19,940	C
Southwest Baptist Univ	MO	15,371	C
Southwest Missouri State Univ	MO	8,918	C
Southwestern Adventist Univ	TX	14,798	C
Southwestern Univ	TX	25,410	HC
Spelman College	GA	19,215	C+
Stanford Univ	CA	37,612	MC
SUNY/College at Old Westbury	NY	12,784	C
SUNY/Univ at Albany	NY	12,951	HC
SUNY/Univ at Stony Brook	NY	12,763	HC
Stetson Univ	FL	29,495	VC
Stillman College	AL	11,370	LC
Stonehill College	MA	30,752	HC
Susquehanna Univ	PA	29,990	VC
Swarthmore College	PA	37,716	MC
Sweet Briar College	VA	27,940	C
Syracuse Univ	NY	34,720	HC
Tabor College	KS	19,500	NC
Temple Univ	PA	15,912	C
Texas A&M Univ at Commerce	TX	8,994	C
Texas Christian Univ	TX	23,410	VC
Texas Wesleyan Univ	TX	16,245	C
Thiel College	PA	20,970	C
Thomas Edison State College	NJ	3,325	SP
Toccoa Falls College	GA	15,600	C
Towson Univ	MD	12,694	VC
Transylvania Univ	KY	23,780	VC+
Trevecca Nazarene Univ	TN	17,548	C
Trinity College	CT	38,040	HC+
Trinity Univ	TX	26,466	HC+
Truman State Univ	MO	9,728	HC+
Tufts Univ	MA	38,233	MC
Tulane Univ	LA	37,451	HC+
Union College	NE	17,130	C
Union Univ	TN	18,800	VC
Universidad Adventista de las Antillas	PR	5,460	
Univ of Alabama	AL	9,040	C+
Univ of Arizona	AZ	10,413	VC
Univ of Bridgeport	CT	25,924	LC
Univ of Calif at Berkeley	CA	15,563	MC
Univ of Calif at Davis	CA	14,995	VC
Univ of Calif at Los Angeles	CA	15,330	MC
Univ of Calif at Riverside	CA	15,330	C
Univ of Calif at San Diego	CA	14,127	HC
Univ of Calif at Santa Barbara	CA	11,732	VC
Univ of Calif at Santa Cruz	CA	16,505	VC
Univ of Central Arkansas	AR	6,388	C
Univ of Chicago	IL	35,087	MC
Univ of Colo at Boulder	CO	10,774	VC
Univ of Dayton	OH	24,850	VC
Univ of Denver	CO	32,148	VC
Univ of Detroit Mercy	MI	25,582	C
Univ of Dubuque	IA	20,950	C
Univ of Evansville	IN	24,190	VC
Univ of Findlay	OH	23,962	NC
Univ of Florida	FL	8,580	MC
Univ of Georgia	GA	8,656	VC
Univ of Great Falls	MT	15,360	C
Univ of Hawaii at Manoa	HI	9,565	VC
Univ of Illinois at Urbana-Champaign	IL	11,316	HC+
Univ of Indianapolis	IN	22,560	VC
Univ of Iowa	IA	10,923	VC
Univ of Kansas	KS	8,923	VC
Univ of La Verne	CA	28,600	C
Univ of Mary Hardin-Baylor	TX	17,268	C
Univ of Miami	FL	34,608	HC
Univ of Mich/Ann Arbor	MI	13,864	HC+
Univ of Missouri/Columbia	MO	13,782	VC
Univ of Mobile	AL	13,620	C
Univ of N Car at Chapel Hill	NC	10,117	MC
Univ of N Car at Charlotte	NC	8,185	C
Univ of N Car at Greensboro	NC	8,248	C
Univ of N Car at Pembroke	NC	6,929	LC
Univ of N Car at Wilmington	NC	8,940	VC
Univ of N Dak	ND	8,390	C
Univ of Northern Iowa	IA	9,834	C
Univ of Okla	OK	9,226	VC
Univ of Oregon	OR	11,479	VC
Univ of Pennsylvania	PA	37,960	MC
Univ of Pittsburgh at Pittsburgh	PA	16,074	HC
Univ of Puget Sound	WA	31,760	HC
Univ of Redlands	CA	32,576	VC
Univ of Richmond	VA	30,100	MC
Univ of Rochester	NY	32,979	HC
Univ of St. Francis	IN	20,964	C
Univ of San Diego	CA	33,156	HC
Univ of San Francisco	CA	34,700	VC
Univ of Sioux Falls	SD	16,390	C
Univ of S Car at Columbia	SC	10,048	VC
Univ of South Florida	FL	9,454	C
Univ of Southern Calif	CA	37,459	MC
Univ of Tenn at Knoxville	TN	8,214	C
Univ of Texas at Austin	TX	10,630	HC
Univ of the Incarnate Word	TX	21,772	LC
Univ of the Ozarks	AR	16,574	C
Univ of the Pacific	CA	31,090	VC
Univ of the South	TN	30,855	HC
Univ of Tulsa	OK	22,090	VC+
Univ of Vermont	VT	16,316	VC
Univ of Virginia	VA	11,740	MC
Univ of Washington	WA	10,361	VC
Univ of West Florida	FL	8,470	C
Univ of Wisc/Eau Claire	WI	8,463	VC
Univ of Wisc/Milwaukee	WI	9,427	LC
Univ of Wisc/Oshkosh	WI	6,130	LC
Ursinus College	PA	34,400	VC
Ursuline College	OH	22,728	LC
Valparaiso Univ	IN	26,118	VC+
Vanderbilt Univ	TN	37,897	MC
Vassar College	NY	37,030	MC
Villanova Univ	PA	35,050	HC
Virginia Commonwealth Univ	VA	9,030	C
Virginia Intermont College	VA	19,800	C
Virginia Union Univ	VA	15,358	LC
Virginia Wesleyan College	VA	25,350	C
Viterbo Univ	WI	20,430	C
Wabash College	IN	27,932	VC
Wake Forest Univ	NC	34,090	MC
Walla Walla College	WA	21,600	NC
Walsh Univ	OH	20,890	C
Wartburg College	IA	21,165	VC
Washburn Univ of Topeka	KS	8,984	NC
Washington and Lee Univ	VA	29,663	MC
Washington State Univ	WA	11,334	C
Washington Univ in St. Louis	MO	38,293	MC
Wayland Baptist Univ	TX	11,919	NC
Webster Univ	MO	21,848	VC
Wellesley College	MA	36,516	MC
Wells College	NY	21,122	VC
Wesleyan College	GA	17,870	VC
Wesleyan Univ	CT	35,139	MC
West Chester Univ of Pennsylvania	PA	11,164	C
West Virginia Wesleyan College	WV	22,920	C
Western Kentucky Univ	KY	6,834	C
Western Mich Univ	MI	12,031	C
Westminster College	MO	18,150	C+
Westminster College	PA	22,960	C
Westmont College	CA	33,062	VC+
Wheaton College	IL	21,934	HC
Wheaton College	MA	36,330	HC
Wheeling Jesuit Univ	WV	22,660	C
Whitman College	WA	32,526	HC+
Whittier College	CA	29,108	C
Whitworth College	WA	26,428	VC+
Wiley College	TX	8,100	LC
Willamette Univ	OR	32,032	VC+
William Carey College	MS	10,150	LC
William Jewell College	MO	21,320	VC
Williams Baptist College	AR	11,950	C
Williams College	MA	32,270	MC
Wilmington College	OH	24,172	LC
Wilson College	PA	23,912	C
Wingate Univ	NC	21,200	C
Winthrop Univ	SC	11,302	C
Wittenberg Univ	OH	31,316	VC
Wofford College	SC	26,710	HC
Wright State Univ	OH	11,490	LC
Yale Univ	CT	37,000	MC
Yeshiva Univ	NY	21,400	C
Youngstown State Univ	OH	11,148	NC

RELIGIOUS EDUCATION

School	ST	$IS	SR
Andrews Univ	MI	19,550	C
Baylor Univ	TX	23,864	VC
Brown Univ	RI	38,174	MC
Campbellsville Univ	KY	17,680	C
Clearwater Christian College	FL	13,160	LC
College of Mount St. Joseph	OH	22,785	C
Concordia Univ/St.Paul	MN	24,486	C
Cornerstone Univ and Grand Rapids Theological Seminary	MI	19,846	C
Dallas Baptist Univ	TX	15,300	VC
Franciscan Univ of Steubenville	OH	20,300	VC
Grace Bible College	MI	15,890	C
Huntingdon College	AL	18,400	VC
Kansas Wesleyan Univ	KS	18,900	VC
La Roche College	PA	22,094	C
Lee Univ	TN	13,780	NC
Lenoir-Rhyne College	NC	19,186	C
Louisiana College	LA	13,450	C
Loyola Univ New Orleans	LA	31,036	VC+
Marian College	IN	23,030	C
Mercyhurst College	PA	20,694	C
Missouri Baptist Univ	MO	18,010	C
Morris College	SC	10,974	LC
Mount Vernon Nazarene Univ	OH	18,925	C
Muskingum College	OH	20,680	C
North Central Univ	MN	14,904	C
Northwest College	WA	18,854	C
Nyack College	NY	18,540	C
Oakwood College	AL	14,904	C
Okla Christian Univ	OK	17,690	NC
Oral Roberts Univ	OK	18,490	C
Pfeiffer Univ	NC	18,980	C
Point Loma Nazarene Univ	CA	21,380	VC
Quincy Univ	IL	22,330	C
St. Edward's Univ	TX	20,428	C
St. Mary-of-the-Woods College	IN	23,280	C
St. Mary's College	MI	13,314	LC
St. Vincent College	PA	25,530	VC
Seattle Pacific Univ	WA	25,944	VC
Simpson College	CA	20,500	C
Southern Adventist Univ	TN	17,080	C
Southern Nazarene Univ	OK	14,634	NC
Southwest Baptist Univ	MO	15,371	C
Sterling College	KS	18,763	C
Tenn Wesleyan College	TN	16,540	C
Thiel College	PA	20,970	C
Trinity Bible College	ND		
Union College	NE	17,130	C
Vanguard Univ of Southern Calif	CA	22,208	C
Wayland Baptist Univ	TX	11,919	NC
West Virginia Wesleyan College	WV	22,920	C
Williams Baptist College	AR	11,950	C

RELIGIOUS MUSIC

School	ST	$IS	SR
Alderson-Broaddus College	WV	19,640	C
Baylor Univ	TX	23,864	VC
Belhaven College	MS	16,040	C+
Bethel College	IN	19,670	C
Campbellsville Univ	KY	17,680	C
Cedarville Univ	OH	19,954	VC
Centenary College of Louisiana	LA	23,100	VC+
Charleston Southern Univ	SC	17,122	C
Clearwater Christian College	FL	13,160	LC
College of the Ozarks	MO	3,500	VC+
Columbia College	SC	22,658	LC
Concordia College	NY	19,200	VC
Concordia Univ at Austin	TX	20,450	LC
Concordia Univ Wisc	WI	16,600	C
Concordia Univ/St.Paul	MN	24,486	C
Cumberland College	KY	16,384	C
Drake Univ	IA	25,120	VC+
East Texas Baptist Univ	TX	13,914	C
Eastern Nazarene College	MA	19,433	LC
Evangel Univ	MO	15,435	C
Furman Univ	SC	28,976	HC+
Gardner-Webb Univ	NC	19,300	C
Georgetown College	KY	22,000	VC
Grand Canyon Univ	AZ	30,000	LC
Greenville College	IL	21,342	C
Grove City College	PA	14,228	HC
Hannibal-LaGrange College	MO	13,940	C
Houston Baptist Univ	TX	16,905	C
Indiana Wesleyan Univ	IN	19,900	C+
Johnson C. Smith Univ	NC	18,108	C
Kentucky Christian College	KY	13,472	C
LaGrange College	GA	20,500	C
Lenoir-Rhyne College	NC	19,186	C
Louisiana College	LA	13,450	C
Madonna Univ	MI	11,504	VC
Malone College	OH	20,995	C
Marywood Univ	PA	26,050	C
McKendree College	IL	21,120	VC
Milligan College	TN	19,860	C+
Miss College	MS	14,574	C
Missouri Baptist Univ	MO	18,010	C
North Central Univ	MN	14,904	C
Northwest College	WA	18,854	C
Northwestern College of Iowa	IA	19,640	C+
Nyack College	NY	18,540	C
Okla Wesleyan Univ	OK	14,100	LC
Oral Roberts Univ	OK	18,490	C
Palm Beach Atlantic Univ	FL	20,690	C
Pfeiffer Univ	NC	18,980	C
St. Olaf College	MN	28,500	HC
Samford Univ	AL	18,648	VC
Seton Hill Univ	PA	24,930	C
Shenandoah Univ	VA	25,190	NC
Shorter College	GA	17,370	C
Southeastern College	FL	11,648	LC
Southwest Baptist Univ	MO	15,371	C
Susquehanna Univ	PA	29,990	VC
Tenn Wesleyan College	TN	16,540	C
Texas Christian Univ	TX	23,410	VC
Toccoa Falls College	GA	15,600	C
Trevecca Nazarene Univ	TN	17,548	C
Union Univ	TN	18,800	VC
Univ of Hartford	CT	31,080	C
Warner Pacific College	OR	21,900	C
Warner Southern College	FL	16,738	LC
Wartburg College	IA	21,165	VC
Wayland Baptist Univ	TX	11,919	NC
Westminster Choir College of Rider Univ	NJ	25,400	SP
Westminster College	PA	22,960	C
William Carey College	MS	10,150	LC
William Tyndale College	MI	12,170	NC
Williams Baptist College	AR	11,950	C

RESPIRATORY THERAPY

School	ST	$IS	SR
Armstrong Atlantic State Univ	GA	7,102	C
Bellarmine Univ	KY	24,110	VC
Boise State Univ	ID	7,657	LC
College of St. Catherine	MN	24,010	VC
Columbia Union College	MD	20,543	C
Dakota State Univ	SD	7,466	C
Gannon Univ	PA	23,260	C
Georgia State Univ	GA	10,658	C
Gwynedd-Mercy College	PA	24,225	C
Indiana Univ Kokomo	IN	4,463	LC
Indiana Univ of Pennsylvania	PA	10,489	C

School	ST	$IS	SR
Indiana Univ-Purdue Univ Indianapolis	IN	8,257	LC
La Roche College	PA	22,094	C
Midwestern State Univ	TX	8,045	LC
Mountain State Univ	WV	10,212	NC
National-Louis Univ	IL	16,240	LC
Nebr Methodist College of Nursing and Allied Health	NE	11,900	SP
N Dak State Univ	ND	8,435	C
Ohio State Univ	OH	13,080	VC+
Point Park Univ	PA	21,840	C
Quinnipiac Univ	CT	30,570	VC
Salisbury Univ	MD	12,664	VC
Shenandoah Univ	VA	25,190	NC
Southern Illinois Univ Carbondale	IL	10,407	C
Southwest Missouri State Univ	MO	8,918	C
SUNY/Univ at Stony Brook	NY	12,763	HC
Tenn State Univ	TN	9,048	LC
Texas Southern Univ	TX	8,920	NC
Texas State Univ	TX	9,320	VC
Thomas Edison State College	NJ	3,325	SP
Univ of Alabama at Birmingham	AL	12,901	C
Univ of Bridgeport	CT	25,924	LC
Univ of Central Florida	FL	10,038	VC
Univ of Hartford	CT	31,080	C
Univ of Indianapolis	IN	22,560	VC
Univ of Kansas	KS	8,923	VC
Univ of Mary	ND	12,900	C+
Univ of Missouri/Columbia	MO	13,782	VC
Univ of South Alabama	AL	7,760	LC
Univ of the Ozarks	AR	16,574	C
Wheeling Jesuit Univ	WV	22,660	C
York College of Pennsylvania	PA	14,500	VC
Youngstown State Univ	OH	11,148	NC

RETAILING

School	ST	$IS	SR
Central Mich Univ	MI	11,142	C
David N. Myers College	OH	9,475	C
Johnson and Wales Univ	RI	22,965	LC
Marymount Univ	VA	23,668	C
Montclair State Univ	NJ	13,790	C
Mount Ida College	MA	25,596	LC
New Jersey City Univ	NJ	11,850	LC
Philadelphia Univ	PA	27,354	C
Purdue Univ/West Lafayette	IN	12,560	VC
Siena Heights Univ	MI	16,140	LC
Southern New Hampshire Univ	NH	26,242	C
Syracuse Univ	NY	34,720	HC
Thomas Edison State College	NJ	3,325	SP
Univ of Arizona	AZ	10,413	VC
Univ of Memphis	TN	8,560	C
Univ of Minn/Twin Cities	MN	13,160	VC
Univ of S Car at Columbia	SC	10,048	VC
Univ of Tenn at Knoxville	TN	8,214	C
Univ of Wisc/Madison	WI	8,262	VC
Univ of Wisc/Stout	WI	9,718	C
Youngstown State Univ	OH	11,148	NC

ROMANCE LANGUAGES AND LITERATURE

School	ST	$IS	SR
Boston College	MA	33,284	MC
Bowdoin College	ME	37,790	MC
Bryn Mawr College	PA	36,890	HC+
Cameron Univ	OK	5,692	NC
Carleton College	MN	34,395	MC
CUNY/City College	NY	4,230	C+
Clark Univ	MA	32,115	VC
Colo College	CO	36,860	HC
Dartmouth College	NH	37,770	MC
DePauw Univ	IN	31,500	HC
Dowling College	NY	23,870	LC
Haverford College	PA	37,900	MC
Johns Hopkins Univ	MD	38,372	MC
Manhattanville College	NY	32,420	C+
Mount Holyoke College	MA	37,918	HC+
New York Univ	NY	39,406	MC
Oberlin College	OH	36,938	MC
Olivet Nazarene Univ	IL	20,480	C
Point Loma Nazarene Univ	CA	21,380	VC
Princeton Univ	NJ	36,649	MC
St. Thomas Aquinas College	NY	20,590	LC
Univ of Chicago	IL	35,087	MC
Univ of Georgia	GA	8,656	VC
Univ of Maine	ME	12,080	C+
Univ of Maryland/College Park	MD	14,227	HC
Univ of Mich/Ann Arbor	MI	13,864	HC+
Univ of Nevada/Las Vegas	NV	11,566	C
Univ of N Car at Chapel Hill	NC	10,117	MC
Univ of Notre Dame	IN	34,442	MC
Univ of Oregon	OR	11,479	VC
Univ of Pennsylvania	PA	37,960	MC
Univ of PR/Rio Piedras	PR	5,730	
Washington and Lee Univ	VA	29,663	MC
Washington Univ in St. Louis	MO	38,293	MC
Wesleyan Univ	CT	35,139	MC
Wheeling Jesuit Univ	WV	22,660	C

RURAL ECONOMICS

School	ST	$IS	SR
Univ of Alaska Fairbanks	AK	9,295	C
Univ of Idaho	ID	8,216	C

RURAL SOCIOLOGY

School	ST	$IS	SR
Auburn Univ	AL	10,396	VC
Cornell Univ	NY	38,253	MC
S Dak State Univ	SD	7,782	C
Univ of Wisc/Madison	WI	8,262	VC

RUSSIAN

School	ST	$IS	SR
Amherst College	MA	37,470	MC
Arizona State Univ-Main	AZ	10,048	C
Bard College	NY	37,352	HC+
Bates College	ME	37,500	MC
Baylor Univ	TX	23,864	VC
Beloit College	WI	29,864	HC
Bowdoin College	ME	37,790	MC
Bowling Green State Univ	OH	13,036	C
Brandeis Univ	MA	38,198	MC
Brigham Young Univ	UT	8,504	HC
Bryn Mawr College	PA	36,890	HC+
Bucknell Univ	PA	35,262	HC+
Carleton College	MN	34,395	MC
Central Washington Univ	WA	9,768	C
CUNY/Brooklyn College	NY	4,353	C+
CUNY/Herbert H. Lehman College	NY	3,320	LC
CUNY/Hunter College	NY	6,729	C+
CUNY/Queens College	NY	4,362	C
Colgate Univ	NY	37,095	MC
College of the Holy Cross	MA	36,451	MC
Colo College	CO	36,860	HC
Columbia Univ/Barnard College	NY	36,990	MC
Columbia Univ/Columbia College	NY	38,590	MC
Cornell College	IA	27,825	VC+
Cornell Univ	NY	38,253	MC
Dartmouth College	NH	37,770	MC
Dickinson College	PA	35,825	HC
Drew Univ/College of Liberal Arts	NJ	35,550	VC
Eckerd College	FL	28,744	C+
Ferrum College	VA	21,240	LC
Florida State Univ	FL	9,028	HC
Gallaudet Univ	DC	16,554	SP
George Washington Univ	DC	41,030	MC
Georgetown Univ	DC	38,242	MC
Goucher College	MD	32,650	HC
Grace College	IN	19,825	VC
Grinnell College	IA	31,060	HC+
Gustavus Adolphus College	MN	27,120	VC+
Harvard Univ/Harvard College	MA	37,928	MC
Haverford College	PA	37,900	MC
Hofstra Univ	NY	27,112	VC
Howard Univ	DC	16,505	C
Illinois Wesleyan Univ	IL	30,380	HC+
Indiana State Univ	IN	10,719	LC
Indiana Univ of Pennsylvania	PA	10,489	C
Iowa State Univ	IA	10,768	VC
Juniata College	PA	29,080	VC
Kent State Univ	OH	12,932	C
Knox College	IL	30,294	VC+
La Salle Univ	PA	31,260	VC
Lawrence Univ	WI	30,900	HC
Lincoln Univ	PA	13,320	C+
Loyola Univ New Orleans	LA	31,036	VC+
Macalester College	MN	31,944	MC
Marlboro College	VT	29,055	VC+
Miami Univ	OH	15,033	HC
Mich State Univ	MI	11,933	VC
Middlebury College	VT	38,100	MC
Mount Holyoke College	MA	37,918	HC+
New York Univ	NY	39,406	MC
Northern Illinois Univ	IL	11,472	C
Oakland Univ	MI	10,800	C
Oberlin College	OH	36,938	MC
Ohio State Univ	OH	13,080	VC+
Ohio Univ	OH	14,448	C
Okla State Univ	OK	9,216	VC
Penn State Univ/Univ Park Campus	PA	15,646	HC
Pomona College	CA	33,960	MC
Portland State Univ	OR	12,453	C
Purdue Univ/West Lafayette	IN	12,560	VC
Rider Univ	NJ	30,900	C
Rutgers, The State Univ of New Jersey/New Brunswick/Piscataway Campus	NJ	15,800	HC
St. Louis Univ	MO	29,780	VC+
St. Olaf College	MN	28,500	HC
San Diego State Univ	CA	10,321	C
San Francisco State Univ	CA	12,070	C
Sarah Lawrence College	NY	41,218	HC
Seattle Pacific Univ	WA	25,944	VC
Smith College	MA	37,034	HC+
Southern Illinois Univ Carbondale	IL	10,407	C
Southern Methodist Univ	TX	34,210	HC
SUNY/Univ at Albany	NY	12,951	HC
Swarthmore College	PA	37,716	MC
Syracuse Univ	NY	34,720	HC
Temple Univ	PA	15,912	C
Texas A&M Univ	TX	11,081	HC
Trinity College	CT	38,040	HC+
Trinity Univ	TX	26,466	HC+
Truman State Univ	MO	9,728	HC+
Tufts Univ	MA	38,233	MC
Tulane Univ	LA	37,451	HC+
Univ of Akron	OH	13,134	NC
Univ of Alabama	AL	9,040	C+
Univ of Arizona	AZ	10,413	VC
Univ of Calif at Davis	CA	14,995	VC
Univ of Calif at Riverside	CA	15,300	C
Univ of Chicago	IL	35,087	MC
Univ of Florida	FL	8,580	MC
Univ of Hawaii at Manoa	HI	9,565	VC
Univ of Illinois at Chicago	IL	13,418	C
Univ of Iowa	IA	10,923	VC
Univ of Kentucky	KY	7,765	C
Univ of Maryland/Baltimore County	MD	14,668	VC+
Univ of Maryland/College Park	MD	14,227	HC
Univ of Mass Boston	MA	6,227	C
Univ of Mich/Ann Arbor	MI	13,864	HC+
Univ of Minn/Twin Cities	MN	13,160	VC
Univ of Missouri/Columbia	MO	13,782	VC
Univ of Montana	MT	9,395	C
Univ of Nebr at Lincoln	NE	9,975	C+
Univ of New Hampshire	NH	14,828	VC
Univ of N Car at Chapel Hill	NC	10,117	MC
Univ of Notre Dame	IN	34,442	MC
Univ of Okla	OK	9,226	VC
Univ of Oregon	OR	11,479	VC
Univ of Pittsburgh at Pittsburgh	PA	16,074	HC
Univ of Rochester	NY	32,979	HC
Univ of St. Thomas	MN	26,918	VC
Univ of South Florida	FL	9,454	C
Univ of Southern Calif	CA	37,459	MC
Univ of Tenn at Knoxville	TN	8,214	C
Univ of Texas at Arlington	TX	7,192	LC
Univ of Texas at Austin	TX	10,630	HC
Univ of the South	TN	30,855	HC
Univ of Utah	UT	9,205	C
Univ of Vermont	VT	16,316	VC
Univ of Wisc/Madison	WI	8,262	VC
Univ of Wisc/Milwaukee	WI	9,427	LC
Univ of Wyoming	WY	8,636	C
Vanderbilt Univ	TN	37,897	MC
Washington State Univ	WA	11,334	C
Washington Univ in St. Louis	MO	38,293	MC
Wayne State Univ	MI	11,774	C
Wellesley College	MA	36,516	MC
Wesleyan Univ	CT	35,139	MC
West Chester Univ of Pennsylvania	PA	11,164	C
Wheaton College	MA	36,330	HC
Williams College	MA	32,270	MC
Wittenberg Univ	OH	31,316	VC
Yale Univ	CT	37,000	MC

RUSSIAN AND SLAVIC STUDIES

School	ST	$IS	SR
American Univ	DC	34,585	VC+
Augsburg College	MN	25,298	C
Bard College	NY	37,352	HC+
Baylor Univ	TX	23,864	VC
Boston College	MA	33,284	MC
Brown Univ	RI	38,174	MC
Cal State, Fullerton	CA	6,648	C
Colgate Univ	NY	37,095	MC
College of the Holy Cross	MA	36,451	MC
College of Wooster	OH	31,300	HC
Columbia Univ/Columbia College	NY	38,590	MC
Concordia College: Moorhead	MN	22,460	VC+
Conn College	CT	37,900	MC
Cornell Univ	NY	38,253	MC
Dartmouth College	NH	37,770	MC
DePauw Univ	IN	31,500	HC
Dickinson College	PA	35,825	HC
Emory Univ	GA	36,872	MC
Florida State Univ	FL	9,028	HC
George Mason Univ	VA	9,732	VC
Hamilton College	NY	37,560	MC
Harvard Univ/Harvard College	MA	37,928	MC
Hobart and William Smith Colleges	NY	36,536	HC
Indiana Univ Bloomington	IN	12,389	VC
Kent State Univ	OH	12,932	C
Knox College	IL	30,294	VC+
Lafayette College	PA	35,746	MC
Lehigh Univ	PA	37,570	HC+
Louisiana State Univ and A&M College	LA	9,126	VC
Macalester College	MN	31,944	MC
Mass Inst of Technology	MA	38,310	MC
Middlebury College	VT	38,100	MC
Muhlenberg College	PA	31,485	HC
Oakland Univ	MI	10,800	C
Randolph-Macon Woman's College	VA	28,430	VC+
Rhodes College	TN	26,466	HC+
Rice Univ	TX	27,550	MC
Rutgers, The State Univ of New Jersey/New Brunswick/Piscataway Campus	NJ	15,800	HC
St. Olaf College	MN	28,500	HC
San Diego State Univ	CA	10,321	C
Sarah Lawrence College	NY	41,218	HC
Simon's Rock College of Bard	MA	36,580	HC
Smith College	MA	37,034	HC+
Southern Methodist Univ	TX	34,210	HC
SUNY/Univ at Albany	NY	12,951	HC
Stetson Univ	FL	29,495	VC
Syracuse Univ	NY	34,720	HC
Texas State Univ	TX	9,320	VC
Texas Tech Univ	TX	10,768	VC
Tufts Univ	MA	38,233	MC
Tulane Univ	LA	37,451	HC+
Union College	NY	36,005	HC
Univ of Alaska Fairbanks	AK	9,295	C
Univ of Calif at Los Angeles	CA	15,330	MC
Univ of Calif at San Diego	CA	14,127	HC
Univ of Calif at Santa Cruz	CA	16,505	VC
Univ of Colo at Boulder	CO	10,774	VC
Univ of Denver	CO	32,148	VC
Univ of Houston	TX	9,818	C
Univ of Illinois at Urbana-Champaign	IL	11,316	HC+
Univ of Iowa	IA	10,923	VC
Univ of Kansas	KS	8,923	VC
Univ of Maryland/College Park	MD	14,227	HC
Univ of Mass Amherst	MA	13,980	C+
Univ of Mich/Ann Arbor	MI	13,864	HC+
Univ of Minn/Twin Cities	MN	13,160	VC
Univ of N Car at Chapel Hill	NC	10,117	MC
Univ of Northern Iowa	IA	9,834	C
Univ of St. Thomas	MN	26,918	VC
Univ of Tenn at Knoxville	TN	8,214	C
Univ of Texas at Austin	TX	10,630	HC
Univ of the South	TN	30,855	HC
Univ of Tulsa	OK	22,090	VC+
Univ of Vermont	VT	16,316	VC
Univ of Washington	WA	10,361	VC
Villanova Univ	PA	35,050	HC
Washington Univ in St. Louis	MO	38,293	MC
Wesleyan Univ	CT	35,139	MC
Wheaton College	MA	36,330	HC

RUSSIAN LANGUAGES AND LITERATURE

School	ST	$IS	SR
New College of Florida	FL	8,906	HC+
Ouachita Baptist Univ	AR	18,900	VC
Reed College	OR	36,950	MC
SUNY/Univ at Stony Brook	NY	12,763	HC
Univ of Calif at Los Angeles	CA	15,330	MC
Univ of Illinois at Urbana-Champaign	IL	11,316	HC+
Washington and Lee Univ	VA	29,663	MC
Wellesley College	MA	36,516	MC

SAFETY AND SECURITY TECHNOLOGY

School	ST	$IS	SR
Farmingdale SUNY	NY	12,891	C
Indiana Univ of Pennsylvania	PA	10,489	C
Lewis Univ	IL	22,950	C+
Madonna Univ	MI	11,504	VC
Marshall Univ	WV	9,116	C
St. John's Univ	NY	30,180	C
Univ of Wisc/Whitewater	WI	8,626	C
Youngstown State Univ	OH	11,148	NC

SAFETY MANAGEMENT

School	ST	$IS	SR
Central Missouri State Univ	MO	9,776	C
CUNY/John Jay College of Criminal Justice	NY	4,259	C
College of the Ozarks	MO	3,500	VC+
Franklin Univ	OH	6,720	SP
Illinois State Univ	IL	10,944	C+
Indiana State Univ	IN	10,719	LC
Keene State College	NH	12,212	C
S Dak State Univ	SD	7,782	C
Southern Christian Univ	AL	9,440	LC

SAFETY SCIENCE

School	ST	$IS	SR
Central Washington Univ	WA	9,768	C
Embry-Riddle Aeronautical Univ	AZ	27,710	C+

ST = STATE $IS = IN-STATE COSTS SR = SELECTOR RATING

School	ST	$IS	SR
Embry-Riddle Aeronautical Univ	FL	27,730	C+

SANSKRIT AND INDIAN STUDIES

School	ST	$IS	SR
Harvard Univ/Harvard College	MA	37,928	MC

SCANDINAVIAN LANGUAGES

School	ST	$IS	SR
Augsburg College	MN	25,298	C
Augustana College	IL	26,610	VC+
Gustavus Adolphus College	MN	27,120	VC+
Pacific Lutheran Univ	WA	25,715	VC
Univ of Calif at Berkeley	CA	15,563	MC
Univ of Calif at Los Angeles	CA	15,330	MC
Univ of Minn/Twin Cities	MN	13,160	VC
Univ of N Dak	ND	8,390	C
Univ of Texas at Austin	TX	10,630	HC
Univ of Washington	WA	10,361	VC

SCANDINAVIAN STUDIES

School	ST	$IS	SR
Augsburg College	MN	25,298	C
Concordia College: Moorhead	MN	22,460	VC+
Luther College	IA	25,700	VC
Pacific Lutheran Univ	WA	25,715	VC
Univ of Mich/Ann Arbor	MI	13,864	HC+
Univ of Wisc/Madison	WI	8,262	VC

SCHOOL PSYCHOLOGY

School	ST	$IS	SR
Crichton College	TN	15,215	C
Eastern Mich Univ	MI	11,478	C
Southwestern Okla State Univ	OK	4,801	C

SCIENCE

School	ST	$IS	SR
Alfred Univ	NY	28,290	C
Alvernia College	PA	23,212	LC
Alverno College	WI	18,898	C
American International College	MA	24,690	LC
Arcadia Univ	PA	29,890	C
Brandeis Univ	MA	38,198	MC
Buena Vista Univ	IA	25,406	C
Caribbean Univ	PR	3,000	
Cheyney Univ of Pennsylvania	PA	9,993	C
Clarkson Univ	NY	32,226	VC
Coe College	IA	27,385	VC
Colo Christian Univ	CO	21,182	VC
Concordia Univ	MI	24,095	C
Drexel Univ	PA	27,655	VC
East Stroudsburg Univ of Pennsylvania	PA	10,336	C
Eastern Nazarene College	MA	19,433	LC
Elizabethtown College	PA	28,800	C
Fairleigh Dickinson Univ/ Metropolitan Campus	NJ	28,584	C
Ferrum College	VA	21,240	LC
Fordham Univ	NY	35,066	HC
Fort Hays State Univ	KS	7,363	C
Frostburg State Univ	MD	11,114	C
Gannon Univ	PA	23,260	C
Grace College	IN	19,825	VC
Graceland Univ	IA	19,550	C
Grinnell College	IA	31,060	HC+
Hampshire College	MA	37,037	HC
Hawaii Pacific Univ	HI	19,218	C
Heritage College	WA	6,720	NC
Houghton College	NY	23,984	VC
Indiana Wesleyan Univ	IN	19,900	C+
John Brown Univ	AR	15,080	VC
Johnson C. Smith Univ	NC	18,108	C
Kent State Univ	OH	12,932	C
Kentucky Christian College	KY	13,472	C
King's College	PA	26,990	C
La Salle Univ	PA	31,260	VC
Le Moyne College	NY	26,400	VC
Lee Univ	TN	13,780	NC
LeMoyne-Owen College	TN	13,070	LC
Lincoln Univ	PA	13,320	C+
Linfield College	OR	27,090	VC
Loras College	IA	24,233	C
Lyndon State College	VT	12,646	LC
Madonna Univ	MI	11,504	VC
Malone College	OH	20,995	C
Marygrove College	MI	17,550	C
Marylhurst Univ	OR	18,465	NC
Maryville Univ of St. Louis	MO	22,090	VC
Mayville State Univ	ND	7,325	NC
Middle Tenn State Univ	TN	8,534	C
Miss State Univ	MS	9,139	C
Missouri Baptist Univ	MO	18,010	C
Montana Tech of The Univ of Montana	MT	9,314	NC
National-Louis Univ	IL	16,240	LC
Northwest Missouri State Univ	MO	9,334	C
Okla City Univ	OK	19,580	VC
Okla Wesleyan Univ	OK	14,100	LC
Oregon State Univ	OR	11,055	C
Penn State Univ at Erie/ Behrend College	PA	12,326	C
Penn State Univ/Altoona	PA	12,578	C
Penn State Univ/Univ Park Campus	PA	15,646	HC
Philander Smith College	AR	7,380	NC
Piedmont College	GA	16,900	C
Pitzer College	CA	37,590	HC
Pomona College	CA	33,960	MC
Purdue Univ/West Lafayette	IN	12,560	VC
Rochester College	MI	16,718	C
Rockford College	IL	28,310	VC
Rutgers, The State Univ of New Jersey/Camden Campus	NJ	14,990	VC
Samford Univ	AL	18,648	VC
San Francisco State Univ	CA	12,070	C
Santa Clara Univ	CA	34,701	HC
Seattle Univ	WA	24,183	VC
Sierra Nevada College	NV	26,136	C
Simon's Rock College of Bard	MA	36,580	HC
Southern Oregon Univ	OR	10,362	C
SUNY/Empire State College	NY	4,505	SP
Trevecca Nazarene Univ	TN	17,548	C
Troy State Univ Dothan	AL	3,842	C
Union College	NE	17,130	C
United States Air Force Academy	CO		HC+
United States Naval Academy	MD		MC
Univ of Alaska Fairbanks	AK	9,295	C
Univ of Denver	CO	32,148	VC
Univ of Findlay	OH	23,962	NC
Univ of Great Falls	MT	15,360	C
Univ of Mass Amherst	MA	13,980	C+
Univ of Mich/Dearborn	MI	6,843	VC
Univ of Northern Iowa	IA	9,834	C
Univ of Oregon	OR	11,479	VC
Univ of St. Francis	IN	20,964	C
Univ of Texas at El Paso	TX	5,799	NC
Univ of Wisc/Parkside	WI	6,160	LC
Univ of Wisc/Platteville	WI	8,450	C
Univ of Wisc/River Falls	WI	8,358	LC
Univ of Wisc/Stout	WI	9,718	C
Upper Iowa Univ	IA	20,076	C
Urbana Univ	OH	19,115	C
Valley City State Univ	ND	7,281	LC
Villanova Univ	PA	35,050	HC
Walsh Univ	OH	20,890	C
Washburn Univ of Topeka	KS	8,984	NC
Washington State Univ	WA	11,334	C
Wayland Baptist Univ	TX	11,919	NC
West Virginia Univ	WV	9,370	C
Western New Mexico Univ	NM	5,950	LC
Wheeling Jesuit Univ	WV	22,660	C
Wilberforce Univ	OH	14,937	LC
William Woods Univ	MO	20,120	C
Youngstown State Univ	OH	11,148	NC

SCIENCE AND MANAGEMENT

School	ST	$IS	SR
Pitzer College	CA	37,590	HC
Scripps College	CA	35,700	HC+
Texas A&M Univ at Galveston	TX	9,948	C+

SCIENCE AND SOCIETY

School	ST	$IS	SR
Northwestern Univ	IL	37,491	MC
Rutgers, The State Univ of New Jersey/Newark Campus	NJ	15,624	VC

SCIENCE EDUCATION

School	ST	$IS	SR
Abilene Christian Univ	TX	18,370	VC
Adams State College	CO	7,468	C
Adelphi Univ	NY	26,300	VC
Alabama A&M Univ	AL	5,100	LC
Albany State Univ	GA	5,764	C+
Alcorn State Univ	MS	7,290	C
Alfred Univ	NY	28,290	C
Alverno College	WI	18,898	C
American International College	MA	24,690	LC
Anderson Univ	IN	19,430	LC
Andrews Univ	MI	19,550	C
Appalachian State Univ	NC	7,637	VC
Arkansas State Univ	AR	8,450	C
Asbury College	KY	20,704	VC
Ashland Univ	OH	24,464	C
Auburn Univ	AL	10,396	VC
Averett Univ	VA	23,010	LC
Baldwin-Wallace College	OH	24,678	C
Ball State Univ	IN	8,660	C
Baylor Univ	TX	23,864	VC
Belmont Univ	TN	21,986	VC
Bemidji State Univ	MN	9,103	C
Bennett College	NC	11,200	C
Bethany College	KS	18,675	LC
Bethany College	WV	19,845	VC
Bethel College	IN	19,670	C
Bethel College	MN	25,180	VC
Bethune-Cookman College	FL	16,480	LC
Black Hills State Univ	SD	7,743	LC
Bloomsburg Univ of Pennsylvania	PA	10,844	C
Blue Mountain College	MS	10,226	C
Boston Univ	MA	38,194	HC+
Bowie State Univ	MD	10,873	C+
Brewton-Parker College	GA	14,200	LC
Brigham Young Univ	UT	8,504	HC
Brigham Young Univ/Hawaii	HI	7,240	VC+
Bryan College	TN	17,900	VC
Buena Vista Univ	IA	25,406	C
Cal State, Long Beach	CA	8,762	C+
Calif Univ of Pennsylvania	PA	10,388	C
Canisius College	NY	28,163	C+
Caribbean Univ	PR	3,000	
Carroll College	WI	22,740	C
Carson-Newman College	TN	16,760	C
Catawba College	NC	20,500	C
Cedar Crest College	PA	25,145	C+
Cedarville Univ	OH	19,954	VC
Centenary College of Louisiana	LA	23,100	VC+
Central Methodist College	MO	16,460	C
Central Mich Univ	MI	11,142	C
Central Missouri State Univ	MO	9,776	C
Central Univ of Bayamon	PR	3,335	
Central Washington Univ	WA	9,768	C
Chadron State College	NE	6,286	NC
Charleston Southern Univ	SC	17,122	C
Christopher Newport Univ	VA	8,862	VC
CUNY/Brooklyn College	NY	4,353	C+
CUNY/Herbert H. Lehman College	NY	3,320	LC
CUNY/Hunter College	NY	6,729	C+
Coker College	SC	21,491	C
Colby-Sawyer College	NH	27,850	LC
College of Mount St. Joseph	OH	22,785	C
College of New Jersey	NJ	15,950	MC
College of Notre Dame of Maryland	MD	27,700	C
College of Our Lady of the Elms	MA	20,644	C
College of St. Rose	NY	22,864	C
College of Santa Fe	NM	25,293	C+
Concord College	WV	8,136	C
Concordia College: Moorhead	MN	22,460	VC+
Concordia Univ Nebr	NE	20,302	C+
Concordia Univ, River Forest	IL	23,600	C
Concordia Univ/St.Paul	MN	24,486	C
Conn College	CT	37,900	MC
Converse College	SC	24,710	VC
Cornell College	IA	27,825	VC+
Cornerstone Univ and Grand Rapids Theological Seminary	MI	19,846	C
Crichton College	TN	15,215	C
Cumberland College	KY	16,384	C
Daemen College	NY	22,120	C
Dana College	NE	20,280	C
David Lipscomb Univ	TN	16,158	VC
Defiance College	OH	22,615	C
Delaware State Univ	DE	8,104	LC
Delta State Univ	MS	6,618	C
Dickinson State Univ	ND	6,338	NC
Doane College	NE	20,000	C
Dominican College	NY	24,810	LC
Duquesne Univ	PA	26,907	VC
East Carolina Univ	NC	8,671	C
East Central Univ	OK	4,968	C
East Texas Baptist Univ	TX	13,914	C
Eastern Mich Univ	MI	11,478	C
Eastern Nazarene College	MA	19,433	LC
Eastern Washington Univ	WA	9,012	C
Edgewood College	WI	20,520	C
Edinboro Univ of Pennsylvania	PA	10,850	LC
Elmira College	NY	33,820	VC
Elon Univ	NC	22,240	VC
Eureka College	IL	24,980	LC
Evangel Univ	MO	15,435	C
Fairmont State	WV	8,280	LC
Florida A&M Univ	FL	7,564	C
Florida Inst of Technology	FL	28,740	VC
Florida International Univ	FL	9,912	VC
Florida Southern College	FL	23,592	C
Florida State Univ	FL	9,028	HC
Franciscan Univ	IA	19,300	C
Franklin College	IN		C
Freed-Hardeman Univ	TN		NC
Fresno Pacific Univ	CA	22,462	C
Friends Univ	KS	15,962	LC
George Fox Univ	OR	26,110	VC
Georgia Southwestern State Univ	GA	6,013	C
Gettysburg College	PA	35,646	HC
Glenville State College	WV	7,812	NC
Goshen College	IN	22,450	VC
Grace College	IN	19,825	VC
Grambling State Univ	LA	6,538	NC
Grand Canyon Univ	AZ	30,000	LC
Grand Valley State Univ	MI	11,022	VC
Greensboro College	NC	21,750	C
Greenville College	IL	21,342	C
Grove City College	PA	14,228	HC
Gustavus Adolphus College	MN	27,120	VC+
Gwynedd-Mercy College	PA	24,225	C
Hamline Univ	MN	27,052	VC
Hardin-Simmons Univ	TX	14,165	C
Hastings College	NE	19,928	VC
Heidelberg College	OH	20,266	NC
Heritage College	WA	6,720	NC
Hillsdale College	MI	22,450	HC
Hofstra Univ	NY	27,112	VC
Holy Family College	PA	13,710	LC
Hood College	MD	27,795	VC
Hope College	MI	25,340	VC
Houghton College	NY	23,984	VC
Humboldt State Univ	CA	9,400	C
Huntington College	IN	23,590	C
Huron Univ	SD	10,450	C
Illinois College	IL	19,100	VC
Immaculata Univ	PA	25,200	C
Indiana State Univ	IN	10,719	LC
Indiana Univ Bloomington	IN	12,389	VC
Indiana Univ of Pennsylvania	PA	10,489	C
Indiana Univ South Bend	IN	4,571	LC
Indiana Univ-Purdue Univ Fort Wayne	IN	5,108	LC
Indiana Univ-Purdue Univ Indianapolis	IN	8,257	LC
Indiana Wesleyan Univ	IN	19,900	C+
Inter American Univ of PR/ San German	PR	6,716	
Iona College	NY	27,988	VC
Iowa Wesleyan College	IA	19,990	C
John Brown Univ	AR	15,080	VC
Johnson State College	VT	11,819	LC
Judson College	AL	14,650	C
Judson College	IL	22,050	LC
Juniata College	PA	29,080	VC
Keene State College	NH	12,212	C
Kennesaw State Univ	GA	2,724	C
Kent State Univ	OH	12,932	C
King's College	PA	26,990	C
Knoxville College	TN	6,200	LC
La Roche College	PA	22,094	C
La Salle Univ	PA	31,260	VC
Lamar Univ	TX	6,816	LC
Langston Univ	OK	2,308	LC
Le Moyne College	NY	26,400	VC
Lenoir-Rhyne College	NC	19,186	C
LeTourneau Univ	TX	21,080	C
Limestone College	SC	17,700	LC
Lincoln Memorial Univ	TN	16,400	LC
Lindenwood Univ	MO	17,050	VC
Livingstone College	NC	18,101	LC
Lock Haven Univ of Pennsylvania	PA	11,098	LC
LIU/Brooklyn Campus	NY	24,790	C
LIU/C.W. Post Campus	NY	28,282	C
Loras College	IA	24,233	C
Louisiana College	LA	13,450	C
Lubbock Christian Univ	TX	15,832	C
Lyndon State College	VT	12,646	LC
MacMurray College	IL	20,005	LC
Malone College	OH	20,995	C
Manhattan College	NY	27,400	VC
Mansfield Univ	PA	11,220	C
Mars Hill College	NC	18,600	LC
Mary Baldwin College	VA	24,939	C
Marymount College of Fordham Univ	NY	27,686	C
Maryville College	TN	25,960	VC
Marywood Univ	PA	26,050	C
Mayville State Univ	ND	7,325	NC
McNeese State Univ	LA	5,259	LC
Mercyhurst College	PA	20,694	C
Messiah College	PA	25,890	VC+
Miami Univ	OH	15,033	HC
MidAmerica Nazarene Univ	KS	18,688	C
Midland Lutheran College	NE	18,600	C
Miles College	AL	7,870	NC
Millikin Univ	IL	25,555	C
Minn State Univ, Mankato	MN	8,803	LC
Minn State Univ, Moorehead	MN	7,000	LC
Minot State Univ	ND	6,602	LC
Miss Valley State Univ	MS	6,765	NC
Missouri Southern State Univ	MO	8,316	C
Monmouth Univ	NJ	26,334	C
Montana State Univ-Billings	MT	9,550	C
Montana State Univ- Northern	MT	8,600	NC
Morningside College	IA	21,610	C
Morris College	SC	10,974	LC
Mount Holyoke College	MA	37,918	HC+
Mount Mary College	WI	20,370	C
Mount Vernon Nazarene Univ	OH	18,925	C
Muskingum College	OH	20,680	C
Nazareth College of Rochester	NY	24,936	VC
Nebr Wesleyan Univ	NE	21,197	C+
New Mexico Highlands Univ	NM	6,182	LC
New York Inst of Technology	NY	24,205	VC

School	ST	$IS	SR
New York Univ	NY	39,406	MC
Niagara Univ	NY	25,050	C
N Car State Univ	NC	9,886	VC
North Georgia College and State Univ	GA	6,984	C
Northeastern State Univ	OK	4,950	LC
Northern Arizona Univ	AZ	9,002	C
Northern Kentucky Univ	KY	6,352	NC
Northern Mich Univ	MI	10,834	C
Northern State Univ	SD	7,117	LC
Northwest Missouri State Univ	MO	9,334	C
Northwest Nazarene Univ	ID	20,360	VC
Northwestern College of Iowa	IA	19,640	C+
Northwestern Okla State Univ	OK	5,433	NC
Oakland City Univ	IN	16,980	NC
Oakwood College	AL	14,904	C
Ohio Univ	OH	14,448	C
Ohio Wesleyan Univ	OH	32,550	VC+
Okla Baptist Univ	OK	15,220	VC
Okla Christian Univ	OK	17,690	NC
Okla City Univ	OK	19,580	VC
Okla Panhandle State Univ	OK	5,370	C
Okla Wesleyan Univ	OK	14,100	LC
Old Dominion Univ	VA	10,441	C
Oral Roberts Univ	OK	18,490	C
Ouachita Baptist Univ	AR	18,900	VC
Palm Beach Atlantic Univ	FL	20,690	C
Peru State College	NE	6,342	NC
Pfeiffer Univ	NC	18,980	C
Philander Smith College	AR	7,380	NC
Plymouth State Univ	NH	12,298	LC
Pontifical Catholic Univ of PR/Ponce	PR	7,298	
Providence College	RI	30,604	HC
Purdue Univ/Calumet	IN	6,630	NC
Purdue Univ/West Lafayette	IN	12,560	VC
Quincy Univ	IL	22,330	C
Rhode Island College	RI	11,565	C
Rider Univ	NJ	30,900	C
Rocky Mountain College	MT	19,015	C
Rowan Univ	NJ	14,506	VC
Rust College	MS	8,200	C+
St. Augustine's College	NC	12,990	LC
St. Cloud State Univ	MN	8,362	C
St. Edward's Univ	TX	20,428	C
St. John Fisher College	NY	24,870	C
St. John's Univ	NY	30,180	C
St. Mary-of-the-Woods College	IN	23,280	C
St. Mary's Univ of Minn	MN	21,535	C
St. Mary's Univ of San Antonio	TX	22,444	C
St. Michael's College	VT	30,100	VC
St. Thomas Aquinas College	NY	20,590	LC
St. Vincent College	PA	25,530	VC
St. Xavier Univ	IL	23,144	C
Salem State College	MA	8,592	C
Schreiner Univ	TX	20,440	C
Seattle Pacific Univ	WA	25,944	VC
Seton Hill Univ	PA	24,930	C
Shaw Univ	NC	14,882	C+
Sheldon Jackson College	AK	14,940	LC
Shepherd College	WV	8,608	C
Slippery Rock Univ of Pennsylvania	PA	10,343	LC
Southeast Missouri State Univ	MO	9,704	C
Southeastern Louisiana Univ	LA	6,791	LC
Southeastern Okla State Univ	OK	6,147	C
Southern Arkansas Univ	AR	6,956	C
Southern Conn State Univ	CT	10,310	C
Southern Illinois Univ Edwardsville	IL	8,724	C
Southern Univ at New Orleans	LA	995	NC
Southern Utah Univ	UT	8,194	C
Southwest Missouri State Univ	MO	8,918	C
Southwestern College	KS	19,560	C
Southwestern Okla State Univ	OK	4,801	C
Springfield College	MA	24,520	C
SUNY at Potsdam	NY	12,160	C
SUNY/College at Buffalo	NY	8,025	C
SUNY/College at Fredonia	NY	11,562	VC
SUNY/College at Old Westbury	NY	12,784	C
SUNY/College at Oneonta	NY	11,870	VC
SUNY/College at Plattsburgh	NY	11,700	C
SUNY/College of Environmental Science and Forestry	NY	14,167	VC
SUNY/Univ at Albany	NY	12,951	HC
SUNY/Univ at New Paltz	NY	11,565	VC
Syracuse Univ	NY	34,720	HC
Tabor College	KS	19,500	NC
Taylor Univ	IN	23,820	VC+
Temple Univ	PA	15,912	C
Texas A&M Univ at Commerce	TX	8,994	C
Texas Christian Univ	TX	23,410	VC
Texas State Univ	TX	9,320	VC
Trevecca Nazarene Univ	TN	17,548	C
Tri-State Univ-Main Campus	IN	23,600	C
Troy State Univ	AL	7,696	C
Troy State Univ Dothan	AL	3,842	C
Turabo Univ	PR	4,110	
Univ of Akron	OH	13,134	NC
Univ of Arizona	AZ	10,413	VC
Univ of Arkansas at Pine Bluff	AR	7,925	C
Univ of Calif at San Diego	CA	14,127	HC
Univ of Central Arkansas	AR	6,388	C
Univ of Central Florida	FL	10,038	VC
Univ of Central Okla	OK	9,434	C
Univ of Charleston	WV	23,620	C
Univ of Cincinnati	OH	14,736	C
Univ of Conn	CT	14,608	VC
Univ of Delaware	DE	12,616	HC
Univ of Evansville	IN	24,190	VC
Univ of Georgia	GA	8,656	VC
Univ of Great Falls	MT	15,360	C
Univ of Idaho	ID	8,216	C
Univ of Illinois at Chicago	IL	13,418	C
Univ of Indianapolis	IN	22,560	VC
Univ of Iowa	IA	10,923	VC
Univ of Kentucky	KY	7,765	C
Univ of Louisiana at Lafayette	LA	5,826	C
Univ of Louisiana at Monroe	LA	5,207	NC
Univ of Louisville	KY	8,762	VC
Univ of Mary	ND	12,900	C+
Univ of Mary Hardin-Baylor	TX	17,268	C
Univ of Maryland/College Park	MD	14,227	HC
Univ of Maryland/Eastern Shore	MD	9,964	C
Univ of Mich/Dearborn	MI	6,843	VC
Univ of Minn/Duluth	MN	12,470	C
Univ of Minn/Twin Cities	MN	13,160	VC
Univ of Miss	MS	7,666	C
Univ of Montana	MT	9,395	C
Univ of Montana--Western	MT	8,073	NC
Univ of Nebr at Kearney	NE	8,286	NC
Univ of Nebr at Lincoln	NE	9,975	C+
Univ of New Hampshire	NH	14,828	VC
Univ of New Mexico	NM	9,223	C
Univ of New Orleans	LA	7,356	C
Univ of North Alabama	AL	7,972	NC
Univ of N Car at Charlotte	NC	8,185	C
Univ of N Car at Greensboro	NC	8,248	C
Univ of N Car at Pembroke	NC	6,929	LC
Univ of N Dak	ND	8,390	C
Univ of North Florida	FL	8,769	VC
Univ of Northern Colo	CO	8,987	C
Univ of Northern Iowa	IA	9,834	C
Univ of Notre Dame	IN	34,442	MC
Univ of Okla	OK	9,226	VC
Univ of Pittsburgh at Johnstown	PA	15,216	LC
Univ of Rio Grande	OH	8,728	NC
Univ of St. Francis	IN	20,964	C
Univ of St. Thomas	MN	26,918	VC
Univ of Scranton	PA	30,836	VC
Univ of Sioux Falls	SD	16,390	C
Univ of South Florida	FL	9,454	C
Univ of Southern Indiana	IN	9,025	LC
Univ of Southern Miss	MS	8,324	LC
Univ of the Incarnate Word	TX	21,772	LC
Univ of Toledo	OH	12,479	NC
Univ of Vermont	VT	16,316	VC
Univ of West Alabama	AL	6,048	C
Univ of Wisc/Eau Claire	WI	8,463	VC
Univ of Wisc/La Crosse	WI	8,991	VC
Univ of Wisc/Oshkosh	WI	6,130	LC
Univ of Wisc/Platteville	WI	8,450	C
Univ of Wisc/Superior	WI	7,051	C+
Univ of Wisc/Whitewater	WI	8,626	C
Utah State Univ	UT	7,371	C
Vanguard Univ of Southern Calif	CA	22,208	C
Viterbo Univ	WI	20,430	C
Warner Southern College	FL	16,738	LC
Wartburg College	IA	21,165	VC
Washington Univ in St. Louis	MO	38,293	MC
Wayne State College	NE	7,352	NC
Wayne State Univ	MI	11,774	C
Weber State Univ	UT	7,945	NC
West Liberty State College	WV	7,868	LC
West Texas A&M Univ	TX	7,533	C
Western Carolina Univ	NC	6,742	C
Western Kentucky Univ	KY	6,834	C
Western New Mexico Univ	NM	5,950	LC
Western State College of Colo	CO	9,014	C
Western Washington Univ	WA	10,119	VC
Westfield State College	MA	10,147	C
Wheaton College	IL	21,934	HC
Whitworth College	WA	26,428	VC+
Widener Univ	PA	27,020	C
William Penn Univ	IA	17,575	LC
Wingate Univ	NC	21,200	C
Winona State Univ	MN		C
Wittenberg Univ	OH	31,316	VC
Wright State Univ	OH	11,490	LC
Xavier Univ	OH	26,850	VC+
Xavier Univ of Louisiana	LA	17,600	C
York College of Pennsylvania	PA	14,500	VC
Youngstown State Univ	OH	11,148	NC

SCIENCE TECHNOLOGY

School	ST	$IS	SR
Claremont McKenna College	CA	36,880	MC
Colby College	ME	37,570	MC
Cornell Univ	NY	38,253	MC
James Madison Univ	VA	10,794	VC
Lehigh Univ	PA	37,570	HC+
Marshall Univ	WV	9,116	C
Olivet Nazarene Univ	IL	20,480	C
Rensselaer Polytechnic Inst	NY	37,579	HC+
St. John Fisher College	NY	24,870	C
Scripps College	CA	35,700	HC+
Stevens Inst of Technology	NJ	35,300	HC+
Wesleyan Univ	CT	35,139	MC

SCULPTURE

School	ST	$IS	SR
Aquinas College	MI	21,894	C
Arizona State Univ-Main	AZ	10,048	C
Atlanta College of Art	GA	18,600	SP
Bard College	NY	37,352	HC+
Birmingham-Southern College	AL	25,364	VC+
Boston Univ	MA	38,194	HC+
Bradley Univ	IL	22,910	VC
Calif College of the Arts	CA	31,530	SP
Cal State, Fullerton	CA	6,648	C
Cal State, San Bernardino	CA	15,238	LC
Cal State, Stanislaus	CA	9,874	C
Catholic Univ of America	DC	34,248	VC
College for Creative Studies	MI	23,298	SP
College of Santa Fe	NM	25,293	C+
College of Visual Arts	MN		SP
Edinboro Univ of Pennsylvania	PA	10,850	LC
Escuela de Artes Plasticas de PR	PR		
Indiana Univ-Purdue Univ Indianapolis	IN	8,257	LC
Kansas City Art Inst	MO	26,850	SP
Kendall College of Art and Design of Ferris State Univ	MI	10,784	SP
Maine College of Art	ME	28,812	SP
Maryland Inst College of Art	MD	30,890	SP
Mass College of Art	MA	15,568	SP
Milwaukee Inst of Art and Design	WI	24,388	SP
Minneapolis College of Art and Design	MN	28,950	SP
Montserrat College of Art	MA	22,790	SP
Moore College of Art and Design	PA	27,096	SP
Northwest Nazarene Univ	ID	20,360	VC
Pacific Northwest College of Art	OR	14,890	SP
Rhode Island School of Design	RI	33,569	SP
Rochester Inst of Technology	NY	29,217	VC+
San Francisco Art Inst	CA	19,300	SP
School of the Art Inst of Chicago	IL	27,800	SP
Shepherd College	WV	8,608	C
SUNY at Potsdam	NY	12,160	C
SUNY/College at Buffalo	NY	8,025	C
Syracuse Univ	NY	34,720	HC
Univ of Dallas	TX	25,898	VC+
Univ of Hartford	CT	31,080	C
Univ of Houston	TX	9,818	C
Univ of Illinois at Urbana-Champaign	IL	11,316	HC+
Univ of Kansas	KS	8,923	VC
Univ of Mass Dartmouth	MA	12,835	C
Univ of Miami	FL	34,608	HC
Univ of Mich/Ann Arbor	MI	13,864	HC+
Univ of North Texas	TX	7,629	C
Univ of Oregon	OR	11,479	VC
Univ of the Arts	PA	29,510	SP
Univ of Washington	WA	10,361	VC
Washington Univ in St. Louis	MO	38,293	MC

SECONDARY EDUCATION

School	ST	$IS	SR
Abilene Christian Univ	TX	18,370	VC
Adams State College	CO	7,468	C
Adelphi Univ	NY	26,300	VC
Adrian College	MI	21,950	C
Alabama A&M Univ	AL	5,100	LC
Alabama State Univ	AL	6,404	C
Albright College	PA	30,579	C
Alderson-Broaddus College	WV	19,640	C
Alfred Univ	NY	28,290	C
Alice Lloyd College	KY	4,040	C
Alma College	MI	25,566	VC
Alvernia College	PA	23,212	LC
Alverno College	WI	18,898	C
American International College	MA	24,690	LC
American Univ	DC	34,585	VC+
Andrews Univ	MI	19,550	C
Appalachian State Univ	NC	7,637	VC
Arcadia Univ	PA	29,890	C
Arizona State Univ-Main	AZ	10,048	C
Arkansas Tech Univ	AR	7,299	C
Armstrong Atlantic State Univ	GA	7,102	C
Asbury College	KY	20,704	VC
Ashland Univ	OH	24,464	C
Auburn Univ	AL	10,396	VC
Auburn Univ Montgomery	AL	9,020	NC
Augsburg College	MN	25,298	C
Augustana College	IL	26,610	VC+
Augustana College	SD	21,998	VC
Averett Univ	VA	23,010	LC
Baker Univ	KS	19,860	VC
Baldwin-Wallace College	OH	24,678	C
Ball State Univ	IN	8,660	C
Baylor Univ	TX	23,864	VC
Bellarmine Univ	KY	24,110	VC
Belmont Abbey College	NC	23,742	C
Bemidji State Univ	MN	9,103	C
Benedictine College	KS	20,603	C
Bennett College	NC	11,200	C
Berea College	KY	5,030	VC+
Bethany College	KS	18,675	LC
Bethany College	WV	19,845	VC
Bethel College	IN	19,670	C
Bethel College	MN	25,180	VC
Birmingham-Southern College	AL	25,364	VC+
Black Hills State Univ	SD	7,743	LC
Blackburn College	IL	13,690	C
Bloomsburg Univ of Pennsylvania	PA	10,844	C
Blue Mountain College	MS	10,226	C
Bluefield College	VA	15,575	C
Boise State Univ	ID	7,657	LC
Boston College	MA	33,284	MC
Bowling Green State Univ	OH	13,036	C
Bradley Univ	IL	22,910	VC
Brewton-Parker College	GA	14,200	LC
Briar Cliff Univ	IA	21,660	C
Brigham Young Univ	UT	8,504	HC
Bucknell Univ	PA	35,262	HC+
Buena Vista Univ	IA	25,406	C
Butler Univ	IN	28,250	VC+
Calif Univ of Pennsylvania	PA	10,388	C
Calumet College of St. Joseph	IN	9,000	LC
Calvin College	MI	22,615	NC
Canisius College	NY	28,163	C+
Capital Univ	OH	26,550	C
Cardinal Stritch Univ	WI	17,620	C
Caribbean Univ	PR	3,000	
Carlow College	PA	21,334	C
Carroll College	MT	20,576	VC
Carson-Newman College	TN	16,760	C
Carthage College	WI	25,000	C
Catholic Univ of America	DC	34,248	VC
Cedar Crest College	PA	25,145	C+
Centenary College	NJ	25,370	LC
Central College	IA	21,206	C
Central Mich Univ	MI	11,142	C
Central Missouri State Univ	MO	9,776	C
Central State Univ	OH	8,922	C+
Central Univ of Bayamon	PR	3,335	
Central Washington Univ	WA	9,768	C
Chadron State College	NE	6,286	NC
Chaminade Univ of Honolulu	HI	21,430	LC
Cheyney Univ of Pennsylvania	PA	9,993	C
Chicago State Univ	IL	10,882	C+
Christopher Newport Univ	VA	8,862	VC
Citadel, The	SC	12,295	C+
CUNY/Brooklyn College	NY	4,353	C+
CUNY/City College	NY	4,230	C+
CUNY/Herbert H. Lehman College	NY	3,320	LC
CUNY/Hunter College	NY	6,729	C+
Clarion Univ of Pennsylvania	PA	11,272	LC
Clarke College	IA	23,165	C
Clearwater Christian College	FL	13,160	LC
Clemson Univ	SC	11,972	HC
Cleveland State Univ	OH	12,308	LC
Coastal Carolina Univ	SC	11,040	C
Coe College	IA	27,385	VC
College Misericordia	PA	26,350	C
College of Notre Dame of Maryland	MD	27,700	C
College of Our Lady of the Elms	MA	20,644	C
College of St. Joseph	VT	19,100	C
College of Santa Fe	NM	25,293	C+
College of the Ozarks	MO	3,500	VC+
College of the Southwest	NM	9,320	C+

ST = STATE $IS = IN-STATE COSTS SR = SELECTOR RATING

School	ST	$IS	SR
Colo Christian Univ	CO	21,182	VC
Columbia College	MO	16,139	C
Columbus State Univ	GA	7,846	C
Concord College	WV	8,136	C
Concordia College	NY	19,200	VC
Concordia College: Moorhead	MN	22,460	VC+
Concordia Univ	MI	24,095	C
Concordia Univ	OR	22,450	C
Concordia Univ at Austin	TX	20,450	LC
Concordia Univ Nebr	NE	20,302	C+
Concordia Univ Wisc	WI	16,600	C
Concordia Univ, River Forest	IL	23,600	C
Concordia Univ/St.Paul	MN	24,486	C
Converse College	SC	24,710	VC
Cornell College	IA	27,825	VC+
Cornerstone Univ and Grand Rapids Theological Seminary	MI	19,846	C
Creighton Univ	NE	26,748	VC+
Crichton College	TN	15,215	C
Cumberland Univ	TN	16,910	C
Dakota State Univ	SD	7,466	C
Dakota Wesleyan Univ	SD	17,832	C
Dana College	NE	20,280	C
Davis and Elkins College	WV	20,594	C
Defiance College	OH	22,615	C
Delaware Valley College	PA	26,676	C
Delta State Univ	MS	6,618	C
DePaul Univ	IL	27,580	VC
Dickinson State Univ	ND	6,338	NC
Dillard Univ	LA	17,325	VC
Dominican College	NY	24,810	LC
Dordt College	IA	20,170	VC
Dowling College	NY	23,870	LC
Drake Univ	IA	25,120	VC+
Drury Univ	MO	18,085	VC+
Duquesne Univ	PA	26,907	VC
East Central Univ	OK	4,968	C
East Stroudsburg Univ of Pennsylvania	PA	10,336	C
East Texas Baptist Univ	TX	13,914	C
Eastern Illinois Univ	IL	11,192	C
Eastern Kentucky Univ	KY	7,708	C
Eastern Mennonite Univ	VA	22,980	LC
Eastern Mich Univ	MI	11,478	C
Eastern Univ	PA	24,020	C
Eastern Washington Univ	WA	9,012	C
Edinboro Univ of Pennsylvania	PA	10,850	LC
Elizabethtown College	PA	28,800	C
Elmhurst College	IL	24,630	C
Elmira College	NY	33,820	VC
Elon Univ	NC	22,240	VC
Emmanuel College	MA	27,600	C+
Emporia State Univ	KS	6,998	C
Eureka College	IL	24,980	LC
Evangel Univ	MO	15,435	C
Fairmont State	WV	8,280	LC
Faulkner Univ	AL	14,500	C
Fayetteville State Univ	NC	5,590	LC
Fitchburg State College	MA	9,622	C
Flagler College	FL	11,860	VC+
Florida Memorial College	FL	6,000	LC
Florida Southern College	FL	23,592	C
Fort Valley State Univ	GA	6,960	C
Franklin College	IN		C
Franklin Pierce College	NH	28,980	LC
Freed-Hardeman Univ	TN		NC
Friends Univ	KS	15,962	LC
Gallaudet Univ	DC	16,554	SP
Gannon Univ	PA	23,260	C
Gardner-Webb Univ	NC	19,300	C
George Fox Univ	OR	26,110	VC
Georgia Southwestern State Univ	GA	6,013	C
Gettysburg College	PA	35,646	HC
Glenville State College	WV	7,812	NC
Gordon College	MA	25,982	VC+
Goshen College	IN	22,450	VC
Grace Bible College	MI	15,890	C
Grand Canyon Univ	AZ	30,000	LC
Grand Valley State Univ	MI	11,022	VC
Grand View College	IA	19,748	LC
Green Mountain College	VT	24,130	C
Greensboro College	NC	21,750	C
Greenville College	IL	21,342	C
Grove City College	PA	14,228	HC
Gustavus Adolphus College	MN	27,120	VC+
Gwynedd-Mercy College	PA	24,225	C
Hamline Univ	MN	27,052	VC
Hannibal-LaGrange College	MO	13,940	C
Harding Univ	AR	14,890	VC
Hardin-Simmons Univ	TX	14,165	C
Hastings College	NE	19,928	VC
Heidelberg College	OH	20,266	NC
Heritage College	WA	6,720	NC
High Point Univ	NC	22,480	C
Hillsdale College	MI	22,450	HC
Hofstra Univ	NY	27,112	VC
Holy Family College	PA	13,710	LC
Hood College	MD	27,795	VC
Hope College	MI	25,340	VC
Hope International Univ	CA	16,940	NC
Houghton College	NY	23,984	VC
Houston Baptist Univ	TX	16,905	C
Howard Payne Univ	TX	15,176	C
Howard Univ	DC	16,505	C
Humboldt State Univ	CA	9,400	C
Huron Univ	SD	10,450	C
Idaho State Univ	ID	8,128	C
Illinois College	IL	19,100	VC
Immaculata Univ	PA	25,200	C
Indiana State Univ	IN	10,719	LC
Indiana Univ East	IN	4,433	LC
Indiana Univ Northwest	IN	4,538	LC
Indiana Univ South Bend	IN	4,571	LC
Indiana Univ Southeast	IN	4,504	LC
Indiana Univ-Purdue Univ Fort Wayne	IN	5,108	LC
Indiana Univ-Purdue Univ Indianapolis	IN	8,257	LC
Inter American Univ of PR/ Aguadilla Campus	PR	3,544	
Inter American Univ of PR/ Arecibo Campus	PR	3,300	
Inter American Univ of PR/ Barranquitas Regional College	PR	3,300	
Inter American Univ of PR/ Fajardo Campus	PR	4,000	
Inter American Univ of PR/ Metropolitan Campus	PR		
Inter American Univ of PR/ Ponce Regional College	PR	3,700	
Inter American Univ of PR/ San German	PR	6,716	
Iona College	NY	27,988	VC
Iowa State Univ	IA	10,768	VC
Iowa Wesleyan College	IA	19,990	C
Ithaca College	NY	31,730	HC
Jacksonville State Univ	AL	6,844	LC
Jarvis Christian College	TX	9,035	NC
John Brown Univ	AR	15,080	VC
John Carroll Univ	OH	27,658	C+
Johnson C. Smith Univ	NC	18,108	C
Johnson State College	VT	11,819	LC
Judson College	AL	14,650	C
Judson College	IL	22,050	LC
Juniata College	PA	29,080	VC
Kansas State Univ	KS	8,728	VC
Kansas Wesleyan Univ	KS	18,900	VC
Keene State College	NH	12,212	C
Kent State Univ	OH	12,932	C
Kentucky State Univ	KY	9,062	NC
Kentucky Wesleyan College	KY	17,250	C
Keuka College	NY	21,170	C
King College	TN	22,500	VC
King's College	PA	26,990	C
Knox College	IL	30,294	VC+
Kutztown Univ of Pennsylvania	PA	10,786	C
La Salle Univ	PA	31,260	VC
La Sierra Univ	CA	19,260	LC
Lake Superior State Univ	MI	9,034	LC
Lakeland College	WI	17,950	C
Lamar Univ	TX	6,816	LC
Lambuth Univ	TN	16,520	C
Lasell College	MA	26,000	C
Lawrence Univ	WI	30,900	HC
Le Moyne College	NY	26,400	VC
Lebanon Valley College	PA	28,870	VC
Lenoir-Rhyne College	NC	19,186	C
LeTourneau Univ	TX	21,080	C
Lewis Univ	IL	22,950	C+
Lewis-Clark State College	ID	6,981	C
Lincoln Memorial Univ	TN	16,400	LC
Lincoln Univ	PA	13,320	C+
Lindenwood Univ	MO	17,050	VC
Lindsey Wilson College	KY	16,392	LC
Livingstone College	NC	18,101	LC
Lock Haven Univ of Pennsylvania	PA	11,098	LC
LIU/Brooklyn Campus	NY	24,790	C
LIU/C.W. Post Campus	NY	28,282	C
Loras College	IA	24,233	C
Louisiana College	LA	13,450	C
Louisiana State Univ and A&M College	LA	9,126	VC
Louisiana State Univ in Shreveport	LA	2,884	NC
Louisiana Tech Univ	LA	7,361	C
Lubbock Christian Univ	TX	15,832	C
Lynn Univ	FL	30,750	C
MacMurray College	IL	20,005	LC
Madonna Univ	MI	11,504	VC
Malone College	OH	20,995	C
Manchester College	IN	23,390	C
Manhattan College	NY	27,400	VC
Mansfield Univ	PA	11,220	C
Marian College of Fond du Lac	WI	19,625	C
Marquette Univ	WI	27,594	VC
Marymount College of Fordham Univ	NY	27,686	C
Marymount Manhattan College	NY	27,292	C
Maryville College	TN	25,960	VC
Maryville Univ of St. Louis	MO	22,090	VC
Marywood Univ	PA	26,050	C
Master's College and Seminary	CA	23,250	VC
Mayville State Univ	ND	7,325	NC
McMurry Univ	TX	17,846	LC
McPherson College	KS	20,265	C
Mercer Univ	GA	27,516	VC+
Mercyhurst College	PA	20,694	C
Merrimack College	MA	29,625	C
Methodist College	NC	19,526	C
Miami Univ	OH	15,033	HC
Midland Lutheran College	NE	18,600	C
Miles College	AL	7,870	NC
Millikin Univ	IL	25,555	C
Minn State Univ, Mankato	MN	8,803	LC
Minn State Univ, Moorehead	MN	7,000	LC
Miss State Univ	MS	9,139	C
Missouri Southern State Univ	MO	8,316	C
Missouri Western State College	MO	8,522	NC
Molloy College	NY	15,180	C
Monmouth College	IL	23,600	C
Monmouth Univ	NJ	26,334	C
Montana State Univ-Billings	MT	9,550	C
Montana State Univ-Bozeman	MT	9,515	C
Montana State Univ-Northern	MT	8,600	NC
Moravian College	PA	28,903	VC
Mount Marty College	SD	15,656	LC
Mount Mary College	WI	20,370	C
Mount Olive College	NC	14,410	LC
Mount St. Mary College	NY	21,270	C
Mount St. Mary's College	CA	28,307	VC
Mount St. Mary's College	MD	28,400	C
Mount Vernon Nazarene Univ	OH	18,925	C
Murray State Univ	KY	7,816	VC
Muskingum College	OH	20,680	C
New England College	NH	28,860	LC
New Jersey City Univ	NJ	11,850	LC
New Mexico State Univ	NM	7,932	C
New York Inst of Technology	NY	24,205	VC
New York Univ	NY	39,406	MC
Newman Univ	KS	18,018	C
Niagara Univ	NY	25,050	C
Nicholls State Univ	LA	6,395	NC
N Car State Univ	NC	9,886	VC
North Central College	IL	25,656	VC
N Dak State Univ	ND	8,435	C
North Georgia College and State Univ	GA	6,984	C
North Park Univ	IL	24,030	C
Northeastern Illinois Univ	IL	2,898	NC
Northeastern State Univ	OK	4,950	LC
Northern Arizona Univ	AZ	9,002	C
Northern Kentucky Univ	KY	6,352	NC
Northern Mich Univ	MI	10,834	C
Northern State Univ	SD	7,117	LC
Northland College	WI	22,170	C+
Northwest College	WA	18,854	C
Northwest Missouri State Univ	MO	9,334	C
Northwestern College of Iowa	IA	19,640	C+
Northwestern Okla State Univ	OK	5,433	NC
Northwestern State Univ of Louisiana	LA	6,331	NC
Northwestern Univ	IL	37,491	MC
Notre Dame College	OH	20,425	C
Nyack College	NY	18,540	C
Oakland City Univ	IN	16,980	NC
Oglethorpe Univ	GA	26,000	VC
Ohio Univ	OH	14,448	C
Ohio Valley College	WV	16,036	C+
Ohio Wesleyan Univ	OH	32,550	VC+
Okla Baptist Univ	OK	15,220	VC
Okla State Univ	OK	9,216	VC
Okla Wesleyan Univ	OK	14,100	LC
Old Dominion Univ	VA	10,441	C
Olivet College	MI	19,984	C+
Ouachita Baptist Univ	AR	18,900	VC
Our Lady of Holy Cross College	LA	5,900	C
Paine College	GA	13,022	LC
Palm Beach Atlantic Univ	FL	20,690	C
Paul Quinn College	TX	8,150	LC
Penn State Univ/Univ Park Campus	PA	15,646	HC
Pepperdine Univ	CA	32,830	VC
Peru State College	NE	6,342	NC
Pfeiffer Univ	NC	18,980	C
Philander Smith College	AR	7,380	NC
Pikeville College	KY	14,900	NC
Point Park Univ	PA	21,840	C
Pontifical Catholic Univ of PR/Ponce	PR	7,298	
Presbyterian College	SC	25,920	VC
Prescott College	AZ	13,430	C
Providence College	RI	30,604	HC
Purdue Univ/Calumet	IN	6,630	NC
Purdue Univ/West Lafayette	IN	12,560	VC
Quincy Univ	IL	22,330	C
Rhode Island College	RI	11,565	C
Rider Univ	NJ	30,900	C
Ripon College	WI	24,995	VC
Rivier College	NH	26,217	C
Rockhurst Univ	MO	22,960	C+
Roger Williams Univ	RI	30,296	C
Roosevelt Univ	IL	22,580	VC
Rosemont College	PA	26,175	C
Rust College	MS	8,200	C+
St. Ambrose Univ	IA	22,800	C
St. Anselm College	NH	30,250	C
St. Cloud State Univ	MN	8,362	C
St. Francis College	NY	10,880	LC
St. Francis Univ	PA	25,876	LC
St. John Fisher College	NY	24,870	C
St. John's Univ	NY	30,180	C
St. Joseph's, Brooklyn,	NY	10,902	C
St. Joseph's College	IN	24,250	C
St. Joseph's Univ	PA	33,590	VC
St. Mary-of-the-Woods College	IN	23,280	C
St. Mary's Univ of San Antonio	TX	22,444	C
St. Michael's College	VT	30,100	VC
St. Paul's College	VA	14,344	NC
St. Peter's College	NJ	22,292	LC
St. Thomas Aquinas College	NY	20,590	LC
St. Thomas Univ	FL	21,400	LC
St. Xavier Univ	IL	23,144	C
Salem International Univ	WV	19,770	C
Salem State College	MA	8,592	C
Salve Regina Univ	RI	29,210	C
Samford Univ	AL	18,648	VC
San Francisco State Univ	CA	12,070	C
Schreiner Univ	TX	20,440	C
Seton Hall Univ	NJ	30,130	VC
Seton Hill Univ	PA	24,930	C
Shaw Univ	NC	14,882	C+
Sheldon Jackson College	AK	14,940	LC
Shepherd College	WV	8,608	C
Silver Lake College of the Holy Family	WI	18,450	LC
Simmons College	MA	33,000	VC
Simpson College	CA	20,500	C
Slippery Rock Univ of Pennsylvania	PA	10,343	LC
S Dak State Univ	SD	7,782	C
Southeast Missouri State Univ	MO	9,704	C
Southeastern College	FL	11,648	LC
Southeastern Okla State Univ	OK	6,147	C
Southern Conn State Univ	CT	10,310	C
Southern Nazarene Univ	OK	14,634	NC
Southern Univ and A&M College	LA	7,372	LC
Southern Univ at New Orleans	LA	995	NC
Southwest Missouri State Univ	MO	8,918	C
Southwestern Adventist Univ	TX	14,798	C
Southwestern Okla State Univ	OK	4,801	C
Spring Hill College	AL	25,868	VC
Springfield College	MA	24,520	C
St. Joseph's, Suffolk	NY	11,297	C
SUNY at Oswego	NY	12,650	C
SUNY at Potsdam	NY	12,160	C
SUNY/College at Buffalo	NY	8,025	C
SUNY/College at Cortland	NY	12,095	C
SUNY/College at Fredonia	NY	11,562	VC
SUNY/College at Old Westbury	NY	12,784	C
SUNY/College at Oneonta	NY	11,870	VC
SUNY/College at Plattsburgh	NY	11,700	C
SUNY/Univ at Albany	NY	12,951	HC
SUNY/Univ at New Paltz	NY	11,565	VC
Stetson Univ	FL	29,495	VC
Syracuse Univ	NY	34,720	HC
Tabor College	KS	19,500	NC
Temple Univ	PA	15,912	C
Tenn Tech Univ	TN	8,670	VC
Texas A&M Univ	TX	11,081	HC
Texas A&M Univ at Commerce	TX	8,994	C
Texas A&M Univ at Kingsville	TX	6,740	LC
Texas State Univ	TX	9,320	VC
Texas Wesleyan Univ	TX	16,245	C
Thiel College	PA	20,970	C
Thomas More College	KY	21,350	C
Thomas Univ	GA	11,490	NC
Toccoa Falls College	GA	15,600	C
Trinity International Univ	IL	22,980	C+
Tri-State Univ-Main Campus	IN	23,600	C
Troy State Univ	AL	7,696	C
Troy State Univ Dothan	AL	3,842	C
Turabo Univ	PR	4,110	
Tuskegee Univ	AL	17,250	LC
Union College	KY	15,920	C
Union College	NE	17,130	NC
Union Univ	TN	18,800	VC

ST = STATE $IS = IN-STATE COSTS SR = SELECTOR RATING

School	ST	$IS	SR
Universidad Adventista de las Antillas	PR	5,460	
Universidad Metropolitana	PR	3,324	
Univ of Akron	OH	13,134	NC
Univ of Alabama	AL	9,040	C+
Univ of Alabama at Birmingham	AL	12,901	C
Univ of Alaska Anchorage	AK	9,100	NC
Univ of Arizona	AZ	10,413	VC
Univ of Central Arkansas	AR	6,388	C
Univ of Cincinnati	OH	14,736	C
Univ of Dayton	OH	24,850	VC
Univ of Delaware	DE	12,616	HC
Univ of Detroit Mercy	MI	25,582	C
Univ of Evansville	IN	24,190	VC
Univ of Findlay	OH	23,962	NC
Univ of Great Falls	MT	15,360	C
Univ of Hartford	CT	31,080	C
Univ of Hawaii at Manoa	HI	9,565	VC
Univ of Houston-Downtown	TX	2,594	NC
Univ of Idaho	ID	8,216	C
Univ of Illinois at Chicago	IL	13,418	C
Univ of Illinois at Urbana-Champaign	IL	11,316	HC+
Univ of Indianapolis	IN	22,560	VC
Univ of Iowa	IA	10,923	VC
Univ of Kansas	KS	8,923	VC
Univ of Kentucky	KY	7,765	C
Univ of Louisiana at Lafayette	LA	5,826	C
Univ of Louisville	KY	8,762	VC
Univ of Maine	ME	12,080	C+
Univ of Maine at Farmington	ME	10,108	C
Univ of Maine at Presque Isle	ME	9,155	LC
Univ of Mary Hardin-Baylor	TX	17,268	C
Univ of Maryland/College Park	MD	14,227	HC
Univ of Maryland/Eastern Shore	MD	9,964	C
Univ of Mass Amherst	MA	13,980	C+
Univ of Miami	FL	34,608	HC
Univ of Mich/Ann Arbor	MI	13,864	HC+
Univ of Mich/Dearborn	MI	6,843	VC
Univ of Mich/Flint	MI	5,548	C
Univ of Minn/Morris	MN	12,896	VC
Univ of Missouri/Columbia	MO	13,782	VC
Univ of Missouri/Kansas City	MO	13,416	VC
Univ of Missouri/Rolla	MO	12,292	HC
Univ of Missouri/St. Louis	MO	11,656	VC
Univ of Mobile	AL	13,620	C
Univ of Montana	MT	9,395	C
Univ of Montana--Western	MT	8,073	NC
Univ of Nebr at Kearney	NE	8,286	NC
Univ of Nebr at Lincoln	NE	9,975	C+
Univ of Nebr at Omaha	NE	8,080	C
Univ of Nevada/Las Vegas	NV	11,566	C
Univ of Nevada/Reno	NV	9,792	C
Univ of New England	ME	27,200	LC
Univ of New Orleans	LA	7,356	C
Univ of North Alabama	AL	7,972	NC
Univ of N Car at Chapel Hill	NC	10,117	MC
Univ of N Car at Greensboro	NC	8,248	C
Univ of N Car at Pembroke	NC	6,929	LC
Univ of N Car at Wilmington	NC	8,940	VC
Univ of North Florida	FL	8,769	VC
Univ of Pittsburgh at Johnstown	PA	15,216	LC
Univ of Portland	OR	28,500	VC
Univ of PR/Cayey Univ College	PR	1,245	
Univ of PR/Rio Piedras	PR	5,730	
Univ of Rhode Island	RI	13,720	VC
Univ of Rio Grande	OH	8,728	NC
Univ of St. Francis	IN	20,964	C
Univ of St. Thomas	MN	26,918	VC
Univ of San Diego	CA	33,156	HC
Univ of San Francisco	CA	34,700	VC
Univ of Scranton	PA	30,836	VC
Univ of Sioux Falls	SD	16,390	C
Univ of South Alabama	AL	7,760	LC
Univ of S Car at Aiken	SC	7,828	LC
Univ of S Car at Columbia	SC	10,048	VC
Univ of S Car at Spartanburg	SC	9,936	C+
Univ of S Dak	SD	7,710	C+
Univ of Southern Indiana	IN	9,025	LC
Univ of Southern Miss	MS	8,324	LC
Univ of Tampa	FL	23,982	VC
Univ of Tenn at Chattanooga	TN	7,783	C
Univ of Tenn at Martin	TN	7,748	C
Univ of Texas-Pan American	TX	5,954	LC
Univ of the Incarnate Word	TX	21,772	LC
Univ of Toledo	OH	12,479	NC
Univ of Vermont	VT	16,316	VC
Univ of West Alabama	AL	6,048	C
Univ of West Florida	FL	8,470	C
Univ of Wisc/Eau Claire	WI	8,463	VC
Univ of Wisc/La Crosse	WI	8,991	VC
Univ of Wisc/Madison	WI	8,262	VC
Univ of Wisc/Oshkosh	WI	6,130	LC
Univ of Wisc/Platteville	WI	8,450	C
Univ of Wisc/River Falls	WI	8,358	LC
Univ of Wisc/Superior	WI	7,051	C+
Univ of Wisc/Whitewater	WI	8,626	C
Univ of Wyoming	WY	8,636	C
Urbana Univ	OH	19,115	C
Ursinus College	PA	34,400	VC
Ursuline College	OH	22,728	LC
Utah State Univ	UT	7,371	C
Valdosta State Univ	GA	7,798	C
Valparaiso Univ	IN	26,118	VC+
Vanderbilt Univ	TN	37,897	MC
Vanguard Univ of Southern Calif	CA	22,208	C
Villanova Univ	PA	35,050	HC
Virginia Intermont College	VA	19,800	C
Virginia Union Univ	VA	15,358	LC
Wagner College	NY	29,900	VC
Walsh Univ	OH	20,890	C
Wartburg College	IA	21,165	VC
Washburn Univ of Topeka	KS	8,984	NC
Washington State Univ	WA	11,334	C
Washington Univ in St. Louis	MO	38,293	MC
Weber State Univ	UT	7,945	NC
Wesley College	DE	19,905	C
West Chester Univ of Pennsylvania	PA	11,164	C
West Liberty State College	WV	7,868	LC
West Virginia State College	WV	6,264	NC
West Virginia Wesleyan College	WV	22,920	C
Western Carolina Univ	NC	6,742	C
Western Conn State Univ	CT	11,625	C
Western Mich Univ	MI	12,031	C
Western New England College	MA	28,924	C
Western New Mexico Univ	NM	5,950	LC
Western State College of Colo	CO	9,014	C
Western Washington Univ	WA	10,119	VC
Westfield State College	MA	10,147	C
Westminster College	MO	18,150	C+
Westminster College	PA	22,960	C
Westminster College	UT	17,226	C
Wheaton College	IL	21,934	HC
Whitworth College	WA	26,428	VC+
Wichita State Univ	KS	8,092	C
Wiley College	TX	8,100	LC
William Jewell College	MO	21,320	VC
William Penn Univ	IA	17,575	LC
Williams Baptist College	AR	11,950	C
Wilmington College	OH	24,172	LC
Winona State Univ	MN		C
Winthrop Univ	SC	11,302	C
Wittenberg Univ	OH	31,316	VC
Wright State Univ	OH	11,490	LC
Xavier Univ of Louisiana	LA	17,600	C
York College of Pennsylvania	PA	14,500	VC
Youngstown State Univ	OH	11,148	NC

SECRETARIAL STUDIES/ OFFICE MANAGEMENT

School	ST	$IS	SR
Bennett College	NC	11,200	C
Caribbean Univ	PR	3,000	
David N. Myers College	OH	9,475	C
Delta State Univ	MS	6,618	C
Eastern Mich Univ	MI	11,478	C
Inter American Univ of PR/Aguadilla Campus	PR	3,544	
Inter American Univ of PR/Barranquitas Regional College	PR	3,300	
Inter American Univ of PR/Bayamon Univ College	PR	3,522	
Inter American Univ of PR/Fajardo Campus	PR	4,000	
Inter American Univ of PR/Metropolitan Campus	PR		
Inter American Univ of PR/Ponce Regional College	PR	3,700	
Inter American Univ of PR/San German	PR	6,716	
Johnson and Wales Univ	RI	22,965	LC
Southeastern Okla State Univ	OK	6,147	C
Southern Univ at New Orleans	LA	995	NC
Turabo Univ	PR	4,110	
Univ of PR at Humacao	PR	1,245	
Univ of PR/Arecibo	PR	1,095	
Univ of PR/Cayey Univ College	PR	1,245	
Univ of PR/Rio Piedras	PR	5,730	
Univ of the Sacred Heart	PR	5,590	
Youngstown State Univ	OH	11,148	NC

SLAVIC LANGUAGES

School	ST	$IS	SR
Columbia Univ/School of General Studies	NY	35,000	C
Duke Univ	NC	37,555	MC
Northwestern Univ	IL	37,491	MC
Princeton Univ	NJ	36,649	MC
St. Olaf College	MN	28,500	HC
Stanford Univ	CA	37,612	MC
Univ of Calif at Berkeley	CA	15,563	MC
Univ of Calif at Los Angeles	CA	15,330	MC
Univ of Calif at Santa Barbara	CA	11,732	VC
Univ of Kansas	KS	8,923	VC
Univ of Pennsylvania	PA	37,960	MC
Univ of Texas at Austin	TX	10,630	HC
Univ of Virginia	VA	11,740	MC
Univ of Washington	WA	10,361	VC
Wayne State Univ	MI	11,774	C

SMALL BUSINESS MANAGEMENT

School	ST	$IS	SR
Adams State College	CO	7,468	C
Cal State, San Bernardino	CA	15,238	LC
Concord College	WV	8,136	C
Ferris State Univ	MI	12,512	C
Florida Atlantic Univ	FL	8,543	C
Florida State Univ	FL	9,028	HC
Hawaii Pacific Univ	HI	19,218	C
Johnson and Wales Univ	RI	22,965	LC
Johnson State College	VT	11,819	LC
Lawrence Tech Univ	MI	20,487	C
Mount Ida College	MA	25,596	LC
Rowan Univ	NJ	14,506	VC
Thomas Edison State College	NJ	3,325	SP
Tusculum College	TN	19,990	C
Union College	NE	17,130	C
Univ of Colo at Boulder	CO	10,774	VC
Univ of Montana	MT	9,395	C
Univ of North Texas	TX	7,629	C
Waynesburg College	PA	19,370	C

SOCIAL FOUNDATIONS

School	ST	$IS	SR
Eastern Mich Univ	MI	11,478	C
Lehigh Univ	PA	37,570	HC+
Southern Christian Univ	AL	9,440	LC
Univ of Wisc/Green Bay	WI	8,154	C

SOCIAL PSYCHOLOGY

School	ST	$IS	SR
Bard College	NY	37,352	HC+
Florida Atlantic Univ	FL	8,543	C
Our Lady of Holy Cross College	LA	5,900	C
Park Univ	MO	10,780	C+
Wheaton College	MA	36,330	HC

SOCIAL SCIENCE

School	ST	$IS	SR
Abilene Christian Univ	TX	18,370	VC
Adelphi Univ	NY	26,300	VC
Alverno College	WI	18,898	C
Anna Maria College	MA	26,140	LC
Arkansas State Univ	AR	8,450	C
Ashland Univ	OH	24,464	C
Averett Univ	VA	23,010	LC
Azusa Pacific Univ	CA	24,720	VC
Bard College	NY	37,352	HC+
Bellevue Univ	NE	4,440	NC
Bemidji State Univ	MN	9,103	C
Benedict College	SC	12,662	LC
Benedictine College	KS	20,603	C
Benedictine Univ	IL	23,840	C
Bennington College	VT	35,910	HC
Berry College	GA	21,410	VC
Bethany College	KS	18,675	LC
Bethel College	IN	19,670	C
Bethel College	KS	19,800	C+
Biola Univ	CA	25,964	VC
Black Hills State Univ	SD	7,743	LC
Bloomsburg Univ of Pennsylvania	PA	10,844	C
Blue Mountain College	MS	10,226	C
Bluefield State College	WV	2,806	LC
Bluffton College	OH	23,694	C
Boise State Univ	ID	7,657	LC
Bowling Green State Univ	OH	13,036	C
Brewton-Parker College	GA	14,200	LC
Buena Vista Univ	IA	25,406	C
Calif Baptist Univ	CA	19,924	C
Calif Inst of Technology	CA	31,677	MC
Calif Lutheran Univ	CA	27,600	LC
Calif Polytechnic State Univ	CA	8,747	VC
Calif State Polytechnic Univ, Pomona	CA	8,793	C+
Cal State, Chico	CA	8,598	LC
Cal State, Los Angeles	CA	5,778	C
Cal State, Monterey Bay	CA	6,683	LC
Cal State, Sacramento	CA	9,543	C
Cal State, San Bernardino	CA	15,238	LC
Cal State, San Marcos	CA	1,736	LC
Cal State, Stanislaus	CA	9,874	C
Calif Univ of Pennsylvania	PA	10,388	C
Canisius College	NY	28,163	C+
Cardinal Stritch Univ	WI	17,620	C
Caribbean Univ	PR	3,000	
Carnegie Mellon Univ	PA	32,682	MC
Carroll College	MT	20,576	VC
Carson-Newman College	TN	16,760	C
Carthage College	WI	25,000	C
Castleton State College	VT	11,820	C
Cazenovia College	NY	23,940	C
Central Washington Univ	WA	9,768	C
Chadron State College	NE	6,286	NC
Chapman Univ	CA	33,118	VC
Charleston Southern Univ	SC	17,122	C
Cheyney Univ of Pennsylvania	PA	9,993	C
CUNY/Hunter College	NY	6,729	C+
Clarion Univ of Pennsylvania	PA	11,272	LC
Clarkson Univ	NY	32,226	VC
Cleveland State Univ	OH	12,308	LC
Colgate Univ	NY	37,095	MC
College of St. Benedict	MN	26,672	VC
Colo Christian Univ	CO	21,182	VC
Concord College	WV	8,136	C
Concordia Univ Wisc	WI	16,600	C
Concordia Univ, River Forest	IL	23,600	C
Coppin State College	MD	10,191	LC
Cumberland Univ	TN	16,910	C
Dana College	NE	20,280	C
Daniel Webster College	NH	24,875	C
Dartmouth College	NH	37,770	MC
David N. Myers College	OH	9,475	C
Delta State Univ	MS	6,618	C
DePaul Univ	IL	27,580	VC
Dominican College	NY	24,810	LC
Dominican Univ	IL	23,610	C
Dordt College	IA	20,170	VC
Dowling College	NY	23,870	LC
Eastern Conn State Univ	CT	10,362	C
Eastern Mennonite Univ	VA	22,990	C
Eastern Mich Univ	MI	11,478	C
Eastern Washington Univ	WA	9,012	C
Edinboro Univ of Pennsylvania	PA	10,850	LC
Elizabeth City State Univ	NC	5,550	LC
Emporia State Univ	KS	6,998	C
Eugene Lang College/New School Univ	NY	34,940	C
Eureka College	IL	24,980	LC
Evangel Univ	MO	15,435	C
Fayetteville State Univ	NC	5,590	LC
Flagler College	FL	11,860	VC+
Florida A&M Univ	FL	7,564	C
Florida Atlantic Univ	FL	8,543	C
Florida Southern College	FL	23,592	C
Florida State Univ	FL	9,028	HC
Fordham Univ	NY	35,066	HC
Franciscan Univ	IA	19,300	C
Fresno Pacific Univ	CA	22,462	C
Frostburg State Univ	MD	11,114	C
Gannon Univ	PA	23,260	C
Gardner-Webb Univ	NC	19,300	C
Goddard College	VT	21,056	C+
Goucher College	MD	32,650	HC
Graceland Univ	IA	19,550	C
Grand Canyon Univ	AZ	30,000	LC
Grand Valley State Univ	MI	11,022	VC
Gustavus Adolphus College	MN	27,120	VC+
Hamline Univ	MN	27,052	VC
Harding Univ	AR	14,890	VC
Hardin-Simmons Univ	TX	14,165	C
Harvard Univ/Harvard College	MA	37,928	MC
Hastings College	NE	19,928	VC
Hawaii Pacific Univ	HI	19,218	C
Heidelberg College	OH	20,266	NC
Hillsdale College	MI	22,450	HC
Hofstra Univ	NY	27,112	VC
Hope International Univ	CA	16,940	NC
Humboldt State Univ	CA	9,400	C
Illinois State Univ	IL	10,944	C+
Immaculata Univ	PA	25,200	C
Indiana Univ Kokomo	IN	4,463	LC
Indiana Univ of Pennsylvania	PA	10,489	C
Indiana Univ-Purdue Univ Fort Wayne	IN	5,108	LC
Iona College	NY	27,988	VC
James Madison Univ	VA	10,794	VC
Johns Hopkins Univ	MD	38,372	MC
Johnson C. Smith Univ	NC	18,108	C
Juniata College	PA	29,080	VC
Kansas State Univ	KS	8,728	VC
Keene State College	NH	12,212	C
Lake Erie College	OH	23,550	C
Lake Superior State Univ	MI	9,034	LC
Lamar Univ	TX	6,816	LC
Langston Univ	OK	2,308	LC
Lee Univ	TN	13,780	NC
LeMoyne-Owen College	TN	13,070	LC
Lesley Univ	MA	30,695	C
Lewis-Clark State College	ID	6,981	C
Liberty Univ	VA	17,220	C
Lincoln Memorial Univ	TN	16,400	LC
Lindsey Wilson College	KY	16,392	LC
Lock Haven Univ of Pennsylvania	PA	11,098	LC
LIU/Brooklyn Campus	NY	24,790	C
LIU/Southampton College	NY	29,370	C+

School	ST	$IS	SR
Louisiana State Univ and A&M College	LA	9,126	VC
Loyola Univ New Orleans	LA	31,036	VC+
Lyndon State College	VT	12,646	LC
Madonna Univ	MI	11,504	VC
Mansfield Univ	PA	11,220	C
Marlboro College	VT	29,055	VC+
Marygrove College	MI	17,550	C
Marylhurst Univ	OR	18,465	NC
Maryville College	TN	25,960	VC
Marywood Univ	PA	26,050	C
Mayville State Univ	ND	7,325	NC
McKendree College	IL	21,120	VC
MCP Hahnemann Univ	PA	18,510	SP
Medaille College	NY	20,060	C
Mercer Univ	GA	27,516	VC+
Mesa State College	CO	8,051	C
Metropolitan State Univ	MN	3,852	SP
Miami Univ	OH	15,033	HC
Mich State Univ	MI	11,933	VC
Mich Tech Univ	MI	13,235	VC
Midland Lutheran College	NE	18,600	C
Millikin Univ	IL	25,555	C
Minn State Univ, Moorehead	MN	7,000	LC
Minot State Univ	ND	6,602	LC
Miss Univ for Women	MS	5,446	LC
Missouri Baptist Univ	MO	18,010	C
Missouri Southern State Univ	MO	8,316	C
Montana State Univ-Northern	MT	8,600	NC
Moravian College	PA	28,903	VC
Morehead State Univ	KY	7,464	C
Mount Marty College	SD	15,656	LC
Mount St. Mary College	NY	21,270	C
Mount St. Mary's College	CA	28,307	VC
Mount Union College	OH	21,120	C
Muhlenberg College	PA	31,485	HC
Muskingum College	OH	20,680	C
National-Louis Univ	IL	16,240	LC
Nazareth College of Rochester	NY	24,936	VC
New College of Calif	CA	8,900	NC
New College of Florida	FL	8,906	HC+
New York Univ	NY	39,406	MC
Niagara Univ	NY	25,050	C
N Car State Univ	NC	9,886	VC
North Central College	IL	25,656	VC
N Dak State Univ	ND	8,435	C
North Georgia College and State Univ	GA	6,984	C
Northeastern State Univ	OK	4,950	LC
Northern Kentucky Univ	KY	6,352	NC
Northern State Univ	SD	7,117	LC
Northwest Christian College	OR	21,860	C
Northwest Missouri State Univ	MO	9,334	C
Northwestern College	MN	22,820	C+
Northwestern Okla State Univ	OK	5,433	NC
Northwestern State Univ of Louisiana	LA	6,331	NC
Notre Dame de Namur Univ	CA	26,932	LC
Nyack College	NY	18,540	C
Ohio Wesleyan Univ	OH	32,550	VC+
Okla Baptist Univ	OK	15,220	VC
Olivet Nazarene Univ	IL	20,480	C
Our Lady of Holy Cross College	LA	5,900	C
Pace Univ	NY	28,652	VC
Pepperdine Univ	CA	32,830	VC
Peru State College	NE	6,342	NC
Piedmont College	GA	16,900	C
Pikeville College	KY	14,900	NC
Pittsburg State Univ	KS	7,128	NC
Plymouth State Univ	NH	12,298	LC
Point Loma Nazarene Univ	CA	21,380	VC
Polytechnic Univ/Brooklyn	NY	33,770	VC
Pontifical Catholic Univ of PR/Ponce	PR	7,298	
Providence College	RI	30,604	HC
Quinnipiac Univ	CT	30,570	VC
Radford Univ	VA	8,500	C
Ramapo College of New Jersey	NJ	15,203	VC
Rhode Island College	RI	11,565	C
Robert Morris Univ	PA	20,438	C
Rockford College	IL	28,310	VC
Roger Williams Univ	RI	30,296	C
Roosevelt Univ	IL	22,580	VC
Rosemont College	PA	26,175	C
St. Bonaventure Univ	NY	24,455	LC
St. Cloud State Univ	MN	8,362	C
St. John's Univ	MN	26,473	VC
St. John's Univ	NY	30,180	C
St. Joseph's, Brooklyn,	NY	10,902	C
St. Joseph's Univ	PA	33,590	VC
St. Louis Univ	MO	29,780	VC+
St. Mary-of-the-Woods College	IN	23,280	C
St. Mary's College	MI	13,314	LC
St. Mary's Univ of Minn	MN	21,535	C
St. Paul's College	VA	14,344	NC
St. Peter's College	NJ	22,292	LC
St. Thomas Aquinas College	NY	20,590	LC
St. Xavier Univ	IL	23,144	C
Samford Univ	AL	18,648	VC
San Diego State Univ	CA	10,321	C
San Jose State Univ	CA	8,187	C
Seton Hall Univ	NJ	30,130	VC
Shawnee State Univ	OH	11,031	NC
Shimer College	IL	19,655	LC
Shorter College	GA	17,370	C
Siena Heights Univ	MI	16,140	LC
Silver Lake College of the Holy Family	WI	18,450	LC
Simpson College	CA	20,500	C
Skidmore College	NY	37,930	HC
Slippery Rock Univ of Pennsylvania	PA	10,343	LC
Southeastern Okla State Univ	OK	6,147	C
Southern Illinois Univ Carbondale	IL	10,407	C
Southern Methodist Univ	TX	34,210	HC
Southern Nazarene Univ	OK	14,634	NC
Southern New Hampshire Univ	NH	26,242	C
Southern Oregon Univ	OR	10,362	C
Southern Wesleyan Univ	SC	19,940	C
Southwest Missouri State Univ	MO	8,918	C
Southwestern Adventist Univ	TX	14,798	C
Spalding Univ	KY	17,985	C
Spring Arbor Univ	MI	20,206	C
St. Joseph's, Suffolk	NY	11,297	C
SUNY/Univ at Buffalo	NY	12,563	VC
SUNY/Univ at New Paltz	NY	11,565	VC
SUNY/Univ at Stony Brook	NY	12,763	HC
Stephens College	MO	24,260	C+
Stetson Univ	FL	29,495	VC
Suffolk Univ	MA	29,200	C
Sul Ross State Univ	TX	6,582	LC
Syracuse Univ	NY	34,720	HC
Tabor College	KS	19,500	NC
Temple Univ	PA	15,912	C
Texas State Univ	TX	9,320	VC
Texas Wesleyan Univ	TX	16,245	C
Thomas Edison State College	NJ	3,325	SP
Thomas Univ	GA	11,490	NC
Touro College	NY	15,250	VC
Towson Univ	MD	12,694	VC
Trevecca Nazarene Univ	TN	17,548	C
Trinity International Univ	IL	22,980	C+
Tri-State Univ-Main Campus	IN	23,600	C
Troy State Univ	AL	7,696	C
Troy State Univ Dothan	AL	3,842	C
Troy State Univ Montgomery	AL	3,600	NC
Turabo Univ	PR	4,110	
Union College	NE	17,130	C
Union Inst and Univ	OH	7,848	SP
United States Air Force Academy	CO		HC+
Universidad Metropolitana	PR	3,324	
Univ of Akron	OH	13,134	NC
Univ of Alaska Southeast	AK	7,900	LC
Univ of Arizona	AZ	10,413	VC
Univ of Bridgeport	CT	25,924	LC
Univ of Calif at Berkeley	CA	15,563	MC
Univ of Calif at Davis	CA	14,995	VC
Univ of Calif at Irvine	CA	19,808	HC
Univ of Calif at Riverside	CA	15,300	C
Univ of Central Florida	FL	10,038	VC
Univ of Chicago	IL	35,087	MC
Univ of Cincinnati	OH	14,736	C
Univ of Denver	CO	32,148	VC
Univ of Georgia	GA	8,656	VC
Univ of Great Falls	MT	15,360	C
Univ of Houston	TX	9,818	C
Univ of Houston-Downtown	TX	2,594	NC
Univ of Indianapolis	IN	22,560	VC
Univ of Iowa	IA	10,923	VC
Univ of La Verne	CA	28,600	C
Univ of Maine at Augusta	ME	4,065	C
Univ of Maine at Fort Kent	ME	9,770	LC
Univ of Mary	ND	12,900	C+
Univ of Mary Hardin-Baylor	TX	17,268	C
Univ of Maryland/Univ College	MD	5,910	SP
Univ of Mich/Ann Arbor	MI	13,864	HC+
Univ of Mich/Dearborn	MI	6,843	VC
Univ of Mich/Flint	MI	5,548	C
Univ of Minn/Morris	MN	12,896	VC
Univ of Missouri/Columbia	MO	13,782	VC
Univ of Montana--Western	MT	8,073	NC
Univ of Montevallo	AL	8,478	C
Univ of Nebr at Kearney	NE	8,286	NC
Univ of Nevada/Las Vegas	NV	11,566	C
Univ of N Dak	ND	8,390	C
Univ of North Texas	TX	7,629	C
Univ of Northern Colo	CO	8,987	C
Univ of Northern Iowa	IA	9,834	C
Univ of Pittsburgh at Bradford	PA	15,294	C
Univ of Pittsburgh at Greensburg	PA	15,984	C
Univ of Pittsburgh at Johnstown	PA	15,216	LC
Univ of Pittsburgh at Pittsburgh	PA	16,074	HC
Univ of PR/Mayaguez	PR		
Univ of PR/Rio Piedras	PR	5,730	
Univ of St. Thomas	MN	26,918	VC
Univ of South Florida	FL	9,454	C
Univ of Southern Calif	CA	37,459	MC
Univ of Southern Colo	CO	7,821	LC
Univ of Southern Miss	MS	8,324	LC
Univ of Tampa	FL	23,982	VC
Univ of the Ozarks	AR	16,574	C
Univ of the Pacific	CA	31,090	VC
Univ of the South	TN	30,855	HC
Univ of Utah	UT	9,205	C
Univ of Virginia's College at Wise	VA	10,116	C
Univ of West Alabama	AL	6,048	C
Univ of West Florida	FL	8,470	C
Univ of Wisc/Eau Claire	WI	8,463	VC
Univ of Wisc/Platteville	WI	8,450	C
Univ of Wisc/Stevens Point	WI	8,116	VC
Univ of Wyoming	WY	8,636	C
Upper Iowa Univ	IA	20,076	C
Valley City State Univ	ND	7,281	LC
Virginia Wesleyan College	VA	25,350	C
Warner Pacific College	OR	21,900	C
Washington State Univ	WA	11,334	C
Washington Univ in St. Louis	MO	38,293	MC
Wayland Baptist Univ	TX	11,919	NC
Wayne State College	NE	7,352	NC
Waynesburg College	PA	19,370	C
Webster Univ	MO	21,848	VC
Wesleyan College	GA	17,870	VC
West Liberty State College	WV	7,868	LC
West Texas A&M Univ	TX	7,533	C
West Virginia Wesleyan College	WV	22,920	C
Western Baptist College	OR	21,808	C
Western Carolina Univ	NC	6,742	C
Western Conn State Univ	CT	11,625	C
Western New Mexico Univ	NM	5,950	LC
Western Oregon Univ	OR	10,281	C
Westminster College	PA	22,960	C
Westminster College	UT	17,226	C
Westmont College	CA	33,062	VC+
Wheaton College	IL	21,934	HC
Wilberforce Univ	OH	14,937	LC
Wiley College	TX	8,100	LC
William Carey College	MS	10,150	LC
William Tyndale College	MI	12,170	NC
Wilmington College	OH	24,172	LC
Winona State Univ	MN		C
Wisc Lutheran College	WI	21,430	VC
Worcester Polytechnic Inst	MA	37,404	HC
Youngstown State Univ	OH	11,148	NC

SOCIAL SCIENCE EDUCATION

School	ST	$IS	SR
Appalachian State Univ	NC	7,637	VC
Armstrong Atlantic State Univ	GA	7,102	C
Auburn Univ	AL	10,396	VC
Averett Univ	VA	23,010	LC
Baylor Univ	TX	23,864	VC
Bethune-Cookman College	FL	16,480	LC
Blackburn College	IL	13,690	C
Blue Mountain College	MS	10,226	C
Brigham Young Univ	UT	8,504	HC
Brigham Young Univ/Hawaii	HI	7,240	VC+
Central Methodist College	MO	16,460	C
Coker College	SC	21,491	C
College of St. Scholastica	MN	24,970	C+
College of Santa Fe	NM	25,293	C+
Dana College	NE	20,280	C
Delta State Univ	MS	6,618	C
Doane College	NE	20,000	C
Eastern Illinois Univ	IL	11,192	C
Eastern Mich Univ	MI	11,478	C
Eastern Nazarene College	MA	19,433	LC
Eastern Washington Univ	WA	9,012	C
Elon Univ	NC	22,240	VC
Fayetteville State Univ	NC	5,590	LC
Florida State Univ	FL	9,028	HC
Fresno Pacific Univ	CA	22,462	C
Friends Univ	KS	15,962	LC
Georgia Southern Univ	GA	8,540	C
Georgia Southwestern State Univ	GA	6,013	C
Hope International Univ	CA	16,940	NC
Humboldt State Univ	CA	9,400	C
Indiana Univ of Pennsylvania	PA	10,489	C
Jackson State Univ	MS	8,382	C
Lincoln Univ	MO	7,158	NC
Mercyhurst College	PA	20,694	C
Miles College	AL	7,870	NC
Miss Valley State Univ	MS	6,765	NC
Missouri Southern State Univ	MO	8,316	C
Montana State Univ-Billings	MT	9,550	C
Montana State Univ-Northern	MT	8,600	NC
Mount Holyoke College	MA	37,918	HC+
Nebr Wesleyan Univ	NE	21,197	C+
N Car Agricultural and Technical State Univ	NC	6,659	LC
North Georgia College and State Univ	GA	6,984	C
Northwest Nazarene Univ	ID	20,360	VC
Oakwood College	AL	14,904	C
Palm Beach Atlantic Univ	FL	20,690	C
Rocky Mountain College	MT	19,015	C
Rust College	MS	8,200	C+
St. John's Univ	NY	30,180	C
St. Mary's Univ of Minn	MN	21,535	C
Schreiner Univ	TX	20,440	C
Seattle Pacific Univ	WA	25,944	VC
Seton Hill Univ	PA	24,930	C
Sheldon Jackson College	AK	14,940	LC
Southern Utah Univ	UT	8,194	C
Southwest Baptist Univ	MO	15,371	C
Southwestern Okla State Univ	OK	4,801	C
SUNY/College at Oneonta	NY	11,870	VC
Stetson Univ	FL	29,495	VC
Toccoa Falls College	GA	15,600	C
Tri-State Univ-Main Campus	IN	23,600	C
Troy State Univ	AL	7,696	C
Troy State Univ Dothan	AL	3,842	C
Turabo Univ	PR	4,110	
Union College	NE	17,130	C
Univ of Arkansas at Pine Bluff	AR	7,925	C
Univ of Central Florida	FL	10,038	VC
Univ of Georgia	GA	8,656	VC
Univ of Mary	ND	12,900	C+
Univ of Maryland/Eastern Shore	MD	9,964	C
Univ of Miss	MS	7,666	C
Univ of North Alabama	AL	7,972	NC
Univ of N Car at Greensboro	NC	8,248	C
Univ of Pittsburgh at Johnstown	PA	15,216	LC
Univ of Rio Grande	OH	8,728	NC
Univ of Wisc/Milwaukee	WI	9,427	LC
Univ of Wisc/Oshkosh	WI	6,130	LC
Warner Southern College	FL	16,738	LC
Washington Univ in St. Louis	MO	38,293	MC
Weber State Univ	UT	7,945	NC
Western Carolina Univ	NC	6,742	C
Westmont College	CA	33,062	VC+
Wiley College	TX	8,100	LC
Youngstown State Univ	OH	11,148	NC

SOCIAL STUDIES

School	ST	$IS	SR
Alvernia College	PA	23,212	LC
Alverno College	WI	18,898	C
Andrews Univ	MI	19,550	C
Barton College	NC	19,314	C
Bluefield College	VA	15,575	C
Brescia Univ	KY	14,225	C
Caldwell College	NJ	24,060	LC
Carlow College	PA	21,334	C
Chaminade Univ of Honolulu	HI	21,430	LC
Christian Brothers Univ	TN	22,290	VC
Cleveland State Univ	OH	12,308	LC
College of St. Catherine	MN	24,010	VC
Concordia Univ	MI	24,095	C
DePaul Univ	IL	27,580	VC
East Stroudsburg Univ of Pennsylvania	PA	10,336	C
Eastern Nazarene College	MA	19,433	LC
Eastern New Mexico Univ	NM	6,762	LC
Elizabethtown College	PA	28,800	C
Erskine College	SC	23,166	VC
Ferrum College	VA	21,240	LC
Grand Canyon Univ	AZ	30,000	LC
Harvard Univ/Harvard College	MA	37,928	MC
Hiram College	OH	28,234	VC
Indiana Wesleyan Univ	IN	19,900	C+
Ithaca College	NY	31,730	HC
John Brown Univ	AR	15,080	VC
Kent State Univ	OH	12,932	C
Methodist College	NC	19,526	C
Minn State Univ, Mankato	MN	8,803	LC
Miss College	MS	14,574	C
Missouri Southern State Univ	MO	8,316	C
Mount St. Mary's College	MD	28,400	C
New York Inst of Technology	NY	24,205	VC
Ohio Northern Univ	OH	27,765	VC
Ohio Univ	OH	14,448	C
Okla Panhandle State Univ	OK	5,370	C
Okla Wesleyan Univ	OK	14,100	LC
Olivet College	MI	19,984	C+
Our Lady of the Lake Univ of San Antonio	TX	17,336	C
Pacific Union College	CA	22,065	C+
Pfeiffer Univ	NC	18,980	C

School	ST	$IS	SR
St. Francis College	NY	10,880	LC
Shippensburg Univ of Pennsylvania	PA	10,826	C
S Car State Univ	SC	6,586	LC
Southern Illinois Univ Carbondale	IL	10,407	C
Southwestern Adventist Univ	TX	14,798	C
Spring Arbor Univ	MI	20,206	C
Univ of Arizona	AZ	10,413	VC
Univ of St. Thomas	MN	26,918	VC
Univ of Wisc/River Falls	WI	8,358	LC
Univ of Wisc/Superior	WI	7,051	C+
Utica College	NY	28,340	C
Vassar College	NY	37,030	MC
Virginia Wesleyan College	VA	25,350	C
Viterbo Univ	WI	20,430	C
Washington State Univ	WA	11,334	C
Wayland Baptist Univ	TX	11,919	NC
Western Kentucky Univ	KY	6,834	C
Youngstown State Univ	OH	11,148	NC

SOCIAL STUDIES EDUCATION

School	ST	$IS	SR
Adams State College	CO	7,468	C
Adelphi Univ	NY	26,300	VC
Alabama State Univ	AL	6,404	C
Alfred Univ	NY	28,290	C
Alice Lloyd College	KY	4,040	C
Anderson Univ	IN	19,430	LC
Andrews Univ	MI	19,550	C
Asbury College	KY	20,704	VC
Augustana College	SD	21,998	VC
Averett Univ	VA	23,010	LC
Ball State Univ	IN	8,660	C
Baylor Univ	TX	23,864	VC
Bethel College	IN	19,670	C
Bloomsburg Univ of Pennsylvania	PA	10,844	C
Boston Univ	MA	38,194	HC+
Brewton-Parker College	GA	14,200	LC
Brigham Young Univ	UT	8,504	HC
Calif Univ of Pennsylvania	PA	10,388	C
Canisius College	NY	28,163	C+
Catawba College	NC	20,500	C
Cedarville Univ	OH	19,954	VC
Centenary College of Louisiana	LA	23,100	VC+
Central Missouri State Univ	MO	9,776	C
Central Washington Univ	WA	9,768	C
CUNY/Brooklyn College	NY	4,353	C+
CUNY/City College	NY	4,230	C+
Clearwater Christian College	FL	13,160	LC
Colby-Sawyer College	NH	27,850	LC
College of New Jersey	NJ	15,950	MC
College of St. Rose	NY	22,864	C
College of the Ozarks	MO	3,500	VC+
Concordia College: Moorhead	MN	22,460	VC+
Concordia Univ/St.Paul	MN	24,486	C
Cumberland College	KY	16,384	C
Daemen College	NY	22,120	C
Dana College	NE	20,280	C
Defiance College	OH	22,615	C
Delta State Univ	MS	6,618	C
Duquesne Univ	PA	26,907	VC
East Carolina Univ	NC	8,671	C
East Texas Baptist Univ	TX	13,914	C
Edgewood College	WI	20,520	C
Edinboro Univ of Pennsylvania	PA	10,850	LC
Florida International Univ	FL	9,912	VC
Franklin College	IN		C
George Fox Univ	OR	26,110	VC
Green Mountain College	VT	24,130	C
Greensboro College	NC	21,750	C
Greenville College	IL	21,342	C
Gwynedd-Mercy College	PA	24,225	C
Heritage College	WA	6,720	NC
Hofstra Univ	NY	27,112	VC
Huntington College	IN	23,590	C
Indiana State Univ	IN	10,719	LC
Indiana Univ Bloomington	IN	12,389	VC
Indiana Univ South Bend	IN	4,571	LC
Indiana Univ Southeast	IN	4,504	LC
Indiana Univ-Purdue Univ Indianapolis	IN	8,257	LC
Indiana Wesleyan Univ	IN	19,900	C+
Ithaca College	NY	31,730	HC
Johnson C. Smith Univ	NC	18,108	C
Judson College	AL	14,650	C
Juniata College	PA	29,080	VC
Kennesaw State Univ	GA	2,724	C
Kent State Univ	OH	12,932	C
Kentucky State Univ	KY	9,062	NC
La Salle Univ	PA	31,260	VC
Le Moyne College	NY	26,400	VC
Limestone College	SC	17,700	C
Louisiana College	LA	13,450	C
Malone College	OH	20,995	C
Mansfield Univ	PA	11,220	C
Mars Hill College	NC	18,600	LC
Mary Baldwin College	VA	24,939	C
Marygrove College	MI	17,550	C
Messiah College	PA	25,890	VC+
MidAmerica Nazarene Univ	KS	18,688	C
Millersville Univ of Pennsylvania	PA	11,269	C
Minn State Univ, Moorehead	MN	7,000	LC
Missouri Southern State Univ	MO	8,316	C
Missouri Valley College	MO	18,500	C
Montana State Univ-Billings	MT	9,550	C
Morningside College	IA	21,610	C
Morris College	SC	10,974	LC
Mount Vernon Nazarene Univ	OH	18,925	C
Nazareth College of Rochester	NY	24,936	VC
New York Univ	NY	39,406	MC
Niagara Univ	NY	25,050	C
N Car State Univ	NC	9,886	VC
Northwestern College	MN	22,820	C+
Notre Dame de Namur Univ	CA	26,932	LC
Okla Christian Univ	OK	17,690	NC
Okla Panhandle State Univ	OK	5,370	C
Okla Wesleyan Univ	OK	14,100	LC
Old Dominion Univ	VA	10,441	C
Oral Roberts Univ	OK	18,490	C
Pontifical Catholic Univ of PR/Ponce	PR	7,298	
Providence College	RI	30,604	HC
Purdue Univ/West Lafayette	IN	12,560	VC
Rider Univ	NJ	30,900	C
Rivier College	NH	26,217	C
Rocky Mountain College	MT	19,015	C
St. Augustine's College	NC	12,990	LC
St. Edward's Univ	TX	20,428	C
St. John Fisher College	NY	24,870	C
St. John's Univ	NY	30,180	C
St. Martin's College	WA	23,245	C
St. Olaf College	MN	28,500	HC
St. Thomas Univ	FL	21,400	LC
Shaw Univ	NC	14,882	C+
Shepherd College	WV	8,608	C
Southeast Missouri State Univ	MO	9,704	C
Southeastern Louisiana Univ	LA	6,791	LC
Southeastern Okla State Univ	OK	6,147	C
Southern Univ at New Orleans	LA	995	NC
Southern Utah Univ	UT	8,194	C
SUNY at Potsdam	NY	12,160	C
SUNY/College at Old Westbury	NY	12,784	C
SUNY/College at Plattsburgh	NY	11,700	C
SUNY/Univ at Albany	NY	12,951	HC
Syracuse Univ	NY	34,720	HC
Taylor Univ	IN	23,820	VC+
Temple Univ	PA	15,912	C
Texas Christian Univ	TX	23,410	VC
Univ of Central Okla	OK	9,434	C
Univ of Charleston	WV	23,620	C
Univ of Conn	CT	14,608	VC
Univ of Evansville	IN	24,190	VC
Univ of Great Falls	MT	15,360	C
Univ of Indianapolis	IN	22,560	VC
Univ of Kentucky	KY	7,765	C
Univ of Louisiana at Lafayette	LA	5,826	C
Univ of Louisiana at Monroe	LA	5,207	NC
Univ of Mich/Dearborn	MI	6,843	VC
Univ of Minn/Duluth	MN	12,470	C
Univ of Minn/Twin Cities	MN	13,160	VC
Univ of N Car at Chapel Hill	NC	10,117	MC
Univ of N Car at Charlotte	NC	8,185	C
Univ of N Car at Pembroke	NC	6,929	LC
Univ of N Dak	ND	8,390	C
Univ of Okla	OK	9,226	VC
Univ of Rio Grande	OH	8,728	NC
Univ of St. Francis	IN	20,964	C
Univ of S Car at Spartanburg	SC	9,936	C+
Univ of South Florida	FL	9,454	C
Univ of Vermont	VT	16,316	VC
Univ of Wisc/La Crosse	WI	8,991	VC
Univ of Wisc/Whitewater	WI	8,626	C
Wartburg College	IA	21,165	VC
Washington Univ in St. Louis	MO	38,293	MC
Wesley College	DE	19,905	C
West Chester Univ of Pennsylvania	PA	11,164	C
West Texas A&M Univ	TX	7,533	C
Whitworth College	WA	26,428	VC+
Xavier Univ of Louisiana	LA	17,600	C
Youngstown State Univ	OH	11,148	NC

SOCIAL WORK

School	ST	$IS	SR
Abilene Christian Univ	TX	18,370	VC
Adams State College	CO	7,468	C
Adelphi Univ	NY	26,300	VC
Alabama A&M Univ	AL	5,100	LC
Alabama State Univ	AL	6,404	C
Albany State Univ	GA	5,764	C+
Alvernia College	PA	23,212	LC
Anderson Univ	IN	19,430	LC
Andrews Univ	MI	19,550	C
Anna Maria College	MA	26,140	LC
Appalachian State Univ	NC	7,637	VC
Arizona State Univ-Main	AZ	10,048	C
Arkansas State Univ	AR	8,450	C
Asbury College	KY	20,704	VC
Ashland Univ	OH	24,464	C
Atlantic Union College	MA	18,868	C
Auburn Univ	AL	10,396	VC
Augsburg College	MN	25,298	C
Augustana College	SD	21,998	VC
Aurora Univ	IL	20,631	C
Austin Peay State Univ	TN	5,814	LC
Avila Univ	MO	20,300	C
Azusa Pacific Univ	CA	24,720	VC
Ball State Univ	IN	8,660	C
Barton College	NC	19,314	C
Baylor Univ	TX	23,864	VC
Belhaven College	MS	16,040	C+
Belmont Univ	TN	21,986	VC
Bemidji State Univ	MN	9,103	C
Benedict College	SC	12,662	LC
Bennett College	NC	11,200	C
Bethany College	KS	18,675	LC
Bethany College	WV	19,845	VC
Bethel College	KS	19,800	C+
Bethel College	MN	25,180	VC
Bloomsburg Univ of Pennsylvania	PA	10,844	C
Bluffton College	OH	23,694	C
Boise State Univ	ID	7,657	LC
Bowie State Univ	MD	10,873	C+
Bowling Green State Univ	OH	13,036	C
Bradley Univ	IL	22,910	VC
Brescia Univ	KY	14,225	C
Briar Cliff Univ	IA	21,660	C
Bridgewater State College	MA	10,482	C
Brigham Young Univ	UT	8,504	HC
Brigham Young Univ/Hawaii	HI	7,240	VC+
Buena Vista Univ	IA	25,406	C
Cabrini College	PA	29,020	C
Cal State, Chico	CA	8,598	LC
Cal State, Fresno	CA	8,414	LC
Cal State, Los Angeles	CA	5,778	C
Cal State, Sacramento	CA	9,543	C
Cal State, San Bernardino	CA	15,238	LC
Cal State, Stanislaus	CA	9,874	C
Calif Univ of Pennsylvania	PA	10,388	C
Calvin College	MI	22,615	NC
Campbell Univ	NC	18,268	VC
Campbellsville Univ	KY	17,680	C
Capital Univ	OH	26,550	C
Caribbean Univ	PR	3,000	
Carlow College	PA	21,334	C
Carroll College	MT	20,576	VC
Carthage College	WI	25,000	C
Castleton State College	VT	11,820	C
Catholic Univ of America	DC	34,248	VC
Cedar Crest College	PA	25,145	C+
Cedarville Univ	OH	19,954	VC
Central Conn State Univ	CT	12,090	C
Central Missouri State Univ	MO	9,776	C
Central State Univ	OH	8,922	C+
Central Univ of Bayamon	PR	3,335	
Central Washington Univ	WA	9,768	C
Chadron State College	NE	6,286	NC
Champlain College	VT	22,030	C
Chatham College	PA	27,266	C+
Christopher Newport Univ	VA	8,862	VC
CUNY/College of Staten Island	NY	4,308	NC
CUNY/Herbert H. Lehman College	NY	3,320	LC
CUNY/Queens College	NY	4,362	C
CUNY/York College	NY	3,292	NC
Clark Atlanta Univ	GA	19,300	C+
Clarke College	IA	23,165	C
Cleveland State Univ	OH	12,308	LC
Coker College	SC	21,491	C
College Misericordia	PA	26,350	C
College of Mount St. Joseph	OH	22,785	C
College of New Rochelle	NY	21,800	C
College of Our Lady of the Elms	MA	20,644	C
College of St. Benedict	MN	26,672	VC
College of St. Catherine	MN	24,010	VC
College of St. Rose	NY	22,864	C
College of St. Scholastica	MN	24,970	C+
College of the Ozarks	MO	3,500	VC+
Colo State Univ	CO	9,964	VC
Columbia College	MO	16,139	C
Columbia College	SC	22,658	LC
Concord College	WV	8,136	C
Concordia College	NY	19,200	VC
Concordia College: Moorhead	MN	22,460	VC+
Concordia Univ	OR	22,450	C
Concordia Univ Wisc	WI	16,600	C
Concordia Univ, River Forest	IL	23,600	C
Coppin State College	MD	10,191	LC
Cornerstone Univ and Grand Rapids Theological Seminary	MI	19,846	C
Creighton Univ	NE	26,748	VC+
Cumberland College	KY	16,384	C
Daemen College	NY	22,120	C
Dana College	NE	20,280	C
David Lipscomb Univ	TN	16,158	VC
De Sales Univ	PA	25,470	C
Defiance College	OH	22,615	C
Delaware State Univ	DE	8,104	LC
Delta State Univ	MS	6,618	C
Dickinson State Univ	ND	6,338	NC
Dominican College	NY	24,810	LC
Dordt College	IA	20,170	VC
East Carolina Univ	NC	8,671	C
East Central Univ	OK	4,968	C
East Tenn State Univ	TN	8,497	C
Eastern Conn State Univ	CT	10,362	C
Eastern Kentucky Univ	KY	7,708	C
Eastern Mennonite Univ	VA	22,990	C
Eastern Mich Univ	MI	11,478	C
Eastern Nazarene College	MA	19,433	LC
Eastern Univ	PA	24,020	C
Eastern Washington Univ	WA	9,012	C
Edinboro Univ of Pennsylvania	PA	10,850	LC
Elizabeth City State Univ	NC	5,550	LC
Elizabethtown College	PA	28,800	C
Evangel Univ	MO	15,435	C
Ferris State Univ	MI	12,512	C
Ferrum College	VA	21,240	LC
Florida A&M Univ	FL	7,564	C
Florida Atlantic Univ	FL	8,543	C
Florida International Univ	FL	9,912	VC
Florida State Univ	FL	9,028	HC
Fordham Univ	NY	35,066	HC
Fort Hays State Univ	KS	7,363	C
Fort Valley State Univ	GA	6,960	C
Franciscan Univ of Steubenville	OH	20,300	VC
Franklin Pierce College	NH	28,980	LC
Freed-Hardeman Univ	TN		NC
Fresno Pacific Univ	CA	22,462	C
Frostburg State Univ	MD	11,114	C
Gallaudet Univ	DC	16,554	SP
Gannon Univ	PA	23,260	C
George Fox Univ	OR	26,110	VC
George Mason Univ	VA	9,732	VC
Georgia Southern Univ	GA	8,540	C
Georgia State Univ	GA	10,658	C
Georgian Court College	NJ	19,040	LC
Gordon College	MA	25,982	VC+
Goshen College	IN	22,450	VC
Grace College	IN	19,825	VC
Grambling State Univ	LA	6,538	NC
Grand Valley State Univ	MI	11,022	VC
Greenville College	IL	21,342	C
Gwynedd-Mercy College	PA	24,225	C
Harding Univ	AR	14,890	VC
Hardin-Simmons Univ	TX	14,165	C
Hawaii Pacific Univ	HI	19,218	C
Heritage College	WA	6,720	NC
Holy Family College	PA	13,710	LC
Hood College	MD	27,795	VC
Hope College	MI	25,340	VC
Howard Payne Univ	TX	15,176	C
Humboldt State Univ	CA	9,400	C
Idaho State Univ	ID	8,128	C
Illinois State Univ	IL	10,944	C+
Indiana State Univ	IN	10,719	LC
Indiana Univ Bloomington	IN	12,389	VC
Indiana Univ East	IN	4,433	LC
Indiana Univ South Bend	IN	4,571	LC
Indiana Univ-Purdue Univ Indianapolis	IN	8,257	LC
Indiana Wesleyan Univ	IN	19,900	C+
Inter American Univ of PR/ Arecibo Campus	PR	3,300	
Inter American Univ of PR/ Fajardo Campus	PR	4,000	
Inter American Univ of PR/ Metropolitan Campus	PR		
Inter American Univ of PR/ Ponce Regional College	PR	3,700	
Iona College	NY	27,988	VC
Jackson State Univ	MS	8,382	C
Jacksonville State Univ	AL	6,844	LC
James Madison Univ	VA	10,794	VC
Johnson C. Smith Univ	NC	18,108	C
Juniata College	PA	29,080	VC
Kansas State Univ	KS	8,728	VC
Kean Univ	NJ	14,479	C
Kentucky Christian College	KY	13,472	C
Kentucky State Univ	KY	9,062	NC
Keuka College	NY	21,170	C
Kutztown Univ of Pennsylvania	PA	10,786	C
La Salle Univ	PA	31,260	VC
La Sierra Univ	CA	19,260	LC
LaGrange College	GA	20,500	C
Lamar Univ	TX	6,816	LC
LeMoyne-Owen College	TN	13,070	LC
Lewis Univ	IL	22,950	C+
Lewis-Clark State College	ID	6,981	C
Limestone College	SC	17,700	C
Lincoln Memorial Univ	TN	16,400	LC
Lindenwood Univ	MO	17,050	VC
Livingstone College	NC	18,101	LC

ST = STATE $IS = IN-STATE COSTS SR = SELECTOR RATING

School	ST	$IS	SR
Beloit College	WI	29,864	HC
Bemidji State Univ	MN	9,103	C
Benedictine College	KS	20,603	C
Benedictine Univ	IL	23,840	C
Bennett College	NC	11,200	C
Bennington College	VT	35,910	HC
Berea College	KY	5,030	VC+
Berry College	GA	21,410	VC
Bethel College	IN	19,670	C
Bethel College	TN	12,980	C
Bethune-Cookman College	FL	16,480	LC
Biola Univ	CA	25,964	VC
Birmingham-Southern College	AL	25,364	VC+
Black Hills State Univ	SD	7,743	LC
Bloomfield College	NJ	19,250	LC
Bloomsburg Univ of Pennsylvania	PA	10,844	C
Bluffton College	OH	23,694	C
Boise State Univ	ID	7,657	LC
Boston College	MA	33,284	MC
Boston Univ	MA	38,194	HC+
Bowdoin College	ME	37,790	MC
Bowie State Univ	MD	10,873	C+
Bowling Green State Univ	OH	13,036	C
Bradley Univ	IL	22,910	VC
Brandeis Univ	MA	38,198	MC
Brewton-Parker College	GA	14,200	LC
Briar Cliff Univ	IA	21,660	C
Bridgewater College	VA	25,150	C
Bridgewater State College	MA	10,482	C
Brigham Young Univ	UT	8,504	HC
Brown Univ	RI	38,174	MC
Bryn Mawr College	PA	36,890	HC+
Bucknell Univ	PA	35,262	HC+
Butler Univ	IN	28,250	VC+
Cabrini College	PA	29,020	C
Caldwell College	NJ	24,060	LC
Calif Baptist Univ	CA	19,924	C
Calif Lutheran Univ	CA	27,600	LC
Calif State Polytechnic Univ, Pomona	CA	8,793	C+
Cal State, Bakersfield	CA	6,090	LC
Cal State, Chico	CA	8,598	LC
Cal State, Dominguez Hills	CA	5,840	LC
Cal State, Fresno	CA	8,414	LC
Cal State, Fullerton	CA	6,648	C
Cal State, Hayward	CA	8,871	LC
Cal State, Long Beach	CA	8,762	C+
Cal State, Los Angeles	CA	5,778	C
Cal State, Northridge	CA	7,757	LC
Cal State, Sacramento	CA	9,543	C
Cal State, San Bernardino	CA	15,238	LC
Cal State, San Marcos	CA	1,736	LC
Cal State, Stanislaus	CA	9,874	C
Calif Univ of Pennsylvania	PA	10,388	C
Calvin College	MI	22,615	NC
Cameron Univ	OK	5,692	NC
Campbellsville Univ	KY	17,680	C
Canisius College	NY	28,163	C+
Capital Univ	OH	26,550	C
Cardinal Stritch Univ	WI	17,620	C
Carleton College	MN	34,395	MC
Carlow College	PA	21,334	C
Carroll College	MT	20,576	VC
Carroll College	WI	22,740	C
Carson-Newman College	TN	16,760	C
Carthage College	WI	25,000	C
Case Western Reserve Univ	OH	32,002	MC
Castleton State College	VT	11,820	C
Catawba College	NC	20,500	C
Catholic Univ of America	DC	34,248	VC
Cedar Crest College	PA	25,145	C+
Cedarville Univ	OH	19,954	VC
Centenary College	NJ	25,370	LC
Centenary College of Louisiana	LA	23,100	VC+
Central College	IA	21,206	C
Central Conn State Univ	CT	12,090	C
Central Methodist College	MO	16,460	C
Central Mich Univ	MI	11,142	C
Central Missouri State Univ	MO	9,776	C
Central State Univ	OH	8,922	C+
Central Univ of Bayamon	PR	3,335	
Central Washington Univ	WA	9,768	C
Centre College	KY	27,300	HC
Chadron State College	NE	6,286	NC
Chapman Univ	CA	33,118	VC
Charleston Southern Univ	SC	17,122	C
Chestnut Hill College	PA	26,450	LC
Chicago State Univ	IL	10,882	C+
Christopher Newport Univ	VA	8,862	VC
CUNY/Baruch College	NY	3,275	VC+
CUNY/Brooklyn College	NY	4,353	C+
CUNY/City College	NY	4,230	C+
CUNY/College of Staten Island	NY	4,308	NC
CUNY/Herbert H. Lehman College	NY	3,320	LC
CUNY/Hunter College	NY	6,729	C+
CUNY/Queens College	NY	4,362	C
CUNY/York College	NY	3,292	NC
Claflin Univ	SC	14,838	C+
Clarion Univ of Pennsylvania	PA	11,272	LC
Clark Atlanta Univ	GA	19,300	C+
Clark Univ	MA	32,115	VC
Clarke College	IA	23,165	C
Clarkson Univ	NY	32,226	VC
Clemson Univ	SC	11,972	HC
Cleveland State Univ	OH	12,308	LC
Coastal Carolina Univ	SC	11,040	C
Coe College	IA	27,385	VC
Coker College	SC	21,491	C
Colby College	ME	37,570	MC
Colgate Univ	NY	37,095	MC
College of Charleston	SC	11,887	HC
College of Mount St. Vincent	NY	26,800	C
College of Mount St. Joseph	OH	22,785	C
College of New Jersey	NJ	15,950	MC
College of New Rochelle	NY	21,800	C
College of Our Lady of the Elms	MA	20,644	C
College of St. Benedict	MN	26,672	VC
College of St. Catherine	MN	24,010	VC
College of St. Elizabeth	NJ	25,460	C
College of St. Rose	NY	22,864	C
College of the Holy Cross	MA	36,451	MC
College of the Ozarks	MO	3,500	VC+
College of the Southwest	NM	9,320	C+
College of William and Mary	VA	12,224	MC
College of Wooster	OH	31,300	HC
Colo College	CO	36,860	HC
Colo State Univ	CO	9,964	VC
Columbia College	MO	16,139	C
Columbia College	SC	22,658	LC
Columbia Univ/Barnard College	NY	36,990	MC
Columbia Univ/Columbia College	NY	38,590	MC
Columbia Univ/School of General Studies	NY	35,000	C
Columbus State Univ	GA	7,846	C
Concord College	WV	8,136	C
Concordia College: Moorhead	MN	22,460	VC+
Concordia Univ, River Forest	IL	23,600	C
Concordia Univ/St.Paul	MN	24,486	C
Conn College	CT	37,900	MC
Cornell College	IA	27,825	VC+
Cornell Univ	NY	38,253	MC
Cornerstone Univ and Grand Rapids Theological Seminary	MI	19,846	C
Covenant College	GA	23,830	VC+
Creighton Univ	NE	26,748	VC+
Culver-Stockton College	MO	17,850	C
Cumberland Univ	TN	16,910	C
Curry College	MA	26,025	LC
Dakota Wesleyan Univ	SD	17,832	C
Dallas Baptist Univ	TX	15,300	VC
Dana College	NE	20,280	C
Dartmouth College	NH	37,770	MC
Davidson College	NC	33,274	MC
Davis and Elkins College	WV	20,594	C
Delaware State Univ	DE	8,104	LC
Delta State Univ	MS	6,618	C
Denison Univ	OH	33,050	HC
DePaul Univ	IL	27,580	VC
DePauw Univ	IN	31,500	HC
Dickinson College	PA	35,825	HC
Dickinson State Univ	ND	6,338	NC
Dillard Univ	LA	17,325	VC
Doane College	NE	20,000	C
Dominican Univ	IL	23,610	C
Dordt College	IA	20,170	VC
Dowling College	NY	23,870	LC
Drake Univ	IA	25,120	VC+
Drew Univ/College of Liberal Arts	NJ	35,550	VC
Drexel Univ	PA	27,655	VC
Drury Univ	MO	18,085	VC+
Duke Univ	NC	37,555	MC
Duquesne Univ	PA	26,907	VC
D'Youville College	NY	21,080	C
Earlham College	IN	29,976	VC+
East Carolina Univ	NC	8,671	C
East Central Univ	OK	4,968	C
East Stroudsburg Univ of Pennsylvania	PA	10,336	C
East Tenn State Univ	TN	8,497	C
East Texas Baptist Univ	TX	13,914	C
Eastern Conn State Univ	CT	10,362	C
Eastern Illinois Univ	IL	11,192	C
Eastern Kentucky Univ	KY	7,708	C
Eastern Mennonite Univ	VA	22,990	C
Eastern Mich Univ	MI	11,478	C
Eastern Nazarene College	MA	19,433	LC
Eastern New Mexico Univ	NM	6,762	LC
Eastern Oregon Univ	OR	10,080	NC
Eastern Univ	PA	24,020	C
Eastern Washington Univ	WA	9,012	C
Eckerd College	FL	28,744	C+
Edgewood College	WI	20,520	C
Edinboro Univ of Pennsylvania	PA	10,850	LC
Edward Waters College	FL	14,374	LC
Elizabeth City State Univ	NC	5,550	LC
Elizabethtown College	PA	28,800	C
Elmhurst College	IL	24,630	C
Elmira College	NY	33,820	VC
Elon Univ	NC	22,240	VC
Emmanuel College	MA	27,600	C+
Emory & Henry College	VA	21,950	C
Emory Univ	GA	36,872	MC
Emporia State Univ	KS	6,998	C
Eugene Lang College/New School Univ	NY	34,940	C
Eureka College	IL	24,980	LC
Evangel Univ	MO	15,435	C
Fairfield Univ	CT	35,505	HC
Fairleigh Dickinson Univ/College at Florham	NJ	30,130	C
Fairleigh Dickinson Univ/Metropolitan Campus	NJ	28,584	C
Fairmont State	WV	8,280	LC
Fayetteville State Univ	NC	5,590	LC
Fisk Univ	TN	17,305	LC
Fitchburg State College	MA	9,622	C
Florida A&M Univ	FL	7,564	C
Florida Atlantic Univ	FL	8,543	C
Florida International Univ	FL	9,912	VC
Florida Memorial College	FL	6,000	LC
Florida Southern College	FL	23,592	C
Florida State Univ	FL	9,028	HC
Fordham Univ	NY	35,066	HC
Fort Hays State Univ	KS	7,363	C
Fort Lewis College	CO	8,353	C
Fort Valley State Univ	GA	6,960	C
Framingham State College	MA	9,381	C
Francis Marion Univ	SC	9,364	C
Franciscan Univ of Steubenville	OH	20,300	VC
Franklin and Marshall College	PA	35,930	HC+
Franklin College	IN		C
Franklin Pierce College	NH	28,980	LC
Frostburg State Univ	MD	11,114	C
Furman Univ	SC	28,976	HC+
Gardner-Webb Univ	NC	19,300	C
Geneva College	PA	21,850	C
George Fox Univ	OR	26,110	VC
George Mason Univ	VA	9,732	VC
George Washington Univ	DC	41,030	MC
Georgetown College	KY	22,000	VC
Georgetown Univ	DC	38,242	MC
Georgia College and State Univ	GA	9,878	C
Georgia Southern Univ	GA	8,540	C
Georgia Southwestern State Univ	GA	6,013	C
Georgia State Univ	GA	10,658	C
Georgian Court College	NJ	19,040	LC
Gettysburg College	PA	35,646	HC
Gonzaga Univ	WA	26,766	HC
Gordon College	MA	25,982	VC+
Goshen College	IN	22,450	VC
Goucher College	MD	32,650	HC
Grace College	IN	19,825	VC
Graceland Univ	IA	19,550	C
Grambling State Univ	LA	6,538	NC
Grand Canyon Univ	AZ	30,000	LC
Grand Valley State Univ	MI	11,022	VC
Greensboro College	NC	21,750	C
Greenville College	IL	21,342	C
Grinnell College	IA	31,060	HC+
Guilford College	NC	24,960	VC
Gustavus Adolphus College	MN	27,120	VC+
Gwynedd-Mercy College	PA	24,225	C
Hamilton College	NY	37,560	MC
Hamline Univ	MN	27,052	VC
Hampshire College	MA	37,037	HC
Hampton Univ	VA	17,112	C+
Hannibal-LaGrange College	MO	13,940	C
Hanover College	IN	25,200	VC
Harding Univ	AR	14,890	VC
Hardin-Simmons Univ	TX	14,165	C
Hartwick College	NY	34,650	C+
Harvard Univ/Harvard College	MA	37,928	MC
Hastings College	NE	19,928	VC
Haverford College	PA	37,900	MC
Hawaii Pacific Univ	HI	19,218	C
Henderson State Univ	AR	7,386	C
Hendrix College	AR	20,970	VC+
Heritage College	WA	6,720	NC
High Point Univ	NC	22,480	C
Hillsdale College	MI	22,450	HC
Hiram College	OH	28,234	VC
Hobart and William Smith Colleges	NY	36,536	HC
Hofstra Univ	NY	27,112	VC
Hollins Univ	VA	27,965	VC
Holy Family College	PA	13,710	LC
Holy Names College	CA	27,980	NC
Hood College	MD	27,795	VC
Hope College	MI	25,040	VC
Houghton College	NY	23,984	VC
Houston Baptist Univ	TX	16,905	C
Howard Payne Univ	TX	15,176	C
Howard Univ	DC	16,505	C
Humboldt State Univ	CA	9,400	C
Huntington College	IN	23,590	C
Huston-Tillotson College	TX	14,232	NC
Idaho State Univ	ID	8,128	C
Illinois College	IL	19,100	VC
Illinois State Univ	IL	10,944	C+
Illinois Wesleyan Univ	IL	30,380	HC+
Immaculata Univ	PA	25,200	C
Indiana State Univ	IN	10,719	LC
Indiana Univ Bloomington	IN	12,389	VC
Indiana Univ Kokomo	IN	4,463	LC
Indiana Univ Northwest	IN	4,538	LC
Indiana Univ of Pennsylvania	PA	10,489	C
Indiana Univ South Bend	IN	4,571	LC
Indiana Univ Southeast	IN	4,504	LC
Indiana Univ-Purdue Univ Fort Wayne	IN	5,108	LC
Indiana Univ-Purdue Univ Indianapolis	IN	8,257	LC
Indiana Wesleyan Univ	IN	19,900	C+
Inter American Univ of PR/Fajardo Campus	PR	4,000	
Inter American Univ of PR/Metropolitan Campus	PR		
Inter American Univ of PR/Ponce Regional College	PR	3,700	
Inter American Univ of PR/San German	PR	6,716	
Iona College	NY	27,988	VC
Iowa State Univ	IA	10,768	VC
Iowa Wesleyan College	IA	19,990	C
Ithaca College	NY	31,730	HC
Jackson State Univ	MS	8,382	C
Jacksonville State Univ	AL	6,844	LC
Jacksonville Univ	FL	24,040	C
James Madison Univ	VA	10,794	VC
Jarvis Christian College	TX	9,035	NC
John Carroll Univ	OH	27,658	C+
Johns Hopkins Univ	MD	38,372	MC
Johnson C. Smith Univ	NC	18,108	C
Johnson State College	VT	11,819	LC
Judson College	IL	22,050	LC
Juniata College	PA	29,080	VC
Kalamazoo College	MI	26,955	HC+
Kansas State Univ	KS	8,728	VC
Kansas Wesleyan Univ	KS	18,900	VC
Kean Univ	NJ	14,479	C
Keene State College	NH	12,212	C
Kennesaw State Univ	GA	2,724	C
Kent State Univ	OH	12,932	C
Kentucky State Univ	KY	9,062	NC
Kentucky Wesleyan College	KY	17,250	C
Kenyon College	OH	35,370	HC+
Keuka College	NY	21,170	C
King's College	PA	26,990	C
Knox College	IL	30,294	VC+
Knoxville College	TN	6,200	LC
Kutztown Univ of Pennsylvania	PA	10,786	C
La Roche College	PA	22,094	C
La Salle Univ	PA	31,260	VC
La Sierra Univ	CA	19,260	LC
Lafayette College	PA	35,746	MC
Lake Forest College	IL	30,270	VC
Lake Superior State Univ	MI	9,034	LC
Lakeland College	WI	17,950	C
Lamar Univ	TX	6,816	LC
Lambuth Univ	TN	16,520	C
Lander Univ	SC	10,496	C
Lane College	TN	11,178	C+
Langston Univ	OK	2,308	LC
Lasell College	MA	26,000	C
Le Moyne College	NY	26,400	VC
Lebanon Valley College	PA	28,870	VC
Lee Univ	TN	13,780	NC
Lees-McRae College	NC	17,106	LC
Lehigh Univ	PA	37,570	HC+
LeMoyne-Owen College	TN	13,070	LC
Lenoir-Rhyne College	NC	19,186	C
Lewis and Clark College	OR	30,620	VC
Lewis Univ	IL	22,950	C+
Lincoln Univ	MO	7,158	NC
Lincoln Univ	PA	13,320	C+
Lindenwood Univ	MO	17,050	VC
Linfield College	OR	27,090	VC
Livingstone College	NC	18,101	LC
Lock Haven Univ of Pennsylvania	PA	11,098	LC
LIU/Brooklyn Campus	NY	24,790	C
LIU/Southampton College	NY	29,370	C+
Longwood Univ	VA	11,175	C
Loras College	IA	24,233	C
Louisiana College	LA	13,450	C
Louisiana State Univ and A&M College	LA	9,126	VC
Louisiana State Univ in Shreveport	LA	2,884	NC
Louisiana Tech Univ	LA	7,361	C
Lourdes College	OH	15,300	LC
Loyola College in Maryland	MD	34,560	HC
Loyola Marymount Univ	CA	32,194	VC
Loyola Univ Chicago	IL	31,164	VC
Loyola Univ New Orleans	LA	31,036	VC+
Luther College	IA	25,700	VC
Lycoming College	PA	27,589	C+
Lynchburg College	VA	26,815	C
Lynn Univ	FL	30,750	C
Macalester College	MN	31,944	MC

ST = STATE **$IS** = IN-STATE COSTS **SR** = SELECTOR RATING

School	ST	$IS	SR
Madonna Univ	MI	11,504	VC
Manchester College	IN	23,390	C
Manhattan College	NY	27,400	VC
Manhattanville College	NY	32,420	C+
Mansfield Univ	PA	11,220	C
Marian College	IN	23,030	C
Marian College of Fond du Lac	WI	19,625	C
Marlboro College	VT	29,055	VC+
Marquette Univ	WI	27,594	VC
Mars Hill College	NC	18,600	LC
Marshall Univ	WV	9,116	C
Martin Univ	IN	10,200	SP
Mary Baldwin College	VA	24,939	C
Mary Washington College	VA	10,166	HC
Marymount College of Fordham Univ	NY	27,686	C
Marymount Manhattan College	NY	27,292	C
Marymount Univ	VA	23,668	C
Maryville College	TN	25,960	VC
Maryville Univ of St. Louis	MO	22,090	VC
Marywood Univ	PA	26,050	C
Mass College of Liberal Arts	MA	8,717	LC
McDaniel College	MD	28,440	VC
McKendree College	IL	21,120	VC
McMurry Univ	TX	17,846	LC
McNeese State Univ	LA	5,259	LC
McPherson College	KS	20,265	C
Mercer Univ	GA	27,516	VC+
Mercy College	NY	19,200	NC
Mercyhurst College	PA	20,694	C
Meredith College	NC	23,065	C
Merrimack College	MA	29,625	C
Mesa State College	CO	8,051	C
Messiah College	PA	25,890	VC+
Methodist College	NC	19,526	C
Metropolitan State College of Denver	CO	2,338	LC
Miami Univ	OH	15,033	HC
Mich State Univ	MI	11,933	VC
MidAmerica Nazarene Univ	KS	18,688	C
Middle Tenn State Univ	TN	8,534	C
Middlebury College	VT	38,100	MC
Midland Lutheran College	NE	18,600	C
Midwestern State Univ	TX	8,045	LC
Millersville Univ of Pennsylvania	PA	11,269	C
Milligan College	TN	19,860	C+
Millikin Univ	IL	25,555	C
Mills College	CA	33,371	VC
Millsaps College	MS	25,182	VC
Minn State Univ, Mankato	MN	8,803	LC
Minn State Univ, Moorehead	MN	7,000	LC
Minot State Univ	ND	6,602	LC
Miss College	MS	14,574	C
Miss State Univ	MS	9,139	C
Miss Valley State Univ	MS	6,765	NC
Missouri Southern State Univ	MO	8,316	C
Missouri Valley College	MO	18,500	C
Molloy College	NY	15,180	C
Monmouth College	IL	23,600	C
Montana State Univ-Billings	MT	9,550	C
Montana State Univ-Bozeman	MT	9,515	C
Montclair State Univ	NJ	13,790	C
Moravian College	PA	28,903	VC
Morehead State Univ	KY	7,464	C
Morehouse College	GA	22,728	C
Morgan State Univ	MD	11,470	C
Morris College	SC	10,974	LC
Mount Holyoke College	MA	37,918	HC+
Mount Mercy College	IA	21,400	C
Mount St. Mary College	NY	21,270	C
Mount St. Mary's College	CA	28,307	VC
Mount St. Mary's College	MD	28,400	C
Mount Union College	OH	21,120	C
Mount Vernon Nazarene Univ	OH	18,925	C
Muhlenberg College	PA	31,485	HC
Murray State Univ	KY	7,816	VC
Muskingum College	OH	20,680	C
Nazareth College of Rochester	NY	24,936	VC
Nebr Wesleyan Univ	NE	21,197	C+
New College of Florida	FL	8,906	HC+
New England College	NH	28,860	LC
New Jersey City Univ	NJ	11,850	LC
New Mexico Highlands Univ	NM	6,182	LC
New Mexico State Univ	NM	7,932	C
New York Inst of Technology	NY	24,205	VC
New York Univ	NY	39,496	MC
Newberry College	SC	22,871	LC
Newman Univ	KS	18,018	C
Niagara Univ	NY	25,050	C
Nicholls State Univ	LA	6,395	NC
Norfolk State Univ	VA	9,722	LC
N Car Agricultural and Technical State Univ	NC	6,659	LC
N Car Central Univ	NC	7,534	LC
N Car State Univ	NC	9,886	VC
N Car Wesleyan College	NC	17,998	C
North Central College	IL	25,656	VC
N Dak State Univ	ND	8,435	C
North Georgia College and State Univ	GA	6,984	C
North Park Univ	IL	24,030	C
Northeastern Illinois Univ	IL	2,898	NC
Northeastern State Univ	OK	4,950	LC
Northeastern Univ	MA	35,650	HC
Northern Arizona Univ	AZ	9,002	C
Northern Illinois Univ	IL	11,472	C
Northern Kentucky Univ	KY	6,352	NC
Northern Mich Univ	MI	10,834	C
Northern State Univ	SD	7,117	LC
Northland College	WI	22,170	C+
Northwest Missouri State Univ	MO	9,334	C
Northwestern College of Iowa	IA	19,640	C+
Northwestern Okla State Univ	OK	5,433	NC
Northwestern State Univ of Louisiana	LA	6,331	NC
Northwestern Univ	IL	37,491	MC
Notre Dame de Namur Univ	CA	26,932	LC
Oakland Univ	MI	10,800	C
Oberlin College	OH	36,938	MC
Occidental College	CA	35,922	HC
Oglala Lakota College	SD	1,950	NC
Oglethorpe Univ	GA	26,000	VC
Ohio Dominican Univ	OH	22,700	C
Ohio Northern Univ	OH	27,765	VC
Ohio State Univ	OH	13,080	VC+
Ohio Univ	OH	14,448	C
Ohio Wesleyan Univ	OH	32,550	VC+
Okla Baptist Univ	OK	15,220	VC
Okla City Univ	OK	19,580	VC
Okla State Univ	OK	9,216	VC
Okla Wesleyan Univ	OK	14,100	LC
Old Dominion Univ	VA	10,441	C
Olivet College	MI	19,984	C+
Olivet Nazarene Univ	IL	20,480	C
Oregon State Univ	OR	11,055	C
Ottawa Univ	KS	11,800	LC
Otterbein College	OH	26,085	C
Ouachita Baptist Univ	AR	18,900	VC
Our Lady of the Lake Univ of San Antonio	TX	17,336	C
Pace Univ	NY	28,652	VC
Pacific Lutheran Univ	WA	25,715	VC
Pacific Union College	CA	22,065	C+
Pacific Univ	OR	24,250	C
Paine College	GA	13,022	LC
Park Univ	MO	10,780	C+
Paul Quinn College	TX	8,150	LC
Penn State Univ/Univ Park Campus	PA	15,646	HC
Pepperdine Univ	CA	32,830	VC
Peru State College	NE	6,342	NC
Pfeiffer Univ	NC	18,980	C
Philander Smith College	AR	7,380	NC
Piedmont College	GA	16,900	C
Pikeville College	KY	14,900	NC
Pittsburg State Univ	KS	7,128	NC
Pitzer College	CA	37,590	HC
Point Loma Nazarene Univ	CA	21,380	VC
Pomona College	CA	33,960	MC
Pontifical Catholic Univ of PR/Ponce	PR	7,298	
Portland State Univ	OR	12,453	C
Prairie View A&M Univ	TX	9,418	NC
Presbyterian College	SC	25,920	VC
Prescott College	AZ	13,430	C
Princeton Univ	NJ	36,649	MC
Principia College	IL	25,044	C+
Providence College	RI	30,604	HC
Purdue Univ/Calumet	IN	6,630	NC
Purdue Univ/West Lafayette	IN	12,560	VC
Quinnipiac Univ	CT	30,570	VC
Radford Univ	VA	8,500	C
Ramapo College of New Jersey	NJ	15,203	VC
Randolph-Macon College	VA	27,190	C
Randolph-Macon Woman's College	VA	28,430	VC+
Reed College	OR	36,950	MC
Regis College	MA	29,000	C
Regis Univ	CO	25,740	C+
Rhode Island College	RI	11,565	C
Rhodes College	TN	26,466	HC+
Rice Univ	TX	27,550	MC
Rider Univ	NJ	30,900	C
Ripon College	WI	24,995	VC
Rivier College	NH	26,217	C
Roanoke College	VA	27,393	C
Roberts Wesleyan College	NY	23,190	C+
Rockford College	IL	28,310	VC
Rockhurst Univ	MO	22,960	C+
Rocky Mountain College	MT	19,015	C
Rollins College	FL	34,300	VC
Roosevelt Univ	IL	22,580	VC
Rosemont College	PA	26,175	C
Rowan Univ	NJ	14,506	VC
Russell Sage College	NY	26,811	C
Rust College	MS	8,200	C+
Rutgers, The State Univ of New Jersey/Camden Campus	NJ	14,990	VC
Rutgers, The State Univ of New Jersey/New Brunswick/Piscataway Campus	NJ	15,800	HC
Rutgers, The State Univ of New Jersey/Newark Campus	NJ	15,624	VC
Sacred Heart Univ	CT	29,178	C
Saginaw Valley State Univ	MI	11,055	C
St. Ambrose Univ	IA	22,800	C
St. Anselm College	NH	30,250	C
St. Augustine's College	NC	12,990	LC
St. Bonaventure Univ	NY	24,455	LC
St. Cloud State Univ	MN	8,362	C
St. Edward's Univ	TX	20,428	C
St. Francis College	NY	10,880	LC
St. Francis Univ	PA	25,876	LC
St. John Fisher College	NY	24,870	C
St. John's Univ	MN	26,473	VC
St. John's Univ	NY	30,180	C
St. Joseph College	CT	29,685	C
St. Joseph's College	IN	24,250	C
St. Joseph's College of Maine	ME	25,600	C
St. Joseph's Univ	PA	33,590	VC
St. Lawrence Univ	NY	35,945	VC
St. Leo Univ	FL	20,600	C
St. Louis Univ	MO	29,780	VC+
St. Mary's College	IN	24,474	VC
St. Mary's College	MI	13,314	LC
St. Mary's College of Maryland	MD	15,908	VC+
St. Mary's Univ of Minn	MN	21,535	C
St. Mary's Univ of San Antonio	TX	22,444	C
St. Michael's College	VT	30,100	VC
St. Norbert College	WI	25,810	C
St. Olaf College	MN	28,500	HC
St. Paul's College	VA	14,344	NC
St. Peter's College	NJ	22,292	LC
St. Thomas Univ	FL	21,400	LC
St. Vincent College	PA	25,530	VC
St. Xavier Univ	IL	23,144	C
Salem College	NC	24,595	VC
Salem State College	MA	8,592	C
Salisbury Univ	MD	12,664	VC
Salve Regina Univ	RI	29,210	C
Sam Houston State Univ	TX	7,142	C
Samford Univ	AL	18,648	VC
San Diego State Univ	CA	10,321	C
San Francisco State Univ	CA	12,070	C
San Jose State Univ	CA	8,187	C
Santa Clara Univ	CA	34,701	HC
Sarah Lawrence College	NY	41,218	HC
Savannah State Univ	GA	7,328	LC
Seattle Pacific Univ	WA	25,944	VC
Seattle Univ	WA	24,183	VC
Seton Hall Univ	NJ	30,130	VC
Seton Hill Univ	PA	24,930	C
Shaw Univ	NC	14,882	C+
Shawnee State Univ	OH	11,031	NC
Shenandoah Univ	VA	25,190	NC
Shepherd College	WV	8,608	C
Shippensburg Univ of Pennsylvania	PA	10,826	C
Shorter College	GA	17,370	C
Siena College	NY	25,310	VC
Simmons College	MA	33,000	VC
Simpson College	IA	23,658	C+
Skidmore College	NY	37,930	HC
Slippery Rock Univ of Pennsylvania	PA	10,343	LC
Smith College	MA	37,034	HC+
Sonoma State Univ	CA	10,421	C
S Car State Univ	SC	6,586	LC
S Dak State Univ	SD	7,782	C
Southeast Missouri State Univ	MO	9,704	C
Southeastern Louisiana Univ	LA	6,791	LC
Southeastern Okla State Univ	OK	6,147	C
Southern Arkansas Univ	AR	6,956	C
Southern Conn State Univ	CT	10,310	C
Southern Illinois Univ Carbondale	IL	10,407	C
Southern Illinois Univ Edwardsville	IL	8,724	C
Southern Methodist Univ	TX	34,210	HC
Southern Nazarene Univ	OK	14,634	NC
Southern Oregon Univ	OR	10,362	C
Southern Univ and A&M College	LA	7,372	LC
Southern Univ at New Orleans	LA	995	NC
Southern Utah Univ	UT	8,194	C
Southwest Baptist Univ	MO	15,371	C
Southwest Minn State Univ	MN	9,106	VC
Southwest Missouri State Univ	MO	8,918	C
Southwestern Univ	TX	25,410	HC
Spelman College	GA	19,215	C+
Spring Arbor Univ	MI	20,206	C
Springfield College	MA	24,520	C
Stanford Univ	CA	37,612	MC
SUNY at Oswego	NY	12,650	C
SUNY at Potsdam	NY	12,160	C
SUNY/College at Brockport	NY	12,111	C
SUNY/College at Buffalo	NY	8,025	C
SUNY/College at Cortland	NY	12,095	C
SUNY/College at Fredonia	NY	11,562	VC
SUNY/College at Geneseo	NY	11,330	HC
SUNY/College at Old Westbury	NY	12,784	C
SUNY/College at Oneonta	NY	11,870	VC
SUNY/College at Plattsburgh	NY	11,700	C
SUNY/College at Purchase	NY	10,587	VC
SUNY/Empire State College	NY	4,505	SP
SUNY/Univ at Albany	NY	12,951	HC
SUNY/Univ at Binghamton	NY	12,787	HC
SUNY/Univ at Buffalo	NY	12,563	VC
SUNY/Univ at New Paltz	NY	11,565	VC
SUNY/Univ at Stony Brook	NY	12,763	HC
State Univ of West Georgia	GA	7,622	C
Stephen F. Austin State Univ	TX	7,552	C
Stetson Univ	FL	29,495	VC
Stonehill College	MA	30,752	HC
Suffolk Univ	MA	29,200	C
Susquehanna Univ	PA	29,990	VC
Swarthmore College	PA	37,716	MC
Sweet Briar College	VA	27,940	C
Syracuse Univ	NY	34,720	HC
Tabor College	KS	19,500	NC
Talladega College	AL	10,110	LC
Tarleton State Univ	TX	7,576	C
Taylor Univ	IN	23,820	VC+
Teikyo Post Univ	CT	24,875	C
Temple Univ	PA	15,912	C
Tenn State Univ	TN	9,048	LC
Tenn Tech Univ	TN	8,670	VC
Texas A&M Univ	TX	11,081	HC
Texas A&M Univ at Commerce	TX	8,994	C
Texas A&M Univ at Corpus Christi	TX	10,269	C
Texas A&M Univ at Kingsville	TX	6,740	LC
Texas Christian Univ	TX	23,410	VC
Texas Lutheran Univ	TX	20,370	C
Texas Southern Univ	TX	8,920	NC
Texas State Univ	TX	9,320	VC
Texas Tech Univ	TX	10,768	VC
Texas Woman's Univ	TX	7,804	LC
Thiel College	PA	20,970	C
Thomas Edison State College	NJ	3,325	SP
Thomas More College	KY	21,350	C
Tougaloo College	MS	9,200	NC
Touro College	NY	15,250	VC
Towson Univ	MD	12,694	VC
Transylvania Univ	KY	23,780	VC+
Trinity Christian College	IL	21,640	VC
Trinity College	CT	38,040	HC+
Trinity College	DC	24,150	LC
Trinity Univ	TX	26,466	HC+
Troy State Univ Dothan	AL	3,842	C
Truman State Univ	MO	9,728	HC+
Tufts Univ	MA	38,233	MC
Tulane Univ	LA	37,451	HC+
Turabo Univ	PR	4,110	
Tuskegee Univ	AL	17,250	LC
Union College	NY	36,005	HC
Union Univ	TN	18,800	VC
Universidad Metropolitana	PR	3,324	
Univ of Akron	OH	13,134	NC
Univ of Alabama at Birmingham	AL	12,901	C
Univ of Alabama in Huntsville	AL	9,126	VC
Univ of Alaska Anchorage	AK	9,100	NC
Univ of Alaska Fairbanks	AK	9,295	C
Univ of Arizona	AZ	10,413	VC
Univ of Arkansas	AR	9,855	VC
Univ of Arkansas at Little Rock	AR	5,637	NC
Univ of Arkansas at Pine Bluff	AR	7,925	C
Univ of Calif at Berkeley	CA	15,563	MC
Univ of Calif at Davis	CA	14,995	VC
Univ of Calif at Irvine	CA	19,808	HC
Univ of Calif at Los Angeles	CA	15,330	MC
Univ of Calif at Riverside	CA	15,300	C
Univ of Calif at San Diego	CA	14,127	HC
Univ of Calif at Santa Barbara	CA	11,732	VC
Univ of Calif at Santa Cruz	CA	16,505	VC
Univ of Central Arkansas	AR	6,388	C
Univ of Central Florida	FL	10,038	VC
Univ of Central Okla	OK	9,434	C
Univ of Chicago	IL	35,087	MC
Univ of Cincinnati	OH	14,736	C
Univ of Colo at Boulder	CO	10,774	VC
Univ of Colo at Colo Springs	CO	10,667	C
Univ of Colo at Denver	CO	3,302	C
Univ of Conn	CT	14,608	VC
Univ of Dayton	OH	24,850	VC

ST = STATE $IS = IN-STATE COSTS SR = SELECTOR RATING

INDEX OF COLLEGE MAJORS

SOFTWARE ENGINEERING

SOIL SCIENCE

SOUTH ASIAN STUDIES

SOUTHWEST AMERICAN STUDIES

SPANISH

ST = STATE **$IS** = IN-STATE COSTS **SR** = SELECTOR RATING

School	ST	$IS	SR
Otterbein College	OH	26,085	C
Ouachita Baptist Univ	AR	18,900	VC
Our Lady of the Lake Univ of San Antonio	TX	17,336	C
Pace Univ	NY	28,652	VC
Pacific Lutheran Univ	WA	25,715	VC
Pacific Union College	CA	22,065	C+
Pacific Univ	OR	24,250	C
Park Univ	MO	10,780	C+
Penn State Univ/Univ Park Campus	PA	15,646	HC
Pepperdine Univ	CA	32,830	VC
Piedmont College	GA	16,900	C
Pittsburg State Univ	KS	7,128	HC
Pitzer College	CA	37,590	HC
Plymouth State Univ	NH	12,298	LC
Point Loma Nazarene Univ	CA	21,380	VC
Pomona College	CA	33,960	MC
Pontifical Catholic Univ of PR/Ponce	PR	7,298	
Portland State Univ	OR	12,453	C
Prairie View A&M Univ	TX	9,418	NC
Presbyterian College	SC	25,920	VC
Prescott College	AZ	13,430	C
Principia College	IL	25,044	C+
Providence College	RI	30,604	HC
Purdue Univ/Calumet	IN	6,630	NC
Purdue Univ/West Lafayette	IN	12,560	VC
Queens Univ of Charlotte	NC	21,840	C
Quinnipiac Univ	CT	30,570	VC
Randolph-Macon College	VA	27,190	C
Randolph-Macon Woman's College	VA	28,430	VC+
Regis College	MA	29,000	C
Regis Univ	CO	25,740	C+
Rhode Island College	RI	11,565	C
Rhodes College	TN	26,466	HC+
Rider Univ	NJ	30,900	C
Ripon College	WI	24,995	VC
Roanoke College	VA	27,393	C
Rockford College	IL	28,310	VC
Rockhurst Univ	MO	22,960	C+
Rollins College	FL	34,300	VC
Roosevelt Univ	IL	22,580	VC
Rosemont College	PA	26,175	C
Rowan Univ	NJ	14,506	VC
Russell Sage College	NY	26,811	C
Rutgers, The State Univ of New Jersey/Camden Campus	NJ	14,990	VC
Rutgers, The State Univ of New Jersey/New Brunswick/Piscataway Campus	NJ	15,800	HC
Rutgers, The State Univ of New Jersey/Newark Campus	NJ	15,624	VC
Sacred Heart Univ	CT	29,178	C
Saginaw Valley State Univ	MI	11,055	C
St. Ambrose Univ	IA	22,800	C
St. Anselm Univ	NH	30,250	C
St. Augustine's College	NC	12,990	NC
St. Bonaventure Univ	NY	24,455	LC
St. Edward's Univ	TX	20,428	C
St. Francis Univ	PA	25,876	LC
St. John Fisher College	NY	24,872	C
St. John's Univ	MN	26,473	VC
St. John's Univ	NY	30,180	C
St. Joseph College	CT	29,685	C
St. Joseph's, Brooklyn,	NY	10,902	C
St. Joseph's Univ	PA	33,590	VC
St. Lawrence Univ	NY	35,945	VC
St. Louis Univ	MO	29,780	VC+
St. Mary-of-the-Woods College	IN	23,280	C
St. Mary's College	IN	24,474	VC
St. Mary's College of Calif	CA	32,850	VC
St. Mary's Univ of Minn	MN	21,535	C
St. Mary's Univ of San Antonio	TX	22,444	C
St. Michael's College	VT	30,100	VC
St. Norbert College	WI	25,810	C
St. Olaf College	MN	28,500	VC
St. Peter's College	NJ	22,292	LC
St. Thomas Aquinas College	NY	20,590	LC
St. Thomas Univ	FL	21,400	LC
St. Vincent College	PA	25,530	VC
St. Xavier Univ	IL	23,144	C
Salem College	NC	24,595	VC
Salisbury Univ	MD	12,664	VC
Salve Regina Univ	RI	29,210	C
Sam Houston State Univ	TX	7,142	C
Samford Univ	AL	18,648	VC
San Diego State Univ	CA	10,321	C
San Jose State Univ	CA	8,187	C
Santa Clara Univ	CA	34,701	HC
Sarah Lawrence College	NY	41,218	HC
Seattle Pacific Univ	WA	25,944	VC
Seattle Univ	WA	24,183	VC
Seton Hall Univ	NJ	30,130	VC
Seton Hill Univ	PA	24,930	C
Shenandoah Univ	VA	25,190	NC
Shippensburg Univ of Pennsylvania	PA	10,826	C
Shorter College	GA	17,370	C
Siena College	NY	25,310	VC
Siena Heights Univ	MI	16,140	LC
Simmons College	MA	33,000	VC
Simon's Rock College of Bard	MA	36,580	HC
Simpson College	IA	23,658	C+
Skidmore College	NY	37,930	HC
Slippery Rock Univ of Pennsylvania	PA	10,343	LC
Smith College	MA	37,034	HC+
Sonoma State Univ	CA	10,421	C
S Car State Univ	SC	6,586	LC
S Dak State Univ	SD	7,782	C
Southeast Missouri State Univ	MO	9,704	C
Southeastern Louisiana Univ	LA	6,791	LC
Southern Arkansas Univ	AR	6,956	C
Southern Conn State Univ	CT	10,310	C
Southern Illinois Univ Carbondale	IL	10,407	C
Southern Methodist Univ	TX	34,210	HC
Southern Nazarene Univ	OK	14,634	NC
Southern Oregon Univ	OR	10,362	C
Southern Univ and A&M College	LA	7,372	LC
Southern Univ at New Orleans	LA	995	NC
Southern Utah Univ	UT	8,194	C
Southwest Baptist Univ	MO	15,371	C
Southwest Minn State Univ	MN	9,106	VC
Southwest Missouri State Univ	MO	8,918	C
Southwestern College	KS	19,560	C
Southwestern Univ	TX	25,410	HC
Spelman College	GA	19,215	C+
Spring Arbor Univ	MI	20,206	C
Spring Hill College	AL	25,868	VC
Stanford Univ	CA	37,612	MC
SUNY at Oswego	NY	12,650	C
SUNY at Potsdam	NY	12,160	C
SUNY/College at Brockport	NY	12,111	C
SUNY/College at Buffalo	NY	8,025	C
SUNY/College at Fredonia	NY	11,562	VC
SUNY/College at Geneseo	NY	11,330	VC
SUNY/College at Old Westbury	NY	12,784	C
SUNY/College at Oneonta	NY	11,870	VC
SUNY/College at Plattsburgh	NY	11,700	C
SUNY/Univ at Albany	NY	12,951	VC
SUNY/Univ at Binghamton	NY	12,787	HC
SUNY/Univ at Buffalo	NY	12,563	VC
SUNY/Univ at New Paltz	NY	11,565	VC
State Univ of West Georgia	GA	7,622	C
Stephen F. Austin State Univ	TX	7,552	C
Stephens College	MO	24,260	C+
Stetson Univ	FL	29,495	VC
Suffolk Univ	MA	29,200	C
Sul Ross State Univ	TX	6,582	LC
Susquehanna Univ	PA	29,990	VC
Swarthmore College	PA	37,716	MC
Sweet Briar College	VA	27,940	C
Syracuse Univ	NY	34,720	HC
Tarleton State Univ	TX	7,576	C
Taylor Univ	IN	23,820	VC+
Temple Univ	PA	15,912	C
Tenn Tech Univ	TN	8,670	VC
Texas A&M Univ	TX	11,081	HC
Texas A&M Univ at Commerce	TX	8,994	C
Texas A&M Univ at Corpus Christi	TX	10,269	C
Texas A&M Univ at Kingsville	TX	6,740	LC
Texas Christian Univ	TX	23,410	VC
Texas Lutheran Univ	TX	20,370	C
Texas Southern Univ	TX	8,920	NC
Texas State Univ	TX	9,320	VC
Texas Tech Univ	TX	10,768	VC
Texas Wesleyan Univ	TX	16,245	C
Thiel College	PA	20,970	C
Towson Univ	MD	12,694	VC
Transylvania Univ	KY	23,780	VC+
Trinity Christian College	IL	21,640	VC
Trinity College	CT	38,040	HC+
Trinity College	DC	24,150	LC
Trinity Univ	TX	26,466	HC+
Truman State Univ	MO	9,728	HC+
Tufts Univ	MA	38,233	MC
Tulane Univ	LA	37,451	HC+
Turabo Univ	PR	4,110	
Union College	NE	17,130	C
Union Univ	TN	18,800	VC
Universidad Adventista de las Antillas	PR	5,460	
Univ of Akron	OH	13,134	NC
Univ of Alabama	AL	9,040	C+
Univ of Alabama at Birmingham	AL	12,901	C
Univ of Arizona	AZ	10,413	VC
Univ of Arkansas	AR	9,855	VC
Univ of Arkansas at Little Rock	AR	5,637	NC
Univ of Calif at Berkeley	CA	15,563	MC
Univ of Calif at Davis	CA	14,995	VC
Univ of Calif at Irvine	CA	19,808	VC
Univ of Calif at Los Angeles	CA	15,330	MC
Univ of Calif at Riverside	CA	15,300	C
Univ of Calif at Santa Barbara	CA	11,732	VC
Univ of Central Arkansas	AR	6,388	C
Univ of Central Florida	FL	10,038	VC
Univ of Central Okla	OK	9,434	C
Univ of Cincinnati	OH	14,736	C
Univ of Colo at Boulder	CO	10,774	VC
Univ of Colo at Colo Springs	CO	10,667	C
Univ of Colo at Denver	CO	3,302	C
Univ of Conn	CT	14,608	VC
Univ of Dallas	TX	25,898	VC+
Univ of Dayton	OH	24,850	VC
Univ of Denver	CO	32,148	VC
Univ of Evansville	IN	24,190	VC
Univ of Findlay	OH	23,962	NC
Univ of Florida	FL	8,580	MC
Univ of Georgia	GA	8,656	VC
Univ of Hawaii at Manoa	HI	9,565	VC
Univ of Houston	TX	9,818	C
Univ of Idaho	ID	8,216	C
Univ of Illinois at Chicago	IL	13,418	C
Univ of Illinois at Urbana-Champaign	IL	11,316	HC+
Univ of Indianapolis	IN	22,560	VC
Univ of Iowa	IA	10,923	VC
Univ of Kansas	KS	8,923	VC
Univ of Kentucky	KY	7,765	C
Univ of La Verne	CA	28,600	C
Univ of Louisiana at Lafayette	LA	5,826	C
Univ of Louisiana at Monroe	LA	5,207	NC
Univ of Louisville	KY	8,762	VC
Univ of Maine	ME	12,080	C+
Univ of Mary Hardin-Baylor	TX	17,268	C
Univ of Maryland/Baltimore County	MD	14,668	VC+
Univ of Maryland/College Park	MD	14,227	HC
Univ of Mass Amherst	MA	13,980	C+
Univ of Mass Boston	MA	6,227	C
Univ of Mass Dartmouth	MA	12,835	C
Univ of Miami	FL	34,608	HC
Univ of Mich/Ann Arbor	MI	13,864	HC+
Univ of Mich/Flint	MI	5,548	C
Univ of Minn/Duluth	MN	12,470	C
Univ of Minn/Morris	MN	12,896	VC
Univ of Minn/Twin Cities	MN	13,160	VC
Univ of Miss	MS	7,666	C
Univ of Missouri/Columbia	MO	13,782	VC
Univ of Missouri/Kansas City	MO	13,416	VC
Univ of Missouri/St. Louis	MO	11,656	VC
Univ of Montana	MT	9,395	C
Univ of Montevallo	AL	8,478	C
Univ of Nebr at Kearney	NE	8,286	NC
Univ of Nebr at Lincoln	NE	9,975	C+
Univ of Nebr at Omaha	NE	8,080	C
Univ of Nevada/Las Vegas	NV	11,566	C
Univ of Nevada/Reno	NV	9,792	C
Univ of New Hampshire	NH	14,828	VC
Univ of New Mexico	NM	9,223	C
Univ of New Orleans	LA	7,356	C
Univ of North Alabama	AL	7,972	NC
Univ of N Car at Asheville	NC	8,079	VC
Univ of N Car at Charlotte	NC	8,185	C
Univ of N Car at Greensboro	NC	8,248	C
Univ of N Car at Wilmington	NC	8,940	VC
Univ of N Dak	ND	8,390	C
Univ of North Florida	FL	8,769	VC
Univ of North Texas	TX	7,629	C
Univ of Northern Colo	CO	8,987	C
Univ of Northern Iowa	IA	9,834	VC
Univ of Notre Dame	IN	34,442	MC
Univ of Okla	OK	9,226	VC
Univ of Oregon	OR	11,479	VC
Univ of Pennsylvania	PA	37,960	MC
Univ of Pittsburgh at Pittsburgh	PA	16,074	HC
Univ of Portland	OR	28,500	VC
Univ of Puget Sound	WA	31,760	HC
Univ of Redlands	CA	32,576	VC
Univ of Rhode Island	RI	13,720	VC
Univ of Richmond	VA	30,100	MC
Univ of Rochester	NY	32,979	HC
Univ of St. Thomas	MN	26,918	VC
Univ of St. Thomas	TX	21,952	VC
Univ of San Diego	CA	33,156	HC
Univ of San Francisco	CA	34,700	VC
Univ of Scranton	PA	30,836	VC
Univ of S Car at Columbia	SC	10,048	VC
Univ of S Car at Spartanburg	SC	9,936	C+
Univ of S Dak	SD	7,710	C+
Univ of South Florida	FL	9,454	C
Univ of Southern Calif	CA	37,459	MC
Univ of Southern Colo	CO	7,821	LC
Univ of Southern Indiana	IN	9,025	LC
Univ of Tampa	FL	23,982	VC
Univ of Tenn at Chattanooga	TN	7,783	C
Univ of Tenn at Knoxville	TN	8,214	C
Univ of Tenn at Martin	TN	7,748	C
Univ of Texas at Arlington	TX	7,192	LC
Univ of Texas at Austin	TX	10,630	HC
Univ of Texas at El Paso	TX	5,799	LC
Univ of Texas at San Antonio	TX	9,088	NC
Univ of Texas-Pan American	TX	5,954	LC
Univ of the District of Columbia	DC	2,070	LC
Univ of the Incarnate Word	TX	21,772	LC
Univ of the Pacific	CA	31,090	VC
Univ of the South	TN	30,855	HC
Univ of Toledo	OH	12,479	NC
Univ of Tulsa	OK	22,090	VC+
Univ of Utah	UT	9,205	C
Univ of Vermont	VT	16,316	VC
Univ of Virginia	VA	11,740	MC
Univ of Virginia's College at Wise	VA	10,116	C
Univ of Washington	WA	10,361	VC
Univ of Wisc/Eau Claire	WI	8,463	VC
Univ of Wisc/Green Bay	WI	8,154	C
Univ of Wisc/La Crosse	WI	8,991	C
Univ of Wisc/Madison	WI	8,262	VC
Univ of Wisc/Milwaukee	WI	9,427	LC
Univ of Wisc/Oshkosh	WI	6,130	LC
Univ of Wisc/Parkside	WI	6,160	LC
Univ of Wisc/Platteville	WI	8,450	C
Univ of Wisc/Stevens Point	WI	8,116	VC
Univ of Wisc/Whitewater	WI	8,626	C
Univ of Wyoming	WY	8,636	C
Ursinus College	PA	34,400	VC
Utah State Univ	UT	7,371	C
Valdosta State Univ	GA	7,798	C
Valley City State Univ	ND	7,281	LC
Valparaiso Univ	IN	26,118	VC+
Vanderbilt Univ	TN	37,897	MC
Vanguard Univ of Southern Calif	CA	22,208	C
Villanova Univ	PA	35,050	HC
Virginia Polytechnic Inst and State Univ	VA	9,179	C
Virginia Wesleyan College	VA	25,350	C
Viterbo Univ	WI	20,430	C
Wabash College	IN	27,932	VC
Wake Forest Univ	NC	34,090	MC
Walla Walla College	WA	21,600	NC
Walsh Univ	OH	20,890	C
Warren Wilson College	NC	21,794	VC
Wartburg College	IA	21,165	VC
Washburn Univ of Topeka	KS	8,984	NC
Washington and Jefferson College	PA	29,570	VC
Washington and Lee Univ	VA	29,663	MC
Washington College	MD	30,540	VC
Washington State Univ	WA	11,334	C
Washington Univ in St. Louis	MO	38,293	MC
Wayland Baptist Univ	TX	11,919	NC
Wayne State College	NE	7,352	NC
Wayne State Univ	MI	11,774	C
Weber State Univ	UT	7,945	NC
Webster Univ	MO	21,848	VC
Wellesley College	MA	36,546	MC
Wells College	NY	21,122	VC
Wesleyan College	GA	17,870	VC
Wesleyan Univ	CT	35,139	MC
West Chester Univ of Pennsylvania	PA	11,164	C
West Texas A&M Univ	TX	7,533	C
Western Carolina Univ	NC	6,742	C
Western Conn State Univ	CT	11,625	C
Western Illinois Univ	IL	10,363	C
Western Kentucky Univ	KY	6,834	C
Western Mich Univ	MI	12,031	C
Western New Mexico Univ	NM	5,950	LC
Western Oregon Univ	OR	10,281	C
Western State College of Colo	CO	9,014	C
Western Washington Univ	WA	10,119	VC
Westminster College	MO	18,150	C+
Westminster College	PA	22,960	C
Westmont College	CA	33,062	VC+
Wheaton College	IL	21,934	HC
Wheeling Jesuit Univ	WV	22,660	C
Whitman College	WA	32,526	HC+
Whittier College	CA	29,108	C
Whitworth College	WA	26,428	VC+
Wichita State Univ	KS	8,092	C
Wilkes Univ	PA	28,060	C
Willamette Univ	OR	32,032	VC+
William Carey College	MS	10,150	LC
William Jewell College	MO	21,320	VC
William Paterson Univ of New Jersey	NJ	14,450	C
Williams College	MA	32,270	MC
Wilmington College	OH	24,172	LC
Wilson College	PA	23,912	C
Wingate Univ	NC	21,200	C
Winona State Univ	MN		
Winston-Salem State Univ	NC	8,926	LC
Winthrop Univ	SC	11,302	C
Wisc Lutheran College	WI	21,430	VC
Wittenberg Univ	OH	31,316	VC

ST = STATE $IS = IN-STATE COSTS   SR = SELECTOR RATING

School	ST	$IS	SR
Wofford College	SC	26,710	HC
Worcester State College	MA	10,005	C
Wright State Univ	OH	11,490	LC
Xavier Univ	OH	26,850	VC+
Xavier Univ of Louisiana	LA	17,600	C
Yale Univ	CT	37,000	MC
York College of Pennsylvania	PA	14,500	VC
Youngstown State Univ	OH	11,148	NC

SPANISH STUDIES

School	ST	$IS	SR
American Univ	DC	34,585	VC+
Assumption College	MA	29,375	C
Bard College	NY	37,352	HC+
Barton College	NC	19,314	C
Cal State, San Bernardino	CA	15,238	LC
Dartmouth College	NH	37,770	MC
Fairleigh Dickinson Univ/College at Florham	NJ	30,130	C
Fairleigh Dickinson Univ/Metropolitan Campus	NJ	28,584	C
Fordham Univ	NY	35,066	HC
Hobart and William Smith Colleges	NY	36,536	HC
Holy Names College	CA	27,980	NC
Montana State Univ-Billings	MT	9,550	C
New College of Florida	FL	8,906	HC+
Reed College	OR	36,950	MC
SUNY/Univ at Stony Brook	NY	12,763	HC
Sweet Briar College	VA	27,940	C
Univ of Calif at San Diego	CA	14,127	HC
Vassar College	NY	37,030	MC

SPECIAL EDUCATION

School	ST	$IS	SR
Alabama A&M Univ	AL	5,100	LC
Alabama State Univ	AL	6,404	C
Albany State Univ	GA	5,764	C+
Albright College	PA	30,579	C
Alcorn State Univ	MS	7,290	C
American International College	MA	24,690	LC
Appalachian State Univ	NC	7,637	VC
Aquinas College	MI	21,894	C
Arcadia Univ	PA	29,890	C
Arizona State Univ-Main	AZ	10,048	C
Arkansas State Univ	AR	8,450	C
Armstrong Atlantic State Univ	GA	7,102	C
Auburn Univ	AL	10,396	VC
Augusta State Univ	GA	2,592	C
Augustana College	SD	21,998	VC
Austin Peay State Univ	TN	5,814	LC
Avila Univ	MO	20,300	C
Ball State Univ	IN	8,660	C
Baylor Univ	TX	23,864	VC
Bellarmine Univ	KY	24,110	VC
Benedictine College	KS	20,603	C
Benedictine Univ	IL	23,840	C
Bennett College	NC	11,200	C
Bethany College	WV	19,845	VC
Black Hills State Univ	SD	7,743	LC
Bloomsburg Univ of Pennsylvania	PA	10,844	C
Boston College	MA	33,284	MC
Boston Univ	MA	38,194	HC+
Bowling Green State Univ	OH	13,036	C
Bradley Univ	IL	22,910	VC
Brenau Univ Women's College	GA	21,800	C
Brescia Univ	KY	14,225	C
Briar Cliff Univ	IA	21,660	C
Bridgewater State College	MA	10,482	C
Brigham Young Univ	UT	8,504	HC
Brigham Young Univ/Hawaii	HI	7,240	VC+
Buena Vista Univ	IA	25,406	C
Cabrini College	PA	29,020	C
Cal State, Long Beach	CA	8,762	C+
Calif Univ of Pennsylvania	PA	10,388	C
Calvin College	MI	22,615	NC
Canisius College	NY	28,163	C+
Cardinal Stritch Univ	WI	17,620	C
Caribbean Univ	PR	3,000	
Carlow College	PA	21,334	C
Cedarville Univ	OH	19,954	VC
Central Mich Univ	MI	11,142	C
Central Missouri State Univ	MO	9,776	C
Central State Univ	OH	8,922	C+
Central Washington Univ	WA	9,768	C
Cheyney Univ of Pennsylvania	PA	9,993	C
CUNY/City College	NY	4,230	C+
CUNY/Medgar Evers College	NY	4,232	NC
Claflin Univ	SC	14,838	C+
Clarion Univ of Pennsylvania	PA	11,272	LC
Clarke College	IA	23,165	C
Clearwater Christian College	FL	13,160	LC
Clemson Univ	SC	11,972	HC
Cleveland State Univ	OH	12,308	LC
Coastal Carolina Univ	SC	11,040	C
College Misericordia	PA	26,350	C
College of Charleston	SC	11,887	HC
College of Mount St. Vincent	NY	26,800	C
College of Mount St. Joseph	OH	22,785	C
College of New Jersey	NJ	15,950	MC
College of Notre Dame of Maryland	MD	27,700	C
College of Our Lady of the Elms	MA	20,644	C
College of St. Elizabeth	NJ	25,460	C
College of St. Joseph	VT	19,100	C
College of St. Mary	NE	21,510	C
College of St. Rose	NY	22,864	C
College of the Southwest	NM	9,320	C+
Columbia College	SC	22,658	LC
Columbus State Univ	GA	7,846	C
Concord College	WV	8,136	C
Concordia Univ Nebr	NE	20,302	C+
Coppin State College	MD	10,191	LC
Creighton Univ	NE	26,748	VC+
Cumberland College	KY	16,384	C
Cumberland Univ	TN	16,910	C
Curry College	MA	26,025	LC
Daemen College	NY	22,120	C
Dana College	NE	20,280	C
Delaware State Univ	DE	8,104	LC
Delta State Univ	MS	6,618	C
Dillard Univ	LA	17,325	VC
Doane College	NE	20,000	C
Dominican College	NY	24,810	LC
Dowling College	NY	23,870	LC
Duquesne Univ	PA	26,907	VC
D'Youville College	NY	21,080	C
East Carolina Univ	NC	8,671	C
East Central Univ	OK	4,968	C
East Stroudsburg Univ of Pennsylvania	PA	10,336	C
East Tenn State Univ	TN	8,497	C
Eastern Illinois Univ	IL	11,192	C
Eastern Kentucky Univ	KY	7,708	C
Eastern Mennonite Univ	VA	22,990	C
Eastern Mich Univ	MI	11,478	C
Eastern New Mexico Univ	NM	6,762	LC
Eastern Univ	PA	24,020	C
Edinboro Univ of Pennsylvania	PA	10,850	LC
Elizabeth City State Univ	NC	5,550	LC
Elmhurst College	IL	24,630	C
Elon Univ	NC	22,240	VC
Erskine College	SC	23,166	VC
Evangel Univ	MO	15,435	C
Felician College	NJ	24,300	C
Fitchburg State College	MA	9,622	C
Florida Atlantic Univ	FL	8,543	C
Florida Gulf Coast Univ	FL	9,908	C
Florida International Univ	FL	9,912	VC
Florida Southern College	FL	23,592	C
Fontbonne Univ	MO	21,508	C
Freed-Hardeman Univ	TN		NC
Gannon Univ	PA	23,260	C
Georgia College and State Univ	GA	9,878	C
Georgia Southern Univ	GA	8,540	C
Georgia Southwestern State Univ	GA	6,013	C
Georgian Court College	NJ	19,040	LC
Glenville State College	WV	7,812	NC
Gonzaga Univ	WA	26,766	HC
Gordon College	MA	25,982	VC+
Goucher College	MD	32,650	HC
Grace College	IN	19,825	VC
Grambling State Univ	LA	6,538	NC
Grand Canyon Univ	AZ	30,000	LC
Green Mountain College	VT	24,130	C
Greensboro College	NC	21,750	C
Greenville College	IL	21,342	C
Gwynedd-Mercy College	PA	24,225	C
Hastings College	NE	19,928	VC
High Point Univ	NC	22,480	C
Holy Family College	PA	13,710	LC
Hood College	MD	27,795	VC
Hope College	MI	25,340	VC
Houston Baptist Univ	TX	16,905	C
Idaho State Univ	ID	8,128	C
Illinois State Univ	IL	10,944	C+
Indiana State Univ	IN	10,719	LC
Indiana Univ Bloomington	IN	12,389	VC
Indiana Univ of Pennsylvania	PA	10,489	C
Indiana Univ South Bend	IN	4,571	LC
Indiana Univ Southeast	IN	4,504	LC
Inter American Univ of PR/Arecibo Campus	PR	3,300	
Inter American Univ of PR/Fajardo Campus	PR	4,000	
Inter American Univ of PR/Metropolitan Campus	PR		
Inter American Univ of PR/Ponce Regional College	PR	3,700	
Inter American Univ of PR/San German	PR	6,716	
Jackson State Univ	MS	8,382	C
Jacksonville State Univ	AL	6,844	LC
Jarvis Christian College	TX	9,035	NC
Juniata College	PA	29,080	VC
Kansas Wesleyan Univ	KS	18,900	VC
Kean Univ	NJ	14,479	C
Keene State College	NH	12,212	C
Kent State Univ	OH	12,932	C
Kutztown Univ of Pennsylvania	PA	10,786	C
La Salle Univ	PA	31,260	VC
Lamar Univ	TX	6,816	LC
Lambuth Univ	TN	16,520	C
Lander Univ	SC	10,496	C
LeMoyne-Owen College	TN	13,070	LC
Lesley Univ	MA	30,695	C
Lewis Univ	IL	22,950	C+
Lincoln Univ	MO	7,158	NC
Lincoln Univ	PA	13,320	C+
Lock Haven Univ of Pennsylvania	PA	11,098	LC
LIU/Brooklyn Campus	NY	24,790	C
Longwood Univ	VA	11,175	C
Loras College	IA	24,233	C
Louisiana College	LA	13,450	C
Louisiana Tech Univ	LA	7,361	C
Loyola Univ Chicago	IL	31,164	VC
MacMurray College	IL	20,005	LC
Malone College	OH	20,995	C
Manhattan College	NY	27,400	VC
Mansfield Univ	PA	11,220	C
Marian College	IN	23,030	C
Marist College	NY	27,596	VC
Marygrove College	MI	17,550	C
Marymount College of Fordham Univ	NY	27,686	C
Marymount Manhattan College	NY	27,292	C
Marywood Univ	PA	26,050	C
McNeese State Univ	LA	5,259	LC
McPherson College	KS	20,265	C
Mercer Univ	GA	27,516	VC+
Mercy College	NY	19,200	NC
Mercyhurst College	PA	20,694	C
Methodist College	NC	19,526	C
Miami Univ	OH	15,033	HC
Mich State Univ	MI	11,933	VC
Middle Tenn State Univ	TN	8,534	C
Millersville Univ of Pennsylvania	PA	11,269	C
Minn State Univ, Moorehead	MN	7,000	LC
Miss College	MS	14,574	C
Miss State Univ	MS	9,139	C
Missouri Southern State Univ	MO	8,316	C
Molloy College	NY	15,180	C
Monmouth Univ	NJ	26,334	C
Montana State Univ-Billings	MT	9,550	C
Morehead State Univ	KY	7,464	C
Morningside College	IA	21,610	C
Mount Marty College	SD	15,656	LC
Mount St. Mary College	NY	21,270	C
Mount Vernon Nazarene Univ	OH	18,925	C
Murray State Univ	KY	7,816	VC
Muskingum College	OH	20,680	C
Nazareth College of Rochester	NY	24,936	VC
Nebr Wesleyan Univ	NE	21,197	C+
New England College	NH	28,860	LC
New Jersey City Univ	NJ	11,850	LC
New Mexico Highlands Univ	NM	6,182	LC
New Mexico State Univ	NM	7,932	C
New York Univ	NY	39,406	MC
Nicholls State Univ	LA	6,395	NC
N Car Agricultural and Technical State Univ	NC	6,659	LC
North Georgia College and State Univ	GA	6,984	C
Northeastern Illinois Univ	IL	2,898	NC
Northeastern State Univ	OK	4,950	LC
Northern Arizona Univ	AZ	9,002	C
Northern Illinois Univ	IL	11,472	C
Northern State Univ	SD	7,117	LC
Northwest College	WA	18,854	C
Northwest Missouri State Univ	MO	9,334	C
Northwestern College of Iowa	IA	19,640	C+
Northwestern Okla State Univ	OK	5,433	NC
Northwestern State Univ of Louisiana	LA	6,331	NC
Ohio Dominican Univ	OH	22,700	C
Okla Christian Univ	OK	17,690	NC
Oral Roberts Univ	OK	18,490	C
Our Lady of the Lake Univ of San Antonio	TX	17,336	C
Penn State Univ/Univ Park Campus	PA	15,646	HC
Peru State College	NE	6,342	NC
Pfeiffer Univ	NC	18,980	C
Philander Smith College	AR	7,380	NC
Piedmont College	GA	16,900	C
Pontifical Catholic Univ of PR/Ponce	PR	7,298	
Presbyterian College	SC	25,920	VC
Prescott College	AZ	13,430	C
Providence College	RI	30,604	HC
Purdue Univ/West Lafayette	IN	12,560	VC
Quincy Univ	IL	22,330	C
Rhode Island College	RI	11,565	C
Saginaw Valley State Univ	MI	11,055	C
St. John Fisher College	NY	24,870	C
St. John's Univ	NY	30,180	C
St. Joseph College	CT	29,685	C
St. Joseph's, Brooklyn,	NY	10,902	C
St. Joseph's Univ	PA	33,590	VC
St. Martin's College	WA	23,245	C
St. Mary-of-the-Woods College	IN	23,280	C
St. Thomas Aquinas College	NY	20,590	LC
Salve Regina Univ	RI	29,210	C
San Francisco State Univ	CA	12,070	C
Seattle Pacific Univ	WA	25,944	VC
Seton Hall Univ	NJ	30,130	VC
Seton Hill Univ	PA	24,930	C
Shaw Univ	NC	14,882	C+
Silver Lake College of the Holy Family	WI	18,450	LC
Simmons College	MA	33,000	VC
Slippery Rock Univ of Pennsylvania	PA	10,343	LC
S Car State Univ	SC	6,586	LC
Southeast Missouri State Univ	MO	9,704	C
Southeastern Louisiana Univ	LA	6,791	LC
Southern Conn State Univ	CT	10,310	C
Southern Illinois Univ Carbondale	IL	10,407	C
Southern Illinois Univ Edwardsville	IL	8,724	C
Southern Univ and A&M College	LA	7,372	LC
Southern Utah Univ	UT	8,194	C
Southern Wesleyan Univ	SC	19,940	C
Southwest Missouri State Univ	MO	8,918	C
Southwestern Okla State Univ	OK	4,801	C
Spring Arbor Univ	MI	20,206	C
SUNY/College at Buffalo	NY	8,025	C
SUNY/College at Geneseo	NY	11,330	HC
SUNY/College at Old Westbury	NY	12,784	C
SUNY/College at Plattsburgh	NY	11,700	C
State Univ of West Georgia	GA	7,622	C
Syracuse Univ	NY	34,720	HC
Tabor College	KS	19,500	NC
Tenn State Univ	TN	9,048	LC
Tenn Tech Univ	TN	8,670	VC
Texas Southern Univ	TX	8,920	NC
Texas State Univ	TX	9,320	VC
Touro College	NY	15,250	VC
Towson Univ	MD	12,694	VC
Trinity Christian College	IL	21,640	VC
Troy State Univ	AL	7,696	C
Troy State Univ Dothan	AL	3,842	C
Turabo Univ	PR	4,110	
Tusculum College	TN	19,990	C
Tuskegee Univ	AL	17,250	LC
Union College	KY	15,920	C
Union Univ	TN	18,800	VC
Univ of Akron	OH	13,134	NC
Univ of Alabama	AL	9,040	C+
Univ of Alabama at Birmingham	AL	12,901	C
Univ of Arizona	AZ	10,413	VC
Univ of Arkansas	AR	9,855	VC
Univ of Arkansas at Monticello	AR	5,940	NC
Univ of Arkansas at Pine Bluff	AR	7,925	C
Univ of Central Arkansas	AR	6,388	C
Univ of Central Florida	FL	10,038	VC
Univ of Central Okla	OK	9,434	C
Univ of Cincinnati	OH	14,736	C
Univ of Conn	CT	14,608	VC
Univ of Dayton	OH	24,850	VC
Univ of Delaware	DE	12,616	HC
Univ of Detroit Mercy	MI	25,582	C
Univ of Evansville	IN	24,190	VC
Univ of Georgia	GA	8,656	VC
Univ of Great Falls	MT	15,360	C
Univ of Hartford	CT	31,080	C
Univ of Idaho	ID	8,216	C
Univ of Illinois at Urbana-Champaign	IL	11,316	HC+
Univ of Kentucky	KY	7,765	C
Univ of Louisiana at Lafayette	LA	5,826	C
Univ of Louisiana at Monroe	LA	5,207	NC
Univ of Maine at Farmington	ME	10,108	C
Univ of Mary	ND	12,900	C+
Univ of Mary Hardin-Baylor	TX	17,268	C
Univ of Maryland/College Park	MD	14,227	HC
Univ of Memphis	TN	8,560	C
Univ of Miami	FL	34,608	HC
Univ of Miss	MS	7,666	C
Univ of Missouri/St. Louis	MO	11,656	VC
Univ of Nebr at Kearney	NE	8,286	NC

ST = STATE $IS = IN-STATE COSTS SR = SELECTOR RATING

School	ST	$IS	SR
Univ of Nebr at Lincoln	NE	9,975	C+
Univ of Nevada/Las Vegas	NV	11,566	C
Univ of Nevada/Reno	NV	9,792	C
Univ of New Mexico	NM	9,223	C
Univ of N Car at Pembroke	NC	6,929	LC
Univ of N Car at Wilmington	NC	8,940	VC
Univ of North Florida	FL	8,769	VC
Univ of Northern Iowa	IA	9,834	C
Univ of Okla	OK	9,226	VC
Univ of PR/Cayey Univ College	PR	1,245	
Univ of PR/Rio Piedras	PR	5,730	
Univ of St. Francis	IN	20,964	C
Univ of Scranton	PA	30,836	VC
Univ of South Alabama	AL	7,760	LC
Univ of S Car at Spartanburg	SC	9,936	C+
Univ of S Dak	SD	7,710	C+
Univ of South Florida	FL	9,454	C
Univ of Southern Indiana	IN	9,025	LC
Univ of Tenn at Chattanooga	TN	7,783	C
Univ of Tenn at Knoxville	TN	8,214	C
Univ of the Incarnate Word	TX	21,772	LC
Univ of Toledo	OH	12,479	NC
Univ of West Alabama	AL	6,048	C
Univ of Wisc/Eau Claire	WI	8,463	VC
Univ of Wisc/Oshkosh	WI	6,130	LC
Univ of Wisc/Whitewater	WI	8,626	C
Univ of Wyoming	WY	8,636	C
Ursuline College	OH	22,728	LC
Utah State Univ	UT	7,371	C
Valdosta State Univ	GA	7,798	C
Vanderbilt Univ	TN	37,897	MC
Virginia Union Univ	VA	15,358	LC
Walla Walla College	WA	21,600	NC
Walsh Univ	OH	20,890	C
Washburn Univ of Topeka	KS	8,984	NC
Wayne State College	NE	7,352	NC
Wayne State Univ	MI	11,774	C
Waynesburg College	PA	19,370	C
West Chester Univ of Pennsylvania	PA	11,164	C
West Liberty State College	WV	7,868	LC
West Texas A&M Univ	TX	7,533	C
Western Carolina Univ	NC	6,742	C
Western Illinois Univ	IL	10,363	C
Western Kentucky Univ	KY	6,834	C
Western Mich Univ	MI	12,031	C
Western New Mexico Univ	NM	5,950	LC
Westfield State College	MA	10,147	C
Wheelock College	MA	29,000	C
Wichita State Univ	KS	8,092	C
Wiley College	TX	8,100	LC
William Paterson Univ of New Jersey	NJ	14,450	C
William Penn Univ	IA	17,575	LC
William Woods Univ	MO	20,120	C
Winona State Univ	MN		C
Winston-Salem State Univ	NC	8,926	LC
Winthrop Univ	SC	11,302	C
Wittenberg Univ	OH	31,316	VC
Wright State Univ	OH	11,490	LC
Xavier Univ	OH	26,850	VC+
York College of Pennsylvania	PA	14,500	VC
Youngstown State Univ	OH	11,148	NC

SPECIFIC LEARNING DISABILITIES

School	ST	$IS	SR
Baldwin-Wallace College	OH	24,678	C
Barton College	NC	19,314	C
Florida International Univ	FL	9,912	VC
Florida State Univ	FL	9,028	HC
Northwest Missouri State Univ	MO	9,334	C
Palm Beach Atlantic Univ	FL	20,690	C
Univ of South Florida	FL	9,454	C
Youngstown State Univ	OH	11,148	NC

SPEECH CORRECTION

School	ST	$IS	SR
Columbia College	SC	22,658	LC
Ithaca College	NY	31,730	HC
Lewis Univ	IL	22,950	C+
MidAmerica Nazarene Univ	KS	18,688	C
Univ of N Car at Greensboro	NC	8,248	C
Western Carolina Univ	NC	6,742	C

SPEECH PATHOLOGY/AUDIOLOGY

School	ST	$IS	SR
Abilene Christian Univ	TX	18,370	VC
Adelphi Univ	NY	26,300	VC
Alabama A&M Univ	AL	5,100	LC
Andrews Univ	MI	19,550	C
Arizona State Univ-Main	AZ	10,048	C
Arkansas State Univ	AR	8,450	C
Armstrong Atlantic State Univ	GA	7,102	C
Auburn Univ	AL	10,396	VC
Augustana College	IL	26,610	VC+
Augustana College	SD	21,998	VC
Baldwin-Wallace College	OH	24,678	C
Ball State Univ	IN	8,660	C
Baylor Univ	TX	23,864	VC
Biola Univ	CA	25,964	VC
Bloomsburg Univ of Pennsylvania	PA	10,844	C
Boston Univ	MA	38,194	HC+
Bowling Green State Univ	OH	13,036	C
Brescia Univ	KY	14,225	C
Brigham Young Univ	UT	8,504	HC
Butler Univ	IN	28,250	VC+
Cal State, Chico	CA	8,598	LC
Cal State, Fresno	CA	8,414	LC
Cal State, Fullerton	CA	6,648	C
Cal State, Hayward	CA	8,871	LC
Cal State, Los Angeles	CA	5,778	C
Cal State, Northridge	CA	7,757	LC
Cal State, Sacramento	CA	9,543	C
Calif Univ of Pennsylvania	PA	10,388	C
Calvin College	MI	22,615	NC
Case Western Reserve Univ	OH	32,002	MC
Central Mich Univ	MI	11,142	C
Central Missouri State Univ	MO	9,776	C
CUNY/Brooklyn College	NY	4,353	C+
CUNY/Herbert H. Lehman College	NY	3,320	LC
Clarion Univ of Pennsylvania	PA	11,272	LC
Clemson Univ	SC	11,972	HC
College of Our Lady of the Elms	MA	20,644	C
College of St. Rose	NY	22,864	C
College of the Ozarks	MO	3,500	VC+
Delta State Univ	MS	6,618	C
Duquesne Univ	PA	26,907	VC
East Carolina Univ	NC	8,671	C
East Stroudsburg Univ of Pennsylvania	PA	10,336	C
Eastern Illinois Univ	IL	11,192	C
Eastern Mich Univ	MI	11,478	C
Eastern New Mexico Univ	NM	6,762	LC
Eastern Washington Univ	WA	9,012	C
Edinboro Univ of Pennsylvania	PA	10,850	LC
Elmhurst College	IL	24,630	C
Elmira College	NY	33,820	VC
Emerson College	MA	32,205	HC
Florida State Univ	FL	9,028	HC
Fontbonne Univ	MO	21,508	C
Fort Hays State Univ	KS	7,363	C
Geneva College	PA	21,850	C
George Washington Univ	DC	41,030	MC
Georgia Southern Univ	GA	8,540	C
Grambling State Univ	LA	6,538	NC
Hampton Univ	VA	17,112	C+
Harding Univ	AR	14,890	VC
Hardin-Simmons Univ	TX	14,165	C
Hofstra Univ	NY	27,112	VC
Howard Univ	DC	16,505	C
Idaho State Univ	ID	8,128	C
Illinois State Univ	IL	10,944	C+
Indiana State Univ	IN	10,719	LC
Indiana Univ Bloomington	IN	12,389	VC
Indiana Univ of Pennsylvania	PA	10,489	C
Indiana Univ-Purdue Univ Fort Wayne	IN	5,108	LC
Iona College	NY	27,988	VC
Ithaca College	NY	31,730	HC
James Madison Univ	VA	10,794	VC
Kean Univ	NJ	14,479	C
Kent State Univ	OH	12,932	C
Kutztown Univ of Pennsylvania	PA	10,786	C
La Salle Univ	PA	31,260	VC
Lamar Univ	TX	6,816	LC
Lambuth Univ	TN	16,520	C
LIU/C.W. Post Campus	NY	28,282	C
Louisiana State Univ and A&M College	LA	9,126	VC
Louisiana Tech Univ	LA	7,361	C
Loyola College in Maryland	MD	34,560	HC
Marquette Univ	WI	27,594	VC
Marymount Manhattan College	NY	27,292	C
Marywood Univ	PA	26,050	C
Miami Univ	OH	15,033	HC
Mich State Univ	MI	11,933	VC
Minn State Univ, Mankato	MN	8,803	LC
Minn State Univ, Moorehead	MN	7,000	LC
Minot State Univ	ND	6,602	LC
Miss Univ for Women	MS	5,446	LC
Molloy College	NY	15,180	C
Murray State Univ	KY	7,816	VC
Nazareth College of Rochester	NY	24,936	VC
New Mexico State Univ	NM	7,932	C
New York Univ	NY	39,406	MC
Nicholls State Univ	LA	6,395	NC
N Car State Univ	NC	9,886	VC
Northeastern Univ	MA	35,650	HC
Northern Arizona Univ	AZ	9,002	C
Northern Illinois Univ	IL	11,472	C
Northern Mich Univ	MI	10,834	C
Northern State Univ	SD	7,117	LC
Northwestern Univ	IL	37,491	MC
Ohio State Univ	OH	13,080	VC+
Okla State Univ	OK	9,216	VC
Old Dominion Univ	VA	10,441	C
Ouachita Baptist Univ	AR	18,900	VC
Our Lady of the Lake Univ of San Antonio	TX	17,336	C
Penn State Univ/Univ Park Campus	PA	15,646	HC
Purdue Univ/West Lafayette	IN	12,560	VC
Radford Univ	VA	8,500	C
Richard Stockton College of New Jersey	NJ	12,972	VC
Rockhurst Univ	MO	22,960	C+
St. Cloud State Univ	MN	8,362	C
St. John's Univ	NY	30,180	C
St. Louis Univ	MO	29,780	VC+
St. Xavier Univ	IL	23,144	C
San Diego State Univ	CA	10,321	C
San Francisco State Univ	CA	12,070	C
San Jose State Univ	CA	8,187	C
Shaw Univ	NC	14,882	C+
S Car State Univ	SC	6,586	LC
Southeast Missouri State Univ	MO	9,704	C
Southeastern Louisiana Univ	LA	6,791	LC
Southern Illinois Univ Carbondale	IL	10,407	C
Southern Illinois Univ Edwardsville	IL	8,724	C
Southern Univ and A&M College	LA	7,372	LC
Southwest Missouri State Univ	MO	8,918	C
SUNY/College at Buffalo	NY	8,025	C
SUNY/College at Cortland	NY	12,095	C
SUNY/College at Fredonia	NY	11,562	VC
SUNY/College at Geneseo	NY	11,330	HC
SUNY/Univ at Buffalo	NY	12,563	VC
SUNY/Univ at New Paltz	NY	11,565	VC
State Univ of West Georgia	GA	7,622	C
Syracuse Univ	NY	34,720	HC
Tenn State Univ	TN	9,048	LC
Texas A&M Univ at Kingsville	TX	6,740	LC
Texas Christian Univ	TX	23,410	VC
Texas State Univ	TX	9,320	VC
Thiel College	PA	20,970	C
Towson Univ	MD	12,694	VC
Truman State Univ	MO	9,728	HC+
Univ of Akron	OH	13,134	NC
Univ of Arizona	AZ	10,413	VC
Univ of Arkansas	AR	9,855	VC
Univ of Arkansas at Little Rock	AR	5,637	NC
Univ of Central Arkansas	AR	6,388	C
Univ of Central Florida	FL	10,038	VC
Univ of Central Okla	OK	9,434	C
Univ of Cincinnati	OH	14,736	C
Univ of Colo at Boulder	CO	10,774	VC
Univ of Florida	FL	8,580	MC
Univ of Georgia	GA	8,656	VC
Univ of Hawaii at Manoa	HI	9,565	VC
Univ of Illinois at Urbana-Champaign	IL	11,316	HC+
Univ of Iowa	IA	10,923	VC
Univ of Kansas	KS	8,923	VC
Univ of Louisiana at Lafayette	LA	5,826	C
Univ of Louisiana at Monroe	LA	5,207	NC
Univ of Maine	ME	12,080	C+
Univ of Mass Amherst	MA	13,980	C+
Univ of Minn/Duluth	MN	12,470	C
Univ of Minn/Twin Cities	MN	13,160	VC
Univ of Miss	MS	7,666	C
Univ of Montevallo	AL	8,478	C
Univ of Nebr at Lincoln	NE	9,975	C+
Univ of Nevada/Reno	NV	9,792	C
Univ of New Hampshire	NH	14,828	VC
Univ of New Mexico	NM	9,223	C
Univ of N Car at Greensboro	NC	8,248	C
Univ of N Dak	ND	8,390	C
Univ of North Texas	TX	7,629	C
Univ of Northern Colo	CO	8,987	C
Univ of Northern Iowa	IA	9,834	C
Univ of Oregon	OR	11,479	VC
Univ of Rhode Island	RI	13,720	VC
Univ of Science and Arts of Okla	OK	5,982	C
Univ of South Alabama	AL	7,760	LC
Univ of S Dak	SD	7,710	C+
Univ of Southern Colo	CO	7,821	LC
Univ of Southern Miss	MS	8,324	LC
Univ of Tenn at Knoxville	TN	8,214	C
Univ of Texas at Austin	TX	10,630	HC
Univ of Texas at Dallas	TX	10,234	HC
Univ of Texas-Pan American	TX	5,954	LC
Univ of the District of Columbia	DC	2,070	LC
Univ of the Pacific	CA	31,090	VC
Univ of Toledo	OH	12,479	NC
Univ of Tulsa	OK	22,090	VC+
Univ of Utah	UT	9,205	C
Univ of Vermont	VT	16,316	VC
Univ of Virginia	VA	11,740	MC
Univ of Washington	WA	10,361	VC
Univ of Wisc/Eau Claire	WI	8,463	VC
Univ of Wisc/Madison	WI	8,262	VC
Univ of Wisc/Milwaukee	WI	9,427	LC
Univ of Wisc/Oshkosh	WI	6,130	LC
Univ of Wisc/River Falls	WI	8,358	LC
Univ of Wisc/Stevens Point	WI	8,116	VC
Univ of Wyoming	WY	8,636	C
Utah State Univ	UT	7,371	C
Valdosta State Univ	GA	7,798	C
Washington State Univ	WA	11,334	C
Wayne State Univ	MI	11,774	C
West Chester Univ of Pennsylvania	PA	11,164	C
West Liberty State College	WV	7,868	LC
West Texas A&M Univ	TX	7,533	C
West Virginia Univ	WV	9,370	C
Western Illinois Univ	IL	10,363	C
Western Kentucky Univ	KY	6,834	C
Western Mich Univ	MI	12,031	C
Western Washington Univ	WA	10,119	VC
Wichita State Univ	KS	8,092	C
Winthrop Univ	SC	11,302	C
Worcester State College	MA	10,005	C
Xavier Univ of Louisiana	LA	17,600	C

SPEECH THERAPY

School	ST	$IS	SR
Baylor Univ	TX	23,864	VC
Cal State, Fresno	CA	8,414	LC
Cleveland State Univ	OH	12,308	LC
College Misericordia	PA	26,350	C
Ithaca College	NY	31,730	HC
Southern Univ and A&M College	LA	7,372	LC
Stephen F. Austin State Univ	TX	7,552	C
Univ of Miss	MS	7,666	C

SPEECH/DEBATE/RHETORIC

School	ST	$IS	SR
Abilene Christian Univ	TX	18,370	VC
Adams State College	CO	7,468	C
Albany State Univ	GA	5,764	C+
Albion College	MI	25,224	VC
Arkansas State Univ	AR	8,450	C
Arkansas Tech Univ	AR	7,299	C
Ashland Univ	OH	24,464	C
Auburn Univ	AL	10,396	VC
Augsburg College	MN	25,298	C
Augustana College	IL	26,610	VC+
Austin Peay State Univ	TN	5,814	LC
Ball State Univ	IN	8,660	C
Bates College	ME	37,500	MC
Baylor Univ	TX	23,864	VC
Beloit College	WI	29,864	HC
Berea College	KY	5,030	VC+
Bethel College	MN	25,180	VC
Black Hills State Univ	SD	7,743	LC
Bloomsburg Univ of Pennsylvania	PA	10,844	C
Blue Mountain College	MS	10,226	C
Brewton-Parker College	GA	14,200	LC
Buena Vista Univ	IA	25,406	C
Butler Univ	IN	28,250	VC+
Cal State, Fresno	CA	8,414	LC
Cal State, Fullerton	CA	6,648	C
Cal State, Hayward	CA	8,871	LC
Cal State, Los Angeles	CA	5,778	C
Cal State, Northridge	CA	7,757	LC
Capital Univ	OH	26,550	C
Central Missouri State Univ	MO	9,776	C
Central Washington Univ	WA	9,768	C
Chadron State College	NE	6,286	NC
Charleston Southern Univ	SC	17,122	C
Chicago State Univ	IL	10,882	C+
CUNY/Herbert H. Lehman College	NY	3,320	LC
CUNY/York College	NY	3,292	NC
Clarion Univ of Pennsylvania	PA	11,272	LC
Clark Atlanta Univ	GA	19,300	C+
College of St. Catherine	MN	24,010	VC
College of William and Mary	VA	12,224	MC
Colo State Univ	CO	9,964	VC
Concordia College: Moorhead	MN	22,460	VC+
Concordia Univ Nebr	NE	20,302	C+
Concordia Univ Wisc	WI	16,600	C
Cornerstone Univ and Grand Rapids Theological Seminary	MI	19,846	C
Creighton Univ	NE	26,748	VC+
Denison Univ	OH	33,050	HC
Dickinson State Univ	ND	6,338	NC
Doane College	NE	20,000	C
Dordt College	IA	20,170	VC
Dowling College	NY	23,870	LC
Drake Univ	IA	25,120	VC+
Drury Univ	MO	18,085	VC+
Duquesne Univ	PA	26,907	VC
East Central Univ	OK	4,968	C
East Tenn State Univ	TN	8,497	C

School	ST	$IS	SR
East Texas Baptist Univ	TX	13,914	C
Eastern Kentucky Univ	KY	7,708	C
Eastern Mich Univ	MI	11,478	C
Eastern Nazarene College	MA	19,433	LC
Eastern New Mexico Univ	NM	6,762	LC
Eastern Washington Univ	WA	9,012	C
Edinboro Univ of Pennsylvania	PA	10,850	LC
Emerson College	MA	32,205	HC
Evangel Univ	MO	15,435	C
Fairmont State	WV	8,280	LC
Fayetteville State Univ	NC	5,590	LC
Fisk Univ	TN	17,305	LC
Florida State Univ	FL	9,028	HC
Freed-Hardeman Univ	TN		NC
Geneva College	PA	21,850	C
Georgia College and State Univ	GA	9,878	C
Georgia State Univ	GA	10,658	C
Gonzaga Univ	WA	26,766	HC
Graceland Univ	IA	19,550	C
Grand Canyon Univ	AZ	30,000	LC
Greenville College	IL	21,342	C
Gustavus Adolphus College	MN	27,120	VC+
Hannibal-LaGrange College	MO	13,940	C
Hastings College	NE	19,928	VC
Hillsdale College	MI	22,450	HC
Hofstra Univ	NY	27,112	VC
Houston Baptist Univ	TX	16,905	C
Humboldt State Univ	CA	9,400	C
Huntingdon College	AL	18,400	VC
Idaho State Univ	ID	8,128	C
Illinois College	IL	19,100	VC
Illinois State Univ	IL	10,944	C+
Indiana Univ Bloomington	IN	12,389	VC
Indiana Univ South Bend	IN	4,571	LC
Indiana Univ-Purdue Univ Fort Wayne	IN	5,108	LC
Iona College	NY	27,988	VC
Iowa State Univ	IA	10,768	VC
Ithaca College	NY	31,730	HC
Jackson State Univ	MS	8,382	C
James Madison Univ	VA	10,794	VC
Kansas Wesleyan Univ	KS	18,900	VC
Kent State Univ	OH	12,932	C
Kutztown Univ of Pennsylvania	PA	10,786	C
Lamar Univ	TX	6,816	LC
Lander Univ	SC	10,496	C
Langston Univ	OK	2,308	LC
Lock Haven Univ of Pennsylvania	PA	11,098	LC
LIU/Brooklyn Campus	NY	24,790	C
Loras College	IA	24,233	C
Louisiana College	LA	13,450	C
Louisiana State Univ and A&M College	LA	9,126	VC
Louisiana State Univ in Shreveport	LA	2,884	NC
Louisiana Tech Univ	LA	7,361	C
Luther College	IA	25,700	VC
Mansfield Univ	PA	11,220	C
Marietta College	OH	27,047	C
McKendree College	IL	21,120	VC
McNeese State Univ	LA	5,259	LC
McPherson College	KS	20,265	C
Metropolitan State College of Denver	CO	2,338	LC
Miami Univ	OH	15,033	HC
Minn State Univ, Mankato	MN	8,803	LC
Minn State Univ, Moorehead	MN	7,000	LC
Miss Valley State Univ	MS	6,765	NC
Missouri Southern State Univ	MO	8,316	C
Missouri Valley College	MO	18,500	C
Missouri Western State College	MO	8,522	NC
Montclair State Univ	NJ	13,790	C
Morehead State Univ	KY	7,464	C
Morgan State Univ	MD	11,470	C
Mount Mercy College	IA	21,400	C
Murray State Univ	KY	7,816	VC
Muskingum College	OH	20,680	C
New York Univ	NY	39,406	MC
N Car Agricultural and Technical State Univ	NC	6,659	LC
North Central College	IL	25,656	VC
Northeastern Illinois Univ	IL	2,898	NC
Northeastern State Univ	OK	4,950	LC
Northern Arizona Univ	AZ	9,002	C
Northern Kentucky Univ	KY	6,352	NC
Northern Mich Univ	MI	10,834	C
Northwest Missouri State Univ	MO	9,334	C
Northwestern Okla State Univ	OK	5,433	NC
Ohio Univ	OH	14,448	C
Okla Baptist Univ	OK	15,220	VC
Okla City Univ	OK	19,580	VC
Olivet Nazarene Univ	IL	20,480	C
Oral Roberts Univ	OK	18,490	C
Oregon State Univ	OR	11,055	C
Otterbein College	OH	26,085	C
Ouachita Baptist Univ	AR	18,900	VC
Penn State Univ/Univ Park Campus	PA	15,646	HC
Pepperdine Univ	CA	32,830	VC
Point Loma Nazarene Univ	CA	21,380	VC
Portland State Univ	OR	12,453	C
Prairie View A&M Univ	TX	9,418	NC
Radford Univ	VA	8,500	C
Rowan Univ	NJ	14,506	VC
St. Ambrose Univ	IA	22,800	C
St. Cloud State Univ	MN	8,362	C
St. John's Univ	NY	30,180	C
St. Joseph's, Brooklyn,	NY	10,902	C
St. Mary's Univ of San Antonio	TX	22,444	C
Sam Houston State Univ	TX	7,142	C
San Francisco State Univ	CA	12,070	C
San Jose State Univ	CA	8,187	C
Shippensburg Univ of Pennsylvania	PA	10,826	C
Simpson College	IA	23,658	C+
Southeastern Okla State Univ	OK	6,147	C
Southern Illinois Univ Carbondale	IL	10,407	C
Southern Illinois Univ Edwardsville	IL	8,724	C
Southern Nazarene Univ	OK	14,634	NC
Southern Univ at New Orleans	LA	995	NC
Southwest Missouri State Univ	MO	8,918	C
Southwestern Adventist Univ	TX	14,798	C
Spring Arbor Univ	MI	20,206	C
St. Joseph's, Suffolk	NY	11,297	C
SUNY at Potsdam	NY	12,160	C
SUNY/College at Oneonta	NY	11,870	VC
SUNY/Univ at Binghamton	NY	12,787	HC
SUNY/Univ at New Paltz	NY	11,565	VC
State Univ of West Georgia	GA	7,622	C
Stephen F. Austin State Univ	TX	7,552	C
Suffolk Univ	MA	29,200	C
Syracuse Univ	NY	34,720	HC
Tarleton State Univ	TX	7,576	C
Temple Univ	PA	15,912	C
Tenn State Univ	TN	9,048	LC
Texas A&M Univ	TX	11,081	HC
Texas A&M Univ at Corpus Christi	TX	10,269	C
Texas Christian Univ	TX	23,410	VC
Texas Southern Univ	TX	8,920	NC
Texas State Univ	TX	9,320	VC
Thomas More College	KY	21,350	C
Touro College	NY	15,250	VC
Trinity Univ	TX	26,466	HC+
Troy State Univ	AL	7,696	C
Truman State Univ	MO	9,728	HC+
Univ of Akron	OH	13,134	NC
Univ of Alaska Southeast	AK	7,900	LC
Univ of Arkansas at Monticello	AR	5,940	NC
Univ of Arkansas at Pine Bluff	AR	7,925	C
Univ of Calif at Berkeley	CA	15,563	MC
Univ of Calif at Davis	CA	14,995	VC
Univ of Central Arkansas	AR	6,388	C
Univ of Central Okla	OK	9,434	C
Univ of Dubuque	IA	20,950	C
Univ of Florida	FL	8,580	MC
Univ of Georgia	GA	8,656	VC
Univ of Hawaii at Manoa	HI	9,565	VC
Univ of Houston	TX	9,818	C
Univ of Illinois at Chicago	IL	13,418	C
Univ of Illinois at Urbana-Champaign	IL	11,316	HC+
Univ of Indianapolis	IN	22,560	VC
Univ of Iowa	IA	10,923	VC
Univ of Kansas	KS	8,923	VC
Univ of La Verne	CA	28,600	C
Univ of Louisiana at Monroe	LA	5,207	NC
Univ of Maine	ME	12,080	C+
Univ of Mary Hardin-Baylor	TX	17,268	C
Univ of Mich/Ann Arbor	MI	13,864	HC+
Univ of Minn/Morris	MN	12,896	VC
Univ of Minn/Twin Cities	MN	13,160	VC
Univ of Missouri/Kansas City	MO	13,416	VC
Univ of Nebr at Kearney	NE	8,286	NC
Univ of Nebr at Lincoln	NE	9,975	C+
Univ of Nebr at Omaha	NE	8,080	C
Univ of Nevada/Reno	NV	9,792	C
Univ of N Car at Chapel Hill	NC	10,117	MC
Univ of N Car at Wilmington	NC	8,940	VC
Univ of Northern Iowa	IA	9,834	C
Univ of Pittsburgh at Pittsburgh	PA	16,074	HC
Univ of Rhode Island	RI	13,720	VC
Univ of Richmond	VA	30,100	MC
Univ of Sioux Falls	SD	16,390	C
Univ of S Car at Columbia	SC	10,048	VC
Univ of South Florida	FL	9,454	C
Univ of Southern Indiana	IN	9,025	LC
Univ of Southern Miss	MS	8,324	LC
Univ of Tenn at Knoxville	TN	8,214	C
Univ of Texas at Arlington	TX	7,192	LC
Univ of Texas at Austin	TX	10,630	HC
Univ of Texas at El Paso	TX	5,799	NC
Univ of Washington	WA	10,361	VC
Univ of Wisc/La Crosse	WI	8,991	VC
Univ of Wisc/Oshkosh	WI	6,130	LC
Univ of Wisc/Platteville	WI	8,450	C
Univ of Wisc/River Falls	WI	8,358	LC
Univ of Wisc/Superior	WI	7,051	C+
Univ of Wisc/Whitewater	WI	8,626	C
Valdosta State Univ	GA	7,798	C
Wabash College	IN	27,932	VC
Walla Walla College	WA	21,600	NC
Washburn Univ of Topeka	KS	8,984	NC
Wayne State College	NE	7,352	NC
West Chester Univ of Pennsylvania	PA	11,164	C
West Texas A&M Univ	TX	7,533	C
West Virginia Univ	WV	9,370	C
West Virginia Wesleyan College	WV	22,920	C
Western Carolina Univ	NC	6,742	C
Western Kentucky Univ	KY	6,834	C
Western Oregon Univ	OR	10,281	C
Whitworth College	WA	26,428	VC+
Willamette Univ	OR	32,032	VC+
Winona State Univ	MN		C
Winthrop Univ	SC	11,302	C
Yeshiva Univ	NY	21,400	C
York College of Pennsylvania	PA	14,500	VC
Youngstown State Univ	OH	11,148	NC

SPORTS MANAGEMENT

School	ST	$IS	SR
Adams State College	CO	7,468	C
Albertson College of Idaho	ID	19,415	VC
Alvernia College	PA	23,212	LC
Anderson Univ	IN	19,430	LC
Arkansas State Univ	AR	8,450	C
Averett Univ	VA	23,010	LC
Baldwin-Wallace College	OH	24,678	C
Ball State Univ	IN	8,660	C
Barry Univ	FL	24,100	LC
Barton College	NC	19,314	C
Becker College	MA	23,710	LC
Belmont Abbey College	NC	23,742	C
Bethel College	IN	19,670	C
Bluffton College	OH	23,694	C
Bowling Green State Univ	OH	13,036	C
Buena Vista Univ	IA	25,406	C
Campbell Univ	NC	18,268	VC
Catawba College	NC	20,500	C
Cedarville Univ	OH	19,954	VC
Colby-Sawyer College	NH	27,850	LC
College Misericordia	PA	26,350	C
College of St. Joseph	VT	19,100	C
Concordia Univ Nebr	NE	20,302	C+
Coppin State College	MD	10,191	LC
Dakota Wesleyan Univ	SD	17,832	C
Daniel Webster College	NH	24,870	C
De Sales Univ	PA	25,470	C
Defiance College	OH	22,615	C
Dowling College	NY	23,870	LC
Drury Univ	MO	18,085	VC+
Edinboro Univ of Pennsylvania	PA	10,850	LC
Elon Univ	NC	22,240	VC
Endicott College	MA	25,266	C+
Erskine College	SC	23,166	VC
Faulkner Univ	AL	14,500	C
Ferrum College	VA	21,240	LC
Flagler College	FL	11,860	VC+
Florida State Univ	FL	9,028	HC
Fontbonne Univ	MO	21,508	C
Franciscan Univ	IA	19,300	C
Franklin Pierce College	NH	28,980	LC
Fresno Pacific Univ	CA	22,462	C
Gardner-Webb Univ	NC	19,300	C
George Mason Univ	VA	9,732	VC
Georgia Southern Univ	GA	8,540	C
Guilford College	NC	24,960	VC
Gwynedd-Mercy College	PA	24,225	C
Hampton Univ	VA	17,112	C+
Harding Univ	AR	14,890	VC
Heidelberg College	OH	20,266	NC
High Point Univ	NC	22,480	C
Huron Univ	SD	10,450	C
Husson College	ME	16,300	LC
Indiana Inst of Technology	IN	21,620	C
Indiana State Univ	IN	10,719	LC
Indiana Univ Bloomington	IN	12,389	VC
Iowa Wesleyan College	IA	19,990	C
Ithaca College	NY	31,730	HC
Johnson and Wales Univ	RI	22,965	LC
Judson College	IL	22,050	LC
Kennesaw State Univ	GA	2,724	C
Lasell College	MA	26,000	C
Lewis Univ	IL	22,950	C+
Liberty Univ	VA	17,220	C
Limestone College	SC	17,700	C
Lindenwood Univ	MO	17,050	VC
Loras College	IA	24,233	C
Lubbock Christian Univ	TX	15,832	C
Lynchburg College	VA	26,815	C
Lyndon State College	VT	12,646	LC
Lynn Univ	FL	30,750	C
MacMurray College	IL	20,005	LC
Malone College	OH	20,995	C
Marian College	IN	23,030	C
Marian College of Fond du Lac	WI	19,625	C
Medaille College	NY	20,060	C
Menlo College	CA	24,000	LC
Methodist College	NC	19,526	C
Miami Univ	OH	15,033	HC
Miss Univ for Women	MS	5,446	LC
Missouri Baptist Univ	MO	18,010	C
Mitchell College	CT	26,396	C
Mount Union College	OH	21,120	C
Mount Vernon Nazarene Univ	OH	18,925	C
Mountain State Univ	WV	10,212	NC
Nebr Wesleyan Univ	NE	21,197	C+
Neumann College	PA	23,890	LC
New England College	NH	28,860	LC
New York Univ	NY	39,406	MC
Nichols College	MA	27,562	LC
N Dak State Univ	ND	8,435	C
Northwestern College	MN	22,820	C+
Northwood Univ	FL	21,040	C
Northwood Univ	MI	20,265	LC
Northwood Univ	TX	20,135	LC
Nova Southeastern Univ	FL	23,346	C
Ohio Northern Univ	OH	27,765	VC
Ohio Univ	OH	14,448	C
Old Dominion Univ	VA	10,441	C
Peru State College	NE	6,342	NC
Pfeiffer Univ	NC	18,980	C
Piedmont College	GA	16,900	C
Point Park Univ	PA	21,840	C
Principia College	IL	25,044	C+
Quincy Univ	IL	22,330	C
Robert Morris Univ	PA	20,438	C
St. Ambrose Univ	IA	22,800	C
St. John Fisher College	NY	24,870	C
St. John's Univ	NY	30,180	C
St. Leo Univ	FL	20,600	C
St. Thomas Univ	FL	21,400	LC
Salem International Univ	WV	19,770	C
Seton Hall Univ	NJ	30,130	VC
Shawnee State Univ	OH	11,031	NC
Shepherd College	WV	8,608	C
Simpson College	IA	23,658	C+
Southern Nazarene Univ	OK	14,634	NC
Southern New Hampshire Univ	NH	26,242	C
Southwest Baptist Univ	MO	15,371	C
Southwestern College	KS	19,560	C
Springfield College	MA	24,520	C
Stetson Univ	FL	29,495	VC
Taylor Univ	IN	23,820	VC+
Temple Univ	PA	15,912	C
Tenn Wesleyan College	TN	16,540	C
Thomas College	ME	19,960	LC
Towson Univ	MD	12,694	VC
Trinity International Univ	IL	22,980	C+
Tri-State Univ-Main Campus	IN	23,600	C
Tusculum College	TN	19,990	C
Union College	KY	15,920	C
Union Univ	TN	18,800	VC
Univ of Charleston	WV	23,620	C
Univ of Dayton	OH	24,850	VC
Univ of Houston	TX	9,818	C
Univ of Idaho	ID	8,216	C
Univ of Indianapolis	IN	22,560	VC
Univ of Kansas	KS	8,923	VC
Univ of Louisville	KY	8,762	VC
Univ of Mary Hardin-Baylor	TX	17,268	C
Univ of Mass Amherst	MA	13,980	C+
Univ of Miami	FL	34,608	HC
Univ of Mich/Ann Arbor	MI	13,864	HC+
Univ of Minn/Crookston	MN	9,626	NC
Univ of New England	ME	27,200	LC
Univ of New Haven	CT	28,650	C
Univ of Pittsburgh at Bradford	PA	15,294	C
Univ of St. Mary	KS	18,868	C
Univ of S Car at Columbia	SC	10,048	VC
Univ of Tenn at Knoxville	TN	8,214	C
Univ of the Incarnate Word	TX	21,772	LC
Univ of the Pacific	CA	31,090	VC
Univ of Tulsa	OK	22,090	VC+
Urbana Univ	OH	19,115	C
Valparaiso Univ	IN	26,118	VC+
Virginia Intermont College	VA	19,800	C
Warner Southern College	FL	16,738	LC
Washington State Univ	WA	11,334	C
Wayne State College	NE	7,352	NC
West Virginia Univ	WV	9,370	C
Western Carolina Univ	NC	6,742	C
Western New England College	MA	28,924	C
Wheeling Jesuit Univ	WV	22,660	C
Wichita State Univ	KS	8,092	C
William Penn Univ	IA	17,575	LC
Wilmington College	DE	5,594	NC
Wilmington College	OH	24,172	LC
Wingate Univ	NC	21,200	C
Winston-Salem State Univ	NC	8,926	LC
Winthrop Univ	SC	11,302	C
Xavier Univ	OH	26,850	VC+

ST = STATE **$IS** = IN-STATE COSTS **SR** = SELECTOR RATING

School	ST	$IS	SR
York College of Pennsylvania	PA	14,500	VC

SPORTS MEDICINE

School	ST	$IS	SR
Averett Univ	VA	23,010	LC
Avila Univ	MO	20,300	C
Baldwin-Wallace College	OH	24,678	C
Cabrini College	PA	29,020	C
Calif Lutheran Univ	CA	27,600	LC
Campbellsville Univ	KY	17,680	C
Capital Univ	OH	26,550	C
Castleton State College	VT	11,820	C
Central Mich Univ	MI	11,142	C
Concordia Univ Wisc	WI	16,600	C
De Sales Univ	PA	25,470	C
Eastern Mich Univ	MI	11,478	C
Eastern Nazarene College	MA	19,433	LC
Elon Univ	NC	22,240	VC
Florida State Univ	FL	9,028	HC
Georgia Southern Univ	GA	8,540	C
High Point Univ	NC	22,480	C
Hope International Univ	CA	16,940	NC
Ithaca College	NY	31,730	HC
John Brown Univ	AR	15,080	VC
Johnson State College	VT	11,819	LC
King's College	PA	26,990	C
Lander Univ	SC	10,496	C
Lees-McRae College	NC	17,106	LC
Lynchburg College	VA	26,815	C
Marietta College	OH	27,047	C
Mercyhurst College	PA	20,694	C
Merrimack College	MA	29,625	C
Missouri Baptist Univ	MO	18,010	C
Northwestern College	MN	22,820	C+
Norwich Univ	VT	21,064	LC
Ohio Univ	OH	14,448	C
Pepperdine Univ	CA	32,830	VC
Pfeiffer Univ	NC	18,980	C
Samford Univ	AL	18,648	VC
Southeast Missouri State Univ	MO	9,704	C
Towson Univ	MD	12,694	VC
Trinity International Univ	IL	22,980	C+
Tusculum College	TN	19,990	C
Union Univ	TN	18,800	VC
Univ of Charleston	WV	23,620	C
Univ of Detroit Mercy	MI	25,582	C
Univ of Evansville	IN	24,190	VC
Univ of Nevada/Las Vegas	NV	11,566	C
Univ of Pittsburgh at Bradford	PA	15,294	C
Univ of Southern Maine	ME	11,212	C
Univ of the Pacific	CA	31,090	VC
Urbana Univ	OH	19,115	C
Valdosta State Univ	GA	7,798	C
Wingate Univ	NC	21,200	C

STATISTICS

School	ST	$IS	SR
American Univ	DC	34,585	VC+
Appalachian State Univ	NC	7,637	VC
Bowling Green State Univ	OH	13,036	C
Brigham Young Univ	UT	8,504	HC
Brown Univ	RI	38,174	MC
Calif Polytechnic State Univ	CA	8,747	VC
Cal State, Hayward	CA	8,871	LC
Cal State, Long Beach	CA	8,762	C+
Carnegie Mellon Univ	PA	32,682	MC
Case Western Reserve Univ	OH	32,002	MC
Central Mich Univ	MI	11,142	C
CUNY/Baruch College	NY	3,275	VC+
CUNY/Hunter College	NY	6,729	C+
College of New Jersey	NJ	15,950	MC
Colo State Univ	CO	9,964	VC
Columbia Univ/Barnard College	NY	36,990	MC
Columbia Univ/Columbia College	NY	38,590	MC
Columbia Univ/School of General Studies	NY	35,000	C
Cornell Univ	NY	38,253	MC
Eastern Kentucky Univ	KY	7,708	C
Eastern Mich Univ	MI	11,478	C
Eastern New Mexico Univ	NM	6,762	LC
Florida International Univ	FL	9,912	VC
Florida State Univ	FL	9,028	HC
George Washington Univ	DC	41,030	MC
Harvard Univ/Harvard College	MA	37,928	MC
Indiana Univ Bloomington	IN	12,389	VC
Iowa State Univ	IA	10,768	VC
James Madison Univ	VA	10,794	VC
Kansas State Univ	KS	8,728	VC
Lehigh Univ	PA	37,570	HC+
Luther College	IA	25,700	VC
Marquette Univ	WI	27,594	VC
Miami Univ	OH	15,033	HC
Mich State Univ	MI	11,933	VC
Mount Holyoke College	MA	37,918	HC+
New York Univ	NY	39,406	MC
N Car State Univ	NC	9,886	VC
N Dak State Univ	ND	8,435	C
Northwest Missouri State Univ	MO	9,334	C
Northwestern Univ	IL	37,491	MC
Oakland Univ	MI	10,800	C
Ohio Northern Univ	OH	27,765	VC
Okla State Univ	OK	9,216	VC
Penn State Univ/Univ Park Campus	PA	15,646	HC
Purdue Univ/West Lafayette	IN	12,560	VC
Rice Univ	TX	27,550	MC
Rochester Inst of Technology	NY	29,217	VC+
Roosevelt Univ	IL	22,580	VC
Rutgers, The State Univ of New Jersey/New Brunswick/Piscataway Campus	NJ	15,800	HC
St. Cloud State Univ	MN	8,362	C
San Diego State Univ	CA	10,321	C
San Francisco State Univ	CA	12,070	C
San Jose State Univ	CA	8,187	C
Southern Methodist Univ	TX	34,210	HC
SUNY/College at Oneonta	NY	11,870	VC
SUNY/Univ at Buffalo	NY	12,563	VC
Syracuse Univ	NY	34,720	HC
Temple Univ	PA	15,912	C
Univ of Akron	OH	13,134	NC
Univ of Alaska Fairbanks	AK	9,295	C
Univ of Calif at Berkeley	CA	15,563	MC
Univ of Calif at Davis	CA	14,995	VC
Univ of Calif at Riverside	CA	15,300	C
Univ of Calif at Santa Barbara	CA	11,732	VC
Univ of Central Florida	FL	10,038	VC
Univ of Chicago	IL	35,087	MC
Univ of Conn	CT	14,608	VC
Univ of Denver	CO	32,148	VC
Univ of Florida	FL	8,580	MC
Univ of Georgia	GA	8,656	VC
Univ of Houston	TX	9,818	C
Univ of Illinois at Chicago	IL	13,418	C
Univ of Illinois at Urbana-Champaign	IL	11,316	HC+
Univ of Iowa	IA	10,923	VC
Univ of Louisiana at Lafayette	LA	5,826	C
Univ of Maryland/Baltimore County	MD	14,668	VC+
Univ of Mich/Ann Arbor	MI	13,864	HC+
Univ of Minn/Morris	MN	12,896	VC
Univ of Minn/Twin Cities	MN	13,160	VC
Univ of Missouri/Columbia	MO	13,782	VC
Univ of Missouri/Rolla	MO	12,292	HC
Univ of Nebr at Kearney	NE	8,286	NC
Univ of N Car at Wilmington	NC	8,940	VC
Univ of North Florida	FL	8,769	VC
Univ of Northern Colo	CO	8,987	C
Univ of Pennsylvania	PA	37,960	MC
Univ of Pittsburgh at Pittsburgh	PA	16,074	HC
Univ of Rhode Island	RI	13,720	VC
Univ of Rochester	NY	32,979	HC
Univ of S Car at Columbia	SC	10,048	VC
Univ of Southern Miss	MS	8,324	LC
Univ of Tenn at Knoxville	TN	8,214	C
Univ of Texas at Dallas	TX	10,234	HC
Univ of Texas at El Paso	TX	5,799	NC
Univ of Vermont	VT	16,316	VC
Univ of Washington	WA	10,361	VC
Univ of West Florida	FL	8,470	C
Univ of Wisc/Eau Claire	WI	8,463	VC
Univ of Wisc/Madison	WI	8,262	VC
Univ of Wyoming	WY	8,636	C
Utah State Univ	UT	7,371	C
Virginia Polytechnic Inst and State Univ	VA	9,179	C
Washington Univ in St. Louis	MO	38,293	MC
Western Mich Univ	MI	12,031	C
Winona State Univ	MN		C
Xavier Univ of Louisiana	LA	17,600	C

STRINGS

School	ST	$IS	SR
Central Washington Univ	WA	9,768	C
Florida State Univ	FL	9,028	HC
Juilliard School	NY	30,385	SP
Manhattan School of Music	NY	31,500	SP
Northwestern Univ	IL	37,491	MC
Roosevelt Univ	IL	22,580	VC
Temple Univ	PA	15,912	C
Univ of Mich/Ann Arbor	MI	13,864	HC+

STUDIO ART

School	ST	$IS	SR
Allegheny College	PA	30,280	VC
American Univ	DC	34,585	VC+
Anna Maria College	MA	26,140	LC
Appalachian State Univ	NC	7,637	VC
Augsburg College	MN	25,298	C
Augusta State Univ	GA	2,592	C
Augustana College	IL	26,610	VC+
Baker Univ	KS	19,860	VC
Baldwin-Wallace College	OH	24,678	C
Barton College	NC	19,314	C
Baylor Univ	TX	23,864	VC
Beloit College	WI	29,864	HC
Benedictine Univ	IL	23,840	C
Berry College	GA	21,410	VC
Birmingham-Southern College	AL	25,364	VC+
Bloomsburg Univ of Pennsylvania	PA	10,844	C
Boston College	MA	33,284	MC
Bowdoin College	ME	37,790	MC
Bradley Univ	IL	22,910	VC
Brenau Univ Women's College	GA	21,800	C
Caldwell College	NJ	24,060	LC
Cal State, Fullerton	CA	6,648	C
Carleton College	MN	34,395	MC
Carthage College	WI	25,000	C
Cazenovia College	NY	23,940	C
Central Missouri State Univ	MO	9,776	C
Central Washington Univ	WA	9,768	C
Chapman Univ	CA	33,118	VC
CUNY/Queens College	NY	4,362	C
CUNY/York College	NY	3,292	NC
Clark Univ	MA	32,115	VC
Clarke College	IA	23,165	C
Cleveland Inst of Art	OH	30,371	SP
Coastal Carolina Univ	SC	11,040	C
Colgate Univ	NY	37,095	MC
College of Charleston	SC	11,887	HC
College of Notre Dame of Maryland	MD	27,700	C
College of St. Rose	NY	22,864	C
College of Santa Fe	NM	25,293	C+
College of the Holy Cross	MA	36,451	MC
College of the Ozarks	MO	3,500	VC+
Colo College	CO	36,860	HC
Columbia College	SC	22,658	LC
Concordia College: Moorhead	MN	22,460	VC+
Concordia Univ Nebr	NE	20,302	C+
Concordia Univ/St.Paul	MN	24,486	C
Denison Univ	OH	33,050	HC
DePauw Univ	IN	31,500	HC
Drake Univ	IA	25,120	VC+
Duquesne Univ	PA	26,907	VC
East Carolina Univ	NC	8,671	C
Eastern Univ	PA	24,020	C
Eastern Washington Univ	WA	9,012	C
Emmanuel College	MA	27,600	C+
Florida State Univ	FL	9,028	HC
Framingham State College	MA	9,381	C
Franklin and Marshall College	PA	35,930	HC+
Gallaudet Univ	DC	16,554	SP
George Mason Univ	VA	9,732	VC
Georgia State Univ	GA	10,658	C
Gettysburg College	PA	35,646	HC
Goucher College	MD	32,650	HC
Graceland Univ	IA	19,550	C
Grand Canyon Univ	AZ	30,000	LC
Hamilton College	NY	37,560	MC
Henderson State Univ	AR	7,386	C
Hobart and William Smith Colleges	NY	36,536	HC
Hollins Univ	VA	27,965	VC
Indiana State Univ	IN	10,719	LC
Indiana Univ Bloomington	IN	12,389	VC
Indiana Univ of Pennsylvania	PA	10,489	C
Indiana Wesleyan Univ	IN	19,900	C+
Ithaca College	NY	31,730	HC
Jacksonville Univ	FL	24,040	C
Johnson State College	VT	11,819	LC
Juniata College	PA	29,080	VC
Kansas Wesleyan Univ	KS	18,900	VC
Kean Univ	NJ	14,479	C
Kentucky State Univ	KY	9,062	NC
Kenyon College	OH	35,370	HC+
Knox College	IL	30,294	VC+
Lawrence Univ	WI	30,900	HC
Lewis and Clark College	OR	30,620	VC
Lewis Univ	IL	22,950	C+
Limestone College	SC	17,700	C
Lincoln Univ	PA	13,320	C+
Lindenwood Univ	MO	17,050	VC
Loras College	IA	24,233	C
Louisiana College	LA	13,450	C
Loyola Marymount Univ	CA	32,194	VC
Loyola Univ New Orleans	LA	31,036	VC+
Lycoming College	PA	27,589	C+
Mansfield Univ	PA	11,220	C
Marian College	IN	23,030	C
Marietta College	OH	27,047	C
Mary Washington College	VA	10,166	HC
Maryville Univ of St. Louis	MO	22,090	VC
Marywood Univ	PA	26,050	C
Mass College of Art	MA	15,568	SP
Mercyhurst College	PA	20,694	C
Messiah College	PA	25,890	VC+
Mich State Univ	MI	11,933	VC
Middle Tenn State Univ	TN	8,534	C
Middlebury College	VT	38,100	MC
Mills College	CA	33,371	VC
Minneapolis College of Art and Design	MN	28,950	SP
Montclair State Univ	NJ	13,790	C
Moravian College	PA	28,903	VC
Mount Holyoke College	MA	37,918	HC+
Nebr Wesleyan Univ	NE	21,197	C+
New York Univ	NY	39,406	MC
Northern Illinois Univ	IL	11,472	C
Northwestern College	MN	22,820	C+
Notre Dame College	OH	20,425	C
Oakland Univ	MI	10,800	C
Old Dominion Univ	VA	10,441	C
Oral Roberts Univ	OK	18,490	C
Parsons School of Design	NY	32,242	SP
Pomona College	CA	33,960	MC
Principia College	IL	25,044	C+
Providence College	RI	30,604	HC
Randolph-Macon College	VA	27,190	C
Rivier College	NH	26,217	C
Rochester Inst of Technology	NY	29,217	VC+
Rollins College	FL	34,300	VC
St. Louis Univ	MO	29,780	VC+
St. Mary's Univ of Minn	MN	21,535	C
St. Olaf College	MN	28,500	HC
St. Vincent College	PA	25,530	VC
Salem College	NC	24,595	VC
Salve Regina Univ	RI	29,210	C
Santa Clara Univ	CA	34,701	HC
Scripps College	CA	35,700	HC+
Seton Hill Univ	PA	24,930	C
Silver Lake College of the Holy Family	WI	18,450	LC
Simon's Rock College of Bard	MA	36,580	HC
Smith College	MA	37,034	HC+
Southern Conn State Univ	CT	10,310	C
Southern Methodist Univ	TX	34,210	HC
Spring Hill College	AL	25,868	VC
SUNY at Potsdam	NY	12,160	C
SUNY/College at Brockport	NY	12,111	C
SUNY/College at Geneseo	NY	11,330	HC
SUNY/Univ at Binghamton	NY	12,787	HC
SUNY/Univ at Buffalo	NY	12,563	VC
SUNY/Univ at Stony Brook	NY	12,763	HC
Sweet Briar College	VA	27,940	C
Texas Christian Univ	TX	23,410	VC
Texas State Univ	TX	9,320	VC
Texas Tech Univ	TX	10,768	VC
Transylvania Univ	KY	23,780	VC+
Trinity Christian College	IL	21,640	VC
Trinity College	CT	38,040	HC+
Tulane Univ	LA	37,451	HC+
Union College	NE	17,130	C
Union College	NY	36,005	HC
Univ of Arizona	AZ	10,413	VC
Univ of Calif at Davis	CA	14,995	VC
Univ of Calif at Irvine	CA	19,808	HC
Univ of Calif at San Diego	CA	14,127	HC
Univ of Evansville	IN	24,190	VC
Univ of Findlay	OH	23,962	NC
Univ of Georgia	GA	8,656	VC
Univ of Houston	TX	9,818	C
Univ of Idaho	ID	8,216	C
Univ of Illinois at Chicago	IL	13,418	C
Univ of Indianapolis	IN	22,560	VC
Univ of Maine	ME	12,080	C+
Univ of Maryland/College Park	MD	14,227	HC
Univ of Mass Amherst	MA	13,980	C+
Univ of Miami	FL	34,608	HC
Univ of Minn/Morris	MN	12,896	VC
Univ of Minn/Twin Cities	MN	13,160	VC
Univ of Missouri/Kansas City	MO	13,416	VC
Univ of Montevallo	AL	8,478	C
Univ of New Hampshire	NH	14,828	VC
Univ of New Mexico	NM	9,223	C
Univ of N Car at Chapel Hill	NC	10,117	MC
Univ of N Car at Greensboro	NC	8,248	C
Univ of N Car at Wilmington	NC	8,940	VC
Univ of Northern Iowa	IA	9,834	C
Univ of Notre Dame	IN	34,442	MC
Univ of Pittsburgh at Pittsburgh	PA	16,074	HC
Univ of Richmond	VA	30,100	MC
Univ of Rochester	NY	32,979	HC
Univ of St. Thomas	TX	21,952	VC
Univ of S Car at Columbia	SC	10,048	VC
Univ of Southern Calif	CA	37,459	MC
Univ of Tenn at Knoxville	TN	8,214	C
Univ of Texas at Arlington	TX	7,192	LC
Univ of Texas at Austin	TX	10,630	HC
Univ of the Pacific	CA	31,090	VC
Univ of Washington	WA	10,361	VC
Univ of West Florida	FL	8,470	C
Univ of Wisc/Superior	WI	7,051	C+
Viterbo Univ	WI	20,430	C
Washington and Lee Univ	VA	29,663	MC
Washington Univ in St. Louis	MO	38,293	MC
Wellesley College	MA	36,516	MC
Wesleyan College	GA	17,870	VC
Wesleyan Univ	CT	35,139	MC
West Chester Univ of Pennsylvania	PA	11,164	C
West Texas A&M Univ	TX	7,533	C
Western Carolina Univ	NC	6,742	C
Western Conn State Univ	CT	11,625	C
Western Kentucky Univ	KY	6,834	C
Wheaton College	MA	36,330	HC

ST = STATE $IS = IN-STATE COSTS SR = SELECTOR RATING

School	ST	$IS	SR
Wichita State Univ	KS	8,092	C
Willamette Univ	OR	32,032	VC+
William Paterson Univ of New Jersey	NJ	14,450	C
William Woods Univ	MO	20,120	C
Youngstown State Univ	OH	11,148	NC

SURVEY AND MAPPING TECHNOLOGY

School	ST	$IS	SR
East Tenn State Univ	TN	8,497	C
Metropolitan State College of Denver	CO	2,338	LC
Pennsylvania College of Technology	PA	15,126	NC
Southern Polytechnic State Univ	GA	7,620	VC
SUNY/College of Environmental Science and Forestry	NY	14,167	VC
SUNY/College of Technology at Alfred	NY	12,416	C
Thomas Edison State College	NJ	3,325	SP
Univ of Akron	OH	13,134	NC
Univ of Alaska Anchorage	AK	9,100	NC

SURVEYING ENGINEERING

School	ST	$IS	SR
Cal State, Fresno	CA	8,414	LC
Ferris State Univ	MI	12,512	C
Metropolitan State College of Denver	CO	2,338	LC
Mich Tech Univ	MI	13,235	VC
New Mexico State Univ	NM	7,932	C
Oregon Inst of Technology	OR	8,718	C
Pennsylvania College of Technology	PA	15,126	NC
Purdue Univ/West Lafayette	IN	12,560	VC
Universidad Metropolitana	PR	3,324	
Universidad Politecnica de PR	PR	5,370	
Univ of Arkansas at Little Rock	AR	5,637	NC
Univ of Maine	ME	12,080	C+
Univ of PR/Mayaguez	PR		

SYSTEMS ANALYSIS

School	ST	$IS	SR
George Washington Univ	DC	41,030	MC
Johnson and Wales Univ	RI	22,965	LC
Rochester Inst of Technology	NY	29,217	VC+
Univ of Miami	FL	34,608	HC

SYSTEMS ENGINEERING

School	ST	$IS	SR
Case Western Reserve Univ	OH	32,002	MC
George Mason Univ	VA	9,732	VC
Huron Univ	SD	10,450	C
Oakland Univ	MI	10,800	C
Point Park Univ	PA	21,840	C
Purdue Univ/West Lafayette	IN	12,560	VC
SUNY/Univ at Binghamton	NY	12,787	HC
Stevens Inst of Technology	NJ	35,300	HC+
Texas A&M Univ at Galveston	TX	9,948	C+
United States Military Academy	NY		MC
United States Naval Academy	MD		MC
Univ of Arizona	AZ	10,413	VC
Univ of Missouri/Rolla	MO	12,292	HC
Univ of Pennsylvania	PA	37,960	MC
Univ of Virginia	VA	11,740	MC
Washington Univ in St. Louis	MO	38,293	MC
West Virginia Univ	WV	9,370	C
Wright State Univ	OH	11,490	LC
Youngstown State Univ	OH	11,148	NC

SYSTEMS SCIENCE

School	ST	$IS	SR
Johnson and Wales Univ	RI	22,965	LC
Stanford Univ	CA	37,612	MC
State Univ of West Georgia	GA	7,622	C
Washington Univ in St. Louis	MO	38,293	MC

TEACHING ENGLISH AS A SECOND/FOREIGN LANGUAGE (TESOL/TEFOL)

School	ST	$IS	SR
Abilene Christian Univ	TX	18,370	VC
Andrews Univ	MI	19,550	C
Brigham Young Univ	UT	8,504	HC
Brigham Young Univ/Hawaii	HI	7,240	VC+
Caribbean Univ	PR	3,000	
Carroll College	MT	20,576	VC
College of Our Lady of the Elms	MA	20,644	C
Earlham College	IN	29,976	VC+
Eastern Mich Univ	MI	11,478	C
Hawaii Pacific Univ	HI	19,218	C
Houston Baptist Univ	TX	16,905	C
Howard Payne Univ	TX	15,176	C
Inter American Univ of PR/Arecibo.Campus	PR	3,300	
Inter American Univ of PR/San German	PR	6,716	
LIU/Brooklyn Campus	NY	24,790	C
Mercy College	NY	19,200	NC
Northern Arizona Univ	AZ	9,002	C
Northwestern College	MN	22,820	C+
Nyack College	NY	18,540	C
Ohio Dominican Univ	OH	22,700	C
Okla Christian Univ	OK	17,690	NC
Pontifical Catholic Univ of PR/Ponce	PR	7,298	
San Jose State Univ	CA	8,187	C
Temple Univ	PA	15,912	C
Texas Wesleyan Univ	TX	16,245	C
Union Univ	TN	18,800	VC
Univ of Louisville	KY	8,762	VC
Univ of Minn/Twin Cities	MN	13,160	VC
Univ of Nebr at Kearney	NE	8,286	NC
Univ of New Mexico	NM	9,223	C
Univ of Northern Iowa	IA	9,834	C
Univ of PR/Mayaguez	PR		

TECHNICAL AND BUSINESS WRITING

School	ST	$IS	SR
Bowling Green State Univ	OH	13,036	C
Carlow College	PA	21,334	C
Cedarville Univ	OH	19,954	VC
Clarkson Univ	NY	32,226	VC
College of Santa Fe	NM	25,293	C+
Colo State Univ	CO	9,964	VC
Doane College	NE	20,000	C
Dominican Univ	IL	23,610	C
Illinois Inst of Technology	IL	26,456	HC+
Lawrence Tech Univ	MI	20,487	C
Madonna Univ	MI	11,504	VC
Marylhurst Univ	OR	18,465	NC
Metropolitan State Univ	MN	3,852	SP
Mich Tech Univ	MI	13,235	VC
Milwaukee School of Engineering	WI	28,479	VC+
Mount Mary College	WI	20,370	C
New Jersey Inst of Technology	NJ	16,396	VC
New Mexico Inst of Mining and Technology	NM	7,580	NC
New York Inst of Technology	NY	24,205	VC
Ohio Dominican Univ	OH	22,700	C
Pennsylvania College of Technology	PA	15,126	NC
Polytechnic Univ/Brooklyn	NY	33,770	VC
Southern Polytechnic State Univ	GA	7,620	VC
Southwest Missouri State Univ	MO	8,918	C
Tenn Tech Univ	TN	8,670	VC
Univ of Arkansas at Little Rock	AR	5,637	NC
Univ of Findlay	OH	23,962	NC
Univ of Hartford	CT	31,080	C
Univ of Houston-Downtown	TX	2,594	NC
Univ of Mass Dartmouth	MA	12,835	C
Univ of Missouri/Rolla	MO	12,292	HC
Univ of Montana--Western	MT	8,073	NC
Univ of New Mexico	NM	9,223	C
Univ of Washington	WA	10,361	VC
Waynesburg College	PA	19,370	C
Wheeling Jesuit Univ	WV	22,660	C
Youngstown State Univ	OH	11,148	NC

TECHNICAL EDUCATION

School	ST	$IS	SR
Andrews Univ	MI	19,550	C
Ball State Univ	IN	8,660	C
Bowling Green State Univ	OH	13,036	C
Brigham Young Univ	UT	8,504	HC
Central Conn State Univ	CT	12,090	C
CUNY/New York City College of Technology	NY	4,269	NC
College of New Jersey	NJ	15,950	MC
College of St. Rose	NY	22,864	C
College of the Ozarks	MO	3,500	VC+
Eastern Kentucky Univ	KY	7,708	C
Elizabeth City State Univ	NC	5,550	LC
Ferris State Univ	MI	12,512	C
Fort Hays State Univ	KS	7,363	C
Georgia Southern Univ	GA	8,540	C
Kean Univ	NJ	14,479	C
Kent State Univ	OH	12,932	C
Millersville Univ of Pennsylvania	PA	11,269	C
Miss State Univ	MS	9,139	C
Montana State Univ-Bozeman	MT	9,515	C
New Mexico Highlands Univ	NM	6,182	LC
New York Inst of Technology	NY	24,205	VC
Norfolk State Univ	VA	9,722	LC
N Car State Univ	NC	9,886	VC
Ohio State Univ	OH	13,080	VC+
Okla State Univ	OK	9,216	VC
Southwestern Okla State Univ	OK	4,801	C
Tuskegee Univ	AL	17,250	LC
Univ of Akron	OH	13,134	NC
Univ of Northern Iowa	IA	9,834	C
Univ of Southern Maine	ME	11,212	C
Univ of Wisc/Platteville	WI	8,450	C
Univ of Wisc/Stout	WI	9,718	C
Valley City State Univ	ND	7,281	LC
Virginia Polytechnic Inst and State Univ	VA	9,179	C
Wayne State Univ	MI	11,774	C
Western Illinois Univ	IL	10,363	C

TECHNOLOGICAL MANAGEMENT

School	ST	$IS	SR
Arkansas State Univ	AR	8,450	C
Champlain College	VT	22,030	C
Clayton College and State Univ	GA	2,441	LC
Colo Technical Univ	CO	9,500	LC
DeVry Univ/Addison (DuPage County)	IL	10,790	LC
DeVry Univ/Alpharetta	GA	10,670	LC
DeVry Univ/Chicago	IL	10,790	LC
DeVry Univ/Colo Springs	CO	11,310	LC
DeVry Univ/Columbus	OH	10,670	LC
DeVry Univ/Crystal City	VA	11,860	C
DeVry Univ/Dallas	TX	10,640	LC
DeVry Univ/Decatur	GA	10,670	LC
DeVry Univ/Fort Washington	PA	11,860	LC
DeVry Univ/Fremont	CA	11,860	LC
DeVry Univ/Kansas City	MO	10,670	LC
DeVry Univ/Long Beach	CA	11,310	LC
DeVry Univ/Miramar	FL	11,310	LC
DeVry Univ/Orlando	FL	11,310	LC
DeVry Univ/Phoenix	AZ	10,670	LC
DeVry Univ/Pomona	CA	11,310	LC
DeVry Univ/Seattle	WA	11,860	LC
DeVry Univ/Tinley Park	IL	10,790	LC
DeVry Univ/West Hills	CA	11,310	LC
DeVry Univ/Westminster	CO	11,310	LC
Excelsior College	NY	975	SP
Franklin Univ	OH	6,720	SP
Golden Gate Univ	CA	11,232	NC
Johnson and Wales Univ	RI	22,965	LC
Lawrence Tech Univ	MI	20,487	C
Murray State Univ	KY	7,816	VC
New Jersey Inst of Technology	NJ	16,396	VC
New York Inst of Technology	NY	24,205	VC
Northern Illinois Univ	IL	11,472	C
Ohio Northern Univ	OH	27,765	VC
Pennsylvania College of Technology	PA	15,126	NC
Southern Illinois Univ Carbondale	IL	10,407	C
Southern New Hampshire Univ	NH	26,242	C
Southern Univ at New Orleans	LA	995	NC
SUNY at Oswego	NY	12,650	C
State Univ of West Georgia	GA	7,622	C
Univ of Alaska Anchorage	AK	9,100	NC
Univ of Alaska Fairbanks	AK	9,295	C
Univ of Findlay	OH	23,962	NC
Univ of Minn/Crookston	MN	9,626	NC
Vermont Technical College	VT	13,684	C
Washburn Univ of Topeka	KS	8,984	NC
Wayne State College	NE	7,352	NC
Wentworth Inst of Technology	MA	23,000	C

TECHNOLOGY AND PUBLIC AFFAIRS

School	ST	$IS	SR
Cameron Univ	OK	5,692	NC
Georgia Inst of Technology	GA	10,340	HC+
Kent State Univ	OH	12,932	C
New Jersey Inst of Technology	NJ	16,396	VC
Pomona College	CA	33,960	MC
Univ of Georgia	GA	8,656	VC
Vassar College	NY	37,030	MC
Washington Univ in St. Louis	MO	38,293	MC
Wheeling Jesuit Univ	WV	22,660	C

TELECOMMUNICATIONS

School	ST	$IS	SR
Alabama A&M Univ	AL	5,100	LC
Ball State Univ	IN	8,660	C
Baylor Univ	TX	23,864	VC
Bowling Green State Univ	OH	13,036	C
Butler Univ	IN	28,250	VC+
Cal State, Monterey Bay	CA	6,683	LC
Capitol College	MD	21,250	C
Champlain College	VT	22,030	C
CUNY/New York City College of Technology	NY	4,269	NC
Colo Technical Univ	CO	9,500	LC
Concordia Univ Wisc	WI	16,600	C
DeVry College of Technology/North Brunswick	NJ	10,100	LC
DeVry/New York	NY	11,860	LC
DeVry Univ/Addison (DuPage County)	IL	10,790	LC
DeVry Univ/Alpharetta	GA	10,670	LC
DeVry Univ/Chicago	IL	10,790	LC
DeVry Univ/Colo Springs	CO	11,310	LC
DeVry Univ/Columbus	OH	10,670	LC
DeVry Univ/Crystal City	VA	11,860	C
DeVry Univ/Dallas	TX	10,640	LC
DeVry Univ/Decatur	GA	10,670	LC
DeVry Univ/Fort Washington	PA	11,860	LC
DeVry Univ/Fremont	CA	11,860	LC
DeVry Univ/Kansas City	MO	10,670	LC
DeVry Univ/Long Beach	CA	11,310	LC
DeVry Univ/Miramar	FL	11,310	LC
DeVry Univ/Orlando	FL	11,310	LC
DeVry Univ/Phoenix	AZ	10,670	LC
DeVry Univ/Pomona	CA	11,310	LC
DeVry Univ/Seattle	WA	11,860	LC
DeVry Univ/Tinley Park	IL	10,790	LC
DeVry Univ/West Hills	CA	11,310	LC
Eastern Mich Univ	MI	11,478	C
Fort Hays State Univ	KS	7,363	C
George Fox Univ	OR	26,110	VC
Illinois State Univ	IL	10,944	C+
Indiana Univ Bloomington	IN	12,389	VC
Indiana Univ-Purdue Univ Fort Wayne	IN	5,108	LC
Ithaca College	NY	31,730	HC
Kean Univ	NJ	14,479	C
Kent State Univ	OH	12,932	C
Kutztown Univ of Pennsylvania	PA	10,786	C
Marywood Univ	PA	26,050	C
Miami Univ	OH	15,033	HC
Mich State Univ	MI	11,933	VC
Morgan State Univ	MD	11,470	C
Murray State Univ	KY	7,816	VC
New York Inst of Technology	NY	24,205	VC
Northern Arizona Univ	AZ	9,002	C
Ohio Univ	OH	14,448	C
Okla Baptist Univ	OK	15,220	VC
Pepperdine Univ	CA	32,830	VC
Purdue Univ/West Lafayette	IN	12,560	VC
Rochester Inst of Technology	NY	29,217	VC+
Roosevelt Univ	IL	22,580	VC
Syracuse Univ	NY	34,720	HC
Temple Univ	PA	15,912	C
Texas Tech Univ	TX	10,768	VC
Univ of Alabama	AL	9,040	C+
Univ of Colo at Boulder	CO	10,774	VC
Univ of Florida	FL	8,580	MC
Univ of Georgia	GA	8,656	VC
Univ of Idaho	ID	8,216	C
Univ of Kentucky	KY	7,765	C
Univ of Louisiana at Lafayette	LA	5,826	C
Univ of Miami	FL	34,608	HC
Univ of Nebr at Kearney	NE	8,286	NC
Univ of Northern Colo	CO	8,987	C
Univ of PR/Arecibo	PR	1,095	
Univ of Texas at Dallas	TX	10,234	HC
Univ of the Sacred Heart	PR	5,590	
Univ of Wisc/Stout	WI	9,718	C
Valdosta State Univ	GA	7,798	C
Western Mich Univ	MI	12,031	C
Youngstown State Univ	OH	11,148	NC

TEXTILE ENGINEERING

School	ST	$IS	SR
Auburn Univ	AL	10,396	VC
Georgia Inst of Technology	GA	10,340	HC+
N Car State Univ	NC	9,886	VC
Philadelphia Univ	PA	27,354	C
Texas Tech Univ	TX	10,768	VC

TEXTILE TECHNOLOGY

School	ST	$IS	SR
Auburn Univ	AL	10,396	VC
Clemson Univ	SC	11,972	HC
Fashion Inst of Technology/SUNY	NY	11,169	C+
Mich State Univ	MI	11,933	VC
Philadelphia Univ	PA	27,354	C
Univ of Mass Dartmouth	MA	12,835	C
Univ of Wisc/Madison	WI	8,262	VC

TEXTILES AND CLOTHING

School	ST	$IS	SR
Albright College	PA	30,579	C
Auburn Univ	AL	10,396	VC
Calif College of the Arts	CA	31,530	SP
Central Missouri State Univ	MO	9,776	C
College for Creative Studies	MI	23,298	SP
Cornell Univ	NY	38,253	MC
Fashion Inst of Technology/SUNY	NY	11,169	C+

School	ST	$IS	SR
Framingham State College	MA	9,381	C
Georgia Inst of Technology	GA	10,340	HC+
Indiana State Univ	IN	10,719	LC
Indiana Univ Bloomington	IN	12,389	VC
Iowa State Univ	IA	10,768	VC
Kansas State Univ	KS	8,728	VC
Louisiana State Univ and A&M College	LA	9,126	VC
Middle Tenn State Univ	TN	8,534	C
Moore College of Art and Design	PA	27,096	SP
N Car State Univ	NC	9,886	VC
N Dak State Univ	ND	8,435	C
Northern Illinois Univ	IL	11,472	C
Northwest Missouri State Univ	MO	9,334	C
Oregon State Univ	OR	11,055	C
Rhode Island School of Design	RI	33,569	SP
Syracuse Univ	NY	34,720	HC
Univ of Calif at Davis	CA	14,995	VC
Univ of Delaware	DE	12,616	HC
Univ of Idaho	ID	8,216	C
Univ of Kentucky	KY	7,765	C
Univ of Minn/Twin Cities	MN	13,160	VC
Univ of Missouri/Columbia	MO	13,782	VC
Univ of Nebr at Lincoln	NE	9,975	C+
Univ of N Car at Greensboro	NC	8,248	C
Univ of Rhode Island	RI	13,720	VC
Univ of Tenn at Knoxville	TN	8,214	C
Univ of Texas at Austin	TX	10,630	HC
Univ of Wisc/Madison	WI	8,262	VC
Virginia Polytechnic Inst and State Univ	VA	9,179	C
Western Kentucky Univ	KY	6,834	C
Western Mich Univ	MI	12,031	C

THEATER DESIGN

School	ST	$IS	SR
Adelphi Univ	NY	26,300	VC
Arcadia Univ	PA	29,890	C
Baylor Univ	TX	23,864	VC
Boston Univ	MA	38,194	HC+
Central Missouri State Univ	MO	9,776	C
College of Santa Fe	NM	25,293	C+
College of the Ozarks	MO	3,500	VC
Cornish College of the Arts	WA	19,900	SP
DePaul Univ	IL	27,580	VC
Dickinson College	PA	35,825	HC
Emerson College	MA	32,205	HC
Florida State Univ	FL	9,028	HC
Franklin Pierce College	NH	28,980	LC
Hofstra Univ	NY	27,112	VC
Ithaca College	NY	31,730	HC
Johnson State College	VT	11,819	LC
Montclair State Univ	NJ	13,790	C
N Car School of the Arts	NC	8,565	SP
Pace Univ	NY	28,652	VC
Purdue Univ/West Lafayette	IN	12,560	VC
Roosevelt Univ	IL	22,580	VC
Seton Hill Univ	PA	24,930	C
Shenandoah Univ	VA	25,190	NC
SUNY/College at Purchase	NY	10,587	VC
Syracuse Univ	NY	34,720	HC
Texas Tech Univ	TX	10,768	VC
Towson Univ	MD	12,694	VC
Univ of Arizona	AZ	10,413	VC
Univ of Cincinnati	OH	14,736	C
Univ of Conn	CT	14,608	VC
Univ of Evansville	IN	24,190	VC
Univ of Florida	FL	8,580	MC
Univ of Kansas	KS	8,923	VC
Univ of Maryland/Baltimore County	MD	14,668	VC+
Univ of Miami	FL	34,608	HC
Univ of Northern Iowa	IA	9,834	C
Univ of Southern Calif	CA	37,459	MC
Vanderbilt Univ	TN	37,897	MC
Washburn Univ of Topeka	KS	8,984	NC
Webster Univ	MO	21,848	VC
Western Mich Univ	MI	12,031	C
Wright State Univ	OH	11,490	LC

THEATER MANAGEMENT

School	ST	$IS	SR
Barry Univ	FL	24,100	LC
Benedictine College	KS	20,603	C
Boston Univ	MA	38,194	HC+
Catawba College	NC	20,500	C
CUNY/Brooklyn College	NY	4,353	C+
College of Santa Fe	NM	25,293	C+
Emerson College	MA	32,205	HC
Hardin-Simmons Univ	TX	14,165	C
Hofstra Univ	NY	27,112	VC
Ithaca College	NY	31,730	HC
Johnson State College	VT	11,819	LC
Luther College	IA	25,700	VC
Roosevelt Univ	IL	22,580	VC
Salisbury Univ	MD	12,664	VC
Seton Hill Univ	PA	24,930	C
Syracuse Univ	NY	34,720	HC
Texas Tech Univ	TX	10,768	VC
Trinity College	CT	38,040	HC+
Univ of Delaware	DE	12,616	HC
Univ of Evansville	IN	24,190	VC
Univ of Hartford	CT	31,080	C
Univ of Miami	FL	34,608	HC
Univ of Portland	OR	28,500	VC
Univ of Southern Calif	CA	37,459	MC
Univ of Texas at El Paso	TX	5,799	NC
Viterbo Univ	WI	20,430	C
Yale Univ	CT	37,000	MC

THEOLOGICAL STUDIES

School	ST	$IS	SR
Alvernia College	PA	23,212	LC
Andrews Univ	MI	19,550	C
Aquinas College	MI	21,894	C
Assumption College	MA	29,375	C
Atlantic Union College	MA	18,868	C
Averett Univ	VA	23,010	LC
Avila Univ	MO	20,300	C
Barry Univ	FL	24,100	LC
Bellarmine Univ	KY	24,110	VC
Belmont Abbey College	NC	23,742	C
Boston College	MA	33,284	MC
Brewton-Parker College	GA	14,200	LC
Briar Cliff Univ	IA	21,660	C
Caldwell College	NJ	24,060	LC
Calumet College of St. Joseph	IN	9,000	LC
Carlow College	PA	21,334	C
Christendom College	VA	18,410	VC+
College of Mount St. Joseph	OH	22,785	C
College of St. Benedict	MN	26,672	VC
College of St. Catherine	MN	24,010	VC
College of St. Elizabeth	NJ	25,460	C
Colo Christian Univ	CO	21,182	VC
Concordia Univ	OR	22,450	C
Concordia Univ Nebr	NE	20,302	C+
Concordia Univ Wisc	WI	16,600	C
Concordia Univ, River Forest	IL	23,600	C
Concordia Univ/St.Paul	MN	24,486	C
Creighton Univ	NE	26,748	VC+
De Sales Univ	PA	25,470	C
Duquesne Univ	PA	26,907	VC
Eastern Mennonite Univ	VA	22,990	C
Eastern Univ	PA	24,020	C
Fordham Univ	NY	35,066	HC
Franciscan Univ of Steubenville	OH	20,300	VC
Gannon Univ	PA	23,260	C
Hanover College	IN	25,200	VC
Hardin-Simmons Univ	TX	14,165	C
Immaculata Univ	PA	25,200	C
John Brown Univ	AR	15,080	VC
Juniata College	PA	29,080	VC
King's College	PA	26,990	C
Lenoir-Rhyne College	NC	19,186	C
Loyola College in Maryland	MD	34,560	HC
Loyola Marymount Univ	CA	32,194	VC
Loyola Univ Chicago	IL	31,164	VC
Malone College	OH	20,995	C
Marian College	IN	23,030	C
Marquette Univ	WI	27,594	VC
Marymount Univ	VA	23,668	C
Molloy College	NY	15,180	C
Mount Mary College	WI	20,370	C
Mount St. Mary's College	MD	28,400	C
Newman Univ	KS	18,018	C
Northwest College	WA	18,854	C
Notre Dame College	OH	20,425	C
Ouachita Baptist Univ	AR	18,900	VC
Pacific Union College	CA	22,065	C+
Pontifical Catholic Univ of PR/Ponce	PR	7,298	
Providence College	RI	30,604	HC
Quincy Univ	IL	22,330	C
Roanoke College	VA	27,393	C
Rockhurst Univ	MO	22,960	C+
St. Ambrose Univ	IA	22,800	C
St. Anselm College	NH	30,250	C
St. John's Univ	MN	26,473	VC
St. John's Univ	NY	30,180	C
St. Joseph's College of Maine	ME	25,600	C
St. Louis Univ	MO	29,780	VC+
St. Mary-of-the-Woods College	IN	23,280	C
St. Mary's College	MI	13,314	LC
St. Mary's Univ of Minn	MN	21,535	C
St. Mary's Univ of San Antonio	TX	22,444	C
St. Peter's College	NJ	22,292	LC
St. Vincent College	PA	25,530	VC
Seattle Pacific Univ	WA	25,944	VC
Southern Adventist Univ	TN	17,080	C
Southwestern Adventist Univ	TX	14,798	C
Spring Hill College	AL	25,868	VC
Sterling College	KS	18,763	C
Texas Lutheran Univ	TX	20,370	C
Thomas More College	KY	21,350	C
Trinity Christian College	IL	21,640	VC
Union College	NE	17,130	C
Universidad Adventista de las Antillas	PR	5,460	
Univ of Arizona	AZ	10,413	VC
Univ of Dallas	TX	25,898	VC+
Univ of Evansville	IN	24,190	VC
Univ of Great Falls	MT	15,360	C
Univ of Notre Dame	IN	34,442	MC
Univ of Portland	OR	28,500	VC
Univ of St. Francis	IL	22,850	C
Univ of St. Mary	KS	18,868	C
Univ of St. Thomas	MN	26,918	VC
Univ of St. Thomas	TX	21,952	VC
Univ of San Francisco	CA	34,700	VC
Univ of Scranton	PA	30,836	VC
Valparaiso Univ	IN	26,118	VC+
Villanova Univ	PA	35,050	HC
Walla Walla College	WA	21,600	NC
Walsh Univ	OH	20,890	C
Waynesburg College	PA	19,370	C
William Tyndale College	MI	12,170	NC
Wisc Lutheran College	WI	21,430	VC
Xavier Univ	OH	26,850	VC+
Xavier Univ of Louisiana	LA	17,600	C

THERAPEUTIC RIDING

School	ST	$IS	SR
St. Andrews Presbyterian College	NC	20,525	C

THIRD WORLD STUDIES

School	ST	$IS	SR
Pitzer College	CA	37,590	HC
Univ of Calif at San Diego	CA	14,127	HC
Univ of the South	TN	30,855	HC

TOURISM

School	ST	$IS	SR
Alliant International Univ	CA	23,640	C
Bowling Green State Univ	OH	13,036	C
Brigham Young Univ	UT	8,504	HC
Brigham Young Univ/Hawaii	HI	7,240	VC+
Cal State, Dominguez Hills	CA	5,840	LC
Cal State, Fullerton	CA	6,648	C
Central Missouri State Univ	MO	9,776	C
Central Washington Univ	WA	9,768	C
Champlain College	VT	22,030	C
Dowling College	NY	23,870	LC
Eastern Mich Univ	MI	11,478	C
Florida International Univ	FL	9,912	VC
George Washington Univ	DC	41,030	MC
Georgia Southern Univ	GA	8,540	C
Hawaii Pacific Univ	HI	19,218	C
Indiana Univ Bloomington	IN	12,389	VC
Indiana Univ-Purdue Univ Indianapolis	IN	8,257	LC
James Madison Univ	VA	10,794	VC
Johnson and Wales Univ	RI	22,965	LC
Johnson State College	VT	11,819	LC
Lasell College	MA	26,000	C
Lynn Univ	FL	30,750	C
Mansfield Univ	PA	11,220	C
Mich State Univ	MI	11,933	VC
Montclair State Univ	NJ	13,790	C
National American Univ	SD	13,680	NC
New Mexico State Univ	NM	7,932	C
Niagara Univ	NY	25,050	C
Rochester Inst of Technology	NY	29,217	VC+
St. Leo Univ	FL	20,600	C
St. Thomas Univ	FL	21,400	LC
Seton Hill Univ	PA	24,930	C
Sojourner-Douglass College	MD	4,170	LC
Southern New Hampshire Univ	NH	26,242	C
Temple Univ	PA	15,912	C
Texas State Univ	TX	9,320	VC
Univ of Colo at Boulder	CO	10,774	VC
Univ of Hawaii at Manoa	HI	9,565	VC
Univ of Missouri/Columbia	MO	13,782	VC
Univ of Nebr at Kearney	NE	8,286	NC
Univ of New Hampshire	NH	14,828	VC
Univ of New Haven	CT	28,650	C
Univ of New Mexico	NM	9,223	C
Univ of New Orleans	LA	7,356	C
Univ of Tenn at Knoxville	TN	8,214	C
Univ of Texas at San Antonio	TX	9,088	NC
Univ of the Sacred Heart	PR	5,590	
Webber International Univ	FL	16,510	C
West Liberty State College	WV	7,868	LC
West Virginia Univ	WV	9,370	C
Western Mich Univ	MI	12,031	C

TOXICOLOGY

School	ST	$IS	SR
Ashland Univ	OH	24,464	C
CUNY/John Jay College of Criminal Justice	NY	4,259	C
College of St. Elizabeth	NJ	25,460	C
Northeastern Univ	MA	35,650	HC
St. John's Univ	NY	30,180	C
Univ of Calif at Davis	CA	14,995	VC
Univ of Louisiana at Monroe	LA	5,207	NC
Univ of the Sciences in Philadelphia	PA	29,310	VC
Univ of Wisc/Madison	WI	8,262	VC
Xavier Univ of Louisiana	LA	17,600	C

TOY DESIGN

School	ST	$IS	SR
Fashion Inst of Technology/ SUNY	NY	11,169	C+
Otis College of Art and Design	CA	23,420	SP

TRADE AND INDUSTRIAL EDUCATION

School	ST	$IS	SR
Alabama A&M Univ	AL	5,100	LC
Kent State Univ	OH	12,932	C
New York Inst of Technology	NY	24,205	VC
Univ of Georgia	GA	8,656	VC
Univ of Houston	TX	9,818	C
Univ of Nevada/Las Vegas	NV	11,566	C
Univ of N Dak	ND	8,390	C
Univ of Wyoming	WY	8,636	C
Valdosta State Univ	GA	7,798	C
Virginia State Univ	VA	10,358	C
Western Kentucky Univ	KY	6,834	C

TRADE AND INDUSTRIAL SUPERVISION AND MANAGEMENT

School	ST	$IS	SR
Metropolitan State Univ	MN	3,852	SP
Minn State Univ, Moorehead	MN	7,000	LC
Miss State Univ	MS	9,139	C
Washington Univ in St. Louis	MO	38,293	MC

TRANSPORTATION AND TRAVEL MARKETING

School	ST	$IS	SR
Johnson and Wales Univ	RI	22,965	LC
Northwood Univ	FL	21,040	C
Northwood Univ	MI	20,265	LC
Northwood Univ	TX	20,135	LC

TRANSPORTATION ENGINEERING

School	ST	$IS	SR
Purdue Univ/West Lafayette	IN	12,560	VC
Texas A&M Univ at Galveston	TX	9,948	C+

TRANSPORTATION MANAGEMENT

School	ST	$IS	SR
Arkansas State Univ	AR	8,450	C
Auburn Univ	AL	10,396	VC
Calif Maritime Academy	CA	14,296	C
Dowling College	NY	23,870	LC
Elmhurst College	IL	24,630	C
Embry-Riddle Aeronautical Univ	FL	27,730	C+
Florida International Univ	FL	9,912	VC
Florida Memorial College	FL	6,000	LC
Iowa State Univ	IA	10,768	VC
Mass Maritime Academy	MA	10,472	C
Niagara Univ	NY	25,050	C
Ohio State Univ	OH	13,080	VC+
Penn State Univ/Univ Park Campus	PA	15,646	HC
Robert Morris Univ	PA	20,438	C
St. John's Univ	NY	30,180	C
San Francisco State Univ	CA	12,070	C
Southern Univ at New Orleans	LA	995	NC
SUNY/Maritime College	NY	10,025	LC
Texas A&M Univ at Galveston	TX	9,948	C+
Thomas Edison State College	NJ	3,325	SP
United States Merchant Marine Academy	NY	6,250	HC+
Univ of Alaska Anchorage	AK	9,100	NC
Univ of Arkansas	AR	9,855	VC
Univ of N Dak	ND	8,390	C
Univ of North Florida	FL	8,769	VC
Univ of Pennsylvania	PA	37,960	MC
Univ of Tenn at Knoxville	TN	8,214	C

TRANSPORTATION TECHNOLOGY

School	ST	$IS	SR
Maine Maritime Academy	ME	12,380	C
Pennsylvania College of Technology	PA	15,126	NC
United States Merchant Marine Academy	NY	6,250	HC+

ULTRASOUND TECHNOLOGY

School	ST	$IS	SR
Barry Univ	FL	24,100	LC
Mountain State Univ	WV	10,212	NC
Nebr Methodist College of Nursing and Allied Health	NE	11,900	SP
Newman Univ	KS	18,018	C
Oregon Inst of Technology	OR	8,718	C

ST = STATE **$IS** = IN-STATE COSTS **SR** = SELECTOR RATING

School	ST	$IS	SR
Rochester Inst of Technology	NY	29,217	VC+
Seattle Univ	WA	24,183	VC

URBAN DESIGN

School	ST	$IS	SR
Arizona State Univ-Main	AZ	10,048	C
New York Univ	NY	39,406	MC
Oregon State Univ	OR	11,055	C
SUNY/Univ at Albany	NY	12,951	HC

URBAN PLANNING TECHNOLOGY

School	ST	$IS	SR
Arizona State Univ-Main	AZ	10,048	C
Ball State Univ	IN	8,660	C
Eastern Mich Univ	MI	11,478	C
Florida Atlantic Univ	FL	8,543	C
Mass Inst of Technology	MA	38,310	MC
Mich State Univ	MI	11,933	VC
Southwest Missouri State Univ	MO	8,918	C
Univ of Nevada/Las Vegas	NV	11,566	C
Univ of Utah	UT	9,205	C

URBAN STUDIES

School	ST	$IS	SR
Adams State College	CO	7,468	C
Albertus Magnus College	CT	23,130	LC
Augsburg College	MN	25,298	C
Baylor Univ	TX	23,864	VC
Bellevue Univ	NE	4,440	NC
Boston Univ	MA	38,194	HC+
Brown Univ	RI	38,174	MC
Bryn Mawr College	PA	36,890	HC+
Calif State Polytechnic Univ, Pomona	CA	8,793	C+
Cal State, Northridge	CA	7,757	LC
Cal State, Stanislaus	CA	9,874	C
Calumet College of St. Joseph	IN	9,000	LC
Canisius College	NY	28,163	C+
Carnegie Mellon Univ	PA	32,682	MC
CUNY/City College	NY	4,230	C+
CUNY/Hunter College	NY	6,729	C+
CUNY/Queens College	NY	4,362	C
Cleveland State Univ	OH	12,308	LC
College of Charleston	SC	11,887	HC
College of Mount St. Vincent	NY	26,800	C
College of Wooster	OH	31,300	HC
Columbia Univ/Barnard College	NY	36,990	MC
Columbia Univ/Columbia College	NY	38,590	MC
Columbia Univ/School of General Studies	NY	35,000	C
Conn College	CT	37,900	MC
Cornell Univ	NY	38,253	MC
David Lipscomb Univ	TN	16,158	VC
DePaul Univ	IL	27,580	VC
Dillard Univ	LA	17,325	VC
Eastern Univ	PA	24,020	C
Eastern Washington Univ	WA	9,012	C
Elmhurst College	IL	24,630	C
Eugene Lang College/New School Univ	NY	34,940	C
Florida International Univ	FL	9,912	VC
Fordham Univ	NY	35,066	HC
Furman Univ	SC	28,976	HC+
Georgia State Univ	GA	10,658	C
Hamline Univ	MN	27,052	VC
Hampshire College	MA	37,037	HC
Haverford College	PA	37,900	MC
Hobart and William Smith Colleges	NY	36,536	HC
Indiana State Univ	IN	10,719	LC
Indiana Univ Bloomington	IN	12,389	VC
Jackson State Univ	MS	8,382	C
Johns Hopkins Univ	MD	38,372	MC
Langston Univ	OK	2,308	LC
Lehigh Univ	PA	37,570	HC+
Loyola Marymount Univ	CA	32,194	VC
Macalester College	MN	31,944	MC
Manhattan College	NY	27,400	VC
Metropolitan State College of Denver	CO	2,338	LC
Miami Univ	OH	15,033	HC
Minn State Univ, Mankato	MN	8,803	LC
Morehouse College	GA	22,728	C
Mount Mercy College	IA	21,400	C
New College of Florida	FL	8,906	HC+
New York Univ	NY	39,406	MC
Northwestern Univ	IL	37,491	MC
Occidental College	CA	35,922	HC
Ohio Univ	OH	14,448	C
Purdue Univ/West Lafayette	IN	12,560	VC
Rhodes College	TN	26,466	HC+
Rockford College	IL	28,310	VC
Roosevelt Univ	IL	22,580	VC
Rutgers, The State Univ of New Jersey/Camden Campus	NJ	14,990	VC

School	ST	$IS	SR
Rutgers, The State Univ of New Jersey/New Brunswick/Piscataway Campus	NJ	15,800	HC
St. Augustine's College	NC	12,990	LC
St. Cloud State Univ	MN	8,362	C
St. Louis Univ	MO	29,780	VC+
St. Peter's College	NJ	22,292	LC
San Diego State Univ	CA	10,321	C
San Francisco State Univ	CA	12,070	C
Stanford Univ	CA	37,612	MC
SUNY/College at Buffalo	NY	8,025	C
Temple Univ	PA	15,912	C
Trinity Univ	TX	26,466	HC+
Univ of Calif at Berkeley	CA	15,563	MC
Univ of Calif at San Diego	CA	14,127	HC
Univ of Cincinnati	OH	14,736	C
Univ of Conn	CT	14,608	VC
Univ of Mich/Flint	MI	5,548	C
Univ of Minn/Duluth	MN	12,470	C
Univ of Minn/Twin Cities	MN	13,160	VC
Univ of Missouri/Kansas City	MO	13,416	VC
Univ of New Orleans	LA	7,356	C
Univ of Pennsylvania	PA	37,960	MC
Univ of Pittsburgh at Pittsburgh	PA	16,074	HC
Univ of Richmond	VA	30,100	MC
Univ of San Diego	CA	33,156	HC
Univ of Tampa	FL	23,982	VC
Univ of Tenn at Knoxville	TN	8,214	C
Univ of Texas at Austin	TX	10,630	HC
Univ of the District of Columbia	DC	2,070	LC
Univ of the Sacred Heart	PR	5,590	
Univ of Wisc/Green Bay	WI	8,154	C
Univ of Wisc/Oshkosh	WI	6,130	LC
Vanderbilt Univ	TN	37,897	MC
Vassar College	NY	37,030	MC
Virginia Commonwealth Univ	VA	9,030	C
Virginia Polytechnic Inst and State Univ	VA	9,179	C
Washington Univ in St. Louis	MO	38,293	MC
Wayne State Univ	MI	11,774	C
Westfield State College	MA	10,147	C
Worcester State College	MA	10,005	C
Wright State Univ	OH	11,490	LC

VETERINARY SCIENCE

School	ST	$IS	SR
Becker College	MA	23,710	LC
Fort Valley State Univ	GA	6,960	C
Lincoln Memorial Univ	TN	16,400	LC
Medaille College	NY	20,060	C
Mercy College	NY	19,200	NC
Mich State Univ	MI	11,933	VC
Mount Ida College	MA	25,596	LC
Murray State Univ	KY	7,816	VC
National American Univ	SD	13,680	NC
Newberry College	SC	22,871	LC
N Dak State Univ	ND	8,435	C
Purdue Univ/West Lafayette	IN	12,560	VC
Quinnipiac Univ	CT	30,570	VC
Tuskegee Univ	AL	17,250	LC
Univ of Arizona	AZ	10,413	VC
Univ of Idaho	ID	8,216	C
Univ of Illinois at Urbana-Champaign	IL	11,316	HC+
Univ of Nebr at Lincoln	NE	9,975	C+
Utah State Univ	UT	7,371	C
Washington State Univ	WA	11,334	C
West Virginia Univ	WV	9,370	C
Wilson College	PA	23,912	C

VIDEO

School	ST	$IS	SR
American InterContinental Univ	GA	12,000	NC
Art Inst of Atlanta	GA	23,205	SP
Atlanta College of Art	GA	18,600	SP
Bethel College	IN	19,670	C
Bloomfield College	NJ	19,250	LC
CUNY/City College	NY	4,230	C+
Drexel Univ	PA	27,655	VC
Fairleigh Dickinson Univ/ College at Florham	NJ	30,130	C
Five Towns College	NY	21,050	SP
Hampshire College	MA	37,037	HC
Hofstra Univ	NY	27,112	VC
Iona College	NY	27,988	VC
Ithaca College	NY	31,730	HC
Kansas City Art Inst	MO	26,850	SP
Madonna Univ	MI	11,504	VC
Maryland Inst College of Art	MD	30,890	SP
Middlebury College	VT	38,100	MC
Minneapolis College of Art and Design	MN	28,950	SP
Point Park Univ	PA	21,840	C
Rochester Inst of Technology	NY	29,217	VC+
San Francisco Art Inst	CA	19,300	SP
Savannah College of Art and Design	GA	27,560	SP

School	ST	$IS	SR
School of the Art Inst of Chicago	IL	27,800	SP
School of Visual Arts	NY	30,200	SP
Syracuse Univ	NY	34,720	HC
Univ of Hartford	CT	31,080	C
Univ of Miami	FL	34,608	HC
Univ of Okla	OK	9,226	VC
Webster Univ	MO	21,848	VC
Wilmington College	DE	5,594	NC

VISUAL AND PERFORMING ARTS

School	ST	$IS	SR
Adelphi Univ	NY	26,300	VC
Albion College	MI	25,224	VC
Alverno College	WI	18,898	C
Andrews Univ	MI	19,550	C
Antioch College	OH	29,269	C
Armstrong Atlantic State Univ	GA	7,102	C
Assumption College	MA	29,375	C
Bennett College	NC	11,200	C
Bennington College	VT	35,910	HC
Bowdoin College	ME	37,790	MC
Bradley Univ	IL	22,910	VC
Brigham Young Univ	UT	8,504	HC
Brown Univ	RI	38,174	MC
Cabrini College	PA	29,020	C
Calif Baptist Univ	CA	19,924	C
Calif College of the Arts	CA	31,530	SP
Cal State, Monterey Bay	CA	6,683	LC
Cal State, San Marcos	CA	1,736	LC
Central Washington Univ	WA	9,768	C
Chatham College	PA	27,266	C+
CUNY/Brooklyn College	NY	4,353	C+
Clark Univ	MA	32,115	VC
College of Visual Arts	MN		SP
Columbia Univ/Columbia College	NY	38,590	MC
Columbia Univ/School of General Studies	NY	35,000	C
Columbus State Univ	GA	7,846	C
Curry College	MA	26,025	LC
Dowling College	NY	23,870	LC
Duke Univ	NC	37,555	MC
Eckerd College	FL	28,744	C+
Erskine College	SC	23,166	VC
Fairfield Univ	CT	35,505	HC
Fayetteville State Univ	NC	5,590	LC
Fordham Univ	NY	35,066	HC
Franciscan Univ	IA	19,300	C
Goddard College	VT	21,056	C+
Grand View College	IA	19,748	LC
Green Mountain College	VT	24,130	C
Haverford College	PA	37,900	MC
Hendrix College	AR	20,970	VC+
Hofstra Univ	NY	27,112	VC
Illinois Wesleyan Univ	IL	30,380	HC+
Indiana Univ Bloomington	IN	12,389	VC
Inter American Univ of PR/ Bayamon Univ College	PR	3,522	
Inter American Univ of PR/ Fajardo Campus	PR	4,000	
Inter American Univ of PR/ Ponce Regional College	PR	3,700	
Ithaca College	NY	31,730	HC
Johnson State College	VT	11,819	LC
Kent State Univ	OH	12,932	C
Keystone College	PA	21,405	LC
King College	TN	22,500	VC
Kutztown Univ of Pennsylvania	PA	10,786	C
Lambuth Univ	TN	16,520	C
Lander Univ	SC	10,496	C
Longwood Univ	VA	11,175	C
Loyola Univ New Orleans	LA	31,036	VC+
McNeese State Univ	LA	5,259	LC
Medaille College	NY	20,060	C
Mount Mercy College	IA	21,400	C
Naropa Univ	CO	23,364	SP
New England Conservatory of Music	MA	35,000	SP
Notre Dame College	OH	20,425	C
Ohio Univ	OH	14,448	C
Oregon State Univ	OR	11,055	C
Otterbein College	OH	26,085	C
Presbyterian College	SC	25,920	VC
Ramapo College of New Jersey	NJ	15,203	NC
Rice Univ	TX	27,550	MC
Roger Williams Univ	RI	30,296	C
Rutgers, The State Univ of New Jersey/New Brunswick/Piscataway Campus	NJ	15,800	HC
Rutgers, The State Univ of New Jersey/Newark Campus	NJ	15,624	VC
St. Andrews Presbyterian College	NC	20,525	C
St. Augustine's College	NC	12,990	LC
St. Bonaventure Univ	NY	24,455	LC
St. Vincent College	PA	25,530	VC
Sarah Lawrence College	NY	41,218	HC
School of the Art Inst of Chicago	IL	27,800	SP

School	ST	$IS	SR
Schreiner Univ	TX	20,440	C
Seattle Pacific Univ	WA	25,944	VC
Shaw Univ	NC	14,882	C+
Siena College	NY	25,310	VC
Simon's Rock College of Bard	MA	36,580	HC
Sonoma State Univ	CA	10,421	C
Southern Oregon Univ	OR	10,362	C
SUNY/College at Old Westbury	NY	12,784	C
SUNY/College at Purchase	NY	10,587	VC
SUNY/Univ at New Paltz	NY	11,565	VC
Texas Tech Univ	TX	10,768	VC
Univ of Alabama	AL	9,040	C+
Univ of Arkansas at Little Rock	AR	5,637	NC
Univ of Calif at San Diego	CA	14,127	HC
Univ of Conn	CT	14,608	VC
Univ of Florida	FL	8,580	MC
Univ of Maine at Farmington	ME	10,108	C
Univ of Maryland/Baltimore County	MD	14,668	VC+
Univ of N Dak	ND	8,390	C
Univ of North Texas	TX	7,629	C
Univ of San Francisco	CA	34,700	VC
Univ of Texas at Austin	TX	10,630	HC
Univ of Texas at Dallas	TX	10,234	HC
Univ of the Sacred Heart	PR	5,590	
Virginia State Univ	VA	10,358	C
Washington State Univ	WA	11,334	C
Washington Univ in St. Louis	MO	38,293	MC
Wells College	NY	21,122	VC
West Virginia Univ	WV	9,370	C
Wichita State Univ	KS	8,092	C

VOCATIONAL EDUCATION

School	ST	$IS	SR
Auburn Univ	AL	10,396	VC
Cal State, Los Angeles	CA	5,778	C
Cal State, San Bernardino	CA	15,238	LC
Central Conn State Univ	CT	12,090	C
Chicago State Univ	IL	10,882	C+
CUNY/New York City College of Technology	NY	4,269	NC
College of New Jersey	NJ	15,950	MC
College of the Ozarks	MO	3,500	VC+
Florida International Univ	FL	9,912	VC
Idaho State Univ	ID	8,128	C
Indiana Univ of Pennsylvania	PA	10,489	C
Kent State Univ	OH	12,932	C
Louisiana State Univ and A&M College	LA	9,126	VC
Martin Univ	IN	10,200	SP
N Car State Univ	NC	9,886	VC
Pennsylvania College of Technology	PA	15,126	NC
Pittsburg State Univ	KS	7,128	NC
San Diego State Univ	CA	10,321	C
San Francisco State Univ	CA	12,070	C
S Dak State Univ	SD	7,782	C
Southern Illinois Univ Carbondale	IL	10,407	C
SUNY at Oswego	NY	12,650	C
Univ of Arkansas	AR	9,855	VC
Univ of Central Florida	FL	10,038	VC
Univ of Idaho	ID	8,216	C
Univ of N Dak	ND	8,390	C
Univ of North Texas	TX	7,629	C
Univ of South Florida	FL	9,454	C
Univ of Toledo	OH	12,479	NC
Univ of Wisc/Stout	WI	9,718	C
Valley City State Univ	ND	7,281	LC
Virginia Polytechnic Inst and State Univ	VA	9,179	C
Wayland Baptist Univ	TX	11,919	NC
Western Mich Univ	MI	12,031	C
Western New Mexico Univ	NM	5,950	LC
Youngstown State Univ	OH	11,148	NC

VOICE

School	ST	$IS	SR
Ball State Univ	IN	8,660	C
Catholic Univ of America	DC	34,248	VC
Central Washington Univ	WA	9,768	C
East Central Univ	OK	4,968	C
East Texas Baptist Univ	TX	13,914	C
Florida State Univ	FL	9,028	HC
Grand Canyon Univ	AZ	30,000	LC
Illinois Wesleyan Univ	IL	30,380	HC+
Indiana Univ Bloomington	IN	12,389	VC
Indiana Univ South Bend	IN	4,571	LC
Juilliard School	NY	30,385	SP
Manhattan School of Music	NY	31,500	SP
Mannes College of Music	NY	31,930	SP
McMurry Univ	TX	17,846	LC
Miss College	MS	14,574	C
New York Univ	NY	39,406	MC
Northwestern Univ	IL	37,491	MC
Nyack College	NY	18,540	C
Ohio Univ	OH	14,448	C
Pacific Lutheran Univ	WA	25,715	VC
Palm Beach Atlantic Univ	FL	20,690	C
Roosevelt Univ	IL	22,580	VC

ST = STATE $IS = IN-STATE COSTS   SR = SELECTOR RATING

School	ST	$IS	SR
Samford Univ	AL	18,648	VC
Shorter College	GA	17,370	C
Southern Nazarene Univ	OK	14,634	NC
Stetson Univ	FL	29,495	VC
Temple Univ	PA	15,912	C
Union Univ	TN	18,800	VC
Univ of Cincinnati	OH	14,736	C
Univ of Illinois at Urbana-Champaign	IL	11,316	HC+
Univ of Kansas	KS	8,923	VC
Univ of Miami	FL	34,608	HC
Univ of Mich/Ann Arbor	MI	13,864	HC+
Univ of New Hampshire	NH	14,828	VC
Univ of Tulsa	OK	22,090	VC+
Weber State Univ	UT	7,945	NC
Westminster Choir College of Rider Univ	NJ	25,400	SP
Youngstown State Univ	OH	11,148	NC

WATER AND WASTEWATER TECHNOLOGY

School	ST	$IS	SR
Texas State Univ	TX	9,320	VC
Wright State Univ	OH	11,490	LC

WATER RESOURCES

School	ST	$IS	SR
Central State Univ	OH	8,922	C+
Colo State Univ	CO	9,964	VC
Heidelberg College	OH	20,266	NC
Northern Mich Univ	MI	10,834	C
Ohio Univ	OH	14,448	C
SUNY/College at Brockport	NY	12,111	C
SUNY/College at Oneonta	NY	11,870	VC
Tarleton State Univ	TX	7,576	C
Texas A&M Univ at Galveston	TX	9,948	C+
Univ of Arizona	AZ	10,413	VC
Univ of Nebr at Lincoln	NE	9,975	C+
Univ of New Hampshire	NH	14,828	VC
Univ of Rhode Island	RI	13,720	VC
Univ of Wisc/Stevens Point	WI	8,116	VC

WEB SERVICES

School	ST	$IS	SR
Champlain College	VT	22,030	C
Indiana Inst of Technology	IN	21,620	C
Johnson and Wales Univ	RI	22,965	LC
Limestone College	SC	17,700	C
Maharishi Univ of Management	IA	29,230	VC
Mercyhurst College	PA	20,694	C
Southern Adventist Univ	TN	17,080	C
Southern Wesleyan Univ	SC	19,940	C
SUNY/College of Technology at Alfred	NY	12,416	C
Univ of Wisc/Stevens Point	WI	8,116	VC

WEB TECHNOLOGY

School	ST	$IS	SR
Bethel College	IN	19,670	C
Cabrini College	PA	29,020	C
Cogswell Polytechnical College	CA	14,400	LC
Davenport Univ	MI	11,636	NC
Duquesne Univ	PA	26,907	VC
Illinois Inst of Technology	IL	26,456	HC+
Mercyhurst College	PA	20,694	C
Strayer Univ	DC	8,789	SP
Tenn Tech Univ	TN	8,670	VC

WELDING ENGINEERING

School	ST	$IS	SR
LeTourneau Univ	TX	21,080	C
Ohio State Univ	OH	13,080	VC+
Pennsylvania College of Technology	PA	15,126	NC

WESTERN CIVILIZATION/ CULTURE

School	ST	$IS	SR
St. John's College	MD	36,360	HC+

WESTERN EUROPEAN STUDIES

School	ST	$IS	SR
Denison Univ	OH	33,050	HC
St. John's College	MD	36,360	HC+
Univ of Mich/Ann Arbor	MI	13,864	HC+
Univ of Nebr at Lincoln	NE	9,975	C+
Washington Univ in St. Louis	MO	38,293	MC

WILDLIFE BIOLOGY

School	ST	$IS	SR
Auburn Univ	AL	10,396	VC
Baker Univ	KS	19,860	VC
Ball State Univ	IN	8,660	C
Colo State Univ	CO	9,964	VC
Humboldt State Univ	CA	9,400	C
Kansas State Univ	KS	8,728	VC
Murray State Univ	KY	7,816	VC
New Mexico State Univ	NM	7,932	C
Ohio Univ	OH	14,448	C
Oregon State Univ	OR	11,055	C
Penn State Univ/Univ Park Campus	PA	15,646	HC
Tarleton State Univ	TX	7,576	C
Texas State Univ	TX	9,320	VC
Unity College	ME	19,845	LC
Univ of Alaska Fairbanks	AK	9,295	C
Univ of Arizona	AZ	10,413	VC
Univ of Calif at Davis	CA	14,995	VC
Univ of Florida	FL	8,580	MC
Univ of Mich/Ann Arbor	MI	13,864	HC+
Univ of Minn/Twin Cities	MN	13,160	VC
Univ of Montana	MT	9,395	C
Univ of Tenn at Martin	TN	7,748	C
Univ of Vermont	VT	16,316	VC
Univ of Wisc/Madison	WI	8,262	VC
Univ of Wisc/Stevens Point	WI	8,116	VC
Washington State Univ	WA	11,334	C
West Texas A&M Univ	TX	7,533	C

WILDLIFE MANAGEMENT

School	ST	$IS	SR
Arkansas State Univ	AR	8,450	C
Brigham Young Univ	UT	8,504	HC
Delaware Valley College	PA	26,676	C
Eastern Kentucky Univ	KY	7,708	C
Eastern New Mexico Univ	NM	6,762	LC
Frostburg State Univ	MD	11,114	C
Lake Superior State Univ	MI	9,034	LC
Lincoln Memorial Univ	TN	16,400	LC
Louisiana Tech Univ	LA	7,361	C
McNeese State Univ	LA	5,259	LC
Mich State Univ	MI	11,933	VC
Miss State Univ	MS	9,139	C
Northwest Missouri State Univ	MO	9,334	C
Peru State College	NE	6,342	NC
Purdue Univ/West Lafayette	IN	12,560	VC
Southwest Missouri State Univ	MO	8,918	C
Sterling College	VT	21,114	C+
Sul Ross State Univ	TX	6,582	LC
Tenn Tech Univ	TN	8,670	VC
Texas A&M Univ at Commerce	TX	8,994	C
Texas Tech Univ	TX	10,768	VC
Univ of Alaska Fairbanks	AK	9,295	C
Univ of Arkansas at Monticello	AR	5,940	NC
Univ of Georgia	GA	8,656	VC
Univ of Idaho	ID	8,216	C
Univ of Maine	ME	12,080	C+
Univ of Mass Amherst	MA	13,980	C+
Univ of New Hampshire	NH	14,828	VC
Univ of PR at Humacao	PR	1,245	
Univ of Rhode Island	RI	13,720	VC
Univ of Wyoming	WY	8,636	C
Utah State Univ	UT	7,371	C
Washington State Univ	WA	11,334	C

WINDS

School	ST	$IS	SR
Florida State Univ	FL	9,028	HC
Juilliard School	NY	30,385	SP
Miss College	MS	14,574	C
Northwestern Univ	IL	37,491	MC
Roosevelt Univ	IL	22,580	VC
Stetson Univ	FL	29,495	VC
Temple Univ	PA	15,912	C
Univ of Mich/Ann Arbor	MI	13,864	HC+
Youngstown State Univ	OH	11,148	NC

WOMEN'S STUDIES

School	ST	$IS	SR
Agnes Scott College	GA	28,230	HC
Allegheny College	PA	30,280	VC
American Univ	DC	34,585	VC+
Amherst College	MA	37,470	MC
Arizona State Univ-Main	AZ	10,048	C
Augsburg College	MN	25,298	C
Bates College	ME	37,500	MC
Beloit College	WI	29,864	HC
Berea College	KY	5,030	VC+
Bowdoin College	ME	37,790	MC
Bowling Green State Univ	OH	13,036	C
Brown Univ	RI	38,174	MC
Bucknell Univ	PA	35,262	HC+
Cal State, Fresno	CA	8,414	LC
Cal State, Fullerton	CA	6,648	C
Cal State, Long Beach	CA	8,762	C+
Cal State, Northridge	CA	7,757	LC
Cal State, San Marcos	CA	1,736	LC
Carleton College	MN	34,395	MC
Case Western Reserve Univ	OH	32,002	MC
Chatham College	PA	27,266	C+
CUNY/Brooklyn College	NY	4,353	C+
CUNY/College of Staten Island	NY	4,308	NC
CUNY/Hunter College	NY	6,729	C+
CUNY/Queens College	NY	4,362	C
Claremont McKenna College	CA	36,880	HC
Coe College	IA	27,385	VC
Colby College	ME	37,570	MC
Colgate Univ	NY	37,095	MC
College of Mount St. Joseph	OH	22,785	C
College of New Jersey	NJ	15,950	MC
College of New Rochelle	NY	21,800	C
College of St. Catherine	MN	24,010	VC
College of Wooster	OH	31,300	HC
Colo College	CO	36,860	HC
Columbia Univ/Barnard College	NY	36,990	MC
Columbia Univ/Columbia College	NY	38,590	MC
Columbia Univ/School of General Studies	NY	35,000	C
Cornell College	IA	27,825	VC+
Cornell Univ	NY	38,253	MC
Dartmouth College	NH	37,770	MC
Denison Univ	OH	33,050	HC
DePaul Univ	IL	27,580	VC
DePauw Univ	IN	31,500	HC
Dickinson College	PA	35,825	HC
Drew Univ/College of Liberal Arts	NJ	35,550	VC
Duke Univ	NC	37,555	MC
Earlham College	IN	29,976	VC+
East Carolina Univ	NC	8,671	C
Eastern Mich Univ	MI	11,478	C
Eckerd College	FL	28,744	C+
Emory Univ	GA	36,872	MC
Eugene Lang College/New School Univ	NY	34,940	C
Florida International Univ	FL	9,912	VC
Florida State Univ	FL	9,028	HC
Fordham Univ	NY	35,066	HC
Gettysburg College	PA	35,646	HC
Goddard College	VT	21,056	C+
Goucher College	MD	32,650	HC
Guilford College	NC	24,960	VC
Gustavus Adolphus College	MN	27,120	VC+
Hamilton College	NY	37,560	MC
Hamline Univ	MN	27,052	VC
Hampshire College	MA	37,037	HC
Harvard Univ/Harvard College	MA	37,928	MC
Hobart and William Smith Colleges	NY	36,536	HC
Hollins Univ	VA	27,965	VC
Indiana Univ South Bend	IN	4,571	LC
Indiana Univ-Purdue Univ Fort Wayne	IN	5,108	LC
Knox College	IL	30,294	VC+
Louisiana State Univ and A&M College	LA	9,126	VC
Macalester College	MN	31,944	MC
Mass Inst of Technology	MA	38,310	MC
Metropolitan State Univ	MN	3,852	SP
Miami Univ	OH	15,033	HC
Mich State Univ	MI	11,933	VC
Middlebury College	VT	38,100	MC
Mills College	CA	33,371	VC
Minn State Univ, Mankato	MN	8,803	LC
Montclair State Univ	NJ	13,790	C
Mount Holyoke College	MA	37,918	HC+
Nebr Wesleyan Univ	NE	21,197	C+
New College of Florida	FL	8,906	HC+
New England College	NH	28,860	LC
Oakland Univ	MI	10,800	C
Oberlin College	OH	36,938	MC
Occidental College	CA	35,922	HC
Ohio State Univ	OH	13,080	VC+
Ohio Wesleyan Univ	OH	32,550	VC+
Old Dominion Univ	VA	10,441	C
Pacific Lutheran Univ	WA	25,715	VC
Penn State Univ/Univ Park Campus	PA	15,646	HC
Pitzer College	CA	37,590	HC
Pomona College	CA	33,960	MC
Portland State Univ	OR	12,453	C
Randolph-Macon College	VA	27,190	C
Rhode Island College	RI	11,565	C
Rice Univ	TX	27,550	MC
Roosevelt Univ	IL	22,580	VC
Rosemont College	PA	26,175	C
Rutgers, The State Univ of New Jersey/New Brunswick/Piscataway Campus	NJ	15,800	HC
Rutgers, The State Univ of New Jersey/Newark Campus	NJ	15,624	VC
St. Joseph College	CT	29,685	C
St. Louis Univ	MO	29,780	VC+
St. Olaf College	MN	28,500	HC
San Diego State Univ	CA	10,321	C
San Francisco State Univ	CA	12,070	C
Sarah Lawrence College	NY	41,218	HC
Scripps College	CA	35,700	HC+
Simmons College	MA	33,000	VC
Skidmore College	NY	37,930	HC
Smith College	MA	37,034	HC+
Sonoma State Univ	CA	10,421	C
Southwestern Univ	TX	25,410	HC
Spelman College	GA	19,215	C+
Stanford Univ	CA	37,612	MC
SUNY at Oswego	NY	12,650	C
SUNY/College at Brockport	NY	12,111	C
SUNY/College at Purchase	NY	10,587	VC
SUNY/Univ at Albany	NY	12,951	HC
SUNY/Univ at Buffalo	NY	12,563	VC
SUNY/Univ at New Paltz	NY	11,565	VC
SUNY/Univ at Stony Brook	NY	12,763	HC
Syracuse Univ	NY	34,720	HC
Temple Univ	PA	15,912	C
Towson Univ	MD	12,694	VC
Trinity College	CT	38,040	HC+
Tufts Univ	MA	38,233	MC
Tulane Univ	LA	37,451	HC+
Union College	NY	36,005	HC
Univ of Arizona	AZ	10,413	VC
Univ of Calif at Berkeley	CA	15,563	MC
Univ of Calif at Davis	CA	14,995	VC
Univ of Calif at Irvine	CA	19,808	HC
Univ of Calif at Los Angeles	CA	15,330	MC
Univ of Calif at Riverside	CA	15,300	C
Univ of Calif at Santa Barbara	CA	11,732	VC
Univ of Calif at Santa Cruz	CA	16,505	VC
Univ of Colo at Boulder	CO	10,774	VC
Univ of Conn	CT	14,608	VC
Univ of Delaware	DE	12,616	HC
Univ of Denver	CO	32,148	VC
Univ of Hartford	CT	31,080	C
Univ of Hawaii at Manoa	HI	9,565	VC
Univ of Kansas	KS	8,923	VC
Univ of Louisville	KY	8,762	VC
Univ of Maine	ME	12,080	C+
Univ of Maine at Farmington	ME	10,108	C
Univ of Maryland/College Park	MD	14,227	HC
Univ of Mass Amherst	MA	13,980	C+
Univ of Mass Boston	MA	6,227	C
Univ of Miami	FL	34,608	HC
Univ of Mich/Ann Arbor	MI	13,864	HC+
Univ of Minn/Duluth	MN	12,470	C
Univ of Minn/Morris	MN	12,896	VC
Univ of Minn/Twin Cities	MN	13,160	VC
Univ of Montana	MT	9,395	C
Univ of Nebr at Lincoln	NE	9,975	C+
Univ of Nevada/Las Vegas	NV	11,566	C
Univ of New Hampshire	NH	14,828	VC
Univ of N Car at Chapel Hill	NC	10,117	MC
Univ of N Car at Greensboro	NC	8,248	C
Univ of Okla	OK	9,226	VC
Univ of Oregon	OR	11,479	VC
Univ of Pennsylvania	PA	37,960	MC
Univ of Puget Sound	WA	31,760	HC
Univ of Rhode Island	RI	13,720	VC
Univ of Richmond	VA	30,100	MC
Univ of Rochester	NY	32,979	HC
Univ of St. Thomas	MN	26,918	VC
Univ of S Car at Columbia	SC	10,048	VC
Univ of South Florida	FL	9,454	C
Univ of Southern Calif	CA	37,459	MC
Univ of Southern Maine	ME	11,212	C
Univ of Tenn at Chattanooga	TN	7,783	C
Univ of Tenn at Knoxville	TN	8,214	C
Univ of Toledo	OH	12,479	NC
Univ of Utah	UT	9,205	C
Univ of Vermont	VT	16,316	VC
Univ of Washington	WA	10,361	VC
Univ of Wisc/Madison	WI	8,262	VC
Univ of Wisc/Whitewater	WI	8,626	C
Univ of Wyoming	WY	8,636	C
Vassar College	NY	37,030	MC
Villanova Univ	PA	35,050	HC
Warren Wilson College	NC	21,794	VC
Washington State Univ	WA	11,334	C
Washington Univ in St. Louis	MO	38,293	MC
Wayne State Univ	MI	11,774	C
Wellesley College	MA	36,516	MC
Wells College	NY	21,122	VC
Wesleyan Univ	CT	35,139	MC
West Chester Univ of Pennsylvania	PA	11,164	C
Western Mich Univ	MI	12,031	C
Wheaton College	MA	36,330	HC
Whitworth College	WA	26,428	VC+
Wichita State Univ	KS	8,092	C
Yale Univ	CT	37,000	MC

WOOD SCIENCE

School	ST	$IS	SR
N Car State Univ	NC	9,886	VC
SUNY/College of Environmental Science and Forestry	NY	14,167	VC
Univ of Maine	ME	12,080	C+
Univ of Washington	WA	10,361	VC

WOODWORKING

School	ST	$IS	SR
Edinboro Univ of Pennsylvania	PA	10,850	LC
Kendall College of Art and Design of Ferris State Univ	MI	10,784	SP
Rochester Inst of Technology	NY	29,217	VC+

ST = STATE $IS = IN-STATE COSTS SR = SELECTOR RATING

School	ST	$IS	SR
Univ of Rio Grande	OH	8,728	NC

YOUTH MINISTRY

School	ST	$IS	SR
Andrews Univ	MI	19,550	C
Benedictine College	KS	20,603	C
Bethel College	IN	19,670	C
Bethel College	MN	25,180	VC
Cascade College	OR	16,700	NC
Charleston Southern Univ	SC	17,122	C
Colo Christian Univ	CO	21,182	VC
Concordia Univ	OR	22,450	C
Cornerstone Univ and Grand Rapids Theological Seminary	MI	19,846	C
Crichton College	TN	15,215	C
Dakota Wesleyan Univ	SD	17,832	C
Dordt College	IA	20,170	VC
Eastern Univ	PA	24,020	C
Georgetown College	KY	22,000	VC
Gordon College	MA	25,982	VC+
Grace Bible College	MI	15,890	C
Grace College	IN	19,825	VC
Greenville College	IL	21,342	C
Hope International Univ	CA	16,940	VC
Huntington College	IN	23,590	C
John Brown Univ	AR	15,080	VC
Judson College	IL	22,050	LC
Kentucky Christian College	KY	13,472	C
King College	TN	22,500	VC
MacMurray College	IL	20,005	LC
Malone College	OH	20,995	C
Mount Vernon Nazarene Univ	OH	18,925	C

School	ST	$IS	SR
Northwest College	WA	18,854	C
Northwestern College	MN	22,820	C+
Northwestern College of Iowa	IA	19,640	C+
Nyack College	NY	18,540	C
Ohio Northern Univ	OH	27,765	VC
Okla Christian Univ	OK	17,690	NC
Okla Wesleyan Univ	OK	14,100	LC
St. Mary's Univ of Minn	MN	21,535	C
Simpson College	CA	20,500	C
Southeastern College	FL	11,648	LC
Spring Arbor Univ	MI	20,206	C
Toccoa Falls College	GA	15,600	C
Trinity International Univ	IL	22,980	C+
Union Univ	TN	18,800	C
Univ of Indianapolis	IN	22,560	VC
Washington State Univ	WA	11,334	C
William Tyndale College	MI	12,170	NC

ZOOLOGY

School	ST	$IS	SR
Alabama A&M Univ	AL	5,100	LC
Andrews Univ	MI	19,550	C
Auburn Univ	AL	10,396	VC
Ball State Univ	IN	8,660	C
Bethel College	TN	12,980	C
Brigham Young Univ	UT	8,504	HC
Calif State Polytechnic Univ, Pomona	CA	8,793	C+
Cal State, Long Beach	CA	8,762	C+
Cal State, Stanislaus	CA	9,874	C
Colo State Univ	CO	9,964	VC
Conn College	CT	37,900	MC
Eastern Mich Univ	MI	11,478	C

School	ST	$IS	SR
Eastern Washington Univ	WA	9,012	C
Florida State Univ	FL	9,028	HC
Fort Valley State Univ	GA	6,960	C
Friends Univ	KS	15,962	LC
Howard Univ	DC	16,505	C
Humboldt State Univ	CA	9,400	C
Idaho State Univ	ID	8,128	C
Iowa State Univ	IA	10,768	VC
Juniata College	PA	29,080	VC
Kent State Univ	OH	12,932	C
Mars Hill College	NC	18,600	LC
Miami Univ	OH	15,033	HC
Mich State Univ	MI	11,933	VC
N Car State Univ	NC	9,886	VC
N Dak State Univ	ND	8,435	C
Northeastern State Univ	OK	4,950	LC
Northern Arizona Univ	AZ	9,002	C
Northern Mich Univ	MI	10,834	C
Northwest Missouri State Univ	MO	9,334	C
Ohio State Univ	OH	13,080	VC+
Ohio Wesleyan Univ	OH	32,550	VC+
Okla State Univ	OK	9,216	VC
Olivet Nazarene Univ	IL	20,480	C
Oregon State Univ	OR	11,055	C
Purdue Univ/Calumet	IN	6,630	NC
Rutgers, The State Univ of New Jersey/Newark Campus	NJ	15,624	VC
San Francisco State Univ	CA	12,070	C
San Jose State Univ	CA	8,187	C
Southern Illinois Univ Carbondale	IL	10,407	C
SUNY at Oswego	NY	12,650	C

School	ST	$IS	SR
Texas A&M Univ	TX	11,081	HC
Texas State Univ	TX	9,320	VC
Texas Tech Univ	TX	10,768	VC
Univ of Akron	OH	13,134	NC
Univ of Arkansas	AR	9,855	VC
Univ of Calif at Davis	CA	14,995	VC
Univ of Calif at Santa Barbara	CA	11,732	VC
Univ of Florida	FL	8,580	MC
Univ of Georgia	GA	8,656	VC
Univ of Hawaii at Manoa	HI	9,565	VC
Univ of Idaho	ID	8,216	C
Univ of Kentucky	KY	7,765	C
Univ of Maine	ME	12,080	C+
Univ of Maryland/College Park	MD	14,227	HC
Univ of Mich/Ann Arbor	MI	13,864	HC+
Univ of Montana	MT	9,395	C
Univ of New Hampshire	NH	14,828	VC
Univ of Okla	OK	9,226	VC
Univ of Rhode Island	RI	13,720	VC
Univ of Texas at Austin	TX	10,630	HC
Univ of Vermont	VT	16,316	VC
Univ of Washington	WA	10,361	VC
Univ of Wisc/Madison	WI	8,262	VC
Univ of Wisc/Milwaukee	WI	9,427	LC
Univ of Wyoming	WY	8,636	C
Washington State Univ	WA	11,334	C
Weber State Univ	UT	7,945	NC
Western New Mexico Univ	NM	5,950	LC

A CLOSE LOOK AT

THE COLLEGES

This section will help you understand the college Profiles that are at the heart of this directory, so you can get the most out of them.

The College Admissions Selector explains Barron's unique system of comparing every school's degree of admissions competitiveness. Colleges are rated from Most Competitive to Less Competitive, and more.

Explanations of the ratings are followed by an in-depth look at the college capsule and essay.

Next comes the Profiles—some 1600 four-year accredited colleges and universities in the United States—followed by encapsulated descriptions of about fifty religious schools. Universities outside the boundaries of this country are profiled here, too, including Canadian, European, and more.

COLLEGE ADMISSIONS SELECTOR

This index groups all the colleges listed in this book according to degree of admissions competitiveness. The *Selector* is not a rating of colleges by academic standards or quality of education; it is rather an attempt to describe, in general terms, the situation a prospective student will meet when applying for admission.

THE CRITERIA USED

The factors used in determining the category for each college were: median entrance examination scores for the 2003–2004 freshman class (the SAT I score used was derived by averaging the median verbal reasoning and the median mathematics reasoning scores; the ACT score used was the median composite score); percentages of 2003–2004 freshmen scoring 500 and above and 600 and above on both the verbal reasoning and mathematics reasoning sections of the SAT I; percentages of 2003–2004 freshmen scoring 21 and above and 27 and above on the ACT; percentage of 2003–2004 freshmen who ranked in the upper fifth and the upper two-fifths of their high school graduating classes; minimum class rank and grade point average required for admission (if any); and percentage of applicants to the 2003–2004 freshman class who were accepted. The *Selector* cannot and does not take into account all the other factors that each college considers when making admissions decisions. Colleges place varying degrees of emphasis on the factors that comprise each of these categories.

USING THE SELECTOR

To use the *Selector* effectively, the prospective student's records should be compared realistically with the freshmen enrolled by the colleges in each category, as shown by the SAT I or ACT scores, the quality of high school record emphasized by the colleges in each category, and the kinds of risks that the applicant wishes to take.

The student should also be aware of what importance a particular school places on various nonacademic factors; when available, this information is presented in the profile of the school. If a student has unusual qualifications that may compensate for exam scores or high school record, the student should examine admissions policies of the colleges in the next higher category than the one that encompasses his or her score and consider those colleges that give major consideration to factors other than exam scores and high school grades. The "safety" college should usually be chosen from the next lower category, where the student can be reasonably sure that his or her scores and high school record will fall above the median scores and records of the freshmen enrolled in the college.

The listing within each category is alphabetical and not in any qualitative order. State-supported institutions have been classified according to the requirements for state residents, but standards for admission of out-of-state students are usually higher. Colleges that are experimenting with the admission of students of higher potential but lower achievement may appear in a less competitive category because of this fact.

A WORD OF CAUTION

The *Selector* is intended primarily for preliminary screening, to eliminate the majority of colleges that are not suitable for a particular student. Be sure to examine the admissions policies spelled out in the *Admissions* section of each profile. And remember that many colleges have to reject *qualified* students; the *Selector* will tell you what your chances are, not which college will accept you.

MOST COMPETITIVE

Even superior students will encounter a great deal of competition for admission to the colleges in this category. In general, these colleges require high school rank in the top 10% to 20% and grade averages of A to B+. Median freshman test scores at these colleges are generally between 655 and 800 on the SAT I and 29 and above on the ACT. In addition, many of these colleges admit only a small percentage of those who apply—usually fewer than one third.

Amherst College, MA
Bates College, ME
Boston College, MA
Bowdoin College, ME
Brandeis University, MA
Brown University, RI
California Institute of Technology, CA
Carleton College, MN
Carnegie Mellon University, PA
Case Western Reserve University, OH
Claremont McKenna College, CA
Colby College, ME
Colgate University, NY
College of New Jersey, The, NJ
College of the Holy Cross, MA
College of William and Mary, VA
Columbia University/Barnard College, NY
Columbia University/Columbia College, NY
Columbia University/Fu Foundation School of Engineering and
    Applied Science, NY
Connecticut College, CT
Cooper Union for the Advancement of Science and Art, NY
Cornell University, NY
Dartmouth College, NH
Davidson College, NC
Duke University, NC
Emory University, GA
George Washington University, DC
Georgetown University, DC
Hamilton College, NY
Harvard University/Harvard College, MA

Harvey Mudd College, CA
Haverford College, PA
Johns Hopkins University, MD
Lafayette College, PA
Macalester College, MN
Massachusetts Institute of Technology, MA
Middlebury College, VT
New York University, NY
Northwestern University, IL
Oberlin College, OH
Pomona College, CA
Princeton University, NJ
Reed College, OR
Rice University, TX
Stanford University, CA
Swarthmore College, PA
Tufts University, MA
United States Coast Guard Academy, CT
United States Military Academy, NY
United States Naval Academy, MD
University of California at Berkeley, CA
University of California at Los Angeles, CA
University of Chicago, IL
University of Florida, FL
University of North Carolina at Chapel Hill, NC
University of Notre Dame, IN
University of Pennsylvania, PA
University of Richmond, VA
University of Southern California, CA
University of Virginia, VA
Vanderbilt University, TN

Vassar College, NY
Wake Forest University, NC
Washington and Lee University, VA
Washington University in St. Louis, MO
Webb Institute, NY

Wellesley College, MA
Wesleyan University, CT
Williams College, MA
Yale University, CT

HIGHLY COMPETITIVE

Colleges in this group generally look for students with grade averages of B+ to B and accept most of their students from the top 20% to 35% of the high school class. Median freshman test scores at these colleges generally range from 620 to 654 on the SAT I and 27 or 28 on the ACT. These schools generally accept between one third and one half of their applicants.

To provide for finer distinctions within this admissions category, a plus (+) symbol has been placed before some entries. These are colleges with median freshman scores of 645 or more on the SAT I or 28 or more on the ACT (depending on which test the college prefers), and colleges that accept fewer than one quarter of their applicants.

Agnes Scott College, GA
+Albert A. List College of Jewish Studies, NY
Austin College, TX
Babson College, MA
+Bard College, NY
Beloit College, WI
Bennington College, VT
+Boston University, MA
Brigham Young University, UT
+Bryn Mawr College, PA
+Bucknell University, PA
Centre College, KY
Clemson University, SC
College of Charleston, SC
College of Wooster, OH
Colorado College, CO
Colorado School of Mines, CO
Denison University, OH
DePauw University, IN
Dickinson College, PA
Emerson College, MA
Fairfield University, CT
Florida State University, FL
Fordham University, NY
+Franklin and Marshall College, PA
+Furman University, SC
+Georgia Institute of Technology, GA
Gettysburg College, PA
Gonzaga University, WA
Goucher College, MD
+Grinnell College, IA
Grove City College, PA
Hampshire College, MA
Hillsdale College, MI
Hobart and William Smith Colleges, NY
+Illinois Institute of Technology, IL
+Illinois Wesleyan University, IL
Ithaca College, NY
+Kalamazoo College, MI
+Kenyon College, OH
Kettering University, MI
Lawrence University, WI
+Lehigh University, PA
Loyola College in Maryland, MD
Mary Washington College, VA
Miami University, OH
+Mount Holyoke College, MA
Muhlenberg College, PA
+New College of Florida, FL
Northeastern University, MA
Occidental College, CA
Penn State University/University Park Campus, PA
Pitzer College, CA

Providence College, RI
+Rensselaer Polytechnic Institute, NY
+Rhodes College, TN
+Rose-Hulman Institute of Technology, IN
Rutgers, The State University of New Jersey/New
    Brunswick/Piscataway Campus
+Saint John's College, MD
Saint Olaf College, MN
Santa Clara University, CA
Sarah Lawrence College, NY
+Scripps College, CA
Simon's Rock College of Bard, MA
Skidmore College, NY
+Smith College, MA
Southern Methodist University, TX
Southwestern University, TX
State University of New York/College at Geneseo, NY
State University of New York/University at Albany, NY
State University of New York/University at Binghamton, NY
State University of New York/University at Stony Brook, NY
+Stevens Institute of Technology, NJ
Stonehill College, MA
Syracuse University, NY
Texas A&M University, TX
+Trinity College, CT
+Trinity University, TX
+Truman State University, MO
+Tulane University, LA
Union College, NY
+United States Air Force Academy, CO
+United States Merchant Marine Academy, NY
University of California at Irvine, CA
University of California at San Diego, CA
University of Delaware, DE
+University of Illinois at Urbana-Champaign, IL
University of Maryland/College Park, MD
University of Miami, FL
+University of Michigan/Ann Arbor, MI
University of Missouri/Rolla, MO
University of Pittsburgh at Pittsburgh, PA
University of Puget Sound, WA
University of Rochester, NY
University of San Diego, CA
University of Texas at Austin, TX
University of Texas at Dallas, TX
University of the South, TN
Villanova University, PA
Wheaton College, IL
Wheaton College, MA
+Whitman College, WA
Wofford College, SC
Worcester Polytechnic Institute, MA

VERY COMPETITIVE

The colleges in this category generally admit students whose averages are no less than B- and who rank in the top 35% to 50% of their graduating class. They generally report median freshman test scores in the 573 to 619 range on the SAT I and from 24 to 26 on the ACT. These schools generally accept between one half and three quarters of their applicants.

The plus (+) has been placed before colleges with median freshman scores of 610 or above on the SAT I or 26 or better on the ACT (depending on which test the college prefers), and colleges that accept fewer than one third of their applicants.

Abilene Christian University, TX
Adelphi University, NY
Albertson College of Idaho, ID
Albion College, MI
Allegheny College, PA
Alma College, MI
+American University, DC
Appalachian State University, NC
Asbury College, KY
Auburn University, AL
+Augustana College, IL
Augustana College, SD
Azusa Pacific University, CA
Baker University, KS
Baylor University, TX
Bellarmine University, KY
Belmont University, TN
Bentley College, MA
+Berea College, KY
Berry College, GA
Bethany College, WV
Bethel College, MN
Biola University, CA
+Birmingham-Southern College, AL
Bradley University, IL
+Brigham Young University/Hawaii, HI
Bryan College, TN
Bryant College, RI
+Butler University, IN
California Polytechnic State University, CA
Campbell University, NC
Carroll College, MT
Catholic University of America, DC
Cedarville University, OH
+Centenary College of Louisiana, LA
Chapman University, CA
+Christendom College, VA
Christian Brothers University, TN
Christopher Newport University, VA
+City University of New York/Baruch College, NY
Clark University, MA
Clarkson University, NY
Coe College, IA
College of Saint Benedict, MN
College of Saint Catherine, MN
+College of the Atlantic, ME
+College of the Ozarks, MO
Colorado Christian University, CO
Colorado State University, CO
Concordia College, NY
+Concordia College: Moorhead, MN
Converse College, SC
+Cornell College, IA
+Covenant College, GA
+Creighton University, NE
Dallas Baptist University, TX
David Lipscomb University, TN
DePaul University, IL
Dillard University, LA
Dordt College, IA
+Drake University, IA
Drew University/College of Liberal Arts, NJ
Drexel University, PA
+Drury University, MO
Duquesne University, PA
+Earlham College, IN
Elmira College, NY

Elon University, NC
Erskine College, SC
+Flagler College, FL
Florida Institute of Technology, FL
Florida International University, FL
Franciscan University of Steubenville, OH
George Fox University, OR
George Mason University, VA
Georgetown College, KY
+Gordon College, MA
Goshen College, IN
Grace College, IN
Grand Valley State University, MI
Guilford College, NC
+Gustavus Adolphus College, MN
Hamline University, MN
Hampden-Sydney College, VA
Hanover College, IN
Harding University, AR
Hastings College, NE
+Hendrix College, AR
Hiram College, OH
Hofstra University, NY
Hollins University, VA
Hood College, MD
Hope College, MI
Houghton College, NY
Huntingdon College, AL
Illinois College, IL
Indiana University Bloomington, IN
Iona College, NY
Iowa State University, IA
James Madison University, VA
John Brown University, AR
Juniata College, PA
Kansas State University, KS
Kansas Wesleyan University, KS
King College, TN
+Knox College, IL
La Salle University, PA
Lake Forest College, IL
Le Moyne College, NY
Lebanon Valley College, PA
Lewis and Clark College, OR
Lindenwood University, MO
Linfield College, OR
Louisiana State University and Agricultural and Mechanical
    College, LA
Loyola Marymount University, CA
Loyola University Chicago, IL
+Loyola University New Orleans, LA
Luther College, IA
Lyon College, AR
Madonna University, MI
Maharishi University of Management, IA
Manhattan College, NY
Marist College, NY
+Marlboro College, VT
Marquette University, WI
Maryville College, TN
Maryville University of Saint Louis, MO
Master's College and Seminary, The, CA
McDaniel College, MD
McKendree College, IL
+Mercer University, GA
+Messiah College, PA
Michigan State University, MI

Michigan Technological University, MI
Mills College, CA
Millsaps College, MS
+Milwaukee School of Engineering, WI
Moravian College, PA
Mount Saint Mary's College, CA
Murray State University, KY
Nazareth College of Rochester, NY
New Jersey Institute of Technology, NJ
New York Institute of Technology, NY
North Carolina State University, NC
North Central College, IL
Northwest Nazarene University, ID
Oglethorpe University, GA
Ohio Northern University, OH
+Ohio State University, OH
+Ohio Wesleyan University, OH
Oklahoma Baptist University, OK
Oklahoma City University, OK
Oklahoma State University, OK
Ouachita Baptist University, AR
Pace University, NY
Pacific Lutheran University, WA
Pepperdine University, CA
Point Loma Nazarene University, CA
Polytechnic University/Brooklyn, NY
Presbyterian College, SC
Purdue University/West Lafayette, IN
Quinnipiac University, CT
Ramapo College of New Jersey, NJ
+Randolph-Macon Woman's College, VA
Richard Stockton College of New Jersey, NJ
Ripon College, WI
+Rochester Institute of Technology, NY
Rockford College, IL
Rollins College, FL
Roosevelt University, IL
Rowan University, NJ
Rutgers, The State University of New Jersey/Camden Campus, NJ
Rutgers, The State University of New Jersey/Newark Campus, NJ
+Saint John's College, NM
Saint John's University, MN
Saint Joseph's University, PA
Saint Lawrence University, NY
+Saint Louis University, MO
Saint Mary's College, IN
Saint Mary's College of California, CA
+Saint Mary's College of Maryland, MD
Saint Michael's College, VT
Saint Vincent College, PA
Salem College, NC
Salisbury University, MD
Samford University, AL
Seattle Pacific University, WA
Seattle University, WA
Seton Hall University, NJ
Siena College, NY
Simmons College, MA
Southern Polytechnic State University, GA
Southwest Minnesota State University, MN
Spring Hill College, AL
State University of New York/College at Fredonia, NY
State University of New York/College at Oneonta, NY
State University of New York/College at Purchase, NY
State University of New York/College of Environmental Science and Forestry, NY
State University of New York/University at Buffalo, NY
State University of New York/University at New Paltz, NY
Stetson University, FL
Susquehanna University, PA
+Taylor University, IN
Tennessee Technological University, TN
Texas Christian University, TX
Texas State University, TX
Texas Tech University, TX

+Thomas Aquinas College, CA
Touro College, NY
Towson University, MD
+Transylvania University, KY
Trinity Christian College, IL
Union University, TN
University of Alabama in Huntsville, AL
University of Arizona, AZ
University of Arkansas, AR
University of California at Davis, CA
University of California at Santa Barbara, CA
University of California at Santa Cruz, CA
University of Central Florida, FL
University of Colorado at Boulder, CO
University of Connecticut, CT
+University of Dallas, TX
University of Dayton, OH
University of Denver, CO
University of Evansville, IN
University of Georgia, GA
University of Hawaii at Manoa, HI
University of Indianapolis, IN
University of Iowa, IA
University of Kansas, KS
University of Louisville, KY
+University of Maryland/Baltimore County, MD
University of Massachusetts Lowell, MA
University of Michigan/Dearborn, MI
University of Minnesota/Morris, MN
University of Minnesota/Twin Cities, MN
University of Missouri/Columbia, MO
University of Missouri/Kansas City, MO
University of Missouri/St. Louis, MO
University of New Hampshire, NH
University of North Carolina at Asheville, NC
University of North Carolina at Wilmington, NC
University of North Florida, FL
University of Oklahoma, OK
University of Oregon, OR
University of Portland, OR
University of Redlands, CA
University of Rhode Island, RI
University of Saint Thomas, MN
University of Saint Thomas, TX
University of San Francisco, CA
University of Scranton, PA
University of South Carolina at Columbia, SC
University of Tampa, FL
University of the Pacific, CA
University of the Sciences in Philadelphia, PA
+University of Tulsa, OK
University of Vermont, VT
University of Washington, WA
University of Wisconsin/Eau Claire, WI
University of Wisconsin/La Crosse, WI
University of Wisconsin/Madison, WI
University of Wisconsin/Stevens Point, WI
Ursinus College, PA
+Valparaiso University, IN
Wabash College, IN
Wagner College, NY
Warren Wilson College, NC
Wartburg College, IA
Washington and Jefferson College, PA
Washington College, MD
Webster University, MO
Wells College, NY
Wesleyan College, GA
Western Washington University, WA
+Westmont College, CA
+Whitworth College, WA
+Willamette University, OR
William Jewell College, MO
Wisconsin Lutheran College, WI
Wittenberg University, OH
+Xavier University, OH
York College of Pennsylvania, PA

COMPETITIVE

This category is a very broad one, covering colleges that generally have median freshman test scores between 500 and 572 on the SAT I and between 21 and 23 on the ACT. Some of these colleges require that students have high school averages of B- or better, although others state a minimum of C+ or C. Generally, these colleges prefer students in the top 50% to 65% of the graduating class and accept between 75% and 85% of their applicants.

Colleges with a plus (+) are those with median freshman SAT I scores of 563 or more or median freshman ACT scores of 24 or more (depending on which test the colleges prefers), and those that admit fewer than half of their applicants.

Adams State College, CO
Adrian College, MI
Alabama State University, AL
Alaska Pacific University, AK
+Albany State University, GA
Albright College, PA
Alcorn State University, MS
Alderson-Broaddus College, WV
Alfred University, NY
Alice Lloyd College, KY
Alliant International University, CA
Alverno College, WI
Andrews University, MI
Antioch College, OH
Aquinas College, MI
Arcadia University, PA
Arizona State University-Main, AZ
Arkansas State University, AR
Arkansas Tech University, AR
Armstrong Atlantic State University, GA
Ashland University, OH
Assumption College, MA
Atlantic Union College, MA
Augsburg College, MN
Augusta State University, GA
Aurora University, IL
Avila University, MO
Baldwin-Wallace College, OH
Ball State University, IN
Barton College, NC
Bay Path College, MA
+Belhaven College, MS
Belmont Abbey College, NC
Bemidji State University, MN
Benedictine College, KS
Benedictine University, IL
Bennett College, NC
Bethel College, IN
+Bethel College, KS
Bethel College, TN
Blackburn College, IL
Bloomsburg University of Pennsylvania, PA
Blue Mountain College, MS
Bluefield College, VA
Bluffton College, OH
Boricua College, NY
+Bowie State University, MD
Bowling Green State University, OH
Brenau University Women's College, GA
Brescia University, KY
Briar Cliff University, IA
Bridgewater College, VA
Bridgewater State College, MA
Buena Vista University, IA
Cabrini College, PA
California Baptist University, CA
California Maritime Academy, CA
+California State Polytechnic University, Pomona, CA
California State University, Fullerton, CA
+California State University, Long Beach, CA
California State University, Los Angeles, CA
California State University, Sacramento, CA
California State University, Stanislaus, CA
California University of Pennsylvania, PA
Campbellsville University, KY
+Canisius College, NY
Capital University, OH
Capitol College, MD
Cardinal Stritch University, WI
Carlos Albizu University, FL

Carlow College, PA
Carroll College, WI
Carson-Newman College, TN
Carthage College, WI
Castleton State College, VT
Catawba College, NC
Cazenovia College, NY
+Cedar Crest College, PA
Central College, IA
Central Connecticut State University, CT
Central Methodist College, MO
Central Michigan University, MI
Central Missouri State University, MO
+Central State University, OH
Central Washington University, WA
Champlain College, VT
Charleston Southern University, SC
+Chatham College, PA
Cheyney University of Pennsylvania, PA
+Chicago State University, IL
Christian Heritage College, CA
+Citadel, The, SC
+City University of New York/Brooklyn College, NY
+City University of New York/City College, NY
+City University of New York/Hunter College, NY
City University of New York/John Jay College of Criminal
    Justice, NY
City University of New York/Queens College, NY
+Claflin University, SC
+Clark Atlanta University, GA
Clarke College, IA
Clarkson College, NE
Coastal Carolina University, SC
Coker College, SC
College Misericordia, PA
College of Mount Saint Vincent, NY
College of Mount St. Joseph, OH
College of New Rochelle, NY
College of Notre Dame of Maryland, MD
College of Our Lady of the Elms, MA
College of Saint Elizabeth, NJ
College of Saint Joseph, VT
College of Saint Mary, NE
College of Saint Rose, NY
+College of Saint Scholastica, MN
+College of Santa Fe, NM
+College of the Southwest, NM
Columbia College, MO
Columbia Union College, MD
Columbia University/School of General Studies, NY
Columbus State University, GA
Concord College, WV
Concordia University, CA
Concordia University, MI
Concordia University, OR
+Concordia University Nebraska, NE
Concordia University Wisconsin, WI
Concordia University, River Forest, IL
Concordia University/St.Paul, MN
Cornerstone University and Grand Rapids Theological
    Seminary, MI
Crichton College, TN
Culver-Stockton College, MO
Cumberland College, KY
Cumberland University, TN
Daemen College, NY
Dakota State University, SD
Dakota Wesleyan University, SD
Dana College, NE
Daniel Webster College, NH

David N. Myers College, OH
Davis and Elkins College, WV
De Sales University, PA
Defiance College, OH
Delaware Valley College, PA
Delta State University, MS
DeVry University/Crystal City, VA
Doane College, NE
Dominican University, IL
Dominican University of California, CA
D'Youville College, NY
East Carolina University, NC
East Central University, OK
East Stroudsburg University of Pennsylvania, PA
East Tennessee State University, TN
East Texas Baptist University, TX
Eastern Connecticut State University, CT
Eastern Illinois University, IL
Eastern Kentucky University, KY
Eastern Mennonite University, VA
Eastern Michigan University, MI
Eastern University, PA
Eastern Washington University, WA
+Eckerd College, FL
Edgewood College, WI
Elizabethtown College, PA
Elmhurst College, IL
+Embry-Riddle Aeronautical University, AZ
+Embry-Riddle Aeronautical University, FL
+Emmanuel College, MA
Emory & Henry College, VA
Emporia State University, KS
+Endicott College, MA
Eugene Lang College/New School University, NY
Evangel University, MO
+Evergreen State College, WA
Fairleigh Dickinson University/College at Florham, NJ
Fairleigh Dickinson University/Metropolitan Campus, NJ
Farmingdale State University of New York, NY
+Fashion Institute of Technology/State University of New York, NY
Faulkner University, AL
Felician College, NJ
Ferris State University, MI
Fisher College, MA
Fitchburg State College, MA
Florida Agricultural and Mechanical University, FL
Florida Atlantic University, FL
Florida Gulf Coast University, FL
Florida Southern College, FL
Fontbonne University, MO
Fort Hays State University, KS
Fort Lewis College, CO
Fort Valley State University, GA
Framingham State College, MA
Francis Marion University, SC
Franciscan University, IA
Franklin College, IN
Fresno Pacific University, CA
Friends World Program, NY
Frostburg State University, MD
Gannon University, PA
Gardner-Webb University, NC
Geneva College, PA
Georgia College and State University, GA
Georgia Southern University, GA
Georgia Southwestern State University, GA
Georgia State University, GA
Globe Institute of Technology, NY
+Goddard College, VT
Goldey-Beacom College, DE
Grace Bible College, MI
Graceland University, IA
Green Mountain College, VT
Greensboro College, NC
Greenville College, IL
Gwynedd-Mercy College, PA
+Hampton University, VA
Hannibal-LaGrange College, MO
Hardin-Simmons University, TX
+Hartwick College, NY
Hawaii Pacific University, HI
Hellenic College/Holy Cross Greek Orthodox School of
     Theology, MA

Henderson State University, AR
High Point University, NC
Houston Baptist University, TX
Howard Payne University, TX
Howard University, DC
Humboldt State University, CA
Huntington College, IN
Huron University, SD
Idaho State University, ID
+Illinois State University, IL
Immaculata University, PA
Indiana Institute of Technology, IN
Indiana University of Pennsylvania, PA
+Indiana Wesleyan University, IN
Iowa Wesleyan College, IA
Jackson State University, MS
Jacksonville University, FL
+John Carroll University, OH
Johnson C. Smith University, NC
Judson College, AL
Kean University, NJ
Keene State College, NH
Kennesaw State University, GA
Kent State University, OH
Kentucky Christian College, KY
Kentucky Wesleyan College, KY
Keuka College, NY
King's College, PA
Kutztown University of Pennsylvania, PA
La Roche College, PA
LaGrange College, GA
Lake Erie College, OH
Lakeland College, WI
Lambuth University, TN
Lander University, SC
+Lane College, TN
Lasell College, MA
Lawrence Technological University, MI
Lenoir-Rhyne College, NC
Lesley University, MA
LeTourneau University, TX
+Lewis University, IL
Lewis-Clark State College, ID
Liberty University, VA
Limestone College, SC
+Lincoln University, PA
Long Island University/Brooklyn Campus, NY
Long Island University/C.W. Post Campus, NY
+Long Island University/Southampton College, NY
Longwood University, VA
Loras College, IA
Louisiana College, LA
Louisiana Tech University, LA
Lubbock Christian University, TX
+Lycoming College, PA
Lynchburg College, VA
Lynn University, FL
Maine Maritime Academy, ME
Malone College, OH
Manchester College, IN
+Manhattanville College, NY
Mansfield University, PA
Marian College, IN
Marian College of Fond du Lac, WI
Marietta College, OH
Marshall University, WV
Mary Baldwin College, VA
Marygrove College, MI
Marymount College of Fordham University, NY
Marymount Manhattan College, NY
Marymount University, VA
Marywood University, PA
Massachusetts Maritime Academy, MA
McPherson College, KS
Medaille College, NY
Mercyhurst College, PA
Meredith College, NC
Merrimack College, MA
Mesa State College, CO
Methodist College, NC
Metropolitan College of New York, NY
MidAmerica Nazarene University, KS
Middle Tennessee State University, TN

Midland Lutheran College, NE
Midway College, KY
Millersville University of Pennsylvania, PA
+Milligan College, TN
Millikin University, IL
Mississippi College, MS
Mississippi State University, MS
Missouri Baptist University, MO
Missouri Southern State University, MO
Missouri Valley College, MO
Mitchell College, CT
Molloy College, NY
Monmouth College, IL
Monmouth University, NJ
Montana State University-Billings, MT
Montana State University-Bozeman, MT
Montclair State University, NJ
Montreat College, NC
Morehead State University, KY
Morehouse College, GA
Morgan State University, MD
Morningside College, IA
Mount Mary College, WI
Mount Mercy College, IA
Mount Saint Mary College, NY
Mount Saint Mary's College, MD
Mount Union College, OH
Mount Vernon Nazarene University, OH
Muskingum College, OH
+Nebraska Wesleyan University, NE
New Mexico State University, NM
Newbury College, MA
Newman University, KS
Niagara University, NY
North Carolina Wesleyan College, NC
North Central University, MN
North Dakota State University, ND
North Georgia College and State University, GA
North Park University, IL
Northern Arizona University, AZ
Northern Illinois University, IL
Northern Michigan University, MI
+Northland College, WI
Northwest Christian College, OR
Northwest College, WA
Northwest Missouri State University, MO
+Northwestern College, MN
+Northwestern College of Iowa, IA
Northwood University, FL
Notre Dame College, OH
Nova Southeastern University, FL
Nyack College, NY
Oakland University, MI
Oakwood College, AL
Ohio Dominican University, OH
Ohio University, OH
+Ohio Valley College, WV
Oklahoma Panhandle State University, OK
Old Dominion University, VA
+Olivet College, MI
Olivet Nazarene University, IL
Oral Roberts University, OK
Oregon Institute of Technology, OR
Oregon State University, OR
Otterbein College, OH
Our Lady of Holy Cross College, LA
Our Lady of the Lake University of San Antonio, TX
+Pacific Union College, CA
Pacific University, OR
Palm Beach Atlantic University, FL
+Park University, MO
Penn State University at Erie/Behrend College, PA
Penn State University/Altoona, PA
Pfeiffer University, NC
Philadelphia Biblical University, PA
Philadelphia University, PA
Piedmont College, GA
Point Park University, PA
Portland State University, OR
Prescott College, AZ
+Principia College, IL
Queens University of Charlotte, NC
Quincy University, IL

Radford University, VA
Randolph-Macon College, VA
Regis College, MA
+Regis University, CO
Reinhardt College, GA
Rhode Island College, RI
Rider University, NJ
Rivier College, NH
Roanoke College, VA
Robert Morris University, PA
+Roberts Wesleyan College, NY
Rochester College, MI
+Rockhurst University, MO
Rocky Mountain College, MT
Roger Williams University, RI
Rosemont College, PA
Russell Sage College, NY
+Rust College, MS
Sacred Heart University, CT
Saginaw Valley State University, MI
Saint Ambrose University, IA
Saint Andrews Presbyterian College, NC
Saint Anselm College, NH
Saint Cloud State University, MN
Saint Edward's University, TX
Saint John Fisher College, NY
Saint John's University, NY
Saint Joseph College, CT
Saint Joseph's College, IN
Saint Joseph's College of Maine, ME
Saint Joseph's College, New York, Brooklyn Campus
Saint Joseph's College, New York, Suffolk Campus
Saint Leo University, FL
Saint Martin's College, WA
Saint Mary-of-the-Woods College, IN
Saint Mary's University of Minnesota, MN
Saint Mary's University of San Antonio, TX
Saint Norbert College, WI
Saint Xavier University, IL
Salem International University, WV
Salem State College, MA
Salve Regina University, RI
Sam Houston State University, TX
San Diego State University, CA
San Francisco State University, CA
San Jose State University, CA
Schreiner University, TX
Seton Hill University, PA
+Shaw University, NC
Shepherd College, WV
Shippensburg University of Pennsylvania, PA
Shorter College, GA
Sierra Nevada College, NV
Simpson College, CA
+Simpson College, IA
Sonoma State University, CA
+South Dakota School of Mines and Technology, SD
South Dakota State University, SD
Southeast Missouri State University, MO
Southeastern Oklahoma State University, OK
Southern Adventist University, TN
Southern Arkansas University, AR
Southern Connecticut State University, CT
Southern Illinois University Carbondale, IL
Southern Illinois University Edwardsville, IL
Southern New Hampshire University, NH
Southern Oregon University, OR
Southern Utah University, UT
Southern Wesleyan University, SC
Southwest Baptist University, MO
Southwest Missouri State University, MO
Southwestern Adventist University, TX
Southwestern College, KS
Southwestern Oklahoma State University, OK
Spalding University, KY
+Spelman College, GA
Spring Arbor University, MI
Springfield College, MA
State University of New York at Oswego, NY
State University of New York at Potsdam, NY
State University of New York/College at Brockport, NY
State University of New York/College at Buffalo, NY
State University of New York/College at Cortland, NY

State University of New York/College at Old Westbury, NY
State University of New York/College at Plattsburgh, NY
+State University of New York/College of Agriculture and
   Technology at Cobleskill, NY
State University of New York/College of Technology at Alfred, NY
State University of West Georgia, GA
Stephen F. Austin State University, TX
+Stephens College, MO
Sterling College, KS
+Sterling College, VT
Suffolk University, MA
Sweet Briar College, VA
Tarleton State University, TX
Teikyo Post University, CT
Temple University, PA
Tennessee Wesleyan College, TN
Texas A&M University at Commerce, TX
Texas A&M University at Corpus Christi, TX
+Texas A&M University at Galveston, TX
Texas Lutheran University, TX
Texas Wesleyan University, TX
Thiel College, PA
Thomas More College, KY
Thomas More College of Liberal Arts, NH
Toccoa Falls College, GA
Trevecca Nazarene University, TN
+Trinity International University, IL
Tri-State University-Main Campus, IN
Troy State University, AL
Troy State University Dothan, AL
Tusculum College, TN
Union College, KY
Union College, NE
+University of Alabama, AL
University of Alabama at Birmingham, AL
University of Alaska Fairbanks, AK
University of Arkansas at Pine Bluff, AR
University of California at Riverside, CA
University of Central Arkansas, AR
University of Central Oklahoma, OK
University of Charleston, WV
University of Cincinnati, OH
University of Colorado at Colorado Springs, CO
University of Colorado at Denver, CO
University of Detroit Mercy, MI
University of Dubuque, IA
University of Great Falls, MT
University of Hartford, CT
University of Hawaii at Hilo, HI
University of Houston, TX
University of Idaho, ID
University of Illinois at Chicago, IL
University of Judaism College of Arts and Sciences, CA
University of Kentucky, KY
University of La Verne, CA
University of Louisiana at Lafayette, LA
+University of Maine, ME
University of Maine at Augusta, ME
University of Maine at Farmington, ME
+University of Mary, ND
University of Mary Hardin-Baylor, TX
University of Maryland/Eastern Shore, MD
+University of Massachusetts Amherst, MA
University of Massachusetts Boston, MA
University of Massachusetts Dartmouth, MA
University of Memphis, TN
University of Michigan/Flint, MI
University of Minnesota/Duluth, MN
University of Mississippi, MS
University of Mobile, AL
University of Montana, MT
University of Montevallo, AL
+University of Nebraska at Lincoln, NE
University of Nebraska at Omaha, NE
University of Nevada/Las Vegas, NV
University of Nevada/Reno, NV
University of New Haven, CT
University of New Mexico, NM
University of New Orleans, LA
University of North Carolina at Charlotte, NC
University of North Carolina at Greensboro, NC
University of North Dakota, ND
University of North Texas, TX
University of Northern Colorado, CO

University of Northern Iowa, IA
University of Pittsburgh at Bradford, PA
University of Pittsburgh at Greensburg, PA
University of Saint Francis, IL
University of Saint Francis, IN
University of Saint Mary, KS
University of Science and Arts of Oklahoma, OK
University of Sioux Falls, SD
+University of South Carolina at Spartanburg, SC
+University of South Dakota, SD
University of South Florida, FL
University of Southern Maine, ME
University of Tennessee at Chattanooga, TN
University of Tennessee at Knoxville, TN
University of Tennessee at Martin, TN
University of the Ozarks, AR
University of Utah, UT
University of Virginia's College at Wise, VA
University of West Alabama, AL
University of West Florida, FL
University of Wisconsin/Green Bay, WI
University of Wisconsin/Platteville, WI
University of Wisconsin/Stout, WI
+University of Wisconsin/Superior, WI
University of Wisconsin/Whitewater, WI
University of Wyoming, WY
Upper Iowa University, IA
Urbana University, OH
Utah State University, UT
Utica College, NY
Valdosta State University, GA
Vanguard University of Southern California, CA
Vermont Technical College, VT
Villa Julie College, MD
Virginia Commonwealth University, VA
Virginia Intermont College, VA
+Virginia Military Institute, VA
Virginia Polytechnic Institute and State University, VA
Virginia State University, VA
Virginia Wesleyan College, VA
Viterbo University, WI
Walsh University, OH
Warner Pacific College, OR
Washington State University, WA
Wayne State University, MI
Waynesburg College, PA
Webber International University, FL
Wentworth Institute of Technology, MA
Wesley College, DE
West Chester University of Pennsylvania, PA
West Texas A&M University, TX
West Virginia University, WV
West Virginia Wesleyan College, WV
Western Baptist College, OR
Western Carolina University, NC
Western Connecticut State University, CT
Western Illinois University, IL
Western Kentucky University, KY
Western Michigan University, MI
Western New England College, MA
Western Oregon University, OR
Western State College of Colorado, CO
Westfield State College, MA
+Westminster College, MO
Westminster College, PA
Westminster College, UT
Wheeling Jesuit University, WV
Wheelock College, MA
Whittier College, CA
Wichita State University, KS
Widener University, PA
Wilkes University, PA
William Paterson University of New Jersey, NJ
William Woods University, MO
Williams Baptist College, AR
Wilson College, PA
Wingate University, NC
Winona State University, MN
Winthrop University, SC
Worcester State College, MA
Xavier University of Louisiana, LA
Yeshiva University, NY
York College, NE

LESS COMPETITIVE

Included in this category are colleges with median freshman test scores generally below 500 on the SAT I and below 21 on the ACT; some colleges that require entrance examinations but do not report median scores; and colleges that admit students with averages generally below C who rank in the top 65% of the graduating class. These colleges usually admit 85% or more of their applicants.

Alabama Agricultural and Mechanical University, AL
Albertus Magnus College, CT
Alvernia College, PA
American Indian College of the Assemblies of God, AZ
American International College, MA
Anderson University, IN
Anna Maria College, MA
Aquinas College, TN
Austin Peay State University, TN
Averett University, VA
Barber-Scotia College, NC
Barry University, FL
Beacon College, FL
Becker College, MA
Benedict College, SC
Berkeley College, NY
Berkeley College of New York City, NY
Bethany College, KS
Bethune-Cookman College, FL
Black Hills State University, SD
Bloomfield College, NJ
Bluefield State College, WV
Boise State University, ID
Brewton-Parker College, GA
Caldwell College, NJ
California Lutheran University, CA
California State University, Bakersfield, CA
California State University, Chico, CA
California State University, Dominguez Hills, CA
California State University, Fresno, CA
California State University, Hayward, CA
California State University, Monterey Bay, CA
California State University, Northridge, CA
California State University, San Bernardino, CA
California State University, San Marcos, CA
Calumet College of St. Joseph, IN
Centenary College, NJ
Chaminade University of Honolulu, HI
Chestnut Hill College, PA
City University of New York/Herbert H. Lehman College, NY
Clarion University of Pennsylvania, PA
Clayton College and State University, GA
Clearwater Christian College, FL
Cleary College, MI
Cleveland State University, OH
Cogswell Polytechnical College, CA
Colby-Sawyer College, NH
Colorado Technical University, CO
Columbia College, SC
Columbia College Chicago, IL
Concordia University at Austin, TX
Coppin State College, MD
Curry College, MA
Delaware State University, DE
DeVry College of Technology/North Brunswick, NJ
DeVry Institute of Technology/New York, NY
DeVry University/Addison (DuPage County), IL
DeVry University/Alpharetta, GA
DeVry University/Chicago, IL
DeVry University/Colorado Springs, CO
DeVry University/Columbus, OH
DeVry University/Dallas, TX
DeVry University/Decatur, GA
DeVry University/Fort Washington, PA
DeVry University/Fremont, CA
DeVry University/Kansas City, MO
DeVry University/Long Beach, CA
DeVry University/Miramar, FL
DeVry University/Orlando, FL
DeVry University/Phoenix, AZ
DeVry University/Pomona, CA

DeVry University/Seattle, WA
DeVry University/Tinley Park, IL
DeVry University/West Hills, CA
DeVry University/Westminster, CO
Dominican College, NY
Dowling College, NY
Eastern Nazarene College, MA
Eastern New Mexico University, NM
East-West University, IL
Edinboro University of Pennsylvania, PA
Edward Waters College, FL
Elizabeth City State University, NC
Eureka College, IL
Fairmont State, WV
Fayetteville State University, NC
Ferrum College, VA
Fisk University, TN
Florida Memorial College, FL
Franklin Pierce College, NH
Friends University, KS
Georgian Court College, NJ
Grand Canyon University, AZ
Grand View College, IA
Hesser College, NH
Hilbert College, NY
Holy Family College, PA
Husson College, ME
Indiana State University, IN
Indiana University East, IN
Indiana University Kokomo, IN
Indiana University Northwest, IN
Indiana University South Bend, IN
Indiana University Southeast, IN
Indiana University-Purdue University Fort Wayne, IN
Indiana University-Purdue University Indianapolis, IN
International College, FL
Jacksonville State University, AL
Johnson and Wales University, RI
Johnson State College, VT
Judson College, IL
Keystone College, PA
Knoxville College, TN
La Sierra University, CA
Lake Superior State University, MI
Lamar University, TX
Langston University, OK
Lees-McRae College, NC
LeMoyne-Owen College, TN
Lincoln Memorial University, TN
Lindsey Wilson College, KY
Livingstone College, NC
Lock Haven University of Pennsylvania, PA
Lourdes College, OH
Lyndon State College, VT
MacMurray College, IL
Mars Hill College, NC
Massachusetts College of Liberal Arts, MA
McMurry University, TX
McNeese State University, LA
Menlo College, CA
Metropolitan State College of Denver, CO
Midwestern State University, TX
Minnesota State University, Mankato, MN
Minnesota State University, Moorhead, MN
Minot State University, ND
Mississippi University for Women, MS
Monroe College, NY
Morris College, SC
Mount Aloysius College, PA
Mount Ida College, MA
Mount Marty College, SD

Mount Olive College, NC
National-Louis University, IL
Neumann College, PA
New England College, NH
New Jersey City University, NJ
New Mexico Highlands University, NM
Newberry College, SC
Nichols College, MA
Norfolk State University, VA
North Carolina Agricultural and Technical State University, NC
North Carolina Central University, NC
Northeastern State University, OK
Northern State University, SD
Northwood University, MI
Northwood University, TX
Norwich University, VT
Notre Dame de Namur University, CA
Oklahoma Wesleyan University, OK
Ottawa University, KS
Paine College, GA
Paul Quinn College, TX
Pine Manor College, MA
Plymouth State University, NH
Presentation College, SD
Saint Augustine's College, NC
Saint Bonaventure University, NY
Saint Francis College, NY
Saint Francis University, PA
Saint Mary's College, MI
Saint Peter's College, NJ
Saint Thomas Aquinas College, NY
Saint Thomas University, FL
Savannah State University, GA
Sheldon Jackson College, AK
Shimer College, IL
Siena Heights University, MI
Silver Lake College of the Holy Family, WI
Slippery Rock University of Pennsylvania, PA
Sojourner-Douglass College, MD
South Carolina State University, SC
South College, GA
Southeastern College, FL
Southeastern Louisiana University, LA
Southeastern University, DC
Southern Christian University, AL
Southern University and A&M College, LA
Southern Vermont College, VT
State University of New York/Maritime College, NY

Stillman College, AL
Sul Ross State University, TX
Talladega College, AL
Tennessee State University, TN
Texas A&M University at Kingsville, TX
Texas Woman's University, TX
Thomas College, ME
Tiffin University, OH
Trinity College, DC
Tuskegee University, AL
Unity College, ME
University of Alaska Southeast, AK
University of Bridgeport, CT
University of Maine at Fort Kent, ME
University of Maine at Machias, ME
University of Maine at Presque Isle, ME
University of New England, ME
University of North Carolina at Pembroke, NC
University of Pittsburgh at Johnstown, PA
University of South Alabama, AL
University of South Carolina at Aiken, SC
University of Southern Colorado, CO
University of Southern Indiana, IN
University of Southern Mississippi, MS
University of Texas at Arlington, TX
University of Texas-Pan American, TX
University of the District of Columbia, DC
University of the Incarnate Word, TX
University of Wisconsin/Milwaukee, WI
University of Wisconsin/Oshkosh, WI
University of Wisconsin/Parkside, WI
University of Wisconsin/River Falls, WI
Ursuline College, OH
Valley City State University, ND
Virginia Union University, VA
Voorhees College, SC
Warner Southern College, FL
West Liberty State College, WV
Western New Mexico University, NM
Wilberforce University, OH
Wiley College, TX
William Carey College, MS
William Penn University, IA
Wilmington College, OH
Winston-Salem State University, NC
Woodbury College, VT
Woodbury University, CA
Wright State University, OH

NONCOMPETITIVE

The colleges in this category generally only require evidence of graduation from an accredited high school (although they may also require completion of a certain number of high school units). Some require that entrance examinations be taken for placement purposes only, or only by graduates of unaccredited high schools or only by out-of-state students. In some cases, insufficient capacity may compel a college in this category to limit the number of students that are accepted; generally, however, if a college accepts 98% or more of its applicants, it automatically falls in this category. Colleges are also rated Noncompetitive if they admit all state residents, but have some requirements for nonresidents.

Allen University, SC
American InterContinental University, GA
Angelo State University, TX
Arkansas Baptist College, AR
Auburn University Montgomery, AL
Baker College of Flint, MI
Bellevue University, NE
Bryn Athyn College of the New Church, PA
Calvin College, MI
Cameron University, OK
Cascade College, OR
Chadron State College, NE
City University, WA
City University of New York/College of Staten Island, NY
City University of New York/Medgar Evers College, NY
City University of New York/New York City College of
    Technology, NY
City University of New York/York College, NY
Concordia College, AL
Davenport University, MI
Dickinson State University, ND
Eastern Oregon University, OR
Freed-Hardeman University, TN
Glenville State College, WV
Golden Gate University, CA
Grambling State University, LA
Heidelberg College, OH
Heritage College, WA
Holy Names College, CA
Hope International University, CA
Humphreys College, CA
Huston-Tillotson College, TX
Jamestown College, ND
Jarvis Christian College, TX
Kendall College, IL
Kentucky State University, KY
Lee University, TN
Lincoln University, MO
Louisiana State University in Shreveport, LA
Marylhurst University, OR
Mayville State University, ND
Mercy College, NY
Miles College, AL
Mississippi Valley State University, MS
Missouri Western State College, MO
Montana State University-Northern, MT
Montana Tech of The University of Montana, MT
Mountain State University, WV
National American University, SD
New College of California, CA
New Mexico Institute of Mining and Technology, NM
Nicholls State University, LA
Northeastern Illinois University, IL
Northern Kentucky University, KY

Northwestern Oklahoma State University, OK
Northwestern State University of Louisiana, LA
Oakland City University, IN
Oglala Lakota College, SD
Ohio State University at Lima, OH
Ohio State University at Mansfield, OH
Ohio State University at Marion, OH
Ohio State University at Newark, OH
Oklahoma Christian University, OK
Peirce College, PA
Pennsylvania College of Technology, PA
Peru State College, NE
Philander Smith College, AR
Pikeville College, KY
Pittsburg State University, KS
Prairie View A&M University, TX
Purdue University/Calumet, IN
Saint Gregory's University, OK
Saint Paul's College, VA
Shawnee State University, OH
Shenandoah University, VA
Sinte Gleska University, SD
Southern Nazarene University, OK
Southern University at New Orleans, LA
Tabor College, KS
Texas Southern University, TX
Thomas University, GA
Tougaloo College, MS
Troy State University Montgomery, AL
University of Akron, OH
University of Alaska Anchorage, AK
University of Arkansas at Little Rock, AR
University of Arkansas at Monticello, AR
University of Findlay, OH
University of Houston-Downtown, TX
University of Louisiana at Monroe, LA
University of Minnesota/Crookston, MN
University of Montana—Western, MT
University of Nebraska at Kearney, NE
University of North Alabama, AL
University of Rio Grande, OH
University of Texas at El Paso, TX
University of Texas at San Antonio, TX
University of Toledo, OH
Walla Walla College, WA
Washburn University of Topeka, KS
Wayland Baptist University, TX
Wayne State College, NE
Weber State University, UT
West Virginia State College, WV
West Virginia University Institute of Technology, WV
William Tyndale College, MI
Wilmington College, DE
Youngstown State University, OH

SPECIAL

Listed here are colleges whose programs of study are specialized; professional schools of art, music, nursing, and other disciplines. In general, the admissions requirements are not based primarily on academic criteria, but on evidence of talent or special interest in the field. Many other colleges and universities offer special-interest programs *in addition* to regular academic curricula, but such institutions have been given a regular competitive rating based on academic criteria. Schools oriented toward working adults have also been assigned this rating.

Albany College of Pharmacy, NY
Allen College, IA
Art Academy of Cincinnati, OH
Art Center College of Design, CA
Art Institute of Atlanta, GA
Art Institute of Boston at Lesley University, MA
Art Institute of Portland, OR
Art Institute of Southern California, CA
Atlanta College of Art, GA
Baltimore Hebrew University, MD
Benjamin Franklin Institute of Technology, MA
Berklee College of Music, MA
Boston Architectural Center, MA
Boston Conservatory, MA
Burlington College, VT
Cabarrus College of Health Sciences, NC
California College of the Arts, CA
California Institute of the Arts, CA
Cambridge College, MA
Charter Oak State College, CT
Cincinnati College of Mortuary Science, OH
Cleveland Institute of Art, OH
Cleveland Institute of Music, OH
College for Creative Studies, MI
College for Lifelong Learning, NH
College of Aeronautics, NY
College of New Rochelle - School of New Resources, NY
College of Visual Arts, MN
Columbus College of Art and Design, OH
Corcoran School of Art and Design, DC
Cornish College of the Arts, WA
Curtis Institute of Music, PA
Deaconess College of Nursing, MO
Eastman School of Music, NY
Excelsior College, NY
Five Towns College, NY
Florida Hospital College of Health Sciences, FL
Franklin University, OH
Gallaudet University, DC
Harris-Stowe State College, MO
Henry Cogswell College, WA
Jewish Hospital College of Nursing and Allied Health, MO
Juilliard School, NY
Kansas City Art Institute, MO
Kendall College of Art and Design of Ferris State University, MI
Laboratory Institute of Merchandising, NY

Lester L. Cox College of Nursing and Health Sciences, MO
Maine College of Art, ME
Manhattan School of Music, NY
Mannes College of Music, NY
Martin University, IN
Maryland Institute College of Art, MD
Massachusetts College of Art, MA
Massachusetts College of Pharmacy and Health Sciences, MA
MCP Hahnemann University, PA
Memphis College of Art, TN
Mercy College of Health Sciences, IA
Metropolitan State University, MN
Milwaukee Institute of Art and Design, WI
Minneapolis College of Art and Design, MN
Montserrat College of Art, MA
Moore College of Art and Design, PA
NAES College, IL
Naropa University, CO
National University, CA
Nebraska Methodist College of Nursing and Allied Health, NE
New England Conservatory of Music, MA
North Carolina School of the Arts, NC
Otis College of Art and Design, CA
Pacific Northwest College of Art, OR
Parsons School of Design, NY
Pratt Institute, NY
Research College of Nursing, MO
Rhode Island School of Design, RI
Ringling School of Art and Design, FL
Samuel Merritt College, CA
San Francisco Art Institute, CA
San Francisco Conservatory of Music, CA
Savannah College of Art and Design, GA
School of the Art Institute of Chicago, IL
School of Visual Arts, NY
State University of New York/Empire State College, NY
Strayer University, DC
Thomas Edison State College, NJ
Trinity College of Nursing and Health Sciences, IL
Union Institute and University, OH
University of Maryland/University College, MD
University of the Arts, PA
VanderCook College of Music, IL
West Suburban College of Nursing, IL
Westminster Choir College of Rider University, NJ

THE BASICS

Some 1700 U.S. colleges and universities, public and private college systems, and Canadian and other foreign universities are described in detail in the Profiles that follow.

The Choice of Schools

Colleges and universities in this country may achieve recognition from a number of professional organizations, but we have based our choice of U.S. colleges on accreditation from the U.S. regional accrediting associations.

Accreditation amounts to a stamp of approval given to a college. The accreditation process evaluates institutions and programs to determine whether they meet established standards of educational quality. The regional associations listed below supervise an aspect of the accrediting procedure—the study of a detailed report submitted by the institution applying for accreditation, and then an inspection visit by members of the accrediting agency. The six agencies are associated with the Commission on Recognition of Postsecondary Accreditation (CORPA). They include:

Middle States Association of Colleges and Schools
New England Association of Schools and Colleges
North Central Association of Colleges and Schools
Northwest Commission on Colleges and Universities
Southern Association of Colleges and Schools
Western Association of Schools and Colleges

Getting accreditation for the first time can take a school several years. To acknowledge that schools have begun this process, the agencies accord them candidate status. Most candidates eventually are awarded full accreditation.

The U.S. schools included in this book are fully accredited or are candidates for that status. If the latter is the case, it is indicated below the address of the school. Because the U.S. regional accrediting bodies do not officially accredit Canadian colleges and universities, and because there is no equivalent accrediting system in Canada, we have chosen to include only the larger, English-language Canadian schools—those with total full-time undergraduate enrollment of more than 10,000. It should be understood that size in no way relates to quality; there are many excellent Canadian colleges and universities with fewer than 10,000 students.

Four-Year Colleges Only

This book presents Profiles for all accredited four-year colleges that grant bachelor's degrees and admit freshmen with no previous college experience. Most of these colleges also accept transfer students. Profiles of upper-division schools, which offer only the junior or senior year of undergraduate study, are not included, nor are junior or community colleges.

Consistent Entries

Each Profile of a U.S. college is organized in the same way; the only Profiles that vary are those of Canada, schools abroad, and religious schools. The following discussion applies to the U.S. college Profiles, but refers to the other Profiles as well.

Every Profile begins with a capsule and is followed by separate sections covering the campus environment, student life, programs of study, admissions, financial aid, information for international students, computers, graduates, and the admissions contact. These categories are always introduced in the same sequence, so you can find data and compare specific points easily. The following commentary will help you evaluate and interpret the information given for each college.

Data Collection

Barron's *Profiles of American Colleges* was first published in 1964. Since then, it has been revised almost every year; comprehensive revisions are undertaken every two years. Such frequent updating is necessary because so much information about colleges—particularly enrollment figures, costs, programs of study, and admissions standards—changes rapidly.

The facts in the capsule portion of each Profile in this edition were gathered in the fall of 2003 and apply to the 2003–2004 academic year. Figures on tuition and room-and-board costs generally change soon after the book is published. For the most up-to-date information on such items, you should always check with the colleges. Other information—such as the basic nature of the school, its campus, and the educational goals of its students—changes less rapidly. A few new programs of study might be added or new services made available, but the basic educational offerings generally will remain constant.

THE CAPSULE

The capsule of each Profile provides basic information about the college at a glance. An explanation of the standard capsule is shown in the accompanying box.

All toll-free phone numbers are presumed to be out-of-state or both in-state and out-of-state, unless noted.

A former name is given if the name has been changed recently. To use the map code to the right of the college name, turn to the appropriate college-locator map at the beginning of each chapter. Wherever "n/av" is used in the capsule, it means the information was not available. The abbreviation "n/app" means not applicable.

Full-time, Part-time, Graduate

Enrollment figures are the clearest indication of the size of a college, and show whether or not it is coeducational and what the

---

COMPLETE NAME OF SCHOOL
(Former Name, if any)
City, State, Zip Code
(Accreditation Status, if a candidate)

MAP CODE

Fax and Phone Numbers

Full-time: Full-time undergraduate enrollment
Part-time: Part-time undergraduate enrollment
Graduate: Graduate enrollment
Year: Semesters, quarters, summer sessions
Application Deadline: Fall admission deadline

Freshman Class: Number of students who applied, number accepted, number enrolled
SAT I: Median Verbal, Median Math

Faculty: Number of full-time faculty; AAUP category of school, salary-level symbol
Ph.D.s: Percentage of faculty holding Ph.D.
Student/Faculty: Full-time student/full-time faculty ratio
Tuition: Yearly tuition and fees (out-of-state if different)
Room & Board: Yearly room-and-board costs

ACT: Median composite ACT

ADMISSIONS SELECTOR RATING

male-female ratio is. Graduate enrollment is presented to give a better idea of the size of the entire student body; some schools have far more graduate students enrolled than undergraduates.

Year

Some of the more innovative college calendars include the 4-1-4, 3-2-3, 3-3-1, and 1-3-1-4-3 terms. College administrators sometimes utilize various intersessions or interims—special short terms—for projects, independent study, short courses, or travel programs. The early semester calendar, which allows students to finish spring semesters earlier than those of the traditional semester calendar, gives students a head start on finding summer jobs. A modified semester (4-1-4) system provides a January or winter term, approximately four weeks long, for special projects that usually earn the same credit as one semester-long course. The trimester calendar divides the year into three equal parts; students may attend college during all three but generally take a vacation during any one. The quarter calendar divides the year into four equal parts; students usually attend for three quarters each year. The capsule also indicates schools that offer a summer session.

Application Deadline

Indicated here is the deadline for applications for admission to the fall semester. If there are no specific deadlines, it will say "open." Application deadlines for admission to other semesters are, where available, given in the admissions section of the profile.

Faculty

The first number given refers to the number of full-time faculty members at the college or university.

The Roman numeral and symbol that follow represent the salary level of faculty at the school as compared with faculty salaries nationally. This information is based on the salary report* published by the American Association of University Professors (AAUP). The Roman numeral refers to the AAUP category to which the particular college or university is assigned. (This allows for comparison of faculty salaries at the same types of schools.) Category I includes "institutions that offer the doctorate degree, and that conferred in the most recent three years an annual average of fifteen or more earned doctorates covering a minimum of three nonrelated disciplines." Category IIA includes "institutions awarding degrees above the baccalaureate, but not included in Category I." Category IIB includes "institutions awarding only the baccalaureate or equivalent degree." Category III includes "institutions with academic ranks, mostly two-year institutions." Category IV includes "institutions without academic ranks." (With the exception of a few liberal arts colleges, this category includes mostly two-year institutions.)

The symbol that follows the Roman numeral indicates into which percentile range the average salary of professors, associate professors, assistant professors, and instructors at the school falls, as compared with other schools in the same AAUP category. The symbols used in this book represent the following:

++$	95th percentile
+$	80th percentile
av$	60th percentile
–$	40th percentile
––$	20th percentile and below

If the school is not a member of AAUP, nothing will appear.

Ph.D.s

The figure here indicates the percentage of full-time faculty who have Ph.D.s or the highest terminal degree.

*Source: Annual Report on the Economic Status of the Profession published in the March-April 2003 issue of Academe: Bulletin of the AAUP, 1012 Fourteenth St. N.W., Suite 500, Washington, D.C. 20005.

Student/Faculty

Student/faculty ratios may be deceptive because the faculties of many large universities include scholars and scientists who do little or no teaching. Nearly every college has some large lecture classes, usually in required or popular subjects, and many small classes in advanced or specialized fields. Here, the ratio reflects full-time students and full-time faculty, and some colleges utilize the services of a large part-time faculty. Additionally, some institutions factor in an FTE component in determining this ratio. We do not, and thus the Student/Faculty ratio that we report may differ somewhat from what the college reports. In general, a student/faculty ratio of 10 to 1 is very good.

If the faculty and student body are both mostly part-time, the entry will say "n/app."

Tuition

It is important to remember that tuition costs change continually and that in many cases, these changes are substantial. Particularly heavy increases have occurred recently and will continue to occur. On the other hand, some smaller colleges are being encouraged to lower tuitions, in order to make higher education more affordable. Students are therefore urged to contact individual colleges for the most current tuition figures.

The figure given here includes tuition and student fees for the school's standard academic year. If costs differ for state residents and out-of-state residents, the figure for nonresidents is given in parentheses. Where tuition costs are listed per credit hour (p/c), per course (p/course), or per unit (p/unit), student fees are not included. In some university systems, tuition is the same for all schools. However, student fees, and therefore the total tuition figure, may vary from school to school.

Room and Board

It is suggested that students check with individual schools for the most current room-and-board figures because, like tuition figures, they increase continually. The room-and-board figures given here represent the annual cost of a double room and all meals. The word "none" indicates that the college does not charge for room and board; "n/app" indicates that room and board are not provided.

Freshman Class

The numbers apply to the number of students who applied, were accepted, and enrolled in the 2003–2004 freshman class or in a recent class.

SAT I, ACT

Whenever available, the median SAT I scores—both Verbal and Mathematics—and the median ACT composite score for the 2003–2004 freshman class are given. If the school has not reported median SAT I or ACT scores, the capsule indicates whether the SAT I or ACT is required. Note: Test scores are reported for mainstream students.

Admissions Selector Rating

The College Admissions Selector Rating indicates the degree of competitiveness of admission to the college.

THE GENERAL DESCRIPTION

The Introductory Paragraph

This paragraph indicates, in general, what types of programs the college offers, when it was founded, whether it is public or private, and its religious affiliation. Baccalaureate program accreditation and information on the size of the school's library collection are also provided.

In evaluating the size of the collection, keep in mind the difference between college and university libraries: A university's graduate and professional schools require many specialized books that would be of no value to an undergraduate. For a university, a ratio of one undergraduate to 500 books generally means an outstanding library, one to 200 an adequate library, one to 100 an inferior library. For a college, a ratio of one to 400 is outstanding, one to 300 superior, one to 200 adequate, one to 50 inferior.

These figures are somewhat arbitrary, because a large university with many professional schools or campuses requires more books than a smaller university. Furthermore, a recently founded college would be expected to have fewer books than an older school, since it has not inherited from the past what might be a great quantity of outdated and useless books. Most libraries can make up for deficiencies through interlibrary loans.

The ratio of students to the number of subscriptions to periodicals is less meaningful, and again, a university requires more periodicals than a college. But for a university, subscription to more than 1500 periodicals is outstanding, and 6000 is generally more than adequate. For a college, 15,000 subscriptions are exceptional, 700 very good, and 400 adequate. Subscription to fewer than 200 periodicals generally implies an inferior library with a very tight budget. Microform items are assuming greater importance within a library's holdings, and this information is included when available. Services of a Learning Resource Center and special facilities, such as a museum, radio or TV station, and Internet access are also described in this paragraph.

This paragraph also provides information on the campus: its size, the type of area in which it is located, and its proximity to a large city.

At most institutions, the existence of classrooms, administrative offices, and dining facilities may be taken for granted, and they generally are not mentioned in the entries unless they have been recently constructed or are considered exceptional.

Student Life

This section, with subdivisions that detail housing, campus activities, sports, facilities for disabled students, services offered to students, and campus safety concentrates on the everyday life of students.

The introductory paragraph, which includes various characteristics of the student body, gives an idea of the mix of attitudes and backgrounds. It includes, where available, percentages of students from out-of-state and from private or public high schools. It also indicates what percentage of the students belong to minority groups and what percentages are Protestant, Catholic, and Jewish. Finally, it tells the average age of all enrolled freshmen and of all undergraduates, and gives data on the freshman dropout rate and the percentage of freshmen who remain to graduate.

Housing. Availability of on-campus housing is described here. If you plan to live on campus, note the type, quantity, and capacity of the dormitory accommodations. Some colleges provide dormitory rooms for freshmen, but require upperclass students to make their own arrangements to live in fraternity or sorority houses, off-campus apartments, or rented rooms in private houses. Some small colleges require all students who do not live with parents or other relatives to live on campus. And some colleges have no residence halls.

This paragraph tells whether special housing is available and whether campus housing is single-sex or coed. It gives the percentage of those who live on campus and those who remain on campus on weekends. Finally, it states if alcohol is not permitted on campus and whether students may keep cars on campus.

Activities. Campus organizations play a vital part in students' social lives. This subsection lists types of activities, including student government, special interest or academic clubs, fraternities and sororities, and cultural and popular campus events sponsored at the college.

Sports. Sports are important on campus, so we indicate the extent of the athletic program by giving the number of intercollegiate and intramural sports offered for men and for women. We have also included the athletic and recreation facilities and campus stadium seating capacity.

Disabled Students. The colleges' own estimates of how accessible their campuses are to the physically disabled are provided. This information should be considered along with the specific kinds of special facilities available. If a Profile does not include a subsection on the disabled, the college did not provide the information.

Services. Services that may be available to students—free or for a fee—include counseling, tutoring, remedial instruction, and reader service for the blind.

Safety. This section lists the safety and security measures that are in place on the campus. These vary among schools, but may include 24-hour foot and vehicle patrol, self-defense education, security escort services, shuttle buses, informal discussions, pamphlets/posters/films, emergency telephones, and lighted pathways/sidewalks.

Programs of Study

Listed here are the bachelor's degrees granted, strongest and most popular majors, and whether associate, master's, and doctoral degrees are awarded. Major areas of study have been included under broader general areas (shown in capital letters in the profiles) for quicker reference; however, the general areas do not necessarily correspond to the academic divisions of the college or university but are more career-oriented.

Required. Wherever possible, information on specific required courses and distribution requirements is supplied, in addition to the number of credits or hours required for graduation. If the college requires students to maintain a certain grade point average (GPA) or pass comprehensive exams to graduate, that also is given.

Special. Special programs are described here. Students at almost every college now have the opportunity to study abroad, either through their college or through other institutions. Internships with businesses, schools, hospitals, and public agencies permit students to gain work experience as they learn. The pass/fail grading option, now quite prevalent, allows students to take courses in unfamiliar areas without threatening their academic average. Many schools offer students the opportunity to earn a combined B.A.-B.S. degree, pursue a general studies (no major) degree, or design their own major. Frequently students may take advantage of a cooperative program offered by two or more universities. Such a program might be referred to, for instance, as a 3-2 engineering program; a student in this program would spend three years at one institution and two at another. The number of national honor societies represented on campus is included. Schools also may conduct honors programs for qualified students, either university-wide or in specific major fields, and these also are listed.

Faculty/Classroom. The percentage of male and female faculty are mentioned here if provided by the college, along with the percentage of introductory courses taught by graduate students (if any). The average class size in an introductory lecture, laboratory, and regular class offering may also be indicated.

Admissions

The admissions section gives detailed information on standards so you can evaluate your chances for acceptance. Where the SAT I or ACT scores of the 2003–2004 freshman class are broken down, you may compare your own scores. Because the role of standardized tests in the admissions process has been subject to criticism, more colleges are considering other factors such as recommendations from high school officials, leadership record, special talents, extracurricular activities, and advanced placement or honors courses completed. A few schools may consider education of parents, ability to pay for college, and relationship to alumni. Some give preference to state residents; others seek a geographically diverse student body.

If a college indicates that it follows an open admissions policy, it is noncompetitive and generally accepts all applicants who meet certain basic requirements, such as graduation from an accredited high school. If a college has rolling admissions, it decides on each application as soon as possible if the applicant's file is complete and does not specify a notification deadline. As a general rule, it is best to submit applications as early as possible.

Some colleges offer special admissions programs for nontraditional applicants. Early admissions programs allow students to begin college either during the summer before their freshman year or during what would have been their last year of high school; in the latter case, a high school diploma is not required. These programs are designed for students who are emotionally and educationally prepared for college at an earlier age than usual.

Deferred admissions plans permit students to spend a year at another activity, such as working or traveling, before beginning college. Students who take advantage of this option can relax during the year off, because they already have been accepted at a college and have a space reserved. During the year off from study, many students become clearer about their educational goals, and they perform better when they do begin study.

Early decision plans allow students to be notified by their first-choice school during the first term of the senior year. This plan may eliminate the anxiety of deciding whether or not to send a deposit to a second-choice college that offers admission before the first-choice college responds.

Requirements. This subsection specifies the minimum high school class rank and GPA, if any, required by the college for freshman applicants. It indicates what standardized tests (if any) are required, specifically the SAT I or ACT, or for Puerto Rican schools, the CEEB (the Spanish-language version of the SAT I). Additional requirements are given such as whether an essay, interview, or audition is necessary, and if AP*/CLEP credit is given. If a college accepts applications on computer disk or on-line, those facts are so noted and described. Other factors used by the school in the admissions decision are also listed.

Procedure. This subsection indicates when you should take entrance exams, the application deadlines for various sessions, the application fee, and when students are notified of the admissions decision. Some schools note that their application deadlines are open; this can mean either that they will consider applications until a class is filled, or that applications are considered right up until registration for the term in which the student wishes to enroll. If a waiting list is an active part of the admissions procedure, the college may indicate the number of applicants placed on that list and the number of wait-listed applicants accepted.

Transfer. Nearly every college admits some transfer students. These students may have earned associate degrees at two-year colleges and want to continue their education at a four-year college or wish to attend a different school. One important thing to consider when transferring is how many credits earned at one school will be accepted at another, so entire semesters won't be spent making up lost work. Because most schools require students to spend a specified number of hours in residence to earn a degree, it is best not to wait too long to transfer if you decide to do so.

Visiting. Some colleges hold special orientation programs for prospective students to give them a better idea of what the school is like. Many also will provide guides for informal visits, often allowing students to spend a night in the residence halls. You should make arrangements with the college before visiting.

Financial Aid

This paragraph in each Profile describes the availability of financial aid. It includes the percentage of freshmen and continuing students who receive aid, the average scholarship, loan, and work contract aid to freshmen, the average amount of need-based scholarships from all sources and the types and sources of aid available, such as scholarships, grants, loans, and work-study. Aid application deadlines and required forms are also indicated.

International Students

This section begins by telling how many of the school's students come from outside the United States. It tells which English proficiency exam, if any, applicants must take and the minimum score required, if there is one. Any necessary college entrance exams, including SAT II: Subject tests, are listed, as are any minimum scores required on those exams.

Computers

This section details the scope of computerized facilities that are available for academic use. Limitations (if any) on student use of computer facilities are outlined. It also gives information on the required or recommended ownership of a PC.

Graduates

This section gives the number of graduates in the 2003 class, the most popular majors and percentage of graduates earning degrees in those fields, and the percentages of men and women in the 2002 class who enrolled in graduate school or found employment within 6 months of graduation.

Admissions Contact

This is the name or title of the person to whom all correspondence regarding your application should be sent. Internet addresses are included here, along with the availability of a video of the campus.

---

* Advanced Placement and AP are registered trademarks owned by the College Entrance Examination Board. No endorsement of this product is implied or given.

PROFILES OF

AMERICAN

COLLEGES

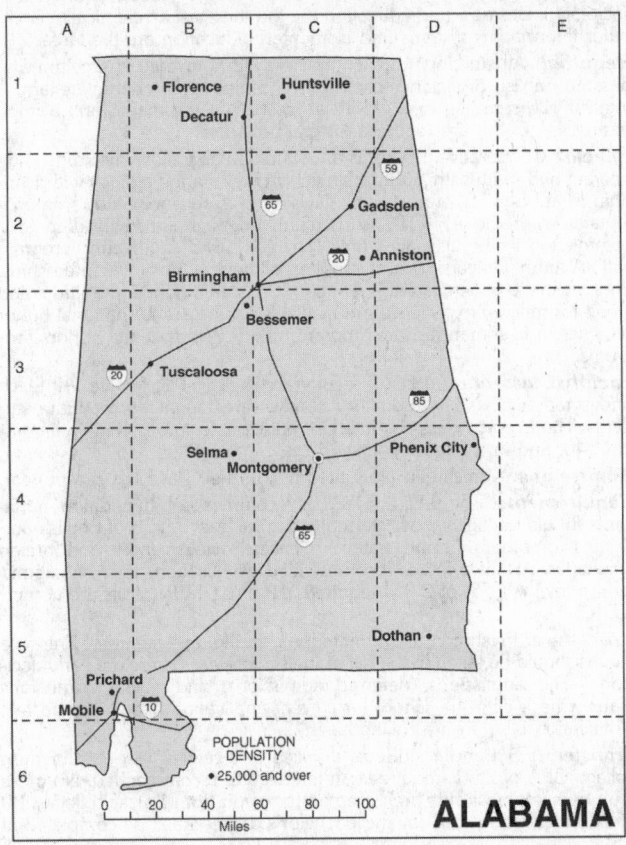

ALABAMA

POPULATION DENSITY
● 25,000 and over

Miles: 0 20 40 60 80 100

ALABAMA AGRICULTURAL AND MECHANICAL UNIVERSITY   C-1
Normal, AL 35762

(256) 372-5245
(800) 553-0816; Fax: (256) 372-9747

Full-time: 1950 men, 2020 women	**Faculty:** 150; IIA, --$
Part-time: 160 men, 190 women	**Ph.D.s:** 70%
Graduate: 360 men, 800 women	**Student/Faculty:** 27 to 1
Year: semesters, summer session	**Tuition:** $2400 ($4300)
Application Deadline: July 15	**Room & Board:** $2700
Freshman Class: n/av	
SAT I: n/av	**ACT:** required
	LESS COMPETITIVE

Alabama Agricultural and Mechanical University, founded in 1875, is a public land-grant institution offering undergraduate and graduate studies in agriculture, home economics, arts and sciences, business, education, engineering, and technology. There are 5 undergraduate schools and 1 graduate school. Figures in above capsule and in this profile are approximate. In addition to regional accreditation, A&M has baccalaureate program accreditation with ABET, ADA, AHEA, CSWE, FIDER, and NCATE. The library contains 253,620 volumes, 48,300 microform items, and 3010 audio/video tapes/CDs, and subscribes to 2070 periodicals. Computerized library services include the card catalog, interlibrary loans, and database searching. Special learning facilities include a learning resource center, art gallery, radio station, TV station, and State Black Archives. The 2001-acre campus is in a suburban area 90 miles north of Birmingham and 95 miles south of Nashville. Including any residence halls, there are 55 buildings.

Student Life: 70% of undergraduates are from Alabama. Students are from 42 states, 29 foreign countries, and Canada. 90% are from public schools. 90% are African American. Most are Protestant. The average age of freshmen is 18; all undergraduates, 20. 30% do not continue beyond their first year; 60% remain to graduate.

Housing: 3100 students can be accommodated in college housing, which includes single-sex dorms. On-campus housing is guaranteed for all 4 years. 60% of students live on campus; of those, 60% remain on campus on weekends. Alcohol is not permitted. All students may keep cars.

Activities: 7% of men belong to 4 national fraternities; 9% of women belong to 4 national sororities. There are 109 groups on campus, including band, cheerleading, choir, chorus, computers, dance, debate, drama, drill team, ethnic, forensics, honors, international, jazz band, marching band, newspaper, orchestra, pep band, political, professional, radio and TV, religious, social, student government, symphony, and yearbook. Popular campus events include Magic City Classic, Women's Week, and Men's Week.

Sports: There are 7 intercollegiate sports for men and 7 for women, and 7 intramural sports for men and 7 for women. Facilities include a 7000-seat gym, an Olympic-size pool, track and playing fields, and a 21,000-seat stadium/health education complex.

Disabled Students: 95% of the campus is accessible. Wheelchair ramps, elevators, special parking, specially equipped rest rooms, and lowered drinking fountains are available.

Services: Counseling and information services are available, as is tutoring in most subjects. There is a reader service for the blind.

Campus Safety and Security: Measures include 24-hour foot and vehicle patrol, self-defense education, security escort services, and informal discussions. There are pamphlets/posters/films and lighted pathways/sidewalks.

Programs of Study: A&M confers B.A., B.S., B.S.C.E., B.S.E.E., B.S.E.T., B.S.M.E., and B.S.W. degrees. Associate, master's, and doctoral degrees are also awarded. Bachelor's degrees are awarded in AGRICULTURE (agricultural business management, agricultural economics, agronomy, animal science, forestry and related sciences, horticulture, and soil science), BIOLOGICAL SCIENCE (biology/biological science, nutrition, and zoology), BUSINESS (accounting, banking and finance, business administration and management, marketing/retailing/merchandising, and office supervision and management), COMMUNICATIONS AND THE ARTS (art, dramatic arts, English, French, linguistics, and telecommunications), COMPUTER AND PHYSICAL SCIENCE (chemistry, computer science, mathematics, and physics), EDUCATION (agricultural, art, early childhood, elementary, home economics, industrial arts, middle school, music, physical, science, secondary, special, and trade and industrial), ENGINEERING AND ENVIRONMENTAL DESIGN (city/community/regional planning, civil engineering, civil engineering technology, drafting and design technology, electrical/electronics engineering, electrical/electronics engineering technology, environmental science, industrial engineering technology, mechanical engineering, and mechanical engineering technology), HEALTH PROFESSIONS (medical laboratory technology, preveterinary science, and speech pathology/audiology), SOCIAL SCIENCE (economics, family/consumer studies, food science, history, human development, political science/government, psychology, social work, and sociology). Physics, food science, and teacher education are the strongest academically. Business administration, education, and computer science are the largest.

Required: All students are required to take at least 52 hours of general studies, including phys ed, music, and art, and to maintain a minimum GPA of 2.0. Students must complete a total of 120 to 126 credit hours, with 30 to 36 in the major. A comprehensive exam is required for some majors.

Special: Co-op programs with Georgia Institute of Technology and Tuskegee University, cross-registration with the University of Alabama in Huntsville, Oakwood College, Calhoun Community College, and Athens State College, internships with various government agencies, dual majors, and work-study programs are available. There is a 3-2 engineering degree program with Georgia Institute of Technology. There are 5 national honor societies, a freshman honors program, and 5 departmental honors programs.

Faculty/Classroom: 70% of faculty are male; 30%, female. 50% teach undergraduates, 30% do research, and 30% do both. No introductory courses are taught by graduate students. The average class size in an introductory lecture is 90; in a laboratory, 20; and in a regular course, 30.

Requirements: The SAT I or ACT is required, with a minimum score of 18 on the ACT. Applicants must have 4 years each of English, math, science, social studies, and history. An interview is recommended. The GED is accepted. A GPA of 2.0 is required. AP and CLEP credits are accepted. Important factors in the admissions decision are advanced placement or honor courses, leadership record, and recommendations by school officials.

Procedure: Freshmen are admitted to all sessions. There are early decision, early admissions, deferred admissions, and rolling admissions plans. Check with the school for current application deadlines. The fall 2003 application fee was $10. Notification is sent on a rolling basis. Applications are accepted on-line at the university's web site.

Transfer: Transfer students must have a minimum GPA of 2.0 and have earned at least 12 semester credit hours. 30 of 128 credits required for the bachelor's degree must be completed at A&M.

Visiting: There are regularly scheduled orientations for prospective students, consisting of sessions in June, July, and November. There are guides for informal visits and visitors may stay overnight. To schedule a visit, contact Antonio Boyle, Director of Admissions at (256) 851-5248.

Financial Aid: 50% of undergraduates work part time. Average annual earnings from campus work are $3600. The CSS Profile, FAFSA, FFS, or SFS and the college's own financial statement are required. Check with the school for current deadlines.

International Students: The school actively recruits these students. They must score 500 on the written TOEFL.

Computers: The mainframe is an IBM. In addition to the Mac/IBM computer center, there are IBM PCs located in the library, computer labs, and language and writing centers. All students may access the system. There are no time limits. The fee is $50. It is strongly recommended that all students have a personal computer.

Graduates: In an average class, 54% graduate in 6 years or less.

Admissions Contact: Antonio Boyle, Director of Admissions. A video is available. E-mail: *aboyle@asnaam.aamu.edu* Web: *www.aamu.edu*

ALABAMA STATE UNIVERSITY
Montgomery, AL 36101-0271

C-4

(334) 229-4291
(800) 410-3522; Fax: (334) 229-4984

Full-time: 1760 men, 2380 women	**Faculty:** 223
Part-time: 210 men, 365 women	**Ph.D.s:** 57%
Graduate: 215 men, 670 women	**Student/Faculty:** 18 to 1
Year: semesters, summer session	**Tuition:** $2905 ($5810)
Application Deadline: July 30	**Room & Board:** $3500
Freshman Class: n/av	
SAT I or ACT: recommended	COMPETITIVE

Alabama State University, founded in 1867, is a state-assisted institution offering undergraduate programs in liberal arts and sciences, business administration, education, music, social work, aerospace studies, and health science. There are 6 undergraduate schools and 1 graduate school. Figures in the above capsule and this profile are approximate. In addition to regional accreditation, ASU has baccalaureate program accreditation with ACBSP, ACOTE, CSWE, NASDTEC, NASM, and NCATE. The library contains 396,871 volumes, 2,559,000 microform items, and 42,319 audio/video tapes/CDs, and subscribes to 1307 periodicals. Computerized library services include the card catalog, interlibrary loans, and database searching. Special learning facilities include a learning resource center, art gallery, and radio station. The 168-acre campus is in an urban area 91 miles south of Birmingham. Including any residence halls, there are 64 buildings.

Student Life: 70% of undergraduates are from Alabama. Students are from 39 states, 16 foreign countries, and Canada. 90% are African American. The average age of freshmen is 19; all undergraduates, 23. 36% do not continue beyond their first year; 21% remain to graduate.

Housing: 2330 students can be accommodated in college housing, which includes single-sex dorms and on-campus apartments. In addition, there are honors houses. On-campus housing is available on a first-come, first-served basis. 62% of students commute. Alcohol is not permitted. All students may keep cars.

Activities: 8% of men belong to 4 national fraternities; 6% of women belong to 4 national sororities. There are 50 groups on campus, including art, band, cheerleading, choir, chorus, dance, debate, drama, drum and bugle corps, honors, international, jazz band, marching band, musical theater, newspaper, orchestra, pep band, political, professional, radio and TV, social service, student government, symphony, and yearbook. Popular campus events include Founders Day, Fall Convocation, and Honors Day Program.

Sports: There are 8 intercollegiate sports for men and 9 for women, and 6 intramural sports for men and 5 for women. Facilities include an 8000-seat acadome, a stadium, a gym, 12 tennis courts, a swimming pool, an 8-lane indoor track, and 2 weight rooms.

Disabled Students: 80% of the campus is accessible. Wheelchair ramps, elevators, special parking, specially equipped rest rooms, special class scheduling, lowered drinking fountains, lowered telephones, and semiautomatic doors are available.

Services: Counseling and information services are available, as is tutoring in some subjects, including math and English. There is remedial math, reading, and writing.

Campus Safety and Security: Measures include 24-hour foot and vehicle patrol, self-defense education, security escort services, and informal discussions. There are pamphlets/posters/films, emergency telephones, lighted pathways/sidewalks, and a campus police department with 24 officers.

Programs of Study: ASU confers B.A., B.S., B.M.E., B.S.Ed., and B.S.W. degrees. Master's degrees are also awarded. Bachelor's degrees are awarded in BIOLOGICAL SCIENCE (biology/biological science), BUSINESS (accounting, banking and finance, business administration and management, business economics, and marketing/retailing/merchandising), COMMUNICATIONS AND THE ARTS (broadcasting, communications, English, fine arts, French, music, and Spanish), COMPUTER AND PHYSICAL SCIENCE (chemistry, information sciences and systems, mathematics, and physics), EDUCATION (art, business,

early childhood, elementary, English, foreign languages, music, secondary, social studies, and special), ENGINEERING AND ENVIRONMENTAL DESIGN (engineering), SOCIAL SCIENCE (criminal justice, history, political science/government, psychology, social work, and sociology). Business and education are the strongest academically. Computer information systems and elementary education are the largest.

Required: All students must complete a 42-hour core curriculum and pass an English proficiency exam and a senior comprehensive exam. A total of 120 semester hours, with at least 27 in the major, and a minimum GPA of 2.0 are required for graduation.

Special: Cooperative programs are offered in all majors, including engineering and math with Auburn University and marine biology with Dauphin Island Sea Laboratory. The Division of Aerospace Studies, in conjunction with the AFROTC curriculum, offers programs leading to a commission in the U.S. Air Force. There is a 3-2 engineering program with Auburn University, and cross-enrollment is possible. Internships, dual majors, a general studies degree, work study, nondegree study, and credit for military experience are available. There are 16 national honor societies, a freshman honors program, and 9 departmental honors programs.

Faculty/Classroom: 49% of faculty are male; 51%, female. All teach undergraduates. No introductory courses are taught by graduate students. The average class size in an introductory lecture is 40; in a laboratory, 40; and in a regular course, 40.

Admissions: 4 freshmen graduated first in their class in a recent year.

Requirements: The SAT I or ACT is recommended. In addition, applicants should be high school graduates with at least 3 units of English and 8 units combined in math, natural sciences, social sciences, and foreign languages. An interview is recommended. Applications may be submitted on-line. A GPA of 2.0 is required. AP and CLEP credits are accepted.

Procedure: Freshmen are admitted fall, spring, and summer. Entrance exams should be taken in the fall of the senior year. There are early decision, early admissions, deferred admissions, and rolling admissions plans. Check with the school for current application deadlines and fee. Notification is sent on a rolling basis.

Transfer: 171 transfer students enrolled in a recent year. A minimum college GPA of 2.0 is required. An interview is recommended. No more than 64 semester hours are accepted for credit from 2-year colleges. 30 of 120 credits required for the bachelor's degree must be completed at ASU.

Visiting: There are regularly scheduled orientations for prospective students. There are guides for informal visits. To schedule a visit, contact the Office of Admissions and Recruitment.

Financial Aid: In a recent year, 93% of all full-time freshmen and 98% of continuing full-time students received some form of financial aid. 94% of full-time freshmen and 75% of continuing full-time students received need-based aid. The average freshman award was $9660. Average annual earnings from campus work are $1984. The average financial indebtedness of a recent graduate was $25,000. ASU is a member of CSS. The FAFSA and Alabama Student Data Form are required. Check with the school for current deadlines.

International Students: There were 11 international students enrolled in a recent year. They must score 500 on the written TOEFL or complete ESL Level 109 and also take the SAT I or the ACT.

Computers: The mainframe is a multiprise 2003-225. About 350 PCs and Macs are available in student labs. All students may access the system 24 hours a day.

Graduates: In a recent year, 437 bachelor's degrees were awarded. The most popular majors were computer information systems (12%), criminal justice (10%), and elementary education (6%). 278 companies recruited on campus in a recent year. Of a recent graduating class, 21% were enrolled in graduate school within 6 months of graduation.

Admissions Contact: Danielle Kennedy-Lamar, Director of Admissions. A video is available. E-mail: *dlamar@asunet.alasu.edu* Web: *www.alasu.edu*

AUBURN UNIVERSITY SYSTEM

The Auburn University System, established in 1856, is a public system in Alabama. It is governed by a board of trustees, whose chief administrator is the president. The primary goal of the system is service through its instruction, research, and extension divisions. The main priorities are to provide a high-quality undergraduate degree at minimal cost, to expand and diversify overall research effort, and to disseminate and apply knowledge for Alabama residents through extension and public service programs. The total enrollment of both campuses is usually about 28,000; there were 1500 faculty members. Altogether there are some 160 baccalaureate, 74 master's, 10 educational specialist, and 39 doctoral programs offered in Auburn University System. There is a 4-year campus located in Auburn and Montgomery. Profiles of the 4-year campuses are included in this section.

AUBURN UNIVERSITY
Auburn, AL 36849-5145 **D-3**

(334) 844-4080; (800) 282-8769

Full-time: 9169 men, 9136 women
Part-time: 1051 men, 692 women
Graduate: 1664 men, 1440 women
Year: semesters, summer session
Application Deadline: August 1
Freshman Class: 12,439 applied, 9653 accepted, 3706 enrolled
SAT I Verbal/Math: 550/570

Faculty: 1028; I, -$
Ph.Ds: 93%
Student/Faculty: 18 to 1
Tuition: $4426 ($12,886)
Room & Board: $5970

ACT: 24 **VERY COMPETITIVE**

Auburn University, founded in 1856, is a state-supported land grant institution offering undergraduate, first professional, and graduate degrees in agriculture, business, education, engineering, liberal arts, sciences and math, veterinary medicine, architecture/design and construction, forestry, human sciences, nursing, and pharmacy. There are 12 undergraduate schools and 1 graduate school. In addition to regional accreditation, Auburn has baccalaureate program accreditation with AACSB, AAFCS, ABET, ACEJMC, ACPE, ACS, ADA, AHEA, ASLA, CAA, CSAB, CSWE, FIDER, NAAB, NASAD, NASM, NCATE, NLN, and SAF. The 3 libraries contain 2,724,011 volumes, 2,592,641 microform items, and 158,580 audio/video tapes/CDs, and subscribe to 35,015 periodicals. Computerized library services include the card catalog, interlibrary loans, database searching, and Internet access. Special learning facilities include a learning resource center, art gallery, radio station, TV station, and a nuclear science center, an arboretum, electron microscopy labs, and a museum of fine arts. The 1875-acre campus is in a small town 110 miles southwest of Atlanta, Georgia. Including any residence halls, there are 144 buildings.

Student Life: 67% of undergraduates are from Alabama. Students are from 45 states, 98 foreign countries, and Canada. 78% are from public schools. 85% are white. The average age of freshmen is 18; all undergraduates, 20. 16% do not continue beyond their first year; 68% remain to graduate.

Housing: 3114 students can be accommodated in college housing, which includes single-sex and coed dorms, on-campus apartments, married-student housing, and fraternity houses. In addition, there are honors houses. On-campus housing is available on a first-come, first-served basis. 85% of students commute. Alcohol is not permitted. All students may keep cars.

Activities: 18% of men and about 1% of women belong to 32 national fraternities; 34% of women belong to 18 national sororities. There are 300 groups on campus, including art, band, cheerleading, chess, choir, chorale, chorus, computers, dance, drama, drill team, ethnic, film, gay, honors, international, jazz band, literary magazine, marching band, musical theater, newspaper, opera, orchestra, pep band, photography, political, professional, radio and TV, religious, social, social service, student government, symphony, and yearbook. Popular campus events include Hey Day, ODK Cake Race, and pep rallies.

Sports: There are 7 intercollegiate sports for men and 9 for women, and 15 intramural sports for men and 15 for women. Facilities include a stadium, a coliseum, an athletic complex, a women's sports center, a track, a park, a student activities center, intramural field houses, racquetball, tennis, and basketball courts, a swim center, a fitness/weight room, and an aerobics-cardio theater.

Disabled Students: 80% of the campus is accessible. Wheelchair ramps, elevators, special parking, specially equipped rest rooms, special class scheduling, lowered drinking fountains, special housing, braille elevators, and wheelchair lifts are available.

Services: Counseling and information services are available, as is tutoring in every subject. There is a reader service for the blind.

Campus Safety and Security: Measures include 24-hour foot and vehicle patrol, self-defense education, security escort services, and shuttle buses. There are informal discussions, pamphlets/posters/films, emergency telephones, and lighted pathways/sidewalks.

Programs of Study: Auburn confers B.A., B.S., B.Arch., B.A.E., B.B.E., B.C.E., B.Che.E., B.E.E., B.F.A., B.Int. Arch., B.Int.Design, B.I.S.E., B.MH.E., B.Mus.Ed., and B.T.M.T. degrees. Master's and doctoral degrees are also awarded. Bachelor's degrees are awarded in AGRICULTURE (agricultural business management, agriculture, animal science, fishing and fisheries, forest engineering, forestry production and processing, horticulture, poultry science, and soil science), BIOLOGICAL SCIENCE (biochemistry, biology/biological science, botany, entomology, marine biology, microbiology, molecular biology, nutrition, wildlife biology, and zoology), BUSINESS (accounting, banking and finance, business administration and management, business economics, fashion merchandising, hotel/motel and restaurant management, international business management, marketing/retailing/merchandising, personnel management, and transportation management), COMMUNICATIONS AND THE ARTS (communications, design, dramatic arts, English, French, German, industrial design, journalism, languages, public relations, Spanish, and speech/debate/rhetoric), COMPUTER AND PHYSICAL SCIENCE (applied mathematics, chemistry, computer science, geology, mathematics, and physics), EDUCATION (business, early childhood, elementary, English, foreign languages, health, home eco-

nomics, industrial arts, mathematics, middle school, physical, science, secondary, social science, special, and vocational), ENGINEERING AND ENVIRONMENTAL DESIGN (aeronautical engineering, agricultural engineering, architecture, aviation administration/management, chemical engineering, civil engineering, computer engineering, construction management, electrical/electronics engineering, environmental science, interior design, landscape architecture/design, mechanical engineering, textile engineering, and textile technology), HEALTH PROFESSIONS (health care administration, medical laboratory technology, nursing, predentistry, premedicine, preoptometry, preveterinary science, and speech pathology/audiology), SOCIAL SCIENCE (anthropology, criminology, economics, food science, geography, history, home furnishings and equipment management/production/services, human development, parks and recreation management, philosophy, physical fitness/movement, political science/government, psychology, public administration, rural sociology, social work, sociology, and textiles and clothing). Engineering, business, and architecture are the strongest academically. Business, engineering, and education are the largest.

Required: All students must complete a core curriculum of 6 semester hours each in English composition, history, literature, and social science, 8 in science, and 3 each in math, philosophy, and fine arts. Students must choose a curriculum and complete its requirements and those of the college or school with at least a 2.0 average in all Auburn courses attempted, on transfer credits accepted for a degree program, and in all course work in the major.

Special: Opportunities are available for co-op programs in most majors, and there are internships, work-study programs, and dual majors. A 3-2 engineering degree with several area institutions, credit by examination, nondegree study, pass/fail options, and study abroad in more than 25 countries are also available. There are 57 national honor societies, including Phi Beta Kappa, a freshman honors program, and honors programs in all departments.

Faculty/Classroom: 73% of faculty are male; 27%, female. 89% teach undergraduates. Graduate students teach 21% of introductory courses. The average class size in an introductory lecture is 43; in a laboratory, 21; and in a regular course, 36.

Admissions: 78% of the 2003-2004 applicants were accepted. The SAT I scores for the 2003-2004 freshman class were: Verbal--21% below 500, 52% between 500 and 599, 23% between 600 and 700, and 4% above 700; Math--16% below 500, 47% between 500 and 599, 32% between 600 and 700, and 5% above 700. The ACT scores were 13% below 21, 31% between 21 and 23, 29% between 24 and 26, 13% between 27 and 28, and 14% above 28. 47% of the current freshmen were in the top fifth of their class; 75% were in the top two fifths. There were 27 National Merit finalists and 4 semifinalists. 148 freshmen graduated first in their class.

Requirements: The SAT I or ACT is required. In addition, graduation from an accredited secondary school is required; a GED will be accepted. Applicants must have completed 4 years of high school English, 3 each of math and social studies, and 2 of science. It is recommended that students also complete 2 years each of a foreign language, an additional science course, and an additional social science course. Admission is equally based on test scores and the GPA in completed core requirements. AP and CLEP credits are accepted. Important factors in the admissions decision are advanced placement or honor courses, evidence of special talent, and parents or siblings attending the school.

Procedure: Freshmen are admitted to all sessions. Entrance exams should be taken in the spring of the junior year. There are early admissions, rolling admissions, and deferred admissions plans. Early decision applications should be filed by November 1; regular applications, by August 1 for fall entry, December 10 for spring entry, and May 1 for summer entry, along with a $25 fee. The fee for international applicants is $50. Notification is sent on a rolling basis. A waiting list is an active part of the admissions procedure. Applications are accepted on-line through the school's web site.

Transfer: 1314 transfer students enrolled in 2002-2003. Students who have attempted 48 quarter hours or 32 semester hours must have earned a cumulative 2.5 GPA in at least 30 quarter hours or 20 semester hours of standard academic courses as required in the core curriculum. These hours must include at least one course in each of the following areas: English (college-level composition or literature), history, math (college-level algebra or higher), and natural science with a lab. 25 of 120 credits required for the bachelor's degree must be completed at Auburn.

Visiting: There are regularly scheduled orientations for prospective students, including Camp War Eagle, minority recruitment weekends, and informal visits. Agendas vary, but normally include campus tours, meetings with admissions counselors, tours of housing, and meetings with faculty in various academic areas as desired. There are guides for informal visits and visitors may sit in on classes and stay overnight. To schedule a visit, contact Admissions Office at *admissions@auburn.edu*.

Financial Aid: In 2003-2004, 51% of all full-time freshmen received some form of financial aid. 33% of full-time freshmen and 41% of continuing full-time students received need-based aid. The average freshman award was $5709. Need-based scholarships or need-based grants averaged $3113; need-based self-help aid (loans and jobs) averaged

$3127; non-need-based athletic scholarships averaged $11,410; and other non-need-based awards and non-need-based scholarships averaged $3385. 15% of undergraduates work part time. Average annual earnings from campus work are $3733. The average financial indebtedness of the 2003 graduate was $18,535. The FAFSA is required. The deadline for filing freshman financial aid applications for fall entry is March 1.

International Students: There are 153 international students enrolled. The school actively recruits these students. They must score 550 on the written TOEFL or 213 on the electronic version and also take the SAT I or the ACT.

Computers: The mainframe is an IBM 9672/EO3. More than 700 networked PCs and terminals are available in various academic buildings and the library. Student computer labs include spreadsheet, word processing, statistical, and other software programs. Students may also access the university's mainframe computers, the Internet, and the Alabama Supercomputer. All students may access the system 24 hours a day. There are no time limits and no fees.

Graduates: From July 1, 2002 to June 30, 2003, 3697 bachelor's degrees were awarded. The most popular majors were business (29%), engineering (11%), and education (9%). In an average class, 37% graduate in 4 years or less, 61% graduate in 5 years or less, and 68% graduate in 6 years or less. Of the 2002 graduating class, 35% were enrolled in graduate school within 6 months of graduation.

Admissions Contact: Doyle Bickers, Director of Admissions. A video is available. E-mail: admissions@auburn.edu Web: www.auburn.edu

---

AUBURN UNIVERSITY MONTGOMERY   C-4
Montgomery, AL 36124-4023   (334) 244-3611
                              (800) 227-2649; Fax: (334) 244-3795

Full-time: 983 men, 1863 women	**Faculty:** 182; IIA, -$
Part-time: 612 men, 1034 women	**Ph.D.s:** n/av
Graduate: 230 men, 576 women	**Student/Faculty:** 16 to 1
Year: semesters, summer session	**Tuition:** $4130 ($11,930)
Application Deadline: open	**Room & Board:** $4890
Freshman Class: 962 applied, 954 accepted, 906 enrolled	
SAT I or ACT: required	**NONCOMPETITIVE**

Auburn University Montgomery, founded in 1967, is a public institution. There are 5 undergraduate and 4 graduate schools. In addition to regional accreditation, AUM has baccalaureate program accreditation with AACSB and NCATE. The library contains 320,039 volumes, 2,417,713 microform items, and 25,053 audio/video tapes/CDs, and subscribes to 2076 periodicals. Computerized library services include the card catalog, interlibrary loans, database searching, and Internet access. Special learning facilities include a learning resource center, art gallery, a graphic arts center, and a mass communication lab. The 500-acre campus is in an urban area 7 miles east of downtown Montgomery. Including any residence halls, there are 50 buildings.

Student Life: 95% of undergraduates are from Alabama. Students are from 34 states, 21 foreign countries, and Canada. 61% are white; 33% African American. The average age of freshmen is 20; all undergraduates, 25.

Housing: 952 students can be accommodated in college housing, which includes single-sex and coed on-campus apartments and married-student housing. On-campus housing is available on a first-come, first-served basis. 90% of students commute. Alcohol is not permitted. All students may keep cars.

Activities: 5% of men belong to 5 national fraternities; 4% of women belong to 7 national sororities. There are 66 groups on campus, including campus activities board, cheerleading, computers, drama, ethnic, honors, international, literary magazine, newspaper, professional, social service and student government. Popular campus events include AUM Fest and Mardi Gras Parade.

Sports: There are 4 intercollegiate sports for men and 3 for women, and 9 intramural sports for men and 7 for women. Facilities include a multipurpose gym-auditorium, an indoor jogging and walking track, baseball and soccer fields, and tennis courts.

Disabled Students: 95% of the campus is accessible. Wheelchair ramps, elevators, special parking, specially equipped rest rooms, special class scheduling, lowered drinking fountains, lowered telephones, and special housing are available.

Services: Counseling and information services are available, as is tutoring in every subject. There is a reader service for the blind, remedial math, reading, and writing, and help with study skills.

Campus Safety and Security: Measures include 24-hour foot and vehicle patrol, security escort services, informal discussions, and pamphlets/posters/films. There are emergency telephones and lighted pathways/sidewalks.

Programs of Study: AUM confers B.A., B.S., B.L.A., B.S.B.A., and B.S.N. degrees. Master's and doctoral degrees are also awarded. Bachelor's degrees are awarded in BIOLOGICAL SCIENCE (biology/biological science), BUSINESS (accounting, banking and finance, business administration and management, business economics, marketing/retailing/

merchandising, and personnel management), COMMUNICATIONS AND THE ARTS (communications, English, and fine arts), COMPUTER AND PHYSICAL SCIENCE (information sciences and systems, mathematics, and physical sciences), EDUCATION (elementary and secondary), HEALTH PROFESSIONS (nursing), SOCIAL SCIENCE (criminal justice, history, international studies, liberal arts/general studies, political science/government, psychology, and sociology). Education and liberal arts are the strongest academically. Elementary education, general business, and general studies are the largest.

Required: To graduate, students must complete a minimum of 120 credit hours with a minimum GPA of 2.0 in the major and overall. All students must fulfill English composition requirements and liberal education program requirements.

Special: AUM offers co-op programs in all majors, cross-registration with Alabama State University, Huntingdon College, and Faulkner University, and study abroad in England and other countries. There are 13 national honor societies, a freshman honors program, and 9 departmental honors programs.

Faculty/Classroom: 51% of faculty are male; 49%, female. The average class size in a laboratory is 22 and in a regular course, 20.

Admissions: 99% of the 2003-2004 applicants were accepted. The ACT scores for the 2003-2004 freshman class were: 65% below 21, 19% between 21 and 23, 10% between 24 and 26, 2% between 27 and 28, and 2% above 28.

Requirements: The ACT or SAT I is required. In addition, high school preparation should include English, math, social studies, science, and foreign language. The GED may be used for admission. A GPA of 2.3 is required. AP and CLEP credits are accepted.

Procedure: Freshmen are admitted to all sessions. Entrance exams should be taken in the junior year. There are early admissions and deferred admissions plans. Application deadlines are open. Application fee is $25. Notification is sent on a rolling basis. Applications are accepted on-line through the school's web site.

Transfer: Applicants for transfer must have a C average and be in good standing at their last school. 30 of 120 credits required for the bachelor's degree must be completed at AUM.

Visiting: There are regularly scheduled orientations for prospective students, including meetings with faculty, staff, advising, and registration. There are guides for informal visits and visitors may sit in on classes. To schedule a visit, contact the Office of Enrollment Services at (334) 244-3668 or vsamuel@mail.aum.edu.

Financial Aid: In 2003-2004, 83% of all full-time freshmen received some form of financial aid. 72% of full-time freshmen received need-based aid. The average freshman award was $5503. Need-based scholarships or need-based grants averaged $3425; need-based self-help aid (loans and jobs) averaged $2560; and non-need-based awards and non-need-based scholarships averaged $3377. 79% of undergraduates work part time. Average annual earnings from campus work are $3882. The FAFSA and the college's own financial statement are required. The priority date for freshman financial aid applications for fall entry is March 1.

International Students: There are 2 international students enrolled. The school actively recruits these students. They must score 500 on the written TOEFL or 173 on the electronic version and also take the ACT or SAT I, scoring 17 on the ACT or 820 on the SAT I.

Computers: The mainframe is an NCR 4300 with a Gateway server. There are 200 PCs available to students throughout the campus, with network access via Ethernet, TCP, or IP. All students may access the system from 7 A.M. to 1 A.M. There are no time limits and no fees. It is strongly recommended that all students have a personal computer.

Graduates: From July 1, 2002 to June 30, 2003, 879 bachelor's degrees were awarded. The most popular majors were business marketing (33%), education (25%), and professional services/public administration (10%). 125 companies recruited on campus in 2002-2003.

Admissions Contact: George Hill, Director/University Registrar. A video is available. E-mail: auminfo@mail.aum.edu Web: www.aum.edu

---

BIRMINGHAM-SOUTHERN COLLEGE   C-2
Birmingham, AL 35254   (205) 226-4696
                              (800) 523-5793; Fax: (205) 226-3074

Full-time: 534 men, 742 women	**Faculty:** 96; IIB, +$
Part-time: 13 men, 14 women	**Ph.D.s:** 97%
Graduate: 35 men, 50 women	**Student/Faculty:** 13 to 1
Year: 4-1-4, summer session	**Tuition:** $18,964
Application Deadline: January 15	**Room & Board:** $6400
Freshman Class: 1080 applied, 960 accepted, 356 enrolled	
SAT I Verbal/Math: 610/600	**ACT:** 27 **VERY COMPETITIVE+**

Birmingham-Southern College, founded in 1856, is a private liberal arts college affiliated with the United Methodist Church. In addition to regional accreditation, BSC has baccalaureate program accreditation with AACSB, NASM, and NCATE. The library contains 231,815 volumes, 175,038 microform items, and 26,914 audio/video tapes/CDs, and subscribes to 955 periodicals. Computerized library services include the card catalog, interlibrary loans, and database searching. Special learning facilities include a learning resource center, art gallery, planetarium, environmental center, and outdoor educational center. The 198-acre campus is in an urban area 3 miles west of downtown Birmingham. Including any residence halls, there are 28 buildings.

Student Life: 70% of undergraduates are from Alabama. Students are from 29 states, 20 foreign countries, and Canada. 90% are white. 85% are Protestant; 12% Catholic. The average age of freshmen is 18; all undergraduates, 24. 16% do not continue beyond their first year; 79% remain to graduate.

Housing: 1220 students can be accommodated in college housing, which includes single-sex dorms, on-campus apartments, married-student housing, fraternity houses, sorority houses, and honors houses. On-campus housing is guaranteed for all 4 years. 85% of students live on campus; of those, 70% remain on campus on weekends. All students may keep cars.

Activities: 54% of men belong to 6 national fraternities; 60% of women belong to 7 national sororities. There are 70 groups on campus, including art, band, choir, chorale, chorus, computers, dance, drama, drill team, ethnic, gay, honors, international, jazz band, literary magazine, musical theater, newspaper, opera, orchestra, pep band, political, professional, religious, social, social service, student government, and yearbook. Popular campus events include Southern Comfort, Honors Day, and Community Day.

Sports: There are 6 intercollegiate sports for men and 8 for women, and 17 intramural sports for men and 17 for women. Facilities include a coliseum, a baseball field, racquetball and tennis courts, 2 soccer fields, a weight room, an intramural athletic field, an indoor pool, a game room, an indoor jogging track, 3 gyms, and an aerobics studio.

Disabled Students: 80% of the campus is accessible. Wheelchair ramps, elevators, special parking, specially equipped rest rooms, special class scheduling, lowered drinking fountains, and lowered telephones are available.

Services: Counseling and information services are available, as is tutoring in some subjects, including math, English, computer science, and other subjects as requested. Tutoring is arranged on an individual basis; assistance in finding teachers is provided upon request.

Campus Safety and Security: Measures include 24-hour foot and vehicle patrol, self-defense education, security escort services, and shuttle buses. There are informal discussions, pamphlets/posters/films, emergency telephones, and lighted pathways/sidewalks.

Programs of Study: BSC confers B.A., B.S., B.F.A., B.Mus., and B.Mus.Ed. degrees. Master's degrees are also awarded. Bachelor's degrees are awarded in BIOLOGICAL SCIENCE (biology/biological science), BUSINESS (accounting and business administration and management), COMMUNICATIONS AND THE ARTS (art history and appreciation, dance, dramatic arts, English, French, German, music, musical theater, painting, photography, printmaking, sculpture, Spanish, and studio art), COMPUTER AND PHYSICAL SCIENCE (chemistry, computer science, mathematics, and physics), EDUCATION (art, dance, elementary, music, and secondary), SOCIAL SCIENCE (Asian/Oriental studies, economics, history, international relations, philosophy, political science/government, psychology, religion, and sociology). Biology, English, and psychology are the strongest academically. Business administration is the largest.

Required: All students must complete 32 regular units with courses in English composition and literature, lab sciences, math, fine arts, foreign language, social sciences, history, philosophy, and religion as well as 4 (January) interim projects. A total of 128 credits with a GPA of at least 2.0 is required to graduate.

Special: There is cross-registration with the University of Alabama at Birmingham, Miles College, the University of Montevallo, and Samford University. Student-designed, dual, and interdisciplinary majors, a Washington semester, internships, work-study programs, and study abroad are offered. There is a 3-2 nursing program with Vanderbilt University and a 3-2 environmental studies program wih Duke University. A 3-2 engineering degree is offered with the University of Alabama at Birmingham, Auburn University, Columbia University, and Washington University at St. Louis. Limited pass/fail options are available. There are 22 national honor societies, including Phi Beta Kappa, a freshman honors program, and 1 departmental honors program.

Faculty/Classroom: 62% of faculty are male; 38%, female. 95% teach undergraduates and 80% both teach and do research. No introductory courses are taught by graduate students. The average class size in an introductory lecture is 21.

Admissions: 89% of the 2003-2004 applicants were accepted. The SAT I scores for the 2003-2004 freshman class were: Verbal--9% below 500, 33% between 500 and 599, 46% between 600 and 700, and 12% above 700; Math--12% below 500, 36% between 500 and 700, 42% between 600 and 700, and 10% above 700. 78% of the current freshmen were in the top fifth of their class; 90% were in the top two fifths. There were 17 National Merit finalists and 50 semifinalists. 24 freshmen graduated first in their class.

Requirements: The SAT I or ACT is required. The minimum SAT I score should be 970 combined, and the minimum ACT score, 21. Appli-

cants should have graduated from an accredited secondary school with 4 courses in English, 4 each in math, science, and social studies, and a recommended 2 in foreign language. The GED is also accepted. An essay is required and an interview is recommended. Fine arts majors are advised to submit a portfolio or arrange an audition. BSC requires applicants to be in the upper 50% of their class. A GPA of 2.0 is required. AP and CLEP credits are accepted. Important factors in the admissions decision are advanced placement or honor courses, leadership record, and recommendations by school officials.

Procedure: Freshmen are admitted fall, spring, and summer. Entrance exams should be taken in the spring of the junior year. There is a rolling admissions plan. There are early admissions and deferred admissions plans. Applications should be filed by January 15 for fall entry, December 15 for winter entry, January 15 for spring entry, and May 1 for summer entry. The fall 2003 application fee was $25. Notification is sent on a rolling basis. Applications are accepted on-line through the college's web site and Common App.

Transfer: 42 transfer students enrolled in 2002-2003. Transfer applicants must have a minimum GPA of 2.0 and leave their former school in good standing. An essay and a school recommendation are required. An interview is recommended. 64 of 128 credits required for the bachelor's degree must be completed at BSC.

Visiting: There are regularly scheduled orientations for prospective students, including Preview Days, Scholarship Days, and individual visits. There are guides for informal visits and visitors may sit in on classes and stay overnight. To schedule a visit, contact the Office of Admission.

Financial Aid: In 2003-2004, 98% of all full-time students received some form of financial aid. 42% of all full-time students received need-based aid. The average freshman award was $13,422. Need-based scholarships or need-based grants averaged $2186 ($4050 maximum); need-based self-help aid (loans and jobs) averaged $4600 ($8125 maximum); non-need-based athletic scholarships averaged $16,648 ($27,700 maximum); and other non-need-based awards and non-need-based scholarships averaged $7985 ($29,530 maximum). 25% of undergraduates work part time. Average annual earnings from campus work are $750. The average financial indebtedness of the 2003 graduate was $13,000. BSC is a member of CSS. The FAFSA is required. The priority date for freshman financial aid applications for fall entry is March 1.

International Students: There are 35 international students enrolled. The school actively recruits these students. They must score 500 on the written TOEFL or 173 on the electronic version. The SAT I or ACT is required instead of the TOEFL for students whose primary language is English, with minimum English or verbal scores of 21 or 475.

Computers: The mainframe is an HP 9000/Series 835. There are 520 PCs in the computer center and other buildings on campus. All residence halls are wired to accept 2 PCs per room. All residence halls have computer labs. All students may access the system 24 hours a day. There are no time limits. The fee is $100. It is strongly recommended that all students have a personal computer.

Graduates: From July 1, 2002 to June 30, 2003, 297 bachelor's degrees were awarded. The most popular majors were business administration (17%), education (11%), and English (8%). In an average class, 1% graduate in 3 years or less, 69% graduate in 4 years or less, 77% graduate in 5 years or less, and 79% graduate in 6 years or less. Of the 2002 graduating class, 48% were enrolled in graduate school within 6 months of graduation and 42% were employed.

Admissions Contact: Sheri S. Salmon, Associate Vice President for Admissions Services. A video is available. E-mail: *ssalmon@bsc.edu* Web: *www.bsc.edu*

CONCORDIA COLLEGE
Selma, AL 36701

B-4

(334) 874-5700; Fax: (334) 874-5755

Full-time: 170 men, 535 women	**Faculty:** 17
Part-time: 11 men, 135 women	**Ph.D.s:** 47%
Graduate: none	**Student/Faculty:** 41 to 1
Year: semesters	**Tuition:** $6174
Application Deadline: August 8	**Room & Board:** $3600
Freshman Class: n/av	
SAT I: n/av	**ACT:** required
	NONCOMPETITIVE

Concordia College, founded in 1922, is a historically black institution, where the Christian faith as taught from the Holy Scriptures and subscribed to by the Lutheran Church-Missouri Synod is the foundation and guide for all programs, activities, and relationships. The library contains 50,328 volumes, 4405 microform items, and 2015 audio/video tapes/CDs, and subscribes to 170 periodicals. Computerized library services include the card catalog, interlibrary loans, and database searching. Special learning facilities include a learning resource center. The 22-acre campus is in a small town 50 miles west of Montgomery. Including any residence halls, there are 13 buildings.

Student Life: 91% of undergraduates are from Alabama. Students are from 12 states and 6 foreign countries. 93% are African American. 57% are Baptist; 17% claim no religious affiliation. The average age of freshmen is 18.

Housing: 350 students can be accommodated in college housing, which includes single-sex dorms. On-campus housing is guaranteed for all 4 years. 79% of students commute. Alcohol is not permitted. All students may keep cars.

Activities: There are no fraternities or sororities. There are 11 groups on campus, including cheerleading, choir, drama, international, religious, and student government. Popular campus events include Spiritual Enrichment Week.

Sports: There are 3 intercollegiate sports for men and 2 for women, and 3 intramural sports for men and 2 for women. Facilities include a gym, a swimming pool, a health and fitness center, and a game room.

Disabled Students: 80% of the campus is accessible. Wheelchair ramps, elevators, special parking, specially equipped rest rooms, lowered drinking fountains, and lowered telephones are available.

Services: Counseling and information services are available, as is tutoring in most subjects. There is remedial math, reading, and writing.

Campus Safety and Security: Measures include informal discussions, lighted pathways/sidewalks, security guards, security gates, and 24-hour foot patrol.

Programs of Study: CC confers B.A. and B.S. degrees. Associate degrees are also awarded. Bachelor's degrees are awarded in BUSINESS (business administration and management), EDUCATION (early childhood and elementary). Education is the strongest academically and has the largest enrollment.

Required: To graduate, students must complete 126 to 137 credit hours, depending on the major, with a minimum 2.0 GPA and pass a comprehensive exam. General education requirements include 18 hours of humanities, 12 of social sciences, 9 of math, 6 of religion, 3 each of computer science and health/phys ed, and 1 of orientation to college.

Special: CC offers internships, a Lutheran teacher diploma program, and cross-registration with other schools in the Concordia University system. There is 1 national honor society and a freshman honors program.

Faculty/Classroom: 59% of faculty are male; 41%, female. All teach undergraduates. The average class size in an introductory lecture is 25; in a laboratory, 15; and in a regular course, 30.

Admissions: 5% of the current freshmen were in the top fifth of their class; 18% were in the top two fifths. 4 freshmen graduated first in their class in a recent year.

Requirements: The ACT is required. A GPA of 2.0 is required. AP and CLEP credits are accepted. Important factors in the admissions decision are advanced placement or honor courses, evidence of special talent, and leadership record.

Procedure: Freshmen are admitted fall and spring. Entrance exams should be taken at the beginning of fall and spring semesters. There is a deferred admissions plan. Applications should be filed by August 8 for fall entry and January 15 for spring entry. The college accepts all applicants. Notification is sent in August.

Transfer: 122 transfer students enrolled in a recent year. Courses completed with a passing grade of C or better at an accredited postsecondary institution will be accepted for transfer, but only work at Concordia is included in the cumulative GPA. 36 of 126 to 137 credits required for the bachelor's degree must be completed at CC.

Visiting: There are regularly scheduled orientations for prospective students. There are guides for informal visits and visitors may sit in on classes and stay overnight. To schedule a visit, contact Evelyn Pickens, Director of Enrollment Management at (334) 874-5700 ext. 171 or *epickens@concordiaselma.edu.*

Financial Aid: In a recent year, all full-time freshmen received some form of financial aid. All full-time students received need-based aid. The average freshman award was $4410. 15% of undergraduates work part time. Average annual earnings from campus work are $700. The FAFSA is required. The deadline for filing freshman financial aid applications for fall entry is April 15.

International Students: There were 33 international students enrolled in a recent year. They must score 500 on the written TOEFL or 173 on the electronic version and also take the college's own test.

Computers: Students may access the network in the computer labs, in the library, or on their own computers. Approximately 100 terminals are available for student use. All students may access the system. There are no time limits. The fee is $10.

Graduates: From July 1, 2002 to June 30, 2003, 35 bachelor's degrees were awarded. The most popular majors were business administration (38%) and education (22%).

Admissions Contact: Evelyn Pickens, Director of Enrollment Management. A video is available. E-mail: *epickens@concordiaselma.edu* Web: *www.concordiaselma.edu*

FAULKNER UNIVERSITY   C-4
Montgomery, AL 36109-3398   (334) 386-7200
(800) 879-9816; Fax: (334) 386-7137

Full-time: 613 men, 984 women	**Faculty:** 58
Part-time: 180 men, 454 women	**Ph.D.s:** 63%
Graduate: 154 men, 130 women	**Student/Faculty:** 28 to 1
Year: semesters, summer session	**Tuition:** $9750
Application Deadline: open	**Room & Board:** $4750
Freshman Class: 400 applied, 316 accepted, 247 enrolled	
ACT: 20	**COMPETITIVE**

Faulkner University, founded in 1942, is a private, multicampus university affiliated with the Church of Christ, offering undergraduate programs in Bible studies, business, education, and liberal arts and sciences. There are 4 undergraduate and 2 graduate schools. The 2 libraries contain 220,610 volumes, 170,939 microform items, and 1447 audio/video tapes/CDs, and subscribe to 3323 periodicals. Computerized library services include the card catalog, interlibrary loans, and database searching. Special learning facilities include a learning resource center and stellar observatory. The 92-acre campus is in an urban area. Including any residence halls, there are 20 buildings.

Student Life: 88% of undergraduates are from Alabama. Others are from 26 states and 6 foreign countries. 91% are from public schools. 56% are white; 42% African American. 93% are Protestant; 18% claim no religious affiliation. The average age of freshmen is 18; all undergraduates, 28. 45% do not continue beyond their first year; 25% remain to graduate.

Housing: 416 students can be accommodated in college housing, which includes single-sex dorms and on-campus apartments. On-campus housing is available on a first-come, first-served basis. Priority is given to out-of-town students. 82% of students commute. Alcohol is not permitted. All students may keep cars.

Activities: There are 4 local fraternities and 4 local sororities. There are 11 groups on campus, including cheerleading, chorus, drama, honors, literary magazine, musical theater, newspaper, religious, social, social service, student government, and yearbook. Popular campus events include the Annual Bible Lectureship, Jamboree, and Fall Visitation Weekend.

Sports: There are 3 intercollegiate sports for men and 3 for women, and 6 intramural sports for men and 6 for women. Facilities include a gym, a weight room, baseball and softball fields, and lighted tennis courts.

Disabled Students: All of the campus is accessible. Wheelchair ramps, elevators, special parking, specially equipped rest rooms, special housing are available. Special needs are met.

Services: Counseling and information services are available, as is tutoring in some subjects, including basic math, English, and reading comprehension. There is remedial math, reading, and writing.

Campus Safety and Security: Measures include 24-hour foot and vehicle patrol, informal discussions, pamphlets/posters/films, and lighted pathways/sidewalks.

Programs of Study: Faulkner confers B.A. and B.S. degrees. Associate, master's, and doctoral degrees are also awarded. Bachelor's degrees are awarded in BIOLOGICAL SCIENCE (biology/biological science), BUSINESS (business administration and management, business data processing, personnel management, and sports management), COMMUNICATIONS AND THE ARTS (English), EDUCATION (elementary, physical, and secondary), SOCIAL SCIENCE (biblical studies, liberal arts/general studies, and prelaw). Business, criminal justice, and education are the largest.

Required: Students must complete a 52-semester-hour core curriculum, including courses in Bible, history, social science, English composition, literature, art/music appreciation, speech communication, physical and natural science, math, computer literacy, and phys ed. B.A. students must take 2 semesters of foreign language. At least 120 semester hours with a minimum GPA of 2.0 are required to graduate.

Special: A second bachelor's degree in a separate major may be completed with a minimum of 24 semester hours earned beyond the first degree. Cross-registration with Auburn University at Montgomery and Huntingdon College, dual majors, credit for life/military/work experience, and nondegree study are offered. Internships in education, psychology, criminal justice, Bible, and sports management are available, as are accelerated degree programs in some majors. There are 4 national honor societies, a freshman honors program, and honors programs in every department.

Faculty/Classroom: 61% of faculty are male; 39%, female. All teach undergraduates and 10% both teach and do research. No introductory courses are taught by graduate students. The average class size in an introductory lecture is 27; in a laboratory, 15; and in a regular course, 20.

Admissions: 79% of the 2003-2004 applicants were accepted.

Requirements: The ACT is required and the SAT I is recommended, with minimum composite scores of 735 on the SAT I or 17 on the ACT. Candidates must be graduates of an accredited secondary school, or have the GED equivalent, with a minimum of 15 academic units, including 3 in English. A GPA of 2.0 is required. AP and CLEP credits are accepted.

Procedure: Freshmen are admitted to all sessions. Application deadlines are open and the application fee is $10. Applications are accepted on computer disk and on-line through at the school's web site.

Transfer: 71 transfer students enrolled in 2003-2004. Applicants must be in good academic standing from another accredited college. 30 of 120 credits required for the bachelor's degree must be completed at Faulkner.

Visiting: There are regularly scheduled orientations for prospective students. There are guides for informal visits and visitors may sit in on classes and stay overnight. To schedule a visit, contact the Admissions Office at *admissions@faulkner.edu.*

Financial Aid: In 2003-2004, 95% of all full-time students received some form of financial aid. 80% of full-time freshmen and 77% of continuing full-time students received need-based aid. The average freshman award was $6500. Need-based scholarships or need-based grants averaged $4000 ($6000 maximum); need-based self-help aid (loans and jobs) averaged $4500 ($5000 maximum); and non-need-based athletic scholarships averaged $5500 ($14,000 maximum). 59% of undergraduates work part time. Average annual earnings from campus work are $1200. The average financial indebtedness of the 2003 graduate was $15,500. Faulkner is a member of CSS. The FAFSA or FFS and the college's own financial statement are required. The deadline for filing freshman financial aid applications for fall entry is May 1.

International Students: There are 6 international students enrolled. They must score 450 on the written TOEFL and also take the ACT, scoring 17.

Computers: The mainframes are an IBM 486 and Pentiums. PCs and Macs are available in the computer lab. All students may access the system. There are no time limits and no fees. It is strongly recommended that all students have a personal computer.

Graduates: From July 1, 2002 to June 30, 2003, 611 bachelor's degrees were awarded. The most popular majors were business administration (42%), management of human resources (18%), and criminal justice (6%). In an average class, 25% graduate in 6 years or less.

Admissions Contact: Keith Mock, Director of Admissions. E-mail: *kmock@faulkner.edu*

HUNTINGDON COLLEGE
Montgomery, AL 36106-2148

C-4

(334) 833-4497
(800) 763-0313; Fax: (334) 833-4347

Full-time: 205 men, 370 women	**Faculty:** 46; IIB, --$
Part-time: 15 men, 25 women	**Ph.Ds:** 80%
Graduate: none	**Student/Faculty:** 13 to 1
Year: 4-1-4, summer session	**Tuition:** $14,560
Application Deadline: open	**Room & Board:** $5940
Freshman Class: n/av	
SAT I or ACT: required	**VERY COMPETITIVE**

Huntingdon College, founded in 1854, is a private liberal arts institution related to the United Methodist Church. In addition to regional accreditation, Huntingdon has baccalaureate program accreditation with NASM. The library contains 102,074 volumes, 47,443 microform items, and 1517 audio/video tapes/CDs, and subscribes to 391 periodicals. Computerized library services include interlibrary loans and database searching. Special learning facilities include a learning resource center, art gallery, and recital hall and theater. The 58-acre campus is in a suburban area 90 miles south of Birmingham. Including any residence halls, there are 18 buildings.

Student Life: 66% of undergraduates are from Alabama. Students are from 24 states, 12 foreign countries, and Canada. 75% are from public schools. 86% are white. 78% are Protestant; 12% claim no religious affiliation; 10% Catholic. The average age of freshmen is 18; all undergraduates, 20. 27% do not continue beyond their first year; 48% remain to graduate.

Housing: 656 students can be accommodated in college housing, which includes coed dorms. On-campus housing is guaranteed for all 4 years. 72% of students live on campus; of those, 80% remain on campus on weekends. Alcohol is not permitted. All students may keep cars.

Activities: 29% of men belong to 2 national fraternities; 32% of women belong to 3 national sororities. There are 50 groups on campus, including art, cheerleading, choir, chorale, chorus, computers, dance, drama, ethnic, forensics, gay, honors, international, jazz band, literary magazine, musical theater, newspaper, opera, photography, political, professional, religious, social, social service, student government, and yearbook. Popular campus events include Stallworth Lecture Series, Performing Arts Series, and Madrigal Dinner.

Sports: There are 6 intercollegiate sports for men and 6 for women, and 16 intramural sports for men and 16 for women. Facilities include a student center with a 1500-seat gym for volleyball, basketball, and badminton, a swimming pool, weight and training rooms, Ping-Pong tables, pool tables, video games, 2 dance studios, and sports medicine fa-

cilities. There are also outdoor tennis courts, softball, baseball, and soccer fields, and an outdoor volleyball court.

Disabled Students: 80% of the campus is accessible. Wheelchair ramps, elevators, special parking, specially equipped rest rooms, special class scheduling, lowered drinking fountains, and lowered telephones are available.

Services: Counseling and information services are available, as is tutoring in most subjects. There is also a reading and writing lab.

Campus Safety and Security: Measures include 24-hour foot and vehicle patrol, self-defense education, security escort services, and informal discussions. There are pamphlets/posters/films, emergency telephones, lighted pathways/sidewalks, controlled access to residence halls, and weather alert broadcasts.

Programs of Study: Huntingdon confers the B.A. degree. Associate degrees are also awarded. Bachelor's degrees are awarded in AGRICULTURE (soil science), BIOLOGICAL SCIENCE (biology/biological science), BUSINESS (accounting and business administration and management), COMMUNICATIONS AND THE ARTS (art, arts administration/management, communications, dance, dramatic arts, English, music, musical theater, and speech/debate/rhetoric), COMPUTER AND PHYSICAL SCIENCE (chemistry, computer science, digital arts/technology, and mathematics), EDUCATION (art, athletic training, dance, music, and physical), ENGINEERING AND ENVIRONMENTAL DESIGN (computer graphics), HEALTH PROFESSIONS (exercise science and prepharmacy), SOCIAL SCIENCE (American studies, European studies, history, international studies, political science/government, psychology, public administration, public affairs, religion, and religious education). Biology, chemistry, and psychology are the strongest academically. Biology, business, and education are the largest.

Required: Huntingdon's core curriculum includes a 12-hour liberal arts symposium, a 3-hour rhetoric seminar, up to 9 hours of foreign languages, and a 3-hour senior capstone course. Additionally, students take 9 hours each of aesthetic expression and science and technology, and 12 hours of social and self-awareness. Students must maintain a minimum GPA of 2.0 over 124 credits for the B.A. Major requirements range from 30 to 42 hours.

Special: The Huntingdon plan includes an opportunity for travel/study experiences offered as part of regular educational costs, hands-on learning experiences in every program of study, dual majors, internships, and co-op programs in business and computer science. The public affairs trisubject major combines politics with 2 other areas, including history, philosophy, psychology, and communications. Cross-registration is available with Auburn University Montgomery, Faulkner University, and the Marine Environmental Sciences Consortium in Dauphin Island. There are 14 national honor societies and 13 departmental honors programs.

Faculty/Classroom: 67% of faculty are male; 33%, female. The average class size in an introductory lecture is 16; in a laboratory, 13; and in a regular course, 13.

Requirements: The SAT I or ACT is required. In addition, applicants should have completed 4 years of high school English, 3 credits each in math and history, 2 credits of science, 2 credits of foreign language, and 2 credits in humanities. An interview is recommended. A portfolio or audition may be required. A GPA of 2.25 is required. AP and CLEP credits are accepted. Important factors in the admissions decision are evidence of special talent, leadership record, and advanced placement or honor courses. Students can apply on-line via CollegeView and by using the Apply CD-ROM

Procedure: Freshmen are admitted fall and spring. Entrance exams should be taken in the spring of the junior year. There is an early admissions and a rolling admissions plan. Application deadlines are open. The application fee is $25, or $15 if submitted on-line.

Transfer: High school and college transcripts are required. An interview is recommended. 31 of 124 credits required for the bachelor's degree must be completed at Huntingdon.

Visiting: There are regularly scheduled orientations for prospective students, consisting of class visitation, a campus tour, a meeting with an admissions counselor, and student panel, financial aid, and faculty presentations. There are guides for informal visits and visitors may sit in on classes and stay overnight. To schedule a visit, contact the Office of Admission.

Financial Aid: 79% of undergraduates work part time. Average annual earnings from campus work are $850. The FAFSA and the college's own financial statement are required. The deadline for filing freshman financial aid applications for fall entry is April 15.

International Students: The school actively recruits these students. They must score 500 on the written TOEFL. The SAT I or ACT is required only for students whose first language is English.

Computers: The mainframe is a network of powerful PCs. All residence hall rooms, classrooms, and faculty and administrative offices have direct access to the Internet. All students may access the system 24 hours a day, 7 days a week.

Graduates: In an average class, 1% graduate in 3 years or less, 45% graduate in 4 years or less, 66% graduate in 5 years or less, and 70% graduate in 6 years or less.

Admissions Contact: Laura Duncan, Director of Admission.
E-mail: *admiss@huntingdon.edu* Web: *www.huntingdon.edu*

JACKSONVILLE STATE UNIVERSITY   D-2
Jacksonville, AL 36265   **(256) 782-5400**
                                    (800) 231-5291; Fax: (256) 782-5121

Full-time: 2463 men, 3308 women	**Faculty:** 294; IIA, -$
Part-time: 590 men, 928 women	**Ph.Ds:** 70%
Graduate: 584 men, 1158 women	**Student/Faculty:** 20 to 1
Year: semesters, summer session	**Tuition:** $3540 ($7080)
Application Deadline: open	**Room & Board:** $3304
Freshman Class: 2452 applied, 2188 accepted, 1078 enrolled	
ACT: 17	**LESS COMPETITIVE**

Jacksonville State University, founded in 1883, is a public institution offering programs in business, arts and sciences, criminal justice, education, and nursing. There are 4 undergraduate schools and 1 graduate school. In addition to regional accreditation, JSU has baccalaureate program accreditation with AACSB, ADA, CSWE, NASAD, NASM, NCATE, and NLN. The library contains 654,849 volumes, 1,370,774 microform items, and 34,089 audio/video tapes/CDs, and subscribes to 2692 periodicals. Computerized library services include the card catalog, interlibrary loans, database searching, and Internet access. Special learning facilities include a learning resource center, radio station, TV station, and stellar observatory. The 318-acre campus is in a small town 75 miles east of Birmingham. Including any residence halls, there are 58 buildings.

Student Life: 83% of undergraduates are from Alabama. Others are from 47 states, 72 foreign countries, and Canada. 95% are from public schools. 73% are white; 21% African American. The average age of freshmen is 20; all undergraduates, 24. 34% do not continue beyond their first year; 66% remain to graduate.

Housing: 1505 students can be accommodated in college housing, which includes single-sex and coed dormitories, on-campus apartments, off-campus apartments, married-student housing, fraternity houses, and sorority houses. There is an international house for students on Rotary Club scholarships. On-campus housing is available on a first-come, first-served basis. 80% of students commute. Alcohol is not permitted. All students may keep cars.

Activities: 10% of men belong to 9 national fraternities; 10% of women belong to 8 national sororities. There are 100 groups on campus, including art, band, cheerleading, chess, choir, chorus, computers, dance, drama, drill team, ethnic, honors, international, jazz band, marching band, musical theater, newspaper, orchestra, pep band, political, professional, radio and TV, religious, social, social service, student government, symphony, and yearbook. Popular campus events include Visitation Day and Parents Day.

Sports: There are 7 intercollegiate sports for men and 8 for women, and 15 intramural sports for men and 15 for women. Facilities include a 15,000-seat football stadium, indoor and outdoor courts, athletic fields, a 5,000-seat indoor gym, an indoor pool, a weight room, and a fitness center.

Disabled Students: 85% of the campus is accessible. Wheelchair ramps, elevators, special parking, specially equipped rest rooms, lowered drinking fountains, and lowered telephones are available.

Services: Counseling and information services are available, as is tutoring in most subjects. There is remedial math, reading, and writing.

Campus Safety and Security: Measures include 24-hour foot and vehicle patrol, security escort services, informal discussions, and pamphlets/posters/films. There are emergency telephones and lighted pathways/sidewalks.

Programs of Study: JSU confers B.A., B.S., B.F.A., B.S.Ed., and B.S.W. degrees. Master's degrees are also awarded. Bachelor's degrees are awarded in BIOLOGICAL SCIENCE (biology/biological science), BUSINESS (accounting, banking and finance, and marketing/retailing/merchandising), COMMUNICATIONS AND THE ARTS (communications, dramatic arts, English, and music), COMPUTER AND PHYSICAL SCIENCE (chemistry, computer science, mathematics, and physics), EDUCATION (early childhood, elementary, health, home economics, music, secondary, and special), HEALTH PROFESSIONS (nursing), SOCIAL SCIENCE (criminal justice, economics, geography, history, political science/government, psychology, social work, and sociology).

Required: All students are required to complete a core curriculum of 46 semester hours, including 15 hours in fine arts and humanities, 8 each in communications and natural sciences, 6 each in analysis and social sciences, and 3 in wellness. English competency and courses in computer literacy are required. A total of 128 semester hours, with at least 52 hours in courses numbered 300 or above and a minimum GPA of 2.0, are required to graduate. At least 32 semester hours must be completed in residence at JSU with no more than 12 hours in correspondence work.

Special: Co-op programs with major area employees are available. JSU has cross-registration with the Marine Environmental Sciences Consortium and internships in education, political science, communication, journalism, and criminal justice. Work-study programs, dual majors in

most programs, and credit for military experience are offered. There are 13 national honor societies.

Faculty/Classroom: 50% of faculty are male; 50%, female. 99% teach undergraduates, 1% do research, and 70% do both. No introductory courses are taught by graduate students. The average class size in an introductory lecture is 50; in a laboratory, 25; and in a regular course, 25.

Admissions: 89% of the 2003-2004 applicants were accepted. The ACT scores for the 2003-2004 freshman class were: 71% below 21, and 29% between 21 and 23.

Requirements: The SAT I or ACT is required. Applicants should be graduates of an accredited high school; the GED is also accepted. 19 on the ACT or 900 on the SAT I is required for unconditional admission; 16 to 18 on the ACT or 750 to 890 on the SAT I is required for conditional admission. AP and CLEP credits are accepted.

Procedure: Freshmen are admitted to all sessions. Application deadlines are open. Applications are accepted on-line through the school's web site. The fall 2003 application fee was $20. Notification is sent on a rolling basis.

Transfer: 750 transfer students enrolled in 2003-2004. Transfer applicants must be eligible to return to the last institution attended. 32 of 128 credits required for the bachelor's degree must be completed at JSU.

Visiting: There are regularly scheduled orientations for prospective students, consisting of 2-day orientations scheduled during the summer. There are guides for informal visits. To schedule a visit, contact Tracy Phillips at (800) 231-5291 ext. 6 or *phillips@jsucc.jsu.edu.*

Financial Aid: In a recent year, 80% of all full-time freshmen and 78% of continuing full-time students received some form of financial aid. 66% of full-time freshmen and 68% of continuing full-time students received need-based aid. The average freshman award was $3500. 55% of undergraduates work part time. Average annual earnings from campus work are $2500. The average financial indebtedness of the 2003 graduate was $17,125. The FAFSA is required. The deadline for filing freshman financial aid applications for fall entry is March 15.

International Students: There are 97 international students enrolled. They must score 500 on the written TOEFL. The SAT I or ACT may be substituted with the scores listed above.

Computers: The mainframe is an IBM 2003 Model 207. The mainframe is accessed via computer labs at various locations on campus. All students may access the system during specific lab hours. There are no time limits and no fees.

Graduates: From July 1, 2002 to June 30, 2003, 1046 bachelor's degrees were awarded. The most popular majors were elementary education (14%), criminal justice (7%), and nursing (7%). 147 companies recruited on campus in 2002-2003.

Admissions Contact: Martha Mitchell, Director of Admissions.
E-mail: *info@jsucc.jsu.edu* Web: *www.jsu.edu*

JUDSON COLLEGE   B-3
Marion, AL 36756   **(334) 683-5110**
                                    (800) 447-9472; Fax: (334) 683-5147

Full-time: 7 men, 304 women	**Faculty:** 28
Part-time: 8 men, 50 women	**Ph.Ds:** 71%
Graduate: none	**Student/Faculty:** 11 to 1
Year: semesters, summer session	**Tuition:** $9020
Application Deadline: open	**Room & Board:** $5630
Freshman Class: 271 applied, 212 accepted, 83 enrolled	
ACT: 23	**COMPETITIVE**

Judson College, founded in 1838, is a private women's liberal arts college affiliated with the Alabama Baptist Convention. In addition to regional accreditation, Judson has baccalaureate program accreditation with NASM. The library contains 55,383 volumes, 2035 microform items, and 7215 audio/video tapes/CDs, and subscribes to 429 periodicals. Computerized library services include the card catalog, interlibrary loans, database searching, and Internet access. Special learning facilities include a learning resource center and the Alabama Women's Hall of Fame. The 80-acre campus is in a small town 27 miles west of Selma. Including any residence halls, there are 18 buildings.

Student Life: 77% of undergraduates are from Alabama. Students are from 24 states, 5 foreign countries, and Canada. 70% are from public schools. 80% are white; 15% African American. 90% are Protestant; 6% claim no religious affiliation. The average age of freshmen is 19; all undergraduates, 24. 35% do not continue beyond their first year; 45% remain to graduate.

Housing: 264 students can be accommodated in college housing, which includes dorms. On-campus housing is guaranteed for all 4 years. 63% of students live on campus; of those, 33% remain on campus on weekends. Alcohol is not permitted. All students may keep cars.

Activities: There are no fraternities or sororities. There are 29 groups on campus, including art, band, cheerleading, choir, chorale, chorus, computers, dance, drama, environmental, honors, literary magazine, marching band, musical theater, newspaper, orchestra, photography, political, professional, religious, social, social service, student government, woodwind ensemble, and yearbook. Popular campus events include Winter Ball, Junior-Sophomore Dance, and Hockey Day.

Sports: Facilities include an indoor swimming pool, riding stables and a riding arena, tennis courts, a wellness center, a gym, an aerobics room, a weight training facility, a hockey field, and a game room.

Disabled Students: 75% of the campus is accessible. Elevators, special parking, specially equipped rest rooms, lowered drinking fountains, and lowered telephones are available.

Services: Counseling and information services are available, as is tutoring in most subjects. There is remedial math and writing.

Campus Safety and Security: Measures include 24-hour foot and vehicle patrol, self-defense education, informal discussions, and pamphlets/posters/films. There are emergency telephones and lighted pathways/sidewalks.

Programs of Study: Judson confers B.A. and B.S. degrees. Bachelor's degrees are awarded in BIOLOGICAL SCIENCE (biology/biological science), BUSINESS (business administration and management), COMMUNICATIONS AND THE ARTS (applied music, art, English, languages, and music), COMPUTER AND PHYSICAL SCIENCE (chemistry and mathematics), EDUCATION (elementary, English, mathematics, middle school, music, science, secondary, and social studies), SOCIAL SCIENCE (criminal justice, history, interdisciplinary studies, psychology, and religion). Biology, education, and psychology are the strongest academically. Biology, elementary education, and business are the largest.

Required: All students are required to complete courses in women's studies, English, history, multicultural studies, speech, religion, social science, math, science, humanities, computer literacy, and health/phys ed. A total of 128 credit hours, with a minimum GPA of 2.0, (2.5 for education majors) is required to graduate. To graduate, all students must complete a minimum of 30 hours in the major with a minimum GPA of 2.0. B.A. students must also complete at least 6 hours of foreign languages at the 200-level or above; B.S. students must complete at least 12 hours of math or science electives in addition to the core competency. A passing score is required on the English Proficiency Usage Test.

Special: Cross-registration with the Marion Military Institute is available for ROTC students. B.A.-B.S. degrees are offered in criminal justice, fashion merchandising, math, business, biology, business and management information systems, psychology, and chemistry. Study abroad in 7 countries, dual majors, an accelerated degree program, an interdisciplinary major, a 3-2 engineering degree with the University of Alabama, work-study programs, and internships are offered. There are preprofessional programs in health, engineering, and law. The Distance Learning program offers credit for prior learning experience and provides individually paced instruction leading to a baccalaureate degree. There are 7 national honor societies and 15 departmental honors programs.

Faculty/Classroom: 50% of faculty are male; 50%, female. All teach undergraduates. The average class size in an introductory lecture is 18; in a laboratory, 11; and in a regular course, 7.

Admissions: 78% of the 2003-2004 applicants were accepted. The SAT I scores for the 2003-2004 freshman class were: Verbal--20% below 500, 20% between 600 and 700, and 60% above 700; Math--20% below 500, 60% between 500 and 599, and 20% above 700. The ACT scores were 36% below 21, 30% between 21 and 23, 23% between 24 and 26, 4% between 27 and 28, and 7% above 28. 28% of the current freshmen were in the top fifth of their class; 62% were in the top two fifths.

Requirements: The SAT I or ACT is required, with a minimum composite score of 18 on the ACT. Applicants should have completed 17 high school credits, including 4 in English, with at least a 2.0 GPA. Non-high school graduates must provide the GED equivalent. An interview is required. AP and CLEP credits are accepted. Important factors in the admissions decision are advanced placement or honor courses, evidence of special talent, and leadership record.

Procedure: Freshmen are admitted fall, winter, and summer. Entrance exams should be taken in the spring of the junior year. There is a rolling admissions plan and an early admissions plan. Application deadlines are open. The fall 2003 application fee was $25. Applications are accepted on-line.

Transfer: 12 transfer students enrolled in 2002-2003. Transfer students must have a minimum GPA of 2.0 and be eligible to return to the school from which they transfer. 32 of 128 credits required for the bachelor's degree must be completed at Judson.

Visiting: There are regularly scheduled orientations for prospective students, consisting of 2 college Preview Days, 1 in June and 1 in August. There are guides for informal visits and visitors may sit in on classes and stay overnight. To schedule a visit, contact Admissions at *admissions@future.judson.edu.*

Financial Aid: In 2003-2004, 98% of all full-time freshmen and 96% of continuing full-time students received some form of financial aid. 93% of full-time freshmen and 66% of continuing full-time students received need-based aid. The average freshman award was $9758. Need-based scholarships or need-based grants averaged $6534; need-based self-help aid (loans and jobs) averaged $3648; non-need-based athletic scholarships averaged $1500; and other non-need-based awards and non-

need-based scholarships averaged $3905. 53% of undergraduates work part time. Average annual earnings from campus work are $1000. The average financial indebtedness of the 2003 graduate was $15,339. The FAFSA, the state aid form, and the college's own financial statement are required. The deadline for filing freshman financial aid applications for fall entry is March 1.

International Students: There were 2 international students enrolled in a recent year. They must score 500 on the written TOEFL or 173 on the electronic version.

Computers: There are 2 general computer centers with 30 PCs available for student use. Access is provided to the campus network and the Internet. The library has 11 for general use. Additionally, specialized computer centers for music and technical writing students bring the total to 61 PCs. All students may access the system 8 A.M. to 1 A.M. Monday to Friday, Saturday, 12 P.M. to 5 P.M., Sunday, 5 P.M. to 1 A.M. There are no time limits and no fees.

Graduates: From July 1, 2002 to June 30, 2003, 53 bachelor's degrees were awarded. The most popular majors were biology (23%), psychology (21%), and education (15%). In an average class, 9% graduate in 3 years or less, 41% graduate in 4 years or less, and 45% graduate in 5 years or less. Of the 2002 graduating class, 14% were enrolled in graduate school within 6 months of graduation and 84% were employed.

Admissions Contact: Michael Scotto, Director of Admissions. E-mail: *admissions@future.judson.edu* Web: *home.judson.edu*

MILES COLLEGE
C-2
Birmingham, AL 35208
(205) 929-1656
(800) 445-0708; Fax: (205) 929-1668

Full-time: 1400 men and women	**Faculty:** 46
Part-time: none	**Ph.D.s:** 50%
Graduate: none	**Student/Faculty:** 30 to 1
Year: semesters, summer session	**Tuition:** $4770
Application Deadline: open	**Room & Board:** $3100
Freshman Class: n/av	
SAT I or ACT: required	**NONCOMPETITIVE**

Miles College, founded in 1908, is a private institution affiliated with and controlled by the Christian Methodist Episcopal Church. The college offers undergraduate programs in the liberal arts and sciences, business, and education. There are 5 undergraduate schools. Figures given in above capsule and in this profile are approximate. The library contains 180,000 volumes and 850 microform items, and subscribes to 250 periodicals. Special learning facilities include a learning resource center, an Afro-American materials center, and a media center. The 35-acre campus is in an urban area 7 miles from downtown Birmingham. Including any residence halls, there are 17 buildings.

Student Life: 98% are African American. The average age of freshmen is 18; all undergraduates, 22. 15% do not continue beyond their first year.

Housing: 490 students can be accommodated in college housing, which includes single-sex dorms. On-campus housing is available on a first-come, first-served basis. Priority is given to out-of-town students. Alcohol is not permitted. All students may keep cars.

Activities: 15% of men belong to 4 local and 4 national fraternities; 15% of women belong to 4 local and 4 national sororities. There are 12 groups on campus, including choir, drama, ethnic, honors, international, literary magazine, newspaper, professional, radio and TV, religious, student government, and yearbook. Popular campus events include Senior Class Day, Spring Festival, and Honors Day.

Sports: There are 6 intercollegiate sports for men and 4 for women, and 5 intramural sports for men and 5 for women. Facilities include a 2000-seat football field, a 1500-seat gym, a weight room, and a baseball field.

Services: Counseling and information services are available, as is tutoring in every subject. There is remedial math, reading, and writing. Miles offers a Student Support Services Program for students with an academically challenged developmental background.

Programs of Study: Miles confers B.A., B.S., and B.S.W. degrees. Associate degrees are also awarded. Bachelor's degrees are awarded in BIOLOGICAL SCIENCE (biology/biological science), BUSINESS (accounting and business administration and management), COMMUNICATIONS AND THE ARTS (communications, English, and language arts), COMPUTER AND PHYSICAL SCIENCE (chemistry, computer science, and mathematics), EDUCATION (early childhood, elementary, science, secondary, and social science), ENGINEERING AND ENVIRONMENTAL DESIGN (environmental science and preengineering), HEALTH PROFESSIONS (predentistry, premedicine, and preveterinary science), SOCIAL SCIENCE (political science/government and social work). Business is the strongest academically. Early childhood and elementary education are the largest.

Required: To graduate, all students must complete a minimum of 51 hours of general education requirements, including the 33-hour freshman studies program. A minimum of 124 credit hours is required for a bachelor's degree, with a minimum GPA of 2.0 in the major. All students must pass English proficiency and exit exams.

Special: Miles offers co-op programs in all majors, internships, federal work-study, and cross-registration with the University of Alabama at Birmingham and other area colleges and universities. There are cooperative programs in allied health sciences with the University of Alabama at Birmingham, and in engineering, physics, veterinary medicine, and Asian studies. There is 1 national honor society and a freshman honors program.

Faculty/Classroom: All teach. undergraduates.

Requirements: The SAT I or ACT is required. In addition, students should be graduates of an accredited high school or hold a GED. A personal interview is recommended. A GPA of 2.0 is required.

Procedure: Freshmen are admitted to all sessions. Application deadlines are open. The fall 2003 application fee was $25.

Transfer: 32 of 124 credits required for the bachelor's degree must be completed at Miles.

Visiting: There are guides for informal visits and visitors may sit in on classes. To schedule a visit, contact Admissions.

Financial Aid: Miles is a member of CSS. The FAFSA is required. Check with the school for current deadlines.

International Students: They must score 450 on the written TOEFL or take the MELAB and also take the SAT I or the ACT.

Computers: All students may access the system. There are no time limits. The fee is $20.

Admissions Contact: Admissions Director. A video is available. Web: *www.miles.edu*

OAKWOOD COLLEGE
C-1
Huntsville, AL 35896

(256) 726-7000
(800) 824-5312; Fax: (256) 726-7154

Full-time: 665 men, 900 women	**Faculty:** 96; IIB, --$
Part-time: 90 men, 105 women	**Ph.D.s:** 54%
Graduate: none	**Student/Faculty:** 16 to 1
Year: semesters, summer session	**Tuition:** $9420
Application Deadline: open	**Room & Board:** $5485
Freshman Class: n/av	
SAT I or ACT: recommended	**COMPETITIVE**

Oakwood College, founded in 1896, is a private, historically black, Seventh-day Adventist institution offering undergraduate programs in business and education, humanities, natural sciences and math, religion and theology, and social sciences. Figures in the above capsule and in this profile are approximate. In addition to regional accreditation, Oakwood has baccalaureate program accreditation with ACBSP, ADA, CSWE, and NCATE. The library contains 125,373 volumes, 2140 microform items, and 4816 audio/video tapes/CDs, and subscribes to 630 periodicals. Computerized library services include the card catalog and database searching. Special learning facilities include a learning resource center, radio station, and a black history museum. The 105-acre campus is in a suburban area 5 miles northwest of Huntsville. Including any residence halls, there are 30 buildings.

Student Life: 79% of undergraduates are from out of state, mostly the South. Students are from 39 states, 22 foreign countries, and Canada. 52% are from public schools. 79% are African American; 12% foreign nationals. The average age of freshmen is 19; all undergraduates, 23. 27% do not continue beyond their first year.

Housing: 1173 students can be accommodated in college housing, which includes single-sex dorms and married-student housing. On-campus housing is available on a first-come, first-served basis. Priority is given to out-of-town students. 71% of students live on campus; of those, 98% remain on campus on weekends. Alcohol is not permitted. Upperclassmen may keep cars.

Activities: There are no fraternities or sororities. There are 20 groups on campus, including band, choir, chorale, drama, honors, international, newspaper, professional, radio and TV, religious, student government, and yearbook. Popular campus events include Convocations, the Arts and Lecture Series, and Centennial.

Sports: There are 4 intramural sports for men and 3 for women. Facilities include a gym, a skating rink, an Olympic-size pool, tennis courts, playing fields, racquetball courts, and a weight room.

Disabled Students: 80% of the campus is accessible. Wheelchair ramps, elevators, special parking, and specially equipped rest rooms are available.

Services: Counseling and information services are available, as is tutoring in most subjects. There is remedial math, reading, and writing. Testing, counseling, and developmental guidance services are available through the counseling center.

Campus Safety and Security: Measures include 24-hour foot and vehicle patrol, security escort services, informal discussions, and pamphlets/posters/films. There are lighted pathways/sidewalks.

Programs of Study: Oakwood confers B.A., B.S., B.B.A., B.M., and B.S.W. degrees. Associate degrees are also awarded. Bachelor's degrees are awarded in BIOLOGICAL SCIENCE (biochemistry and biology/biological science), BUSINESS (accounting and business administration

and management), COMMUNICATIONS AND THE ARTS (communications, English, French, music, music business management, music performance, and Spanish), COMPUTER AND PHYSICAL SCIENCE (chemistry, computer mathematics, computer science, information sciences and systems, mathematics, and natural sciences), EDUCATION (business, elementary, English, home economics, mathematics, music, physical, science, and social science), HEALTH PROFESSIONS (medical technology and nursing), SOCIAL SCIENCE (dietetics, family/consumer studies, history, home economics, human development, international studies, ministries, physical fitness/movement, psychology, religion, religious education, and social work). Biochemistry, chemistry, and nursing are the strongest academically. Business and biology are the largest.

Required: To graduate, students must complete 128 semester hours, including 30 in the major and 40 in upper-division courses, with a GPA of 2.0. Regular chapel attendance is required. All students must complete a liberal arts core, and must meet English oral and written proficiency requirements.

Special: Students may cross-register with Alabama A&M, Athens State, or the University of Alabama at Huntsville. The college offers a student missionary abroad program as well as a study abroad program through the Adventist College Consortium. Internships, work-study, dual majors, independent study, life experience credit, and pass/fail options are also available. A second bachelor's degree is offered to students completing at least 160 semester credits. There is 1 national honor society and 2 departmental honors program.

Faculty/Classroom: 51% of faculty are male; 49%, female. All teach undergraduates. The average class size in an introductory lecture is 30; in a laboratory, 30; and in a regular course, 40.

Admissions: 1 freshman graduated first in the class in a recent year.

Requirements: The SAT I or ACT is recommended. In addition, applicants should be high school graduates with a minimum GPA of 2.0 and at least 11 academic units, distributed as follows: 4 in English, 2 each in math, science, and social studies, and 1 in typing. The GED is accepted. Two character references are required. Students with GPAs between 1.7 and 2.0 may be admitted on probation. Applicants admitted without test scores must take the ACT during freshman orientation. AP and CLEP credits are accepted. Important factors in the admissions decision are recommendations by school officials, ability to finance college education, and leadership record.

Procedure: Freshmen are admitted to all sessions. Entrance exams should be taken before high school graduation. There is an early decision plan and a rolling admissions plan. Application deadlines are open. The application fee is $20.

Transfer: Applicants must submit a college transcript and a statement of honorable dismissal. Grades of C minus or better transfer for credit. 32 of 128 credits required for the bachelor's degree must be completed at Oakwood.

Visiting: There are guides for informal visits and visitors may sit in on classes and stay overnight. To schedule a visit, contact Fred Pullins, Enrollment Management at (256) 726-7030.

Financial Aid: Oakwood is a member of CSS. The FAFSA, the college's own financial statement, and student and parent federal income tax returns are required. Check with the school for current deadlines.

International Students: They must score 500 on the written TOEFL and also take the college's own test and the SAT I or ACT. Students may take the ACT on campus prior to registration.

Computers: PCs are available in various departmental computer labs. A public computer lab is available in the library. There are no time limits. Fees vary.

Admissions Contact: Fred Pullins, Enrollment Management Director. E-mail: *admission@oakwood.edu* Web: *www.oakwood.edu*

SAMFORD UNIVERSITY
C-2
Birmingham, AL 35229

(205) 726-3673
(800) 888-7218; Fax: (205) 726-2171

Full-time: 977 men, 1683 women	**Faculty:** 181; IIA, +$
Part-time: 50 men, 126 women	**Ph.D.s:** 80%
Graduate: 146 men, 248 women	**Student/Faculty:** 15 to 1
Year: 4-1-4, summer session	**Tuition:** $13,154
Application Deadline: March 1	**Room & Board:** $5494
Freshman Class: 2074 applied, 1859 accepted, 680 enrolled	
SAT I or ACT: required	**VERY COMPETITIVE**

Samford University, founded in 1841, is a private, liberal arts school and maintains a close relationship with the Alabama Baptist Convention. There are 5 undergraduate and 8 graduate schools. In addition to regional accreditation, Samford has baccalaureate program accreditation with AACSB, CAAHEP, CCNE, FIDER, NASM, and NCATE. The 5 libraries contain 446,272 volumes, 1,318,119 microform items, and 15,181 audio/video tapes/CDs, and subscribe to 3522 periodicals. Computerized library services include the card catalog, interlibrary loans, and database searching. Special learning facilities include a learning resource center, art gallery, planetarium, radio station, TV station, global center, drug information center, and conservatory. The 180-acre campus is in a suburban area 4 miles south of Birmingham. Including any residence halls, there are 62 buildings.

Student Life: 54% of undergraduates are from out of state, mostly the South. Students are from 41 states, 17 foreign countries, and Canada. 65% are from public schools. 89% are white. Most are Protestant. The average age of freshmen is 18; all undergraduates, 20. 11% do not continue beyond their first year; 89% remain to graduate.

Housing: 1860 students can be accommodated in college housing, which includes single-sex dorms, fraternity houses, and sorority houses. In addition, there is a university-owned facility for study in England. On-campus housing is available on a first-come, first-served basis. 65% of students live on campus. Alcohol is not permitted. All students may keep cars.

Activities: 29% of men belong to 7 national fraternities; 38% of women belong to 8 national sororities. There are 102 groups on campus, including band, cheerleading, choir, chorale, chorus, computers, dance, debate, drama, drill team, ethnic, honors, international, jazz band, literary magazine, marching band, musical theater, newspaper, opera, orchestra, pep band, political, professional, radio and TV, religious, social, social service, student government, symphony, and yearbook. Popular campus events include Step Sing, Spring Fling, and Family Weekend.

Sports: There are 8 intercollegiate sports for men and 9 for women, and 12 intramural sports for men and 12 for women. Facilities include a 6700-seat stadium, a 4000-seat gym, intramural fields, tennis and racquetball courts, practice fields, baseball, soccer, and softball fields, and a swimming pool.

Disabled Students: Most of the campus is accessible. Wheelchair ramps, elevators, special parking, specially equipped rest rooms, special class scheduling, lowered drinking fountains, lowered telephones, and special housing are available.

Services: Counseling and information services are available, as is tutoring in most subjects. There is a reader service for the blind.

Campus Safety and Security: Measures include 24-hour foot and vehicle patrol, self-defense education, security escort services, and informal discussions. There are pamphlets/posters/films, emergency telephones, and lighted pathways/sidewalks.

Programs of Study: Samford confers B.A., B.S., B.G.S., B.Mus., B.S.B.A., B.S.Ed., and B.S.N. degrees. Associate, master's, and doctoral degrees are also awarded. Bachelor's degrees are awarded in BIOLOGICAL SCIENCE (biochemistry, biology/biological science, marine science, and nutrition), BUSINESS (accounting, business administration and management, and human resources), COMMUNICATIONS AND THE ARTS (classics, communications, dramatic arts, English, fine arts, French, German, graphic design, Greek, journalism, language arts, Latin, music, music performance, music theory and composition, musical theater, piano/organ, Spanish, and voice), COMPUTER AND PHYSICAL SCIENCE (chemistry, computer science, mathematics, physics, and science), EDUCATION (athletic training, early childhood, elementary, music, physical, and secondary), ENGINEERING AND ENVIRONMENTAL DESIGN (engineering physics, environmental science, and interior design), HEALTH PROFESSIONS (exercise science, health, nursing, and sports medicine), SOCIAL SCIENCE (Asian/Oriental studies, biblical studies, community services, counseling/psychology, family/consumer studies, geography, history, international relations, Latin American studies, liberal arts/general studies, philosophy, political science/government, psychology, public administration, religion, religious music, social science, and sociology). Teacher education, business, and music are the strongest academically. Nursing, business management, and early childhood education are the largest.

Required: All students must receive an overall GPA of at least 2.0 and take at least 128 credits, including 30 semester hours in their major. Distribution requirements include 8 semester hours in cultural perspectives, 8 semester hours in communication arts, 4 hours in Biblical Perspectives, and 2 hours in phys ed. Students also must demonstrate writing proficiency. 50% of credits must be in the degree field, with 15 credits in the major field.

Special: A 3-2 engineering degree is available with Auburn, Washington (St. Louis), and Mercer Universities and the University of Alabama. The School of Arts and Sciences offers an interdisciplinary core curriculum with team teaching. Cross-registration with Birmingham-Southern College, the University of Alabama at Birmingham, the University of Montevallo, and Miles College, study abroad in England and 16 other countries, additional major options, internships, credit for life experience, and pass/fail options are also offered. Accelerated degree programs are possible in some majors. There are 28 national honor societies, a freshman honors program, and 17 departmental honors programs.

Faculty/Classroom: 54% of faculty are male; 46%, female. 72% teach undergraduates. No introductory courses are taught by graduate students. The average class size in an introductory lecture is 21; in a laboratory, 25; and in a regular course, 21.

Admissions: 90% of the 2003-2004 applicants were accepted. The ACT scores for the 2003-2004 freshman class were: 14% below 21, 23% between 21 and 23, 30% between 24 and 26, 15% between 27 and 28,

and 18% above 28. 55% of the current freshmen were in the top fifth of their class; 80% were in the top two fifths. There were 7 National Merit finalists and 2 semifinalists. 27 freshmen graduated first in their class.

Requirements: The SAT I or ACT is required. In addition, applicants need 18 academic credits and 16 Carnegie units, including 4 in English, 3 each in math and science, and 2 each in social studies and history. 2 units in foreign language are recommended. An essay is required and an interview suggested. The GED is accepted. AP and CLEP credits are accepted. Important factors in the admissions decision are advanced placement or honor courses, leadership record, and recommendations by school officials.

Procedure: Freshmen are admitted fall, spring, and summer. Entrance exams should be taken in the junior year. There is a rolling admissions plan. There are early admissions and deferred admissions plans. Priority applications should be filed by March 1 for fall entry. The fall 2003 application fee was $25. Notification is sent on a rolling basis. Applications are accepted on-line through the school's web site at http://www.applyweb.com/aw?samu.

Transfer: 79 transfer students enrolled in 2002-2003. A minimum of 15 credits in the major field must be earned at Samford. 64 of 128 credits required for the bachelor's degree must be completed at Samford.

Visiting: There are regularly scheduled orientations for prospective students, consisting of a 2-day program during which students stay on campus, take placement tests, meet advisers, and register for classes. There are guides for informal visits and visitors may sit in on classes and stay overnight. To schedule a visit, contact the Admissions Office.

Financial Aid: In 2002-2003, 40% of all full-time freshmen and 41% of continuing full-time students received some form of financial aid. At least 38% of all full-time students received need-based aid. The average freshman award was $9977. Need-based scholarships or need-based grants averaged $7527; need-based self-help aid (loans and jobs) averaged $3211; non-need-based athletic scholarships averaged $9168; and other institutional non-need-based awards and non-need-based scholarships averaged $5584. 30% of undergraduates work part time. Average annual earnings from campus work are $1500. The average financial indebtedness of the 2003 graduate was $15,801. The FAFSA is required. The priority date for freshman financial aid applications for fall entry is March 1.

International Students: There were 24 international students enrolled in a recent year. They must score 550 on the written TOEFL or 213 on the electronic version and also take the SAT I or the ACT.

Computers: The mainframe is an IBM RISC/6000 7026 H70. There are 6 computer labs available for general academic and student use. Near semester's end, hours of operation may be extended. PCs include Dell and Power Mac. There is a voice/data connection for every resident student. All students may access the system. There are no time limits and no fees.

Graduates: From July 1, 2002 to June 30, 2003, 626 bachelor's degrees were awarded. The most popular majors were business (16%), development and family studies (9%), and education (8%). In an average class, 51% graduate in 4 years or less, and 69% graduate in 5 years or less. 187 companies recruited on campus in 2002-2003.

Admissions Contact: Phil Kimrey, Dean of Admission and Financial Aid. E-mail: *admiss@samford.edu* Web: *www.samford.edu*

SOUTHERN CHRISTIAN UNIVERSITY   C-4
Montgomery, AL 36117-3553   (334) 387-3877, ext. 213
(800) 351-4040; Fax: (334) 387-3878

Full-time: 180 men, 149 women	**Faculty:** 50
Part-time: 6 men, 6 women	**Ph.D.s:** 63%
Graduate: 184 men, 124 women	**Student/Faculty:** 7 to 1
Year: semesters, summer session	**Tuition:** $9440
Application Deadline: open	**Room & Board:** n/app
Freshman Class: n/av	
SAT I or ACT: n/av	**LESS COMPETITIVE**

Southern Christian University, founded in 1967 and affiliated with the Church of Christ, merges traditional and on-line education; 90% of its students access SCU programs via Distance Learning. There is 1 undergraduate and 2 graduate schools. The library contains 73,000 volumes, 500 microform items, and 800 audio/video tapes/CDs, and subscribes to 1200 periodicals. Computerized library services include the card catalog, interlibrary loans, database searching, and Internet access. Special learning facilities include a learning resource center. The 9-acre campus is in an urban area in Montgomery. There is one building.

Student Life: 65% of undergraduates are from out of state. Students are from 50 states and 3 foreign countries. 68% are white; 30% African American. Most are Protestant. The average age of freshmen is 28; all undergraduates, 35.

Housing: There are no residence halls. Alcohol is not permitted. All students may keep cars.

Activities: There are no fraternities or sororities. There are some groups and organizations on campus, including student government.

Disabled Students: Wheelchair ramps and special parking are available. All classrooms and the learning resource center are accessible.

Programs of Study: SCU confers B.A. and B.S. degrees. Master's and doctoral degrees are also awarded. Bachelor's degrees are awarded in BUSINESS (human resources and management information systems), EDUCATION (social foundations), SOCIAL SCIENCE (biblical studies, human development, law enforcement and corrections, liberal arts/general studies, ministries, and safety management). Human and social development, management communication, and ministry/Bible are the largest.

Required: Students must complete at least 128 credit hours, with 36 in the major and a minimum GPA of 2.0.

Faculty/Classroom: 77% of faculty are male; 23%, female. No introductory courses are taught by graduate students.

Requirements: CLEP credit is accepted.

Procedure: Freshmen are admitted to all sessions. Application deadlines are open. Application fee is $50. Applications are accepted on-line through *www.southernchristian.edu*. Notification is sent on a rolling basis.

Transfer: Unconditional admission requires a 2.0 GPA on prior course work; below 2.0, students are admitted on a conditional basis. 32 of 128 credits required for the bachelor's degree must be completed at SCU.

Visiting: On-line orientation is available at the school's web site.

Financial Aid: In a recent year, 90% of all full-time freshmen received some form of financial aid. 85% of full-time freshmen received need-based aid. The average freshman award was $9725. The average financial indebtedness of a recent graduate was $30,000. The FAFSA and the college's own financial statement are required. Check with the school for current deadlines.

International Students: There are 4 international students enrolled. They must score 440 on the written TOEFL and also take the SAT I or the ACT.

Computers: On-campus students may use PCs in the library. All students may access the system. All students are required to have personal computers. A Windows 200MHz Intel Pentium Processor or equivalent Mac OS 8.1 is required.

Graduates: From July 1, 2002 to June 30, 2003, 95 bachelor's degrees were awarded. The most popular majors were ministry/Bible (41%), human development (34%), and management communication (23%). Of the 2002 graduating class, 50% were enrolled in graduate school within 6 months of graduation and 90% were employed.

Admissions Contact: Rick Johnson, Director of Enrollment Management. E-mail: *rickkjohnson@southernchristian.edu*
Web: *www.southernchristian.edu*

SPRING HILL COLLEGE
A-5
Mobile, AL 36608

(251) 380-3030
(800) 742-6704; Fax: (251) 460-2186

Full-time: 403 men, 640 women	**Faculty:** 66; IIA, --$
Part-time: 52 men, 116 women	**Ph.Ds:** 92%
Graduate: 90 men, 178 women	**Student/Faculty:** 16 to 1
Year: semesters, summer session	**Tuition:** $19,000
Application Deadline: July 1	**Room & Board:** $6868
Freshman Class: 1122 applied, 892 accepted, 312 enrolled	
SAT I Verbal/Math: 560/540	**ACT:** 24 **VERY COMPETITIVE**

Spring Hill College, founded in 1830, is a private Catholic liberal arts and sciences college. There is 1 undergraduate and 4 graduate schools. In addition to regional accreditation, Spring Hill has baccalaureate program accreditation with ACBSP and CCNE. The 2 libraries contain 169,755 volumes, 301,110 microform items, and 100 audio/video tapes/CDs, and subscribe to 548 periodicals. Computerized library services include the card catalog, interlibrary loans, database searching, and Internet access. Special learning facilities include a theater. The 450-acre campus is in a suburban area in Mobile. Including any residence halls, there are 32 buildings.

Student Life: 51% of undergraduates are from Alabama. Students are from 35 states, 15 foreign countries, and Canada. 76% are white; 15% African American. 57% are Catholic; 23% Protestant. The average age of freshmen is 18; all undergraduates, 22. 19% do not continue beyond their first year; 58% remain to graduate.

Housing: 852 students can be accommodated in college housing, which includes single-sex and coed dorms and on-campus apartments. On-campus housing is guaranteed for all 4 years. 69% of students live on campus; of those, 90% remain on campus on weekends. All students may keep cars.

Activities: 22% of men belong to 3 national fraternities; 25% of women belong to 4 national sororities. There are 30 groups on campus, including art, cheerleading, chorale, computers, dance, drama, ethnic, honors, international, literary magazine, musical theater, newspaper, photography, political, professional, religious, social, social service, student government, and yearbook. Popular campus events include Mardi Gras, Oktoberfest, and Christmas on the Hill.

Sports: There are 7 intercollegiate sports for men and 8 for women, and 8 intramural sports for men and 8 for women. Facilities include an 18-hole golf course; tennis and basketball courts; an outdoor sand volleyball area; and baseball, softball, football, rugby, and soccer fields. A recreation center houses the intercollegiate basketball arena, 2 basketball courts, 2 racquetball courts, a cardiovascular exercise room, an indoor pool, and a running track.

Disabled Students: 80% of the campus is accessible. Wheelchair ramps, elevators, special parking, specially equipped rest rooms, special class scheduling, lowered drinking fountains, and lowered telephones are available.

Services: Counseling and information services are available, as is tutoring in some subjects, including English, theology, math, languages, philosophy, economics, biology, and accounting. There is remedial math, reading, and writing.

Campus Safety and Security: Measures include 24-hour foot and vehicle patrol, self-defense education, security escort services, and informal discussions. There are pamphlets/posters/films, emergency telephones, and lighted pathways/sidewalks.

Programs of Study: Spring Hill confers B.A., B.S., and B.S.N. degrees. Associate and master's degrees are also awarded. Bachelor's degrees are awarded in BIOLOGICAL SCIENCE (biochemistry, biology/biological science, and marine biology), BUSINESS (accounting, banking and finance, business administration and management, electronic business, international business management, marketing management, and organizational behavior), COMMUNICATIONS AND THE ARTS (arts administration/management, communications, creative writing, dramatic arts, English, graphic design, journalism, Spanish, and studio art), COMPUTER AND PHYSICAL SCIENCE (chemistry, computer science, and mathematics), EDUCATION (early childhood, elementary, and secondary), ENGINEERING AND ENVIRONMENTAL DESIGN (engineering and environmental science), HEALTH PROFESSIONS (art therapy, nursing, predentistry, premedicine, and preveterinary science), SOCIAL SCIENCE (economics, history, humanities, international studies, liberal arts/general studies, philosophy, political science/government, psychology, and theological studies). Theology, English, and business are the strongest academically. Business administration, biology, and psychology are the largest.

Required: All students must take core curriculum courses in English composition and literature, history, philosophy, theology, math, science, social science, fine art, and foreign language. Students must also take one cultural diversity course and at least 3 writing-enriched courses (including one in the major) beyond the required 4 core curriculum English courses. Graduation requirements include completion of a minimum of 128 semester hours with a minimum GPA of 2.0 and 30-36 upper-division semester hours in the major with a minimum grade of 2.0.

Special: SHC offers 3-2 engineering programs with the University of Alabama-Birmingham, Auburn University, the University of Florida, Marquette University, and Texas A & M University. It also offers 3-3 occupational therapy and physical therapy programs with Rockhurst University and Nova Southeastern University. The college is a member of the Marine Environmental Sciences Consortium and offers marine biology courses at the Dauphin Island Sea Lab. Several study-abroad options are available. Internships are also available in many majors. An accelerated degree program is offered in organizational leadership, and most majors may be completed in 3 years by taking summer courses. Also available are dual majors, student-designed majors, a Washington semester, and pass/fail options. There are 8 national honor societies, a freshman honors program, and 5 departmental honors programs.

Faculty/Classroom: 61% of faculty are male; 39%, female. All teach undergraduates. No introductory courses are taught by graduate students. The average class size in an introductory lecture is 23; in a laboratory, 20; and in a regular course, 16.

Admissions: 80% of the 2003-2004 applicants were accepted. The SAT I scores for the 2003-2004 freshman class were: Verbal--27% below 500, 33% between 500 and 599, 37% between 600 and 700, and 3% above 700; Math--27% below 500, 44% between 500 and 599, 26% between 600 and 700, and 3% above 700. The ACT scores were 26% below 21, 23% between 21 and 23, 21% between 24 and 26, 17% between 27 and 28, and 13% above 28. 42% of the current freshmen were in the top fifth of their class; 71% were in the top two fifths. 6 freshmen graduated first in their class.

Requirements: The SAT I or ACT is required; the ACT is preferred. Applicants should have completed at least 16 high school units, including 4 in English, 3 each in math, science, and social studies, and 3 in other academic areas. The GED equivalent is accepted. An essay is required and an interview is recommended. Spring Hill requires applicants to be in the upper 50% of their class. A GPA of 2.5 is required. AP and CLEP credits are accepted. Important factors in the admissions decision are advanced placement or honor courses, recommendations by school officials, and leadership record.

Procedure: Freshmen are admitted fall, spring, and summer. Entrance exams should be taken in spring of the junior year or fall of the senior year. There is a rolling admissions plan and a deferred admissions plan. Applications should be filed by July 1 for fall entry and December 15 for spring entry, along with a $25 fee. Notification is sent on a rolling basis. Applications are accepted on-line through the college's web site.

Transfer: 47 transfer students enrolled in 2002-2003. Transfer applicants must have at least 20 semester hours of college credit, a minimum cumulative GPA of 2.5, good academic standing at the last college or university attended, and satisfactory recommendation. 32 of 128 credits required for the bachelor's degree must be completed at Spring Hill.

Visiting: There are regularly scheduled orientations for prospective students, including a campus tour, faculty appointment, attending a class, lunch with a student, and an interview with an admission counselor. There are guides for informal visits and visitors may sit in on classes and stay overnight. To schedule a visit, contact the Office of Admissions at *admit@shc.edu*.

Financial Aid: In 2003-2004, 96% of all full-time freshmen and 95% of continuing full-time students received some form of financial aid. 67% of all full-time students received need-based aid. The average freshman award was $15,655. Need-based scholarships or need-based grants averaged $7353 ($20,100 maximum); need-based self-help aid (loans and jobs) averaged $3863 ($7195 maximum); non-need-based athletic scholarships averaged $5034 ($21,368 maximum); and other non-need-based awards and non-need-based scholarships averaged $8807 ($17,830 maximum). 27% of undergraduates work part time. Average annual earnings from campus work are $847. The average financial indebtedness of the 2003 graduate was $17,092. Spring Hill is a member of CSS. The FAFSA, the state aid form, and the college's own financial statement are required. The priority date for freshman financial aid applications for fall entry is March 1.

International Students: There are 19 international students enrolled. The school actively recruits these students. They must score 550 on the written TOEFL or 213 on the electronic version or take the MELAB. The SAT I or ACTis required of students with English as their first language.

Computers: The mainframe is an HP9000 minicomputer. The minicomputer supports interactive users as well as servers for the academic network of PCs and Macs. The academic network is connected to the Internet. Approximately 141 PCs and 14 Macs are available for general student use; these include machines in instructional labs that support teaching needs. All students may access the system. Students may access the system from residence halls all the time. Computer labs are open Monday to Thursday, 8 A.M. to midnight; Friday, 8 A.M. to 10 P.M.; Saturday, 10 A.M. to 5 P.M.; Sunday, noon to midnight. There are no time limits and no fees.

Graduates: From July 1, 2002 to June 30, 2003, 202 bachelor's degrees were awarded. The most popular majors were business administration (22%), communication arts (21%), and biology and psychology (9%). In an average class, 2% graduate in 3 years or less, 47% graduate in 4 years or less, 57% graduate in 5 years or less, and 58% graduate in 6 years or less. 7 companies recruited on campus in 2002-2003. Of the 2002 graduating class, 28% were enrolled in graduate school within 6 months of graduation and 71% were employed.

Admissions Contact: Florence Hines, Vice President of Enrollment Management. E-mail: *admit@shc.edu*
Web: *http://www.shc.edu/admission*

STILLMAN COLLEGE
B-3
Tuscaloosa, AL 35403-9990
(205) 366-8156
(800) 841-5722; Fax: (205) 366-8817

Full-time: 640 men, 780 women	**Faculty:** 52
Part-time: 20 men, 20 women	**Ph.D.s:** 70%
Graduate: none	**Student/Faculty:** 27 to 1
Year: semesters, summer session	**Tuition:** $7848
Application Deadline: open	**Room & Board:** $4000
Freshman Class: n/av	
SAT I or ACT: required	**LESS COMPETITIVE**

Stillman College, founded in 1876, is a small, private liberal arts institution affiliated with the Presbyterian Church (U.S.A.). Figures in the above capsule and in this profile are approximate. The library contains 113,120 volumes, 7240 microform items, and 3550 audio/video tapes/CDs, and subscribes to 360 periodicals. Computerized library services include the card catalog, interlibrary loans, and database searching. Special learning facilities include a learning resource center, art gallery, and radio station. The 100-acre campus is in a small town 60 miles from Birmingham and 105 miles from Montgomery. Including any residence halls, there are 26 buildings.

Student Life: 70% of undergraduates are from Alabama. Students are from 27 states and 8 foreign countries. 95% are from public schools. 98% are African American. Most are Protestant. The average age of freshmen is 19.

Housing: 750 students can be accommodated in college housing, which includes single-sex dorms and off-campus apartments. On-campus housing is available on a first-come, first-served basis. 50% of students live on campus. Alcohol is not permitted. All students may keep cars.

Activities: 10% of men belong to 4 national fraternities; 20% of women belong to 4 national sororities. There are 19 groups on campus, including art, band, cheerleading, choir, chorus, dance, debate, drama, honors, international, jazz band, marching band, newspaper, pep band, radio and TV, religious, social, social service, student government, and yearbook. Popular campus events include "S" Day, Founder's Day, and Coffee House.

Sports: There are 6 intercollegiate sports for men and 6 for women. Facilities include a college center, tennis courts, a stress center, bowling lanes, billiards, a swimming pool, a gym, a football field, and a weight room.

Disabled Students: Wheelchair ramps, elevators, special parking, and specially equipped rest rooms are available.

Services: Counseling and information services are available, as is tutoring in some subjects, including reading, writing, math, physics, and chemistry. There is remedial math, reading, and writing.

Campus Safety and Security: Measures include 24-hour foot and vehicle patrol, self-defense education, security escort services, and informal discussions. There are pamphlets/posters/films and lighted pathways/sidewalks.

Programs of Study: Stillman confers B.A. and B.S. degrees. Bachelor's degrees are awarded in BIOLOGICAL SCIENCE (biology/biological science), BUSINESS (business administration and management), COMMUNICATIONS AND THE ARTS (art, English, and music), COMPUTER AND PHYSICAL SCIENCE (computer science and mathematics), EDUCATION (elementary and physical), HEALTH PROFESSIONS (premedicine), SOCIAL SCIENCE (history, prelaw, and religion).

Required: To graduate, students must complete a minimum of 124 credit hours, with at least 30 in the major, and maintain a minimum GPA of 2.0 overall and in the major. The 53-credit-hour general education core includes courses in religion, logic, English composition, public speaking, African heritage, African American experience, history, social science, physical and life sciences, math, computer literacy, health, and phys ed. All students must submit a senior thesis and take a senior departmental exam.

Special: Stillman offers local, national, and international opportunites for cooperative education and internships. Cross-registration is possible with the University of Alabama at Birmingham, with which there also are cooperative degree programs in nursing and allied health. Federal work-study is available on and off campus, and students may earn credit for prior learning experiences. There are 3 national honor societies.

Faculty/Classroom: 40% of faculty are male; 60%, female. All teach undergraduates. The average class size in an introductory lecture is 40; in a laboratory, 40; and in a regular course, 35.

Requirements: The SAT I or ACT is required. In addition, applicants should be high school graduates or have earned the GED. Secondary preparation should include 4 units of English and 1 unit each of math, science, and history. All applicants must have an interview. Music majors must audition. A GPA of 2.0 is required. AP and CLEP credits are accepted.

Procedure: Freshmen are admitted to all sessions. There is a rolling admissions plan. Notification is sent on a rolling basis. Application deadlines are open. The application fee is $25.

Transfer: Transfer applicants should present at least a C average in previous college work and must plan to spend at least a year in residence. 64 of 124 credits required for the bachelor's degree must be completed at Stillman.

Visiting: There are regularly scheduled orientations for prospective students. To schedule a visit, contact the director of recruitment.

Financial Aid: The CSS Profile, FAFSA, FFS, or SFS and the college's own financial statement are required. Check with the school for current deadlines.

International Students: The school actively recruits these students. They must take the SAT I or the ACT. Applicants whose native language is not English must take the TOEFL.

Computers: The mainframe is a DEC Alpha server. Terminals and PCs are available in computer labs and residence halls. Student accounts and e-mail addresses are issued. All students may access the system 8 A.M. to 9 P.M. Monday through Saturday. There are no fees.

Admissions Contact: Mason Bonner, Director of Admissions.
E-mail: *mbonner@www.stillman.edu* Web: *www.stillman.edu*

TALLADEGA COLLEGE
C-2
Talladega, AL 35160
(256) 761-6416; (800) 633-2440

Full-time: 230 men, 400 women	**Faculty:** 40
Part-time: 10 men, 20 women	**Ph.D.s:** 60%
Graduate: none	**Student/Faculty:** 16 to 1
Year: semesters	**Tuition:** $6810
Application Deadline: open	**Room & Board:** $3300
Freshman Class: n/av	
SAT I or ACT: required	**LESS COMPETITIVE**

Talladega College, founded in 1867, is a private liberal arts institution offering emphases on business, sciences, and social work. Figures given in above capsule and in this profile are approximate. In addition to regional accreditation, Dega has baccalaureate program accreditation with

CSWE. The library contains 87,960 volumes and 350 audio/video tapes/CDs, and subscribes to 330 periodicals. Computerized library services include the card catalog and interlibrary loans. Special learning facilities include a learning resource center, art gallery, science drop-in center, curriculum and writing labs, and financial computer lab. The 130-acre campus is in a small town 55 miles east of Birmingham and 115 miles west of Atlanta. Including any residence halls, there are 42 buildings.

Student Life: 60% of undergraduates are from Alabama. Students are from 29 states and 2 foreign countries. 99% are African American. Most are Protestant. The average age of freshmen is 18; all undergraduates, 20. 22% do not continue beyond their first year; 45% remain to graduate.

Housing: 580 students can be accommodated in college housing, which includes single-sex dorms and on-campus apartments. In addition, there are honors houses. On-campus housing is guaranteed for all 4 years. 70% of students live on campus; of those, 90% remain on campus on weekends. Alcohol is not permitted. All students may keep cars.

Activities: 14% of men belong to 4 national fraternities; 40% of women belong to 4 national sororities. There are 23 groups on campus, including art, cheerleading, choir, chorus, computers, dance, drama, honors, jazz band, newspaper, professional, social, student government, and yearbook. Popular campus events include Spring Concert, Carnival, and Coronation.

Sports: There are 4 intercollegiate sports for men and 4 for women, and 8 intramural sports for men and 3 for women. Facilities include a swimming pool, a 150-seat gym, lounges, game rooms, tennis courts, and a baseball field.

Disabled Students: 50% of the campus is accessible. Wheelchair ramps, elevators, special parking, and specially equipped rest rooms are available.

Services: Counseling and information services are available, as is tutoring in every subject. There is remedial math, reading, and writing.

Campus Safety and Security: Measures include 24-hour foot and vehicle patrol, security escort services, informal discussions, and pamphlets/posters/films. There are lighted pathways/sidewalks.

Programs of Study: Dega confers the B.A. degree. Bachelor's degrees are awarded in BIOLOGICAL SCIENCE (biology/biological science), BUSINESS (accounting, banking and finance, and business administration and management), COMMUNICATIONS AND THE ARTS (English and music performance), COMPUTER AND PHYSICAL SCIENCE (chemistry, computer science, mathematics, and physics), EDUCATION (music), SOCIAL SCIENCE (economics, history, psychology, public administration, social work, and sociology). Business, biology, and chemistry are the strongest academically. Biology is the largest.

Required: To graduate, students must maintain a minimum GPA of 2.5 while taking 124 to 127 total semester hours, including 60 in the major and completion of a core curriculum. Distribution requirements at the freshman level include 8 semester hours in natural sciences, 6 each in communications, social sciences, and humanities, 2 in phys ed, and 1 in freshman orientation; additional hours in these subjects vary by major at the sophomore level.

Special: Talladega offers co-op programs with other schools through individual departments, a 3-2 engineering degree with Auburn University, internships involving historic preservation work, work-study plans with Adopt-a-Family and Adult Literacy, and B.A.-B.S. degrees in biology, business administration, chemistry, and computer science. There are dual majors available in law, nursing, engineering, and allied health. There are 4 national honor societies.

Faculty/Classroom: 60% of faculty are male; 40%, female. All teach undergraduates and 25% both teach and do research. The average class size in an introductory lecture is 30; in a laboratory, 20; and in a regular course, 18.

Requirements: The SAT I or ACT is required. In addition, applicants must be graduates of an accredited secondary school with 22 academic units, including 4 in English, 3 in social studies, and 2 each in math, science, health/phys ed, and electives. The GED is considered. An essay and interview are recommended. An audition is required for music majors. A GPA of 2.5 is required. CLEP credit is accepted. Important factors in the admissions decision are advanced placement or honor courses, recommendations by school officials, and recommendations by alumni. Applications are accepted on-line through the school's web site.

Procedure: Freshmen are admitted fall and spring. Entrance exams should be taken in the junior year. There is a deferred admissions plan and a rolling admissions plan. Application deadlines are open. The fall 2003 application fee was $10.

Transfer: Applicants must have a cumulative GPA of 2.0 in college work. The SAT I or ACT is recommended. 60 of 124 credits required for the bachelor's degree must be completed at Dega.

Visiting: There are guides for informal visits and visitors may sit in on classes and stay overnight. To schedule a visit, contact the Admissions Office.

Financial Aid: The CSS Profile, FAFSA, FFS, or SFS and the college's own financial statement are required. Check with the school for current deadlines.

International Students: The school actively recruits these students. They must take the TOEFL or the college's own test and the SAT I or the ACT.

Computers: The mainframes are a DEC VAX 750 and an HP 835/41. Student computer labs in the library and in a classroom building provide 30 PCs and 3 mainframe terminals. All students may access the system from 8 A.M. to 4:30 P.M. and 7 P.M. to 10 P.M. daily. There are no time limits and no fees.

Admissions Contact: Admissions Office.
E-mail: *admissions@talladega.edu* Web: *www.talladega.edu*

TROY STATE UNIVERSITY SYSTEM

The Troy State University System, established in 1887, is a private system in Alabama. It is governed by a board of trustees, whose chief administrator is chancellor. The primary goal of the system is to provide an academic, cultural, and social environment conducive to the development of students as well as productive, individual members of society. The main priorities are the preprofessional and professional preparation of students in the arts and sciences, fine arts, business, education, communication, applied science, nursing, and allied health sciences. The total enrollment of the main campus is about 7000; there were about 654 faculty members. Altogether there are 38 baccalaureate, and 14 master's programs offered in Troy State University System. Profiles of the 4-year campuses are included in this section.

TROY STATE UNIVERSITY	C-4
Troy, AL 36082	(334) 670-3179
	(800) 551-9716; Fax: (334) 670-3733

Full-time: 1510 men, 2070 women	Faculty: 209; IIA, --$
Part-time: 350 men, 680 women	Ph.D.s: 53%
Graduate: 850 men, 1325 women	Student/Faculty: 17 to 1
Year: semesters, summer session	Tuition: $3530 ($7060)
Application Deadline: open	Room & Board: $4580
Freshman Class: n/av	
SAT I or ACT: required	COMPETITIVE

Troy State University, founded in 1887, is a liberal arts institution that is part of the public Troy State University system. There are 5 undergraduate and 3 graduate schools. Figures in the above capsule and in this profile are approximate. In addition to regional accreditation, TSU has baccalaureate program accreditation with AACSB, ACBSP, CSWE, NASM, NCATE, and NLN. The library contains 389,524 volumes, 1,362,063 microform items, and 10,065 audio/video tapes/CDs, and subscribes to 4190 periodicals. Computerized library services include the card catalog, interlibrary loans, and database searching. Special learning facilities include a learning resource center, art gallery, TV station, and arboretum. The 577-acre campus is in a small town 50 miles south of Montgomery. Including any residence halls, there are 73 buildings.

Student Life: 83% of undergraduates are from Alabama. Students are from 49 states, 55 foreign countries, and Canada. 62% are white; 25% African American.

Housing: 1527 students can be accommodated in college housing, which includes single-sex and coed dorms, on-campus apartments, off-campus apartments, married-student housing, fraternity houses, and sorority houses. In addition, there are honors houses, special-interest houses, an international house, and substance-free housing. On-campus housing is guaranteed for all 4 years. 72% of students commute. Alcohol is not permitted. All students may keep cars.

Activities: 18% of men belong to 11 national fraternities; 19% of women belong to 8 national sororities. There are 110 groups on campus, including art, band, cheerleading, choir, chorale, chorus, computers, dance, drama, drill team, ethnic, film, honors, international, jazz band, literary magazine, marching band, musical theater, newspaper, opera, orchestra, pep band, photography, political, professional, radio and TV, religious, social, social service, student government, symphony, and yearbook. Popular campus events include Greek Week, winter formals, and spring break weekends.

Sports: There are 7 intercollegiate sports for men and 9 for women, and 11 intramural sports for men and 11 for women. Facilities include a 17,500-seat football stadium, a 4000-seat gym, a natatorium, a baseball field, a golf course, and tennis courts.

Disabled Students: 95% of the campus is accessible. Wheelchair ramps, elevators, special parking, specially equipped rest rooms, special class scheduling, lowered drinking fountains, lowered telephones, graded inclines, and specially equipped apartments are available.

Services: Counseling and information services are available, as is tutoring in most subjects. There is a reader service for the blind and remedial math, reading, and writing.

Campus Safety and Security: Measures include 24-hour foot and vehicle patrol, self-defense education, security escort services, and pamphlets/posters/films. There are lighted pathways/sidewalks.

Programs of Study: TSU confers B.A., B.S., B.A.Ed., B.Applied Sc., B.S.Ed., and B.S.N. degrees. Associate and master's degrees are also awarded. Bachelor's degrees are awarded in BIOLOGICAL SCIENCE (biology/biological science and marine biology), BUSINESS (accounting, banking and finance, business administration and management, and marketing/retailing/merchandising), COMMUNICATIONS AND THE ARTS (art history and appreciation, broadcasting, communications, dramatic arts, English, journalism, and speech/debate/rhetoric), COMPUTER AND PHYSICAL SCIENCE (chemistry, computer science, and mathematics), EDUCATION (art, early childhood, elementary, English, foreign languages, health, mathematics, music, physical, science, secondary, social science, and special), HEALTH PROFESSIONS (medical technology and nursing), SOCIAL SCIENCE (criminal justice, history, human services, international relations, political science/government, psychology, social science, and social work). Business and education are the strongest academically. Business is the largest.

Required: All students must maintain a minimum GPA of 2.0 while taking 120 to 140 semester credit hours, 54 of which must be in their major field. Distribution requirements include 48 hours of general studies, covering such subjects as English, math, history, science, and fine arts.

Special: Cross-registration with the Marine Biological Consortium, internships in education, journalism, and nursing, study abroad in 2 countries, work-study programs at the university, and student-designed majors in public relations, advertising, and other fields are offered. Credit for life experience and nondegree study are also offered. There are 21 national honor societies, including Phi Beta Kappa, a freshman honors program, and 8 departmental honors programs.

Faculty/Classroom: 52% of faculty are male; 48%, female. All teach undergraduates.

Requirements: The SAT I or ACT is required, with recommended composite scores of 870 or 18, respectively. Applicants must have earned at least 15 Carnegie units, with 11 in academic courses and 3 to 4 in English. An interview is recommended, along with a portfolio or audition for some programs. The GED is accepted. A GPA of 2.0 is required. AP and CLEP credits are accepted. Important factors in the admissions decision are ability to finance college education, evidence of special talent, and extracurricular activities record. Applications are accepted on-line.

Procedure: Freshmen are admitted to all sessions. Entrance exams should be taken in the fall of the senior year. There is a rolling admissions plan. Application deadlines are open. The fall 2003 application fee was $20.

Transfer: 372 transfer students enrolled in a recent year. Transfer applicants need 20 semester hours attempted at their previous institution, with a GPA of at least 2.0.

Visiting: There are regularly scheduled orientations for prospective students, including a campus tour, classroom visitation, academic consultation, and interviews. There are guides for informal visits and visitors may sit in on classes. To schedule a visit, contact the Office of Enrollment Services.

Financial Aid: TSU is a member of CSS. The CSS Profile, FAFSA, FFS, or SFS and the college's own financial statement are required. The deadline for filing freshman financial aid applications for fall entry is May 1.

International Students: There were 224 international students enrolled in a recent year. The school actively recruits these students. They must score 500 on the written TOEFL or 175 on the electronic version and also take the SAT I or the ACT, scoring 18 on the ACT or 870 on the SAT I.

Computers: The mainframes are an IBM ES 9000 and an IBM 9375. All students may access the system 7 days a week. There are no time limits and no fees.

Graduates: In a recent year, 827 bachelor's degrees were awarded. The most popular majors were business (26%), education (24%), and nursing (7%). In an average class, 40% graduate in 4 years or less, and 52% graduate in 5 years or less.

Admissions Contact: Buddy Starling, Dean of Enrollment Services. A video is available. E-mail: *bstar@trojan.troyst.edu* Web: *www.troyst.edu*

TROY STATE UNIVERSITY DOTHAN   D-5
Dothan, AL 36304   (334) 983-6556; Fax: (334) 983-6322

Full-time: 253 men, 539 women	Faculty: 59
Part-time: 304 men, 485 women	Ph.D.s: 81%
Graduate: 66 men, 252 women	Student/Faculty: 13 to 1
Year: semesters, summer session	Tuition: $3842 ($7372)
Application Deadline: open	Room & Board: n/app
Freshman Class: 139 applied, 97 accepted, 77 enrolled	
ACT: 22	COMPETITIVE

Troy State University Dothan, founded in 1965, is a public liberal arts school. As part of the Troy State University System, it established a permanent campus in Dothan in 1977 to serve the tri-state region. It continues to offer degree completion studies for the military at Fort Rucker. There are 3 undergraduate and 3 graduate schools. In addition to regional accreditation, TSUD has baccalaureate program accreditation with ACBSP and NCATE. The library contains 101,136 volumes, 283,829 microform items, and 14,311 audio/video tapes/CDs, and subscribes to 455 periodicals. Computerized library services include the card catalog, interlibrary loans, database searching, and Internet access. Special learning facilities include a learning resource center. The 250-acre campus is in an urban area 90 miles southeast of Montgomery. There are 3 buildings.

Student Life: 93% of undergraduates are from Alabama. Others are from 7 states. 95% are from public schools. 71% are white; 21% African American. The average age of freshmen is 24; all undergraduates, 30. 48% do not continue beyond their first year; 31% remain to graduate.

Housing: There are no residence halls. All students commute. Alcohol is not permitted. All students may keep cars.

Activities: There are no fraternities or sororities. There are 19 groups on campus, including band, computers, ethnic, honors, literary magazine, professional, religious, social, and student government. Popular campus events include Spring Picnic, Heritage Week, and Black History Program.

Sports: There is no sports program at TSUD.

Disabled Students: All of the campus is accessible. Wheelchair ramps, elevators, special parking, specially equipped rest rooms, lowered drinking fountains, and lowered telephones are available.

Services: Counseling and information services are available, as is tutoring in most subjects. There is remedial math and writing.

Campus Safety and Security: Measures include 24-hour foot and vehicle patrol, pamphlets/posters/films, and lighted pathways/sidewalks.

Programs of Study: TSUD confers B.A., B.S., B.A.Ed., B.A.S., and B.S.Ed degrees. Associate and master's degrees are also awarded. Bachelor's degrees are awarded in BIOLOGICAL SCIENCE (biology/ biological science), BUSINESS (accounting, banking and finance, business administration and management, business economics, marketing management, and personnel management), COMMUNICATIONS AND THE ARTS (English), COMPUTER AND PHYSICAL SCIENCE (chemistry, computer science, mathematics, and science), EDUCATION (early childhood, elementary, English, mathematics, science, secondary, social science, and special), SOCIAL SCIENCE (criminal justice, psychology, social science, and sociology). Education is the strongest academically. Computer information systems, accounting, and elementary education are the largest.

Required: All students must take a minimum of 120 semester hours, including 30 in their major, and must maintain an overall GPA of at least 2.0. Distribution requirements include English composition I and II, 6 hours each of literature, history, and social science, 3 hours each of music and art, microcomputing and speech, math, biology, philosophy, and science.

Special: Internships in the accounting and education programs, nondegree study, and pass/fail options are available. There are 4 national honor societies.

Faculty/Classroom: 68% of faculty are male; 32%, female. All teach undergraduates. No introductory courses are taught by graduate students. The average class size in a regular course is 15.

Admissions: 70% of the 2003-2004 applicants were accepted. The ACT scores for the 2003-2004 freshman class were: 29% below 21, 52% between 21 and 23, and 19% between 24 and 26.

Requirements: The SAT I or ACT is required. In addition, applicants must be graduates of an accredited high school. Beginning freshmen under age 21 must have a minimum ACT score of 19. The GED is accepted. A GPA of 2.0 is required. AP and CLEP credits are accepted.

Procedure: Freshmen are admitted fall, spring, and summer. Entrance exams should be taken during the junior year of high school. Application deadlines are open and the application fee is $20. Applications are accepted on-line through *http://www.tsud.edu/admissions/admissionapp.htm.*

Transfer: 347 transfer students enrolled in 2003-2004. Transfer applicants receive unconditional acceptance if their GPA is 2.0 or above. 30 of 120 credits required for the bachelor's degree must be completed at TSUD.

Visiting: There are regularly scheduled orientations for prospective students, including review of program and services, introduction of department deans, and meetings with advisers. There are guides for informal visits and visitors may sit in on classes. To schedule a visit, contact Taylor Barbaree at (334) 983-6556 ext. 207 or *tbarbaree@tsud.edu.*

Financial Aid: In 2003-2004, 53% of all full-time freshmen and 64% of continuing full-time students received some form of financial aid. 53% of full-time freshmen and 64% of continuing full-time students received need-based aid. Need-based scholarships or need-based grants averaged $3082; and need-based self-help aid (loans and jobs) averaged $1896. 1% of undergraduates work part time. The FAFSA is required. The deadline for filing freshman financial aid applications for fall entry is July 1.

International Students: They must score 550 on the written TOEFL or 213 on the electronic version.

Computers: The mainframe is an IBM 4331. There are 120 PCs in 3 labs and the library. All students may access the system between 8 A.M.

and 9 P.M., Monday through Thursday and on weekends. There are no time limits and no fees.

Graduates: From July 1, 2002 to June 30, 2003, 292 bachelor's degrees were awarded. The most popular majors were general business (31%), computer and information science (13%), and elementary education (12%). 56 companies recruited on campus in 2002-2003.

Admissions Contact: Bob Willis, Enrollment Services.
E-mail: *rwillis@troyst.edu* Web: *www.tsud.edu*

TROY STATE UNIVERSITY MONTGOMERY

		C-4
Montgomery, AL 36103-4419		(334) 241-9506
	(800) 355-TSUM; Fax: (334) 241-9714	

Full-time: 380 men, 707 women	**Faculty:** 37
Part-time: 609 men, 1486 women	**Ph.D.s:** n/av
Graduate: 178 men, 398 women	**Student/Faculty:** 29 to 1
Year: semesters, summer session	**Tuition:** $3600 ($7130)
Application Deadline: open	**Room & Board:** n/app
Freshman Class: n/av	
SAT I or ACT: not required	**NONCOMPETITIVE**

Troy State University Montgomery, founded in 1965 as a branch of the Troy State University System, is a public evening commuter institution offering undergraduate and graduate degrees in arts and sciences, education, and business. There are 3 undergraduate schools and 1 graduate school. In addition to regional accreditation, TSUM has baccalaureate program accreditation with ACBSP. The library contains 36,504 volumes, 78,323 microform items, and 9166 audio/video tapes/CDs, and subscribes to 484 periodicals. Computerized library services include the card catalog, interlibrary loans, and database searching. Special learning facilities include a learning resource center, planetarium, radio station, TV station, and the Rosa L. Parks Library and Museum. The 6-acre campus is in an urban area in downtown Montgomery. There are 7 buildings.

Student Life: 99% of undergraduates are from Alabama. 52% are African American; 44% white. The average age of all undergraduates is 28.

Housing: There are no residence halls. All students commute. Alcohol is not permitted.

Activities: There are no fraternities or sororities. There are 7 groups on campus, including honors, professional, social service, and student government. Popular campus events include Golf Classic.

Sports: There is no sports program at TSUM.

Disabled Students: 95% of the campus is accessible. Wheelchair ramps, elevators, special parking, specially equipped rest rooms, lowered drinking fountains, and lowered telephones are available.

Services: Counseling and information services are available, as is tutoring in some subjects. There is a reader service for the blind, and remedial math, reading, and writing. Tutors may be provided for students upon request.

Campus Safety and Security: Measures include security escort services, informal discussions, pamphlets/posters/films, and lighted pathways/sidewalks. There are foot and vehicle patrols during class hours.

Programs of Study: TSUM confers B.A. and B.S. degrees. Associate and master's degrees are also awarded. Bachelor's degrees are awarded in BUSINESS (accounting, banking and finance, business administration and management, management science, and marketing management), COMMUNICATIONS AND THE ARTS (English), COMPUTER AND PHYSICAL SCIENCE (computer science and mathematics), SOCIAL SCIENCE (history, political science/government, psychology, and social science). Computer and information science is the strongest academically. Resources management is the largest.

Required: Students must complete a minimum of 120 semester hours, with 36 hours within the TSU system in the major area, and maintain a minimum GPA of 2.0. At least half of the required total hours must be composed of traditional credits, excluding credit by correspondence or by exam.

Special: TSUM offers an external degree program in professional studies for those unable to attend regularly scheduled classes because of handicap, work, or family restrictions. Credit may be granted for military service and experiential learning. Guided independent study/research, accelerated degree programs, nondegree study, and pass/fail options are possible. Flexible schedules and televised courses are available to meet the needs of adult students. Cross-registration with Alabama State University is offered. There are 2 national honor societies.

Faculty/Classroom: No introductory courses are taught by graduate students.

Requirements: Graduates from accredited secondary schools should have 15 Carnegie units, with 3 or more in English and 11 others in academic courses. Graduates from nonaccredited secondary schools may be admitted if they meet the same requirements and are deemed capable of performing satisfactorily. The GED is accepted. Other applicants may be admitted as unclassified, nondegree-seeking students. For students under 21, the high school GPA and SAT I or ACT scores are used in a formula to determine admissions eligibility; those applicants not having a test score may be admitted with conditional status. For students

over 21, requirements include a minimum high school GPA of 2.0. Applicants with a lower GPA may be admitted conditionally.

Procedure: Freshmen are admitted to all sessions. Entrance exams should be taken by the fall of the senior year. There is an early admissions plan. There is a rolling admissions plan. Application deadlines are open. Application fee is $20. Applications are accepted on-line through the school's web site.

Transfer: Transfer students must submit college transcripts from each college attended. Those with fewer than 15 quarter hours (or 9 semester hours) of credit are required to submit a high school transcript as well. Applicants should have a college GPA of at least 2.0 and be in good standing; others may be admitted conditionally.

Visiting: There are guides for informal visits and visitors may sit in on classes.

Computers: The mainframes are a DEC Alpha server 2000, a DEC Alpha server 1000, and 4 Gateway ALR 7200 Series. Students may access compilers and other utilities via DEC terminals and PCs in several locations as well as through dial-up capability. Approximately 300 PCs have access to the Internet and the Web. Students taking computer and information science courses may access the system 7 days a week.

Graduates: From July 1, 2002 to June 30, 2003, 302 bachelor's degrees were awarded. The most popular majors were human resources management (28%), psychology (16%), and general business (15%).

Admissions Contact: Larry Hawkins, Director of Enrollment Management. E-mail: *admit@tsum.edu* Web: *www.tsum.edu*

TUSKEGEE UNIVERSITY

		D-4
Tuskegee, AL 36088		(334) 727-8500
	(800) 622-6531; Fax: (334) 724-4402	

Full-time: 1004 men, 1292 women	**Faculty:** 231
Part-time: 46 men, 49 women	**Ph.D.s:** 70%
Graduate: 151 men, 221 women	**Student/Faculty:** 10 to 1
Year: semesters, summer session	**Tuition:** $11,310
Application Deadline: open	**Room & Board:** $5940
Freshman Class: n/av	
SAT I or ACT: required	**LESS COMPETITIVE**

Tuskegee University, founded in 1881 by Booker T. Washington, is an independent professional and technical institution offering degree programs in liberal arts and sciences, agriculture, architecture, business, education, engineering, and health professions. Some information in this capsule and profile is approximate. There are 5 undergraduate and 4 graduate schools. In addition to regional accreditation, Tuskegee has baccalaureate program accreditation with ABET, CSWE, NAAB, NCATE, and NLN. The 3 libraries contain 293,660 volumes and 300 microform items, and subscribe to 1150 periodicals. Computerized library services include the card catalog, interlibrary loans, and database searching. Special learning facilities include a learning resource center, the Carver Museum, a child development center, and special engineering labs. The 5200-acre campus is in a rural area 40 miles east of Montgomery. Including any residence halls, there are 150 buildings.

Student Life: 70% of undergraduates are from out of state, mostly the South. Students are from 41 states, 31 foreign countries, and Canada. 90% are from public schools. 90% are African American. The average age of freshmen is 18; all undergraduates, 22. 29% do not continue beyond their first year; 51% remain to graduate.

Housing: 2300 students can be accommodated in college housing, which includes single-sex dorms, on-campus apartments, and married-student housing. In addition, there are honors houses. On-campus housing is guaranteed for the freshman year only. 60% of students live on campus. Alcohol is not permitted. All students may keep cars.

Activities: 4% of men belong to 6 local and 4 national fraternities; 4% of women belong to 5 local and 4 national sororities. There are 60 groups on campus, including band, cheerleading, choir, chorus, drama, honors, international, jazz band, marching band, newspaper, orchestra, religious, social service, and student government. Popular campus events include Spring Pageant, Campus All-Star Challenge, and Student Leadership Retreat.

Sports: There are 5 intercollegiate sports for men and 5 for women, and 7 intramural sports for men and 6 for women. Facilities include a 10,000-seat stadium, a 5000-seat arena, a student center, tennis courts, a rifle range, playing fields, and an Olympic-size natatorium.

Disabled Students: Wheelchair ramps, elevators, special parking, specially equipped rest rooms, special class scheduling, lowered drinking fountains, and lowered telephones are available.

Services: Counseling and information services are available, as is tutoring in some subjects. There is a reader service for the blind.

Campus Safety and Security: Measures include 24-hour foot and vehicle patrol, security escort services, informal discussions, and lighted pathways/sidewalks.

Programs of Study: Tuskegee confers B.A., B.S., and B.S.N. degrees. Master's and doctoral degrees are also awarded. Bachelor's degrees are awarded in AGRICULTURE (animal science and horticulture), BIOLOGICAL SCIENCE (biology/biological science), BUSINESS (accounting, banking and finance, business administration and management, business economics, hospitality management services, management science, and marketing/retailing/merchandising), COMMUNICATIONS AND THE ARTS (English), COMPUTER AND PHYSICAL SCIENCE (chemistry, computer science, mathematics, and physics), EDUCATION (early childhood, elementary, physical, secondary, special, and technical), ENGINEERING AND ENVIRONMENTAL DESIGN (chemical engineering, construction management, electrical/electronics engineering, and mechanical engineering), HEALTH PROFESSIONS (nursing, occupational therapy, and veterinary science), SOCIAL SCIENCE (dietetics, food science, history, political science/government, psychology, social work, and sociology). Engineering, biology, and veterinary science are the largest.

Required: All students must complete a general education curriculum, including courses in history, sociology, philosophy, art, English, humanities, political science, math, natural sciences, and phys ed. A minimum of 124 semester credits with a GPA of 2.0 is required for graduation.

Special: Cooperative programs, internships, work-study programs, dual majors, nondegree study, and a B.A.-B.S. degree are offered. There are 17 national honor societies, a freshman honors program, and 9 departmental honors programs.

Faculty/Classroom: 70% of faculty are male; 30%, female. No introductory courses are taught by graduate students.

Requirements: The SAT I or ACT is required, with the SAT I preferred. The recommended minimum composite score is 900 on the SAT I or 18 on the ACT. A GPA of 2.5 is recommended. Applicants should be graduates of an accredited secondary school or hold the GED. They should have completed 4 units of English, 3 each of social science and math, and 1 each of physical science and biological science. SAT II: Subject tests in mathematics (level I or II) and 1 other subject are recommended. An essay is required. A GPA of 2.0 is required. AP and CLEP credits are accepted.

Procedure: Freshmen are admitted to all sessions. There is an early admissions plan. Application deadlines are open. Notification is sent on a rolling basis.

Transfer: Applicants must be in good standing at all previously attended institutions and have completed 12 or more semester hours with a GPA of 2.0. 44 of 124 credits required for the bachelor's degree must be completed at Tuskegee.

Visiting: Visitors may sit in on classes and stay overnight. To schedule a visit, contact the Office of Admissions.

Financial Aid: Tuskegee is a member of CSS. The CSS Profile and federal tax returns are required. Check with the school for current deadlines.

International Students: These students must take the TOEFL and the SAT I or the ACT.

Computers: The mainframe is a DEC VAX 6420. There are more than 150 PCs and terminals in various campus departments. All students may access the system. There are no time limits and no fees.

Graduates: From July 1, 2002 to June 30, 2003, 472 bachelor's degrees were awarded. The most popular majors were engineering (13%), veterinary medicine (12%), and biology (11%). In an average class, 25% graduate in 4 years or less, 6% graduate in 5 years or less, and 20% graduate in 6 years or less. Of the 2002 graduating class, 22% were enrolled in graduate school within 6 months of graduation and 80% were employed.

Admissions Contact: Monette Evans, Vice President/Director for Admissions and Enrollment Management.
E-mail: *admi@acd.tuskegee.edu* Web: *www.tuskegee.edu*

UNIVERSITY OF ALABAMA SYSTEM

The University of Alabama System, established in 1969, is a public system in Alabama. It is governed by a board of trustees, whose chief administrator is the chancellor. The primary goal of the system is to serve all the people of the state through teaching, research, and public service. The main priorities are to promote the economic, cultural, and social welfare of Alabama through higher education; to educate and train the leaders and citizens of tomorrow; and to conduct research in all fields that address the critical needs of mankind. The total enrollment of all 3 campuses is usually about 40,000; there were 3000 faculty members. Altogether there are some 175 baccalaureate, 150 master's, and 90 doctoral programs offered in University of Alabama System. There is a 4-year campus located in Tuscaloosa, Birmingham, and Huntsville. Profiles of the 4-year campuses are included in this section.

UNIVERSITY OF ALABAMA
Tuscaloosa, AL 35487

B-3
(205) 348-5666
(800) 933-BAMA; Fax: (205) 348-9046

Full-time: 6578 men, 7672 women	**Faculty:** 649; I, --$
Part-time: 782 men, 836 women	**Ph.D.s:** 98%
Graduate: 1954 men, 2448 women	**Student/Faculty:** 22 to 1
Year: semesters, summer session	**Tuition:** $4134 ($11,294)
Application Deadline: August 1	**Room & Board:** $4906
Freshman Class: 8298 applied, 7194 accepted, 3077 enrolled	
SAT I Verbal/Math: 554/553	**ACT:** 24 COMPETITIVE+

The University of Alabama, founded in 1831, is a public comprehensive research institution and part of the University of Alabama system. There are 8 undergraduate and 10 graduate schools. In addition to regional accreditation, UA has baccalaureate program accreditation with AACSB, AAFCS, ABET, ACEJMC, ADA, AHEA, CCNE, CSAB, CSWE, FIDER, NASAD, NASM, NCATE, and NLN. The 8 libraries contain 2,302,472 volumes, 3,832,832 microform items, and 516,079 audio/video tapes/CDs, and subscribe to 20,763 periodicals. Computerized library services include the card catalog, interlibrary loans, database searching, and Internet access. Special learning facilities include a learning resource center, art gallery, natural history museum, radio station, TV station, special collections department, map library, observatory, specialized computer labs, and archeological site. The 1000-acre campus is in a suburban area 50 miles southwest of Birmingham. Including any residence halls, there are 253 buildings.

Student Life: 78% of undergraduates are from Alabama. Students are from 50 states, 79 foreign countries, and Canada. 89% are from public schools. 80% are white; 13% African American. 56% are Protestant; 32% claim no religious affiliation; 8% Catholic. The average age of freshmen is 18; all undergraduates, 21. 17% do not continue beyond their first year; 62% remain to graduate.

Housing: 5000 students can be accommodated in college housing, which includes single-sex and coed dorms, on-campus apartments, married-student housing, fraternity houses, and sorority houses. In addition, there are honors houses, language houses, and special-interest houses. On-campus housing is available on a first-come, first-served basis. 76% of students commute. All students may keep cars.

Activities: 16% of men belong to 1 local and 25 national fraternities; 25% of women belong to 20 national sororities. There are 274 groups on campus, including art, band, cheerleading, chess, choir, chorale, chorus, computers, dance, debate, drama, drill team, ethnic, film, forensics, gay, honors, international, jazz band, literary magazine, marching band, musical theater, newspaper, opera, orchestra, pep band, photography, political, professional, radio and TV, religious, social, social service, student government, symphony, and yearbook. Popular campus events include Honors Week, Get on Board Day, and Family Weekend.

Sports: There are 8 intercollegiate sports for men and 11 for women, and 17 intramural sports for men and 16 for women. Facilities include an 83,000-seat football stadium, a 15,000-seat basketball arena, a track and field facility, a 6100-seat baseball stadium, a 1600-foot softball stadium, an indoor football practice facility, lighted varsity and public tennis courts, an aquatic complex with Olympic-size and standard pools and a weight-lifting facility, a soccer field, racquetball, basketball, and volleyball courts, weight and exercise rooms, an indoor/outdoor pool, an 18-hole golf course with clubhouse and driving range, an outdoor Olympic-size pool, and fitness centers in the residence halls.

Disabled Students: 90% of the campus is accessible. Wheelchair ramps, elevators, special parking, specially equipped rest rooms, special class scheduling, lowered drinking fountains, lowered telephones, automatic doors, TDD, adaptive technology, and Areas of Refuge are available.

Services: Counseling and information services are available, as is tutoring in some subjects, including math, chemistry, physics, computer science, accounting, finance, economics, and foreign languages. There is a reader service for the blind, remedial math, reading, and writing, a center for teaching and learning, a writing lab, a career center, computer-based self-tutoring, and a math computer lab.

Campus Safety and Security: Measures include 24-hour foot and vehicle patrol, self-defense education, security escort services, and informal discussions. There are pamphlets/posters/films, emergency telephones, lighted pathways/sidewalks, community-oriented police service (COPS), UA Police Bike Patrol, Project Hope, educational awareness for personal safety, alcohol awareness, and domestic violence awareness programs.

Programs of Study: UA confers B.A., B.S., B.A.Com., B.F.A., B.M., B.S.A.E., B.S.C.B.A., B.S.C.E., B.S.Ch.E., B.S.Chem., B.S.C.S., B.S.Ed., B.S.E.E., B.S.Geo., B.S.H.E.S., B.S.I.E., B.S.M.E., B.S.Met., B.S.N., and B.S.W. degrees. Master's and doctoral degrees are also awarded. Bachelor's degrees are awarded in BIOLOGICAL SCIENCE (biology/biological science, marine science, and microbiology), BUSINESS (accounting, banking and finance, and management information systems), COMMUNICATIONS AND THE ARTS (advertising, art history and appreciation, classics, dance, English, French, German, journalism, music, public relations, Russian, Spanish, telecommunications, and visual and performing arts), COMPUTER AND PHYSICAL SCIENCE (chemistry, computer science, geology, mathematics, and physics), EDUCATION (athletic training, early childhood, education of the multiply handicapped, elementary, health, music, physical, secondary, and special), ENGINEERING AND ENVIRONMENTAL DESIGN (aerospace studies, chemical engineering, civil engineering, electrical/electronics engineering, environmental science, industrial administration/management, industrial engineering, interior design, mechanical engineering, and metallurgical engineering), HEALTH PROFESSIONS (health care administration, music therapy, and nursing), SOCIAL SCIENCE (American studies, anthropology, clothing and textiles management/production/services, criminal justice, economics, family/consumer resource management, food production/management/services, food science, geography, history, home economics, human development, interdisciplinary studies, international studies, philosophy, physical fitness/movement, political science/government, psychology, religion, and social work). Advertising, accounting, and engineering are the strongest academically. Public relations, finance, and marketing are the largest.

Required: To graduate, all students must complete a minimum of 120 semester hours, including at least 27 in the major, with a minimum GPA of 2.0. Core curriculum requirements include 12 hours each of humanities/fine arts and history/social science, 11 of natural science/math, 6 of computer studies or a foreign language, 6 of English composition, and 6 of upper-level courses with a writing component.

Special: UA offers cross-registration with Stillman College and Shelton State Community College, internships, international study programs, a Washington semester, a 3-week May-June interim term, exchange study within the United States, work-study, co-op programs, accelerated programs in business, B.A.-B.S. degrees, dual majors, student-designed majors, interdisciplinary majors in the New College arts and sciences program, credit for life experiences, nondegree study, and pass/fail options. There are 3-2 engineering degree programs with the University of Montevallo, as well as cross-registration within the Engineering Foundation Coalition. There are 66 national honor societies, including Phi Beta Kappa, a freshman honors program, and 13 departmental honors programs.

Faculty/Classroom: 64% of faculty are male; 36%, female. 73% teach undergraduates, 6% do research, and 4% do both. Graduate students teach 34% of introductory courses. The average class size in an introductory lecture is 52; in a laboratory, 17; and in a regular course, 24.

Admissions: 87% of the 2003-2004 applicants were accepted. The SAT I scores for the 2003-2004 freshman class were: Verbal--26% below 500, 43% between 500 and 599, 24% between 600 and 700, and 8% above 700; Math--24% below 500, 46% between 500 and 599, 25% between 600 and 700, and 5% above 700. The ACT scores were 23% below 21, 30% between 21 and 23, 24% between 24 and 26, 12% between 27 and 28, and 11% above 28. 41% of the current freshmen were in the top fifth of their class; 69% were in the top two fifths. There were 34 National Merit finalists.

Requirements: The SAT I or ACT is required. In addition, a minimum GPA of 2.0 is required; admission is based on a sliding scale of test scores and high school GPA. The GED is accepted. High school preparation should include 4 units each of English and social studies, 3 each of math and science, 1 of foreign language, and 5 of academic electives. Students with a 2.5 academic GPA and a 20 ACT composite or 970 SAT I combined score will generally be admitted. A GPA of 2.0 is required. AP and CLEP credits are accepted. Important factors in the admissions decision are advanced placement or honor courses, evidence of special talent, and leadership record.

Procedure: Freshmen are admitted to all sessions. Entrance exams should be taken in the spring of the junior year. There is a rolling admissions plan and an early admissions plan. Applications should be filed by August 1 for fall entry and May 1 for summer entry, along with a $25 fee. Notification is sent on a rolling basis within 2 weeks of completed application. Applications are accepted on-line through *apply@ua.edu*.

Transfer: 1795 transfer students enrolled in 2002-2003. Applicants need an overall minimum GPA of 2.0 with at least 24 semester hours earned. Those with fewer than 24 hours must meet freshman standards. 32 of 120 credits required for the bachelor's degree must be completed at UA.

Visiting: There are regularly scheduled orientations for prospective students, consisting of a campus tour followed by meetings with admissions counselors and faculty and staff. Customized visits to suit student and parent needs are possible. University Day (4 times a year) offers tours and information sessions. There are guides for informal visits and visitors may sit in on classes and stay overnight. To schedule a visit, contact the Office of Undergraduate Admissions at *admissions@ua.edu*.

Financial Aid: In 2003-2004, 68% of all full-time freshmen and 66% of continuing full-time students received some form of financial aid. 30% of full-time freshmen and 35% of continuing full-time students received need-based aid. The average freshman award was $7260. Need-based scholarships or need-based grants averaged $3169 ($6750 maximum); need-based self-help aid (loans and jobs) averaged $3178 ($8735 maximum); non-need-based athletic scholarships averaged $10,903 ($18,462 maximum); and other non-need-based awards and non-need-based scholarships averaged $6081 ($27,159 maximum). Average an-

nual earnings from campus work are $3110. The average financial indebtedness of the 2003 graduate was $19,319. The FAFSA is required. The priority date for freshman financial aid applications for fall entry is March 1.

International Students: There are 295 international students enrolled. The school actively recruits these students. They must score 500 on the written TOEFL or 173 on the electronic version or earn a proficiency certificate from the university's English Language Institute. The SAT I or ACTis required only for scholarship consideration.

Computers: The mainframes are an R26, Sun V880. More than 60 computer labs with more than 1450 PCs are located on campus to provide network access. All students may access the system 24 hours a day.

Graduates: From July 1, 2002 to June 30, 2003, 2892 bachelor's degrees were awarded. The most popular majors were marketing (8%), finance (8%), and management (6%). In an average class, 1% graduate in 3 years or less, 35% graduate in 4 years or less, 56% graduate in 5 years or less, and 62% graduate in 6 years or less. 596 companies recruited on campus in 2002-2003.

Admissions Contact: Roger Thompson, Assistant Vice President of Enrollment Management. A video is available.
E-mail: *admissions@ua.edu* Web: *http://www.ua.edu*

UNIVERSITY OF ALABAMA AT BIRMINGHAM C-2
Birmingham, AL 35294 (205) 934-8221
(800) 421-8743; Fax: (205) 975-7114

Full-time: 2959 men, 4623 women	**Faculty:** I, --$
Part-time: 1122 men, 1677 women	**Ph.D.s:** 86%
Graduate: 1466 men, 2170 women	**Student/Faculty:** n/av
Year: semesters, summer session	**Tuition:** $4274 ($9494)
Application Deadline: July 1	**Room & Board:** $8627
Freshman Class: 4710 applied, 3807 accepted, 1619 enrolled	
ACT: 22	**COMPETITIVE**

The University of Alabama at Birmingham, founded in 1969, is a public institution offering degrees in the arts and humanities, business, education, engineering, natural sciences and math, health-related professions, and social and behavioral sciences. There are 9 undergraduate and 13 graduate schools. In addition to regional accreditation, UAB has baccalaureate program accreditation with AACSB, ABET, CAHEA, CSWE, NASAD, NASM, NCATE, and NLN. The 2 libraries contain 1,224,842 volumes, 1,293,397 microform items, and 76,079 audio/video tapes/CDs, and subscribe to 3538 periodicals. Computerized library services include the card catalog, interlibrary loans, database searching, and Internet access. Special learning facilities include an art gallery, radio station, Reynolds Historical Library, and Alabama Museum of the Health Sciences. The 180-acre campus is in an urban area in Birmingham. Including any residence halls, there are 110 buildings.

Student Life: 94% of undergraduates are from Alabama. Students are from 43 states, 105 foreign countries, and Canada. 92% are from public schools. 57% are white; 32% African American. The average age of freshmen is 19; all undergraduates, 22. 25% do not continue beyond their first year.

Housing: 1911 students can be accommodated in college housing, which includes single-sex and coed dorms, on-campus apartments, and married-student housing. On-campus housing is available on a first-come, first-served basis. 89% of students commute. Alcohol is not permitted. All students may keep cars.

Activities: 6% of men belong to 9 national fraternities; 6% of women belong to 8 national sororities. There are 150 groups on campus, including band, cheerleading, chess, choir, dance, drama, ethnic, honors, international, jazz band, literary magazine, marching band, musical theater, newspaper, pep band, political, professional, radio and TV, religious, social, social service, student government, and yearbook. Popular campus events include Springfest and Madrigal Feaste.

Sports: There are 6 intercollegiate sports for men and 9 for women, and 11 intramural sports for men and 11 for women. Facilities include 11 tennis courts; 3 enclosed, lighted fields; a quarter-mile running track; and a physical education complex, which includes 2 gyms, 3 basketball courts, 4 volleyball courts, 6 racquetball/handball courts, 2 wallyball courts, a squash court, fitness weight areas, 2 cardio-fitness rooms with equipment, an indoor track, an indoor heated swimming pool, and equipment.

Disabled Students: 80% of the campus is accessible. Wheelchair ramps, elevators, special parking, specially equipped rest rooms, lowered drinking fountains, and lowered telephones are available.

Services: Counseling and information services are available, as is tutoring in most subjects. There is a reader service for the blind and remedial math, reading, and writing.

Campus Safety and Security: Measures include 24-hour foot and vehicle patrol, self-defense education, security escort services, and shuttle buses. There are informal discussions, pamphlets/posters/films, emergency telephones, lighted pathways/sidewalks, a bike and mounted patrol, and a campus watch program.

Programs of Study: UAB confers B.A., B.S., B.F.A., B.S.B.M.E., B.S.C.E., B.S.E.E., B.S.M.E., B.S.Mt.E., B.S.N., and B.S.S.W. degrees. Master's and doctoral degrees are also awarded. Bachelor's degrees are awarded in BIOLOGICAL SCIENCE (biology/biological science), BUSINESS (accounting, banking and finance, business administration and management, and marketing/retailing/merchandising), COMMUNICATIONS AND THE ARTS (art, communications, dramatic arts, English, French, music, and Spanish), COMPUTER AND PHYSICAL SCIENCE (chemistry, computer science, information sciences and systems, mathematics, natural sciences, and physics), EDUCATION (early childhood, elementary, health, physical, secondary, and special), ENGINEERING AND ENVIRONMENTAL DESIGN (biomedical engineering, civil engineering, electrical/electronics engineering, industrial administration/management, materials engineering, and mechanical engineering), HEALTH PROFESSIONS (cytotechnology, health science, medical records administration/services, medical technology, nuclear medical technology, nursing, physician's assistant, radiological science, and respiratory therapy), SOCIAL SCIENCE (African American studies, anthropology, criminal justice, economics, history, international studies, philosophy, political science/government, psychology, social work, and sociology). Biology, psychology, and communication studies are the largest.

Required: All students must complete a core curriculum that includes courses in math, computers, English, history, science, social sciences, philosophy, fine arts, foreign language or culture, and literature. To receive a bachelor's degree, students must complete 128 semester hours for most programs, with a GPA of at least 2.0.

Special: UAB offers student-designed majors, cross-registration with the Birmingham Area Consortium for Higher Education, internships, study abroad in 12 countries, work-study programs, nondegree study, pass/fail options, and credit by exam and for life experience. Cooperative education programs in the student's area of interest provide full-time or part-time work. There are 28 national honor societies, a freshman honors program, and several departmental honors programs.

Faculty/Classroom: 64% of faculty are male; 36%, female.

Admissions: 81% of the 2003-2004 applicants were accepted. The ACT scores for the 2003-2004 freshman class were: 46% below 21, 24% between 21 and 23, 15% between 24 and 26, 7% between 27 and 28, and 8% above 28. 37% of the current freshmen were in the top fifth of their class; 65% were in the top two fifths. There were 10 National Merit finalists. 28 freshmen graduated first in their class.

Requirements: The SAT I or ACT is required. In addition, applicants should have completed 12 Carnegie units, including 4 in English and 2 each in math, science, and social studies. The GED is accepted if the student's score on the test is at least 52. A GPA of 2.0 is required. AP and CLEP credits are accepted.

Procedure: Freshmen are admitted to all sessions. Entrance exams should be taken by the beginning of the senior year. There is a rolling admissions plan.There are early admissions and deferred admissions plans. Applications should be filed by July 1 for fall entry, December 1 for spring entry, and April 15 for summer entry. The fall 2003 application fee was $25. Notification is sent on a rolling basis. Applications are accepted on-line through *www.uab.edu/Enrollment.*

Transfer: 1025 transfer students enrolled in 2002-2003. Applicants should have earned at least 24 semester hours at an accredited institution with a minimum GPA of 2.0. College transcripts and statements of good standing from prior colleges are required of all transfer students. 64 of 128 credits required for the bachelor's degree must be completed at UAB.

Visiting: There are regularly scheduled orientations for prospective students, including a question-and-answer session, academic advising, sessions for parents, and presentations on student life, financial aid, housing, and student development. There are guides for informal visits and visitors may sit in on classes. To schedule a visit, contact Yolanda Tait at (205) 934-8142.

Financial Aid: In 2002-2003, 48% of all full-time freshmen and 49% of continuing full-time students received some form of financial aid. At least 47% of full-time freshmen and 48% of continuing full-time students received need-based aid. The average freshman award was $7829. Need-based scholarships or need-based grants averaged $3215; need-based self-help aid (loans and jobs) averaged $3310; non-need-based athletic scholarships averaged $10,285; and other institutional non-need-based awards and non-need-based scholarships averaged $4289. The average financial indebtedness of the 2003 graduate was $18,299. UAB is a member of CSS. The FAFSA and the college's own financial statement are required. The priority date for freshman financial aid applications for fall entry is April 1.

International Students: International students must score 500 on the written TOEFL.

Computers: The mainframes is composed of a Hitachi DataSystems operating in IBM System/ESA/370 mode. An IBM 4381 is used as a server for Internet and Suranet, with access to the Alabama Supercomputer Cray X-MP24. PCs are available in various schools and labs for student use; dorms are wired for Internet access. All students may access the system. There are no time limits and no fees.

Graduates: From July 1, 2002 to June 30, 2003, 1464 bachelor's degrees were awarded. The most popular majors were psychology (9%), management (8%), and nursing (7%). In an average class, 13% graduate in 4 years or less, 29% graduate in 5 years or less, and 38% graduate in 6 years or less. 60 companies recruited on campus in 2002-2003.

Admissions Contact: Office of Undergraduate Admissions.
E-mail: *undergradadmit@uab.edu* Web: *www.uab.edu*

UNIVERSITY OF ALABAMA IN HUNTSVILLE   C-1
Huntsville, AL 35899 (256) 824-6070
(800) UAH-CALL; Fax: (256) 824-6073

Full-time: 1984 men, 1889 women	**Faculty:** 277; I, --$
Part-time: 790 men, 818 women	**Ph.D.s:** 87%
Graduate: 921 men, 649 women	**Student/Faculty:** 14 to 1
Year: semesters, summer session	**Tuition:** $4126 ($8702)
Application Deadline: August 15	**Room & Board:** $5000
Freshman Class: 1785 applied, 1563 accepted, 798 enrolled	
SAT I Verbal/Math: 570/570	**ACT:** 24 **VERY COMPETITIVE**

The University of Alabama in Huntsville, founded in 1950 and part of the University of Alabama system, is a public institution offering programs in liberal arts and sciences, business, nursing, and engineering. There are 5 undergraduate schools and 1 graduate school. In addition to regional accreditation, UAH has baccalaureate program accreditation with AACSB, ABET, CCNE, CSAB, NASM, and NLN. The library contains 326,399 volumes, 579,663 microform items, and 2677 audio/video tapes/CDs, and subscribes to 1169 periodicals. Computerized library services include the card catalog, interlibrary loans, and database searching. Special learning facilities include an art gallery and radio station. The 376-acre campus is in a suburban area 100 miles north of Birmingham and 90 miles south of Nashville. Including any residence halls, there are 34 buildings.

Student Life: 86% of undergraduates are from Alabama. Students are from 45 states, 55 foreign countries, and Canada. 85% are from public schools. 74% are white; 14% African American. 71% are Protestant; 13% Catholic; 7% claim no religious affiliation. The median age of freshmen is 18; all undergraduates, 21. 24% do not continue beyond their first year; 44% remain to graduate.

Housing: 1042 students can be accommodated in college housing, which includes coed dorms, on-campus apartments, and married-student housing. Suites for fraternities and sororities are also available. On-campus housing is available on a first-come, first-served basis. 83% of students commute. Alcohol is not permitted. All students may keep cars.

Activities: 7% of men belong to 6 national fraternities; 6% of women belong to 4 national sororities. There are 110 groups on campus, including art, cheerleading, chess, choir, chorale, chorus, computers, dance, drama, ethnic, film, gay, honors, international, jazz band, literary magazine, newspaper, pep band, photography, political, professional, radio and TV, religious, social, social service, student government, and symphony. Popular campus events include FallFest, SpringFest, and Frosh Mosh.

Sports: There are 8 intercollegiate sports for men and 8 for women, and 16 intramural sports for men and 16 for women. Facilities include a 2800-seat gym, a swimming pool, racquetball and tennis courts, soccer fields, softball diamonds, and a fitness center with cardio equipment, indoor track, weight room, fitness classes, aquatics, sand volleyball, and sports nutrition center.

Disabled Students: 98% of the campus is accessible. Wheelchair ramps, elevators, special parking, specially equipped rest rooms, special class scheduling, lowered drinking fountains, special housing, and a swimming pool lift are available.

Services: Counseling and information services are available, as is tutoring in most subjects. There is a reader service for the blind, and remedial math, reading, and writing. Study skills classes are also offered.

Campus Safety and Security: Measures include 24-hour foot and vehicle patrol, security escort services, informal discussions, and pamphlets/posters/films. There are lighted pathways/sidewalks and and card-controlled dorm access.

Programs of Study: UAH confers B.A., B.S., B.S.B.A., B.S.E., and B.S.N. degrees. Master's and doctoral degrees are also awarded. Bachelor's degrees are awarded in BIOLOGICAL SCIENCE (biology/biological science), BUSINESS (accounting, banking and finance, business administration and management, management information systems, and marketing/retailing/merchandising), COMMUNICATIONS AND THE ARTS (communications, English, fine arts, languages, and music), COMPUTER AND PHYSICAL SCIENCE (chemistry, computer science, mathematics, and physics), EDUCATION (education), ENGINEERING AND ENVIRONMENTAL DESIGN (chemical engineering, civil engineering, computer engineering, electrical/electronics engineering, industrial engineering, mechanical engineering, and optical engineering), HEALTH PROFESSIONS (nursing), SOCIAL SCIENCE (history, philosophy, political science/government, psychology, and sociology). Engineering, nursing, and computer science are the largest.

Required: All students must earn a minimum GPA of 2.0 over 128 to 137 credit hours, including 21 to 36 in their major. The core curriculum includes courses in English composition, literature, world history, foreign language and communications, fine arts, math, science, and social sciences.

Special: UAH offers co-op programs in all majors, cross-registration with Alabama Agricultural and Mechanical University, Athens State University, and Calhoun Community College, and internships in administrative science, communications, education, and political science. A 3-2 engineering degree is available with Oakwood College. Dual majors, B.A.-B.S. degrees in math and biology, nondegree study, and a pass/fail option are also offered. There are 23 national honor societies and a freshman honors program.

Faculty/Classroom: 64% of faculty are male; 36%, female. All teach and do research. Graduate students teach 5% of introductory courses. The average class size in an introductory lecture is 29; in a laboratory, 14; and in a regular course, 23.

Admissions: 88% of the 2003-2004 applicants were accepted. The SAT I scores for the 2003-2004 freshman class were: Verbal--17% below 500, 46% between 500 and 599, 31% between 600 and 700, and 5% above 700; Math--18% below 500, 45% between 500 and 599, 32% between 600 and 700, and 5% above 700. The ACT scores were 14% below 21, 25% between 21 and 23, 31% between 24 and 26, 15% between 27 and 28, and 15% above 28. 53% of the current freshmen were in the top fifth of their class; 83% were in the top two fifths. There were 6 National Merit finalists. 2 freshmen graduated first in their class.

Requirements: The SAT I or ACT is required. In addition, a sliding scale with the GPA determines the minimum test score needed. The GED is accepted. Students should present a minimum of 20 Carnegie units, including 4 years of English and social studies, and 3 each of math and science. AP and CLEP credits are accepted.

Procedure: Freshmen are admitted fall, spring, and summer. Entrance exams should be taken during the junior year. There are early admissions, rolling admissions, and deferred admissions plans. Applications should be filed by August 15 for fall entry, December 15 for spring entry, and May 15 for summer entry, along with a $20 fee. Notification is sent on a rolling basis. Applications are accepted on-line through *http://register.uah.edu*.

Transfer: 641 transfer students enrolled in 2002-2003. Applicants need a minimum GPA of 2.0, in 18 hours of credit from an accredited college or university. 32 of 128 credits required for the bachelor's degree must be completed at UAH.

Visiting: There are regularly scheduled orientations for prospective students, including new student orientation, held prior to the beginning of each semester or during the first week of classes. There are guides for informal visits and visitors may sit in on classes and stay overnight. To schedule a visit, contact Ann Lee, Recruiting Coordinator at (256) 824-7142 or *leev@uah.edu*.

Financial Aid: In 2003-2004, 82% of all full-time freshmen and 68% of continuing full-time students received some form of financial aid. 41% of full-time freshmen and 47% of continuing full-time students received need-based aid. The average freshman award was $3633. Need-based scholarships or need-based grants averaged $3386 ($15,500 maximum); need-based self-help aid (loans and jobs) averaged $4219 ($14,625 maximum); and non-need-based athletic scholarships averaged $6157. 10% of undergraduates work part time. Average annual earnings from campus work are $4115. The average financial indebtedness of the 2003 graduate was $17,058. The FAFSA is required. The priority date for freshman financial aid applications for fall entry is April 1. The deadline for filing freshman financial aid applications for fall entry is July 31.

International Students: In a recent year, there were 151 international students enrolled. The school actively recruits these students. They must score 500 on the written TOEFL or 173 on the electronic version and also take the college's own test and the SAT I or the ACT.

Computers: The mainframe is an HP Alpha server 4000. Terminals are located in 13 buildings across campus. The campus is served by Ethernet and provides access to the Alabama Supercomputer. All students may access the system 24 hours a day. There are no time limits and no fees.

Graduates: From July 1, 2002 to June 30, 2003, 807 bachelor's degrees were awarded. The most popular majors were nursing (18%), management information systems (12%), and mechanical engineering (7%). In an average class, 13% graduate in 4 years or less, 36% graduate in 5 years or less, and 44% graduate in 6 years or less. 296 companies recruited on campus in 2002-2003.

Admissions Contact: Scott Verzyl, Associate Vice President for Enrollment Svc, Reg. And Dir of Adm. E-mail: *admitme@email.uah.edu* Web: *www.uah.edu*

UNIVERSITY OF MOBILE
A-5
Mobile, AL 36663-0220
(251) 675-5990
(800) 946-7267; Fax: (251) 675-6329

Full-time: 390 men, 848 women	**Faculty:** 87
Part-time: 95 men, 336 women	**Ph.D.s:** 72%
Graduate: 41 men, 139 women	**Student/Faculty:** 14 to 1
Year: semesters, summer session	**Tuition:** $8770
Application Deadline: September 10	**Room & Board:** $4850
Freshman Class: 413 applied, 276 accepted, 204 enrolled	
ACT: 22	**COMPETITIVE**

University of Mobile, founded in 1961, is a private liberal arts institution affiliated with the Southern Baptists. There are 6 undergraduate and 4 graduate schools. In addition to regional accreditation, Mobile has baccalaureate program accreditation with ACBSP, NASM, and NLN. The library contains 70,000 volumes, 260 microform items, and 3000 audio/video tapes/CDs, and subscribes to 600 periodicals. Computerized library services include the card catalog, interlibrary loans, database searching, and Internet access. Special learning facilities include a learning resource center, art gallery, and a forest learning center. The 830-acre campus is in a suburban area 10 miles northwest of Mobile. Including any residence halls, there are 52 buildings.

Student Life: 83% of undergraduates are from Alabama. Students are from 21 states, 19 foreign countries, and Canada. 86% are from public schools. 73% are white; 19% African American. 84% are Protestant; 9% Catholic; 6% claim no religious affiliation. The average age of freshmen is 18; all undergraduates, 26. 45% do not continue beyond their first year; 33% remain to graduate.

Housing: 372 students can be accommodated in college housing, which includes single-sex dorms. On-campus housing is guaranteed for the freshman year only and is available on a first-come, first-served basis. 80% of students commute. Alcohol is not permitted. All students may keep cars.

Activities: There are no fraternities or sororities. There are 52 groups on campus, including art, band, cheerleading, choir, chorale, chorus, computers, dance, drama, ethnic, honors, international, musical theater, newspaper, orchestra, pep band, political, professional, religious, social, social service, student government, and symphony. Popular campus events include College Preview Day, Upper Room Dinner Theater, and Starlight Pageant.

Sports: There are 6 intercollegiate sports for men and 7 for women, and 7 intramural sports for men and 6 for women. Facilities include an 800-seat gym, a tennis complex with 10 courts, a swimming pool, a track, baseball, softball, and soccer fields, and a golf driving range with 2 putting greens.

Disabled Students: All of the campus is accessible. Wheelchair ramps, elevators, special parking, specially equipped rest rooms, special class scheduling, lowered drinking fountains, and lowered telephones are available.

Services: Counseling and information services are available, as is tutoring in some subjects, including writing, English, and math. There is remedial math, reading, and writing.

Campus Safety and Security: Measures include 24-hour foot and vehicle patrol, self-defense education, informal discussions, and pamphlets/posters/films. There are emergency telephones, lighted pathways/sidewalks, and a professional campus security service available 24 hours per day.

Programs of Study: Mobile confers B.A., B.S., B.M., and B.S.N. degrees. Associate and master's degrees are also awarded. Bachelor's degrees are awarded in BIOLOGICAL SCIENCE (biology/biological science), BUSINESS (accounting, business administration and management, and marketing/retailing/merchandising), COMMUNICATIONS AND THE ARTS (communications, English, and music), COMPUTER AND PHYSICAL SCIENCE (chemistry, computer science, and mathematics), EDUCATION (early childhood, elementary, physical, and secondary), HEALTH PROFESSIONS (nursing), SOCIAL SCIENCE (economics, history, liberal arts/general studies, psychology, religion, and sociology). Education and nursing are the strongest academically. Business administration, elementary education, and nursing are the largest.

Required: All students are required to complete 128 credit hours, with at least 30 in their major field, and earn a minimum GPA of 2.0. Distribution requirements include 12 hours in English, 8 hours in lab science, 6 hours each in religion and history, 6 hours from the following subjects: business, computer science, economics, political science, psychology, and sociology, 4 hours in health/phys ed and recreation, 3 hours each in speech and math, and 3 hours in art, music, or philosophy. Computer literacy must be demonstrated. Chapel attendance is also required.

Special: A variety of internships and work-study programs, B.A.-B.S. degrees, an accelerated degree program, and dual majors are available, as is a 3-2 engineering degree with Auburn University and the University of South Alabama. There are 11 national honor societies, a freshman honors program, and 7 departmental honors programs.

Faculty/Classroom: 47% of faculty are male; 53%, female. All teach undergraduates. No introductory courses are taught by graduate stu-

dents. The average class size in an introductory lecture is 25; in a laboratory, 16; and in a regular course, 20.

Admissions: 67% of the 2003-2004 applicants were accepted. The ACT scores for the 2003-2004 freshman class were: 49% below 21, 21% between 21 and 23, 15% between 24 and 26, 7% between 27 and 28, and 8% above 28. 42% of the current freshmen were in the top fifth of their class; 70% were in the top two fifths.

Requirements: The ACT is required. In addition, applicants must have 22 Carnegie units and a minimum composite score of 19 on the ACT. An essay, portfolio, and interview are recommended. The GED is accepted. The ACT is not required of applicants over age 30. A GPA of 2.0 is required. AP and CLEP credits are accepted. Important factors in the admissions decision are advanced placement or honor courses, ability to finance college education, and leadership record.

Procedure: Freshmen are admitted fall, spring, and summer. Entrance exams should be taken in August before the junior year. There are early decision and deferred admissions plans. Early decision applications should be filed by October 31; regular applications, by September 10 for fall entry, January 24 for spring entry, and May 1 for summer entry. Notification of early decision is sent November 1; regular decision, on a rolling basis. Applications are accepted on-line through *www.umobile.edu*.

Transfer: 172 transfer students enrolled in 2002-2003. Transfer students need to have earned a minimum GPA of 2.0 for previous college work. If fewer than 30 semester hours are accepted, a minimum score of 19 on the ACT and a high school transcript, or GED, are required. 35 of 128 credits required for the bachelor's degree must be completed at Mobile.

Visiting: There are regularly scheduled orientations for prospective students, including financial aid seminars, academic seminars, faculty advising, campus tours, and admissions counseling. There are guides for informal visits and visitors may sit in on classes and stay overnight. To schedule a visit, contact Brian Boyle, Director of Admissions at (251) 442-2287.

Financial Aid: In 2003-2004, 98% of all full-time freshmen and 97% of continuing full-time students received some form of financial aid. 36% of full-time freshmen and 32% of continuing full-time students received need-based aid. The average freshman award was $6800. Need-based scholarships or need-based grants averaged $3725 ($12,374 maximum); need-based self-help aid (loans and jobs) averaged $4470 ($10,500 maximum); and non-need-based athletic scholarships averaged $8246 ($16,220 maximum). 15% of undergraduates work part time. Average annual earnings from campus work are $1545. The average financial indebtedness of the 2003 graduate was $8683. The FAFSA and the college's own financial statement are required.

International Students: There are 31 international students enrolled. The school actively recruits these students. They must score 500 on the written TOEFL and also take the ACT, scoring 19.

Computers: The mainframe is an HP 9000/800/L3000-5X running HP-UX. Students use the terminals located in 6 computer labs. All students may access the system 8 A.M. to 9 P.M. Monday through Friday and a half day Saturday. There are no time limits. The fee is $35 per semester. It is strongly recommended that all students have a personal computer.

Graduates: From July 1, 2002 to June 30, 2003, 275 bachelor's degrees were awarded. The most popular majors were education (29%), interdisciplinary studies (21%), and religion (10%). 45 companies recruited on campus in 2002-2003.

Admissions Contact: Brian Boyle, Director of Admissions.
E-mail: *brianb@mail.umobile.edu* Web: *www.umobile.edu*

UNIVERSITY OF MONTEVALLO
Montevallo, AL 35115-6000

C-3

(205) 665-6030
(800) 292-4349; Fax: (205) 665-6032

Full-time: 778 men, 1568 women	**Faculty:** 137; IIA, --$
Part-time: 66 men, 184 women	**Ph.D.s:** 81%
Graduate: 86 men, 331 women	**Student/Faculty:** 17 to 1
Year: semesters, summer session	**Tuition:** $4784 ($9284)
Application Deadline: August 1	**Room & Board:** $3694
Freshman Class: 1334 applied, 1050 accepted, 524 enrolled	
SAT I or ACT: required	**COMPETITIVE**

The University of Montevallo, founded in 1896, is a public, liberal arts institution offering courses in business, fine arts, music, preprofessional training, and teacher preparation. There are 4 undergraduate schools and 1 graduate school. In addition to regional accreditation, UM has baccalaureate program accreditation with AACSB, ADA, AHEA, CSWE, NASAD, NASM, and NCATE. The library contains 258,152 volumes, 795,344 microform items, and 3733 audio/video tapes/CDs, and subscribes to 748 periodicals. Computerized library services include the card catalog, interlibrary loans, and database searching. Special learning facilities include a learning resource center, art gallery, TV station, and university theater. The 160-acre campus is in a small town 35 miles south of Birmingham. Including any residence halls, there are 37 buildings.

Student Life: 96% of undergraduates are from Alabama. Students are from 18 states, 22 foreign countries, and Canada. 94% are from public

schools. 82% are white; 12% African American. The average age of freshmen is 18; all undergraduates, 21. 24% do not continue beyond their first year; 42% remain to graduate.

Housing: 1276 students can be accommodated in college housing, which includes single-sex and coed dorms and on-campus apartments. On-campus housing is available on a first-come, first-served basis. 58% of students commute. All students may keep cars.

Activities: 20% of men belong to 7 national fraternities; 16% of women belong to 7 national sororities. There are 74 groups on campus, including art, cheerleading, choir, chorus, dance, debate, drama, ethnic, forensics, gay, honors, international, jazz band, literary magazine, musical theater, newspaper, pep band, photography, political, professional, radio and TV, religious, social, social service, student government, and yearbook. Popular campus events include College Night, Springfest, and Honors Day.

Sports: There are 4 intercollegiate sports for men and 5 for women, and 7 intramural sports for men and 4 for women. Facilities include a 2200-seat gym, an indoor swimming pool, soccer and other playing fields, a golf course, a walking track, and tennis courts.

Disabled Students: 90% of the campus is accessible. Wheelchair ramps, elevators, special parking, specially equipped rest rooms, special class scheduling, lowered drinking fountains, and lowered telephones are available.

Services: Counseling and information services are available, as is tutoring in some subjects, including study skills. There is a reader service for the blind, remedial math, reading, and writing, and a speech and hearing center.

Campus Safety and Security: Measures include 24-hour foot and vehicle patrol, security escort services, informal discussions, and pamphlets/posters/films. There are lighted pathways/sidewalks, campus lighting, and electronic access into residence halls.

Programs of Study: UM confers B.A., B.S., B.B.A., B.F.A., B.M., and B.M.E. degrees. Master's degrees are also awarded. Bachelor's degrees are awarded in BIOLOGICAL SCIENCE (biology/biological science), BUSINESS (accounting, banking and finance, business administration and management, management science, and marketing/retailing/merchandising), COMMUNICATIONS AND THE ARTS (art, communications, dramatic arts, English, French, journalism, music, Spanish, and studio art), COMPUTER AND PHYSICAL SCIENCE (chemistry and mathematics), EDUCATION (art, early childhood, education of the deaf and hearing impaired, elementary, home economics, music, and physical), HEALTH PROFESSIONS (speech pathology/audiology), SOCIAL SCIENCE (history, political science/government, psychology, social science, social work, and sociology). Elementary/early childhood education, speech pathology, and English are the largest.

Required: To graduate, students must complete a minimum of 130 semester hours with an overall 2.0 GPA while meeting core, major, and minor requirements. Core requirements include 12 hours of writing reinforcement courses (usually met with literature and major/minor courses), 7 hours of sciences (2 branches), 6 hours each of foundations in writing, world literature, world civilizations, and institutions and issues courses, 4 hours of health/phys ed, and 3 hours each of oral communications, math, computer science, fine arts, and human behavior and inquiry courses.

Special: A 3-2 engineering degree is offered with Auburn University and the University of Alabama at Birmingham. Internships, study abroad, work-study, an accelerated degree plan, B.A.-B.S. degrees, dual degrees, and pass/fail options are available. There are 22 national honor societies and a freshman honors program.

Faculty/Classroom: 46% of faculty are male; 54%, female. 99% teach undergraduates. No introductory courses are taught by graduate students. The average class size in an introductory lecture is 27; in a laboratory, 24; and in a regular course, 24.

Admissions: 79% of the 2003-2004 applicants were accepted.

Requirements: The SAT I or ACT is required; the ACT is preferred. In addition, applicants must be high school graduates with a minimum of 16 academic credits, including 4 units each of English, social studies, and academic electives and 2 each of math and science. 1 year each of algebra and plane geometry is recommended. The GED is accepted with a minimum standard score average of 50. A GPA of 2.0 is required. AP and CLEP credits are accepted. Important factors in the admissions decision are advanced placement or honor courses, evidence of special talent, and geographic diversity.

Procedure: Freshmen are admitted to all sessions. Entrance exams should be taken in April or June of the junior year or October of the senior year. There is a rolling admissions plan. There are early admissions and deferred admissions plans. Applications should be filed by August 1 for fall entry, December 1 for spring entry, and May 1 for summer entry. Notification is sent on a rolling basis beginning September 1. Applications are accepted on-line through *www.montevallo.edu/admissions*.

Transfer: 284 transfer students enrolled in 2002-2003. Applicants need a minimum GPA of 2.0 on previous college study attempted. 30 of 130 credits required for the bachelor's degree must be completed at UM.

Visiting: There are regularly scheduled orientations for prospective students, consisting of 1 day of preregistration in July and 2 days of orientation in August, including on-site visits, mentor groups, play activities, and career and learning style assessments. There are guides for informal visits and visitors may sit in on classes and stay overnight. To schedule a visit, contact the Office of Admissions.

Financial Aid: In 2003-2004, 59% of all full-time freshmen and 55% of continuing full-time students received some form of financial aid. 38% of full-time freshmen and 39% of continuing full-time students received need-based aid. The average freshman award was $5867. Need-based scholarships or need-based grants averaged $4425; need-based self-help aid (loans and jobs) averaged $1953; institutional non-need-based athletic scholarships averaged $6497; and other institutional non-need-based awards and non-need-based scholarships averaged $3910. The average financial indebtedness of the 2003 graduate was $14,265. The FAFSA is required. The priority date for freshman financial aid applications for fall entry is April 15.

International Students: There were 47 international students enrolled in a recent year. They must score 525 on the written TOEFL.

Computers: The mainframe is a Compaq Alpha DS20E. About 170 Pentium-class machines and 130 Power Macs are available in 9 computer labs. All students may access the system 7 A.M. to 11 P.M. Monday through Friday; hours vary on weekends. There are no time limits and no fees.

Graduates: From July 1, 2002 to June 30, 2003, 474 bachelor's degrees were awarded. The most popular majors were business/marketing (15%), social sciences and history (14%), and education (14%). In an average class, 28% graduate in 4 years or less, 41% graduate in 5 years or less, and 43% graduate in 6 years or less. 80 companies recruited on campus in a recent year.

Admissions Contact: Lynn Gurganus, Director of Admissions. E-mail: *admissions@montevallo.edu* Web: *www.montevallo.edu*

UNIVERSITY OF NORTH ALABAMA

B-1

Florence, AL 35632-0001

(256) 765-4608

(800) TALKUNA; Fax: (256) 765-4960

Full-time: 1724 men, 2392 women	**Faculty:** 195; IIA, --$
Part-time: 355 men, 524 women	**Ph.D's:** 72%
Graduate: 215 men, 420 women	**Student/Faculty:** 21 to 1
Year: semesters, summer session	**Tuition:** $3700 ($6904)
Application Deadline: July 1	**Room & Board:** $4272
Freshman Class: 1298 applied, 1298 accepted, 753 enrolled	
ACT: 21	**NONCOMPETITIVE**

The University of North Alabama, founded in 1872, is a public institution offering degree programs in arts and sciences, business, education, and nursing. There are 4 undergraduate and 3 graduate schools. In addition to regional accreditation, UNA has baccalaureate program accreditation with AACSB, ACBSP, CSWE, NASAD, NASM, NCATE, and NLN. The 2 libraries contain 358,393 volumes, 1,006,142 microform items, and 9898 audio/video tapes/CDs, and subscribe to 3126 periodicals. Computerized library services include the card catalog, interlibrary loans, database searching, and Internet access. Special learning facilities include a learning resource center, art gallery, planetarium, and radio station. The 125-acre campus is in an urban area 116 miles north of Birmingham. Including any residence halls, there are 68 buildings.

Student Life: 75% of undergraduates are from Alabama. Others are from 38 states, 31 foreign countries, and Canada. 89% are from public schools. 77% are white. The average age of freshmen is 19; all undergraduates, 23. 45% do not continue beyond their first year; 35% remain to graduate.

Housing: 1010 students can be accommodated in college housing, which includes single-sex and coed dorms, on-campus apartments, off-campus apartments, married-student housing, an international house, fraternity houses, and sorority houses. On-campus housing is available on a first-come, first-served basis. 81% of students commute. Alcohol is not permitted. All students may keep cars.

Activities: 4% of men belong to 6 national fraternities; 7% of women belong to 6 national sororities. There are 91 groups on campus, including band, cheerleading, choir, chorus, computers, debate, drama, drill team, ethnic, film, honors, international, jazz band, literary magazine, marching band, musical theater, newspaper, pep band, photography, political, professional, radio and TV, religious, social, social service, student government, and yearbook. Popular campus events include Spring Fling and George Lindsey Film Festival.

Sports: There are 6 intercollegiate sports for men and 6 for women, and 19 intramural sports for men and 19 for women. Facilities include a 13,500-seat football stadium, a 4000-seat gym, a baseball field, an outdoor track, an indoor swimming pool, and tennis courts.

Disabled Students: 96% of the campus is accessible. Wheelchair ramps, elevators, special parking, specially equipped rest rooms, special class scheduling, lowered drinking fountains, and lowered telephones are available.

Services: Counseling and information services are available, as is tutoring in some subjects, including math, English, history, biology, chemistry, accounting, finance, and economics. There is a reader service for the blind and remedial math and writing, and an academic resource center that features computer-assisted tutoring and faculty mentoring.

Campus Safety and Security: Measures include 24-hour foot and vehicle patrol, shuttle buses, informal discussions, and pamphlets/posters/films. There are emergency telephones and lighted pathways/sidewalks.

Programs of Study: UNA confers B.A., B.S., B.A.M., B.B.A., B.F.A., B.G.S., B.M.M.Ed., B.S.Ed., B.S.M., B.S.N., and B.S.W. degrees. Master's degrees are also awarded. Bachelor's degrees are awarded in BIOLOGICAL SCIENCE (biology/biological science and environmental biology), BUSINESS (accounting, banking and finance, business economics, and marketing/retailing/merchandising), COMMUNICATIONS AND THE ARTS (art, communications, dramatic arts, English, French, German, journalism, music, public relations, and Spanish), COMPUTER AND PHYSICAL SCIENCE (chemistry, computer science, geology, information sciences and systems, mathematics, and physics), EDUCATION (art, business, early childhood, elementary, foreign languages, home economics, music, physical, science, secondary, and social science), ENGINEERING AND ENVIRONMENTAL DESIGN (interior design), HEALTH PROFESSIONS (industrial hygiene and nursing), SOCIAL SCIENCE (criminal justice, geography, history, political science/government, psychology, social work, and sociology). Physical sciences, biological sciences, and math are the strongest academically. Management, accounting, and marketing are the largest.

Required: Students must complete a core curriculum, which includes 12 semester hours in history, social and behavioral sciences, humanities, and fine arts, 11 in natural sciences and math, and 6 in language composition. Total number of hours in majors vary. Passing grades in 1 writing emphasis and 1 computer course also are needed. A minimum of 128 semester hours and a minimum GPA of 2.0 are required to graduate.

Special: UNA offers cooperative programs in all majors, work-study programs, various B.A.-B.S. degrees, dual majors, and a general studies degree. Nondegree study is possible. There are 13 national honor societies, including Phi Beta Kappa, and 2 departmental honors programs.

Faculty/Classroom: 59% of faculty are male; 41%, female. All teach undergraduates. No introductory courses are taught by graduate students.

Admissions: All of the 2003-2004 applicants were accepted. The ACT scores for the 2003-2004 freshman class were: 49% below 21, 22% between 21 and 23, 19% between 24 and 26, 6% between 27 and 28, and 4% above 28. 37% of the current freshmen were in the top fifth of their class; 72% were in the top two fifths.

Requirements: The SAT I or ACT is required. In addition, applicants should be graduates of an accredited high school or have earned a GED. A GPA of 2.0 is required. AP and CLEP credits are accepted.

Procedure: Freshmen are admitted fall, spring, and summer. Entrance exams should be taken in the senior year. There is a deferred admissions plan. Applications should be filed by July 1 for fall entry, December 1 for spring entry, and May 25 for summer entry. Notification is sent on a rolling basis. Applications are accepted on-line.

Transfer: 594 transfer students enrolled in 2003-2004. Applicants should be eligible to return to the school last attended. 30 of 128 credits required for the bachelor's degree must be completed at UNA.

Visiting: There are regularly scheduled orientations for prospective students, including orientation programs conducted each summer prior to the fall semester. There are guides for informal visits.

Financial Aid: In 2003-2004, 51% of all full-time freshmen and 54% of continuing full-time students received some form of financial aid. 50% of full-time freshmen and 45% of continuing full-time students received need-based aid. Need-based scholarships or need-based grants averaged $2098; need-based self-help aid (loans and jobs) averaged $3033; and non-need-based athletic scholarships averaged $6961. 8% of undergraduates work part time. Average annual earnings from campus work are $2250. The FAFSA is required. The deadline for filing freshman financial aid applications for fall entry is April 1.

International Students: There are 158 international students enrolled. The school actively recruits these students. They must score 500 on the written TOEFL or 173 on the electronic version.

Computers: The mainframe is an IBM 4300 series. Terminals are located in the computer center and in computer labs in the Colleges of Business and Education. Macs and PCs are available in the academic resource center, with additional units in faculty and departmental offices. Computer labs are also in each dorm. All students may access the system. There are no time limits and no fees. It is strongly recommended that all students have a personal computer.

Graduates: From July 1, 2002 to June 30, 2003, 794 bachelor's degrees were awarded. The most popular majors were business (29%), education (16%), and nursing (12%). In an average class, 12% graduate in 4 years or less, 28% graduate in 5 years or less, and 36% graduate in 6 years or less. 100 companies recruited on campus in 2002-2003.

Admissions Contact: Kim Mauldin, Director of Admissions. A video is available. E-mail: *admissions@una.edu* Web: *http://www.una.edu*

UNIVERSITY OF SOUTH ALABAMA
A-5
Mobile, AL 36688
(334) 460-6141
(800) 872-5247; Fax: (334) 460-7023

Full-time: 3044 men, 4498 women	Faculty: 678; IIA, -$
Part-time: 1081 men, 1548 women	Ph.D.s: 79%
Graduate: 794 men, 1876 women	Student/Faculty: 11 to 1
Year: semesters, summer session	Tuition: $3770 ($7160)
Application Deadline: August 10	Room & Board: $3990
Freshman Class: 2683 applied, 2485 accepted, 1195 enrolled	
ACT: 22	LESS COMPETITIVE

The University of South Alabama, a state-supported institution established in 1963, offers undergraduate and graduate degrees in the allied health professions, arts and sciences, business and management studies, education, engineering, nursing, computer and information sciences, and medicine. There are 8 undergraduate and 8 graduate schools. In addition to regional accreditation, USA has baccalaureate program accreditation with AACSB, ABET, ACOTE, AHEA, APTA, ARCEPA, ASLHA, CAAHEP, CAHEA, CCNE, CSAB, JRCERT, LCME, NAACLS, NASAD, NASM, NCATE, and NLN. The 2 libraries contain 517,293 volumes and 1,480,330 microform items, and subscribe to 5215 periodicals. Computerized library services include the card catalog, interlibrary loans, and database searching. Special learning facilities include a learning resource center, art gallery, radio station, TV station, and the Dauphin Island Sea Lab. The 1224-acre campus is in a suburban area 150 miles east of New Orleans. Including any residence halls, there are 114 buildings.

Student Life: 78% of undergraduates are from Alabama. Students are from 40 states, 100 foreign countries, and Canada. 67% are white; 16% African American. The average age of all undergraduates is 24. 29% do not continue beyond their first year.

Housing: 1966 students can be accommodated in college housing, which includes coed dorms, on-campus apartments, married-student housing, fraternity houses, and sorority houses. On-campus housing is available on a first-come, first-served basis. 80% of students commute. Alcohol is not permitted. All students may keep cars.

Activities: 10% of men belong to 12 national fraternities; 7% of women belong to 8 national sororities. There are 130 groups on campus, including art, band, cheerleading, chess, choir, chorale, chorus, dance, debate, drama, ethnic, film, gay, honors, international, jazz band, literary magazine, musical theater, newspaper, opera, orchestra, pep band, political, professional, radio and TV, religious, social, social service, student government, and symphony. Popular campus events include Club South, Greek Week, and Chi Omega Songfest.

Sports: There are 7 intercollegiate sports for men and 8 for women, and 13 intramural sports for men and 12 for women. Facilities include a 10,000-seat arena; a 49,000-square-foot student recreation center, including 6 handball courts, fitness rooms, 2 basketball/volleyball courts, and an indoor track; several intramural fields; and an outdoor swimming pool.

Disabled Students: 90% of the campus is accessible. Wheelchair ramps, elevators, special parking, specially equipped rest rooms, lowered drinking fountains, and lowered telephones are available.

Services: Counseling and information services are available, as is tutoring in some subjects. There is a reader service for the blind, and remedial math, reading, and writing.

Campus Safety and Security: Measures include 24-hour foot and vehicle patrol, self-defense education, security escort services, and informal discussions. There are pamphlets/posters/films, emergency telephones, and lighted pathways/sidewalks.

Programs of Study: USA confers B.A., B.S., B.F.A., B.Mus., B.S.B.A., B.S.Cardioresp.Sc., B.S.C.E., B.S.Ch.E., B.S.C.L.S., B.S.Comp.Eng., B.S.Ed., B.S.E.E., B.S.M.E., B.S.N., B.S.Preprof.Hlth.Sc., B.S.R.S., and B.S.Sp.Hear.Sc. degrees. Master's and doctoral degrees are also awarded. Bachelor's degrees are awarded in BIOLOGICAL SCIENCE (biology/biological science), BUSINESS (accounting, banking and finance, business administration and management, business economics, electronic business, marketing/retailing/merchandising, and recreation and leisure services), COMMUNICATIONS AND THE ARTS (communications, dramatic arts, English, fine arts, languages, and music), COMPUTER AND PHYSICAL SCIENCE (atmospheric sciences and meteorology, chemistry, computer science, geology, mathematics, and physics), EDUCATION (early childhood, education, elementary, health, physical, secondary, and special), ENGINEERING AND ENVIRONMENTAL DESIGN (chemical engineering, civil engineering, computer engineering, electrical/electronics engineering, and mechanical engineering), HEALTH PROFESSIONS (biomedical science, clinical science, nursing, radiological science, respiratory therapy, and speech pathology/audiology), SOCIAL SCIENCE (anthropology, criminal justice, geography, history, international studies, philosophy, political science/government, psychology, and sociology). Business administration, nursing, and elementary education are the largest.

Required: General education requirements consist of 12 hours each in written composition, humanities, and fine arts, 11 hours in natural science and math, and at least 12 hours in history and the social and behavioral sciences. A minimum of 128 semester hours, with a minimum GPA of 2.0, are required for graduation.

Special: USA offers co-op programs in most majors, federal work-study, internships, study abroad in 4 countries, dual majors, an adult degree program, and a personalized studies program. There are 43 national honor societies and a freshman honors program.

Faculty/Classroom: 65% of faculty are male; 35%, female. No introductory courses are taught by graduate students. The average class size in an introductory lecture is 76; in a laboratory, 31; and in a regular course, 32.

Admissions: 93% of the 2003-2004 applicants were accepted.

Requirements: The ACT or SAT I is required, with a minimum ACT score of 19 required for regular admission. In addition, applicants should be high school graduates or have a GED certificate. AP and CLEP credits are accepted.

Procedure: Freshmen are admitted to all sessions. Entrance exams should be taken during the junior year or early in the senior year. There is an early admissions plan and a rolling admissions plan. Applications should be filed by August 10 for fall entry, December 15 for spring entry, and May 20 for summer entry. The fall 2003 application fee was $25. Notification is sent on a rolling basis.

Transfer: 1060 transfer students enrolled in fall 2002. Transfer applicants must have at least a 2.0 GPA on all college work attempted for regular admission. 32 credits of 128 required for the bachelor's degree must be completed at USA.

Visiting: There are regularly scheduled orientations for prospective students, including 3 Saturday visiting days in November, February, and April. There are guides for informal visits and visitors may sit in on classes. To schedule a visit, contact Melissa Haab, Director of Admissions.

Financial Aid: In 2003-2004, 65% of all full-time students received some form of financial aid. 65% of all full-time students received need-based aid. The average freshman award was $10,000. 35% of undergraduates work part time. Average annual earnings from campus work are $4000. The average financial indebtedness of the 2003 graduate was $11,000. The FAFSA and the college's own financial statement are required. The deadline for filing freshman financial aid applications for fall entry is May 1.

International Students: There are 976 international students enrolled. The school actively recruits these students. They must score 500 on the written TOEFL.

Computers: The mainframe is a Sun SPARC server 10 model 512. Students may access the academic host Sun SPARC server through terminals in the terminal lab or through modem connections. Access to the Internet is provided through PCs on campus or via modem for computers off campus. All students may access the system at various times. All students are required to have access to personal computers. Students enrolled in the entry-level programming sequence are required to have laptops.

Graduates: From July 1, 2002 to June 30, 2003, 1371 bachelor's degrees were awarded. The most popular majors were nursing (11%), elementary education (8%), and marketing (6%). In an average class, 12% graduate in 4 years or less, 25% graduate in 5 years or less, and 32% graduate in 6 years or less. 283 companies recruited on campus in 2002-2003. Of the 2002 graduating class, 67% were employed within 6 months of graduation.

Admissions Contact: Melissa Haab, Director of Admissions.
E-mail: admiss@usouthal.edu Web: www.southalabama.edu

UNIVERSITY OF WEST ALABAMA
A-3
Livingston, AL 35470
(205) 652-3578
(888) 636-8800; Fax: (205) 652-3522

Full-time: 660 men, 790 women	Faculty: 87; IIA, --$
Part-time: 55 men, 90 women	Ph.D.s: 65%
Graduate: 70 men, 260 women	Student/Faculty: 17 to 1
Year: semesters, summer session	Tuition: $3245 ($6490)
Application Deadline: open	Room & Board: $3425
Freshman Class: n/av	
SAT I or ACT: required	COMPETITIVE

University of West Alabama, founded in 1835, is a state-controlled institution offering programs in liberal arts and sciences, business and commerce, general studies, and education. There are 5 undergraduate schools and 1 graduate school. Figures in the above capsule and in this profile are approximate. In addition to regional accreditation, UWA has baccalaureate program accreditation with NCATE and NLN. The 2 libraries contain 135,000 volumes, 500,000 microform items, and 7500 audio/video tapes/CDs, and subscribe to 700 periodicals. Computerized library services include interlibrary loans and database searching. Special learning facilities include a learning resource center, art gallery, and TV station. The 600-acre campus is in a small town 35 miles east of Meridian, Mississippi. Including any residence halls, there are 36 buildings.

Student Life: 80% of undergraduates are from Alabama. Students are from 21 states, 9 foreign countries, and Canada. 88% are from public schools. 61% are white; 37% African American. The average age of freshmen is 18; all undergraduates, 22. 39% do not continue beyond their first year.

Housing: 903 students can be accommodated in college housing, which includes single-sex dorms, on-campus apartments, and married-student housing. In addition, there are honors houses. On-campus housing is guaranteed for all 4 years. Alcohol is not permitted. All students may keep cars.

Activities: 10% of men belong to 6 national fraternities; 6% of women belong to 4 national sororities. There are 30 groups on campus, including band, cheerleading, choir, chorus, drama, drill team, ethnic, honors, international, jazz band, marching band, newspaper, pep band, photography, political, professional, radio and TV, religious, social, student government, symphony, and yearbook. Popular campus events include Springfest and Club Luie.

Sports: There are 5 intercollegiate sports for men and 5 for women, and 8 intramural sports for men and 8 for women. Facilities include an 800-seat gym, a 7500-seat football stadium, a baseball field, tennis and racquetball courts, a pool, weight rooms, a lake, and hiking trails.

Disabled Students: 95% of the campus is accessible. Wheelchair ramps, elevators, special parking, specially equipped rest rooms, special class scheduling, and lowered drinking fountains are available.

Services: Counseling and information services are available, as is tutoring in most subjects. There is remedial math, reading, and writing.

Campus Safety and Security: Measures include 24-hour foot and vehicle patrol, informal discussions, pamphlets/posters/films, and lighted pathways/sidewalks.

Programs of Study: UWA confers B.A., B.S., B.B.A., and B.T. degrees. Associate and master's degrees are also awarded. Bachelor's degrees are awarded in BIOLOGICAL SCIENCE (biology/biological science and marine biology), BUSINESS (accounting and business administration and management), COMMUNICATIONS AND THE ARTS (English), COMPUTER AND PHYSICAL SCIENCE (chemistry, computer science, mathematics, and physics), EDUCATION (athletic training, early childhood, elementary, middle school, physical, science, secondary, and special), ENGINEERING AND ENVIRONMENTAL DESIGN (environmental science and industrial engineering technology), HEALTH PROFESSIONS (predentistry and premedicine), SOCIAL SCIENCE (history, prelaw, psychology, social science, and sociology). English, business, and sciences are the strongest academically. Education and business are the largest.

Required: To graduate, all students must complete at least 120 semester hours with a minimum GPA of 2.0.

Special: There is a 3-2 engineering program with Auburn University and the University of Alabama at Birmingham. The 2-year technical division offers programs leading to a possible B.T. degree. B.A.-B.S. degrees, a co-op program in environmental science, and an accelerated degree are available. Nondegree study is possible. There are 5 national honor societies, a freshman honors program, and 4 departmental honors programs.

Faculty/Classroom: 60% of faculty are male; 40%, female. 90% teach undergraduates. Graduate students teach 4% of introductory courses. The average class size in an introductory lecture is 30; in a laboratory, 18; and in a regular course, 15.

Requirements: The SAT I or ACT is required, with a minimum composite score of 18 on the ACT for unconditional admission. In addition, applicants should have completed 15 high school credits or the GED equivalent. Applications are accepted on-line via the school's web site. AP and CLEP credits are accepted.

Procedure: Freshmen are admitted to all sessions. Entrance exams should be taken during the junior or senior year. There are early admissions, deferred admissions, and rolling admissions plans. Application deadlines are open. The application fee is $20.

Transfer: Transfer applicants must have maintained a minimum GPA of 2.0 in all previous college courses. 30 of 120 credits required for the bachelor's degree must be completed at UWA.

Visiting: There are regularly scheduled orientations for prospective students. There are guides for informal visits and visitors may sit in on classes and stay overnight. To schedule a visit, contact the Admissions Office.

Financial Aid: The CSS Profile, FAFSA, FFS, or SFS is required. Check with the school for current deadlines.

International Students: They must score 500 on the written TOEFL and also take the SAT I or the ACT, scoring 18 on the ACT.

Computers: The mainframe is an IBM 9375. All students may access the system. There are no time limits. The fee is $45 per semester. It is strongly recommended that all students have a personal computer.

Graduates: In an average class, 17% graduate in 3 years or less, 28% graduate in 4 years or less, 33% graduate in 5 years or less, and 37% graduate in 6 years or less.

Admissions Contact: Richard Hester, Director of Admissions. A video is available. E-mail: *rhester@uwa.edu* Web: *www.uwa.edu*

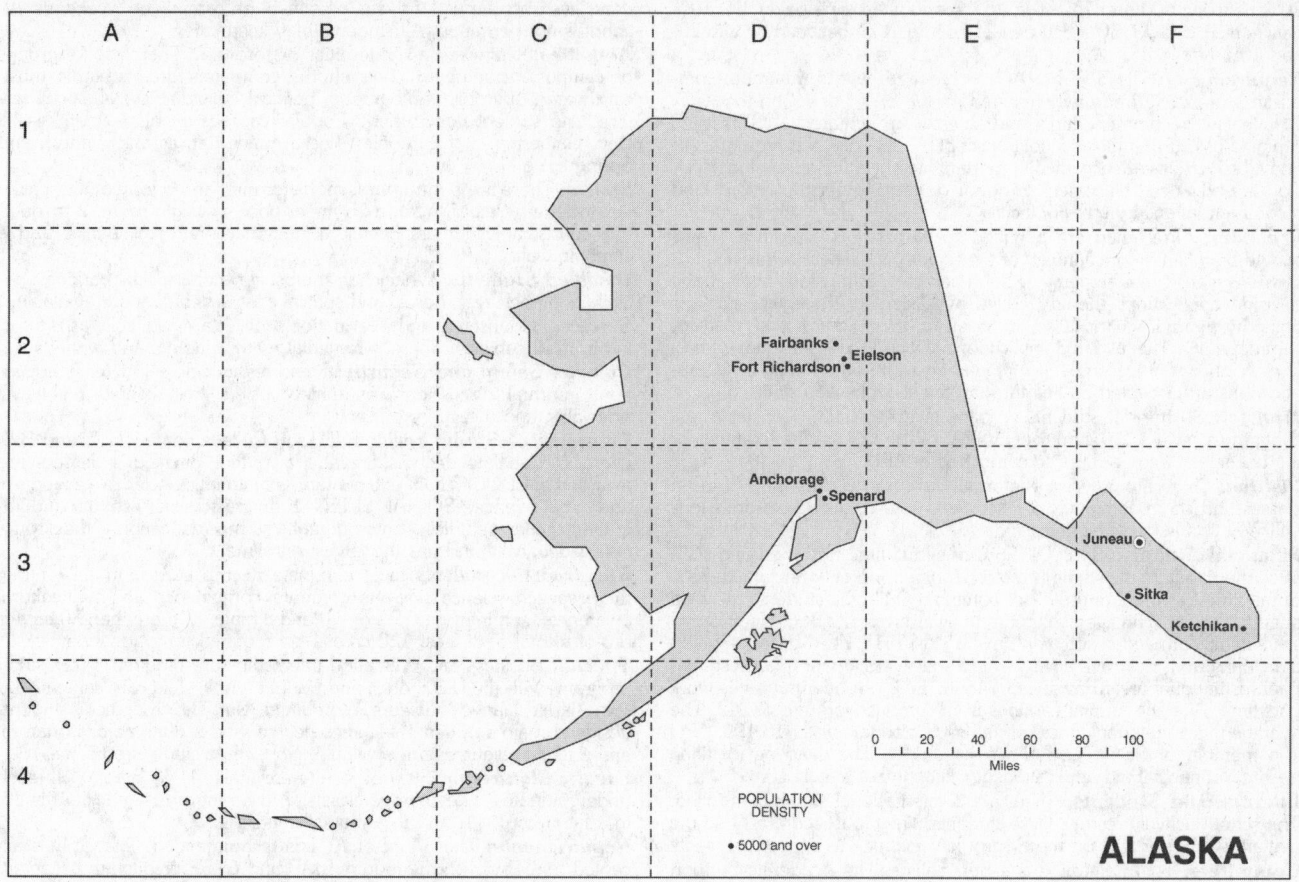

POPULATION DENSITY

• 5000 and over

0   20   40   60   80   100
Miles

ALASKA

ALASKA PACIFIC UNIVERSITY   D-3
Anchorage, AK 99508-4672
**(907) 564-8248
(800) 252-7528; Fax: (907) 564-8317**

Full-time: 102 men, 182 women	**Faculty:** 30
Part-time: 56 men, 138 women	**Ph.D.s:** 77%
Graduate: 71 men, 124 women	**Student/Faculty:** 9 to 1
Year: 4-1-4, summer session	**Tuition:** $12,410 ($16,328)
Application Deadline: February 1	**Room & Board:** $5500

Freshman Class: 117 applied, 107 accepted, 28 enrolled
SAT I Verbal/Math: 540/520   **ACT:** 22   **COMPETITIVE**

Alaska Pacific University, founded in 1957, is a private institution offering undergraduate programs in business administration, elementary and middle school education, environmental science and outdoor studies, liberal studies, and psychology. The library contains 760,423 volumes, 559,496 microform items, and 1032 audio/video tapes/CDs, and subscribes to 3430 periodicals. Computerized library services include the card catalog and interlibrary loans. Special learning facilities include a learning resource center, art gallery, radio station, TV station, and an Alaskana Collection. The 200-acre campus is in a suburban area in midtown Anchorage. Including any residence halls, there are 7 buildings.

Student Life: 74% of undergraduates are from Alaska. Students are from 34 states and 6 foreign countries. 67% are white; 16% Native American/Eskimo. The average age of freshmen is 21; all undergraduates, 30. 21% do not continue beyond their first year; 30% remain to graduate.

Housing: 120 students can be accommodated in college housing, which includes coed dorms, on-campus apartments, and married-student housing. In addition, there are special-interest houses. On-campus housing is guaranteed for the freshman year only, is available on a first-come, first-served basis, and is available on a lottery system for upperclassmen. 81% of students commute. Alcohol is not permitted. All students may keep cars.

Activities: There are no fraternities or sororities. There are 21 groups on campus, including band, chorus, drama, environmental, ethnic, gay, international, newspaper, professional, religious, student government, Students in Free Enterprise, and yearbook. Popular campus events include Earth Day, Spring Honors Convocation, and Fall Academic Convocation.

Sports: There are 5 intramural sports for men and 5 for women. Facilities include a 300-seat sports center, an indoor swimming pool, cross-country skiing and running trails, a climbing wall, a soccer field, a lake for boating, and a weight/exercise room.

Disabled Students: 75% of the campus is accessible. Wheelchair ramps, elevators, special parking, specially equipped rest rooms, lowered drinking fountains, and lowered telephones are available.

Services: Counseling and information services are available, as is tutoring in most subjects, including math, writing, and other subjects as needed. There is remedial math and writing.

Campus Safety and Security: Measures include informal discussions, pamphlets/posters/films, emergency telephones, and lighted pathways/sidewalks. Safety signs are posted as needed.

Programs of Study: APU confers B.A. and B.S. degrees. Associate and master's degrees are also awarded. Bachelor's degrees are awarded in AGRICULTURE (natural resource management), BIOLOGICAL SCIENCE (marine biology), BUSINESS (business administration and management and recreational facilities management), EDUCATION (elementary), ENGINEERING AND ENVIRONMENTAL DESIGN (environmental science), SOCIAL SCIENCE (human services, liberal arts/general studies, and psychology). Environmental science/outdoor studies and elementary education are the largest.

Required: All students must complete 4 semester hours each in an Orientation to Active Learning class, a lab science, a course in social/behavioral science, and a course in ethics or religion; 2 courses in humanities; a sophomore seminar in major; and an American Sign Language course. Courses to meet writing, speech, and quantitative skills competencies are also required, as well as a 3-semester-hour practicum and a portfolio.

Special: The internship program is very strong. The Degree Completion Program for working adults leads to a B.A. in organizational management, accounting, or human services. There are 2 national honor societies and 2 departmental honors programs.

Faculty/Classroom: 61% of faculty are male; 39%, female. 98% teach undergraduates. No introductory courses are taught by graduate students. The average class size in an introductory lecture is 10; in a laboratory, 10; and in a regular course, 9.

Admissions: 91% of the 2003-2004 applicants were accepted. The SAT I scores for the 2003-2004 freshman class were: Verbal--50% below 500, 20% between 500 and 599, 20% between 600 and 700, and 10% above 700; Math--30% below 500, 50% between 500 and 599, and 20% between 600 and 700. The ACT scores were 40% below 21, 10% between 21 and 23, 30% between 24 and 26, 10% between 27 and 28, and 10% above 28.

Requirements: The SAT I or ACT is required, with a minimum composite score of 920 normally required on the SAT I or 19 on the ACT. Two teacher recommendations and an essay are required. A GED is acceptable in lieu of a high school transcript. A GPA of 2.5 is required. AP and CLEP credits are accepted. Important factors in the admissions decision are advanced placement or honor courses, leadership record, and recommendations by school officials.

Procedure: Freshmen are admitted to all sessions. Entrance exams should be taken before January of the senior year. There is a rolling admissions plan. There are early decision and early admissions plans. Early decision applications should be filed by December 1; regular applications, by February 1 for fall entry, open for spring entry, and open for summer entry. The fall 2003 application fee was $25. Notification of early decision is sent December 15; regular decision, on a rolling basis. Applications are accepted on-line through the school's web site.

Transfer: 80 transfer students enrolled in 2002-2003. Transfer applicants must have a 2.0 cumulative GPA. 32 of 128 credits required for the bachelor's degree must be completed at APU.

Visiting: There are guides for informal visits and visitors may sit in on classes and stay overnight. To schedule a visit, contact the Admissions Office at *admissions@alaskapacific.edu*.

Financial Aid: In 2003-2004, 96% of all full-time freshmen and 83% of continuing full-time students received some form of financial aid. 75% of full-time freshmen and 59% of continuing full-time students received need-based aid. The average freshman award was $23,366. Need-based scholarships or need-based grants averaged $3515; need-based self-help aid (loans and jobs) averaged $4711; and average first-time freshman total institutional award averaged $4840. 17% of undergraduates work part time. Average annual earnings from campus work are $1242. The average financial indebtedness of the 2003 graduate was $18,195. APU is a member of CSS. The FAFSA is required. The deadline for filing freshman financial aid applications for fall entry is March 15.

International Students: There are 3 international students enrolled. The school actively recruits these students. They must score 500 on the written TOEFL or 213 on the electronic version.

Computers: The mainframe is a Sun Solaris. The Academic Support Center provides 40 PCs for student and faculty use. Internet and web access is provided free of charge to enrolled students and is available in faculty and administrative offices. All students may access the system.

Graduates: From July 1, 2002 to June 30, 2003, 95 bachelor's degrees were awarded. The most popular majors were business administration (50%), environmental science (11%), and liberal studies (10%). In an average class, 3% graduate in 3 years or less, 18% graduate in 4 years or less, 19% graduate in 5 years or less, and 35% graduate in 6 years or less.

Admissions Contact: Michael Warner and Jessica Carr, Codirectors of Admissions. E-mail: *admissions@alaskapacific.edu*
Web: *http://www.alaskapacific.edu*

SHELDON JACKSON COLLEGE   F-3
Sitka, AK 99835   (907) 747-5221
(800) 478-4556; Fax: (907) 747-6366

Full-time: 165 men and women	**Faculty:** 17
Part-time: 75 men and women	**Ph.D.s:** 71%
Graduate: none	**Student/Faculty:** 10 to 1
Year: semesters	**Tuition:** $8020
Application Deadline: open	**Room & Board:** $6920
Freshman Class: n/av	
SAT I or ACT: recommended	**LESS COMPETITIVE**

Sheldon Jackson College, founded in 1878, is a private liberal arts college, offering emphases in natural and aquatic resources, outdoor recreation, fisheries, marine biology, business, elementary and secondary education, and interdisciplinary studies. Figures in the above capsule and in this profile are approximate. In addition to regional accreditation, Sheldon Jackson College has baccalaureate program accreditation with NASDTEC. The library contains 80,000 volumes, and subscribes to 500 periodicals. Computerized library services include the card catalog, interlibrary loans, and database searching. Special learning facilities include a learning resource center, natural history museum, state-owned museum, and salmon hatchery. The 345-acre campus is in a small town in southeast Alaska. Including any residence halls, there are 23 buildings.

Student Life: 70% of undergraduates are from out of state, mostly the Northwest. Students are from 35 states and 4 foreign countries. 99% are from public schools. 70% are white; 26% Native American/Eskimo. The average age of freshmen is 20; all undergraduates, 24. 18% do not continue beyond their first year; 21% remain to graduate.

Housing: 240 students can be accommodated in college housing, which includes single-sex dorms, on-campus apartments, and married-student housing. On-campus housing is guaranteed for the freshman year only and is available on a first-come, first-served basis. 75% of students live on campus; of those, all remain on campus on weekends. Alcohol is not permitted. All students may keep cars.

Activities: There are no fraternities or sororities. There are 14 groups on campus, including art, choir, chorus, computers, drama, ethnic, musical theater, outdoor, photography, political, religious, social, social service, and student government. Popular campus events include Alaska Day, Gathering of the People (Alaska native dances and dinner), and Spring Expo.

Sports: There are 5 intramural sports for men and 5 for women. Facilities include a 2-court gym, a 25-meter pool, a weight room, 2 racquetball courts, a wilderness center, a student center, sea kayaks, and a climbing wall.

Disabled Students: Wheelchair ramps, elevators, special parking, specially equipped rest rooms, and special class scheduling are available.

Services: Counseling and information services are available, as is tutoring in most subjects. There is remedial math, reading, and writing.

Campus Safety and Security: Measures include self-defense education, informal discussions, pamphlets/posters/films, lighted pathways/sidewalks, and a security officer.

Programs of Study: Sheldon Jackson College confers B.A. and B.S. degrees. Associate degrees are also awarded. Bachelor's degrees are awarded in EDUCATION (elementary, mathematics, science, secondary, and social science), SOCIAL SCIENCE (interdisciplinary studies and liberal arts/general studies). Environmental science/education is the strongest academically and has the largest enrollment.

Required: All students must complete a core curriculum in writing, math, speech, science, fine arts, computer competence, and multicultural awareness. A minimum GPA of 2.0 and a major of more than 30 credits out of a total of at least 120 credits are required for graduation.

Special: Business and education internships are required. Work-study programs with the U.S. Forest and Park Services, child care centers, and the Alaska Native Museum, combined B.A.-B.S. degrees, student-designed majors, a general studies degree, and a dual major in natural and aquatic resources are available. Nondegree study is possible.

Faculty/Classroom: 59% of faculty are male; 41%, female. All teach undergraduates. The average class size in an introductory lecture is 32; in a laboratory, 11; and in a regular course, 13.

Requirements: The SAT I or ACT is recommended. The GED is accepted. A GPA of 2.0 is required. AP and CLEP credits are accepted. Applications are accepted on-line.

Procedure: Freshmen are admitted fall and spring. There is a rolling admissions plan. Application deadlines are open. The application fee is $25.

Transfer: The college follows a nonselective admissions policy for transfer applicants with a 2.0 GPA. 30 of 120 credits required for the bachelor's degree must be completed at Sheldon Jackson College.

Visiting: There are regularly scheduled orientations for prospective students, including campus tour visits to classrooms and meetings with financial aid counselors. There are guides for informal visits and visitors may sit in on classes and stay overnight. To schedule a visit, contact the Admissions Office.

Financial Aid: 90% of undergraduates work part time. Average annual earnings from campus work are $1500. The FAFSA is required. Check with the school for current deadlines.

International Students: They must score 550 on the written TOEFL or 250 on the electronic version.

Computers: The mainframe is a Dell. A 20-unit center housing PCs and Macs is open from 8 A.M. to 10 P.M. weekdays, and part of the weekend. Hookups are available in every dorm room. All students may access the system. There are no time limits. The fee is $370 per year. It is strongly recommended that all students have a personal computer.

Graduates: In a recent year, 20 bachelor's degrees were awarded. The most popular majors were aquatic resources (60%), elementary education (30%), and natural resource management (10%). In an average class, 40% graduate in 4 years or less, 50% graduate in 5 years or less, and 60% graduate in 6 years or less. Of a recent graduating class, 10% were enrolled in graduate school within 6 months of graduation and 80% were employed.

Admissions Contact: Elizabeth Lower, Director of Admissions. E-mail: *elower@sj-alaska.edu* Web: *http://www.sj-alaska.edu*

UNIVERSITY OF ALASKA SYSTEM

The University of Alaska is the only public institution of higher learning in the state of Alaska. It is a statewide system consisting of three multimission main campuses located in Anchorage, Fairbanks, and Juneau, with extended satellite colleges and sites throughout Alaska. The university was established at Fairbanks in 1917 as the Alaska Agricultural College and School of Mines; in 1935 it was renamed the University of Alaska. The university now includes full-service universities in Fairbanks, Anchorage, and Juneau; lower division college centers in Bethel, Dillington, Ketchikan, Kodiak, Kotzebue, Nome, Palmer, Sitka, and Soldotna; a community college at Valdez; and vocational, rural education, and extension sites through the state. The university is governed by an eleven-member Board of Regents. The board is an autonomous organization and the highest authority in the administration of the university, governed by the Alaska Statutes, which provides for the appointment of the regents by the governor for overlapping terms of eight years. Since 1975, students have been represented on the board; they are appointed for two-year terms.

UNIVERSITY OF ALASKA ANCHORAGE
D-3

Anchorage, AK 99508   (907) 786-1480; Fax: (907) 786-4888

Full-time: 2100 men, 2900 women	Faculty: 331; IIA, -$
Part-time: 2800 men, 4800 women	Ph.D.s: 80%
Graduate: 200 men, 400 women	Student/Faculty: 16 to 1
Year: semesters, summer session	Tuition: $2500 ($6800)
Application Deadline: open	Room & Board: $6600
Freshman Class: n/av	
SAT I or ACT: recommended	NONCOMPETITIVE

The University of Alaska Anchorage, founded in 1954, is a public institution and a major unit of the University of Alaska statewide system. Its baccalaureate programs are administered through the Colleges of Arts and Sciences, Business and Public Policy, Health, Education, and Social Welfare, and the School of Engineering, and the Community and Technical College. Tuition is based on the level of course work and number of credits taken; fees also vary by credits. There are 5 undergraduate and 5 graduate schools. Figures in the above capsule and in this profile are approximate. In addition to regional accreditation, UAA has baccalaureate program accreditation with AACSB, ABET, ACEJMC, ADA, CAHEA, CSWE, NASAD, NASDTEC, and NLN. The library contains 676,750 volumes, 574,010 microform items, and 7080 audio/video tapes/CDs, and subscribes to 3480 periodicals. Computerized library services include interlibrary loans and database searching. Special learning facilities include a learning resource center, art gallery, radio station, TV station, a dental clinic, a welding lab, an auto-diesel garage, a theater, photography labs, and a student art museum show case. The 428-acre campus is in an urban area. Including any residence halls, there are 27 buildings.

Student Life: 90% of undergraduates are from Alaska. 80% are white. The average age of all undergraduates is 29. 37% do not continue beyond their first year.

Housing: 388 students can be accommodated in college housing, which includes single-sex and coed on-campus apartments. There is also a house for Alaska natives or American Indians who are engineering majors. On-campus housing is available on a first-come, first-served basis. Priority is given to out-of-town students. 97% of students commute. Alcohol is not permitted. All students may keep cars.

Activities: There are no fraternities or sororities. There are 75 groups on campus, including art, band, cheerleading, chess, choir, chorus, computers, dance, debate, drama, ethnic, film, gay, honors, international, jazz band, literary magazine, newspaper, orchestra, photography, political, professional, radio and TV, religious, social, social service, student government, and yearbook. Popular campus events include Great Alaska Shoot-Out, Northern Lights Invitational, and Student Showcase.

Sports: There are 6 intercollegiate sports for men and 4 for women, and 10 intramural sports for men and 10 for women. Facilities include an ice rink, an indoor jogging track, a gym, a swimming/diving pool, a weight room, and racquetball/squash courts.

Disabled Students: All of the campus is accessible. Wheelchair ramps, elevators, special parking, specially equipped rest rooms, lowered drinking fountains, and lowered telephones are available.

Services: Counseling and information services are available, as is tutoring in most subjects. There is a reader service for the blind and remedial math, reading, and writing. Sign language, interpreters, and note takers are available.

Campus Safety and Security: Measures include 24-hour foot and vehicle patrol, self-defense education, security escort services, and informal discussions. There are pamphlets/posters/films, emergency telephones, and lighted pathways/sidewalks.

Programs of Study: UAA confers B.A., B.S., B.B.A., B.Ed., B.F.A., B.Mus., and B.S.W. degrees. Associate and master's degrees are also awarded. Bachelor's degrees are awarded in BIOLOGICAL SCIENCE (biology/biological science), BUSINESS (accounting, banking and finance, business administration and management, hotel/motel and restaurant management, management information systems, marketing/retailing/merchandising, and transportation management), COMMUNICATIONS AND THE ARTS (art, communications, dramatic arts, English, fine arts, journalism, languages, and music), COMPUTER AND PHYSICAL SCIENCE (chemistry, computer science, mathematics, and natural sciences), EDUCATION (elementary, music, physical, and secondary), ENGINEERING AND ENVIRONMENTAL DESIGN (aeronauti-

cal technology, civil engineering, survey and mapping technology, and technological management), HEALTH PROFESSIONS (nursing), SOCIAL SCIENCE (anthropology, criminal justice, economics, history, human services, interdisciplinary studies, political science/government, psychology, social work, and sociology). Education, nursing, and social sciences are the strongest academically. Elementary education, accounting, and nursing are the largest.

Required: General education requirements include 7 credits in natural science, 6 each in written communications, humanities, and social sciences, and 3 each in oral communication, quantitative skills, and fine arts. A total of 120 to 132 credits, with 48 upper-division courses, and a minimum GPA of 2.0 are required to graduate.

Special: UAA participates in the National Student Exchange Program and offers study abroad. UAA also offers B.A.-B.S. degrees, student-designed and dual majors, internships, pass/fail options, a 3-2 electrical engineering degree, a general studies degree, nondegree study, and credit for life experience. The Community and Technical College provides educational and vocational courses for career development. There are 2 national honor societies and 3 departmental honors programs.

Faculty/Classroom: 60% of faculty are male; 40%, female. The average class size in an introductory lecture is 50; in a laboratory, 20; and in a regular course, 35.

Requirements: The SAT I or ACT is recommended. In addition, applicants should be graduates of an accredited secondary school or have a high school or GED certificate. A GPA of 2.5 is required. AP and CLEP credits are accepted. Applications are accepted on-line through the university's web site.

Procedure: Freshmen are admitted to all sessions. Entrance exams should be taken by May of the senior year. There are early admissions, deferred admissions, and rolling admissions plans. The college accepts all applicants. Check with the school for current application guidelines. The fall 2003 application fee was $35. Notification is sent on a rolling basis.

Transfer: Applicants must meet admission requirements and must have a minimum GPA of 2.0 and at least 30 credit hours earned at an accredited postsecondary institution. 30 of 120 credits required for the bachelor's degree must be completed at UAA.

Visiting: There are regularly scheduled orientations for prospective students, consisting of registration orientation, application process, campus tours, student appointments, and classes. There are guides for informal visits and visitors may sit in on classes. To schedule a visit, contact the Office of Admissions.

Financial Aid: UAA is a member of CSS. The FAFSA and the college's own financial statement are required. Check with the school for current deadlines.

International Students: They must score 450 on the written TOEFL and also take the SAT I or the ACT.

Computers: The mainframe is a DEC AXP 2100 Alpha open VMS system. There are also 120 Mac and IBM PCs available in various academic departments, the Learning Resource Center, the Reading and Writing Center, and the Campus Center. All students may access the system. There are no time limits and no fees.

Graduates: In an average class, 5% graduate in 4 years or less, 14% graduate in 5 years or less, and 20% graduate in 6 years or less.

Admissions Contact: Enrollment Services. A video is available. Web: *www.uaa.alaska.edu*

UNIVERSITY OF ALASKA FAIRBANKS
D-2

Fairbanks, AK 99775-7480   (907) 474-7500
(800) 478-1823; Fax: (907) 474-5379

Full-time: 1695 men, 1842 women	Faculty: 507; I, --$
Part-time: 1505 men, 2678 women	Ph.D.s: n/av
Graduate: 496 men, 520 women	Student/Faculty: 7 to 1
Year: semesters, summer session	Tuition: $4165 ($11,095)
Application Deadline: August 1	Room & Board: $5130
Freshman Class: 1895 applied, 1587 accepted, 1021 enrolled	
SAT I Verbal/Math: 510/510	ACT: 21 COMPETITIVE

The University of Alaska Fairbanks, founded in 1917 and the nation's northernmost Land, Sea, and Space Grant university and international research center, advances and disseminates knowledge through creative teaching, research, and public service with an emphasis on Alaska, the North, and their diverse peoples. There are 8 undergraduate and 9 graduate schools. In addition to regional accreditation, UAF has baccalaureate program accreditation with AACSB, ABET, ACEJMC, ACS, CAAHEP, CSAB, CSWE, NASDTEC, NASM, and SAF. The 3 libraries contain 608,575 volumes, 1,131,516 microform items, and 664,448 audio/video tapes/CDs, and subscribe to 2754 periodicals. Computerized library services include the card catalog, interlibrary loans, and database searching. Special learning facilities include a learning resource center, art gallery, natural history museum, radio station, and TV station. Several research institutes and labs for study in the physical and natural sciences are associated with the university. The 2250-acre campus is in a small town 4 miles northwest of Fairbanks. Including any residence halls, there are 175 buildings.

Student Life: 87% of undergraduates are from Alaska. Students are from 48 states, 29 foreign countries, and Canada. 62% are white; 21% Native American/Eskimo. The average age of freshmen is 21; all undergraduates, 26. 30% do not continue beyond their first year.

Housing: 1554 students can be accommodated in college housing, which includes coed dorms, on-campus apartments, and married-student housing. In addition, there are honors floors, a first-year experience residence, and a healthy lifestyle residence. On-campus housing is available on a first-come, first-served basis. 72% of students commute. All students may keep cars.

Activities: There is 1 national fraternity and 1 national sorority. There are 86 groups on campus, including art, band, cheerleading, chess, choir, chorus, computers, dance, drama, ethnic, film, gay, honors, international, jazz band, literary magazine, musical theater, newspaper, opera, orchestra, pep band, political, professional, radio and TV, religious, social, student government, and symphony. Popular campus events include All-Campus Day, Alcohol Awareness Week, and Meltdown (spring event).

Sports: There are 4 intercollegiate sports for men and 4 for women, and 21 intramural sports for men and 21 for women. Facilities include a 2500-seat arena, a 2000-seat gym, a 1500-seat skating rink, 2 racquetball courts, 2 weight rooms, 4 basketball courts, an Olympic-size swimming pool, a small-bore rifle range, and a lighted 30-mile ski trail.

Disabled Students: 90% of the campus is accessible. Wheelchair ramps, elevators, special parking, specially equipped rest rooms, special class scheduling, lowered drinking fountains, lowered telephones, a shuttle bus, and a swimming pool equipped with hydraulic lifts are available. Special residence hall accommodations are coordinated by the Disabled Student Service Office.

Services: Counseling and information services are available, as is tutoring in some subjects, including chemistry, calculus, languages, biology, math, physics, geology, and English. There is a reader service for the blind and remedial math, reading, and writing.

Campus Safety and Security: Measures include 24-hour foot and vehicle patrol, self-defense education, security escort services, and shuttle buses. There are informal discussions, pamphlets/posters/films, emergency telephones, lighted pathways/sidewalks, a 24-hour dorm lockup, a 24-hour crisis line, evening patrols inside dorms, residence hall check-in, and security escort service.

Programs of Study: UAF confers B.A., B.S., B.B.A., B.Ed., B.F.A., B.M., and B.T. degrees. Associate, master's, and doctoral degrees are also awarded. Bachelor's degrees are awarded in AGRICULTURE (fishing and fisheries, natural resource management, and wildlife management), BIOLOGICAL SCIENCE (biology/biological science and wildlife biology), BUSINESS (accounting, business administration and management, and business economics), COMMUNICATIONS AND THE ARTS (art, communications, dramatic arts, English, Eskimo, journalism, linguistics, modern language, music, and music performance), COMPUTER AND PHYSICAL SCIENCE (applied physics, chemistry, computer science, earth science, geology, mathematics, physics, science, and statistics), EDUCATION (elementary and music), ENGINEERING AND ENVIRONMENTAL DESIGN (civil engineering, electrical/electronics engineering, environmental science, geological engineering, mechanical engineering, mining and mineral engineering, petroleum/natural gas engineering, and technological management), SOCIAL SCIENCE (anthropology, area studies, criminal justice, ethnic studies, geography, history, interdisciplinary studies, Japanese studies, Native American studies, philosophy, political science/government, psychology, rural economics, Russian and Slavic studies, social work, and sociology). Engineering, fisheries, and wildlife management are the strongest academically. Biological sciences, business administration, and computer science are the largest.

Required: All students must complete core courses in English and oral communication, library skills, humanities, social science, natural science, and math. A minimum of 120 credit hours, with 27 to 30 in the major, and a 2.0 GPA are required for graduation. Courses in English and speech communication are required.

Special: The university's College of Rural Alaska offers satellite education programs to Alaska residents to reach students at remote sites. Study abroad is offered in 8 countries, and B.A.-B.S. degrees are available in 8 majors (anthropology, biological sciences, chemistry, physics, interdisciplinary studies, math, psychology, and sociology). Internships are offered through the Rural Alaska Honors Institute. Student-designed majors, credit/no credit options, nondegree study, and credit for life, military, and work experience are also available. There are 10 national honor societies and a freshman honors program.

Faculty/Classroom: 61% of faculty are male; 39%, female. The average class size in a regular course is 15.

Admissions: 84% of the 2003-2004 applicants were accepted. The SAT I scores for the 2003-2004 freshman class were: Verbal--42% below 500, 35% between 500 and 599, 18% between 600 and 700, and 5% above 700; Math--43% below 500, 36% between 500 and 599, 19% between 600 and 700, and 3% above 700. The ACT scores were 48% below 21, 22% between 21 and 23, 17% between 24 and 26, 5% between 27 and 28, and 8% above 28. 26% of the current freshmen were in the top fifth of their class; 50% were in the top two fifths.

Requirements: The SAT I or ACT is required. In addition, applicants should be graduates of an accredited secondary school with 16 academic credits, including 4 in English and 3 each in math, natural or physical sciences, and social sciences, with a minimum GPA of 2.5 in these courses. The GED or its equivalent is accepted. A GPA of 2.0 is required. AP and CLEP credits are accepted.

Procedure: Freshmen are admitted to all sessions. Applications should be filed by August 1 for fall entry and December 1 for spring entry. There is a rolling admissions plan. The college accepts all applicants. Notification is sent on a rolling basis. The fall 2003 application fee was $35. Applications are accepted on-line.

Transfer: 509 transfer students enrolled in 2002-2003. A GPA of 2.0 in all previous college work and an honorable dismissal from all schools attended are required. Applicants with fewer than 30 semester hours of transferable credit also must have a high school GPA of 2.0 and ACT or SAT I scores. 30 of 120 credits required for the bachelor's degree must be completed at UAF.

Visiting: There are regularly scheduled orientations for prospective students. There are guides for informal visits and visitors may sit in on classes and stay overnight. To schedule a visit, contact the Admissions Counseling Office at *admissions@uaf.edu*.

Financial Aid: In 2003-2004, 38% of all full-time freshmen and 42% of continuing full-time students received some form of financial aid. 26% of full-time freshmen and 29% of continuing full-time students received need-based aid. Need-based scholarships or need-based grants averaged $4516; and need-based self-help aid (loans and jobs) averaged $7242. 16% of undergraduates work part time. Average annual earnings from campus work are $5950. The FAFSA is required. The deadline for filing freshman financial aid applications for fall entry is May 15.

International Students: There are 184 international students enrolled. They must score 550 on the written TOEFL and also take the SAT I or the ACT.

Computers: The mainframe is a DEC Alpha 7000-640. PCs and Macs are available for student use in the library, the Bunnell Building, and various academic departments. All students may access the system 24 hours per day. There are no time limits and no fees.

Graduates: From July 1, 2002 to June 30, 2003, 395 bachelor's degrees were awarded. The most popular majors were biological sciences (12%), education (7%), and business administration (6%). In an average class, 7% graduate in 4 years or less, 18% graduate in 5 years or less, and 24% graduate in 6 years or less.

Admissions Contact: Nancy Dix, Director of Admissions. A video is available. E-mail: *admissions@uaf.edu* Web: *www.uaf.edu*

UNIVERSITY OF ALASKA SOUTHEAST   F-3
Juneau, AK 99801

(907) 465-6457
(877) 465-4827; Fax: (907) 465-6365

Full-time: 250 men, 310 women	**Faculty:** 60; IIA, --$
Part-time: 580 men, 850 women	**Ph.D.s:** 52%
Graduate: 40 men, 50 women	**Student/Faculty:** 50 to 1
Year: semesters, summer session	**Tuition:** $2500 ($7000)
Application Deadline: open	**Room & Board:** $5400
Freshman Class: n/av	
SAT I or ACT: recommended	**LESS COMPETITIVE**

The University of Alaska Southeast, a multicampus institution founded in 1972, is part of the University of Alaska statewide system, with baccalaureate programs offered in business and public administration, education, and liberal arts and science. There are 3 undergraduate and 2 graduate schools. Figures in the above capsule and in this profile are approximate.The library contains 250,000 volumes, 250,000 microform items, and 1850 audio/video tapes/CDs, and subscribes to 1500 periodicals. Computerized library services include the card catalog, interlibrary loans, and database searching. Special learning facilities include a learning resource center and media and educational technology classrooms. The 198-acre campus is in a suburban area 10 miles north of Juneau. Including any residence halls, there are 18 buildings.

Student Life: 75% of undergraduates are from Alaska. Students are from 37 states, 12 foreign countries, and Canada. 95% are from public schools. 70% are white; 17% Native American/Eskimo. The average age of freshmen is 18; all undergraduates, 24.

Housing: 250 students can be accommodated in college housing, which includes single-sex dorms, on-campus apartments, and married-student housing. On-campus housing is available on a first-come, first-served basis. Priority is given to out-of-town students. 90% of students commute. All students may keep cars.

Activities: There are no fraternities or sororities. There are 16 groups on campus, including choir, ethnic, gay, honors, literary magazine, newspaper, political, professional, religious, and student government.

Popular campus events include Ski Day, whale-watching, and Eagle Preserve field trips.

Sports: There are 3 intramural sports for men and 3 for women. Facilities include a community gym and pool, an activity center, and access to health club facilities.

Disabled Students: 95% of the campus is accessible. Wheelchair ramps, elevators, special parking, specially equipped rest rooms, lowered drinking fountains, and lowered telephones are available.

Services: Counseling and information services are available, as is tutoring in most subjects. There is a reader service for the blind and remedial math, reading, and writing.

Campus Safety and Security: Measures include shuttle buses, informal discussions, pamphlets/posters/films, and emergency telephones. There are lighted pathways/sidewalks and late-night security at student housing.

Programs of Study: UAS confers B.A., B.S., B.B.A., B.Ed., and B.L.A. degrees. Associate and master's degrees are also awarded. Bachelor's degrees are awarded in BIOLOGICAL SCIENCE (biology/biological science and marine biology), BUSINESS (accounting and business administration and management), COMMUNICATIONS AND THE ARTS (art, communications, literature, and speech/debate/rhetoric), COMPUTER AND PHYSICAL SCIENCE (mathematics), EDUCATION (elementary), ENGINEERING AND ENVIRONMENTAL DESIGN (environmental science), SOCIAL SCIENCE (liberal arts/general studies, political science/government, public administration, and social science). Accounting, marine biology, and environmental science are the strongest academically. Liberal arts is the largest.

Required: All students are required to complete general education courses, including 15 credits in humanities and social science, 10 in math and natural sciences, 6 in written communication skills, and 3 in speech. A total of 120 semester credits, with at least 36 in the major, and a minimum GPA of 2.0 are required in order to graduate. In the liberal arts program, a portfolio is required.

Special: UAS offers cross-registration through the National Student Exchange and internships with federal and state agencies. Study abroad, work-study, dual and student-designed majors, credit/no credit options, and credit for military experience are also available. The School of Career and Continuing Education offers courses and certificate programs in technological skills.

Faculty/Classroom: 98% teach undergraduates. No introductory courses are taught by graduate students. The average class size in an introductory lecture is 20 and in a laboratory, 12.

Requirements: The SAT I or ACT is recommended. In addition, applicants should be graduates of an accredited secondary school or have the GED. A GPA of 2.0 is required. AP and CLEP credits are accepted.

Procedure: Freshmen are admitted fall and spring. There are early admissions, deferred admissions, and rolling admissions plans. Application deadlines are open. The fall 2003 application fee was $35.

Transfer: A minimum GPA of 2.0 from an accredited institution is required. 30 of 120 credits required for the bachelor's degree must be completed at UAS.

Visiting: There are regularly scheduled orientations for prospective students. There are guides for informal visits and visitors may sit in on classes. To schedule a visit, contact Greg Wagner.

Financial Aid: UAS is a member of CSS. The FAFSA and the college's own financial statement are required. Check with the school for current deadlines.

International Students: They must score 550 on the written TOEFL and also take the SAT I or the ACT.

Computers: The mainframe is a DEC VAX 8600. There are 2 computer labs with 15 terminals each. There are also 68 IBM and Mac PCs. All students may access the system. There are no time limits and no fees.

Admissions Contact: Greg Wagner, Director of Admissions. E-mail: *jyuas@alaska.edu* Web: *http://www.jun.alaska.edu*

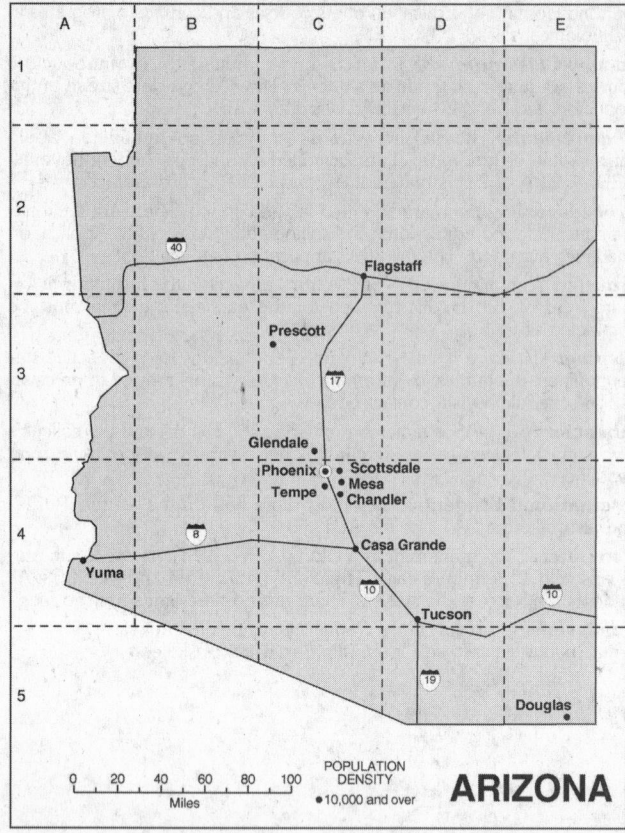

ARIZONA

POPULATION
DENSITY
● 10,000 and over

0 20 40 60 80 100
Miles

AMERICAN INDIAN COLLEGE OF THE ASSEMBLIES OF GOD
C-4

Phoenix, AZ 85021

(602) 944-3335 x 235
(800) 933-3828; Fax: (602) 943-8299

Full-time: 33 men, 29 women	**Faculty:** 5
Part-time: 5 men, 7 women	**Ph.D.s:** 10%
Graduate: none	**Student/Faculty:** 12 to 1
Year: semesters	**Tuition:** $5425
Application Deadline: open	**Room & Board:** $3850
Freshman Class: 31 applied, 22 accepted, 15 enrolled	
SAT I Verbal/Math: 380/430	**ACT:** 14 **LESS COMPETITIVE**

American Indian College of the Assemblies of God, founded in 1957, is a Christian college with a specific mission of preparing American Indians for leadership in churches, education, and the community. The library contains 20,000 volumes and 35 audio/video tapes/CDs, and subscribes to 102 periodicals. Computerized library services include the card catalog and Internet access. Special learning facilities include a learning resource center and a student-led chapel. The 10-acre campus is in an urban area in north Phoenix, just east of I17 and the Metrocenter area. Including any residence halls, there are 9 buildings.

Student Life: 72% of undergraduates are from Arizona. Others are from 10 states and 1 foreign country. 85% are from public schools. 67% are Native American/Eskimo; 18% white. Most are Protestant. The average age of freshmen is 23; all undergraduates, 26.

Housing: 80 students can be accommodated in college housing, which includes single-sex dorms and off-campus apartments. 52% of students live on campus; of those, all remain on campus on weekends. Alcohol is not permitted. All students may keep cars.

Activities: There are no fraternities or sororities. There are some groups and organizations on campus, including band, cheerleading, drama, ethnic, religious, student government, and yearbook. Popular campus events include missions conventions and College Days.

Sports: There is no sports program at AIC. Facilities include a full-size gym with a locker room and a weight room.

Disabled Students: All of the campus is accessible. Wheelchair ramps, special parking, specially equipped rest rooms, and lowered drinking fountains are available.

Services: Counseling and information services are available, as is tutoring in most subjects. There is remedial math, reading, and writing.

Campus Safety and Security: Measures include informal discussions, pamphlets/posters/films, lighted pathways/sidewalks, and night security.

Programs of Study: AIC confers the B.A. degree. Associate degrees are also awarded. Bachelor's degrees are awarded in EDUCATION (elementary), SOCIAL SCIENCE (ministries).

Required: To graduate, all students must maintain a GPA of 2.0 and complete 128 total credits. Students must complete courses in history, science, math, computer, and bible studies. A comprehensive bible exam is required.

Special: Internships and dual majors are available.

Faculty/Classroom: 65% of faculty are male; 35%, female. All teach undergraduates and 1% both teach and do research. The average class size in an introductory lecture is 11; in a laboratory, 6; and in a regular course, 6.

Admissions: 71% of the 2003-2004 applicants were accepted. The ACT scores for the 2003-2004 freshman class were: 100% below 21.

Requirements: The SAT I or ACT is required. In addition, transcripts from high school and any other secondary schools attended are required along with a pastor's reference form. Applicants are required to take placement tests with satisfactory results. A 2.0 GPA is required and the GED is accepted. A GPA of 2.0 is required. AP and CLEP credits are accepted. Important factors in the admissions decision are advanced placement or honor courses, evidence of special talent, and extracurricular activities record.

Procedure: Freshmen are admitted to all sessions. Entrance exams should be taken prior to acceptance. There are early decision, early admissions, and deferred admissions plans. Application deadlines are open. 1 early decision candidate was accepted for the 2003-2004 class.

Transfer: 31 transfer students enrolled in 2003-2004. Official transcripts from high school and each college attended, plus a pastor's reference form are required. Students must demonstrate proficiency in English, writing, math, and reading. 30 of 128 credits required for the bachelor's degree must be completed at AIC.

Visiting: There are regularly scheduled orientations for prospective students, consisting of College Days in the fall and spring semesters that include class visits, overnight stays in dorms, and meals in the cafeteria for 2 days. There are guides for informal visits and visitors may sit in on classes and stay overnight. To schedule a visit, contact Admissions at aicadm@aicag.edu.

Financial Aid: In 2003-2004, 88% of all full-time freshmen and 96% of continuing full-time students received some form of financial aid. 88% of full-time freshmen and 90% of continuing full-time students received need-based aid. The average freshman award was $4924. 34% of undergraduates work part time. Average annual earnings from campus work are $1489. The average financial indebtedness of the 2003 graduate was $6772. The FAFSA is required. The deadline for filing freshman financial aid applications for fall entry is August.

International Students: There is 1 international student enrolled. They must score 500 on the written TOEFL and also take the SAT I or the ACT.

Computers: A computer lab with 39 computers is open every day. Students sign in on the network with passwords. All computers have access to the Internet and the Web. All students may access the system. There are no time limits and no fees. It is strongly recommended that all students have a personal computer.

Graduates: In a recent year, 11 bachelor's degrees were awarded. The most popular majors were elementary education (57%) and Christian ministry (43%). In an average class, 35% graduate in 6 years or less.

Admissions Contact: Steve Clindaniel, Admissions Director.
E-mail: aicadm@aicag.edu Web: www.aicag.edu

ARIZONA BOARD OF REGENTS

The Arizona Board of Regents, established in 1945, is a private system in Arizona. It is governed by a Board of Regents, whose chief administrator is executive director and chief executive officer. The primary goal of the system is teaching, research, and service. The main priorities are to provide strong undergraduate instruction programs; to conduct extensive research and graduate instruction programs; and to ensure access for qualified Arizona residents, especially underrepresented ethnic minorities. The total enrollment of all 3 campuses is usually about 104,000; there were 3500 faculty members. Altogether there are some 325 baccalaureate, 250 master's, and 140 doctoral programs offered in Arizona Board of Regents. Profiles of the 4-year campuses are included in this section.

ARIZONA STATE UNIVERSITY-MAIN

Tempe, AZ 85287-0112

C-4

(480) 965-7788

Full-time: 14,876 men, 16,059 women	**Faculty:** 1722; I, -$
Part-time: 3788 men, 3904 women	**Ph.D.s:** 84%
Graduate: 4877 men, 5397 women	**Student/Faculty:** 18 to 1
Year: semesters, summer session	**Tuition:** $3595 ($12,115)
Application Deadline: open	**Room & Board:** $6453
Freshman Class: 19,785 applied, 17,490 accepted, 7126 enrolled	
SAT I Verbal/Math: 542/553	**ACT:** 23 **COMPETITIVE**

Arizona State University-Main, founded in 1885, is a publicly funded institution offering undergraduate programs in the arts and sciences, business, education, engineering, nursing, public programs, architecture and environmental design, social work, and fine arts. There are 9 undergraduate and 10 graduate schools. In addition to regional accreditation, ASU-Main has baccalaureate program accreditation with AACSB, ABET, ACCE, ACEJMC, ADA, CSAB, CSWE, FIDER, NAAB, NASM, NLN, and NRPA. The 5 libraries contain 3,360,166 volumes, 5,882,115 microform items, and 1,192,455 audio/video tapes/CDs, and subscribe to 32,805 periodicals. Computerized library services include the card catalog, interlibrary loans, database searching, and Internet access. Special learning facilities include an art gallery, planetarium, radio station, and TV station. The 814-acre campus is in an urban area 10 miles east of Phoenix. Including any residence halls, there are 72 buildings.

Student Life: 74% of undergraduates are from Arizona. Students are from 50 states, 108 foreign countries, and Canada. 70% are white; 12% Hispanic. The average age of freshmen is 18; all undergraduates, 22. 23% do not continue beyond their first year; 52% remain to graduate.

Housing: 6000 students can be accommodated in college housing, which includes coed dorms, on-campus apartments, and fraternity houses. In addition, there are honors houses, special-interest houses, and a residence for freshman. On-campus housing is available on a first-come, first-served basis. 85% of students commute. All students may keep cars.

Activities: 6% of men belong to 24 national fraternities; 7% of women belong to 19 national sororities. There are 498 groups on campus, including academic, adult reentry, art, band, cheerleading, chess, choir, chorus, computers, dance, drama, ethnic, film, gay, honors, international, jazz band, literary magazine, marching band, musical theater, newspaper, opera, orchestra, photography, political, professional, radio and TV, religious, social, social service, student government, student leadership, and symphony. Popular campus events include World Fest international food and cultural festival and Fiesta Bowl.

Sports: There are 10 intercollegiate sports for men and 11 for women, and 35 intramural sports for men and 35 for women. Facilities include 4 stadiums (including football and baseball), a tennis center, an aquatic complex, a golf course, 2 activity centers, a student recreation complex, and a track.

Disabled Students: 98% of the campus is accessible. Wheelchair ramps, elevators, special parking, specially equipped rest rooms, special class scheduling, lowered drinking fountains, lowered telephones, and flashing alarms for the deaf, braille maps, modified residence hall rooms, and an adaptive exercise program and facility are available.

Services: Counseling and information services are available, as is tutoring in most subjects, including 125 different courses. There is a reader service for the blind, and remedial math, reading, and writing. There is also on-line tutoring and graduate test preparation.

Campus Safety and Security: Measures include 24-hour foot and vehicle patrol, self-defense education, security escort services, and shuttle buses. There are informal discussions, pamphlets/posters/films, emergency telephones, and lighted pathways/sidewalks.

Programs of Study: ASU-Main confers B.A., B.S., B.A.E., B.F.A., B.I.S., B.Mus., B.S.D., B.S.E., B.S.L.A., B.S.N., B.S.P., and B.S.W. degrees. Master's and doctoral degrees are also awarded. Bachelor's degrees are awarded in AGRICULTURE (plant science), BIOLOGICAL SCIENCE (biochemistry, biology/biological science, environmental biology, microbiology, and molecular biology), BUSINESS (accounting, banking and finance, management science, marketing/retailing/merchandising, purchasing/inventory management, real estate, and recreation and leisure services), COMMUNICATIONS AND THE ARTS (art, art history and appreciation, broadcasting, ceramic art and design, Chinese, communications, dance, dramatic arts, drawing, English, French, German, graphic design, industrial design, Italian, Japanese, journalism, media arts, metal/jewelry, music, music performance, music theory and composition, painting, photography, printmaking, Russian, sculpture, and Spanish), COMPUTER AND PHYSICAL SCIENCE (chemistry, computer science, geology, information sciences and systems, mathematics, and physics), EDUCATION (early childhood, elementary, music, secondary, and special), ENGINEERING AND ENVIRONMENTAL DESIGN (aeronautical engineering, architecture, bioengineering, chemical engineering, civil engineering, computer engineering, construction engineering, electrical/electronics engineering, engineering, industrial engineering, interior design, landscape architecture/design, materials science, mechanical engineering, urban design, and urban planning technology), HEALTH PROFESSIONS (clinical science, music therapy, nursing, and

speech pathology/audiology), SOCIAL SCIENCE (African American studies, American Indian studies, anthropology, criminal justice, economics, family/consumer resource management, geography, Hispanic American studies, history, humanities, interdisciplinary studies, philosophy, physical fitness/movement, political science/government, psychology, religion, social work, sociology, and women's studies). Engineering, architecture, and computer science are the strongest academically. Business, psychology, and communication are the largest.

Required: To graduate, students must have a minimum GPA of 2.0 and a total of at least 120 credit hours, including 50 hours of upper-level work. The number of hours in the major varies by degree program. All students must take English composition and fulfill the general studies requirement of 35 hours in the areas of numeracy, literacy and critical inquiry, humanities and fine arts, social and behavioral sciences, natural sciences, global awareness, and historical awareness.

Special: ASU offers internships in many disciplines, study abroad in 41 countries, and a variety of interdisciplinary undergraduate programs. Students may participate in educational programs supported by several institutes and centers, such as the National Center for Electron Microscopy, the American Indian Institute, and the Center for Medieval and Renaissance Studies. Also available are continuing education programs and a summer math and science program for high school students. There are 28 national honor societies, including Phi Beta Kappa, and a freshman honors program. Most departments have honors programs.

Faculty/Classroom: 61% of faculty are male; 39%, female. The average class size in an introductory lecture is 40 and in a laboratory, 22.

Admissions: 88% of the 2003-2004 applicants were accepted. The SAT I scores for the 2003-2004 freshman class were: Verbal--30% below 500, 44% between 500 and 599, 21% between 600 and 700, and 5% above 700; Math--27% below 500, 41% between 500 and 599, 26% between 600 and 700, and 6% above 700. The ACT scores were 27% below 21, 27% between 21 and 23, 24% between 24 and 26, 11% between 27 and 28, and 11% above 28. 44% of the current freshmen were in the top fifth of their class; 72% were in the top two fifths. There were 173 National Merit finalists.

Requirements: The SAT I or ACT is required. The minimum composite score on the ACT is 22 for in-state students, 24 for out-of-state students; on the SAT I, 1040 for in-state students, 1110 for out-of-state students. Graduation from an accredited secondary school must include 4 years each of English and math, 3 years of lab science, 2 years each of social science (including American history) and the same foreign language, and 1 year of fine arts. The GED, minimum score 50, is also accepted. ASU-Main requires applicants to be in the upper 25% of their class. A GPA of 3.0 is required. AP and CLEP credits are accepted.

Procedure: Freshmen are admitted to all sessions. Entrance exams should be taken late in the junior year. There is an early admissions plan. There is a rolling admissions plan. Application deadlines are open. There is an admissions fee of $50 for nonresidents only. Applications are accepted on-line.

Transfer: 3978 transfer students enrolled in 2002-2003. Applicants with fewer than 36 transferable hours must meet the requirements for freshman admission. A minimum GPA of 2.0 is required for in-state applicants; 2.5 for out-of-state applicants. 30 of 120 credits required for the bachelor's degree must be completed at ASU-Main.

Visiting: There are regularly scheduled orientations for prospective students. There are guides for informal visits and visitors may sit in on classes. To schedule a visit, contact Undergraduate Admissions at (480) 727-7013 or asuvisit@asu.edu.

Financial Aid: In 2003-2004, 68% of all full-time freshmen and 66% of continuing full-time students received some form of financial aid. 36% of full-time freshmen and 39% of continuing full-time students received need-based aid. The average freshman award was $6264. Need-based scholarships or need-based grants averaged $4570; need-based self-help aid (loans and jobs) averaged $2457; and non-need-based athletic scholarships averaged $8936. The average financial indebtedness of the 2003 graduate was $17,780. ASU-Main is a member of CSS. The CSS Profile, FAFSA, FFS, or SFS is required. The deadline for filing freshman financial aid applications for fall entry is March 1.

International Students: There are 1038 international students enrolled. They must score 500 on the written TOEFL or 173 on the electronic version.

Computers: There are IBM RS/6000/390s and 590s and an SGI Power Challenge as computer servers, HP 9000/735s as statistical servers, IBM RS/6000 and HP 9000/735 as file servers, Sun SPARC20s, Sun SPARC10s, HP 9000/712s, and IBM RS/6000/250s as translators, HP T500 and HP K200 for development as transaction servers, and Sun SPARC20s and Sun SPARC 10s as miscellaneous servers. Also available are 770 Rycom, MAG, HAL, Zenith, and Mac PCs in 7 areas on campus, 1 site is open 24 hours per day. All students may access the system. There are no time limits and no fees.

Graduates: From July 1, 2002 to June 30, 2003, 6765 bachelor's degrees were awarded. The most popular majors were interdisciplinary studies (9%), communication (6%), and psychology (5%). In an average class, 1% graduate in 3 years or less, 26% graduate in 4 years or less,

47% graduate in 5 years or less, and 52% graduate in 6 years or less. 515 companies recruited on campus in 2002-2003.

Admissions Contact: Tim Desch, Director Undergraduate Admissions. E-mail: *ugrading@asu.edu* Web: *www.asu.edu*

DEVRY UNIVERSITY/PHOENIX
Phoenix, AZ 85021-2995
C-4

(602) 870-9201
(800) 528-0250; Fax: (602) 331-1494

Full-time: 1177 men, 333 women	**Faculty:** n/av
Part-time: 368 men, 132 women	**Ph.D.s:** n/av
Graduate: n/av	**Student/Faculty:** n/av
Year: semesters, summer session	**Tuition:** $10,670
Application Deadline: open	**Room & Board:** n/app
Freshman Class: n/av	
SAT I or ACT: n/av	**LESS COMPETITIVE**

DeVry University/Phoenix is a private institution opened in 1967; there are 66 other DeVry University locations in the United States and Canada. The school offers a hands-on technology-based curriculum in business administration, computer information systems, electronics, technical management, information technology, computer engineering technology, and telecommunications. In addition to regional accreditation, DeVry has baccalaureate program accreditation with ABET. The library contains 22,500 volumes and subscribes to 7230 periodicals. Computerized library services include database searching. Special learning facilities include a learning resource center and electronics and other labs. The 18-acre campus is in a suburban area in Phoenix. There is one building.

Student Life: 63% of students are white; 17% Hispanic. The average age of all undergraduates is 25.

Housing: There are no residence halls. Housing referrals may be obtained through the Student Housing Office. There are private apartments, student-plan housing, and private rooms. All students commute. Alcohol is not permitted. All students may keep cars.

Activities: There are no fraternities or sororities. There are 13 groups on campus, including ethnic, honors, professional, radio and TV, religious, social, and yearbook. Popular campus events include Thanksgiving Dinner, Ethnic Day, and Cinco de Mayo.

Sports: There is 1 intramural sport for men and 1 for women. Facilities include a game room. Students can obtain free passes for a fitness center.

Disabled Students: All of the campus is accessible. Wheelchair ramps, elevators, special parking, specially equipped rest rooms, special class scheduling, lowered drinking fountains, and lowered telephones are available.

Services: Counseling and information services are available, as is tutoring in every subject.

Campus Safety and Security: Measures include security escort services, informal discussions, pamphlets/posters/films, and emergency telephones. There are lighted pathways/sidewalks and a security guard service Monday through Friday 8 A.M. to 11 P.M. and from 12 noon to 6 P.M. on Sunday. The building is guarded during hours of closure by a motion-detector system.

Programs of Study: DeVry confers the B.S. degree. Associate and master's degrees are also awarded. Bachelor's degrees are awarded in BIOLOGICAL SCIENCE (bioinformatics), BUSINESS (business administration and management), COMMUNICATIONS AND THE ARTS (telecommunications), COMPUTER AND PHYSICAL SCIENCE (information sciences and systems), ENGINEERING AND ENVIRONMENTAL DESIGN (biomedical engineering, computer engineering, electrical/electronics engineering technology, and technological management). Computer information systems and electronics engineering technology are the largest.

Required: To graduate, students must achieve a GPA of at least 2.0 and satisfactorily complete all curriculum requirements. Course requirements vary according to program. All first-semester students take courses in business organization, computer applications, algebra, psychology, and student success strategies.

Special: Accelerated degrees, co-op programs, nondegree study, distance learning, and evening and weekend classes are possible. There is 1 national honor society.

Faculty/Classroom: All teach undergraduates.

Requirements: Admissions requirements include graduation from a secondary school; the GED is also accepted. Applicants must pass the DeVry entrance exam or present satisfactory ACT or SAT I scores. An interview is required. CLEP credit is accepted.

Procedure: Freshmen are admitted fall, spring, and summer. There is a rolling admissions plan. There are early admissions and deferred admissions plans. Application deadlines are open. Application fee is $50. Applications are accepted on-line through *https://apply.embark.com/UGrad/DeVry/21.*

Transfer: 256 transfer students enrolled in a recent year. Applicants must present passing grades in all completed college course work, demonstrate language skills proficiency with at least 24 completed semester

hours, and present evidence of math proficiency by appropriate college-level credits. 25% of 48 to 154 credits required for the bachelor's degree must be completed at DeVry.

Visiting: There are regularly scheduled orientations for prospective students. There are guides for informal visits and visitors may sit in on classes. To schedule a visit, contact the Director of Admissions.

Financial Aid: In 2002-2003, 49% of all full-time freshmen and 75% of continuing full-time students received some form of financial aid. At least 48% of full-time freshmen and at least 73% of continuing full-time students received need-based aid. The average freshman award was $6765. Need-based scholarships or need-based grants averaged $3997; need-based self-help aid (loans and jobs) averaged $4108; and institutional non-need-based awards and non-need-based scholarships averaged $9288. The FAFSA is required. The deadline for freshman financial aid applications is rolling.

International Students: There were 26 international students enrolled in a recent year They must score 550 on the written TOEFL or 173 on the electronic version and also take DeVry's computerized placement test, achieving a minimum score that varies by program.

Computers: The mainframe is an IBM 3081K. Lab facilities include IBM PCs in stand-alone and network configurations with access to the mainframe. LANs provide access to a wide range of applications software. Hard copy from the mainframe is provided through a local minicomputer and medium- and high-speed printers. Students in the computer information systems program may access the system during published lab hours. There are no time limits and no fees. Students in the information technology program have DeVry-issued laptop computers.

Graduates: From July 1, 2002 to June 30, 2003, 892 bachelor's degrees were awarded. The most popular majors among recent graduates were computer information systems (49%), business (28%), and electronics engineering technology (23%). 210 companies recruited on campus in a recent year.

Admissions Contact: Director of Admissions. E-mail: *admissions@phx.devry.edu* Web: *www.devry-phx.edu*

EMBRY-RIDDLE AERONAUTICAL UNIVERSITY
Prescott, AZ 86301-3720
C-3

(928) 777-6692
(800) 442-ERAU; Fax: 9928) 777-6606

Full-time: 1181 men, 244 women	**Faculty:** 87; IIB, av$
Part-time: 184 men, 22 women	**Ph.D.s:** 74%
Graduate: 29 men, 9 women	**Student/Faculty:** 16 to 1
Year: semesters, summer session	**Tuition:** $21,340
Application Deadline: open	**Room & Board:** $6370
Freshman Class: 1250 applied, 1001 accepted, 304 enrolled	
SAT I Verbal/Math: 540/580	**ACT:** 24 **COMPETITIVE+**

Embry-Riddle Aeronautical University, founded in 1926, is a private institution offering undergraduate programs in aviation, engineering, business, and professional training on 2 campuses: the Prescott campus, founded in 1978, and the Daytona Beach, Florida, campus. Graduate programs are also offered at both campuses. There are 3 undergraduate schools and 1 graduate school. In addition to regional accreditation, ERAU has baccalaureate program accreditation with ABET and CAA. The library contains 26,264 volumes, 192,027 microform items, and 2518 audio/video tapes/CDs, and subscribes to 629 periodicals. Computerized library services include the card catalog, interlibrary loans, database searching, and Internet access. Special learning facilities include a learning resource center, radio station, 4 wind tunnels, an aviation safety center, and an aircraft structures lab. The Flight Training Center at Ernest A. Love Field offers a simulator lab and flight operations center. The 547-acre campus is in a rural area 100 miles north of Phoenix. Including any residence halls, there are 91 buildings.

Student Life: 22% of undergraduates are from Arizona. Others are from 48 states, 20 foreign countries, and Canada. 74% are white. The average age of freshmen is 18; all undergraduates, 21. 25% do not continue beyond their first year; 51% remain to graduate.

Housing: 849 students can be accommodated in college housing, which includes coed dorms and on-campus apartments. On-campus housing is guaranteed for the freshman year only and is available on a first-come, first-served basis. 53% of students commute. Alcohol is not permitted. All students may keep cars.

Activities: 8% of men belong to 4 national fraternities; 7% of women belong to 1 national sorority. There are 58 groups on campus, including ethnic, gay, honors, international, jazz band, literary magazine, newspaper, political, professional, radio and TV, religious, social, social service, and student government. Popular campus events include Octoberwest, Spring Fling, and Hawaii Luau Club.

Sports: There are 2 intercollegiate sports for men and 1 for women, and 19 intramural sports for men and 19 for women. Facilities include an activity center with 3 basketball courts and 3 volleyball courts, a gym/weight room, a multipurpose athletic playing field, a game room, a swimming pool complex, and a fitness facility.

Disabled Students: 20% of the campus is accessible. Wheelchair ramps, special parking, specially equipped rest rooms, special class scheduling, lowered drinking fountains, lowered telephones, special housing, and pneumatic doors are available.

Services: Counseling and information services are available, as is tutoring in most subjects. There is remedial math, reading, and writing.

Campus Safety and Security: Measures include 24-hour foot and vehicle patrol, self-defense education, security escort services, and shuttle buses. There are informal discussions, pamphlets/posters/films, emergency telephones, and lighted pathways/sidewalks.

Programs of Study: ERAU confers the B.S. degree. Master's degrees are also awarded. Bachelor's degrees are awarded in COMMUNICATIONS AND THE ARTS (communications), COMPUTER AND PHYSICAL SCIENCE (atmospheric sciences and meteorology, computer science, and software engineering), ENGINEERING AND ENVIRONMENTAL DESIGN (aeronautical engineering, aeronautical science, aerospace studies, aviation administration/management, aviation maintenance management, civil engineering, computer engineering, electrical/electronics engineering, and engineering physics), SOCIAL SCIENCE (safety science). Aeronautics is the strongest academically. Aeronautical Science is the largest.

Required: All students must complete 36 credits of general education requirements, including courses in communication skills, technical report writing, humanities/social sciences, math, physical science, economics, and computer science. A total of 120 to 136 credit hours with a minimum GPA of 2.0 is required to graduate.

Special: Cooperative and work-study programs, nondegree study, internships in all majors, and study abroad in 19 countries are offered. Flight training may be taken in conjunction with aeronautical science and other degree programs. Credit is given for life and military experience. There are 4 national honor societies.

Faculty/Classroom: 77% of faculty are male; 23%, female. All teach undergraduates. No introductory courses are taught by graduate students. The average class size in an introductory lecture is 22; in a laboratory, 13; and in a regular course, 21.

Admissions: 80% of the 2003-2004 applicants were accepted. The SAT I scores for the 2003-2004 freshman class were: Verbal--29% below 500, 38% between 500 and 599, 28% between 600 and 700, and 4% above 700; Math--20% below 500, 36% between 500 and 599, 37% between 600 and 700, and 7% above 700. The ACT scores were 20% below 21, 23% between 21 and 23, 26% between 24 and 26, 13% between 27 and 28, and 18% above 28. 41% of the current freshmen were in the top fifth of their class; 74% were in the top two fifths. 9 freshmen graduated first in their class.

Requirements: The SAT I or ACT is required. In addition, applicants must be graduates of an accredited secondary school or have a GED equivalent. All admissions items are processed at Daytona Beach headquarters. AP and CLEP credits are accepted. Important factors in the admissions decision are advanced placement or honor courses, recommendations by school officials, and evidence of special talent.

Procedure: Freshmen are admitted to all sessions. Entrance exams should be taken during the fall of the senior year. There is a deferred admissions plan. Application deadlines are open, but early decision applications are due December 1. Notification is on a rolling basis. 44 early decision candidates were accepted for the 2003-2004 class. Applications are accepted on-line through the ERAU web site.

Transfer: 96 transfer students enrolled in 2003-2004. Applicants must have a minimum GPA of 2.0 in at least 12 credit hours earned. 30 of 120 to 136 credits required for the bachelor's degree must be completed at ERAU.

Visiting: There are regularly scheduled orientations for prospective students. There are guides for informal visits. To schedule a visit, contact Bill Thompson at (928) 777-6600 or *pradmit@erau.edu*.

Financial Aid: In 2003-2004, 80% of all full-time freshmen and 64% of continuing full-time students received some form of financial aid. 78% of full-time freshmen and 51% of continuing full-time students received need-based aid. The average freshman award was $13,483. Need-based scholarships or need-based grants averaged $4363 ($10,000 maximum); need-based self-help aid (loans and jobs) averaged $4856 ($6000 maximum); and other non-need-based awards and non-need-based scholarships averaged $5410 ($10,000 maximum). 40% of undergraduates work part time. Average annual earnings from campus work are $1859. The average financial indebtedness of the 2003 graduate was $33,433. ERAU is a member of CSS. The FAFSA is required. The deadline for filing freshman financial aid applications for fall entry is April 15.

International Students: There are 33 international students enrolled. The school actively recruits these students. They must score 500 on the written TOEFL and also take the SAT I or the ACT.

Computers: The mainframes are a Linux, Solaris, Windows 2000, and Novell NetWare Servers. The single-user log-in allows access to network printers, storage space, academic servers, course management and community portal services (Blackboard), DS3 Internet, e-mail via web client, and personal web space. All students may access the system. There are no time limits and no fees. It is highly recommended that students in computer science have personal computers.

Graduates: From July 1, 2002 to June 30, 2003, 316 bachelor's degrees were awarded. The most popular majors were aeronautical science (45%), aerospace engineering (19%), and aerospace studies (2%). In an average class, 31% graduate in 4 years or less, 47% graduate in 5 years or less, and 51% graduate in 6 years or less. 21 companies recruited on campus in 2002-2003. Of the 2002 graduating class, 5% were enrolled in graduate school within 6 months of graduation and 98% were employed.

Admissions Contact: Bill Thompson, Director of Admissions.
E-mail: *admit@pr.erau.edu* Web: *www.embryriddle.edu*

GRAND CANYON UNIVERSITY
Phoenix, AZ 85061-1097
C-4
(602) 589-2855
(800) 800-9776, ext. 2855; Fax: (602) 589-2580

Full-time: 450 men, 880 women	**Faculty:** 96; IIB, --$
Part-time: 125 men, 155 women	**Ph.D.s:** 80%
Graduate: 570 men, 1935 women	**Student/Faculty:** 14 to 1
Year: semesters, summer session	**Tuition:** $21,000
Application Deadline: open	**Room & Board:** $9000
Freshman Class: n/av	
SAT I or ACT: required	**LESS COMPETITIVE**

Grand Canyon University, founded in 1949, is a small, private, nonsectarian liberal arts institution. There are 5 undergraduate and 2 graduate schools. Figures in the above capsule and in this profile are approximate. In addition to regional accreditation, Canyon has baccalaureate program accreditation with NLN. The library contains 166,000 volumes, 97,324 microform items, and 4100 audio/video tapes/CDs, and subscribes to 700 periodicals. Computerized library services include the card catalog, interlibrary loans, and database searching. Special learning facilities include an art gallery. The 90-acre campus is in a suburban area in Phoenix. Including any residence halls, there are 32 buildings.

Student Life: 81% of undergraduates are from Arizona. Students are from 43 states, 6 foreign countries, and Canada. 77% are white; 10% Hispanic. 87% are Protestant; 9% Catholic. The average age of freshmen is 19; all undergraduates, 25.

Housing: 600 students can be accommodated in college housing, which includes single-sex dorms and on-campus apartments. On-campus housing is available on a first-come, first-served basis. 52% of students live on campus. Alcohol is not permitted. All students may keep cars.

Activities: There are no fraternities or sororities. There are many groups and organizations on campus, including art, band, cheerleading, choir, chorale, chorus, computers, drama, ethnic, honors, international, jazz band, literary magazine, musical theater, newspaper, opera, orchestra, pep band, photography, political, professional, religious, social service, student government, and yearbook. Popular campus events include Spiritual Emphasis Week, Harvest Festival, and Spring Formal.

Sports: There are 5 intercollegiate sports for men and 4 for women. Facilities include a baseball field, a 500-seat gym, a 1750-seat gym, a 3000-seat stadium, 6 tennis courts, a weight room, and a swimming pool.

Disabled Students: All of the campus is accessible. Wheelchair ramps, elevators, special parking, and specially equipped rest rooms are available.

Services: Counseling and information services are available, as is tutoring in most subjects. There is a reader service for the blind and remedial reading and writing. Tutors are also trained in test-taking techniques, study skills, and time management.

Campus Safety and Security: Measures include 24-hour foot and vehicle patrol, self-defense education, security escort services, and informal discussions. There are emergency telephones, lighted pathways/sidewalks, and a university safety committee that provides controlled after-hours access to residence halls.

Programs of Study: Canyon confers B.A., B.S., B.B.A., B.L.S., B.M., and B.S.N. degrees. Master's degrees are also awarded. Bachelor's degrees are awarded in BIOLOGICAL SCIENCE (biology/biological science and environmental biology), BUSINESS (accounting, banking and finance, business administration and management, human resources, international business management, marketing/retailing/merchandising, and personnel management), COMMUNICATIONS AND THE ARTS (applied music, communications, dramatic arts, English, fine arts, graphic design, music, piano/organ, Spanish, speech/debate/rhetoric, studio art, and voice), COMPUTER AND PHYSICAL SCIENCE (chemistry, computer science, and mathematics), EDUCATION (art, business, elementary, music, physical, science, secondary, and special), HEALTH PROFESSIONS (nursing), SOCIAL SCIENCE (Christian studies, criminal justice, economics, history, physical fitness/movement, psychology, religious music, social science, social studies, and sociology). Natural sciences, elementary education, and nursing are the strongest academically and have the largest enrollments.

Required: All students are required to complete 39 hours of general studies, including 3 hours each in Old Testament history and New Testament history, 6 each in English and humanities, 9 in social studies, 10 in science, and 2 in phys ed. Chapel attendance is required. A writing proficiency exam along with a total of 128 semester hours, with a minimum GPA of 2.0, are required to graduate.

Special: Co-op programs with several schools in the Christian College Coalition are available. Internships are offered for most majors through organizations, corporations, and agencies in the Phoenix area. Dual majors, study abroad in 5 countries, and a Washington semester are possible. A 3-2 engineering degree with Arizona State University is available. There is 1 national honor society, Phi Beta Kappa, a freshman honors program, and 1 departmental honors program.

Faculty/Classroom: 50% of faculty are male; 50%, female. All teach undergraduates. The average class size in an introductory lecture is 25; in a laboratory, 10; and in a regular course, 25.

Requirements: The SAT I or ACT is required. In addition, applicants should be graduates of an accredited high school or have a GED. A GPA of 2.14 is required. AP and CLEP credits are accepted. Important factors in the admissions decision are evidence of special talent, extracurricular activities record, and leadership record.

Procedure: Freshmen are admitted to all sessions. Entrance exams should be taken during the junior or senior year of high school. There is a rolling admissions plan. Application deadlines are open. The application fee is $50.

Transfer: 305 transfer students enrolled in a recent year. Transfer applicants must have a minimum GPA of 2.0 and a minimum of 24 transferable hours. 30 of 128 credits required for the bachelor's degree must be completed at Canyon.

Visiting: There are regularly scheduled orientations for prospective students, including High School Preview Days in February and Transfer Preview Days in March. There are guides for informal visits and visitors may sit in on classes and stay overnight. To schedule a visit, contact the Admission Office.

Financial Aid: In a recent year, 60% of all full-time freshmen and 66% of continuing full-time students received some form of financial aid. The average freshman award was $8405. The FAFSA is recommended. Check with the school for current deadlines.

International Students: The school actively recruits these students. They must score 500 on the written TOEFL, and the SAT I or ACT is required of students with English as their first language, with a 50 national percentile score or higher required.

Computers: The mainframe is a DEC Alpha 4100 server. The computer lab facilities also include a large network of Macs and PCs, and a Motorola 6000 system. All students may access the system usually from morning until midnight. There are no time limits. The fee is $85 per semester.

Graduates: In a recent year, 340 bachelor's degrees were awarded. The most popular majors were business (25%), health professions (18%), and education (12%). In an average class, 27% graduate in 4 years or less, 40% graduate in 5 years or less, and 47% graduate in 6 years or less.

Admissions Contact: April Chapman, Director of Admissions. A video is available. E-mail: *admiss@grand-canyon.edu* Web: *www.grand-canyon.edu*

NORTHERN ARIZONA UNIVERSITY
Flagstaff, AZ 86011

C-2

(928) 523-5511
(888) MORE-NAU; Fax: (928) 523-8483

Full-time: 4468 men, 6566 women	**Faculty:** 711; I, --$
Part-time: 802 men, 1179 women	**Ph.D.s:** 83%
Graduate: 1745 men, 4064 women	**Student/Faculty:** 16 to 1
Year: semesters, summer session	**Tuition:** $3628 ($12,028)
Application Deadline: March 1	**Room & Board:** $5374
Freshman Class: 2352 enrolled	
SAT I Verbal/Math: 524/520	**ACT:** 22 **COMPETITIVE**

Northern Arizona University, founded in 1899, is a public institution offering undergraduate and graduate degrees in a full range of disciplines from liberal arts and sciences to professional and career-related fields. There are 10 undergraduate and 8 graduate schools. In addition to regional accreditation, NAU has baccalaureate program accreditation with AACSB, ABET, ADA, AHEA, APTA, CAPTE, NASM, NCATE, NLN, NRPA, and SAF. The library contains 633,623 volumes, 547,849 microform items, and 32,774 audio/video tapes/CDs, and subscribes to 6816 periodicals. Computerized library services include the card catalog, interlibrary loans, database searching, and Internet access. Special learning facilities include a learning resource center, art gallery, radio station, TV station, an observatory, research centers, and the Institute for Human Development. The 738-acre campus is in a rural area 140 miles north of Phoenix. Including any residence halls, there are 94 buildings.

Student Life: 85% of undergraduates are from Arizona. Students are from 50 states, 67 foreign countries, and Canada. 76% are white; 11% Hispanic. The average age of freshmen is 19; all undergraduates, 23. 31% do not continue beyond their first year; 69% remain to graduate.

Housing: 6106 students can be accommodated in college housing, which includes single-sex and coed dorms, on-campus apartments, mar-

ried-student housing, fraternity houses, and sorority houses. In addition, there are honors houses. On-campus housing is guaranteed for the freshman year only and is available on a first-come, first-served basis. 52% of students commute. Alcohol is not permitted. All students may keep cars.

Activities: 3% of men belong to 13 national fraternities; 6% of women belong to 9 national sororities. There are 157 groups on campus, including art, band, cheerleading, chess, choir, chorale, chorus, computers, dance, debate, drama, drill team, ethnic, film, forensics, gay, honors, international, jazz band, marching band, musical theater, newspaper, opera, orchestra, pep band, photography, political, professional, radio and TV, religious, social, social service, student government, and symphony. Popular campus events include Martin Luther King, Jr. Day, Luminario Lighting, and Parents Weekend.

Sports: There are 5 intercollegiate sports for men and 8 for women, and 32 intramural sports for men and 32 for women. Facilities include the Skydome for football, basketball, and indoor track and field, 3 recreation centers with basketball and racquetball courts and weight rooms, a 50-meter indoor swimming pool with diving facilities, and numerous outdoor grass fields for soccer, rugby, and lacrosse.

Disabled Students: 90% of the campus is accessible. Wheelchair ramps, elevators, special parking, specially equipped rest rooms, special class scheduling, lowered drinking fountains, and lowered telephones are available.

Services: Counseling and information services are available, as is tutoring in most subjects. There is a reader service for the blind and remedial math, reading, and writing. Most counseling and tutoring is done by volunteers and student interns.

Campus Safety and Security: Measures include 24-hour foot and vehicle patrol, self-defense education, security escort services, and shuttle buses. There are informal discussions, pamphlets/posters/films, emergency telephones, and lighted pathways/sidewalks.

Programs of Study: NAU confers B.A., B.S., B.F.A., B.Mus., B.Mus.Ed., B.S.B.A., B.S.C.S.E., B.S.D.H., B.S.E., B.S.Ed., B.S.F., B.S.J., B.S.N., and B.S.W. degrees. Master's and doctoral degrees are also awarded. Bachelor's degrees are awarded in AGRICULTURE (forestry and related sciences), BIOLOGICAL SCIENCE (biology/biological science, botany, microbiology, and zoology), BUSINESS (accounting, banking and finance, business administration and management, business economics, hotel/motel and restaurant management, and marketing/retailing/merchandising), COMMUNICATIONS AND THE ARTS (advertising, art history and appreciation, arts administration/management, broadcasting, communications, design, dramatic arts, English, fine arts, French, German, journalism, music, Spanish, speech/debate/rhetoric, and telecommunications), COMPUTER AND PHYSICAL SCIENCE (chemistry, computer science, geology, information sciences and systems, mathematics, and physics), EDUCATION (art, business, early childhood, elementary, foreign languages, health, industrial arts, music, science, secondary, special, and teaching English as a second/foreign language (TESOL/TEFOL)), ENGINEERING AND ENVIRONMENTAL DESIGN (civil engineering, computer engineering, electrical/electronics engineering, engineering, environmental engineering, and mechanical engineering), HEALTH PROFESSIONS (nursing, predentistry, premedicine, and speech pathology/audiology), SOCIAL SCIENCE (anthropology, criminal justice, economics, geography, history, international relations, parks and recreation management, philosophy, political science/government, prelaw, psychology, public administration, religion, social work, and sociology). Health professions, engineering, and business are the strongest academically. Education, hotel/restaurant management, and psychology are the largest.

Required: To graduate, students must have at least 120 credit hours, including 45 to 60 in the major, with a minimum GPA of 2.0; some majors require a higher GPA. Students must complete a 44-hour liberal studies curriculum, consisting of discipline courses (9 hours each of creative arts and letters and behavioral science and 8 each of natural science and math), and foundation courses (6 hours of English and 3 hours of college algebra).

Special: NAU offers co-op programs in business and hotel/restaurant management, cross-registration with many universities through the National Student Exchange, and internships in most majors. Legislative internships are offered through the Arizona State Senate and House of Representatives. Students may study abroad in 19 countries. Work-study programs are available in numerous fields, including engineering, business, park services, and arts management. Accelerated degrees in more than 50 majors, a general studies degree, dual majors, nondegree study, and pass/fail options are possible. There are 7 national honor societies and a freshman honors program.

Faculty/Classroom: 50% of faculty are male; 50%, female. All both teach and do research. The average class size in a laboratory is 22 and in a regular course, 33.

Admissions: The SAT I scores for the 2003-2004 freshman class were: Verbal--33% below 500, 44% between 500 and 599, 20% between 600 and 700, and 3% above 700; Math--37% below 500, 41% between 500 and 599, 20% between 600 and 700, and 2% above 700. The ACT scores were 39% below 21, 29% between 21 and 23, 20% between 24 and 26, 8% between 27 and 28, and 4% above 28.

Requirements: The SAT I or ACT is required. In addition, students must have a minimum GPA of 2.5 or rank in the top 50% of their class, or have minimum composite SAT I scores of 1040 for in-state and 1110 for out-of-state applicants, or minimum ACT scores of 22 for in-state and 24 for out-of-state applicants. Students should be graduates of an accredited secondary school or hold the GED. Requirements include 16 academic credits, with a grade of C or better in each class of 4 years of English, 3 each of algebra and lab science, 2 of foreign language, and 1 each of geometry, social studies, fine art, and American history. AP and CLEP credits are accepted.

Procedure: Freshmen are admitted fall, spring, and summer. Entrance exams should be taken before the last semester of the senior year. There is a rolling admissions plan. Applications should be filed by March 1 for fall entry, October 1 for spring entry, and May 15 for summer entry. The fall 2003 application fee was $25. Notification is sent on a rolling basis.

Transfer: 1266 transfer students enrolled in 2002-2003. Transfer students must be eligible to reenter the institution last attended. Requirements vary with the number of college credits being transferred. Generally, in-state applicants must have a minimum GPA of 2.0 and submit high school and/or college transcripts. Nonresident transfer students with a GPA below 2.5 are admitted on a space-available basis. 30 credits of 120 required for the bachelor's degree must be completed at NAU.

Visiting: There are regularly scheduled orientations for prospective students, including 8 2-day orientation/registration sessions for new students held mid-June through mid-July, and a 4-day program held the week before the fall and spring semesters. There are guides for informal visits and visitors may sit in on classes and stay overnight. To schedule a visit, contact the Office of Undergraduate Admissions at *undergraduate.admissions@nau.edu.*

Financial Aid: In 2003-2004, 75% of all full-time freshmen and 68% of continuing full-time students received some form of financial aid. 57% of full-time freshmen received need-based aid. The average freshman award was $5168. Need-based scholarships or need-based grants averaged $5168; need-based self-help aid (loans and jobs) averaged $5026; and non-need-based athletic scholarships averaged $9768. 65% of undergraduates work part time. Average annual earnings from campus work are $1447. The average financial indebtedness of the 2003 graduate was $16,319. The FAFSA is required. The deadline for filing freshman financial aid applications for fall entry is April 15.

International Students: There are 316 international students enrolled. The school actively recruits these students. They must score 500 on the written TOEFL or 173 on the electronic version or take the MELAB.

Computers: PCs are available to students at various campus locations. All students may access the system. There are no time limits and no fees. It is strongly recommended that all students have personal computers.

Graduates: From July 1, 2002 to June 30, 2003, 2867 bachelor's degrees were awarded. The most popular majors were elementary education (26%), business administration (19%), and liberal arts (8%). In an average class, 1% graduate in 3 years or less, 3% graduate in 4 years or less, 26% graduate in 5 years or less, and 50% graduate in 6 years or less.

Admissions Contact: David Bousquet, Director of Admissions. A video is available. E-mail: *undergraduate.admissions@nau.edu* Web: *www.nau.edu*

PRESCOTT COLLEGE C-3
Prescott, AZ 86301

(928) 778-2090, ext. 2101
(800) 628-6364; Fax: (928) 776-5137

Full-time: 305 men, 435 women	**Faculty:** 49
Part-time: 40 men, 55 women	**Ph.D.s:** 43%
Graduate: 65 men, 120 women	**Student/Faculty:** 15 to 1
Year: trimesters, summer session	**Tuition:** $13,430
Application Deadline: open	**Room & Board:** n/app
Freshman Class: n/av	
SAT I or ACT: not required	**COMPETITIVE**

Prescott College, founded in 1966, is a private commuter institution offering a nontraditional undergraduate program in the liberal arts. The curriculum is organized into multidisciplinary courses that allow students to pursue individual areas of competency. Evaluations of a student's work are conducted through a portfolio/contract system and an ongoing series of student self-evaluations. There are 3 undergraduate schools and 1 graduate school. Figures in the above capsule and in this profile are approximate. The library contains 22,417 volumes, 125 microform items, and 1304 audio/video tapes/CDs, and subscribes to 270 periodicals. Computerized library services include the card catalog, interlibrary loans, and database searching. Special learning facilities include a learning resource center, art gallery, a greenhouse, a weather station, and a recycling center. The 4-acre campus is in a small town 100 miles north of Phoenix. There are 16 buildings.

Student Life: 89% of undergraduates are from out of state, mostly the Northeast. Students are from 43 states, 5 foreign countries, and Canada.

96% are white. The average age of freshmen is 20; all undergraduates, 28.5% do not continue beyond their first year; 78% remain to graduate.

Housing: There are no residence halls. All students commute. Alcohol is not permitted. All students may keep cars.

Activities: There are no fraternities or sororities. There are 10 groups on campus, including agriculture/garden, Amnesty International, art, arts and activism, dance, drama, environmental, gay, indigenous rights, literary magazine, martial arts, newspaper, photography, political, social, social service, student government, and student union. Popular campus events include Earth Day, Southwest Writers Series, and Student-Directed Days.

Sports: There is no sports program at Prescott. There are no sports facilities on campus, but students have access to the local community pool, weight room, gym, and city league sports.

Disabled Students: 60% of the campus is accessible. Wheelchair ramps, special parking, and specially equipped rest rooms are available.

Services: There is remedial math and writing. There is a learning specialist on staff and untimed tests are available.

Campus Safety and Security: Measures include self-defense education, informal discussions, pamphlets/posters/films, and emergency telephones.

Programs of Study: Prescott confers the B.A. degree. Master's degrees are also awarded. Bachelor's degrees are awarded in AGRICULTURE (environmental studies), BIOLOGICAL SCIENCE (biology/biological science), COMMUNICATIONS AND THE ARTS (communications, English, fine arts, journalism, photography, and Spanish), COMPUTER AND PHYSICAL SCIENCE (earth science and geology), EDUCATION (art, early childhood, education, elementary, environmental, foreign languages, guidance, middle school, recreation, secondary, and special), ENGINEERING AND ENVIRONMENTAL DESIGN (environmental science), SOCIAL SCIENCE (anthropology, community services, criminal justice, economics, peace studies, psychology, social work, and sociology). Environmental studies is the strongest academically. Education is the largest.

Required: Prescott does not specify any formal graduation requirements. Students may design an individual program of studies within 4 multidisciplinary areas: environmental studies, adventure education, arts and letters, and integrative studies. Each student is required to submit a graduation proposal at the end of the junior year to the Graduation Review Committee.

Special: Student-coordinated internships, study abroad in almost any country, dual majors, a general studies degree, pass/fail options, and credit for life experience are offered. All majors are student-designed.

Faculty/Classroom: 55% of faculty are male; 45%, female. All teach undergraduates. The average class size in an introductory lecture is 12; in a laboratory, 12; and in a regular course, 12.

Requirements: The GED is accepted. The school requires essays, transcripts, and letters of recommendation. Students may also submit portfolios and writing samples. Important factors in the admissions decision are extracurricular activities record, personality/intangible qualities, and leadership record.

Procedure: Freshmen are admitted fall and spring. Application deadlines are open. There is a rolling admissions plan. The fall 2003 application fee was $25.

Transfer: 170 transfer students enrolled in a recent year. Transfer applicants must meet the same requirements as entering freshmen and must also submit official college transcripts. Students who successfully completed 2 years of college work (60 semester hours or 90 quarter credits) need not submit high school transcripts. There is a 2-year residency requirement. 90 of 186 credits required for the bachelor's degree must be completed at Prescott.

Visiting: There are regularly scheduled orientations for prospective students, including a college video, a campus tour, and an interview with an admissions counselor. There are guides for informal visits and visitors may sit in on classes. To schedule a visit, contact the RDP Admissions Office.

Financial Aid: In a recent year, 33% of all full-time freshmen and 73% of continuing full-time students received some form of financial aid. 33% of full-time freshmen and 73% of continuing full-time students received need-based aid. The average freshman award was $3264. 17% of undergraduates work part time. Average annual earnings from campus work are $1780. The average financial indebtedness of a recent graduate was $15,891. The FAFSA is required.

International Students: In a recent year there were 8 international students enrolled. They must score 500 on the written TOEFL.

Computers: The Learning Center has 20 PCs for student use. All students may access the system 100 hours per week. There are no time limits and no fees.

Graduates: In a recent year, 264 bachelor's degrees were awarded. The most popular majors were environmental studies (40%), integrative studies (30%), and arts and letters (23%). In an average class, 25% graduate in 3 years or less, 45% graduate in 4 years or less, 52% graduate in 5 years or less, and 52% graduate in 6 years or less.

Admissions Contact: Shari Sterling, Director of Admissions. E-mail: *rdpadmissions@prescott.edu* Web: *www.prescott.edu*

UNIVERSITY OF ARIZONA
Tucson, AZ 85721

D-4

(520) 621-3237; Fax: (520) 621-9799

Full-time: 11,283 men, 12,822 women	**Faculty:** 1495; I, av$
Part-time: 1738 men, 1921 women	**Ph.D.s:** 94%
Graduate: 3177 men, 3266 women	**Student/Faculty:** 16 to 1
Year: semesters, summer session	**Tuition:** $3603 ($12,373)
Application Deadline: April 1	**Room & Board:** $6810
Freshman Class: 21,185 applied, 18,021 accepted, 5958 enrolled	
SAT I Verbal/Math: 552/563	**ACT:** 24 **VERY COMPETITIVE**

The University of Arizona, founded in 1885, is a public land-grant institution controlled by the state of Arizona. Undergraduate programs are offered in agriculture, architecture, arts and sciences, business and public administration, education, engineering and mines, and nursing, pharmacy, and other health-related professions. There are 13 undergraduate and 5 graduate schools. In addition to regional accreditation, UA has baccalaureate program accreditation with AACSB, ABET, ACPE, ADA, ASLA, NAAB, NASAD, NASM, NCATE, and NLN. The 7 libraries contain 4,918,178 volumes, 5,992,439 microform items, and 55,173 audio/video tapes/CDs, and subscribe to 26,711 periodicals. Computerized library services include the card catalog, interlibrary loans, and database searching. Special learning facilities include a learning resource center, art gallery, natural history museum, planetarium, radio station, TV station, the Ansel Adams Center for creative photography, and the Integrated Learning Center. The 357-acre campus is in an urban area in Tucson. Including any residence halls, there are 172 buildings.

Student Life: 72% of undergraduates are from Arizona. Others are from 49 states, 131 foreign countries, and Canada. 90% are from public schools. 65% are white; 13% Hispanic. The average age of freshmen is 19; all undergraduates, 21. 23% do not continue beyond their first year; 55% remain to graduate.

Housing: 4600 students can be accommodated in college housing, which includes single-sex and coed dorms, on-campus apartments, off-campus apartments, fraternity houses, and sorority houses. In addition, there are honors houses and special-interest houses. On-campus housing is available on a first-come, first-served basis. 82% of students commute. Alcohol is not permitted. All students may keep cars.

Activities: 7% of men belong to 24 national fraternities; 11% of women belong to 21 national sororities. There are 375 groups on campus, including art, band, cheerleading, chess, choir, chorale, chorus, computers, dance, drama, drill team, ethnic, film, gay, honors, international, jazz band, literary magazine, marching band, musical theater, newspaper, orchestra, pep band, photography, political, professional, radio and TV, religious, social, social service, student government, and yearbook. Popular campus events include the Spring Fling carnival and cultural programs.

Sports: There are 8 intercollegiate sports for men and 10 for women, and 27 intramural sports for men and 26 for women. Facilities include an athletic center, a 53,000-seat stadium, a 13,500-seat arena, and a student recreation facility with a weight room, a waveless swimming pool, two gyms, aerobics facilities, treadmills, stairclimbers, stationary bicycles, and racquetball, squash, and handball courts. Hiking, backpacking, and skiing trails as well as facilities for kayaking, caving, and scuba diving are available.

Disabled Students: 95% of the campus is accessible. Wheelchair ramps, elevators, special parking, specially equipped rest rooms, lowered drinking fountains, lowered telephones, physical therapy, counseling, interpreters, note taking, equipment maintenance, and an adaptive athletics program are available.

Services: Counseling and information services are available, as is tutoring in most subjects. There is a reader service for the blind and remedial writing.

Campus Safety and Security: Measures include 24-hour foot and vehicle patrol, self-defense education, security escort services, and shuttle buses. There are emergency telephones and lighted pathways/sidewalks.

Programs of Study: UA confers B.A., B.S., B.Arch., B.F.A., B.L.A., B.M., B.S.B.A., B.S.H.S., B.S.N., and B.S.P.A. degrees. Master's and doctoral degrees are also awarded. Bachelor's degrees are awarded in AGRICULTURE (agricultural economics, animal science, natural resource management, plant science, range/farm management, and soil science), BIOLOGICAL SCIENCE (biochemistry, biology/biological science, ecology, evolutionary biology, microbiology, molecular biology, nutrition, physiology, and wildlife biology), BUSINESS (accounting, banking and finance, business administration and management, business economics, entrepreneurial studies, human resources, management information systems, management science, marketing/retailing/merchandising, and retailing), COMMUNICATIONS AND THE ARTS (art history and appreciation, classics, communications, creative writing, dance, dramatic arts, English, fine arts, French, German, Italian, journalism, language arts, Latin, linguistics, media arts, music, music performance, music theory and composition, musical theater, performing arts, Portuguese, Russian, Spanish, studio art, and theater design), COMPUTER AND PHYSICAL SCIENCE (applied science, astronomy, atmospheric sciences, chemistry, computer science, earth science,

geology, geoscience, hydrology, mathematics, natural sciences, and physics), EDUCATION (agricultural, art, drama, early childhood, elementary, health, home economics, music, physical, science, secondary, and special), ENGINEERING AND ENVIRONMENTAL DESIGN (aeronautical engineering, aerospace studies, agricultural engineering technology, architecture, bioengineering, chemical engineering, city/community/regional planning, civil engineering, computer engineering, electrical/electronics engineering, engineering, engineering physics, environmental science, geological engineering, industrial engineering, landscape architecture/design, materials engineering, mechanical engineering, mining and mineral engineering, nuclear engineering, optical engineering, and systems engineering), HEALTH PROFESSIONS (health care administration, medical technology, nursing, pharmacy, speech pathology/audiology, and veterinary science), SOCIAL SCIENCE (anthropology, child care/child and family studies, criminal justice, East Asian studies, economics, ethnic studies, family/consumer resource management, family/consumer studies, geography, German area studies, history, humanities, interdisciplinary studies, Judaic studies, Latin American studies, liberal arts/general studies, Mexican-American/Chicano studies, Near Eastern studies, philosophy, political science/government, psychology, public administration, religion, social science, social studies, sociology, theological studies, water resources, and women's studies). Sciences, social sciences, and management information systems are the strongest academically. Social sciences and business are the largest.

Required: All students must complete a core curriculum of courses in natural sciences, traditions and cultures, individuals and societies, math, English, art, and a foreign language. A total of 125 credits, with a minimum GPA of 2.0, is required to graduate.

Special: Co-op programs are available in almost all majors. B.A.-B.S. degrees, dual majors, interdisciplinary degrees such as engineering-math and theater arts-education, a 3-2 arts and sciences-business degree, and student-designed majors are offered. Internships in almost all disciplines, a Washington semester, study abroad in numerous countries, work-study programs on campus, a general studies degree, and pass/fail options are offered. Nondegree study is possible. There are 19 national honor societies, including Phi Beta Kappa, and a freshman honors program.

Faculty/Classroom: 67% of faculty are male; 33%, female. 62% teach undergraduates and 94% do research. Graduate students teach 42% of introductory courses. The average class size in an introductory lecture is 45; in a laboratory, 22; and in a regular course, 34.

Admissions: 85% of the 2003-2004 applicants were accepted. The SAT I scores for the 2003-2004 freshman class were: Verbal--26% below 500, 44% between 500 and 599, 26% between 600 and 700, and 4% above 700; Math--23% below 500, 41% between 500 and 599, 31% between 600 and 700, and 5% above 700. The ACT scores were 23% below 21, 25% between 21 and 23, 28% between 24 and 26, 12% between 27 and 28, and 12% above 28. 56% of the current freshmen were in the top fifth of their class; 82% were in the top two fifths. There were 58 National Merit finalists. 366 freshmen graduated in the top 1% of their class.

Requirements: The SAT I or ACT is required. In addition, applicants should have completed 4 years each in high school English and math, 3 in science, 2 of a foreign language, and 1 each in history, fine arts, and social studies. A GED may be considered in place of a high school diploma. Some fine arts programs require auditions prior to admission. A GPA of 3.0 is required. AP and CLEP credits are accepted. Important factors in the admissions decision are advanced placement or honor courses, leadership record, and extracurricular activities record.

Procedure: Freshmen are admitted to all sessions. Entrance exams should be taken from March of the junior year through December of the senior year. There is an early admissions plan. Applications should be filed by April 1 for fall entry, October 1 for spring entry, and May 1 for summer entry, along with a $50 fee. Notification is sent on a rolling basis beginning November 1. Applications are accepted on-line through the school's web site at http://admissions.arizona.edu.

Transfer: 1845 transfer students enrolled in 2002-2003. Resident transfer applicants must have a minimum GPA of 2.0; nonresidents, 2.5. Some university divisions have higher requirements. Admission is competitive for out-of-state students. 30 of 125 credits required for the bachelor's degree must be completed at UA.

Visiting: There are regularly scheduled orientations for prospective students, consisting of an admissions presentation and tour. There are guides for informal visits and visitors may sit in on classes. To schedule a visit, contact the Tour Desk at (520) 621-3641 or visitua@arizona.edu.

Financial Aid: UA is a member of CSS. The FAFSA is required. The priority date for freshman financial aid applications for fall entry is March 1.

International Students: There are 2732 international students enrolled. The school actively recruits these students. They must score 500 on the written TOEFL or 173 on the electronic version or take the Comprehensive English Language Test. The SAT I, with a score of 1110, or the ACT is required only if the applicant is a graduate of a U.S. high school.

Computers: The mainframes are an IBM 9672 and UNIX systems using IBM and HP. There are 1913 terminals, all with Internet access. All students may access the system 18 hours a day. Students may access the system depending on course work. There are no fees.

Graduates: From July 1, 2002 to June 30, 2003, 5352 bachelor's degrees were awarded. The most popular majors were business/marketing (17%), social sciences and history (11%), and communications/communication technologies (9%). In an average class, 1% graduate in 3 years or less, 29% graduate in 4 years or less, 49% graduate in 5 years or less, and 55% graduate in 6 years or less. 250 companies recruited on campus in 2002-2003.

Admissions Contact: Lori Goldman, Director of Admissions. A video is available. E-mail: *appinfo@arizona.edu* Web: *www.arizona.edu*

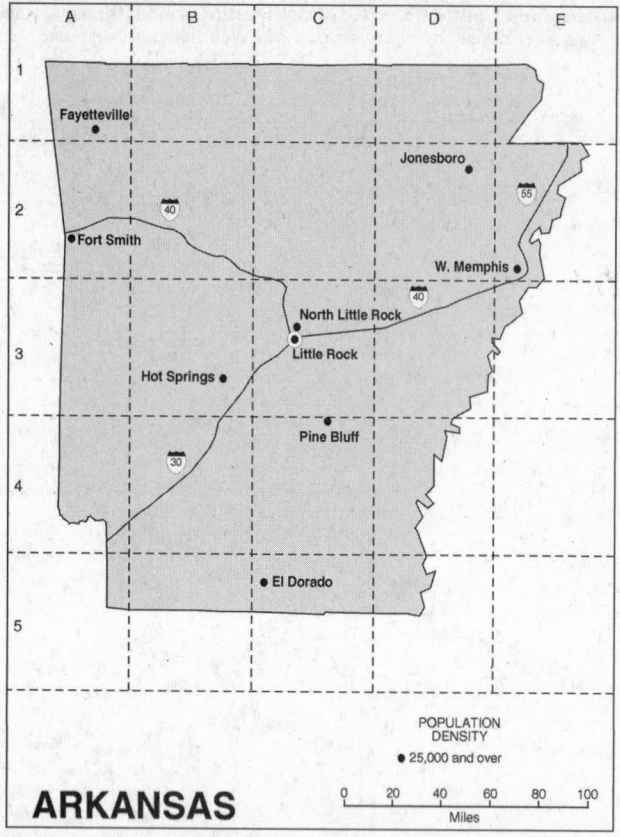

ARKANSAS

POPULATION
DENSITY

● 25,000 and over

0 20 40 60 80 100
Miles

(accounting and business administration and management), COMPUTER AND PHYSICAL SCIENCE (computer science), EDUCATION (elementary), SOCIAL SCIENCE (human services and religion). Business administration is the strongest academically and is the largest.

Required: Students must complete a minimim of 124 credit hours, with 45 in upper-division courses, and must maintain a minimum GPA of 2.0 overall and in the major. Required courses include the Old Testament, theology, humanities, liberal arts, and art or music appreciation.

Special: The college offers a co-op program with Ouachita Baptist University, work-study programs, combined B.A.-B.S. degrees, dual majors, and 1 general studies degree.

Admissions: All of the 2003-2004 applicants were accepted.

Requirements: For unconditional admission, applicants must be graduates of an accredited high school or have a GED. Others may be admitted conditionally. A GPA of 2.0 is required. Important factors in the admissions decision are ability to finance college education, evidence of special talent, and parents or siblings attending the school.

Procedure: Freshmen are admitted fall, spring, and summer. Entrance exams should be taken during the registration/orientation period of each semester. Applications should be filed by July 16 for fall entry, January 31 for spring entry, and May 15 for summer entry, along with a $25 fee. The college accepts all applicants. Notification is sent in July.

Transfer: 50 transfer students enrolled in 2002-2003. For unconditional admission, transfer applicants must have a cumulative GPA of 2.0 and not have been suspended from the previously attended institution. Others may be admitted conditionally.

Visiting: There are regularly scheduled orientations for prospective students, including a tour of campus. There are guides for informal visits and visitors may sit in on classes. To schedule a visit, contact the Admissions and Enrollment Office at (501) 244-5160.

Financial Aid: In 2003-2004, 90% of all full-time students received some form of financial aid. 90% of all full-time students received need-based aid. The average freshman award was $2025. 15% of undergraduates work part time. Average annual earnings from campus work are $816. The average financial indebtedness of the 2003 graduate was $5600. The FAFSA is required. The priority date for freshman financial aid applications for fall entry is February 1. The deadline for filing freshman financial aid applications for fall entry is August 1.

International Students: They must score 500 on the written TOEFL and also take the college's own entrance exam.

Computers: There are approximately 40 computers located in various areas on campus for student use. All students may access the system.

Graduates: From July 1, 2002 to June 30, 2003, 15 bachelor's degrees were awarded. The most popular majors were business administration (20%), human resources (10%), and teacher education (10%). Of the 2002 graduating class, 5% were enrolled in graduate school within 6 months of graduation and 30% were employed.

Admissions Contact: Freddie M. Fox, Registrar.
Web: *www.arbaptcol.edu*

ARKANSAS BAPTIST COLLEGE

C-3

Little Rock, AR 72202-6099

(501) 374-7856, ext. 19
Fax: (501) 375-9257

Full-time: 360 men and women	**Faculty:** n/av
Part-time: none	**Ph.D.s:** n/av
Graduate: none	**Student/Faculty:** 23 to 1
Year: semesters, summer session	**Tuition:** $2530
Application Deadline: July 16	**Room & Board:** $3000
Freshman Class: 57 applied, 57 accepted, 57 enrolled	
SAT I or ACT: not required	**NONCOMPETITIVE**

Arkansas Baptist College, founded in 1884, is a private liberal arts institution affiliated with American Baptist Churches, U.S.A. The library contains 32,000 volumes, 10,000 microform items, and 2000 audio/video tapes/CDs, and subscribes to 75 periodicals. Computerized library services include the card catalog, interlibrary loans, database searching, and Internet access. The campus is in an urban area in downtown Little Rock. Including any residence halls, there are 9 buildings.

Student Life: 90% of undergraduates are from Arkansas. All are African American. Most are Protestant. The average age of freshmen is 18; all undergraduates, 22.

Housing: 160 students can be accommodated in college housing, which includes single-sex dorms. On-campus housing is guaranteed for all 4 years. 50% of students live on campus; of those, 30% remain on campus on weekends. Alcohol is not permitted. All students may keep cars.

Activities: 10% of men belong to 3 local fraternities; 10% of women belong to 2 local sororities. There are 5 groups on campus, including cheerleading, computers, religious, social, and student government. Popular campus events include Ms. ABC and Mr. ABC Pageants.

Sports: There are 2 intercollegiate sports for men and 2 for women. Facilities include a gym.

Disabled Students: 40% of the campus is accessible. Wheelchair ramps and special parking are available.

Services: There is remedial math, reading, and writing.

Campus Safety and Security: Measures include 24-hour foot and vehicle patrol, informal discussions, and lighted pathways/sidewalks.

Programs of Study: ABC confers B.A. and B.S. degrees. Associate degrees are also awarded. Bachelor's degrees are awarded in BUSINESS

ARKANSAS STATE UNIVERSITY

D-2

State University, AR 72467

(870) 972-3024
(800) 382-3030; Fax: (870) 910-8094

Full-time: 3119 men, 4338 women	**Faculty:** 397; IIA, --$
Part-time: 726 men, 1230 women	**Ph.D.s:** 62%
Graduate: 413 men, 747 women	**Student/Faculty:** 19 to 1
Year: semesters, summer session	**Tuition:** $4810 ($10,720)
Application Deadline: see profile	**Room & Board:** $3640
Freshman Class: 3088 applied, 2039 accepted, 1525 enrolled	
ACT: 21	**COMPETITIVE**

Arkansas State University, founded in 1909 and part of the Arkansas State University System, is a state-supported institution offering undergraduate and graduate degrees in agriculture, humanities and social sciences, business, communications, education, engineering, sciences and mathematics, fine arts, nursing, and health professions. There are 10 undergraduate schools and 1 graduate school. In addition to regional accreditation, ASU has baccalaureate program accreditation with AACSB, ABET, ACEJMC, ASLA, CSAB, CSWE, NASAD, NASM, NCATE, NLN, CAPTE, NAACLS,, and NASPAA. The library contains 578,164 volumes, 562,574 microform items, and 14,508 audio/video tapes/CDs, and subscribes to 1675 periodicals. Computerized library services include the card catalog, interlibrary loans, and database searching. Special learning facilities include a learning resource center, art gallery, natural history museum, radio station, TV station, facilities for agriculture and environmental ecotoxicology research, a geographic information system facility, an electron microscope lab, and the Delta Studies Center. The 942-acre campus is in a small town 70 miles west of Memphis, Tennessee. Including any residence halls, there are 85 buildings.

Student Life: 89% of undergraduates are from Arkansas. Others are from 46 states, 56 foreign countries, and Canada. 93% are from public schools. 81% are white; 14% African American. The average age of freshmen is 20; all undergraduates, 24. 30% do not continue beyond their first year; 39% remain to graduate.

Housing: 2315 students can be accommodated in college housing, which includes single-sex dorms, an honors wing and first-year experience wing, on-campus apartments, married-student housing, and fraternity houses. On-campus housing is available on a first-come, first-served basis. 80% of students commute. Alcohol is not permitted. All students may keep cars.

Activities: 18% of men belong to 12 national fraternities; 10% of women belong to 9 national sororities. There are 192 groups on campus, including academic, art, cheerleading, choir, computers, dance, debate, drama, drill team, ethnic, forensics, gay, honors, international, jazz band, marching band, musical theater, newspaper, pep band, photography, political, professional, radio and TV, religious, social service, student government, symphony, and yearbook. Popular campus events include Springfest, Convocation of Scholars Week, and International Night.

Sports: There are 7 intercollegiate sports for men and 8 for women, and 28 intramural sports for men and 28 for women. Facilities include a 10,563-seat convocation center, a 30,708-seat football stadium, a 1,200-seat baseball complex, a 1,200-seat track facility, and a soccer field.

Disabled Students: 95% of the campus is accessible. Wheelchair ramps, elevators, special parking, specially equipped rest rooms, special class scheduling, lowered drinking fountains, lowered telephones, and automatic doors are available.

Services: Counseling and information services are available, as is tutoring in some subjects. There is a reader service for the blind, and remedial math, reading, and writing. Tutoring is available in basic courses.

Campus Safety and Security: Measures include 24-hour foot and vehicle patrol, pamphlets/posters/films, emergency telephones, and lighted pathways/sidewalks.

Programs of Study: ASU confers B.A., B.S., B.F.A., B.Mus., B.Mus.Ed., B.S.A.E., B.S.Ag., B.S.E., B.S.Ed., B.S. in Eng., B.S.N., B.S.R.S., and B.S.W. degrees. Associate, master's, and doctoral degrees are also awarded. Bachelor's degrees are awarded in AGRICULTURE (agricultural business management, agriculture, animal science, plant science, and wildlife management), BIOLOGICAL SCIENCE (biology/biological science), BUSINESS (accounting, banking and finance, business administration and management, business economics, business systems analysis, international business management, management information systems, marketing/retailing/merchandising, sports management, and transportation management), COMMUNICATIONS AND THE ARTS (dramatic arts, English, fine arts, French, graphic design, journalism, media arts, music, music performance, radio/television technology, Spanish, and speech/debate/rhetoric), COMPUTER AND PHYSICAL SCIENCE (chemistry, computer science, mathematics, and physics), EDUCATION (agricultural, art, athletic training, business, early childhood, elementary, English, foreign languages, health, mathematics, middle school, music, physical, science, and special), ENGINEERING AND ENVIRONMENTAL DESIGN (engineering, manufacturing technology, printing technology, and technological management), HEALTH PROFESSIONS (exercise science, medical laboratory technology, nursing, public health, radiological science, and speech pathology/audiology), SOCIAL SCIENCE (community services, criminology, economics, geography, history, liberal arts/general studies, philosophy, political science/government, psychology, social science, social work, and sociology). Early childhood education, engineering, and nursing are the strongest academically. Nursing, early childhood education, and biological sciences are the largest.

Required: All students must complete a 44-credit distribution of general education courses. A total of at least 124 credits, with a minimum GPA of 2.0, is required to graduate. All students must take a state-administered comprehensive exam.

Special: An interdisciplinary studies degree, co-op programs, study abroad in 17 countries, and work-study programs are offered. Dual majors and internships are available in many areas. Nondegree study is possible. There are 42 national honor societies, a freshman honors program, and 1 departmental honors program.

Faculty/Classroom: 56% of faculty are male; 44%, female. 89% teach undergraduates, 19% do research, and 17% do both. Graduate students teach 3% of introductory courses. The average class size in an introductory lecture is 24; in a laboratory, 24; and in a regular course, 27.

Admissions: 66% of the 2003-2004 applicants were accepted. The ACT scores for the 2003-2004 freshman class were: 43% below 21, 22% between 21 and 23, 23% between 24 and 26, 7% between 27 and 28, and 5% above 28.

Requirements: ACT, SAT I, ASSET, or COMPASS scores are required, with ACT scores recommended. Applicants should have completed 18 high school units, including 4 in English, 3 in social studies, 3 each in math and science, and 2 in 1 foreign language. The university places those applicants scoring below 19 on the ACT in developmental or re-

medial courses. A high school transcript is also required. A GPA of 2.0 is required. AP and CLEP credits are accepted.

Procedure: Freshmen are admitted to all sessions. Entrance exams should be taken before April 1 of the high school senior year. There are early admissions and deferred admissions plans. Applications are due before the first class day. Notification is sent on a rolling basis. Applications are accepted on-line through the school's web site. The 2003-2004 fee was $15.

Transfer: 924 transfer students enrolled in 2003-2004. Transfer applicants should have a minimum GPA of 2.0. Those having completed 12 or fewer credit hours will be admitted on the same basis as freshmen. Official transcripts from every institution attended are required. 32 of at least 124 credits required for the bachelor's degree must be completed at ASU.

Visiting: There are regularly scheduled orientations for prospective students, consisting of sessions in March, September, and November. There are guides for informal visits and visitors may sit in on classes and stay overnight. To schedule a visit, contact the Office of Admissions.

Financial Aid: In 2003-2004, 83% of all full-time freshmen and 68% of continuing full-time students received some form of financial aid. 78% of full-time freshmen and 61% of continuing full-time students received need-based aid. The average freshman award was $2600. Need-based scholarships or need-based grants averaged $2400 ($3000 maximum); need-based self-help aid (loans and jobs) averaged $1200 ($2400 maximum); and non-need-based athletic scholarships averaged $3200 ($3600 maximum). 12% of undergraduates work part time. Average annual earnings from campus work are $3600. The average financial indebtedness of the 2003 graduate was $14,900. The FAFSA and the college's own financial statement are required. The deadline for filing freshman financial aid applications for fall entry is July 1.

International Students: There are 86 international students enrolled. The school actively recruits these students. They must score 500 on the written TOEFL or 173 on the electronic version and also take the SAT I or the ACT, scoring 19 on the ACT.

Graduates: From July 1, 2002 to June 30, 2003, 1604 bachelor's degrees were awarded. The most popular majors were early childhood education (11%), business administration (7%), and management information systems (5%). In an average class, 1% graduate in 3 years or less, 19% graduate in 4 years or less, 32% graduate in 5 years or less, and 39% graduate in 6 years or less. 153 companies recruited on campus in 2002-2003. Of the 2002 graduating class, 97% were employed within 6 months of graduation.

Admissions Contact: Paula James Lynn, Director of Admissions. A video is available. E-mail: *admissions@astate.edu* Web: *www.astate.edu/admissions.htm*

ARKANSAS TECH UNIVERSITY   B-2
Russellville, AR 72801-2222   (479) 968-0343
                                    (800) 582-6953; Fax: (479) 964-0522

Full-time: 2457 men, 2669 women	**Faculty:** IIB, -$
Part-time: 330 men, 433 women	**Ph.D.s:** 68%
Graduate: 109 men, 251 women	**Student/Faculty:** n/av
Year: semesters, summer session	**Tuition:** $3574 ($6886)
Application Deadline: open	**Room & Board:** $3725
Freshman Class: 2854 applied, 1547 accepted, 1508 enrolled	
ACT: 22	**COMPETITIVE**

Arkansas Tech University, founded in 1909, is a state-supported institution offering undergraduate instruction in the liberal and fine arts, business, education, physical and life sciences, information technology, systems science, and other technical fields. Graduate instruction is offered in education, liberal arts, instructional technology, information technology, and fisheries and wildlife. There are 7 undergraduate schools and 1 graduate school. In addition to regional accreditation, Tech has baccalaureate program accreditation with AACSB, ABET, ACS, CAHEA, NASM, NCATE, NLN, and NRPA. The library contains 247,869 volumes, 842,936 microform items, and 6041 audio/video tapes/CDs, and subscribes to 1107 periodicals. Computerized library services include the card catalog, interlibrary loans, database searching, and Internet access. Special learning facilities include a learning resource center, art gallery, natural history museum, radio station, TV station, energy center, and library with distance learning classrooms, satellite downlink, and 400 data drops for laptop computers. The 516-acre campus is in a small town 75 miles east of Little Rock. Including any residence halls, there are 50 buildings.

Student Life: 96% of undergraduates are from Arkansas. Students are from 35 states, 32 foreign countries, and Canada. 90% are white. The average age of freshmen is 22; all undergraduates, 23. 34% do not continue beyond their first year; 41% remain to graduate.

Housing: 1587 students can be accommodated in college housing, which includes single-sex and coed dorms and on-campus apartments. On-campus housing is guaranteed for all 4 years. 73% of students commute. Alcohol is not permitted. All students may keep cars.

Activities: 5% of men belong to 4 national fraternities; 3% of women belong to 2 national sororities. There are 97 groups on campus, including art, band, cheerleading, chess, choir, chorale, chorus, computers, dance, debate, drama, drill team, ethnic, film, honors, international, jazz band, literary magazine, marching band, musical theater, newspaper, orchestra, pep band, photography, political, professional, radio and TV, social, social service, student government, and yearbook. Popular campus events include Greek Week, Family Day, and Spring Fling and Fall Fest.

Sports: There are 4 intercollegiate sports for men and 5 for women, and 28 intramural sports for men and 28 for women. Facilities include a coliseum, fields, an Olympic-size indoor pool, racquetball courts, and a 10,000-seat stadium. The Student Activities Building is the hub of indoor recreational activities.

Disabled Students: All of the campus is accessible. Wheelchair ramps, elevators, special parking, specially equipped rest rooms, lowered drinking fountains, and lowered telephones are available.

Services: Counseling and information services are available, as is tutoring in most subjects. There is a reader service for the blind and remedial math, reading, and writing.

Campus Safety and Security: Measures include 24-hour foot and vehicle patrol, self-defense education, security escort services, informal discussions, and lighted pathways/sidewalks,

Programs of Study: Tech confers B.A., B.S., B.F.A., B.M.E., B.S.B.A., B.S.E.E., B.S.E.G., B.S.M.E., and B.S.N. degrees. Associate and master's degrees are also awarded. Bachelor's degrees are awarded in AGRICULTURE (agricultural business management), BIOLOGICAL SCIENCE (biology/biological science), BUSINESS (accounting, business administration and management, hotel/motel and restaurant management, office supervision and management, and recreation and leisure services), COMMUNICATIONS AND THE ARTS (art, creative writing, English, journalism, languages, music, and speech/debate/rhetoric), COMPUTER AND PHYSICAL SCIENCE (chemistry, computer science, geology, mathematics, natural sciences, and physical sciences), EDUCATION (art, business, elementary, health, middle school, music, and secondary), ENGINEERING AND ENVIRONMENTAL DESIGN (emergency/disaster science and engineering), HEALTH PROFESSIONS (medical laboratory technology, nursing, and rehabilitation therapy), SOCIAL SCIENCE (economics, history, international studies, parks and recreation management, psychology, and sociology). Elementary education, management marketing, and computer science are the strongest academically and are the largest.

Required: Students must complete at least 124 semester hours, including 40 hours of upper-level courses to fulfill a major, and maintain a minimum GPA of 2.0. General education requirements include 12 hours of social studies, 8 to 12 of science, 6 of communications, 3 each of math, fine arts, and the humanities, and 2 of phys ed or military science. Activity credits are limited to 4 semester hours.

Special: Special academic features include internships and work-study programs, as well as study abroad, accelerated programs, B.A.-B.S. degrees, and dual majors. Independent study is available to seniors. Off-campus courses and on-line telecourses are also offered. There are 4 national honor societies and a freshman honors program.

Faculty/Classroom: 58% of faculty are male; 42%, female.

Admissions: 54% of the 2003-2004 applicants were accepted. The ACT scores for the 2003-2004 freshman class were: 38% below 21, 23% between 21 and 23, 23% between 24 and 26, 11% between 27 and 28, and 5% above 28.

Requirements: The ACT is required and the SAT I is recommended. In addition, applicants must be graduates of a secondary school on the Arkansas preparatory track. Academic ability must be demonstrated by one of the following: a high school GPA of at least 2.0 on a 4.0 scale; a minimum ACT score of 15; attainment of Freshman Placement test score standards; or completion of 6 semester hours with a cumulative average of C or better in summer sessions or as a part-time student in regular sessions, with at least 3 of the hours being in English, math, social studies, or science. AP and CLEP credits are accepted.

Procedure: Freshmen are admitted to all sessions. Entrance exams should be taken no later than the second semester of the senior year of high school. There is a rolling admissions plan. Application deadlines are open. Applications are accepted on-line through *http:// admissions.atu.edu/newapply.htm.*

Transfer: 676 transfer students enrolled in 2002-2003. Transfers are accepted for second-semester freshman, sophomore, and junior classes. A C average is required; no D grades are accepted. 30 of 124 credits required for the bachelor's degree must be completed at Tech.

Visiting: There are regularly scheduled orientations for prospective students, including the opportunity to visit with or attend presentations by faculty in each academic discipline. There are guides for informal visits and visitors may sit in on classes. To schedule a visit, contact the Admissions Office at *tech.enroll@mail.atu.edu.*

Financial Aid: In a recent year, 55% of all full-time freshmen and 53% of continuing full-time students received some form of financial aid. 50% of full-time freshmen and 44% of continuing full-time students received need-based aid. The average freshman award was $3585. 11% of undergraduates work part time. Average annual earnings from campus work are $1258. The average financial indebtedness of a recent graduate was $14,762. The FAFSA and the college's own financial statement are required. The deadline for filing freshman financial aid applications for fall entry is May 1.

International Students: There are 153 international students enrolled. The school actively recruits these students. They must score 500 on the written TOEFL and also take the SAT I or the ACT.

Computers: All students may access the system. There are no time limits and no fees.

Graduates: From July 1, 2002 to June 30, 2003, 758 bachelor's degrees were awarded. The most popular majors were early childhood education (11%), computer science (9%), and management marketing (8%). In an average class, 15% graduate in 4 years or less, 32% graduate in 5 years or less, and 41% graduate in 6 years or less.

Admissions Contact: Shauna Donnell, Director of Enrollment Management. A video is available. E-mail: *tech.enroll@mail.atu.edu* Web: *www.atu.edu*

HARDING UNIVERSITY
C-2

Searcy, AR 72149-0001

(501) 279-4407
(800) 477-4407; Fax: (501) 279-4076

Full-time: 1739 men, 2120 women	**Faculty:** 186
Part-time: 97 men, 80 women	**Ph.D.s:** 65%
Graduate: 233 men, 841 women	**Student/Faculty:** 21 to 1
Year: semesters, summer session	**Tuition:** $10,120
Application Deadline: July 1	**Room & Board:** $4770
Freshman Class: 1750 applied, 1020 accepted, 967 enrolled	
SAT I Verbal/Math: 550/540	**ACT:** 24 **VERY COMPETITIVE**

Harding University, founded in 1924, is a private Christian institution comprised of the Colleges of Arts and Sciences and Bible and Religion and the Schools of Business, Education, and Nursing. Some information in the above capsule is approximate. There are 7 undergraduate and 5 graduate schools. In addition to regional accreditation, Harding has baccalaureate program accreditation with ACBSP, CSWE, NASM, NCATE, and NLN. The library contains 459,351 volumes, 153,000 microform items, and 6750 audio/video tapes/CDs, and subscribes to 1442 periodicals. Computerized library services include the card catalog, interlibrary loans, and database searching. Special learning facilities include a learning resource center, art gallery, natural history museum, radio station, and TV station. The 200-acre campus is in a small town 50 miles northeast of Little Rock. Including any residence halls, there are 50 buildings.

Student Life: 69% of undergraduates are from out of state, mostly the Southwest. Students are from 50 states, 48 foreign countries, and Canada. 73% are from public schools. 87% are white. Most are Protestant. The average age of freshmen is 18; all undergraduates, 21. 22% do not continue beyond their first year; 60% remain to graduate.

Housing: 2400 students can be accommodated in college housing, which includes single-sex dorms, on-campus apartments, off-campus apartments, and married-student housing. On-campus housing is guaranteed for all 4 years. 71% of students live on campus; of those, 80% remain on campus on weekends. Alcohol is not permitted. All students may keep cars.

Activities: 50% of men belong to 14 local fraternities; 39% of women belong to 14 local sororities. There are 40 groups on campus, including art, band, cheerleading, choir, chorale, chorus, computers, debate, drama, drill team, ethnic, film, forensics, honors, international, jazz band, literary magazine, marching band, musical theater, newspaper, orchestra, pep band, photography, political, professional, radio and TV, religious, social, social service, student government, symphony, and yearbook. Popular campus events include Spring Sing, Parents Weekend, and Youth Forum.

Sports: There are 7 intercollegiate sports for men and 5 for women, and 10 intramural sports for men and 10 for women. Facilities include baseball and softball fields, racquetball, handball, and tennis courts, a football stadium, an indoor and outdoor track, a golf practice range, a gymnastics room, 2 weight rooms, 2 Olympic-size swimming pools, and 2 gyms. Harding owns a 2000-acre camp in the Ozark Mountains with horses, 25 rustic cabins, streams, and hiking trails.

Disabled Students: 95% of the campus is accessible. Wheelchair ramps, elevators, special parking, specially equipped rest rooms, special class scheduling, lowered drinking fountains, and lowered telephones are available.

Services: Counseling and information services are available, as is tutoring in every subject. There is a reader service for the blind and remedial math, reading, and writing.

Campus Safety and Security: Measures include 24-hour foot and vehicle patrol, self-defense education, security escort services, and informal discussions. There are pamphlets/posters/films, emergency telephones, and lighted pathways/sidewalks.

Programs of Study: Harding confers B.A., B.S., B.B.A., B.F.A, B.M.E., B.Mus., B.S.M.T., B.S.N., and B.S.W. degrees. Master's degrees are also awarded. Bachelor's degrees are awarded in BIOLOGICAL SCIENCE (biochemistry and biology/biological science), BUSINESS (accounting, business administration and management, business economics, human resources, international business management, marketing/retailing/merchandising, and sports management), COMMUNICATIONS AND THE ARTS (advertising, art, broadcasting, communications, design, dramatic arts, English, fine arts, French, graphic design, music, painting, and Spanish), COMPUTER AND PHYSICAL SCIENCE (chemistry, computer science, mathematics, and physics), EDUCATION (early childhood, elementary, foreign languages, music, and secondary), ENGINEERING AND ENVIRONMENTAL DESIGN (interior design), HEALTH PROFESSIONS (medical technology, nursing, predentistry, premedicine, and speech pathology/audiology), SOCIAL SCIENCE (American studies, dietetics, economics, history, home economics, international studies, liberal arts/general studies, ministries, political science/government, psychology, public administration, religion, social science, social work, and sociology). Business, premedicine, and sciences are the strongest academically. Business and education are the largest.

Required: All students must complete 54 hours of general education courses, including religion, English composition, history, speech communications, social sciences, biology, physical science, math, Western literature, music and art appreciation, and phys ed. A total of 128 semester hours, with a minimum GPA of 2.0, is required to graduate.

Special: The Harding campus in Florence, Italy, and programs in Greece, England, and Australia offer international studies. Internships are given in in social work, teaching, nursing, and international missions. Co-op programs in all majors, work-study programs, dual majors, a general studies degree, nondegree study, and pass/fail options are available. A 3-2 engineering degree is offered with the University of Missouri, Georgia Institute of Technology, and the University of Southern California. There are 3 national honor societies, a freshman honors program, and 13 departmental honors programs.

Faculty/Classroom: 64% of faculty are male; 36%, female. All teach undergraduates and 20% do research. No introductory courses are taught by graduate students. The average class size in an introductory lecture is 39; in a laboratory, 15; and in a regular course, 24.

Admissions: 58% of the 2003-2004 applicants were accepted. The SAT I scores for the 2003-2004 freshman class were: Verbal--26% below 500, 45% between 500 and 599, 24% between 600 and 700, and 6% above 700; Math--35% below 500, 34% between 500 and 599, 25% between 600 and 700, and 6% above 700. The ACT scores were 26% below 21, 27% between 21 and 23, 20% between 24 and 26, 10% between 27 and 28, and 17% above 28. 55% of the current freshmen were in the top fifth of their class; 80% were in the top two fifths. There were 24 National Merit finalists and 20 semifinalists and 41 freshmen graduated first in their class in a recent year.

Requirements: The SAT I or ACT is required. A lower GPA can be offset by higher test scores. Applicants should be graduates of an accredited secondary school and have completed 19 high school hours, including 4 each in English and math, 3 each in science and social studies, 3 in art, history, or music, and 2 in a foreign language. An interview is highly recommended. Harding requires applicants to be in the upper 50% of their class. A GPA of 3.0 is required. AP and CLEP credits are accepted. Important factors in the admissions decision are leadership record, recommendations by school officials, and advanced placement or honor courses.

Procedure: Freshmen are admitted to all sessions. Entrance exams should be taken in the junior year or early in the senior year. There are early admissions and deferred admissions plans. There is a rolling admissions plan. Applications should be filed by July 1 for fall entry and November 1 for spring entry. Notification is sent on a rolling basis beginning May 1. A waiting list is an active part of the admissions procedure. The fall 2003 application fee was $35.

Transfer: 249 transfer students enrolled in a recent year. Applicants with a minimum GPA of 2.0 and at least 14 semester hours earned are considered for admission. An interview is highly recommended. 32 of 128 credits required for the bachelor's degree must be completed at Harding.

Visiting: There are regularly scheduled orientations for prospective students. There are guides for informal visits and visitors may sit in on classes and stay overnight. To schedule a visit, contact the Admissions Office at *mwilliams@harding.edu.*

Financial Aid: In 2003-2004, 93% of all full-time freshmen and 91% of continuing full-time students received some form of financial aid. 52% of full-time freshmen and 57% of continuing full-time students received need-based aid. The average freshman award was $8687. Need-based scholarships or need-based grants averaged $5828 ($13,500 maximum); need-based self-help aid (loans and jobs) averaged $3879 ($14,500 maximum); and non-need-based athletic scholarships averaged $7000 ($14,000 maximum). 33% of undergraduates work part time. Average annual earnings from campus work are $866. The average financial indebtedness of a recent graduate was $19,711. Harding is a member of CSS. The CSS Profile or FFS is required. Check with the school for current deadlines.

International Students: There were 228 international students enrolled in a recent year. The school actively recruits these students. They must score 500 on the written TOEFL.

Computers: The mainframe is a DEC VAX 3600. There are numerous terminals for accessing the mainframe and 200 PCs available for student use. Many students have their own computers. All students may access the system. The fee is $100. It is strongly recommended that all students have a personal computer.

Graduates: In a recent year, 629 bachelor's degrees were awarded. The most popular majors were elementary education (10%), nursing (6%), and accounting (6%). In an average class, 10% graduate in 3 years or less, 39% graduate in 4 years or less, 48% graduate in 5 years or less, and 56% graduate in 6 years or less. 330 companies recruited on campus in a recent year. Of a recent graduating class, 10% were enrolled in graduate school within 6 months of graduation and 98% were employed.

Admissions Contact: Glen Dillard, Director of Enrollment Management. A video is available. E-mail: *gdillard@harding.edu* Web: *www.harding.edu*

HENDERSON STATE UNIVERSITY
Arkadelphia, AR 71999-0001
B-4
(870) 230-5028
Fax: (870) 230-5066

Full-time: 1203 men, 1536 women	**Faculty:** 168; IIA, --$
Part-time: 120 men, 193 women	**Ph.D.s:** 71%
Graduate: 128 men, 301 women	**Student/Faculty:** 16 to 1
Year: semesters, summer session	**Tuition:** $3850 ($7209)
Application Deadline: open	**Room & Board:** $3536
Freshman Class: 631 enrolled	
SAT I Verbal/Math: 539/522	**ACT:** 21 COMPETITIVE

Henderson State University began in 1890 as Arkadelphia Methodist College, an affiliate of the Methodist Church. In 1929 it became a state institution offering liberal arts courses. There are 3 undergraduate schools and 1 graduate school. In addition to regional accreditation, HSU has baccalaureate program accreditation with AACSB, NASM, NCATE, and NLN. The library contains 636,952 volumes, 213,922 microform items, and 18,983 audio/video tapes/CDs, and subscribes to 1519 periodicals. Computerized library services include the card catalog, interlibrary loans, database searching, and Internet access. Special learning facilities include an art gallery, planetarium, radio station, and TV station. The 157-acre campus is in a small town 60 miles southwest of Little Rock. Including any residence halls, there are 32 buildings.

Student Life: 77% of undergraduates are from Arkansas. Students are from 24 states, 28 foreign countries, and Canada. 80% are white; 15% African American. The average age of freshmen is 18; all undergraduates, 23.

Housing: 878 students can be accommodated in college housing, which includes single-sex and coed dorms and off-campus apartments. In addition, there are honors houses and apartments on campus that are managed by an outside group. On-campus housing is available on a first-come, first-served basis. 71% of students commute. Alcohol is not permitted. All students may keep cars.

Activities: There are 8 national fraternities and 8 national sororities. There are 70 groups on campus, including art, band, cheerleading, choir, chorale, chorus, dance, drama, ethnic, gay, honors, international, jazz band, marching band, musical theater, newspaper, pep band, political, professional, radio and TV, religious, social, social service, student government, and yearbook. Popular campus events include Spring Fling, orientation, and Family Day.

Sports: There are 5 intercollegiate sports for men and 6 for women, and 5 intramural sports for men and 5 for women. Facilities include a 9600-seat football stadium, a gym, an auxiliary gym, a weight room, an intramural practice field for football, a swimming pool, 6 tennis courts, baseball and softball fields, and a track.

Disabled Students: 72% of the campus is accessible. Wheelchair ramps, elevators, special parking, specially equipped rest rooms, special class scheduling, lowered drinking fountains, and lowered telephones are available.

Services: Counseling and information services are available, as is tutoring in most subjects. There is a reader service for the blind and remedial math and reading.

Campus Safety and Security: Measures include 24-hour foot and vehicle patrol, informal discussions, and lighted pathways/sidewalks.

Programs of Study: HSU confers B.A., B.S., B.B.A., B.F.A., B.M., B.S.E., and B.S.N. degrees. Associate and master's degrees are also awarded. Bachelor's degrees are awarded in BIOLOGICAL SCIENCE (biology/biological science), BUSINESS (accounting, business administration and management, and recreation and leisure services), COMMUNICATIONS AND THE ARTS (communications, dramatic arts, English, music, Spanish, and studio art), COMPUTER AND PHYSICAL SCIENCE (chemistry, computer science, mathematics, and physics), EDUCATION (athletic training, business, elementary, music, and physical), ENGINEERING AND ENVIRONMENTAL DESIGN (aviation administration/management), HEALTH PROFESSIONS (nursing), SOCIAL SCIENCE (family/consumer studies, history, human services, political science/government, psychology, public administration, and sociology). Elementary education, business administration, and nursing are the largest.

Required: All students must complete a total of 124 credit hours, including 30 in the major, with a minimum GPA of 2.0. Core requirements include 12 semester hours in social science, 11 in natural science, 9 in English, 6 in humanities, 3 each in non-Western culture, math, and oral communication, and 2 in phys ed or military science. Students must take the comprehensive Rising Junior Examination.

Special: HSU offers co-op programs and cross-registration with Ouachita Baptist University, internships in business, psychology, political science, recreation, and education, work-study programs, credit for military experience, nondegree study, and pass/fail options. There are 11 national honor societies and a freshman honors program.

Faculty/Classroom: 62% of faculty are male; 38%, female. All teach undergraduates and 30% both teach and do research. Graduate students teach 1% of introductory courses. The average class size in an introductory lecture is 50; in a laboratory, 20; and in a regular course, 30.

Admissions: The SAT I scores for the 2003-2004 freshman class were: Verbal--35% below 500, 35% between 500 and 599, and 30% between 600 and 700; Math--40% below 500, 40% between 500 and 599, and 20% between 600 and 700. The ACT scores were 41% below 21, 22% between 21 and 23, 22% between 24 and 26, 10% between 27 and 28, and 5% above 28. 37% of the current freshmen were in the top fifth of their class; 64% were in the top two fifths. 6 freshmen graduated first in their class.

Requirements: The ACT is required. In addition, applicants need at least 15 academic credits or 15 Carnegie units. Students with a predicted GPA of 1.5 or below will be admitted conditionally. 4 units of English, 3 of history, civics, or American government, 2 each of natural science, math, and foreign language, and a half unit of computer science are recommended. HSU requires applicants to be in the upper 50% of their class. A GPA of 3.13 is required. AP and CLEP credits are accepted.

Procedure: Freshmen are admitted fall, spring, and summer. Entrance exams should be taken during the senior year. Application deadlines are open. Notification is sent on a rolling basis. Applications are accepted on-line through *www.hsu.edu/dept/ura/application.html*.

Transfer: 294 transfer students enrolled in a recent year. Applicants with a cumulative GPA below 2.0 will be admitted conditionally. The entire academic record is considered. 30 of 124 credits required for the bachelor's degree must be completed at HSU.

Visiting: There are regularly scheduled orientations for prospective students. There are guides for informal visits and visitors may stay overnight. To schedule a visit, contact Vikita Hardwrick at *buckg@hsu.edu*.

Financial Aid: In a recent year, 80% of all full-time freshmen and 61% of continuing full-time students received some form of financial aid. 52% of full-time freshmen and 56% of continuing full-time students received need-based aid. The average freshman award was $3725. 10% of undergraduates work part time. The FAFSA or FFS is required. The deadline for filing freshman financial aid applications for fall entry is March 1.

International Students: There are 110 international students enrolled. The school actively recruits these students. They must score 500 on the written TOEFL or 173 on the electronic version or take the MELAB. They must also take the ACT or SAT I.

Computers: The mainframe is a Compaq DS2. The campus is networked for student access to the mainframe and LAN. Students have full access to the Internet, Telnet access to computer services mainframe, and network access to file servers from all dorms to 10 labs. About 175 lab computers are available, not including computers in dorms. All students may access the system. There are no time limits and no fees.

Graduates: From July 1, 2002 to June 30, 2003, 402 bachelor's degrees were awarded. The most popular majors were education (19%), business administration (19%), and psychology (8%). In an average class, 1% graduate in 3 years or less, 17% graduate in 4 years or less, 22% graduate in 5 years or less, and 27% graduate in 6 years or less. 100 companies recruited on campus in 2002-2003.

Admissions Contact: Vikita Hardwrick, Director of University Relations/Admissions. E-mail: *hardwrv@hsu.edu*
Web: *www.hsu.edu/dept/ura/index.html*

HENDRIX COLLEGE
C-3
Conway, AR 72032
(501) 450-1362
(800) 277-9017; Fax: (501) 450-3843

Full-time: 443 men, 588 women	Faculty: 81; IIB, av$
Part-time: 13 men, 6 women	Ph.D.s: 100%
Graduate: 3 men, 6 women	Student/Faculty: 13 to 1
Year: semesters	Tuition: $15,630
Application Deadline: open	Room & Board: $5340
Freshman Class: 891 applied, 770 accepted, 267 enrolled	
SAT I Verbal/Math: 632/610	ACT: 27 VERY COMPETITIVE+

Hendrix College, founded in 1876, is a private liberal arts college affiliated with the United Methodist Church. There is 1 graduate school. In addition to regional accreditation, Hendrix has baccalaureate program accreditation with NASM and NCATE. The library contains 212,767 volumes, 182,229 microform items, and 1628 audio/video tapes/CDs, and subscribes to 736 periodicals. Computerized library services include the card catalog, interlibrary loans, and database searching. Special learning facilities include an art gallery, radio station, and a writing lab. The 65-acre campus is in a suburban area 25 miles northwest of Little Rock. Including any residence halls, there are 39 buildings.

Student Life: 61% of undergraduates are from Arkansas. Students are from 35 states, 12 foreign countries, and Canada. 71% are white. 48% are Protestant; 30% claim no religious affiliation; 9% Catholic. The average age of freshmen is 18; all undergraduates, 20. 15% do not continue beyond their first year; 85% remain to graduate.

Housing: 901 students can be accommodated in college housing, which includes single-sex and coed dorms, on-campus apartments, and off-campus apartments. In addition, there are language houses and a substance-free house. On-campus housing is guaranteed for all 4 years. 80% of students live on campus; of those, 80% remain on campus on weekends. All students may keep cars.

Activities: There are no fraternities or sororities. There are 56 groups on campus, including art, band, cheerleading, choir, chorale, chorus, dance, debate, drama, ethnic, gay, honors, international, jazz band, literary magazine, musical theater, newspaper, opera, orchestra, pep band, photography, political, professional, radio and TV, religious, social, social service, student government, and yearbook. Popular campus events include Candlelight Carol Service, Basketball Homecoming, and Kampus Kitty Week.

Sports: There are 8 intercollegiate sports for men and 9 for women, and 20 intramural sports for men and 20 for women. Facilities include a 1600-seat gym, an indoor activity center with tennis and racquetball courts, intramural football and softball fields, a nature fitness trail, and NCAA regulation baseball and soccer fields.

Disabled Students: 95% of the campus is accessible. Wheelchair ramps, elevators, special parking, specially equipped rest rooms, and push-button door openers are available.

Services: Counseling and information services are available, as is tutoring in some subjects, including math, biology, writing, chemistry, foreign languages, accounting, physics, and psychology.

Campus Safety and Security: Measures include 24-hour foot and vehicle patrol, self-defense education, security escort services, and informal discussions. There are pamphlets/posters/films, emergency telephones, and lighted pathways/sidewalks.

Programs of Study: Hendrix confers the B.A. degree. Master's degrees are also awarded. Bachelor's degrees are awarded in AGRICULTURE (environmental studies), BIOLOGICAL SCIENCE (biology/biological science), BUSINESS (accounting and business economics), COMMUNICATIONS AND THE ARTS (art, dramatic arts, English, French, German, music, Spanish, and visual and performing arts), COMPUTER AND PHYSICAL SCIENCE (chemistry, computer science, mathematics, and physics), EDUCATION (elementary), HEALTH PROFESSIONS (exercise science), SOCIAL SCIENCE (anthropology, history, interdisciplinary studies, international relations, philosophy, political science/government, psychology, religion, and sociology). Chemistry, psychology, and religion are the strongest academically. Biology, psychology, and English are the largest.

Required: To graduate, students must complete a total of 32 courses with a minimum 2.0 GPA. General education requirements consist of 3 components: (1) Collegiate Center, (2) Learning Domains, and (3) Capacities. The Collegiate Center includes Journeys (first-year common course), 1 course from Explorations, and 1 course from Challenges of the Contemporary World. Students must also take 7 courses across 3 distinct Learning Domains and meet basic skill standards in 4 Capacities sections (writing skills, foreign language, quantitative skills, and physical activity).

Special: Internships and work-study may be arranged in all fields. The college offers 3-2 engineering programs with Columbia, Vanderbilt, and Washington Universities. Also available are a Washington semester, study abroad, dual majors, and student-designed interdisciplinary studies. Students can pursue minors in all academic departments, as well as gender studies and cultural anthropology. There are 6 national honor societies, including Phi Beta Kappa.

Faculty/Classroom: 65% of faculty are male; 35%, female. All teach undergraduates, 78% both teach and do research. No introductory courses are taught by graduate students. The average class size in an introductory lecture is 20; in a laboratory, 26; and in a regular course, 17.

Admissions: 86% of the 2003-2004 applicants were accepted. The SAT I scores for the 2003-2004 freshman class were: Verbal--7% below 500, 27% between 500 and 599, 47% between 600 and 700, and 19% above 700; Math--8% below 500, 31% between 500 and 599, 48% between 600 and 700, and 13% above 700. The ACT scores were 6% below 21, 17% between 21 and 23, 20% between 24 and 26, 21% between 27 and 28, and 36% above 28. 60% of the current freshmen were in the top fifth of their class; 84% were in the top two fifths. There were 7 National Merit finalists and 11 semifinalists. 11 freshmen graduated first in their class.

Requirements: The SAT I or ACT is required. In addition, Hendrix recommends that applicants have completed 4 high school units in English, 3 to 4 each in math and social studies, 2 to 3 in science, and 2 in a foreign language. The GED is accepted. AP and CLEP credits are accepted. Important factors in the admissions decision are leadership record, advanced placement or honor courses, and extracurricular activities record.

Procedure: Freshmen are admitted fall and spring. Entrance exams should be taken during the junior and senior years. There is a deferred admissions plan. Application deadlines are open. Application fee is $40. Notification is sent on a rolling basis. 2 applicants were on the 2003 waiting list; 2 were admitted. Applications are accepted on-line through www.hendrix.edu/admission/application/online.htm.

Transfer: 34 transfer students enrolled in 2002-2003. Official transcripts from all colleges previously attended must be submitted. 16 of 32 courses required for the bachelor's degree must be completed at Hendrix.

Visiting: There are regularly scheduled orientations for prospective students, including attending a class, visits with students and faculty, a campus tour, and a luncheon with speakers. Students may also stay overnight in a residence hall. There are guides for informal visits and visitors may sit in on classes and stay overnight. To schedule a visit, contact the Office of Admission at adm@hendrix.edu.

Financial Aid: In 2003-2004, 98% of all full-time freshmen and 94% of continuing full-time students received some form of financial aid. 59% of full-time freshmen and 42% of continuing full-time students received need-based aid. The average freshman award was $12,417. Need-based scholarships or need-based grants averaged $3070 ($13,400 maximum); need-based self-help aid (loans and jobs) averaged $4420 ($8125 maximum); and non-need-based awards and non-need-based scholarships averaged $7562 ($24,058 maximum). 40% of undergraduates work part time. Average annual earnings from campus work are $1326. The average financial indebtedness of the 2003 graduate was $9807. Hendrix is a member of CSS. The FAFSA and the college's own financial statement are required. The deadline for filing freshman financial aid applications for fall entry is February 15.

International Students: There are 14 international students enrolled. The school actively recruits these students. They must score 550 on the written TOEFL or 223 on the electronic version.

Computers: The mainframe is a Windows NT server. There are computer labs utilizing 45 Macs and 47 PCs. In addition, all dorm rooms are wired for computer hookup. All students may access the system 24 hours a day, 7 days a week. There are no time limits and no fees.

Graduates: From July 1, 2002 to June 30, 2003, 207 bachelor's degrees were awarded. The most popular majors were biology (15%), psychology (14%), and economics and business/history (12%). In an average class, 2% graduate in 3 years or less, 55% graduate in 4 years or less, 66% graduate in 5 years or less, and 64% graduate in 6 years or less. 86 companies recruited on campus in 2002-2003. Of the 2002 graduating class, 40% were enrolled in graduate school within 6 months of graduation and 38% were employed.

Admissions Contact: Karen Foust, Vice President for Enrollment. E-mail: adm@hendrix.edu Web: www.hendrix.edu

JOHN BROWN UNIVERSITY
Siloam Springs, AR 72761

A-1
(501) 524-7190
(877) JBU-INFO; Fax: (479) 524-4196

Full-time: 655 men, 795 women	Faculty: 60; IIB, -$
Part-time: 55 men, 50 women	Ph.D.s: 73%
Graduate: 60 men, 80 women	Student/Faculty: 17 to 1
Year: semesters	Tuition: $10,605 ($12,375)
Application Deadline: see profile	Room & Board: $4480 ($4660)
Freshman Class: n/av	
SAT I or ACT: recommended	VERY COMPETITIVE

John Brown University, founded in 1919, is a private, nondenominational Christian institution offering undergraduate programs in arts and literature, Bible studies, business, communication, engineering and technology, general studies, health promotion and human performance, natural science, social studies, and teacher education. Figures in above capsule and this profile are approximate. In addition to regional accreditation, JBU has baccalaureate program accreditation with NCATE. The library contains 95,000 volumes, 30,000 microform items, and 3000 audio/video tapes/CDs, and subscribes to 450 periodicals. Computerized library services include interlibrary loans and database searching. Special learning facilities include a learning resource center, radio station, TV station, and a wellness assessment laboratory. The 200-acre campus is in a small town 80 miles east of Tulsa, Oklahoma. Including any residence halls, there are 15 buildings.

Student Life: 58% of undergraduates are from out of state, mostly the Southwest. Students are from 44 states, 35 foreign countries, and Canada. 88% are white; 10% foreign nationals. Most are Protestant. The average age of freshmen is 19; all undergraduates, 21. 24% do not continue beyond their first year; 45% remain to graduate.

Housing: 750 students can be accommodated in college housing, which includes single-sex dorms, on-campus apartments, off-campus apartments, and married-student housing. On-campus housing is guaranteed for the freshman year only. 75% of students live on campus; of those, 80% remain on campus on weekends. Alcohol is not permitted. All students may keep cars.

Activities: There are no fraternities or sororities. There are many groups and organizations on campus, including band, cheerleading, choir, chorale, chorus, drama, ethnic, honors, newspaper, pep band, photography, radio and TV, religious, student government, and yearbook. Popular campus events include Christmas Candlelight Service, Spiritual Emphasis Week, Welcome banquet, and Marriage and Family Emphasis Week.

Sports: There are 4 intercollegiate sports for men and 4 for women, and 8 intramural sports for men. Facilities include a 1500-seat gym, soccer and softball fields, a baseball diamond, a training room, and a swimming pool. The Lifetime Health Complex includes an indoor track, 4 racquetball courts, a Nautilus fitness center, an aerobics room, and a 3-court recreation center.

Disabled Students: 70% of the campus is accessible. Wheelchair ramps, elevators, special parking, specially equipped rest rooms, special class scheduling, lowered drinking fountains, and lowered telephones are available.

Services: Counseling and information services are available, as is tutoring in most subjects. There is remedial math, reading, and writing.

Campus Safety and Security: Measures include security escort services, informal discussions, and lighted pathways/sidewalks.

Programs of Study: JBU confers B.A., B.S., B.E., B.Mus.Ed., and B.S.E. degrees. Associate degrees are also awarded. Bachelor's degrees are awarded in BIOLOGICAL SCIENCE (biochemistry and biology/biological science), BUSINESS (accounting, business administration and management, and office supervision and management), COMMUNICATIONS AND THE ARTS (art, broadcasting, design, English, journalism, music, and public relations), COMPUTER AND PHYSICAL SCIENCE (chemistry, mathematics, and science), EDUCATION (business, early childhood, elementary, music, physical, science, and secondary), ENGINEERING AND ENVIRONMENTAL DESIGN (construction management, electrical/electronics engineering, and engineering), HEALTH PROFESSIONS (community health work, medical laboratory technology, and sports medicine), SOCIAL SCIENCE (biblical studies, crosscultural studies, family and community services, history, interdisciplinary studies, international studies, ministries, pastoral studies, prelaw, psychology, social studies, theological studies, and youth ministry). Engineering and teacher education are the strongest academically. Business, broadcasting, and psychology are the largest.

Required: All students must complete 12 hours in Bible studies, 9 hours in general education, 6 hours each in English and science, and 3 hours each in American history and humanities, as well as competencies in communication and quantitative skills, physical fitness concepts, and health and hygiene. A total of 124 semester hours, with a minimum GPA of 2.0 (2.25 in teacher education and engineering), is required in order to graduate.

Special: Internships or field experiences are available in most majors. Study abroad in 3 countries, a Washington semester, and pass/fail options are offered. There is 1 national honor society and a freshman honors program.

Faculty/Classroom: 70% of faculty are male; 30%, female. 94% teach undergraduates. The average class size in an introductory lecture is 40; in a laboratory, 25; and in a regular course, 30.

Requirements: The SAT I or ACT is recommended. In addition, applicants should have completed 14 high school units, including 4 in English, 3 in math, 2 each in science, history, and foreign language, and 1 in social studies. Two references are required: one from a high school counselor or teacher, the other from a pastor or church leader. An essay and an interview are recommended. Applicants 21 years of age or older may be admitted without ACT or SAT I scores. JBU requires applicants to be in the upper 50% of their class. A GPA of 2.5 is required. AP and CLEP credits are accepted. Important factors in the admissions decision are advanced placement or honor courses, leadership record, and evidence of special talent.

Procedure: Freshmen are admitted fall and spring. Entrance exams should be taken during the spring of the junior year or fall of the senior year. There is an early admissions plan and a rolling admissions plan. Check with the school for current deadlines. Notification is sent on a rolling basis. The fall 2003 application fee was $25. A waiting list is an active part of the admissions procedure.

Transfer: Transfer applicants must have completed at least 12 units of college work, with at least 9 transferable, and a minimum 2.0 GPA. 36 of 124 credits required for the bachelor's degree must be completed at JBU.

Visiting: There are regularly scheduled orientations for prospective students, including campus tours, consultations with faculty and coaches, and examination of financial aid opportunities. There are guides for informal visits and visitors may sit in on classes and stay overnight. To schedule a visit, contact the Admissions Office.

Financial Aid: In a recent year, 72% of all full-time freshmen and 81% of continuing full-time students received some form of financial aid. 47% of full-time freshmen and 44% of continuing full-time students received need-based aid. The average freshman award was $10,060. The average financial indebtedness of the 2003 graduate was $12,260. JBU is a member of CSS. The CSS Profile or FFS is required.

International Students: They must score 550 on the written TOEFL.

Computers: There are 80 IBM PCs and 20 Macintoshes in 4 computer rooms, and local area networks are available. All students may access the system from 7:30 A.M. to 10:30 P.M. daily. There are no time limits. The fee is $15 per semester.

Admissions Contact: Nate Mouttet, Director of Admissions. A video is available. E-mail: *jbuinfo@jbu.edu* Web: *www.jbu.edu*

LYON COLLEGE
Batesville, AR 72503-2317

C-2

(870) 698-4250
(800) 423-2542; Fax: (870) 793-1791

Full-time: 219 men, 232 women	**Faculty:** 44; IIB, -$
Part-time: 8 men, 13 women	**Ph.D.s:** 91%
Graduate: none	**Student/Faculty:** 10 to 1
Year: semesters, summer session	**Tuition:** $13,130
Application Deadline: August	**Room & Board:** $5920
Freshman Class: 427 applied, 309 accepted, 120 enrolled	
SAT I Verbal/Math: 560/550	**ACT:** 24 **VERY COMPETITIVE**

Lyon College, founded in 1872, is a selective, private, residential, liberal arts college affiliated with the Presbyterian Church (U.S.A.). In addition to regional accreditation, Lyon has baccalaureate program accreditation with NCATE. The library contains 158,392 volumes, 2921 microform items, and 5587 audio/video tapes/CDs, and subscribes to 1324 periodicals. Computerized library services include the card catalog, interlibrary loans, database searching, and Internet access. Special learning facilities include a learning resource center, language lab, and computer lab. The 136-acre campus is in a small town 90 miles north of Little Rock. Including any residence halls, there are 28 buildings.

Student Life: 86% of undergraduates are from Arkansas. Students are from 18 states, 15 foreign countries, and Canada. 85% are white. The average age of freshmen is 18; all undergraduates, 21. 20% do not continue beyond their first year; 52% remain to graduate.

Housing: 409 students can be accommodated in college housing, which includes single-sex dorms. On-campus housing is guaranteed for all 4 years. 78% of students live on campus; of those, 75% remain on campus on weekends. All students may keep cars.

Activities: 17% of men belong to 3 national fraternities; 28% of women belong to 2 national sororities. There are 48 groups on campus, including art, bagpipe band, band, cheerleading, choir, drama, ethnic, honors, international, literary magazine, newspaper, political, professional, religious, social, social service, student government, and yearbook. Popular campus events include LyonFest, Arkansas Scottish Festival, and Service Day.

Sports: There are 6 intercollegiate sports for men and 6 for women, and 25 intramural sports for men and 25 for women. Facilities include an 1100-seat gym, softball, baseball, and soccer fields, a cross-country trail, a swimming pool, 6 tennis courts, and a weight room.

Disabled Students: 80% of the campus is accessible. Wheelchair ramps, elevators, special parking, specially equipped rest rooms, and lowered drinking fountains are available.

Services: Counseling and information services are available, as is tutoring in some subjects, including foreign language. There are remedial math and writing. Writing and math labs are available.

Campus Safety and Security: Measures include 24-hour foot and vehicle patrol, security escort services, informal discussions, pamphlets/posters/films, and lighted pathways/sidewalks.

Programs of Study: Lyon confers B.A. and B.S. degrees. Bachelor's degrees are awarded in AGRICULTURE (environmental studies), BIOLOGICAL SCIENCE (biology/biological science), BUSINESS (accounting and business administration and management), COMMUNICATIONS AND THE ARTS (art, dramatic arts, English, music, and Spanish), COMPUTER AND PHYSICAL SCIENCE (chemistry, computer science, and mathematics), SOCIAL SCIENCE (economics, history,

political science/government, psychology, and religion). Biology, psychology, and business administration are the largest.

Required: All students are required to demonstrate proficiency in English composition, math, and foreign language; meet distribution requirements in social sciences, arts and literature, natural science and math, and religion and philosophy; take the 2-semester Western Tradition course sequence; complete the freshman orientation program; and take 1 semester of phys ed in each of the 4 years. A total of 120 credits, with a minimum GPA of 2.0, are required to graduate.

Special: Internships are offered and cross-registration (for certain courses) with the University of Arkansas Community College at Batesville and Ozarka College. A 2-2 engineering program is offered with the University of Missouri in Rolla, and a 3-2 program is offered with the University of Arkansas at Fayetteville. Work-study courses, study abroad in 4 countries, dual majors, student-designed majors, pass/fail options, and credit for military experience are available. There are 9 national honor societies.

Faculty/Classroom: 67% of faculty are male; 33%, female. All both teach and do research. The average class size in an introductory lecture is 18; in a laboratory, 13; and in a regular course, 14.

Admissions: 72% of the 2003-2004 applicants were accepted. 46% of the current freshmen were in the top fifth of their class; 82% were in the top two fifths. 9 freshmen graduated first in their class.

Requirements: The SAT I or ACT is required. In addition, applicants should have completed a minimum of 16 high school units, including 4 in English, 3 each in science and math, 3 in social sciences, and 2 in a foreign language. A letter of recommendation and an admission interview are recommended. AP credits are accepted.

Procedure: Freshmen are admitted fall and spring. Entrance exams should be taken in the spring of junior year and the fall of senior year. There is a rolling admissions plan and a deferred admissions plan. Applications should be filed by August for fall entry and January for spring entry. The fall 2003 application fee was $25. Notification is sent on a rolling basis. Applications are accepted on computer disk and on-line through the college's web site *www.lyon.edu/apply/applyonline.html.*

Transfer: 30 transfer students enrolled in 2002-2003. Transfer applicants with 24 or more semester hours must submit a transcript and statement of good standing from each institution attended. Students with fewer than 24 semester hours must submit their final high school transcript and ACT or SAT I scores. 24 of 120 credits required for the bachelor's degree must be completed at Lyon.

Visiting: There are regularly scheduled orientations for prospective students, consisting of a campus tour, admission and financial aid orientation, and information sessions with faculty and students. There are guides for informal visits and visitors may sit in on classes and stay overnight. To schedule a visit, contact the Admission Office.

Financial Aid: In 2003-2004, 93% of all full-time freshmen and 96% of continuing full-time students received some form of financial aid. 64% of full-time freshmen and 66% of continuing full-time students received need-based aid. The average freshman award was $13,728. Need-based scholarships or need-based grants averaged $11,078; need-based self-help aid (loans and jobs) averaged $3606; non-need-based athletic scholarships averaged $9348; and other non-need-based awards and non-need-based scholarships averaged $9625. 40% of undergraduates work part time. Average annual earnings from campus work are $1250. The average financial indebtedness of the 2003 graduate was $15,383. The FAFSA is required. The priority date for freshman financial aid applications for fall entry is March 1.

International Students: There are 19 international students enrolled. They must score 550 on the written TOEFL or 213 on the electronic version and also take the SAT I or the ACT.

Computers: The mainframe includes an IBM RISC 6000, 1 DEC Alpha, and several Intel-based NT servers. Students have access to campus information resources from 54 computers in classrooms, residence hall lounges, the Union, and the library. Students may also access these resources in residence hall rooms using their own PCs. Access to the Internet is available from any network access point with a user ID and password. All students may access the system. There are no time limits. The fee is $200.

Graduates: From July 1, 2002 to June 30, 2003, 128 bachelor's degrees were awarded. The most popular majors were business administration (13%), biology (13%), and psychology (10%). In an average class, 52% graduate in 4 years or less, 52% graduate in 5 years or less, and 52% graduate in 6 years or less. Of the 2002 graduating class, 29% were enrolled in graduate school within 6 months of graduation and 60% were employed.

Admissions Contact: Denny Bardos, Vice President for Enrollment Services. E-mail: *admissions@lyon.edu* Web: *www.lyon.edu*

OUACHITA BAPTIST UNIVERSITY
Arkadelphia, AR 71998-0001

B-4

(870) 245-5110
(800) 342-5628; Fax: (870) 245-5500

Full-time: 681 men, 814 women	**Faculty:** 111; IIB, -$
Part-time: 27 men, 16 women	**Ph.Ds:** 76%
Graduate: none	**Student/Faculty:** 13 to 1
Year: semesters, summer session	**Tuition:** $14,100
Application Deadline: open	**Room & Board:** $4800
Freshman Class: 879 applied, 704 accepted, 418 enrolled	
SAT I Verbal/Math: 560/590	**ACT:** 25 **VERY COMPETITIVE**

Ouachita Baptist University, founded in 1886, is a private liberal arts institution affiliated with the Arkansas Baptist State Convention. Some information in the above capsule is approximate. There are 7 undergraduate schools. In addition to regional accreditation, Ouachita has baccalaureate program accreditation with NASM and NCATE. The 2 libraries contain 117,517 volumes, 205,614 microform items, and 3159 audio/video tapes/CDs, and subscribe to 1067 periodicals. Computerized library services include the card catalog, interlibrary loans, and database searching. Special learning facilities include a learning resource center, art gallery, and planetarium. The 60-acre campus is in a small town 65 miles southwest of Little Rock. Including any residence halls, there are 33 buildings.

Student Life: 53% of undergraduates are from Arkansas. Students are from 32 states and 62 foreign countries. 95% are from public schools. 90% are white. Most are Protestant. The average age of freshmen is 18; all undergraduates, 21. 25% do not continue beyond their first year.

Housing: 1352 students can be accommodated in college housing, which includes single-sex dorms, on-campus apartments, off-campus apartments, and married-student housing. On-campus housing is guaranteed for the freshman year only and is available on a first-come, first-served basis. 90% of students live on campus; of those, 60% remain on campus on weekends. Alcohol is not permitted. All students may keep cars.

Activities: 30% of men belong to 5 local fraternities; 30% of women belong to 5 local sororities. There are 30 groups on campus, including band, cheerleading, choir, chorale, chorus, computers, debate, drama, drill team, ethnic, film, honors, international, jazz band, marching band, musical theater, newspaper, opera, orchestra, pep band, photography, political, professional, religious, social, social service, student government, and yearbook. Popular campus events include International Student Fair, Tiger Tunes, and Tiger Traks.

Sports: There are 9 intercollegiate sports for men and 5 for women, and 4 intramural sports for men and 3 for women. Facilities include a 6000-seat football stadium, an athletic complex featuring a 2500-seat basketball arena, a swimming pool, a weight room, and tennis, racquetball, and volleyball courts.

Disabled Students: 95% of the campus is accessible. Wheelchair ramps, elevators, special parking, specially equipped rest rooms, and special class scheduling are available.

Services: Counseling and information services are available, as is tutoring in most subjects. There is a reader service for the blind and remedial math, reading, and writing.

Campus Safety and Security: Measures include 24-hour foot and vehicle patrol, informal discussions, pamphlets/posters/films, and emergency telephones. There are lighted pathways/sidewalks.

Programs of Study: Ouachita confers B.A., B.S., B.M., B.M.E., and B.S.E. degrees. Associate degrees are also awarded. Bachelor's degrees are awarded in BIOLOGICAL SCIENCE (biology/biological science), BUSINESS (accounting, business administration and management, and business economics), COMMUNICATIONS AND THE ARTS (communications, dramatic arts, English, French, music, musical theater, Russian languages and literature, Spanish, and speech/debate/rhetoric), COMPUTER AND PHYSICAL SCIENCE (chemistry, computer science, mathematics, and physics), EDUCATION (art, business, early childhood, elementary, foreign languages, health, home economics, middle school, music, science, and secondary), HEALTH PROFESSIONS (medical laboratory technology, predentistry, premedicine, and speech pathology/audiology), SOCIAL SCIENCE (biblical studies, dietetics, economics, history, ministries, philosophy, political science/government, prelaw, psychology, religion, sociology, and theological studies). Education, business, and religion are the largest.

Required: All students must fulfill 44 semester hours of general education courses, including 2 semesters of 1 foreign language, 7 chapel credits, and 2 semester hours of phys ed. A total of 128 semester hours, with a minimum GPA of 2.0, is required for graduation.

Special: Ouachita offers cross-registration with Henderson State University, a Washington semester for political science majors, internships and co-op programs for business majors, B.A.-B.S. degrees, dual majors, pass/fail options, and nondegree study. Study-abroad opportunities are available in Germany, England, France, Italy, Russia, Japan, China, Hong Kong, Kazakhstan, Austria, Israel, Belize, and Morocco. There is a freshman honors program.

Faculty/Classroom: 73% of faculty are male; 27%, female. All teach undergraduates. The average class size in an introductory lecture is 30; in a laboratory, 11; and in a regular course, 13.

Admissions: 80% of the 2003-2004 applicants were accepted. The SAT I scores for the 2003-2004 freshman class were: Verbal--29% below 500, 39% between 500 and 599, 24% between 600 and 700, and 8% above 700; Math--26% below 500, 45% between 500 and 599, 22% between 600 and 700, and 7% above 700. The ACT scores were 23% below 21, 27% between 21 and 23, 26% between 24 and 26, 13% between 27 and 28, and 11% above 28. 53% of the current freshmen were in the top fifth of their class; 80% were in the top two fifths. There were 6 National Merit finalists and 25 freshmen graduated first in their class in a recent year.

Requirements: The SAT I or ACT is required. In addition, applicants should have completed 19 high school units, including 4 in English, 3 in social science, and 2 each in natural science and math; 2 in a foreign language and 1/2 in computer science are also recommended. A GPA of 2.75 is required. AP and CLEP credits are accepted.

Procedure: Freshmen are admitted to all sessions. Entrance exams should be taken in the junior year. There are early decision, early admissions, and deferred admissions plans. There is a rolling admissions plans. Application deadlines are open. Application fee is $25. 10 early decision candidates were accepted for the 2003-2004 class. Check with the school for current deadlines.

Transfer: 53 transfer students enrolled in a recent year. Applicants must be eligible to return to their previous school. 60 of 128 credits required for the bachelor's degree must be completed at Ouachita.

Visiting: There are regularly scheduled orientations for prospective students, including a campus tour, a question-and-answer session, and meetings with professors and students. There are guides for informal visits and visitors may sit in on classes and stay overnight. To schedule a visit, contact the Admissions Counseling Office at *jonesr@obu.edu.*

Financial Aid: In 2003-2004, 97% of all full-time freshmen and 94% of continuing full-time students received some form of financial aid. 32% of full-time freshmen and 35% of continuing full-time students received need-based aid. The average freshman award was $12,418. Need-based scholarships or need-based grants averaged $3630 ($7650 maximum); need-based self-help aid (loans and jobs) averaged $3815 ($14,000 maximum); non-need-based athletic scholarships averaged $8326 ($19,460 maximum); and other non-need-based awards and non-need-based scholarships averaged $4098 ($10,000 maximum). 52% of undergraduates work part time. Average annual earnings from campus work are $1500. The average financial indebtedness of a recent graduate was $6130. The FAFSA and the college's own financial statement are required.

International Students: There were 78 international students enrolled in a recent year. The school actively recruits these students. They must score 550 on the written TOEFL and also take the SAT I or the ACT, scoring 20.

Computers: The mainframe is an AS/400. There are 5 computer labs available to students. All academic departments have PCs. All students may access the system. There are no time limits and no fees.

Graduates: In a recent year, 312 bachelor's degrees were awarded. The most popular majors were education (20%), religion (14%), and business related (14%). In an average class, 30% graduate in 4 years or less, 45% graduate in 5 years or less, and 50% graduate in 6 years or less. 17 companies recruited on campus in a recent year. Of a recent graduating class, 10% were enrolled in graduate school within 6 months of graduation and 90% were employed.

Admissions Contact: David Goodman, Director of Admissions Counseling. E-mail: *admissions@alpha.obu.edu* Web: *www.obu.edu*

PHILANDER SMITH COLLEGE
Little Rock, AR 72202

C-3

(501) 370-5221
(800) 446-6772; Fax: (501) 370-5225

Full-time: 800 men and women	**Faculty:** 32
Part-time: 200 men and women	**Ph.Ds:** 20%
Graduate: none	**Student/Faculty:** 24 to 1
Year: semesters, summer session	**Tuition:** $4330
Application Deadline: see profile	**Room & Board:** $3050
Freshman Class: n/av	
ACT: required	**NONCOMPETITIVE**

Philander Smith College, founded in 1877, is affiliated with the United Methodist Church. The college offers undergraduate degrees in education, humanities, natural and physical sciences, business, and social science. Figures given in the above capsule and in this profile are approximate. The library contains 83,000 volumes, 170 microform items, and 60 audio/video tapes/CDs, and subscribes to 370 periodicals. Computerized library services include interlibrary loans. The 25-acre campus is in an urban area in Little Rock. There are 14 buildings.

Student Life: n/av

Housing: n/av

Programs of Study: PSC confers B.A., B.S., and B.A.M. degrees. Bachelor's degrees are awarded in BIOLOGICAL SCIENCE (biology/

biological science), BUSINESS (accounting, business administration and management, hospitality management services, and office supervision and management), COMMUNICATIONS AND THE ARTS (music), COMPUTER AND PHYSICAL SCIENCE (chemistry, computer science, and science), EDUCATION (business, early childhood, education administration, English, mathematics, physical, science, secondary, and special), SOCIAL SCIENCE (political science/government, psychology, social work, and sociology).

Required: To graduate, all students must complete at least 124 credit hours with a minimum 2.0 GPA and satisfy general education requirements, which include courses in speech, English composition, literature, philosophy and religion, physical and life science, math, computing, psychology, political science or sociology, economics, U.S. history, phys ed, and health.

Special: There are 2 national honor societies.

Requirements: The ACT is required. In addition, the SAT I is accepted. Applicants must be graduates of an accredited secondary school or have a GED certificate. A GPA of 2.0 is required for unconditional admission. Students should have completed 16 academic credits, including 4 units of English, 2 of math, and 2 from 2 of the following: foreign language, science, or social studies. AP and CLEP credits are accepted.

Procedure: There is an early admissions plan and a rolling admissions plan. Check with the school for current application deadlines. The fall 2003 application fee was $10.

Transfer: 22 of 32 credits required for the bachelor's degree must be completed at PSC.

Visiting: To schedule a visit, contact the Admissions Office.

Financial Aid: In a recent year, 90% of all full-time freshmen and 80% of continuing full-time students received some form of financial aid. PSC is a member of CSS. The FFS is required. Check with the school for current deadlines.

International Students: They must score 500 on the written TOEFL or 213 on the electronic version or take IELP, or present an ESL certificate and also take the ACT.

Computers: There are no time limits and no fees.

Admissions Contact: Office of Admissions.
Web: *www.philander.edu*

SOUTHERN ARKANSAS UNIVERSITY
Magnolia, AR 71754

B-5

(870) 235-4040
(800) 332-SAUM; Fax: (870) 235-4931

Full-time: 1123 men, 1326 women	**Faculty:** 136; IIB, -$
Part-time: 97 men, 258 women	**Ph.D.s:** 54%
Graduate: 39 men, 165 women	**Student/Faculty:** 18 to 1
Year: semesters, summer session	**Tuition:** $3496 ($5186)
Application Deadline: open	**Room & Board:** $3460
Freshman Class: 1155 applied, 939 accepted, 565 enrolled	
SAT I: n/av	**ACT:** required **COMPETITIVE**

Southern Arkansas University, founded in 1909, is a state-supported liberal arts institution offering degrees in business administration, education, liberal and performing arts, and science and technology. There are 4 undergraduate schools and 1 graduate school. In addition to regional accreditation, SAU has baccalaureate program accreditation with CSWE, NASAD, NASM, NCATE, and NLN. The library contains 150,341 volumes, 669,721 microform items, and 12,214 audio/video tapes/CDs, and subscribes to 725 periodicals. Computerized library services include the card catalog, interlibrary loans, database searching, and Internet access. Special learning facilities include a learning resource center, art gallery, radio station, biological field station, and university farm. The 781-acre campus is in a small town. Including any residence halls, there are 27 buildings.

Student Life: 71% of undergraduates are from Arkansas. Students are from 22 states, 40 foreign countries, and Canada. 97% are from public schools. 69% are white; 24% African American. The average age of freshmen is 18; all undergraduates, 28. 32% do not continue beyond their first year.

Housing: 1043 students can be accommodated in college housing, which includes single-sex and coed dorms. In addition, there are honors houses and an international house. On-campus housing is guaranteed for all 4 years. 66% of students commute. Alcohol is not permitted. All students may keep cars.

Activities: 10% of men belong to 7 national fraternities; 13% of women belong to 7 national sororities. There are 78 groups on campus, including art, band, cheerleading, choir, chorale, computers, dance, drama, drill team, ethnic, honors, international, jazz band, literary magazine, marching band, musical theater, newspaper, pep band, photography, political, professional, radio and TV, religious, social, student government, and yearbook. Popular campus events include Spring Fling and Celebration of Lights (Christmas).

Sports: There are 6 intercollegiate sports for men and 6 for women, and 15 intramural sports for men and 15 for women. Facilities include a 6500-seat stadium, a 1450-seat gym, 10 lighted tennis courts, baseball and softball fields, a track, an indoor pool, a dance studio, a multipurpose building with basketball and volleyball courts, and a wellness center.

Disabled Students: 95% of the campus is accessible. Wheelchair ramps, elevators, special parking, specially equipped rest rooms, special class scheduling, lowered drinking fountains, lowered telephones, and automatic doors are available.

Services: Counseling and information services are available, as is tutoring in most subjects. There is remedial math, reading, and writing, and supplemental instruction in courses with high drop/failure rates.

Campus Safety and Security: Measures include 24-hour foot and vehicle patrol, security escort services, informal discussions, and pamphlets/posters/films. There are emergency telephones and lighted pathways/sidewalks.

Programs of Study: SAU confers B.A., B.S., B.A.S., B.B.A., B.M.E., B.S.E., and B.S.W. degrees. Associate and master's degrees are also awarded. Bachelor's degrees are awarded in AGRICULTURE (agricultural business management and agriculture), BIOLOGICAL SCIENCE (biology/biological science), BUSINESS (accounting and business administration and management), COMMUNICATIONS AND THE ARTS (art, broadcasting, communications, English, journalism, and Spanish), COMPUTER AND PHYSICAL SCIENCE (chemistry, computer science, and mathematics), EDUCATION (agricultural, art, business, elementary, health, middle school, music, and science), ENGINEERING AND ENVIRONMENTAL DESIGN (manufacturing technology), HEALTH PROFESSIONS (medical laboratory technology), SOCIAL SCIENCE (community services, history, political science/government, psychology, and sociology). Accounting and physical science are the strongest academically. Business administration and health education/kinesiology are the largest.

Required: All students must complete 43 semester hours of general education courses, including 18 in humanities, 12 in social sciences, 4 each in biological and physical science, 3 in math, and 2 to 3 in physical and health education. A minimum of 124 total semester hours, with a minimum GPA of 2.0, is required to graduate.

Special: Work-study programs at SAU, business and Spanish internships, study abroad in Russia, and a general studies degree are offered. There is 1 national honor society, a freshman honors program, and 6 departmental honors programs.

Faculty/Classroom: 54% of faculty are male; 46%, female. 94% teach undergraduates, 10% do research, and 10% do both. No introductory courses are taught by graduate students. The average class size in an introductory lecture is 35; in a laboratory, 25; and in a regular course, 20.

Admissions: 81% of the 2003-2004 applicants were accepted. The ACT scores for the 2003-2004 freshman class were: 57% below 21, 22% between 21 and 23, 15% between 24 and 26, 4% between 27 and 28, and 2% above 28.

Requirements: The ACT is required, with a minimum composite of 19. Applicants should have completed 4 high school units in English, 3 each in math and social studies, and 2 each in natural science and a foreign language. The GED is accepted. AP and CLEP credits are accepted.

Procedure: Freshmen are admitted to all sessions. Entrance exams should be taken in the fall prior to enrollment. There is a rolling admissions plan and a deferred admissions plan. Application deadlines are open. Applications are accepted on-line through the university's web site *www.saumag.edu*.

Transfer: 208 transfer students enrolled in 2002-2003. Applicants must be eligible to return to their previous school and meet GPA requirements. Those with fewer than 24 credit hours must submit ACT or SAT I scores and a high school transcript or GED. 30 of 124 credits required for the bachelor's degree must be completed at SAU.

Visiting: There are regularly scheduled orientations for prospective students. There are guides for informal visits and visitors may sit in on classes and stay overnight. To schedule a visit, contact the Admissions Office at *muleriders@saumag.edu*.

Financial Aid: In 2003-2004, 75% of all full-time freshmen and 79% of continuing full-time students received some form of financial aid. 74% of full-time freshmen and 76% of continuing full-time students received need-based aid. The average freshman award was $3498. Need-based scholarships or need-based grants averaged $3472 ($6050 maximum); need-based self-help aid (loans and jobs) averaged $3440 ($5325 maximum); non-need-based athletic scholarships averaged $3590 ($7040 maximum); and other non-need-based awards and non-need-based scholarships averaged $5406 ($7710 maximum). 49% of undergraduates work part time. Average annual earnings from campus work are $2116. The average financial indebtedness of the 2003 graduate was $16,281. The FAFSA is required. The priority date for freshman financial aid applications for fall entry is July 1.

International Students: There are 125 international students enrolled. The school actively recruits these students. They must score 500 on the written TOEFL or 173 on the electronic version and also take the SAT I or the ACT.

Computers: Computer resources are located in the library, 3 computer labs, and 3 computer classrooms. All students may access the system. There are no time limits and no fees.

Graduates: From July 1, 2002 to June 30, 2003, 335 bachelor's degrees were awarded. The most popular majors were business administration (27%), elementary teacher education (8%), and agricultural business management (7%). In an average class, 1% graduate in 3 years or less, 10% graduate in 4 years or less, 11% graduate in 5 years or less, and 28% graduate in 6 years or less.

Admissions Contact: Sarah Jennings, Dean of Enrollment Services. E-mail: *sejennings@saumag.edu* Web: *www.saumag.edu*

UNIVERSITY OF ARKANSAS SYSTEM

The University of Arkansas System, established in 1871, is a system in Arkansas. It is governed by a board of trustees, whose chief administrator is president. The primary goal of the system is teaching, research, and public service. The total enrollment of all 5 campuses is usually about 32,071; there were 2334 faculty members. Altogether there are some 236 baccalaureate, 112 master's, and 30 doctoral programs offered in University of Arkansas System. Profiles of the 4-year campuses are included in this section.

UNIVERSITY OF ARKANSAS
Fayetteville, AR 72701

A-1

(479) 575-5346
(800) 377-8632; Fax: (479) 575-7515

Full-time: 5637 men, 5400 women	**Faculty:** 765; I, --$
Part-time: 1015 men, 1031 women	**Ph.D.s:** 92%
Graduate: 1721 men, 1601 women	**Student/Faculty:** 14 to 1
Year: semesters, summer session	**Tuition:** $4768 ($11,518)
Application Deadline: August 15	**Room & Board:** $5087
Freshman Class: 4919 applied, 4661 accepted, 2357 enrolled	
SAT I Verbal/Math: 580/590	**ACT:** 24 **VERY COMPETITIVE**

The University of Arkansas, founded in 1871, is a land-grant institution offering undergraduate and graduate programs in liberal arts and sciences, agricultural, food, social and natural sciences, life sciences, business administration, engineering, architecture, education, law, and human environmental sciences. There are 8 undergraduate and 2 graduate schools. In addition to regional accreditation, U of A has baccalaureate program accreditation with AACSB, ABET, ACEJMC, ADA, ASLA, CSWE, FIDER, NAAB, NASM, NCATE, and NLN. The 5 libraries contain 1,689,976 volumes, 3,336,025 microform items, and 24,776 audio/video tapes/CDs, and subscribe to 11,461 periodicals. Computerized library services include the card catalog, interlibrary loans, and database searching. Special learning facilities include an art gallery, natural history museum, planetarium, radio station, TV station, and numerous research centers. The 357-acre campus is in an urban area 190 miles northwest of Little Rock. Including any residence halls, there are 187 buildings.

Student Life: 88% of undergraduates are from Arkansas. Students are from 47 states, 109 foreign countries, and Canada. 95% are from public schools. 83% are white. The average age of freshmen is 18; all undergraduates, 22. 17% do not continue beyond their first year.

Housing: 3830 students can be accommodated in college housing, which includes single-sex and coed dorms, on-campus apartments, and married-student housing. In addition, there are honors and special-interest floors, apartments for students with dependent children, and a First-year Experience Program area. On-campus housing is guaranteed for the freshman year only and is available on a first-come, first-served basis. All students may keep cars.

Activities: 14% of men belong to 15 national fraternities; 19% of women belong to 12 national sororities. There are 273 groups on campus, including art, band, cheerleading, chess, choir, chorale, chorus, computers, dance, debate, drama, drill team, ethnic, film, gay, honors, international, jazz band, literary magazine, marching band, musical theater, newspaper, opera, orchestra, pep band, photography, political, professional, radio and TV, religious, social, social service, student government, symphony, and yearbook. Popular campus events include Academic Festival, Native American Pow Wow, and Martin Luther King, Jr. Event.

Sports: There are 8 intercollegiate sports for men and 11 for women, and 51 intramural sports for men and 51 for women. Facilities include a 72,000-seat stadium, a 20,000-seat basketball arena, a 3300-seat baseball stadium, a 9000-seat volleyball arena, a 1500-seat soccer stadium, a 1500-seat softball stadium, a 3000-seat indoor running-track, 4 gyms, indoor and outdoor jogging tracks, 2 dance studios, 10 racquetball courts, a fitness and weight training center, a swimming pool, an outdoor recreation center, 20 outdoor and 6 indoor tennis courts, 10 multipurpose playing fields, an indoor practice football field, and a gym/weight training and conditioning facility.

Disabled Students: All of the campus is accessible. Wheelchair ramps, elevators, special parking, specially equipped rest rooms, special class scheduling, lowered drinking fountains, lowered telephones, and automatic doors on entrances to buildings are available.

Services: Counseling and information services are available, as is tutoring in some subjects. There is a reader service for the blind, remedial

math, reading, and writing, a math resource center, a writing center, and Student Support Services. Individual colleges have labs and other facilities.

Campus Safety and Security: Measures include 24-hour foot and vehicle patrol, self-defense education, security escort services, and shuttle buses. There are informal discussions, pamphlets/posters/films, emergency telephones, lighted pathways/sidewalks, crime prevention lectures, a rape defense program, property engraving, bicycle patrol, and electronic card access in residence halls.

Programs of Study: U of A confers B.A., B.S., B.Arch., B.I.D., B.L.A., B.M., B.S.A., B.S.B.A., B.S.B.A.E., B.S.C.E., B.S.Ch.E., B.S.C.S.E, B.S.E., B.S.E.E., B.S.E.M., B.S.H.E.S., B.S.I.B., B.S.I.E., B.S.I.M., B.S.M.E., B.S.N., and B.S.P.A. degrees. Master's and doctoral degrees are also awarded. Bachelor's degrees are awarded in AGRICULTURE (agricultural business management, agricultural economics, animal science, horticulture, plant protection (pest management), and poultry science), BIOLOGICAL SCIENCE (biology/biological science, botany, microbiology, nutrition, and zoology), BUSINESS (accounting, apparel and accessories marketing, banking and finance, business administration and management, business economics, international business management, marketing management, marketing/retailing/merchandising, and transportation management), COMMUNICATIONS AND THE ARTS (art, classics, communications, dramatic arts, English, French, German, journalism, music, and Spanish), COMPUTER AND PHYSICAL SCIENCE (chemistry, computer science, earth science, geology, mathematics, and physics), EDUCATION (agricultural, early childhood, elementary, middle school, music, recreation, special, and vocational), ENGINEERING AND ENVIRONMENTAL DESIGN (agricultural engineering, architecture, bioengineering, chemical engineering, civil engineering, computer engineering, electrical/electronics engineering, environmental science, industrial engineering, interior design, landscape architecture/design, and mechanical engineering), HEALTH PROFESSIONS (exercise science, health science, medical science, nursing, predentistry, premedicine, preoptometry, prepharmacy, prepodiatry, and speech pathology/audiology), SOCIAL SCIENCE (American studies, anthropology, criminal justice, economics, food science, geography, history, human development, international relations, Middle Eastern studies, philosophy, political science/government, prelaw, psychology, public administration, social work, and sociology). Business, chemical and electrical engineering, and computer science are the strongest academically. Childhood education, accounting, and kinesiology are the largest.

Required: To graduate, all students must complete 35 hours of general education courses, including 9 in social sciences, 8 in science, 6 in English, and 3 each in fine arts, math, humanities, and history/government. No more than 25% of the minimum total of 124 hours may be D or below.

Special: Co-op programs and internships are available, as well as dual majors and B.A.-B.S. degrees in many majors, and study abroad in 16 countries. There are 3-2 engineering degrees with several universities, a combined medical/dental degree, and a 6-year B.S./J.D. degree for highly qualified students. Nondegree study is possible. There are 60 national honor societies, including Phi Beta Kappa, a freshman honors program, and 30 departmental honors programs.

Faculty/Classroom: 68% of faculty are male; 32%, female. 96% teach undergraduates. The average class size in an introductory lecture is 38; in a laboratory, 18; and in a regular course, 29.

Admissions: 95% of the 2003-2004 applicants were accepted. The SAT I scores for the 2003-2004 freshman class were: Verbal--16% below 500, 38% between 500 and 599, 37% between 600 and 700, and 9% above 700; Math--17% below 500, 34% between 500 and 599, 39% between 600 and 700, and 10% above 700. The ACT scores were 17% below 21, 25% between 21 and 23, 25% between 24 and 26, 13% between 27 and 28, and 20% above 28. 57% of the current freshmen were in the top fifth of their class; 80% were in the top two fifths. There were 29 National Merit finalists and 23 semifinalists. 177 freshmen graduated first in their class.

Requirements: The SAT I or ACT is required. U of A recommends 4 years each of English and math and 3 years each of social science and natural science. AP and honors level courses will enhance the applicant's opportunity for admission. A GPA of 3.0 is required. AP and CLEP credits are accepted. Important factors in the admissions decision are advanced placement or honor courses, leadership record, and evidence of special talent.

Procedure: Freshmen are admitted fall, spring, and summer. Entrance exams should be taken in the junior year or in October or December of the senior year. There are early admissions and deferred admissions plans. There is a rolling admissions plan. Early decision applications should be filed by February 15; regular applications, by August 15 for fall entry and January 1 for spring entry. The fall 2003 application fee was $30. Notification is sent on a rolling basis. Applications are accepted on computer disk and on-line.

Transfer: 1264 transfer students enrolled in 2002-2003. Applicants must present a GPA of 2.0 on all college course work attempted and be in good standing at the last institution attended. Those with fewer than 24 transferable semester credits must meet the requirements of entering freshmen. 30 credits of 124 required for the bachelor's degree must be completed at U of A.

Visiting: There are regularly scheduled orientations for prospective students, consisting of individual or group campus tours, meetings with an academic adviser, residence hall tours, and a meeting with an admissions counselor. Appointments are recommended, but not required. There are guides for informal visits and visitors may sit in on classes. To schedule a visit, contact the Admissions Office at *jreimer@uark.edu*.

Financial Aid: In 2003-2004, 78% of all full-time freshmen and 71% of continuing full-time students received some form of financial aid. 28% of full-time freshmen and 40% of continuing full-time students received need-based aid. The average freshman award was $7171. Need-based scholarships or need-based grants averaged $3282 ($8150 maximum); need-based self-help aid (loans and jobs) averaged $3337 ($8625 maximum); non-need-based athletic scholarships averaged $7834 ($12,241 maximum); and other non-need-based awards and non-need-based scholarships averaged $5860 ($19,525 maximum). 4% of undergraduates work part time. Average annual earnings from campus work are $1887. The average financial indebtedness of the 2003 graduate was $8337. U of A is a member of CSS. The FAFSA is required. The deadline for filing freshman financial aid applications for fall entry is March 1.

International Students: There are 340 international students enrolled. The school actively recruits these students. They must score 550 on the written TOEFL or 213 on the electronic version. Electrical engineering and computer systems engineering require a composite score of 1000 on the SAT I or 25 on the ACT, and a score of 5 on the TSE.

Computers: The mainframe is an IBM 9672 with a Sun Enterprise 5000. More than 600 Macs and PCs are available for academic use in student labs and in the computer center. E-mail and access to the Internet is available to all students. Networked servers provide access to word processing, spreadsheet, database, graphics, and statistical package applications. Dial-up password resets are available through a web interface. All students may access the system 24 hours daily. There are no time limits and no fees. It is recommended that students in architecture have personal computers.

Graduates: From July 1, 2002 to June 30, 2003, 2291 bachelor's degrees were awarded. The most popular majors were marketing and transportation (7%), finance (7%), and curriculum and instruction (4%). In an average class, 23% graduate in 4 years or less, 19% graduate in 5 years or less, and 49% graduate in 6 years or less. 200 companies recruited on campus in 2002-2003. Of the 2002 graduating class, 25% were enrolled in graduate school within 6 months of graduation and 40% were employed.

Admissions Contact: Dawn Medley, Director. A video is available. E-mail: *uafadmis@uark.edu* Web: *http://www.uark.edu*

UNIVERSITY OF ARKANSAS AT LITTLE ROCK

Little Rock, AR 72204-1099

C-3

(501) 569-3492
(800) 482-8892; Fax: (501) 569-8956

Full-time: 2140 men, 3310 women	**Faculty:** IIA, -$
Part-time: 1350 men, 2390 women	**Ph.D.s:** 45%
Graduate: 505 men, 1255 women	**Student/Faculty:** n/av
Year: semesters, summer session	**Tuition:** $3040 ($6295)
Application Deadline: open	**Room & Board:** $2600
Freshman Class: n/av	
SAT I or ACT: required	**NONCOMPETITIVE**

The University of Arkansas at Little Rock began in 1927 as Little Rock Junior College, took the name of Little Rock University in 1957, and joined the University of Arkansas system in 1969. There are 5 undergraduate and 2 graduate schools. Figures in the above capsule and in this profile are approximate. In addition to regional accreditation, UALR has baccalaureate program accreditation with AACSB, ABET, ACEJMC, ASLA, CSWE, NASAD, NASM, NCATE, and NLN. The library contains 394,780 volumes, 691,612 microform items, and 8300 audio/video tapes/CDs, and subscribes to 2626 periodicals. Computerized library services include the card catalog, interlibrary loans, and database searching. Special learning facilities include a learning resource center, art gallery, planetarium, radio station, TV station, and a speech and hearing clinic. The 150-acre campus is in an urban area in Little Rock. Including any residence halls, there are 38 buildings.

Student Life: 93% of undergraduates are from Arkansas. Students are from 44 states, 62 foreign countries, and Canada. 70% are white; 24% African American. The average age of freshmen is 19; all undergraduates, 26. 41% do not continue beyond their first year.

Housing: 306 students can be accommodated in college housing, which includes coed dorms, on-campus apartments, and university-owned rental houses. On-campus housing is available on a first-come, first-served basis. 97% of students commute. Alcohol is not permitted. All students may keep cars.

Activities: 5% of men belong to 6 national fraternities; 3% of women belong to 6 national sororities. There are 75 groups on campus, including cheerleading, chess, chorale, dance, drama, honors, jazz band, literary magazine, musical theater, newspaper, opera, pep band, political,

professional, radio and TV, religious, social service, and student government. Popular campus events include International Week, Sunshine Days, and Art Spree.

Sports: There are 6 intercollegiate sports for men and 7 for women, and 18 intramural sports for men and 18 for women. Facilities include a 2000-seat gym, a swimming pool, tennis courts, baseball and intramural fields, a horseshoe pit, a bowling alley, a fitness and weight room, an indoor jogging track, basketball, volleyball, and racquetball courts, a steam room, and a sauna.

Disabled Students: 85% of the campus is accessible. Wheelchair ramps, elevators, special parking, specially equipped rest rooms, special class scheduling, lowered drinking fountains, and study rooms are available.

Services: Counseling and information services are available, as is tutoring in every subject. There is a reader service for the blind and remedial math, reading, and writing. Also available are a braille dictionary, typewriter, reading machine, and interpreters.

Campus Safety and Security: Measures include 24-hour foot and vehicle patrol, self-defense education, security escort services, and informal discussions. There are emergency telephones, lighted pathways/sidewalks, emergency phones, and a student patrol crime prevention unit.

Programs of Study: UALR confers B.A., B.S., B.B.A., and B.S.W. degrees. Associate, master's, and doctoral degrees are also awarded. Bachelor's degrees are awarded in BIOLOGICAL SCIENCE (biology/biological science), BUSINESS (accounting, banking and finance, business administration and management, management science, and marketing/retailing/merchandising), COMMUNICATIONS AND THE ARTS (advertising, art, art history and appreciation, dramatic arts, English, French, journalism, music, radio/television technology, Spanish, technical and business writing, and visual and performing arts), COMPUTER AND PHYSICAL SCIENCE (chemistry, computer science, geology, information sciences and systems, mathematics, and physics), EDUCATION (early childhood, education of the deaf and hearing impaired, elementary, and health), ENGINEERING AND ENVIRONMENTAL DESIGN (computer technology, construction technology, electrical/electronics engineering technology, industrial administration/management, manufacturing engineering, mechanical engineering technology, and surveying engineering), HEALTH PROFESSIONS (environmental health science, health science, and speech pathology/audiology), SOCIAL SCIENCE (criminal justice, economics, history, international studies, interpreter for the deaf, liberal arts/general studies, philosophy, political science/government, psychology, and sociology). Psychology, biology, and liberal arts are the largest.

Required: All students must complete a minimum of 124 credit hours, including 45 at the upper level, while maintaining a GPA of 2.0. A minimum 44-hour core curriculum must be completed, and distribution requirements include freshman composition, speech and history, 3 hours of math, and 2 hours of leisure science. Each student must complete a major and a minor or a double major. There also is an exam in written English. Language proficiency is required for the B.A. degree.

Special: Study abroad in Mexico, France, Spain, and Austria is available; UALR has exchange relationships with more than 30 countries. In addition, internships, work-study programs with the university, cross-registration with the University of Arkansas Medical School, B.A.-B.S. degrees, a general studies degree, student-designed majors, nondegree study, and pass/fail options are offered. There are 3 national honor societies, including Phi Beta Kappa, a freshman honors program, and 5 departmental honors programs.

Faculty/Classroom: 53% of faculty are male; 47%, female.

Requirements: The SAT I or ACT is required. In addition, 2 or more of the following criteria must be met: a high school GPA of at least 2.5 or a passing GED test score; an ACT composite score of at least 21 or a combined verbal/math SAT I score of 990 taken within the past 5 years; completion of a college preparatory core in high school that includes 4 units of English, 3 each of math and social studies, and 2 each of natural science and a single foreign language. Students with test subscores below the state minimum requirement will be placed in the appropriate development courses. A GPA of 2.5 is required. AP and CLEP credits are accepted.

Procedure: Freshmen are admitted to all sessions. Entrance exams should be taken during the fall of the senior year. There are early admissions, deferred admissions, and rolling admissions plans. Application deadlines are open.

Transfer: 939 transfer students enrolled in 2002-2003. Applicants must have a minimum college GPA of 2.0. They must submit official transcripts from each college previously attended. Students who have 12 or fewer acceptable transfer credits must meet all the admission requirements for entering freshmen. 30 of 124 credits required for the bachelor's degree must be completed at UALR.

Visiting: There are regularly scheduled orientations for prospective students, which take place before each semester and at which attendance is required. There are guides for informal visits and visitors may sit in on classes. To schedule a visit, contact the Admissions Office.

Financial Aid: In a recent year, 65% of all full-time freshmen received some form of financial aid. 4% of undergraduates work part time. Average annual earnings from campus work are $1400. The FAFSA is required. Check with the school for current deadlines.

International Students: There were 387 international students enrolled in a recent year. They must score 525 on the written TOEFL and also take the college's own test and the Test of Written English (TWE), with a score of at least 4 points.

Computers: The mainframe is a DEC VAX 11/780. About 750 PCs and computer terminals are available for student use and are located throughout the campus. Students have access to e-mail, FTP, Telnet, Gopher, and World Wide Web. All students may access the system 24 hours daily. There are no time limits and no fees.

Graduates: In a recent year, 978 bachelor's degrees were awarded.

Admissions Contact: John Noah, Director.

Web: *www.ualr.edu/~adminfo/*

UNIVERSITY OF ARKANSAS AT MONTICELLO C-4
Monticello, AR 71656-3596 (870) 460-1026
(800) 844-1826; Fax: (870) 460-1933

Full-time: 840 men, 1000 women	**Faculty:** 116
Part-time: 100 men, 190 women	**Ph.D.s:** 60%
Graduate: 50 men, 90 women	**Student/Faculty:** 16 to 1
Year: semesters, summer session	**Tuition:** $2950 ($6040)
Application Deadline: open	**Room & Board:** $2990
Freshman Class: n/av	
SAT I or ACT: required	**NONCOMPETITIVE**

The University of Arkansas at Monticello was established in 1909 as the Fourth District Agricultural School. Made part of the public University of Arkansas System in 1971, UAM offers liberal arts undergraduate courses and graduate programs. Figures in the above capsule and in this profile are approximate. There are 6 undergraduate and 2 graduate schools. In addition to regional accreditation, UAM has baccalaureate program accreditation with NASM, NCATE, NLN, and SAF. The library contains 146,000 volumes, 221,000 microform items, and 640 audio/video tapes/CDs, and subscribes to 1140 periodicals. Computerized library services include the card catalog, interlibrary loans, and database searching. Special learning facilities include a learning resource center, natural history museum, planetarium, a university forest, and a university farm. The 1556-acre campus is in a small town 90 miles south of Little Rock. Including any residence halls, there are 37 buildings.

Student Life: 90% of undergraduates are from Arkansas. Students are from 20 states and 3 foreign countries. 99% are from public schools. 75% are white; 20% African American. The average age of freshmen is 19; all undergraduates, 23. 44% do not continue beyond their first year; 26% remain to graduate.

Housing: 600 students can be accommodated in college housing, which includes single-sex dorms, on-campus apartments, and married-student housing. On-campus housing is guaranteed for all 4 years. 75% of students commute. Alcohol is not permitted. All students may keep cars.

Activities: 10% of men belong to 6 national fraternities; 9% of women belong to 5 national sororities. There are 56 groups on campus, including art, band, cheerleading, chess, choir, chorus, debate, ethnic, honors, jazz band, literary magazine, marching band, musical theater, newspaper, pep band, political, professional, religious, social, social service, and student government. Popular campus events include Forestry Festival, Special Olympics, and All-Campus Talent Show.

Sports: There are 5 intercollegiate sports for men and 5 for women, and 6 intramural sports for men and 6 for women. Facilities include a 4000-seat stadium, a 2500-seat gym, a swimming pool, tennis and racquetball courts, and facilities for numerous intramural sports.

Disabled Students: All of the campus is accessible. Wheelchair ramps, elevators, special parking, specially equipped rest rooms, special class scheduling, lowered drinking fountains, lowered telephones, extended test times, books on tape, note takers, quiet test facilites, and word processing assistance are available.

Services: Counseling and information services are available, as is tutoring in some subjects, including general education. There is a reader service for the blind and remedial math, reading, and writing.

Campus Safety and Security: Measures include 24-hour foot and vehicle patrol, informal discussions, pamphlets/posters/films, and emergency telephones. There are lighted pathways/sidewalks.

Programs of Study: UAM confers B.A., B.S., B.B.A., B.M.Ed., and B.S.N. degrees. Associate and master's degrees are also awarded. Bachelor's degrees are awarded in AGRICULTURE (agriculture, forestry and related sciences, and wildlife management), BIOLOGICAL SCIENCE (biology/biological science), BUSINESS (accounting, business administration and management, and management information systems), COMMUNICATIONS AND THE ARTS (art, English, music, and speech/debate/rhetoric), COMPUTER AND PHYSICAL SCIENCE (chemistry, geodetic science, mathematics, and physical sciences), EDUCATION (business, elementary, health, music, physical, and special), HEALTH PROFESSIONS (nursing), SOCIAL SCIENCE (criminal justice, history, political science/government, psychology, and social work). Forestry and sciences are the strongest academically. Business administration, elementary education, and computer information systems are the largest.

Required: All students are required to complete 124 total semester hours, approximately 30 within their major, and maintain a minimum GPA of 2.0 (2.75 in education). Distribution requirements include 11 hours in basic sciences, 6 hours each in composition and humanities, and 3 hours each in fine arts, speech, U.S. history or government, psychology or sociology, social science, and math.

Special: A work-study program in forestry, a general studies degree, cross-registration within the University of Arkansas system, credit for military experience, dual majors, and nondegree study are available. There is 1 national honor society and a freshman honors program.

Faculty/Classroom: 65% of faculty are male; 35%, female. All teach undergraduates and 11% do research. No introductory courses are taught by graduate students. The average class size in an introductory lecture is 27; in a laboratory, 15; and in a regular course, 20.

Requirements: The SAT I or ACT is required. In addition, a high school diploma or GED is required. The Arkansas high school core curriculum is recommended. State law requires proof of immunization. AP and CLEP credits are accepted.

Procedure: Freshmen are admitted to all sessions. Entrance exams should be taken by December of the senior year. Application deadlines are open. There is a rolling admissions plan. Applications are accepted on-line at the university's web site.

Transfer: Transfer students must be in good academic standing at the previous college. ACT or SAT I test scores are required only if the student has not successfully completed Freshman Composition I and College Algebra. 30 of 124 credits required for the bachelor's degree must be completed at UAM.

Visiting: There are regularly scheduled orientations for prospective students, a review of admission requirements and financial aid opportunities and a visit to academic departments and faculty in the field of interest. There are guides for informal visits and visitors may sit in on classes and stay overnight. To schedule a visit, contact the Office of Admissions.

Financial Aid: UAM is a member of CSS. The FAFSA is required. Check with the school for current deadlines.

International Students: They must score 500 on the written TOEFL or 173 on the electronic version and also take the SAT I or the ACT.

Computers: The mainframe is a DEC Alpha DS20. There are approximately 275 PCs in public computer labs for students use. Residence halls are wired for network access. All campus computers have access to the campus network and the Internet. All students are eligible for e-mail accounts and have web access to their grades, financial aid, and demographic information. All students may access the system. There are no time limits and no fees. It is strongly recommended that all students have a personal computer.

Admissions Contact: Mary Whiting, Director of Admissions. A video is available. E-mail: *whitingm@uamont.edu* Web: *www.uamont.edu*

UNIVERSITY OF ARKANSAS AT PINE BLUFF C-4
Pine Bluff, AR 71601-2799 (870) 575-8492
(800) 264-6585; Fax: (870) 543-8014

Full-time: 1235 men, 1495 women	**Faculty:** 171; IIB, --$
Part-time: 125 men, 200 women	**Ph.D.s:** 57%
Graduate: 25 men, 70 women	**Student/Faculty:** 16 to 1
Year: semesters, summer session	**Tuition:** $3210 ($6510)
Application Deadline: open	**Room & Board:** $4720
Freshman Class: n/av	
SAT I or ACT: required	**COMPETITIVE**

The University of Arkansas at Pine Bluff, established in 1873, is a historically black land-grant institution providing a liberal arts education as part of the public University of Arkansas system. There are 5 undergraduate schools and 1 graduate school. Figures in the above capsule and in this profile are approximate. In addition to regional accreditation, UAPB has baccalaureate program accreditation with AHEA, CSWE, NASM, NCATE, and NLN. The library contains 271,547 volumes, 119,205 microform items, and 4299 audio/video tapes/CDs, and subscribes to 1050 periodicals. Computerized library services include the card catalog, interlibrary loans, and database searching. Special learning facilities include a learning resource center, art gallery, radio station, and TV station. The 318-acre campus is in a small town 40 miles southeast of Little Rock and approximately 142 miles southwest of Memphis. Including any residence halls, there are 49 buildings.

Student Life: 80% of undergraduates are from Arkansas. Students are from 28 states, 17 foreign countries, and Canada. 94% are African American. The average age of freshmen is 18; all undergraduates, 22. 61% do not continue beyond their first year.

Housing: 1099 students can be accommodated in college housing, which includes single-sex dorms and honors clusters in the dorms. On-campus housing is guaranteed for all 4 years. 65% of students commute. Alcohol is not permitted. All students may keep cars.

Activities: There are 4 local and 4 national fraternities and 4 local and 4 national sororities. There are 65 groups on campus, including art, band, cheerleading, choir, computers, drama, drill team, honors, jazz band, marching band, newspaper, orchestra, photography, political, professional, radio and TV, religious, social, social service, student government, and yearbook. Popular campus events include Founders Day, Spring Emphasis, and Unity Fest.

Sports: There are 7 intercollegiate sports for men and 8 for women, and 20 intramural sports for men and 19 for women. Facilities include a phys ed complex that provides activities such as flag football, basketball, volleyball, softball, tennis, handball, racquetball, track and field, and badminton. There is also a swimming pool and a 6000-seat football stadium.

Disabled Students: 98% of the campus is accessible. Wheelchair ramps, elevators, special parking, specially equipped rest rooms, special class scheduling, lowered drinking fountains, and lowered telephones are available.

Services: Counseling and information services are available, as is tutoring in most subjects. There is a reader service for the blind and remedial math, reading, and writing.

Campus Safety and Security: Measures include 24-hour foot and vehicle patrol, self-defense education, security escort services, and informal discussions. There are pamphlets/posters/films, emergency telephones, lighted pathways/sidewalks, and there is a department of public safety and security on campus.

Programs of Study: UAPB confers B.A. and B.S. degrees. Associate and master's degrees are also awarded. Bachelor's degrees are awarded in AGRICULTURE (agriculture, conservation and regulation, and fishing and fisheries), BIOLOGICAL SCIENCE (biology/biological science), BUSINESS (accounting and business administration and management), COMMUNICATIONS AND THE ARTS (art, English, journalism, music, and speech/debate/rhetoric), COMPUTER AND PHYSICAL SCIENCE (applied mathematics, chemistry, computer science, mathematics, and physics), EDUCATION (agricultural, art, business, early childhood, English, home economics, industrial arts, mathematics, middle school, music, physical, science, social science, and special), ENGINEERING AND ENVIRONMENTAL DESIGN (industrial engineering technology and preengineering), HEALTH PROFESSIONS (nursing, predentistry, premedicine, prepharmacy, and rehabilitation therapy), SOCIAL SCIENCE (criminal justice, family/consumer studies, gerontology, history, liberal arts/general studies, parks and recreation management, political science/government, psychology, social work, and sociology). Business administration, biology, and computer science are the strongest academically and are the largest.

Required: All students must complete at least 124 hours of credit, including 30 hours in their major, while earning an overall 2.0 GPA (2.5 for teacher education majors) and a C or better in all major courses. Distribution requirements include English, math, social and natural science, and phys ed courses. Students must pass a comprehensive exam in their major.

Special: The university offers formal co-op education and work-study programs, concurrent registration with members of the University of Arkansas system, internships, B.A.-B.S. degrees, and dual and student-designed majors. Also offered are credit for military experience, nondegree study, individualized programs of study for honors college students, and study abroad. There are 4 national honor societies, a freshman honors program, and 6 departmental honors programs.

Faculty/Classroom: 54% of faculty are male; 46%, female. The average class size in a laboratory is 20 and in a regular course, 21.

Requirements: The SAT I or ACT is required. The ACT, with a minimum composite score of 19, is preferred. Applicants must have earned 15 credits, including 4 units of English and 3 each in social studies, math, and science. The GED is accepted. Students not meeting these requirements may apply for conditional admission. A GPA of 2.0 is required. AP and CLEP credits are accepted.

Procedure: Freshmen are admitted fall, spring, and summer. Entrance exams should be taken during the junior or senior year. There are early admissions, deferred admissions, and rolling admissions plans. Notification is sent on a rolling basis. Check with the school for current application deadlines and fees.

Transfer: 210 transfer students enrolled in a recent year. Transfer students must have a minimum GPA of 2.0. Applicants with fewer than 60 semester hours of college credit must submit an application, ACT or SAT I scores, and all college transcripts. 30 of 124 credits required for the bachelor's degree must be completed at UAPB.

Visiting: There are regularly scheduled orientations for prospective students. There are guides for informal visits and visitors may sit in on classes and stay overnight. To schedule a visit, contact the Director of Recruitment at (501) 575-8961 or (800) 525-5272.

Financial Aid: In a recent year, 70% of undergraduates worked part time. Average annual earnings from campus work were $800. UAPB is a member of CSS. The FAFSA is required.

International Students: In a recent year, there were 44 international students enrolled. They must score 550 on the written TOEFL and also take the SAT I or ACT. The ACT, with a minimum score of 19, is preferred. SAT I scores may be used.

Computers: The mainframe is a Dec VAX 4500. The academic computer center is networked to the mainframe with a capacity for 60 PCs. All students may access the system 7 A.M. to 11 P.M. Monday through Friday, and during special weekend hours. There are no time limits. There is a $15 lab fee.

Graduates: In a recent year, 332 bachelor's degrees were awarded. The most popular majors were general studies (13%), business administration (13%), and criminal justice (9%). In an average class, 1% graduate in 3 years or less, 9% graduate in 4 years or less, 20% graduate in 5 years or less, and 26% graduate in 6 years or less. 21 companies recruited on campus in a recent year. Of a recent graduating class, 10% were enrolled in graduate school within 6 months of graduation and 42% were employed.

Admissions Contact: Erica Fulton, Director of Admissions and Academic Records. E-mail: *fulton_e@4500.uapb.edu* Web: *www.uapb.edu*

UNIVERSITY OF CENTRAL ARKANSAS   C-3
Conway, AR 72035-0001

Full-time: 2670 men, 4190 women	Faculty: 398; IIA, --$
Part-time: 340 men, 450 women	Ph.D.s: 68%
Graduate: 270 men, 770 women	Student/Faculty: n/av
Year: semesters, summer session	Tuition: $3240 ($5905)
Application Deadline: August 1	Room & Board: $3150
Freshman Class: n/av	
SAT I or ACT: required	COMPETITIVE

(501) 450-3128; (800) 243-8245

The University of Central Arkansas, established in 1907, is a comprehensive public institution offering undergraduate and graduate degrees in liberal arts, business, health-related sciences, and education. Figures in the above capsule and in this profile are approximate. There are 7 undergraduate schools and 1 graduate school. In addition to regional accreditation, UCA has baccalaureate program accreditation with AACSB, ADA, APTA, CAHEA, NASAD, NASM, NCATE, and NLN. The library contains 405,200 volumes, 866,600 microform items, and 6200 audio/video tapes/CDs, and subscribes to 2000 periodicals. Computerized library services include the card catalog, interlibrary loans, and database searching. Special learning facilities include a learning resource center, art gallery, planetarium, radio station, and TV station. The 262-acre campus is in a small town 29 miles north of Little Rock. Including any residence halls, there are 52 buildings.

Student Life: 90% of undergraduates are from Arkansas. Students are from 35 states, 52 foreign countries, and Canada. 96% are from public schools. 90% are white; 10% African American. The average age of freshmen is 19; all undergraduates, 22. 38% do not continue beyond their first year; 30% remain to graduate.

Housing: 2120 students can be accommodated in college housing, which includes single-sex and coed dorms. In addition, there are honors houses and an international student residence hall. On-campus housing is available on a first-come, first-served basis. 75% of students commute. Alcohol is not permitted. All students may keep cars.

Activities: 10% of men belong to 9 national fraternities; 10% of women belong to 9 national sororities. There are 95 groups on campus, including art, band, cheerleading, choir, chorale, chorus, dance, drama, ethnic, gay, honors, international, jazz band, literary magazine, marching band, musical theater, newspaper, orchestra, pep band, photography, political, professional, radio and TV, religious, social, social service, student government, symphony, and yearbook. Popular campus events include Bear Facts Day.

Sports: There are 4 intercollegiate sports for men and 6 for women, and 18 intramural sports for men and 18 for women. Facilities include a gym, a swimming pool, a fitness center, racquetball and tennis courts, a track, soccer fields, and softball fields.

Disabled Students: 98% of the campus is accessible. Wheelchair ramps, elevators, special parking, specially equipped rest rooms, special class scheduling, lowered drinking fountains, lowered telephones, and special dorm rooms are available.

Services: Counseling and information services are available, as is tutoring in some subjects. There is a reader service for the blind and remedial math, reading, and writing.

Campus Safety and Security: Measures include 24-hour foot and vehicle patrol, security escort services, informal discussions, and pamphlets/posters/films. There are emergency telephones, lighted pathways/sidewalks, and security checkpoints.

Programs of Study: UCA confers B.A., B.S., B.B.A., B.M., B.M.E., and B.S.E. degrees. Associate, master's, and doctoral degrees are also awarded. Bachelor's degrees are awarded in BIOLOGICAL SCIENCE (biology/biological science), BUSINESS (accounting, banking and finance, business administration and management, business economics, insurance and risk management, and marketing/retailing/merchandising), COMMUNICATIONS AND THE ARTS (communications, English, French, journalism, music, Spanish, and speech/debate/rhetoric), COMPUTER AND PHYSICAL SCIENCE (chemistry, computer science, information sciences and systems, mathematics, and physics), EDUCATION (art, athletic training, early childhood, education of the exceptional child, elementary, foreign languages, guidance, library science, middle school, music, physical, science, secondary, and special), ENGINEERING AND ENVIRONMENTAL DESIGN (environmental science, interior design, and preengineering), HEALTH PROFESSIONS (exercise science, health care administration, health science, medical technology, nuclear medical technology, nursing, occupational therapy, physical therapy, predentistry, premedicine, preoptometry, prepharmacy, preveterinary science, radiological science, and speech pathology/audiology), SOCIAL SCIENCE (dietetics, economics, family/consumer studies, geography, gerontology, history, philosophy, political science/government, psychology, public administration, religion, and sociology). Business, health-related sciences, and education are the strongest academically. Business and health-related sciences are the largest.

Required: All students must earn a minimum of 124 semester hours, including 40 in upper-division courses. Distribution requirements include 7 hours in science, and 6 hours each in the humanities and social sciences. A minimum GPA of 2.25 is needed for the B.B.A., 2.5 for most education programs. Minimum requirements also include 2 semester hours in physical education.

Special: Study abroad, work-study programs, a B.S.-B.A. degree, a 3-2 engineering degree with Arkansas State University, dual majors, nondegree study, and pass/fail options are available. Co-op programs in business, computer science, and health sciences and internships in education are also possible. There are 18 national honor societies, a freshman honors program, and 25 departmental honors programs.

Faculty/Classroom: 60% of faculty are male; 40%, female. No introductory courses are taught by graduate students. The average class size in a laboratory is 20 and in a regular course, 34.

Requirements: The SAT I or ACT is required, with a minimum ACT score of 19. The GED is accepted. UCA requires applicants to be in the upper 33% of their class. A GPA of 3.0 is required. AP and CLEP credits are accepted. Important factors in the admissions decision are advanced placement or honor courses, evidence of special talent, and recommendations by school officials.

Procedure: Freshmen are admitted to all sessions. Thee is a rolling admissions plan. Notification is sent on a rolling basis. Check with the school for current deadlines and fees.

Transfer: Applicants need, on UCA's scale, a minimum cumulative GPA of 2.0. 24 of 124 credits required for the bachelor's degree must be completed at UCA.

Visiting: There are regularly scheduled orientations for prospective students, including tours at 11 A.M. and 2 P.M.; departments and dorms may be visited. There are also special visitation days that include a campus tour, departmental session, lunch, parents' session, optional residence hall tour, and classroom visit or planetarium show. Visitors may sit in on classes. To schedule a visit, contact the Admissions Office.

Financial Aid: 10% of undergraduates work part time. The FAFSA is required. Check with the school for current deadlines.

International Students: The school actively recruits these students. They must score 500 on the written TOEFL or 173 on the electronic version.

Computers: The mainframes are an IBM 5390, Multipurpose 2000. There are also 110 PCs and Macs available in academic buildings, the library, and dorms. All students may access the system. There are no time limits and no fees. It is strongly recommended that all students have a personal computer.

Admissions Contact: Director of Admissions.
E-mail: *admissions@ecom.uca.edu* Web: *http://www.uca.edu*

UNIVERSITY OF THE OZARKS
Clarksville, AR 72830
B-2
(479) 979-1421
(800) 264-8636; Fax: (479) 979-1355

Full-time: 309 men, 381 women	Faculty: 45; IIB, -$
Part-time: 10 men, 31 women	Ph.D.s: 87%
Graduate: none	Student/Faculty: 15 to 1
Year: semesters, summer session	Tuition: $11,894
Application Deadline: April 1	Room & Board: $4680
Freshman Class: 482 applied, 469 accepted, 214 enrolled	
SAT I Verbal/Math: 548/490	ACT: 23 COMPETITIVE

The University of the Ozarks, founded in 1834, is a private, comprehensive liberal arts institution affiliated with the Presbyterian Church, (U.S.A.). There are 4 undergraduate schools. In addition to regional accreditation, Ozarks has baccalaureate program accreditation with IACBE and NCATE. The library contains 69,960 volumes, 6927 microform items, and 2955 audio/video tapes/CDs, and subscribes to 611 periodicals. Computerized library services include the card catalog, interlibrary loans, database searching, and Internet access. Special learning facilities include a learning resource center, art gallery, radio station, TV station, and the Jones Learning Center for students with diagnosed learning disabilities. The 35-acre campus is in a small town 100 miles northwest of Little Rock. Including any residence halls, there are 16 buildings.

Student Life: 59% of undergraduates are from Arkansas. Students are from 22 states and 20 foreign countries. 92% are from public schools. 73% are white; 16% foreign nationals. 56% are Protestant; 27% claim no religious affiliation; 16% Catholic. The average age of freshmen is 18; all undergraduates, 20. 34% do not continue beyond their first year.

Housing: 500 students can be accommodated in college housing, which includes single-sex and coed dorms. On-campus housing is guaranteed for the freshman year only and is available on a first-come, first-served basis. Priority is given to out-of-town students. 67% of students live on campus; of those, 51% remain on campus on weekends. Alcohol is not permitted. All students may keep cars.

Activities: There are no fraternities or sororities. There are 30 groups on campus, including art, cheerleading, choir, chorale, chorus, dance, debate, drama, film, forensics, honors, international, literary magazine, newspaper, political, professional, radio and TV, religious, social, social service, student government, and yearbook. Popular campus events include International Fair and Banquet, Family Weekend, and Freshman Matriculation Ceremony.

Sports: There are 6 intercollegiate sports for men and 5 for women, and 6 intramural sports for men and 5 for women. Facilities include a sports complex housing racquetball courts, a pool, and a 2200-seat basketball arena. In addition, there are softball, soccer, and baseball fields, a quarter-mile track, tennis courts, and a 700-seat stadium.

Disabled Students: 90% of the campus is accessible. Elevators, special parking, specially equipped rest rooms, special class scheduling, and lowered drinking fountains are available.

Services: Counseling and information services are available, as is tutoring in every subject. There is remedial math, reading, and writing.

Campus Safety and Security: Measures include 24-hour foot and vehicle patrol, informal discussions, emergency telephones, and lighted pathways/sidewalks.

Programs of Study: Ozarks confers B.A., B.S., and B.G.S. degrees. Bachelor's degrees are awarded in BIOLOGICAL SCIENCE (biology/biological science), BUSINESS (accounting, business administration and management, and marketing/retailing/merchandising), COMMUNICATIONS AND THE ARTS (art, communications, dramatic arts, English, and music), COMPUTER AND PHYSICAL SCIENCE (chemistry and mathematics), EDUCATION (business, early childhood, middle school, and physical), ENGINEERING AND ENVIRONMENTAL DESIGN (environmental science and materials science), HEALTH PROFESSIONS (respiratory therapy), SOCIAL SCIENCE (economics, history, liberal arts/general studies, political science/government, psychology, religion, social science, and sociology). Chemistry, English, and business are the strongest academically. Business and biology are the largest.

Required: Students are required to earn 124 hours, with 30 to 54 in the major, and maintain a minimum GPA of 2.0. Distribution requirements include 7 hours in math and science and 6 hours each in foreign language, the humanities and fine arts, and social science or business. Students must also take 4 hours in phys ed, 3 hours of composition, and a computer literacy exam.

Special: Internships, study abroad in 8 countries including Japan, numerous work-study programs, dual majors, a general studies degree, and a 3-2 engineering degree with the University of Arkansas are available. There is 1 national honor society.

Faculty/Classroom: 76% of faculty are male; 24%, female. All teach undergraduates. The average class size in an introductory lecture is 17; in a laboratory, 20; and in a regular course, 17.

Admissions: 97% of the 2003-2004 applicants were accepted. The SAT I scores for the 2003-2004 freshman class were: Verbal--6% below 500, 77% between 500 and 599, 11% between 600 and 700, and 6% above 700; Math--57% below 500, 33% between 500 and 599, 7% between 600 and 700, and 3% above 700. The ACT scores were 34% below 21, 35% between 21 and 23, 16% between 24 and 26, 8% between 27 and 28, and 7% above 28. 39% of the current freshmen were in the top fifth of their class; 67% were in the top two fifths. There was 1 National Merit finalist and 5 semifinalists. 7 freshmen graduated first in their class.

Requirements: The SAT I or ACT is required, with a minimum composite score of 800 on the SAT I or 18 on the ACT. An interview is recommended. The GED is accepted. A GPA of 2.0 is required. AP and CLEP credits are accepted. Important factors in the admissions decision are personality/intangible qualities, advanced placement or honor courses, and evidence of special talent.

Procedure: Freshmen are admitted to all sessions. Entrance exams should be taken as early as possible. There is a deferred admissions plan and a rolling admissions plan. For priority consideration, applications should be filed by April 1 for fall entry and December 1 for spring entry. Notification is sent on a rolling basis. The fall 2003 application fee was $10. Applications are accepted on-line through the school's web site.

Transfer: 37 transfer students enrolled in 2002-2003. A GPA of 2.0 and college transcripts are required. Applicants with a GPA of less than 2.0 or fewer than 30 hours of college work must furnish high school transcripts and ACT or SAT I results. 30 credits of 124 required for the bachelor's degree must be completed at Ozarks.

Visiting: There are regularly scheduled orientations for prospective students, including a campus tour and meetings with faculty and students, admissions, and financial aid. In most cases, prospective students may meet with the president and coaches as requested, and may sit in on classes. There are guides for informal visits and visitors may stay overnight. To schedule a visit, contact the Admissions Office at *admiss@ozarks.edu.*

Financial Aid: In 2003-2004, 82% of all full-time freshmen and 92% of continuing full-time students received some form of financial aid. 48% of full-time freshmen and 50% of continuing full-time students received need-based aid. The average freshman award was $11,000. Need-based scholarships or need-based grants averaged $10,400 ($20,000 maximum); need-based self-help aid (loans and jobs) averaged $5349 ($7300 maximum); and non-need-based awards and non-need-based scholarships averaged $11,237. 43% of undergraduates work part time. Average annual earnings from campus work are $1700. The average financial indebtedness of the 2003 graduate was $13,900. The FAFSA is required. The deadline for filing freshman financial aid applications for fall entry is February 15.

International Students: There are 116 international students enrolled. The school actively recruits these students. They must score 500 on the written TOEFL and also take the college's own test.

Computers: The university provides 100 networked PCs with Internet access in computer labs. Each residence hall room has 2 Internet ports. All students may access the system. There are no time limits. The fee is $100. It is strongly recommended that all students have a personal computer.

Graduates: From July 1, 2002 to June 30, 2003, 112 bachelor's degrees were awarded. The most popular majors were business administration (21%), management (21%), and marketing (10%). In an average class, 28% graduate in 4 years or less, 43% graduate in 5 years or less, and 47% graduate in 6 years or less. 50 companies recruited on campus in 2002-2003. Of the 2002 graduating class, 11% were enrolled in graduate school within 6 months of graduation and 68% were employed.

Admissions Contact: Jim Decker, Director of Admissions. E-mail: *jdecker@ozarks.edu.* Web: *www.ozarks.edu*

WILLIAMS BAPTIST COLLEGE
Walnut Ridge, AR 72476

D-1

(870) 759-4121
(800) 722-4434; Fax: (870) 886-3924

Full-time: 220 men, 291 women	**Faculty:** 28
Part-time: 70 men, 72 women	**Ph.D.s:** n/av
Graduate: none	**Student/Faculty:** 18 to 1
Year: semesters, summer session	**Tuition:** $8150
Application Deadline: open	**Room & Board:** $3800
Freshman Class: 407 applied, 281 accepted, 121 enrolled	
ACT: 21	**COMPETITIVE**

Williams Baptist College, founded in 1941, is a private liberal arts institution providing undergraduate education in business, education, humanities, natural sciences, religion, and social sciences. WBC is affiliated with the Southern Baptist Church and is sponsored by the Arkansas Baptist Convention. In addition to regional accreditation, WBC has baccalaureate program accreditation with NCATE. The library contains 67,807 volumes and 18,626 microform items, and subscribes to 206 periodicals. Computerized library services include the card catalog, interlibrary loans, database searching, and Internet access. Special learning facilities include a learning resource center, art gallery, and an education curriculum lab. The 180-acre campus is in a rural area 100 miles northwest of Memphis, Tennessee, and 125 miles north of Little Rock. Including any residence halls, there are 40 buildings.

Student Life: 84% of undergraduates are from Arkansas. Students are from 14 states and 3 foreign countries. 94% are from public schools. 93% are white. Most are Protestant. The average age of freshmen is 18; all undergraduates, 24. 31% do not continue beyond their first year; 46% remain to graduate.

Housing: 419 students can be accommodated in college housing, which includes single-sex dorms, on-campus apartments, and married-student housing. On-campus housing is guaranteed for all 4 years. 63% of students live on campus; of those, 35% remain on campus on weekends. Alcohol is not permitted. All students may keep cars.

Activities: There are no fraternities or sororities. There are 32 groups on campus, including art, cheerleading, chess, choir, chorale, chorus, drama, honors, international, literary magazine, pep band, professional, religious, social, social service, student government, symphony, and yearbook. Popular campus events include Harvest Fest, Winter Formal Banquet, and Wow days.

Sports: There are 4 intercollegiate sports for men and 3 for women, and 4 intramural sports for men and 4 for women. Facilities include a gym, a weight room, racquetball and tennis courts, a jogging track, and a student center.

Disabled Students: 90% of the campus is accessible. Wheelchair ramps, special parking, specially equipped rest rooms, special class scheduling, and lowered drinking fountains are available.

Services: Counseling and information services are available, as is tutoring in some subjects, including English, math, and science. There is a reader service for the blind, and remedial math, reading, and writing.

Campus Safety and Security: Measures include lighted pathways/sidewalks and vehicle and foot patrols.

Programs of Study: WBC confers B.A., B.S., B.F.A., B.S.B.A., and B.S.Ed. degrees. Associate degrees are also awarded. Bachelor's degrees are awarded in BIOLOGICAL SCIENCE (biology/biological science), BUSINESS (business administration and management), COMMUNICATIONS AND THE ARTS (art, English, and music), COMPUTER AND PHYSICAL SCIENCE (computer science), EDUCATION (elementary, physical, and secondary), SOCIAL SCIENCE (counseling/psychology, history, psychology, religion, religious education, and religious music). Education, psychology, and religion are the strongest academically. Education, religion, and phys ed are the largest.

Required: To graduate, all students must follow a core curriculum including humanities, social science and religion, natural science and math, and physical activity. Chapel attendance is mandatory. A total of 128 credits, with 36 to 64 hours in the major, and a minimum GPA of 2.0 are required to graduate.

Special: WBC offers study abroad in England, Latin America, the Middle East, and Russia, a Washington semester through the American Studies Program, and a general studies major. There are 8 national honor societies.

Faculty/Classroom: 44% of faculty are male; 56%, female. All both teach and do research. The average class size in an introductory lecture is 21; in a laboratory, 23; and in a regular course, 9.

Admissions: 69% of the 2003-2004 applicants were accepted. The ACT scores for the 2003-2004 freshman class were: 45% below 21, 23% between 21 and 23, 23% between 24 and 26, 4% between 27 and 28, and 5% above 28. 8 freshmen graduated first in their class.

Requirements: The ACT is required. In addition, applicants must be graduates of an accredited secondary school. A minimum of 16 academic credits is required and should include at least 12 in the areas of English, math, social science, and natural science. A GPA of 2.5 is required. AP and CLEP credits are accepted.

Procedure: Freshmen are admitted to all sessions. Application deadlines are open. There is a rolling admissions plan. Application fee is $20. Notification is sent on a rolling basis. Applications are accepted on-line through the college's web site.

Transfer: 66 transfer students enrolled in 2002-2003. Transfer students must have a GPA of 2.0 for unconditional admission. 32 credits of 128 required for the bachelor's degree must be completed at WBC.

Visiting: There are regularly scheduled orientations for prospective students, including visits with faculty in fields of interest, mock classes, financial aid sessions, campus tours, and a student panel discussion. There are guides for informal visits and visitors may sit in on classes and stay overnight. To schedule a visit, contact the Director of Admissions.

Financial Aid: In 2003-2004, all full-time freshmen and 99% of continuing full-time students received some form of financial aid. 71% of full-time freshmen and 77% of continuing full-time students received need-based aid. The average freshman award was $8574. Need-based scholarships or need-based grants averaged $3128 ($4650 maximum); need-based self-help aid (loans and jobs) averaged $3062 ($4544 maximum); non-need-based athletic scholarships averaged $3862 ($11,400 maximum); and other non-need-based awards and non-need-based scholarships averaged $4127 ($9722 maximum). 46% of undergraduates work part time. Average annual earnings from campus work are $1346. The average financial indebtedness of the 2003 graduate was $12,752. The FAFSA is required. The deadline for filing freshman financial aid applications for fall entry is May 1.

International Students: There are 6 international students enrolled. They must score 500 on the written TOEFL, also take the SAT I or ACT, scoring 19 on the ACT, and take the college's own interest inventory test.

Computers: WBC uses PCs for all computing, and a computer lab is available to students. All students may access the system. There are no time limits. The fee is $125.

Graduates: From July 1, 2002 to June 30, 2003, 90 bachelor's degrees were awarded. The most popular majors were psychology (17%), religion (14%), and physical education (14%). In an average class, 24% graduate in 4 years or less, 42% graduate in 5 years or less, and 46% graduate in 6 years or less.

Admissions Contact: Angela Flippo, Director of Admissions. A video is available. E-mail: *admissions@wbclab.edu* Web: *www.wbcoll.edu*

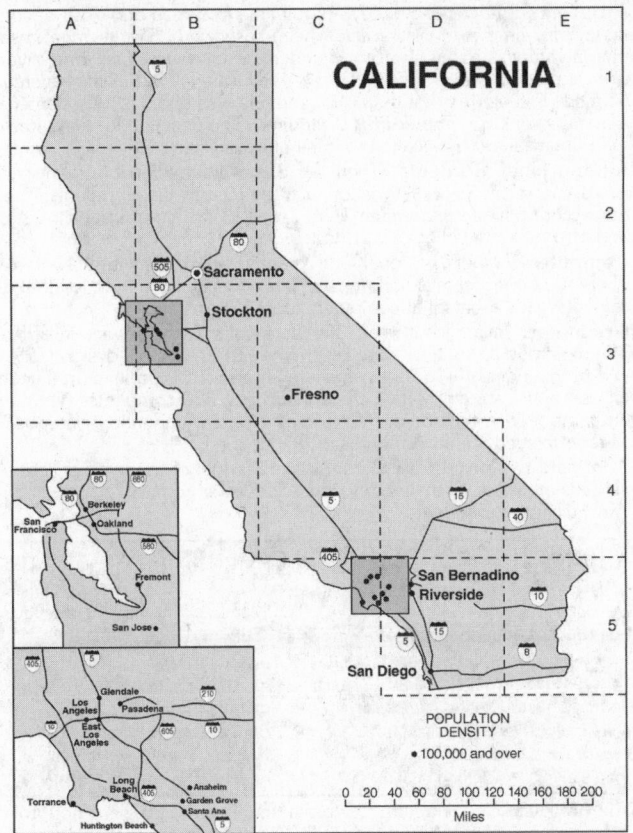

CALIFORNIA

POPULATION
DENSITY
● 100,000 and over

0 20 40 60 80 100 120 140 160 180 200
Miles

ALLIANT INTERNATIONAL UNIVERSITY
(Formerly United States International University)   **D-5**

San Diego, CA 92131-1799

(858) 635-4772
(866) 825-5426; Fax: (858) 635-4739

Full-time: 163 men, 201 women	**Faculty:** 36
Part-time: 27 men, 28 women	**Ph.D.s:** 96%
Graduate: 756 men, 2294 women	**Student/Faculty:** 10 to 1
Year: semesters, summer session	**Tuition:** $16,760
Application Deadline: March 1	**Room & Board:** $6880
Freshman Class: 475 applied, 367 accepted, 130 enrolled	
SAT I or ACT: recommended	**COMPETITIVE**

Alliant International University, formerly United States International University, established in 1952, is a private institution offering undergraduate and graduate programs in business, psychology, and international studies. The university has campuses in San Diego, Fresno, Irvine, Los Angeles, San Francisco Bay, and Sacramento. There are 2 undergraduate and 5 graduate schools. The library contains 191,549 volumes, 351,656 microform items, and 3097 audio/video tapes/CDs, and subscribes to 1149 periodicals. Computerized library services include the card catalog, interlibrary loans, database searching, and Internet access. Special learning facilities include a learning resource center and a curriculum lab for education. The 60-acre campus is in a suburban area 15 miles north of downtown San Diego. Including any residence halls, there are 68 buildings.

Student Life: 40% of undergraduates are from California. Others are from 47 states, 69 foreign countries, and Canada. 65% are from public schools. 30% are white; 28% foreign nationals; 19% Hispanic; 14% African American. The average age of freshmen is 18; all undergraduates, 22.

Housing: 600 students can be accommodated in college housing, which includes single-sex dorms. On-campus housing is guaranteed for all 4 years. 70% of students commute. All students may keep cars.

Activities: There are no fraternities or sororities. There are 15 to 20 groups on campus, including ethnic, gay, honors, international, literary magazine, newspaper, professional, social, social service, student government, and yearbook. Popular campus events include harbor cruises, beach parties, and the International Friendship Festival.

Sports: There are 4 intercollegiate sports for men and 5 for women, and 7 intramural sports for men and 7 for women. Facilities include weight and exercise rooms, tennis courts, softball, baseball, and soccer fields, 4 swimming pools, an all-purpose playing field, and a basketball/volleyball indoor recreational facility.

Disabled Students: 80% of the campus is accessible. Wheelchair ramps, elevators, special parking, and specially equipped rest rooms are available.

Services: Counseling and information services are available, as is tutoring in most subjects. There is a reader service for the blind, and remedial math, reading, and writing.

Campus Safety and Security: Measures include 24-hour foot and vehicle patrol, security escort services, pamphlets/posters/films, and lighted pathways/sidewalks.

Programs of Study: AIU confers B.A. and B.S. degrees. Master's and doctoral degrees are also awarded. Bachelor's degrees are awarded in BUSINESS (business administration and management, hotel/motel and restaurant management, international business management, and tourism), SOCIAL SCIENCE (international relations and psychology). Business and psychology are the largest.

Required: To graduate, students must complete 120 semester units, including 48 in the major, with a minimum GPA of 2.0. The general education curriculum includes symbolic systems and intellectual skills, quantitative and technological skills; global and multicultural perspectives; global perspectives though the humanities, social sciences and natural sciences; and community service.

Special: AIU offers internships, study abroad at the university's international campuses, an accelerated degree program, a general studies degree, B.A.-B.S. degrees, and nondegree study. There is a freshman honors program.

Faculty/Classroom: 58% of faculty are male; 42%, female. 15% teach undergraduates and 42% do research. No introductory courses are taught by graduate students. The average class size in an introductory lecture is 25 and in a regular course, 18.

Admissions: 77% of the 2003-2004 applicants were accepted.

Requirements: The SAT I or ACT is recommended. In addition, applicants should be graduates of a regionally accredited secondary school with a GPA of 2.0. International students must demonstrate proficiency in English if it is not their first language. A GPA of 2.0 is required. AP and CLEP credits are accepted. Important factors in the admissions decision are advanced placement or honor courses, leadership record, and evidence of special talent.

Procedure: Freshmen are admitted fall, spring, and summer. Entrance exams should be taken by the end of senior year, but earlier is recommended. There are early decision and deferred admissions plans. Students should apply 30 days before the upcoming term; applying by March 1 for fall entry is recommended. The application fee is $40. Notification is sent on a rolling basis. Applications are accepted on computer disk and on-line through the university's web site.

Transfer: 73 transfer students enrolled in 2003-2004. A college GPA of 2.0 is required. All applicants must submit high school as well as college transcripts. 30 of 120 credits required for the bachelor's degree must be completed at AIU.

Visiting: There are regularly scheduled orientations for prospective students, including admissions and financial aid counseling, meeting with a student panel, an information fair, a campus tour, and dinner. There are guides for informal visits and visitors may sit in on classes and stay overnight. To schedule a visit, contact the Admissions Office at *admissions@alliant.edu.*

Financial Aid: In 2003-2004, 78% of all full-time freshmen and 68% of continuing full-time students received some form of financial aid. 69% of full-time freshmen and 60% of continuing full-time students received need-based aid. The average freshman award was $11,800. Need-based scholarships or need-based grants averaged $7100 ($22,310 maximum); need-based self-help aid (loans and jobs) averaged $6300 ($10,000 maximum); non-need-based athletic scholarships averaged $8140 ($20,900 maximum); other non-need-based awards and non-need-based scholarships averaged $1400 ($10,000 maximum); and outside/alternative loans averaged $15,000 ($29,000 maximum). 50% of undergraduates work part time. Average annual earnings from campus work are $3850. The average financial indebtedness of the 2003 graduate was $13,310. The FAFSA and the college's own financial statement are required. The priority date for freshman financial aid applications for fall entry is March 1. The deadline for filing freshman financial aid applications for fall entry is August 1.

International Students: There are 117 international students enrolled. The school actively recruits these students. They must score 550 on the written TOEFL and also take the college's own test.

Computers: All students may access the system. There are no time limits and no fees. It is strongly recommended that all students have a personal computer.

Graduates: From July 1, 2002 to June 30, 2003, 97 bachelor's degrees were awarded. The most popular majors were international business administration (43%), psychology (17%), and business administration (9%). Of the 2002 graduating class, 25% were enrolled in graduate school within 6 months of graduation and 85% were employed.

Admissions Contact: Hernan Bucheli, Director of Enrollment Management. E-mail: *admissions@alliant.edu* Web: *www.alliant.edu*

ART CENTER COLLEGE OF DESIGN C-5

Pasadena, CA 91103 (626) 396-2373; Fax: (626) 795-0578

Full-time: 823 men, 589 women	**Faculty:** 66
Part-time: none	**Ph.D.s:** n/av
Graduate: 66 men, 55 women	**Student/Faculty:** 21 to 1
Year: trimesters, summer session	**Tuition:** $23,450
Application Deadline: open	**Room & Board:** n/app
Freshman Class: 949 applied, 687 accepted, 518 enrolled	
SAT I or ACT: required	SPECIAL

Art Center College of Design, founded in 1930, is a private, nonprofit institution offering programs in fine arts and design. In addition to regional accreditation, Art Center has baccalaureate program accreditation with NASAD. The library contains 64,000 volumes, 60,000 microform items, and 4000 audio/video tapes/CDs, and subscribes to 400 periodicals. Computerized library services include the card catalog and database searching. Special learning facilities include an art gallery. The 175-acre campus is in a suburban area 10 miles northwest of Los Angeles. There is one building.

Student Life: 53% of undergraduates are from California. Students are from 43 states, 36 foreign countries, and Canada. 45% are Asian American; 42% white; 21% foreign nationals; 10% Hispanic. The average age of freshmen is 23; all undergraduates, 24. 5% do not continue beyond their first year; 78% remain to graduate.

Housing: There are no residence halls. All students commute. Alcohol is not permitted. All students may keep cars.

Activities: There are no fraternities or sororities. There are 12 groups on campus, including ethnic, gay, international, religious, social, and student government.

Sports: There is no sports program at Art Center. Students have access to athletic facilities at Occidental College and California Institute of Technology.

Disabled Students: All of the campus is accessible. Wheelchair ramps, elevators, special parking, specially equipped rest rooms, lowered drinking fountains, and lowered telephones are available.

Services: Counseling and information services are available, as is tutoring in some subjects, including some art classes.

Campus Safety and Security: Measures include 24-hour foot and vehicle patrol, emergency telephones, and lighted pathways/sidewalks.

Programs of Study: Art Center confers B.S. and B.F.A. degrees. Master's degrees are also awarded. Bachelor's degrees are awarded in COMMUNICATIONS AND THE ARTS (advertising, design, film arts, fine arts, graphic design, illustration, industrial design, and photography), ENGINEERING AND ENVIRONMENTAL DESIGN (environmental design). Illustration, graphic design, and industrial design are the largest.

Required: To graduate, students must complete a total of 135 credit hours, with 90 in the major, and 45 units of liberal arts and sciences. Course requirements vary by the program. A minimum GPA of 2.5 and a core curriculum of English Composition and Introduction to Modernism are also required.

Special: The college offers cross-registration with Occidental College, the California Institute of Technology, and the Southern California Institute of Architecture, internships, and nondegree study.

Faculty/Classroom: 74% of faculty are male; 26%, female. 99% teach undergraduates. No introductory courses are taught by graduate students. The average class size in an introductory lecture is 22 and in a regular course, 30.

Admissions: 72% of the 2003-2004 applicants were accepted.

Requirements: The SAT I or ACT is required. In addition, applicants must be graduates of an accredited secondary school or have a GED. Official transcripts and a portfolio must be submitted. An interview is recommended. A GPA of 2.5 is required. AP credits are accepted. Important factors in the admissions decision are evidence of special talent, advanced placement or honor courses, and extracurricular activities record.

Procedure: Freshmen are admitted fall, spring, and summer. Entrance exams should be taken in the senior year. Application deadlines are open. Application fee is $45.

Transfer: 486 transfer students enrolled in 2002-2003. Transfer applicants must have a minimum 2.5 GPA and provide official transcripts from all colleges attended. Up to 60 units of liberal arts and studio credits may be transferred. Portfolios are required, and interviews are recommended. Up to 32 of the 45 liberal arts and science units required for graduation may be transferred. There is a 4-semester residency requirement. 75 of 135 credits required for the bachelor's degree must be completed at Art Center.

Visiting: There are regularly scheduled orientations for prospective students. There are guides for informal visits. To schedule a visit, contact Admissions.

Financial Aid: In 2003-2004, 70% of all full-time freshmen received some form of financial aid. 57% of full-time freshmen and 76% of continuing full-time students received need-based aid. The average freshman award was $14,471. 16% of undergraduates work part time. Average annual earnings from campus work are $2325. The average financial indebtedness of the 2003 graduate was $55,810. Art Center is a member of CSS. The FAFSA is required. The deadline for filing freshman financial aid applications for fall entry is March 1.

International Students: There were 249 international students enrolled in a recent year. The school actively recruits these students. They must score 550 on the written TOEFL or 213 on the electronic version and also take the college's own test.

Computers: Many personal and graphics computers are available. There are no time limits and no fees. It is strongly recommended that all students have a personal computer, specifically a Mac.

Graduates: In a recent year, 354 bachelor's degrees were awarded. The most popular majors were illustration (20%), graphic design (19%), and product design (16%). In an average class, 70% graduate in 4 years or less, and 77% graduate in 5 years or less. 200 companies recruited on campus in a recent year. Of a recent year's graduating class, 94% were employed within 6 months of graduation.

Admissions Contact: Kit Baron, Vice President of Student Services. A video is available. E-mail: *admissions@artcenter.edu* Web: *www.artcenter.edu*

ART INSTITUTE OF SOUTHERN CALIFORNIA D-5

Laguna Beach, CA 92651 (949) 376-6000
(800) 255-0762; Fax: (949) 376-6009

Full-time: 100 men, 60 women	**Faculty:** 8
Part-time: 20 men, 30 women	**Ph.D.s:** 85%
Graduate: none	**Student/Faculty:** 20 to 1
Year: semesters, summer session	**Tuition:** $14,500
Application Deadline: March 2	**Room & Board:** n/app
Freshman Class: n/av	
SAT I or ACT: required	SPECIAL

The Art Institute of Southern California, founded in 1961, is a nonprofit, independent, institution offering full- and part-time undergraduate art programs leading to the Bachelor of Fine Arts. Figures in the above capsule and this profile are approximate. In addition to regional accreditation, AISC has baccalaureate program accreditation with NASAD. The library contains 15,000 volumes and 300 audio/video tapes/CDs, and subscribes to 90 periodicals. Computerized library services include the card catalog and interlibrary loans. Special learning facilities include a learning resource center and art gallery. The 9-acre campus is in a small town 47 miles southeast of Los Angeles. There are 11 buildings.

Student Life: 60% of undergraduates are from California. Students are from 33 states, 13 foreign countries, and Canada. 85% are from public schools. 66% are white; 13% foreign nationals; 11% Asian American. The average age of freshmen is 19; all undergraduates, 23. 15% do not continue beyond their first year; 60% remain to graduate.

Housing: There are no residence halls. The institute will assist in the location of off-campus housing. All students commute. Alcohol is not permitted. All students may keep cars.

Activities: There are no fraternities or sororities. There are 2 groups on campus, including art and student government.

Sports: There is no sports program at AISC.

Disabled Students: 90% of the campus is accessible. Special parking, specially equipped rest rooms, special class scheduling, and lowered drinking fountains are available.

Services: There is remedial reading and writing.

Campus Safety and Security: Measures include security escort services and night security.

Programs of Study: AISC confers the B.F.A. degree. Bachelor's degrees are awarded in COMMUNICATIONS AND THE ARTS (animation, drawing, graphic design, illustration, and painting).

Required: All students must complete 122 credit hours, with approximately 55 in the major, including studio electives. General education requirements include 30 hours in liberal arts and 15 in art history. 22 hours of studio foundation courses are required, in which students explore all artistic medium.

Special: Internships are possible, and work-study is available on campus. Students may petition the registrar if they wish to attempt more than 15 semester units.

Faculty/Classroom: 65% of faculty are male; 35%, female. All teach undergraduates. The average class size in an introductory lecture is 15 and in a regular course, 12.

Requirements: The SAT I or ACT is required for applicants currently in high school. Students must be high school graduates or hold a GED. A personal essay and letter of recommendation are required, as is a personal or telephone interview, and a 10-piece portfolio. A GPA of 2.5 is required. AP and CLEP credits are accepted. Important factors in the admissions decision are evidence of special talent, recommendations by school officials, and ability to finance college education.

Procedure: Freshmen are admitted fall and spring. There is a deferred admissions plan and a rolling admissions plan. Notification is sent on a rolling basis. Check with the school for current deadlines. The fall 2003 application fee was $35. Applications are accepted on-line at the institution's web site.

Transfer: In addition to freshman requirements, transfer students must submit all prior college transcripts. 45 of 122 credits required for the bachelor's degree must be completed at AISC.

Visiting: There are regularly scheduled orientations for prospective students, consisting of national portfolio days and open house. There are guides for informal visits and visitors may sit in on classes. To schedule a visit, contact the Admissions Office.

Financial Aid: AISC is a member of CSS. The CSS Profile, FAFSA, or FFS and SAAC for California grants are required. Check with the school for current deadlines.

International Students: The school actively recruits these students. They must score 550 on the written TOEFL or 213 on the electronic version and also take the college's own test.

Computers: There are 30 Macs available in a network for student use, with all necessary software for multimedia and full color computer animation. All students may access the system. There are no time limits and no fees. It is strongly recommended that all students have a personal computer.

Admissions Contact: Anthony Padilla, Dean of Admissions. A video is available. E-mail: *admissions@aisc.edu* Web: *http://www.aisc.edu*

AZUSA PACIFIC UNIVERSITY
Azusa, CA 91702-7000

D-5

(626) 812-3016
(800) TALK-APU; Fax: (626) 812-3096

Full-time: 1487 men, 2736 women	Faculty: 268; IIA, -$
Part-time: 89 men, 90 women	Ph.D.s: 73%
Graduate: 1368 men, 2448 women	Student/Faculty: 16 to 1
Year: semesters, summer session	Tuition: $19,024
Application Deadline: March 1	Room & Board: $5696
Freshman Class: 2472 applied, 2042 accepted, 912 enrolled	
SAT I or ACT: required	VERY COMPETITIVE

Azusa Pacific University, founded in 1899, is a private, interdenominational Christian institution offering undergraduate and graduate programs in the liberal arts and emphasizing spiritual growth. There are 6 undergraduate and 6 graduate schools. In addition to regional accreditation, APU has baccalaureate program accreditation with CSWE and NLN. The 2 libraries contain 184,092 volumes, 613,038 microform items, and 14,829 audio/video tapes/CDs, and subscribe to 1800 periodicals. Computerized library services include the card catalog, interlibrary loans, and database searching. Special learning facilities include a learning resource center, art gallery, radio station, and TV station. The 60-acre campus is in an urban area 26 miles east of Los Angeles. Including any residence halls, there are 67 buildings.

Student Life: 81% of undergraduates are from California. Students are from 44 states, 53 foreign countries, and Canada. 73% are white; 12% Hispanic. 38% are nondenominational or Christian; 12% claim no religious affiliation; 6% are Catholic. The average age of freshmen is 18; all undergraduates, 20. 19% do not continue beyond their first year.

Housing: 2807 students can be accommodated in college housing, which includes single-sex and coed dorms, on-campus apartments, off-campus apartments, and married-student housing. On-campus housing is available on a first-come, first-served basis and is available on a lottery system for upperclassmen. 63% of students live on campus; of those, 50% remain on campus on weekends. Alcohol is not permitted. All students may keep cars.

Activities: There are no fraternities or sororities. There are 32 groups on campus, including art, band, cheerleading, choir, chorale, chorus, computers, drama, ethnic, honors, international, jazz band, newspaper, orchestra, pep band, photography, political, religious, social, student government, and yearbook. Popular campus events include Missions Week, Mega Weekend-Homecoming/Dinner Rally, and Night of Champions.

Sports: There are 7 intercollegiate sports for men and 7 for women, and 6 intramural sports for men and 4 for women. Facilities include an all-weather track, a 3000-seat football stadium, a baseball field, a 1200-seat gym, a residence hall lounge, and a recreation room.

Disabled Students: All of the campus is accessible. Wheelchair ramps, elevators, special parking, specially equipped rest rooms, lowered drinking fountains, and lowered telephones are available.

Services: Counseling and information services are available, as is tutoring in most subjects. There is remedial math, reading, and writing.

Campus Safety and Security: Measures include 24-hour foot and vehicle patrol, security escort services, shuttle buses, and informal discussions. There are pamphlets/posters/films, emergency telephones, and lighted pathways/sidewalks.

Programs of Study: APU confers B.A. and B.S. degrees. Master's and doctoral degrees are also awarded. Bachelor's degrees are awarded in BIOLOGICAL SCIENCE (biochemistry and biology/biological science), BUSINESS (accounting, business administration and management, and marketing/retailing/merchandising), COMMUNICATIONS AND THE ARTS (communications, English, music, and Spanish), COMPUTER AND PHYSICAL SCIENCE (chemistry, computer science, information sciences and systems, mathematics, and physics), EDUCATION (art, music, and physical), HEALTH PROFESSIONS (nursing and premedicine), SOCIAL SCIENCE (biblical studies, history, international studies, liberal arts/general studies, ministries, philosophy, political science/government, psychology, religion, social science, social work, and sociology). Nursing, education, and religion are the strongest academically. Liberal studies is the largest.

Required: All students must take 126 semester units and earn a minimum GPA of 2.0. 18 units of Bible courses, 120 hours of community ministry, and 2 units of health are required. General education requirements include courses in public speaking, fine arts, religion and philosophy, English, algebra, foreign language, and phys ed. Heritage and Institution, Identity and Relationships, and Nature are also required courses.

Special: Internships in ministerial and American studies, study abroad in Japan, Latin America, Taiwan, and England, and a Washington semester are available. In addition, work-study with the university, a B.A.-B.S. degree, dual majors in all programs, and a 3-2 engineering degree are offered. APU awards credit for life experience and allows nondegree study. There are 2 national honor societies and a freshman honors program.

Faculty/Classroom: 54% of faculty are male; 46%, female. No introductory courses are taught by graduate students. The average class size in an introductory lecture is 40 and in a regular course, 35.

Admissions: 83% of the 2003-2004 applicants were accepted. The SAT I scores for the 2003-2004 freshman class were: Verbal--33% below 500, 43% between 500 and 599, 21% between 600 and 700, and 3% above 700; Math--33% below 500, 40% between 500 and 599, 25% between 600 and 700, and 3% above 700. The ACT scores were 55% below 21, 37% between 24 and 26, and 8% above 28. 60% of the current freshmen were in the top fifth of their class; 86% were in the top two fifths.

Requirements: The SAT I or ACT is required, but no minimum score is necessary. An essay is required. A portfolio and an interview are recommended for certain programs. The GED is accepted. A GPA of 2.5 is required. AP and CLEP credits are accepted. Important factors in the admissions decision are personality/intangible qualities, evidence of special talent, and advanced placement or honor courses.

Procedure: Freshmen are admitted to all sessions. Entrance exams should be taken prior to enrollment. There are early admissions and deferred admissions plans. Applications should be filed by March 1 for fall entry, along with a $45 fee. Notification is sent on a rolling basis. A waiting list is an active part of the admissions procedure. Applications are accepted on-line through the school's web site.

Transfer: 473 transfer students enrolled in 2002-2003. Applicants must have a minimum GPA of 2.0 on previous college work. The SAT I or ACT is not required if 30 or more semester units have been completed. An associate degree and an interview are recommended. 30 of 126 credits required for the bachelor's degree must be completed at APU.

Visiting: There are regularly scheduled orientations for prospective students, including Seniors Only Day in November, and a brother/sister weekend in February that is open to both juniors and seniors. There are guides for informal visits and visitors may sit in on classes and stay overnight. To schedule a visit, contact the Admissions Office at (626) 815-6000, ext. 3016.

Financial Aid: In 2003-2004, 60% of all full-time freshmen and 55% of continuing full-time students received some form of financial aid. 73% of full-time freshmen received need-based aid. The average freshman award was $9143. 34% of undergraduates work part time. The average financial indebtedness of the 2003 graduate was $18,440. The FAFSA and the college's own financial statement are required. The deadline for filing freshman financial aid applications for fall entry is July 1.

International Students: There are 72 international students enrolled. The school actively recruits these students. They must score 500 on the written TOEFL.

Computers: 268 computer workstations are available on campus. All students may access the system Monday through Friday 8 A.M. to 11 P.M., Saturday 8:30 A.M. to 8 P.M., and Sunday 1 P.M. to 6 P.M. There are no time limits and no fees. It is recommended that students in Human Development (degree completion program) have personal computers.

Graduates: From July 1, 2002 to June 30, 2003, 1076 bachelor's degrees were awarded. The most popular majors were liberal arts (9%), communication studies (7%), and nursing (6%).

Admissions Contact: David Burke, Director of Undergraduate Admissions. A video is available. E-mail: *admissions@apu.edu* Web: *http://www.apu.edu*

BIOLA UNIVERSITY
D-5
La Mirada, CA 90639-0001

(562) 903-4752
(800) OK-BIOLA; Fax: (562) 903-4709

Full-time: 1060 men, 1844 women	**Faculty:** 161; IIA, -$
Part-time: 48 men, 60 women	**Ph.Ds:** n/av
Graduate: 984 men, 633 women	**Student/Faculty:** 18 to 1
Year: 4-1-4, summer session	**Tuition:** $19,564
Application Deadline: June 1	**Room & Board:** $6400
Freshman Class: 1901 applied, 1483 accepted, 700 enrolled	
SAT I Verbal/Math: 563/555	**ACT:** 24 **VERY COMPETITIVE**

Biola University, founded in 1908, is a private, interdenominational Christian institution offering undergraduate and graduate degrees in arts and sciences, psychology, theology, intercultural studies, and business. There are 6 undergraduate and 6 graduate schools. In addition to regional accreditation, Biola has baccalaureate program accreditation with ACBSP, APA, ATS, NASAD, NASM, and NLN. The library contains 286,231 volumes, 554,610 microform items, and 14,347 audio/video tapes/CDs, and subscribes to 14,609 periodicals. Computerized library services include the card catalog, interlibrary loans, database searching, and Internet access. Special learning facilities include a learning resource center, art gallery, radio station, TV station, film studio and 3-D art facility, MIDI lab for music composition majors, electronic piano lab, listening lab with music archives, physical science labs, and scanning electron microscope. The 95-acre campus is in a suburban area 22 miles southeast of Los Angeles. Including any residence halls, there are 39 buildings.

Student Life: 70% of students are white; 11% Asian American. Most are Protestant. The average age of freshmen is 18; all undergraduates, 20. 17% do not continue beyond their first year; 60% remain to graduate.

Housing: 2184 students can be accommodated in college housing, which includes single-sex and coed dorms, on-campus apartments, and off-campus apartments. On-campus housing is available on a first-come, first-served basis. 69% of students live on campus; of those, 73% remain on campus on weekends. Alcohol is not permitted. All students may keep cars.

Activities: There are no fraternities or sororities. There are 52 groups on campus, including band, cheerleading, chess, chorale, dance, debate, drama, ethnic, film, forensics, gospel choir, honors, international, jazz band, ministries, missionary, musical theater, newspaper, orchestra, political, professional, radio and TV, religious, social, social service, student government, symphony, and yearbook. Popular campus events include Multicultural Week, Christmas Celebration, and Harvest Festival.

Sports: There are 7 intercollegiate sports for men and 8 for women, and 5 intramural sports for men and 5 for women. Facilities include a gym-swimming complex, a 450-seat auditorium, athletic fields, including one for soccer, a quarter-mile track, a baseball diamond, tennis, sand volleyball, and basketball courts, and a fitness center.

Disabled Students: 88% of the campus is accessible. Wheelchair ramps, elevators, special parking, specially equipped rest rooms, special class scheduling, lowered drinking fountains, and lowered telephones are available.

Services: Counseling and information services are available, as is tutoring in most subjects. There is a reader service for the blind and a writing center.

Campus Safety and Security: Measures include 24-hour foot and vehicle patrol, self-defense education, security escort services, and informal discussions. There are pamphlets/posters/films, emergency telephones, lighted pathways/sidewalks, and a bike patrol.

Programs of Study: Biola confers B.A., B.S., and B.M. degrees. Master's and doctoral degrees are also awarded. Bachelor's degrees are awarded in BIOLOGICAL SCIENCE (biochemistry and biology/biological science), BUSINESS (accounting, business administration and management, management science, and marketing management), COMMUNICATIONS AND THE ARTS (art, broadcasting, communications, English, journalism, music, music performance, music theory and composition, and Spanish), COMPUTER AND PHYSICAL SCIENCE (applied mathematics, computer science, information sciences and systems, mathematics, and physical sciences), EDUCATION (Christian, mathematics, music, and physical), HEALTH PROFESSIONS (nursing and speech pathology/audiology), SOCIAL SCIENCE (anthropology, biblical studies, crosscultural studies, history, humanities, liberal arts/general studies, philosophy, psychology, social science, and sociology). Business administration, biological science, and chemistry are the strongest academically. Business, organizational leadership, and liberal studies are the largest.

Required: To graduate, students must pass a writing competency exam, complete 30 units of biblical studies and theology, and fulfill the general education and phys ed requirements. At least 130 semester hours must be completed, with 30 hours in the major and 24 of these in upper-division work. Other requirements vary by major. A minimum 2.0 GPA is required.

Special: Cross-registration with the Au Sable Institute of Environmental Studies is possible. Biola offers internships, summer travel tours, study

abroad, and an American studies program in Washington D.C., sponsored by the Christian College Coalition. Special programs include L.A. Film Studies, a semester in Hollywood working in the film industry; Biola Baja, a 3-week program at Vermillion Sea Field, Baja; a family studies course at Focus on the Family Institute in Colorado Springs; a China studies program at Fudan University in Shanghai, China; and a development theory studies program in Honduras. Also available are on- and off-campus work-study programs, a B.A.- B.S. degree, a 3-2 engineering degree with the University of Southern California, dual majors, and non-degree study. There are several preprofessional programs available, including prelaw, prephysical therapy, and prechiropractic. A 3-1 program with Los Angeles College of Chiropractic is offered. There are 2 national honor societies, a freshman honors program, and 7 departmental honors programs.

Faculty/Classroom: 75% of faculty are male; 25%, female. 76% teach undergraduates. No introductory courses are taught by graduate students. The average class size in an introductory lecture is 35 and in a laboratory, 15.

Admissions: 78% of the 2003-2004 applicants were accepted. The SAT I scores for the 2003-2004 freshman class were: Verbal--22% below 500, 42% between 500 and 599, 30% between 600 and 700, and 8% above 700; Math--27% below 500, 41% between 500 and 599, 26% between 600 and 700, and 6% above 700. The ACT scores were 25% below 21, 21% between 21 and 23, 25% between 24 and 26, 14% between 27 and 28, and 15% above 28. 68% of the current freshmen were in the top fifth of their class; 89% were in the top two fifths. 39 freshmen graduated first in their class in a recent year.

Requirements: The SAT I or ACT is required. Applicants need not be graduates of an accredited secondary school. The GED is accepted. Students should have completed 15 academic credits, including 4 years of English and foreign language, 3 years of math, and 2 each of social studies and science. All students must be evangelical Christians who can demonstrate Christian character, leadership ability, and the aptitude for possible success in college. Applicants must submit 2 personal references: 1 from their pastor or someone on the pastoral staff, and 1 from the school last attended, or from an employer if they have been out of school for a year and have been working. An essay and an interview are required. A GPA of 3.0 is required. AP and CLEP credits are accepted. Important factors in the admissions decision are personality/intangible qualities, recommendations by school officials, and leadership record.

Procedure: Freshmen are admitted to all sessions. There is a deferred admissions plan and a rolling admissions plan. Early decision applications should be filed by December 1; regular applications, by June 1 for fall entry and January 1 for spring entry, along with a $45 fee. Notification of early decision is sent December 24; regular decision, on a rolling basis. Applications are accepted on-line through the school's web site.

Transfer: 238 transfer students enrolled in a recent year. Applicants with fewer than 27 credit hours must submit both college transcripts and SAT I scores. All students must provide high school transcripts. A minimum 2.0 GPA and an interview are required. 30 credits of 130 required for the bachelor's degree must be completed at Biola.

Visiting: There are regularly scheduled orientations for prospective students, including class visits; orientation with the departments of admissions, financial aid, and student affairs; chapel; a sporting event; and a Disneyland or Knott's Berry Farm visit. There are guides for informal visits and visitors may sit in on classes and stay overnight. To schedule a visit, contact the Admissions Office.

Financial Aid: In 2003-2004, 80% of all full-time freshmen and 77% of continuing full-time students received some form of financial aid. 63% of full-time freshmen and 65% of continuing full-time students received need-based aid. The average freshman award was $12,900. Need-based scholarships or need-based grants averaged $11,323 ($19,564 maximum); need-based self-help aid (loans and jobs) averaged $3565 ($5625 maximum); non-need-based athletic scholarships averaged $7528 ($19,564 maximum); and other non-need-based awards and non-need-based scholarships averaged $4315 ($7000 maximum). 34% of undergraduates work part time. Average annual earnings from campus work are $3318. The average financial indebtedness of the 2003 graduate was $22,000. The FAFSA and the college's own financial statement are required. California residents should submit the Cal Grant GPA verification form. The deadline for filing freshman financial aid applications for fall entry is March 2.

International Students: There are 128 international students enrolled. The school actively recruits these students. They must score 600 on the written TOEFL or 250 on the electronic version, take the college's own test, and also take the SAT I or the ACT, scoring 920 on the SAT I.

Computers: The mainframes are an HP 9000/Series 300, a DEC VAX 3100, and a DEC VAX 2100. There is 1 main computer center for the HP and VAX terminals. In addition, Mac and PC labs are located throughout the campus. All residence hall rooms have Internet access. All students may access the system every day. There are no time limits and no fees.

Graduates: From July 1, 2002 to June 30, 2003, 686 bachelor's degrees were awarded. The most popular majors were business administration (8%), psychology (7%), and liberal studies (7%). In an average class, 2% graduate in 3 years or less, 42% graduate in 4 years or less, 45% graduate in 5 years or less, and 51% graduate in 6 years or less. 90 companies recruited on campus in 2002-2003. Of the 2002 graduating class, 45% were employed within 6 months of graduation.

Admissions Contact: Gregory G. Vaughan, Director of Enrollment Management. E-mail: *admissions@biola.edu* Web: *www.biola.edu*

CALIFORNIA BAPTIST UNIVERSITY
Riverside, CA 92504-3297

D-5
(909) 343-4212
(877) 228-8866; Fax: (909) 343-4525

Full-time: 490 men, 954 women	**Faculty:** 76
Part-time: 111 men, 198 women	**Ph.D.s:** 65%
Graduate: 151 men, 455 women	**Student/Faculty:** 19 to 1
Year: semesters, summer session	**Tuition:** $14,684
Application Deadline: open	**Room & Board:** $5240
Freshman Class: 705 applied, 594 accepted, 305 enrolled	
SAT I Verbal/Math: 508/503	**ACT:** 20 COMPETITIVE

California Baptist University, founded in 1950, is a private institution supported by the California Southern Baptist Convention and offering degree programs in the arts and sciences, business, and religious studies. There are 6 undergraduate and 5 graduate schools. In addition to regional accreditation, Cal Baptist has baccalaureate program accreditation with ACBSP and NASM. The library contains 86,381 volumes, 50,949 microform items, and 4992 audio/video tapes/CDs, and subscribes to 349 periodicals. Computerized library services include the card catalog, interlibrary loans, database searching, and Internet access. Special learning facilities include a learning resource center and art gallery. The 80-acre campus is in a suburban area 60 miles east of Los Angeles. Including any residence halls, there are 25 buildings.

Student Life: 95% of undergraduates are from California. Students are from 19 states, 15 foreign countries, and Canada. 76% are from public schools. 66% are white; 14% Hispanic. 80% are Protestant; 13% claim no religious affiliation; 7% Catholic. The average age of freshmen is 19; all undergraduates, 25. 14% do not continue beyond their first year; 56% remain to graduate.

Housing: 905 students can be accommodated in college housing, which includes single-sex dorms, on-campus apartments, off-campus apartments, and married-student housing. On-campus housing is guaranteed for all 4 years. 52% of students commute. Alcohol is not permitted. All students may keep cars.

Activities: There are no fraternities or sororities. There are 16 groups on campus, including art, band, choir, chorale, chorus, computers, debate, drama, ethnic, forensics, honors, international, musical theater, newspaper, orchestra, pep band, political, professional, religious, social service, student government, and yearbook. Popular campus events include Campus Day, Twirp Week, and Octoberfest.

Sports: There are 8 intercollegiate sports for men and 6 for women, and 8 intramural sports for men and 8 for women. Facilities include a 950-seat gym, baseball, soccer, and softball fields, tennis and sand volleyball courts, an Olympic swimming facility, fitness center, and activity center.

Disabled Students: 95% of the campus is accessible. Wheelchair ramps, elevators, special parking, specially equipped rest rooms, and lowered drinking fountains are available.

Services: Counseling and information services are available, as is tutoring in most subjects. There is remedial math, reading, and writing.

Campus Safety and Security: Measures include 24-hour foot and vehicle patrol, self-defense education, security escort services, and informal discussions. There are pamphlets/posters/films, emergency telephones, and lighted pathways/sidewalks.

Programs of Study: Cal Baptist confers B.A., B.S., and B.B.A. degrees. Master's degrees are also awarded. Bachelor's degrees are awarded in BIOLOGICAL SCIENCE (biology/biological science), BUSINESS (business administration and management and management science), COMMUNICATIONS AND THE ARTS (applied art, communications, English, music, and visual and performing arts), COMPUTER AND PHYSICAL SCIENCE (information sciences and systems and mathematics), EDUCATION (physical), HEALTH PROFESSIONS (exercise science), SOCIAL SCIENCE (behavioral science, Christian studies, criminal justice, history, liberal arts/general studies, philosophy, political science/government, psychology, social science, and sociology). Liberal studies (education) is the strongest academically. Business, psychology, and kinesiology are the largest.

Required: All students must complete courses in fine arts, humanities, natural sciences, religion, social sciences, and phys ed. A total of 124 units, with a minimum GPA of 2.0, is required to graduate.

Special: Cal Baptist offers an accelerated program in several disciplines. Study abroad in at least 6 countries, internships, work-study programs, a Washington semester, B.A.-B.S. degrees, dual majors, and credit for military/work experience are available. There are 2 national honor societies.

Faculty/Classroom: 63% of faculty are male; 37%, female. 92% teach undergraduates. No introductory courses are taught by graduate students. The average class size in an introductory lecture is 33; in a laboratory, 11; and in a regular course, 22.

Admissions: 84% of the 2003-2004 applicants were accepted. The SAT I scores for the 2003-2004 freshman class were: Verbal--47% below 500, 35% between 500 and 599, 17% between 600 and 700, and 1% above 700; Math--44% below 500, 46% between 500 and 599, and 10% between 600 and 700. The ACT scores were 49% below 21, 34% between 21 and 23, 11% between 24 and 26, 4% between 27 and 28, and 2% above 28.

Requirements: The SAT I or ACT is required. In addition, applicants should be graduates of an accredited high school or have a GED. An essay and interview are recommended, and 2 references, preferably from a church leader and an official of an academic institution, are required. A GPA of 2.5 is required. AP and CLEP credits are accepted. Important factors in the admissions decision are recommendations by school officials, leadership record, and advanced placement or honor courses.

Procedure: Freshmen are admitted fall and spring. Entrance exams should be taken during the junior year. There is a rolling admissions plan a deferred admissions plan. Application deadlines are open. Application fee is $45. Applications are accepted on-line through the university's web site *www.calbaptist.edu*.

Transfer: 100 transfer students enrolled in 2002-2003. Applicants must have a minimum GPA of 2.0, if they are transferring at least 30 transferable semester units. Only courses with a grade of C- or better may transfer. If less than 30 units, their high school GPA must be at least 2.5 and they must submit SAT I or ACT scores. 36 of 124 credits required for the bachelor's degree must be completed at Cal Baptist.

Visiting: There are regularly scheduled orientations for prospective students, consisting of a welcome, orientation, academic fair, and tours. There are guides for informal visits and visitors may sit in on classes and stay overnight. To schedule a visit, contact the Admissions Office.

Financial Aid: In a recent year, 89% of all full-time freshmen and 95% of continuing full-time students received some form of financial aid. 65% of full-time freshmen and 79% of continuing full-time students received need-based aid. The average freshman award was $8400. 21% of undergraduates work part time. Average annual earnings from campus work are $3800. The average financial indebtedness of a recent graduate was $18,300. The FAFSA is required.

International Students: There are 21 international students enrolled. The school actively recruits these students. They must score 520 on the written TOEFL and also take the SAT I or ACT, with a minimum score of 920 on the SAT I or 19 on the ACT.

Computers: The mainframe is an HP 9000/Model K-460 (HP-UNIX). Academic computer labs house 175 computers available for student use. All students may access the system during open lab and library hours. There are no time limits and no fees.

Graduates: From July 1, 2002 to June 30, 2003, 364 bachelor's degrees were awarded. The most popular majors were liberal studies (education) (39%), psychology/behavioral science (14%), and business (11%). In an average class, 7% graduate in 3 years or less, 44% graduate in 4 years or less, 52% graduate in 5 years or less, and 54% graduate in 6 years or less. 210 companies recruited on campus in 2002-2003.

Admissions Contact: Allen Johnson, Director, Undergraduate Admissions. E-mail: *admissions@calbaptist.edu* Web: *www.calbaptist.edu*

CALIFORNIA COLLEGE OF THE ARTS
San Francisco, CA 94107

B-3
(415) 703-9535
(800) 447-1ART; Fax: (415) 703-9539

Full-time: 470 men, 679 women	**Faculty:** 34
Part-time: 35 men, 85 women	**Ph.D.s:** 63%
Graduate: 60 men, 129 women	**Student/Faculty:** 34 to 1
Year: semesters, summer session	**Tuition:** $23,500
Application Deadline: February 15	**Room & Board:** $8030
Freshman Class: 620 applied, 490 accepted, 165 enrolled	
SAT I Verbal/Math: 547/507	**ACT:** 22 SPECIAL

California College of the Arts, formerly California College of Arts and Crafts, established in 1907, is a private professional arts institution offering programs in fine arts, design, and architecture studies. There is 1 undergraduate and 6 graduate schools. In addition to regional accreditation, CCA has baccalaureate program accreditation with FIDER, NAAB, and NASAD. The 2 libraries contain 39,000 volumes, 50 microform items, and 520 audio/video tapes/CDs, and subscribe to 340 periodicals. Computerized library services include the card catalog, interlibrary loans, and database searching. Special learning facilities include a learning resource center and art gallery. The 4-acre campus is in an urban area. Including any residence halls, there are 15 buildings.

Student Life: 73% of undergraduates are from California. Students are from 39 states, 21 foreign countries, and Canada. 82% are from public schools. 58% are white; 10% Asian American. The average age of freshmen is 18; all undergraduates, 25. 21% do not continue beyond their first year.

Housing: 275 students can be accommodated in college housing, which includes coed dorms, on-campus apartments, and an off-campus residence hall. On-campus housing is guaranteed for the freshman year only, is available on a first-come, first-served basis, and is available on a lottery system for upperclassmen. Priority is given to out-of-town students. 84% of students commute. Alcohol is not permitted. No one may keep cars.

Activities: There are no fraternities or sororities. There are 18 groups on campus, including art, ethnic, gay, honors, international, newspaper, professional, and student government. Popular campus events include All-College Honors, Holiday and Spring Fair, and Student Gala.

Sports: There is no sports program at CCA.

Disabled Students: 80% of the campus is accessible. Wheelchair ramps, elevators, special parking, specially equipped rest rooms, special class scheduling, lowered drinking fountains, and lowered telephones are available.

Services: Counseling and information services are available, as is tutoring in some subjects, including humanities and sciences.

Campus Safety and Security: Measures include self-defense education, security escort services, shuttle buses, and informal discussions. There are pamphlets/posters/films, emergency telephones, and lighted pathways/sidewalks.

Programs of Study: CCA confers B.A., B.Arch, and B.F.A. degrees. Master's degrees are also awarded. Bachelor's degrees are awarded in COMMUNICATIONS AND THE ARTS (ceramic art and design, creative writing, film arts, glass, graphic design, illustration, industrial design, metal/jewelry, painting, photography, printmaking, sculpture, and visual and performing arts), ENGINEERING AND ENVIRONMENTAL DESIGN (architecture, furniture design, and interior design), SOCIAL SCIENCE (fashion design and technology and textiles and clothing). Design, painting/drawing, and illustration are the largest.

Required: Students must successfully complete 126 credits for the B.F.A. and B.A., with 57 in the major, and 162 for the B.Arch., with 96 in the major. Distribution requirements are 51 credits in humanities and science plus 75 in studio work for fine arts majors and 111 in studio work for architecture majors. All students must complete the core curriculum and maintain a minimum GPA of 2.0.

Special: Co-op programs in design are available. Cross-registration is permitted with Mills and Holy Names colleges in Oakland and with the University of San Francisco in San Francisco. Opportunities are provided for internships, study abroad in 11 countries, student-designed majors, and nondegree study. The Association of Independent Colleges of Art and Design Mobility Program is also possible.

Faculty/Classroom: 54% of faculty are male; 46%, female. 94% teach undergraduates. No introductory courses are taught by graduate students. The average class size in an introductory lecture is 18 and in a regular course, 18.

Admissions: 79% of the 2003-2004 applicants were accepted. The SAT I scores for the 2003-2004 freshman class were: Verbal--26% below 500, 50% between 500 and 599, 19% between 600 and 700, and 5% above 700; Math--45% below 500, 37% between 500 and 599, and 18% between 600 and 700. The ACT scores were 14% below 21, 50% between 21 and 23, 27% between 24 and 26, and 9% between 27 and 28.

Requirements: The SAT I or ACT is recommended. In addition, graduation from an accredited secondary school is required; a GED will be accepted. An essay, portfolio, and letters of recommendation are required. An interview is strongly recommended. A GPA of 2.0 is required. AP credits are accepted. Important factors in the admissions decision are evidence of special talent, recommendations by school officials, and extracurricular activities record.

Procedure: Freshmen are admitted fall and spring. There is a rolling admissions plan. Applications should be filed by February 15 for fall entry and October 1 for spring entry, along with a $50 fee. Notification is sent on a rolling basis. Applications are accepted on-line through *www.cca.edu.*

Transfer: 204 transfer students enrolled in 2002-2003. Applicants must submit a portfolio. 30 of 126 credits required for the bachelor's degree must be completed at CCA.

Visiting: There are regularly scheduled orientations for prospective students, including fall and spring open houses and orientation for admitted students a week prior to start of the semester. There are guides for informal visits and visitors may sit in on classes. To schedule a visit, contact the Office of Enrollment Services at (415) 703-9523.

Financial Aid: In 2003-2004, 57% of all full-time freshmen and 65% of continuing full-time students received some form of financial aid. 53% of full-time freshmen and 63% of continuing full-time students received need-based aid. The average freshman award was $17,645. Need-based scholarships or need-based grants averaged $9801; need-based self-help aid (loans and jobs) averaged $3456; and non-need-based awards and non-need-based scholarships averaged $2250. All undergraduates work part time. Average annual earnings from campus work are $1500. The average financial indebtedness of the 2003 graduate was $25,361. The FAFSA and the college's own financial statement are required. The deadline for filing freshman financial aid applications for fall entry is March 1.

International Students: There are 34 international students enrolled. They must score 550 on the written TOEFL or 213 on the electronic version.

Computers: The mainframe is an HP 3000. Mulitmedia computer labs on both campuses house Mac Power PCs and Quadras, scanners, printers, removable media drives, CD recorders, and Quick Cam cameras. Various software is available. The labs are networked to the Internet. All students may access the system. There are no time limits and no fees.

Graduates: From July 1, 2002 to June 30, 2003, 198 bachelor's degrees were awarded. The most popular majors were painting/drawing (14%) and individualized major (9%). In an average class, 39% graduate in 6 years or less.

Admissions Contact: Sheri Sivin McKenzie, Vice President for Enrollment Management. E-mail: *smckenzie@cca.edu* Web: *www.cca.edu*

CALIFORNIA INSTITUTE OF TECHNOLOGY   C-5
Pasadena, CA 91125   (626) 395-6341; Fax: (626) 683-3026

Full-time: 594 men, 297 women	**Faculty:** 295
Part-time: none	**Ph.D.s:** 100%
Graduate: 936 men, 345 women	**Student/Faculty:** 3 to 1
Year: quarters	**Tuition:** $24,117
Application Deadline: January 1	**Room & Board:** $7560
Freshman Class: 3072 applied, 520 accepted, 189 enrolled	
SAT I Verbal/Math: 740/790	**MOST COMPETITIVE**

California Institute of Technology, founded in 1891, is a private institution offering programs in engineering, science, and math. In addition to regional accreditation, Caltech has baccalaureate program accreditation with ABET and ACS. The 16 libraries contain 705,350 volumes, 613,155 microform items (601,681 microfiche, 11,474 film), and 920 audio/video tapes/CDs, and subscribe to 3901 periodicals. Computerized library services include the card catalog, interlibrary loans, database searching, and Internet access. Special learning facilities include a learning resource center. The 124-acre campus is in a suburban area 12 miles northeast of Los Angeles. Including any residence halls, there are 103 buildings.

Student Life: 65% of undergraduates are from out of state, mostly the West. Students are from 46 states, 28 foreign countries, and Canada. 85% are from public schools. 51% are white; 31% Asian American. The average age of freshmen is 18; all undergraduates, 20. 5% do not continue beyond their first year; 89% remain to graduate.

Housing: 820 students can be accommodated in college housing, which includes coed dorms, off-campus apartments, and married-student housing. On-campus housing is guaranteed for all 4 years. 90% of students live on campus. Alcohol is not permitted. All students may keep cars.

Activities: There are no fraternities or sororities. There are 85 groups on campus, including art, band, cheerleading, chess, choir, chorale, chorus, computers, dance, drama, ethnic, film, gay, honors, international, jazz band, literary magazine, musical theater, newspaper, opera, orchestra, pep band, photography, political, professional, religious, social, social service, student government, symphony, and yearbook. Popular campus events include Ditch Day, International Day, and Pre-Frosh Weekend.

Sports: There are 10 intercollegiate sports for men and 8 for women, and 16 intramural sports for men and 13 for women. Facilities include 2 Olympic-size swimming pools, a 300-seat gym, a 440-meter track, a football field, 4 baseball fields, and 8 tennis courts. Another athletic facility includes a gym, a 4000-square-foot exercise room with equipment, and racquetball courts.

Disabled Students: 98% of the campus is accessible. Wheelchair ramps, elevators, special parking, specially equipped rest rooms, and lowered telephones are available.

Services: Counseling and information services are available, as is tutoring in every subject. There is a reader service for the blind.

Campus Safety and Security: Measures include 24-hour foot and vehicle patrol, self-defense education, security escort services, and informal discussions. There are pamphlets/posters/films, emergency telephones, and lighted pathways/sidewalks.

Programs of Study: Caltech confers the B.S. degree. Master's and doctoral degrees are also awarded. Bachelor's degrees are awarded in BIOLOGICAL SCIENCE (biology/biological science), COMMUNICATIONS AND THE ARTS (literature), COMPUTER AND PHYSICAL SCIENCE (astronomy, chemistry, geochemistry, geology, geophysics and seismology, mathematics, physics, and planetary and space science), ENGINEERING AND ENVIRONMENTAL DESIGN (aeronautical engineering, chemical engineering, civil engineering, electrical/electronics engineering, engineering, engineering and applied science, and mechanical engineering), SOCIAL SCIENCE (economics, history, political science/government, and social science). Engineering, applied science, and electrical engineering are the largest.

Required: All students must complete 108 units in humanities and social science, 90 each in math and physics, 21 in chemistry, 9 in biology, 6 in lab, 9 in additional science courses, and 3 terms of phys ed. A total of 780 quarter units, including 516 in the major, and a minimum GPA of 1.9 are required to graduate.

Special: Caltech offers cross-registration with Scripps College, Occidental College, and Art Center College of Design, various work-study programs, including those with NASA's Jet Propulsion Laboratory, dual majors in any major, and independent studies degrees with faculty-approved student-designed majors. A 3-2 engineering degree is possible with several institutions. Pass/fail options are available for freshmen. A summer undergraduate research fellowship program is offered. Study abroad at University College in London, Cambridge University, and University of Copenhagen in Denmark is possible.

Faculty/Classroom: 85% of faculty are male; 15%, female. All both teach and do research. No introductory courses are taught by graduate students. The average class size in an introductory lecture is 150 and in a regular course, 12.

Admissions: 17% of the 2003-2004 applicants were accepted. The SAT I scores for the 2003-2004 freshman class were: Verbal--1% below 500, 5% between 500 and 599, 17% between 600 and 700, and 77% above 700; Math--4% between 600 and 700, and 96% above 700. 99% of the current freshmen were in the top fifth of their class; all were in the top two fifths. There were 53 National Merit finalists. 85 freshmen graduated first in their class.

Requirements: The SAT I or ACT is required. In addition, SAT II: Subject tests in writing, math level II, and one in physics, biology, or chemistry are required. Applicants should have completed 4 years of high school math, 3 of English, 1 each of chemistry and history, and 5 units from other concentrations. Important factors in the admissions decision are advanced placement or honor courses, recommendations by school officials, and evidence of special talent.

Procedure: Freshmen are admitted in the fall. Entrance exams should be taken through December of the senior year. There are early decision, early admissions, and deferred admissions plans. Early decision applications should be filed by November 1; regular applications, by January 1 for fall entry, along with a $50 fee. Notification of early decision is sent December 31; regular decision, April 1. 151 early decision candidates were accepted for the 2003-2004 class. A waiting list is an active part of the admissions procedure. Applications are accepted on-line through *embark.com*.

Transfer: 23 transfer students enrolled in 2002-2003. Transfers, admitted only into sophomore and junior classes, need a minimum GPA of 3.0. Applicants must have completed 1 year (2 years for juniors) of calculus and calculus-based physics, and must take Caltech's entrance exams in math and physics. Chemistry or chemical engineering majors also should have completed 1 year of chemistry and must take an additional entrance exam. 216 quarter units of 780 required for the bachelor's degree must be completed at Caltech.

Visiting: There are regularly scheduled orientations for prospective students, including a 1:30 P.M. video screening and a 2 P.M. student-led tour, followed by an information session with an admissions counselor. There are guides for informal visits and visitors may sit in on classes. To schedule a visit, contact the Admissions Office.

Financial Aid: In 2003-2004, 60% of all full-time freshmen and 58% of continuing full-time students received some form of financial aid. 51% of continuing full-time students received need-based aid. The average freshman award was $21,687. The average financial indebtedness of the 2003 graduate was $10,244. Caltech is a member of CSS. The CSS Profile and FAFSA are required. The deadline for filing freshman financial aid applications for fall entry is January 15.

International Students: There are 92 international students enrolled. They must take the SAT I or the ACT, as well as SAT II: Subject tests in math level IIC, writing, and chemistry, physics, or biology.

Computers: The mainframe is a Sun/UNIX cluster. Terminals are located in all buildings, including student housing. The mainframe computer can also be accessed from student-owned PCs. All students may access the system any time. There are no time limits and no fees. It is strongly recommended that all students have a personal computer.

Graduates: From July 1, 2002 to June 30, 2003, 248 bachelor's degrees were awarded. The most popular majors were engineering and applied science (50%), physical sciences (33%), and biology (9%). In an average class, 89% graduate in 6 years or less. 85 companies recruited on campus in 2002-2003. Of the 2002 graduating class, 45% were enrolled in graduate school within 6 months of graduation and 30% were employed.

Admissions Contact: Dan Langdale, Director of Admissions. E-mail: *ugadmissions@caltech.edu* Web: *www.admissions.caltech.edu*

CALIFORNIA INSTITUTE OF THE ARTS   C-5
Valencia, CA 91355   (661) 255-1050
(800) 545-ARTS; Fax: (805) 254-8352

Full-time: 449 men, 339 women	**Faculty:** n/av
Part-time: 8 men, 10 women	**Ph.D.s:** n/av
Graduate: 243 men, 236 women	**Student/Faculty:** 7 to 1
Year: semesters	**Tuition:** $24,695
Application Deadline: January 5	**Room & Board:** $5995
Freshman Class: 2838 applied, 1033 accepted, 498 enrolled	
SAT I or ACT: not required	**SPECIAL**

California Institute of the Arts, founded in 1961, is a private institution offering undergraduate and graduate programs in art, dance, film and video, music, and theater, and graduate majors in directing, integrated media, and writing. There are 6 undergraduate and 6 graduate schools. In addition to regional accreditation, Cal Arts has baccalaureate program accreditation with NASAD, NASM, NASD, and NAST. The library contains 96,306 volumes, 5320 microform items, and 17,718 audio/video tapes/CDs, and subscribes to 382 periodicals. Computerized library services include the card catalog, interlibrary loans, and database searching. Special learning facilities include an art gallery, radio station, TV station, movie theater, sound stages, scenery construction shops, and slide and film libraries. The 60-acre campus is in a suburban area 30 miles north of Los Angeles. Including any residence halls, there are 3 buildings.

Student Life: 63% of undergraduates are from out of state, mostly the Midwest. Students are from 48 states, 39 foreign countries, and Canada. 69% are white; 14% foreign nationals; 12% Asian American. The average age of freshmen is 19; all undergraduates, 22. 13% do not continue beyond their first year; 94% remain to graduate.

Housing: 450 students can be accommodated in college housing, which includes coed dorms and on-campus apartments. On-campus housing is available on a first-come, first-served basis and is available on a lottery system for upperclassmen. Priority is given to out-of-town students. 53% of students live on campus. All students may keep cars.

Activities: There are no fraternities or sororities. There are 17 groups on campus, including art, chess, dance, drama, ethnic, film, gay, international, jazz band, literary magazine, newspaper, opera, orchestra, photography, political, radio and TV, sports clubs, student government, and symphony. Popular campus events include music festivals, theater productions, and poetry readings.

Sports: There is no sports program at Cal Arts. Facilities include tennis courts, sand volleyball courts, and a swimming pool.

Disabled Students: 95% of the campus is accessible. Wheelchair ramps, elevators, special parking, specially equipped rest rooms, special class scheduling, lowered drinking fountains, lowered telephones, and special housing are available.

Services: Counseling and information services are available, as is tutoring in some subjects, including ESL. There is a reader service for the blind. All computerized media systems are used in the 6 major departments, and other subjects, which vary each year.

Campus Safety and Security: Measures include 24-hour foot and vehicle patrol, security escort services, informal discussions, pamphlets/posters/films, and lighted pathways/sidewalks.

Programs of Study: Cal Arts confers the B.F.A. degree. Master's degrees are also awarded. Bachelor's degrees are awarded in COMMUNICATIONS AND THE ARTS (dance, dramatic arts, film arts, fine arts, and music). Art, music, and acting are the strongest academically. Art, film/video, and theater are the largest.

Required: To graduate, all students must complete a total of 120 credit hours, with 48 in critical studies and 72 in the major, and must satisfy all curriculum and degree requirements of the particular school.

Special: Cal Arts offers internships with local and national companies, student-designed majors, interdisciplinary studies, study abroad in 6 countries, and a cooperative education program.

Faculty/Classroom: 62% of faculty are male; 38%, female. No introductory courses are taught by graduate students. The average class size in an introductory lecture is 15 and in a regular course, 8.

Admissions: 36% of the 2003-2004 applicants were accepted. There was 1 National Merit semifinalist.

Requirements: Applicants must be graduates of an accredited secondary school or have a GED certificate. They must submit an official transcript and an essay. Portfolios and auditions are required and an interview is recommended. AP credits are accepted. Important factors in the admissions decision are evidence of special talent and advanced placement or honor courses.

Procedure: Freshmen are admitted fall and spring. There is a rolling admissions plan. Applications should be filed by January 5 for fall entry and November 15 for spring entry, along with a $60 fee. Notification is sent on a rolling basis. A waiting list is an active part of the admissions procedure.

Transfer: 87 transfer students enrolled in 2002-2003. Applicants must submit official college and high school transcripts. An audition or a portfolio is required. Depending on the program, at least 1 or 2 years, including the final semester, must be completed in residence.

Visiting: There are regularly scheduled orientations for prospective students, including tours held Monday through Friday at 12 P.M. throughout the academic year. Visitors may sit in on classes. To schedule a visit, contact the Office of Admissions at *admiss@calarts.edu*.

Financial Aid: In a recent year, 72% of all full-time freshmen and 79% of continuing full-time students received some form of financial aid. 62% of full-time freshmen and 68% of continuing full-time students received need-based aid. The average freshman award was $18,688. 23% of undergraduates work part time. Average annual earnings from campus work are $1536. The average financial indebtedness of a recent graduate was $25,069. Cal Arts is a member of CSS. The FAFSA is required. The deadline for filing freshman financial aid applications for fall entry is March 2.

International Students: There were 176 international students enrolled in a recent year. They must score 550 on the written TOEFL.

Computers: In addition to the library's computer center, the graphic design school has a Mac computer-imaging, text, and visual motion lab. The film and video school offers computer animation labs and editing equipment. The theater and dance schools feature computerized lighting facilities, and the music school has computerized composition and digital synthesis systems. All students may access the system. There are no time limits and no fees.

Graduates: In a recent year, 151 bachelor's degrees were awarded. The most popular majors were animation (20%), art/photography (20%), and music performance (20%). In an average class, 52% graduate in 4 years or less. 25 companies recruited on campus in 2002-2003.

Admissions Contact: Carol Kim, Director of Enrollment Services. E-mail: *admiss@calarts.edu* Web: *www.calarts.edu*

CALIFORNIA LUTHERAN UNIVERSITY   C-5
Thousand Oaks, CA 91360-2700   (805) 493-3135
(877) 258-3678; Fax: (805) 493-3114

Full-time: 744 men, 970 women	**Faculty:** 100; IIA, av$
Part-time: 105 men, 100 women	**Ph.D.s:** 94%
Graduate: 291 men, 709 women	**Student/Faculty:** 17 to 1
Year: semesters, summer session	**Tuition:** $20,400
Application Deadline: March 15	**Room & Board:** $7200
Freshman Class: n/av	
SAT I or ACT: required	**LESS COMPETITIVE**

California Lutheran University, founded in 1959, is a private, nonprofit liberal arts institution affiliated with the Evangelical Lutheran Church of America. The comprehensive university offers undergraduate programs in arts and sciences, business, and education. There are 3 undergraduate and 4 graduate schools. The library contains 114,280 volumes, 18,080 microform items, and 1140 audio/video tapes/CDs, and subscribes to 610 periodicals. Computerized library services include the card catalog, interlibrary loans, and database searching. Special learning facilities include a learning resource center, art gallery, radio station, TV station, and a state-of-the-art science center. The 290-acre campus is in a suburban area 45 miles north of downtown Los Angeles in Ventura County, 50 miles south of Santa Barbara. Including any residence halls, there are 41 buildings.

Student Life: 67% of undergraduates are from California. Students are from 35 states, 33 foreign countries, and Canada. 70% are from public schools. 67% are white; 12% Hispanic. 48% are Protestant; 26% claim no religious affiliation; 21% Catholic. The average age of freshmen is 18; all undergraduates, 20. 18% do not continue beyond their first year; 60% remain to graduate.

Housing: 1300 students can be accommodated in college housing, which includes coed dorms and on-campus apartments. In addition, there are honors houses, a quiet hall, graduate housing, and senior singles. On-campus housing is guaranteed for all 4 years. 82% of students live on campus; of those, 75% remain on campus on weekends. Alcohol is not permitted. All students may keep cars.

Activities: There are no fraternities or sororities. There are 36 groups on campus, including art, band, cheerleading, choir, chorale, chorus, computers, dance, debate, drama, drum and bugle corps, environmental, ethnic, film, forensics, gay, honors, international, jazz band, literary magazine, marching band, musical theater, newspaper, orchestra, pep band, photography, political, professional, radio and TV, religious, social, social service, student alumni, student government, symphony, and yearbook. Popular campus events include Santa Lucia, Scandinavian Day, and the Pulitzer Prize Symposium.

Sports: There are 11 intercollegiate sports for men and 10 for women, and 10 intramural sports for men and 10 for women. Facilities include a 400-seat gym, 2 fields, a swimming pool, tennis courts, and a 2000-seat stadium.

Disabled Students: 75% of the campus is accessible. Wheelchair ramps, elevators, special parking, specially equipped rest rooms, lowered drinking fountains, and lowered telephones are available.

Services: Counseling and information services are available, as is tutoring in every subject. The learning resources and writing centers offer help with study and writing skills. There is remedial math, reading, and writ-

ing. A student support services program helps low-income first-generation students adapt to the academic and social life of the campus.

Campus Safety and Security: Measures include 24-hour foot and vehicle patrol, security escort services, shuttle buses, and informal discussions. There are pamphlets/posters/films, emergency telephones, and lighted pathways/sidewalks. All residence halls are equipped with security systems.

Programs of Study: CLU confers B.A. and B.S. degrees. Master's and doctoral degrees are also awarded. Bachelor's degrees are awarded in BIOLOGICAL SCIENCE (biochemistry and biology/biological science), BUSINESS (accounting, business administration and management, and marketing/retailing/merchandising), COMMUNICATIONS AND THE ARTS (art, communications, dramatic arts, English, French, German, multimedia, music, and Spanish), COMPUTER AND PHYSICAL SCIENCE (chemistry, computer science, geology, information sciences and systems, mathematics, and physics), EDUCATION (education and physical), HEALTH PROFESSIONS (predentistry, premedicine, and sports medicine), SOCIAL SCIENCE (criminal justice, economics, history, interdisciplinary studies, international studies, liberal arts/general studies, philosophy, political science/government, prelaw, psychology, religion, social science, and sociology). Biology, accounting, and humanities are the strongest academically. Business, psychology, and communication arts are the largest.

Required: To graduate, all students must complete a core curriculum including 16 to 20 units in social science, 8 each in religion, foreign language, and science, 7 in English, 4 to 6 in creative arts, 4 in math, and 3 in phys ed. Students must also fulfill content requirements of a freshman cluster and take 2 writing-intensive courses, global studies, gender and ethnic studies, and a senior level capstone course. Also needed are a total of 124 units, 40 of which must be upper division with 32 hours in the major for a B.A. and a minimum of 36 hours for a B.S. The final 30 credits before graduation must be completed at CLU. Students must have a minimum 2.0 GPA, with 2.25 in the major.

Special: CLU offers co-op programs, cross-registration with Wagner College, internships, a Washington semester, and study abroad in 20 countries. Also available are work-study, accelerated degrees in business, computer science, and accounting, a general studies degree, and dual and student-designed interdisciplinary degree majors. A 3-2 engineering degree with Washington University of St. Louis, credit for experiential learning, special student status for nondegree study, pass/fail options, continuing education, English as a second language, and an adult degree evening program are also offered. There are 6 national honor societies, a freshman honors program, and honors programs in all departments.

Faculty/Classroom: 56% of faculty are male; 44%, female. 94% teach undergraduates. No introductory courses are taught by graduate students. The average class size in an introductory lecture is 35; in a laboratory, 17; and in a regular course, 22.

Requirements: The SAT I or ACT is required. In addition, minimum composite scores are 800 for the SAT I (400 verbal) and 19 for the ACT. Applicants must be graduates of an accredited secondary school and have completed a minimum of 4 years of English, 2 years each of math, foreign language, and social studies, and 1 of lab science. The GED is accepted. An essay is required and an interview is recommended. AP and CLEP credits are accepted. Important factors in the admissions decision are advanced placement or honor courses, recommendations by school officials, and evidence of special talent.

Procedure: Freshmen are admitted fall and spring. Entrance exams should be taken in the fall. There are early decision and deferred admissions plans. Early decision applications should be filed by November 15; regular applications, by March 15 for fall entry, and October 1 for spring entry, along with a $45 fee. Notification of early decision is sent December 1; regular decision, on a rolling basis. A waiting list is an active part of the admissions procedure. Applications are accepted on computer disk and on-line through *www.callutheran.edu* and the Common Application.

Transfer: 182 transfer students enrolled in 2002-2003. Transfers must have a minimum 2.25 GPA and at least 24 credit hours earned. An application is required. An interview is recommended. Applicants must be in good standing at the previous college and may submit a recommendation from a college professor in lieu of a high school recommendation. 32 of 124 credits required for the bachelor's degree must be completed at CLU.

Visiting: There are regularly scheduled orientations for prospective students, including an admission and financial aid interview, a tour, visits with faculty or coaches, and lunch. There are guides for informal visits and visitors may sit in on classes and stay overnight. To schedule a visit, contact the Admission Office at *admissions@callutheran.edu*.

Financial Aid: In 2003-2004, 90% of all full-time freshmen and 85% of continuing full-time students received some form of financial aid. The average freshman award was $16,729. 45% of undergraduates work part time. Average annual earnings from campus work are $1000. The FAFSA is required. The deadline for filing freshman financial aid applications for fall entry is March 1.

International Students: The school actively recruits these students. They must score 530 on the written TOEFL, take the college's own test, and also take the SAT I or the ACT.

Computers: The mainframes are an HP 9000-825, and a DEC VAX 11/750. Students may access the network through 72 terminals in the library and labs. Mac and IBM labs are in the computer science building. The Ahmanson Science Center has a hypermedia lab with 14 Macs. 6 halls contain 3 Macs with printers. All students may access the system any time. There are no time limits and no fees.

Admissions Contact: Darryl Calkins, Dean of Admission.
E-mail: *dcalkins@clunet.edu* Web: *www.clunet.edu*

CALIFORNIA MARITIME ACADEMY B-3
Vallejo, CA 94590-0644

(707) 654-1330
(800) 561-1945; Fax: (707) 654-1336

Full-time: 460 men, 120 women	**Faculty:** 49; IIB, +$
Part-time: 20 men, 65 women	**Ph.Ds:** 31%
Graduate: none	**Student/Faculty:** 12 to 1
Year: semesters, summer session	**Tuition:** $7546 ($16,006)
Application Deadline: see profile	**Room & Board:** $6750
Freshman Class: n/av	
SAT I or ACT: required	**COMPETITIVE**

California Maritime Academy, founded in 1929, is a public college that awards undergraduate degrees in marine transportation, business, engineering, and technology. Some information in this capsule and profile is approximate. In addition to regional accreditation, Cal Maritime has baccalaureate program accreditation with ABET. The library contains 25,000 volumes and 15,000 microform items, and subscribes to 225 periodicals. Computerized library services include the card catalog, interlibrary loans, and database searching. Special learning facilities include a learning resource center, a training ship, navigation, steam plant, and diesel engine simulators, and a fluid dynamics lab with wind tunnels and a miniature jet turbine engine. The 67-acre campus is in a suburban area 30 miles northeast of San Francisco. Including any residence halls, there are 26 buildings.

Student Life: 80% of undergraduates are from California. Students are from 19 states and 14 foreign countries. 70% are from public schools. 55% are white; 13% Asian American. The average age of freshmen is 21; all undergraduates, 22. 7% do not continue beyond their first year.

Housing: 457 students can be accommodated in college housing, which includes single-sex and coed dorms. In addition, there are 24-hour quiet residences. On-campus housing is guaranteed for all 4 years. 65% of students live on campus; of those, 30% remain on campus on weekends. Alcohol is not permitted. All students may keep cars.

Activities: There are no fraternities or sororities. There are 16 groups on campus, including auto shop, drill team, engineering, ethnic, international, photography, professional, religious, social, social service, student government, and surf club. Popular campus events include movie nights, cave exploring, and cafe night.

Sports: There are 7 intercollegiate sports for men and 5 for women, and 10 intramural sports for men and 8 for women. Facilities include a gym, a weight room, physical therapy and exercise rooms, a 25-meter pool, tennis and racquetball courts, and a sports field.

Disabled Students: 70% of the campus is accessible. Wheelchair ramps, special parking, specially equipped rest rooms, lowered drinking fountains, and lowered telephones are available.

Services: Counseling and information services are available, as is tutoring in some subjects, including math, English, engineering, and science. There is remedial math, reading, and writing.

Campus Safety and Security: Measures include 24-hour foot and vehicle patrol, self-defense education, security escort services, and informal discussions. There are pamphlets/posters/films, lighted pathways/sidewalks, and surveillance cameras.

Programs of Study: Cal Maritime confers the B.S degree. Bachelor's degrees are awarded in BUSINESS (business administration and management and transportation management), ENGINEERING AND ENVIRONMENTAL DESIGN (engineering technology, marine engineering, maritime science, and mechanical engineering). Mechanical engineering is the strongest academically. Marine transportation is the largest.

Required: Graduation requirements for all students include a minimum 2.0 GPA and completion of English composition, American government, U.S. history, algebra and trigonometry, computer science, and survival swimming courses. All students must participate in at least one 2-month training cruise. A total of 129 to 187 credits is required for graduation.

Special: The Academy has simulator training and requires a 2-month session aboard the Academy's ship. Lab time is a major part of each program. Industry internships are available during the summer. Dual majors and co-op programs are available, as is cross-registration with other Cal State institutions. There are B.A.-B.S. degrees in mechanical engineering, business, marine transportation, facilities engineering, global studies, and marine engineering.

Faculty/Classroom: 85% of faculty are male; 15%, female. All teach undergraduates. The average class size in an introductory lecture is 20; in a laboratory, 9; and in a regular course, 20.

Requirements: The SAT I or ACT is required. In addition, secondary school courses must include 4 years of English, 3 each of math and electives, 2 of language, and 1 each of lab science, history, and a visual or performing art. A GPA of 2.0 is required. AP and CLEP credits are accepted. Important factors in the admissions decision are leadership record, advanced placement or honor courses, and evidence of special talent.

Procedure: Freshmen are admitted in the fall. Entrance exams should be taken by December of the senior year. Early decision applications should be filed by November. Check with the school for application deadline and fee. Notification is sent on a rolling basis. Applications are accepted on-line through *www.csumentor.edu*.

Transfer: 50 transfer students enrolled in a recent year. Applicants must have a 2.0 GPA, provide SAT I or ACT scores, and be in good standing at the last institution attended.

Visiting: There are regularly scheduled orientations for prospective students. There are guides for informal visits. To schedule a visit, contact the Admissions Office.

Financial Aid: In a recent year, 59% of all full-time freshmen and 69% of continuing full-time students received some form of financial aid. 59% of full-time freshmen and 60% of continuing full-time students received need-based aid. The average freshman award was $8042. 80% of undergraduates work part time. Average annual earnings from campus work were $700. The average financial indebtedness of a recent graduate was $5147. The FAFSA is required. Check with the school for current deadlines.

International Students: There are 20 international students enrolled. They must score 550 on the written TOEFL or 213 on the electronic version and also take the SAT I or the ACT.

Computers: There are 22 self-contained PCs in the computer center and 4 PCs in the library. There are also 5 Macs in the residence halls. All students may access the system. There are no time limits and no fees.

Graduates: In a recent year, 64 bachelor's degrees were awarded. The most popular majors were marine transportation (31%), business administration (28%), and mechanical engineering (23%). In an average class, 49% graduate in 4 years or less, 8% graduate in 5 years or less, and 3% graduate in 6 years or less. 30 companies recruited on campus in a recent year. Of a recent graduating class, 1% were enrolled in graduate school within 6 months of graduation and all were employed.

Admissions Contact: Chris Krzak, Director of Admissions and Outreach. E-mail: *admission@csum.edu* Web: *www.csum.edu*

CALIFORNIA POLYTECHNIC STATE UNIVERSITY B-4
San Luis Obispo, CA 93407

(805) 756-2311
Fax: (805) 756-5400

Full-time: 8885 men, 7215 women	**Faculty:** 654; IIA, ++$
Part-time: 565 men, 410 women	**Ph.Ds:** 73%
Graduate: 450 men, 570 women	**Student/Faculty:** 20 to 1
Year: quarters, summer session	**Tuition:** $2155 ($9535)
Application Deadline: November 30	**Room & Board:** $7403
Freshman Class: n/av	
SAT I or ACT: required	**VERY COMPETITIVE**

California Polytechnic State University, founded in 1901, is a public institution that is part of the California State University system. It offers programs in agriculture, architecture and environmental design, business, education, engineering, liberal arts, sciences and math, and preprofessional studies. There are 6 undergraduate and 19 graduate schools. Figures in the above capsule and this profile are approximate. In addition to regional accreditation, Cal Poly has baccalaureate program accreditation with AACSB, ABET, ACCE, ADA, AHEA, ASLA, CSAB, NAAB, NRPA, and SAF. The library contains 1,206,340 volumes, 2,055,543 microform items, and 37,256 audio/video tapes/CDs, and subscribes to 3198 periodicals. Computerized library services include the card catalog, interlibrary loans, and database searching. Special learning facilities include a learning resource center, art gallery, radio station, and TV station. The 6000-acre campus is in a suburban area 200 miles from both San Francisco and Los Angeles. Including any residence halls, there are 130 buildings.

Student Life: 96% of undergraduates are from California. Students are from 48 states, 41 foreign countries, and Canada. 61% are white; 11% Asian American; 10% Hispanic. The average age of freshmen is 19; all undergraduates, 22. 11% do not continue beyond their first year.

Housing: 2783 students can be accommodated in college housing, which includes single-sex and coed dorms. In addition, there are special-interest houses and living/learning centers with an academic theme. On-campus housing is available on a first-come, first-served basis. 83% of students commute. Alcohol is not permitted. All students may keep cars.

Activities: 8% of men belong to 1 local and 26 national fraternities; 9% of women belong to 8 national sororities. There are 400 groups on campus, including art, band, cheerleading, chess, choir, chorale, chorus, computers, dance, drama, ethnic, film, gay, honors, international, jazz band, literary magazine, marching band, musical theater, newspaper, orchestra, pep band, photography, political, professional, radio and TV, religious, social, social service, student government, and symphony. Popular campus events include Rose Float, Week of Welcome (WOW), and Civil Rights Awareness Week.

Sports: There are 9 intercollegiate sports for men and 8 for women, and 19 intramural sports for men and 19 for women. Facilities include an indoor/outdoor swimming pool, volleyball, tennis, basketball, and racquetball courts, weight rooms, playing fields, and a track.

Disabled Students: 95% of the campus is accessible. Wheelchair ramps, elevators, special parking, specially equipped rest rooms, and lowered telephones are available.

Services: Counseling and information services are available, as is tutoring in most subjects. There is a reader service for the blind, a writing skills lab, and a test office. Psychological and career services are available.

Campus Safety and Security: Measures include 24-hour foot and vehicle patrol, security escort services, pamphlets/posters/films, and emergency telephones. There are lighted pathways/sidewalks.

Programs of Study: Cal Poly confers B.A., B.S., and B.Arch. degrees. Master's degrees are also awarded. Bachelor's degrees are awarded in AGRICULTURE (agricultural business management, agriculture, dairy science, horticulture, natural resource management, and soil science), BIOLOGICAL SCIENCE (biochemistry, biology/biological science, ecology, and microbiology), BUSINESS (business administration and management, and recreation and leisure services), COMMUNICATIONS AND THE ARTS (English, graphic design, and journalism), COMPUTER AND PHYSICAL SCIENCE (chemistry, computer science, mathematics, physical sciences, physics, and statistics), EDUCATION (industrial arts and physical), ENGINEERING AND ENVIRONMENTAL DESIGN (aeronautical engineering, agricultural engineering, architectural engineering, architecture, city/community/regional planning, civil engineering, computer engineering, construction management, electrical/electronics engineering, engineering, environmental engineering, industrial engineering, landscape architecture/design, manufacturing engineering, materials engineering, mechanical engineering, and metallurgical engineering), SOCIAL SCIENCE (economics, food science, history, human development, philosophy, political science/government, psychology, and social science). Agricultural management, architecture, and business administration are the largest.

Required: Students must have a minimum 2.0 GPA and complete general education and breadth requirements, including the following: 18 units each of physical and life sciences, social sciences, and literature and the arts; 14 units of English; and 5 units of psychology and health. Math and computer literacy courses and a senior project are required. 186 to 263 quarter units are needed to graduate.

Special: Cal Poly offers work-study programs, co-op programs in numerous majors, study abroad in 11 countries, dual majors, and internships in many majors. Credit for military experience and pass/fail options are available.

Faculty/Classroom: 69% of faculty are male; 31%, female.

Requirements: The SAT I or ACT is required. In addition, applicants must be graduates of an accredited high school or have a GED. 15 academic credits are required, including 4 years of English, 3 each of math and science, 2 of a foreign language, and 1 each of history and visual or performing arts. A GPA of 2.0 is required. AP and CLEP credits are accepted.

Procedure: Freshmen are admitted fall and summer. Entrance exams should be taken January 15. There are early decision and early admissions plans. Early decision applications should be filed by October 31; regular applications, by November 30 for fall entry and February 28 for summer entry, along with a $55 fee. Notification of early decision is sent December 15; regular decision, March 1. Applications are accepted online.

Transfer: 1030 transfer students enrolled in a recent year. Applicants must have completed 56 semester or 84 quarter units with a minimum GPA of 2.0. 50 of 186 credits required for the bachelor's degree must be completed at Cal Poly.

Visiting: There are regularly scheduled orientations for prospective students, held on Mondays and Wednesdays at 10 A.M. and 2 P.M. There are guides for informal visits and visitors may stay overnight. To schedule a visit, contact the Admissions Office at (805) 756-2792.

Financial Aid: In a recent year, 29% of all full-time freshmen and 34% of continuing full-time students received some form of financial aid. The average freshman award was $6299. The average financial indebtedness of the 2003 graduate was $12,908. The FAFSA and the college's own financial statement are required. The deadline for filing freshman financial aid applications for fall entry is March 2.

International Students: In a recent year there were 79 international students enrolled. The school actively recruits these students. They must score 550 on the written TOEFL.

Computers: The mainframe is an IBM ES/9000 Model 732. There are also more than 1000 Macs and PCs available throughout campus. All students may access the system. There are no time limits and no fees. It is strongly recommended that all students have a personal computer.

Graduates: In a recent year, 2838 bachelor's degrees were awarded. The most popular majors were engineering (22%), business (18%), and agriculture (15%). In an average class, 64% graduate in 6 years or less.

Admissions Contact: James L. Maraviglia, Director of Admissions. E-mail: *admprosp@calpoly.edu* Web: *www.calpoly.edu*

CALIFORNIA STATE POLYTECHNIC UNIVERSITY, POMONA

D-5

Pomona, CA 91768-4019	(909) 869-3427; Fax: (909) 869-4529
Full-time: 8238 men, 6373 women	Faculty: 672; IIA, ++$
Part-time: 1779 men, 1260 women	Ph.D.s: 60%
Graduate: 952 men, 1202 women	Student/Faculty: 22 to 1
Year: quarters, summer session	Tuition: $2046 ($10,500)
Application Deadline: November 1	Room & Board: $6747
Freshman Class: 11,040 applied, 3345 accepted, 2284 enrolled	
SAT I Verbal/Math: 485/518	ACT: 21 COMPETITIVE+

California State Polytechnic University, Pomona, an occupationally oriented institution founded in 1938, is part of the state-supported university system. It offers undergraduate and graduate programs in agriculture, liberal arts and sciences, business, engineering, and technical and professional training. There are 8 undergraduate and 7 graduate schools. In addition to regional accreditation, Cal Poly Pomona has baccalaureate program accreditation with AACSB, ABET, ADA, ASLA, CSAB, and NAAB. The library contains 756,131 volumes, 2,502,023 microform items, and 10,553 audio/video tapes/CDs, and subscribes to 5430 periodicals. Computerized library services include the card catalog, interlibrary loans, and database searching. Special learning facilities include a learning resource center, art gallery, TV station, and interactive TV studio. The 1438-acre campus is in a suburban area 30 miles east of Los Angeles. Including any residence halls, there are 80 buildings.

Student Life: 97% of undergraduates are from California. Students are from 50 states, 54 foreign countries, and Canada. 87% are from public schools. 37% are Asian American; 30% white; 28% Hispanic. The average age of freshmen is 18; all undergraduates, 22. 18% do not continue beyond their first year; 45% remain to graduate.

Housing: 1800 students can be accommodated in college housing, which includes coed dorms. In addition, there are special-interest houses and a center for regenerative studies. On-campus housing is available on a first-come, first-served basis. 91% of students commute. All students may keep cars.

Activities: 1% of men belong to 6 local and 11 national fraternities; 1% of women belong to 3 local and 4 national sororities. There are 220 groups on campus, including art, band, cheerleading, choir, chorale, chorus, computers, ethnic, film, gay, honors, international, literary magazine, musical theater, newspaper, pep band, photography, political, professional, religious, social, social service, student government, and yearbook. Popular campus events include Rose Float, Broncofest, and Founder's Day.

Sports: There are 6 intercollegiate sports for men and 6 for women. Facilities include a 5000-seat stadium, tennis and racquetball courts, basketball and volleyball courts, soccer, baseball, and softball fields, a track, a swimming pool, gymnastics and weight rooms, a horse arena, and dance studios.

Disabled Students: 96% of the campus is accessible. Wheelchair ramps, elevators, special parking, specially equipped rest rooms, special class scheduling, lowered drinking fountains, lowered telephones, and specialized tram, van, and shuttle transportation are available.

Services: Counseling and information services are available, as is tutoring in most subjects. There is a reader service for the blind and remedial math and writing.

Campus Safety and Security: Measures include 24-hour foot and vehicle patrol, self-defense education, security escort services, and shuttle buses. There are informal discussions, pamphlets/posters/films, emergency telephones, lighted pathways/sidewalks, vehicle assists, and crime prevention programs.

Programs of Study: Cal Poly Pomona confers B.A. and B.S. degrees. Master's degrees are also awarded. Bachelor's degrees are awarded in AGRICULTURE (agricultural business management, agriculture, agronomy, animal science, and horticulture), BIOLOGICAL SCIENCE (biology/biological science, biotechnology, botany, microbiology, plant physiology, and zoology), BUSINESS (accounting, apparel and accessories marketing, banking and finance, business administration and management, hotel/motel and restaurant management, human resources, international business management, marketing/retailing/merchandising, operations research, and real estate), COMMUNICATIONS AND THE ARTS (art, communications, dramatic arts, English, music, and Spanish), COMPUTER AND PHYSICAL SCIENCE (chemistry, computer science, geology, information sciences and systems, mathematics, and physics), ENGINEERING AND ENVIRONMENTAL DESIGN (aeronautical engineering, architecture, chemical engineering, civil engineering, computer technology, construction technology, electrical/electronics engineering, engineering technology, industrial engineering, landscape architecture/design, manufacturing engineering, materials engineering, and mechanical engineering), SOCIAL SCIENCE (anthropology, behavioral science, economics, food science, geography, history, liberal arts/general studies, philosophy, physical fitness/movement, political science/government, psychology, social science, sociology, and urban studies). Engineering, architecture, and business are the strongest academically. Computer information systems, electrical engineering, and mechanical engineering are the largest.

Required: All students must complete general education requirements, including courses in written and oral communications, critical thinking, math, humanities, natural sciences, and social sciences, and must pass a graduation writing test. A total of 186 (B.A.) to 198 (B.S.) quarter units with a minimum GPA of 2.0 is required to graduate.

Special: Cross-registration is possible with any California State University school. Internships and co-op programs are available in agriculture, business, environmental design, engineering, science, political science, behavioral science, and phys ed. An international study program in 17 countries, work-study programs, B.A.-B.S. degrees, a liberal studies degree, credit for military experience, an external degree program, and credit/no credit options are offered. Nondegree study is possible. There are 30 national honor societies and a freshman honors program.

Faculty/Classroom: 61% of faculty are male; 39%, female. The average class size in a regular course is 25.

Admissions: 30% of the 2003-2004 applicants were accepted. The SAT I scores for the 2003-2004 freshman class were: Verbal--54% below 500, 34% between 500 and 599, 11% between 600 and 700, and 1% above 700; Math--36% below 500, 39% between 500 and 599, 23% between 600 and 700, and 3% above 700. The ACT scores were 50% below 21, 26% between 21 and 23, 16% between 24 and 26, 6% between 27 and 28, and 2% above 28.

Requirements: The SAT I or ACT is recommended. In addition, applicants must be graduates of an accredited secondary school or have a GED equivalent. Secondary school courses must include 4 years of high school English, 3 each of math and electives, 2 of foreign language, and 1 each of science, history, and art. A GPA of 2.0 is required. AP and CLEP credits are accepted.

Procedure: Freshmen are admitted to all sessions. Entrance exams should be taken during the fall of the senior year. There is a rolling admissions plan and a deferred admissions plan. Applications should be filed by November 1 for fall entry, June 1 for winter entry, August 1 for spring entry, and February 1 for summer entry, along with a $55 fee. Notification is sent on a rolling basis. Applications are accepted on computer disk and on-line through XAPplication and *www.csumentor.edu*.

Transfer: 1250 transfer students enrolled in 2002-2003. Applicants must have completed 56 semester or 84 quarter units including college preparatory subjects. A 2.0 GPA (2.4 for nonresidents) is required. 50 of 186 to 198 credits required for the bachelor's degree must be completed at Cal Poly Pomona.

Visiting: There are regularly scheduled orientations for prospective students, consisting of tours of the campus led by current undergraduate students and a 90 minute walking tour. There are guides for informal visits and visitors may sit in on classes and stay overnight. To schedule a visit, contact Visitor Services at (909) 869-3529.

Financial Aid: In 2003-2004, 41% of all full-time freshmen and 54% of continuing full-time students received some form of financial aid. 38% of full-time freshmen and 48% of continuing full-time students received need-based aid. The average freshman award was $7332. Average annual earnings from campus work are $1560. The average financial indebtedness of the 2003 graduate was $11,258. The FAFSA is required. The deadline for filing freshman financial aid applications for fall entry is March 2.

International Students: There are 911 international students enrolled. They must score 525 on the written TOEFL and also take the SAT I or the ACT.

Computers: The mainframe is a DEC Alpha 7000-620. PC clusters are available in labs on campus. All students may access the system 24 hours per day. There are no time limits and no fees. It is recommended that students in environmental design have personal computers.

Graduates: From July 1, 2002 to June 30, 2003, 3348 bachelor's degrees were awarded. The most popular majors were marketing management (8%), management/human resources (7%), and computer information systems (6%). In an average class, 8% graduate in 4 years or less, 30% graduate in 5 years or less, and 45% graduate in 6 years or less. 230 companies recruited on campus in 2002-2003.

Admissions Contact: Dr. George R. Bradshaw, Director of Admissions and Outreach. A video is available.
E-mail: *grbradshaw@csupomona.edu* Web: *www.csupomona.edu*

CALIFORNIA STATE UNIVERSITY SYSTEM

The California State University System, established in 1961, is a public system in California. It is governed by a board of trustees, whose chief administrator is the chancellor. The primary goal of the system is teaching. The main priorities are to emphasize quality in instruction; to provide an environment in which scholarship, research, creative, artistic, and professional activity are valued and supported; and to stress the importance of the liberal arts and sciences. The total enrollment of all 22 campuses is usually about 350,000; there were 19,500 faculty members. Altogether there are some 965 baccalaureate, 600 master's, and 14 joint doctoral programs offered in the California State University System. 4-year campuses are located in Bakersfield, Chico, Dominguez Hills, Fresno, Fullerton, Hayward, Humboldt, Long Beach, Los Angeles, Northridge, Pomona, Sacramento, San Bernadino, San Diego, San Francisco, San Jose, San Luis Obispo, and Sonoma. Profiles of the 4-year campuses are included in this section.

CALIFORNIA STATE UNIVERSITY, BAKERSFIELD   C-4
Bakersfield, CA 93311-1099   **(661) 664-2160**
                                   (800) 788-2782; Fax: (661) 664-3389

Full-time: 1440 men, 2700 women	**Faculty:** 234; IIA, +$
Part-time: 395 men, 705 women	**Ph.D.s:** 50%
Graduate: 570 men, 1260 women	**Student/Faculty:** 14 to 1
Year: quarters, summer session	**Tuition:** $1960 ($9340)
Application Deadline: open	**Room & Board:** $4130
Freshman Class: n/av	
SAT I or ACT: required	**LESS COMPETITIVE**

California State University/Bakersfield, founded in 1965, is part of the California State University System. It offers graduate and undergraduate programs in liberal arts and sciences, business, public administration, education, health fields, preengineering, and preprofessional training. Figures given in the above capsule and in this profile are approximate. There are 3 undergraduate and 10 graduate schools. In addition to regional accreditation, Cal State Bakersfield has baccalaureate program accreditation with AACSB, NCATE, and NLN. The library contains 339,900 volumes, 603,300 microform items, and 5180 audio/video tapes/CDs, and subscribes to 2700 periodicals. Computerized library services include the card catalog, interlibrary loans, and database searching. Special learning facilities include a learning resource center, art gallery, natural history museum, geological data sample repository, archeological information center, an instructional television network, applied research center, and animal care and treatment facility. The 375-acre campus is in an urban area in southwest Bakersfield. Including any residence halls, there are 30 buildings.

Student Life: 98% of undergraduates are from California. Students are from 25 states, 50 foreign countries, and Canada. 98% are from public schools. 51% are white; 25% Hispanic. The average age of freshmen is 19; all undergraduates, 25. 15% do not continue beyond their first year.

Housing: 330 students can be accommodated in college housing, which includes single-sex and coed dorms. On-campus housing is guaranteed for all 4 years. 98% of students commute. Alcohol is not permitted. All students may keep cars.

Activities: 2% of men belong to 3 national fraternities; 2% of women belong to 4 national sororities. There are 74 groups on campus, including art, band, cheerleading, chess, choir, chorale, computers, dance, drama, ethnic, film, gay, honors, international, jazz band, literary magazine, musical theater, newspaper, opera, orchestra, pep band, photography, political, professional, radio and TV, religious, social, social service, student government, and symphony. Popular campus events include Cinco de Mayo, Open Campus, and Jazz Festival.

Sports: There are 7 intercollegiate sports for men and 6 for women, and 12 intramural sports for men and 12 for women. Facilities include a 4000-seat gymn, a wrestling sport center, an aquatic center, tennis and racquetball courts, and softball and soccer fields.

Disabled Students: Wheelchair ramps, elevators, special parking, specially equipped rest rooms, special class scheduling, lowered drinking fountains, and lowered telephones are available.

Services: Counseling and information services are available, as is tutoring in most subjects, as well as in study skills. There is a reader service for the blind and remedial math, reading, and writing.

Campus Safety and Security: Measures include 24-hour foot and vehicle patrol, self-defense education, security escort services, and informal discussions. There are pamphlets/posters/films, emergency telephones, and lighted pathways/sidewalks.

Programs of Study: Cal State Bakersfield confers B.A. and B.S. degrees. Master's degrees are also awarded. Bachelor's degrees are awarded in BIOLOGICAL SCIENCE (biology/biological science), BUSINESS (business administration and management), COMMUNICATIONS AND THE ARTS (art, communications, dramatic arts, English, music, and Spanish), COMPUTER AND PHYSICAL SCIENCE (chemistry, computer science, geology, mathematics, and physics), ENGINEERING AND ENVIRONMENTAL DESIGN (land use management and reclamation), HEALTH PROFESSIONS (clinical science and nursing), SOCIAL SCIENCE (anthropology, child psychology/development, criminal justice, economics, history, liberal arts/general studies, philosophy, political science/government, psychology, public administration, religion, and sociology). Business, education, and public administration are the strongest academically. Business is the largest.

Required: All students must complete 72 quarter units of general education requirements in basic skills, Western civilization, non-Western culture, philosophy, fine arts, literature, technology, and physical, social, and life sciences. They must also take a comprehensive writing examination or complete an upper-division writing course with a grade of C or better, demonstrate understanding of American history and government institutions, and complete a senior seminar. A total of 186 quarter units with a minimum GPA of 2.0 is required in order to graduate.

Special: Cal State Bakersfield offers co-op programs in education and business administration, cross-registration through the National Student Exchange Program, study abroad at 36 universities in 16 countries, a 3-2 engineering degree with California Polytechnic State University/San Luis Obispo, and student-designed majors. Credit for life experience, pass/fail options, and nondegree study are available. Students may also earn credits as interns and participate in work-study programs on and off campus. There is a freshman honors program.

Faculty/Classroom: 62% of faculty are male; 38%, female. All both teach and do research. No introductory courses are taught by graduate students. The average class size in an introductory lecture is 40; in a laboratory, 24; and in a regular course, 30.

Requirements: The SAT I or ACT is required if the GPA is below 3.0. (3.6 for nonresidents). Admission is based on an eligibility index that weights the GPA and standardized test scores. In addition, applicants must be graduates of an accredited secondary school or GED equivalent, and have a total of 15 academic units, including 4 years of English, 3 of math, 2 of foreign language, 1 each of lab science, U.S. history/government, and visual and performing arts, and 3 of electives. Cal State Bakersfield requires applicants to be in the upper 33% of their class. A GPA of 2.0 is required. AP and CLEP credits are accepted.

Procedure: Freshmen are admitted fall, winter, and spring. Entrance exams should be taken by December of the senior year. There are early decision, early admissions, deferred admissions, and rolling admissions plans. Application deadlines are open. Application fee is $55.

Transfer: 682 transfer students enrolled in a recent year. A 2.0 GPA (2.4 for nonresidents) is required in a minimum of 56 semester or 84 quarter units earned, including English and math. 45 of 186 credits required for the bachelor's degree must be completed at Cal State Bakersfield.

Visiting: There are regularly scheduled orientations for prospective students, consisting of a day-long orientation that includes meetings with faculty advisers and school deans. There are guides for informal visits and visitors may sit in on classes. To schedule a visit, contact the Office of Outreach Services at (805) 664-3138.

Financial Aid: In a recent year, 50% of all full-time freshmen received some form of financial aid. 9% of undergraduates work part time. Cal State Bakersfield is a member of CSS. The FAFSA is required. Check with the school for current deadlines.

International Students: The school actively recruits these students. They must score 500 on the written TOEFL and also the SAT I or ACT is required if the GPA is below 3.0.

Computers: The mainframes are a CDC CYBER 830 and a DEC VAX 8350. There are about 300 PCs available in student labs located throughout the campus. All students may access the system. There are no time limits and no fees.

Graduates: In a recent year, 804 bachelor's degrees were awarded. The most popular majors were education (16%), business (13%), and public administration (4%). In an average class, 28% graduate in 5 years or less.

Admissions Contact: Dr. Homer Montalvo, Dean of Admissions.
E-mail: hmontalvo@csubak.edu

CALIFORNIA STATE UNIVERSITY, CHICO   B-2
Chico, CA 95929-0722

(530) 898-4428
(800) 542-4426; Fax: (530) 898-6456

Full-time: 6180 men, 6995 women	**Faculty:** 615; IIA, +$
Part-time: 685 men, 780 women	**Ph.D.s:** 62%
Graduate: 825 men, 1250 women	**Student/Faculty:** 21 to 1
Year: semesters, summer session	**Tuition:** $2070 ($9450)
Application Deadline: November 30	**Room & Board:** $6528
Freshman Class: n/av	
SAT I or ACT: required	**LESS COMPETITIVE**

California State University/Chico, founded in 1887, is a public institution offering undergraduate programs in behavioral and social sciences, business, communication and education, engineering, computer science and technology, humanities and fine arts, natural sciences, agriculture, and nursing. The university offers web-based classes. There are 7 undergraduate schools and 1 graduate school. The figures in the above capsule and in this profile are approximate. In addition to regional accreditation, CSU has baccalaureate program accreditation with AACSB, ABET, ACCE, ADA, CSAB, CSWE, NASAD, NASM, NLN, and NRPA. The library contains 948,564 volumes, 1,140,465 microform items, and 22,968 audio/video tapes/CDs, and subscribes to 20,404 periodicals. Computerized library services include the card catalog, interlibrary loans, and database searching. Special learning facilities include a learning resource center, art gallery, planetarium, radio station, an instructional media center, university farm, biological field station, anthropology museum, media preparation lab, computer graphics lab, and recording arts studio. The 130-acre campus is in a small town 100 miles north of Sacramento. Including any residence halls, there are 72 buildings.

Student Life: 99% of undergraduates are from California. Students are from 44 states, 48 foreign countries, and Canada. 94% are from public schools. 67% are white; 10% Hispanic. The average age of freshmen is 18; all undergraduates, 22. 21% do not continue beyond their first year; 64% remain to graduate.

Housing: 1700 students can be accommodated in college housing, which includes coed dorms, on-campus apartments, and off-campus apartments. In addition, there are honors houses, language houses, special-interest houses, and thematic housing for minorities in engineering and science, math, business, and agriculture.. On-campus housing is available on a first-come, first-served basis. 90% of students commute. Alcohol is not permitted. All students may keep cars.

Activities: 8% of men belong to 4 local and 14 national fraternities; 8% of women belong to 8 local and 10 national sororities. There are 200 groups on campus, including art, band, cheerleading, chess, choir, chorale, chorus, computers, dance, debate, departmental, drama, drill team, ethnic, film, forensics, gay, honors, international, intramural and club sports, jazz band, literary magazine, musical theater, newspaper, opera, orchestra, pep band, political, professional, radio and TV, re-entry, religious, social, social service, student government, symphony, and yearbook. Popular campus events include International Festival, Greek Week, and Fun Without Alcohol Fair.

Sports: There are 6 intercollegiate sports for men and 7 for women, and 17 intramural sports for men and 16 for women. Facilities include 2 gyms, athletic training rooms, a dance studio, swimming and diving pools, a par course, putting greens and sand trap, handball /racquetball courts, baseball/softball fields, an all-weather track, a soccer stadium, a 7500-seat football stadium, and a residence hall sports center.

Disabled Students: 95% of the campus is accessible. Wheelchair ramps, elevators, special parking, specially equipped rest rooms, special class scheduling, lowered drinking fountains, lowered telephones, sign language interpreters, on-campus transportation, Braille signage, books on tape, adaptive computer lab, and disability support services are available.

Services: Counseling and information services are available, as is tutoring in every subject. There is a reader service for the blind and remedial math, reading, and writing. A student learning center offers a tutorial program, study skills development, and learning assistance workshops.

Campus Safety and Security: Measures include 24-hour foot and vehicle patrol, self-defense education, security escort services, and shuttle buses. There are informal discussions, pamphlets/posters/films, emergency telephones, lighted pathways/sidewalks, a victim awareness program, and crime prevention workshops.

Programs of Study: CSU confers B.A., B.S., and B.F.A. degrees. Master's degrees are also awarded. Bachelor's degrees are awarded in AGRICULTURE (agricultural business management and agriculture), BIOLOGICAL SCIENCE (biology/biological science, microbiology, and nutrition), BUSINESS (business administration and management), COMMUNICATIONS AND THE ARTS (art, communications, dramatic arts, English, fine arts, French, German, journalism, music, musical theater, and Spanish), COMPUTER AND PHYSICAL SCIENCE (chemistry, computer science, geology, geoscience, information sciences and systems, mathematics, physical sciences, and physics), EDUCATION (physical), ENGINEERING AND ENVIRONMENTAL DESIGN (civil engineering, computer engineering, construction management, electrical/electronics engineering, environmental science, industrial engineering technology, and mechanical engineering), HEALTH PROFESSIONS (exercise science, health science, nursing, and speech pathology/audiology), SOCIAL SCIENCE (American studies, anthropology, Asian/Oriental studies, child psychology/development, economics, ethnic studies, geography, history, humanities, international relations, Latin American studies, liberal arts/general studies, parks and recreation management, philosophy, political science/government, psychology, public administration, religion, social science, social work, and sociology). Nursing, accounting, and biology are the strongest academically. Business administration, liberal studies, and communications are the largest.

Required: Graduation requirements for all students include the completion of math, writing proficiency, ethnic studies, non-Western studies, U.S. history, U.S. Constitution, and U.S./California government courses. Also required are a 48-unit general education program, a 2.0 minimum GPA, 124 to 132 total credit hours, and 24 to 115 hours in the major.

Special: The university offers co-op programs and cross-registration as part of the National Student Exchange. Internships, distance learning, teacher certification, study abroad in 16 countries, work-study, student-designed majors, independent study, credit for experience, nondegree study, and pass/fail options are available. There are 4 national honor societies, a freshman honors program, and 28 departmental honors programs.

Faculty/Classroom: 59% of faculty are male; 41%, female. All teach undergraduates. Graduate students teach 2% of introductory courses. The average class size in an introductory lecture is 25; in a laboratory, 21; and in a regular course, 22.

Requirements: The SAT I or ACT is required. An index combining GPA and SAT I and ACT scores is used to determine eligibility for admission. Applicants must be graduates of secondary school or have a GED and have completed 4 years of English, 3 years each of math and college preparatory electives, 2 years of a foreign language, and 1 year each of history, science, art and/or music. AP and CLEP credits are accepted.

Procedure: Freshmen are admitted fall and spring. Entrance exams should be taken in fall of the senior year. There is a deferred admissions plan and a rolling admissions plan. Applications should be filed by November 30 for fall entry, along with a $55 fee. Applications are accepted on-line at *www.csumentor.edu*.

Transfer: 1660 transfer students enrolled in a recent year. Transfer students who are California residents must have a minimum 2.0 GPA, and nonresidents need 2.4. A minimum of 56 transferable credit hours are needed, and students must have made up any missing college preparatory subjects and provide a statement of good standing from prior institutions. 30 of 124 credits required for the bachelor's degree must be completed at CSU.

Visiting: There are guides for informal visits and visitors may sit in on classes. To schedule a visit, contact University Outreach.

Financial Aid: The FAFSA is required. The deadline for filing freshman financial aid applications for fall entry is March 2.

International Students: In a recent year there were 282 international students enrolled. The school actively recruits these students. They must score 500 on the written TOEFL or 173 on the electronic version.

Computers: The mainframes are an IBM 4381, an IBM 3090, and a DEC VAX 6310. There are 1000 PCs available, with about 200 networked. There are also more than 50 terminals. In addition, there are large department-based central computers. All students may access the system. There are no time limits and no fees. It is strongly recommended that all students have a personal computer.

Graduates: In a recent year, 2696 bachelor's degrees were awarded. The most popular majors were business administration (16%), liberal studies (13%), and psychology (5%). In an average class, 10% graduate in 4 years or less, 38% graduate in 5 years or less, and 49% graduate in 6 years or less. 282 companies recruited on campus in a recent year.

Admissions Contact: John Swiney, Director of Admissions.
E-mail: *info@csuchico.edu* Web: *http://www.csuchico.edu*

CALIFORNIA STATE UNIVERSITY, DOMINGUEZ HILLS C-5
Carson, CA 90747-0005   (310) 243-3696

Full-time: 1470 men, 3140 women	**Faculty:** 290; IIA, +$
Part-time: 790 men, 2280 women	**Ph.D.s:** 80%
Graduate: 1480 men, 3360 women	**Student/Faculty:** 16 to 1
Year: semesters, summer session	**Tuition:** $1740 ($9140)
Application Deadline: see profile	**Room & Board:** $4100
Freshman Class: n/av	
SAT I or ACT: required	**LESS COMPETITIVE**

California State University Dominguez Hills, founded in 1960 as part of the state-supported university system, offers graduate and undergraduate programs in liberal arts and sciences, business, fine arts, health sciences, and technology to a primarily commuter student body. Figures in above capsule and in this profile are approximate. There are 4 undergraduate and 4 graduate schools. In addition to regional accreditation, CSU Dominguez Hills has baccalaureate program accreditation with CAHEA, NASAD, NASM, NCATE, and NLN. The library contains 396,520 volumes, 569,630 microform items, and 17,130 audio/video tapes/CDs, and subscribes to 4740 periodicals. Computerized library services include the card catalog and database searching. Special learning facilities include a learning resource center, art gallery, planetarium, and TV station. The 350-acre campus is in an urban area 10 miles south of Los Angeles. There are 40 buildings.

Student Life: 98% of undergraduates are from California. Students are from 29 states, 79 foreign countries, and Canada. 98% are from public schools. 30% are African American; 30% Hispanic; 20% white; 10% Asian American. The average age of freshmen is 19; all undergraduates, 29. 30% do not continue beyond their first year; 30% remain to graduate.

Housing: There are no residence halls. 710 students can be accommodated in college housing, which includes single-sex and coed on-campus apartments. On-campus housing is guaranteed for all 4 years. 96% of students commute. All students may keep cars.

Activities: There are 4 national fraternities and 1 local and 2 national sororities. There are 69 groups on campus, including art, band, cheerleading, choir, chorale, computers, dance, drama, drill team, ethnic, gay, honors, international, jazz band, literary magazine, musical theater,

newspaper, orchestra, photography, political, professional, radio and TV, religious, social, social service, student government, symphony, and yearbook. Popular campus events include .

Sports: There are 4 intercollegiate sports for men and 4 for women. Facilities include the Olympic Velodrome (bicycle racing stadium), a gym, tennis courts, a baseball field, a track, a weight room, a swimming pool, and a soccer field.

Disabled Students: Wheelchair ramps, elevators, special parking, specially equipped rest rooms, lowered drinking fountains, and lowered telephones are available.

Services: Counseling and information services are available, as is tutoring in most subjects. There is a reader service for the blind and remedial math, reading, and writing.

Campus Safety and Security: Measures include 24-hour foot and vehicle patrol, security escort services, informal discussions, and pamphlets/posters/films. There are emergency telephones and lighted pathways/sidewalks.

Programs of Study: CSU Dominguez Hills confers B.A. and B.S. degrees. Master's degrees are also awarded. Bachelor's degrees are awarded in BIOLOGICAL SCIENCE (biology/biological science), BUSINESS (business administration and management, labor studies, recreation and leisure services, and tourism), COMMUNICATIONS AND THE ARTS (art, communications, dramatic arts, English, music, and Spanish), COMPUTER AND PHYSICAL SCIENCE (chemistry, computer science, digital arts/technology, geology, mathematics, and physics), EDUCATION (physical), HEALTH PROFESSIONS (clinical science, health science, nursing, and occupational therapy), SOCIAL SCIENCE (African studies, anthropology, behavioral science, economics, geography, history, human services, interdisciplinary studies, liberal arts/general studies, Mexican-American/Chicano studies, philosophy, political science/government, psychology, public administration, and sociology). Liberal studies is the strongest academically. Business administration is the largest.

Required: To graduate, students must complete 120 to 132 semester units, including 54 to 60 units in general education, 40 units in upper-division courses, and specific courses or proficiency tests in U.S. history and politics, math, and writing. A minimum GPA of 2.0 must be maintained.

Special: Cross-registration is offered with 7 other California State University schools. Study abroad in 15 countries, co-op programs in all majors, on-campus work-study, internships, B.A.-B.S. degrees, dual and student-designed majors, credit for life experience, and pass/fail options are available. A B.A. in interdisciplinary studies, in which an accelerated degree is possible, and in liberal studies is offered. Many majors have evening programs. There are 2 national honor societies, a freshman honors program, and 13 departmental honors programs.

Faculty/Classroom: 50% of faculty are male; 50%, female. 95% teach undergraduates. The average class size in an introductory lecture is 45; in a laboratory, 19; and in a regular course, 32.

Requirements: The SAT I or ACT is required, except of those with a GPA of at least 3.0 (3.6 for nonresidents). Students must be high school graduates with a GPA of at least 2.0 and 15 academic units, including 4 in English, 3 in math, 2 in foreign language, and 1 each in U.S. history, lab science, and visual and performing arts. The GED is accepted. CSU Dominguez Hills requires applicants to be in the upper 33% of their class. AP and CLEP credits are accepted.

Procedure: Freshmen are admitted fall and spring. Entrance exams should be taken prior to submitting an application. There are early decision and early admissions plans and a rolling admissions plan. Check with the school for current application deadlines. The fall 2003 application fee was $55. On-line applications are accepted at *www.csumentor.edu*.

Transfer: Applicants should have a college GPA of at least 2.0 (2.4 for nonresidents) and submit SAT I or ACT scores if transferring fewer than 56 semester or 84 quarter units. 30 of 120 credits required for the bachelor's degree must be completed at CSU Dominguez Hills.

Visiting: There are regularly scheduled orientations for prospective students. There are guides for informal visits and visitors may sit in on classes. To schedule a visit, contact the Outreach Office for group visits at (310) 516-3699 or the Information at Center for individual visits at (310) 516-3696.

Financial Aid: The FAFSA is required. Check with the school for current deadlines.

International Students: The school actively recruits these students. They must score 550 on the written TOEFL and also take the SAT I or the ACT.

Computers: The mainframes are a CDC CYBER 960 and a DEC VAX 6500. About 450 Mac and IBM PCs are available in the library, student labs, and individual departments. All students may access the system. There are no time limits and no fees. It is strongly recommended that all students have a personal computer.

Admissions Contact: Information and Services Center.
Web: *www.csudh.edu*

CALIFORNIA STATE UNIVERSITY, FRESNO   C-3
Fresno, CA 93740-8027   (559) 278-2261; Fax: (559) 278-4812

Full-time: 5834 men, 8460 women	Faculty: 681; IIA, +$
Part-time: 1968 men, 2312 women	Ph.D.s: n/av
Graduate: 1359 men, 2415 women	Student/Faculty: 21 to 1
Year: semesters, summer session	Tuition: $2414 ($9182)
Application Deadline: May 15	Room & Board: $6000
Freshman Class: n/av	
SAT I Verbal/Math: 470/490	ACT: 18 LESS COMPETITIVE

California State University, Fresno, founded in 1911, is part of the state-supported university system. The school offers undergraduate and graduate programs in agriculture and technology, liberal arts and sciences, business administration, education, engineering, health fields, and pre-professional training. There are 8 undergraduate and 8 graduate schools. In addition to regional accreditation, Fresno State has baccalaureate program accreditation with AACSB, ABET, ACCE, ACEJMC, ADA, AHEA, APTA, ASLA, CSWE, FIDER, NASM, NCATE, NLN, and NRPA. The library contains 977,198 volumes, 1,207,118 microform items, and 71,482 audio/video tapes/CDs, and subscribes to 2559 periodicals. Computerized library services include the card catalog, interlibrary loans, and database searching. Special learning facilities include a learning resource center, art gallery, planetarium, radio station, and various farm lab units. The 327-acre campus is in a suburban area 300 miles southeast of San Francisco. Including any residence halls, there are 47 buildings.

Student Life: 96% of undergraduates are from California. Others are from 48 states, 89 foreign countries, and Canada. 99% are from public schools. 36% are white; 26% Hispanic; 14% Asian American. The average age of freshmen is 18; all undergraduates, 23. 20% do not continue beyond their first year; 55% remain to graduate.

Housing: 1100 students can be accommodated in college housing, which includes single-sex and coed dorms. In addition, there are special-interest houses. On-campus housing is available on a first-come, first-served basis. 94% of students commute. Alcohol is not permitted. All students may keep cars.

Activities: 3% of men belong to 4 local and 15 national fraternities; 3% of women belong to 4 local and 9 national sororities. There are 270 groups on campus, including art, band, cheerleading, chess, choir, chorale, chorus, computers, dance, drama, drill team, ethnic, film, gay, honors, international, jazz band, marching band, musical theater, newspaper, orchestra, pep band, photography, political, professional, radio and TV, religious, social, social service, and student government. Popular campus events include Vintage Days, International Week, and Black History Month.

Sports: There are 10 intercollegiate sports for men and 12 for women, and 4 intramural sports for men and 4 for women. Facilities include 2 gyms, an indoor/outdoor swimming pool, 12 tennis courts, 6 indoor handball/racquetball courts, and 2 putting greens and driving areas. There are sports clubs in cycling, fencing, judo, karate, rodeo, and rugby. The campus stadium seats 41,031, the baseball stadium seats 6575, and the softball stadium seats 5467. There is also a 10,800-square-foot strength and conditioning center.

Disabled Students: All of the campus is accessible. Wheelchair ramps, elevators, special parking, specially equipped rest rooms, special class scheduling, lowered drinking fountains, and lowered telephones are available.

Services: Counseling and information services are available, as is tutoring in most subjects. There is a reader service for the blind, and remedial math, reading, and writing.

Campus Safety and Security: Measures include 24-hour foot and vehicle patrol, self-defense education, security escort services, and informal discussions. There are pamphlets/posters/films, emergency telephones, lighted pathways/sidewalks, closed-circuit television cameras, and bicycle safety patrols.

Programs of Study: Fresno State confers B.A. and B.S. degrees. Master's and doctoral degrees are also awarded. Bachelor's degrees are awarded in AGRICULTURE (agricultural business management, animal science, and plant science), BIOLOGICAL SCIENCE (biology/biological science), BUSINESS (business administration and management and recreational facilities management), COMMUNICATIONS AND THE ARTS (art, communications, dramatic arts, English, French, graphic design, journalism, linguistics, music, Spanish, and speech/debate/rhetoric), COMPUTER AND PHYSICAL SCIENCE (chemistry, computer science, geology, mathematics, natural sciences, and physics), EDUCATION (agricultural), ENGINEERING AND ENVIRONMENTAL DESIGN (civil engineering, computer engineering, construction management, electrical/electronics engineering, industrial engineering, industrial engineering technology, interior design, mechanical engineering, and surveying engineering), HEALTH PROFESSIONS (health science, nursing, speech pathology/audiology, and speech therapy), SOCIAL SCIENCE (African American studies, anthropology, child psychology/development, criminology, economics, family/consumer studies, food science, geography, history, liberal arts/general studies, Mexican-American/Chicano studies,

philosophy, physical fitness/movement, political science/government, psychology, public administration, social work, sociology, and women's studies). Business and liberal arts are the largest.

Required: All students must complete general education requirements. A minimum of 124 to 137 semester units, with a GPA of 2.0, is required to graduate. The number of required hours in the major varies.

Special: Study abroad in London, New Zealand, China, and the South Pacific (17 countries in total), co-op programs, internships, work-study programs, B.A.-B.S. degrees, dual majors, and student-designed majors are offered. A liberal studies major, credit for military experience, pass/fail options, and nondegree study are available. There are 22 national honor societies, a freshman honors program, and 2 departmental honors programs.

Faculty/Classroom: 57% of faculty are male; 43%, female. All both teach and do research. The average class size in an introductory lecture is 28; in a laboratory, 20; and in a regular course, 26.

Admissions: The SAT I scores for the 2003-2004 freshman class were: Verbal--62% below 500, 28% between 500 and 599, 9% between 600 and 700, and 1% above 700; Math--54% below 500, 34% between 500 and 599, 11% between 600 and 700, and 1% above 700. The ACT scores were 68% below 21, 17% between 21 and 23, 10% between 24 and 26, 3% between 27 and 28, and 2% above 28.

Requirements: Only students with a GPA below 3.0 are required to submit SAT I or ACT scores. Applicants must be graduates of an accredited secondary school or have a GED. Secondary school courses must include 15 academic credits: 4 years of high school English, 3 each of math and electives, 2 of a foreign language, and 1 each of science, history/government, and visual/performing arts. A GPA of 2.0 is required. AP and CLEP credits are accepted.

Procedure: Freshmen are admitted fall and spring. Entrance exams should be taken as early as possible, by the first semester of the senior year. Applications should be filed by May 15 for fall entry and October 15 for spring entry. The fall 2003 application fee was $55. Notification is sent on a rolling basis. Applications are accepted on-line through the school's web site via CSUMentor.

Transfer: 1993 transfer students enrolled in 2003-2004. Transfer applicants must have a minimum GPA of 2.0 and 56 transferable semester units earned, including English and math. 30 of 124 to 137 credits required for the bachelor's degree must be completed at Fresno State.

Visiting: There are regularly scheduled orientations for prospective students, including 1- and 2-day overnight programs for entering students. There are guides for informal visits and visitors may stay overnight. To schedule a visit, contact Orientation and Transition Services or University Outreach Services at (559) 278-7533 or (559) 278-2048.

Financial Aid: In a recent year, 61% of all full-time freshmen and 78% of continuing full-time students received some form of financial aid. 23% of full-time freshmen and 50% of continuing full-time students received need-based aid. The average freshman award was $5312. 3% of undergraduates work part time. Average annual earnings from campus work are $3000. The average financial indebtedness of a recent year's graduate was $14,458. Fresno State is a member of CSS. The FAFSA is required. The deadline for filing freshman financial aid applications for fall entry is March 2.

International Students: There were 392 international students enrolled in a recent year. The school actively recruits these students. They must score 500 on the written TOEFL and also take the SAT I or the ACT.

Computers: The mainframe is an IBM 3090. There are 1500 PCs and Macs available for student use. All students may access the system any time. There are no time limits and no fees. All students are required to have personal computers.

Graduates: From July 1, 2002 to June 30, 2003, 2922 bachelor's degrees were awarded. The most popular majors were liberal studies (23%), business administration (16%), and criminology (5%). In an average class, 11% graduate in 4 years or less, 31% graduate in 5 years or less, and 40% graduate in 6 years or less. 259 companies recruited on campus in 2002-2003.

Admissions Contact: Vivian Franco, Director of Admissions. E-mail: *vivian-franco@csufresno.edu* Web: *www.csufresno.edu*

CALIFORNIA STATE UNIVERSITY, FULLERTON   D-5
Fullerton, CA 92834   (714) 278-2370

Full-time: 7419 men, 11,237 women	Faculty: IIA, +$
Part-time: 3373 men, 4867 women	Ph.D.s: n/av
Graduate: 1990 men, 3706 women	Student/Faculty: n/av
Year: semesters, summer session	Tuition: $2516 ($10,976)
Application Deadline: November 30	Room & Board: $4132
Freshman Class: 17,503 applied, 11,524 accepted, 3150 enrolled	
SAT I Verbal/Math: 480/500	ACT: 19 COMPETITIVE

California State University, Fullerton, founded in 1957, is part of the California State University system. The school offers programs in the arts, business and economics, communications, engineering and computer science, human development and community services, humanities and social science, and natural science and math. There are 7 undergraduate and 7 graduate schools. In addition to regional accreditation, Cal State Fullerton has baccalaureate program accreditation with AACSB, ABET, ACEJMC, NASAD, NASM, NCATE, and NLN. The library contains 654,790 volumes, 964,340 microform items, and 15,790 audio/video tapes/CDs, and subscribes to 2500 periodicals. Computerized library services include the card catalog, interlibrary loans, and database searching. Special learning facilities include a learning resource center, art gallery, an arboretum, an herbarium, a center for economic education, a developmental research center, a foreign language lab, an institute for economic and environmental studies, an institute for molecular biology and nutrition, a phonetic research lab, a social science research center, and a sport and movement institute. The 225-acre campus is in a suburban area 30 miles east of Los Angeles. Including any residence halls, there are 22 buildings.

Student Life: 96% of undergraduates are from California. Students are from 40 states, 105 foreign countries, and Canada. 40% are white; 20% Asian American; 20% Hispanic. The average age of freshmen is 18; all undergraduates, 23. 20% do not continue beyond their first year; 60% remain to graduate.

Housing: 400 students can be accommodated in college housing, which includes coed on-campus apartments, fraternity houses, and sorority houses. On-campus housing is available on a first-come, first-served basis. 98% of students commute. All students may keep cars.

Activities: There are 5 local and 13 national fraternities and 1 local sorority and 8 national sororities. There are 200 groups on campus, including art, band, cheerleading, choir, chorus, computers, dance, drama, ethnic, gay, honors, international, jazz band, literary magazine, musical theater, newspaper, orchestra, pep band, photography, political, professional, religious, social, social service, student government, and yearbook.

Sports: There are 7 intercollegiate sports for men and 9 for women, and 7 intramural sports for men and 9 for women. Facilities include a gym, a swimming pool, tennis and racquetball courts, baseball/softball, track, and soccer fields, a bowling alley, and a stadium.

Disabled Students: All of the campus is accessible. Wheelchair ramps, elevators, special parking, specially equipped rest rooms, lowered drinking fountains, lowered telephones, and automatic doors are available.

Services: Counseling and information services are available, as is tutoring in some subjects, including English and math. There is a reader service for the blind and remedial math, reading, and writing.

Campus Safety and Security: Measures include 24-hour foot and vehicle patrol, self-defense education, security escort services, and shuttle buses. There are pamphlets/posters/films, emergency telephones, and lighted pathways/sidewalks.

Programs of Study: Cal State Fullerton confers B.A., B.S., B.F.A., and B.M. degrees. Master's degrees are also awarded. Bachelor's degrees are awarded in BIOLOGICAL SCIENCE (biochemistry and biology/ biological science), BUSINESS (accounting, banking and finance, business administration and management, business economics, international business management, management information systems, management science, marketing/retailing/merchandising, and tourism), COMMUNICATIONS AND THE ARTS (advertising, animation, art history and appreciation, broadcasting, ceramic art and design, communications, comparative literature, crafts, dance, dramatic arts, drawing, English, film arts, fine arts, French, German, graphic design, illustration, Japanese, journalism, linguistics, music, photography, printmaking, public relations, sculpture, Spanish, speech/debate/rhetoric, and studio art), COMPUTER AND PHYSICAL SCIENCE (chemistry, computer science, geology, mathematics, and physics), EDUCATION (art, music, and physical), ENGINEERING AND ENVIRONMENTAL DESIGN (civil engineering, electrical/electronics engineering, engineering and applied science, and mechanical engineering), HEALTH PROFESSIONS (health science, nursing, and speech pathology/audiology), SOCIAL SCIENCE (African American studies, American studies, anthropology, Asian/American studies, child psychology/development, criminal justice, economics, geography, history, human services, Latin American studies, liberal arts/ general studies, Mexican-American/Chicano studies, philosophy, political science/government, psychology, public administration, religion, Russian and Slavic studies, sociology, and women's studies). Business administration, communications, and psychology are the largest.

Required: Graduation requirements for all students include the completion of a minimum of 51 units of general education courses, a 2.0 GPA, and an upper-division writing course designated by the major department. 120 to 135 credit hours must be completed for graduation, and students must pass a writing proficiency exam.

Special: The university offers cross-registration with other schools in the California State University system, the University of California, and California Community Colleges, internships and co-op programs in 45 academic areas, study abroad in 18 countries, and work-study programs both on and off campus. A B.A.-B.S. degree in chemistry, dual and student-designed majors, and pass/fail options are also available. There are 16 national honor societies, a freshman honors program, and 13 departmental honors programs.

Faculty/Classroom: No introductory courses are taught by graduate students. The average class size in an introductory lecture is 50; in a laboratory, 24; and in a regular course, 25.

Admissions: 66% of the 2003-2004 applicants were accepted. The SAT I scores for the 2003-2004 freshman class were: Verbal--58% below 500, 33% between 500 and 599, and 8% between 600 and 700; Math--48% below 500, 37% between 500 and 599, 13% between 600 and 700, and 1% above 700. The ACT scores were 60% below 21, 23% between 21 and 23, 13% between 24 and 26, 2% between 27 and 28, and 3% above 28. 43% of the current freshmen were in the top fourth of their class; 81% were in the top half.

Requirements: The SAT I or ACT is required. In addition, applicants must be graduates of an accredited secondary school or have a GED certificate. Secondary school courses must include 4 years of English, 3 of math, 2 each of a foreign language, science, and history, and 1 of visual or performing arts. Admission is based on the Qualifiable Eligibility Index, a combination of the high school GPA and either the SAT I or ACT score. Auditions are required for music majors. A GPA of 2.0 is required. AP and CLEP credits are accepted.

Procedure: Freshmen are admitted fall and spring. Entrance exams should be taken during the senior year of high school. There is an early admissions plan. Applications should be filed by November 30 for fall entry, along with a $55 fee. Notification is sent on a rolling basis. Applications are accepted on-line.

Transfer: Applicants must have a minimum 2.0 GPA. The SAT I or ACT is required for students with fewer than 56 transferable units earned. Students with 56 transferable units or more must have 30 units of general education completed with a C or better, including English composition, math, speech, and critical thinking. 30 of 120 credits required for the bachelor's degree must be completed at Cal State Fullerton.

Visiting: There are regularly scheduled orientations for prospective students. There are guides for informal visits. To schedule a visit, contact New Student Orientation at (714) 278-3120.

Financial Aid: In 2002-2003, 39% of all full-time freshmen and 36% of continuing full-time students received some form of financial aid. 34% of full-time freshmen and 28% of continuing full-time students received need-based aid. The average freshman award was $6592. Need-based scholarships or need-based grants averaged $6404; need-based self-help aid (loans and jobs) averaged $2862; non-need-based athletic scholarships averaged $6369; and other non-need-based awards and non-need-based scholarships averaged $3123. Cal State Fullerton is a member of CSS. The FAFSA is required. The priority date for freshman financial aid applications for fall entry is March 2.

International Students: They must score 500 on the written TOEFL or 173 on the electronic version.

Computers: The mainframes are a DEC VAX 8550 and an IBM 3090/ 150E. Students may access the mainframe via school-based and computer center labs. All students may access the system 24 hours a day. There are no time limits and no fees.

Graduates: In an average class, 8% graduate in 4 years or less, and 23% graduate in 5 years or less.

Admissions Contact: Director of Admissions.
Web: *www.fullerton.edu*

CALIFORNIA STATE UNIVERSITY, HAYWARD
Hayward, CA 94542-3095

B-3
(510) 885-2784

Full-time: 2743 men, 4639 women	Faculty: 370; IIA, ++$
Part-time: 741 men, 1264 women	Ph.D.s: 90%
Graduate: 1473 men, 2607 women	Student/Faculty: 20 to 1
Year: quarters, summer session	Tuition: $2418 ($10,878)
Application Deadline: June 30	Room & Board: $6453
Freshman Class: n/av	
SAT I or ACT: recommended	LESS COMPETITIVE

California State University, Hayward, founded in 1957, is part of the California State University system. The institution offers degree programs in the arts, sciences, business and economics, and education to a primarily commuter student body. Some information in the above capsule and in this profile is approximate. There are 4 undergraduate and 4 graduate schools. In addition to regional accreditation, CSUH has baccalaureate program accreditation with AACSB, NASAD, NASM, NCATE, and NLN. The library contains 850,000 volumes, 700,000 microform items, and 26,000 audio/video tapes/CDs, and subscribes to 2000 periodicals. Computerized library services include the card catalog, interlibrary loans, and database searching. Special learning facilities include a learning resource center, art gallery, natural history museum, radio station, TV station, and marine biology lab, and geology summer field camp. The 342-acre campus is in a suburban area 20 miles southeast of San Francisco in the Hayward Hills. Including any residence halls, there are 17 buildings.

Student Life: 90% of undergraduates are from California. 85% are from public schools. 50% are white; 25% Asian American; 10% African American; 10% Hispanic. The average age of freshmen is 20; all under-

graduates, 25. 15% do not continue beyond their first year; 60% remain to graduate.

Housing: 400 students can be accommodated in college housing, which includes coed on-campus apartments. On-campus housing is guaranteed for the freshman year only and is available on a first-come, first-served basis. 94% of students commute. All students may keep cars.

Activities: 1% of men belong to 4 national fraternities; 1% of women belong to 3 national sororities. There are 90 groups on campus, including art, cheerleading, chorale, chorus, computers, dance, drama, ethnic, film, gay, honors, international, jazz band, literary magazine, musical theater, newspaper, opera, orchestra, pep band, photography, political, professional, radio and TV, religious, social, social service, student government, symphony, and yearbook. Popular campus events include Science Fair and several leadership conferences.

Sports: There are 4 intercollegiate sports for men and 7 for women. Facilities include tennis and racquetball courts, 2 swimming pools, a track, a football field, a martial arts facility, a gymnastics center, a dance studio, baseball and softball diamonds, a 9000-seat stadium, a 5000-seat gym, and a 500-seat theater.

Disabled Students: 90% of the campus is accessible. Wheelchair ramps, elevators, special parking, specially equipped rest rooms, lowered drinking fountains, and lowered telephones are available. The Disabled Student Services Center provides scribe, interpretive, and translation services.

Services: Counseling and information services are available, as is tutoring in most subjects. There is a reader service for the blind and remedial math, reading, and writing.

Campus Safety and Security: Measures include 24-hour foot and vehicle patrol, self-defense education, security escort services, and shuttle buses. There are informal discussions, pamphlets/posters/films, emergency telephones, and lighted pathways/sidewalks.

Programs of Study: CSUH confers B.A. and B.S. degrees. Master's degrees are also awarded. Bachelor's degrees are awarded in AGRICULTURE (environmental studies), BIOLOGICAL SCIENCE (biochemistry and biology/biological science), BUSINESS (accounting, business administration and management, marketing/retailing/merchandising, and recreation and leisure services), COMMUNICATIONS AND THE ARTS (advertising, art, arts administration/management, broadcasting, communications, dramatic arts, English, French, journalism, music, Spanish, and speech/debate/rhetoric), COMPUTER AND PHYSICAL SCIENCE (chemistry, computer science, geology, mathematics, physical sciences, physics, and statistics), ENGINEERING AND ENVIRONMENTAL DESIGN (engineering, environmental science, and industrial engineering), HEALTH PROFESSIONS (health science, nursing, and speech pathology/audiology), SOCIAL SCIENCE (anthropology, criminal justice, economics, ethnic studies, geography, history, human development, international studies, Latin American studies, liberal arts/general studies, philosophy, physical fitness/movement, political science/government, psychology, and sociology). Business administration, liberal studies, and computer science are the strongest academically. Business administration and liberal studies are the largest.

Required: In order to graduate, students must fulfill the university writing skills requirement, have a 2.0 minimum GPA, and complete 186 quarter units, including 72 in distribution requirements. The number of hours in the major varies by program from 56 to 153 quarter units.

Special: CSUH offers cross-registration with local community colleges, other CSU campuses, and the University of California/Berkeley. Internships, study abroad in 15 countries, work-study programs, and student-designed majors are also available. The PACE program provides degree opportunities in liberal studies and in human development to working adults. There is 1 national honor society, a freshman honors program, and 1 departmental honors program.

Requirements: The SAT I or ACT is recommended. In addition, all students must meet the eligibility index, a combination of the high school GPA and SAT I or ACT scores. Applicants must be graduates of an accredited secondary school or have a GED certificate. Secondary school courses must include 4 years of English, 3 of math, 2 each of foreign language, history, and science, and 1 each of art, dance, drama/theater, or music, and electives. A GPA of 2.0 is required. AP and CLEP credits are accepted. Important factors in the admissions decision are advanced placement or honor courses, leadership record, and evidence of special talent.

Procedure: Freshmen are admitted to all sessions. There are early decision, early admissions, and deferred admissions plans. Applications should be filed by June 30 for fall entry, October 31 for winter entry, January 12 for spring entry, and April 6 for summer entry. Notification is sent on a rolling basis beginning March 15. Check with the school for current application fee. Applications are accepted on-line through CSU-Mentor.

Transfer: Applicants must have a minimum 2.0 GPA (2.45 for nonresidents), be in good standing at the last college attended, and either meet freshman admission requirements or have completed at least 56 transferable semester (84 quarter) units. 45 of 186 quarter units required for the bachelor's degree must be completed at CSUH.

Visiting: There are regularly scheduled orientations for prospective students. There are guides for informal visits. To schedule a visit, contact Enrollment Services at (510) 885-2556.

Financial Aid: In 2003-2004, 43% of all full-time freshmen and 42% of continuing full-time students received some form of financial aid. 43% of full-time freshmen and 42% of continuing full-time students received need-based aid. The average freshman award was $6918. Need-based scholarships or need-based grants averaged $6494; and need-based self-help aid (loans and jobs) averaged $2413. All undergraduates work part time. CSUH is a member of CSS. The FAFSA is required. Check with the school for current application deadlines.

International Students: They must score 525 on the written TOEFL or 197 on the electronic version. Graduates of a U.S. high school must also take the SAT I or ACT.

Computers: The mainframes are an E/XSI and an IBM 9370. There are 300 IBM, AT&T, and Mac PCs available throughout campus. All students may access the system on a 24-hour basis from home and 16 hours per day on campus. There are no time limits and no fees.

Admissions Contact: Admissions. E-mail: *askes@csuhayward.edu* Web: *www.csuhayward.edu*

CALIFORNIA STATE UNIVERSITY, LONG BEACH   D-5
Long Beach, CA 90840-0106   (562) 985-4141
Fax: (562) 985-4973

Full-time: 8534 men, 13,145 women	Faculty: 1087; IIA, +$
Part-time: 2803 men, 3585 women	Ph.D.s: 82%
Graduate: 2333 men, 4315 women	Student/Faculty: 20 to 1
Year: semesters, summer session	Tuition: $2362 ($10,822)
Application Deadline: November 30	Room & Board: $6400
Freshman Class: 26,821 applied, 11,807 accepted, 3526 enrolled	
SAT I or ACT: required	COMPETITIVE+

California State University, Long Beach, founded in 1949, is a nonprofit institution that is part of the California State University system. The commuter university offers undergraduate programs through the Colleges of Health and Human Services, Liberal Arts, Natural Sciences and Math, Business Administration, Engineering, the Arts, and Education. There are 7 undergraduate and 7 graduate schools. In addition to regional accreditation, CSULB has baccalaureate program accreditation with AACSB, ABET, ACEJMC, AHEA, APTA, CSWE, FIDER, NASAD, NASM, NLN, and NRPA. The library contains 1,469,280 volumes, 1,489,266 microform items, and 27,573 audio/video tapes/CDs, and subscribes to 7890 periodicals. Computerized library services include the card catalog, interlibrary loans, database searching, and Internet access. Special learning facilities include a learning resource center, art gallery, radio station, and TV station. The 322-acre campus is in a suburban area 25 miles southeast of Los Angeles. Including any residence halls, there are 84 buildings.

Student Life: 94% of undergraduates are from California. Students are from Canada. 90% are from public schools. 34% are white; 30% Asian American; 23% Hispanic. The average age of freshmen is 18; all undergraduates, 22. 12% do not continue beyond their first year; 44% remain to graduate.

Housing: 1830 students can be accommodated in college housing, which includes single-sex and coed dorms. On-campus housing is available on a first-come, first-served basis. 95% of students commute. All students may keep cars.

Activities: 4% of men belong to 17 national fraternities; 4% of women belong to 14 national sororities. There are 150 groups on campus, including art, band, cheerleading, choir, chorale, chorus, computers, dance, drama, drill team, ethnic, film, gay, honors, international, jazz band, literary magazine, musical theater, newspaper, opera, orchestra, pep band, photography, political, professional, radio and TV, religious, social, social service, student government, symphony, and yearbook. Popular campus events include the Kaleidoscope Spring Festival and Engineering Day, Blues Festival, and Odyssey Theme Year.

Sports: There are 10 intercollegiate sports for men and 9 for women, and 14 intramural sports for men and 12 for women. Facilities include the Long Beach Arena (seats 11,500 for basketball), a baseball field (seats 1500), the Pyramid Sports Arena (seats 5000) and an indoor gym (seats 2000).

Disabled Students: 99% of the campus is accessible. Wheelchair ramps, elevators, special parking, specially equipped rest rooms, special class scheduling, lowered drinking fountains, and lowered telephones are available. The university also offers registration and mobility assistance, adaptive equipment, counseling, community referrals, and services to the learning-disabled.

Services: Counseling and information services are available, as is tutoring in most subjects. There is a reader service for the blind and remedial math, reading, and writing.

Campus Safety and Security: Measures include 24-hour foot and vehicle patrol, security escort services, shuttle buses, and informal discussions. There are pamphlets/posters/films, emergency telephones, and lighted pathways/sidewalks.

Programs of Study: CSULB confers B.A., B.S., B.F.A., B.M., and B.Voc.Ed. degrees. Master's degrees are also awarded. Bachelor's degrees are awarded in BIOLOGICAL SCIENCE (biochemistry, biology/biological science, botany, cell biology, ecology, physiology, and zoology), BUSINESS (accounting, banking and finance, business administration and management, international business management, management information systems, marketing/retailing/merchandising, and personnel management), COMMUNICATIONS AND THE ARTS (art, communications, comparative literature, dance, design, dramatic arts, English, film arts, French, German, Japanese, journalism, music, and Spanish), COMPUTER AND PHYSICAL SCIENCE (applied mathematics, chemistry, computer science, earth science, geology, mathematics, physics, and statistics), EDUCATION (elementary, mathematics, science, and special), ENGINEERING AND ENVIRONMENTAL DESIGN (aerospace studies, chemical engineering, civil engineering, computer engineering, electrical/electronics engineering, engineering technology, and mechanical engineering), HEALTH PROFESSIONS (health care administration and health science), SOCIAL SCIENCE (African American studies, anthropology, Asian/Oriental studies, economics, geography, Hispanic American studies, history, human development, interdisciplinary studies, international studies, philosophy, political science/government, psychology, religion, sociology, and women's studies). Art, biological sciences, and music are the strongest academically. Business administration, psychology, and liberal studies are the largest.

Required: Graduation requirements for all students include the completion of 51 units in general education (45 for engineering majors), 40 units of upper-division course work, and 30 units in residence at the university. Students must have a minimum 2.0 GPA and a total of 124 to 140 credit hours, depending on the major. Required courses include University 100: The University in Your Future.

Special: The university offers cross-registration with California State University, Dominguez Hills for courses not offered at CSULB. Internships, study abroad in 22 countries, dual majors in engineering, a 3-2 engineering degree, student-designed majors, and pass/fail options are also available. There are 23 national honor societies, including Phi Beta Kappa, and a freshman honors program.

Faculty/Classroom: 54% of faculty are male; 46%, female. All teach undergraduates, 60% do research, and 60% do both. Graduate students teach 3% of introductory courses. The average class size in an introductory lecture is 68; in a laboratory, 24; and in a regular course, 26.

Admissions: 44% of the 2003-2004 applicants were accepted. The SAT I scores for the 2003-2004 freshman class were: Verbal--50% below 500, 37% between 500 and 599, 12% between 600 and 700, and 1% above 700; Math--38% below 500, 43% between 500 and 599, 18% between 600 and 700, and 2% above 700. There were 13 National Merit finalists and 2 semifinalists. 53 freshmen graduated first in their class.

Requirements: The SAT I or ACT is required. In addition, applicants must be graduates of an accredited secondary school and have completed 4 years of English, 3 years each of math and electives, 2 years of foreign language, and 1 year each of lab science, U.S. history or U.S. history and government, and 1 visual and performing arts. Students are admitted on the basis of the eligibility index, which is computed from the secondary school GPA and the SAT I or ACT scores. California residents with a minimum 3.0 GPA are automatically admissible. A portfolio is required for art and design students. An audition is required for dance, music, and theater students. A GPA of 2.0 is required. AP and CLEP credits are accepted.

Procedure: Freshmen are admitted fall and spring. Entrance exams should be taken during the fall semester of the senior year. Applications should be filed by November 30 for fall entry and August 31 for spring entry. There is a rolling admissions plan. Notification is sent on a rolling basis. The fall 2003 application fee was $55. Applications are accepted on computer disk and on-line through the school's web site.

Transfer: 3346 transfer students enrolled in 2002-2003. Upper-division students must have completed a minimum of 60 semester units, and have a minimum 2.0 GPA, lower division students must meet the same requirements as entering freshmen. 30 of 120 to 140 credits required for the bachelor's degree must be completed at CSULB.

Visiting: There are regularly scheduled orientations for prospective students, consisting of Student Orientation, Advising, and Registration (SOAR) sessions. Students may participate in SOAR I, which consists of advising and registration, or SOAR II, which involves a campus tour and an orientation to activities. There are guides for informal visits. To schedule a visit, contact the Office of School Relations at (562) 985-5358.

Financial Aid: CSULB is a member of CSS. The FAFSA is required. The deadline for filing freshman financial aid applications for fall entry is March 2.

International Students: The school actively recruits these students. They must score 500 on the written TOEFL and also take the SAT I or the ACT.

Computers: Four main labs with a total of approximately 550 PC-based or Mac-based systems, plus 54 college-based labs with a total of between 550 and 1100 PC or Mac-based systems, are open for student use 5 or more days a week. Internet and Web access are automatically available on most of the available systems. All students may access the

system during open lab hours, which vary across campus. There are no time limits and no fees.

Graduates: From July 1, 2002 to June 30, 2003, 5055 bachelor's degrees were awarded. The most popular majors were liberal studies (9%), psychology (7%), and information systems (6%). In an average class, 11% graduate in 4 years or less, and 44% graduate in 6 years or less.

Admissions Contact: Thomas Enders, Assistant Vice President, Enrollment Services. Web: www.csulb.edu

CALIFORNIA STATE UNIVERSITY, LOS ANGELES   C-5

Los Angeles, CA 90032   (323) 343-3940; Fax: (323) 343-3945

Full-time: 3913 men, 6542 women	Faculty: 565; IIA, +$
Part-time: 1556 men, 2410 women	Ph.D.s: n/av
Graduate: 2166 men, 4050 women	Student/Faculty: 19 to 1
Year: quarters, summer session	Tuition: $2440 ($9208)
Application Deadline: June 15	Room & Board: $3338
Freshman Class: 11,395 applied, 6366 accepted, 1370 enrolled	
SAT I or ACT: required	COMPETITIVE

California State University, Los Angeles, founded in 1947 as part of the state system, offers undergraduate and graduate programs in liberal arts and sciences, business education, engineering, health science, and professional training. There are 6 undergraduate schools. In addition to regional accreditation, Cal State, LA has baccalaureate program accreditation with AACSB, ABET, ACS, ADA, ASHA, CACREP, COA, CORE, CSWE, NASAD, NASM, NASPAA, NCATE, and NLN.The library contains 1,127,398 volumes, 1,080,781 microform items, and 5498 audio/video tapes/CDs, and subscribes to 2110 periodicals. Computerized library services include the card catalog, interlibrary loans, database searching, and Internet access. Special learning facilities include a learning resource center, art gallery, and TV station. The 173-acre campus is in an urban area 5 miles east of downtown Los Angeles. Including any residence halls, there are 22 buildings.

Student Life: 95% of undergraduates are from California. Students are from Canada and foreign countries. 52% are Hispanic; 22% Asian American; 16% white. The average age of freshmen is 18; all undergraduates, 25.

Housing: 1006 students can be accommodated in college housing, which includes single-sex and coed on-campus apartments. In addition, there are special-interest houses and an international house. On-campus housing is available on a first-come, first-served basis. 60% of students live on campus. All students may keep cars.

Activities: There are 8 national fraternities and 2 local and 6 national sororities. There are 115 groups on campus, including band, chess, choir, chorale, chorus, computers, dance, drama, ethnic, forensics, gay, honors, international, jazz band, literary magazine, musical theater, newspaper, opera, orchestra, political, professional, radio and TV, religious, social, social service, student government, symphony, and yearbook. Popular campus events include Christmas Toy and Food Drive, Earth Week, and Career Day.

Sports: There are 6 intercollegiate sports for men and 6 for women, and 9 intramural sports for men and 7 for women. Facilities include a 4800-seat stadium, a 5500-seat gym, a swimming pool, tennis and racquetball courts, a track, and athletic fields.

Disabled Students: 95% of the campus is accessible. Wheelchair ramps, elevators, special parking, specially equipped rest rooms, and lowered telephones are available.

Services: Counseling and information services are available, as is tutoring in most subjects. There is a reader service for the blind and remedial math, reading, and writing.

Campus Safety and Security: Measures include 24-hour foot and vehicle patrol, self-defense education, security escort services, and shuttle buses. There are informal discussions, pamphlets/posters/films, emergency telephones, and lighted pathways/sidewalks.

Programs of Study: Cal State, LA confers B.A., B.S., B.M., and B.Voc.Ed. degrees. Master's and doctoral degrees are also awarded. Bachelor's degrees are awarded in BIOLOGICAL SCIENCE (biochemistry, biology/biological science, and microbiology), BUSINESS (business administration and management), COMMUNICATIONS AND THE ARTS (dramatic arts, English, French, graphic design, Japanese, media arts, music, music performance, Spanish, and speech/debate/rhetoric), COMPUTER AND PHYSICAL SCIENCE (chemistry, computer science, geology, information sciences and systems, mathematics, natural sciences, and physics), EDUCATION (industrial arts, physical, and vocational), ENGINEERING AND ENVIRONMENTAL DESIGN (civil engineering, electrical/electronics engineering, engineering, industrial engineering technology, and mechanical engineering), HEALTH PROFESSIONS (health science, nursing, rehabilitation therapy, and speech pathology/audiology), SOCIAL SCIENCE (African American studies, anthropology, child psychology/development, criminal justice, dietetics, economics, fire protection, geography, history, interdisciplinary studies, Latin American studies, liberal arts/general studies, Mexican-American/Chicano studies, philosophy, political science/government, psychology, social science, social work, and sociology). Child development, computer information systems, and criminal justice are the largest.

Required: To graduate, students must complete 186 to 203 quarter units, with a minimum 2.0 GPA, and must demonstrate skills in math and oral and written communications. General education requirements include 72 quarter units in the social sciences, natural sciences, and humanities.

Special: Cross-registration is offered with other California State University schools. The school, as part of the state university system, is part of the California Desert Studies Consortium, which provides a field facility in the Mojave Desert to develop desert studies educational programs. It is also part of the Ocean Studies Institute, which facilitates marine educational and research activities. Students may design their own majors. Internships, study-abroad in 18 countries, work-study programs, B.A.-B.S. degrees, dual majors, pass/fail options, and credit for life experience are available. An accelerated degree program in nursing is offered. There are 21 national honor societies, including Phi Beta Kappa, a freshman honors program, and 5 departmental honors programs.

Faculty/Classroom: 55% of faculty are male; 45%, female. All teach undergraduates. No introductory courses are taught by graduate students. The average class size in an introductory lecture is 40; in a laboratory, 8; and in a regular course, 40.

Admissions: 56% of the 2003-2004 applicants were accepted.

Requirements: The SAT I or ACT is required. In addition, applicants should be graduates of accredited secondary schools or have a GED equivalent. 15 academic credits are required, including 4 years of English, 3 of math, 2 of the same foreign language, 1 each of biological and physical science with lab, 1 each of U.S. history and social science, and 1 year in electives and the visual and performing arts. A GPA of 2.0 is required. AP and CLEP credits are accepted.

Procedure: Freshmen are admitted to all sessions. Entrance exams should be taken during the junior year or senior year. Applications should be filed by June 15 for fall entry, November 1 for winter entry, February 1 for spring entry, and April 1 for summer entry. There is a rolling admissions plan. Notification is sent on a rolling basis. The fall 2003 application fee was $55. Applications are accepted on-line through CSU-Mentor.

Transfer: 1592 transfer students enrolled in 2002-2003. Applicants must have 56 semester units (84 quarter units), a 2.0 GPA (2.4 GPA for nonresidents), and have completed the CSU graduation requirements in English compostion, speech communication, critical thinking, and quantitative reasoning. 45 of 186 to 203 credits required for the bachelor's degree must be completed at Cal State, LA.

Visiting: There are guides for informal visits.

Financial Aid: The CSS Profile or FAFSA and the SAAC (in-state) are required. The deadline for filing freshman financial aid applications for fall entry is March 1.

International Students: They must score 550 on the written TOEFL or 213 on the electronic version and also take the SAT I or the ACT.

Computers: The mainframe is a 35-server network of Sun servers. Students use the network system through both general access computing labs and electronic classrooms, and have remote access via modems. Currently, there are 1500 workstations available to students, including PCs, Sun UNIX workstations, and Macs. All students may access the system 24 hours a day. There is a 2-hour limit in the open access labs during peak demand periods. There are no fees.

Graduates: From July 1, 2002 to June 30, 2003, 2899 bachelor's degrees were awarded. The most popular majors were child development (12%), computer information systems (8%), and psychology (7%). 376 companies recruited on campus in 2002-2003.

Admissions Contact: Joan Woosley, Director of Admission and University Registrar.

CALIFORNIA STATE UNIVERSITY, MONTEREY BAY   B-3

Seaside, CA 93955   (831) 582-5100, ext.3; Fax: (831) 582-5110

Full-time: 1243 men, 1717 women	**Faculty:** 142; IIA, +$
Part-time: 146 men, 221 women	**Ph.D.s:** n/av
Graduate: 41 men, 86 women	**Student/Faculty:** 21 to 1
Year: semesters, summer session	**Tuition:** $2473 ($10,933)
Application Deadline: March 15	**Room & Board:** $4210
Freshman Class: 4149 applied, 2781 accepted, 944 enrolled	
SAT I Verbal/Math: 470/460	**ACT:** 20 **LESS COMPETITIVE**

California State University, Monterey Bay, founded in 1994, is a public institution with 13 undergraduate divisions, including arts and sciences, communications, education and professional training, and science and technology. There are 13 undergraduate and 4 graduate schools. The library contains 50,000 volumes and 1250 audio/video tapes/CDs, and subscribes to 10,000 periodicals. Computerized library services include interlibrary loans, database searching, and Internet access. Special learning facilities include a learning resource center. The 1397-acre campus is in a suburban area 90 miles south of San Francisco. Including any residence halls, there are 58 buildings.

Student Life: 98% of undergraduates are from California. Students are from 33 states and 21 foreign countries. 92% are from public schools. 46% are white; 27% Hispanic. The average age of freshmen is 19; all

undergraduates, 23. 25% do not continue beyond their first year; 40% remain to graduate.

Housing: 4172 students can be accommodated in college housing, which includes single-sex and coed dorms, on-campus apartments, and married-student housing. On-campus housing is available on a first-come, first-served basis. 62% of students live on campus. Alcohol is not permitted. All students may keep cars.

Activities: There are no fraternities or sororities. There are 50 groups on campus, including choir, chorus, computers, dance, disabilities, drama, ethnic, gay, international, musical theater, photography, political, professional, religious, social, social service, student government, and yearbook. Popular campus events include Capstone Festival.

Sports: There are 4 intercollegiate sports for men and 5 for women, and 5 intramural sports for men and 5 for women. Facilities include 3 racquetball courts, a 2500-square-foot fitness room, saunas, and a 10,000-square-foot gym with facilities for basketball, volleyball, badminton, indoor soccer, aerobics, and dance. There is also a soccer complex, an aquatic center, a disc golf course, a stadium track, and a baseball field.

Disabled Students: All of the campus is accessible. Wheelchair ramps, elevators, special parking, specially equipped rest rooms, and special class scheduling are available.

Services: Counseling and information services are available, as is tutoring in some subjects, including computer skills and others by demand. There is a reader service for the blind and remedial math, reading, and writing.

Campus Safety and Security: Measures include 24-hour vehicle patrol, self-defense education, security escort services, and shuttle buses. There are informal discussions, pamphlets/posters/films, emergency telephones, and lighted pathways/sidewalks.

Programs of Study: CSUMB confers B.A. and B.S. degrees. Master's degrees are also awarded. Bachelor's degrees are awarded in BUSINESS (management science), COMMUNICATIONS AND THE ARTS (communications technology, telecommunications, and visual and performing arts), COMPUTER AND PHYSICAL SCIENCE (computer science and earth science), EDUCATION (education), SOCIAL SCIENCE (behavioral science, international studies, liberal arts/general studies, and social science). Computer science and technology, liberal studies, and business administration are the strongest academically. Liberal studies, business administration, and earth systems are the largest.

Required: To graduate, students must complete 124 credit hours, including general education requirements and at least 24 hours in the major.

Special: Study abroad in 18 countries and an integrated studies major are available.

Faculty/Classroom: 51% of faculty are male; 49%, female. All teach undergraduates. The average class size in an introductory lecture is 23; in a laboratory, 17; and in a regular course, 22.

Admissions: 67% of the 2003-2004 applicants were accepted. The SAT I scores for the 2003-2004 freshman class were: Verbal--54% below 500, 36% between 500 and 599, and 10% between 600 and 700; Math--58% below 500, 35% between 500 and 599, and 7% between 600 and 700. The ACT scores were 62% below 21, 22% between 21 and 23, 12% between 24 and 26, 2% between 27 and 28, and 2% above 28.

Requirements: The SAT I or ACT is required. A GPA of 2.0 is required. AP and CLEP credits are accepted.

Procedure: Freshmen are admitted fall and spring. Entrance exams should be taken March, April, or May of each year. Applications should be filed by March 15 for fall entry and November 30 for spring entry, along with a $55 fee. Notification is sent November 30 for fall entry and September 30 for spring entry. Applications are accepted on-line through XAP.

Transfer: 670 transfer students enrolled in 2002-2003. Applicants must have a college GPA of 2.0 and 56 transferable semester units, including 30 units of general education courses. 30 of 124 credits required for the bachelor's degree must be completed at CSUMB.

Visiting: There are regularly scheduled orientations for prospective students, including onsite advising and registration, campus tours, and faculty one-on-one sessions. There are guides for informal visits and visitors may sit in on classes and stay overnight. To schedule a visit, contact Valarie E. Brown at valarie_brown@csumb.edu.

Financial Aid: In 2003-2004, 53% of all full-time freshmen and 47% of continuing full-time students received some form of financial aid. 51% of full-time freshmen and 49% of continuing full-time students received need-based aid. The average freshman award was $6558. Need-based scholarships or need-based grants averaged $6041 ($12,147 maximum); need-based self-help aid (loans and jobs) averaged $4075 ($15,952 maximum); non-need-based athletic scholarships averaged $1575 ($2000 maximum); and other non-need-based awards and non-need-based scholarships averaged $1918 ($2473 maximum). The average financial indebtedness of the 2003 graduate was $7400. The FAFSA is required. The priority date for freshman financial aid applications for fall entry is March 2.

International Students: There are 19 international students enrolled. They must score 525 on the written TOEFL or 197 on the electronic version and also take the SAT I or the ACT.

Computers: The mainframe is an IBM. All students have their own web page, e-mail account, and space on the campuswide server. All students may access the system. There are no time limits and no fees. It is strongly recommended that all students have a personal computer.

Graduates: From July 1, 2002 to June 30, 2003, 200 bachelor's degrees were awarded. The most popular majors were liberal studies (24%), human communication (12%), and telecommunication (12%). In an average class, 11% graduate in 4 years or less, 29% graduate in 5 years or less, and 40% graduate in 6 years or less. 42 companies recruited on campus in 2002-2003.

Admissions Contact: Campus Service Center, One-Stop-Shop. A video is available. E-mail: *onestop@csumb.edu*
Web: *http://onestop.csumb.edu*

CALIFORNIA STATE UNIVERSITY, NORTHRIDGE C-5
Northridge, CA 91330 (818) 677-3700; Fax: (818) 677-3766

Full-time: 8120 men, 11,485 women	**Faculty:** 865; IIA, +$
Part-time: 2428 men, 3447 women	**Ph.D.s:** 84%
Graduate: 2512 men, 5005 women	**Student/Faculty:** 23 to 1
Year: semesters, summer session	**Tuition:** $1892 ($8660)
Application Deadline: November 30	**Room & Board:** $5865
Freshman Class: 13,211 applied, 10,092 accepted, 3610 enrolled	
SAT I Verbal/Math: 460/470	**LESS COMPETITIVE**

California State University, Northridge, founded in 1958, is part of the state-supported university system offering degree programs in the liberal arts and sciences, business administration, education, engineering, music, health fields, and fine arts. There are 8 undergraduate schools and 1 graduate school. In addition to regional accreditation, CSUN has baccalaureate program accreditation with AACSB, ABET, ACEJMC, AHEA, APTA, CAHEA, CSAB, NASAD, NASM, NCATE, and NRPA. The library contains 1,274,351 volumes, 3,128,169 microform items, and 17,677 audio/video tapes/CDs, and subscribes to 16,973 periodicals. Computerized library services include the card catalog, interlibrary loans, and database searching. Special learning facilities include a learning resource center, art gallery, planetarium, radio station, TV station, observatory, anthropological museum, botanical gardens, urban archives center, Natural Center on Deafness, and Center for the Study of Cancer and Development Biology. The 353-acre campus is in a suburban area 25 miles north of Los Angeles. Including any residence halls, there are 76 buildings.

Student Life: 93% of undergraduates are from California. Students are from 46 states and Canada. 93% are from public schools. 32% are white; 23% Hispanic. The average age of freshmen is 18; all undergraduates, 24.

Housing: 2400 students can be accommodated in college housing, which includes coed on-campus apartments and an international house. On-campus housing is guaranteed for all 4 years and is available on a first-come, first-served basis. All students may keep cars.

Activities: There are 5 local and 13 national fraternities and 6 local and 8 national sororities. There are 181 groups on campus, including art, band, cheerleading, choir, chorale, chorus, computers, dance, drama, ethnic, film, gay, honors, international, jazz band, literary magazine, marching band, musical theater, newspaper, opera, orchestra, photography, political, professional, radio and TV, religious, social, social service, student government, symphony, and yearbook. Popular campus events include International Student Days, Campus Community Day, and Welcome Week.

Sports: There are 8 intercollegiate sports for men and 10 for women, and 9 intramural sports for men and 9 for women. Facilities include 2 gyms, 2 swimming pools, softball and soccer fields, handball, racquetball, and tennis courts, a baseball field, and a track.

Disabled Students: 98% of the campus is accessible. Wheelchair ramps, elevators, special parking, specially equipped rest rooms, special class scheduling, lowered drinking fountains, lowered telephones, and electric doors are available.

Services: Counseling and information services are available, as is tutoring in some subjects, including English and math. There is a reader service for the blind and remedial math, reading, and writing. Student tutors are available for other selected subjects as well.

Campus Safety and Security: Measures include 24-hour foot and vehicle patrol, security escort services, shuttle buses, and informal discussions. There are pamphlets/posters/films, emergency telephones, and lighted pathways/sidewalks.

Programs of Study: CSUN confers B.A., B.S., and B.M. degrees. Master's degrees are also awarded. Bachelor's degrees are awarded in BIOLOGICAL SCIENCE (biochemistry, biology/biological science, environmental biology, and microbiology), BUSINESS (accounting, banking and finance, business administration and management, management information systems, marketing/retailing/merchandising, and recreation and leisure services), COMMUNICATIONS AND THE ARTS (art, dance, dramatic arts, English, film arts, French, German, journalism, linguistics, music, Spanish, and speech/debate/rhetoric), COMPUTER AND PHYSICAL SCIENCE (astrophysics, chemistry, computer science, earth science, geology, mathematics, physics, and radiological technology), EDUCATION (business, education of the deaf and hearing impaired, home economics, and physical), ENGINEERING AND ENVIRONMENTAL DESIGN (engineering), HEALTH PROFESSIONS (biomedical science, exercise science, health, health care administration, medical laboratory technology, nursing, physical therapy, recreation therapy, and speech pathology/audiology), SOCIAL SCIENCE (African American studies, anthropology, Asian/American studies, child psychology/development, criminology, economics, family/consumer studies, geography, history, humanities, liberal arts/general studies, Mexican-American/Chicano studies, philosophy, political science/government, psychology, sociology, urban studies, and women's studies). Liberal studies is the strongest academically. Business administration and economics, social and behavioral sciences, and arts, media, and communication are the largest.

Required: All students must complete 52 units of general education requirements in 6 areas, including courses in American history, U.S. Constitution, state and local government, English, math, logic, and oral and written communication. A total of 124 semester units for the B.A., 128 to 132 for the B.S., and 132 for the B.M., with a minimum GPA of 2.0, is required to graduate. At least 30 semester units must be completed in residence.

Special: Cross-registration is offered through the Intra System Visitor Program. Study abroad in 16 countries, internships, university work-study programs, dual majors, student-designed majors, credit for military experience, and pass/fail options for elective courses are offered. There are 4 national honor societies, a freshman honors program, and 5 departmental honors programs.

Faculty/Classroom: 60% of faculty are male; 40%, female. All teach undergraduates. Graduate students teach 12% of introductory courses. The average class size in an introductory lecture is 33 and in a laboratory, 20.

Admissions: 76% of the 2003-2004 applicants were accepted. The SAT I scores for the 2003-2004 freshman class were: Verbal--65% below 500, 27% between 500 and 599, 7% between 600 and 700, and 1% above 700; Math--61% below 500, 28% between 500 and 599, 11% between 600 and 700, and 1% above 700.

Requirements: The SAT I or ACT is required for students with a GPA below 3.0 (3.6 for nonresidents). Applicants should have completed 4 years of high school English, 3 each of math and academic electives, 2 of foreign language, and 1 each of lab science, U.S. history/government, and visual/performing arts. CSUN requires applicants to be in the upper 33% of their class. A GPA of 2.0 is required. AP and CLEP credits are accepted. Important factors in the admissions decision are recommendations by school officials, evidence of special talent, and leadership record.

Procedure: Freshmen are admitted fall and spring. Entrance exams should be taken by December of the senior year. There is an early decision plan. Applications should be filed by November 30 for fall entry, June 30 for winter entry, August 31 for spring entry, and February 28 for summer entry. The fall 2003 fee was $55. Notification is sent on a rolling basis. Applications are accepted on-line through CSU Mentor.

Transfer: A GPA of 2.0 (2.4 for nonresidents) is required in a minimum of 56 transferable semester units. Basic courses in writing, math, speech, and logic must be completed with a grade of C or better. 30 of 124 credits required for the bachelor's degree must be completed at CSUN.

Visiting: There are regularly scheduled orientations for prospective students, held in June and July for fall entrance and in November for spring entrance. There are guides for informal visits and visitors may sit in on classes and stay overnight. To schedule a visit, contact Student Outreach and Recruitment at (818) 677-2879 or *jason.roberts@csun.edu*.

Financial Aid: The average financial indebtedness of a recent graduate was $12,000. CSUN is a member of CSS. The SAAC is required. The deadline for filing freshman financial aid applications for fall entry is March 2.

International Students: There are 1019 international students enrolled. They must score 500 on the written TOEFL.

Computers: The mainframe is an IBM 4381. There are 1700 PCs on campus; 300 are networked by DOS and UNIX. The computers are located in some labs and classrooms, libraries, and student housing. All students may access the system 24 hours a day, 7 days a week.

Graduates: From July 1, 2002 to June 30, 2003, 6142 bachelor's degrees were awarded. The most popular majors were business administration (18%), liberal studies (9%), and psychology (8%). In an average class, 3% graduate in 4 years or less, 15% graduate in 5 years or less, and 25% graduate in 6 years or less. 400 companies recruited on campus in 2002-2003.

Admissions Contact: Eric Forbes, Registrar and Director of Operations, Admissions, and Records. Web: *http://www.csun.edu/index.html*

CALIFORNIA STATE UNIVERSITY, SACRAMENTO   B-3
Sacramento, CA 95819-6048   (916) 278-7362
(800) 722-4748; Fax: (916) 278-5603

Full-time: 7210 men, 9990 women	Faculty: 683; IIA, +$
Part-time: 2361 men, 3001 women	Ph.Ds: 77%
Graduate: 1954 men, 3859 women	Student/Faculty: 25 to 1
Year: semesters, summer session	Tuition: $2980 ($11,440)
Application Deadline: open	Room & Board: $6563
Freshman Class: 11,214 applied, 5864 accepted, 2437 enrolled	
SAT I Verbal/Math: 470/490	ACT: 19 COMPETITIVE

California State University/Sacramento, founded in 1947, is part of the state-supported university system. The school offers graduate and undergraduate programs in the liberal arts and sciences, business administration, education, engineering, music, and health and human service fields. There are 8 undergraduate and 7 graduate schools. In addition to regional accreditation, Sac State has baccalaureate program accreditation with AACSB, ABET, AHEA, CSWE, NASAD, NASM, NLN, and NRPA. The library contains 967,418 volumes, 2,317,727 microform items, and 135,074 audio/video tapes/CDs, and subscribes to 4071 periodicals. Computerized library services include the card catalog, interlibrary loans, database searching, and Internet access. Special learning facilities include a learning resource center, art gallery, radio station, TV station, aquatic center, and anthropology museum. The 282-acre campus is in a suburban area 90 miles northeast of San Francisco. Including any residence halls, there are 51 buildings.

Student Life: 98% of undergraduates are from California. Students are from 40 states, 54 foreign countries, and Canada. 94% are from public schools. 45% are white; 17% Asian American; 13% Hispanic. The average age of freshmen is 18; all undergraduates, 23. 19% do not continue beyond their first year; 52% remain to graduate.

Housing: 1299 students can be accommodated in college housing, which includes coed dorms. On-campus housing is available on a first-come, first-served basis. 95% of students commute. All students may keep cars.

Activities: 7% of men belong to 1 local and 18 national fraternities; 5% of women belong to 2 local and 8 national sororities. There are 250 groups on campus, including art, band, cheerleading, chess, choir, chorale, chorus, computers, dance, drama, ethnic, film, gay, honors, international, jazz band, marching band, musical theater, newspaper, opera, orchestra, pep band, photography, political, professional, radio and TV, religious, social, social service, student government, and symphony. Popular campus events include Greek Week, Festival of New American Music, and River City Days.

Sports: There are 8 intercollegiate sports for men and 8 for women, and 13 intramural sports for men and 13 for women. Facilities include a 15,000-seat stadium, 2 gyms, 2 swimming pools, an all-weather outdoor track, baseball, softball, and soccer fields, and an aquatic center, with sailing, wind-surfing, rowing, and canoeing.

Disabled Students: 90% of the campus is accessible. Wheelchair ramps, elevators, special parking, specially equipped rest rooms, special class scheduling, lowered drinking fountains, and lowered telephones are available.

Services: Counseling and information services are available, as is tutoring in most subjects. There is a reader service for the blind and remedial math, reading, and writing.

Campus Safety and Security: Measures include 24-hour foot and vehicle patrol, self-defense education, security escort services, and shuttle buses. There are informal discussions, pamphlets/posters/films, emergency telephones, and lighted pathways/sidewalks.

Programs of Study: Sac State confers B.A., B.S., and B.M. degrees. Master's and doctoral degrees are also awarded. Bachelor's degrees are awarded in BIOLOGICAL SCIENCE (biology/biological science and microbiology), BUSINESS (accounting, banking and finance, business administration and management, insurance, international business management, management information systems, marketing/retailing/merchandising, and real estate), COMMUNICATIONS AND THE ARTS (communications, dramatic arts, English, French, German, journalism, music, and Spanish), COMPUTER AND PHYSICAL SCIENCE (chemistry, computer science, geology, mathematics, physical sciences, and physics), EDUCATION (business, early childhood, and health), ENGINEERING AND ENVIRONMENTAL DESIGN (civil engineering, computer engineering, electrical/electronics engineering, engineering technology, and mechanical engineering), HEALTH PROFESSIONS (environmental health science, medical laboratory technology, nursing, physical therapy, and speech pathology/audiology), SOCIAL SCIENCE (anthropology, criminal justice, economics, geography, history, international relations, parks and recreation management, philosophy, psychology, public administration, social science, social work, and sociology). Nursing, criminal justice, and business administration are the strongest academically. Business administration, communications, and criminal justice are the largest.

Required: In order to graduate, students must complete a minimum of 124 semester hours, including 30 to 86 hours in the major, with a mini-

mum 2.0 GPA. Students must complete 51 units in general education requirements and take proficiency examinations in writing and a foreign language. A course in race and ethnicity in American society is required.

Special: The university offers cross-registration with other California State University schools, co-op programs in many academic programs, internships, a Washington semester, study abroad in 12 countries, and dual and student-designed majors. There are 12 national honor societies, including Phi Beta Kappa.

Faculty/Classroom: 53% of faculty are male; 47%, female. All both teach and do research. The average class size in an introductory lecture is 40; in a laboratory, 20; and in a regular course, 40.

Admissions: 52% of the 2003-2004 applicants were accepted. The SAT I scores for the 2003-2004 freshman class were: Verbal--60% below 500, 31% between 500 and 599, 8% between 600 and 700, and 1% above 700; Math--51% below 500, 38% between 500 and 599, 10% between 600 and 700, and 1% above 700. The ACT scores were 61% below 21, 23% between 21 and 23, 13% between 24 and 26, 2% between 27 and 28, and 1% above 28.

Requirements: The SAT I or ACT is required of applicants with a high school GPA below 3.0. Applicants should have completed 4 years of high school English, 3 years of math, 2 years of a foreign language, 1 year each of lab science, history, and visual/performing arts and 3 years of college preparatory electives. A GPA of 2.0 is required. AP and CLEP credits are accepted.

Procedure: Freshmen are admitted fall and spring. Entrance exams should be taken before December of the senior year. There is a rolling admissions plan and an early admissions plan. Application deadlines are open. Notification is sent in December for fall entry and in September for spring entry. Applications are accepted on-line through www.csumentor.edu.

Transfer: 4439 transfer students enrolled in 2002-2003. Applicants must have a 2.0 GPA and 56 transferable semester units, including 30 units of specific general education courses to include oral and written communication, critical thinking, and math. 50 of 120 credits required for the bachelor's degree must be completed at Sac State.

Visiting: There are regularly scheduled orientations for prospective students. There are guides for informal visits and visitors may sit in on classes. To schedule a visit, contact the University Outreach Services Office at outreach@csus.edu.

Financial Aid: In 2003-2004, 48% of all full-time freshmen and 47% of continuing full-time students received some form of financial aid. 65% of full-time freshmen and 70% of continuing full-time students received need-based aid. The average freshman award was $1912. Need-based scholarships or need-based grants averaged $1662 ($7774 maximum); need-based self-help aid (loans and jobs) averaged $1868 ($7600 maximum); and non-need-based awards and non-need-based scholarships averaged $3784 ($12,549 maximum). 75% of undergraduates work part time. Average annual earnings from campus work are $1678. The average financial indebtedness of the 2003 graduate was $17,288. Sac State is a member of CSS. The FAFSA and SAAC are required. The deadline for filing freshman financial aid applications for fall entry is March 2.

International Students: There are 708 international students enrolled. They must score 510 on the written TOEFL or 180 on the electronic version and also take the SAT I or the ACT.

Computers: There are 700 terminals or PC workstations located throughout the campus. All students may obtain accounts to access e-mail and Internet services and all campus computers. All students may access the system. There are no fees. It is strongly recommended that all students have a personal computer.

Graduates: From July 1, 2002 to June 30, 2003, 4223 bachelor's degrees were awarded. The most popular majors were business management (11%), criminal justice (8%), and communication studies (8%). In an average class, 1% graduate in 3 years or less, 13% graduate in 4 years or less, 30% graduate in 5 years or less, and 38% graduate in 6 years or less. Of the 2002 graduating class, 20% were enrolled in graduate school within 6 months of graduation.

Admissions Contact: Emiliano Diaz, Director of University Outreach Services. E-mail: outreach@csus.edu Web: http://www.csus.edu/admr/

CALIFORNIA STATE UNIVERSITY, SAN BERNARDINO   D-5
San Bernardino, CA 92407-2397   (909) 880-5188
Fax: (909) 880-7034

Full-time: 3382 men, 6514 women	Faculty: IIA, +$
Part-time: 820 men, 1403 women	Ph.Ds: 100%
Graduate: 1610 men, 3198 women	Student/Faculty: 20 to 1
Year: quarters, summer session	Tuition: $9855
Application Deadline: open	Room & Board: $5383
Freshman Class: 6463 applied, 3948 accepted, 1383 enrolled	
SAT I Verbal/Math: 440/450	ACT: 18 LESS COMPETITIVE

California State University, San Bernardino, founded in 1965, is a public, comprehensive regional university offering programs in business and public administration, natural sciences, education, arts and letters, and social and behavioral sciences. There are 5 undergraduate and 19 graduate schools. In addition to regional accreditation, CSUSB has baccalaureate program accreditation with AACSB, ADA, CSAB, CSWE, NASAD, and NLN. The library contains 761,862 volumes, 652,814 microform items, and 15,484 audio/video tapes/CDs, and subscribes to 1658 periodicals. Computerized library services include the card catalog, interlibrary loans, and database searching. Special learning facilities include a learning resource center, art gallery, and radio station. The 430-acre campus is in a suburban area 60 miles east of Los Angeles. Including any residence halls, there are 45 buildings.

Student Life: 99% of undergraduates are from California. Students are from 29 states, 49 foreign countries, and Canada. 83% are from public schools. 35% are white; 31% Hispanic; 12% African American. The average age of freshmen is 18; all undergraduates, 22. 19% do not continue beyond their first year.

Housing: 747 students can be accommodated in college housing, which includes single-sex and coed dorms and on-campus apartments. On-campus housing is available on a first-come, first-served basis. 93% of students commute. All students may keep cars.

Activities: 4% of men belong to 1 local and 8 national fraternities; 3% of women belong to 6 national sororities. There are 80 groups on campus, including art, band, cheerleading, choir, chorale, chorus, computers, dance, drama, ethnic, gay, honors, international, jazz band, musical theater, newspaper, orchestra, political, professional, radio and TV, religious, social, social service, and student government. Popular campus events include Dia de los Muertos, California Indian Cultural Awareness Conference, and Around the World.

Sports: There are 4 intercollegiate sports for men and 7 for women. Facilities include an arena for basketball and volleyball, baseball, softball, and soccer fields, tennis courts, swimming pools for water polo and recreational swimming, and a gym for recreational workouts.

Disabled Students: 98% of the campus is accessible. Wheelchair ramps, elevators, special parking, specially equipped rest rooms, lowered drinking fountains, lowered telephones, student assistants, cart service, and special equipment such as TSS, phonic ear, and VisualTek are available.

Services: Counseling and information services are available, as is tutoring in most subjects. There is a reader service for the blind and remedial math and writing.

Campus Safety and Security: Measures include 24-hour foot and vehicle patrol, self-defense education, security escort services, and emergency telephones. There are lighted pathways/sidewalks and e-mail and web site alerts.

Programs of Study: CSUSB confers B.A., B.S., and B.V.E. degrees. Master's degrees are also awarded. Bachelor's degrees are awarded in AGRICULTURE (environmental studies), BIOLOGICAL SCIENCE (biochemistry and biology/biological science), BUSINESS (accounting, banking and finance, business administration and management, business economics, human resources, international business management, management information systems, management science, and small business management), COMMUNICATIONS AND THE ARTS (advertising, art, art history and appreciation, ceramic art and design, communications, dance, dramatic arts, English, French, graphic design, music, music history and appreciation, music performance, music technology, musicology/ethnomusicology, painting, photography, printmaking, sculpture, and Spanish), COMPUTER AND PHYSICAL SCIENCE (applied physics, chemistry, computer science, geology, mathematics, and physics), EDUCATION (bilingual/bicultural, health, music, and vocational), ENGINEERING AND ENVIRONMENTAL DESIGN (furniture design), HEALTH PROFESSIONS (environmental health science, exercise science, health care administration, health science, nursing, and premedicine), SOCIAL SCIENCE (American studies, anthropology, child psychology/development, criminal justice, economics, ethnic studies, food science, geography, gerontology, history, human development, human services, humanities, liberal arts/general studies, paralegal studies, philosophy, political science/government, psychology, public administration, social science, social work, sociology, and Spanish studies). Liberal arts and business administration are the largest.

Required: To graduate, students must complete 180 to 198 quarter hours, including 60 in upper-division courses and requirements for the major, with a minimum GPA of 2.0. The 82-credit general education program includes courses in basic skills, natural sciences, humanities, social and behavioral sciences, lifelong understanding, upper-division writing, multicultural/gender studies, and electives. Students must also demonstrate an understanding of the U.S. Constitution, American history, and California government.

Special: The university offers cross-registration with other CSU campuses and with the University of California in Riverdale, and study abroad in 18 countries. Also available are internships, accelerated study, campus and community work-study programs, B.A.-B.S. degrees, dual and student-designed majors, credit for vocational education and military experience, and nondegree study. There is 1 national honor society, including Phi Beta Kappa, and a freshman honors program.

Faculty/Classroom: 56% of faculty are male; 44%, female. The average class size in an introductory lecture is 40; in a laboratory, 18; and in a regular course, 24.

Admissions: 61% of the 2003-2004 applicants were accepted. The SAT I scores for the 2003-2004 freshman class were: Verbal--76% below 500, 20% between 500 and 599, and 4% between 600 and 700; Math--70% below 500, 24% between 500 and 599, and 6% between 600 and 700. The ACT scores were 71% below 21, 17% between 21 and 23, 8% between 24 and 26, 2% between 27 and 28, and 1% above 28.

Requirements: The SAT I or ACT is required for some programs. In addition, applicants must be graduates of an accredited secondary school. Preparatory work should include 4 years of English, 3 of math, 2 of foreign language, 1 each of U.S. history/government, lab science, and visual and performing arts, and 3 of electives. Admission is based on an eligibility index that weighs the high school GPA and the SAT I or ACT score. Students with GPAs of 3.0 or better (3.6 for nonresidents) are exempt from test score requirements. AP and CLEP credits are accepted. Important factors in the admissions decision are advanced placement or honor courses, recommendations by school officials, and leadership record.

Procedure: Freshmen are admitted to all sessions. Entrance exams should be taken prior to applying. There is a rolling admissions plan and an early admissions plan. Applications are accepted beginning October 1. The fall 2003 application fee was $55. Applications are accepted online through *www.csumentor.edu*.

Transfer: 1717 transfer students enrolled in 2002-2003. Applicants must have a minimum college GPA of 2.0 (2.4 for nonresidents) and be in good standing at the previously attended institution. Those with fewer than 56 transferable semester units must submit ACT or SAT I scores. 45 of 180 credits required for the bachelor's degree must be completed at CSUSB.

Visiting: There are regularly scheduled orientations for prospective students, including sessions on admissions requirements, financial aid information, and campus (student) life information. There are guides for informal visits and visitors may sit in on classes and stay overnight. To schedule a visit, contact the Outreach Services Office.

Financial Aid: The FAFSA is required. The deadline for filing freshman financial aid applications for fall entry is March 2.

International Students: There were 626 international students enrolled in a recent year. The school actively recruits these students. They must score 500 on the written TOEFL or 173 on the electronic version.

Computers: The mainframes are an IBM 4381 and a DEC VAX 3500. Macs and PCs are available in various buildings. All students may access the system. There are no time limits and no fees.

Graduates: From July 1, 2002 to June 30, 2003, 2331 bachelor's degrees were awarded. The most popular majors were business administration (23%), liberal studies (23%), and social science/history (10%). Of the 2002 graduating class, 17% were enrolled in graduate school within 6 months of graduation.

Admissions Contact: Enrollment Services. A video is available.
E-mail: *www.moreinfo@mail.csusb.edu*
Web: *http://enrollment.csusb.edu*

CALIFORNIA STATE UNIVERSITY, SAN MARCOS
San Marcos, CA 92096-0001

D-5
(760) 750-4848
Fax: (760) 750-3248

Full-time: 5760 men and women	**Faculty:** 170; IIA, av$
Part-time: none	**Ph.D.s:** 92%
Graduate: 750 men and women	**Student/Faculty:** n/av
Year: semesters, summer session	**Tuition:** $1740 ($10,000)
Application Deadline: see profile	**Room & Board:** n/app
Freshman Class: n/av	
SAT I or ACT: recommended	**LESS COMPETITIVE**

California State University, San Marcos, founded in 1989, is a public commuter institution that is part of the California State University system. There are 2 undergraduate and 3 graduate schools. Figures in the above capsule and in this profile are approximate. In addition to regional accreditation, Cal State San Marcos has baccalaureate program accreditation with NCATE. The library contains 148,114 volumes, 755,260 microform items, and 5668 audio/video tapes/CDs, and subscribes to 1871 periodicals. Computerized library services include the card catalog, interlibrary loans, and database searching. Special learning facilities include a learning resource center. The 304-acre campus is in a suburban area 32 miles northeast of San Diego. There are 8 buildings.

Student Life: 98% of undergraduates are from California. Students are from Canada. 55% are white; 18% Hispanic. The average age of freshmen is 19; all undergraduates, 25.

Housing: There are no residence halls. All students commute. Alcohol is not permitted.

Activities: 3% of men belong to 2 national fraternities; 2% of women belong to 2 national sororities. There are 35 groups on campus, including computers, ethnic, gay, honors, international, political, professional, religious, social, student government, and yearbook. Popular campus events include Admissions Day, San Marcos Grand Festival, and Preview Day.

Sports: There are 3 intercollegiate sports for men and 3 for women, and 5 intramural sports for men and 5 for women. Facilities include an Olympic-quality track.

Disabled Students: All of the campus is accessible. Wheelchair ramps, elevators, special parking, specially equipped rest rooms, special class scheduling, lowered drinking fountains, and lowered telephones are available.

Services: There is a reader service for the blind, and remedial math, reading, and writing. There is a writing center, and math, accounting, and computer labs.

Campus Safety and Security: Measures include 24-hour foot and vehicle patrol, security escort services, informal discussions, and pamphlets/posters/films. There are emergency telephones and lighted pathways/sidewalks.

Programs of Study: Cal State San Marcos confers B.A. and B.S. degrees. Master's degrees are also awarded. Bachelor's degrees are awarded in BIOLOGICAL SCIENCE (biology/biological science), BUSINESS (business administration and management), COMMUNICATIONS AND THE ARTS (communications, creative writing, literature, Spanish, and visual and performing arts), COMPUTER AND PHYSICAL SCIENCE (chemistry, computer science, and mathematics), SOCIAL SCIENCE (economics, history, human development, liberal arts/general studies, political science/government, psychology, social science, sociology, and women's studies). Business administration, psychology, and liberal studies are the largest.

Required: To graduate, students must attain foreign language proficiency at the intermediate level, demonstrate computer competency, fulfill a writing requirement, and maintain a GPA of 2.0. The number of credits required for graduation varies from 124 to 132 depending on the major.

Special: There is cross-registration with other CSU campuses. Internships, study abroad in 16 countries, and work-study programs are available.

Faculty/Classroom: 53% of faculty are male; 47%, female. Graduate students teach 5% of introductory courses. The average class size in an introductory lecture is 25; in a laboratory, 25; and in a regular course, 25.

Requirements: The SAT I or ACT is recommended. A GPA of 2.0 is required. AP and CLEP credits are accepted.

Procedure: Freshmen are admitted fall and spring. Check with the school for current deadlines. The application fee is $55. Applications are accepted on-line at www.csumentor.edu

Transfer: 1086 transfer students enrolled in a recent year. Requirements include 56 units completed and a 2.0 GPA for California residents, 2.4 for nonresidents. 30 of 124 credits required for the bachelor's degree must be completed at Cal State San Marcos.

Visiting: There are regularly scheduled orientations for prospective students, including workshops and a campus tour. There are guides for informal visits and visitors may sit in on classes. To schedule a visit, contact the Office of Admissions.

Financial Aid: In a recent year, 39% of all full-time freshmen and 50% of continuing full-time students received some form of financial aid. 32% of full-time freshmen and 36% of continuing full-time students received need-based aid. The average freshman award was $5046. The average financial indebtedness of a recent graduate was $15,027. Cal State San Marcos is a member of CSS. The FAFSA is required. Check with the school for current deadlines.

International Students: The school actively recruits these students. They must score 550 on the written TOEFL.

Computers: All students may access the system. There are no time limits and no fees. It is strongly recommended that all students have a personal computer.

Graduates: In a recent year, 1100 bachelor's degrees were awarded. Of the 2002 graduating class, 33% were enrolled in graduate school within 6 months of graduation and 79% were employed.

Admissions Contact: Cherine Heckman, Director of Admissions. A video is available. E-mail: apply@csusm.edu Web: www.csusm.edu

---

CALIFORNIA STATE UNIVERSITY, STANISLAUS   B-3
Turlock, CA 95382   (209) 667-3070
(800) 828-7733; Fax: (209) 667-3788

Full-time: 1421 men, 2756 women	Faculty: 292; IIA, +$
Part-time: 660 men, 1317 women	Ph.D.s: 56%
Graduate: 519 men, 1399 women	Student/Faculty: 14 to 1
Year: 4-1-4, summer session	Tuition: $2503 ($8989)
Application Deadline: May 1	Room & Board: $7371
Freshman Class: 2687 applied, 1733 accepted, 653 enrolled	
SAT I Verbal/Math: 470/490	ACT: 19 COMPETITIVE

California State University, Stanislaus, founded in 1957, is a state-supported institution offering undergraduate and graduate programs in liberal and fine arts, business, health science, and teacher preparation. There are 3 undergraduate schools and 1 graduate school. In addition to regional accreditation, CSU/Stanislaus has baccalaureate program accreditation with AACSB, ABA, ACS, CCNE, CCTC, CSWE, NASAD,

NASM, NASPAA, and NCATE. The library contains 353,827 volumes, 1,280,144 microform items, and 3587 audio/video tapes/CDs, and subscribes to 1816 periodicals. Computerized library services include the card catalog, interlibrary loans, database searching, and Internet access. Special learning facilities include a learning resource center, art gallery, radio station, and laser lab, marine sciences station, greenhouse, art gallery, mainstage theater, recital hall, observatory, art complex, and distance learning studios. The 225-acre campus is in a rural area in the San Joaquin Valley, about 100 miles from San Francisco. Including any residence halls, there are 23 buildings.

Student Life: 99% of undergraduates are from California. Students are from 22 states, 20 foreign countries, and Canada. 96% are from public schools. 50% are white; 23% Hispanic; 10% foreign nationals. The average age of freshmen is 18; all undergraduates, 25. 60% of freshmen remain to graduate.

Housing: 650 students can be accommodated in college housing, which includes coed dorms and on-campus apartments. On-campus housing is available on a first-come, first-served basis. 92% of students commute. All students may keep cars.

Activities: 5% of men belong to 5 national fraternities; 3% of women belong to 9 national sororities. There are 72 groups on campus, including art, band, cheerleading, choir, chorale, chorus, computers, dance, drama, ethnic, gay, honors, international, jazz band, marching band, newspaper, opera, orchestra, pep band, photography, political, professional, radio, religious, social, student government, and symphony. Popular campus events include College Day, Warrior Day, and Wellness Day.

Sports: There are 6 intercollegiate sports for men and 6 for women, and 9 intramural sports for men and 9 for women. Facilities include a field house, a 2300-seat gym, softball and baseball diamonds, a soccer field, tennis courts, an all-weather track, a swimming pool, and a weight room.

Disabled Students: 99% of the campus is accessible. Wheelchair ramps, elevators, special parking, specially equipped rest rooms, lowered drinking fountains, lowered telephones, tutors, and note taking are available.

Services: Counseling and information services are available, as is tutoring in most subjects. There is a reader service for the blind and remedial math, reading, and writing.

Campus Safety and Security: Measures include 24-hour foot and vehicle patrol, self-defense education, security escort services, and shuttle buses. There are informal discussions, pamphlets/posters/films, emergency telephones, and lighted pathways/sidewalks. There are also 24-hour security officers, safety awareness programs, motorist assistance, and CPR and first-aid training.

Programs of Study: CSU/Stanislaus confers B.A., B.S., B.F.A., and B.M. degrees. Master's degrees are also awarded. Bachelor's degrees are awarded in AGRICULTURE (agriculture), BIOLOGICAL SCIENCE (biology/biological science, botany, ecology, entomology, genetics, marine biology, microbiology, and zoology), BUSINESS (accounting, banking and finance, business administration and management, management science, and marketing and distribution), COMMUNICATIONS AND THE ARTS (art, art history and appreciation, communications, dramatic arts, English, fine arts, French, media arts, music, music performance, music technology, music theory and composition, painting, printmaking, sculpture, and Spanish), COMPUTER AND PHYSICAL SCIENCE (applied physics, chemistry, computer science, earth science, geology, information sciences and systems, mathematics, physical sciences, and physics), EDUCATION (bilingual/bicultural, health, music, and physical), HEALTH PROFESSIONS (clinical science and nursing), SOCIAL SCIENCE (addiction studies, anthropology, archeology, child psychology/development, cognitive science, corrections, criminal justice, criminology, developmental psychology, economics, ethnic studies, experimental psychology, forensic studies, geography, history, human services, interdisciplinary studies, international studies, law enforcement and corrections, liberal arts/general studies, philosophy, political science/government, psychology, public administration, social science, social work, sociology, and urban studies). Liberal studies, business and psychology are the strongest academically. Liberal studies is the largest.

Required: To graduate, students must complete at least 120 semester units, including 51 in the general education program and 40 in upper-division courses, with a minimum GPA of 2.0. Distribution requirements consist of 12 units of social science, 9 each of communication skills, natural science and math, and humanities, and 3 of computer study or health.

Special: Numerous co-op programs and internships are offered. Cross-registration with the Higher Education Consortium of Central California, study abroad in 19 countries, work-study programs, nondegree study, a Washington semester, an accelerated degree program, B.A.-B.S. degrees, dual majors, student-designed majors, and pass/fail options are also available. There are 10 national honor societies and a freshman honors program.

Faculty/Classroom: 55% of faculty are male; 45%, female. All teach undergraduates and 80% both teach and do research. Graduate students teach 1% of introductory courses. The average class size in an introductory lecture is 50; in a laboratory, 25; and in a regular course, 30.

Admissions: 64% of the 2003-2004 applicants were accepted. The SAT I scores for the 2003-2004 freshman class were: Verbal--44% below 500, 46% between 500 and 599, 9% between 600 and 700, and 1% above 700; Math--42% below 500, 46% between 500 and 599, 11% between 600 and 700, and 1% above 700. The ACT scores were 62% below 21, 18% between 21 and 23, 14% between 24 and 26, 3% between 27 and 28, and 3% above 28.

Requirements: The SAT I or ACT is recommended. In addition, admission is based on an eligibility index that weights GPA and the SAT I or ACT scores. Applicants with a GPA of 3.0 (3.4 for nonresidents) are exempt from test score requirements. Applicants should be graduates of an accredited secondary school. Preparatory course work should include 4 years of English, 3 of math, 2 each of foreign language, history, social sciences, and lab science, 1 of visual and performing arts, and 1 elective. A GPA of 3.0 is required. AP and CLEP credits are accepted. Important factors in the admissions decision are advanced placement or honor courses, evidence of special talent, and geographic diversity.

Procedure: Freshmen are admitted to all sessions. Entrance exams should be taken in fall of the senior year. There is an early decision plan. Early decision applications should be filed by November 30; regular applications, by May 1 for fall entry, November 30 for winter entry, November 30 for spring entry, and April 30 for summer entry, along with a $55 fee. Notification of early decision and regular decision is sent on a rolling basis. Applications are accepted on-line through *www.csumentor.edu.*

Transfer: Applicants must have a college GPA of 2.0 (2.4 for nonresidents) and have completed their lower-division general education English and math courses. Those with fewer than 56 transferable semester credits must meet freshman entrance requirements. 30 of 120 credits required for the bachelor's degree must be completed at CSU/Stanislaus.

Visiting: There are regularly scheduled orientations for prospective students. There are guides for informal visits and visitors may sit in on classes. To schedule a visit, contact University Outreach Services at *outreach_help_desk@csustan.edu.*

Financial Aid: In 2003-2004, 54% of all full-time freshmen and 55% of continuing full-time students received some form of financial aid. 47% of all full-time students received need-based aid. The average freshman award was $6126. Need-based scholarships or need-based grants averaged $4548; need-based self-help aid (loans and jobs) averaged $2253; institutional non-need-based athletic scholarships averaged $2026; and other institutional non-need-based awards and non-need-based scholarships averaged $1010. 15% of undergraduates work part time. The average financial indebtedness of the 2003 graduate was $12,750. CSU/Stanislaus is a member of CSS. The FAFSA and the SAAC for California residents are required. The deadline for filing freshman financial aid applications for fall entry is March 2.

International Students: They must score 500 on the written TOEFL or 173 on the electronic version and also take the SAT I or the ACT.

Computers: The mainframe is an IBM. Terminals are located for student access and may be used for class assignments and personal business. All students may access the system. There are no time limits and no fees.

Graduates: From July 1, 2002 to June 30, 2003, 1241 bachelor's degrees were awarded. The most popular majors were liberal studies (30%), business (14%), and social sciences (13%). In an average class, 22% graduate in 4 years or less, 42% graduate in 5 years or less, and 50% graduate in 6 years or less.

Admissions Contact: Lisa M. Bernardo, Director of Admissions and Records. A video is available.
E-mail: *outreach_help_desk@csustan.edu* Web: *http://www.csustan.edu*

CHAPMAN UNIVERSITY
Orange, CA 92866

D-5

(714) 997-6711
(888) CUAPPLY; Fax: (714) 997-6713

Full-time: 1385 men, 1876 women	Faculty: 199; IIA, +$
Part-time: 92 men, 90 women	Ph.D.s: 90%
Graduate: 412 men, 812 women	Student/Faculty: 16 to 1
Year: 4-1-4, summer session	Tuition: $24,590
Application Deadline: January 31	Room & Board: $8528
Freshman Class: 3084 applied, 1902 accepted, 823 enrolled	
SAT I Verbal/Math: 593/594	ACT: 25 **VERY COMPETITIVE**

Chapman University, founded in 1861, is an independent institution affiliated with the Disciples of Christ Christian Church, offering degree programs in liberal and fine arts, business, education, and the health sciences. There are 7 undergraduate and 8 graduate schools. In addition to regional accreditation, Chapman has baccalaureate program accreditation with AACSB, APTA, and NASM. The library contains 178,986 volumes, 423,569 microform items, and 5421 audio/video tapes/CDs, and subscribes to 1196 periodicals. Computerized library services include the card catalog, interlibrary loans, database searching, and Internet access. Special learning facilities include a learning resource center,

art gallery, radio station, TV station, and a food science sensory lab. The 60-acre campus is in a suburban area 35 miles southeast of Los Angeles. Including any residence halls, there are 25 buildings.

Student Life: 74% of undergraduates are from California. Students are from 40 states, 45 foreign countries, and Canada. 62% are from public schools. 65% are white. 26% are Protestant; 23% declined to state; 22% Catholic. The average age of freshmen is 19; all undergraduates, 22. 13% do not continue beyond their first year.

Housing: 1450 students can be accommodated in college housing, which includes coed dorms, on-campus apartments, and married-student housing. In addition, there are special-interest houses and women's communities. On-campus housing is guaranteed for the freshman year only, is available on a first-come, first-served basis, and is available on a lottery system for upperclassmen. Priority is given to out-of-town students. 57% of students commute. All students may keep cars.

Activities: 14% of men belong to 5 national fraternities; 17% of women belong to 5 national sororities. There are 60 groups on campus, including art, band, cheerleading, choir, chorale, chorus, community service, dance, debate, drama, ethnic, film, forensics, gay, honors, international, jazz band, literary magazine, newspaper, opera, orchestra, pep band, photography, political, professional, radio and TV, religious, social, social service, student government, symphony, and yearbook. Popular campus events include lunchtime concerts, Spring Sizzle, and All University Formal.

Sports: There are 10 intercollegiate sports for men and 10 for women, and 10 intramural sports for men and 10 for women. Facilities include a gym, a weight room, 3 practice fields, and 4 tennis courts. Baseball and softball fields, a track, and a pool are available for student use nearby in the city of Orange.

Disabled Students: 75% of the campus is accessible. Wheelchair ramps, elevators, special parking, specially equipped rest rooms, special class scheduling, lowered drinking fountains, lowered telephones, and special housing are available.

Services: Counseling and information services are available, as is tutoring in most subjects, including math, sciences, business, and English. There is a reader service for the blind, and remedial math, reading, and writing. In addition, there are note takers, readers, and tapes for deaf, blind, and international students; special study skills workshops; and help for the learning disabled.

Campus Safety and Security: Measures include 24-hour foot and vehicle patrol, self-defense education, security escort services, and informal discussions. There are pamphlets/posters/films, emergency telephones, lighted pathways/sidewalks, and rape awareness and victim assistance programs.

Programs of Study: Chapman confers B.A., B.S., B.F.A., B.M., and B.S.B.A. degrees. Master's and doctoral degrees are also awarded. Bachelor's degrees are awarded in BIOLOGICAL SCIENCE (biology/biological science), BUSINESS (accounting, business administration and management, and organizational behavior), COMMUNICATIONS AND THE ARTS (art, art history and appreciation, communications, creative writing, dance, dramatic arts, English, film arts, French, graphic design, music, music performance, public relations, Spanish, and studio art), COMPUTER AND PHYSICAL SCIENCE (chemistry, computer science, information sciences and systems, and mathematics), EDUCATION (athletic training and music), ENGINEERING AND ENVIRONMENTAL DESIGN (environmental science), HEALTH PROFESSIONS (health science and music therapy), SOCIAL SCIENCE (economics, food science, history, law, liberal arts/general studies, peace studies, philosophy, physical fitness/movement, political science/government, psychology, religion, social science, and sociology). Business is the strongest academically. Business, communications, and film and television are the largest.

Required: Students in the B.A., B.F.A., B.S., and B.S.B.A. programs must complete a total of 124 credits with at least a 2.0 GPA. In addition, students must meet requirements in basic subjects such as writing, oral communication, freshman seminar, math, and phys ed through course work, advanced credit, or exam. General education requirements include 10 credits in natural sciences and 9 each in humanities and social sciences. Also required are 6 credits each of cultural heritage/human diversity and foreign language, and a junior writing proficiency exam.

Special: Cooperative and internship programs are available. Students may study abroad for a semester or spend a semester in Washington, D.C. Dual and student-designed majors are possible. A general studies degree, B.A.-B.S. degrees, nondegree study options, and pass/fail options are also permitted. A 3-2 engineering degree with the University of California, Irvine, is possible. There is 1 national honor society and a freshman honors program.

Faculty/Classroom: 60% of faculty are male; 40%, female. 96% teach undergraduates. No introductory courses are taught by graduate students. The average class size in an introductory lecture is 23; in a laboratory, 17; and in a regular course, 21.

Admissions: 62% of the 2003-2004 applicants were accepted. The SAT I scores for the 2003-2004 freshman class were: Verbal--6% below 500, 51% between 500 and 599, 36% between 600 and 700, and 7% above 700; Math--5% below 500, 50% between 500 and 599, 40% be-

tween 600 and 700, and 5% above 700. 41% of the current freshmen were in the top fifth of their class; 83% were in the top two fifths. There was 1 National Merit finalist and 26 semifinalists. 9 freshmen graduated first in their class.

Requirements: The SAT I or ACT is required. In addition, applicants should be graduates of accredited high schools or have earned the GED. Secondary preparation should include 4 years of English, 3 each of math and social science or electives, and 2 each of science and a foreign language. Prospective art or music majors should show some preparation in those fields. A personal essay is required. An on-campus interview is recommended. A GPA of 2.75 is required. AP and CLEP credits are accepted. Important factors in the admissions decision are advanced placement or honor courses, evidence of special talent, and leadership record.

Procedure: Freshmen are admitted fall and spring. Entrance exams should be taken by fall of the senior year. There is an early admissions plan. Applications should be filed by January 31 for fall entry, November 15 for spring entry, and June 1 for summer entry, along with a $50 fee. Notification is sent February 28. 153 applicants were on the 2003 waiting list. Applications are accepted on-line through the school's web site.

Transfer: 304 transfer students enrolled in 2002-2003. Transfer applicants should have completed at least 12 credits of transferable college work with a 2.25 minimum GPA. High school records and SAT I or ACT scores should be submitted if fewer than 30 transferable credits have been completed. 24 of 124 credits required for the bachelor's degree must be completed at Chapman.

Visiting: There are regularly scheduled orientations for prospective students, consisting of Fall and Spring Campus Exploration Day events. Weekday appointments and campus tours are also available. There are guides for informal visits and visitors may sit in on classes. To schedule a visit, contact the Office of Admissions.

Financial Aid: In 2003-2004, 90% of all full-time freshmen and 86% of continuing full-time students received some form of financial aid. 64% of full-time freshmen and 61% of continuing full-time students received need-based aid. The average freshman award was $23,422. Need-based scholarships or need-based grants averaged $16,363 ($34,050 maximum); need-based self-help aid (loans and jobs) averaged $4433 ($10,625 maximum); and other non-need-based awards and non-need-based scholarships averaged $14,271 ($37,200 maximum). 60% of undergraduates work part time. Average annual earnings from campus work are $1695. The average financial indebtedness of the 2003 graduate was $18,574. Chapman is a member of CSS. The FAFSA and the state aid form are required. The priority date for freshman financial aid applications for fall entry is March 2.

International Students: There are 88 international students enrolled. The school actively recruits these students. They must score 500 on the written TOEFL or 213 on the electronic version and also take the SAT I or the ACT.

Computers: The mainframe is an HP 3000/957. There are 46 Mac IIsi and SE computers, 50 other PCs, 3 DEC MicroVAX II UNIX-based minicomputers, 2 DEC workstations that are networked and have access to the Internet, 25 Power Mac 6100/60s, 1 DEC Alpha, and 1 SGT. All students may access the system 8 A.M. to 11 P.M. There are no time limits and no fees. It is strongly recommended that all students have a personal computer.

Graduates: From July 1, 2002 to June 30, 2003, 695 bachelor's degrees were awarded. The most popular majors were business administration (16%), film and television (13%), and liberal studies (8%). In an average class, 49% graduate in 4 years or less, and 59% graduate in 6 years or less. 80 companies recruited on campus in 2002-2003. Of the 2002 graduating class, 40% were enrolled in graduate school within 6 months of graduation and 93% were employed.

Admissions Contact: Mike Drummy, Assistant Vice President of Enrollment Services and Chief Admission Officer.
E-mail: *admit@chapman.edu* Web: *www.chapman.edu*

CHRISTIAN HERITAGE COLLEGE	D-5
El Cajon, CA 92019-1157	(619) 588-7747
	(800) 676-2242; Fax: (619) 590-1739

Full-time: 500 men and women	**Faculty:** 30
Part-time: 100 men and women	**Ph.D.s:** 50%
Graduate: none	**Student/Faculty:** 17 to 1
Year: semesters, summer session	**Tuition:** $14,000
Application Deadline: open	**Room & Board:** $5990
Freshman Class: n/av	
SAT I or ACT: required	COMPETITIVE

Christian Heritage College is a small, private institution founded in 1970 by the Scott Memorial Baptist Church of San Diego, with which it is still affiliated. It offers programs in the liberal arts, business, and education. Some information in this capsule and profile is approximate. The library contains 70,000 volumes, 80 microform items, and 3820 audio/video tapes/CDs, and subscribes to 250 periodicals. Computerized library services include database searching. Special learning facilities include the nearby Institute for Creation Research. The 32-acre campus is in a sub-

urban area 15 miles east of San Diego. Including any residence halls, there are 14 buildings.

Student Life: 80% of undergraduates are from California. 75% are from public schools. 70% are white; 10% African American; 10% Hispanic. Most are Protestant. The average age of freshmen is 18; all undergraduates, 21. 40% do not continue beyond their first year; 30% remain to graduate.

Housing: 200 students can be accommodated in college housing, which includes single-sex dorms and off-campus apartments. In addition, there are language houses. On-campus housing is guaranteed for all 4 years and is available on a first-come, first-served basis. 50% of students live on campus; of those, 30% remain on campus on weekends. Alcohol is not permitted. All students may keep cars.

Activities: There are no fraternities or sororities. There are 16 groups on campus, including art, cheerleading, choir, chorale, chorus, computers, drama, honors, international, musical theater, newspaper, pep band, political, religious, social, student government, and yearbook. Popular campus events include spring, winter, and Valentine's Day banquets, and the Missions Conference.

Sports: There are 3 intercollegiate sports for men and 4 for women, and 5 intramural sports for men and 4 for women. Facilities include a swimming pool, a gym, outdoor courts for tennis, volleyball, and basketball, and soccer and softball fields.

Disabled Students: 90% of the campus is accessible. Wheelchair ramps, elevators, and special parking are available.

Services: Counseling and information services are available, as is tutoring in some subjects.

Campus Safety and Security: Measures include 24-hour foot and vehicle patrol, lighted pathways/sidewalks, and a fenced campus.

Programs of Study: CHC confers B.A. and B.S. degrees. Associate degrees are also awarded. Bachelor's degrees are awarded in BIOLOGICAL SCIENCE (biology/biological science), BUSINESS (business administration and management), COMMUNICATIONS AND THE ARTS (communications, English, and music), COMPUTER AND PHYSICAL SCIENCE (mathematics), EDUCATION (education), ENGINEERING AND ENVIRONMENTAL DESIGN (aviation administration/management), SOCIAL SCIENCE (biblical studies, history, human development, interdisciplinary studies, liberal arts/general studies, physical fitness/movement, and psychology). Counseling psychology, education, and business are the strongest academically. Business, education, and human development are the largest.

Required: The required credits for graduation vary by degree program and major. All students must take 46 to 52 credits in sciences and math, social science, and humanities; 20 credits in personal Christian development and biblical studies; and the balance in major field requirements and electives. A 2.0 GPA is required for graduation.

Special: Students attend chapel 3 times each week, participate in an annual Bible conference, and complete a student ministry assignment each semester. Independent study for 1 to 3 credits can be arranged. There are internships in psychology, pastoral studies, and education.

Faculty/Classroom: 60% of faculty are male; 40%, female. All teach undergraduates. The average class size in an introductory lecture is 40; in a laboratory, 15; and in a regular course, 16.

Requirements: The SAT I or ACT is required; the ACT is preferred. Applicants must have a high school diploma or the GED, or have successfully completed the California State High School Proficiency Exam. Secondary preparation should include 4 units of English, 3 each of math, natural science, and social studies, and 2 of a single foreign language. A personal essay is also required. In addition, applicants must meet certain spiritual requirements. CHC requires applicants to be in the upper 50% of their class. A GPA of 2.25 is required. AP and CLEP credits are accepted. Important factors in the admissions decision are recommendations by school officials, leadership record, and extracurricular activities record.

Procedure: Freshmen are admitted fall and spring. Entrance exams should be taken during the junior year. Application deadlines are open. Notification is sent on a rolling basis. Check with the school for current application fee.

Transfer: 30 of 124 credits required for the bachelor's degree must be completed at CHC.

Visiting: There are regularly scheduled orientations for prospective students, including a campus tour, cafeteria meal, and class and chapel attendance. There are guides for informal visits and visitors may sit in on classes and stay overnight. To schedule a visit, contact the Admissions Office.

Financial Aid: 70% of undergraduates work part time. CHC is a member of CSS. The FAFSA and the college's own financial statement are required. Check with the school for current deadlines.

International Students: The school actively recruits these students. They must score 500 on the written TOEFL and also take the college's own test. The SAT I (score of 900) or the ACT (score of 19) is also required.

Computers: The mainframe is a Dell. There are 32 networked PCs at 3 campus locations, all with e-mail, Internet, and web access. All students may access the system. There are no time limits and no fees.

Graduates: In an average class, 1% graduate in 3 years or less, 78% graduate in 4 years or less, 97% graduate in 5 years or less, and 99% graduate in 6 years or less.

Admissions Contact: Misty Chappelle, Director of Admissions.
E-mail: *chcadm@adm.christianheritage.edu*
Web: *www.christianheritage.edu*

CLAREMONT COLLEGES, THE

Established in 1925, this prestigious group of seven private colleges is a consortium of higher education institutions. It is comprised of five undergraduate liberal arts colleges: Claremont McKenna, Harvey Mudd, Pitzer, Pomona, and Scripps; and two graduate institutions: Claremont Graduate University and Keck Graduate Institute of Applied Life Sciences. Collectively, the seven institutions serve nearly 6000 students from 50 states and more than 80 foreign countries. 2500 courses are taught each year by 600 professors, often with class sizes under 20. Six contiguous campuses with 175 buildings are spread over 350 acres of land with the seventh campus located nearby. Each institution is independent, with its own faculty, student body, administration, curricular emphasis, and distinctive style. However, each is enriched by the presence of the others. The consortium offers students a variety of intellectual, cultural, and social activities in facilities and shared academic resources. Claremont University Consortium (CUC) is the central coordinating and support organization for The Claremont Colleges. Some of the 28 services include campus safety, libraries, health and counseling services, ethnic student centers, an interfaith office of chaplains, a centralized bookstore, food services, information technology, human resources, real estate, risk management, and employee benefits. In the words of the founding father, Dr. Robert J. Bernard, "This pioneering enterprise has given national leadership in demonstrating how the advantages of small colleges and the advantages of a university can be combined to build a notable center of learning."

CLAREMONT MCKENNA COLLEGE — D-5

Claremont, CA 91711-6425   (909) 621-8088; Fax: (909) 621-8516

Full-time: 580 men, 470 women	**Faculty:** 135; IIB, ++$
Part-time: 3 men	**Ph.D.s:** 97%
Graduate: none	**Student/Faculty:** 8 to 1
Year: semesters	**Tuition:** $27,700
Application Deadline: January 1	**Room & Board:** $9180
Freshman Class: 2892 applied, 897 accepted, 284 enrolled	
SAT I Verbal/Math: 690/700	**ACT:** 30 **MOST COMPETITIVE**

Claremont McKenna College, founded in 1946, is a highly selective liberal arts college with a curricular emphasis on economics, government, international relations, and public affairs. The 5 libraries contain 2,008,476 volumes, 1,448,021 microform items, and 15,400 audio/video tapes/CDs, and subscribe to 5592 periodicals. Computerized library services include the card catalog, interlibrary loans, and database searching. Special learning facilities include a learning resource center, art gallery, radio station, and 10 research institutes. The 50-acre campus is in a small town 35 miles east of downtown Los Angeles. Including any residence halls, there are 29 buildings.

Student Life: 52% of undergraduates are from out of state, mostly the Northwest. Students are from 44 states, 21 foreign countries, and Canada. 73% are from public schools. 65% are white; 14% Asian American. 36% claim no religious affiliation; 25% Protestant; 19% Catholic; 6% Jewish. The average age of freshmen is 18; all undergraduates, 20. 3% do not continue beyond their first year; 86% remain to graduate.

Housing: 984 students can be accommodated in college housing, which includes coed dorms, on-campus apartments, and substance-free housing. On-campus housing is guaranteed for all 4 years. 96% of students live on campus; of those, 80% remain on campus on weekends. All students may keep cars.

Activities: There are no fraternities or sororities. There are 185 groups on campus, including art, band, cheerleading, choir, chorale, chorus, computers, dance, debate, drama, ethnic, film, forensics, gay, honors, international, jazz band, literary magazine, musical theater, newspaper, orchestra, photography, political, professional, radio and TV, religious, social, social service, student government, symphony, and yearbook. Popular campus events include International Festival, Madrigal Dinners, and Monte Carlo Night.

Sports: There are 10 intercollegiate sports for men and 10 for women, and 10 intramural sports for men and 9 for women. Facilities include basketball courts, weight room, fitness center, track and football field, aquatic center, tennis courts, baseball, softball, and soccer fields, archery range, squash and volleyball courts, and lacrosse and intramural fields.

Disabled Students: 90% of the campus is accessible. Wheelchair ramps, elevators, special parking, specially equipped rest rooms, special class scheduling, and special housing are available. The campus complies with ADA requirements and reasonably accommodates students with physical disabilities as necessary to meet their access needs.

Services: Counseling and information services are available, as is tutoring in most subjects. There is remedial writing. The Writing Center offers writing help and specialized workshops.

Campus Safety and Security: Measures include 24-hour foot and vehicle patrol, self-defense education, security escort services, and informal discussions. There are pamphlets/posters/films, emergency telephones, and lighted pathways/sidewalks.

Programs of Study: CMC confers the B.A. degree. Bachelor's degrees are awarded in AGRICULTURE (environmental studies), BIOLOGICAL SCIENCE (biochemistry, biology/biological science, and neurosciences), BUSINESS (business economics and management engineering), COMMUNICATIONS AND THE ARTS (dramatic arts, English literature, French, German, literature, and Spanish), COMPUTER AND PHYSICAL SCIENCE (chemistry, mathematics, physics, and science technology), ENGINEERING AND ENVIRONMENTAL DESIGN (environmental science), SOCIAL SCIENCE (African American studies, American studies, Asian/Oriental studies, economics, history, interdisciplinary studies, international relations, Latin American studies, law, Mexican-American/Chicano studies, philosophy, political science/government, psychology, religion, and women's studies). Economics, government, and international relations are strongest academically and have the largest enrollments.

Required: All students must complete 32 courses (128 semester hours) with a C average. Required courses include a minimum of 3 semesters each of social science and phys ed; 2 each of sciences and humanities; 1 each of English, calculus, and civilization; and foreign language proficiency equal to 3 college semesters. A thesis is required of all students. At least 16 courses must be taken in residence.

Special: CMC students may cross-register at any of the Claremont Colleges and may participate in exchange programs with Haverford, Spelman, or Colby Colleges. Students may study abroad in 43 countries or spend a semester in Washington, D.C. Part-time and full-time internships and dual and student-designed majors are available. There is a 3-2 economic-engineering program with Harvey Mudd College and a 3-2 management-engineering program. A multidisciplinary program in leadership studies and an interdisciplinary program in legal studies are offered. There are limited pass/fail options. There are 5 national honor societies, including Phi Beta Kappa, and a freshman honors program.

Faculty/Classroom: 66% of faculty are male; 34%, female. All both teach and do research. The average class size in a laboratory is 18 and in a regular course, 16.

Admissions: 31% of the 2003-2004 applicants were accepted. The SAT I scores for the 2003-2004 freshman class were: Verbal--7% between 500 and 599, 47% between 600 and 700, and 46% above 700; Math--5% between 500 and 599, 51% between 600 and 700, and 44% above 700. The ACT scores were 2% between 21 and 23, 10% between 24 and 26, 19% between 27 and 28, and 69% above 28. 97% of the current freshmen were in the top fifth of their class. There were 14 National Merit finalists. 20 freshmen graduated first in their class.

Requirements: The SAT I is required. In addition, applicants must be graduates of an accredited high school or have earned the GED. Secondary preparation must include 4 years of English, 3 years (preferably 4) of math, at least 2 years of a foreign language and science, and 1 year of history. A personal essay is required, and an interview is recommended. AP credits are accepted. Important factors in the admissions decision are advanced placement or honor courses, leadership record, and extracurricular activities record.

Procedure: Freshmen are admitted fall and spring. Entrance exams should be taken during the junior year or between October and January of the senior year. There is an early decision plan. Early decision applications should be filed by November 15; regular applications, by January 1 for fall entry and November 1 for spring entry. The fall 2003 application fee was $50. Notification of early decision is sent December 15; regular decision, April 1. 55 early decision candidates were accepted for the 2003-2004 class. 277 applicants were on the 2003 waiting list; none were accepted. Applications are accepted on computer disk and on-line through the school's web site.

Transfer: 70 transfer students enrolled in a recent year. Applicants must submit the SAT I or ACT scores, high school and college transcripts, essays, a college report form, midsemester grades, and recommendations from a college professor or counselor. 64 of 128 credits required for the bachelor's degree must be completed at CMC.

Visiting: There are regularly scheduled orientations for prospective students, including a campus tour, faculty presentations, student discussions, and admissions and financial aid workshops. There are guides for informal visits and visitors may sit in on classes and stay overnight. To schedule a visit, contact the Admissions Office at *admission@claremontmckenna.edu.*

Financial Aid: In 2003-2004, 67% of all full-time freshmen and 70% of continuing full-time students received some form of financial aid. 50% of full-time freshmen and 56% of continuing full-time students received need-based aid. The average freshman award was $24,119. 50% of undergraduates work part time. Average annual earnings from campus work are $2240. The average financial indebtedness of the 2003 graduate was $13,100. CMC is a member of CSS. The CSS Profile or FAFSA is required. The deadline for filing freshman financial aid applications for fall entry is February 1.

International Students: There are 31 international students enrolled. The school actively recruits these students. They must score 550 on the written TOEFL and also take the SAT I or the ACT.

Computers: The mainframe is an HP9000. Students have access to 3 computer labs, run by several Windows 2000 and UNIX servers. All dorm rooms and classrooms are wired for network access. Students have access to grades, class, and personal information via a web portal. Faculty utilize WebCT for many courses, an on-line access system offering bulletin boards, real-time chats, on-line testing, and connection to additional resource materials. All students may access the system. There are no time limits and no fees.

Graduates: From July 1, 2002 to June 30, 2003, 288 bachelor's degrees were awarded. The most popular majors were government (25%), economics (24%), and psychology (13%). In an average class, 84% graduate in 4 years or less, 86% graduate in 5 years or less, and 87% graduate in 6 years or less. 80 companies recruited on campus in 2002-2003. Of the 2002 graduating class, 20% were enrolled in graduate school at the time of graduation and 47% were employed.

Admissions Contact: Richard C. Vos, VP, Dean of Admission and Financial Aid. E-mail: *admission@claremontmckenna.edu* Web: *www.mckenna.edu*

COGSWELL POLYTECHNICAL COLLEGE B-3
Sunnyvale, CA 94089 (408) 541-0100, ext. 152
(800)-264-7955 (COGSWLL); Fax: (408) 747-0764

Full-time: 200 men and women	**Faculty:** 10
Part-time: 300 men and women	**Ph.D.s:** 35%
Graduate: none	**Student/Faculty:** 20 to 1
Year: trimesters, summer session	**Tuition:** $14,400
Application Deadline: open	**Room & Board:** n/app
Freshman Class: n/av	
SAT I or ACT: not required	**LESS COMPETITIVE**

Cogswell Polytechnical College, founded in 1887, is a small, independent engineering and arts college. Figures in the above capsule and in this profile are approximate. The library contains 13,000 volumes, 250 microform items, and 200 audio/video tapes/CDs, and subscribes to 125 periodicals. Computerized library services include the card catalog and database searching. Special learning facilities include an art gallery and commercial studio, and video postproduction company. The 4-acre campus is in a suburban area 40 miles south of San Francisco in California's Silicon Valley. There is one building.

Student Life: 70% of undergraduates are from California. 65% are from public schools. The average age of freshmen is 19; all undergraduates, 28. 10% do not continue beyond their first year; 70% remain to graduate.

Housing: There are no residence halls. Arrangements can be made to accommodate students in private houses or at nearby corporate apartments. Alcohol is not permitted. All students may keep cars.

Activities: There are no fraternities or sororities. There are 7 groups on campus, including art, computers, honors, international, jazz band, professional, and student government. Popular campus events include Founders Day, club competitions, and ski trips.

Sports: There is no sports program at Cogswell College. Facilities include a game room, a student lounge, and access to community athletic facilities.

Disabled Students: Wheelchair ramps, special parking, specially equipped rest rooms, special class scheduling, lowered drinking fountains, and lowered telephones are available.

Services: Counseling and information services are available, as is tutoring in every subject. There is remedial writing.

Campus Safety and Security: Measures include pamphlets/posters/films, lighted pathways/sidewalks, an emergency evacuation plan, and maps in the classrooms.

Programs of Study: Cogswell College confers B.A.C.V.I. (Computer and Video Imaging), B.S.E.E., B.S.F.S. (Fire Science), and B.S.S.W.E. (Software Engineering) degrees. Bachelor's degrees are awarded in COMMUNICATIONS AND THE ARTS (animation, audio technology, and music technology), COMPUTER AND PHYSICAL SCIENCE (computer programming, digital arts/technology, and web technology), ENGINEERING AND ENVIRONMENTAL DESIGN (computer engineering, computer graphics, and electrical/electronics engineering), SOCIAL SCIENCE (fire control and safety technology and fire protection). Engineering and animation are the strongest academically. Computer video imaging is the largest.

Required: To graduate, students must complete a total of 120 to 128 credits with 18 to 27 in the major and have a 2.0 GPA. 45 to 56 credits in general education core courses are required, depending on the major, and include courses in English, math, natural sciences, social sciences, and humanities.

Special: Cogswell offers various internships and work-study programs. The college administers the Open Learning for the Fire Service (OLFS)

program for Arizona, California, and Nevada, through which nonresident students can earn a B.S. in fire science. Nondegree study and pass/fail options are possible. There is a freshman honors program.

Faculty/Classroom: 65% of faculty are male; 35%, female. The average class size in an introductory lecture is 15; in a laboratory, 8; and in a regular course, 25.

Requirements: Applicants must be high school graduates or have the GED. Secondary preparation must include 3 years of English, 2 to 3 of math, including algebra, geometry, and trigonometry, and 1 year of science. Cogswell requires a personal essay and recommends a personal interview. A portfolio is required for computer and video imaging programs. A GPA of 2.7 is required. AP and CLEP credits are accepted. Important factors in the admissions decision are advanced placement or honor courses, recommendations by school officials, and ability to finance college education.

Procedure: Freshmen are admitted to all sessions. There are early decision and early admissions plans. Check with the school for current application deadlines and fee.

Transfer: Applicants must have completed at least 12 college credits with a 2.2 GPA. An interview is recommended. 27 of 120 credits required for the bachelor's degree must be completed at Cogswell College.

Visiting: Visitors may sit in on classes. To schedule a visit, contact the dean of marketing and recruiting.

Financial Aid: Cogswell College is a member of CSS. The FAFSA and the college's own financial statement are required. Check with the school for current application deadlines.

International Students: The school actively recruits these students. They must score 550 on the written TOEFL.

Computers: The mainframe is a DEC VAX 11/780. There are also 35 PCs available in computer labs and the library. The Internet is accessible in computer labs. All students may access the system during school hours. There are no time limits and no fees. It is strongly recommended that all students have a personal computer.

Admissions Contact: Patricia DelRio, Director of Admissions. E-mail: *admin@cogswell.edu* Web: *www.cogswell.edu*

CONCORDIA UNIVERSITY D-5
Irvine, CA 92612-3299 (949) 854-8002 ext. 1118
(800) 229-1200; Fax: (949) 854-6894

Full-time: 433 men, 824 women	**Faculty:** 67
Part-time: 58 men, 105 women	**Ph.D.s:** 57%
Graduate: 112 men, 215 women	**Student/Faculty:** 19 to 1
Year: semesters	**Tuition:** $17,990
Application Deadline: May 1	**Room & Board:** $6430
Freshman Class: 986 applied, 656 accepted, 270 enrolled	
SAT I Verbal/Math: 530/540	**ACT:** 22 **COMPETITIVE**

Concordia University, founded in 1972, is a private liberal arts institution affiliated with the Lutheran Church-Missouri Synod. There are 5 undergraduate and 3 graduate schools. The library contains 90,467 volumes, 42,718 microform items, and 3237 audio/video tapes/CDs, and subscribes to 379 periodicals. Computerized library services include the card catalog, interlibrary loans, database searching, and Internet access. Special learning facilities include a learning resource center, art gallery, and radio station. The 70-acre campus is in a suburban area 40 miles south of Los Angeles. Including any residence halls, there are 24 buildings.

Student Life: 79% of undergraduates are from California. Students are from 35 states and 8 foreign countries. 77% are white; 10% Hispanic. 18% claim no religious affiliation; 12% Protestant; 10% Catholic. The average age of freshmen is 18; all undergraduates, 22. 23% do not continue beyond their first year; 77% remain to graduate.

Housing: 1000 students can be accommodated in college housing, which includes single-sex dorms. On-campus housing is guaranteed for all 4 years. 69% of students live on campus. All students may keep cars.

Activities: There are no fraternities or sororities. There are 17 groups on campus, including art, choir, chorale, chorus, dance, debate, drama, ethnic, film, literary magazine, newspaper, radio and TV, religious, social, social service, student government, and yearbook. Popular campus events include Closing Banquet, Christmas Dance, and Octoberfest.

Sports: There are 5 intercollegiate sports for men and 6 for women, and 5 intramural sports for men and 5 for women. Facilities include a 1500-seat gym, a soccer field, a baseball/softball diamond, volleyball, tennis, and racquetball courts, a track field, a weight room, a dance room, team rooms, and locker rooms.

Disabled Students: 90% of the campus is accessible. Wheelchair ramps, special parking, specially equipped rest rooms, and lowered drinking fountains are available.

Services: Counseling and information services are available, as is tutoring in some subjects, including math, chemistry, critical thinking, Spanish, biology, and calculus.

Campus Safety and Security: Measures include 24-hour foot and vehicle patrol, security escort services, informal discussions, pamphlets/posters/films, and lighted pathways/sidewalks.

Programs of Study: Concordia Irvine confers the B.A. degree. Associate and master's degrees are also awarded. Bachelor's degrees are awarded in BIOLOGICAL SCIENCE (biology/biological science), BUSINESS (business administration and management), COMMUNICATIONS AND THE ARTS (art, communications, dramatic arts, English, and music), COMPUTER AND PHYSICAL SCIENCE (mathematics), EDUCATION (Christian and early childhood), HEALTH PROFESSIONS (exercise science), SOCIAL SCIENCE (behavioral science, history, humanities, liberal arts/general studies, psychology, and religion). Education, social science, and business administration are the strongest academically and are the largest.

Required: All students must complete 49 semester hours of general education requirements, including courses in humanities and fine arts, math and science, social science, religion, and exercise and sport science. A total of 128 credits, including 36 to 45 in the major, is required to graduate. A GPA of 2.0 in major and program course work must be maintained.

Special: Cross-registration is possible with 9 Concordia Universities/Colleges nationwide. Internships, an accelerated degree program in the liberal arts major with an emphasis on business and teacher education, and dual and student-designed majors are available. There are 2 national honor societies, a freshman honors program, and 2 departmental honors programs.

Faculty/Classroom: 57% of faculty are male; 43%, female. 92% teach undergraduates. No introductory courses are taught by graduate students. The average class size in a laboratory is 24 and in a regular course, 26.

Admissions: 67% of the 2003-2004 applicants were accepted. The SAT I scores for the 2003-2004 freshman class were: Verbal--34% below 500, 43% between 500 and 599, 21% between 600 and 700, and 2% above 700; Math--32% below 500, 46% between 500 and 599, 19% between 600 and 700, and 3% above 700. The ACT scores were 40% below 21, 25% between 21 and 23, 20% between 24 and 26, 6% between 27 and 28, and 9% above 28. 45% of the current freshmen were in the top fifth of their class; 80% were in the top two fifths.

Requirements: The SAT I or ACT is required. In addition, applicants should be high school graduates with 4 years of English, 3 each of math and science, and 2 each of social studies and a foreign language. The GED is accepted. A school reference is also required. Concordia Irvine requires applicants to be in the upper 50% of their class. A GPA of 2.8 is required. AP and CLEP credits are accepted. Important factors in the admissions decision are leadership record, extracurricular activities record, and evidence of special talent.

Procedure: Freshmen are admitted fall and spring. Entrance exams should be taken by the fall of the senior year. There is a rolling admissions plan and a deferred admissions plan. Applications should be filed by May 1 for fall entry and December 1 for spring entry. The fall 2003 application fee was $50. Notification is sent on a rolling basis. Applications are accepted on computer disk and on-line through XAPplication.

Transfer: 132 transfer students enrolled in 2002-2003. A GPA of 2.3 is required in a minimum of 24 semester or 36 quarter units completed. An academic reference is required, as are official high school transcripts. 32 of 128 credits required for the bachelor's degree must be completed at Concordia Irvine.

Visiting: There are regularly scheduled orientations for prospective students. There are guides for informal visits and visitors may sit in on classes and stay overnight. To schedule a visit, contact the Admission Office at (949) 854-8002, ext. 1106 or admission@cui.edu.

Financial Aid: In 2003-2004, 70% of all full-time freshmen and 71% of continuing full-time students received some form of financial aid. 40% of full-time freshmen and 38% of continuing full-time students received need-based aid. The average freshman award was $14,511. Need-based scholarships or need-based grants averaged $6974; need-based self-help aid (loans and jobs) averaged $2520; non-need-based athletic scholarships averaged $5780; and other non-need-based awards and non-need-based scholarships averaged $6147. 25% of undergraduates work part time. Average annual earnings from campus work are $2000. The average financial indebtedness of the 2003 graduate was $16,500. The FAFSA and the college's own financial statement are required. The deadline for filing freshman financial aid applications for fall entry is March 2.

International Students: There are 81 international students enrolled. The school actively recruits these students. They must score 550 on the written TOEFL or 213 on the electronic version and also take the SAT I or the ACT.

Computers: The mainframe is a VAX. Students have access to 69 computers, e-mail to on-campus addresses, the Internet and Web, and a campuswide network. All students may access the system. There are no time limits and no fees.

Graduates: From July 1, 2002 to June 30, 2003, 235 bachelor's degrees were awarded. The most popular majors were liberal studies (18%), business administration (16%), and applied liberal arts (15%). In an average class, 2% graduate in 3 years or less, 89% graduate in 4 years or less, 7% graduate in 5 years or less, and 2% graduate in 6 years or less. 47 companies recruited on campus in 2002-2003.

Admissions Contact: Paul Marquardt, Director of Admission. E-mail: paul.marquardt@cui.edu Web: www.cui.edu

DEVRY UNIVERSITY/FREMONT
Fremont, CA 94555

B-3
(510) 574-1200
(888) 201-9941; Fax: (510) 742-0868

Full-time: 998 men, 269 women	**Faculty:** n/av
Part-time: 276 men, 108 women	**Ph.D.s:** n/av
Graduate: n/av	**Student/Faculty:** n/av
Year: semesters, summer session	**Tuition:** $11,860
Application Deadline: open	**Room & Board:** n/app
Freshman Class: n/av	
SAT I or ACT: n/av	**LESS COMPETITIVE**

DeVry University/Fremont, founded in 1998, is a private institution offering hands-on programs in electronics, business administration, computer information systems, telecommunications management, computer engineering technology, and technical management. The school is 1 of 67 DeVry University locations throughout the United States and Canada. In addition to regional accreditation, DeVry has baccalaureate program accreditation with ABET. The library contains 27,000 volumes and 3000 audio/video tapes/CDs, and subscribes to 60 periodicals. Computerized library services include the card catalog, interlibrary loans, and database searching. Special learning facilities include a learning resource center and electronic labs. The 17-acre campus is in a suburban area. There is one building.

Student Life: 36% of students are Asian American; 23% white; 17% Hispanic. The average age of all undergraduates is 24.

Housing: There are no residence halls. Housing referrals can be obtained through the Student Housing Office. There are private apartments, student-plan housing, and private rooms. All students commute. Alcohol is not permitted. All students may keep cars.

Activities: There are no fraternities or sororities. There are 6 groups on campus, including chess, ethnic, professional, and religious. Popular campus events include Thanksgiving Dinner, Summer BBQ, and Book Fair.

Sports: There is no sports program at DeVry.

Disabled Students: 90% of the campus is accessible. Wheelchair ramps, elevators, special parking, specially equipped rest rooms, and lowered drinking fountains are available.

Services: Counseling and information services are available, as is tutoring in every subject.

Campus Safety and Security: Measures include 24-hour foot and vehicle patrol, self-defense education, security escort services, and informal discussions. There are pamphlets/posters/films, emergency telephones, and lighted pathways/sidewalks.

Programs of Study: DeVry confers the B.S. degree. Associate and master's degrees are also awarded. Bachelor's degrees are awarded in BIOLOGICAL SCIENCE (bioinformatics), BUSINESS (business administration and management), COMMUNICATIONS AND THE ARTS (telecommunications), COMPUTER AND PHYSICAL SCIENCE (information sciences and systems), ENGINEERING AND ENVIRONMENTAL DESIGN (biomedical engineering, computer engineering, electrical/electronics engineering technology, and technological management). Electronics, telecommunications, and computer information systems are the largest.

Required: To graduate, students must achieve a cumulative GPA of at least 2.0 and satisfactorily complete all curriculum requirements. Course requirements vary according to program. All first-semester students take courses in business organization, computer applications, algebra, psychology, and student success strategies.

Special: Accelerated degrees, co-op programs, nondegree study, and evening and weekend classes are possible.

Faculty/Classroom: All teach undergraduates.

Requirements: Admissions requirements include graduation from a secondary school; the GED is also accepted. Applicants must pass the DeVry entrance exam or present satisfactory ACT or SAT I scores. An interview is required. CLEP credit is accepted.

Procedure: Freshmen are admitted fall, spring, and summer. There is a rolling admissions plan. There are early admissions and deferred admissions plans. Application deadlines are open. Application fee is $50. Applications are accepted on-line through https://apply.embark.com/UGrad/DeVry/21.

Transfer: 28 transfer students enrolled in a recent year. Applicants must present passing grades in all completed college course work, demonstrate language skills proficiency in at least 24 completed semester hours, and present evidence of math proficiency by appropriate college-level credits. 25% of 48 to 154 credits required for the bachelor's degree must be completed at DeVry.

Visiting: There are regularly scheduled orientations for prospective students. There are guides for informal visits and visitors may sit in on classes. To schedule a visit, contact Choo Yaz, New Student Coordinator.

Financial Aid: In 2002-2003, 59% of all full-time freshmen and 80% of continuing full-time students received some form of financial aid. At least 58% of full-time freshmen and at least 78% of continuing full-time students received need-based aid. The average freshman award was $8061. Need-based scholarships or need-based grants averaged $5933; need-based self-help aid (loans and jobs) averaged $4577; and institutional non-need-based awards and non-need-based scholarships averaged $10,077. The FAFSA is required. The deadline for filing freshman financial aid applications for fall is rolling.

International Students: There were 55 international students enrolled in a recent year. They must score 500 on the written TOEFL or 173 on the electronic version and also take the college's own entrance exam.

Computers: Lab facilities include PCs in stand-alone and network configurations with access to the mainframe. LANs provide access to a wide range of applications software. Hard copy from the mainframe is provided through a local minicomputer and medium- and high-speed printers. All students may access the system. Students may access the system during lab hours. There are no fees. It is strongly recommended that all students have a personal computer. Students in the information technology program have DeVry-issued laptop computers.

Graduates: From July 1, 2002 to June 30, 2003, 387 bachelor's degrees were awarded. The most popular majors were computer information systems (65%), business (18%), and electronics engineering technology (17%). 40 companies recruited on campus in a recent year.

Admissions Contact: Mark Martin, Director of Admissions.
Web: *www.fre.devry.edu*

DEVRY UNIVERSITY/LONG BEACH
Long Beach, CA 90806-2449

C-5

(562) 427-4162
(800) 597-0444; Fax: (562) 997-5371

Full-time: 880 men, 302 women	**Faculty:** n/av
Part-time: 548 men, 198 women	**Ph.D.s:** n/av
Graduate: n/av	**Student/Faculty:** n/av
Year: semesters, summer session	**Tuition:** $11,310
Application Deadline: open	**Room & Board:** n/app
Freshman Class: n/av	
SAT I or ACT: n/av	**LESS COMPETITIVE**

DeVry University/Long Beach is 1 of 67 DeVry University locations in the United States and Canada. The school offers programs in business administration, computer information systems, electronics, telecommunications management, technical management, information technology, and computer engineering technology. There is 1 undergraduate school. In addition to regional accreditation, DeVry has baccalaureate program accreditation with ABET. The library contains 13,251 volumes and 2069 audio/video tapes/CDs, and subscribes to 76 periodicals. Computerized library services include the card catalog, interlibrary loans, and database searching. Special learning facilities include a learning resource center and electronics and other labs. The 11-acre campus is in an urban area midway between Los Angeles and Orange County. There is one building.

Student Life: 33% of students are Hispanic; 27% Asian American; 19% white; 13% African American. The average age of all undergraduates is 24.

Housing: There are no residence halls. Housing referrals may be obtained through the Student Housing Office. There are private apartments, student-plan housing, and private rooms. All students commute. Alcohol is not permitted. All students may keep cars.

Activities: There are no fraternities or sororities. There are 13 groups on campus, including ethnic and professional. Popular campus events include Welcome BBQ, Cleo's Cafe, and Winter Formal.

Sports: There is 1 intramural sport for men and 1 for women.

Disabled Students: 90% of the campus is accessible. Wheelchair ramps, elevators, special parking, specially equipped rest rooms, lowered drinking fountains, and lowered telephones are available.

Services: Counseling and information services are available, as is tutoring in every subject.

Campus Safety and Security: Measures include security escort services, informal discussions, pamphlets/posters/films, emergency telephones, and lighted pathways/sidewalks. A DeVry employee patrols the building from 4 P.M. to midnight, and a guard service patrols the lot from 6:30 A.M. to midnight.

Programs of Study: DeVry confers the B.S. degree. Associate and master's degrees are also awarded. Bachelor's degrees are awarded in BIOLOGICAL SCIENCE (bioinformatics), BUSINESS (business administration and management), COMMUNICATIONS AND THE ARTS (telecommunications), COMPUTER AND PHYSICAL SCIENCE (information sciences and systems), ENGINEERING AND ENVIRONMENTAL DESIGN (computer engineering, electrical/electronics engineering technology, and technological management). Computer information systems, telecommunications, and business are the largest.

Required: To graduate, students must achieve a cumulative GPA of at least 2.0 and satisfactorily complete all curriculum requirements. Course requirements vary according to program. All first-semester students take courses in business organization, computer applications, algebra, psychology, and student success strategies.

Special: Evening and weekend classes, co-op programs, distance learning, and nondegree study are possible. There is 1 national honor society.

Faculty/Classroom: All teach undergraduates.

Requirements: Admissions requirements include graduation from a secondary school; the GED is also accepted. Applicants must pass the DeVry entrance exam or present satisfactory ACT or SAT I scores. An interview is required. CLEP credit is accepted.

Procedure: Freshmen are admitted fall, spring, and summer. There is a rolling admissions plan. There are early admissions and deferred admissions plans. Application deadlines are open. Application fee is $50. Applications are accepted on-line through *https://apply.embark.com/UGrad/DeVry/21.*

Transfer: 1 transfer student enrolled in a recent year. Applicants must present passing grades in all completed college course work, demonstrate language skills proficiency with at least 24 completed semester hours, and present evidence of math proficiency by appropriate college-level credits. 25% of 48 to 154 credits required for the bachelor's degree must be completed at DeVry.

Visiting: There are regularly scheduled orientations for prospective students. There are guides for informal visits and visitors may sit in on classes. To schedule a visit, contact the New Student Coordinator.

Financial Aid: In 2002-2003, 49% of all full-time freshmen and 73% of continuing full-time students received some form of financial aid. At least 48% of full-time freshmen and at least 71% of continuing full-time students received need-based aid. The average freshman award was $7322. Need-based scholarships or need-based grants averaged $4637; need-based self-help aid (loans and jobs) averaged $4038; and institutional non-need-based awards and non-need-based scholarships averaged $12,342. DeVry is a member of CSS. The FAFSA is required.

International Students: There were 51 international students enrolled in a recent year. They must score 500 on the written TOEFL or 173 on the electronic version and also take the college's own entrance exam.

Computers: Lab facilities include PCs in stand-alone and network configurations, with access to the mainframe. LANs provide access to a wide range of applications software. Hard copy from the mainframe is provided through a local minicomputer and medium- and high-speed printers. Computer information systems students may access the system during published lab hours. There are no fees.

Graduates: From July 1, 2002 to June 30, 2003, 530 bachelor's degrees were awarded. The most popular majors were computer information systems (66%), business (22%), and electronics engineering technology (11%). 86 companies recruited on campus in a recent year.

Admissions Contact: Alex Kotoyantz, Director of Admissions.
E-mail: *cblas@socal.devry.edu* Web: *www.lb.devry.edu*

DEVRY UNIVERSITY/POMONA
Pomona, CA 91768-2642

D-5

(909) 622-9800
(800) 882-7536; Fax: (909) 623-4165

Full-time: 1144 men, 347 women	**Faculty:** n/av
Part-time: 637 men, 249 women	**Ph.D.s:** n/av
Graduate: n/av	**Student/Faculty:** n/av
Year: semesters, summer session	**Tuition:** $11,310
Application Deadline: open	**Room & Board:** n/app
Freshman Class: n/av	
SAT I or ACT: n/av	**LESS COMPETITIVE**

DeVry University/Pomona is 1 of 67 DeVry University locations in the United States and Canada. The school offers programs in business administration, computer information systems, electronics, telecommunications management, technical management, information technology, and computer engineering technology. In addition to regional accreditation, DeVry has baccalaureate program accreditation with ABET. The library contains 15,580 volumes, more than 11,000 e-books, and 875 audio/video tapes/CDs, and subscribes to more than 90 periodicals. Computerized library services include the card catalog, interlibrary loans, and database searching. Special learning facilities include a learning resource center and electronics and other labs. The 11-acre campus is in an urban area 30 miles east of Los Angeles. There is 1 building.

Student Life: 40% of students are Hispanic; 26% Asian American; 21% white. The average age of all undergraduates is 24.

Housing: There are no residence halls. Housing referrals may be obtained through the Student Housing Office. There are private apartments, student-run housing, and private rooms. All students commute. Alcohol is not permitted. All students may keep cars.

Activities: There are no fraternities or sororities. There are 14 groups on campus, including computers, ethnic, honors, professional, and social. Popular campus events include Welcome Barbecue, Winter Formal, and Part-time Jobs Fair.

Sports: There is 1 intramural sport for men and 1 for women.

Disabled Students: 90% of the campus is accessible. Wheelchair ramps, elevators, special parking, specially equipped rest rooms, lowered drinking fountains, and lowered telephones are available.

Services: Counseling and information services are available, as is tutoring in every subject.

Campus Safety and Security: Measures include security escort services, informal discussions, pamphlets/posters/films, and emergency telephones. There are lighted pathways/sidewalks. A DeVry employee patrols the building from 4 P.M. to midnight, and a guard service patrols the lot from 6:30 A.M. to midnight.

Programs of Study: DeVry confers the B.S. degree. Associate and master's degrees are also awarded. Bachelor's degrees are awarded in BUSINESS (business administration and management), COMMUNICATIONS AND THE ARTS (telecommunications), COMPUTER AND PHYSICAL SCIENCE (computer programming and information sciences and systems), ENGINEERING AND ENVIRONMENTAL DESIGN (biomedical engineering, computer engineering, electrical/electronics engineering technology, and technological management). Computer information systems and telecommunications are the largest.

Required: To graduate, students must achieve a cumulative GPA of at least 2.0 and satisfactorily complete all curriculum requirements. Course requirements vary according to program. All first-semester students take courses in business organization, computer applications, algebra, psychology, and student success strategies.

Special: Evening and weekend classes, nondegree study, distance learning, and co-op programs in all majors are possible. There are 5 national honor societies.

Faculty/Classroom: All teach undergraduates.

Requirements: Admissions requirements include graduation from a secondary school; the GED is also accepted. Applicants must pass the DeVry entrance exam or present satisfactory ACT or SAT I scores. An interview is required. CLEP credit is accepted.

Procedure: Freshmen are admitted fall, spring, and summer. There are early admissions and deferred admissions plans. There is a rolling admissions plan. Application deadlines are open. Application fee is $50. Notification is sent on a rolling basis. Applications are accepted on-line through *https://apply.embark.com/UGrad/DeVry/21/*.

Transfer: 1 transfer student enrolled in a recent year. Applicants must present passing grades in all completed college course work, demonstrate language skills proficiency with at least 24 completed semester hours, and evidence of math proficiency by appropriate college-level credits. A minimum 2.0 GPA is required. 25% of 48 to 154 credits required for the bachelor's degree must be completed at DeVry.

Visiting: There are regularly scheduled orientations for prospective students. There are guides for informal visits and visitors may sit in on classes. To schedule a visit, contact Linda Flores or Martha Irias, New Student Coordinators.

Financial Aid: In 2002-2003, 53% of all full-time freshmen and 76% of continuing full-time students received some form of financial aid. At least 52% of full-time freshmen and 74% of continuing full-time students received need-based aid. The average freshman award was $6813. Need-based scholarships or need-based grants averaged $4377; need-based self-help aid (loans and jobs) averaged $3814; and institutional non-need-based awards and non-need-based scholarships averaged $11,356. DeVry is a member of CSS. The FAFSA is required.

International Students: There were 89 international students enrolled in a recent year. They must score 500 on the written TOEFL or 173 on the electronic version and also take the college's own entrance exam.

Computers: The mainframe is an IBM. Lab facilities include PCs in stand-alone and network configurations, with access to the mainframe. LANs provide access to a wide range of applications software. Hard copy from the mainframe is provided through a local minicomputer and medium- and high-speed printers. Computer information systems students may access the system during published lab hours. There are no time limits and no fees.

Graduates: From July 1, 2002 to June 30, 2003, 651 bachelor's degrees were awarded. The most popular majors were computer information systems (65%), business (25%), and electronics engineering technology (10%). 16 companies recruited on campus in a recent year.

Admissions Contact: Jere Thrasher, Director of Admissions.
Web: *www.pom.devry.edu*

DEVRY UNIVERSITY/WEST HILLS
West Hills, CA 91304-3200

C-5

(818) 932-3001
(888) 610-0800; Fax: (818) 868-4165

Full-time: 487 men, 156 women	**Faculty:** n/av
Part-time: 369 men, 149 women	**Ph.D.s:** n/av
Graduate: n/av	**Student/Faculty:** n/av
Year: semesters, summer session	**Tuition:** $11,310
Application Deadline: open	**Room & Board:** n/app
Freshman Class: n/av	
SAT I or ACT: n/av	**LESS COMPETITIVE**

DeVry University/West Hills, founded in 1999, is a private institution offering hands-on programs in electronics, business administration, computer information systems, telecommunications management, information technology, computer engineering technology, and technical management. The school is 1 of 67 DeVry University locations throughout the United States and Canada. The library contains 14,728 volumes

and 411 audio/video tapes/CDs, and subscribes to 130 periodicals. Computerized library services include the card catalog, interlibrary loans, and database searching. Special learning facilities include a learning resource center and electronics and other labs. The 15-acre campus is in a suburban area in the San Fernando Valley. There is 1 building.

Student Life: 32% of students are white; 26% Asian American; 26% Hispanic. The average age of all undergraduates is 24.

Housing: All students commute. Housing referrals can be obtained through the Student Housing Office. There are private apartments, student-plan housing, and private rooms. Alcohol is not permitted. All students may keep cars.

Activities: There are no fraternities or sororities. There are 10 groups on campus, including computers, ethnic, international, professional, religious, and social. Popular campus events include Welcome BBQ, Cosmic Bowling, and Winter Formal.

Sports: There are 3 intramural sports for men and 3 for women.

Disabled Students: All of the campus is accessible. Wheelchair ramps, elevators, special parking, specially equipped rest rooms, lowered drinking fountains, and lowered telephones are available.

Services: Counseling and information services are available, as is tutoring in every subject.

Campus Safety and Security: Measures include emergency telephones and lighted pathways/sidewalks.

Programs of Study: DeVry confers the B.S. degree. Associate and master's degrees are also awarded. Bachelor's degrees are awarded in BUSINESS (business administration and management), COMMUNICATIONS AND THE ARTS (telecommunications), COMPUTER AND PHYSICAL SCIENCE (information sciences and systems), ENGINEERING AND ENVIRONMENTAL DESIGN (biomedical engineering, computer engineering, electrical/electronics engineering technology, and technological management). Computer information systems and business are the largest.

Required: To graduate, students must achieve a cumulative GPA of at least 2.0 and satisfactorily complete all curriculum requirements. Course requirements vary according to program. All first-semester students take courses in business organization, computer applications, algebra, psychology, and student success strategies.

Special: Co-op programs, nondegree study, distance learning, and evening and weekend classes are possible.

Faculty/Classroom: All teach undergraduates.

Requirements: Admissions requirements include graduation from a secondary school; the GED is also accepted. Applicants must pass the DeVry entrance exam or present satisfactory ACT or SAT I scores. An interview is required. CLEP credit is accepted.

Procedure: Freshmen are admitted fall, spring, and summer. There are early admissions and deferred admissions plans. There is a rolling admissions plan. Application deadlines are open. Application fee is $50. Notification is sent on a rolling basis. Applications are accepted on-line through *https://apply.embark.com/UGrad/DeVry/21/*.

Transfer: 1 transfer student enrolled in a recent year. Applicants must present passing grades in all completed college course work, demonstrate language skills proficiency in at least 24 completed semester hours, and present evidence of math proficiency by appropriate college-level credits. 25% of 48 to 154 credits required for the bachelor's degree must be completed at DeVry.

Visiting: There are regularly scheduled orientations for prospective students. There are guides for informal visits and visitors may sit in on classes. To schedule a visit, contact the New Student Coordinator.

Financial Aid: In 2002-2003, 45% of all full-time freshmen and 74% of continuing full-time students received some form of financial aid. At least 44% of full-time freshmen and 72% of continuing full-time students received need-based aid. The average freshman award was $6485. Need-based scholarships or need-based grants averaged $4699; need-based self-help aid (loans and jobs) averaged $3568; and institutional non-need-based awards and non-need-based scholarships averaged $10,824. The FAFSA is required.

International Students: There were 10 international students enrolled in a recent year. They must score 500 on the written TOEFL or 173 on the electronic version and also take the college's own entrance exam.

Computers: Lab facilities include PCs in stand-alone and network configurations, with access to the mainframe. LANs provide access to a wide range of applications software. Hard copy from the mainframe is provided through a local microcomputer and medium- and high-speed printers. Computer information students may access the system during published lab hours. Students may access the system. There are no fees.

Graduates: From July 1, 2002 to June 30, 2003, 217 bachelor's degrees were awarded. The most popular majors were business (64%), electronics engineering technology (21%), and computer information systems (15%). 7 companies recruited on campus in a recent year.

Admissions Contact: Dewey McGuirk, Director of Admissions.
E-mail: *admissions@devry.edu* Web: *www.wh.devry.edu*

DOMINICAN UNIVERSITY OF CALIFORNIA
B-3
San Rafael, CA 94901-2298
(415) 485-3204
(888) 323-6763; Fax: (415) 485-3214

Full-time: 215 men, 639 women	**Faculty:** 58
Part-time: 69 men, 223 women	**Ph.D.s:** 71%
Graduate: 159 men, 461 women	**Student/Faculty:** 15 to 1
Year: semesters, summer session	**Tuition:** $22,650
Application Deadline: March 2	**Room & Board:** $9020
Freshman Class: 1792 applied, 980 accepted, 245 enrolled	
SAT I Verbal/Math: 527/515	**ACT:** 22 COMPETITIVE

Dominican University of California, founded in 1890, is an independent, international, learner-centered university of Catholic heritage. There are 5 undergraduate and 4 graduate schools. In addition to regional accreditation, Dominican has baccalaureate program accreditation with AOTA and NLN. The library contains 88,325 volumes, 3121 microform items, and 775 audio/video tapes/CDs, and subscribes to 409 periodicals. Computerized library services include the card catalog, interlibrary loans, and database searching. Special learning facilities include a learning resource center, art gallery, radio station, music library, and art history slide and print collection. The 80-acre campus is in a suburban area 11 miles north of San Francisco. Including any residence halls, there are 21 buildings.

Student Life: 89% of undergraduates are from California. Students are from 20 states and 24 foreign countries. 68% are from public schools. 55% are white; 10% Asian American; 10% Hispanic. 31% are Catholic; 6% claim no religious affiliation. The average age of freshmen is 18; all undergraduates, 26. 18% do not continue beyond their first year; 37% remain to graduate.

Housing: 491 students can be accommodated in college housing, which includes coed dorms. On-campus housing is available on a first-come, first-served basis and is available on a lottery system for upperclassmen. 57% of students commute. All students may keep cars.

Activities: There are no fraternities or sororities. There are 15 groups on campus, including art, cheerleading, choir, computers, drama, ethnic, film, honors, international, literary magazine, radio and TV, religious, social service, student government, and yearbook. Popular campus events include Shield Day (welcoming the freshman class) and student congregation.

Sports: There are 3 intercollegiate sports for men and 3 for women. Facilities include a gym, a fitness center, a swimming pool, tennis courts, a soccer field, and a sand volleyball court.

Disabled Students: 50% of the campus is accessible. Wheelchair ramps, elevators, special parking, specially equipped rest rooms, special class scheduling, and lowered drinking fountains are available.

Services: Counseling and information services are available, as is tutoring in some subjects, including writing, math, chemistry, economics, time management, and study skills. There is remedial math and writing.

Campus Safety and Security: Measures include 24-hour foot and vehicle patrol, security escort services, informal discussions, and emergency telephones. There are lighted pathways/sidewalks.

Programs of Study: Dominican confers B.A., B.S., B.F.A., and B.S.N. degrees. Master's degrees are also awarded. Bachelor's degrees are awarded in AGRICULTURE (environmental studies), BIOLOGICAL SCIENCE (biology/biological science), BUSINESS (electronic business, human resources, and international business management), COMMUNICATIONS AND THE ARTS (art, art history and appreciation, communications, creative writing, English literature, and music), COMPUTER AND PHYSICAL SCIENCE (digital arts/technology), HEALTH PROFESSIONS (nursing, occupational therapy, and premedicine), SOCIAL SCIENCE (history, humanities, international studies, liberal arts/general studies, political science/government, psychology, and religion). Biology, psychology, and nursing are the strongest academically. Nursing, psychology, and business management are the largest.

Required: All students must complete 124 credit hours, including at least 24 in upper-division work, with a minimum 2.0 GPA. Core requirements include a cultural heritage colloquium of 12 units; 6 units in religious heritage; 3 units each in human nature, verbal expression, quantitative reasoning, cultural perspectives, human relationships, and creativity in the arts; and 3 to 4 units in the natural world. A senior thesis, project, recital, or comprehensive exam is required.

Special: There is a semester interchange program with colleges in Michigan, Florida, or New York. Dominican also offers study abroad, dual majors, student-designed majors, internships, pass/fail options outside of major and general education courses, and an evening/weekend bachelor's degree program. There is a freshman honors program.

Faculty/Classroom: 35% of faculty are male; 65%, female. 83% teach undergraduates. No introductory courses are taught by graduate students. The average class size in an introductory lecture is 19; in a laboratory, 10; and in a regular course, 11.

Admissions: 55% of the 2003-2004 applicants were accepted. The SAT I scores for the 2003-2004 freshman class were: Verbal--36% below 500, 44% between 500 and 599, 16% between 600 and 700, and 4%

above 700; Math--42% below 500, 40% between 500 and 599, 16% between 600 and 700, and 2% above 700. 40% of the current freshmen were in the top fifth of their class; 80% were in the top two fifths.

Requirements: The SAT I is required. In addition, applicants must be graduates of an accredited high school or have earned the GED. Secondary preparation must include 4 years of English, 2 each of math and a foreign language, and 1 each of lab science and history. An essay and a recommendation are required. An interview and a visit to the campus are highly recommended. Prospective music majors are encouraged to schedule an audition. A GPA of 2.0 is required. AP and CLEP credits are accepted. Important factors in the admissions decision are recommendations by school officials, extracurricular activities record, and evidence of special talent.

Procedure: Freshmen are admitted fall and spring. Entrance exams should be taken in the late fall or early spring of the senior year. There is a deferred admissions plan. Applications should be filed by March 2 for fall entry, December 15 for spring entry, and May 1 for summer entry, along with a $40 fee. Notification is sent on a rolling basis. Applications are accepted on-line through the school's web site.

Transfer: 93 transfer students enrolled in 2003-2004. Applicants must have a 2.0 GPA at an accredited college. They must also submit official high school and college transcripts and a letter of recommendation from a professor, academic dean, or counselor. 30 of 124 credits required for the bachelor's degree must be completed at Dominican.

Visiting: There are regularly scheduled orientations for prospective students, including financial aid conferences, math and writing placement testing, meeting with the prospective academic adviser, and a campus tour. There are guides for informal visits and visitors may sit in on classes and stay overnight. To schedule a visit, contact the Admissions Office at (415) 457-4440 or enroll@dominican.edu.

Financial Aid: In 2003-2004, 98% of all full-time freshmen and 85% of continuing full-time students received some form of financial aid. 86% of full-time freshmen and 70% of continuing full-time students received need-based aid. The average freshman award was $20,852. 4% of undergraduates work part time. Average annual earnings from campus work are $2750. The FAFSA and the college's own financial statement are required. The deadline for filing freshman financial aid applications for fall entry is March 2.

International Students: There are 44 international students enrolled. The school actively recruits these students. They must score 550 on the written TOEFL or 213 on the electronic version and also take the SAT I or the ACT.

Computers: The mainframe is an IBM RF/6000 Model 530H. Students have access to 120 PCs, laser printers, an optical scanner, Ethernet and TCP/IP running on a Novell network, and numerous software programs. They also have access to e-mail, the Internet, and the Web, from computer labs, residence halls, the library, and the student center. All students may access the system. There is a 2-hour time limit only when other students are waiting. There are no fees.

Graduates: From July 1, 2002 to June 30, 2003, 226 bachelor's degrees were awarded. The most popular majors were nursing (19%), psychology (17%), and humanities (12%). In an average class, 37% graduate in 4 years or less, 51% graduate in 5 years or less, and 47% graduate in 6 years or less.

Admissions Contact: Art Cross, Director of Admissions (Day Program). E-mail: enroll@dominican.edu Web: www.dominican.edu

FRESNO PACIFIC UNIVERSITY
C-3
Fresno, CA 93702
(559) 453-2231
(800) 660-6089; Fax: (559) 453-2007

Full-time: 306 men, 638 women	**Faculty:** 53
Part-time: 45 men, 66 women	**Ph.D.s:** 63%
Graduate: 230 men, 668 women	**Student/Faculty:** 18 to 1
Year: semesters, summer session	**Tuition:** $17,592
Application Deadline: July 31	**Room & Board:** $4870
Freshman Class: 618 applied, 377 accepted, 202 enrolled	
SAT I Verbal/Math: 510/490	**ACT:** 19 COMPETITIVE

Fresno Pacific University, founded in 1944, is a private Christian liberal arts college affiliated with the Mennonite Brethren. There are 3 undergraduate schools and 1 graduate school. The library contains 163,061 volumes, 312,000 microform items, and 10,320 audio/video tapes/CDs, and subscribes to 10,227 periodicals. Computerized library services include the card catalog, interlibrary loans, database searching, and Internet access. Special learning facilities include a learning resource center, the Center for Mennonite Brethren Studies, the Center for Conflict Studies and Peacemaking, and the Center for Degree Completion. The 42-acre campus is in a suburban area 150 miles southeast of San Francisco. Including any residence halls, there are 18 buildings.

Student Life: 97% of undergraduates are from California. Students are from 14 states, 12 foreign countries, and Canada. 86% are from public schools. 65% are white; 19% Hispanic. 89% are Protestant; 7% Catholic. The average age of freshmen is 21; all undergraduates, 22. 18% do not continue beyond their first year; 54% remain to graduate.

Housing: 560 students can be accommodated in college housing, which includes single-sex dorms, on-campus apartments, off-campus apartments, and married-student housing. On-campus housing is available on a first-come, first-served basis and is available on a lottery system for upperclassmen. Priority is given to out-of-town students. 54% of students live on campus; of those, 32% remain on campus on weekends. Alcohol is not permitted. All students may keep cars.

Activities: There are no fraternities or sororities. There are 17 groups on campus, including art, choir, chorale, chorus, drama, ethnic, honors, international, jazz band, newspaper, pep band, professional, religious, social, social service, student government, and yearbook. Popular campus events include Carol Sing, Winter Ball, and Junior/Senior Banquet.

Sports: There are 4 intercollegiate sports for men and 5 for women, and 6 intramural sports for men and 6 for women. Facilities include a gym, 2 soccer fields, a swimming pool, a track and field facility, a weight room, and 2 racquetball courts.

Disabled Students: All of the campus is accessible. Wheelchair ramps, elevators, special parking, specially equipped rest rooms, lowered drinking fountains, lowered telephones, and special housing are available.

Services: Counseling and information services are available, as is tutoring in every subject. There is a reader service for the blind, and remedial math, reading, and writing.

Campus Safety and Security: Measures include 24-hour foot and vehicle patrol, self-defense education, security escort services, and shuttle buses. There are informal discussions, pamphlets/posters/films, emergency telephones, lighted pathways/sidewalks, and 24-hour monitoring by closed-circuit security cameras. 18 cameras create a virtual perimeter patrol of the campus.

Programs of Study: FPU confers the B.A. degree. Associate and master's degrees are also awarded. Bachelor's degrees are awarded in BIOLOGICAL SCIENCE (biology/biological science), BUSINESS (accounting, business administration and management, and sports management), COMMUNICATIONS AND THE ARTS (English, music, and Spanish), COMPUTER AND PHYSICAL SCIENCE (chemistry, mathematics, and natural sciences), EDUCATION (English, mathematics, music, physical, science, and social science), ENGINEERING AND ENVIRONMENTAL DESIGN (environmental science), HEALTH PROFESSIONS (premedicine), SOCIAL SCIENCE (history, ministries, missions, philosophy, prelaw, psychology, religion, social science, and social work). Business, education, and religion are the strongest academically. Business, education, and psychology are the largest.

Required: Students must complete 124 semester units, 40 of which are in upper-division courses, with at least a 2.0 GPA. General education requirements include a biblical studies/world civilization series, 2 courses each in humanities, natural sciences, social sciences, and phys ed and math. Students are required to attend College Hour, a twice-weekly program of lectures, films, and concerts. Students are encouraged to volunteer 2 hours of community service per week. Several majors require internships.

Special: Internships are available, as is a 1-semester cooperative program with the University of California, Davis. Cross-registration is possible with San Joaquin College of Law and California State University, Fresno. A B.A. in management and organizational development is offered to working adults. Other off-campus learning opportunities include programs in American studies in Washington, D.C., urban studies in Chicago, and study abroad in Israel, Japan, Costa Rica, and Brethren Colleges in England, Spain, France, Germany, or China. A summer semester in Mexico is offered. There is 1 national honor society and a freshman honors program.

Faculty/Classroom: 58% of faculty are male; 42%, female. 54% teach undergraduates. No introductory courses are taught by graduate students. The average class size in a regular course is 18.

Admissions: 61% of the 2003-2004 applicants were accepted. The SAT I scores for the 2003-2004 freshman class were: Verbal--43% below 500, 41% between 500 and 599, 15% between 600 and 700, and 1% above 700; Math--51% below 500, 32% between 500 and 599, 15% between 600 and 700, and 2% above 700. The ACT scores were 59% below 21, 24% between 21 and 23, 16% between 24 and 26, and 1% between 27 and 28.

Requirements: The SAT I or ACT is required. In addition, applicants should be graduates of an accredited high school or have the GED. Required secondary preparation includes 4 years of college prep English, 2 years of social studies, algebra 1 and 2, and geometry, and at least 1 year of a lab science. The college recommends that applicants also take courses in art, music, and 2 years of the same foreign language, all with a grade of C or better. An essay is required, and an audition is recommended for prospective music majors. A GPA of 3.1 is required. AP and CLEP credits are accepted. Important factors in the admissions decision are recommendations by school officials, advanced placement or honor courses, and extracurricular activities record.

Procedure: Freshmen are admitted fall and spring. Entrance exams should be taken during the fall of the senior year. Early decision applications should be filed by January 31; regular applications, by July 31 for fall entry and December 5 for spring entry, along with a $40 fee. Notifi-

cation is sent on a rolling basis. Applications are accepted on-line through the school's web site.

Transfer: 129 transfer students enrolled in 2002-2003. Applicants should have completed at least 24 transferable units of college work with a 2.4 GPA. Those with fewer credits may apply any time but must meet freshman admission requirements. SAT I or ACT scores are recommended. 30 of 124 credits required for the bachelor's degree must be completed at FPU.

Visiting: There are regularly scheduled orientations for prospective students. There are guides for informal visits and visitors may sit in on classes and stay overnight. To schedule a visit, contact Dina Gonzales Pina, Director of College Admissions, at ugadmis@fresno.edu.

Financial Aid: In 2003-2004, 99% of all full-time freshmen and 93% of continuing full-time students received some form of financial aid. 85% of full-time freshmen and 79% of continuing full-time students received need-based aid. The average freshman award was $14,500. The average financial indebtedness of the 2003 graduate was $14,000. The FAFSA and the college's own financial statement are required. The deadline for filing freshman financial aid applications for fall entry is May 1.

International Students: There are 34 international students enrolled. The school actively recruits these students. They must score 500 on the written TOEFL.

Computers: The mainframe is an Amax Dual Xeon. The college provides student access to the Internet and Web as follows: 12 PCs in the library, 75 PCs in computer labs, and 4 PCs in the commuter house. Students may access university systems through dial-up procedures. All students may access the system 8 A.M. to 12 P.M. weekdays, 1 to 4 P.M. weekends. There are no time limits and no fees. It is strongly recommended that all students have a personal computer.

Graduates: From July 1, 2002 to June 30, 2003, 285 bachelor's degrees were awarded. The most popular majors were business (39%), liberal studies (27%), and biblical studies (5%). Of the 2002 graduating class, 41% were enrolled in graduate school within 6 months of graduation.

Admissions Contact: Dina Gonzales Pina, Director of College Admissions. A video is available. E-mail: dgonzale@fresno.edu
Web: www.fresno.edu

GOLDEN GATE UNIVERSITY
San Francisco, CA 94105-2968

B-3
(415) 442-7800
(800) 448-4968; Fax: (415) 442-7807

Full-time: 72 men, 76 women	**Faculty:** n/av
Part-time: 250 men, 288 women	**Ph.D.s:** n/av
Graduate: 1717 men, 1896 women	**Student/Faculty:** n/av
Year: trimesters, summer session	**Tuition:** $11,232
Application Deadline: June 1	**Room & Board:** n/app
Freshman Class: n/av	
SAT I or ACT: not required	**NONCOMPETITIVE**

Golden Gate University, founded in 1901, is a private, nonprofit, independent, commuter institution offering undergraduate and graduate degrees in business administration, accounting, human and social sciences, and special programs. There are 3 undergraduate and 4 graduate schools. The 2 libraries contain 300,000 volumes, and subscribe to 2500 periodicals. Computerized library services include interlibrary loans and database searching. Special learning facilities include a learning resource center and an English as a Second Language center. The 1-acre campus is in an urban area in San Francisco. There are 2 buildings.

Student Life: 51% of students are white; 19% Asian American; 18% foreign nationals; 10% African American; 10% Hispanic. The average age of freshmen is 21; all undergraduates, 37. 12% do not continue beyond their first year.

Housing: There are no residence halls. All students commute. Alcohol is not permitted.

Activities: There are no fraternities or sororities. There are 5 groups on campus, including ethnic, international, newspaper, professional, and social. Popular campus events include Commencement Ball and other social functions.

Sports: There is no sports program at Golden Gate.

Disabled Students: All of the campus is accessible. Wheelchair ramps, elevators, special parking, and specially equipped rest rooms are available.

Services: Counseling and information services are available, as is tutoring in some subjects. There is remedial math, reading, and writing.

Campus Safety and Security: Measures include security escort services, informal discussions, and pamphlets/posters/films.

Programs of Study: Golden Gate confers B.S. and B.B.A. degrees. Master's and doctoral degrees are also awarded. Bachelor's degrees are awarded in BUSINESS (accounting, banking and finance, human resources, and international business management), ENGINEERING AND ENVIRONMENTAL DESIGN (technological management). Accounting, finance, and information systems are the strongest academically. Finance, accounting, and management are the largest.

Required: A total of 123 trimester hours, with 21 to 33 in the major, are required to graduate. A minimum GPA of 2.0 is also required.

Special: The university offers cooperative programs, cross-registration with the San Francisco Consortium, internships, an accelerated degree program, dual majors, credit for military experience, nondegree study, and credit/no credit options. Also available are weekend classes and 10-week terms.

Faculty/Classroom: All teach undergraduates. No introductory courses are taught by graduate students. The average class size in an introductory lecture is 25; in a laboratory, 15; and in a regular course, 20.

Requirements: Applicants must be graduates of an accredited secondary school or have a GED. A GPA of 2.5 is required. AP and CLEP credits are accepted.

Procedure: Freshmen are admitted fall, spring, and summer. There are early admissions and deferred admissions plans. Applications should be filed by June 1 for fall entry, October 1 for spring entry, and February 1 for summer entry. The fall 2003 application fee was $55 ($90 international). Notification is sent on a rolling basis. Applications are accepted on-line through the school's web site and CollegeNET.

Transfer: 50 transfer students enrolled in a recent year. At least 24 transferable units and a 2.0 overall GPA are required. A minimum of 30 units out of 123, including 21 in the major, must be completed at GGU.

Visiting: Visitors may sit in on classes. To schedule a visit, contact the Admissions Office.

Financial Aid: The FAFSA is required. The deadline for filing freshman financial aid applications for fall entry is open.

International Students: There were 226 international students enrolled in a recent year. The school actively recruits these students. They must score 525 on the written TOEFL or 197 on the electronic version. Check the web site for further information.

Computers: The mainframe is an HP 3000/Series 64. PCs are available in the computer center. All students may access the system at designated hours. There are no time limits and no fees.

Graduates: In a recent year, 201 bachelor's degrees were awarded. The most popular majors were management (25%), accounting (15%), and human relations (8%). 74 companies recruited on campus in a recent year. Of a recent year's graduating class, 9% were enrolled in graduate school within 6 months of graduation and 64% were employed.

Admissions Contact: Office of Enrollment Services.
E-mail: *info@ggu.edu* Web: *www.ggu.edu*

HARVEY MUDD COLLEGE   D-5
Claremont, CA 91711   (909) 621-8011; Fax: (909) 607-7046

Full-time: 473 men, 227 women	**Faculty:** 77; IIB, ++$
Part-time: 3 men, 1 woman	**Ph.D.s:** 100%
Graduate: none	**Student/Faculty:** 9 to 1
Year: semesters	**Tuition:** $28,660
Application Deadline: January 15	**Room & Board:** $9420
Freshman Class: 1535 applied, 709 accepted, 191 enrolled	
SAT I Verbal/Math: 700/750	**MOST COMPETITIVE**

Harvey Mudd College, founded in 1955, is one of the Claremont Colleges. It is a private college specializing in engineering and physical science education within a liberal arts tradition. There are 5 undergraduate and 2 graduate schools. In addition to regional accreditation, Harvey Mudd has baccalaureate program accreditation with ABET and ACS. The library contains 1.9 million volumes, and subscribes to 6800 periodicals. Computerized library services include the card catalog, interlibrary loans, database searching, and Internet access. Special learning facilities include an art gallery, planetarium, and radio station. The 30-acre campus is in a suburban area 35 miles east of Los Angeles. Including any residence halls, there are 19 buildings.

Student Life: 52% of undergraduates are from out of state, mostly the Northwest. Students are from 31 states, 12 foreign countries, and Canada. 80% are from public schools. 72% are white; 22% Asian American. The average age of freshmen is 18; all undergraduates, 20. 3% do not continue beyond their first year.

Housing: 632 students can be accommodated in college housing, which includes single-sex and coed dorms and on-campus apartments. On-campus housing is guaranteed for the freshman year only, is available on a first-come, first-served basis, and is available on a lottery system for upperclassmen. 95% of students live on campus; of those, 94% remain on campus on weekends. All students may keep cars.

Activities: There are no fraternities or sororities. There are 74 groups on campus, including art, band, chess, choir, chorale, chorus, computers, dance, drama, ethnic, gay, international, jazz band, literary magazine, musical theater, newspaper, orchestra, pep band, photography, political, professional, radio and TV, religious, social, social service, student government, symphony, and yearbook. Popular campus events include 5-class competition relay races, Wednesday night lecture/dinner series, and film nights.

Sports: There are 10 intercollegiate sports for men and 10 for women, and 6 intramural sports for men and 6 for women. Facilities include an athletic facility housing 2 gym floors, a weight room, a 400-meter track,

a swimming pool, 9 tennis courts, and sports fields. The campus recreation facility houses a full-size gym floor, an aerobic/dance room, and a fitness room with treadmills, steppers, exercycles, and weight equipment.

Disabled Students: 99% of the campus is accessible. Wheelchair ramps, elevators, special parking, specially equipped rest rooms, special class scheduling, and lowered drinking fountains are available.

Services: Counseling and information services are available, as is tutoring in most subjects. Support is offered on a case-by-case basis.

Campus Safety and Security: Measures include 24-hour foot and vehicle patrol, self-defense education, security escort services, and informal discussions. There are pamphlets/posters/films, emergency telephones, lighted pathways/sidewalks, and a biweekly, electronic newsletter on campus security issues.

Programs of Study: Harvey Mudd confers the B.S. degree. Bachelor's degrees are awarded in BIOLOGICAL SCIENCE (biology/biological science), COMPUTER AND PHYSICAL SCIENCE (chemistry, computer science, mathematics, and physics), ENGINEERING AND ENVIRONMENTAL DESIGN (engineering). Physics and chemistry are the strongest academically. Engineering and computer science are the largest.

Required: To graduate, all students must have a 2.0 GPA and complete a total of 128 hours, including 45 hours in a common core. This consists of 4 semesters of math, 3 semesters of physics, 2 semesters of chemistry, and courses in biology, programming, and system engineering, plus 2 electives chosen from core offerings. Another 37 hours are required in humanities and social sciences, including literature, psychology, philosophy, history, and institutions, and 46 in the major and electives. All students take 3 semesters of noncredit phys ed courses. A senior research or corporate clinic project is required.

Special: Students may cross-register at any of the other Claremont Colleges. Internships are available for engineering and math majors. Study abroad, a Washington semester, work-study, computer science/math and math/biology majors, and student-designed majors are available. A 3-2 engineering degree with Claremont McKenna College is possible, as is a 4-1 B.S./M.B.A. with Claremont Graduate University. Some courses may be audited. The first semester for freshmen is taken on a pass/fail basis; thereafter, only 1 noncore and nonmajor course per semester may be taken on that basis. There is 1 national honor society and 7 departmental honors programs.

Faculty/Classroom: 78% of faculty are male; 22%, female. All both teach and do research. The average class size in an introductory lecture is 75; in a laboratory, 10; and in a regular course, 15.

Admissions: 46% of the 2003-2004 applicants were accepted. The SAT I scores for the 2003-2004 freshman class were: Verbal--1% below 500, 9% between 500 and 599, 41% between 600 and 700, and 49% above 700; Math--1% between 500 and 599, 17% between 600 and 700, and 82% above 700. 99% of the current freshmen were in the top fifth of their class; all were in the top two fifths. There were 44 National Merit finalists and 7 semifinalists. 33 freshmen graduated first in their class.

Requirements: The SAT I is required. In addition, applicants must be graduates of an accredited secondary school and have completed 4 years each of English and math (including algebra, demonstrative and analytic geometry, trigonometry, and calculus) and 1 year each of physics and chemistry. The college strongly recommends that applicants take 2 years of a foreign language and 1 year each of history and biology. SAT II: Subject tests in math II, writing, and 1 other subject are required. Applicants must submit 2 personal essays and are encouraged to seek an interview. AP credits are accepted. Important factors in the admissions decision are leadership record, recommendations by school officials, and advanced placement or honor courses.

Procedure: Freshmen are admitted in the fall. Entrance exams should be taken by January of the senior year. There are early decision and deferred admissions plans. Early decision applications should be filed by November 15; regular applications, by January 15 for fall entry, along with a $50 fee. Notification of early decision is sent December 15; regular decision, April 1. 47 early decision candidates were accepted for the 2003-2004 class. 236 applicants were on the 2003 waiting list. Applications are accepted on-line through Common App.

Transfer: 7 transfer students enrolled in 2002-2003. Applicants must submit SAT II: Subject test scores, transcripts, course descriptions, and references from a college math, science, or engineering teacher and from a counselor. An interview is recommended. Students must have completed courses in calculus, physics, chemistry, and English composition. 64 of 128 credits required for the bachelor's degree must be completed at Harvey Mudd.

Visiting: There are regularly scheduled orientations for prospective students, including tours and interviews conducted Monday through Friday and Saturday mornings in the fall. There are guides for informal visits and visitors may sit in on classes and stay overnight. To schedule a visit, contact the Admission Office.

Financial Aid: In 2003-2004, 84% of all full-time freshmen and 83% of continuing full-time students received some form of financial aid. 53% of full-time freshmen and 58% of continuing full-time students received need-based aid. The average freshman award was $21,389. Need-based

scholarships or need-based grants averaged $20,127 ($33,175 maximum); need-based self-help aid (loans and jobs) averaged $4435 ($8500 maximum); non-need-based awards and non-need-based scholarships averaged $4697 ($38,080 maximum); and non-need-based loans (parent loans and PLUS loans) averaged $14,611 ($37,000 maximum). 27% of undergraduates work part time. Average annual earnings from campus work are $924. The average financial indebtedness of the 2003 graduate was $17,313. Harvey Mudd is a member of CSS. The CSS Profile or FAFSA is required. The deadline for filing freshman financial aid applications for fall entry is February 1.

International Students: There are 21 international students enrolled. Students must take the SAT I and SAT II: Subject tests in math, writing, and 1 other subject.

Computers: Students may access systems from dorm rooms, academic labs, classrooms, and via wireless network. Nearly 300 systems ranging from Mac and Windows PCs to SGI, Sun, and HP UNIX workstations are available on the network for student use. All students may access the system 24 hours a day. There are no time limits and no fees. It is strongly recommended that all students have a personal computer.

Graduates: From July 1, 2002 to June 30, 2003, 152 bachelor's degrees were awarded. The most popular majors were engineering (35%), computer science (26%), and mathematics (15%). In an average class, 77% graduate in 4 years or less, 82% graduate in 5 years or less, and 84% graduate in 6 years or less. 69 companies recruited on campus in 2002-2003. Of the 2002 graduating class, 47% were enrolled in graduate school within 6 months of graduation and 34% were employed.

Admissions Contact: Deren Finks, Vice President, Dean of Admissions and Financial Aid. E-mail: *admission@hmc.edu*
Web: *www.hmc.edu*

HOLY NAMES COLLEGE
Oakland, CA 94619

B-3

(510) 436-1321
(800) 430-1321; Fax: (510) 436-1325

Full-time: 103 men, 288 women	**Faculty:** 22
Part-time: 26 men, 176 women	**Ph.D.s:** 90%
Graduate: 58 men, 292 women	**Student/Faculty:** 18 to 1
Year: semesters, summer session	**Tuition:** $20,180
Application Deadline: August 1	**Room & Board:** $7800
Freshman Class: 134 applied, 131 accepted, 58 enrolled	
SAT I Verbal/Math: 490/470	**NONCOMPETITIVE**

Holy Names College, founded in 1868, is an independent college affiliated with the Roman Catholic Church. It offers education in the liberal arts and preparation for some professions. In addition to regional accreditation, Holy Names has baccalaureate program accreditation with NASM and NLN. The library contains 111,472 volumes, 50,931 microform items, and 5142 audio/video tapes/CDs, 25,000 e-books, and subscribes to 190 periodicals. Computerized library services include database searching and Internet access. Special learning facilities include a learning resource center, art gallery, a performing arts center, a 400-seat theater, and a black box theater. The 60-acre campus is in an urban area 20 miles east of San Francisco. Including any residence halls, there are 15 buildings.

Student Life: 96% of undergraduates are from California. Students are from 14 states, 12 foreign countries, and Canada. 62% are from public schools. 32% are African American; 28% white; 16% Hispanic. The average age of freshmen is 18; all undergraduates, 32. 38% do not continue beyond their first year; 46% remain to graduate.

Housing: 351 students can be accommodated in college housing, which includes coed dorms. On-campus housing is guaranteed for all 4 years. 67% of students commute. All students may keep cars.

Activities: There are no fraternities or sororities. There are 10 groups on campus, including choir, chorale, computers, drama, ethnic, gay, honors, international, orchestra, religious, social service, and student government. Popular campus events include Humanistic Studies Days and Founders Day.

Sports: There are 4 intercollegiate sports for men and 4 for women. Facilities include a gym, a pool, a fitness center, locker rooms and training rooms, and an outdoor fitness course.

Disabled Students: 60% of the campus is accessible. Elevators, special parking, specially equipped rest rooms, lowered drinking fountains, lowered telephones, a learning disability program, and special accommodations based on student need and eligibility are available.

Services: Counseling and information services are available, as is tutoring in most subjects. There is remedial math and writing. Note takers and extended time for tests may be arranged.

Campus Safety and Security: Measures include self-defense education, security escort services, informal discussions, and lighted pathways/sidewalks. There is a 24-hour manned entrance gate and a nighttime foot patrol.

Programs of Study: Holy Names confers B.A., B.S., B.Mus., and B.S.N. degrees. Master's degrees are also awarded. Bachelor's degrees are awarded in BIOLOGICAL SCIENCE (biology/biological science), BUSINESS (business administration and management and human re-

sources), COMMUNICATIONS AND THE ARTS (communications, English, English as a second/foreign language, and music), COMPUTER AND PHYSICAL SCIENCE (computer science), HEALTH PROFESSIONS (nursing), SOCIAL SCIENCE (history, human services, humanities, liberal arts/general studies, philosophy, psychology, religion, sociology, and Spanish studies). Business administration, nursing, and psychology are the largest.

Required: Students must have a 2.0 GPA and complete at least 120 hours with 24 to 36 in the major and 20 upper-division hours taken outside the major field. Students must complete a core curriculum, including foundation courses in critical thinking and communication, and courses in disciplinary studies, integrative studies across cultures, and writing across the curriculum. In some cases these requirements may be satisfied by secondary record, advanced placement, or challenge test. All students must take multidisciplinary courses in humanistic studies and a senior colloquium.

Special: Students may cross-register for 1 course per semester at any of 9 members of the Regional Association of East Bay Colleges and Universities. Internships, study abroad, and cooperative exchange programs with Central College in Iowa, Anna Maria College in Massachusetts, the Center for Bilingual Multicultural Studies in Mexico, and Kansai University of Foreign Studies in Japan are available. Dual and student-designed majors and interdisciplinary majors, including business administration and communication and business administration and philosophy, are offered. Accelerated degrees are available in all B.A. programs. A weekend college for adults, limited nondegree study, and pass/fail options are available. There are 10 national honor societies and 1 departmental honors program.

Faculty/Classroom: 36% of faculty are male; 64%, female. 61% teach undergraduates. No introductory courses are taught by graduate students. The average class size in an introductory lecture is 22; in a laboratory, 13; and in a regular course, 15.

Admissions: 98% of the 2003-2004 applicants were accepted. The SAT I scores for the 2003-2004 freshman class were: Verbal--58% below 500, 35% between 500 and 599, and 7% between 600 and 700; Math--58% below 500, 35% between 500 and 599, and 7% between 600 and 700. 30% of the current freshmen were in the top fifth of their class; 74% were in the top two fifths. 1 freshman graduated first in the class.

Requirements: The SAT I or ACT is required. In addition, applicants must be graduates of an accredited secondary school or have earned the GED. Secondary preparation should include at least 4 years of English, 3 years of math, 2 years of a single foreign language, 1 year each of lab science and U.S. history, 1 additional year of advanced courses in math, lab science, or foreign language, and 3 other 1-year college preparatory electives. In addition, the college requires a personal essay. Music auditions are required for scholarship applicants and recommended for others. AP and CLEP credits are accepted. Important factors in the admissions decision are advanced placement or honor courses, leadership record, and recommendations by school officials.

Procedure: Freshmen are admitted fall and spring. Entrance exams should be taken during the fall of the senior year. There is a deferred admissions plan. There is a rolling admissions plan. Applications should be filed by August 1 for fall entry and December 1 for spring entry, along with a $35 fee. Notification is sent on a rolling basis. Applications are accepted on computer disk and on-line through *www.hnc.edu*.

Transfer: 97 transfer students enrolled in 2002-2003. Applicants must have at least a 2.2 GPA in college work or a minimum of 30 transferable units. They must submit college records, a letter of recommendation from a college teacher or counselor, and a personal statement of their educational goals. 24 of 120 credits required for the bachelor's degree must be completed at Holy Names.

Visiting: There are guides for informal visits and visitors may sit in on classes and stay overnight. To schedule a visit, contact the Admissions Office at (510) 436-1351.

Financial Aid: In 2003-2004, 79% of all full-time freshmen and 65% of continuing full-time students received some form of financial aid. 74% of full-time freshmen and 65% of continuing full-time students received need-based aid. The average freshman award was $22,883. Need-based scholarships or need-based grants averaged $9918 (maximum); need-based self-help aid (loans and jobs) averaged $2625 (maximum); non-need-based athletic scholarships averaged $7715 ($19,970 maximum); and other non-need-based awards and non-need-based scholarships averaged $9370 ($19,970 maximum). 25% of undergraduates work part time. Average annual earnings from campus work are $2000. The average financial indebtedness of the 2003 graduate was $21,000. The FAFSA is required. The priority date for freshman financial aid applications for fall entry is March 2. The deadline for filing freshman financial aid applications for fall entry is August 1.

International Students: There are 16 international students enrolled. The school actively recruits these students. They must score 490 on the written TOEFL or 163 on the electronic version or take the MELAB.

Computers: The mainframe is A DEC Alpha 4000. 24 IBM PCs and 12 Macs are available in 2 large computer labs open to all students. Additional computers are located in the music resource lab, the nursing department, and the library. There are 16 PCs in a lab in the residence hall.

Microsoft Office and Internet access is available. The entire campus has fiber optic cable connection. All students may access the system 8 A.M. to 10 P.M. daily in the labs. Network access is available 24 hours a day. There are no time limits and no fees.

Graduates: From July 1, 2002 to June 30, 2003, 113 bachelor's degrees were awarded. The most popular majors were nursing (27%), business and marketing (22%), and liberal studies (10%). In an average class, 30% graduate in 4 years or less, 41% graduate in 5 years or less, and 46% graduate in 6 years or less. 14 companies recruited on campus in 2002-2003.

Admissions Contact: Jeffrey Miller, Vice President for Enrollment Management. E-mail: *admissions@hnc.edu* Web: *www.hnc.edu*

HOPE INTERNATIONAL UNIVERSITY D-5
Fullerton, CA 92831 (714) 879-3901, ext. 2215
(800) 762-1294; Fax: (714) 524-0231

Full-time: 300 men, 400 women	**Faculty:** 29
Part-time: 40 men, 100 women	**Ph.D.s:** 48%
Graduate: 80 men, 80 women	**Student/Faculty:** 24 to 1
Year: 4-1-4, summer session	**Tuition:** $12,500
Application Deadline: see profile	**Room & Board:** $4440
Freshman Class: n/av	
SAT I or ACT: required	**NONCOMPETITIVE**

Hope International University, founded in 1928, is a small, private liberal arts institution affiliated with the Independent Christian Church/Churches of Christ. Figures given in the above capsule and in this profile are approximate. There are 2 undergraduate schools and 1 graduate school. The library contains 65,000 volumes, 100 microform items, and 3300 audio/video tapes/CDs, and subscribes to 300 periodicals. Computerized library services include the card catalog and database searching. Special learning facilities include a learning resource center and a 1000-seat theater. The 15-acre campus is in an urban area 45 miles southeast of Los Angeles. Including any residence halls, there are 9 buildings.

Student Life: 53% of undergraduates are from California. Students are from 25 states, 27 foreign countries, and Canada. 88% are from public schools. 61% are white; 20% foreign nationals. Most are Protestant. The average age of freshmen is 18; all undergraduates, 21. 19% do not continue beyond their first year; 48% remain to graduate.

Housing: 450 students can be accommodated in college housing, which includes single-sex dorms. On-campus housing is guaranteed for all 4 years. 52% of students live on campus; of those, 75% remain on campus on weekends. Alcohol is not permitted. All students may keep cars.

Activities: There are no fraternities or sororities. There are 17 groups on campus, including band, cheerleading, choir, chorale, chorus, drama, international, literary magazine, newspaper, orchestra, religious, social service, student government, and yearbook. Popular campus events include Sadie Hawkins, Spring Formal, and Service on Saturday (community outreach).

Sports: There are 4 intercollegiate sports for men and 5 for women, and 10 intramural sports for men and 8 for women. Facilities include a swimming pool and game rooms.

Disabled Students: 95% of the campus is accessible. Elevators, special parking, and specially equipped rest rooms are available. Priority is given to disabled students for first-floor housing.

Services: Counseling and information services are available, as is tutoring in most subjects. There is a reader service for the blind, and remedial math, reading, and writing.

Campus Safety and Security: Measures include 24-hour foot and vehicle patrol, security escort services, and lighted pathways/sidewalks.

Programs of Study: Hope confers B.A., B.S., B.M., and B.M.E. degrees. Associate and master's degrees are also awarded. Bachelor's degrees are awarded in BUSINESS (business administration and management), COMMUNICATIONS AND THE ARTS (music and Spanish), EDUCATION (education, music, secondary, and social science), HEALTH PROFESSIONS (health science and sports medicine), SOCIAL SCIENCE (biblical studies, child psychology/development, crosscultural studies, human services, interdisciplinary studies, liberal arts/general studies, ministries, psychology, social science, and youth ministry). Education, business, and church ministry are the largest.

Required: Regular attendance at convocation and Christian service is required. To graduate, students must complete at least 124 credit units with 36 to 51 in the major, and demonstrate 80% or better competency on the university placement test. A minimum GPA of 2.0 must be maintained. Distribution requirements include 18 credits in biblical studies and 55 in general education courses.

Special: Hope International offers co-op programs and cross-registration with California State University, Fullerton. Internships, study abroad in 3 countries, work-study programs, dual and student-designed majors, nondegree study, pass/fail options, and credit for life, military, and work experience are also offered. There is a freshman honors program.

Faculty/Classroom: 69% of faculty are male; 31%, female. 83% teach undergraduates. No introductory courses are taught by graduate students. The average class size in an introductory lecture is 33; in a laboratory, 20; and in a regular course, 30.

Requirements: The SAT I or ACT is required. In addition, applicants must be high school graduates with a GPA of 2.5. The GED is accepted. A personal essay and references from a church leader and an academic counselor are required. AP and CLEP credits are accepted.

Procedure: Freshmen are admitted fall and spring. Entrance exams should be taken before enrolling. There are early admissions, deferred admissions, and rolling admissions plans. The college accepts all applicants. Check with the school for current deadlines. The fall 2003 application fee was $30.

Transfer: Transfer students must submit copies of college transcripts and SAT I scores if fewer than 30 college units have been completed. A minimum GPA of 2.0 is required. 30 of 124 credits required for the bachelor's degree must be completed at Hope.

Visiting: There are regularly scheduled orientations for prospective students. There are guides for informal visits and visitors may sit in on classes and stay overnight. To schedule a visit, contact the Admissions Office.

Financial Aid: In a recent year, 80% of undergraduates worked part time. The FAFSA and the college's own financial statement are required. Check with the school for current deadlines.

International Students: The school actively recruits these students. They must score 500 on the written TOEFL and also take the college's own entrance exam.

Computers: PC facilities are available for student use at the campus learning center. All students may access the system at any time. There are no time limits and no fees. It is strongly recommended that all students have a personal computer.

Graduates: In a recent year, in an average class, 42% graduated in 4 years or less, 54% graduated in 5 years or less, and 56% graduated in 6 years or less.

Admissions Contact: Kaylene Carr, Director of Admissions. A video is available. E-mail: *twinston@hiu.edu* Web: *www.hiu.ed*

HUMBOLDT STATE UNIVERSITY A-1
Arcata, CA 95521-8299 (707) 826-4402; Fax: (707) 826-6194

Full-time: 2689 men, 3258 women	**Faculty:** 290; IIA, +$
Part-time: 345 men, 390 women	**Ph.D.s:** 82%
Graduate: 420 men, 623 women	**Student/Faculty:** 21 to 1
Year: semesters, summer session	**Tuition:** $2539 ($9307)
Application Deadline: June 1	**Room & Board:** $6861
Freshman Class: 5521 applied, 3677 accepted, 867 enrolled	
SAT I Verbal/Math: 530/520	**ACT:** 21 **COMPETITIVE**

Humboldt State University, founded in 1913, is a liberal arts institution and the northernmost campus of the California State University system. There are 3 undergraduate schools and 1 graduate school. In addition to regional accreditation, Humboldt has baccalaureate program accreditation with ABET, ACEJMC, CSWE, NASAD, NASM, NLN, and SAF. The library contains 594,735 volumes, 603,251 microform items, and 19,363 audio/video tapes/CDs, and subscribes to 2517 periodicals. Computerized library services include the card catalog, interlibrary loans, database searching, and Internet access. Special learning facilities include an art gallery, natural history museum, radio station, observatory, greenhouse, solar hydrogen project, wildlife sanctuaries, the Center for Appropriate Technology, child development lab, ceramics lab, jewelry lab, marine lab, fish hatchery, and wildlife care center. The 161-acre campus is in a small town 275 miles north of San Francisco. Including any residence halls, there are 90 buildings.

Student Life: 83% of undergraduates are from California. Students are from 50 states, 29 foreign countries, and Canada. 95% are from public schools. 62% are white. The average age of freshmen is 19; all undergraduates, 24. 28% do not continue beyond their first year.

Housing: 1356 students can be accommodated in college housing, which includes single-sex and coed dormitories and on-campus apartments. In addition, there are living learning houses. On-campus housing is available on a first-come, first-served basis. 82% of students commute. Alcohol is not permitted. All students may keep cars.

Activities: There are 2 national fraternities and 4 local sororities. There are 124 groups on campus, including art, band, cheerleading, chorale, chorus, computers, dance, debate, drama, environmental, ethnic, film, gay, honors, international, jazz band, literary magazine, marching band, musical theater, newspaper, opera, orchestra, pep band, photography, political, professional, radio and TV, religious, social, social service, student government, and symphony. Popular campus events include Native American Motivation Day, Cinco de Mayo, and Latino Week.

Sports: There are 5 intercollegiate sports for men and 7 for women, and 5 intramural sports for men and 5 for women. Facilities include a 7000-seat stadium, all-weather track, swimming pool, field house, tennis and racquetball courts, playing fields, 2 gyms, weight room, and rock-climbing wall.

Disabled Students: 60% of the campus is accessible. Wheelchair ramps, elevators, special parking, specially equipped rest rooms, special class scheduling, lowered drinking fountains, lowered telephones, wheelchair-accessible transportation, and a study center are available.

Services: Counseling and information services are available, as is tutoring in every subject. There is a reader service for the blind and remedial math, reading, and writing.

Campus Safety and Security: Measures include 24-hour foot and vehicle patrol, self-defense education, security escort services, and informal discussions. There are pamphlets/posters/films, emergency telephones, lighted pathways/sidewalks, and emergency transportation services.

Programs of Study: Humboldt confers B.A. and B.S. degrees. Master's degrees are also awarded. Bachelor's degrees are awarded in AGRICULTURE (fishing and fisheries, forestry and related sciences, and natural resource management), BIOLOGICAL SCIENCE (biology/biological science, botany, wildlife biology, and zoology), BUSINESS (business administration and management and business economics), COMMUNICATIONS AND THE ARTS (art, communications, dramatic arts, English, fine arts, French, German, journalism, music, Spanish, and speech/debate/rhetoric), COMPUTER AND PHYSICAL SCIENCE (chemistry, geology, information sciences and systems, mathematics, oceanography, and physics), EDUCATION (business, elementary, English, industrial arts, mathematics, middle school, music, physical, science, secondary, and social science), ENGINEERING AND ENVIRONMENTAL DESIGN (environmental engineering, environmental science, industrial engineering technology, and land use management and reclamation), HEALTH PROFESSIONS (nursing, predentistry, and premedicine), SOCIAL SCIENCE (anthropology, child psychology/development, geography, history, liberal arts/general studies, Native American studies, parks and recreation management, philosophy, physical fitness/movement, political science/government, prelaw, psychology, religion, social science, social work, and sociology). Environmental resources engineering, natural resources, and performing arts are the strongest academically. Biological sciences is the largest.

Required: To graduate, students must complete 120 to 132 semester credits, including 48 in general education courses and at least 24 to 36 in the major, including up to 40 units in electives, with a minimum overall GPA of 2.0. Requirements in freshman reading and composition, American institutions, U.S. history and the Constitution, and California government may be met through course work or exams. Also required are 2 courses in Diversity and Common Ground as well as a graduation writing proficiency exam.

Special: HSU offers campus work-study programs and co-op programs with a variety of public and private agencies, including the areas of fisheries, biology, geology, botany, engineering, soil science, hydrology, and range and soil conservation. Internships and study abroad in 25 countries, with semesters in London, China, and Greece are also offered. Dual majors, student-designed majors, credit for life and military experience, and credit/no credit grading options are also available. There are 5 national honor societies and 6 departmental honors programs.

Faculty/Classroom: 57% of faculty are male; 43%, female. The average class size in an introductory lecture is 33; in a laboratory, 21; and in a regular course, 24.

Admissions: 67% of the 2003-2004 applicants were accepted. The SAT I scores for the 2003-2004 freshman class were: Verbal--37% below 500, 39% between 500 and 599, 22% between 600 and 700, and 2% above 700; Math--39% below 500, 42% between 500 and 599, 17% between 600 and 700, and 2% above 700. The ACT scores were 46% below 21, 26% between 21 and 23, 17% between 24 and 26, 7% between 27 and 28, and 4% above 28.

Requirements: The SAT I or ACT is recommended. In addition, applicants must be high school graduates with a minimium GPA of 2.0 and 15 academic credits, to include 4 years in English, 3 years in college prep math, 2 years each in foreign language, social science, and lab science, including 1 year physical and 1 year life science, and 1 year each of U.S. history/government and visual and performing arts. The GED is accepted. HSU uses an eligibility index that combines GPA and ACT or SAT I scores for admission. Requirements are higher for out-of-state applicants. Contact the Office of Admissions for further information. AP and CLEP credits are accepted.

Procedure: Freshmen are admitted fall and spring. Entrance exams should be taken prior to admission. There are early decision and early admissions plans. There is a rolling admissions plan. Applications should be filed by June 1 for fall entry. Notification is sent on a rolling basis. The fall 2003 application fee was $55. Applications are accepted on-line through CSUMentor.

Transfer: 908 transfer students enrolled in 2002-2003. Applicants must have a minimum college GPA of 2.0 (2.4 for nonresidents). To enter, students need 30 general education units with a grade of C or better, including courses in written and speech communication, critical thinking, and math. Students with fewer than 56 transferable semester units must meet freshman requirements. 30 of 120 to 132 credits required for the bachelor's degree must be completed at Humboldt.

Visiting: There are regularly scheduled orientations for prospective students, including Preview Day in the spring and mandatory summer orientation for new students, which provides peer and academic counseling, registration, and a variety of social activities. There are guides for informal visits and visitors may sit in on classes and stay overnight. To schedule a visit, contact the Office of Admissions at hsuinfo@humboldt.edu.

Financial Aid: The average freshman award was $8050. Humboldt is a member of CSS. The FAFSA is required. The deadline for filing freshman financial aid applications for fall entry is March 2.

International Students: There are 42 international students enrolled. The school actively recruits these students. They must score 550 on the written TOEFL.

Computers: The mainframe is an HPES 40. More than 308 Macs and PCs are available in numerous locations. Students also have access to the Internet, academic specialty centers, and specialized software programs. All students may access the system 24 hours a day. There are no time limits and no fees. It is strongly recommended that all students have a personal computer.

Graduates: From July 1, 2002 to June 30, 2003, 1391 bachelor's degrees were awarded. The most popular majors were liberal studies (11%), art (7%), and biology (7%). In an average class, 8% graduate in 4 years or less, 27% graduate in 5 years or less, and 38% graduate in 6 years or less.

Admissions Contact: Rebecca Kalal, Assistant Director, Admissions. A video is available. E-mail: hsuinfo@.humboldt.edu
Web: www.humboldt.edu

HUMPHREYS COLLEGE
B-3
Stockton, CA 95207   (209) 478-0800; Fax: (209) 478-8721

Full-time: 260 men, 400 women	**Faculty:** 22
Part-time: 30 men, 70 women	**Ph.Ds:** 46%
Graduate: 40 men, 20 women	**Student/Faculty:** 30 to 1
Year: quarters, summer session	**Tuition:** $7000
Application Deadline: open	**Room & Board:** n/av
Freshman Class: n/a	
SAT I or ACT: not required	**NONCOMPETITIVE**

Humphreys College, founded in 1896, is an independent institution offering undergraduate degrees in business management, accounting, paralegal studies, computer management, and liberal arts to a primarily commuter student body. Some information in this capsule and profile is approximate. The library contains 21,000 volumes and 1000 audio/video tapes/CDs, and subscribes to 110 periodicals. Computerized library services include the card catalog and database searching. The 10-acre campus is in a suburban area 40 miles south of Sacramento. Including any residence halls, there are 9 buildings.

Student Life: 97% of undergraduates are from California. Students are from 4 states and 5 foreign countries. 97% are from public schools. 70% are white; 17% Hispanic. The average age of freshmen is 23; all undergraduates, 25. 20% do not continue beyond their first year; 50% remain to graduate.

Housing: 64 students can be accommodated in college housing, which includes single-sex on-campus apartments and married-student housing. On-campus housing is available on a first-come, first-served basis. Priority is given to out-of-town students. 90% of students commute. Alcohol is not permitted. All students may keep cars.

Activities: There are no fraternities or sororities. There are 4 groups on campus, including professional and student government. Popular campus events include a Halloween party, a Christmas dinner, and a quarterly Hot Dog Day barbecue.

Sports: There is no sports program at Humphreys. Facilities include a swimming pool, a basketball court, a tennis court, and sports fields.

Disabled Students: All of the campus is accessible. Wheelchair ramps, special parking, specially equipped rest rooms, special class scheduling, lowered drinking fountains, and lowered telephones are available.

Services: Counseling and information services are available, as is tutoring in some subjects, including accounting. There is remedial math and writing.

Campus Safety and Security: Measures include 24-hour foot and vehicle patrol, security escort services, and lighted pathways/sidewalks.

Programs of Study: Humphreys confers the B.S. degree. Associate and doctoral degrees are also awarded. Bachelor's degrees are awarded in BUSINESS (accounting, business administration and management, court reporting, and management information systems), EDUCATION (early childhood), SOCIAL SCIENCE (community services and paralegal studies). Paralegal studies is the largest.

Required: To graduate, students must complete a total of 180 quarter units, including 56 in the major and 72 in general education courses, with a minimum GPA of 2.0.

Special: Local internship positions are available for students of paralegal studies and business administration. Dual majors in business studies are possible.

Faculty/Classroom: 51% of faculty are male; 49%, female. All teach undergraduates. No introductory courses are taught by graduate students. The average class size in an introductory lecture is 17.

Requirements: Applicants must be graduates of an accredited secondary school or have earned a GED. AP and CLEP credits are accepted.

Procedure: Freshmen are admitted to all sessions. Entrance exams should be taken at any time. There are early admissions and deferred admissions plans. Application deadlines are open. Check with the school for current fee. Notification is sent on a rolling basis.

Transfer: Applicants must submit official transcripts and have a GPA of at least 2.0. 36 of 180 credits required for the bachelor's degree must be completed at Humphreys.

Visiting: There are regularly scheduled orientations for prospective students, including a campus tour, classroom visits, and meetings with admissions, financial aid, and academic advisers. There are guides for informal visits and visitors may sit in on classes. To schedule a visit, contact Santa Lopez in Admissions.

Financial Aid: 64% of undergraduates work part time. Average annual earnings from campus work are $1200. Humphreys is a member of CSS. The FAFSA is required. Check with the school for current deadlines.

International Students: They must score 450 on the written TOEFL or take the MELAB.

Computers: The mainframe is an IBM AS/400. There are 30 PCs available in 2 campus labs. All students may access the system when a lab aide or instructor is present or with an instructor's permission. There are no time limits and no fees.

Graduates: From July 1, 2002 to June 30, 2003, 48 bachelor's degrees were awarded.

Admissions Contact: Santa Lopez, Director of Admissions.
Web: *www.humphreys.edu*

LA SIERRA UNIVERSITY D-5
Riverside, CA 92515-8247

(909) 785-2176
(800) 874-5587; Fax: (909) 785-2447

Full-time: 440 men, 490 women	**Faculty:** 98; IIA, --$
Part-time: 50 men, 70 women	**Ph.D.s:** 76%
Graduate: 70 men, 80 women	**Student/Faculty:** 10 to 1
Year: quarters, summer session	**Tuition:** $15,060
Application Deadline: see profile	**Room & Board:** $4200
Freshman Class: n/av	
SAT I or ACT: required	**LESS COMPETITIVE**

La Sierra University, founded originally as La Sierra Academy in 1922, is a Seventh-day Adventist, private university, offering undergraduate and graduate programs in applied and liberal arts and sciences, business and management, religion, and education. Figures in the above capsule and in this profile are approximate. There are 5 undergraduate and 4 graduate schools. In addition to regional accreditation, La Sierra has baccalaureate program accreditation with ABET. The library contains 230,000 volumes and 285,000 microform items, and subscribes to 1500 periodicals. Computerized library services include the card catalog, interlibrary loans, and database searching. Special learning facilities include a learning resource center, art gallery, natural history museum, radio station, an observatory, a missionary museum, an arboretum. The 300-acre campus is in a suburban area 40 miles east of Los Angeles. Including any residence halls, there are 48 buildings.

Student Life: 71% of undergraduates are from California. Students are from 34 states, 58 foreign countries, and Canada. 39% are from public schools. 35% are white; 31% Asian American; 19% Hispanic. 90% are Protestant; 12% claim no religious affiliation. The average age of freshmen is 19; all undergraduates, 22.

Housing: 650 students can be accommodated in college housing, which includes single-sex dorms, on-campus apartments, off-campus apartments, and married-student housing. In addition, there are honors houses. On-campus housing is available on a first-come, first-served basis. 56% of students commute. Alcohol is not permitted. All students may keep cars.

Activities: There are no fraternities or sororities. There are 30 groups on campus, including band, choir, chorus, computers, drama, ethnic, international, literary magazine, newspaper, orchestra, professional, religious, social service, student government, and yearbook. Popular campus events include University Experience, Academic Expo, and Community Service Day.

Sports: There are 3 intercollegiate sports for men and 2 for women, and 9 intramural sports for men and 9 for women. Facilities include a gym, soccer and flag football fields, a running track, a swimming pool, and a fitness center.

Disabled Students: 99% of the campus is accessible. Wheelchair ramps, elevators, special parking, specially equipped rest rooms, and special class scheduling are available.

Services: Counseling and information services are available, as is tutoring in most subjects. There is a reader service for the blind, and remedial math, reading, and writing, and a learning support center.

Campus Safety and Security: Measures include 24-hour foot and vehicle patrol, security escort services, informal discussions, and lighted pathways/sidewalks.

Programs of Study: La Sierra confers B.A., B.S., B.B.A., B.F.A., B.Mus., and B.S.W. degrees. Associate, master's, and doctoral degrees are also awarded. Bachelor's degrees are awarded in BIOLOGICAL SCIENCE (biochemistry, biology/biological science, biometrics and biostatistics, and biophysics), BUSINESS (accounting, banking and finance, business administration and management, electronic business, international business management, and marketing management), COMMUNICATIONS AND THE ARTS (art, communications, English, English as a second/foreign language, fine arts, graphic design, music, music performance, and Spanish), COMPUTER AND PHYSICAL SCIENCE (chemistry, computer science, information sciences and systems, mathematics, and physics), EDUCATION (elementary, music, physical, and secondary), HEALTH PROFESSIONS (exercise science and health science), SOCIAL SCIENCE (history, liberal arts/general studies, political science/government, psychobiology, psychology, religion, social work, and sociology). English and history are the strongest academically. Biology, psychology, and business are the largest.

Required: To graduate, students must complete 190 units, at least 60 of which must be upper-division, with a GPA of 2.0. All students must complete a University Studies curriculum consisting of a 29-unit core curriculum and the distribution requirements, and 15 clock hours of community service per year.

Special: Cross-registration with Walla Walla College is necessary for engineering students. Study abroad is available in 3 countries through the Adventist Colleges Abroad Consortium. Liberal studies students work with an adviser to design their own major. There is a freshman honors program.

Faculty/Classroom: 71% of faculty are male; 29%, female. All teach undergraduates, 70% do research, and 70% do both. Graduate students teach 1% of introductory courses. The average class size in an introductory lecture is 30; in a laboratory, 21; and in a regular course, 20.

Requirements: The SAT I or ACT is required. In addition, prospective students should have a high school diploma or equivalent. Test scores above the 50th percentile and a personal interview are recommended. Provisional acceptance may be considered with lesser credentials, following a more exhaustive examination. A GPA of 2.5 is required. AP and CLEP credits are accepted. Important factors in the admissions decision are recommendations by school officials, leadership record, and evidence of special talent.

Procedure: Freshmen are admitted to all sessions. Entrance exams should be taken during the senior year. There is a rolling admissions plan. Check with the school for current deadlines. The fall 2003 application fee was $30.

Transfer: Transcripts from all previous colleges are required. 36 of 190 credits required for the bachelor's degree must be completed at La Sierra.

Visiting: There are regularly scheduled orientations for prospective students, including a tour and meetings with faculty and administrators. There are guides for informal visits and visitors may sit in on classes and stay overnight. To schedule a visit, contact Recruitment/Admissions.

Financial Aid: La Sierra is a member of CSS. The FAFSA is required. Check with the school for current deadlines.

International Students: The school actively recruits these students. They must score 550 on the written TOEFL or take the MELAB and also take the SAT I or the ACT.

Computers: The mainframe is a Sun SPARC 1000. Terminals accessing the mainframe are available in every building on campus, and Mac, AT&T, and IBM PCs are available in the PC lab. All systems are connected to an Ethernet network and a Micom Dataswitch. All students may access the system 24 hours a day. There are no time limits and no fees.

Admissions Contact: C. Tom Smith, Associate Vice Preseident, Enrollment Services. E-mail: *admissions@lasierra.edu*
Web: *www.lasierra.edu*

LOYOLA MARYMOUNT UNIVERSITY C-5
Los Angeles, CA 90045

(310) 338-2750
(800) LMU-INFO; Fax: (310) 338-2797

Full-time: 2082 men, 3186 women	**Faculty:** 419; IIA, ++$
Part-time: 91 men, 106 women	**Ph.D.s:** 86%
Graduate: 629 men, 1177 women	**Student/Faculty:** 13 to 1
Year: semesters, summer session	**Tuition:** $23,934
Application Deadline: February 1	**Room & Board:** $8260
Freshman Class: 7716 applied, 4568 accepted, 1335 enrolled	
SAT I Verbal/Math: 571/583	**VERY COMPETITIVE**

Loyola Marymount University, a private institution founded in 1911 and affiliated with the Roman Catholic Church, offers programs in liberal arts, business administration, fine arts, science, engineering, and law. There are 5 undergraduate schools and 1 graduate school. In addition to regional accreditation, LMU has baccalaureate program accreditation with AACSB, ABET, ACS, NASAD, NASDTEC, and NCATE. The 2 libraries contain 943,637 volumes, 1,560,619 microform items, and 20,880 audio/video tapes/CDs, and subscribe to 10,086 periodicals.

Computerized library services include the card catalog, interlibrary loans, database searching, and Internet access. Special learning facilities include a learning resource center, art gallery, radio station, the Burns Fine Arts Center, and the Little Theatre. The 128-acre campus is in a suburban area 15 miles southwest of downtown Los Angeles on a mesa overlooking Marina del Rey. Including any residence halls, there are 40 buildings.

Student Life: 76% of undergraduates are from California. Students are from 50 states, 72 foreign countries, and Canada. 51% are white; 17% Hispanic; 13% Asian American. 53% are Catholic; 25% Christian, Buddhist, or other. The average age of freshmen is 18; all undergraduates, 20. 13% do not continue beyond their first year; 72% remain to graduate.

Housing: 2897 students can be accommodated in college housing, which includes single-sex and coed dorms and on-campus apartments. In addition, there are honors houses and special-interest houses. On-campus housing is available on a lottery system for upperclassmen. 54% of students live on campus; of those, 50% remain on campus on weekends. All students may keep cars.

Activities: 14% of men belong to 5 national fraternities; 6% of women belong to 7 national sororities. There are 120 groups on campus, including art, cheerleading, chess, choir, chorale, chorus, computers, dance, drama, ethnic, film, gay, honors, international, literary magazine, newspaper, orchestra, pep band, political, professional, radio and TV, religious, social, social service, student government, and yearbook. Popular campus events include Cinco de Mayo, Special Games (disabled children), and the ASLMU Formal Dance.

Sports: There are 8 intercollegiate sports for men and 9 for women, and 6 intramural sports for men and 6 for women. Facilities include an athletic pavilion, a 4166-seat gym, a swimming pool, tennis, handball, and racquetball courts, a baseball stadium, a floating crew shell house, soccer, rugby, and football fields, and a recreation center.

Disabled Students: 95% of the campus is accessible. Wheelchair ramps, elevators, special parking, specially equipped rest rooms, special class scheduling, lowered drinking fountains, and lowered telephones are available. Special arrangements are possible for placement tests and registration. Hearing aid equipment is provided for disabled students in the library.

Services: Counseling and information services are available, as is tutoring in most subjects. There is a reader service for the blind and remedial math, reading, and writing. There is an extensive learning resource center with full-time specialists in reading, writing, and study skills as well as a peer tutoring staff and computer-aided instruction. Note takers and special equipment and materials are available.

Campus Safety and Security: Measures include 24-hour foot and vehicle patrol, security escort services, informal discussions, and emergency telephones. There are lighted pathways/sidewalks.

Programs of Study: LMU confers B.A., B.S., B.B.A., B.S.A., and B.S.E. degrees. Master's degrees are also awarded. Bachelor's degrees are awarded in BIOLOGICAL SCIENCE (biochemistry and biology/biological science), BUSINESS (accounting and business administration and management), COMMUNICATIONS AND THE ARTS (art history and appreciation, classics, communications, dance, dramatic arts, English, French, media arts, music, Spanish, and studio art), COMPUTER AND PHYSICAL SCIENCE (chemistry, computer science, mathematics, natural sciences, and physics), ENGINEERING AND ENVIRONMENTAL DESIGN (civil engineering, computer graphics, electrical/electronics engineering, engineering physics, environmental science, and mechanical engineering), SOCIAL SCIENCE (African American studies, Asian/Oriental studies, classical/ancient civilization, economics, European studies, history, humanities, philosophy, political science/government, psychology, sociology, theological studies, and urban studies). Communication arts, political science, and engineering are the strongest academically. Psychology, communication studies, and business administration are the largest.

Required: The core curriculum required for all students in the liberal arts college includes 6 hours each of communication skills, history, science/technology, philosophy, and theology, and 3 hours of fine arts, literature/psychology, and social studies. A minimum 2.0 GPA is required, as are at least 120 semester credits, with at least 40 hours in the major. The last 30 semester hours of academic work and at least 12 hours of the major must be completed at LMU.

Special: LMU offers internships and volunteer work experience with local firms, study abroad in Europe, Mexico, Japan, and China, a Washington semester, dual majors, work-study, student-designed and individualized studies majors, accelerated degree programs in all majors, a general studies degree, nondegree study, and pass/fail options for electives. There are 2 national honor societies and a freshman honors program.

Faculty/Classroom: 60% of faculty are male; 40%, female. All both teach and do research. No introductory courses are taught by graduate students. The average class size in an introductory lecture is 19 and in a regular course, 19.

Admissions: 59% of the 2003-2004 applicants were accepted. The SAT I scores for the 2003-2004 freshman class were: Verbal--13% below 500, 51% between 500 and 599, 32% between 600 and 700, and 4% above 700; Math--13% below 500, 46% between 500 and 599, 36% between 600 and 700, and 5% above 700.

Requirements: The SAT I is required and the ACT is recommended. In addition, prospective students must be graduates of an accredited secondary school and have completed 4 years of English, 3 each of a foreign language, math, and social studies, 2 of science, and 1 of an academic elective. A recommendation from an official of a previous school and essays are required. An interview is recommended. A GPA of 2.9 is required. AP credits are accepted. Important factors in the admissions decision are recommendations by school officials, advanced placement or honor courses, and evidence of special talent.

Procedure: Freshmen are admitted fall and spring. Entrance exams should be taken during the spring of the junior year or fall of the senior year. There is a deferred admissions plan and a rolling admissions plan. Applications should be filed by February 1 for fall entry and December 1 for spring entry, along with a $50 fee. Notification is sent on a rolling basis. A waiting list is an active part of the admissions procedure. Applications are accepted on-line.

Transfer: 193 transfer students enrolled in 2002-2003. Applicants must have a minimum 2.75 GPA and at least 30 credit hours earned. No minimum credit hours are necessary for students who meet freshman requirements. The SAT I and an interview are recommended. 30 credits of 120 required for the bachelor's degree must be completed at LMU.

Visiting: There are regularly scheduled orientations for prospective students, consisting of an open house in the fall. There are guides for informal visits and visitors may sit in on classes. To schedule a visit, contact the Admissions Office.

Financial Aid: In a recent year, 52% of all full-time freshmen and 64% of continuing full-time students received some form of financial aid. 41% of full-time freshmen and 63% of continuing full-time students received need-based aid. The average freshman award was $16,180. 32% of undergraduates work part time. Average annual earnings from campus work are $3000. The average financial indebtedness of a recent graduate was $20,893. The CSS Profile and FAFSA are required. The deadline for filing freshman financial aid applications for fall entry is February 15.

International Students: There are 181 international students enrolled. They must score 550 on the written TOEFL.

Computers: The mainframe is an IBM 4381. There are 40 PCs in a student lab networked with Internet access. The library houses 30 PCs with Internet access. Residence halls are wired for access to a campuswide network through students' personal computers. The system may be accessed through a 24-hour dial-in service. Labs are available more than 60 hours per week. All students may access the system; 2 hours for remote access. There are no fees. It is strongly recommended that all students have a personal computer.

Graduates: From July 1, 2002 to June 30, 2003, 1188 bachelor's degrees were awarded. The most popular majors were business administration (25%), psychology (7%), and communication studies (7%). In an average class, 1% graduate in 3 years or less, 57% graduate in 4 years or less, 69% graduate in 5 years or less, and 73% graduate in 6 years or less. 112 companies recruited on campus in 2002-2003.

Admissions Contact: Matthew Fissinger, Director of Undergraduate Admissions. A video is available. E-mail: *admissions@lmu.edu* Web: *www.lmu.edu*

MASTER'S COLLEGE AND SEMINARY, THE   C-5
Santa Clarita, CA 91321-1200   (661) 259-3540 ext 3365
(800) 568-6248; Fax: (661) 288-1037

Full-time: 440 men, 547 women	**Faculty:** 52
Part-time: 111 men, 92 women	**Ph.D.s:** 70%
Graduate: 389 men, 40 women	**Student/Faculty:** 19 to 1
Year: semesters, summer session	**Tuition:** $17,200
Application Deadline: March 6	**Room & Board:** $6050
Freshman Class: 773 applied, 639 accepted, 340 enrolled	
SAT I Verbal/Math: 580/560	**ACT:** 25 **VERY COMPETITIVE**

The Master's College, founded in 1927, is a private, nondenominational Christian liberal arts institution. The library contains 133,199 volumes, 35,129 microform items, and 6100 audio/video tapes/CDs, and subscribes to 505 periodicals. Computerized library services include the card catalog, interlibrary loans, database searching, and Internet access. Special learning facilities include a learning resource center. The 110-acre campus is in a rural area 35 miles north of Los Angeles. Including any residence halls, there are 27 buildings.

Student Life: 67% of undergraduates are from California. Students are from 42 states, 23 foreign countries, and Canada. 46% are from public schools. 85% are white. Most are Protestant. The average age of freshmen is 19; all undergraduates, 20. 17% do not continue beyond their first year; 58% remain to graduate.

Housing: 805 students can be accommodated in college housing, which includes single-sex dorms and off-campus apartments. In addition, there are special-interest houses. On-campus housing is guaranteed for the freshman year only and is available on a first-come, first-served basis. 72% of students live on campus; of those, 95% remain on campus on weekends. Alcohol is not permitted. All students may keep cars.

Activities: There are no fraternities or sororities. There are 15 groups on campus, including band, choir, chorale, drama, film, jazz band, musical theater, opera, orchestra, pep band, radio and TV, religious, social service, and student government. Popular campus events include College View Weekend, Community Day, and Mission Conference.

Sports: There are 5 intercollegiate sports for men and 5 for women, and 7 intramural sports for men and 7 for women. Facilities include a gym, a sports field, tennis and volleyball courts, an intramural field, a swimming pool, and a fitness center.

Disabled Students: All of the campus is accessible. Wheelchair ramps, special parking, specially equipped rest rooms, lowered drinking fountains, and lowered telephones are available.

Services: Counseling and information services are available, as is tutoring in most subjects. There is remedial math.

Campus Safety and Security: Measures include 24-hour foot and vehicle patrol, shuttle buses, and lighted pathways/sidewalks.

Programs of Study: TMC confers B.A., B.S., and B.Th. degrees. Master's degrees are also awarded. Bachelor's degrees are awarded in BIOLOGICAL SCIENCE (biology/biological science), BUSINESS (business administration and management), COMMUNICATIONS AND THE ARTS (communications, English, and music), COMPUTER AND PHYSICAL SCIENCE (information sciences and systems, mathematics, and natural sciences), EDUCATION (elementary, physical, and secondary), SOCIAL SCIENCE (biblical studies, history, home economics, liberal arts/general studies, and political science/government). Biological sciences, biblical studies, and business administration are the strongest academically. Biblical studies, education, and business administration are the largest.

Required: Students must complete at least 122 semester hours, including 78 distributed as follows: 24 hours in biblical studies, 18 in social sciences, 9 in English, 7 in natural science, 6 in cross-cultural studies, and 3 each in communication, business, logical reasoning, and fine arts. Students must complete at least 40 semester hours in upper-division courses and at least 40 in the major and must maintain a minimum GPA of 2.0.

Special: Students may cross-register with the Coalition of Christian Colleges and Universities and may participate in a co-op program with the College of the Canyons. Internships are offered with local churches, radio stations, and newspapers. A Washington semester, study abroad, dual majors in music plus a second discipline, and a general studies degree are available. The Master's Institute, a 1-year certificate Bible program, is also offered.

Faculty/Classroom: 80% of faculty are male; 20%, female. All teach undergraduates. No introductory courses are taught by graduate students. The average class size in an introductory lecture is 42; in a laboratory, 16; and in a regular course, 14.

Admissions: 83% of the 2003-2004 applicants were accepted. The SAT I scores for the 2003-2004 freshman class were: Verbal--19% below 500, 41% between 500 and 599, 34% between 600 and 700, and 6% above 700; Math--20% below 500, 48% between 500 and 599, 27% between 600 and 700, and 5% above 700. The ACT scores were 19% below 21, 21% between 21 and 23, 31% between 24 and 26, 14% between 27 and 28, and 15% above 28. 52% of the current freshmen were in the top fifth of their class; 82% were in the top two fifths. 7 freshmen graduated first in their class.

Requirements: The SAT I or ACT is required. In addition, applicants must have completed 4 years of English, 3 each of math and science, 2 of history, and 8 units of electives. A GPA of 2.5 is required. AP and CLEP credits are accepted. Important factors in the admissions decision are personality/intangible qualities, recommendations by school officials, and leadership record.

Procedure: Freshmen are admitted fall and spring. Entrance exams should be taken in the fall. There is a deferred admissions plan. Applications should be filed by March 6 for fall entry; deadlines are open for spring entry. The fee is $35. Notification is sent April 1. Applications are accepted on-line.

Transfer: 119 transfer students enrolled in 2002-2003. Applicants must meet freshman requirements. A maximum of 70 units can be transferred from a junior college; 94 units from a 4-year college. 28 of 122 credits required for the bachelor's degree must be completed at TMC.

Visiting: There are regularly scheduled orientations for prospective students, including class visitation, meetings with faculty, interviews, athletic events, an overnight stay, and college activities. There are guides for informal visits and visitors may sit in on classes and stay overnight. To schedule a visit, contact the Enrollment Office at (800) 568-6428, ext. 3363 or jbhughes@masters.edu.

Financial Aid: In 2003-2004, 70% of all full-time freshmen and 85% of continuing full-time students received some form of financial aid. 61% of full-time freshmen and 67% of continuing full-time students received need-based aid. The average freshman award was $14,326. 21% of undergraduates work part time. Average annual earnings from campus work are $2413. The average financial indebtedness of the 2003 graduate was $13,130. TMC is a member of CSS. The FAFSA and the college's own financial statement are required. The priority date for freshman financial aid applications for fall entry is March 2.

International Students: There are 39 international students enrolled. They must score 525 on the written TOEFL or 197 on the electronic version.

Computers: Computer access is available in the library, the business center, the math lab, and the computer center. All students may access the system. There are no time limits and no fees. All students are required to have personal computers.

Graduates: From July 1, 2002 to June 30, 2003, 239 bachelor's degrees were awarded. The most popular majors were biblical studies (29%), business (21%), and education (13%). In an average class, 4% graduate in 3 years or less, 51% graduate in 4 years or less, 54% graduate in 5 years or less, and 58% graduate in 6 years or less.

Admissions Contact: Yaphet N. Peterson, Director of Enrollment Management. A video is available. E-mail: *enrollment@masters.edu* Web: *http://www.masters.edu*

MENLO COLLEGE
Atherton, CA 94027   **B-3**

(650) 688-3762
(800) 55-MENLO; Fax: (650) 617-2395

Full-time: 290 men, 200 women	**Faculty:** 21; IIB, +$
Part-time: 60 men, 80 women	**Ph.D.s:** 80%
Graduate: none	**Student/Faculty:** 23 to 1
Year: semesters, summer session	**Tuition:** $17,000
Application Deadline: open	**Room & Board:** $7000
Freshman Class: n/av	
SAT I or ACT: required	**LESS COMPETITIVE**

Menlo College, founded in 1927, is a private college offering preprofessional programs in the liberal arts and management. Figures in the above capsule and in this profile are approximate. The library contains 61,000 volumes, 670 microform items, and 330 audio/video tapes/CDs, and subscribes to 740 periodicals. Computerized library services include the card catalog, interlibrary loans, and database searching. Special learning facilities include a learning resource center, radio station, TV station, a photo lab, a newspaper production facility, and an observation room for the psychology program. The 62-acre campus is in a suburban area 30 miles south of San Francisco. Including any residence halls, there are 16 buildings.

Student Life: 75% of undergraduates are from California. Students are from 18 states and 17 foreign countries. 60% are from public schools. 54% are white; 13% Asian American; 12% foreign nationals. The average age of freshmen is 18; all undergraduates, 23. 51% do not continue beyond their first year; 33% remain to graduate.

Housing: 400 students can be accommodated in college housing, which includes single-sex and coed dorms and on-campus apartments. In addition, there are special-interest houses. On-campus housing is guaranteed for all 4 years. 62% of students live on campus; of those, 55% remain on campus on weekends. All students may keep cars.

Activities: There are no fraternities or sororities. There are 14 groups on campus, including cheerleading, chess, computers, debate, drama, ethnic, honors, international, newspaper, professional, radio and TV, social, social service, and student government. Popular campus events include Spring Fest, SBA Day, and Communication Career Day.

Sports: There are 8 intercollegiate sports for men and 6 for women, and 4 intramural sports for men and 4 for women. Facilities include 2 swimming pools, a soccer field, tennis courts, a track, and a 600-seat gym. The campus stadium seats 1000, the largest auditorium/arena, 220.

Disabled Students: 95% of the campus is accessible. Wheelchair ramps, elevators, special parking, specially equipped rest rooms, lowered drinking fountains, and lowered telephones are available.

Services: Counseling and information services are available, as is tutoring in every subject. There is a reader service for the blind.

Campus Safety and Security: Measures include 24-hour foot and vehicle patrol, informal discussions, pamphlets/posters/films, and lighted pathways/sidewalks.

Programs of Study: Menlo confers B.A. and B.S. degrees. Bachelor's degrees are awarded in BUSINESS (business administration and management, international business management, management information systems, and sports management), COMMUNICATIONS AND THE ARTS (communications), SOCIAL SCIENCE (liberal arts/general studies and psychology). Management and mass communications are the strongest academically and are the largest.

Required: All students must complete 59 units in the general education curriculum, including 9 units each of English, math, management, and economics, 7 of science, 6 of diversity, 4 of quantitative skills, and 3 each of American institutions and computer competency. A total of 124 units, including 21 to 30 in the major and 18 in a concentration, and a minimum 2.0 GPA are required to graduate.

Special: Students may earn up to 12 credits through internships. Menlo also offers study abroad in England, China, and Chile, dual and student-designed majors, B.A.-B.S. degrees, and an accelerated degree program in management. There are 2 national honor societies and 1 departmental honors program.

Faculty/Classroom: 59% of faculty are male; 41%, female. All teach undergraduates. The average class size in an introductory lecture is 23; in a laboratory, 20; and in a regular course, 16.

Requirements: The SAT I or ACT is required. In addition, a personal essay and letter of recommendation should be submitted. The GED is accepted. A GPA of 2.5 is required. AP and CLEP credits are accepted. Important factors in the admissions decision are advanced placement or honor courses, evidence of special talent, and leadership record.

Procedure: Freshmen are admitted fall and spring. Entrance exams should be taken during the junior or senior year. There are early decision, early admissions, deferred admissions, and rolling admissions plans. Application deadlines are open. 35 early decision candidates were accepted for the 2003-2004 class. Check with the school for current fees. Applications are available on-line.

Transfer: Transfer applicants must show potential for success indicated by a 2.5 GPA at the college level. Those with fewer than 24 credits must meet freshman requirements. 30 of 124 credits required for the bachelor's degree must be completed at Menlo.

Visiting: There are regularly scheduled orientations for prospective students, including a fall preview with an introduction to college life and college decision making. The spring visit for accepted students provides an in-depth view of Menlo. There are guides for informal visits and visitors may sit in on classes and stay overnight. To schedule a visit, contact the Office of Admissions at (650) 688-3753 or (800) 55-Menlo.

Financial Aid: In a recent year, 40% of undergraduates worked part time. Average annual earnings from campus work were $2000. Menlo is a member of CSS. The CSS Profile or FAFSA is required. Check with the school for current deadlines.

International Students: The school actively recruits these students. They must score 500 on the written TOEFL or take the SAT I or ACT if English is their first language.

Computers: The mainframes are an HP 3000/Series 44 and an HP 9000/Series 300. There are 56 HP PCs and 10 Macs located in academic buildings. All students may access the system 8 A.M. to 11 P.M. daily. There are no time limits and no fees.

Admissions Contact: Sara Sargent, Director of Admissions Outreach Programs. E-mail: *ssargent@menlo.edu* Web: *www.menlo.edu*

MILLS COLLEGE
Oakland, CA 94613

B-3

(510) 430-2135
(800) 87-MILLS; Fax: (510) 430-3314

Full-time: 726 women	**Faculty:** 87; II A, +$
Part-time: none	**Ph.D.s:** 90%
Graduate: 80 men, 471 women	**Student/Faculty:** 8 to 1
Year: semesters	**Tuition:** $24,441
Application Deadline: February 1	**Room & Board:** $8930
Freshman Class: 558 applied, 409 accepted, 139 enrolled	
SAT I or ACT: required	**VERY COMPETITIVE**

Mills College, founded in 1852, is a private women's college offering instruction in liberal and fine arts, sciences, and teacher preparation. Graduate programs are coed. The library contains 206,600 volumes, 7700 microform items, and 5000 audio/video tapes/CDs, and subscribes to 700 periodicals. Computerized library services include the card catalog, interlibrary loans, database searching, and Internet access. Special learning facilities include an art gallery, a children's school, a small book press, an electronic/computer music studio, a botanical garden, and a computer learning studio. The 135-acre campus is in an urban area 12 miles east of San Francisco. Including any residence halls, there are 84 buildings.

Student Life: 73% of undergraduates are from California. Students are from 37 states, 8 foreign countries, and Canada. 80% are from public schools. 56% are white; 12% Hispanic; 11% African American. The average age of freshmen is 19; all undergraduates, 22. 20% do not continue beyond their first year; 60% remain to graduate.

Housing: 780 students can be accommodated in college housing, which includes single-sex and coed dorms, on-campus apartments, and married-student housing. Married-student housing is offered on an equal basis to domestic partners of lesbian and gay students, and a student co-op house is available for juniors and seniors. In addition, there are language houses and special-interest houses. On-campus housing is guaranteed for all 4 years. 57% of students live on campus; of those, 75% remain on campus on weekends. All students may keep cars.

Activities: There are no sororities. There are 30 groups on campus, including art, band, choir, chorale, chorus, dance, drama, ethnic, gay, honors, international, literary magazine, newspaper, political, professional, religious, social, social service, student government, and yearbook. Popular campus events include Black and White Ball, Fine Arts Festival, and Writer's Harvest.

Sports: Facilities include an 872-seat gym, a weight room/fitness center, athletic fields, a pool, and 6 tennis courts.

Disabled Students: 90% of the campus is accessible. Wheelchair ramps, elevators, special parking, specially equipped rest rooms, special class scheduling, lowered telephones, and special housing are available.

Services: Counseling and information services are available, as is tutoring in every subject. There is a reader service for the blind.

Campus Safety and Security: Measures include 24-hour foot and vehicle patrol, self-defense education, security escort services, and shuttle buses. There are informal discussions, pamphlets/posters/films, emergency telephones, and lighted pathways/sidewalks.

Programs of Study: Mills confers the B.A. degree. Master's and doctoral degrees are also awarded. Bachelor's degrees are awarded in AGRICULTURE (environmental studies), BIOLOGICAL SCIENCE (biochemistry and biology/biological science), BUSINESS (business economics), COMMUNICATIONS AND THE ARTS (art history and appreciation, comparative literature, creative writing, dance, English, French, media arts, modern language, music, and studio art), COMPUTER AND PHYSICAL SCIENCE (chemistry, computer science, and mathematics), ENGINEERING AND ENVIRONMENTAL DESIGN (environmental science), SOCIAL SCIENCE (American studies, anthropology, biopsychology, child psychology/development, economics, ethnic studies, Hispanic American studies, history, international relations, liberal arts/general studies, philosophy, political science/government, psychology, public administration, public affairs, sociology, and women's studies). Art, biology, and computer science are the strongest academically. English and psychology are the largest.

Required: All students must fullfill a core curriculum that includes 4 courses in Disciplinary Experiences, 3 courses in Perspectives, an English writing requirement, 1 course in quantitative and computational reasoning, and 1 information literacy/information technology skills course. A total of 34 semester course credits is required, with 10 to 17 in the major. The minimum GPA is 2.0. A comprehensive exam/thesis may be required in some majors.

Special: There is cross-registration with the University of California at Berkeley and California State University, among others. Mills offers co-op programs, internships, study abroad, a Washington semester, work-study programs, dual, student-designed, and interdisciplinary majors, including political, legal, and economic analysis, accelerated degree programs, including 3-2 engineering, 4+1 MBA, and 4+1 interdisciplinary computer science, a general studies degree, credit by exam, and pass/fail options. There is 1 national honor society, and Phi Beta Kappa.

Faculty/Classroom: 46% of faculty are male; 54%, female. All both teach and do research. No introductory courses are taught by graduate students. The average class size in a laboratory is 15 and in a regular course, 12.

Admissions: 73% of the 2003-2004 applicants were accepted. The SAT I scores for the 2003-2004 freshman class were: Verbal--14% below 500, 40% between 500 and 599, 38% between 600 and 700, and 8% above 700; Math--27% below 500, 40% between 500 and 599, 29% between 600 and 700, and 4% above 700. 62% of the current freshmen were in the top fifth of their class; 97% were in the top two fifths.

Requirements: The SAT I or ACT is required. In addition, SAT II: Subject tests are recommended. Applicants should graduate from an accredited secondary school or have a GED. An essay is required; an interview, recommended. Mills requires applicants to be in the upper 50% of their class. A GPA of 3.0 is required. AP credits are accepted. Important factors in the admissions decision are advanced placement or honor courses, personality/intangible qualities, and recommendations by school officials.

Procedure: Freshmen are admitted fall and spring. Entrance exams should be taken at least 1 month prior to application. There are early action and deferred admissions plans. Early action applications should be filed by November 15; regular applications, by February 1 for fall entry and November 1 for spring entry, along with a $40 fee. Notification of early action is sent December 20; regular decision, March 30. Applications are accepted on-line through Common Application.

Transfer: 103 transfer students enrolled in 2002-2003. Transfer applicants with fewer than 24 transferable semester hours should take the SAT I or ACT. 12 of 34 Mills course credits required for the bachelor's degree must be completed at Mills.

Visiting: There are regularly scheduled orientations for prospective students, consisting of class visits, campus tours, lunch with faculty, financial aid workshops, an admissions interview, and an overnight stay. There are guides for informal visits and visitors may sit in on classes and stay overnight. To schedule a visit, contact the Admission Office.

Financial Aid: Mills is a member of CSS. The FAFSA and the college's own financial statement are required. The priority date for freshman financial aid applications for fall entry is February 15.

International Students: There are 12 international students enrolled. The school actively recruits these students. They must score 550 on the written TOEFL or 213 on the electronic version and also take the SAT I.

Computers: The mainframe is a Sun SPARC 10. Students can access any 1 of 3 central system servers from many locations on campus. The 3 systems provide e-mail services, file storage and sharing, and student

financial and academic records. A mix of 132 Macs and PCs in residence halls, computing labs, academic departmental labs, the library, and student lounges give students access to the Internet and Web. All students may access the system 24 hours a day, year-round. There are no time limits. The fee is $140. It is recommended that students in computer science and book arts have personal computers. A Mac is recommended.
Admissions Contact: Muriel Whitcomb, Acting Dean of Admission. A video is available. E-mail: *admission@mills.edu* Web: *www.mills.edu*

MOUNT SAINT MARY'S COLLEGE　　　　C-5
Los Angeles, CA 90049
　　　　　　　　　　　　　　　　(310) 954-4250
　　　　　　　　(800) 999-9893; Fax: (310) 954-4259

Full-time: 19 men, 896 women	**Faculty:** 74; IIB, -$
Part-time: 2 men, 33 women	**Ph.Ds:** 51%
Graduate: 72 men, 337 women	**Student/Faculty:** 12 to 1
Year: semesters	**Tuition:** $20,456
Application Deadline: February 15	**Room & Board:** $7851
Freshman Class: n/av	
SAT I or ACT: required	**VERY COMPETITIVE**

Mount Saint Mary's College, founded in 1925 and affiliated with the Catholic Church, is a private, primarily women's institution that offers programs in the liberal arts and sciences. In addition to regional accreditation, The Mount has baccalaureate program accreditation with NASM and NLN. The library contains 132,000 volumes, 320 microform items, and 2520 audio/video tapes/CDs, and subscribes to 690 periodicals. Computerized library services include the card catalog, interlibrary loans, and database searching. Special learning facilities include a learning resource center and art gallery. The 72-acre campus is in an urban area 10 miles west of Los Angeles. Including any residence halls, there are 26 buildings.
Student Life: 89% of undergraduates are from California. Students are from 19 states and 1 foreign country. 74% are from public schools. 44% are Hispanic; 20% Asian American; 18% white. 71% claim no religious affiliation; 23% are Catholic. The average age of freshmen is 18; all undergraduates, 23.
Housing: 482 students can be accommodated in college housing, which includes single-sex dorms. On-campus housing is guaranteed for all 4 years. 56% of students live on campus. All students may keep cars.
Activities: 66% of women belong to 2 local sororities and 1 national sorority. There are no fraternities. There are 29 groups on campus, including art, choir, chorale, chorus, computers, dance, departmental, drama, ethnic, honors, musical theater, newspaper, political, professional, religious, social, social service, student government, and yearbook. Popular campus events include Mary's Day (honors and awards), Horizon's Day, and Spring Sing.
Sports: There are 4 intramural sports for women. Facilities include a pool, tennis courts, exercise and weight rooms, and cardiovascular equipment.
Disabled Students: Wheelchair ramps, elevators, and special parking are available.
Services: Counseling and information services are available, as is tutoring in most subjects. A peer tutoring program is available.
Campus Safety and Security: Measures include 24-hour foot and vehicle patrol, self-defense education, shuttle buses, and informal discussions. There are pamphlets/posters/films and lighted pathways/sidewalks.
Programs of Study: The Mount confers B.A., B.S., and B.A.M. degrees. Associate and master's degrees are also awarded. Bachelor's degrees are awarded in BIOLOGICAL SCIENCE (biochemistry and biology/biological science), BUSINESS (business administration and management), COMMUNICATIONS AND THE ARTS (art, English, French, music, and Spanish), COMPUTER AND PHYSICAL SCIENCE (chemistry and mathematics), EDUCATION (elementary and secondary), HEALTH PROFESSIONS (nursing), SOCIAL SCIENCE (American studies, child psychology/development, gerontology, history, liberal arts/general studies, philosophy, political science/government, psychology, religion, social science, and sociology). Premedicine is the strongest academically. Nursing and biological science are the largest.
Required: Requirements for graduation include completion of 59 units of distribution requirements and 124 total credit hours, with the number of hours in the major varying by department. English courses and a minimum 2.0 GPA are required.
Special: The Mount offers cross-registration with UCLA, internships within the business department, study abroad in Spain, England, and France, a Washington semester through American University, dual and student-designed majors, credit for prior experiences, and pass/fail options. There are 11 national honor societies, a freshman honors program, and 9 departmental honors programs.
Faculty/Classroom: 25% of faculty are male; 75%, female. No introductory courses are taught by graduate students. The average class size in an introductory lecture is 20; in a laboratory, 20; and in a regular course, 19.
Admissions: The SAT I scores for the 2003-2004 freshman class were: Verbal--43% below 500, 46% between 500 and 599, and 11% between

600 and 700; Math--43% below 500, 48% between 500 and 599, and 9% between 600 and 700.
Requirements: The SAT I or ACT is required. In addition, applicants must be graduates of an accredited secondary school or have earned the GED, with 16 academic credits and 16 Carnegie units, including 4 years of English literature and composition, 2 or 3 years each of math, science, and social studies, and 1 or 2 years of history. An essay is required, and an interview is recommended. A GPA of 3.25 is required. AP and CLEP credits are accepted. Important factors in the admissions decision are recommendations by school officials, recommendations by alumni, and advanced placement or honor courses.
Procedure: Freshmen are admitted in the fall. Entrance exams should be taken at the end of the junior year or the beginning of the senior year. Applications should be filed by February 15 for priority consideration for fall entry and November 1 for spring entry. The fall 2003 application fee was $40. Notification is sent on a rolling basis.
Transfer: 76 transfer students enrolled in 2002-2003. Transfer students must have a minimum 2.25 GPA with at least 24 completed credit hours. 30 of 124 credits required for the bachelor's degree must be completed at The Mount.
Visiting: There are regularly scheduled orientations for prospective students, including workshops, student panels, tours, class visits, and faculty presentations. There are guides for informal visits and visitors may sit in on classes. To schedule a visit, contact the Admissions Office.
Financial Aid: In 2003-2004, 96% of all full-time freshmen and 92% of continuing full-time students received some form of financial aid. The average freshman award was $14,500. 45% of undergraduates work part time. Average annual earnings from campus work are $1800. The Mount is a member of CSS. The FAFSA is required.
International Students: There were 3 international students enrolled in a recent year. They must score 550 on the written TOEFL.
Computers: The mainframe is a Sequent S27. There are 40 PCs available in a lab for word processing, database use, computer programming, and Internet access. All students may access the system during regular working hours, 4 nights per week, and from 3 P.M. to 11 P.M. on Sunday. There are no time limits and no fees.
Graduates: The most popular majors among 2003 graduates were nursing (32%), liberal studies (11%), and business (9%). In an average class, 66% graduate in 5 years or less.
Admissions Contact: Dean Kilgour, Dean of Admissions.
E-mail: *admissions@msmc.la.edu* Web: *www.msmc.la.edu*

NATIONAL UNIVERSITY　　　　　　　D-5
La Jolla, CA 92037
　　　　　　　　　　　　　　　　(858) 541-7701
　　　　　　　　(800) NAT-UNIV; Fax: (858) 541-7792

Full-time: 822 men, 1134 women	**Faculty:** 197; IIA, av$
Part-time: 1100 men, 1344 women	**Ph.Ds:** 94%
Graduate: 5036 men, 8066 women	**Student/Faculty:** 10 to 1
Year: quarters, summer session	**Tuition:** $9690
Application Deadline: open	**Room & Board:** n/app
Freshman Class: 168 applied, 168 accepted, 63 enrolled	
SAT I or ACT: not required	**SPECIAL**

National University, founded in 1971, is a private, nonprofit institution offering lifelong learning opportunities to adult learners in 11 major metropolitan areas. Disciplines include business, technology, criminal justice, computers, education, human services, nursing, counseling, arts and sciences, and math. There are 3 undergraduate and 4 graduate schools. In addition to regional accreditation, National has baccalaureate program accreditation with CCNE, CCTC, and IACBE. The library contains 210,916 volumes, 2,696,789 microform items, and 6322 audio/video tapes/CDs, and subscribes to 2232 periodicals. Computerized library services include the card catalog, interlibrary loans, database searching, and Internet access. Special learning facilities include a learning resource center. The 15-acre campus is in an urban area 3 miles northeast of downtown San Diego. There are 8 buildings.
Student Life: All students are from California. 58% are white; 16% Hispanic; 10% African American. The average age of freshmen is 29; all undergraduates, 32. 32% do not continue beyond their first year.
Housing: There are no residence halls. All students commute. Alcohol is not permitted. All students may keep cars.
Activities: There are no fraternities or sororities. There is an honors group on campus.
Sports: There is no sports program at National.
Disabled Students: All of the campus is accessible. Wheelchair ramps, elevators, special parking, specially equipped rest rooms, special class scheduling, lowered drinking fountains, and lowered telephones are available.
Services: Counseling and information services are available. Instruction is offered in math and English through the Writing Center. There is remedial math, reading, and writing.
Campus Safety and Security: Measures include 24-hour foot and vehicle patrol and lighted pathways/sidewalks.

Programs of Study: National confers B.A., B.S., B.B.A., and B.S.N. degrees. Associate and master's degrees are also awarded. Bachelor's degrees are awarded in BIOLOGICAL SCIENCE (life science), BUSINESS (accounting, banking and finance, business administration and management, management information systems, and organizational behavior), COMMUNICATIONS AND THE ARTS (communications, English, and media arts), COMPUTER AND PHYSICAL SCIENCE (computer science, earth science, information sciences and systems, and mathematics), HEALTH PROFESSIONS (nursing), SOCIAL SCIENCE (behavioral science, criminal justice, interdisciplinary studies, international studies, law, liberal arts/general studies, and psychology). Computer science, accounting, and psychology are the strongest academically. Business and computer science are the largest.

Required: To graduate, students must complete a total of 180 quarter hours, including 36 upper-division quarter units, with a minimum GPA of 2.0. A minimum of 45 hours in the major and 67 quarter units in general education are required.

Special: There are 3 national honor societies, and 2 departmental honors programs.

Faculty/Classroom: 67% of faculty are male; 33%, female. All both teach and do research. No introductory courses are taught by graduate students. The average class size in an introductory lecture is 18 and in a regular course, 18.

Admissions: All of the 2003-2004 applicants were accepted.

Requirements: Graduation from an accredited secondary school or satisfactory scores on the GED are required for admission. Applicants are generally expected to have 5 or more years of successful work experience. National requires an interview. AP and CLEP credits are accepted. Important factors in the admissions decision are leadership record, evidence of special talent, and advanced placement or honor courses.

Procedure: Freshmen are admitted to all sessions. There is a deferred admissions plan. Application deadlines are open. Application fee is $60. Notification is sent on a rolling basis. Applications are accepted on-line through *www.nu.edu/getmoreinfo.html.*

Transfer: 4949 transfer students enrolled in 2002-2003. Transfer applicants must have a minimum GPA of 2.0. Transcripts from all previous institutions attended must be submitted. 45 of 180 credits required for the bachelor's degree must be completed at National.

Visiting: There are guides for informal visits and visitors may sit in on classes. To schedule a visit, contact the Associate Regional Dean at *nrohland@nu.edu.*

Financial Aid: In a recent year, 70% of continuing full-time students received some form of financial aid, including need-based aid. National is a member of CSS. The CSS/Profile or FAFSA and the college's own financial statement are required. Application deadlines are open.

International Students: There were 222 international students enrolled in a recent year. The school actively recruits these students. They must score 525 on the written TOEFL or take the MELAB.

Computers: The mainframe is an IBM 3081-GX. Students have access to National's PC labs. All students may access the system Monday through Friday, 8 A.M. to 9 P.M., and Saturday, 8 A.M. to 2 P.M. There are no time limits and no fees.

Graduates: From July 1, 2002 to June 30, 2003, 1349 bachelor's degrees were awarded. The most popular majors were education (23%), arts/reading (14%), and science/special education (7%).

Admissions Contact: Nancy Rohland, Associate Regional Dean.
E-mail: *admissions@nu.edu* Web: *www.nu.edu*

Activities: There are no fraternities or sororities. There are 10 groups on campus, including band, drama, ethnic, film, gay, literary magazine, newspaper, political, professional, social, social service, and student government. Popular campus events include an arts and social change showcase, movie nights, and acoustic band nights.

Sports: There is 1 intercollegiate sports program for men.

Disabled Students: 60% of the campus is accessible. Wheelchair ramps, specially equipped rest rooms, and special class scheduling are available.

Services: There is remedial math, reading, and writing.

Campus Safety and Security: Measures include front-desk security in all buildings.

Programs of Study: New College confers the B.A. degree. Master's degrees are also awarded. Bachelor's degrees are awarded in COMMUNICATIONS AND THE ARTS (dramatic arts, English, film arts, fine arts, music, and Spanish), SOCIAL SCIENCE (anthropology, political science/government, psychology, and social science). Humanities is the strongest academically and is the largest.

Required: To graduate, students must complete at least 120 credit hours, including 30 in the major. Requirements include 6 units of core humanities and 3 units each of arts, literature or writing, social sciences, scientific reasoning, quantitative reasoning, research methods, a practicum, and a senior project. A minimum GPA of 2.0 is required.

Special: Internships include a required 3-unit practicum on or off campus. New College offers work-study programs, independent study, study abroad in Mexico and Nepal, an accelerated degree program, student-designed majors, and pass/fail options. Students can earn up to 30 units of credit for prior life, military, and work experience.

Faculty/Classroom: 60% of faculty are male; 40%, female. 80% teach undergraduates. The average class size in an introductory lecture is 12; in a laboratory, 10; and in a regular course, 12.

Requirements: New College requires graduation from an accredited secondary school; the GED is also accepted. An essay is required. AP and CLEP credits are accepted.

Procedure: Freshmen are admitted fall and spring. There is a deferred admissions plan and a rolling admissions plan. The college accepts all applicants. Check with the school for current deadlines and fees.

Transfer: 30 of 120 credits required for the bachelor's degree must be completed at New College.

Visiting: There are regularly scheduled orientations for prospective students, consisting of monthly open houses. There are guides for informal visits and visitors may sit in on classes. To schedule a visit, contact the Admissions Coordinator.

Financial Aid: In a recent year, 85% of undergraduates worked part time. Average annual earnings from campus work were $3500. New College is a member of CSS. The FAFSA and the college's own financial statement are required. Check with the school for current deadlines.

International Students: They must score 500 on the written TOEFL.

Computers: The mainframe is a Prime unit. Terminals are located in the library. IBMs and Macs are available for word processing and layout and design. All students may access the system. There are no time limits and no fees.

Graduates: In an average class, 50% graduate in 4 years or less, 80% graduate in 5 years or less, and 100% graduate in 6 years or less. Of the 2002 graduating class, 30% were enrolled in graduate school within 6 months of graduation and 75% were employed.

Admissions Contact: Admissions Coordinator.
E-mail: *admissions@newcollege.edu* Web: *www.newcollege.edu*

NEW COLLEGE OF CALIFORNIA
B-3
San Francisco, CA 94110
(415) 437-3460
(888) 437-3460; Fax: (415) 437-3417

Full-time: 60 men, 80 women	Faculty: 16
Part-time: 10 women	Ph.D.s: 20%
Graduate: 10 men, 10 women	Student/Faculty: 11 to 1
Year: semesters, summer session	Tuition: $8900
Application Deadline: see profile	Room & Board: n/app
Freshman Class: n/av	
SAT I or ACT: not required	NONCOMPETITIVE

New College of California, founded in 1971, is a private college offering a liberal arts program. Figures in the above capsule and in this profile are approximate. The library contains 30,000 volumes. Computerized library services include the card catalog, interlibrary loans, and database searching. Special learning facilities include a learning resource center a video-editing lab, and a theater. The 2-acre campus is in an urban area in the mission district of San Francisco. There are 3 buildings.

Student Life: 70% of undergraduates are from California. Students are from 10 states, 5 foreign countries, and Canada. 80% are from public schools. 61% are white; 16% African American; 10% Hispanic. The average age of freshmen is 25; all undergraduates, 28. 30% do not continue beyond their first year; 70% remain to graduate.

Housing: There are no residence halls. All students commute. Alcohol is not permitted.

NOTRE DAME DE NAMUR UNIVERSITY
B-3
Belmont, CA 94002
(650) 508-3607
(800) 263-0545; Fax: (650) 508-3426

Full-time: 175 men, 420 women	Faculty: 44; IIA, av$
Part-time: 105 men, 275 women	Ph.D.s: 75%
Graduate: 160 men, 445 women	Student/Faculty: 14 to 1
Year: semesters, summer session	Tuition: $18,460
Application Deadline: see profile	Room & Board: $8480
Freshman Class: n/av	
SAT I or ACT: required	LESS COMPETITIVE

The College of Notre Dame, founded in 1851, is an independent liberal arts institution affiliated with the Roman Catholic Church. Figures in the above capsule and in this profile are approximate. There is 1 graduate school. In addition to regional accreditation, CND has baccalaureate program accreditation with NASM and NCATE. The library contains 100,000 volumes, 68,975 microform items, and 7960 audio/video tapes/CDs, and subscribes to 750 periodicals. Computerized library services include the card catalog, interlibrary loans, and database searching. Special learning facilities include an art gallery and and the Archives of Modern Christian Art. The 80-acre campus is in a suburban area 25 miles south of San Francisco. Including any residence halls, there are 23 buildings.

Student Life: 80% of undergraduates are from California. Students are from 23 states, 18 foreign countries, and Canada. 70% are from public schools. 38% are white; 25% Asian American; 17% foreign nationals; 13% Hispanic. 55% are Catholic; 30% claim no religious affiliation. The average age of freshmen is 18; all undergraduates, 24. 19% do not continue beyond their first year; 60% remain to graduate.

Housing: 300 students can be accommodated in college housing, which includes coed dorms and on-campus apartments. On-campus housing is guaranteed for all 4 years. 63% of students commute. All students may keep cars.

Activities: There are no fraternities or sororities. There are 27 groups on campus, including academic, art, band, cheerleading, choir, chorale, chorus, computers, dance, drama, ethnic, gay, honors, international, jazz band, literary magazine, musical theater, newspaper, orchestra, photography, political, professional, religious, social, social service, student government, symphony, and yearbook. Popular campus events include Honors Day, Ralston Concert Series, and Fiesta Latina.

Sports: There are 5 intercollegiate sports for men and 6 for women, and 2 intramural sports for men and 2 for women. Facilities include a gym, a recreation center, tennis courts, a soccer field, a weight room, a swimming pool, a par course, an arcade, and pool and Ping-Pong tables.

Disabled Students: 90% of the campus is accessible. Wheelchair ramps, special parking, specially equipped rest rooms, and special class scheduling are available.

Services: Counseling and information services are available, as is tutoring in every subject. There is remedial math, reading, and writing.

Campus Safety and Security: Measures include 24-hour foot and vehicle patrol, security escort services, informal discussions, and pamphlets/posters/films. There are lighted pathways/sidewalks.

Programs of Study: CND confers B.A., B.S., B.F.A., and B.Mus. degrees. Associate and master's degrees are also awarded. Bachelor's degrees are awarded in BIOLOGICAL SCIENCE (biochemistry and biology/biological science), BUSINESS (accounting, banking and finance, business administration and management, business economics, international business management, and marketing/retailing/merchandising), COMMUNICATIONS AND THE ARTS (art, communications, dramatic arts, English, fine arts, French, graphic design, and music), COMPUTER AND PHYSICAL SCIENCE (computer science, information sciences and systems, and mathematics), EDUCATION (social studies), HEALTH PROFESSIONS (predentistry, premedicine, prepharmacy, and preveterinary science), SOCIAL SCIENCE (history, human services, humanities, Latin American studies, liberal arts/general studies, philosophy, political science/government, prelaw, psychology, religion, social science, and sociology). Biology, premedicine, and English are the strongest academically. Business administration, liberal studies, and psychology are the largest.

Required: All students must complete general education requirements, 3 units of career development, and a writing proficiency exam. American history is required for those students who have not completed this course in an American high school. A total of 124 semester units with an overall GPA of 2.0 is required in order to graduate.

Special: The college offers a Washington semester through Trinity College as well as an exchange program with Emmanuel College in Boston. Internships, accelerated degree programs in business administration and human service, B.A.-B.S. degrees in biology and biochemistry, a 3-2 engineering degree with Boston University, dual and student-designed majors, a general studies degree, credit for military experience, and pass/fail options are offered. Study abroad is available in 7 countries. Nondegree study is possible. There are 3 national honor societies and a freshman honors program.

Faculty/Classroom: 46% of faculty are male; 54%, female. 71% teach undergraduates. No introductory courses are taught by graduate students. The average class size in an introductory lecture is 25; in a laboratory, 10; and in a regular course, 15.

Admissions: 1 freshman graduated first in the class in a recent year.

Requirements: The SAT I or ACT is required. The average GPA is a 3.2. The average combined SAT I is approximately 1000. In addition, applicants should have completed 13 Carnegie units, including 4 years of high school English, 2 each of math, history/social studies, foreign language, and 1 of lab science. In addition, students should have 1 year in 3 of these areas beyond the basic requirements. An essay is required. An audition is required for music majors. A GPA of 2.0 is required. AP and CLEP credits are accepted. Important factors in the admissions decision are advanced placement or honor courses, evidence of special talent, and leadership record.

Procedure: Freshmen are admitted to all sessions. Entrance exams should be taken by the December test date of the senior year. There is a deferred admissions plan and a rolling admissions plan. Check with the school for current deadlines. The application fee is $40.

Transfer: Transfer applicants must have a 2.0 GPA to be considered for admission. 24 of 124 credits required for the bachelor's degree must be completed at CND.

Visiting: There are regularly scheduled orientations for prospective students, consisting of tours and information on student life, financial aid, and academics. There are guides for informal visits and visitors may sit in on classes and stay overnight. To schedule a visit, contact the Admission Office.

Financial Aid: In a recent year, the average freshman award was $19,753. 25% of undergraduates work part time. Average annual earnings from campus work are $1168. CND is a member of CSS. The FAFSA and the college's own financial statement are required. Check with the school for current deadlines.

International Students: The school actively recruits these students. They must score 500 on the written TOEFL or 173 on the electronic version.

Computers: The mainframe is an IBM AS/400. 3 computer labs are available offering Mac and DOS workstations. All students may access the system 7 days a week. There are no time limits and no fees.

Graduates: In a recent year, in an average class, 56% graduated in 4 years or less.

Admissions Contact: Katy Murphy, Dean of Enrollment.
E-mail: *admiss@ndnu.edu* Web: *www.ndnu.edu*

OCCIDENTAL COLLEGE

Los Angeles, CA 90041

C-5

(323) 259-2700
(800) 825-5262; Fax: (323) 259-2958

Full-time: 764 men, 1059 women	Faculty: 136; IIB, ++$
Part-time: 7 men, 10 women	Ph.D.s: 98%
Graduate: 6 men, 12 women	Student/Faculty: 13 to 1
Year: semesters, summer session	Tuition: $28,092
Application Deadline: January 10	Room & Board: $7830
Freshman Class: 4513 applied, 1964 accepted, 441 enrolled	
SAT I Verbal/Math: 630/630	HIGHLY COMPETITIVE

Occidental College, founded in 1887, is a private nonsectarian school of liberal arts and sciences. The library contains 497,161 volumes, 413,190 microform items, and 17,408 audio/video tapes/CDs, and subscribes to 903 periodicals. Computerized library services include the card catalog, interlibrary loans, database searching, and Internet access. Special learning facilities include a learning resource center, art gallery, radio station, theater, art studio, ornithology collection, and physics, plasma, and optic labs. The 120-acre campus is in an urban area in Los Angeles. Including any residence halls, there are 44 buildings.

Student Life: 56% of undergraduates are from California. Students are from 45 states, 24 foreign countries, and Canada. 61% are from public schools. 53% are white; 15% Hispanic; 12% Asian American. 32% are Protestant; 25% claim no religious affiliation; 22% Catholic; 14% Muslim, Hindu, Buddhist, and Orthodox; 7% Jewish. The average age of freshmen is 18; all undergraduates, 20. 9% do not continue beyond their first year; 78% remain to graduate.

Housing: 1320 students can be accommodated in college housing, which includes single-sex and coed dorms and fraternity houses. In addition, there are special-interest houses. On-campus housing is guaranteed for the freshman year only and is available on a lottery system for upperclassmen. 70% of students live on campus; of those, 60% remain on campus on weekends. All students may keep cars.

Activities: 5% of men belong to 1 national fraternity; 11% of women belong to 2 local sororities. There are 104 groups on campus, including art, cheerleading, chess, choir, chorale, dance, debate, drama, ethnic, film, gay, honors, international, investment, jazz band, literary magazine, musical theater, newspaper, orchestra, photography, political, professional, radio and TV, religious, social, social service, student government, symphony, and yearbook. Popular campus events include Da Getaway, Asian Pacific Heritage Week, and World Music Festival.

Sports: There are 9 intercollegiate sports for men and 9 for women, and 3 intramural sports for men and 3 for women. Facilities include football, soccer, baseball, and softball fields, an all-weather track, tennis courts, an outdoor pool, a dance studio, a sports medicine center, gyms, and a weight room.

Disabled Students: 80% of the campus is accessible. Wheelchair ramps, elevators, special parking, specially equipped rest rooms, lowered drinking fountains, and lowered telephones are available.

Services: Counseling and information services are available, as is tutoring in most subjects. Peer and faculty advisers are available through the Center for Teaching and Learning. Academic success workshops, individual counseling, and learning disability services are also available.

Campus Safety and Security: Measures include 24-hour foot and vehicle patrol, security escort services, shuttle buses, and informal discussions. There are pamphlets/posters/films, emergency telephones, and lighted pathways/sidewalks. Residence halls are always locked; a whistle alert program is available.

Programs of Study: Oxy confers the A.B. degree. Master's degrees are also awarded. Bachelor's degrees are awarded in BIOLOGICAL SCIENCE (biochemistry and biology/biological science), COMMUNICATIONS AND THE ARTS (art history and appreciation, comparative literature, dramatic arts, French, German, languages, music, and Spanish), COMPUTER AND PHYSICAL SCIENCE (chemistry, geochemistry, geology, geophysics and seismology, mathematics, and physics), ENGINEERING AND ENVIRONMENTAL DESIGN (environmental science), SOCIAL SCIENCE (American studies, anthropology, Asian/Oriental studies, cognitive science, economics, history, international relations, philosophy, physical fitness/movement, political science/government, psychobiology, psychology, religion, sociology, urban studies, and women's studies). Social sciences, biology, and chemistry are the strongest academically. Social sciences, English, and diplomacy and world affairs are the largest.

Required: To graduate, students must complete 32 courses of 4 semester hours each and maintain a minimum GPA of 2.0. In addition, all students must fulfill core course requirements in foreign language, fine arts, and writing proficiency; 12 units are required in science and math and cultural studies. To graduate, all students must complete a comprehensive exam; some majors require a thesis.

Special: Cross-registration is permitted with the California Institute of Technology and the Art Center College of Design. Cooperative programs are available with Columbia University. Students may study abroad in 29 countries in Europe, Asia, Africa, and Latin America. Opportunities are provided for internships, a Washington semester, a U.N. semester in New York City, work-study programs, B.A.-B.S. degrees, dual and student-designed majors, a 3-2 engineering degree with the California Institute of Technology, a 3-3 law program with Columbia, a 4-2 biotech program with Keck, an exchange program with Spelman and Morehouse, credit by exam, nondegree study, and pass/fail options. There are 8 national honor societies, including Phi Beta Kappa. All departments have honors programs.

Faculty/Classroom: 57% of faculty are male; 43%, female. All both teach and do research. No introductory courses are taught by graduate students. The average class size in an introductory lecture is 22; in a laboratory, 15; and in a regular course, 20.

Admissions: 44% of the 2003-2004 applicants were accepted. 81% of the current freshmen were in the top fifth of their class; 98% were in the top two fifths. 23 freshmen graduated first in their class.

Requirements: The SAT I or ACT is required. In addition, applicants should be high school graduates of high academic standing with 4 years each of English and math, 3 each of foreign language and science, and 2 each of social studies and history. The GED is accepted. An essay is required, and an interview is recommended. AP credits are accepted. Important factors in the admissions decision are extracurricular activities record, advanced placement or honor courses, and recommendations by school officials.

Procedure: Freshmen are admitted in the fall. Entrance exams should be taken no later than December of the senior year. There are early decision and deferred admissions plans. Early decision applications should be filed by November 15; regular applications, by January 10 for fall entry, along with a $50 fee. Notification of early decision is sent December 15; regular decision, April 1. 45 early decision candidates were accepted for the 2003-2004 class. 592 applicants were on the 2003 waiting list; 99 were admitted. Applications are accepted on-line through Common App or the school's web site.

Transfer: 53 transfer students enrolled in 2002-2003. Students must have at least a B average (3.0 GPA) in all courses submitted for transfer credit. The SAT I or ACT is required. The application deadline is March 15 for the fall, November 1 for the spring. 64 of 128 credits required for the bachelor's degree must be completed at Oxy.

Visiting: There are regularly scheduled orientations for prospective students, including campus tours Monday through Friday at 10:30 A.M. and 3 P.M., followed by information sessions with an admission officer at 11:30 A.M. and 4 P.M. There are guides for informal visits and visitors may sit in on classes and stay overnight. To schedule a visit, contact the Office of Admission.

Financial Aid: In 2002-2003, 61% of all full-time freshmen and 70% of continuing full-time students received some form of financial aid. 60% of full-time freshmen and 70% of continuing full-time students received need-based aid. The average freshman award was $25,878. 59% of undergraduates work part time. The average financial indebtedness of the 2003 graduate was $13,591. Oxy is a member of CSS. The CSS/Profile or FAFSA, noncustodial parent's statement, and business farm supplement are required. The deadline for filing freshman financial aid applications for fall entry is February 1.

International Students: There are 77 international students enrolled. The school actively recruits these students. They must score 600 on the written TOEFL or 250 on the electronic version and also take the SAT I or the ACT.

Computers: The mainframe is an Enterprise E420R. Macs and PCs are available in the library's computer center. 206 PCs are available in library and dorm labs, and the entire campus has wireless access to the campus network and the Internet. All students may access the system at any time. There are no time limits and no fees.

Graduates: From July 1, 2002 to June 30, 2003, 404 bachelor's degrees were awarded. The most popular majors were economics (12%), psychology (9%), and English (9%). In an average class, 75% graduate in 4 years or less, 78% graduate in 5 years or less, and 79% graduate in 6 years or less. Of the 2002 graduating class, 28% were enrolled in graduate school within 6 months of graduation.

Admissions Contact: Vince Cuseo, Director of Admission.
E-mail: *admission@oxy.edu* Web: *www.oxy.edu*

OTIS COLLEGE OF ART AND DESIGN
Los Angeles, CA 90045

C-2
(310) 665-6820
(800) 527-6847; Fax: (310) 665-6821

Full-time: 352 men, 653 women	**Faculty:** 38
Part-time: 6 men, 12 women	**Ph.D.s:** 71%
Graduate: 13 men, 30 women	**Student/Faculty:** 26 to 1
Year: semesters, summer session	**Tuition:** $23,420
Application Deadline: open	**Room & Board:** n/app
Freshman Class: 557 accepted, 250 enrolled	
SAT I Verbal/Math: 488/513	**ACT:** 22 **SPECIAL**

Otis College of Art and Design, founded in 1918, is a private, not-for-profit college offering undergraduate programs in fine arts, ceramics, graphic design and illustration, environmental design, fashion design, toy design, and digital media design and graduate programs in fine arts and writing. As part of their instruction, students work directly with professional artists, designers, critics, and writers. There are 3 undergraduate schools and 1 graduate school. In addition to regional accreditation, Otis has baccalaureate program accreditation with NASAD. The library contains 42,000 volumes and 2500 audio/video tapes/CDs, and subscribes to 150 periodicals. Computerized library services include the card catalog and database searching. Special learning facilities include an art gallery, a photographic darkroom, printmaking studios, a fine books press room, a woodworking studio, a digital imaging room, a metalworking shop, and multiuse studios. The 5-acre campus is in an urban area on the west side of Los Angeles. There are 3 buildings.

Student Life: 72% of undergraduates are from California. Students are from 50 states, 32 foreign countries, and Canada. 75% are from public schools. 33% are white; 30% Asian American; 12% nonresidential aliens; 12% Hispanic. The average age of all undergraduates is 22. 31% do not continue beyond their first year.

Housing: There are no residence halls. All students commute. Alcohol is not permitted. All students may keep cars.

Activities: There are no fraternities or sororities. There are some groups and organizations on campus, including literary magazine, newspaper, and student government. Popular campus events include gallery openings, a yearly fashion design show, and a student leadership retreat.

Sports: There is no sports program at Otis.

Disabled Students: All of the campus is accessible. Wheelchair ramps, elevators, special parking, specially equipped rest rooms, lowered drinking fountains, and lowered telephones are available.

Services: Counseling and information services are available, as is tutoring in most subjects. There is remedial math, reading, and writing.

Campus Safety and Security: Measures include 24-hour foot and vehicle patrol, self-defense education, security escort services, and informal discussions. There are pamphlets/posters/films, emergency telephones, and lighted pathways/sidewalks.

Programs of Study: Otis confers the B.F.A. degree. Master's degrees are also awarded. Bachelor's degrees are awarded in COMMUNICATIONS AND THE ARTS (advertising, design, graphic design, illustration, painting, photography, and toy design), COMPUTER AND PHYSICAL SCIENCE (digital arts/technology), ENGINEERING AND ENVIRONMENTAL DESIGN (environmental design), SOCIAL SCIENCE (fashion design and technology). Graphic design and digital media are the strongest academically. Digital media design, communication arts (graphic design and illustration) and fashion design are the largest.

Required: The Bachelor of Fine Arts is awarded to students in good academic standing who have successfully completed no less than 130 credits, of which a minimum of 30 are in the liberal arts, and 12 in the history of art and design. Graduation requirements include course work in computer literacy, English, humanities, math, biological or physical sciences, and social science.

Special: Study abroad is available in London, Paris, and Stockholm. Internships and independent study are also available. There is a freshman honors program.

Faculty/Classroom: 45% of faculty are male; 55%, female. All teach undergraduates.

Admissions: The SAT I scores for the 2003-2004 freshman class were: Verbal--53% below 500, 28% between 500 and 599, 16% between 600 and 700, and 3% above 700; Math--44% below 500, 40% between 500 and 599, 13% between 600 and 700, and 3% above 700. The ACT scores were 48% below 21, 13% between 21 and 23, 13% between 24 and 26, 13% between 27 and 28, and 13% above 28.

Requirements: The SAT I or ACT is required. In addition, applicants must be graduates of an accredited secondary school or have a GED certificate, and submit a portfolio. Interviews are recommended for students, and essays are required. Applicants must have 4 units of English, 3 of math, 2 each of science (1 lab) and history, and 1 of social studies. A GPA of 2.5 is required. AP credits are accepted.

Procedure: Freshmen are admitted fall and spring. Entrance exams should be taken in the fall. Application deadlines are open. There is a rolling admissions plan. Notification is sent on a rolling basis. Application fee is $50. Applications are accepted on-line through the school's web site.

Transfer: 170 transfer students enrolled in 2002-2003. Transfer students must have a minimum 2.5 GPA and submit high school and college transcripts, an essay, and a statement of good standing from prior institutions. A portfolio is required. An interview is recommended. 62 of 130 credits required for the bachelor's degree must be completed at Otis.

Visiting: There are regularly scheduled orientations for prospective students, including a campus tour and departmental, portfolio, and financial aid presentations. There are guides for informal visits and visitors may sit in on classes. To schedule a visit, contact the Admissions Office.

Financial Aid: In 2003-2004, 72% of all full-time freshmen and 74% of continuing full-time students received some form of financial aid. At least 64% of full-time freshmen and 63% of continuing full-time students received need-based aid. The average freshman award was $9899. Need-based scholarships or need-based grants averaged $7927; need-based self-help aid (loans and jobs) averaged $2340; and other non-need-based awards and non-need-based scholarships averaged $3558. The average financial indebtedness of the 2003 graduate was $25,700. The FAFSA and the state aid form are required. The priority date for freshman financial aid applications for fall entry is February 15.

International Students: There were 106 international students enrolled in a recent year. The school actively recruits these students. They must score 550 on the written TOEFL or 213 on the electronic version. Students from countries where English is the official language should take the ACT or SAT I, not the TOEFL.

Computers: The computer center consists of the Open Access Media Lab and 3 computer classrooms. All students must pass a computer literacy exam prior to gaining access to computer labs and software. All students may access the system. There are no time limits and no fees. It is strongly recommended that all students have a personal computer.

Graduates: From July 1, 2002 to June 30, 2003, 163 bachelor's degrees were awarded. In an average class, 35% graduate in 4 years or less, 3% graduate in 5 years or less, and 2% graduate in 6 years or less.

Admissions Contact: Marc D. Meredith, Dean of Admissions.
E-mail: *admissions@otis.edu* Web: *http://www.otis.edu*

PACIFIC UNION COLLEGE
Angwin, CA 94508-9707

B-2

(707) 965-6336
(800) 862-7080; Fax: (707) 965-6432

Full-time: 649 men, 784 women	**Faculty:** 100
Part-time: 2 men, 3 women	**Ph.D.s:** 56%
Graduate: 8 women	**Student/Faculty:** 14 to 1
Year: quarters, summer session	**Tuition:** $17,115
Application Deadline: open	**Room & Board:** $4950
Freshman Class: 1690 applied, 583 accepted, 318 enrolled	
SAT I Verbal/Math: 512/498	**ACT:** 22 **COMPETITIVE+**

Pacific Union College, founded in 1888, is a private college affiliated with the Seventh-day Adventist Church offering programs in liberal arts, religion, business, health science, and teacher preparation, among others. In addition to regional accreditation, PUC has baccalaureate program accreditation with CAADE, CCTC, CSWE, IACBE, NASM, and NLN. The library contains 137,148 volumes, 121,991 microform items, and 5394 audio/video tapes/CDs, and subscribes to 827 periodicals. Computerized library services include the card catalog, interlibrary loans, database searching, and Internet access. Special learning facilities include a learning resource center, art gallery, natural history museum, radio station, and video production studio, and an observatory. The 2000-acre campus is in a small town 70 miles north of San Francisco. Including any residence halls, there are 60 buildings.

Student Life: 72% of undergraduates are from California. Students are from 18 states, 19 foreign countries, and Canada. 47% are white; 19% Asian American; 10% foreign nationals; 10% Hispanic. Most claim no religious affiliation. The average age of freshmen is 19.

Housing: 1344 students can be accommodated in college housing, which includes single-sex dorms and married-student housing. On-campus housing is guaranteed for all 4 years. 80% of students live on campus. Alcohol is not permitted. All students may keep cars.

Activities: There are no fraternities or sororities. There are 50 groups on campus, including academic, art, band, campus ministries, chess, choir, chorale, computers, drama, ethnic, film, honors, jazz band, literary magazine, newspaper, orchestra, photography, political, radio and TV, religious, social, student government, symphony, and yearbook. Popular campus events include picnic and ski days, All-College Get-Acquainted Party, and Fall Festival.

Sports: There are 3 intercollegiate sports for men and 3 for women, and 6 intramural sports for men and 6 for women. Facilities include a gym, a pool, a stadium, lighted tennis courts, and 3 athletic fields for softball, soccer, volleyball, flagball, and track and field.

Disabled Students: 95% of the campus is accessible. Wheelchair ramps, elevators, special parking, specially equipped rest rooms, and special class scheduling are available.

Services: Counseling and information services are available, as is tutoring in most subjects. There is a reader service for the blind and remedial math and writing.

Campus Safety and Security: Measures include 24-hour foot and vehicle patrol, self-defense education, security escort services, and informal discussions. There are pamphlets/posters/films, emergency telephones, lighted pathways/sidewalks, and a safety committee.

Programs of Study: PUC confers B.A., B.S., B.B.A., B.Mus., B.S.Med.Tech., and B.S.W. degrees. Associate and master's degrees are also awarded. Bachelor's degrees are awarded in BIOLOGICAL SCIENCE (biology/biological science and biophysics), BUSINESS (business administration and management and recreation and leisure services), COMMUNICATIONS AND THE ARTS (communications, English, fine arts, French, graphic design, journalism, music, public relations, and Spanish), COMPUTER AND PHYSICAL SCIENCE (applied mathematics, chemistry, computer science, digital arts/technology, mathematics, natural sciences, and physics), EDUCATION (early childhood and physical), ENGINEERING AND ENVIRONMENTAL DESIGN (airline piloting and navigation, electrical/electronics engineering technology, engineering technology, and graphic arts technology), HEALTH PROFESSIONS (medical laboratory technology and nursing), SOCIAL SCIENCE (behavioral science, history, psychology, religion, social studies, social work, sociology, and theological studies). Sciences and behavioral science are the strongest academically. Nursing and business administration are the largest.

Required: To graduate, a student must complete a minimum of 192 quarter hours, including 60 in upper-level courses. The student must maintain a minimum GPA of 2.0. The required total hours in the major and the general education requirements vary according to the major. A religion course is required, as is a thesis in some programs.

Special: Students may study abroad in Austria, Spain, France, Argentina, and Italy, earn B.A.-B.S. degrees, take dual majors, and pursue a major in interdisciplinary studies. Internships and accelerated degree programs are also offered. The college offers nondegree study and credit for life, military, and work experience. There are 5 national honor societies and a freshman honors program.

Faculty/Classroom: 61% of faculty are male; 39%, female. 99% teach undergraduates. The average class size in an introductory lecture is 19; in a laboratory, 18; and in a regular course, 17.

Admissions: 34% of the 2003-2004 applicants were accepted. The SAT I scores for the 2003-2004 freshman class were: Verbal--38% below 500, 38% between 500 and 599, 19% between 600 and 700, and 5% above 700; Math--42% below 500, 35% between 500 and 599, 20% between 600 and 700, and 3% above 700. The ACT scores were 38% below 21, 25% between 21 and 23, 22% between 24 and 26, 7% between 27 and 28, and 8% above 28. 21% of the current freshmen were in the top fifth of their class; 50% were in the top two fifths.

Requirements: The ACT is recommended. Scores are used only for advising purposes. Candidates for admission should have completed 4 years of English, 2 of math, and 1 each of science and history. A GPA of 2.3 is required. AP and CLEP credits are accepted. Important factors in the admissions decision are recommendations by school officials, leadership record, and advanced placement or honor courses.

Procedure: Freshmen are admitted to all sessions. Entrance exams should be taken in the junior or senior year. Application deadlines are open. Application fee is $30. Applications are accepted on-line through the school's web site.

Transfer: 183 transfer students enrolled in a recent year. Admission requirements are the same as for nontransfer students. 36 of 192 credits required for the bachelor's degree must be completed at PUC.

Visiting: There are regularly scheduled orientations for prospective students. There are guides for informal visits and visitors may sit in on classes and stay overnight. To schedule a visit, contact the Admissions Office at (707) 965-6425.

Financial Aid: In a recent year, 99% of all full-time students received some form of financial aid. 96% of full-time freshmen and 95% of continuing full-time students received need-based aid. The average freshman award was $13,136. 80% of undergraduates work part time. Average annual earnings from campus work are $1500. The average financial indebtedness of a recent graduate was $12,000. The FAFSA and the college's own financial statement are required. The deadline for filing freshman financial aid applications for fall entry is March 2.

International Students: There are 114 international students enrolled. They must score 450 on the written TOEFL or 133 on the electronic version and also take the SAT I or the ACT.

Computers: Campus-wide access is available in dorms, labs, and the library. All students may access the system at any time. There are no time limits and no fees. It is strongly recommended that all students have a personal computer.

Graduates: The most popular majors were nursing (11%), early childhood education (9%), and business (7%). In an average class, 12% graduate in 4 years or less, 19% graduate in 5 years or less, and 21% graduate in 6 years or less.

Admissions Contact: Sean Kootsey, Director of Enrollment Services. A video is available. E-mail: *enroll@puc.edu* Web: *www.puc.edu*

PEPPERDINE UNIVERSITY

Malibu, CA 90263-4392

C-5

(310) 506-4392; Fax: (310) 506-4861

Full-time: 1050 men, 1610 women	Faculty: 167; IIA, ++$
Part-time: 50 men, 80 women	Ph.D.s: 100%
Graduate: 2270 men, 2380 women	Student/Faculty: 16 to 1
Year: semesters, summer session	Tuition: $25,250
Application Deadline: January 15	Room & Board: $8650
Freshman Class: n/av	
SAT I or ACT: required	VERY COMPETITIVE

Pepperdine University, founded in 1937, is a private liberal arts university affiliated with the Church of Christ. Figures in the above capsule and in this profile are approximate. The library contains 470,236 volumes, 455,162 microform items, and 5817 audio/video tapes/CDs, and subscribes to 3134 periodicals. Computerized library services include the card catalog, interlibrary loans, and database searching. Special learning facilities include an art gallery, radio station, TV station, writing center, and Japanese tea ceremony room. The 830-acre campus is in a suburban area 35 miles northwest of Los Angeles, overlooking the Pacific Ocean. Including any residence halls, there are 76 buildings.

Student Life: 51% of undergraduates are from California. Students are from 49 states, 53 foreign countries, and Canada. 65% are from public schools. 60% are white. 65% are Protestant; 17% Catholic; 17% 12% undeclared, 6% other, 1% Islamic, 1% Orthodox, 1% Buddist. The average age of freshmen is 18; all undergraduates, 20. 15% do not continue beyond their first year; 70% remain to graduate.

Housing: 1863 students can be accommodated in college housing, which includes single-sex dorms, on-campus apartments, and married-student housing. On-campus housing is guaranteed for all 4 years. 65% of students live on campus; of those, 55% remain on campus on weekends. Alcohol is not permitted. All students may keep cars.

Activities: 25% of men belong to 6 national fraternities; 25% of women belong to 8 national sororities. There are 50 groups on campus, including art, band, cheerleading, chess, choir, chorale, chorus, computers, cycling, dance, debate, drama, equestrian, ethnic, honors, international, jazz band, literary magazine, musical theater, newspaper, opera, orchestra, pep band, photography, political, professional, radio and TV, religious, social, social service, student government, symphony, and yearbook. Popular campus events include Midnight Madness, Songfest, and Parents Weekend.

Sports: There are 7 intercollegiate sports for men and 7 for women, and 11 intramural sports for men and 11 for women. Facilities include a field house, a pool, a weight room, basketball, racquetball, and tennis courts, playing fields, an all-weather track, an aerobics room, and a whirlpool/hot tub.

Disabled Students: Wheelchair ramps, elevators, special parking, specially equipped rest rooms, special class scheduling, lowered drinking fountains, and lowered telephones are available.

Services: Counseling and information services are available, as is tutoring in most subjects.

Campus Safety and Security: Measures include 24-hour foot and vehicle patrol, self-defense education, security escort services, and shuttle buses. There are informal discussions, pamphlets/posters/films, emergency telephones, lighted pathways/sidewalks, guarded entrances to campus, security cameras, late-night escort service, and campus crimewatch program.

Programs of Study: Pepperdine confers B.A., B.S., and B.S.M. degrees. Master's and doctoral degrees are also awarded. Bachelor's degrees are awarded in BIOLOGICAL SCIENCE (biology/biological science and nutrition), BUSINESS (accounting, business administration and management, and international business management), COMMUNICATIONS AND THE ARTS (advertising, art, communications, dramatic arts, English, French, German, journalism, music, public relations, Spanish, speech/debate/rhetoric, and telecommunications), COMPUTER AND PHYSICAL SCIENCE (chemistry, computer science, mathematics, and natural sciences), EDUCATION (elementary, physical, and secondary), ENGINEERING AND ENVIRONMENTAL DESIGN (engineering), HEALTH PROFESSIONS (sports medicine), SOCIAL SCIENCE (economics, history, humanities, international studies, liberal arts/general studies, philosophy, political science/government, psychology, religion, social science, and sociology). Natural sciences (premedical), sports medicine, and political science are the strongest academically. Communication and business are the largest.

Required: To graduate, students must complete 128 units, including 64 units of general education requirements. 2 years of a broad liberal arts core curriculum are needed. Courses are required in English, religion, Western heritage, non-Western heritage, American heritage, behavioral science, foreign language, lab science, math, speech and rhetoric, freshman seminar, and phys ed. Students must take at least 40 upper-division units and complete a 28-unit residency requirement. Pepperdine requires a minimum GPA of 2.0 for graduation.

Special: Students may earn 1 to 4 units for an internship, available in most majors, participate in a Washington or a Sacramento semester, and study abroad in 8 countries. The school offers a 3-2 engineering degree

with Washington University in St. Louis, the University of Southern California, and Boston University. There are dual majors in any discipline, student-designed contract majors, federal work-study programs, nondegree study, and pass/fail options. There are 12 national honor societies, a freshman honors program, and 3 departmental honors programs.

Faculty/Classroom: All teach undergraduates. No introductory courses are taught by graduate students. The average class size in an introductory lecture is 18; in a laboratory, 15; and in a regular course, 17.

Requirements: The SAT I or ACT is required. In addition, it is strongly recommended that candidates for admission present a college preparatory program that includes 4 years of English, 3 of math, 2 each of foreign language and science, and courses in speech communication, humanities, and social science. AP and CLEP credits are accepted. Important factors in the admissions decision are advanced placement or honor courses, recommendations by school officials, and evidence of special talent.

Procedure: Freshmen are admitted fall and spring. Entrance exams should be taken in the fall. There are early decision and deferred admissions plans. Check with the school for current application deadlines. The application fee is $55. Applications are available on-line at *www.wavelink.edu.* A waiting-list is an active part of the admissions procedure.

Transfer: Transfer applicants should have a minimum GPA of 2.7 from an accredited college. SAT I or ACT scores are required for applicants who have completed fewer than 30 transferable semester hours at an accredited college. 28 of 128 credits required for the bachelor's degree must be completed at Pepperdine.

Visiting: There are regularly scheduled orientations for prospective students, including tours of the campus, meetings with faculty and current students, and sessions on admission and financial aid; interviews may be arranged on the hour with admission counselors. There are guides for informal visits and visitors may sit in on classes and stay overnight. To schedule a visit, contact the Admissions Office.

Financial Aid: 97% of undergraduates work part time. Average annual earnings from campus work are $1500. Pepperdine is a member of CSS. The FAFSA, the college's own financial statement, the federal income tax form, state scholarship/grant form (California residents), and W-2 wage statement are required. Check with the school for current deadlines.

International Students: The school actively recruits these students. They must score 550 on the written TOEFL and also take the college's own test and the SAT I or the ACT.

Computers: The mainframe is an IBM ES/9000 Model 210. 292 PCs are available to students in residence halls, computer labs, electronic classrooms, the library, and the student center. Access to the minicomputer and mainframe, the library system, and the Internet is available. Students may access the system with permission from the faculty. Word-processing labs are open to all students. There are no time limits and no fees.

Graduates: In an average class, 4% graduate in 3 years or less, 67% graduate in 4 years or less, 65% graduate in 5 years or less, and 75% graduate in 6 years or less.

Admissions Contact: Paul A. Long, Dean of Admission and Enrollment Management. A video is available.
E-mail: *admission-seaver@pepperdine.edu* Web: *www.pepperdine.edu*

PITZER COLLEGE

Claremont, CA 91711-6101

D-5

(909) 621-8129

(800) PITZER-1; Fax: (909) 621-8770

Full-time: 368 men, 524 women	Faculty: 71; IIB, ++$
Part-time: 13 men, 37 women	Ph.D.s: 98%
Graduate: none	Student/Faculty: 13 to 1
Year: semesters	Tuition: $29,794
Application Deadline: January 15	Room & Board: $7796
Freshman Class: 2425 applied, 1215 accepted, 229 enrolled	
SAT I Verbal/Math: 615/620	ACT: 25 HIGHLY COMPETITIVE

Pitzer College, founded in 1963, is a private liberal arts college emphasizing the social and behavioral sciences. It is one of the Claremont Colleges. There are 5 undergraduate and 2 graduate schools. The library contains 2,280,000 volumes, 1.5 million microform items, and 17,000 audio/video tapes/CDs, and subscribes to 5900 periodicals. Computerized library services include the card catalog, interlibrary loans, and database searching. Special learning facilities include an art gallery, radio station, TV station, a social science lab, and an arboretum. The 30-acre campus is in a suburban area 35 miles east of Los Angeles. Including any residence halls, there are 13 buildings.

Student Life: 54% of undergraduates are from California. Students are from 44 states, 14 foreign countries, and Canada. 45% are white; 13% Hispanic; 10% Asian American. The average age of freshmen is 18. 16% do not continue beyond their first year; 70% remain to graduate.

Housing: 601 students can be accommodated in college housing, which includes single-sex and coed dorms and off-campus apartments. In addition, there is a quiet hall, an involvement tower, an A-1 food co-op, and substance-free residences. On-campus housing is guaranteed for the freshman year only. 71% of students live on campus. All students may keep cars.

Activities: There are no fraternities or sororities. There are 25 groups on campus, including art, band, chess, choir, chorale, chorus, computers, dance, debate, drama, ethnic, film, gay, honors, international, jazz band, literary magazine, newspaper, orchestra, photography, political, professional, radio and TV, religious, social, social service, and student government. Popular campus events include the Kohoutek Festival, Atherton dinners, and Marquis Library Firesides.

Sports: There are 10 intercollegiate sports for men and 9 for women. Facilities include 3 gyms, 5 swimming pools, 20 tennis courts, numerous playing fields, and lighted volleyball courts. The campus stadium seats 1200. There are also shared intercollegiate sports with Pomona College. The Gold Student Center features a fitness room, a lap pool, a Frisbee field, and basketball and volleyball courts.

Disabled Students: 95% of the campus is accessible. Wheelchair ramps, elevators, special parking, specially equipped rest rooms, lowered drinking fountains, and lowered telephones are available.

Services: Counseling and information services are available, as is tutoring in every subject and tutoring software and programs for the learning disabled. There is a reader service for the blind and remedial writing.

Campus Safety and Security: Measures include 24-hour foot and vehicle patrol, self-defense education, security escort services, and informal discussions. There are pamphlets/posters/films, emergency telephones, and lighted pathways/sidewalks.

Programs of Study: Pitzer confers the B.A. degree. Bachelor's degrees are awarded in BIOLOGICAL SCIENCE (biochemistry, biology/biological science, and neurosciences), BUSINESS (management engineering and organizational behavior), COMMUNICATIONS AND THE ARTS (art, classics, dance, dramatic arts, English, film arts, French, linguistics, media arts, music, and Spanish), COMPUTER AND PHYSICAL SCIENCE (chemistry, mathematics, physics, science, and science and management), ENGINEERING AND ENVIRONMENTAL DESIGN (environmental science), SOCIAL SCIENCE (African American studies, American studies, anthropology, Asian/American studies, Asian/Oriental studies, Caribbean studies, economics, European studies, history, international relations, Latin American studies, Mexican-American/Chicano studies, philosophy, political science/government, psychology, sociology, Third World studies, and women's studies). Social and behavioral sciences are the strongest academically and the largest.

Required: Students must complete a total of 32 courses with a 2.0 GPA. Although requirements vary according to major, most students take introductory or preparatory courses in their first 2 years and courses in or related to their major in the last 2 years. All students must fulfill educational objectives in the following areas: interdisciplinary and intercultural exploration; social responsibility and the ethical implications of knowledge and action; breadth of knowledge; and written expression.

Special: Students may cross-register at any of the other Claremont Colleges, or study abroad in Africa, Asia, Europe, Latin America, North America, or Oceania. There are co-op programs, work-study, internships, dual majors, student-designed majors, an extensive first-year seminar program, and interdisciplinary study offered in science and technology, and international or intercultural studies. Joint advanced degrees are offered in math, business administration, and public policy, as is a 7-year B.A./D.O. program with the College of Western Health Sciences. There are independent study and limited pass/fail options. Most departments have honors programs.

Faculty/Classroom: 60% of faculty are male; 40%, female. All both teach and do research. The average class size in an introductory lecture is 35; in a laboratory, 50; and in a regular course, 17.

Admissions: 50% of the 2003-2004 applicants were accepted. The SAT I scores for the 2003-2004 freshman class were: Verbal--8% below 500, 32% between 500 and 599, 46% between 600 and 700, and 15% above 700; Math--10% below 500, 30% between 500 and 599, 48% between 600 and 700, and 12% above 700. The ACT scores were 2% between 12 and 17, 32% between 18 and 23, 52% between 24 and 29, and 14% between 30 and 36. 61% of the current freshmen were in the top fifth of their class; 89% were in the top two fifths.

Requirements: The SAT I or ACT is recommended. Starting in fall 2004, Pitzer implemented a 3-year trial that exempts students in the top 10% of their class, or those with an unweighted GPA in academic subjects of 3.5, from submitting ACT or SAT I scores. Students without these qualifications must submit either ACT, SAT I, 2 SAT II, 2 AP test scores over 4 (1 in English, 1 in math or science), 2 IB exams (1 in English, 1 in math) or a higher-level math course, or one recent graded writing sample from a humanities or social science course and a graded advanced math exam, both including teacher's comments and grades. In addition, applicants must be graduates of an accredited secondary school or have earned the GED. Secondary school courses must include 4 years of English courses requiring extensive writing and 3 years each of social and behavioral sciences including history, lab science, foreign language, and math. A personal essay is required, and a personal interview is recommended. AP credits are accepted. Important factors in the

admissions decision are advanced placement or honor courses, leadership record, and evidence of special talent.

Procedure: Freshmen are admitted fall and spring. Entrance exams should be taken by January 15. There are early admissions and deferred admissions plans. Early decision applications should be filed by December 1; regular applications, by January 15 for fall entry and October 15 for spring entry. The fall 2003 application fee was $50. Notification of early decision is sent January 1; regular decision, April 1. 195 applicants were on the 2003 waiting list. Applications are accepted on-line through Common App.

Transfer: 19 transfer students enrolled in 2002-2003. No more than 2 years of previous credits may be transferred. 16 of 32 courses required for the bachelor's degree must be completed at Pitzer.

Visiting: There are regularly scheduled orientations for prospective students. There are guides for informal visits and visitors may sit in on classes and stay overnight. To schedule a visit, contact the Office of Admissions at (909) 621-8889 or campus_visit@pitzer.edu.

Financial Aid: In 2003-2004, 37% of all full-time freshmen and 41% of continuing full-time students received some form of financial aid. 35% of full-time freshmen and 41% of continuing full-time students received need-based aid. The average freshman award was $28,282. 60% of undergraduates work part time. Average annual earnings from campus work are $2300. The average financial indebtedness of the 2003 graduate was $20,900. Pitzer is a member of CSS. The CSS/Profile or FAFSA is required. The deadline for filing freshman financial aid applications for fall entry is February 1.

International Students: There are 37 international students enrolled. The school actively recruits these students. They must score 587 on the written TOEFL or 240 on the electronic version and also take the SAT I or the ACT.

Computers: Macs and PCs are available in labs. All students may access the system. There are no time limits and no fees.

Graduates: From July 1, 2002 to June 30, 2003, 244 bachelor's degrees were awarded. The most popular majors were psychology (15%), sociology (14%), and art/art history (10%). In an average class, 1% graduate in 3 years or less, 64% graduate in 4 years or less, and 9% graduate in 5 years or less. 25 companies recruited on campus in 2002-2003.

Admissions Contact: Arnaldo Rodriguez, Vice President, Admission and Financial Aid. E-mail: admission@pitzer.edu Web: www.pitzer.edu

POINT LOMA NAZARENE UNIVERSITY   D-5
San Diego, CA 92106-2899   (619) 849-2565
(800) 733-7770; Fax: (619) 849-2601

Full-time: 920 men, 1365 women	Faculty: 115; IIB, av$
Part-time: 35 men, 40 women	Ph.D.s: 61%
Graduate: 195 men, 340 women	Student/Faculty: 20 to 1
Year: semesters, summer session	Tuition: $18,000
Application Deadline: March 1	Room & Board: $6630
Freshman Class: n/av	
SAT I or ACT: required	VERY COMPETITIVE

Point Loma Nazarene University, founded in 1902, is a private liberal arts university affiliated with the Church of the Nazarene. In addition to regional accreditation, PLNU has baccalaureate program accreditation with ACBSP and NLN. Figures in the above capsule and in this profile are approximate. The library contains 143,577 volumes, 35,037 microform items, and 10,700 audio/video tapes/CDs, and subscribes to 613 periodicals. Computerized library services include the card catalog, interlibrary loans, and database searching. Special learning facilities include a learning resource center, radio station, and a laboratory preschool. The 90-acre campus is in a suburban area 5 miles southwest of San Diego. Including all residence halls, there are 42 buildings.

Student Life: 77% of undergraduates are from California. Students are from 36 states, 14 foreign countries, and Canada. 82% are from public schools. 84% are white. Most are Protestant. The average age of freshmen is 18; all undergraduates, 20. 21% do not continue beyond their first year; 89% remain to graduate.

Housing: 1460 students can be accommodated in college housing, which includes single-sex dorms, on-campus apartments, off-campus apartments, and married-student housing. On-campus housing is available on a first-come, first-served basis and is available on a lottery system for upperclassmen. 67% of students live on campus. Alcohol is not permitted. Upperclassmen may keep cars.

Activities: There are 3 local fraternities and 1 national and 2 local sororities. There are 41 groups on campus, including art, band, cheerleading, choir, chorale, computers, debate, drama, ethnic, forensics, honors, international, jazz band, literary magazine, newspaper, opera, orchestra, pep band, political, professional, radio and TV, religious, social, social service, student government, and yearbook. Popular campus events include Spiritual Emphasis Week and Christmas Messiah Concert.

Sports: There are 7 intercollegiate sports for men and 5 for women, and 18 intramural sports for men and 17 for women. Facilities include a gym, baseball and soccer fields, a track, tennis courts, dorm lounges, and table tennis and pool tables.

Disabled Students: 75% of the campus is accessible. Wheelchair ramps, elevators, special parking, specially equipped rest rooms, special class scheduling, lowered drinking fountains, and lowered telephones are available.

Services: Counseling and information services are available, as is tutoring in most subjects. There is a reader service for the blind, and remedial math, reading, and writing.

Campus Safety and Security: Measures include 24-hour foot and vehicle patrol, self-defense education, security escort services, and shuttle buses. There are informal discussions, pamphlets/posters/films, emergency telephones, and lighted pathways/sidewalks.

Programs of Study: PLNU confers B.A., B.S., and B.S.N. degrees. Master's degrees are also awarded. Bachelor's degrees are awarded in BIOLOGICAL SCIENCE (biology/biological science), BUSINESS (accounting, business administration and management, and management information systems), COMMUNICATIONS AND THE ARTS (art, communications, dramatic arts, journalism, literature, music, music business management, romance languages and literature, Spanish, and speech/debate/rhetoric), COMPUTER AND PHYSICAL SCIENCE (chemistry, computer science, mathematics, and physics), EDUCATION (physical), ENGINEERING AND ENVIRONMENTAL DESIGN (engineering physics), HEALTH PROFESSIONS (nursing), SOCIAL SCIENCE (child psychology/development, dietetics, economics, family and community services, history, home economics, industrial and organizational psychology, liberal arts/general studies, philosophy, political science/government, psychology, religion, religious education, social science, social work, and sociology). Biology, chemistry, and art are the strongest academically. Liberal studies and business are the largest.

Required: To graduate, students must complete a minimum of 128 semester units. At least 24 upper-division semester units are needed for the major. A minimum GPA of 2.0 is required. Students must complete the general education requirements, though B.S.N. candidates need not take a foreign language. General education requirements include 9 courses in cultural studies, 5 in the sciences, 4 in cognitive studies, and 3 in religious studies. Students must demonstrate proficiency in writing and math.

Special: PLNU offers internships in the church, in state and national governments, in journalism, in small business, and in the film industry. Students may study abroad in several world capitals and in Russia, the Middle East, and Costa Rica. There are Washington and United Nations semester programs. Various dual or interdepartmental majors are offered, including biology-chemistry, graphic communications, human environmental science-business, and church music-youth ministries. There are preprofessional programs in medicine/dentistry, law, and engineering. A general studies degree in liberal studies is available, as is credit for life, military, and work experience for nursing students. PLNU also offers nondegree study and credit/no credit options. There is 1 national honor society, a freshman honors program, and 1 departmental honors program.

Faculty/Classroom: 55% of faculty are male; 45%, female. 95% teach undergraduates and 10% both teach and do research. No introductory courses are taught by graduate students. The average class size in an introductory lecture is 75; in a laboratory, 18; and in a regular course, 25.

Admissions: 18 freshmen graduated first in their class in a recent year.

Requirements: The SAT I or ACT is required. In addition, candidates for admission should have completed 4 years of English, 2 years each of foreign language and math, and 1 year each of history and science. A GPA of 2.8 is required. AP and CLEP credits are accepted. Important factors in the admissions decision are personality/intangible qualities, leadership record, and advanced placement or honor courses.

Procedure: Freshmen are admitted to all sessions. Entrance exams should be taken in the junior year or early in the senior year. There are early action and deferred admissions plans. Early action applications should be filed by December 1; regular applications by March 1 for fall entry. The fall 2003 application fee was $45. Notification is sent on a rolling basis.

Transfer: 165 transfer students enrolled in a recent year. Transfer students must have a C average in all college work and present transcripts, including certificates of honorable dismissal. Credits submitted from non-accredited schools will be evaluated individually. Advanced standing is provisional for at least 1 term, in which the student must maintain at least a C average. 24 of 128 credits required for the bachelor's degree must be completed at PLNU.

Visiting: There are regularly scheduled orientations for prospective students, including campus tours and appointments with major advisers. There are guides for informal visits and visitors may sit in on classes and stay overnight. To schedule a visit, contact the Admissions Office at (619) 221-2273.

Financial Aid: In a recent year, 85% of all full-time students received some form of financial aid. 28% of undergraduates work part time. PLNU is a member of CSS. The CSS Profile or FAFSA and the college's own financial statement are required. The deadline for filing freshman financial aid applications for fall entry is March 2.

International Students: There were 19 international students enrolled in a recent year. They must score 550 on the written TOEFL or 216 on the electronic version and also take the SAT I.

Computers: The mainframes are a Data General MV/10,000. Terminals are located in the computer center and the business and science areas. There are 125 PCs and 20 Apples in computer labs available for classes and for general use. All students may access the system when computer labs are open. There are no time limits and no fees, but there is a 1-hour limit when other students are waiting. It is recommended that students in business administration have personal computers.

Graduates: In a recent year, 447 bachelor's degrees were awarded. The most popular majors were business (21%), liberal studies (17%), and nursing (13%). In an average class, 31% graduate in 4 years or less, 46% graduate in 5 years or less, and 52% graduate in 6 years or less. 140 companies recruited on campus in a recent year.

Admissions Contact: Scott Shoemaker, Director, Admissions. A video is available. E-mail: *admissions@ptloma.edu* Web: *www.ptloma.edu/admissions*

POMONA COLLEGE   D-5
Claremont, CA 91711   (909) 621-8134; Fax: (909) 621-8952

Full-time: 785 men, 755 women	Faculty: 155; IIB, ++$
Part-time: 20 men, 15 women	Ph.D.s: 100%
Graduate: none	Student/Faculty: 10 to 1
Year: semesters	Tuition: $26,890
Application Deadline: January 2	Room & Board: $9980
Freshman Class: n/av	
SAT I or ACT: required	**MOST COMPETITIVE**

Pomona College, the oldest and largest of the Claremont Colleges (a consortium of colleges) is an independent, national liberal arts and sciences institution founded in 1887. There are 5 undergraduate and 2 graduate schools. Figures in the above capsules and in this profile are approximate. The 3 libraries contain 2,022,481 volumes, 1,382,687 microform items, and 777 audio/video tapes/CDs, and subscribe to 6624 periodicals. Computerized library services include the card catalog, interlibrary loans, and database searching. Special learning facilities include an art gallery, radio station, observatory, and modern languages and international relations center. The 140-acre campus is in a suburban area 35 miles east of Los Angeles, and 20 miles east of Pasadena. Including any residence halls, there are 47 buildings.

Student Life: 61% of undergraduates are from out of state, mostly the Northwest. Students are from 49 states, 31 foreign countries, and Canada. 69% are from public schools. 51% are white; 21% Asian American; 10% Hispanic. The average age of freshmen is 18; all undergraduates, 20. 1% do not continue beyond their first year; 94% remain to graduate.

Housing: 1335 students can be accommodated in college housing, which includes coed dorms and on-campus apartments. In addition, there are language houses. On-campus housing is guaranteed for all 4 years. 97% of students live on campus; of those, 95% remain on campus on weekends. All students may keep cars.

Activities: 6% of men and about 4% of women belong to 6 local fraternities. There are no sororities. There are 280 groups on campus, including art, band, chess, choir, chorus, dance, debate, drama, ethnic, film, gay, honors, international, jazz band, literary magazine, musical theater, newspaper, orchestra, pep band, photography, political, professional, radio and TV, religious, social, social service, student government, symphony, and yearbook.

Sports: There are 10 intercollegiate sports for men and 10 for women, and 13 intramural sports for men and 13 for women. Facilities include an all-weather track, 2 swimming pools, a weight room, a fitness center, a dance studio, various playing fields, and courts for tennis, squash, racquetball, basketball, volleyball, and badminton.

Disabled Students: 80% of the campus is accessible. Wheelchair ramps, elevators, special parking, specially equipped rest rooms, special class scheduling, lowered drinking fountains, and lowered telephones are available.

Services: Counseling and information services are available, as is tutoring in most subjects. There is a reader service for the blind.

Campus Safety and Security: Measures include 24-hour foot and vehicle patrol, self-defense education, security escort services, and informal discussions. There are pamphlets/posters/films, emergency telephones, and lighted pathways/sidewalks.

Programs of Study: Pomona confers the B.A. degree. Bachelor's degrees are awarded in BIOLOGICAL SCIENCE (biology/biological science, molecular biology, and neurosciences), COMMUNICATIONS AND THE ARTS (art history and appreciation, Chinese, classics, dramatic arts, English, fine arts, French, German, Japanese, languages, linguistics, literature, media arts, music, Russian, Spanish, and studio art), COMPUTER AND PHYSICAL SCIENCE (chemistry, computer science, geology, mathematics, physics, and science), ENGINEERING AND ENVIRONMENTAL DESIGN (technology and public affairs), SOCIAL SCIENCE (African American studies, American studies, anthropology, Asian/Oriental studies, economics, German area studies, history, international relations, Latin American studies, philosophy, political science/government, psychology, public affairs, religion, sociology, and women's studies). Social sciences and sciences are the largest.

Required: Students must pass 1 course in each of the following categories: read literature critically, use and understand scientific method, use and understand formal reasoning, understand and analyze data, analyze creative art critically, perform or produce creative art, explore and understand human behavior, explore and understand historical culture, compare and contrast contemporary culture, and think critically about values and rationality. In all, 32 semester courses must be completed with a 6.0 GPA on a 12.0 scale.

Special: Students may cross-register at any of the Claremont Colleges, study abroad in 22 countries, and spend a semester in Washington, D.C. Dual and student-designed majors, internships, and independent study are possible. A 3-2 engineering program is offered with California Institute of Technology or Washington University in St. Louis. Students may study for 1 semester at Colby, Smith, Spelman, or Swarthmore Colleges. There are pass/fail options. There are 9 national honor societies, including Phi Beta Kappa.

Faculty/Classroom: 58% of faculty are male; 42%, female. All both teach undergraduates and do research. The average class size in an introductory lecture is 30; in a laboratory, 14; and in a regular course, 14.

Requirements: The SAT I or ACT is required. In addition, although applicants need not be graduates of accredited high schools (some may be admitted after the junior year), most are, or have earned the GED. Secondary preparation must include 4 years of English, 3 years each of math and foreign languages, and 2 years each of lab and social sciences. An essay is required and an interview is strongly recommended. AP credits are accepted. Important factors in the admissions decision are recommendations by school officials, leadership record, and recommendations by alumni.

Procedure: Freshmen are admitted in the fall. Entrance exams should be taken before December of the senior year. There are early decision, early admissions, and deferred admissions plans. Early decision applications should be filed by November 15; (phase I) or December 28 (phase II); regular applications, by January 2 for fall entry. Notification of early decision is sent December 15 (phase I) or February 15 (phase II); regular decision, April 10. The application fee is $60. Applications are accepted on-line at CollegeLink, Embark, Apply, Common Application, and the College Board's "Next Stop College." A waiting list is an active part of the admissions procedure.

Transfer: 16 transfer students enrolled in a recent year. Applicants must have completed at least 1 year (24 semester hours) of college-level courses at the time of enrollment. 16 of 32 credits required for the bachelor's degree must be completed at Pomona.

Visiting: There are regularly scheduled orientations for prospective students, including interviews, information sessions, and tours. There are guides for informal visits and visitors may sit in on classes and stay overnight. To schedule a visit, contact the Admissions Office.

Financial Aid: In a recent year, 53% of all full-time freshmen and 52% of continuing full-time students received some form of financial aid. 49% of full-time freshmen and 52% of continuing full-time students received need-based aid. The average freshman award was $21,310. 65% of undergraduates work part time. Average annual earnings from campus work are $2000. The average financial indebtedness of a recent graduate was $15,800. Pomona is a member of CSS. The CSS Profile or FAFSA and tax returns are required. The deadline for filing freshman financial aid applications for fall entry is February 1.

International Students: There were 35 international students enrolled in a recent year. The school actively recruits these students. They must score 600 on the written TOEFL or 250 on the electronic version and also take the SAT I and the ACT.

Computers: The mainframe is a DEC Alpha. Students may access the mainframe computer at several public facilities and from dorm rooms. Macs and PCs are available in public work areas. All students may access the system. There are no time limits and no fees.

Graduates: In an average class, 94% graduate in 4 years or less, and 96% graduate in 5 years or less.

Admissions Contact: Bruce J. Poch, Vice President and Dean of Admissions. E-mail: *admissions@pomona.edu* Web: *www.pomona.edu*

SAINT MARY'S COLLEGE OF CALIFORNIA
B-3
Moraga, CA 94575-4800
(925) 631-4224
(800) 800-4SMC; Fax: (925) 376-7193

Full-time: 1003 men, 1403 women	**Faculty:** 208; IIA, +$
Part-time: 44 men, 44 women	**Ph.D.s:** 90%
Graduate: 352 men, 797 women	**Student/Faculty:** 12 to 1
Year: 4-1-4	**Tuition:** $23,775
Application Deadline: February 1	**Room & Board:** $9075
Freshman Class: 3172 applied, 2590 accepted, 562 enrolled	
SAT I Verbal/Math: 540/550	**ACT:** 22 **VERY COMPETITIVE**

Saint Mary's College of California, founded in 1863, is a private, independent, liberal arts college affiliated with the Roman Catholic Church.

The school offers undergraduate and graduate programs in liberal arts, nursing, economics and business administration, education, and pre-professional studies. There are 5 undergraduate and 5 graduate schools. In addition to regional accreditation, Saint Mary's College of California has baccalaureate program accreditation with NLN. The library contains 210,516 volumes, 470,596 microform items, and 11,062 audio/video tapes/CDs, and subscribes to 1042 periodicals. Computerized library services include the card catalog, interlibrary loans, and database searching. Special learning facilities include an art gallery, radio station, and TV station. The 420-acre campus is in a suburban area 20 miles east of San Francisco. Including any residence halls, there are 58 buildings.

Student Life: 86% of undergraduates are from California. Others are from 25 states, 14 foreign countries, and Canada. 57% are from public schools. 61% are white; 18% Hispanic; 10% Asian American. 58% are Catholic; 17% claim no religious affiliation. The average age of freshmen is 18; all undergraduates, 20. 11% do not continue beyond their first year; 67% remain to graduate.

Housing: 1576 students can be accommodated in college housing, which includes single-sex and coed dorms and on-campus apartments. On-campus housing is guaranteed for the freshman year only and is available on a lottery system for upperclassmen. 61% of students live on campus; of those, 68% remain on campus on weekends. All students may keep cars.

Activities: There are no fraternities or sororities. There are 42 groups on campus, including art, cheerleading, choir, chorus, dance, drama, ethnic, gay, honors, international, jazz band, literary magazine, musical theater, newspaper, pep band, political, professional, radio and TV, religious, social, social service, student government, and yearbook. Popular campus events include Welcome Back Dance, OASIS, and St. Mary's Day Off.

Sports: There are 7 intercollegiate sports for men and 8 for women, and 9 intramural sports for men and 9 for women. Facilities include a gym, football and baseball fields, a swimming pool, lighted tennis courts, a soccer field and rugby pitch, a weight room, and a workout facility.

Disabled Students: 90% of the campus is accessible. Wheelchair ramps, elevators, special parking, specially equipped rest rooms, special class scheduling, lowered drinking fountains, and lowered telephones are available.

Services: Counseling and information services are available, as is tutoring in most subjects. Tutoring is available in 1-on-1 sessions or group workshops. Readers, note takers, and other services are provided to learning or physically disabled students.

Campus Safety and Security: Measures include 24-hour foot and vehicle patrol, security escort services, informal discussions, and pamphlets/posters/films. There are emergency telephones and lighted pathways/sidewalks.

Programs of Study: Saint Mary's College of California confers B.A., B.S., and B.S.N. degrees. Master's and doctoral degrees are also awarded. Bachelor's degrees are awarded in BIOLOGICAL SCIENCE (biology/biological science), BUSINESS (accounting and business administration and management), COMMUNICATIONS AND THE ARTS (art, classical languages, communications, English, French, performing arts, and Spanish), COMPUTER AND PHYSICAL SCIENCE (chemistry, mathematics, and physics), EDUCATION (health, physical, and recreation), ENGINEERING AND ENVIRONMENTAL DESIGN (preengineering), HEALTH PROFESSIONS (health science and nursing), SOCIAL SCIENCE (anthropology, economics, history, liberal arts/general studies, philosophy, political science/government, psychology, and religion). Business administration, communications, and psychology are the largest.

Required: To graduate, students must complete 36 course credits, including 17 at the upper-division level, with a GPA of 2.0 overall and in the major. Specific requirements include 4 Great Books seminars and 2 courses each in religious studies, humanities, math/science, and social sciences. All students must demonstrate competence in written English.

Special: Saint Mary's College and Samuel Merritt College confer the B.S.N. degree to students completing the Intercollegiate Nursing Program. The college offers seminars in all fields, dual and student-designed majors, study abroad in 10 countries, a Washington semester, cross-registration with the Regional Association of East Bay Colleges and Universities, and an integral liberal arts degree. There are 3-2 engineering programs with Washington University, the University of Southern California, and Boston University.

Faculty/Classroom: 52% of faculty are male; 48%, female. All both teach and do research. No introductory courses are taught by graduate students. The average class size in an introductory lecture is 25; in a laboratory, 16; and in a regular course, 20.

Admissions: 82% of the 2003-2004 applicants were accepted. The SAT I scores for the 2003-2004 freshman class were: Verbal--25% below 500, 53% between 500 and 599, 19% between 600 and 700, and 3% above 700; Math--24% below 500, 49% between 500 and 599, 25% between 600 and 700, and 2% above 700. The ACT scores were 29% below 21, 28% between 21 and 23, 19% between 24 and 26, 11% between 27 and 28, and 13% above 28. 66% of the current freshmen were in the top fifth of their class; 83% were in the top two fifths.

Requirements: The SAT I or ACT is required. In addition, candidates should be graduates of an accredited secondary school, with 16 academic units, including 4 in English and 1 each in algebra, advanced algebra, geometry, and U.S. history. It is recommended that the remaining units be made up of foreign language, lab science, and additional academic electives in the student's areas of strength. The GED is accepted. An essay is required. AP and CLEP credits are accepted. Important factors in the admissions decision are recommendations by school officials, advanced placement or honor courses, and parents or siblings attending the school.

Procedure: Freshmen are admitted to all sessions. Entrance exams should be taken by December of the senior year. There is a deferred admissions plan. Applications should be filed by February 1 for fall entry and January 1 for spring entry. Notification of early decision is sent January 1; regular decision, April 1. 208 were on the 2003 waiting list; 49 were admitted. Applications are accepted on computer disk and on-line through the Apply Technologies CD-ROM, Apply, and the college's web site.

Transfer: 153 transfer students enrolled in 2003-2004. Applicants must have a GPA of 2.3 and a minimum of 23 transferable academic semester units. 9 of 36 course credits required for the bachelor's degree must be completed at Saint Mary's College of California.

Visiting: There are regularly scheduled orientations for prospective students. There are guides for informal visits and visitors may sit in on classes and stay overnight. To schedule a visit, contact the Admissions Office at (925) 631-4106.

Financial Aid: In 2003-2004, 75% of all full-time freshmen and 74% of continuing full-time students received some form of financial aid. 60% of full-time freshmen and 63% of continuing full-time students received need-based aid. The average freshman award was $18,979. Need-based scholarships or need-based grants averaged $15,904 ($23,640 maximum); need-based self-help aid (loans and jobs) averaged $4323 ($8625 maximum); non-need-based athletic scholarships averaged $16,455 ($33,215 maximum); and other non-need-based awards and non-need-based scholarships averaged $9033 ($16,000 maximum). 55% of undergraduates work part time. Average annual earnings from campus work are $1696. The average financial indebtedness of the 2003 graduate was $21,165. Saint Mary's College of California is a member of CSS. The FAFSA and California GPA verification form for residents only are required. The deadline for filing freshman financial aid applications for fall entry is March 2.

International Students: There are 78 international students enrolled. The school actively recruits these students. Nonnative English speakers who submit a score of 525 or higher on the written TOEFL (197 on the electronic version) may be admitted as full-time undergraduates. Others may be accepted conditionally and enrolled in the college's Intensive English Program.

Computers: There are 250 college-owned workstations available for general student use in the library, computer center, and dorms. All students may access the system. There are no time limits and no fees.

Graduates: From July 1, 2002 to June 30, 2003, 768 bachelor's degrees were awarded. The most popular majors were business administration (31%), psychology (12%), and communications (12%). In an average class, 64% graduate in 4 years or less, 66% graduate in 5 years or less, and 67% graduate in 6 years or less. 74 companies recruited on campus in 2002-2003. Of the 2002 graduating class, 14% were enrolled in graduate school within 6 months of graduation and 64% were employed.

Admissions Contact: Dorothy Jones, Dean of Admissions. A video is available. E-mail: *smcadmit@stmarys-ca.edu* Web: *http://www.stmarys-ca.edu*

SAMUEL MERRITT COLLEGE   B-3
Oakland, CA 94609-9954   **(510) 869-6576**
      (800) 607-6377; Fax: (510) 869-6525

Full-time: 16 men, 233 women	**Faculty:** 26
Part-time: 5 men, 31 women	**Ph.D.s:** 52%
Graduate: 180 men, 431 women	**Student/Faculty:** 10 to 1
Year: semesters	**Tuition:** $21,790
Application Deadline: March 1	**Room & Board:** $8829
Freshman Class: 19 applied, 19 accepted, 15 enrolled	
SAT I Verbal/Math: 515/490	**ACT:** 22 **SPECIAL**

Samuel Merritt College, founded in 1909, is a private, independent college offering a nursing program in cooperation with St. Mary's College of California. Graduate degrees are offered in nursing, physical therapy, podiatric medicine, physician assistant, and occupational therapy. In addition to regional accreditation, Samuel Merritt College has baccalaureate program accreditation with APTA and NLN. The library contains 16,000 volumes and 1437 audio/video tapes/CDs, and subscribes to 437 periodicals. Computerized library services include the card catalog, interlibrary loans, and database searching. Special learning facilities include a health education center, television studio, and nursing resource, physical therapy, and occupational therapy labs. The 1-acre campus is in an

urban area in Oakland, 10 miles east of San Francisco. Including any residence halls, there are 3 buildings.

Student Life: All undergraduates are from California. 41% are white; 22% Asian American; 15% Hispanic; 12% African American. The average age of freshmen is 19; all undergraduates, 26.

Housing: 103 students can be accommodated in college housing, which includes coed dorms. On-campus housing is available on a first-come, first-served basis. 92% of students commute. Alcohol is not permitted. All students may keep cars.

Activities: There are no fraternities or sororities. There are 15 groups on campus, including ethnic, gay, honors, professional, religious, social, social service, student government, and yearbook. Popular campus events include Career Fair, Beginning and End of Year Bar-B-Cues, and Multicultural Spring Fair.

Sports: There is no sports program at Samuel Merritt College.

Disabled Students: All of the campus is accessible. Wheelchair ramps, elevators, special parking, specially equipped rest rooms, and lowered drinking fountains are available.

Services: Counseling and information services are available, as is tutoring in every subject. There is remedial math, reading, and writing.

Campus Safety and Security: Measures include 24-hour foot and vehicle patrol, self-defense education, security escort services, and shuttle buses. There are informal discussions, pamphlets/posters/films, emergency telephones, and lighted pathways/sidewalks.

Programs of Study: Samuel Merritt College confers the B.S.N. degree. Master's and doctoral degrees are also awarded. Bachelor's degrees are awarded in HEALTH PROFESSIONS (nursing).

Required: Students must take a basic core curriculum with a minimum of 129 total credit hours, including 69 lower-division and 60 upper-division courses. Students must take at least 60 hours in the major. A minimum GPA of 2.0 overall and in the nursing major is necessary.

Special: There is 1 national honor society and 1 departmental honors program.

Faculty/Classroom: 26% of faculty are male; 74%, female. 30% teach undergraduates. No introductory courses are taught by graduate students. The average class size in a laboratory is 9 and in a regular course, 27.

Admissions: All of the 2003-2004 applicants were accepted. The SAT I scores for the 2003-2004 freshman class were: Verbal--33% below 500, 42% between 500 and 599, and 25% between 600 and 700; Math--50% below 500, 42% between 500 and 599, and 8% between 600 and 700. The ACT scores were 25% below 21, and 75% between 21 and 23.

Requirements: The SAT I is required. In addition, students must be high school graduates or hold a GED. Candidates for admission should have completed 3 years of English and 2 years each of math, science, and social studies. A GPA of 2.5 is required. AP and CLEP credits are accepted. Important factors in the admissions decision are advanced placement or honor courses, leadership record, and extracurricular activities record.

Procedure: Freshmen are admitted fall and spring. Entrance exams should be taken within 3 to 4 months of admission. The priority date for filing applications is March 1 for fall entry, October 1 for spring. The fall 2003 application fee was $35. Notification is sent on a rolling basis. A waiting list is an active part of the admissions procedure.

Transfer: 51 transfer students enrolled in 2003-2004. A minimum college GPA of 2.5 is required for students with more than 30 prior credits, as well as completion of specified prerequisite courses. 18 of 129 credits required for the bachelor's degree must be completed at Samuel Merritt College.

Visiting: There are regularly scheduled orientations for prospective students, including a campus tour and meetings with students and faculty. There are guides for informal visits. To schedule a visit, contact the Office of Admission.

Financial Aid: In 2003-2004, 90% of all full-time freshmen and 79% of continuing full-time students received some form of financial aid. 80% of full-time freshmen and 74% of continuing full-time students received need-based aid. The average freshman award was $13,603, with $9818 ($15,100 maximum) from need-based scholarships or need-based grants and $3785 ($9625 maximum) from need-based self-help aid (loans and jobs). 83% of undergraduates work part time. Average annual earnings from campus work are $1000. The average financial indebtedness of the 2003 graduate was $31,000. Samuel Merritt College is a member of CSS. The FAFSA is required. The priority date for freshman financial aid applications for fall entry is March 3. The deadline for filing freshman financial aid applications for fall entry is August 2.

International Students: They must score 550 on the written TOEFL and also take the SAT I or the ACT.

Computers: The mainframe is an IBM RS/6000 Model 970. The academic computer lab at St. Mary's College is available to Samuel Merritt students. All students may access the system. There are no time limits and no fees.

Graduates: From July 1, 2002 to June 30, 2003, 61 bachelor's degrees were awarded. In an average class, 78% graduate in 4 years or less.

Admissions Contact: Admission Office.
E-mail: *admissions@samuelmerritt.edu* Web: *http://samuelmerritt.edu*

SAN DIEGO STATE UNIVERSITY D-5
San Diego, CA 92182 (619) 594-7800; Fax: (619) 594-1250

Full-time: 9452 men, 12,868 women	**Faculty:** 1050; IIA, +$
Part-time: 2361 men, 3165 women	**Ph.D.s:** 90%
Graduate: 2432 men, 4026 women	**Student/Faculty:** 21 to 1
Year: semesters, summer session	**Tuition:** $2014 ($8902)
Application Deadline: November 30	**Room & Board:** $8307
Freshman Class: 29,129 applied, 14,454 accepted, 3730 enrolled	
SAT I Verbal/Math: 530/550	**ACT:** 22	**COMPETITIVE**

San Diego State University, founded in 1897, is a public liberal arts university that is part of the California State University system. There are 8 undergraduate schools. In addition to regional accreditation, SDSU has baccalaureate program accreditation with ACEJMC, ADA, ASLA, CSWE, FIDER, NASAD, NASM, NCATE, NLN, and NRPA. The library contains 1,342,735 volumes, 4,262,210 microform items, and 12,616 audio/video tapes/CDs, and subscribes to 8245 periodicals. Computerized library services include the card catalog, interlibrary loans, and database searching. Special learning facilities include a learning resource center, art gallery, planetarium, radio station, TV station, theater, and recital hall. The 282-acre campus is in an urban area 8 miles east of downtown San Diego. Including any residence halls, there are 56 buildings.

Student Life: 96% of undergraduates are from California. Others are from 50 states, 82 foreign countries, and Canada. 45% are white; 20% Hispanic; 15% Asian American. The average age of freshmen is 18; all undergraduates, 22. 21% do not continue beyond their first year.

Housing: 3087 students can be accommodated in college housing, which includes coed dorms, on-campus apartments, fraternity houses, and sorority houses. In addition, there are honors houses, special-interest houses, and international housing. On-campus housing is available on a first-come, first-served basis. 87% of students commute. All students may keep cars.

Activities: 7% of men belong to 15 national fraternities; 6% of women belong to 9 national sororities. There are 300 groups on campus, including art, band, cheerleading, choir, chorale, chorus, dance, drama, drill team, ethnic, film, gay, honors, international, jazz band, marching band, musical theater, newspaper, opera, orchestra, pep band, political, professional, radio and TV, religious, social, social service, student government, and symphony. Popular campus events include Ethnic Pride and PowWow.

Sports: There are 6 intercollegiate sports for men and 11 for women, and 7 intramural sports for men and 7 for women. Facilities include a gym, basketball, racquetball, tennis, and volleyball courts, a swimming pool, a track, soccer, softball, baseball, and football fields, an aquatic center, a weight room, bowling and gymnastic equipment, a cardio room, and a 30-foot climbing wall.

Disabled Students: 95% of the campus is accessible. Wheelchair ramps, elevators, special parking, specially equipped rest rooms, special class scheduling, lowered drinking fountains, lowered telephones, orientation, counseling, transportation, books on tape, sign language interpreters, testing assistance, support equipment for loan, special computers, and note-taking services are available.

Services: Counseling and information services are available, as is tutoring in most subjects. There is a reader service for the blind, and remedial math, reading, and writing.

Campus Safety and Security: Measures include 24-hour foot and vehicle patrol, self-defense education, security escort services, and informal discussions. There are pamphlets/posters/films, emergency telephones, and lighted pathways/sidewalks.

Programs of Study: SDSU confers B.A., B.S., and B.M. degrees. Master's and doctoral degrees are also awarded. Bachelor's degrees are awarded in BIOLOGICAL SCIENCE (biology/biological science, microbiology, and nutrition), BUSINESS (accounting, banking and finance, business administration and management, international business management, marketing/retailing/merchandising, and real estate), COMMUNICATIONS AND THE ARTS (broadcasting, classics, communications, comparative literature, dance, dramatic arts, English, fine arts, French, German, Japanese, journalism, linguistics, music, Russian, and Spanish), COMPUTER AND PHYSICAL SCIENCE (astronomy, chemistry, computer science, geology, information sciences and systems, mathematics, physical sciences, physics, and statistics), EDUCATION (vocational), ENGINEERING AND ENVIRONMENTAL DESIGN (aeronautical engineering, civil engineering, computer engineering, electrical/electronics engineering, environmental engineering, and mechanical engineering), HEALTH PROFESSIONS (exercise science, health science, nursing, and speech pathology/audiology), SOCIAL SCIENCE (African studies, American studies, anthropology, Asian/Oriental studies, child psychology/development, criminal justice, economics, European studies, geography, gerontology, history, humanities, Latin American studies, Mexican-American/Chicano studies, parks and recreation management, peace studies, philosophy, political science/government, psychology, public administration, religion, Russian and Slavic studies, social science, social work, sociology, urban studies, and women's studies). Business administration is the strongest academically and the largest.

Required: To graduate, students must complete 124 to 133 credit hours, including 49 general education units. The number of hours in the major varies by program. A 2.0 or higher GPA must be maintained, depending on the major. Students must demonstrate math and writing competency and fulfill requirements in upper-division writing and in American Institutions. History majors must complete a senior thesis.

Special: Students may study abroad in London and Paris and receive credit for life, military, and work experience. Cross-registration with the University of California, community colleges, and California State University, internships, dual majors, an interdisciplinary major, a political science internship in Sacramento or Washington, D.C., an off-campus public administration program, and a prelaw program in cooperation with California Western School of Law are available. There are 30 national honor societies, including Phi Beta Kappa, a freshman honors program, and 24 departmental honors programs.

Faculty/Classroom: 53% of faculty are male; 47%, female. Graduate students teach 13% of introductory courses. The average class size in an introductory lecture is 32 and in a regular course, 29.

Admissions: 50% of the 2003-2004 applicants were accepted. The SAT I scores for the 2003-2004 freshman class were: Verbal--34% below 500, 49% between 500 and 599, 16% between 600 and 700, and 1% above 700; Math--25% below 500, 49% between 500 and 599, 24% between 600 and 700, and 2% above 700. The ACT scores were 32% below 21, 29% between 21 and 23, 26% between 24 and 26, 9% between 27 and 28, and 4% above 28.

Requirements: The SAT I or ACT is required. In addition, applicants must have a qualifying CSU eligibility index, based on a combination of GPA and standardized test scores. Candidates for admission should have completed 4 years of English, 3 of math, 2 of a foreign language, 1 each of science with lab, U.S. history, and visual and performing arts, and 3 of electives. A GPA of 2.5 is required.

Procedure: Freshmen are admitted fall and spring. Entrance exams should be taken by October of the senior year. Applications should be filed by November 30 for fall entry and August 31 for spring entry. The fall 2003 application fee was $55. Notification is sent on a rolling basis. Applications are accepted on-line through the admissions web site.

Transfer: 2898 transfer students enrolled in 2003-2004. A minimum 2.0 GPA is required. Students with fewer than 56 transferable semester units must complete the regular admission procedure. Any number of units are accepted from a 4-year institution, but a maximum of 70 units may transfer from a 2-year institution. 30 of 124 to 133 credits required for the bachelor's degree must be completed at SDSU.

Visiting: There are regularly scheduled orientations for prospective students, including tours that can be scheduled with SDSU ambassadors. Visitors may stay overnight. To schedule a visit, contact Housing and Residential Life at (619) 594-6868.

Financial Aid: In 2003-2004, 45% of all full-time freshmen and 40% of continuing full-time students received some form of financial aid. The average freshman award was $5600. Need-based scholarships or need-based grants averaged $4500; need-based self-help aid (loans and jobs) averaged $3200; non-need-based athletic scholarships averaged $7400; and other non-need-based awards and non-need-based scholarships averaged $2500. The average financial indebtedness of the 2003 graduate was $13,000. SDSU is a member of CSS. The FAFSA and the state aid form are required.

International Students: There are 840 international students enrolled. They must score 550 on the written TOEFL and also take the college's own test.

Computers: The mainframes are an IBM-390 MVS System, a VAX Sun SPARC-1000E, and a SPARC-20. Student accounts are available by application; there is both on-campus and off-campus access. Various labs on campus with approximately 2000 computers are available. All students may access the system. There are no time limits and no fees.

Graduates: From July 1, 2002 to June 30, 2003, 5390 bachelor's degrees were awarded. The most popular majors were business/marketing (16%), social sciences and history (12%), and physical sciences (10%). In an average class, 7% graduate in 4 years or less, 20% graduate in 5 years or less, and 38% graduate in 6 years or less.

Admissions Contact: Kathleen Deaver, Director of Admissions.
E-mail: *arweb.sdsu.edu/es/admissions* Web: *www.csumentor.edu*

SAN FRANCISCO ART INSTITUTE B-3
San Francisco, CA 94133 (415) 749-4500
(800) 345-SFAI; Fax: (415) 749-4592

Full-time: 225 men, 195 women	**Faculty:** 35
Part-time: 40 men, 45 women	**Ph.D.s:** 99%
Graduate: 50 men, 80 women	**Student/Faculty:** 12 to 1
Year: semesters, summer session	**Tuition:** $19,300
Application Deadline: see profile	**Room & Board:** n/app
Freshman Class: n/av	
SAT I or ACT: required	**SPECIAL**

San Francisco Art Institute, founded in 1871, is a private, commuter college devoted solely to the fine arts. In addition to regional accreditation,

SFAI has baccalaureate program accreditation with NASAD. Figures in the above capsule and in this profile are approximate. The library contains 22,000 volumes and 1500 audio/video tapes/CDs, and subscribes to 210 periodicals. Special learning facilities include a learning resource center and art gallery. The 3-acre campus is in an urban area. There is 1 building.

Student Life: 66% of students are white; 11% foreign nationals. The average age of freshmen is 26; all undergraduates, 26. 12% do not continue beyond their first year; 15% remain to graduate.

Housing: There are no residence halls. All students commute. Alcohol is not permitted.

Activities: There are no fraternities or sororities. There are 7 groups on campus, including art, ethnic, gay, international, newspaper, and student government. Popular campus events include visiting artist lectures, symposia, and graduate open studios.

Sports: There is no sports program at SFAI.

Disabled Students: 70% of the campus is accessible. Wheelchair ramps, elevators, special parking, specially equipped rest rooms, and special class scheduling are available.

Services: Counseling and information services are available, as is tutoring in most subjects. There is remedial math, reading, and writing.

Campus Safety and Security: Measures include 24-hour foot and vehicle patrol, emergency telephones, and video security cameras.

Programs of Study: SFAI confers the B.F.A. degree. Master's degrees are also awarded. Bachelor's degrees are awarded in COMMUNICATIONS AND THE ARTS (film arts, fine arts, painting, photography, printmaking, sculpture, and video). Painting and photography are the largest.

Required: Students are required to complete at least 120 credit hours, 36 of which must be in the major. 6 liberal arts units, 24 studio units, and 15 art history units must be completed, as well as 33 units in the Letters and Science Program. SFAI requires a minimum GPA of 2.0.

Special: Students may participate in off-campus internships for credit. There are study-abroad opportunities in 9 countries. There is an interdisciplinary program in which studio curricula are chosen that best support specific artistic direction. The institute offers dual majors in all subjects, nondegree study, work-study with SFAI, and pass/fail options in the senior year.

Faculty/Classroom: 52% of faculty are male; 48%, female. 96% teach undergraduates. No introductory courses are taught by graduate students. The average class size in an introductory lecture is 100; in a laboratory, 17; and in a regular course, 17.

Requirements: The SAT I or ACT is required, with a minimum required score of 20 on the ACT or 420 on the SAT I verbal. A GPA of 2.5 is required. AP and CLEP credits are accepted. Important factors in the admissions decision are evidence of special talent, recommendations by school officials, and recommendations by alumni.

Procedure: Freshmen are admitted to all sessions. There are deferred admissions and rolling admissions plans. Check with the school for current application deadlines. The fall 2003 application fee was $60. Notification is sent on a rolling basis.

Transfer: Transfer students must have satisfactory prior college performance and a portfolio appropriate to their level of experience. College transcripts and an essay are required. 30 of 120 credits required for the bachelor's degree must be completed at SFAI.

Visiting: There are guides for informal visits and visitors may sit in on classes. To schedule a visit, contact the Office of Admissions.

Financial Aid: The FAFSA is required. Check with the school for current deadlines.

International Students: The school actively recruits these students. They must score 500 on the written TOEFL.

Computers: The mainframe is an HP. Students have access to 3 computer labs. 6 Macs are for students in the tutoring center, and 6 Amigas can be used for video processing. 24 Macs are available in the Center for Digital Media. All students may access the system. Students registered in CDM classes may access the system from 9 A.M. to 10 P.M. There are no time limits. The fee is $50.

Graduates: In an average class, 33% graduate in 5 years or less.

Admissions Contact: Mark Takiguchi, Director of Admissions.
E-mail: *admissions@sfai.edu* Web: *www.sfai.edu*

SAN FRANCISCO CONSERVATORY OF MUSIC   B-3
San Francisco, CA 94122   (415) 759-3431; Fax: (415) 759-3499

Full-time: 60 men, 75 women	Faculty: 24
Part-time: 5 men, 5 women	Ph.D.s: 21%
Graduate: 45 men, 85 women	Student/Faculty: 6 to 1
Year: semesters	Tuition: $20,780
Application Deadline: see profile	Room & Board: n/app
Freshman Class: n/av	
SAT I or ACT: required	SPECIAL

San Francisco Conservatory of Music, founded in 1917, is a private institution offering undergraduate, graduate, and nondegree programs in

music. There is 1 graduate school. Figures in the above capsule and in this profile are approximate. In addition to regional accreditation, SFCM has baccalaureate program accreditation with NASM. The library contains 44,782 volumes and 15,538 audio/video tapes/CDs, and subscribes to 72 periodicals. Computerized library services include the card catalog, interlibrary loans, and database searching. The 5-acre campus is in an urban area in a residential neighborhood of San Francisco. There are 3 buildings.

Programs of Study: SFCM confers the B.Mus. degree. Master's degrees are also awarded. Bachelor's degrees are awarded in COMMUNICATIONS AND THE ARTS (music). Voice, piano, and violin are the largest.

Required: Students must complete 130 credit hours, 100 of which must be music related, and the remainder in general education courses, including courses in fine arts, English, history, and humanities. Specific required courses and total number of hours in the major vary by instrument. Students must also pass the senior recital and maintain a minimum GPA of 2.0.

Special: Work-study programs and accelerated degree programs are available.

Faculty/Classroom: 67% of faculty are male; 33%, female. All teach undergraduates. No introductory courses are taught by graduate students. The average class size in an introductory lecture is 15 and in a regular course, 7.

Requirements: The SAT I or ACT is required. In addition, all applicants must have reached a high level of musical proficiency. An audition is required. A GPA of 2.5 is required. AP and CLEP credits are accepted. Important factors in the admissions decision are evidence of special talent, personality/intangible qualities, and extracurricular activities record.

Procedure: Freshmen are admitted fall and spring. Entrance exams should be taken by the late fall or early spring. There is an early admissions plan. Check with the school for current application deadlines. The fall 2003 application fee was $70. A waiting list is an active part of the admissions procedure.

Transfer: Transfer students must demonstrate a high level of musical proficiency, submit 2 letters of recommendation, and have a good academic record. An audition is required. 30 of 130 credits required for the bachelor's degree must be completed at SFCM.

Visiting: There are guides for informal visits and visitors may sit in on classes. To schedule a visit, contact Alex Brose in the Admissions Office.

Financial Aid: 85% of undergraduates work part time. Average annual earnings from campus work are $1700. The FAFSA and the college's own financial statement are required. Check with the school for current deadlines.

International Students: They must score 500 on the written TOEFL or 173 on the electronic version and also take the SAT I or the ACT.

Computers: Students have access to a computer lab equipped with Mac PCs, electronic keyboards, and a laser printer. Software includes class tutorials and a variety of commercially available music programs. All students may access the system when the building is open. There are no time limits and no fees.

Graduates: In an average class, 61% graduate in 4 years or less, 64% graduate in 5 years or less, and 64% graduate in 6 years or less.

Admissions Contact: Alex Brose, Admissions Office.
E-mail: *admit@sfcm.edu* Web: *www.sfcm.edu*

SAN FRANCISCO STATE UNIVERSITY   B-3
San Francisco, CA 94132   (415) 338-2355; Fax: (415) 338-0903

Full-time: 20,828 men and women	Faculty: 977; IIA, ++$
Part-time: none	Ph.D.s: n/av
Graduate: 7550 men and women	Student/Faculty: 21 to 1
Year: semesters, summer session	Tuition: $2500 ($10,960)
Application Deadline: see profile	Room & Board: $9570
Freshman Class: 14,531 applied, 9571 accepted, 1480 enrolled	
SAT I or ACT: required	COMPETITIVE

San Francisco State University, founded in 1899, is a public liberal arts institution offering graduate and undergraduate programs as part of the California State University system. There are 8 undergraduate and 8 graduate schools. In addition to regional accreditation, San Francisco State has baccalaureate program accreditation with AACSB, ACEJMC, ADA, AHEA, NASM, and NLN. The library contains 780,230 volumes, 2,209,455 microform items, and 72,245 audio/video tapes/CDs, and subscribes to 5679 periodicals (3677 electronic). Computerized library services include the card catalog, interlibrary loans, database searching, and Internet access. Special learning facilities include a learning resource center, art gallery, natural history museum, planetarium, radio station, TV station, a field campus, the Labor Archives and Research Center, a Media Access Center, and an anthropology museum. The 130-acre campus is in an urban area in San Francisco. Including any residence halls, there are 23 buildings.

Student Life: 78% of undergraduates are from California. Students are from 17 states, 12 foreign countries, and Canada. 48% are white; 28%

Asian American; 10% Hispanic. The average age of all undergraduates is 24. 17% do not continue beyond their first year; 62% remain to graduate.

Housing: College housing includes coed dorms. On-campus housing is available on a first-come, first-served basis. 95% of students commute. Alcohol is not permitted. All students may keep cars.

Activities: There are 12 national fraternities and 4 local and 8 national sororities. There are 200 groups on campus, including art, band, cheerleading, choir, chorale, chorus, dance, debate, drama, ethnic, film, gay, honors, jazz band, literary magazine, musical theater, newspaper, opera, orchestra, pep band, political, professional, radio and TV, social service, student government, symphony, and yearbook. Popular campus events include Activities Fair and Crafts Festival, Morrison Artists' Series Chamber Music Program, and the Alexander String Quartet.

Sports: There are 8 intercollegiate sports for men and 7 for women, and 10 intramural sports for men and 10 for women. Facilities include a 6500-seat stadium, 2 gyms, an indoor pool, a weight room, a training room, wrestling and gymnastics areas, an all-weather track, 14 tennis courts, softball and baseball fields, and auxiliary practice fields.

Disabled Students: Wheelchair ramps, elevators, special parking, specially equipped rest rooms, lowered drinking fountains, lowered telephones, readers, interpreters, an equipment loan, on-campus transportation, and priority registration are available.

Services: Counseling and information services are available, as is tutoring in every subject.

Campus Safety and Security: Measures include 24-hour foot and vehicle patrol, self-defense education, security escort services, and shuttle buses. There are informal discussions, pamphlets/posters/films, emergency telephones, and lighted pathways/sidewalks.

Programs of Study: San Francisco State confers B.A., B.S., B.M., and B.Voc.Ed. degrees. Associate, master's, and doctoral degrees are also awarded. Bachelor's degrees are awarded in BIOLOGICAL SCIENCE (biochemistry, biology/biological science, botany, cell biology, ecology, marine biology, microbiology, physiology, and zoology), BUSINESS (accounting, banking and finance, business administration and management, international business management, labor studies, management science, marketing/retailing/merchandising, personnel management, real estate, and transportation management), COMMUNICATIONS AND THE ARTS (broadcasting, Chinese, classics, comparative literature, dance, dramatic arts, English, film arts, fine arts, French, German, Italian, Japanese, journalism, music, Russian, and speech/debate/rhetoric), COMPUTER AND PHYSICAL SCIENCE (applied mathematics, chemistry, computer science, geology, information sciences and systems, mathematics, physics, science, and statistics), EDUCATION (early childhood, elementary, home economics, industrial arts, physical, recreation, secondary, special, and vocational), ENGINEERING AND ENVIRONMENTAL DESIGN (civil engineering, electrical/electronics engineering, engineering, industrial administration/management, interior design, and mechanical engineering), HEALTH PROFESSIONS (allied health, clinical science, health science, medical laboratory technology, nursing, physical therapy, public health, and speech pathology/audiology), SOCIAL SCIENCE (African American studies, American studies, anthropology, clothing and textiles management/production/services, dietetics, economics, geography, history, humanities, interdisciplinary studies, international relations, liberal arts/general studies, philosophy, political science/government, psychology, social work, sociology, urban studies, and women's studies).

Required: To graduate, students must complete 124 to 132 credits with a minimum GPA of 2.0. The required general education core includes 27 credits in arts and sciences, 12 in basic skills subjects, and 9 in upper-division courses. English composition and U.S. history and government competency requirements may be fulfilled by either exam or course work.

Special: Students may cross-register with the California College of Podiatric Medicine, the City College of San Francisco, Cogswell College of Engineering, and several other area universities. Study abroad in numerous countries, a Washington semester, campus work-study, a general studies degree, dual and student-designed majors, credit for life experience, nondegree study, and pass/fail options are also offered. There is a chapter of Phi Beta Kappa and a freshman honors program.

Faculty/Classroom: 61% of faculty are male; 39%, female. No introductory courses are taught by graduate students.

Admissions: 66% of the 2003-2004 applicants were accepted. The ACT scores for the 2003-2004 freshman class were: 33% below 17, 46% between 18 and 23, 20% between 24 and 29, and 2% above 29.

Requirements: The SAT I or ACT is required. In addition, applicants should be graduates of an accredited secondary school with a minimum GPA of 2.0. The GED is accepted. High school courses should include 4 years of English, 3 of math, 2 of foreign language, and 1 each of U.S. history or government, lab science, and visual and performing arts. A GPA of 2.0 is required. AP and CLEP credits are accepted.

Procedure: Freshmen are admitted fall and spring. The priority application filing period for fall entry is October 1 to November 30 prior to the fall in which the student plans to attend; students may still apply after November 30 as long as space remains in their chosen major. Nursing, radio/TV, and film majors have firm application deadlines; check with the school for those deadlines. The application fee is $55. Notification is sent on a rolling basis. Applications are accepted on-line.

Transfer: Applicants must have a college GPA of 2.0 (2.4 for nonresidents). Those with fewer than 56 transferable semester credits must meet freshman entrance requirements. 30 of 124 credits required for the bachelor's degree must be completed at San Francisco State.

Visiting: There are regularly scheduled orientations for prospective students. There are guides for informal visits and visitors may sit in on classes. To schedule a visit, contact Student Outreach Services.

Financial Aid: In 2003-2004, need-based scholarships or need-based grants averaged $4652; and need-based self-help aid (loans and jobs) averaged $1855. The average financial indebtedness of the 2003 graduate was $15,265. San Francisco State is a member of CSS. The CSS/Profile or FFS is required.

International Students: They must score 500 on the written TOEFL.

Computers: The mainframes are a DEC VAX 6420 and an IBM 4381/R22. There are 46 dial-in modems, 50 CD-ROM and on-line databases, more than 100 networked terminals, and more than 1000 IBM, Mac, and other PCs available for student use. All students may access the system 24 hours daily. There are no time limits and no fees.

Graduates: From July 1, 2002 to June 30, 2003, 7344 bachelor's degrees were awarded. The most popular majors were business/marketing (25%), social sciences/history (10%), and visual and performing arts (9%). 33 companies recruited on campus in 2002-2003.

Admissions Contact: Student Outreach Services.
E-mail: *outreach@sfsu.edu* Web: *www.sfsu.edu*

SAN JOSE STATE UNIVERSITY   B-3
San Jose, CA 95192   (408) 924-2000; Fax: (408) 924-2050

Full-time: 6975 men, 7615 women	**Faculty:** 868; IIA, +$
Part-time: 3435 men, 3395 women	**Ph.D.s:** 84%
Graduate: 1975 men, 3550 women	**Student/Faculty:** 17 to 1
Year: semesters, summer session	**Tuition:** $1940 ($7845)
Application Deadline: open	**Room & Board:** $6250
Freshman Class: n/av	
SAT I or ACT: required	**COMPETITIVE**

San Jose State University, founded in 1857 and part of the California State University system, is a public institution offering undergraduate and graduate programs in applied arts and science, social science, and social work to a primarily commuter student body. There are 8 undergraduate and 8 graduate schools. Figures in the above capsules and in this profile are approximate. In addition to regional accreditation, SJSU has baccalaureate program accreditation with AACSB, ABET, ACEJMC, ADA, ASLA, NASAD, NASM, NCATE, and NLN. The 2 libraries contain 1,101,995 volumes, 1,621,426 microform items, and 37,146 audio/video tapes/CDs, and subscribe to 2504 periodicals. Computerized library services include the card catalog, interlibrary loans, and database searching. Special learning facilities include a learning resource center, art gallery, radio station, and TV station. The 104-acre campus is in an urban area in the center of San Jose. Including any residence halls, there are 55 buildings.

Student Life: Students are from 40 states, 114 foreign countries, and Canada. 89% are from public schools. 36% are Asian American; 30% white; 14% Hispanic. The average age of freshmen is 20; all undergraduates, 25.

Housing: 2014 students can be accommodated in college housing, which includes coed dorms, on-campus apartments, fraternity houses, and sorority houses. In addition, there are special-interest houses and an international students center. On-campus housing is available on a first-come, first-served basis. Alcohol is not permitted. All students may keep cars.

Activities: 8% of men belong to 6 local and 15 national fraternities; 4% of women belong to 3 local and 9 national sororities. There are 175 groups on campus, including art, band, cheerleading, choir, chorale, chorus, dance, drama, ethnic, film, gay, international, literary magazine, marching band, musical theater, newspaper, photography, political, radio and TV, social, student government, and symphony. Popular campus events include International Food Bazaar, Welcome Day, and National Collegiate Alcohol Awareness Week.

Sports: There are 6 intercollegiate sports for men and 10 for women, and 17 intramural sports for men and 13 for women. Facilities include a gym, a pool, a track, a football field, and a recreation center with racquetball courts and a bowling alley.

Disabled Students: 95% of the campus is accessible. Wheelchair ramps, elevators, special parking, specially equipped rest rooms, special class scheduling, lowered drinking fountains, lowered telephones, and preadmission assistance are available.

Services: Counseling and information services are available, as is tutoring in most subjects. There is a reader service for the blind. There are also test accommodations, sign-language interpreters, liaisons to faculty, and note takers.

Campus Safety and Security: Measures include 24-hour foot and vehicle patrol, self-defense education, security escort services, and shuttle buses. There are informal discussions, pamphlets/posters/films, emergency telephones, lighted pathways/sidewalks, and a canine patrol.

Programs of Study: SJSU confers B.A., B.S., B.F.A., and B.Mus. degrees. Master's degrees are also awarded. Bachelor's degrees are awarded in BIOLOGICAL SCIENCE (biochemistry, biology/biological science, botany, microbiology, and zoology), BUSINESS (accounting, banking and finance, business administration and management, international business management, and marketing/retailing/merchandising), COMMUNICATIONS AND THE ARTS (advertising, broadcasting, dance, design, dramatic arts, English, film arts, fine arts, French, German, journalism, music, Spanish, and speech/debate/rhetoric), COMPUTER AND PHYSICAL SCIENCE (chemistry, computer science, geology, mathematics, physics, and statistics), EDUCATION (early childhood and teaching English as a second/foreign language (TESOL/TEFOL)), ENGINEERING AND ENVIRONMENTAL DESIGN (aeronautical engineering, chemical engineering, civil engineering, computer engineering, electrical/electronics engineering, engineering, industrial engineering, interior design, materials engineering, and mechanical engineering), HEALTH PROFESSIONS (nursing, occupational therapy, and speech pathology/audiology), SOCIAL SCIENCE (anthropology, criminal justice, economics, food science, geography, history, philosophy, political science/government, psychology, religion, social science, social work, and sociology). Accounting is the strongest academically. Accounting, electrical engineering, and management are the largest.

Required: Students must complete 39 units of core general education, including 12 units of upper-division courses in residence and 6 units of American history and institutions. A minimum of 124 credits, with at least 24 in the major, a minimum GPA of 2.0, and the successful completion of writing, English, and entry-level math tests are required to graduate.

Special: SJSU has opportunities for cooperative programs in business, science, engineering, arts, and the humanities, work-study with many employers, internships (some required, some optional), study abroad in 16 countries, field experiences, and student teaching. An accelerated program is offered in nursing, and the B.A.-B.S. degree and dual majors are available in various areas of study. A general studies degree, student-designed majors, nondegree study, and credit/no-credit options are possible. There are 3 national honor societies and 18 departmental honors programs.

Faculty/Classroom: 66% of faculty are male; 34%, female. The average class size in an introductory lecture is 30; in a laboratory, 20; and in a regular course, 25.

Requirements: The SAT I or ACT is required. Scores are used to calculate an eligibility index rating, which determines qualification for admission. Graduation from an accredited secondary school is required; the GED is accepted. Applicants must have completed 4 years of English, 3 each of math and electives, 2 of a foreign language, and 1 each of history, science, and art. AP and CLEP credits are accepted. Important factors in the admissions decision are personality/intangible qualities, recommendations by alumni, and recommendations by school officials.

Procedure: Freshmen are admitted fall and spring. Entrance exams should be taken prior to the fall semester. There are early admissions, deferred admissions, and rolling admissions plans. Application deadlines are open. Applications are accepted on-line. The fall 2003 application fee was $55.

Transfer: Applicants must have a minimum GPA of 2.0. The student's rating in the eligibility index is also considered in determining qualification for transfer. 30 of 124 credits required for the bachelor's degree must be completed at SJSU.

Visiting: There are regularly scheduled orientations for prospective students. There are guides for informal visits and visitors may sit in on classes. To schedule a visit, contact the Office of Relations with Schools at (408) 924-2564.

Financial Aid: SJSU is a member of CSS. The FAFSA is required. Check with the school for current deadlines.

International Students: There were 498 international students enrolled in a recent year. The school actively recruits these students. They must score 500 on the written TOEFL and also take the SAT I or the ACT.

Computers: The mainframe is an IBM 3090. About 50% of students use the 1597 PCs available, about 300 of which are networked. All students may access the system 9 A.M. to 8 P.M. Monday through Friday and 9 A.M. to 5 P.M. Saturday. There are no time limits and no fees.

Graduates: In an average class, 9% graduate in 4 years or less, 39% graduate in 5 years or less, and 70% graduate in 6 years or less.

Admissions Contact: John Bradbury, Director of Admissions. E-mail: *contact@anrnet.sjsu.edu*

SANTA CLARA UNIVERSITY B-3
Santa Clara, CA 95053 (408) 554-4700; Fax: (408) 554-5255

Full-time: 1898 men, 2341 women	**Faculty:** IIA, ++$
Part-time: 71 men, 53 women	**Ph.D.s:** 91%
Graduate: 1189 men, 1000 women	**Student/Faculty:** n/av
Year: quarters, summer session	**Tuition:** $25,365
Application Deadline: January 15	**Room & Board:** $9336
Freshman Class: 6388 applied, 4224 accepted, 897 enrolled	
SAT I Verbal/Math: 580/610	**ACT:** 25 **HIGHLY COMPETITIVE**

Santa Clara University, founded in 1851 by Jesuit priests, is a private institution offering undergraduate and graduate degrees in arts and sciences, engineering, business law, education, and counseling. Enrollment figures in the above capsule are for fall 2002. There are 3 undergraduate and 5 graduate schools. In addition to regional accreditation, Santa Clara University has baccalaureate program accreditation with AACSB, ABET, and NASM. The 2 libraries contain 639,691 volumes, 2,007,913 microform items, and 12,622 audio/video tapes/CDs, and subscribe to 11,952 periodicals. Computerized library services include the card catalog, interlibrary loans, and database searching. Special learning facilities include a learning resource center, art gallery, planetarium, radio station, TV station, and California Mission (archeology lab). The 104-acre campus is in a suburban area 46 miles south of San Francisco. Including any residence halls, there are 51 buildings.

Student Life: 66% of undergraduates are from California. Students are from 32 states, 10 foreign countries, and Canada. 52% are from public schools. 57% are white; 20% Asian American; 13% Hispanic. 51% are Catholic; 18% Protestant; 17% claim no religious affiliation. The average age of freshmen is 18; all undergraduates, 20. 8% do not continue beyond their first year; 80% remain to graduate.

Housing: 1803 students can be accommodated in college housing, which includes coed dorms, on-campus apartments, and off-campus apartments. All freshman students select 1 of 9 residential learning communities (RLCs). Approximately 75% of sophomores participate in RLCs. Juniors and seniors can apply for the Sobrato apartment-style learning community. On-campus housing is guaranteed for the freshman year only, is available on a first-come, first-served basis, and is available on a lottery system for upperclassmen. Priority is given to out-of-town students. 52% of students commute. All students may keep cars.

Activities: There are no fraternities or sororities. There are 55 groups on campus, including art, cheerleading, choir, chorale, chorus, computers, dance, debate, drama, ethnic, film, forensics, gay, gospel choir, honors, international, jazz band, literary magazine, major-specific, musical theater, newspaper, opera, orchestra, pep band, photography, political, professional, radio and TV, religious, social, social service, student government, symphony, and yearbook. Popular campus events include Bronco Bust (Spirit Week), Special Olympics, and Cinco de Mayo.

Sports: There are 8 intercollegiate sports for men and 9 for women, and 6 intramural sports for men and 11 for women. Facilities include an activities center with a basketball pavilion, volleyball courts, a swimming pool, a weight-training section, and a sauna. There is also a 6800-seat stadium with practice fields nearby, and several fields for general recreation and intramurals.

Disabled Students: All of the campus is accessible. Wheelchair ramps, elevators, special parking, specially equipped rest rooms, special class scheduling, lowered drinking fountains, lowered telephones, and a TTY phone system are available. Residence halls have been restructured to allow disabled students to open all doors with a remote control. Scribes and note takers are also provided.

Services: Counseling and information services are available, as is tutoring in most subjects.

Campus Safety and Security: Measures include 24-hour foot and vehicle patrol, security escort services, informal discussions, and pamphlets/posters/films. There are emergency telephones and lighted pathways/sidewalks.

Programs of Study: Santa Clara University confers B.A., B.S., B.S.C., and B.S.Ch. degrees. Master's and doctoral degrees are also awarded. Bachelor's degrees are awarded in AGRICULTURE (environmental studies), BIOLOGICAL SCIENCE (biology/biological science), BUSINESS (accounting, banking and finance, business administration and management, business economics, management information systems, and marketing/retailing/merchandising), COMMUNICATIONS AND THE ARTS (art history and appreciation, classical languages, classics, communications, dramatic arts, English, French, German, Greek, Italian, music, Spanish, and studio art), COMPUTER AND PHYSICAL SCIENCE (chemistry, computer science, information sciences and systems, mathematics, physics, and science), ENGINEERING AND ENVIRONMENTAL DESIGN (civil engineering, computer engineering, electrical/electronics engineering, engineering, engineering physics, environmental science, and mechanical engineering), SOCIAL SCIENCE (anthropology, classical/ancient civilization, economics, history, interdisciplinary studies, liberal arts/general studies, philosophy, political science/government, psychology, religion, and sociology). Social sciences and engineering are the strongest academically. Social sciences and business are the largest.

Required: All students are required to maintain a GPA of at least 2.0 in both major and minor subjects. Students must take 175 quarter units for most bachelor's degrees. Core requirements include composition and literature, Western culture, foreign language, social sciences, math and natural sciences, technology, ethics, religious studies, United States, and World Cultures/Societies.

Special: Study abroad in 26 countries at 75 sites is offered, as are international internship and volunteer opportunities. A co-op program in engineering, dual majors, internships in business, government, and nonprofit agencies, a general studies degree, student-designed majors, work-study, a Washington semester, and pass/fail options also are available. There are 21 national honor societies, including Phi Beta Kappa, a freshman honors program, and 4 departmental honors programs.

Faculty/Classroom: 62% of faculty are male; 38%, female. 74% teach undergraduates, and all both teach and do research. No introductory courses are taught by graduate students. The average class size in an introductory lecture is 29; in a laboratory, 13; and in a regular course, 22.

Admissions: 66% of the 2003-2004 applicants were accepted. The SAT I scores for the 2003-2004 freshman class were: Verbal--13% below 500, 44% between 500 and 599, 39% between 600 and 700, and 4% above 700; Math--7% below 500, 36% between 500 and 599, 49% between 600 and 700, and 8% above 700. The ACT scores were 9% below 21, 22% between 21 and 23, 34% between 24 and 26, 17% between 27 and 28, and 18% above 28. 56% of the current freshmen were in the top fifth of their class; 87% were in the top two fifths. There were 54 National Merit finalists in a recent year. 42 freshmen graduated first in their class in a recent year.

Requirements: The SAT I or ACT is required. In addition, applicants should have 18 academic units, including 4 years each of English and math, 3 each of foreign language and science, 1 or 2 of which are a lab, 1 each in social studies and history, and 2 in electives. An essay is required. An audition is recommended for theater arts majors. The GED is not accepted. AP credits are accepted. Important factors in the admissions decision are extracurricular activities record, advanced placement or honor courses, and recommendations by school officials.

Procedure: Freshmen are admitted fall, winter, and spring. Entrance exams should be taken by February 1. There are early action and deferred admissions plans. Early action applications should be filed by November 15; regular applications, by January 15 for fall entry, along with a $55 fee. Notification of early action is sent December 20; regular decision, on a rolling basis. 164 applicants were on the 2003 waiting list; 89 were admitted. Applications are accepted on-line.

Transfer: 220 transfer students enrolled in 2002-2003. Transfer students need a minimum GPA of 3.0. 87 of 175 credits required for the bachelor's degree must be completed at Santa Clara University.

Visiting: There are regularly scheduled orientations for prospective students, including an open house in October, with overviews of academic programs and student activities, and preview weekend in April for accepted students. There are guides for informal visits and visitors may sit in on classes and stay overnight. To schedule a visit, contact the Undergraduate Admissions Office.

Financial Aid: In a recent year, 64% of all full-time freshmen and 61% of continuing full-time students received some form of financial aid. 42% of full-time freshmen and 45% of continuing full-time students received need-based aid. The average freshman award was $14,826. Need-based scholarships or need-based grants averaged $12,292; need-based self-help aid (loans and jobs) averaged $2899; non-need-based athletic scholarships averaged $7887; and other non-need-based awards and non-need-based scholarships averaged $4689. 57% of undergraduates work part time. Average annual earnings from campus work are $1324. The average financial indebtedness of the 2002 graduate was $22,869. Santa Clara University is a member of CSS. The CSS/Profile or FAFSA is required. The priority date for freshman financial aid applications for fall entry is February 1.

International Students: There were 120 international students enrolled in a recent year. They must score 550 on the written TOEFL or 213 on the electronic version and also take the SAT I or the ACT.

Computers: The mainframes are an IBM 4381, a DEC VAX 8650, and a 750 DEC VAX. There are also PCs available in computer labs. All students may access the system. There are no time limits and no fees.

Graduates: From July 1, 2001 to June 30, 2002, 1112 bachelor's degrees were awarded. The most popular majors were business/marketing (33%), social studies and history (15%), and engineering/engineering technologies (10%). In an average class, 75% graduate in 4 years or less, 80% graduate in 5 years or less, and 81% graduate in 6 years or less. 230 companies recruited on campus in a recent year. Of a recent year's graduating class, 18% were enrolled in graduate school within 6 months of graduation.

Admissions Contact: Sandra Hayes, Dean of Admissions. A video is available. E-mail: *ugadmissions@scu.edu* Web: *www.scu.edu*

SCRIPPS COLLEGE
Claremont, CA 91711-3948

D-5
(909) 621-8149
(800) 770-1333; Fax: (909) 607-7508

Full-time: 804 women	**Faculty:** 59; IIB, ++$
Part-time: 6 women	**Ph.D.s:** 98%
Graduate: none	**Student/Faculty:** 14 to 1
Year: semesters	**Tuition:** $27,100
Application Deadline: January 15	**Room & Board:** $8600
Freshman Class: 1378 applied, 747 accepted, 210 enrolled	
SAT I Verbal/Math: 670/650	**ACT:** 30

HIGHLY COMPETITIVE+

Scripps College, founded in 1926, is a private liberal arts institution for women. A member of the Claremont Colleges, Scripps emphasizes a challenging core curriculum based on interdisciplinary humanistic studies. The 4 libraries contain 2,232,086 volumes, 719 microform items, and 5508 audio/video tapes/CDs, and subscribe to 5733 periodicals. Computerized library services include the card catalog, interlibrary loans, and database searching. Special learning facilities include an art gallery, radio station, TV station, humanities museum, and biological field station. The 30-acre campus is in a suburban area 35 miles east of Los Angeles. Including any residence halls, there are 27 buildings.

Student Life: 56% of undergraduates are from out of state, mostly the Northwest. Students are from 45 states and 19 foreign countries. 63% are from public schools. 61% are white; 13% Asian American. The average age of freshmen is 18; all undergraduates, 20. 12% do not continue beyond their first year; 76% remain to graduate.

Housing: 733 students can be accommodated in college housing, which includes single-sex dorms and on-campus apartments. In addition, there are foreign language corridors. On-campus housing is guaranteed for all 4 years. 96% of students live on campus; of those, 80% remain on campus on weekends. All students may keep cars.

Activities: There are no sororities. There are 200 groups on campus, including art, band, chess, choir, chorale, chorus, computers, dance, debate, drama, ethnic, film, gay, honors, international, jazz band, literary magazine, musical theater, newspaper, opera, orchestra, photography, political, professional, radio and TV, religious, social, social service, student government, symphony, and yearbook. Popular campus events include Break Away Series, Scripps Outdoor Adventure Program, and Freshman Mugging.

Sports: Facilities include 2 gyms, tennis and squash courts, 4 swimming pools, a climbing wall, a workout room, 2 outdoor tracks, and fields for baseball, softball, and soccer.

Disabled Students: 70% of the campus is accessible. Wheelchair ramps, elevators, special parking, specially equipped rest rooms, special class scheduling, lowered drinking fountains, and special housing are available.

Services: Counseling and information services are available, as is tutoring in every subject. There is a reader service for the blind.

Campus Safety and Security: Measures include 24-hour foot and vehicle patrol, self-defense education, security escort services, and informal discussions. There are pamphlets/posters/films, emergency telephones, and lighted pathways/sidewalks.

Programs of Study: Scripps confers the B.A. degree. Bachelor's degrees are awarded in BIOLOGICAL SCIENCE (biology/biological science and neurosciences), COMMUNICATIONS AND THE ARTS (art history and appreciation, classical languages, dance, dramatic arts, English, Germanic languages and literature, Italian, languages, music, and studio art), COMPUTER AND PHYSICAL SCIENCE (chemistry, mathematics, physics, science and management, and science technology), ENGINEERING AND ENVIRONMENTAL DESIGN (engineering, environmental science, and preengineering), SOCIAL SCIENCE (African American studies, American studies, anthropology, Asian/American studies, Asian/Oriental studies, classical/ancient civilization, economics, European studies, French studies, German area studies, Hispanic American studies, history, humanities, Italian studies, Judaic studies, Latin American studies, Mexican-American/Chicano studies, philosophy, political science/government, prelaw, psychology, religion, and women's studies). English, studio art, and biology are the strongest academically. Social science, politics, and international relations are the largest.

Required: To graduate, students must complete a total of 128 credits, or 32 courses with a minimum C average. Core requirements include the 3-semester humanities core, 2 additional courses in humanities, and 1 course each in fine arts, letters, natural sciences, social sciences, and math. All students must also fulfill language and thesis requirements.

Special: Students may cross-register with any of the other Claremont Colleges. Scripps also offers internships, work-study programs, study abroad in 35 countries, a Washington semester, and student-designed, dual, and interdisciplinary majors, including organizational studies and science, technology, and society. Many courses are offered as seminars. There are 3-2 accelerated degree programs in the arts and business administration. A 3-2 engineering program (B.A.-B.S.) is offered with Harvey Mudd College, Washington University in St. Louis, USC, UC Berkeley, and Columbia, Stanford, and Boston Universities. There are 3 national honor societies, including Phi Beta Kappa, and 16 departmental honors programs.

Faculty/Classroom: 37% of faculty are male; 63%, female. All both teach and do research. The average class size in an introductory lecture is 30; in a laboratory, 20; and in a regular course, 17.

Admissions: 54% of the 2003-2004 applicants were accepted. The SAT I scores for the 2003-2004 freshman class were: Verbal--13% between 500 and 599, 52% between 600 and 700, and 35% above 700; Math--2% below 500, 16% between 500 and 599, 58% between 600 and 700, and 24% above 700. The ACT scores were 1% below 21, 9% between 21 and 23, 17% between 24 and 26, 26% between 27 and 28, and 47% above 28. 89% of the current freshmen were in the top fifth of their class; 99% were in the top two fifths. There were 14 National Merit finalists and 1 semifinalist. 5 freshmen graduated first in their class.

Requirements: The SAT I or ACT is required. In addition, applicants must have completed 4 units each of high school English and math, 3 each of lab science and social studies, and either 3 of a single foreign language or 2 each of 2 languages. SAT II: Subject tests and an interview are recommended. An essay and a graded writing assignment from the junior or senior year are required. Scripps requires applicants to be in the upper 50% of their class. A GPA of 3.0 is required. AP and CLEP credits are accepted. Important factors in the admissions decision are advanced placement or honor courses, evidence of special talent, and leadership record.

Procedure: Freshmen are admitted fall and spring. Entrance exams should be taken by December of the senior year. There are early decision, early admissions, and deferred admissions plans. Early decision applications should be filed by November 1; regular applications, by January 15 for fall entry and November 15 for spring entry. The fall 2003 application fee was $50. Notification of early decision is sent December 15; regular decision, April 1. 47 early decision candidates were accepted for the 2003-2004 class. 287 were on the 2003 waiting list; 8 were admitted.

Transfer: 18 transfer students enrolled in 2002-2003. A cumulative college GPA of 3.0 is required. 64 of 128 credits required for the bachelor's degree must be completed at Scripps.

Visiting: There are guides for informal visits and visitors may sit in on classes and stay overnight. To schedule a visit, contact the Admission Office at *admission@scrippscollege.edu*.

Financial Aid: In a recent year, 63% of all full-time freshmen and 62% of continuing full-time students received some form of financial aid. 51% of all full-time students received need-based aid. The average freshman award for 2002-2003 was $23,046. Average annual earnings from campus work are $1024. The average financial indebtedness of a recent year's graduate was $13,394. Scripps is a member of CSS. The CSS/Profile or FAFSA is required. The deadline for filing freshman financial aid applications for fall entry is February 1.

International Students: There are 15 international students enrolled. The school actively recruits these students. They must score 600 on the written TOEFL and also take the SAT I or the ACT.

Computers: The mainframe is a DEC VAX. PCs and Macs are available in computer labs and dorms. Students are served by the Novell Network, with access to the Internet, including direct access from their rooms. All students may access the system. There are no time limits and no fees.

Graduates: From July 1, 2002 to June 30, 2003, 198 bachelor's degrees were awarded. The most popular majors were politics and international relations (11%), psychology (10%), and studio art (10%). In an average class, 1% graduate in 3 years or less, 81% graduate in 4 years or less, 73% graduate in 5 years or less, and 77% graduate in 6 years or less. 160 companies recruited on campus in 2002-2003. Of the 2002 graduating class, 36% were enrolled in graduate school within 6 months of graduation and 55% were employed.

Admissions Contact: Patricia F. Goldsmith, Vice President and Dean of Admissions, Financial Aid. E-mail: *admission@scrippscollege.edu* Web: *www.scrippscol.edu*

SIMPSON COLLEGE
Redding, CA 96003

B-3
(530) 224-5600
(800) 598-2493; Fax: (530) 226-4861

Full-time: 348 men, 587 women	Faculty: 40
Part-time: 13 men, 16 women	Ph.D.s: 58%
Graduate: 74 men, 137 women	Student/Faculty: 23 to 1
Year: semesters, summer session	Tuition: $14,760
Application Deadline: open	Room & Board: $5740
Freshman Class: 784 applied, 743 accepted, 154 enrolled	
SAT I Verbal/Math: 510/487	ACT: 21 COMPETITIVE

Simpson College, founded in 1921, is a private Christian liberal arts college. An official institution of the Christian and Missionary Alliance, the student population represents more than 25 evangelical denominations. In addition to regional accreditation, Simpson has baccalaureate program accreditation with WASC. The library contains 90,000 volumes, 221,045 microform items, and 2240 audio/video tapes/CDs, and sub-

scribes to 328 periodicals, with on-line access to more than 8000 periodicals. Computerized library services include the card catalog, interlibrary loans, database searching, and Internet access. Special learning facilities include a learning resource center. The 92-acre campus is in a suburban area in the northeast city limits of Redding. Including any residence halls, there are 11 buildings.

Student Life: 86% of undergraduates are from California. Students are from 24 states, 6 foreign countries, and Canada. 86% are white. Most are Protestant. The average age of freshmen is 18; all undergraduates, 25. 40% do not continue beyond their first year; 60% remain to graduate.

Housing: 590 students can be accommodated in college housing, which includes single-sex dorms, off-campus apartments, and married-student housing. On-campus housing is guaranteed for all 4 years. 66% of students live on campus; of those, 90% remain on campus on weekends. Alcohol is not permitted. All students may keep cars.

Activities: There are no fraternities or sororities. There are 20 groups on campus, including art, cheerleading, choir, chorale, Commuter Students Association, drama, ethnic, golf, jazz band, literary magazine, newspaper, pep band, photography, professional, psychology, religious, social, social service, student government, and yearbook. Popular campus events include Spring and Winter Banquet, Missions Emphasis Week, and Multicultural Appreciation Day.

Sports: There are 3 intercollegiate sports for men and 3 for women, and 4 intramural sports for men and 4 for women. Facilities include a soccer field, a 1450-seat gym, weight and training rooms, a softball field, and outdoor volleyball and basketball courts. Students have access to nearby facilities for swimming, boating, mountain climbing, and skiing.

Disabled Students: 95% of the campus is accessible. Wheelchair ramps, elevators, special parking, specially equipped rest rooms, lowered drinking fountains, lowered telephones, and special housing are available.

Services: Counseling and information services are available, as is tutoring in every subject.

Campus Safety and Security: Measures include 24-hour foot and vehicle patrol, security escort services, informal discussions, and emergency telephones. There are lighted pathways/sidewalks, an emergency whistle program, local police patrols, and monthly campus safety meetings.

Programs of Study: Simpson confers the B.A. degree. Associate and master's degrees are also awarded. Bachelor's degrees are awarded in BUSINESS (accounting, business administration and management, human resources, and institutional management), COMMUNICATIONS AND THE ARTS (communications, English, and music), COMPUTER AND PHYSICAL SCIENCE (mathematics), EDUCATION (elementary and secondary), SOCIAL SCIENCE (biblical studies, history, liberal arts/general studies, ministries, missions, pastoral studies, psychology, religion, religious education, social science, and youth ministry). Psychology, education, and human resources are the largest.

Required: Students must complete at least 124 credits, with a minimum of 36 upper division credits and at least 30 major credits (of which 24 must be upper division). A minimum GPA of 2.0 must be maintained. Foundational studies requirements include 24 credits in Biblical Christianity and its foundations and 48 credits in human expression, human history and behavior, and global environment. Additionally, graduation requirements include the completion of an application for degree and recommendation by the undergraduate faculty.

Special: Off-campus educational programs are offered through the China Studies Program, Contemporary Music Program in Martha's Vineyard, Latin American Studies Program, Los Angeles Film Studies Center, Middle East Studies Program, Oxford Honors Program, and the Russian Studies Program. Students may study abroad in a variety of countries. Internships are available in Christian education, pastoral studies, youth ministries business, and psychology. Work-study programs in elementary education and with the federal government are also available. There is also a 1-year, nondegree certificate program in Bible and contemporary church music. Accelerated degree programs in business and human resources management, liberal arts, psychology, organizational leadership, and Christian ministry leadership are also available for students with 60 college credits and 5 years of full-time experience. There is 1 national honor society.

Faculty/Classroom: 80% of faculty are male; 20%, female. All teach undergraduates. The average class size in an introductory lecture is 25; in a laboratory, 13; and in a regular course, 14.

Admissions: 95% of the 2003-2004 applicants were accepted. The SAT I scores for the 2003-2004 freshman class were: Verbal--43% below 500, 42% between 500 and 599, 13% between 600 and 700, and 2% above 700; Math--56% below 500, 33% between 500 and 599, 11% between 600 and 700, and 1% above 700. The ACT scores were 42% below 21, 32% between 21 and 23, 16% between 24 and 26, 6% between 27 and 28, and 3% above 28. 44% of the current freshmen were in the top fifth of their class; 67% were in the top two fifths. 1 freshman graduated first in the class.

Requirements: The SAT I or ACT is required. In addition, applicants must be graduates of an accredited high school or have a GED. It is recommended that applicants have completed 4 years of high school English, 3 each of math, science, and social studies/history, and 2 of a foreign language. A GPA of 2.0 is required. AP and CLEP credits are accepted. Important factors in the admissions decision are leadership record, personality/intangible qualities, and recommendations by school officials.

Procedure: Freshmen are admitted to all sessions. Entrance exams should be taken during the junior year or in the fall of the senior year. There is a deferred admissions plan. Application deadlines are open. Application fee is $20. Notification is sent on a rolling basis. Applications are accepted on-line through *www.simpsonca.edu*.

Transfer: 101 transfer students enrolled in 2002-2003. Transfer applicants with at least 30 semester college credits need not submit SAT I or ACT scores. 30 of 124 credits required for the bachelor's degree must be completed at Simpson.

Visiting: There are regularly scheduled orientations for prospective students, consisting of College Days weekend, offered each spring. There are guides for informal visits and visitors may sit in on classes and stay overnight. To schedule a visit, contact Matthew Bridgen, Assistant Director of Undergraduate Recruitment, at *admissions@simpsonca.edu*.

Financial Aid: In 2003-2004, 95% of all full-time freshmen and 94% of continuing full-time students received some form of financial aid. 78% of full-time freshmen and 79% of continuing full-time students received need-based aid. The average freshman award was $11,915, with $4779 ($13,758 maximum) from need-based scholarships or need-based grants, $3125 ($3625 maximum) from need-based self-help aid (loans and jobs), and $4011 ($7500 maximum) from non-need-based awards and non-need-based scholarships. 32% of undergraduates work part time. Average annual earnings from campus work are $1007. The average financial indebtedness of the 2003 graduate was $17,600. Simpson is a member of CSS. The FAFSA and the college's own financial statement are required. The priority date for freshman financial aid applications for fall entry is March 2.

International Students: There are 5 international students enrolled. They must score 500 on the written TOEFL and also take the SAT I or the ACT.

Computers: The mainframe is an IBM AS/400 B-70. The college administrative system is accessible via the Web at any time. 65 computers with Internet and network access are available in various locations throughout the campus for student use. All students may access the system. Students may access the system only during hours of operation of the specific facility. There are no fees. It is strongly recommended that all students have a personal computer.

Graduates: From July 1, 2002 to June 30, 2003, 296 bachelor's degrees were awarded. The most popular majors were liberal arts (25%), psychology (20%), and human resources management (18%). In an average class, 1% graduate in 3 years or less, 4% graduate in 4 years or less, 36% graduate in 5 years or less, and 45% graduate in 6 years or less.

Admissions Contact: Matthew Bridgen, Assistant Director of Undergraduate Recruitment. E-mail: *admissions@simpsonca.edu* Web: *www.simpsonca.edu*

SONOMA STATE UNIVERSITY

Rohnert Park, CA 94928   B-3
(707) 664-2778; Fax: (707) 664-2060

Full-time: 2175 men, 3844 women	**Faculty:** 246; IIA, +$
Part-time: 415 men, 562 women	**Ph.D.s:** 95%
Graduate: 399 men, 976 women	**Student/Faculty:** 24 to 1
Year: semesters, summer session	**Tuition:** $6020 ($11,470)
Application Deadline: November	**Room & Board:** $7411
Freshman Class: 6366 applied, 5361 accepted, 1303 enrolled	
SAT I Verbal/Math: 520/520	**ACT:** 21 COMPETITIVE

Sonoma State University, founded in 1960 and part of the California State University system, offers undergraduate programs in business and economics, natural sciences, social sciences, and arts and humanities, and graduate programs in education, counseling, business, and other fields. There are 4 undergraduate schools and 1 graduate school. In addition to regional accreditation, Sonoma State has baccalaureate program accreditation with ACS, NASAD, NASM, and NLN. The library contains 706,537 volumes, 1,669,872 microform items, and 27,895 audio/video tapes/CDs, and subscribes to 1085 periodicals. Computerized library services include the card catalog, interlibrary loans, and database searching. Special learning facilities include a learning resource center, art gallery, radio station, observatory, and natural preserve. The 275-acre campus is in a suburban area 45 miles north of San Francisco. Including any residence halls, there are 62 buildings.

Student Life: 97% of undergraduates are from California. Students are from 39 states, 36 foreign countries, and Canada. 93% are from public schools. 64% are white; 10% Hispanic. The average age of freshmen is 18; all undergraduates, 23. 20% do not continue beyond their first year; 50% remain to graduate.

Housing: 2341 students can be accommodated in college housing, which includes single-sex and coed dorms and on-campus apartments.

In addition, there are special-interest, women-in-science, substance-free, and intensive study houses. On-campus housing is guaranteed for the freshman year only and is available on a first-come, first-served basis. 62% of students commute. All students may keep cars.

Activities: 6% of men belong to 5 national fraternities; 5% of women belong to 4 national sororities. There are 100 groups on campus, including art, cheerleading, chess, choir, chorale, chorus, computers, dance, drama, ethnic, gay, honors, international, jazz band, literary magazine, musical theater, newspaper, orchestra, pep band, political, professional, radio and TV, religious, social, social service, student government, and video. Popular campus events include Science Night, Parents Day, and Unity Through Diversity Week.

Sports: There are 4 intercollegiate sports for men and 7 for women, and 10 intramural sports for men and 10 for women. Facilities include a 5000-seat stadium, a 3000-seat gym, a field house, tennis courts, a pool, a 500-seat auditorium, and various playing fields.

Disabled Students: All of the campus is accessible. Wheelchair ramps, elevators, special parking, specially equipped rest rooms, special class scheduling, lowered drinking fountains, and lowered telephones are available. A reading machine, phonic listening devices, PC and mainframe access, and interpreters are also available.

Services: Counseling and information services are available, as is tutoring in most subjects. There is a reader service for the blind and remedial math, reading, and writing. Learning disability assessment is also available.

Campus Safety and Security: Measures include 24-hour foot and vehicle patrol, self-defense education, security escort services, and pamphlets/posters/films. There are emergency telephones and lighted pathways/sidewalks.

Programs of Study: Sonoma State confers B.A., B.S., and B.F.A. degrees. Master's degrees are also awarded. Bachelor's degrees are awarded in BIOLOGICAL SCIENCE (biology/biological science), BUSINESS (business administration and management), COMMUNICATIONS AND THE ARTS (art, communications, English, fine arts, French, music, Spanish, and visual and performing arts), COMPUTER AND PHYSICAL SCIENCE (chemistry, computer science, geology, mathematics, and physics), ENGINEERING AND ENVIRONMENTAL DESIGN (environmental science), HEALTH PROFESSIONS (nursing), SOCIAL SCIENCE (African American studies, American Indian studies, anthropology, criminal justice, economics, ethnic studies, gender studies, geography, history, human development, interdisciplinary studies, international studies, Latin American studies, liberal arts/general studies, Mexican-American/Chicano studies, philosophy, physical fitness/movement, political science/government, psychology, sociology, and women's studies). Liberal arts, physics, and math are the strongest academically. Business, psychology, and liberal studies are the largest.

Required: Undergraduate students must complete 120 to 132 units, depending on the degree program, consisting of 48 to 51 units of general education, a concentration of study in a specific major, and electives. General education programs require experience in oral and written communications, critical thinking, natural science and math, arts and humanities, social sciences, and personal integration. All students must take an ethnic studies course and the equivalent of courses in U.S. government, U.S. history, and California government.

Special: Students may cross-register at Mills College, Oakland, and University of California, Berkeley. Study-abroad programs are available in 17 countries. Community service internships, work-study, nondegree study through Open University, and pass/fail grading options are available. B.A. and B.S. options in biology, chemistry, environmental studies, geology, interdisciplinary studies, math, and physics are offered. The Hutchins School B.A. in liberal studies offers small seminar classes and an interdisciplinary curriculum. Distance learning programs in nursing are available at 3 off-site centers. There are 6 national honor societies, and 5 departmental honors programs.

Faculty/Classroom: 58% of faculty are male; 42%, female. 99% teach undergraduates. Graduate students teach 1% of introductory courses. The average class size in an introductory lecture is 45; in a laboratory, 20; and in a regular course, 26.

Admissions: 84% of the 2003-2004 applicants were accepted. The SAT I scores for the 2003-2004 freshman class were: Verbal--39% below 500, 44% between 500 and 599, 15% between 600 and 700, and 2% above 700; Math--37% below 500, 47% between 500 and 599, 15% between 600 and 700, and 1% above 700. The ACT scores were 39% below 21, 35% between 21 and 23, 21% between 24 and 26, 3% between 27 and 28, and 2% above 28.

Requirements: The SAT I or ACT is required, unless the applicant has a 3.0 GPA. Applicants should be graduates of accredited high schools or have earned the GED. Secondary school preparation should include 4 years each of arts and humanities, 3 each of English, math, social science, and academic electives, and 1 each of music, history, and a lab science. A GPA of 2.0 is required. AP and CLEP credits are accepted. Geographic diversity is an important factor in the admission decision.

Procedure: Freshmen are admitted fall and spring. Applications should be filed by November for fall entry and August for spring entry. There is a rolling admissions plan. Notification is sent on a rolling basis. The fall 2003 application fee was $55. Applications are accepted on-line.

Transfer: 646 transfer students enrolled in 2002-2003. Applicants must have a minimum 2.0 GPA. The maximum number of transferable credits is 70. 30 of 120 to 132 credits required for the bachelor's degree must be completed at Sonoma State.

Visiting: There are regularly scheduled orientations for prospective students, consisting of programs in the spring and summer. There are guides for informal visits and visitors may sit in on classes. To schedule a visit, contact the Admissions Development Office at (707) 664-3032.

Financial Aid: In 2003-2004, 66% of all full-time freshmen received some form of financial aid. 36% of full-time freshmen received need-based aid. The average freshman award was $12,548. Need-based scholarships or need-based grants averaged $5858; need-based self-help aid (loans and jobs) averaged $2865; and non-need-based awards and non-need-based scholarships averaged $2120. 5% of undergraduates work part time. Average annual earnings from campus work are $1919. The average financial indebtedness of the 2003 graduate was $7848. The FAFSA is required. The priority date for freshman financial aid applications for fall entry is January 31.

International Students: There are 101 international students enrolled. The school actively recruits these students. They must score 500 on the written TOEFL or 173 on the electronic version.

Computers: Students may access the network via any of 30 computer labs or personal computers with wired ports throughout campus. Information about labs can be found at *http://www.sonoma.edu/it/labs/*. All students may access the system. There are no time limits and no fees. It is strongly recommended that all students have a personal computer.

Graduates: From July 1, 2002 to June 30, 2003, 1372 bachelor's degrees were awarded. The most popular majors were business administration (16%), psychology (11%), and liberal studies (10%). In an average class, 2% graduate in 3 years or less, 20% graduate in 4 years or less, 42% graduate in 5 years or less, and 49% graduate in 6 years or less. 275 companies recruited on campus in 2002-2003.

Admissions Contact: Gustavo Flores, Admissions Office. A video is available. E-mail: *gustavo.flores@sonoma.edu* Web: *www.sonoma.edu*

STANFORD UNIVERSITY
Stanford, CA 94305-3005

B-3
(650) 723-2091; Fax: (650) 723-6050

Full-time: 3340 men, 3102 women	**Faculty:** I, ++$
Part-time: none	**Ph.D.s:** 99%
Graduate: 5007 men, 2793 women	**Student/Faculty:** n/av
Year: quarters, summer session	**Tuition:** $28,563
Application Deadline: December 15	**Room & Board:** $9049
Freshman Class: 18,628 applied, 2343 accepted, 1640 enrolled	
SAT I or ACT: required	**MOST COMPETITIVE**

Stanford University, founded in 1885, is a private research-intensive university offering a broad curriculum in undergraduate liberal arts, graduate education, and professional training. There are 3 undergraduate and 7 graduate schools. In addition to regional accreditation, Stanford has baccalaureate program accreditation with AACSB and ABET. The 19 libraries contain 7,803,988 volumes, 4,900,000 microform items, and 378,657 audio/video tapes/CDs, and subscribe to 30,000 periodicals. Computerized library services include the card catalog, interlibrary loans, database searching, and Internet access. Special learning facilities include a learning resource center, art gallery, radio station, TV station, an art museum, a biological preserve, and a linear accelerator. The 8180-acre campus is in a suburban area 30 miles south of San Francisco. Including any residence halls, there are 678 buildings.

Student Life: 54% of undergraduates are from out of state, mostly the Middle Atlantic. Students are from 50 states, 65 foreign countries, and Canada. 72% are from public schools. 46% are white; 25% Asian American; 12% Hispanic; 10% African American. The average age of freshmen is 18; all undergraduates, 20. 3% do not continue beyond their first year; 93% remain to graduate.

Housing: 10,290 students can be accommodated in college housing, which includes single-sex and coed dormitories, on-campus apartments, off-campus apartments, married-student housing, fraternity houses, and sorority houses. In addition, there are language houses, and special-interest houses, and ethnic theme houses. On-campus housing is guaranteed for all 4 years. 94% of students live on campus; of those, 95% remain on campus on weekends. Upperclassmen may keep cars.

Activities: 13% of men belong to 15 national fraternities; 13% of women belong to 10 national sororities. There are 600 groups on campus, including art, band, cheerleading, chess, choir, chorale, computers, dance, debate, drama, ethnic, film, gay, honors, international, jazz band, literary magazine, marching band, musical theater, newspaper, orchestra, pep band, photography, political, professional, radio and TV, religious, social, social service, student government, symphony, and yearbook. Popular campus events include the Big Game, Full Moon on the Quad, and Pow Wow.

Sports: There are 15 intercollegiate sports for men, 18 for women, and 1 coed and 37 intramural sports for men and 37 for women. Facilities

include athletic fields, gyms, swimming pools, volleyball courts, lighted tennis courts, dance studios, an 18-hole golf course, a sailing center, a rowing facility, handball, racquetball and squash courts, a baseball diamond, a football stadium, a softball stadium, and field hockey, lacrosse, and soccer fields.

Disabled Students: 90% of the campus is accessible. Wheelchair ramps, elevators, special parking, specially equipped rest rooms, special class scheduling, lowered drinking fountains, lowered telephones, and a Diversity and Access Office are available.

Services: Counseling and information services are available, as is tutoring in most subjects. There is a reader service for the blind. The Disability Resource Center provides many services to learning disabled students. The Schwab Learning Center serves students with learning differences and attention deficit hyperactivity disorder.

Campus Safety and Security: Measures include 24-hour foot and vehicle patrol, self-defense education, security escort services, and shuttle buses. There are informal discussions, pamphlets/posters/films, emergency telephones, and lighted pathways/sidewalks.

Programs of Study: Stanford confers B.S., A.B., and B.A.S. degrees. Master's and doctoral degrees are also awarded. Bachelor's degrees are awarded in BIOLOGICAL SCIENCE (biology/biological science), COMMUNICATIONS AND THE ARTS (art, Chinese, classics, communications, comparative literature, dramatic arts, English, fine arts, French, Italian, Japanese, linguistics, music, Slavic languages, and Spanish), COMPUTER AND PHYSICAL SCIENCE (chemistry, computer science, earth science, geology, geophysics and seismology, geoscience, mathematics, and physics), ENGINEERING AND ENVIRONMENTAL DESIGN (aeronautical science, chemical engineering, civil engineering, electrical/electronics engineering, engineering, industrial engineering, materials science, mechanical engineering, and petroleum/natural gas engineering), SOCIAL SCIENCE (African American studies, American studies, anthropology, archeology, crosscultural studies, East Asian studies, economics, German area studies, history, international relations, philosophy, political science/government, psychology, religion, sociology, systems science, urban studies, and women's studies). Biology, economics, and computer science are the largest.

Required: To graduate, students must complete 180 units, including requirements for the major, a writing requirement, 1 year of a foreign language, 1 year of Introduction to the Humanities, 3 courses in natural sciences, applied science and technology, and math, 3 courses in humanities and social sciences, and 2 courses in world cultures, American cultures, and Gender Studies.

Special: Internships, study abroad, a Washington semester, student-designed majors, dual majors, a B.A.-B.S. degree, pass/no credit options, and numerous research opportunities are offered. There are many national honor societies, including Phi Beta Kappa. Almost all departments have honors programs.

Faculty/Classroom: 78% of faculty are male; 22%, female. All both teach and do research. Graduate students teach 5% of undergraduate class sections.

Admissions: 13% of the 2003-2004 applicants were accepted. The SAT I scores for the 2003-2004 freshman class were: Verbal--8% between 500 and 599, 28% between 600 and 700, and 63% above 700; Math--5% between 500 and 599, 25% between 600 and 700, and 69% above 700. 96% of the current freshmen were in the top fifth of their class; 99% were in the top two fifths.

Requirements: The SAT I or ACT is required; the SAT I is preferred. The university recommends that applicants have strong preparation in high school English, math, a foreign language, science, and social studies. SAT II: Subject tests are strongly recommended. AP credits are accepted. Important factors in the admissions decision are advanced placement or honor courses, personality/intangible qualities, and recommendations by school officials.

Procedure: Freshmen are admitted in the fall. Entrance exams should be taken before December of the application year. There are early action and deferred admissions plans. Early action applications should be filed by November 1; regular applications, by December 15 for fall entry, along with a $75 fee. Notification of early action is sent mid-December; regular decision, early April. 598 early action candidates were accepted for the 2003-2004 class. A waiting list is an active part of the admissions procedure. Applications are accepted on-line.

Transfer: 81 transfer students enrolled in 2003-2004. Transfer students must complete 1 full year of academic work prior to enrollment. There is only fall quarter enrollment for transfer students. The application deadline is March 15. 90 of 180 credits required for the bachelor's degree must be completed at Stanford.

Visiting: There are regularly scheduled orientations for prospective students, including group information sessions and campus tours. There are guides for informal visits and visitors may sit in on classes. To schedule a visit, contact the Office of Undergraduate Admission at *admission@stanford.edu*.

Financial Aid: In 2003-2004, 74% of all full-time freshmen and 73% of continuing full-time students received some form of financial aid. 47% of full-time freshmen received need-based aid. The average freshman award was $29,861. Need-based scholarships or need-based grants averaged $24,399; and need-based self-help aid (loans and jobs) averaged $3015. The average financial indebtedness of the 2003 graduate was $16,045. Stanford is a member of CSS. The CSS/Profile or FAFSA is required. The deadline for filing freshman financial aid applications for fall entry is February 1.

International Students: There were 332 international students enrolled in a recent year. The school actively recruits these students. They must take the TOEFL as well as the SAT I or the ACT. SAT II: Subject tests are strongly recommended.

Computers: Macs and other PCs are available in residences, libraries, and other campus clusters. All students may access the system. There are no time limits and no fees.

Graduates: From July 1, 2002 to June 30, 2003, 1788 bachelor's degrees were awarded. The most popular majors were biology/human biology (16%), economics (8%), and computer science (8%). In an average class, 93% graduate in 6 years or less. 325 companies recruited on campus in 2002-2003.

Admissions Contact: Robin Mamlet, Director of Admission. A video is available. E-mail: *rmamlet@stanford.edu* Web: *www.stanford.edu*

THOMAS AQUINAS COLLEGE   C-5
Santa Paula, CA 93060   (805) 525-4417, ext. 361
(800) 634-9797; Fax: (805) 525-0620

Full-time: 153 men, 179 women	**Faculty:** 30
Part-time: none	**Ph.D.s:** 73%
Graduate: none	**Student/Faculty:** 11 to 1
Year: semesters	**Tuition:** $16,800
Application Deadline: open	**Room & Board:** $5200
Freshman Class: 184 applied, 144 accepted, 101 enrolled	
SAT I Verbal/Math: 670/610	**ACT:** 28 **VERY COMPETITIVE+**

Thomas Aquinas College, founded in 1969 and affiliated with the Roman Catholic Church, is a small, private, liberal arts college offering an integrated studies curriculum based on the Great Books. All classes are conducted as conversations directed by teachers using the Socratic method. In addition to regional accreditation, TAC has baccalaureate program accreditation with AALE. The library contains 52,000 volumes and 7800 audio/video tapes/CDs, and subscribes to 55 periodicals. Computerized library services include the card catalog, interlibrary loans, database searching, and Internet access. Special learning facilities include a learning resource center and art gallery. The 170-acre campus is in a rural area 60 miles northwest of Los Angeles. Including any residence halls, there are 22 buildings.

Student Life: 63% of undergraduates are from out of state, mostly the Midwest. Students are from 42 states, 7 foreign countries, and Canada. 20% are from public schools. 82% are white. 92% are Catholic; 6% Protestant. The average age of freshmen is 19; all undergraduates, 20. 11% do not continue beyond their first year; 79% remain to graduate.

Housing: 382 students can be accommodated in college housing, which includes single-sex dorms. On-campus housing is guaranteed for all 4 years. 99% of students live on campus; of those, all remain on campus on weekends. Alcohol is not permitted. All students may keep cars.

Activities: There are no fraternities or sororities. There are some groups and organizations on campus, including choir, drama, literary magazine, and religious. Popular campus events include St. Thomas Aquinas Day, President's Day, and Alumni Day.

Sports: There are 4 intramural sports for men and 2 for women. Facilities include tennis, basketball, and volleyball courts, a soccer field, a swimming area, a weight-lifting room, and a softball field.

Disabled Students: All of the campus is accessible. Wheelchair ramps, elevators, special parking, specially equipped rest rooms, and lowered drinking fountains are available.

Services: All students may be tutored by the full-time teaching faculty.

Campus Safety and Security: Measures include lighted pathways/sidewalks.

Programs of Study: TAC confers the B.A. degree. Bachelor's degrees are awarded in SOCIAL SCIENCE (liberal arts/general studies).

Required: The entire curriculum is required of all students: 4 years of seminars in literature, history, and social sciences, 4 years each of philosophy, theology, math, and lab science, 2 years of language, and 1 year of music. A total of 146 semester hours, with a minimum GPA of 2.0, is required to graduate. A senior thesis is also required.

Special: There are no electives, majors, or minors. Students read original writings of Western civilization and discuss them in small seminarstyle groups. Many exams are oral.

Faculty/Classroom: 91% of faculty are male; 9%, female. All teach undergraduates. The average class size in an introductory lecture is 17; in a laboratory, 17; and in a regular course, 17.

Admissions: 78% of the 2003-2004 applicants were accepted. The SAT I scores for the 2003-2004 freshman class were: Verbal--12% between 500 and 599, 59% between 600 and 700, and 29% above 700; Math--1% below 500, 38% between 500 and 599, 52% between 600

and 700, and 9% above 700. The ACT scores were 7% between 21 and 23, 41% between 24 and 26, 11% between 27 and 28, and 41% above 28. 58% of the current freshmen were in the top fifth of their class; 79% were in the top two fifths. There were 2 National Merit finalists and 1 semifinalist. 4 freshmen graduated first in their class.

Requirements: The SAT I or ACT is required. In addition, candidates for admission should have completed 4 years of English, 3 of math, and 2 each of a foreign language, history, and science. Important factors in the admissions decision are personality/intangible qualities, advanced placement or honor courses, and recommendations by school officials.

Procedure: Freshmen are admitted in the fall. Entrance exams should be taken by March. There are early admissions and deferred admissions plans. Application deadlines are open. Notification is sent on a rolling basis.

Transfer: Transfers are not accepted.

Visiting: There are regularly scheduled orientations for prospective students, including hosting of prospective students by current students. Visits are for up to 5 days and consist of observing classes and attending lectures, concerts, and meals. There are guides for informal visits and visitors may sit in on classes and stay overnight. To schedule a visit, contact the Admissions Office at (800) 634-9797, ext. 360 or *admissions@thomasaquinas.edu*.

Financial Aid: In 2003-2004, 71% of all full-time students received some form of financial aid. 66% of full-time freshmen and 71% of continuing full-time students received need-based aid. The average freshman award was $13,800, with $8724 ($16,688 maximum) from need-based scholarships or need-based grants, $4321 ($6460 maximum) from need-based self-help aid (loans and jobs), and other $755 ($6350 maximum) from other non-need-based awards and non-need-based scholarships. 60% of undergraduates work part time. Average annual earnings from campus work are $2960. The average financial indebtedness of the 2003 graduate was $13,250. TAC is a member of CSS. The FAFSA, the college's own financial statement, and parent and student federal tax returns are required. The deadline for filing freshman financial aid applications for fall entry is July 1.

International Students: There are 25 international students enrolled. They must score 570 on the written TOEFL or 230 on the electronic version and also take the SAT I.

Computers: 2 PCs are available for student use in 1 women's dorm and 1 men's dorm; there are 6 student computers in the library for e-mail and word processing, 3 of which have full Internet access. All students may access the system whenever available, or during library hours. There are no time limits and no fees.

Graduates: From July 1, 2002 to June 30, 2003, 77 bachelor's degrees were awarded. The most popular major was liberal arts (100%). In an average class, 61% graduate in 4 years or less, 68% graduate in 5 years or less, and 70% graduate in 6 years or less. 7 companies recruited on campus in 2002-2003. Of the 2002 graduating class, 17% were enrolled in graduate school within 6 months of graduation and 62% were employed.

Admissions Contact: Thomas J. Susanka, Director of Admission. A video is available. E-mail: *admissions@thomasaquinas.edu* Web: *thomasaquinas.edu*

UNITED STATES INTERNATIONAL UNIVERSITY
(See Alliant International University)

UNIVERSITY OF CALIFORNIA SYSTEM

The University of California System, established in 1868, is a public system in California. It is governed by a Board of Regents, whose chief administrator is the president. The primary goal of the system is teaching, research, and public service. The total enrollment of all 9 campuses is usually about 163,000; there were 7000 faculty members. Altogether there are some 565 baccalaureate, 250 master's, and 200 doctoral programs offered in the University of California System. 4-year campuses are located in Berkeley, Davis, Irvine, Los Angeles, Riverside, San Diego, and Santa Barbara. Profiles of the 4-year campuses are included in this section.

UNIVERSITY OF CALIFORNIA AT BERKELEY   B-3
Berkeley, CA 94720-5800   (510) 642-3175; Fax: (510) 642-7333

Full-time: 10,185 men, 12,100 women	**Faculty:** 1462; I, ++$
Part-time: 798 men, 751 women	**Ph.D.s:** 98%
Graduate: 4981 men, 4429 women	**Student/Faculty:** 15 to 1
Year: semesters, summer session	**Tuition:** $5250 ($19,460)
Application Deadline: November 30	**Room & Board:** $10,313
Freshman Class: 36,472 applied, 8710 accepted, 3655 enrolled	
SAT I Verbal/Math: 629/671	**MOST COMPETITIVE**

The University of California at Berkeley, founded in 1868, is a public institution offering a wide variety of programs in the social and physical sciences, liberal arts, and professional fields. It is the oldest campus of the

University of California system. Enrollment figures in the above capsule are for fall 2002. There are 7 undergraduate and 14 graduate schools. In addition to regional accreditation, Cal has baccalaureate program accreditation with AACSB, ABET, ADA, ASLA, CSWE, NAAB, and SAF. The 30 libraries contain 9,388,785 volumes, 6,548,043 microform items, and 118,353 audio/video tapes/CDs, and subscribe to 83,089 periodicals. Computerized library services include the card catalog, interlibrary loans, and database searching. Special learning facilities include a learning resource center, art gallery, natural history museum, radio station, TV station, a botanical garden, an anthropology museum, a hall of science, the University Art Museum and Pacific Film Archive, a seismographic station, herbaria, the Hall for the Performing Arts, an observatory, and many off-campus facilities. The 1232-acre campus is in an urban area 10 miles east of San Francisco. Including any residence halls, there are 100 buildings.

Student Life: 90% of undergraduates are from California. Others are from 50 states, 130 foreign countries, and Canada. 85% are from public schools. 42% are Asian American; 30% white; 10% Hispanic. The average age of freshmen is 19; all undergraduates, 21. 5% do not continue beyond their first year; 84% remain to graduate.

Housing: 10,000 students can be accommodated in college housing, which includes single-sex and coed dormitories, off-campus apartments, married-student housing, fraternity houses, and sorority houses. In addition, there are honors houses, language houses, special-interest houses, substance-free housing, an international house, and co-ops. Honor students are given priority choice for housing. On-campus housing is guaranteed for the freshman year only and is available on a lottery system for upperclassmen. All students may keep cars.

Activities: 11% of men belong to 14 local and 38 national fraternities; 10% of women belong to 7 local and 13 national sororities. There are more than 400 groups on campus, including art, band, cheerleading, chess, choir, chorale, chorus, computers, dance, debate, drama, ethnic, film, forensics, gay, honors, international, jazz band, literary magazine, marching band, musical theater, newspaper, orchestra, pep band, photography, political, professional, radio and TV, religious, social, social service, student government, symphony, and yearbook. Popular campus events include the Big Game, Cal Performances, and E-Week.

Sports: There are 13 intercollegiate sports for men and 13 for women, and 14 intramural sports for men and 14 for women. Facilities include a football stadium, a track stadium, a basketball pavilion, 4 gyms, a martial arts room, 7 swimming pools, 3 weight rooms, squash, racquetball, handball, volleyball, and tennis courts, and baseball and softball fields.

Disabled Students: 95% of the campus is accessible. Wheelchair ramps, elevators, special parking, specially equipped rest rooms, special class scheduling, lowered drinking fountains, lowered telephones, and a disabled students program are available.

Services: Counseling and information services are available, as is tutoring in most subjects. There is a reader service for the blind, a workshop in study strategy and note taking, counseling, and an athletic study center.

Campus Safety and Security: Measures include 24-hour foot and vehicle patrol, self-defense education, security escort services, and shuttle buses. There are informal discussions, pamphlets/posters/films, emergency telephones, lighted pathways/sidewalks, a rape prevention peer education program, and an earthquake emergency preparedness program.

Programs of Study: Cal confers B.A. and B.S. degrees. Master's and doctoral degrees are also awarded. Bachelor's degrees are awarded in AGRICULTURE (conservation and regulation and forestry and related sciences), BIOLOGICAL SCIENCE (biology/biological science, microbiology, molecular biology, nutrition, and plant genetics), BUSINESS (business administration and management), COMMUNICATIONS AND THE ARTS (art history and appreciation, Chinese, classical languages, communications, comparative literature, dance, dramatic arts, Dutch, English, film arts, French, German, Greek, Italian, Japanese, Latin, linguistics, music, Scandinavian languages, Slavic languages, Spanish, and speech/debate/rhetoric), COMPUTER AND PHYSICAL SCIENCE (applied mathematics, astrophysics, chemistry, computer science, earth science, mathematics, physical sciences, physics, and statistics), ENGINEERING AND ENVIRONMENTAL DESIGN (architecture, bioengineering, chemical engineering, civil engineering, computer engineering, electrical/electronics engineering, engineering and applied science, engineering physics, environmental engineering, environmental science, industrial engineering, landscape architecture/design, manufacturing engineering, materials engineering, materials science, mechanical engineering, and nuclear engineering), HEALTH PROFESSIONS (optometry and public health), SOCIAL SCIENCE (African American studies, American studies, anthropology, Asian/American studies, Asian/Oriental studies, Celtic studies, classical/ancient civilization, cognitive science, economics, ethnic studies, geography, Hispanic American studies, history, interdisciplinary studies, Latin American studies, law, Middle Eastern studies, Native American studies, Near Eastern studies, peace studies, philosophy, political science/government, psychology, religion, social science, social work, sociology, South Asian studies, urban studies, and women's studies). Electrical engineering and computer science, political science, and architecture are the largest.

Required: All undergraduate students are required to satisfy the general university requirements of English and writing proficiency, and integrative and comparative courses in American history, institutions, and cultures. Students must complete 120 units with a minimum GPA of 2.0.

Special: Co-op programs, cross-registration with many area schools, internships, work-study programs, and study abroad in 33 countries are available. Interdisciplinary majors are also available. Students may double-major, earn dual degrees, design their own majors, study independently, and choose pass/fail options. Students have opportunities for independent or team research. There are 6 national honor societies, including Phi Beta Kappa.

Faculty/Classroom: 67% of faculty are male; 33%, female. All teach undergraduates and 80% do research. The average class size in a regular course is 40.

Admissions: 24% of the 2003-2004 applicants were accepted. The SAT I scores for the 2003-2004 freshman class were: Verbal--10% below 500, 23% between 500 and 599, 40% between 600 and 700, and 27% above 700; Math--4% below 500, 15% between 500 and 599, 35% between 600 and 700, and 46% above 700. 95% of the current freshmen were in the top fifth of their class; all were in the top two fifths.

Requirements: The SAT I or ACT is required, as well as 3 SAT II: Subject tests. Also required are 4 years of English, 3 of math (4 recommended), 2 each of history/social sciences, lab science (3 recommended), foreign language (3 recommended), and college preparatory electives. A GPA of 2.8 is required. AP credits are accepted. Important factors in the admissions decision are advanced placement or honor courses, evidence of special talent, and leadership record.

Procedure: Freshmen are admitted in the fall. Entrance exams should be taken no later than December test dates in the senior year. There is a deferred admissions plan. Applications should be filed by November 30 for fall entry. The fall 2003 application fee was $40. Notification is sent March 30. Applications are accepted on-line through www.ucop.edu/pathways.

Transfer: 1703 transfer students enrolled in 2003-2004. A minimum GPA of 2.4 generally is required for in-state students and 2.8 for out-of-state students. Admission is competitive, so meeting the minimum does not guarantee admission. Students must have completed at least 60 transferable semester units and no more than 80 to 90 semester units (depending upon the specific college). They must complete all lower-division courses for their intended major prior to admission. 24 of 120 credits required for the bachelor's degree must be completed at Cal.

Visiting: There are regularly scheduled orientations for prospective students, including student-led tours by the visitor information center and group advising from the Office of Undergraduate Admission and Relations with Schools. There are guides for informal visits and visitors may sit in on classes. To schedule a visit, contact the Visitor Information Center at (510) 642-5215.

Financial Aid: In 2002-2003, 48% of all full-time freshmen and 46% of continuing full-time students received some form of financial aid. 45% of full-time freshmen and 42% of continuing full-time students received need-based aid. The average freshman award was $13,360. Need-based scholarships or need-based grants averaged $9663; need-based self-help aid (loans and jobs) averaged $5164; non-need-based athletic scholarships averaged $8894; and other non-need-based awards and non-need-based scholarships averaged $2682. 26% of undergraduates work part time. Average annual earnings from campus work are $1948. The average financial indebtedness of the 2002 graduate was $14,990. The FAFSA is required. The deadline for filing freshman financial aid applications for fall entry is March 2.

International Students: There are 704 international students enrolled. They must score 550 on the written TOEFL. They must also take SAT II: Subject tests in writing, math level I or IC, or IIC and 1 test in one of the following areas: English literature, foreign languages, science, or social studies.

Computers: The mainframes are an IBM 3090 and a DEC UNIX. There are 12 general-access computer facilities on campus, with about 600 computers, including Macs, PCs, and UNIX workstations. Additional computer labs are located in residence halls, libraries, and academic departments. Internet access and e-mail accounts are available. Home computers can be linked to the campus data network. All students may access the system. There are no time limits and no fees.

Graduates: From July 1, 2001 to June 30, 2002, 6198 bachelor's degrees were awarded. The most popular majors were political science (7%), electrical engineering and computer science (7%), and economics (7%). In an average class, 52% graduate in 4 years or less, 79% graduate in 5 years or less, and 84% graduate in 6 years or less. 630 companies recruited on campus in 2002-2003.

Admissions Contact: Pamela Burnett, Director, Undergraduate Admission. E-mail: ouars@uclink.berkeley.edu Web: www.berkeley.edu

UNIVERSITY OF CALIFORNIA AT DAVIS
Davis, CA 95616-8507

B-2

(530) 752-2971; Fax: (530) 752-1280

Total Enrollment: 27,114 students	**Faculty:** I, +$
Year: quarters, summer session	**Ph.D.s:** n/av
Application Deadline: see profile	**Student/Faculty:** n/av
	Tuition: $5852 ($20,062)
	Room & Board: $9143

Freshman Class: 32,531 applied, 18,528 accepted, 4786 enrolled
SAT I Verbal/Math: 568/616   **ACT:** 24   **VERY COMPETITIVE**

University of California at Davis, founded in 1905, is a public, comprehensive institution offering programs in arts and science, agricultural and environmental sciences, and engineering. There are 3 undergraduate and 5 graduate schools. In addition to regional accreditation, UCD has baccalaureate program accreditation with ABET, ADA, and ASLA. The 5 libraries contain 3,180,865 volumes, 3,948,731 microform items, and 14,047 audio/video tapes/CDs, and subscribe to 44,232 periodicals. Computerized library services include the card catalog and database searching. Special learning facilities include a learning resource center, art gallery, radio station, experimental farms, a 150-acre arboretum, a raptor center, an equestrian center, a primate research center, and the Crocker Nuclear Laboratory. The 5980-acre campus is in a suburban area 15 miles west of Sacramento and 72 miles northeast of San Francisco. Including any residence halls, there are 1083 buildings.

Student Life: 96% of undergraduates are from California. Students are from 47 states, 113 foreign countries, and Canada. 90% are from public schools. 45% are white; 35% Asian American; 10% Hispanic. The average age of freshmen is 18; all undergraduates, 21. 1% do not continue beyond their first year; 76% remain to graduate.

Housing: 6062 students can be accommodated in college housing, which includes single-sex and coed dorms, on-campus apartments, off-campus apartments, and married-student housing. In addition, there are honors houses, language houses, and special-interest houses. On-campus housing is guaranteed for the freshman year only. 81% of students commute. Alcohol is not permitted. All students may keep cars.

Activities: 9% of men belong to 28 national fraternities; 9% of women belong to 20 national sororities. There are 320 groups on campus, including art, band, cheerleading, chess, choir, chorus, computers, dance, drama, ethnic, film, gay, honors, international, jazz band, literary magazine, marching band, musical theater, newspaper, orchestra, pep band, photography, political, professional, radio and TV, religious, social, social service, student government, symphony, and yearbook. Popular campus events include Picnic Day, Whole Earth Festival, and Asian Pacific Cultural Week.

Sports: There are 11 intercollegiate sports for men and 9 for women, and 18 intramural sports for men and 18 for women. Facilities include a football stadium, tennis and basketball courts, equestrian trails, a track field, baseball, soccer, and softball fields, a recreation hall, 2 gyms, 2 swimming pools, bowling alleys, weight-training facilities, and an outdoor roller hockey rink.

Disabled Students: 99% of the campus is accessible. Wheelchair ramps, elevators, special parking, specially equipped rest rooms, special class scheduling, lowered drinking fountains, lowered telephones, and lowered automatic teller machines are available.

Services: Counseling and information services are available, as is tutoring in most subjects. There is a reader service for the blind and remedial math and writing.

Campus Safety and Security: Measures include 24-hour foot and vehicle patrol, self-defense education, security escort services, and shuttle buses. There are informal discussions, pamphlets/posters/films, emergency telephones, and lighted pathways/sidewalks. There is also a rape prevention program, a crime prevention unit, a bike patrol unit, and a K-9 program.

Programs of Study: UCD confers B.S., A.B., and B.A.S. degrees. Master's and doctoral degrees are also awarded. Bachelor's degrees are awarded in AGRICULTURE (agricultural business management, agricultural economics, animal science, international agriculture, plant science, range/farm management, and soil science), BIOLOGICAL SCIENCE (avian sciences, bacteriology, biochemistry, biology/biological science, botany, ecology, entomology, environmental biology, genetics, microbiology, nutrition, physiology, toxicology, wildlife biology, and zoology), BUSINESS (organizational behavior), COMMUNICATIONS AND THE ARTS (art history and appreciation, Chinese, communications, comparative literature, design, dramatic arts, English, fine arts, French, German, Greek, Italian, Japanese, Latin, linguistics, music, Russian, Spanish, speech/debate/rhetoric, and studio art), COMPUTER AND PHYSICAL SCIENCE (atmospheric sciences and meteorology, chemistry, computer science, geology, hydrology, mathematics, physics, polymer science, and statistics), EDUCATION (physical), ENGINEERING AND ENVIRONMENTAL DESIGN (aeronautical engineering, agricultural engineering, bioengineering, chemical engineering, civil engineering, computer engineering, electrical/electronics engineering, environmental design, environmental science, landscape architecture/design, materials engineering, and mechanical engineering), HEALTH PROFESSIONS (community

health work and environmental health science), SOCIAL SCIENCE (African studies, American studies, anthropology, behavioral science, classical/ancient civilization, dietetics, East Asian studies, economics, food science, geography, history, human development, human ecology, international relations, medieval studies, Mexican-American/Chicano studies, Native American studies, philosophy, political science/government, psychology, religion, social science, sociology, textiles and clothing, and women's studies). Agricultural, biological, and biotechnical sciences are the strongest academically. Biological science, biochemistry, and psychology are the largest.

Required: General education requirements vary by college but are based on 3 components: topical breadth, social-cultural diversity, and writing experience. A minimum of 180 quarter units with a minimum GPA of 2.0 are required for graduation, as is proficiency in English composition and an American History and Institutions requirement.

Special: There are credit and noncredit internship programs. Study abroad in more than 32 countries and a Washington semester are offered. Students may participate in college work-study, federal work-study, and California work-study programs. Several A.B.-B.S. degrees are offered. Students may design their own majors, take dual majors, and elect pass/fail options. Interdisciplinary majors are offered in African American and African studies, American studies, Chicana/Chicano (Mexican American) studies, comparative literature, East Asian studies, exercise science, international relations, linguistics, medieval studies, Native American studies, religious studies, and women's studies. There are 24 national honor societies, including Phi Beta Kappa, a freshman honors program, and 3 departmental honors programs.

Faculty/Classroom: The average class size in a laboratory is 21 and in a regular course, 56.

Admissions: 57% of the 2003-2004 applicants were accepted. The SAT I scores for the 2003-2004 freshman class were: Verbal--20% below 500, 39% between 500 and 599, 33% between 600 and 700, and 8% above 700; Math--8% below 500, 29% between 500 and 599, 47% between 600 and 700, and 16% above 700.

Requirements: The SAT I or ACT is required. In addition, candidates for admission should have completed 4 units of English, 3 of math, and 2 each of foreign language, history/social science, lab science, and college preparatory electives, for a total of 15 units. SAT II: Subject tests are required in writing, math, and 1 other subject chosen from English literature, foreign language, science, or social studies. A GPA of 3.3 is required. AP credits are accepted. Important factors in the admissions decision are advanced placement or honor courses, evidence of special talent, and leadership record.

Procedure: Freshmen are admitted fall, winter, and spring. Entrance exams should be taken no later than December of the senior year. There is a deferred admissions plan. Check with the school for current application deadlines and fees. Applications are accepted on-line.

Transfer: 2251 transfer students enrolled in 2002-2003. Junior-level transfers have priority. Requirements vary by college, discipline, and major.

Visiting: There are regularly scheduled orientations for prospective students, including weekend tours of the campus, weekday tours by appointment, and drop-in counseling with staff and faculty. The campus also offers a 1-day preview for prospective students and their families. There are guides for informal visits and visitors may sit in on classes and stay overnight. To schedule a visit, contact UC Davis Visitor Services at (530) 752-8111.

Financial Aid: 44% of undergraduates work part time. The average financial indebtedness of the 2003 graduate was $8300. UCD is a member of CSS. The CSS/Profile or FFS is required.

International Students: International students must score 500 on the written TOEFL. They must also take SAT II: Subject tests in writing, math, and 1 other subject.

Computers: There are hundreds of PCs and terminals located in numerous computer labs and classrooms throughout the campus. In addition, many PCs are provided for student use in the residence halls. All students may access the system. There are no time limits and no fees. It is strongly recommended that all students have a personal computer.

Graduates: From July 1, 2002 to June 30, 2003, 5166 bachelor's degrees were awarded. In an average class, 1% graduate in 3 years or less, 28% graduate in 4 years or less, 65% graduate in 5 years or less, and 75% graduate in 6 years or less. Of the 2002 graduating class, 38% were enrolled in graduate school within 6 months of graduation and 79% were employed.

Admissions Contact: Admissions Officer.
E-mail: *freshmanadmission@ucdavis.edu* Web: *http://why.ucdavis.edu*

UNIVERSITY OF CALIFORNIA AT IRVINE D-5
Irvine, CA 92697-1075 (949) 824-6703; Fax: (949) 824-2711

Full-time: 8840 men, 9574 women	Faculty: I, +$
Part-time: 442 men, 323 women	Ph.D.s: 98%
Graduate: 2064 men, 1328 women	Student/Faculty: n/av
Year: quarters, summer session	Tuition: $5804 ($19,284)
Application Deadline: November 30	Room & Board: $8200
Freshman Class: 34,287 applied, 18,360 accepted, 4043 enrolled	
SAT I Verbal/Math: 570/620	HIGHLY COMPETITIVE

The University of California, Irvine, founded in 1965, is a public research university and part of the University of California System. Enrollment figures in the above capsule are for fall 2002. There are 8 undergraduate and 3 graduate schools. In addition to regional accreditation, UCI has baccalaureate program accreditation with AACSB and ABET. The 3 libraries contain 2,560,259 volumes, 2,584,114 microform items, and 101,335 audio/video tapes/CDs, and subscribe to 28,416 periodicals. Computerized library services include the card catalog, interlibrary loans, and database searching. Special learning facilities include a learning resource center, art gallery, planetarium, radio station, freshwater marsh reserve, arboretum, laser institute, and numerous research centers. The 1489-acre campus is in a suburban area 40 miles south of Los Angeles. Including any residence halls, there are 418 buildings.

Student Life: 98% of undergraduates are from California. Students are from 49 states, 59 foreign countries, and Canada. 88% are from public schools. 51% are Asian American; 24% white; 11% Hispanic. The average age of freshmen is 18; all undergraduates, 21. 8% do not continue beyond their first year.

Housing: 4645 students can be accommodated in college housing, which includes single-sex and coed dorms, on-campus apartments, and married-student housing. In addition, there are honors houses, language houses, special-interest houses, academic theme houses, an 80-space RV park (vehicles not provided), and houses for lease to fraternities and sororities. On-campus housing is guaranteed for the freshman year only, is available on a first-come, first-served basis, and is available on a lottery system for upperclassmen. 74% of students commute. Alcohol is not permitted. All students may keep cars.

Activities: 8% of men belong to 12 national fraternities; 8% of women belong to 9 national sororities. There are 275 groups on campus, including art, band, cheerleading, choir, chorale, chorus, computers, dance, drama, ethnic, film, gay, honors, international, jazz band, literary magazine, musical theater, newspaper, opera, orchestra, pep band, political, professional, radio and TV, religious, social, social service, student government, symphony, and yearbook. Popular campus events include Celebrate UCI, Rainbow Festival, and Engineering Week.

Sports: There are 11 intercollegiate sports for men and 9 for women, and 23 intramural sports for men and 20 for women. Facilities include a 2500-seat track stadium, a 5000-seat events center, a 1000-seat soccer field, a 500-seat tennis stadium, baseball and other fields, a swimming pool, 6 indoor handball/racquetball/squash courts, and an activities hall with areas for badminton, basketball, volleyball, combatives, fencing, and weight training. A sailing and crew base is located in nearby Newport Beach.

Disabled Students: 99% of the campus is accessible. Wheelchair ramps, elevators, special parking, specially equipped rest rooms, special class scheduling, lowered drinking fountains, lowered telephones, special housing, automatic doors, and transportation on and off campus are available.

Services: Counseling and information services are available, as is tutoring in most subjects. There is a reader service for the blind and remedial math, reading, and writing.

Campus Safety and Security: Measures include 24-hour foot and vehicle patrol, self-defense education, security escort services, and shuttle buses. There are informal discussions, pamphlets/posters/films, emergency telephones, and lighted pathways/sidewalks.

Programs of Study: UCI confers B.A., B.S., B.F.A., and B.Mus. degrees. Master's and doctoral degrees are also awarded. Bachelor's degrees are awarded in BIOLOGICAL SCIENCE (biology/biological science and ecology), COMMUNICATIONS AND THE ARTS (art history and appreciation, Chinese, classics, comparative literature, dance, dramatic arts, English, film arts, French, German, Japanese, linguistics, music, Spanish, and studio art), COMPUTER AND PHYSICAL SCIENCE (chemistry, information sciences and systems, mathematics, and physics), ENGINEERING AND ENVIRONMENTAL DESIGN (aeronautical engineering, chemical engineering, civil engineering, computer engineering, electrical/electronics engineering, engineering, environmental design, environmental engineering, and mechanical engineering), SOCIAL SCIENCE (anthropology, classical/ancient civilization, criminology, crosscultural studies, East Asian studies, economics, history, human ecology, humanities, international studies, philosophy, political science/government, psychology, social science, sociology, and women's studies). Biological sciences, political science, and economics are the strongest academically. Biological sciences, social ecology, and economics are the largest.

Required: To graduate, students must maintain a GPA of at least 2.0, earn 180 quarter units, and fulfill requirements in English composition and in American history and institutions. Under distribution requirements, 3 courses each must be completed in writing beyond the introductory level, natural sciences, social and behavioral sciences, humanistic inquiry, and math and symbolic systems, and 1 course each in multicultural studies and global issues.

Special: Students may study abroad in Spain, England, India, Kenya, Sweden, and Egypt. UCI also offers internships, a Washington semester, work-study programs with the university, B.A.-B.S. degrees, dual majors, and pass/fail options. There are 3 national honor societies, including Phi Beta Kappa, a freshman honors program, and 14 departmental honors programs.

Faculty/Classroom: 67% of faculty are male; 33%, female. All both teach and do research. The average class size in an introductory lecture is 250; in a laboratory, 24; and in a regular course, 37.

Admissions: 54% of the 2003-2004 applicants were accepted. The SAT I scores for the 2003-2004 freshman class were: Verbal--13% below 500, 48% between 500 and 599, 34% between 600 and 700, and 5% above 700; Math--5% below 500, 32% between 500 and 599, 47% between 600 and 700, and 16% above 700. All of the current freshmen were in the top fifth of their class.

Requirements: The SAT I or ACT is required; required minimum scores are determined by an eligibility index. In addition, SAT II: Subject tests in writing, math, and a third chosen from science, social science, foreign language, or English literature are required. Applicants need 15 academic credits, including 4 years of English, 3 in math, and 2 each in foreign language, history/social science, lab science, and electives. An additional year each in foreign language, math, and science is recommended. An essay also is needed. The GED is accepted. AP credits are accepted.

Procedure: Freshmen are admitted in the fall. Entrance exams should be taken no later than December of the senior year. Applications should be filed by November 30 for fall entry. The fall 2003 application fee was $40. Notification is sent March 30. Applications are accepted on-line through www.ucop.edu/pathways/.

Transfer: 1447 transfer students enrolled in 2002-2003. Applicants must have completed 60 transferable units, including 2 semesters of English composition and 1 semester of math. Some majors require completion of prerequisites. California Community College transfers receive preference. 36 of 180 quarter units required for the bachelor's degree must be completed at UCI.

Visiting: There are regularly scheduled orientations for prospective students. There are guides for informal visits and visitors may sit in on classes and stay overnight. To schedule a visit, contact the Office of Admissions and Relations with Schools and Colleges.

Financial Aid: Average annual earnings from campus work are $1640. UCI is a member of CSS. The FAFSA and GPA verification form to state agency are required. The priority date for freshman financial aid applications for fall entry is March 2. The deadline for filing freshman financial aid applications for fall entry is May 1.

International Students: International students must score 550 on the written TOEFL and also take the SAT I or the ACT, as well as SAT II: Subject tests in writing and math, and a third in an area of the student's choice.

Computers: There are approximately 500 computer terminals/PCs located in the computer center, the student center, the library, and departmental computer labs. All students may access the system 24 hours a day. Students may access the system in 2-hour sessions. There are no fees.

Graduates: From July 1, 2001 to June 30, 2002, 3630 bachelor's degrees were awarded. The most popular majors were social sciences and history (30%), biological/life sciences (14%), and psychology (11%). In an average class, 37% graduate in 4 years or less, 70% graduate in 5 years or less, and 76% graduate in 6 years or less.

Admissions Contact: Marguerite Bonous-Hammarth, Director, Admissions. Web: www.uci.edu

UNIVERSITY OF CALIFORNIA AT LOS ANGELES C-5
Los Angeles, CA 90095 (310) 825-3101; Fax: (310) 206-1206

Full-time: 10,678 men, 13,920 women	Faculty: 1871; I, ++$
Part-time: 532 men, 585 women	Ph.D.s: 98%
Graduate: 5877 men, 5118 women	Student/Faculty: 13 to 1
Year: quarters, summer session	Tuition: $4878 ($17,257)
Application Deadline: November 30	Room & Board: $10,452
Freshman Class: 44,994 applied, 10,581 accepted, 4268 enrolled	
SAT I Verbal/Math: 630/670	ACT: 26 MOST COMPETITIVE

University of California at Los Angeles (UCLA), founded in 1919, is a public institution offering undergraduate and graduate degrees in arts and sciences, engineering, applied science, nursing, theater, film, and television. There are 5 undergraduate and 12 graduate schools. In addition to regional accreditation, UCLA has baccalaureate program accreditation with AACSB, ABET, ADA, CSWE, NAAB, and NLN. The 13 libraries contain 8,265,189 volumes, 6,098,847 microform items, and 251,761 audio/video tapes/CDs, and subscribe to 79,283 periodicals. Computerized library services include the card catalog, interlibrary loans, database searching, and Internet access. Special learning facilities include a learning resource center, art gallery, natural history museum, planetarium, and radio station. The 419-acre campus is in an urban area in Los Angeles. Including any residence halls, there are 272 buildings.

Student Life: 94% of undergraduates are from California. Students are from 50 states, 100 foreign countries, and Canada. 81% are from public schools. 38% are Asian American; 33% white; 15% Hispanic. The average age of freshmen is 18; all undergraduates, 21. 3% do not continue beyond their first year; 87% remain to graduate.

Housing: 7320 students can be accommodated in college housing, which includes coed dorms, off-campus apartments, married-student housing, fraternity houses, and sorority houses. On-campus housing is guaranteed for the freshman year only and is available on a lottery system for upperclassmen. 73% of students commute. Alcohol is not permitted.

Activities: 12% of men belong to 5 local and 23 national fraternities; 9% of women belong to 3 local and 17 national sororities. There are more than 700 groups on campus, including band, cheerleading, choir, chorale, chorus, computers, dance, drama, ethnic, film, gay, honors, international, literary magazine, marching band, newspaper, photography, political, professional, radio and TV, religious, social, social service, student government, and yearbook.

Sports: There are 10 intercollegiate sports for men and 11 for women, and 21 intramural sports for men and 17 for women. Facilities include a pavilion, a stadium, a tennis center, and a recreation and sports center.

Disabled Students: All of the campus is accessible. Wheelchair ramps, elevators, special parking, specially equipped rest rooms, special class scheduling, lowered drinking fountains, and lowered telephones are available.

Services: Counseling and information services are available, as is tutoring in most subjects. There is a reader service for the blind and remedial math, reading, and writing.

Campus Safety and Security: Measures include 24-hour foot and vehicle patrol, self-defense education, security escort services, and shuttle buses. There are informal discussions, pamphlets/posters/films, emergency telephones, and lighted pathways/sidewalks.

Programs of Study: UCLA confers B.A. and B.S. degrees. Master's and doctoral degrees are also awarded. Bachelor's degrees are awarded in BIOLOGICAL SCIENCE (biochemistry, biology/biological science, botany, marine biology, microbiology, molecular biology, neurosciences, and physiology), BUSINESS (business economics and international economics), COMMUNICATIONS AND THE ARTS (African languages, Arabic, art, art history and appreciation, Chinese, communications, comparative literature, design, dramatic arts, English, film arts, French, German, Greek, Hebrew, Italian, Japanese, Korean, Latin, linguistics, music, music history and appreciation, Portuguese, Russian languages and literature, Scandinavian languages, Slavic languages, and Spanish), COMPUTER AND PHYSICAL SCIENCE (applied mathematics, applied physics, astrophysics, atmospheric sciences and meteorology, chemistry, computer mathematics, computer science, cybernetics, earth science, geology, geophysics and seismology, mathematics, paleontology, and physics), ENGINEERING AND ENVIRONMENTAL DESIGN (aeronautical engineering, chemical engineering, civil engineering, computer engineering, electrical/electronics engineering, geological engineering, geophysical engineering, materials engineering, and mechanical engineering), HEALTH PROFESSIONS (nursing), SOCIAL SCIENCE (African American studies, American studies, anthropology, Asian/American studies, classical/ancient civilization, cognitive science, crosscultural studies, East Asian studies, economics, European studies, geography, Hispanic American studies, history, human ecology, interdisciplinary studies, international studies, Italian studies, Judaic studies, Latin American studies, Near Eastern studies, philosophy, political science/government, psychobiology, psychology, religion, Russian and Slavic studies, sociology, and women's studies). Biology, psychology, and economics are the largest.

Required: Students must complete a minimum of 180 quarter units and maintain a minimum GPA of 2.0 in all courses. All students must demonstrate a proficiency in English composition, or take specific courses to achieve this proficiency, and must also meet course requirements in American history and institutions. Other requirements vary by major and college or school.

Special: Opportunities are provided for internships, work-study programs, study abroad in 33 countries, B.A.-B.S. degrees, student-designed majors, dual majors, and interdisciplinary majors, including chemistry and materials science, Chicana and Chicano studies, and math and engineering. There is a Washington, D.C. program for 20 to 30 students selected each fall and spring. There are 4 national honor societies, including Phi Beta Kappa, a freshman honors program, and 7 departmental honors programs.

Faculty/Classroom: 69% of faculty are male; 31%, female. All both teach and do research.

Admissions: 24% of the 2003-2004 applicants were accepted. The SAT I scores for the 2003-2004 freshman class were: Verbal--9% below 500, 26% between 500 and 599, 43% between 600 and 700, and 22% above 700; Math--5% below 500, 19% between 500 and 599, 37% between 600 and 700, and 39% above 700. The ACT scores were 2% below 21, 26% between 21 and 23, 48% between 24 and 28, and 24% above 28.

Requirements: The SAT I or ACT is required. In addition, graduation from an accredited secondary school is required. Applicants must submit a challenging academic program, including honors and AP-level courses in English, math, a language other than English, science, and history and social science; most students complete at least 42 semester courses in these areas. SAT II: Subject tests in writing, math, and 1 subject of the student's choice are required. An essay is required, and a portfolio and audition are required for all art, theater, and film and television majors. UCLA requires applicants to be in the upper 13% of their class. A GPA of 3.3 is required. AP credits are accepted. Important factors in the admissions decision are advanced placement or honors courses, evidence of special talent, and leadership record.

Procedure: Freshmen are admitted in the fall. Entrance exams should be taken preferably in the junior year, but no later than December of the senior year. Applications should be filed by November 30 for fall entry. The fall 2003 application fee was $40. Notification is sent March 31. Applications are accepted on-line through UC Application or *www.ucop.edu/pathways.*

Transfer: 3256 transfer students enrolled in 2002-2003. For minimum requirements, transfer students must have earned 90 quarter units at the previous college and have completed preparatory courses for the selected major. Most students selected present a GPA of 3.0 or better. 68 of 180 credits required for the bachelor's degree must be completed at UCLA.

Visiting: There are regularly scheduled orientations for prospective students, including campus tours by current UCLA students, offered weekdays at 10:15 A.M. and 2:15 P.M. Reservations are required. Visitors may sit in on classes. To schedule a visit, contact Tours in Undergraduate Admissions at (310) 825-8764.

Financial Aid: In a recent year, 59% of all full-time freshmen and 61% of continuing full-time students received some form of financial aid. 45% of full-time freshmen and 60% of continuing full-time students received need-based aid. The average freshman award was $11,180. Need-based scholarships or need-based grants averaged $8834; need-based self-help aid (loans and jobs) averaged $4052; non-need-based athletic scholarships averaged $12,234; and other non-need-based awards and non-need-based scholarships averaged $2387. 41% of undergraduates work part time. Average annual earnings from campus work are $3436. The average financial indebtedness of the 2003 graduate was $12,775. The FAFSA and the college's own financial statement are required. The deadline for filing freshman financial aid applications for fall entry is March 2.

International Students: There are 877 international students enrolled. They must score 550 on the written TOEFL and also take the SAT I or the ACT. Students must take SAT II: Subject tests in writing, math, and a choice of literature, foreign language, science, or social science.

Computers: The mainframe is an IBM 3090 Model 600S. There are also IBM, HP, Zenith, and DEC VAX PCs available throughout the campus. All students may access the system 24 hours a day, 7 days a week. Time limits vary by individual departments. There are no fees.

Graduates: From July 1, 2002 to June 30, 2003, 6919 bachelor's degrees were awarded. The most popular majors were psychology (13%), economics (13%), and political science (8%). In an average class, 3% graduate in 3 years or less, 57% graduate in 4 years or less, 84% graduate in 5 years or less, and 87% graduate in 6 years or less. 396 companies recruited on campus in 2002-2003.

Admissions Contact: Director of Undergraduate Admissions and Relations with Schools. E-mail: *ugadm@saonet.ucla.edu* Web: *http://www.ucla.edu*

UNIVERSITY OF CALIFORNIA AT RIVERSIDE   D-5
Riverside, CA 92521   (909) 787-3411; Fax: (909) 787-6344

Full-time: 6718 men, 8030 women	Faculty: 660; I, av$
Part-time: 267 men, 267 women	Ph.D.s: 98%
Graduate: 1009 men, 1005 women	Student/Faculty: 22 to 1
Year: quarters, summer session	Tuition: $5950 ($19,681)
Application Deadline: November 30	Room & Board: $9350
Freshman Class: 20,060 applied, 15,862 accepted, 3891 enrolled	
SAT I Verbal/Math: 510/550	ACT: 21 COMPETITIVE

University of California at Riverside, founded in 1954, is a public liberal arts institution with undergraduate programs in engineering, humanities, arts, social sciences, and natural and agricultural sciences. There are 3 undergraduate and 5 graduate schools. In addition to regional accreditation, UCR has baccalaureate program accreditation with ABET. The 4 libraries contain 2,193,630 volumes, 1,816,170 microform items, and 41,892 audio/video tapes/CDs, and subscribe to 11,848 periodicals.

Computerized library services include the card catalog, interlibrary loans, database searching, and Internet access. Special learning facilities include a learning resource center, art gallery, radio station, a museum of photography, botanical gardens, and various research centers. The 1200-acre campus is in an urban area 50 miles east of Los Angeles. Including any residence halls, there are 476 buildings.

Student Life: 99% of undergraduates are from California. Students are from 40 states, 21 foreign countries, and Canada. 89% are from public schools. 41% are Asian American; 24% Hispanic; 22% white. The average age of freshmen is 18; all undergraduates, 21. 15% do not continue beyond their first year; 66% remain to graduate.

Housing: 4354 students can be accommodated in college housing, which includes coed dorms, on-campus apartments, off-campus apartments, married-student housing, and fraternity houses. In addition, there are honors houses, special-interest houses, and an international village. On-campus housing is guaranteed for the freshman year only and is available on a first-come, first-served basis. 72% of students commute. All students may keep cars.

Activities: 3% of men belong to 4 local and 15 national fraternities; 3% of women belong to 6 local and 14 national sororities. There are 214 groups on campus, including art, bagpipe band, band, cheerleading, chess, choir, chorale, chorus, computers, dance, drama, ethnic, gay, honors, international, jazz band, literary magazine, marching band, musical theater, newspaper, orchestra, pep band, photography, political, professional, radio and TV, religious, social, social service, student government, and yearbook. Popular campus events include Highlander Days, Oktoberfest, and Winter Arts Festival.

Sports: There are 8 intercollegiate sports for men and 9 for women, and 10 intramural sports for men, 5 for women, and 6 that are co-ed. Facilities include a heated Olympic-size pool, weight rooms, a track, a vita course, racquetball, tennis, basketball, and volleyball courts, a gym, an aerobics room, a roller hockey rink, and a student recreation center.

Disabled Students: 90% of the campus is accessible. Wheelchair ramps, elevators, special parking, specially equipped rest rooms, special class scheduling, lowered drinking fountains, lowered telephones, and automatic doors are available.

Services: Counseling and information services are available, as is tutoring in every subject, including individual and group tutoring. There is a reader service for the blind, and remedial math, reading, and writing. There are also study skills classes, preparation sessions for graduate entrance exams, study groups, individual counseling and lab work, speedreading classes, and English as a Second Language classes.

Campus Safety and Security: Measures include 24-hour foot and vehicle patrol, self-defense education, security escort services, and shuttle buses. There are informal discussions, pamphlets/posters/films, emergency telephones, lighted pathways/sidewalks, and a ride-along program.

Programs of Study: UCR confers B.A. and B.S. degrees. Master's and doctoral degrees are also awarded. Bachelor's degrees are awarded in BIOLOGICAL SCIENCE (biochemistry, biology/biological science, botany, entomology, and neurosciences), BUSINESS (business administration and management and business economics), COMMUNICATIONS AND THE ARTS (art, art history and appreciation, Chinese, classics, comparative literature, creative writing, dance, dramatic arts, English, French, German, languages, linguistics, music, Russian, and Spanish), COMPUTER AND PHYSICAL SCIENCE (chemistry, computer science, geology, geophysics and seismology, information sciences and systems, mathematics, physical sciences, physics, and statistics), ENGINEERING AND ENVIRONMENTAL DESIGN (chemical engineering, electrical/electronics engineering, environmental engineering, environmental science, and mechanical engineering), HEALTH PROFESSIONS (premedicine), SOCIAL SCIENCE (African American studies, anthropology, Asian/Oriental studies, classical/ancient civilization, community services, economics, ethnic studies, history, human development, humanities, Latin American studies, liberal arts/general studies, Mexican-American/Chicano studies, Native American studies, philosophy, political science/government, psychobiology, psychology, religion, social science, sociology, and women's studies). Biomedical sciences is the strongest academically. Business administration, biology, and psychology are the largest.

Required: Students must demonstrate proficiency in English, a knowledge of American history and institutions, and complete a maximum of 6 phys ed units. A total of 180 quarter credit hours with a minimum GPA of 2.0 is required in order to graduate. The number of hours in the major varies. All students must complete a 1-year sequence in English composition, in computers, math, or statistics, and in concepts/issues of ethnicity. There are breadth requirements in humanities, social sciences, and natural sciences/math for all students; the number of units/courses in each group depends on the student's college and major. A thesis is required for honors program students.

Special: Internships, work-study programs with various agencies and employers on and off campus, study abroad in 35 countries, and a semester in Washington in conjunction with the College of William and Mary are available. An accelerated degree in biomedical science is offered in conjunction with UCLA. Student-designed majors, dual majors, opportunities for undergraduate research, and pass/fail options in elective subjects are possible. Grants are available for research, fieldwork, or other creative activity. Academic internships and co-op programs are offered in all majors. There are 9 national honor societies, including Phi Beta Kappa, a freshman honors program, and 13 departmental honors programs.

Faculty/Classroom: 68% of faculty are male; 32%, female. All teach undergraduates; 68% both teach and do research. No introductory courses are taught by graduate students. The average class size in an introductory lecture is 25; in a laboratory, 20; and in a regular course, 22.

Admissions: 79% of the 2003-2004 applicants were accepted. The SAT I scores for the 2003-2004 freshman class were: Verbal--44% below 500, 40% between 500 and 599, 14% between 600 and 700, and 2% above 700; Math--28% below 500, 39% between 500 and 599, 27% between 600 and 700, and 6% above 700. The ACT scores were 47% below 21, 28% between 21 and 23, 17% between 24 and 26, 5% between 27 and 28, and 3% above 28.

Requirements: The SAT I or ACT is required. The minimum GPA varies depending on SAT I or ACT scores, but a GPA of 2.8 is required. Candidates for admission should have completed 4 years of English, 3 of math, and 2 of foreign language, history, science, and electives. SAT II: Subject tests are required in writing, math, and 1 subject chosen from English literature, foreign language, science, or social studies. AP credits are accepted. Advanced placement or honor courses is an important factor in the admission decision.

Procedure: Freshmen are admitted fall, winter, and spring. Entrance exams should be taken no later than December of the senior year. There is an early admissions plan. Applications should be filed by November 30 for fall entry, July 31 for winter entry, and October 31 for spring entry. The fall 2003 application fee was $40. Notification is sent March 31. Applications are accepted on-line through the university's web site.

Transfer: 874 transfer students enrolled in 2002-2003. Applicants need a minimum college GPA of 2.4 and must complete a 7-course pattern. Some majors require additional course completion and a higher GPA. 35 credits of 180 required for the bachelor's degree must be completed at UCR.

Visiting: There are regularly scheduled orientations for prospective students. Along with University Preview Day in October, tours are available throughout the year on weekdays and some Saturdays. There are guides for informal visits and visitors may sit in on classes and stay overnight. To schedule a visit, contact the Office of Relations with Schools at (909) 787-5045 or *tourucr@pop.ucr.edu.*

Financial Aid: In 2003-2004, 70% of all full-time students received some form of financial aid. 60% of all full-time students received need-based aid. The average freshman award was $13,562. The average financial indebtedness of the 2003 graduate was $13,216. The FAFSA is required. The deadline for filing freshman financial aid applications for fall entry is March 2.

International Students: There are 262 international students enrolled. They must score 550 on the written TOEFL.

Computers: The mainframe is a DEC 2100 Alpha Server cluster (VM-SAXP) with an IBM ES/9000-311 (MVS/ESA). There are more than 600 terminals and PCs, including NeXT, PowerMac, and high-end DOS/Windows PCs, plus more than 150 printers. They are located in dorms, the student center, and various campus buildings. All terminals have Internet access, including on-line access to the UC library system, computer classes, and e-mail accounts. All students may access the system. There are no time limits and no fees.

Graduates: From July 1, 2002 to June 30, 2003, 1966 bachelor's degrees were awarded. The most popular majors were business administration (25%), psychology (8%), and liberal studies (7%). In an average class, 37% graduate in 4 years or less, 60% graduate in 5 years or less, and 66% graduate in 6 years or less. 280 companies recruited on campus in 2002-2003. Of the 2002 graduating class, 35% were enrolled in graduate school within 6 months of graduation and 61% were employed.

Admissions Contact: LaRae Lundgren, Director of Undergraduate Admissions. E-mail: *discover@pop.ucr.edu* Web: *http://www.ucr.edu*

UNIVERSITY OF CALIFORNIA AT SAN DIEGO D-5
La Jolla, CA 92093 (858) 534-4831

Full-time: 9513 men, 10,359 women	Faculty: 946; I, +$
Part-time: none	Ph.D.s: 98%
Graduate: 2076 men, 1368 women	Student/Faculty: 21 to 1
Year: quarters, summer session	Tuition: $5507 ($19,237)
Application Deadline: November 30	Room & Board: $8620
Freshman Class: 43,438 applied, 17,618 accepted, 3799 enrolled	
SAT I Verbal/Math: 600/650	ACT: 26 HIGHLY COMPETITIVE

University of California at San Diego, founded in 1960, is a public liberal arts institution. There are 6 undergraduate and 5 graduate schools. In addition to regional accreditation, UCSD has baccalaureate program accreditation with ABET. The 10 libraries contain 2,616,776 volumes, 2,880,645 microform items, and 87,625 audio/video tapes/CDs, and subscribe to 24,986 periodicals. Computerized library services include the card catalog, interlibrary loans, database searching, and Internet access. Special learning facilities include an art gallery, radio station, TV station, aquarium-museum, supercomputer center, and theater. The 1976-acre campus is in a suburban area 12 miles north of downtown San Diego. Including any residence halls, there are 501 buildings.

Student Life: 98% of undergraduates are from California. Students are from 70 foreign countries and Canada. 88% are from public schools. 38% are Asian American; 36% white; 10% Hispanic. The average age of freshmen is 18; all undergraduates, 21. 7% do not continue beyond their first year; 93% remain to graduate.

Housing: 6352 students can be accommodated in college housing, which includes coed dorms, on-campus apartments, off-campus apartments, and married-student housing. In addition, there are language houses, special-interest houses, and an international house. On-campus housing is available on a lottery system for upperclassmen. 64% of students commute. All students may keep cars.

Activities: 10% of men belong to 14 national fraternities; 10% of women belong to 19 national sororities. There are 380 groups on campus, including academic, art, band, cheerleading, chess, choir, chorale, chorus, computers, dance, debate, drama, enterprise, ethnic, film, gay, honors, international, jazz band, literary magazine, musical theater, newspaper, opera, orchestra, pep band, photography, political, professional, radio and TV, religious, social, social service, student government, symphony, and yearbook. Popular campus events include Fall Festival on the Green, Spring Sun God Festival, and Asian Pacific Awareness Week.

Sports: There are 12 intercollegiate sports for men and 12 for women, and 27 intramural sports for men and 23 for women. Facilities include a 9-lane, all-weather track, soccer and softball fields, an athletic training facility, 2 pools, a spa, a weight room, tennis courts, playing fields, and a golf driving range. An 188,000-square-foot recreation complex features a 5000-seat arena, 8 handball/racquetball courts, 2 squash courts, a 12,000-square-foot weight-training facility, a climbing wall, and basketball, volleyball, and badminton courts.

Disabled Students: 95% of the campus is accessible. Wheelchair ramps, elevators, special parking, specially equipped rest rooms, special class scheduling, lowered drinking fountains, lowered telephones, special accommodations, and administrative support services are available.

Services: Counseling and information services are available, as is tutoring in most subjects. There is a reader service for the blind.

Campus Safety and Security: Measures include 24-hour foot and vehicle patrol, self-defense education, security escort services, and shuttle buses. There are informal discussions, pamphlets/posters/films, emergency telephones, lighted pathways/sidewalks, a student safety awareness program, peer educators, and an on-campus police department.

Programs of Study: UCSD confers B.A. and B.S. degrees. Master's and doctoral degrees are also awarded. Bachelor's degrees are awarded in AGRICULTURE (animal science and environmental studies), BIOLOGICAL SCIENCE (biochemistry, bioinformatics, biology/biological science, biophysics, biotechnology, ecology, microbiology, molecular biology, and physiology), BUSINESS (management science), COMMUNICATIONS AND THE ARTS (art history and appreciation, Chinese, classics, communications, dance, dramatic arts, English literature, Germanic languages and literature, linguistics, literature, music, music history and appreciation, music technology, studio art, and visual and performing arts), COMPUTER AND PHYSICAL SCIENCE (applied mathematics, applied physics, chemistry, computer science, earth science, information sciences and systems, mathematics, physical chemistry, and physics), EDUCATION (mathematics and science), ENGINEERING AND ENVIRONMENTAL DESIGN (aerospace studies, bioengineering, chemical engineering, computer engineering, electrical/electronics engineering, engineering, engineering physics, environmental engineering, environmental science, and mechanical engineering), SOCIAL SCIENCE (anthropology, cognitive science, economics, ethnic studies, French studies, gender studies, history, human development, international studies, Italian studies, Japanese studies, Judaic studies, Latin American studies, philosophy, political science/government, psychology, religion, Russian and Slavic studies, sociology, Spanish studies, Third World studies, and urban studies). Sciences, the arts, and social sciences are the strongest academically. Biology, economics, and electrical and computer engineering are the largest.

Required: Graduation requirements vary by college but students must complete 180 to 184 total quarter units or 45 to 46 courses, with a minimum of 60 credit hours or 12 to 22 courses in the major. Students must maintain a minimum GPA of 2.0.

Special: Internships in many fields, work-study, study abroad in more than 30 countries, and a Washington semester are offered. B.A.-B.S. degrees, an accelerated degree, dual majors, student-designed majors, and exchange programs with Dartmouth College, Spelman College, and Morehouse College are available. Nondegree study, credit for military experience, and pass/fail options are possible. There are 2 national honor societies, including Phi Beta Kappa, a freshman honors program, and 14 departmental honors programs.

Faculty/Classroom: 73% of faculty are male; 27%, female. 98% teach undergraduates and all do research. Graduate students teach 2% of introductory courses. The average class size in an introductory lecture is 300; in a laboratory, 40; and in a regular course, 100.

Admissions: 41% of the 2003-2004 applicants were accepted. The SAT I scores for the 2003-2004 freshman class were: Verbal--12% below 500, 33% between 500 and 599, 46% between 600 and 700, and 9% above 700; Math--5% below 500, 19% between 500 and 599, 52% between 600 and 700, and 25% above 700. The ACT scores were 15% below 21, 15% between 21 and 23, 32% between 24 and 26, 22% between 27 and 28, and 26% above 28. All of the current freshmen were in the top fifth of their class.

Requirements: The SAT I or ACT is required. In addition, 3 SAT II: Subject tests, including writing, math I or II, and a choice of English literature, foreign language, science, or social studies, are required. Candidates for admission should have completed 4 years of English, 3 of math, and 2 each of a foreign language, lab science, history, and college preparatory electives. A GPA of 2.8 is required. AP credits are accepted. Important factors in the admissions decision are advanced placement or honor courses, leadership record, and extracurricular activities record.

Procedure: Freshmen are admitted in the fall. Entrance exams should be taken by December of the senior year. Applications should be filed by November 30 for fall entry, along with a $40 fee. Notification is sent March 30. Applications are accepted on-line.

Transfer: 1498 transfer students enrolled in 2002-2003. California residents should have a competitive GPA; average 2001 GPA was 3.35. Transfers should have completed 90 quarter units. Preference is given to applicants from state community colleges. 36 of 180 credits required for the bachelor's degree must be completed at UCSD.

Visiting: There are regularly scheduled orientations for prospective students. There are guides for informal visits and visitors may sit in on classes. To schedule a visit, contact Campus Tours at (858) 822-1455 or *campustours@ucsd.edu*.

Financial Aid: In 2003-2004, 50% of all full-time freshmen and 46% of continuing full-time students received some form of financial aid. 47% of full-time freshmen and 42% of continuing full-time students received need-based aid. In 2002-2003, the average freshman award was $10,426. Need-based scholarships or need-based grants averaged $7109; need-based self-help aid (loans and jobs) averaged $4609; and non-need-based awards and non-need-based scholarships averaged $2413. 75% of undergraduates work part time. Average annual earnings from campus work are $1878. The average financial indebtedness of the 2002 graduate was $13,800. UCSD is a member of CSS. The FAFSA and the state aid form are required. The priority date for freshman financial aid applications for fall entry is March 2. The deadline for filing freshman financial aid applications for fall entry is May 1.

International Students: There are 400 international students enrolled. They must score 550 on the written TOEFL and also take the SAT I or the ACT, as well as SAT II: Subject tests in writing, math I or II, and either English literature, foreign language, science, or social studies.

Computers: There are 1500 computer terminals available for student use in computer labs, libraries, the student center, and each undergraduate college. Students have access to e-mail, the Internet, and the World Wide Web. There is a campuswide network. All students may access the system 24 hours every day. There are no time limits and no fees. It is strongly recommended that all students have a personal computer.

Graduates: The most popular majors were psychology (8%), communications (6%), and economics (6%). In an average class, 1% graduate in 3 years or less, 52% graduate in 4 years or less, 88% graduate in 5 years or less, and 96% graduate in 6 years or less. 600 companies recruited on campus in a recent year. Of the 2002 graduating class, 33% were enrolled in graduate school within 6 months of graduation and 65% were employed.

Admissions Contact: Mae Brown, Assistant Vice Chancellor, Admissions and Enrollment Services. E-mail: *admissionsinfo@ucsd.edu* Web: *http://admissions.ucsd.edu/*

UNIVERSITY OF CALIFORNIA AT SANTA BARBARA   C-5

Santa Barbara, CA 93106   (805) 893-2881; Fax: (805) 893-2676

Full-time: 7785 men, 9210 women	**Faculty:** 792; I, +$
Part-time: 390 men, 350 women	**Ph.Ds:** 100%
Graduate: 1460 men, 1190 women	**Student/Faculty:** 21 to 1
Year: quarters, summer session	**Tuition:** $3850 ($14,915)
Application Deadline: see profile	**Room & Board:** $7895
Freshman Class: n/av	
SAT I: required	**ACT:** recommended
	VERY COMPETITIVE

The University of California at Santa Barbara, founded in 1909, is a public liberal arts institution offering programs in creative studies, engineering, and letters and science. There are 3 undergraduate schools and 1 graduate school. Figures in the above capsule and in this profile are approximate. In addition to regional accreditation, UCSB has baccalaureate program accreditation with ABET and CSAB. The library contains 2,674,331 volumes, 3,669,358 microform items, and 103,495 audio/video tapes/CDs, and subscribes to 18,898 periodicals. Computerized library services include the card catalog, interlibrary loans, and database searching. Special learning facilities include a learning resource center, art gallery, radio station, language and learning lab, and numerous national and multicampus research institutes. The 813-acre campus is in a suburban area 10 miles west of Santa Barbara. Including any residence halls, there are 300 buildings.

Student Life: 94% of undergraduates are from California. Students are from 48 states, 45 foreign countries, and Canada. 86% are from public schools. 56% are white; 15% Hispanic; 14% Asian American. The average age of freshmen is 18; all undergraduates, 21. 12% do not continue beyond their first year; 67% remain to graduate.

Housing: 4069 students can be accommodated in college housing, which includes coed dorms, on-campus apartments, off-campus apartments, married-student housing, and special-interest floors. On-campus housing is available on a first-come, first-served basis. 79% of students commute. All students may keep cars.

Activities: 15% of men belong to 2 local and 20 national fraternities; 16% of women belong to 4 local and 14 national sororities. There are 300 groups on campus, including band, cheerleading, chess, choir, chorale, chorus, computers, dance, drama, ethnic, film, gay, honors, international, jazz band, literary magazine, newspaper, pep band, photography, political, professional, radio and TV, religious, social, social service, student government, and yearbook. Popular campus events include Club Day, Activities Fair, and UCEN Cultural Festival.

Sports: There are 11 intercollegiate sports for men and 10 for women, and 18 intramural sports for men and 18 for women. Facilities include a football stadium, a track, 24 tennis courts, an aquatics complex plus a campus swimming pool, 2 gyms, a gymnastics area, a weight room, a Nautilus facility, a wellness institute, an aerobics studio, outdoor basketball courts, softball and baseball fields, a ropes course and climbing wall, and a sailing center.

Disabled Students: 98% of the campus is accessible. Wheelchair ramps, elevators, special parking, specially equipped rest rooms, special class scheduling, lowered drinking fountains, and lowered telephones are available.

Services: Counseling and information services are available, as is tutoring in most subjects. There is a reader service for the blind and remedial reading and writing.

Campus Safety and Security: Measures include 24-hour foot and vehicle patrol, self-defense education, security escort services, and emergency telephones. There are lighted pathways/sidewalks.

Programs of Study: UCSB confers B.A., B.S., B.F.A., and B.M. degrees. Master's and doctoral degrees are also awarded. Bachelor's degrees are awarded in BIOLOGICAL SCIENCE (biochemistry, biology/biological science, cell biology, evolutionary biology, marine biology, microbiology, physiology, and zoology), BUSINESS (business economics), COMMUNICATIONS AND THE ARTS (art, art history and appreciation, Chinese, classics, communications, comparative literature, dance, dramatic arts, English, film arts, French, German, Germanic languages and literature, Japanese, linguistics, literature, music, music performance, music theory and composition, Portuguese, Slavic languages, and Spanish), COMPUTER AND PHYSICAL SCIENCE (chemistry, computer science, geology, geophysics and seismology, hydrology, mathematics, physics, and statistics), ENGINEERING AND ENVIRONMENTAL DESIGN (chemical engineering, electrical/electronics engineering, environmental science, and mechanical engineering), HEALTH PROFESSIONS (pharmacy), SOCIAL SCIENCE (African American studies, anthropology, Asian/American studies, Asian/Oriental studies, biopsychology, economics, geography, history, interdisciplinary studies, Islamic studies, Italian studies, Latin American studies, law, medieval studies, Mexican-American/Chicano studies, philosophy, political science/government, psychology, public affairs, religion, sociology, and women's studies). Business economics, political science, and biological science are the largest.

Required: Graduation requirements vary by college. Generally, students will take one third of their distribution in the major subject, one third in general education courses, and one third in elective courses. General subject requirements include courses in English, foreign language, science/math/technology, social sciences, civilization and thought, literature, and the arts; specific subject requirements include 6 writing-intensive courses and 1 course each in non-Western culture, quantitative relationships, and ethnic studies. To graduate, students must earn at least 180 quarter units, with a minimum GPA of 2.0, and have completed the American History and Institutions requirement.

Special: A Washington semester, internships, study abroad in 32 countries, work-study programs, student-designed majors, the B.A.-B.S. degree, and an accelerated degree program in electrical engineering are offered. There are 6 national honor societies, including Phi Beta Kappa, and a freshman honors program.

Faculty/Classroom: 69% of faculty are male; 31%, female. All both teach and do research. The average class size in an introductory lecture is 60; in a laboratory, 24; in a regular course, 30.

Requirements: The SAT I is required and the ACT is recommended, as well as SAT II: Subject tests in writing, math, and 1 other choice. Candidates for admission must have completed 4 years of English, 3 of math, and 2 each of foreign language, lab science, history/social science,

and college-preparatory electives. An additional year each in foreign language, math, and science is recommended. AP and CLEP credits are accepted.

Procedure: Freshmen are admitted in the fall. Entrance exams should be taken by November of the senior year. Check with the school for current deadlines. The fall 2003 application fee was $40. Applications are accepted on-line.

Transfer: 1291 transfer students enrolled in a recent year. California residents should have a minimum 2.0 GPA in transferable course work; nonresidents, a 2.8 GPA. Students with fewer than 12 quarter or semester units of transferable course work must provide standardized test scores. 35 of 180 credits required for the bachelor's degree must be completed at UCSB.

Visiting: There are regularly scheduled orientations for prospective students, consisting of a campus film, an information session, and a walking tour of the campus led by a student guide. There are guides for informal visits and visitors may sit in on classes and stay overnight. To schedule a visit, contact the Office of Relations with Schools at (805) 893-2485.

Financial Aid: In a recent year, 45% of all full-time freshmen and 42% of continuing full-time students received some form of financial aid. 36% of full-time freshmen and 33% of continuing full-time students received need-based aid. The average freshman award was $9446. The average financial indebtedness of a recent graduate was $16,426. UCSB is a member of CSS. The FAFSA is required. Check with the school for current deadlines.

International Students: They must score 500 on the written TOEFL and also take the SAT I or the ACT. Students must take SAT II: Subject tests in in writing, math, and 1 other choice.

Computers: They are accessed via numerous systems and networks on campus. There are more than 1800 terminals available in PC and departmental labs. All students may access the system at any time, if students have their own computer and modem.

Graduates: In a recent year the most popular majors were social sciences/history (24%), business/marketing (12%), and visual and performing arts (8%).

Admissions Contact: Undergraduate Admissions Office.
E-mail: *appinfo@sa.ucsb.edu* Web: *www.ucsb.edu*

UNIVERSITY OF CALIFORNIA AT SANTA CRUZ B-3
Santa Cruz, CA 95064 (831) 459-4008; Fax: (831) 459-4452

Full-time: 5820 men, 7182 women	Faculty: 516; I, av$
Part-time: 348 men, 310 women	Ph.D.s: 98%
Graduate: 614 men, 723 women	Student/Faculty: 25 to 1
Year: quarters, summer session	Tuition: $6191 ($20,401)
Application Deadline: November 30	Room & Board: $10,314
Freshman Class: 21,525 applied, 17,284 accepted, 3429 enrolled	
SAT I Verbal/Math: 572/577	ACT: 23 **VERY COMPETITIVE**

University of California, Santa Cruz, opened in 1965, is a public institution with a small-college setting and the academic resources of a major university, offering programs in the arts, engineering, humanities, physical and biological sciences, and social sciences. There are 10 undergraduate schools and 1 graduate school. In addition to regional accreditation, UCSC has baccalaureate program accreditation with ABET. The 10 libraries contain 1,302,295 volumes, 831,193 microform items, and 41,187 audio/video tapes/CDs, and subscribe to 9023 periodicals. Computerized library services include the card catalog, interlibrary loans, database searching, and Internet access. Special learning facilities include a learning resource center, art gallery, radio station, agroecology program farm, arboretum, Long Marine Lab, and Lick Observatory on Mt. Hamilton. The 2000-acre campus is in a small town 30 miles southwest of San Jose and 75 miles south of San Francisco. Including any residence halls, there are 471 buildings.

Student Life: 94% of undergraduates are from California. Students are from 50 states, 22 foreign countries, and Canada. 80% are from public schools. 52% are white; 17% Asian American; 14% Hispanic. The average age of freshmen is 18; all undergraduates, 21. 13% do not continue beyond their first year; 65% remain to graduate.

Housing: 5932 students can be accommodated in college housing, which includes single-sex and coed dorms, on-campus apartments, off-campus apartments, and married-student housing. In addition, there are language houses, special-interest houses, and multicultural residence halls. On-campus housing is available on a lottery system for upperclassmen. 58% of students commute. Alcohol is not permitted. Upperclassmen may keep cars.

Activities: 1% of men belong to 4 national fraternities; 1% of women belong to 3 local and 3 national sororities. There are several groups on campus, including art, band, cheerleading, chess, choir, chorale, chorus, computers, dance, debate, drama, ethnic, film, gay, honors, international, jazz band, literary magazine, musical theater, orchestra, photography, political, professional, radio and TV, religious, social, social service, student government, symphony, and yearbook. Popular campus events include Multicultural Festival and Martin Luther King, Jr. Convocation.

Sports: There are 15 intercollegiate sports for men and 17 for women, and 10 intramural sports for men and 11 for women. Facilities include a 50-meter pool, 2 playing fields, a weight room, an all-weather jogging track, fully equipped gyms, a fitness course, racquetball, tennis and basketball courts, and a 12,000-square-foot fitness center.

Disabled Students: 90% of the campus is accessible. Wheelchair ramps, elevators, special parking, specially equipped rest rooms, special class scheduling, lowered drinking fountains, lowered telephones, and wheelchair lift-equipped transportation are available.

Services: Counseling and information services are available, as is tutoring in some subjects, including writing. There is a reader service for the blind. A learning center helps SAA/EOP students with math and writing skills.

Campus Safety and Security: Measures include 24-hour foot and vehicle patrol, self-defense education, security escort services, and shuttle buses. There are informal discussions, pamphlets/posters/films, emergency telephones, lighted pathways/sidewalks, a rape prevention program, seminars for residential staff, and guards at each entrance from 8 P.M. until dawn.

Programs of Study: UCSC confers B.A., B.S., and B.M. degrees. Master's and doctoral degrees are also awarded. Bachelor's degrees are awarded in AGRICULTURE (environmental studies), BIOLOGICAL SCIENCE (biochemistry, bioinformatics, biology/biological science, and marine biology), BUSINESS (business economics and international economics), COMMUNICATIONS AND THE ARTS (art, art history and appreciation, classical languages, dramatic arts, film arts, French, linguistics, literature, and music), COMPUTER AND PHYSICAL SCIENCE (chemistry, computer science, earth science, geology, information sciences and systems, mathematics, and physics), ENGINEERING AND ENVIRONMENTAL DESIGN (computer engineering), HEALTH PROFESSIONS (health science), SOCIAL SCIENCE (American studies, anthropology, community services, economics, German area studies, history, Italian studies, Latin American studies, law, philosophy, political science/government, psychobiology, psychology, religion, Russian and Slavic studies, sociology, South Asian studies, and women's studies). Psychology, business management economics, and biology are the largest.

Required: In order to graduate, all students must complete 36 full-credit courses (180 quarter units) with a minimum GPA of 2.0. Courses are required in arts, English, history, writing-intensive, ethnic/third world, humanities, math, sciences, and social sciences. They must satisfy university requirements in American history and institutions and in English composition, the residence requirement, the core course, and a comprehensive exam or equivalent body of work, or a senior thesis. Particular college requirements and those of an approved major vary. All students must also satisfy each of the UCSC general education requirements with a course graded C or better.

Special: Cross-registration is possible with other University of California campuses, Hampshire College, the University of New Hampshire, and the University of New Mexico. UCSC also offers work-study, a Washington semester, internships in many arenas, study abroad in 34 countries, student-designed majors, dual majors, a 3-2 engineering degree with the University of California, Berkeley, and a B.A.-B.S. degree in earth sciences, chemistry and biochemistry, and computer science. There is a chapter of Phi Beta Kappa, a freshman honors program, and several honors programs.

Faculty/Classroom: 60% of faculty are male; 40%, female. All both teach and do research. Graduate students teach 1% of introductory courses. The average class size in an introductory lecture is 100.

Admissions: 80% of the 2003-2004 applicants were accepted. The SAT I scores for the 2003-2004 freshman class were: Verbal--21% below 500, 40% between 500 and 599, 32% between 600 and 700, and 8% above 700; Math--17% below 500, 42% between 500 and 599, 36% between 600 and 700, and 6% above 700. The ACT scores were 9% between 12 and 17, 38% between 18 and 23, 46% between 24 and 29, and 7% between 30 and 36. 90% of the current freshmen were in the top tenth of their class.

Requirements: The SAT I or ACT is required, as are SAT II: Subject tests in writing, math, and a choice of English literature, social science, foreign language, or science. Applicants must be graduates of an accredited secondary school or have a GED certificate. They should have completed 15 academic credits, including 4 years of English, 3 of math, and 2 each of foreign language, history, lab science, and college preparatory electives. Auditions are required for music majors, and portfolios are recommended for art majors. All students must submit a personal statement. Nonresidents must meet additional requirements. A GPA of 2.8 is required. AP credits are accepted. Important factors in the admissions decision are advanced placement or honor courses, evidence of special talent, and extracurricular activities record.

Procedure: Freshmen are admitted in the fall. Entrance exams should be taken by December of the senior year. Applications should be filed by November 30 for fall entry. Notification is sent in March and April. The fall 2003 application fee was $40. Applications are accepted on-line through *http://www.universityofcalifornia.edu/admissions/undergradapp*.

Transfer: 885 transfer students enrolled in 2003-2004. Applicants should have completed 84 quarter credits, with a GPA of 2.4 required for California residents and 2.8 for nonresidents, and all subject areas must be completed. No senior transfers are accepted. 35 of 180 credits required for the bachelor's degree must be completed at UCSC.

Visiting: There are guides for informal visits and visitors may sit in on classes. To schedule a visit, contact the Office of Admissions at *ucscvisits@ucsc.edu*.

Financial Aid: The FAFSA is required. The deadline for filing freshman financial aid applications for fall entry is March 2.

International Students: There are 120 international students enrolled. They must score 550 on the written TOEFL or 220 on the electronic version and also take the SAT I or the ACT. Students must also take SAT II: Subject tests in writing, math and 1 other area (not math).

Computers: The mainframe is a Sun SPARC Station 10. There are Macs and PCs available in 13 open-access computer labs and in classrooms throughout the campus, providing e-mail and Internet access. ResNet provides Internet access to all students in university-sponsored housing. All students may sign up for e-mail addresses. All students may access the system. There are no time limits and no fees. It is strongly recommended that all students have a personal computer.

Graduates: From July 1, 2002 to June 30, 2003, 2931 bachelor's degrees were awarded. In an average class, 1% graduate in 3 years or less, 42% graduate in 4 years or less, 61% graduate in 5 years or less, and 65% graduate in 6 years or less.

Admissions Contact: Kevin M. Browne, Executive Director of Admissions and University Registrar. E-mail: *admissions@ucsc.edu* Web: *admissions.ucsc.edu*

UNIVERSITY OF JUDAISM COLLEGE OF ARTS AND SCIENCES   C-5

Bel Air, CA 90077

(310) 476-9777, ext. 261
(888) UJ FOR ME; Fax: (310) 471-3657

Full-time: 45 men, 60 women	**Faculty:** 10
Part-time: 5 men, 5 women	**Ph.D.s:** 100%
Graduate: 60 men, 70 women	**Student/Faculty:** 10 to 1
Year: semesters	**Tuition:** $15,550
Application Deadline: see profile	**Room & Board:** $8680
Freshman Class: n/av	
SAT I or ACT: required	**COMPETITIVE**

The College of Arts and Sciences at the University of Judaism is distinguished by its core curriculum integrating the study of Western and Jewish civilizations. It prepares students for careers and graduate studies in law, business, psychology, education and other fields. There are 3 graduate schools. Figures in the above capsule and in this profile are approximate. The library contains 105,000 volumes, and subscribes to 400 periodicals. Computerized library services include the card catalog and interlibrary loans. Special learning facilities include a learning resource center, art gallery, and radio station. The 28-acre campus is in a suburban area. Including any residence halls, there are 9 buildings.

Student Life: 71% of undergraduates are from California. Students are from 22 states and 2 foreign countries. 80% are from public schools. 81% are white; 10% Hispanic. Most are Jewish. The average age of freshmen is 18; all undergraduates, 23. 5% do not continue beyond their first year; 90% remain to graduate.

Housing: 192 students can be accommodated in college housing, which includes coed dorms, on-campus apartments, and married-student housing. On-campus housing is guaranteed for all 4 years. 85% of students live on campus; of those, 80% remain on campus on weekends. All students may keep cars.

Activities: There are no fraternities or sororities. There are many groups and organizations on campus, including art, chorus, dance, drama, literary magazine, newspaper, political, radio and TV, religious, social, social service, student government, and yearbook.

Sports: Facilities include a weight room, basketball and volleyball courts, and a soccer field.

Disabled Students: All of the campus is accessible. Elevators, special parking, specially equipped rest rooms, lowered drinking fountains, lowered telephones, and specially equipped dorm rooms are available.

Services: Counseling and information services are available, as is tutoring in most subjects. There is remedial math and writing.

Campus Safety and Security: Measures include 24-hour foot and vehicle patrol, self-defense education, informal discussions, and pamphlets/posters/films. There are lighted pathways/sidewalks.

Programs of Study: UJ confers the B.A. degree. Master's degrees are also awarded. Bachelor's degrees are awarded in BUSINESS (business administration and management), COMMUNICATIONS AND THE ARTS (journalism and literature), HEALTH PROFESSIONS (premedicine), SOCIAL SCIENCE (ethics, politics, and social policy, Judaic studies, liberal arts/general studies, political science/government, and psychology).

Required: All students must complete a core curriculum combining the study of Jewish and Western civilizations, as well as courses in communications and foreign language, and 1 in computer science. There are distribution requirements in math, natural and behavioral sciences, and fine arts. Other requirements vary according to the major, with at least 32 to 36 upper-division credits needed. A total of 127 semester units, with a minimum GPA of 2.0, is required to graduate.

Special: There is a 5-year joint business management program with University of Judaism's Lieber School of Graduate Studies. Student-designed and dual majors are available. Internships in all available majors, study abroad, work-study programs, accelerated degree programs, and pass/fail options are offered. Students may apply for independent study projects.

Faculty/Classroom: 75% of faculty are male; 25%, female. All teach undergraduates and all both teach and do research. No introductory courses are taught by graduate students. The average class size in an introductory lecture is 13; in a laboratory, 6; and in a regular course, 9.

Requirements: The SAT I or ACT is required, with scores of at least 1100 on the SAT I or 23 on the ACT preferred. Applicants must be graduates of an accredited secondary school or have the GED. A visit and an interview are recommended for all students. Two recommendations from teachers, an autobiographical essay, and a secondary school report/recommendation from an academic counselor also are required. Students scoring below 500 verbal on the SAT I or earning below a 3.2 GPA are occasionally admitted if their essay, recommendations, and grades in English and other humanities courses are exceptionally strong. A GPA of 3.2 is required. AP credits are accepted.

Procedure: Freshmen are admitted fall and spring. Entrance exams should be taken no later than November of the year prior to enrollment. There are early decision and deferred admissions plans and a rolling admissions plan. Check with the school for current deadlines. The fall 2003 application fee was $15.

Transfer: 19 transfer students enrolled in a recent year. Previous college work should be at the B level to transfer. Students with fewer than 60 college credits should also have a minimum 3.0 high school GPA, at least 1100 on the SAT I or 23 on the ACT, 2 recommendations, and an autobiographical essay. The SAT I or ACT requirement is waived if the applicant has 60 or more transferable credits. A visit and an interview are recommended. 34 of 127 credits required for the bachelor's degree must be completed at UJ.

Visiting: There are regularly scheduled orientations for prospective students, including meetings with admissions representatives and campus tours. There are guides for informal visits and visitors may sit in on classes and stay overnight. To schedule a visit, contact Amnon Finkelstein, Dean of Admissions at (310) 476-9777, ext. 252 or finaid@uj.edu.

Financial Aid: In a recent year, 74% of all full-time freshmen and 78% of continuing full-time students received some form of financial aid. 68% of full-time freshmen and 75% of continuing full-time students received need-based aid. 78% of undergraduates work part time. Average annual earnings from campus work are $1694. The average financial indebtedness of a recent graduate was $8932. UJ is a member of CSS. The FAFSA, the college's own financial statement, tax returns, and W2s are required. Check with the school for current deadlines.

International Students: In a recent year, there were 2 international students enrolled. They must score 550 on the written TOEFL or 213 on the electronic version and also take the SAT I or the ACT, scoring 1100.

Computers: In total, there are 4 computer rooms housing 30 IBMs, and Macs, and several printers. All students may access the system. There are no time limits and no fees.

Graduates: In a recent year, 22 bachelor's degrees were awarded. The most popular majors were psychology (46%), literature (23%), and Judaic studies (15%). In an average class, 75% graduate in 4 years or less, and 25% graduate in 5 years or less. Of a recent graduating class, 65% were enrolled in graduate school within 6 months of graduation.

Admissions Contact: Dr. Amnon Finkelstein, Dean of Admissions. E-mail: afinkelstein@uj.edu Web: www.uj.edu

---

UNIVERSITY OF LA VERNE
La Verne, CA 91750-4443

D-5

(909) 392-2800
(800) 876-4658; Fax: (909) 392-2714

Full-time: 494 men, 849 women	**Faculty:** 126; I, --$
Part-time: 25 men, 28 women	**Ph.D.s:** 71%
Graduate: 782 men, 1426 women	**Student/Faculty:** 11 to 1
Year: 4-1-4, summer session	**Tuition:** $20,500
Application Deadline: February 1	**Room & Board:** $8100
Freshman Class: 1072 applied, 793 accepted, 303 enrolled	
SAT I Verbal/Math: 490/500	**ACT:** 20 COMPETITIVE

The University of La Verne, founded in 1891, is an independent, liberal arts and graduate studies university. There are 3 undergraduate and 4 graduate schools. The library contains 215,000 volumes, and subscribes to 4500 periodicals. Computerized library services include the card catalog, interlibrary loans, and database searching. Special learning facilities include a learning resource center, art gallery, natural history museum, radio station, TV station, theater, and archeology lab. The 26-acre campus is in a suburban area 35 miles east of Los Angeles. Including any residence halls, there are 26 buildings.

Student Life: 94% of undergraduates are from California. Students are from 13 states. 36% are Hispanic; 36% white; 10% African American. 35% are Catholic; 31% Protestant; 27% claim no religious affiliation. The average age of freshmen is 18; all undergraduates, 20. 12% do not continue beyond their first year.

Housing: 518 students can be accommodated in college housing, which includes single-sex and coed dorms. In addition, there are special-interest houses and an international floor. On-campus housing is available on a first-come, first-served basis and is available on a lottery system for upperclassmen. Priority is given to out-of-town students. 65% of students commute. Alcohol is not permitted. All students may keep cars.

Activities: 18% of men belong to 1 local and 2 national fraternities; 15% of women belong to 1 local and 3 national sororities. There are 40 groups on campus, including art, cheerleading, choir, chorale, chorus, computers, dance, debate, departmental, drama, environmental, ethnic, forensics, gay, honors, international, jazz band, literary magazine, musical theater, newspaper, photography, political, professional, radio and TV, religious, social, social service, student government, and yearbook. Popular campus events include Cinco de Mayo, International Week, and Commuter Day.

Sports: There are 11 intercollegiate sports for men and 9 for women, and 6 intramural sports for men and 6 for women. Facilities include a football stadium, 2 gyms, a pool, a weight and fitness center, tennis courts, an outdoor track, and soccer and other playing fields.

Disabled Students: 95% of the campus is accessible. Wheelchair ramps, elevators, special parking, specially equipped rest rooms, and lowered telephones are available.

Services: Counseling and information services are available, as is tutoring in most subjects. There is a reader service for the blind and remedial math, reading, and writing. Students may use the computerized Learning Enhancement Center or schedule tutoring free of charge.

Campus Safety and Security: Measures include 24-hour foot and vehicle patrol, security escort services, informal discussions, and pamphlets/posters/films. There are emergency telephones and lighted pathways/sidewalks.

Programs of Study: ULV confers B.A. and B.S. degrees. Associate, master's, and doctoral degrees are also awarded. Bachelor's degrees are awarded in BIOLOGICAL SCIENCE (biology/biological science and environmental biology), BUSINESS (accounting, business administration and management, business economics, electronic business, institutional management, international business management, and marketing and distribution), COMMUNICATIONS AND THE ARTS (art, art history and appreciation, broadcasting, communications, comparative literature, dramatic arts, English, French, German, journalism, music, Spanish, and speech/debate/rhetoric), COMPUTER AND PHYSICAL SCIENCE (chemistry, computer science, mathematics, natural sciences, and physics), EDUCATION (athletic training and education), ENGINEERING AND ENVIRONMENTAL DESIGN (computer engineering and environmental science), HEALTH PROFESSIONS (health care administration), SOCIAL SCIENCE (anthropology, behavioral science, child psychology/development, criminology, history, international studies, liberal arts/general studies, paralegal studies, philosophy, physical fitness/movement, political science/government, psychology, public administration, religion, social science, and sociology). Natural science, education, and psychology are the strongest academically. Business, liberal studies, and psychology are the largest.

Required: To graduate, students must complete a minimum of 128 credit hours, with a minimum GPA of 2.0. 32 hours in the major are required, and 6 in general education. Required core courses include Values and Critical Thinking, Service Learning, International/Intercultural Experience, The Human Condition, and Toward a Sustainable Planet.

Special: Internships, study abroad in 10 countries, work-study programs, B.A.-B.S. degrees, dual majors, and nondegree study are available. Pass/fail options are also available. There are 9 national honor societies and a freshman honors program.

Faculty/Classroom: 57% of faculty are male; 43%, female. 91% teach undergraduates. No introductory courses are taught by graduate students. The average class size in an introductory lecture is 12; in a laboratory, 10; and in a regular course, 14.

Admissions: 74% of the 2003-2004 applicants were accepted. The SAT I scores for the 2003-2004 freshman class were: Verbal--50% below 500, 43% between 500 and 599, 6% between 600 and 700, and 1% above 700; Math--46% below 500, 45% between 500 and 599, and 9% between 600 and 700. The ACT scores were 58% below 21, 32% between 21 and 23, 6% between 24 and 26, and 3% between 27 and 28. 55% of the current freshmen were in the top fifth of their class; 87% were in the top two fifths.

Requirements: The SAT I or ACT is required. In addition, applicants must be graduates of an accredited secondary school. An essay is required, and an interview is recommended. AP and CLEP credits are accepted. Important factors in the admissions decision are advanced placement or honor courses, recommendations by school officials, and extracurricular activities record.

Procedure: Freshmen are admitted fall and spring. Entrance exams should be taken in the junior or senior year. There is a rolling admissions plan and a deferred admissions plan. Applications should be filed by February 1 for fall entry and December 1 for spring entry, along with a $50 fee. Notification is sent on a rolling basis. Applications are accepted on-line through Princeton Review at *apply.embark.com/ugrad/ulaverne/2/*, the College Board at *www.collegeboard.com*, or the Association of Independent Colleges and Universities at *www.aiccumentor.org/admissionApp/*.

Transfer: 107 transfer students enrolled in 2002-2003. Applicants must demonstrate academic ability at all previous colleges attended. Students with fewer than 32 transferable semester credits must submit SAT I or ACT scores and a high school transcript. 32 of 128 credits required for the bachelor's degree must be completed at ULV.

Visiting: There are regularly scheduled orientations for prospective students, including campus tours, faculty and student panels, and meals. There are guides for informal visits and visitors may sit in on classes and stay overnight. To schedule a visit, contact the Admissions Office.

Financial Aid: In 2003-2004, 96% of all full-time freshmen and 94% of continuing full-time students received some form of financial aid. 70% of full-time freshmen and 66% of continuing full-time students received need-based aid. The average freshman award was $19,839. Need-based scholarships or need-based grants averaged $10,315 ($23,258 maximum); need-based self-help aid (loans and jobs) averaged $10,257 ($23,008 maximum); and non-need-based awards and non-need-based scholarships averaged $8092 ($24,375 maximum). 56% of undergraduates work part time. Average annual earnings from campus work are $1999. The FAFSA and Cal Grant Application are required. The deadline for filing freshman financial aid applications for fall entry is March 2.

International Students: There are 30 international students enrolled. The school actively recruits these students. International applicants must demonstrate English proficiency by presenting either a TOEFL score of 500, an SAT I verbal score of 480, a grade of 3.0 on ULV's own test, or 30 transferable college credits, including the equivalent of English 110.

Computers: The mainframe is an HP 9000. 10 labs and a campuswide network offer a variety of hardware, software, and operating environments. All students may access the system 24 hours, 7 days a week. There are no time limits and no fees.

Graduates: From July 1, 2002 to June 30, 2003, 272 bachelor's degrees were awarded. The most popular majors were business administration (17%), liberal studies (15%), and criminology (8%). In an average class, 31% graduate in 4 years or less, 48% graduate in 5 years or less, and 50% graduate in 6 years or less. 62 companies recruited on campus in 2002-2003.

Admissions Contact: Ana Liza V. Zell, Director of Admissions. E-mail: *admissions@ulv.edu* Web: *www.ulv.edu*

UNIVERSITY OF REDLANDS   D-5
Redlands, CA 92373-0999

(909) 335-4074
(800) 455-5064; Fax: (909) 335-4089

Full-time: 901 men, 1291 women	**Faculty:** 156; IIA, av$
Part-time: 15 men, 16 women	**Ph.D.s:** 86%
Graduate: 28 men, 60 women	**Student/Faculty:** 14 to 1
Year: 4-1-4	**Tuition:** $24,096
Application Deadline: February 1	**Room & Board:** $8480
Freshman Class: 2669 applied, 1890 accepted, 574 enrolled	
SAT I Verbal/Math: 580/570	**ACT:** 24 **VERY COMPETITIVE**

University of Redlands, founded in 1907, is a private institution that offers programs in liberal and fine arts, business, and teacher preparation. There are 2 undergraduate and 4 graduate schools. The library contains 421,996 volumes, 308,205 microform items, and 10,885 audio/video tapes/CDs, and subscribes to 8347 periodicals. Computerized library services include the card catalog, interlibrary loans, and database searching. Special learning facilities include an art gallery, a language lab, a computer center, and a geographic information systems lab. The 160-acre campus is in a small town 60 miles east of Los Angeles. Including any residence halls, there are 86 buildings.

Student Life: 73% of undergraduates are from California. Students are from 42 states, 10 foreign countries, and Canada. 62% are white; 12% Hispanic. The average age of freshmen is 18; all undergraduates, 20. 14% do not continue beyond their first year.

Housing: 1670 students can be accommodated in college housing, which includes single-sex and coed dorms, on-campus apartments, off-campus apartments, married-student housing, fraternity houses, and sorority houses. In addition, there are honors houses and special-interest houses. On-campus housing is guaranteed for all 4 years. 75% of students live on campus. All students may keep cars.

Activities: 10% of men belong to 7 local fraternities; 13% of women belong to 5 local sororities. There are 105 groups on campus, including art, band, cheerleading, chess, choir, chorale, chorus, dance, debate, drama, drill team, ethnic, film, gay, honors, international, jazz band, literary magazine, musical theater, newspaper, opera, orchestra, pep band, photography, political, professional, radio and TV, religious, social, social service, student government, symphony, and yearbook. Popular campus events include Mayfest, Multicultural Festival, and Feast of Lights.

Sports: There are 10 intercollegiate sports for men and 10 for women, and 7 intramural sports for men and 7 for women. Facilities include a fitness center, an aquatic center, a football stadium, tennis courts, and baseball, softball, soccer, and lacrosse fields.

Disabled Students: 25% of the campus is accessible. Wheelchair ramps, elevators, special parking, specially equipped rest rooms, special class scheduling, lowered drinking fountains, and lowered telephones are available.

Services: Counseling and information services are available, as is tutoring in every subject. There is a reader service for the blind.

Campus Safety and Security: Measures include 24-hour foot and vehicle patrol, self-defense education, security escort services, and shuttle buses. There are informal discussions, pamphlets/posters/films, emergency telephones, lighted pathways/sidewalks, and safety whistles.

Programs of Study: Redlands confers B.A., B.S., and B.Mus. degrees. Master's degrees are also awarded. Bachelor's degrees are awarded in BIOLOGICAL SCIENCE (biochemistry, biology/biological science, and molecular biology), BUSINESS (accounting and business administration and management), COMMUNICATIONS AND THE ARTS (art, English, French, German, music, and Spanish), COMPUTER AND PHYSICAL SCIENCE (chemistry, computer science, mathematics, and physics), ENGINEERING AND ENVIRONMENTAL DESIGN (environmental science), SOCIAL SCIENCE (anthropology, Asian/Oriental studies, economics, history, international relations, liberal arts/general studies, philosophy, political science/government, psychology, religion, and sociology). Liberal arts is the strongest academically. Business is the largest.

Required: Requirements for graduation vary according to the degree and major. Students must complete at least 132 units with a minimum of 44 in the major, and maintain a minimum GPA of 2.0. Students pursuing a B.S. degree must fulfill an additional field requirement. A capstone in the major is required.

Special: Cross-registration with sister colleges, various internships, and study abroad in 50 countries are offered. A Washington semester, a Sacramento program, various work-study programs, B.A.-B.S. degrees, a liberal studies degree, dual majors, and accelerated degree programs are available. Students may pursue nondegree study, take advantage of pass/fail options, and receive credit for life or work experience. At the Johnston Center for Integrative studies, students design their own majors and courses of study. There are 4 national honor societies, including Phi Beta Kappa, a freshman honors program, and 23 departmental honors programs.

Faculty/Classroom: 48% of faculty are male; 52%, female. All teach undergraduates. No introductory courses are taught by graduate students. The average class size in an introductory lecture is 20; in a laboratory, 10; and in a regular course, 12.

Admissions: 71% of the 2003-2004 applicants were accepted. The SAT I scores for the 2003-2004 freshman class were: Verbal--11% below 500, 50% between 500 and 599, 34% between 600 and 700, and 5% above 700; Math--12% below 500, 51% between 500 and 599, 32% between 600 and 700, and 6% above 700. The ACT scores were 15% below 21, 29% between 21 and 23, 25% between 24 and 26, 17% between 27 and 28, and 14% above 28. There were 4 National Merit finalists.

Requirements: The SAT I or ACT is required. In addition, Redlands recommends that applicants have completed a minimum of 16 units in solid academic areas. The student should have completed at least 4 years of high school English, 2 to 3 years each of math, lab sciences, and social science, and 2 years of a foreign language. AP and CLEP credits are accepted. Important factors in the admissions decision are advanced placement or honor courses, leadership record, and personality/intangible qualities.

Procedure: Freshmen are admitted to all sessions. Entrance exams should be taken prior to application. There are rolling and deferred admissions plans. Early decision applications should be filed by December 15; regular applications, by February 1 for fall entry, and January 1 for spring entry. Notification is sent on a rolling basis. The fall 2003 application fee was $40. Applications are accepted on-line through the Common Application and the school's web site.

Transfer: 127 transfer students enrolled in 2002-2003. The SAT I or the ACT may be required of transfer applicants, depending on how many units are accepted. 30 of 132 credits required for the bachelor's degree must be completed at Redlands.

Visiting: There are regularly scheduled orientations for prospective students, including campus tours at 10 A.M., 1 P.M., and 4 P.M., on weekdays and 11 A.M. and 1 P.M. on Saturdays during the school year. There are guides for informal visits and visitors may sit in on classes and stay overnight. To schedule a visit, contact the Visit Coordinator at (909) 793-2121, ext. 4573 or *Tamie_Fawcett@redlands.edu*.

Financial Aid: In 2003-2004, 90% of all full-time freshmen and 91% of continuing full-time students received some form of financial aid. 73% of full-time freshmen and 78% of continuing full-time students received need-based aid. The average freshman award was $22,814. Need-based scholarships or need-based grants averaged $13,268 ($19,400 maximum); need-based self-help aid (loans and jobs) averaged $6077 ($11,625 maximum); non-need-based awards and non-need-based scholarships averaged $1708 ($6934 maximum); and outside aid, state, Pell, and SEOG averaged $8721 ($20,409 maximum). 54% of undergraduates work part time. Average annual earnings from campus work are $1291. The FAFSA, the college's own financial statement, and the GPA verification form for California residents are required.

International Students: There are 19 international students enrolled. The school actively recruits these students. They must score 550 on the written TOEFL or 213 on the electronic version.

Computers: The academic computing center provides 150 networked Mac and Windows computers connecting to Mac, NT, and UNIX servers and the Internet. These include specialized graphics/desktop publishing and geographic information systems (GIS) labs as well as general-purpose teaching and drop-in labs. All students may access the system. There are no time limits. The fee is $300.

Graduates: From July 1, 2002 to June 30, 2003, 420 bachelor's degrees were awarded. The most popular majors were liberal studies (22%), social sciences/history (17%), and business (10%). In an average class, 54% graduate in 4 years or less, 57% graduate in 5 years or less, and 57% graduate in 6 years or less.

Admissions Contact: Paul M. Driscoll, Dean of Admissions.
E-mail: *admissions@uor.edu* Web: *www.redlands.edu*

UNIVERSITY OF SAN DIEGO   D-5
San Diego, CA 92110
(619) 260-4506
(800) 248-4873; Fax: (619) 260-6836

Full-time: 1777 men, 2869 women	**Faculty:** 314; I, av$
Part-time: 56 men, 101 women	**Ph.D.s:** 97%
Graduate: 1146 men, 1313 women	**Student/Faculty:** 15 to 1
Year: 4-1-4, summer session	**Tuition:** $23,594
Application Deadline: January 5	**Room & Board:** $9562
Freshman Class: 7273 applied, 3709 accepted, 1064 enrolled	
SAT I Verbal/Math: 600/620	**ACT:** 26 **HIGHLY COMPETITIVE**

The University of San Diego, founded in 1949, is a private, Catholic liberal arts university. There are 4 undergraduate and 5 graduate schools. In addition to regional accreditation, USD has baccalaureate program accreditation with AACSB and ABET. The 2 libraries contain 714,082 volumes, 839,992 microform items, and 8624 audio/video tapes/CDs, and subscribe to 10,451 periodicals. Computerized library services include the card catalog, interlibrary loans, and database searching. Special learning facilities include a learning resource center, art gallery, TV station, media center, and child development center. The 180-acre campus is in an urban area 10 miles north of downtown San Diego. Including any residence halls, there are 101 buildings.

Student Life: 60% of undergraduates are from California. Students are from 50 states, 63 foreign countries, and Canada. 57% are from public schools. 68% are white; 16% Hispanic. 55% are Catholic; 10% Protestant. The average age of freshmen is 18; all undergraduates, 21. 14% do not continue beyond their first year; 72% remain to graduate.

Housing: 1900 students can be accommodated in college housing, which includes single-sex and coed dorms and on-campus apartments. In addition, there are honors houses and special-interest houses. On-campus housing is guaranteed for all 4 years. 52% of students live on campus; of those, 70% remain on campus on weekends. All students may keep cars.

Activities: 14% of men belong to 4 national fraternities; 19% of women belong to 4 national sororities. There are 60 groups on campus, including academic, art, cheerleading, choir, chorus, dance, drama, ethnic, gay, honors, international, jazz band, newspaper, opera, orchestra, political, professional, religious, social, social service, student government, and yearbook. Popular campus events include Walk on Water Contest, Orientation Week, and sponsored concerts and events.

Sports: There are 8 intercollegiate sports for men and 8 for women, and 15 intramural sports for men and 15 for women. Facilities include a sports center, a stadium, tennis courts, a swimming pool, soccer, baseball, and softball fields, and the Mission Bay Aquatic Center.

Disabled Students: 80% of the campus is accessible. Wheelchair ramps, elevators, special parking, specially equipped rest rooms, and lowered drinking fountains are available. Individual needs can be accommodated.

Services: Counseling and information services are available, as is tutoring in most subjects.

Campus Safety and Security: Measures include 24-hour foot and vehicle patrol, self-defense education, security escort services, and shuttle buses. There are informal discussions, pamphlets/posters/films, emergency telephones, and lighted pathways/sidewalks.

Programs of Study: USD confers B.A., B.A./B.S., B.Acc., B.B.A., and B.S.N. degrees. Master's and doctoral degrees are also awarded. Bachelor's degrees are awarded in BIOLOGICAL SCIENCE (biology/biological science and marine science), BUSINESS (accounting, business administration and management, and business economics), COMMUNICA-TIONS AND THE ARTS (communications, English, fine arts, French, music, and Spanish), COMPUTER AND PHYSICAL SCIENCE (chemistry, computer science, mathematics, oceanography, and physics), EDUCATION (elementary and secondary), ENGINEERING AND ENVIRONMENTAL DESIGN (electrical/electronics engineering and industrial engineering), HEALTH PROFESSIONS (nursing), SOCIAL SCIENCE (anthropology, economics, history, humanities, international relations, liberal arts/general studies, philosophy, political science/government, psychology, religion, sociology, and urban studies). Business administration and communication studies are the largest.

Required: All students must take 124 credit hours, including 36 to 72 in their major, while maintaining a minimum GPA of 2.0. Distribution requirements include 9 units each of religious studies and humanities and fine arts, 6 each of philosophy, natural sciences, and social sciences, 3 or 4 of math, 3 of composition and literature, as well as 3 semesters of foreign language.

Special: A B.A.-B.S. degree is offered in electrical, industrial, and mechanical engineering. Internships in all disciplines, study abroad in 9 countries, and work-study programs on campus are available. There are 15 national honor societies, including Phi Beta Kappa, and a freshman honors program.

Faculty/Classroom: 57% of faculty are male; 43%, female. 90% teach undergraduates, 50% do research, and 50% do both. No introductory courses are taught by graduate students. The average class size in an introductory lecture is 25; in a laboratory, 15; and in a regular course, 22.

Admissions: 51% of the 2003-2004 applicants were accepted. The SAT I scores for the 2003-2004 freshman class were: Verbal--7% below 500, 42% between 500 and 599, 44% between 600 and 700, and 7% above 700; Math--4% below 500, 33% between 500 and 599, 53% between 600 and 700, and 10% above 700. The ACT scores were 3% below 21, 16% between 21 and 23, 34% between 24 and 26, 25% between 27 and 28, and 23% above 28. 75% of the current freshmen were in the top fifth of their class; 96% were in the top two fifths. 56 freshmen graduated first in their class.

Requirements: The SAT I is required. Admission is highly selective. Applicants should present a well-balanced secondary school program of college preparatory courses in English, foreign language, math, laboratory science, history, and social science. Both the content of the academic program as well as the quality of performance is considered. In addition, SAT I/ ACT results are used to broaden understanding of the applicant's potential. AP and CLEP credits are accepted. Important factors in the admissions decision are recommendations by school officials, extracurricular activities record, and advanced placement or honor courses.

Procedure: Freshmen are admitted fall, spring, and summer. Entrance exams should be taken before December 30 for early action and before March 1 for regular consideration. There is an early admissions plan. Applications should be filed by January 5 for fall entry and November 1 for spring entry, along with a $55 fee. Notification is sent April 15. 97 applicants were on the 2003 waiting list; 8 were admitted. Applications are accepted on-line through the university's web site at *www.sandiego.edu/ ugadmiss/apply.html*.

Transfer: 341 transfer students enrolled in 2002-2003. Transfer students must have a minimum GPA of 3.0 and have earned 24 credit hours. 30 of 124 credits required for the bachelor's degree must be completed at USD.

Visiting: There are regularly scheduled orientations for prospective students, including tours and information sessions offered by the Admissions Office Monday through Friday at 10 A.M. and 2 P.M., and Saturday from November through April at 10 A.M. and noon. There are guides for informal visits and visitors may sit in on classes. To schedule a visit, contact the Admissions Office.

Financial Aid: In 2003-2004, 74% of all full-time freshmen and 71% of continuing full-time students received some form of financial aid. 55% of full-time freshmen and 64% of continuing full-time students received need-based aid. The average freshman award in 2002-2003 was $17,508. Need-based scholarships or need-based grants averaged $17,508; need-based self-help aid (loans and jobs) averaged $3507; non-need-based athletic scholarships averaged $15,398; and other non-need-based awards and non-need-based scholarships averaged $6268. 21% of undergraduates work part time. Average annual earnings from campus work are $18,000. The average financial indebtedness of the 2003 graduate was $25,631. The FAFSA is required. The deadline for filing freshman financial aid applications for fall entry is February 20.

International Students: There are 125 international students enrolled. The school actively recruits these students. They must score 550 on the written TOEFL or 213 on the electronic version and also take the SAT I or the ACT. Students must take SAT II: Subject tests in writing.

Computers: The mainframe is an IBM M80. There are 300 Macs and PCs located in buildings across campus. All students may access the system. There are no time limits and no fees. It is strongly recommended that all students have a personal computer.

Graduates: From July 1, 2002 to June 30, 2003, 1176 bachelor's degrees were awarded. The most popular majors were business administration (34%), communication (12%), and psychology (7%). In an average class, 59% graduate in 4 years or less, 70% graduate in 5 years or less, and 68% graduate in 6 years or less. 115 companies recruited on campus in 2002-2003. Of the 2002 graduating class, 36% were enrolled in graduate school within 6 months of graduation and 96% were employed.

Admissions Contact: Stephen Pultz, Director of Admissions.
E-mail: *admissions@sandiego.edu* Web: *www.sandiego.edu*

UNIVERSITY OF SAN FRANCISCO	**B-3**
San Francisco, CA 94117-1080	(415) 422-6563
	(800) CALLUSF; Fax: (415) 422-2217
Full-time: 1567 men, 2926 women	Faculty: 270; I, +$
Part-time: 101 men, 124 women	Ph.D.s: 93%
Graduate: 1361 men, 2080 women	Student/Faculty: 17 to 1
Year: 4-1-4, summer session	Tuition: $24,920
Application Deadline: February 1	Room & Board: $9780
Freshman Class: 4634 applied, 3798 accepted, 921 enrolled	
SAT I Verbal/Math: 550/560	ACT: 23 VERY COMPETITIVE

The University of San Francisco, founded in 1855, is a private Roman Catholic institution run by the Jesuit Fathers and offering degree programs in the arts and sciences, business, education, nursing, and law. Cost figures in the above capsule are for 2004-2005. There are 5 undergraduate and 6 graduate schools. In addition to regional accreditation, USF has baccalaureate program accreditation with AACSB, ACS, APA, CSAB, and NLN. The 2 libraries contain 915,000 volumes, 900,000 microform items, and 5420 audio/video tapes/CDs, and subscribe to 2500 periodicals. Computerized library services include the card catalog, interlibrary loans, and database searching. Special learning facilities include a learning resource center, art gallery, radio station, rare book room, the Institute for Chinese-Western Cultural History, and the Center for Pacific Rim Studies. The 55-acre campus is in an urban area in the heart of the city. Including any residence halls, there are 17 buildings.

Student Life: 69% of undergraduates are from California. Students are from 50 states, 53 foreign countries, and Canada. 44% are from public schools. 39% are white; 25% Asian American; 13% Hispanic. 48% are Catholic; 33% Buddhist, Hindu, or Muslim. The average age of freshmen is 18; all undergraduates, 21. 20% do not continue beyond their first year; 67% remain to graduate.

Housing: 2250 students can be accommodated in college housing, which includes single-sex and coed dorms, on-campus apartments, and off-campus apartments. In addition, there are special-interest houses, a multicultural floor, an academic interest floor, a freshman experiences floor, and a quiet floor. On-campus housing is guaranteed for the freshman year only. Alcohol is not permitted. All students may keep cars.

Activities: 1% of men belong to 2 local and 1 national fraternity; 2% of women belong to 4 local and 2 national sororities. There are 75 groups on campus, including cheerleading, choir, chorale, chorus, computers, drama, ethnic, honors, international, literary magazine, musical theater, newspaper, orchestra, pep band, political, professional, radio and TV, religious, social, social service, and student government. Popular campus events include Founders Day and International Week.

Sports: There are 7 intercollegiate sports for men and 7 for women, and 8 intramural sports for men and 8 for women. Facilities include a 600-seat soccer stadium, a recreation center with a 50-meter swimming pool, a multipurpose gym, a weight room, a dance and aerobics room, a martial arts room, and 5 racquetball/handball courts.

Disabled Students: 95% of the campus is accessible. Wheelchair ramps, elevators, special parking, specially equipped rest rooms, lowered drinking fountains, and exam accommodations are available.

Services: Counseling and information services are available, as is tutoring in every subject. There is a reader service for the blind. There is a full-time counselor for learning-disabled students, as well as a learning and writing center for students in need of academic assistance.

Campus Safety and Security: Measures include 24-hour foot and vehicle patrol, self-defense education, security escort services, and shuttle buses. There are informal discussions, pamphlets/posters/films, emergency telephones, and lighted pathways/sidewalks.

Programs of Study: USF confers B.A., B.S., B.Arch., B.F.A., B.P.A., B.S.B.A., and B.S.N. degrees. Master's and doctoral degrees are also awarded. Bachelor's degrees are awarded in BIOLOGICAL SCIENCE (biology/biological science), BUSINESS (accounting, banking and finance, business administration and management, hospitality management services, hotel/motel and restaurant management, international business management, management information systems, marketing/retailing/merchandising, and organizational behavior), COMMUNICATIONS AND THE ARTS (art history and appreciation, arts administration/management, communications, drawing, English, fine arts, French, graphic design, illustration, media arts, painting, performing arts, Spanish, and visual and performing arts), COMPUTER AND PHYSICAL SCIENCE (chemistry, computer science, information sciences and systems, mathematics, and physics), EDUCATION (athletic training, elementary, middle school, and secondary), ENGINEERING AND ENVIRONMENTAL DESIGN (architecture and environmental science), HEALTH PRO-

FESSIONS (exercise science and nursing), SOCIAL SCIENCE (economics, history, Latin American studies, law enforcement and corrections, philosophy, political science/government, psychology, public administration, religion, sociology, and theological studies). Sciences and business are the strongest academically. Communications, nursing, and psychology are the largest.

Required: All students must maintain a GPA of at least 2.0 and take 128 credit hours, including 58 in upper-division courses. 36 to 58 hours are required in the major. The current general education requirements include 9 units each of basic skills and history/social science, 6 each of philosophy, religious studies, cultural perspectives, natural science, and literature and fine arts, and 3 of ethics.

Special: Cross-registration with the San Francisco Consortium, and internships with local business, social services, and research opportunities are available. Study abroad in Europe and Japan, work-study programs both on and off campus, and with social service agencies, a B.A.-B.S. degree in exercise and sports science, dual majors in liberal arts and education, 3-2 engineering degrees with the University of Southern California, student-designed majors, nondegree study, and limited pass/fail options are also available. The College of Professional Studies is a degree completion program for working adults. There are 5 national honor societies, a freshman honors program, and 1 departmental honors program.

Faculty/Classroom: 60% of faculty are male; 40%, female. 90% teach undergraduates, 75% do research, and 90% do both. No introductory courses are taught by graduate students. The average class size in an introductory lecture is 28; in a laboratory, 13; and in a regular course, 20.

Admissions: 82% of the 2003-2004 applicants were accepted. The SAT I scores for the 2003-2004 freshman class were: Verbal--24% below 500, 48% between 500 and 599, 25% between 600 and 700, and 3% above 700; Math--21% below 500, 47% between 500 and 599, 28% between 600 and 700, and 4% above 700. The ACT scores were 22% below 21, 33% between 21 and 23, 25% between 24 and 26, 10% between 27 and 28, and 10% above 28. 49% of the current freshmen were in the top fifth of their class; 79% were in the top two fifths. 2 freshmen graduated first in their class.

Requirements: The SAT I or ACT is required. In addition, applicants are required to have 20 academic units, based on 6 years of academic electives, 4 of English, 3 each of math and social studies, and 2 each of foreign language and lab science. An essay is required. The GED is accepted. A GPA of 3.0 is required. AP and CLEP credits are accepted. Important factors in the admissions decision are extracurricular activities record, evidence of special talent, and leadership record.

Procedure: Freshmen are admitted fall and spring. Entrance exams should be taken during the first half of the senior year. There are early admissions and deferred admissions plans. There is a rolling admissions plan. Early decision applications should be filed by November 15; regular applications, by February 1 for fall entry and December 15 for spring entry, along with a $55 fee. Notification of early decision is sent January 1; regular decision, on a rolling basis. Applications are accepted on computer disk and on-line through the school's web site, *www.usfca.edu*, and ApplyWeb.

Transfer: 359 transfer students enrolled in 2002-2003. Applicants need a minimum GPA of 2.0, or 2.8 if they have earned fewer than 24 semester units. 45 credits of 128 required for the bachelor's degree must be completed at USF.

Visiting: There are regularly scheduled orientations for prospective students, including a tour of campus, academic buildings, library, residence halls, recreation centers, and a group information session hosted by an admissions staff member. There are guides for informal visits and visitors may sit in on classes and stay overnight. To schedule a visit, contact the Office of Admissions at *admissions@usfca.edu*.

Financial Aid: In 2003-2004, 71% of all full-time freshmen and 57% of continuing full-time students received some form of financial aid. 62% of full-time freshmen and 57% of continuing full-time students received need-based aid. The average freshman award was $19,976. 29% of undergraduates work part time. Average annual earnings from campus work are $2900. The average financial indebtedness of the 2003 graduate was $19,958. The FAFSA is required. The deadline for filing freshman financial aid applications for fall entry is February 15.

International Students: There are 347 international students enrolled. The school actively recruits these students. They must score 550 on the written TOEFL or 213 on the electronic version and also take the SAT I. Students must take the SAT II: Writing test for placement only.

Computers: The mainframe is a DEC Alpha/VMS administrative computer. There are 200 PCs available in 10 locations operating on a LAN system. Each residence room is linked to the network, allowing e-mail and other applications. All students may access the system. There are no time limits and no fees. Refer to *http://www.usfca.edu/its/support/supported-systems.html* for information on supported computers.

Graduates: From July 1, 2002 to June 30, 2003, 1192 bachelor's degrees were awarded. The most popular majors were communication (10%), business administration (9%), and psychology (8%). In an average class, 1% graduate in 3 years or less, 47% graduate in 4 years or

less, 63% graduate in 5 years or less, and 67% graduate in 6 years or less. 110 companies recruited on campus in 2002-2003. Of the 2002 graduating class, 15% were enrolled in graduate school within 6 months of graduation and 70% were employed.

Admissions Contact: Thomas Matos, Director of Admissions.
E-mail: *admissions@usfca.edu* Web: *http://www.usfca.edu/*

UNIVERSITY OF SOUTHERN CALIFORNIA   C-5
Los Angeles, CA 90089-   (213) 740-1111; Fax: (213) 740-6364

Full-time: 7707 men, 7980 women	**Faculty:** 1304; I, +$
Part-time: 407 men, 287 women	**Ph.D.s:** 87%
Graduate: 8204 men, 7021 women	**Student/Faculty:** 10 to 1
Year: semesters, summer session	**Tuition:** $28,827
Application Deadline: January 10	**Room & Board:** $8632
Freshman Class: 29,278 applied, 8753 accepted, 2975 enrolled	
SAT I Verbal/Math: 655/680	**ACT:** 29 **MOST COMPETITIVE**

University of Southern California, founded in 1880, is a private institution offering undergraduate and graduate programs in liberal arts, fine arts, education, business, law, dentistry, engineering, communications, health professions, and more. There are 14 undergraduate and 18 graduate schools. In addition to regional accreditation, USC has baccalaureate program accreditation with AACSB, ABET, ACEJMC, ACPE, ACS, ADA, AOTA, APTA, CAHEA, CSAB, CSWE, NAAB, NASM, NLN, and NASPAA. The 25 libraries contain 3,800,702 volumes, 6,113,659 microform items, and 51,522 audio/video tapes/CDs, and subscribe to 30,335 periodicals. Computerized library services include the card catalog, interlibrary loans, database searching, and Internet access. Special learning facilities include a learning resource center, art gallery, natural history museum, radio station, TV station, labs, state-of-the-art cinema/film-making facilities, wind tunnel, and marine science center. The 155-acre campus is in an urban area 3 miles south of the Los Angeles Civic Center. Including any residence halls, there are 166 buildings.

Student Life: 69% of undergraduates are from California. Students are from 50 states, 108 foreign countries, and Canada. 60% are from public schools. 48% are white; 21% Asian American; 13% Hispanic. The average age of freshmen is 18; all undergraduates, 20. 6% do not continue beyond their first year; 81% remain to graduate.

Housing: 6400 students can be accommodated in college housing, which includes coed dorms, on-campus apartments, off-campus apartments, married-student housing, fraternity houses, and sorority houses. In addition, there are special-interest houses, a Greek honors house, Latino, African American, multicultural, environmental, and cinema floors, and an international residential hall. On-campus housing is guaranteed for the freshman year only, is available on a first-come, first-served basis, and is available on a lottery system for upperclassmen. 65% of students commute. All students may keep cars.

Activities: 16% of men belong to 4 local and 21 national fraternities; 17% of women belong to 8 local and 10 national sororities. There are more than 600 groups on campus, including art, band, cheerleading, chess, choir, chorale, chorus, computers, dance, debate, drama, drill team, ethnic, film, gay, honors, international, jazz band, literary magazine, marching band, musical theater, newspaper, opera, orchestra, pep band, photography, political, professional, radio and TV, religious, social, social service, student government, symphony, and yearbook. Popular campus events include Springfest, International Food and Cultural Fair, and Spectrum concert series.

Sports: There are 10 intercollegiate sports for men and 10 for women, and 24 intramural sports for men and 20 for women. Facilities include a student athletic center, a track, a gym, 2 Olympic pools, and tennis, swimming, and baseball stadiums.

Disabled Students: 95% of the campus is accessible. Wheelchair ramps, elevators, special parking, specially equipped rest rooms, special class scheduling, lowered drinking fountains, lowered telephones, and special housing are available.

Services: Counseling and information services are available, as is tutoring in every subject. There is a reader service for the blind. Accommodations are made for students with disabilities.

Campus Safety and Security: Measures include 24-hour foot and vehicle patrol, self-defense education, security escort services, and shuttle buses. There are informal discussions, pamphlets/posters/films, emergency telephones, and lighted pathways/sidewalks. The safety department patrols an area 5 times the area of the campus.

Programs of Study: USC confers B.A., B.S., B.Arch., B.F.A., B.Land.Arch., and B.M. degrees. Master's and doctoral degrees are also awarded. Bachelor's degrees are awarded in BIOLOGICAL SCIENCE (biology/biological science and biophysics), BUSINESS (accounting and business administration and management), COMMUNICATIONS AND THE ARTS (art history and appreciation, broadcasting, classics, communications, comparative literature, dramatic arts, English, film arts, fine arts, French, German, jazz, journalism, linguistics, music, music business management, music performance, music theory and composition, public relations, Russian, Spanish, studio art, theater design, and theater management), COMPUTER AND PHYSICAL SCIENCE (astronomy, chem-

istry, computer science, geology, mathematics, physical sciences, physics, and polymer science), EDUCATION (music), ENGINEERING AND ENVIRONMENTAL DESIGN (aeronautical engineering, aerospace studies, architecture, biomedical engineering, chemical engineering, civil engineering, computer engineering, electrical/electronics engineering, engineering and applied science, environmental engineering, environmental science, and mechanical engineering), HEALTH PROFESSIONS (nursing and occupational therapy), SOCIAL SCIENCE (African American studies, American studies, anthropology, Asian/American studies, economics, geography, gerontology, history, international relations, philosophy, political science/government, psychology, public administration, religion, social science, sociology, and women's studies). Business, engineering, and communications are the largest.

Required: All students must satisfy requirements in foreign language, freshman writing, and general education and take 1 multicultural course. Graduation requirements include a minimum of 128 credit hours and a minimum GPA of 2.0.

Special: Cross-registration is permitted with Hebrew Union College and Howard University. Internships in various majors, a Washington semester, work-study programs, study abroad in 28 countries, dual majors, a general studies degree, student-designed majors, a 3-2 engineering degree, and pass/fail options are available. Students are encouraged to pursue interdisciplinary study linking core art and science disciplines to professional programs. There are 41 national honor societies, including Phi Beta Kappa, and a freshman honors program.

Faculty/Classroom: 69% of faculty are male; 31%, female. All do research. No introductory courses are taught by graduate students. The average class size in an introductory lecture is 30; in a laboratory, 24; and in a regular course, 28.

Admissions: 30% of the 2003-2004 applicants were accepted. The SAT I scores for the 2003-2004 freshman class were: Verbal--1% below 500, 18% between 500 and 599, 53% between 600 and 700, and 28% above 700; Math--9% between 500 and 599, 49% between 600 and 700, and 42% above 700. The ACT scores were 4% between 18 and 23, 53% between 24 and 29, and 43% between 30 and 36. 85% of the current freshmen were in the top fifth of their class; 95% were in the top two fifths. There were 158 National Merit finalists.

Requirements: The SAT I or ACT is required. In addition, graduation from an accredited secondary school is required. Applicants must have completed 16 high school courses, including 4 years of English, 3 of math, 2 each of a foreign language, science, and social studies, plus 3 academic electives. An essay is required, and an interview is recommended. AP credits are accepted. Important factors in the admissions decision are advanced placement or honor courses, recommendations by school officials, and evidence of special talent.

Procedure: Freshmen are admitted fall and spring. Entrance exams should be taken by November of the senior year for scholarship applicants; by December for all others. Applications should be filed by January 10 for fall entry, along with a $65 fee. Notification is sent April 1. Applications are accepted on-line.

Transfer: 1164 transfer students enrolled in 2002-2003. Transfer applicants must submit 30 units of transferable work. Admission is highly competitive and the average GPA for entering transfer students is 3.5. 64 of 128 credits required for the bachelor's degree must be completed at USC.

Visiting: There are regularly scheduled orientations for prospective students. There are guides for informal visits and visitors may sit in on classes and stay overnight. To schedule a visit, contact the Admission Office at (213) 740-6616.

Financial Aid: In 2003-2004, 68% of all full-time freshmen and 65% of continuing full-time students received some form of financial aid. 45% of full-time freshmen and 48% of continuing full-time students received need-based aid. The average freshman award was $19,952. Need-based scholarships or need-based grants averaged $21,859; need-based self-help aid (loans and jobs) averaged $5095; non-need-based athletic scholarships averaged $28,999; and other non-need-based awards and non-need-based scholarships averaged $11,732. The average financial indebtedness of the 2003 graduate was $19,176. USC is a member of CSS. The CSS Profile or FAFSA and tax forms are required. The deadline for filing freshman financial aid applications for fall entry is January 22.

International Students: There are 1332 international students enrolled. The school actively recruits these students. They must take the college's own test and also take the SAT I or the ACT.

Computers: There are approximately 2500 PCs available for student use on campus. These are linked via USCnet to the Internet. They are located in labs, residence halls, and libraries. All student rooms in university housing are wired for direct connection to the Internet. Most of the campus has wireless connectivity as well. All students may access the system. There are no time limits and no fees.

Graduates: From July 1, 2002 to June 30, 2003, 3824 bachelor's degrees were awarded. In an average class, 61% graduate in 4 years or less, 77% graduate in 5 years or less, and 81% graduate in 6 years or less. 600 companies recruited on campus in 2002-2003.

Admissions Contact: J. Michael Thompson, Dean of Admission and Financial Aid. A video is available. Web: *www.usc.edu*

UNIVERSITY OF THE PACIFIC
Stockton, CA 95211-0197

B-3

(209) 946-2211
(800) 959-2867; Fax: (209) 946-2413

Full-time: 1355 men, 1884 women	Faculty: 235; IIA, +$
Part-time: 66 men, 52 women	Ph.D.s: 91%
Graduate: 1306 men, 1458 women	Student/Faculty: 14 to 1
Year: semesters, summer session	Tuition: $23,600
Application Deadline: February 15	Room & Board: $7490
Freshman Class: 4501 applied, 3173 accepted, 818 enrolled	
SAT I Verbal/Math: 570/550	ACT: 24 VERY COMPETITIVE

The University of the Pacific, founded in 1851, is a private nonreligious institution. It offers undergraduate and graduate programs in arts and sciences, and professional programs in pharmacy, law, and dentistry. There are 8 undergraduate schools and 1 graduate school. In addition to regional accreditation, Pacific has baccalaureate program accreditation with AACSB, ABET, ACS, and CAAHEP. The 2 libraries contain 281,769 volumes, 689,462 microform items, and 10,676 audio/video tapes/CDs, and subscribe to 1361 periodicals. Computerized library services include the card catalog, interlibrary loans, database searching, and Internet access. Special learning facilities include a learning resource center, art gallery, radio station, and the Brubeck Institute. The 175-acre campus is in a suburban area 80 miles east of San Francisco and 40 miles south of Sacramento. Including any residence halls, there are 85 buildings.

Student Life: 84% of undergraduates are from California. 45% are white; 30% Asian American; 10% Hispanic. The average age of freshmen is 18; all undergraduates, 21. 12% do not continue beyond their first year.

Housing: 2183 students can be accommodated in college housing, which includes coed dorms, on-campus apartments, off-campus apartments, married-student housing, fraternity houses, and sorority houses. In addition, there are honors houses, special-interest houses, and intercultural, wellness, pharmacy, and learning involvement theme houses. On-campus housing is guaranteed for the freshman year only, is available on a first-come, first-served basis, and is available on a lottery system for upperclassmen. Priority is given to out-of-town students. 59% of students live on campus. Alcohol is not permitted. All students may keep cars.

Activities: 20% of men belong to 1 local fraternity and 4 national fraternities; 21% of women belong to 4 national sororities. There are 100 groups on campus, including art, band, cheerleading, choir, chorale, chorus, club sports, computers, dance, debate, drama, ethnic, forensics, gay, honors, international, jazz band, literary magazine, musical theater, newspaper, opera, orchestra, pep band, photography, political, professional, radio and TV, religious, social, social service, student government, and symphony. Popular campus events include men's basketball games, Pacific Boardwalk Carnival, and Cultural Diversity Week.

Sports: There are 7 intercollegiate sports for men and 9 for women, and 30 intramural sports for men and 30 for women. Facilities include a 6000-seat sports arena, an Olympic-size pool, tennis courts, a softball field, and a fitness center.

Disabled Students: 90% of the campus is accessible. Wheelchair ramps, elevators, special parking, specially equipped rest rooms, special class-scheduling, lowered drinking fountains, and lowered telephones are available.

Services: Counseling and information services are available, as is tutoring in every subject. There is a reader service for the blind, and remedial math, reading, and writing.

Campus Safety and Security: Measures include 24-hour foot and vehicle patrol, security escort services, informal discussions, and pamphlets/posters/films. There are emergency telephones and lighted pathways/sidewalks.

Programs of Study: Pacific confers B.A., B.S., B.F.A., B.M., B.S.B.A., B.S.B.E., B.S.C.E., B.S.E.E., B.S.E.M., B.S.E.P., and B.S.M.E. degrees. Master's and doctoral degrees are also awarded. Bachelor's degrees are awarded in BIOLOGICAL SCIENCE (biochemistry and biology/biological science), BUSINESS (business administration and management and sports management), COMMUNICATIONS AND THE ARTS (art, art history and appreciation, classics, communications, dramatic arts, English, French, German, graphic design, Japanese, music, music business management, music history and appreciation, music performance, music theory and composition, Spanish, and studio art), COMPUTER AND PHYSICAL SCIENCE (applied mathematics, chemistry, computer science, geology, geophysics and seismology, information sciences and systems, mathematics, and physics), EDUCATION (education, music, and physical), ENGINEERING AND ENVIRONMENTAL DESIGN (civil engineering, computer engineering, electrical/electronics engineering, engineering management, engineering physics, environmental science, and mechanical engineering), HEALTH PROFESSIONS (music therapy, prepharmacy, speech pathology/audiology, and sports

medicine), SOCIAL SCIENCE (economics, history, international relations, international studies, liberal arts/general studies, philosophy, political science/government, psychology, religion, social science, and sociology). Natural sciences and the professions are the strongest academically. Arts and sciences, pharmacy, and business are the largest.

Required: Students must complete at least 124 credit hours to graduate. The required general education program consists of 3 "mentor seminars" and 6 to 9 other courses chosen from categories such as the Individual and Society, the Human Heritage, and the Natural World and Formal Systems of Thought.

Special: The engineering school requires and guarantees a co-op program for specialized training in the field. Internships for credit or pay in all majors, more than 230 study-abroad programs in more than 80 countries, a Washington semester, and more than 20 work-study programs also are available. Student-designed majors, B.A./B.S. degrees, dual majors in most disciplines, and pass/fail options are possible. There are 18 national honor societies and a freshman honors program. All departments have honors programs.

Faculty/Classroom: 63% of faculty are male; 37%, female. All teach undergraduates. No introductory courses are taught by graduate students. The average class size in a regular course is 19.

Admissions: 70% of the 2003-2004 applicants were accepted. The SAT I scores for the 2003-2004 freshman class were: Verbal--18% below 500, 47% between 500 and 599, 33% between 600 and 700, and 2% above 700; Math--10% below 500, 40% between 500 and 599, 40% between 600 and 700, and 10% above 700. The ACT scores were 14% below 21, 28% between 21 and 23, 29% between 24 and 26, 20% between 27 and 28, and 9% above 28. 60% of the current freshmen were in the top fifth of their class; 87% were in the top two fifths.

Requirements: The SAT I or ACT is required. In addition, applicants must have 16 academic credits, including a recommended 4 years of high school English, 3 of math, 2 in the same foreign language, 2 of lab science, 1 of U.S history or government, 1 of fine or performing arts, and 4 additional academic courses. An essay is required; an interview is recommended. An audition is necessary for music students. The GED is accepted. A GPA of 2.0 is required. AP and CLEP credits are accepted.

Procedure: Freshmen are admitted fall and spring. Entrance exams should be taken in the spring of the junior year or fall of the senior year. There are early decision and deferred admissions plans. Early decision applications should be filed by December 15; regular applications, by February 15 for fall entry and December 15 for spring entry. The fall 2003 application fee was $50. Notification of early decision is sent January 15; regular decision, on a rolling basis. Applications are accepted online through CollegeNET.

Transfer: 257 transfer students enrolled in 2003-2004. Applicants should have a minimum GPA of 2.5 and at least 16 credit hours. The SAT I or ACT and high school transcripts are required if fewer than 30 units of college work have been completed. 32 of 124 credits required for the bachelor's degree must be completed at Pacific.

Visiting: There are regularly scheduled orientations for prospective students, including a tour, appointments with faculty, admissions, and financial aid personnel, and class visits. There are guides for informal visits and visitors may sit in on classes and stay overnight. To schedule a visit, contact Admissions at *admissions@pacific.edu*.

Financial Aid: In a recent year, 82% of all full-time freshmen and 88% of continuing full-time students received some form of financial aid. 81% of full-time freshmen and 67% of continuing full-time students received need-based aid. The average freshman award for the 2003-2004 school year was $19,845. 36% of undergraduates work part time. Average annual earnings from campus work are $1300. Pacific is a member of CSS. The FAFSA is required. The deadline for filing freshman financial aid applications for fall entry is February 15.

International Students: There are 88 international students enrolled. The school actively recruits these students. They must score 475 on the written TOEFL or 150 on the electronic version. The SAT I or ACT is required if the student has attended a U.S.-style high school.

Computers: The mainframe is a Sun Enterprise 450. 350 PCs, primarily IBMs, Macs, and Sun Rays are available for student use in residence halls, computer labs, and the library. All students may access the system any time. There are no time limits and no fees. It is recommended that students in pharmacy have personal computers.

Graduates: From July 1, 2002 to June 30, 2003, 681 bachelor's degrees were awarded. The most popular majors were business (22%), biology (12%), and sports science (7%). In an average class, 1% graduate in 3 years or less, 44% graduate in 4 years or less, 64% graduate in 5 years or less, and 69% graduate in 6 years or less.

Admissions Contact: Marc McGee, Director of Admissions. E-mail: *admissions@pacific.edu* Web: *www.pacific.edu*

VANGUARD UNIVERSITY OF SOUTHERN CALIFORNIA

Costa Mesa, CA 92626

D-5

(714) 556-3610
(800) 722-6279; Fax: (714) 966-5471

Full-time: 471 men, 838 women	Faculty: 56; IIB, av$
Part-time: 16 men, 15 women	Ph.D.s: 74%
Graduate: 169 men, 195 women	Student/Faculty: 23 to 1
Year: semesters, summer session	Tuition: $16,328
Application Deadline: December 1	Room & Board: $5880
Freshman Class: 746 applied, 599 accepted, 350 enrolled	
SAT I Verbal/Math: 517/497	ACT: 22 COMPETITIVE

Vanguard University of Southern California, founded in 1920, is a private Christian comprehensive university of liberal arts and profesional studies affiliated with the Assemblies of God. The library contains 147,212 volumes, 18,459 microform items, and 5952 audio/video tapes/CDs, and subscribes to 850 periodicals. Computerized library services include the card catalog, interlibrary loans, and database searching. Special learning facilities include a learning resource center. The 38-acre campus is in a suburban area 40 miles southeast of Los Angeles and 5 miles north of Newport Beach. Including any residence halls, there are 25 buildings.

Student Life: 80% of undergraduates are from California. Students are from 39 states, 18 foreign countries, and Canada. 75% are from public schools. 72% are white; 17% Hispanic. Most are Protestant. The average age of freshmen is 18; all undergraduates, 20. 26% do not continue beyond their first year; 46% remain to graduate.

Housing: 1028 students can be accommodated in college housing, which includes single-sex dorms, on-campus apartments, off-campus apartments, and married-student housing. On-campus housing is available on a first-come, first-served basis and is available on a lottery system for upperclassmen. Priority is given to out-of-town students. 82% of students live on campus; of those, 75% remain on campus on weekends. Alcohol is not permitted. All students may keep cars.

Activities: There are no fraternities or sororities. There are 50 groups on campus, including art, band, choir, chorale, chorus, debate, drama, ethnic, forensics, international, jazz band, musical theater, newspaper, orchestra, pep band, political, religious, social service, student government, student ministries, and yearbook. Popular campus events include Harvest Party, International Missions Week, and Christmas Party.

Sports: There are 6 intercollegiate sports for men and 7 for women, and 15 intramural sports for men and 15 for women. Facilities include a gym, baseball, softball, and soccer fields, a weight room, and contracted off-campus tennis courts and track course.

Disabled Students: 95% of the campus is accessible. Wheelchair ramps, elevators, special parking, specially equipped rest rooms, special class scheduling, and special housing are available.

Services: Counseling and information services are available, as is tutoring in most subjects.

Campus Safety and Security: Measures include 24-hour foot and vehicle patrol, security escort services, pamphlets/posters/films, and emergency telephones. There are lighted pathways/sidewalks and room and vehicle unlocks.

Programs of Study: VU confers B.A. and B.S. degrees. Master's degrees are also awarded. Bachelor's degrees are awarded in BIOLOGICAL SCIENCE (biology/biological science), BUSINESS (accounting, banking and finance, business administration and management, international business management, marketing/retailing/merchandising, and personnel management), COMMUNICATIONS AND THE ARTS (communications, dramatic arts, English, music, and Spanish), COMPUTER AND PHYSICAL SCIENCE (chemistry and mathematics), EDUCATION (elementary, physical, science, and secondary), HEALTH PROFESSIONS (premedicine), SOCIAL SCIENCE (anthropology, biblical studies, history, ministries, political science/government, prelaw, psychology, religious education, and sociology). Religion, social sciences, and natural sciences are the strongest academically. Business, liberal studies, and religion are the largest.

Required: Students must complete a minimum of 124 credits, with 40 to 70 in the major. General education requirements include 16 credits in religion, 15 in humanities and fine arts, 12 in social science, 7 in natural sciences and math, and 2 in phys ed. VU requires a minimum GPA of 2.0.

Special: Study abroad in Costa Rica, Australia, China, England, Egypt, and Russia, internships, a Washington semester, a general studies degree, work-study, accelerated degree programs in business, psychology, and religion, and pass/fail options are available. 3 summer sessions are offered. There are 4 national honor societies and 4 departmental honors programs.

Faculty/Classroom: 67% of faculty are male; 33%, female. 81% teach undergraduates. No introductory courses are taught by graduate students. The average class size in an introductory lecture is 40; in a laboratory, 12; and in a regular course, 19.

Admissions: 80% of the 2003-2004 applicants were accepted. The SAT I scores for the 2003-2004 freshman class were: Verbal--43% below 500, 35% between 500 and 599, 20% between 600 and 700, and 2% above 700; Math--48% below 500, 38% between 500 and 599, 13% between 600 and 700, and 1% above 700. 46% of the current freshmen were in the top fifth of their class; 75% were in the top two fifths. 1 freshman graduated first in the class.

Requirements: The SAT I or ACT is required. In addition, high school courses should include 4 years of English, 3 of social studies, and 2 of math and science. Applicants are required to write an application essay and submit references from a pastor/minister. A GPA of 2.8 is required. AP and CLEP credits are accepted. Important factors in the admissions decision are leadership record, advanced placement or honor courses, and evidence of special talent.

Procedure: Freshmen are admitted fall and spring. Entrance exams should be taken in the junior year. There is a rolling admissions plan. Applications should be filed by December 1 for fall entry, along with a $45 fee. Notification is sent on a rolling basis. A waiting list is an active part of the admissions procedure. Applications are accepted on-line through www.vanguard.edu.

Transfer: 165 transfer students enrolled in 2002-2003. Transfer applicants must submit college transcripts and have a minimum college GPA of 2.0. 24 of 124 credits required for the bachelor's degree must be completed at VU.

Visiting: There are regularly scheduled orientations for prospective students, consisting of University PreVU on Veterans Day each year and Sneak PreVU in spring. There are guides for informal visits and visitors may sit in on classes and stay overnight. To schedule a visit, contact Undergraduate Admissions.

Financial Aid: 21% of undergraduates work part time. Average annual earnings from campus work are $3025. The FAFSA and state scholarship/grant forms are required. The deadline for filing freshman financial aid applications for fall entry is March 2.

International Students: There are 11 international students enrolled. They must score 550 on the written TOEFL or 213 on the electronic version.

Computers: The mainframe is an HP3000. There are 110 academic PCs in 10 locations on campus. All network computers have access to the Internet. Students may bring their PCs and connect to the LAN in the dorms. All students may access the system 24 hours a day 7 days a week. There are no time limits and no fees. Gateway Pentium III (minimum) is recommended as a personal computer.

Graduates: From July 1, 2002 to June 30, 2003, 378 bachelor's degrees were awarded. The most popular majors were business (32%), psychology (21%), and religion (15%). In an average class, 35% graduate in 4 years or less, 43% graduate in 5 years or less, and 46% graduate in 6 years or less. 30 companies recruited on campus in 2002-2003.

Admissions Contact: Jennifer Purga, Director of Admissions. A video is available. E-mail: admissions@vanguard.edu
Web: www.vanguard.edu/admissions

WESTMONT COLLEGE

Santa Barbara, CA 93108

C-5

(805) 565-6005
(800) 777-9011; Fax: (805) 565-6234

Full-time: 462 men, 869 women	Faculty: 83; IIB, +$
Part-time: 4 men, 8 women	Ph.D.s: 92%
Graduate: none	Student/Faculty: 16 to 1
Year: semesters, summer session	Tuition: $24,890
Application Deadline: February 15	Room & Board: $8172
Freshman Class: 1404 applied, 1188 accepted, 355 enrolled	
SAT I Verbal/Math: 610/600	ACT: 26 VERY COMPETITIVE+

Westmont College, founded in 1937, is a selective, nondenominational Christian college devoted to the intellectual and spiritual development of students through a rigorous liberal arts curriculum. The library contains 162,274 volumes, 20,687 microform items, and 7926 audio/video tapes/CDs, and subscribes to 3211 periodicals. Computerized library services include the card catalog, interlibrary loans, database searching, and Internet access. Special learning facilities include a learning resource center, art gallery, radio station, observatory, science center with a premedical center, physiology lab, and a fitness center. The 111-acre campus is in a suburban area 90 miles north of Los Angeles. Including any residence halls, there are 30 buildings.

Student Life: 66% of undergraduates are from California. Students are from 35 states, 8 foreign countries, and Canada. 70% are from public schools. 84% are white. Most are Protestant. The average age of freshmen is 18; all undergraduates, 20. 11% do not continue beyond their first year; 70% remain to graduate.

Housing: 1148 students can be accommodated in college housing, which includes single-sex and coed dorms, off-campus apartments, and married-student housing. On-campus housing is guaranteed for all 4 years. 85% of students live on campus; of those, 65% remain on campus on weekends. Alcohol is not permitted. Upperclassmen may keep cars.

Activities: There are no fraternities or sororities. There are 50 groups on campus, including art, band, cheerleading, chess, choir, chorale, chorus, computers, dance, debate, drama, ethnic, film, honors, international, jazz band, leadership, literary magazine, musical theater, newspaper, opera, orchestra, pep band, photography, political, professional, radio and TV, religious, social, social service, student government, symphony, and yearbook. Popular campus events include Community Service Day, Multicultural Fellowship Week, and theatrical and musical productions.

Sports: There are 6 intercollegiate sports for men and 6 for women, and 11 intramural sports for men and 11 for women. Facilities include a 2133-seat gym, a soccer/baseball field, a swimming pool, a fitness room, a dance studio, a track, and volleyball, tennis, basketball, and racquetball courts.

Disabled Students: 60% of the campus is accessible. Wheelchair ramps, elevators, special parking, specially equipped rest rooms, special class scheduling, lowered drinking fountains, lowered telephones, and special housing are available.

Services: Counseling and information services are available, as is tutoring in every subject. There is a reader service for the blind and remedial math. A writers' corner supervised by tutors is available.

Campus Safety and Security: Measures include 24-hour foot and vehicle patrol, self-defense education, security escort services, and shuttle buses. There are informal discussions, pamphlets/posters/films, emergency telephones, and lighted pathways/sidewalks.

Programs of Study: Westmont confers B.A. and B.S. degrees. Bachelor's degrees are awarded in BIOLOGICAL SCIENCE (biology/biological science and neurosciences), BUSINESS (business economics), COMMUNICATIONS AND THE ARTS (art, communications, dramatic arts, English, French, modern language, music, and Spanish), COMPUTER AND PHYSICAL SCIENCE (chemistry, computer science, mathematics, and physics), EDUCATION (art, English, mathematics, music, physical, and social science), ENGINEERING AND ENVIRONMENTAL DESIGN (engineering physics), HEALTH PROFESSIONS (exercise science), SOCIAL SCIENCE (European studies, history, liberal arts/general studies, philosophy, political science/government, psychology, religion, social science, and sociology). Biology, communication studies, and economics/business are the largest.

Required: All students must earn a minimum GPA of 2.0 while taking at least 124 credit hours, including 36 to 66 in the major. A total of 60 units in general education courses is required, with 16 units in religious studies and 4 units in phys ed. Also required are courses in the history of Western civilization, English composition, and math.

Special: Westmont offers cross-registration with 12 Christian colleges, internships in local businesses and social agencies, study abroad in 11 countries, and semesters in Washington, D.C., San Francisco, and Los Angeles. B.A.-B.S. degrees, student-designed majors, work-study programs, a 3-2 engineering program with several California universities, University of Washington, and Boston University, and pass/fail options also are available. There are also preprofessional programs in dentistry, law, medicine, ministry/missions, optometry, pharmacology, physical therapy, and veterinary medicine. There are 7 national honor societies, a freshman honors program, and 9 departmental honors programs.

Faculty/Classroom: 62% of faculty are male; 38%, female. All both teach and do research. The average class size in an introductory lecture is 30; in a laboratory, 15; and in a regular course, 20.

Admissions: 85% of the 2003-2004 applicants were accepted. The SAT I scores for the 2003-2004 freshman class were: Verbal--8% below 500, 35% between 500 and 599, 45% between 600 and 700, and 12% above 700; Math--6% below 500, 32% between 500 and 599, 41% between 600 and 700, and 21% above 700. The ACT scores were 3% below 21, 20% between 21 and 23, 33% between 24 and 26, 23% between 27 and 28, and 21% above 28. 62% of the current freshmen were in the top fifth of their class; 89% were in the top two fifths. There were 12 National Merit finalists. 21 freshmen graduated first in their class.

Requirements: The SAT I or ACT is required. In addition, SAT I scores of 500 verbal and 500 math or an ACT composite score of 25 is recommended. Applicants need 16 academic credits, including 4 years of high school English, 3 of math, 2 each of a foreign language, social science, and physical science, and 1 each of history and biological science. Interviews are recommended. Essays are required. The GED is accepted. A GPA of 3.0 is required. AP and CLEP credits are accepted. Important factors in the admissions decision are advanced placement or honor courses, leadership record, and extracurricular activities record.

Procedure: Freshmen are admitted fall and spring. Entrance exams should be taken during the spring of the junior year or the beginning of the senior year. Early decision applications should be filed by December 1; regular applications, by February 15 for fall entry and November 1 for spring entry. Notification of early decision is sent January 20; regular decision, April 1. The fall 2003 application fee was $40 (on-line) or $50 (paper). Applications are accepted on-line through CollegeLink, XAP, Princeton Review, and Westmont's web site.

Transfer: 60 transfer students enrolled in 2002-2003. Transfer students from 2-year colleges must have a minimum GPA of 2.8, and those students from 4-year colleges or universities, a 2.5. The college will not accept more than 64 transferable units from a community college; there is no maximum number of transferable units from a 4-year college. High school transcripts and test scores are required if the student has fewer than 24 transferable units. 32 of 124 credits required for the bachelor's degree must be completed at Westmont.

Visiting: There are regularly scheduled orientations for prospective students, consisting of meeting faculty and administrators and attending classes, academic seminars, student/parent panels, academic open houses, admission and financial aid sessions, student led small groups, campus tours, and various cultural events. There are guides for informal visits and visitors may sit in on classes and stay overnight. To schedule a visit, contact Admissions/Campus Visit Coordinator at (805) 565-6200.

Financial Aid: In 2003-2004, 76% of all full-time freshmen and 83% of continuing full-time students received some form of financial aid. 75% of full-time freshmen and 82% of continuing full-time students received need-based aid. The average freshman award was $16,571. 54% of undergraduates work part time. Average annual earnings from campus work are $872. The average financial indebtedness of the 2003 graduate was $19,548. The FAFSA is required. The deadline for filing freshman financial aid applications for fall entry is March 2.

International Students: There are 16 international students enrolled. They must score 560 on the written TOEFL or 260 on the electronic version and also take the SAT I or the ACT.

Computers: The mainframe is a 3 IBM RS/6000s. There are 30 PCs and 47 Macs available in the library. There are Ethernet connections in every office, every dorm room, and many classrooms. The complete network has access to the Internet. All students may access the system. There are no time limits and no fees. It is strongly recommended that all students have a personal computer.

Graduates: From July 1, 2002 to June 30, 2003, 308 bachelor's degrees were awarded. The most popular majors were communication studies (15%), economics/business (14%), and English (12%). In an average class, 5% graduate in 3 years or less, 62% graduate in 4 years or less, 70% graduate in 5 years or less, and 71% graduate in 6 years or less. 50 companies recruited on campus in 2002-2003. Of the 2002 graduating class, 48% were enrolled in graduate school within 6 months of graduation and 85% were employed.

Admissions Contact: Joyce M. Luy, Director of Admissions. A video is available. E-mail: *admissions@westmont.edu* Web: *http://www.westmont.edu*

WHITTIER COLLEGE
Whittier, CA 90608

	D-5
Full-time: 535 men, 700 women	(562) 907-4238; Fax: (562) 907-4870
Part-time: 30 men, 15 women	Faculty: 96; IIB, ++$
Graduate: 335 men, 495 women	Ph.D.s: 88%
Year: 4-1-4, summer session	Student/Faculty: 13 to 1
Application Deadline: see profile	Tuition: $22,070
Freshman Class: n/av	Room & Board: $7045
SAT I or ACT: required	COMPETITIVE

Whittier College, founded in 1887 by the Society of Friends, is an independent, liberal arts institution with no religious affiliation. There are 2 graduate schools. Figures in the above capsule and in this profile are approximate. In addition to regional accreditation, Whittier has baccalaureate program accreditation with CSWE. The 2 libraries contain 225,337 volumes, 33,729 microform items, and 4650 audio/video tapes/CDs, and subscribe to 700 periodicals. Computerized library services include the card catalog, interlibrary loans, and database searching. Special learning facilities include a learning resource center, art gallery, radio station, and the Fairchild Aerial Photography Collection, a performing arts center, and a writing center. The 95-acre campus is in a suburban area 18 miles southeast of Los Angeles, in the foothills of the San Gabriel Mountains. Including any residence halls, there are 50 buildings.

Student Life: 73% of undergraduates are from California. Students are from 27 states, 20 foreign countries, and Canada. 69% are from public schools. 50% are white; 30% Hispanic; 10% Asian American. The average age of freshmen is 18; all undergraduates, 21. 26% do not continue beyond their first year; 54% remain to graduate.

Housing: 813 students can be accommodated in college housing, which includes coed dorms. In addition, there are special-interest houses, a multicultural community residence hall, and a substance-free living environment residence hall. On-campus housing is guaranteed for all 4 years. 60% of students live on campus; of those, 75% remain on campus on weekends. All students may keep cars.

Activities: 15% of men belong to 4 local fraternities; 15% of women belong to 5 local sororities. There are 54 groups on campus, including art, band, cheerleading, choir, chorale, chorus, computers, dance, drama, ethnic, film, gay, honors, international, jazz band, literary magazine, musical theater, newspaper, photography, political, professional, radio and TV, religious, social, social service, student government, and yearbook. Popular campus events include the Spring Sing (annual talent show), Hawaiian Islander Club Luau, and Asian Night.

Sports: There are 11 intercollegiate sports for men and 10 for women, and 10 intramural sports for men and 10 for women. Facilities include a 7000-seat stadium, a 2000-seat gym, 3 playing fields, an athletics center, an aquatics center, a fitness center, and tennis courts.

Disabled Students: 75% of the campus is accessible. Wheelchair ramps, elevators, special parking, specially equipped rest rooms, special class scheduling, lowered drinking fountains, and lowered telephones are available.

Services: Counseling and information services are available, as is tutoring in every subject.

Campus Safety and Security: Measures include 24-hour foot and vehicle patrol, self-defense education, security escort services, and informal discussions. There are pamphlets/posters/films, emergency telephones, and lighted pathways/sidewalks.

Programs of Study: Whittier confers the B.A. degree. Master's and doctoral degrees are also awarded. Bachelor's degrees are awarded in BIOLOGICAL SCIENCE (biochemistry and biology/biological science), BUSINESS (business administration and management), COMMUNICATIONS AND THE ARTS (art, dramatic arts, English, French, music, and Spanish), COMPUTER AND PHYSICAL SCIENCE (chemistry, earth science, mathematics, and physics), EDUCATION (physical), SOCIAL SCIENCE (child psychology/development, economics, history, international studies, philosophy, political science/government, psychology, religion, social work, and sociology). Business administration, political science, and English are the largest.

Required: All students must take a total of 120 credits, including at least 30 in the major field, with a minimum GPA of 2.0. Distribution requirements include 3 credits in college writing, 6 in paired courses from European and North American civilizations, Asian, African, and Latin American civilizations, or contemporary society and the individual, 8 in natural sciences, and 3 each in humanities, math, and fine arts.

Special: Internships are possible in business, counseling, teaching, and other areas. Study abroad is offered in 5 countries, with additional opportunities with 36 universities overseas through the University of Miami consortium. A Washington semester in January is optional. The Whittier Scholars Program offers self-designed interdisciplinary curricula. Nondegree study and pass/fail options are available. Whittier offers a 3-2 engineering program with University of Southern California, Dartmouth College, and Columbia, Washington, Case Western Reserve, and Colorado State universities. There are 10 national honor societies.

Faculty/Classroom: 60% of faculty are male; 40%, female. All teach undergraduates. No introductory courses are taught by graduate students. The average class size in an introductory lecture is 20; in a laboratory, 24; and in a regular course, 22.

Requirements: The SAT I or ACT is required, the SAT I is preferred. The college recommends that applicants have 4 years of high school English, 3 years each of history, math, science, and 2 years of a foreign language. An essay is required. An interview is recommended. A GPA of 2.0 is required. AP credits are accepted. Important factors in the admissions decision are advanced placement or honor courses, recommendations by school officials, and leadership record.

Procedure: Freshmen are admitted in the fall. Entrance exams should be taken during the junior year or fall of the senior year. There is a deferred admissions plan and a rolling admissions plan. Check with the school for current deadlines. There is a $35 application fee. Whittier provides Windows or Mac versions to any student wishing to apply via computer disk. On-line applications may be accessed via the school's web site.

Transfer: 117 transfer students enrolled in a recent year. Transfer applicants are considered on a case-by-case basis, but a minimum GPA of 2.5 is recommended in academic course work. The SAT or the ACT is required for students with fewer than 30 academic units. The GED is accepted for transfer applicants with at least 30 academic units. 30 of 120 credits required for the bachelor's degree must be completed at Whittier.

Visiting: There are regularly scheduled orientations for prospective students, consisting of an interview with an admission officer and a campus tour. Customized visits can be arranged to include faculty, coaches, extracurricular activities, class visits, and residence hall tours. There are guides for informal visits and visitors may sit in on classes and stay overnight. To schedule a visit, contact the Office of Admissions.

Financial Aid: In a recent year, 83% of all full-time freshmen and 75% of continuing full-time students received some form of financial aid. 67% of full-time freshmen and 64% of continuing full-time students received need-based aid. The average freshman award was $16,587. 64% of undergraduates work part time. Average annual earnings from campus work are $1280. The average financial indebtedness of a recent graduate was $22,466. Whittier is a member of CSS. The CSS Profile or FAFSA is required. Check with the school for current deadlines.

International Students: In a recent year, there were 50 international students enrolled. The school actively recruits these students. They must score 550 on the written TOEFL or 217 on the electronic version and also take the SAT I or the ACT.

Computers: The mainframe is a Digital UNIX Alpha server. Computers are accessible in several labs around campus, in the library, and in many residence halls. Through the college network, students have access to the library OPAC, e-mail, other on-line resources, and the Internet. All students may access the system 24 hours daily. There are no time limits and no fees.

Graduates: In a recent year, 308 bachelor's degrees were awarded. The most popular majors were business (14%), biology (10%), and English (10%). In an average class, 51% graduate in 4 years or less, 57% graduate in 5 years or less, and 58% graduate in 6 years or less. 38 companies recruited on campus in a recent year. Of a recent graduating class, 20% were enrolled in graduate school within 6 months of graduation and 74% were employed.

Admissions Contact: Urmi Kar, Dean of Enrollment.
E-mail: *admission@whittier.edu* Web: *www.whittier.edu*

WOODBURY UNIVERSITY C-5
Burbank, CA 91510-7846 (818) 767-0888
(800) 784-9663; Fax: (818) 767-7520

Full-time: 790 men and women	**Faculty:** 24; IIA, av$
Part-time: 230 men and women	**Ph.D.s:** 88%
Graduate: 150 men and women	**Student/Faculty:** 26 to 1
Year: semesters, summer session	**Tuition:** $18,350
Application Deadline: open	**Room & Board:** $7000
Freshman Class: n/av	
SAT I: required	**LESS COMPETITIVE**

Woodbury University, founded in 1884, is a private institution that emphasizes business and professional design education. Figures in the above capsule and in this profile are approximate. There are 3 undergraduate schools and 1 graduate school. In addition to regional accreditation, Woodbury has baccalaureate program accreditation with FIDER and NAAB. The library contains 70,699 volumes, 89,785 microform items, and 1341 audio/video tapes/CDs, and subscribes to 1500 periodicals. Computerized library services include the card catalog, interlibrary loans, and database searching. Special learning facilities include a learning resource center, art gallery, and architecture gallery. The 23-acre campus is in a suburban area 17 miles north of Los Angeles. Including any residence halls, there are 15 buildings.

Student Life: Students are from 32 foreign countries. 33% are white; 24% Hispanic; 19% Asian American; 15% foreign nationals. The average age of freshmen is 18; all undergraduates, 21.

Housing: 198 students can be accommodated in college housing, which includes single-sex, coed dorms, and non-smoking suites. On-campus housing is guaranteed for all 4 years. 80% of students commute. All students may keep cars.

Activities: 5% of men belong to 1 local and 1 national fraternity; 5% of women belong to 2 local and 1 national sorority. There are 36 groups on campus, including computers, drama, ethnic, fashion, gay, international, newspaper, political, professional, religious, social, social service, and student government. Popular campus events include Chinese New Year, Black History Dinner, and Winter Formal.

Sports: There are 4 intramural sports for men and 4 for women. Facilities include a gym, basketball and volleyball courts, weight training and aerobics rooms, an outdoor swimming pool, a quarter-mile track, and a field for soccer and other sports.

Disabled Students: 90% of the campus is accessible. Wheelchair ramps, elevators, special parking, specially equipped rest rooms, and special class scheduling are available.

Services: Counseling and information services are available, as is tutoring in some subjects, including accounting, physics, architectural structures. There is remedial math and writing. Books on tape are available for the blind.

Campus Safety and Security: Measures include 24-hour foot and vehicle patrol, self-defense education, security escort services, and informal discussions. There are pamphlets/posters/films, emergency telephones, and lighted pathways/sidewalks.

Programs of Study: Woodbury confers B.S. and B.Arch. degrees. Master's degrees are also awarded. Bachelor's degrees are awarded in BUSINESS (accounting, banking and finance, business administration and management, fashion merchandising, international business management, management science, and marketing/retailing/merchandising), COMPUTER AND PHYSICAL SCIENCE (information sciences and systems), ENGINEERING AND ENVIRONMENTAL DESIGN (architecture, computer graphics, and interior design), SOCIAL SCIENCE (fashion design and technology, history, humanities, political science/government, and psychology). Business and architecture are the strongest academically and have the largest enrollments.

Required: To graduate with a B.S., students must complete 126 semester units, including 44 to 66 in the major; with a B.Arch., 160 semester units, including 98 in the major. All students must maintain a minimum GPA of 2.0 and take freshman composition, comparative literature, computer literacy, and public speaking courses. Course work in behavioral sciences, economics, fine arts, history, natural science, math, and philosophy is also part of the curriculum.

Special: Internships are required for architecture, interior design, arts and sciences, fashion design, and fashion marketing majors and encouraged for all others. Current registration with area institutions, work-study programs, study abroad in France, dual majors, and pass/fail options also are offered. There are interdisciplinary majors in humanities and management and psychology and management.

Faculty/Classroom: 66% of faculty are male; 34%, female. 89% teach undergraduates, 3% do research, and 3% do both. No introductory courses are taught by graduate students. The average class size in an introductory lecture is 17; in a laboratory, 15; and in a regular course, 14.

Requirements: The SAT I is required. In addition, application form, essay, 2 academic references, official high school transcripts, and official SAT I or ACT scores are required for all applicants. Students applying to the animation arts major are also required to submit a portfolio. A GPA of 2.0 is required. AP and CLEP credits are accepted. Important factors in the admissions decision are advanced placement or honor courses, evidence of special talent, and recommendations by school officials.

Procedure: Freshmen are admitted fall, spring, and summer. Entrance exams should be taken prior to application (SAT I or ACT). There is a deferred admissions plan and a rolling admissions plan. Application deadlines are open. Application fee is $35.

Transfer: Applicants are required to have maintained a minimum GPA of 2.0 and to take the SAT I or ACT if they have completed fewer than 30 semester units. The priority application deadline for fall entry is April 15. 45 credits required for the bachelor's degree must be completed at Woodbury.

Visiting: There are regularly scheduled orientations for prospective students, consisting of meeting with admissions counselors, the president, faculty members, students, financial aid counselors, and student services staff. There are guides for informal visits and visitors may sit in on classes and stay overnight. To schedule a visit, contact the Admissions Office.

Financial Aid: Woodbury is a member of CSS. The FAFSA and the college's own financial statement are required. Check with the school for current application deadlines.

International Students: The school actively recruits these students. They must score 550 on the written TOEFL.

Computers: The mainframes are 2 DEC VAX 4200s. All full-time freshman are required to have and are provided with a multimedia notebook computer that allows access to the Internet and Web. Many PCs are available throughout campus. Because students have their own computers, there is 24-hour access. There are no time limits. The fee is $850.

Admissions Contact: Kyle Lynn Matthews.
E-mail: *admit@vaxb.woodbury.edu* Web: *www.woodburyu.edu*

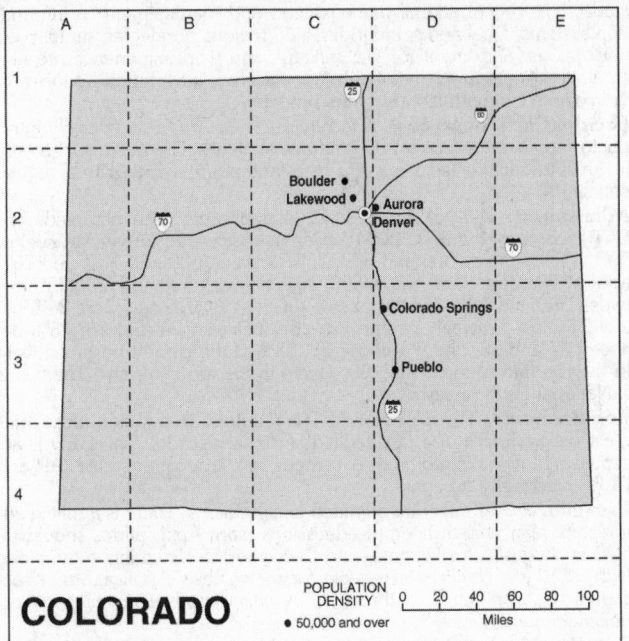

COLORADO

POPULATION DENSITY
● 50,000 and over

0 20 40 60 80 100
Miles

ADAMS STATE COLLEGE
Alamosa, CO 81102

C-4

(719) 587-7712
(800) 824-6494; Fax: (719) 587-7522

Full-time: 855 men, 900 women	**Faculty:** 103; IIB, --$
Part-time: 85 men, 215 women	**Ph.D.s:** 91%
Graduate: 115 men, 280 women	**Student/Faculty:** 17 to 1
Year: semesters, summer session	**Tuition:** $2280 ($6915)
Application Deadline: see profile	**Room & Board:** $5190
Freshman Class: n/av	
SAT I or ACT: recommended	**COMPETITIVE**

Adams State College, founded in 1921, is a public liberal arts college awarding undergraduate and graduate degrees. There are 4 undergraduate schools and 1 graduate school. Figures in the above capsule and in this profile are approximate. In addition to regional accreditation, Adams State has baccalaureate program accreditation with NASM and NCATE. The library contains 154,603 volumes, 703,115 microform items, and 2090 audio/video tapes/CDs, and subscribes to 1086 periodicals. Computerized library services include the card catalog, interlibrary loans, and database searching. Special learning facilities include a learning resource center, art gallery, planetarium, and radio station. The 90-acre campus is in a small town 220 miles south of Denver and 200 miles north of Albuquerque, New Mexico. Including any residence halls, there are 52 buildings.

Student Life: 85% of undergraduates are from Colorado. Students are from 38 states, 6 foreign countries, and Canada. 95% are from public schools. 67% are white; 27% Hispanic. The average age of freshmen is 19; all undergraduates, 23. 42% do not continue beyond their first year; 33% remain to graduate.

Housing: 1052 students can be accommodated in college housing, which includes single-sex and coed dormitories, on-campus apartments, and married-student housing. In addition, there is freshmen interest-group housing. On-campus housing is guaranteed for the freshman year only, is available on a first-come, first-served basis, and is available on a lottery system for upperclassmen. 50% of students commute. Alcohol is not permitted. All students may keep cars.

Activities: There are no fraternities or sororities. There are 40 groups on campus, including band, cheerleading, chess, choir, chorale, computers, drama, ethnic, gay, honors, international, jazz band, literary magazine, marching band, musical theater, pep band, photography, political, radio and TV, religious, social service, student government, and yearbook. Popular campus events include Student Appreciation Breakfast, Spud Bowl, and Snow Daze.

Sports: There are 6 intercollegiate sports for men and 5 for women, and 5 intramural sports for men and 5 for women. Facilities include a swimming pool, handball, racquetball, and tennis courts, horseshoe pits, indoor and outdoor tracks, a weight room, free weights and weight ma-

chines, an 1800-square-foot climbing wall, an aerobics studio, a cardiovascular area, and game facilities.

Disabled Students: 95% of the campus is accessible. Wheelchair ramps, elevators, special parking, specially equipped rest rooms, special class scheduling, lowered drinking fountains, and lowered telephones are available.

Services: Counseling and information services are available, as is tutoring in every subject. There is remedial math, reading, and writing.

Campus Safety and Security: Measures include 24-hour foot and vehicle patrol, security escort services, informal discussions, and pamphlets/posters/films. There are emergency telephones, lighted pathways/sidewalks, and formal safety seminars.

Programs of Study: Adams State confers B.A. and B.S. degrees. Associate and master's degrees are also awarded. Bachelor's degrees are awarded in BIOLOGICAL SCIENCE (biology/biological science and ecology), BUSINESS (accounting, banking and finance, business administration and management, business economics, international business management, management information systems, marketing/retailing/merchandising, office supervision and management, small business management, and sports management), COMMUNICATIONS AND THE ARTS (advertising, art, dramatic arts, English, journalism, music, music performance, Spanish, and speech/debate/rhetoric), COMPUTER AND PHYSICAL SCIENCE (chemistry, computer science, earth science, geology, and mathematics), EDUCATION (art, athletic training, business, elementary, English, foreign languages, mathematics, music, physical, science, secondary, and social studies), ENGINEERING AND ENVIRONMENTAL DESIGN (preengineering), HEALTH PROFESSIONS (allied health, predentistry, premedicine, preoptometry, prepharmacy, and preveterinary science), SOCIAL SCIENCE (criminology, history, interdisciplinary studies, political science/government, prelaw, psychology, social work, sociology, and urban studies). Biology and allied health sciences are the strongest academically. Business and education are the largest.

Required: All students must maintain a GPA of at least 2.0 and complete 120 credit hours, including 24 in the major. General education requirements total 40 semester hours, with 6 in communication arts, 6 in human behavior and institutions, 6 in history and culture, 6 in arts and literature, 3 in quantitative thinking, and 2 in health and fitness. Students are also required to take 3 seminars in science foundations/issues and pass a technology proficiency exam.

Special: Cross-registration through the State Colleges of Colorado consortium is available. Work-study programs with the college, dual majors, a general studies degree, and student-designed majors are possible. Nondegree study is offered.

Faculty/Classroom: 63% of faculty are male; 37%, female. All teach undergraduates. No introductory courses are taught by graduate students. The average class size in an introductory lecture is 24; in a laboratory, 14; and in a regular course, 25.

Requirements: The SAT I or ACT is recommended. In addition, applicants are required to have at least 15 academic credits with 4 in English, 3 in social science, 2 each in math, lab science, and foreign language, and 1/2 in computer applications. The GED is accepted. Adams State requires applicants to be in the upper 67% of their class. A GPA of 2.5 is required. AP and CLEP credits are accepted. Important factors in the admissions decision are advanced placement or honor courses, leadership record, and recommendations by school officials.

Procedure: Freshmen are admitted to all sessions. Entrance exams should be taken during the junior year. There is a deferred admissions plan and a rolling admissions plan. The fee is $25. Check with the school for current deadlines. Applications are accepted on-line via Colorado Mentor or the college's web site.

Transfer: 157 transfer students enrolled in a recent year. Applicants must have a minimum GPA of 2.0. If they have fewer than 12 credits, the SAT I or ACT test scores and official high school transcripts are also required. 30 of 120 credits required for the bachelor's degree must be completed at Adams State.

Visiting: There are regularly scheduled orientations for prospective students, including a meeting with academic faculty, a campus tour, information on financial aid and housing, and a free ticket to an athletic event (when applicable). There are guides for informal visits and visitors may sit in on classes and stay overnight. To schedule a visit, contact the Admissions Office.

Financial Aid: The FAFSA is required. Check with the school for current deadlines.

International Students: In a recent year, there were 11 international students enrolled. The school actively recruits these students. They must score 550 on the written TOEFL or 213 on the electronic version and also take the SAT I or the ACT.

Computers: The mainframes are a network of 13 Dell and Compaq Servers. There are 30 stand-alone Pentium PCs and 75 networked Pentium clients located in 7 labs throughout the campus and supported by 13 file servers. All students may access the system. The fee is $50.

Graduates: In a recent year, 299 bachelor's degrees were awarded. The most popular majors were business (29%), education (14%), and psychology (9%). In an average class, 2% graduate in 3 years or less, 12% graduate in 4 years or less, 40% graduate in 5 years or less, and 50% graduate in 6 years or less. 78 companies recruited on campus in a recent year. Of a recent graduating class, 93% were employed within 6 months of graduation.

Admissions Contact: Lori Lee Laske, Assistant Director of Admissions. A video is available. E-mail: *ascadmit@adams.edu*
Web: *www.adams.edu*

COLORADO CHRISTIAN UNIVERSITY　　　C-2
Lakewood, CO 80226-7499　　　　　　　(303) 963-3410
　　　　　　　　　(800) 44 FAITH; Fax: (303) 963-3401

Full-time: 424 men, 711 women	**Faculty:** n/av
Part-time: 162 men, 165 women	**Ph.D.s:** 85%
Graduate: 43 men, 78 women	**Student/Faculty:** 28 to 1
Year: semesters, summer session	**Tuition:** $15,140
Application Deadline: August 1	**Room & Board:** $6042
Freshman Class: 1185 applied, 877 accepted, 324 enrolled	
SAT I Verbal/Math: 550/550	**ACT:** 24　**VERY COMPETITIVE**

Colorado Christian University, founded in 1914, is a private, Christian interdenominational institution offering undergraduate and graduate programs in the arts and sciences, biblical studies, music and education. There are 4 undergraduate and 3 graduate schools. The library contains 53,532 volumes, 281,234 microform items, and 3917 audio/video tapes/CDs, and subscribes to 415 periodicals. Computerized library services include the card catalog, interlibrary loans, database searching, and Internet access. Special learning facilities include a learning resource center and art gallery. The 29-acre campus is in a suburban area 10 miles west of Denver. Including any residence halls, there are 21 buildings.

Student Life: 59% of undergraduates are from Colorado. Students are from 44 states, 16 foreign countries, and Canada. 81% are white. Most are Protestant. The average age of freshmen is 19; all undergraduates, 20. 33% do not continue beyond their first year.

Housing: 732 students can be accommodated in college housing, which includes single-sex dorms, on-campus apartments, off-campus apartments, and married-student housing. In addition, there are special-interest houses. On-campus housing is guaranteed for the freshman year only, is available on a first-come, first-served basis, and is available on a lottery system for upperclassmen. Priority is given to out-of-town students. 65% of students live on campus; of those, 38% remain on campus on weekends. Alcohol is not permitted. All students may keep cars.

Activities: There are no fraternities or sororities. There are 21 groups on campus, including band, cheerleading, choir, chorus, computers, drama, honors, international, jazz band, literary magazine, musical theater, newspaper, orchestra, photography, professional, religious, social, social service, student government, symphony, and yearbook. Popular campus events include Preview Days, Spring Retreat, and New Student Retreat.

Sports: There are 5 intercollegiate sports for men and 5 for women, and 6 intramural sports for men and 6 for women. Facilities include a gym and soccer and practice fields.

Disabled Students: 85% of the campus is accessible. Wheelchair ramps, special parking, specially equipped rest rooms, special class scheduling, lowered drinking fountains, lowered telephones, and special housing are available.

Services: Counseling and information services are available, as is tutoring in every subject. There is remedial math, reading, and writing.

Campus Safety and Security: Measures include 24-hour foot and vehicle patrol, security escort services, emergency telephones, and lighted pathways/sidewalks.

Programs of Study: CCU confers B.A., B.S., and B.M. degrees. Associate and master's degrees are also awarded. Bachelor's degrees are awarded in BIOLOGICAL SCIENCE (biology/biological science), BUSINESS (accounting, business administration and management, human resources, management information systems, and management science), COMMUNICATIONS AND THE ARTS (art, communications, English, and music), COMPUTER AND PHYSICAL SCIENCE (computer management and science), EDUCATION (elementary, music, and secondary), SOCIAL SCIENCE (biblical studies, history, liberal arts/general studies, psychology, social science, theological studies, and youth ministry). Science, biology, and education are the strongest academically. Human resources management, computer/information technology, and liberal arts are the largest.

Required: To graduate, students must complete at least 128 semester hours, including the 48-hour general education requirement and courses specified for the major, with a minimum cumulative GPA of 2.0; 2.5 in the major. The university requires 4 semesters of Christian service and regular chapel attendance. All students must complete 12 credits in biblical studies.

Special: The school offers an ROTC program in cooperation with CU Boulder, cross-registration with the Focus on the Family Institute, internships, study abroad in 7 countries, a Washington semester, and work-study programs. Accelerated degree programs are available in Christian leadership, organizational management, and management of information systems. Dual and student-designed majors, nondegree study, pass/fail options, and credit for life, military, and work experience are also available. There are 2 national honor societies, a freshman honors program, and 1 departmental honors program.

Faculty/Classroom: 65% of faculty are male; 35%, female. No introductory courses are taught by graduate students. The average class size in an introductory lecture is 25; in a laboratory, 18; and in a regular course, 30.

Admissions: 74% of the 2003-2004 applicants were accepted. The SAT I scores for the 2003-2004 freshman class were: Verbal--18% below 500, 47% between 500 and 599, 25% between 600 and 700, and 10% above 700; Math--31% below 500, 40% between 500 and 599, 25% between 600 and 700, and 4% above 700. The ACT scores were 24% below 21, 25% between 21 and 23, 28% between 24 and 26, 15% between 27 and 28, and 8% above 28. 53% of the current freshmen were in the top fifth of their class; 80% were in the top two fifths. There was 1 National Merit finalist.

Requirements: The SAT I or ACT is required. In addition, applicants must be graduates of an accredited secondary school. The GED is accepted. An essay is required. A campus visit is recommended. AP and CLEP credits are accepted.

Procedure: Freshmen are admitted to all sessions. There is a rolling admissions plan and a deferred admissions plan. Applications should be filed by August 1 for fall entry and December 15 for spring entry, along with a $40 fee. Notification is sent on a rolling basis. Applications are accepted on-line through *www.applyweb.com/apply/ccu/newmainmenu.html*.

Transfer: Applicants for transfer should have completed 12 college credits with a minimum GPA of 2.0. 30 of 128 credits required for the bachelor's degree must be completed at CCU.

Visiting: There are regularly scheduled orientations for prospective students. There are guides for informal visits and visitors may sit in on classes and stay overnight. To schedule a visit, contact the Office of Admissions at *admission@ccu.edu*.

Financial Aid: In 2003-2004, 64% of all full-time students received some form of financial aid. 59% of full-time freshmen and 56% of continuing full-time students received need-based aid. The average freshman award was $9712. Need-based scholarships or need-based grants averaged $7355; need-based self-help aid (loans and jobs) averaged $3105; institutional non-need-based athletic scholarships averaged $6616; and other institutional non-need-based awards and non-need-based scholarships averaged $15,070. 5% of undergraduates work part time. Average annual earnings from campus work are $1720. The average financial indebtedness of the 2003 graduate was $20,390. The FAFSA is required. The deadline for filing freshman financial aid applications for fall entry is March 15.

International Students: There are 13 international students enrolled. The school actively recruits these students. They must score 500 on the written TOEFL and also take the college's own test and the SAT I or the ACT.

Computers: The mainframe is a VAX cluster. PCs are available in the computer lab and in the library. Dorm apartments are wired for the Internet. All students may access the system.

Graduates: From July 1, 2002 to June 30, 2003, 463 bachelor's degrees were awarded. The most popular majors were business/marketing (69%), liberal arts (9%), and philosophy/religion/theology (5%). In an average class, 31% graduate in 4 years or less, and 6% graduate in 5 years or less.

Admissions Contact: Waynette Moreland, Director of Admission Operations. A video is available. E-mail: *wmoreland@ccu.edu*
Web: *www.ccu.edu*

COLORADO COLLEGE　　　　　　　　D-3
Colorado Springs, CO 80903　　　　　(719) 389-6344
　　　　　　　　(800) 542-7214; Fax: (719) 389-6816

Full-time: 877 men, 1052 women	**Faculty:** 166; IIB, ++$
Part-time: none	**Ph.D.s:** 96%
Graduate: 10 men, 17 women	**Student/Faculty:** 12 to 1
Year: see profile, summer session	**Tuition:** $28,644
Application Deadline: January 15	**Room & Board:** $7216
Freshman Class: 3533 applied, 1975 accepted, 593 enrolled	
SAT I or ACT: required	**HIGHLY COMPETITIVE**

Colorado College, founded in 1874, is an independent liberal arts and sciences institution. The academic year is based on the Block Plan, under which students take only 1 course during each of the 8 3-1/2-week-long blocks of study; there is also a 9-week 3-block summer session. The library contains 579,362 volumes, 122,707 microform items, and 2189 audio/video tapes/CDs, and subscribes to 2328 periodicals. Computerized library services include the card catalog, interlibrary loans, and database searching. Special learning facilities include a learning resource center, art gallery, radio station, an electronic music studio, a telescope dome, multimedia computer lab, the Colorado College Press, an herbarium, a Fourier transform nuclear magnetic resonance spectrometer, a scanning electronic microscope and transmission electronic microscope, and an environmental service van equipped for field research. The 90-acre campus is in a suburban area 70 miles south of Denver. Including any residence halls, there are 52 buildings.

Student Life: 72% of undergraduates are from out of state, mostly the West. Students are from 49 states, 25 foreign countries, and Canada. 70% are from public schools. 78% are white. The average age of freshmen is 18; all undergraduates, 20. 6% do not continue beyond their first year; 82% remain to graduate.

Housing: 1476 students can be accommodated in college housing, which includes single-sex and coed dorms and on-campus apartments. In addition, there are language houses, substance-free, smoke-free, diversity, community arts, arts and crafts, sustainable living, and special-interest houses. On-campus housing is guaranteed for all 4 years. 83% of students live on campus. Upperclassmen may keep cars.

Activities: 16% of men belong to 3 national fraternities; 18% of women belong to 3 national sororities. There are 80 groups on campus, including art, band, chess, choir, chorale, chorus, computers, dance, drama, ethnic, film, forensics, gay, honors, international, jazz band, literary magazine, musical theater, newspaper, orchestra, photography, political, professional, radio and TV, religious, social, social service, student government, symphony, and yearbook. Popular campus events include an afternoon and evening concert, an annual arts and crafts sale, and Division I men's ice hockey games.

Sports: There are 9 intercollegiate sports for men and 9 for women, and 17 intramural sports for men and 17 for women. Facilities include a sports center with 2 gyms, weight and exercise rooms, squash, tennis, and racquetball courts, a pool, an ice rink, and playing fields.

Disabled Students: 80% of the campus is accessible. Wheelchair ramps, elevators, special parking, specially equipped rest rooms, lowered drinking fountains, and lowered telephones are available.

Services: Counseling and information services are available, as is tutoring in most subjects. There is a writing center.

Campus Safety and Security: Measures include 24-hour foot and vehicle patrol, self-defense education, security escort services, and shuttle buses. There are informal discussions, pamphlets/posters/films, emergency telephones, and lighted pathways/sidewalks.

Programs of Study: CC confers the B.A. degree. Master's degrees are also awarded. Bachelor's degrees are awarded in BIOLOGICAL SCIENCE (biochemistry, biology/biological science, and neurosciences), BUSINESS (international economics), COMMUNICATIONS AND THE ARTS (art history and appreciation, classics, comparative literature, creative writing, dance, dramatic arts, English, film arts, French, German, music, romance languages and literature, Russian, Spanish, and studio art), COMPUTER AND PHYSICAL SCIENCE (chemistry, computer mathematics, geology, mathematics, and physics), ENGINEERING AND ENVIRONMENTAL DESIGN (environmental science), SOCIAL SCIENCE (anthropology, Asian/Oriental studies, economics, history, history of philosophy, liberal arts/general studies, philosophy, political science/government, psychology, religion, sociology, Southwest American studies, and women's studies). Biology, English, and psychology are the largest.

Required: Students must complete 32 units, with at least 9 units outside the division of the major, 18 outside the major department, and 4 in Alternative Perspectives. At least 3 courses in each division are required. Students must take 3 units of natural science with 1 lab science, 3 of social science, and 3 of humanities. Major requirements vary from 8 to 14 units. Students must earn a 2.0 GPA and achieve intermediate-level proficiency in a foreign language. Most majors offer (if not require) a comprehensive exam or a thesis.

Special: CC offers co-op programs with Columbia University School of Law, study abroad in several countries, and 3-2 engineering degrees. There are 3 national honor societies, including Phi Beta Kappa, and 100 departmental honors programs.

Faculty/Classroom: 41% of full-time faculty are male; 59%, female. All both teach and do research. No introductory courses are taught by graduate students. The average class size in an introductory lecture is 20; in a laboratory, 17; and in a regular course, 14.

Admissions: 56% of the 2003-2004 applicants were accepted. In a recent year, there were 12 National Merit finalists and 31 freshmen graduated first in their class.

Requirements: The SAT I or ACT is required. In addition, applicants should have completed at least 16 (18 to 20 recommended) high school academic credits. The GED is accepted. An essay is required. AP credits are accepted. Important factors in the admissions decision are advanced placement or honor courses, extracurricular activities record, and evidence of special talent.

Procedure: Freshmen are admitted fall and spring. Entrance exams should be taken by the fall of the senior year. There are early action and deferred admissions plans. Early action applications should be filed by November 15; regular applications, by January 15 for fall entry and November 1 for spring entry. Notification of early action is sent January 1; regular decision, by April 1. 546 early action candidates were accepted for the 2003-2004 class. 467 applicants were on the 2003 waiting list; 14 were admitted. Applications are accepted on-line through Common App and College Board.

Transfer: 44 transfer students enrolled in 2003-2004. Transfer candidates who are not submitting 3 semesters or 4 quarters of college work must submit their high school record. A letter of recommendation from a professor or teacher and a dean's form are required, as well as an application essay. 16 of 32 units (1 unit = 4 semester hours) required for the bachelor's degree must be completed at CC.

Visiting: There are regularly scheduled orientations for prospective students, including a class visit, an information session with an admissions director, and a student-led tour. There are guides for informal visits and visitors may sit in on classes and stay overnight. To schedule a visit, contact the Admission Office.

Financial Aid: In 2003-2004, 47% of all full-time freshmen and 45% of continuing full-time students received some form of financial aid. At least 43% of all full-time students received need-based aid. The average freshman award was $22,299. Need-based scholarships or need-based grants averaged $20,035; need-based self-help aid (loans and jobs) averaged $3381; institutional non-need-based athletic scholarships averaged $28,335; and other institutional non-need-based awards and non-need-based scholarships averaged $12,279. The average financial indebtedness of the 2003 graduate was $13,850. CC is a member of CSS. The CSS Profile or FAFSA and noncustodial (divorced/separated) parents' statement are required. The priority date for freshman financial aid applications for fall entry is February 15.

International Students: There were 46 international students enrolled in a recent year The school actively recruits these students. They must score 550 on the written TOEFL and also take the SAT I or ACT.

Computers: The mainframes are a Data General 8520 and 4605, used for administrative purposes. Academic computing is supported by a distributed network of PCs and Macs. There are 116 machines in public labs and 161 in departmental labs. The local area network is 10/100 Mb with a Gb backbone. All students may access the system. There are no time limits and no fees. It is strongly recommended that all students have a personal computer.

Graduates: From July 1, 2002 to June 30, 2003, 500 bachelor's degrees were awarded. The most popular majors were social studies and history (38%), biological/life sciences (11%), and English (9%). In an average class, 70% graduate in 4 years or less, 77% graduate in 5 years or less, and 77% graduate in 6 years or less. 47 companies recruited on campus in a recent year. Of a recent graduating class, 22% were enrolled in graduate school within 6 months of graduation and 80% were employed.

Admissions Contact: Dean of Admission and Financial Aid. A video is available. E-mail: *admission@coloradocollege.edu* Web: *www.coloradocollege.edu*

COLORADO SCHOOL OF MINES   C-2
Golden, CO 80401-1842   **(303) 273-3220**
(800) 446-9488; Fax: (303) 273-3509

Full-time: 1990 men, 623 women	**Faculty:** 171; I, av$
Part-time: 44 men, 10 women	**Ph.D.s:** 71%
Graduate: 518 men, 216 women	**Student/Faculty:** 15 to 1
Year: semesters, summer session	**Tuition:** $6433 ($19,763)
Application Deadline: June 1	**Room & Board:** $6100
Freshman Class: 2890 applied, 2422 accepted, 688 enrolled	
SAT I Verbal/Math: 595/650	**ACT:** 27 **HIGHLY COMPETITIVE**

The Colorado School of Mines, founded in 1874, is a public institution offering programs in science, economics, and engineering. In addition to regional accreditation, CSM has baccalaureate program accreditation with ABET. The library contains 356,000 volumes and 236,000 microform items, and subscribes to 2700 periodicals. Computerized library services include the card catalog, interlibrary loans, and database searching. Special learning facilities include a geology museum. The 373-acre campus is in a small town 15 miles west of Denver. Including any residence halls, there are 35 buildings.

Student Life: 74% of undergraduates are from Colorado. Others are from 50 states, 62 foreign countries, and Canada. 90% are from public schools. 82% are white. 52% are Protestant; 21% Catholic; 20% claim no religious affiliation. The average age of freshmen is 18; all undergraduates, 20. 17% do not continue beyond their first year; 60% remain to graduate.

Housing: 620 students can be accommodated in college housing, which includes coed dorms, on-campus apartments, and married-student housing. On-campus housing is guaranteed for the freshman year only and is available on a first-come, first-served basis. All students may keep cars.

Activities: 19% of men belong to 7 national fraternities; 19% of women belong to 3 national sororities. There are 95 groups on campus, including band, cheerleading, choir, chorus, computers, drama, ethnic, honors, international, literary magazine, marching band, musical theater, newspaper, political, professional, religious, social, social service, student government, and yearbook. Popular campus events include International Day, Winter Carnival, and Parents Day.

Sports: There are 11 intercollegiate sports for men and 6 for women, and 13 intramural sports for men and 12 for women. Facilities include a 10,000-seat stadium, a gym, numerous intramural fields, tennis courts, and a field house.

Disabled Students: All of the campus is accessible. Wheelchair ramps, elevators, special parking, specially equipped rest rooms, special class scheduling, and lowered drinking fountains are available.

Services: Counseling and information services are available, as is tutoring in most subjects. There is remedial math and writing.

Campus Safety and Security: Measures include 24-hour foot and vehicle patrol, informal discussions, emergency telephones, and lighted pathways/sidewalks.

Programs of Study: CSM confers the B.S. degree. Master's and doctoral degrees are also awarded. Bachelor's degrees are awarded in COMPUTER AND PHYSICAL SCIENCE (chemistry, mathematics, and physics), ENGINEERING AND ENVIRONMENTAL DESIGN (chemical engineering, engineering, geological engineering, geophysical engineering, metallurgical engineering, mining and mineral engineering, and petroleum/natural gas engineering), SOCIAL SCIENCE (economics). Chemical engineering, geological engineering, and petroleum engineering are the strongest academically. General engineering, chemical engineering, and mathematical and computing sciences are the largest.

Required: Students must complete 138 to 148 credit hours, with 35 to 40 hours in the major and a GPA of 2.0. Required courses include humanities, calculus, physics, computer science, chemistry, and phys ed.

Special: Co-op programs, internships in the humanities, accelerated degree programs in all majors, dual majors, study abroad in 7 countries, and nondegree study are offered. There is 1 national honor society, including Phi Beta Kappa, a freshman honors program, and 3 departmental honors programs.

Faculty/Classroom: 80% of faculty are male; 20%, female. 93% teach undergraduates, and 50% both teach and do research. No introductory courses are taught by graduate students. The average class size in an introductory lecture is 75; in a laboratory, 22; and in a regular course, 35.

Admissions: 84% of the 2003-2004 applicants were accepted. The SAT I scores for the 2003-2004 freshman class were: Verbal--10% below 500, 38% between 500 and 599, 41% between 600 and 700, and 11% above 700; Math--2% below 500, 19% between 500 and 599, 54% between 600 and 700, and 25% above 700. The ACT scores were 1% below 21, 11% between 21 and 23, 27% between 24 and 26, 22% between 27 and 28, and 39% above 28. 90% of the current freshmen were in the top fifth of their class; all were in the top two fifths. 57 freshmen graduated first in their class.

Requirements: The SAT I or ACT is required. In addition, applicants must be graduates of an accredited secondary school. The GED is accepted. Students should have completed 16 high school academic credits, including 4 credits each of English and math, 3 of science, 2 of social studies, and 3 academic electives. AP credits are accepted. Important factors in the admissions decision are advanced placement or honor courses, leadership record, and recommendations by school officials.

Procedure: Freshmen are admitted to all sessions. Entrance exams should be taken by late in the junior year or early in the senior year. There is a deferred admissions plan. Applications should be filed by June 1 for fall entry, December 1 for spring entry, and June 10 for summer entry, along with a $45 fee. Notification is sent on a rolling basis. Applications are accepted on computer disk and on-line through CollegeLink, Apply, and Peterson's, as well as CSM's web site.

Transfer: 77 transfer students enrolled in 2003-2004. Transfer applicants must have a minimum GPA of 2.75. 30 of 138 credits required for the bachelor's degree must be completed at CSM.

Visiting: There are regularly scheduled orientations for prospective students, including a daylong visitation program twice each fall where students may visit departments and talk with faculty. Sessions in admissions and financial aid also are given. There are guides for informal visits and visitors may sit in on classes. To schedule a visit, contact Carmen Brenner at (303) 273-3226; (800) 446-9488, ext. 3220; or cbrenner@mines.edu.

Financial Aid: In 2003-2004, 85% of all full-time students received some form of financial aid. 74% of all full-time students received need-based aid. The average freshman award was $12,900. 70% of undergraduates work part time. Average annual earnings from campus work are $750. The average financial indebtedness of the 2003 graduate was $17,500. CSM is a member of CSS. The FAFSA is required. The deadline for filing freshman financial aid applications for fall entry is March 1.

International Students: There are 97 international students enrolled. The school actively recruits these students. They must score 550 on the written TOEFL and also take the SAT I or the ACT.

Computers: The mainframe is IBM RS/6000 systems running AIX. Students can use all public computer systems managed by the CSM Com-

puting Center. This includes central UNIX servers, UNIX workstations, PCs, terminals, and special devices. About 150 systems of various types are available in public (campus) access labs. All students may access the system 24 hours through dial-in access and direct network connection. Computer labs are open 7 A.M. to midnight Monday to Thursday, 7 A.M. to 6 P.M. on Friday, 9 A.M. to 5:30 P.M. on Saturday, and 9 A.M. to midnight on Sunday. There are no time limits and no fees.

Graduates: From July 1, 2002 to June 30, 2003, 437 bachelor's degrees were awarded. The most popular majors were general engineering (39%), chemical engineering (20%), and metallurgical and materials engineering (8%). In an average class, 1% graduate in 3 years or less, 30% graduate in 4 years or less, 55% graduate in 5 years or less, and 62% graduate in 6 years or less. 151 companies recruited on campus in 2002-2003. Of the 2002 graduating class, 10% were enrolled in graduate school within 6 months of graduation and 95% were employed.

Admissions Contact: Bill Young, Director of Enrollment Management. E-mail: admit@mines.edu Web: www.mines.edu

COLORADO STATE UNIVERSITY
Fort Collins, CO 80523-0015

C-1
(970) 491-6909
Fax: (970) 491-7799

Full-time: 9098 men, 9665 women	**Faculty:** 865; I, +$
Part-time: 1012 men, 903 women	**Ph.D.s:** 99%
Graduate: 1963 men, 1874 women	**Student/Faculty:** 22 to 1
Year: semesters, summer session	**Tuition:** $3919 ($14,391)
Application Deadline: July 1	**Room & Board:** $6045
Freshman Class: 12,026 applied, 9520 accepted, 3802 enrolled	
SAT I Verbal/Math: 550/560	**ACT:** 24 VERY COMPETITIVE

Colorado State University, founded in 1870 and part of the Colorado State University system, is a public, land-grant institution, offering 66 undergraduate majors in 51 departments within 8 colleges. There are 8 undergraduate schools and 1 graduate school. In addition to regional accreditation, Colorado State has baccalaureate program accreditation with AACSB, ABET, ACCE, ACEJMC, ADA, ASLA, CSWE, FIDER, NASM, NCATE, NRPA, and SAF. The 4 libraries contain 1,909,882 volumes, 2,520,216 microform items, and 9535 audio/video tapes/CDs, and subscribe to 20,712 periodicals. Computerized library services include the card catalog, interlibrary loans, and database searching. Special learning facilities include a learning resource center, art gallery, radio station, TV station, environmental learning center, and plant environmental research center. The 666-acre campus is in a suburban area in Fort Collins, 65 miles north of Denver. Including any residence halls, there are 100 buildings.

Student Life: 81% of undergraduates are from Colorado. Students are from 50 states, 96 foreign countries, and Canada. 81% are white. The average age of freshmen is 18; all undergraduates, 21. 18% do not continue beyond their first year; 63% remain to graduate.

Housing: 4550 students can be accommodated in college housing, which includes coed dorms, on-campus apartments, married-student housing, fraternity houses, and sorority houses. In addition, there are honors floors and 20 other special-interest floors. On-campus housing is guaranteed for the freshman year only and is available on a first-come, first-served basis. 70% of students commute. All students may keep cars.

Activities: 8% of men belong to 20 national fraternities; 9% of women belong to 15 national sororities. There are 300 groups on campus, including art, band, cheerleading, chess, choir, chorale, chorus, computers, dance, debate, drama, drill team, ethnic, film, forensics, gay, honors, international, jazz band, literary magazine, marching band, musical theater, newspaper, opera, orchestra, pep band, photography, political, professional, radio and TV, religious, social, social service, student government, symphony, and yearbook. Popular campus events include Centertainment, International Poster Exhibition, and Summer Outdoor Theater.

Sports: There are 5 intercollegiate sports for men and 9 for women, and 16 intramural sports for men and 16 for women. Facilities include a 9,000-seat arena, indoor and outdoor tracks, a football stadium, a baseball diamond, intramural fields, indoor swimming pools, a comprehensive student recreation center, and an obstacle course for personal development.

Disabled Students: 90% of the campus is accessible. Wheelchair ramps, elevators, special parking, specially equipped rest rooms, special class scheduling, lowered drinking fountains, lowered telephones, special housing, an advocacy office for disabled students, telecommunication devices for the deaf, and special transportation are available.

Services: Counseling and information services are available, as is tutoring in most subjects. There is a reader service for the blind. There are interpreters and note takers available.

Campus Safety and Security: Measures include 24-hour foot and vehicle patrol, self-defense education, security escort services, and shuttle buses. There are informal discussions, pamphlets/posters/films, emergency telephones, lighted pathways/sidewalks, lectures by campus police on a variety of safety issues, a crime victim support unit, and a bike patrol.

Programs of Study: Colorado State confers B.A., B.S., B.F.A., and B.M. degrees. Master's and doctoral degrees are also awarded. Bachelor's degrees are awarded in AGRICULTURE (agricultural business management, agricultural economics, agronomy, animal science, equine science, fishing and fisheries, forestry and related sciences, horticulture, natural resource management, and range/farm management), BIOLOGICAL SCIENCE (biochemistry, biology/biological science, botany, microbiology, nutrition, wildlife biology, and zoology), BUSINESS (accounting, apparel and accessories marketing, banking and finance, business administration and management, hotel/motel and restaurant management, marketing/retailing/merchandising, and recreational facilities management), COMMUNICATIONS AND THE ARTS (art, English, French, German, journalism, music, performing arts, Spanish, speech/debate/rhetoric, and technical and business writing), COMPUTER AND PHYSICAL SCIENCE (chemistry, computer science, geology, information sciences and systems, mathematics, physical sciences, physics, and statistics), EDUCATION (agricultural, home economics, and physical), ENGINEERING AND ENVIRONMENTAL DESIGN (agricultural engineering, chemical engineering, civil engineering, construction management, electrical/electronics engineering, engineering and applied science, industrial engineering technology, interior design, landscape architecture/design, and mechanical engineering), HEALTH PROFESSIONS (environmental health science and occupational therapy), SOCIAL SCIENCE (anthropology, economics, history, home economics, human development, liberal arts/general studies, philosophy, political science/government, psychology, social work, sociology, and water resources). Engineering and applied science, chemistry, and microbiology are the strongest academically. Business, psychology, and exercise and sport science are the largest.

Required: To graduate, students must complete at least 120 credit hours, 27 of them in the major, with a minimum GPA of 2.0. Students must complete the All University Core described in the catalog.

Special: Colorado State offers co-op programs with Metropolitan State College and Universidad Autonoma in Mexico and participates in cross-registration with AIMS Community College. Study abroad in more than 30 countries, a semester at sea, work-study programs, internships, B.A.-B.S. degrees, and pass/fail options are available. Teaching certification students receive a bachelor's degree in their chosen subject and also complete a certification sequence through the School of Education. There are 43 national honor societies, including Phi Beta Kappa, and a freshman honors program.

Faculty/Classroom: 75% of faculty are male; 25%, female. All both teach and do research. Graduate students teach 10% of introductory courses. The average class size in an introductory lecture is 46; in a laboratory, 21; and in a regular course, 25.

Admissions: 79% of the 2003-2004 applicants were accepted. The SAT I scores for the 2003-2004 freshman class were: Verbal--23% below 500, 48% between 500 and 599, 26% between 600 and 700, and 4% above 700; Math--19% below 500, 48% between 500 and 599, 28% between 600 and 700, and 5% above 700. The ACT scores were 13% below 21, 33% between 21 and 23, 31% between 24 and 26, 12% between 27 and 28, and 11% above 28. 41% of the current freshmen were in the top fifth of their class; 76% were in the top two fifths. There were 14 National Merit finalists and 9 semifinalists. 121 freshmen graduated first in their class.

Requirements: The SAT I or ACT is required; the average freshman has a composite SAT I score of 1114 and an ACT composite of 24. Graduation from secondary school is required. The GED is accepted. Students should have completed 18 high school credits, 15 of which are academic credits, including 4 years of English, 3 of math, including algebra I, geometry, and algebra II, 2 of natural science, 2 of social science, 1 additional year of natural or social science, and 2 years of the same foreign language. An essay is recommended. AP and CLEP credits are accepted. Important factors in the admissions decision are advanced placement or honor courses, leadership record, and recommendations by school officials.

Procedure: Freshmen are admitted to all sessions. Entrance exams should be taken during the junior year or early fall of the senior year. There is a rolling admissions plan. Applications should be filed by July 1 for fall entry and December 1 for spring entry, along with a $50 fee. Notification is sent on a rolling basis. Applications are accepted on-line through the school's web site.

Transfer: 1791 transfer students enrolled in 2002-2003. Applicants must have a minimum cumulative 2.0 GPA. However, at least 13 semester credits and a 2.7 cumulative GPA are required to be considered strong candidates for admission. Admission is subject to satisfactory completion of current courses, submission of current courses, and submission of a final, complete, official transcript. Students holding an associate degree from an accredited Colorado institution are guaranteed admission providing that it is the last institution attended and that a cumulative 2.0 GPA has been achieved from all institutions attended. Specific majors may require prerequisites and enrollment may be limited. 32 of 120 credits required for the bachelor's degree must be completed at Colorado State.

Visiting: There are regularly scheduled orientations for prospective students, including Visit Days, which provide information about admissions, financial aid, and housing. A presentation on admissions, financial aid, and student life is offered each weekday, followed by a campus tour guided by student volunteers. The presentations start at 9:15 A.M. and 1:15 P.M. There are guides for informal visits and visitors may sit in on classes. To schedule a visit, contact Andrea Moss in the Office of Admissions at (970) 491-6393.

Financial Aid: In a recent year, 70% of all full-time freshmen and 65% of continuing full-time students received some form of financial aid. 41% of all full-time students received need-based aid. The average freshman award was $6200. 47% of undergraduates work part time. Average annual earnings from campus work are $2000. The average financial indebtedness of a recent graduate was $15,736. The FAFSA is required. The deadline for filing freshman financial aid applications for fall entry is March 1.

International Students: There were 243 international students enrolled in a recent year. The school actively recruits these students. They must score 525 on the written TOEFL or 197 on the electronic version. Scores from other English language proficiency exams may be considered in lieu of the TOEFL. They must also take the SAT I or the ACT.

Computers: The mainframes are an IBM 9672 Model R22 and 4 IBM/6000 servers (production servers) and 4 additional network servers. There are numerous student computer labs on campus, including some in residence halls, dial-up modems, and access to the Internet. Every residence hall room has high-speed Internet access. All students may access the system 24 hours a day. There are no time limits and no fees.

Graduates: From July 1, 2002 to June 30, 2003, 3998 bachelor's degrees were awarded. The most popular majors were business (14%), technical journalism (4%), and psychology (4%). In an average class, 34% graduate in 4 years or less, 58% graduate in 5 years or less, and 63% graduate in 6 years or less. 149 companies recruited on campus in 2002-2003.

Admissions Contact: Admissions Counselor. A video is available.
E-mail: admissions@vines.colostate.edu
Web: www.colostate.edu/depts/admission/

COLORADO TECHNICAL UNIVERSITY
Colorado Springs, CO 80907-3896

D-3
(719) 590-6810
Fax: (719) 590-3740

Full-time: 319 men, 111 women	**Faculty:** 30
Part-time: 527 men, 249 women	**Ph.D.s:** 50%
Graduate: 509 men, 189 women	**Student/Faculty:** 14 to 1
Year: quarters, summer session	**Tuition:** $9500
Application Deadline: open	**Room & Board:** n/app
Freshman Class: n/av	
SAT I or ACT: recommended	**LESS COMPETITIVE**

Colorado Technical University, founded in 1965, is a private commuter institution offering programs with technical and management emphasis in computer science, electronic engineering technology, management, computer engineering, and electrical engineering. A large percentage of the students are working adults who have transferred from other colleges. There are branch campuses in Sioux Falls, South Dakota and Denver, Colorado. There are 3 undergraduate and 3 graduate schools. In addition to regional accreditation, Colorado Tech has baccalaureate program accreditation with ABET and CAAHEP. The library contains 33,000 volumes, 15,000 microform items, and 400 audio/video tapes/CDs, and subscribes to 362 periodicals. Computerized library services include the card catalog, interlibrary loans, and database searching. Special learning facilities include a learning resource center. The 5-acre campus is in a suburban area in Colorado Springs. There are 2 buildings.

Student Life: 95% of undergraduates are from Colorado. Students are from 14 foreign countries. 76% are white; 11% African American.

Housing: There are no residence halls. Alcohol is not permitted.

Activities: There are no fraternities or sororities. There are 6 groups on campus, including computers, honors, international, professional, and student government. Popular campus events include a summer picnic.

Sports: There is no sports program at Colorado Tech. Facilities include a high-tech workout facility.

Disabled Students: All of the campus is accessible. Wheelchair ramps, special parking, specially equipped rest rooms, and lowered drinking fountains are available.

Services: Counseling and information services are available, as is tutoring in most subjects, including English, math, and computer science. Taped tutorials are offered as well. There is remedial math and writing. Upon entry to Colorado Tech, students are assigned a counselor/mentor who can assist them throughout their academic career.

Campus Safety and Security: Measures include informal discussions, pamphlets/posters/films, emergency telephones, and lighted pathways/sidewalks. There is a security service.

Programs of Study: Colorado Tech confers the B.S. degree. Associate, master's, and doctoral degrees are also awarded. Bachelor's degrees are awarded in BUSINESS (business administration and management, management information systems, and management science), COMMUNICATIONS AND THE ARTS (telecommunications), COMPUTER AND PHYSICAL SCIENCE (computer science and information sciences and systems), ENGINEERING AND ENVIRONMENTAL DESIGN (computer engineering, electrical/electronics engineering, electrical/electronics engineering technology, graphic arts technology, and technological management), SOCIAL SCIENCE (criminal justice). Engineering, computer science, and engineering technology are the strongest academically.

Required: All students must complete a core of general education courses, including math, engineering science, English, and humanities/social sciences. An average of 180 quarter hours, with a cumulative GPA of 2.0, is required to graduate, as is a course in career development.

Special: Internships are possible with several local technology companies. Work-study programs are available with social services, the public library, and the university. Nondegree study, co-op programs, study abroad in London, and credit for life, military, and work experience are possible.

Faculty/Classroom: 67% of faculty are male; 33%, female. All teach undergraduates. No introductory courses are taught by graduate students. The average class size in an introductory lecture is 19; in a laboratory, 19; and in a regular course, 19.

Requirements: The SAT I or ACT is recommended, with suggested minimum composite scores of 1050 (550 math) on the SAT I or 24 on the ACT. Applicants should be graduates of an accredited high school. The GED is accepted. An essay is required for scholarships. An interview is recommended. Students without transfer of credit or an ACT or SAT I test report must pass Colorado Tech's entrance exams in math and English. AP and CLEP credits are accepted. Important factors in the admissions decision are ability to finance college education, personality/intangible qualities, and recommendations by school officials.

Procedure: Freshmen are admitted to all sessions. Entrance exams should be taken prior to the student's desired entry date. There are early admissions and deferred admissions plans. There is a rolling admissions plan. Application deadlines are open. The fall 2003 application fee was $50. Notification is sent on a rolling basis.

Transfer: 800 transfer students enrolled in 2002-2003. Most new students are transfers. They must meet the same criteria as entering freshmen. The university uses placement tests in math and English for acceptance and placement. 45 quarter hours of 180 required for the bachelor's degree must be completed at Colorado Tech.

Visiting: There are regularly scheduled orientations for prospective students, consisting of a tour and an admissions overview program. There are guides for informal visits and visitors may sit in on classes. To schedule a visit, contact the Admissions Director.

Financial Aid: In 2003-2004, 20% of all full-time freshmen and 33% of continuing full-time students received some form of financial aid. 50% of full-time freshmen and 60% of continuing full-time students received need-based aid. The average freshman award was $7000, with $3000 ($4050 maximum) from need-based scholarships or need-based grants, and $4000 ($6625 maximum) from need-based self-help aid (loans and jobs). 2% of undergraduates work part time. Average annual earnings from campus work are $1500. The average financial indebtedness of the 2003 graduate was $30,000. The FAFSA and the state aid form are required. The priority date for freshman financial aid applications for fall entry is March 15.

International Students: There are 14 international students enrolled. They must score 550 on the written TOEFL or provide satisfactory evidence of completion of ELS or college-level English, and also take the SAT I, ACT, or the college's own entrance exam, scoring 1050 on the SAT I.

Computers: The mainframe is a 3X HP DL 380 server. There are 14 labs with 186 systems in support of various academic programs on campus, as well as 15 systems available for student use in the library and 5 in the student lounge. Most have Internet access. All students may access the system 8 A.M. to 9 P.M. Monday through Thursday, and 8 A.M. to 5 P.M. Friday and Saturday. There are no time limits and no fees.

Graduates: From July 1, 2002 to June 30, 2003, 147 bachelor's degrees were awarded. The most popular majors were information technology/information technology management (33%), management (26%), and computer science (15%). 72 companies recruited on campus in 2002-2003.

Admissions Contact: Rob Dillman, Vice President of Admissions. A video is available. E-mail: rdillman@coloradotech.edu Web: http://www.coloradotech.edu

---

DEVRY UNIVERSITY/COLORADO SPRINGS D-3
Colorado Springs, CO 80910-3124
(719) 632-3000
Fax: (719) 632-1909

Full-time: 123 men, 43 women	**Faculty:** n/av
Part-time: 93 men, 41 women	**Ph.D.s:** n/av
Graduate: n/av	**Student/Faculty:** n/av
Year: semesters, summer session	**Tuition:** $11,310
Application Deadline: open	**Room & Board:** n/app
Freshman Class: n/av	
SAT I or ACT: n/av	**LESS COMPETITIVE**

DeVry University/Colorado Springs, founded in 2001, is 1 of 67 DeVry University locations throughout the United States and Canada. The private institution offers career-oriented degree programs with hands-on training in various fields of business and technology. The library contains 1800 volumes and 20 audio/video tapes/CDs, and subscribes to 20 periodicals. Computerized library services include the card catalog, interlibrary loans, and database searching. Special learning facilities include a learning resource center and electronics and other labs.

Student Life: 60% of students are white; 14% African American. The average age of all undergraduates is 27.

Housing: There are no residence halls. Housing referrals can be obtained through the Student Housing Office. There are private apartments, student-plan housing, and private rooms. All students commute. Alcohol is not permitted. All students may keep cars.

Activities: There are no fraternities or sororities. There is 1 professional group on campus. Popular campus events include various food events.

Sports: There is no sports program at DeVry.

Disabled Students: 90% of the campus is accessible. Wheelchair ramps, elevators, special parking, specially equipped rest rooms, and lowered telephones are available.

Services: Counseling and information services are available, as is tutoring in every subject.

Campus Safety and Security: Measures include 24-hour foot and vehicle patrol, security escort services, informal discussions, and pamphlets/posters/films. There are emergency telephones and full-time security personnel.

Programs of Study: DeVry confers the B.S. degree. Associate and master's degrees are also awarded. Bachelor's degrees are awarded in BUSINESS (business administration and management), COMMUNICATIONS AND THE ARTS (telecommunications), COMPUTER AND PHYSICAL SCIENCE (information sciences and systems), ENGINEERING AND ENVIRONMENTAL DESIGN (technological management). Computer information systems and business administration are the largest.

Required: To graduate, students must achieve a GPA of at least 2.0 and satisfactorily complete all curriculum requirements. Course requirements vary according to program. All first-semester students take courses in business organization, algebra, psychology, and student success strategies.

Special: Accelerated degree programs are offered in computer information systems and business administration. Co-op programs, nondegree study, distance learning, and evening and weekend classes are possible.

Faculty/Classroom: All teach undergraduates.

Requirements: Admissions requirements include graduation from a secondary school; the GED is also accepted. Applicants must pass the DeVry entrance exam or present satisfactory ACT or SAT I scores. An interview is also required. CLEP credit is accepted.

Procedure: Freshmen are admitted to all sessions. There is a rolling admissions plan. There are early admissions and deferred admissions plans. Application deadlines are open. Application fee is $50. Applications are accepted on-line through https://apply.embark.com/UGrad/DeVry/21.

Transfer: Applicants for transfer must submit official transcripts from all previous colleges attended indicating passing grades in all completed course work, demonstrate language skills proficiency in at least 24 completed semester hours, and present evidence of math proficiency by appropriate college-level credits. A minimum GPA of 2.0 is required. 25% of 48 to 154 credits required for the bachelor's degree must be completed at DeVry.

Visiting: There are regularly scheduled orientations for prospective students. There are guides for informal visits and visitors may sit in on classes. To schedule a visit, contact Mare App, New Student Coordinator.

Financial Aid: In 2002-2003, 62% of all full-time freshmen and 73% of continuing full-time students received some form of financial aid. 62% of full-time freshmen and 73% of continuing full-time students received need-based aid. The average freshman award was $7137. Need-based scholarships or need-based grants averaged $4149; need-based self-help aid (loans and jobs) averaged $4172; and institutional non-need-based awards and non-need-based scholarships averaged $8712. The FAFSA is required.

International Students: There was 1 international student enrolled in a recent year. They must score 500 on the written TOEFL or 173 on the electronic version and also take the college's own entrance exam.

Graduates: From July 1, 2002 to June 30, 2003, 2 bachelor's degrees were awarded. The most popular major was computer information systems (100%).

Admissions Contact: Pam Smith, Director of Admissions.
E-mail: *admitcs@cs.devry.edu* Web: *www.cs.devry.edu*

DEVRY UNIVERSITY/WESTMINSTER   C-2
Westminster, CO 80234-2010   (303) 280-7600
(888) 212-1857; Fax: (303) 280-7606

Full-time: 350 men, 107 women	Faculty: n/av
Part-time: 144 men, 69 women	Ph.D.s: n/av
Graduate: none	Student/Faculty: n/av
Year: semesters, summer session	Tuition: $11,310
Application Deadline: open	Room & Board: n/app
Freshman Class: n/av	
SAT I or ACT: n/av	LESS COMPETITIVE

DeVry University/Westminster, founded in 2001, is a private institution offering hands-on programs in electronics, business administration, computer information systems, information technology, and computer engineering technology. The school is 1 of 67 DeVry University locations throughout the United States and Canada. The library contains 500 volumes and 150 audio/video tapes/CDs, and subscribes to 50 periodicals. Computerized library services include the card catalog, interlibrary loans, and database searching. Special learning facilities include a learning resource center and electronics and other labs.

Student Life: 58% of students are white. The average age of all undergraduates is 24.

Housing: Housing referrals can be obtained through the Student Housing Office. There are private apartments, student-plan housing, and private rooms. All students commute. All students may keep cars.

Activities: There are no fraternities or sororities. There are 3 groups on campus, including professional and yearbook. Popular campus events include BBQ and other food events.

Sports: There is no sports program at DeVry University/Westminster.

Disabled Students: 90% of the campus is accessible. Wheelchair ramps, elevators, special parking, specially equipped rest rooms, and lowered telephones are available.

Services: Counseling and information services are available, as is tutoring in every subject.

Campus Safety and Security: Measures include security escort services, informal discussions, pamphlets/posters/films, emergency telephones, and lighted pathways/sidewalks.

Programs of Study: DeVry University/Westminster confers the B.S. degree. Associate degrees are also awarded. Bachelor's degrees are awarded in BIOLOGICAL SCIENCE (bioinformatics), BUSINESS (business administration and management), COMPUTER AND PHYSICAL SCIENCE (information sciences and systems), ENGINEERING AND ENVIRONMENTAL DESIGN (biomedical engineering, computer engineering, electrical/electronics engineering technology, and technological management). Electronics is the largest.

Required: To graduate, students must achieve a GPA of 2.0 and satisfactorily complete all curriculum requirements. Course requirements vary according to program. All first-semester students take courses in business organization, computer applications, algebra, psychology, and student success strategies.

Special: Accelerated degrees, co-op programs, nondegree study, distance learning, and evening and weekend classes are possible.

Faculty/Classroom: All teach undergraduates.

Requirements: Admissions requirements include graduation from a secondary school; the GED is also accepted. Applicants must pass the DeVry entrance exam or present satisfactory ACT or SAT I scores. An interview is required. CLEP credit is accepted.

Procedure: Freshmen are admitted fall, spring, and summer. There is a rolling admissions plan. There are early admissions and deferred admissions plans. Application deadlines are open. Application fee is $50. Applications are accepted on-line through *https://apply.embark.com/UGrad/DeVry/21/*.

Transfer: Applicants for transfer must present passing grades in all completed college course work, demonstrate language proficiency in at least 24 completed semester hours, and present evidence of math proficiency by appropriate college-level credits. 25% of 48 to 154 credits required for the bachelor's degree must be completed at DeVry University/Westminster.

Visiting: There are regularly scheduled orientations for prospective students. There are guides for informal visits and visitors may sit in on classes. To schedule a visit, contact Pam Smith, Dean of Admissions.

Financial Aid: In 2002-2003, 59% of all full-time freshmen and 67% of continuing full-time students received some form of financial aid. At least 58% of full-time freshmen and at least 66% of continuing full-time students received need-based aid. The average freshman award was $5618. Need-based scholarships or need-based grants averaged $3687; need-based self-help aid (loans and jobs) averaged $3764; and institu-

tional non-need-based awards and non-need-based scholarships averaged $12,266. The FAFSA is required.

International Students: There were 5 international students enrolled in a recent year. They must score 500 on the written TOEFL or 173 on the electronic version and also take the college's own entrance exam.

Admissions Contact: Pam Smith, Dean of Admissions.
E-mail: *Denver-admissions@den.devry.edu* Web: *www.den.devry.edu*

FORT LEWIS COLLEGE   B-4
Durango, CO 81301   (970) 247-7184; Fax: (970) 247-7179

Full-time: 1991 men, 1837 women	Faculty: 172; IIB, -$
Part-time: 175 men, 179 women	Ph.D.s: 81%
Graduate: none	Student/Faculty: 22 to 1
Year: trimesters, summer session	Tuition: $2789 ($11,329)
Application Deadline: August 1	Room & Board: $5564
Freshman Class: 3146 applied, 2440 accepted, 923 enrolled	
SAT I Verbal/Math: 500/500	ACT: 20 COMPETITIVE

Fort Lewis College, founded in 1911, is a public institution with undergraduate programs in arts and sciences, business, and education. There are 3 undergraduate schools. In addition to regional accreditation, FLC has baccalaureate program accreditation with AACSB, NASM, and TEAC. The library contains 181,944 volumes, 344,071 microform items, and 4801 audio/video tapes/CDs, and subscribes to 580 periodicals. Computerized library services include the card catalog, interlibrary loans, database searching, and Internet access. Special learning facilities include a learning resource center, art gallery, radio station, and a center for Southwest Studies. The 600-acre campus is in a small town 350 miles southwest of Denver and 250 miles northwest of Albuquerque, New Mexico. Including any residence halls, there are 43 buildings.

Student Life: 68% of undergraduates are from Colorado. Others are from 49 states, 15 foreign countries, and Canada. 99% are from public schools. 71% are white; 17% Native American/Eskimo. The average age of freshmen is 18; all undergraduates, 22. 44% do not continue beyond their first year.

Housing: 1540 students can be accommodated in college housing, which includes single-sex and coed dorms, on-campus apartments, and married-student housing. There is a Hispanic center, a Native American center, and an environmental center. On-campus housing is guaranteed for the freshman year only and is available on a first-come, first-served basis. 69% of students commute. Alcohol is not permitted. All students may keep cars.

Activities: There are no fraternities or sororities. There are 58 groups on campus, including art, band, cheerleading, chess, choir, chorale, chorus, computers, dance, drama, drill team, ethnic, gay, honors, international, jazz band, literary magazine, musical theater, newspaper, orchestra, political, professional, radio and TV, religious, social, social service, student government, and symphony. Popular campus events include Weekend Wipeout and Hozhoni Days.

Sports: There are 5 intercollegiate sports for men and 5 for women, and 10 intramural sports for men and 10 for women. Facilities include a field house, an outdoor sports complex, an indoor swimming pool, and a student life center, which includes a 3-court gym, a racquetball court, an aerobic/dance studio, a track, a climbing wall, and a cardio/weight area.

Disabled Students: 80% of the campus is accessible. Wheelchair ramps, elevators, special parking, specially equipped rest rooms, lowered drinking fountains, lowered telephones, and workstations modified for individual needs are available.

Services: Counseling and information services are available, as is tutoring in most subjects. There is a reader service for the blind and remedial math and writing.

Campus Safety and Security: Measures include 24-hour foot and vehicle patrol, self-defense education, security escort services, and informal discussions. There are pamphlets/posters/films, emergency telephones, and lighted pathways/sidewalks.

Programs of Study: FLC confers B.A. and B.S. degrees. Associate degrees are also awarded. Bachelor's degrees are awarded in BIOLOGICAL SCIENCE (biology/biological science), BUSINESS (accounting and business administration and management), COMMUNICATIONS AND THE ARTS (art, dramatic arts, English, music, and Spanish), COMPUTER AND PHYSICAL SCIENCE (chemistry, geology, information sciences and systems, mathematics, and physics), HEALTH PROFESSIONS (exercise science), SOCIAL SCIENCE (anthropology, economics, history, humanities, philosophy, political science/government, psychology, sociology, and Southwest American studies). Business, chemistry, and geology are the strongest academically. Business is the largest.

Required: To graduate, students must complete 120 semester hours with 30 to 40 hours in the major, 50 credits outside the major, and a minimum GPA of 2.0 overall and within the major. A total of 32 to 44 hours in general distribution courses is required.

Special: The college offers cooperative programs in most majors, numerous internships, a Washington semester for political science majors, study abroad in 23 countries, student-designed majors, a general studies degree, nondegree study, pass/fail options, and B.A.-B.S. degrees. There are 3-2 engineering degrees with 4 universities and a preforestry degree with Colorado State and Northern Arizona Universities. There are 14 national honor societies and a freshman honors program.

Faculty/Classroom: In fall 2002, 54% of faculty were male; 46%, female. All teach undergraduates and 15% both teach and do research. The average class size in an introductory lecture is 27; in a laboratory, 15; and in a regular course, 12.

Admissions: 78% of the 2003-2004 applicants were accepted. The SAT I scores for the 2003-2004 freshman class were: Verbal--49% below 500, 36% between 500 and 599, and 14% between 600 and 700; Math--46% below 500, 42% between 500 and 599, and 11% between 600 and 700. The ACT scores were 53% below 21, 28% between 21 and 23, 13% between 24 and 26, 3% between 27 and 28, and 3% above 28. 16% of the current freshmen were in the top fifth of their class; 37% were in the top two fifths. 6 freshmen graduated first in their class.

Requirements: The SAT I or ACT is required, with recommended minimum composite scores of 800 and 17 (20 enhanced), respectively. Applicants must be graduates of an accredited secondary school or have a GED certificate. An interview is recommended. A GPA of 2.0 is required. AP and CLEP credits are accepted.

Procedure: Freshmen are admitted to all sessions. Entrance exams should be taken in the spring of the junior year in high school. Applications should be filed by August 1 for fall entry, December 1 for winter entry, and April 1 for summer entry. The fall 2003 application fee was $20. Notification is sent on a rolling basis. Applications are accepted on-line through the college's web site.

Transfer: 349 transfer students enrolled in 2003-2004. Applicants for transfer should have completed a minimum of 12 credit hours and have a GPA of 2.0. Courses completed with a grade of C- or better may transfer. An interview is recommended. 28 of 120 credits required for the bachelor's degree must be completed at FLC.

Visiting: There are regularly scheduled orientations for prospective students. There are guides for informal visits and visitors may sit in on classes and stay overnight. To schedule a visit, contact the Office of Admission at *admission@fortlewis.edu.*

Financial Aid: In a recent year, 61% of the full-time freshmen and 66% of the continuing full-time students received some form of financial aid. 49% of all full-time students received need-based aid. The average freshman award was $5755. 20% of undergraduates work part time. Average annual earnings from campus work are $1650. The average financial indebtedness of a recent year's graduate was $14,102. The FAFSA is required. The deadline for filing freshman financial aid applications for fall entry is February 15.

International Students: There are 60 international students enrolled. They must score 500 on the written TOEFL or 173 on the electronic version.

Computers: The mainframe is a Windows network. There are more than 500 student-accessible computers on campus, with full Internet access and free e-mail and web page hosting. All students may access the system. There are no time limits and no fees.

Graduates: From July 1, 2002 to June 30, 2003, 726 bachelor's degrees were awarded. The most popular majors were business/marketing (23%), social science and history (14%), and English (10%). In an average class, 1% graduate in 3 years or less, 9% graduate in 4 years or less, 26% graduate in 5 years or less, and 31% graduate in 6 years or less. 75 companies recruited on campus in 2002-2003. Of the 2002 graduating class, 20% were enrolled in graduate school within 6 months of graduation and 90% were employed.

Admissions Contact: Gretchen Foster, Director, Admission and Development. A video is available. E-mail: *admission@fortlewis.edu* Web: *www.fortlewis.edu*

MESA STATE COLLEGE
Grand Junction, CO 81501

	A-2
	(970) 248-1698
(800) 982-MESA; Fax: (970) 248-1973	
Full-time: 1750 men, 2235 women	Faculty: 204; IIB, --$
Part-time: 490 men, 830 women	Ph.D.s: 72%
Graduate: 25 men, 25 women	Student/Faculty: 20 to 1
Year: semesters, summer session	Tuition: $2290 ($7115)
Application Deadline: see profile	Room & Board: $5765
Freshman Class: n/av	
SAT I or ACT: required	COMPETITIVE

Mesa State College, founded in 1925, is a public institution offering undergraduate programs in liberal arts, sciences, business, and preprofessional areas. There are 3 undergraduate schools and 1 graduate school. Figures in the above capsule and in this profile are approximate. In addition to regional accreditation, Mesa State has baccalaureate program accreditation with CAHEA and NLN. The library contains 189,000 volumes, 803,012 microform items, and 25,578 audio/video tapes/CDs, and subscribes to 1035 periodicals. Computerized library services include the card catalog, interlibrary loans, and database searching. Special learning facilities include a learning resource center, art gallery, radio

station, and TV studio. The 42-acre campus is in a small town 250 miles west of Denver. Including any residence halls, there are 26 buildings.

Student Life: 90% of undergraduates are from Colorado. Students are from 30 states, 43 foreign countries, and Canada. 86% are white. The average age of freshmen is 20; all undergraduates, 25. 39% do not continue beyond their first year; 53% remain to graduate.

Housing: 918 students can be accommodated in college housing, which includes coed dorms and on-campus apartments. On-campus housing is available on a first-come, first-served basis. 81% of students commute. Alcohol is not permitted. All students may keep cars.

Activities: There are no fraternities or sororities. There are 50 groups on campus, including art, cheerleading, choir, chorus, computers, dance, ethnic, honors, international, jazz band, literary magazine, musical theater, newspaper, outdoors, political, professional, radio and TV, religious, social, social service, and student government. Popular campus events include Unity Fest, spring series, and art shows.

Sports: There are 4 intercollegiate sports for men and 7 for women, and 18 intramural sports for men and 18 for women. Facilities include a weight room, tennis courts, a swimming pool, and a recreation center with climbing walls, racquetball courts, an elevated running track, and workout facilities.

Disabled Students: 98% of the campus is accessible. Wheelchair ramps, elevators, special parking, specially equipped rest rooms, special class scheduling, lowered drinking fountains, and lowered telephones are available.

Services: Counseling and information services are available, as is tutoring in every subject, except accounting. There is a reader service for the blind and remedial math, reading, and writing.

Campus Safety and Security: Measures include 24-hour foot and vehicle patrol, self-defense education, security escort services, and informal discussions. There are pamphlets/posters/films, lighted pathways/sidewalks, a crime watch program, an emergency contact service, and first-aid and CPR courses.

Programs of Study: Mesa State confers B.A., B.S., B.B.A., and B.S.N. degrees. Associate and master's degrees are also awarded. Bachelor's degrees are awarded in BIOLOGICAL SCIENCE (biology/biological science), BUSINESS (accounting and business administration and management), COMMUNICATIONS AND THE ARTS (communications, English, and fine arts), COMPUTER AND PHYSICAL SCIENCE (computer science, mathematics, and physical sciences), ENGINEERING AND ENVIRONMENTAL DESIGN (environmental engineering technology), HEALTH PROFESSIONS (nursing), SOCIAL SCIENCE (history, liberal arts/general studies, physical fitness/movement, political science/government, psychology, social science, and sociology). Nursing and allied health, natural science, and math are the strongest academically. Business, natural science, and math are the largest.

Required: To graduate, students must complete a minimum of 123 credits, with 40 hours in upper-level courses in the emphasis area and a minimum GPA of 2.0. All students must take English 111 and 112 as well as 33 hours of general education courses and 3 hours of phys ed. A comprehensive exam is required.

Special: Mesa State offers internships in many of its programs, including one in the state legislature, a Washington semester, work-study programs, student-designed majors in selected studies, and the B.A.-B.S. degree in several majors. Nondegree study for students over 20 years of age and credit for life, military, and work experience are available. There are 10 national honor societies, a freshman honors program, and 5 departmental honors programs.

Faculty/Classroom: 62% of faculty are male; 38%, female. All teach undergraduates. No introductory courses are taught by graduate students. The average class size in an introductory lecture is 30; in a laboratory, 20; and in a regular course, 30.

Requirements: The SAT I or ACT is required, with a minimum composite score of 940 on the SAT I or 21 on the ACT. Applicants must be graduates of an accredited secondary school or hold the GED. The college prefers that students complete 4 years of high school English, 3 each of math, science, and social studies, 2 of foreign language, and 1 of history. An essay, an interview, and an audition for some classes are recommended. Mesa State requires applicants to be in the upper 75% of their class. A GPA of 2.6 is required. AP and CLEP credits are accepted. Important factors in the admissions decision are recommendations by school officials, personality/intangible qualities, and evidence of special talent.

Procedure: Freshmen are admitted to all sessions. Entrance exams should be taken late in the junior year or early in the senior year. There is a deferred admissions plan and a rolling admissions plan. Check with the school for current deadlines. The fall 2003 application fee was $30. Applications are accepted on computer disk and on-line.

Transfer: Applicants must have a minimum GPA of 2.0 with 30 semester hours; otherwise, they must meet the criteria for entering freshmen.

Visiting: There are regularly scheduled orientations for prospective students, including advising sessions. There are guides for informal visits and visitors may sit in on classes. To schedule a visit, contact the Admissions Office.

Financial Aid: The FAFSA is required. Check with the school for current deadlines.

International Students: They must score 525 on the written TOEFL or the MELAB and the Comprehensive English Language Test. They must also take the SAT I or the ACT.

Computers: The mainframe is a DEC VAX. All enrolled students have access to the network and more than 260 computers in 6 labs plus other locations. All students may access the system. There are no time limits. Check with the school for current fee. It is strongly recommended that all students have a personal computer.

Admissions Contact: Tyre Bush, Director of Admissions and Recruitment. A video is available. E-mail: *tbush@mesastate.edu* Web: *www.mesastate.edu*

METROPOLITAN STATE COLLEGE OF DENVER C-2
Denver, CO 80217-3362   (303) 556-3058; Fax: (303) 556-6345

Full-time: 4540 men, 5820 women	**Faculty:** 446
Part-time: 3325 men, 4765 women	**Ph.D.s:** n/av
Graduate: none	**Student/Faculty:** 23 to 1
Year: semesters, summer session	**Tuition:** $2340 ($8190)
Application Deadline: see profile	**Room & Board:** n/app
Freshman Class: n/av	
SAT I or ACT: required	**LESS COMPETITIVE**

Metropolitan State College of Denver, founded in 1963, is a public commuter institution offering degree programs in the liberal arts and sciences, business, and professional studies, as well as individualized degree programs. There are 3 undergraduate schools. Figures in the above capsule and in this profile are approximate. In addition to regional accreditation, Metro State has baccalaureate program accreditation with ABET, CSWE, NASM, NCATE, NLN, and NRPA. The library contains 692,677 volumes, 1,053,419 microform items, and 16,975 audio/video tapes/CDs, and subscribes to 4150 periodicals. Computerized library services include the card catalog, interlibrary loans, and database searching. Special learning facilities include a learning resource center, art gallery, radio station, a world indoor airport, a writing center, and student support services. The 175-acre campus is in an urban area in Denver. There are 38 buildings.

Student Life: 99% of undergraduates are from Colorado. Students are from 40 states, 66 foreign countries, and Canada. 96% are from public schools. 71% are white; 12% Hispanic. The average age of freshmen is 22; all undergraduates, 26. 38% do not continue beyond their first year.

Housing: There are no residence halls. All students commute. All students may keep cars.

Activities: There are no fraternities or sororities. There are 100 groups on campus, including art, band, cheerleading, chess, choir, chorale, chorus, computers, debate, drama, ethnic, gay, honors, international, jazz band, literary magazine, musical theater, newspaper, orchestra, political, professional, radio and TV, religious, social, social service, student government, and symphony. Popular campus events include Club Day, World Friendship Festival, and Family Night.

Sports: There are 5 intercollegiate sports for men and 5 for women, and 10 intramural sports for men and 6 for women. Facilities include playing fields, volleyball, basketball, badminton, racquetball, handball, squash, and tennis courts, a swimming pool, a dance studio, a weight room, a fitness center and green room, a 3500-seat events center, an auxiliary gym, and a three-quarter-mile jogging path.

Disabled Students: 90% of the campus is accessible. Wheelchair ramps, elevators, special parking, specially equipped rest rooms, special class scheduling, lowered drinking fountains, and lowered telephones are available. There are also telephones, tapes, and classroom aids for the hearing impaired, an adaptive computer lab, testing accommodations, sign-language and oral interpreters, priority registration, and a resource and referral library available.

Services: Counseling and information services are available, as is tutoring in most subjects. ESL services and an adult learning services office are available.

Campus Safety and Security: Measures include 24-hour foot and vehicle patrol, self-defense education, security escort services, and shuttle buses. There are informal discussions, pamphlets/posters/films, emergency telephones, lighted pathways/sidewalks, bicycle registration, and date/acquaintance rape education seminars.

Programs of Study: Metro State confers B.A., B.S., and B.F.A. degrees. Bachelor's degrees are awarded in BIOLOGICAL SCIENCE (biology/biological science), BUSINESS (accounting, banking and finance, hospitality management services, management science, marketing/retailing/merchandising, and recreation and leisure services), COMMUNICATIONS AND THE ARTS (art, communications, English, fine arts, industrial design, journalism, modern language, music performance, Spanish, and speech/debate/rhetoric), COMPUTER AND PHYSICAL SCIENCE (atmospheric sciences and meteorology, chemistry, computer management, computer science, information sciences and systems, mathematics, and physics), EDUCATION (music and physical), ENGINEERING AND ENVIRONMENTAL DESIGN (airline piloting and navi-

gation, aviation administration/management, aviation computer technology, civil engineering technology, electrical/electronics engineering technology, environmental science, industrial administration/management, industrial engineering technology, land use management and reclamation, mechanical engineering technology, survey and mapping technology, and surveying engineering), HEALTH PROFESSIONS (health care administration and nursing), SOCIAL SCIENCE (African American studies, anthropology, behavioral science, criminal justice, economics, history, human services, Mexican-American/Chicano studies, philosophy, physical fitness/movement, political science/government, psychology, social work, sociology, and urban studies). Criminal justice, psychology, and computer information systems are the largest.

Required: To graduate, students must complete at least 120 credit hours, 40 of which must be upper division, and 30 in the major, with a minimum overall GPA of 2.0. There are 3 levels of general studies requirements, totaling 33 hours and including a multicultural requirement and a senior experience.

Special: Metro State offers co-op and service-learning programs in most majors, and cross-registration with a consortium of state colleges and the University of Colorado at Denver. Internships, study abroad, work-study programs, dual majors, student-designed majors, nondegree study, and pass/fail options are available. There are 9 national honor societies, a freshman honors program, and 10 departmental honors programs.

Faculty/Classroom: 56% of faculty are male; 44%, female. All teach undergraduates. The average class size in an introductory lecture is 25; in a laboratory, 14; and in a regular course, 19.

Admissions: 3 freshmen graduated first in their class.

Requirements: The SAT I or ACT is required. In addition, applicants should be graduates of an accredited secondary school, with 15 Carnegie units. The GED is accepted. AP and CLEP credits are accepted. Important factors in the admissions decision are recommendations by school officials, extracurricular activities record, and evidence of special talent.

Procedure: Freshmen are admitted to all sessions. Entrance exams should be taken prior to application. There is a rolling admissions plan. Check with the school for current deadlines. The application fee is $25. Applications are accepted on-line.

Transfer: 2126 transfer students enrolled in a recent year. Applicants must have a 2.0 GPA and be in good standing at their previous school. Some probationary transfers are considered. 30 of 120 credits required for the bachelor's degree must be completed at Metro State.

Visiting: There are regularly scheduled orientations for prospective students, including class scheduling and registration, college services and resources, transfer of credit, academic advising, choice of major, career counseling, and assessment testing if needed. There are guides for informal visits and visitors may sit in on classes. To schedule a visit, contact the Office of Admissions.

Financial Aid: In a recent year, 47% of undergraduates worked part time. Average annual earnings from campus work were $5000. The average financial indebtedness of a recent graduate was $18,222. Metro State is a member of CSS. The FAFSA is required. Check with the school for current deadlines.

International Students: In a recent year, there were 128 international students enrolled. They must score 500 on the written TOEFL. The SAT I or ACT is required if the applicant is under 20 and has graduated from a U.S. high school.

Computers: The mainframe is a Hitachi EX027. There is a DEC ALPHA mini computer along with about 450 PCs housed in 24 different labs. NeXT, Pentium II, and Mac systems are available. All students may access the system. Labs are open 96 hours a week, and 64 call-up lines are available 24 hours a day. There are no time limits. Check with the school for current fee.

Graduates: In a recent year, 2050 bachelor's degrees were awarded. The most popular majors were behavioral science (9%), computer information systems (7%), and criminal justice (7%). In an average class, 4% graduate in 4 years or less, 13% graduate in 5 years or less, and 20% graduate in 6 years or less. 181 companies recruited on campus in a recent year. Of a recent graduating class, 72% were employed within 6 months of graduation.

Admissions Contact: Office of Admissions. A video is available. Web: *www.mscd.edu* or *gopher://mscdgopher*

NAROPA UNIVERSITY
Boulder, CO 80302-6697

C-2

(303) 546-5295
(800) 772-6951; Fax: (303) 546-3572

Full-time: 164 men, 233 women
Part-time: 20 men, 32 women
Graduate: 223 men, 500 women
Year: semesters
Application Deadline: January 15
Freshman Class: 100 applied, 95 accepted, 39 enrolled
SAT I Verbal/Math: 560/555

Faculty: 35
Ph.D.s: 40%
Student/Faculty: 11 to 1
Tuition: $15,764
Room & Board: $7600

ACT: 19

SPECIAL

Naropa University, founded in 1974, is a private, nonprofit, nonsectarian, Buddhist-inspired, experiential liberal arts institution. It offers undergraduate and graduate degrees in the arts, social sciences, and the humanities. The library contains 28,000 volumes and 2000 audio/video tapes/CDs, and subscribes to 125 periodicals. Computerized library services include the card catalog, interlibrary loans, database searching, and Internet access. Special learning facilities include an art gallery, 2 meditation halls, a writing center, a volunteer center, a community arts center, and a career center. The 12-acre campus is in an urban area in Boulder. Including any residence halls, there are 19 buildings.

Student Life: 74% of undergraduates are from out of state, mostly the West. Students are from 46 states, 16 foreign countries, and Canada. 74% are white. The average age of freshmen is 22; all undergraduates, 24. 32% do not continue beyond their first year.

Housing: 26 students can be accommodated in college housing, which includes coed dormitories. On-campus housing is guaranteed for the freshman year only and is available on a first-come, first-served basis. 99% of students commute. Alcohol is not permitted. All students may keep cars.

Activities: There are no fraternities or sororities. There are 20 groups on campus, including chorus, dance, drama, environmental, ethnic, gay, international, literary magazine, newspaper, political, professional, religious, social, social service, and student government. Popular campus events include African dance and drumming, Gay Pride Week, and cultural festivals.

Sports: There is 1 intramural sport for men and 1 for women.

Disabled Students: 65% of the campus is accessible. Wheelchair ramps, elevators, special parking, specially equipped rest rooms, special class scheduling, lowered drinking fountains, and lowered telephones are available.

Services: Counseling and information services are available, as is tutoring in some subjects, including writing. There is a reader service for the blind.

Campus Safety and Security: Measures include self-defense education, security escort services, informal discussions, and pamphlets/posters/films. There are lighted pathways/sidewalks and an evening foot and vehicle patrol.

Programs of Study: Naropa confers B.A. and B.F.A. degrees. Master's degrees are also awarded. Bachelor's degrees are awarded in COMMUNICATIONS AND THE ARTS (creative writing, literature, performing arts, and visual and performing arts), EDUCATION (early childhood), ENGINEERING AND ENVIRONMENTAL DESIGN (environmental science), SOCIAL SCIENCE (interdisciplinary studies, psychology, and religion). Psychology, interdisciplinary studies, and religious studies are the largest.

Required: Students must complete 120 credits, 27 to 37 in the major, with a 2.0 average GPA. An extensive core curriculum includes courses in contemplative practices, world wisdom studies, cultural and historical studies, artistic process, leadership and service, healing arts, communication arts, and complex systems. A writing proficiency exam is required.

Special: Cross-registration with the University of Colorado, work-study programs, internships, dual majors, and student-designed majors are available, as well as study abroad in Bali, Nepal, India, the Czech Republic, and Costa Rica. Volunteer opportunities are also available.

Faculty/Classroom: 40% of faculty are male; 60%, female. 56% teach undergraduates. No introductory courses are taught by graduate students. The average class size in a regular course is 12.

Admissions: 95% of the 2003-2004 applicants were accepted. The SAT I scores for the 2003-2004 freshman class were: Math--33% below 500, 50% between 500 and 599, and 17% between 600 and 700. The ACT scores for the 2003-2004 freshman class were: 66% below 21, and 33% between 21 and 23.

Requirements: A high school transcript, an interview, 2 recommendations, and an essay are required. The GED is accepted. A GPA of 2.5 is required. AP and CLEP credits are accepted. Important factors in the admissions decision are personality/intangible qualities, evidence of special talent, and recommendations by school officials.

Procedure: Freshmen are admitted fall and spring. There is a deferred admissions plan. Applications should be filed by January 15 for fall entry and October 15 for spring entry, along with a $35 fee. Notification is sent on a rolling basis. Applications are accepted on-line through the university web site *www.naropa.edu.*

Transfer: 100 transfer students enrolled in 2003-2004. Requirements for transfer students are unique to each academic department. 60 of 120 credits required for the bachelor's degree must be completed at Naropa.

Visiting: There are regularly scheduled orientations for prospective students, including daily tours, class visitation, and meetings with counselors. There are guides for informal visits and visitors may sit in on classes. To schedule a visit, contact the Visitation Coordinator at (303) 546-3548 or *admissions@naropa.edu.*

Financial Aid: In 2003-2004, 67% of all full-time students received some form of financial aid. 64% of full-time freshmen and 67% of continuing full-time students received need-based aid. The average freshman award was $16,957. Need-based scholarships or need-based grants averaged $7323 ($15,000 maximum); and need-based self-help aid (loans and jobs) averaged $9090 ($12,625 maximum). 22% of undergraduates work part time. Average annual earnings from campus work are $1762. The average financial indebtedness of the 2003 graduate was $20,000. The FAFSA is required. The priority date for freshman financial aid applications for fall entry is March 1.

International Students: There are 19 international students enrolled. They must score 550 on the written TOEFL.

Computers: 70 PCs are available for student use in 2 lab locations with Internet access. Students can access the mainframe for web registration and student information. All students may access the system. There are no time limits and no fees. It is strongly recommended that all students have a personal computer.

Graduates: From July 1, 2002 to June 30, 2003, 94 bachelor's degrees were awarded. The most popular majors were psychology (42%), performing arts (15%), and writing and literature (14%). In an average class, 4% graduate in 3 years or less, 24% graduate in 4 years or less, and 32% graduate in 5 years or less.

Admissions Contact: Susan Boyle, Assistant Vice President of Admissions and Marketing. E-mail: *admissions@naropa.edu*
Web: *www.naropa.edu*

REGIS UNIVERSITY
Denver, CO 80221-1099

C-2

(303) 458-4900
(800) 388-2366, ext. 4900; Fax: (303) 964-5534

Full-time: 425 men, 675 women
Part-time: none
Graduate: none
Year: semesters, summer session
Application Deadline: open
Freshman Class: n/av
SAT I or ACT: required

Faculty: 68
Ph.D.s: 95%
Student/Faculty: 15 to 1
Tuition: $20,950
Room & Board: $7600

COMPETITIVE+

Regis University, founded in 1877, is a private, Roman Catholic liberal arts institution operated by the Jesuits. There are 3 undergraduate schools. Figures in the above capsule and in this profile are approximate. In addition to regional accreditation, Regis has baccalaureate program accreditation with CAHEA, NCATE, and NLN. The library contains 420,799 volumes, 136,379 microform items, and 104,698 audio/video tapes/CDs, and subscribes to 3979 periodicals. Computerized library services include the card catalog, interlibrary loans, and database searching. Special learning facilities include a learning resource center and radio station. The 90-acre campus is in a suburban area in north Denver. Including any residence halls, there are 12 buildings.

Student Life: 57% of undergraduates are from Colorado. Students are from 40 states, 23 foreign countries, and Canada. 77% are white. 56% are Catholic; 55% Buddhist, Latter-day Saints, and unknown; 9% Protestant. The average age of freshmen is 18; all undergraduates, 21. 50% of freshmen remain to graduate.

Housing: 600 students can be accommodated in college housing, which includes coed dorms. On-campus housing is guaranteed for all 4 years and is available on a first-come, first-served basis. 63% of students commute. All students may keep cars.

Activities: There are no fraternities or sororities. There are 30 groups on campus, including cheerleading, choir, chorus, dance, ethnic, forensics, gay, honors, international, leadership, literary magazine, newspaper, political, professional, radio and TV, religious, social, social service, student government, and yearbook. Popular campus events include Mistletoe Madness, Ranger Week, and Hall Olympics.

Sports: There are 6 intercollegiate sports for men and 6 for women, and 8 intramural sports for men and 8 for women. Facilities include a 2800-seat gym, a pool, tennis courts, and playing fields.

Disabled Students: 80% of the campus is accessible. Wheelchair ramps, elevators, special parking, specially equipped rest rooms, special class scheduling, lowered drinking fountains, and lowered telephones are available.

Services: Counseling and information services are available, as is tutoring in every subject. There is a reader service for the blind.

Campus Safety and Security: Measures include 24-hour foot and vehicle patrol, self-defense education, security escort services, and pamphlets/posters/films. There are emergency telephones and lighted pathways/sidewalks.

Programs of Study: Regis confers B.A., B.S., and B.S.N. degrees. Master's degrees are also awarded. Bachelor's degrees are awarded in BIOLOGICAL SCIENCE (biochemistry, biology/biological science, and neurosciences), BUSINESS (accounting, business administration and management, business economics, international business management, and marketing/retailing/merchandising), COMMUNICATIONS AND THE ARTS (communications, English, French, and Spanish), COMPUTER AND PHYSICAL SCIENCE (chemistry, computer science, and mathematics), ENGINEERING AND ENVIRONMENTAL DESIGN (engineering), HEALTH PROFESSIONS (medical records administration/services and nursing), SOCIAL SCIENCE (economics, history, philosophy, political science/government, prelaw, psychology, religion, and sociology). Business is the largest.

Required: Students must complete 128 credit hours with a minimum GPA of 2.0. Required courses include 58 credit hours in the core curriculum, of which 12 are seminars, 7 to 8 are math and natural science, 6 are in literature/humanities, social science, religious studies, and philosophy, and 3 each are in economics, communication arts, and fine arts.

Special: Cross-registration is possible with Denver University and Metropolitan State. Internships, study abroad, and work-study programs with Regis are available. The college offers B.A.-B.S. degrees, dual majors, student-designed majors, a 3-2 engineering degree with Washington University, and pass/fail options. There is 1 national honor society and a freshman honors program.

Faculty/Classroom: 57% of faculty are male; 43%, female. All both teach and do research. The average class size in an introductory lecture is 30; in a laboratory, 15; and in a regular course, 30.

Admissions: 8 freshmen graduated first in their class.

Requirements: The SAT I or ACT is required. In addition, applicants should be graduates of an accredited secondary school. The GED is accepted. Students should have completed 16 high school academic credits, including 4 years of English, 3 each of math, science, and history, 2 of a foreign language, and 1 to 2 of social studies. A recommendation from the high school counselor and an essay are required. An interview is recommended. A GPA of 2.3 is required. AP and CLEP credits are accepted. Important factors in the admissions decision are recommendations by school officials, leadership record, and extracurricular activities record.

Procedure: Freshmen are admitted fall and spring. Entrance exams should be taken in the fall. There is a deferred admissions plan and a rolling admissions plan. Applications are accepted on-line or on computer disk. Application deadlines are open. Application fee is $40. A waiting list is an active part of the admissions procedure.

Transfer: Applicants must have a GPA of 2.5. All previous college work is considered. The college reviews each applicant individually. 30 of 128 credits required for the bachelor's degree must be completed at Regis.

Visiting: There are guides for informal visits and visitors may sit in on classes and stay overnight. To schedule a visit, contact the Admissions Office.

Financial Aid: In a recent year, 90% of all full-time students received some form of financial aid. The FAFSA and the college's own financial statement are required. Check with the school for current deadlines.

International Students: The school actively recruits these students. They must score 550 on the written TOEFL or 213 on the electronic version or take the MELAB, and the ELS/ALA.

Computers: The mainframe is a DEC VAX 11/785. The mainframe and PCs systems are available 24 hours a day in the computer labs. All students may access the system. There are no time limits and no fees. It is strongly recommended that all students have a personal computer.

Admissions Contact: Vic Davolt, Director of Admissions. A video is available. E-mail: *regisadm@regis.edu*

UNITED STATES AIR FORCE ACADEMY
USAFA, CO 80840-5025 D-3

(719) 333-2520
(800) 443-9266; Fax: (719) 333-3012

Full-time: 3450 men, 707 women	**Faculty:** 577; IIB, +$
Part-time: none	**Ph.D.s:** 57%
Graduate: none	**Student/Faculty:** 8 to 1
Year: semesters, summer session	**Tuition:** 0
Application Deadline: January 31	**Room & Board:** 0
Freshman Class: 10,780 applied, 1631 accepted, 1270 enrolled	
SAT I Verbal/Math: 630/663	**HIGHLY COMPETITIVE+**

The United States Air Force Academy, the newest of the United States service academies, was founded in 1954 and is a public institution. Graduates receive the B.S. degree and a second lieutenant's commission in the regular Air Force. All graduates are obligated to serve at least 5 years of active duty military service. Tuition, room, board, medical, and dental expenses are paid by the U.S. government. Each cadet receives a monthly salary from which to pay for uniforms, supplies, and personal expenses. Entering freshmen are required to deposit $2,500 to defray the initial costs of uniforms and personal expenses incurred upon entry. Students who are unable to submit the full deposit will receive a reduced monthly cash allotment until prescribed levels are reached. In addition

to regional accreditation, USAFA has baccalaureate program accreditation with ABET and CSAB. The 3 libraries contain 688,801 volumes, 621,792 microform items, and 4860 audio/video tapes/CDs, and subscribe to 2106 periodicals. Computerized library services include the card catalog, interlibrary loans, and database searching. Special learning facilities include a learning resource center, art gallery, planetarium, radio station, TV station, a field engineering and readiness lab, and an aeronautics lab/aeronautical research center. The 18,000-acre campus is in a suburban area 70 miles south of downtown Denver and 8 miles north of downtown Colorado Springs. Including any residence halls, there are 13 buildings.

Student Life: 95% of undergraduates are from out of state. Students are from 50 states and 26 foreign countries. 81% are white. 63% are Protestant; 30% Catholic; 12% claim no religious affiliation. The average age of freshmen is 18; all undergraduates, 20. 18% do not continue beyond their first year; 71% remain to graduate.

Housing: 4400 students can be accommodated in college housing, which includes coed dorms. On-campus housing is guaranteed for all 4 years. All students live on campus. Alcohol is not permitted. Upperclassmen may keep cars.

Activities: There are no fraternities or sororities. There are 87 groups on campus, including band, chamber music, cheerleading, chess, choir, chorale, chorus, computers, drama, drill team, drum and bugle corps, ethnic, film, forensics, honors, literary magazine, marching band, musical theater, newspaper, pep band, photography, professional, radio and TV, religious, show choir, social, social service, student government, and yearbook. Popular campus events include Acceptance Parade, Christmas "Messiah" program, and Graduation Week.

Sports: There are 17 intercollegiate sports for men and 10 for women, and 13 intramural sports for men and 12 for women. Facilities include a 47,000-seat stadium, a cadet gym, a field house, 143 acres of athletic facilities and recreational areas, 3 basketball gyms, 4 indoor tennis courts, an Olympic-size swimming pool, a water polo pool, 3 squash and 19 racquetball/handball courts, and 2 weight training rooms.

Disabled Students: Wheelchair ramps, elevators, special parking, specially equipped rest rooms, and lowered drinking fountains are available.

Services: Counseling and information services are available, as is tutoring in every subject, including studying techniques and English as a second language. There is remedial math, reading, and writing.

Campus Safety and Security: Measures include 24-hour foot and vehicle patrol, self-defense education, security escort services, and informal discussions. There are pamphlets/posters/films, emergency telephones, and lighted pathways/sidewalks.

Programs of Study: USAFA confers the B.S. degree. Bachelor's degrees are awarded in BIOLOGICAL SCIENCE (biology/biological science), BUSINESS (management science and operations research), COMMUNICATIONS AND THE ARTS (English), COMPUTER AND PHYSICAL SCIENCE (atmospheric sciences and meteorology, chemistry, computer science, mathematics, physics, and science), ENGINEERING AND ENVIRONMENTAL DESIGN (aeronautical engineering, aerospace studies, civil engineering, computer engineering, electrical/electronics engineering, engineering, engineering and applied science, engineering mechanics, environmental engineering, mechanical engineering, and military science), SOCIAL SCIENCE (behavioral science, economics, geography, history, humanities, international studies, law, political science/government, psychology, and social science). Engineering and basic sciences are the strongest academically. Engineering, management, and social sciences are the largest.

Required: Cadets must complete the requirements for the core curriculum and for an academic major. They must be proficient in phys ed and military training, and demonstrate an aptitude for commissioned service and leadership. A total of 145 to 161 semester hours is required, with a minimum GPA of 2.0, to graduate. The required curriculum includes 9 hours of military arts and sciences, 6 hours of phys ed, and 1 hour of aviation.

Special: All cadets receive orientation flights in Air Force aircraft and take aviation science courses. A semester exchange program is available with the French Air Force Academy and U.S. Army, Naval, and Coast Guard academies. Freshman classes start in June, and basic cadet training must be completed before academics begin in August. Work-study programs are available, and dual majors are possible in all areas. There is an interdisciplinary space operations major. There are 2 national honor societies.

Faculty/Classroom: 85% of faculty are male; 15%, female. All teach undergraduates and 10% also do research. The average class size in an introductory lecture is 17; in a laboratory, 17; and in a regular course, 17.

Admissions: 15% of the 2003-2004 applicants were accepted. The SAT I scores for the 2003-2004 freshman class were: Verbal--2% below 500, 32% between 500 and 599, 51% between 600 and 700, and 15% above 700; Math--1% below 500, 20% between 500 and 599, 54% between 600 and 700, and 25% above 700. 80% of the current freshmen were in the top fifth of their class; 85% were in the top two fifths. 133 freshmen graduated first in their class.

Requirements: The SAT I or ACT is required. In addition, candidates must be U.S. citizens between 17 and 22 years of age, unmarried, with no dependents, and nominated from a legal source. Students should have completed 4 years each of English, math, and lab sciences, and 2 years each of social sciences and foreign languages. A computer course is recommended. A personal interview is required, as is an essay and a drug and alcohol abuse certificate. A GPA of 2.0 is required. AP credits are accepted. Important factors in the admissions decision are advanced placement or honor courses, leadership record, and personality/intangible qualities.

Procedure: Freshmen are admitted in the summer. Entrance exams should be taken in the spring of the junior year. Applications should be filed by January 31 for fall entry. Notification of early decision is sent beginning in November; regular decision, in March.

Transfer: All students must enter as freshmen and attend 4 years. All 145 to 161 credits required for the bachelor's degree must be completed at USAFA.

Visiting: There are regularly scheduled orientations for prospective students, consisting of a 2-day orientation held in March and April. Students are given briefings by the superintendent, the commandant of cadets, the dean of cadets, and the director of athletics. Students stay overnight in the dorms and shadow their escort cadets the second day, attending classes, training, and meals. There is also a daily tour. There are guides for informal visits. To schedule a visit, contact the Director of Admissions.

International Students: There are 48 international students enrolled. They must take the SAT I or the ACT.

Computers: The mainframes are a Unisys and an HP. All cadets reimburse the academy for a PC upon entry. These PCs are all networked to a 10,000 drop fiber-optic LAN called USAFANET. Gateways to the Internet are provided as well, and cadets have limited access to the Unisys. All students may access the system 24 hours per day. There are no time limits and no fees. All students are required to have personal computers.

Graduates: The most popular majors were engineering (30%), management (19%), and social sciences (11%). In an average class, 71% graduate in 4 years or less, and 77% graduate in 5 years or less. Of the 2002 graduating class, 3% were enrolled in graduate school within 6 months of graduation and all were employed.

Admissions Contact: Rolland Stoneman, Associate Director, Admissions/Selections. Web: *www.usafa.edu/rr/*

UNIVERSITY OF COLORADO SYSTEM

The University of Colorado System, established in 1876, is a public system. It is governed by an elected board of regents and the chief administrator is the president. The primary goal of the system is comprehensive research, instruction, and public service. The total enrollment of all four campuses is about 55,000, with 5000 faculty members. The University of Colorado at Boulder ranks fourth among public universities and colleges in overall research expenditures per faculty member. 1 of only 34 public universities belonging to the prestigious Association of American Universities, the University of Colorado at Boulder is the only member institution in the Rocky Mountain area. Profiles of the 4-year campuses in Boulder, Colorado Springs, and Denver are included in this section.

UNIVERSITY OF COLORADO AT BOULDER   C-2
Boulder, CO 80309-0552   **(303) 492-6301; Fax: (303) 492-7115**

Full-time: 12,464 men, 11,398 women	**Faculty:** 1176; I, av$
Part-time: 1295 men, 1029 women	**Ph.D.s:** 90%
Graduate: 3163 men, 2692 women	**Student/Faculty:** 20 to 1
Year: semesters, summer session	**Tuition:** $4020 ($19,508)
Application Deadline: February 15	**Room & Board:** $6754
Freshman Class: 20,920 applied, 16,790 accepted, 5592 enrolled	
SAT I Verbal/Math: 570/600	**ACT:** 25 **VERY COMPETITIVE**

The University of Colorado at Boulder, established in 1876, is a public institution offering undergraduate and graduate programs in arts and sciences, business, engineering, architecture and planning, music, education, and journalism. There are 7 undergraduate and 3 graduate schools. In addition to regional accreditation, CU-Boulder has baccalaureate program accreditation with AACSB, ABET, ACEJMC, NASM, and NCATE. The 5 libraries contain 3,314,432 volumes, 6,507,734 microform items, and 76,041 audio/video tapes/CDs, and subscribe to 24,012 periodicals. Computerized library services include the card catalog, interlibrary loans, and database searching. Special learning facilities include a learning resource center, art gallery, natural history museum, planetarium, radio station, TV station, interactive foreign language video center, mountain research station, and integrated teaching and learning lab in engineering. The 600-acre campus is in a suburban area 30 miles northwest of Denver. Including any residence halls, there are 200 buildings.

Student Life: 67% of undergraduates are from Colorado. Students are from 50 states, more than 100 foreign countries, and Canada. 79% are

white. The average age of freshmen is 19; all undergraduates, 21. 17% do not continue beyond their first year; 83% remain to graduate.

Housing: 6000 students can be accommodated in college housing, which includes coed dorms, on-campus apartments, and married-student housing. In addition, there are honors houses, special-interest houses, and 5 residential academic programs that include housing. On-campus housing is guaranteed for the freshman year only and is available on a first-come, first-served basis. 77% of students commute. All students may keep cars.

Activities: 9% of men belong to 15 national fraternities; 14% of women belong to 4 local and 10 national sororities. There are 293 groups on campus, including art, band, cheerleading, chess, choir, chorale, chorus, computers, dance, drama, drill team, environmental, ethnic, film, gay, honors, international, jazz band, literary magazine, marching band, musical theater, opera, orchestra, pep band, photography, political, professional, radio and TV, religious, social, social service, special interest, student government, symphony, and yearbook. Popular campus events include World Affairs Conference, International Women's Week, and Trivia Bowl.

Sports: There are 7 intercollegiate sports for men and 8 for women, and 16 intramural sports for men and 15 for women. Facilities include a 52,000-seat stadium and an 8700-seat events center, a recreation center that includes an 8-lane swimming pool, diving pool, ice rink, handball and racquetball courts, basketball and squash courts, outdoor tennis courts, weight-training rooms, an indoor running track, and an indoor climbing wall.

Disabled Students: 77% of the campus is accessible. Wheelchair ramps, elevators, special parking, specially equipped rest rooms, special class scheduling, lowered drinking fountains, lowered telephones, assisted classroom listening devices, and TTY, TDD, and TT phone support systems are available.

Services: Counseling and information services are available, as is tutoring in most subjects, including a learning disabilities program and an interpreter for the deaf (curricular and non-curricular). There is a reader service for the blind and remedial writing. There is also a Multicultural Center for Counseling and Community Development, which includes counselors for individuals and groups.

Campus Safety and Security: Measures include 24-hour foot and vehicle patrol, self-defense education, security escort services, and shuttle buses. There are informal discussions, pamphlets/posters/films, emergency telephones, and lighted pathways/sidewalks. Campus police are academy-trained and commissioned officers of the Boulder police force. Additional safety programs and services are detailed on the CU-Boulder police home page: *http://www.colorado.edu/police/*.

Programs of Study: CU-Boulder confers B.A., B.S., B.Env.D., B.F.A., B.Mus., and B.Mus.Ed. degrees. Master's and doctoral degrees are also awarded. Bachelor's degrees are awarded in BIOLOGICAL SCIENCE (biochemistry, cell biology, environmental biology, and molecular biology), BUSINESS (accounting, banking and finance, business administration and management, international business management, management science, marketing management, small business management, and tourism), COMMUNICATIONS AND THE ARTS (advertising, art history and appreciation, broadcasting, Chinese, classics, communications, dance, dramatic arts, English, film arts, fine arts, French, Germanic languages and literature, Italian, Japanese, journalism, linguistics, music, Spanish, and telecommunications), COMPUTER AND PHYSICAL SCIENCE (applied mathematics, astronomy, chemistry, computer science, geology, information sciences and systems, mathematics, and physics), EDUCATION (music), ENGINEERING AND ENVIRONMENTAL DESIGN (aeronautical engineering, architectural engineering, chemical engineering, civil engineering, computer engineering, electrical/electronics engineering, engineering, engineering physics, environmental design, environmental engineering, environmental science, and mechanical engineering), HEALTH PROFESSIONS (exercise science and speech pathology/audiology), SOCIAL SCIENCE (anthropology, Asian/Oriental studies, economics, ethnic studies, geography, German area studies, history, humanities, international relations, philosophy, political science/government, psychology, religion, Russian and Slavic studies, sociology, and women's studies). Engineering, biological sciences, and psychology are the strongest academically. Psychology, biology, and pre-journalism and mass communication are the largest.

Required: For graduation, students must complete at least 120 credits, including a minimum of 30 in the major. A GPA of at least 2.0 is required. Other requirements vary by undergraduate college and program.

Special: Sewall, Farrand, and other residential programs for freshmen and sophomores offer a small liberal arts college atmosphere while taking advantage of the resources of a major university. A residential program in Baker Hall Village offers courses in the environmental sciences. Student-designed and dual majors, internships, 5-year B.A.- M.A. degrees, and cooperative programs in business and engineering are available. Study abroad in more than 60 countries, work-study programs in federal labs, internships, a 3-2 engineering degree, and cross registration with other University of Colorado campuses are offered. There are 15 national honor societies, including Phi Beta Kappa, a freshman honors program, and 47 departmental honors programs.

Faculty/Classroom: 62% of faculty are male; 38%, female. All both teach and do research. Graduate students teach 20% of introductory courses. The average class size in an introductory lecture is 42; in a laboratory, 17; and in a regular course, 25.

Admissions: 80% of the 2003-2004 applicants were accepted. The SAT I scores for the 2003-2004 freshman class were: Verbal--12% below 500, 48% between 500 and 599, 35% between 600 and 700, and 6% above 700; Math--9% below 500, 40% between 500 and 599, 42% between 600 and 700, and 9% above 700. The ACT scores were 9% below 21, 24% between 21 and 23, 33% between 24 and 26, 19% between 27 and 28, and 16% above 28. 44% of the current freshmen were in the top fifth of their class; 80% were in the top two fifths. There were 6 National Merit finalists. 155 freshmen graduated first in their class.

Requirements: The SAT I or ACT is required. In addition, applicants must have completed 16 credits of high school work as identified by the University of Colorado minimum Academic Preparation Standards. Students are asked to write a personal statement. Interviews are not used in the decision-making process. Auditions are required for consideration to the College of Music. Portfolios are discouraged. Students with a GED are considered on an individual basis. A GPA of 2.0 is required. AP and CLEP credits are accepted. Important factors in the admissions decision are advanced placement or honor courses, geographic diversity, and leadership record.

Procedure: Freshmen are admitted to all sessions. Entrance exams should be taken no later than December of the senior year. There is a rolling admissions plan and a deferred admissions plan. Applications should be filed by February 15 for fall entry, October 1 for spring entry, and February 15 for summer entry, along with a $50 fee. Notification is sent on a rolling basis. 1007 applicants were on the 2003 waiting list; 186 were admitted. Applications are accepted on-line through *www.colorado.edu/prospective*.

Transfer: 1386 transfer students enrolled in 2002-2003. All applicants must submit official high school and college transcripts. Students who have completed fewer than 30 semester hours must also submit SAT I or ACT results. 30 of 120 credits required for the bachelor's degree must be completed at CU-Boulder.

Visiting: There are regularly scheduled orientations for prospective students, including advising, placement testing, registration, social and campus orientation, and meetings with college deans and faculty. Parents are invited. There are guides for informal visits and visitors may sit in on classes. To schedule a visit, contact the Admissions/Campus Visit Programs at *www.colorado.edu*.

Financial Aid: The information in this section is approximate. In 2003-2004, 58% of all full-time freshmen and 47% of continuing full-time students received some form of financial aid. 30% of full-time freshmen and 29% of continuing full-time students received need-based aid. Need-based scholarships or need-based grants averaged $5847 ($34,123 maximum); need-based self-help aid (loans and jobs) averaged $3151 ($12,420 maximum); and non-need-based athletic scholarships averaged $17,937 ($30,740 maximum). 61% of undergraduates work part time. Average annual earnings from campus work are $2445. The average financial indebtedness of the 2003 graduate was $16,002. The FAFSA and tax returns are required. The deadline for filing freshman financial aid applications for fall entry is March 1.

International Students: There are 332 international students enrolled. They must score 500 on the written TOEFL or 173 (220 for engineering) on the electronic version or take the MELAB. Other tests or verification of proficiency will be considered on an individual basis.

Computers: The mainframe is an Hitachi Data Systems 3090. More than 1200 public access PCs are available in the computer labs, classroom buildings, dorms, and libraries. All have Internet, Web, and Personal Lookup access. All students have e-mail and Internet accounts on the academic mainframe. All students may access the system 24 hours a day. There are no time limits and no fees. It is strongly recommended that all students have a personal computer.

Graduates: From July 1, 2002 to June 30, 2003, 5003 bachelor's degrees were awarded. The most popular majors were psychology (8%), finance (5%), and communication (5%). In an average class, 37% graduate in 4 years or less, 63% graduate in 5 years or less, and 68% graduate in 6 years or less. 400 companies recruited on campus in 2002-2003.

Admissions Contact: Barbara Schneider, Executive Director of Admissions. Web: *www.colorado.edu/admissions/apply.html*

UNIVERSITY OF COLORADO AT COLORADO SPRINGS   D-3
Colorado Springs, CO 80933-7150

(719) 262-3383
(800) 990-8227

Full-time: 1732 men, 2837 women	**Faculty:** 273; IIA, av$
Part-time: 525 men, 781 women	**Ph.D.s:** 89%
Graduate: 727 men, 1018 women	**Student/Faculty:** 17 to 1
Year: semesters, summer session	**Tuition:** $4378 ($19,210)
Application Deadline: July 1	**Room & Board:** $6289
Freshman Class: 2915 applied, 1953 accepted, 911 enrolled	
SAT I Verbal/Math: 531/540	**ACT:** 23 **COMPETITIVE**

The University of Colorado at Colorado Springs, established in 1965, is a public institution with programs in liberal arts, business, engineering, education, and nursing. There are 4 undergraduate and 5 graduate schools. In addition to regional accreditation, UCCS has baccalaureate program accreditation with AACSB, ABET, CSAB, NCATE, and NLN. The library contains 669,757 volumes, 432,872 microform items, and 5979 audio/video tapes/CDs, and subscribes to 2247 periodicals. Computerized library services include the card catalog, interlibrary loans, database searching, and Internet access. Special learning facilities include a learning resource center, art gallery, a center for excellence in oral communication, a math learning center, a science learning center, a writing center, and a language technology center. The 504-acre campus is in an urban area 70 miles south of Denver. Including any residence halls, there are 24 buildings.

Student Life: 92% of undergraduates are from Colorado. Others are from 48 states, 35 foreign countries, and Canada. 78% are white. The average age of freshmen is 18; all undergraduates, 27. 35% do not continue beyond their first year; 40% remain to graduate.

Housing: 600 students can be accommodated in college housing, which includes single-sex and coed dorms. On-campus housing is available on a first-come, first-served basis. 90% of students commute. All students may keep cars.

Activities: 1% of men and about 1% of women belong to 1 national fraternity; 1% of women belong to 1 local sorority. There are 50 groups on campus, including art, choir, computers, dance, drama, ethnic, film, gay, honors, international, literary magazine, newspaper, photography, political, professional, radio and TV, religious, social, and student government. Popular campus events include Winter Holiday Festival and Comedy Night.

Sports: There are 5 intercollegiate sports for men and 5 for women, and 13 intramural sports for men and 12 for women. Facilities include a gym, softball and soccer fields, a multipurpose field, tennis and volleyball courts, and a fitness center.

Disabled Students: 95% of the campus is accessible. Wheelchair ramps, elevators, special parking, specially equipped rest rooms, lowered drinking fountains, and lowered telephones are available.

Services: Counseling and information services are available, as is tutoring in most subjects. There is a reader service for the blind.

Campus Safety and Security: Measures include 24-hour foot and vehicle patrol, self-defense education, security escort services, and shuttle buses. There are informal discussions, pamphlets/posters/films, emergency telephones, and lighted pathways/sidewalks.

Programs of Study: UCCS confers B.A. and B.S. degrees. Master's and doctoral degrees are also awarded. Bachelor's degrees are awarded in BIOLOGICAL SCIENCE (biology/biological science), BUSINESS (business administration and management), COMMUNICATIONS AND THE ARTS (communications, English, fine arts, and Spanish), COMPUTER AND PHYSICAL SCIENCE (chemistry, computer science, mathematics, and physics), ENGINEERING AND ENVIRONMENTAL DESIGN (electrical/electronics engineering), HEALTH PROFESSIONS (health care administration and nursing), SOCIAL SCIENCE (anthropology, economics, geography, history, philosophy, political science/government, psychology, and sociology). Business, engineering, and psychology are the strongest academically.

Required: To graduate, students must complete 124 credit hours, with at least 30 of them in the major, with a minimum GPA of 2.0. All students must take English and a computer literacy course. Other requirements vary with the program.

Special: The university offers work-study, dual majors, nondegree study, and pass/fail options. There are 3 national honor societies, including Phi Beta Kappa.

Faculty/Classroom: 53% of faculty are male; 47%, female. 93% teach undergraduates, and 80% both teach and do research. Graduate students teach 1% of introductory courses. The average class size in an introductory lecture is 32; in a laboratory, 45; and in a regular course, 22.

Admissions: 67% of the 2003-2004 applicants were accepted. The SAT I scores for the 2003-2004 freshman class were: Verbal--29% below 500, 47% between 500 and 599, 19% between 600 and 700, and 5% above 700; Math--28% below 500, 41% between 500 and 599, 29% between 600 and 700, and 2% above 700. The ACT scores were 24% below 21, 21% between 21 and 23, 38% between 24 and 26, 9% between

27 and 28, and 8% above 28. 34% of the current freshmen were in the top fifth of their class; 65% were in the top two fifths.

Requirements: The SAT I or ACT is required, with recommended minimum composite scores of 850 and 18, respectively. Applicants must be graduates of an accredited secondary school. The GED is accepted. Secondary school courses must include 15 high school credits, including 4 years of English, 3 years each of math and science, 2 years each of foreign language and social studies, and 1 academic elective. AP and CLEP credits are accepted. Important factors in the admissions decision are advanced placement or honor courses, evidence of special talent, and recommendations by school officials.

Procedure: Freshmen are admitted to all sessions. Entrance exams should be taken during the senior year. There is a deferred admissions plan. Early decision applications should be filed by April 1; regular applications, by July 1 for fall entry, December 1 for spring entry, and May 1 for summer entry. The fall 2003 application fee was $45. Notification is sent on a rolling basis. Applications are accepted on-line through www.uccs.edu.

Transfer: 732 transfer students enrolled in 2003-2004. Applicants must have a minimum GPA of 2.5 and a minimum of 12 credit hours earned. The school recommends minimum composite scores of 850 on the SAT I or 18 on the ACT. 30 of 124 credits required for the bachelor's degree must be completed at UCCS.

Visiting: There are regularly scheduled orientations for prospective students. There are guides for informal visits and visitors may sit in on classes. To schedule a visit, contact the Marketing Office at (719) 262-3084 or visitcu@uccs.edu.

Financial Aid: In 2003-2004, 70% of all full-time freshmen and 63% of continuing full-time students received some form of financial aid. 47% of full-time freshmen and 54% of continuing full-time students received need-based aid. The average freshman award was $5630. Need-based scholarships or need-based grants averaged $2680 ($10,196 maximum); need-based self-help aid (loans and jobs) averaged $3600 ($25,000 maximum); non-need-based athletic scholarships averaged $2330 ($19,700 maximum); and other non-need-based awards and non-need-based scholarships averaged $2260 ($28,990 maximum). 9% of undergraduates work part time. Average annual earnings from campus work are $3905. The average financial indebtedness of the 2003 graduate was $14,203. UCCS is a member of CSS. The FAFSA is required. The deadline for filing freshman financial aid applications for fall entry is April 1.

International Students: There are 59 international students enrolled. They must score 550 on the written TOEFL and also take the SAT I or the ACT.

Computers: The mainframes are a DEC VAX 4000, 2 DEC VAX Station 3100s, 4 DEC Alphas, 4 DEC Stations, and 6 HP servers running NT/3 UNIX servers. There are 4 labs with a total of 111 PCs and 3 labs with a total of 30 Macs. There are 7 technology classrooms with a total of 240 PCs. All labs and classrooms can access the Web and the campus network. All students may access the system 8 A.M. to 10 P.M. daily. There are no time limits and no fees. It is strongly recommended that all students have a personal computer.

Graduates: From July 1, 2002 to June 30, 2003, 1360 bachelor's degrees were awarded. The most popular majors were business (17%), psychology (14%), and communications (13%). In an average class, 12% graduate in 4 years or less, 20% graduate in 5 years or less, and 29% graduate in 6 years or less. 120 companies recruited on campus in 2002-2003.

Admissions Contact: Admissions Office. E-mail: admrec@uccs.edu. Web: www.uccs.edu

UNIVERSITY OF COLORADO AT DENVER	C-2
Denver, CO 80217-3364	(303) 556-3287; Fax: (303) 556-4838
Full-time: 2171 men, 2652 women	Faculty: 457; IIA, +$
Part-time: 1696 men, 2384 women	Ph.D.s: n/av
Graduate: 2694 men, 3999 women	Student/Faculty: 11 to 1
Year: semesters, summer session	Tuition: $3302 ($14,930)
Application Deadline: July 22	Room & Board: n/app
Freshman Class: 1778 applied, 1244 accepted, 631 enrolled	
SAT I or ACT: required	COMPETITIVE

The University of Colorado at Denver, established in 1912, is a public, commuter institution with programs in the liberal arts and sciences, business, engineering and applied sciences, music, architecture and planning, and education. The enrollment figures in the above capsule are for fall 2002. There are 4 undergraduate and 6 graduate schools. In addition to regional accreditation, CU-Denver has baccalaureate program accreditation with AACSB, ABET, NAAB, NASM, and NCATE. The library contains 607,971 volumes, 1,042,081 microform items, and 16,309 audio/video tapes/CDs, and subscribes to 2380 periodicals. Computerized library services include the card catalog, interlibrary loans, database searching, and Internet access. Special learning facilities include a learning resource center, art gallery, TV station, and a writing center. The campus is in an urban area in downtown Denver.

Student Life: 90% of undergraduates are from Colorado. Students are from 50 states, 82 foreign countries, and Canada. 90% are from public schools. 28% are white. The average age of freshmen is 18; all undergraduates, 25. 33% do not continue beyond their first year; 44% remain to graduate.

Housing: There are no residence halls, but there are off-campus apartments. All students commute. Alcohol is not permitted. All students may keep cars.

Activities: There are no fraternities or sororities. There are 60 groups on campus, including art, chorale, computers, dance, drama, ethnic, gay, honors, international, jazz band, musical theater, newspaper, political, professional, religious, social, social service, and student government. Popular campus events include Fall Festival.

Sports: Facilities include a phys ed building with a pool including a diving well, a weight room, squash, racquetball/handball, and tennis courts, and a basketball half-court, a dance studio, 3 gym arenas, a fitness center and a green room, a 400-meter track, a football/rugby/lacrosse field, softball fields, a baseball field, a soccer field, and a sand volleyball court.

Disabled Students: All of the campus is accessible. Wheelchair ramps, elevators, special parking, specially equipped rest rooms, special class scheduling, lowered drinking fountains, lowered telephones, a transit system, and an adaptive computer lab are available.

Services: Counseling and information services are available, as is tutoring in most subjects. There is a reader service for the blind. There are ESL classes and study skills courses.

Campus Safety and Security: Measures include 24-hour foot and vehicle patrol, self-defense education, security escort services, and shuttle buses. There are informal discussions, pamphlets/posters/films, emergency telephones, lighted pathways/sidewalks, crime prevention programs, and emergency response.

Programs of Study: CU-Denver confers B.A., B.S., and B.F.A degrees. Master's and doctoral degrees are also awarded. Bachelor's degrees are awarded in BIOLOGICAL SCIENCE (biology/biological science), BUSINESS (business administration and management), COMMUNICATIONS AND THE ARTS (communications, creative writing, dramatic arts, English, fine arts, French, music, and Spanish), COMPUTER AND PHYSICAL SCIENCE (applied mathematics, chemistry, computer science, mathematics, and physics), ENGINEERING AND ENVIRONMENTAL DESIGN (civil engineering, electrical/electronics engineering, and mechanical engineering), SOCIAL SCIENCE (anthropology, economics, geography, history, interdisciplinary studies, philosophy, political science/government, psychology, and sociology). Business, engineering, and psychology are the strongest academically. Business administration, biology, and psychology are the largest.

Required: To graduate, students must complete 120 credit hours with a minimum GPA of 2.0. All students must complete the core curriculum courses in addition to the requirements for the major.

Special: Cross-registration is possible with Metropolitan State College, Community College of Denver, and Red Rocks Commmunity College. Concurrent enrollment with any University of Colorado campus is possible. Cooperative programs, 1-semester internships, study abroad in 12 countries, work-study programs, an accelerated degree program in Liberal Arts and Arts and Media, and B.A.-B.S. degrees are available. The university offers dual majors, a general studies degree, nondegree study, and pass/fail options. There are small individualized classes, peer advocates, and workshops. There are 8 national honor societies.

Faculty/Classroom: 62% of faculty are male; 38%, female. The average class size in an introductory lecture is 35; in a laboratory, 16; and in a regular course, 24.

Admissions: 70% of the 2003-2004 applicants were accepted. The SAT I scores for the 2003-2004 freshman class were: Verbal--39% below 500, 43% between 500 and 599, 17% between 600 and 700, and 2% above 700; Math--37% below 500, 42% between 500 and 599, 20% between 600 and 700, and 1% above 700. 17% of the current freshmen were in the top fifth of their class; 41% were in the top two fifths.

Requirements: The SAT I or ACT is required. In addition, preference for admission is given to applicants who rank in the top 30% of their high school graduating class and present a composite score of 21 or higher on the ACT or a combined score of 950 or higher on the SAT I. CU-Denver requires applicants to be in the upper 30% of their class. A GPA of 2.5 is required. AP and CLEP credits are accepted. Important factors in the admissions decision are advanced placement or honor courses, evidence of special talent, and extracurricular activities record.

Procedure: Freshmen are admitted to all sessions. Entrance exams should be taken in the junior or senior year of high school. There is a deferred admissions plan. Applications should be filed by July 22 for fall entry, December 1 for spring entry, and May 3 for summer entry, along with a $40 fee. Notification is sent on a rolling basis.

Transfer: 969 transfer students enrolled in 2002-2003. Applicants for transfer must have earned at least 12 credit hours for admission to liberal arts and sciences and music programs, and 24 credit hours for admission to business and engineering. A minimum GPA of 2.5 is required, or 2.0 if transferring from Colorado School of Mines, Colorado State University, or the University of Colorado at Boulder and Colorado Springs. 30 of 120 credits required for the bachelor's degree must be completed at CU-Denver.

Visiting: There are regularly scheduled orientations for prospective students, including a mini-lecture, a tour of campus, and financial aid and academic advising. There are guides for informal visits and visitors may sit in on classes. To schedule a visit, contact the Office of Admissions.

Financial Aid: In 2003-2004, 33% of all full-time freshmen and 38% of continuing full-time students received some form of financial aid. 17% of full-time freshmen and 29% of continuing full-time students received need-based aid. The average freshman award was $5188. Need-based scholarships or need-based grants averaged $4256; need-based self-help aid (loans and jobs) averaged $2530; and other non-need-based awards and non-need-based scholarships averaged $1272. The average financial indebtedness of the 2003 graduate was $16,075. CU-Denver is a member of CSS. The FAFSA, the college's own financial statement, and tax returns are required. The priority date for freshman financial aid applications for fall entry is April 1.

International Students: There are 239 international students enrolled. The school actively recruits these students. They must score 525 on the written TOEFL or 197 on the electronic version.

Computers: The Denver campus maintains a communications network with more than 2,500 connections. This network provides access to all campus minicomputers and connection to the Auraria Library Online Information System, the World Wide Web, and the Internet. There are more than 2500 PCs located on the campus in 21 teaching labs, 2 public labs, individual labs, and offices. All students may access the system any time. There are no time limits and no fees.

Graduates: From July 1, 2002 to June 30, 2003, 1384 bachelor's degrees were awarded. The most popular majors were business administration (26%), economics (11%), and communications (10%). In an average class, 14% graduate in 4 years or less, 21% graduate in 5 years or less, and 9% graduate in 6 years or less.

Admissions Contact: Barbara Edwards, Director of Admissions.
E-mail: *admissions@cudenver.edu*
Web: *www.cudenver.edu/Admissions/default.htm*

UNIVERSITY OF DENVER
Denver, CO 80208

C-2
(303) 871-2036
(800) 525-9495; Fax: (303) 871-3301

Full-time: 1804 men, 2002 women	**Faculty:** 408; I, -$
Part-time: 82 men, 369 women	**Ph.D.s:** 92%
Graduate: 2239 men, 2733 women	**Student/Faculty:** 9 to 1
Year: quarters, summer session	**Tuition:** $24,873
Application Deadline: February 1	**Room & Board:** $7275
Freshman Class: 4334 applied, 3405 accepted, 1021 enrolled	
SAT I Verbal/Math: 555/567	**ACT:** 24 **VERY COMPETITIVE**

The University of Denver, established in 1864, is a private institution offering degrees in arts and sciences, fine arts, music, business, engineering, and education. Enrollment figures in the above capsule are from fall 2002. There are 7 undergraduate and 6 graduate schools. In addition to regional accreditation, DU has baccalaureate program accreditation with AACSB, ABET, ACS, CSWE, NASAD, and NASM. The 3 libraries contain 1,155,981 volumes, 970,022 microform items, and 1736 audio/video tapes/CDs, and subscribe to 5788 periodicals. Computerized library services include the card catalog, interlibrary loans, and database searching. Special learning facilities include a learning resource center, art gallery, radio station, high-altitude research field station, observatory, and elementary, middle, and high schools. The 123-acre campus is in a suburban area 8 miles southeast of the Denver business district. Including any residence halls, there are 90 buildings.

Student Life: 56% of undergraduates are from out of state, mostly the West. Students are from 50 states, 94 foreign countries, and Canada. 67% are from public schools. 76% are white. The average age of freshmen is 18; all undergraduates, 20. 14% do not continue beyond their first year; 86% remain to graduate.

Housing: 1511 students can be accommodated in college housing, which includes single-sex and coed dorms, on-campus apartments, married-student housing, fraternity houses, and sorority houses. There are honors and special-interest floors. On-campus housing is guaranteed for all 4 years. 57% of students commute. All students may keep cars.

Activities: 28% of men belong to 9 national fraternities; 21% of women belong to 5 national sororities. There are 120 groups on campus, including art, band, cheerleading, chess, choir, chorale, chorus, computers, dance, drama, ethnic, film, gay, honors, international, jazz band, literary magazine, musical theater, newspaper, opera, orchestra, pep band, photography, political, professional, radio and TV, religious, social, social service, student government, symphony, and yearbook. Popular campus events include Winter Carnival, Festival of Nations Celebration, and Pioneers in the Rockies Freshman Camp.

Sports: There are 10 intercollegiate sports for men and 11 for women, and 33 intramural sports for men and 32 for women. Facilities include a sports and wellness center with an ice arena, a community skating rink, a gym, a multipurpose field house, an Olympic-size swimming pool, exercise facilities, a health clinic, a yoga studio, tennis courts, and a playing field.

Disabled Students: Wheelchair ramps, elevators, special parking, specially equipped rest rooms, special class scheduling, lowered drinking fountains, and lowered telephones are available.

Services: Counseling and information services are available, as is tutoring in most subjects. There is a reader service for the blind and remedial math and writing.

Campus Safety and Security: Measures include 24-hour foot and vehicle patrol, security escort services, shuttle buses, and informal discussions. There are pamphlets/posters/films, emergency telephones, lighted pathways/sidewalks, and a bicycle patrol.

Programs of Study: DU confers B.A., B.S., B.F.A., B.M., B.S.Acc., B.S.A.T., B.S.B.A., B.S.Ch., B.S.Comp.E., B.S.E., B.S.E.E., and B.S.M.E. degrees. Master's and doctoral degrees are also awarded. Bachelor's degrees are awarded in AGRICULTURE (animal science), BIOLOGICAL SCIENCE (biochemistry and biology/biological science), BUSINESS (accounting, banking and finance, business administration and management, business economics, hospitality management services, international business management, marketing/retailing/merchandising, and real estate), COMMUNICATIONS AND THE ARTS (art, art history and appreciation, communications, dramatic arts, English, French, German, Italian, jazz, journalism, languages, music, music performance, and Spanish), COMPUTER AND PHYSICAL SCIENCE (astronomy, chemistry, computer science, digital arts/technology, mathematics, physics, science, and statistics), ENGINEERING AND ENVIRONMENTAL DESIGN (computer engineering, construction management, electrical/electronics engineering, environmental science, and mechanical engineering), SOCIAL SCIENCE (anthropology, Asian/Oriental studies, cognitive science, economics, geography, history, international studies, philosophy, political science/government, psychology, public affairs, religion, Russian and Slavic studies, social science, sociology, and women's studies). Communications, psychology, and business are the strongest academically. Communications, accounting, and political science are the largest.

Required: For graduation, students must complete 183 to 204 quarter hours, including 42 to 135 in the major, with a minimum GPA of 2.0. All students must take 12 quarter hours each of English, natural sciences, arts and humanities, and social sciences, 8 of math and computer science, and 4 of oral communication.

Special: DU offers co-op programs, study abroad in more than 45 countries, internships, a Washington quarter, work-study programs, accelerated degree programs, dual majors, a 3-2 engineering program, and a 3-2 business program. Nondegree study and pass/fail options are also available. There are 13 national honor societies, including Phi Beta Kappa, a freshman honors program, and 13 departmental honors programs.

Faculty/Classroom: 68% of faculty are male; 32%, female. Graduate students teach 5% of introductory courses. The average class size in an introductory lecture is 40; in a laboratory, 17; and in a regular course, 20.

Admissions: 79% of the 2003-2004 applicants were accepted. 64% of a recent freshman class were in the top fifth of their class; 78% were in the top two fifths.

Requirements: The SAT I or ACT is required. In addition, applicants must be graduates of an accredited secondary school. The GED is accepted. The university recommends that applicants have 15 to 20 high school academic credits, including 4 in English, 3 to 4 in math, and 2 to 4 each in foreign language, social science, and natural sciences (2 with lab). Course work in the arts is encouraged. An essay is required of all students. A Hyde interview is required of early action applicants only. An audition is required for music applicants, and a portfolio is recommended for art students. AP and CLEP credits are accepted. Important factors in the admissions decision are advanced placement or honor courses, personality/intangible qualities, and evidence of special talent.

Procedure: Freshmen are admitted to all sessions. Entrance exams should be taken by January of the senior year. There are early action, early admissions, and deferred admissions plans. Early action applications should be filed by November 15; regular applications, by February 1 for fall entry, December 1 for winter entry, February 15 for spring entry, and May 15 for summer entry. The fall 2003 application fee was $50. Notification of early action is sent January 15; regular decision, on a rolling basis. Applications are accepted on-line through the university's web site as well as through Common App, CollegeLink, and CollegeView.

Transfer: 229 transfer students enrolled in a recent year. Applicants must submit a transcript from all colleges attended. Those students with fewer than 30 semester hours of college credit must submit a high school record as well. A minimum GPA of 2.0 is required, but a GPA of 3.0 is recommended. 45 of the 183 to 204 quarter credits required for the bachelor's degree must be completed at DU.

Visiting: There are regularly scheduled orientations for prospective students, including an information session and campus tour. Visitors may sit in on classes and stay overnight. To schedule a visit, contact the Appointment Desk in Undergraduate Admissions.

Financial Aid: In a recent year, 74% of all full-time freshmen and 60% of continuing full-time students received some form of financial aid. 38% of full-time freshmen received need-based aid. The average freshman award was $16,314. 26% of undergraduates worked part time. Average annual earnings from campus work were $1400. The average financial indebtedness of a recent graduate was $9700. The FAFSA is required. The deadline for filing freshman financial aid applications for fall entry is February 15.

International Students: In a recent year, there were 526 international students enrolled. The school actively recruits these students. They must score 500 on the written TOEFL or 173 on the electronic version and also take the college's own test and the SAT I or the ACT. The university offers conditional admission.

Computers: The mainframe consists of DEC Alpha 4000 and 4100 servers running both VMS and UNIX. There are more than 500 PCs available in dorms, computer labs, the library, and most classrooms. Internet access is widely available on and off campus. All students may access the system 24 hours a day. There are no time limits and no fees. All students are required to have personal laptop computers.

Graduates: In a recent year, 660 bachelor's degrees were awarded. The most popular majors were communication (8%), biology (7%), and marketing (6%). In an average class, 2% graduate in 3 years or less, 58% graduate in 4 years or less, 68% graduate in 5 years or less, and 69% graduate in 6 years or less. In a recent year, 165 companies recruited on campus. Of a recent graduating class, 33% were enrolled in graduate school within 6 months of graduation and 40% were employed.

Admissions Contact: The Office of Admission.
E-mail: *admission@du.edu* Web: *www.du.edu*

UNIVERSITY OF NORTHERN COLORADO
Greeley, CO 80639

D-1

(970) 351-2881
(888) 700-4UNC; Fax: (970) 351-2984

Full-time: 3624 men, 5642 women	**Faculty:** 439; I, --$
Part-time: 354 men, 591 women	**Ph.D.s:** 78%
Graduate: 600 men, 1623 women	**Student/Faculty:** 21 to 1
Year: semesters, summer session	**Tuition:** $3205 ($12,331)
Application Deadline: August 1	**Room & Board:** $5782
Freshman Class: 7172 applied, 5063 accepted, 2138 enrolled	
SAT I Verbal/Math: 520/520	**ACT:** 22 COMPETITIVE

The University of Northern Colorado, founded in 1890, is a state-supported public institution offering undergraduate and graduate programs in liberal arts and sciences, business, education, health and human sciences, and performing and visual arts. The enrollment and financial aid figures are from 2002. There are 4 undergraduate schools and 1 graduate school. In addition to regional accreditation, UNC has baccalaureate program accreditation with AACSB, ADA, NASM, NCATE, and NLN. The 2 libraries contain 1,002,163 volumes, 1,213,058 microform items, and 44,843 audio/video tapes/CDs, and subscribe to 3621 periodicals. Computerized library services include the card catalog, interlibrary loans, database searching, and Internet access. Special learning facilities include a learning resource center, art gallery, radio station, TV station, and more than 30 partner schools. The 240-acre campus is in a suburban area 50 miles north of Denver. Including any residence halls, there are 46 buildings.

Student Life: 90% of undergraduates are from Colorado. Others are from 48 states, 48 foreign countries, and Canada. 93% are from public schools. 81% are white. The average age of freshmen is 18; all undergraduates, 21. 30% do not continue beyond their first year; 47% remain to graduate.

Housing: 3101 students can be accommodated in college housing, which includes single-sex and coed dormitories, on-campus apartments, off-campus apartments, married-student housing, fraternity houses, and sorority houses. In addition, there are off-campus houses, graduate women's houses, and special-interest floors. On-campus housing is guaranteed for the freshman year only, is available on a first-come, first-served basis, and is available on a lottery system for upperclassmen. 71% of students commute. All students may keep cars.

Activities: 6% of men belong to 7 national fraternities; 4% of women belong to 8 national sororities. There are 93 groups on campus, including art, band, cheerleading, chess, choir, chorale, computers, dance, drama, drill team, ethnic, film, gay, honors, international, jazz band, literary magazine, marching band, musical theater, opera, orchestra, pep band, photography, political, professional, radio and TV, religious, social, social service, student government, symphony, and yearbook. Popular campus events include Hawaiian Luau, Academic Excellence Week, and International Dinner.

Sports: There are 7 intercollegiate sports for men and 9 for women, and 12 intramural sports for men and 10 for women. Facilities include a stadium and a recreation center with 5 gyms, 3 racquetball courts, a weight room and aerobics room, and an indoor track.

Disabled Students: All of the campus is accessible. Wheelchair ramps, elevators, special parking, specially equipped rest rooms, special class scheduling, lowered drinking fountains, lowered telephones, and academic support services such as note taking, transportation, interpreters, adaptive computer instruction, and library assistance are available.

Services: Counseling and information services are available, as is tutoring in most subjects. There is a reader service for the blind, and remedial math, reading, and writing.

Campus Safety and Security: Measures include 24-hour foot and vehicle patrol, security escort services, shuttle buses, and pamphlets/posters/films. There are emergency telephones and lighted pathways/sidewalks.

Programs of Study: UNC confers B.A., B.S., B.A.S., B.A.T., B.M., and B.M.E. degrees. Master's and doctoral degrees are also awarded. Bachelor's degrees are awarded in AGRICULTURE (natural resource management), BIOLOGICAL SCIENCE (biochemistry and biology/biological science), BUSINESS (accounting, business administration and management, management science, and marketing/retailing/merchandising), COMMUNICATIONS AND THE ARTS (advertising, art, communications, dance, dramatic arts, English, fine arts, French, German, graphic design, journalism, music, public relations, Spanish, and telecommunications), COMPUTER AND PHYSICAL SCIENCE (actuarial science, atmospheric sciences and meteorology, chemistry, computer science, earth science, geology, information sciences and systems, mathematics, physics, and statistics), EDUCATION (physical and science), HEALTH PROFESSIONS (allied health, community health work, nursing, rehabilitation therapy, and speech pathology/audiology), SOCIAL SCIENCE (African American studies, criminal justice, dietetics, economics, geography, gerontology, history, interdisciplinary studies, international relations, Mexican-American/Chicano studies, philosophy, physical fitness/movement, political science/government, psychology, social science, and sociology). Business, music, and nursing are the strongest academically. Business, interdisciplinary studies, and nursing are the largest.

Required: Students must earn a minimum of 120 semester hours (some majors require additional hours) with a minimum GPA of 2.0. All students must complete 40 semester hours in required general education courses and meet all degree requirements in the major.

Special: UNC offers internships and co-op programs in many majors and study abroad in England, Australia, Spain, France, and Germany or through the International Student Exchange Program. Dual majors, student-designed majors, credit by exam, and pass/fail options are also available. Cross-registration is available with Aims Community College, and there are accelerated degree programs in nursing and business. There are 8 national honor societies and a freshman honors program.

Faculty/Classroom: 50% of faculty are male; 50%, female. All both teach and do research. Graduate students teach 17% of introductory courses. The average class size in an introductory lecture is 42; in a laboratory, 24; and in a regular course, 28.

Admissions: 71% of the 2003-2004 applicants were accepted. The SAT I scores for the 2003-2004 freshman class were: Verbal--38% below 500, 42% between 500 and 599, 18% between 600 and 700, and 2% above 700; Math--37% below 500, 44% between 500 and 599, 18% between 600 and 700, and 1% above 700. The ACT scores were 31% below 21, 34% between 21 and 23, 24% between 24 and 26, 8% between 27 and 28, and 4% above 28. 28% of the current freshmen were in the top fifth of their class; 59% were in the top two fifths. 14 freshmen graduated first in their class.

Requirements: The SAT I or ACT is required. Admission standards are set by the Colorado Commission on Higher Education, but each applicant is evaluated on an individual basis. In general, an ACT score of 22, or an SAT I composite score of 1000, and a cumulative GPA of 2.9, are required. Graduation from an accredited high school is required. AP and CLEP credits are accepted. Important factors in the admissions decision are recommendations by school officials, evidence of special talent, and advanced placement or honor courses.

Procedure: Freshmen are admitted fall, spring, and summer. Entrance exams should be taken as early as possible. There is a deferred admissions plan. Applications should be filed by August 1 for fall entry, December 20 for spring entry, and May 1 for summer entry. The fall 2003 application fee was $40. Notification is sent on a rolling basis. Applications are accepted on-line through *www.catalog.unco.edu/decide.html.*

Transfer: 953 transfer students enrolled in 2003-2004. Applicants with 30 or more credit hours must have a minimum college GPA of 2.0. Transfer students who have completed fewer than 12 credit hours of college must meet the same criteria for admission as entering freshmen. Transfers with 12 to 29 semester hours must have a minimum 2.5 GPA. 30 of 120 credits required for the bachelor's degree must be completed at UNC.

Visiting: There are regularly scheduled orientations for prospective students, including academic advising, registration, tours, and special activities. There are guides for informal visits and visitors may sit in on classes. To schedule a visit, contact the UNC Visitors Center at (970) 351-2097 or *www.unco.edu/admissions/tourform.html.*

Financial Aid: In 2001-2002, 74% of all full-time freshmen and 69% of continuing full-time students received some form of financial aid. 56% of full-time freshmen and 59% of continuing full-time students received need-based aid. The average freshman award was $6517. Need-based scholarships or need-based grants averaged $3525 ($18,612 maximum); need-based self-help aid (loans and jobs) averaged $6217 ($18,305 maximum); and non-need-based athletic scholarships averaged $3503 ($12,500 maximum). 16% of undergraduates work part time. Average annual earnings from campus work are $1614. The FAFSA is required. The deadline for filing freshman financial aid applications for fall entry is March 1.

International Students: There are 34 international students enrolled. They must score 520 on the written TOEFL or take the MELAB; they must also take the SAT I or the ACT, scoring 1000 on the SAT I or 22 on the ACT.

Computers: The mainframe is an IBM Multiprise 3000H30. Students may access the mainframe from a variety of computer labs, including those in academic buildings, the library, the student center, and residence halls. UNC's 15 computer labs (most with access to networks) include terminals with Macs and PCs. All students may access the system. There are no time limits. The fee is $4.50 per credit hour.

Graduates: From July 1, 2002 to June 30, 2003, 1896 bachelor's degrees were awarded. The most popular majors were business management (16%), psychology (9%), and health services (8%). In an average class, 1% graduate in 3 years or less, 26% graduate in 4 years or less, 43% graduate in 5 years or less, and 47% graduate in 6 years or less. 452 companies recruited on campus in 2002-2003. Of the 2002 graduating class, 12% were enrolled in graduate school within 6 months of graduation and 81% were employed.

Admissions Contact: Gary Gullickson, Director of Admissions. A video is available. E-mail: *unc@mail.unco.edu* Web: *http://www.unco.edu*

UNIVERSITY OF SOUTHERN COLORADO
Pueblo, CO 81001-4901

D-3
(719) 549-2462
(877) 872-9653; Fax: (719) 549-2419

Full-time: 1510 men, 1850 women	**Faculty:** 159; IIA, --$
Part-time: 770 men, 1205 women	**Ph.D.s:** 70%
Graduate: 55 men, 115 women	**Student/Faculty:** 21 to 1
Year: semesters, summer session	**Tuition:** $2450 ($9730)
Application Deadline: see profile	**Room & Board:** $5375
Freshman Class: n/av	
SAT I or ACT: required	**LESS COMPETITIVE**

The University of Southern Colorado, founded in 1933, is part of the Colorado State University System. The public institution offers undergraduate programs in humanities and social sciences, business administration, nursing, applied science, technology, engineering, and education. There are 5 undergraduate and 3 graduate schools. Figures in the above capsule and in this profile are approximate. In addition to regional accreditation, USC has baccalaureate program accreditation with ABET, ACS, CSWE, NASM, and NLN. The library contains 180,000 volumes, 10,000 microform items, and 16,862 audio/video tapes/CDs, and subscribes to 1327 periodicals. Computerized library services include the card catalog, interlibrary loans, and database searching. Special learning facilities include a learning resource center, art gallery, radio station, TV station, and nature center. The 275-acre campus is in an urban area 100 miles south of Denver. Including any residence halls, there are 15 buildings.

Student Life: 87% of undergraduates are from Colorado. Students are from 41 states, 32 foreign countries, and Canada. 59% are white; 26% Hispanic. The average age of freshmen is 19; all undergraduates, 26. 39% do not continue beyond their first year; 27% remain to graduate.

Housing: 652 students can be accommodated in college housing, which includes coed dorms and on-campus apartments. On-campus housing is guaranteed for the freshman year only and is available on a first-come, first-served basis. 81% of students commute. Alcohol is not permitted. All students may keep cars.

Activities: 1% of men belong to 2 national fraternities; 1% of women belong to 1 local sorority. There are 68 groups on campus, including art, cheerleading, choir, chorale, computers, drama, ethnic, gay, honors, international, jazz band, literary magazine, newspaper, pep band, political, professional, radio and TV, religious, social, social service, student government, and symphony. Popular campus events include the Town and Gown series, Teacher Career Fair, and departmental lecture series.

Sports: There are 5 intercollegiate sports for men and 5 for women, and 5 intramural sports for men and 3 for women. Facilities include an arena with an indoor swimming pool, a weight room, a rock climbing wall, and racquetball, basketball, and volleyball courts; a sports complex with tennis courts, and baseball, softball, and soccer fields; bike trails; a rope course; and a nature center.

Disabled Students: All of the campus is accessible. Wheelchair ramps, elevators, special parking, specially equipped rest rooms, special class scheduling, lowered drinking fountains, and lowered telephones are available.

Services: Counseling and information services are available, as is tutoring in most subjects. Remedial math and English are available on-campus from a local community college.

Campus Safety and Security: Measures include 24-hour foot and vehicle patrol, self-defense education, security escort services, and informal discussions. There are pamphlets/posters/films, emergency telephones, and lighted pathways/sidewalks.

Programs of Study: USC confers B.A., B.S., B.S.B.A., B.S.C.E.T., B.S.E.E.T., B.S.I.En., B.S.M.E.T., B.S.N., and B.S.W. degrees. Master's degrees are also awarded. Bachelor's degrees are awarded in BIOLOGICAL SCIENCE (biochemistry, biology/biological science, and biotechnology), BUSINESS (accounting, business administration and management, and recreation and leisure services), COMMUNICATIONS AND THE ARTS (art, broadcasting, communications, English, journalism, music performance, music theory and composition, and Spanish), COMPUTER AND PHYSICAL SCIENCE (chemistry, information sciences and systems, mathematics, and physics), EDUCATION (music), ENGINEERING AND ENVIRONMENTAL DESIGN (automotive technology, civil engineering technology, electrical/electronics engineering technology, industrial administration/management, industrial engineering, mechanical engineering technology, and preengineering), HEALTH PROFESSIONS (chiropractic, environmental health science, exercise science, medical technology, nursing, occupational therapy, physician's assistant, predentistry, premedicine, preoptometry, preosteopathy, prepharmacy, prepodiatry, preveterinary science, and speech pathology/audiology), SOCIAL SCIENCE (criminology, economics, history, political science/government, prelaw, psychology, social science, social work, and sociology). Business, engineering technology, and nursing are the strongest academically. Accounting, biology, and management are the largest.

Required: To graduate, all students must complete at least 120 semester hours, including 40 in upper-division courses and 30 to 48 in the major, with a minimum GPA of 2.0. General education requirements include a 14-credit skills component of courses in communication, computer literacy, and quantitative skills, as well as a 19-credit knowledge component of courses in humanities, social sciences, and science and technology. Other requirements vary with the major.

Special: USC offers co-op programs, internships, study abroad in 8 countries, and on-campus work-study programs. Also available are 5-year combined B.S.B.A./M.B.A. degrees, a 3-2 engineering degree with Colorado State University, dual majors, nondegree study, and preprofessional programs in forestry, physical therapy, and wildlife management. USC is a member of the National Student Exchange. There are 10 national honor societies, including Phi Beta Kappa, a freshman honors program, and 10 departmental honors programs.

Faculty/Classroom: 60% of faculty are male; 39%, female. 99% teach undergraduates, 10% do research, and 4% do both. No introductory courses are taught by graduate students. The average class size in an introductory lecture is 70; in a laboratory, 24; and in a regular course, 22.

Admissions: 14 freshmen graduated first in their class.

Requirements: The SAT I or ACT is required. In addition, applicants must be graduates of an accredited secondary school or have a GED certificate with a minimum score of 45. USC computes a CCHE admission index, comprised of the high school GPA and SAT I or ACT scores. Students scoring below 80 will still be considered by an admissions committee. Academic preparation should consist of 4 years of English, 3 of math including algebra and geometry, 2 of natural science including physical science, 2 of social studies including American government, and 2 of a foreign language. AP and CLEP credits are accepted. Important factors in the admissions decision are advanced placement or honor courses, leadership record, and recommendations by school officials.

Procedure: Freshmen are admitted to all sessions. Entrance exams should be taken during spring of the junior year or fall of the senior year. Check with the school for current deadlines and fee. Notification is sent on a rolling basis.

Transfer: A minimum GPA of 2.0 and official transcripts of previous college work are required. Applicants with fewer than 30 credit hours must submit ACT or SAT I scores and high school transcripts. 30 of 120 credits required for the bachelor's degree must be completed at USC.

Visiting: There are regularly scheduled orientations for prospective students, including a tour, lunch, and mini-sessions on financial aid, athletics, scholarships, and student services. There are guides for informal visits and visitors may sit in on classes. To schedule a visit, contact the Admissions Office at *info@uscolo.edu*.

Financial Aid: The FAFSA is required. Check with the school for current deadlines.

International Students: The school actively recruits these students. They must score 500 on the written TOEFL or 173 on the electronic version and also take the MELAB.

Computers: Approximately 400 IBM PCs and Macs are available for student use in the library, the administration and technology buildings, and several departments. All students may access the system 24 hours a day. There are no time limits. Check with the school for current fee.

Admissions Contact: Pam Anastassiou, Director of Admissions and Records. E-mail: *info@uscolo.edu* Web: *www.uscolo.edu*

WESTERN STATE COLLEGE OF COLORADO
Gunnison, CO 81231

B-3

(970) 943-2119
(800) 876-5309; Fax: (970) 943-2212

Full-time: 1320 men, 862 women	**Faculty:** 107; IIB, -$
Part-time: 100 men, 103 women	**Ph.Ds:** 85%
Graduate: none	**Student/Faculty:** 20 to 1
Year: semesters, summer session	**Tuition:** $2564 ($9746)
Application Deadline: June 1	**Room & Board:** $6450
Freshman Class: 1972 applied, 1648 accepted, 634 enrolled	
SAT I Verbal/Math: 510/500	**ACT:** 21 COMPETITIVE

Western State College of Colorado, founded in 1901, is a public institution offering undergraduate programs in liberal arts and sciences, business, recreation, and education. There are 8 undergraduate schools. In addition to regional accreditation, Western has baccalaureate program accreditation with NASM. The library contains 156,000 volumes, 1 million microform items, and 5000 audio/video tapes/CDs, and subscribes to 650 periodicals. Computerized library services include the card catalog, interlibrary loans, and database searching. Special learning facilities include a learning resource center, art gallery, radio station, TV station, and botanical gardens. The 228-acre campus is in a rural area 210 miles southwest of Denver. Including any residence halls, there are 30 buildings.

Student Life: 76% of undergraduates are from Colorado. Others are from 49 states, 12 foreign countries, and Canada. 85% are from public schools. 90% are white. 66% are claim no religious affiliation; 8% Protestant. The average age of freshmen is 18; all undergraduates, 21. 41% do not continue beyond their first year; 35% remain to graduate.

Housing: 1200 students can be accommodated in college housing, which includes single-sex and coed dorms, on-campus apartments, and married-student housing. In addition, there are special-interest houses and theme floors on art, science, and outdoor pursuits. On-campus housing is guaranteed for the freshman year only and is available on a first-come, first-served basis. 55% of students commute. All students may keep cars.

Activities: 3% of men belong to 1 local fraternity and 2 national fraternities; 2% of women belong to 2 local sororities and 1 national sorority. There are 60 groups on campus, including art, band, cheerleading, choir, chorale, chorus, dance, drama, ethnic, gay, honors, international, jazz band, literary magazine, marching band, musical theater, opera, orchestra, outdoors/wilderness, pep band, photography, political, professional, radio and TV, religious, social, social service, student government, symphony, and yearbook. Popular campus events include Parents Weekend, Spring Carnival, and weekly entertainment programs.

Sports: There are 6 intercollegiate sports for men and 5 for women, and 10 intramural sports for men and 10 for women. Facilities include a fitness center, 2 gyms, a 5000-seat football stadium, an all-weather track, a number of playing fields, a weight room, an indoor swimming pool, a par course, a games/pool area with a bowling alley, and racquetball, tennis, and volleyball courts.

Disabled Students: 75% of the campus is accessible. Wheelchair ramps, elevators, special parking, specially equipped rest rooms, lowered drinking fountains, lowered telephones, and an audio device to increase telephone volume are available.

Services: Counseling and information services are available, as is tutoring in most subjects. There is a reader service for the blind and remedial math and writing.

Campus Safety and Security: Measures include security escort services, informal discussions, pamphlets/posters/films, and emergency telephones. There are lighted pathways/sidewalks and van shuttle service during special events to prevent students' drinking and driving.

Programs of Study: Western confers B.A. and B.F.A. degrees. Bachelor's degrees are awarded in BIOLOGICAL SCIENCE (biology/biological science), BUSINESS (accounting, business administration and management, and recreation and leisure services), COMMUNICATIONS AND THE ARTS (art, communications, dramatic arts, English, fine arts, music, and Spanish), COMPUTER AND PHYSICAL SCIENCE (chemistry, computer science, geology, and mathematics), EDUCATION (art, elementary, foreign languages, music, science, and secondary), ENGINEERING AND ENVIRONMENTAL DESIGN (preengineering), HEALTH PROFESSIONS (physical therapy and predentistry), SOCIAL SCIENCE (anthropology, economics, history, physical fitness/movement, political science/government, prelaw, psychology, and sociology). Business, biological sciences, and communications are the strongest academically. Kinesiology and education are the largest.

Required: For graduation, students must complete 120 credit hours with a minimum GPA of 2.0. There are liberal arts requirements of 27 credits in human relationships, natural sciences, and creative arts, as well as competencies in written expression, oral communication, and math.

Special: The Department of Business and Accounting offers a co-op program. Students may cross-register with Mesa, Adams, and Metro State Colleges. Study abroad, internships, work-study programs, an accelerated degree program in teacher education, dual and student-designed majors, and credit for military and work experience are available. There are 9 national honor societies, a freshman honors program, and 2 departmental honors programs.

Faculty/Classroom: 58% of faculty are male; 42%, female. All both teach and do research. The average class size in an introductory lecture is 22; in a laboratory, 15; and in a regular course, 19.

Admissions: 84% of the 2003-2004 applicants were accepted. The SAT I scores for the 2003-2004 freshman class were: Verbal--48% below 500, 40% between 500 and 599, and 12% between 600 and 700; Math--50% below 500, 38% between 500 and 599, and 12% between 600 and 700. The ACT scores were 52% below 21, 31% between 21 and 23, 14% between 24 and 26, 3% between 27 and 28, and 1% above 28. 17% of the current freshmen were in the top fifth of their class; 45% were in the top two fifths. 12 freshmen graduated first in their class.

Requirements: The SAT I or ACT is required. A minimum composite score of 950 on the SAT I or 20 on the ACT is recommended, as are an essay and an interview. Applicants must be graduates of an accredited secondary school. Western recommends that in high school students complete 4 years of English, 3 of math, and 2 each of natural and social science. Course work in a foreign language and computer science is strongly recommended. Western requires applicants to be in the upper 67% of their class. A GPA of 2.5 is required. AP and CLEP credits are accepted. Important factors in the admissions decision are advanced placement or honor courses, leadership record, and extracurricular activities record.

Procedure: Freshmen are admitted to all sessions. Entrance exams should be taken during spring of the junior year or fall of the senior year. There is a deferred admissions plan. Applications should be filed by June 1 for fall entry, November 1 for spring entry, and March 1 for summer entry, along with a $40 fee. Notification is sent on a rolling basis. Applications are accepted on-line through the school's web site www.western.edu.

Transfer: Applicants for transfer must have a minimum GPA of 2.0 and may be asked to submit SAT I or ACT test scores. 30 of 120 credits required for the bachelor's degree must be completed at Western.

Visiting: There are regularly scheduled orientations for prospective students. There are guides for informal visits and visitors may sit in on classes. To schedule a visit, contact the Admissions Office at (800) 876-5309 or discover@western.edu.

Financial Aid: In 2003-2004, 80% of all full-time freshmen and 85% of continuing full-time students received some form of financial aid. 65% of full-time freshmen and 70% of continuing full-time students received need-based aid. The average freshman award was $4000. Need-based scholarships or need-based grants averaged $500 ($4000 maximum); need-based self-help aid (loans and jobs) averaged $3000 ($5000 maximum); non-need-based athletic scholarships averaged $450 ($5000 maximum); and other non-need-based awards and non-need-based scholarships averaged $500 ($3000 maximum). 35% of undergraduates work part time. Average annual earnings from campus work are $1500. The average financial indebtedness of the 2003 graduate was $12,000. The FAFSA is required. The priority date for freshman financial aid applications for fall entry is March 1. The deadline for filing freshman financial aid applications for fall entry is April 1.

International Students: There are 38 international students enrolled. They must score 525 on the written TOEFL or 213 on the electronic version.

Computers: The mainframes are a DEC Alpha cluster, consisting of an Alpha 1000, an Alpha Server 3600, an Alpha Server 2100, and a VAX Alpha 3600. There are more than 150 PCs and terminals available to students in labs and the library. Students have access to word processing, database, and spreadsheet software and the Internet. All students may access the system at all times. There are no time limits. The fee is $25 per year.

Graduates: From July 1, 2002 to June 30, 2003, 441 bachelor's degrees were awarded. The most popular majors were business/accounting (20%), biology (10%), and history (9%). 15 companies recruited on campus in 2002-2003. Of the 2002 graduating class, 4% were enrolled in graduate school within 6 months of graduation and 95% were employed.

Admissions Contact: Tonya Van Hee, Assistant Director. A video is available. E-mail: tvanhee@western.edu Web: www.western.edu

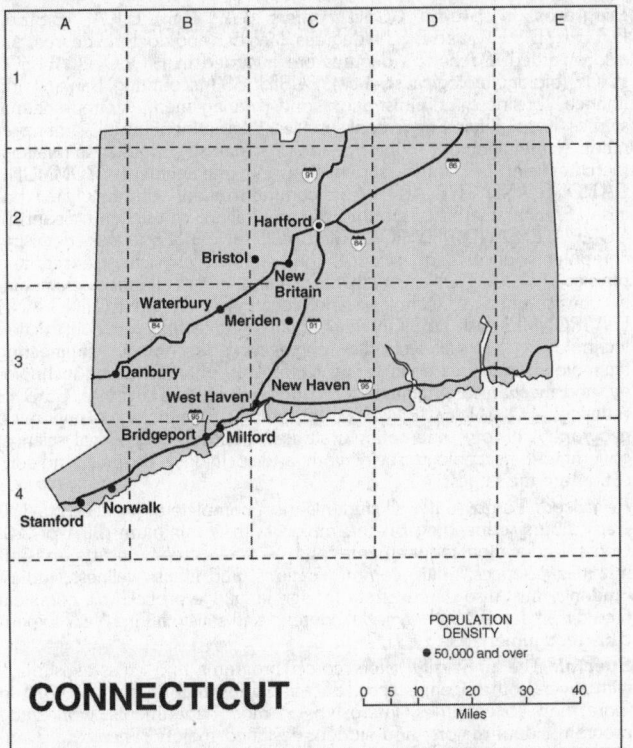

POPULATION DENSITY
● 50,000 and over

CONNECTICUT

0   5 10   20   30   40
Miles

ALBERTUS MAGNUS COLLEGE
New Haven, CT 06511-1189

C-3
(203) 773-8501
(800) 578-9160; Fax: (203) 773-9539

Full-time: 580 men, 1075 women	**Faculty:** 41; IIB, av$
Part-time: 28 men, 105 women	**Ph.D.s:** 90%
Graduate: 247 men, 192 women	**Student/Faculty:** 40 to 1
Year: semesters, summer session	**Tuition:** $15,800
Application Deadline: open	**Room & Board:** $7330
Freshman Class: 537 applied, 504 accepted, 136 enrolled	
SAT I Verbal/Math: 455/450	**LESS COMPETITIVE**

Albertus Magnus College, founded in 1925, is a private college affiliated with the Roman Catholic Church and sponsored by the Dominican Sisters of St. Mary of the Springs. The college offers undergraduate and graduate degrees in the liberal arts and sciences and in business. In addition to regional accreditation, Albertus Magnus has baccalaureate program accreditation with IACBE. The library contains 120,000 volumes, 7000 microform items, and 1200 audio/video tapes/CDs, and subscribes to 720 periodicals. Computerized library services include the card catalog, interlibrary loans, database searching, and Internet access. Special learning facilities include a learning resource center, art gallery, theater, and an academic skill center. The 55-acre campus is in a suburban area 80 miles from New York City. Including any residence halls, there are 16 buildings.

Student Life: 95% of undergraduates are from Connecticut. Students are from 10 states and 6 foreign countries. 50% are from public schools. 66% are white; 19% African American. Most are Catholic. The average age of freshmen is 19; all undergraduates, 22. 10% do not continue beyond their first year; 70% remain to graduate.

Housing: 320 students can be accommodated in college housing, which includes single-sex and coed dorms. Residence halls are mainly old mansions that have been converted into student housing. Each building houses 15 to 65 studetns. On-campus housing is guaranteed for all 4 years. 60% of students live on campus; of those, 70% remain on campus on weekends. All students may keep cars.

Activities: There are no fraternities or sororities. There are 20 groups on campus, including art, computers, dance, debate, drama, ethnic, film, honors, international, literary magazine, musical theater, photography, political, professional, religious, social, social service, student government, and yearbook. Popular campus events include Fall Candlelight Ceremony, Christmas events, and Laurel Day.

Sports: There are 5 intercollegiate sports for men and 6 for women. Facilities include an Olympic-size pool, a gym, indoor and outdoor tracks,

racquetball and volleyball courts, weight and dance rooms, 4 tennis courts, a game room, and soccer and softball fields.

Disabled Students: All of the campus is accessible. Wheelchair ramps, elevators, special parking, specially equipped rest rooms, special class scheduling, lowered drinking fountains, and lowered telephones are available.

Services: Counseling and information services are available, as is tutoring in every subject. There is remedial math, reading, and writing.

Campus Safety and Security: Measures include 24-hour foot and vehicle patrol, security escort services, shuttle buses, and informal discussions. There are pamphlets/posters/films and lighted pathways/sidewalks.

Programs of Study: Albertus Magnus confers B.A., B.S., and B.F.A. degrees. Associate and master's degrees are also awarded. Bachelor's degrees are awarded in BIOLOGICAL SCIENCE (biology/biological science), BUSINESS (accounting, business administration and management, and management information systems), COMMUNICATIONS AND THE ARTS (communications, dramatic arts, English, and fine arts), COMPUTER AND PHYSICAL SCIENCE (mathematics), HEALTH PROFESSIONS (art therapy, predentistry, premedicine, and preveterinary science), SOCIAL SCIENCE (criminology, history, human services, humanities, industrial and organizational psychology, liberal arts/general studies, philosophy, political science/government, prelaw, psychology, religion, sociology, and urban studies). Liberal arts, business, and computer technology are the strongest academically. Business/economics, sociology, and psychology are the largest.

Required: To graduate, all students must complete at least 120 credit hours, including 60 outside the major and at least 30 in the major. General education requirements, including 6 credits each in English and humanities, and 3 each in fine arts, math, science, and senior humanities, must be fulfilled. Distribution requirements include 3 credits each of history, social science, philosophy, religion, and literature. Service learning or career explorations are also required. A minimum 2.0 GPA is required.

Special: The college offers junior- and senior-year internships allowing up to 12 credits, study abroad, a Washington semester, work-study programs, and accelerated degree programs in business and information technology, psychology, criminal justice, communications, English, humanities, and general studies. Also available are dual and student-designed majors, nondegree study, pass/fail options, independent study, and preprofessional programs. Students may take accelerated degree programs in the evening or take weekend courses. There are 5 national honor societies, a freshman honors program, and 12 departmental honors programs.

Faculty/Classroom: 46% of faculty are male; 54%, female. All both teach and do research. No introductory courses are taught by graduate students. The average class size in an introductory lecture is 20; in a laboratory, 10; and in a regular course, 15.

Admissions: 94% of the 2003-2004 applicants were accepted. The SAT I scores for the 2003-2004 freshman class were: Verbal--69% below 500, 25% between 500 and 599, 5% between 600 and 700, and 1% above 700; Math--72% below 500, 21% between 500 and 599, 7% between 600 and 700, and 1% above 700. 19% of the current freshmen were in the top fifth of their class; 42% were in the top two fifths. There were 7 National Merit semifinalists. 4 freshmen graduated first in their class.

Requirements: The SAT I is required, with a minimum recommended composite score of 800. Applicants must be graduates of an accredited secondary school or have a GED certificate and have completed 16 academic credits, including 4 years of English, 2 or 3 years each of foreign language, math, and science, 2 years of history, and 1 year of social studies. High school transcripts, rank, and 2 letters of recommendation are required. The SAT II: Subject test in writing and an interview are recommended. Albertus Magnus requires applicants to be in the upper 50% of their class. A GPA of 2.5 is required. AP and CLEP credits are accepted. Important factors in the admissions decision are advanced placement or honor courses, recommendations by school officials, and leadership record.

Procedure: Freshmen are admitted to all sessions. Entrance exams should be taken between April of the junior year and November of the senior year. There is a rolling admissions plan and a deferred admissions plan. Application deadlines are open. The fall 2003 application fee was $35. Notification is sent on a rolling basis beginning December 15. Applications are accepted on-line through the university's website or CollegeNET.

Transfer: 31 transfer students enrolled in 2002-2003. Transfer students must present a minimum 2.0 overall GPA and a 2.0 GPA for all transferable, compatible course work. 30 of 120 credits required for the bachelor's degree must be completed at Albertus Magnus.

Visiting: There are regularly scheduled orientations for prospective students, consisting of registration, a general introduction, a financial aid/major introduction, lunch, a campus tour, and an interview. There are guides for informal visits and visitors may sit in on classes and stay overnight. To schedule a visit, contact the Admissions Office.

Financial Aid: In a recent year, 83% of all full-time freshmen and 87% of continuing full-time students received some form of financial aid. 83% of full-time freshmen and 87% of continuing full-time students received need-based aid. The average freshman award was $8500. 10% of undergraduates worked part time. Average annual earnings from campus work were $1000. The average financial indebtedness of a recent graduate was $13,000. Albertus Magnus is a member off CSS. The CSS Profile or FAFSA and the college's own financial statement are required. The deadline for filing freshman financial aid applications for fall entry is March 15.

International Students: The school actively recruits these students. They must score 550 on the written TOEFL.

Computers: The mainframe is a Prime 2450. There are also 48 terminals and 26 PCs available for student use in the computer center and the library. All students may access the system 9 A.M. to 10 P.M. There are no time limits and no fees. It is strongly recommended that all students have a personal computer.

Graduates: From July 1, 2002 to June 30, 2003, 648 bachelor's degrees were awarded. The most popular majors were management (69%), psychology (9%), and sociology (7%). In an average class, 80% graduate in 4 years or less, and 100% graduate in 5 years or less. 10 companies recruited on campus in 2002-2003. Of the 2002 graduating class, 25% were enrolled in graduate school within 6 months of graduation and 70% were employed.

Admissions Contact: Richard Lolatte, Dean of Admissions and Financial Aid. E-mail: *admissions@albertus.edu* Web: *www.albertus.edu*

CENTRAL CONNECTICUT STATE UNIVERSITY C-2
New Britain, CT 06050

(860) 832-2278
(888) 733-2278; Fax: (860) 832-2522

Full-time: 3344 men, 3434 women	**Faculty:** 395; IIA, +$
Part-time: 1278 men, 1343 women	**Ph.D.s:** 77%
Graduate: 949 men, 1781 women	**Student/Faculty:** 17 to 1
Year: semesters, summer session	**Tuition:** $5384 ($12,372)
Application Deadline: May 1	**Room & Board:** $6706
Freshman Class: 5503 applied, 3024 accepted, 1178 enrolled	
SAT I Verbal/Math: 514/515	**COMPETITIVE**

Central Connecticut State University, founded in 1849, offers degree programs in liberal arts, engineering technology, business, and education. It is part of the Connecticut State University system. There are 4 undergraduate schools and 1 graduate school. In addition to regional accreditation, CCSU has baccalaureate program accreditation with ABET, ACS, CSAB, CSWE, NAIT, NCATE, and NLN. The library contains 665,605 volumes, 554,168 microform items, and 7259 audio/video tapes/CDs, and subscribes to 2772 periodicals. Computerized library services include the card catalog, interlibrary loans, and database searching. Special learning facilities include a learning resource center, art gallery, planetarium, radio station, and writing and math centers. The 294-acre campus is in a suburban area 10 miles west of Hartford. Including any residence halls, there are 39 buildings.

Student Life: 93% of undergraduates are from Connecticut. Students are from 26 states, 54 foreign countries, and Canada. 75% are white. 56% claim no religious affiliation; 30% Catholic. The average age of freshmen is 18; all undergraduates, 21. 24% do not continue beyond their first year; 42% remain to graduate.

Housing: 2200 students can be accommodated in college housing, which includes single-sex and coed dorms. On-campus housing is guaranteed for all 4 years. 70% of students commute. All students may keep cars.

Activities: 1% of men belong to 2 national fraternities; 1% of women belong to 1 national sorority. There are 100 groups on campus, including art, band, cheerleading, choir, chorale, chorus, computers, dance, drama, ethnic, gay, honors, international, jazz band, literary magazine, marching band, newspaper, orchestra, pep band, photography, political, professional, radio and TV, religious, social, social service, student government, and yearbook. Popular campus events include Winter and Spring Weekends, First Week, and Vance Lectures.

Sports: There are 7 intercollegiate sports for men and 9 for women, and 8 intramural sports for men and 8 for women. Facilities include a 3800-seat gym, 8 tennis courts, a 6000-seat football stadium, a 37,000-square-foot air-supported recreation facility, a natatorium, weight training rooms, and softball, baseball, touch football, and soccer fields.

Disabled Students: 90% of the campus is accessible. Wheelchair ramps, elevators, special parking, specially equipped rest rooms, special class scheduling, lowered drinking fountains, and lowered telephones are available. Personal care attendants serve as roommates for physically disabled resident students.

Services: Counseling and information services are available, as is tutoring in some subjects. There is a reader service for the blind and remedial math, reading, and writing.

Campus Safety and Security: Measures include 24-hour foot and vehicle patrol, self-defense education, security escort services, and shuttle buses. There are informal discussions, pamphlets/posters/films, emergency telephones, and lighted pathways/sidewalks.

Programs of Study: CCSU confers B.A., B.S., B.F.A., B.S.Ed., B.S.E.T., B.S.I.T., and B.S.N. degrees. Master's and doctoral degrees are also awarded. Bachelor's degrees are awarded in BIOLOGICAL SCIENCE (biology/biological science), BUSINESS (accounting, banking and finance, business administration and management, entrepreneurial studies, hospitality management services, international business management, management information systems, marketing/retailing/merchandising, and office supervision and management), COMMUNICATIONS AND THE ARTS (art, communications, dramatic arts, English, French, German, graphic design, Italian, music, and Spanish), COMPUTER AND PHYSICAL SCIENCE (actuarial science, chemistry, computer science, earth science, mathematics, physical sciences, and physics), EDUCATION (art, athletic training, early childhood, elementary, music, physical, technical, and vocational), ENGINEERING AND ENVIRONMENTAL DESIGN (civil engineering technology, construction technology, electrical/electronics engineering technology, engineering technology, industrial engineering technology, manufacturing technology, and mechanical engineering technology), HEALTH PROFESSIONS (nursing), SOCIAL SCIENCE (anthropology, criminology, economics, geography, history, international studies, philosophy, political science/government, psychology, social work, and sociology). Business and education are the largest.

Required: To graduate, all students must complete at least 122 to 130 credit hours, depending on the major, with a minimum GPA of 2.0. General education requirements total 44 to 46 credits in arts and humanities, sciences, math, communications, and fitness/wellness studies. Students must also demonstrate foreign language proficiency, complete 6 credits in courses with a global context, and satisfy a First-Year Experience requirement.

Special: The university offers co-op programs and cross-registration with several other Connecticut educational institutions, study abroad in more than 45 countries, internships in most departments, work-study programs, dual majors, and student-designed majors. There are 7 national honor societies, a freshman honors program, and 1 departmental honors program.

Faculty/Classroom: 61% of faculty are male; 39%, female. All teach undergraduates. No introductory courses are taught by graduate students. The average class size in an introductory lecture is 35; in a laboratory, 20; and in a regular course, 25.

Admissions: 55% of the 2003-2004 applicants were accepted. The SAT I scores for the 2003-2004 freshman class were: Verbal--39% below 500, 49% between 500 and 599, 12% between 600 and 700, and 1% above 700; Math--41% below 500, 47% between 500 and 599, 11% between 600 and 700, and 1% above 700.

Requirements: The SAT I is required, with recommended minimum scores of 480 verbal and 450 math. Applicants must be graduates of an accredited secondary school or have earned a GED. An interview is recommended. CCSU also recommends that applicants have 14 academic credits: 4 in English, 3 each in math and a foreign language, and 2 each in science and social sciences, including 1 in U.S. history. AP and CLEP credits are accepted. Important factors in the admissions decision are extracurricular activities record, recommendations by school officials, and advanced placement or honor courses.

Procedure: Freshmen are admitted fall and spring. Entrance exams should be taken in May of the junior year or November of the senior year. There is a deferred admissions plan. Applications should be filed by May 1 for fall entry and November 1 for spring entry. Notification is sent on a rolling basis. The fall 2003 application fee was $40.

Transfer: 699 transfer students enrolled in 2002-2003. Applicants must have a minimum of 12 transferable credits and a GPA of 2.0 and must submit official transcripts from previous schools attended. 45 of 122 credits required for the bachelor's degree must be completed at CCSU.

Visiting: There are regularly scheduled orientations for prospective students, including a fall open house in October and daily and select Saturday visits throughout the fall and spring. There are guides for informal visits and visitors may sit in on classes. To schedule a visit, contact the Admissions Office at *admissions@ccsu.edu*.

Financial Aid: In 2003-2004, 46% of all full-time freshmen and 67% of continuing full-time students received some form of financial aid. 44% of full-time freshmen and 64% of continuing full-time students received need-based aid. The average freshman award was $4730. Need-based scholarships or need-based grants averaged $3583 ($6000 maximum); need-based self-help aid (loans and jobs) averaged $2373 ($4000 maximum); non-need-based athletic scholarships averaged $10,949 ($19,000 maximum); and other non-need-based awards and non-need-based scholarships averaged $1914 ($2700 maximum). 40% of undergraduates work part time. Average annual earnings from campus work are $1000. The average financial indebtedness of the 2003 graduate was $13,500. CCSU is a member of CSS. The FAFSA and federal income tax returns are required. The priority date for freshman financial aid applications for fall entry is March 1. The deadline for filing freshman financial aid applications for fall entry is September 1.

International Students: There are 158 international students enrolled. The school actively recruits these students. They must score 500 on the written TOEFL.

Computers: All PCs on campus have access to the Internet. There are approximately 1200 PCs and Macs in labs and classrooms. The main computer lab is the only open, general purpose lab for outside classroom computer use. There are approximately 230 computers in that lab for student use. All students may access the system 8:30 A.M. to 12 P.M., Monday to Thursday; 8:30 A.M. to 6 P.M., Friday; 9 A.M. to 6 P.M., Saturday; and 1 P.M. to 10 P.M., Sunday. There are no time limits and no fees.

Graduates: In a recent year, 1167 bachelor's degrees were awarded. The most popular majors were education (18%), psychology (10%), and marketing (6%). In an average class, 42% graduate in 6 years or less. 63 companies recruited on campus in 2002-2003.

Admissions Contact: Myrna Garcia-Bowen, Director of Admissions.
E-mail: *admissions@ccsu.edu* Web: *www.ccsu.edu*

CHARTER OAK STATE COLLEGE C-2
New Britain, CT 06053-2142
(860) 832-3800
Fax: (860) 832-3999

Full-time: none	**Faculty:** n/av
Part-time: 697 men, 881 women	**Ph.D.s:** 77%
Graduate: none	**Student/Faculty:** n/av
Year: see profile	**Tuition:** $940 ($1140)
Application Deadline: open	**Room & Board:** n/app
Freshman Class: n/av	
SAT I or ACT: not required	**SPECIAL**

Charter Oak State College, founded in 1973, is a public liberal arts institution offering degree programs for adult students who cannot complete a college degree by conventional means because of family, job, or financial considerations. Credits may be earned by transfer, testing, portfolio review, contract learning, or by taking Charter Oak's online and video courses. Matriculation and admission fees are $940 in state ($1140 out of state) for the first year and $375 in state ($549 out of state) for continuing students. Charter Oak course tuition is $140 per credit in state ($195 out of state) plus a $25 registration fee. 3-credit courses run for 8 or 15 weeks. The offices are in a suburban area 7 miles south of Hartford. There is one building.

Student Life: 62% of undergraduates are from Connecticut. Students are from 50 states, 5 foreign countries, and Canada. 70% are white; 10% African American. The average age of all undergraduates is 40.

Housing: There are no residence halls.

Disabled Students: All of the office complex is accessible. Wheelchair ramps, elevators, special parking, specially equipped rest rooms, and lowered drinking fountains are available. The program is a distance-learning one that does not require students to come to the facility. They can obtain services by phone, fax, and e-mail.

Services: Counseling and information services are available, as is tutoring in some subjects, including writing, math, and psychology. Tutoring is available online.

Programs of Study: Charter Oak confers B.A. and B.S. degrees. Associate degrees are also awarded. Bachelor's degrees are awarded in SOCIAL SCIENCE (liberal arts/general studies).

Required: All baccalaureate students must complete 120 total credits, at least 60 of which must be in liberal arts for the B.S. and 90 for the B.A.; 36 credits must be in the field of concentration.

Special: Student-designed concentrations and accelerated degree programs are available in all majors.

Faculty/Classroom: There are 69 part-time faculty. 50% of faculty are male; 50%, female.

Requirements: Charter Oak State College requires applicants to have earned at least 9 college credits. AP and CLEP credits are accepted.

Procedure: Freshmen are admitted to all sessions. There is a rolling admissions plan. Application deadlines are open. The fall 2003 application fee was $50.

Transfer: Most students who enroll in Charter Oak State College have attended college previously.

Financial Aid: The average financial indebtedness of the 2003 graduate was $4828. Charter Oak is a member of CSS. The FAFSA and the college's own financial statement are required. The deadline for filing freshman financial aid applications for fall entry is June 30.

International Students: Students must meet COSC English competency requirements before they are admitted.

Computers: There are no time limits and no fees.

Graduates: From July 1, 2002 to June 30, 2003, 421 bachelor's degrees were awarded.

Admissions Contact: Lori Gagne Pendleton, Director of Admissions.
E-mail: *info@charteroak.edu* Web: *www.charteroak.edu*

CONNECTICUT COLLEGE E-3
New London, CT 06320-4196
(860) 439-2200
Fax: (860) 439-4301

Full-time: 724 men, 1026 women	**Faculty:** 155; IIB, +$
Part-time: 21 men, 66 women	**Ph.D.s:** 90%
Graduate: 4 men, 8 women	**Student/Faculty:** 11 to 1
Year: semesters	**Tuition:** $37,900
Application Deadline: January 1	**Room & Board:** see profile
Freshman Class: 4396 applied, 1536 accepted, 511 enrolled	
SAT I Verbal/Math: 660/650	**ACT:** 27 **MOST COMPETITIVE**

Connecticut College, founded in 1911, is a private institution offering degree programs in the liberal arts and sciences. Tuition and room and board are combined in a comprehensive fee of $37,900 per year. The 2 libraries contain 652,509 volumes, 151,979 microform items, and 153,156 audio/video tapes/CDs, and subscribe to 3458 periodicals. Computerized library services include the card catalog, interlibrary loans, database searching, and Internet access. Special learning facilities include an art gallery, radio station, an observatory, and an arboretum. The 702-acre campus is in a small town midway between Boston and New York City. Including any residence halls, there are 51 buildings.

Student Life: 87% of undergraduates are from out of state, mostly the Northeast. Students are from 50 states, 57 foreign countries, and Canada. 49% are from public schools. 73% are white. 27% are Protestant; 26% Catholic; 17% claim no religious affiliation; 14% Jewish. The average age of freshmen is 18; all undergraduates, 21. 8% do not continue beyond their first year; 83% remain to graduate.

Housing: 1750 students can be accommodated in college housing, which includes coed dorms. In addition, there are language houses and special-interest houses. On-campus housing is guaranteed for all 4 years. 98% of students live on campus; of those, 85% remain on campus on weekends. All students may keep cars.

Activities: There are no fraternities or sororities. There are 55 groups on campus, including a cappella, art, band, chess, choir, chorale, chorus, computers, dance, drama, ethnic, film, gay, honors, international, jazz band, literary magazine, newspaper, opera, orchestra, photography, political, radio and TV, religious, social, social service, student government, symphony, and yearbook. Popular campus events include Eclipse Weekend, Harvestfest, and Floralia.

Sports: There are 12 intercollegiate sports for men and 14 for women, and 12 intramural sports for men and 10 for women. Facilities include an 800-seat gym, playing fields, an ice rink, a boat house, a weight training room, an indoor pool, a dance studio, 12 tennis courts, and courts for squash, racquetball, badminton, basketball, and volleyball. There is also a track and field facility with an all-weather, 8-lane, 400-meter track, facilities for all field events, and a game field.

Disabled Students: 25% of the campus is accessible. Wheelchair ramps, elevators, special parking, specially equipped rest rooms, special class scheduling, lowered drinking fountains, and lowered telephones are available.

Services: Counseling and information services are available, as is tutoring in most subjects.

Campus Safety and Security: Measures include 24-hour foot and vehicle patrol, security escort services, informal discussions, and pamphlets/posters/films. There are emergency telephones, lighted pathways/sidewalks, and an electronic access system in student residences.

Programs of Study: Connecticut College confers the B.A. degree. Master's degrees are also awarded. Bachelor's degrees are awarded in BIOLOGICAL SCIENCE (biochemistry, biology/biological science, botany, neurosciences, and zoology), COMMUNICATIONS AND THE ARTS (art, art history and appreciation, Chinese, classics, comparative literature, dance, dramatic arts, English, French, German, Italian, Japanese, music, and music technology), COMPUTER AND PHYSICAL SCIENCE (astrophysics, chemistry, mathematics, and physics), EDUCATION (foreign languages, music, and science), ENGINEERING AND ENVIRONMENTAL DESIGN (architecture, engineering physics, and environmental science), SOCIAL SCIENCE (African studies, American studies, anthropology, East Asian studies, economics, gender studies, Hispanic American studies, history, human development, humanities and social science, international relations, Italian studies, Latin American studies, medieval studies, philosophy, political science/government, psychology, religion, Russian and Slavic studies, sociology, and urban studies). Government, history, and psychology are the largest.

Required: To graduate, students must complete at least 128 credit hours with a minimum GPA of 2.0. Distribution requirements cover 7 courses from 7 academic areas, plus a foreign language. Students must also complete 2 courses designated as writing intensive or writing enhanced.

Special: Cross-registration with 12 area colleges, internships in government, human services, and other fields, a Washington semester at American University, dual majors, student-designed majors, a 3-2 engineering degree with Washington University in St. Louis or Boston University, nondegree study, and satisfactory/unsatisfactory options are available. One third of the junior class studies abroad. An international studies certificate program is available, which combines competency in a foreign language, an internship, and study abroad. There are also certificate programs in museum studies, community action and public policy, conservation biology and environmental studies, arts and technology, and education. There are 4 national honor societies, including Phi Beta Kappa; all departments have honors programs.

Faculty/Classroom: 55% of faculty are male; 45%, female. All teach undergraduates. No introductory courses are taught by graduate students. The average class size in an introductory lecture is 27; in a laboratory, 15; and in a regular course, 20.

Admissions: 35% of the 2003-2004 applicants were accepted. The SAT I scores for the 2003-2004 freshman class were: Verbal--2% below 500, 16% between 500 and 599, 56% between 600 and 700, and 26% above 700; Math--2% below 500, 10% between 500 and 599, 65% between 600 and 700, and 23% above 700. 83% of the current freshmen were in the top fifth of their class; 99% were in the top two fifths.

Requirements: Any 3 SAT II: Subject tests or the ACT is required. In addition, applicants must be graduates of an accredited secondary school. An essay is required and an interview is recommended. AP credits are accepted. Important factors in the admissions decision are advanced placement or honor courses, leadership record, and evidence of special talent.

Procedure: Freshmen are admitted fall and spring. Entrance exams should be taken by January of the senior year. There are early decision, early admissions, and deferred admissions plans. Early decision applications should be filed by November 15; regular applications, by January 1 for fall entry and December 1 for spring entry, along with a $55 fee. Notification of early decision is sent December 15; regular decision, April 1. 329 early decision candidates were accepted for the 2003-2004 class. A waiting list is an active part of the admissions procedure. Applications are accepted on-line.

Transfer: 29 transfer students enrolled in 2002-2003. Applicants must have a minimum college GPA of 3.0 and be in good standing at the previous school attended. SAT I or ACT scores are required and an interview is recommended. 64 credits of 128 required for the bachelor's degree must be completed at Connecticut College.

Visiting: There are regularly scheduled orientations for prospective students, including an introduction to the college, student perspectives, academic programs, a luncheon for parents and students, tours, and a reception. There are guides for informal visits and visitors may sit in on classes and stay overnight. To schedule a visit, contact the Admissions Office.

Financial Aid: In 2003-2004, 44% of all full-time freshmen and 50% of continuing full-time students received some form of financial aid. 42% of full-time freshmen and 50% of continuing full-time students received need-based aid. The average freshman award was $22,748. 63% of undergraduates work part time. Average annual earnings from campus work are $693. The average financial indebtedness of the 2003 graduate was $18,602. Connecticut College is a member of CSS. The CSS/Profile, FAFSA, and parent and student tax forms, including noncustodial parent's statement or business supplement when applicable, are required. The deadline for filing freshman financial aid applications for fall entry is January 15.

International Students: There are 150 international students enrolled. The school actively recruits these students. They must score 600 on the written TOEFL or 250 on the electronic version and also take the SAT I or the ACT. Students must also take SAT II: Subject tests in any 3 subjects.

Computers: The mainframes are a DEC MicroVAX 3900, a DEC System 5500, and a DEC Alpha server. There are 3 public terminal rooms for the mainframe system. Macs and PCs are available for student use in computer labs and individual departments. Laser printers, plotters, and scanners are also available. A campuswide network links computer clusters, classrooms, labs, dorm rooms, and the library with voice data and video transmission capabilities. All students may access the system 24 hours a day. There are no time limits and no fees. It is strongly recommended that all students have a personal computer.

Graduates: From July 1, 2002 to June 30, 2003, 475 bachelor's degrees were awarded. The most popular majors were economics (9%), English (9%), and government international relations (8%). In an average class, 75% graduate in 4 years or less, 81% graduate in 5 years or less, and 82% graduate in 6 years or less. 266 companies recruited on campus in 2002-2003. Of the 2002 graduating class, 18% were enrolled in graduate school within 6 months of graduation and 81% were employed.

Admissions Contact: Martha Merrill, Dean of Admissions.
E-mail: *admission@conncoll.edu*
Web: *www.connecticutcollege.edu/admissions*

CONNECTICUT STATE UNIVERSITY SYSTEM

The Connecticut State University System is the largest public system of higher education in Connecticut. CSU consists of 4 comprehensive universities and a system office serving more than 36,000 students. The CS universities, which are governed by an 18-member board of trustees, are: Central Connecticut State University in New Britain, Eastern Connecticut State University in Willimantic, Southern Connecticut State University in New Haven, and Western Connecticut State University in Danbury. The universities offer academic programs in more than 160 subject areas at the bachelor's, master's, sixth-year certificate, and doctoral levels. Students may enroll on a full- or part-time basis during fall, spring, and summer terms. The CS universities are teaching institutions.Their main priorities are access to education with emphasis on a multicultural experience, quality within a context of curriculum diversity and a range of delivery systems, and public service, including linkages with schools, state government, and private enterprise. Profiles of the four universities are included here.

EASTERN CONNECTICUT STATE UNIVERSITY   D-2
Willimantic, CT 06226   (860) 465-5286; Fax: (860) 465-4382

Full-time: 1560 men, 2015 women	**Faculty:** IIA, av$
Part-time: 570 men, 875 women	**Ph.D.s:** 87%
Graduate: 70 men, 255 women	**Student/Faculty:** 18 to 1
Year: semesters, summer session	**Tuition:** $4095 ($9950)
Application Deadline: see profile	**Room & Board:** $6270
Freshman Class: n/av	
SAT I or ACT: required	**COMPETITIVE**

Eastern Connecticut State University, founded in 1889, is the state's public liberal arts institution. There are 3 undergraduate schools and 1 graduate school. Figures in the above capsule and in this profile are approximate. The library contains 287,040 volumes, 60,373 microform items, and 3657 audio/video tapes/CDs, and subscribes to 2068 periodicals. Computerized library services include the card catalog, interlibrary loans, and database searching. Special learning facilities include a learning resource center, art gallery, planetarium, radio station, and TV station. The 177-acre campus is in a suburban area 29 miles east of Hartford and 90 miles southwest of Boston. Including any residence halls, there are 47 buildings.

Student Life: 92% of undergraduates are from Connecticut. Students are from 29 states and 28 foreign countries. 82% are white. The average age of freshmen is 19; all undergraduates, 26.

Housing: 1966 students can be accommodated in college housing, which includes single-sex and coed dorms and on-campus apartments. In addition, there are special-interest houses. On-campus housing is available on a first-come, first-served basis and is available on a lottery system for upperclassmen. Priority is given to out-of-town students. 65% of students live on campus. Alcohol is not permitted. Upperclassmen may keep cars.

Activities: There are no fraternities or sororities. There are 48 groups on campus, including art, band, cheerleading, choir, chorus, computers, dance, drama, ethnic, gay, honors, international, jazz band, literary magazine, musical theater, newspaper, orchestra, photography, political, professional, radio and TV, religious, social, social service, student government, and yearbook. Popular campus events include Spring Weekend, Parents Day, and International Festival.

Sports: There are 6 intercollegiate sports for men and 9 for women, and 17 intramural sports for men and 14 for women. Facilities include a 2800-seat field house, a 6-lane swimming pool, a soccer field, a baseball complex, a softball stadium, and tennis, basketball, racquetball, and squash courts.

Disabled Students: 90% of the campus is accessible. Wheelchair ramps, elevators, special parking, specially equipped rest rooms, special class scheduling, lowered drinking fountains, and lowered telephones are available.

Services: Counseling and information services are available, as is tutoring in most subjects. There is a reader service for the blind and remedial math, reading, and writing.

Campus Safety and Security: Measures include 24-hour foot and vehicle patrol, self-defense education, security escort services, and shuttle buses. There are informal discussions, pamphlets/posters/films, emergency telephones, and lighted pathways/sidewalks.

Programs of Study: ECSU confers B.A., B.S. and B.G.S. degrees. Associate and master's degrees are also awarded. Bachelor's degrees are awarded in BIOLOGICAL SCIENCE (biology/biological science), BUSINESS (accounting, business administration and management, and recreation and leisure services), COMMUNICATIONS AND THE ARTS (communications, English, fine arts, and Spanish), COMPUTER AND PHYSICAL SCIENCE (computer science and mathematics), EDUCATION (early childhood, library science, middle school, and physical), ENGINEERING AND ENVIRONMENTAL DESIGN (environmental science), SOCIAL SCIENCE (American studies, economics, history, liberal arts/general studies, political science/government, psychology, social science, social work, and sociology). Biology, Spanish, and math are the strongest academically. Psychology, business administration, and sociology and applied social relations are the largest.

Required: To graduate, students must complete 120 credit hours, including 30 to 48 hours in the major, with a GPA of 2.0. General education requirements include 12 credits in interdisciplinary studies, 9 in social sciences, 7 in natural sciences, and 3 each in math, fine arts, literature, writing, health and phys ed, and computer literacy. Students must also fulfill a foreign language requirement.

Special: ECSU offers co-op programs in all majors, cross-registration with the University of Connecticut, internships, study abroad in 22 countries, a Washington semester, work-study programs, accelerated degree programs, dual majors, a general studies degree, nondegree study, pass/fail options, and credit for military experience. In addition to the B.S./certification programs for early childhood and elementary education, teacher certification is available for middle school and secondary education studies. There are 5 national honor societies, a freshman honors program, and 4 departmental honors programs.

Faculty/Classroom: All teach undergraduates. No introductory courses are taught by graduate students. The average class size in a laboratory is 18 and in a regular course, 25.

Requirements: The SAT I or ACT is required. In addition, applicants must be graduates of an accredited secondary school or have a GED. They should have completed 13 high school academic credits, including 4 years of English, 3 of math, and 2 each of foreign language, social studies, and science (including 1 of lab science). An interview is recommended. ECSU requires applicants to be in the upper 50% of their class. A GPA of 2.5 is required. AP and CLEP credits are accepted. Important factors in the admissions decision are recommendations by school officials, advanced placement or honor courses, and leadership record.

Procedure: Freshmen are admitted fall and spring. Entrance exams should be taken in November or December of the senior year. There are early admissions, deferred admissions, and rolling admissions plans. Check with the school for current deadlines. The application fee is $40.

Transfer: 274 transfer students enrolled in a recent year. Applicants should have completed a minimum of 12 credit hours with a GPA of 2.5. Official college and high school transcripts are required, and an associate degree and an interview are recommended. 30 of 120 credits required for the bachelor's degree must be completed at ECSU.

Visiting: There are regularly scheduled orientations for prospective students, including small group discussions, a tour of the campus, and a personal interview. There are guides for informal visits and visitors may sit in on classes. To schedule a visit, contact the Office of Admissions at (860) 465-5286 or www.admissions@easternct.edu.

Financial Aid: The FAFSA is required. Check with the school for current deadlines.

International Students: In a recent year there were 71 international students enrolled. The school actively recruits these students. They must score 550 on the written TOEFL or 213 on the electronic version and also take the SAT I or the ACT, scoring 1020.

Computers: The mainframe is a DEC VAX 7620 minicomputer. The main lab houses approximately 100 PC stations, comprised of IBM, Mac, and Zenith equipment. Other computer labs are located in the Media Center Building and in the Learning Center. All systems are connected to the campus Ethernet network. All students may access the system. There are no time limits and no fees.

Admissions Contact: A video is available.
E-mail: admissions@ecsu.ctstateu.edu Web: ecsu.ctstateu.edu

FAIRFIELD UNIVERSITY
Fairfield, CT 06824-5195

B-4
(203) 254-4100; Fax: (203) 254-4199

Full-time: 1400 men, 1981 women	Faculty: 205; IIA, ++$
Part-time: 281 men, 358 women	Ph.D.s: 94%
Graduate: 393 men, 640 women	Student/Faculty: 16 to 1
Year: semesters, summer session	Tuition: $26,585
Application Deadline: January 15	Room & Board: $8920
Freshman Class: 7655 applied, 3782 accepted, 789 enrolled	
SAT I Verbal/Math: 590/607	ACT: 26 HIGHLY COMPETITIVE

Fairfield University, founded by the Jesuits in 1942, is a private, Roman Catholic Jesuit institution. There are 5 undergraduate and 5 graduate schools. In addition to regional accreditation, Fairfield has baccalaureate program accreditation with AACSB, AAMFT, ABET, ACS, GACREP, and NLN. The library contains 317,335 volumes, 858,916 microform items, and 13,239 audio/video tapes/CDs, and subscribes to 1796 periodicals. Computerized library services include the card catalog, interlibrary loans, and database searching. Special learning facilities include an art gallery, radio station, TV station, a media center, a 750-seat concert hall/theater, and a rehearsal and improvisation theater. The 200-acre campus is in a suburban area 60 miles northeast of New York City. Including any residence halls, there are 34 buildings.

Student Life: Undergraduates are from 33 states, 29 foreign countries, and Canada. 60% are from public schools. 87% are white. 80% are Catholic; 18% Protestant. The average age of freshmen is 18; all undergraduates, 20. 12% do not continue beyond their first year; 80% remain to graduate.

Housing: 2593 students can be accommodated in college housing, which includes coed dorms and on-campus apartments. In addition, there are special-interest houses and a substance-free floor. On-campus housing is guaranteed for all 4 years. 80% of students live on campus; of those, 85% remain on campus on weekends. Upperclassmen may keep cars.

Activities: There are no fraternities or sororities. There are 100 groups on campus, including art, band, cheerleading, chorale, computers, dance, debate, drama, ethnic, film, gay, honors, international, jazz band, literary magazine, musical theater, newspaper, orchestra, pep band, political, professional, radio and TV, religious, social, social service, student government, and yearbook. Popular campus events include Dogwood Festival, Martin Luther King Week, and Harvest Weekend.

Sports: There are 8 intercollegiate sports for men and 11 for women, and 15 intramural sports for men and 15 for women. Facilities include a gym, a 25-meter swimming pool, weight rooms, indoor and outdoor tennis courts, racquetball and volleyball courts, indoor and outdoor tracks, a sauna, a whirlpool, and fitness equipment.

Disabled Students: All of the campus is accessible. Wheelchair ramps, elevators, special parking, specially equipped rest rooms, special class scheduling, lowered drinking fountains, lowered telephones, and special housing are available. Accommodations for seeing-eye dogs and a library computer station for physically challenged students are also available.

Services: Counseling and information services are available, as is tutoring in every subject. There is a reader service for the blind.

Campus Safety and Security: Measures include 24-hour foot and vehicle patrol, self-defense education, security escort services, and shuttle buses. There are informal discussions, pamphlets/posters/films, emergency telephones, lighted pathways/sidewalks, EMT security officers, and a bike patrol.

Programs of Study: Fairfield confers B.A. and B.S. degrees. Associate and master's degrees are also awarded. Bachelor's degrees are awarded in BIOLOGICAL SCIENCE (biology/biological science and neurosciences), BUSINESS (accounting, banking and finance, business administration and management, international business management, and marketing/retailing/merchandising), COMMUNICATIONS AND THE ARTS (communications, English, fine arts, French, German, Italian, Spanish, and visual and performing arts), COMPUTER AND PHYSICAL SCIENCE (chemistry, computer science, information sciences and systems, mathematics, physics, and software engineering), ENGINEERING AND ENVIRONMENTAL DESIGN (computer engineering, electrical/electronics engineering, and mechanical engineering), HEALTH PROFESSIONS (nursing), SOCIAL SCIENCE (American studies, economics, history, international studies, philosophy, political science/government, psychology, religion, and sociology). Finance and biology are the strongest academically. Biology, psychology, and communications are the largest.

Required: To graduate, students must complete 120 credits, 60 of them in general education core requirements, with a minimum GPA of 2.0. Distribution requirements include 15 credits in philosophy, religious studies, and ethics, 15 credits in English and fine arts, 12 credits in math and natural sciences, 12 credits in history and social sciences, and 6 credits in foreign languages. First-year students are required to take a course in multiculturalism.

Special: Fairfield participates in CIEE and offers study abroad in 6 countries, a Washington semester, a federal work-study program, B.A.-B.S. degrees in economics, international studies, and psychology, student-designed majors, and dual majors in all subjects. A 3-2 engineering degree is offered with the University of Connecticut, Rensselaer Polytechnic Institute, Columbia University, and Stevens Institute of Technology. A general studies degree and credit for life, military, and work experience are available through the School of Continuing Education. Internships, both credit and noncredit, are offered at area corporations, publications, banks, and other businesses. Minors include women's studies, marine science, black studies, environmental studies, jazz, classical studies, Russian and Eastern studies, biochemistry, and Judaic studies. There are 14 national honor societies, including Phi Beta Kappa, and a freshman honors program. There is a university-wide honors program.

Faculty/Classroom: 57% of faculty are male; 43%, female. All both teach and do research. No introductory courses are taught by graduate students. The average class size in an introductory lecture is 29; in a laboratory, 13; and in a regular course, 23.

Admissions: 49% of the 2003-2004 applicants were accepted. The SAT I scores for the 2003-2004 freshman class were: Verbal--6% below 500, 47% between 500 and 599, 41% between 600 and 700, and 6% above 700; Math--4% below 500, 39% between 500 and 599, 50% between 600 and 700, and 7% above 700. 64% of the current freshmen were in the top fifth of their class; 91% were in the top two fifths. There were 6 National Merit semifinalists. 6 freshmen graduated first in their class.

Requirements: The SAT I is required. In addition, applicants must be graduates of an accredited secondary school. A B average is required. Students should have completed 15 academic credits, including 4 credits of English, 3 to 4 credits each of history, math, and lab science, and 2 to 4 credits of a foreign language. The school recommends SAT II: Subject tests in writing, literature, language, and math, and, for nursing and science majors, in the sciences. An interview is recommended. Fairfield requires applicants to be in the upper 30% of their class. A GPA of 3.0 is required. AP and CLEP credits are accepted. Important factors in the admissions decision are advanced placement or honor courses, leadership record, and evidence of special talent.

Procedure: Freshmen are admitted in the fall. Entrance exams should be taken in the spring of the junior year or fall of the senior year. There are early decision and deferred admissions plans. Early decision applications should be filed by November 15; regular applications, by January 15 for fall entry. The fall 2003 application fee was $55. Notification of early decision is sent December 15; regular decision, April 1. 135 early decision candidates were accepted for the 2003-2004 class. 773 applicants were on the 2003 waiting list; 121 were admitted. Applications are accepted on-line.

Transfer: 70 transfer students enrolled in 2002-2003. The SAT I and a college GPA of 2.5 (2.8 in business) are required. 60 of 120 credits required for the bachelor's degree must be completed at Fairfield.

Visiting: There are regularly scheduled orientations for prospective students, consisting of a summer orientation the third week in June and a fall program 2 days before classes begin. There are guides for informal visits and visitors may sit in on classes and stay overnight. To schedule a visit, contact the Admissions Office.

Financial Aid: In 2003-2004, 71% of all full-time freshmen and 51% of continuing full-time students received some form of financial aid. 48% of full-time freshmen and 36% of continuing full-time students received need-based aid. The average freshman award was $13,841. Need-based scholarships or need-based grants averaged $10,216 ($20,000 maximum); need-based self-help aid (loans and jobs) averaged $4104 ($6125 maximum); non-need-based athletic scholarships averaged $15,814 ($35,770 maximum); and other non-need-based awards and non-need-based scholarships averaged $10,936 ($26,100 maximum). 14% of undergraduates work part time. Average annual earnings from campus work are $1028. The average financial indebtedness of the 2003 graduate was $25,194. Fairfield is a member of CSS. The CSS/Profile or FAFSA, parent and student tax returns, and a verification statement from first-time applicants are required. The deadline for filing freshman financial aid applications for fall entry is February 15.

International Students: There are 47 international students enrolled. The school actively recruits these students. They must score 550 on the written TOEFL or 213 on the electronic version and also take the SAT I or the ACT, scoring 1150 on the SAT I.

Computers: The mainframe is a VAX 6430. Staffed computer labs are maintained in all academic buildings. Mac and IBM PS/2 PCs are available. Terminals are networked throughout campus for access to Netscape and the mainframe. All students may access the system daily until midnight. There are no time limits and no fees. It is strongly recommended that all students have a personal computer.

Graduates: From July 1, 2002 to June 30, 2003, 832 bachelor's degrees were awarded. The most popular majors were marketing (12%), communications (11%), and English (11%). In an average class, 76% graduate in 4 years or less, 78% graduate in 5 years or less, and 80% graduate in 6 years or less. 117 companies recruited on campus in 2002-2003. Of the 2002 graduating class, 20% were enrolled in graduate school within 6 months of graduation and 60% were employed.

Admissions Contact: Marianne Gumpper, Interim Director. A video is available. E-mail: *admis@mail.fairfield.edu* Web: *www.fairfield.edu*

MITCHELL COLLEGE
New London, CT 06320

	(800) 443-2811
	(800) 443-2811; Fax: (860) 444-1209
Full-time: 631 men and women	**Faculty:** 24
Part-time: 114 men and women	**Ph.D.s:** 55%
Graduate: none	**Student/Faculty:** 26 to 1
Year: semesters, summer session	**Tuition:** $18,128
Application Deadline: August 30	**Room & Board:** $8268
Freshman Class: n/av	
SAT I or ACT: required	**COMPETITIVE**

Mitchell College, founded in 1938, is a private institution offering associate and bachelor degree programs in the liberal arts and professional areas. Some information in this capsule and profile is approximate. The 2 libraries contain 45,000 volumes, 38,928 microform items, and 50 audio/video tapes/CDs, and subscribe to 90 periodicals. Computerized library services include the card catalog, interlibrary loans, and database searching. Special learning facilities include a learning resource center. The 65-acre campus is in a suburban area on the shore of the Thames River where it meets Long Island Sound. Including any residence halls, there are 19 buildings.

Student Life: 54% of undergraduates are from Connecticut. Students are from 17 states, 5 foreign countries, and Canada. 50% are from public schools. 60% are white; 10% African American. 44% are Catholic; 31% claim no religious affiliation; 16% Protestant; 7% Jewish. The average age of freshmen is 18; all undergraduates, 20. 35% do not continue beyond their first year; 65% remain to graduate.

Housing: 450 students can be accommodated in college housing, which includes single-sex and coed dorms. On-campus housing is guaranteed for all 4 years. 85% of students live on campus; of those, 68% remain on campus on weekends. Alcohol is not permitted. All students may keep cars.

Activities: There are no fraternities or sororities. There are 35 groups on campus, including art, cheerleading, choir, chorus, computers, dance, drama, ethnic, gay, honors, international, newspaper, professional, religious, social, social service, student government, and yearbook.

Sports: There are 9 intercollegiate sports for men and 9 for women, and 15 intramural sports for men and 15 for women. Facilities include a basketball court, a fitness center, 2 beaches, natural and groomed trails, woods, tennis courts, and athletic fields for all varsity teams.

Disabled Students: 50% of the campus is accessible. Wheelchair ramps, elevators, special parking, specially equipped rest rooms, and special class scheduling are available.

Services: Counseling and information services are available, as is tutoring in every subject. There is a reader service for the blind.

Campus Safety and Security: Measures include 24-hour foot and vehicle patrol, security escort services, shuttle buses, and informal discussions. There are emergency telephones and lighted pathways/sidewalks.

Programs of Study: Mitchell College confers B.A. and B.S. degrees. Associate degrees are also awarded. Bachelor's degrees are awarded in BUSINESS (business administration and management and sports management), EDUCATION (early childhood), SOCIAL SCIENCE (criminal justice, human development, liberal arts/general studies, and psychology). Early childhood education is the strongest academically. Business administration and liberal and professional studies are the largest.

Required: To graduate, students must complete 120 credits with a minimum GPA of 2.0; 2.67 for early childhood education. A first-year seminar and a course in computer systems is required. A capstone is required in human development.

Special: Numerous internships are available through department heads. Work-study programs and B.A.-B.S. degrees are available. Student-designed majors are possible in liberal and professional studies. There are 2 national honor societies, including Phi Beta Kappa, and 1 departmental honors program.

Faculty/Classroom: 46% of faculty are male; 54%, female. All teach undergraduates. The average class size in an introductory lecture is 12; in a laboratory, 10; and in a regular course, 12.

Requirements: The SAT I or ACT is required. In addition, the GED is accepted. A recommendation and a personal statement are required. A GPA of 2.0 is required. AP and CLEP credits are accepted. Important factors in the admissions decision are extracurricular activities record, recommendations by school officials, and personality/intangible qualities.

Procedure: Freshmen are admitted fall and spring. Entrance exams should be taken during summer orientation. There are early decision and deferred admissions plans. Early decision applications should be filed by November 15; regular applications, by August 30 for fall entry and January 15 for spring entry, along with a $30 fee. Notification of early decision is sent December 15; regular decision, on a rolling basis. 35 early decision candidates were accepted for the 2003-2004 class. Applications are accepted on computer disk and on-line.

Transfer: 45 transfer students enrolled in 2002-2003. Applicants must submit college transcripts and a letter of good standing, in addition to fulfilling regular application requirements. 30 of 120 credits required for the bachelor's degree must be completed at Mitchell College.

Visiting: There are regularly scheduled orientations for prospective students, including a student-guided tour and an interview with an admissions counselor. There are guides for informal visits and visitors may sit in on classes. To schedule a visit, contact the Admissions Office at *admissions@mitchell.edu*.

Financial Aid: In a recent year, 77% of all full-time freshmen and 80% of continuing full-time students received some form of financial aid. 70% of all full-time students received need-based aid. The average freshman award was $9000. The FAFSA is required. The priority date for freshman financial aid applications for fall entry is March 1. The deadline for filing freshman financial aid applications for fall entry is May 1.

International Students: There are 12 international students enrolled. The school actively recruits these students. They must score 500 on the written TOEFL or 173 on the electronic version and also take the APIEL and the SAT I or the ACT.

Computers: Mitchell offers a computer for every 4 students. Computers are available in 4 labs, all residence halls, the library, and the Academic Success Center. All students may access the system at all times. There are no time limits and no fees. It is strongly recommended that all students have a personal computer.

Graduates: In a recent year, 6 bachelor's degrees were awarded. The most popular major was human development and family studies (100%). In an average class, 60% graduate in 4 years or less. 20 companies recruited on campus in a recent year.

Admissions Contact: Kathleen Neal, Director of Admissions. A video is available. E-mail: *neal_k@mitchell.edu* Web: *www.mitchell.edu*

QUINNIPIAC UNIVERSITY
Hamden, CT 06518

C-3
(203) 582-8600
(800) 462-1944; Fax: (203) 582-8906

Full-time: 1953 men, 3136 women	**Faculty:** 225; IIA, ++$
Part-time: 152 men, 229 women	**Ph.D.s:** 78%
Graduate: 709 men, 942 women	**Student/Faculty:** 23 to 1
Year: semesters, summer session	**Tuition:** $21,120
Application Deadline: February 1	**Room & Board:** $9450
Freshman Class: 8881 applied, 5503 accepted, 1318 enrolled	
SAT I Verbal/Math: 540/550	**ACT:** 25 **VERY COMPETITIVE**

Quinnipiac University, founded in 1929, is a private institution offering undergraduate and graduate degrees in health sciences, business, communications, liberal arts, education, and law. There are 4 undergraduate and 3 graduate schools. In addition to regional accreditation, Quinnipiac has baccalaureate program accreditation with AACSB, ABA, AOTA, APTA, CAHEA, and NLN. The 2 libraries contain 304,875 volumes, 9100 microform items, and 1890 audio/video tapes/CDs, and subscribe to 3900 periodicals. Computerized library services include interlibrary loans and database searching. Special learning facilities include a learning resource center, radio station, TV station, and a critical care nursing lab. The 400-acre campus is in a suburban area 8 miles north of New Haven and 35 miles south of Hartford. Including any residence halls, there are 35 buildings.

Student Life: 66% of undergraduates are from out of state, mostly the Northeast. Students are from 26 states, 12 foreign countries, and Canada. 75% are from public schools. 90% are white. 58% are Catholic; 20% Protestant; 12% claim no religious affiliation; 8% Jewish. The average age of freshmen is 19; all undergraduates, 21. 13% do not continue beyond their first year; 69% remain to graduate.

Housing: 3450 students can be accommodated in college housing, which includes coed dorms, on-campus apartments, and off-campus apartments. Housing is guaranteed for 3 years to incoming freshmen and 2 years for incoming transfer students. All seniors live off campus. 75% of students live on campus; of those, 70% remain on campus on weekends. Upperclassmen may keep cars.

Activities: 5% of men belong to 1 local and 1 national fraternity; 6% of women belong to 1 local and 2 national sororities. There are 65 groups on campus, including cheerleading, chorale, dance, drama, ethnic, film, gay, honors, international, literary magazine, music society, musical theater, newspaper, pep band, photography, political, professional, radio and TV, religious, science, social, social service, student government, women's, and yearbook. Popular campus events include May Weekend, Lip Sync Contest, and Parents Weekend.

Sports: There are 9 intercollegiate sports for men and 10 for women, and 6 intramural sports for men and 6 for women. Facilities include more than 20 acres of playing fields, a 1500-seat gym, 2 basketball courts, a weight training room, a steam room, and a state-of-the-art fitness facility with a large multipurpose room for indoor tennis, basketball, volleyball, and aerobics, and a suspended indoor track.

Disabled Students: All of the campus is accessible. Wheelchair ramps, elevators, special parking, specially equipped rest rooms, special class scheduling, lowered drinking fountains, lowered telephones, and special housing are available.

Services: Counseling and information services are available, as is tutoring in most subjects, including all freshman-level courses and others by request. Special workshops on work study skills, library resources, and time management are available.

Campus Safety and Security: Measures include 24-hour foot and vehicle patrol, self-defense education, security escort services, and shuttle buses. There are informal discussions, pamphlets/posters/films, emergency telephones, lighted pathways/sidewalks, perimeter security in the form of contract security officers at all entrances, and vehicle and occupant check-in identification.

Programs of Study: Quinnipiac confers B.A., B.S., and B.H.S. degrees. Master's degrees are also awarded. Bachelor's degrees are awarded in BIOLOGICAL SCIENCE (biochemistry, biology/biological science, biotechnology, and microbiology), BUSINESS (accounting, banking and finance, business administration and management, business economics, entrepreneurial studies, international business management, management science, and marketing/retailing/merchandising), COMMUNICATIONS AND THE ARTS (advertising, communications, English, journalism, public relations, and Spanish), COMPUTER AND PHYSICAL SCIENCE (chemistry, computer science, digital arts/technology, and mathematics), HEALTH PROFESSIONS (health care administration, health science, nursing, occupational therapy, predentistry, premedicine, radiological science, respiratory therapy, and veterinary science), SOCIAL SCIENCE (criminal justice, economics, gerontology, history, liberal arts/general studies, paralegal studies, political science/government, prelaw, psychobiology, psychology, social science, and sociology). Psychology and physical therapy are the strongest academically. Mass communications, physical therapy, and accounting are the largest.

Required: All students must complete 50 semester hours of the core curriculum, which includes competency in English, math, oral communi-

cations, and computer information systems. Courses in arts, behavioral and social sciences, humanities, physical and biological sciences, economics, and management are also part of the core. To graduate, students must maintain a minimum GPA of 2.0 over 120 total semester hours.

Special: Internships in all majors, study abroad in more than 25 countries, a Washington semester with American University, work-study programs, dual and student-designed majors, B.A.-B.S. degrees, credit for life experience, and nondegree study are available. A 5 1/2-year freshman entry-level master's in physical therapy and occupational therapy is offered, as well as a 6-year freshman entry-level, physician assistant master's program, and a 5-year master of arts in education for those interested in teaching at the elementary, middle, or high school level. There are 8 national honor societies, a freshman honors program, and 9 departmental honors programs.

Faculty/Classroom: 58% of faculty are male; 42%, female. 85% teach undergraduates, 58% do research, and 53% do both. No introductory courses are taught by graduate students. The average class size in an introductory lecture is 24; in a laboratory, 15; and in a regular course, 22.

Admissions: 62% of the 2003-2004 applicants were accepted. The SAT I scores for the 2003-2004 freshman class were: Verbal--23% below 500, 58% between 500 and 599, 17% between 600 and 700, and 1% above 700; Math--16% below 500, 57% between 500 and 599, 25% between 600 and 700, and 2% above 700. The ACT scores were 10% below 21, 29% between 21 and 23, 30% between 24 and 26, 25% between 27 and 28, and 6% above 28. 44% of the current freshmen were in the top fifth of their class; 78% were in the top two fifths. 35 freshmen graduated first in their class.

Requirements: The SAT I or ACT is required. In addition, a minimum composite score of 1000 on the SAT I or 23 on the ACT is recommended. All students must have completed 16 academic credits, including 4 in English, 3 in math, 2 each in science and social studies, and 5 in electives. The GED is accepted. An interview is recommended, and an essay is required. Quinnipiac requires applicants to be in the upper 50% of their class. A GPA of 2.5 is required. AP and CLEP credits are accepted. Important factors in the admissions decision are advanced placement or honor courses, extracurricular activities record, and leadership record.

Procedure: Freshmen are admitted fall and spring. Entrance exams should be taken in the junior year and early in the senior year. There is a deferred admissions plan. Applications should be filed by February 1 for fall entry and December 15 for spring entry, along with a $45 fee. Notification is sent on a rolling basis. 600 applicants were on the 2003 waiting list; 30 were admitted. Applications are accepted on-line through CollegeNET and the school's web site.

Transfer: 148 transfer students enrolled in a recent year. Transfer students must have a minimum college GPA of 2.5 and must submit SAT I scores and high school or college transcripts. An interview is recommended. 45 of 120 credits required for the bachelor's degree must be completed at Quinnipiac.

Visiting: There are regularly scheduled orientations for prospective students, consisting of interviews, a group information session, student-guided tours, financial aid sessions, an opportunity to speak with faculty, and open houses. There are guides for informal visits and visitors may sit in on classes. To schedule a visit, contact the Admissions Office.

Financial Aid: In 2003-2004, 70% of all full-time students received some form of financial aid. 55% of all full-time students received need-based aid. The average freshman award was $12,800. 28% of undergraduates work part time. Average annual earnings from campus work are $1800. The average financial indebtedness of the 2003 graduate was $17,170. The FAFSA is required. The deadline for filing freshman financial aid applications for fall entry is March 1.

International Students: In a recent year, there were 35 international students enrolled. The school actively recruits these students. They must score 550 on the written TOEFL or 213 on the electronic version and also take the SAT I or the ACT.

Computers: The mainframes are a DEC Alpha 2100 and a Sun Server 450. 45 networked PCs are available to all students in the computer center, with an additional 90 PCs in various labs and classrooms for students in specific majors. Residence halls are networked to the central system, and all students have access to e-mail, the Internet, and support software. All students may access the system 24 hours a day. There are no time limits and no fees. All students are required to have personal computers.

Graduates: From July 1, 2002 to June 30, 2003, 1040 bachelor's degrees were awarded. The most popular majors were mass communications (11%), occupational therapy (10%), and physical therapy (9%). In an average class, 60% graduate in 4 years or less, 64% graduate in 5 years or less, and 69% graduate in 6 years or less. 75 companies recruited on campus in 2002-2003. Of the 2002 graduating class, 15% were enrolled in graduate school within 6 months of graduation and 88% were employed.

Admissions Contact: Joan Isaac Mohr, Dean of Admissions. A video is available. E-mail: *admissions@quinnipiac.edu* Web: *www.quinnipiac.edu*

SACRED HEART UNIVERSITY
B-4

Fairfield, CT 06825   (203) 371-7880; Fax: (203) 365-7607

Full-time: 1233 men, 1807 women	**Faculty:** IIA, av$
Part-time: 314 men, 695 women	**Ph.D.s:** 83%
Graduate: 539 men, 1142 women	**Student/Faculty:** 18 to 1
Year: semesters, summer session	**Tuition:** $20,268
Application Deadline: open	**Room & Board:** $8910
Freshman Class: 4701 applied, 3219 accepted, 817 enrolled	
SAT I Verbal/Math: 520/530	**COMPETITIVE**

Sacred Heart University, founded in 1963, is a private Catholic institution that offers majors within health sciences, liberal arts and sciences, business, education, and information technology. There are 4 undergraduate and 3 graduate schools. In addition to regional accreditation, SHU has baccalaureate program accreditation with APTA, CSWE, and NLN. The library contains 121,064 volumes, 770 microform items, and 1125 audio/video tapes/CDs, and subscribes to 4568 periodicals. Computerized library services include the card catalog, interlibrary loans, and database searching. Special learning facilities include a learning resource center, art gallery, radio station, and center for performing arts. The 56-acre campus is in a suburban area in southwestern Connecticut, 55 miles northeast of New York City. Including any residence halls, there are 19 buildings.

Student Life: 50% of undergraduates are from out of state, mostly the Northeast. Students are from 27 states, 45 foreign countries, and Canada. 67% are from public schools. 85% are white. 75% are Catholic; 17% Protestant. The average age of freshmen is 18; all undergraduates, 20. 20% do not continue beyond their first year; 80% remain to graduate.

Housing: 1700 students can be accommodated in college housing, which includes coed dorms, on-campus apartments, and off-campus apartments. In addition, there are honors floors and wellness floors. On-campus housing is guaranteed for all 4 years and is available on a first-come, first-served basis. 66% of students live on campus; of those, 75% remain on campus on weekends. Alcohol is not permitted. Upperclassmen may keep cars.

Activities: 8% of men belong to 4 local fraternities; 7% of women belong to 6 local sororities. There are 70 groups on campus, including art, band, cheerleading, choir, chorale, chorus, computers, dance, debate, drama, drill team, ethnic, film, gay, honors, international, jazz band, literary magazine, marching band, musical theater, newspaper, orchestra, pep band, photography, political, professional, radio and TV, religious, social, social service, student government, and yearbook. Popular campus events include Harvest Weekend, Black History Month, and Latino Month.

Sports: There are 15 intercollegiate sports for men and 17 for women, and 7 intramural sports for men and 7 for women. Facilities include a health and recreation center with 4 multipurpose athletic courts, seating for 2200, and a fitness center. There is a field turf football field, an all-weather track, 6 championship tennis courts, and a softball field.

Disabled Students: 90% of the campus is accessible. Wheelchair ramps, elevators, special parking, specially equipped rest rooms, special class scheduling, lowered drinking fountains, lowered telephones, and room nameplates are available.

Services: There is a reader service for the blind and remedial math, reading, and writing.

Campus Safety and Security: Measures include 24-hour foot and vehicle patrol, self-defense education, security escort services, and shuttle buses. There are informal discussions, pamphlets/posters/films, emergency telephones, and lighted pathways/sidewalks. All campus-owned residence halls have sprinklers and alarms and are designated nonsmoking.

Programs of Study: SHU confers B.A. and B.S. degrees. Associate and master's degrees are also awarded. Bachelor's degrees are awarded in BIOLOGICAL SCIENCE (biology/biological science), BUSINESS (accounting, banking and finance, business administration and management, international business management, and management science), COMMUNICATIONS AND THE ARTS (art, English, media arts, and Spanish), COMPUTER AND PHYSICAL SCIENCE (chemistry, computer science, and mathematics), ENGINEERING AND ENVIRONMENTAL DESIGN (environmental science), HEALTH PROFESSIONS (medical technology and nursing), SOCIAL SCIENCE (criminal justice, economics, history, international studies, liberal arts/general studies, philosophy, physical fitness/movement, political science/government, psychology, religion, social work, and sociology). Business, biology, and psychology are the strongest academically. Business, computer science, and psychology are the largest.

Required: All students must complete 120 credit hours, including 30 to 58 in the major, while maintaining a minimum 2.0 GPA. Distribution requirements include an 18-credit required core consisting of freshman writing, oral communication, college math, and literature and civilizations, and a 30- to 32-credit elective core consisting of 9 credits of social science, 9 of philosophy and religious studies, 6 of arts and humanities, and 6 of science and math. B.S. candidates need an additional course each of math and science; B.A. candidates, an additional 6 credits of foreign language.

Special: SHU offers co-op programs in all majors, paid and unpaid internships at area corporations, including Fortune 500 companies, hospitals, newspapers, and social service agencies, study abroad worldwide, legislative internships, and on-campus work-study. There are 11 national honor societies, a freshman honors program, and 1 departmental honors program.

Faculty/Classroom: 51% of faculty are male; 49%, female. All teach undergraduates and 80% do research. No introductory courses are taught by graduate students. The average class size in an introductory lecture is 20; in a laboratory, 10; and in a regular course, 20.

Admissions: 68% of the 2003-2004 applicants were accepted. The SAT I scores for the 2003-2004 freshman class were: Verbal--34% below 500, 54% between 500 and 599, 11% between 600 and 700, and 1% above 700; Math--14% below 500, 51% between 500 and 599, 31% between 600 and 700, and 1% above 700. 33% of the current freshmen were in the top fifth of their class; 65% were in the top two fifths. 5 freshmen graduated first in their class.

Requirements: The SAT I or ACT is required. In addition, an application, essay, and 1 letter of recommendation are required. An interview is recommended. Required are 4 years of English and 3 years of math, science, history, and language, with 4 years preferred. SHU requires applicants to be in the upper 50% of their class. A GPA of 3.0 is required. AP and CLEP credits are accepted. Important factors in the admissions decision are advanced placement or honor courses, leadership record, and recommendations by school officials.

Procedure: Freshmen are admitted fall and spring. Entrance exams should be taken in May of the junior year and/or November of the senior year. There are early decision, early admissions, and deferred admissions plans. Early decision applications should be filed by October 1; regular applications, are processed on a rolling basis for fall entry. There is a $50 application fee. Notification of early decision is sent October 15; regular decision, on a rolling basis beginning January 1. 159 early decision candidates were accepted for the 2003-2004 class. 369 applicants were on the 2003 waiting list; 20 were admitted. Applications are accepted on computer disk and on-line through Common Application, CTMentor, Catholic Application, Next Stop College, and SHU online appplication.

Transfer: 175 transfer students enrolled in 2002-2003. Applicants require a minimum GPA of 2.7. 30 of 120 credits required for the bachelor's degree must be completed at SHU.

Visiting: There are regularly scheduled orientations for prospective students, including Monday-Friday tours and interviews, Saturday tours, interviews and information sessions, and open house programs. There are guides for informal visits and visitors may sit in on classes and stay overnight. To schedule a visit, contact the Office of Admissions.

Financial Aid: In 2003-2004, 88% of all full-time freshmen and 83% of continuing full-time students received some form of financial aid. 73% of full-time freshmen and 70% of continuing full-time students received need-based aid. The average freshman award was $13,441, with $5094 ($24,550 maximum) from need-based scholarships or grants, $3837 ($9125 maximum) from need-based self-help aid (loans and jobs), $823 ($29,639 maximum) from non-need-based athletic scholarships, and $2310 ($11,000 maximum) from other non-need-based awards and non-need-based scholarships. Private scholarships/grants and alternative loans averaged $1377 ($28,630 maximum). 27% of undergraduates work part time. Average annual earnings from campus work are $1320. The average financial indebtedness of the 2003 graduate was $18,213. SHU is a member of CSS. The CSS Profile or FAFSA is required. The priority date for freshman financial aid applications for fall entry is February 15.

International Students: There are 47 international students enrolled. The school actively recruits these students. They must score 550 on the written TOEFL or 270 on the electronic version and also take the SAT I or the ACT.

Computers: Students access the Internet via laptops. There are also 17 computer labs/classrooms with 300 accessible terminals. Each student also has 15MB on a web server to host student web pages. A Dell laptop is included in the tuition. Students receive a new laptop in their junior year. All students may access the system 24 hours a day. There are no time limits and no fees. All students are required to have personal computers.

Graduates: The most popular majors were business/finance (37%), psychology (20%), and computer science (5%). In an average class, 47% graduate in 4 years or less, 55% graduate in 5 years or less, and 56% graduate in 6 years or less. 147 companies recruited on campus in 2002-2003. Of the 2002 graduating class, 33% were enrolled in graduate school within 6 months of graduation and 61% were employed.

Admissions Contact: Karen N. Guastelle, Dean of Undergraduate Admissions. E-mail: *enroll@sacredheart.edu* Web: *www.sacredheart.edu*

SAINT JOSEPH COLLEGE
West Hartford, CT 06117

C-2

(860) 231-5216; Fax: (860) 233-5695

Full-time: 2 men, 845 women	Faculty: 73; IIA, av$
Part-time: 16 men, 330 women	Ph.D.s: 82%
Graduate: 85 men, 558 women	Student/Faculty: 12 to 1
Year: semesters, summer session	Tuition: $20,900
Application Deadline: rolling	Room & Board: $8785
Freshman Class: 709 applied, 485 accepted, 190 enrolled	
SAT I Verbal/Math: 490/470	COMPETITIVE

Saint Joseph College, founded in 1932 and affiliated with the Roman Catholic Church, is a private primarily women's college offering a liberal arts education with preprofessional programs in nursing, education, and business at the undergraduate level. The Weekend College and graduate school offer coeducational studies. In addition to regional accreditation, SJC has baccalaureate program accreditation with ADA, CSWE, and NLN. The library contains 122,357 volumes, 58,772 microform items, and 3000 audio/video tapes/CDs, and subscribes to 557 periodicals. Computerized library services include the card catalog, interlibrary loans, and database searching. Special learning facilities include a learning resource center, art gallery, academic resources center, and 2 lab schools: the Gengras Center for Exceptional Children and the School for Young Children. The 84-acre campus is in a suburban area 3 miles west of Hartford. Including any residence halls, there are 13 buildings.

Student Life: 91% of undergraduates are from Connecticut. Students are from 9 states. 88% are from public schools. 75% are white; 12% African American; 11% Hispanic. Most are Catholic. The average age of freshmen is 18; all undergraduates, 21. 20% do not continue beyond their first year; 65% remain to graduate.

Housing: 428 students can be accommodated in college housing, which includes single-sex dorms. On-campus housing is guaranteed for all 4 years. 52% of students commute. Alcohol is not permitted. All students may keep cars.

Activities: There are no fraternities or sororities. There are 20 groups on campus, including art, cheerleading, choir, chorale, chorus, dance, drama, ethnic, honors, international, literary magazine, musical theater, political, professional, religious, social, social service, student government, and yearbook. Popular campus events include Convocation, Cultural Awareness Day, and Symposium Day.

Sports: There are 8 intercollegiate sports for women and 8 intramural sports for women. Facilities include an all-weather track, a gym, an exercise room, tennis courts, a dance studio, and a pool.

Disabled Students: 75% of the campus is accessible. Wheelchair ramps, elevators, special parking, specially equipped rest rooms, special class scheduling, lowered drinking fountains, and lowered telephones are available. Other needs are met on a case-by-case basis.

Services: Counseling and information services are available, as is tutoring in most subjects, including ESL. There is remedial math, reading, and writing. Other services are arranged as needed through the Academic Resource Center.

Campus Safety and Security: Measures include 24-hour foot and vehicle patrol, self-defense education, security escort services, and shuttle buses. There are informal discussions, pamphlets/posters/films, emergency telephones, and lighted pathways/sidewalks.

Programs of Study: SJC confers B.A., B.S., and B.S.N. degrees. Master's degrees are also awarded. Bachelor's degrees are awarded in BIOLOGICAL SCIENCE (biology/biological science, and nutrition), BUSINESS (business economics and management science), COMMUNICATIONS AND THE ARTS (art history and appreciation, English, and Spanish), COMPUTER AND PHYSICAL SCIENCE (chemistry and mathematics), EDUCATION (special), ENGINEERING AND ENVIRONMENTAL DESIGN (environmental science), HEALTH PROFESSIONS (nursing), SOCIAL SCIENCE (American studies, child psychology/development, dietetics, family/consumer studies, history, international studies, liberal arts/general studies, philosophy, psychology, religion, social work, sociology, and women's studies). Psychology, education, and sciences are the strongest academically. Education, psychology, and English are the largest.

Required: All students must maintain a minimum GPA of 2.0, pass a written or oral comprehensive exam, and take 120 total credit hours including a minimum of 30 in the major and liberal arts requirements of 12 credits in 4 core areas, plus 6 credits in religion, 9 in humanities, 9 in social studies, 7 to 8 in natural science/math, and 1 in phys ed.

Special: The college offers cross-registration through the Hartford consortium, numerous internships, study abroad in Great Britain, Europe, Japan, and Spain, accelerated degree programs in business administration, interdisciplinary majors, student-designed majors, and a dual major in biology-chemistry. Credit for life experience, nondegree study, and pass/fail options are available. There is 1 national honor society and a freshman honors program.

Faculty/Classroom: 34% of faculty are male; 66%, female. 92% teach undergraduates. No introductory courses are taught by graduate students. The average class size in an introductory lecture is 30; in a laboratory, 20; and in a regular course, 20.

Admissions: 68% of the 2003-2004 applicants were accepted. The SAT I scores for the 2003-2004 freshman class were: Verbal--54% below 500, 34% between 500 and 599, 11% between 600 and 700, and 1% above 700; Math--66% below 500, 28% between 500 and 599, and 6% between 600 and 700. 38% of the current freshmen were in the top fifth of their class; 73% were in the top two fifths.

Requirements: The SAT I is required. In addition, applicants need 16 academic credits distributed among English, foreign language, history, math, science, and social studies. The GED is accepted, and an interview is recommended. A GPA of 2.5 is required. AP and CLEP credits are accepted. Important factors in the admissions decision are advanced placement or honor courses, recommendations by school officials, and evidence of special talent.

Procedure: Freshmen are admitted fall and spring. Entrance exams should be taken. There are early decision, rolling, and deferred admissions plans. Early decision applications should be filed by November 15. There is a $35 application fee. Notification is sent on a rolling basis. 69 early decision candidates were accepted for the 2003-2004 class. Applications are accepted on-line.

Transfer: 120 transfer students enrolled in 2002-2003. Saint Joseph accepts transfers up to the beginning of the junior year. Applicants need a minimum college GPA of 2.7. 45 of 120 credits required for the bachelor's degree must be completed at SJC.

Visiting: There are regularly scheduled orientations for prospective students, including open houses, preview days, overnights, individual appointments, and campus tours. There are guides for informal visits and visitors may sit in on classes and stay overnight. To schedule a visit, contact Mary Yuskis, Director of Admissions at (860) 231-5216 or *admissions@sjc.edu*.

Financial Aid: In 2003-2004, 94% of all full-time freshmen and 86% of continuing full-time students received some form of financial aid. 86% of full-time freshmen and 85% of continuing full-time students received need-based aid. The average freshman award was $17,898, with $6531 ($18,000 maximum) from need-based scholarships or grants, $4295 ($8425 maximum) from need-based self-help aid (loans and jobs), and $7071 ($12,000 maximum) from non-need-based awards and scholarships. 61% of undergraduates work part time. Average annual earnings from campus work are $1670. The average financial indebtedness of the 2003 graduate was $17,649. SJC is a member of CSS. The FAFSA is required. The priority date for freshman financial aid applications for fall entry is February 15. The deadline for filing freshman financial aid applications for fall entry is March 15.

International Students: They must score 530 on the written TOEFL and also take the SAT I or the ACT.

Computers: The mainframe is a Microsoft NT 4.0 network. The McDonough network center houses 92 Dell Pentium PCs and 12 Power Macs. Access to the Internet, e-mail, and various software packages and educational tools are available. All students may access the system any time. There are no time limits and no fees.

Graduates: From July 1, 2002 to June 30, 2003, 205 bachelor's degrees were awarded. The most popular majors were social work (12%), child study (12%), and nursing (10%). In an average class, 1% graduate in 3 years or less, 60% graduate in 4 years or less, 5% graduate in 5 years or less, and 5% graduate in 6 years or less. 140 companies recruited on campus in 2002-2003. Of the 2002 graduating class, 21% were enrolled in graduate school within 6 months of graduation and 79% were employed.

Admissions Contact: Mary Yuskis, Director of Admissions. A video is available. E-mail: *admissions@mercy.sjc.edu* Web: *www.sjc.edu*

SOUTHERN CONNECTICUT STATE UNIVERSITY
New Haven, CT 06515

C-3

(203) 392-5649; Fax: (203) 392-5727

Full-time: 2480 men, 3815 women	Faculty: 328; IIA,
Part-time: 885 men, 1190 women	Ph.D.s: 83%
Graduate: 1015 men, 2925 women	Student/Faculty: 17 to 1
Year: semesters, summer session	Tuition: $4030 ($10,000)
Application Deadline: open	Room & Board: $6285
Freshman Class: n/av	
SAT I: required	COMPETITIVE

Southern Connecticut State University, founded in 1893, provides undergraduate and graduate liberal arts programs in the arts, business, education, professional studies, and the sciences. It is part of the Connecticut State University system. Figures given in this capsule and in this profile are approximate. There are 5 undergraduate and 6 graduate schools. In addition to regional accreditation, SCSU has baccalaureate program accreditation with CSWE and NLN. The library contains 495,660 volumes, 753,033 microform items, and 4689 audio/video tapes/CDs, and subscribes to 3549 periodicals. Computerized library services include the card catalog, interlibrary loans, and database searching. Special learning facilities include a learning resource center, art gallery, planetarium, radio station, and TV station. The 168-acre campus is in an urban area 35 miles south of Hartford and 90 miles from New York City. Including any residence halls, there are 28 buildings.

Student Life: 92% of undergraduates are from Connecticut. Students are from 20 states, 36 foreign countries, and Canada. 90% are from public schools. 77% are white. 64% are Catholic; 18% Protestant. The average age of freshmen is 19; all undergraduates, 22. 25% do not continue beyond their first year; 48% remain to graduate.

Housing: 2100 students can be accommodated in college housing, which includes single-sex dorms and on-campus apartments. On-campus housing is guaranteed for all 4 years. 72% of students commute. Upperclassmen may keep cars.

Activities: 1% of men belong to 3 local and 3 national fraternities; 1% of women belong to 1 local and 2 national sororities. There are 70 groups on campus, including art, band, cheerleading, choir, chorale, chorus, computers, dance, drama, drill team, ethnic, gay, honors, international, jazz band, literary magazine, marching band, musical theater, newspaper, pep band, photography, political, professional, radio and TV, religious, social, social service, student government, and yearbook. Popular campus events include Springfest, Parents Day, and Octoberfest.

Sports: There are 9 intercollegiate sports for men and 8 for women. Facilities include a 6000-seat artificial-surface playing complex for football, soccer, field hockey, and track; field house and gym facilities for basketball, gymnastics, badminton, tennis, track and field, volleyball, and indoor baseball; and an 8-lane swimming pool.

Disabled Students: 80% of the campus is accessible. Wheelchair ramps, elevators, special parking, specially equipped rest rooms, special class scheduling, lowered drinking fountains, lowered telephones, and special computer facilities are available.

Services: Counseling and information services are available, as is tutoring in every subject. There is a reader service for the blind and remedial math, reading, and writing.

Campus Safety and Security: Measures include 24-hour foot and vehicle patrol, self-defense education, security escort services, and shuttle buses. There are informal discussions, pamphlets/posters/films, emergency telephones, and lighted pathways/sidewalks. Campus security is provided by a campus-based police force.

Programs of Study: SCSU confers B.A., B.S., B.S.Bus.Adm., and B.S.Ed. degrees. Associate and master's degrees are also awarded. Bachelor's degrees are awarded in BIOLOGICAL SCIENCE (biochemistry and biology/biological science), BUSINESS (accounting, banking and finance, business administration and management, business economics, marketing/retailing/merchandising, and recreation and leisure services), COMMUNICATIONS AND THE ARTS (art history and appreciation, communications, dramatic arts, English, fine arts, French, German, Italian, journalism, Spanish, and studio art), COMPUTER AND PHYSICAL SCIENCE (chemistry, computer science, earth science, mathematics, and physics), EDUCATION (art, early childhood, elementary, foreign languages, health, library science, physical, science, secondary, and special), HEALTH PROFESSIONS (nursing and public health), SOCIAL SCIENCE (economics, geography, history, philosophy, political science/government, psychology, social work, and sociology). Psychology, communications, and elementary education are the largest.

Required: All students must complete distribution requirements that include 6 credits each in English composition and speech, natural sciences, and social sciences, 3 credits each in American politics, fine arts, foreign languages, math, literature, philosophy, and Western civilization, and 1 credit each in phys ed and health. Students must take 122 total credits, with a minimum of 30 hours in the major field, and maintain a minimum overall GPA of 2.0.

Special: SCSU offer co-op programs in all academic majors, internships in many departments, study abroad in a variety of countries, a combined B.A.-B.S. degree, dual majors, a general studies degree, student-designed majors in liberal studies, and pass/fail options. There are 2 national honor societies, a freshman honors program, and 1 departmental honors program.

Faculty/Classroom: 61% of faculty are male; 39%, female. 96% teach undergraduates. No introductory courses are taught by graduate students. The average class size in an introductory lecture is 30; in a laboratory, 25; and in a regular course, 22.

Requirements: The SAT I is required. A minimum composite score of 900 on the SAT I, with at least 450 each in verbal and math, or a composite score of 15 on the ACT, is needed. In addition, applicants should be in the upper 50% of their high school class and should graduate with 4 years in English, 3 in math, and 2 each in natural sciences and social sciences, including American history. The GED is accepted. 2 years of foreign language are recommended. An essay also is needed. SCSU requires applicants to be in the upper 50% of their class. A GPA of 2.5 is required. AP and CLEP credits are accepted. Important factors in the admissions decision are advanced placement or honor courses, recommendations by school officials, and leadership record.

Procedure: Freshmen are admitted fall and spring. There are early decision, early admissions, and rolling admissions plans. Application deadlines are open. The fall 2003 application fee was $40.

Transfer: 774 transfer students enrolled in a recent year. Transfer applicants must have a minimum of 6 college credits with a grade of C or better and an overall GPA of 2.0. The SAT I is required for applicants with fewer than 24 college credits. 30 of 122 credits required for the bachelor's degree must be completed at SCSU.

Visiting: There are regularly scheduled orientations for prospective students. Visitors may sit in on classes. To schedule a visit, contact Admissions Office.

Financial Aid: In a recent year, 70% of all full-time freshmen and 60% of continuing full-time students received some form of financial aid. 38% of full-time freshmen and 48% of continuing full-time students received need-based aid. The average freshman award was $4800. 10% of undergraduates work part time. Average annual earnings from campus work are $1800. The average financial indebtedness of a recent graduate was $10,000. SCSU is a member of CSS. The FAFSA and the college's own financial statement are required. Check with the school for current deadlines.

International Students: In a recent year, there were 60 international students enrolled. They must score 525 on the written TOEFL and also take the SAT I or the ACT, scoring 900.

Computers: The mainframe is a DEC VAX 8650. More than 300 PCs are available for student use in various campus locations. All are networkable. All students may access the system 17 hours a day. There are no time limits and no fees.

Graduates: In a recent year, 1162 bachelor's degrees were awarded. The most popular majors were communications (12%), psychology (11%), and sociology (6%). In an average class, 13% graduate in 4 years or less, 29% graduate in 5 years or less, and 34% graduate in 6 years or less. 150 companies recruited on campus in a recent year. Of a recent graduating class, 31% were enrolled in graduate school within 6 months of graduation and 94% were employed.

Admissions Contact: Heather Stearns, Assistant Director of Admissions.

TEIKYO POST UNIVERSITY   B-3
Waterbury, CT 06723-2540   (203) 596-4520
                              (800) 345-2562; Fax: (203) 756-5810

Full-time: 306 men, 361 women	**Faculty:** 33; II B, av$
Part-time: 150 men, 420 women	**Ph.D.s:** 61%
Graduate: none	**Student/Faculty:** 20 to 1
Year: semesters, summer session	**Tuition:** $17,500
Application Deadline: open	**Room & Board:** $7375
Freshman Class: 1115 applied, 734 accepted, 204 enrolled	
SAT I or ACT: recommended	**COMPETITIVE**

Teikyo Post University, founded in 1890, is a private institution offering liberal arts and business programs with an international focus. There are 2 undergraduate schools. The library contains 116,019 volumes, 76,221 microform items, and 1065 audio/video tapes/CDs, and subscribes to 427 periodicals. Computerized library services include the card catalog, interlibrary loans, and database searching. Special learning facilities include a learning resource center and a tutorial center. The 70-acre campus is in an urban area 1 mile west of Waterbury. Including any residence halls, there are 13 buildings.

Student Life: 76% of undergraduates are from Connecticut. Students are from 12 states, 20 foreign countries, and Canada. 75% are from public schools. 63% are white; 17% African American. The average age of freshmen is 19; all undergraduates, 26. 23% do not continue beyond their first year; 39% remain to graduate.

Housing: 424 students can be accommodated in college housing, which includes coed dorms and off-campus apartments. On-campus housing is guaranteed for all 4 years. 58% of students live on campus; of those, 60% remain on campus on weekends. All students may keep cars.

Activities: There are no fraternities or sororities. There are 30 groups on campus, including cheerleading, chorale, chorus, computers, drama, ethnic, gay, honors, international, literary magazine, musical theater, social, social service, student government, and yearbook. Popular campus events include dances, concerts, and international food festivals.

Sports: There are 5 intercollegiate sports for men and 5 for women, and 4 intramural sports for men and 4 for women. Facilities include a soccer field, a fitness center, a weight room, a racquetball court, a swimming pool, and tennis courts.

Disabled Students: 70% of the campus is accessible. Wheelchair ramps, elevators, special parking, specially equipped rest rooms, and special class scheduling are available.

Services: Counseling and information services are available, as is tutoring in most subjects. There is a reader service for the blind and remedial math, reading, and writing.

Campus Safety and Security: Measures include 24-hour foot and vehicle patrol, self-defense education, security escort services, and shuttle buses. There are informal discussions, pamphlets/posters/films, and lighted pathways/sidewalks.

Programs of Study: TPU confers B.A. and B.S. degrees. Associate degrees are also awarded. Bachelor's degrees are awarded in BUSINESS (accounting, banking and finance, business administration and management, management science, and marketing/retailing/merchandising), COMMUNICATIONS AND THE ARTS (English), SOCIAL SCIENCE (criminal justice, history, liberal arts/general studies, psychology, and sociology). Biology is the strongest academically. Management and general studies are the largest.

Required: To graduate, all students must maintain a minimum GPA of 2.0, earn a total of 120 credits, including at least 33 in the major, and take a computer course.

Special: Co-op programs in all majors, cross-registration with Naugatuck Valley Community College, study abroad in England, the Netherlands, and Japan, internships with area businesses, general studies degrees, accelerated degree programs, B.A.-B.S. degrees, and credit for life experience are available. There are 2 national honor societies and 1 departmental honors program.

Faculty/Classroom: 57% of faculty are male; 43%, female. All teach undergraduates. The average class size in an introductory lecture is 20; in a laboratory, 15; and in a regular course, 35.

Admissions: 66% of the 2003-2004 applicants were accepted.

Requirements: The SAT I or ACT is recommended. In addition, applicants must be graduates of an accredited secondary school, with 4 years of English and at least 16 total academic credits. The GED is accepted. TPU requires applicants to be in the upper 50% of their class. A GPA of 2.0 is required. AP and CLEP credits are accepted. Important factors in the admissions decision are personality/intangible qualities, extracurricular activities record, and recommendations by school officials.

Procedure: Freshmen are admitted to all sessions. There are early decision, early admissions, and deferred admissions plans. Early decision applications should be filed by November 1. There is a $40 application fee. Notification of early decision is sent December 15; regular decision, on a rolling basis. Applications are accepted on-line through *www.teikyopost.edu.*

Transfer: 68 transfer students enrolled in 2002-2003. Applicants must have a minimum college GPA of 2.0, submit an official college transcript, and have an interview. The SAT I is recommended. 30 of 120 credits required for the bachelor's degree must be completed at TPU.

Visiting: There are regularly scheduled orientations for prospective students, including tours, interviews with admissions counselors, and meetings with faculty and students. There are guides for informal visits and visitors may sit in on classes and stay overnight. To schedule a visit, contact the Admissions Office at (203) 596-4620 or *arossiter@teikyopost.edu.*

Financial Aid: In 2003-2004, 94% of all full-time freshmen and 90% of continuing full-time students received some form of financial aid. 87% of full-time freshmen and 85% of continuing full-time students received need-based aid. The average freshman award was $18,500. 62% of undergraduates work part time. Average annual earnings from campus work are $1005. The average financial indebtedness of the 2003 graduate was $19,875. TPU is a member of CSS. The FAFSA, the college's own financial statement, and parent and student federal tax returns are required. The priority date for freshman financial aid applications for fall entry is May 1. Freshman financial aid applications for fall entry are processed on a rolling basis.

International Students: There are 65 international students enrolled. The school actively recruits these students. They must score 550 on the written TOEFL.

Computers: The mainframe is a DEC. PCs are available for student use in the computer lab, the library, and the tutorial center. All have Internet capabilities. Residence halls are also connected to the Internet for students who have their own computers. All students may access the system. There are no time limits and no fees. It is strongly recommended that all students have a personal computer.

Graduates: From July 1, 2002 to June 30, 2003, 204 bachelor's degrees were awarded. The most popular majors were management (27%), general studies (15%), and marketing (10%). In an average class, 36% graduate in 4 years or less, 31% graduate in 5 years or less, and 5% graduate in 6 years or less. 43 companies recruited on campus in 2002-2003. Of the 2002 graduating class, 10% were enrolled in graduate school within 6 months of graduation and 75% were employed.

Admissions Contact: Aline Rossiter, Dean of Admissions. A video is available. E-mail: *tpuadmis@teikyopost.edu* Web: *http://teikyopost.edu*

TRINITY COLLEGE	C-2
Hartford, CT 06106	**(860) 297-2180; Fax: (860) 297-2287**
Full-time: 1002 men, 999 women	**Faculty:** 187; IIB, ++$
Part-time: 75 men, 112 women	**Ph.D.s:** 90%
Graduate: 92 men, 70 women	**Student/Faculty:** 11 to 1
Year: semesters	**Tuition:** $30,230
Application Deadline: January 15	**Room & Board:** $7810
Freshman Class: 5510 applied, 1993 accepted, 550 enrolled	
SAT I Verbal/Math: 650/660	**ACT:** 27
	HIGHLY COMPETITIVE+

Founded in 1823, Trinity College in Hartford is an independent, nonsectarian liberal arts college of the highest quality. Its rigorous curriculum is

firmly grounded in the traditional liberal arts disciplines and marked by an array of interdisciplinary studies, exceptional offerings in science and engineering, and distinctive educational connections with Connecticut's capital city and cities around the world. There is 1 graduate school. In addition to regional accreditation, Trinity has baccalaureate program accreditation with ABET. The library contains 992,817 volumes, 399,394 microform items, and 225,477 audio/video tapes/CDs, and subscribes to 2438 periodicals. Computerized library services include the card catalog, interlibrary loans, database searching, and Internet access. Special learning facilities include an art gallery, radio station, TV station, and Connecticut Public Television and Radio. The 100-acre campus is in an urban area southwest of downtown Hartford. Including any residence halls, there are 78 buildings.

Student Life: 79% of undergraduates are from out of state, mostly the Northeast. Students are from 44 states, 28 foreign countries, and Canada. 43% are from public schools. 79% are white. 32% are Protestant; 28% Catholic; 25% claim no religious affiliation; 8% are Jewish; 7%, miscellaneous. The average age of freshmen is 18; all undergraduates, 20. 8% do not continue beyond their first year; 84% remain to graduate.

Housing: 1861 students can be accommodated in college housing, which includes coed dorms, on-campus apartments, and fraternity houses. In addition, there are special-interest houses. On-campus housing is guaranteed for all 4 years. 93% of students live on campus; of those, 70% remain on campus on weekends. Upperclassmen may keep cars.

Activities: 20% of men and about 16% of women belong to 3 local and 4 national fraternities. There are no sororities. There are 112 groups on campus, including art, bagpipe band, band, cheerleading, chess, choir, chorale, chorus, dance, debate, drama, ethnic, film, gay, honors, international, jazz band, literary magazine, musical theater, newspaper, pep band, photography, political, professional, radio and TV, religious, social, social service, student government, and yearbook. Popular campus events include Human Rights Lecture Series, Black History Month, and Latino Heritage Week.

Sports: There are 15 intercollegiate sports for men and 13 for women, and 14 intramural sports for men and 14 for women. Facilities include a pool, outdoor and indoor tracks, playing fields, a weight room, a fitness center, and tennis, squash, and basketball courts.

Disabled Students: 60% of the campus is accessible. Wheelchair ramps, elevators, special parking, specially equipped rest rooms, special class scheduling, lowered drinking fountains, and lowered telephones are available.

Services: Counseling and information services are available, as is tutoring in every subject. There is a reader service for the blind. The writing center offers instruction in all forms of writing, and the math center provides individual tutoring on topics related to math and other courses involving quantitative reasoning.

Campus Safety and Security: Measures include 24-hour foot and vehicle patrol, self-defense education, security escort services, and shuttle buses. There are informal discussions, pamphlets/posters/films, emergency telephones, and lighted pathways/sidewalks.

Programs of Study: Trinity confers B.A. and B.S. degrees. Master's degrees are also awarded. Bachelor's degrees are awarded in BIOLOGICAL SCIENCE (biochemistry, biology/biological science, and neurosciences), COMMUNICATIONS AND THE ARTS (art history and appreciation, classics, comparative literature, dance, dramatic arts, English, fine arts, French, German, Italian, modern language, music, Russian, Spanish, studio art, and theater management), COMPUTER AND PHYSICAL SCIENCE (chemistry, computer science, mathematics, and physics), EDUCATION (education), ENGINEERING AND ENVIRONMENTAL DESIGN (engineering and environmental science), SOCIAL SCIENCE (American studies, anthropology, classical/ancient civilization, economics, history, interdisciplinary studies, international studies, Judaic studies, philosophy, political science/government, psychology, public affairs, religion, sociology, and women's studies). Political science, economics, and English are the largest.

Required: All students must complete 36 course credits, including 10 to 15 in the major and 1 from each of 5 distribution areas: arts, humanities, natural sciences, numerical and symbolic reasoning, and social sciences. Students must maintain at least a C average overall.

Special: Trinity offers special freshman programs for exceptional students, including interdisciplinary programs in the sciences and the humanities. There is an intensive study program under which students can devote a semester to 1 subject. Cross-registration through such programs as the Hartford Consortium and the Twelve-College Exchange Program, hundreds of internships (some with Connecticut Public Radio and TV on campus), study abroad virtually worldwide, including San Francisco, Rome, South Africa, Trinidad, Russia, and Nepal, a Washington semester, dual majors in all disciplines, student-designed majors, nondegree study, and pass/fail options also are offered. A 5-year advanced degree in electrical or mechanical engineering with Rensselaer Polytechnic Institute also is available. There are 4 national honor societies, including Phi Beta Kappa, and most departments have an honors program.

Faculty/Classroom: 60% of faculty are male; 40%, female. All both teach and do research. No introductory courses are taught by graduate students. The average class size in an introductory lecture is 21; in a laboratory, 15; and in a regular course, 13.

Admissions: 36% of the 2003-2004 applicants were accepted. The SAT I scores for the 2003-2004 freshman class were: Verbal--3% below 500, 26% between 500 and 599, 54% between 600 and 700, and 15% above 700; Math--4% below 500, 22% between 500 and 599, 55% between 600 and 700, and 20% above 700. The ACT scores were 5% below 21, 12% between 21 and 23, 23% between 24 and 26, 25% between 27 and 28, and 35% above 28. 73% of the current freshmen were in the top fifth of their class; 91% were in the top two fifths.

Requirements: The SAT I or ACT is required, along with the SAT II: Subject test in writing, or SAT II: Subject tests in writing and 2 additional subjects. Trinity strongly emphasizes individual character and personal qualities in admission. Consequently, an interview and essay are recommended. The college requires 4 years of English, 2 years each in foreign language and algebra, and 1 year each in geometry, history, and lab science. AP credits are accepted. Important factors in the admissions decision are advanced placement or honor courses, extracurricular activities record, and evidence of special talent.

Procedure: Freshmen are admitted in the fall. Entrance exams should be taken in the fall of the senior year. There are early decision and deferred admissions plans. Early decision applications should be filed by November 15; regular applications, by January 15 for fall entry. The fall 2003 application fee was $50. Notification of early decision is sent December 15; regular decision, April 1. 271 early decision candidates were accepted for the 2003-2004 class. 364 applicants were on the 2003 waiting list; 7 were admitted. Applications are accepted on-line through *Embark.com*, Common App, or *nextstopcollege.org*.

Transfer: 21 transfer students enrolled in 2002-2003. Transfer applicants must take the SAT I or ACT. A minimum college GPA of 3.0 is recommended. 18 of 36 credits required for the bachelor's degree must be completed at Trinity.

Visiting: There are regularly scheduled orientations for prospective students. There are guides for informal visits and visitors may sit in on classes and stay overnight. To schedule a visit, contact the Admissions Office at *admissions.office@trincoll.edu*.

Financial Aid: In 2003-2004, 36% of all full-time freshmen and 45% of continuing full-time students received some form of financial aid. 35% of full-time freshmen and 41% of continuing full-time students received need-based aid. The average freshman award was $23,630. Need-based scholarships or need-based grants averaged $21,694 ($39,740 maximum); need-based self-help aid (loans and jobs) averaged $3800 ($8325 maximum); and non-need-based awards and non-need-based scholarships averaged $6088 ($10,461 maximum). 30% of undergraduates work part time. Average annual earnings from campus work are $1624. The average financial indebtedness of the 2003 graduate was $13,792. Trinity is a member of CSS. The CSS/Profile or FAFSA is required. The deadline for filing freshman financial aid applications for fall entry is February 1.

International Students: In a recent year, there were 67 international students enrolled. The school actively recruits these students. They must score 550 on the written TOEFL and also take the SAT I or the ACT.

Computers: The mainframe is a Peoplesoft on Microsoft NT servers. All dorm rooms are equipped with Ethernet connections. In addition, more than 200 public workstations of various types are available for student use; all can access the Internet and campus-based network resources. The campus network supports UNIX, Windows and Mac workstations. All students have e-mail accounts, and all are entitled to a personal home page on a campus server. All students may access the system 24 hours daily. There are no time limits and no fees. It is strongly recommended that all students have a personal computer. A Windows portable is recommended.

Graduates: From July 1, 2002 to June 30, 2003, 553 bachelor's degrees were awarded. The most popular majors were political science (16%), economics (12%), and history (10%). In an average class, 82% graduate in 4 years or less, 89% graduate in 5 years or less, and 90% graduate in 6 years or less.

Admissions Contact: Larry R. Dow, Dean of Admissions/Financial Aid. E-mail: *admissions.office@mail.trincoll.edu* Web: *http://www.trincoll.edu*

UNITED STATES COAST GUARD ACADEMY
New London, CT 06320-8103

E-3

(860) 444-8500
(800) 883-8724; Fax: (860) 701-6700

Full-time: 683 men, 302 women	**Faculty:** 112
Part-time: none	**Ph.D.s:** 30%
Graduate: none	**Student/Faculty:** 9 to 1
Year: semesters, summer session	**Tuition:** 0
Application Deadline: January 31	**Room & Board:** n/app
Freshman Class: 2085 applied, 405 accepted, 300 enrolled	
SAT I Verbal/Math: 620/640	**ACT:** 27 **MOST COMPETITIVE**

The U.S. Coast Guard Academy, founded in 1876, is an Armed Forces Service Academy for men and women. Appointments are made solely on the basis of an annual nationwide competition. Except for an entrance fee of $3000, the federal government covers all cadet expenses by providing a monthly allowance of $600 plus a daily food allowance. In addition to regional accreditation, the Academy has baccalaureate program accreditation with ABET. The library contains 150,000 volumes, 60,000 microform items, and 1500 audio/video tapes/CDs, and subscribes to 850 periodicals. Computerized library services include the card catalog, interlibrary loans, and database searching. Special learning facilities include the Coast Guard Museum, a $5 million ship's bridge simulator, and the Leadership Development Center for the Coast Guard. The 110-acre campus is in a suburban area 45 miles southeast of Hartford. Including any residence halls, there are 25 buildings.

Student Life: 93% of undergraduates are from out of state, mostly the Northeast. Students are from 50 states and 14 foreign countries. 79% are white. 33% are Catholic; 30% claim no religious affiliation; 29% Protestant. The average age of freshmen is 18; all undergraduates, 21. 21% do not continue beyond their first year; 67% remain to graduate.

Housing: 1000 students can be accommodated in college housing, which includes coed dorms. On-campus housing is guaranteed for all 4 years. All students live on campus. Alcohol is not permitted. Upperclassmen may keep cars.

Activities: There are no fraternities or sororities. There are many groups and organizations on campus, including bagpipe band, band, cheerleading, choir, chorale, chorus, dance, debate, drama, drill team, drum and bugle corps, ethnic, international, jazz band, marching band, musical theater, newspaper, pep band, political, professional, religious, social, social service, student government, and yearbook. Popular campus events include Parents Weekend, Coast Guard Day, and Hispanic Heritage and Black History months.

Sports: There are 13 intercollegiate sports for men and 11 for women, and 13 intramural sports for men and 13 for women. Facilities include a field house with 3 basketball courts, a 6-lane swimming pool, 5 racquetball courts, and facilities for track meets, tennis matches, and baseball and softball games; an additional athletic facility with wrestling and weight rooms, basketball courts, gymnastics areas, a swimming pool, and saunas; a 4500-seat stadium; and practice and playing fields, outdoor tennis courts, and rowing and seamanship-sailing centers.

Disabled Students: 24% of the campus is accessible. Wheelchair ramps, elevators, special parking, and specially equipped rest rooms are available.

Services: Counseling and information services are available, as is tutoring in every subject.

Campus Safety and Security: Measures include 24-hour foot and vehicle patrol, self-defense education, and lighted pathways/sidewalks.

Programs of Study: the Academy confers the B.S. degree. Bachelor's degrees are awarded in BIOLOGICAL SCIENCE (marine science), BUSINESS (management science and operations research), ENGINEERING AND ENVIRONMENTAL DESIGN (civil engineering, electrical/electronics engineering, mechanical engineering, and naval architecture and marine engineering), SOCIAL SCIENCE (political science/government). Political science/government is the largest.

Required: To graduate, cadets must pass at least 37 courses, of which 25 are core; accumulate a minimum of 126 credit hours, with at least 90 credits of C or better, exclusive of phys ed; complete the academic requirements for one of the approved majors and attain a minimum GPA of 2.0 in all required upper-division courses in the major; successfully complete all professional development and phys ed requirements; and maintain a high sense of integrity.

Special: Cross-registration with Connecticut College, summer cruises to foreign ports, 6-week internships with various government agencies and some engineering and science organizations, and a 1-semester exchange program with the 3 other military academies are available. All graduates are commissioned in the U.S. Coast Guard. There are 2 national honor societies, a freshman honors program, and 3 departmental honors programs.

Faculty/Classroom: 90% of faculty are male; 10%, female. The average class size in an introductory lecture is 28; in a laboratory, 18; and in a regular course, 20.

Admissions: 19% of the 2003-2004 applicants were accepted. The SAT I scores for the 2003-2004 freshman class were: Verbal--2% below 500, 35% between 500 and 599, 51% between 600 and 700, and 12% above 700; Math--1% below 500, 22% between 500 and 599, 57% between 600 and 700, and 20% above 700. 80% of the current freshmen were in the top fifth of their class; 95% were in the top two fifths. 12% of freshmen graduated first in their class.

Requirements: The SAT I or ACT is required. In addition, applicants must have reached the age of 17 but not the age of 23 by July 1 of the year of admission, be citizens of the United States, and be single at the time of appointment and remain single while attending the academy. Required secondary school courses include 4 years each of English and math. AP credits are accepted. Important factors in the admissions decision are advanced placement or honor courses, recommendations by school officials, and leadership record.

Procedure: Freshmen are admitted in the summer. Entrance exams should be taken by December 15. There is an early admissions plan. Applications should be filed by January 31 for fall entry. Notification is sent on a rolling basis. 400 applicants were on the 2003 waiting list; 130 were admitted. Applications are accepted on-line through the Coast Guard web site *www.cga.edu*.

Transfer: All transfer students must meet the same standards as incoming freshmen and must begin as freshmen no matter how many semesters or years of college they have completed. All of the 126 credits required for the bachelor's degree must be completed at the Academy.

Visiting: There are regularly scheduled orientations for prospective students, including an admissions briefing and tour of the academy every Friday. To schedule a visit contact the Director of Admissions.

International Students: They must score 550 on the written TOEFL and also take the SAT I or the ACT scoring 1100 on the SAT I.

Computers: Students may use computer rooms in the dorms and academic building. All students receive a laptop upon entering the Academy. All rooms are wired for Internet access. All students may access the system 24 hours a day. There are no time limits and no fees. All students are required to have personal computers.

Graduates: In a recent year, 165 bachelor's degrees were awarded. The most popular majors were management (21%), marine science (19%), and government (17%). In an average class, 60% graduate in 4 years or less, and 1% graduate in 5 years or less.

Admissions Contact: Susan D. Bibeau, Director of Admissions. A video is available. E-mail: *admissions@cga.uscg.mil* Web: *www.cga.edu*

UNIVERSITY OF BRIDGEPORT
Bridgeport, CT 06602   B-4

(203) 576-4552
(800) EXCEL-UB; Fax: (203) 576-4941

Full-time: 428 men, 575 women	**Faculty:** 66; IIA, -$
Part-time: 83 men, 175 women	**Ph.Ds:** 90%
Graduate: 892 men, 1012 women	**Student/Faculty:** 15 to 1
Year: semesters, summer session	**Tuition:** $17,924
Application Deadline: April 1	**Room & Board:** $8000

Freshman Class: 1796 applied, 1514 accepted, 293 enrolled
SAT I Verbal/Math: 450/460   **LESS COMPETITIVE**

The University of Bridgeport, founded in 1927, is a private, independent, nonsectarian university offering programs in the arts, humanities, social sciences, business, engineering and design, natural sciences, human services, dental hygiene, chiropractic and naturopathic medicine, and teacher preparation. There are 10 undergraduate and 7 graduate schools. In addition to regional accreditation, UB has baccalaureate program accreditation with ABET, ADA, and NASAD. The library contains 275,000 volumes, 1million microform items, and 5000 audio/video tapes/CDs, and subscribes to 1700 periodicals. Computerized library services include interlibrary loans and database searching. Special learning facilities include a learning resource center and art gallery. The 86-acre campus is in an urban area 60 miles northeast of New York City. Including any residence halls, there are 30 buildings.

Student Life: 62% of undergraduates are from Connecticut. Students are from 37 states, 52 foreign countries, and Canada. 89% are from public schools. 32% are African American; 27% white; 20% foreign nationals; 13% Hispanic. 69% claim no religious affiliation; 14% Catholic. The average age of freshmen is 19; all undergraduates, 24. 32% do not continue beyond their first year; 50% remain to graduate.

Housing: 1014 students can be accommodated in college housing, which includes coed dorms. In addition, there are special-interest houses and alcohol- and tobacco-free buildings. On-campus housing is guaranteed for all 4 years. 54% of students commute. All students may keep cars.

Activities: 1% of men belong to 2 local fraternities; 2% of women belong to 1 local sorority. There are 44 groups on campus, including art, cheerleading, computers, debate, ethnic, honors, international, literary magazine, newspaper, photography, political, professional, radio and TV, religious, social, social service, student government, and yearbook. Popular campus events include International Festival, Winter Prelude, and Wisteria Ball.

Sports: There are 4 intercollegiate sports for men and 6 for women, and 8 intramural sports for men and 8 for women. Facilities include a gym, athletic fields, tennis and racquetball courts, and a recreation center with an indoor pool.

Disabled Students: 80% of the campus is accessible. Wheelchair ramps, elevators, special parking, specially equipped rest rooms, and special class scheduling are available.

Services: Counseling and information services are available, as is tutoring in every subject. There is a reader service for the blind, and remedial math, reading, and writing.

Campus Safety and Security: Measures include 24-hour foot and vehicle patrol, security escort services, informal discussions, and pamphlets/posters/films. There are emergency telephones, lighted pathways/sidewalks, and campus security systems.

Programs of Study: UB confers B.A., B.S., B.F.A., and B.M. degrees. Associate, master's, and doctoral degrees are also awarded. Bachelor's degrees are awarded in BIOLOGICAL SCIENCE (biology/biological sci-

ence), BUSINESS (accounting, banking and finance, business administration and management, fashion merchandising, international business management, international economics, management information systems, management science, and marketing/retailing/merchandising), COMMUNICATIONS AND THE ARTS (communications, English, graphic design, illustration, industrial design, journalism, literature, and music), COMPUTER AND PHYSICAL SCIENCE (computer science and mathematics), ENGINEERING AND ENVIRONMENTAL DESIGN (computer engineering and interior design), HEALTH PROFESSIONS (dental hygiene, predentistry, premedicine, and respiratory therapy), SOCIAL SCIENCE (economics, human services, interdisciplinary studies, international studies, prelaw, psychology, religion, and social science). Computer science/engineering, business, and dental hygiene are the strongest academically. Dental hygiene, psychology, and computer science/engineering are the largest.

Required: All students are required to complete at least 120 credit hours, including at least 30 in the major field. A minimum GPA of 2.0 is necessary. Distribution requirements cover 33 core credits and are composed of skills, heritage, and capstone sections, including 3 hours each in English composition and quantitative skills, and 24 semester hours consisting of 6 hours each in humanities, natural science, and social science and 3 each in integrated studies and fine arts.

Special: UB offers co-op programs with several local institutions, cross-registration with Sacred Heart and Fairfield Universities, internships in many degree programs, study abroad in England, Switzerland, or Spain, a Washington semester, and work-study programs. In addition, a general studies accelerated degree program, dual majors, student-designed majors, and B.A.-B.S. degrees are available. Credit for life experience, non-degree study, and pass/fail options are offered. There are 11 national honor societies and 1 departmental honors program.

Faculty/Classroom: 79% of faculty are male; 21%, female. All both teach and do research. No introductory courses are taught by graduate students. The average class size in an introductory lecture is 14; in a laboratory, 10; and in a regular course, 14.

Admissions: 84% of the 2003-2004 applicants were accepted. The SAT I scores for the 2003-2004 freshman class were: Verbal--69% below 500, 22% between 500 and 599, 8% between 600 and 700, and 1% above 700; Math--65% below 500, 25% between 500 and 599, 8% between 600 and 700, and 2% above 700. 20% of the current freshmen were in the top fifth of their class; 43% were in the top two fifths.

Requirements: The SAT I or ACT is required. In addition, applicants are required to have 16 academic credits or Carnegie units, including 4 units of English, 3 of math, 2 each in social studies and a lab science, and 5 electives. A portfolio is required for B.F.A. students and an audition for B.M. candidates. UB requires applicants to be in the upper 40% of their class. A GPA of 2.0 is required. AP and CLEP credits are accepted. Important factors in the admissions decision are advanced placement or honor courses, extracurricular activities record, and recommendations by school officials.

Procedure: Freshmen are admitted fall and spring. Entrance exams should be taken during the senior year. There are early decision, early admissions, and deferred admissions plans. There is a rolling admissions plan. Applications should be filed by April 1 for fall entry and December 1 for spring entry, along with a $25 fee. Notification is sent on a rolling basis. Applications are accepted on computer disk and on-line through the school's web site.

Transfer: 133 transfer students enrolled in 2002-2003. Transfer applicants need a minimum GPA of 2.5 and at least 12 earned credit hours. The SAT I or ACT and an interview are recommended. 30 credits of 120 required for the bachelor's degree must be completed at UB.

Visiting: There are regularly scheduled orientations for prospective students. There are guides for informal visits and visitors may sit in on classes and stay overnight. To schedule a visit, contact the Admissions Office at *admit@bridgeport.edu*.

Financial Aid: The FAFSA and the college's own financial statement are required. The deadline for filing freshman financial aid applications for fall entry is April 15.

International Students: There are 199 international students enrolled. The school actively recruits these students. They must score 500 on the written TOEFL or take the MELAB, the Comprehensive English Language Test, or the college's own test.

Computers: The mainframe is an HP. Computer systems available to students throughout campus include Sun Microsystems workstations, Apollo workstations, 7 all-purpose PC labs, and a specialized microprocessor lab. All students may access the system 8 A.M. to 11 P.M. daily. UB-net is available 24 hours a day from dorm rooms or dial-ups. There are no time limits and no fees.

Graduates: From July 1, 2002 to June 30, 2003, 180 bachelor's degrees were awarded. The most popular majors were elective studies (23%), business administration (9%), and human services (8%). In an average class, 40% graduate in 4 years or less, 45% graduate in 5 years or less, and 50% graduate in 6 years or less. Of the 2002 graduating class, 10% were enrolled in graduate school within 6 months of graduation and 60% were employed.

Admissions Contact: Barbara L. Maryak, Dean of Admissions. A video is available. E-mail: *admit@bridgeport.edu*
Web: *www.bridgeport.edu*

UNIVERSITY OF CONNECTICUT
Storrs, CT 06269-3088

D-2

(860) 486-3137; Fax: (860) 486-1476

Full-time: 6762 men, 7489 women	**Faculty:** 842; I, +$
Part-time: 252 men, 254 women	**Ph.Ds:** 95%
Graduate: 2586 men, 2840 women	**Student/Faculty:** 17 to 1
Year: semesters, summer session	**Tuition:** $7308 ($19,036)
Application Deadline: February 1	**Room & Board:** $7300
Freshman Class: 16,442 applied, 9128 accepted, 3165 enrolled	
SAT I Verbal/Math: 572/593	**VERY COMPETITIVE**

The University of Connecticut, founded in 1881, is a public, land-grant, sea-grant, multicampus research institution offering degree programs in liberal arts and sciences and professional studies. There are 12 undergraduate and 5 graduate schools. In addition to regional accreditation, UConn has baccalaureate program accreditation with AACSB, ABET, ACPE, ADA, APTA, ASLA, CAAHEP, CCNE, CSAB, NAACLS, NASAD, NASM, NAST, NCATE, and NLN. The library contains 2,334,581 volumes, 2,602,161 microform items, and 5067 audio/video tapes/CDs, and subscribes to 35,263 periodicals. Computerized library services include the card catalog, interlibrary loans, database searching, and Internet access. Special learning facilities include a learning resource center, art gallery, natural history museum, planetarium, radio station, and TV station. The 4104-acre campus is in a rural area 25 miles east of Hartford. Including any residence halls, there are 350 buildings.

Student Life: 76% of undergraduates are from Connecticut. Students are from 50 states, 53 foreign countries, and Canada. 74% are white. The average age of freshmen is 18; all undergraduates, 21. 12% do not continue beyond their first year; 70% remain to graduate.

Housing: About 9000 students can be accommodated in college housing, which includes single-sex and coed dorms, on-campus apartments, off-campus apartments, married-student housing, fraternity houses, and sorority houses. In addition, there are honors houses, language houses, special-interest houses, substance-free dorms, a floor for older students, a living/learning center, and facilities for international and engineering students. On-campus housing is guaranteed for the freshman year only. 75% of students live on campus; of those, 70% remain on campus on weekends. Upperclassmen may keep cars.

Activities: 8% of men belong to 18 national fraternities; 6% of women belong to 9 national sororities. There are 238 groups on campus, including art, band, cheerleading, chess, choir, chorale, chorus, computers, dance, debate, drama, drill team, ethnic, film, gay, honors, international, jazz band, literary magazine, marching band, musical theater, newspaper, opera, orchestra, pep band, photography, political, professional, radio and TV, religious, social, social service, student government, symphony, and yearbook. Popular campus events include Spring Weekend, "UConn Do It" campus clean-up day, and Winter Weekend.

Sports: There are 11 intercollegiate sports for men and 13 for women, and 28 intramural sports for men and 28 for women. Facilities include a sports center, a field house, a 16,000-seat football stadium, a 10,000-seat basketball stadium, and a student, faculty, and staff workout center.

Disabled Students: 80% of the campus is accessible. Wheelchair ramps, elevators, special parking, specially equipped rest rooms, special class scheduling, lowered drinking fountains, lowered telephones, special housing, a tactile map, and 4 specially equipped transportation vans are available.

Services: Counseling and information services are available, as is tutoring in most subjects. There is a reader service for the blind. Also available are a Braille printer, a Kurzweil reading machine and Mac computer with voice synthesizer, a machine to enlarge printed material, a talking calculator, and a TDD.

Campus Safety and Security: Measures include 24-hour foot and vehicle patrol, self-defense education, security escort services, and shuttle buses. There are informal discussions, pamphlets/posters/films, emergency telephones, and lighted pathways/sidewalks.

Programs of Study: UConn confers B.A., B.S., B.F.A., B.G.S., B.Mus., B.S.E., and B.S.Pharm. degrees. Associate, master's, and doctoral degrees are also awarded. Bachelor's degrees are awarded in AGRICULTURE (agricultural economics, agriculture, agronomy, animal science, horticulture, and natural resource management), BIOLOGICAL SCIENCE (biology/biological science, biophysics, evolutionary biology, genetics, marine science, molecular biology, nutrition, and physiology), BUSINESS (accounting, banking and finance, business administration and management, insurance and risk management, management information systems, marketing/retailing/merchandising, and real estate), COMMUNICATIONS AND THE ARTS (art, art history and appreciation, classics, communications, dramatic arts, English, French, German, journalism, linguistics, music, Portuguese, Spanish, theater design, and visual and performing arts), COMPUTER AND PHYSICAL SCIENCE (chemistry, computer science, geology, mathematics, physics, and statistics), EDUCATION (agricultural, athletic training, education, elementary,

English, foreign languages, mathematics, music, recreation, science, social studies, and special), ENGINEERING AND ENVIRONMENTAL DESIGN (biomedical engineering, chemical engineering, civil engineering, computer engineering, electrical/electronics engineering, environmental engineering, environmental science, landscape architecture/design, manufacturing engineering, materials engineering, and mechanical engineering), HEALTH PROFESSIONS (cytotechnology, exercise science, health care administration, medical laboratory technology, nursing, pharmacy, and physical therapy), SOCIAL SCIENCE (anthropology, dietetics, Eastern European studies, economics, geography, history, human development, Italian studies, Latin American studies, Middle Eastern studies, philosophy, political science/government, psychology, sociology, urban studies, and women's studies). Psychology, political science, and preteaching are the largest.

Required: To graduate, students must complete 120 credits with a GPA of 2.0. There are general education requirements in foreign language, expository writing, math, literature and the arts, culture and modern society, philosophical and ethical analysis, social scientific and comparative analysis, and science and technology. Students must complete a course that provides hands-on experience in a major computer application.

Special: UConn offers co-op programs in most majors, internships, study abroad in 28 countries, dual majors, general studies degrees, student-designed majors, work-study programs, nondegree study, and pass/fail options. There are 24 national honor societies, including Phi Beta Kappa, and a freshman honors program.

Faculty/Classroom: 69% of faculty are male; 31%, female. All both teach and do research. Graduate students teach 36% of introductory courses. The average class size in an introductory lecture is 46; in a laboratory, 19; and in a regular course, 39.

Admissions: 56% of the 2003-2004 applicants were accepted. The SAT I scores for the 2003-2004 freshman class were: Verbal--11% below 500, 52% between 500 and 599, 32% between 600 and 700, and 5% above 700; Math--9% below 500, 43% between 500 and 599, 40% between 600 and 700, and 8% above 700. 60% of the current freshmen were in the top fifth of their class; 94% were in the top two fifths. There were 2 National Merit semifinalists. 38 freshmen graduated first in their class.

Requirements: The SAT I or ACT is required. In addition, applicants must be graduates of an approved secondary school and should rank in the upper range of their class. The GED is accepted. Students must complete 16 high school academic units, including 4 years of English, 3 of math, 2 each of foreign language, science, and social studies, and 3 of electives. An essay is required. An audition is required for music and theater students and a portfolio for art students. AP credits are accepted. Important factors in the admissions decision are advanced placement or honor courses, evidence of special talent, and leadership record.

Procedure: Freshmen are admitted fall and spring. Entrance exams should be taken in the spring of the junior year or fall of the senior year. There are early admissions and deferred admissions plans. There is a rolling admissions plan. Applications should be filed by February 1 for fall entry and October 15 for spring entry, along with a $70 fee. Notification is sent on a rolling basis. 2096 applicants were on the 2003 waiting list; 837 were admitted. Applications are accepted on-line through CollegeLink, Apply, and CollegeView.

Transfer: 666 transfer students enrolled in 2002-2003. Applicants should have a minimum GPA of 2.5 and submit official transcripts from all colleges previously attended, the high school transcript, and SAT I or ACT scores as needed. An associate degree or a minimum of 54 credit hours is recommended. 30 credits of 120 required for the bachelor's degree must be completed at UConn.

Visiting: There are regularly scheduled orientations for prospective students, including daily tours and information sessions. Visitors may sit in on classes. To schedule a visit, contact the Lodewick Visitors Center at (860) 486-4900 or *tours@lvc.pr.uconn.edu*.

Financial Aid: In 2003-2004, 93% of all full-time freshmen and 78% of continuing full-time students received some form of financial aid. 75% of full-time freshmen and 73% of continuing full-time students received need-based aid. The average freshman award was $8142. Need-based scholarships or need-based grants averaged $5086 ($14,600 maximum); need-based self-help aid (loans and jobs) averaged $2989 ($4925 maximum); and non-need-based athletic scholarships averaged $10,997 ($24,482 maximum). Average annual earnings from campus work are $1800. The average financial indebtedness of the 2003 graduate was $17,185. The FAFSA is required. The priority date for freshman financial aid applications for fall entry is March 1.

International Students: There are 113 international students enrolled. The school actively recruits these students. They must score 550 on the written TOEFL or 213 on the electronic version and also take the college's own test and either the SAT I or the ACT.

Computers: The mainframes are IBM 3090s, Models 150E and 180E. There are more than 1300 terminals on campus located in the computer center, the library, the various schools and colleges, and some residence halls. All students may access the system 24 hours weekdays; 8 A.M. to 12 P.M. weekends. There are no time limits and no fees.

Graduates: From July 1, 2002 to June 30, 2003, 3477 bachelor's degrees were awarded. The most popular majors were general studies (8%), human development and family studies (7%), and psychology (7%). In an average class, 50% graduate in 4 years or less, 67% graduate in 5 years or less, and 70% graduate in 6 years or less. 200 companies recruited on campus in 2002-2003. Of the 2002 graduating class, 35% were enrolled in graduate school within 6 months of graduation and 81% were employed.

Admissions Contact: James D. Morales, Director of Admissions. E-mail: *beahusky@uconnvm.uconn.edu* Web: *www.uconn.edu*

UNIVERSITY OF HARTFORD
West Hartford, CT 06117

C-2

(860) 243-4296
(800) 947-4303; Fax: (860) 768-4961

Full-time: 2266 men, 2267 women	**Faculty:** 319; IIA, av$
Part-time: 435 men, 644 women	**Ph.D.s:** 79%
Graduate: 665 men, 968 women	**Student/Faculty:** 14 to 1
Year: semesters, summer session	**Tuition:** $22,470
Application Deadline: open	**Room & Board:** $8610
Freshman Class: 12,009 applied, 7658 accepted, 1448 enrolled	
SAT I Verbal/Math: 520/520	**ACT:** 22 COMPETITIVE

The University of Hartford, founded in 1877, is an independent, nonsectarian institution offering extensive undergraduate and graduate programs ranging from liberal arts to business. There are 7 undergraduate and 6 graduate schools. In addition to regional accreditation, University of Hartford has baccalaureate program accreditation with AACSB, ABET, APTA, CAHEA, NASAD, NASM, NCATE, and NLN. The 3 libraries contain 578,672 volumes and 336,304 microform items, and subscribe to 3447 periodicals. Computerized library services include the card catalog, interlibrary loans, and database searching. Special learning facilities include a learning resource center, art gallery, radio station, TV station, and the Museum of American Political Life. The 320-acre campus is in a suburban area 4 miles northwest of Hartford. Including any residence halls, there are 32 buildings.

Student Life: 61% of undergraduates are from out of state, mostly the Northeast. Students are from 45 states, 42 foreign countries, and Canada. 74% are from public schools. 78% are white; 11% African American. 67% are claim no religious affiliation; 19% Catholic; 7% Protestant; 6% Jewish. The average age of freshmen is 18; all undergraduates, 22. 24% do not continue beyond their first year; 55% remain to graduate.

Housing: 3472 students can be accommodated in college housing, which includes coed dorms and on-campus apartments. In addition, there are honors houses, special-interest houses, the Residential College for the Arts, and the International Residential College. On-campus housing is guaranteed for all 4 years. 66% of students live on campus; of those, 85% remain on campus on weekends. All students may keep cars.

Activities: 17% of men belong to 7 national fraternities; 21% of women belong to 7 national sororities. There are 45 groups on campus, including art, band, cheerleading, choir, chorale, chorus, computers, drama, ethnic, gay, honors, international, jazz band, literary magazine, musical theater, newspaper, opera, orchestra, pep band, political, professional, radio and TV, religious, social, social service, student government, symphony, and yearbook. Popular campus events include Welcome Weekend, Spring Weekend, and Winter Carnival.

Sports: There are 9 intercollegiate sports for men and 9 for women, and 16 intramural sports for men and 16 for women. Facilities include playing fields, a 25-meter outdoor pool, tennis courts, golf practice cages, a fitness trail, and a sports center with a 4600-seat multipurpose court, an 8-lane swimming pool, a weight room, racquetball courts, a squash court, and saunas.

Disabled Students: Wheelchair ramps, elevators, special parking, specially equipped rest rooms, lowered drinking fountains, lowered telephones, and special housing are available.

Services: Counseling and information services are available, as is tutoring in most subjects. There is a reader service for the blind, and remedial math, reading, and writing. The health education office offers peer counseling and workshops on health-related topics. Professional counseling is available.

Campus Safety and Security: Measures include 24-hour foot and vehicle patrol, self-defense education, security escort services, and shuttle buses. There are informal discussions, pamphlets/posters/films, emergency telephones, lighted pathways/sidewalks, and a bicycle patrol.

Programs of Study: University of Hartford confers B.A., B.F.A., B.Mus., B.S.A.E.T., B.S.B.A., B.S.C.E., B.S.Comp.E., B.S.Ed., B.S.E.E., B.S.E.E.T., B.S.M.E., and B.S.N. degrees. Associate, master's, and doctoral degrees are also awarded. Bachelor's degrees are awarded in BIOLOGICAL SCIENCE (biology/biological science), BUSINESS (accounting, banking and finance, business administration and management, entrepreneurial studies, insurance, management information systems, management science, and marketing/retailing/merchandising), COMMUNICATIONS AND THE ARTS (art history and appreciation, audio technology, ceramic art and design, communications, dance, design, dramatic arts, drawing, English, film arts, fine arts, illustration, jazz, languages,

media arts, music, music business management, music history and appreciation, music performance, music technology, music theory and composition, musical theater, painting, photography, printmaking, sculpture, technical and business writing, theater management, and video), COMPUTER AND PHYSICAL SCIENCE (chemistry, computer science, information sciences and systems, mathematics, physics, and radiological technology), EDUCATION (early childhood, elementary, music, secondary, and special), ENGINEERING AND ENVIRONMENTAL DESIGN (architectural engineering, biomedical engineering, chemical engineering technology, civil engineering, computer engineering, electrical/electronics engineering, electrical/electronics engineering technology, engineering, engineering technology, manufacturing engineering, mechanical engineering, and mechanical engineering technology), HEALTH PROFESSIONS (chiropractic, health science, medical laboratory technology, nursing, occupational therapy, physical therapy, predentistry, premedicine, preoptometry, and respiratory therapy), SOCIAL SCIENCE (criminal justice, economics, history, human services, interdisciplinary studies, international studies, Judaic studies, philosophy, political science/government, psychology, religious music, sociology, and women's studies). Computer science, engineering, and physical therapy are the strongest academically. Communication, psychology, and elementary education are the largest.

Required: To graduate, students must complete at least 120 credit hours, fulfill the university's core curriculum requirements, and maintain an overall GPA of 2.0. Specific core and course requirements vary with the major.

Special: Cross-registration with the Greater Hartford Consortium, internships in all majors, study abroad, a Washington semester, work-study programs, credit for life experience, nondegree study, and pass/fail options are available. In addition, students may pursue accelerated degrees, B.A.-B.S. degrees, dual majors, or their own individually designed majors. There are interdisciplinary majors in acoustics and music and in experimental studio combining performing, literary, and visual arts. Also available are preprofessional programs in biology/preoptometry with the New England College of Optometry, predentistry with the New York University School of Dentistry, and prechiropractic with the New York Chiropractic College. There are 19 national honor societies and a freshman honors program. All undergraduate colleges have honors programs.

Faculty/Classroom: 64% of faculty are male; 36%, female. All teach undergraduates and 97% do research. No introductory courses are taught by graduate students. The average class size in an introductory lecture is 23; in a laboratory, 14; and in a regular course, 18.

Admissions: 64% of the 2003-2004 applicants were accepted. The SAT I scores for the 2003-2004 freshman class were: Verbal--32% below 500, 49% between 500 and 599, 17% between 600 and 700, and 1% above 700; Math--29% below 500, 52% between 500 and 599, 17% between 600 and 700, and 2% above 700. The ACT scores were 35% below 21, 24% between 21 and 23, 25% between 24 and 26, 9% between 27 and 28, and 7% above 28. 19% of the current freshmen were in the top fifth of their class; 48% were in the top two fifths.

Requirements: The SAT I is required. In addition, applicants should have 16 academic high school credits and 16 Carnegie units, including 4 units in English, 3 in math (3.5 for B.S. candidates), and 2 each in foreign language, science, and social studies. A portfolio and an audition are required for B.F.A. and B.Mus. candidates, respectively. A personal statement is required, and an interview is recommended for all students. AP and CLEP credits are accepted. Important factors in the admissions decision are advanced placement or honor courses, recommendations by school officials, and leadership record.

Procedure: Freshmen are admitted fall and spring. Entrance exams should be taken in the spring of the junior year or the fall of the senior year. There are early admissions and deferred admissions plans. Application deadlines are open. The fall 2003 application fee was $35. Notification is sent on a rolling basis.

Transfer: 245 transfer students enrolled in 2002-2003. Transfer students must have a minimum college GPA of 2.25, with 2.5 recommended, and must submit SAT I or ACT scores if they have fewer than 30 transferable college-level credits. An interview is also recommended. 30 of 120 credits required for the bachelor's degree must be completed at University of Hartford.

Visiting: There are regularly scheduled orientations for prospective students. There are guides for informal visits and visitors may sit in on classes and stay overnight. To schedule a visit, contact the Office of Admissions.

Financial Aid: In 2003-2004, 97% of all full-time freshmen and 92% of continuing full-time students received some form of financial aid. 69% of full-time freshmen and 72% of continuing full-time students received need-based aid. The average freshman award was $15,953. Need-based scholarships or need-based grants averaged $6309; need-based self-help aid (loans and jobs) averaged $4253; non-need-based athletic scholarships averaged $26,329; and other non-need-based awards and non-need-based scholarships averaged $6234. 22% of undergraduates work part time. Average annual earnings from campus work are $1043. The average financial indebtedness of the 2003 graduate was $22,297. The

FAFSA is required. The deadline for filing freshman financial aid applications for fall entry is February 1.

International Students: There are 156 international students enrolled. The school actively recruits these students. They must score 550 on the written TOEFL. The SAT I or the ACT is recommended.

Computers: The mainframe is a DEC VAX 6610. Approximately 400 PCs, terminals, and workstations are available for student use in a variety of university locations, some of which are open 8 A.M. to midnight. All students may access the system. There are no time limits and no fees. It is strongly recommended that all students have a personal computer.

Graduates: From July 1, 2002 to June 30, 2003, 954 bachelor's degrees were awarded. The most popular majors were communications (10%), health science/radiology technology (6%), and psychology (5%). In an average class, 42% graduate in 4 years or less, 55% graduate in 5 years or less, and 55% graduate in 6 years or less. 316 companies recruited on campus in 2002-2003. Of the 2002 graduating class, 20% were enrolled in graduate school within 6 months of graduation and 87% were employed.

Admissions Contact: Richard A. Zeiser, Dean of Admissions.
E-mail: *admission@hartford.edu* Web: *www.hartford.edu*

UNIVERSITY OF NEW HAVEN
West Haven, CT 06516

C-3

(203) 932-7319
(800) DIAL-UNH; Fax: (203) 931-6093

Full-time: 1080 men, 920 women	**Faculty:** IIA, +$
Part-time: 354 men, 273 women	**Ph.D.s:** 92%
Graduate: 835 men, 924 women	**Student/Faculty:** 11 to 1
Year: 4-1-4, summer session	**Tuition:** $20,150
Application Deadline: open	**Room & Board:** $8500

Freshman Class: 3025 applied, 2039 accepted, 631 enrolled
SAT I Verbal/Math: 510/510

COMPETITIVE

The University of New Haven, founded in 1920, is a private institution offering undergraduate programs in arts and sciences, business, engineering, public safety and professional studies, and hotel, restaurant, and tourism administration. There are 5 undergraduate schools and 1 graduate school. In addition to regional accreditation, UNH has baccalaureate program accreditation with ABET. The library contains 383,969 volumes, 511,144 microform items, and 1066 audio/video tapes/CDs, and subscribes to 1321 periodicals. Computerized library services include the card catalog, interlibrary loans, database searching, and Internet access. Special learning facilities include a learning resource center, art gallery, radio station, and TV station. The 78-acre campus is in a suburban area 5 miles west of New Haven. Including any residence halls, there are 31 buildings.

Student Life: 63% of undergraduates are from Connecticut. Students are from 30 states, 58 foreign countries, and Canada. 85% are from public schools. 72% are white; 11% African American. The average age of freshmen is 18; all undergraduates, 20. 22% do not continue beyond their first year; 40% remain to graduate.

Housing: 1300 students can be accommodated in college housing, which includes coed dorms and on-campus apartments. On-campus housing is available on a first-come, first-served basis and is available on a lottery system for upperclassmen. Priority is given to out-of-town students. 73% of students live on campus; of those, 70% remain on campus on weekends. All students may keep cars.

Activities: 4% of men belong to 2 local and 1 national fraternity; 4% of women belong to 3 local and 1 national sorority. There are 50 groups on campus, including cheerleading, chorus, dance, drama, ethnic, forensics, gay, honors, international, jazz band, newspaper, pep band, photography, political, professional, radio and TV, religious, social, social service, student government, and yearbook. Popular campus events include Family Day, Snow Ball Formal, and Spring Weekend.

Sports: There are 9 intercollegiate sports for men and 10 for women, and 10 intramural sports for men and 9 for women. Facilities include baseball, softball, and intramural playing fields; tennis courts; a gym with basketball courts, weight training room, racquetball court, and gymnastics area; and a stadium for football, soccer, and lacrosse.

Disabled Students: 82% of the campus is accessible. Wheelchair ramps, elevators, special parking, specially equipped rest rooms, special class scheduling, lowered drinking fountains, lowered telephones, and special door handles are available.

Services: Counseling and information services are available, as is tutoring in most subjects. There is remedial math, reading, and writing.

Campus Safety and Security: Measures include 24-hour foot, bicycle, and vehicle patrol, security escort services, informal discussions, and pamphlets/posters/films. There are emergency telephones, lighted pathways/sidewalks, and required programs during orientation for new students.

Programs of Study: UNH confers B.A. and B.S. degrees. Associate and master's degrees are also awarded. Bachelor's degrees are awarded in BIOLOGICAL SCIENCE (biology/biological science, biotechnology, and marine biology), BUSINESS (accounting, banking and finance, business administration and management, business economics, hotel/

motel and restaurant management, international business management, marketing/retailing/merchandising, sports management, and tourism), COMMUNICATIONS AND THE ARTS (art, audio technology, communications, creative writing, English, graphic design, literature, music, and music business management), COMPUTER AND PHYSICAL SCIENCE (applied mathematics, chemistry, computer management, computer science, mathematics, and natural sciences), ENGINEERING AND ENVIRONMENTAL DESIGN (aviation administration/management, chemical engineering, civil engineering, computer engineering, electrical/electronics engineering, engineering, environmental science, fire protection engineering, industrial engineering, industrial engineering technology, interior design, materials science, mechanical engineering, and occupational safety and health), HEALTH PROFESSIONS (dental hygiene, predentistry, premedicine, and preveterinary science), SOCIAL SCIENCE (clinical psychology, community psychology, corrections, criminal justice, dietetics, fire control and safety technology, fire science, forensic studies, history, law enforcement and corrections, liberal arts/general studies, political science/government, and psychology). Criminal justice, business administration, and fire protection are the strongest academically. Business and marketing, criminal justice, and engineering are the largest.

Required: To graduate, all students must maintain a GPA of 2.0, pass a writing proficiency exam, and complete a total of 120 to 136 credits, depending on the major. Students must complete the Freshman Experience Seminar and take at least 34 credits from the university core curriculum, including a total of 19 in lab science, social sciences, history, literature or philosophy, and art, music, or theater, 6 in communication skills, and 3 each in quantitative skills, computers, and scientific methodology.

Special: UNH offers co-op programs in most majors, internships, work-study programs, student-designed majors in the School of Professional Studies, interdisciplinary majors including biomedical computing, B.A.-B.S. degrees, a 5-year B.S.-M.S. program in environmental science, and nondegree study. Study-abroad programs are available. There are 5 national honor societies and a freshman honors program.

Faculty/Classroom: 72% of faculty are male; 28%, female. 90% teach undergraduates. No introductory courses are taught by graduate students. The average class size in an introductory lecture is 20; in a laboratory, 15; and in a regular course, 20.

Admissions: 67% of the 2003-2004 applicants were accepted. The SAT I scores for the 2003-2004 freshman class were: Verbal--44% below 500, 40% between 500 and 599, 15% between 600 and 700, and 1% above 700; Math--43% below 500, 39% between 500 and 599, 16% between 600 and 700, and 2% above 700. 29% of the current freshmen were in the top fifth of their class; 56% were in the top two fifths. 9 freshmen graduated first in their class.

Requirements: The SAT I or ACT is required. The SAT I is preferred, with a minimum combined score of 900. The GED is accepted. In addition, applicants should be graduates of an accredited secondary school. An interview is recommended. A letter of recommendation is required along with a personal essay. A GPA of 2.0 is required. AP and CLEP credits are accepted.

Procedure: Freshmen are admitted fall and spring. Entrance exams should be taken in the fall or winter of the senior year. There are rolling and deferred admissions plans. Application deadlines are open. The fall 2003 application fee was $50. Applications are accepted on-line.

Transfer: 158 transfer students enrolled in 2002-2003. Applicants should have a minimum college GPA of 2.0 and should submit all official transcripts. An interview is recommended, and the SAT I is required for students with fewer than 30 college credits. 30 of 120 credits required for the bachelor's degree must be completed at UNH.

Visiting: There are regularly scheduled orientations for prospective students, including daily information sessions, Open House, Accepted Student Days, and Junior Open House. There are guides for informal visits and visitors may sit in on classes and stay overnight. To schedule a visit, contact the Admissions Office at *adminfo@newhaven.edu*.

Financial Aid: In a recent year, 81% of all full-time freshmen and 73% of continuing full-time students received some form of financial aid. 76% of full-time freshmen and 68% of continuing full-time students received need-based aid. The average freshman award was $12,315. 15% of undergraduates work part time. Average annual earnings from campus work are $882. The average financial indebtedness of a recent graduate was $16,868. UNH is a member of CSS. The FAFSA, the college's own financial statement, and the student's and parents' 1040 tax form are required. The deadline for filing freshman financial aid applications for fall entry is March 15.

International Students: There are 93 international students enrolled. The school actively recruits these students. They must score 520 on the written TOEFL or 190 on the electronic version. English-speaking students may submit SAT I or ACT scores instead.

Computers: The mainframe is a DEC Alpha. There are 600 PCs located in the computer center, the library, and academic and administrative buildings. All students may access the system 24 hours a day. There are no time limits and no fees.

Graduates: In a recent year, 322 bachelor's degrees were awarded. The most popular majors were criminal justice/law enforcement (24%), forensic science (10%), and business administration (10%). In an average class, 40% graduate in 6 years or less. Of a recent graduating class, 5% were enrolled in graduate school within 6 months of graduation and 94% were employed.

Admissions Contact: Jane Sangeloty, Director of Undergraduate Admissions. E-mail: *adminfo@newhaven.edu*
Web: *http://www.newhaven.edu*

WESLEYAN UNIVERSITY
Middletown, CT 06459-4890

C-3
(860) 685-3000
Fax: (860) 685-3001

Full-time: 1282 men, 1422 women	**Faculty:** 329; IIA, ++$
Part-time: 8 men, 10 women	**Ph.D.s:** 91%
Graduate: 164 men, 226 women	**Student/Faculty:** 8 to 1
Year: semesters	**Tuition:** $30,001
Application Deadline: January 1	**Room & Board:** $5138
Freshman Class: 6955 applied, 1854 accepted, 718 enrolled	
SAT I Verbal/Math: 700/690	**ACT:** 31 **MOST COMPETITIVE**

Wesleyan University, founded in 1831, is an independent institution offering programs in the liberal arts and sciences. The 4 libraries contain 1,224,750 volumes, 255,164 microform items, and 43,865 audio/video tapes/CDs, and subscribe to 4281 periodicals. Computerized library services include the card catalog, interlibrary loans, and database searching. Special learning facilities include a learning resource center, art gallery, radio station, and an observatory. The 170-acre campus is in a suburban area 15 miles south of Hartford, and 2 hours from both Boston and New York City. Including any residence halls, there are 90 buildings.

Student Life: 91% of undergraduates are from out of state, mostly the Northeast. Students are from 47 states, 45 foreign countries, and Canada. 56% are from public schools. 67% are white. 20% are Jewish; 15% Catholic. The average age of freshmen is 19; all undergraduates, 20.

Housing: 2600 students can be accommodated in college housing, which includes single-sex and coed dorms, on-campus apartments, off-campus apartments, married-student housing, and fraternity houses. In addition, there are language houses and special-interest houses. On-campus housing is guaranteed for all 4 years. 96% of students live on campus; of those, 95% remain on campus on weekends. All students may keep cars.

Activities: 5% of men and about 3% of women belong to 2 local and 5 national fraternities; 1% of women belong to 2 local sororities. There are 190 groups on campus, including art, band, cheerleading, chess, choir, chorale, chorus, computers, dance, debate, drama, ethnic, film, gay, honors, international, jazz band, literary magazine, musical theater, newspaper, opera, orchestra, pep band, photography, political, professional, radio and TV, religious, social, social service, student government, symphony, and yearbook. Popular campus events include Fall Ball and Spring Fling.

Sports: There are 15 intercollegiate sports for men and 14 for women, and 14 intramural sports for men and 13 for women. Facilities include a 5000-seat stadium, a 3000-seat gym, a 50-meter Olympic-size pool, a 400-meter outdoor track, a 200-meter indoor track, a hockey arena, a strength and fitness center, 16 tennis courts, 14 squash courts, 4 soccer fields, 2 football practice fields, 2 rugby pitches, a boathouse, and field hockey, ultimate Frisbee, baseball, and softball fields.

Disabled Students: 25% of the campus is accessible. Wheelchair ramps, elevators, special parking, specially equipped rest rooms, special class scheduling, lowered drinking fountains, and lowered telephones are available.

Services: Counseling and information services are available, as is tutoring in most subjects. There is remedial math and writing.

Campus Safety and Security: Measures include 24-hour foot and vehicle patrol, self-defense education, security escort services, and shuttle buses. There are informal discussions, pamphlets/posters/films, emergency telephones, and lighted pathways/sidewalks.

Programs of Study: Wesleyan confers the B.A. degree. Master's and doctoral degrees are also awarded. Bachelor's degrees are awarded in BIOLOGICAL SCIENCE (biochemistry, biology/biological science, molecular biology, and neurosciences), COMMUNICATIONS AND THE ARTS (art history and appreciation, classics, dance, dramatic arts, English, film arts, French, German, Italian, music, romance languages and literature, Russian, Spanish, and studio art), COMPUTER AND PHYSICAL SCIENCE (astronomy, chemistry, computer science, earth science, mathematics, physics, and science technology), SOCIAL SCIENCE (African American studies, American studies, anthropology, archeology, Asian/Oriental studies, classical/ancient civilization, economics, French studies, history, Latin American studies, medieval studies, philosophy, political science/government, psychology, religion, Russian and Slavic studies, sociology, and women's studies). Sciences, economics, and history are the strongest academically. English, government, and history are the largest.

Required: To graduate, all students must complete 128 credit hours. Distribution requirements include 3 courses each in humanities and arts, social and behavioral sciences, and natural science and math. A mini-

mum academic average of 74 must be maintained, with at least 6 semesters of full-time residency.

Special: Wesleyan offers exchange programs with 11 northeastern colleges, cross-registration with 2 area colleges, study abroad in 41 countries on 6 continents, internships, a Washington semester, dual and student-designed majors, and pass/fail options. 3-2 engineering programs with Cal Tech and Columbia University are also available. There are 2 national honor societies, including Phi Beta Kappa, and 40 departmental honors programs.

Faculty/Classroom: 59% of faculty are male; 41%, female. All both teach and do research. No introductory courses are taught by graduate students. The average class size in an introductory lecture is 40; in a laboratory, 15; and in a regular course, 24.

Admissions: 27% of the 2003-2004 applicants were accepted. The SAT I scores for the 2003-2004 freshman class were: Verbal--1% below 500, 12% between 500 and 599, 36% between 600 and 700, and 51% above 700; Math--8% between 500 and 599, 48% between 600 and 700, and 44% above 700. The ACT scores were 1% below 21, 2% between 21 and 23, 11% between 24 and 26, 15% between 27 and 28, and 70% above 28. 91% of the current freshmen were in the top fifth of their class. There were 72 National Merit semifinalists.

Requirements: The SAT I or ACT is required, as are SAT II: Subject tests in writing and 2 other subjects. In addition, applicants should have 20 academic credits, including 4 years each of English, foreign language, math, science, and social studies. An essay is necessary. AP credits are accepted. Important factors in the admissions decision are advanced placement or honor courses, recommendations by school officials, and leadership record.

Procedure: Freshmen are admitted in the fall. Entrance exams should be taken in the spring of the junior year or the fall of the senior year. There are early decision and deferred admissions plans. Early decision applications should be filed by November 15; regular applications, by January 1 for fall entry. The fall 2003 application fee was $55. Notification of early decision is sent December 15; regular decision, April 1. 290 early decision candidates were accepted for the 2003-2004 class. A waiting list is an active part of the admissions procedure. Applications are accepted on-line through CommonApp, Next Stop College, Embark, Apply!, and CollegeLink.

Transfer: 63 transfer students enrolled in 2002-2003. Applicants need a strong academic record and scores submitted from either the SAT I or ACT. An interview is recommended.

Visiting: There are regularly scheduled orientations for prospective students, including 1-hour long campus tours and group information sessions. There are guides for informal visits and visitors may sit in on classes and stay overnight. To schedule a visit, contact the Admissions Office.

Financial Aid: In 2003-2004, 47% of all full-time freshmen and 50% of continuing full-time students received some form of financial aid. 47% of full-time freshmen and 50% of continuing full-time students received need-based aid. The average freshman award was $27,776, with $23,613 from need-based scholarships or need-based grants; and $4163 from need-based self-help aid (loans and jobs). 89% of undergraduates work part time. Average annual earnings from campus work are $1350. The average financial indebtedness of the 2003 graduate was $21,389. Wesleyan is a member of CSS. The CSS/Profile or FAFSA is required. The deadline for filing freshman financial aid applications for fall entry is February 1.

International Students: The school actively recruits these students. They must score 600 on the written TOEFL or 250 on the electronic version or take the IELTS. They must also take the SAT I or the ACT and the SAT II: Subject tests in writing and 2 other areas.

Computers: The mainframes are a DEC Alpha and a Sun Ultra-SPARC. More than 150 PCs and Macs are connected to the mainframe at various campus locations. Students use a variety of public servers for e-mail, web access, and other applications. Software for word processing and statistical analysis is also available. All students may access the system. There are no time limits. The fee is $10 per month for dorm connectivity. It is strongly recommended that all students have a personal computer.

Graduates: From July 1, 2002 to June 30, 2003, 724 bachelor's degrees were awarded. The most popular majors were social sciences and history (31%), visual and performing arts (13%), and area and ethnic studies (12%). In an average class, 1% graduate in 3 years or less, 82% graduate in 4 years or less, 87% graduate in 5 years or less, and 88% graduate in 6 years or less. 60 companies recruited on campus in a recent year. Of the 2002 graduating class, 24% were enrolled in graduate school within 6 months of graduation and 58% were employed.

Admissions Contact: Nancy Hargrave-Meislahn, Dean of Admissions and Financial Aid. E-mail: *admissions@wesleyan.edu*
Web: *www.wesleyan.edu*

WESTERN CONNECTICUT STATE UNIVERSITY
A-3
Danbury, CT 06810-6855
(203) 837-9000
(877) 837-9278; Fax: (203) 837-8276

Full-time: 1734 men, 2080 women	**Faculty:** 186; IIA, +$
Part-time: 609 men, 813 women	**Ph.Ds:** 80%
Graduate: 279 men, 564 women	**Student/Faculty:** 21 to 1
Year: semesters, summer session	**Tuition:** $5045 ($12,033)
Application Deadline: open	**Room & Board:** $6580
Freshman Class: 3603 applied, 2010 accepted, 820 enrolled	
SAT I Verbal/Math: 490/480	**COMPETITIVE**

Western Connecticut State University, founded in 1903, is a public institution offering programs in business, arts and sciences, and professional studies. It is part of the Connecticut State University system. There are 3 undergraduate schools and 1 graduate school. In addition to regional accreditation, West Conn has baccalaureate program accreditation with CSWE and NLN. The 2 libraries contain 182,915 volumes, 471,099 microform items, and 8654 audio/video tapes/CDs, and subscribe to 1273 periodicals. Computerized library services include the card catalog, interlibrary loans, and database searching. Special learning facilities include a learning resource center, art gallery, radio station, an observatory, electron microscope, and photography studio. The 346-acre campus is in a suburban area 65 miles north of New York City. Including any residence halls, there are 19 buildings.

Student Life: 90% of undergraduates are from Connecticut. Students are from 20 states, 21 foreign countries, and Canada. 91% are from public schools. 77% are white. The average age of freshmen is 18; all undergraduates, 23. 30% do not continue beyond their first year.

Housing: 1264 students can be accommodated in college housing, which includes single-sex and coed dorms and on-campus apartments. On-campus housing is guaranteed for all 4 years. 70% of students commute. All students may keep cars.

Activities: 3% of men belong to 3 national fraternities; 2% of women belong to 3 local and 2 national sororities. There are 50 groups on campus, including art, band, cheerleading, chess, choir, chorale, chorus, computers, dance, drama, ethnic, film, gay, honors, international, jazz band, literary magazine, musical theater, newspaper, opera, orchestra, photography, political, professional, radio and TV, religious, social, social service, student government, and yearbook. Popular campus events include West Fest, Midnight Breakfast, and Student Leadership Banquet.

Sports: There are 5 intercollegiate sports for men and 8 for women, and 6 intramural sports for men and 5 for women. Facilities include 2 gyms, a weight training area, 4 tennis courts, 5 playing fields, an indoor swimming pool, and a field house with an indoor running track.

Disabled Students: 95% of the campus is accessible. Wheelchair ramps, elevators, special parking, specially equipped rest rooms, special class scheduling, lowered drinking fountains, and lowered telephones are available.

Services: Counseling and information services are available, as is tutoring in some subjects. There is a reader service for the blind, and remedial math, reading, and writing, and a computer science clinic.

Campus Safety and Security: Measures include 24-hour foot and vehicle patrol, security escort services, shuttle buses, and informal discussions. There are pamphlets/posters/films, emergency telephones, and lighted pathways/sidewalks.

Programs of Study: West Conn confers B.A., B.S., B.B.A., and B. Music degrees. Associate and master's degrees are also awarded. Bachelor's degrees are awarded in BIOLOGICAL SCIENCE (biology/biological science), BUSINESS (accounting, banking and finance, business administration and management, management information systems, and marketing management), COMMUNICATIONS AND THE ARTS (art, communications, dramatic arts, English, graphic design, illustration, music, music performance, photography, Spanish, and studio art), COMPUTER AND PHYSICAL SCIENCE (atmospheric sciences and meteorology, chemistry, computer mathematics, computer science, earth science, and mathematics), EDUCATION (elementary, health, music, and secondary), ENGINEERING AND ENVIRONMENTAL DESIGN (environmental science), HEALTH PROFESSIONS (community health work, medical laboratory technology, and nursing), SOCIAL SCIENCE (American studies, anthropology, criminal justice, economics, history, law enforcement and corrections, paralegal studies, political science/government, psychology, social science, social work, and sociology). Education, business, justice and law administration, psychology, and communications are the largest.

Required: To graduate, students must complete 122 credit hours, with a minimum GPA of 2.0 or higher for some programs. All students must also fulfill the General Education distribution requirements, including phys ed, and the foreign language requirement.

Special: The university offers co-op programs with local corporations and the New England Regional Student Program. Student-designed majors, dual majors, study abroad, and pass/fail options are available. Non-degree study is offered at the University Center for Adult Education. There are 7 national honor societies, a freshman honors program, and 2 departmental honors programs.

Faculty/Classroom: 57% of faculty are male; 43%, female. All teach undergraduates, 25% do research, and 25% do both. No introductory courses are taught by graduate students. The average class size in an introductory lecture is 38; in a laboratory, 17; and in a regular course, 23.

Admissions: 56% of the 2003-2004 applicants were accepted. The SAT I scores for the 2003-2004 freshman class were: Verbal--54% below 500, 38% between 500 and 599, 7% between 600 and 700, and 1% above 700; Math--58% below 500, 33% between 500 and 599, 9% between 600 and 700, and 1% above 700. 11% of the current freshmen were in the top fifth of their class; 37% were in the top two fifths.

Requirements: The SAT I is required. The ACT accepted in lieu of SAT I scores. Applicants must be graduates of an accredited secondary school. The GED is accepted. Students should have completed 13 high school academic credits, including 4 in English, 3 in math, 2 to 3 in foreign language, 2 in science, and 1 each in history and social studies. Additional credits in art, music, and computer science are highly recommended. An essay and an interview are recommended. A GPA of 2.5 is required. AP and CLEP credits are accepted. Important factors in the admissions decision are advanced placement or honor courses, evidence of special talent, and recommendations by school officials.

Procedure: Freshmen are admitted fall and spring. Entrance exams should be taken by December of the senior year. There is a deferred admissions plan. There is a rolling admissions plan. Application deadlines are open. Application fee is $40. Applications are accepted on-line through *www.wcsu.edu/admissions/ugrad.asp*.

Transfer: 308 transfer students enrolled in 2002-2003. Transfers must have a minimum of 12 college credits. Applicants must have a cumulative GPA of 2.0 for all college course work. A higher GPA is requied fort some programs. 30 of 122 credits required for the bachelor's degree must be completed at West Conn.

Visiting: There are regularly scheduled orientations for prospective students, including campus tours on weekdays when classes are in session. There is an Open House on a Sunday in early November. There are guides for informal visits and visitors may sit in on classes. To schedule a visit, contact the Office of Admissions.

Financial Aid: In 2003-2004, 58% of all full-time freshmen and 55% of continuing full-time students received some form of financial aid. 44% of full-time freshmen and 40% of continuing full-time students received need-based aid. The average freshman award was $4680 with $2325 ($8998 maximum) from need-based scholarships or need-based grants, $995 ($15,000 maximum) from need-based self-help aid (loans and jobs), and $1360 ($16,904 maximum) from other non-need-based awards and non-need-based scholarships. 93% of undergraduates work part time. Average annual earnings from campus work are $1722. The FAFSA and the college's own financial statement are required. The deadline for filing freshman financial aid applications for fall entry is March 15.

International Students: There were 32 international students enrolled in a recent year. They must score 550 on the written TOEFL or 213 on the electronic version and also take the SAT I or the ACT.

Computers: 400 IBM and Mac PCs are available for student use in various campus locations. All students may access the system at any time. There are no time limits and no fees.

Graduates: From July 1, 2002 to June 30, 2003, 559 bachelor's degrees were awarded. The most popular majors were business (26%), education (11%), and justice and law (7%). In an average class, 1% graduate in 3 years or less, 19% graduate in 4 years or less, 36% graduate in 5 years or less, and 41% graduate in 6 years or less. 108 companies recruited on campus in 2002-2003. Of the 2002 graduating class, 24% were enrolled in graduate school within 6 months of graduation and 92% were employed.

Admissions Contact: William Hawkins, Director of University Admissions/Enrollment Planning. A video is available.
Web: *www.wcsu.edu/admissions*

YALE UNIVERSITY
C-3
New Haven, CT 06520-8234
(203) 432-9316
Fax: (203) 432-9392

Full-time: 2652 men, 2640 women	**Faculty:** 2028; I, ++$
Part-time: 29 men, 33 women	**Ph.Ds:** 96%
Graduate: 3039 men, 3078 women	**Student/Faculty:** 3 to 1
Year: semesters, summer session	**Tuition:** $28,400
Application Deadline: December 31	**Room & Board:** $8600
Freshman Class: 17,735 applied, 2014 accepted, 1353 enrolled	
SAT I Verbal/Math: 750/750	**ACT:** 32 **MOST COMPETITIVE**

Yale University, founded in 1701, is a private liberal arts institution. In addition to regional accreditation, Yale has baccalaureate program accreditation with AACSB, ABET, AMA, APA, ATS, CAAHEP, CAHEA, CCNE, LMCE, NAAB, NASM, NLN, and SAF among others. The 43 libraries contain 10.9 million volumes, 6.5 million microform items, and 215,554 audio/video tapes/CDs, and subscribe to 69,664 periodicals. Computerized library services include the card catalog, interlibrary loans, and database searching. Special learning facilities include an art gallery, natural history museum, planetarium, radio station, and Beinecke Rare Books and Manuscript Library, Marsh Botanical Gardens and Yale Natural Preserves, and several research centers. The 200-acre campus is in an urban area 75 miles northeast of New York City. Including any residence halls, there are 200 buildings.

Student Life: 92% of undergraduates are from out of state, mostly the Middle Atlantic. Students are from 49 states, 74 foreign countries, and Canada. 60% are from public schools. 49% are white; 17% foreign nationals; 11% Asian American. The average age of freshmen is 18; all undergraduates, 20. 2% do not continue beyond their first year; 98% remain to graduate.

Housing: 4690 students can be accommodated in college housing, which includes coed dorms and on-campus apartments. On-campus housing is guaranteed for the freshman year only and is available on a lottery system for upperclassmen. 84% of students live on campus. All students may keep cars.

Activities: There are 300 groups on campus, including art, band, cheerleading, chess, choir, chorale, chorus, computers, dance, debate, drama, ethnic, film, gay, honors, international, jazz band, literary magazine, marching band, musical theater, newspaper, opera, orchestra, pep band, photography, political, professional, radio and TV, religious, social, social service, student government, symphony, and yearbook. Popular campus events include Communiversity Day, fall and spring concerts, and the East/West Film Festival.

Sports: There are 16 intercollegiate sports for men and 18 for women, and 25 intramural sports for men and 21 for women. Facilities include the 71,000-seat Yale Bowl, a sports complex, a gym, a swimming pool, a skating rink, a sailing center, an equestrian center, and golf courses.

Disabled Students: Wheelchair ramps, elevators, special parking, specially equipped rest rooms, special class scheduling, lowered drinking fountains, lowered telephones, and a door-to-door lift-van service are available.

Services: Counseling and information services are available, as is tutoring in every subject. There is a reader service for the blind.

Campus Safety and Security: Measures include 24-hour foot and vehicle patrol, self-defense education, security escort services, and shuttle buses. There are informal discussions, pamphlets/posters/films, emergency telephones, and lighted pathways/sidewalks.

Programs of Study: Yale confers B.A., B.S., and B.L.S. degrees. Master's and doctoral degrees are also awarded. Bachelor's degrees are awarded in BIOLOGICAL SCIENCE (biochemistry, biology/biological science, and biophysics), COMMUNICATIONS AND THE ARTS (art, art history and appreciation, Chinese, classics, dramatic arts, English, film arts, French, German, Italian, Japanese, linguistics, literature, music, Portuguese, Russian, Spanish, and theater management), COMPUTER AND PHYSICAL SCIENCE (applied mathematics, astronomy, chemistry, computer science, geology, mathematics, and physics), ENGINEERING AND ENVIRONMENTAL DESIGN (architecture, biomedical engineering, chemical engineering, electrical/electronics engineering, engineering, engineering and applied science, and mechanical engineering), SOCIAL SCIENCE (African American studies, American studies, anthropology, archeology, classical/ancient civilization, East Asian studies, Eastern European studies, economics, ethics, politics, and social policy, ethnic studies, German area studies, history, history of science, humanities, Judaic studies, Latin American studies, Near Eastern studies, philosophy, political science/government, psychology, religion, sociology, and women's studies). History, political science, and economics are the largest.

Required: To graduate, students must complete 36 semester courses, including at least 3 courses in each of 4 distributional groups and at least 12 courses from outside the distributional group that includes their major. Foreign language proficiency must be demonstrated.

Special: The university offers study abroad in several countries including England, Russia, Germany, and Japan, and cooperates with other study-abroad opportunities. It also offers an accelerated degree program, B.A.-B.S. degrees, dual majors, and student-designed majors. Directed Studies, a special freshman program in the humanities, affords outstanding students the opportunity to survey the Western cultural tradition. Programs in the residential colleges allow students with special interests to pursue them in a more informal atmosphere. There is a chapter of Phi Beta Kappa.

Faculty/Classroom: 65% of faculty are male; 35%, female.

Admissions: 11% of the 2003-2004 applicants were accepted. The SAT I scores for the 2003-2004 freshman class were: Verbal--3% between 500 and 599, 23% between 600 and 700, and 74% above 700; Math--1% between 500 and 599, 24% between 600 and 700, and 74% above 700.

Requirements: The SAT I or ACT is required. In addition, only those applicants submitting SAT I scores must also take any 3 SAT II: Subject tests. Most successful applicants rank in the top 10% of their high school class. All students must have completed a rigorous high school program encompassing all academic disciplines. 2 essays are required and an interview is recommended. AP credits are accepted. Important factors in the admissions decision are advanced placement or honor courses, leadership record, and extracurricular activities record.

Procedure: Freshmen are admitted in the fall. Entrance exams should be taken at any time up to and including the January test date in the year of application. There are early action, early admissions, and deferred admissions plans. Early action applications should be filed by November 1; regular applications, by December 31 for fall entry. The fall 2003 application fee was $65. Notification of early action is sent mid-December; regular decision, April 1. A waiting list is an active part of the admissions procedure. Applications are accepted on-line through the College Board's EXPAN program only.

Transfer: 29 transfer students enrolled in 2002-2003. Applicants must take either the SAT I or ACT and have 1 full year of credit. An essay and 3 letters of recommendation are required. 18 of 36 credits required for the bachelor's degree must be completed at Yale.

Visiting: There are regularly scheduled orientations for prospective students. There are guides for informal visits and visitors may sit in on classes and stay overnight. To schedule a visit, contact the Admissions Office.

Financial Aid: In 2003-2004, 55% of all full-time students received some form of financial aid. 38% of all full-time students received need-based aid. The average freshman award was $17,430. Yale is a member of CSS. The CSS Profile or FAFSA and student and parent tax returns, as well as the CSS Divorced/Separated Parents Statement and Business/Farm Supplement, if applicable, are required. The deadline for filing freshman financial aid applications for fall entry is February 1.

International Students: There are 463 international students enrolled. The school actively recruits these students. They must score 600 on the written TOEFL and also take the SAT I and 3 SAT II: Subject tests, or the ACT.

Computers: The mainframe consists of almost 300 servers. Dozens of machines provide a complement of student computing services including comprehensive networking, e-mail, web space, and a shared file system. There are also PCs and Macs available in dorms, libraries, classrooms, and the computer center. All students may access the system 24 hours a day. There are no time limits and no fees. It is strongly recommended that all students have a personal computer.

Graduates: From July 1, 2002 to June 30, 2003, 1380 bachelor's degrees were awarded. The most popular majors were history (15%), political science (11%), and economics (9%). Of the 2002 graduating class, 31% were enrolled in graduate school within 6 months of graduation and 64% were employed.

Admissions Contact: Dan O'Neill, Assistant Director.
E-mail: *daniel.j.oneill@yale.edu* Web: *www.yale.edu/admit*

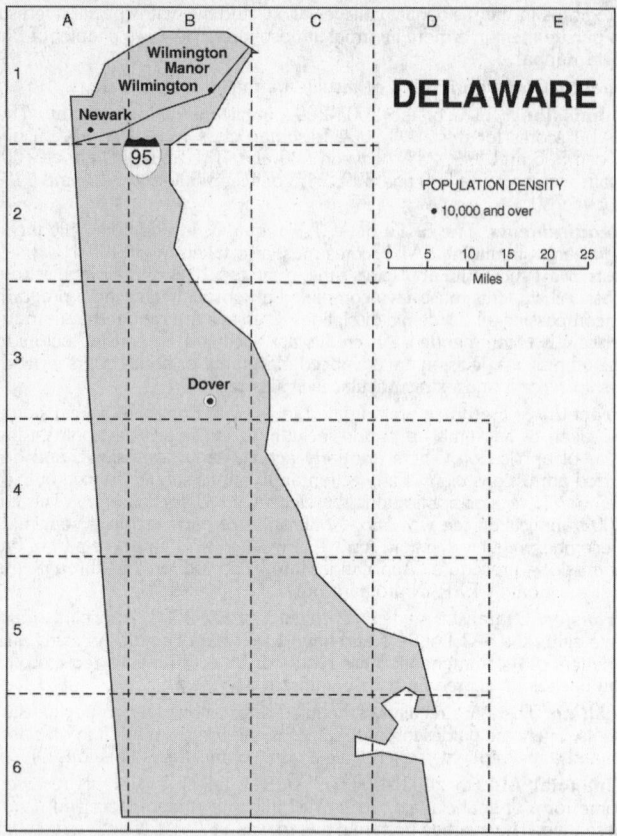

DELAWARE

POPULATION DENSITY

• 10,000 and over

0 5 10 15 20 25
Miles

DELAWARE STATE UNIVERSITY

Dover, DE 19901   B-3

(302) 739-4917

Full-time: 970 men, 1300 women	**Faculty:** 184; IIA, av$
Part-time: 240 men, 400 women	**Ph.D.s:** 74%
Graduate: 80 men, 170 women	**Student/Faculty:** 12 to 1
Year: semesters, summer session	**Tuition:** $3415 ($7165)
Application Deadline: see profile	**Room & Board:** $4690
Freshman Class: n/av	
SAT I or ACT: required	**LESS COMPETITIVE**

Delaware State University, founded in 1891, is a publicly assisted institution offering programs in agricultural and technical fields, business, engineering, liberal and fine arts, health science, professional training, and teacher preparation. There are 4 undergraduate schools and 1 graduate school. Figures in the above capsule and in this profile are approximate. In addition to regional accreditation, DSU has baccalaureate program accreditation with ACBSP and NCATE. The library contains 201,550 volumes, 76,096 microform items, and 13,652 audio/video tapes/CDs, and subscribes to 3058 periodicals. Computerized library services include the card catalog, interlibrary loans, and database searching. Special learning facilities include a learning resource center, art gallery, planetarium, and radio station. The 400-acre campus is in a suburban area 45 miles south of Wilmington. Including any residence halls, there are 31 buildings.

Student Life: 56% of undergraduates are from Delaware. Students are from 29 states, 40 foreign countries, and Canada. 90% are from public schools. 64% are African American; 32% white. The average age of freshmen is 18; all undergraduates, 21. 32% do not continue beyond their first year; 28% remain to graduate.

Housing: 1334 students can be accommodated in college housing, which includes single-sex dorms. In addition, there are honors houses and an honors dorm. On-campus housing is available on a first-come, first-served basis. 54% of students commute. Alcohol is not permitted. All students may keep cars.

Activities: 50% of men belong to 4 national fraternities; 50% of women belong to 4 national sororities. There are 53 groups on campus, including cheerleading, choir, drama, ethnic, honors, international, jazz band, marching band, newspaper, pep band, radio and TV, religious, social service, student government, and yearbook. Popular campus events include Parent's Day, Annual Career Fair, and Annual Pride Day.

Sports: There are 8 intercollegiate sports for men and 7 for women, and 20 intramural sports for men and 20 for women. Facilities include an indoor swimming pool, a dance studio, racquetball and handball courts, 2 gyms, a football stadium, a baseball field, an outdoor track, and tennis courts.

Disabled Students: Wheelchair ramps, elevators, special parking, and specially equipped rest rooms are available. The Office of Disabilities Services provides assistance to students with all types of disabilities.

Services: Counseling and information services are available, as is tutoring in every subject. There is remedial math, reading, and writing. A university tutoring program is available with a tutoring lab and tutorial service available in residence halls. A supplemental instruction program is available for challenging courses.

Campus Safety and Security: Measures include 24-hour foot and vehicle patrol, shuttle buses, informal discussions, and pamphlets/posters/films. There are emergency telephones and lighted pathways/sidewalks.

Programs of Study: DSU confers B.A., B.S., B.S.W., and B.Tech. degrees. Master's degrees are also awarded. Bachelor's degrees are awarded in AGRICULTURE (agricultural business management, fish and game management, and natural resource management), BIOLOGICAL SCIENCE (biology/biological science and botany), BUSINESS (accounting, business administration and management, fashion merchandising, hotel/motel and restaurant management, and marketing/retailing/merchandising), COMMUNICATIONS AND THE ARTS (English, French, journalism, music, and Spanish), COMPUTER AND PHYSICAL SCIENCE (chemistry, computer science, mathematics, and physics), EDUCATION (agricultural, art, business, early childhood, elementary, health, home economics, music, physical, science, and special), ENGINEERING AND ENVIRONMENTAL DESIGN (chemical engineering, civil engineering, electrical/electronics engineering, and mechanical engineering), HEALTH PROFESSIONS (community health work, environmental health science, and nursing), SOCIAL SCIENCE (economics, history, parks and recreation management, political science/government, psychology, social work, and sociology). Education is the strongest academically. Business administration, education, and English are the largest.

Required: 52 hours of general education requirements must be completed, distributed as follows: 16 hours of core courses, 3 hours of arts and humanities, 6 hours of foreign languages, 6 hours of literature, 6 hours of math, 6 hours of natural sciences, and a minimum 3-hour Senior Capstone Experience course. A total of 121 credit hours and a minimum GPA of 2.0 are required.

Special: The university offers accelerated degrees, combined B.A.-B.S. degrees, student-designed majors, and a 3-2 engineering program with the University of Delaware. Work-study is available on campus. There are assisted internships in airway science and nursing, and co-op programs in business, education, home economics, social work, and agriculture. There are 6 national honor societies, including Phi Beta Kappa, and a freshman honors program.

Faculty/Classroom: 61% of faculty are male; 39%, female. No introductory courses are taught by graduate students. The average class size in a regular course is 16.

Admissions: 6 freshmen graduated first in their class.

Requirements: The SAT I or ACT is required. In addition, applicants should graduate from an accredited secondary school or have a GED. 16 academic credits are required, including 4 units of English and 3 of math, of which 2 must be in algebra and 1 must be in geometry, 3 of science courses with a lab, 2 of history and/or social studies, and 4 of electives, including foreign language or computer science courses. A GPA of 2.0 is required. CLEP credit is accepted. Important factors in the admissions decision are extracurricular activities record, advanced placement or honor courses, and recommendations by school officials.

Procedure: Freshmen are admitted fall and spring. Entrance exams should be taken in December or January of the senior year. There is an early admissions plan and a rolling admissions plan. Check with the school for current deadlines and application fee.

Transfer: Applicants must submit a statement of honorable withdrawal and high school and college transcripts. 30 of 121 credits required for the bachelor's degree must be completed at DSU.

Visiting: There are regularly scheduled orientations for prospective students, including a High School Day Program. There are guides for informal visits. To schedule a visit, contact Jethro Williams.

Financial Aid: In a recent year, 77% of all full-time freshmen and 75% of continuing full-time students received some form of financial aid. 72% of full-time freshmen and 71% of continuing full-time students received need-based aid. The average freshman award was $7047. 4% of undergraduates work part time. Average annual earnings from campus work are $2376. DSU is a member of CSS. The CSS Profile or FFS is required. Check with the school for current deadlines.

International Students: They must score 500 on the written TOEFL and also take the SAT I or the ACT.

Computers: The mainframe is an IBM RS/6000. There are computer labs specifically for students, and students may also use terminals in the library. Students may access the university network from their own PC from residence halls. Applications include e-mail, Internet access, word processing, spreadsheets, graphics packages, and others. All students may access the system 24 hours a day. There are no time limits and no fees.

Admissions Contact: Jethro Williams, Admissions Director.
E-mail: *jwilliam@dsc.edu* Web: *www.dsc.edu*

GOLDEY-BEACOM COLLEGE   B-1
Wilmington, DE 19808   (302) 998-8814
(800) 833-4877; Fax: (302) 996-5408

Full-time: 300 men, 440 women	**Faculty:** 24
Part-time: 230 men, 340 women	**Ph.D.s:** 49%
Graduate: 70 men, 70 women	**Student/Faculty:** 30 to 1
Year: semesters, summer session	**Tuition:** $7955
Application Deadline: open	**Room & Board:** $3495
Freshman Class: n/av	
SAT I: required	**COMPETITIVE**

Goldey-Beacom College, founded in 1886, is a private business college that provides undergraduate training and education for careers in business, industry, and government. The figures in the above capsule and in this profile are approximate. There is 1 graduate school. In addition to regional accreditation, Goldey-Beacom College has baccalaureate program accreditation with AACSB and ACBSP. The library contains 48,000 volumes, 27,283 microform items, and 693 audio/video tapes/CDs, and subscribes to 800 periodicals. Computerized library services include interlibrary loans and database searching. Special learning facilities include a learning resource center. The 28-acre campus is in a suburban area 10 miles west of Wilmington. Including any residence halls, there are 8 buildings.

Student Life: 60% of undergraduates are from Delaware. Students are from 22 states, 50 foreign countries, and Canada. 75% are from public schools. 81% are white; 10% African American. The average age of freshmen is 19; all undergraduates, 21. 30% do not continue beyond their first year; 70% remain to graduate.

Housing: 300 students can be accommodated in college housing, which includes coed on-campus apartments. In addition, there are special-interest houses. On-campus housing is guaranteed for all 4 years. 80% of students commute. All students may keep cars.

Activities: 10% of men belong to 2 national fraternities; 10% of women belong to 2 national sororities. There are 23 groups on campus, including cheerleading, chorus, computers, drama, ethnic, honors, international, literary magazine, newspaper, professional, religious, social service, and student government. Popular campus events include Goldey-Beacom Follies, Spring Fest, and International Night.

Sports: Facilities include soccer and softball fields, and tennis, basketball, and handball courts.

Disabled Students: All of the campus is accessible. Wheelchair ramps, elevators, special parking, specially equipped rest rooms, lowered drinking fountains, and lowered telephones are available.

Services: Counseling and information services are available, as is tutoring in most subjects. There is a reader service for the blind, remedial math, reading, and writing, and computer-based tutorials.

Campus Safety and Security: Measures include 24-hour foot and vehicle patrol, self-defense education, informal discussions, and pamphlets/posters/films. There are lighted pathways/sidewalks and security from 6 P.M. to 6 A.M. on the small campus.

Programs of Study: Goldey-Beacom College confers the B.S. degree. Associate and master's degrees are also awarded. Bachelor's degrees are awarded in BUSINESS (accounting, banking and finance, international business management, and marketing/retailing/merchandising), COMPUTER AND PHYSICAL SCIENCE (computer programming). Accounting and computer science are the strongest academically. Accounting and management are the largest.

Required: To graduate, students must complete a minimum of 136 credit hours with an overall GPA of 2.0. Students must also fulfill the college's core requirements in English, math, and computer science.

Special: Co-op programs in all majors, an accelerated degree program, a 5-year advanced business degree, dual majors, internships, study abroad, and work-study programs are available. There is 1 national honor society, a freshman honors program, and 3 departmental honors programs.

Faculty/Classroom: 66% of faculty are male; 34%, female. All teach undergraduates. No introductory courses are taught by graduate students. The average class size in an introductory lecture is 35 and in a regular course, 25.

Requirements: The SAT I is required. In addition, applicants must be high school graduates or have a GED. A GPA of 2.0 is required. AP and CLEP credits are accepted. Important factors in the admissions decision are leadership record, evidence of special talent, and recommendations by school officials.

Procedure: Freshmen are admitted to all sessions. There are early admissions, deferred admissions, and rolling admissions plans. Application deadlines are open. Application fee is $30.

Transfer: Transfer applicants must submit high school and college transcripts. 65 of 136 credits required for the bachelor's degree must be completed at Goldey-Beacom College.

Visiting: There are regularly scheduled orientations for prospective students, including an open house. There are guides for informal visits and visitors may sit in on classes and stay overnight. To schedule a visit, contact the Admissions Office.

Financial Aid: Goldey-Beacom College is a member of CSS. The FAFSA is required. Check with the school for current deadlines.

International Students: In a recent year, there were 145 international students enrolled. The school actively recruits these students. They must score 500 on the written TOEFL.

Computers: The mainframes are an IBM Series 4361 and a VM/SP Release 5. The college's 4 computer labs contain more than 160 IBM PS/2 Model 50 terminals. Modems may access the mainframe from off campus 24 hours a day. There are no fees.

Admissions Contact: Kevin M. McIntyre, Director of Admissions and Associate Dean. A video is available.
E-mail: *mcintyrk@goldey.gbc.edu* Web: *www.goldey.gbc.edu*

UNIVERSITY OF DELAWARE   A-1
Newark, DE 19716   (302) 831-8123; Fax: (302) 831-6905

Full-time: 6218 men, 8598 women	**Faculty:** 1119; I, av$
Part-time: 406 men, 586 women	**Ph.D.s:** 85%
Graduate: 1535 men, 11,941 women	**Student/Faculty:** 13 to 1
Year: 4-1-4, summer session	**Tuition:** $6498 ($15,420)
Application Deadline: February 15	**Room & Board:** $6118
Freshman Class: 22,020 applied, 9267 accepted, 3450 enrolled	
SAT I or ACT: required	**HIGHLY COMPETITIVE**

The University of Delaware, founded in 1743 and chartered in 1833, is a privately controlled, state-assisted institution, offering programs in agricultural and natural resources, liberal arts and sciences, business, education, human services, health and nursing sciences, and engineering. There are 6 undergraduate and 7 graduate schools. In addition to regional accreditation, Delaware has baccalaureate program accreditation with AACSB, ABET, ADA, APTA, CAHEA, NASDTEC, NASM, NCATE, and NLN. The 5 libraries contain 3,019,990 volumes, 3,346,374 microform items, and 16,461 audio/video tapes/CDs, and subscribe to 12,496 periodicals. Computerized library services include the card catalog, interlibrary loans, database searching, and Internet access. Special learning facilities include a learning resource center, art gallery, radio station, TV station, and a preschool lab, development ice skating science center, computer-controlled greenhouse, nursing practice labs, physical therapy clinic, 400-acre agricultural research complex, exercise physiology biomechanics labs, foreign language media center, and composite materials center. The 1000-acre campus is in a small town 12 miles southwest of Wilmington; centered on the east coast between New York City and Washington, D.C. Including any residence halls, there are 400 buildings.

Student Life: 59% of undergraduates are from out of state, mostly the Middle Atlantic. Students are from 50 states, 100 foreign countries, and Canada. 79% are from public schools. 87% are white. 34% are Catholic; 30% claim no religious affiliation; 23% Protestant; 10% Jewish. The average age of freshmen is 18; all undergraduates, 20. 10% do not continue beyond their first year; 70% remain to graduate.

Housing: 7100 students can be accommodated in college housing, which includes single-sex and coed dorms, on-campus apartments, married-student housing, fraternity houses, and sorority houses. In addition, there are honors houses, language houses, special-interest houses, alcohol/smoke-free residence halls, and suites. On-campus housing is guaranteed for all 4 years. 50% of students live on campus; of those, 75% remain on campus on weekends. All students may keep cars.

Activities: 15% of men belong to 1 local and 17 national fraternities; 15% of women belong to 2 local and 14 national sororities. There are 203 groups on campus, including art, band, cheerleading, chess, choir, chorale, chorus, computers, dance, drama, drill team, ethnic, film, gay, honors, international, jazz band, literary magazine, marching band, musical theater, newspaper, opera, orchestra, pep band, political, professional, radio and TV, religious, social, social service, student government, and symphony. Popular campus events include Greek Week and Convocation Commencement, and Parents and Family Day.

Sports: There are 11 intercollegiate sports for men and 12 for women, and 15 intramural sports for men and 15 for women. Facilities include a 23,000-seat football stadium, 3 multipurpose gyms, 6 outdoor multipurpose fields, 8 outdoor basketball courts, 2 squash courts, 15 racquetball courts, 21 outdoor tennis courts, indoor and outdoor pools, a universal weight room, a 6000-seat basketball arena, a rock climbing wall, a high-ropes challenge course, 4 student fitness centers, a strength and conditioning room with free weights, outdoor and indoor tracks, softball, baseball, lacrosse, and soccer fields, 2 ice arenas, an outdoor hockey rink, and 4 wallyball courts.

Disabled Students: 95% of the campus is accessible. Wheelchair ramps, elevators, special parking, specially equipped rest rooms, special class scheduling, lowered drinking fountains, lowered telephones, and special housing are available.

Services: Counseling and information services are available, as is tutoring in every subject. There is a reader service for the blind, and remedial math, reading, and writing. There is also a writing center, a math center, and an academic services center for assistance with academic self-management development, critical thinking, and problem solving, and for individual assistance for learning-disabled students.

Campus Safety and Security: Measures include 24-hour foot and vehicle patrol, self-defense education, security escort services, and shuttle buses. There are informal discussions, pamphlets/posters/films, emergency telephones, lighted pathways/sidewalks, ongoing student-awareness programs in the residence halls, community policing, and keycard access to residence halls.

Programs of Study: Delaware confers B.A., B.S., B.A. Liberal Studies, B.A.S., B.C.E., B.Ch.E., B.C.P.E., B.E.E., B.E.N.E., B.F.A., B.M.E., B.Mus., B.S.Acc., B.S.Ag., B.S.A.T., B.S.B.A., B.S.Ed., B.S.N., and B.S.P.E. degrees. Associate, master's, and doctoral degrees are also awarded. Bachelor's degrees are awarded in AGRICULTURE (agricultural business management, agricultural economics, agriculture, animal science, natural resource management, plant science, and soil science), BIOLOGICAL SCIENCE (biochemistry, biology/biological science, biotechnology, entomology, nutrition, and plant pathology), BUSINESS (accounting, banking and finance, business administration and management, hotel/motel and restaurant management, management science, marketing/retailing/merchandising, and recreation and leisure services), COMMUNICATIONS AND THE ARTS (art, art history and appreciation, communications, comparative literature, English, fine arts, historic preservation, Italian, journalism, languages, music, music theory and composition, and theater management), COMPUTER AND PHYSICAL SCIENCE (astronomy, chemistry, computer science, geology, geophysics and seismology, information sciences and systems, mathematics, and physics), EDUCATION (agricultural, athletic training, early childhood, education, elementary, English, foreign languages, mathematics, music, physical, psychology, science, secondary, and special), ENGINEERING AND ENVIRONMENTAL DESIGN (bioengineering, chemical engineering, civil engineering, computer engineering, electrical/electronics engineering, engineering technology, environmental engineering, environmental science, landscape architecture/design, and mechanical engineering), HEALTH PROFESSIONS (medical laboratory technology and nursing), SOCIAL SCIENCE (anthropology, community services, consumer services, criminal justice, dietetics, economics, family and community services, fashion design and technology, food science, geography, history, human development, interdisciplinary studies, international relations, Latin American studies, parks and recreation management, philosophy, physical fitness/movement, political science/government, psychology, sociology, textiles and clothing, and women's studies). Engineering, all sciences, and business are the strongest academically. Biological sciences, elementary teacher education, and engineering are the largest.

Required: For graduation, students must complete at least 120 credits with a minimum GPA of 2.0. All students must take freshman English and 3 credits of course work with multicultural or multiethnic content. Most majors require more than 120 credits. Most degree programs require that half of the courses be in the major field of study.

Special: Students may participate in cooperative programs, internships, study abroad in 25 countries, a Washington semester, and work-study programs. The university offers accelerated degree programs, B.A.-B.S. degrees, dual majors, 68 minors, student-designed majors (Bachelor of Arts in Liberal Studies), and pass/fail options. There are 4-1 degree programs in engineering and hotel and restaurant management. Nondegree study is available through the Division of Continuing Education. There is an extensive undergraduate research program. Students may earn an enriched degree through the University Honors Program. There are 37 national honor societies, including Phi Beta Kappa, and a freshman honors program.

Faculty/Classroom: 62% of faculty are male; 38%, female. All teach undergraduates. Graduate students teach 5% of introductory courses. The average class size in a laboratory is 18 and in a regular course, 35.

Admissions: 42% of the 2003-2004 applicants were accepted. The SAT I scores for the 2003-2004 freshman class were: Verbal--12% below 500, 46% between 500 and 599, 36% between 600 and 700, and 6% above 700; Math--9% below 500, 37% between 500 and 599, 45% between 600 and 700, and 9% above 700. 50% of the current freshmen were in the top fifth of their class; 86% were in the top two fifths.

Requirements: The SAT I or ACT is required. In addition, applicants should be graduates of an accredited secondary school. The GED is accepted. Students should have completed a minimum of 16 high school academic credits, including 4 years of English, 2 years each of math, science, foreign language, and history, 1 year of social studies, and 3 years of academic course electives. SAT II: Subject tests are recommended, especially for honors program applicants. A writing sample and at least 1 letter of recommendation are required for all applicants. AP credits are accepted. Important factors in the admissions decision are advanced placement or honor courses, recommendations by school officials, and personality/intangible qualities.

Procedure: Freshmen are admitted fall and spring. Entrance exams should be taken at the end of the junior year or the beginning of the senior year. There are early decision and deferred admissions plans. Early decision applications should be filed by November 15; regular applications, by February 15 for fall entry and November 15 for spring entry, along with a $60 fee. Notification of early decision is sent December 15; regular decision, mid-March. 792 early decision candidates were accepted for the 2003-2004 class. 1601 applicants were on the 2003 waiting list; 138 were admitted. Applications are accepted on-line through an in-house application at *www.udel.edu/apply.*

Transfer: 579 transfer students enrolled in 2002-2003. Applicants for transfer should have completed at least 36 credits with a minimum GPA of 2.5 for most majors; some majors require a GPA of 3.0 or better and/or specific course work. 30 of 120 credits required for the bachelor's degree must be completed at Delaware.

Visiting: There are regularly scheduled orientations for prospective students, consisting of a 30-minute admissions information session and a 90-minute walking tour of campus. There are guides for informal visits and visitors may sit in on classes. To schedule a visit, contact the Admissions Office at *admissions@udel.edu.*

Financial Aid: In a recent year, 70% of all full-time freshmen and 64% of continuing full-time students received some form of financial aid. 42% of full-time freshmen and 35% of continuing full-time students received need-based aid. The average freshman award was $5500. 20% of undergraduates work part time. Average annual earnings from campus work are $1000. The average financial indebtedness of a recent graduate was $13,967. The FAFSA is required. The priority date for freshman financial aid applications for fall entry is February 1. The deadline for filing freshman financial aid applications for fall entry is March 15.

International Students: There are 140 international students enrolled. The school actively recruits these students. They must score 550 on the written TOEFL or 213 on the electronic version and also take the ELPT. The SAT I is recommended.

Computers: The mainframes consist of 2 IBM RS/6000-990, 1 Silicon Graphics Power Challenge, 1 Cray Research J916/8-1024, 2 Sun Microsystems Ultra Enterprise 4,000, and 1 Sun Microsystems Ultra Enterprise 5,000. 35 computing sites are available to students, offering more than 900 terminals, PCs, and Macs. All residence hall rooms and many classrooms are equipped with data outlets for network connection. All students may access the system 24 hours a day. There are no time limits and no fees.

Graduates: From July 1, 2002 to June 30, 2003, 3192 bachelor's degrees were awarded. The most popular majors were elementary teacher education (6%), psychology (6%), and finance (5%). In an average class, 1% graduate in 3 years or less, 55% graduate in 4 years or less, 70% graduate in 5 years or less, and 72% graduate in 6 years or less. 500 companies recruited on campus in 2002-2003. Of the 2002 graduating class, 20% were enrolled in graduate school within 6 months of graduation and 79% were employed.

Admissions Contact: Lou Hirsh, Director of Admissions.
E-mail: *admissions@udel.edu* Web: *www.udel.edu*

WESLEY COLLEGE B-3
Dover, DE 19901-3875 (302) 736-2400
(800) 937-5398; Fax: (302) 736-2301

Full-time: 594 men, 667 women	**Faculty:** 57; IIB, -$
Part-time: 139 men, 191 women	**Ph.Ds:** 75%
Graduate: 17 men, 103 women	**Student/Faculty:** 22 to 1
Year: semesters, summer session	**Tuition:** $13,705
Application Deadline: open	**Room & Board:** $6200
Freshman Class: 1842 applied, 1253 accepted, 501 enrolled	
SAT I Verbal/Math: 495/500	**COMPETITIVE**

Wesley College, founded in 1873, is a private liberal arts institution affiliated with the United Methodist Church. In addition to regional accreditation, Wesley has baccalaureate program accreditation with ABA, NCATE, and NLN. The library contains 100,842 volumes, 172,548 microform items, and 940 audio/video tapes/CDs, and subscribes to 232 periodicals. Computerized library services include interlibrary loans, database searching, and Internet access. Special learning facilities include a learning resource center. The 26-acre campus is in a small town 75 miles south of Philadelphia. Including any residence halls, there are 20 buildings.

Student Life: 60% of undergraduates are from out of state, mostly the Middle Atlantic. Students are from 18 states and 9 foreign countries. 85% are from public schools. 78% are white; 17% African American. 61% are Protestant; 35% Catholic. The average age of freshmen is 18; all undergraduates, 20. 23% do not continue beyond their first year; 53% remain to graduate.

Housing: 778 students can be accommodated in college housing, which includes single-sex and coed dorms and on-campus apartments.

In addition, there are honors houses. On-campus housing is guaranteed for all 4 years. 62% of students live on campus; of those, 30% remain on campus on weekends. Alcohol is not permitted. All students may keep cars.

Activities: 15% of men belong to 3 national fraternities; 15% of women belong to 3 local sororities. There are 30 groups on campus, including band, cheerleading, choir, chorale, chorus, drama, ethnic, honors, international, jazz band, literary magazine, newspaper, photography, political, professional, religious, social, social service, student government, and yearbook. Popular campus events include Family Day, International Fair, and Spring Fling.

Sports: There are 8 intercollegiate sports for men and 8 for women, and 4 intramural sports for men and 4 for women. Facilities include a swimming pool, tennis courts, a football stadium, athletic fields, a gym, a game room, and an exercise room.

Disabled Students: 65% of the campus is accessible. Wheelchair ramps, elevators, special parking, specially equipped rest rooms, special class scheduling, and lowered drinking fountains are available.

Services: Counseling and information services are available, as is tutoring in every subject. There is remedial math, reading, and writing.

Campus Safety and Security: Measures include 24-hour foot and vehicle patrol, security escort services, informal discussions, and pamphlets/posters/films. There are emergency telephones and lighted pathways/sidewalks.

Programs of Study: Wesley confers B.A. and B.S. degrees. Associate and master's degrees are also awarded. Bachelor's degrees are awarded in BIOLOGICAL SCIENCE (biology/biological science), BUSINESS (accounting, business administration and management, management science, and marketing/retailing/merchandising), COMMUNICATIONS AND THE ARTS (communications and English), EDUCATION (elementary, English, physical, secondary, and social studies), ENGINEERING AND ENVIRONMENTAL DESIGN (environmental science), HEALTH PROFESSIONS (medical laboratory technology and nursing), SOCIAL SCIENCE (American studies, history, liberal arts/general studies, paralegal studies, political science/government, and psychology). Education, psychology, and business are the strongest academically and have the largest enrollments.

Required: For graduation, students must complete 124 credit hours, with at least 15 hours in the major and a minimum GPA of 2.0. 50 hours of core courses, including English, religion, science, math, American culture, non-American culture, and phys ed are required.

Special: Wesley offers internships in business and industry, environmental science, medical technology, and government agencies. Study abroad in 5 countries, work-study programs, dual majors, pass/fail options, and credit for life, military, and work experience are available. There are 2 national honor societies and 1 departmental honors program.

Faculty/Classroom: 58% of faculty are male; 42%, female. All teach undergraduates, 3% do research, and 3% do both. No introductory courses are taught by graduate students. The average class size in an introductory lecture is 20; in a laboratory, 12; and in a regular course, 20.

Admissions: 68% of the 2003-2004 applicants were accepted. The SAT I scores for the 2003-2004 freshman class were: Verbal--50% below 500, 39% between 500 and 599, 10% between 600 and 700, and 1% above 700; Math--50% below 500, 39% between 500 and 599, 10% between 600 and 700, and 1% above 700. 5 freshmen graduated first in their class.

Requirements: The SAT I is required. In addition, applicants must be graduates of an accredited secondary school; the GED is accepted. Students should have completed 12 academic credits or 16 Carnegie units, including 4 units of English and 2 units each of math, history, science, and social studies. An interview is recommended. Wesley requires applicants to be in the upper 80% of their class. A GPA of 2.2 is required. AP and CLEP credits are accepted. Important factors in the admissions decision are recommendations by school officials, extracurricular activities record, and leadership record.

Procedure: Freshmen are admitted fall and winter. Entrance exams should be taken in the junior year. There are early decision, rolling, and deferred admissions plans. Application deadlines are open. Application fee is $20. 20 early decision candidates were accepted for the 2003-2004 class. Applications are accepted on-line.

Transfer: 30 transfer students enrolled in 2002-2003. Applicants must have a minimum GPA of 2.0 and a minimum composite SAT I score of 800. 36 of 124 credits required for the bachelor's degree must be completed at Wesley.

Visiting: There are regularly scheduled orientations for prospective students. There are guides for informal visits and visitors may sit in on classes and stay overnight. To schedule a visit, contact the Office of Admissions at (800) WESLEYU or *admissions@wesley.edu.*

Financial Aid: In a recent year, 80% of all full-time freshmen and 78% of continuing full-time students received some form of financial aid. 80% of full-time freshmen and 78% of continuing full-time students received need-based aid. The average freshman award was $6500. 24% of undergraduates work part time. Average annual earnings from campus

work are $1000. The average financial indebtedness of a recent graduate was $16,000. The FAFSA or SFS and the college's own financial statement are required. The deadline for filing freshman financial aid applications for fall entry is April 15.

International Students: There are 20 international students enrolled. The school actively recruits these students. They must score 550 on the written TOEFL and also take the SAT I.

Computers: The mainframe may be accessed from more than 120 terminals across campus for use in word processing, programming, accounting, and statistics. PCs are available for student use in the writing center, computer center, and accounting lab. All students may access the system 24 hours a day, 7 days a week. There are no time limits and no fees. It is strongly recommended that all students have a personal computer.

Graduates: From July 1, 2002 to June 30, 2003, 214 bachelor's degrees were awarded. The most popular majors were education (16%), psychology (14%), and management (12%). In an average class, 1% graduate in 3 years or less, 48% graduate in 4 years or less, 50% graduate in 5 years or less, and 53% graduate in 6 years or less. 30 companies recruited on campus in 2002-2003. Of a recent graduating class, 16% were enrolled in graduate school within 6 months of graduation and 62% were employed.

Admissions Contact: Arthur Jacobs, Director of Admissions. A video is available. E-mail: *jacobsar@wesley.edu* Web: *www.wesley.edu*

WILMINGTON COLLEGE
New Castle, DE 19720

B-1
(302) 328-9407
(877) 967-5464; Fax: (302) 328-5902

Full-time: 713 men, 1303 women	Faculty: 41; IIA, -$
Part-time: 567 men, 1394 women	Ph.D.s: 55%
Graduate: 723 men, 1724 women	Student/Faculty: 49 to 1
Year: semesters, summer session	Tuition: $5594
Application Deadline: open	Room & Board: n/app
Freshman Class: 1500 applied, 1500 accepted	
SAT I or ACT: not required	NONCOMPETITIVE

Wilmington College, founded in 1967, is a private, liberal arts commuter college offering admission to students from varied academic backgrounds. There are 6 undergraduate and 7 graduate schools. In addition to regional accreditation, Wilmington has baccalaureate program accreditation with NASDTEC and NLN. The library contains 191,885 volumes, 93,545 microform items, and 2611 audio/video tapes/CDs, and subscribes to 468 periodicals. Computerized library services include the card catalog, interlibrary loans, database searching, and Internet access. Special learning facilities include a learning resource center, radio station, and TV station. The 18-acre campus is in an urban area 7 miles south of Wilmington. There are 18 buildings.

Student Life: 87% of undergraduates are from Delaware. Students are from 12 states, 5 foreign countries, and Canada. 85% are from public schools. 45% are white; 12% African American. The average age of freshmen is 27; all undergraduates, 30. 8% do not continue beyond their first year; 76% remain to graduate.

Housing: There are no residence halls. All students commute. The college provides a list of housing accommodations in the community and makes recommendations for off-campus apartments. Alcohol is not permitted. All students may keep cars.

Activities: There is 1 national fraternity. There are no sororities. There are 11 groups on campus, including behavioral science division club, cheerleading, criminal justice club, film, honors, International Reading Association, newspaper, photography, radio and TV, student government, and yearbook.

Sports: There are 4 intercollegiate sports for men and 5 for women. Facilities include a 1000-seat gym and a recreation room.

Disabled Students: All of the campus is accessible. Wheelchair ramps, elevators, special parking, specially equipped rest rooms, lowered drinking fountains, and lowered telephones are available.

Services: Counseling and information services are available, as is tutoring in some subjects, including math and English. There is remedial math and reading. Staff members also are available to assist students with study skills such as test taking, reading, concentration development, and time management.

Campus Safety and Security: Measures include 24-hour foot and vehicle patrol, security escort services, emergency telephones, and lighted pathways/sidewalks.

Programs of Study: Wilmington confers B.A., B.S., and B.S.N. degrees. Associate, master's, and doctoral degrees are also awarded. Bachelor's degrees are awarded in BUSINESS (accounting, banking and finance, business administration and management, personnel management, and sports management), COMMUNICATIONS AND THE ARTS (communications technology, media arts, multimedia, and video), EDUCATION (early childhood and elementary), ENGINEERING AND ENVIRONMENTAL DESIGN (aeronautical science and aviation administration/management), HEALTH PROFESSIONS (nursing), SOCIAL SCIENCE (behavioral science and criminal justice). Nursing and elementary education are the strongest academically. Business, nursing, and elementary education are the largest.

Required: To graduate, students must complete a total of 120 hours with a minimum GPA of 2.0. 54 hours are required in the major. The 36-hour general studies core requirement includes 12 hours of social science, 9 each of English and humanities, and 3 each of math and science. At least 45 credit hours of upper-division course work are required, as is demonstrated competence in verbal and written communication and computational skills. At least 3 credits must be taken in computer operations. Nursing students must also submit official transcripts verifying graduation from a diploma or associate degree nursing program. Candidates for the B.S.N. degree must possess an R.N. license.

Special: The school offers practicums for education students, co-op programs, work-study programs with area employers, internships, a general studies degree, an accelerated degree program, dual majors, pass/fail options, credit for life experience, and by-challenge exam. There is 1 national honor society and 2 departmental honors programs.

Faculty/Classroom: 70% of faculty are male; 30%, female. 66% teach undergraduates. The average class size in an introductory lecture is 25; in a laboratory, 10; and in a regular course, 17.

Admissions: All of the 2003-2004 applicants were accepted.

Requirements: Graduation from an accredited secondary school or satisfactory scores on the GED are required for admission. An interview may be required of some students, and an essay is recommended. A GPA of 2.0 is required. AP and CLEP credits are accepted.

Procedure: Freshmen are admitted to all sessions. There are rolling and deferred admissions plans. Application deadlines are open. Application fee is $25. The college accepts all applicants.

Transfer: 2736 transfer students enrolled in 2002-2003. Applicants must have a 2.0 GPA; those with a lower GPA must have an interview. Some applicants may be required to submit SAT I or ACT scores. Those with fewer than 15 semester credits must submit high school transcripts. No more than 75 semester credits will be accepted for transfer credit. 45 of 120 credits required for the bachelor's degree must be completed at Wilmington.

Visiting: There are guides for informal visits and visitors may sit in on classes. To schedule a visit, contact the Admissions Office.

Financial Aid: In 2003-2004, 33% of all full-time freshmen received some form of financial aid. 10% of full-time freshmen received need-based aid. The average freshman award was $5034. The FAFSA is required. The deadline for filing freshman financial aid applications for fall entry is August 15.

International Students: There are 40 international students enrolled. They must score 500 on the written TOEFL or they may submit a transcript of successful completion of at least 12 credit hours from a U.S. institution of higher education.

Computers: The mainframe is a DEC MicroVAX 3300. Macs, IBM models 25, PC, XT, and AT are available in the library and in the faculty study. Only students matriculated in communications technology majors may access the system during designated class/lab time. There are no time limits and no fees.

Graduates: 128 companies recruited on campus in 2002-2003.

Admissions Contact: Andrey Mattern, Manager of Admissions. E-mail: *apara@wilmcoll.edu* Web: *www.wilmcoll.edu*

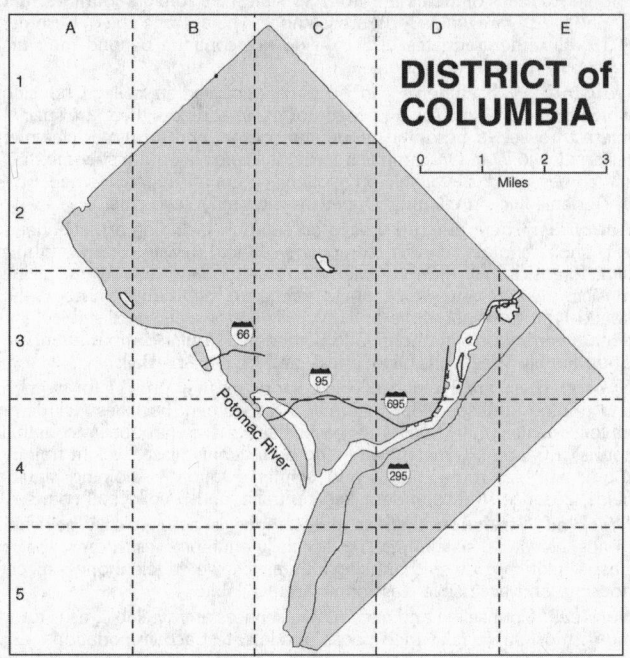

DISTRICT of COLUMBIA

0 1 2 3
Miles

AMERICAN UNIVERSITY
Washington, DC 20016-8001

A-2

(202) 885-6000
Fax: (202) 885-1025

Full-time: 2059 men, 3368 women	**Faculty:** 476; I, +$
Part-time: 136 men, 189 women	**Ph.D.s:** 96%
Graduate: 1449 men, 2386 women	**Student/Faculty:** 11 to 1
Year: semesters, summer session	**Tuition:** $24,839
Application Deadline: February 1	**Room & Board:** $9746
Freshman Class: 9101 applied, 5973 accepted, 1249 enrolled	
SAT I Verbal/Math: 620/600	**ACT:** 27 **VERY COMPETITIVE+**

American University, founded in 1893, is a private liberal arts institution affiliated with the United Methodist Church. There are 5 undergraduate and 6 graduate schools. In addition to regional accreditation, AU has baccalaureate program accreditation with AACSB, ACEJMC, ACS, NASDTEC, NASM, and NCATE. The library contains 776,900 volumes, more than 1 million microform items, and 57,335 audio/video tapes/CDs, and subscribes to 3214 periodicals. Computerized library services include the card catalog, interlibrary loans, database searching, and Internet access. Special learning facilities include a learning resource center, art gallery, radio station, TV station, language resource center, multimedia design and development lab, national center for health fitness, audiotechnology lab, broadcast newsroom, journalism center, and UNIX, intelligent systems, and Oracle development labs. The 78-acre campus is in a suburban area 5 miles northwest of downtown Washington D.C. Including any residence halls, there are 37 buildings.

Student Life: 87% of undergraduates are from out of state, mostly the Middle Atlantic. Students are from 50 states, 97 foreign countries, and Canada. 65% are white; 12% foreign nationals; 10% African American. The average age of freshmen is 18; all undergraduates, 20. 13% do not continue beyond their first year; 66% remain to graduate.

Housing: 4000 students can be accommodated in college housing, which includes single-sex and coed dorms and off-campus apartments. In addition, there is an international-intercultural hall, honors floors, and special-interest floors, including a service floor. All dorms are smoke-free. On-campus housing is guaranteed for all 4 years. 65% of students live on campus. Alcohol is not permitted. Upperclassmen may keep cars.

Activities: 14% of men belong to 10 national fraternities; 16% of women belong to 13 national sororities. There are 150 groups on campus, including art, band, cheerleading, chess, choir, chorale, chorus, computers, dance, drama, ethnic, film, forensics, gay, honors, international, jazz band, Kennedy Political Union, literary magazine, musical theater, newspaper, orchestra, pep band, photography, political, professional, radio and TV, religious, social, social service, student government, symphony, and yearbook. Popular campus events include Family Weekend, Founders Day Ball, and campus Beautification Day.

Sports: There are 9 intercollegiate sports for men and 10 for women, and 15 intramural sports for men and 16 for women. Facilities include a 6000-seat gym, 2 swimming pools, hockey and soccer fields, a softball diamond, an all-purpose field, cardiovascular and strength training equipment, weight rooms, courts for tennis, basketball, and volleyball, an aerobics studio, an indoor jogging track, and an outdoor, 6-lane tartan track.

Disabled Students: 94% of the campus is accessible. Wheelchair ramps, elevators, special parking, specially equipped rest rooms, special class scheduling, lowered drinking fountains, lowered telephones, special housing, and university shuttle equipped to accommodate students in wheelchairs are available.

Services: Counseling and information services are available, as is tutoring in every subject. There is a reader service for the blind, and remedial math, reading, and writing. A math and statistics tutoring lab, a writing center, a foreign language resource center, and a writing lab are available.

Campus Safety and Security: Measures include 24-hour foot and vehicle patrol, self-defense education, security escort services, and shuttle buses. There are informal discussions, pamphlets/posters/films, emergency telephones, lighted pathways/sidewalks, safety orientation programs, alarms and closed-circuit cameras, and posted crime alerts.

Programs of Study: AU confers B.A., B.S., B.F.A., and B.S.B.A. degrees. Associate, master's, and doctoral degrees are also awarded. Bachelor's degrees are awarded in BIOLOGICAL SCIENCE (biochemistry, biology/biological science, and marine science), BUSINESS (banking and finance, business administration and management, international business management, management information systems, and marketing management), COMMUNICATIONS AND THE ARTS (art history and appreciation, audio technology, communications, dramatic arts, film arts, fine arts, graphic design, journalism, literature, music, performing arts, public relations, and studio art), COMPUTER AND PHYSICAL SCIENCE (applied mathematics, chemistry, computer science, information sciences and systems, mathematics, physics, and statistics), EDUCATION (elementary and secondary), ENGINEERING AND ENVIRONMENTAL DESIGN (computer graphics and environmental science), HEALTH PROFESSIONS (health science), SOCIAL SCIENCE (American studies, anthropology, area studies, criminal justice, economics, French studies, German area studies, history, interdisciplinary studies, international studies, Judaic studies, Latin American studies, law, philosophy, political science/government, psychology, religion, Russian and Slavic studies, sociology, Spanish studies, and women's studies). Political science, business administration, and international studies are the strongest academically and are the largest.

Required: To graduate, students must complete 120 credit hours with a minimum GPA of 2.0. In addition, students must complete 30 credit hours of general education requirements in 5 curricular areas and fulfill the school's competency requirements in English composition and math by either passing an exam or taking a course in each area. Many majors require internships and senior seminars.

Special: AU offers internships in all majors, study abroad in more than 20 countries, and a Washington semester program. Work-study is available on campus and with local community service agencies. Dual majors, interdisciplinary programs, student-designed majors, 3-2 engineering degrees, and B.A.-B.S. degrees are also available. Combined bachelor's/master's programs are available in most majors. Cross-registration may be arranged through the Consortium of Universities of the Washington Metropolitan Area. Credit for life experience, nondegree study, and pass/fail options are available. There are preprofessional programs in dentistry, engineering, law, medicine, optometry, osteopathy, pharmacy, and veterinary medicine. There are 17 national honor societies, including Phi Beta Kappa, a freshman honors program, and 27 departmental honors programs.

Faculty/Classroom: 56% of faculty are male; 44%, female. No introductory courses are taught by graduate students. The average class size in an introductory lecture is 27 and in a regular course, 20.

Admissions: 66% of the 2003-2004 applicants were accepted. The SAT I scores for the 2003-2004 freshman class were: Verbal--5% below 500, 32% between 500 and 599, 46% between 600 and 700, and 17% above 700; Math--5% below 500, 42% between 500 and 599, 44% between 600 and 700, and 9% above 700. The ACT scores were 2% below 21, 12% between 21 and 23, 34% between 24 and 26, 18% between 27 and 28, and 33% above 28. 66% of the current freshmen were in the top fifth of their class; 94% were in the top two fifths. There were 11 National Merit finalists.

Requirements: The SAT I or ACT is required. In addition, students must have graduated from an accredited secondary school with at least 16 Carnegie units, including at least 4 units in English, 3 units in college preparatory math (including the equivalent of 2 units in algebra), 3 units in social sciences/history, 2 units in foreign language(s), and 2 units in natural or lab science. Applicants who have satisfactory scores on the GED may also apply. All students must submit an essay and 2 letters of recommendation. Interviews are recommended. A GPA of 2.0 is required. AP and CLEP credits are accepted. Important factors in the admissions decision are advanced placement or honor courses, extracurricular activities record, and recommendations by school officials.

Procedure: Freshmen are admitted to all sessions. Entrance exams should be taken in the spring of the junior year or the fall of the senior year. There are early decision and deferred admissions plans. Early decision applications should be filed by November 15; regular applications, by February 1 for fall entry, December 1 for spring entry, and April 1 for summer entry, along with a $45 fee. Notification of early decision is sent December 31; regular decision, April 1. 195 early decision candidates were accepted for the 2003-2004 class. 545 applicants were on the 2003 waiting list; none were accepted. Applications are accepted on-line through the school's web site or Common App.

Transfer: 367 transfer students enrolled in 2002-2003. Transfer applicants must be in good academic and social standing at the school previously attended and have a minimum GPA of 2.5 to be considered competitive for admission. 45 of 120 credits required for the bachelor's degree must be completed at AU.

Visiting: There are regularly scheduled orientations for prospective students, including daily tours and information sessions, open houses, and overnight programs. There are guides for informal visits and visitors may sit in on classes and stay overnight. To schedule a visit, contact the Welcome Center.

Financial Aid: In 2003-2004, 80% of all full-time freshmen and 60% of continuing full-time students received some form of financial aid. 53% of full-time freshmen and 42% of continuing full-time students received need-based aid. Need-based scholarships or need-based grants averaged $16,044; need-based self-help aid (loans and jobs) averaged $10,993; and non-need-based athletic scholarships averaged $13,604. 15% of undergraduates work part time. Average annual earnings from campus work are $1534. The average financial indebtedness of the 2003 graduate was $18,716. AU is a member of CSS. The FAFSA and the college's own financial statement are required. The deadline for filing freshman financial aid applications for fall entry is March 1 (November 15 early decision).

International Students: There are 400 international students enrolled. The school actively recruits these students. They must score 550 on the written TOEFL or 213 on the electronic version; or the SAT I with a score of 530 or higher on the verbal section; or the SAT II: English Language Proficiency Test with a score of 970 or higher; or the IELTS with a score of 6.5 or higher.

Computers: More than 550 IBM, Mac, and other PCs are available for student use in various campus locations. All residence hall rooms are fully networked.The entire university is wireless for laptops, PDAs, and cell phones. Students have space on the network web servers for personal web pages, a personal network drive for saving files, and access to an antivirus package. All students may access the system. There are no time limits and no fees. It is strongly recommended that all students have a personal computer.

Graduates: From July 1, 2002 to June 30, 2003, 1227 bachelor's degrees were awarded. The most popular majors were international studies and business administration (18%), political science (9%), and public communication (8%). In an average class, 2% graduate in 3 years or less, 60% graduate in 4 years or less, 68% graduate in 5 years or less, and 71% graduate in 6 years or less. 40 companies recruited on campus in 2002-2003. Of the 2002 graduating class, 71% were enrolled in graduate school within 6 months of graduation and 63% were employed.

Admissions Contact: Dr. Sharon Alston, Director of Admissions. E-mail: *afa@american.edu* Web: *admissions@american.edu*

CATHOLIC UNIVERSITY OF AMERICA	**C-2**
Washington, DC 20064	**(202) 319-5305**
	(800) 673-2772; Fax: (202) 319-6171

Full-time: 1127 men, 1350 women	**Faculty:** 232; I, -$
Part-time: 94 men, 188 women	**Ph.D.s:** 96%
Graduate: 1440 men, 1541 women	**Student/Faculty:** 11 to 1
Year: semesters, summer session	**Tuition:** $24,750
Application Deadline: February 15	**Room & Board:** $9498
Freshman Class: 2748 applied, 2251 accepted, 673 enrolled	
SAT I Verbal/Math: 584/577	**ACT:** 25 **VERY COMPETITIVE**

Catholic University of America, founded in 1887 and affiliated with the Roman Catholic Church, offers undergraduate programs through the schools of arts and sciences, engineering, architecture, nursing, philosophy, the Benjamin T. Rome School of Music, and the Metropolitan College. There are 7 undergraduate and 10 graduate schools. In addition to regional accreditation, CUA has baccalaureate program accreditation with ABET, ACPE, APA, ATS, CSWE, NAAB, NASM, NCATE, and NLN. The 3 libraries contain 1,580,282 volumes, 1,139,773 microform items, and 39,136 audio/video tapes/CDs, and subscribe to 5907 periodicals. Computerized library services include the card catalog, interlibrary loans, database searching, and Internet access. Special learning facilities include a learning resource center, art gallery, radio station, an archeology lab, a rare book collection, and electronic/computer classrooms. The

144-acre campus is in an urban area in Washington, D.C. Including any residence halls, there are 52 buildings.

Student Life: 94% of undergraduates are from out of state, mostly the Middle Atlantic. Students are from 50 states, 32 foreign countries, and Canada. 72% are white. Most are Catholic. The average age of freshmen is 19; all undergraduates, 22. 15% do not continue beyond their first year; 69% remain to graduate.

Housing: 1928 students can be accommodated in college housing, which includes single-sex and coed dorms. In addition, there are special-interest houses, a freshman residential college, and an upper classmen residential college. On-campus housing is available on a first-come, first-served basis and is available on a lottery system for upperclassmen. 66% of students live on campus. Upperclassmen may keep cars.

Activities: There are 100 groups on campus, including art, cheerleading, choir, chorale, chorus, computers, dance, debate, drama, ethnic, film, forensics, gay, honors, international, jazz band, literary magazine, musical theater, newspaper, opera, orchestra, pep band, photography, political, professional, radio and TV, religious, social, social service, student government, symphony, and yearbook. Popular campus events include Family Weekend, Oktoberfest, and Beaux Arts Ball.

Sports: There are 10 intercollegiate sports for men and 11 for women, and 6 intramural sports for men and 5 for women. Facilities include an athletic center that houses 4 basketball and 5 handball/racquetball courts, a 6-lane, 25-meter swimming pool, tennis plaza, weight training room, aerobics room, men's and women's saunas, adjoining playing fields, 2 dance studios, indoor jogging track, and 3 volleyball courts.

Disabled Students: 65% of the campus is accessible. Wheelchair ramps, elevators, special parking, specially equipped rest rooms, special class scheduling, lowered drinking fountains, lowered telephones, special housing, and accessible classrooms are available.

Services: Counseling and information services are available, as is tutoring in most subjects. Taped books, readers, test accommodations, and sign language interpreters are available. There is a reader service for the blind and remedial math, reading, and writing.

Campus Safety and Security: Measures include 24-hour foot and vehicle patrol, self-defense education, security escort services, and shuttle buses. There are informal discussions, pamphlets/posters/films, emergency telephones, lighted pathways/sidewalks, and fixed security posts, emergency whistles, watch captains in every building, and an access control system.

Programs of Study: CUA confers B.A., B.S., B.A.G.S., B.B.E., B.C.E., B.E.E., B.M., B.M.E., B.S.C.S., B.S.N., B.Arch, and B.S.Arch degrees. Master's and doctoral degrees are also awarded. Bachelor's degrees are awarded in BIOLOGICAL SCIENCE (biochemistry and biology/biological science), BUSINESS (accounting, banking and finance, business administration and management, human resources, international economics, and management science), COMMUNICATIONS AND THE ARTS (art, art history and appreciation, classics, communications, dramatic arts, English, French, German, Latin, music, music history and appreciation, music performance, music theory and composition, musical theater, painting, piano/organ, sculpture, Spanish, and voice), COMPUTER AND PHYSICAL SCIENCE (chemistry, computer science, elementary particle physics, mathematics, and physics), EDUCATION (art, drama, early childhood, education, elementary, English, mathematics, music, and secondary), ENGINEERING AND ENVIRONMENTAL DESIGN (architecture, biomedical engineering, civil engineering, electrical/electronics engineering, engineering, environmental science, and mechanical engineering), HEALTH PROFESSIONS (medical laboratory technology and nursing), SOCIAL SCIENCE (anthropology, economics, history, liberal arts/general studies, medieval studies, philosophy, political science/government, psychology, religion, social work, and sociology). Politics is the strongest academically. Architecture is the largest.

Required: To graduate, students must complete 120 credit hours, including 42 hours in the major, with a minimum GPA of 2.0. Courses must meet distribution requirements in English composition, philosophy, religion and religious study, language and literature, humanities, math and natural sciences, and social and behavioral sciences. A comprehensive exam is required in most majors.

Special: Cross-registration is available with the Consortium of Universities of the Washington Metropolitan Area. Opportunities are also provided for internships, accelerated degree programs, dual majors, B.A./B.S. degrees, pass/fail options, and study abroad in 10 countries. There are 15 national honor societies, including Phi Beta Kappa, and a freshman honors program.

Faculty/Classroom: 64% of faculty are male; 36%, female. 80% teach undergraduates and all do research. Graduate students teach 20% of introductory courses. The average class size in an introductory lecture is 21; in a laboratory, 20; and in a regular course, 19.

Admissions: 82% of the 2003-2004 applicants were accepted. The SAT I scores for the 2003-2004 freshman class were: Verbal--13% below 500, 41% between 500 and 599, 38% between 600 and 700, and 8% above 700; Math--14% below 500, 42% between 500 and 599, 40% between 600 and 700, and 4% above 700. The ACT scores were 16% below 21, 18% between 21 and 23, 29% between 24 and 26, 16% between 27 and 28, and 21% above 28. 49% of the current freshmen were in the top fifth of their class; 83% were in the top two fifths.

Requirements: The SAT I or ACT is required. In addition, the SAT II: Writing test is required for placement, and the SAT II: Foreign Language test is recommended. Applicants must be graduates of an accredited secondary school. The GED is accepted. Students should present 17 academic credits, including 4 each in English, and social studies, 3 each in math and science, 2 in foreign languages, and 1 in fine arts or humanities. An essay is required. An audition is required for music applicants and a portfolio for architecture applicants is recommended. AP credits are accepted. Important factors in the admissions decision are extracurricular activities record, leadership record, and advanced placement or honor courses.

Procedure: Freshmen are admitted fall and spring. Entrance exams should be taken by February of the senior year of high school. There are early decision and deferred admissions plans. Early decision applications should be filed by December 1; regular applications, by February 15 for fall entry, along with a $55 fee. Notification of early decision is sent January 15; regular decision, March 20. Applications are accepted on-line through *admissions.cua.edu/application/*.

Transfer: 175 transfer students enrolled in 2002-2003. Applicants must submit a high school transcript, SAT I or ACT scores, and a college transcript. A letter of recommendation and an essay are required. Terms of admission are finalized by the dean of the appropriate school. 30 of 120 credits required for the bachelor's degree must be completed at CUA.

Visiting: There are regularly scheduled orientations for prospective students, including an information session with an admissions counselor and a guided campus tour. There are guides for informal visits and visitors may sit in on classes and stay overnight. To schedule a visit, contact the Admissions Office.

Financial Aid: In 2003-2004, 96% of all full-time freshmen and 87% of continuing full-time students received some form of financial aid. 80% of full-time freshmen and 81% of continuing full-time students received need-based aid. 45% of undergraduates work part time. Average annual earnings from campus work are $1500. CUA is a member of CSS. The FAFSA is required. The priority date for freshman financial aid applications for fall entry is January 15. The deadline for filing freshman financial aid applications for fall entry is February 1.

International Students: There are 57 international students enrolled. The school actively recruits these students. They must score 550 on the written TOEFL or 213 on the electronic version.

Computers: The mainframes are a Sun E4500, Sun V880, Sun V480, and Compaq 6400. There are 500 networked PCs spread across the campus for student use. All dorms are wired and students have access to the Internet and Web. All students may access the system 24 hours a day. There are no time limits and no fees. It is strongly recommended that all students have personal computers. Dell or Gateway is recommended.

Graduates: From July 1, 2002 to June 30, 2003, 491 bachelor's degrees were awarded. The most popular majors were social science and history (17%), architecture (15%), and business and economics (10%). In an average class, 59% graduate in 4 years or less, 68% graduate in 5 years or less, and 69% graduate in 6 years or less. More than 100 companies recruited on campus in 2002-2003. Of the 2002 graduating class, 36% were enrolled in graduate school within 6 months of graduation and 91% were employed.

Admissions Contact: Shahin R. Mafaher, Interim Dean of Enrollment Services. A video is available. E-mail: *cua-admissions@cua.edu*

CORCORAN SCHOOL OF ART AND DESIGN C-3
(Formerly Corcoran School of Art)
Washington, DC 20006

(202) 639-1814
(888) CORCORAN; Fax: (202) 639-1830

Full-time: 110 men, 180 women	Faculty: 34
Part-time: 10 men, 20 women	Ph.D.s: 63%
Graduate: none	Student/Faculty: 8 to 1
Year: semesters, summer session	Tuition: $15,520
Application Deadline: open	Room & Board: $5515
Freshman Class: n/av	
SAT I or ACT:	SPECIAL

Established in 1890, the Corcoran School of Art and Design, formerly Corcoran School of Art, is a private professional art college offering undergraduate programs in fine art, design, and photography. Figures in the above capsule and in this profile are approximate. In addition to regional accreditation, Corcoran has baccalaureate program accreditation with NASAD. The library contains 19,000 volumes, and subscribes to 130 periodicals. Computerized library services include interlibrary loans. Special learning facilities include a learning resource center and art gallery. The 7-acre campus is in an urban area in Washington, D.C. There are 3 buildings.

Student Life: 72% of undergraduates are from out of state, mostly the Middle Atlantic. Students are from 24 states, 32 foreign countries, and Canada. 75% are from public schools. 55% are white; 21% foreign nationals; 10% African American. The average age of freshmen is 19; all undergraduates, 23. 3% do not continue beyond their first year; 60% remain to graduate.

Housing: There are no residence halls. On-campus housing is guaranteed for the freshman year only and is available on a first-come, first-served basis. Priority is given to out-of-town students. 84% of students commute. Alcohol is not permitted. No one may keep cars.

Activities: There are no fraternities or sororities. There are 4 groups on campus, including art, literary magazine, newspaper, and student government. Popular campus events include student art openings, museum and gallery openings, and visiting artists' lectures.

Sports: There is no sports program at Corcoran.

Disabled Students: 70% of the campus is accessible. Wheelchair ramps, elevators, special parking, specially equipped rest rooms, lowered drinking fountains, and lowered telephones are available.

Services: Counseling and information services are available, as is tutoring in most subjects, including art history, writing, humanities, and general academic subjects. There is remedial writing.

Campus Safety and Security: Measures include 24-hour foot and vehicle patrol, informal discussions, and pamphlets/posters/films.

Programs of Study: Corcoran confers the B.F.A. degree. Associate degrees are also awarded. Bachelor's degrees are awarded in COMMUNICATIONS AND THE ARTS (fine arts, graphic design, and photography). Fine arts is the largest.

Required: Students must complete 126 credits, with 65 to 70 of these in the major, and 23 in the core curriculum, and must maintain a minimum GPA of 2.0. Course distribution must involve the disciplines of art history, humanities, liberal arts, and writing. Curricula will include courses in drawing, design, idea resources, and media. Seniors must present thesis exhibitions.

Special: Cooperative programs are permitted with the ACE and AICA art college consortiums. Opportunities are provided for internships in graphic design and photography, credit by exam, work-study programs with the Corcoran Gallery of Art, and nondegree study.

Faculty/Classroom: 50% of faculty are male; 50%, female. All teach undergraduates. The average class size in an introductory lecture is 23; in a laboratory, 10; and in a regular course, 10.

Requirements: The SAT I or ACT is required. In addition, applicants must have graduated from an approved secondary school; a GED will be accepted. A portfolio is required, and an interview is recommended. A GPA of 2.5 is required. AP credits are accepted. Important factors in the admissions decision are evidence of special talent, personality/intangible qualities, and advanced placement or honor courses.

Procedure: Freshmen are admitted fall and spring. Entrance exams should be taken prior to January 30 of the senior year. There is a deferred admissions plan and a rolling admissions plan. Application deadlines are open. Application fee is $30.

Transfer: A review of studio art transcripts will be considered for the level of entry of transfer students. A portfolio review will be the final determining factor. 63 of 126 credits required for the bachelor's degree must be completed at Corcoran.

Visiting: There are regularly scheduled orientations for prospective students, consisting of personal visit with admissions staff. There are guides for informal visits and visitors may sit in on classes. To schedule a visit, contact the Admissions Department.

Financial Aid: Corcoran is a member of CSS. The CSS Profile and the college's own financial statement are required. Check with the school for current deadlines.

International Students: The school actively recruits these students. They must score 550 on the written TOEFL and also take the SAT I or the ACT.

Computers: In labs, the student lounge, and the library there are Macs, Power Macs, and PCs as well as workstations and servers. Internet access is available. All students may access the system. Students may access the system during lab hours in Computer Graphics. There are no fees.

Admissions Contact: Anne Bowman, Director of Admissions. E-mail: *admofc.corcoran.org* Web: *www.corcoran.edu*

GALLAUDET UNIVERSITY C-3
Washington, DC 20002-3695

(202) 651-5114 (TTY) or (202) 651-5750 (
(800) 995-0550 (TTY/V); Fax: (202) 651-5744

Full-time: 480 men, 570 women	Faculty: 300; IIA, +$
Part-time: 100 men, 100 women	Ph.D.s: 66%
Graduate: 90 men, 330 women	Student/Faculty: 4 to 1
Year: semesters, summer session	Tuition: $10,528
Application Deadline: open	Room & Board: $8030
Freshman Class: n/av	
SAT I or ACT: not required	SPECIAL

Gallaudet University, founded in 1864 as a university designed exclusively for deaf and hard-of-hearing students, offers programs in liberal and fine arts, teacher preparation, and professional training. Figures in the above capsule and in this profile are approximate. There are 4 undergraduate and 4 graduate schools. In addition to regional accreditation, Gallaudet has baccalaureate program accreditation with CSWE and NCATE. The library contains 215,500 volumes, 371,000 microform items, and 4530 audio/video tapes/CDs, and subscribes to 1415 periodicals. Computerized library services include the card catalog, interlibrary loans, and database searching. Special learning facilities include a learning resource center, TV station, child development center, national and international centers on deafness, and a research institute on deafness. The 99-acre campus is in an urban area in Washington, D.C. Including any residence halls, there are 30 buildings.

Student Life: 95% of undergraduates are from out of state, mostly the Northeast. Students are from 50 states and Canada. 74% are white; 14% foreign nationals.

Housing: Campus housing includes single-sex and coed dorms. On-campus housing is guaranteed for the freshman year only and is available on a first-come, first-served basis. 51% of students live on campus; of those, 51% remain on campus on weekends. Alcohol is not permitted. All students may keep cars.

Activities: 15% of men belong to 1 local and 3 national fraternities; 20% of women belong to 2 local and 3 national sororities. There are 32 groups on campus, including art, cheerleading, computers, dance, drama, ethnic, gay, honors, international, literary magazine, newspaper, political, religious, social, social service, student government, and yearbook. Popular campus events include rock festival, drama productions, and lecture series.

Sports: There are 9 intercollegiate sports for men and 8 for women, and 12 intramural sports for men and 12 for women. Facilities include a field house, a gym, a swimming pool, tennis and racquetball courts, weight training rooms, playing fields, and bowling alleys.

Disabled Students: Wheelchair ramps, elevators, special parking, specially equipped rest rooms, special class scheduling, lowered drinking fountains, lowered telephones, and phones with TTY. Sign language skills are required of all faculty and professional staff.

Services: Counseling and information services are available, as is tutoring in every subject, including throughout the tutorial, English, and writing centers. There is remedial math, reading, and writing. An information-on-deafness center is also available.

Campus Safety and Security: Measures include 24-hour foot and vehicle patrol, security escort services, shuttle buses, and informal discussions. There are pamphlets/posters/films and lighted pathways/sidewalks.

Programs of Study: Gallaudet confers B.A. and B.S. degrees. Associate, master's, and doctoral degrees are also awarded. Bachelor's degrees are awarded in BIOLOGICAL SCIENCE (biology/biological science), BUSINESS (accounting, business administration and management, entrepreneurial studies, management science, and recreation and leisure services), COMMUNICATIONS AND THE ARTS (apparel design, art history and appreciation, communications, dramatic arts, English, French, German, graphic design, media arts, Russian, Spanish, and studio art), COMPUTER AND PHYSICAL SCIENCE (chemical technology, chemistry, computer science, mathematics, and physics), EDUCATION (art, early childhood, elementary, home economics, physical, and secondary), ENGINEERING AND ENVIRONMENTAL DESIGN (engineering technology), HEALTH PROFESSIONS (recreation therapy), SOCIAL SCIENCE (child care/child and family studies, economics, family/consumer studies, history, interpreter for the deaf, parks and recreation management, philosophy, political science/government, psychology, religion, and social work).

Required: The core curriculum requires 12 hours each of social science and English, 9 of literature and humanities, 8 of lab science, 5 of communication arts, 4 of phys ed, and 3 of philosophy, plus demonstrated proficiency in a foreign language. A total of 124 credits, with 30 to 60 in the major, and a minimum 2.0 GPA are required for graduation.

Special: Gallaudet offers co-op programs with Oberlin College in Ohio and Western Maryland College, cross-registration with the Consortium of Universities of the Washington Metropolitan Area, and a 3-2 engineering degree with George Washington University. Internships, study abroad, dual majors, work-study programs, and B.A.-B.S. degrees are available. There is a chapter of Phi Beta Kappa and a freshman honors program.

Faculty/Classroom: No introductory courses are taught by graduate students.

Requirements: Applicants must submit a recent audiogram and results of the most recent edition of the Stanford Achievement Test. SAT I or ACT scores may be submitted. High school transcripts, letters of recommendation, and writing samples are also required. The GED is accepted. AP and CLEP credits are accepted. Important factors in the admissions decision are advanced placement or honor courses, recommendations by school officials, and leadership record.

Procedure: Freshmen are admitted fall and spring. Entrance exams should be taken in October or November of the senior year. There is a deferred admissions plan and a rolling admissions plan. Application deadlines are open. Application fee is $35.

Transfer: Deaf and hard-of-hearing transfer applicants must submit a recent audiogram, official college transcripts from all schools attended, and at least 2 letters of recommendation. Students should have completed 12 or more credit hours with at least a 2.0 GPA; those who do not meet these requirements must submit recent SAT I or ACT scores and a final high school transcript.

Visiting: There are regularly scheduled orientations for prospective students, including a tour of campus, classroom observations, and interviews with selected offices and programs. There are guides for informal visits and visitors may sit in on classes. To schedule a visit, contact the Gallaudet University Visitor's Center at (202) 651-5050.

Financial Aid: The FAFSA and the college's own financial statement are required. Check with the school for current deadlines.

International Students: They must take the TOEFL, or the MELAB, or the Comprehensive English Language Test, or the college's own test. They must also take the college's own entrance exam and the most recent edition of the Stanford Achievement Test; SAT I or ACT scores may be submitted.

Computers: The mainframes are a 2 DEC VAX 6250s and 2 DEC VAX 8650s. There are about 1100 PCs, including 145 in public user areas. All residence halls have VT terminals, with Benson Hall housing a computer lab. There is national network access via BITnet, NSFnet, and the Internet. All students may access the system 24 hours a day. There are no time limits and no fees.

Admissions Contact: Director of Admissions.
E-mail: *admission@gallua.gallaudet.edu*

GEORGE WASHINGTON UNIVERSITY   B-3
Washington, DC 20052
(202) 994-6040
(800) 447-3765; Fax: (202) 994-0325

Full-time: 3868 men, 5355 women	**Faculty:** I, +$
Part-time: 396 men, 334 women	**Ph.Ds:** 92%
Graduate: 4490 men, 5417 women	**Student/Faculty:** n/av
Year: semesters, summer session	**Tuition:** $30,820
Application Deadline: January 15	**Room & Board:** $10,210
Freshman Class: 18,442 applied, 7103 accepted, 2260 enrolled	
SAT I Verbal/Math: 640/640	**ACT:** 28 **MOST COMPETITIVE**

George Washington University, founded in 1821, is a private institution providing degree programs in arts and sciences, business, engineering, international affairs, health sciences, education, law, and public health. Tuition and fees for first-year students are $34,030. There are 6 undergraduate and 8 graduate schools. In addition to regional accreditation, GW has baccalaureate program accreditation with AACSB, ABET, CAHEA, CSAB, NASAD, NASM, and NCATE. The 3 libraries contain 2,104,962 volumes, 2,771,235 microform items, and 206,826 audio/video tapes/CDs, and subscribe to 1098 periodicals. Computerized library services include the card catalog, interlibrary loans, and database searching. Special learning facilities include a learning resource center, art gallery, radio station, and TV station. The 37-acre campus is in an urban area 3 blocks west of the White House. Including any residence halls, there are 123 buildings.

Student Life: 98% of undergraduates are from out of state, mostly the Middle Atlantic. Students are from 50 states, 137 foreign countries, and Canada. 70% are from public schools. 65% are white. The average age of freshmen is 19; all undergraduates, 20.

Housing: 4243 students can be accommodated in college housing, which includes single-sex and coed dorms, on-campus apartments, sorority floors, and fraternity houses. In addition, there are special-interest houses. On-campus housing is available on a lottery system for upperclassmen. 68% of students live on campus. All students may keep cars.

Activities: 16% of men belong to 11 national fraternities; 13% of women belong to 7 national sororities. There are 257 groups on campus, including art, band, cheerleading, chess, choir, chorale, chorus, computers, dance, debate, drama, ethnic, film, folk life, forensics, gay, geology, honors, international, jazz band, literary magazine, marching band, musical theater, newspaper, opera, orchestra, pep band, photography, political, professional, radio and TV, religious, social, social service, student government, symphony, and yearbook. Popular campus events include a yearly benefit auction, Spring Fling, and Fall Fest.

Sports: There are 9 intercollegiate sports for men and 8 for women, and 16 intramural sports for men and 16 for women. Facilities include a 5000-seat gym with 2 auxiliary gyms, an AAU swimming pool, weight rooms, a jogging track, squash and racquetball courts, and soccer and baseball fields.

Disabled Students: 95% of the campus is accessible. Wheelchair ramps, elevators, special parking, specially equipped rest rooms, special class scheduling, lowered drinking fountains, and lowered telephones are available.

Services: Counseling and information services are available, as is tutoring in every subject. There is a reader service for the blind.

Campus Safety and Security: Measures include 24-hour foot and vehicle patrol, self-defense education, security escort services, and informal

discussions. There are pamphlets/posters/films, emergency telephones, lighted pathways/sidewalks, and a bike patrol.

Programs of Study: GW confers B.A., B.S., B.Accy., B.B.A., B.Mus., B.S.C.E., B.S.C.Eng., B.S.C.S., B.S.E.E., B.S.H.S., B.S.M.E., and B.S.S.A. degrees. Associate, master's, and doctoral degrees are also awarded. Bachelor's degrees are awarded in BIOLOGICAL SCIENCE (biology/biological science), BUSINESS (accounting, banking and finance, business administration and management, business economics, human resources, international business management, marketing management, and tourism), COMMUNICATIONS AND THE ARTS (art history and appreciation, broadcasting, Chinese, classics, communications, dance, dramatic arts, English, fine arts, French, German, Japanese, journalism, literature, multimedia, music, music performance, public relations, Russian, and Spanish), COMPUTER AND PHYSICAL SCIENCE (applied mathematics, chemistry, computer science, geology, information sciences and systems, mathematics, physics, statistics, and systems analysis), ENGINEERING AND ENVIRONMENTAL DESIGN (civil engineering, computer engineering, electrical/electronics engineering, engineering, environmental science, and mechanical engineering), HEALTH PROFESSIONS (clinical science, emergency medical technologies, medical laboratory technology, nuclear medical technology, physician's assistant, premedicine, radiological science, and speech pathology/audiology), SOCIAL SCIENCE (American studies, anthropology, archeology, criminal justice, East Asian studies, economics, European studies, geography, history, human services, humanities, interdisciplinary studies, international relations, Judaic studies, Latin American studies, liberal arts/general studies, Middle Eastern studies, philosophy, physical fitness/movement, political science/government, psychology, religion, and sociology). Political communication, international affairs, and biological sciences are the strongest academically. Psychology, political science, and international affairs are the largest.

Required: Students must complete 120 semester hours with a minimum GPA of 2.0 for most majors. Arts and sciences majors must meet general curriculum requirements that include literacy, quantitative and logical reasoning, natural sciences, social and behavioral sciences, creative and performing arts, literature, Western civilization, and foreign languages or culture. Other specific course requirements vary with the different divisions of the university.

Special: Cross-registration is available through the Consortium of Colleges and Universities. There are co-op programs in education, business, engineering, arts and sciences, and international affairs, and internships throughout the Washington metropolitan area. Study abroad in locations throughout the world, work-study programs, dual majors, student-designed majors, and a 3-2 engineering degree program with 8 colleges are also available. Nondegree study, a general studies degree, credit by exam, and pass/fail options are possible. There are 12 national honor societies, including Phi Beta Kappa, a freshman honors program, and 21 departmental honors programs.

Faculty/Classroom: 68% of faculty are male; 32%, female. Graduate students teach 2% of introductory courses. The average class size in an introductory lecture is 32 and in a regular course, 22.

Admissions: 39% of the 2003-2004 applicants were accepted. The SAT I scores for the 2003-2004 freshman class were: Verbal--3% below 500, 25% between 500 and 599, 52% between 600 and 700, and 20% above 700; Math--2% below 500, 25% between 500 and 599, 55% between 600 and 700, and 18% above 700. The ACT scores were 2% below 21, 10% between 21 and 23, 24% between 24 and 26, 26% between 27 and 28, and 37% above 28. 86% of the current freshmen were in the top fifth of their class; 99% were in the top two fifths.

Requirements: The SAT I or ACT is required. In addition, students must have successfully completed a strong academic program in high school. SAT II: Subject tests are strongly recommended. An essay, 1 teacher recommendation, and 1 counselor recommendation are required. An interview is encouraged. AP and CLEP credits are accepted. Important factors in the admissions decision are advanced placement or honor courses, recommendations by school officials, and leadership record.

Procedure: Freshmen are admitted to all sessions. Entrance exams should be taken in the junior year and the fall semester of the senior year. There are early decision, early admissions, and deferred admissions plans. Early decision applications should be filed by December 1; regular applications, by January 15 for fall entry. Notification of early decision is sent December 15; regular decision, on a rolling basis beginning March 15. 875 early decision candidates were accepted for the 2003-2004 class. A waiting list is an active part of the admissions procedure. Applications are accepted on computer disk and on-line through Common App and CollegeLink.

Transfer: 385 transfer students enrolled in 2002-2003. In addition to a record of high marks and exam scores, applicants must submit official transcripts of all postsecondary work. Minimum GPA requirements vary from 2.5 to 3.0, depending on the major. The SAT I or ACT is required, and an interview is encouraged. 30 to 45 of 120 credits required for the bachelor's degree must be completed at GW.

Visiting: There are regularly scheduled orientations for prospective students, including group information sessions and campus tours. Class visi-

tation, lunch with current students, and other activities can be arranged, if requested in advance. There are guides for informal visits and visitors may sit in on classes and stay overnight. To schedule a visit, contact the University Visitor Center at (202) 994-6602.

Financial Aid: In 2002-2003, 39% of all full-time freshmen and 38% of continuing full-time students received some form of financial aid. At least 38% of full-time freshmen and 37% of continuing full-time students received need-based aid. The average freshman award was $26,888. Need-based scholarships or need-based grants averaged $15,651; need-based self-help aid (loans and jobs) averaged $6004; institutional non-need-based athletic scholarships averaged $19,977; and other institutional non-need-based awards and non-need-based scholarships averaged $13,836. The average financial indebtedness of the 2003 graduate was $25,943. GW is a member of CSS. The CSS Profile or FAFSA and the college's own financial statement are required. The priority date for freshman financial aid applications for fall entry is February 1.

International Students: The school actively recruits these students. They must score 550 on the written TOEFL and also take the college's own test, and the SAT I or the ACT.

Computers: The mainframes are an IBM 4381/R14, a Sun SPARC Station 2000, and 7 Citrix servers. All residence halls have computer rooms, and the campus computer center is open 24 hours a day. In addition, 7 computer classrooms are available as walk-in labs when classes are not scheduled. Modems are available on the campus network. There is a 24-hour computer lab in the library. All dorm rooms are networked fiber-optically. All students may access the system all the time. There are no time limits and no fees. It is strongly recommended that all students have a personal computer. An IBM, Mac, Dell, or Compaq is recommended.

Graduates: From July 1, 2002 to June 30, 2003, 2007 bachelor's degrees were awarded. The most popular majors were social sciences and history (33%), business/marketing (16%), and psychology (8%). In an average class, 69% graduate in 4 years or less, 74% graduate in 5 years or less, and 75% graduate in 6 years or less.

Admissions Contact: Dr. Kathryn M. Napper, Director of Admissions. E-mail: *gwadm@gwu.edu* Web: *www.gwu.edu*

GEORGETOWN UNIVERSITY
Washington, DC 20057

B-3
(202) 687-3600; Fax: (202) 687-5084

Full-time: 2940 men, 3386 women	Faculty: 655; I, +$
Part-time: 77 men, 147 women	Ph.D.s: 98%
Graduate: 3278 men, 3336 women	Student/Faculty: 10 to 1
Year: semesters, summer session	Tuition: $28,209
Application Deadline: January 10	Room & Board: $10,033
Freshman Class: 15,420 applied, 3505 accepted, 1528 enrolled	
SAT I or ACT: required	MOST COMPETITIVE

Georgetown University, founded in 1789, is a private institution affiliated with the Roman Catholic Church and offers programs in arts and sciences, business administration, foreign service, languages and linguistics, and nursing. There are 4 undergraduate and 3 graduate schools. In addition to regional accreditation, Georgetown has baccalaureate program accreditation with AACSB and NLN. The 6 libraries contain 2,293,259 volumes, 3,598,609 microform items, and 29,882 audio/video tapes/CDs, and subscribe to 26,521 periodicals. Computerized library services include the card catalog, interlibrary loans, database searching, and Internet access. Special learning facilities include a learning resource center, art gallery, planetarium, radio station, and TV station. The 110-acre campus is in an urban area 1.5 miles northwest of downtown Washington D.C. Including any residence halls, there are 64 buildings.

Student Life: 97% of undergraduates are from out of state, mostly the Middle Atlantic. Students are from 50 states, 92 foreign countries, and Canada. 47% are from public schools. 67% are white. 52% are Catholic; 24% Protestant; 12% claim no religious affiliation; 7% Hindu, Buddhist, Islamic, unspecified. The average age of freshmen is 18; all undergraduates, 20. 5% do not continue beyond their first year; 93% remain to graduate.

Housing: 5181 students can be accommodated in college housing, which includes coed dorms and on-campus apartments. Special-interest floors are available in some residence halls. On-campus housing is available on a lottery system for upperclassmen. 79% of students live on campus; of those, 95% remain on campus on weekends. No one may keep cars.

Activities: There are no fraternities or sororities. There are 129 groups on campus, including art, band, cheerleading, chess, choir, chorale, chorus, computers, dance, debate, drama, ethnic, gay, honors, international, jazz band, literary magazine, musical theater, newspaper, orchestra, pep band, photography, political, professional, radio and TV, religious, social, social service, student government, symphony, and yearbook. Popular campus events include GU Day and Career Week.

Sports: There are 12 intercollegiate sports for men and 13 coed, and 22 intramural sports for men and 22 coed. Facilities include a field house, a 150000-square-foot underground facility with a swimming pool, handball/racquetball/squash courts, a jogging track, weight training equipment, and multipurpose courts for basketball, volleyball, and tennis.

Disabled Students: 94% of the campus is accessible. Wheelchair ramps, elevators, special parking, specially equipped rest rooms, special class scheduling, lowered drinking fountains, lowered telephones, special housing, a special map of the campus with accessibility routes, a tactile map of the campus for visually disabled students, and a paratransit vehicle for mobility on the main campus are available.

Services: Counseling and information services are available, as is tutoring in every subject. There is a reader service for the blind.

Campus Safety and Security: Measures include 24-hour foot and vehicle patrol, security escort services, shuttle buses, and informal discussions. There are pamphlets/posters/films, emergency telephones, and lighted pathways/sidewalks.

Programs of Study: Georgetown confers B.A.B., B.S., B.A.L.S., B.L.S., B.S.B.A., B.S.F.S., B.S.L.A., B.S.L.I., and B.S.N. degrees. Master's and doctoral degrees are also awarded. Bachelor's degrees are awarded in BIOLOGICAL SCIENCE (biochemistry and biology/ biological science), BUSINESS (accounting, banking and finance, business administration and management, international business management, and marketing/retailing/merchandising), COMMUNICATIONS AND THE ARTS (Arabic, Chinese, classics, comparative literature, English, fine arts, French, German, Italian, Japanese, linguistics, Portuguese, Russian, and Spanish), COMPUTER AND PHYSICAL SCIENCE (chemistry, computer science, mathematics, and physics), HEALTH PROFESSIONS (health and nursing), SOCIAL SCIENCE (American studies, economics, history, interdisciplinary studies, international relations, philosophy, political science/government, psychology, religion, and sociology). English, international politics, and government are the strongest academically. International affairs, government, and English are the largest.

Required: Students must complete 120 credits and maintain a minimum GPA of 2.0. A core of liberal arts courses is required, consisting of 2 courses each in philosophy and theology. Computer science is required of students majoring in math and computer science.

Special: Cross-registration is available with a consortium of universities in the Washington metropolitian area. Opportunities are provided for internships, study abroad in 33 countries, work-study programs, student-designed majors, and dual majors. A general studies degree, B.A.-B.S. degrees, nondegree study, credit by examination, and pass/fail options are also offered. There are 15 national honor societies, including Phi Beta Kappa, a freshman honors program, and 16 departmental honors programs.

Faculty/Classroom: 60% of faculty are male; 40%, female. Graduate students teach 9% of introductory courses. The average class size in an introductory lecture is 33; in a laboratory, 13; and in a regular course, 27.

Admissions: 23% of the 2003-2004 applicants were accepted. 94% of the current freshmen were in the top fifth of their class; 99% were in the top two fifths. 147 freshmen graduated first in their class.

Requirements: The SAT I or ACT is required. In addition, graduation from an accredited secondary school is required, with 4 years of English, a minimum of 2 each of a foreign language, math, and social studies, and 1 of natural science. An additional 2 years each of math and science is required for students intending to major in math, science, nursing, or business. SAT II: Subject tests are strongly recommended. Applicants to the Walsh School of Foreign Service and the Faculty of Languages and Linguistics are required to submit results of an SAT II: Subject test in a modern foreign language. AP credits are accepted. Important factors in the admissions decision are evidence of special talent and leadership record.

Procedure: Freshmen are admitted in the fall. Entrance exams should be taken in the junior year and again at the beginning of the senior year. There are early admissions and deferred admissions plans. Early decision applications should be filed by November 1; regular applications, by January 10 for fall entry, along with a $60 fee. Notification of early decision is sent December 15; regular decision, April 1. 1216 applicants were on the 2003 waiting list; 138 were admitted. Applications are accepted on computer disk and on-line through MacApply, but must also be submitted in paper form.

Transfer: 261 transfer students enrolled in 2002-2003. Transfer students must have successfully completed a minimum of 12 credit hours with a minimum GPA of 3.0. Either the SAT I or the ACT is required. An interview is recommended. Transfers must complete their last 2 years at Georgetown. 60 of 120 credits required for the bachelor's degree must be completed at Georgetown.

Visiting: There are regularly scheduled orientations for prospective students throughout the year, including a question and answer period led by an admissions officer, followed by a campus tour led by a student guide. There are guides for informal visits and visitors may sit in on classes. To schedule a visit, contact the Office of Undergraduate Admissions at Student Financial Services: (202) 687-4547.

Financial Aid: Average annual earnings from campus work are $3000. Georgetown is a member of CSS. The CSS/Profile or FAFSA is required. The deadline for filing freshmen financial aid applications for fall entry is February 1.

International Students: There are 483 international students enrolled. The school actively recruits these students. They must score 550 on the written TOEFL or 213 on the electronic version and also take the SAT I or the ACT. Students must take SAT II: Subject tests in writing and 2 others of the student's choice.

Computers: The mainframe is an IBM Multiprise 2003/224. In addition, there are about 360 terminals and PCs in the library, computer labs, and the School of Business. All students may access the system. There are no time limits and no fees.

Graduates: From July 1, 2002 to June 30, 2003, 1636 bachelor's degrees were awarded. The most popular majors were international affairs (21%), government (10%), and English (10%). In an average class, 1% graduate in 3 years or less, 90% graduate in 4 years or less, 93% graduate in 5 years or less, and 93% graduate in 6 years or less. 985 companies recruited on campus in 2002-2003. Of the 2002 graduating class, 26% were enrolled in graduate school within 6 months of graduation and 51% were employed.

Admissions Contact: Charles A. Deacon, Dean of Admissions. Web: *www.georgetown.edu/undergrad/admissions/*

HOWARD UNIVERSITY
Washington, DC 20059

C-3

(202) 806-2700
(800) 822-6363; Fax: (202) 806-2740

Full-time: 2176 men, 4472 women	**Faculty:** 669; I, --$
Part-time: 126 men, 285 women	**Ph.Ds:** 78%
Graduate: 1330 men, 2269 women	**Student/Faculty:** 10 to 1
Year: semesters, summer session	**Tuition:** $10,935
Application Deadline: February 2	**Room & Board:** $5570
Freshman Class: 7057 applied, 3982 accepted, 1460 enrolled	
SAT I or ACT: required	**COMPETITIVE**

Howard University, founded in 1867, is a private, nonsectarian institution and the largest predominantly black university in the United States. There are 6 undergraduate and 11 graduate schools. In addition to regional accreditation, Howard has baccalaureate program accreditation with AACSB, ABA, ABET, ACEJMC, ACPE, ADA, AHEA, AOTA, APTA, ASLA, ATS, CAHEA, CSAB, CSWE, NAAB, NAACLS, NASAD, NASDTEC, NASM, NCATE, and NLN. The 8 libraries contain 2,200,000 volumes and 3,400,000 microform items, and subscribe to 26,280 periodicals. Computerized library services include the card catalog, interlibrary loans, database searching, and Internet access. Special learning facilities include a learning resource center, art gallery, radio station, TV station, and history and culture research centers. The 256-acre campus is in an urban area in Washington, D.C. and Silver Spring and Beltsville, MD. Including any residence halls, there are 116 buildings.

Student Life: 86% of undergraduates are from out of state, mostly the Middle Atlantic. Students are from 50 states, 61 foreign countries, and Canada. 78% are from public schools. 86% are African American. The average age of freshmen is 18; all undergraduates, 21. 11% do not continue beyond their first year; 63% remain to graduate.

Housing: 4748 students can be accommodated in college housing, which includes coed dorms, on-campus apartments, off-campus apartments, and married-student housing. On-campus housing is guaranteed for the freshman year only, is available on a first-come, first-served basis, and is available on a lottery system for upperclassmen. Priority is given to out-of-town students. 55% of students commute. All students may keep cars.

Activities: There are 4 national fraternities; 1% of women belong to 4 national sororities. There are 150 groups on campus, including art, bagpipe band, band, cheerleading, chess, choir, chorale, chorus, computers, dance, debate, drama, drill team, drum and bugle corps, film, gay, honors, international, jazz band, literary magazine, marching band, musical theater, newspaper, orchestra, pep band, political, professional, radio and TV, religious, social, social service, student government, and yearbook. Popular campus events include Spring Festival, Opening Convocation, and Charter Day.

Sports: There are 15 intercollegiate sports for men and 15 for women, and 5 intramural sports for men and 5 for women. Facilities include a sports center, a gym, and practice fields.

Disabled Students: All of the campus is accessible. Wheelchair ramps, elevators, special parking, specially equipped rest rooms, special class scheduling, lowered drinking fountains, and lowered telephones are available.

Services: Counseling and information services are available, as is tutoring in most subjects. There is a reader service for the blind and remedial math, reading, and writing.

Campus Safety and Security: Measures include 24-hour foot and vehicle patrol, security escort services, shuttle buses, and informal discussions. There are pamphlets/posters/films, emergency telephones, and lighted pathways/sidewalks.

Programs of Study: Howard confers B.A., B.S., B.Arch., B.B.A., B.F.A., B.M., B.M.E., B.S.C.E., B.S.C.L.S., B.S.Ch.E., B.S. Comp.Eng., B.S. Comp. Sci., B.S.E.E., B.S.M.E., B.S.N., B.S.N.S., B.S.O.T., B.S.P.T., B.S. in P.A., and B.S. in R.T.T. degrees. Master's and doctoral degrees are also awarded. Bachelor's degrees are awarded in BIOLOGICAL SCIENCE (biology/biological science, microbiology, and zoology), BUSINESS (accounting, banking and finance, business administration and management, hospitality management services, insurance, international business management, and marketing/retailing/merchandising), COMMUNICATIONS AND THE ARTS (art history and appreciation, classics, communications, dance, design, dramatic arts, English, French, German, Greek, jazz, journalism, music, music business management, music history and appreciation, musical theater, photography, printmaking, Russian, and Spanish), COMPUTER AND PHYSICAL SCIENCE (chemistry, computer science, information sciences and systems, mathematics, and physics), EDUCATION (art, early childhood, elementary, health, music, physical, recreation, and secondary), ENGINEERING AND ENVIRONMENTAL DESIGN (architecture, chemical engineering, civil engineering, electrical/electronics engineering, and mechanical engineering), HEALTH PROFESSIONS (medical laboratory technology, music therapy, nursing, occupational therapy, pharmacy, physical therapy, physician's assistant, predentistry, premedicine, radiograph medical technology, and speech pathology/audiology), SOCIAL SCIENCE (African American studies, African studies, anthropology, criminal justice, dietetics, economics, history, philosophy, political science/government, psychology, and sociology). Psychology, business, and engineering are the strongest academically. Accounting, finance, and electrical engineering are the largest.

Required: To graduate, students must complete 121 to 171 credit hours, including 21 to 78 in a major and 12 to 39 in a minor, with a minimum GPA of 2.0. General requirements include 4 courses in phys ed, 2 in freshman English, 1 in writing, and in Afro-American studies; 1 year of college-level math; demonstrated proficiency in a foreign language; and successful completion of a comprehensive exam in the major.

Special: Cross-registration is available with the Consortium of Universities in the Washington Metropolitan Area. Opportunities are also provided for internships, work-study, and co-op programs, study abroad in 5 countries in Europe and Africa, B.A.-B.S. degrees in engineering and business, student-designed majors, pass/fail options, and accelerated degree programs in medicine and dentistry. There are 15 national honor societies, including Phi Beta Kappa, a freshman honors program, and 15 departmental honors programs.

Faculty/Classroom: 68% of faculty are male; 32%, female. The average class size in an introductory lecture is 40; in a laboratory, 20; and in a regular course, 20.

Admissions: 56% of the 2003-2004 applicants were accepted. 55% of the current freshmen were in the top fifth of their class; 70% were in the top two fifths. 15 freshmen graduated first in their class.

Requirements: The SAT I or ACT is required, with a minimum composite score of 800 on the SAT I (400 verbal, 400 math) or 21 on the ACT. Graduation from an accredited secondary school is required. The GED is accepted. Students must have a minimum of 16 academic credits, including 4 in English, 2 each in foreign language, math, science, and either history or social studies, and 4 in electives. Students must submit letters of recommendation from 2 high school teachers and 1 high school counselor. Other requirements vary by college. Engineering majors must take the SAT II: Subject test in math I. Art majors must submit a portfolio, and music and theater majors must audition. A GPA of 2.0 is required. AP credits are accepted. Important factors in the admissions decision are recommendations by school officials and advanced placement or honor courses.

Procedure: Freshmen are admitted fall, spring, and summer. Entrance exams should be taken in the fall of the senior year. There are early admissions and deferred admissions plans. Applications should be filed by February 2 for fall entry, November 1 for spring entry, and April 1 for summer entry, along with a $45 fee. Notification is sent on a rolling basis.

Transfer: 331 transfer students enrolled in 2002-2003. All applicants must submit 2 official transcripts from each college or university attended. Students transferring to the School of Business must have successfully completed 18 semester hours or 23 quarter hours of courses, with a minimum GPA of 2.5. For many other majors, the requirement is 12 semester hours or 18 quarter hours, with a minimum GPA of 2.0. Applicants to the College of Arts and Sciences need 3 credits each in English composition and college-level algebra. 30 of 121 credits required for the bachelor's degree must be completed at Howard.

Visiting: There are regularly scheduled orientations for prospective students, including an admissions interview, classroom and dorm visits, and conversations with faculty and students. There are guides for informal visits and visitors may sit in on classes and stay overnight. To schedule a visit, contact the Office of Enrollment Management/Recruitment at (202) 806-2900 or *www.howard.edu/enrollmentmanagement*.

Financial Aid: In 2003-2004, 72% of all full-time freshmen and 54% of continuing full-time students received some form of financial aid. 80% of full-time freshmen and 82% of continuing full-time students received need-based aid. The average freshman award was $16,879. Need-based scholarships or need-based grants averaged $3417; need-based self-help aid (loans and jobs) averaged $3079; non-need-based awards and non-

need-based scholarships averaged $3466; and other awards averaged $12,501. 9% of undergraduates work part time. Average annual earnings from campus work are $3700. The average financial indebtedness of the 2003 graduate was $17,548. Howard is a member of CSS. The FAFSA is required. The priority date for freshman financial aid applications for fall entry is February 2.

International Students: There are 668 international students enrolled. They must score 500 on the written TOEFL and also take the SAT I or the ACT. Students must also take SAT II: Subject tests in Writing.

Computers: The mainframe is an IBM9672 RA 4. There are 1823 workstations for students and 3850 network CPUs. There are 28 smart classrooms in various academic buildings, and each student has wired network services, cable TV, and telephone service in their dorm. All students may access the system. Facilities are open 24 hours a day. There are no time limits and no fees. It is strongly recommended that all students have a personal computer.

Graduates: From July 1, 2002 to June 30, 2003, 1187 bachelor's degrees were awarded. The most popular majors were biology (8%), psychology (7%), and marketing (6%). In an average class, 58% graduate in 4 years or less, 91% graduate in 5 years or less, and 99% graduate in 6 years or less. More than 300 companies recruited on campus in 2002-2003. Of the 2002 graduating class, 35% were enrolled in graduate school within 6 months of graduation and 40% were employed.

Admissions Contact: Ann-Marie Waterman, Acting Director, Office of Enrollment Management/Admissions. A video is available.
E-mail: *admission@howard.edu* Web: *www.howard.edu*

SOUTHEASTERN UNIVERSITY   D-4
Washington, DC 20024   (202) 265-5343; Fax: (202) 488-8093

Full-time: 50 men, 75 women	**Faculty:** 13
Part-time: 110 men, 280 women	**Ph.D.s:** 62%
Graduate: 185 men, 285 women	**Student/Faculty:** 11 to 1
Year: quarters, summer session	**Tuition:** $8505
Application Deadline: open	**Room & Board:** n/app
Freshman Class: n/av	
SAT I or ACT: recommended	**LESS COMPETITIVE**

Southeastern University, founded as Washington School for Accountancy in 1879, is a private, commuter college offering programs in business administration, accounting, computer information systems, finance, banking, and marketing to a student body comprised primarily of working adults. There is 1 undergraduate school. Figures in the above capsule and in this profile are approximate. The library contains 40,000 volumes, and subscribes to 1200 periodicals. Computerized library services include the card catalog and database searching. Special learning facilities include a learning resource center. The 3-acre campus is in an urban area in a residential part southwest of Washington, D.C. There is one building.

Student Life: 56% of undergraduates are from District of Columbia. Students are from 4 states, 40 foreign countries, and Canada. 58% are African American; 35% foreign nationals. The average age of freshmen is 29; all undergraduates, 30.

Housing: There are no residence halls. Referral listings of long- and short-term housing are available. Alcohol is not permitted. No one may keep cars.

Activities: There is 1 local fraternity. There are some groups and organizations on campus, including chess, computers, newspaper, and student government. Popular campus events include Annual Awards Ceremony, a chess tournament, and International Week.

Sports: There is no sports program at Southeastern.

Disabled Students: All of the campus is accessible. Wheelchair ramps, special parking, specially equipped rest rooms, special class scheduling, and lowered telephones are available.

Services: Counseling and information services are available, as is tutoring in most subjects. There is remedial math, reading, and writing. There are also individualized learning programs for students in upper-level courses.

Campus Safety and Security: Measures include 24-hour foot and vehicle patrol, security escort services, shuttle buses, and lighted pathways/sidewalks.

Programs of Study: Southeastern confers the B.S. degree. Associate and master's degrees are also awarded. Bachelor's degrees are awarded in BUSINESS (accounting, banking and finance, business administration and management, and marketing/retailing/merchandising), COMPUTER AND PHYSICAL SCIENCE (information sciences and systems), SOCIAL SCIENCE (law, liberal arts/general studies, and public administration). Business and computer science are the strongest academically. Business and computer science/information systems are the largest.

Required: To graduate, students must complete 120 credit hours, maintaining a 2.0 GPA, including the general studies core curriculum, which consists of 30 hours in the fields of English, information systems, math, humanities, and social science. Also required are 24 hours in the general studies electives, 27 hours of major requirements, 27 hours in the professional core, 6 hours of professional electives, and 6 hours of general electives. All students must take an orientation course and a computer course.

Special: Southeastern offers extensive co-op programs, internships, work-study, accelerated degree programs, B.A.-B.S.degrees, dual majors, and credit by exam and for life/military/work experience. The Add-a-Degree program allows any student with a bachelor's degree to add a second area of expertise, add professional qualifications, or prepare for graduate study by completing necessary foundation courses. There is 1 national honor society.

Faculty/Classroom: 81% of faculty are male; 19%, female. All teach undergraduates. No introductory courses are taught by graduate students. The average class size in a regular course is 11.

Requirements: The SAT I or ACT is recommended. In addition, students must be graduates of an accredited secondary school or have a GED and must pass Southeastern's placement test for regular admission. CLEP credit is accepted.

Procedure: Freshmen are admitted to all sessions. There is a rolling admissions plan. Application deadlines are open. Application fee is $45.

Transfer: 23 transfer students enrolled in a recent year. All transfer applicants must submit transcripts. Up to 60 credits, with a grade of C or better, may be transferred. 60 of 120 credits required for the bachelor's degree must be completed at Southeastern.

Visiting: To schedule a visit, contact Jack Flinter at (202) 488-8162.

Financial Aid: In a recent year, 54% of all full-time freshmen and 63% of continuing full-time students received some form of financial aid. 43% of full-time freshmen and 54% of continuing full-time students received need-based aid. 3% of undergraduates work part time. Average annual earnings from campus work are $2900. The average financial indebtedness of a recent graduate was $17,125. The FAFSA and the college's own financial statement are required. Check with the school for current deadlines.

International Students: In a recent year, there were 70 international students enrolled. They must score 500 on the written TOEFL. Applicants scoring below 550 are required to take 2 English courses. Those scoring below 500 are required to enroll in the university's Language Institute.

Computers: Southeastern's computer center has an IBM mainframe. The PC network is fully available to students. Those students required to use computing in their major may access the system. There are no time limits and no fees.

Graduates: In a recent year, 69 bachelor's degrees were awarded. The most popular majors were liberal studies (28%), information systems management (23%), and management (17%). In an average class, 20% graduate in 4 years or less, 40% graduate in 5 years or less, and 40% graduate in 6 years or less. 24 companies recruited on campus in a recent year.

Admissions Contact: Jack Flinter, Director of Admissions. E-mail: jflinter@admin.seu.edu

STRAYER UNIVERSITY
C-3
Washington, DC 20005
(202) 408-2400
(888) 4-STRAYER; Fax: (202) 289-1831

Full-time: 1240 men, 1270 women	**Faculty:** 117
Part-time: 3820 men, 5455 women	**Ph.D.s:** 51%
Graduate: 1060 men, 1165 women	**Student/Faculty:** 22 to 1
Year: quarters, summer session	**Tuition:** $8790
Application Deadline: open	**Room & Board:** n/app
Freshman Class: n/av	
SAT I or ACT: recommended	**SPECIAL**

Strayer University, founded in 1892, is an independent commuter institution with 17 campuses in Washington, D.C., Maryland, and Virginia, as well as a distance learning program via the Internet. All programs are computer or business related. Figures in this capsule and in this profile are approximate. The library contains 35,000 volumes and 2813 audio/video tapes/CDs, and subscribes to 550 periodicals. Computerized library services include the card catalog, interlibrary loans, and database searching. Special learning facilities include a learning resource center. The campus is in an urban area. 2 of the campuses are located in Washington D.C. and 6 campuses are in suburban Virginia.There are 13 buildings.

Student Life: 97% of undergraduates are from District of Columbia. Students are from 26 states, 124 foreign countries, and Canada. 42% are African American; 32% white. The average age of all undergraduates is 33.

Housing: There are no residence halls. All students commute. Alcohol is not permitted. All students may keep cars.

Activities: There are no fraternities or sororities. There are 13 groups on campus, including computers, debate, ethnic, honors, international, newspaper, professional, and religious.

Sports: The sports program is an athletic club, which uses intercollegiate athletic participation to promote education and student development.

Disabled Students: All of the campus is accessible. Wheelchair ramps, elevators, special parking, specially equipped rest rooms, lowered drinking fountains, and lowered telephones are available.

Services: Counseling and information services are available, as is tutoring in some subjects, including accounting, computer information systems, English, and math at the introductory course level. There is remedial reading and writing.

Campus Safety and Security: Measures include security escort services, informal discussions, pamphlets/posters/films, and lighted pathways/sidewalks. There are security guards at all the urban campuses and during evening hours at other campuses, crime seminars held regularly for students and employees, and a campus crime awareness booklet is published annually or available via the school's web site.

Programs of Study: Strayer confers the B.S. degree. Associate and master's degrees are also awarded. Bachelor's degrees are awarded in BUSINESS (accounting, business administration and management, and international business management), COMPUTER AND PHYSICAL SCIENCE (information sciences and systems and web technology), SOCIAL SCIENCE (economics). Computer information systems, business administration, and accounting are the strongest academically. Computer information systems and business administration are the largest.

Required: To graduate, students must complete 180 quarter hours, including 54 in the major, with a minimum GPA of 2.0. There is a core general studies component to each undergraduate degree, as well as a general business component.

Special: Strayer offers co-op programs in all majors, dual majors, internships with area businesses, accelerated diploma programs in computer information systems and accounting, and credit for military and work experience. There are 2 national honor societies.

Faculty/Classroom: 71% of faculty are male; 29%, female. All teach undergraduates. No introductory courses are taught by graduate students.

Requirements: The SAT I or ACT is recommended. Applicants must either submit SAT I scores of at least 400 verbal and/or 400 math or take Stayer's placement tests. Students must have earned a high school diploma or a GED. AP and CLEP credits are accepted.

Procedure: Freshmen are admitted to all sessions. Entrance exams should be taken by the beginning of the first quarter of attendance. There is a deferred admissions plan and a rolling admissions plan. Application deadlines are open. The application fee is $35. Applications are accepted on-line via the school's web site.

Transfer: Requirements are the same as for freshmen. 54 of 180 credits required for the bachelor's degree must be completed at Strayer.

Visiting: There are regularly scheduled orientations for prospective students. Scheduled orientations for prospective students rotate among the campuses. There are guides for informal visits. To schedule a visit, contact the Campus Manager at info45@strayer.edu.

Financial Aid: The FAFSA is required. Check with the school for current deadlines.

International Students: In a recent year, there were 585 international students enrolled. The school actively recruits these students. They must score 500 on the written TOEFL or 173 on the electronic version.

Computers: The mainframe is a Sun SPARC 1000. There are 750 PCs available for student use, some located in the library and 8 learning resource centers. Students have access to the Internet and other on-line services through these terminals. Additionally, each campus has at least 1 PC lab and 1 networking UNIX lab. All students may access the system. There are no time limits and no fees.

Graduates: In a recent year, 1379 bachelor's degrees were awarded. The most popular majors were computer information systems (36%), business administration (26%), and computer networking (25%). 200 companies recruited on campus in a recent year. Of the 2002 graduating class, 14% were enrolled in graduate school within 6 months of graduation and 86% were employed.

Admissions Contact: Melvin Menns, Washington Campus Manager. E-mail: info45@strayer.edu Web: www.strayer.edu

TRINITY COLLEGE
C-2
Washington, DC 20017
(202) 884-9400
(800) 492-6882; Fax: (202) 884-9403

Full-time: 6 men, 555 women	**Faculty:** 48; IIB, -$
Part-time: 16 men, 434 women	**Ph.D.s:** 98%
Graduate: 93 men, 533 women	**Student/Faculty:** 12 to 1
Year: semesters	**Tuition:** $16,860
Application Deadline: open	**Room & Board:** $7290
Freshman Class: 423 applied, 331 accepted, 160 enrolled	
SAT I Verbal/Math: 430/410	**ACT:** 16 **LESS COMPETITIVE**

Trinity College, founded in 1897, is a private, women's liberal arts college affiliated with the Roman Catholic Church. The school year consists of traditional semesters plus 1-week courses during January and May. There are 2 undergraduate and 2 graduate schools. In addition to regional accreditation, Trinity has baccalaureate program accreditation with NASDTEC. The library contains 215,338 volumes, 6826 microform items, and 13,797 audio/video tapes/CDs, and subscribes to 509 periodicals. Computerized library services include the card catalog, interlibrary loans, and database searching. Special learning facilities include a learning resource center, art gallery, and computer center, writing center, and career and counseling center. The 26-acre campus is in an urban area 2 1/2 miles north of the U.S. Capitol. Including any residence halls, there are 7 buildings.

Student Life: 50% of undergraduates are from out of state, mostly the Middle Atlantic. Students are from 24 states and 22 foreign countries. 60% are from public schools. 67% are African American. 61% are Protestant; 23% Catholic; 13% claim no religious affiliation. The average age of freshmen is 18; all undergraduates, 22. 30% do not continue beyond their first year; 50% remain to graduate.

Housing: 250 students can be accommodated in college housing, which includes single-sex dorms. On-campus housing is guaranteed for all 4 years. 78% of students commute. All students may keep cars.

Activities: There are no fraternities. There are 23 groups on campus, including choir, chorale, computers, dance, drama, ethnic, Future Female Attorneys of America, gay, honors, international, literary magazine, newspaper, photography, political, professional, psychology, religious, social, social service, student government, and yearbook. Popular campus events include Founders Day, Class Days, and Junior Ring Day.

Sports: Facilities include 2 athletic fields for soccer and field hockey, a fitness center, 6 tennis courts, an outdoor sand volleyball court, and a state-of-the-art sports center with pool, weight room, and basketball court.

Disabled Students: 80% of the campus is accessible. Wheelchair ramps, elevators, special parking, specially equipped rest rooms, and lowered telephones are available.

Services: Counseling and information services are available, as is tutoring in every subject. There is a reader service for the blind and signing for hearing-impaired students.

Campus Safety and Security: Measures include 24-hour foot and vehicle patrol, self-defense education, security escort services, and shuttle buses. There are informal discussions, pamphlets/posters/films, emergency telephones, and lighted pathways/sidewalks.

Programs of Study: Trinity confers B.A. and B.S. degrees. Master's degrees are also awarded. Bachelor's degrees are awarded in BIOLOGICAL SCIENCE (biochemistry and biology/biological science), BUSINESS (business administration and management and business economics), COMMUNICATIONS AND THE ARTS (communications, English, languages, and Spanish), COMPUTER AND PHYSICAL SCIENCE (chemistry, computer science, mathematics, and physical sciences), EDUCATION (elementary), ENGINEERING AND ENVIRONMENTAL DESIGN (engineering and environmental science), HEALTH PROFESSIONS (premedicine), SOCIAL SCIENCE (criminal justice, economics, history, human services, international studies, political science/government, prelaw, psychology, and sociology). English, history, and political science are the strongest academically. Psychology, business administration, and communication are the largest.

Required: To graduate, students must complete a total of 128 credit hours with a minimum GPA of 2.0. Between 42 and 50 hours are required in the major. All students must take the courses required in the Foundation for Leadership curriculum and must complete a senior seminar.

Special: Cross-registration is offered through the Consortium of Universities of the Washington Area. Trinity offers internships in all majors and minors, as well as work-study programs. Students may study in France, Italy, and various other countries by arrangement with their faculty adviser. B.A.-B.S. degrees, a 5-year accelerated degree in teaching, a 3-2 engineering degree with George Washington University, dual and student-designed majors, a general studies degree, credit for life experience, nondegree study, and pass/fail options are also available. There are 2 national honor societies, including Phi Beta Kappa, and a freshman honors program.

Faculty/Classroom: 35% of faculty are male; 65%, female. 72% teach undergraduates. No introductory courses are taught by graduate students. The average class size in an introductory lecture is 16; in a laboratory, 16; and in a regular course, 13.

Admissions: 78% of the 2003-2004 applicants were accepted. The SAT I scores for the 2003-2004 freshman class were: Verbal--78% below 500, 17% between 500 and 599, and 5% between 600 and 700; Math--81% below 500, 18% between 500 and 599, and 1% between 600 and 700. The ACT scores were 83% below 21, and 17% between 21 and 23.

Requirements: The SAT I or ACT is recommended. In addition, graduation from an accredited secondary school or satisfactory scores on the GED are required for admission. A total of 16 academic credits is required, including 4 years of English and 3 to 4 years each of a foreign language, history, math, and science. AP examinations and SAT II: Subject tests are recommended. An interview and an essay or graded writing sample are required. A GPA of 2.0 is required. AP and CLEP credits are accepted. Important factors in the admissions decision are leadership record, extracurricular activities record, and recommendations by school officials.

Procedure: Freshmen are admitted fall, spring, and summer. Entrance exams should be taken in the junior year. There are early admissions and deferred admissions plans. Application deadlines are open. Application fee is $35. Applications are accepted on computer disk. Notification is usually within 2 weeks of receipt of the completed application and on a rolling basis thereafter.

Transfer: 28 transfer students enrolled in 2002-2003. Transfer applicants must have a GPA of 2.5. An interview is recommended; an essay is required. 45 of 128 credits required for the bachelor's degree must be completed at Trinity.

Visiting: There are regularly scheduled orientations for prospective students, consisting of a full-day program, including an overview of the college, the curriculum, financing, and student life. There are guides for informal visits and visitors may sit in on classes and stay overnight. To schedule a visit, contact the Office of Admissions at *admissions@trinitydc.edu*.

Financial Aid: In 2003-2004, 84% of all full-time freshmen and 87% of continuing full-time students received some form of financial aid. 83% of full-time freshmen and 82% of continuing full-time students received need-based aid. The average freshman award was $14,537. Need-based scholarships or need-based grants averaged $6771; need-based self-help aid (loans and jobs) averaged $5828; and non-need-based awards and non-need-based scholarships averaged $10,558. 8% of undergraduates work part time. Average annual earnings from campus work are $1000. The average financial indebtedness of the 2003 graduate was $24,093. Trinity is a member of CSS. The FAFSA is required. The priority date for freshman financial aid applications for fall entry is March 1.

International Students: There are 38 international students enrolled. The school actively recruits these students. They must score 550 on the written TOEFL. The SAT I or ACT is recommended.

Computers: Students may use the 28 PCs and 13 Macs located in the 3 computer labs. All have printer access. There are an additional 67 PCs in 3 classrooms, 2 PCs in the CyberCafe, and 2 PCs in Enrollment Services for on-line record access. All students may access the system. There are no time limits and no fees. It is strongly recommended that all students have a personal computer.

Graduates: The most popular majors were psychology (29%), business administration (25%), and communication (14%).

Admissions Contact: Lori Janowski, Director of Admissions. E-mail: *admissions@trinitydc.edu* Web: *www.trinitydc.edu*

UNIVERSITY OF THE DISTRICT OF COLUMBIA C-2
Washington, DC 20008 (202) 274-6069; Fax: (202) 274-6341

Full-time: 787 men, 1113 women	**Faculty:** 343
Part-time: 1061 men, 2045 women	**Ph.D.s:** 52%
Graduate: 83 men, 152 women	**Student/Faculty:** 6 to 1
Year: semesters, summer session	**Tuition:** $2070 ($4626)
Application Deadline: open	**Room & Board:** n/app
Freshman Class: 2074 applied, 1684 accepted, 562 enrolled	
SAT I: n/av	**ACT:** required
	LESS COMPETITIVE

The University of the District of Columbia, founded in 1977, is a publicly funded, land-grant commuter institution offering programs in liberal arts, business, education, and technical fields. Some figures given in above capsule and in this profile are approximate. There are 5 undergraduate schools and 1 graduate school. In addition to regional accreditation, UDC has baccalaureate program accreditation with ABET, CAHEA, CSWE, NASDTEC, NASM, and NLN. The 4 libraries contain 470,330 volumes, 623,991 microform items, and 21,207 audio/video tapes/CDs, and subscribe to 2787 periodicals. Computerized library services include database searching. Special learning facilities include a learning resource center, art gallery, radio station, TV station, and early childhood learning center. The 22-acre campus is in a suburban area in northwest Washington, D.C. There are 26 buildings.

Student Life: 87% of undergraduates are from District of Columbia. Students are from 49 states and 55 foreign countries. 85% are from public schools. 72% are African American. The average age of freshmen is 18; all undergraduates, 27. 35% do not continue beyond their first year; 65% remain to graduate.

Housing: There are no residence halls. All students commute. Alcohol is not permitted.

Activities: 2% of men belong to 7 national fraternities; 2% of women belong to 5 national sororities. There are 139 groups on campus, including art, band, cheerleading, chess, choir, chorale, computers, dance, drama, drum and bugle corps, ethnic, film, honors, international, jazz band, marching band, newspaper, orchestra, pep band, photography, political, professional, radio and TV, religious, social, social service, student government, and yearbook. Popular campus events include the Cross-Cultural Extended Family Program and International Multicultural Recognition Day.

Sports: There are 6 intercollegiate sports for men and 6 for women, and 8 intramural sports for men and 6 for women. Facilities include a

3000-seat gym, a swimming pool, a weight room, and racquetball and tennis courts.

Disabled Students: All of the campus is accessible. Wheelchair ramps, elevators, special parking, specially equipped rest rooms, lowered drinking fountains, and lowered telephones are available.

Services: Counseling and information services are available, as is tutoring in every subject. There is a reader service for the blind and remedial math and reading.

Campus Safety and Security: Measures include 24-hour foot and vehicle patrol, emergency telephones, and lighted pathways/sidewalks.

Programs of Study: UDC confers B.A. and B.S. degrees. Associate and master's degrees are also awarded. Bachelor's degrees are awarded in BIOLOGICAL SCIENCE (biology/biological science), BUSINESS (accounting, banking and finance, business administration and management, marketing/retailing/merchandising, and office supervision and management), COMMUNICATIONS AND THE ARTS (dramatic arts, English, fine arts, French, media arts, music, and Spanish), COMPUTER AND PHYSICAL SCIENCE (chemistry, computer science, mathematics, and physics), EDUCATION (early childhood, elementary, health, and physical), ENGINEERING AND ENVIRONMENTAL DESIGN (architecture, aviation administration/management, civil engineering, construction engineering, electrical/electronics engineering, electromechanical technology, environmental science, and mechanical engineering), HEALTH PROFESSIONS (nursing and speech pathology/audiology), SOCIAL SCIENCE (criminal justice, economics, fire science, food science, geography, history, philosophy, political science/government, psychology, public administration, social work, sociology, and urban studies). Business is the strongest academically. Fine arts is the largest.

Required: To graduate, students must complete 120 to 130 semester hours with a minimum GPA of 2.0. All students must take 6 hours each of English composition, literature and advanced writing, foreign language, social science, math, and natural sciences, 4 of personal and community health, and 3 each of philosophy and fine arts.

Special: Cross-registration may be arranged through the Consortium of Universities of the Washington Metropolitan Area. Co-op programs with the federal government, internships, study abroad in 4 countries, work-study programs, and B.A.-B.S. degrees in administration of justice, chemistry, and physics are offered. Nondegree study and credit for life experience are also available. There are 4 national honor societies and a freshman honors program.

Faculty/Classroom: 66% of faculty are male; 34%, female. 89% teach undergraduates, 3% do research, and 20% do both. No introductory courses are taught by graduate students. The average class size in an introductory lecture is 23; in a laboratory, 23; and in a regular course, 23.

Admissions: 81% of the 2003-2004 applicants were accepted.

Requirements: The ACT is required. In addition, a high school diploma or GED is required for admission, along with an interview. High school courses must include 4 years of English and 2 each of foreign language, social science, lab science, and math (algebra and geometry). AP and CLEP credits are accepted. Important factors in the admissions decision are ability to finance college education, advanced placement or honor courses, and recommendations by school officials.

Procedure: Freshmen are admitted to all sessions. Application deadlines are open. The fall 2003 application fee was $20.

Transfer: Applicants must have a minimum GPA of 2.0. Those with fewer than 30 hours of college credit must submit a high school transcript along with college records. 30 of 120 credits required for the bachelor's degree must be completed at UDC.

Visiting: There are guides for informal visits and visitors may sit in on classes. To schedule a visit, contact the Office of Student Recruitment at (202) 282-3350.

Financial Aid: In 2003-2004, 25% of all full-time freshmen and 35% of continuing full-time students received some form of financial aid. 35% of full-time freshmen and 33% of continuing full-time students received need-based aid. Need-based scholarships or need-based grants averaged $3000 ($19,000 maximum); need-based self-help aid (loans and jobs) averaged $8512; non-need-based athletic scholarships averaged $9000 ($16,370 maximum); and other non-need-based awards and non-need-based scholarships averaged $1000 ($15,000 maximum). UDC is a member of CSS. The CSS Profile or FFS is required. Check with the school for current application deadlines

International Students: They must score 550 on the written TOEFL and also take the university's own English, math, and reading tests.

Computers: The mainframes are an IBM 4381 and a DEC VAX 8650. PCs are also available. All students may access the system 24 hours a day. There are no time limits and no fees.

Admissions Contact: LaVerne Hill-Flanagan, Director of Recruitment and Admissions. E-mail: *lflanagan@udc.edu* Web: *universityofdc.org*

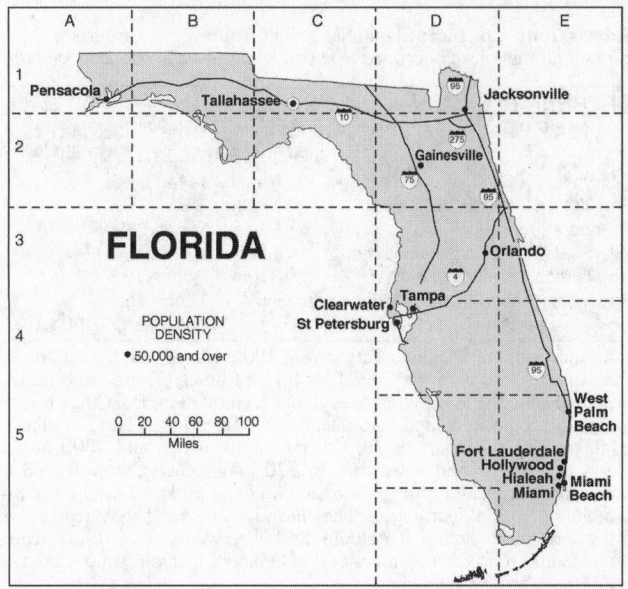

FLORIDA

POPULATION DENSITY
• 50,000 and over

0 20 40 60 80 100
Miles

BARRY UNIVERSITY
Miami Shores, FL 33161

E-5

(305) 899-3100
(800) 695-2279; Fax: (305) 899-2971

Full-time: 1010 men, 2270 women	**Faculty:** 167; IIA, -$
Part-time: 1135 men, 1600 women	**Ph.D.s:** 80%
Graduate: 855 men, 1930 women	**Student/Faculty:** 15 to 1
Year: semesters, summer session	**Tuition:** $17,500
Application Deadline: open	**Room & Board:** $6600
Freshman Class: n/av	
SAT I or ACT: required	**LESS COMPETITIVE**

Barry University is an independent Roman Catholic institution of liberal arts and professional studies. Figures in the above capsule and in this profile are approximate. There are 6 undergraduate and 10 graduate schools. In addition to regional accreditation, Barry has baccalaureate program accreditation with CAHEA and NLN. The library contains 290,590 volumes, 512,192 microform items, and 3593 audio/video tapes/CDs, and subscribes to 1851 periodicals. Computerized library services include the card catalog, interlibrary loans, and database searching. Special learning facilities include a learning resource center, radio station, human performance lab, biotechnology lab, photography studios, TV studio, theater, biomechanics lab, and multimedia business classrooms. The 122-acre campus is in a suburban area 14 miles from Fort Lauderdale and 7 miles north of downtown Miami. Including any residence halls, there are 26 buildings.

Student Life: 67% of undergraduates are from Florida. Students are from 46 states, 70 foreign countries, and Canada. 75% are from public schools. 39% are white; 30% Hispanic; 17% African American. 24% are Catholic; 8% Protestant. The average age of freshmen is 19; all undergraduates, 25. 28% do not continue beyond their first year; 48% remain to graduate.

Housing: 715 students can be accommodated in college housing, which includes single-sex and coed dorms and off-campus apartments. In addition, there are special-interest houses. On-campus housing is guaranteed for the freshman year only, is available on a first-come, first-served basis, and is available on a lottery system for upperclassmen. Priority is given to out-of-town students. 71% of students commute. All students may keep cars.

Activities: 13% of men belong to 3 national fraternities; 4% of women belong to 2 national sororities. There are 82 groups on campus, including cheerleading, chorale, computers, dance, drama, ethnic, honors, international, literary magazine, musical theater, newspaper, photography, political, professional, radio and TV, religious, social, social service, and student government. Popular campus events include Halloween Dance, Festival of Nations, and World AIDS Day.

Sports: There are 5 intercollegiate sports for men and 7 for women. Facilities include baseball, softball, and soccer fields, a health and sports center with an indoor gym, outdoor basketball courts, and racquetball and tennis courts, an outdoor swimming pool, a strength and conditioning center, an athletic training room, a human performance lab, and a biomechanics lab.

Disabled Students: 85% of the campus is accessible. Wheelchair ramps, elevators, special parking, specially equipped rest rooms, special class scheduling, lowered drinking fountains, and lowered telephones are available.

Services: Counseling and information services are available, as is tutoring in most subjects. There is remedial math, reading, and writing.

Campus Safety and Security: Measures include 24-hour foot and vehicle patrol, self-defense education, security escort services, and shuttle buses. There are informal discussions, pamphlets/posters/films, emergency telephones, and lighted pathways/sidewalks.

Programs of Study: Barry confers B.A., B.S., B.F.A., B.L.S., B.P.A., B.P.S., B.S.L.S., B.S.N., B.S.T., and B.S.W. degrees. Master's and doctoral degrees are also awarded. Bachelor's degrees are awarded in BIOLOGICAL SCIENCE (biology/biological science and marine biology), BUSINESS (accounting, international business management, management information systems, management science, marketing/retailing/merchandising, and sports management), COMMUNICATIONS AND THE ARTS (advertising, art, broadcasting, communications, dramatic arts, English, French, music performance, photography, public relations, Spanish, and theater management), COMPUTER AND PHYSICAL SCIENCE (chemistry, computer science, and mathematics), EDUCATION (early childhood and physical), ENGINEERING AND ENVIRONMENTAL DESIGN (preengineering), HEALTH PROFESSIONS (cytotechnology, medical technology, nuclear medical technology, nursing, occupational therapy, predentistry, premedicine, prepharmacy, and ultrasound technology), SOCIAL SCIENCE (criminology, economics, history, international studies, liberal arts/general studies, philosophy, political science/government, prelaw, psychology, sociology, and theological studies). Biology, chemistry, and elementary and early childhood education are the strongest academically. Nursing, elementary and early childhood education, and biology are the largest.

Required: To graduate, students must complete 120 credit hours, including at least 48 in upper-division courses, 40 to 60 in the major, and 45 distributed in these curricular divisions: theology and philosophy, written and oral communication, physical or natural science and math, social and behavior sciences, and humanities and the arts. A minimum GPA of 2.0 must be maintained.

Special: Barry offers junior- or senior-year internships, a Washington semester for prelaw/political science students, on-campus work-study programs in all departments, dual majors, a liberal studies degree, an accelerated degree program in nursing, nondegree study, and pass/fail options. Students may study in 5 European countries. Barry is a member of the College Consortium for International Studies; students can participate in more than 50 programs offered by members. There are 15 national honor societies and a freshman honors program.

Faculty/Classroom: 44% of faculty are male; 56%, female. 69% teach undergraduates. No introductory courses are taught by graduate students. The average class size in an introductory lecture is 17; in a laboratory, 14; and in a regular course, 17.

Requirements: The SAT I or ACT is required. In addition, graduation from an accredited secondary school or satisfactory scores on the GED are required for admission. A GPA of 2.0 is required. AP and CLEP credits are accepted.

Procedure: Freshmen are admitted to all sessions. Entrance exams should be taken as early as possible. There is an early admissions plan and a rolling admissions plan. Application deadlines are open. The fall 2003 application fee was $30. Applications are accepted on computer disk and on-line.

Transfer: Applicants must have earned at least 12 acceptable credit hours with a minimum GPA of 2.0. 30 of 120 credits required for the bachelor's degree must be completed at Barry.

Visiting: There are guides for informal visits and visitors may sit in on classes. To schedule a visit, contact Undergraduate Admissions at (305) 899-3113 or (800) 695-2279.

Financial Aid: Barry is a member of CSS. The FAFSA is required. Check with the school for current deadlines.

International Students: The school actively recruits these students. They must score 550 on the written TOEFL.

Computers: The mainframe is a DEC Alpha 2100. The system may be accessed via dial-up modems or networked PCs in labs and residence halls. All students may access the system 24 hours a day. There are no time limits and no fees. It is strongly recommended that all students have a personal computer. It is required that students in anesthesiology program (graduate degree) have personal computers. IBM ThinkPad or Dell is recommended.

Graduates: In a recent year, 951 bachelor's degrees were awarded. The most popular majors were biology (21%), education (13%), and nursing (9%). In an average class, 49% graduate in 4 years or less, 48% graduate in 5 years or less, and 48% graduate in 6 years or less. 125 companies recruited on campus in a recent year.

Admissions Contact: Tracy Fontaine, Director of Admissions.
E-mail: *admissions@mail.barry.edu* Web: *www.barry.edu*

BEACON COLLEGE
Leesburg, FL 34748   **(352) 787-7660; Fax: (352) 787-0721**

Full-time: 51 men, 34 women	**Faculty:** 10
Part-time: none	**Ph.D.s:** 45%
Graduate: none	**Student/Faculty:** 9 to 1
Year: semesters, summer session	**Tuition:** $19,700
Application Deadline: open	**Room & Board:** $6200
Freshman Class: 49 applied, 45 accepted, 30 enrolled	
SAT I or ACT: not required	**LESS COMPETITIVE**

Beacon College, founded in 1989, is a private institution that offers undergraduate degrees in liberal studies and human services exclusively for students with learning disabilities. The library contains 20,075 volumes and 554 audio/video tapes/CDs, and subscribes to 182 periodicals. Computerized library services include the card catalog, interlibrary loans, database searching, and Internet access. Special learning facilities include a learning resource center and art gallery. The 2-acre campus is in a small town in the downtown historic district. Including any residence halls, there are 11 buildings.

Student Life: 84% of undergraduates are from out of state, mostly the South. Students are from 25 states and 1 foreign country. 48% are from public schools. 81% are white; 14% African American. The average age of freshmen is 20. 23% do not continue beyond their first year; 76% remain to graduate.

Housing: 130 students can be accommodated in college housing, which includes coed on-campus apartments and off-campus apartments. On-campus housing is guaranteed for all 4 years. All students live on campus; of those, 97% remain on campus on weekends. Alcohol is not permitted. All students may keep cars.

Activities: 38% of women belong to 1 local sorority. There are no fraternities. There are 15 groups on campus, including art, choir, computers, drama, literary magazine, musical theater, newspaper, social, social service, student government, and yearbook.

Disabled Students: 90% of the campus is accessible. Wheelchair ramps, special parking, specially equipped rest rooms, special class scheduling, and special housing are available.

Services: Counseling and information services are available, as is tutoring in every subject. There is remedial math, reading, and writing. There is an Academic Mentoring Program.

Campus Safety and Security: Measures include lighted pathways/sidewalks and school van transportation.

Programs of Study: Beacon College confers the B.A. degree. Associate degrees are also awarded. Bachelor's degrees are awarded in SOCIAL SCIENCE (human services and liberal arts/general studies).

Required: To graduate, students must have 120 credit hours, including 33 credit hours of general education and at least 63 credit hours in their major, and a 2.0 GPA. Students in the liberal studies program must write a thesis and take a comprehensive exam.

Special: Internships, B.A.-B.S. degrees, dual majors, and study abroad are possible.

Faculty/Classroom: 55% of faculty are male; 45%, female. All teach undergraduates, 15% do research, and 15% do both. The average class size in an introductory lecture is 8; in a laboratory, 10; and in a regular course, 8.

Admissions: 92% of the 2003-2004 applicants were accepted.

Requirements: CLEP credit is accepted.

Procedure: Freshmen are admitted fall and spring. Entrance exams should be taken within 3 years prior to application. There are early decision and deferred admissions plans. Application deadlines are open. Application fee is $50.

Transfer: 10 transfer students enrolled in 2002-2003. 78 of 120 credits required for the bachelor's degree must be completed at Beacon College.

Visiting: There are regularly scheduled orientations for prospective students. There are guides for informal visits and visitors may sit in on classes. To schedule a visit, contact Stephanie Knight at *admissions@beaconcollege.edu*.

Financial Aid: In 2003-2004, 43% of all full-time freshmen received some form of financial aid. 43% of full-time freshmen received need-based aid. The average freshman award was $6200. Need-based scholarships or need-based grants averaged $6200 (maximum). The FAFSA and the college's own financial statement are required. The priority date for freshman financial aid applications for fall entry is May 1. The deadline for filing freshman financial aid applications for fall entry is July 1.

International Students: There is 1 international student enrolled. They must take the TOEFL and the college's own entrance exam, and WAIS subtests with the GLE in reading, writing, and math.

Computers: All students may access the system during school hours. There are no time limits and no fees. It is strongly recommended that all students have a personal computer.

Graduates: From July 1, 2002 to June 30, 2003, 24 bachelor's degrees were awarded. The most popular majors were liberal studies (80%) and human services (20%). In an average class, 50% graduate in 4 years or less, 40% graduate in 5 years or less, and 10% graduate in 6 years or less.

Admissions Contact: Stephanie Knight, Admissions Counselor.
E-mail: *admissions@beaconcollege.edu* Web: *www.beaconcollege.edu*

BETHUNE-COOKMAN COLLEGE   D-2
Daytona Beach, FL 32114-3099   **(386) 481-2600**
(800) 448-0228; Fax: (386) 481-2601

Full-time: 1582 men, 1036 women	**Faculty:** 141; IIB, --$
Part-time: 58 men, 118 women	**Ph.D.s:** 57%
Graduate: none	**Student/Faculty:** 19 to 1
Year: semesters, summer session	**Tuition:** $10,106
Application Deadline: July 30	**Room & Board:** $6374
Freshman Class: 2523 applied, 1804 accepted, 620 enrolled	
SAT I Verbal/Math: 410/410	**LESS COMPETITIVE**

Bethune-Cookman College, founded in 1904, is a private liberal arts institution affiliated with the United Methodist Church. There are 6 undergraduate schools. In addition to regional accreditation, B-CC has baccalaureate program accreditation with NCATE and NLN. The library contains 170,272 volumes, 50,125 microform items, and 4500 audio/video tapes/CDs, and subscribes to 770 periodicals. Computerized library services include the card catalog, interlibrary loans, and database searching. Special learning facilities include a learning resource center, art gallery, radio station, TV studio, and observatory. The 70-acre campus is in an urban area 65 miles east of Orlando. Including any residence halls, there are 37 buildings.

Student Life: 66% of undergraduates are from Florida. Students are from 39 states, 35 foreign countries, and Canada. 90% are from public schools. 90% are African American. 93% are Protestant; 6% Catholic. The average age of freshmen is 18; all undergraduates, 20. 23% do not continue beyond their first year; 76% remain to graduate.

Housing: 1772 students can be accommodated in college housing, which includes single-sex dorms. In addition, there are honor student dorms and wings for Greek letter organizations. On-campus housing is guaranteed for the freshman year only and is available on a first-come, first-served basis. Priority is given to out-of-town students. 59% of students live on campus; of those, 85% remain on campus on weekends. Alcohol is not permitted. Upperclassmen may keep cars.

Activities: 3% of men belong to 5 national fraternities; 5% of women belong to 4 national sororities. There are 35 groups on campus, including band, cheerleading, choir, chorale, computers, dance, drama, drill team, honors, international, literary magazine, marching band, newspaper, political, professional, radio and TV, religious, social, student government, and yearbook. Popular campus events include Religious Outreach, Career Day, and Futurism Seminar.

Sports: There are 7 intercollegiate sports for men and 8 for women, and 6 intramural sports for men and 7 for women. Facilities include a gym, a weight room, a practice field, and tennis and racquetball courts.

Disabled Students: 30% of the campus is accessible. Wheelchair ramps, elevators, special parking, specially equipped rest rooms, lowered drinking fountains, and lowered telephones are available.

Services: Counseling and information services are available, as is tutoring in most subjects. There is remedial math, reading, and writing.

Campus Safety and Security: Measures include 24-hour foot and vehicle patrol, security escort services, informal discussions, and pamphlets/posters/films. There are lighted pathways/sidewalks.

Programs of Study: B-CC confers B.A. and B.S. degrees. Bachelor's degrees are awarded in BIOLOGICAL SCIENCE (biology/biological science), BUSINESS (accounting, business administration and management, hotel/motel and restaurant management, and international business management), COMMUNICATIONS AND THE ARTS (communications, dramatic arts, English, modern language, and music), COMPUTER AND PHYSICAL SCIENCE (chemistry, computer science, information sciences and systems, mathematics, and physics), EDUCATION (business, education of the exceptional child, elementary, English, mathematics, music, physical, science, and social science), ENGINEERING AND ENVIRONMENTAL DESIGN (computer engineering), HEALTH PROFESSIONS (clinical science and nursing), SOCIAL SCIENCE (criminal justice, gerontology, history, international studies, liberal arts/general studies, political science/government, psychology, religion, and sociology). Business administration, elementary education, and nursing are the strongest academically. Business administration, elementary education, and criminal justice are the largest.

Required: To graduate, students must have a total of 124 credit hours with a minimum GPA of 2.0. All students must complete a total of 49 hours in general education requirements, pass all parts of the College-Level Academic Skills Test (CLAST), and pass at a specified level 9 senior exit exams that may include a standardized exam and/or senior area comprehensive exam. They must also complete a senior seminar and senior research paper.

Special: Students may take courses at other institutions with the approval of the area adviser or registrar. B-CC offers cooperative courses in all divisions, internships related to the student's major, work-study programs, nondegree-study, and 3-2 engineering degrees with the Universities of Florida and Central Florida, Tuskegee and Florida Atlantic Universities, and Florida Agriculture and Mechanical University-Florida State University. Study abroad is available in Spain, France, and Germany. There are 6 national honor societies, including Phi Beta Kappa and a freshman honors program.

Faculty/Classroom: 52% of faculty are male; 48%, female. 93% teach undergraduates and 7% both teach and do research. The average class size in an introductory lecture is 20; in a laboratory, 20; and in a regular course, 18.

Admissions: 72% of the 2003-2004 applicants were accepted. The SAT I scores for the 2003-2004 freshman class were: Verbal--85% below 500, 12% between 500 and 599, 2% between 600 and 700, and 1% above 700; Math--85% below 500, 12% between 500 and 599, 2% between 600 and 700, and 1% above 700. The ACT scores were 77% below 21, 21% between 21 and 23, and 2% between 24 and 26. 18% of the current freshmen were in the top fifth of their class; 40% were in the top two fifths.

Requirements: The SAT I or ACT is required. In addition, graduation from an accredited secondary school or satisfactory scores on the GED are required for admission. High school courses must include 24 credits with 4 of English, 3 each of math and science, 2 of history, 1/2 each of government, economics, vocational ed, art, management skills, and phys ed, and 9 of electives; 2 years of a modern language are strongly recommended. Students must submit an essay and a letter of recommendation. A GPA of 2.25 is required. AP and CLEP credits are accepted. Important factors in the admissions decision are extracurricular activities record, leadership record, and geographic diversity.

Procedure: Freshmen are admitted to all sessions. Entrance exams should be taken during the fall prior to application. There is a deferred admissions plan. Applications should be filed by July 30 for fall entry, November 30 for spring entry, and April 30 for summer entry, along with a $25 fee. Notification is sent on a rolling basis.

Transfer: 84 transfer students enrolled in 2002-2003. Applicants must submit transcripts from previous institutions attended and a statement of good standing and eligibility to return. A minimum GPA of 2.25 is required. Students having fewer than 12 credit hours must meet the requirements for entering freshmen. 30 of 124 credits required for the bachelor's degree must be completed at B-CC.

Visiting: There are guides for informal visits and visitors may sit in on classes. To schedule a visit, contact the Admissions Office at *ferrierL@cookman.edu.*

Financial Aid: The average freshman award was $14,500. Need-based scholarships or need-based grants averaged $7100 ($8000 maximum); need-based self-help aid (loans and jobs) averaged $2845 ($3500 maximum); non-need-based athletic scholarships averaged $12,470 ($13,000 maximum); and other non-need-based awards and non-need-based scholarships averaged $7100 ($8000 maximum). 75% of undergraduates work part time. Average annual earnings from campus work are $1400. The average financial indebtedness of the 2003 graduate was $25,900. B-CC is a member of CSS. The FAFSA is required. The deadline for filing freshman financial aid applications for fall entry is March 1.

International Students: There are 173 international students enrolled. The school actively recruits these students. They must score 550 on the written TOEFL or 213 on the electronic version and also take the SAT I or the ACT.

Computers: The mainframe is an IBM AS400. Each academic building is equipped with computer facilities. More than 650 computer keyboards are available for student use. All students may access the system. There are no time limits and no fees.

Graduates: From July 1, 2002 to June 30, 2003, 351 bachelor's degrees were awarded. The most popular majors were criminal justice (17%), business administration (11%), and psychology (8%). In an average class, 3% graduate in 3 years or less, 10% graduate in 4 years or less, 23% graduate in 5 years or less, and 30% graduate in 6 years or less. 150 companies recruited on campus in 2002-2003. Of the 2002 graduating class, 26% were enrolled in graduate school within 6 months of graduation and 75% were employed.

Admissions Contact: Les Ferrier, Director of Admissions. A video is available. E-mail: *ferrierl@cookman.edu*
Web: *www.bethune.cookman.edu*

CARLOS ALBIZU UNIVERSITY

E-5
Miami, FL 33172-2209
(305) 593-1223 ext 160
(800) 672-3246; Fax: (305) 593-1854

Full-time: 34 men, 116 women	**Faculty:** 4
Part-time: 50 men, 157 women	**Ph.D.s:** n/av
Graduate: 131 men, 365 women	**Student/Faculty:** 37 to 1
Year: trimesters, summer session	**Tuition:** $10,569
Application Deadline: open	**Room & Board:** n/app
Freshman Class: 93 applied, 83 accepted, 73 enrolled	
SAT I or ACT: not required	**COMPETITIVE**

Carlos Albizu University is a private, specialized institution of higher learning offering degrees at the undergraduate, graduate, and doctoral levels. CAU has campuses in San Juan, Puerto Rico, and Miami, Florida, founded in 1966 and 1980 respectively. There are 3 undergraduate and 3 graduate schools. The library contains 23,000 volumes and 1026 audio/video tapes/CDs, and subscribes to 350 periodicals. Computerized library services include the card catalog, interlibrary loans, database searching, and Internet access. Special learning facilities include a learning resource center and an ESOL lab. The 18-acre campus is in an urban area in Miami. There are 2 buildings.

Student Life: 98% of undergraduates are from Florida. Students are from 22 states, 42 foreign countries, and Canada. 72% are Hispanic; 11% African American. The average age of freshmen is 28; all undergraduates, 35. 1% do not continue beyond their first year; 37% remain to graduate.

Housing: There are no residence halls. All students commute. Alcohol is not permitted. All students may keep cars.

Activities: There are no fraternities or sororities. There are 5 groups on campus, including ethnic, gay, honors, newsletter, and student government. Popular campus events include the Excellent Student Award Banquet, the Student Council Initiation Event, and the Student Support Services Cultural Event.

Disabled Students: All of the campus is accessible. Wheelchair ramps, special parking, specially equipped rest rooms, and lowered drinking fountains are available.

Services: Counseling and information services are available, as is tutoring in most subjects. There is a mentoring program and student support services center.

Campus Safety and Security: Measures include 24-hour foot and vehicle patrol, security escort services, emergency telephones, and lighted pathways/sidewalks. There is an annual report on crime statistics.

Programs of Study: CAU confers B.A., B.S., and B.B.A. degrees. Master's and doctoral degrees are also awarded. Bachelor's degrees are awarded in BUSINESS (business administration and management), EDUCATION (elementary), SOCIAL SCIENCE (psychology). Psychology is the largest.

Required: To graduate, students must earn 120 to 124 credits, with 30 to 48 in the major. Foundation courses include English composition, oral communication, math, behavioral life, physical sciences, humanities, cross-cultural studies, literature, liberal arts, and computing, for a total of 48 credits.

Special: CAU offers cross-registration with other area colleges, internships or practicums in psychology and elementary education, federal work-study, an accelerated degree program in business administration, and dual majors in psychology and elementary education. There is 1 national honor society.

Faculty/Classroom: 43% of faculty are male; 57%, female. 100% both teach and do research. Graduate students teach 15% of introductory courses. The average class size in an introductory lecture is 12; in a laboratory, 10; and in a regular course, 15.

Admissions: 89% of the 2003-2004 applicants were accepted.

Requirements: A GPA of 2.0 is required. AP and CLEP credits are accepted. Important factors in the admissions decision are advanced placement or honor courses and ability to finance college education.

Procedure: Freshmen are admitted fall, spring, and summer. Application deadlines are open. Application fee is $25.

Transfer: 31 transfer students enrolled in 2002-2003. Transfer applicants must have an overall GPA of 2.0 and must submit official transcripts from all colleges/universities previously attended. 30 of 120 credits required for the bachelor's degree must be completed at CAU.

Visiting: There are regularly scheduled orientations for prospective students, consisting of 2 open houses per session. There are guides for informal visits and visitors may sit in on classes. To schedule a visit, contact Dr. Arturo Tigera at (305) 593-1223 ext. 149 or *atigera@albizu.edu.*

Financial Aid: In 2003-2004, 75% of all full-time freshmen and 79% of continuing full-time students received some form of financial aid. 73% of full-time freshmen and 76% of continuing full-time students received need-based aid. The average freshman award was $10,000. 12% of undergraduates work part time. Average annual earnings from campus work are $1500. The average financial indebtedness of the 2003 graduate was $25,000. The FAFSA and the college's own financial statement are required. The deadline for filing freshman financial aid applications for fall entry is June 1.

Computers: The mainframe is an HP 9000 Model L2000. There are 17 PCs in the library, 23 in a computer lab, and 14 in an educational technology lab, all available for student use. All students may access the system from 10 A.M. to 9 P.M. Monday through Friday, and from 9 A.M. to 3 P.M. Saturdays. There are no time limits and no fees. It is strongly recommended that all students have a personal computer.

Graduates: From July 1, 2002 to June 30, 2003, 37 bachelor's degrees were awarded. Of the 2002 graduating class, 53% were enrolled in graduate school within 6 months of graduation.

Admissions Contact: Rafael Vasquez, Assistant Director of Recruitment, Admissions, and Outreach. E-mail: *rvasquez@albizu.edu* Web: *www.albizu.edu*

CLEARWATER CHRISTIAN COLLEGE

D-4

Clearwater, FL 33759

(727) 726-1153, ext. 228
(800) 348-4463; Fax: (727) 726-8597

Full-time: 270 men, 350 women	**Faculty:** 34
Part-time: 10 men, 10 women	**Ph.D.s:** 56%
Graduate: none	**Student/Faculty:** 18 to 1
Year: semesters, summer session	**Tuition:** $10,420
Application Deadline: see profile	**Room & Board:** $4580
Freshman Class: n/av	
SAT I or ACT: recommended	**LESS COMPETITIVE**

Clearwater Christian College, founded in 1966, is a private, fundamentalist, nonsectarian institution offering programs in Bible, liberal arts, business, and teacher preparation. Figures in the above capsule and in this profile are approximate. The library contains 103,000 volumes, 198,000 microform items, and 2100 audio/video tapes/CDs, and subscribes to 1050 periodicals. Computerized library services include the card catalog, interlibrary loans, and database searching. Special learning facilities include a learning resource center. The 130-acre campus is in a small town 10 miles west of Tampa. Including any residence halls, there are 7 buildings.

Student Life: 47% of undergraduates are from Florida. Students are from 37 states, 14 foreign countries, and Canada. 27% are from public schools. 89% are white. Most are Protestant. The average age of freshmen is 18; all undergraduates, 20. 39% do not continue beyond their first year; 41% remain to graduate.

Housing: 600 students can be accommodated in college housing, which includes single-sex dorms. On-campus housing is guaranteed for all 4 years. 81% of students live on campus; of those, all remain on campus on weekends. Alcohol is not permitted. All students may keep cars.

Activities: There are no fraternities or sororities. There are 8 groups on campus, including band, cheerleading, choir, chorale, drama, honors, newspaper, orchestra, pep band, political, professional, religious, student government, and yearbook.

Sports: There are 3 intercollegiate sports for men and 3 for women, and 3 intramural sports for men and 3 for women. Facilities include a gym and a playing field.

Disabled Students: All of the campus is accessible. Wheelchair ramps, elevators, special parking, specially equipped rest rooms, lowered drinking fountains, and lowered telephones are available.

Services: There is a reader service for the blind as needed.

Campus Safety and Security: Measures include 24-hour foot and vehicle patrol, self-defense education, informal discussions, and pamphlets/posters/films. There are emergency telephones and lighted pathways/sidewalks.

Programs of Study: CCC confers B.A. and B.S. degrees. Associate degrees are also awarded. Bachelor's degrees are awarded in BIOLOGICAL SCIENCE (biology/biological science), BUSINESS (accounting and business administration and management), COMMUNICATIONS AND THE ARTS (communications, English, and music), COMPUTER AND PHYSICAL SCIENCE (mathematics), EDUCATION (elementary, music, physical, secondary, social studies, and special), HEALTH PROFESSIONS (premedicine), SOCIAL SCIENCE (biblical studies, history, humanities, ministries, pastoral studies, prelaw, psychology, religious education, and religious music). Education and business are the largest.

Required: General education requirements include 25 hours of human adjustment, 19 each of social science and humanities, 12 of arts and communication, and 10 of science and math. Computer science courses are required. A total of 128 credit hours is required, including more than 60 in the major, with a minimum GPA of 2.0. Students must have no grade lower than a C- in any major requirement and maintain satisfactory Christian service involvement throughout the college career.

Special: On occasion, credit from an approved correspondence school may be accepted, or registration at another school for a course to complete degree requirements at CCC may be permitted. Internships are offered in teacher education, business, and psychology. Work-study programs and nondegree study are possible. There is 1 national honor society.

Faculty/Classroom: 68% of faculty are male; 32%, female. All teach undergraduates. The average class size in an introductory lecture is 50; in a laboratory, 20; and in a regular course, 25.

Requirements: The SAT I or ACT is recommended, with a minimum score of 870 on the SAT I or 18 on the ACT. Applicants must be high school graduates or have a GED certificate. An essay is required, and an interview is recommended. A GPA of 2.0 is required. AP and CLEP credits are accepted.

Procedure: Freshmen are admitted to all sessions. Entrance exams should be taken in the fall of the senior year. There is a deferred admissions plan and a rolling admissions plan. The application fee is $35. Check with the school for current deadlines.

Transfer: Transfer applicants must submit transcripts from all postsecondary schools attended. Grades of C or better transfer. Applicants must have a minimum cumulative postsecondary GPA of 2.0. 32 of 128 credits required for the bachelor's degree must be completed at CCC.

Visiting: There are regularly scheduled orientations for prospective students. There are guides for informal visits and visitors may sit in on classes and stay overnight. To schedule a visit, contact the Admissions Office.

Financial Aid: The CSS Profile, FAFSA, or FFS are required; the FFS is preferred.

International Students: They must score 500 on the written TOEFL and also take Applicants must also submit a Foreign Student Data Form. and also take the SAT I or the ACT, scoring 18.

Computers: The mainframe is an IBM AS/400. Internet access through an on-campus server is available through residence hall rooms, the library, public terminals in residence halls, and the computer lab. All students may access the system. There are no time limits. The annual fee is $30. It is strongly recommended that all students have a personal computer.

Admissions Contact: Benjamin J. Puckett, Dean of Enrollment Services. A video is available. E-mail: *benpuckett@clearwater.edu* Web: *clearwater.edu*

DEVRY UNIVERSITY/MIRAMAR

Miramar, FL 33027-4150

(954) 499-9700
(866) 793-3879; Fax: (954) 499-9723

Full-time: 239 men, 82 women	**Faculty:** n/av
Part-time: 307 men, 148 women	**Ph.D.s:** n/av
Graduate: n/av	**Student/Faculty:** n/av
Year: semesters, summer session	**Tuition:** $11,310
Application Deadline: open	**Room & Board:** n/app
Freshman Class: n/av	
SAT I or ACT: n/av	**LESS COMPETITIVE**

Devry University/Miramar, 1 of 67 DeVry University locations in the United States and Canada, opened in 2002. It offers programs in business administration, computer engineering technology, computer information systems, electronics engineering technology, network and communications management, and technical management. The library contains 8100 volumes and 550 audio/video tapes/CDs, and subscribes to 125 periodicals. The size of the campus is 16 acres.

Student Life: 39% are African American; 38% Hispanic; 11% white.

Housing: There are no residence halls. All students commute.

Activities: There are no fraternities or sororities.

Programs of Study: DeVry confers B.A. degrees. Associate and master's degrees are also awarded. Bachelor's degrees are awarded in BUSINESS (business administration and management), COMMUNICATIONS AND THE ARTS (telecommunications), COMPUTER AND PHYSICAL SCIENCE (information sciences and systems), ENGINEERING AND ENVIRONMENTAL DESIGN (computer engineering, electrical/electronics engineering technology, and technological management).

Required: To graduate, students must achieve a GPA of at least 2.0, complete 48 to 154 credit hours, and satisfactorily complete all curriculum requirements. Course requirements vary according to program. All first-semester students take courses in business organization, computer applications, algebra, psychology, and student success strategies.

Special: Accelerated degree programs, co-op programs, and distance learning are available.

Requirements: Admissions requirements include graduation from a secondary school; the GED is accepted. Applicants must pass the DeVry entrance exam or present satisfactory SAT I or ACT scores. An interview is required.

Procedure: Freshmen are admitted fall, spring, and summer. There are early admissions and deferred admissions plans. Application deadlines are open. Application fee is $50. Applications are accepted on-line through *https://apply.embark.com/UGrad/DeVry/21/*.

Transfer: 25 of 48 credits required for the bachelor's degree must be completed at DeVry University/Miramar.

Financial Aid: In 2003-2004, 69% of all full-time students received some form of financial aid. At least 65% of full-time freshmen and at least 64% of continuing full-time students received need-based aid. The average freshman award was $6506. Need-based scholarships or need-based grants averaged $4035; need-based self-help aid (loans and jobs) averaged $3416; and other institutional non-need-based awards and non-need-based scholarships averaged $6562. The FAFSA is required.

The deadline for filing freshman financial aid applications for fall entry is rolling.

International Students: Students must score 500 on the written TOEFL or 173 on the electronic version and also take the college's own entrance exam.

Graduates: In a recent year, the most popular major was engineering/engineering technologies (100%).

Admissions Contact: Martin Najarro, Director of Admissions.
E-mail: *openhouse@mir.devry.edu* Web: *www.devry.edu/miramar*

DEVRY UNIVERSITY/ORLANDO
D-3
Orlando, FL 32839-2426
(407) 370-3131
(866) 353-3879; Fax: (407) 370-3198

Full-time: 577 men, 231 women	**Faculty:** n/av
Part-time: 372 men, 166 women	**Ph.Ds:** n/av
Graduate: n/av	**Student/Faculty:** n/av
Year: semesters, summer session	**Tuition:** $11,310
Application Deadline: open	**Room & Board:** n/app
Freshman Class: n/av	
SAT I or ACT: n/av	**LESS COMPETITIVE**

DeVry University/Orlando, founded in 2000, is a private institution offering hands-on programs in electronics, business administration, computer information systems, telecommunications management, information technology, and computer engineering technology. The school is 1 of 67 DeVry University locations throughout the United States and Canada. The library contains 14,000 volumes, 8000 e-books, and 950 audio/video tapes/CDs, and subscribes to 62 periodicals. Computerized library services include the card catalog, interlibrary loans, and database searching. Special learning facilities include a learning resource center and electronics and other labs.

Student Life: 30% of students are white; 26% African American; 16% Hispanic. The average age of all undergraduates is 25.

Housing: There are no residence halls. Housing referrals can be obtained through the Student Housing Office. There are private apartments, student-plan housing, and private rooms. All students commute. Alcohol is not permitted. All students may keep cars.

Activities: There are no fraternities or sororities. There are 11 groups on campus, including professional, social, and yearbook. Popular campus events include Model Car Competition, Fun Flicks, and Welcome Picnic.

Sports: There is no sports program at DeVry.

Disabled Students: 98% of the campus is accessible. Special parking, specially equipped rest rooms, lowered drinking fountains, and lowered telephones are available.

Services: Counseling and information services are available, as is tutoring in every subject.

Campus Safety and Security: Measures include security escort services, informal discussions, pamphlets/posters/films, and emergency telephones. There are lighted pathways/sidewalks and off-duty police as security.

Programs of Study: DeVry confers the B.S. degree. Associate and master's degrees are also awarded. Bachelor's degrees are awarded in BUSINESS (business administration and management), COMMUNICATIONS AND THE ARTS (telecommunications), COMPUTER AND PHYSICAL SCIENCE (information sciences and systems), ENGINEERING AND ENVIRONMENTAL DESIGN (computer engineering, electrical/electronics engineering technology, and technological management). Electronics, computer information systems, and telecommunications are the largest.

Required: To graduate, students must achieve a GPA of at least 2.0 and satisfactorily complete all curriculum requirements. Course requirements vary according to program. All first-semester students take courses in business organization, computer applications, algebra, psychology, and student success strategies.

Special: Accelerated degrees, co-op programs, nondegree study, distance learning, and evening and weekend classes are possible.

Faculty/Classroom: All teach undergraduates.

Requirements: Admissions requirements include graduation from a secondary school; the GED is also accepted. Applicants must pass the DeVry entrance exam or present satisfactory ACT or SAT I scores. An interview is required. CLEP credit is accepted.

Procedure: Freshmen are admitted fall, winter, and summer. There are early admissions and deferred admissions plans. Application deadlines are open. Application fee is $50. Notification is sent on a rolling basis. Applications are accepted on-line through *https://apply.embark.com/UGrad/DeVry/21/*.

Transfer: 3 transfer students enrolled in a recent year. Applicants must present passing grades in all completed college course work, demonstrate language skills proficiency in at least 24 completed semester hours, and present evidence of math proficiency by appropriate college-level credits. A minimum GPA of 2.0 is required. 25% of 48 to 154 credits required for the bachelor's degree must be completed at DeVry.

Visiting: There are regularly scheduled orientations for prospective students. There are guides for informal visits and visitors may sit in on classes. To schedule a visit, contact the New Student Coordinator.

Financial Aid: In 2002-2003, 68% of all full-time freshmen and 79% of continuing full-time students received some form of financial aid. At least 67% of full-time freshmen and 77% of continuing full-time students received need-based aid. The average freshman award was $6351. Need-based scholarships or need-based grants averaged $3859; need-based self-help aid (loans and jobs) averaged $3673; and institutional non-need-based awards and non-need-based scholarships averaged $10,000. The FAFSA is required. There is a rolling deadline for filing freshman financial aid applications for fall entry.

International Students: They must score 500 on the written TOEFL or 173 on the electronic version and also take the college's own entrance exam.

Graduates: From July 1, 2002 to June 30, 2003, 11 bachelor's degrees were awarded. The most popular majors were business (91%) and electronics engineering technology (9%).

Admissions Contact: Director of Admissions.
E-mail: *krochford@orl.devry.edu* Web: *www.orl.devry.edu*

ECKERD COLLEGE
D-4
St. Petersburg, FL 33711
(727) 864-8331
(800) 456-9009; Fax: (727) 866-2304

Full-time: 727 men, 877 women	**Faculty:** 102; IIB, av$
Part-time: 13 men, 14 women	**Ph.Ds:** 94%
Graduate: none	**Student/Faculty:** 16 to 1
Year: 4-1-4, summer session	**Tuition:** $22,774
Application Deadline: April 1	**Room & Board:** $5970
Freshman Class: 2046 applied, 1569 accepted, 435 enrolled	
SAT I Verbal/Math: 573/570	**COMPETITIVE+**

Eckerd College, founded in 1958, is a private liberal arts institution affiliated with the Presbyterian Church (U.S.A.). Interdisciplinary programs are an important part of the school's curriculum. This is reflected in the organization of the faculty into collegia, rather than into traditional departments. The college also fosters and encourages strong faculty-student mentoring, service learning, volunteerism, other types of hands-on, practical learning, and environmental and global perspectives. In addition to regional accreditation, Eckerd has baccalaureate program accreditation with AALE. The library contains 113,850 volumes, 14,606 microform items, and 1941 audio/video tapes/CDs, and subscribes to 3009 periodicals. Computerized library services include the card catalog, interlibrary loans, and database searching. Special learning facilities include an art gallery, radio station, TV station, and a sea mammal necropsy lab. The 267-acre campus is in a suburban area on 1 1/4 miles of waterfront, 5 miles south of St. Petersburg. Including any residence halls, there are 67 buildings.

Student Life: 69% of undergraduates are from out of state, mostly the Northeast. Students are from 50 states, 49 foreign countries, and Canada. 75% are from public schools. 77% are white. 52% are claim no religious affiliation; 24% Protestant; 18% Catholic; 7% Muslim, Hindu, Buddhist, and Greek Orthodox. The average age of freshmen is 18; all undergraduates, 20. 16% do not continue beyond their first year; 64% remain to graduate.

Housing: 1209 students can be accommodated in college housing, which includes single-sex and coed dorms and on-campus apartments. In addition, there are language houses and substance-free houses. On-campus housing is guaranteed for the freshman year only, is available on a first-come, first-served basis, and is available on a lottery system for upperclassmen. 76% of students live on campus; of those, 95% remain on campus on weekends. All students may keep cars.

Activities: There are no fraternities or sororities. There are 74 groups on campus, including cheerleading, chess, choir, chorale, chorus, computers, drama, ethnic, film, gay, honors, international, literary magazine, musical theater, newspaper, photography, political, professional, radio and TV, religious, social, social service, student government, water search and rescue, and yearbook. Popular campus events include the Festival of Cultures, Kon-Tiki, and the Festival of Hope.

Sports: There are 6 intercollegiate sports for men and 7 for women, and 11 intramural sports for men and 10 for women. Facilities include a gym, a baseball and softball complex, soccer fields, tennis courts, a weight room, a renovated and modernized fitness room, a swimming pool, and waterfront facilities.

Disabled Students: 90% of the campus is accessible. Wheelchair ramps, elevators, special parking, specially equipped rest rooms, special class scheduling, lowered drinking fountains, lowered telephones are available. Readers are available for the visually impaired, as are magnifiers in the library.

Services: Counseling and information services are available, as is tutoring in some subjects, including math, sciences, and foreign languages.

Campus Safety and Security: Measures include 24-hour foot and vehicle patrol, security escort services, informal discussions, and pamphlets/posters/films. There are emergency telephones, lighted pathways/ sidewalks, and a security gate at the entrance to the campus.

Programs of Study: Eckerd confers B.A. and B.S. degrees. Bachelor's degrees are awarded in AGRICULTURE (environmental studies), BIOLOGICAL SCIENCE (biology/biological science and marine science), BUSINESS (business administration and management, international business management, and management science), COMMUNICATIONS AND THE ARTS (communications, comparative literature, creative writing, dramatic arts, English, French, German, music, Russian, Spanish, and visual and performing arts), COMPUTER AND PHYSICAL SCIENCE (chemistry, computer science, mathematics, and physics), HEALTH PROFESSIONS (predentistry and premedicine), SOCIAL SCIENCE (American studies, anthropology, economics, history, human development, humanities, international relations, philosophy, political science/government, prelaw, psychology, religion, sociology, and women's studies). Marine science, management, and environmental studies are the largest.

Required: To graduate, students must complete a total of 36 courses or 126 semester hours with a minimum GPA of 2.0. Required courses include 1each in the arts, humanities, natural and social sciences, and environmental and global perspectives. Students must also demonstrate competencies in writing, speaking, foreign language, computation, and technology, and must take a comprehensive exam or submit a thesis or project in the senior year.

Special: Eckerd offers internships, study abroad, work-study programs, and dual majors in all subjects, interdisciplinary majors in international relations and environmental studies, student-designed majors, nondegree study, and pass/fail options. Students may earn B.A.-B.S. degrees in biology, chemistry, and marine science. A 3-2 engineering degree is offered with Auburn, Washington, and Columbia Universities and the University of Miami. The Program for Experienced Learners (students 25 and older) offers independent study, weekend courses, and credit for experiential learning. There are 8 national honor societies, including Phi Beta Kappa, a freshman honors program, and 30 departmental honors programs.

Faculty/Classroom: 66% of faculty are male; 34%, female. All both teach and do research. The average class size in an introductory lecture is 20; in a laboratory, 15; and in a regular course, 20.

Admissions: 77% of the 2003-2004 applicants were accepted. The SAT I scores for the 2003-2004 freshman class were: Verbal--20% below 500, 37% between 500 and 599, 32% between 600 and 700, and 8% above 700. 40% of the current freshmen were in the top fifth of their class; 73% were in the top two fifths. There were 3 National Merit finalists and 5 semifinalists. 15 freshmen graduated first in their class.

Requirements: The SAT I or ACT is required. In addition, graduation from an accredited secondary school or satisfactory scores on the GED are required. High school courses must include 4 years of English, 3 each of math and science, 2 each of a foreign language and social studies, and 1 of history. SAT II: subject tests in writing, literature, and math are recommended. An essay is required and an interview is recommended. A GPA of 2.0 is required. AP and CLEP credits are accepted. Important factors in the admissions decision are advanced placement or honor courses, leadership record, and personality/intangible qualities.

Procedure: Freshmen are admitted fall, winter, and spring. Entrance exams should be taken in October, November, or December. There are early admissions and deferred admissions plans. Applications should be filed by April 1 for fall entry, December 1 for winter entry, and December 1 for spring entry. Notification is sent on a rolling basis. A waiting list is an active part of the admissions procedure.

Transfer: 86 transfer students enrolled in 2002-2003. Applicants must have a minimum GPA of 2.5. The SAT I or ACT is required. An interview is recommended. A faculty recommendation is required. 63 of 126 credits required for the bachelor's degree must be completed at Eckerd.

Visiting: There are regularly scheduled orientations for prospective students, consisting of an interview and a tour. There are guides for informal visits and visitors may sit in on classes and stay overnight. To schedule a visit, contact the Admissions Office.

Financial Aid: In 2003-2004, 87% of all full-time students received some form of financial aid. 65% of full-time freshmen and 64% of continuing full-time students received need-based aid. The average freshman award was $17,200. 75% of undergraduates work part time. Average annual earnings from campus work are $1500. The average financial indebtedness of the 2003 graduate was $17,500. The FAFSA is required. The deadline for filing freshman financial aid applications for fall entry is March 15.

International Students: There are 144 international students enrolled. The school actively recruits these students. They must score 550 on the written TOEFL or 213 on the electronic version.

Computers: The mainframe consists of 2 Sun SPARC computers. There are 20 PCs in a Novell Network in the computer lab and 40 PCs in the science lab through which students may access the mainframe. Students with their own PCs may access the mainframe through modems or Ethernet from their dorm rooms. Each dorm has a lab with 3 computers connected to the network. All students may access the sys-

tem at any time. There are no time limits and no fees. It is strongly recommended that all students have a personal computer.

Graduates: From July 1, 2002 to June 30, 2003, 345 bachelor's degrees were awarded. The most popular majors were marine science (13%), management (11%), and international business (11%). In an average class, 1% graduate in 3 years or less, 64% graduate in 4 years or less, 65% graduate in 5 years or less, and 67% graduate in 6 years or less. 110 companies recruited on campus in a recent year. Of the 2002 graduating class, 28% were enrolled in graduate school within 6 months of graduation and 64% were employed.

Admissions Contact: Richard Hallin, Dean of Admissions.
E-mail: *hallinrr@eckerd.edu* Web: *http://www.eckerd.edu*

EDWARD WATERS COLLEGE
Jacksonville, FL 32209

D-1

(904) 470-8202
(888) 898-3191; Fax: (904) 470-8048

Full-time: 661 men, 600 women	Faculty: 44
Part-time: 20 men, 19 women	Ph.D.s: 18%
Graduate: none	Student/Faculty: 29 to 1
Year: semesters, summer session	Tuition: $8344
Application Deadline: n/av	Room & Board: $6030
Freshman Class: 2374 applied, 800 accepted, 511 enrolled	
SAT I Verbal/Math: 390/380	ACT: 16 LESS COMPETITIVE

Edward Waters College, founded in 1866, is the oldest independent institution of higher learning in Florida. Affiliated with the African Methodist Episcopal Church, the college offers programs in the arts and sciences, business, and education. The library contains 65,798 volumes and 2900 audio/video tapes/CDs, and subscribes to 1350 periodicals. Computerized library services include the card catalog, interlibrary loans, database searching, and Internet access. Special learning facilities include a learning resource center, an art gallery, and a museum of African art. The 50-acre campus is in an urban area in Jacksonville. Including any residence halls, there are 25 buildings.

Student Life: 90% of undergraduates are from Florida. Students are from 12 states, 4 foreign countries, and Canada. 90% are from public schools. 95% are African American. The average age of freshmen is 18; all undergraduates, 20. 40% do not continue beyond their first year; 60% remain to graduate.

Housing: 584 students can be accommodated in college housing, which includes single-sex dorms. In addition, there are honors dorms. 53% of students live on campus; of those, 45% remain on campus on weekends. Alcohol is not permitted. All students may keep cars.

Activities: 20% of men belong to 4 national fraternities; 35% of women belong to 4 national sororities. There are 20 groups on campus, including band, cheerleading, choir, chorus, dance, drama, drill team, honors, international, jazz band, marching band, newspaper, pep band, photography, political, professional, religious, social service, student government, and yearbook. Popular campus events include Fall and Spring Convocations, Religious Emphasis Week, and African American History Celebration.

Sports: There are 6 intercollegiate sports for men and 5 for women, and 3 intramural sports for men and 3 for women. Facilities are off campus.

Disabled Students: 75% of the campus is accessible. Wheelchair ramps, elevators, special parking, specially equipped rest rooms, and lowered drinking fountains are available.

Services: Counseling and information services are available, as is tutoring in every subject. There is remedial math, reading, and writing. There is a student support services program for students who are academically disadvantaged. Academic career counseling employment services are available.

Campus Safety and Security: Measures include 24-hour foot and vehicle patrol, security escort services, informal discussions, and emergency telephones. There are lighted pathways/sidewalks.

Programs of Study: EWC confers B.A., B.S., and B.B.A. degrees. Bachelor's degrees are awarded in BIOLOGICAL SCIENCE (biology/ biological science), BUSINESS (accounting and business administration and management), COMMUNICATIONS AND THE ARTS (communications and English), COMPUTER AND PHYSICAL SCIENCE (computer science and mathematics), EDUCATION (early childhood, elementary, and physical), SOCIAL SCIENCE (criminal justice, history, philosophy, political science/government, psychology, religion, and sociology). Education is the strongest academically. Business administration is the largest.

Required: To graduate, all students must complete at least 120 credit hours, including 30 in the major, with a 2.0 GPA overall and in the major. Weekly chapel service attendance is required.

Special: EWC offers co-op programs, internships in communications, political science, education, and criminal justice, dual and student-designed majors, and work-study programs. A dual law degree with Florida Coastal School of Law and a 3-2 engineering degree with Florida A&M University are offered. There is a freshman honors program.

Faculty/Classroom: 50% of faculty are male; 50%, female. All teach undergraduates.

Admissions: 34% of the 2003-2004 applicants were accepted. The SAT I scores for the 2003-2004 freshman class were: Verbal--98% below 500, and 2% between 500 and 599; Math--98% below 500, and 2% between 500 and 599. The ACT scores were 99% below 21. 10% of the current freshmen were in the top fifth of their class; 58% were in the top two fifths. There were 3 National Merit finalists.

Requirements: The SAT I or ACT is required for some programs. In addition, SAT I or ACT scores are necessary for unconditional admission. Applicants must be graduates of an accredited secondary school or have a GED certificate, and have taken the California Achievement Test. EWC requires applicants to be in the upper 20% of their class. A GPA of 2.0 is required. AP and CLEP credits are accepted. Important factors in the admissions decision are advanced placement or honor courses, ability to finance college education, and recommendations by school officials.

Procedure: Freshmen are admitted fall and spring. The college accepts all applicants. Check with the school for current application deadlines. Notification is sent on a rolling basis. The 2003 fall application fee was $25. There is a rolling admissions plan. Applications are accepted online.

Transfer: 30 of 120 credits required for the bachelor's degree must be completed at EWC.

Visiting: There are guides for informal visits. To schedule a visit, contact the Admissions Office.

Financial Aid: In 2003-2004, 80% of all full-time freshmen and 86% of continuing full-time students received some form of financial aid. 82% of full-time freshmen and 91% of continuing full-time students received need-based aid. The average freshman award was $9550, with $2400 ($5830 maximum) from need-based scholarships or need-based grants, $2950 ($9125 maximum) from need-based self-help aid (loans and jobs); $2095 ($7187 maximum) from non-need-based athletic scholarships; and $2105 ($4250 maximum) from other non-need-based awards and non-need-based scholarships. 23% of undergraduates work part time. Average annual earnings from campus work are $1790. The average financial indebtedness of the 2003 graduate was $9500. EWC is a member of CSS. The FAFSA is required. The priority date for freshman financial aid applications for fall entry is April 15.

International Students: There are 39 international students enrolled. The school actively recruits these students. They must take an English proficiency exam and are encouraged to take the TOEFL.

Computers: The mainframe is an AS400. There are computer labs in 3 academic buildings and 3 in the library. All students may access the system. There are no time limits and no fees.

Graduates: From July 1, 2002 to June 30, 2003, 126 bachelor's degrees were awarded. The most popular majors were organizational management (69%), business administration (11%), and criminal justice (5%). In an average class, 20% graduate in 4 years or less, 23% graduate in 5 years or less, and 25% graduate in 6 years or less. 250 companies recruited on campus in 2002-2003.

Admissions Contact: Tony Baldwin, Director of Enrollment. A video is available. E-mail: *tabaldwin@ewc.edu* Web: *www.ewc.edu*

EMBRY-RIDDLE AERONAUTICAL UNIVERSITY   D-2
Daytona Beach, FL 32114   (386) 226-6112
                                  (800) 862-2416; Fax: (386) 226-7070

Full-time: 3435 men, 724 women	**Faculty:** 207; IIA, av$
Part-time: 287 men, 72 women	**Ph.D.s:** 91%
Graduate: 303 men, 105 women	**Student/Faculty:** 20 to 1
Year: semesters, summer session	**Tuition:** $21,360
Application Deadline: July 1	**Room & Board:** $6370
Freshman Class: 3073 applied, 2507 accepted, 1017 enrolled	
SAT I Verbal/Math: 550/570	**ACT:** 24 **COMPETITIVE+**

Embry-Riddle Aeronautical University, founded in 1926, is a private institution offering undergraduate programs in aviation, engineering, and business on 2 campuses: one in Daytona Beach and the other, founded in 1978, in Prescott, Arizona. There are 4 undergraduate schools and 1 graduate school. In addition to regional accreditation, ERAU has baccalaureate program accreditation with ABET and ACBSP. The library contains 143,515 volumes, 779 microform items, and 7534 audio/video tapes/CDs, and subscribes to 761 periodicals. Computerized library services include the card catalog, interlibrary loans, and database searching. Special learning facilities include a learning resource center, radio station, an airway science simulation lab, and a College of Aviation Building. The 164-acre campus is in an urban area 48 miles northeast of Orlando. Including any residence halls, there are 48 buildings.

Student Life: 71% of undergraduates are from out of state, mostly the South. Students are from 50 states, 94 foreign countries, and Canada. 66% are white; 10% foreign nationals. The average age of freshmen is 18; all undergraduates, 21. 23% do not continue beyond their first year; 47% remain to graduate.

Housing: 1889 students can be accommodated in college housing, which includes coed dorms, on-campus apartments, off-campus apartments, and married-student housing. On-campus housing is guaranteed for the freshman year only, is available on a first-come, first-served basis, and is available on a lottery system for upperclassmen. 57% of students commute. All students may keep cars.

Activities: 9% of men belong to 12 national fraternities; 9% of women belong to 3 national sororities. There are 124 groups on campus, including cheerleading, chess, choir, computers, dance, debate, drama, drill team, ethnic, film, gay, honors, international, literary magazine, musical theater, newspaper, pep band, photography, political, professional, radio and TV, religious, social, social service, student government, and yearbook. Popular campus events include Spring Concert and Hypnotist.

Sports: There are 6 intercollegiate sports for men and 5 for women, and 18 intramural sports for men and 17 for women. Facilities include a field house with a full-size basketball court and 2 practice courts, a fitness center, a weight room, softball and soccer fields, a swimming pool, a Nautilus/weight room, racquetball and tennis courts, and a fitness trail.

Disabled Students: 95% of the campus is accessible. Wheelchair ramps, elevators, special parking, specially equipped rest rooms, lowered drinking fountains, lowered telephones, and ADA-compliant signage and reception counters are available.

Services: Counseling and information services are available, as is tutoring in most subjects. There is remedial math, reading, and writing.

Campus Safety and Security: Measures include 24-hour foot and vehicle patrol, self-defense education, security escort services, and shuttle buses. There are informal discussions, pamphlets/posters/films, emergency telephones, lighted pathways/sidewalks, and "Call A Ride And Live" (CARAL).

Programs of Study: ERAU confers the B.S. degree. Associate and master's degrees are also awarded. Bachelor's degrees are awarded in BUSINESS (business administration, management, and transportation management), COMMUNICATIONS AND THE ARTS (communications), COMPUTER AND PHYSICAL SCIENCE (atmospheric sciences and meteorology, computer science, and software engineering), ENGINEERING AND ENVIRONMENTAL DESIGN (aeronautical engineering, aeronautical science, aeronautical technology, aerospace studies, air traffic control, aviation maintenance management, civil engineering, computer engineering, computer graphics, electrical/electronics engineering, engineering physics, and engineering technology), SOCIAL SCIENCE (safety science). Aeronautics is the strongest academically. Aeronautical science (flight) is the largest.

Required: To graduate, students must complete a total of 120 to 136 credit hours, including 60 in the major, with a minimum GPA of 2.0. All students must complete 36 credits of general education requirements, including courses in communication skills, technical report writing, humanities/social sciences, math, physical science, economics, and computer science.

Special: ERAU offers co-op programs and internships in all majors, study abroad in 19 countries, work-study programs, credit for life experience, and nondegree study. There are 6 national honor societies.

Faculty/Classroom: 78% of faculty are male; 22%, female. All teach undergraduates, 8% do research, and 8% do both. No introductory courses are taught by graduate students. The average class size in an introductory lecture is 30; in a laboratory, 16; and in a regular course, 28.

Admissions: 82% of the 2003-2004 applicants were accepted. The SAT I scores for the 2003-2004 freshman class were: Verbal--27% below 500, 45% between 500 and 599, 25% between 600 and 700, and 3% above 700; Math--17% below 500, 42% between 500 and 599, 35% between 600 and 700, and 5% above 700. The ACT scores were 19% below 21, 24% between 21 and 23, 31% between 24 and 26, 14% between 27 and 28, and 12% above 28. 40% of the current freshmen were in the top fifth of their class; 68% were in the top two fifths. 11 freshmen graduated first in their class.

Requirements: The SAT I or ACT is required. In addition, students should complete a competitive academic program in high school, including 16 Carnegie units with at least 3 years of math. Admissions decisions are based on the strength of the academic record, rank in class, standardized test scores, recommendations, and the written statement. AP and CLEP credits are accepted. Important factors in the admissions decision are advanced placement or honor courses, recommendations by school officials, and evidence of special talent.

Procedure: Freshmen are admitted to all sessions. Entrance exams should be taken during spring of the junior year or fall of the senior year. There is a rolling admissions plan and an early decision plan. Early decision applications should be filed by December 1; regular applications, by July 1 for fall entry, November 1 for spring entry, and April 1 for summer entry. Notification of early decision is sent December ; regular decision, on a rolling basis. 151 early decision candidates were accepted for the 2003-2004 class. The 2003 fall applications fee was $30. Applications are accepted on computer disk and on-line through *www.db.erau.edu/application.html.*

Transfer: 273 transfer students enrolled in 2002-2003. A GPA of 2.5 is preferred. 30 of 120 to 136 credits required for the bachelor's degree must be completed at ERAU.

Visiting: There are regularly scheduled orientations for prospective students. There are guides for informal visits and visitors may sit in on classes and stay overnight. To schedule a visit, contact the Admissions Office at (386) 226-6100 or *dbadmit@erau.edu.*

Financial Aid: In 2003-2004, 70% of all full-time freshmen and 66% of continuing full-time students received some form of financial aid. 87% of full-time freshmen and 80% of continuing full-time students received need-based aid. The average freshman award was $13,641. Need-based scholarships or need-based grants averaged $3727 ($10,000 maximum); need-based self-help aid (loans and jobs) averaged $5794 ($6000 maximum); non-need-based athletic scholarships averaged $11,556 ($13,000 maximum); and other non-need-based awards and non-need-based scholarships averaged $4567 ($10,000 maximum). 37% of undergraduates work part time. Average annual earnings from campus work are $2435. The average financial indebtedness of the 2003 graduate was $36,022. ERAU is a member of CSS. The FAFSA is required. The deadline for filing freshman financial aid applications for fall entry is April 15.

International Students: There are 402 international students enrolled. The school actively recruits these students. They must score 500 on the written TOEFL and also take the SAT I or the ACT.

Computers: The mainframes are IBM, Solaris, and Compaq servers. The campus network has two parts: academic/administrative facilities and the residence hall network. The academic facilities have direct access to network applications, printing, and the university intranet (ERAU Online) where many course materials are located. The residence hall network is structured so that every resident student has a network port. It is through this connection that students access the university Intranet, the Internet; Internet2; a software application installation server; game servers; and other academic-and entertainment-oriented network items. There are currently 1,800 student-owned computers registered in ResNet. All students may access the system at any time. There are no time limits and no fees. It is recommended that students in the computer science program have personal computers.

Graduates: From July 1, 2002 to June 30, 2003, 835 bachelor's degrees were awarded. The most popular majors were aeronautical science (40%), aerospace engineering (14%), and aviation business administration (7%). In an average class, 21% graduate in 4 years or less, 42% graduate in 5 years or less, and 47% graduate in 6 years or less. 175 companies recruited on campus in 2002-2003. Of the 2002 graduating class, 14% were enrolled in graduate school within 6 months of graduation and 92% were employed.

Admissions Contact: Michael Novak, Director of Admissions. A video is available. E-mail: *admit@db.erau.edu* Web: *www.embryriddle.edu*

FLAGLER COLLEGE
St. Augustine, FL 32084   D-2

(904) 829-6481
(800) 304-4208; Fax: (904) 826-0094

Full-time: 763 men, 1223 women	**Faculty:** 62
Part-time: 15 men, 32 women	**Ph.D.s:** 65%
Graduate: none	**Student/Faculty:** 32 to 1
Year: semesters, summer session	**Tuition:** $7410
Application Deadline: March 1	**Room & Board:** $4450
Freshman Class: 1897 applied, 628 accepted, 443 enrolled	
SAT I Verbal/Math: 570/560	**ACT:** 23 **VERY COMPETITIVE+**

Flagler College, founded in 1968, is an independent liberal arts college. Some information in the above capsule is approximate. The library contains 80,522 volumes, 70,020 microform items, and 2880 audio/video tapes/CDs, and subscribes to 458 periodicals. Computerized library services include the card catalog, interlibrary loans, and database searching. Special learning facilities include a learning resource center, art gallery, and radio station. The 35-acre campus is in a small town 35 miles south of Jacksonville and 45 miles north of Daytona Beach. Including any residence halls, there are 13 buildings.

Student Life: 67% of undergraduates are from Florida. Students are from 46 states, 23 foreign countries, and Canada. 93% are white. The average age of freshmen is 18; all undergraduates, 21. 32% do not continue beyond their first year.

Housing: 720 students can be accommodated in college housing, which includes single-sex dorms. On-campus housing is guaranteed for the freshman year only and is available on a first-come, first-served basis. 62% of students commute. Alcohol is not permitted. All students may keep cars.

Activities: There are no fraternities or sororities. There are 25 groups on campus, including art, cheerleading, choir, chorus, dance, drama, film, honors, literary magazine, newspaper, photography, professional, radio and TV, religious, social service, and student government. Popular campus events include Flagler Forum; Fall, Spring, Parents, and Luau Weekends; and Spirit Week.

Sports: There are 6 intercollegiate sports for men and 6 for women, and 9 intramural sports for men and 10 for women. Facilities include a 17-acre complex for baseball and soccer, 8 tennis courts, a swimming pool, and a multipurpose gym.

Disabled Students: 80% of the campus is accessible. Wheelchair ramps, elevators, special parking, specially equipped rest rooms, lowered drinking fountains, lowered telephones, and special housing are available.

Services: Counseling and information services are available. Tutoring is available only by referral and based upon private contract between tutor and student. There is a reader service for the blind and remedial math, reading, and writing.

Campus Safety and Security: Measures include 24-hour foot and vehicle patrol, self-defense education, informal discussions, and pamphlets/posters/films. There are emergency telephones and lighted pathways/sidewalks.

Programs of Study: Flagler confers the B.A. degree. Bachelor's degrees are awarded in BUSINESS (accounting, business administration and management, and sports management), COMMUNICATIONS AND THE ARTS (art, communications, dramatic arts, English, fine arts, graphic design, and Spanish), EDUCATION (art, education of the deaf and hearing impaired, elementary, and secondary), SOCIAL SCIENCE (history, Latin American studies, philosophy, political science/government, psychology, religion, and social science). Business, education, and Latin American studies are the strongest academically. Business, education, and communications are the largest.

Required: To graduate, students must complete a minimum of 120 semester hours, including 30 to 90 hours in the major, with a minimum GPA of 2.0. All students must take 6 hours in English composition, 6 hours in math, and 3 hours in speech communication. In addition, students must take 15 hours of courses required by the general education program in humanities, social sciences, and math/natural sciences. Students must demonstrate basic computer skills, complete a career planning program, and pass all subtests of the College Level Academic Skills Test (CLAST).

Special: The school offers internships, work-study, and dual majors. Students may participate in study-abroad programs in almost any country. Students majoring in deaf education can work directly with students at the Florida State School for the Deaf and Blind. Students in the fashion buying, merchandising, or design programs participate in the visiting student program at the Fashion Institute of Technology in New York City. There are 4 national honor societies and 2 departmental honors programs.

Faculty/Classroom: 63% of faculty are male; 37%, female. All teach undergraduates. The average class size in an introductory lecture is 30; in a laboratory, 12; and in a regular course, 22.

Admissions: 33% of the 2003-2004 applicants were accepted. The SAT I scores for the 2003-2004 freshman class were: Verbal--12% below 500, 56% between 500 and 599, 30% between 600 and 700, and 3% above 700; Math--13% below 500, 60% between 500 and 599, 26% between 600 and 700, and 2% above 700. The ACT scores were 11% below 21, 41% between 21 and 23, 30% between 24 and 26, 13% between 27 and 28, and 6% above 28. 45% of the current freshmen were in the top fifth of their class; 79% were in the top two fifths. 3 freshmen graduated first in their class in a recent year.

Requirements: The SAT I or ACT is required. In addition, graduation from an accredited secondary school, or a satisfactory score on the GED, is required for admission. Students must have a total of 19 academic credits. High school courses must include 4 credits of English, 3 credits each of math and science, and 2 credits of a foreign language. An essay is required, and an interview is recommended. Flagler requires applicants to be in the upper 50% of their class. A GPA of 2.75 is required. AP and CLEP credits are accepted. Important factors in the admissions decision are advanced placement or honor courses, leadership record, and extracurricular activities record.

Procedure: Freshmen are admitted fall and spring. Entrance exams should be taken during the fall of the senior year at the latest. There are early decision and deferred admissions plans. Early decision applications should be filed by January 15; regular applications, by March 1 for fall entry and October 15 for winter entry, along with a $20 fee. Notification of early decision is sent February 1; regular decision, March 15. Applications are accepted on computer disk and on-line through CollegeNET.

Transfer: 100 transfer students enrolled in a recent year. Transfer students must have a minimum of 24 semester hours with a minimum GPA of 2.5. Transfers must also score at least 1010 on the SAT I or 21 on the ACT. 45 of 120 credits required for the bachelor's degree must be completed at Flagler.

Visiting: There are guides for informal visits and visitors may sit in on classes and stay overnight. To schedule a visit, contact the Office of Admissions.

Financial Aid: In 2003-2004, 81% of all full-time freshmen and 87% of continuing full-time students received some form of financial aid. 36% of full-time freshmen and 42% of continuing full-time students received need-based aid. The average freshman award was $7109. Need-based scholarships or need-based grants averaged $2942 ($11,860 maximum); need-based self-help aid (loans and jobs) averaged $2461 ($3625 maximum); non-need-based athletic scholarships averaged $2604 ($11,860 maximum); and other non-need-based awards and non-need-based scholarships averaged $4529 ($12,195 maximum). 60% of undergraduates work part time. Average annual earnings from campus work are

$487. The average financial indebtedness of a recent graduate was $15,988. The FAFSA and the college's own financial statement are required. Check with the school for current deadlines.

International Students: There were 58 international students enrolled in a recent year. They must score 550 on the written TOEFL.

Computers: The mainframe is a DEC PDP 11/34A. The college has a ratio of 1 computer to every 8 students. All have access to the Internet and the Web. All students may access the system during library hours. There are no time limits and no fees.

Graduates: In a recent year, 361 bachelor's degrees were awarded. The most popular majors were business administration (24%), education (19%), and communication (14%). In an average class, 41% graduate in 4 years or less, 54% graduate in 5 years or less, and 54% graduate in 6 years or less. 2 companies recruited on campus in 2002-2003. Of the 2002 graduating class, 12% were enrolled in graduate school within 6 months of graduation and 24% were employed.

Admissions Contact: Marc G. Williar, Director of Admissions. A video is available. E-mail: *admiss@flagler.edu* Web: *www.flagler.edu*

FLORIDA AGRICULTURAL AND MECHANICAL UNIVERSITY

C-1

Tallahassee, FL 32307-3200

(850) 599-3796
Fax: (850) 599-3069

Full-time: 4348 men, 6138 women	**Faculty:** 607; IIA, +$
Part-time: 590 men, 725 women	**Ph.D.s:** 76%
Graduate: 348 men, 654 women	**Student/Faculty:** 17 to 1
Year: semesters, summer session	**Tuition:** $3013 ($13,368)
Application Deadline: May 15	**Room & Board:** $4551
Freshman Class: 5467 applied, 3875 accepted, 2143 enrolled	
SAT I or ACT: required	COMPETITIVE

Florida Agricultural and Mechanical University, founded in 1887 and a public institution within the state university system of Florida, offers undergraduate programs in agriculture, allied health science, architecture, the arts and sciences, business and industry, education, engineering, journalism, pharmacy and pharmaceutical sciences, upper-level nursing, and technology. There are 14 undergraduate schools and 1 graduate school. In addition to regional accreditation, Florida A&M has baccalaureate program accreditation with AACSB, ABET, ACEJMC, ACPE, APTA, CSWE, NAAB, NCATE, and NLN. The 6 libraries contain 781,408 volumes, 171,926 microform items, and 75,622 audio/video tapes/CDs, and subscribe to 10,137 periodicals. Computerized library services include the card catalog, interlibrary loans, database searching, and Internet access. Special learning facilities include a learning resource center, art gallery, radio station, TV station, black archives, and an observatory. The 422-acre campus is in an urban area 169 miles east of Jacksonville. Including any residence halls, there are 155 buildings.

Student Life: 79% of undergraduates are from Florida. Students are from 46 states, 49 foreign countries, and Canada. 95% are from public schools. 94% are African American. The average age of freshmen is 19; all undergraduates, 22. 20% do not continue beyond their first year.

Housing: 3356 students can be accommodated in college housing, which includes single-sex dorms, on-campus apartments, and married-student housing. On-campus housing is guaranteed for the freshman year only and is available on a first-come, first-served basis. Priority is given to out-of-town students. 51% of students commute. Alcohol is not permitted. Upperclassmen may keep cars.

Activities: There are 5 national fraternities and 4 national sororities. There are 147 groups on campus, including cheerleading, choir, chorus, dance, drama, drill team, ethnic, honors, international, jazz band, marching band, newspaper, orchestra, pep band, political, professional, radio and TV, religious, social, social service, student government, symphony, and yearbook. Popular campus events include FAMU Essence Theater, FAMU Orchesis Dance Theater, and Ebony Fashion Fair.

Sports: There are 9 intercollegiate sports for men and 8 for women and 14 intramural sports for men and women. Facilities include a 3300-seat gym, a 1600-seat auditorium, a 25,559-seat football stadium, swimming pools, baseball diamonds, softball and track fields, tennis courts, a bowling alley, a pool hall, a student activities center, and a fitness center.

Disabled Students: 90% of the campus is accessible. Wheelchair ramps, elevators, special parking, and specially equipped rest rooms are available.

Services: Counseling and information services are available, as is tutoring in some subjects, including math, English, and reading. There is remedial math, reading, and writing.

Campus Safety and Security: Measures include 24-hour foot and vehicle patrol, self-defense education, security escort services, and informal discussions. There are pamphlets/posters/films and lighted pathways/sidewalks.

Programs of Study: Florida A&M confers B.A., B.S., B.Arch., B.C.J., B.S.Arch. and Constr.E.T., B.S.Arch.E.T., B.S.Studies., B.S.C.E., B.S.C.E.T., B.S.Ch.E., B.S.Constr.E.T., B.S.E.E., B.S.Elect.E.T., B.S.H.C.M., B.S.I.E., B.S.J., B.S.M.E., B.S.M.R.A., B.S.N., B.S.Pharm., B.S.P.T., B.S.R.T., B.S.T., and B.S.W. degrees. Associate, master's, and doctoral degrees are also awarded. Bachelor's degrees are awarded in AGRICULTURE (animal science and horticulture), BIOLOGICAL SCIENCE (biology/biological science), BUSINESS (accounting, banking and finance, business administration and management, and business economics), COMMUNICATIONS AND THE ARTS (dramatic arts, English, fine arts, journalism, and music), COMPUTER AND PHYSICAL SCIENCE (actuarial science, chemistry, computer science, mathematics, and physics), EDUCATION (art, business, early childhood, elementary, industrial arts, music, and science), ENGINEERING AND ENVIRONMENTAL DESIGN (chemical engineering, civil engineering, electrical/electronics engineering, engineering technology, industrial engineering, and mechanical engineering), HEALTH PROFESSIONS (nursing, occupational therapy, pharmacy, physical therapy, predentistry, and premedicine), SOCIAL SCIENCE (criminal justice, economics, history, political science/government, psychology, public administration, social science, social work, and sociology). Business, engineering, and pharmacy are the strongest academically. Business, pharmacy, and arts and sciences are the largest.

Required: General education requirements include 36 credit hours in English, humanities, social science, natural science, American history, foreign language, and math at the college algebra level or above. In order to graduate, students must complete at least 120 credit hours, including 30 in a major field, with a minimum GPA of 2.0.

Special: Cooperative programs and cross-registration are offered in conjunction with Florida State University. Internships are available either on or off campus. Florida A&M also offers a Washington semester for architecture majors, a B.A.-B.S. degree, credit for life experience, and pass/fail options. Nondegree study is possible. There are 10 national honor societies and a freshman honors program.

Faculty/Classroom: 33% of faculty are male; 37%, female. No introductory courses are taught by graduate students. The average class size in an introductory lecture is 40; in a laboratory, 15; and in a regular course, 40.

Admissions: 71% of the 2003-2004 applicants were accepted. The ACT scores for the 2003-2004 freshman class were: 69% below 20, 23% between 21 and 24, 6% between 25 and 28, 1% between 29 and 32, and 1% above 33.

Requirements: The SAT I or ACT is required, with a minimum composite score of 900 on the SAT I, or 450 on each part, or 19 on the ACT. Applicants must be graduates of accredited secondary schools or have earned a GED. The university requires 19 academic credits, including 4 each in English and academic electives, 3 each in math, science, and social studies, and 2 in foreign language. A GPA of 2.0 is required. AP and CLEP credits are accepted. Important factors in the admissions decision are recommendations by school officials, extracurricular activities record, and evidence of special talent.

Procedure: Freshmen are admitted to all sessions. Entrance exams should be taken by the fall of the senior year. There is a deferred admissions plan. Applications should be filed by May 15 for fall entry, November 15 for spring entry, and April 1 for summer entry. The fall 2003 application fee was $20. Notification is sent on a rolling basis.

Transfer: Applicants must present a minimum GPA of 2.0 in at least 60 semester hours or 90 quarter hours earned. 30 of 120 credits required for the bachelor's degree must be completed at Florida A&M.

Visiting: There are regularly scheduled orientations for prospective students. There are guides for informal visits and visitors may sit in on classes. To schedule a visit, contact Ms. Sheryl Cooper at (850) 599-3869.

Financial Aid: 1% of undergraduates work part time. Average annual earnings from campus work are $1800. The average financial indebtedness of the 2003 graduate was $23,000. The university prefers the FAFSA but will accept the CSS Profile. The priority date for freshman financial aid applications for fall entry is March 1. The deadline for filing freshman financial aid applications for fall entry is June 30.

International Students: There are 113 international students enrolled. They must score 500 on the written TOEFL and also take the SAT I or the ACT.

Computers: The mainframe is an IBM 4381 model 13. The school provides more than 100 PCs and Macs for academic use. All students may access the system. There are no time limits and no fees.

Graduates: From July 1, 2002 to June 30, 2003, 1437 bachelor's degrees were awarded. The most popular majors were business administration (16%), psychology (7%), and elementary education (6%). 600 companies recruited on campus in a recent year.

Admissions Contact: Mitchie Stewart, Interim Director. E-mail: *mitchie.stewart@famu.edu* Web: *www.famu.edu*

FLORIDA ATLANTIC UNIVERSITY
Boca Raton, FL 33431-0991

E-5

(561) 297-3040
(800) 299-4FAU; Fax: (561) 297-2758

Full-time: 4411 men, 6288 women	**Faculty:** 895; I, --$
Part-time: 3748 men, 6625 women	**Ph.D.s:** 94%
Graduate: 1563 men, 2383 women	**Student/Faculty:** 12 to 1
Year: semesters, summer session	**Tuition:** $2943 ($13,955)
Application Deadline: June 1	**Room & Board:** $5600
Freshman Class: 7898 applied, 5612 accepted, 2178 enrolled	
SAT I Verbal/Math: 511/515	**ACT:** 20 COMPETITIVE

Florida Atlantic University, founded in 1961, is a publicly funded liberal arts institution in the state university system of Florida. There are 8 undergraduate and 8 graduate schools. In addition to regional accreditation, FAU has baccalaureate program accreditation with AACSB, ABET, ACS, ASLHA, CSAB, CSWE, NAAB, NAACLS, NASM, NASPAA, NCATE, and NLN. The library contains 902,834 volumes, 1,915,696 microform items, and 11,107 audio/video tapes/CDs, and subscribes to 3836 periodicals. Computerized library services include the card catalog, interlibrary loans, and database searching. Special learning facilities include a learning resource center, art gallery, radio station, TV station, engineering research labs, a marine sciences research center, a K-8 developmental research school, a nonnative fish research lab, and an environmental sciences center. The 860-acre campus is in a suburban area 17 miles north of Fort Lauderdale, 45 miles north of Miami, and 22 miles south of Palm Beach. Including any residence halls, there are 88 buildings.

Student Life: 92% of undergraduates are from Florida. Students are from 49 states, 144 foreign countries, and Canada. 59% are white; 17% African American; 14% Hispanic. The average age of freshmen is 19; all undergraduates, 25. 34% do not continue beyond their first year; 38% remain to graduate.

Housing: 2200 students can be accommodated in college housing, which includes single-sex and coed dorms, on-campus apartments, and married-student housing. In addition, there are honors houses, wellness and quiet floors, and apartments for students age 21 and older. On-campus housing is guaranteed for the freshman year only and is available on a first-come, first-served basis. 92% of students commute. All students may keep cars.

Activities: 1% of men belong to 12 national fraternities; 1% of women belong to 9 national sororities. There are 170 groups on campus, including art, band, cheerleading, chess, choir, chorale, chorus, computers, dance, drama, ethnic, film, gay, honors, international, jazz band, literary magazine, marching band, musical theater, newspaper, opera, orchestra, pep band, political, professional, radio and TV, religious, social, social service, and student government. Popular campus events include Luau, African American Festival, and Earth Day.

Sports: There are 8 intercollegiate sports for men and 9 for women, and 10 intramural sports for men and 10 for women. Facilities include an athletic center, a gym, a weight room, baseball and softball stadiums, a lighted soccer field, a 25-meter swimming pool with 1- and 10-meter diving boards, lighted outdoor jai alai, a dance area, and 8 tennis, 5 racquetball, 4 badminton, 3 volleyball, and 2 basketball courts.

Disabled Students: All of the campus is accessible. Wheelchair ramps, elevators, special parking, specially equipped rest rooms, lowered drinking fountains, and lowered telephones are available.

Services: Counseling and information services are available, as is tutoring in most subjects. There is a reader service for the blind. Remedial work must be taken at the community college level.

Campus Safety and Security: Measures include 24-hour foot and vehicle patrol, self-defense education, security escort services, and shuttle buses. There are informal discussions, pamphlets/posters/films, emergency telephones, and lighted pathways/sidewalks.

Programs of Study: FAU confers B.A., B.S., B.A.E., B.Arch., B.B.A., B.F.A., B.H.S., B.Mus., B.P.M., B.S.C.E., B.S.C.V., B.S.E., B.S.E.E., B.S.H.S., B.S.M.E., B.S.M.T., B.S.N., B.S.O.E., B.S.W., and B.U.R.P. degrees. Associate, master's, and doctoral degrees are also awarded. Bachelor's degrees are awarded in BIOLOGICAL SCIENCE (biology/biological science and marine biology), BUSINESS (accounting, banking and finance, business administration and management, international business management, marketing/retailing/merchandising, real estate, and small business management), COMMUNICATIONS AND THE ARTS (art, communications, dramatic arts, English, fine arts, French, German, graphic design, Italian, journalism, linguistics, music, and Spanish), COMPUTER AND PHYSICAL SCIENCE (chemistry, computer science, geology, information sciences and systems, mathematics, and physics), EDUCATION (elementary, English, foreign languages, physical, and special), ENGINEERING AND ENVIRONMENTAL DESIGN (architecture, computer engineering, electrical/electronics engineering, mechanical engineering, ocean engineering, and urban planning technology), HEALTH PROFESSIONS (health care administration, health science, medical laboratory technology, and nursing), SOCIAL SCIENCE (anthropology, criminal justice, economics, geography, history, interdisciplinary studies, Judaic studies, liberal arts/general studies, phi-

losophy, political science/government, psychobiology, psychology, public administration, social psychology, social science, social work, and sociology). Engineering, education, and business are the strongest academically. Elementary education, management, and accounting are the largest.

Required: All students must take the College Level Academic Skills Test (CLAST) required by the state. To graduate, students must complete a total of 120 credit hours, with a minimum GPA of 2.0. All students must take the required courses in the core curriculum, including 9 credits each of humanities and social sciences, and 6 each of math, communication, and natural sciences, and must demonstrate proficiency in a foreign language.

Special: FAU offers cooperative programs and internships in most majors. Work-study programs, dual and student-designed majors, a general studies degree, credit for military experience, nondegree study, and pass/fail options are available. The school offers a Washington semester, study abroad through all state university system of Florida programs, and an exchange program in ocean engineering with the Polytechnic University of Madrid, Spain; there is also a study-abroad center in Salamanca, Spain. Cross-registration is available with all Florida state universities, in science and engineering with Palm Beach and Broward Community Colleges, and in military science with the University of Miami. Students may earn a second baccalaureate degree with 30 additional hours in a number of subjects. There are 15 national honor societies, a freshman honors program, and 9 departmental honors programs.

Faculty/Classroom: 59% of faculty are male; 41%, female. All both teach and do research. Graduate students teach 5% of introductory courses. The average class size in an introductory lecture is 50; in a laboratory, 15; and in a regular course, 25.

Admissions: 71% of the 2003-2004 applicants were accepted. The SAT I scores for the 2003-2004 freshman class were: Verbal--44% below 500, 43% between 500 and 599, 12% between 600 and 700, and 1% above 700; Math--40% below 500, 44% between 500 and 599, 14% between 600 and 700, and 1% above 700. The ACT scores were 57% below 21, 25% between 21 and 23, 11% between 24 and 26, 5% between 27 and 28, and 3% above 28. There were 4 National Merit finalists and 1 semifinalist in a recent year.

Requirements: The SAT I or ACT is required, with a minimum composite score of 1000 on the SAT I or 23 on the ACT. In addition, graduation from an accredited secondary school or satisfactory scores on the GED are required. Students must have 19 academic credits, including 4 units of English, 3 each of math (algebra I and higher), science (including 2 with substantial lab work), and social studies, and 2 of a foreign language, plus 4 of electives in computer science, fine arts, or humanities. A portfolio or an audition may be requested by individual departments. An essay and an interview are required. A GPA of 2.0 is required. AP and CLEP credits are accepted. Important factors in the admissions decision are advanced placement or honor courses, evidence of special talent, and recommendations by school officials.

Procedure: Freshmen are admitted to all sessions. Entrance exams should be taken by June. There are early decision, early admissions, and deferred admissions plans. Applications should be filed by June 1 for fall entry, October 15 for spring entry, and March 15 for summer entry. There is a rolling admissions plan. Notification is sent on a rolling basis. The fall 2003 application fee was $20. 11 early decision candidates were accepted for a recent class. Applications are accepted on-line.

Transfer: Students must have a minimum GPA of 2.0, submit official transcripts from the previous schools attended, and be in good standing at those institutions. Applicants from a community or junior college in Florida with an associate degree are automatically admitted. Students with fewer than 60 transferable hours must meet the same criteria as entering freshmen. 30 credits of 120 required for the bachelor's degree must be completed at FAU.

Visiting: There are regularly scheduled orientations for prospective students, consisting of a group tour. There are guides for informal visits. To schedule a visit, contact the Admissions Office.

Financial Aid: In a recent year, 61% of all full-time freshmen and 34% of continuing full-time students received some form of financial aid. 52% of full-time freshmen and 29% of continuing full-time students received need-based aid. The average freshman award was $1731. 5% of undergraduates work part time. Average annual earnings from campus work are $3200. FAU is a member of CSS. The FAFSA is required. The deadline for filing freshman financial aid applications for fall entry is March 1.

International Students: There were 747 international students enrolled in a recent year. The school actively recruits these students. They must score 550 on the written TOEFL or 213 on the electronic version and also take the SAT I or the ACT.

Computers: The mainframe is a DEC VAX 6320. There are more than 400 on-campus PCs available for student use. Students may access the mainframe at various sites on campus or via modem. In addition, there is an on-campus network, including e-mail, Bitnet, and common software. All students may access the system. Labs are open from 8 A.M. to 11 P.M. weekdays and various hours on weekends; there is modem access 24 hours a day. There are no time limits and no fees.

Graduates: From July 1, 2002 to June 30, 2003, 3591 bachelor's degrees were awarded. The most popular majors were elementary education (11%), finance (5%), and accounting (5%). In an average class, 16% graduate in 4 years or less, 32% graduate in 5 years or less, and 38% graduate in 6 years or less. 200 companies recruited on campus in 2002-2003.

Admissions Contact: Albert Colom, Director of Admissions. A video is available. E-mail: *admisweb@fau.edu* Web: *www.fau.edu*

FLORIDA GULF COAST UNIVERSITY
H-6
Fort Myers, FL 33965-6565
(941) 590-7891
(888) 889-1095; Fax: (941) 590-7894

Full-time: 1273 men, 2099 women	**Faculty:** 192; IIA, -$
Part-time: 670 men, 1190 women	**Ph.D.s:** 83%
Graduate: 264 men, 482 women	**Student/Faculty:** 18 to 1
Year: semesters, summer session	**Tuition:** $2908 ($13,263)
Application Deadline: March 1	**Room & Board:** $7000
Freshman Class: 2578 applied, 1854 accepted, 885 enrolled	
SAT I Verbal/Math: 520/510	**ACT:** 21 **COMPETITIVE**

Florida Gulf Coast University, founded in 1991, is part of the State University System of Florida. There are 5 undergraduate schools. In addition to regional accreditation, FGCU has baccalaureate program accreditation with AOTA, APTA, and NLN. The library contains 282,357 volumes, 527,687 microform items, and 2295 audio/video tapes/CDs, and subscribes to 1429 periodicals. Computerized library services include the card catalog, interlibrary loans, database searching, and Internet access. Special learning facilities include a learning resource center, art gallery, radio station, TV station, chickee huts, computer labs, and family resource center. The 760-acre campus is in a rural area in southwest Florida in southern Lee County. Including any residence halls, there are 44 buildings.
Student Life: 91% of undergraduates are from Florida. Students are from 49 states, 66 foreign countries, and Canada. 81% are white. The average age of freshmen is 18; all undergraduates, 25. 30% do not continue beyond their first year; 31% remain to graduate.
Housing: 1374 students can be accommodated in college housing, which includes coed on-campus apartments. On-campus housing is available on a first-come, first-served basis. 76% of students commute. Alcohol is not permitted. All students may keep cars.
Activities: 1% of men belong to 1 national fraternity; 1% of women belong to 1 national sorority. There are 89 groups on campus, including cheerleading, chess, choir, dance, debate, drama, ethnic, honors, international, newspaper, professional, religious, social, social service, and student government. Popular campus events include Jazz on the Green and Eagle Expo.
Sports: There are 6 intercollegiate sports for men and 6 for women, and 4 intramural sports for men and 4 for women. Facilities include a fitness center, a lakefront, a 4500-seat teaching gym, 2 playing fields, and 12 tennis courts.
Disabled Students: All of the campus is accessible. Wheelchair ramps, elevators, special parking, specially equipped rest rooms, special class scheduling, lowered drinking fountains, and lowered telephones are available.
Services: Counseling and information services are available, as is tutoring in most subjects.
Campus Safety and Security: Measures include 24-hour foot and vehicle patrol, self-defense education, security escort services, and shuttle buses. There are informal discussions, pamphlets/posters/films, emergency telephones, and lighted pathways/sidewalks.
Programs of Study: FGCU confers B.A. and B.S. degrees. Associate and master's degrees are also awarded. Bachelor's degrees are awarded in BUSINESS (accounting, banking and finance, management science, and marketing and distribution), COMPUTER AND PHYSICAL SCIENCE (computer science and information sciences and systems), EDUCATION (early childhood, elementary, and special), HEALTH PROFESSIONS (health science, nursing, and physical therapy), SOCIAL SCIENCE (criminal justice, human services, liberal arts/general studies, paralegal studies, and political science/government). Management and elementary education are the largest.
Required: To graduate, students must have a 2.0 minimum GPA and 120 credit hours that include courses in phys ed, computer science, general education, service learning, and university colloquium.
Special: The university offers cross-registration with the University of Central Florida, study abroad in China, a Washington semester, and work-study programs. There is 1 national honor society, including Phi Beta Kappa, a freshman honors program, and 1 departmental honors program.
Faculty/Classroom: 48% of faculty are male; 52%, female. All both teach and do research. No introductory courses are taught by graduate students. The average class size in an introductory lecture is 25; in a laboratory, 23; and in a regular course, 21.
Admissions: 72% of the 2003-2004 applicants were accepted. The SAT I scores for the 2003-2004 freshman class were: Verbal--39% below

500, 47% between 500 and 599, 12% between 600 and 700, and 1% above 700; Math--41% below 500, 44% between 500 and 599, 15% between 600 and 700, and 1% above 700. The ACT scores were 43% below 21, 34% between 21 and 23, 16% between 24 and 26, 4% between 27 and 28, and 2% above 28. 37% of the current freshmen were in the top fifth of their class; 71% were in the top two fifths. 1 freshman graduated first in the class.
Requirements: The SAT I or ACT is recommended. A GPA of 2.0 is required. AP and CLEP credits are accepted. Important factors in the admissions decision are recommendations by school officials, leadership record, and evidence of special talent.
Procedure: Freshmen are admitted fall, spring, and summer. Entrance exams should be taken in the junior year. Applications should be filed by March 1 for fall entry, October 15 for spring entry, and March 1 for summer entry, along with a $30 fee. Applications are accepted on-line through the university's web site.
Transfer: 615 transfer students enrolled in 2002-2003. Lower level transfers must meet the same requirements as regular admissions. Upper level transfers must have a 2.0 GPA and 60 hours of transferable credit, and be in good standing at their last institution. 30 of 120 credits required for the bachelor's degree must be completed at FGCU.
Visiting: There are regularly scheduled orientations for prospective students. There are guides for informal visits and visitors may sit in on classes. To schedule a visit, contact the Admissions Office at (888) 889-1095 or (239) 590-7878 or *admissions@fgcu.edu*.
Financial Aid: In 2003-2004, 84% of all full-time freshmen and 74% of continuing full-time students received some form of financial aid. 42% of all full-time students received need-based aid. The average freshman award was $5860. Need-based scholarships or need-based grants averaged $3501 ($7650 maximum); need-based self-help aid (loans and jobs) averaged $2566 ($4950 maximum); non-need-based athletic scholarships averaged $2207 ($5500 maximum); and other non-need-based awards and non-need-based scholarships averaged $3501 ($22,625 maximum). 80% of undergraduates work part time. Average annual earnings from campus work are $6000. The average financial indebtedness of the 2003 graduate was $17,125. The FAFSA is required. The priority date for freshman financial aid applications for fall entry is April 1.
International Students: There are 51 international students enrolled. The school actively recruits these students. They must score 550 on the written TOEFL or 213 on the electronic version and also take the SAT I or the ACT, scoring 880 (SAT I) or 16 (ACT).
Computers: 14 computer labs/classrooms and 313 university-owned computers are available for classroom and personal use and for on-line admissions and course schedules. All students may access the system any time. There are no time limits and no fees.
Graduates: From July 1, 2002 to June 30, 2003, 621 bachelor's degrees were awarded. The most popular majors were liberal arts/liberal studies (24%), elementary education (13%), and nursing (11%).
Admissions Contact: F. Larry Stiles, Director of Admissions.
E-mail: *oar@fgcu.edu* Web: *http://www.fgcu.edu*

FLORIDA HOSPITAL COLLEGE OF HEALTH SCIENCES
D-3
Orlando, FL 32803
(407) 303-5548
(800) 500-7747; Fax: (407) 303-9408

Full-time: 129 men, 478 women	**Faculty:** 37
Part-time: 214 men, 580 women	**Ph.D.s:** 5%
Graduate: none	**Student/Faculty:** 16 to 1
Year: semesters, summer session	**Tuition:** $5300
Application Deadline: July 13	**Room & Board:** $1600
Freshman Class: 12 applied, 12 accepted, 11 enrolled	
SAT I: n/av	**ACT:** required **SPECIAL**

Florida Hospital College of Health Sciences, founded in 1992 and affiliated with the Seventh-day Adventist Church, is a private institution offering programs in allied health, nursing, and preprofessional studies. In addition to regional accreditation, Florida Hospital College of Health Sciences has baccalaureate program accreditation with NLN and JR-CERT. The library contains 13,857 volumes and 1720 audio/video tapes/CDs, and subscribes to 167 periodicals. Computerized library services include the card catalog, interlibrary loans, database searching, and Internet access. Special learning facilities include a learning resource center. The 9-acre campus is in an urban area in Orlando. Including any residence halls, there are 6 buildings.
Student Life: 75% of undergraduates are from Florida. Students are from 46 states, 4 foreign countries, and Canada. 78% are from public schools. 57% are white; 15% Hispanic; 14% African American. 34% claim no religious affiliation; 20% Protestant; 14% Catholic. The average age of freshmen is 29; all undergraduates, 29.
Housing: 124 students can be accommodated in college housing, which includes single-sex and coed dorms and off-campus apartments. On-campus housing is available on a first-come, first-served basis. Priori-

ty is given to out-of-town students. 90% of students commute. Alcohol is not permitted. No one may keep cars.

Activities: There are no fraternities or sororities. There are 12 groups on campus, including drama, newspaper, religious, student government, and yearbook. Popular campus events include Fall Festival, International Food Festival, and Spring Picnic.

Sports: There are 3 intramural sports for men and 3 for women. Facilities include an outdoor sports court, canoes, a game room, and billiards.

Disabled Students: All of the campus is accessible. Wheelchair ramps, elevators, special parking, specially equipped rest rooms, and lowered drinking fountains are available.

Services: Counseling and information services are available, as is tutoring in some subjects, including English, math, chemistry, anatomy and physiology, and statistics. There is remedial math and writing.

Campus Safety and Security: Measures include 24-hour foot and vehicle patrol, security escort services, shuttle buses, and informal discussions. There are pamphlets/posters/films and lighted pathways/sidewalks.

Programs of Study: Florida Hospital College of Health Sciences confers the B.S. degree. Associate degrees are also awarded. Bachelor's degrees are awarded in HEALTH PROFESSIONS (health science, nursing, and radiological science). Nursing and radiography are the strongest academically. Nursing and radiological sciences are the largest.

Required: Students must take at least 127 credits and maintain a GPA of 2.0.

Faculty/Classroom: 36% of faculty are male; 64%, female. All teach undergraduates. The average class size in an introductory lecture is 27; in a laboratory, 22; and in a regular course, 22.

Admissions: All of the 2003-2004 applicants were accepted.

Requirements: The ACT is required. A GPA of 2.5 is required. AP and CLEP credits are accepted.

Procedure: Freshmen are admitted to all sessions. Applications should be filed by July 13 for fall entry, November 25 for winter entry, and March 22 for summer entry, along with a $20 fee. A waiting list is an active part of the admissions procedure.

Transfer: 1160 transfer students enrolled in 2002-2003. Applicants must submit the completed application, the application fee, all previous transcripts, and ACT scores, if applicable. 86 of 127 credits required for the bachelor's degree must be completed at Florida Hospital College of Health Sciences.

Visiting: There are regularly scheduled orientations for prospective students, including fall and spring open houses. There are guides for informal visits and visitors may sit in on classes. To schedule a visit, contact Yvette Saliba at (407) 303-1878 or *yvette.saliba@fhchs.edu.*

Financial Aid: In 2003-2004, 77% of all full-time freshmen and 70% of continuing full-time students received some form of financial aid. 40% of full-time freshmen and 39% of continuing full-time students received need-based aid. The average freshman award was $2650. Need-based scholarships or need-based grants averaged $1739 ($2650 maximum); need-based self-help aid (loans and jobs) averaged $1313 (maximum); and non-need-based awards and non-need-based scholarships averaged $451 ($2226 maximum). 10% of undergraduates work part time. Average annual earnings from campus work are $2000. The FAFSA and the college's own financial statement are required. The deadline for filing freshman financial aid applications for fall entry is April 12.

International Students: There are 47 international students enrolled. They must score 550 on the written TOEFL or 213 on the electronic version and also take the SAT I or the ACT, scoring 19.

Computers: The mainframe is an IBM AS400. Students have access to 50 PCs in the learning resource center, computer lab, and library. All students may access the system during regular hours of operation. There are no time limits and no fees. It is strongly recommended that all students have a personal computer.

Graduates: From July 1, 2002 to June 30, 2003, 28 bachelor's degrees were awarded. The most popular majors were radiography (53%) and nursing (46%). In an average class, 36% graduate in 3 years or less, and 39% graduate in 4 years or less.

Admissions Contact: Fiona Ghosn, Director of Admissions.
E-mail: *fiona.ghosn@fhchs.edu* Web: *www.fhchs.edu*

FLORIDA INSTITUTE OF TECHNOLOGY E-3
Melbourne, FL 32901-6975 (321) 674-8030
(800) 888-4348; Fax: (321) 723-9468

Full-time: 1546 men, 671 women	Faculty: 180
Part-time: 90 men, 39 women	Ph.D.s: 94%
Graduate: 1456 men, 887 women	Student/Faculty: 12 to 1
Year: semesters, summer session	Tuition: $22,600
Application Deadline: open	Room & Board: $6140
Freshman Class: 2657 applied, 2196 accepted, 551 enrolled	
SAT I Verbal/Math: 560/600	ACT: 25 VERY COMPETITIVE

Florida Institute of Technology, founded in 1958, offers undergraduate degrees in engineering and science, liberal arts, management, psychology, and aeronautics. There are 5 undergraduate and 6 graduate schools.

In addition to regional accreditation, Florida Tech has baccalaureate program accreditation with ABET, ACS, APA, CAA, and CSAB. The library contains 407,492 volumes, 304,937 microform items, and 3176 audio/video tapes/CDs, and subscribes to 6567 periodicals. Computerized library services include the card catalog, interlibrary loans, and database searching. Special learning facilities include a learning resource center, radio station, and TV station. The 130-acre campus is in a small town 70 miles east of Orlando. Including any residence halls, there are 75 buildings.

Student Life: 46% of undergraduates are from out of state, mostly the Northeast. Students are from 46 states, 88 foreign countries, and Canada. 73% are from public schools. 55% are white; 21% foreign nationals. The average age of freshmen is 18; all undergraduates, 21. 21% do not continue beyond their first year; 54% remain to graduate.

Housing: 1347 students can be accommodated in college housing, which includes single-sex and coed dorms and on-campus apartments. On-campus housing is guaranteed for the freshman year only and is available on a first-come, first-served basis. 53% of students live on campus; of those, 78% remain on campus on weekends. All students may keep cars.

Activities: 15% of men belong to 6 national fraternities; 15% of women belong to 1 local and 2 national sororities. There are 107 groups on campus, including band, cheerleading, chess, chorus, computers, dance, drama, drill team, environmental, ethnic, gay, honors, international, jazz band, literary magazine, newspaper, pep band, political, professional, radio and TV, religious, science fiction, social, social service, student government, and yearbook. Popular campus events include Basketball games, Poor Man's Mardi Gras, and Big Man on Campus.

Sports: There are 5 intercollegiate sports for men and 5 for women, and 28 intramural sports for men and 28 for women. Facilities include a sports and recreation center, with 2 basketball courts, a racquetball court, and a 5000-square-foot weight and fitness area with cardiovascular machines, free weights, and specialized weight equipment.

Disabled Students: 90% of the campus is accessible. Wheelchair ramps, elevators, special parking, specially equipped rest rooms, special class scheduling, lowered drinking fountains, and lowered telephones are available.

Services: Counseling and information services are available, as is tutoring in every subject. There is a reader service for the blind, and remedial math, reading, and writing.

Campus Safety and Security: Measures include 24-hour foot and vehicle patrol, self-defense education, security escort services, and informal discussions. There are pamphlets/posters/films, emergency telephones, lighted pathways/sidewalks, and formal "Personal Safety and Security" sessions are given to all University Experience classes by security staff.

Programs of Study: Florida Tech confers B.A. and B.S. degrees. Master's and doctoral degrees are also awarded. Bachelor's degrees are awarded in BIOLOGICAL SCIENCE (biochemistry, biology/biological science, ecology, marine biology, and molecular biology), BUSINESS (accounting, business administration and management, and management information systems), COMMUNICATIONS AND THE ARTS (communications), COMPUTER AND PHYSICAL SCIENCE (applied mathematics, astrophysics, atmospheric sciences and meteorology, chemistry, computer science, information sciences and systems, oceanography, physics, and planetary and space science), EDUCATION (computer, mathematics, and science), ENGINEERING AND ENVIRONMENTAL DESIGN (aeronautical engineering, aeronautical science, aviation administration/management, aviation computer technology, chemical engineering, civil engineering, computer engineering, electrical/electronics engineering, environmental science, mechanical engineering, military science, and ocean engineering), HEALTH PROFESSIONS (premedicine), SOCIAL SCIENCE (forensic studies, humanities, interdisciplinary studies, and psychology). Engineering, science, and aeronautics are the strongest academically. Computer engineering, aerospace engineering, and aviation management are the largest.

Required: To graduate, students must have a minimum 2.0 GPA and 120 to 135 credit hours. The required number of hours in the major varies. All students must take 9 hours in communication and humanities and 3 in English composition. The core curriculum also requires 6 credit hours each in physical or life sciences and math, and 3 hours in computer science and social sciences.

Special: Florida Tech offers co-op programs in all majors. Students may choose to pursue more than 1 degree by completing degree requirements for each major. Internships are available in the senior year for many majors, including psychology, engineering, and aeronautics. Study abroad and work-study programs are available. There are 9 national honor societies.

Faculty/Classroom: 81% of faculty are male; 19%, female. 7% teach undergraduates, 5% do research, and 88% do both. Graduate students teach 15% of introductory courses. The average class size in an introductory lecture is 29; in a laboratory, 19; and in a regular course, 24.

Admissions: 83% of the 2003-2004 applicants were accepted. The SAT I scores for the 2003-2004 freshman class were: Verbal--20% below 500, 43% between 500 and 599, 33% between 600 and 700, and 4%

above 700; Math--10% below 500, 36% between 500 and 599, 44% between 600 and 700, and 10% above 700. The ACT scores were 17% below 21, 20% between 21 and 23, 32% between 24 and 26, 18% between 27 and 28, and 13% above 28. 50% of the current freshmen were in the top fifth of their class; 79% were in the top two fifths. There were 2 National Merit finalists. 12 freshmen graduated first in their class.

Requirements: The SAT I or ACT is required. In addition, applicants must be graduates of an accredited secondary school or have a GED certificate. At least 18 academic credits or Carnegie units are required, including 4 years each of English, math, and science. An experiential essay is required and an interview is recommended. A GPA of 2.8 is required. AP and CLEP credits are accepted. Important factors in the admissions decision are advanced placement or honor courses, recommendations by school officials, and extracurricular activities record.

Procedure: Freshmen are admitted fall and spring. Entrance exams should be taken during the junior year or the beginning of the senior year of high school. There are early admissions, deferred admissions, and rolling admission plans. Application deadlines are open. The fall 2003 application fee was $40. Applications are accepted on-line through *www.fit.edu/ugrad/apply.htm.*

Transfer: 172 transfer students enrolled in 2002-2003. Applicants must have a minimum 2.5 GPA. If transfer students have fewer than 30 semester hours, high school transcripts and SAT I or ACT scores are required. A personal statement is recommended. 30 of 120 credits required for the bachelor's degree must be completed at Florida Tech.

Visiting: There are regularly scheduled orientations for prospective students, including tours and interviews with admissions staff, faculty, or department heads upon request. There are guides for informal visits and visitors may sit in on classes. To schedule a visit, contact the Admissions Office at *admission@fit.edu.*

Financial Aid: In 2003-2004, all full-time freshmen and 89% of continuing full-time students received some form of financial aid. 74% of full-time freshmen and 68% of continuing full-time students received need-based aid. The average freshman award was $16,434. Need-based scholarships or need-based grants averaged $13,759 ($30,841 maximum); need-based self-help aid (loans and jobs) averaged $4838 ($11,125 maximum); non-need-based athletic scholarships averaged $11,477 ($23,387 maximum); and other non-need-based awards and non-need-based scholarships averaged $8713 ($29,441 maximum). 29% of undergraduates work part time. Average annual earnings from campus work was $1475. The average financial indebtedness of the 2003 graduate was $20,644. The FAFSA is required. The deadline for filing freshman financial aid applications for fall entry is March 15.

International Students: There are 460 international students enrolled. The school actively recruits these students. They must score 550 on the written TOEFL or 213 on the electronic version and also take a math entrance qualifying exam. If students score below 550 on the TOEFL, they take language courses on campus. They also take the SAT I (minimum 950) or the ACT.

Computers: Students may access the system through more than 250 workstations located in general public or department labs. All student residence halls on the central campus have direct network access in their rooms. Students have access internally to the Florida Tech web-based intranet and externally to the Internet. All students may access the system 24 hours per day. There are no time limits and no fees.

Graduates: The most popular majors were aviation management (10%), computer engineering (9%), and business administration (8%). In an average class, 35% graduate in 4 years or less, 52% graduate in 5 years or less, and 54% graduate in 6 years or less. 72 companies recruited on campus in 2002-2003. Of the 2002 graduating class, 28% were enrolled in graduate school within 6 months of graduation and 56% were employed.

Admissions Contact: Judi Marino, Director, Undergraduate Admissions. A video is available. E-mail: *jmarino@fit.edu*
Web: *http://www.fit.edu*

FLORIDA INTERNATIONAL UNIVERSITY E-5

Miami, FL 33199 (305) 348-2363; Fax: (305) 348-3648

Full-time: 6852 men, 9383 women	Faculty: 745; I, --$
Part-time: 4820 men, 6114 women	Ph.D.s: 97%
Graduate: 2439 men, 3520 women	Student/Faculty: 22 to 1
Year: semesters, summer session	Tuition: $2889 ($13,917)
Application Deadline: open	Room & Board: $7023
Freshman Class: 8450 applied, 3634 accepted, 1739 enrolled	
SAT I Verbal/Math: 570/570	ACT: 25 VERY COMPETITIVE

Florida International University, founded in 1965, is part of the State University System of Florida. Undergraduate degrees are offered through the Colleges of Arts and Sciences, Business Administration, Education, Engineering, Health, Science, and Urban and Public Affairs; and the Schools of Accounting, Computer Science, Architecture, Hospitality Management, Music, and Journalism and Mass Communication. The North and University Park campuses are in Miami, and there are 2 edu-

cational centers in Fort Lauderdale. There are 14 undergraduate and 15 graduate schools. In addition to regional accreditation, FIU has baccalaureate program accreditation with AACSB, ABET, ACCE, ACEJMC, ADA, APTA, ASLA, CSWE, NAAB, NASM, NCATE, and NLN. The 2 libraries contain 1,673,224 volumes, 3,442,044 microform items, and 142,029 audio/video tapes/CDs, and subscribe to 8666 periodicals. Computerized library services include the card catalog, interlibrary loans, and database searching. Special learning facilities include a learning resource center, radio station, and an art museum. The 573-acre campus is in an urban area 10 miles west of downtown Miami. Including any residence halls, there are 24 buildings.

Student Life: 91% of undergraduates are from Florida. Students are from 50 states, 126 foreign countries, and Canada. 61% are from public schools. 54% are Hispanic; 21% white; 14% African American. The average age of freshmen is 19; all undergraduates, 24. 5% do not continue beyond their first year; 63% remain to graduate.

Housing: 2200 students can be accommodated in college housing, which includes coed dorms, on-campus apartments, and married-student housing. On-campus housing is available on a first-come, first-served basis. 95% of students commute. All students may keep cars.

Activities: 9% of men belong to 10 national fraternities; 10% of women belong to 1 local and 9 national sororities. There are 150 groups on campus, including band, cheerleading, chorus, drama, ethnic, gay, honors, international, marching band, newspaper, political, professional, radio and TV, religious, social, social service, student government, and yearbook.

Sports: There are 6 intercollegiate sports for men and 9 for women, and 14 intramural sports for men and 10 for women. Facilities include a 5000-seat arena with basketball and racquetball courts, an aquatic center, baseball and soccer fields, a fitness center with Nautilus machines, and a racquet sports center with lighted tennis and racquetball courts.

Disabled Students: 96% of the campus is accessible. Wheelchair ramps, elevators, special parking, specially equipped rest rooms, special class scheduling, lowered drinking fountains, and lowered telephones are available. There is also accessible computer equipment for visually impaired students, including talking and large-print computers.

Services: Counseling and information services are available, as is tutoring in most subjects. There is a reader service for the blind and remedial math, reading, and writing. Note taking, adapted testing, and special registration may be arranged for disabled students.

Campus Safety and Security: Measures include 24-hour foot and vehicle patrol, security escort services, informal discussions, and pamphlets/posters/films. There are emergency telephones and lighted pathways/sidewalks.

Programs of Study: FIU confers B.A., B.S., B.Ac., B.B.A., B.F.A., B.H.S.A., B.M., B.P.A., and B.S.N. degrees. Associate, master's, and doctoral degrees are also awarded. Bachelor's degrees are awarded in BIOLOGICAL SCIENCE (biology/biological science and marine biology), BUSINESS (accounting, banking and finance, business administration and management, hospitality management services, international business management, management information systems, management science, marketing/retailing/merchandising, personnel management, real estate, tourism, and transportation management), COMMUNICATIONS AND THE ARTS (art, art history and appreciation, communications, dance, dramatic arts, English, French, German, music, Portuguese, and Spanish), COMPUTER AND PHYSICAL SCIENCE (applied mathematics, chemistry, computer science, geology, information sciences and systems, mathematics, physics, and statistics), EDUCATION (art, education of the emotionally handicapped, education of the mentally handicapped, elementary, English, foreign languages, health, home economics, mathematics, music, physical, science, social studies, special, specific learning disabilities, and vocational), ENGINEERING AND ENVIRONMENTAL DESIGN (architectural technology, biomedical engineering, chemical engineering, civil engineering, computer engineering, construction management, electrical/electronics engineering, environmental science, industrial engineering, interior design, and mechanical engineering), HEALTH PROFESSIONS (health care administration, health science, nursing, occupational therapy, and rehabilitation therapy), SOCIAL SCIENCE (Asian/Oriental studies, criminal justice, dietetics, economics, geography, history, humanities, international relations, Italian studies, liberal arts/general studies, parks and recreation management, philosophy, political science/government, psychology, public administration, religion, social work, sociology, urban studies, and women's studies). Accounting, engineering, and biology are the strongest academically. Accounting, hospitality management, and elementary education are the largest.

Required: To graduate, students must complete between 120 and 152 hours with a 2.0 GPA. There are also general education and writing requirements. Students admitted with fewer than 48 hours must complete the core curriculum.

Special: FIU offers co-op and work-study programs, and study abroad in 6 countries. Accelerated degree programs, nondegree study, dual majors, and B.A.-B.S. degrees in chemistry, enviromental studies, and geology may also be arranged. There are 25 national honor societies, a freshman honors program, and 18 departmental honors programs.

Faculty/Classroom: 66% of faculty are male; 34%, female. All both teach and do research. Graduate students teach 32% of introductory courses. The average class size in an introductory lecture is 41; in a laboratory, 15; and in a regular course, 23.

Admissions: 43% of the 2003-2004 applicants were accepted. The SAT I scores for the 2003-2004 freshman class were: Verbal--8% below 500, 58% between 500 and 599, 30% between 600 and 700, and 4% above 700; Math--6% below 500, 59% between 500 and 599, 31% between 600 and 700, and 4% above 700. The ACT scores were 1% below 21, 24% between 21 and 23, 50% between 24 and 26, 14% between 27 and 28, and 11% above 28. 9 freshmen graduated first in their class.

Requirements: The SAT I or ACT is required. In addition, applicants must be graduates of an accredited secondary school or have a GED certificate. The required academic courses include 4 units in English, 3 each in math, natural science, and social studies, 2 in a foreign language, and 4 in academic electives. The university's placement tests must be taken the semester before attending. An interview may be required. A GPA of 2.0 is required. AP and CLEP credits are accepted. Important factors in the admissions decision are advanced placement or honor courses, evidence of special talent, and recommendations by school officials.

Procedure: Freshmen are admitted fall, spring, and summer. Entrance exams should be taken during the spring of the junior year. There are early admissions and deferred admissions plans. There is a rolling admissions plan. Application deadlines are open. Application fee is $25. Applications are accepted on-line.

Transfer: 2370 transfer students enrolled in 2002-2003. Applicants with fewer than 60 semester credits must meet regular freshman admissions requirements. All students must pass the CLAST or take the pre-CLAST testing program during the first term of enrollment, fulfill core curriculum or general education requirements, and have a 2.0 GPA. 30 of 120 to 152 credits required for the bachelor's degree must be completed at FIU.

Visiting: There are regularly scheduled orientations for prospective students, including placement tests, advising, a tour, and student activities. There are guides for informal visits and visitors may sit in on classes. To schedule a visit, contact the Office of Admissions.

Financial Aid: In a recent year, 52% of all full-time freshmen and 40% of continuing full-time students received some form of financial aid. 72% of full-time freshmen and 73% of continuing full-time students received need-based aid. The average freshman award was $4191. 6% of undergraduates work part time. Average annual earnings from campus work are $2000. The average financial indebtedness of a recent graduate was $4650. FIU is a member of CSS. The FAFSA is required. The deadline for filing freshman financial aid applications for fall entry is March 1.

International Students: There are 1219 international students enrolled. The school actively recruits these students. They must score 500 on the written TOEFL or 173 on the electronic version and also take the SAT I or the ACT.

Computers: The mainframes are a DEC VAX 8800 and a Sun 4/280. Students may access the campus Ethernet network through terminals and PCs and through dial-up access from home. All students may access the system 8 A.M. to 4 A.M. There are no time limits and no fees.

Graduates: From July 1, 2002 to June 30, 2003, 4708 bachelor's degrees were awarded. The most popular majors were business (41%), education (8%), and psychology (6%). In an average class, 1% graduate in 3 years or less, 19% graduate in 4 years or less, 39% graduate in 5 years or less, and 50% graduate in 6 years or less. 180 companies recruited on campus in a recent year. Of a recent graduating class, 37% were enrolled in graduate school within 6 months of graduation and 70% were employed.

Admissions Contact: Carmen Brown, Admissions Director.
E-mail: *brownc@fiu.edu* Web: *www.fiu.edu*

FLORIDA MEMORIAL COLLEGE
E-5
Miami, FL 33054
(305) 626-3750
(800) 822-1362; Fax: (305) 626-3769

Full-time: n/av none	Faculty: 80
Part-time: n/av none	Ph.D.s: 40%
Graduate: n/av none	Student/Faculty: 18 to 1
Year: , summer session	Tuition: $6000
Application Deadline: open	Room & Board: n/app
Freshman Class: n/av	
SAT I or ACT: required	LESS COMPETITIVE

Florida Memorial College, founded in 1879, is a private liberal arts institution affiliated with the American Baptist Church. Figures given in above capsule and in this profile are approximate. There are 6 undergraduate schools. The library contains 88,000 volumes, and subscribes to 400 periodicals. Special learning facilities include an aviation center. The 77-acre campus is in an urban area in northwestern Miami. There are 12 buildings.

Programs of Study: Florida Memorial confers B.A., and B.S. degrees. Bachelor's degrees are awarded in BIOLOGICAL SCIENCE (biology/ biological science), BUSINESS (accounting, business administration and management, and transportation management), COMMUNICATIONS AND THE ARTS (English, fine arts, and music), COMPUTER AND PHYSICAL SCIENCE (chemistry, computer science, and mathematics), EDUCATION (elementary, physical, and secondary), ENGINEERING AND ENVIRONMENTAL DESIGN (air traffic control, aviation administration/management, and aviation computer technology), SOCIAL SCIENCE (criminal justice, philosophy, political science/government, psychology, public administration, religion, and sociology).

Required: To graduate, all students must complete at least 124 credit hours, including 62 hours of general education requirements, with a minimum overall GPA of 2.0. Students must successfully complete all 4 subtests of the Florida College-Level Academic Skills Test by their junior year.

Special: Private sector and college internships, work-study, and a 3-2 engineering program with the University of Miami are available. Pass/fail credit and nondegree options are possible. There is a freshman honors program.

Requirements: The SAT I or ACT is required. A minimum composite score of 840 is required on the SAT I or 17 on the ACT for education majors. Applicants must be graduates of an accredited secondary school or have a GED certificate. 1 faculty and 2 personal recommendations, an autobiography, and a health certificate are required. Up to 20% of a freshman class may be admitted for 1 semester on a conditional basis to demonstrate their abilities. A GPA of 2.0 is required.

Procedure: Freshmen are admitted fall and spring. Application deadlines are open. The application fee is $15.

Transfer: Transcripts must be submitted for all previous college work, as well as high school transcripts for students with fewer than 3 credits. The SAT I or ACT is recommended. 30 of 124 credits required for the bachelor's degree must be completed at Florida Memorial.

Financial Aid: The CSS Profile or FFS is required. Check with the school for current deadlines.

International Students: They must take the TOEFL.

Computers: The mainframes are an IBM 9375 Model 60 and a DEC VAX 6210. There is an IBM PS/2 microcomputer lab in the aviation center, and another computer lab in the classroom building. All students may access the system. There are no time limits and no fees.

Admissions Contact: Peggy Kelly, Director of Admissions.
Web: *http://www.fmc.edu*

FLORIDA SOUTHERN COLLEGE
D-4
Lakeland, FL 33801-5698
(863) 680-3909
(800) 274-4131; Fax: (863) 680-4120

Full-time: 707 men, 1060 women	Faculty: 106; IIB, av$
Part-time: 37 men, 37 women	Ph.D.s: 90%
Graduate: 15 men, 24 women	Student/Faculty: 17 to 1
Year: semesters, summer session	Tuition: $17,542
Application Deadline: August 1	Room & Board: $6050
Freshman Class: 1735 applied, 1295 accepted, 439 enrolled	
SAT I Verbal/Math: 508/514	ACT: 21 COMPETITIVE

Florida Southern College, founded in 1885, is a private institution affiliated with the United Methodist Church offering undergraduate programs through the divisions of humanities, social sciences, and natural sciences. The library contains 192,684 volumes, 458,541 microform items, and 12,798 audio/video tapes/CDs, and subscribes to 641 periodicals. Computerized library services include the card catalog, interlibrary loans, and database searching. Special learning facilities include a learning resource center, art gallery, and planetarium. The 100-acre campus is in a suburban area 30 miles east of Tampa. Including any residence halls, there are 40 buildings.

Student Life: 70% of undergraduates are from Florida. Students are from 38 states, 43 foreign countries, and Canada. 75% are from public schools. 82% are white. 26% claim no religious affiliation; 24% Protestant; 17% Catholic. The average age of freshmen is 18; all undergraduates, 20. 32% do not continue beyond their first year; 55% remain to graduate.

Housing: 1242 students can be accommodated in college housing, which includes single-sex dorms, married-student housing, fraternity houses, and sorority houses. On-campus housing is guaranteed for all 4 years. 64% of students live on campus; of those, 60% remain on campus on weekends. Alcohol is not permitted. All students may keep cars.

Activities: 21% of men belong to 5 national fraternities; 20% of women belong to 5 national sororities. There are 49 groups on campus, including art, band, cheerleading, choir, chorale, chorus, dance, drama, ethnic, extensive volunteer program, film, honors, international, jazz band, literary magazine, musical theater, newspaper, opera, orchestra, pep band, photography, political, professional, religious, social, student government, and yearbook. Popular campus events include theater productions, a jazz festival, and the Festival of Fine Art series.

Sports: There are 7 intercollegiate sports for men and 8 for women, and 6 intramural sports for men and 6 for women. Facilities include a 2500-seat air-conditioned field house for basketball and volleyball; fields for soccer, softball, and intramurals; 9 lighted tennis courts and a sand volleyball court; aerobics, weight, and fitness facilities; an intramural gym; a heated competitive-size pool; a boathouse for water-skiing equipment. Facilities for baseball games and golf matches are off campus.

Disabled Students: 20% of the campus is accessible. Wheelchair ramps, elevators, special parking, specially equipped rest rooms, special class scheduling, lowered drinking fountains, and lowered telephones are available.

Services: Counseling and information services are available, as is tutoring in some subjects, including math and English.

Campus Safety and Security: Measures include 24-hour foot and vehicle patrol, security escort services, informal discussions, and pamphlets/posters/films. There are emergency telephones and lighted pathways/sidewalks.

Programs of Study: Florida Southern confers B.A., B.S., B.M.E., B.S.M., and B.S.N. degrees. Master's degrees are also awarded. Bachelor's degrees are awarded in AGRICULTURE (horticulture), BIOLOGICAL SCIENCE (biology/biological science), BUSINESS (accounting, banking and finance, business administration and management, business economics, hotel/motel and restaurant management, international business management, marketing/retailing/merchandising, and personnel management), COMMUNICATIONS AND THE ARTS (advertising, communications, dramatic arts, English, journalism, music, public relations, and Spanish), COMPUTER AND PHYSICAL SCIENCE (chemistry, information sciences and systems, and mathematics), EDUCATION (art, athletic training, early childhood, elementary, foreign languages, middle school, music, science, secondary, and special), ENGINEERING AND ENVIRONMENTAL DESIGN (environmental science), SOCIAL SCIENCE (criminal justice, economics, history, humanities, political science/government, psychology, religion, social science, and sociology). Biology, music, and business/economics are the strongest academically. Business, education, and biology are the largest.

Required: To graduate, all students must have completed 124 semester hours of credit, with no more than 42 hours in the major for most programs and a minimum 2.0 GPA. Core requirements include 9 hours of humanities, 8 of natural science, 6 each of English, social sciences, and math, 3 each of history and fine arts, 2 of phys ed, and attendance at faith and life convocation.

Special: Florida Southern offers study abroad in 8 countries, a Washington semester with American University, and a 3-2 engineering degree with Washington University/St. Louis and the University of Miami. Students may choose the United Nations semester in cooperation with Drew University in New Jersey, or the May Option Program, which combines study and travel in England for course credit. Internships with corporations in Tampa, Lakeland, and Orlando are offered through most academic departments and are required by many. Credit for military experience and pass/fail options are available. There are 17 national honor societies and a freshman honors program.

Faculty/Classroom: 61% of faculty are male; 39%, female. All teach undergraduates. No introductory courses are taught by graduate students. The average class size in an introductory lecture is 20; in a laboratory, 15; and in a regular course, 19.

Admissions: 75% of the 2003-2004 applicants were accepted. The SAT I scores for the 2003-2004 freshman class were: Verbal--48% below 500, 36% between 500 and 599, 15% between 600 and 700, and 1% above 700; Math--42% below 500, 43% between 500 and 599, 13% between 600 and 700, and 2% above 700. The ACT scores were 43% below 21, 33% between 21 and 23, 18% between 24 and 26, 5% between 27 and 28, and 1% above 28. 45% of the current freshmen were in the top fifth of their class; 73% were in the top two fifths. 2 freshmen graduated first in their class.

Requirements: The SAT I or ACT is required. A minimum composite score of 950 is required on the SAT I or 20 on the ACT. Applicants must be graduates of an accredited secondary school or have a GED certificate. An essay is required and an interview is recommended. AP and CLEP credits are accepted.

Procedure: Freshmen are admitted to all sessions. Entrance exams should be taken starting in the junior year of high school. There is a deferred admissions plan and a rolling admissions plan. Applications should be filed by August 1 for fall entry and December 1 for spring entry. Notification is sent on a rolling basis. The fall 2003 fall application fee was $30. Applications are accepted on computer disk and on-line through the school's web site.

Transfer: 140 transfer students enrolled in 2002-2003. Transfer students must have a minimum 2.5 GPA and must submit SAT I or ACT scores. An associate degree and an interview are recommended. 31 of 124 credits required for the bachelor's degree must be completed at Florida Southern.

Visiting: There are regularly scheduled orientations for prospective students, including campuswide open houses. There are guides for informal visits and visitors may sit in on classes and stay overnight. To schedule a visit, contact the Admissions Office at *fscadm@flsouthern.edu*.

Financial Aid: In 2003-2004, 96% of all full-time freshmen and 91% of continuing full-time students received some form of financial aid. 72% of full-time freshmen and 74% of continuing full-time students received need-based aid. The average freshman award was $15,924. 78% of undergraduates work part time. Average annual earnings from campus work are $1200. The average financial indebtedness of the 2003 graduate was $13,703. The FAFSA, the college's own financial statement, and the parents' and student's tax returns are required. The deadline for filing freshman financial aid applications for fall entry is March 1.

International Students: There are 74 international students enrolled. The school actively recruits these students. They must score 550 on the written TOEFL.

Computers: The mainframe is an IBM AS/400 ESO. 15 PCs are available in the library for students' academic and word processing needs, and there are 12 specialized computer labs (both PC and Mac) for the courses that require computer use. In addition, a central computer lab has been established with 30 PCs and 6 Macs with extended hours for campuswide use. All students may access the system during lab hours. There are no time limits and no fees. It is strongly recommended that all students have a personal computer.

Graduates: From July 1, 2002 to June 30, 2003, 443 bachelor's degrees were awarded. The most popular majors were business (33%), education (10%), and biology (7%). In an average class, 7% graduate in 3 years or less, 45% graduate in 4 years or less, 55% graduate in 5 years or less, and 56% graduate in 6 years or less. 70 companies recruited on campus in 2002-2003. Of the 2002 graduating class, 15% were enrolled in graduate school within 6 months of graduation and 74% were employed.

Admissions Contact: Barry Connors, Director of Admissions. A video is available. E-mail: *fscadm@flsouthern.edu*
Web: *http://www.flsouthern.edu*

FLORIDA STATE UNIVERSITY
Tallahassee, FL 32306-   C-1   (850) 644-6200; Fax: (850) 644-0197

Full-time: 11,204 men, 14,755 women	**Faculty:** 1403; I, -$
Part-time: 1674 men, 1997 women	**Ph.D.s:** 92%
Graduate: 3201 men, 4053 women	**Student/Faculty:** 19 to 1
Year: semesters, summer session	**Tuition:** $2860 ($13,888)
Application Deadline: March 1	**Room & Board:** $6168
Freshman Class: 18,561 applied, 10,971 accepted, 4111 enrolled	
SAT I Verbal/Math: 590/600	**ACT:** 25 **HIGHLY COMPETITIVE**

Florida State University, a public institution founded in 1851, is a residential university designated as a Doctoral Research (Extensive) University by the Carnegie Foundation for the Advancement of Teaching. There are 15 undergraduate and 16 graduate schools. In addition to regional accreditation, FSU has baccalaureate program accreditation with AACSB, ABET, ADA, AHEA, ASLA, CSWE, FIDER, NASM, NCATE, NLN, and NRPA. The 6 libraries contain 2,620,296 volumes, 9,029,029 microform items, and 73,519 audio/video tapes/CDs, and subscribe to 21,598 periodicals. Computerized library services include the card catalog, interlibrary loans, database searching, and Internet access. Special learning facilities include a learning resource center, art gallery, planetarium, radio station, TV station, nuclear accelerator, x-ray emission lab, marine lab, supercomputers, and the National High Magnetic Field Laboratory. The 448-acre campus is in a suburban area 163 miles west of Jacksonville. Including any residence halls, there are 215 buildings.

Student Life: 82% of undergraduates are from Florida. Students are from 50 states, 118 foreign countries, and Canada. 82% are from public schools. 71% are white; 12% African American. The average age of freshmen is 19; all undergraduates, 21. 16% do not continue beyond their first year.

Housing: 6000 students can be accommodated in college housing, which includes single-sex and coed dorms, on-campus apartments, married-student housing, fraternity houses, and sorority houses. In addition, there are honors houses, special-interest houses, living and learning centers, scholarship houses, academic discipline houses, and music residences. On-campus housing is available on a first-come, first-served basis. All students may keep cars.

Activities: 15% of men belong to 28 national fraternities; 13% of women belong to 21 national sororities. There are 266 groups on campus, including art, band, cheerleading, chess, choir, chorale, chorus, computers, dance, debate, drama, drill team, ethnic, forensics, gay, honors, international, jazz band, literary magazine, marching band, musical theater, newspaper, opera, orchestra, pep band, political, professional, radio and TV, religious, social, social service, student government, symphony, and yearbook. Popular campus events include Twelve Days of Dance, Parents Weekend, and Seven Days of Opening Nights.

Sports: There are 9 intercollegiate sports for men and 10 for women, and 27 intramural sports for men and 27 for women. Facilities include an 80000-seat stadium, an aquatic center with a heated outdoor swimming pool, a golf course, a track, courts for basketball, tennis, racquetball, and handball, a student recreation center with an indoor Olympic-size swimming pool, 2 Jacuzzis, a steam room, a sauna, 10 racquetball courts, a squash court, a multipurpose gym, a 3-lane jogging track, aerobic rooms, aerobic exercise machines, and free and fixed weights, and a lakefront recreation area for outdoor water sports.

Disabled Students: 99% of the campus is accessible. Wheelchair ramps, elevators, special parking, specially equipped rest rooms, special class scheduling, lowered drinking fountains, and lowered telephones are available.

Services: Counseling and information services are available, as is tutoring in most subjects. There is a reader service for the blind, and remedial math, reading, and writing.

Campus Safety and Security: Measures include 24-hour foot and vehicle patrol, self-defense education, security escort services, and shuttle buses. There are informal discussions, pamphlets/posters/films, emergency telephones, lighted pathways/sidewalks, a full time police force, a bicycle identification program, a valuables identification program, and a victim advocate program.

Programs of Study: FSU confers B.A., B.S., B.F.A, B.M., B.M.Ed., and B.S.N. degrees. Associate, master's, and doctoral degrees are also awarded. Bachelor's degrees are awarded in AGRICULTURE (environmental studies and plant science), BIOLOGICAL SCIENCE (biochemistry, biology/biological science, cell biology, ecology, evolutionary biology, genetics, marine biology, molecular biology, nutrition, physiology, and zoology), BUSINESS (accounting, banking and finance, business administration and management, entrepreneurial studies, fashion merchandising, hotel/motel and restaurant management, insurance and risk management, international business management, management information systems, management science, marketing/retailing/ merchandising, personnel management, recreation and leisure services, recreational facilities management, small business management, and sports management), COMMUNICATIONS AND THE ARTS (advertising, American literature, apparel design, art history and appreciation, broadcasting, classics, communications, creative writing, dance, dramatic arts, English, fiber/textiles/weaving, film arts, French, German, Greek, Italian, jazz, Latin, linguistics, music, music history and appreciation, music performance, music theory and composition, musical theater, piano/ organ, public relations, Russian, Spanish, speech/debate/rhetoric, strings, studio art, theater design, voice, and winds), COMPUTER AND PHYSICAL SCIENCE (actuarial science, applied mathematics, atmospheric sciences and meteorology, chemical technology, chemistry, computer science, geology, information sciences and systems, mathematics, physics, and statistics), EDUCATION (art, athletic training, early childhood, education of the emotionally handicapped, education of the mentally handicapped, education of the visually handicapped, elementary, English, foreign languages, health, home economics, mathematics, music, physical, reading, science, social science, and specific learning disabilities), ENGINEERING AND ENVIRONMENTAL DESIGN (bioengineering, biomedical engineering, chemical engineering, civil engineering, computer engineering, electrical/electronics engineering, environmental engineering, environmental science, graphic arts technology, industrial engineering, interior design, materials engineering, and mechanical engineering), HEALTH PROFESSIONS (community health work, music therapy, nursing, predentistry, premedicine, preoptometry, prepharmacy, preveterinary science, rehabilitation therapy, speech pathology/audiology, and sports medicine), SOCIAL SCIENCE (American studies, anthropology, Asian/Oriental studies, Caribbean studies, child care/child and family studies, classical/ancient civilization, clothing and textiles management/ production/services, criminology, dietetics, Eastern European studies, economics, family/consumer studies, fashion design and technology, food science, geography, history, home economics, humanities, international relations, Latin American studies, philosophy, political science/ government, prelaw, psychology, religion, Russian and Slavic studies, social science, social work, sociology, and women's studies). Biology, meteorology, and physics are the strongest academically. Biology, psychology, and business are the largest.

Required: Students must take the Florida College Level Academic Skills Test (CLAST) for admission to upper-division status. The required core curriculum includes 6 semester hours in English composition, 6 to 12 history/social science, 5 to 11 humanities/fine arts, and 7 in natural sciences. All academic areas require at least 120 semester hours for graduation.

Special: Cross-registration with Florida Agricultural and Mechanical University and Tallahassee Community College is possible, as is study at FSU centers in London or Florence and in programs in Costa Rica, France, Russia, Spain, Switzerland, and Vietnam, among other countries. FSU offers cooperative programs in engineering, computer science, business, and communication, work-study programs, general studies and combined B.A.-B.S. degrees, dual majors, and accelerated degree programs. Internships are required in criminology, human science, education, nursing, and social work. There are preprofessional programs in health and law. There are 47 national honor societies, including Phi Beta Kappa, a freshman honors program, and 60 departmental honors programs.

Faculty/Classroom: 62% of faculty are male; 38%, female. Graduate students teach 51% of introductory courses. The average class size in an introductory lecture is 41; in a laboratory, 18; and in a regular course, 35.

Admissions: 59% of the 2003-2004 applicants were accepted. The SAT I scores for the 2003-2004 freshman class were: Verbal--8% below 500, 50% between 500 and 599, 38% between 600 and 700, and 4% above 700; Math--9% below 500, 48% between 500 and 599, 40% between 600 and 700, and 4% above 700. The ACT scores were 5% below 21, 28% between 21 and 23, 34% between 24 and 26, 18% between 27 and 28, and 14% above 28. 87% of the current freshmen were in the top fifth of their class; 95% were in the top two fifths. There were 19 National Merit finalists.

Requirements: The SAT I or ACT is required. In addition, it is recommended that in-state students have at least an A-/B+ weighted average and a minimum composite SAT I score of 1100, or 25 on the ACT. Out-of-state students must meet higher standards. Applicants should have at least the following high school units; 4 in English, 3 in math, natural science, and social science, and 2 in a foreign language. Other factors include the number of honors, AP, and IB classes, strength of academic curriculum, class rank, and others. AP and CLEP credits are accepted. Important factors in the admissions decision are advanced placement or honor courses, evidence of special talent, and recommendations by school officials.

Procedure: Freshmen are admitted fall, spring, and summer. Entrance exams should be taken beginning in the second semester of the junior year. There is an early admissions plan and a rolling admissions plan. Applications should be filed by March 1 for fall entry, November 1 for spring entry, and March 1 for summer entry, along with a $30 fee. Notification is sent on a rolling basis. Applications are accepted on-line through the school's web site.

Transfer: 1875 transfer students enrolled in 2002-2003. Transfer applicants should present at least a 2.5 cumulative college GPA unless transferring from a Florida public community college with an associate in arts degree, in which case the minimum college GPA needed varies according to major. Applicants with less than 60 semester hours of transferable credit must also meet freshman admission requirements. All transfers must have completed 2 years of the same foreign language in high school or have 8 semester hours at the college level. Students must pass the Florida CLAST Examination. 30 of 120 credits required for the bachelor's degree must be completed at FSU.

Visiting: There are regularly scheduled orientations for prospective students, including campus tours several times daily on weekdays. Walking and riding tours are available and tours are coordinated around an 11:00 admissions information session. There are guides for informal visits and visitors may sit in on classes. To schedule a visit, contact Visitor Services at (850) 644-3246 or visitorservices@admin.fsu.edu.

Financial Aid: In 2003-2004, 41% of all full-time students received some form of financial aid. 31% of all full-time students received need-based aid. The average freshman award was $4147. Need-based scholarships or need-based grants averaged $3608; need-based self-help aid (loans and jobs) averaged $2839; non-need-based athletic scholarships averaged $5514; and other non-need-based awards and non-need-based scholarships averaged $2601. 2% of undergraduates work part time. Average annual earnings from campus work are $1778. The average financial indebtedness of the 2003 graduate was $17,112. The FAFSA and the college's own financial statement are required. The priority date for freshman financial aid applications for fall entry is February 15. The deadline for filing freshman financial aid applications for fall entry is March 1.

International Students: There are 341 international students enrolled. They must score 550 on the written TOEFL or 213 on the electronic version and also take the SAT I or the ACT.

Computers: The mainframes are an IBM SP3, an IBM P690 cluster, an IBM Z900, and 2064-105 Z series with 5 processors. The campus is fully wired and wireless in many locations. All students may access the system, although use of some machines is restricted to particular majors or graduate students. There are no time limits and no fees. It is strongly recommended that all students have a personal computer. It is recommended that students in engineering programs have personal computers. A PC with a 1.8 GHz Pentium 4, 128 MB of RAM 606B hard drive, or a Mac 700MHz G4 is recommended.

Graduates: From July 1, 2002 to June 30, 2003, 6335 bachelor's degrees were awarded. The most popular majors were finance (5%), psychology (5%), and criminology (5%). In an average class, 4% graduate in 3 years or less, 42% graduate in 4 years or less, 58% graduate in 5 years or less, and 63% graduate in 6 years or less.

Admissions Contact: Admissions.
E-mail: admissions@admin.fsu.edu Web: http://admissions.fsu.edu

INTERNATIONAL COLLEGE
D-5
Naples, FL 34119-7932

(239) 513-1122
(800) 466-8017; Fax: (239) 513-9054

Full-time: 352 men, 632 women	**Faculty:** 51
Part-time: 136 men, 207 women	**Ph.Ds:** 64%
Graduate: 63 men, 104 women	**Student/Faculty:** 19 to 1
Year: trimesters, summer session	**Tuition:** $8060
Application Deadline: open	**Room & Board:** n/app
Freshman Class: 606 applied, 507 accepted, 486 enrolled	
SAT I or ACT: not required	**LESS COMPETITIVE**

International College, founded in 1990, is a private institution offering undergraduate and graduate degree programs in business and public administration, accounting, criminal justice, health administration and allied health, computer technology, and paralegal studies. There are 4 undergraduate and 3 graduate schools. The library contains 27,859 volumes and 545 audio/video tapes/CDs, and subscribes to 254 periodicals. Computerized library services include the card catalog, interlibrary loans, database searching, and Internet access. Special learning facilities include an art gallery. The 10-acre campus is in a suburban area 100 miles west of Fort Lauderdale. There is 1 building.

Student Life: All students are from Florida. 70% are white; 14% Hispanic; 13% African American. The average age of freshmen is 31; all undergraduates, 33.

Housing: There are no residence halls. 99% of students commute.

Activities: There are no fraternities or sororities. There are some groups and organizations on campus, including literary magazine and student government.

Disabled Students: All of the campus is accessible. Elevators, specially equipped rest rooms, and lowered drinking fountains are available.

Services: There is remedial math and writing.

Campus Safety and Security: Measures include security escort services and lighted pathways/sidewalks.

Programs of Study: International College confers the B.S. degree. Associate and master's degrees are also awarded. Bachelor's degrees are awarded in BUSINESS (accounting and business administration and management), COMPUTER AND PHYSICAL SCIENCE (information sciences and systems), ENGINEERING AND ENVIRONMENTAL DESIGN (computer technology), HEALTH PROFESSIONS (health and health care administration), SOCIAL SCIENCE (criminal justice, interdisciplinary studies, and paralegal studies). Management is the largest.

Required: To graduate, students must complete a minimum of 120 semester hours, with at least 60 in the major and a minimum GPA of 2.0. At least 48 hours must be upper-division courses. A comprehensive exam is required.

Special: Dual majors, internships, work study, an accelerated degree in management, on-line classes, and credit for life experience are possible.

Faculty/Classroom: 68% of faculty are male; 31%, female. All teach undergraduates. No introductory courses are taught by graduate students. The average class size in an introductory lecture is 14; in a laboratory, 14; and in a regular course, 14.

Admissions: 84% of the 2003-2004 applicants were accepted.

Requirements: An essay and interview are required. AP and CLEP credits are accepted.

Procedure: Freshmen are admitted fall, winter, and summer. Entrance exams should be taken any time. Application deadlines are open. There is a rolling admissions plan. Application fee is $20. Notification is sent on a rolling basis. Applications are accepted on-line through the college's web site.

Transfer: 645 transfer students enrolled in 2002-2003. Applicants must submit previous transcripts. Only credits completed with a C or better will transfer. 32 credits of 120 required for the bachelor's degree must be completed at International College.

Visiting: There are regularly scheduled orientations for prospective students.

Financial Aid: In 2003-2004, 94% of all full-time freshmen and 93% of continuing full-time students received some form of financial aid. 84% of all full-time students received need-based aid. The average freshman award was $7888 with $1400 ($4050 maximum) from need-based scholarships or need-based grants, $3500 ($6625 maximum) from need-based self-help aid (loans and jobs), and $2988 from non-need-based awards and non-need-based scholarships. 1% of undergraduates work part time. Average annual earnings from campus work are $4000. The average financial indebtedness of the 2003 graduate was $17,000. The FAFSA is required. The deadline for filing freshman financial aid applications for fall entry is September 10.

International Students: The school actively recruits these students. They must score 500 on the written TOEFL or 173 on the electronic version and also take the CPAT, scoring 130.

Computers: There are 12 classrooms and 2 labs networked with access to the Internet and Web. There are 220 workstations in the library and computer center. E-mail accounts are available. All students may access the system. There are no time limits and no fees.

Graduates: From July 1, 2002 to June 30, 2003, 379 bachelor's degrees were awarded. The most popular majors were management/business (40%), criminal justice (16%), and legal studies (15%). 12 companies recruited on campus in 2002-2003. Of the 2002 graduating class, 5% were enrolled in graduate school within 6 months of graduation and 94% were employed.

Admissions Contact: Rita Lampus, Director of Admissions.
E-mail: *rlampus@internationalcollege.edu*
Web: *www.internationalcollege.edu*

JACKSONVILLE UNIVERSITY
D-1
Jacksonville, FL 32211

(904) 256-7000
(800) 225-2027; Fax: (904) 256-7012

Full-time: 988 men, 912 women	**Faculty:** 125; IIA, -$
Part-time: 119 men, 195 women	**Ph.Ds:** 75%
Graduate: 188 men, 230 women	**Student/Faculty:** 15 to 1
Year: semesters, summer session	**Tuition:** $17,940
Application Deadline: open	**Room & Board:** $6100
Freshman Class: 1684 applied, 1179 accepted, 418 enrolled	
SAT I Verbal/Math: 520/520	**ACT:** 22 **COMPETITIVE**

Jacksonville University, founded in 1934, is a private institution offering undergraduate and graduate degree programs in the arts and sciences, fine arts, and business. There are 3 undergraduate and 4 graduate schools. In addition to regional accreditation, JU has baccalaureate program accreditation with CCNE, NASAD, NASM, and NLN. The library contains 328,900 volumes, 352,608 microform items, and 33,366 audio/video tapes/CDs, and subscribes to 326 periodicals. Computerized library services include the card catalog, interlibrary loans, database searching, and Internet access. Special learning facilities include a learning resource center, art gallery, planetarium, radio station, TV station, a chemistry research lab, and a marine science center. The 260-acre campus is in a suburban area 10 minutes from downtown Jacksonville, near the St. Johns River. Including any residence halls, there are 48 buildings.

Student Life: 66% of undergraduates are from Florida. Students are from 46 states, 61 foreign countries, and Canada. 72% are white; 16% African American. 23% are Protestant; 20% Catholic. The average age of freshmen is 19; all undergraduates, 22. 31% do not continue beyond their first year; 44% remain to graduate.

Housing: 1061 students can be accommodated in college housing, which includes single-sex dorms and on-campus apartments. On-campus housing is guaranteed for all 4 years. 59% of students live on campus. All students may keep cars.

Activities: 18% of men belong to 6 national fraternities; 15% of women belong to 4 national sororities. There are more than 50 groups and organizations on campus, including art, band, cheerleading, choir, chorale, chorus, dance, debate, drama, drill team, ethnic, film, honors, international, jazz band, literary magazine, musical theater, newspaper, orchestra, pep band, photography, political, professional, radio and TV, religious, social, social service, student government, symphony, and yearbook.

Sports: There are 7 intercollegiate sports for men and 10 for women. Facilities include a 1500-seat stadium, a gym, a swimming pool, a boat house, baseball and softball diamonds, soccer and football fields, and an archery range. There are also tennis, basketball, handball/racquetball, volleyball, and shuffleboard courts, an all-purpose playing field, a 440-yard track, a 540-seat auditorium, a 220-seat recital hall, and a dance pavilion.

Disabled Students: Wheelchair ramps, elevators, special parking, specially equipped rest rooms, special class scheduling, and lowered drinking fountains are available. Accommodation is made for all students regardless of disability.

Services: Counseling and information services are available, as is tutoring in most subjects. There is a reader service for the blind, and remedial math, reading, and writing. There also is a writer service for note taking in class.

Campus Safety and Security: Measures include 24-hour foot and vehicle patrol, self-defense education, security escort services, and informal discussions. There are pamphlets/posters/films, emergency telephones, and lighted pathways/sidewalks.

Programs of Study: JU confers B.A., B.S., B.F.A., B.G.S., B.Mus., B.Mus.Ed., and B.S.N. degrees. Master's degrees are also awarded. Bachelor's degrees are awarded in BIOLOGICAL SCIENCE (biology/biological science and marine science), BUSINESS (accounting, banking and finance, business administration and management, international business management, and marketing/retailing/merchandising), COMMUNICATIONS AND THE ARTS (art history and appreciation, communications, dance, dramatic arts, English, French, music, music performance, music theory and composition, Spanish, and studio art), COMPUTER AND PHYSICAL SCIENCE (chemistry, computer science, information sciences and systems, mathematics, and physics), EDUCATION (art, dance, education of the exceptional child, elementary, music, and physical), ENGINEERING AND ENVIRONMENTAL DESIGN (aviation administration/management, computer graphics, electrical/

electronics engineering, engineering physics, environmental science, and mechanical engineering), HEALTH PROFESSIONS (nursing), SOCIAL SCIENCE (economics, geography, history, humanities, international studies, philosophy, political science/government, psychology, and sociology). Business administration, nursing, and biology are the largest.

Required: All students must complete a core curriculum, including 9 hours of English and literature, 4 hours of lab science, 3 hours each of technology, social science, math, philosophy, information systems, humanities, history, foreign language, fine arts, and economics, and 1 hour of phys ed. A total of 128 hours, with a minimum GPA of 2.0, is needed to graduate.

Special: Internships and work-study are available, as are student-designed majors, and a dual major in music and business. There is a co-op program in art, and a 3-2 engineering degree is available with 7 other universities and technological institutes. There is a Washington semester and study abroad in 12 countries. Credit is granted for military experience. There are 12 national honor societies, including Phi Beta Kappa, and a freshman honors program.

Faculty/Classroom: 57% of faculty are male; 43%, female. No introductory courses are taught by graduate students. The average class size in an introductory lecture is 17; in a laboratory, 16; and in a regular course, 14.

Admissions: 70% of the 2003-2004 applicants were accepted. The SAT I scores for the 2003-2004 freshman class were: Verbal--38% below 500, 44% between 500 and 599, 16% between 600 and 700, and 2% above 700; Math--35% below 500, 41% between 500 and 599, 21% between 600 and 700, and 3% above 700. The ACT scores were 28% below 21, 41% between 21 and 23, 13% between 24 and 26, 13% between 27 and 28, and 5% above 28. 38% of the current freshmen were in the top fifth of their class; 66% were in the top two fifths.

Requirements: The SAT I or ACT is required. In addition, applicants must be graduates of an accredited secondary school and provide an official copy of their secondary school transcript, or have a GED. At least 18 academic credits are required, including 4 in English, 3 each in math, natural science, and social sciences, and 2 of the same foreign language. Art students must submit a portfolio. Music, theater, and dance students must audition. A GPA of 2.0 is required. AP and CLEP credits are accepted. Important factors in the admissions decision are advanced placement or honor courses, extracurricular activities record, and leadership record.

Procedure: Freshmen are admitted to all sessions. Entrance exams should be taken in the spring of the junior year or the fall or spring of the senior year. There are early admissions and deferred admissions plans. There is a rolling admissions plan. Application deadlines are open. The fall 2003 application fee was $30. Notification is sent on a rolling basis beginning October 1. Applications are accepted on-line through the university's web site.

Transfer: 216 transfer students enrolled in 2002-2003. Transfer students must submit official transcripts from all colleges attended. Art students must submit a portfolio; music and dance students must audition. Transfer applicants must have completed at least 1 semester at an accredited college or university, be in good standing at the last institution attended, and have a minimum GPA of 2.0. 32 credits of 128 required for the bachelor's degree must be completed at JU.

Visiting: There are regularly scheduled orientations for prospective students, consisting of an interview, a campus tour, advisement, area presentations, registration, a parents program, and mock classes. There are guides for informal visits and visitors may sit in on classes and stay overnight. To schedule a visit, contact the Admissions office.

Financial Aid: In 2003-2004, 98% of all full-time freshmen received some form of financial aid. 80% of full-time freshmen received need-based aid. JU is a member of CSS. The FAFSA, the college's own financial statement, a federal tax return, and W-2 are required. The priority date for freshman financial aid applications for fall entry is January 15.

International Students: There are 64 international students enrolled. The school actively recruits these students. They must score 540 on the written TOEFL or 207 on the electronic version and also take the SAT I or the ACT.

Computers: The mainframes are an HP 3000 Series 957 and a DEC Alpha server. There are 350 campus computers available for student use. These are contained in various computer labs and computerized classrooms. Access to the Internet is provided, as are wireless connection areas on campus. All students may access the system during lab hours, 7 days a week, with dial-in access. There are no time limits and no fees. It is strongly recommended that all students have a personal computer.

Graduates: From July 1, 2002 to June 30, 2003, 399 bachelor's degrees were awarded. The most popular majors were business (29%), nursing (14%), and communications (7%). In an average class, 31% graduate in 4 years or less, 41% graduate in 5 years or less, and 44% graduate in 6 years or less. 50 companies recruited on campus in 2002-2003. Of the 2002 graduating class, 23% were enrolled in graduate school within 6 months of graduation and 51% were employed.

Admissions Contact: John P. Grundig, Director of Admissions. E-mail: *admissions@ju.edu* Web: *www.ju.edu*

LYNN UNIVERSITY
Boca Raton, FL 33431

E-5

(561) 237-7900
(800) 888-LYNN; Fax: (561) 237-7100

Full-time: 847 men, 804 women	**Faculty:** 57
Part-time: 88 men, 164 women	**Ph.Ds:** 80%
Graduate: 175 men, 172 women	**Student/Faculty:** 29 to 1
Year: semesters, summer session	**Tuition:** $22,750
Application Deadline: open	**Room & Board:** $8000
Freshman Class: 2608 applied, 2013 accepted, 658 enrolled	
ACT: 22	**COMPETITIVE**

Lynn University, founded in 1962, is a private, nonsectarian liberal arts college offering graduate and undergraduate programs in the arts and sciences, business, education, hospitality, and preprofessional studies. There are 6 undergraduate and 2 graduate schools. In addition to regional accreditation, LU has baccalaureate program accreditation with ABFSE. The library contains 95,000 volumes, 2000 microform items, and 3500 audio/video tapes/CDs, 2000 film reels, and subscribes to 400 periodicals. Computerized library services include the card catalog, interlibrary loans, and database searching. Special learning facilities include a learning resource center, art gallery, radio station, and an academic resource center. The 123-acre campus is in a suburban area midway between Fort Lauderdale and Palm Beach. Including any residence halls, there are 17 buildings.

Student Life: 50% of undergraduates are from out of state, mostly the Northeast. Students are from 46 states, 77 foreign countries, and Canada. 34% are from public schools. 27% are white; 17% foreign nationals. The average age of freshmen is 19; all undergraduates, 20. 40% do not continue beyond their first year; 60% remain to graduate.

Housing: 680 students can be accommodated in college housing, which includes single-sex and coed dorms. On-campus housing is guaranteed for all 4 years. 65% of students live on campus; of those, 74% remain on campus on weekends. All students may keep cars.

Activities: 1% of men belong to 1 national fraternity; 1% of women belong to 1 national sorority. There are 25 groups on campus, including cheerleading, choir, community service, debate, drama, drill team, ethnic, film, honors, international, literary magazine, newspaper, photography, political, professional, radio and TV, religious, social, social service, student government, and yearbook. Popular campus events include Holiday Formal, International Day, and Spring Fling.

Sports: There are 5 intercollegiate sports for men and 7 for women, and 10 intramural sports for men and 6 for women. Facilities include softball, baseball and soccer fields, tennis courts, indoor and outdoor basketball courts, 2 outdoor pools, and a weight facility.

Disabled Students: 90% of the campus is accessible. Wheelchair ramps, elevators, special parking, specially equipped rest rooms, special class scheduling, and lowered drinking fountains are available.

Services: Counseling and information services are available, as is tutoring in most subjects. There are services for learning disabled students. There is remedial math, reading, and writing.

Campus Safety and Security: Measures include 24-hour foot and vehicle patrol, self-defense education, security escort services, and informal discussions. There are pamphlets/posters/films and lighted pathways/sidewalks.

Programs of Study: LU confers B.A. and B.S. degrees. Associate, master's, and doctoral degrees are also awarded. Bachelor's degrees are awarded in BUSINESS (accounting, business administration and management, fashion merchandising, hotel/motel and restaurant management, marketing/retailing/merchandising, recreational facilities management, sports management, and tourism), COMMUNICATIONS AND THE ARTS (communications, design, fine arts, and graphic design), EDUCATION (early childhood, education, elementary, and secondary), ENGINEERING AND ENVIRONMENTAL DESIGN (aviation administration/management), HEALTH PROFESSIONS (health care administration), SOCIAL SCIENCE (history, human services, humanities, political science/government, prelaw, psychology, and sociology). Accounting, international management, and education are the strongest academically. Business administration and hotel restaurant management are the largest.

Required: Students are required to complete 120 to 128 credits, with 45 to 50 in the major, and must maintain a minimum GPA of 2.0. In addition, all students must complete a core curriculum of 39 semester hours. To graduate, students must complete courses in public forum, academic adventure, and first year experience.

Special: Opportunities are provided for internships, which are required in many majors. There is study abroad in Ireland, Japan, and France. Credit by exam, credit for life experience, and pass/fail options are available. There is a freshman honors program.

Faculty/Classroom: 56% of faculty are male; 44%, female. All teach undergraduates. No introductory courses are taught by graduate students. The average class size in an introductory lecture is 26; in a laboratory, 20; and in a regular course, 22.

Admissions: 77% of the 2003-2004 applicants were accepted. The SAT I scores for the 2003-2004 freshman class were: Verbal--69% below

500, 27% between 500 and 599, 4% between 600 and 700, and 1% above 700; Math--68% below 500, 26% between 500 and 599, 6% between 600 and 700, and 1% above 700. The ACT scores were 45% below 21, and 55% between 24 and 26. 16% of the current freshmen were in the top fifth of their class; 34% were in the top two fifths. 4 freshmen graduated first in their class in a recent year.

Requirements: The SAT I or ACT is required. In addition, graduation from an accredited secondary school is required; a GED will be accepted. Applicants must have a minimum high school GPA of 2.0. An essay and an interview are recommended. A GPA of 2.5 is required. AP and CLEP credits are accepted. Important factors in the admissions decision are recommendations by school officials, personality/intangible qualities, and extracurricular activities record.

Procedure: Freshmen are admitted fall and spring. Entrance exams should be taken during the junior or senior year. There are early admissions and deferred admissions plans. Notification of regular decision is sent on a rolling basis. Application deadlines are open. Application fee is $35. Applications are accepted on-line.

Transfer: 178 transfer students enrolled in 2002-2003. Transfer students must submit an official transcript from each previous college attended, plus a recommendation from the dean of students. The student must have maintained a minimum GPA of 2.0. An interview is recommended. Most complete an essay and a personal statement. 30 of 120 to 130 credits required for the bachelor's degree must be completed at LU.

Visiting: There are guides for informal visits and visitors may sit in on classes. To schedule a visit, contact the Office of Admissions at *admissions@lynn.edu*.

Financial Aid: In 2003-2004, 75% of all full-time freshmen and 50% of continuing full-time students received some form of financial aid. 53% of full-time freshmen and 34% of continuing full-time students received need-based aid. The average freshman award was $16,662. Need-based scholarships or need-based grants averaged $9713 ($20,550 maximum); need-based self-help aid (loans and jobs) averaged $17,505 ($42,625 maximum); non-need-based athletic scholarships averaged $15,940 ($30,000 maximum); and other non-need-based awards and non-need-based scholarships averaged $7677 ($30,000 maximum). 77% of undergraduates work part time. Average annual earnings from campus work are $683. The average financial indebtedness of the 2003 graduate was $12,572. LU is a member of CSS. The FAFSA or FFS is required. The priority date for freshman financial aid applications for fall entry is March 1.

International Students: There are 265 international students enrolled. The school actively recruits these students. They must score 500 on the written TOEFL or 173 on the electronic version.

Computers: Apple and IBM PCs are available in the library and computer classroom. All students may access the system. There are no time limits and no fees.

Graduates: From July 1, 2002 to June 30, 2003, 355 bachelor's degrees were awarded. The most popular majors were business administration/general management (11%), hospitality (8%), and international business (6%). In an average class, 6% graduate in 3 years or less, 30% graduate in 4 years or less, 35% graduate in 5 years or less, and 35% graduate in 6 years or less. 98 companies recruited on campus in 2002-2003.

Admissions Contact: Alejandra Carvajal, Associate Director of Admission. A video is available. E-mail: *admission@lynn.edu* Web: *www.lynn.edu*

NEW COLLEGE OF FLORIDA   D-4
Sarasota, FL 34243-2197   (941) 359-4269; Fax: (941) 359-4435

Full-time: 262 men, 409 women	Faculty: 60; IIB, av$
Part-time: none	Ph.D.s: 100%
Graduate: none	Student/Faculty: 11 to 1
Year: 4-1-4	Tuition: $3246 ($16,484)
Application Deadline: May 1	Room & Board: $5660
Freshman Class: 445 applied, 343 accepted, 157 enrolled	
SAT I Verbal/Math: 682/630	ACT: 28
	HIGHLY COMPETITIVE+

New College of Florida, established in 1960, is the honors college of the State University System of Florida. The library contains 257,047 volumes, 548,156 microform items, and 4195 audio/video tapes/CDs, and subscribes to 1850 periodicals. Computerized library services include the card catalog, interlibrary loans, database searching, and Internet access. Special learning facilities include an art gallery, a media and educational technology center, writing resource center, math reading room, marine biology research center, and a living ecosystem teaching and research aquarium. The 144-acre campus is in a suburban area 50 miles south of Tampa, on Sarasota Bay. Including any residence halls, there are 46 buildings.

Student Life: 74% of undergraduates are from Florida. Students are from 39 states, 12 foreign countries, and Canada. 81% are from public schools. 83% are white. The average age of freshmen is 19; all under-

graduates, 20. 19% do not continue beyond their first year; 72% remain to graduate.

Housing: 460 students can be accommodated in college housing, which includes single-sex and coed dorms and on-campus apartments. In addition, there are apartment-style dorms, food co-op housing, and a wellness dorm. On-campus housing is guaranteed for the freshman year only. 70% of students live on campus; of those, 70% remain on campus on weekends. All students may keep cars.

Activities: There are no fraternities or sororities. There are 43 groups on campus, including chess, choir, dance, debate, drama, ethnic, film, gay, international, literary magazine, newspaper, political, religious, social, social service, and student government. Popular campus events include Halloween and graduation parties, a student/faculty softball game, and a diversity discussion service (Campus Week of Dialog).

Sports: There is no sports program at New College. Facilities include a soccer field, a softball diamond, a fitness path, outdoor tennis and basketball courts, a volleyball pit, playground equipment, a swimming pool, and a fitness center with Nautilus equipment and indoor facilities for racquetball, aerobics, dance, and yoga.

Disabled Students: 80% of the campus is accessible. Wheelchair ramps, elevators, special parking, specially equipped rest rooms, special class scheduling, lowered drinking fountains, lowered telephones, and special housing are available.

Services: Counseling and information services are available, as is tutoring in most subjects. There is a reader service for the blind. A writing resouce center provides assistance in developing writing skills and strategies.

Campus Safety and Security: Measures include 24-hour foot and vehicle patrol, self-defense education, security escort services, and informal discussions. There are pamphlets/posters/films, emergency telephones, lighted pathways/sidewalks, and 24-hour dispatch/information services, and fire/smoke alarm systems in all dorms.

Programs of Study: New College confers the B.A. degree. Bachelor's degrees are awarded in BIOLOGICAL SCIENCE (biology/biological science), COMMUNICATIONS AND THE ARTS (art history and appreciation, classics, dramatic arts, English, fine arts, Germanic languages and literature, languages, literature, music, and Russian languages and literature), COMPUTER AND PHYSICAL SCIENCE (chemistry, mathematics, natural sciences, and physics), ENGINEERING AND ENVIRONMENTAL DESIGN (environmental science), SOCIAL SCIENCE (anthropology, economics, French studies, history, humanities, international studies, medieval studies, philosophy, political science/government, psychology, public administration, religion, social science, sociology, Spanish studies, urban studies, and women's studies). Psychology, humanities, and anthropology are the largest.

Required: An academic credit system is not used. To qualify for graduation, students must complete 7 semester contracts, which are designed by the student in consultation with faculty; 3 independent study projects completed during January each year, between the fall and spring semesters; a senior thesis, which involves original research or creative work and includes working closely with a faculty committee of the student's choice; and an oral baccalaureate exam, which is primarily a defense of the senior thesis. To fulfill the liberal arts curriculum requirements, students must complete 8 LAC-designated courses, including 1 each in humanities, natural sciences, and social sciences. Exemptions from the LAC requirements are possible through AP exam scores of 4 and 5, IB higher level exam scores of 5 to 7, and transferable college course work at the general education level. Students also must use on-line training to sign up for a college e-mail account and complete the College Level Academic Skills Test or be exempted by appropriate college course work or SAT I or ACT scores.

Special: Domestic and international internships, study abroad in 39 countries, accelerated degree programs, student-designed, interdisciplinary and dual majors, and independent study are available. There is a freshman honors program and all departments have honors programs.

Faculty/Classroom: 57% of faculty are male; 43%, female. All teach undergraduates, 95% do research, and 95% do both. The average class size in a regular course is 16.

Admissions: 77% of the 2003-2004 applicants were accepted. The SAT I scores for the 2003-2004 freshman class were: Verbal--1% below 500, 7% between 500 and 599, 57% between 600 and 700, and 35% above 700; Math--3% below 500, 25% between 500 and 599, 60% between 600 and 700, and 13% above 700. The ACT scores were 6% between 21 and 23, 26% between 24 and 26, 29% between 27 and 28, and 39% above 28. 61% of the current freshmen were in the top fifth of their class; 93% were in the top two fifths. There were 8 National Merit finalists and 2 semifinalists. 6 freshmen graduated first in their class.

Requirements: The SAT I or ACT is required. In addition, graduation from an accredited secondary school (preferred) or the GED is required. High school students should pursue at least 5 academic courses each year, at the most rigorous level available, with a minimum distribution of 4 years of English; 3 years each of math, sciences, and social sciences; 2 consecutive years of the same foreign language; and 3 other academic courses. Application essays must be submitted. A formal interview is recommended for all applicants. A GPA of 3.0 is required. Important factors in the admissions decision are advanced placement or honor courses, evidence of special talent, and recommendations by school officials.

Procedure: Freshmen are admitted fall and spring. Entrance exams should be taken by fall of the senior year. There are early admissions, deferred admissions, and a rolling admission plan. Applications should be filed by May 1 for fall entry and December 31 for spring entry, along with a $30 fee. Notification is sent on a rolling basis. 23 students were on the 2003 waiting list; 15 were admitted. Applications are accepted on-line through Embark.com, FACTS.org, College Board's Next Stop College, and the Common Application.

Transfer: 50 transfer students enrolled in 2002-2003. Transfers must be in good academic and financial standing with their previous college(s). Transfers with less than 60 semester hours must submit SAT I or ACT scores. A minimum of 4 semesters and 2 indpendent study projects must be completed at New College. 7 semesters and 3 independent study projects are required for the bachelor's degree.

Visiting: There are regularly scheduled orientations for prospective students, including a campus tour, admissions information session, and/or class visits, which must be scheduled individually by the student through Admissions. Visitors may sit in on classes and stay overnight. To schedule a visit, contact the Office of Admissions at *admissions@ncf.edu*.

Financial Aid: In 2003-2004, 94% of all full-time freshmen and 96% of continuing full-time students received some form of financial aid. 30% of full-time freshmen and 34% of continuing full-time students received need-based aid. The average freshman award was $7723. Need-based scholarships or need-based grants averaged $2507 ($6615 maximum); need-based self-help aid (loans and jobs) averaged $2771 ($6125 maximum); and other non-need-based awards and non-need-based scholarships averaged $5820 ($18,800 maximum). 4% of undergraduates work part time. Average annual earnings from campus work are $2049. The average financial indebtedness of the 2003 graduate was $16,645. The FAFSA is required. The deadline for filing freshman financial aid applications for fall entry is March 1.

International Students: There are 16 international students enrolled. The school actively recruits these students. They must score 560 on the written TOEFL or 220 on the electronic version and also take the SAT I or the ACT.

Computers: The campus has 5 computer labs, including an open-use lab (15 computers), a teaching lab (24 computers), and a teaching lab with 25 computers used in conjunction with the college's mentoring program. The other 2 labs are an open-use Mac lab (11 computers) and Mac publications lab (3 computers) run by students. All computer labs provide access to the Internet and Ethernet connections are available in all residence hall rooms, at the student run café, the auditorium, and the library. There are free student e-mail accounts, free dial-up Internet access, and personal web page hosting. All students may access the system 24 hours a day. There are no time limits and no fees.

Graduates: From July 1, 2002 to June 30, 2003, 138 bachelor's degrees were awarded. The most popular majors were political science (9%), psychology (9%), and humanities (8%). In an average class, 47% graduate in 4 years or less, 71% graduate in 5 years or less, and 72% graduate in 6 years or less. 60 companies recruited on campus in 2002-2003. Of the 2002 graduating class, 25% were enrolled in graduate school within 6 months of graduation.

Admissions Contact: Joel Bauman, Dean of Admissions and Financial Aid. E-mail: *admissions@ncf.edu* Web: *www.ncf.edu*

NORTHWOOD UNIVERSITY
E-5
West Palm Beach, FL 33409-2911 (561) 478-5500
(800) 458-8325; Fax: (561) 640-3328

Full-time: 398 men, 256 women	**Faculty:** 14
Part-time: 23 men, 8 women	**Ph.D.s:** 36%
Graduate: none	**Student/Faculty:** 47 to 1
Year: quarters, summer session	**Tuition:** $13,995
Application Deadline: August 1	**Room & Board:** $7045
Freshman Class: 818 applied, 532 accepted, 163 enrolled	
SAT I Verbal/Math: 470/480	**ACT:** 19 **COMPETITIVE**

Northwood University, founded in 1959, is a private institution offering undergraduate degrees in business administration and management. Campuses are located in Florida, Michigan, and Texas. The Florida campus opened in 1982. The library contains 23,000 volumes and 450 audio/video tapes/CDs, and subscribes to 130 periodicals. Computerized library services include the card catalog, database searching, and Internet access. Special learning facilities include a learning resource center, art gallery, and the Ethics Center for Business. The 84-acre campus is in a suburban area 70 miles north of Miami. Including any residence halls, there are 10 buildings.

Student Life: 62% of undergraduates are from out of state, mostly the South. Students are from 35 states, 47 foreign countries, and Canada. 70% are from public schools. 57% are white; 23% foreign nationals. The average age of freshmen is 18; all undergraduates, 21. 40% do not continue beyond their first year; 41% remain to graduate.

Housing: 432 students can be accommodated in college housing, which includes single-sex on-campus apartments. On-campus housing is guaranteed for the freshman year only. 56% of students commute. All students may keep cars.

Activities: There are no fraternities or sororities. There are 15 groups on campus, including art, computers, debate, drama, ethnic, honors, international, newspaper, photography, political, professional, social, social service, student government, and yearbook. Popular campus events include Automotive Industry Show, Diversity Month, and carnival.

Sports: There are 4 intercollegiate sports for men and 5 for women, and 6 intramural sports for men and 6 for women. Facilities include baseball, softball, and soccer fields, a student center, and a recreation center with an outdoor swimming pool and basketball, tennis, and handball/racquetball courts.

Disabled Students: 80% of the campus is accessible. Wheelchair ramps, elevators, special parking, specially equipped rest rooms, special class scheduling, lowered drinking fountains, and lowered telephones are available.

Services: Counseling and information services are available, as is tutoring in every subject, including accounting, math, English, and computers. There is remedial math and writing.

Campus Safety and Security: Measures include 24-hour foot and vehicle patrol, informal discussions, pamphlets/posters/films, and emergency telephones. There are lighted pathways/sidewalks.

Programs of Study: Northwood confers the B.B.A. degree. Associate degrees are also awarded. Bachelor's degrees are awarded in BUSINESS (accounting, banking and finance, business administration and management, hotel/motel and restaurant management, international business management, management information systems, marketing management, sports management, and transportation and travel marketing), COMMUNICATIONS AND THE ARTS (advertising). Accounting and management information systems are the strongest academically. Business management and automotive marketing are the largest.

Required: To graduate, all students must complete a minimum of 180 credit hours, with 36 credit hours in the major. A minimum GPA of 2.0 must be maintained, and 6 credits of computer science management and 2 credits of executive fitness must be completed. Internships for 1 to 6 credits are required in some majors.

Special: Northwood offers cooperative programs and cross-registration with Georgian College in Canada, internships with various automotive and fashion marketing corporations, study abroad in 20 countries, and various work-study programs. Externships are available for all programs and required in 4. Also available are accelerated degree programs in all majors, dual majors, credit for military experience, and nondegree study. There is a freshman honors program.

Faculty/Classroom: 65% of faculty are male; 35%, female. All teach undergraduates. The average class size in an introductory lecture is 27; in a laboratory, 13; and in a regular course, 18.

Admissions: 65% of the 2003-2004 applicants were accepted. The SAT I scores for the 2003-2004 freshman class were: Verbal--66% below 500, 30% between 500 and 599, and 4% between 600 and 700; Math--55% below 500, 32% between 500 and 599, and 13% between 600 and 700. The ACT scores were 63% below 21, 21% between 21 and 23, 12% between 24 and 26, and 4% between 27 and 28. 16% of the current freshmen were in the top fifth of their class; 32% were in the top two fifths.

Requirements: The SAT I or ACT is required. In addition, applicants must be graduates of an accredited secondary school or have a GED certificate. An interview is recommended. A GPA of 2.0 is required. AP and CLEP credits are accepted. Important factors in the admissions decision are advanced placement or honor courses, evidence of special talent, and leadership record.

Procedure: Freshmen are admitted to all sessions. Entrance exams should be taken in the fall of the senior year. There are early admissions, rolling admissions, and deferred admissions plans. Applications should be filed by August 1 for fall entry, November 1 for winter entry, February 15 for spring entry, and June 1 for summer entry, along with a $25 fee. Notification is sent on a rolling basis. Applications are accepted on-line.

Transfer: 139 transfer students enrolled in 2002-2003. Applicants must have a minimum 2.0 GPA, with at least 15 credit hours earned and official transcripts of all completed college-level work. Good academic and social standing are required. An interview is recommended. 45 of 180 credits required for the bachelor's degree must be completed at Northwood.

Visiting: There are regularly scheduled orientations for prospective students, including a fall and spring open house, campus tours, and meetings with students and financial aid and academic staff. There are guides for informal visits and visitors may sit in on classes and stay overnight. To schedule a visit, contact the Admissions Office at *fladmit@northwood.edu*.

Financial Aid: In 2003-2004, 91% of all full-time freshmen and 86% of continuing full-time students received some form of financial aid. 55% of full-time freshmen and 50% of continuing full-time students received need-based aid. The average freshman award was $13,030. Need-based

scholarships or need-based grants averaged $9183 ($15,434 maximum); need-based self-help aid (loans and jobs) averaged $4318 ($4725 maximum); non-need-based athletic scholarships averaged $4044 ($12,500 maximum); and other non-need-based awards and non-need-based scholarships averaged $1799 ($24,491 maximum). 9% of undergraduates work part time. Average annual earnings from campus work are $1050. The average financial indebtedness of the 2003 graduate was $13,495. The FAFSA is required. The priority date for freshman financial aid applications for fall entry is April 15.

International Students: There are 149 international students enrolled. The school actively recruits these students. They must score 500 on the written TOEFL or 173 on the electronic version.

Computers: The mainframe is an IBM RS/6000. There are 42 PCs in computer classrooms available to all students when classes are not in session, plus 6 in the student center, 14 in the library, and 13 tied to special automotive software for those academic majors. All students may access the system. There are no time limits and no fees.

Graduates: From July 1, 2002 to June 30, 2003, 140 bachelor's degrees were awarded. The most popular majors were marketing/management (26%), automotive marketing (23%), and international business (19%). In an average class, 22% graduate in 4 years or less, and 41% graduate in 6 years or less.

Admissions Contact: Jack Letvinchuk, Admissions Director. A video is available. E-mail: *fladmit@northwood.edu* Web: *www.northwood.edu*

NOVA SOUTHEASTERN UNIVERSITY   E-5
Fort Lauderdale, FL 33314   (954) 262-8000
(800) 338-4723, ext. 8000

Full-time: 814 men, 2317 women	**Faculty:** 70
Part-time: 502 men, 1590 women	**Ph.Ds:** n/av
Graduate: 5882 men, 12,417 women	**Student/Faculty:** 45 to 1
Year: trimesters, summer session	**Tuition:** $15,220
Application Deadline: open	**Room & Board:** $8126
Freshman Class: n/av	
SAT I Verbal/Math: 480/500	**ACT:** 20 **COMPETITIVE**

Nova Southeastern University, founded in 1964, is a private institution offering degree programs in liberal arts, sciences, business, health sciences, and education, and preprofessional studies. There are 3 undergraduate and 8 graduate schools. The 3 libraries contain 597,200 volumes, 1,347,411 microform items, and 19,878 audio/video tapes/CDs, and subscribe to 11,455 periodicals. Computerized library services include the card catalog, interlibrary loans, database searching, and Internet access. Special learning facilities include a learning resource center and radio station. The 300-acre campus is in a suburban area 10 miles west of downtown Fort Lauderdale. Including any residence halls, there are 39 buildings.

Student Life: 80% of undergraduates are from Florida. Students are from 38 states, 20 foreign countries, and Canada. 45% are white; 26% African American; 16% Hispanic. The average age of all undergraduates is 30. 25% do not continue beyond their first year.

Housing: 553 students can be accommodated in college housing, which includes coed dorms, on-campus apartments, and married-student housing. On-campus housing is guaranteed for the freshman year only and is available on a first-come, first-served basis. 94% of students commute. Alcohol is not permitted. All students may keep cars.

Activities: There are 4 national fraternities and 3 national sororities. There are 34 groups on campus, including cheerleading, chorus, drama, environmental, ethnic, honors, international, newspaper, political, professional, radio and TV, religious, social, and student government. Popular campus events include Hollywood Squares, Life 101, and Student Life Achievement Awards.

Sports: There are 5 intercollegiate sports for men and 8 for women, and 11 intramural sports for men and 11 for women. Facilities include baseball and soccer fields and a recreational complex with a swimming pool and basketball and tennis courts.

Disabled Students: Wheelchair ramps, elevators, special parking, specially equipped rest rooms, lowered drinking fountains, special housing, and wheelchair lifts in some buildings are available.

Services: Counseling and information services are available, as is tutoring in most subjects. There is remedial math, reading, and writing. Availability of remedial tutoring is contingent on registration in specific courses.

Campus Safety and Security: Measures include 24-hour foot and vehicle patrol, security escort services, shuttle buses, and informal discussions. There are pamphlets/posters/films, emergency telephones, and lighted pathways/sidewalks.

Programs of Study: NSU confers B.A., B.S., B.H. Sc., and B.S.N. degrees. Associate, master's, and doctoral degrees are also awarded. Bachelor's degrees are awarded in BIOLOGICAL SCIENCE (biology/biological science and marine biology), BUSINESS (accounting, banking and finance, business administration and management, and sports management), COMMUNICATIONS AND THE ARTS (English), COMPUT-

ER AND PHYSICAL SCIENCE (computer science and information sciences and systems), EDUCATION (athletic training, early childhood, education of the exceptional child, and elementary), HEALTH PROFESSIONS (health science, nursing, and physician's assistant), SOCIAL SCIENCE (history, humanities, paralegal studies, prelaw, and psychology). Business and education are the largest.

Required: To graduate, all students must complete at least 120 credit hours. A minimum 2.25 GPA is needed for courses in the major, and a 2.0 for all other courses.

Special: NSU offers internships, study abroad in 5 countries, work-study and accelerated degree programs, and nondegree study. Combined bachelor-professional degree programs and a dual admission program are also available. There are 4 national honor societies, a freshman honors program, and 3 departmental honors programs.

Faculty/Classroom: 57% of faculty are male; 43%, female. No introductory courses are taught by graduate students. The average class size in a regular course is 19.

Admissions: The SAT I scores for the 2003-2004 freshman class were: Verbal--57% below 500, 34% between 500 and 599, 8% between 600 and 700, and 1% above 700; Math--46% below 500, 37% between 500 and 599, 14% between 600 and 700, and 3% above 700. The ACT scores were 56% below 21, 25% between 21 and 23, 11% between 24 and 26, 5% between 27 and 28, and 3% above 28.

Requirements: The SAT I or ACT is required. In addition, applicants must be graduates of an accredited secondary school or have a GED certificate. An interview is recommended. AP and CLEP credits are accepted. Important factors in the admissions decision are advanced placement or honor courses, leadership record, and recommendations by alumni.

Procedure: Freshmen are admitted to all sessions. Entrance exams should be taken Scores must be received by June 15 for the fall semester. There are early admissions, rolling admissions, and deferred admissions plans. Application deadlines are open. The fall 2003 application fee was $50. Applications are accepted on-line through *http://www.undergrad.nova.edu/admissions/applyonline.cfm*.

Transfer: 117 transfer students enrolled in a recent year. Applicants must have a minimum 2.5 GPA from a regionally accredited institution. An interview is recommended. At least 50% of credits in the major or specialty must be earned at NSU. 30 of 120 credits required for the bachelor's degree must be completed at NSU.

Visiting: There are regularly scheduled orientations for prospective students. There are guides for informal visits and visitors may sit in on classes. To schedule a visit, contact the Admissions Office at *ncsinfo@nova.edu*.

Financial Aid: In 2003-2004, 78% of all full-time freshmen and 76% of continuing full-time students received some form of financial aid. 77% of full-time freshmen and 73% of continuing full-time students received need-based aid. The average freshman award was $15,197. Need-based scholarships or need-based grants averaged $9211; need-based self-help aid (loans and jobs) averaged $6308; non-need-based athletic scholarships averaged $6255; and other non-need-based awards and non-need-based scholarships averaged $2491. The average financial indebtedness of the 2003 graduate was $21,607. NSU is a member of CSS. The FAFSA and the college's own financial statement are required. The priority date for freshman financial aid applications for fall entry is April 15.

International Students: There are 143 international students enrolled. The school actively recruits these students. They must score 550 on the written TOEFL or 213 on the electronic version or take the MELAB. The SAT I, with a minimum verbal score of 480, may replace the TOEFL/MELAB.

Computers: The mainframe is a Sun Microsystems Enterprise 5000. There are 32 microlabs with access to the Internet, and 1,510 computers are available to students. All students may access the system. There are no time limits and no fees. It is strongly recommended that all students have a personal computer.

Graduates: From July 1, 2002 to June 30, 2003, 942 bachelor's degrees were awarded. The most popular majors were business (47%), education (20%), and health professions (8%).

Admissions Contact: Maria Dillard, Director of Enrollment Management. E-mail: *ncsinfo@nova.edu* Web: *undergrad.nova.edu/admissions*

PALM BEACH ATLANTIC UNIVERSITY E-5
West Palm Beach, FL 33416-4708
(561) 803-2100
(888) GO TO PBA; Fax: (561) 803-2115

Full-time: 781 men, 1435 women	Faculty: 103
Part-time: 64 men, 140 women	Ph.Ds: 75%
Graduate: 220 men, 356 women	Student/Faculty: 22 to 1
Year: semesters, summer session	Tuition: $14,890
Application Deadline: open	Room & Board: $5800
Freshman Class: 970 applied, 846 accepted, 444 enrolled	
SAT I Verbal/Math: 550/530	ACT: 23	COMPETITIVE

Palm Beach Atlantic University, formerly Palm Beach Atlantic College and founded in 1968, is a comprehensive Christian university. There are 8 undergraduate and 5 graduate schools. In addition to regional accreditation, PBA has baccalaureate program accreditation with NASM. The library contains 215,105 volumes, 26,477 microform items, and 4499 audio/video tapes/CDs, and subscribes to 44,766 periodicals. Computerized library services include the card catalog, interlibrary loans, database searching, and Internet access. Special learning facilities include a children's literature collection. The 25-acre campus is in an urban area 60 miles north of Miami. Including any residence halls, there are 18 buildings.

Student Life: 74% of undergraduates are from Florida. Students are from 47 states, 25 foreign countries, and Canada. 69% are white; 15% African American. 81% are Protestant; 10% Catholic. The average age of freshmen is 20; all undergraduates, 21. 27% do not continue beyond their first year; 42% remain to graduate.

Housing: 1000 students can be accommodated in college housing, which includes single-sex dorms and on-campus apartments. 59% of students commute. Alcohol is not permitted. All students may keep cars.

Activities: There are no fraternities or sororities. There are 38 groups on campus, including art, cheerleading, chess, choir, chorale, chorus, computers, concert band, dance, drama, ethnic, film, honors, international, jazz band, literary magazine, music ensembles, musical theater, newspaper, orchestra, pep band, photography, political, professional, radio and TV, religious, social, social service, student government, symphony, and yearbook. Popular campus events include American Free Enterprise Day and Christival.

Sports: There are 6 intercollegiate sports for men and 6 for women, and 25 intramural sports for men and 25 for women. Facilities include a 60,000-square-foot sports and recreation center, a 1750-seat main arena, and an auxiliary gym for basketball, volleyball, and badminton. Racquetball courts, a weight room, a fitness room, a dance room, and an indoor jogging track are also available.

Disabled Students: 80% of the campus is accessible. Wheelchair ramps, elevators, special parking, and specially equipped rest rooms are available.

Services: Counseling and information services are available, as is tutoring in most subjects. There is remedial math, reading, and writing.

Campus Safety and Security: Measures include 24-hour foot and vehicle patrol, self-defense education, security escort services, and informal discussions. There are pamphlets/posters/films, emergency telephones, and lighted pathways/sidewalks.

Programs of Study: PBA confers B.A., B.S., B.G.S., B.Mus., and B.S.N. degrees. Associate, master's, and doctoral degrees are also awarded. Bachelor's degrees are awarded in BIOLOGICAL SCIENCE (biology/biological science), BUSINESS (banking and finance, business administration and management, entrepreneurial studies, international business management, management science, and marketing management), COMMUNICATIONS AND THE ARTS (art, communications, dance, dramatic arts, English, music, music performance, music theory and composition, musical theater, and voice), COMPUTER AND PHYSICAL SCIENCE (computer science and mathematics), EDUCATION (art, athletic training, drama, elementary, English, mathematics, music, physical, science, secondary, social science, and specific learning disabilities), HEALTH PROFESSIONS (exercise science), SOCIAL SCIENCE (biblical studies, history, liberal arts/general studies, ministries, philosophy, political science/government, prelaw, psychology, religion, and religious music). Business, psychology, and education are the strongest academically and have the largest enrollments.

Required: Students must complete core requirements and 120 credit hours, with a minimum of 30 credit hours in the major and 42 upper-level hours. A minimum 2.0 GPA is required.

Special: PBA offers work-study, internships, an interdisciplinary major, dual majors, student-designed majors, accelerated degree programs in organizational management and ministry, and a Washington semester and study abroad through the Coalition of Christian Colleges and Universities. A 2-2 engineering degree with the University of Florida, ESL, and teacher certification are also offered. There is a freshman honors program.

Faculty/Classroom: 37% of faculty are male; 63%, female. 85% teach undergraduates. No introductory courses are taught by graduate students. The average class size in an introductory lecture is 30; in a laboratory, 24; and in a regular course, 20.

Admissions: 87% of the 2003-2004 applicants were accepted. The SAT I scores for the 2003-2004 freshman class were: Verbal--24% below 500, 52% between 500 and 599, 21% between 600 and 700, and 3% above 700; Math--30% below 500, 49% between 500 and 599, 20% between 600 and 700, and 1% above 700. The ACT scores were 29% below 21, 27% between 21 and 23, 27% between 24 and 26, 12% between 27 and 28, and 5% above 28. 39% of the current freshmen were in the top fifth of their class; 65% were in the top two fifths.

Requirements: The SAT I or ACT is required for some programs. In addition, applicants must be graduates of an accredited secondary school or have a GED certificate, and have completed 18 academic credits—4 in English, 3 in math, science, social studies, and history, and 2 in a foreign language. A minimum composite score of 960 on the SAT I or 21 on the ACT, an essay, and an interview are required. A portfolio is recommended for art students. A GPA of 2.0 is required. AP and CLEP credits are accepted. Important factors in the admissions decision are advanced placement or honor courses, leadership record, and personality/intangible qualities.

Procedure: Freshmen are admitted to all sessions. Entrance exams should be taken in the junior year of high school. There are early admissions and deferred admissions plans. Application deadlines are open and notification is sent on a rolling basis beginning December 8. Applications are accepted on-line through the university's web site.

Transfer: 360 transfer students enrolled in 2002-2003. Transfer students must have a minimum 2.0 GPA, a minimum of 12 credit hours, and 2 letters of recommendation. An interview is encouraged. 32 of 120 credits required for the bachelor's degree must be completed at PBA.

Visiting: There are regularly scheduled orientations for prospective students, including a general open house and a school-specific open house. There are guides for informal visits and visitors may sit in on classes and stay overnight. To schedule a visit, contact the Admissions Office at (561) 803-2100 or admit@pba.edu.

Financial Aid: In 2003-2004, all full-time freshmen and 98% of continuing full-time students received some form of financial aid. 15% of undergraduates work part time. Average annual earnings from campus work are $1000. PBA is a member of CSS. The FAFSA, the state aid form, and the college's own financial statement are required. The deadline for filing freshman financial aid applications for fall entry is April 1.

International Students: There are 87 international students enrolled. The school actively recruits these students. They must score 500 on the written TOEFL.

Computers: Computer labs are available and there is 1 computer per dorm room. All campus computers are networked to the central student and web servers. No mainframe access is available, although all students have drive space and server space just for web pages. Dial-up connections provide off-campus access. All students may access the system. There are no time limits and no fees. It is strongly recommended that all students have a personal computer.

Graduates: From July 1, 2002 to June 30, 2003, 350 bachelor's degrees were awarded. The most popular majors were business/management (58%), education (14%), and psychology (11%). In an average class, 2% graduate in 3 years or less, 31% graduate in 4 years or less, 38% graduate in 5 years or less, and 42% graduate in 6 years or less.

Admissions Contact: Buck James, Vice President of Enrollment Services. E-mail: admit@pba.edu Web: www.pba.edu

RINGLING SCHOOL OF ART AND DESIGN D-4
Sarasota, FL 34234-5896
(941) 351-5100
(800) 255-7695; Fax: (941) 359-7517

Full-time: 514 men, 448 women	Faculty: 62
Part-time: 12 men, 15 women	Ph.Ds: 65%
Graduate: none	Student/Faculty: 16 to 1
Year: semesters	Tuition: $19,060
Application Deadline: open	Room & Board: $8470
Freshman Class: 1030 applied, 686 accepted, 298 enrolled	
SAT I Verbal/Math: 520/510	ACT: 23	SPECIAL

Ringling School of Art and Design, founded in 1931, is a private art college. In addition to regional accreditation, Ringling School has baccalaureate program accreditation with FIDER and NASAD. The library contains 44,237 volumes and 4505 audio/video tapes/CDs, and subscribes to 310 periodicals. Computerized library services include interlibrary loans, database searching, and Internet access. Special learning facilities include a learning resource center, art gallery, and a total of 113,000 slides. The 37-acre campus is in an urban area 50 miles south of Tampa. Including any residence halls, there are 60 buildings.

Student Life: 51% of undergraduates are from out of state, mostly the South. Students are from 46 states and 33 foreign countries. 78% are white. The average age of freshmen is 19; all undergraduates, 21. 22% do not continue beyond their first year; 72% remain to graduate.

Housing: 474 students can be accommodated in college housing, which includes single-sex and coed dorms, on-campus apartments, and married-student housing. On-campus housing is available on a first-come, first-served basis and is available on a lottery system for upperclassmen. Priority is given to out-of-town students. 52% of students commute. Alcohol is not permitted. All students may keep cars.

Activities: 3% of men belong to 2 national fraternities; 2% of women belong to 1 national sorority. There are 22 groups on campus, including art, computers, drama, ethnic, gay, international, literary magazine, professional, religious, social, social service, and student government. Popular campus events include All School Welcome Back Beach Party, Valentines Dance, and Latin Ball.

Sports: There are 4 intramural sports for men and 4 for women. Facilities include a basketball court and a recreation room with pool tables.

Disabled Students: 80% of the campus is accessible. Wheelchair ramps, elevators, special parking, specially equipped rest rooms, special class scheduling, lowered telephones, and interpreters for the hearing-impaired are available.

Services: Counseling and information services are available, as is tutoring in some subjects, including English, art history, and history. There is remedial writing.

Campus Safety and Security: Measures include 24-hour foot and vehicle patrol, security escort services, informal discussions, and emergency telephones. There are lighted pathways/sidewalks.

Programs of Study: Ringling School confers the B.F.A. degree. Bachelor's degrees are awarded in COMMUNICATIONS AND THE ARTS (fine arts, graphic design, illustration, and photography), ENGINEERING AND ENVIRONMENTAL DESIGN (computer graphics and interior design). Illustration is the largest.

Required: To graduate, all students must complete 123 semester hours, including the CORE studio program, 75 hours of studio art, 30 hours of liberal arts, and 12 hours of art history, with 75 hours in the major. A minimum 2.0 GPA and courses in drawing, 2- and 3-dimensional design, art history, and written communication are required.

Special: The college offers cross-registration with the Art College Exchange, internships with Walt Disney Animation and Home Box Office, and study abroad in France, England, and Ireland. Also available are credit by portfolio, and a nondegree, continuing education program.

Faculty/Classroom: 64% of faculty are male; 36%, female. All teach undergraduates. The average class size in an introductory lecture is 25 and in a regular course, 19.

Admissions: 67% of the 2003-2004 applicants were accepted. The SAT I scores for the 2003-2004 freshman class were: Verbal--35% below 500, 47% between 500 and 599, 17% between 600 and 700, and 1% above 700; Math--39% below 500, 51% between 500 and 599, and 10% between 600 and 700.

Requirements: The SAT I or ACT is recommended. In addition, applicants must have received either a standard high school diploma from an accredited secondary school or a GED. Admission is based on the academic record, letters of recommendation, and a portfolio. An essay is required and an interview is recommended. A GPA of 2.0 is required. AP and CLEP credits are accepted. Important factors in the admissions decision are evidence of special talent, advanced placement or honor courses, and recommendations by school officials.

Procedure: Freshmen are admitted in the fall. Application deadlines are open for fall entry. Applications for computer animation should be filed January 15 along with a $35 fee. Notification is sent on a rolling basis. 40 students were on the 2003 waiting list; 10 were admitted. Applications are accepted on-line.

Transfer: 115 transfer students enrolled in 2002-2003. Transfer students must meet the same criteria as freshmen and must also submit college transcripts. 45 of 123 credits required for the bachelor's degree must be completed at Ringling School.

Visiting: There are guides for informal visits and visitors may sit in on classes. To schedule a visit, contact the Admissions Office.

Financial Aid: In 2003-2004, 73% of all full-time freshmen and 72% of continuing full-time students received some form of financial aid. 66% of full-time freshmen and 61% of continuing full-time students received need-based aid. The average freshman award was $14,224. Need-based scholarships or need-based grants averaged $1517 ($4500 maximum); need-based self-help aid (loans and jobs) averaged $2608 ($8625 maximum); other non-need-based awards and non-need-based scholarships averaged $14,000; and outside scholarships averaged $3670 ($25,920 maximum). 35% of undergraduates work part time. Average annual earnings from campus work are $2500. The average financial indebtedness of the 2003 graduate was $16,500. The FAFSA and the college's own financial statement are required. The priority date for freshman financial aid applications for fall entry is March 1.

International Students: There are 56 international students enrolled. The school actively recruits these students. They must score 500 on the written TOEFL or 173 on the electronic version and submit a portfolio.

Computers: There is a student/computer ratio of better than 2 to 1, with an array of computing services and resources. All students may access the system. There are no time limits and no fees.

Graduates: From July 1, 2002 to June 30, 2003, 206 bachelor's degrees were awarded. The most popular majors were illustration (39%), graphic and interactive communication (18%), and computer animation

(17%). In an average class, 60% graduate in 4 years or less, 63% graduate in 5 years or less, and 64% graduate in 6 years or less. 35 companies recruited on campus in 2002-2003. Of the 2002 graduating class, 7% were enrolled in graduate school within 6 months of graduation and 85% were employed.

Admissions Contact: James H. Dean, Dean of Admissions.
E-mail: *admissions@ringling.edu* Web: *ringling.edu*

ROLLINS COLLEGE D-3

Winter Park, FL 32789	(407) 646-2161; Fax: (407) 646-1502
Full-time: 676 men, 1057 women	**Faculty:** 149; IIA, +$
Part-time: none	**Ph.D.s:** 89%
Graduate: 358 men, 474 women	**Student/Faculty:** 9 to 1
Year: semesters	**Tuition:** $26,250
Application Deadline: February 15	**Room & Board:** $8050
Freshman Class: 2271 applied, 1510 accepted, 497 enrolled	
SAT I Verbal/Math: 570/580	**ACT:** 24 **VERY COMPETITIVE**

Rollins College, founded in 1885, is a private, liberal arts institution. In addition to regional accreditation, Rollins has baccalaureate program accreditation with NASM and ACS. The library contains 290,934 volumes, 42,435 microform items, and 3361 audio/video tapes/CDs, and subscribes to 10,600 periodicals. Computerized library services include the card catalog, interlibrary loans, database searching, and Internet access. Special learning facilities include a learning resource center, art gallery, radio station, TV station, art museum, theaters, writing center, and student resource center. The 70-acre campus is in a suburban area 5 miles north of Orlando. Including any residence halls, there are 70 buildings.

Student Life: 57% of undergraduates are from out of state, mostly the Northeast. Students are from 46 states, 51 foreign countries, and Canada. 49% are from public schools. 74% are white. The average age of freshmen is 18; all undergraduates, 20. 17% do not continue beyond their first year; 62% remain to graduate.

Housing: 1250 students can be accommodated in college housing, which includes coed dorms, on-campus apartments, fraternity houses, and sorority houses. In addition, there are honors houses and special-interest houses. On-campus housing is guaranteed for all 4 years. 62% of students live on campus; of those, 63% remain on campus on weekends. Upperclassmen may keep cars.

Activities: 38% of men belong to 1 local and 4 national fraternities; 40% of women belong to 1 local and 4 national sororities. There are 122 groups on campus, including art, brass ensemble, cheerleading, choir, chorale, chorus, computers, dance, drama, ethnic, film, gay, honors, international, jazz band, literary magazine, musical theater, newspaper, photography, political, professional, radio and TV, religious, social, social service, student government, and yearbook. Popular campus events include Rollins Autumn Art Festival, World Hunger Concert, and the Bach Festival.

Sports: There are 10 intercollegiate sports for men and 12 for women, and 20 intramural sports for men and 20 for women. Facilities include a 2500-seat auditorium, a 600-seat stadium, tennis courts, baseball and soccer fields, a field house with a gym that seats 2500, a weight room, a boat house, and a swimming pool.

Disabled Students: 55% of the campus is accessible. Wheelchair ramps, elevators, special parking, specially equipped rest rooms, special class scheduling, lowered drinking fountains, and lowered telephones are available.

Services: Counseling and information services are available, as is tutoring in every subject. There is a reader service for the blind, and remedial math, reading, and writing.

Campus Safety and Security: Measures include 24-hour foot and vehicle patrol, self-defense education, security escort services, and informal discussions. There are pamphlets/posters/films, emergency telephones, lighted pathways/sidewalks, and 24-hour locked residential units.

Programs of Study: Rollins confers the A.B. degree. Master's degrees are also awarded. Bachelor's degrees are awarded in BIOLOGICAL SCIENCE (biology/biological science), BUSINESS (international business management), COMMUNICATIONS AND THE ARTS (art history and appreciation, dramatic arts, English, French, music history and appreciation, music performance, Spanish, and studio art), COMPUTER AND PHYSICAL SCIENCE (chemistry, computer science, mathematics, and physics), EDUCATION (elementary), ENGINEERING AND ENVIRONMENTAL DESIGN (environmental science), SOCIAL SCIENCE (anthropology, classical/ancient civilization, economics, European studies, history, international relations, Latin American studies, philosophy, political science/government, psychology, religion, and sociology). Psychology, international business, and economics are the largest.

Required: All students must complete at least 6 skills, including at least 4 cognitive, and at least 2 affective courses, a values requirement, and 4 phys ed courses. A minimum of 35 course units, with 12 to 16 in the course major, and a minimum GPA of 2.0 are required to graduate.

Special: Rollins offers cross-registration with the evening studies division, co-op programs with American University in Washington, D.C., and Paris and the Duke University School of Forestry and Environmen-

458 FLORIDA

tal Studies, departmental and professional internships, study abroad in 9 countries, and a Washington semester. Also available are accelerated degree programs, a B.A.-B.S. degree in preengineering, an interdepartmental biochemistry/molecular biology major, dual majors in any combination, and student-designed majors. A 3-2 engineering degree with Washington University in St. Louis and Auburn, Case Western Reserve and Columbia Universities is offered. Nondegree study and pass/fail options are possible. There are 3 national honor societies, a freshman honors program, and 28 departmental honors programs.

Faculty/Classroom: 62% of faculty are male; 38%, female. No introductory courses are taught by graduate students. The average class size in an introductory lecture is 17; in a laboratory, 17; and in a regular course, 17.

Admissions: 66% of the 2003-2004 applicants were accepted. The SAT I scores for the 2003-2004 freshman class were: Verbal--11% below 500, 49% between 500 and 599, 35% between 600 and 700, and 4% above 700; Math--10% below 500, 48% between 500 and 599, 37% between 600 and 700, and 6% above 700. The ACT scores were 12% below 21, 30% between 21 and 23, 31% between 24 and 26, 16% between 27 and 28, and 10% above 28. 60% of the current freshmen were in the top fifth of their class; 82% were in the top two fifths. 3 freshmen graduated first in their class.

Requirements: The SAT I or ACT is required. In addition, applicants must be graduates of an accredited secondary school or have a GED certificate, and have completed 4 years of English, 3 of math, and 2 each of foreign language, science, and social studies. An essay is required. SAT II: Subject tests in writing, math, and foreign language and an interview are recommended. AP credits are accepted. Important factors in the admissions decision are advanced placement or honor courses, evidence of special talent, and extracurricular activities record.

Procedure: Freshmen are admitted fall and spring. Entrance exams should be taken by the first semester of the senior year. There are early decision, early admissions, and deferred admissions plans. Early decision applications should be filed by January 15; regular applications by February 15 for fall entry and December 1 for spring entry. Notification of early decision is sent February 1; regular decision, April 1. The fall 2003 application fee was $40. 175 students were on the 2003 waiting list; 17 were admitted. Applications are accepted on computer disk.

Transfer: Transfer students must satisfy all regular admission requirements and submit official transcripts of college and high school work and SAT I or ACT scores. A recommended 2.5 GPA and a year's worth of credit hours earned are required. An interview is recommended. 16 of 35 credits required for the bachelor's degree must be completed at Rollins.

Visiting: There are regularly scheduled orientations for prospective students, including 2 all-campus previews in the fall. There are guides for informal visits and visitors may sit in on classes and stay overnight. To schedule a visit, contact the Office of Admissions.

Financial Aid: In 2003-2004, 67% of all full-time freshmen and 73% of continuing full-time students received some form of financial aid. 36% of full-time freshmen and 42% of continuing full-time students received need-based aid. The average freshman award was $18,866, with $7035 from need-based scholarships or need-based grants, $2616 from need-based self-help aid (loans and jobs), $1296 from non-need-based athletic scholarships, and $7919 from other non-need-based awards and non-need-based scholarships. 15% of undergraduates work part time. Average annual earnings from campus work are $891. The average financial indebtedness of the 2003 graduate is $14,500. Rollins is a member of CSS. The CSS/Profile or FAFSA and the college's own financial statement are required. The deadline for filing freshman financial aid applications for fall entry is March 1.

International Students: There are 65 international students enrolled. The school actively recruits these students. They must score 550 on the written TOEFL and also take the SAT I or the ACT.

Computers: The student computing center is open 24 hours. More than 150 terminals and PCs for student use are located in the writing center, residence halls, the library, and departmental lounges. Students may bring their own PC and, with a modem, access the mainframe 24 hours per day. All students may access the system. There are no time limits and no fees. It is strongly recommended that all students have a personal computer.

Graduates: From July 1, 2002 to June 30, 2003, 383 bachelor's degrees were awarded. The most popular majors were international business (11%), psychology (10%), and English (9%). Of the 2002 graduating class, 24% were enrolled in graduate school within 6 months of graduation and 62% were employed.

Admissions Contact: David G. Erdmann, Dean of Admission and Student Financial Planning. A video is available.
E-mail: *admission@rollins.edu*
Web: *http://www.rollins/admission/index.shtml*

SAINT LEO UNIVERSITY — D-3
Saint Leo, FL 33574-6665 (352) 588-8283
(800) 334-5532; Fax: (352) 588-8257

Full-time: 471 men, 561 women	**Faculty:** 68; IIB, --$
Part-time: 18 men, 33 women	**Ph.D.s:** 81%
Graduate: 178 men, 257 women	**Student/Faculty:** 15 to 1
Year: semesters, summer session	**Tuition:** $13,570
Application Deadline: open	**Room & Board:** $7030
Freshman Class: 1933 applied, 1145 accepted, 382 enrolled	
SAT I Verbal/Math: 490/490	**ACT:** 21 COMPETITIVE

Saint Leo University, a private institution, was founded in 1889 by the Benedictine Order of the Catholic Church. The university offers undergraduate programs in business administration, the humanities, natural sciences, social sciences, education, and preprofessional studies There are 3 undergraduate and 2 graduate schools. In addition to regional accreditation, Saint Leo has baccalaureate program accreditation with CSWE and IACBE. The library contains 141,521 volumes, 28,290 microform items, and 6437 audio/video tapes/CDs, and subscribes to 700 periodicals. Computerized library services include the card catalog, interlibrary loans, database searching, and Internet access. Special learning facilities include a learning resource center and TV station. The 186-acre campus is in a rural area 40 miles north of Tampa. Including any residence halls, there are 23 buildings.

Student Life: 69% of undergraduates are from Florida. Students are from 33 states, 35 foreign countries, and Canada. 68% are from public schools. 66% are white. 51% are Catholic; 29% Protestant; 15% claim no religious affiliation. The average age of freshmen is 18; all undergraduates, 22. 33% do not continue beyond their first year; 40% remain to graduate.

Housing: 797 students can be accommodated in college housing, which includes single-sex and coed dorms, on-campus apartments, fraternity houses, and sorority houses. On-campus housing is available on a first-come, first-served basis and is available on a lottery system for upperclassmen. 69% of students live on campus; of those, 80% remain on campus on weekends. All students may keep cars.

Activities: 10% of men belong to 3 local and 2 national fraternities; 6% of women belong to 1 local sorority and 4 national sororities. There are 43 groups on campus, including band, cheerleading, chorus, drama, ethnic, honors, international, literary magazine, newspaper, political, professional, radio and TV, religious, social, social service, student government, and yearbook. Popular campus events include Fall Festival, Spring Fling, and Winter Formal.

Sports: There are 6 intercollegiate sports for men and 7 for women, and 13 intramural sports for men and 13 for women. Facilities include a 2000-seat indoor gym, a fitness center, an outdoor swimming pool, a golf course, soccer, softball, baseball, and practice fields, basketball, volleyball, lighted tennis, and racquetball courts, and sailing and canoeing.

Disabled Students: 95% of the campus is accessible. Wheelchair ramps, elevators, special parking, specially equipped rest rooms, and lowered drinking fountains are available. Accommodations for persons with disabilities are available on a case-by-case basis with proper documentation.

Services: Counseling and information services are available, as is tutoring in most subjects. There is remedial math and writing.

Campus Safety and Security: Measures include 24-hour foot and vehicle patrol, security escort services, informal discussions, and pamphlets/posters/films. There are emergency telephones and lighted pathways/sidewalks.

Programs of Study: Saint Leo confers B.A., B.S., and B.S.W. degrees. Associate and master's degrees are also awarded. Bachelor's degrees are awarded in BIOLOGICAL SCIENCE (biology/biological science), BUSINESS (accounting, business administration and management, hospitality management services, human resources, sports management, and tourism), COMMUNICATIONS AND THE ARTS (English), COMPUTER AND PHYSICAL SCIENCE (information sciences and systems), EDUCATION (elementary), ENGINEERING AND ENVIRONMENTAL DESIGN (environmental science), HEALTH PROFESSIONS (health care administration and medical technology), SOCIAL SCIENCE (criminal justice, history, human services, international studies, political science/government, psychology, religion, social work, and sociology). Biology, English, and environmental science are the strongest academically. Business administration, elementary education, and criminal justice are the largest.

Required: To graduate, all students must complete a minimum of 120 academic credits, with 30 to 60 hours in the major, all the requirements of their division and major, and 53 to 56 hours in the general education program. The honors program may be substituted for general education requirements. A minimum 2.0 GPA and capstone course are required, and there is a 30-hour residency requirement.

Special: Saint Leo offers internships in most majors, study abroad in 8 countries, work-study programs on campus, dual majors, and credit for military experience. There is a prelaw program, preprofessional programs in medicine, dentistry, and veterinary science, Liberal Arts in Management Program (LAMP), Learning Enhancement for Academic Progress (LEAP), and Air Force and Army ROTC programs. There are 9 national honor societies and a freshman honors program.

Faculty/Classroom: 61% of faculty are male; 39%, female. All teach undergraduates. No introductory courses are taught by graduate students. The average class size in an introductory lecture is 25; in a laboratory, 10; and in a regular course, 20.

Admissions: 59% of the 2003-2004 applicants were accepted. The SAT I scores for the 2003-2004 freshman class were: Verbal--51% below 500, 40% between 500 and 599, 7% between 600 and 700, and 1% above 700; Math--52% below 500, 41% between 500 and 599, and 7% between 600 and 700. The ACT scores were 44% below 21, 33% between 21 and 23, 16% between 24 and 26, 2% between 27 and 28, and 5% above 28. 22% of the current freshmen were in the top fifth of their class; 60% were in the top two fifths.

Requirements: The SAT I or ACT is required. In addition, applicants must be graduates of an accredited secondary school or have a GED certificate, and have completed 4 credits each in English and electives, 3 each in math and social studies, and 2 in science. A GPA of 2.3 is required. AP and CLEP credits are accepted. Important factors in the admissions decision are advanced placement or honor courses, personality/intangible qualities, and recommendations by school officials.

Procedure: Freshmen are admitted fall and spring. Entrance exams should be taken by the fall of the senior year. There is a deferred admissions plan. Application deadlines are open. The fall 2003 application fee was $35. Notification is sent on a rolling basis. Applications are accepted on-line through CollegeLink, Catholic College Application, and the school's web site.

Transfer: 132 transfer students enrolled in 2002-2003. Applicants must submit an official transcript from each previously attended college, a recommendation from the dean of students of the last institution attended, and a writing sample. A minimum 2.5 GPA is required. If transferring fewer than 24 academic credits, a high school transcript (or GED) and standardized test scores are required. 30 of 120 credits required for the bachelor's degree must be completed at Saint Leo.

Visiting: There are regularly scheduled orientations for prospective students, consisting of overnight campus visitation programs. There are guides for informal visits and visitors may sit in on classes and stay overnight. To schedule a visit, contact the Office of Admission at *admission@saintleo.edu*.

Financial Aid: In 2003-2004, 99% of all full-time freshmen and 90% of continuing full-time students received some form of financial aid. 84% of full-time freshmen and 82% of continuing full-time students received need-based aid. The average freshman award was $13,375. Need-based scholarships or need-based grants averaged $9200 ($23,600 maximum); and non-need-based athletic scholarships averaged $3000. 21% of undergraduates work part time. Average annual earnings from campus work are $2500. The average financial indebtedness of the 2003 graduate was $15,000. Saint Leo is a member of CSS. The FAFSA is required. The priority date for freshman financial aid applications for fall entry is March 1.

International Students: There are 49 international students enrolled. The school actively recruits these students. They must score 550 on the written TOEFL or 213 on the electronic version. They must also take the SAT I or the ACT, scoring a minimum of 450 on the SAT I verbal section.

Computers: The mainframe is a Compaq ES40. All students may use the 65 PCs that are located throughout the library, with more than 100 total on campus available for student use. In addition, students living in university residences are provided notebook computers for the wireless network throughout campus. Students register for courses, check schedules, interact with faculty, and participate in many other essential activities on-line using the university's web portal. All students may access the system. There are no time limits and no fees.

Graduates: From July 1, 2002 to June 30, 2003, 192 bachelor's degrees were awarded. The most popular majors were business administration (20%), elementary education (15%), and psychology (9%). In an average class, 30% graduate in 4 years or less, 39% graduate in 5 years or less, and 40% graduate in 6 years or less. 18 companies recruited on campus in 2002-2003. Of the 2002 graduating class, 57% were enrolled in graduate school within 6 months of graduation and 91% were employed.

Admissions Contact: Gary Bracken, Vice President for Enrollment. E-mail: *admission@saintleo.edu* Web: *www.saintleo.edu*

SAINT THOMAS UNIVERSITY   E-5
Miami, FL 33054   (305) 628-6546
(800) 367-9010; Fax: (305) 628-6591

Full-time: 451 men, 720 women	Faculty: n/av
Part-time: none	Ph.D.s: n/av
Graduate: 582 men, 767 women	Student/Faculty: n/av
Year: semesters, summer session	Tuition: $16,200
Application Deadline: open	Room & Board: $5200
Freshman Class: 1290 applied, 549 accepted, 338 enrolled	
SAT I Verbal/Math: 440/445	ACT: 17 LESS COMPETITIVE

Saint Thomas University, founded in 1961, is a private, liberal arts university affiliated with the Roman Catholic Church and sponsored by the Archdiocese of Miami. There are 2 undergraduate and 2 graduate schools. The 2 libraries contain 200,000 volumes and subscribe to 1000 periodicals. Computerized library services include the card catalog, interlibrary loans, and database searching. Special learning facilities include a learning resource center and TV station. The 140-acre campus is in a suburban area 10 miles from Miami and Fort Lauderdale. Including any residence halls, there are 15 buildings.

Student Life: 85% of undergraduates are from Florida. Students are from 23 states, 49 foreign countries, and Canada. 70% are from public schools. 37% are Hispanic; 23% African American; 21% white; 18% foreign nationals. 50% are Catholic; 12% claim no religious affiliation. The average age of freshmen is 19; all undergraduates, 25. 30% do not continue beyond their first year; 42% remain to graduate.

Housing: 350 students can be accommodated in college housing, which includes coed dorms. In addition, there are special-interest houses. On-campus housing is guaranteed for all 4 years. 80% of students commute. All students may keep cars.

Activities: 10% of men and about 2% of women belong to 1 local and 1 national fraternity; 5% of women belong to 1 national sorority. There are 20 groups on campus, including art, cheerleading, choir, computers, drama, ethnic, honors, international, literary magazine, newspaper, photography, political, professional, radio and TV, religious, social, social service, student government, and yearbook. Popular campus events include Senior Capping Ceremony, Freshman Investiture Ceremony, and Land and Water Olympics.

Sports: There are 5 intercollegiate sports for men and 4 for women, and 12 intramural sports for men and 12 for women. Facilities include basketball, soccer, and softball fields, tennis courts, a weight room, and a swimming pool.

Disabled Students: 90% of the campus is accessible. Wheelchair ramps, elevators, special parking, specially equipped rest rooms, and special class scheduling are available.

Services: Counseling and information services are available, as is tutoring in most subjects. There is remedial math, reading, and writing. Computer-assisted instruction is available.

Campus Safety and Security: Measures include 24-hour foot and vehicle patrol, self-defense education, security escort services, and informal discussions. There are pamphlets/posters/films, emergency telephones, and lighted pathways/sidewalks.

Programs of Study: STU confers B.A. and B.B.A. degrees. Master's degrees are also awarded. Bachelor's degrees are awarded in BIOLOGICAL SCIENCE (biology/biological science), BUSINESS (accounting, banking and finance, business administration and management, hospitality management services, hotel/motel and restaurant management, human resources, international business management, marketing/retailing/merchandising, sports management, and tourism), COMMUNICATIONS AND THE ARTS (communications, English, and Spanish), COMPUTER AND PHYSICAL SCIENCE (chemistry, computer programming, and computer science), EDUCATION (elementary, secondary, and social studies), HEALTH PROFESSIONS (predentistry and premedicine), SOCIAL SCIENCE (American studies, criminal justice, economics, history, human services, international relations, liberal arts/general studies, political science/government, prelaw, psychology, public administration, religion, and sociology). Sports administration and accounting are the strongest academically. Business management, psychology, and communications are the largest.

Required: All students must complete at least 120 semester credits (126 for business), with 30 to 60 in the major, and specific courses, including 12 credits in English, 9 each in math/physical science, philosophy, and religion, and 6 each in history, social science, and humanities. Students must maintain a 2.0 overall GPA and a 2.25 GPA in the major subject.

Special: Communication arts, hospitality management, and sports administration internships, study abroad in Italy and Spain, and a general studies degree are available. The university grants credit for life, military, and work experience via the Life Experience Portfolio. There are 2 national honor societies, a freshman honors program, and 1 departmental honors program.

Admissions: 43% of the 2003-2004 applicants were accepted.

Requirements: The SAT I or ACT is required. In addition, applicants should have completed 18 high school units, including 4 units in English,

3 each in math and social science, and 2 in science. A GPA of 2.0 is required. AP and CLEP credits are accepted. Important factors in the admissions decision are recommendations by school officials, advanced placement or honor courses, and evidence of special talent.

Procedure: Freshmen are admitted to all sessions. Entrance exams should be taken in December of the senior year of high school. There is a rolling admissions plan and a deferred admissions plan. Application deadlines are open. Application fee is $40.

Transfer: Maximum credit hours accepted are 60 from a junior college and 90 from a 4-year institution. No grade of D is acceptable in courses beyond sophomore level or in the major. Students with fewer than 30 credits must submit a high school transcript and SAT I or ACT scores. 30 of 120 credits required for the bachelor's degree must be completed at STU.

Visiting: There are guides for informal visits and visitors may sit in on classes and stay overnight. To schedule a visit, contact the Admissions Office.

Financial Aid: The CSS Profile or FAFSA and the college's own financial statement are required. The priority date for freshman financial aid applications for fall entry is April 1.

International Students: There are 221 international students enrolled. The school actively recruits these students. They must score 525 on the written TOEFL or 193 on the electronic version and also take the college's own test, as well as the SAT I or ACT, scoring 440 on the verbal section of the SAT I and 440 on the math section, or 18 on the ACT.

Computers: The mainframe is a Prime 9755. There are 30 IBM PS/2 Model 30-286 and 55SX PCs available for academic use in the computer lab. All students may access the system any time it is available. There are no time limits and no fees.

Admissions Contact: Andre Lightbourn, Associate Director of Admissions. A video is available. E-mail: *alightbo@stu.edu* Web: *www.stu.edu*

SOUTHEASTERN COLLEGE

D-3

Lakeland, FL 33801

(863) 667-5018

(800) 500-8760; Fax: (863) 667-5200

Full-time: 600 men, 650 women	**Faculty:** 43
Part-time: 50 men, 70 women	**Ph.D.s:** 48%
Graduate: none	**Student/Faculty:** 29 to 1
Year: semesters, summer session	**Tuition:** $7545
Application Deadline: see profile	**Room & Board:** $4110
Freshman Class: n/av	
SAT I or ACT: required	**LESS COMPETITIVE**

Southeastern College, founded in 1935 is a Christian liberal arts institution offering 25 degree programs that equip students to serve in both professional careers and ministry-related fields. Figures in the above capsule and in this profile are approximate. The 2 libraries contain 94,000 volumes, 1658 microform items, and 2850 audio/video tapes/CDs, and subscribe to 431 periodicals. Computerized library services include the card catalog, interlibrary loans, and database searching. Special learning facilities include a learning resource center, radio station, TV station, and Pentecostal Research Library. The 56-acre campus is in a small town 30 miles east of Tampa and 45 miles west of Orlando. Including any residence halls, there are 32 buildings.

Student Life: 58% of undergraduates are from Florida. Students are from 40 states, 8 foreign countries, and Canada. 79% are white; 10% Hispanic. Most are Protestant. The average age of freshmen is 18; all undergraduates, 21. 19% do not continue beyond their first year; 35% remain to graduate.

Housing: 910 students can be accommodated in college housing, which includes single-sex dorms and on-campus apartments. On-campus housing is guaranteed for all 4 years. 60% of students live on campus. Alcohol is not permitted. All students may keep cars.

Activities: There are no fraternities or sororities. There are 20 groups on campus, including band, cheerleading, choir, chorale, chorus, computers, drama, ethnic, honors, international, jazz band, newspaper, radio and TV, religious, social service, student government, and yearbook. Popular campus events include Fall Festival, Christmas Social, and Junior-Senior Banquet.

Sports: There are 4 intercollegiate sports for men and 4 for women, and 8 intramural sports for men and 6 for women. Facilities include a gym, baseball and soccer fields, tennis, racquetball, and beach volleyball courts, a weight room, and intramural fields.

Disabled Students: 90% of the campus is accessible. Wheelchair ramps, elevators, special parking, specially equipped rest rooms, special class scheduling, and lowered drinking fountains are available.

Services: Counseling and information services are available, as is tutoring in some subjects, including math, reading, and English. There is remedial math, reading, and writing.

Campus Safety and Security: Measures include 24-hour foot and vehicle patrol, informal discussions, pamphlets/posters/films, lighted pathways/sidewalks, and a main entrance security booth attendant.

Programs of Study: SoutheasternCollege confers B.A., B.S., B.M., and B.S.W. degrees. Bachelor's degrees are awarded in BIOLOGICAL SCIENCE (biology/biological science), BUSINESS (accounting, business administration and management, and marketing/retailing/merchandising), COMMUNICATIONS AND THE ARTS (communications, English, and music), EDUCATION (Christian, education of the exceptional child, elementary, psychology, pastoral studies, Christian education, and business. There are accelerated degree programs in Church leadership and in education, middle school, music, and secondary), SOCIAL SCIENCE (biblical studies, interdisciplinary studies, ministries, pastoral studies, psychology, religion, religious music, social work, and youth ministry). Religion, education, and psychology are the strongest academically. Religion is the largest.

Required: Every degree student must complete 125 to 130 hours, including 36 hours of general education and at least 20 hours of religion. Distribution requirements include 6 to 12 hours each in arts and communications, human adjustment, science and math, social sciences, and humanities and fine arts. A minimum GPA of 2.0 must be maintained.

Special: Internships are available in communications, education, ministry, psychology, pastoral studies, Christian education, and business. There are 2 national honor societies and 2 departmental honors programs.

Faculty/Classroom: 66% of faculty are male; 34%, female. 96% teach undergraduates. The average class size in an introductory lecture is 60; in a laboratory, 20; and in a regular course, 28.

Requirements: The SAT I or ACT is required. The GED is accepted. A GPA of 1.5 is required. AP and CLEP credits are accepted.

Procedure: Freshmen are admitted to all sessions. Entrance exams should be taken prior to enrollment. There is an early admissions plan and a rolling admissions plan. Check with the school for current deadlines. The fall 2003 application fee was $40. Southeastern accepts applications on-line.

Transfer: 137 transfer students enrolled in a recent year. Admission requirements for transfer applicants are the same as for first-time students. 30 of 130 credits required for the bachelor's degree must be completed at SoutheasternCollege.

Visiting: There are regularly scheduled orientations for prospective students, including College Days (fall and spring), which consist of a 24 hour overview of campus life with class visits, faculty reception, admission/financial aid workshops, a student panel discussion, and a worship service. There are guides for informal visits and visitors may sit in on classes and stay overnight. To schedule a visit, contact the Admission Office.

Financial Aid: In a recent year, 58% of all full-time freshmen and 71% of continuing full-time students received some form of financial aid. 51% of full-time freshmen and 62% of continuing full-time students received need-based aid. The average freshman award was $6961. 20% of undergraduates work part time. Average annual earnings from campus work are $1500. The FAFSA and the college's own financial statement are required. Check with the school for current deadlines.

International Students: In a recent year, there were 8 international students enrolled. The school actively recruits these students. They must score 500 on the written TOEFL and also take the SAT I or the ACT.

Computers: The mainframe is an IBM AS/400. PCs and Macs are available for student use in the computer lab, e-mail, Internet access, voice mail, and cable are available from each dorm room. All students may access the system during designated lab hours or from their residence hall. There are no time limits and no fees.

Graduates: In a recent year, 222 bachelor's degrees were awarded. In an average class, 30% graduate in 6 years or less.

Admissions Contact: Omar Rashed, Director of Admission. E-mail: *admission@secollege.edu* Web: *http://www.secollege.edu*

STATE UNIVERSITY SYSTEM OF FLORIDA

Florida's State University System comprises 11 institutions serving a highly diverse enrollment of more than 261,000 students and employing more than 14,400 full- and part-time faculty. The Florida Board of Governors sets policy and provides leadership for the system, while a president and a Board of Trustees administers each university. The SUS institutions also engage Florida's leading private colleges and universities in numerous research and academic partnerships. In 2002-2003, Florida's State University System granted a total of 53,887 bachelor's, master's, doctoral, and professional degrees. In 2003, the system established three Centers of Excellence — in biomedical and marine biotechnology at Florida Atlantic University, in Boca Raton; in photonics at the University of Central Florida in Orlando; and in regenerative health biotechnology at the University of Florida in Gainesville. The system is also home to the National High Magnetic Field Laboratory at Florida State University, in Tallahassee. Other institutions include Florida A&M University, the University of West Florida, the University of North Florida, the University of South Florida, New College of Florida, Florida International University, and Florida Gulf Coast University.

STETSON UNIVERSITY
Deland, FL 32723

D-2

(386) 822-7100
(800) 688-0101; Fax: (386) 822-7112

Full-time: 885 men, 1185 women	Faculty: 186; IIA, +$
Part-time: 35 men, 56 women	Ph.Ds: 90%
Graduate: 151 men, 232 women	Student/Faculty: 11 to 1
Year: semesters, summer session	Tuition: $22,640
Application Deadline: March 1	Room & Board: $6855
Freshman Class: 1992 applied, 1510 accepted, 529 enrolled	
SAT I Verbal/Math: 572/564	ACT: 24 VERY COMPETITIVE

Stetson University, founded in 1883, is an independent institution offering undergraduate programs in liberal arts and sciences, music, and business administration and graduate programs. There are 3 undergraduate and 2 graduate schools. In addition to regional accreditation, Stetson has baccalaureate program accreditation with AACSB, NASM, and NCATE. The 3 libraries contain 389,942 volumes, 413,506 microform items, and 18,789 audio/video tapes/CDs, and subscribe to 1145 periodicals. Computerized library services include the card catalog, interlibrary loans, database searching, and Internet access. Special learning facilities include an art gallery and a museum of minerals. The 170-acre campus is in a small town 35 miles north of Orlando and 25 miles west of Daytona Beach. Including any residence halls, there are 64 buildings.

Student Life: 77% of undergraduates are from Florida. Students are from 40 states, 35 foreign countries, and Canada. 83% are white. 47% are claim no religious affiliation; 31% Protestant; 15% Catholic. The average age of freshmen is 19; all undergraduates, 21. 19% do not continue beyond their first year; 60% remain to graduate.

Housing: 1524 students can be accommodated in college housing, which includes single-sex and coed dorms, fraternity houses, and sorority houses. In addition, there are honors houses, language houses, and special-interest houses. On-campus housing is guaranteed for all 4 years. 65% of students live on campus; of those, 60% remain on campus on weekends. All students may keep cars.

Activities: 33% of men belong to 8 national fraternities; 29% of women belong to 6 national sororities. There are 93 groups on campus, including band, cheerleading, chess, choir, chorale, chorus, computers, dance, drama, ethnic, gay, honors, international, jazz band, literary magazine, musical theater, newspaper, opera, orchestra, political, professional, radio and TV, religious, social, social service, student government, symphony, and yearbook. Popular campus events include Caribbean Week, Asian Week, and Black History Month.

Sports: There are 7 intercollegiate sports for men and 8 for women, and 14 intramural sports for men and 14 for women. Facilities include 4 racquetball, 6 volleyball, and 8 tennis courts, basketball courts, weight and training rooms, baseball and soccer fields, 2 softball fields, a multipurpose field, a training and exercise science facility, a swimming pool, and a 5000-seat auditorium.

Disabled Students: 80% of the campus is accessible. Wheelchair ramps, elevators, special parking, specially equipped rest rooms, special class scheduling, lowered drinking fountains, and lowered telephones are available.

Services: Counseling and information services are available, as is tutoring in most subjects. There is a reader service for the blind.

Campus Safety and Security: Measures include 24-hour foot and vehicle patrol, self-defense education, security escort services, and informal discussions. There are pamphlets/posters/films, emergency telephones, and lighted pathways/sidewalks.

Programs of Study: Stetson confers B.A., B.S., B.B.A., B.M., and B.M.E. degrees. Master's degrees are also awarded. Bachelor's degrees are awarded in BIOLOGICAL SCIENCE (biochemistry, biology/biological science, marine biology, and molecular biology), BUSINESS (accounting, banking and finance, business administration and management, business economics, electronic business, international business management, management science, marketing/retailing/merchandising, and sports management), COMMUNICATIONS AND THE ARTS (art, communications, dramatic arts, English, French, German, guitar, music, music performance, music theory and composition, piano/organ, Spanish, voice, and winds), COMPUTER AND PHYSICAL SCIENCE (chemistry, computer science, digital arts/technology, mathematics, and physics), EDUCATION (elementary, music, secondary, and social science), ENGINEERING AND ENVIRONMENTAL DESIGN (environmental science), HEALTH PROFESSIONS (health science, medical technology, and rehabilitation therapy), SOCIAL SCIENCE (American studies, economics, geography, history, humanities, international studies, Latin American studies, philosophy, political science/government, prelaw, psychology, religion, Russian and Slavic studies, social science, and sociology). Business, psychology, and education are the largest.

Required: To graduate, all students must complete 120 total credit hours, including 30 to 40 in the major, with a minimum GPA of 2.0. A freshman English sequence and courses in religious studies or philosophy, humanities, natural sciences, and social sciences are required.

Special: Stetson offers co-op programs in preengineering, prelaw, premedicine, forestry, environmental studies, and medical technology, internships in most disciplines, study abroad in France, Germany, Spain, Russia, Mexico, Hong Kong, and United Kingdom, and a Washington semester at American University. B.A.-B.S. degrees, dual majors, student-designed majors through the honors programs, 3-2 engineering degrees, a 3-3 law degree with Stetson College of Law, and pass/fail options are also offered. There is also the Leadership Development Program, the Roland George Investments Program, in which students manage an actual investment portfolio exceeding $2.5 million, and the Family Business Center. There are 6 national honor societies, including Phi Beta Kappa, and a freshman honors program.

Faculty/Classroom: 62% of faculty are male; 38%, female. 97% teach undergraduates and 50% do research. No introductory courses are taught by graduate students. The average class size in an introductory lecture is 23; in a laboratory, 14; and in a regular course, 19.

Admissions: 76% of the 2003-2004 applicants were accepted. The SAT I scores for the 2003-2004 freshman class were: Verbal--15% below 500, 50% between 500 and 599, 27% between 600 and 700, and 7% above 700; Math--18% below 500, 49% between 500 and 599, 29% between 600 and 700, and 4% above 700. The ACT scores were 20% below 21, 24% between 21 and 23, 30% between 24 and 26, 15% between 27 and 28, and 12% above 28. 52% of the current freshmen were in the top fifth of their class; 78% were in the top two fifths. 17 freshmen graduated first in their class.

Requirements: The SAT I or ACT is required. In addition, applicants must be graduates of an accredited secondary school or have a GED, and have completed 4 years of English, 3 of math and science, and 2 each of foreign language, social sciences, and electives. Auditions are required for music students. A GPA of 2.0 is required. AP and CLEP credits are accepted. Important factors in the admissions decision are advanced placement or honor courses, leadership record, and evidence of special talent.

Procedure: Freshmen are admitted fall, spring, and summer. Entrance exams should be taken in the spring of the junior year or the fall of the senior year. There are early decision, early admissions, and deferred admissions plans. Early decision applications should be filed by November 1; regular applications, by March 1 for fall entry, along with a $40 fee. Notification of early decision is sent November 15 and then on a rolling basis; regular decision, on a rolling basis. 63 early decision candidates were accepted for the 2003-2004 class. Applications are accepted on computer disk and on-line.

Transfer: 131 transfer students enrolled in 2002-2003. Transfer students must have completed a semester of academic work in good standing at an accredited college with a minimum 2.0 GPA. A 2.8 GPA and an interview are recommended. 45 of 120 credits required for the bachelor's degree must be completed at Stetson.

Visiting: There are regularly scheduled orientations for prospective students, consisting of a campus tour and orientation, interviews, class visits, and presentations. There are guides for informal visits and visitors may sit in on classes and stay overnight. To schedule a visit, contact the Admissions Office.

Financial Aid: In 2003-2004, 99% of all full-time freshmen and 97% of continuing full-time students received some form of financial aid. 58% of full-time freshmen and 56% of continuing full-time students received need-based aid. The average freshman award was $19,687. Need-based scholarships or need-based grants averaged $16,751 ($32,602 maximum); need-based self-help aid (loans and jobs) averaged $5056 ($9025 maximum); non-need-based athletic scholarships averaged $12,615 ($30,314 maximum); and other non-need-based awards and non-need-based scholarships averaged $8093 ($19,286 maximum). 30% of undergraduates work part time. Average annual earnings from campus work are $2321. The average financial indebtedness of the 2003 graduate was $20,000. Stetson is a member of CSS. The FAFSA is required. The priority date for freshman financial aid applications for fall entry is March 15.

International Students: There are 74 international students enrolled. The school actively recruits these students. They must score 550 on the written TOEFL and also take the SAT I or the ACT.

Computers: The mainframe is a Sun V880. There are several general-access computer labs with PCs and Macs networked to each other and to the mainframe. All students may access the system. There are no time limits and no fees.

Graduates: From July 1, 2002 to June 30, 2003, 454 bachelor's degrees were awarded. The most popular majors were business (37%), education (8%), and psychology (7%). In an average class, 50% graduate in 4 years or less, 59% graduate in 5 years or less, and 60% graduate in 6 years or less. 80 companies recruited on campus in 2002-2003.

Admissions Contact: Deborah Thompson, Vice President for Enrollment Management. E-mail: admissions@stetson.edu
Web: www.stetson.edu/admissions

UNIVERSITY OF CENTRAL FLORIDA

D-3

Orlando, FL 32816-0111   (407) 823-3000; Fax: (407) 823-3419

Full-time: 11,606 men, 14,151 women	**Faculty:** 1152; I, --$
Part-time: 3799 men, 4614 women	**Ph.D.s:** 78%
Graduate: 3011 men, 3921 women	**Student/Faculty:** 22 to 1
Year: semesters, summer session	**Tuition:** $3013 ($14,041)
Application Deadline: May 1	**Room & Board:** $7025
Freshman Class: 20,533 applied, 12,289 accepted, 5965 enrolled	
SAT I Verbal/Math: 583/593	**ACT:** 25 **VERY COMPETITIVE**

University of Central Florida, founded in 1963 and part of the State University System of Florida, offers programs in liberal and fine arts, business, engineering, health science, professional training, and teacher preparation, and graduate and research programs in optics, biotechnology, simulation, computer science, and other areas. There are 7 undergraduate and 7 graduate schools. In addition to regional accreditation, UCF has baccalaureate program accreditation with AACSB, ABET, CSAB, CSWE, NASM, NCATE, and NLN. The library contains 1,487,913 volumes, 2,821,936 microform items, and 37,780 audio/video tapes/CDs, and subscribes to 11,665 periodicals. Computerized library services include the card catalog, interlibrary loans, database searching, and Internet access. Special learning facilities include a learning resource center, art gallery, FM and AM radio stations, an observatory, an arboretum, a center for research and education in optics and lasers, an institute for simulation and training, and the Florida Solar Energy Center. The 1415-acre campus is in an urban area 13 miles northeast of downtown Orlando. Including any residence halls, there are 151 buildings.

Student Life: 94% of undergraduates are from Florida. Students are from 50 states, 131 foreign countries, and Canada. 71% are white; 12% Hispanic. The average age of freshmen is 18; all undergraduates, 23. 17% do not continue beyond their first year; 54% remain to graduate.

Housing: 7911 students can be accommodated in college housing, which includes single-sex and coed dorms, on-campus apartments, off-campus apartments, fraternity houses, and sorority houses. In addition, there are honors houses and special-interest houses. On-campus housing is available on a first-come, first-served basis. 80% of students commute. All students may keep cars.

Activities: 13% of men belong to 24 national fraternities; 12% of women belong to 17 national sororities. There are 329 groups on campus, including art, band, cheerleading, choir, chorus, computers, dance, debate, drama, drill team, ethnic, film, forensics, gay, honors, international, jazz band, literary magazine, marching band, musical theater, newspaper, orchestra, pep band, photography, political, pre-professional Medical Society, professional, radio and TV, religious, social, social service, student government, volunteer UCF, and yearbook. Popular campus events include Student Showcase Week, Wellness Fair, and ethnic awareness festivals.

Sports: There are 7 intercollegiate sports for men and 10 for women, and 51 intramural sports for men and 51 for women. Facilities include a recreation center with cardiovascular and weight training equipment, a climbing tower, basketball, tennis, disc golf, and badminton courts, a softball field, a swimming pool, a golf driving range, a 400-meter track, a dance/exercise studio, weight rooms, and a 92,000-square-foot arena.

Disabled Students: 95% of the campus is accessible. Wheelchair ramps, elevators, special parking, specially equipped rest rooms, special class scheduling, lowered drinking fountains, and lowered telephones are available.

Services: Counseling and information services are available, as is tutoring in most subjects, including math, English, reading, physics, statistics, Spanish, biology, chemistry, and economics. There is a reader service for the blind, and remedial math, reading, and writing. A review program for the College-Level Academic Skills Test (CLAST) is also available.

Campus Safety and Security: Measures include 24-hour foot and vehicle patrol, self-defense education, security escort services, and shuttle buses. There are informal discussions, pamphlets/posters/films, emergency telephones, and lighted pathways/sidewalks. There is also a college-sponsored transportation system that buses students to and from apartment complexes within a 2- or 3-mile radius of the school.

Programs of Study: UCF confers B.A., B.S., B.F.A., B.M., B.M.E., B.S.A.E., B.S.B.A., B.S.C.E., B.S.Cp.E., B.S.E.E., B.S.E.E.T., B.S.Env.E., B.S.E.T., B.S.I.E., B.S.M.E., B.S.N., and B.S.W. degrees. Associate, master's, and doctoral degrees are also awarded. Bachelor's degrees are awarded in BIOLOGICAL SCIENCE (biology/biological science and microbiology), BUSINESS (accounting, banking and finance, business administration and management, hospitality management services, management information systems, management science, and marketing/retailing/merchandising), COMMUNICATIONS AND THE ARTS (advertising, art, broadcasting, communications, dramatic arts, English, film arts, fine arts, French, journalism, languages, music, public relations, and Spanish), COMPUTER AND PHYSICAL SCIENCE (chemistry, computer science, digital arts/technology, mathematics, physics, and statistics), EDUCATION (art, business, early childhood, education of the ex-

ceptional child, elementary, English, foreign languages, mathematics, music, physical, science, social science, special, and vocational), ENGINEERING AND ENVIRONMENTAL DESIGN (aeronautical engineering, aerospace studies, civil engineering, computer engineering, electrical/electronics engineering, electrical/electronics engineering technology, engineering technology, environmental engineering, industrial engineering technology, and mechanical engineering), HEALTH PROFESSIONS (health care administration, health science, medical laboratory technology, nursing, radiological science, respiratory therapy, and speech pathology/audiology), SOCIAL SCIENCE (anthropology, criminal justice, economics, forensic studies, history, humanities, law, liberal arts/general studies, philosophy, political science/government, psychology, public administration, social science, social work, and sociology). Engineering, business administration, and computer science are the strongest academically. Business, education, and psychology are the largest.

Required: To graduate, students must complete at least 120 semester hours, with 36 hours in general education program courses, including 9 each in communication foundations and cultural and historical foundations, and 6 each in math foundations, science foundations, and social foundations. Students must maintain a minimum GPA of 2.0. There is a 30 hour residency requirement and the last semester is required in residence.

Special: Internships are available in most majors through UCF's extensive partnerships with area businesses and industries such as NASA, Disney, Universal Studios, and AT&T. Students may participate in study abroad and co-op and work-study programs, earn B.A.-B.S. degrees or a liberal studies degree, or pursue dual majors. Nondegree study and pass/fail options are available. There is a 3-4 accelerated degree program with the University of South Florida. There are 36 national honor societies, a freshman honors program, and 47 departmental honors programs.

Faculty/Classroom: 62% of faculty are male; 38%, female. All teach undergraduates, 95% do research, and 95% do both. No introductory courses are taught by graduate students. The average class size in an introductory lecture is 58; in a laboratory, 28; and in a regular course, 34.

Admissions: 60% of the 2003-2004 applicants were accepted. The SAT I scores for the 2003-2004 freshman class were: Verbal--9% below 500, 50% between 500 and 599, 37% between 600 and 700, and 4% above 700; Math--7% below 500, 45% between 500 and 599, 43% between 600 and 700, and 5% above 700. The ACT scores were 7% below 21, 16% between 21 and 23, 42% between 24 and 26, 21% between 27 and 28, and 14% above 28. 84% of the current freshmen were in the top fifth of their class; 87% were in the top two fifths. There were 34 National Merit finalists and 6 semifinalists. 55 freshmen graduated first in their class.

Requirements: The SAT I or ACT is required. In addition, GPA and standardized test scores are rated on a sliding scale. A high school diploma or GED is required. Applicants should have completed 4 units of English, 3 each of math, science (2 with labs), and social studies, and 2 of a foreign language, plus 4 of academic electives. A GPA of 2.0 is required. AP and CLEP credits are accepted. Important factors in the admissions decision are advanced placement or honor courses, evidence of special talent, and leadership record.

Procedure: Freshmen are admitted to all sessions. Entrance exams should be taken during the junior year or the first semester of the senior year. Applications should be filed by May 1 for fall entry, November 1 for spring entry, and March 1 for summer entry, along with a $30 fee. There is a rolling admissions plan, and notification is sent on a rolling basis. 629 applicants were on the 2003 waiting list. Applications are accepted on-line through the school's web site.

Transfer: 5639 transfer students enrolled in 2002-2003. A minimum GPA of 2.0 is required in all college work. Either the SAT I or the ACT is required of applicants with fewer than 60 credit hours. Other transfer requirements vary widely depending on credits already earned. 30 of 120 credits required for the bachelor's degree must be completed at UCF.

Visiting: There are regularly scheduled orientations for prospective students, including tours offered twice a day, Monday through Friday, followed by a group information session or personal interview. There are guides for informal visits and visitors may sit in on classes. To schedule a visit, contact Undergraduate Admissions office.

Financial Aid: In 2003-2004, 85% of all full-time freshmen and 74% of continuing full-time students received some form of financial aid. 23% of full-time freshmen and 26% of continuing full-time students received need-based aid. The average freshman award was $4078. Need-based scholarships or need-based grants averaged $3378 ($4000 maximum); need-based self-help aid (loans and jobs) averaged $2388 ($5335 maximum); non-need-based athletic scholarships averaged $3731 ($9412 maximum); and other non-need-based awards and non-need-based scholarships averaged $2851 ($18,782 maximum). 49% of undergraduates work part time. Average annual earnings from campus work are $5735. The average financial indebtedness of the 2003 graduate was $12,780. UCF is a member of CSS. The FAFSA is required. The deadline for filing freshman financial aid applications for fall entry is March 1.

International Students: There are 329 international students enrolled. They must score 500 on the written TOEFL or 220 on the electronic version. Students with fewer than 60 semester hours of college credit must take either the SAT I or the ACT.

Computers: The mainframe is a Sun 6800. Many public-access computer labs with 2535 terminals are available. Students use e-mail to communicate with faculty and classmates, and have free Internet access. All students may access the system at all times. There are no time limits and no fees. It is strongly recommended that all students have a personal computer, especially students in Digital Media.

Graduates: From July 1, 2002 to June 30, 2003, 6732 bachelor's degrees were awarded. The most popular majors were business (27%), education (10%), and health (9%). In an average class, 2% graduate in 3 years or less, 27% graduate in 4 years or less, 48% graduate in 5 years or less, and 54% graduate in 6 years or less. 118 companies recruited on campus in 2002-2003. Of the 2002 graduating class, 21% were enrolled in graduate school within 6 months of graduation and 71% were employed.

Admissions Contact: Gordon Chavis Jr. J.D., Executive Director. E-mail: *admission@mail.ucf.edu* Web: *http://www.ucf.edu/*

UNIVERSITY OF FLORIDA	D-2
Gainesville, FL 32611-4000	(352) 392-1365

Full-time: 14,373 men, 16,844 women	**Faculty:** 1686; I, av$
Part-time: 1469 men, 1296 women	**Ph.D.s:** 94%
Graduate: 6585 men, 6888 women	**Student/Faculty:** 19 to 1
Year: semesters, summer session	**Tuition:** $2780 ($13,808)
Application Deadline: January 13	**Room & Board:** $5800
Freshman Class: 24,821 applied, 12,028 accepted, 6658 enrolled	
SAT I Verbal/Math: 625/642	**ACT:** 27 **MOST COMPETITIVE**

The University of Florida, founded in 1853, is a public liberal arts institution that is part of the state university system of Florida. There are 14 undergraduate and 17 graduate schools. In addition to regional accreditation, UF has baccalaureate program accreditation with AACSB, ABET, ACCE, ACEJMC, ACPE, ADA, AHEA, APTA, ASLA, FIDER, NAAB, NASAD, NASM, NCATE, NLN, and SAF. The 15 libraries contain 5,024,637 volumes, 6,701,512 microform items, and 36,078 audio/video tapes/CDs, and subscribe to 28,103 periodicals. Computerized library services include the card catalog, interlibrary loans, and database searching. Special learning facilities include a learning resource center, art gallery, natural history museum, radio station, TV station, a performing arts center, and a teaching hospital. The 2000-acre campus is in a suburban area 75 miles from Jacksonville. Including any residence halls, there are 850 buildings.

Student Life: 95% of undergraduates are from Florida. Students are from 50 states, 114 foreign countries, and Canada. 76% are white; 13% Hispanic. The average age of freshmen is 18; all undergraduates, 21. 7% do not continue beyond their first year; 64% remain to graduate.

Housing: 7351 students can be accommodated in college housing, which includes single-sex and coed dorms, on-campus apartments, off-campus apartments, married-student housing, fraternity houses, and sorority houses. In addition, there are honors houses, special-interest houses, quiet floors, wellness floors, and first-year floors. On-campus housing is available on a first-come, first-served basis and is available on a lottery system for upperclassmen. 79% of students commute. All students may keep cars.

Activities: 15% of men belong to 29 national fraternities; 15% of women belong to 18 national sororities. There are more than 500 groups on campus, including art, band, cheerleading, chess, choir, chorale, chorus, computers, dance, drama, drill team, ethnic, film, gay, honors, international, jazz band, literary magazine, marching band, musical theater, newspaper, orchestra, pep band, photography, political, professional, radio and TV, religious, social, social service, student government, symphony, and yearbook. Popular campus events include Madrigal dinners, student-sponsored cultural programs, and Gator Growl, a student-produced variety show.

Sports: There are 8 intercollegiate sports for men and 10 for women. Facilities include tennis, volleyball, and basketball courts, a 12,000-seat athletic center, a 60,000-square-foot fitness park, an Olympic-size swimming pool, a running track, weight rooms, intramural fields, an 83,000-seat stadium, and lakefront facilities.

Disabled Students: 95% of the campus is accessible. Wheelchair ramps, elevators, special parking, specially equipped rest rooms, special class scheduling, lowered drinking fountains, lowered telephones, and special housing are available. There is computer access for blind and visually impaired students.

Services: Counseling and information services are available, as is tutoring in every subject. There is a reader service for the blind and a counseling center.

Campus Safety and Security: Measures include 24-hour foot and vehicle patrol, self-defense education, security escort services, and shuttle buses. There are informal discussions, pamphlets/posters/films, emergency telephones, lighted pathways/sidewalks, and an apartment safety program in cooperation with local law enforcement.

Programs of Study: UF confers B.A., B.S., B.A.E., B.F.A., B.H.S., B.M.E., B.Mus., B.S.A., B.S.B.A., B.S.F., B.S.N., and B.S.P. degrees. Master's and doctoral degrees are also awarded. Bachelor's degrees are awarded in AGRICULTURE (agricultural business management, agronomy, animal science, dairy science, forestry and related sciences, horticulture, natural resource management, plant science, and soil science), BIOLOGICAL SCIENCE (botany, entomology, microbiology, wildlife biology, and zoology), BUSINESS (accounting, banking and finance, business administration and management, human resources, insurance, management science, marketing/retailing/merchandising, and recreation and leisure services), COMMUNICATIONS AND THE ARTS (advertising, art, art history and appreciation, dance, East Asian languages and literature, English, French, German, graphic design, journalism, linguistics, music, performing arts, photography, Portuguese, public relations, Russian, Spanish, speech/debate/rhetoric, telecommunications, theater design, and visual and performing arts), COMPUTER AND PHYSICAL SCIENCE (astronomy, chemistry, computer science, earth science, geology, information sciences and systems, mathematics, physics, and statistics), EDUCATION (agricultural, art, elementary, health, and music), ENGINEERING AND ENVIRONMENTAL DESIGN (aeronautical engineering, agricultural engineering, architecture, chemical engineering, civil engineering, computer engineering, construction engineering, electrical/electronics engineering, emergency/disaster science, engineering and applied science, environmental engineering, industrial engineering technology, interior design, landscape architecture/design, materials engineering, mechanical engineering, nuclear engineering, and nuclear engineering technology), HEALTH PROFESSIONS (allied health, exercise science, health science, nursing, occupational therapy, physical therapy, prepharmacy, rehabilitation therapy, and speech pathology/audiology), SOCIAL SCIENCE (American studies, anthropology, Asian/Oriental studies, classical/ancient civilization, criminology, economics, food science, geography, history, home economics, interdisciplinary studies, Judaic studies, philosophy, physical fitness/movement, political science/government, psychology, religion, and sociology). Engineering, pharmacy, and tax law are the strongest academically. Business, finance, and psychology are the largest.

Required: Requirements for graduation vary depending on the major elected, but all students are required to complete a minimum of 120 credits and maintain a minimum 2.0 GPA.

Special: UF offers many internships, dual and student-designed majors, and study abroad in 32 countries. Cross-registration is possible through the Undergraduate Inter-institutional Registration program. Work-study programs, accelerated degree programs, co-op programs, and B.A.-B.S. degrees are available. There are 53 national honor societies, including Phi Beta Kappa and a freshman honors program.

Faculty/Classroom: 77% of faculty are male; 23%, female. Graduate students teach 10% of introductory courses.

Admissions: 48% of the 2003-2004 applicants were accepted. The SAT I scores for the 2003-2004 freshman class were: Verbal--4% below 500, 30% between 500 and 599, 52% between 600 and 700, and 14% above 700; Math--2% below 500, 23% between 500 and 599, 56% between 600 and 700, and 19% above 700. The ACT scores were 1% below 21, 10% between 21 and 23, 24% between 24 and 26, 27% between 27 and 28, and 38% above 28. 84% of the current freshmen were in the top fifth of their class; 97% were in the top two fifths. There were 205 National Merit finalists.

Requirements: The SAT I or ACT is required; the SAT I is preferred. Minimum composite scores are 950 on the SAT I and 19 on the ACT. Candidates should have graduated from an accredited secondary school or have a GED, and have completed 4 years of English, 3 years each of math, science, and social studies, 2 years of a foreign language, and 4 units of academic electives. AP and CLEP credits are accepted. Important factors in the admissions decision are advanced placement or honor courses, parents or siblings attending the school, and recommendations by school officials.

Procedure: Freshmen are admitted to all sessions. Entrance exams should be taken in the junior year. There is an early decision plan. Early decision applications should be filed by October 1; regular applications, by January 13 for fall entry, September 15 for spring entry, and January 12 for summer entry. The fall 2003 application was $30. Notification of early decision is sent December; regular decision on a rolling basis. Applications are accepted on-line through the school's web site.

Transfer: 2031 transfer students enrolled in 2002-2003. Admission requirements for transfer students vary by college. The lower division is highly competitive; applicants are encouraged to apply at the upper-division level. Students should try to complete their associate degrees or 60 semester hours before applying. 30 of 120 credits required for the bachelor's degree must be completed at UF.

Visiting: There are regularly scheduled orientations for prospective students, consisting of general information sessions at 10 A.M. and 2 P.M. Monday through Friday (excluding holidays) and a student-guided walking tour of the central campus. There are guides for informal visits and visitors may sit in on classes and stay overnight. To schedule a visit, contact the Admissions Office.

Financial Aid: In 2003-2004, 34% of all full-time students received some form of financial aid. 18% of full-time freshmen and 22% of continuing full-time students received need-based aid. The average freshman award was $7873. Need-based scholarships or need-based grants averaged $4036; need-based self-help aid (loans and jobs) averaged $2341; and non-need-based athletic scholarships averaged $8357. 17% of undergraduates work part time. Average annual earnings from campus work are $1800. The average financial indebtedness of the 2003 graduate was $14,449. The FAFSA is required. The priority date for freshman financial aid applications for fall entry is March 15.

International Students: They must score 550 on the written TOEFL or 213 on the electronic version. Freshmen and lower-division transfers must take the SAT I or ACT.

Computers: The mainframes are an IBM ES9000-831/3VF, an IBM RS6000/SP (9 nodes), and a DEC Alpha cluster. There are also 353 PCs and 100 Macs available for general student use. Upper-division teaching labs restricted to department majors add several hundred more. All students may access the system via 151 terminals for general student use. There is a limit on the IBM systems but no limit on the DEC cluster. There are no fees. All students are required to have personal computers.

Graduates: From July 1, 2002 to June 30, 2003, 7975 bachelor's degrees were awarded. The most popular majors were business/marketing (21%), engineering (11%), and social sciences/history (11%). In an average class, 77% graduate in 6 years or less.

Admissions Contact: Bill Kolb, Director of Admissions.
Web: *www.reg.ufl.edu/regadmi.htm*

UNIVERSITY OF MIAMI
Coral Gables, FL 33124

	E-5
	(305) 284-4323; Fax: (305) 284-2507
Full-time: 3909 men, 5280 women	Faculty: 685; I, av$
Part-time: 279 men, 535 women	Ph.D.s: 97%
Graduate: 2596 men, 2649 women	Student/Faculty: 13 to 1
Year: semesters, summer session	Tuition: $26,280
Application Deadline: February 1	Room & Board: $8328
Freshman Class: 16,844 applied, 7483 accepted, 2072 enrolled	
SAT I Verbal/Math: 560/580	ACT: 26 HIGHLY COMPETITIVE

The University of Miami, founded in 1925, is a private university that offers degrees in more than 130 majors and areas of study. There are 8 undergraduate and 10 graduate schools. In addition to regional accreditation, UM has baccalaureate program accreditation with AACSB, ABET, ACEJMC, APTA, NAAB, NASM, NCATE, and NLN. The 4 libraries contain 2,399,584 volumes, 3,750,839 microform items, and 51,348 audio/video tapes/CDs, and subscribe to 19,407 periodicals. Computerized library services include the card catalog, interlibrary loans, database searching, and Internet access. Special learning facilities include a learning resource center, art gallery, radio station, TV station, a state-of-the-art research vessel, a sound stage and film studios, a film theater, a performing arts theater, a concert hall, a wellness center, an arboretum, and a palmetum. The 260-acre campus is in a suburban area 6 miles south of Miami. Including any residence halls, there are 101 buildings.

Student Life: 57% of undergraduates are from Florida. Students are from 49 states, 99 foreign countries, and Canada. 68% are from public schools. 51% are white; 25% Hispanic; 10% African American. 48% are Catholic; 29% Protestant; 14% Jewish. The average age of freshmen is 18; all undergraduates, 21. 13% do not continue beyond their first year; 69% remain to graduate.

Housing: 4211 students can be accommodated in college housing, which includes single-sex and coed dormitories, on-campus apartments, and fraternity houses. All freshmen living on campus live in residential colleges with live-in resident faculty. On-campus housing is guaranteed for all 4 years. 59% of students commute. All students may keep cars.

Activities: 14% of men belong to 17 national fraternities; 13% of women belong to 11 national sororities. There are 175 groups on campus, including art, band, cheerleading, chess, choir, chorale, chorus, dance, debate, drama, drill team, ethnic, film, gay, honors, international, jazz band, literary magazine, marching band, musical theater, newspaper, opera, orchestra, pep band, political, professional, radio and TV, religious, social, social service, student government, symphony, and yearbook. Popular campus events include International Week, Cinematic Arts Commission (CAC) Film Festival, and Gusman Concert Hall – Festivale Miami.

Sports: There are 8 intercollegiate sports for men and 10 for women, and 20 intramural sports for men and 20 for women. Facilities include a baseball stadium seating 6000, a soccer stadium, a sports complex, a tennis center, a track and field facility, an athletic center, lighted tennis courts, 4 sports fields, and an Olympic-size swimming pool. A 149,000-square-foot indoor/outdoor recreational facility includes a multipurpose room, a courtyard, 4 basketball/volleyball courts, an aerobics room, an atrium/fitness room, a floor hockey/indoor soccer gym, a swimming pool, an elevated jogging track, 6 racquetball and 2 squash courts, a spa, and 2 saunas.

Disabled Students: 95% of the campus is accessible. Wheelchair ramps, elevators, special parking, specially equipped rest rooms, special class scheduling, lowered drinking fountains, lowered telephones, and lowered elevator controls are available.

Services: Counseling and information services are available, as is tutoring in most subjects. There is a reader service for the blind, and remedial math, reading, and writing.

Campus Safety and Security: Measures include 24-hour foot and vehicle patrol, self-defense education, security escort services, and shuttle buses. There are informal discussions, pamphlets/posters/films, emergency telephones, and lighted pathways/sidewalks. There has been a comprehensive crime prevention program since 1981, including security card access to all residential colleges, office crimewatch, and an adopt a cop program in the residence halls.

Programs of Study: UM confers B.A., B.S., B.Arch., B.B.A., B.C.S., B.F.A., B.G.S., B.H.S., B.M., B.S.A.E., B.S.B.E., B.S.C., B.S.C.E., B.S.Cp.E., B.S.E.E., B.S.E.S., B.S.I.E., B.S.I.T., B.S.M.E., B.S.N., and B.S.S.A. degrees. Master's and doctoral degrees are also awarded. Bachelor's degrees are awarded in BIOLOGICAL SCIENCE (biochemistry, biology/biological science, marine science, and microbiology), BUSINESS (accounting, banking and finance, business administration and management, entrepreneurial studies, human resources, international business management, management information systems, marketing management, and sports management), COMMUNICATIONS AND THE ARTS (advertising, art, art history and appreciation, audio technology, broadcasting, ceramic art and design, communications, creative writing, dramatic arts, English, film arts, fine arts, French, German, graphic design, guitar, Italian, jazz, journalism, music, music performance, music theory and composition, musical theater, painting, percussion, photography, piano/organ, printmaking, public relations, sculpture, Spanish, studio art, telecommunications, theater design, theater management, video, and voice), COMPUTER AND PHYSICAL SCIENCE (applied mathematics, chemistry, computer science, geology, mathematics, physics, and systems analysis), EDUCATION (athletic training, elementary, music, secondary, and special), ENGINEERING AND ENVIRONMENTAL DESIGN (aeronautical engineering, architectural engineering, architecture, biomedical engineering, civil engineering, computer engineering, electrical/electronics engineering, engineering, environmental engineering, environmental science, industrial engineering, manufacturing engineering, and mechanical engineering), HEALTH PROFESSIONS (health science, music therapy, nursing, predentistry, premedicine, prepharmacy, and preveterinary science), SOCIAL SCIENCE (African American studies, American studies, anthropology, criminology, economics, geography, history, international studies, Judaic studies, Latin American studies, philosophy, political science/government, prelaw, psychobiology, psychology, religion, sociology, and women's studies). Marine science, international finance and marketing, and music are the strongest academically. Biology, psychology, and business management and organization are the largest.

Required: Requirements for each degree vary, but all students must complete at least 120 credit hours. All students must fulfill general education requirements in English composition, math, writing across the curriculum, natural sciences, social sciences, and arts and humanities. Students must complete 24 to 36 hours in the major and maintain a minimum GPA of 2.0.

Special: UM offers co-op programs in engineering and internships in communications, business, engineering, architecture, and science. There is on- and off-campus work-study and study abroad in 25 countries. Also available are 3-2 engineering degrees with Jacksonville University and Eckerd College. There are 45 national honor societies, including Phi Beta Kappa, and a freshman honors program. All departments have honors programs.

Faculty/Classroom: 65% of faculty are male; 35%, female. 77% of faculty in undergraduate schools teach undergraduates. Graduate students teach 24% of introductory courses. The average class size in an introductory lecture is 30; in a laboratory, 17; and in a regular course, 20.

Admissions: 44% of the 2003-2004 applicants were accepted. The SAT I scores for the 2003-2004 freshman class were: Verbal--9% below 500, 40% between 500 and 599, 41% between 600 and 700, and 11% above 700; Math--4% below 500, 33% between 500 and 599, 47% between 600 and 700, and 15% above 700. 80% of the current freshmen were in the top fifth of their class; 96% were in the top two fifths.

Requirements: The SAT I or ACT is required. In addition, it is recommended that applicants have completed 4 years of English, 3 each of math, science, and social sciences, and 2 of foreign language. Also considered in the admissions decision are a recommendation from a high school counselor and an essay. The GED is accepted. AP and CLEP credits are accepted. Important factors in the admissions decision are advanced placement or honor courses, recommendations by school officials, and evidence of special talent.

Procedure: Freshmen are admitted fall and spring. Entrance exams should be taken in the fall of the senior year or earlier. There are early decision and deferred admissions plans. Early decision applications should be filed by November 1; regular applications, by February 1 for fall entry and November 1 for spring entry, along with a $55 fee. Notification of early decision is sent December 15; regular decision, April 1. 300 early decision candidates were accepted for the 2003-2004 class. A waiting list is an active part of the admissions procedure. Applications are accepted on-line through the school's web site at *www.miami.edu/apply*.

Transfer: 573 transfer students enrolled in 2002-2003. Transfer applicants must have a GPA of at least 2.8; higher admission standards are in effect for most programs. College transcripts and a statement of good standing from previous institutions attended are required. Courses with grades of C or higher may transfer for credit. 45 of 120 credits required for the bachelor's degree must be completed at UM.

Visiting: There are regularly scheduled orientations for prospective students, consisting of several open house programs that enable students to tour the campus and meet with representatives from admission, financial aid, and various university departments. Daily information sessions are offered on campus. There are guides for informal visits and visitors may sit in on classes. To schedule a visit, contact the Admission Office or the specific school or college.

Financial Aid: In 2003-2004, 88% of all full-time freshmen and 84% of continuing full-time students received some form of financial aid. 57% of full-time freshmen and 55% of continuing full-time students received need-based aid. The average freshman award was $23,902. Need-based scholarships or need-based grants averaged $15,455 ($37,875 maximum); need-based self-help aid (loans and jobs) averaged $7056 ($33,325 maximum); non-need-based athletic scholarships averaged $20,728 ($36,688 maximum); other non-need-based awards and non-need-based scholarships averaged $13,874 ($44,221 maximum); and need-based parent loans, need-based tuition remission, and need-based athletic scholarships averaged $12,047 ($36,064 maximum). 27% of undergraduates work part time. Average annual earnings from campus work are $2000. The average financial indebtedness of the 2003 graduate was $29,046. The FAFSA and the state aid form are required. The deadline for filing freshman financial aid applications for fall entry is February 15.

International Students: There are 711 international students enrolled. The school actively recruits these students. They must take the TOEFL if English is not their native language scoring 550 on the written TOEFL or 213 on the electronic version. Students from American schools or IB curriculums must also take the SAT I ot the ACT.

Computers: The mainframes are an IBM 9672-RB6, an open VMS cluster running on 2 AlphaServer 5/4100s, and a main UNIX system running Tru64 on an AlphaServer 5/4100. Numerous workstations and more than 40 computer labs are located in residential colleges, libraries, and schools across campus. More than 1000 PCs, workstations, and terminals are available to students. Each residential college has a computer lab with PCs running Windows, laser printers, scanners, and connections to the campuswide network. All students may access the system 24 hours a day. There are no time limits and no fees.

Graduates: From July 1, 2002 to June 30, 2003, 2053 bachelor's degrees were awarded. The most popular majors were biology (7%), finance (7%), and psychology (6%). 110 companies recruited on campus in 2002-2003. Of the 2002 graduating class, 29% were enrolled in graduate school within 6 months of graduation and 36% were employed.

Admissions Contact: Edward M. Gillis, Associate Dean, Enrollments/Director, Admission. A video is available.
E-mail: *admission@miami.edu* Web: *www.miami.edu/admission*

UNIVERSITY OF NORTH FLORIDA
Jacksonville, FL 32224   D-1
    (904) 620-2624; Fax: (904) 620-2414

Full-time: 3440 men, 4769 women	**Faculty:** 357; II A, -$
Part-time: 1794 men, 2443 women	**Ph.D.s:** 95%
Graduate: 562 men, 1110 women	**Student/Faculty:** 23 to 1
Year: semesters, summer session	**Tuition:** $2913 ($13,268)
Application Deadline: July 2	**Room & Board:** $5856
Freshman Class: 6104 applied, 3804 accepted, 1576 enrolled	
SAT I Verbal/Math: 576/576	**ACT:** 22 **VERY COMPETITIVE**

The University of North Florida, founded in 1965, is a public university that is part of the state university system. There are 5 undergraduate and 5 graduate schools. In addition to regional accreditation, UNF has baccalaureate program accreditation with AACSB, ABET, ACCE, CAAHEP, CAPTE, NASM, NCATE, and NLN. The library contains 746,604 volumes, 1.3 million microform items, and 67,208 audio/video tapes/CDs, and subscribes to 3466 periodicals. Computerized library services include the card catalog, interlibrary loans, and database searching. Special learning facilities include a learning resource center, art gallery, radio station, TV station, theater, auditorium, and nature preserve. The 1300-acre campus is in an urban area 12 miles southeast of downtown Jacksonville. Including any residence halls, there are 67 buildings.

Student Life: 94% of undergraduates are from Florida. Students are from 47 states, 96 foreign countries, and Canada. 77% are white; 10% African American. Most claim no religious affiliation. The average age of freshmen is 19; all undergraduates, 24. 24% do not continue beyond their first year; 54% remain to graduate.

Housing: 2000 students can be accommodated in college housing, which includes coed dorms, on-campus apartments, and married-

student housing. In addition, there are honors houses. On-campus housing is available on a first-come, first-served basis. 86% of students commute. All students may keep cars.

Activities: 6% of men belong to 8 national fraternities; 6% of women belong to 7 national sororities. There are 172 groups on campus, including art, band, cheerleading, choir, chorale, chorus, computers, dance, drama, ethnic, film, gay, honors, international, jazz band, literary magazine, newspaper, orchestra, pep band, photography, political, professional, radio and TV, religious, social, social service, and student government. Popular campus events include Clubfest, Spring Bash, and Earth Music Fest.

Sports: There are 8 intercollegiate sports for men and 9 for women, and 12 intramural sports for men and 12 for women. Facilities include a baseball stadium, softball, soccer, and multipurpose fields, an aquatic center, a fitness center, jogging trails, racquetball, basketball, volleyball, and tennis courts, a 6000-seat multipurpose arena, and lakes for canoeing and fishing.

Disabled Students: Wheelchair ramps, elevators, special parking, specially equipped rest rooms, special class scheduling, lowered drinking fountains, and lowered telephones are available. The Disabled Services Office provides specialized assistance and equipment, including priority registration, interpreters for the hearing impaired, and proctored testing.

Services: Counseling and information services are available, as is tutoring in some subjects including reading, writing, math, business, accounting, physics, biology, chemistry, Spanish, French, and English as a second language.

Campus Safety and Security: Measures include 24-hour foot and vehicle patrol, self-defense education, security escort services, and informal discussions. There are pamphlets/posters/films, emergency telephones, lighted pathways/sidewalks, and university police presentations at new student orientation.

Programs of Study: UNF confers B.A., B.S., B.A.E., B.B.A., B.F.A., B.M., B.S.E.E., B.S.H., and B.S.N. degrees. Associate, master's, and doctoral degrees are also awarded. Bachelor's degrees are awarded in BIOLOGICAL SCIENCE (biology/biological science), BUSINESS (accounting, banking and finance, business administration and management, business economics, marketing management, and transportation management), COMMUNICATIONS AND THE ARTS (art, communications, English, fine arts, jazz, music, music performance, and Spanish), COMPUTER AND PHYSICAL SCIENCE (chemistry, computer science, information sciences and systems, mathematics, physics, and statistics), EDUCATION (art, athletic training, elementary, mathematics, middle school, music, physical, science, secondary, and special), ENGINEERING AND ENVIRONMENTAL DESIGN (civil engineering, construction management, electrical/electronics engineering, and mechanical engineering), HEALTH PROFESSIONS (health science, nursing, and pre-dentistry), SOCIAL SCIENCE (anthropology, criminal justice, economics, history, philosophy, political science/government, prelaw, psychology, and sociology). Nursing, special education, and elementary education are the strongest academically. Communications, psychology, and business management are the largest.

Required: Students are required to take general education distribution requirements, including 9 hours of composition and humanities and 6 each of natural science, math, and social science. A minimum 2.0 GPA and 120 credit hours, with a minimum of 60 hours in the major, are needed for graduation. All students must take the state-required college-level academic skills test unless exempt.

Special: There are cooperative programs for internships in most majors and work-study programs with several Jacksonville businesses. Study abroad, a Washington semester, accelerated degree program in nursing, B.A.-B.S. degrees in math, statistics, and psychology, dual majors, and student-designed majors also are available. Credit is given for military experience. There are 5 national honor societies, a freshman honors program, and 27 departmental honors programs.

Faculty/Classroom: 60% of faculty are male; 40%, female. 91% teach undergraduates, 78% do research, and 69% do both. No introductory courses are taught by graduate students. The average class size in an introductory lecture is 38; in a laboratory, 17; and in a regular course, 35.

Admissions: 62% of the 2003-2004 applicants were accepted. The SAT I scores for the 2003-2004 freshman class were: Verbal--10% below 500, 56% between 500 and 599, 31% between 600 and 700, and 4% above 700; Math--9% below 500, 54% between 500 and 599, 35% between 600 and 700, and 2% above 700. The ACT scores were 31% below 21, 47% between 21 and 23, 17% between 24 and 26, 4% between 27 and 28, and 1% above 28. 46% of the current freshmen were in the top fifth of their class; 77% were in the top two fifths. 14 freshmen graduated first in their class.

Requirements: The SAT I or ACT is required, with minimum acceptable composite scores of 970 on the SAT I; 20 on the ACT. In addition, applicants must be graduates of an accredited secondary school or have a GED. A total of 15 academic credits plus 4 additional academic electives or 19 Carnegie units is required. Secondary school course work must include 4 years of English, 3 each of math, science, and social studies, and 2 of foreign language. A GPA of 2.5 is required. AP and CLEP credits are accepted. Important factors in the admissions decision are advanced placement or honor courses, recommendations by school officials, and evidence of special talent.

Procedure: Freshmen are admitted to all sessions. Entrance exams should be taken during the spring of the junior year or the fall of the senior year. There are early admissions and deferred admissions plans. Applications should be filed by July 2 for fall entry, November 2 for spring entry, and April 8 for summer entry. The fall 2003 application fee was $20. Notification is sent on a rolling basis. Applications are accepted on-line.

Transfer: 6313 transfer students enrolled in 2002-2003. Transfer applicants with fewer than 60 credit hours must take either the SAT I or the ACT and achieve a minimum composite score of 970 on the SAT I or 20 on the ACT, and must meet all high school unit requirements. The minimum college GPA for transfers is 2.0. Some programs require 2.5. 30 of 120 credits required for the bachelor's degree must be completed at UNF.

Visiting: There are regularly scheduled orientations for prospective students, consisting of open houses, which include tours of the campus and housing, a general information session, financial aid sessions, academic advising, and personal interviews by request. There are guides for informal visits and visitors may sit in on classes. To schedule a visit, contact the Admissions Office at (904) 620-2625.

Financial Aid: In 2003-2004, 85% of all full-time freshmen and 72% of continuing full-time students received some form of financial aid. 34% of full-time freshmen and 35% of continuing full-time students received need-based aid. The average freshman award was $2073. Need-based scholarships or need-based grants averaged $1753 ($4050 maximum); need-based self-help aid (loans and jobs) averaged $2380 ($4000 maximum); non-need-based athletic scholarships averaged $3454 ($9900 maximum); and other non-need-based awards and non-need-based scholarships averaged $2212 ($19,645 maximum). 5% of undergraduates work part time. Average annual earnings from campus work are $6476. The average financial indebtedness of the 2003 graduate was $12,346. The FAFSA is required. The deadline for filing freshman financial aid applications for fall entry is April 1.

International Students: There are 83 international students enrolled. The school actively recruits these students. They must score 500 on the written TOEFL and also take the SAT I or the ACT.

Computers: Internet and e-mail are accessible via dial-up and network connections in labs and residence halls. There are approximately 600 Pentium-level PCs in general-purpose and distributed labs with application software, including statistics and graphics packages. All students may access the system. The general-purpose labs are open more than 100 hours per week. There are no time limits and no fees. It is recommended that students in building construction management have personal computers. A Pentium 200 Notebook with 128 MB RAM and a 6 GB hard drive is recommended.

Graduates: From July 1, 2002 to June 30, 2003, 2107 bachelor's degrees were awarded. The most popular majors were communications (9%), psychology (8%), and health science (8%). In an average class, 2% graduate in 3 years or less, 20% graduate in 4 years or less, 46% graduate in 5 years or less, and 54% graduate in 6 years or less. 281 companies recruited on campus in 2002-2003.

Admissions Contact: John Yancey, Director of Admissions. A video is available. E-mail: *osprey@unf.edu* Web: *www.unf.edu*

UNIVERSITY OF SOUTH FLORIDA
Tampa, FL 33620

D-1

(813) 974-3350; Fax: (813) 974-9689

Full-time: 8798 men, 12,792 women	Faculty: 1530; I, --$
Part-time: 4491 men, 6382 women	Ph.D.s: 93%
Graduate: 3473 men, 5456 women	Student/Faculty: 14 to 1
Year: semesters, summer session	Tuition: $2946 ($13,974)
Application Deadline: May 1	Room & Board: $6508
Freshman Class: 15,491 applied, 9567 accepted, 4715 enrolled	
SAT I Verbal/Math: 540/540	ACT: 22 COMPETITIVE

The University of South Florida, founded in 1956, is a comprehensive public institution, part of the Florida Division of Colleges and Universities, offering programs in liberal and fine arts, business, engineering, health science, and education. USF also maintains campuses at Lakeland, Sarasota, and St. Petersburg. There are 6 undergraduate and 9 graduate schools. In addition to regional accreditation, USF has baccalaureate program accreditation with AACSB, ABET, ACEJMC, ASLA, CSAB, CSWE, NAAB, NASAD, NASM, NCATE, and NLN. The 5 libraries contain 1,912,874 volumes, 4,287,300 microform items, and 148,986 audio/video tapes/CDs, and subscribe to 16,698 periodicals. Computerized library services include the card catalog, interlibrary loans, database searching, and Internet access. Special learning facilities include a learning resource center, art gallery, radio station, TV station, mock broadcasting studio, anthropology museum, and botanical gardens. The 1913-acre campus is in an urban area 10 miles northeast of downtown Tampa. Including any residence halls, there are 359 buildings.

Student Life: 96% of undergraduates are from Florida. Students are from 50 states, 112 foreign countries, and Canada. 91% are from public schools. 69% are white; 12% African American; 10% Hispanic. The average age of freshmen is 19; all undergraduates, 22. 19% do not continue beyond their first year; 44% remain to graduate.

Housing: 4143 students can be accommodated in college housing, which includes single-sex and coed dorms, on-campus apartments, married-student housing, fraternity houses, and sorority houses. In addition, there are honors houses, special-interest houses, and an international hall. On-campus housing is available on a first-come, first-served basis. 87% of students commute. All students may keep cars.

Activities: 6% of men belong to 19 national fraternities; 4% of women belong to 11 national sororities. There are more than 200 groups on campus, including art, band, cheerleading, chess, choir, chorale, chorus, computers, dance, drama, drill team, ethnic, film, gay, honors, international, jazz band, literary magazine, marching band, musical theater, newspaper, opera, orchestra, pep band, photography, political, professional, radio and TV, religious, social, social service, student government, and symphony. Popular campus events include Women's Awareness Week, Bull Blast, and Week of Welcome.

Sports: There are 8 intercollegiate sports for men and 8 for women, and 14 intramural sports for men and 13 for women. Facilities include a 10,000-seat multipurpose arena, 4 pools, tennis and indoor racquetball courts, a track, a jogging course, an indoor recreation center with weight-training and aerobics rooms, a soccer stadium, a softball complex, a baseball stadium, and an 18-hole golf course.

Disabled Students: All of the campus is accessible. Wheelchair ramps, elevators, special parking, specially equipped rest rooms, special class scheduling, lowered drinking fountains, and lowered telephones are available.

Services: Counseling and information services are available, as is tutoring in most subjects. There is a reader service for the blind.

Campus Safety and Security: Measures include 24-hour foot and vehicle patrol, self-defense education, security escort services, and shuttle buses. There are informal discussions, pamphlets/posters/films, emergency telephones, lighted pathways/sidewalks, and university police.

Programs of Study: USF confers B.A., B.S., B.F.A., B.I.S., B.M., B.S.W., and several engineering degrees. Associate, master's, and doctoral degrees are also awarded. Bachelor's degrees are awarded in BIOLOGICAL SCIENCE (biology/biological science and microbiology), BUSINESS (accounting, banking and finance, business administration and management, business economics, management information systems, management science, and marketing/retailing/merchandising), COMMUNICATIONS AND THE ARTS (art, classics, communications, dance, dramatic arts, English literature, French, German, Italian, languages, music, Russian, Spanish, and speech/debate/rhetoric), COMPUTER AND PHYSICAL SCIENCE (chemistry, geology, mathematics, physical sciences, and physics), EDUCATION (art, business, education, education of the emotionally handicapped, education of the mentally handicapped, elementary, English, foreign languages, mathematics, music, physical, science, social studies, special, specific learning disabilities, and vocational), ENGINEERING AND ENVIRONMENTAL DESIGN (chemical engineering, civil engineering, computer engineering, electrical/electronics engineering, engineering, environmental science, industrial engineering, and mechanical engineering), HEALTH PROFESSIONS (medical technology and nursing), SOCIAL SCIENCE (African American studies, American studies, anthropology, criminology, economics, geography, gerontology, history, humanities, international relations, liberal arts/general studies, philosophy, political science/government, psychology, religion, social science, social work, sociology, and women's studies). Education, fine arts, and sciences are the strongest academically. Business and education are the largest.

Required: To graduate, all students are required to complete at least 120 credit hours, including 36 distributed among English, math, science, social science, historical perspectives, fine arts, and humanities and 9 of exit requirements in major works/major issues and literature/writing. The number of hours required for each major varies. Students must maintain a minimum GPA of 2.0.

Special: USF offers co-op programs in business and engineering, study abroad, cross-registration, work-study programs, accelerated degree programs in public health and medicine, internships, a Washington semester, dual and student-designed majors, a liberal arts degree, nondegree study, and pass/fail options for some courses. There are 21 national honor societies, a freshman honors program, and 18 departmental honors programs.

Faculty/Classroom: 57% of faculty are male; 43%, female. 48% teach undergraduates and 16% do research. The average class size in an introductory lecture is 37; in a laboratory, 21; and in a regular course, 31.

Admissions: 62% of the 2003-2004 applicants were accepted. The SAT I scores for the 2003-2004 freshman class were: Verbal--29% below 500, 49% between 500 and 599, 20% between 600 and 700, and 2% above 700; Math--26% below 500, 48% between 500 and 599, 23% between 600 and 700, and 3% above 700. The ACT scores were 6% below 18, 59% between 18 and 23, 32% between 24 and 29, and 4%

above 29. 44% of the current freshmen were in the top fifth of their class. There were 7 National Merit finalists.

Requirements: The SAT I or ACT is required. In addition, candidates for admission should have completed 4 units each of English and academic electives, 3 each of math, science, and social studies, and 2 of a foreign language. The GED is accepted. Applicants who do not meet minimum requirements but have important attributes, special talents, or unique circumstances are considered for admission by an academic faculty committee. A GPA of 2.0 is required. AP and CLEP credits are accepted. Important factors in the admissions decision are advanced placement or honor courses, evidence of special talent, and recommendations by school officials.

Procedure: Freshmen are admitted to all sessions. Entrance exams should be taken at the end of the junior year or the beginning of the senior year. Applications should be filed by May 1 for fall entry, October 1 for spring entry, and March 1 for summer entry, along with a $30 fee. Notification is sent on a rolling basis. Applications are accepted on-line.

Transfer: 4063 transfer students enrolled in 2002-2003. Students with fewer than 60 transferable hours must meet freshman requirements. Additionally, applicants must have a cumulative college GPA of 2.0 and be in good standing at their last institution. 30 of 120 credits required for the bachelor's degree must be completed at USF.

Visiting: There are regularly scheduled orientations for prospective students, including a 2-day program. There are guides for informal visits and visitors may sit in on classes. To schedule a visit, contact the Admissions Office/New Student Orientation at (813) 974-3060 or *orassist@admin.usf.edu*.

Financial Aid: In 2003-2004, 72% of all full-time students received some form of financial aid. 48% of all full-time students received need-based aid. The average freshman award was $6337. 23% of undergraduates work part time. The FAFSA is required. The priority date for freshman financial aid applications for fall entry is January 1. The deadline for filing freshman financial aid applications for fall entry is March 1.

International Students: There are 788 international students enrolled. The school actively recruits these students. They must score 550 on the written TOEFL and also take the SAT I or the ACT.

Computers: The mainframe is an IBM 9672-R32 Enterpriser server MVS OS/390. Student computer labs exist throughout campus. All students may access the system. There are no time limits and no fees.

Graduates: From July 1, 2002 to June 30, 2003, 4974 bachelor's degrees were awarded. The most popular majors were business (27%), education (14%), and social science (12%). In an average class, 1% graduate in 3 years or less, 20% graduate in 4 years or less, 40% graduate in 5 years or less, and 47% graduate in 6 years or less. 692 companies recruited on campus in 2002-2003. Of the 2002 graduating class, 22% were enrolled in graduate school within 6 months of graduation and 71% were employed.

Admissions Contact: Dewey Holleman, Director of Admissions. A video is available. E-mail: *dhollema@admin.usf.edu*
Web: *http://usfweb.usf.edu/enroll/admiss/admiss.htm*

UNIVERSITY OF TAMPA
Tampa, FL 33606-1490

D-4
(813) 253-6211
(888) 646-2738; Fax: (813) 258-7398

Full-time: 1356 men, 2271 women	**Faculty:** 191; IIB, av$
Part-time: 190 men, 308 women	**Ph.D's:** 91%
Graduate: 252 men, 284 women	**Student/Faculty:** 19 to 1
Year: semesters, summer session	**Tuition:** $17,572
Application Deadline: open	**Room & Board:** $6410
Freshman Class: 5269 applied, 3202 accepted, 1044 enrolled	
SAT I Verbal/Math: 545/548	**ACT:** 23 **VERY COMPETITIVE**

The University of Tampa, founded in 1931, is a comprehensive, independent institution that offers degree programs in more than 65 undergraduate and preprofessional areas of study, and graduate and evening programs. There are 2 undergraduate and 2 graduate schools. In addition to regional accreditation, UT has baccalaureate program accreditation with AACSB, NASM, and NLN. The library contains 252,000 volumes, 36,000 microform items, and 5200 audio/video tapes/CDs, and subscribes to 11,300 periodicals. Computerized library services include the card catalog, interlibrary loans, database searching, and Internet access. Special learning facilities include a learning resource center, art gallery, radio station, TV station, a fully equipped research vessel for marine science studies, music facility, writing and language labs, academic center for excellence, graphic design studio, marine science lab, and art studios. The 95-acre campus is in an urban area in Tampa. Including any residence halls, there are 45 buildings.

Student Life: 60% of undergraduates are from out of state, mostly the Northeast. Students are from 50 states, 101 foreign countries, and Canada. 75% are from public schools. 63% are white; 13% foreign nationals. The average age of freshmen is 19; all undergraduates, 24. 23% do not continue beyond their first year; 52% remain to graduate.

Housing: 2504 students can be accommodated in college housing, which includes single-sex and coed dorms and on-campus apartments.

In addition, there is a special honors floor and a substance-free floor. 70% of students live on campus; of those, 85% remain on campus on weekends. All students may keep cars.

Activities: 12% of men belong to 8 national fraternities; 14% of women belong to 9 national sororities. There are 110 groups on campus, including academic art, band, cheerleading, chess, chorale, chorus, computers, dance, debate, drama, ethnic, gay, honors, international, jazz band, leadership, literary magazine, musical theater, newspaper, orchestra, pep band, political, professional, radio and TV, religious, social, social service, special interest, student government, symphony, and yearbook. Popular campus events include Into the Streets (volunteer program), Homecoming, and Global Village Day.

Sports: There are 6 intercollegiate sports for men and 8 for women, and 7 intramural sports for men and 7 for women. Facilities include a sports center, a stadium, baseball, softball, practice, and intramural fields, a boat house, an Olympic-size pool, 6 lighted tennis courts, volleyball and basketball courts, activity and fitness centers, a dance studio, the student union, and recreation rooms in each residence hall.

Disabled Students: All of the campus is accessible. Wheelchair ramps, elevators, special parking, specially equipped rest rooms, lowered drinking fountains, lowered telephones, and special housing are available.

Services: Counseling and information services are available, as is tutoring in every subject. There is remedial math, reading, and writing.

Campus Safety and Security: Measures include 24-hour foot and vehicle patrol, self-defense education, security escort services, and shuttle buses. There are informal discussions, pamphlets/posters/films, emergency telephones, lighted pathways/sidewalks, and a full-service, on-campus security office.

Programs of Study: UT confers B.A., B.S., B.F.A., B.L.S., B.M., and B.S.N. degrees. Associate and master's degrees are also awarded. Bachelor's degrees are awarded in BIOLOGICAL SCIENCE (biochemistry, biology/biological science, and marine science), BUSINESS (accounting, banking and finance, business administration and management, business economics, international business management, and marketing/retailing/merchandising), COMMUNICATIONS AND THE ARTS (art, communications, creative writing, English, fine arts, graphic design, music, performing arts, and Spanish), COMPUTER AND PHYSICAL SCIENCE (chemistry, information sciences and systems, and mathematics), EDUCATION (elementary and secondary), ENGINEERING AND ENVIRONMENTAL DESIGN (computer graphics and environmental science), HEALTH PROFESSIONS (exercise science and nursing), SOCIAL SCIENCE (criminology, economics, history, international studies, liberal arts/general studies, political science/government, psychology, social science, sociology, and urban studies). Biology and chemistry are the strongest academically. Business, biology, and communication are the largest.

Required: To graduate, students must maintain a minimum GPA of 2.0 in at least 124 credit hours, including the 2-year Learning Community, 11 each in humanities/fine arts and social science, 6 in natural science, global issues, non-Western studies, and writing-intensive course work. The requirements for individual majors vary.

Special: Students may participate in internships, work-study programs on campus, study abroad in 7 countries, a Washington semester, and an Oxford semester program. UT also offers summer marine science courses at the Gulf Coast Research Laboratory, nondegree study, pass/fail options, and credit for life, military, and work experience. There are 22 national honor societies, a freshman honors program, and 16 departmental honors programs.

Faculty/Classroom: 61% of faculty are male; 39%, female. All teach undergraduates. No introductory courses are taught by graduate students. The average class size in an introductory lecture is 19; in a laboratory, 19; and in a regular course, 21.

Admissions: 61% of the 2003-2004 applicants were accepted. The SAT I scores for the 2003-2004 freshman class were: Math--37% below 500, 48% between 500 and 599, 14% between 600 and 700, and 1% above 700. The ACT scores for the 2003-2004 freshman class were: 3% below 21, 48% between 21 and 23, 45% between 27 and 28, and 4% above 28. 23% of the current freshmen were in the top fifth of their class; 85% were in the top two fifths.

Requirements: The SAT I or ACT is required. In addition, candidates for admission should have completed 4 credits in English, 2 each in math, science, and social studies, and 5 in college-preparatory electives. The GED is accepted. A portfolio or an audition is required for specific art and music programs. A GPA of 2.5 is required. AP and CLEP credits are accepted. Important factors in the admissions decision are personality/intangible qualities, evidence of special talent, and recommendations by school officials.

Procedure: Freshmen are admitted fall, spring, and summer. Entrance exams should be taken by the end of the junior year or early in the senior year. There is a deferred admissions plan. Application deadlines are open. Notification is sent on a rolling basis after September 15. Application fee is $35. Applications are accepted on computer disk and on-line through the university's web site.

Transfer: 366 transfer students enrolled in 2002-2003. Applicants should have earned 17 college credits with a minimum GPA of 2.0. 31

of 124 credits required for the bachelor's degree must be completed at UT.

Visiting: There are regularly scheduled orientations for prospective students, including a campus tour and an interview with an admissions counselor, faculty, and others as requested. There are guides for informal visits and visitors may sit in on classes and stay overnight. To schedule a visit, contact the Admissions Office at *admissions@ut.edu*.

Financial Aid: In 2003-2004, 87% of all full-time freshmen and 88% of continuing full-time students received some form of financial aid. 79% of full-time freshmen and 80% of continuing full-time students received need-based aid. The average freshman award was $15,472. Need-based scholarships or need-based grants averaged $6813; need-based self-help aid (loans and jobs) averaged $3055 ($5125 maximum); and non-need-based awards and non-need-based scholarships averaged $2000 (maximum). 22% of undergraduates work part time. Average annual earnings from campus work are $2000. The average financial indebtedness of the 2003 graduate was $22,791. UT is a member of CSS. The FAFSA is required.

International Students: There are 310 international students enrolled. The school actively recruits these students. They must score 550 on the written TOEFL or 213 on the electronic version and also take the SAT I or the ACT.

Computers: Students may use Macs and PCs in the computer labs in the computer center, student union, and classroom buildings, a Sun lab with workstations, a multimedia decision support center, and several discipline-specific labs. All students may access the system. There are no time limits and no fees.

Graduates: From July 1, 2002 to June 30, 2003, 667 bachelor's degrees were awarded. The most popular majors were business (24%), social science and history (13%), and education (12%). In an average class, 40% graduate in 4 years or less, 50% graduate in 5 years or less, and 52% graduate in 6 years or less. 174 companies recruited on campus in 2002-2003. Of the 2002 graduating class, 14% were enrolled in graduate school within 6 months of graduation and 100% were employed.

Admissions Contact: Barbara P. Strickler, Vice President, Enrollment. E-mail: *admissions@ut.edu* Web: *www.ut.edu*

UNIVERSITY OF WEST FLORIDA
Pensacola, FL 32514-5750

A-1

(850) 474-2230
(800) 263-1074; Fax: (850) 474-3360

Full-time: 2100 men, 2900 women	**Faculty:** IIA, -$
Part-time: 1100 men, 1400 women	**Ph.D.s:** n/av
Graduate: 610 men, 1025 women	**Student/Faculty:** n/av
Year: semesters, summer session	**Tuition:** $2470 ($10,660)
Application Deadline: June 30	**Room & Board:** $6000
Freshman Class: 2569 applied, 2000 accepted, 896 enrolled	
SAT I or ACT: required	**COMPETITIVE**

The University of West Florida, founded in 1967, is a public, liberal arts institution that is part of the State University system of Florida. Enrollment figures in the above capsule are approximate. There are 3 undergraduate and 3 graduate schools. In addition to regional accreditation, UWF has baccalaureate program accreditation with AACSB, ABET, CSWE, NCATE, and NLN. The library contains 416,380 volumes, 1,635,474 microform items, and 7311 audio/video tapes/CDs, and subscribes to 5032 periodicals. Computerized library services include the card catalog, interlibrary loans, and database searching. Special learning facilities include a learning resource center, art gallery, radio station, TV station, and an archeology museum. The 1600-acre campus is in a suburban area 10 miles north of downtown Pensacola. Including any residence halls, there are 71 buildings.

Student Life: 87% of undergraduates are from Florida. Students are from 49 states, 82 foreign countries, and Canada. 78% are white; 10% African American. The average age of freshmen is 19; all undergraduates, 25.

Housing: 1250 students can be accommodated in college housing, which includes coed dorms and on-campus apartments. In addition, there are honors houses. On-campus housing is available on a first-come, first-served basis. 85% of students commute. All students may keep cars.

Activities: There are 6 national fraternities and 5 national sororities. There are 85 groups on campus, including art, band, cheerleading, choir, chorale, chorus, debate, drama, ethnic, film, forensics, gay, honors, international, jazz band, literary magazine, newspaper, orchestra, political, professional, radio and TV, religious, social, social service, student government, and symphony.

Sports: There are 6 intercollegiate sports for men and 7 for women, and 16 intramural sports for men and 16 for women. There are facilities for baseball, track, tennis, racquetball, handball, softball, soccer, swimming, diving, weight lifting, and aerobics.

Disabled Students: All of the campus is accessible. Wheelchair ramps, elevators, special parking, specially equipped rest rooms, special class

scheduling, lowered drinking fountains, and special housing are available.

Services: Counseling and information services are available, as is tutoring in most subjects. There is remedial math, reading, and writing. Remedial courses are offered on campus by the local community college.

Campus Safety and Security: Measures include 24-hour foot and vehicle patrol, security escort services, informal discussions, and pamphlets/posters/films. There are emergency telephones, lighted pathways/sidewalks, and a trolley system.

Programs of Study: UWF confers B.A., B.S., B.F.A., B.S.B.A., B.S.C.E., B.S.E.E., and B.S.N degrees. Associate, master's, and doctoral degrees are also awarded. Bachelor's degrees are awarded in BIOLOGICAL SCIENCE (biology/biological science and marine biology), BUSINESS (accounting, banking and finance, business administration and management, business economics, and marketing/retailing/merchandising), COMMUNICATIONS AND THE ARTS (communications, English, music, and studio art), COMPUTER AND PHYSICAL SCIENCE (chemistry, computer science, mathematics, physics, and statistics), EDUCATION (art, early childhood, elementary, health, middle school, music, and secondary), ENGINEERING AND ENVIRONMENTAL DESIGN (computer engineering and electrical/electronics engineering), HEALTH PROFESSIONS (medical laboratory technology, nursing, predentistry, and premedicine), SOCIAL SCIENCE (criminal justice, history, philosophy, political science/government, prelaw, psychology, religion, social science, and social work). Accounting, communication arts, and management are the strongest academically. Communication arts, psychology, and business are the largest.

Required: To graduate, students must maintain a 2.0 GPA and complete 120 semester hours with a minimum of 24 hours in the major and 24 hours in upper-division courses.

Special: Internships are arranged on an individual basis through a student's major department. The college offers pass/fail options and credit for military experience. A 3-2 engineering degree is also offered. There are 5 national honor societies and a freshman honors program.

Admissions: 78% of the 2003-2004 applicants were accepted.

Requirements: The SAT I or ACT is required. In addition, students must have completed 4 years of English, 3 each of math, science, and social studies, and 2 of a foreign language. A GPA of 2.0 is required. AP and CLEP credits are accepted. Important factors in the admissions decision are advanced placement or honor courses, evidence of special talent, and geographic diversity.

Procedure: Freshmen are admitted to all sessions. Entrance exams should be taken by the fall of the senior year. There are early admissions and deferred admissions plans. Applications should be filed by June 30 for fall entry, December 1 for spring entry, and April 1 for summer entry, along with a $20 fee. Notification is sent on a rolling basis. Applications are accepted on-line through the school's web site.

Transfer: 1054 transfer students enrolled in a recent year. Applicants must have a 2.0 GPA and a 2.0 at their last institution. Transfer students with fewer than 60 semester hours of transferable credit must meet freshman admission requirements. 30 of 120 credits required for the bachelor's degree must be completed at UWF.

Visiting: There are regularly scheduled orientations for prospective students, including 5 Open House Programs per year. There are guides for informal visits and visitors may sit in on classes. To schedule a visit, contact the Admissions Office.

Financial Aid: The CSS/Profile, the University of West Florida Request for Financial Aid Consideration form, and SAR are required. Check with the school for current application deadlines.

International Students: There were 271 international students enrolled in a recent year. They must score 525 on the written TOEFL or 193 on the electronic version or take the MELAB. They must also take the SAT I or the ACT, scoring 970 on the SAT I or 20 on the ACT.

Computers: The mainframe is an IBM 4381. All students may access the system. There are no time limits and no fees.

Graduates: In a recent year, 1286 bachelor's degrees were awarded. The most popular majors were business (22%), education (19%), and psychology (9%).

Admissions Contact: Matthew Hulett, Director of Admissions. E-mail: *admissions@uwf.edu* Web: *www.uwf.edu*

WARNER SOUTHERN COLLEGE
Lake Wales, FL 33859

D-4

(863) 638-7212
(800) 309-9563; Fax: (863) 638-7290

Full-time: 336 men, 443 women	**Faculty:** 52
Part-time: 65 men, 231 women	**Ph.D.s:** 54%
Graduate: 36 men, 18 women	**Student/Faculty:** 15 to 1
Year: semesters, summer session	**Tuition:** $11,380
Application Deadline: open	**Room & Board:** $5358
Freshman Class: 260 applied, 183 accepted, 115 enrolled	
SAT I Verbal/Math: 470/450	**ACT:** 19 **LESS COMPETITIVE**

Warner Southern College is a Christian college in the liberal arts tradition committed to the search for truth in the context of Christian faith and academic excellence. There are 2 undergraduate schools and 1 graduate school. The library contains 74,000 volumes, 7267 microform items, and 15,200 audio/video tapes/CDs, and subscribes to 178 periodicals. Computerized library services include the card catalog, interlibrary loans, database searching, and Internet access. Special learning facilities include a learning resource center. The 380-acre campus is in a rural area 5 miles south of Lake Wales. Including any residence halls, there are 20 buildings.

Student Life: 88% of undergraduates are from Florida. Students are from 26 states, 18 foreign countries, and Canada. 68% are white; 17% African American. 61% are Protestant; 29% claim no religious affiliation; 7% Catholic. The average age of freshmen is 19; all undergraduates, 22. 62% do not continue beyond their first year; 50% remain to graduate.

Housing: 235 students can be accommodated in college housing, which includes single-sex dorms and off-campus apartments. On-campus housing is guaranteed for all 4 years. 58% of students commute. Alcohol is not permitted. All students may keep cars.

Activities: There are no fraternities or sororities. There are 14 groups on campus, including band, cheerleading, choir, chorale, chorus, computers, honors, newspaper, pep band, photography, religious, social, social service, and student government. Popular campus events include Christmas banquet, Barn Party, and Spring banquet.

Sports: There are 7 intercollegiate sports for men and 8 for women, and 4 intramural sports for men and 3 for women. Facilities include the Turner Athletic Center.

Disabled Students: 90% of the campus is accessible. Wheelchair ramps, special parking, specially equipped rest rooms, lowered drinking fountains, and lowered telephones are available.

Services: Counseling and information services are available, as is tutoring in most subjects. There is remedial math, reading, and writing.

Campus Safety and Security: Measures include 24-hour foot and vehicle patrol, security escort services, shuttle buses, and informal discussions. There are pamphlets/posters/films, emergency telephones, lighted pathways/sidewalks, and special training in CPR/First Aid and emergency response.

Programs of Study: Warner Southern College confers the B.A. degree. Associate and master's degrees are also awarded. Bachelor's degrees are awarded in BIOLOGICAL SCIENCE (biology/biological science), BUSINESS (accounting, banking and finance, business administration and management, business law, institutional management, marketing management, and sports management), COMMUNICATIONS AND THE ARTS (communications and English), COMPUTER AND PHYSICAL SCIENCE (information sciences and systems), EDUCATION (business, education of the exceptional child, elementary, English, music, physical, science, and social science), HEALTH PROFESSIONS (exercise science), SOCIAL SCIENCE (biblical studies, history, pastoral studies, psychology, religious music, and social work). Biblical studies, social work, and teacher education are the strongest academically. Organizational management, church ministry, and teacher education are the largest.

Required: To graduate, students must complete 128 credit hours with a GPA of 2.0 to 2.5, depending on the major. 30 to 80 hours are required in the major. 48 hours of upper-division courses are required, as is a computer application course in the major.

Special: Internships are required in many majors, including teacher education, social work, sports management, and church ministry. An accelerated degree program is available in organizational management. HEART (Hunger Education and Resource Training) is a missionary training program designed to equip students to serve in missions, community development work, or crosscultural assignments in developing countries. There are 5 national honor societies and 1 departmental honors program.

Faculty/Classroom: 72% of faculty are male; 28%, female. All teach undergraduates, 20% do research, and 20% do both. No introductory courses are taught by graduate students. The average class size in an introductory lecture is 28; in a laboratory, 20; and in a regular course, 18.

Admissions: 70% of the 2003-2004 applicants were accepted. The SAT I scores for the 2003-2004 freshman class were: Verbal--69% below 500, 27% between 500 and 599, 21% between 600 and 700, and 2% above 700; Math--69% below 500, 27% between 500 and 599, 2% between 600 and 700, and 2% above 700. The ACT scores were 66% below 21, 16% between 21 and 23, 13% between 24 and 26, 2% between 27 and 28, and 3% above 28. 19% of the current freshmen were in the top fifth of their class; 54% were in the top two fifths. There was 1 National Merit finalist and 1 semifinalist. 2 freshmen graduated first in their class.

Requirements: The SAT I or ACT is required. Warner Southern College requires applicants to be in the upper 50% of their class. A GPA of 2.25 is required. AP and CLEP credits are accepted.

Procedure: Freshmen are admitted fall and spring. Entrance exams should be taken in the junior or senior year. There is a rolling admissions plan. There are early admissions and deferred admissions plans. Application deadlines are open. Application fee is $20. Applications are accepted on-line.

Transfer: 39 transfer students enrolled in 2002-2003. Applicants may transfer 24 or more hours from a regionally accredited school and must

present a GPA of 2.0 or higher. 36 of 128 credits required for the bachelor's degree must be completed at Warner Southern College.

Visiting: There are regularly scheduled orientations for prospective students, consisting of Warner Weekend held in the spring. There are guides for informal visits and visitors may sit in on classes and stay overnight. To schedule a visit, contact Deanna Frazier at *admissions@warner.edu.*

Financial Aid: In 2003-2004, 93% of all full-time freshmen and 98% of continuing full-time students received some form of financial aid. 91% of full-time freshmen and 52% of continuing full-time students received need-based aid. Need-based scholarships or need-based grants averaged $12,401; need-based self-help aid (loans and jobs) averaged $14,000; non-need-based athletic scholarships averaged $3736; and other non-need-based awards and non-need-based scholarships averaged $7802. 47% of undergraduates work part time. Average annual earnings from campus work are $1528. The FAFSA and the state aid form are required. The priority date for freshman financial aid applications for fall entry is May 10. The deadline for filing freshman financial aid applications for fall entry is October 1.

International Students: There are 31 international students enrolled. The school actively recruits these students. They must score 500 on the written TOEFL or 173 on the electronic version and also take the SAT I or ACT, scoring 870 or 18, respectively.

Computers: There are 75 computers available in 3 computer labs. All students may access the system 7:30 A.M. to 10:45 P.M., Monday to Friday, and some weekend hours. There are no time limits and no fees. It is strongly recommended that all students have a personal computer. It is recommended that students in on-line majors have personal computers.

Graduates: From July 1, 2002 to June 30, 2003, 368 bachelor's degrees were awarded. The most popular majors were organizational management (63%), elementary education (6%), and business administration (3%). In an average class, 25% graduate in 4 years or less, 32% graduate in 5 years or less, and 35% graduate in 6 years or less.

Admissions Contact: Jason Roe, Director of Admissions. E-mail: *admissions@warner.edu* Web: *www.warner.edu*

WEBBER COLLEGE
(See Webber International University)

WEBBER INTERNATIONAL UNIVERSITY
Babson Park, FL 33827

D-3
(863) 638-2930
(800) 741-1844; Fax: (863) 638-1317

Full-time: 326 men, 204 women	**Faculty:** 16
Part-time: 25 men, 33 women	**Ph.D.s:** 54%
Graduate: 31 men, 37 women	**Student/Faculty:** 33 to 1
Year: semesters, summer session	**Tuition:** $12,000
Application Deadline: August 1	**Room & Board:** $4510
Freshman Class: 418 applied, 209 accepted, 85 enrolled	
SAT I Verbal/Math: 477/487	**ACT:** 18 COMPETITIVE

Webber International University, formerly Webber College, is a privately endowed, nonprofit institution founded in 1927, and offering undergraduate and graduate degrees in business. Some information in the above capsule is approximate. In addition to regional accreditation, Webber has baccalaureate program accreditation with IACBE. The library contains 28,000 volumes, 105 microform items, and 529 audio/video tapes/CDs, and subscribes to 63 periodicals. Computerized library services include the card catalog, interlibrary loans, and database searching. Special learning facilities include a learning resource center and an Audubon Society museum. The 110-acre campus is in a small town 50 miles east of Tampa and 50 miles south of Orlando. Including any residence halls, there are 10 buildings.

Student Life: 64% of undergraduates are from Florida. Students are from 12 states, 36 foreign countries, and Canada. 76% are from public schools. 57% are white; 26% foreign nationals; 10% African American. The average age of freshmen is 19; all undergraduates, 21. 42% do not continue beyond their first year.

Housing: 210 students can be accommodated in college housing, which includes single-sex dorms. On-campus housing is guaranteed for the freshman year only and is available on a first-come, first-served basis. 55% of students commute. All students may keep cars.

Activities: There are no fraternities or sororities. There are 11 groups on campus, including debate, honors, international, newspaper, political, professional, religious, social, social service, and student government. Popular campus events include Webber Weekend, Christmas Party, and Beach Party.

Sports: There are 7 intercollegiate sports for men and 8 for women, and 4 intramural sports for men and 4 for women. Facilities include 2 gyms, a weight room, tennis courts, 2 racquetball courts, a swimming pool, softball, baseball, and soccer fields, beach volleyball courts, and a lake for water sports.

Disabled Students: 72% of the campus is accessible. Wheelchair ramps, special parking, specially equipped rest rooms, special class scheduling, lowered drinking fountains, and lowered telephones are available.

Services: Counseling and information services are available, as is tutoring in most subjects. There is remedial math, reading, and writing.

Campus Safety and Security: Measures include security escort services, informal discussions, pamphlets/posters/films, and lighted pathways/sidewalks. There is a security patrol nights and all weekend.

Programs of Study: Webber confers the B.S. degree. Associate and master's degrees are also awarded. Bachelor's degrees are awarded in BUSINESS (accounting, banking and finance, business administration and management, hotel/motel and restaurant management, international business management, marketing/retailing/merchandising, recreational facilities management, and tourism), SOCIAL SCIENCE (prelaw). Business administration is the strongest academically and has the largest enrollment.

Required: To graduate, all students must complete 120 credit hours, including courses in their major, a 40-credit general curriculum, and a 30-credit business core. A GPA of 2.0 or better must be maintained. Students must pass the college's required English courses and meet its writing requirements. All students must take at least 3 computer courses.

Special: Cross-registration with other schools may be arranged. Internships are required for international tourism, hospitality management, and sport management majors. Study abroad is available in 2 countries. There is 1 national honor society and 1 departmental honors program.

Faculty/Classroom: 77% of faculty are male; 23%, female. All teach undergraduates, 15% do research, and 15% do both. The average class size in an introductory lecture is 35; in a laboratory, 10; and in a regular course, 21.

Admissions: 50% of the 2003-2004 applicants were accepted. The SAT I scores for the 2003-2004 freshman class were: Verbal--81% below 500, and 18% between 500 and 599; Math--79% below 500, 19% between 500 and 599, and 3% between 600 and 700. The ACT scores were 76% below 21, 19% between 21 and 23, 4% between 24 and 26, and 1% between 27 and 28.

Requirements: The SAT I or ACT is required, with a minimum composite score of 860 on the SAT I or 18 on the ACT. Applicants should be graduates of accredited secondary schools and have completed 3 years each of English, math, and science and 2 years of social studies. An essay is also required. The GED is accepted. A GPA of 2.0 is required. AP and CLEP credits are accepted. Important factors in the admissions decision are personality/intangible qualities, recommendations by school officials, and leadership record.

Procedure: Freshmen are admitted to all sessions. Entrance exams should be taken during the senior year. There are early decision, early admissions, and deferred admissions plans. There is a rolling admissions plan. Applications should be filed by August 1 for fall entry and December 1 for spring entry, along with a $35 fee. Notification is sent on a rolling basis. Applications are accepted on-line through the school's web site.

Transfer: Applicants must have a minimum GPA of 2.0 with 15 credit hours, leave their previous institution in good academic standing, and submit a letter of recommendation and a student essay. Students with fewer than 15 credits must meet freshman requirements. 30 of 120 credits required for the bachelor's degree must be completed at Webber.

Visiting: There are guides for informal visits and visitors may sit in on classes and stay overnight. To schedule a visit, contact the Director of Admissions at (863) 638-2911.

Financial Aid: In 2003-2004, 97% of all full-time freshmen and 96% of continuing full-time students received some form of financial aid. 61% of full-time freshmen and 60% of continuing full-time students received need-based aid. The average freshman award was $10,742. Need-based scholarships or need-based grants averaged $8377 ($16,000 maximum); need-based self-help aid (loans and jobs) averaged $2480 ($7625 maximum); non-need-based athletic scholarships averaged $4659 ($8000 maximum); and other non-need-based awards and non-need-based scholarships averaged $2041 ($5000 maximum). 46% of undergraduates work part time. Average annual earnings from campus work are $1000. The average financial indebtedness of a recent graduate was $11,813. Webber is a member of CSS. The FAFSA is required. Check with the school for current deadlines.

International Students: There were 115 international students enrolled in a recent year. The school actively recruits these students. They must score 500 on the written TOEFL or 173 on the electronic version, and also take the SAT I or the ACT, scoring 860 (SAT I).

Computers: There are 35 PCs located at the computer center and direct connections to the Internet. All students may access the system. There are no time limits and no fees. It is strongly recommended that all students have a personal computer.

Graduates: In a recent year, 125 bachelor's degrees were awarded.

Admissions Contact: Kathy Wilson, Registrar. A video is available. E-mail: *wilson@webber.edu* Web: *www.webber.edu*

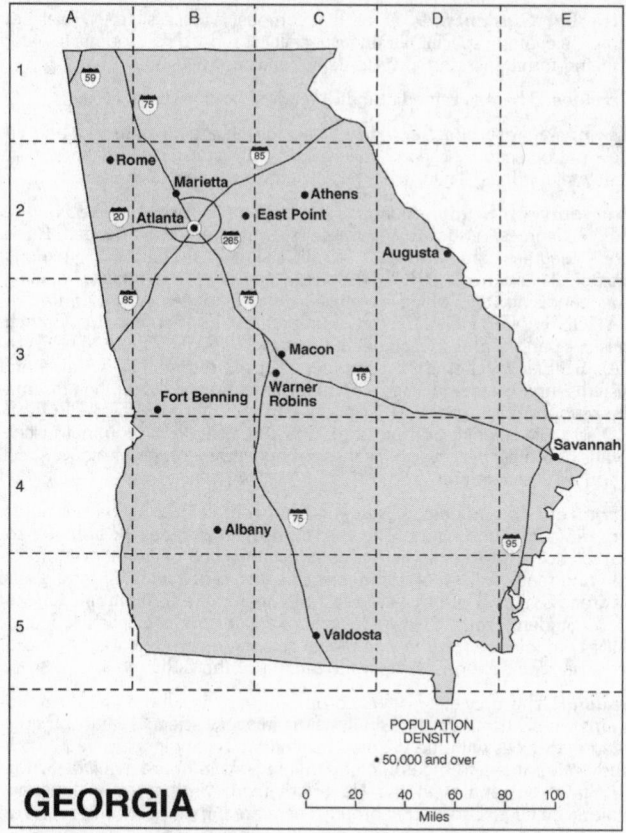

GEORGIA

POPULATION
DENSITY

• 50,000 and over

0 20 40 60 80 100
Miles

AGNES SCOTT COLLEGE
Decatur, GA 30030

B-2

(404) 471-6285
(800) 868-8602; Fax: (404) 471-6414

Full-time: 852 women	**Faculty:** 77; IIB, +$
Part-time: 46 women	**Ph.D.s:** 100%
Graduate: 4 men, 21 women	**Student/Faculty:** 11 to 1
Year: semesters	**Tuition:** $20,470
Application Deadline: March 1	**Room & Board:** $7760
Freshman Class: 782 applied, 514 accepted, 213 enrolled	
SAT I Verbal/Math: 620/590	**ACT:** 26 **HIGHLY COMPETITIVE**

Agnes Scott College, founded in 1889, is an independent liberal arts college for women, and is affiliated with the Presbyterian Church (U.S.A.). There is 1 undergraduate and 1 graduate school. The library contains 217,759 volumes, 32,677 microform items, and 18,758 audio/video tapes/CDs, and subscribes to 1458 periodicals. Computerized library services include the card catalog, interlibrary loans, database searching, and Internet access. Special learning facilities include a learning resource center, art gallery, planetarium, an educational technology center, multimedia classrooms, and centers for writing and speaking. The 100-acre campus is in an urban area 6 miles from downtown Atlanta. Including any residence halls, there are 25 buildings.

Student Life: 53% of undergraduates are from Georgia. Students are from 41 states and 29 foreign countries. 77% are from public schools. 56% are white; 35% Hispanic; 20% African American. 57% are Protestant; 19% Catholic; 8% Islamic and various others; 6% claim no religious affiliation. The average age of freshmen is 18; all undergraduates, 21. 16% do not continue beyond their first year; 65% remain to graduate.

Housing: 737 students can be accommodated in college housing, which includes single-sex dorms and on-campus apartments. In addition, there are special-interest houses, language wings for French and German, and CHOICE housing (Choosing Healthy Options In a Community Environment). On-campus housing is guaranteed for all 4 years. 89% of students live on campus; of those, 65% remain on campus on weekends. All students may keep cars.

Activities: There are no fraternities. There are 79 groups on campus, including art, choir, chorale, dance, drama, ethnic, gay, honors, international, literary magazine, marching band, musical theater, newspaper, orchestra, political, professional, religious, social, social service, student

government, and yearbook. Popular campus events include Black Cat, holiday parties, and Senior Investiture.

Sports: Facilities include a gym with a regulation basketball court, an 8-lane indoor pool, a soccer field, a tennis facility, a weight room, a track, an aerobics room, and dance studios.

Disabled Students: 90% of the campus is accessible. Wheelchair ramps, elevators, special parking, specially equipped rest rooms, special class scheduling, lowered drinking fountains, lowered telephones, special housing, and lifts are available.

Services: Counseling and information services are available, as is tutoring in some subjects, including classical languages, English, math, physics, biology, psychology, chemistry, and economics. There is a reader service for the blind and centers for writing and speaking.

Campus Safety and Security: Measures include 24-hour foot and vehicle patrol, self-defense education, security escort services, and informal discussions. There are pamphlets/posters/films, emergency telephones, lighted pathways/sidewalks, and reimbursement for emergency taxi service.

Programs of Study: Agnes Scott confers the B.A. degree. Master's degrees are also awarded. Bachelor's degrees are awarded in BIOLOGICAL SCIENCE (biochemistry and biology/biological science), COMMUNICATIONS AND THE ARTS (classical languages, classics, creative writing, dramatic arts, English, fine arts, French, German, music, and Spanish), COMPUTER AND PHYSICAL SCIENCE (astrophysics, chemistry, mathematics, and physics), SOCIAL SCIENCE (anthropology, classical/ancient civilization, economics, history, international relations, philosophy, political science/government, psychology, religion, sociology, and women's studies). Biology, English, and psychology are the largest.

Required: Requirements for graduation include first-year seminar and courses in English composition and reading, foreign language, and phys ed, as well as courses in literature and fine arts, religious or philosophical thought, historical studies or classical civilization, natural science, math, social science, and social and cultural analysis. Students must complete 130 credit hours, including 32 to 52 in the major, with a 2.0 GPA.

Special: There is cross-registration through ARCHE (a 19-member consortium), and more than 300 credit and noncredit internships are available. There is a 3-2 engineering program with the Georgia Institute of Technology, and the college offers dual, student-designed, and interdisciplinary majors. Pass/fail options are also available. Opportunities for study abroad include exchange programs, a Global Awareness program, and Global Connections. Also offered are a Washington semester, an Atlanta semester, the PLEN Public Policy Semester, the Mills College Exchange, a 3-4 architecture degree with Washington University, and work-study programs. Teacher certification and Language Across the Curriculum programs are offered. B.A. degree requirements may be completed in 3 years. There are 13 national honor societies, including Phi Beta Kappa.

Faculty/Classroom: 40% of faculty are male; 60%, female. All both teach and do research. No introductory courses are taught by graduate students. The average class size in an introductory lecture is 20; in a laboratory, 13; and in a regular course, 15.

Admissions: 66% of the 2003-2004 applicants were accepted. The SAT I scores for the 2003-2004 freshman class were: Verbal--9% below 500, 29% between 500 and 599, 46% between 600 and 700, and 16% above 700; Math--17% below 500, 40% between 500 and 599, 40% between 600 and 700, and 4% above 700. The ACT scores were 8% below 21, 16% between 21 and 23, 30% between 24 and 26, 12% between 27 and 28, and 34% above 28. 78% of the current freshmen were in the top fifth of their class; 93% were in the top two fifths. There was 1 National Merit semifinalist. 7 freshmen graduated first in their class.

Requirements: The SAT I or ACT is required. In addition, applicants (except early admission) must graduate from an accredited secondary school or have a GED. A total of 16 academic credits is recommended, including 4 years of English, 3 of math, and 2 each of a foreign language, science, and social studies. An essay is required, and an interview is recommended. An audition is required for those seeking a music scholarship. AP credits are accepted. Important factors in the admissions decision are advanced placement or honor courses, recommendations by school officials, and leadership record.

Procedure: Freshmen are admitted fall and spring. Entrance exams should be taken late in the junior year or by January of the senior year. There are early decision, early admissions, and deferred admissions plans. Early decision applications should be filed by November 15; regular applications, by March 1 for fall entry and November 1 for spring entry, along with a $35 fee. Notification of early decision is sent December 15; regular decision, March 1. 34 early decision candidates were accepted for the 2003-2004 class. 18 applicants were on the 2003 waiting list; 3 were admitted. Applications are accepted on-line through CollegeLink, Apply, Common Application, Peterson's, EXPAN, Next Stop College, CollegeNET, Georgia Mentor and at *www.agnesscott.edu/online-application/login.asp.*

Transfer: 9 transfer students enrolled in 2002-2003. A minimum college GPA of 3.0 is recommended, as is an interview and a letter of recommendation from a professor. 64 of 130 credits required for the bachelor's degree must be completed at Agnes Scott.

Visiting: There are regularly scheduled orientations for prospective students, including classes, tours, interviews, residence hall experiences, and informational sessions. There are guides for informal visits and visitors may sit in on classes and stay overnight. To schedule a visit, contact the Office of Admission at (800) 868-8602, ext. 6285 or admission@agnesscott.edu.

Financial Aid: In 2003-2004, 97% of all full-time freshmen and 96% of continuing full-time students received some form of financial aid. 71% of full-time freshmen and 63% of continuing full-time students received need-based aid. The average freshman award was $22,038 with $13,115 from need-based scholarships or need-based grants, $3806 from need-based self-help aid (loans and jobs), $3448 from non-need-based awards and non-need-based scholarships, and $1669 from tuition remission and outside scholarships. 61% of undergraduates work part time. Average annual earnings from campus work are $2000. The average financial indebtedness of the 2003 graduate was $17,627. Agnes Scott is a member of CSS. The FAFSA and the college's own financial statement are required. The CSS/Profile is required for early decision financial aid applicants. The priority date for freshman financial aid applications for fall entry is February 15. The deadline for filing freshman financial aid applications for fall entry is May 1.

International Students: There are 69 international students enrolled. The school actively recruits these students. They must take the TOEFL, with a score of 600 recommended, and also take the SAT I or the ACT.

Computers: The mainframe is an IBM RS/6000. There are more than 500 computers on the campus for student use, with more than 60 PCs located in 4 computer centers and 3 satellite centers in the residence halls, 8 Macs located in the fine arts building, and 5 in the language lab, and more than 240 computers in classrooms. All computers on campus are a part of the campus network, which provides Internet access to all students. All students may access the system. There are no time limits and no fees.

Graduates: From July 1, 2002 to June 30, 2003, 184 bachelor's degrees were awarded. The most popular majors were English/creative writing (13%), psychology (13%), and economics/business (12%). In an average class, 2% graduate in 3 years or less, 58% graduate in 4 years or less, 62% graduate in 5 years or less, and 63% graduate in 6 years or less. 21 companies recruited on campus in 2002-2003. Of the 2002 graduating class, 35% were enrolled in graduate school within 6 months of graduation and 52% were employed.

Admissions Contact: Stephanie Balmer, Associate VP for Enrollment/ Dean of Admission. A video is available.
E-mail: admission@agnesscott.edu Web: http://www.agnesscott.edu

---

ALBANY STATE UNIVERSITY   B-4
Albany, GA 31705-2796

(229) 430-7862
(800) 822-RAMS; Fax: (229) 430-3936

Full-time: 855 men, 1610 women	**Faculty:** 128
Part-time: 150 men, 410 women	**Ph.D.s:** 52%
Graduate: 115 men, 330 women	**Student/Faculty:** 19 to 1
Year: semesters, summer session	**Tuition:** $2400 ($8030)
Application Deadline: see profile	**Room & Board:** $3370
Freshman Class: 2663 applied, 1310 accepted, 417 enrolled	
SAT I Verbal/Math: required	**ACT:** required **COMPETITIVE+**

Albany State University, founded in 1903, is a state-supported institution within the University System of Georgia, offering programs in liberal arts, business, health fields, and teacher education. There are 4 undergraduate schools and 1 graduate school. Figures in the above capsule and in this profile are approximate. In addition to regional accreditation, Albany State has baccalaureate program accreditation with ACBSP, NCATE, and NLN. The library contains 351,467 volumes, 743,621 microform items, and 3431 audio/video tapes/CDs, and subscribes to 169,097 periodicals. Computerized library services include the card catalog, interlibrary loans, and database searching. Special learning facilities include a radio station. The 144-acre campus is in an urban area 175 miles south of Atlanta. Including any residence halls, there are 28 buildings.

Student Life: 98% of undergraduates are from Georgia. 91% are African American. The average age of all undergraduates is 24.

Housing: College housing includes single-sex dorms. On-campus housing is available on a first-come, first-served basis and is available on a lottery system for upperclassmen. Alcohol is not permitted. All students may keep cars.

Activities: There are 3 national fraternities and 3 national sororities. There are many groups and organizations on campus, including art, band, cheerleading, choir, chorale, computers, dance, debate, drama, drill team, honors, jazz band, marching band, musical theater, pep band, political, professional, religious, social, social service, student government, and yearbook. Popular campus events include Honors Day and Founders Day.

Sports: There are 5 intercollegiate sports for men and 6 for women, and 2 intramural sports for men and 1 for women. Facilities include tennis courts, baseball and softball fields, an Olympic-size pool, a recreation room, and an all-weather track.

Disabled Students: 90% of the campus is accessible. Wheelchair ramps, elevators, special parking, specially equipped rest rooms, lowered drinking fountains, and lowered telephones are available.

Services: There is remedial math, reading, and writing.

Campus Safety and Security: Measures include 24-hour foot and vehicle patrol, security escort services, pamphlets/posters/films, and emergency telephones. There are lighted pathways/sidewalks.

Programs of Study: Albany State confers B.A., B.S., B.S.N., and B.S.W. degrees. Associate and master's degrees are also awarded. Bachelor's degrees are awarded in BIOLOGICAL SCIENCE (biology/ biological science), BUSINESS (accounting, marketing/retailing/ merchandising, and office supervision and management), COMMUNICATIONS AND THE ARTS (art, dramatic arts, English, fine arts, French, music, Spanish, and speech/debate/rhetoric), COMPUTER AND PHYSICAL SCIENCE (chemistry, computer science, information sciences and systems, and mathematics), EDUCATION (early childhood, health, middle school, music, physical, science, and special), HEALTH PROFESSIONS (allied health and nursing), SOCIAL SCIENCE (criminal justice, forensic studies, history, political science/government, psychology, social work, and sociology).

Required: To graduate, all students must complete 120 semester hours, including 30 in the major. The core curriculum includes 12 hours of social science, 10 to 11 of science/math/technology, 9 of essential composition and math skills, 6 of humanities/fine arts, 5 of leadership and global awareness, and 3 of phys ed. Most majors require a minimum GPA of 2.25. Students must take a Regents exam to assess English language skills competency, pass a comprehensive exam in their major, and/or score satisfactorily on the aptitude section of the GRE.

Special: The university offers co-op programs in all majors, 2+2 programs with Darton College, dual majors in social sciences, and 3-2 engineering degrees with the Georgia Institute of Technology. Several work-study programs and a gerontology training program are available. Albany State participates in the Georgian Intern Programs. All language majors are eligible to study abroad. There are 5 national honor societies, a freshman honors program, and 4 departmental honors programs.

Faculty/Classroom: 56% of faculty are male; 44%, female.

Requirements: The SAT I or ACT is required. The student must have a minimum verbal score of 430 and a math score of 400 on the SAT I, or English score of 17 and a math score of 16 on the ACT. Applicants must be graduates of an accredited secondary school and have completed 4 years each of English and math, 3 each of science and social sciences, and 2 of a foreign language. A GED is accepted; however, GED students must take and pass SAT II: Subject tests in areas where college-preparatory courses are deficient. A GPA of 2.0 is required. AP and CLEP credits are accepted.

Procedure: Freshmen are admitted to all sessions. Entrance exams should be taken by December of the senior year. There is an early admissions plan and a rolling admissions plan. Check with the school for current deadlines. The fall 2003 application fee was $20.

Transfer: Students must provide official transcripts of all previous college work. Students with fewer than 30 transferable semester hours must meet freshman requirements. 30 of 120 credits required for the bachelor's degree must be completed at Albany State.

Visiting: There are regularly scheduled orientations for prospective students, consisting of summer and fall orientations and planned campus visitations. There are guides for informal visits and visitors may sit in on classes. To schedule a visit, contact the Office of Student Affairs at (229) 430-4742.

Financial Aid: The FAFSA is required. Check with the school for current deadlines.

International Students: They must score 500 on the written TOEFL and also take the SAT I, ACT, or the college's own entrance exam, scoring 830.

Computers: The mainframe is an HP 1500. 4 computer labs are available to students including a 24-hour lab. Students can access the Internet and World Wide Web. All students may access the system. There are no time limits and no fees.

Graduates: In a recent year, 485 bachelor's degrees were awarded. The most popular majors were criminal justice (9%), sociology (7%), and allied health science (6%).

Admissions Contact: Fred Suttles, Assistant Director of Recruitment. A video is available. E-mail: fsuttles@asurams.edu
Web: www.asurams.edu

AMERICAN INTERCONTINENTAL UNIVERSITY B-2
(Formerly American College)
Atlanta, GA 30326

(404) 965-5721
(800) 999-4248; Fax: (404) 965-5701

Full-time: 280 men, 710 women	**Faculty:** 37
Part-time: none	**Ph.D.s:** 99%
Graduate: none	**Student/Faculty:** 15 to 1
Year: quarters, summer session	**Tuition:** $12,000
Application Deadline: open	**Room & Board:** n/app
Freshman Class: n/av	
SAT I or ACT: not required	**NONCOMPETITIVE**

American InterContinental University is a private institution founded in 1977. AIU offers undergraduate programs in interior design, visual communication, fashion design, fashion marketing, business, video production, and information technology. Figures in the above capsule and in this profile are approximate. In addition to regional accreditation, AIU has baccalaureate program accreditation with FIDER. The library contains 23,000 volumes, 17 microform items, and 600 audio/video tapes/CDs, and subscribes to 300 periodicals. Computerized library services include the card catalog, interlibrary loans, and database searching. Special learning facilities include a learning resource center and art gallery. The 1-acre campus is in an urban area in north Atlanta. Including any residence halls, there is 1 building.

Student Life: 62% of undergraduates are from out of state, mostly the South. Students are from 40 states, 54 foreign countries, and Canada. 45% are white; 25% African American; 25% foreign nationals. The average age of freshmen is 19; all undergraduates, 24.

Housing: 200 students can be accommodated in college housing, which includes single-sex off-campus apartments. On-campus housing is available on a first-come, first-served basis. Alcohol is not permitted. All students may keep cars.

Activities: There are no fraternities or sororities. There are 6 groups on campus, including newspaper, professional, social, and student government. Popular campus events include International Day, Career Days, and Fashion Association Bazaar.

Sports: There is no sports program at AIU.

Disabled Students: Wheelchair ramps, elevators, special parking, specially equipped rest rooms, special class scheduling, and lowered telephones are available.

Services: There is remedial math, reading, and writing.

Campus Safety and Security: Measures include 24-hour foot and vehicle patrol, security escort services, informal discussions, and pamphlets/posters/films. There are emergency telephones and lighted pathways/sidewalks.

Programs of Study: AIU confers B.B.A. and B.F.A. degrees. Associate degrees are also awarded. Bachelor's degrees are awarded in BUSINESS (business administration and management and fashion merchandising), COMMUNICATIONS AND THE ARTS (video), COMPUTER AND PHYSICAL SCIENCE (information sciences and systems), ENGINEERING AND ENVIRONMENTAL DESIGN (commercial art and interior design), SOCIAL SCIENCE (fashion design and technology). Interior design and visual communication are the strongest academically and are the largest.

Required: In addition to specific requirements for individual programs of study, all students must complete 25 credit hours each in humanities and social sciences and 5 credit hours in math. Students may substitute 10 hours of a foreign language for 10 hours of social science. 190 quarter credit hours are required to graduate, with 140 in the major and a minimum GPA of 2.0.

Special: Students may earn up to 20 credit hours in internships. Study abroad in London and Dubai is offered. All majors offer accelerated degree opportunities. A dual major in fashion marketing and design is available. There is a freshman honors program.

Faculty/Classroom: 39% of faculty are male; 61%, female. All teach undergraduates. The average class size in an introductory lecture is 25; in a laboratory, 16; and in a regular course, 18.

Requirements: Applicants should be graduates of a secondary school and should submit 2 personal references. The GED is accepted. A GPA of 2.0 is required. AP and CLEP credits are accepted. Important factors in the admissions decision are personality/intangible qualities, leadership record, and evidence of special talent.

Procedure: Freshmen are admitted to all sessions. There is an early admissions plan. Application deadlines are open. The fall 2003 application fee was $35.

Transfer: Transfer students must have a minimum 2.0. GPA. 2 personal references must be submitted. 60 of 190 credits required for the bachelor's degree must be completed at AIU.

Visiting: There are regularly scheduled orientations for prospective students. There are guides for informal visits and visitors may sit in on classes. To schedule a visit, contact Suzanne McBride in Admissions.

Financial Aid: In a recent year, 76% of undergraduates worked part time. Average annual earnings from campus work were $900. AIU is a member of CSS. The CSS Profile or FAFSA and the college's own financial statement are required. Check with the school for current deadlines.

International Students: The school actively recruits these students. They must score 500 on the written TOEFL and also take the college's own test.

Computers: There are 76 PCs available to students, 40 in a classroom setting and 36 in a computer lab. All students may access the system. There are no time limits and no fees.

Admissions Contact: Marita Carey, Director of Admissions. E-mail: mcarey@aiuniv.edu

ARMSTRONG ATLANTIC STATE UNIVERSITY E-4
Savannah, GA 31419-1997

(912) 927-5277
(800) 633-2349; Fax: (912) 921-5462

Full-time: 1186 men, 2260 women	**Faculty:** 267
Part-time: 662 men, 1635 women	**Ph.D.s:** 67%
Graduate: 203 men, 707 women	**Student/Faculty:** 13 to 1
Year: semesters, summer session	**Tuition:** $2602 ($9238)
Application Deadline: July 1	**Room & Board:** $4500
Freshman Class: n/av	
SAT I Verbal/Math: 520/500	**ACT:** 20 **COMPETITIVE**

Armstrong Atlantic State University, founded in 1935, is a public institution within the University System of Georgia, offering programs in the arts and sciences, education, computing, and the health professions. There are 4 undergraduate and 4 graduate schools. In addition to regional accreditation, AASU has baccalaureate program accreditation with ABET, ACS, ADA, CAHEA, CAPTE, JRCERT, NAACLS, NASM, NCATE, and NLN. The library contains 222,024 volumes, 681,657 microform items, and 11,215 audio/video tapes/CDs, and subscribes to 1150 periodicals. Computerized library services include the card catalog, interlibrary loans, database searching, and Internet access. Special learning facilities include a learning resource center and art gallery. The 250-acre campus is in an urban area. Including any residence halls, there are 30 buildings.

Student Life: 89% of undergraduates are from Georgia. Students are from 46 states, 71 foreign countries, and Canada. 69% are white; 21% African American. The average age of freshmen is 23; all undergraduates, 26. 35% do not continue beyond their first year; 19% remain to graduate.

Housing: 600 students can be accommodated in college housing, which includes single-sex on-campus apartments. On-campus housing is available on a first-come, first-served basis. 90% of students commute. Alcohol is not permitted. All students may keep cars.

Activities: There is 1 local fraternity and 2 national fraternities and 1 national sorority. There are 58 groups on campus, including band, cheerleading, choir, chorus, computers, dance, debate, drama, ethnic, gay, honors, international, jazz band, literary magazine, musical theater, newspaper, orchestra, pep band, political, professional, religious, social, social service, student government, and yearbook. Popular campus events include AASU Celebrates and International Culture Day.

Sports: There are 4 intercollegiate sports for men and 4 for women. Facilities include an indoor pool, a gym, a weight room, an indoor running track, tennis courts, and playing fields.

Disabled Students: 80% of the campus is accessible. Wheelchair ramps, elevators, special parking, specially equipped rest rooms, special class scheduling, lowered drinking fountains, and special housing are available.

Services: Counseling and information services are available, as is tutoring in most subjects. There is a reader service for the blind, and remedial math, reading, and writing.

Campus Safety and Security: Measures include 24-hour foot and vehicle patrol, self-defense education, security escort services, and pamphlets/posters/films. There are emergency telephones and lighted pathways/sidewalks.

Programs of Study: AASU confers B.A., B.S., B.F.A., B.G.S., B.Health Science, B.I.T., B.Mus.Ed., B.S.D.H., B.S.Ed., B.S.M.T., and B.S.N. degrees. Associate and master's degrees are also awarded. Bachelor's degrees are awarded in BIOLOGICAL SCIENCE (biology/biological science), COMMUNICATIONS AND THE ARTS (art, dramatic arts, English, music, Spanish, and visual and performing arts), COMPUTER AND PHYSICAL SCIENCE (applied physics, chemistry, computer science, information sciences and systems, and mathematics), EDUCATION (art, business, elementary, middle school, music, physical, secondary, social science, and special), HEALTH PROFESSIONS (dental hygiene, health science, medical technology, nursing, physical therapy, radiological science, respiratory therapy, and speech pathology/audiology), SOCIAL SCIENCE (criminal justice, economics, history, liberal arts/general studies, political science/government, and psychology). Nursing and education are the largest.

Required: The core curriculum consists of 60 hours in humanities, math, natural sciences, and social sciences and 3 in phys ed. A minimum GPA of 2.0 overall and a grade of C or better in each major course is required. Each student must complete 123 hours, with 29 hours in the major, and must take a comprehensive exam.

Special: AASU offers co-op programs in engineering, study abroad in 26 countries, many dual-degree programs, including a 3-2 degree in forestry and environmental science with Duke University, and 3-2 engineering programs with several colleges, including Georgia Tech. A general studies degree, cross-registration with Savannah State University and Georgia Southern University, on-campus work-study, and credit for military experience are also offered. There are 10 national honor societies, a freshman honors program, and 6 departmental honors programs.

Faculty/Classroom: 50% of faculty are male; 50%, female. 90% both teach and do research. No introductory courses are taught by graduate students. The average class size in an introductory lecture is 22; in a laboratory, 18; and in a regular course, 19.

Admissions: The SAT I scores for the 2003-2004 freshman class were: Verbal--36% below 500, 48% between 500 and 599, 15% between 600 and 700, and 1% above 700; Math--47% below 500, 41% between 500 and 599, 11% between 600 and 700, and 1% above 700. The ACT scores were 52% below 21, 29% between 21 and 23, 14% between 24 and 26, 4% between 27 and 28, and 1% above 28.

Requirements: The SAT I is required, with a the minimum score of 420 on each section. Art students must submit a portfolio. Applicants should graduate from an accredited secondary school. A GED may be accepted. College preparatory work should include 4 units of English, 3 each of math, science, and social studies, and 2 of foreign language. A GPA of 2.0 is required. AP and CLEP credits are accepted.

Procedure: Freshmen are admitted to all sessions. There is an early admissions plan. Applications should be filed by July 1 for fall entry, November 1 for spring entry, and May 1 for summer entry, along with a $20 fee. Applications are accepted on-line.

Transfer: 991 transfer students enrolled in 2002-2003. Transfer applicants must submit all transcripts and must be in good standing at the last college attended. 30 of 123 credits required for the bachelor's degree must be completed at AASU.

Visiting: There are regularly scheduled orientations for prospective students, including a tour of the campus and departments. There are guides for informal visits. To schedule a visit, contact Melanie Mirande at (912) 921-5424.

Financial Aid: In 2003-2004, 80% of all full-time freshmen and 85% of continuing full-time students received some form of financial aid. 60% of full-time freshmen and 69% of continuing full-time students received need-based aid. The average freshman award was $4000. Need-based scholarships or need-based grants averaged $4000; need-based self-help aid (loans and jobs) averaged $2000; non-need-based athletic scholarships averaged $4000; and other non-need-based awards and non-need-based scholarships averaged $3500. Average annual earnings from campus work are $4500. The average financial indebtedness of the 2003 graduate was $8000. The FAFSA and the college's own financial statement are required. The priority date for freshman financial aid applications for fall entry is March 15. The deadline for filing freshman financial aid applications for fall entry is May 1.

International Students: There are 164 international students enrolled. The school actively recruits these students. They must score 500 on the written TOEFL and also take the SAT I or the ACT.

Computers: The mainframe is a DEC VAX 4/750. There are AT&T, Zenith, and Mac PCs for student use in the library and a central computer lab. There are also several computer labs in academic buildings, and all dorms are wired for Internet access. All students may access the system. There are no time limits and no fees.

Graduates: From July 1, 2002 to June 30, 2003, 549 bachelor's degrees were awarded. The most popular majors were nursing (15%), elementary education (13%), and general studies (12%). 71 companies recruited on campus in 2002-2003.

Admissions Contact: Jill H. Bell-Marriott, Associate Director of Admissions. Web: *www.armstrong.edu*

ART INSTITUTE OF ATLANTA
Atlanta, GA 30328   B-2
                                          (770) 394-8300
                        (800) 275-4242; Fax: (770) 394-0008

Full-time: 1241 men, 1097 women	**Faculty:** 91
Part-time: 178 men, 183 women	**Ph.D.s:** 51%
Graduate: none	**Student/Faculty:** 26 to 1
Year: quarters, summer session	**Tuition:** $16,560
Application Deadline: open	**Room & Board:** n/app
Freshman Class: n/av	
SAT I or ACT: not required	SPECIAL

The Art Institute of Atlanta, founded in 1949, seeks to educate creative professionals. It offers bachelor's degree programs in advertising, media arts and animation, digital media production, game art and design, graphic design, interior design, multimedia and web design, photographic imaging, and culinary arts management and associate degree programs in culinary arts, graphic design, multimedia and web design, photographic imaging, and video production. In addition to regional accreditation, The Art Institute has baccalaureate program accreditation with FIDER and ACF. The library contains 38,780 volumes and 6100 audio/video tapes/CDs, and subscribes to 135 periodicals. Computerized library services include the card catalog, interlibrary loans, database searching, and Internet access. Special learning facilities include a learning resource center, art gallery, and academic support center. The 7-acre campus is in a suburban area in the Metro-Atlanta community of Dunwoody, approximately 5 miles north of the city limits. Including any residence halls, there are 2 buildings.

Student Life: 73% of undergraduates are from Georgia. Students are from 44 states, 38 foreign countries, and Canada. 49% are white; 34% African American. The average age of freshmen is 20; all undergraduates, 23.

Housing: College-sponsored housing includes coed off-campus apartments. All students commute. All students may keep cars.

Activities: There are no fraternities or sororities. There are 16 groups on campus, including art, dance, gay, international, photography, professional, social service, and student government. Popular campus events include gallery openings, Quarterly Welcome Week, and Quarterly Portfolio Show.

Sports: There is no sports program at The Art Institute. Facilities include basketball courts and fields for touch football, a swimming pool, and a weight room in student housing.

Disabled Students: All of the campus is accessible. Wheelchair ramps, elevators, special parking, specially equipped rest rooms, lowered drinking fountains, lowered telephones, and special housing are available.

Services: Counseling and information services are available, as is tutoring in most subjects. There is remedial math, reading, and writing. Tutoring is available in computer classes.

Campus Safety and Security: Measures include 24-hour foot and vehicle patrol, self-defense education, shuttle buses, and informal discussions. There are pamphlets/posters/films and lighted pathways/sidewalks.

Programs of Study: The Art Institute confers B.A., B.S., and B.F.A. degrees. Associate degrees are also awarded. Bachelor's degrees are awarded in COMMUNICATIONS AND THE ARTS (advertising, animation, graphic design, multimedia, photography, and video), ENGINEERING AND ENVIRONMENTAL DESIGN (computer graphics and interior design), SOCIAL SCIENCE (culinary arts). Graphic design, culinary arts, and video production are the largest.

Required: The Art Institute requires 192 credit hours for the B.F.A., with a minimum GPA of 2.0. Students in design-based majors complete a portfolio of work prior to graduation. The core curriculum includes foundation art, English, art history, humanties, math, and science courses. Foundation art classes are not required for culinary arts students.

Special: Internships in all programs, independent study, work-study programs, and study abroad are possible.

Faculty/Classroom: 53% of faculty are male; 47%, female. All teach undergraduates. The average class size in a regular course is 16.

Requirements: Students must submit SAT I, ACT, ASSET, or COMPASS test scores. (COMPASS testing is offered free at the college to any applicant needing it.) Preference is given to applicants with GPAs of 3.0 or above; a minimum GPA of 2.5 for bachelor's degree applicants is highly recommended. An official transcript showing high school GPA is required; the GED is accepted. An essay and an interview are required. AP and CLEP credits are accepted.

Procedure: Freshmen are admitted to all sessions. Entrance exams should be taken prior to the application closing date. There is a rolling admissions plan. There are early admissions and deferred admissions plans. Application deadlines are open. Application fee is $50. Applications are accepted on-line through *www.applyweb.com/aw?aia.*

Transfer: In addition to fulfilling general admission requirements, transfer students must also submit all previous college transcripts. 96 of 192 credits required for the bachelor's degree must be completed at The Art Institute.

Visiting: There are regularly scheduled orientations for prospective students, including individual tours and interviews. There are guides for informal visits and visitors may sit in on classes with prior approval. To schedule a visit, contact the Office of Admissions.

Financial Aid: 1% of undergraduates work part time. The FAFSA and the state aid form are required. The deadline for filing freshman financial aid applications for fall entry is rolling.

International Students: There are 84 international students enrolled. The school actively recruits these students. They must score 480 on the written TOEFL or 157 on the electronic version. ASSET, COMPASS, or SAT I or ACT scores can be submitted instead.

Computers: Students are allowed full Internet access in each of the college's 16 computer labs. There are 382 PCs for student use. All students may access the system. There are no time limits and no fees.

Graduates: From July 1, 2002 to June 30, 2003, 127 bachelor's degrees were awarded. The most popular majors were graphic design (22%), culinary arts (17%), and video production (8%). 174 companies recruited on campus in 2002-2003. Of the 2002 graduating class, 90% were employed within 6 months of graduation.

Admissions Contact: Donna Scott, Director of Admissions. A video is available. E-mail: aiaadm@aii.edu Web: www.aia.artinstitutes.edu

ATLANTA COLLEGE OF ART
Atlanta, GA 30309

B-2

(404) 733-5100
(800) 832-2104; Fax: (404) 733-5107

Full-time: 220 men, 200 women	Faculty: 23
Part-time: 10 men, 10 women	Ph.D.s: 87%
Graduate: none	Student/Faculty: 18 to 1
Year: semesters, summer session	Tuition: $13,000
Application Deadline: open	Room & Board: $5600
Freshman Class: n/av	
SAT I or ACT: required	SPECIAL

The Atlanta College of Art, founded in 1928, is a private professional art college offering programs in the fine arts, design, and electronic arts. Figures given in the above capsule and in this profile are approximate. In addition to regional accreditation, ACA has baccalaureate program accreditation with NASAD. The library contains 29,000 volumes and 100 audio/video tapes/CDs, and subscribes to 200 periodicals. Computerized library services include interlibrary loans and database searching. Special learning facilities include a learning resource center, art gallery, printmaking studio, photography darkrooms, computer labs, and experimental sound lab. There is also a sculpture building with a foundry, forge, and woodworking shop. The 6-acre campus is in an urban area in Atlanta. Including any residence halls, there are 3 buildings.

Student Life: 52% of undergraduates are from out of state, mostly the South. Students are from 21 states and 6 foreign countries. 80% are from public schools. 62% are white; 18% African American. 62% are Muslim and Russian Orthodox; 26% Protestant; 9% Catholic. The average age of freshmen is 18; all undergraduates, 21. 30% do not continue beyond their first year; 55% remain to graduate.

Housing: 120 students can be accommodated in college housing, which includes coed on-campus apartments. On-campus housing is guaranteed for the freshman year only and is available on a first-come, first-served basis. Priority is given to out-of-town students. 70% of students commute. Alcohol is not permitted. All students may keep cars.

Activities: There are no fraternities or sororities. There are 15 groups on campus, including art, ethnic, film, gay, international, photography, social, social service, student government, and yearbook. Popular campus events include Welcome Week, student gallery openings, and Thanksgiving Feast.

Sports: There is no sports program at ACA.

Disabled Students: 95% of the campus is accessible. Wheelchair ramps, elevators, special parking, specially equipped rest rooms, lowered drinking fountains, and lowered telephones are available.

Services: Counseling and information services are available, as is tutoring in some subjects, including liberal arts subjects. A writing lab is available.

Campus Safety and Security: Measures include 24-hour foot and vehicle patrol, self-defense education, security escort services, and informal discussions. There are pamphlets/posters/films, emergency telephones, and lighted pathways/sidewalks.

Programs of Study: ACA confers the B.F.A. degree. Bachelor's degrees are awarded in COMMUNICATIONS AND THE ARTS (advertising, design, drawing, fine arts, graphic design, illustration, painting, photography, printmaking, sculpture, and video), ENGINEERING AND ENVIRONMENTAL DESIGN (computer graphics and interior design). Communication design and electronic arts are the largest.

Required: To graduate, the student must complete 42 credits in liberal arts and 78 in studio art for a total of 120 credit hours. Of the 78 studio credits, 33 to 36 must be in the major. The student must also complete 12 credits each in world cultures and art history, 6 in composition, and 3 each in math, science, social science, and humanities. A GPA of 2.0 in the major and overall and a senior exit review are required.

Special: Students may design their own majors, combining 2 or 3 areas of the arts. Special academic programs include cross-registration with the colleges of the University Center of Georgia and other art schools, highly supervised internships, and a dual degree program with Oglethorpe University.

Faculty/Classroom: 65% of faculty are male; 35%, female. All both teach and do research. The average class size in an introductory lecture is 25 and in a regular course, 12.

Requirements: The SAT I or ACT is required. In addition, applicants must have graduated from an accredited secondary school and must submit an essay and portfolio. Either 2 letters of recommendation or 1 letter and an on-campus interview are required. The GED is accepted. ACA requires applicants to be in the upper 50% of their class. A GPA of 2.0 is required. AP credits are accepted. Important factors in the admissions decision are evidence of special talent, personality/intangible qualities, and recommendations by alumni.

Procedure: Freshmen are admitted fall and spring. Entrance exams should be taken during the senior year. There are early admissions, deferred admissions, and rolling admissions plans. Application deadlines are open. Application fee is $30. Applications are accepted on-line via ACA's web site.

Transfer: Applicants must have a GPA of at least 2.0 and must submit a portfolio and transcripts from previously attended colleges from which credit was earned. Either 2 letters of recommendation or 1 letter and an on-campus interview are required. 39 of 120 credits required for the bachelor's degree must be completed at ACA.

Visiting: There are regularly scheduled orientations for prospective students, including open houses, general information sessions, workshops, and special events for prospective students. There are guides for informal visits and visitors may sit in on classes. To schedule a visit, contact the Admissions Office.

Financial Aid: In a recent year, 20% of undergraduates worked part time. Average annual earnings from campus work were $1700. ACA is a member of CSS. The FAFSA and the college's own financial statement are required. Check with the school for current deadlines.

International Students: The school actively recruits these students. They must score 500 on the written TOEFL.

Computers: There are 24 computers for student use in the computer center and the electronic arts studio. All students may access the system during scheduled hours. There are no time limits and no fees.

Admissions Contact: Carol Lee Conchar, Director of Enrollment Management. E-mail: acainfo@woodruff-arts.org Web: www.aca.edu

AUGUSTA STATE UNIVERSITY
Augusta, GA 30904-2200

D-2

(706) 737-1632; Fax: (706) 667-4355

Full-time: 1297 men, 2204 women	Faculty: 198; IIA, -$
Part-time: 578 men, 1197 women	Ph.D.s: 70%
Graduate: 261 men, 598 women	Student/Faculty: 18 to 1
Year: semesters, summer session	Tuition: $2592 ($9228)
Application Deadline: July 21	Room & Board: n/app
Freshman Class: 1714 applied, 1106 accepted, 839 enrolled	
SAT I Verbal/Math: 490/480	COMPETITIVE

Augusta State University, founded in 1925, is a liberal arts commuter institution within the University System of Georgia. There are 3 undergraduate and 3 graduate schools. In addition to regional accreditation, Augusta State University has baccalaureate program accreditation with AACSB, NASM, NCATE, and NLN. The library contains 503,000 volumes, 948,693 microform items, and 7844 audio/video tapes/CDs, and subscribes to 924 periodicals. Computerized library services include the card catalog, interlibrary loans, and database searching. Special learning facilities include a learning resource center, art gallery, and radio station. The 72-acre campus is in an urban area 140 miles east of Atlanta on the Georgia-South Carolina border. There are 35 buildings.

Student Life: 85% of undergraduates are from Georgia. Students are from 46 states, 59 foreign countries, and Canada. 95% are from public schools. 67% are white; 24% African American. The average age of freshmen is 19; all undergraduates, 25. 34% do not continue beyond their first year; 21% remain to graduate.

Housing: There are no residence halls. All of students commute. Alcohol is not permitted. All students may keep cars.

Activities: 2% of men belong to 3 national fraternities; 2% of women belong to 4 national sororities. There are 58 groups on campus, including art, band, cheerleading, choir, chorus, drama, ethnic, honors, international, jazz band, literary magazine, newspaper, orchestra, pep band, photography, political, professional, religious, social, social service, and student government. Popular campus events include Lyceum, Midnight Madness, and SOS.

Sports: There are 5 intercollegiate sports for men and 6 for women, and 2 intramural sports for men and 2 for women. Facilities include a 2000-seat gym, baseball, soccer, and softball fields, a tennis center, and an 18-hole golf course.

Disabled Students: 90% of the campus is accessible. Wheelchair ramps, elevators, special parking, specially equipped rest rooms, special class scheduling, lowered drinking fountains, and lowered telephones are available.

Services: Counseling and information services are available, as is tutoring in most subjects. There is a reader service for the blind, and remedial math, reading, and writing.

Campus Safety and Security: Measures include 24-hour foot and vehicle patrol, security escort services, shuttle buses, and informal discussions. There are pamphlets/posters/films and lighted pathways/sidewalks.

Programs of Study: Augusta State University confers B.A., B.S., B.B.A., B.F.A., B.M., and B.S.Ed. degrees. Associate and master's degrees are also awarded. Bachelor's degrees are awarded in BIOLOGICAL SCIENCE (biology/biological science), BUSINESS (accounting, banking and finance, business administration and management, and marketing/retailing/merchandising), COMMUNICATIONS AND THE ARTS (art, communications, English, French, music, Spanish, and studio art), COMPUTER AND PHYSICAL SCIENCE (chemistry, computer science, mathematics, and physics), EDUCATION (early childhood, education of the mentally handicapped, elementary, health, middle school, music, and special), SOCIAL SCIENCE (criminal justice, history, political science/government, psychology, and sociology). Biology, early childhood education, and computer science are the largest.

Required: Students must complete 125 hours, with a minimum GPA of 2.0. All students are required to take 6 courses in phys ed; pass the Regents test in reading and composition; and demonstrate, through course completion or exam, a knowledge of U.S. and Georgia history and their constitutions.

Special: A Washington semester and study abroad may be arranged. The school offers co-op programs with area companies, internships, work-study programs, dual majors, nondegree study, and cross-registration with Paine College. There are 5 national honor societies, a freshman honors program, and 7 departmental honors programs.

Faculty/Classroom: 54% of faculty are male; 46%, female. All teach undergraduates. No introductory courses are taught by graduate students. The average class size in an introductory lecture is 30; in a laboratory, 19; and in a regular course, 27.

Admissions: 65% of the 2003-2004 applicants were accepted. The SAT I scores for the 2003-2004 freshman class were: Verbal--54% below 500, 35% between 500 and 599, 10% between 600 and 700, and 1% above 700; Math--55% below 500, 35% between 500 and 599, 9% between 600 and 700, and 1% above 700.

Requirements: The SAT I or ACT is required, with a verbal score of 430 and math score of 400 on the SAT I or a comparable score on the ACT. Applicants must be graduates of an accredited secondary school. The GED is accepted. Secondary school courses must include 4 units each of English and math, 3 each of science and social science, and 2 of a foreign language. A GPA of 2.0 is required. AP and CLEP credits are accepted.

Procedure: Freshmen are admitted fall, spring, and summer. There is a deferred admissions plan. Applications should be filed by July 21 for fall entry and December 6 for spring entry, along with a $20 fee. Notification is sent on a rolling basis. Applications are accepted on-line through the school's web site.

Transfer: 430 transfer students enrolled in 2002-2003. Applicants must have completed 30 semester or 45 quarter hours. If fewer than 15 semester hours have been completed, students are considered as entering freshmen and are required to submit appropriate paperwork. 30 of 125 credits required for the bachelor's degree must be completed at Augusta State University.

Visiting: There are regularly scheduled orientations for prospective students. There are guides for informal visits and visitors may sit in on classes. To schedule a visit, contact the Admissions Office.

Financial Aid: In 2003-2004, 76% of all full-time freshmen and 84% of continuing full-time students received some form of financial aid. 48% of full-time freshmen and 62% of continuing full-time students received need-based aid. The average freshman award was $7350, with $2225 ($4650 maximum) from need-based scholarships or need-based grants, $2313 ($4625 maximum) from need-based self-help aid (loans and jobs), $1110 ($3392 maximum) from non-need-based athletic scholarships, and $1712 ($2750 maximum) from other non-need-based awards and non-need-based scholarships. 94% of undergraduates work part time. Average annual earnings from campus work are $3000. The average financial indebtedness of the 2003 graduate was $14,986. Augusta State University is a member of CSS. The FAFSA is required. The deadline for filing freshman financial aid applications for fall entry is June 1.

International Students: There are 120 international students enrolled. They must score 540 on the written TOEFL and also take the SAT I.

Computers: The mainframe is a DEC VAX 4200. Access to the Internet and the Web is available from 600 computers in 6 campus labs, plus remote dial-in access from off-campus locations. All students may access the system. There are no time limits and no fees.

Graduates: From July 1, 2002 to June 30, 2003, 534 bachelor's degrees were awarded. The most popular majors were psychology (9%), sociology (9%), and biology (7%). In an average class, 1% graduate in 3 years or less, 8% graduate in 4 years or less, 17% graduate in 5 years or less, and 21% graduate in 6 years or less. 100 companies recruited on campus in 2002-2003.

Admissions Contact: Katherine Sweeney, Registrar and Director of Admissions. E-mail: *admissions@aug.edu*
Web: *www.aug.edu/admissions*

BERRY COLLEGE	A-2
Mount Berry, GA 30149-0159	**(706) 236-2215**
	(800) BERRYGA; Fax: (706) 290-2178
Full-time: 672 men, 1176 women	Faculty: 148; IIA, --$
Part-time: 17 men, 20 women	Ph.D.s: 96%
Graduate: 39 men, 111 women	Student/Faculty: 12 to 1
Year: semesters, summer session	Tuition: $15,220
Application Deadline: February 1	Room & Board: $6190
Freshman Class: n/av	
SAT I or ACT: required	VERY COMPETITIVE

Berry College, founded in 1902, is a private nonsectarian college offering programs in fine and liberal arts and preprofessional programs in education and business. There are 4 undergraduate schools and 1 graduate school. In addition to regional accreditation, Berry has baccalaureate program accreditation with NASM and NCATE. The library contains 707,000 volumes, 525,000 microform items, and 5000 audio/video tapes/CDs, and subscribes to 1595 periodicals. Computerized library services include the card catalog, interlibrary loans, database searching, and Internet access. Special learning facilities include a learning resource center, art gallery, TV station, equine center, forestry center, and beef- and dairy-cattle operations. The 28,000-acre campus is in a suburban area 65 miles northwest of Atlanta. Including any residence halls, there are 38 buildings.

Student Life: 84% of undergraduates are from Georgia. Students are from 34 states, 22 foreign countries, and Canada. 91% are white. 75% are Protestant; 15% Catholic. The average age of freshmen is 18; all undergraduates, 22. 24% do not continue beyond their first year; 62% remain to graduate.

Housing: 1424 students can be accommodated in college housing, which includes single-sex and coed dorms and on-campus apartments. On-campus housing is guaranteed for the freshman year only and is available on a first-come, first-served basis. 84% of students live on campus; of those, 60% remain on campus on weekends. Alcohol is not permitted. All students may keep cars.

Activities: There are no fraternities or sororities. There are 67 groups on campus, including cheerleading, chess, choir, chorus, computers, dance, drama, ethnic, forensics, honors, international, jazz band, literary magazine, musical theater, newspaper, orchestra, pep band, political, professional, radio and TV, religious, social, social service, student government, and yearbook. Popular campus events include Mountain Day, Conson Wilson Lecture Series, and BCTC Theater Season.

Sports: There are 7 intercollegiate sports for men and 6 for women, and 15 intramural sports for men and 14 for women. Facilities include running and biking trails, 10 tennis courts, intramural fields, 2 gyms, a weight-training room, an indoor swimming pool, 3 sand volleyball courts, and an equestrian center.

Disabled Students: 90% of the campus is accessible. Wheelchair ramps, elevators, special parking, specially equipped rest rooms, lowered drinking fountains, and special housing are available.

Services: Counseling and information services are available, as is tutoring in most subjects. There is a reader service for the blind.

Campus Safety and Security: Measures include 24-hour foot and vehicle patrol, self-defense education, informal discussions, and pamphlets/posters/films. There are lighted pathways/sidewalks and a gated campus.

Programs of Study: Berry confers B.A., B.S., and B.Mu. degrees. Master's degrees are also awarded. Bachelor's degrees are awarded in AGRICULTURE (animal science), BIOLOGICAL SCIENCE (biology/biological science), BUSINESS (accounting, banking and finance, business administration and management, and marketing management), COMMUNICATIONS AND THE ARTS (art, communications, dramatic arts, English, French, German, music, music performance, Spanish, and studio art), COMPUTER AND PHYSICAL SCIENCE (chemistry, computer science, mathematics, and physics), EDUCATION (art, early childhood, mathematics, middle school, music, and physical), ENGINEERING AND ENVIRONMENTAL DESIGN (environmental science and preengineering), HEALTH PROFESSIONS (predentistry, premedicine, preoptometry, prepharmacy, and preveterinary science), SOCIAL SCIENCE (economics, history, interdisciplinary studies, international studies, philosophy, political science/government, prelaw, psychology, religion, social science, and sociology). Business, education, and communication are the largest.

Required: General education requirements include 5 courses in the humanities and fine arts, 3 each in behavioral science, math and natural sciences, communication, and health and phys ed, and 2 in electives. A 2.0 GPA and a total of 124 credits, including at least 30 hours in the major, are required for graduation. All students are also required to attend at least 3 approved cultural events per semester and pass a comprehensive exam or other senior assessment in the major.

Special: The college offers internships, a Washington semester, study abroad in 17 countries, plus others through consortia, work-study programs, student-designed majors, co-op programs, cross-registration with Shorter College, dual majors, credit by exam, and nondegree study. There are 3-2 engineering degrees and dual degree programs in several fields with the Georgia Institute of Technology and Mercer University. There is also a dual degree program in nursing with Emory University. There are 17 national honor societies, a freshman honors program, and 5 departmental honors programs.

Faculty/Classroom: 65% of faculty are male; 35%, female. 99% teach undergraduates, 99% do research, and 99% do both. No introductory courses are taught by graduate students. The average class size in an introductory lecture is 29; in a laboratory, 20; and in a regular course, 20.

Requirements: The SAT I or ACT is required. In addition, applicants should be graduates of an accredited high school or have a GED. 20 academic credits are required, including 4 units each of English and math (to include algebra I, algebra II, and either geometry or trigonometry), 3 each of science and social studies, and 2 of a foreign language. A GPA of 2.0 is required. AP credits are accepted. Important factors in the admissions decision are advanced placement or honor courses, leadership record, and recommendations by school officials.

Procedure: Freshmen are admitted to all sessions. Entrance exams should be taken by the fall of the senior year. There are early decision and early admissions plans. There is a rolling admissions plan. Applications should be filed by February 1 for fall entry, along with a $25 fee. Notification is sent on a rolling basis. A waiting list is an active part of the admissions procedure. Applications are accepted on computer disk and on-line through Apply, College Board, or Peterson's.

Transfer: 80 transfer students enrolled in 2002-2003. Applicants must submit official transcripts from all colleges previously attended, have a minimum GPA of 2.5 and be in good standing at the last school attended. 32 of 124 credits required for the bachelor's degree must be completed at Berry.

Visiting: There are regularly scheduled orientations for prospective students, including weekdays and Saturday mornings. Students should schedule their campus visit in advance. Several "Discover Berry" days are held during fall and spring. There are guides for informal visits and visitors may sit in on classes and stay overnight. To schedule a visit, contact the Admissions Office at *admissions@berry.edu*.

Financial Aid: In 2003-2004, 99% of all full-time students received some form of financial aid. 60% of full-time freshmen and 55% of continuing full-time students received need-based aid. The average freshman award was $13,919. 78% of undergraduates work part time. Average annual earnings from campus work are $2750. The average financial indebtedness of the 2003 graduate was $12,000. Berry is a member of CSS. The FAFSA and the college's own financial statement are required. The priority date for freshman financial aid applications for fall entry is April 1.

International Students: There are 37 international students enrolled. The school actively recruits these students. They must score 550 on the written TOEFL or 213 on the electronic version and also take the SAT I or ACT if the student is from an English-speaking country.

Computers: PCs and Macs are located in 4 computer labs and in the library. Internet access is provided. Each residence hall room has Internet access. All students may access the system. There are no time limits and no fees.

Graduates: From July 1, 2002 to June 30, 2003, 345 bachelor's degrees were awarded. The most popular majors were early childhood education (16%), business and marketing (14%), and social sciences and history (13%). In an average class, 1% graduate in 3 years or less, 50% graduate in 4 years or less, 60% graduate in 5 years or less, and 63% graduate in 6 years or less. 137 companies recruited on campus in 2002-2003. Of the 2002 graduating class, 25% were enrolled in graduate school within 6 months of graduation and 99% were employed.

Admissions Contact: Garreth Johnson, Dean of Admissions. A video is available. E-mail: *admissions@berry.edu* Web: *www.berry.edu*

BRENAU UNIVERSITY WOMEN'S COLLEGE   B-2
Gainesville, GA 30501

(770) 534-6100
(800) 252-5119; Fax: (770) 538-4306

Full-time: 538 women	**Faculty:** 81; IIA, --$
Part-time: 48 women	**Ph.D.s:** n/av
Graduate: 21 women	**Student/Faculty:** 7 to 1
Year: semesters, summer session	**Tuition:** $14,040
Application Deadline: open	**Room & Board:** $7760
Freshman Class: n/av	
SAT I or ACT: required	**COMPETITIVE**

Brenau University Women's College, founded in 1878, is a private undergraduate and graduate liberal arts institution for women. Coeducational programs are offered as part of the university, in an evening and weekend format. There are 4 undergraduate schools. In addition to regional accreditation, Brenau has baccalaureate program accreditation with FIDER and NLN. The library contains 103,740 volumes, 350,328 microform items, and 16,023 audio/video tapes/CDs, and subscribes to 2000 periodicals. Computerized library services include the card catalog, interlibrary loans, database searching, and Internet access. Special learning facilities include a learning resource center, art gallery, natural history museum, radio station, TV station, and TV studio. The 57-acre campus is in a suburban area 50 miles northeast of Atlanta. Including any residence halls, there are 50 buildings.

Student Life: 87% of undergraduates are from Georgia. Students are from 19 states and 19 foreign countries. 89% are from public schools. 79% are white; 10%, African American. The average age of freshmen is 18; all undergraduates, 22. 27% do not continue beyond their first year.

Housing: 330 students can be accommodated in college housing, which includes dorms, on-campus apartments, off-campus apartments, and sorority houses. In addition, there are special-interest houses. On-campus housing is guaranteed for all 4 years. 50% of students live on campus. Alcohol is not permitted. All students may keep cars.

Activities: 50% of women belong to 9 national sororities. There are 55 groups on campus, including art, choir, chorale, chorus, dance, drama,

film, honors, international, literary magazine, musical theater, newspaper, opera, photography, political, professional, radio and TV, religious, social, social service, student government, symphony, and yearbook. Popular campus events include Remember All the Traditions Week, May Day, and Spade Hunt.

Sports: Facilities include a tennis center, a recreation field, a gym, and a natatorium.

Disabled Students: 90% of the campus is accessible. Wheelchair ramps, elevators, special parking, specially equipped rest rooms, special class scheduling, lowered drinking fountains, and lowered telephones are available.

Services: There is remedial math, reading, and writing, and there are professional degreed tutors for diagnosed learning-disabled students.

Campus Safety and Security: Measures include 24-hour foot and vehicle patrol, self-defense education, security escort services, and informal discussions. There are pamphlets/posters/films and lighted pathways/sidewalks.

Programs of Study: Brenau confers B.A., B.S., B.B.A., B.F.A., B.M., and B.S.N. degrees. Master's degrees are also awarded. Bachelor's degrees are awarded in AGRICULTURE (environmental studies), BIOLOGICAL SCIENCE (biology/biological science), BUSINESS (accounting, business administration and management, fashion merchandising, and marketing/retailing/merchandising), COMMUNICATIONS AND THE ARTS (arts administration/management, communications, dance, dramatic arts, English, fine arts, music performance, musical theater, and studio art), EDUCATION (art, dance, early childhood, middle school, music, and special), ENGINEERING AND ENVIRONMENTAL DESIGN (commercial art, environmental science, graphic and printing production, and interior design), HEALTH PROFESSIONS (nursing and occupational therapy), SOCIAL SCIENCE (history, international studies, liberal arts/general studies, paralegal studies, political science/government, and psychology). Occupational therapy, fine arts, and performing arts are the strongest academically. Nursing, occupational therapy, and performing arts are the largest.

Required: To graduate, all students must complete at least 120 semester hours of work including 48 to 69 hours in the major. Requirements for each degree vary, but students must maintain a 2.0 GPA overall and a 2.5 GPA in course work required by the major. Most majors either require or encourage internships. In addition to specific requirements, students must take phys ed courses and demonstrate computer as well as oral and written communication proficiency. Courses in women's health and leisure studies are also required.

Special: Cross-registration is possible with the Atlanta Regional Consortium for Higher Education. Students may study abroad in 10 foreign countries. Brenau offers B.A.-B.S. degrees, work study programs, internships, a Washington semester, a general studies degree, and student-designed majors. Students may receive credit for life, military, and work experience. There are 8 national honor societies, a freshman honors program, and 4 departmental honors programs.

Faculty/Classroom: 37% of faculty are male; 63%, female. All teach undergraduates. No introductory courses are taught by graduate students. The average class size in an introductory lecture is 19; in a laboratory, 12; and in a regular course, 14.

Requirements: The SAT I or ACT is required. In addition, candidates for admission should have completed 4 units of English, 3 of math, 2 of science, 2 to 3 of social studies, and 7 to 9 of electives. A GPA of 2.0 is required. AP and CLEP credits are accepted. Important factors in the admissions decision are advanced placement or honor courses, extracurricular activities record, and evidence of special talent.

Procedure: Freshmen are admitted fall and spring. Entrance exams should be taken in the fall of the senior year or the spring of the junior year. Application deadlines are open. The fall 2003 application fee was $35. There is a rolling admissions plan. Applications are accepted on-line through the school's web site.

Transfer: 94 transfer students enrolled in 2002-2003. A minimum GPA of 2.0 on transfer credits is required, and transfer students must submit high school transcripts and SAT I scores if fewer than 30 hours were earned. The last 45 semester hours, including at least 30 in the major, must be taken at Brenau. Students must maintain a minimum GPA of 2.0 and 2.5 in the major. 45 of 120 credits required for the bachelor's degree must be completed at Brenau.

Visiting: There are regularly scheduled orientations for prospective students, consisting of a campus tour, information sessions, and an interview. There are guides for informal visits and visitors may sit in on classes and stay overnight. To schedule a visit, contact the Admissions Office at *wcadmissions@lib.brenau.edu*.

Financial Aid: In 2003-2004, 97% of all full-time freshmen and 94% of continuing full-time students received some form of financial aid. 74% of full-time freshmen and 65% of continuing full-time students received need-based aid. The average freshman award was $16,385. Need-based scholarships or need-based grants averaged $7249 ($10,550 maximum); need-based self-help aid (loans and jobs) averaged $2594 ($4625 maximum); non-need-based athletic scholarships averaged $5175 ($19,500 maximum); and other non-need-based awards and non-need-based scholarships averaged $12,274 ($19,534 maximum). 22% of undergraduates work part time. Average annual earnings from campus work are $1835. The average financial indebtedness of the 2003 graduate was $9757. The FAFSA is required. The priority date for freshman financial aid applications for fall entry is May 1. The deadline for filing freshman financial aid applications for fall entry is July 15.

International Students: There are 14 international students enrolled. The school actively recruits these students. They must score 500 on the written TOEFL or 173 on the electronic or complete level 109 at an ELS language center. They must take the SAT I or ACTonly if the TOEFL is not taken, scoring 900 on the SAT I.

Computers: There are 112 Pentium and 486 PCs located in labs and residence halls around campus. All are attached to the campuswide network for use of library resources, the Internet (via a T-1 connection), and e-mail. All students may access the system 24 hours per day. There are no time limits and no fees.

Graduates: In a recent year, 130 bachelor's degrees were awarded. The most popular majors were occupational therapy (21%), nursing (16%), and teacher education (13%). In an average class, 30% graduate in 4 years or less, 35% graduate in 5 years or less, and 40% graduate in 6 years or less. 20 companies recruited on campus in a recent year.

Admissions Contact: Christina Cochran, Coordinator of Women's College Admissions. E-mail: *ccochran@lib.brenau.edu* or at *wcadmissions* Web: *www.brenau.edu*

BREWTON-PARKER COLLEGE   C-4
Mt. Vernon, GA 30445-0197   **(912) 583-3264**
(800) 342-1087; Fax: (912) 583-4498

Full-time: 345 men, 584 women	**Faculty:** 60; IIB, --$
Part-time: 45 men, 135 women	**Ph.Ds:** 54%
Graduate: none	**Student/Faculty:** 15 to 1
Year: semesters, summer session	**Tuition:** $9900
Application Deadline: open	**Room & Board:** $4300
Freshman Class: 602 applied, 319 accepted, 274 enrolled	
SAT I Verbal/Math: 479/463	**ACT:** 18 **LESS COMPETITIVE**

Brewton-Parker College, founded in 1904, is a private institution offering instruction in the liberal arts and sciences. It is affiliated with the Georgia Baptist Convention. The library contains 80,871 volumes, 2985 microform items, and 5575 audio/video tapes/CDs, and subscribes to 350 periodicals. Computerized library services include the card catalog, interlibrary loans, database searching, and Internet access. Special learning facilities include a learning resource center, art gallery, and a living history museum. The 270-acre campus is in a rural area 90 miles west of Savannah. Including any residence halls, there are 46 buildings.

Student Life: 95% of undergraduates are from Georgia. Students are from 13 states, 11 foreign countries, and Canada. 85% are from public schools. 77% are white; 19% African American. 74% are Protestant; 14% claim no religious affiliation. The average age of freshmen is 19; all undergraduates, 23. 38% do not continue beyond their first year; 17% remain to graduate.

Housing: 450 students can be accommodated in college housing, which includes single-sex dorms. On-campus housing is guaranteed for all 4 years. 68% of students commute. Alcohol is not permitted. All students may keep cars.

Activities: 5% of men belong to 2 local fraternities; 7% of women belong to 3 local sororities. There are 26 groups on campus, including band, cheerleading, choir, chorus, dance, drama, ethnic, honors, international, jazz band, musical theater, newspaper, pep band, professional, religious, social, social service, student government, and yearbook. Popular campus events include Road Rally, Fun Flicks, and the Fine Arts Series.

Sports: There are 3 intercollegiate sports for men and 4 for women, and 6 intramural sports for men and 6 for women. Facilities include softball, baseball, and soccer fields, tennis courts, a swimming pool, a gym, a track, an intramural field, an outdoor volleyball court, a physical fitness building, a game room, and a campus lake.

Disabled Students: 80% of the campus is accessible. Wheelchair ramps, special parking, specially equipped rest rooms, lowered telephones, and special housing are available.

Services: Counseling and information services are available, as is tutoring in most subjects. There is remedial math, reading, and writing. Tutoring in Spanish is available.

Campus Safety and Security: Measures include self-defense education, informal discussions, emergency telephones, and lighted pathways/sidewalks.

Programs of Study: BPC confers B.A., B.S., B.Min., and B.Mu. degrees. Associate degrees are also awarded. Bachelor's degrees are awarded in BIOLOGICAL SCIENCE (biology/biological science), BUSINESS (accounting and business administration and management), COMMUNICATIONS AND THE ARTS (English, music, music performance, and speech/debate/rhetoric), COMPUTER AND PHYSICAL SCIENCE (mathematics), EDUCATION (early childhood, education, health, mathematics, middle school, music, physical, science, secondary,

and social studies), SOCIAL SCIENCE (Christian studies, history, liberal arts/general studies, political science/government, psychology, religion, social science, sociology, and theological studies). Education degree programs have the largest enrollments.

Required: The required core curriculum consists of humanities, math and natural science, social science, phys ed, and computer science. Students must maintain a minimum 2.0 GPA with half of the major taken at BPC.

Special: The college offers internships, a general studies degree, B.A.-B.S. degrees, and nondegree study.

Faculty/Classroom: All teach undergraduates. The average class size in an introductory lecture is 28; in a laboratory, 15; and in a regular course, 14.

Admissions: 53% of the 2003-2004 applicants were accepted. The SAT I scores for the 2003-2004 freshman class were: Verbal--55% below 500, 32% between 500 and 599, 9% between 600 and 700, and 4% above 700; Math--60% below 500, 32% between 500 and 599, 6% between 600 and 700, and 2% above 700. The ACT scores were 46% below 21, 51% between 21 and 23, 2% between 24 and 26, and 1% between 27 and 28. 26% of the current freshmen were in the top fifth of their class; 73% were in the top two fifths.

Requirements: The SAT I is required for some programs and the ACT is recommended. A GED is accepted. Students should prepare with 4 years of English, 3 of social studies, and 2 each of foreign language, math, and science. A GPA of 2.0 is required. AP credits are accepted. Important factors in the admissions decision are personality/intangible qualities, leadership record, and advanced placement or honor courses.

Procedure: Freshmen are admitted to all sessions. Entrance exams should be taken during the senior year of high school. There are early decision and early admissions plans. Application deadlines are open. Application fee is $25. 201 early decision candidates were accepted for the 2003-2004 class. Applications are accepted on-line through the school's web site.

Transfer: 39 transfer students enrolled in 2002-2003. Applicants must submit transcripts from previously attended institutions, along with high school transcripts, if they have completed fewer than 30 semester hours. 60 credits required for the bachelor's degree must be completed at BPC.

Visiting: There are regularly scheduled orientations for prospective students, consisting of a campus tour and academic and financial aid sessions. There are guides for informal visits and visitors may sit in on classes and stay overnight. To schedule a visit, contact the Office of Admissions at *admissions@bpc.edu.*

Financial Aid: The average freshman award for 2003-2004 was $8900. Need-based scholarships or need-based grants averaged $2600 ($4850 maximum); need-based self-help aid (loans and jobs) averaged $1124 ($8325 maximum); non-need-based athletic scholarships averaged $1860 ($10,000 maximum); and other non-need-based awards and non-need-based scholarships averaged $1650 ($6000 maximum). 18% of undergraduates work part time. Average annual earnings from campus work are $750. The average financial indebtedness of the 2003 graduate was $5000. BPC is a member of CSS. The FAFSA and the college's own financial statement are required. The priority date for freshman financial aid applications for fall entry is April 3.

International Students: There are 30 international students enrolled. They must take the SAT I, scoring 860.

Computers: The mainframe is an HP 9000. 51 PCs are available in computer labs, which are accessible to all students. Students have e-mail accounts and can take on-line classes. All students may access the system. There are no time limits and no fees.

Graduates: From July 1, 2002 to June 30, 2003, 208 bachelor's degrees were awarded. The most popular majors were education (36%), business administration (23%), and psychology (9%). In an average class, 9% graduate in 4 years or less, 14% graduate in 5 years or less, and 16% graduate in 6 years or less. 23 companies recruited on campus in 2002-2003. Of the 2002 graduating class, 23% were enrolled in graduate school within 6 months of graduation and 51% were employed.

Admissions Contact: Brad Kissell, Dean of Enrollment Management. E-mail: *admissions@bpc.edu* Web: bpc.edu

---

CLARK ATLANTA UNIVERSITY   B-2
Atlanta, GA 30314   **(404) 880-8918**
(800) 668-3228; Fax: (404) 880-6174

Full-time: 1096 men, 2698 women	**Faculty:** 242
Part-time: 35 men, 92 women	**Ph.D.s:** 78%
Graduate: 330 men, 665 women	**Student/Faculty:** 16 to 1
Year: semesters, summer session	**Tuition:** $12,862
Application Deadline: June 1	**Room & Board:** $6438
Freshman Class: 6940 applied, 3220 accepted, 902 enrolled	
SAT I Verbal/Math: 460/470	**ACT:** 20 **COMPETITIVE+**

Clark Atlanta University was formed in 1988 from the consolidation of Clark College (1869) and Atlanta University (1865). A private, predominantly black college affiliated with the United Methodist Church, CAU offers programs in arts and sciences, business administration, education, and social work. There are 5 undergraduate and 4 graduate schools. In addition to regional accreditation, CAU has baccalaureate program accreditation with AACSB, CAHEA, CSWE, and NCATE. The library contains 742,257 volumes, 836,593 microform items, and 10,555 audio/video tapes/CDs, and subscribes to 1410 periodicals. Computerized library services include interlibrary loans and database searching. Special learning facilities include a learning resource center, art gallery, radio station, TV station, and a distance learning instructional technology education center. The 113-acre campus is in an urban area 3 miles southwest of Atlanta. Including any residence halls, there are 30 buildings.

Student Life: 62% of undergraduates are from out of state, mostly the South. Students are from 42 states, 14 foreign countries, and Canada. 97% are African American. Most are Protestant. The average age of freshmen is 18; all undergraduates, 20. 22% do not continue beyond their first year; 50% remain to graduate.

Housing: 1682 students can be accommodated in college housing, which includes single-sex and coed dorms, on-campus apartments, and off-campus apartments. On-campus housing is available on a first-come, first-served basis and is available on a lottery system for upperclassmen. 63% of students live on campus. Alcohol is not permitted. All students may keep cars.

Activities: 20% of men belong to 4 national fraternities; 30% of women belong to 4 national sororities. There are 75 groups on campus, including art, band, cheerleading, choir, chorale, chorus, computers, dance, drama, drill team, ethnic, film, honors, international, jazz band, marching band, musical theater, newspaper, orchestra, pep band, photography, political, professional, radio and TV, religious, social, social service, student government, symphony, and yearbook. Popular campus events include Commencement and Alumni Weekend, Founders Week, and convocations.

Sports: Facilities include a gym, a stadium, and a student center.

Disabled Students: 70% of the campus is accessible. Wheelchair ramps, elevators, special parking, and specially equipped rest rooms are available.

Services: Counseling and information services are available, as is tutoring in every subject. There is remedial math, reading, and writing.

Campus Safety and Security: Measures include 24-hour foot and vehicle patrol, security escort services, shuttle buses, and informal discussions. There are pamphlets/posters/films, emergency telephones, and lighted pathways/sidewalks.

Programs of Study: CAU confers B.A., B.S., and B.S.W. degrees. Master's and doctoral degrees are also awarded. Bachelor's degrees are awarded in BIOLOGICAL SCIENCE (biology/biological science), BUSINESS (accounting and business administration and management), COMMUNICATIONS AND THE ARTS (art, communications, English, languages, music, and speech/debate/rhetoric), COMPUTER AND PHYSICAL SCIENCE (chemistry, computer science, mathematics, and physics), EDUCATION (business, early childhood, middle school, and physical), ENGINEERING AND ENVIRONMENTAL DESIGN (engineering), HEALTH PROFESSIONS (allied health), SOCIAL SCIENCE (economics, history, philosophy, political science/government, psychology, religion, social work, and sociology). Business administration, physical and biological sciences, and communications are the strongest academically. Biology, business, and communications are the largest.

Required: To graduate, students must complete a minimum of 122 hours of course work, including a prescribed major sequence, with a minimum 2.0 GPA. Beyond the general education core requirements, at least 60% of courses must represent work at or above the 300 level.

Special: Clark Atlanta offers co-op programs, internships, study abroad in 12 countries, accelerated degree programs, and a Washington semester. There is cross-registration with Atlanta University Center, Georgia Institute of Technology, Georgia State University, and Paine College. B.A.-B.S. degrees may be obtained in business and management, education, and social and natural sciences. Dual majors in allied health and engineering and a 3-2 engineering degree with 7 universities are also available. There are 10 national honor societies and a freshman honors program.

Faculty/Classroom: 64% of faculty are male; 36%, female. 83% teach undergraduates. The average class size in an introductory lecture is 34; in a laboratory, 12; and in a regular course, 17.

Admissions: 46% of the 2003-2004 applicants were accepted. The SAT I scores for the 2003-2004 freshman class were: Verbal--73% below 500, 21% between 500 and 599, 5% between 600 and 700, and 1% above 700; Math--68% below 500, 27% between 500 and 599, and 5% between 600 and 700. The ACT scores were 70% below 21, 16% between 21 and 23, 12% between 24 and 26, 1% between 27 and 28, and 1% above 28.

Requirements: The SAT I or ACT is required. In addition, applicants must be high school graduates or hold the GED. A letter of recommendation is required. A GPA of 2.5 is required. AP and CLEP credits are accepted. Important factors in the admissions decision are academic background, advanced placement or honor courses, and recommendations by school officials.

Procedure: Freshmen are admitted fall and spring. Entrance exams should be taken by January. There are early admissions and deferred

admissions plans. Applications should be filed by June 1 for fall entry and October 1 for spring entry, along with a $35 fee. Notification of early decision is sent January 1; regular decision, on a rolling basis. Applications are accepted on-line through the school's web site.

Transfer: 295 transfer students enrolled in 2002-2003. Applicants must have a 2.3 GPA, be in good standing at the institution previously attended, and have completed at least 12 semester hours. 30 of 122 credits required for the bachelor's degree must be completed at CAU.

Visiting: There are regularly scheduled orientations for prospective students. There are guides for informal visits and visitors may sit in on classes. To schedule a visit, contact Robin Reid, Admission Counselor at (404) 880-8782 or rreid@cau.edu.

Financial Aid: In 2003-2004, 94% of all full-time freshmen and 95% of continuing full-time students received some form of financial aid. 79% of full-time freshmen and 78% of continuing full-time students received need-based aid. The average freshman award was $15,853. Need-based scholarships or need-based grants averaged $3492 ($4000 maximum); need-based self-help aid (loans and jobs) averaged $2988 ($4000 maximum); non-need-based athletic scholarships averaged $11,353 ($18,391 maximum); and other non-need-based awards and non-need-based scholarships averaged $11,307 ($23,062 maximum). 6% of undergraduates work part time. Average annual earnings from campus work are $3705. The average financial indebtedness of the 2003 graduate was $17,768. CAU is a member of CSS. The FAFSA is required. The priority date for freshman financial aid applications for fall entry is April 1. The deadline for filing freshman financial aid applications for fall entry is July 15.

International Students: There are 38 international students enrolled. The school actively recruits these students. They must score 500 on the written TOEFL or 173 on the electronic version.

Computers: The mainframes are an HP 9000 and a Sun 3800. Students may access the mainframe through the academic student computer lab. Those students with assigned user identification codes may access the system any time. There are no time limits and no fees. It is strongly recommended that all students have a personal computer.

Graduates: From July 1, 2002 to June 30, 2003, 443 bachelor's degrees were awarded. The most popular majors were business administration (22%), mass media arts (18%), and social work (11%). In an average class, 10% graduate in 3 years or less, 36% graduate in 4 years or less, 81% graduate in 5 years or less, and 92% graduate in 6 years or less. 300 companies recruited on campus in 2002-2003.

Admissions Contact: Julius Dodds, Director of Admissions. E-mail: jdodds@cau.edu Web: www.cau.edu

CLAYTON COLLEGE AND STATE UNIVERSITY   B-2
Morrow, GA 30260-0285   (770) 961-5100; Fax: (770) 961-3752

Full-time: 819 men, 1608 women	**Faculty:** 169
Part-time: 914 men, 1873 women	**Ph.D.s:** 51%
Graduate: none	**Student/Faculty:** 14 to 1
Year: semesters, summer session	**Tuition:** $2441 ($9077)
Application Deadline: July 1	**Room & Board:** n/app
Freshman Class: 3424 applied, 2621 accepted, 1554 enrolled	
SAT I Verbal/Math: 490/480	**ACT:** 19 **LESS COMPETITIVE**

Clayton College and State University, founded in 1969 as a public junior college, has been a 4-year undergraduate college in the University System of Georgia since 1985. The first baccalaureate degrees were awarded in 1989. There are 5 undergraduate schools. In addition to regional accreditation, Clayton State has baccalaureate program accreditation with ADA, NCATE, and NLN. The library contains 97,835 volumes, 254,014 microform items, and 5113 audio/video tapes/CDs, and subscribes to 750 periodicals. Computerized library services include the card catalog, interlibrary loans, and database searching. Special learning facilities include a learning resource center and a concert facility. The 160-acre campus is in a suburban area 17 miles south of downtown Atlanta near Hartsfield International Airport. There are 12 buildings.

Student Life: 92% of undergraduates are from Georgia. Students are from 28 states, 42 foreign countries, and Canada. The average age of all undergraduates is 28. 37% do not continue beyond their first year.

Housing: There are no residence halls. All of students commute. Alcohol is not permitted. All students may keep cars.

Activities: There are no fraternities or sororities. There are 20 groups on campus, including art, band, cheerleading, choir, chorale, chorus, computers, drama, ethnic, gay, honors, international, jazz band, musical theater, newspaper, professional, religious, social, social service, and student government. Popular campus events include Southern Crescent Festival and Spring Fling.

Sports: There are 4 intercollegiate sports for men and 4 for women. Facilities include a gym, jogging trails, a circuit training facility, a weight room, soccer fields, and tennis, badminton, volleyball, and basketball courts.

Disabled Students: All of the campus is accessible. Wheelchair ramps, elevators, special parking, specially equipped rest rooms, special class scheduling, lowered drinking fountains, and lowered telephones are available.

Services: Counseling and information services are available, as is tutoring in most subjects. There is remedial math, reading, and writing.

Campus Safety and Security: Measures include 24-hour foot and vehicle patrol, self-defense education, security escort services, and pamphlets/posters/films. There are emergency telephones and lighted pathways/sidewalks.

Programs of Study: Clayton State confers B.A., B.S., B.A.S., B.B.A., B.M., and B.S.N. degrees. Associate degrees are also awarded. Bachelor's degrees are awarded in BUSINESS (accounting, business administration and management, and marketing and distribution), COMMUNICATIONS AND THE ARTS (music, music performance, and music theory and composition), COMPUTER AND PHYSICAL SCIENCE (information sciences and systems), EDUCATION (middle school), ENGINEERING AND ENVIRONMENTAL DESIGN (technological management), HEALTH PROFESSIONS (allied health, dental hygiene, health care administration, and nursing), SOCIAL SCIENCE (history and interdisciplinary studies). Nursing, middle school education, and music performance are the strongest academically. Management is the largest.

Required: Students in the baccalaureate program must complete 120 to 126 semester hours, including a 60-hour core curriculum in English and humanities, math or sciences, and social sciences. A 2.0 minimum GPA is required for graduation.

Special: Co-op programs and internships can be arranged in all majors except middle school education. The B.A.S. career program enables associate degree holders to complete the baccalaureate degree. Cross-registration is offered through the University Center Consortium. Dual majors, B.A.-B.S. degrees, study abroad, student-designed majors, and work-study programs are offered. Distance learning opportunities are possible. There are 2 national honor societies and a freshman honors program.

Faculty/Classroom: 51% of faculty are male; 49%, female. All teach undergraduates.

Admissions: 77% of the 2003-2004 applicants were accepted. The SAT I scores for the 2003-2004 freshman class were: Verbal--53% below 500, 37% between 500 and 599, and 9% between 600 and 700; Math--57% below 500, 35% between 500 and 599, 8% between 600 and 700, and 1% above 700. The ACT scores were 65% below 21, 16% between 21 and 23, 15% between 24 and 26, 3% between 27 and 28, and 2% above 28.

Requirements: The SAT I or ACT is required, with minimum SAT I scores of 430 verbal and 400 math, or a minimum ACT score of 17 English and 17 math. Applicants should be graduates of accredited secondary schools. High school preparation should include 4 courses each in English and math, 3 each in science, history, and social studies, and 2 in a foreign language. Students may also be admitted on the strength of their high school academic records. AP and CLEP credits are accepted.

Procedure: Freshmen are admitted to all sessions. Entrance exams should be taken before registration. There are early admissions and deferred admissions plans. Applications should be filed by July 1 for fall entry, December 1 for spring entry, and April 1 for summer entry, along with a $40 fee. The on-line application fee is $5. Notification is sent on a rolling basis. Applications are accepted on-line through http://www.clayton.edu.

Transfer: 578 transfer students enrolled in 2002-2003. Applicants with fewer than 30 semester hours or 45 quarter credits must meet the same criteria as entering freshmen. 30 of 120 credits required for the bachelor's degree must be completed at Clayton State.

Visiting: There are regularly scheduled orientations for prospective students, including tours of the campus and the opportunity to meet faculty and staff and learn about the athletic programs, the notebook computers, and campus life. There are guides for informal visits and visitors may sit in on classes. To schedule a visit, contact the Office of Admissions at (770) 961-3500 or ccsu-info@mail.clayton.edu.

Financial Aid: In 2003-2004, 32% of all full-time freshmen and 48% of continuing full-time students received some form of financial aid. Clayton State is a member of CSS. The FAFSA and the college's own financial statement are required. The deadline for filing freshman financial aid applications for fall entry is April 1.

International Students: There are 328 international students enrolled. The school actively recruits these students. They must score 550 on the written TOEFL or 210 on the electronic version and also take the Georgia State Test for English Proficiency (G-STEP) and the SAT I or the ACT.

Computers: The mainframe is an HP 9000. Universal Personal Information Technology Access is a program to provide each CCSU student with a Microquest notebook computer and Internet access. All students may access the system. All students are required to have personal computers.

Graduates: From July 1, 2002 to June 30, 2003, 399 bachelor's degrees were awarded. The most popular majors were business/marketing (36%), nursing/health (29%), and computer information science (17%). 99 companies recruited on campus in 2002-2003.

Admissions Contact: Jeff Hammer, Director of Admissions.
E-mail: ccsu-info@mail.clayton.edu Web: www.clayton.edu

COLUMBUS STATE UNIVERSITY   A-3
Columbus, GA 31907-5645   (706) 568-2035
(866) 264-2035; Fax: (706) 568-2462

Full-time: 1521 men, 2460 women	Faculty: 222; IIA, -$
Part-time: 793 men, 1250 women	Ph.D.s: 70%
Graduate: 430 men, 513 women	Student/Faculty: 18 to 1
Year: semesters, summer session	Tuition: $2676 ($9312)
Application Deadline: July 28	Room & Board: $5170
Freshman Class: 2150 applied, 1500 accepted, 1009 enrolled	
SAT I Verbal/Math: 493/482	ACT: 20 COMPETITIVE

Columbus State University, established in 1958, is a public liberal arts institution within the University System of Georgia. There are 4 undergraduate and 4 graduate schools. In addition to regional accreditation, Columbus State has baccalaureate program accreditation with APTA, CACREP, NASAD, NASM, NCATE, and NLN. The library contains 263,486 volumes, 933,488 microform items, and 8957 audio/video tapes/CDs, and subscribes to 1487 periodicals. Computerized library services include the card catalog, interlibrary loans, and database searching. Special learning facilities include a learning resource center, art gallery, and archives. The 132-acre campus is in a suburban area 100 miles south of Atlanta. Including any residence halls, there are 26 buildings.

Student Life: 86% of undergraduates are from Georgia. 62% are white; 29% African American. The average age of freshmen is 20; all undergraduates, 22. 30% do not continue beyond their first year; 27% remain to graduate.

Housing: 594 students can be accommodated in college housing, which includes single-sex on-campus apartments and off-campus apartments. In addition, there are special-interest houses. On-campus housing is guaranteed for all 4 years. 91% of students commute. Alcohol is not permitted. All students may keep cars.

Activities: 1% of men belong to 1 local fraternity and 6 national fraternities; 1% of women belong to 2 local and 5 national sororities. There are 50 groups on campus, including art, band, cheerleading, choir, chorale, chorus, computers, dance, drama, drill team, ethnic, film, honors, international, jazz band, literary magazine, musical theater, newspaper, orchestra, pep band, photography, political, professional, religious, social, social service, student government, and symphony. Popular campus events include Black History Month, Halloween, and Greek Week.

Sports: There are 5 intercollegiate sports for men and 4 for women, and 16 intramural sports for men and 16 for women. Facilities include a gym, a weight room, tennis courts, baseball, soccer, softball, and intramural multipurpose fields, a walking trail, and volleyball and basketball courts.

Disabled Students: All of the campus is accessible. Wheelchair ramps, elevators, special parking, specially equipped rest rooms, lowered drinking fountains, lowered telephones, and specially equipped electronic doors are available.

Services: Counseling and information services are available, as is tutoring in most subjects. There is a reader service for the blind, and remedial math, reading, and writing. Scribe and braille services are also available.

Campus Safety and Security: Measures include 24-hour foot and vehicle patrol, self-defense education, security escort services, and shuttle buses. There are informal discussions, pamphlets/posters/films, emergency telephones, lighted pathways/sidewalks, and shuttles for evening students.

Programs of Study: Columbus State confers B.A., B.S., B.B.A., B.F.A., B.M., B.S.Ed. and B.S.N. degrees. Associate and master's degrees are also awarded. Bachelor's degrees are awarded in BIOLOGICAL SCIENCE (biology/biological science), BUSINESS (accounting, banking and finance, business administration and management, management information systems, and marketing/retailing/merchandising), COMMUNICATIONS AND THE ARTS (art, communications, dramatic arts, English, music, music performance, and visual and performing arts), COMPUTER AND PHYSICAL SCIENCE (chemistry, computer science, geology, and mathematics), EDUCATION (art, drama, early childhood, foreign languages, health, middle school, music, secondary, and special), HEALTH PROFESSIONS (exercise science, health science, and nursing), SOCIAL SCIENCE (criminal justice, history, political science/government, psychology, and sociology). Business, education, and music are the strongest academically. Business, education, and nursing are the largest.

Required: To graduate, all students must maintain a 2.0 GPA and complete a minimum of 123 semester hours, 63 of them in a core curriculum and 60 in the major. 3 semester hours of phys ed are required. All students must pass the Georgia Regents Test for competency in reading and writing, complete English 101 and 102 with a C or better, and satisfy the Georgia History and Constitution and U.S. History and Constitution requirement by taking specified courses at a University System of Georgia institution or, for transfers from outside the system, by passing an exemption test. Some majors require a comprehensive exam.

Special: Cooperative programs in computer programming, engineering, nursing, and business, internships, a Washington semester, work-study, and study abroad in Asia, Europe, and the Americas are possible. A 3-2 engineering degree with the Georgia Institute of Technology and a B.A.-B.S. degree in political science, biology, chemistry, math, or psychology are also available. There are 13 national honor societies and a freshman honors program.

Faculty/Classroom: 67% of faculty are male; 33%, female. Graduate students teach 1% of introductory courses. The average class size in an introductory lecture is 24; in a laboratory, 17; and in a regular course, 20.

Admissions: 70% of the 2003-2004 applicants were accepted. The SAT I scores for the 2003-2004 freshman class were: Verbal--58% below 500, 32% between 500 and 599, 9% between 600 and 700, and 1% above 700; Math--60% below 500, 31% between 500 and 599, 8% between 600 and 700, and 1% above 700.

Requirements: The SAT I or ACT is required; the SAT I is preferred, with a minimum verbal score of 440 and math score of 410. A minimum ACT score of 17 English and 17 math is accepted. Applicants must be graduates of accredited secondary schools. 16 academic credits are required, including 4 each in English and math, 3 each in science and social studies, and 2 in a foreign language. AP and CLEP credits are accepted.

Procedure: Freshmen are admitted to all sessions. Entrance exams should be taken in the fall of the senior year. There are early decision and early admissions plans. Early decision applications should be filed by July 3; regular applications, by July 28 for fall entry, December 12 for spring entry, and May 25 for summer entry, along with a $25 fee. Notification is sent on a rolling basis. Applications are accepted on-line through CollegeNET.

Transfer: 481 transfer students enrolled in 2002-2003. Transfer students with fewer than 30 hours of credit must meet the same requirements as entering freshmen. Transfer students must have a 2.0 GPA and be eligible to return to the institution last attended. 30 of a minimum of 123 credits required for the bachelor's degree must be completed at Columbus State.

Visiting: There are regularly scheduled orientations for prospective students, During the fall and spring semesters, there are college visitation programs. Prospective students may arrange a tour on any weekday. There are guides for informal visits and visitors may sit in on classes. To schedule a visit, contact the Admissions Office at *www.admission@colstate.edu.*

Financial Aid: In 2002-2003, 77% of all full-time freshmen and 55% of continuing full-time students received some form of financial aid. 61% of full-time freshmen and 53% of continuing full-time students received need-based aid. The average freshman award was $3723. Need-based scholarships or need-based grants averaged $2875; need-based self-help aid (loans and jobs) averaged $2813; and non-need-based athletic scholarships averaged $2107. The average financial indebtedness of the 2003 graduate was $11,859. The CSS/Profile or FAFSA is required. The priority date for freshman financial aid applications for fall entry is May 1.

International Students: There are 84 international students enrolled. The school actively recruits these students. They must score 550 on the written TOEFL or 213 on the electronic version and also take the SAT I or the ACT, scoring 970 on the SAT I.

Computers: The mainframe is an IBM 4361. Computers are available in the computer center, library, business and education departments, and learning labs. All students may access the system. There are no time limits. The fee is $76.

Graduates: From July 1, 2002 to June 30, 2003, 580 bachelor's degrees were awarded. The most popular majors were computer science (9%), early childhood (9%), and criminal justice (7%). In an average class, 27% graduate in 6 years or less. 150 companies recruited on campus in 2002-2003.

Admissions Contact: Susan Lovell, Associate Director of Admissions. A video is available. E-mail: *lovell_susan@colstate.edu*
Web: *www.colstate.edu*

COVENANT COLLEGE D-4
Lookout Mountain, GA 30750 (706) 820-2398
(888) 451-2683; Fax: (706) 820-0893

Full-time: 338 men, 507 women	**Faculty:** 53; IIB, av$
Part-time: 16 men, 11 women	**Ph.D.s:** 77%
Graduate: 26 men, 47 women	**Student/Faculty:** 16 to 1
Year: semesters, summer session	**Tuition:** $18,230
Application Deadline: May 1	**Room & Board:** $5600
Freshman Class: 715 applied, 262 enrolled	
SAT I Verbal/Math: 610/590	**ACT:** 26 **VERY COMPETITIVE+**

Covenant College, founded in 1955, is a private liberal arts college affiliated with the Presbyterian Church in America (P.C.A.). The library contains 100,000 volumes, 5000 microform items, and 4500 audio/video tapes/CDs, and subscribes to 400 periodicals. Computerized library services include interlibrary loans and database searching. The 310-acre campus is in a suburban area 12 miles southwest of Chattanooga, Tennessee. Including any residence halls, there are 10 buildings.

Student Life: 70% of undergraduates are from out of state, mostly the South. Students are from 49 states, 7 foreign countries, and Canada. 93% are white. Most are Protestant. The average age of freshmen is 18; all undergraduates, 20. 21% do not continue beyond their first year; 60% remain to graduate.

Housing: 774 students can be accommodated in college housing, which includes single-sex dorms and on-campus apartments. On-campus housing is guaranteed for all 4 years. 88% of students live on campus; of those, 85% remain on campus on weekends. Alcohol is not permitted. All students may keep cars.

Activities: There are no fraternities or sororities. There are 48 groups on campus, including cheerleading, choir, chorale, dance, drama, honors, international, literary magazine, newspaper, photography, professional, religious, social, social service, student government, symphony, and yearbook. Popular campus events include Madrigal Dinner, Spring Banquet, and Kilter Night.

Sports: There are 3 intercollegiate sports for men and 4 for women, and 7 intramural sports for men and 7 for women. Facilities include a gym, a weight room, a swimming pool, tennis courts, 3 soccer fields, running trails, an aerobics room, and a wellness room equipped with a variety of fitness machines.

Disabled Students: All of the campus is accessible. Wheelchair ramps, elevators, special parking, specially equipped rest rooms, lowered drinking fountains, lowered telephones, and special doors for wheelchair access are available.

Services: Counseling and information services are available, as is tutoring in some subjects, including math and writing.

Campus Safety and Security: Measures include lighted pathways/sidewalks and a watchman who maintains campus security at night.

Programs of Study: Covenant confers B.A., B.S., and B.Mus. degrees. Associate and master's degrees are also awarded. Bachelor's degrees are awarded in BIOLOGICAL SCIENCE (biology/biological science), BUSINESS (business administration and management and management science), COMMUNICATIONS AND THE ARTS (applied music, English, and music), COMPUTER AND PHYSICAL SCIENCE (chemistry, information sciences and systems, mathematics, natural sciences, and physics), EDUCATION (elementary), SOCIAL SCIENCE (biblical studies, economics, history, interdisciplinary studies, missions, philosophy, psychology, religion, and sociology). Education, business, and biology are the strongest academically. Business, English, and education are the largest.

Required: All students must complete 55 to 63 hours of core and distribution requirements, including course work in Bible studies, interdisciplinary studies, English composition, cross-cultural experience, speech, language, phys ed, computers, lab science, social science, and history. A minimum total of 126 credits and a GPA of 2.0 are required for graduation. All students must also complete an oral interview and a senior integration project, in which they explore a problem in their major field in light of Christian philosophy.

Special: Cross-registration is possible with the Council for Christian Colleges and Universities (CCCU) as are internships in business, psychology, and biology. Students may study abroad in 9 countries or spend a semester in Washington. There is a 3-2 engineering program with Georgia Tech and other universities and technical institutes and a 13-month degree-completion program for students with 2 years of previous college experience. Juniors and seniors may take classes on a pass/fail basis. There are 2 national honor societies, a freshman honors program, and 2 departmental honors programs.

Faculty/Classroom: 87% of faculty are male; 13%, female. All teach undergraduates. No introductory courses are taught by graduate students. The average class size in an introductory lecture is 19; in a laboratory, 16; and in a regular course, 18.

Admissions: The SAT I scores for the 2003-2004 freshman class were: Verbal--14% below 500, 28% between 500 and 599, 42% between 600 and 700, and 16% above 700; Math--19% below 500, 32% between 500 and 599, 39% between 600 and 700, and 10% above 700. The ACT scores were 18% below 21, 17% between 21 and 23, 22% between 24 and 26, 21% between 27 and 28, and 25% above 28. 36% of the current freshmen were in the top fifth of their class; 60% were in the top two fifths. 9 freshmen graduated first in their class in a recent year.

Requirements: The SAT I or ACT is required, with a minimum composite score of 1000 on the SAT I or 21 on the ACT. Applicants must graduate from an accredited high school or have a GED. Applicants should have 4 years of high school English, 3 years of math, and 2 years each of foreign language, history, science, and social studies. An essay and an interview are required. A GPA of 2.5 is required. AP and CLEP credits are accepted. Important factors in the admissions decision are advanced placement or honor courses, extracurricular activities record, and leadership record.

Procedure: Freshmen are admitted fall and spring. Entrance exams should be taken by January of the senior year. Applications should be filed by May 1 for fall entry and November 1 for spring entry, along with a $25 fee. Notification is sent on a rolling basis.

Transfer: 58 transfer students enrolled in a recent year. Transfer applicants must take either the SAT I, with a minimum composite score of 1000, or the ACT, with a minimum composite of 21. Courses with a grade of C or better that apply toward the selected Covenant program will receive transfer credit. 30 of 126 credits required for the bachelor's degree must be completed at Covenant.

Visiting: There are regularly scheduled orientations for prospective students, consisting of a campus preview weekend during which high school students stay in dorms and attend classes, seminars, and other college activities. There are guides for informal visits and visitors may sit in on classes and stay overnight. To schedule a visit, contact Beth Nedelisky, Admissions Assistant Director, at (706) 419-1656.

Financial Aid: In a recent year, 87% of all full-time freshmen and 92% of continuing full-time students received some form of financial aid. 71% of full-time freshmen and 66% of continuing full-time students received need-based aid. The average freshman award was $11,678. 38% of undergraduates work part time. Average annual earnings from campus work are $1854. The FAFSA and the college's own financial statement are required. The priority date for freshman financial aid applications for fall entry is March 1. The deadline for filing freshman financial aid applications for fall entry is March 31.

International Students: There are 7 international students enrolled. The school actively recruits these students. They must score 540 on the written TOEFL or 207 on the electronic version. Applicants are encouraged to take the SAT I or ACT if it is available in their country.

Computers: 135 PCs are available for student use in 3 computer labs, the library, and dorm clusters. All students may access the system 8 A.M. to 12 A.M. Monday through Thursday and Saturday and 8 A.M. to 6 P.M. on Friday. There are no time limits. The fee is $60 per semester.

Graduates: From July 1, 2002 to June 30, 2003, 165 bachelor's degrees were awarded. The most popular majors were English (11%), psychology (9%), and biology, history, and Bible studies (8%). In an average class, 1% graduate in 3 years or less, 49% graduate in 4 years or less, 58% graduate in 5 years or less, and 60% graduate in 6 years or less. 25 companies recruited on campus in a recent year.

Admissions Contact: Bryan Pierce, Director, Student Recruitment. E-mail: *admissions@covenant.edu* Web: *covenant.edu*

DEVRY UNIVERSITY/ALPHARETTA
Alpharetta, GA 30004-2232

B-2

(770) 664-9520
(800) 221-4771; Fax: (770) 664-8824

Full-time: 530 men, 287 women	**Faculty:** n/av
Part-time: 315 men, 154 women	**Ph.D.s:** n/av
Graduate: n/av	**Student/Faculty:** n/av
Year: semesters, summer session	**Tuition:** $10,670
Application Deadline: open	**Room & Board:** n/app
Freshman Class: n/av	
SAT I or ACT: n/av	**LESS COMPETITIVE**

DeVry University/Alpharetta, founded in 1997, is a private institution offering hands-on programs in electronics, business administration, computer information systems, telecommunications management, technical management, information technology, and computer engineering technology. The school is 1 of 67 DeVry University locations throughout the United States and Canada. In addition to regional accreditation, DeVry has baccalaureate program accreditation with ABET. The library contains 3517 volumes and 221 audio/video tapes/CDs, and subscribes to 75 periodicals. Computerized library services include the card catalog, interlibrary loans, and database searching. Special learning facilities include a learning resource center and electronics and other labs. The 9-acre campus is in a suburban area. There is 1 building.

Student Life: 32% of students are African American; 28% white. The average age of all undergraduates is 27.

Housing: There are no residence halls. Housing referrals may be obtained through the Student Housing Office. There are private apartments, student-plan housing, and private rooms. All students commute. Alcohol is not permitted. All students may keep cars.

Activities: There are no fraternities or sororities. There are 12 groups on campus, including international, newspaper, professional, programming, social, and toastmasters. Popular campus events include Fall Festival, Spring Fling, and Thanksgiving Dinner.

Sports: There are 4 intramural sports for men and 4 for women.

Disabled Students: 98% of the campus is accessible. Wheelchair ramps, elevators, special parking, specially equipped rest rooms, lowered drinking fountains, and lowered telephones are available.

Services: Counseling and information services are available, as is tutoring in every subject.

Campus Safety and Security: Measures include security escort services, informal discussions, pamphlets/posters/films, and emergency telephones. There is CCTV and video recording.

Programs of Study: DeVry confers the B.S. degree. Associate and master's degrees are also awarded. Bachelor's degrees are awarded in BIOLOGICAL SCIENCE (bioinformatics), BUSINESS (business administration and management), COMMUNICATIONS AND THE ARTS (tele-

communications), COMPUTER AND PHYSICAL SCIENCE (information sciences and systems), ENGINEERING AND ENVIRONMENTAL DESIGN (computer engineering, electrical/electronics engineering technology, and technological management). Telecommunications, computer information systems, and business administration are the largest.

Required: To graduate, students must achieve a cumulative GPA of at least 2.0 and satisfactorily complete all curriculum requirements. Course requirements vary according to program. All first-semester students take courses in business organization, computer applications, algebra, psychology, and student success strategies.

Special: Accelerated degrees, co-op programs, nondegree study, distance learning, and evening classes are possible. There are 5 national honor societies.

Faculty/Classroom: All teach undergraduates.

Requirements: Admissions requirements include graduation from a secondary school; the GED is also accepted. Applicants must pass the DeVry entrance exam or present satisfactory ACT or SAT I scores. An interview is required. CLEP credit is accepted.

Procedure: Freshmen are admitted fall, spring, and summer. There are early admissions and deferred admissions plans. There is a rolling admissions plan. Application deadlines are open. Application fee is $50. Notification is sent on a rolling basis. Applications are accepted on-line through *https://apply.embark.com/UGrad/DeVry/21/*.

Transfer: 133 transfer students enrolled in a recent year. Applicants must present passing grades in all completed college course work, demonstrate language skills proficiency with at least 24 completed semester hours, and present evidence of math proficiency by appropriate college-level credits. A minimum GPA of 2.0 is required. 25% of 48 to 154 credits required for the bachelor's degree must be completed at DeVry.

Visiting: There are regularly scheduled orientations for prospective students. There are guides for informal visits and visitors may sit in on classes. To schedule a visit, contact the New Student Coordinator.

Financial Aid: In 2002-2003, 51% of all full-time freshmen and 71% of continuing full-time students received some form of financial aid. At least 49% of full-time freshmen and 68% of continuing full-time students received need-based aid. The average freshman award was $7008. Need-based scholarships or need-based grants averaged $3741; need-based self-help aid (loans and jobs) averaged $3549; and institutional non-need-based awards and non-need-based scholarships averaged $6349. The FAFSA is required. There is a rolling deadline for filing freshman financial aid applications for fall entry.

International Students: There were 39 international students enrolled in a recent year. They must score 500 on the written TOEFL or 173 on the electronic version and also take the college's own entrance exam.

Computers: Lab facilities include PCs in stand-alone and network configurations with access to the mainframe. LANs provide access to a wide range of applications software. Hard copy from the mainframe is provided through a local minicomputer and medium- and high-speed printers. All students may access the system during lab hours. There are no fees. It is strongly recommended that all students have a personal computer.

Graduates: From July 1, 2002 to June 30, 2003, 283 bachelor's degrees were awarded. The most popular majors were computer information systems (66%), business (27%), and electronics engineering technology (7%). 65 companies recruited on campus in a recent year.

Admissions Contact: Gerry Purcell, Director of Admissions. E-mail: *admissions@devry.edu* Web: *www.atl.devry.edu/alpharetta/*

DEVRY UNIVERSITY/DECATUR
Decatur, GA 30030-2198

B-2

(404) 292-2645
(800) 221-4771; Fax: (404) 292-7011

Full-time: 1034 men, 768 women	**Faculty:** n/av
Part-time: 411 men, 348 women	**Ph.D.s:** n/av
Graduate: n/av	**Student/Faculty:** n/av
Year: semesters, summer session	**Tuition:** $10,670
Application Deadline: open	**Room & Board:** n/app
Freshman Class: n/av	
SAT I or ACT: n/av	**LESS COMPETITIVE**

DeVry University/Decatur, a private institution, was established in 1969; there are 66 other DeVry University locations in the United States and Canada. The school offers technology-based undergraduate programs in business administration, electronics, computer information systems, telecommunications management, technical management, information technology, and computer engineering technology. In addition to regional accreditation, DeVry has baccalaureate program accreditation with ABET. The library contains 22,094 volumes, 12,000 e-books, and 1380 audio/video tapes/CDs. Computerized library services include the card catalog, interlibrary loans, and database searching. Special learning facilities include a learning resource center and electronics and other labs. The 18-acre campus is in a suburban area 6 miles from downtown Atlanta. There is 1 building.

Student Life: The average age of all undergraduates is 27.

Housing: There are no residence halls. Housing referrals may be obtained through the Student Housing Office. There are private apartments, student-plan housing, and private rooms. All students commute. Alcohol is not permitted. All students may keep cars.

Activities: There are no fraternities or sororities. There are 12 groups on campus, including electronics, environmental, ethnic, film, fitness, ham radio, honors, international, newspaper, professional, social, and toastmasters (speech). Popular campus events include Fall Festival, Spring Fling, and Thanksgiving Dinner.

Sports: There is 1 intercollegiate sport for men, and 4 intramural sports for men and 4 for women.

Disabled Students: 98% of the campus is accessible. Wheelchair ramps, elevators, special parking, specially equipped rest rooms, lowered drinking fountains, and lowered telephones are available.

Services: Counseling and information services are available, as is tutoring in every subject.

Campus Safety and Security: Measures include security escort services, informal discussions, pamphlets/posters/films, and emergency telephones. There are lighted pathways/sidewalks. The campus is patrolled by county police 7:30 A.M. to 8 P.M. Monday through Friday and by DeVry security 6:30 A.M. to 11:30 P.M. Monday through Friday and 8 A.M. to 5 P.M. Saturday.

Programs of Study: DeVry confers the B.S. degree. Associate and master's degrees are also awarded. Bachelor's degrees are awarded in BIOLOGICAL SCIENCE (bioinformatics), BUSINESS (business administration and management), COMMUNICATIONS AND THE ARTS (telecommunications), COMPUTER AND PHYSICAL SCIENCE (information sciences and systems), ENGINEERING AND ENVIRONMENTAL DESIGN (biomedical engineering, computer engineering, electrical/electronics engineering technology, and technological management). Computer information systems and telecommunications are the largest.

Required: To graduate, students must achieve a cumulative GPA of at least 2.0 and satisfactorily complete all curriculum requirements. Course requirements vary according to program. All first-semester students take courses in business organization, computer applications, algebra, psychology, and student success strategies.

Special: Evening and weekend classes, co-op programs, an accelerated degree program, distance learning, and nondegree study are possible. There are 4 national honor societies and 3 departmental honors programs.

Faculty/Classroom: All teach undergraduates.

Requirements: Admissions requirements include graduation from a secondary school; the GED is also accepted. Applicants must pass the DeVry entrance exam or present satisfactory ACT or SAT I scores. An interview is required. CLEP credit is accepted.

Procedure: Freshmen are admitted fall, spring, and summer. There are early admissions and deferred admissions plans. There is a rolling admissions plan. Application deadlines are open. Application fee is $50. Notification is sent on a rolling basis. Applications are accepted on-line through https://apply.embark.com/UGrad/DeVry/21/.

Transfer: 746 transfer students enrolled in a recent year. Applicants must present passing grades in all completed college course work, demonstrate language skills proficiency with at least 24 completed semester hours, and evidence math proficiency by appropriate college-level credits. A minimum GPA of 2.0 is required. 25% of 48 to 154 credits required for the bachelor's degree must be completed at DeVry.

Visiting: There are regularly scheduled orientations for prospective students. There are guides for informal visits and visitors may sit in on classes. To schedule a visit, contact the New Student Coordinator.

Financial Aid: In 2002-2003, 76% of all full-time freshmen and 85% of continuing full-time students received some form of financial aid. At least 74% of full-time freshmen and 83% of continuing full-time students received need-based aid. The average freshman award was $8075. Need-based scholarships or need-based grants averaged $4535; need-based self-help aid (loans and jobs) averaged $3915; and institutional non-need-based awards and non-need-based scholarships averaged $7861. The FAFSA is required. There is a rolling deadline for filing freshman financial aid applications for fall entry.

International Students: There were 68 international students enrolled in a recent year. They must score 500 on the written TOEFL or 173 on the electronic version and also take the college's own entrance exam.

Computers: The mainframe is an IBM 3081K. Lab facilities include PCs in stand-alone and network configurations, with access to the mainframe. LANs provide access to a wide range of applications software. Hard copy from the mainframe is provided through a local minicomputer and medium- and high-speed printers. Students in the computer information systems program may access the system during published lab hours. There are no fees.

Graduates: From July 1, 2002 to June 30, 2003, 454 bachelor's degrees were awarded. The most popular majors were computer information systems (63%), business (31%), and electronics engineering technology (8%). 49 companies recruited on campus in a recent year.

Admissions Contact: Tonya Gibson, Director of Admissions.
E-mail: *dsilva@admin.atl.devry.edu* Web: *www.atl.devry.edu*

EMORY UNIVERSITY
B-2
Atlanta, GA 30322
(800) 727-6036

Full-time: 2468 men, 3123 women	Faculty: 699; I, ++$
Part-time: 42 men, 84 women	Ph.D.s: 99%
Graduate: 2324 men, 3012 women	Student/Faculty: 8 to 1
Year: semesters, summer session	Tuition: $27,952
Application Deadline: January 15	Room & Board: $8920
Freshman Class: 10,372 applied, 4357 accepted, 1260 enrolled	
SAT I Verbal/Math: 640/660	ACT: 29 MOST COMPETITIVE

Emory University, founded in 1836, is a private institution affiliated with the United Methodist Church. There are 4 undergraduate and 7 graduate schools. The 7 libraries contain 2,700,000 volumes, 3,580,981 microform items, and 32,603 audio/video tapes/CDs, and subscribe to 27,426 periodicals. Computerized library services include the card catalog, interlibrary loans, database searching, and Internet access. Special learning facilities include a learning resource center, art gallery, planetarium, radio station, TV station, and , the Michael C. Carlos Museum, and the Carter Center. The 631-acre campus is in a suburban area 5 miles northeast of downtown Atlanta. Including any residence halls, there are 121 buildings.

Student Life: 82% of undergraduates are from out of state, mostly the South. Others are from 50 states, 65 foreign countries, and Canada. 65% are from public schools. 65% are white; 16% Asian American; 10% African American. The average age of freshmen is 18; all undergraduates, 20. 6% do not continue beyond their first year.

Housing: 4014 students can be accommodated in college housing, which includes single-sex and coed dormitories, on-campus apartments, married-student housing, fraternity houses, and sorority houses. In addition, there are honors houses, language houses, and special-interest houses. On-campus housing is guaranteed for all 4 years. 70% of students live on campus; of those, 95% remain on campus on weekends. Upperclassmen may keep cars.

Activities: 35% of men belong to 14 national fraternities; 35% of women belong to 10 national sororities. There are 220 groups on campus, including art, bagpipe band, band, cheerleading, chess, choir, chorale, chorus, computers, dance, debate, drama, ethnic, film, gay, honors, international, jazz band, literary magazine, musical theater, newspaper, orchestra, pep band, photography, political, professional, radio and TV, religious, social, social service, student government, symphony, and yearbook. Popular campus events include Heritage Ball, Festival of Nine Lessons, and Martin Luther King Week.

Sports: There are 9 intercollegiate sports for men and 9 for women, and 40 intramural sports for men and 40 for women. Facilities include a phys ed center, which contains a 3000-seat gym with 4 basketball courts, an Olympic-size swimming pool, 2 Nautilus weight rooms, and tennis, racquetball, and squash courts. In addition, there is a soccer field and a 400-meter track, with seating for 2000 spectators.

Disabled Students: 90% of the campus is accessible. Wheelchair ramps, elevators, special parking, specially equipped rest rooms, special class scheduling, lowered drinking fountains, and lowered telephones are available.

Services: Counseling and information services are available, as is tutoring in most subjects. There is a reader service for the blind.

Campus Safety and Security: Measures include 24-hour foot and vehicle patrol, self-defense education, security escort services, and shuttle buses. There are informal discussions, pamphlets/posters/films, emergency telephones, lighted pathways/sidewalks, and The campus patrol is a fully accredited police department.

Programs of Study: Emory confers B.A., B.S., B.B.A., and B.S.N. degrees. Associate, master's, and doctoral degrees are also awarded. Bachelor's degrees are awarded in BIOLOGICAL SCIENCE (biology/biological science, and neurosciences), BUSINESS (accounting, banking and finance, business administration and management, business economics, and marketing/retailing/merchandising), COMMUNICATIONS AND THE ARTS (art history and appreciation, classics, comparative literature, creative writing, dance, dramatic arts, English, film arts, French, Latin, modern language, music, and Spanish), COMPUTER AND PHYSICAL SCIENCE (chemistry, computer science, mathematics, and physics), EDUCATION (educational statistics and research), HEALTH PROFESSIONS (nursing), SOCIAL SCIENCE (African studies, anthropology, Asian/Oriental studies, classical/ancient civilization, economics, European studies, French studies, German area studies, history, international studies, Judaic studies, Latin American studies, medieval studies, Middle Eastern studies, philosophy, political science/government, psychology, religion, Russian and Slavic studies, sociology, and women's studies). All programs are equally strong academically is the strongest academically. Business administration, psychology, and economics are the largest.

Required: To graduate, students must complete 132 semester hours, including courses during the first 2 years in English, science, math, history, the social sciences, health, and phys ed. Students must have a GPA of 1.9 for the first 3 years and 2.0 in the senior year. The number of hours required for the major varies by department. A thesis is required for students in honors or dual B.A./M.A. or B.S./M.S. programs.

Special: Special academic programs include cross-registration with Atlanta area colleges and universities, departmental internships, work-study programs, dual majors, 3-2 and 4-2 engineering degrees with Georgia Tech, and pass/fail options. A Washington semester and B.A.-B.S. degrees are available, and students may study abroad in many countries. There are accelerated degree programs offered in biology, chemistry, math, physics, English, history, philosophy, political science, sociology, and computer science. There are 25 national honor societies, including Phi Beta Kappa.

Faculty/Classroom: 67% of faculty are male; 33%, female. 100% both teach and do research. Graduate students teach 10% of introductory courses. The average class size in an introductory lecture is 25; in a laboratory, 10; and in a regular course, 18.

Admissions: 42% of the 2003-2004 applicants were accepted. The SAT I scores for the 2003-2004 freshman class were: Verbal--10% between 500 and 599, 50% between 600 and 700, and 40% above 700; Math--5% between 500 and 599, 44% between 600 and 700, and 51% above 700. The ACT scores were 8% between 24 and 26, 39% between 27 and 28, and 54% above 28. 87% of the current freshmen were in the top fifth of their class; 95% were in the top two fifths. There were 53 National Merit finalists.

Requirements: The SAT I or ACT is required. In addition, and 1 SAT II: Subject test is recommended. The student must have acquired 16 academic credits in secondary school, including 4 years of English, 3 of math, and 2 each of history and science. The university requires the student to submit an essay. AP credits are accepted. Important factors in the admissions decision are advanced placement or honor courses, recommendations by school officials, and extracurricular activities record.

Procedure: Freshmen are admitted in the fall. Entrance exams should be taken prior to applying. There are early decision, early admissions, and deferred admissions plans. Early decision applications should be filed by November 1; regular applications, by January 15 for fall entry. Notification of early decision is sent December 15; regular decision, April 1. 437 early decision candidates were accepted for the 2003-2004 class. 500 applicants were on the 2003 waiting list; 70 were admitted. Applications are accepted on-line through the school's web site.

Transfer: 89 transfer students enrolled in 2002-2003. Applicants must have taken the SAT I or ACT and completed at least 1 year of college, with a GPA of 3.0. 64 of 132 credits required for the bachelor's degree must be completed at Emory.

Visiting: There are regularly scheduled orientations for prospective students, including a group information session and a campus tour. There are guides for informal visits and visitors may sit in on classes and stay overnight. To schedule a visit, contact the Admission Office.

Financial Aid: In 2003-2004, 57% of all full-time freshmen and 63% of continuing full-time students received some form of financial aid. 37% of full-time freshmen and 38% of continuing full-time students received need-based aid. The average freshman award was $23,016. Need-based scholarships or need-based grants averaged $18,049; need-based self-help aid (loans and jobs) averaged $3367; and other non-need-based awards and non-need-based scholarships averaged $1600. 70% of undergraduates work part time. The average financial indebtedness of the 2003 graduate was $18,606. Emory is a member of CSS. The CSS/Profile or FAFSA is required. The deadline for filing freshman financial aid applications for fall entry is February 15.

International Students: There are 240 international students enrolled. The school actively recruits these students. and also take the SAT I or the ACT.

Computers: The mainframes are an IBM 9672-E01 and a SunSPARC 20J. There are about 600 PCs located in the library, dorms, computing centers, and some academic departments. All students may access the system 24 hours a day. There are no time limits and no fees.

Graduates: From July 1, 2002 to June 30, 2003, 1422 bachelor's degrees were awarded. The most popular majors were business (17%), economics (10%), and psychology (9%). In an average class, 2% graduate in 3 years or less, 82% graduate in 4 years or less, 90% graduate in 5 years or less, and 90% graduate in 6 years or less. 250 companies recruited on campus in 2002-2003. Of the 2002 graduating class, 65% were enrolled in graduate school within 6 months of graduation.

Admissions Contact: Daniel C. Walls, Dean of Admission. A video is available. E-mail: *admiss@emory.edu* Web: *www.emory.edu/admissions*

FORT VALLEY STATE UNIVERSITY   B-3
Fort Valley, GA 31030-3298   (478) 822-7594
(877) 462-3878; Fax: (478) 822-7595

Full-time: 899 men, 1080 women	**Faculty:** 133
Part-time: 111 men, 201 women	**Ph.D.s:** 60%
Graduate: 59 men, 187 women	**Student/Faculty:** 15 to 1
Year: semesters, summer session	**Tuition:** $2782 ($9418)
Application Deadline: see profile	**Room & Board:** $4178
Freshman Class: 2484 applied, 1194 accepted, 511 enrolled	
SAT I or ACT: required	**COMPETITIVE**

Fort Valley State University, founded in 1895, is a public land-grant member of the University System of Georgia. The university offers undergraduate programs in the arts and sciences, business, education, agriculture, engineering, and other vocational and technical fields. Graduate programs are offered in early childhood, middle grades education, mental health and rehabilitation counseling, and guidance and counseling. Some information in this capsule and profile is approximate. There are 3 undergraduate schools and 1 graduate school. In addition to regional accreditation, FVSU has baccalaureate program accreditation with NCATE. The library contains 250,000 volumes and 172,000 microform items, and subscribes to 1168 periodicals. Computerized library services include the card catalog, interlibrary loans, and database searching. Special learning facilities include a learning resource center, radio station, TV station, experimental agricultural plots, animal research centers, and a greenhouse complex. The 1375-acre campus is in a rural area 30 miles southwest of Macon. Including any residence halls, there are 35 buildings.

Student Life: 92% of undergraduates are from Georgia. Students are from 29 states and 5 foreign countries. 92% are African American. 50% of freshmen remain to graduate.

Housing: 982 students can be accommodated in college housing, which includes single-sex dorms and on-campus apartments. On-campus housing is guaranteed for the freshman year only and is available on a first-come, first-served basis. 65% of students live on campus. Alcohol is not permitted. All students may keep cars.

Activities: There are 4 national fraternities and 5 national sororities. There are 73 groups on campus, including cheerleading, choir, chorus, dance, drama, honors, international, jazz band, marching band, newspaper, opera, orchestra, political, radio and TV, religious, social service, student government, and yearbook. Popular campus events include Black History month.

Sports: There are 8 intercollegiate sports for men, and 3 intramural sports for men and 3 for women. Facilities include a stadium, a gym, a baseball field, lighted tennis courts, an indoor swimming pool, indoor and outdoor tracks, and shuffleboard courts.

Disabled Students: Wheelchair ramps, elevators, special parking, and specially equipped rest rooms are available.

Services: Counseling and information services are available, as is tutoring in most subjects. There is remedial math, reading, and writing.

Campus Safety and Security: Measures include 24-hour foot and vehicle patrol, informal discussions, and pamphlets/posters/films.

Programs of Study: FVSU confers B.A., B.S., B.B.A., and B.S.W. degrees. Associate and master's degrees are also awarded. Bachelor's degrees are awarded in AGRICULTURE (agricultural economics, animal science, horticulture, and plant science), BIOLOGICAL SCIENCE (biology/biological science, nutrition, and zoology), BUSINESS (accounting, business administration and management, marketing/retailing/merchandising, and office supervision and management), COMMUNICATIONS AND THE ARTS (communications and English), COMPUTER AND PHYSICAL SCIENCE (chemistry, computer science, information sciences and systems, and mathematics), EDUCATION (agricultural, early childhood, home economics, mathematics, middle school, physical, and secondary), ENGINEERING AND ENVIRONMENTAL DESIGN (agricultural engineering technology, commercial art, and electrical/electronics engineering technology), HEALTH PROFESSIONS (veterinary science), SOCIAL SCIENCE (child psychology/development, criminal justice, economics, political science/government, psychology, social work, and sociology).

Required: Students must complete a minimum of 120 credit hours, plus 5 additional hours to satisfy requirements for freshmen orientation and for military science or phys ed. General education requirements include courses in humanities, social science, math/science, and in the major. The bachelor's degree requires a minimum GPA of 2.0 and no grade below C in the major.

Special: Students may participate in cooperative work-study programs with local industries, cross-register for courses at Robins Residence Center, and study abroad. FVSU also offers a 3-2 dual degree program in chemistry/geosciences with University of Oklahoma, in engineering or other technical fields with Georgia Institute of Technology, and a 3-2 engineering degree with University of Nevada, Las Vegas. There are 5 national honor societies and a freshman honors program.

Faculty/Classroom: 60% of faculty are male; 40%, female. The average class size in a regular course is 25.

Admissions: 48% of the 2003-2004 applicants were accepted.

Requirements: The SAT I or ACT is required. In addition, applicants must be graduates of an accredited secondary school or have earned a GED. The university requires at least 17 academic units of study, including 4 in English, 3 each in social science, math, and science, and 2 of foreign language. A GPA of 2.67 is required. AP and CLEP credits are accepted.

Procedure: Freshmen are admitted to all sessions. There is an early admissions plan and a rolling admissions plan. There is a $20 fee. Check with the school for current application deadlines. Notification is sent on a rolling basis. Applications are accepted on-line through the school's web site.

Transfer: In addition to meeting standard admission requirements, transfers must submit transcripts from all colleges previously attended. Transfer credit is accepted based on a 2.0 minimum GPA, and only courses with a C or better will be accepted. 45 credits of a minimum of 125 required for the bachelor's degree must be completed at FVSU.

Visiting: There are regularly scheduled orientations for prospective students, including an overview, an introduction of administration and faculty, and a tour. There are guides for informal visits and visitors may sit in on classes. To schedule a visit, contact the Office of Enrollment Management.

Financial Aid: Need-based scholarships or need-based grants averaged $2700 ($3040 maximum); need-based self-help aid (loans and jobs) averaged $2362 ($2438 maximum); and non-need-based athletic scholarships averaged $944 ($1000 maximum). The FAFSA is required. Check with the school for current deadlines.

International Students: They must take the TOEFL and the college's own test and also take the SAT I or the ACT.

Computers: There are no time limits and no fees. It is strongly recommended that all students have a personal computer.

Admissions Contact: John D. Jones, Assistant Vice President/Assessment and Accountability. E-mail: *jonesj@fvsu.edu*
Web: *www.fvsu.edu*

GEORGIA BAPTIST COLLEGE OF NURSING
(See Mercer University)

GEORGIA COLLEGE AND STATE UNIVERSITY
Milledgeville, GA 31061

C-3

(478) 445-5004
(800) 342-0471; Fax: (478) 445-1914

Full-time: 1608 men, 2394 women	**Faculty:** 270; IIA, -$
Part-time: 250 men, 410 women	**Ph.D.s:** 77%
Graduate: 351 men, 682 women	**Student/Faculty:** 15 to 1
Year: semesters, summer session	**Tuition:** $3596 ($12,602)
Application Deadline: July 15	**Room & Board:** $6282
Freshman Class: 2547 applied, 1590 accepted, 1011 enrolled	
SAT I Verbal/Math: 540/530	**ACT:** 22 **COMPETITIVE**

Georgia College and State University, founded in 1889, is the public liberal arts university of Georgia. There are 4 undergraduate schools and 1 graduate school. In addition to regional accreditation, GC&SU has baccalaureate program accreditation with AACSB, NASM, NCATE, and NLN. The library contains 183,000 volumes, 649,526 microform items, and 4641 audio/video tapes/CDs, and subscribes to 1077 periodicals. Computerized library services include the card catalog, interlibrary loans, and database searching. Special learning facilities include a learning resource center, art gallery, radio station, TV station, and museum. The 590-acre campus is in an urban area 30 miles from Macon. Including any residence halls, there are 61 buildings.

Student Life: 96% of undergraduates are from Georgia. Others are from 23 states, 47 foreign countries, and Canada. 85% are white; 10% African American. The average age of freshmen is 18; all undergraduates, 22. 25% do not continue beyond their first year.

Housing: 1573 students can be accommodated in college housing, which includes single-sex and coed dormitories and off-campus apartments. In addition, there are honors houses. On-campus housing is available on a first-come, first-served basis. 66% of students commute. Alcohol is not permitted. All students may keep cars.

Activities: 10% of men belong to 6 national fraternities; 9% of women belong to 6 national sororities. There are 91 groups on campus, including band, cheerleading, choir, chorale, chorus, dance, debate, drama, ethnic, honors, international, jazz band, literary magazine, musical theater, photography, political, professional, radio and TV, religious, social, social service, student government, and yearbook. Popular campus events include Week of Welcome, Progressive Dinner, and International Week.

Sports: There are 5 intercollegiate sports for men and 4 for women, and 16 intramural sports for men and 16 for women. Facilities include a basketball arena, a gym, a track, racquetball courts, a weight room, aerobics facilities, an indoor rock-climbing wall, a 70-acre phys ed complex, a soccer field, a ball park, a golf course, tennis courts, an indoor and an outdoor pool, a rope/challenge course, and nearby lakes for canoeing, sailing, and skiing.

Disabled Students: 82% of the campus is accessible. Wheelchair ramps, elevators, special parking, specially equipped rest rooms, lowered drinking fountains, lowered telephones, and special housing are available.

Services: Counseling and information services are available, as is tutoring in most subjects. There is a reader service for the blind, and remedial math, reading, and writing.

Campus Safety and Security: Measures include 24-hour foot and vehicle patrol, self-defense education, security escort services, and shuttle buses. There are informal discussions, pamphlets/posters/films, emergency telephones, and lighted pathways/sidewalks.

Programs of Study: GC&SU confers B.A., B.S., B.B.A., B.G.S., B.M., B.M.E. B.M.T., and B.S.N. degrees. Master's degrees are also awarded. Bachelor's degrees are awarded in BIOLOGICAL SCIENCE (biology/biological science), BUSINESS (accounting, business administration and management, international business management, management science, marketing and distribution, and office supervision and management), COMMUNICATIONS AND THE ARTS (art, dramatic arts, English, French, music, Spanish, and speech/debate/rhetoric), COMPUTER AND PHYSICAL SCIENCE (chemistry, computer science, information sciences and systems, and mathematics), EDUCATION (early childhood, health, middle school, music, physical, recreation, and special), ENGINEERING AND ENVIRONMENTAL DESIGN (environmental science), HEALTH PROFESSIONS (music therapy, and nursing), SOCIAL SCIENCE (criminal justice, economics, history, liberal arts/general studies, political science/government, psychology, and sociology). Education is the strongest academically. Education and nursing are the largest.

Required: To graduate, students must complete at least 120 semester hours, including 60 in the major and 39 in upper-level courses, with a minimum GPA of 2.0. Core curriculum requirements include 12 hours of social science, 11 of math/science, 9 of essential skills, 6 of humanities/fine arts, 4 of global and arts awareness, and 18 of courses related to the major. All B.A. candidates and some B.S. candidates must take foreign language. All students must pass an exam on the history and Constitution of both the U.S. and Georgia, the reading and writing sections of the Regents exam, and a senior exit exam in the major. They must also earn a C or better in English 101.

Special: GC&SU has study-abroad agreements with institutions worldwide, co-op programs, internships, work-study programs, dual majors, independent study, and student-designed majors. There is a 3-2 engineering degree program with the Georgia Institute of Technology. There are 10 national honor societies, a freshman honors program.

Faculty/Classroom: 54% of faculty are male; 46%, female. All teach undergraduates. No introductory courses are taught by graduate students.

Admissions: 62% of the 2003-2004 applicants were accepted. The SAT I scores for the 2003-2004 freshman class were: Verbal--21% below 500, 56% between 500 and 599, 20% between 600 and 700, and 1% above 700; Math--24% below 500, 57% between 500 and 599, 18% between 600 and 700, and 1% above 700. The ACT scores were 27% below 21, 44% between 21 and 23, 19% between 24 and 26, 8% between 27 and 28, and 2% above 28.

Requirements: The SAT I or ACT is required. In addition, , with a composite score of 940 (minimum 440 verbal and 400 math) on the SAT I, or 20 (minimum 17 English and 18 math) on the ACT. Applicants must be graduates of an accredited or recognized secondary school and must complete the Georgia college-preparatory curriculum requirements, including 4 units each of English and math, 3 each of social science and science, and 2 of a foreign language. A GPA of 2.22 is required. AP and CLEP credits are accepted.

Procedure: Freshmen are admitted to all sessions. Entrance exams should be taken by January of the senior year. Applications should be filed by July 15 for fall entry, December 1 for spring entry, and May 1 for summer entry, along with a $25 fee. Notification is sent on a rolling basis. Applications are accepted on-line through *www.applyweb.com/aw?gcsu*.

Transfer: 361 transfer students enrolled in 2002-2003. Applicants must have at least a 2.0 GPA, submit official transcripts from all colleges attended, and be eligible to return to their previous institution. Those who have completed fewer than 30 semester hours must meet all freshman admissions requirements. 40 of 120 credits required for the bachelor's degree must be completed at GC&SU.

Visiting: There are regularly scheduled orientations for prospective students, including receptions, tours, school meetings, information sessions, and academic and cocurricular advising and registration. There are guides for informal visits and visitors may sit in on classes. To schedule a visit, contact the Office of Admissions at 478-445-1283 or (in-state) 800-342-0471.

Financial Aid: Need-based scholarships or need-based grants averaged $3739; need-based self-help aid (loans and jobs) averaged $2598; and other non-need-based awards and non-need-based scholarships averaged $3579. The average financial indebtedness of the 2003 graduate was $10,759. GC&SU is a member of CSS. The FAFSA is required. The deadline for filing freshman financial aid applications for fall entry is March 1.

International Students: There are 95 international students enrolled. The school actively recruits these students. They must score 500 on the written TOEFL or 173 on the electronic version and also take or take the IELTS or Cambridge Exam, or they must complete the highest level of an ESL course. and also take the college's own entrance exam.

Computers: The mainframe is an HP N-class. There are 16 labs with 527 computers used for class registration, e-mail, and courses taught via the Web. All students may access the system Lab hours vary. There are no time limits. The fee is $38/per semester. It is strongly recommended that all students have a personal computer.

Graduates: From July 1, 2002 to June 30, 2003, 678 bachelor's degrees were awarded. The most popular majors were psychology (10%), nursing (9%), and management (8%). In an average class, 35% graduate in 6 years or less. 46 companies recruited on campus in 2002-2003.

Admissions Contact: Maryllis Wolfgang, Director of Admissions. E-mail: *maryllis.wolfgan@gcsu.edu* Web: *www.gcsu.edu*

GEORGIA INSTITUTE OF TECHNOLOGY B-2
Atlanta, GA 30332 (404) 894-4154; Fax: (404) 894-9511

Full-time: 7487 men, 2880 women	Faculty: 807; I, ++$
Part-time: 631 men, 259 women	Ph.D.s: 95%
Graduate: 4029 men, 1357 women	Student/Faculty: 13 to 1
Year: semesters, summer session	Tuition: $4076 ($16,002)
Application Deadline: January 15	Room & Board: $6264
Freshman Class: 8573 applied, 5386 accepted, 2237 enrolled	
SAT I Verbal/Math: 644/693	ACT: 28

HIGHLY COMPETITIVE+

Georgia Institute of Technology, founded in 1885, is a public technological institution offering programs in architecture, management, policy, and international affairs, engineering, computing, and science. There are 6 undergraduate and 6 graduate schools. In addition to regional accreditation, Georgia Tech has baccalaureate program accreditation with AACSB, ABET, CSAB, and NAAB. The 2 libraries contain 2,258,892 volumes, 4,257,720 microform items, and 84,941 audio/video tapes/CDs, and subscribe to 21,248 periodicals. Computerized library services include the card catalog, interlibrary loans, and database searching. Special learning facilities include a learning resource center, art gallery, and radio station. The 400-acre campus is in an urban area. Including any residence halls, there are 175 buildings.

Student Life: 65% of undergraduates are from Georgia. Others are from 50 states, 90 foreign countries, and Canada. 85% are from public schools. 69% are white; 15% Asian American. The average age of freshmen is 18; all undergraduates, 21. 10% do not continue beyond their first year.

Housing: 7569 students can be accommodated in college housing, which includes single-sex and coed dormitories, on-campus apartments, married-student housing, fraternity houses, and sorority houses. In addition, there are language houses and special-interest houses. On-campus housing is guaranteed for the freshman year only; is available on a first-come, first-served basis, and is available on a lottery system for upperclassmen. 50% of students live on campus; of those, 67% remain on campus on weekends. Alcohol is not permitted. All students may keep cars.

Activities: 23% of men belong to 32 national fraternities; 25% of women belong to 1 local and 12 national sororities. There are 308 groups on campus, including band, cheerleading, chess, chorale, chorus, computers, dance, drama, drill team, ethnic, gay, honors, international, jazz band, literary magazine, marching band, musical theater, newspaper, orchestra, pep band, photography, political, professional, radio and TV, religious, social, social service, student government, symphony, and yearbook. Popular campus events include Greek Week and the Ramblin' Wreck Parade.

Sports: There are 9 intercollegiate sports for men and 8 for women, and 21 intramural sports for men and 21 for women. Facilities include indoor and outdoor tennis and track facilities, softball fields, a 4000-seat baseball stadium, a 55,000-seat football stadium, a 9100-seat basketball arena, an Olympic aquatic center for swimming and diving, a golf practice facility, and a recreation center with 6 multipurpose indoor courts, strength training and cardio-fitness facilities, and 3 studios for aerobic fitness programs.

Disabled Students: 60% of the campus is accessible. Wheelchair ramps, elevators, special parking, specially equipped rest rooms, special class scheduling, lowered drinking fountains, lowered telephones, and visual alarms in housing, assistive listening devices, adapted furniture in computer labs, adaptable living space, and a paid TDD telephone booth are available.

Services: Counseling and information services are available, as is tutoring in most subjects. There is a reader service for the blind. the Learning Assistance Program/ Freshmen Experience that provides tutors for calculus, chemistry, particle dynamics, and other advanced core classes; the GT Cable Network enables students to call tutors for help in chemistry, physics, math, and computer science; and there are walk-in tutoring services available.

Campus Safety and Security: Measures include 24-hour foot and vehicle patrol, self-defense education, security escort services, and shuttle buses. There are informal discussions, pamphlets/posters/films, emergency telephones, lighted pathways/sidewalks, and foot patrol, bike patrol, limited access to dorms, mobile security patrol, and video cameras.

Programs of Study: Georgia Tech confers B.S. and many specialized bachelor's degrees in science, engineering, and computing fields. degrees. Master's and doctoral degrees are also awarded. Bachelor's degrees are awarded in BIOLOGICAL SCIENCE (biology/biological science), BUSINESS (business administration and management, and management science), COMMUNICATIONS AND THE ARTS (industrial design), COMPUTER AND PHYSICAL SCIENCE (applied mathematics, chemistry, computer science, earth science, mathematics, physics, and polymer science), ENGINEERING AND ENVIRONMENTAL DESIGN (aeronautical engineering, architecture, chemical engineering, civil engineering, computer engineering, construction management, electrical/electronics engineering, industrial engineering, materials engineering, materials science, mechanical engineering, nuclear engineering, technology and public affairs, and textile engineering), SOCIAL SCIENCE (economics, history, international relations, psychology, public affairs, and textiles and clothing). Engineering, computer science, and sciences are the strongest academically. Mechanical engineering, computer science, and management are the largest.

Required: All students must take English, calculus, computer science, social science, and a health science course selected from 2 options. Distribution requirements include 12 hours of humanities, 12 of social science, including specific course work in U.S. and Georgia history and government, 8 of math, 8 of science, 3 of computer science, and 2 of wellness. Students must maintain a 2.0 GPA in 125 hours, and must pass a reading and writing competency exam.

Special: Extensive co-op programs, cross-registration with other Atlanta-area colleges, and internships are available. Study abroad in 22 countries is possible. An engineering transfer program is offered within the university system, and a liberal arts-engineering dual degree program serves area colleges and institutions nationwide. Students have access to multidisciplinary and certificate programs outside their major field of study. The Georgia Tech Regional Engineering Program (GTREP) offers undergraduate and graduate degrees in collaboration with Armstrong Atlantic State University, Georgia Southern University, and Savannah State University. There are 11 national honor societies.

Faculty/Classroom: 83% of faculty are male; 17%, female. All teach undergraduates. Graduate students teach 17% of introductory courses. The average class size in an introductory lecture is 30 and in a laboratory, 19.

Admissions: 63% of the 2003-2004 applicants were accepted. The SAT I scores for the 2003-2004 freshman class were: Verbal--2% below 500, 22% between 500 and 599, 54% between 600 and 700, and 23% above 700; Math--5% between 500 and 599, 45% between 600 and 700, and 50% above 700. 80% of the current freshmen were in the top fifth of their class; 96% were in the top two fifths. There were 100 National Merit finalists.

Requirements: The SAT I or ACT is required. In addition, candidates for admission must have completed 4 years each of English and math, 3 of science, 2 each of history and the same foreign language, and 3 of social studies. AP credits are accepted. Important factors in the admissions decision are leadership record, extracurricular activities record, and evidence of special talent.

Procedure: Freshmen are admitted in the fall. Entrance exams should be taken by the end of the junior year. Applications should be filed by January 15 for fall entry and January 15 for summer entry. Notification is sent March 15. 163 applicants were on the 2003 waiting list; 35 were admitted. Applications are accepted on-line through *www.apply.gatech.edu.*

Transfer: 447 transfer students enrolled in 2002-2003. Transfer applicants must have completed a minimum of 30 semester hours or 45 quarter hours of course work. Grades and academic standing must be satisfactory for the last term of enrollment at the prior college. Competitive GPAs are determined according to the projected major. 36 of 120 credits required for the bachelor's degree must be completed at Georgia Tech.

Visiting: There are regularly scheduled orientations for prospective students, including the Connect with Tech program, which is offered 8 times between September and April by invitation only for high-achieving prospective freshmen and their parents; includes an overnight stay in a freshman hall, a class visit, and a tour. There are guides for informal visits and visitors may sit in on classes and stay overnight. To schedule a visit, contact the Office of Undergraduate Admissions at (404) 894-6809 or *admissions@gatech.edu.*

Financial Aid: In 2003-2004, 83% of all full-time freshmen and 72% of continuing full-time students received some form of financial aid. 41% of full-time freshmen and 40% of continuing full-time students received need-based aid. The average freshman award was $8820. Need-based scholarships or need-based grants averaged $3491 ($14,202 maximum); need-based self-help aid (loans and jobs) averaged $2900 ($6625 maximum); non-need-based athletic scholarships averaged $12,210 ($24,600 maximum); and other non-need-based awards and non-need-based scholarships averaged $4726 ($23,652 maximum). 2% of undergraduates work part time. Average annual earnings from campus work are $2400. The average financial indebtedness of the 2003 graduate was $16,692. The FAFSA and the college's own financial statement are required. The deadline for filing freshman financial aid applications for fall entry is March 1.

International Students: There are 577 international students enrolled. They must score 600 on the written TOEFL or 250 on the electronic version and also take the SAT I, scoring 440.

Computers: The mainframe is a Sun Microsystem servers with an IP Gigabit Ethernet network. Students living on campus can access the Internet and the campus computer network from their residences. All students have access to 4 computing labs on campus that contain approximately 160 general purpose computing workstations and 100 workstations equipped for multimedia projects. There are also school-specific labs and PCs in many classrooms. For students with mobile computing devices, Georgia Tech operates a wireless/walkup network. All students may access the system. There are no time limits and no fees. All students are required to have personal computers. It is recommended that students in all have personal computers. Minimum PC or Mac requirements include Pentium IV/G4 or higher, is recommended.

Graduates: From July 1, 2002 to June 30, 2003, 2417 bachelor's degrees were awarded. The most popular majors were management (14%), computer science (13%), and industrial engineering (12%). In an average class, 24% graduate in 4 years or less, 59% graduate in 5 years or less, and 68% graduate in 6 years or less. 800 companies recruited on campus in 2002-2003.

Admissions Contact: Ingrid Hayes, Director of Undergraduate Admissions. E-mail: *admissions@success.gatech.edu*
Web: *www.admissions.gatech.edu*

GEORGIA SOUTHERN UNIVERSITY
D-3
Statesboro, GA 30460   (912) 681-5391; Fax: (912) 486-7240

Full-time: 6115 men, 6132 women	**Faculty:** 629; IIA, -$
Part-time: 703 men, 746 women	**Ph.D.s:** 77%
Graduate: 578 men, 1430 women	**Student/Faculty:** 19 to 1
Year: semesters, summer session	**Tuition:** $2912 ($9548)
Application Deadline: July 1	**Room & Board:** $5628
Freshman Class: 7921 applied, 4277 accepted, 2761 enrolled	
SAT I Verbal/Math: 520/520	**ACT:** 21 **COMPETITIVE**

Georgia Southern University, founded in 1906, is a member of the public university system of Georgia and offers undergraduate degree programs in education, business, liberal arts and social sciences, science and technology, and health and professional studies. There are 6 undergraduate schools and 1 graduate school. In addition to regional accreditation, Georgia Southern has baccalaureate program accreditation with AACSB, ABET, ACCE, ACS, ADA, CAAHEP, CCNE, CSAB, FIDER, NAIT, NASAD, NASM, NASPAA, NASPE, NCATE, NLN, and NRPA. The library contains 561,413 volumes, 877,364 microform items, and 28,871 audio/video tapes/CDs, and subscribes to 3216 periodicals. Computerized library services include the card catalog, interlibrary loans, database searching, and Internet access. Special learning facilities include a learning resource center, art gallery, natural history museum, planetarium, radio station, wildlife center, botanical gardens, performing arts center, and a continuing education center. The 643-acre campus is in a small town 50 miles northwest of Savannah. Including any residence halls, there are 141 buildings.

Student Life: 95% of undergraduates are from Georgia. Students are from 46 states, 77 foreign countries, and Canada. 72% are white; 24% African American. 50% are Protestant; 43% claim no religious affiliation; 6% Catholic. The average age of freshmen is 18; all undergraduates, 21. 24% do not continue beyond their first year; 37% remain to graduate.

Housing: 3278 students can be accommodated in college housing, which includes single-sex and coed dorms, on-campus apartments, fraternity houses, and sorority houses. In addition, there are honors houses, special-interest houses, and theme halls. On-campus housing is available on a first-come, first-served basis and is available on a lottery system for upperclassmen. 76% of students commute. All students may keep cars.

Activities: 12% of men belong to 14 national fraternities; 11% of women belong to 7 national sororities. There are 150 groups on campus, including art, band, cheerleading, choir, chorale, chorus, computers, dance, debate, drama, drill team, ethnic, gay, honors, international, jazz band, literary magazine, marching band, multicultural, musical theater, newspaper, opera, orchestra, pep band, photography, political, professional, radio, religious, social, social service, student government, and symphony. Popular campus events include Eagle Expo Career Fairs, Welcome Week Activities, and Black History Month.

Sports: There are 6 intercollegiate sports for men and 9 for women, and 9 intramural sports for men and 9 for women. Facilities include football, soccer, and softball fields, basketball, handball, racquetball, tennis, and volleyball courts, a weight training area, golf ranges, an exercise trail, football and baseball stadiums, a field house, swimming pools, a challenge course, an activity center, circuit training and cardiovascular equipment, an indoor walking track, and other facilities.

Disabled Students: 92% of the campus is accessible. Wheelchair ramps, elevators, special parking, specially equipped rest rooms, special class scheduling, lowered drinking fountains, lowered telephones, and special housing are available.

Services: Counseling and information services are available, as is tutoring in most subjects. There is a reader service for the blind, and remedial math, reading, and writing.

Campus Safety and Security: Measures include 24-hour foot and vehicle patrol, self-defense education, security escort services, and informal discussions. There are pamphlets/posters/films, emergency telephones, lighted pathways/sidewalks, bike police, and environmental safety services.

Programs of Study: Georgia Southern confers B.A., B.S., B.A.S., B.B.A., B.F.A., B.G.S., B.M., B.S.B., B.S.C.E.T., B.S.Chem., B.S.Cons., B.S.Ed., B.S.E.E.T., B.S.H.S., B.S.J.S., B.S.K., B.S.Manu., B.S.Mat., B.S.M.E.T., B.S.N., B.S.P., and B.S.P.Mgt. degrees. Master's and doctoral degrees are also awarded. Bachelor's degrees are awarded in BIOLOGICAL SCIENCE (biology/biological science and nutrition), BUSINESS (accounting, banking and finance, fashion merchandising, hotel/motel and restaurant management, human resources, international economics, logistics, management science, marketing and distribution, marketing/retailing/merchandising, recreation and leisure services, recreational facilities management, sports management, and tourism), COMMUNICATIONS AND THE ARTS (art, broadcasting, communications, dramatic arts, English, French, German, journalism, music, performing arts, public relations, and Spanish), COMPUTER AND PHYSICAL SCIENCE (chemistry, computer science, geology, information sciences and systems, mathematics, and physics), EDUCATION (art, business, early childhood, health, middle school, music, social science, special, and technical), ENGINEERING AND ENVIRONMENTAL DESIGN (civil engineering technology, construction management, electrical/electronics engineering technology, engineering technology, industrial administration/management, interior design, mechanical engineering technology, and printing technology), HEALTH PROFESSIONS (community health work, exercise science, health, nursing, recreation therapy, speech pathology/audiology, and sports medicine), SOCIAL SCIENCE (anthropology, child care/child and family studies, criminal justice, economics, family/consumer studies, food production/management/services, food science, geography, history, international studies, philosophy, political science/government, psychology, social work, and sociology). Business, education, and nursing are the largest.

Required: All students must complete a total of 125 semester credit hours, including at least 30 in the major, with a minimum GPA of 2.0. Specific courses must be completed in English, math, history, humanities, science and technology, and social sciences.

Special: GSU offers opportunities for study abroad, internships, work-study programs, B.A.-B.S. degrees, cooperative programs, a general studies degree, cross-registration with Georgia Tech and East Georgia College, and a 3-2 engineering degree with Georgia Institute of Technology, pass/fail options, credit for military service, and nondegree study. There are 14 national honor societies and a freshman honors program.

Faculty/Classroom: 56% of faculty are male; 44%, female. 95% teach undergraduates and 80% do research. No introductory courses are taught by graduate students.

Admissions: 54% of the 2003-2004 applicants were accepted. The SAT I scores for the 2003-2004 freshman class were: Verbal--34% below 500, 52% between 500 and 599, 13% between 600 and 700, and 1% above 700; Math--35% below 500, 49% between 500 and 599, 15% between 600 and 700, and 1% above 700. The ACT scores were 43% below 21, 36% between 21 and 23, 14% between 24 and 26, 4% between 27 and 28, and 3% above 28.

Requirements: The SAT I or ACT is required. In addition, a high school diploma or the equivalent and satisfactory SAT I or ACT scores and GPA are required. A minimum of 18 credits in college preparatory courses should include 4 each in English and math, 3 each in social studies and science, 2 in a foreign language, and 2 additional courses. A GPA of 2.0 is required. AP and CLEP credits are accepted.

Procedure: Freshmen are admitted to all sessions. Entrance exams should be taken during the junior year. There are deferred and rolling admissions plans. Applications should be filed by July 1 for fall entry, December 1 for spring entry, and May 1 for summer entry, along with a $20 fee. Notification is sent on a rolling basis. Applications are accepted on-line through the school's web site.

Transfer: 752 transfer students enrolled in 2002-2003. Applicants must have completed at least 30 semester credit hours of college courses with a minimum GPA of 2.0. Those with fewer than 30 hours must meet freshman requirements. Students transferring with an associate degree must have a minimum GPA of 2.0 in a school with a parallel curriculum. 38 of 125 credits required for the bachelor's degree must be completed at Georgia Southern.

Visiting: There are regularly scheduled orientations for prospective students. There are guides for informal visits and visitors may stay overnight. To schedule a visit, contact the Office of Admissions at *admissions@georgiasouthern.edu*.

Financial Aid: The FAFSA is required. The deadline for filing freshman financial aid applications for fall entry is March 31.

International Students: There are 159 international students enrolled. The school actively recruits these students. They must score 500 on the written TOEFL or 173 on the electronic version and also take the SAT I (scoring 960) or the ACT.

Computers: The mainframe is a Sun 4501. Students may access the campus network through more than 1400 PCs and Macs located in general and departmental labs across campus. These are located in all major academic buildings. All students may access the system 24 hours a day. There are no time limits and no fees.

Graduates: From July 1, 2002 to June 30, 2003, 1864 bachelor's degrees were awarded. The most popular majors were business/marketing (31%), education (10%), and parks and recreation (9%). In an average class, 1% graduate in 3 years or less, 12% graduate in 4 years or less, 30% graduate in 5 years or less, and 37% graduate in 6 years or less. 94 companies recruited on campus in 2002-2003. Of the 2002 graduating class, 17% were enrolled in graduate school within 6 months of graduation and 81% were employed.

Admissions Contact: Dr. Teresa Thompson, Associate Vice President. A video is available. E-mail: *admissions@georgiasouthern.edu* Web: *http://admissions.georgiasouthern.edu/*

GEORGIA SOUTHWESTERN STATE UNIVERSITY   B-4
Americus, GA 31709

(912) 928-1273
(800) 338-0082; Fax: (912) 931-2983

Full-time: 550 men, 900 women	**Faculty:** 128; IIA, --$
Part-time: 165 men, 335 women	**Ph.D.s:** 72%
Graduate: 105 men, 485 women	**Student/Faculty:** 11 to 1
Year: semesters, summer session	**Tuition:** $2225 ($8020)
Application Deadline: see profile	**Room & Board:** $3790
Freshman Class: n/av	
SAT I or ACT: required	**COMPETITIVE**

Georgia Southwestern State University, founded in 1906, is a liberal arts, professional and teachers college that is part of the public University System of Georgia. There are 5 undergraduate and 4 graduate schools. The figures in the above capsule and in this profile are approximate. In addition to regional accreditation, GSW has baccalaureate program accreditation with NCATE and NLN. The library contains 190,000 volumes, 618,842 microform items, and 1849 audio/video tapes/CDs, and subscribes to 825 periodicals. Computerized library services include the card catalog, interlibrary loans, and database searching. Special learning facilities include a learning resource center, art gallery, and TV station. The 225-acre campus is in a small town 38 miles north of Albany. Including any residence halls, there are 37 buildings.

Student Life: 95% of undergraduates are from Georgia. Students are from 18 states, 33 foreign countries, and Canada. 70% are from public schools. 72% are white; 25% African American. The average age of freshmen is 20; all undergraduates, 22. 27% do not continue beyond their first year; 25% remain to graduate.

Housing: 597 students can be accommodated in college housing, which includes single-sex dorms. In addition, there are special-interest houses and independent fraternity and sorority houses. On-campus housing is guaranteed for all 4 years. 62% of students commute. All students may keep cars.

Activities: 13% of men belong to 7 national fraternities; 15% of women belong to 8 national sororities. There are 55 groups on campus, including art, band, cheerleading, choir, chorale, chorus, computers, dance, drama, ethnic, forensics, Habitat for Humanity, honors, international, jazz band, literary magazine, musical theater, newspaper, nursing, orchestra, photography, political, radio and TV, religious, social, social service, and student government. Popular campus events include Convocation Series.

Sports: There are 3 intercollegiate sports for men and 4 for women, and 9 intramural sports for men and 9 for women. Facilities include 2 gyms, tennis courts, an indoor/outdoor pool, a lake for canoeing, and playing fields for baseball, softball, football, and soccer. The larger gym seats 3000; the smaller seats 500.

Disabled Students: 85% of the campus is accessible. Wheelchair ramps, elevators, special parking, specially equipped rest rooms, special class scheduling, lowered drinking fountains, and accessible dorms are available.

Services: Counseling and information services are available, as is tutoring in most subjects. There is a reader service for the blind and remedial math, reading, and writing.

Campus Safety and Security: Measures include 24-hour foot and vehicle patrol, self-defense education, security escort services, and informal discussions. There are pamphlets/posters/films, emergency telephones, and lighted pathways/sidewalks.

Programs of Study: GSW confers B.A., B.S., B.A.S., B.B.A., B.F.A., B.S. Ed., and B.S.N. degrees. Associate and master's degrees are also awarded. Bachelor's degrees are awarded in BIOLOGICAL SCIENCE (biology/biological science), BUSINESS (accounting, business adminis-

tration and management, and marketing/retailing/merchandising), COMMUNICATIONS AND THE ARTS (English, fine arts, and music), COMPUTER AND PHYSICAL SCIENCE (chemistry, computer programming, computer science, geology, and mathematics), EDUCATION (art, business, early childhood, elementary, English, foreign languages, mathematics, middle school, music, recreation, science, secondary, social science, and special), ENGINEERING AND ENVIRONMENTAL DESIGN (computer technology), HEALTH PROFESSIONS (nursing), SOCIAL SCIENCE (history, political science/government, psychology, and sociology). Geology, preprofessional health and nursing, and education are the strongest academically. Business, education, and nursing are the largest.

Required: To graduate, students must complete 120 credit hours, including 18 in the major, with a minimum GPA of 2.0. The core curriculum consists of 12 hours each in English and the humanities, science, math, and social science. The student must also complete 4 courses in health and phys ed, including swimming, and pass tests in reading, writing, and geography.

Special: The college offers a 3-2 engineering degree with the Georgia Institute of Technology, cooperative programs with the South Georgia Technical School, a 2-2 degree program in nursing, internships through the Governor's Intern Program, study abroad, and credit for military phys ed and training. There are 15 national honor societies, a freshman honors program, and 1 departmental honors program.

Faculty/Classroom: 56% of faculty are male; 44%, female. All teach undergraduates and 25% do research. No introductory courses are taught by graduate students. The average class size in an introductory lecture is 22; in a laboratory, 19; and in a regular course, 18.

Admissions: In a recent year, 4 freshmen graduated first in their class.

Requirements: The SAT I or ACT is required, the SAT I is preferred. Students must score at least 430 verbal and 400 math on the SAT I, and no lower than 18 on the verbal part and 17 on the math part of the ACT; those with lower scores may gain acceptance through the Developmental Studies Program. Students must be graduates of an accredited secondary school or have a GED certificate. The college requires 16 academic credits and 21 Carnegie units, based on 4 years of English, 3 of science and 4 of math, 2 each of history and a foreign language, and 1 of social studies. An art portfolio and a music audition are recommended for appropriate majors. A GPA of 2.0 is required. AP and CLEP credits are accepted. Important factors in the admissions decision are advanced placement or honor courses, evidence of special talent, and geographic diversity.

Procedure: Freshmen are admitted to all sessions. Entrance exams should be taken before the end of the senior year. There is a rolling admissions plan. Check with the school for current deadlines. The fall 2003 appplication fee was $20. Applications are accepted on-line at the school's web site.

Transfer: 188 transfer students enrolled in a recent year. Applicants should be in good standing at their former institutions. Those with fewer than 30 hours of transfer credit must meet freshman requirements. 30 of 120 credits required for the bachelor's degree must be completed at GSW.

Visiting: There are regularly scheduled orientations for prospective students. There are guides for informal visits and visitors may sit in on classes and stay overnight. To schedule a visit, contact the Admissions Office.

Financial Aid: In a recent year, 52% of all full-time freshmen and 68% of continuing full-time students received some form of financial aid. 25% of full-time freshmen and 36% of continuing full-time students received need-based aid. The average freshman award was $4930. 8% of undergraduates work part time. Average annual earnings from campus work are $1648. The average financial indebtedness of a recent graduate was $11,500. The FAFSA is required. Check with the school for current deadlines.

International Students: In a recent year, there were 68 international students enrolled. The school actively recruits these students. They must score 524 on the written TOEFL or 190 on the electronic version.

Computers: The mainframe is an IBM RISC 6000 Model 570. Two computer labs are equipped with IBM PCs that are connected to the main computer by a token ring network. All students may access the system 8 A.M. to 12 midnight Monday through Friday and selected hours on weekends. There are no time limits and no fees.

Graduates: In a recent year, 294 bachelor's degrees were awarded. The most popular majors were business (24%), education (23%), and psychology/sociology (17%). 108 companies recruited on campus in a recent year. Of the 2002 graduating class, 96% were employed within 6 months of graduation.

Admissions Contact: Gary Fallis, Director of Admissions. A video is available. E-mail: *gswapps@canes.gsw.edu* Web: *www.gsw.edu*

GEORGIA STATE UNIVERSITY
B-2
Atlanta, GA 30303-3083 (404) 651-2365; Fax: (404) 651-4811

Full-time: 5248 men, 8334 women	**Faculty:** 998; I, -$
Part-time: 2601 men, 4025 women	**Ph.D.s:** 85%
Graduate: 3275 men, 4596 women	**Student/Faculty:** 14 to 1
Year: semesters, summer session	**Tuition:** $3920 ($13,544)
Application Deadline: March 1	**Room & Board:** $6738
Freshman Class: 9296 applied, 5281 accepted, 2455 enrolled	
SAT I Verbal/Math: 530/540	**ACT:** 21 **COMPETITIVE**

Georgia State University, founded in 1913 and a part of the University System of Georgia, is a public residential university offering programs in liberal arts and sciences, business administration, education, law, health sciences, and public policy. There are 5 undergraduate and 6 graduate schools. In addition to regional accreditation, Georgia State has baccalaureate program accreditation with AACSB, ADA, APTA, CAHEA, CSWE, NASAD, NASM, NCATE, and NLN. The 2 libraries contain 1,521,867 volumes, 263,872 microform items, and 22,937 audio/video tapes/CDs, and subscribe to 7531 periodicals. Computerized library services include interlibrary loans and database searching. Special learning facilities include a learning resource center, art gallery, radio station, TV station, digital arts lab, observatory, instructional technology center, and distance learning classrooms. The 44-acre campus is in an urban area in downtown Atlanta. Including any residence halls, there are 48 buildings.

Student Life: 92% of undergraduates are from Georgia. Students are from 48 states, 126 foreign countries, and Canada. 45% are white; 37% African American; 11% Asian American. The average age of freshmen is 20; all undergraduates, 24. 19% do not continue beyond their first year; 32% remain to graduate.

Housing: 2000 students can be accommodated in college housing, which includes single-sex and coed on-campus apartments. In addition, there are honors houses and special-interest houses. On-campus housing is available on a first-come, first-served basis. 90% of students commute. All students may keep cars.

Activities: 3% of men belong to 9 national fraternities; 4% of women belong to 11 national sororities. There are 146 groups on campus, including art, band, cheerleading, chess, chorale, chorus, computers, dance, debate, drama, ethnic, film, gay, honors, international, jazz band, literary magazine, musical theater, newspaper, opera, orchestra, outdoor, pep band, photography, political, professional, radio and TV, religious, social, social service, student government, and yearbook. Popular campus events include International Student Festival, Honors Day, and Greek Week.

Sports: There are 7 intercollegiate sports for men and 7 for women, and 33 intramural sports for men and 33 for women. Facilities include a phys ed complex with 3 gyms, a pool, a diving well, a weight room, indoor and outdoor tennis courts, a climbing wall, a jogging track, exercise rooms, a dance studio, and racquetball courts; the Indian Creek recreation area with a pool, 3 tennis courts, picnic facilities, regular and sand volleyball, basketball courts, and a rope challenge course; and the Panthersville Road athletic fields.

Disabled Students: All of the campus is accessible. Wheelchair ramps, elevators, special parking, specially equipped rest rooms, special class scheduling, lowered drinking fountains, and lowered telephones are available.

Services: Counseling and information services are available, as is tutoring in most subjects. There is a reader service for the blind, and remedial math, reading, and writing. Programs are available in effective studying, reading comprehension, speed reading, test and note taking, test anxiety, fear of public speaking, and organization and planning.

Campus Safety and Security: Measures include 24-hour foot and vehicle patrol, self-defense education, security escort services, and shuttle buses. There are informal discussions, pamphlets/posters/films, emergency telephones, lighted pathways/sidewalks, 24-hour security at university housing, and a bicycle patrol.

Programs of Study: Georgia State confers B.A., B.S., B.B.A., B.F.A., B.I.S., B.M., B.S.Ed., and B.S.W. degrees. Master's and doctoral degrees are also awarded. Bachelor's degrees are awarded in BIOLOGICAL SCIENCE (biology/biological science and nutrition), BUSINESS (accounting, banking and finance, business administration and management, business economics, hospitality management services, human resources, insurance and risk management, management information systems, marketing/retailing/merchandising, real estate, and recreation and leisure services), COMMUNICATIONS AND THE ARTS (art, classics, dance, dramatic arts, English, film arts, fine arts, French, German, journalism, music, Spanish, speech/debate/rhetoric, and studio art), COMPUTER AND PHYSICAL SCIENCE (actuarial science, chemistry, computer science, geology, mathematics, and physics), EDUCATION (art, early childhood, health, and middle school), HEALTH PROFESSIONS (medical technology, nursing, and respiratory therapy), SOCIAL SCIENCE (anthropology, criminal justice, economics, geography, history, interdisciplinary studies, philosophy, physical fitness/movement, political science/government, psychology, religion, social work, sociology, and ur-

ban studies). Management, computer science, and psychology are the largest.

Required: Students must complete distribution requirements, including courses in humanities, natural science and math, and social science. A minimum of 120 hours must be completed for graduation with a minimum GPA of 2.0.

Special: There is cross-registration with the University Center in Georgia. Internships with numerous employers and government agencies can be arranged. Study abroad is available in western Europe, Mexico, Israel, the former Soviet Union, and Canada. Work-study, student-designed majors, and pass/fail options are available. The Summer Scholar program allows high school seniors to take college-level course work. There is a freshman honors program.

Faculty/Classroom: 57% of faculty are male; 43%, female.

Admissions: 57% of the 2003-2004 applicants were accepted. The SAT I scores for the 2003-2004 freshman class were: Verbal--32% below 500, 47% between 500 and 599, 19% between 600 and 700, and 2% above 700; Math--29% below 500, 49% between 500 and 599, 20% between 600 and 700, and 2% above 700. The ACT scores were 40% below 21, 31% between 21 and 23, 20% between 24 and 26, 8% between 27 and 28, and 1% above 28. 46% of the current freshmen were in the top fifth of their class; 86% were in the top two fifths.

Requirements: The SAT I or ACT is required with preferred scores on the SAT I of 500 verbal and 500 math; on the ACT of 22 English and 22 math. Applicants must graduate from a regionally accredited high school. A total of 16 academic credits is required. Students should prepare with 4 years each of English and math, 3 years each of science and social science, and 2 years of the same foreign language. AP and CLEP credits are accepted. Important factors in the admissions decision are evidence of special talent, advanced placement or honor courses, and extracurricular activities record.

Procedure: Freshmen are admitted fall, spring, and summer. Entrance exams should be taken during the first semester of the senior year. There is an early admissions plan. There is a rolling admissions plan. Applications should be filed by March 1 for fall entry, October 1 for spring entry, and March 1 for summer entry, along with a $50 fee. Notification is sent on a rolling basis. Applications are accepted on-line.

Transfer: 3923 transfer students enrolled in 2002-2003. Transfer applicants must submit official transcripts of all college-level work, have a minimum GPA of 2.5, have earned 30 semester hours, and be in good academic standing. Those with fewer than 30 semester hours earned must meet freshman requirements. 39 of 120 credits required for the bachelor's degree must be completed at Georgia State.

Visiting: There are guides for informal visits and visitors may sit in on classes. To schedule a visit, contact Susan Goodroe, Welcome Center at (404) 651-3900 or sgoodroe@gsu.edu.

Financial Aid: In 2003-2004, 77% of all full-time freshmen and 68% of continuing full-time students received some form of financial aid. 33% of full-time freshmen and 41% of continuing full-time students received need-based aid. The average freshman award was $7798. Need-based scholarships or need-based grants averaged $3309 ($4050 maximum); need-based self-help aid (loans and jobs) averaged $5226 ($8625 maximum); non-need-based athletic scholarships averaged $8475 ($24,216 maximum); and other non-need-based awards and non-need-based scholarships averaged $3874 ($16,597 maximum). Average annual earnings from campus work are $2126. The average financial indebtedness of the 2003 graduate was $19,861. Georgia State is a member of CSS. The FAFSA and the college's own financial statement are required. The priority date for freshman financial aid applications for fall entry is April 1. The deadline for filing freshman financial aid applications for fall entry is November 1.

International Students: There are 811 international students enrolled. The school actively recruits these students. They must score 550 on the written TOEFL or 213 on the electronic version and also take the college's own test and also take the SAT I, scoring 830, or the ACT.

Computers: The mainframe is an IBM 2003-124 with an OS390 operating system. There are 722 workstations in 10 PC labs. All PCs are networked for Internet access using Enterprise software. All students may access the system 24 hours per day. There are no time limits and no fees.

Graduates: The most popular majors were management (8%), psychology (8%), and marketing/computer information systems (7%). In an average class, 1% graduate in 3 years or less, 13% graduate in 4 years or less, 31% graduate in 5 years or less, and 32% graduate in 6 years or less.

Admissions Contact: Diane M. Weber, Director of Admissions.
E-mail: admissions@gsu.edu Web: www.gsu.edu

KENNESAW STATE UNIVERSITY
B-2

Kennesaw, GA 30144-5591 (770) 423-6300; Fax: (770) 423-6541

Full-time: 3983 men, 6062 women	**Faculty:** 442; IIA, av$
Part-time: 1911 men, 3633 women	**Ph.D.s:** 74%
Graduate: 763 men, 1133 women	**Student/Faculty:** 23 to 1
Year: semesters, summer session	**Tuition:** $2724 ($9360)
Application Deadline: see profile	**Room & Board:** n/av
Freshman Class: 5738 applied, 4035 accepted, 2190 enrolled	
SAT I Verbal/Math: 539/535	**COMPETITIVE**

Kennesaw State University, founded in 1963, is a public college in the University System of Georgia. There are 6 undergraduate and 4 graduate schools. In addition to regional accreditation, Kennesaw State has baccalaureate program accreditation with AACSB, NASM, NCATE, and NLN. The library contains 550,000 volumes, 1,723,000 microform items, and 9500 audio/video tapes/CDs, and subscribes to 4202 periodicals. Computerized library services include the card catalog, interlibrary loans, and database searching. Special learning facilities include a learning resource center and art gallery. The 185-acre campus is in a suburban area 25 miles north of Atlanta. Including any residence halls, there are 25 buildings.

Student Life: 96% of undergraduates are from Georgia. Students are from 31 states, 129 foreign countries, and Canada. 80% are white; 11% African American. The average age of freshmen is 21; all undergraduates, 25. 30% do not continue beyond their first year.

Housing: 1058 students can be accommodated in college housing, which includes coed on-campus apartments. On-campus housing is available on a first-come, first-served basis. 94% of students commute. Alcohol is not permitted. All students may keep cars.

Activities: 1% of men belong to 3 national fraternities; 7% of women belong to 6 national sororities. There are 112 groups on campus, including art, band, cheerleading, choir, chorale, chorus, computers, drama, ethnic, gay, honors, international, jazz band, literary magazine, newspaper, opera, pep band, political, professional, religious, social, social service, student government, symphony, and yearbook. Popular campus events include KSU Day, Black History Month, and KSU Turkey Trot.

Sports: There are 4 intercollegiate sports for men and 4 for women, and 16 intramural sports for men and 16 for women. Facilities include a gym, a pool, tennis and racquetball courts, and baseball, softball, and soccer fields.

Disabled Students: All of the campus is accessible. Wheelchair ramps, elevators, special parking, specially equipped rest rooms, special class scheduling, lowered drinking fountains, lowered telephones, marked crosswalks with curb cuts, adapted computer equipment with voice synthesizer, a voice-activated computer, screen-enlarging programs, a swimming pool lift, microfilm and microfiche facilities for wheelchair-bound and blind students, a brailler, and enlarged-print machines are available.

Services: Counseling and information services are available, as is tutoring in some subjects, including math, foreign languages, and English. There is a reader service for the blind, and remedial math, reading, and writing.

Campus Safety and Security: Measures include 24-hour foot and vehicle patrol, self-defense education, security escort services, and informal discussions. There are pamphlets/posters/films, emergency telephones, and lighted pathways/sidewalks.

Programs of Study: Kennesaw State confers B.A., B.S., B.B.A., B.F.A., and B.M. degrees. Master's degrees are also awarded. Bachelor's degrees are awarded in BIOLOGICAL SCIENCE (biochemistry, biology/biological science, and biotechnology), BUSINESS (accounting, banking and finance, business economics, management science, marketing/retailing/merchandising, purchasing/inventory management, and sports management), COMMUNICATIONS AND THE ARTS (art, communications, dramatic arts, English, French, music, music performance, and Spanish), COMPUTER AND PHYSICAL SCIENCE (chemistry, computer science, information sciences and systems, and mathematics), EDUCATION (art, early childhood, elementary, English, foreign languages, health, mathematics, middle school, music, physical, science, and social studies), HEALTH PROFESSIONS (nursing), SOCIAL SCIENCE (criminal justice, geography, history, human services, international studies, political science/government, psychology, and sociology). Business, psychology, and education are the strongest academically. Business and education are the largest.

Required: Requirements vary by degree program. Generally, all students must complete 123 semester hours, including 45 to 47 in core curriculum courses and 39 in upper-level courses, with a minimum GPA of 2.0 and grades of C or better in the major and in required English courses. Students must also successfully complete the University System of Georgia Regents' Testing Program and demonstrate (by course or exam) competency in the history and constitutions of the United States and Georgia. 3 hours of Fitness for Living is also required.

Special: Students may register for courses with any of the colleges in the University System of Georgia, study abroad in 2 countries, and participate in work-study programs and internships, some with pass/fail options. Dual majors and nondegree programs also are offered. There are

23 national honor societies, a freshman honors program, and 7 departmental honors programs.

Faculty/Classroom: 50% of faculty are male; 50%, female. 10% both teach and do research. No introductory courses are taught by graduate students. The average class size in an introductory lecture is 38; in a laboratory, 32; and in a regular course, 32.

Admissions: 70% of the 2003-2004 applicants were accepted. The SAT I scores for the 2003-2004 freshman class were: Verbal--35% below 500, 48% between 500 and 599, 16% between 600 and 700, and 1% above 700; Math--40% below 500, 46% between 500 and 599, 13% between 600 and 700, and 1% above 700.

Requirements: The SAT I or ACT is required, with SAT I scores of at least 510 verbal and 470 math, or ACT scores of at least 22 English and 20 math. Applicants should be graduates of accredited secondary schools or have the GED. Secondary preparation should include 4 units each of English and math, 3 each of social science and science, and 2 of a foreign language. A GPA of 2.5 is required. AP and CLEP credits are accepted. Important factors in the admissions decision are advanced placement or honor courses, ability to finance college education, and recommendations by alumni.

Procedure: Freshmen are admitted fall, spring, and summer. Entrance exams should be taken before June 1. Check with the school for current application deadlines. The fall 2003 application fee was $40. Notification is sent on a rolling basis. Applications are accepted on-line.

Transfer: 1278 transfer students enrolled in a recent year. Applicants should have completed 30 semester hours with a GPA of 2.0 or above; those with a lower GPA may be admitted on probation. Grades of D or better (C or better in English) may be transferred by those with a 2.0 cumulative GPA. Students with fewer than 30 hours of credit must meet freshman requirements. 30 of 123 credits required for the bachelor's degree must be completed at Kennesaw State.

Visiting: There are regularly scheduled orientations for prospective students, including Insight Sessions every Tuesday at 4 P.M. and special visits for adult students. There are guides for informal visits. To schedule a visit, contact the Admissions Office at ksuadmit@kennesaw.edu.

Financial Aid: The FAFSA is required. The deadline for filing freshman financial aid applications for fall entry is March 31.

International Students: There are 1472 international students enrolled. The school actively recruits these students. They must score 173 on the electronic TOEFL or take ESL level 109. They must also take the SAT I or the ACT.

Computers: The mainframe is a CDC Cyber 850. There are also 78 networked PCs in an open lab that can access mainframes available to all state institutions. Computers may be used for any work associated with instruction. All students may access the system 24 hours a day. There are no time limits and no fees.

Graduates: In a recent year, 1646 bachelor's degrees were awarded. The most popular majors were early childhood education (12%), management (10%), and communication (7%).

Admissions Contact: Joe F. Head, Dean of Enrollment Services. A video is available. E-mail: ksuadmit@ksumail.kennesaw.edu Web: www.kennesaw.edu

LAGRANGE COLLEGE
A-3

LaGrange, GA 30240 (706) 880-8253
(800) 593-2885; Fax: (706) 880-8010

Full-time: 335 men, 515 women	**Faculty:** 66; IIB, av$
Part-time: 35 men, 86 women	**Ph.D.s:** 78%
Graduate: 16 men, 33 women	**Student/Faculty:** 13 to 1
Year: 4-1-4, summer session	**Tuition:** $14,482
Application Deadline: open	**Room & Board:** $6018
Freshman Class: 549 applied, 440 accepted, 181 enrolled	
SAT I Verbal/Math: 525/500	**ACT:** 22 **COMPETITIVE**

LaGrange College, founded in 1831, is a private liberal arts institution affiliated with the United Methodist Church. Major undergraduate programs include business, art, education, biology, and psychology. In addition to regional accreditation, LaGrange has baccalaureate program accreditation with ACBSP and NLN. The library contains 138,799 volumes, 171,946 microform items, and 3354 audio/video tapes/CDs, and subscribes to 527 periodicals. Computerized library services include the card catalog, interlibrary loans, database searching, and Internet access. Special learning facilities include a learning resource center, art gallery, 2 music technology labs, and a performing arts theater. The 85-acre campus is in a small town 70 miles southwest of Atlanta. Including any residence halls, there are 22 buildings.

Student Life: 86% of undergraduates are from Georgia. Students are from 13 states and 13 foreign countries. 60% are from public schools. 79% are white; 15% African American. 49% are Protestant; 31% claim no religious affiliation. The average age of freshmen is 19; all undergraduates, 21. 12% do not continue beyond their first year; 68% remain to graduate.

Housing: 642 students can be accommodated in college housing, which includes single-sex and coed dorms and on-campus apartments.

On-campus housing is guaranteed for all 4 years. 52% of students live on campus; of those, 50% remain on campus on weekends. Alcohol is not permitted. All students may keep cars.

Activities: 35% of men belong to 3 national fraternities; 30% of women belong to 4 national sororities. There are 48 groups on campus, including art, cheerleading, choir, drama, ethnic, film, honors, international, jazz band, literary magazine, opera, photography, political, professional, religious, social, social service, student government, and yearbook. Popular campus events include Family Weekend, Greek Week, and Celebrate the Servant Week.

Sports: There are 6 intercollegiate sports for men and 6 for women, and 7 intramural sports for men and 7 for women. Facilities include a fitness center, West Point Lake, an auditorium, indoor and outdoor pools, 3 gyms, 10 lighted tennis courts, and lighted softball, baseball, and soccer fields.

Disabled Students: 75% of the campus is accessible. Wheelchair ramps, elevators, special parking, specially equipped rest rooms, special class scheduling, and lowered drinking fountains are available.

Services: Counseling and information services are available, as is tutoring in most subjects.

Campus Safety and Security: Measures include 24-hour foot and vehicle patrol, pamphlets/posters/films, lighted pathways/sidewalks, and and safety awareness seminars during freshman orientation.

Programs of Study: LaGrange confers B.A., B.S., B.B.A., and B.S.N. degrees. Associate and master's degrees are also awarded. Bachelor's degrees are awarded in BIOLOGICAL SCIENCE (biochemistry and biology/biological science), BUSINESS (accounting, and business administration and management), COMMUNICATIONS AND THE ARTS (art, dramatic arts, English, fine arts, music, music performance, music technology, and Spanish), COMPUTER AND PHYSICAL SCIENCE (chemistry, computer science, and mathematics), EDUCATION (early childhood and middle school), HEALTH PROFESSIONS (nursing, predentistry, and premedicine), SOCIAL SCIENCE (history, human services, political science/government, prelaw, psychology, religion, religious music, and social work). Business administration, human services, and nursing are the largest.

Required: To graduate, all students must complete 108 semester hours, including 60 in the major. The core curriculum includes Freshman Cornerstone, rhetoric and compostion, math, world languages and cultures, natural science, laboratory science, quantitative reasoning, humanities, fine arts, religion, and the American experience. All students must have a minimum GPA of 2.0.

Special: Internships are offered in business, social work, and political science, including positions in a congressional office in Washington. Students may study abroad in Ireland, Great Britain, Japan, France. There is an accelerated degree program in organizational leadership. A 3-2 engineering degree is offered with Georgia Institute of Technology and Auburn University. There are 12 national honor societies, a freshman honors program, and 8 departmental honors programs.

Faculty/Classroom: 56% of faculty are male; 44%, female. All teach undergraduates and 30% both teach and do research. No introductory courses are taught by graduate students. The average class size in an introductory lecture is 13; in a laboratory, 16; and in a regular course, 11.

Admissions: 80% of the 2003-2004 applicants were accepted. The SAT I scores for the 2003-2004 freshman class were: Verbal--38% below 500, 42% between 500 and 599, 19% between 600 and 700, and 1% above 700; Math--46% below 500, 38% between 500 and 599, and 16% between 600 and 700. The ACT scores were 41% below 21, 26% between 21 and 23, 17% between 24 and 26, and 16% between 27 and 28.

Requirements: The SAT I or ACT is required. In addition, applicants should be graduates of accredited secondary schools or have a GED certificate. They should have completed a minimum of 4 units of English, 3 of social studies, and 2 each of math and science. A GPA of 2.5 is required. AP credits are accepted. Important factors in the admissions decision are extracurricular activities record, personality/intangible qualities, and leadership record.

Procedure: Freshmen are admitted to all sessions. Application deadlines are open. Application fee is $20.

Transfer: Transfer students must have a minimum 2.0 GPA and be in good standing with the previous college. 65 of 108 credits required for the bachelor's degree must be completed at LaGrange.

Visiting: There are regularly scheduled orientations for prospective students, including admissions workshops, a student panel, and a guided tour of the campus. There are guides for informal visits and visitors may sit in on classes and stay overnight. To schedule a visit, contact the Admission Office at (706) 880-8005 or lgcadmis@lagrange.edu.

Financial Aid: In 2003-2004, 97% of all full-time freshmen and 87% of continuing full-time students received some form of financial aid. 67% of full-time freshmen and 40% of continuing full-time students received need-based aid. The average freshman award was $12,906. Need-based scholarships or need-based grants averaged $15,518 ($25,220 maximum); need-based self-help aid (loans and jobs) averaged $6177 ($18,500 maximum); and non-need-based awards and non-need-based

scholarships averaged $6990 ($23,260 maximum). 28% of undergraduates work part time. Average annual earnings from campus work are $3000. The average financial indebtedness of the 2003 graduate was $15,972. The FAFSA and the college's own financial statement are required. The deadline for filing freshman financial aid applications for fall entry is May 1.

International Students: There are 24 international students enrolled. The school actively recruits these students. They must score 500 on the written TOEFL.

Computers: The mainframe consists of Dell Rackmount Poweredge Servers. Computers are networked via underground fiber-optic cables to dorm rooms and 11 computer labs, with more than 175 terminals available. All students may access the system 24 hours a day. There are no time limits and no fees.

Graduates: From July 1, 2002 to June 30, 2003, 174 bachelor's degrees were awarded. The most popular majors were business (32%), visual and performing arts (14%), and nursing (9%). In an average class, 31% graduate in 4 years or less, 45% graduate in 5 years or less, and 47% graduate in 6 years or less. 10 companies recruited on campus in 2002-2003.

Admissions Contact: Andy Geeter, Director of Admission. E-mail: ageeter@lagrange.edu Web: www.lagrange.edu

MERCER UNIVERSITY   C-3
Macon, GA 31207-0001   (478) 301-2650
(800) 840-8577; Fax: (478) 301-2828

Full-time: 1316 men, 2510 women	Faculty: 282; IIA, av$
Part-time: 207 men, 547 women	Ph.Ds: 92%
Graduate: 990 men, 1630 women	Student/Faculty: 14 to 1
Year: semesters, summer session	Tuition: $20,796
Application Deadline: July 1	Room & Board: $6720
Freshman Class: n/av	
ACT: 28	VERY COMPETITIVE+

Mercer University, founded in 1833, is a private institution affiliated with the Georgia Baptist Convention. The university offers degree programs in liberal arts, business and economics, education, engineering, and professional studies. Mercer also offers a Great Books program as an alternative to the traditional core curriculum. Faculty information in the above capsule is approximate. There are 5 undergraduate and 7 graduate schools. In addition to regional accreditation, Mercer has baccalaureate program accreditation with ABET, CSAB, and NASM. The 2 libraries contain 418,865 volumes, 3,055,812 microform items, and 57,166 audio/video tapes/CDs. Computerized library services include the card catalog, interlibrary loans, and database searching. Special learning facilities include a learning resource center. The 130-acre campus is in a suburban area 85 miles south of Atlanta. Including any residence halls, there are 58 buildings.

Student Life: 77% of undergraduates are from Georgia. Students are from 35 states, 48 foreign countries, and Canada. 73% are white; 19% African American. 62% are Protestant; 19% claim no religious affiliation; 9% Catholic. The average age of freshmen is 18; all undergraduates, 20. 24% do not continue beyond their first year.

Housing: 1208 students can be accommodated in college housing, which includes single-sex and coed dorms, on-campus apartments, married-student housing, fraternity houses, and sorority houses. On-campus housing is guaranteed for the freshman year only, is available on a first-come, first-served basis, and is available on a lottery system for upperclassmen. Priority is given to out-of-town students. 60% of students live on campus; of those, 70% remain on campus on weekends. Alcohol is not permitted. All students may keep cars.

Activities: 15% of men belong to 9 national fraternities; 20% of women belong to 1 local and 7 national sororities. There are 65 groups on campus, including bagpipe band, band, cheerleading, chess, choir, chorale, chorus, computers, dance, debate, drama, ethnic, honors, international, jazz band, literary magazine, musical theater, newspaper, opera, pep band, political, professional, religious, social, social service, student government, and yearbook. Popular campus events include Pilgrimage to Penfield, Spring Concert, and Family Weekend.

Sports: There are 7 intercollegiate sports for men and 7 for women, and 10 intramural sports for men and 10 for women. Facilities include 2 gyms, 3 playing fields, a student center, a swimming pool, a 30-station fitness trail, a lighted intramural complex, and tennis, volleyball, and racquetball courts.

Disabled Students: 85% of the campus is accessible. Wheelchair ramps, elevators, special parking, specially equipped rest rooms, special class scheduling, lowered drinking fountains, lowered telephones, and assistance with registration are available.

Services: Counseling and information services are available, as is tutoring in most subjects. There is a reader service for the blind, and remedial math, reading, and writing.

Campus Safety and Security: Measures include 24-hour foot and vehicle patrol, self-defense education, security escort services, and shuttle buses. There are informal discussions, pamphlets/posters/films, emergency telephones, lighted pathways/sidewalks, and external CCTV cameras monitored by the police department.

Programs of Study: Mercer confers B.A., B.S., B.B.A., B.M., B.M.D., B.M.E., B.S.E., B.S.M., and B.S.N. degrees. Master's and doctoral degrees are also awarded. Bachelor's degrees are awarded in BIOLOGICAL SCIENCE (biology/biological science), BUSINESS (accounting, banking and finance, business administration and management, and marketing/retailing/merchandising), COMMUNICATIONS AND THE ARTS (English, French, German, Greek, Latin, music, and Spanish), COMPUTER AND PHYSICAL SCIENCE (chemistry, computer science, mathematics, natural sciences, and physics), EDUCATION (early childhood, elementary, music, secondary, and special), ENGINEERING AND ENVIRONMENTAL DESIGN (biomedical engineering, electrical/electronics engineering, environmental engineering, industrial engineering, and mechanical engineering), HEALTH PROFESSIONS (predentistry, premedicine, and prepharmacy), SOCIAL SCIENCE (economics, history, philosophy, political science/government, prelaw, psychology, religion, social science, and sociology). Engineering, chemistry, and English are the strongest academically. Business, English, and engineering are the largest.

Required: To graduate, all students must complete at least 120 to 128 semester hours with a minimum GPA of 2.0.

Special: Mercer offers co-op programs in all majors, cross-registration with Wesleyan and Macon State Colleges, B.A.-B.S. degrees in various science and math fields, internships, student-designed majors, work-study programs, and satisfactory-unsatisfactory options for elective courses. Students may study abroad in Spain, France, Great Britain, Australia, Hong Kong, and Morocco. There are 2 national honor societies, a freshman honors program, and 20 departmental honors programs.

Faculty/Classroom: 61% of faculty are male; 39%, female. All teach undergraduates. No introductory courses are taught by graduate students. The average class size in an introductory lecture is 21; in a laboratory, 15; and in a regular course, 17.

Requirements: The SAT I or ACT is required. In addition, applicants must be graduates of an accredited secondary school and have completed 16 academic units. Students should submit their transcript and class rank, a recommendation from a guidance counselor, and a list of extracurricular activities, including employment. A GPA of 3.0 is required. AP and CLEP credits are accepted. Important factors in the admissions decision are advanced placement or honor courses, extracurricular activities record, and evidence of special talent.

Procedure: Freshmen are admitted to all sessions. Entrance exams should be taken in the spring of the junior year or fall of the senior year. There are early admissions and deferred admissions plans. There is a rolling admissins plan. Applications should be filed by July 1 for fall entry and November 1 for spring entry. Notification of early decision is sent December 1; regular decision, on a rolling basis.

Transfer: 132 transfer students enrolled in a recent year. A minimum GPA of 2.0 is required for all transfer students. Applicants with fewer than 9 semester hours must meet freshman entrance requirements. Those with fewer than 20 semester hours must submit a high school transcript and SAT I or ACT scores. Those with more than 20 semester hours must submit transcripts from all colleges attended and be in good academic standing at their present school, or present evidence of satisfactory work in a previously attended college. 30 of 120 to 128 credits required for the bachelor's degree must be completed at Mercer.

Visiting: There are regularly scheduled orientations for prospective students, including 26 regional orientation programs in the spring, 3 preorientation sessions during the summer, and a 4-day orientation prior to the beginning of classes. There are guides for informal visits and visitors may sit in on classes and stay overnight. To schedule a visit, contact the Office of Admissions.

Financial Aid: The FAFSA and the college's own financial statement are required. The deadline for filing freshman financial aid applications for fall entry is April 1.

International Students: The school actively recruits these students. They must score 550 on the written TOEFL or take Mercer's ELI exit examination. They must also take the SAT I, scoring 800, or the ACT.

Computers: The mainframes are comprised of DEC 2100 and VAX 4000 models. Terminals are located in designated public and departmental student computer labs, and they can be accessed from off campus. All students may access the system 24 hours per day if they have dial-in access. There are no time limits and no fees. It is strongly recommended that all students have a personal computer.

Graduates: In a recent year, 900 bachelor's degrees were awarded.

Admissions Contact: Allen S. London, Vice President for University Admissions. A video is available. E-mail: *admissions@mercer.edu* Web: *www.mercer.edu*

MOREHOUSE COLLEGE
B-2
Atlanta, GA 30314
(404) 215-2632
(800) 851-1254; Fax: (404) 524-5635

Full-time: 2716 men	Faculty: 172; IIB, av$
Part-time: 143 men	Ph.D.s: 74%
Graduate: none	Student/Faculty: 16 to 1
Year: semesters, summer session	Tuition: $14,310
Application Deadline: February 15	Room & Board: $8418
Freshman Class: 2196 applied, 1605 accepted, 742 enrolled	
SAT I Verbal/Math: 520/530	ACT: 21 COMPETITIVE

Morehouse College, founded in 1867, is a private men's liberal arts college offering undergraduate programs in the arts and humanities, natural sciences and math, and social sciences and business. In addition to regional accreditation, Morehouse has baccalaureate program accreditation with AACSB. The library contains 550,000 volumes, 15,000 microform items, and 8000 audio/video tapes/CDs, and subscribes to 110 periodicals. Computerized library services include the card catalog, interlibrary loans, and database searching. Special learning facilities include a learning resource center and an academic support center. The 61-acre campus is in an urban area 3 miles southwest of downtown Atlanta. Including any residence halls, there are 36 buildings.

Student Life: 77% of undergraduates are from out of state, mostly the South. Students are from 45 states and 14 foreign countries. 80% are from public schools. 93% are African American. Most are Protestant. The average age of freshmen is 18; all undergraduates, 20. 16% do not continue beyond their first year; 55% remain to graduate.

Housing: 1676 students can be accommodated in college housing, which includes single-sex dorms and on-campus apartments. On-campus housing is guaranteed for the freshman year only, is available on a first-come, first-served basis, and is available on a lottery system for upperclassmen. 55% of students live on campus; of those, all remain on campus on weekends. Alcohol is not permitted. Upperclassmen may keep cars.

Activities: 7% of men belong to 5 national fraternities. There are no sororities. There are 60 groups on campus, including band, chess, choir, chorus, computers, dance, debate, drama, ethnic, glee club, honors, international, jazz band, literary magazine, marching band, musical theater, newspaper, political, professional, religious, social, social service, speech, student government, and yearbook. Popular campus events include Founders Day, Religious Emphasis Week, and Parents Weekend.

Sports: Facilities include a comprehensive health and phys ed center, a 9000-seat football stadium, a track, and a 5700-seat basketball arena.

Disabled Students: 85% of the campus is accessible. Wheelchair ramps, elevators, special parking, specially equipped rest rooms, lowered drinking fountains, and lowered telephones are available.

Services: Counseling and information services are available, as is tutoring in most subjects. There is remedial math, reading, and writing.

Campus Safety and Security: Measures include 24-hour foot and vehicle patrol, security escort services, shuttle buses, and informal discussions. There are pamphlets/posters/films and lighted pathways/sidewalks.

Programs of Study: Morehouse confers B.A. and B.S. degrees. Bachelor's degrees are awarded in BIOLOGICAL SCIENCE (biology/biological science), BUSINESS (accounting, banking and finance, business administration and management, and marketing/retailing/merchandising), COMMUNICATIONS AND THE ARTS (art, English, French, German, music, and Spanish), COMPUTER AND PHYSICAL SCIENCE (chemistry, computer science, mathematics, and physics), EDUCATION (physical), SOCIAL SCIENCE (African American studies, economics, history, international relations, philosophy, political science/government, psychology, religion, sociology, and urban studies). Engineering, business administration, and English are the strongest academically. Business administration, psychology, and computer science are the largest.

Required: Students must complete a minimum of 120 semester hours, including 53 hours in general studies, plus 8 noncredit hours in Freshman Orientation and College Assembly. A 2.0 GPA is required, with no grade below C in the major.

Special: Morehouse is a member of the Atlanta University Center; students may register for courses and even complete a major in any of the 6 member institutions. In addition, students may study abroad in Europe or Africa. A dual-degree program is offered in architecture with the University of Michigan and in engineering with Columbia, Dartmouth, Georgia Tech, Rensselaer, and other schools; students in these programs are offered summer internships. Work study is also available. There are 6 national honor societies, including Phi Beta Kappa, a freshman honors program, and 10 departmental honors programs.

Faculty/Classroom: 71% of faculty are male; 29%, female. All teach undergraduates and 20% do research. The average class size in an introductory lecture is 25; in a laboratory, 30; and in a regular course, 20.

Admissions: 73% of the 2003-2004 applicants were accepted. The SAT I scores for the 2003-2004 freshman class were: Verbal--39% below 500, 40% between 500 and 599, 18% between 600 and 700, and 3% above 700; Math--38% below 500, 42% between 500 and 599, 18% be-

tween 600 and 700, and 2% above 700. The ACT scores were 48% below 21, 24% between 21 and 23, 16% between 24 and 26, 6% between 27 and 28, and 6% above 28. 34% of the current freshmen were in the top fifth of their class; 68% were in the top two fifths. 1 freshman graduated first in the class.

Requirements: The SAT I or ACT is required. The minimum SAT I composite score is 1000. In addition, applicants should be graduates of accredited secondary schools or have the GED. Secondary preparation should include 4 units in English, 3 in math, 2 each in natural and social sciences, and 5 in other disciplines. Applicants must write an essay and are urged to seek an interview. A GPA of 2.8 is required. AP and CLEP credits are accepted. Important factors in the admissions decision are advanced placement or honor courses, leadership record, and recommendations by school officials.

Procedure: Freshmen are admitted fall and spring. Entrance exams should be taken by the fall of the senior year. There are early decision and deferred admissions plans. Early decision applications should be filed by November 15; regular applications, by February 15 for fall entry and October 15 for spring entry. Notification of early decision is sent December 1; regular decision, March 1. A waiting list is an active part of the admissions procedure. Applications are accepted on-line through *www.morehouse.edu.*.

Transfer: Transfer applicants must have at least a 2.5 GPA and a minimum of 26 semester hours of credit. 64 of 120 credits required for the bachelor's degree must be completed at Morehouse.

Visiting: There are regularly scheduled orientations for prospective students. There are guides for informal visits and visitors may sit in on classes. To schedule a visit, contact the Admissions Office.

Financial Aid: In 2003-2004, 51% of all full-time freshmen and 48% of continuing full-time students received some form of financial aid. 49% of full-time freshmen and 39% of continuing full-time students received need-based aid. The average freshman award was $4613. Need-based scholarships or need-based grants averaged $3319 ($6625 maximum); need-based self-help aid (loans and jobs) averaged $2588 ($5528 maximum); non-need-based athletic scholarships averaged $5939 ($9364 maximum); and other non-need-based awards and non-need-based scholarships averaged $5939 ($8403 maximum). 21% of undergraduates work part time. Average annual earnings from campus work are $1500. The average financial indebtedness of the 2003 graduate was $12,000. The FAFSA and the college's own financial statement are required. The deadline for filing freshman financial aid applications for fall entry is April 1.

International Students: There are 100 international students enrolled. The school actively recruits these students. They must score 500 on the written TOEFL.

Computers: PCs are available for student use. All students may access the system.

Graduates: From July 1, 2002 to June 30, 2003, 506 bachelor's degrees were awarded. The most popular majors were business administration (35%), biology (10%), and political science (8%). In an average class, 33% graduate in 4 years or less, 40% graduate in 5 years or less, and 50% graduate in 6 years or less. 60 companies recruited on campus in 2002-2003.

Admissions Contact: Terrance Dixon, Associate Dean, Admissions and Recruitment. E-mail: *tdixon@morehouse.edu*
Web: *www.morehouse.edu*

NORTH GEORGIA COLLEGE AND STATE UNIVERSITY
B-1

Dahlonega, GA 30597

(706) 864-1754
(800) 498-9581; Fax: (706) 864-1478

Full-time: 1265 men, 1880 women	Faculty: n/av
Part-time: 235 men, 566 women	Ph.D.s: 64%
Graduate: 135 men, 436 women	Student/Faculty: n/av
Year: semesters, summer session	Tuition: $2808 ($9444)
Application Deadline: July 1	Room & Board: $4176
Freshman Class: 1793 applied, 1131 accepted, 668 enrolled	
SAT I Verbal/Math: 530/520	ACT: 21 COMPETITIVE

North Georgia College and State University, founded in 1873 as a military college, is today a liberal arts college that is part of the public University System of Georgia. One of 4 colleges in the United States classified as military colleges by the Department of the Army, the school requires all male resident students to join its Corps of Cadets; other students are given an option to join. There are 4 undergraduate schools and 1 graduate school. In addition to regional accreditation, NGCSU has baccalaureate program accreditation with ACBSP, APTA, NCATE, and NLN. The 2 libraries contain 142,807 volumes, 774,482 microform items, and 3118 audio/video tapes/CDs, and subscribe to 2546 periodicals. Computerized library services include the card catalog, interlibrary loans, database searching, and Internet access. Special learning facilities include an art gallery, planetarium, a math lab, a language lab, and a writing center. The 665-acre campus is in a small town 60 miles north of Atlanta. Including any residence halls, there are 25 buildings.

Student Life: 95% of undergraduates are from Georgia. Students are from 33 states, 8 foreign countries, and Canada. 90% are from public schools. 93% are white. The average age of freshmen is 19; all undergraduates, 22.

Housing: 1200 students can be accommodated in college housing, which includes single-sex dorms and on-campus apartments. On-campus housing is available on a first-come, first-served basis. 69% of students commute. Alcohol is not permitted. All students may keep cars.

Activities: 13% of men belong to 2 local and 4 national fraternities; 10% of women belong to 4 national sororities. There are 52 groups on campus, including band, cheerleading, choir, chorale, chorus, drama, drill team, ethnic, honors, jazz band, literary magazine, marching band, newspaper, pep band, political, professional, religious, student government, symphony, and yearbook. Popular campus events include Spring Jam, Frisbee golf, and military reviews.

Sports: There are 5 intercollegiate sports for men and 6 for women, and 7 intramural sports for men and 7 for women. Facilities include a swimming pool, a track, a fully equipped exercise room, a rappeling tower, a confidence course, a picnic area, a 2000-seat gym, and a 250-seat arena.

Disabled Students: 50% of the campus is accessible. Wheelchair ramps, elevators, special parking, specially equipped rest rooms, and lowered drinking fountains are available.

Services: Counseling and information services are available, as is tutoring in most subjects. There is a reader service for the blind, and remedial math, reading, and writing.

Campus Safety and Security: Measures include 24-hour foot and vehicle patrol, security escort services, informal discussions, and emergency telephones. There are lighted pathways/sidewalks.

Programs of Study: NGCSU confers A.B., B.S., B.B.A., and B.S.N. degrees. Associate and master's degrees are also awarded. Bachelor's degrees are awarded in BIOLOGICAL SCIENCE (biology/biological science), BUSINESS (accounting, banking and finance, business administration and management, business economics, marketing/retailing/merchandising, and recreation and leisure services), COMMUNICATIONS AND THE ARTS (art, arts administration/management, English, French, music, and Spanish), COMPUTER AND PHYSICAL SCIENCE (chemistry, computer science, mathematics, and physics), EDUCATION (art, early childhood, elementary, foreign languages, mathematics, middle school, music, physical, science, secondary, social science, and special), ENGINEERING AND ENVIRONMENTAL DESIGN (preengineering), HEALTH PROFESSIONS (nursing, predentistry, premedicine, prepharmacy, and preveterinary science), SOCIAL SCIENCE (criminal justice, history, political science/government, prelaw, psychology, social science, and sociology). Education and premedicine are the strongest academically. Business and teacher education are the largest.

Required: To graduate, students must complete 120 semester credit hours with a minimum GPA of 2.0. English, math, lab sciences, and social sciences are required.

Special: Special academic programs include a co-op program in business, internships, a 3-2 engineering degree with Georgia Institute of Technology, study abroad in Europe, South America, and Canada, dual majors, and credit for life, military, or work experience. There are 9 national honor societies, including Phi Beta Kappa, a freshman honors program, and 8 departmental honors programs.

Faculty/Classroom: 50% of faculty are male; 50%, female. All teach undergraduates. No introductory courses are taught by graduate students. The average class size in an introductory lecture is 30; in a laboratory, 30; and in a regular course, 30.

Admissions: 63% of the 2003-2004 applicants were accepted. The SAT I scores for the 2003-2004 freshman class were: Verbal--29% below 500, 54% between 500 and 599, 16% between 600 and 700, and 1% above 700; Math--33% below 500, 49% between 500 and 599, 17% between 600 and 700, and 1% above 700. The ACT scores were 39% below 21, 36% between 21 and 23, 18% between 24 and 26, 4% between 27 and 28, and 3% above 28.

Requirements: The SAT I is required. In addition, students must have graduated from a secondary school with 4 years of English, 3 each of math, science, and social science, and 2 of a foreign language. The GED is accepted if granted at least 5 years later than expected high school graduation date. SAT II: Subject tests are required of homeschooled students. A GPA of 2.0 is required. AP and CLEP credits are accepted. Important factors in the admissions decision are leadership record, advanced placement or honor courses, and evidence of special talent.

Procedure: Freshmen are admitted fall, spring, and summer. Entrance exams should be taken in the junior year. There is a deferred admissions plan. Applications should be filed by July 1 for fall entry, December 15 for spring entry, and April 15 for summer entry, along with a $25 fee. Notification is sent on a rolling basis. Applications are accepted on-line through Apply or the NGCSU web site.

Transfer: 270 transfer students enrolled in a recent year. Transfer students must have maintained a C average and a clear conduct record and be in good academic standing. Those who have not completed 90 quarter hours of transferable credit must have completed the approved precollege curriculum and must submit high school transcripts and SAT I or ACT results. 45 of 120 credits required for the bachelor's degree must be completed at NGCSU.

Visiting: There are regularly scheduled orientations for prospective students, including an admissions video, a college overview, a tour, and a meeting with an admissions counselor. There are guides for informal visits and visitors may stay overnight. To schedule a visit, contact the Admissions Office at *admissions@ngcsu.edu*.

Financial Aid: The FAFSA and the college's own financial statement are required. The priority date for freshman financial aid applications for fall entry is March 15. The deadline for filing freshman financial aid applications for fall entry is May 1.

International Students: There were 52 international students enrolled in a recent year. They must score 550 on the written TOEFL or 213 on the electronic version and also take the SAT I or ACT.

Computers: The mainframe is a Dell. PCs are available in the library, NHS building, student center, and dorms. All students may access the system 8 A.M. to 10 P.M. There are no time limits and no fees.

Graduates: From July 1, 2002 to June 30, 2003, 691 bachelor's degrees were awarded. The most popular majors were nursing (16%), early childhood education (10%), and marketing (7%). 71 companies recruited on campus in 2002-2003. Of the 2002 graduating class, 6% were enrolled in graduate school within 6 months of graduation and 48% were employed.

Admissions Contact: Robert LaVerriere, Director of Undergraduate Admissions and Recruiting. A video is available.
E-mail: *rlaverriere@ngcsu.edu* Web: *www.ngcsu.edu*

OGLETHORPE UNIVERSITY
B-2
Atlanta, GA 30319-2797

(404) 364-8307
(800) 428-4484; Fax: (404) 364-8500

Full-time: 279 men, 505 women	Faculty: 56; IIB, av$
Part-time: 50 men, 111 women	Ph.D.s: 96%
Graduate: 20 men, 64 women	Student/Faculty: 14 to 1
Year: semesters, summer session	Tuition: $19,640
Application Deadline: open	Room & Board: $6360
Freshman Class: 746 applied, 492 accepted, 173 enrolled	
SAT I or ACT: required	VERY COMPETITIVE

Oglethorpe University, founded in 1835, is an independent institution offering programs in the liberal arts, business, and teacher preparation. Some information in this capsule and profile is approximate. There are 2 undergraduate and 2 graduate schools. In addition to regional accreditation, Oglethorpe has baccalaureate program accreditation with NCATE. The library contains 125,432 volumes, 4189 microform items, and 6786 audio/video tapes/CDs, and subscribes to 775 periodicals. Computerized library services include the card catalog, interlibrary loans, and database searching. Special learning facilities include a learning resource center, art gallery, and radio station. The 118-acre campus is in a suburban area 10 miles northeast of downtown Atlanta. Including any residence halls, there are 25 buildings.

Student Life: 62% of undergraduates are from Georgia. Students are from 36 states and 21 foreign countries. 74% are from public schools. 65% are white; 20% African American. 50% claim no religious affiliation; 44% Protestant; 12% Catholic. The average age of freshmen is 18; all undergraduates, 20. 19% do not continue beyond their first year; 63% remain to graduate.

Housing: 575 students can be accommodated in college housing, which includes single-sex and coed dorms, fraternity houses, and sorority houses. On-campus housing is available on a first-come, first-served basis. Priority is given to out-of-town students. 56% of students live on campus; of those, 60% remain on campus on weekends. All students may keep cars.

Activities: 41% of men belong to 4 national fraternities; 22% of women belong to 2 national sororities. There are 51 groups on campus, including art, cheerleading, choir, chorale, chorus, computers, dance, drama, ethnic, gay, honors, international, literary magazine, newspaper, pep band, photography, political, professional, radio and TV, religious, social, social service, student government, and yearbook. Popular campus events include Boar's Head Ceremony, Oglethorpe Day, and International Night.

Sports: There are 7 intercollegiate sports for men and 6 for women, and 6 intramural sports for men and 6 for women. Facilities include a field house and recreation center, housing basketball and volleyball courts, a running track, handball courts, and a weight room. Outdoor facilities include 6 tennis courts, an all-weather track, an outdoor swimming pool, a sand volleyball court, and soccer, baseball, and intramural fields.

Disabled Students: 90% of the campus is accessible. Wheelchair ramps, elevators, special parking, specially equipped rest rooms, and special class scheduling are available.

Services: Counseling and information services are available, as is tutoring in most subjects, including all core courses, English, writing, accounting, and any subject.

Campus Safety and Security: Measures include 24-hour foot and vehicle patrol, self-defense education, informal discussions, and pamphlets/posters/films. There are lighted pathways/sidewalks.

Programs of Study: Oglethorpe confers B.A., B.S., and B.B.A. degrees. Master's degrees are also awarded. Bachelor's degrees are awarded in BIOLOGICAL SCIENCE (biology/biological science), BUSINESS (accounting and business administration and management), COMMUNICATIONS AND THE ARTS (art, communications, and English), COMPUTER AND PHYSICAL SCIENCE (chemistry, computer science, mathematics, and physics), EDUCATION (early childhood, middle school, and secondary), SOCIAL SCIENCE (American studies, behavioral science, economics, history, international studies, philosophy, political science/government, psychology, social work, and sociology). Accounting, biology, and English are the strongest academically. Business administration, biology, and communications are the largest.

Required: To graduate, all students must complete at least 120 credit hours, fulfilling a major as well as completing the core curriculum, and achieve a minimum GPA of 2.0. The core curriculum includes course work in writing, literature, Western civilization, math, psychology, philosophy, interdisciplinary social sciences, music or art, physical science, and biological science. All freshmen must complete the first-year experience program.

Special: Oglethorpe offers co-op programs in all majors, cross-registration through the University Center in Georgia, international exchange agreements with several universities in Europe, Asia, and South America, and other study-abroad options. Internships are available in all areas of study, earning up to 15 credit hours for upperclassmen with a minimum 2.8 GPA, and a Washington semester offers internships with Georgia senators and others. There is a dual-degree program with the Atlanta College of Art and a 3-2 engineering program with Georgia Institute of Technology, the Universities of Florida and Southern California, and Auburn University. Accelerated degrees, dual majors, student-designed majors, federal work-study programs, and nondegree study are offered. There are 7 national honor societies.

Faculty/Classroom: 68% of faculty are male; 32%, female. All teach undergraduates. No introductory courses are taught by graduate students. The average class size in an introductory lecture is 20; in a laboratory, 20; and in a regular course, 15.

Admissions: 66% of the 2003-2004 applicants were accepted. The SAT I scores for the 2003-2004 freshman class were: Verbal--12% below 500, 34% between 500 and 599, 40% between 600 and 700, and 14% above 700; Math--21% below 500, 39% between 500 and 599, 34% between 600 and 700, and 6% above 700. The ACT scores were 5% below 21, 29% between 21 and 23, 20% between 24 and 26, 33% between 27 and 28, and 13% above 28. 60% of the current freshmen were in the top fifth of their class; 80% were in the top two fifths.

Requirements: The SAT I or ACT is required, with a minimum recommended composite score of 950 on the SAT I or 21 on the ACT. Students should graduate from an accredited high school or have a GED certificate. They should have completed 4 courses in English, 3 each in science and social studies, and a math sequence of algebra I and II and geometry. A counselor's or teacher's recommendation is required, and an essay is required for a scholarship. An interview is recommended. AP and CLEP credits are accepted. Important factors in the admissions decision are recommendations by school officials, extracurricular activities record, and advanced placement or honor courses.

Procedure: Freshmen are admitted to all sessions. Entrance exams should be taken late in the junior year or early in the senior year. There are early decision, early admissions, and deferred admissions plans. Application deadlines are open. Application fee is $35. 25 early decision candidates were accepted in a recent year. Applications are accepted on computer disk through CollegeLink. Notification is sent on a rolling basis.

Transfer: 104 transfer students enrolled in a recent year. Applicants who have completed less than a full year of college work must take the SAT I or ACT. All transfers must be in good academic standing with a minimum GPA of 2.5. An interview is recommended. 48 of 120 credits required for the bachelor's degree must be completed at Oglethorpe.

Visiting: There are regularly scheduled orientations for prospective students, including placement tests, class registration, an activities fair, and group activities. There are guides for informal visits and visitors may sit in on classes and stay overnight. To schedule a visit, contact the Admissions Office.

Financial Aid: In 2003-2004, 96% of all full-time freshmen and 85% of continuing full-time students received some form of financial aid. 69% of full-time freshmen and 58% of continuing full-time students received need-based aid. The average financial indebtedness of the 2003 graduate was $16,250. Oglethorpe is a member of CSS. The FAFSA is required. Check with the school for current deadlines.

International Students: There are 49 international students enrolled. The school actively recruits these students. They must score 500 on the written TOEFL or demonstrate proficiency in English by other means, and also take the SAT I or ACT.

Computers: The university is served by a local area network. All students are provided e-mail accounts and may access the network and the

Internet on their PCs or through the library or computer labs. All students may access the system. There are no time limits and no fees. It is strongly recommended that all students have a personal computer.

Graduates: From July 1, 2002 to June 30, 2003, 252 bachelor's degrees were awarded. In an average class, 2% graduate in 3 years or less, 53% graduate in 4 years or less, 62% graduate in 5 years or less, and 65% graduate in 6 years or less.

Admissions Contact: David Rhodes, Vice President for Enrollment Management. E-mail: *admission@oglethorpe.edu*
Web: *www.oglethorpe.edu*

PAINE COLLEGE
Augusta, GA 30901-3182

D-2

(706) 821-8320
(800) 476-7703; Fax: (706) 821-8691

Full-time: 242 men, 616 women	**Faculty:** 82
Part-time: 48 men, 66 women	**Ph.D.s:** 51%
Graduate: none	**Student/Faculty:** 10 to 1
Year: semesters, summer session	**Tuition:** $9082
Application Deadline: August 1	**Room & Board:** $3940
Freshman Class: n/av	
SAT I Verbal/Math: 400/380	**ACT:** 15 **LESS COMPETITIVE**

Paine College, founded in 1882, is a largely African-American private institution affiliated with the Christian Methodist Episcopal Church and the United Methodist Church. It offers programs in liberal arts, business, and teacher preparation. In addition to regional accreditation, Paine has baccalaureate program accreditation with ACBSP. The library contains 88,900 volumes, 7000 microform items, and 1300 audio/video tapes/CDs, and subscribes to 5350 periodicals. Computerized library services include the card catalog, interlibrary loans, database searching, and Internet access. Special learning facilities include a learning resource center, art gallery, and tutorial and enrichment center. The 55-acre campus is in an urban area 150 miles east of Atlanta and 72 miles west of Columbia, South Carolina. Including any residence halls, there are 25 buildings.

Student Life: 83% of undergraduates are from Georgia. Students are from 30 states and 3 foreign countries. 98% are African American. 84% are Protestant; 10% claim no religious affiliation. The average age of freshmen is 19; all undergraduates, 23. 38% do not continue beyond their first year; 30% remain to graduate.

Housing: 506 students can be accommodated in college housing, which includes single-sex dorms. On-campus housing is available on a first-come, first-served basis. 58% of students live on campus; of those, 2% remain on campus on weekends. Alcohol is not permitted. All students may keep cars.

Activities: 10% of men belong to 4 national fraternities; 10% of women belong to 4 national sororities. There are 36 groups on campus, including band, cheerleading, choir, chorus, dance, drama, honors, international, literary magazine, marching band, NAACP, newspaper, professional, religious, social, student government, and yearbook. Popular campus events include Miss Paine Coronation, Founders Day, and black history activities.

Sports: There are 4 intercollegiate sports for men and 5 for women, and 7 intramural sports for men and 7 for women. Facilities include a gym, a tennis court, a track, a baseball field, and outside basketball and volleyball courts.

Disabled Students: 60% of the campus is accessible. Wheelchair ramps, elevators, special parking, specially equipped rest rooms, and lowered drinking fountains are available.

Services: Counseling and information services are available, as is tutoring in most subjects. There is remedial math, reading, and writing.

Campus Safety and Security: Measures include 24-hour foot and vehicle patrol, security escort services, informal discussions, and pamphlets/posters/films. There are emergency telephones and lighted pathways/sidewalks.

Programs of Study: Paine confers B.A. and B.S. degrees. Bachelor's degrees are awarded in BIOLOGICAL SCIENCE (biology/biological science), BUSINESS (business administration and management), COMMUNICATIONS AND THE ARTS (communications and English), COMPUTER AND PHYSICAL SCIENCE (chemistry and mathematics), EDUCATION (early childhood, middle school, and secondary), SOCIAL SCIENCE (history, philosophy, psychology, and sociology). Education, natural sciences, and math are the strongest academically. Biology, business, and sociology are the largest.

Required: Common curriculum requirements include 18 hours in world citizenship/society, 14 in science/technology, 8 to 10 in fundamentals, 9 in spiritual and social values, and 6 in the aesthetic heritage. From 33 to 71 hours are required in the major. A minimum GPA of 2.5 in the major is needed. To graduate, at least 124 credits must be completed. A thesis in most programs and comprehensive exams in some programs may also be required.

Special: Paine has co-op programs in natural and social sciences and business administration, cross-registration with Augusta State University and Clark Atlanta University, internships for business administration and

sociology majors, and study abroad in France, Africa, and South America. A 3-2 engineering degree is offered with Tuskegee University. There are transfer programs with the Medical University of South Carolina at Charleston School of Nursing and Medical College of Georgia. There are 2 national honor societies and a freshman honors program.

Faculty/Classroom: 60% of faculty are male; 40%, female. All teach undergraduates. The average class size in an introductory lecture is 25; in a laboratory, 20; and in a regular course, 23.

Admissions: The SAT I scores for the 2003-2004 freshman class were: Verbal--91% below 500, 8% between 500 and 599, and 1% between 600 and 700; Math--87% below 500, 12% between 500 and 599, and 1% between 600 and 700. The ACT scores were 95% below 21, 2% between 21 and 23, 2% between 24 and 26, and 1% between 27 and 28.

Requirements: The SAT I is required. In addition, applicants should be graduates of an accredited secondary school or have a GED. A total of 16 academic credits is required, including 4 units of English, and 3 each of math, social studies, and science. A GPA of 2.0 is required. AP and CLEP credits are accepted. Important factors in the admissions decision are recommendations by school officials, advanced placement or honor courses, and evidence of special talent.

Procedure: Freshmen are admitted to all sessions. Entrance exams should be taken during spring and summer testing sessions; they are also offered during each orientation period. There are early admissions and deferred admissions plans. There is a rolling admissions plan. Applications should be filed by August 1 for fall entry, December 1 for spring entry, and June 1 for summer entry, along with a $20 fee ($35 for international applicants). Notification is sent on a rolling basis. Applications are accepted on-line.

Transfer: 39 transfer students enrolled in 2002-2003. Applicants must meet freshman criteria except for the SAT I requirement if they have attained sophomore or higher status. 30 credits of 124 required for the bachelor's degree must be completed at Paine.

Visiting: There are regularly scheduled orientations for prospective students, including meetings with administrators, tours of the city and campus, and placement testing. There are guides for informal visits and visitors may sit in on classes and stay overnight. To schedule a visit, contact Joe Tinsley, Assistant Director of Admissions at *tinsleyj@mail.paine.edu*.

Financial Aid: In 2003-2004, 90% of all full-time students received some form of financial aid, including need-based aid. 60% of undergraduates work part time. Average annual earnings from campus work are $2000. Paine is a member of CSS. The FAFSA is required. The deadline for filing freshman financial aid applications for fall entry is April 15.

International Students: There are 5 international students enrolled. They must score 500 on the written TOEFL and also take the SAT I.

Computers: The mainframe consists of a Compaq supermicrocomputer and 6 servers. Students access e-mail and the Internet from a lab via student servers in the MIS office. There are 100 PCs and Macs in 3 main labs in the Learning Resource Center, 1 science lab (20 systems), the Tutorial and Enrichment Center (20 systems), 2 business administration division labs (15 to 20 systems each), and some faculty offices. All students may access the system. There are no time limits. The fee is included in the comprehensive fee.

Graduates: From July 1, 2002 to June 30, 2003, 114 bachelor's degrees were awarded. The most popular majors were general sociology (18%), counseling psychology (9%), and biology (7%). In an average class, 13% graduate in 4 years or less, 24% graduate in 5 years or less, and 30% graduate in 6 years or less. 15 companies recruited on campus in 2002-2003. Of the 2002 graduating class, 5% were enrolled in graduate school within 6 months of graduation and 90% were employed.

Admissions Contact: Joseph Tinsley, Director of Admissions.
E-mail: *tinsleyj@mail.paine.edu* Web: *www.paine.edu*

PIEDMONT COLLEGE
Demorest, GA 30535

C-1

(706) 778-3000, ext. 1188
(800) 277-7020; Fax: (706) 776-6635

Full-time: 311 men, 547 women	**Faculty:** 76
Part-time: 61 men, 91 women	**Ph.D.s:** 83%
Graduate: 212 men, 937 women	**Student/Faculty:** 11 to 1
Year: semesters, summer session	**Tuition:** $12,500
Application Deadline: open	**Room & Board:** $4400
Freshman Class: 304 applied, 279 accepted, 154 enrolled	
SAT I Verbal/Math: 510/510	**ACT:** 21 **COMPETITIVE**

Piedmont College, founded in 1897, is a private, liberal arts institution affiliated with the Congregational Christian Churches of America and the United Church of Christ. There are 4 undergraduate schools and 1 graduate school. In addition to regional accreditation, Piedmont has baccalaureate program accreditation with NLN. The library contains 122,000 volumes, 42,406 microform items, and 876 audio/video tapes/CDs, and subscribes to 367 periodicals. Computerized library services include the card catalog, interlibrary loans, and database searching. Special learning facilities include a learning resource center, art gallery, radio station, TV station, the Georgia Youth Science and Technology Center, and an observatory. The 300-acre campus is in a small town 75 miles northeast of Atlanta. Including any residence halls, there are 26 buildings.

Student Life: 94% of undergraduates are from Georgia. Students are from 15 states and 24 foreign countries. 93% are from public schools. 89% are white. 55% are Protestant; 41% claim no religious affiliation. The average age of freshmen is 18; all undergraduates, 25. 27% do not continue beyond their first year; 32% remain to graduate.

Housing: 375 students can be accommodated in college housing, which includes coed dorms. On-campus housing is guaranteed for all 4 years. 63% of students commute. Alcohol is not permitted. All students may keep cars.

Activities: There are no fraternities or sororities. There are 20 groups on campus, including art, cheerleading, choir, chorale, chorus, debate, drama, film, honors, jazz band, musical theater, newspaper, orchestra, professional, radio and TV, religious, social, social service, student government, and yearbook. Popular campus events include Halloween Dance, Spring Formal Dance, and cultural activities.

Sports: There are 5 intercollegiate sports for men and 6 for women, and 5 intramural sports for men and 5 for women. Facilities include a gym, 8 tennis courts, beach volleyball courts, and regulation baseball, softball, and soccer fields.

Disabled Students: 85% of the campus is accessible. Wheelchair ramps, elevators, special parking, specially equipped rest rooms, and special class scheduling are available.

Services: Counseling and information services are available, as is tutoring in some subjects, including most general education courses; such as math, English, biology, Spanish, chemistry, and history.

Campus Safety and Security: Measures include 24-hour foot and vehicle patrol, security escort services, informal discussions, and pamphlets/posters/films. There are emergency telephones, lighted pathways/sidewalks, and campus patrol by the local police department.

Programs of Study: Piedmont confers B.A., B.S., and B.S.N. degrees. Master's degrees are also awarded. Bachelor's degrees are awarded in AGRICULTURE (environmental studies), BIOLOGICAL SCIENCE (biology/biological science), BUSINESS (business administration and management and sports management), COMMUNICATIONS AND THE ARTS (art, communications, dramatic arts, English, music, and Spanish), COMPUTER AND PHYSICAL SCIENCE (chemistry, computer mathematics, mathematics, and science), EDUCATION (early childhood, middle school, and special), ENGINEERING AND ENVIRONMENTAL DESIGN (environmental science), HEALTH PROFESSIONS (nursing), SOCIAL SCIENCE (criminal justice, history, interdisciplinary studies, philosophy, political science/government, psychology, religion, social science, and sociology). Sociology, music, and English are the strongest academically. Education, business administration, and social sciences are the largest.

Required: To graduate, a minimum of 120 credit hours is required, with a minimum GPA of 2.0, or higher in some majors. Students must complete 18 to 55 credit hours in their major, 23 to 26 in humanities, 14 to 18 in math and natural science, 9 in social science, 3 in fine arts, and 3 in computer science.

Special: Piedmont offers internships in business, psychology, education, art management, criminal justice, sociology, and political science, study abroad in 3 countries, and student-designed majors. There are 4 national honor societies, a freshman honors program, and 1 departmental honors program.

Faculty/Classroom: 52% of faculty are male; 48%, female. 80% teach undergraduates. No introductory courses are taught by graduate students. The average class size in an introductory lecture is 18; in a laboratory, 12; and in a regular course, 14.

Admissions: 92% of the 2003-2004 applicants were accepted. The SAT I scores for the 2003-2004 freshman class were: Verbal--47% below 500, 31% between 500 and 599, 21% between 600 and 700, and 1% above 700; Math--46% below 500, 37% between 500 and 599, 16% between 600 and 700, and 1% above 700. The ACT scores were 49% below 21, 31% between 21 and 23, 11% between 24 and 26, 7% between 27 and 28, and 2% above 28. 5% of the current freshmen were in the top fifth of their class; 21% were in the top two fifths.

Requirements: The SAT I or ACT is required. In addition, applicants must be graduates of an accredited secondary school or have a GED certificate. Students must have completed a minimum of 21 academic units. Piedmont Scholars are required to submit an essay. A portfolio is required for art scholarship applicants and an audition for music scholarship applicants. An interview is recommended for all students. A GPA of 2.0 is required. AP and CLEP credits are accepted. Important factors in the admissions decision are leadership record, advanced placement or honor courses, and extracurricular activities record.

Procedure: Freshmen are admitted to all sessions. There is a deferred admissions plan. Application deadlines are open. Notification is sent on a rolling basis.

Transfer: 96 transfer students enrolled in 2002-2003. Applicants must have a GPA of 2.0 at each institution attended. An interview is recommended. 30 of 120 credits required for the bachelor's degree must be completed at Piedmont.

Visiting: There are regularly scheduled orientations for prospective students, consisting of student activities, academic assistance and counseling, resident orientation, and a financial aid presentation. There are guides for informal visits and visitors may sit in on classes and stay overnight. To schedule a visit, contact Jim Clement.

Financial Aid: In 2003-2004, 98% of all full-time freshmen and 93% of continuing full-time students received some form of financial aid. 68% of full-time freshmen and 73% of continuing full-time students received need-based aid. The average freshman award was $5870. Need-based scholarships or need-based grants averaged $1166 ($10,400 maximum); need-based self-help aid (loans and jobs) averaged $1990 ($5313 maximum); and non-need-based awards and non-need-based scholarships averaged $2811 ($14,400 maximum). 87% of undergraduates work part time. Average annual earnings from campus work are $1562. The average financial indebtedness of the 2003 graduate was $9585. The FAFSA and the state aid form are required. The priority date for freshman financial aid applications for fall entry is May 1. The deadline for filing freshman financial aid applications for fall entry is July 1.

International Students: There are 39 international students enrolled. They must score 550 on the written TOEFL or 213 on the electronic version and also take the SAT I or the ACT.

Computers: There are 6 PC labs with 78 computers that connect to the network system, with access to the Internet. All students may access the system more than 90 hours per week. There are no time limits and no fees.

Graduates: From July 1, 2002 to June 30, 2003, 228 bachelor's degrees were awarded. The most popular majors were business administration (27%), early childhood education (25%), and sociology (9%). In an average class, 6% graduate in 3 years or less, 34% graduate in 4 years or less, and 42% graduate in 5 years or less.

Admissions Contact: Jim Clement, Director of Undergraduate Admissions. A video is available. E-mail: jclement@piedmont.edu Web: www.piedmont.edu

REINHARDT COLLEGE
Waleska, GA 30183
B-2
(770) 720-5526
1-87REINHARDT; Fax: (770) 720-5899

Full-time: 379 men, 563 women	**Faculty:** 51
Part-time: 60 men, 82 women	**Ph.D.s:** 39%
Graduate: none	**Student/Faculty:** 18 to 1
Year: semesters, summer session	**Tuition:** $11,150
Application Deadline: open	**Room & Board:** $9600
Freshman Class: 675 applied, 543 accepted, 382 enrolled	
SAT I Verbal/Math: 498/481	**ACT:** 19	COMPETITIVE

Reinhardt College, founded in 1883, is a private institution affiliated with the Methodist Church and offering undergraduate degrees. There are 4 undergraduate schools. The library contains 48,000 volumes, 1983 microform items, and 3598 audio/video tapes/CDs, and subscribes to 315 periodicals. Computerized library services include the card catalog, interlibrary loans, database searching, and Internet access. Special learning facilities include an art gallery, natural history museum, radio station, and TV station. The 600-acre campus is in a small town 40 miles north of Atlanta. Including any residence halls, there are 31 buildings.

Student Life: 98% of undergraduates are from Georgia. Students are from 4 states, 6 foreign countries, and Canada. 90% are from public schools. 82% are white. 70% are Protestant; 23% claim no religious affiliation; 6% Catholic. The average age of freshmen is 18; all undergraduates, 23. 36% do not continue beyond their first year; 50% remain to graduate.

Housing: 404 students can be accommodated in college housing, which includes single-sex dorms. On-campus housing is guaranteed for all 4 years. 64% of students commute. Alcohol is not permitted. All students may keep cars.

Activities: There are no fraternities or sororities. There are 14 groups on campus, including cheerleading, honors, newspaper, professional, radio and TV, religious, social, social service, student government, and yearbook. Popular campus events include Spring Day, Spring Formal, and Diversity Days.

Sports: There are 5 intercollegiate sports for men and 4 for women, and 4 intramural sports for men and 4 for women. Facilities include parks, jogging trails, outdoor volleyball, tennis, and basketball courts, soccer and softball fields, a pool, a weight room, a bowling alley, and racquetball courts.

Disabled Students: 90% of the campus is accessible. Wheelchair ramps, elevators, special parking, specially equipped rest rooms, special class scheduling, and lowered drinking fountains are available.

Services: Counseling and information services are available, as is tutoring in every subject.

Campus Safety and Security: Measures include 24-hour foot and vehicle patrol, self-defense education, and lighted pathways/sidewalks.

Programs of Study: Reinhardt confers B.A., B.S., B.F.A., and B.S.B.A. degrees. Associate degrees are also awarded. Bachelor's degrees are awarded in BIOLOGICAL SCIENCE (biology/biological science), BUSI-

NESS (business administration and management), COMMUNICATIONS AND THE ARTS (communications), SOCIAL SCIENCE (liberal arts/general studies). Business and liberal studies are the largest.

Required: To graduate, students must have a core curriculum in the humanities, math and science, social science, language, phys ed, and wellness. A total of 120 semester hours is required, including 65 in the major. A 2.0 GPA must be maintained.

Special: Internships, study abroad, and work-study programs are available. There is an accelerated degree program in organizational leadership. There is 1 national honor society and a freshman honors program.

Faculty/Classroom: 45% of faculty are male; 55%, female. All teach undergraduates. The average class size in an introductory lecture is 17; in a laboratory, 17; and in a regular course, 17.

Admissions: 80% of the 2003-2004 applicants were accepted. The SAT I scores for the 2003-2004 freshman class were: Verbal--52% below 500, 38% between 500 and 599, 8% between 600 and 700, and 1% above 700; Math--61% below 500, 32% between 500 and 599, 7% between 600 and 700, and 1% above 700. The ACT scores were 73% below 21, 16% between 21 and 23, 10% between 24 and 26, and 1% between 27 and 28. 1 freshman graduated first in the class.

Requirements: The SAT I or ACT is required. In addition, the GED is accepted and a placement test may be required. A GPA of 2.0 is required. AP and CLEP credits are accepted. Important factors in the admissions decision are recommendations by alumni, recommendations by school officials, and parents or siblings attending the school.

Procedure: Freshmen are admitted to all sessions. Entrance exams should be taken before acceptance. There is a rolling admissions plan and an early admissions plan. Application deadlines are open. Application fee is $25. Applications are accepted on-line.

Transfer: 60 transfer students enrolled in 2003-2003. A GPA of 2.0 or better may be considered for transfer applicants. 40 of 120 credits required for the bachelor's degree must be completed at Reinhardt.

Visiting: There are regularly scheduled orientations for prospective students. There are guides for informal visits and visitors may sit in on classes.

Financial Aid: In 2003-2004, 96% of all full-time freshmen and 90% of continuing full-time students received some form of financial aid. 30% of full-time freshmen and 40% of continuing full-time students received need-based aid. The average freshman award was $8200. 20% of undergraduates work part time. Average annual earnings from campus work are $4883. The average financial indebtedness of the 2003 graduate was $28,000. Reinhardt is a member of CSS. The FAFSA is required. The priority date for freshman financial aid applications for fall entry is May 1.

International Students: There are 42 international students enrolled. They must score 500 on the written TOEFL.

Computers: There are various computer labs, with network access to each dorm room. All students may access the system. There are no time limits and no fees. It is strongly recommended that all students have a personal computer.

Graduates: The most popular majors were business (23%), education (20%), and communications (7%). In an average class, 37% graduate in 6 years or less.

Admissions Contact: Julie Cook, Director of Admissions.
E-mail: *admissions@reinhardt.edu* Web: *www.reinhardt.edu*

SAVANNAH COLLEGE OF ART AND DESIGN   E-4
Savannah, GA 31401-3146   (912) 525-5100
                               (800) 869-7223; Fax: (912) 525-5995

Full-time: 2452 men, 2369 women	Faculty: 295
Part-time: 263 men, 234 women	Ph.D.s: 71%
Graduate: 445 men, 444 women	Student/Faculty: 16 to 1
Year: quarters, summer session	Tuition: $19,535
Application Deadline: open	Room & Board: $8025
Freshman Class: 3516 applied, 2648 accepted, 1048 enrolled	
SAT I Verbal/Math: 551/532	ACT: 23 SPECIAL

Savannah College of Art and Design, founded in 1978, is a private fine arts university emphasizing career preparation in the visual and performing arts, design, building arts, and the history of art and architecture. There are 7 undergraduate schools. In addition to regional accreditation, SCAD has baccalaureate program accreditation with NAAB. The library contains 113,000 volumes, 6237 microform items, and 4200 audio/video tapes/CDs, and subscribes to 915 periodicals. Computerized library services include the card catalog, interlibrary loans, database searching, and Internet access. Special learning facilities include a learning resource center, art gallery, radio station, TV station, international student center, writing center, Internet labs, and the Earle W. Newton Center for British-American Studies. The campus is in an urban area on the southeast coast of Georgia, midway between Charleston, South Carolina, and Jacksonville, Florida.

Student Life: 78% of undergraduates are from out of state, mostly the South. Students are from 50 states, 77 foreign countries, and Canada. 40% are white. The average age of freshmen is 18; all undergraduates,

21. 18% do not continue beyond their first year; 63% remain to graduate.

Housing: 1900 students can be accommodated in college housing, which includes single-sex and coed dorms and on-campus apartments. Theme housing is also available. On-campus housing is available on a first-come, first-served basis. 70% of students commute. Alcohol is not permitted. All students may keep cars.

Activities: There are no fraternities or sororities. There are 45 groups on campus, including art, cheerleading, chess, chorale, computers, dance, drama, ethnic, film, international, literary magazine, musical theater, newspaper, orchestra, photography, professional, radio and TV, religious, social service, and student government. Popular campus events include Sidewalk Arts Festival, Beaux Arts Ball, and International Student Festival.

Sports: There are 8 intercollegiate sports for men and 9 for women, and 6 intramural sports for men and 6 for women. Facilities include Club SCAD and Turner fitness center.

Disabled Students: 80% of the campus is accessible. Wheelchair ramps, elevators, special parking, specially equipped rest rooms, special class scheduling, lowered drinking fountains, and lowered telephones are available. Facilities vary by building, but individual situations are accommodated.

Services: Counseling and information services are available, as is tutoring in every subject. There is a sign language interpreter for hearing-impaired students and a coordinator of disability services.

Campus Safety and Security: Measures include 24-hour foot and vehicle patrol, self-defense education, security escort services, and shuttle buses. There are informal discussions, pamphlets/posters/films, emergency telephones, lighted pathways/sidewalks, and video surveillance cameras.

Programs of Study: SCAD confers the B.F.A. degree. Master's degrees are also awarded. Bachelor's degrees are awarded in COMMUNICATIONS AND THE ARTS (art, art history and appreciation, fiber/textiles/weaving, graphic design, historic preservation, illustration, industrial design, media arts, metal/jewelry, painting, performing arts, photography, and video), ENGINEERING AND ENVIRONMENTAL DESIGN (architecture, computer graphics, furniture design, and interior design), SOCIAL SCIENCE (fashion design and technology). Graphic design, photography, and architecture are the largest.

Required: To graduate, students need 30 to 45 hours of foundation drawing/design. 65 to 70 of liberal arts, 60 to 70 in the major and 10 to 20 of electives, for a total of 180 quarter hours. All students must earn at least 5 quarter hours in computer courses. Students must maintain a 2.0 GPA overall and a 3.0 in the major.

Special: The college offers study abroad in France and Italy, on-campus work-study programs, dual majors in all disciplines, sessions for credit in New York and other domestic locations, and internships with artists, designers, museums, agencies, and architectural firms in the United States and abroad. There are 2 national honor societies.

Faculty/Classroom: 56% of faculty are male; 44%, female. All teach undergraduates. No introductory courses are taught by graduate students. The average class size in an introductory lecture is 20 and in a regular course, 11.

Admissions: 75% of the 2003-2004 applicants were accepted. The SAT I scores for the 2003-2004 freshman class were: Verbal--27% below 500, 38% between 500 and 599, 31% between 600 and 700, and 3% above 700; Math--33% below 500, 42% between 500 and 599, 24% between 600 and 700, and 1% above 700. The ACT scores were 28% below 21, 28% between 21 and 23, 23% between 24 and 26, 13% between 27 and 28, and 8% above 28.

Requirements: The SAT I or ACT is required. In addition, students must submit a completed application and high school transcript indicating successful completion. Preference is given to students with a 3.0 GPA or above and to students whose SAT I or ACT scores are above the national average (B.F.A. Architecture candidates with math scores below 540 or 23, respectively, may be admitted to architecture on a conditional basis). 3 recommendations, an interview, and a portfolio are encouraged. SCAD requires applicants to be in the upper 50% of their class. AP credits are accepted. Important factors in the admissions decision are evidence of special talent, recommendations by school officials, and leadership record.

Procedure: Freshmen are admitted to all sessions. Entrance exams should be taken by November of the senior year. There is an early admissions plan. There is a rolling admissions plan. Application deadlines are open. Application fee is $50. Applications are accepted on-line.

Transfer: 578 transfer students enrolled in 2002-2003. Transfer students must submit a completed application and college transcripts. (High school transcripts may be required if the number of college credits is insufficient for evaluating performance.) An official report of SAT I or ACT scores (architecture majors only) and 3 recommendations are required. A portfolio and an interview are encouraged but not required. 45 of 180 credits required for the bachelor's degree must be completed at SCAD.

Visiting: There are regularly scheduled orientations for prospective students, including check-in, tours, visits with faculty from areas of interest, portfolio reviews, financial aid counseling, admissions counseling, workshops, and a social event. There are guides for informal visits and visitors may sit in on classes. To schedule a visit, contact the Admission Office at *admission@scad.edu*.

Financial Aid: In 2003-2004, 55% of all full-time freshmen and 49% of continuing full-time students received some form of financial aid. 49% of full-time freshmen and 44% of continuing full-time students received need-based aid. The average freshman award was $7268. 88% of undergraduates work part time. Average annual earnings from campus work are $1500. The average financial indebtedness of the 2003 graduate was $18,000. The FAFSA is required, a customized packet of materials is sent to each applicant interested in financial aid. The priority date for freshman financial aid applications for fall entry is April 1. The deadline for filing freshman financial aid applications for fall entry is September 1.

International Students: There are 286 international students enrolled. The school actively recruits these students. They must score 500 on the written TOEFL or 177 on the electronic version and also take the SAT I or the ACT.

Computers: There are approximately 30 computer labs located across the campus, including Internet labs, homework labs, a video lab, and classroom labs. All students may access the system. Students may access the system at designated times. There are no fees.

Graduates: From July 1, 2002 to June 30, 2003, 841 bachelor's degrees were awarded. The most popular majors were computer art (23%), graphic design (14%), and photography (10%). In an average class, 14% graduate in 3 years or less, 47% graduate in 4 years or less, 60% graduate in 5 years or less, and 63% graduate in 6 years or less. 45 companies recruited on campus in 2002-2003. Of the 2002 graduating class, 10% were enrolled in graduate school within 6 months of graduation.

Admissions Contact: Pamela Poetter, Vice President for Admission. A video is available. E-mail: *admission@scad.edu* Web: *www.scad.edu*

SAVANNAH STATE UNIVERSITY
Savannah, GA 31404
E-4
(912) 356-2181
(800) 788-0478; Fax: (912) 356-2256

Full-time: 942 men, 1260 women	**Faculty:** n/av
Part-time: 142 men, 250 women	**Ph.D.s:** 54%
Graduate: 47 men, 130 women	**Student/Faculty:** 15 to 1
Year: semesters, summer session	**Tuition:** $2830 ($9466)
Application Deadline: June 1	**Room & Board:** $4498
Freshman Class: 2158 applied, 1493 accepted, 609 enrolled	
SAT I Verbal/Math: 440/430	**ACT:** 17 **LESS COMPETITIVE**

Savannah State University, founded in 1890, is a liberal arts institution that is part of the University System of Georgia. Undergraduate and graduate degrees are offered through the colleges of business, liberal arts and social sciences, and sciences and technology. Preprofessional programs are available. Some information in this capsule and profile is approximate. There are 3 undergraduate and 3 graduate schools. In addition to regional accreditation, Savannah State has baccalaureate program accreditation with ABET, CSWE, and NCATE. The library contains 200,000 volumes, 557,690 microform items, and 4173 audio/video tapes/CDs, and subscribes to 832 periodicals. Computerized library services include the card catalog, interlibrary loans, and database searching. Special learning facilities include a learning resource center, radio station, arts center, and marine science lab. The 165-acre campus is in a suburban area 265 miles southeast of Atlanta. Including any residence halls, there are 42 buildings.

Student Life: 80% of undergraduates are from Georgia. Students are from 20 states and 10 foreign countries. 70% are from public schools. 92% are African American. The average age of freshmen is 19; all undergraduates, 23. 62% of freshmen remain to graduate.

Housing: 1260 students can be accommodated in college housing, which includes single-sex dorms, on-campus apartments, and married-student housing. On-campus housing is available on a first-come, first-served basis. 55% of students commute. Alcohol is not permitted. All students may keep cars.

Activities: 15% of men and 3% of women belong to 6 national fraternities; 20% of women belong to 4 national sororities. There are 23 groups on campus, including art, band, cheerleading, choir, chorale, computers, dance, debate, drama, drill team, ethnic, international, jazz band, literary magazine, marching band, newspaper, opera, political, professional, radio and TV, religious, student government, and yearbook. Popular campus events include drama presentations, a Fine Arts Festival, and Christmas and spring concerts.

Sports: There are 5 intercollegiate sports for men and 4 for women, and 1 intramural sport for men. Facilities include a student center, gym complex, swimming pool, stadium, field house, tennis court, track, and field.

Disabled Students: 80% of the campus is accessible. Wheelchair ramps, elevators, special parking, specially equipped rest rooms, and lowered drinking fountains are available.

Services: Counseling and information services are available, as is tutoring in every subject. There is remedial math, reading, and writing.

Campus Safety and Security: Measures include 24-hour foot and vehicle patrol, informal discussions, pamphlets/posters/films, and lighted pathways/sidewalks. The campus police department is staffed with public safety officers, building attendants, security guards, safety inspectors, and telephone operators.

Programs of Study: Savannah State confers B.A., B.S., B.B.A., and B.S.W. degrees. Master's degrees are also awarded. Bachelor's degrees are awarded in BIOLOGICAL SCIENCE (biology/biological science and marine biology), BUSINESS (accounting, management information systems, marketing/retailing/merchandising, and recreational facilities management), COMMUNICATIONS AND THE ARTS (broadcasting, communications, English, and music), COMPUTER AND PHYSICAL SCIENCE (chemistry, computer science, mathematics, and physics), ENGINEERING AND ENVIRONMENTAL DESIGN (chemical engineering, civil engineering, electrical/electronics engineering technology, engineering technology, environmental science, mechanical engineering, and petroleum/natural gas engineering), HEALTH PROFESSIONS (predentistry), SOCIAL SCIENCE (criminal justice, history, political science/government, social work, and sociology). Biology, chemistry, and accounting are the strongest academically. Accounting, criminal justice, and management are the largest.

Required: To graduate, all students must complete 120 credit hours and fulfill the core curriculum requirements of 30 hours in courses appropriate to the major and 20 hours each of humanities, math and science, and social science. Students must maintain a minimum 2.0 GPA. Students must pass the University System of Georgia Language Skills Exam, 6 hours of phys ed courses, and 3 to 5 hours of a freshman orientation course. Exit competency exams and other requirements may be required.

Special: The college offers co-op programs, cross-registration, study abroad, a student exchange program with Armstrong State College, a dual degree program with Georgia Institute of Technology, the Georgia Legislative Internship Program, on- and off-campus work-study programs, correspondence study, credit for military experience, and nondegree study. There are 7 national honor societies and a freshman honors program.

Faculty/Classroom: 67% of faculty are male; 32%, female. All teach undergraduates. The average class size in an introductory lecture is 35; in a laboratory, 22; and in a regular course, 33.

Admissions: 69% of the 2003-2004 applicants were accepted. The SAT I scores for the 2003-2004 freshman class were: Verbal--85% below 500, 12% between 500 and 599, 2% between 600 and 700, and 1% above 700; Math--86% below 500, 12% between 500 and 599, 1% between 600 and 700, and 1% above 700. The ACT scores were 95% below 21, 3% between 21 and 23, 1% between 24 and 26, 1% between 27 and 28, and 1% above 28. 5 freshmen graduated first in their class in a recent year.

Requirements: The SAT I or ACT is required, with a minimum composite score of 830 on the SAT I or 17 on the ACT. In addition, applicants must be graduates of an accredited secondary school. Students should have completed 4 units each of English and math, 3 each of science and social studies, and 2 of 1 foreign language. A GPA of 2.0 is required. AP and CLEP credits are accepted.

Procedure: Freshmen are admitted to all sessions. Entrance exams should be taken early in the senior year. There are early admissions and deferred admissions plans. Applications should be filed by June 1 for fall entry and December 1 for spring entry, along with a $20 fee. Notification is sent on a rolling basis.

Transfer: Applicants with at least 45 quarter hours or 30 semester hours of core curriculum credit do not need to submit high school transcripts, but must have a 2.0 average. All transfers must submit college transcripts, standardized test scores, and proof of good standing at the previous institution. 30 credits of 120 required for the bachelor's degree must be completed at Savannah State.

Visiting: There are guides for informal visits and visitors may sit in on classes. To schedule a visit, contact the Office of Admissions.

Financial Aid: 80% of full-time freshmen and 90% of continuing full-time students received need-based aid. The average freshman award was $3200. Need-based scholarships or need-based grants averaged $3000 ($4050 maximum); need-based self-help aid (loans and jobs) averaged $2625; non-need-based athletic scholarships averaged $1415 ($7328 maximum); and other non-need-based awards and non-need-based scholarships averaged $1000 ($4000 maximum). Savannah State is a member of CSS. The CSS Profile, FAFSA, the college's own financial statement, and the Scholarship Application Form are required. Check with the school for current deadlines.

International Students: They must score 500 on the written TOEFL and also take the SAT I, ACT, the college's own entrance exam, or the Collegiate Placement Exams.

Computers: Students may access Prime systems located in the School of Business and Hubert Technical Sciences Center. All students may access the system 8 A.M. to 10 P.M. There are no time limits and no fees.

Graduates: In an average class, 29% graduate in 6 years or less.

Admissions Contact: Gwendolyn Moore, Associate Director of Admissions. A video is available. E-mail: *MooreG@savstate.edu* Web: *http://www.savstate.edu*

SHORTER COLLEGE
Rome, GA 30165-4298

A-2
(706) 233-7319
(800) 868-6980; Fax: (706) 233-7224

Full-time: 328 men, 513 women	Faculty: 62; IIB, --$
Part-time: 15 men, 28 women	Ph.D.s: 74%
Graduate: none	Student/Faculty: 14 to 1
Year: varies by program, summer session	Tuition: $11,705
	Room & Board: $5665

Application Deadline: open
Freshman Class: 555 applied, 460 accepted, 185 enrolled
SAT I Verbal/Math: 530/530 **ACT:** 22 **COMPETITIVE**

Shorter College, founded in 1873, is a private institution affiliated with the Baptist Church and offering undergraduate degree programs in communications, education, business, fine arts, humanities, social sciences, religion, and natural sciences. There are 6 undergraduate schools. In addition to regional accreditation, Shorter has baccalaureate program accreditation with NASM. The library contains 134,201 volumes, 7334 microform items, and 4645 audio/video tapes/CDs, and subscribes to 596 periodicals. Computerized library services include the card catalog, interlibrary loans, database searching, and Internet access. Special learning facilities include a learning resource center, art gallery, natural history museum, and radio station. The 150-acre campus is in a small town 70 miles northwest of Atlanta. Including any residence halls, there are 18 buildings.

Student Life: 87% of undergraduates are from Georgia. Students are from 16 states, 21 foreign countries, and Canada. 96% are from public schools. 86% are white. 82% are Protestant; 10% claim no religious affiliation. The average age of freshmen is 19; all undergraduates, 21. 26% do not continue beyond their first year; 48% remain to graduate.

Housing: 618 students can be accommodated in college housing, which includes single-sex dorms, on-campus apartments, and married-student housing. On-campus housing is guaranteed for the freshman year only and is available on a first-come, first-served basis. 60% of students live on campus; of those, 56% remain on campus on weekends. Alcohol is not permitted. All students may keep cars.

Activities: 16% of men and about 29% of women belong to 2 national fraternities; 28% of women belong to 1 local and 1 national sorority. There are 44 groups on campus, including art, band, cheerleading, choir, chorale, chorus, dance, drama, ethnic, honors, international, literary magazine, musical theater, newspaper, opera, professional, radio and TV, religious, social service, student government, and yearbook. Popular campus events include Parents Weekend, Christmas Dinners, and ShorterFest.

Sports: There are 6 intercollegiate sports for men and 6 for women, and 12 intramural sports for men and 12 for women. Facilities include a 54,000-square foot activities complex that houses a basketball arena, dance and aerobics studios, racquetball courts, a weight room, and an indoor jogging track. In addition, there are tennis courts and a swimming pool.

Disabled Students: 50% of the campus is accessible. Wheelchair ramps, elevators, special parking, specially equipped rest rooms, and lowered drinking fountains are available.

Services: Counseling and information services are available, as is tutoring in most subjects. There is a reader service for the blind, and remedial math, reading, and writing. Computerized study skills assessment and training is offered.

Campus Safety and Security: Measures include 24-hour foot and vehicle patrol, self-defense education, security escort services, and informal discussions. There are pamphlets/posters/films and lighted pathways/sidewalks. Campus access is controlled via a gatehouse from 6 P.M. to 6 A.M., all weekends and during vacations.

Programs of Study: Shorter confers B.A., B.S., B.B.A., B.C.M., B.F.A., B.M., B.M.Ed., and B.S.E. degrees. Bachelor's degrees are awarded in BIOLOGICAL SCIENCE (biology/biological science), BUSINESS (accounting, business administration and management, and recreational facilities management), COMMUNICATIONS AND THE ARTS (art, communications, dramatic arts, English, French, music, musical theater, piano/organ, public relations, Spanish, and voice), COMPUTER AND PHYSICAL SCIENCE (chemistry, mathematics, and natural sciences), EDUCATION (early childhood, mathematics, middle school, and music), HEALTH PROFESSIONS (medical laboratory technology), SOCIAL SCIENCE (Christian studies, economics, history, parks and recreation management, psychology, religion, religious music, social science, and sociology). Music and natural sciences are the strongest academically. Business, early childhood education, and music are the largest.

Required: To graduate, students must maintain at least a 2.0 overall GPA, or 2.5 for education degrees, in 126 to 138 credits, with grades of C or better in the 27 to 96 credits required for a major. The core curriculum requires 33 hours in English, speech, literature, religion, social sci-

ence, science, math, phys ed, and the arts. Those seeking B.A. and B.S. degrees will have additional core requirements. In addition, students must complete 42 hours in upper-level courses and pass an English writing exam.

Special: Shorter offers internships in most programs, cross-registration with Berry College, and study abroad in England, China, Austria, and Hong Kong. Dual and student-designed majors and pass/fail options are available. There are 5 national honor societies, a freshman honors program, and 4 departmental honors programs.

Faculty/Classroom: 61% of faculty are male; 39%, female. All teach undergraduates and 30% both teach and do research. The average class size in an introductory lecture is 23; in a laboratory, 20; and in a regular course, 17.

Admissions: 83% of the 2003-2004 applicants were accepted. The SAT I scores for the 2003-2004 freshman class were: Verbal--36% below 500, 42% between 500 and 599, 18% between 600 and 700, and 4% above 700; Math--36% below 500, 44% between 500 and 599, 19% between 600 and 700, and 1% above 700. The ACT scores were 36% below 21, 30% between 21 and 23, 22% between 24 and 26, 5% between 27 and 28, and 7% above 28. 54% of the current freshmen were in the top fifth of their class; 75% were in the top two fifths. 5 freshmen graduated first in their class.

Requirements: The SAT I or ACT is required. In addition, applicants should be graduates of accredited secondary schools or have a GED certificate. Secondary preparation should include 4 units in English, 3 each in history or social sciences, math, and natural sciences, and 2 in foreign language. Prospective music majors must audition and take a theory placement test; prospective theater majors must audition. A GPA of 2.25 is required. AP and CLEP credits are accepted. Important factors in the admissions decision are advanced placement or honor courses, evidence of special talent, and extracurricular activities record.

Procedure: Freshmen are admitted to all sessions. Entrance exams should be taken by the fall of the senior year. There is a rolling admissions plan. Application deadlines are open. Application fee is $25.

Transfer: 61 transfer students enrolled in a recent year. Applicants must submit transcripts, a character reference, and catalogs from any out-of-state colleges attended. A minimum 2.0 GPA based on transferable credit is required. 30 of 126 credits required for the bachelor's degree must be completed at Shorter.

Visiting: There are regularly scheduled orientations for prospective students, consisting of entertainment, financial aid workshops, a student-administration panel discussion, faculty consultations, admissions consultations, and campus/residence hall tours. There are guides for informal visits and visitors may sit in on classes and stay overnight. To schedule a visit, contact the Admissions Office.

Financial Aid: In 2003-2004, all full-time freshmen and 99% of continuing full-time students received some form of financial aid. 72% of full-time freshmen and 73% of continuing full-time students received need-based aid. The average freshman award was $14,054, with $5851 ($18,609 maximum) from need-based scholarships or grants, $2172 ($14,000 maximum) from need-based self-help aid (loans and jobs), $213 ($7250 maximum) from non-need-based athletic scholarships, and $5818 ($19034 maximum) from other non-need-based awards and non-need-based scholarships. 60% of undergraduates work part time. Average annual earnings from campus work was $1170. The average financial indebtedness of the 2003 graduate was $16,718. The FAFSA and the college's own financial statement are required. The deadline for filing freshman financial aid applications for fall entry is April 1.

International Students: There are 40 international students enrolled. The school actively recruits these students. They must score 500 on the written TOEFL or 173 on the electronic version or take the MELAB, the ELS English Proficiency Evaluation, and also take the SAT I or the ACT.

Computers: The mainframe is a DEC 486-33. There are 67 PCs and Macs distributed among 3 networked labs, the library, and the counseling center. All students may access the system. There are no time limits and no fees.

Graduates: From July 1, 2002 to June 30, 2003, 176 bachelor's degrees were awarded. The most popular majors were education (20%), biology (11%), and psychology (9%). In an average class, 1% graduate in 3 years or less, 45% graduate in 4 years or less, 51% graduate in 5 years or less, and 51% graduate in 6 years or less. 20 companies recruited on campus in 2002-2003.

Admissions Contact: Dr. John Head, VP for Enrollment Management. E-mail: *admissions@shorter.edu* Web: *www.shorter.edu*

SOUTH COLLEGE
Savannah, GA 31406

E-4

(912) 201-8014; Fax: (912) 201-8072

Full-time: 115 men, 305 women	**Faculty:** 18
Part-time: 40 men, 90 women	**Ph.D.s:** 17%
Graduate: none	**Student/Faculty:** 20 to 1
Year: quarters, summer session	**Tuition:** $8720
Application Deadline: open	**Room & Board:** n/app
Freshman Class: n/av	
SAT I or ACT: recommended	**LESS COMPETITIVE**

South College, a private institution founded in 1899, offers undergraduate programs in business administration and health-related fields. Figures in the above capsule and in this profile are approximate. In addition to regional accreditation, South College has baccalaureate program accreditation with APTA and CAHEA. The library contains 15,000 volumes and 148 audio/video tapes/CDs, and subscribes to 64 periodicals. Computerized library services include interlibrary loans and database searching. Special learning facilities include 2 medical labs, 2 computer labs and a physical therapist assistant lab. The 9-acre campus is in an urban area in Savannah. There are 2 buildings.

Student Life: 98% of undergraduates are from Georgia. Students are from 2 states and 5 foreign countries. 57% are white; 38% African American. The average age of all undergraduates is 30.

Housing: There are no residence halls. All students commute. Alcohol is not permitted. All students may keep cars.

Activities: There are no fraternities or sororities. There are 5 groups on campus, including computers, professional, and student government. Popular campus events include Business week, Health Professions Month, and Paralegal Week.

Sports: There is no sports program at South College.

Disabled Students: All of the campus is accessible. Wheelchair ramps, elevators, special parking, specially equipped rest rooms, and lowered telephones are available.

Services: Counseling and information services are available, as is tutoring in most subjects. There is remedial math and writing.

Campus Safety and Security: Measures include lighted pathways/sidewalks and a safety patrol during evening class hours.

Programs of Study: South College confers B.B.A., and B.S. in Physician Assistant degrees. Associate degrees are also awarded. Bachelor's degrees are awarded in BUSINESS (business administration and management), HEALTH PROFESSIONS (physician's assistant). Paralegal studies, medical assisting, and business administration are the largest.

Required: Students must earn a 2.0 GPA and take courses in algebra, composition, computers or word processing, personal development, and effective speaking. A total of 183 quarter credits must be completed.

Special: Internships are available in paralegal studies, medical assisting, physical therapist assistant, business administration, and physician assistant. Work-study programs are offered with various employers and South College, and there are dual majors.

Faculty/Classroom: 46% of faculty are male; 54%, female. 98% teach undergraduates. The average class size in an introductory lecture is 18; in a laboratory, 9; and in a regular course, 18.

Requirements: The SAT I or ACT is recommended. In addition, students should score a minimum of 830 on the SAT I or 17 on the ACT; they may also take a test administered by the college. Students must have earned a high school diploma or GED. An interview is required. CLEP credit is accepted.

Procedure: Freshmen are admitted to all sessions. Entrance exams should be taken prior to application. There is a rolling admissions plan. Application deadlines are open. The fall 2003 fee was $25.

Transfer: Transfer students must have completed 15 quarter hours or 12 semester hours of academic course work with a minimum 1.5 GPA. 73 of 183 credits required for the bachelor's degree must be completed at South College.

Financial Aid: In a recent year, 85% of all full-time students received some form of financial aid. 85% of all full-time students received need-based aid. The average freshman award was $7035. All undergraduates work part time. Average annual earnings from campus work are $1410. The average financial indebtedness of a recent graduate was $8000. The FAFSA is required. Check with the school for current deadlines.

International Students: The school actively recruits these students. They must score 550 on the written TOEFL and also take the Computerized Placement Test (CPT).

Computers: 50 PCs are available in 2 labs and in the library. Home access is also available. All students may access the system. There are no time limits and no fees.

Graduates: In a recent year, the most popular majors were medical assisting (29%), paralegal studies (24%), and accounting (16%). Of a recent graduating class, 97% were employed within 6 months of graduation.

Admissions Contact: Gus Edwards, Director of Admissions.
Web: *southcollege.edu*

SOUTHERN POLYTECHNIC STATE UNIVERSITY
Marietta, GA 30060

B-2

(770) 528-7281

(800) 635-3204; Fax: (770) 528-7292

Full-time: 1500 men, 300 women	**Faculty:** 139; II A, av$
Part-time: 1000 men, 215 women	**Ph.D.s:** 57%
Graduate: 340 men, 290 women	**Student/Faculty:** 13 to 1
Year: semesters, summer session	**Tuition:** $2754 ($9690)
Application Deadline: August 1	**Room & Board:** $4866
Freshman Class: 781 applied, 667 accepted, 443 enrolled	
SAT I Verbal/Math: 530/570	**ACT:** 22 **VERY COMPETITIVE**

Southern Polytechnic State University, founded in 1948, is a public institution that is part of the university system of Georgia. The university offers degree programs in computer science, management, engineering, technology, and architecture. Enrollment figures in the above capsule are approximate. There are 3 undergraduate schools. In addition to regional accreditation, Southern Polytechnic has baccalaureate program accreditation with ABET, ACCE, and NAAB. The library contains 119,780 volumes, 57,144 microform items, and 82 audio/video tapes/CDs, and subscribes to 1256 periodicals. Computerized library services include the card catalog, interlibrary loans, database searching, and Internet access. Special learning facilities include a learning resource center and radio station. The 120-acre campus is in a suburban area 15 miles northwest of Atlanta. Including any residence halls, there are 23 buildings.

Student Life: 96% of undergraduates are from Georgia. Students are from 22 states, 93 foreign countries, and Canada. The average age of freshmen is 21; all undergraduates, 26. 40% do not continue beyond their first year.

Housing: 476 students can be accommodated in college housing, which includes single-sex and coed dorms. On-campus housing is available on a first-come, first-served basis. 88% of students commute. All students may keep cars.

Activities: 5% of men belong to 1 local and 6 national fraternities; 2% of women belong to 3 national sororities. There are 43 groups on campus, including computers, ethnic, honors, international, political, professional, radio and TV, religious, social, social service, student government, and yearbook. Popular campus events include Fall Party, Spring Fling, and NSBE Awards Dinner.

Sports: There are 3 intercollegiate sports for men and 1 for women, and 23 intramural sports for men and 23 for women. Facilities include a 1000-seat gym, a baseball field, softball fields, 9 tennis courts, a 500-seat auditorium, outdoor areas for basketball and volleyball, a multipurpose soccer field, an outdoor running track, and an indoor recreational facility with a swimming pool, racquetball courts, exercise and weight training rooms, and basketball courts that are suitable for badminton and volleyball.

Disabled Students: 80% of the campus is accessible. Wheelchair ramps, elevators, special parking, specially equipped rest rooms, special class scheduling, lowered drinking fountains, and lowered telephones are available.

Services: Counseling and information services are available, as is tutoring in some subjects, including English, math, and physics. There is a reader service for the blind.

Campus Safety and Security: Measures include 24-hour foot and vehicle patrol, security escort services, informal discussions, and pamphlets/posters/films. There are emergency telephones and lighted pathways/sidewalks.

Programs of Study: Southern Polytechnic confers B.A., B.S., B.Arch., and B.A.S. degrees. Associate and master's degrees are also awarded. Bachelor's degrees are awarded in BIOLOGICAL SCIENCE (biology/biological science), BUSINESS (business administration and management), COMMUNICATIONS AND THE ARTS (technical and business writing), COMPUTER AND PHYSICAL SCIENCE (computer science, information sciences and systems, mathematics, physics, and software engineering), ENGINEERING AND ENVIRONMENTAL DESIGN (architecture, civil engineering technology, computer engineering, construction engineering, electrical/electronics engineering technology, engineering and applied science, industrial engineering technology, manufacturing engineering, mechanical engineering technology, and survey and mapping technology), SOCIAL SCIENCE (international studies). Electrical engineering technology, mechanical engineering technology, and computer science are the strongest academically and have the largest enrollments.

Required: All students must complete a core curriculum of 42 semester hours of English composition, college algebra, humanites and fine arts, math and natural sciences, and social sciences. To graduate students must maintain a minimum 2.0 GPA in 120 to 128 semester hours.

Special: Southern Polytechnic offers cross-registration with the University Center in Georgia, cooperative programs in all majors, dual majors in all disciplines, internships, and study abroad in Germany and Mexico. Credit is given for life experience and by exam. There is 1 national honor society and a freshman honors program.

Faculty/Classroom: 83% of faculty are male; 17%, female. 98% teach undergraduates and 2% do research. No introductory courses are taught by graduate students.

Admissions: 85% of the 2003-2004 applicants were accepted. The SAT I scores for the 2003-2004 freshman class were: Verbal--26% below 500, 53% between 500 and 599, 20% between 600 and 700, and 1% above 700; Math--12% below 500, 53% between 500 and 599, 33% between 600 and 700, and 2% above 700.

Requirements: The SAT I or ACT is required. In addition, applicants must be graduates of an accredited secondary school. Students should have completed 21 academic credits, including 4 years of English and math, 3 of science and social studies, and 2 of a foreign language. A GPA of 2.5 is required. AP and CLEP credits are accepted.

Procedure: Freshmen are admitted to all sessions. Entrance exams should be taken at the end of the junior year. There is a rolling admissions plan. Applications should be filed by August 1 for fall entry, December 1 for spring entry, and May 1 for summer entry, along with a $20 fee. Notification is sent on a rolling basis. Applications are accepted on-line through *www.applyweb.com/aw?spsu* and *www.peachnet.edu/ga-easy/apply.*

Transfer: 622 transfer students enrolled in 2002-2003. Applicants must have a minimum GPA of 2.0. and must submit college transcripts. SAT I or ACT scores may be required for some students. 30 of 120 credits required for the bachelor's degree must be completed at Southern Polytechnic.

Visiting: There are regularly scheduled orientations for prospective students. There are guides for informal visits and visitors may sit in on classes. To schedule a visit, contact Jim Cooper at (770) 528-4188 or *jcooper@spsu.edu.*

Financial Aid: In 2001-2002, 37% of all full-time freshmen and 35% of continuing full-time students received some form of financial aid. The average freshman award was $6954. Need-based scholarships or need-based grants averaged $2700; need-based self-help aid (loans and jobs) averaged $2853; and non-need-based awards and non-need-based scholarships averaged $2430. Southern Polytechnic is a member of CSS. The FAFSA is required. The deadline for filing freshman financial aid applications for fall entry is March 15.

International Students: There are 273 international students enrolled. They must score 550 on the written TOEFL.

Computers: There are more than 15 servers to run applications. There are 60 PCs available in the student lab, and several hundred more in various academic departmental labs for general and specialized uses. All students may access the system. There are no time limits and no fees. It is recommended that students in architecture have personal computers.

Graduates: From July 1, 2002 to June 30, 2003, 386 bachelor's degrees were awarded. The most popular majors were engineering/engineering technology (61%), computer science (22%), and business/marketing (7%). In an average class, 7% graduate in 4 years or less, 18% graduate in 5 years or less, and 27% graduate in 6 years or less. 135 companies recruited on campus in 2002-2003.

Admissions Contact: Virginia A. Head, Director of Admissions. E-mail: *admissions@spsu.edu* Web: *spsu.edu*

SPELMAN COLLEGE	B-2
Atlanta, GA 30314	(404) 681-3643
	(800) 982-2411; Fax: (404) 215-7788
Full-time: 2080 women	**Faculty:** 145
Part-time: none	**Ph.D.s:** 81%
Graduate: none	**Student/Faculty:** 14 to 1
Year: semesters	**Tuition:** $12,165
Application Deadline: see profile	**Room & Board:** $7050
Freshman Class: n/av	
SAT I or ACT: required	COMPETITIVE+

Spelman College, founded in 1881, is a private, nonsectarian, liberal arts college for black women. Figures in the above capsule and in this profile are approximate. In addition to regional accreditation, Spelman has baccalaureate program accreditation with NASM and NCATE. The library contains 500,000 volumes and 385,538 microform items, and subscribes to 1439 periodicals. Special learning facilities include a learning resource center, art gallery, and a language lab, a media center, and music and art studios. The 32-acre campus is in an urban area 3 miles southwest of downtown Atlanta. Including any residence halls, there are 24 buildings.

Student Life: 71% of undergraduates are from out of state, mostly the South. Students are from 46 states, 21 foreign countries, and Canada. 86% are from public schools. 96% are African American. The average age of freshmen is 18; all undergraduates, 20. 10% do not continue beyond their first year; 72% remain to graduate.

Housing: 1169 students can be accommodated in college housing, which includes dorms. In addition, there are honors houses. On-campus housing is guaranteed for the freshman year only, is available on a first-come, first-served basis, and is available on a lottery system for upperclassmen. Priority is given to out-of-town students. 60% of students live

on campus; of those, 67% remain on campus on weekends. Alcohol is not permitted. Upperclassmen may keep cars.

Activities: 88% of women belong to 4 local and 4 national sororitie. There are no fraternities. There are 60 groups on campus, including art, band, cheerleading, choir, chorus, dance, drama, gay, honors, international, jazz band, literary magazine, musical theater, newspaper, political, religious, social, student government, and yearbook. Popular campus events include Founders Day and Martin Luther King Jr.'s Birthday.

Sports: Facilities include a gym, tennis courts, a swimming pool, a weight room, dance studios, and bowling lanes.

Disabled Students: 25% of the campus is accessible. Wheelchair ramps, elevators, special parking, and specially equipped rest rooms are available.

Services: Counseling and information services are available, as is tutoring in every subject.

Campus Safety and Security: Measures include 24-hour foot and vehicle patrol, self-defense education, security escort services, and shuttle buses. There are informal discussions, pamphlets/posters/films, emergency telephones, and lighted pathways/sidewalks.

Programs of Study: Spelman confers B.A. and B.S. degrees. Bachelor's degrees are awarded in BIOLOGICAL SCIENCE (biochemistry and biology/biological science), COMMUNICATIONS AND THE ARTS (art, dramatic arts, English, fine arts, French, music, and Spanish), COMPUTER AND PHYSICAL SCIENCE (chemistry, computer science, mathematics, natural sciences, and physics), EDUCATION (art), ENGINEERING AND ENVIRONMENTAL DESIGN (engineering), SOCIAL SCIENCE (anthropology, child psychology/development, economics, history, philosophy, political science/government, psychology, religion, sociology, and women's studies). Biology and engineering are the strongest academically. Psychology, biology, and English are the largest.

Required: To graduate, students must complete 120 semester hours, including at least 30 or more in the major and maintain a GPA of 2.0. Core requirements include 8 credits of African studies, up to 8 of foreign language, 4 of international or women's studies, up to 4 each of English composition, computer literacy, and math, and 2 to 3 of phys ed, plus freshman orientation and sophmore assembly. Students also must complete 4 credits each of divisional requirements in social science, humanities, natural science, and fine arts. A reading course may be required, based on the placement test scores.

Special: Students may cross-register with Atlanta University Center member institutions. Spelman offers internships, study abroad in several countries, student-designed majors, work-study programs at the school, B.A.-B.S. degrees, and dual majors, as well as a 3-2 engineering degree with Georgia Tech, Rochester Institute of Technology, University of Alabama at Huntsville, Auburn and Boston Universities, and North Carolina Agricultural and Technical State University. The college grants credit for life experience and permits nondegree study. There are 9 national honor societies, including Phi Beta Kappa, and a freshman honors program.

Faculty/Classroom: 36% of faculty are male; 64%, female.

Requirements: The SAT I or ACT is required. In addition, applicants should be high school graduates or have a GED certificate. Students should have earned at least 12 academic credits, including 4 in English, 2 each in foreign language, math (algebra and geometry), social studies, and science (including a lab science). Students with additional years in math, science, and language and with AP and honors courses are considered more competitive. An essay is required. An audition or portfolio is recommended for art majors. A GPA of 2.0 is required. AP and CLEP credits are accepted. Important factors in the admissions decision are advanced placement or honor courses, leadership record, and recommendations by school officials.

Procedure: Freshmen are admitted in the fall. Entrance exams should be taken by December of the senior year. There are early decision and deferred admissions plans. Check with the school for current application deadlines and fee. The fall 2003 application fee was $35.

Transfer: 14 transfer students enrolled in a recent year. A 3.0 GPA is recommended, with a minimum 2.0 required. Applicants must submit high school and college transcripts, as well as 2 recommendations from instructors at the last school attended. Students with fewer than 30 semester hours of credit must also submit SAT I or ACT scores. 32 of 120 credits required for the bachelor's degree must be completed at Spelman.

Visiting: There are regularly scheduled orientations for prospective students, including a general information session and a campus tour. There are also high school senior days and junior days. There are guides for informal visits. To schedule a visit, contact the Admissions Office at (404) 681-3643, ext. 2188.

Financial Aid: The average financial indebtedness of a recent graduate was $18,000. Spelman is a member of CSS. The FAFSA and the college's own financial statement are required. Check with the school for current deadlines.

International Students: The school actively recruits these students. They must score 450 on the written TOEFL and also take the SAT I or the ACT.

Computers: The mainframe is a DEC VAX 11/780. PCs, Macs, and Sun workstations are available. All students may access the system 24 hours a day. There are no time limits. It is strongly recommended that all students have a personal computer.

Graduates: In a recent year, the most popular majors were English (16%), psychology (15%), and economics (10%). In an average class, 2% graduate in 3 years or less, 81% graduate in 4 years or less, 88% graduate in 5 years or less, and 91% graduate in 6 years or less. Of a recent graduating class, 35% were enrolled in graduate school within 6 months of graduation and 51% were employed.

Admissions Contact: Theodora Riley, Interim Director of Admissions and Orientation Services. E-mail: *admiss@spelman.edu*
Web: *www.spelman.edu*

STATE UNIVERSITY OF WEST GEORGIA A-2
Carrollton, GA 30118 (770) 836-6416; Fax: (770) 836-4502

Full-time: 2705 men, 4036 women	**Faculty:** 207; IIA, --$
Part-time: 476 men, 835 women	**Ph.D.s:** 82%
Graduate: 516 men, 1695 women	**Student/Faculty:** 33 to 1
Year: semesters, summer session	**Tuition:** $3216 ($11,178)
Application Deadline: July 3	**Room & Board:** $4406
Freshman Class: 4848 applied, 3026 accepted, 1752 enrolled	
SAT I Verbal/Math: 512/505	**ACT:** 21 **COMPETITIVE**

State University of West Georgia, founded in 1906 as part of the University System of Georgia, is a public institution offering degree programs in liberal arts, business, and teacher preparation. There are 3 undergraduate schools and 1 graduate school. In addition to regional accreditation, West Georgia has baccalaureate program accreditation with AACSB, NASAD, NASM, NCATE, NLN, ACS, CACREP, and NASPAA. The library contains 384,249 volumes, 1,117,611 microform items, and 9872 audio/video tapes/CDs, and subscribes to 1226 periodicals. Computerized library services include the card catalog, interlibrary loans, and database searching. Special learning facilities include a learning resource center, art gallery, radio station, TV station, observatory, state archaeologist office, performing arts center, the Advanced Academy of Georgia, and the Waring Archaeology Laboratory. The 394-acre campus is in a suburban area 50 miles southwest of Atlanta. Including any residence halls, there are 65 buildings.

Student Life: 95% of undergraduates are from Georgia. Students are from 43 states, 68 foreign countries, and Canada. 95% are from public schools. 73% are white; 22% African American. The average age of freshmen is 19; all undergraduates, 22. 30% do not continue beyond their first year; 30% remain to graduate.

Housing: 2300 students can be accommodated in college housing, which includes single-sex and coed dorms and fraternity houses. In addition, there are special-interest houses, a sorority-only residence hall, and housing for the Advanced Academy of Georgia students. On-campus housing is guaranteed for the freshman year only, is available on a first-come, first-served basis, and is available on a lottery system for upperclassmen. Priority is given to out-of-town students. 71% of students commute. All students may keep cars.

Activities: 9% of men belong to 13 national fraternities; 12% of women belong to 10 national sororities. There are 82 groups on campus, including band, cheerleading, choir, chorus, dance, debate, drama, drill team, ethnic, gay, honors, international, jazz band, literary magazine, marching band, musical theater, newspaper, opera, pep band, political, professional, radio and TV, religious, social, social service, student government, and yearbook. Popular campus events include Fine Arts Festival, Spring Fling, and International Student Night.

Sports: There are 5 intercollegiate sports for men and 6 for women, and 15 intramural sports for men and 15 for women. Facilities include 3 gyms, an Olympic-size swimming pool, a weight room, a baseball stadium, an Olympic-size metric track, a football field house, and various intramural and practice fields.

Disabled Students: 65% of the campus is accessible. Wheelchair ramps, elevators, special parking, specially equipped rest rooms, special class scheduling, lowered drinking fountains, and lowered telephones are available.

Services: Counseling and information services are available, as is tutoring in some subjects, including most core subjects. There is a reader service for the blind, and remedial math, reading, and writing. There is also braille equipment and a speech recognition computer.

Campus Safety and Security: Measures include 24-hour foot and vehicle patrol, security escort services, shuttle buses, and informal discussions. There are pamphlets/posters/films, emergency telephones, and lighted pathways/sidewalks.

Programs of Study: West Georgia confers B.A., B.S., B.B.A., B.F.A., B.M., B.S.Ed., B.S.E.S., B.S.N., and B.S.Rec. degrees. Master's and doctoral degrees are also awarded. Bachelor's degrees are awarded in AGRICULTURE (environmental studies), BIOLOGICAL SCIENCE (biology/biological science), BUSINESS (accounting, banking and finance, business economics, international economics, management information systems, management science, marketing/retailing/merchandising, and real estate), COMMUNICATIONS AND THE ARTS (art, communications, English, fine arts, French, music, Spanish, and speech/debate/

rhetoric), COMPUTER AND PHYSICAL SCIENCE (chemistry, computer science, earth science, geology, mathematics, and physics), EDUCATION (art, business, early childhood, middle school, music, physical, and special), ENGINEERING AND ENVIRONMENTAL DESIGN (environmental science and technological management), HEALTH PROFESSIONS (nursing and speech pathology/audiology), SOCIAL SCIENCE (anthropology, criminology, economics, geography, history, international studies, parks and recreation management, philosophy, political science/government, psychology, sociology, and systems science). Administrative systems, early childhood education, and global studies are the strongest academically. Early childhood education, biology, and nursing are the largest.

Required: To graduate, students must have earned 120 semester credit hours with a minimum GPA of 2.0. Distribution requirements include 39 hours in the major, 20 each in the humanities, science, math, and social sciences, and 3 in phys ed.

Special: The university has cooperative and work-study programs with state, regional, national, and international corporations and offers short-term internships and supervised work experience, usually for credit. Cross-registration with the University of Georgia and Dalton College is available. The student may undertake an accelerated-degree program in any major, a dual major in physics/engineering or math/computer science, a 3-2 engineering degree program with Mercer University, Georgia Tech, or Auburn University, nondegree study for teacher certification, and study abroad in Europe, Russia, and China. There are 30 national honor societies, including Phi Beta Kappa, a freshman honors program, and 11 departmental honors programs.

Faculty/Classroom: 51% of faculty are male; 49%, female. 54% teach undergraduates, 74% do research, and 32% do both. No introductory courses are taught by graduate students. The average class size in an introductory lecture is 39; in a laboratory, 24; and in a regular course, 26.

Admissions: 62% of the 2003-2004 applicants were accepted. The SAT I scores for the 2003-2004 freshman class were: Verbal--47% below 500, 42% between 500 and 599, 10% between 600 and 700, and 1% above 700; Math--49% below 500, 40% between 500 and 599, 10% between 600 and 700, and 1% above 700. The ACT scores were 55% below 21, 28% between 21 and 23, 11% between 24 and 26, 5% between 27 and 28, and 1% above 28.

Requirements: The SAT I or ACT is required, with a minimum score of at least 430 on the SAT I verbal section and 400 on the SAT I math section (17 on the ACT English, 17 on the ACT math). Applicants must have completed 16 college preparatory high school units, including 4 each in English and math, 3 each in science and social science, and 2 in foreign language. A GPA of 2.5 is required. AP and CLEP credits are accepted.

Procedure: Freshmen are admitted fall, spring, and summer. Entrance exams should be taken by December of the senior year. There is a rolling admissions plan. Early decision applications should be filed by June 15; regular applications, by July 3 for fall entry, November 1 for spring entry, and April 1 for summer entry. The fall 2003 application was $20. Notification is sent on a rolling basis. Applications are accepted on-line through the university's web site.

Transfer: 401 transfer students enrolled in 2002-2003. Applicants must have a minimum GPA of 2.0 in all work attempted. 30 of 120 credits required for the bachelor's degree must be completed at West Georgia.

Visiting: There are regularly scheduled orientations for prospective students. There are guides for informal visits and visitors may sit in on classes. To schedule a visit, contact Dr. Bobby Johnson, Director of Admissions.

Financial Aid: In 2003-2004, 93% of all full-time freshmen and 82% of continuing full-time students received some form of financial aid. 52% of full-time freshmen and 29% of continuing full-time students received need-based aid. The average freshman award was $3173. Average annual earnings from campus work are $3300. The average financial indebtedness of the 2003 graduate was $17,000. West Georgia is a member of CSS. The FAFSA is required. The priority date for freshman financial aid applications for fall entry is open.

International Students: There are 62 international students enrolled. The school actively recruits these students. They must score 523 on the written TOEFL or 193 on the electronic version and also take the SAT I or the ACT scoring 430 on the verbal section of the SAT I and 400 on the math section (17 on the ACT English and 17 on the ACT math).

Computers: The mainframes are an IBM RS6000 Model J40, a Sun Microsystems 1000, a Sun Enterprise 3000, and an HP 9000 Model G30. More than 1500 PCs support 3 computer labs, as well as the business, arts and sciences, and education departments. All students may access the system. There are no time limits and no fees. It is strongly recommended that all students have a personal computer.

Graduates: From July 1, 2002 to June 30, 2003, 898 bachelor's degrees were awarded. The most popular majors were early childhood education (11%), psychology (10%), and management (9%). In an average class, 11% graduate in 4 years or less, 24% graduate in 5 years or less, and 30% graduate in 6 years or less. 250 companies recruited on campus in 2002-2003.

Admissions Contact: Dr. Bobby Johnson, Director of Admissions.
E-mail: *rjohnson@westga.edu* Web: *www.westga.edu*

THOMAS UNIVERSITY
Thomasville, GA 31792-7499

B-5
(229) 226-1621
(800) 538-9784; Fax: (229) 226-1653

Full-time: 164 men, 341 women	Faculty: 38
Part-time: 44 men, 135 women	Ph.D.s: 65%
Graduate: 32 men, 56 women	Student/Faculty: 13 to 1
Year: semesters, summer session	Tuition: $9090
Application Deadline: open	Room & Board: $2400
Freshman Class: 114 applied, 114 accepted, 62 enrolled	
SAT I Verbal/Math: 490/490	ACT: 17 NONCOMPETITIVE

Thomas University, founded in 1950, is a private institution offering 20 undergraduate degrees and master's programs in business administration and rehabilitation counseling. In addition to regional accreditation, Thomas University has baccalaureate program accreditation with NLN. The library contains 54,209 volumes and 823 audio/video tapes/CDs, and subscribes to 413 periodicals. Computerized library services include the card catalog, interlibrary loans, and database searching. Special learning facilities include a learning resource center. The 25-acre campus is in a rural area 28 miles north of Tallahassee. Including any residence halls, there are 20 buildings.

Student Life: 90% of undergraduates are from Georgia. Students are from 9 states, 11 foreign countries, and Canada. 99% are from public schools. 64% are white; 24% African American. The average age of freshmen is 24; all undergraduates, 27.

Housing: 64 students can be accommodated in college housing, which includes single-sex and coed dorms and off-campus apartments. 89% of students commute. Alcohol is not permitted. All students may keep cars.

Activities: There are no fraternities or sororities. There are 23 groups on campus, including chorus, jazz band, literary magazine, newspaper, religious, social, and student government.

Sports: There are 5 intercollegiate sports for men and 5 for women, and 3 intramural sports for men and 3 for women. The university contracts with the city of Thomasville and other groups to use existing public athletic facilities. On-campus facilities include a soccer field, a tennis court, a beach volleyball court, and an outdoor basketball court.

Disabled Students: 90% of the campus is accessible. Wheelchair ramps, special parking, specially equipped rest rooms, and lowered telephones are available.

Services: Counseling and information services are available, as is tutoring in most subjects. There is a reader service for the blind, and remedial math, reading, and writing.

Campus Safety and Security: Measures include informal discussions, pamphlets/posters/films, lighted pathways/sidewalks, an evening vehicle patrol, and sheriff's deputies on campus.

Programs of Study: Thomas University confers B.A. and B.S. degrees. Associate and master's degrees are also awarded. Bachelor's degrees are awarded in BIOLOGICAL SCIENCE (biology/biological science), BUSINESS (business administration and management), COMMUNICATIONS AND THE ARTS (English), EDUCATION (early childhood, middle school, and secondary), HEALTH PROFESSIONS (nursing and rehabilitation therapy), SOCIAL SCIENCE (criminal justice, humanities, liberal arts/general studies, psychology, social science, and social work). Early childhood education and criminal justice are the largest.

Required: To graduate, students must complete 120 semester hours, including 30 to 60 in the major, with a minimum GPA of 2.0 (2.5 for education majors). Core requirements include 48 to 49 semester hours in English composition, history, biology, math, political science, music or art, and computer science. All students must pass a posttest.

Special: There are 6 national honor societies, including Phi Beta Kappa, and 6 departmental honors programs.

Faculty/Classroom: All teach undergraduates. No introductory courses are taught by graduate students. The average class size in an introductory lecture is 16; in a laboratory, 14; and in a regular course, 12.

Admissions: 100% of the 2003-2004 applicants were accepted. The SAT I scores for the 2003-2004 freshman class were: Verbal--75% below 500, 17% between 500 and 599, and 8% between 600 and 700; Math--67% below 500, 25% between 500 and 599, and 8% between 600 and 700. The ACT scores were 80% below 21, and 20% between 21 and 23.

Requirements: The SAT I or ACT is recommended. In addition, students should be graduates of an accredited high school or its equivalent. AP and CLEP credits are accepted.

Procedure: Freshmen are admitted to all sessions. Entrance exams should be taken prior to enrollment. There is a rolling admissions plan. Application deadlines are open. Application fee is $25. Applications are accepted on-line through the school's web site.

Transfer: 74 transfer students enrolled in a recent year. Applicants should have a minimum college GPA of 2.0 and be in good standing at their current or previous institution. 30 of 120 credits required for the bachelor's degree must be completed at Thomas University.

Visiting: There are regularly scheduled orientations for prospective students. There are guides for informal visits. To schedule a visit, contact Lourena Maxwell at *lmaxwell@thomasu.edu*.

Financial Aid: In 2003-2004, 95% of all full-time freshmen and 96% of continuing full-time students received some form of financial aid. 50% of full-time freshmen and 48% of continuing full-time students received need-based aid. The average freshman award was $5500. 2% of undergraduates work part time. Average annual earnings from campus work are $1593. The average financial indebtedness of the 2003 graduate was $3328. Thomas University is a member of CSS. The FAFSA and the college's own financial statement are required. The deadline for filing freshman financial aid applications for fall entry is open.

International Students: There are 44 international students enrolled. The school actively recruits these students. They must score 550 on the written TOEFL or 213 on the electronic version and also take the college's own entrance exam or the MAPS (Multiple Assessment Program/Services).

Computers: There are 48 Gateways in 4 campus labs. All students may access the system 8 A.M. to 9 P.M. Students may access the system 1 hour. There are no fees. It is strongly recommended that all students have a personal computer.

Graduates: From July 1, 2002 to June 30, 2003, 117 bachelor's degrees were awarded. In an average class, 18% graduate in 4 years or less, and 35% graduate in 5 years or less. 19 companies recruited on campus in 2002-2003.

Admissions Contact: Darla M. Glass, Director of Student Affairs.
Web: *www.thomasu.edu*

TOCCOA FALLS COLLEGE
Toccoa Falls, GA 30598

C-1
(706) 886-6831 ext. 5380
(800) 868-3257; Fax: (706) 282-6012

Full-time: 327 men, 410 women	Faculty: 45; IIB, --$
Part-time: 18 men, 45 women	Ph.D.s: 49%
Graduate: none	Student/Faculty: 16 to 1
Year: semesters, summer session	Tuition: $11,300
Application Deadline: August 1	Room & Board: $4300
Freshman Class: 664 applied, 484 accepted, 253 enrolled	
SAT I Verbal/Math: 540/510	ACT: 20 COMPETITIVE

Toccoa Falls College is a private, interdenominational Christian college founded in 1907 that offers programs in Biblical studies, counseling, Christian education, communications, missions, teacher education, theology, music, business administration, and general studies. In addition to regional accreditation, TFC has baccalaureate program accreditation with NASM and AABC. The library contains 135,546 volumes, 6241 microform items, and 4346 audio/video tapes/CDs, and subscribes to 293 periodicals. Computerized library services include the card catalog, interlibrary loans, database searching, and Internet access. Special learning facilities include a learning resource center and radio station. The 1100-acre campus is in a small town 90 miles northeast of Atlanta. Including any residence halls, there are 45 buildings.

Student Life: 59% of undergraduates are from Georgia. Students are from 39 states, 13 foreign countries, and Canada. 70% are from public schools. 89% are white. Most are Protestant. The average age of freshmen is 21; all undergraduates, 22. 24% do not continue beyond their first year; 46% remain to graduate.

Housing: 629 students can be accommodated in college housing, which includes single-sex dorms, on-campus apartments, off-campus apartments, and married-student housing. On-campus housing is guaranteed for all 4 years. 60% of students live on campus; of those, 60% remain on campus on weekends. Alcohol is not permitted. All students may keep cars.

Activities: There are no fraternities or sororities. There are 10 groups on campus, including band, cheerleading, choir, chorale, chorus, drama, ethnic, international, jazz band, newspaper, orchestra, outdoor club, photography, radio and TV, religious, social, social service, student government, and yearbook. Popular campus events include Artist Series, Spiritual Emphasis Week, and Lecture Series.

Sports: There are 3 intercollegiate sports for men and 3 for women, and 6 intramural sports for men and 6 for women. Facilities include a gymnatorium with racquetball courts and a weight room, tennis courts, and soccer and baseball fields.

Disabled Students: 70% of the campus is accessible. Wheelchair ramps, elevators, special parking, specially equipped rest rooms, special class scheduling, lowered drinking fountains, and lowered telephones are available.

Services: Counseling and information services are available, as is tutoring in most subjects.

Campus Safety and Security: Measures include 24-hour foot and vehicle patrol, security escort services, informal discussions, and pamphlets/posters/films. There are lighted pathways/sidewalks and the campus is closed at night, with a guard at the entrance.

Programs of Study: TFC confers B.A., B.S., and B.M. degrees. Associate degrees are also awarded. Bachelor's degrees are awarded in

BUSINESS (business administration and management), COMMUNICA-TIONS AND THE ARTS (broadcasting, English, journalism, music, music performance, and public relations), EDUCATION (Christian, early childhood, English, middle school, music, secondary, and social science), SOCIAL SCIENCE (biblical languages, biblical studies, counseling/psychology, ministries, missions, pastoral studies, philosophy, religion, religious music, and youth ministry). Teacher education, cross-cultural studies, and business are the strongest academically. Counseling psychology, cross-cultural studies, and youth ministries are the largest.

Required: Students must succesfully complete at least 123 semester hours, with 42 in the major, maintaining a C- or better, to earn a bachelor's degree. All students must also complete a core curriculum of 66 hours, which includes 30 hours of Bible and doctrine. A GPA of at least 2.0 must be maintained. Additional requirements for graduation include 4 semesters of student ministry, a senior oral comprehensive exam, or a thesis.

Special: The college offers dual majors, and B.A.-B.S. degrees are available. An on-campus work-study program and internships for many majors are also provided. There are 2 national honor societies.

Faculty/Classroom: 76% of faculty are male; 24%, female. All teach undergraduates. The average class size in an introductory lecture is 52; in a laboratory, 12; and in a regular course, 26.

Admissions: 73% of the 2003-2004 applicants were accepted. The SAT I scores for the 2003-2004 freshman class were: Verbal--33% below 500, 42% between 500 and 599, 21% between 600 and 700, and 4% above 700; Math--42% below 500, 43% between 500 and 599, 13% between 600 and 700, and 2% above 700. The ACT scores were 53% below 21, 19% between 21 and 23, 14% between 24 and 26, 11% between 27 and 28, and 3% above 28. 31% of the current freshmen were in the top fifth of their class; 57% were in the top two fifths. 4 freshmen graduated first in their class.

Requirements: The SAT I or ACT is required, with a minimum composite score of 1000 on the SAT I or 21.9 on the ACT. High school graduation or a GED certificate is required. A personal reference from the student's pastor and an essay submitted with the student's application are also required. Admission is based on an index found by multiplying high school GPA by the best total standardized test score. A GPA of 2.0 is required. AP and CLEP credits are accepted. Important factors in the admissions decision are personality/intangible qualities, extracurricular activities record, and leadership record.

Procedure: Freshmen are admitted to all sessions. Entrance exams should be taken early in the senior year. There is a rolling admissions plan. Applications should be filed by August 1 for fall entry, January 1 for spring entry, and May 15 for summer entry, along with a $20 fee. Notification is sent on a rolling basis. Applications are accepted on-line through the school's web site.

Transfer: 96 transfer students enrolled in 2002-2003. Transfer students must have successfully completed 12 semester hours of college credit courses and have maintained a minimum GPA of 2.0. Students must also provide 3 references and write an essay. 31 of 123 credits or 25% of the degree, whichever is greater, required for the bachelor's degree must be completed at TFC.

Visiting: There are regularly scheduled orientations for prospective students, including visits to the admissions counselor, school directors, and the financial aid office arranged 2 weeks in advance. There are guides for informal visits and visitors may sit in on classes and stay overnight. To schedule a visit, contact the Office of Admissions at *admissions@tfc.edu.*

Financial Aid: In 2003-2004, 96% of all full-time students received some form of financial aid. 82% of full-time freshmen and 73% of continuing full-time students received need-based aid. The average freshman award was $8871. Need-based scholarships or need-based grants averaged $3929; need-based self-help aid (loans and jobs) averaged $3212; and non-need-based awards and non-need-based scholarships averaged $5212. 34% of undergraduates work part time. Average annual earnings from campus work are $1856. The average financial indebtedness of the 2003 graduate was $14,905. The FAFSA and the state aid form are required. The priority date for freshman financial aid applications for fall entry is May 1. The deadline for filing freshman financial aid applications for fall entry is September 30.

International Students: There are 31 international students enrolled. They must score 500 on the written TOEFL and also take the SAT I or the ACT.

Computers: The college provides 52 PCs for student use, located in an academic computer lab, all of which are Internet-accessible and computers for e-mail and research in the library. All students may access the system. There are no time limits and no fees. It is strongly recommended that all students have a personal computer.

Graduates: From July 1, 2002 to June 30, 2003, 169 bachelor's degrees were awarded. The most popular majors were counseling (24%), teacher education (18%), and world missions (15%). In an average class, 3% graduate in 3 years or less, 36% graduate in 4 years or less, 46% graduate in 5 years or less, and 46% graduate in 6 years or less. 75 companies recruited on campus in 2002-2003.

Admissions Contact: Tristam Addridge, Director of Admissions. E-mail: *admission@tfc.edu* Web: *www.tfc.edu*

UNIVERSITY OF GEORGIA
Athens, GA 30602
C-2
(706) 542-2112; Fax: (706) 542-1466

Full-time: 9690 men, 12,600 women	**Faculty:** 1809; I, av$
Part-time: 1215 men, 1320 women	**Ph.Ds:** 95%
Graduate: 3000 men, 4485 women	**Student/Faculty:** 12 to 1
Year: semesters, summer session	**Tuition:** $3208 ($13,984)
Application Deadline: see profile	**Room & Board:** $5240
Freshman Class: n/av	
SAT I or ACT: required	**VERY COMPETITIVE**

The University of Georgia, chartered in 1785 and part of the University System of Georgia, offers degree programs in the arts and sciences, marine studies, music, business, agricultural and environmental sciences, education, family and consumer sciences, forest resources, journalism, social work, pharmacy, law, veterinary medicine, and preprofessional studies. There are 12 undergraduate schools and 1 graduate school. Figures in the above capsule and in this profile are approximate. In addition to regional accreditation, UGA has baccalaureate program accreditation with AACSB, ABET, ACEJMC, ACPE, ADA, ASLA, CSWE, FIDER, NASAD, NASM, NCATE, NRPA, and SAF. The 3 libraries contain 3,622,094 volumes, 6,001,206 microform items, and 174,967 audio/video tapes/CDs, and subscribe to 39,784 periodicals. Computerized library services include the card catalog, interlibrary loans, and database searching. Special learning facilities include a learning resource center, art gallery, natural history museum, radio station, bioscience learning center, rare book and manuscript library, performing arts center, State Botanical Garden of Georgia, Peabody Awards Archives, and Institute for Newspaper Management Studies. The 605-acre campus is in a small town 80 miles east of Atlanta. Including any residence halls, there are 335 buildings.

Student Life: 82% of undergraduates are from Georgia. Students are from 50 states, 131 foreign countries, and Canada. 87% are from public schools. 83% are white. 43% are Protestant; 42% claim no religious affiliation; 10% Catholic. The average age of freshmen is 19; all undergraduates, 21. 10% do not continue beyond their first year; 66% remain to graduate.

Housing: 7933 students can be accommodated in college housing, which includes single-sex and coed dorms, on-campus apartments, and married-student housing. On-campus housing is available on a first-come, first-served basis. Alcohol is not permitted. All students may keep cars.

Activities: 16% of men belong to 25 national fraternities; 21% of women belong to 22 national sororities. There are 430 groups on campus, including art, band, cheerleading, chess, chorale, chorus, computers, dance, debate, drama, drill team, ethnic, film, gay, honors, international, jazz band, literary magazine, marching band, musical theater, newspaper, orchestra, pep band, photography, political, professional, radio and TV, religious, social, social service, student government, and yearbook. Popular campus events include UGA Health Fair and dance, music, and art series.

Sports: There are 8 intercollegiate sports for men and 8 for women, and 28 intramural sports for men and 27 for women. Facilities include an 82122-seat coliseum, a 12000-seat basketball arena, a 4500-seat tennis stadium, 4 indoor tennis courts, complete football-training facilities, and a sports complex with a lake, a beach, playing fields, and trails. There is also the Ramsey Student Center with 5 gyms, 3 swimming pools, a strength/conditioning room, 10 racquetball courts, an indoor track, and a climbing wall. The Women's Athletic Complex hosts women's soccer and softball programs with 3000-spectator capacity.

Disabled Students: 90% of the campus is accessible. Wheelchair ramps, elevators, special parking, specially equipped rest rooms, special class scheduling, lowered drinking fountains, lowered telephones, and wheelchair vans, auxiliary aides, residence hall accommodations, and an adaptive technology lab are available.

Services: Counseling and information services are available, as is tutoring in every subject, including . There is a reader service for the blind, and remedial math, reading, and writing. Alternate format textbooks and class materials, note takers, modifications for tests and assignments, and counseling and advisement from learning disability specialists. There are also sign language interpreters, text type machines, FM/assistive listening devices, and a pilot closed-captioning program.

Campus Safety and Security: Measures include 24-hour foot and vehicle patrol, self-defense education, security escort services, and shuttle buses. There are informal discussions, pamphlets/posters/films, emergency telephones, and lighted pathways/sidewalks.

Programs of Study: UGA confers B.A., B.S., B.B.A., B.F.A., B.L.A., B.Mus., B.S.A., B.S.A.E., B.S.BioEng., B.S.Chem., B.S.Ed., B.S.E.H., B.S.F.R., B.S.Family and Consumer Services, B.S.H.E., B.S.P.A., B.S.Pcs., B.S.Phr., and B.S.W., A.B.J. degrees. Associate, master's, and doctoral degrees are also awarded. Bachelor's degrees are awarded in AGRICULTURE (agricultural economics, agriculture, dairy science, fishing and fisheries, forestry and related sciences, horticulture, plant protection (pest management), poultry science, and wildlife management), BIOLOGICAL SCIENCE (biochemistry, biology/biological science, botany, ecology, entomology, genetics, microbiology, nutrition, and zoology), BUSINESS (accounting, business administration and management, fashion merchandising, international business management, management information systems, management science, marketing/retailing/merchandising, real estate, and recreation and leisure services), COMMUNICATIONS AND THE ARTS (advertising, art, broadcasting, communications, comparative literature, design, dramatic arts, English, French, German, Germanic languages and literature, Greek, Italian, journalism, Latin, linguistics, music, music performance, music theory and composition, public relations, romance languages and literature, Spanish, speech/debate/rhetoric, studio art, and telecommunications), COMPUTER AND PHYSICAL SCIENCE (astronomy, chemistry, computer science, geology, mathematics, physics, and statistics), EDUCATION (agricultural, art, business, early childhood, elementary, English, foreign languages, health, marketing and distribution, mathematics, middle school, music, science, social science, special, and trade and industrial), ENGINEERING AND ENVIRONMENTAL DESIGN (agricultural engineering, bioengineering, environmental science, interior design, landscape architecture/design, preengineering, and technology and public affairs), HEALTH PROFESSIONS (environmental health science, music therapy, pharmacy, predentistry, premedicine, preveterinary science, and speech pathology/audiology), SOCIAL SCIENCE (anthropology, child care/child and family studies, classical/ancient civilization, clothing and textiles management/production/services, cognitive science, criminal justice, dietetics, economics, family/consumer studies, food science, geography, history, home furnishings and equipment management/production/services, interdisciplinary studies, Japanese studies, philosophy, political science/government, psychology, religion, social science, social work, and sociology). Business, journalism, and genetics are the strongest academically. Finance, marketing, and psychology are the largest.

Required: Students must have a 2.0 GPA to graduate and must complete a maximum of 120 semester hours, with at least 18 in the major and 42 in general education. Required specific disciplines are grammar, composition, literature, math, biological sciences, history, and American government, and environmental literacy. Specific courses include basic phys ed and English 1101 and 1102. UGA also requires all students to pass the Regents Exit Exam, as well as exams on the federal and state constitutions.

Special: UGA offers co-op programs with the Medical College of Georgia and the Georgia Institute of Technology, as well as cross-registration with University Center institutions in urban Atlanta. With the Governor's Intern Program, students may serve a full-time 10-week internship in a state government agency; many other internships are available within the departments, as well as work-study programs within the university and with many area businesses. Students may study abroad in 26 countries. A Washington semester, an accelerated degree program in business, general studies and 3-2 engineering degrees, student-designed majors, dual degrees and double majors, and nondegree study are also available. There are 48 national honor societies, including Phi Beta Kappa, a freshman honors program, and 51 departmental honors programs.

Faculty/Classroom: 67% of faculty are male; 33%, female. 81% teach undergraduates. Graduate students teach 25% of introductory courses. The average class size in an introductory lecture is 75; in a laboratory, 21; and in a regular course, 32.

Requirements: The SAT I or ACT is required. UGA admits freshmen primarily on the basis of high school curriculum, grades earned, and college admissions test scores. The university may consider qualitative information to determine a student's potential for success. Applicants should be high school graduates or present a GED certificate. Students should have taken 4 years of English, 3 each of math, science, and social studies, and 2 of a foreign language. An audition is required for music majors. Applications may be submitted on-line at the UGA web site. AP and CLEP credits are accepted.

Procedure: Freshmen are admitted to all sessions. Entrance exams should be taken in January of the senior year. Check with the school for current application deadlines and fee. The fall 2003 application fee was $50. Notification is sent on a rolling basis.

Transfer: Applicants must have a minimum GPA of 2.3, although transfer GPA requirements vary by program. Students who wish to apply as freshman transfers must meet both transfer GPA admission requirements and the academic requirements for entering freshmen. 40 of 120 credits required for the bachelor's degree must be completed at UGA.

Visiting: There are regularly scheduled orientations for prospective students, consisting of campus tours and meetings with faculty, staff, and students. There are guides for informal visits and visitors may sit in on classes and stay overnight. To schedule a visit, contact the Admissions Office.

Financial Aid: UGA is a member of CSS. The FAFSA is required. Check with the school for current deadlines.

International Students: They must score 550 on the written TOEFL or 213 on the electronic version and also take the SAT I or the ACT, scoring 1000 (SAT I).

Computers: The mainframes are a comprised of an IBM 3090 Model 400; CDC CYBERs 180/850, 180/845, and 205; and a DEC VAX 11/780. Computers for student use are located at various points across campus, including the library, residence halls, the computer center, academic departments, and computer labs. All students may access the system at designated times for the various locations. There are no time limits and no fees.

Admissions Contact: Nancy G. McDuff, Director of Admissions.
E-mail: *undergrad@admissions.uga.edu*
Web: *www.uga.edu/admissions/*

UNIVERSITY SYSTEM OF GEORGIA

The University System of Georgia, established in 1932, is a public system. It is governed by an 18-member Board of Regents whose chief administrator is the chancellor. The primary goals of the system are teaching, research, and public service. The main priorities are to provide broad access to undergraduate education at a high level of excellence, to provide sound programs of graduate education and research addressing state and national problems and advancing the frontiers of knowledge, and to work cooperatively with all levels and sectors of education to improve the social, cultural, and economic welfare of the state's citizens. The total enrollment of all 32 campuses is 247,020, with 8,870 faculty members. There are 921 baccalaureate, 585 master's, and 173 doctoral programs offered through the system.

VALDOSTA STATE UNIVERSITY
Valdosta, GA 31698

C-5
(229) 333-5791
(800) 618-1878; Fax: (229) 333-5482

Full-time: 2929 men, 4546 women	**Faculty:** 427; IIA, -$
Part-time: 965 men, 2107 women	**Ph.D.s:** 75%
Graduate: 304 men, 1368 women	**Student/Faculty:** 18 to 1
Year: semesters, summer session	**Tuition:** $2860 ($9496)
Application Deadline: August 1	**Room & Board:** $4938
Freshman Class: 6850 applied, 4732 accepted, 1733 enrolled	
SAT I Verbal/Math: 511/504	**ACT:** 21 COMPETITIVE

Valdosta State University, founded in 1906 and a unit of the University System of Georgia, is a public liberal arts institution offering degrees in arts and sciences, education, business administration, nursing, and fine arts. There are 5 undergraduate and 4 graduate schools. In addition to regional accreditation, VSU has baccalaureate program accreditation with AACSB, ASLHA, CSWE, NASAD, NASM, NCATE, and NLN. The library contains 453,757 volumes, 1,069,189 microform items, and 49,748 audio/video tapes/CDs, and subscribes to 2833 periodicals. Computerized library services include the card catalog, interlibrary loans, and database searching. Special learning facilities include a learning resource center, art gallery, planetarium, radio station, TV station, and herbarium. The 200-acre campus is in an urban area of southern Georgia, 3 1/2 hours from Atlanta and from Orlando, Florida. Including any residence halls, there are 83 buildings.

Student Life: 94% of undergraduates are from Georgia. Students are from 46 states, 54 foreign countries, and Canada. 70% are from public schools. 73% are white; 21% African American. The average age of freshmen is 18; all undergraduates, 23. 25% do not continue beyond their first year; 30% remain to graduate.

Housing: 1580 students can be accommodated in college housing, which includes single-sex and coed dorms, on-campus apartments, married-student housing, and fraternity houses. In addition, there are honors, wellness, and 24-hour quiet wings in the dorms. On-campus housing is guaranteed for all 4 years. 76% of students commute. Alcohol is not permitted. All students may keep cars.

Activities: 5% of men belong to 12 national fraternities; 3% of women belong to 10 national sororities. There are 108 groups on campus, including art, band, cheerleading, chess, choir, chorale, chorus, computers, dance, debate, drama, drill team, ethnic, gay, honors, international, jazz band, literary magazine, marching band, musical theater, newspaper, orchestra, outdoor, pep band, photography, political, professional, radio and TV, religious, social, social service, student government, and symphony. Popular campus events include Family Day, Beach Trip, and The Happening.

Sports: There are 6 intercollegiate sports for men and 5 for women, and 16 intramural sports for men and 16 for women. Facilities include a phys ed complex with a 5500-seat basketball arena, a health fitness center, a weight training room, and a human performance lab; and a gym with a weight room, training room, dance studio, auxiliary gym, and outdoor pool.

Disabled Students: All of the campus is accessible. Wheelchair ramps, elevators, special parking, specially equipped rest rooms, special class scheduling, lowered drinking fountains, lowered telephones, and modified furnishings in dorm rooms are available.

Services: Counseling and information services are available, as is tutoring in some subjects, including math, reading, and English at no charge. There is a reader service for the blind.

Campus Safety and Security: Measures include 24-hour foot and vehicle patrol, self-defense education, security escort services, and shuttle buses. There are pamphlets/posters/films, emergency telephones, lighted pathways/sidewalks, bicycle patrol, security cameras, and electronically operated dorm entrances.

Programs of Study: VSU confers B.A., B.S., B.A.S., B.B.A., B.F.A., B.G.S., B.M., B.S.Ed., B.S.E.S., and B.S.N. degrees. Associate, master's, and doctoral degrees are also awarded. Bachelor's degrees are awarded in BIOLOGICAL SCIENCE (biology/biological science), BUSINESS (accounting, banking and finance, business administration and management, business economics, and marketing/retailing/merchandising), COMMUNICATIONS AND THE ARTS (art, dramatic arts, English, French, media arts, music, music performance, Spanish, speech/debate/rhetoric, and telecommunications), COMPUTER AND PHYSICAL SCIENCE (applied mathematics, astronomy, chemistry, computer science, information sciences and systems, mathematics, and physics), EDUCATION (art, business, early childhood, health, middle school, music, physical, secondary, special, and trade and industrial), ENGINEERING AND ENVIRONMENTAL DESIGN (environmental science and interior design), HEALTH PROFESSIONS (exercise science, nursing, speech pathology/audiology, and sports medicine), SOCIAL SCIENCE (anthropology, criminal justice, history, liberal arts/general studies, paralegal studies, philosophy, political science/government, psychology, and sociology). Sports medicine, accounting, and nursing are the strongest academically. Education, nursing, and business are the largest.

Required: To graduate, all students must complete a minimum of 120 semester hours, including 60 in the core curriculum and 20 in a major, with a GPA of 2.0. Reasonable proficiency in written and spoken English is also required.

Special: VSU offers more than 30 dual degrees with the Georgia Institute of Technology and has a co-op program with the Medical College of Georgia. Internships are available, as are work-study programs, study abroad, a general studies degree, and credit for life experience. There are 15 national honor societies, including Phi Beta Kappa, and a freshman honors program.

Faculty/Classroom: 61% of faculty are male; 39%, female. No introductory courses are taught by graduate students. The average class size in an introductory lecture is 27; in a laboratory, 18; and in a regular course, 24.

Admissions: 69% of the 2003-2004 applicants were accepted. The SAT I scores for the 2003-2004 freshman class were: Verbal--45% below 500, 45% between 500 and 599, 9% between 600 and 700, and 1% above 700; Math--47% below 500, 42% between 500 and 599, 10% between 600 and 700, and 1% above 700. The ACT scores were 16% between 21 and 23, 70% between 24 and 26, 13% between 27 and 28, and 1% above 28. 34% of the current freshmen were in the top fifth of their class.

Requirements: The SAT I or ACT is required, with a minimum score of 430 verbal and 400 math on the SAT I or 17 English and 17 math on the ACT. Applicants must be graduates of accredited high schools and have completed the college preparatory curriculum including 4 years each of English and math, 3 each of science and social science, and 2 each of a foreign language and academic or arts electives. A GPA of 2.0 is required. AP and CLEP credits are accepted.

Procedure: Freshmen are admitted to all sessions. Entrance exams should be taken so that the results may be received by VSU at least 20 days prior to registration. There is a rolling admissions plan. Applications should be filed by August 1 for fall entry, December 1 for spring entry, and May 1 for summer entry, along with a $20 fee. Notification is sent on a rolling basis. Applications are accepted on-line.

Transfer: 2778 transfer students enrolled in 2002-2003. Applicants with fewer than 30 hours of transferable credit must meet the same qualifications as entering freshmen. Applicants with 30 or more hours must submit transcripts from all previously attended colleges and have earned a minimum GPA of 2.0 in all work attempted. 30 of 120 credits required for the bachelor's degree must be completed at VSU.

Visiting: There are regularly scheduled orientations for prospective students, consisting of a Saturday open house 3 times a year, including an academic and activities carousel, campus tour, and lunch. There are guides for informal visits and visitors may sit in on classes. To schedule a visit, contact the Admissions Office.

Financial Aid: In 2003-2004, 95% of all full-time freshmen and 69% of continuing full-time students received some form of financial aid. 41% of full-time freshmen and 47% of continuing full-time students received need-based aid. The average freshman award was $9736. Average annual earnings from campus work are $2000. The average financial indebtedness of the 2003 graduate was $17,534. VSU is a member of CSS. The FAFSA and the college's own financial statement are required. The deadline for filing freshman financial aid applications for fall entry is June 1.

International Students: There are 214 international students enrolled. They must score 523 on the written TOEFL or 193 on the electronic version.

Computers: The mainframes are comprised of UNIX-based central servers with Novell netware, an HP 9000 model G70 business server, and a Sun SPARC server 1000. VSU also has access to the CDC CYBER 850, IBM 3090, and other computing facilities of the University System of Georgia. There are 24 PC and terminal labs located in educational buildings and the library. Students have access to the Internet, e-mail, and Galileo. All students may access the system. There are no time limits and no fees.

Graduates: From July 1, 2002 to June 30, 2003, 1429 bachelor's degrees were awarded. The most popular majors were early childhood education (9%), business management (7%), and marketing (6%).

Admissions Contact: Walter H. Peacock, Director of Admissions. A video is available. E-mail: *admissions@valdosta.edu* Web: *www.valdosta.edu*

WESLEYAN COLLEGE
C-3
Macon, GA 31210
(912) 757-5206
(800) 447-6610; Fax: (912) 757-4030

Full-time: 525 women	**Faculty:** 47; IIB, --$
Part-time: 136 women	**Ph.D.s:** 89%
Graduate: 16 men, 67 women	**Student/Faculty:** 11 to 1
Year: semesters, summer session	**Tuition:** $10,420
Application Deadline: February 1	**Room & Board:** $7450
Freshman Class: 323 applied, 250 accepted, 89 enrolled	
SAT I or ACT: required	**VERY COMPETITIVE**

Wesleyan College, founded in 1836, is a private, liberal arts college for women, affiliated with the United Methodist Church. It is the world's first college chartered to grant degrees to women. In addition to regional accreditation, Wesleyan has baccalaureate program accreditation with NASM. The library contains 142,579 volumes, 33,216 microform items, and 6552 audio/video tapes/CDs, and subscribes to 630 periodicals. Computerized library services include the card catalog, interlibrary loans, database searching, and Internet access. Special learning facilities include an art gallery, computerized teaching classroom, language and math labs, collaborative research science labs, and arboretum. The 200-acre campus is in a suburban area 90 miles south of Atlanta. Including any residence halls, there are 18 buildings.

Student Life: 67% of undergraduates are from Georgia. Students are from 28 states and 31 foreign countries. 90% are from public schools. 46% are white; 28% African American; 19% foreign nationals. 54% are Protestant; 28% claim no religious affiliation; 9% Catholic; 8% Buddhist, Hindu, Muslim, Eastern Orthodox, and Bahai. The average age of freshmen is 19; all undergraduates, 24. 22% do not continue beyond their first year.

Housing: 622 students can be accommodated in college housing, which includes single-sex dorms and on-campus apartments. On-campus housing is guaranteed for all 4 years. 70% of students live on campus. Alcohol is not permitted. All students may keep cars.

Activities: There are no sororities. There are 40 groups on campus, including art, choir, chorus, computers, dance, debate, drama, ethnic, forensics, gay, honors, international, literary magazine, musical theater, newspaper, photography, political, professional, recreation, religious, social, social service, student government, and yearbook. Popular campus events include Casino Night, Benefit Ball, and Fun Day.

Sports: Facilities include an equestrian arena, softball and soccer fields, an indoor pool, a gym, a dance studio, a weight room, a lake, a fitness trail, and a fitness center.

Disabled Students: 65% of the campus is accessible. Wheelchair ramps, elevators, special parking, specially equipped rest rooms, special class scheduling, lowered drinking fountains, and lowered telephones are available.

Services: Counseling and information services are available, as is tutoring in some subjects. Free tutors are available upon request, and academic counseling is available. In addition, a writing lab, study skills workshops, and sessions with first-year classes conducted by the director of the academic center are available.

Campus Safety and Security: Measures include 24-hour foot and vehicle patrol, self-defense education, security escort services, and informal discussions. There are pamphlets/posters/films, emergency telephones, and lighted pathways/sidewalks. Dorm entrances are kept locked.

Programs of Study: Wesleyan confers A.B. and B.S.B.A. degrees. Master's degrees are also awarded. Bachelor's degrees are awarded in BIOLOGICAL SCIENCE (biology/biological science), BUSINESS (business administration and management and international business management), COMMUNICATIONS AND THE ARTS (advertising, art history and appreciation, communications, English, French, music, Spanish, and studio art), COMPUTER AND PHYSICAL SCIENCE (chemistry, mathematics, physical sciences, and physics), EDUCATION (early childhood and middle school), SOCIAL SCIENCE (American studies, economics, history, humanities, interdisciplinary studies, international relations, philosophy, political science/government, psychology, religion, and social science). Art, biology, and business are the strongest academically. Business, biology, and psychology are the largest.

Required: To graduate, students must complete 120 credit hours with a minimum GPA of 2.0. Requirements include proficiency in writing, math, and modern foreign language, 10 courses distributed with 2 but no more than 3 from fine arts, humanities, science and math, and social sciences. A first-year seminar, a speech-intensive course, cross-cultural and workplace experience, and integrative experience in the major are also required. All classes are seminar based.

Special: Wesleyan offers cross-registration with Mercer University and a 3-2 engineering degree with Georgia Institute of Technology and Auburn and Mercer Universities. More than 150 internships are available, as are interdisciplinary, student-designed, and dual majors, study abroad in 10 countries, a Washington semester, work-study programs, credit for life experience, nondegree study, and pass/fail options. There are 10 national honor societies and a freshman honors program.

Faculty/Classroom: 47% of faculty are male; 53%, female. All teach undergraduates and 75% both teach and do research. No introductory courses are taught by graduate students. The average class size in an introductory lecture is 16; in a laboratory, 12; and in a regular course, 13.

Admissions: 77% of the 2003-2004 applicants were accepted. The SAT I scores for the 2003-2004 freshman class were: Verbal--27% below 500, 40% between 500 and 599, 28% between 600 and 700, and 5% above 700; Math--38% below 500, 38% between 500 and 599, 18% between 600 and 700, and 6% above 700. The ACT scores were 47% below 21, 15% between 21 and 23, 24% between 24 and 26, and 15% between 27 and 28. 53% of the current freshmen were in the top fifth of their class; 77% were in the top two fifths. 3 freshmen graduated first in their class.

Requirements: The SAT I or ACT is required. In addition, each applicant for admission is reviewed on the following: performance in and quality of a college preparatory curriculum, standardized test score, counselor and teacher recommendation, writing ability, and cocurricular involvement. A minimum of 15 Carnegie units is required, including 4 units of English, 3 each of math, natural sciences, and social sciences, and 2 of foreign language. Admitted students must graduate from an accredited secondary school or have a GED certificate. The admission staff does not require but welcomes the opportunity to interview prospective students. Students who wish to be considered for a performance arts scholarship must submit a portfolio or audition. AP and CLEP credits are accepted. Important factors in the admissions decision are advanced placement or honor courses, evidence of special talent, and leadership record.

Procedure: Freshmen are admitted fall and spring. Entrance exams should be taken by the fall of the senior year. There are early decision, early admissions, and deferred admissions plans. Early decision applications should be filed by November 15 (Round II, January 15); regular applications, by February 1 for fall entry priority consideration and December 1 for spring entry. Notification of early decision is sent December 15 (Round II, February 15); regular decision, after March 1. 25 early decision candidates were accepted for the 2003-2004 class. Applications are accepted on-line.

Transfer: 11 transfer students enrolled in 2002-2003. Applicants with fewer than 24 transferable semester hours must submit a final high school transcript and record of standardized test scores in addition to their college transcripts. An interview is recommended. 30 of 120 credits required for the bachelor's degree must be completed at Wesleyan.

Visiting: There are regularly scheduled orientations for prospective students, including a campus tour, parent/student panels, class visits, admission and financial aid sessions, and meals in the dining hall. There are guides for informal visits and visitors may sit in on classes and stay overnight. To schedule a visit, contact Sheri Baucom, Admissions.

Financial Aid: In 2003-2004, all full-time freshmen and 96% of continuing full-time students received some form of financial aid. 62% of full-time freshmen and 58% of continuing full-time students received need-based aid. The average freshman award was $12,300. Need-based scholarships or need-based grants averaged $10,087; need-based self-help aid (loans and jobs) averaged $6333; and non-need-based awards and non-need-based scholarships averaged $12,343. 43% of full-time undergraduates work part time. The average financial indebtedness of the 2003 graduate was $20,200. Wesleyan is a member of CSS. The FAFSA and the college's own financial statement are required. The deadline for filing freshman financial aid applications for fall entry is May 1.

International Students: There are 124 international students enrolled. The school actively recruits these students. They must score 550 on the written TOEFL. It is strongly recommended that the SAT I or ACT be taken.

Computers: The campus is fully networked and connected to the Internet. Students have e-mail access. All students may access the system. There are no time limits and no fees. All students are required to have personal computers. A Compaq 1500C notebook is recommended.

Graduates: From July 1, 2002 to June 30, 2003, 94 bachelor's degrees were awarded. The most popular majors were psychology (25%), biology (15%), and business administration (15%). In an average class, 40% graduate in 4 years or less, 44% graduate in 5 years or less, and 44% graduate in 6 years or less.

Admissions Contact: Patricia M. Gibbs, Vice President of Enrollment Services and Student Affairs. A video is available.
E-mail: *admissions@wesleyancollege.edu*
Web: *www.wesleyancollege.edu*

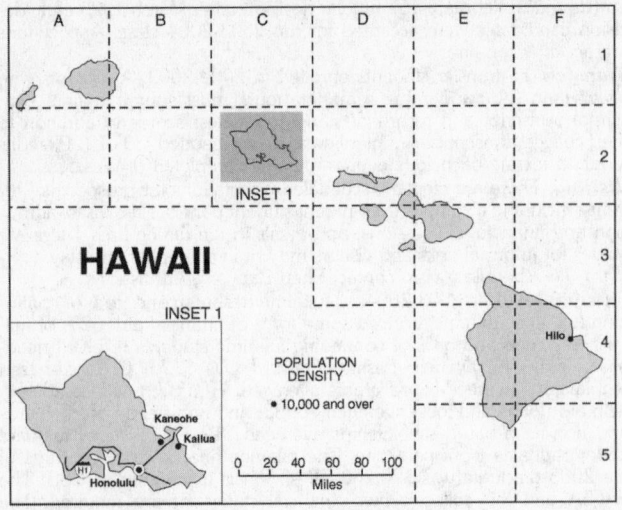

Services: Counseling and information services are available, as is tutoring in most subjects. There is remedial math, reading, and writing.

Campus Safety and Security: Measures include 24-hour foot and vehicle patrol, security escort services, informal discussions, and pamphlets/posters/films. There are emergency telephones and lighted pathways/sidewalks.

Programs of Study: BYUH confers B.A., B.S., B.F.A., and B.S.W. degrees. Associate degrees are also awarded. Bachelor's degrees are awarded in BIOLOGICAL SCIENCE (biology/biological science), BUSINESS (accounting, hospitality management services, international business management, and tourism), COMMUNICATIONS AND THE ARTS (art, English, fine arts, and music), COMPUTER AND PHYSICAL SCIENCE (computer science, information sciences and systems, and mathematics), EDUCATION (art, business, elementary, English, mathematics, science, social science, special, and teaching English as a second/foreign language (TESOL/TEFOL)), HEALTH PROFESSIONS (predentistry and premedicine), SOCIAL SCIENCE (Hawaiian studies, history, interdisciplinary studies, international studies, Pacific area studies, physical fitness/movement, political science/government, psychology, and social work). Biological science, information systems, and education are the strongest academically. International business management, information systems, and psychology are the largest.

Required: Students must complete the 31- to 43-credit general education curriculum, as well as meet English proficiency, religious education, health, and phys ed requirements. A total of 120 credit hours, including 40 in the major, must be earned with a minimum GPA of 2.0 for graduation. A thesis is required in certain areas.

Special: BYUH offers work-study programs with the Polynesian Cultural Center, internships, cooperative programs in most majors, nondegree study, student-designed majors in interdisciplinary studies, dual majors in elementary education and special education, and pass/fail options. There are 5 national honor societies and a freshman honors program.

Faculty/Classroom: 75% of faculty are male; 25%, female. All teach undergraduates and 15% both teach and do research.

Admissions: 29% of the 2003-2004 applicants were accepted. The ACT scores for the 2003-2004 freshman class were: 41% below 21, 31% between 21 and 23, 20% between 24 and 26, 6% between 27 and 28, and 2% above 28. 15% of the current freshmen were in the top fifth of their class; 50% were in the top two fifths. In a recent year, 4 freshmen graduated first in their class.

Requirements: The ACT is required and the SAT I is recommended. In addition, the applicant should be a high school graduate. Homeschooled and other nontraditional students should call for more information. A GPA of 3.0 is required. AP and CLEP credits are accepted. Important factors in the admissions decision are geographic diversity, recommendations by alumni, and personality/intangible qualities.

Procedure: Freshmen are admitted to all sessions. Entrance exams should be taken prior to the application deadline. There is a deferred admissions plan. Applications should be filed by February 15 for fall entry, October 1 for winter entry, February 15 for spring entry, and February 15 for summer entry. Notification is sent April 1 or within 1 to 3 weeks of the date the application is received.

Transfer: 214 transfer students enrolled in a recent year. Applicants must have 30 hours of college credit, with a minimum GPA of 2.5. 30 of 120 credits required for the bachelor's degree must be completed at BYUH.

Visiting: There are guides for informal visits. To schedule a visit, contact the University Relations Office at (808) 293-3660 or toac@byuh.edu.

Financial Aid: 50% of undergraduates work part time. Average annual earnings from campus work are $6000. The FAFSA is required. Check with the school for current deadlines.

International Students: In a recent year, there were 942 international students enrolled. The school actively recruits these students. They must score 400 on the written TOEFL or take the MELAB, and also take the ACT.

Computers: The mainframe is an IBM RS/6000. Students can use the mainframe via the web for registration and access to student information. Students can also log in to network servers to access their e-mail and the Internet from any computer on campus. There are approximately 300 computers available to students in campus labs. All students may access the system 18 hours per day. There are no time limits. The fee is $25.

Graduates: In a recent year, 357 bachelor's degrees were awarded. The most popular majors were information systems (15%), international business management (10%), and social work (7%). 60 companies recruited on campus in a recent year.

Admissions Contact: Jeffrey N. Bunker, Dean for Admissions/Records. A video is available. E-mail: adm@byuh.edu
Web: http://www.byuh.edu

BRIGHAM YOUNG UNIVERSITY/HAWAII
Laie, HI 96762

C-2

(808) 293-3731; Fax: (808) 293-3741

Full-time: 1123 men, 1308 women	**Faculty:** 124
Part-time: 108 men, 164 women	**Ph.D.s:** 63%
Graduate: none	**Student/Faculty:** 20 to 1
Year: semesters, summer session	**Tuition:** $2580 ($3860)
Application Deadline: February 15	**Room & Board:** $4660
Freshman Class: 2989 applied, 860 accepted, 227 enrolled	
SAT I: recommended	**ACT:** required

VERY COMPETITIVE+

Brigham Young University/Hawaii, founded in 1955 by the Church of Jesus Christ of Latter-day Saints (LDS), is a private institution offering programs in liberal arts, business, and education. Admissions priority is given to members of the LDS Church. Tuition is $2580 for LDS students, $3860 for non-LDS students. (See above capsule.) Some information in this capsule is approximate. There are 3 undergraduate schools. In addition to regional accreditation, BYUH has baccalaureate program accreditation with CSWE. The library contains 3179 volumes, 948,000 microform items, and 8053 audio/video tapes/CDs, and subscribes to 2100 periodicals. Computerized library services include the card catalog, interlibrary loans, and database searching. Special learning facilities include a learning resource center, art gallery, and natural history museum. The nearby Polynesian Cultural Center houses an art collection and an artifact collection, and provides valuable research opportunities for students in related programs. The 200-acre campus is in a small town 38 miles from Honolulu. Including any residence halls, there are 42 buildings.

Student Life: Students are from 43 states, 69 foreign countries, and Canada. 41% are foreign nationals; 38% white. The average age of freshmen is 20; all undergraduates, 23. 50% do not continue beyond their first year.

Housing: 1374 students can be accommodated in college housing, which includes single-sex dorms, on-campus apartments, and married-student housing. On-campus housing is guaranteed for the freshman year only and is available on a first-come, first-served basis. 62% of students live on campus. Alcohol is not permitted. All students may keep cars.

Activities: There are no fraternities or sororities. There are 41 groups on campus, including art, band, cheerleading, chess, choir, chorale, computers, dance, drama, ethnic, film, honors, international, jazz band, literary magazine, musical theater, newspaper, pep band, political, professional, religious, social, social service, student government, and yearbook. Popular campus events include International Food Fest, International Cultural Night, and Talent Show.

Sports: There are 4 intercollegiate sports for men and 4 for women, and 10 intramural sports for men and 10 for women. Facilities include 3 softball fields, 2 soccer fields, a rugby field, 10 tennis and 4 racquetball courts, a swimming pool, a weight room, a bowling alley, a dance studio, pool tables, a 5000-seat activity center, and 2 basketball gyms, one of which seats 500.

Disabled Students: 95% of the campus is accessible. Wheelchair ramps, elevators, special parking, specially equipped rest rooms, lowered drinking fountains, and lowered telephones are available.

CHAMINADE UNIVERSITY OF HONOLULU
C-2
Honolulu, HI 96816
(808) 735-4735
(800) 735-3733; Fax: (808) 739-4647

Full-time: 325 men, 702 women	**Faculty:** 69
Part-time: 12 men, 25 women	**Ph.D.s:** 62%
Graduate: 209 men, 492 women	**Student/Faculty:** 15 to 1
Year: semesters, summer session	**Tuition:** $13,500
Application Deadline: open	**Room & Board:** $7930
Freshman Class: 830 applied, 799 accepted, 251 enrolled	
SAT I Verbal/Math: 470/480	**ACT:** 21 **LESS COMPETITIVE**

Chaminade University of Honolulu, founded in 1955, is a private institution affiliated with the Roman Catholic Church. The school is divided into three major programs: the day undergraduate is on the main campus, the evening undergraduate program is off campus, and the evening graduate program is on campus. There are 5 undergraduate and 5 graduate schools. The library contains 68,256 volumes, 134,000 microform items, and 231 audio/video tapes/CDs, and subscribes to 273 periodicals. Computerized library services include interlibrary loans. Special learning facilities include a learning resource center and an observatory. The 62-acre campus is in an urban area 4 miles east of downtown Honolulu. Including any residence halls, there are 14 buildings.

Student Life: 55% of undergraduates are from Hawaii. Others are from 32 states, 10 foreign countries, and Canada. 61% are Asian American; 25% white. 43% are Catholic; 31% Protestant; 25% claim no religious affiliation. The average age of freshmen is 18; all undergraduates, 22. 35% do not continue beyond their first year; 38% remain to graduate.

Housing: 395 students can be accommodated in college housing, which includes single-sex and coed dorms, on-campus apartments, and off-campus apartments. On-campus housing is available on a first-come, first-served basis. 65% of students commute. All students may keep cars.

Activities: There are no fraternities or sororities. There are 38 groups on campus, including art, cheerleading, choir, computers, drama, ethnic, honors, international, literary magazine, newspaper, orchestra, political, professional, religious, social, social service, student government, and yearbook. Popular campus events include Spring Serendipity, International Extravaganza, and Club Fest.

Sports: There are 4 intercollegiate sports for men and 4 for women. Facilities include volleyball, tennis, and basketball courts, and fitness and weight-training facilities.

Disabled Students: 69% of the campus is accessible. Wheelchair ramps, special parking, specially equipped rest rooms, special class scheduling, lowered drinking fountains, and lowered telephones are available.

Services: Counseling and information services are available, as is tutoring in most subjects. There is remedial math, reading, and writing.

Campus Safety and Security: Measures include 24-hour foot and vehicle patrol, self-defense education, security escort services, and informal discussions. There are pamphlets/posters/films, emergency telephones, and lighted pathways/sidewalks.

Programs of Study: Chaminade confers B.A., B.S., and B.F.A. degrees. Associate and master's degrees are also awarded. Bachelor's degrees are awarded in AGRICULTURE (environmental studies), BIOLOGICAL SCIENCE (biology/biological science), BUSINESS (accounting, management science, and marketing/retailing/merchandising), COMMUNICATIONS AND THE ARTS (communications and English), COMPUTER AND PHYSICAL SCIENCE (computer science and information sciences and systems), EDUCATION (early childhood, elementary, and secondary), ENGINEERING AND ENVIRONMENTAL DESIGN (interior design), SOCIAL SCIENCE (behavioral science, criminal justice, forensic studies, history, humanities, international relations, psychology, religion, and social studies). Forsensic science, biology, and education are the strongest academically, and are the largest.

Required: To graduate, students must complete 124 credit hours, including 61 in general education courses and at least 24 in the major at the upper-division level. A 2.0 GPA is required in all majors except criminal justice (2.5), communications (2.5), and education (2.75).

Special: Internships are available with local companies through the Career Development office. Students may design majors toward a B.A. in humanities. There is a sister university exchange program with the University of Dayton and St. Mary's University. There are 7 national honor societies.

Faculty/Classroom: 55% of faculty are male; 45%, female. All teach undergraduates. No introductory courses are taught by graduate students. The average class size in an introductory lecture is 19; in a laboratory, 17; and in a regular course, 17.

Admissions: 96% of the 2003-2004 applicants were accepted. The SAT I scores for the 2003-2004 freshman class were: Verbal--65% below 500, 26% between 500 and 599, and 9% between 600 and 700; Math--56% below 500, 33% between 500 and 599, 10% between 600 and 700, and 1% above 700. The ACT scores were 51% below 21, 30% between 21 and 23, 9% between 24 and 26, 5% between 27 and 28, and

5% above 28. 16% of the current freshmen were in the top fifth of their class; 31% were in the top two fifths. 3 freshmen graduated first in their class.

Requirements: The SAT I or ACT is recommended, with a minimum SAT I score of 460 on each part or a composite ACT score of 18. In addition, students must have earned 16 credits, based on 2 years of science, 3 each of math and social studies, and 4 each of English and college preparatory electives. The GED is accepted. An essay is required, and an interview is recommended. A GPA of 2.0 is required. AP and CLEP credits are accepted. Important factors in the admissions decision are leadership record, personality/intangible qualities, and extracurricular activities record.

Procedure: Freshmen are admitted fall and spring. Entrance exams should be taken during the first semester of the senior year. There is a rolling admissions plan. Application deadlines are open. Application fee is $50. Applications are accepted on-line through the school's web site.

Transfer: 115 transfer students enrolled in 2002-2003. Applicants must have a minimum GPA of 2.0. 30 of 124 credits required for the bachelor's degree must be completed at Chaminade.

Visiting: There are guides for informal visits and visitors may sit in on classes. To schedule a visit, contact the Admissions Office at (800) 735-3733 or *admissions@chaminade.edu*.

Financial Aid: In 2003-2004, 99% of all full-time freshmen and 96% of continuing full-time students received some form of financial aid. 73% of full-time freshmen and 76% of continuing full-time students received need-based aid. The average freshman award was $17,012. Need-based scholarships or need-based grants averaged $2713 ($14,050 maximum); need-based self-help aid (loans and jobs) averaged $3260 ($8125 maximum); non-need-based athletic scholarships averaged $5057 ($15,510 maximum); and other non-need-based awards and non-need-based scholarships averaged $8926 ($20,000 maximum). 5% of undergraduates work part time. Average annual earnings from campus work are $1500. The average financial indebtedness of the 2003 graduate was $26,411. Chaminade is a member of CSS. The FAFSA is required. The priority date for freshman financial aid applications for fall entry is March 1.

International Students: There are 26 international students enrolled. They must score 450 on the written TOEFL or 133 on the electronic version or take the MELAB.

Computers: There is a campus network. PCs are available in the computer lab, library, dining facility, residence halls, and administration office. A wireless network is available in residence halls. Students pay $60 per semester for wireless access. All students may access the system. There are no time limits and no fees.

Graduates: From July 1, 2002 to June 30, 2003, 206 bachelor's degrees were awarded. The most popular majors were criminal justice (17%), management (13%), and elementary education (11%). In an average class, 4% graduate in 3 years or less, 24% graduate in 4 years or less, 37% graduate in 5 years or less, and 39% graduate in 6 years or less. 40 companies recruited on campus in 2002-2003.

Admissions Contact: Ao'Lani Lorenzo, Admissions Counselor. A video is available. E-mail: *admissions@chaminade.edu*
Web: *www.chaminade.edu*

HAWAII PACIFIC UNIVERSITY
C-2
Honolulu, HI 96813
(808) 544-0238
(866) 225-5478; Fax: (808) 544-1136

Full-time: 1605 men, 2447 women	**Faculty:** 221
Part-time: 1367 men, 1316 women	**Ph.D.s:** 77%
Graduate: 579 men, 586 women	**Student/Faculty:** 18 to 1
Year: 4-1-4, summer session	**Tuition:** $10,448
Application Deadline: open	**Room & Board:** $8770
Freshman Class: 2710 applied, 2194 accepted, 591 enrolled	
SAT I Verbal/Math: 520/520	**ACT:** 23 **COMPETITIVE**

Hawaii Pacific University, founded in 1965, is a private institution offering undergraduate and graduate programs in liberal arts, business, computer science, marine science, nursing, and travel industry management. There are 6 undergraduate schools and 1 graduate school. In addition to regional accreditation, HPU has baccalaureate program accreditation with CSWE and NLN. The 2 libraries contain 162,000 volumes, 320,000 microform items, and 7500 audio/video tapes/CDs, and subscribe to 1975 periodicals. Computerized library services include the card catalog, interlibrary loans, database searching, and Internet access. Special learning facilities include a learning resource center, art gallery, and a research vessel (boat). The 135-acre campus is in an urban area downtown Honolulu and suburban Kaneohu on the island of Oahu. Including any residence halls, there are 16 buildings.

Student Life: 60% of undergraduates are from Hawaii. Students are from 50 states, 112 foreign countries, and Canada. 75% are from public schools. 37% are Asian American; 32% white; 23% foreign nationals. The average age of freshmen is 19; all undergraduates, 25. 26% do not continue beyond their first year; 65% remain to graduate.

Housing: 210 students can be accommodated in college housing, which includes single-sex and coed dorms and off-campus apartments, and homestay program. The housing office assists students in finding apartments and other living arrangements in Honolulu. On-campus housing is available on a first-come, first-served basis. Priority is given to out-of-town students. 97% of students commute. Alcohol is not permitted. All students may keep cars.

Activities: There are no fraternities or sororities. There are 85 groups on campus, including art, band, cheerleading, chorale, computers, dance, debate, drama, ethnic, film, gay, honors, international, literary magazine, musical theater, newspaper, pep band, political, professional, religious, social, social service, and student government. Popular campus events include Intercultural Day, Honors Banquet, and Club Carnival.

Sports: There are 4 intercollegiate sports for men and 4 for women, and 5 intramural sports for men and 5 for women. Facilities include soccer and softball fields, tennis courts, and use of a civic basketball arena.

Disabled Students: 75% of the campus is accessible. Wheelchair ramps, elevators, special parking, specially equipped rest rooms, special class scheduling, lowered drinking fountains, and lowered telephones are available.

Services: Counseling and information services are available, as is tutoring in most subjects. There is remedial math, reading, and writing.

Campus Safety and Security: Measures include 24-hour foot and vehicle patrol, security escort services, shuttle buses, and informal discussions. There are pamphlets/posters/films, emergency telephones, and lighted pathways/sidewalks.

Programs of Study: HPU confers B.A., B.S., B.S.B.A., B.S.Comp.Sci., B.S.N., and B.S.W. degrees. Associate and master's degrees are also awarded. Bachelor's degrees are awarded in BIOLOGICAL SCIENCE (biology/biological science and marine science), BUSINESS (accounting, banking and finance, business administration and management, business economics, entrepreneurial studies, human resources, international business management, management science, marketing management, personnel management, small business management, and tourism), COMMUNICATIONS AND THE ARTS (advertising, communications, English, journalism, literature, and public relations), COMPUTER AND PHYSICAL SCIENCE (applied mathematics, computer programming, computer science, oceanography, and science), EDUCATION (teaching English as a second/foreign language (TESOL/TEFOL)), ENGINEERING AND ENVIRONMENTAL DESIGN (environmental science and military science), HEALTH PROFESSIONS (nursing and premedicine), SOCIAL SCIENCE (anthropology, classical/ancient civilization, criminal justice, economics, history, human services, humanities, international relations, international studies, Pacific area studies, political science/government, psychology, public administration, social science, social work, and sociology). Marine biology, nursing, and computer science are the strongest academically. Nursing, computer science, and management are the largest.

Required: To graduate, students must complete a minimum of 124 semester hours in most majors, including 21 to 62 in the major, with a minimum GPA of 2.0. The core curriculum includes English, communications, global systems, quantitative skills, economics, humanities, history, and the behavioral and natural sciences; specific courses include an introduction to computers and a career seminar.

Special: Upperclassmen may participate in internships and work-study programs with numerous companies and study abroad in 4 countries. HPU also offers accelerated degree and co-op programs in all majors, B.A.-B.S. degrees in most majors, student-designed majors, dual majors in all business subjects, a 3-2 engineering degree with Washington University in St. Louis and the University of Southern California, credit for military experience, nondegree study, and pass/fail options. There are 15 national honor societies, a freshman honors program, and 7 departmental honors programs.

Faculty/Classroom: 58% of faculty are male; 42%, female. 87% teach undergraduates, 30% do research, and 30% do both. No introductory courses are taught by graduate students. The average class size in an introductory lecture is 20; in a laboratory, 15; and in a regular course, 19.

Admissions: 81% of the 2003-2004 applicants were accepted. The SAT I scores for the 2003-2004 freshman class were: Verbal--38% below 500, 48% between 500 and 599, 13% between 600 and 700, and 1% above 700; Math--41% below 500, 37% between 500 and 599, 20% between 600 and 700, and 2% above 700. The ACT scores were 36% below 21, 16% between 21 and 23, 20% between 24 and 26, 11% between 27 and 28, and 17% above 28. 40% of the current freshmen were in the top fifth of their class; 66% were in the top two fifths. 20 freshmen graduated first in their class.

Requirements: The SAT I or ACT is required. In addition, applicants must be high school graduates or have a GED certificate. The university prefers completion of 20 credits based on 4 years of English, 2 each of math and social studies, and 2 each of history and science. An essay and an interview are recommended. Certain programs, for example, marine science and nursing, have more specific admission requirements. A GPA of 2.5 is required. AP and CLEP credits are accepted. Important factors in the admissions decision are recommendations by school officials, advanced placement or honor courses, and evidence of special talent.

Procedure: Freshmen are admitted to all sessions. Entrance exams should be taken during the spring or summer of the junior year or the fall of the senior year. There is a rolling admissions plan and a deferred admissions plan. Application deadlines are open. Applications are accepted on-line through Common App, Apply Now, and the school's web site.

Transfer: 861 transfer students enrolled in 2002-2003. Applicants must have a GPA of 2.0 in a minimum of 24 credit hours. The SAT I or ACT and an interview are recommended. 30 of 124 credits required for the bachelor's degree must be completed at HPU.

Visiting: There are regularly scheduled orientations for prospective students. There are guides for informal visits and visitors may sit in on classes and stay overnight. To schedule a visit, contact Scott Stensrud at the Admissions Office at *admissions@hpu.edu*.

Financial Aid: In 2003-2004, 70% of all full-time freshmen and 42% of continuing full-time students received some form of financial aid. 43% of full-time freshmen and 30% of continuing full-time students received need-based aid. The average freshman award was $10,032. Need-based scholarships or need-based grants averaged $4041 ($12,100 maximum); need-based self-help aid (loans and jobs) averaged $4751 ($17,250 maximum); non-need-based athletic scholarships averaged $3351 ($6702 maximum); and other non-need-based awards and non-need-based scholarships averaged $4144 ($8288 maximum). 6% of undergraduates work part time. Average annual earnings from campus work are $1637. The average financial indebtedness of the 2003 graduate was $5150. The FAFSA and the college's own financial statement are required. The priority date for freshman financial aid applications for fall entry is March 1.

International Students: There are 1099 international students enrolled. The school actively recruits these students. They must score 550 on the written TOEFL or 213 on the electronic version and also take the college's own test.

Computers: There are 400 IBM PCs located in the computer center and tutoring labs equipped with the UNIX system and CD-ROMs. All students may access the system 7 days a week during day and evening hours. There are no time limits and no fees. It is strongly recommended that all students have a personal computer.

Graduates: From July 1, 2002 to June 30, 2003, 1038 bachelor's degrees were awarded. The most popular majors were business (40%), nursing (12%), and computer information systems (11%). In an average class, 5% graduate in 3 years or less, 25% graduate in 4 years or less, 36% graduate in 5 years or less, and 39% graduate in 6 years or less. 133 companies recruited on campus in 2002-2003. Of the 2002 graduating class, 63% were enrolled in graduate school within 6 months of graduation and 69% were employed.

Admissions Contact: Cherie Andrade, Director of Admissions. A video is available. E-mail: *admissions@hpu.edu* Web: *http://www.hpu.edu*

UNIVERSITY OF HAWAII SYSTEM

The University of Hawaii System, established in 1907, is a public system in Hawaii. It is governed by a Board of Regents, whose chief administrator is the president and the chancellor. The primary goal of the system is to provide all qualified people in Hawaii an equal opportunity for quality college and university education, to create knowledge and gain insights through research and scholarship, to preserve and contribute to the artistic and cultural heritage of the community, and to provide other public service through the dissemination of current and new ideas and techniques. The main priorities are serving the state of Hawaii, achieving program quality, establishing Pacific/Asian focus, and adapting to scientific change. The total enrollment of all 10 campuses is usually about 45,000; there were 3100 faculty members. Altogether there are some 123 baccalaureate, 88 master's, and 56 doctoral programs offered in University of Hawaii System. There is a 4-year campus located in Hilo and Manoa. Profiles of the 4-year campuses are included in this section.

UNIVERSITY OF HAWAII AT HILO   F-4
Hilo, HI 96720-4091

(808) 974-7414
(800) 897-4456; Fax: (808) 933-0861

Full-time: 870 men, 1330 women	**Faculty:** 162; IIB, av$
Part-time: 235 men, 395 women	**Ph.Ds:** 80%
Graduate: 20 men, 70 women	**Student/Faculty:** 14 to 1
Year: semesters, summer session	**Tuition:** $2376 ($7944)
Application Deadline: see profile	**Room & Board:** $6264
Freshman Class: n/av	
SAT I or ACT: required	**COMPETITIVE**

The University of Hawaii at Hilo, founded in 1970, is part of the public University of Hawaii and offers degree programs through its Colleges of Agriculture, Arts and Sciences, and Hawaiian language. It has a branch campus at Kealakekua, West Hawaii. Major programs include marine science, volcanology, and astronomy. There are 3 undergraduate and 2 graduate schools. Figures in the above capsule and in this profile are approximate. In addition to regional accreditation, UH Hilo has baccalaureate program accreditation with NLN. The library contains 240,000 volumes and 11,000 microform items, and subscribes to 1200 periodicals. Computerized library services include the card catalog, interlibrary loans, and database searching. Special learning facilities include a learning resource center, art gallery, space science center and marine education center. The 115-acre campus is in a small town 200 miles southeast of Honolulu. Including any residence halls, there are 54 buildings.

Student Life: 69% of undergraduates are from Hawaii. Students are from 46 states, 32 foreign countries, and Canada. 76% are from public schools. 31% are white; 27% Asian American; 18% Native American/Eskimo. The average age of all undergraduates is 27. 29% do not continue beyond their first year; 31% remain to graduate.

Housing: 800 students can be accommodated in college housing, which includes coed dorms, on-campus apartments, off-campus apartments, and married-student housing. In addition, there are honors houses, special-interest houses, and an educational/recreational enrichment hall. On-campus housing is available on a first-come, first-served basis. Priority is given to out-of-town students. 79% of students commute. Alcohol is not permitted. All students may keep cars.

Activities: There are no fraternities or sororities. There are 40 groups on campus, including art, band, cheerleading, chess, choir, chorale, chorus, computers, dance, drama, ethnic, gay, honors, international, jazz band, literary magazine, musical theater, newspaper, pep band, political, professional, religious, social, social service, and student government. Popular campus events include International Night, May Day, and dances.

Sports: There are 5 intercollegiate sports for men and 4 for women, and 10 intramural sports for men and 10 for women. Facilities include a student activities center with billiards and a game room, an athletic complex with basketball courts and a weight room, 8 tennis courts, and baseball, softball, and soccer fields.

Disabled Students: 95% of the campus is accessible. Wheelchair ramps, elevators, special parking, specially equipped rest rooms, special class scheduling, lowered drinking fountains, lowered telephones, and specially designed dorm rooms, cassette recorders, talking calculators, a TDY terminal, a magnifier projector, a large-print typewriter, and taped textbooks are available.

Services: Counseling and information services are available, as is tutoring in most subjects. There is remedial math, reading, and writing.

Campus Safety and Security: Measures include 24-hour foot and vehicle patrol, self-defense education, informal discussions, and emergency telephones. There are lighted pathways/sidewalks.

Programs of Study: UH Hilo confers B.A., B.S., B.B.A., and B.S.N. degrees. Master's degrees are also awarded. Bachelor's degrees are awarded in AGRICULTURE (agriculture), BIOLOGICAL SCIENCE (biology/biological science and marine science), BUSINESS (business administration and management), COMMUNICATIONS AND THE ARTS (art, communications, English, linguistics, and music), COMPUTER AND PHYSICAL SCIENCE (astronomy, chemistry, computer science, geology, mathematics, natural sciences, and physics), HEALTH PROFESSIONS (nursing), SOCIAL SCIENCE (anthropology, criminal justice, economics, geography, Hawaiian studies, history, Japanese studies, liberal arts/general studies, philosophy, political science/government, psychology, and sociology). Business, computer science, biology are the strongest academically. Business, psychology, and marine science are the largest.

Required: To graduate, students must earn a minimum of 120 semester hours, including at least 30 in the college from which a degree is sought, with a 2.0 GPA overall and in the major. Students also must complete general education requirements, including 10 semester hours of natural sciences with 1 hour of lab, 9 each of humanitites and social sciences, 6 of world cultures, and 3 each of English composition and quantitative reasoning. 3 writing-intensive sourses and 1 Hawaiian/Asian/Pacific course are also required.

Special: UH Hilo offers cross-registration with Hawaii Community College, a political science legislative internship and other internships in business and psychology, and many work-study programs. Students may study abroad through a variety of programs and other internships in business and psychology. The school permits a student-designed liberal studies major, dual degrees, a 3-2 engineering degree with the University of Hawaii at Manoa, nondegree study, pass/fail options, and credit for military experience. There is a freshman honors program.

Faculty/Classroom: 60% of faculty are male; 40%, female. All both teach and do research. The average class size in an introductory lecture is 25; in a laboratory, 25; and in a regular course, 17.

Admissions: 4 freshmen graduated first in their class in a recent year.

Requirements: The SAT I or ACT is required. In addition, applicants should be high school graduates or present a GED certificate. Students should have earned 22 academic credits, including 4 units of English, 3 of math, 3 of life and physical sciences, and 7 of electives. Applications are accepted on-line. UH Hilo requires applicants to be in the upper 50% of their class. A GPA of 2.5 is required. AP and CLEP credits are accepted. Important factors in the admissions decision are advanced

placement or honor courses, recommendations by school officials, and evidence of special talent.

Procedure: Freshmen are admitted fall and spring. Entrance exams should be taken by November of the senior year. There is an early admissions plan. There is a rolling admissions plan. Check with the school for current deadlines. The application fee is $40. Notification is sent on a rolling basis. Applications are accepted on-line through the school's web site.

Transfer: 577 transfer students enrolled in a recent year. Applicants must have a GPA of 2.0; those with fewer than 24 college credits must submit their high school transcript and SAT I or ACT results. 30 of 120 credits required for the bachelor's degree must be completed at UH Hilo.

Visiting: There are regularly scheduled orientations for prospective students, including a campus tour and a meeting with an admissions counselor. There are guides for informal visits and visitors may sit in on classes. To schedule a visit, contact the Admissions Office at (808) 933-3714.

Financial Aid: In a recent year, 55% of all full-time freshmen and 41% of continuing full-time students received some form of financial aid. 55% of full-time freshmen received need-based aid. The average freshman award was $3853. 70% of undergraduates work part time. Average annual earnings from campus work are $2600. The average financial indebtedness of a recent graduate was $10,698. UH Hilo is a member of CSS. The FAFSA and the college's own financial statement are required. Check with the school for current deadlines.

International Students: There were 311 international students enrolled in a recent year. The school actively recruits these students. They must score 500 on the written TOEFL or 173 on the electronic version and also take the college's own test. The SAT I or ACT is not required, but is recommended.

Computers: The mainframes are a SPARC Center 2000, 2 SPARC Server 690s, and an IBM ES/9000. There are 250 PCs and terminals in various locations on campus. Access to e-mail and the Internet requires a password assignment from the computer center. All students may access the system at posted times in person and any time by modem. There are no time limits and no fees.

Graduates: In a recent year, 419 bachelor's degrees were awarded. The most popular majors were psychology (15%), business administration (11%), and marine science (8%). In an average class, 1% graduate in 3 years or less, 10% graduate in 4 years or less, 25% graduate in 5 years or less, and 31% graduate in 6 years or less. 36 companies recruited on campus in a recent year.

Admissions Contact: Admissions Office. A video is available.
E-mail: *uhhadm@hawaii.edu* Web: *www.uhh.hawaii.edu*

UNIVERSITY OF HAWAII AT MANOA
Honolulu, HI 96822

C-2
(808) 956-8975
(800) 823-9771; Fax: (808) 956-4148

Full-time: 4801 men, 6100 women	**Faculty:** 1193; I, av$
Part-time: 868 men, 1041 women	**Ph.Ds:** 83%
Graduate: 2397 men, 3499 women	**Student/Faculty:** 9 to 1
Year: semesters, summer session	**Tuition:** $3464 ($9944)
Application Deadline: June 1	**Room & Board:** $6101
Freshman Class: 5182 applied, 3633 accepted, 1905 enrolled	
SAT I Verbal/Math: 520/560	**ACT:** 22 VERY COMPETITIVE

The University of Hawaii at Manoa, founded in 1907, is the major research institution in the University of Hawaii system. The undergraduate programs offered include liberal arts and sciences, business, education, engineering, nursing, tropical agriculture, architecture, travel industry management, physical science, technology, Hawaiian, Asian-Pacific Studies, social work, and medicine. There are 13 undergraduate and 11 graduate schools. In addition to regional accreditation, UHM has baccalaureate program accreditation with AACSB, AALE, ABET, ACEJMC, ADA, CSWE, NAAB, NASM, NLN, ABA, ACS, ADA, APA, ASLHA, CACREP, CCNE, LCME, and NAACLS. The 2 libraries contain 3.2 million volumes, 6 million microform items, and 54,590 audio/video tapes/CDs, and subscribe to 27,328 periodicals. Computerized library services include the card catalog, interlibrary loans, database searching, and Internet access. Special learning facilities include a learning resource center, art gallery, radio station, and TV station. The 300-acre campus is in an urban area in Honolulu. Including any residence halls, there are 247 buildings.

Student Life: 80% of undergraduates are from Hawaii. Students are from 50 states, 62 foreign countries, and Canada. 70% are from public schools. 62% are Asian American; 24% white. The average age of freshmen is 18; all undergraduates, 23. 23% do not continue beyond their first year; 64% remain to graduate.

Housing: 2983 students can be accommodated in college housing, which includes single-sex and coed dorms, on-campus apartments, and married-student housing. In addition, there are special-interest houses, substance free/wellness, first-year experience, technology, and 24-hour quiet halls. On-Campus housing is available on a lottery system for upperclassmen. 79% of students commute. All students may keep cars.

Activities: There is 1 local fraternity and 1 local and 1 national sorority. There are 100 groups on campus, including art, band, cheerleading, chess, choir, chorale, chorus, dance, drama, drill team, ethnic, film, gay, honors, international, literary magazine, marching band, musical theater, newspaper, opera, pep band, photography, political, professional, radio and TV, religious, social, social service, student government, and symphony. Popular campus events include noontime concerts, Midnight Madness, and Registered Independent Organization Involvement Fair.

Sports: There are 8 intercollegiate sports for men and 10 for women, and 20 intramural sports for men and 20 for women. Facilities include a 10,000-seat arena, a 4400-seat baseball stadium, swimming facilities, 2 weight rooms, a turf field and rubberized track, 2 grass fields, 3 gyms, and an off-campus football stadium.

Disabled Students: 60% of the campus is accessible. Wheelchair ramps, elevators, special parking, specially equipped rest rooms, special class scheduling, lowered drinking fountains, and lowered telephones. Disability access information is available on request, and auxiliary aids and program adjustments can be arranged on an individual basis.

Services: Counseling and information services are available, as is tutoring in some subjects on a limited basis. There is a reader service for the blind.

Campus Safety and Security: Measures include 24-hour foot and vehicle patrol, security escort services, shuttle buses, and informal discussions. There are pamphlets/posters/films, emergency telephones, and lighted pathways/sidewalks.

Programs of Study: UHM confers B.A., B.S., B.Arch., B.B.A., B.Ed., B.F.A., B.Mus., and B.S.W. degrees. Master's and doctoral degrees are also awarded. Bachelor's degrees are awarded in AGRICULTURE (agricultural economics, agriculture, animal science, plant protection (pest management), and plant science), BIOLOGICAL SCIENCE (biology/biological science, botany, microbiology, physiology, and zoology), BUSINESS (accounting, banking and finance, business administration and management, business economics, human resources, international business management, management information systems, marketing/retailing/merchandising, real estate, recreation and leisure services, and tourism), COMMUNICATIONS AND THE ARTS (apparel design, art, Chinese, classics, communications, dance, dramatic arts, English, English as a second/foreign language, French, German, Hawaiian, Japanese, journalism, Korean, linguistics, music, Russian, Spanish, and speech/debate/rhetoric), COMPUTER AND PHYSICAL SCIENCE (atmospheric sciences and meteorology, chemistry, computer science, geology, geophysics and seismology, information sciences and systems, mathematics, and physics), EDUCATION (athletic training, elementary, physical, recreation, and secondary), ENGINEERING AND ENVIRONMENTAL DESIGN (architecture, bioengineering, civil engineering, electrical/electronics engineering, environmental science, and mechanical engineering), HEALTH PROFESSIONS (dental hygiene, medical laboratory technology, nursing, and speech pathology/audiology), SOCIAL SCIENCE (American studies, anthropology, Asian/Oriental studies, economics, ethnic studies, European studies, family/consumer resource management, food science, geography, Hawaiian studies, history, liberal arts/general studies, Pacific area studies, peace studies, philosophy, political science/government, psychology, religion, social work, sociology, and women's studies). Education, business, and medicine are the strongest academically. Computer science, psychology, and art are the largest.

Required: In most disciplines, a minimum GPA of 2.0 and a total of 124 credit hours are required for graduation. The total number of hours required in the major varies according to discipline. All students must fulfill general education core requirements.

Special: Internships are available with a variety of employers including the state legislature, and through 55 different offices as well as academic departments via career services. Co-op and work-study programs and internships are also offered. Dual majors, nondegree study, and pass/fail options are available. The liberal studies program offers student-designed majors. Students may study abroad in any one of 20 countries for a summer, a semester, or a year. There are 7 national honor societies, including Phi Beta Kappa, a freshman honors program, and 2 departmental honors programs.

Faculty/Classroom: 63% of faculty are male; 37%, female. The average class size in an introductory lecture is 42; in a laboratory, 16; and in a regular course, 21.

Admissions: 70% of the 2003-2004 applicants were accepted. The SAT I scores for the 2003-2004 freshman class were: Verbal--36% below 500, 46% between 500 and 599, 16% between 600 and 700, and 2% above 700; Math--17% below 500, 50% between 500 and 599, 27% between 600 and 700, and 6% above 700. 25 freshmen graduated first in their class.

Requirements: The SAT I or ACT is required. The minimum required score on the SAT I is 510 for each section or on the ACT, 22 composite. Applicants must be graduates of an accredited secondary school. The GED is accepted. UHM requires 22 Carnegie units or 17 academic credits, including 4 units of English and 3 units each of math, science, and social studies, as well as 4 additional units of college preparatory courses and 5 electives. UHM requires applicants to be in the upper 40% of their class. A GPA of 2.8 is required. AP and CLEP credits are accepted. Important factors in the admissions decision are advanced placement or honor courses, recommendations by school officials, and leadership record.

Procedure: Freshmen are admitted to all sessions. Entrance exams should be taken by December of the senior year for fall admission. There is a rolling admissions plan. Applications should be filed by June 1 for fall entry and November 1 for spring entry, along with a $40 fee. Notification is sent on a rolling basis. Applications are accepted on-line through the university's web site.

Transfer: 2115 transfer students enrolled in 2002-2003. Applicants must have a total of 24 semester credits with a minimum GPA of 2.5. 30 of 124 credits required for the bachelor's degree must be completed at UHM.

Visiting: There are regularly scheduled orientations for prospective students, including campus tours and information sessions on areas of study, financial aid, and student employment. There are guides for informal visits and visitors may sit in on classes and stay overnight. To schedule a visit, contact School and College Services at (808) 956-6524 or toll free (877) 447-3233 or *visituhm@hawaii.edu.*

Financial Aid: In 2003-2004, 44% of all full-time freshmen and 41% of continuing full-time students received some form of financial aid. 37% of full-time freshmen and 34% of continuing full-time students received need-based aid. The average freshman award was $7876. Need-based scholarships or need-based grants averaged $3267 ($9062 maximum); need-based self-help aid (loans and jobs) averaged $3750 ($12,325 maximum); non-need-based athletic scholarships averaged $11,063 ($17,697 maximum); and other non-need-based awards and non-need-based scholarships averaged $5496 ($18,503 maximum). 90% of undergraduates work part time. Average annual earnings from campus work are $4200. The average financial indebtedness of the 2003 graduate was $8003. UHM is a member of CSS. The FAFSA and the college's own financial statement are required. The priority date for freshman financial aid applications for fall entry is March 1. The deadline for filing freshman financial aid applications for fall entry is March 15.

International Students: There are 505 international students enrolled. The school actively recruits these students. They must score 500 on the written TOEFL or 173 on the electronic version and also take the SAT I, scoring 510 on each part, or the ACT; the SAT I is preferred.

Computers: The mainframes are an IBM 9672 -RA5 and numerous Sun servers (various models). There are networked IBM and Mac PCs available in labs, academic departments, and offices. Access is also available via modem dial-up or cable modem from home. All students may access the system. There are no time limits and no fees. It is recommended that students in architecture have personal computers.

Graduates: From July 1, 2002 to June 30, 2003, 2393 bachelor's degrees were awarded. The most popular majors were psychology (6%), marketing (5%), and liberal studies (4%). In an average class, 11% graduate in 4 years or less, 38% graduate in 5 years or less, and 53% graduate in 6 years or less. 54 companies recruited on campus in 2002-2003.

Admissions Contact: Jan Heu, Interim Director of Admissions and Records. E-mail: *ar-info@hawaii.edu* Web: *www.hawaii.edu/admrec*

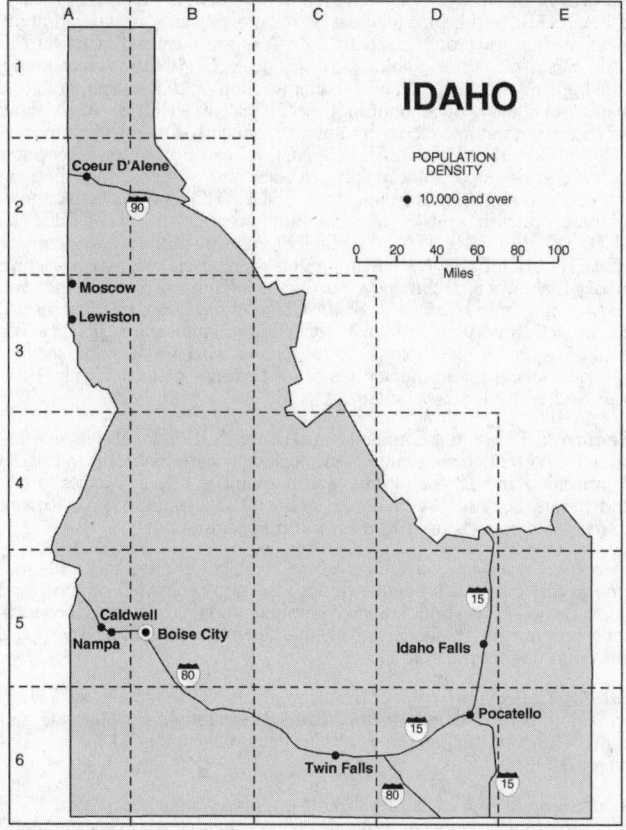

orchestra, pep band, photography, political, professional, religious, social, social service, student government, and yearbook. Popular campus events include Spring Fling, Student-Alumni Career Forum, and Winterfest.

Sports: There are 8 intercollegiate sports for men and 10 for women, and 16 intramural sports for men and 15 for women. Facilities include an activities center with a 3000-seat gym, a weight room, and a swimming pool, as well as a 6500-seat baseball stadium, softball and soccer fields, and an outdoor walking/running path.

Disabled Students: 75% of the campus is accessible. Wheelchair ramps, elevators, special parking, specially equipped rest rooms, and lowered drinking fountains are available.

Services: Counseling and information services are available, as is tutoring in most subjects. There is a reader service for the blind, and remedial math, reading, and writing.

Campus Safety and Security: Measures include 24-hour foot and vehicle patrol, self-defense education, security escort services, and informal discussions. There are pamphlets/posters/films, emergency telephones, and lighted pathways/sidewalks.

Programs of Study: ACI confers B.A. and B.S. degrees. Bachelor's degrees are awarded in AGRICULTURE (environmental studies), BIOLOGICAL SCIENCE (biology/biological science), BUSINESS (business administration and management, international business management, international economics, and sports management), COMMUNICATIONS AND THE ARTS (art, creative writing, dramatic arts, English, music, and Spanish), COMPUTER AND PHYSICAL SCIENCE (chemistry, computer mathematics, and mathematics), EDUCATION (physical), HEALTH PROFESSIONS (exercise science), SOCIAL SCIENCE (anthropology, economics, history, philosophy, political science/government, psychology, and religion). Biology, business, and social sciences/history are the largest.

Required: To graduate, the student must earn 124 credits, including 40 or more in upper-division courses, with a minimum GPA of 2.0. Required disciplines include writing, math, Western civilization, cultural diversity, natural sciences, literature, social sciences, philosophy, religion, fine arts, and phys ed.

Special: ACI offers a 3-2 engineering degree with 4 universities, as well as cross-registration with Northwest Nazarene University. Internships with major corporations, work-study programs on campus, a Washington semester, study abroad, pass/fail options, phys ed credit for military experience, an accelerated degree in business, and nondegree study are also available. The Gipson Scholar Program allows freshmen with superior records to design their own majors. There is 1 national honor society and a freshman honors program.

Faculty/Classroom: 62% of faculty are male; 38%, female. All teach undergraduates and do research. The average class size in an introductory lecture is 18; in a laboratory, 15; and in a regular course, 20.

Admissions: 76% of the 2003-2004 applicants were accepted. The SAT I scores for the 2003-2004 freshman class were: Verbal--18% below 500, 49% between 500 and 599, 27% between 600 and 700, and 6% above 700; Math--21% below 500, 41% between 500 and 599, 35% between 600 and 700, and 4% above 700. 66% of the current freshmen were in the top fifth of their class; 90% were in the top two fifths.

Requirements: The SAT I or ACT is required. In addition, applicants must be high school graduates or present a GED certificate. ACI recommends that students have 4 years of English, 3 each of math, history, and social studies, and 2 of science. An essay and a teacher or guidance counselor recommendation are required. AP and CLEP credits are accepted. Important factors in the admissions decision are extracurricular activities record, leadership record, and recommendations by school officials.

Procedure: Freshmen are admitted to all sessions. Entrance exams should be taken by the fall of the senior year. There is a rolling admissions plan. There are early admissions and deferred admissions plans. Early decision applications should be filed by November 15; regular applications, by June 1 for fall entry, along with a $50 fee. Notification of early decision is sent December 15; regular decision, on a rolling basis.

Transfer: 41 transfer students enrolled in 2002-2003. Applicants must supply official transcripts and clearance reports from colleges attended, as well as an essay and 1 teacher recommendation. They must also have at least 28 semester hours of college credit. 30 of 124 credits required for the bachelor's degree must be completed at ACI.

Visiting: There are regularly scheduled orientations for prospective students, including an overnight stay with student hosts, class visitations, personal appointments with financial aid counselors, professors, and coaches, social events, and a campus tour. Individual tours can also be arranged. There are guides for informal visits and visitors may sit in on classes and stay overnight. To schedule a visit, contact the Admission Office at *www.albertson.edu*.

Financial Aid: In 2003-2004, 97% of all full-time freshmen and 94% of continuing full-time students received some form of financial aid. 65%

ALBERTSON COLLEGE OF IDAHO
Caldwell, ID 83605-4432

A-5

(208) 459-5305
(800) 224-3246; Fax: (208) 459-5757

Full-time: 360 men, 426 women	**Faculty:** 71
Part-time: 7 men, 10 women	**Ph.D.s:** 93%
Graduate: 3 men, 6 women	**Student/Faculty:** 11 to 1
Year: 4-1-4	**Tuition:** $14,400
Application Deadline: June 1	**Room & Board:** $5015
Freshman Class: 950 applied, 720 accepted, 253 enrolled	
ACT: 24	**VERY COMPETITIVE**

Albertson College of Idaho, founded in 1891, is a private institution offering degree programs in liberal arts education and the sciences. The college runs on a 12-6-12 calendar, with a 6-week intercession. In addition to regional accreditation, ACI has baccalaureate program accreditation with NASDTEC. The library contains 183,308 volumes, 17,000 microform items, and 1717 audio/video tapes/CDs, and subscribes to 703 periodicals. Computerized library services include the card catalog, interlibrary loans, and database searching. Special learning facilities include an art gallery, natural history museum, planetarium, and a rock and mineral collection. The 43-acre campus is in a small town 25 miles west of Boise. Including any residence halls, there are 21 buildings.

Student Life: 72% of undergraduates are from Idaho. Students are from 27 states, 13 foreign countries, and Canada. 95% are from public schools. 78% are white. Most claim no religious affiliation. The average age of freshmen is 18; all undergraduates, 20. 23% do not continue beyond their first year; 54% remain to graduate.

Housing: 525 students can be accommodated in college housing, which includes single-sex and coed dorms and on-campus apartments. In addition, there is an honors residence hall and special lifestyle floors (substance free, and so on). On-campus housing is guaranteed for the freshman year only, is available on a first-come, first-served basis, and is available on a lottery system for upperclassmen. 56% of students live on campus; of those, 80% remain on campus on weekends. All students may keep cars.

Activities: 20% of men belong to 3 national fraternities; 15% of women belong to 1 local and 3 national sororities. There are 55 groups on campus, including art, band, cheerleading, choir, chorale, chorus, computers, dance, debate, drama, ethnic, film, gay, honors, international, jazz band, jazz choir, literary magazine, musical theater, newspaper, opera,

of full-time freshmen and 88% of continuing full-time students received need-based aid. Need-based scholarships or need-based grants averaged $4097; need-based self-help aid (loans and jobs) averaged $3760; non-need-based athletic scholarships averaged $3600; and other non-need-based awards and non-need-based scholarships averaged $4080. 40% of undergraduates work part time. Average annual earnings from campus work are $775. The average financial indebtedness of the 2003 graduate was $18,125. ACI is a member of CSS. The FAFSA and the college's own financial statement are required. The priority date for freshman financial aid applications for fall entry is February 15.

International Students: There are 20 international students enrolled. They must score 550 on the written TOEFL or 213 on the electronic version or take the MELAB and also take the SAT I or the ACT.

Computers: The mainframe is an HP 9000. There are 8 computer lab clusters with 120 PCs, all with access to the Internet. There are also mini labs in residence halls, and every room is wired to provide access to the Internet and other campus computer offerings. All students may access the system at designated times in computer labs; 24 hours in residence halls. There are no time limits and no fees. It is strongly recommended that all students have a personal computer.

Graduates: From July 1, 2002 to June 30, 2003, 161 bachelor's degrees were awarded. The most popular majors were history and social science (19%), business (17%), and biology (16%). In an average class, 47% graduate in 4 years or less, 47% graduate in 5 years or less, and 51% graduate in 6 years or less. Of the 2002 graduating class, 14% were enrolled in graduate school within 6 months of graduation and 80% were employed.

Admissions Contact: Brandie Holly, Director of Admissions. A video is available. E-mail: *admissions@albertson.edu*
Web: *www.albertson.edu*

BOISE STATE UNIVERSITY   B-5
Boise, ID 83725

(208) 426-1177
(800) 824-7017; Fax: (208) 426-3765

Full-time: 4913 men, 5542 women	**Faculty:** 475; IIA, -$
Part-time: 2716 men, 3380 women	**Ph.D.s:** 78%
Graduate: 748 men, 1033 women	**Student/Faculty:** 22 to 1
Year: semesters, summer session	**Tuition:** $3251 ($9971)
Application Deadline: July 14	**Room & Board:** $4406
Freshman Class: 3900 applied, 3602 accepted, 2104 enrolled	
SAT I Verbal/Math: 508/505	**ACT:** 21 **LESS COMPETITIVE**

Boise State University, founded in 1932, is part of the Idaho Higher Education System and offers degree programs in the arts and sciences, business, education, health science, public affairs, technology, and vocational technical education. Some figures given in above capsule and in this profile are approximate. There are 7 undergraduate schools and 1 graduate school. In addition to regional accreditation, Boise State has baccalaureate program accreditation with AACSB, CAHEA, CSWE, NASM, NCATE, and NLN. The library contains 505,618 volumes, 1,100,000 microform items, and 58,000 audio/video tapes/CDs, and subscribes to 4797 periodicals. Computerized library services include the card catalog, interlibrary loans, and database searching. Special learning facilities include a learning resource center, art gallery, radio station, and technology center. The 110-acre campus is in an urban area in Boise. Including any residence halls, there are 60 buildings.

Student Life: 92% of undergraduates are from Idaho. Students are from 49 states, 47 foreign countries, and Canada. 85% are white. The average age of freshmen is 21; all undergraduates, 26. 41% do not continue beyond their first year; 59% remain to graduate.

Housing: 929 students can be accommodated in college housing, which includes single-sex and coed dorms, on-campus apartments, and married-student housing. On-campus housing is available on a first-come, first-served basis. 93% of students commute. All students may keep cars.

Activities: 1% of men belong to 4 national fraternities; 1% of women belong to 3 national sororities. There are 136 groups on campus, including art, band, cheerleading, chess, choir, chorale, dance, drama, drill team, ethnic, gay, honors, international, jazz band, literary magazine, marching band, newspaper, orchestra, pep band, political, professional, radio and TV, religious, social, social service, and student government. Popular campus events include Spring Fling, Leadership Quest, and Martin Luther King, Jr. Celebration.

Sports: There are 7 intercollegiate sports for men and 7 for women. Facilities include a 30,000-seat stadium, a 12,000-seat indoor arena, a swimming pool, racquetball courts, indoor and outdoor tennis courts, indoor and outdoor tracks, and a weight room.

Disabled Students: 97% of the campus is accessible. Wheelchair ramps, elevators, special parking, specially equipped rest rooms, special class scheduling, lowered drinking fountains, lowered telephones, and electric doors are available.

Services: Counseling and information services are available, as is tutoring in most subjects. There is a reader service for the blind and remedial math, reading, and writing.

Campus Safety and Security: Measures include 24-hour foot and vehicle patrol, shuttle buses, informal discussions, and pamphlets/posters/films. There are emergency telephones and lighted pathways/sidewalks.

Programs of Study: Boise State confers B.A., B.S., B.A.A.S., B.B.A., B.F.A., B.I.S., and B.Mus. degrees. Associate, master's, and doctoral degrees are also awarded. Bachelor's degrees are awarded in BIOLOGICAL SCIENCE (biology/biological science), BUSINESS (accounting, banking and finance, business administration and management, and marketing/retailing/merchandising), COMMUNICATIONS AND THE ARTS (art, communications, dramatic arts, English, fine arts, and music), COMPUTER AND PHYSICAL SCIENCE (chemistry, geology, geophysics and seismology, information sciences and systems, mathematics, physics, and radiological technology), EDUCATION (art, education, elementary, English, music, physical, and secondary), ENGINEERING AND ENVIRONMENTAL DESIGN (construction management), HEALTH PROFESSIONS (environmental health science, health science, medical laboratory technology, nursing, predentistry, premedicine, and respiratory therapy), SOCIAL SCIENCE (anthropology, criminal justice, economics, history, interdisciplinary studies, philosophy, political science/government, psychology, social science, social work, and sociology). Business, art, and theater arts are the strongest academically. Business and education are the largest.

Required: To graduate, students must complete 128 credits with a minimum GPA of 2.0. Core requirements include 6 semester hours in English composition and 12 each in arts and humanities, social sciences, math, and natural sciences. A minimum grade of C is required in all major courses and courses used to meet the core requirements.

Special: Boise State offers internships, work-study programs, dual majors, a general studies degree, nondegree study, pass/fail options, and study abroad in England, France, Germany, and Italy. There is a cooperative program in engineering with the University of Idaho. There is a freshman honors program.

Faculty/Classroom: 69% of faculty are male; 31%, female. 94% teach undergraduates. No introductory courses are taught by graduate students. The average class size in an introductory lecture is 30 and in a laboratory, 21.

Admissions: 92% of the 2003-2004 applicants were accepted. 23% of the current freshmen were in the top fifth of their class; 35% were in the top two fifths.

Requirements: The SAT I or ACT is required. In addition, students must graduate from an accredited high school and have an appropriate GPA and ACT or SAT I test score (as rated by the school's admission index). Students must have completed 4 years of English, 3 each of math (algebra I and higher) and natural science, 2 1/2 of social science, 1 of humanities or foreign language, and 1 1/2 in other college-preparatory classes. Students who have not completed all the above classes but meet the other admission requirements will be considered for provisional admission status. AP and CLEP credits are accepted.

Procedure: Freshmen are admitted to all sessions. Applications should be filed by July 14 for fall entry and December 2 for spring entry. Notification of both early decision and regular decision is sent on a rolling basis. Check with the school for current application fee.

Transfer: A minimum GPA of 2.0 is required for students with at least 14 college credits. Those students with fewer credits must submit SAT I or ACT scores and a high school transcript. 30 of 128 credits required for the bachelor's degree must be completed at Boise State.

Visiting: There are guides for informal visits and visitors may sit in on classes. To schedule a visit, contact the New Student Information Center at (208) 385-1820 or (800) 824-7017.

Financial Aid: In 2003-2004, 58% of all full-time students received some form of financial aid. 38% of full-time freshmen and 39% of continuing full-time students received need-based aid. The average freshman award was $5801. Need-based scholarships or need-based grants averaged $2891; need-based self-help aid (loans and jobs) averaged $2426; and non-need-based athletic scholarships averaged $8254. Boise State is a member of CSS. The CSS Profile or FAFSA is required. Check with the school for current application deadlines.

International Students: In a recent year, there were 131 international students enrolled. Applicants must score 500 on the written TOEFL.

Computers: The mainframes are an IBM 4341 Model 2 and an HP 3000. There are also 750 PCs and Macs available in labs and faculty offices. All students may access the system. Students may access the system 2 hours at a time in the labs.

Admissions Contact: Barbara Fortin, Director of Admissions. A video is available. E-mail: *bsuinfo@boisestate.edu* Web: *www.boisestate.edu*

IDAHO STATE UNIVERSITY
Pocatello, ID 83209-0009

D-6

(208) 282-5822; Fax: (208) 282-4231

Full-time: 3851 men, 4319 women	**Faculty:** 577; IIA, --$
Part-time: 1418 men, 2095 women	**Ph.D.s:** 68%
Graduate: 778 men, 1160 women	**Student/Faculty:** 13 to 1
Year: semesters, summer session	**Tuition:** $3448 ($10,048)
Application Deadline: August 1	**Room & Board:** $4680
Freshman Class: 3573 applied, 2638 accepted, 2107 enrolled	
SAT I Verbal/Math: 525/530	**ACT:** 20	**COMPETITIVE**

Idaho State University, founded in 1901, is a public institution offering programs in the liberal arts and sciences, business, education, engineering, and health professions. There are 7 undergraduate schools and 1 graduate school. In addition to regional accreditation, ISU has baccalaureate program accreditation with AACSB, ABET, ACPE, ADA, APTA, CSWE, NASDTEC, NASM, and NCATE. The library contains 462,101 volumes, 1,953,720 microform items, and 622 audio/video tapes/CDs, and subscribes to 3559 periodicals. Computerized library services include the card catalog, interlibrary loans, and database searching. Special learning facilities include a learning resource center, art gallery, natural history museum, planetarium, radio station, and TV station. The 972-acre campus is in a small town 150 miles north of Salt Lake City. Including any residence halls, there are 54 buildings. Faculty data is the above capsule is approximate.

Student Life: 94% of undergraduates are from Idaho. Students are from 43 states, 57 foreign countries, and Canada. 96% are from public schools. 88% are white. 42% claim no religious affiliation; 38% Latter Day Saints (Mormon); 6% Catholic. The average age of freshmen is 20; all undergraduates, 26. 39% do not continue beyond their first year.

Housing: 680 students can be accommodated in college housing, which includes single-sex and coed dorms, on-campus apartments, and married-student housing. In addition, there are honors houses and special-interest houses. On-campus housing is available on a first-come, first-served basis. Alcohol is not permitted. All students may keep cars.

Activities: 1% of men belong to 3 local fraternities; 1% of women belong to 3 local sororities. There are 140 groups on campus, including band, choir, chorus, computers, dance, debate, drama, ethnic, film, gay, honors, international, jazz band, marching band, newspaper, outdoor, pep band, photography, political, professional, radio and TV, religious, social, student government, and symphony. Popular campus events include movies, concerts, and art displays.

Sports: There are 6 intercollegiate sports for men and 7 for women, and 14 intramural sports for men and 14 for women. Facilities include playing fields, a field house, a gym, a recreation center, tennis courts, an athletic arena, a fitness/wellness center, and facilities for bowling and billiards.

Disabled Students: All of the campus is accessible. Wheelchair ramps, elevators, special parking, specially equipped rest rooms, lowered drinking fountains, lowered telephones, special housing, electric doors, and handrails are available.

Services: Counseling and information services are available, as is tutoring in every subject. There is a reader service for the blind, and remedial math, reading, and writing.

Campus Safety and Security: Measures include 24-hour foot and vehicle patrol, self-defense education, security escort services, and shuttle buses. There are informal discussions, pamphlets/posters/films, emergency telephones, lighted pathways/sidewalks, and and an e-mail bulletin alert service on campus.

Programs of Study: ISU confers B.A., B.S., B.A.G.S., B.A.T., B.B.A., B.F.A., B.M., B.M.E., and B.U.S. degrees. Associate, master's, and doctoral degrees are also awarded. Bachelor's degrees are awarded in BIOLOGICAL SCIENCE (biochemistry, biology/biological science, botany, ecology, microbiology, and zoology), BUSINESS (accounting, banking and finance, business administration and management, human resources, management science, and marketing/retailing/merchandising), COMMUNICATIONS AND THE ARTS (art, communications, dramatic arts, English, fine arts, French, German, music, music performance, Spanish, and speech/debate/rhetoric), COMPUTER AND PHYSICAL SCIENCE (chemistry, computer science, geology, information sciences and systems, mathematics, and physics), EDUCATION (early childhood, elementary, health, music, physical, secondary, special, and vocational), ENGINEERING AND ENVIRONMENTAL DESIGN (computer technology, engineering, and engineering management), HEALTH PROFESSIONS (dental hygiene, health care administration, medical laboratory technology, nursing, physician's assistant, radiological science, and speech pathology/audiology), SOCIAL SCIENCE (American studies, anthropology, dietetics, economics, history, home economics, international studies, liberal arts/general studies, philosophy, political science/government, psychology, social work, and sociology). Nursing, elementary education, and secondary education are the strongest academically. Biology is the largest.

Required: Students must satisfy general education requirements in the areas of written and spoken English, math, biological and physical sciences, fine arts, literature, philosophy, U.S. and non-U.S. history, government/economics, foreign language, psychology, anthropology, and sociology. To graduate, students must complete 128 credit hours, including 24 to 50 in the major, with a minimum GPA of 2.0.

Special: ISU participates in the Idaho Dental Education Program and several other medical co-op programs. Students may cross-register through the Western Education Exchange. ISU also offers a work-study program, study abroad in 50 countries, dual and student-designed majors, internships, credit by challenge exam or for life/military/work experience, nondegree study, and a general studies degree. As many as 16 credits of correspondence study may be applied toward the bachelor's degree. There are 11 national honor societies and 6 departmental honors programs.

Faculty/Classroom: 58% of faculty are male; 42%, female.

Admissions: 74% of the 2003-2004 applicants were accepted. The SAT I scores for the 2003-2004 freshman class were: Verbal--37% below 500, 42% between 500 and 599, 17% between 600 and 700, and 4% above 700; Math--43% below 500, 30% between 500 and 599, 25% between 600 and 700, and 2% above 700. The ACT scores were 52% below 21, 24% between 21 and 23, 16% between 24 and 26, 5% between 27 and 28, and 3% above 28.

Requirements: The SAT I or ACT is required; the ACT is preferred. Applicants must be graduates of an accredited secondary school or have a GED. They should prepare with 4 units of English, 3 each of math and science, 2.5 of social studies, 2 of college preparation, and 1 of foreign language. A GPA of 2.0 is required. AP and CLEP credits are accepted. Important factors in the admissions decision are advanced placement or honor courses, recommendations by school officials, and parents or siblings attending the school.

Procedure: Freshmen are admitted to all sessions. Entrance exams should be taken early in the senior year. There is a rolling admissions plan. There are early admissions and deferred admissions plans. Applications should be filed by August 1 for fall entry and December 1 for spring entry. The fall 2003 application fee was $30. Notification is sent on a rolling basis. Applications are accepted on-line through *www.isu.edu.*

Transfer: 1210 transfer students enrolled in 2002-2003. Applicants must submit a final, official transcript from each college attended. At least 14 credit hours with a minimum GPA of 2.0 is required; students with fewer credit hours are subject to freshman admission requirements. Applicants with fewer than 25 credits must submit high school transcripts. 32 of 128 credits required for the bachelor's degree must be completed at ISU.

Visiting: There are regularly scheduled orientations for prospective students. There are guides for informal visits. To schedule a visit, contact Enrollment Planning at (208) 282-3277.

Financial Aid: In 2003-2004, 56% of all full-time freshmen received some form of financial aid. 70% of full-time freshmen received need-based aid. 12% of undergraduates work part time. The FAFSA is required. The deadline for filing freshman financial aid applications for fall entry is March 15.

International Students: There are 184 international students enrolled. The school actively recruits these students. They must score 500 on the written TOEFL and also take the SAT I or the ACT.

Computers: The mainframe is an HP 3000. Macs and PCs are available to all students in academic buildings. All students may access the system. There are no time limits. The fee is $10 per semester.

Graduates: From July 1, 2002 to June 30, 2003, 1212 bachelor's degrees were awarded. The most popular majors were education (12%), business administration (7%), and biology (5%). In an average class, 7% graduate in 4 years or less, 15% graduate in 5 years or less, and 26% graduate in 6 years or less. 170 companies recruited on campus in 2002-2003.

Admissions Contact: Nathan Peterson, Assoc. Director, Recruitment. A video is available. E-mail: *petenath@isu.edu*
Web: *www.isu.edu/departments/enroll/*

LEWIS-CLARK STATE COLLEGE
Lewiston, ID 83501-2698

A-3

(208) 792-2210
(800) 933-LCSC; Fax: (208) 792-2876

Full-time: 950 men, 1305 women	**Faculty:** 134; IIB, --$
Part-time: 413 men, 803 women	**Ph.D.s:** 71%
Graduate: none	**Student/Faculty:** 17 to 1
Year: semesters, summer session	**Tuition:** $3126 ($9124)
Application Deadline: open	**Room & Board:** $3855
Freshman Class: 985 applied, 796 accepted, 563 enrolled	
SAT I Verbal/Math: 490/500	**ACT:** 19	**COMPETITIVE**

Lewis-Clark State College, founded in 1893 and today part of the Idaho Higher Education System, offers programs in the arts and sciences, business, education, nursing, and preprofessional and technical training. It is named for the famed explorers, who once camped near what is now the campus. There are 8 undergraduate schools. In addition to regional accreditation, Lewis-Clark has baccalaureate program accreditation with AACSB, NASDTEC, NCATE, and NLN. The library contains 253,000 volumes, 53,000 microform items, and 7000 audio/video tapes/CDs, and subscribes to 4000 periodicals. Computerized library services include the card catalog, interlibrary loans, and database searching. Special learning facilities include a learning resource center, art gallery, planetarium, radio station, TV station, and an educational technology center. The 44-acre campus is in an urban area 100 miles southeast of Spokane. Including any residence halls, there are 29 buildings.

Student Life: 86% of undergraduates are from Idaho. Students are from 20 states, 30 foreign countries, and Canada. 82% are white. The average age of freshmen is 21; all undergraduates, 25. 46% do not continue beyond their first year; 28% remain to graduate.

Housing: 300 students can be accommodated in college housing, which includes single-sex and coed dorms, off-campus apartments, and married-student housing. In addition, there are honors houses and language houses. On-campus housing is available on a first-come, first-served basis. 91% of students commute. Alcohol is not permitted. All students may keep cars.

Activities: There are no fraternities or sororities. There are 46 groups on campus, including art, chess, choir, chorale, chorus, computers, dance, debate, departmental, drama, ethnic, honors, international, jazz band, literary magazine, musical theater, newspaper, orchestra, political, professional, radio and TV, religious, social, and student government. Popular campus events include Artists Series and Dogwood Festival.

Sports: There are 5 intercollegiate sports for men and 5 for women, and 8 intramural sports for men and 7 for women. Facilities include a gym, indoor tennis courts, and a baseball field.

Disabled Students: 99% of the campus is accessible. Wheelchair ramps, elevators, special parking, specially equipped rest rooms, and special class scheduling are available.

Services: Counseling and information services are available, as is tutoring in every subject. There is a reader service for the blind, and remedial math, reading, and writing.

Campus Safety and Security: Measures include 24-hour foot and vehicle patrol, self-defense education, security escort services, shuttle buses, and lighted pathways/sidewalks.

Programs of Study: Lewis-Clark confers B.A., B.S., B.Applied Sc., B.Applied Tech., B.S.N., and B.S.W. degrees. Associate degrees are also awarded. Bachelor's degrees are awarded in BIOLOGICAL SCIENCE (biology/biological science), BUSINESS (business administration and management), COMMUNICATIONS AND THE ARTS (communications and English), COMPUTER AND PHYSICAL SCIENCE (chemistry, computer science, geoscience, mathematics, and natural sciences), EDUCATION (elementary and secondary), HEALTH PROFESSIONS (nursing), SOCIAL SCIENCE (criminal justice, history, liberal arts/general studies, physical fitness/movement, psychology, social science, and social work). Education, business, and nursing are the strongest academically and the largest.

Required: Students must earn 128 credit hours, including 38 to 40 in the core curriculum and 48 in their major, with a minimum GPA of 2.0 to graduate.

Special: Lewis-Clark offers cooperative programs and cross-registration with 3 Idaho universities, on-campus internships, work-study programs, student-designed majors, nondegree study, and pass/fail options. The college grants credit for military experience. There are also between-semester and weekend academic programs, and flexible scheduling in a variety of programs. A 3-2 engineering degree is available at Boise or Idaho State Universities. There is 1 national honor society and a freshman honors program.

Faculty/Classroom: 58% of faculty are male; 42%, female. All teach undergraduates. The average class size in an introductory lecture is 33 and in a laboratory, 25.

Admissions: 81% of the 2003-2004 applicants were accepted. The SAT I scores for the 2003-2004 freshman class were: Verbal--56% below 500, 33% between 500 and 599, 10% between 600 and 700, and 2% above 700; Math--50% below 500, 36% between 500 and 599, 12% between 600 and 700, and 3% above 700. The ACT scores were 62% below 21, 20% between 21 and 23, 13% between 24 and 26, 3% between 27 and 28, and 2% above 28. 19% of the current freshmen were in the top fifth of their class; 48% were in the top two fifths. 5 freshmen graduated first in their class.

Requirements: The SAT I or ACT is required if the applicant is under age 21 at the time of college entrance. Lewis-Clark has a liberal admissions policy, but students must be high school graduates or present a GED certificate. They must have fulfilled requirements in English, math, social and natural sciences, fine arts, and speech, with a minimum GPA of 2.0. AP and CLEP credits are accepted.

Procedure: Freshmen are admitted to all sessions. Entrance exams should be taken before registration. There is a rolling admissions plan. There are early admissions and deferred admissions plans. Application deadlines are open. Application fee is $35. Applications are accepted on-line through *www.lcsc.edu/admissions/forms.*

Transfer: 389 transfer students enrolled in 2002-2003. Applicants who do not have a minimum GPA of 2.0 must submit standardized test scores. 32 of 128 credits required for the bachelor's degree must be completed at Lewis-Clark.

Visiting: There are regularly scheduled orientations for prospective students, including STAR (Student Advising and Registration) and Warrior Discovery Day. There are guides for informal visits and visitors may sit in on classes and stay overnight. To schedule a visit, contact the Office of Recruitment and Retention at (208) 792-2378 or *sspws@lcsc.edu.*

Financial Aid: In 2003-2004, 68% of all full-time freshmen and 62% of continuing full-time students received some form of financial aid. 52% of full-time freshmen and 50% of continuing full-time students received need-based aid. The average freshman award was $4033. Need-based scholarships or need-based grants averaged $2781 ($4500 maximum); need-based self-help aid (loans and jobs) averaged $2652 ($6625 maximum); non-need-based athletic scholarships averaged $4485 ($8562 maximum); and other non-need-based awards and non-need-based scholarships averaged $2873. 10% of undergraduates work part time. Average annual earnings from campus work are $1360. Lewis-Clark is a member of CSS. The FAFSA is required. The priority date for freshman financial aid applications for fall entry is March 1.

International Students: There are 94 international students enrolled. The school actively recruits these students. They must score 500 on the written TOEFL or 173 on the electronic version.

Computers: There are 445 PCs located in computer labs in several buildings including the library. All students may access the system 7 days a week. There are no time limits and no fees.

Graduates: From July 1, 2002 to June 30, 2003, 299 bachelor's degrees were awarded. The most popular majors were business (25%), justice studies (15%), and nursing (14%). Of the 2002 graduating class, 8% were enrolled in graduate school within 6 months of graduation.

Admissions Contact: Steven J. Bussolini, Director of Admission and Market Development. E-mail: *admissions@lcsc.edu* Web: *www.lcsc.edu*

NORTHWEST NAZARENE UNIVERSITY A-5
Nampa, ID 83686 (208) 467-8496; (877) NNU-4-YOU

Full-time: 1163 men and women	**Faculty:** 93; IIA, --$
Part-time: none	**Ph.Ds:** 69%
Graduate: 409 men and women	**Student/Faculty:** 13 to 1
Year: semesters, summer session	**Tuition:** $15,920
Application Deadline: August 8	**Room & Board:** $4440
Freshman Class: 1085 applied, 576 accepted, 259 enrolled	
SAT I Verbal/Math: 551/545	**ACT:** 23 **VERY COMPETITIVE**

Northwest Nazarene University, founded in 1913, is a private liberal arts college affiliated with the Church of the Nazarene. It offers programs in fine arts, language and literature, math and natural science, philosophy and religion, professional studies, and social science. In addition to regional accreditation, NNU has baccalaureate program accreditation with CSWE, NASM, and NCATE. The library contains 120,000 volumes, 19,500 microform items, and 3500 audio/video tapes/CDs, and subscribes to 830 periodicals. Computerized library services include the card catalog, interlibrary loans, database searching, and Internet access. Special learning facilities include a learning resource center, art gallery, and educational media center. The 85-acre campus is in a small town 20 miles west of Boise. Including any residence halls, there are 26 buildings.

Student Life: 65% of undergraduates are from out of state, mostly the Northwest. Students are from 32 states, 8 foreign countries, and Canada. 93% are white. Most are Protestant. The average age of freshmen is 19; all undergraduates, 21. 30% do not continue beyond their first year; 38% remain to graduate.

Housing: 852 students can be accommodated in college housing, which includes single-sex dorms, on-campus apartments, off-campus apartments, and married-student housing. On-campus housing is guaranteed for all 4 years. 60% of students live on campus; of those, 80% remain on campus on weekends. Alcohol is not permitted. All students may keep cars.

Activities: There are no fraternities or sororities. There are more than 30 groups on campus, including art, band, chess, choir, chorale, chorus, computers, debate, drama, drill team, film, forensics, honors, international, jazz band, literary magazine, musical theater, newspaper, orchestra, pep band, photography, political, professional, radio and TV, religious, social, social service, student government, symphony, and yearbook. Popular campus events include Welcome Week, Malibu Days, and Mother-Daughter weekend.

Sports: There are 5 intercollegiate sports for men and 6 for women, and 6 intramural sports for men and 6 for women. Facilities include a lighted baseball field, 2 soccer fields, outdoor basketball, tennis, and sand volleyball courts, a track-and-field facility, a field house, a park, and a softball field.

Disabled Students: 95% of the campus is accessible. Wheelchair ramps, elevators, special parking, specially equipped rest rooms, special class scheduling, lowered drinking fountains, lowered telephones, special housing, and alternate testing and evaluation methods are available.

Services: Counseling and information services are available, as is tutoring in every subject. There is remedial math, reading, and writing.

Campus Safety and Security: Measures include 24-hour foot and vehicle patrol, security escort services, informal discussions, and pamphlets/posters/films. There are emergency telephones, lighted pathways/ sidewalks, a professional security company, student lock-up-unlock and walk-around-campus teams, and a city police substation.

Programs of Study: NNU confers B.A., B.S., and B.S.N. degrees. Associate and master's degrees are also awarded. Bachelor's degrees are awarded in BIOLOGICAL SCIENCE (biochemistry and biology/ biological science), BUSINESS (accounting, business administration and management, international business management, marketing and distribution, and recreation and leisure services), COMMUNICATIONS AND THE ARTS (art, ceramic art and design, communications, English, graphic design, music, painting, sculpture, and Spanish), COMPUTER AND PHYSICAL SCIENCE (chemistry, computer science, mathematics, natural sciences, and physics), EDUCATION (art, elementary, English, foreign languages, mathematics, music, physical, science, and social science), ENGINEERING AND ENVIRONMENTAL DESIGN (engineering physics), HEALTH PROFESSIONS (nursing and premedicine), SOCIAL SCIENCE (economics, history, international studies, liberal arts/general studies, ministries, philosophy, political science/government, psychology, religion, and social work). Biology, education, and business are the strongest academically and are the largest.

Required: All students must complete 124 semester credits, of which 43 must be upper division. Students must show competency in communication and language skills, have a 2.0 GPA, demonstrate math proficiency, complete a major field of study, and take a comprehensive exam. In addition, each student must complete general education requirements, which are divided into three categories: English, speech, wellness, math proficiency, and freshman seminar; Bible history and literature, theology, philosophy, and history; and art history/music literature, literature, science, and social science electives.

Special: There is cross-registration with other Nazarene schools and study abroad in 11 countries. The university also offers internships, a work-study program, a general studies degree, dual and student-designed majors, and credit for military experience. There is a 3-2 engineering program with the University of Idaho, Seattle Pacific University, and Walla Walla College. There is 1 national honor society and a freshman honors program.

Faculty/Classroom: 65% of faculty are male; 35%, female. 97% teach undergraduates, 12% do research, and 12% do both. No introductory courses are taught by graduate students. The average class size in an introductory lecture is 21; in a laboratory, 10; and in a regular course, 16.

Admissions: 53% of the 2003-2004 applicants were accepted. The SAT I scores for the 2003-2004 freshman class were: Verbal--30% below 500, 41% between 500 and 599, 20% between 600 and 700, and 9% above 700; Math--34% below 500, 39% between 500 and 599, 17% between 600 and 700, and 10% above 700. There were 5 National Merit finalists. 14 freshmen graduated first in their class in a recent year.

Requirements: The ACT is required. In addition, applicants should be graduates of an accredited secondary school; the GED may also be accepted. Applicants should prepare with 4 years of English, 3 each of math, science, and history or social science, and 2 of foreign language. A GPA of 2.5 is required. AP and CLEP credits are accepted.

Procedure: Freshmen are admitted fall, spring, and summer. Entrance exams should be taken early in the senior year. There is a rolling admissions plan. Applications should be filed by August 8 for fall entry and December 15 for winter entry, along with a $25 fee. Notification is sent on a rolling basis. Applications are accepted on-line through the school's web site.

Transfer: 70 transfer students enrolled in 2002-2003. Students who have earned the equivalent of 12 semester credits may be admitted as transfer students. Official transcripts from all colleges previously attended must be submitted. 32 of 124 credits required for the bachelor's degree must be completed at NNU.

Visiting: There are regularly scheduled orientations for prospective students, including the opportunity to stay in a dorm and have class visits. There are guides for informal visits and visitors may sit in on classes and stay overnight. To schedule a visit, contact the Campus Visit Coordinator at admissions@nnu.edu.

Financial Aid: In a recent year, 95% of all full-time freshmen and 96% of continuing full-time students received some form of financial aid. 61% of full-time freshmen and 57% of continuing full-time students received need-based aid. The average freshman award was $9645. 66% of undergraduates work part time. Average annual earnings from campus work are $827. The average financial indebtedness of a recent graduate was $15,560. The FAFSA is required. The priority date for freshman financial aid applications for fall entry is February 15. The deadline for filing freshman financial aid applications for fall entry is August 25.

International Students: There were 8 international students enrolled in a recent year. They must score 500 on the written TOEFL or 173 on the electronic version and also take the ACT, scoring 18.

Computers: Mainframe terminals and PCs for student use are available. Languages and software include APL, BASIC, C++, COBOL, FORTRAN, LOGO, MODSIM II, Paradox, Pascal, Powerhouse 4GL, and RPG. WordPerfect and Quattro are installed in all PCs. All students may access the system. There are no time limits and no fees. It is strongly recommended that all students have a personal computer.

Graduates: In a recent year, 198 bachelor's degrees were awarded. The most popular majors were business administration (13%), elementary education (12%), and religion/religious studies (9%). In an average class, 51% graduate in 6 years or less. 100 companies recruited on campus in a recent year.

Admissions Contact: Office of Enrollment Services.
Web: www.nnu.edu

UNIVERSITY OF IDAHO	A-2
Moscow, ID 83844-2282	(208) 885-6326
	(888) 884-3246; Fax: (208) 885-9119

Full-time: 4605 men, 3798 women	Faculty: 545; I, --$
Part-time: 647 men, 557 women	Ph.D.s: 80%
Graduate: 1421 men, 1078 women	Student/Faculty: 15 to 1
Year: semesters, summer session	Tuition: $3348 ($10,740)
Application Deadline: August 1	Room & Board: $4868
Freshman Class: 3973 applied, 3202 accepted, 1663 enrolled	
SAT I Verbal/Math: 550/560	ACT: 23 COMPETITIVE

The University of Idaho, founded in 1889 as a land-grant institution, offers programs in art and architecture, agriculture, business and economics, education, engineering, letters and science, mines and earth resources, and natural resources, forestry, wildlife, and range sciences. There are 8 undergraduate and 2 graduate schools. In addition to regional accreditation, UI has baccalaureate program accreditation with AACSB, ABET, ADA, ASLA, CSAB, FIDER, NAAB, NASAD, NASM, NCATE, NRPA, and SAF. The 2 libraries contain 1,556,788 volumes, 189,048 microform items, and 25,405 audio/video tapes/CDs, and subscribe to 8086 periodicals. Computerized library services include the card catalog, interlibrary loans, and database searching. Special learning facilities include a learning resource center, art gallery, radio station, TV station, and an electron microscopy center, a lab animal facility, research institutes for water resources and for materials and advanced processing, university farms, and experimental forests. The 800-acre campus is in a small town 90 miles southeast of Spokane, Washington. Including any residence halls, there are 147 buildings.

Student Life: 78% of undergraduates are from Idaho. Students are from 50 states, 82 foreign countries, and Canada. 98% are from public schools. 92% are white. The average age of freshmen is 18; all undergraduates, 22. 18% do not continue beyond their first year; 48% remain to graduate.

Housing: 2850 students can be accommodated in college housing, which includes single-sex and coed dorms, on-campus apartments, off-campus apartments, married-student housing, fraternity houses, and sorority houses. In addition, there are honors houses and special-interest houses. On-campus housing is guaranteed for all 4 years. 55% of students commute. Alcohol is not permitted. All students may keep cars.

Activities: 16% of men belong to 18 national fraternities; 13% of women belong to 9 national sororities. There are 132 groups on campus, including art, band, cheerleading, chess, choir, chorale, chorus, computers, dance, drama, drill team, ethnic, film, gay, honors, international, jazz band, literary magazine, marching band, musical theater, newspaper, opera, orchestra, pep band, photography, political, professional, radio and TV, religious, social, social service, student government, symphony, and yearbook. Popular campus events include Lionel Hampton Jazz Festival, the Borah Symposium, and Palousafest.

Sports: There are 6 intercollegiate sports for men and 7 for women, and 28 intramural sports for men and 27 for women. Facilities include an activity center, a 17,000-seat domed stadium for basketball and football games, indoor and outdoor tracks, a 2-pool swim center, 3 gyms, a 500-seat auditorium, an 18-hole championship golf course, and tennis, racquetball, and handball courts, and a student recreation center with a 55-foot climbing wall.

Disabled Students: 87% of the campus is accessible. Wheelchair ramps, elevators, special parking, specially equipped rest rooms, special class scheduling, lowered drinking fountains, lowered telephones, and 2 motorized wheelchairs, plus readers, note takers, and sign language interpreters are available.

Services: Counseling and information services are available, as is tutoring in most subjects. There is a reader service for the blind.

Campus Safety and Security: Measures include 24-hour foot and vehicle patrol, self-defense education, informal discussions, and pamphlets/ posters/films. There are emergency telephones and lighted pathways/ sidewalks.

Programs of Study: UI confers B.A., B.S., B.Arch., B.Dan., B.F.A., B.G.S., B.L.Arch, B.Mus., B.N.S., and B.Tech. degrees. Master's and doctoral degrees are also awarded. Bachelor's degrees are awarded in AGRICULTURE (agricultural business management, agricultural economics, agricultural mechanics, agriculture, animal science, fishing and fisheries, forestry production and processing, horticulture, range/farm management, soil science, and wildlife management), BIOLOGICAL SCIENCE (biology/biological science, botany, entomology, microbiology, molecular biology, and zoology), BUSINESS (accounting, banking and finance, management information systems, marketing/retailing/

merchandising, office supervision and management, personnel management, and sports management), COMMUNICATIONS AND THE ARTS (applied music, art, communications, dance, design, dramatic arts, English, fine arts, French, German, journalism, Latin, music, music history and appreciation, music performance, music theory and composition, photography, Spanish, studio art, and telecommunications), COMPUTER AND PHYSICAL SCIENCE (applied mathematics, chemistry, computer science, geology, information sciences and systems, mathematics, and physics), EDUCATION (agricultural, art, business, early childhood, elementary, foreign languages, home economics, industrial arts, marketing and distribution, music, physical, recreation, science, secondary, special, and vocational), ENGINEERING AND ENVIRONMENTAL DESIGN (agricultural engineering, architectural engineering, bioengineering, cartography, chemical engineering, civil engineering, computer engineering, electrical/electronics engineering, geological engineering, interior design, landscape architecture/design, mechanical engineering, metallurgical engineering, and mining and mineral engineering), HEALTH PROFESSIONS (medical laboratory technology and veterinary science), SOCIAL SCIENCE (American studies, anthropology, classical/ancient civilization, criminal justice, dietetics, economics, food science, geography, history, interdisciplinary studies, international relations, Latin American studies, parks and recreation management, philosophy, political science/government, psychology, rural economics, sociology, and textiles and clothing). Electrical engineering, forestry, and business are the strongest academically. Elementary education, business, and electrical and computer engineering are the largest.

Required: To graduate, students must complete at least 128 credit hours, including 36 in upper-division courses and 40 in the major, with a minimum GPA of 2.0. The core curriculum requires a total of 30 credits in communications, math, natural and applied sciences, humanities, and social sciences.

Special: UI offers cooperative programs and cross-registration with Washington State University, internships, extensive study-abroad programs, work-study programs, B.A.-B.S. degrees, dual and student-designed majors, a general studies degree, accelerated degrees, credit for life and work experience, nondegree study, and pass/fail options. There are 24 national honor societies, including Phi Beta Kappa, and a freshman honors program.

Faculty/Classroom: 73% of faculty are male; 27%, female. Graduate students teach 20% of introductory courses. The average class size in an introductory lecture is 39; in a laboratory, 14; and in a regular course, 16.

Admissions: 81% of the 2003-2004 applicants were accepted. The SAT I scores for the 2003-2004 freshman class were: Verbal--28% below 500, 42% between 500 and 599, 26% between 600 and 700, and 4% above 700; Math--24% below 500, 41% between 500 and 599, 30% between 600 and 700, and 4% above 700. The ACT scores were 31% below 21, 25% between 21 and 23, 21% between 24 and 26, 12% between 27 and 28, and 11% above 28. 39% of the current freshmen were in the top fifth of their class; 68% were in the top two fifths.

Requirements: The SAT I or ACT is required. In addition, applicants must be graduates of an accredited secondary school. GED certificates are accepted for special admissions only. Students must have completed at least 8 credits in English, 6 each in math and natural science, 5 in social science, 3 in electives, and 2 in humanities/foreign language. A GPA of 2.5 is required. AP and CLEP credits are accepted.

Procedure: Freshmen are admitted to all sessions. Entrance exams should be taken during the junior or senior year. There are early admissions and deferred admissions plans. Applications should be filed by August 1 for fall entry, December 15 for spring entry, and May 1 for summer entry, along with a $40 fee. Notification is sent on a rolling basis. Applications are accepted on-line through Netscape.

Transfer: 777 transfer students enrolled in 2002-2003. Applicants must have completed at least 14 credit hours with a minimum GPA of 2.0, or 2.8 for engineering transfers from outside the state of Idaho. 32 of 128 credits required for the bachelor's degree must be completed at UI.

Visiting: There are regularly scheduled orientations for prospective students, including a visit with faculty and financial aid personnel, a tour of campus, and an overnight stay in the dorms or Greek houses. There are guides for informal visits and visitors may sit in on classes and stay overnight. To schedule a visit, contact the Office of New Student Services at (208) 885-6163 or nss@uidaho.edu.

Financial Aid: In 2003-2004, 57% of all full-time freshmen and 58% of continuing full-time students received some form of financial aid. 40% of full-time freshmen and 42% of continuing full-time students received need-based aid. The average freshman award was $8079. Need-based scholarships or need-based grants averaged $3036; need-based self-help aid (loans and jobs) averaged $3627; institutional non-need-based athletic scholarships averaged $10,345; and other institutional non-need-based awards and non-need-based scholarships averaged $3194. All undergraduates work part time. The average financial indebtedness of the 2003 graduate was $19,299. The FAFSA is required. The priority date for freshman financial aid applications for fall entry is February 15. The deadline for filing freshman financial aid applications for fall entry is February 15.

International Students: The school actively recruits these students. They must score 525 on the written TOEFL or 193 on the electronic version and also take the SAT I or the ACT.

Computers: There are more than 600 PCs available in cluster sites across campus and in the PC lab. All students may access the system 23 hours a day in more than 20 labs. There are no time limits and no fees.

Graduates: From July 1, 2002 to June 30, 2003, 1684 bachelor's degrees were awarded. The most popular majors were business/marketing (13%), education (12%), and engineering (10%). In an average class, 19% graduate in 4 years or less, 47% graduate in 5 years or less, and 55% graduate in 6 years or less.

Admissions Contact: Daniel D. Davenport, Director, Admissions and Student Financial Aid. A video is available. E-mail: finaid@uidaho.edu Web: www.its.uidaho.edu/admissions/ugrad/

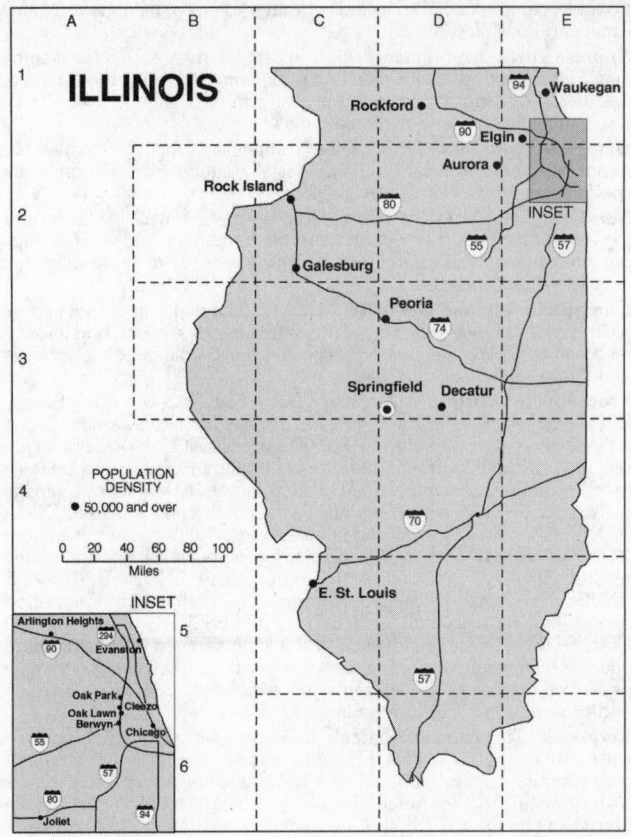

AUGUSTANA COLLEGE

C-2

Rock Island, IL 61201-2296
(309) 794-7341
(800) 798-8100, ext. 7341; Fax: (309) 794-7422

Full-time: 956 men, 1321 women	**Faculty:** 145; IIB, +$
Part-time: 17 men, 15 women	**Ph.Ds:** 94%
Graduate: none	**Student/Faculty:** 16 to 1
Year: quarters, summer session	**Tuition:** $20,829
Application Deadline: open	**Room & Board:** $5781
Freshman Class: 2722 applied, 2060 accepted, 614 enrolled	
ACT: 26	**VERY COMPETITIVE+**

Augustana College, founded in 1860, is a private liberal arts institution affiliated with the Evangelical Lutheran Church in America. In addition to regional accreditation, Augustana has baccalaureate program accreditation with NASM and NCATE. The 3 libraries contain 185,026 volumes, 107,037 microform items, and 1741 audio/video tapes/CDs, and subscribe to 1200 periodicals. Computerized library services include the card catalog, interlibrary loans, database searching, and Internet access. Special learning facilities include a learning resource center, art gallery, natural history museum, radio station, a preschool, a center for communicative disorders, a geology museum, a planetarium/observatory, a map library, a Swedish immigration research center, 2 outdoor environmental labs, and an educational technology building. The 115-acre campus is in a suburban area 165 miles west of Chicago. Including any residence halls, there are 46 buildings.

Student Life: 87% of undergraduates are from Illinois. Students are from 31 states, 23 foreign countries, and Canada. 91% are white. 36% are Protestant; 30% Catholic; 6% claim no religious affiliation. The average age of freshmen is 18; all undergraduates, 20. 14% do not continue beyond their first year; 75% remain to graduate.

Housing: 1539 students can be accommodated in college housing, which includes single-sex and coed dorms, on-campus apartments, and off-campus apartments. In addition, there are special-interest houses. On-campus housing is guaranteed for all 4 years. 68% of students live on campus; of those, 75% remain on campus on weekends. Alcohol is not permitted. All students may keep cars.

Activities: 23% of men belong to 7 local fraternities; 28% of women belong to 6 local sororities. There are 110 groups on campus, including alcohol responsibility, band, cheerleading, choir, chorale, chorus, com-

puters, dance, debate, drama, environmental, ethnic, gay, honors, international, jazz band, literary magazine, musical theater, newspaper, opera, orchestra, pep band, political, professional, radio and TV, religious, social, social service, student government, symphony, volunteer, and yearbook. Popular campus events include Messiah performances, Greek Olympics, and Humanities Festival.

Sports: There are 9 intercollegiate sports for men and 8 for women, and 19 intramural sports for men and 18 for women. Facilities include a recreational center with an indoor 200-meter track, courts for basketball, volleyball, racquetball, and tennis, a weight room, and physical conditioning equipment. A phys ed center has courts for basketball, volleyball, racquetball, and badminton, weight and physical conditioning rooms, wrestling facilities, and a swimming pool. There is a lighted field and an all-weather track for football, soccer, and track and field, including stadium seating for 3500. Facilities also include a baseball field, 10 outdoor tennis courts, and a dance studio.

Disabled Students: 75% of the campus is accessible. Wheelchair ramps, elevators, special parking, specially equipped rest rooms, lowered drinking fountains, lowered telephones, special housing, and automatic door openers are available.

Services: Counseling and information services are available, as is tutoring in every subject. There is a reader service for the blind.

Campus Safety and Security: Measures include 24-hour foot and vehicle patrol, self-defense education, security escort services, and informal discussions. There are pamphlets/posters/films and lighted pathways/sidewalks.

Programs of Study: Augustana confers the B.A. degree. Bachelor's degrees are awarded in BIOLOGICAL SCIENCE (biology/biological science), BUSINESS (accounting and business administration and management), COMMUNICATIONS AND THE ARTS (art, art history and appreciation, classics, dramatic arts, English, French, German, music, music performance, Scandinavian languages, Spanish, speech/debate/rhetoric, and studio art), COMPUTER AND PHYSICAL SCIENCE (chemistry, computer science, earth science, geology, mathematics, and physics), EDUCATION (art, elementary, music, physical, and secondary), ENGINEERING AND ENVIRONMENTAL DESIGN (engineering physics, landscape architecture/design, and preengineering), HEALTH PROFESSIONS (occupational therapy, premedicine, and speech pathology/audiology), SOCIAL SCIENCE (Asian/Oriental studies, economics, geography, history, philosophy, political science/government, psychology, public administration, religion, and sociology). Premedicine, business administration, and biology are the largest.

Required: A total of 123 credits with a minimum GPA of 2.0 is required to graduate. Courses in foreign language, religion, writing, phys ed, fine arts, humanities, literature, and the sciences must be completed.

Special: Cooperative degree programs are offered in engineering, environmental management, forestry, landscape architecture, and occupational therapy with Duke, Iowa State, Northwestern, Purdue, and Washington (St. Louis) Universities and the University of Illinois (Urbana-Champaign). Domestic and international internships are offered. Study abroad is possible in 17 countries, including China, Peru, Sweden, Germany, and France, as is fall term study in East Asia, Europe, and Latin America. Interdisciplinary majors are offered in earth science, teaching, Asian studies, and public administration. A B.A.-B.S. degree in occupational therapy is offered, as well as 3-2 engineering programs with the University of Illinois and Purdue, Washington (St. Louis), and Iowa State Universities. Work-study programs, double majors, phys ed credits, and pass/fail options are available. There are 13 national honor societies, including Phi Beta Kappa, a freshman honors program, and 12 departmental honors programs.

Faculty/Classroom: 62% of faculty are male; 38%, female. All teach undergraduates and 25% do research. The average class size in an introductory lecture is 23; in a laboratory, 17; and in a regular course, 22.

Admissions: 76% of the 2003-2004 applicants were accepted. The ACT scores for the 2003-2004 freshman class were: 8% below 21, 20% between 21 and 23, 31% between 24 and 26, 16% between 27 and 28, and 25% above 28. 56% of the current freshmen were in the top fifth of their class; 87% were in the top two fifths.

Requirements: The SAT I or ACT is required. In addition, applicants should be graduates of an accredited secondary school with 16 academic credits, including 4 in English, 3 in math, 2 each in science and social studies, 1 in foreign language, and other science and math courses for appropriate majors. An audition for music majors and an interview are recommended. The GED is accepted. AP credits are accepted. Important factors in the admissions decision are advanced placement or honor courses, evidence of special talent, and recommendations by school officials.

Procedure: Freshmen are admitted fall, winter, and spring. Entrance exams should be taken by fall of the senior year. There is a deferred admissions plan. Application deadlines are open. The fall 2003 application fee was $25. Notification is sent on a rolling basis. 153 applicants were on the 2003 waiting list; 20 were admitted. Applications are accepted on computer disk and on-line through Common App and CollegeNET, respectively.

Transfer: 77 transfer students enrolled in 2002-2003. A minimum GPA of 2.0 is required. SAT I or ACT scores and an interview are recommended. 60 of 123 credits required for the bachelor's degree must be completed at Augustana.

Visiting: There are regularly scheduled orientations for prospective students, including information sessions with speakers, exhibits, campus tours, meetings with faculty, counselors, and students, and social activities. There are guides for informal visits and visitors may sit in on classes and stay overnight. To schedule a visit, contact Martin Sauer, Director of Admissions.

Financial Aid: In 2003-2004, 96% of all full-time students received some form of financial aid. 67% of full-time freshmen and 66% of continuing full-time students received need-based aid. The average freshman award was $14,123. Need-based scholarships or need-based grants averaged $11,801; need-based self-help aid (loans and jobs) averaged $3355; and other non-need-based awards and non-need-based scholarships averaged $7644. 80% of undergraduates work part time. Average annual earnings from campus work are $900. The average financial indebtedness of the 2003 graduate was $17,076. The FAFSA and the college's own financial statement are required. The deadline for filing freshman financial aid applications for fall entry is April 5.

International Students: There are 22 international students enrolled. The school actively recruits these students. They must score 550 on the written TOEFL and also take the SAT I or the ACT.

Computers: The mainframe is a DEC Alpha Server 800 5/333. More than 1000 college-owned PCs and 1200 student-owned PCs are included in a comprehensive network linking academic and administrative buildings and residence halls. Access to the Internet and supercomputers at the University of Illinois is provided. An educational technology building provides extensive hardware, software, presentation, and help facilities for general and multimedia computing. All students may access the system. There are no time limits and no fees. It is strongly recommended that all students have a personal computer.

Graduates: From July 1, 2002 to June 30, 2003, 518 bachelor's degrees were awarded. The most popular majors were biology/premedicine (22%), business administration (21%), and English (7%). In an average class, 71% graduate in 4 years or less, 75% graduate in 5 years or less, and 77% graduate in 6 years or less. 238 companies recruited on campus in 2002-2003. Of the 2002 graduating class, 34% were enrolled in graduate school within 6 months of graduation and 65% were employed.

Admissions Contact: Martin R. Sauer, Director of Admissions.
E-mail: *admissions@augustana.edu* Web: *www.augustana.edu*

AURORA UNIVERSITY
Aurora, IL 60506-4892

E-2

(630) 844-5533
(800) 742-5281; Fax: (630) 844-5535

Full-time: 538 men, 905 women	**Faculty:** 63; IIA, --$
Part-time: 64 men, 152 women	**Ph.D.s:** 85%
Graduate: 514 men, 1284 women	**Student/Faculty:** 23 to 1
Year: quarters, summer session	**Tuition:** $14,250
Application Deadline: open	**Room & Board:** $6381
Freshman Class: 1263 applied, 834 accepted, 329 enrolled	
SAT I Verbal/Math: 473/527	**ACT:** 20 **COMPETITIVE**

Aurora University, founded in 1893, is a private institution that offers graduate and undergraduate degrees in arts and sciences, education, business and information science, communication, nursing and health, recreation, social work, and a professional/staff program. There are 4 undergraduate and 4 graduate schools. In addition to regional accreditation, AU has baccalaureate program accreditation with CSWE, NLN, and NRPA. The library contains 114,144 volumes, 221,286 microform items, and 6791 audio/video tapes/CDs, and subscribes to 627 periodicals. Computerized library services include the card catalog, interlibrary loans, and database searching. Special learning facilities include a learning resource center, art gallery, TV station, Native-American museum, lake-front campus, and natural study area in Wisconsin. The 27-acre campus is in a suburban area 40 miles west of Chicago. Including any residence halls, there are 19 buildings.

Student Life: 96% of undergraduates are from Illinois. Students are from 17 states. 89% are from public schools. 70% are white; 17% African American; 10% Hispanic. 65% claim no religious affiliation; 17% Catholic; 17% Protestant. The average age of freshmen is 18; all undergraduates, 26. 24% do not continue beyond their first year; 50% remain to graduate.

Housing: 415 students can be accommodated in college housing, which includes single-sex and coed dorms. On-campus housing is available on a first-come, first-served basis. 69% of students commute. Alcohol is not permitted. All students may keep cars.

Activities: 2% of men belong to 1 local and 3 national fraternities; 3% of women belong to 2 local and 2 national sororities. There are 40

groups on campus, including cheerleading, choir, chorus, computers, dance, drama, ethnic, film, gay, honors, international, literary magazine, musical theater, newspaper, photography, political, professional, radio and TV, religious, social service, student government, and yearbook. Popular campus events include Spring Fling and annual Native-American Pow Wow.

Sports: There are 6 intercollegiate sports for men and 5 for women, and 7 intramural sports for men and 6 for women. Facilities include a fitness center, a weight room, a 2000-seat gym, football and soccer fields, a racquetball court, and a climbing wall.

Disabled Students: 95% of the campus is accessible. Wheelchair ramps, elevators, special parking, specially equipped rest rooms, and special class scheduling are available.

Services: Counseling and information services are available, as is tutoring in most subjects. There is remedial math, reading, and writing. There are professional and peer tutors, workshops in word processing, and computer-based tutorials.

Campus Safety and Security: Measures include 24-hour foot and vehicle patrol, self-defense education, security escort services, and informal discussions. There are pamphlets/posters/films, emergency telephones, and lighted pathways/sidewalks.

Programs of Study: AU confers B.A., B.S., B.S.N., B.S.P.S., and B.S.W. degrees. Master's and doctoral degrees are also awarded. Bachelor's degrees are awarded in BIOLOGICAL SCIENCE (biology/biological science), BUSINESS (accounting, business administration and management, business economics, management information systems, management science, and marketing/retailing/merchandising), COMMUNICATIONS AND THE ARTS (communications, English, and literature), COMPUTER AND PHYSICAL SCIENCE (computer science and mathematics), EDUCATION (elementary and physical), ENGINEERING AND ENVIRONMENTAL DESIGN (environmental science and industrial administration/management), HEALTH PROFESSIONS (nursing), SOCIAL SCIENCE (criminal justice, history, humanities, parks and recreation management, philosophy, political science/government, psychology, religion, social work, and sociology). Business, education, and protective services are the largest.

Required: To graduate, students must complete 120 semester hours with a minimum GPA of 2.0. Distribution requirements include 12 semester hours each in humanities, social/behavioral science, and natural science/math, 6 in freshman English, and 3 additional in communication. A minimum of 27 hours is required in the major; most require 36 or more.

Special: AU offers cross-registration with North Central College and Benedictine University, field-related job experience, work-study programs, study abroad in England, Germany, and Mexico, internships, student designed and dual majors, nondegree study, and a B.A.-B.S. degree. Pass/fail options, and credit for life, military, or work experience are also available. There are 3 national honor societies.

Faculty/Classroom: 40% of faculty are male; 60%, female. All teach undergraduates. No introductory courses are taught by graduate students. The average class size in an introductory lecture is 24; in a laboratory, 18; and in a regular course, 16.

Admissions: 66% of the 2003-2004 applicants were accepted. The SAT I scores for the 2003-2004 freshman class were: Verbal--60% below 500, and 40% between 500 and 599; Math--56% below 500, and 45% between 500 and 599. 26% of the current freshmen were in the top fifth of their class; 61% were in the top two fifths. 2 freshmen graduated first in their class.

Requirements: The SAT I or ACT is recommended. In addition, applicants must be graduates of an accredited secondary school or have earned the GED. A GPA of 2.0 is required. AP and CLEP credits are accepted. Important factors in the admissions decision are leadership record, advanced placement or honor courses, and extracurricular activities record.

Procedure: Freshmen are admitted fall, winter, and spring. Entrance exams should be taken by late in the junior year or early in the senior year. There is a rolling admissions plan. There are early decision, early admissions, and deferred admissions plans. Application deadlines are open. The fall 2003 application fee was $25. 60 early decision candidates were accepted for the 2003-2004 class. Applications are accepted on-line through *www.aurora.edu*.

Transfer: 320 transfer students enrolled in 2002-2003. Applicants are required to have a minimum GPA of 2.0 and must have completed at least 15 semester hours. 30 of 120 credits required for the bachelor's degree must be completed at AU.

Visiting: There are regularly scheduled orientations for prospective students. There are guides for informal visits and visitors may sit in on classes and stay overnight. To schedule a visit, contact the Admissions Office at *admission@aurora.edu*.

Financial Aid: In 2003-2004, 97% of all full-time freshmen and 73% of continuing full-time students received some form of financial aid. 79% of full-time freshmen and 62% of continuing full-time students received need-based aid. The average freshman award was $13,855. Need-based scholarships or need-based grants averaged $5886 ($7000 maximum);

need-based self-help aid (loans and jobs) averaged $3275 ($6124 maximum); and non-need-based awards and non-need-based scholarships averaged $7258 ($9000 maximum). 11% of undergraduates work part time. Average annual earnings from campus work are $849. The average financial indebtedness of the 2003 graduate was $6925. The FAFSA is required. The priority date for freshman financial aid applications for fall entry is April 15.

International Students: They must score 550 on the written TOEFL.

Computers: The mainframe is a Tru64 running UNIX. DEC, HP, IBM, and Dell PCs are available in 4 computer labs. All students may access the system until midnight. There are no time limits and no fees. It is strongly recommended that all students have a personal computer.

Graduates: From July 1, 2002 to June 30, 2003, 357 bachelor's degrees were awarded. The most popular majors were business (21%), education (17%), and criminal justice (16%). In an average class, 39% graduate in 4 years or less, 52% graduate in 5 years or less, and 54% graduate in 6 years or less. 41 companies recruited on campus in 2002-2003. Of the 2002 graduating class, 15% were enrolled in graduate school within 6 months of graduation and 90% were employed.

Admissions Contact: Linda Gebhard, Enrollment Information Manager. A video is available. E-mail: *admission@aurora.edu* Web: *http://www.aurora.edu*

BENEDICTINE UNIVERSITY
Lisle, IL 60532

E-2

(630) 829-4306; Fax: (630) 960-1126

Full-time: 582 men, 890 women	**Faculty:** 67
Part-time: 209 men, 433 women	**Ph.D.s:** 85%
Graduate: 255 men, 599 women	**Student/Faculty:** 22 to 1
Year: semesters, summer session	**Tuition:** $17,470
Application Deadline: open	**Room & Board:** $6370
Freshman Class: 869 applied, 797 accepted, 306 enrolled	
ACT: 23	**COMPETITIVE**

Benedictine University, founded in 1887, is a private, Roman Catholic liberal arts and sciences institution. There are 3 undergraduate and 3 graduate schools. In addition to regional accreditation, Benedictine has baccalaureate program accreditation with ADA and NLN. The library contains 176,452 volumes, 331,148 microform items, and 4691 audio/video tapes/CDs, and subscribes to 7270 periodicals. Computerized library services include the card catalog, interlibrary loans, and database searching. Special learning facilities include a learning resource center, art gallery, natural history museum, and TV station. The 108-acre campus is in a suburban area 25 miles west of Chicago. Including any residence halls, there are 11 buildings.

Student Life: 96% of undergraduates are from Illinois. Students are from 25 states and 8 foreign countries. 70% are from public schools. 48% are white; 13% Asian American; 10% African American. The average age of freshmen is 18; all undergraduates, 24. 23% do not continue beyond their first year; 53% remain to graduate.

Housing: 404 students can be accommodated in college housing, which includes single-sex and coed dorms. On-campus housing is available on a first-come, first-served basis. 65% of students commute. All students may keep cars.

Activities: There are no fraternities or sororities. There are 38 groups on campus, including art, band, cheerleading, choir, chorus, computers, dance, debate, ethnic, honors, international, jazz band, literary magazine, musical theater, newspaper, pep band, political, professional, radio and TV, religious, social, social service, and student government. Popular campus events include Family Day, Spring Fest, and Gospel Fest.

Sports: There are 8 intercollegiate sports for men and 8 for women, and 16 intramural sports for men and 16 for women. Facilities include a recreation center housing a main arena, a pool, a weight room, and a dance room; racquetball and tennis courts; and softball, baseball, soccer, and football fields.

Disabled Students: All of the campus is accessible. Wheelchair ramps, elevators, special parking, specially equipped rest rooms, and lowered drinking fountains are available.

Services: Counseling and information services are available, as is tutoring in most subjects. There is remedial math, reading, and writing.

Campus Safety and Security: Measures include 24-hour foot and vehicle patrol, self-defense education, security escort services, and informal discussions. There are pamphlets/posters/films, emergency telephones, and lighted pathways/sidewalks.

Programs of Study: Benedictine confers B.A., B.S., B.B.A., and B.S.N. degrees. Associate, master's, and doctoral degrees are also awarded. Bachelor's degrees are awarded in BIOLOGICAL SCIENCE (biochemistry, biology/biological science, molecular biology, and nutrition), BUSINESS (accounting, banking and finance, business administration and management, business economics, international business management, management information systems, marketing management, marketing/retailing/merchandising, and organizational behavior), COMMUNICATIONS AND THE ARTS (arts administration/management, communications, literature, music, publishing, Spanish, and studio art), COMPUTER AND PHYSICAL SCIENCE (chemistry, computer science, mathematics, and physics), EDUCATION (elementary and special), ENGINEERING AND ENVIRONMENTAL DESIGN (engineering and applied science and environmental science), HEALTH PROFESSIONS (clinical science, health care administration, health science, nuclear medical technology, and nursing), SOCIAL SCIENCE (economics, history, international studies, philosophy, political science/government, psychology, social science, and sociology). Biology, management, and psychology are the largest.

Required: To graduate students must complete 120 semester hours, including 36 in their major, and maintain a minimum GPA of 2.0. They must complete 12 hours in the arts and humanities, 9 each in social sciences, natural sciences, and cultural heritage, 6 in rhetoric, and 3 each in speech, math, and freshman seminar. A thesis, capstone course or project, or comprehensive exam is required in specific departments.

Special: There is cross-registration with North Central College, Aurora University, and the Illinois Institute of Technology. Benedictine offers study abroad in 4 countries, and exchange programs can be arranged through other colleges. There are 3-2 preengineering degrees with Marquette University and the Universities of Illinois, Detroit, and Notre Dame, and an engineering degree with the Illinois Institute of Technology. Preprofessional programs including prepodiatry, pre-physical therapy, and prenursing are offered. Work-study programs with a number of surrounding firms, internships, an accelerated degree program in management, credit for work and life experience, and dual majors are also offered. There are 11 national honor societies and a freshman honors program.

Faculty/Classroom: 66% of faculty are male; 34%, female. All both teach and do research. No introductory courses are taught by graduate students. The average class size in an introductory lecture is 23; in a laboratory, 17; and in a regular course, 18.

Admissions: 92% of the 2003-2004 applicants were accepted. The ACT scores for the 2003-2004 freshman class were: 28% below 21, 26% between 21 and 23, 23% between 24 and 26, 12% between 27 and 28, and 10% above 28. 41% of the current freshmen were in the top fifth of their class; 66% were in the top two fifths. 18 freshmen graduated first in their class.

Requirements: The ACT is required. In addition, to be admitted, students must complete 4 years of English, 3 each of social studies, math, and lab science, and 2 of foreign language. The GED is accepted. AP and CLEP credits are accepted.

Procedure: Freshmen are admitted fall and spring. Application deadlines are open. Application fee is $40. Notification is sent on a rolling basis.

Transfer: Applicants must have a C average. A minimum GPA of 2.0 is necessary, and an interview is required in some cases. Students who have completed fewer than 20 semester hours must submit ACT or SAT I scores. 30 of 120 credits required for the bachelor's degree must be completed at Benedictine.

Visiting: There are regularly scheduled orientations for prospective students, including a regularly scheduled Visit Day and open houses each semester. There are guides for informal visits and visitors may sit in on classes and stay overnight. To schedule a visit, contact the Admissions Office.

Financial Aid: In 2003-2004, 98% of all full-time freshmen and 95% of continuing full-time students received some form of financial aid. The average freshman award was $12,567. Need-based scholarships or need-based grants averaged $5297; need-based self-help aid (loans and jobs) averaged $4871; and other non-need-based awards and non-need-based scholarships averaged $5435. Average annual earnings from campus work are $3000. The average financial indebtedness of the 2002 graduate was $16,895. Benedictine is a member of CSS. The FAFSA and the college's own financial statement are required.

International Students: There are 25 international students enrolled. The school actively recruits these students. They must score 550 on the written TOEFL or 213 on the electronic version and also take the SAT I or the ACT.

Computers: There are 200 PCs available in open labs and classrooms. All students may access the system. Students may use the PC labs 24 hours a day. There are no time limits. The fee is $150.

Graduates: From July 1, 2002 to June 30, 2003, 369 bachelor's degrees were awarded. The most popular majors were biology (10%), psychology (10%), and management and organizational behavior (8%). In an average class, 32% graduate in 4 years or less, 48% graduate in 5 years or less, and 53% graduate in 6 years or less. 150 companies recruited on campus in 2002-2003.

Admissions Contact: Kari A. Cranmer, Director of Admissions. A video is available. E-mail: *admissions@ben.edu* Web: *www.ben.edu*

BLACKBURN COLLEGE

Carlinville, IL 62626

C-4
(217) 854-3231
(800) 233-3550; Fax: (217) 854-3713

Full-time: 250 men, 310 women	**Faculty:** 32
Part-time: 5 men, 10 women	**Ph.D.s:** 72%
Graduate: none	**Student/Faculty:** 17 to 1
Year: semesters, summer session	**Tuition:** $9890
Application Deadline: open	**Room & Board:** $4590
Freshman Class: n/av	
SAT I or ACT: required	COMPETITIVE

Blackburn College, founded in 1837, is a private liberal arts institution affiliated with the Presbyterian Church (U.S.A.). The college is noted for its work program, which allows resident students to reduce their education costs and develop useful skills by managing and administering all essential campus services. Figures in the above capsule and in this profile are approximate. The library contains 80,000 volumes, and subscribes to 400 periodicals. Computerized library services include interlibrary loans and database searching. Special learning facilities include a learning resource center and art gallery. The 80-acre campus is in a rural area 60 miles north of St. Louis. Including any residence halls, there are 13 buildings.

Student Life: 85% of undergraduates are from Illinois. Students are from 12 states and 9 foreign countries. 85% are from public schools. 81% are white; 11% African American. 50% are Protestant; 45% Catholic. The average age of freshmen is 18; all undergraduates, 20. 30% do not continue beyond their first year.

Housing: 480 students can be accommodated in college housing, which includes single-sex and coed dorms. On-campus housing is guaranteed for all 4 years. 76% of students live on campus; of those, 60% remain on campus on weekends. All students may keep cars.

Activities: There are no fraternities or sororities. There are 15 groups on campus, including band, cheerleading, choir, chorale, chorus, drama, ethnic, international, jazz band, literary magazine, newspaper, religious, social, student government, and yearbook.

Sports: There are 6 intercollegiate sports for men and 6 for women, and 9 intramural sports for men and 9 for women. Facilities include a gym, a swimming pool, racquetball and tennis courts, weight and wrestling rooms, an outdoor track, and lighted playing fields.

Disabled Students: 65% of the campus is accessible. Wheelchair ramps, elevators, special parking, specially equipped rest rooms, special class scheduling, lowered drinking fountains, and lowered telephones are available.

Services: Counseling and information services are available, as is tutoring in most subjects.

Campus Safety and Security: Measures include self-defense education, security escort services, lighted pathways/sidewalks, and and student-run security through the work program.

Programs of Study: Blackburn confers the B.A. degree. Bachelor's degrees are awarded in BIOLOGICAL SCIENCE (biology/biological science), BUSINESS (accounting, business administration and management, international business management, and international economics), COMMUNICATIONS AND THE ARTS (American literature, art, English literature, music business management, music performance, and Spanish), COMPUTER AND PHYSICAL SCIENCE (chemistry, computer science, and mathematics), EDUCATION (art, elementary, English, music, physical, secondary, and social science), HEALTH PROFESSIONS (medical laboratory technology), SOCIAL SCIENCE (history, political science/government, psychology, and public administration). Life sciences and physical sciences are the strongest academically. Biology, education, and business are the largest.

Required: To graduate, students must complete 122 semester hours with a minimum 2.0 GPA. Requirements include interdisciplinary courses, intercultural courses in foreign languages or English, and foundation courses in writing, literature, math, philosophy or religion, analysis, fine arts, and phys ed. Work program participation is required of resident students. All students must complete their last year in residence.

Special: Blackburn offers supervised off-campus internships related to student majors, co-op programs, work-study programs, and a semester in Mexico, Great Britain, or Washington, D.C. A 3-2 engineering degree with Washington University in St. Louis is offered. Students may design their own majors. There is 1 national honor society.

Faculty/Classroom: 65% of faculty are male; 35%, female. All teach undergraduates. The average class size in an introductory lecture is 25; in a laboratory, 20; and in a regular course, 18.

Admissions: 4 freshmen graduated first in their class in a recent year.

Requirements: The SAT I or ACT is required. In addition, applicants should be graduates of an accredited secondary school or have a GED certificate. Blackburn recommends completion of 4 years of English, 2 to 4 of math, and 2 each of lab sciences, social sciences, and foreign language. A personal essay is required. Blackburn requires applicants to be in the upper 60% of their class. A GPA of 2.0 is required. AP and CLEP credits are accepted. Important factors in the admissions decision are leadership record, personality/intangible qualities, and recommendations by school officials.

Procedure: Freshmen are admitted fall and spring. Entrance exams should be taken in the junior year or early in the senior year. There is a rolling admissions plan. Application deadlines are open. Applications are accepted on-line through the school's web site.

Transfer: 37 transfer students enrolled in a recent year. Applicants must submit official transcripts of college-level work and be in good standing at the previous institution attended. Students from accredited colleges may receive credit for grades of C or better; those with associate degrees may transfer some D grades. Credit for work at unaccredited institutions may be accepted provisionally. 30 of 122 credits required for the bachelor's degree must be completed at Blackburn.

Visiting: There are regularly scheduled orientations for prospective students, including a campus tour and meetings with an admissions representative, the financial aid director, and a department head. There are guides for informal visits and visitors may sit in on classes and stay overnight. To schedule a visit, contact the Admissions Office.

Financial Aid: In a recent year, 94% of all full-time students received some form of financial aid. 79% of full-time freshmen and 81% of continuing full-time students received need-based aid. The average freshman award was $7728. All undergraduates work part time. Average annual earnings from campus work are $630. The average financial indebtedness of a recent graduate was $11,000. Blackburn is a member of CSS. The FAFSA is required. Check with the school for current deadlines.

International Students: There were 18 international students enrolled in a recent year. The school actively recruits these students. They must score 525 on the written TOEFL or 200 on the electronic version.

Computers: There are PCs and Macs along with 2 HP workstations available in the computer center. All students may access the system every day during lab hours. There are no time limits and no fees.

Graduates: In a recent year, 116 bachelor's degrees were awarded. The most popular majors were business (30%), education (27%), and biology (9%). In an average class, 45% graduate in 4 years or less, 47% graduate in 5 years or less, and 48% graduate in 6 years or less. Of a recent graduating class, 10% were enrolled in graduate school within 6 months of graduation and 90% were employed.

Admissions Contact: John C. Malin, Director of Admissions.
E-mail: *jmali@mail.blackburn.edu* Web: *www.blackburn.edu*

BRADLEY UNIVERSITY

Peoria, IL 61625

D-3
(309) 677-1000
(800) 447-6460; Fax: (309) 677-2797

Full-time: 2276 men, 2651 women	**Faculty:** 332; II A, +$
Part-time: 157 men, 221 women	**Ph.D.s:** 83%
Graduate: 456 men, 376 women	**Student/Faculty:** 15 to 1
Year: semesters, summer session	**Tuition:** $16,930
Application Deadline: open	**Room & Board:** $5980
Freshman Class: 4271 applied, 3570 accepted, 1105 enrolled	
SAT I or ACT: required	VERY COMPETITIVE

Bradley University, founded in 1897, is an independent, privately endowed institution. Bradley offers a full range of baccalaureate and graduate-level programs, as well as personal attention, from a faculty dedicated to student learning. There are 5 undergraduate schools and 1 graduate school. In addition to regional accreditation, Bradley has baccalaureate program accreditation with AACSB, ABET, ACCE, ADA, NASAD, NASM, NCATE, and NLN. The library contains 424,752 volumes, 810,955 microform items, and 9574 audio/video tapes/CDs, and subscribes to 2109 periodicals. Computerized library services include the card catalog, interlibrary loans, and database searching. Special learning facilities include a learning resource center, art gallery, radio station, and TV station. The 75-acre campus is in an urban area 160 miles southwest of Chicago. Including any residence halls, there are 41 buildings.

Student Life: 86% of undergraduates are from Illinois. Students are from 42 states, 55 foreign countries, and Canada. 80% are white. 42% are Protestant; 34% Catholic; 14% claim no religious affiliation; 6% Jewish. The average age of freshmen is 18; all undergraduates, 20. 13% do not continue beyond their first year.

Housing: 2300 students can be accommodated in college housing, which includes single-sex and coed dorms, on-campus apartments, fraternity houses, and sorority houses. Wellness floors are available in residence halls. On-campus housing is guaranteed for all 4 years. 70% of students live on campus; of those, 99% remain on campus on weekends. Upperclassmen may keep cars.

Activities: 36% of men belong to 17 national fraternities; 33% of women belong to 12 national sororities. There are 223 groups on campus, including art, band, cheerleading, chess, choir, chorale, chorus, computers, dance, drama, forensics, gay, honors, international, jazz band, literary magazine, musical theater, newspaper, orchestra, pep band, photography, political, professional, radio and TV, religious, social, social service, student government, symphony, and yearbook. Popular campus events include Founders Day, Greek Week, and Garret Week.

Sports: There are 6 intercollegiate sports for men and 7 for women, and 24 intramural sports for men and 24 for women. Facilities include tennis courts, a civic center, playing fields, a field house, outdoor lighted basketball courts, and a 6500-seat gym.

Disabled Students: 80% of the campus is accessible. Wheelchair ramps, elevators, special parking, specially equipped rest rooms, and lowered drinking fountains are available.

Services: Counseling and information services are available, as is tutoring in most subjects, including introductory subjects and selected higher-level classes. There is remedial math and writing.

Campus Safety and Security: Measures include 24-hour foot and vehicle patrol, security escort services, informal discussions, and pamphlets/posters/films. There are emergency telephones, lighted pathways/sidewalks, engravers for marking personal property, and a medical escort service.

Programs of Study: Bradley confers B.A., B.S., B.F.A., B.M., B.S.C., B.S.C.E., B.S.E.E., B.S.I.E., B.S.M.E., B.S.M.F.E., B.S.M.F.E.T., and B.S.N. degrees. Master's degrees are also awarded. Bachelor's degrees are awarded in BIOLOGICAL SCIENCE (biochemistry, biology/biological science, and molecular biology), BUSINESS (accounting, banking and finance, business administration and management, insurance and risk management, international business management, management information systems, and marketing/retailing/merchandising), COMMUNICATIONS AND THE ARTS (art history and appreciation, communications, dramatic arts, English, French, German, graphic design, multimedia, music, music business management, music performance, music theory and composition, photography, printmaking, sculpture, Spanish, studio art, and visual and performing arts), COMPUTER AND PHYSICAL SCIENCE (actuarial science, chemistry, computer science, geoscience, information sciences and systems, mathematics, and physics), EDUCATION (art, drama, early childhood, elementary, home economics, music, secondary, and special), ENGINEERING AND ENVIRONMENTAL DESIGN (civil engineering, construction engineering, electrical/electronics engineering, engineering physics, environmental science, industrial engineering, manufacturing engineering, manufacturing technology, and mechanical engineering), HEALTH PROFESSIONS (health science, medical technology, nursing, and physical therapy), SOCIAL SCIENCE (criminal justice, dietetics, economics, family/consumer studies, history, international studies, philosophy, political science/government, psychology, religion, social work, and sociology). Business, engineering, and natural sciences are the strongest academically. Communication, elementary education, and psychology are the largest.

Required: To graduate, the student must complete the school's basic skills and general education curriculum. Overall, the university requires 124 total credit hours, with 32 hours in the student's major and a minimum GPA of 2.0.

Special: Special academic programs include an honors program, co-op programs, internships, a Washington semester, work-study programs, study abroad in 30 countries, B.A.-B.S. degrees in most majors, dual majors, and leadership fellowships. There are 31 national honor societies and a freshman honors program.

Faculty/Classroom: 68% of faculty are male; 32%, female. All both teach and do research. No introductory courses are taught by graduate students. The average class size in a laboratory is 14 and in a regular course, 20.

Admissions: 84% of the 2003-2004 applicants were accepted. The SAT I scores for the 2003-2004 freshman class were: Math--23% below 500, 37% between 500 and 599, 35% between 600 and 700, and 5% above 700. The ACT scores for the 2003-2004 freshman class were: 9% below 21, 22% between 21 and 23, 32% between 24 and 26, 19% between 27 and 28, and 18% above 28. 52% of the current freshmen were in the top fifth of their class; 83% were in the top two fifths. There were 14 National Merit finalists in a recent year. 57 freshmen graduated first in their class in a recent year.

Requirements: The SAT I or ACT is required. A GPA of 2.5 is required. AP and CLEP credits are accepted. Important factors in the admissions decision are advanced placement or honor courses, extracurricular activities record, and evidence of special talent.

Procedure: Freshmen are admitted to all sessions. Entrance exams should be taken in the spring of the junior year or the fall of the senior year. There is an early admissions plan. Application deadlines are open. The fall 2003 application fee was $35. Notification is sent on a rolling basis. A waiting list is an active part of the admissions procedure. Applications are accepted on-line.

Transfer: 320 transfer students enrolled in 2002-2003. Transfer students must have a minimum GPA of 2.0. Those with fewer than 15 hours of college credit must submit ACT or SAT I scores and a high school transcript. 30 of 124 credits required for the bachelor's degree must be completed at Bradley.

Visiting: There are regularly scheduled orientations for prospective students, including class visits, campus tours, admissions information, financial assistance seminars, lunch, and student and parent meetings. There are guides for informal visits and visitors may sit in on classes and stay overnight. To schedule a visit, contact the Office of Undergraduate Admissions.

Financial Aid: In 2003-2004, 96% of all full-time freshmen and 85% of continuing full-time students received some form of financial aid. 67% of full-time freshmen and 56% of continuing full-time students received need-based aid. The average freshman award was $14,114. Need-based scholarships or need-based grants averaged $9895 ($10,500 maximum); need-based self-help aid (loans and jobs) averaged $4444 ($5425 maximum); non-need-based athletic scholarships averaged $12,077 ($22,910 maximum); and other non-need-based awards and non-need-based scholarships averaged $9118 ($10,500 maximum). 26% of undergraduates work part time. Average annual earnings from campus work are $950. The average financial indebtedness of the 2003 graduate was $15,941. Bradley is a member of CSS. The FAFSA is required. The deadline for filing freshman financial aid applications for fall entry is March 1.

International Students: There are 96 international students enrolled. The school actively recruits these students. They must score 500 on the written TOEFL or 173 on the electronic version.

Computers: The mainframe is a Control Data CYBER 930. There are about 2000 AT&T, Zenith, IBM, and Mac PCs available throughout the campus. All students may access the system 24 hours a day. There are no time limits and no fees.

Graduates: From July 1, 2002 to June 30, 2003, 1381 bachelor's degrees were awarded. The most popular majors were communications (13%), elementary education (9%), and psychology (6%). In an average class, 49% graduate in 4 years or less, 66% graduate in 5 years or less, and 67% graduate in 6 years or less. 251 companies recruited on campus in 2002-2003. Of the 2002 graduating class, 18% were enrolled in graduate school within 6 months of graduation and 72% were employed.

Admissions Contact: Angela (Nickie) Roberson, Associate Provost for Enrollment Management. A video is available.
E-mail: admissions@bradley.edu Web: www.bradley.edu/admissions/

CHICAGO STATE UNIVERSITY
Chicago, IL 60628
E-2
(773) 995-2513
(800) 278-3011; Fax: (773) 995-3820

Full-time: 907 men, 2296 women	**Faculty:** IIA, --$
Part-time: 411 men, 1290 women	**Ph.D.s:** 62%
Graduate: 670 men, 1466 women	**Student/Faculty:** n/av
Year: semesters, summer session	**Tuition:** $4382 ($10,766)
Application Deadline: July 15	**Room & Board:** $6500
Freshman Class: 1694 applied, 790 accepted, 542 enrolled	
ACT: 18	**COMPETITIVE+**

Chicago State University, founded in 1867, is a public commuter and residential institution controlled by the State of Illinois. It offers day and evening undergraduate programs through the Colleges of Arts and Sciences, Health Sciences, Business Administration, and Education and nontraditional programs. There are 5 undergraduate and 2 graduate schools. In addition to regional accreditation, Chicago State has baccalaureate program accreditation with ADA, CAHEA, NCATE, and NLN. The library contains 26,000 volumes and 388,028 microform items, and subscribes to 1734 periodicals. Computerized library services include the card catalog, interlibrary loans, and database searching. Special learning facilities include a learning resource center, art gallery, radio station, and a TV studio. The 161-acre campus is in an urban area 12 miles south of downtown Chicago. Including any residence halls, there are 11 buildings.

Student Life: 98% of undergraduates are from Illinois. Students are from 24 states, 21 foreign countries, and Canada. 80% are African American; 10% white. The average age of freshmen is 21; all undergraduates, 29.

Housing: 360 students can be accommodated in college housing, which includes coed dorms. On-campus housing is available on a first-come, first-served basis. Alcohol is not permitted. All students may keep cars.

Activities: 12% of men and about 15% of women belong to 4 national fraternities and 4 national sororities. There are 17 groups on campus, including cheerleading, choir, dance, drama, drill team, honors, international, jazz band, literary magazine, musical theater, newspaper, photography, political, professional, radio and TV, religious, social, student government, and yearbook. Popular campus events include Welcome Week activities, Black Writers Conference, and Hispanic Heritage Month.

Sports: There are 6 intercollegiate sports for men and 6 for women, and 4 intramural sports for men and 2 for women. Facilities include tennis courts, indoor/outdoor tracks, an Olympic-size swimming pool, weight rooms, basketball courts, a fitness center, a dance studio, and a baseball field.

Disabled Students: All of the campus is accessible. Wheelchair ramps, elevators, special parking, specially equipped rest rooms, lowered drinking fountains, and lowered telephones are available.

Services: Counseling and information services are available, as is tutoring in some subjects, including math, science, and accounting. There is remedial math, reading, and writing.

Campus Safety and Security: Measures include 24-hour foot and vehicle patrol, security escort services, informal discussions, and pamphlets/posters/films. There are emergency telephones and lighted pathways/sidewalks.

Programs of Study: Chicago State confers B.A., B.S., B.M.E., and B.S.Ed. degrees. Master's degrees are also awarded. Bachelor's degrees are awarded in BIOLOGICAL SCIENCE (biochemistry and biology/biological science), BUSINESS (accounting, banking and finance, business administration and management, management science, marketing/retailing/merchandising, and recreation and leisure services), COMMUNICATIONS AND THE ARTS (art, broadcasting, English, music, Spanish, and speech/debate/rhetoric), COMPUTER AND PHYSICAL SCIENCE (chemistry, computer science, information sciences and systems, mathematics, and physics), EDUCATION (art, bilingual/bicultural, business, early childhood, elementary, industrial arts, music, physical, secondary, and vocational), HEALTH PROFESSIONS (health, health care administration, health science, nursing, predentistry, and premedicine), SOCIAL SCIENCE (African American studies, criminal justice, economics, geography, history, political science/government, prelaw, psychology, and sociology). Business administration and computer science are the strongest academically. Elementary education is the largest.

Required: All students must complete 120 credit hours, including 40 hours in the major, maintain a 2.0 GPA, and fulfill a foreign language requirement. They must complete a 39-hour core curriculum as well as exams in English, math, reading, and the U.S. Constitution.

Special: Chicago State offers a combined B.A.-B.S. degree, a board of governors degree program, a University Without Walls Program, and an individualized curriculum program. Study abroad in Liberia and life experience credits are also provided. There is a freshman honors program.

Faculty/Classroom: 99% teach undergraduates. The average class size in an introductory lecture is 60; in a laboratory, 26; and in a regular course, 35.

Admissions: 47% of the 2003-2004 applicants were accepted. The ACT scores for the 2003-2004 freshman class were: 89% below 21, 8% between 21 and 23, and 3% between 24 and 26. 19% of the current freshmen were in the top fifth of their class; 54% were in the top two fifths.

Requirements: The ACT is required, but scores need not be submitted if the applicant is over 23 years of age. Graduation from an accredited secondary school is required; a GED will be accepted. Minimum credits submitted should include 4 units of English and 3 each of math, science, social sciences. A GPA of 2.0 is required. AP and CLEP credits are accepted.

Procedure: Freshmen are admitted to all sessions. Applications should be filed by July 15 for fall entry, November 1 for spring entry, and May 1 for summer entry, along with a $25 fee. Notification is sent on a rolling basis.

Transfer: 630 transfer students enrolled in 2002-2003. Transfer students must have a minimum GPA of 2.0, and those with fewer than 24 hours must also meet freshman admission requirements. 30 of 120 credits required for the bachelor's degree must be completed at Chicago State.

Visiting: There are regularly scheduled orientations for prospective students, including a tour of campus, an admissions overview, and financial aid information. To schedule a visit, contact the Office of Admissions at ug-admissions@csu.edu.

Financial Aid: In 2003-2004, 68% of all full-time freshmen and 77% of continuing full-time students received some form of financial aid. 67% of full-time freshmen and 75% of continuing full-time students received need-based aid. The average freshman award was $3589. Need-based scholarships or need-based grants averaged $3174 ($5450 maximum); need-based self-help aid (loans and jobs) averaged $1949 ($8002 maximum); and non-need-based athletic scholarships averaged $5431 ($8005 maximum). Average annual earnings from campus work are $2700. The average financial indebtedness of the 2003 graduate was $23,000. The FAFSA is required. The priority date for freshman financial aid applications for fall entry is February 1. The deadline for filing freshman financial aid applications for fall entry is April 15.

International Students: There are 50 international students enrolled. They must score 525 on the written TOEFL or 195 on the electronic version and also take the college's own test. They must also take the SAT I or the ACT, scoring 17 on the ACT.

Computers: There are 40 Zenith PCs available. All students may access the system 8:30 A.M. to 10 P.M. Monday through Friday, 8:30 A.M. to 5 P.M. Saturday, and 1 p.m to 8 P.M. Sunday. There are no time limits. The fee is $5. It is strongly recommended that all students have a personal computer.

Graduates: From July 1, 2002 to June 30, 2003, 1110 bachelor's degrees were awarded. The most popular majors were elementary education (6%), nursing (5%), and criminal justice (5%).

Admissions Contact: Addie Epps, Director of Admissions.
E-mail: ug-admissions@csu.edu Web: www.csu.edu

COLUMBIA COLLEGE CHICAGO
Chicago, IL 60605

E-2

(312) 663-1600, ext. 7133
(800) 838-1226; Fax: (312) 344-8024

Full-time: 3775 men, 4017 women	**Faculty:** 286; IIA, av$
Part-time: 716 men, 757 women	**Ph.Ds:** 35%
Graduate: 171 men, 479 women	**Student/Faculty:** 27 to 1
Year: semesters, summer session	**Tuition:** $15,270
Application Deadline: August 15	**Room & Board:** $9838
Freshman Class: 3025 applied, 2548 accepted, 1523 enrolled	
ACT: 20	**LESS COMPETITIVE**

Columbia College Chicago, founded in 1890, is a private liberal arts institution with special emphasis on educating students for creative occupations in the visual, performing, and media and commununication arts. There are 3 undergraduate schools and 1 graduate school. The library contains 2054 volumes, 128,615 microform items, and 13,772 audio/video tapes/CDs, and subscribes to 1204 periodicals. Computerized library services include the card catalog, interlibrary loans, and database searching. Special learning facilities include a learning resource center, art gallery, radio station, TV station, and contemporary photography museum. The campus is in an urban area in Chicago. Including any residence halls, there are 15 buildings.

Student Life: 75% of undergraduates are from Illinois. Students are from 50 states, 51 foreign countries, and Canada. 80% are from public schools. 63% are white; 16% African American; 11% Hispanic. The average age of freshmen is 19; all undergraduates, 22.

Housing: 500 students can be accommodated in college housing, which includes coed dorms. On-campus housing is available on a first-come, first-served basis. Priority is given to out-of-town students. 95% of students commute. Alcohol is not permitted. All students may keep cars.

Activities: There are no fraternities or sororities. There are 27 groups on campus, including art, chorus, computers, dance, drama, ethnic, film, gay, international, jazz band, literary magazine, musical theater, photography, political, professional, radio and TV, religious, social service, student government, and yearbook. Popular campus events include African Heritage, Dr. Martin Luther King Jr.'s Birthday, and Women in the Arts.

Disabled Students: 95% of the campus is accessible. Wheelchair ramps, elevators, specially equipped rest rooms, special class scheduling, and lowered telephones are available.

Services: Counseling and information services are available, as is tutoring in some subjects. There is a reader service for the blind, and remedial math, reading, and writing.

Campus Safety and Security: Measures include self-defense education, security escort services, informal discussions, and pamphlets/posters/films. There are emergency telephones and lighted pathways/sidewalks.

Programs of Study: Columbia confers B.A. and B.F.A. degrees. Master's degrees are also awarded. Bachelor's degrees are awarded in BUSINESS (marketing management), COMMUNICATIONS AND THE ARTS (advertising, art, audio technology, creative writing, dance, dramatic arts, film arts, journalism, multimedia, music, music business management, photography, and radio/television technology), EDUCATION (early childhood), ENGINEERING AND ENVIRONMENTAL DESIGN (computer graphics), SOCIAL SCIENCE (crosscultural studies and interpreter for the deaf). Art, film/video, and management are the largest.

Required: To graduate, all students must complete 124 semester hours of study with a minimum 2.0 GPA. General studies distribution consists of 9 hours each of literature/humanities and science/math, 6 each of English, history, and social science, and 3 each of computer applications, oral communications, senior seminar, and electives; 1 intensive writing course also is required.

Special: Columbia offers study abroad in 2 countries, independent study, internships, work-study programs, student-designed majors, and a general studies degree.

Faculty/Classroom: 56% of faculty are male; 44%, female. All teach undergraduates. No introductory courses are taught by graduate students. The average class size in a regular course is 16.

Admissions: 84% of the 2003-2004 applicants were accepted.

Requirements: Applicants should be graduates of accredited secondary schools. The GED is also accepted. An interview is recommended. AP and CLEP credits are accepted.

Procedure: Freshmen are admitted to all sessions. There is a deferred admissions plan. Applications should be filed by August 15 for fall entry, along with a $35 fee. The college accepts all applicants. Notification is sent on a rolling basis. Applications are accepted on-line through the school's web site.

Transfer: 1325 transfer students enrolled in 2002-2003. Up to 88 credit hours are accepted with a grade of C or better; up to 62 credit hours from 2-year colleges with a grade of C or better are accepted. 36 of 124 credits required for the bachelor's degree must be completed at Columbia.

Visiting: There are regularly scheduled orientations for prospective students. There are guides for informal visits and visitors may sit in on classes. To schedule a visit, contact the Undergraduate Admissions Office.

Financial Aid: The FAFSA is required.

International Students: There are 250 international students enrolled. The school actively recruits these students. They must score 500 on the written TOEFL or 173 on the electronic version.

Computers: The mainframes are an IBM AS/400 and a P200. PCs are available for student use in the college's computer labs. There are no time limits and no fees.

Graduates: From July 1, 2002 to June 30, 2003, 1370 bachelor's degrees were awarded. The most popular majors were film/video (12%), marketing (9%), and art and design (9%).

Admissions Contact: Murphy Monroe, Director of Admissions. E-mail: *admissions@popmail.colum.edu*

CONCORDIA UNIVERSITY, RIVER FOREST E-1
River Forest, IL 60305
(708) 209-3100
(866) GO-2-CURF; Fax: (708) 209-3473

Full-time: 380 men, 617 women	**Faculty:** 66; IIB, -$
Part-time: 61 men, 145 women	**Ph.D.s:** 65%
Graduate: 110 men, 393 women	**Student/Faculty:** 15 to 1
Year: semesters, summer session	**Tuition:** $18,200
Application Deadline: open	**Room & Board:** $5400
Freshman Class: 670 applied, 611 accepted, 228 enrolled	
SAT I: n/av	**ACT:** required **COMPETITIVE**

Concordia University, founded in 1864, is a private liberal arts institution affiliated with the Lutheran Church, Missouri Synod. There are 3 undergraduate schools and 1 graduate school. In addition to regional accreditation, Concordia University has baccalaureate program accreditation with NCATE and NLN. The library contains 165,000 volumes, 630,000 microform items, and 3894 audio/video tapes/CDs, and subscribes to 470 periodicals. Computerized library services include the card catalog, interlibrary loans, database searching, and Internet access. Special learning facilities include a learning resource center, art gallery, natural history museum, early childhood resource center, human performance lab, language lab, computer center, and weather station. The 40-acre campus is in a suburban area 10 miles west of downtown Chicago. Including any residence halls, there are 40 buildings.

Student Life: 65% of undergraduates are from Illinois. Students are from 26 states, 1 foreign country, and Canada. 66% are from public schools. 53% are white. 51% are Protestant; 39% includes undeclared; 9% Catholic. The average age of freshmen is 18; all undergraduates, 22. 28% do not continue beyond their first year; 60% remain to graduate.

Housing: 750 students can be accommodated in college housing, which includes single-sex and coed dorms and married-student housing. On-campus housing is guaranteed for all 4 years. 50% of students live on campus; of those, 85% remain on campus on weekends. Alcohol is not permitted. All students may keep cars.

Activities: There are no fraternities or sororities. There are 43 groups on campus, including band, cheerleading, choir, chorale, chorus, computers, dance, drama, ethnic, honors, international, jazz band, literary magazine, musical theater, newspaper, pep band, professional, religious, social, social service, student government, symphony, and yearbook. Popular campus events include Orientation Week, Campus Awareness Day, and Family Weekend.

Sports: There are 8 intercollegiate sports for men and 8 for women, and 12 intramural sports for men and 12 for women. Facilities include 2 gyms, an indoor swimming pool, weight training room, human performance lab, football and soccer fields, tennis courts, baseball and softball fields, track, first aid training room, table tennis, billiards, and table games.

Disabled Students: 74% of the campus is accessible. Wheelchair ramps, elevators, special parking, specially equipped rest rooms, special class scheduling, lowered drinking fountains, and lowered telephones are available.

Services: Counseling and information services are available, as is tutoring in every subject. There is remedial math, reading, and writing.

Campus Safety and Security: Measures include 24-hour foot and vehicle patrol, self-defense education, security escort services, and shuttle buses. There are informal discussions, pamphlets/posters/films, emergency telephones, and lighted pathways/sidewalks.

Programs of Study: Concordia University confers B.A., B.Mus., and B.Mus.Ed. degrees. Master's and doctoral degrees are also awarded. Bachelor's degrees are awarded in BIOLOGICAL SCIENCE (biology/biological science), BUSINESS (accounting and business administration and management), COMMUNICATIONS AND THE ARTS (art, communications, English, and music), COMPUTER AND PHYSICAL SCIENCE (chemistry, computer programming, computer science, mathematics, natural sciences, and physical sciences), EDUCATION (computer, early childhood, elementary, middle school, music, physical, science, and secondary), HEALTH PROFESSIONS (premedicine), SOCIAL SCIENCE (geography, history, physical fitness/movement, political science/government, prelaw, psychology, religion, social science, social work, sociology, and theological studies). Teacher education, music, and com-

puter science are the strongest academically. Teacher education, business, and psychology are the largest.

Required: All students are required to take 2 years of liberal arts, including humanities, English, science, religion, and social science, and 5 quarter hours of phys ed. A 2.0 to 2.25 GPA and a total of 128 to 180 quarter hours are required. The number of hours required for the major varies by program.

Special: Cross-registration is possible with Dominican University and the Chicago Consortium of Colleges. Concordia also offers internships for liberal arts majors in the Chicago area, which provides numerous opportunities, study abroad in England, and pass/fail options. Work-study is possible, as is an accelerated degreee program in organizational management. There are 3 national honor societies, including Phi Beta Kappa, and a freshman honors program.

Faculty/Classroom: 56% of faculty are male; 44%, female. 94% teach undergraduates, 31% do research, and 31% do both. No introductory courses are taught by graduate students. The average class size in an introductory lecture is 20; in a laboratory, 18; and in a regular course, 25.

Admissions: 91% of the 2003-2004 applicants were accepted. The ACT scores for the 2003-2004 freshman class were: 37% below 21, 24% between 21 and 23, 22% between 24 and 26, 8% between 27 and 28, and 9% above 28. 22% of the current freshmen were in the top fifth of their class; 30% were in the top two fifths. 7 freshmen graduated first in their class.

Requirements: The ACT is required. In addition, applicants should have 15 units of credit, with 11 units in college preparatory courses, including English, math, lab science, and social studies. A letter of recommendation is required, as is a minimum GPA of 2.0 in the college preparatory subjects and a ranking in the top half of their graduating class. AP and CLEP credits are accepted. Important factors in the admissions decision are advanced placement or honor courses, recommendations by school officials, and leadership record.

Procedure: Freshmen are admitted to all sessions. Entrance exams should be taken in the spring of the junior year or fall of the senior year. There is a rolling admissions plan. Application deadlines are open. Applications are accepted on-line through the college's web site.

Transfer: 76 transfer students enrolled in 2003-2004. A cumulative GPA of 2.0 or higher at all previous colleges plus a letter of recommendation are required. 48 of 128 to 180 credits required for the bachelor's degree must be completed at Concordia University.

Visiting: There are regularly scheduled orientations for prospective students, consisting of daily planned activities during orientation in the first week of the fall semester. There are guides for informal visits and visitors may sit in on classes and stay overnight. To schedule a visit, contact the Office of Admission at *www.crtadmis.edu*.

Financial Aid: In 2003-2004, 93% of all full-time freshmen and 87% of continuing full-time students received some form of financial aid. 85% of full-time freshmen and 67% of continuing full-time students received need-based aid. The average freshman award was $12,000. The average financial indebtedness of the 2003 graduate was $12,000. Concordia University is a member of CSS. The FAFSA, the college's own financial statement, and the student and parent 1040 U.S. tax forms are required.

International Students: There are 4 international students enrolled. They must score 525 on the written TOEFL or take the MELAB, or successfully complete Level 109 at an ELS language center. They must also take the SAT I or the ACT.

Computers: There are 5 Macs and 64 PCs. Computers are available in the computer center, the PC lab, and the library. All students may access the system 24 hours per day. There are no time limits and no fees.

Graduates: From July 1, 2002 to June 30, 2003, 241 bachelor's degrees were awarded. The most popular majors were education (32%), business (25%), and sociology/social work (8%). In an average class, 59% graduate in 6 years or less. Of the 2002 graduating class, 15% were enrolled in graduate school within 6 months of graduation and 96% were employed.

Admissions Contact: E-mail: *crfadmis@curf.edu* Web: *www.curf.edu*

DEPAUL UNIVERSITY E-2
Chicago, IL 60604
(312) 362-8300
(800) 4-DEPAUL; Fax: (312) 362-5749

Full-time: 4585 men, 6262 women	**Faculty:** 685; I, -$
Part-time: 1543 men, 2195 women	**Ph.D.s:** 73%
Graduate: 3884 men, 3989 women	**Student/Faculty:** 16 to 1
Year: quarters, summer session	**Tuition:** $18,790
Application Deadline: February 1	**Room & Board:** $8790
Freshman Class: 9464 applied, 6904 accepted, 2261 enrolled	
SAT I Verbal/Math: 560/540	**ACT:** 22 **VERY COMPETITIVE**

DePaul University, founded by the Vincentian Order in 1898, is a private Catholic institution with 2 main campuses: the Lincoln Park Campus houses undergraduate programs in liberal arts and sciences, education, theater, and music, and the Loop Campus offers programs in commerce, law, and computer science, telecommunications, and information systems (CTI). There are also 6 suburban campuses. There are 8 undergraduate and 9 graduate schools. In addition to regional accreditation, DePaul has baccalaureate program accreditation with AACSB, NASM, NCATE, and NLN. The 8 libraries contain 1,749,558 volumes, 1,598,445 microform items, and 140,947 audio/video tapes/CDs, and subscribe to 10,166 periodicals. Computerized library services include the card catalog, interlibrary loans, and database searching. Special learning facilities include a learning resource center, art gallery, radio station, a performing arts center, a recording studio, and a marketing research center. The 36-acre campus is in an urban area in Chicago. Including any residence halls, there are 39 buildings.

Student Life: 88% of undergraduates are from Illinois. Students are from 50 states, 74 foreign countries, and Canada. 68% are from public schools. 60% are white; 13% Hispanic; 11% African American. 33% are Catholic; 12% claim no religious affiliation. The average age of freshmen is 18; all undergraduates, 21.

Housing: 3500 students can be accommodated in college housing, which includes coed dorms and on-campus apartments. In addition, there are honors houses and limited off-campus apartments and a condominium complex. On-campus housing is available on a first-come, first-served basis and is available on a lottery system for upperclassmen. Priority is given to out-of-town students. 75% of students commute. All students may keep cars.

Activities: 3% of men belong to 9 local fraternities; 3% of women belong to 9 local sororities. There are 140 groups on campus, including cheerleading, choir, chorale, chorus, computers, dance, drama, drill team, ethnic, gay, honors, international, jazz band, marching band, musical theater, opera, pep band, political, professional, radio and TV, religious, social, social service, student government, symphony, and yearbook. Popular campus events include Hispanic Awareness Month, Women's History Month, and Annual Spring Concert (FEST).

Sports: There are 6 intercollegiate sports for men and 7 for women, and 10 intramural sports for men and 8 for women. Facilities include soccer and softball fields, and a 120,000-square-foot fitness and recreation center with a 4-court gym, a 4-lane track, a 6-lane pool, racquetball courts, a weight and fitness area, a spin studio, and a wellness suite.

Disabled Students: 95% of the campus is accessible. Wheelchair ramps, elevators, special parking, specially equipped rest rooms, lowered drinking fountains, lowered telephones, and a disabled student services department are available.

Services: Counseling and information services are available, as is tutoring in most subjects. There is a reader service for the blind and remedial math, reading, and writing. A writing center, a productive learning strategies program, and a student development center are also available.

Campus Safety and Security: Measures include 24-hour foot and vehicle patrol, self-defense education, security escort services, and shuttle buses. There are informal discussions, pamphlets/posters/films, emergency telephones, lighted pathways/sidewalks, and a crime prevention office.

Programs of Study: DePaul confers B.A., B.S., B.F.A, B.M., and B.S.C. degrees. Master's and doctoral degrees are also awarded. Bachelor's degrees are awarded in BIOLOGICAL SCIENCE (biology/biological science), BUSINESS (accounting, banking and finance, business administration and management, business economics, and marketing/retailing/merchandising), COMMUNICATIONS AND THE ARTS (applied music, art, communications, comparative literature, dramatic arts, English, fine arts, French, German, Italian, jazz, music, music business management, Spanish, and theater design), COMPUTER AND PHYSICAL SCIENCE (chemistry, computer science, information sciences and systems, mathematics, and physics), EDUCATION (early childhood, elementary, foreign languages, music, physical, and secondary), ENGINEERING AND ENVIRONMENTAL DESIGN (environmental science), HEALTH PROFESSIONS (medical laboratory technology), SOCIAL SCIENCE (American studies, economics, geography, history, international studies, Judaic studies, Latin American studies, philosophy, political science/government, psychology, religion, social science, social studies, sociology, urban studies, and women's studies). Commerce, liberal arts and science, and computer science are the largest.

Required: All students must complete general education requirements, including 4 courses in behavioral and social sciences, 3 each in natural sciences and math, 2 each in English composition, world civilization, and philosophy and religion, and 1 each in art, music, and literature. A total of 192 quarter hour credits, including a minimum of 52 in the student's major, and a minimum GPA of 2.0 are required to graduate.

Special: A co-op program in Jewish studies is offered with Spertus College of Judaica. Numerous internships in communications, commerce, computer science, and social sciences are possible. Study abroad is offered in 11 countries and in a West European Seminar in Comparative Business Practices. Accelerated degree programs, dual majors, a certificate program in acting and costume construction, pass/fail options, and concentrations within the theater major, including acting, costume design, general theater studies, lighting design, playwriting, production theater management, and theater technology, are available. The School for

New Learning provides evening and weekend degree programs for adult learners, with credit given for life and work experience. There are 21 national honor societies, a freshman honors program, and 29 departmental honors programs.

Faculty/Classroom: 59% of faculty are male; 41%, female. 83% teach undergraduates. No introductory courses are taught by graduate students. The average class size in an introductory lecture is 18; in a laboratory, 18; and in a regular course, 16.

Admissions: 73% of the 2003-2004 applicants were accepted. The SAT I scores for the 2003-2004 freshman class were: Verbal--22% below 500, 44% between 500 and 599, 29% between 600 and 700, and 5% above 700; Math--26% below 500, 47% between 500 and 599, 24% between 600 and 700, and 4% above 700. The ACT scores were 22% below 21, 32% between 21 and 23, 26% between 24 and 26, 12% between 27 and 28, and 8% above 28. 40% of the current freshmen were in the top fifth of their class; 74% were in the top two fifths. 18 freshmen graduated first in their class in a recent year.

Requirements: The SAT I or ACT is required. In addition, applicants should have completed 16 Carnegie units or submit the GED. A portfolio is required for theater majors, and an audition for acting and music majors. DePaul requires applicants to be in the upper 50% of their class. A GPA of 2.5 is required. AP and CLEP credits are accepted. Important factors in the admissions decision are advanced placement or honor courses, leadership record, and personality/intangible qualities.

Procedure: Freshmen are admitted to all sessions. Entrance exams should be taken by the spring of the junior year. There are early admissions and deferred admissions plans. There is a rolling admissions plan. Applications should be filed by February 1 for fall entry, December 1 for winter entry, and February 1 for spring entry. Notification of early decision is sent January 1; regular decision, on a rolling basis. The fall 2003 application fee was $35.

Transfer: 1383 transfer students enrolled in 2002-2003. A 2.0 GPA is required for most programs; a 2.5 in commerce. Applicants with fewer than 30 semester hours or 44 quarter hours should submit high school transcripts and SAT I or ACT scores. An audition is required for music and theater majors. 45 of 192 credits required for the bachelor's degree must be completed at DePaul.

Visiting: There are regularly scheduled orientations for prospective students, including a 2-day program offered throughout the summer that provides academic advising, assessment testing, and registration, in addition to information on social activities and residence life. There are guides for informal visits and visitors may sit in on classes and stay overnight. To schedule a visit, contact the Admissions Office.

Financial Aid: DePaul is a member of CSS. The FAFSA is required.

International Students: They must score 550 on the written TOEFL or 215 on the electronic version and also take the SAT I or the ACT.

Computers: The mainframe is an IBM system/390 Multiprize 2000. There are 200 mainframe terminals and more than 1500 PCs available. All students may access the system 24 hours a day. There are no time limits and no fees. It is strongly recommended that all students have a personal computer.

Graduates: From July 1, 2002 to June 30, 2003, 1686 bachelor's degrees were awarded. The most popular majors were commerce (29%), computer and information science (28%), and education (22%). In an average class, 43% graduate in 5 years or less, and 60% graduate in 6 years or less. 100 companies recruited on campus in 2002-2003.

Admissions Contact: Carlene Klaas, Dean of Admissions.
E-mail: *admitdpu@depaul.edu* Web: *www.depaul.edu*

DEVRY UNIVERSITY/ADDISON (DUPAGE COUNTY)   E-2
Addison, IL 60101-6106   (630) 953-2000
(800) 346-5420; Fax: (630) 953-1236

Full-time: 1652 men, 714 women	**Faculty:** n/av
Part-time: 1537 men, 924 women	**Ph.Ds:** n/av
Graduate: n/av	**Student/Faculty:** n/av
Year: semesters, summer session	**Tuition:** $10,790
Application Deadline: open	**Room & Board:** n/app
Freshman Class: n/av	
SAT I or ACT: n/av	**LESS COMPETITIVE**

DeVry University/Addison (DuPage County), a private institution, opened in 1982; there are 66 other DeVry University locations in the United States and Canada. The school offers hands-on technology-based programs in electronics, business administration, telecommunications management, computer information systems, technical management, information technology, and computer engineering technology. In addition to regional accreditation, DeVry has baccalaureate program accreditation with ABET. The library contains 16,606 volumes and 676 audio/video tapes/CDs, and subscribes to 109 periodicals. Computerized library services include the card catalog, interlibrary loans, and database searching. Special learning facilities include a learning resource center and electronics and other labs. The 15-acre campus is in a suburban area 20 miles west of Chicago. There is one building.

Student Life: 52% of students are white; 13% African American. The average age of all undergraduates is 26.

Housing: There are no residence halls. Housing referrals can be obtained through the Student Housing Office. There are private apartments, student-plan housing, and private rooms. All students commute. Alcohol is not permitted. All students may keep cars.

Activities: There are no fraternities or sororities. There are 11 groups on campus, including computers, ethnic, honors, international, literary magazine, newspaper, professional, religious, and social service. Popular campus events include Summer Fest, Casino Night, and Santa Day.

Sports: There are 5 intramural sports for men and 5 for women. Facilities include a weight room, a gym, an indoor and outdoor track, baseball diamonds, and an outdoor pool, all available not far from DeVry.

Disabled Students: 90% of the campus is accessible. Wheelchair ramps, elevators, special parking, specially equipped rest rooms, and lowered drinking fountains are available.

Services: Counseling and information services are available, as is tutoring in every subject.

Campus Safety and Security: Measures include lighted pathways/ sidewalks. During business hours, the campus is patrolled by student assistants. An alarm system is in operation during other hours.

Programs of Study: DeVry confers the B.S. degree. Associate degrees are also awarded. Bachelor's degrees are awarded in BUSINESS (business administration and management), COMMUNICATIONS AND THE ARTS (telecommunications), COMPUTER AND PHYSICAL SCIENCE (information sciences and systems), ENGINEERING AND ENVIRONMENTAL DESIGN (computer engineering, electrical/electronics engineering technology, and technological management). Computer information systems, telecommunications, and electronics engineering technology are the largest.

Required: To graduate, students must achieve a cumulative GPA of at least 2.0 and satisfactorily complete all curriculum requirements. Course requirements vary according to program. All first-semester students take courses in business organization, computer applications, algebra, psychology, and student success strategies.

Special: Nondegree study, co-op programs, an accelerated degree program, evening and weekend classes, and distance learning are available. There are 3 national honor societies and 3 departmental honors programs.

Faculty/Classroom: All teach undergraduates.

Requirements: Admissions requirements include graduation from a secondary school; the GED is also accepted. Applicants must pass the DeVry entrance exam or present satisfactory ACT or SAT I scores. An interview is required. CLEP credit is accepted.

Procedure: Freshmen are admitted fall, spring, and summer. There is a rolling admissions plan. There are early admissions and deferred admissions plans. Application deadlines are open. Application fee is $50. Applications are accepted on-line through *https://apply.embark.com/ UGrad/DeVry/21.*

Transfer: 60 transfer students enrolled in a recent year. Applicants must present passing grades in all completed college course work, demonstrate language skills proficiency with at least 24 completed semester hours, and present evidence of math proficiency by appropriate college-level credits. A minimum GPA of 2.0 is required. 25% of 48 to 154 credits required for the bachelor's degree must be completed at DeVry.

Visiting: There are regularly scheduled orientations for prospective students. There are guides for informal visits and visitors may sit in on classes. To schedule a visit, contact Billy Bungert, New Student Coordinator at (708) 953-0610.

Financial Aid: In 2002-2003, 24% of all full-time freshmen and 49% of continuing full-time students received some form of financial aid. 24% of full-time freshmen and at least 48% of continuing full-time students received need-based aid. The average freshman award was $6723. Need-based scholarships or need-based grants averaged $5099; need-based self-help aid (loans and jobs) averaged $3495; and institutional non-need-based awards and non-need-based scholarships averaged $6930. DeVry is a member of CSS. The FAFSA is required. The deadline for filing freshman financial aid applications is rolling.

International Students: There were 75 international students enrolled in a recent year. They must score 500 on the written TOEFL or 173 on the electronic version or take the MELAB, the Comprehensive English Language Test, or the college's own test and also take the SAT I, ACT, or the college's own entrance exam.

Computers: The mainframe is an IBM 3081K. Lab facilities include PCs in stand-alone and network configuration, with access to the mainframe. LANs provide access to a wide range of applications software. Hard copy from the mainframe is provided through a local minicomputer and medium- and high-speed printers. Students in the computer information systems program may access the system during published lab hours. There are no time limits and no fees.

Graduates: From July 1, 2002 to June 30, 2003, 719 bachelor's degrees were awarded. The most popular majors were computer information systems (71%), business (17%), and electronics engineering technology (12%). 55 companies recruited on campus in a recent year.

Admissions Contact: Ted Kulawiak, Director of Admissions.
E-mail: *mbutler@dpg.devry.edu* Web: *www.dpg.devry.edu*

DEVRY UNIVERSITY/CHICAGO
E-2
Chicago, IL 60618-5994

(773) 929-6550
(800) 383-3879; Fax: (773) 697-2710

Full-time: 1199 men, 616 women	**Faculty:** n/av
Part-time: 660 men, 421 women	**Ph.D.s:** n/av
Graduate: none	**Student/Faculty:** n/av
Year: semesters, summer session	**Tuition:** $10,790
Application Deadline: open	**Room & Board:** n/app
Freshman Class: n/av	
SAT I or ACT: n/av	**LESS COMPETITIVE**

DeVry University/Chicago, founded in 1931, is a private institution offering hands-on programs in electronics, computer engineering technology, information technology, business administration, telecommunications, technical management, and computer information systems. The school is a part of DeVry University, Inc., an organization administering the 67 DeVry University locations throughout the United States and Canada. In addition to regional accreditation, DeVry has baccalaureate program accreditation with ABET. The library contains 19,524 volumes and 1136 audio/video tapes/CDs, and subscribes to 26 periodicals. Computerized library services include the card catalog, interlibrary loans, and database searching. Special learning facilities include a learning resource center and electronics and other labs. The 14-acre campus is in an urban area in northwest Chicago. There is 1 building.

Student Life: 34% of students are African American; 31% Hispanic; 22% white; 11% Asian American. The average age of all undergraduates is 26.

Housing: There are no residence halls. Housing referrals may be obtained through the Student Housing Office. There are private apartments, student-plan housing, and private rooms. All students commute. Alcohol is not permitted. All students may keep cars.

Activities: There are no fraternities or sororities. There are 16 groups on campus, including computers, ethnic, honors, international, newspaper, professional, and religious. Popular campus events include Megaflicks and Freaky Photos, Taste of Chicago, and Welcome Week.

Sports: There is no sports program at DeVry.

Disabled Students: 70% of the campus is accessible. Elevators, special parking, specially equipped rest rooms, lowered drinking fountains, and lowered telephones are available.

Services: Counseling and information services are available, as is tutoring in every subject.

Campus Safety and Security: Measures include 24-hour foot and vehicle patrol and lighted pathways/sidewalks. Security guards are on duty Monday through Friday 7 A.M. to midnight. There is 24-hour security on weekends and holidays.

Programs of Study: DeVry confers the B.S. degree. Associate degrees are also awarded. Bachelor's degrees are awarded in BUSINESS (business administration and management), COMMUNICATIONS AND THE ARTS (telecommunications), COMPUTER AND PHYSICAL SCIENCE (information sciences and systems), ENGINEERING AND ENVIRONMENTAL DESIGN (computer engineering, electrical/electronics engineering technology, and technological management). Computer information systems and electronics engineering technology are the largest.

Required: To graduate, students must achieve a cumulative GPA of at least 2.0 and satisfactorily complete all curriculum requirements. Course requirements vary according to program. All first-semester students take courses in business organization, computer applications, algebra, psychology, and student success strategies.

Special: Accelerated degrees, co-op programs, evening and weekend classes, and nondegree study are possible. There are 3 national honor societies and 3 departmental honors programs.

Faculty/Classroom: All teach undergraduates.

Requirements: Admission requirements include graduation from a secondary school; the GED is also accepted. Applicants must pass the DeVry entrance exam or present satisfactory ACT or SAT I scores. An interview is required. CLEP credit is accepted.

Procedure: Freshmen are admitted fall, spring, and summer. There are early admissions and deferred admissions plans. There is a rolling admissions plan. Application deadlines are open. Application fee is $50. Notification is sent on a rolling basis. Applications are accepted on-line through *https://apply.embark.com/UGrad/DeVry/21/.*

Transfer: 8 transfer students enrolled in a recent year. Applicants must present passing grades in all completed college course work, demonstrate language skills proficiency with at least 24 completed semester hours, and evidence math proficiency by appropriate college-level credits. A minimum GPA of 2.0 is required. 25% of 48 to 154 credits required for the bachelor's degree must be completed at DeVry.

Visiting: There are regularly scheduled orientations for prospective students. There are guides for informal visits and visitors may sit in on classes. To schedule a visit, contact the Enrollment Services Coordinator at (773) 929-8500.

Financial Aid: In 2002-2003, 35% of all full-time freshmen and 64% of continuing full-time students received some form of financial aid. At least 34% of full-time freshmen and 63% of continuing full-time students received need-based aid. The average freshman award was $9238. Need-based scholarships or need-based grants averaged $6630; need-based self-help aid (loans and jobs) averaged $3792; and institutional non-need-based awards and non-need-based scholarships averaged $7112. The FAFSA is required. There is a rolling deadline for filing freshman financial aid applications for fall entry.

International Students: There were 100 international students enrolled in a recent year. They must score 500 on the written TOEFL or 173 on the electronic version and also take the college's own entrance exam.

Computers: The mainframe is an IBM 3081. Lab facilities include PCs in stand-alone and network configuration, with access to the mainframe. LANs provide access to a wide range of applications software. Hard copy from the mainframe is provided through a local minicomputer and medium- and high-speed printers. Computer information systems students may access the system during lab hours. There are no fees.

Graduates: From July 1, 2002 to June 30, 2003, 577 bachelor's degrees were awarded. The most popular majors were computer information systems (56%), business administration (26%), and electronics technology (18%). 115 companies recruited on campus in a recent year.

Admissions Contact: Christine Hierl, Director of Admissions.
E-mail: *admissions2@devry.edu* Web: *www.chi.devry.edu*

DEVRY UNIVERSITY/TINLEY PARK
Tinley Park, IL 60477-6243

E-2

(708) 342-3100
(877) 305-8184; Fax: (708) 342-3505

Full-time: 696 men, 243 women	**Faculty:** n/av
Part-time: 314 men, 174 women	**Ph.Ds:** n/av
Graduate: n/av	**Student/Faculty:** n/av
Year: semesters, summer session	**Tuition:** $10,790
Application Deadline: open	**Room & Board:** n/app
Freshman Class: n/av	
SAT I or ACT: n/av	**LESS COMPETITIVE**

DeVry University/Tinley Park, founded in 2000, is 1 of 67 DeVry University locations throughout the United States and Canada. The private institution offers career-oriented degree programs with hands-on training in various fields of business and technology. The library contains 11,000 volumes, 10,000 e-books, and 600 audio/video tapes/CDs, and subscribes to 71 periodicals. Computerized library services include the card catalog, interlibrary loans, and database searching. Special learning facilities include a learning resource center and electronics and other labs.

Student Life: 53% of students are white; 30% African American. The average age of all undergraduates is 26.

Housing: There are no residence halls. Housing referrals can be obtained through the Student Housing Office. There are private apartments, student-plan housing, and private rooms. All students commute. All students may keep cars.

Activities: There are no fraternities or sororities. There are 6 groups on campus, including computers, professional, and social. Popular campus events include Anniversary Celebration.

Sports: There is no sports program at DeVry.

Disabled Students: All of the campus is accessible. Wheelchair ramps, elevators, special parking, specially equipped rest rooms, special class scheduling, lowered drinking fountains, and lowered telephones are available.

Services: Counseling and information services are available, as is tutoring in every subject.

Campus Safety and Security: Measures include security escort services, informal discussions, emergency telephones, and lighted pathways/sidewalks. There are 24-hour emergency telephone/alarm devices and 16-hour patrols by trained security personnel.

Programs of Study: DeVry confers the B.S. degree. Associate and master's degrees are also awarded. Bachelor's degrees are awarded in BUSINESS (business administration and management), COMMUNICATIONS AND THE ARTS (telecommunications), COMPUTER AND PHYSICAL SCIENCE (information sciences and systems), ENGINEERING AND ENVIRONMENTAL DESIGN (computer engineering, electrical/electronics engineering technology, and technological management). Telecommunications management and computer information systems are the largest.

Required: To graduate, students must achieve a GPA of at least 2.0 and complete all curriculum requirements. Course requirements may vary according to program. All first-semester students take courses in business organization, computer applications, algebra, psychology, and student success strategies.

Special: Accelerated degree programs are offered in business administration and telecommunications management. Co-op programs, nondegree study, distance learning, and evening and weekend classes are possible.

Faculty/Classroom: All teach undergraduates.

Requirements: Admissions requirements include graduation from a secondary school; the GED is also accepted. Applicants must pass the DeVry entrance exam or present satisfactory ACT or SAT I scores. An interview is required. CLEP credit is accepted.

Procedure: Freshmen are admitted to all sessions. There is a rolling admissions plan. There are early admissions and deferred admissions plans. Application deadlines are open. Application fee is $50. Applications are accepted on-line through *https://apply.embark.com/UGrad/DeVry/21*.

Transfer: 360 transfer students enrolled in a recent year. Applicants must submit official transcripts from all previous colleges attended indicating passing grades in all completed course work, demonstrate language skills proficiency in at least 24 completed semester hours, and present evidence of math proficiency by appropriate college-level credits. A minimum GPA of 2.0 is required. 25% of 48 to 154 credits required for the bachelor's degree must be completed at DeVry.

Visiting: There are regularly scheduled orientations for prospective students. There are guides for informal visits and visitors may sit in on classes. To schedule a visit, contact Kerrie Flynn, New Student Coordinator.

Financial Aid: In 2002-2003, 49% of all full-time freshmen and 72% of continuing full-time students received some form of financial aid. 49% of full-time freshmen and 72% of continuing full-time students received need-based aid. The average freshman award was $7533. Need-based scholarships or need-based grants averaged $5844; need-based self-help aid (loans and jobs) averaged $3747; and institutional non-need-based awards and non-need-based scholarships averaged $8740. The FAFSA is required. The deadline for filing freshman financial aid applications is rolling.

International Students: There were 13 international students enrolled in a recent year. They must score 500 on the written TOEFL or 173 on the electronic version and also take the college's own entrance exam.

Graduates: From July 1, 2002 to June 30, 2003, 180 bachelor's degrees were awarded. The most popular majors were computer information systems (89%), electronics engineering technology (9%), and business (3%).

Admissions Contact: Angela Howard, Director of Admissions.
E-mail: *imccauley@tp.devry.edu* Web: *www.tp.devry.edu*

DOMINICAN UNIVERSITY
River Forest, IL 60305

E-2

(708) 524-6800
(800) 828-8475; Fax: (708) 524-5990

Full-time: 310 men, 700 women	**Faculty:** 83; IIA, -$
Part-time: 69 men, 132 women	**Ph.Ds:** 88%
Graduate: 431 men, 1258 women	**Student/Faculty:** 12 to 1
Year: semesters, summer session	**Tuition:** $17,950
Application Deadline: open	**Room & Board:** $5660
Freshman Class: 665 applied, 548 accepted, 242 enrolled	
ACT: 23	**COMPETITIVE**

Dominican University, founded in 1901, is an independent liberal arts institution affiliated with the Roman Catholic Church and sponsored by the Sinsinawa Dominicans. There are 2 undergraduate and 4 graduate schools. In addition to regional accreditation, Dominican University has baccalaureate program accreditation with ACBSP and ADA. The library contains 300,000 volumes, 46,000 microform items, and 4170 audio/video tapes/CDs, and subscribes to 5800 periodicals. Computerized library services include the card catalog, interlibrary loans, and database searching. Special learning facilities include an art gallery, a language lab, and a writing center. The 30-acre campus is in a suburban area 10 miles west of Chicago. Including any residence halls, there are 8 buildings.

Student Life: 90% of undergraduates are from Illinois. Students are from 23 states and 16 foreign countries. 55% are from public schools. 70% are white; 16% Hispanic. 67% are Catholic; 17% Protestant; 13% claim no religious affiliation. The average age of freshmen is 18; all undergraduates, 23. 15% do not continue beyond their first year; 65% remain to graduate.

Housing: 350 students can be accommodated in college housing, which includes single-sex and coed dorms. On-campus housing is guaranteed for all 4 years. 65% of students commute. All students may keep cars.

Activities: There are no fraternities or sororities. There are 30 groups on campus, including art, cheerleading, choir, computers, dance, drama, ethnic, honors, international, literary magazine, musical theater, newspaper, photography, political, professional, religious, social, social service, and student government. Popular campus events include Founders Day, Spring Fling, and Candle and Rose Ceremony.

Sports: There are 7 intercollegiate sports for men and 7 for women, and 5 intramural sports for men and 5 for women. Facilities include a gym, an indoor running track, an indoor swimming pool, a weight room, a training room, a fitness center, a dance room, racquetball courts, and soccer fields.

Disabled Students: All of the campus is accessible. Wheelchair ramps, elevators, special parking, specially equipped rest rooms, special class scheduling, and lowered drinking fountains are available.

Services: Counseling and information services are available, as is tutoring in most subjects.

Campus Safety and Security: Measures include 24-hour foot and vehicle patrol, security escort services, shuttle buses, and informal discussions. There are pamphlets/posters/films, emergency telephones, lighted pathways/sidewalks, and door alarms.

Programs of Study: Dominican University confers B.A. and B.S. degrees. Master's degrees are also awarded. Bachelor's degrees are awarded in AGRICULTURE (natural resource management), BIOLOGICAL SCIENCE (biochemistry, biology/biological science, and nutrition), BUSINESS (accounting, business administration and management, fashion merchandising, and international business management), COMMUNICATIONS AND THE ARTS (art, communications, dramatic arts, English, fine arts, French, graphic design, Italian, journalism, music, performing arts, photography, Spanish, and technical and business writing), COMPUTER AND PHYSICAL SCIENCE (chemistry, computer science, information sciences and systems, and mathematics), ENGINEERING AND ENVIRONMENTAL DESIGN (computer graphics, engineering, and environmental science), SOCIAL SCIENCE (American studies, criminology, dietetics, fashion design and technology, food production/management/services, food science, history, international relations, philosophy, political science/government, psychology, religion, social science, and sociology). English, psychology, and sciences are the strongest academically. Business administration, psychology, and computer science are the largest.

Required: To graduate, students must complete 124 credit hours with a minimum GPA of 2.0. A total of 30 to 56 hours is required in the major. All students must demonstrate proficiency, through a placement exam or the completion of specified courses, in English composition, math, computer competency, and library skills. In addition, students must take 1 interdisciplinary seminar at each academic level and 1 course each in natural sciences, history, fine arts and literature, social sciences, theology, and philosophy. 1 course must meet the multicultural requirement.

Special: Co-op programs in medical technology and nursing with Rush University, cross-registration with Concordia University, internships, study abroad in 4 countries, and a Washington semester are offered. Student-designed majors and interdisciplinary majors, including computer information systems, math and computer science, environmental science, and environmental management, credit for prior learning, and pass/fail options are possible. There is an accelerated degree program in organizational leadership, and a joint B.A.-B.S. in engineering with the Illinios Institute of Technology, and a dual admission program with Chicago College of Pharmacy. There are 11 national honor societies and a freshman honors program.

Faculty/Classroom: 46% of faculty are male; 54%, female. All both teach and do research. No introductory courses are taught by graduate students. The average class size in an introductory lecture is 25; in a laboratory, 12; and in a regular course, 18.

Admissions: 82% of the 2003-2004 applicants were accepted. The ACT scores for the 2003-2004 freshman class were: 34% below 21, 27% between 21 and 23, 19% between 24 and 26, 12% between 27 and 28, and 8% above 28. 36% of the current freshmen were in the top fifth of their class; 67% were in the top two fifths. 2 freshmen graduated first in their class.

Requirements: The SAT I or ACT is required. In addition, graduation from an accredited secondary school or satisfactory scores on the GED are required for admission. The school requires 14 academic credits or 16 Carnegie units. High school courses should include English, math, foreign language, social science, and lab science. An essay is required and an interview is recommended. Dominican University requires applicants to be in the upper 50% of their class. A GPA of 2.75 is required. AP and CLEP credits are accepted. Important factors in the admissions decision are advanced placement or honor courses, recommendations by school officials, and leadership record.

Procedure: Freshmen are admitted to all sessions. Entrance exams should be taken in the junior year. There is a deferred admissions plan. Application deadlines are open. Application fee is $20. Applications are accepted on-line.

Transfer: 161 transfer students enrolled in 2002-2003. Applicants must have a minimum of 12 credit hours with a GPA of 2.5. An interview is recommended. The high school record will be evaluated if GPA is below 2.5 at the previous college. 34 of 124 credits required for the bachelor's degree must be completed at Dominican University.

Visiting: There are regularly scheduled orientations for prospective students, consisting of 5 visiting days and 2 Sunday open house programs per year. Students attend class, tour the campus, and hear faculty and student presentations on visiting days. There are guides for informal visits and visitors may sit in on classes and stay overnight. To schedule a visit, contact the Undergraduate Admissions Office at *domadmis@dom.edu.*

Financial Aid: In 2003-2004, 93% of all full-time freshmen and 79% of continuing full-time students received some form of financial aid. 84% of full-time freshmen and 75% of continuing full-time students received need-based aid. The average freshman award was $14,773. Need-based scholarships or need-based grants averaged $10,364 ($17,850 maximum); need-based self-help aid (loans and jobs) averaged $3263 ($4625 maximum); and non-need-based awards and non-need-based scholarships averaged $2341 ($6000 maximum). All undergraduates work part time. Average annual earnings from campus work are $2071. The average financial indebtedness of the 2003 graduate was $15,138. Dominican University is a member of CSS. The FAFSA and tax returns are required. The priority date for freshman financial aid applications for fall entry is April 15. The deadline for filing freshman financial aid applications for fall entry is September 1.

International Students: There are 23 international students enrolled. The school actively recruits these students. They must score 550 on the written TOEFL or 213 on the electronic version and also take the ELS. In some cases, a standardized entrance exam will be required.

Computers: The mainframe is a DEC VAX 8400. 105 PCs can access the mainframe, and PCs are available in computer labs and classrooms. All students may access the system 110 hours per week at the computer center or at all times with a modem. There are no time limits and no fees. It is strongly recommended that all students have a personal computer.

Graduates: From July 1, 2002 to June 30, 2003, 279 bachelor's degrees were awarded. The most popular majors were business (15%), psychology (9%), and sociology (5%). In an average class, 55% graduate in 4 years or less, 62% graduate in 5 years or less, and 63% graduate in 6 years or less. Of the 2002 graduating class, 12% were enrolled in graduate school within 6 months of graduation and 95% were employed.

Admissions Contact: Glenn Hamilton, Director of Freshman Admission. E-mail: *domadmis@dom.edu* Web: *www.dom.edu*

EASTERN ILLINOIS UNIVERSITY E-4
Charleston, IL 61920-3099 (217) 581-2223
(800) 252-5711; Fax: (217) 581-7060

Full-time: 3827 men, 5063 women	**Faculty:** 593; IIA, -$
Part-time: 336 men, 619 women	**Ph.D.s:** 71%
Graduate: 650 men, 1027 women	**Student/Faculty:** 15 to 1
Year: semesters, summer session	**Tuition:** $4982 ($12,107)
Application Deadline: open	**Room & Board:** $6210
Freshman Class: 10,036 applied, 7892 accepted, 2964 enrolled	
ACT: 22	**COMPETITIVE**

Eastern Illinois University, founded in 1895, is a state-assisted school offering undergraduate and graduate degrees in arts and sciences and professional studies. There are 4 undergraduate schools and 1 graduate school. In addition to regional accreditation, EIU has baccalaureate program accreditation with AACSB, ACEJMC, ADA, NASAD, NASM, NCATE, and NRPA. The library contains 934,699 volumes, 1,362,881 microform items, and 26,225 audio/video tapes/CDs, and subscribes to 3387 periodicals. Computerized library services include the card catalog, interlibrary loans, and database searching. Special learning facilities include a learning resource center, art gallery, radio station, and TV station. The 320-acre campus is in a small town 50 miles south of Champaign-Urbana. Including any residence halls, there are 90 buildings.

Student Life: 98% of undergraduates are from Illinois. Students are from 38 states, 48 foreign countries, and Canada. 98% are from public schools. 89% are white. The average age of freshmen is 18; all undergraduates, 20. 19% do not continue beyond their first year; 66% remain to graduate.

Housing: 5527 students can be accommodated in college housing, which includes single-sex and coed dorms, on-campus apartments, married-student housing, fraternity houses, and sorority houses. In addition, there are honors houses. On-campus housing is guaranteed for all 4 years. 54% of students commute. Upperclassmen may keep cars.

Activities: 19% of men belong to 12 national fraternities; 19% of women belong to 1 local sorority and 12 national sororities. There are 155 groups on campus, including art, band, cheerleading, choir, chorale, chorus, computers, dance, debate, drama, drill team, ethnic, forensics, gay, honors, international, jazz band, literary magazine, marching band, musical theater, newspaper, orchestra, pep band, political, professional, radio and TV, religious, social, social service, student government, symphony, and yearbook. Popular campus events include Family Weekend, Greek Week, and an arts festival.

Sports: There are 10 intercollegiate sports for men and 10 for women, and 19 intramural sports for men and 19 for women. Facilities include a swimming pool, a gym, a student recreation center, a track, tennis courts, racquetball courts, and a jogging trail.

Disabled Students: 75% of campus housing and 90% of academic buildings are accessible. Wheelchair ramps, elevators, special parking, specially equipped rest rooms, special class scheduling, lowered drinking fountains, and lowered telephones are available.

Services: Counseling and information services are available, as is tutoring in most subjects. There is a reader service for the blind, and remedial math, reading, and writing. An academic assistance center advises freshmen and students with undeclared majors. Term paper clinics, study skills seminars, and stress management workshops are also available.

Campus Safety and Security: Measures include 24-hour foot and vehicle patrol, self-defense education, security escort services, and shuttle buses. There are informal discussions, pamphlets/posters/films, emergency telephones, and lighted pathways/sidewalks.

Programs of Study: EIU confers B.A., B.S., B.M., B.S.Bus., and B.S.Ed. degrees. Master's degrees are also awarded. Bachelor's degrees are awarded in BIOLOGICAL SCIENCE (biology/biological science), BUSINESS (accounting, banking and finance, business administration and management, and marketing/retailing/merchandising), COMMUNICATIONS AND THE ARTS (art, communications, dramatic arts, English, journalism, languages, and music), COMPUTER AND PHYSICAL SCIENCE (chemistry, computer science, geology, mathematics, and physics), EDUCATION (early childhood, elementary, middle school, physical, secondary, social science, and special), ENGINEERING AND ENVIRONMENTAL DESIGN (industrial engineering technology), HEALTH PROFESSIONS (medical laboratory science and speech pathology/audiology), SOCIAL SCIENCE (African American studies, economics, geography, history, philosophy, political science/government, psychology, and sociology). Business and education are the strongest academically. Elementary education, biological science, and phys ed are the largest.

Required: A total of 120 credit hours, with a minimum of 40 hours in upper-division courses, must be completed for graduation. The minimum GPA required for graduation is 2.0 (2.5 in education). A core curriculum of 40 to 46 hours includes courses in language, quantitative reasoning and problem solving, scientific awareness, foreign languages, cultural experience, foundations of civilizations, human behavior, social interaction and well-being, U.S. Constitution, and a senior seminar.

Special: EIU offers a co-op program in clinical laboratory science and an engineering co-op program with the University of Illinois at Champaign-Urbana. Internships, study abroad in 12 countries, dual majors, nondegree study, B.A.-B.S. degrees in athletic training and industrial technology, and pass/fail options are available. Credit for life experience may be granted through the Board of Trustees program and the Career Occupations program. There are 20 national honor societies, a freshman honors program, and 20 departmental honors programs.

Faculty/Classroom: 57% of faculty are male; 43%, female. The average class size in an introductory lecture is 32; in a laboratory, 20; and in a regular course, 23.

Admissions: 79% of the 2003-2004 applicants were accepted. The ACT scores for the 2003-2004 freshman class were: 34% below 21, 37% between 21 and 23, 19% between 24 and 26, 7% between 27 and 28, and 3% above 28. 20% of the current freshmen were in the top fifth of their class; 50% were in the top two fifths.

Requirements: The SAT I or ACT is required. The required minimum composite scores are 18 on the ACT and 860 on the SAT I for those students who rank in the upper 25% of their class, 19 on the ACT and 900 on the SAT I for those in the upper 50%, and 22 on the ACT and 1020 on the SAT I for those in the upper 75%. SAT II: Subject tests are also accepted. Applicants must be graduates of an accredited secondary school. The GED is accepted. 13 academic credits are required and should include 4 years of English and 3 years each of math, science, and social studies, including 1 year of U.S. history. EIU requires applicants to be in the upper 75% of their class. AP and CLEP credits are accepted.

Procedure: Freshmen are admitted to all sessions. Entrance exams should be taken by spring of the junior year. There is an early admissions plan. Application deadlines are open. Application fee is $30. Notification is sent on a rolling basis. Applications are accepted on-line through the university's web site.

Transfer: 1046 transfer students enrolled in 2002-2003. Transfer students must have earned 30 credit hours with a minimum GPA of 2.0. An associate degree is recommended. 42 of 120 credits required for the bachelor's degree must be completed at EIU.

Visiting: There are regularly scheduled orientations for prospective students, including open houses, scheduled several times in the spring and fall, which provide an opportunity to meet with representatives of colleges and academic departments and student services personnel and go on student-led campus tours. There are guides for informal visits and visitors may sit in on classes. To schedule a visit, contact the Office of Orientation.

Financial Aid: In 2003-2004, 46% of all full-time freshmen and 48% of continuing full-time students received some form of financial aid. The average freshman award was $8044. Need-based scholarships or need-based grants averaged $2470; need-based self-help aid (loans and jobs) averaged $2007; non-need-based athletic scholarships averaged $3292; and other institutional non-need-based awards and non-need-based scholarships averaged $5185. 25% of undergraduates work part time. The average financial indebtedness of the 2003 graduate was $13,997. The FAFSA, parent and student income tax forms, and an institutional verification form are required. The priority date for freshman financial

aid applications for fall entry is April 1. The deadline for filing freshman financial aid applications for fall entry is April 15.

International Students: There are 65 international students enrolled. The school actively recruits these students. They must score 500 on the written TOEFL or 173 on the electronic version or achieve a proficiency level of 9 from a U.S. ESL center.

Computers: The mainframe is an IBM 2066-0A1. There are also 1219 IBM and Mac PCs available to students, all networked. All students may access the system. There are no time limits and no fees.

Graduates: From July 1, 2002 to June 30, 2003, 2064 bachelor's degrees were awarded. The most popular majors were elementary education (12%) and family and consumer science (8%). In an average class, 31% graduate in 4 years or less, 59% graduate in 5 years or less, and 69% graduate in 6 years or less. 502 companies recruited on campus in 2002-2003.

Admissions Contact: Dale Wolf, Director of Admissions. A video is available. E-mail: *cdadmit@eiu.edu* Web: *http://www.eiu.edu*

EAST-WEST UNIVERSITY
E-2
Chicago, IL 60605
(312) 939-0111
(877) 398-9376; Fax: (312) 939-0083

Full-time: 366 men, 618 women	**Faculty:** 11
Part-time: 6 men, 16 women	**Ph.D.s:** 8%
Graduate: none	**Student/Faculty:** 89 to 1
Year: quarters, summer session	**Tuition:** $10,365
Application Deadline: open	**Room & Board:** n/app
Freshman Class: n/av	
ACT: required	**LESS COMPETITIVE**

East-West University, founded in 1978, is a private commuter institution offering undergraduate programs in the arts and sciences, business, computer science, and engineering. Some figures given in the above capsule and in this profile are approximate. The library contains 21,500 volumes and 8500 microform items, and subscribes to 95 periodicals. The campus is in an urban area in Chicago. There is one building.

Student Life: 85% of students are from in state. Others are from 9 foreign countries. 97% are from public schools. 75% are African American; 13% Hispanic. The average age of freshmen is 19; all undergraduates, 20.

Housing: There are no residence halls. Alcohol is not permitted.

Activities: There are no fraternities or sororities. There are 3 groups on campus, including drama, international, and student government. Popular campus events include International Day, Mother's Day Banquet, and Black History Celebration.

Sports: There is no sports program at East-West.

Disabled Students: 50% of the campus is accessible. Elevators and specially equipped rest rooms are available.

Services: Counseling and information services are available, as is tutoring in most subjects. There is remedial math, reading, and writing.

Programs of Study: East-West confers B.A. and B.S. degrees. Associate degrees are also awarded. Bachelor's degrees are awarded in BUSINESS (business administration and management), COMMUNICATIONS AND THE ARTS (communications and English), COMPUTER AND PHYSICAL SCIENCE (computer science), ENGINEERING AND ENVIRONMENTAL DESIGN (electrical/electronics engineering technology), SOCIAL SCIENCE (behavioral science). Business administration is the largest.

Required: General education requirements vary according to the degree program. To graduate, students must complete at least 180 quarter hours, including 60 in a major field, with a minimum GPA of 2.0.

Special: East-West offers co-op programs in all majors.

Faculty/Classroom: All teach undergraduates. The average class size in an introductory lecture is 15; in a laboratory, 15; and in a regular course, 15.

Requirements: The ACT is required. In addition, applicants must be graduates of accredited secondary schools or have earned a GED. Placement exams are required in math and English. A GPA of 2.5 is required. AP and CLEP credits are accepted.

Procedure: Freshmen are admitted to all sessions. Application deadlines are open. Notification is sent on a rolling basis. Check with the school for current application fee.

Transfer: East-West accepts only courses with grades of C or better. 48 of 180 quarter hours required for the bachelor's degree must be completed at East-West.

Visiting: There are regularly scheduled orientations for prospective students. There are guides for informal visits and visitors may sit in on classes.

Financial Aid: In 2003-2004, 90% of all full-time students received some form of financial aid. 90% of all full-time students received need-based aid. The average freshman award was $9021. Need-based scholarships or need-based grants averaged $2970; and need-based self-help aid (loans and jobs) averaged $2625. The CSS Profile is required. Check with the school for current application deadlines.

International Students: The school actively recruits these students. They must take the college's own test. Applicants are encouraged, but not required, to submit TOEFL scores.

Computers: The mainframe is a Texas Instruments 930. There are 21 PCs available for student use. There are no time limits.

Admissions Contact: William Link, Director of Admissions. E-mail: *williaml@eastwest.edu* Web: *eastwest.edu*

ELMHURST COLLEGE
Elmhurst, IL 60126-3296

E-2

(630) 617-3400
(800) 697-1871; Fax: (630) 617-5501

Full-time: 699 men, 1369 women	**Faculty:** 110; IIB, +$
Part-time: 121 men, 207 women	**Ph.D.s:** 85%
Graduate: 108 men, 89 women	**Student/Faculty:** 19 to 1
Year: 4-1-4, summer session	**Tuition:** $18,600
Application Deadline: April 1	**Room & Board:** $6030
Freshman Class: 1511 applied, 1100 accepted, 366 enrolled	
ACT: 23	**COMPETITIVE**

Elmhurst College, founded in 1871, is a private liberal arts college affiliated with the United Church of Christ. In addition to regional accreditation, Elmhurst has baccalaureate program accreditation with NCATE and NLN. The library contains 222,441 volumes, 50,605 microform items, and 7532 audio/video tapes/CDs, and subscribes to 2010 periodicals. Computerized library services include the card catalog, interlibrary loans, and database searching. Special learning facilities include a learning resource center, art gallery, radio station, a 16-track, 34-channel board recording studio, an electron microscopy lab, and an accelerator lab. The 38-acre campus is in a suburban area 15 miles west of Chicago. Including any residence halls, there are 23 buildings.

Student Life: 92% of undergraduates are from Illinois. Students are from 26 states, 21 foreign countries, and Canada. 82% are from public schools. 76% are white. 41% are Catholic; 26% claim no religious affiliation; 22% Protestant; 10% Muslim, Hindu, and Buddhist. The average age of freshmen is 18; all undergraduates, 24. 17% do not continue beyond their first year; 70% remain to graduate.

Housing: 805 students can be accommodated in college housing, which includes coed dorms, on-campus apartments, and off-campus apartments. In addition, there are honors houses. On-campus housing is guaranteed for all 4 years. 62% of students commute. All students may keep cars.

Activities: 5% of men belong to 3 national fraternities; 11% of women belong to 2 local and 4 national sororities. There are 100 groups on campus, including art, band, cheerleading, chess, choir, chorale, chorus, computers, dance, drama, ethnic, film, gay, honors, international, jazz band, literary magazine, musical theater, newspaper, orchestra, pep band, political, professional, radio and TV, religious, social, social service, student government, symphony, and yearbook. Popular campus events include Midwest Jazz Festival, Spring Fling, and Family Day.

Sports: There are 8 intercollegiate sports for men and 8 for women, and 7 intramural sports for men and 7 for women. Facilities include a phys ed center, weight rooms, and courts for tennis, racquetball, and handball.

Disabled Students: 95% of the campus is accessible. Wheelchair ramps, elevators, special parking, specially equipped rest rooms, special class scheduling, lowered drinking fountains, and lowered telephones are available.

Services: Counseling and information services are available, as is tutoring in most subjects.

Campus Safety and Security: Measures include 24-hour foot and vehicle patrol, security escort services, informal discussions, and pamphlets/posters/films. There are emergency telephones and lighted pathways/sidewalks.

Programs of Study: Elmhurst confers B.A., B.S., B.L.S., and B.Mus. degrees. Master's degrees are also awarded. Bachelor's degrees are awarded in BIOLOGICAL SCIENCE (biology/biological science), BUSINESS (accounting, banking and finance, business administration and management, international business management, marketing/retailing/merchandising, recreational facilities management, and transportation management), COMMUNICATIONS AND THE ARTS (art, communications, dramatic arts, English, French, German, music, music business management, and Spanish), COMPUTER AND PHYSICAL SCIENCE (chemistry, computer science, information sciences and systems, mathematics, and physics), EDUCATION (art, athletic training, drama, early childhood, elementary, mathematics, music, physical, secondary, and special), ENGINEERING AND ENVIRONMENTAL DESIGN (environmental science), HEALTH PROFESSIONS (nursing and speech pathology/audiology), SOCIAL SCIENCE (American studies, economics, geography, history, liberal arts/general studies, philosophy, political science/government, psychology, religion, sociology, and urban studies). Biology, English, and education are the strongest academically. Business administration, nursing, and education-related programs are the largest.

Required: All students are required to take a minimum of 11 general education courses in the following 11 categories: writing and reasoning;

Western culture; fine arts; literature; people, power, and politics; the natural world; issues and inquiry in science and technology; human behavior; global society; the search for human values; and the Judeo-Christian heritage and religious faith. Students must maintain a 2.0 GPA and complete 128 semester hours. The total number of hours required for the major varies from 32 to 72.

Special: There are cooperative programs in all majors. The Center for Professional Excellence provides internships and mentoring experiences. Internships varying from 1 month to 1 term are available in approximately 20 major fields. Students may study abroad in 10 countries. Elmhurst also offers a Washington semester and a 3-2 engineering degree with the Illinois Institute of Technology, Washington University, and the Universities of Illinois and Southern California. There are accelerated degree programs in business administration, managerial communication, information technology, and psychology. Credit for life, military, and work experience, nondegree study, and pass/fail options are possible. There are 20 national honor societies, a freshman honors program, and 22 departmental honors programs.

Faculty/Classroom: 54% of faculty are male; 46%, female. All both teach and do research. No introductory courses are taught by graduate students. The average class size in an introductory lecture is 19; in a laboratory, 15; and in a regular course, 16.

Admissions: 73% of the 2003-2004 applicants were accepted. The ACT scores for the 2003-2004 freshman class were: 37% below 21, 17% between 21 and 23, 26% between 24 and 26, 11% between 27 and 28, and 9% above 28. 40% of the current freshmen were in the top fifth of their class; 69% were in the top two fifths.

Requirements: The SAT I or ACT is required; the ACT is preferred. Candidates for admission must have completed 16 academic units of credit including at least 3 in English and 2 each of math, social science, and natural science lab courses. 2 years of a foreign language are recommended. AP and CLEP credits are accepted. Important factors in the admissions decision are advanced placement or honor courses, leadership record, and extracurricular activities record.

Procedure: Freshmen are admitted fall and spring. Entrance exams should be taken by the spring of the senior year. There are early admissions and deferred admissions plans. Applications should be filed by April 1 for fall entry and January 15 for spring entry. The fall 2003 application fee was $25. Notification is sent on a rolling basis. Applications are accepted on-line through the college's web site and CollegeNET.

Transfer: 265 transfer students enrolled in 2002-2003. Applicants must have a 2.4 GPA and be in good standing at the most recent college attended. A higher GPA is required for nursing, athletic training, and education. 32 of 128 credits required for the bachelor's degree must be completed at Elmhurst.

Visiting: There are regularly scheduled orientations for prospective students, including an admissions interview, a campus tour, and faculty meetings if desired. There are guides for informal visits and visitors may sit in on classes and stay overnight. To schedule a visit, contact the Office of Admission.

Financial Aid: In 2003-2004, 88% of all full-time freshmen and 75% of continuing full-time students received some form of financial aid. 74% of full-time freshmen and 65% of continuing full-time students received need-based aid. The average freshman award was $15,525. Need-based scholarships or need-based grants averaged $5800 ($14,000 maximum); need-based self-help aid (loans and jobs) averaged $2100 ($4000 maximum); and non-need-based awards and non-need-based scholarships averaged $7300 ($12,400 maximum). 63% of undergraduates work part time. Average annual earnings from campus work are $1160. The average financial indebtedness of the 2003 graduate was $14,700. Elmhurst is a member of CSS. The FAFSA and the college's own financial statement are required. The priority date for freshman financial aid applications for fall entry is April 15.

International Students: There are 31 international students enrolled. The school actively recruits these students. They must score 550 on the written TOEFL or 213 on the electronic version or take the MELAB.

Computers: The mainframes are a Dell Poweredge 4200, a Unisys HS 6000, an IBM 9370, an AS400, a 9402-EO2, Type 9309, and a Harris Nighthawk. Students may access networked systems via network connections on campus and modem. In addition, 200 PCs and 32 Macs are available for student use in multiple student labs. All students may access the system. Remote access is available 7 days a week, 24 hours a day. Labs are available 98 hours per week. There are no time limits and no fees.

Graduates: From July 1, 2002 to June 30, 2003, 608 bachelor's degrees were awarded. The most popular majors were business and marketing (33%), education (16%), and health professions (7%). In an average class, 1% graduate in 3 years or less, 57% graduate in 4 years or less, 69% graduate in 5 years or less, and 72% graduate in 6 years or less. Of the 2002 graduating class, 17% were enrolled in graduate school within 6 months of graduation and 90% were employed.

Admissions Contact: Andrew B. Sison, Director of Admission. E-mail: *admit@elmhurst.edu* Web: *www.elmhurst.edu*

EUREKA COLLEGE
Eureka, IL 61530

D-3

(309) 467-6350
(888) 4-EUREKA; Fax: (309) 467-6576

Full-time: 500 men and women	**Faculty:** 44
Part-time: 10 men and women	**Ph.Ds:** 85%
Graduate: none	**Student/Faculty:** 14 to 1
Year: semesters, summer session	**Tuition:** $19,100
Application Deadline: open	**Room & Board:** $5880
Freshman Class: n/av	
SAT I or ACT: required	**LESS COMPETITIVE**

Eureka College, founded in 1855, is a small, private, liberal arts college affiliated with the Christian Church (Disciples of Christ). Some information in this capsule and profile is approximate. In addition to regional accreditation, Eureka has baccalaureate program accreditation with NCATE. The library contains 85,000 volumes, 4989 microform items, and 977 audio/video tapes/CDs, and subscribes to 343 periodicals. Computerized library services include interlibrary loans and database searching. Special learning facilities include a learning resource center, art gallery, and the Ronald Reagan Museum. The 112-acre campus is in a small town 18 miles east of Peoria, in central Illinois. Including any residence halls, there are 23 buildings.

Student Life: 90% of undergraduates are from Illinois. Students are from 17 states and 1 foreign country. 90% are from public schools. 87% are white. 37% claim no religious affiliation; 31% Protestant; 28% Catholic. The average age of freshmen is 18; all undergraduates, 21. 25% do not continue beyond their first year; 65% remain to graduate.

Housing: 451 students can be accommodated in college housing, which includes single-sex and coed dorms, fraternity houses, and sorority houses. On-campus housing is guaranteed for all 4 years. 80% of students live on campus; of those, 70% remain on campus on weekends. All students may keep cars.

Activities: 35% of men belong to 3 national fraternities; 35% of women belong to 1 local and 2 national sororities. There are 41 groups on campus, including art, cheerleading, choir, chorale, chorus, computers, drama, ethnic, honors, international, literary magazine, musical theater, newspaper, photography, political, professional, religious, social, social service, student government, and yearbook. Popular campus events include Founders Day and Pride Day.

Sports: There are 8 intercollegiate sports for men and 8 for women, and 6 intramural sports for men and 6 for women. Facilities include a gym, a pool, a weight room, tennis courts, and football, softball, and baseball fields.

Disabled Students: 50% of the campus is accessible. Wheelchair ramps, elevators, special parking, and specially equipped rest rooms are available.

Services: Counseling and information services are available, as is tutoring in most subjects. There is remedial reading and writing. There is also a writing center.

Campus Safety and Security: Measures include informal discussions, pamphlets/posters/films, and lighted pathways/sidewalks.

Programs of Study: Eureka confers B.A. and B.S. degrees. Bachelor's degrees are awarded in BIOLOGICAL SCIENCE (biology/biological science), BUSINESS (accounting, business administration and management, business economics, and management information systems), COMMUNICATIONS AND THE ARTS (communications, dramatic arts, English, fine arts, and music), COMPUTER AND PHYSICAL SCIENCE (chemistry, computer science, mathematics, and physical sciences), EDUCATION (athletic training, education, elementary, music, physical, science, and secondary), HEALTH PROFESSIONS (medical laboratory technology), SOCIAL SCIENCE (child care/child and family studies, history, liberal arts/general studies, philosophy, physical fitness/movement, political science/government, psychology, religion, social science, and sociology). Chemistry, biology, and business administration are the strongest academically. Business administration, education, and psychology are the largest.

Required: All students must take English composition, biological and physical sciences, general studies, math, phys ed, Western civilization, 3 humanities courses, and 3 social science courses. A total of at least 124 hours is required for graduation, including 32 hours in the major. A minimum GPA of 2.0 is required.

Special: Cooperative programs include a 3-2 engineering degree with Washington University in St. Louis and Illinois Institute of Technology, a 2-2 B.S.N. with Mennonite College of Nursing or St. Francis College of Nursing, and a 3-1 clinical lab science degree with St. Francis or St. John's School of Clinical Laboratory Science. Students may study abroad in 5 countries. Professional programs in arts management, art therapy, communications, prelaw, premedicine, preministry, and teacher education are offered. An interdisciplinary major in arts and letters combines visual, performing, and literary arts. Internships, student-designed, and dual majors are offered in various areas. A Washington semester is available. There are 7 national honor societies, a freshman honors program, and 4 departmental honors programs.

Faculty/Classroom: 64% of faculty are male; 36%, female. All teach undergraduates. The average class size in an introductory lecture is 20; in a laboratory, 10; and in a regular course, 20.

Admissions: 35% of the current freshmen were in the top fifth of their class; 65% were in the top two fifths.

Requirements: The SAT I or ACT is required. In addition, applicants should be graduates of accredited secondary schools or have the GED. Eureka requires applicants to be in the upper 50% of their class. A GPA of 2.0 is required. AP and CLEP credits are accepted. Important factors in the admissions decision are recommendations by school officials, extracurricular activities record, and leadership record.

Procedure: Freshmen are admitted to all sessions. Entrance exams should be taken by December of the senior year. There is a deferred admissions plan. Application deadlines are open. Notification is sent on a rolling basis. Application fee is $15.

Transfer: Applicants must have at least a 2.0 GPA in previous college work. Those with fewer than 30 hours of transferable credit must submit high school transcripts and ACT scores. Courses with grades below C are not accepted. 30 of 124 credits required for the bachelor's degree must be completed at Eureka.

Visiting: There are regularly scheduled orientations for prospective students, including visits with admissions and financial aid advisers, observing student panels, meetings with faculty and coaches, and campus tours. There are guides for informal visits and visitors may sit in on classes and stay overnight. To schedule a visit, contact Kurt Krile, Office of Admissions at *kkrile@eureka.edu*.

Financial Aid: In a recent year, 98% of all full-time students received some form of financial aid. 93% of full-time freshmen and 91% of continuing full-time students received need-based aid. The average freshman award was $12,563. 49% of undergraduates work part time. Average annual earnings from campus work are $1000. The average financial indebtedness of a recent graduate was $14,500. Eureka is a member of CSS. The FAFSA is required. Check with the school for current deadlines.

International Students: The school actively recruits these students. They must score 550 on the written TOEFL.

Computers: The mainframe is a DEC PDP 11/24. There are 50 PCs available in the computer center, library computer lab (with Internet access), and residence halls. Pillow to Port is available in all dorm rooms. All students may access the system. There are no time limits and no fees.

Graduates: In a recent year, 101 bachelor's degrees were awarded. The most popular majors were education (24%), business (23%), and psychology (15%). In an average class, 58% graduate in 4 years or less, and 5% graduate in 5 years or less. Of a recent graduating class, 20% were enrolled in graduate school within 6 months of graduation and 75% were employed.

Admissions Contact: Dr. Brian Sajko, Dean of Admissions and Financial Aid. E-mail: *admissions@eureka.edu* Web: *www.eureka.edu*

GREENVILLE COLLEGE
Greenville, IL 62246-0159

D-4

(618) 664-7130
(800) 345-4440; Fax: (618) 664-9841

Full-time: 533 men, 575 women	**Faculty:** 63
Part-time: 24 men, 28 women	**Ph.Ds:** 65%
Graduate: 41 men, 75 women	**Student/Faculty:** 18 to 1
Year: 4-1-4, summer session	**Tuition:** $15,776
Application Deadline: open	**Room & Board:** $5566
Freshman Class: 447 applied, 431 accepted, 207 enrolled	
SAT I Verbal/Math: 550/510	**ACT:** 22 **COMPETITIVE**

Greenville College, founded in 1892, is a private liberal arts institution affiliated with the Free Methodist Church. It offers bachelor's degree programs in the humanities; mathematics, natural sciences, and information science technologies; social sciences; and the educational arts and sciences, and master's degrees in leadership and ministry, education, and teaching. The library contains 131,425 volumes, 13,909 microform items, and 3546 audio/video tapes/CDs, and subscribes to 498 periodicals. Computerized library services include the card catalog, interlibrary loans, database searching, and Internet access. Special learning facilities include a learning resource center, art gallery, radio station, and the Bock Museum. The 25-acre campus is in a small town 50 miles east of St. Louis. Including any residence halls, there are 36 buildings.

Student Life: 68% of undergraduates are from Illinois. Students are from 38 states, 13 foreign countries, and Canada. 85% are white. 81% are Protestant; 14% claim no religious affiliation. The average age of freshmen is 18; all undergraduates, 24. 27% do not continue beyond their first year; 54% remain to graduate.

Housing: 740 students can be accommodated in college housing, which includes single-sex dorms and on-campus apartments. In addition, there are language houses. On-campus housing is guaranteed for all 4 years. 63% of students live on campus; of those, 60% remain on campus on weekends. Alcohol is not permitted. All students may keep cars.

Activities: There are no fraternities or sororities. There are 20 groups on campus, including art, band, cheerleading, choir, chorale, chorus, drama, ethnic, honors, jazz band, musical theater, newspaper, pep band, photography, professional, radio and TV, religious, social, social service, student government, and yearbook. Popular campus events include Agape Music Festival, All College Hike, and Back to School Bash.

Sports: There are 7 intercollegiate sports for men and 7 for women, and 6 intramural sports for men and 6 for women. Facilities include a gym, a sports training annex, a recreational center, 6 tennis courts, a fitness pool, an all-weather track, and softball, baseball, football, soccer, and practice fields.

Disabled Students: 25% of the campus is accessible. Wheelchair ramps, elevators, special parking, specially equipped rest rooms, special class scheduling, and lowered drinking fountains are available.

Services: Counseling and information services are available, as is tutoring in most subjects, including lower-division general education courses. There is remedial math, reading, and writing. There is a program for at-risk freshmen.

Campus Safety and Security: Measures include self-defense education, security escort services, informal discussions, and pamphlets/posters/films. There are emergency telephones, lighted pathways/sidewalks, and alarm systems in some buildings.

Programs of Study: Greenville confers B.A., B.S., and B.Mus.Ed. degrees. Master's degrees are also awarded. Bachelor's degrees are awarded in BIOLOGICAL SCIENCE (biology/biological science and environmental biology), BUSINESS (accounting, business administration and management, management information systems, marketing/retailing/merchandising, and recreation and leisure services), COMMUNICATIONS AND THE ARTS (art, communications, dramatic arts, English, French, modern language, music, public relations, Spanish, and speech/debate/rhetoric), COMPUTER AND PHYSICAL SCIENCE (chemistry, computer science, mathematics, and physics), EDUCATION (early childhood, elementary, English, foreign languages, mathematics, music, physical, science, secondary, social studies, and special), SOCIAL SCIENCE (history, liberal arts/general studies, ministries, pastoral studies, philosophy, political science/government, psychology, religion, religious music, social work, sociology, and youth ministry). Biology, chemistry, and math are the strongest academically. Education, music, and information science and technology are the largest.

Required: A minimum of 126 credits and a 2.0 GPA are required for graduation. All students must successfully complete the core requirements in addition to specific courses in communication, English, history, phys ed, and foreign language (B.A. only). Other degree requirements are fulfilled by in-depth study in biblical studies, cross-cultural experience, physical fitness activities, lab science, math, literature, philosophy or sociology, and a writing-intensive course.

Special: The college provides opportunities for dual majors in such areas as psychology/religion and religion/philosophy, B.A.-B.S. degrees, student-designed programs, work-study programs, study abroad, credit by exam, internships, a general studies degree, pass/fail options, and nondegree study. A 3-2 engineering degree with the University of Illinois and Washington University, a 2-2 degree with St. John's College of Nursing, and an American Studies program in Washington, D.C. are also available. Cross-registration is offered within the Wesleyan Urban Coalition, the Christian College Consortium, and the Council of Christian Colleges and Universities. There are 5 national honor societies and a freshman honors program.

Faculty/Classroom: 68% of faculty are male; 32%, female. 95% teach undergraduates. The average class size in an introductory lecture is 22; in a laboratory, 18; and in a regular course, 20.

Admissions: 96% of the 2003-2004 applicants were accepted. The SAT I scores for the 2003-2004 freshman class were: Verbal--31% below 500, 44% between 500 and 599, 22% between 600 and 700, and 3% above 700; Math--31% below 500, 47% between 500 and 599, and 22% between 600 and 700. The ACT scores were 35% below 21, 21% between 21 and 23, 27% between 24 and 26, 9% between 27 and 28, and 8% above 28.

Requirements: The SAT I or ACT is required, with a minimum composite score of 860 on the SAT I or 18 on the ACT. Applicants must have completed a minimum of 16 high school units; recommended are 4 units in English, 2 each in a foreign language and math, and 1 each in a lab science and American history. A GED certificate will be accepted. An essay is also required. Greenville requires applicants to be in the upper 50% of their class. A GPA of 2.0 is required. AP and CLEP credits are accepted. Important factors in the admissions decision are leadership record, advanced placement or honor courses, and personality/intangible qualities.

Procedure: Freshmen are admitted to all sessions. Entrance exams should be taken in the spring of the junior year. Application deadlines are open. Application fee is $25. Notification is sent on a rolling basis. Applications are accepted on-line.

Transfer: 151 transfer students enrolled in 2002-2003. A minimum average grade of C or better is required. An associate degree will be accepted for transfer. 40 of 126 credits required for the bachelor's degree must be completed at Greenville.

Visiting: There are regularly scheduled orientations for prospective students, including campus visits during scheduled preview days. There are

guides for informal visits and visitors may sit in on classes and stay overnight. To schedule a visit, contact the Admissions Office at (800) 345-4440 or (618) 664-7100 or admissions@greenville.edu.

Financial Aid: In 2003-2004, 98% of all full-time freshmen and 97% of continuing full-time students received some form of financial aid. 86% of all full-time students received need-based aid. The average freshman award was $15,236. Need-based scholarships or need-based grants averaged $7285; need-based self-help aid (loans and jobs) averaged $5116; and other non-need-based awards and non-need-based scholarships averaged $4100. 40% of undergraduates work part time. Average annual earnings from campus work are $850. The average financial indebtedness of the 2003 graduate was $17,248. The FAFSA is required. The deadline for filing freshman financial aid applications for fall entry is July 1.

International Students: There are 20 international students enrolled. They must score 500 on the written TOEFL.

Computers: There are 80 PCs available in the library and throughout the campus. Database, spreadsheet, and word processing programs are available. A wireless network is available for use anywhere on campus. Students may purchase a laptop computer at discounted prices from Dell. All students may access the system 24 hours a day. There are no time limits and no fees. It is strongly recommended that all students have a personal computer.

Graduates: From July 1, 2002 to June 30, 2003, 295 bachelor's degrees were awarded. The most popular majors were education (28%), philosophy/religion (9%), and sciences (9%). In an average class, 40% graduate in 4 years or less, 52% graduate in 5 years or less, and 54% graduate in 6 years or less.

Admissions Contact: Michael Ritter, Director of Admissions.
E-mail: *admissions@greenville.edu* Web: *http://www.greenville.edu*

ILLINOIS COLLEGE
Jacksonville, IL 62650-2299

C-3
(217) 245-3030
(866) 464-5265; Fax: (217) 245-3034

Full-time: 440 men, 563 women	Faculty: 61; IIB, av$
Part-time: 7 men, 6 women	Ph.D.s: 85%
Graduate: none	Student/Faculty: 16 to 1
Year: semesters, summer session	Tuition: $13,300
Application Deadline: August 15	Room & Board: $5800
Freshman Class: 970 applied, 726 accepted, 318 enrolled	
SAT I Verbal/Math: 585/595	ACT: 23 VERY COMPETITIVE

Illinois College, founded in 1829, is a private liberal arts institution related to the Presbyterian Church (U.S.A.) and the United Church of Christ. The library contains 160,000 volumes, 7000 microform items, and 3000 audio/video tapes/CDs, and subscribes to 627 periodicals. Computerized library services include the card catalog, interlibrary loans, database searching, and Internet access. Special learning facilities include an art gallery, theater, and television studio. The 62-acre campus is in a small town 35 miles west of Springfield. Including any residence halls, there are 26 buildings.

Student Life: 95% of undergraduates are from Illinois. Students are from 15 states and 7 foreign countries. 93% are white. 60% are Protestant; 26% Catholic; 13% claim no religious affiliation. The average age of freshmen is 18; all undergraduates, 21. 26% do not continue beyond their first year; 55% remain to graduate.

Housing: 772 students can be accommodated in college housing, which includes single-sex and coed dorms. In addition, there are honors houses and language houses. On-campus housing is guaranteed for all 4 years. 72% of students live on campus; of those, 70% remain on campus on weekends. All students may keep cars.

Activities: There are no fraternities or sororities. There are 60 groups on campus, including art, band, cheerleading, chess, choir, chorale, computers, debate, drama, ethnic, forensics, honors, international, literary magazine, newspaper, photography, political, professional, radio and TV, religious, social, social service, student government, and yearbook. Popular campus events include Osage Orange Picnic, Honors Retreat, and McGaw Fine Arts Series.

Sports: There are 9 intercollegiate sports for men and 8 for women, and 4 intramural sports for men and 4 for women. Facilities include a game room, a gym with 2 basketball and 3 squash and handball courts, volleyball and badminton courts, a swimming pool, a fitness center, playing fields, an all-weather track, and 6 tennis courts.

Disabled Students: 80% of the campus is accessible. Wheelchair ramps, elevators, special parking, specially equipped rest rooms, special class scheduling, lowered drinking fountains, lowered telephones, and special housing are available.

Services: Counseling and information services are available, as is tutoring in most subjects. There is a reader service for the blind. Note takers, scribes, and test readers are also available.

Campus Safety and Security: Measures include 24-hour foot and vehicle patrol, self-defense education, security escort services, and shuttle buses. There are informal discussions, pamphlets/posters/films, emergency telephones, and lighted pathways/sidewalks.

Programs of Study: IC confers B.A. and B.S. degrees. Bachelor's degrees are awarded in BIOLOGICAL SCIENCE (biology/biological science), BUSINESS (accounting and business administration and management), COMMUNICATIONS AND THE ARTS (communications, dramatic arts, English, fine arts, French, German, music, Spanish, and speech/debate/rhetoric), COMPUTER AND PHYSICAL SCIENCE (chemistry, computer science, information sciences and systems, mathematics, and physics), EDUCATION (elementary, foreign languages, physical, science, and secondary), ENGINEERING AND ENVIRONMENTAL DESIGN (environmental science), HEALTH PROFESSIONS (medical laboratory technology), SOCIAL SCIENCE (economics, history, international relations, philosophy, political science/government, prelaw, psychology, religion, and sociology). Life sciences is the strongest academically. Business administration, education, and biology are the largest.

Required: To graduate, all students must fulfill general graduation and convocation requirements and complete at least 120 semester hours, including 24 hours of electives outside of the major discipline. A 2.0 GPA is required.

Special: The college offers study abroad in various countries, on- and off-campus work-study programs, and internships through the departments of communication, computer science and information systems, economics and business administration, English, and political science. Also available are student-designed and dual majors, B.A.-B.S. degrees, a 3-2 engineering degree with the University of Illinois, Washington University, or Southern Illinois University-Edwardsville, and a 3-2 occupational therapy program with Washington University. The Intercultural Exchange Program with Ritsumeikan University in Kyoto, Japan, Model United Nations simulations, and the Urban Studies Program of Associated Colleges of the Midwest in Chicago are offered. There are 9 national honor societies, including Phi Beta Kappa.

Faculty/Classroom: 70% of faculty are male; 30%, female. All teach undergraduates. The average class size in an introductory lecture is 48; in a laboratory, 20; and in a regular course, 18.

Admissions: 75% of the 2003-2004 applicants were accepted. The SAT I scores for the 2003-2004 freshman class were: Verbal--12% below 500, 42% between 500 and 599, 38% between 600 and 700, and 8% above 700; Math--8% below 500, 42% between 500 and 599, 38% between 600 and 700, and 12% above 700. The ACT scores were 20% below 21, 31% between 21 and 23, 27% between 24 and 26, 13% between 27 and 28, and 9% above 28. 41% of the current freshmen were in the top fifth of their class; 75% were in the top two fifths. 12 freshmen graduated first in their class.

Requirements: The SAT I or ACT is required. In addition, applicants must be graduates of an accredited secondary school or have a GED certificate. Students should have completed at least 15 academic credits, including 3 in English and 7 from the following: English, foreign language, history, lab science, math, and social studies. 1 recommendation and 1 essay or 2 letters recommendations are required. IC requires applicants to be in the upper 50% of their class. A GPA of 2.5 is required. AP and CLEP credits are accepted.

Procedure: Freshmen are admitted to all sessions. Entrance exams should be taken in the spring of the junior year of high school. Applications should be filed by August 15 for the fall entry, along with a $25 fee. Notification is sent on a rolling basis. A waiting list is an active part of the admissions procedure. Applications are accepted on computer disk and on-line.

Transfer: 55 transfer students enrolled in 2002-2003. Transfer students must have a minimum 2.0 GPA and submit SAT I or ACT scores and transcripts of completed college work. 36 of 120 credits required for the bachelor's degree must be completed at IC.

Visiting: There are regularly scheduled orientations for prospective students, including general information sessions, meetings with faculty, a campus tour, and lunch. There are guides for informal visits and visitors may sit in on classes and stay overnight. To schedule a visit, contact the Admissions Office at *admissions@ic.edu.*

Financial Aid: In 2003-2004, 96% of all full-time students received some form of financial aid. 60% of full-time freshmen and 67% of continuing full-time students received need-based aid. The average freshman award was $12,500. Need-based scholarships or need-based grants averaged $8600 ($13,621 maximum); need-based self-help aid (loans and jobs) averaged $4375 ($8125 maximum); and non-need-based awards and non-need-based scholarships averaged $5077 ($13,300 maximum). 39% of undergraduates work part time. Average annual earnings from campus work are $750. The average financial indebtedness of the 2003 graduate was $11,916. The FAFSA is required. The priority date for freshman financial aid applications for fall entry is March 1. The deadline for filing freshman financial aid applications for fall entry is May 1.

International Students: There are 10 international students enrolled. They must score 550 on the written TOEFL or 213 on the electronic version.

Computers: The mainframe is a digital UNIX Alpha server. There are six computer clusters on campus networking more than 100 machines; all offices and dorm rooms are wired to the network. All students may access the system in labs from 8 A.M. to midnight and any time from dorm rooms. There are no time limits and no fees.

Graduates: From July 1, 2002 to June 30, 2003, 179 bachelor's degrees were awarded. The most popular majors were education (11%), business administration (11%), and accounting (7%). In an average class, 1% graduate in 3 years or less, 44% graduate in 4 years or less, 53% graduate in 5 years or less, and 55% graduate in 6 years or less. Of the 2002 graduating class, 33% were enrolled in graduate school within 6 months of graduation and 70% were employed.

Admissions Contact: Vice President for Enrollment.
Web: *www.ic.edu.*

ILLINOIS INSTITUTE OF TECHNOLOGY   E-2
Chicago, IL 60616
(312) 567-3025
(800) 448-2329; Fax: (312) 567-6939

Full-time: 1245 men, 425 women	**Faculty:** 241
Part-time: 219 men, 52 women	**Ph.D.s:** 99%
Graduate: 2782 men, 1444 women	**Student/Faculty:** 7 to 1
Year: semesters, summer session	**Tuition:** $20,332
Application Deadline: open	**Room & Board:** $6124
Freshman Class: 2538 applied, 1502 accepted, 397 enrolled	
SAT I Verbal/Math: 620/670	**ACT:** 28

HIGHLY COMPETITIVE+

Illinois Institute of Technology, founded in 1890, is a private institution offering undergraduate programs in architecture, engineering, applied math, biology, chemistry, physics, computing, political science, business, and psychology. There are 5 undergraduate and 7 graduate schools. In addition to regional accreditation, IIT has baccalaureate program accreditation with ABET. The 3 libraries contain 594,294 volumes, 184,377 microform items, and 54,274 audio/video tapes/CDs, and subscribe to 666 periodicals. Computerized library services include the card catalog, interlibrary loans, and database searching. Special learning facilities include a learning resource center and radio station. The 120-acre campus is in an urban area 3 miles south of downtown Chicago. Including any residence halls, there are 33 buildings.

Student Life: 53% of undergraduates are from Illinois. Students are from 49 states, 96 foreign countries, and Canada. 80% are from public schools. 43% are white; 33% foreign nationals; 10% Asian American. The average age of freshmen is 19; all undergraduates, 23. 19% do not continue beyond their first year; 62% remain to graduate.

Housing: 1251 students can be accommodated in college housing, which includes single-sex and coed dorms, on-campus apartments, married-student housing, fraternity houses, and sorority houses. On-campus housing is guaranteed for all 4 years. 58% of students live on campus; of those, 80% remain on campus on weekends. All students may keep cars.

Activities: 21% of men belong to 7 national fraternities; 15% of women belong to 2 local sororities and 1 national sorority. There are 80 groups on campus, including art, chess, choir, chorus, commuter, computers, dance, drama, ethnic, film, gay, honors, international, jazz band, literary magazine, musical theater, newspaper, photography, professional, radio and TV, religious, social, social service, student government, union, and yearbook. Popular campus events include International Fest, Greek Week, and Spring Formal.

Sports: There are 5 intercollegiate sports for men and 5 for women, and 6 intramural sports for men and 6 for women. Facilities include tennis, basketball, volleyball, racquetball, and squash courts, soccer and softball fields, a swimming pool, an exercise room, a weight room, a bowling alley, and a game room.

Disabled Students: Wheelchair ramps, elevators, special parking, specially equipped rest rooms, and lowered drinking fountains are available.

Services: Counseling and information services are available, as is tutoring in some subjects, including lower division science, math, engineering, and writing courses. There is a reader service for the blind.

Campus Safety and Security: Measures include 24-hour foot and vehicle patrol, security escort services, shuttle buses, and informal discussions. There are pamphlets/posters/films, emergency telephones, and lighted pathways/sidewalks.

Programs of Study: IIT confers B.S. and B.Arch. degrees. Master's and doctoral degrees are also awarded. Bachelor's degrees are awarded in BIOLOGICAL SCIENCE (biochemistry, biology/biological science, biophysics, and molecular biology), COMMUNICATIONS AND THE ARTS (technical and business writing), COMPUTER AND PHYSICAL SCIENCE (applied mathematics, chemistry, computer science, information sciences and systems, physics, and web technology), ENGINEERING AND ENVIRONMENTAL DESIGN (aeronautical engineering, architectural engineering, architecture, chemical engineering, civil engineering, computer engineering, electrical/electronics engineering, manufacturing technology, mechanical engineering, and metallurgical engineering), SOCIAL SCIENCE (political science/government and psychology). All engineering programs are the strongest academically. Architecture and engineering are the largest.

Required: To graduate, students must have completed a total of 126 to 142 credit hours with a minimum cumulative GPA and a minimum major GPA of 2.0. General education requirements include 21 hours of social studies or humanities, 11 hours of science, 5 hours of math, 1 course each in industrial culture and computer science, and 6 hours of interdisciplinary project work.

Special: IIT offers co-op programs in engineering, dual majors, study abroad, and an accelerated degree program in prelaw. There are 3 national honor societies.

Faculty/Classroom: 86% of faculty are male; 14%, female. No introductory courses are taught by graduate students. The average class size in an introductory lecture is 18; in a laboratory, 12; and in a regular course, 18.

Admissions: 59% of the 2003-2004 applicants were accepted. The SAT I scores for the 2003-2004 freshman class were: Verbal--6% below 500, 28% between 500 and 599, 51% between 600 and 700, and 15% above 700; Math--17% between 500 and 599, 47% between 600 and 700, and 35% above 700. The ACT scores were 6% between 21 and 23, 30% between 24 and 26, 21% between 27 and 28, and 43% above 28. 80% of the current freshmen were in the top fifth of their class; 90% were in the top two fifths.

Requirements: The SAT I or ACT is required. In addition, graduation from an accredited secondary school is required for admission. The school requires 16 academic credits, including 4 units each of English and math, 3 of lab science, and 2 of history or social science. A GPA of 3.0 is required. AP credits are accepted. Important factors in the admissions decision are advanced placement or honor courses, leadership record, and recommendations by school officials.

Procedure: Freshmen are admitted fall and spring. There is a deferred admissions plan. Application deadlines are open. The fall 2003 application fee was $30. Notification is sent on a rolling basis. Applications are accepted on-line through CollegeLink and numerous others, including *Embark.com.*

Transfer: 83 transfer students enrolled in 2002-2003. A minimum 3.0 GPA is required. 45 of 126 credits required for the bachelor's degree must be completed at IIT.

Visiting: There are regularly scheduled orientations for prospective students, including accompanying current students, visiting classes, and attending department receptions. There are guides for informal visits and visitors may sit in on classes and stay overnight. To schedule a visit, contact Emily Staples at (312) 567-5193 or *bangtson@iit.edu.*

Financial Aid: In 2003-2004, 99% of all full-time freshmen and 98% of continuing full-time students received some form of financial aid. 56% of full-time freshmen and 45% of continuing full-time students received need-based aid. The average freshman award was $19,117. Need-based scholarships or need-based grants averaged $2757 ($13,466 maximum); need-based self-help aid (loans and jobs) averaged $2891 ($7625 maximum); non-need-based athletic scholarships averaged $157 ($9000 maximum); and other non-need-based awards and non-need-based scholarships averaged $15,239 ($34,000 maximum). 24% of undergraduates work part time. Average annual earnings from campus work are $2604. The average financial indebtedness of the 2003 graduate was $14,370. IIT is a member of CSS. The FAFSA is required. The priority date for freshman financial aid applications for fall entry is April 15.

International Students: There are 263 international students enrolled. The school actively recruits these students. They must score 550 on the written TOEFL and also take the SAT I or the ACT.

Computers: The mainframes are a DEC VAX 3600 and an SGI Challenge. There are also many Macs and SGI UNIX workstations available in academic buildings. Dorm rooms are linked to the university network, providing Internet and e-mail access. Wireless network access is available at the library, some dorms, and most buildings on campus. All students may access the system. There are no time limits and no fees. It is strongly recommended that all students have a personal computer.

Graduates: From July 1, 2002 to June 30, 2003, 267 bachelor's degrees were awarded. The most popular majors were computer engineering (16%), computer science (15%), and electrical engineering (12%). In an average class, 4% graduate in 3 years or less, 28% graduate in 4 years or less, 63% graduate in 5 years or less, and 67% graduate in 6 years or less. 63 companies recruited on campus in 2002-2003. Of the 2002 graduating class, 43% were enrolled in graduate school within 6 months of graduation and 51% were employed.

Admissions Contact: Brent Benner, Director of Admissions. E-mail: *admission@iit.edu* Web: *www.iit.edu*

ILLINOIS STATE UNIVERSITY
D-3
Normal, IL 61761
(309) 438-2181
(800) 366-2478; Fax: (309) 438-3932

Full-time: 7080 men, 9731 women	**Faculty:** 846; I, --$
Part-time: 606 men, 680 women	**Ph.Ds:** 85%
Graduate: 970 men, 1793 women	**Student/Faculty:** 20 to 1
Year: semesters, summer session	**Tuition:** $5530 ($8593)
Application Deadline: March 1	**Room & Board:** $5414
Freshman Class: 10,075 applied, 7570 accepted, 3097 enrolled	
ACT: 24	**COMPETITIVE+**

Illinois State University, founded in 1857, is a public institution offering instruction through schools of applied science and technology, arts and sciences, business, education, fine arts, and nursing. There are 6 undergraduate schools and 1 graduate school. In addition to regional accreditation, ISU has baccalaureate program accreditation with AACSB, ADA, AHEA, CSWE, NASAD, NASM, NCATE, NLN, and NRPA. The library contains 1,566,327 volumes, 1,882,332 microform items, and 24,716 audio/video tapes/CDs, and subscribes to 12,254 periodicals. Computerized library services include the card catalog, interlibrary loans, and database searching. Special learning facilities include a learning resource center, art gallery, planetarium, radio station, TV station, and a distance-learning classroom. The 850-acre campus is in an urban area 125 miles south of Chicago and 180 miles north of St. Louis. Including any residence halls, there are 153 buildings.

Student Life: 96% of undergraduates are from Illinois. Students are from 48 states, 89 foreign countries, and Canada. 89% are from public schools. 87% are white. The average age of freshmen is 18; all undergraduates, 20. 17% do not continue beyond their first year; 60% remain to graduate.

Housing: 7452 students can be accommodated in college housing, which includes single-sex and coed dorms, on-campus apartments, and married-student housing. In addition, there are honors houses and special-interest houses. On-campus housing is available on a first-come, first-served basis. All students may keep cars.

Activities: 10% of men belong to 21 national fraternities; 9% of women belong to 17 national sororities. There are 250 groups on campus, including art, band, cheerleading, chess, choir, chorale, chorus, computers, dance, debate, drama, drill team, ethnic, film, forensics, gay, honors, international, jazz band, literary magazine, marching band, musical theater, newspaper, opera, orchestra, pep band, photography, political, professional, radio and TV, religious, social, social service, student government, symphony, and yearbook. Popular campus events include Festival ISU, International Fair, and Madrigal Dinners.

Sports: There are 8 intercollegiate sports for men and 11 for women, and 9 intramural sports for men and 9 for women. Facilities include a student recreational building, a basketball arena, a football stadium, a field house, baseball diamonds, tennis courts, Olympic-size pools, an 18-hole golf course, a soccer and softball field, and a bowling and billiards center.

Disabled Students: All of the campus is accessible. Wheelchair ramps, elevators, special parking, specially equipped rest rooms, special class scheduling, lowered drinking fountains, lowered telephones, a telecommunication device, 2 rooms in the library for visually disabled students, and a learning lab with a braille thermoform and a variable speed lexicon are available.

Services: Counseling and information services are available, as is tutoring in every subject. There is a reader service for the blind, remedial math, reading, and writing, interpreters for the hearing impaired, note takers, taped lectures, and braillists.

Campus Safety and Security: Measures include 24-hour foot and vehicle patrol, self-defense education, security escort services, and shuttle buses. There are informal discussions, pamphlets/posters/films, emergency telephones, and lighted pathways/sidewalks.

Programs of Study: ISU confers B.A., B.S., B.F.A., B.Mu., B.Mu.E., B.S.Ed., and B.S.W. degrees. Master's and doctoral degrees are also awarded. Bachelor's degrees are awarded in AGRICULTURE (agriculture), BIOLOGICAL SCIENCE (biochemistry and biology/biological science), BUSINESS (accounting, banking and finance, business administration and management, insurance, international business management, management science, and marketing/retailing/merchandising), COMMUNICATIONS AND THE ARTS (art, communications, dramatic arts, English, French, German, music, music performance, public relations, Spanish, speech/debate/rhetoric, and telecommunications), COMPUTER AND PHYSICAL SCIENCE (chemistry, computer science, digital arts/technology, geology, information sciences and systems, mathematics, and physics), EDUCATION (business, computer, early childhood, elementary, health, middle school, music, physical, and special), ENGINEERING AND ENVIRONMENTAL DESIGN (industrial engineering technology), HEALTH PROFESSIONS (environmental health science, health care administration, medical laboratory technology, nursing, and speech pathology/audiology), SOCIAL SCIENCE (anthropology, criminal justice, economics, fashion design and technology, geography, history, home economics, parks and recreation management, philosophy, political science/government, psychology, safety management, social science, social work, and sociology). Elementary education, business administration, and special education are the largest.

Required: Students must complete 45 hours of General Education and a total of 120 credit hours with a minimum GPA of 2.0. In addition, they must pass a writing exam and exams on the Constitutions of the U.S. and the State of Illinois, and one on the proper use of the American flag.

Special: There are numerous cooperative programs and internships, dual majors, student-designed majors, and work-study programs both on campus and with nonprofit organizations. There is also a general studies degree, a 3-2 engineering program with the University of Illinois, a B.S./M.P.A., and study abroad in 11 countries. Pass/fail options are available, and credit is given for military experience. ISU is part of the National Student Exchange, enabling qualifying juniors and seniors to study for up to 1 year at one of several hundred colleges around the country. There are 25 national honor societies, including Phi Beta Kappa, a freshman honors program, and 43 departmental honors programs.

Faculty/Classroom: 55% of faculty are male; 45%, female. All teach undergraduates. Graduate students teach 13% of introductory courses. The average class size in an introductory lecture is 37; in a laboratory, 22; and in a regular course, 32.

Admissions: 75% of the 2003-2004 applicants were accepted. The ACT scores for the 2003-2004 freshman class were: 15% below 21, 36% between 21 and 23, 32% between 24 and 26, 11% between 27 and 28, and 6% above 28. 29% of the current freshmen were in the top fifth of their class; 68% were in the top two fifths. There were 6 National Merit finalists. 25 freshmen graduated first in their class.

Requirements: The ACT is required. In addition, applicants must be graduates of an accredited secondary school or have a GED. Admission is based on a combination of factors, including class rank and ACT or SAT I score. ISU requires applicants to be in the upper 50% of their class. AP and CLEP credits are accepted.

Procedure: Freshmen are admitted to all sessions. Entrance exams should be taken in the fall of the junior year. Applications should be filed by March 1 for fall entry, along with a $30 fee. Notification is sent on a rolling basis. Applications are accepted on-line through *www.illinoisstate.edu*.

Transfer: 2578 transfer students enrolled in 2002-2003. Graduates of Illinois community colleges holding associate degrees are admitted pending receipt of transcripts. Other students must meet the requirements for beginning freshmen with a minimum 2.0 GPA. 30 of 120 credits required for the bachelor's degree must be completed at ISU.

Visiting: There are regularly scheduled orientations for prospective students. There are guides for informal visits and visitors may sit in on classes; they may stay overnight only during scheduled Preview orientations. To schedule a visit, contact the Admissions Office at (309) 438-8486 or *preview@ilstu.edu* or go to *www.ilstu.edu/preview*.

Financial Aid: In 2003-2004, 39% of all full-time freshmen and 42% of continuing full-time students received some form of financial aid. 26% of full-time freshmen and 29% of continuing full-time students received need-based aid. The average freshman award was $6158. Need-based scholarships or need-based grants averaged $5369; need-based self-help aid (loans and jobs) averaged $2867; non-need-based athletic scholarships averaged $6683; and other non-need-based awards and non-need-based scholarships averaged $2371. Average annual earnings from campus work are $2151. The average financial indebtedness of the 2003 graduate was $13,921. The CSS/Profile, FAFSA, FFS, or SFS is required. The deadline for filing freshman financial aid applications for fall entry is March 1.

International Students: There are 158 international students enrolled. The school actively recruits these students. They must score 550 on the written TOEFL.

Computers: The mainframe is a Hitachi EX/80. Mainframe terminals are in various locations across campus, and 120 terminals are placed for student access. There are also 1039 PCs in labs and dorms across campus. All students have an e-mail address and access to the Internet and Web. The mainframe is available to those taking courses involving its use. Students may access the system 24 hours a day. There are no time limits and no fees.

Graduates: From July 1, 2002 to June 30, 2003, 4202 bachelor's degrees were awarded. The most popular majors were elementary education (11%), business administration (6%), and marketing (5%). In an average class, 1% graduate in 3 years or less, 36% graduate in 4 years or less, 59% graduate in 5 years or less, and 60% graduate in 6 years or less. 261 companies recruited on campus in 2002-2003.

Admissions Contact: Molly Arnold, Interim Director of Admissions. A video is available. E-mail: *ugradadm@ilstu.edu* Web: *www.ilstu.edu*

ILLINOIS WESLEYAN UNIVERSITY
Bloomington, IL 61702-2900

D-3

(309) 556-3031; (800) 332-2498

Full-time: 906 men, 1193 women	**Faculty:** 185; IIB, +$
Part-time: 3 men, 5 women	**Ph.D.s:** 85%
Graduate: none	**Student/Faculty:** 11 to 1
Year: 4-4-1	**Tuition:** $24,540
Application Deadline: March 1	**Room & Board:** $5840
Freshman Class: 3331 applied, 1431 accepted, 579 enrolled	
SAT I Verbal/Math: 630/640	**ACT:** 29

HIGHLY COMPETITIVE+

Illinois Wesleyan University, founded in 1850, is a private institution offering 35 major programs in liberal arts, fine arts, and nursing. There are 5 undergraduate schools. In addition to regional accreditation, Illinois Wesleyan has baccalaureate program accreditation with CCNE and NASM. The library contains 314,894 volumes, 23,297 microform items, and 15,076 audio/video tapes/CDs, and subscribes to 1043 print periodicals and 13,966 full-text electronic database titles. Computerized library services include the card catalog, interlibrary loans, database searching, and Internet access. Special learning facilities include a learning resource center, art gallery, radio station, TV station, observatory, multicultural center, and a 20-acre tract of virgin timberland. The 79-acre campus is in a suburban area 130 miles from Chicago and 160 miles from St. Louis. Including any residence halls, there are 51 buildings.

Student Life: 85% of undergraduates are from Illinois. Students are from 36 states, 20 foreign countries, and Canada. 86% are from public schools. 86% are white. The average age of freshmen is 18; all undergraduates, 19. 8% do not continue beyond their first year; 78% remain to graduate.

Housing: 1758 students can be accommodated in college housing, which includes coed dorms, fraternity houses, and sorority houses. In addition, there are honors houses, language houses, special-interest houses, and an international house. On-campus housing is guaranteed for all 4 years. 83% of students live on campus; of those, 80% remain on campus on weekends. All students may keep cars.

Activities: 40% of men belong to 7 national fraternities; 32% of women belong to 5 national sororities. There are 167 groups on campus, including band, cheerleading, chess, choir, chorale, chorus, computers, dance, drama, ethnic, gay, honors, international, jazz band, literary magazine, marching band, musical theater, newspaper, opera, orchestra, pep band, political, professional, radio and TV, religious, social, social service, student government, symphony, and yearbook. Popular campus events include Family Days, Blue Moon Coffeehouse, and Fine Arts Festival.

Sports: There are 9 intercollegiate sports for men and 9 for women, and 11 intramural sports for men and 11 for women. Facilities include a fitness center with weight/exercise equipment and racquetball courts; a swimming pool with 1- and 3-meter diving boards; an activity center with a 200-meter, 6-lane indoor track and courts for tennis, recreational basketball, and volleyball; a separate gym for intercollegiate and other activities; an outdoor track; and softball, baseball, and soccer fields.

Disabled Students: 95% of the campus is accessible. Wheelchair ramps, elevators, special parking, specially equipped rest rooms, special class scheduling, lowered drinking fountains, lowered telephones, and special housing are available.

Services: Counseling and information services are available, as is tutoring in every subject. There is a reader service for the blind. Assistance in writing and study skills is also available.

Campus Safety and Security: Measures include 24-hour foot and vehicle patrol, self-defense education, security escort services, and informal discussions. There are pamphlets/posters/films, emergency telephones, and lighted pathways/sidewalks. An emergency response team of key executives and staff members has developed policies and procedures for natural disasters and other crises.

Programs of Study: Illinois Wesleyan confers B.A., B.S., B.F.A., B.Mus., B.Mus.Ed., and B.S.N. degrees. Bachelor's degrees are awarded in BIOLOGICAL SCIENCE (biology/biological science), BUSINESS (accounting, business administration and management, insurance and risk management, and international business management), COMMUNICATIONS AND THE ARTS (dramatic arts, English, French, German, music, music theory and composition, musical theater, piano/organ, Russian, Spanish, visual and performing arts, and voice), COMPUTER AND PHYSICAL SCIENCE (chemistry, computer science, mathematics, and physics), EDUCATION (elementary), HEALTH PROFESSIONS (nursing), SOCIAL SCIENCE (American studies, anthropology, economics, Hispanic American studies, history, interdisciplinary studies, international studies, philosophy, political science/government, psychology, religion, and sociology). The life sciences, music, and business and economics are the largest.

Required: A total of 32 course units (128 semester hours) is required for the bachelor's degree with a 2.0 GPA. General education requirements include 2 course units in natural sciences and 1 each in literature, intellectual traditions, formal reasoning, cultural and historical change, contemporary social institutions, the arts, analysis of values, and Gateway colloquium, plus demonstrated proficiency in a foreign language. 2

additional writing-intensive courses are required, as is course work focusing on U.S. and global diversity issues.

Special: There are several combined degree programs, including a 3-2 degree in forestry and environmental studies with Duke University, a 2-2 engineering degree with the University of Illinois, and 3-2 engineering programs with a number of universities. Students may study abroad in many locations throughout the world through the Institute for the International Education of Students (IES), Pembroke College, Keio University, University of Oxford, Arcadia University Center for Study Abroad, and many other programs. The university also offers work-study, internships in many areas, Washington and United Nations semesters, dual and student-designed majors, and pass/fail options. There are 28 national honor societies, including Phi Beta Kappa. All departments have honors programs.

Faculty/Classroom: 56% of faculty are male; 44%, female. All both teach and do research. The average class size in an introductory lecture is 22; in a laboratory, 14; and in a regular course, 16.

Admissions: 43% of the 2003-2004 applicants were accepted. The SAT I scores for the 2003-2004 freshman class were: Verbal--1% below 500, 30% between 500 and 599, 46% between 600 and 700, and 23% above 700; Math--1% below 500, 22% between 500 and 599, 54% between 600 and 700, and 23% above 700. The ACT scores were 5% between 21 and 23, 20% between 24 and 26, 23% between 27 and 28, and 52% above 28. 76% of the current freshmen were in the top fifth of their class; 97% were in the top two fifths. There were 15 National Merit finalists. 38 freshmen graduated first in their class.

Requirements: The SAT I or ACT is required. In addition, applicants should graduate from an accredited secondary school, though a GED may be accepted. 15 academic credits are required. It is strongly recommended that these include 4 units of English, 3 each of natural science, math, and a foreign language, and 2 of social science. An audition is required for theater and music majors and a portfolio for art majors. Illinois Wesleyan requires applicants to be in the upper 35% of their class. A GPA of 3.0 is required. AP credits are accepted. Important factors in the admissions decision are advanced placement or honor courses, evidence of special talent, and leadership record.

Procedure: Freshmen are admitted fall and spring. Entrance exams should be taken in the spring of the junior year. There are early admissions and deferred admissions plans. Applications should be filed by March 1 for fall entry and November 1 for spring entry. Notification is sent on a rolling basis. 837 applicants were on the 2003 waiting list; 7 were admitted. Applications are accepted on computer disk and on-line.

Transfer: 5 transfer students enrolled in 2003-2004. Applicants must submit all high school and college transcripts. A GPA of at least 2.5 is required. 16 course units (64 semester hours) of 32 course units (128 semester hours) required for the bachelor's degree must be completed at Illinois Wesleyan.

Visiting: There are regularly scheduled orientations for prospective students. The First-Year Experience is a weeklong set of activities geared to assist new students in adjusting to campus and academic life. First-year students are housed together to share common challenges and successes in their new environment. There are guides for informal visits and visitors may sit in on classes and stay overnight. To schedule a visit, contact the Admissions Office.

Financial Aid: In 2003-2004, 90% of all full-time freshmen and 89% of continuing full-time students received some form of financial aid. 47% of full-time freshmen and 54% of continuing full-time students received need-based aid. The average freshman award was $14,656. Need-based scholarships or need-based grants averaged $13,904 ($23,971 maximum); need-based self-help aid (loans and jobs) averaged $4885 ($6685 maximum); and other non-need-based awards and non-need-based scholarships averaged $10,675 ($16,700 maximum). 46% of undergraduates work part time. Average annual earnings from campus work are $1853. The average financial indebtedness of the 2003 graduate was $18,617. Illinois Wesleyan is a member of CSS. The CSS/Profile or FAFSA and the college's own financial statement are required. The deadline for filing freshman financial aid applications for fall entry is March 1.

International Students: There are 45 international students enrolled. The school actively recruits these students. They must score 550 on the written TOEFL.

Computers: The mainframe is an IBM AS/400. There are more than 400 Macs and PCs available in various computer labs and dorms. Access to the Internet and World Wide Web is available through the campus network. About 80% of students bring computers to campus. All students may access the system. There are no time limits and no fees.

Graduates: From July 1, 2002 to June 30, 2003, 479 bachelor's degrees were awarded. The most popular majors were business administration (13%), biology (9%), and psychology (8%). In an average class, 1% graduate in 3 years or less, 75% graduate in 4 years or less, 78% graduate in 5 years or less, and 78% graduate in 6 years or less. 75 companies recruited on campus in 2002-2003. Of the 2002 graduating class, 29% were enrolled in graduate school within 6 months of graduation and 67% were employed.

Admissions Contact: Jerry Pope, Dean of Admissions. A video is available. E-mail: *iwuadmit@titan.iwu.edu* Web: *www.iwu.edu*

JUDSON COLLEGE	E-1
Elgin, IL 60123-1498	(847) 628-2500
	(800) 879-5376; Fax: (847) 695-0216

Full-time: 806 men and women	**Faculty:** 40
Part-time: 367 men and women	**Ph.D.s:** 49%
Graduate: none	**Student/Faculty:** 20 to 1
Year: semesters	**Tuition:** $16,050
Application Deadline: open	**Room & Board:** $6000
Freshman Class: n/av	
SAT I or ACT: required	**LESS COMPETITIVE**

Judson College is an evangelical Christian college of the liberal arts, sciences, and professions. Some information in this capsule and profile is approximate. The library contains 90,000 volumes, 27,000 microform items, and 17,000 audio/video tapes/CDs, and subscribes to 500 periodicals. Computerized library services include the card catalog, interlibrary loans, database searching, and Internet access. Special learning facilities include a learning resource center, art gallery, and radio station. The 80-acre campus is in a suburban area 40 miles west of Chicago. Including any residence halls, there are 15 buildings.

Student Life: 75% of undergraduates are from Illinois. Students are from 14 states and 18 foreign countries. 80% are white. 82% are Protestant; 9% Catholic; 7% claim no religious affiliation. The average age of all undergraduates is 20. 26% do not continue beyond their first year.

Housing: 670 students can be accommodated in college housing, which includes single-sex dorms, on-campus apartments, and married-student housing. On-campus housing is guaranteed for all 4 years. 58% of students live on campus; of those, 35% remain on campus on weekends. Alcohol is not permitted. All students may keep cars.

Activities: There are no fraternities or sororities. There are 23 groups on campus, including art, band, business, cheerleading, choir, chorale, chorus, computers, drama, ethnic, honors, international, literary magazine, newspaper, orchestra, photography, political, radio and TV, religious, social, social service, student government, and yearbook. Popular campus events include Spiritual Enrichment Week, Parents Weekend, and Christmas by Candlelight.

Sports: There are 3 intercollegiate sports for men and 4 for women, and 9 intramural sports for men and 8 for women. Facilities include a fitness center, a 1500-seat gym, a soccer field, lighted baseball and softball diamonds, lighted tennis courts, racquetball and handball courts, indoor and outdoor running tracks, and a Nautilus and free-weight facility.

Disabled Students: 80% of the campus is accessible. Wheelchair ramps, elevators, special parking, specially equipped rest rooms, special class scheduling, lowered drinking fountains, and lowered telephones are available.

Services: Counseling and information services are available, as is tutoring in some subjects, including core courses. There is a reader service for the blind and remedial math, reading, and writing.

Campus Safety and Security: Measures include 24-hour foot and vehicle patrol, security escort services, emergency telephones, and lighted pathways/sidewalks.

Programs of Study: Judson confers the B.A. degree. Master's degrees are also awarded. Bachelor's degrees are awarded in BIOLOGICAL SCIENCE (biology/biological science), BUSINESS (accounting, business administration and management, international business management, and sports management), COMMUNICATIONS AND THE ARTS (communications, dramatic arts, English, fine arts, media arts, and music), COMPUTER AND PHYSICAL SCIENCE (chemistry, computer science, and mathematics), EDUCATION (early childhood, elementary, English, mathematics, music, physical, science, and secondary), ENGINEERING AND ENVIRONMENTAL DESIGN (preengineering), HEALTH PROFESSIONS (medical laboratory technology, nursing, predentistry, and premedicine), SOCIAL SCIENCE (anthropology, history, political science/government, prelaw, psychology, sociology, and youth ministry). Architecture, education, and business are the strongest academically. Education, art, and business are the largest.

Required: Most students must have a GPA of 2.0; education majors must have a 2.5. Students must complete at least 126 credit hours, including 45 to 66 in the major, and take the college's core courses of Bible study, writing, speech, literature, math, science, history, fine arts, human relations, and phys ed, as well as a course in either psychology or sociology.

Special: The college has co-op programs with North Park College, Rush University, and the Mennonite College of Nursing, cross-registration with the Christian College Coalition, and work-study programs with many businesses. Students may serve internships in art and business, take a Washington semester, a film studies semester in Hollywood, an ecology studies semester at Sable Institute in Michigan, or study abroad in Russia, Egypt, the Dominican Republic, England, or Israel. The college allows dual majors, student-designed majors, and accelerated degrees in business leadership and management, human services, human resource management, and criminal justice management. There are pass/fail options for courses outside the major. There is 1 national honor society, a freshman honors program, and 2 departmental honors programs.

Faculty/Classroom: 90% of faculty are male; 10%, female. 80% teach undergraduates and 20% both teach and do research. The average class size in an introductory lecture is 28; in a laboratory, 9; and in a regular course, 16.

Requirements: The SAT I or ACT is required, with a minimum score of 18 on the ACT; the ACT is preferred. Graduation from secondary school is required. A minimum of 15 academic units is recommended. The GED is accepted. Judson requires applicants to be in the upper 50% of their class. A GPA of 2.0 is required. AP and CLEP credits are accepted. Important factors in the admissions decision are advanced placement or honor courses, recommendations by school officials, and leadership record.

Procedure: Freshmen are admitted to all sessions. Entrance exams should be taken in the spring of the junior year or the fall of the senior year. There is a deferred admissions plan. Application deadlines are open. Application fee is $30. Applications are accepted on-line through the school's web site, *www.judsoncollege.edu*. Notification is sent on a rolling basis.

Transfer: Students with fewer than 28 hours of college credit must submit high school transcripts showing a GPA of at least 2.0, as well as ACT results with a composite score of at least 18. Transfer students with more than 28 hours must have a GPA of at least 2.0. 30 of 126 credits required for the bachelor's degree must be completed at Judson.

Visiting: There are regularly scheduled orientations for prospective students, including a tour, class visits, a chapel visit, and individual meetings with professors, coaches, and other advisers. There are guides for informal visits and visitors may sit in on classes and stay overnight. To schedule a visit, contact the Enrollment Services Office at *admission@judsoncollege.edu.*

Financial Aid: Judson is a member of CSS. The FAFSA and the college's own financial statement are required. Check with the school for current deadlines.

International Students: The school actively recruits these students. They must score 550 on the written TOEFL or take the MELAB. The SAT I or the ACT (scoring 18) is required.

Computers: There are 30 PCs and 24 Macs available in the computer lab. All students may access the system. There are no time limits and no fees.

Graduates: In an average class, 5% graduate in 5 years or less, and 81% graduate in 6 years or less.

Admissions Contact: Philip G. Guth, Vice President for Enrollment Management and Technology Services. A video is available. E-mail: *admissions@judson-il.edu* Web: *www.judsoncollege.edu*

KENDALL COLLEGE
Evanston, IL 60201

E-1
(847) 448-2304
(877) 588-8860; Fax: (847) 448-2120

Full-time: 233 men, 221 women	**Faculty:** 23
Part-time: 58 men, 116 women	**Ph.D.s:** 18%
Graduate: none	**Student/Faculty:** 20 to 1
Year: quarters, summer session	**Tuition:** $15,497
Application Deadline: open	**Room & Board:** $5853
Freshman Class: n/av	
ACT: required	**NONCOMPETITIVE**

Kendall College, founded in 1934, is a private institution affiliated with the United Methodist Church. It offers programs in liberal arts, business, and professional training, as well as culinary arts. The library contains 41,539 volumes, 200 microform items, and 1500 audio/video tapes/CDs, and subscribes to 210 periodicals. Computerized library services include interlibrary loans, database searching, and Internet access. Special learning facilities include an American Indian museum. The 1-acre campus is in an urban area in Chicago. Including any residence halls, there is 1 building.

Student Life: 89% of undergraduates are from Illinois. Students are from 5 states, 5 foreign countries, and Canada. 70% are from public schools. 65% are white; 14% African American. The average age of freshmen is 30; all undergraduates, 28. 36% do not continue beyond their first year; 25% remain to graduate.

Housing: 241 students can be accommodated in college housing, which includes single-sex and coed dorms. On-campus housing is available on a first-come, first-served basis. 55% of students commute. Alcohol is not permitted. No one may keep cars.

Activities: There are no fraternities or sororities. There are some groups and organizations on campus, including computers, honors, international, newspaper, professional, social service, and student government.

Sports: There is no sports program at Kendall.

Disabled Students: All of the campus is accessible. Wheelchair ramps, elevators, special parking, and specially equipped rest rooms are available.

Services: Counseling and information services are available, as is tutoring in most subjects. There is remedial math, reading, and writing.

Campus Safety and Security: Measures include 24-hour foot and vehicle patrol and lighted pathways/sidewalks.

Programs of Study: Kendall confers the B.A. degree. Associate degrees are also awarded. Bachelor's degrees are awarded in BUSINESS (business administration and management, hospitality management services, and hotel/motel and restaurant management), EDUCATION (early childhood), SOCIAL SCIENCE (food production/management/services and human services). Culinary Arts, early childhood education, and hospitality management are the strongest academically. Culinary arts and hospitality management are the largest.

Required: A 2.0 GPA is required to graduate.

Special: All majors require internships. Study abroad in 3 countries and work-study programs are available. Accelerated degree programs, B.A.-B.S. degrees, and student-designed majors are also possible. There are 2 national honor societies, including Phi Beta Kappa, and 2 departmental honors programs.

Faculty/Classroom: 64% of faculty are male; 36%, female. All teach undergraduates. The average class size in an introductory lecture is 25; in a laboratory, 15; and in a regular course, 13.

Admissions: 6% of the current freshmen were in the top fifth of their class; 25% were in the top two fifths.

Requirements: The ACT is required. Minimum acceptable score on the SAT I is 425 Verbal, 425 math; on the ACT, the minimum score is 18. However, there is a placement test for students who do not meet the minimum requirement. Applicants should be graduates of an accredited secondary school or have a GED. They should prepare with 4 years of high school math, 2 years each of history, science, and social studies, and 1 year of a foreign language. An interview is recommended. A GPA of 2.0 is required. AP and CLEP credits are accepted.

Procedure: Freshmen are admitted to all sessions. Entrance exams should be taken as soon as requested. There is a deferred admissions plan. There is a rolling admissions plan. Application deadlines are open. Application fee is $30. Applications are accepted on-line.

Transfer: 118 transfer students enrolled in 2002-2003. The minimum GPA for transfer applicants is 2.0. An interview is recommended. 84 of 184 credits required for the bachelor's degree must be completed at Kendall.

Visiting: There are regularly scheduled orientations for prospective students. There are guides for informal visits and visitors may sit in on classes and stay overnight. To schedule a visit, contact the Admissions Office at *admissions@kendall.edu.*

Financial Aid: In 2003-2004, 85% of all full-time students received some form of financial aid. Average annual earnings from campus work are $1800. Kendall is a member of CSS. The FAFSA and the college's own financial statement are required.

International Students: They must score 500 on the written TOEFL or 173 on the electronic version and also take the college's own test and the SAT I or the ACT.

Computers: IBM PS/2 PCs are available in the computer lab. All students may access the system. There are no time limits. The fee is $100 per term.

Graduates: From July 1, 2002 to June 30, 2003, 49 bachelor's degrees were awarded. In an average class, 55% graduate in 4 years or less. Of the 2002 graduating class, 95% were employed within 6 months of graduation.

Admissions Contact: Carl Goodmonson, Director of Admissions. E-mail: *admissions@kendall.edu* Web: *www.kendall.edu*

KNOX COLLEGE
Galesburg, IL 61401

C-2
(309) 341-7123
(800) 678-KNOX; Fax: (309) 341-7070

Full-time: 517 men, 588 women	**Faculty:** 94; IIB, av$
Part-time: 8 men, 14 women	**Ph.D.s:** 94%
Graduate: none	**Student/Faculty:** 12 to 1
Year: trimesters	**Tuition:** $24,369
Application Deadline: February 1	**Room & Board:** $5925
Freshman Class: 1414 applied, 1129 accepted, 268 enrolled	
SAT I Verbal/Math: 620/610	**ACT:** 27 **VERY COMPETITIVE+**

Knox College, founded in 1837, is an independent liberal arts college. The 3 libraries contain 304,997 volumes, 96,990 microform items, and 6781 audio/video tapes/CDs, and subscribe to 633 periodicals. Computerized library services include the card catalog, interlibrary loans, database searching, and Internet access. Special learning facilities include a learning resource center, natural history museum, radio station, and a 760-acre biological field station near the campus. The 82-acre campus is in a small town 180 miles southwest of Chicago. Including any residence halls, there are 42 buildings.

Student Life: 56% of undergraduates are from Illinois. Students are from 46 states, 50 foreign countries, and Canada. 88% are from public schools. 71% are white. The average age of freshmen is 18; all under-

graduates, 20. 13% do not continue beyond their first year; 78% remain to graduate.

Housing: 1114 students can be accommodated in college housing, which includes single-sex and coed dorms, on-campus apartments, and fraternity houses. In addition, there are special-interest houses. On-campus housing is guaranteed for all 4 years. 95% of students live on campus; of those, 80% remain on campus on weekends. All students may keep cars.

Activities: 37% of men belong to 4 national fraternities; 15% of women belong to 2 national sororities. There are 102 groups on campus, including art, band, chess, choir, chorus, computers, dance, drama, ethnic, gay, honors, international, jazz band, literary magazine, newspaper, orchestra, photography, political, professional, radio and TV, religious, social, social service, student government, symphony, and yearbook. Popular campus events include International Fair, Black Culture Month, and Flunk Day.

Sports: There are 11 intercollegiate sports for men and 10 for women and 5 coed intramural sports. Facilities include 6 outdoor playing fields, 2 gyms, a swimming pool, tennis courts, and an outdoor track. The campus stadium seats 5000; the gym, 3000. There are club sports in men's volleyball, lacrosse, and water polo. The field house contains a 200-meter indoor track, tennis and volleyball courts, and multiuse space.

Disabled Students: 60% of the campus is accessible. Wheelchair ramps, elevators, special parking, specially equipped rest rooms, and special class scheduling are available.

Services: There is a reader service for the blind. The Center for Teaching and Learning provides academic support to students in most subjects, particularly development of writing skills.

Campus Safety and Security: Measures include 24-hour foot and vehicle patrol, security escort services, informal discussions, and pamphlets/posters/films. There are emergency telephones and lighted pathways/sidewalks.

Programs of Study: Knox confers the B.A. degree. Bachelor's degrees are awarded in BIOLOGICAL SCIENCE (biochemistry and biology/biological science), BUSINESS (banking and finance), COMMUNICATIONS AND THE ARTS (art history and appreciation, classics, creative writing, dramatic arts, English literature, French, German, modern language, music, Russian, Spanish, and studio art), COMPUTER AND PHYSICAL SCIENCE (chemistry, computer science, mathematics, and physics), EDUCATION (elementary and secondary), ENGINEERING AND ENVIRONMENTAL DESIGN (environmental science), SOCIAL SCIENCE (African American studies, American studies, anthropology, economics, German area studies, history, international relations, philosophy, political science/government, psychology, Russian and Slavic studies, sociology, and women's studies). Biology, chemistry, and math are the strongest academically. Economics, biology, and education are the largest.

Required: Students must take a 1-term interdisciplinary preceptorial emphasizing writing and discussion skills. In addition to this, 2 writing-intensive courses and 1 course emphasizing oral presentation are required. 1 course focusing on diversity is also required, as well as documentation of a significant experiental learning project outside the classroom. Breadth requirements include 1 course each in the 4 areas of arts, humanities, math, and natural science, and an additional field of concentration, minor or major, not in the department of the major.

Special: The normal academic load is 3 courses per term, with 3 terms per year. Cooperative programs are offered with Washington University in St. Louis in architecture and engineering; Columbia University in engineering and law; University of Illinois at Urbana-Champaign and Rensselaer Polytechnic Institute in engineering; Rush University in medicine, nursing, and medical technology; Duke University in forestry and environmental management; and University of Chicago in law and social work. Study abroad is available in 20 countries. Other programs include a Washington semester, an urban studies semester, science and library research programs, work-study programs, and numerous internships. Dual majors, student-designed majors, and pass/fail options are available. Early admission to Rush Medical College is possible. Nondegree study is possible. Knox College participates in the Kemper Scholars Program. There are 7 national honor societies, including Phi Beta Kappa. All departments have honors programs.

Faculty/Classroom: 61% of faculty are male; 39%, female. All both teach and do research. The average class size in an introductory lecture is 23; in a laboratory, 12; and in a regular course, 17.

Admissions: 80% of the 2003-2004 applicants were accepted. The SAT I scores for the 2003-2004 freshman class were: Verbal--12% below 500, 29% between 500 and 599, 40% between 600 and 700, and 19% above 700; Math--12% below 500, 32% between 500 and 599, 48% between 600 and 700, and 8% above 700. The ACT scores were 7% below 21, 11% between 21 and 23, 28% between 24 and 26, 19% between 27 and 28, and 35% above 28. 54% of the current freshmen were in the top fifth of their class; 86% were in the top two fifths. There were 3 National Merit finalists and 3 semifinalists. 8 freshmen graduated first in their class.

Requirements: The SAT I or ACT is recommended. In addition, an essay is required of all applicants. Applicants should be graduates of an accredited secondary school with a minimum of 15 academic credits (18 to 20 are recommended). An interview is strongly recommended. AP and CLEP credits are accepted. Important factors in the admissions decision are advanced placement or honor courses, recommendations by school officials, and extracurricular activities record.

Procedure: Freshmen are admitted in the fall. Entrance exams should be taken by December 15. There are early admissions and deferred admissions plans. Early decision applications should be filed by December 1; regular applications, by February 1 for fall entry, November 1 for winter entry, and January 15 for spring entry, along with a $35 fee. Notification of early decision is sent December 31; regular decision, March 31. 34 applicants were on the 2003 waiting list; 20 were admitted. Applications are accepted on-line through Common App.

Transfer: 53 transfer students enrolled in 2002-2003. A 2.75 GPA is required. An interview is recommended. 13 of 36 credits required for the bachelor's degree must be completed at Knox.

Visiting: There are regularly scheduled orientations for prospective students, including a summer open house in early August, fall open houses in October and November, and a winter open house in January. Open house programs include campus tours, class visits, lunch with students and professors, and informational sessions. Interviews are available on request. Students are also welcome to visit at other times of the year that are more convenient to them. There are guides for informal visits and visitors may sit in on classes and stay overnight. To schedule a visit, contact the Admission Office at (309) 341-7100 or admission@knox.edu.

Financial Aid: In 2003-2004, 98% of all full-time freshmen and 96% of continuing full-time students received some form of financial aid. 70% of full-time freshmen and 73% of continuing full-time students received need-based aid. The average freshman award was $20,576. Need-based scholarships or need-based grants averaged $16,328 ($30,000 maximum); need-based self-help aid (loans and jobs) averaged $4920 ($7670 maximum); and other non-need-based awards and non-need-based scholarships averaged $10,872 ($18,900 maximum). 69% of undergraduates work part time. Average annual earnings from campus work are $977. The average financial indebtedness of the 2003 graduate was $18,221. The FAFSA, the college's own financial statement, and student and parent tax returns are required. The priority date for freshman financial aid applications for fall entry is March 1.

International Students: There are 96 international students enrolled. The school actively recruits these students. They must score 550 on the written TOEFL and also take the SAT I or the ACT.

Computers: The mainframes are composed of HP 9000 UNIX servers and NT servers. Virtually every campus building is linked via a fiber-optic Ethernet network. There are 5 public networked computer labs equipped with more than 200 Power Macs and Pentiums. Students may connect PCs from their rooms to the library, e-mail services, software applications, and the Internet. All students may access the system. A large student computer lab is open 24 hours. Others are open until midnight. There are no time limits and no fees.

Graduates: From July 1, 2002 to June 30, 2003, 241 bachelor's degrees were awarded. The most popular majors were economics (14%), psychology (8%), and biology (7%). In an average class, 64% graduate in 4 years or less, 78% graduate in 5 years or less, and 78% graduate in 6 years or less. 105 companies recruited on campus in 2002-2003. Of the 2002 graduating class, 30% were enrolled in graduate school within 6 months of graduation and 68% were employed.

Admissions Contact: Paul Steenis, Director of Admission.
E-mail: admission@knox.edu Web: www.knox.edu

LAKE FOREST COLLEGE
Lake Forest, IL 60045-2399

E-1
(847) 735-5000
(800) 828-4751; Fax: (847) 735-6271

Full-time: 566 men, 758 women	**Faculty:** 87; IIB, +$
Part-time: 8 men, 13 women	**Ph.D.s:** 97%
Graduate: 5 men, 7 women	**Student/Faculty:** 15 to 1
Year: semesters, summer session	**Tuition:** $24,506
Application Deadline: March 1	**Room & Board:** $5764
Freshman Class: 1835 applied, 1240 accepted, 347 enrolled	
SAT I Verbal/Math: 578/584	**ACT:** 25 **VERY COMPETITIVE**

Lake Forest College, founded in 1857, is a private liberal arts institution affiliated by heritage with the Presbyterian Church (U.S.A.). The 2 libraries contain 257,444 volumes, 103,890 microform items, and 5015 audio/video tapes/CDs, and subscribe to 1518 periodicals. Computerized library services include the card catalog, interlibrary loans, database searching, and Internet access. Special learning facilities include a learning resource center, art gallery, radio station, a multimedia language lab, and an electronic music studio with practice rooms. The 107-acre campus is in a suburban area 30 miles north of Chicago. Including any residence halls, there are 30 buildings.

Student Life: 56% of undergraduates are from out of state, mostly the Midwest. Students are from 46 states, 50 foreign countries, and Canada. 64% are from public schools. 75% are white; 11% foreign nationals. The average age of freshmen is 18; all undergraduates, 20. 20% do not continue beyond their first year; 67% remain to graduate.

Housing: 1096 students can be accommodated in college housing, which includes single-sex and coed dorms and on-campus apartments. In addition, there are honors houses, special-interest houses, and options for 24-hour quiet hours and substance-free housing. On-campus housing is guaranteed for all 4 years. 82% of students live on campus; of those, 98% remain on campus on weekends. Upperclassmen may keep cars.

Activities: 19% of men belong to 3 local and 1 national fraternity; 15% of women belong to 3 local and 1 national sorority. There are 67 groups on campus, including art, band, cheerleading, chess, choir, chorus, computers, dance, debate, drama, ethnic, film, gay, honors, international, jazz band, literary magazine, musical theater, newspaper, orchestra, pep band, photography, political, professional, radio and TV, religious, social, social service, student government, and yearbook. Popular campus events include Festival of Ra, Big Chill Weekend, and poet, writer, artist, and scholar-residence programs.

Sports: There are 9 intercollegiate sports for men and 10 for women, and 8 intramural sports for men and 8 for women. Facilities include a gym, tennis courts, indoor and outdoor basketball courts, and racquetball, handball, squash, and outdoor sand volleyball courts. There are also weight and exercise rooms, a pool, an indoor ice rink, and baseball, football, soccer, and intramural fields.

Disabled Students: 80% of the campus is accessible. Wheelchair ramps, elevators, special parking, specially equipped rest rooms, special class scheduling, lowered drinking fountains, and lowered telephones are available.

Services: Counseling and information services are available, as is tutoring in most subjects.

Campus Safety and Security: Measures include 24-hour foot and vehicle patrol, self-defense education, security escort services, and shuttle buses. There are informal discussions, pamphlets/posters/films, emergency telephones, and lighted pathways/sidewalks.

Programs of Study: Lake Forest confers the B.A. degree. Master's degrees are also awarded. Bachelor's degrees are awarded in BIOLOGICAL SCIENCE (biology/biological science), BUSINESS (business economics), COMMUNICATIONS AND THE ARTS (art, communications, English, French, music, and Spanish), COMPUTER AND PHYSICAL SCIENCE (chemistry, computer science, mathematics, and physics), EDUCATION (education), ENGINEERING AND ENVIRONMENTAL DESIGN (environmental science), SOCIAL SCIENCE (American studies, anthropology, area studies, Asian/Oriental studies, economics, history, international relations, Latin American studies, philosophy, political science/government, psychology, and sociology). Economics, politics, and history are the largest.

Required: All students are required to complete 32 courses with a minimum GPA of 2.0. General education requirements include 2 courses in natural science or math, 2 cultural diversity courses, and 1 course each in freshman studies, freshman writing, humanities, social science, and senior studies.

Special: Lake Forest offers cross-registration with Barat College of DePaul University and Associated Colleges of the Midwest, an extensive internship program through Chicago Alliance and Outreach Programs, a student-designed Independent Scholar Program, and study abroad in 14 countries. Dual and interdisciplinary majors, including American studies, Asian studies, area studies, art (studio and art history), and environmental studies, are available. There is a Washington semester with American University and a work-study program. A 3-2 engineering degree with Washington University at St. Louis and a 3-2 extended degree program in social service with the University of Chicago School of Social Service Administration are offered. Several minors and a pass/fail option are available. A program in marine biology is offered in the Bahamas. There are 11 national honor societies, including Phi Beta Kappa, and a freshman honors program.

Faculty/Classroom: 56% of faculty are male; 44%, female. 100% both teach and do research. No introductory courses are taught by graduate students. The average class size in an introductory lecture is 20; in a laboratory, 12; and in a regular course, 17.

Admissions: 68% of the 2003-2004 applicants were accepted. The SAT I scores for the 2003-2004 freshman class were: Verbal--17% below 500, 39% between 500 and 599, 36% between 600 and 700, and 8% above 700; Math--14% below 500, 41% between 500 and 599, 37% between 600 and 700, and 8% above 700. The ACT scores were 15% below 21, 18% between 21 and 23, 29% between 24 and 26, 16% between 27 and 28, and 22% above 28. 45% of the current freshmen were in the top fifth of their class; 65% were in the top two fifths. There were 2 National Merit finalists and 14 semifinalists. 9 freshmen graduated first in their class.

Requirements: The SAT I or ACT is required. In addition, applicants are advised to complete a minimum of 16 academic credits, including 4 in English, 3 in math, 2 to 4 each in social and natural sciences, and study in 1 or more foreign languages. A GED is accepted. An interview is encouraged. AP credits are accepted. Important factors in the admissions decision are advanced placement or honor courses, evidence of special talent, and extracurricular activities record.

Procedure: Freshmen are admitted fall and winter. Entrance exams should be taken in the junior or senior year. There are early decision,

early admissions, and deferred admissions plans. Early decision applications should be filed by January 1; regular applications, by March 1 for fall entry and December 15 for spring entry. The fall 2003 application fee was $40. Notification of early decision is sent January 21; regular decision, March 21. 25 early decision candidates were accepted for the 2003-2004 class. 75 applicants were on the 2003 waiting list; 12 were admitted. Applications are accepted on computer disk and on-line through CollegeLink, the Common Application, ExPAN, and MacApply.

Transfer: 67 transfer students enrolled in 2002-2003. Transfer applicants should have a minimum C average in all college work and should be in good standing with their previous institution. High school and college transcripts and a letter of recommendation from the academic dean or a teacher at the most recent college attended are required. 16 of 32 credits required for the bachelor's degree must be completed at Lake Forest.

Visiting: There are regularly scheduled orientations for prospective students, consisting of class visitation, panel presentations, tours and individual appointments with faculty and/or admission officers. There are guides for informal visits and visitors may sit in on classes and stay overnight. To schedule a visit, contact the Admissions Office at *admissions@lakeforest.edu*.

Financial Aid: In 2003-2004, 89% of all full-time students received some form of financial aid. 79% of full-time freshmen and 76% of continuing full-time students received need-based aid. The average freshman award was $19,209. Need-based scholarships or need-based grants averaged $16,486 ($25,575 maximum); need-based self-help aid (loans and jobs) averaged $3730 ($6300 maximum); and non-need-based awards and non-need-based scholarships averaged $8808 ($24,096 maximum). 85% of undergraduates work part time. Average annual earnings from campus work are $1650. The average financial indebtedness of the 2003 graduate was $17,285. Lake Forest is a member of CSS. The CSS/Profile or FAFSA is required. The deadline for filing freshman financial aid applications for fall entry is March 1.

International Students: There are 130 international students enrolled. The school actively recruits these students. They must score 550 on the written TOEFL or 220 on the electronic version and also take the SAT I or the ACT.

Computers: There are 190 computers that access the mainframe, the majority of which are available for student use. There are also more than 100 PCs in 11 computer labs in residence halls and academic buildings available for student use. The residence hall PCs have word-processing, database-management, and spreadsheet capabilities. Internet network hookups in residence hall rooms are possible at no charge. All students may access the system 24 hours a day, 7 days a week. There are no time limits and no fees.

Graduates: From July 1, 2002 to June 30, 2003, 294 bachelor's degrees were awarded. The most popular majors were business/economics (23%), communications (11%), and psychology (8%). In an average class, 1% graduate in 3 years or less, 61% graduate in 4 years or less, 65% graduate in 5 years or less, and 66% graduate in 6 years or less. 56 companies recruited on campus in 2002-2003. Of the 2002 graduating class, 33% were enrolled in graduate school within 6 months of graduation and 70% were employed.

Admissions Contact: William G. Motzer, Vice President for Admissions and Career Services. E-mail: *admissions@lfc.edu* Web: *http://www.lfc.edu*

LEWIS UNIVERSITY   E-2
Romeoville, IL 60446   **(815) 838-0500, ext. 5250**
                                    (800) 897-9000; Fax: (815) 836-5002

Full-time: 1016 men, 1234 women	**Faculty:** 141; IIA, -$
Part-time: 317 men, 649 women	**Ph.D.s:** 57%
Graduate: 466 men, 788 women	**Student/Faculty:** 16 to 1
Year: semesters, summer session	**Tuition:** $15,950
Application Deadline: open	**Room & Board:** $7000
Freshman Class: 1595 applied, 1056 accepted, 458 enrolled	
SAT I Verbal/Math: 550/590	**ACT:** 24 **COMPETITIVE+**

Lewis University, founded in 1932, is a private institution affiliated with the Roman Catholic Church and sponsored by the De La Salle Christian Brothers. A comprehensive liberal arts university, Lewis offers classes at its main campus and at more than 20 satellite locations in the Chicago metropolitan area. There are 4 undergraduate and 11 graduate schools. In addition to regional accreditation, Lewis has baccalaureate program accreditation with NCATE and NLN. The library contains 180,000 volumes, 13,100 microform items, and 2300 audio/video tapes/CDs, and subscribes to 800 periodicals. Computerized library services include the card catalog, interlibrary loans, database searching, and Internet access. Special learning facilities include a learning resource center, art gallery, radio station, TV station, and aviation building and airport. The 350-acre campus is in a suburban area 30 miles southwest of downtown Chicago. Including any residence halls, there are 21 buildings.

Student Life: 97% of undergraduates are from Illinois. Students are from 24 states, 30 foreign countries, and Canada. 75% are from public schools. 71% are white; 14% African American. Most are Catholic. The average age of freshmen is 19; all undergraduates, 28. 19% do not continue beyond their first year.

Housing: 900 students can be accommodated in college housing, which includes single-sex and coed dorms. On-campus housing is available on a first-come, first-served basis and is available on a lottery system for upperclassmen. Priority is given to out-of-town students. 73% of students commute. All students may keep cars.

Activities: 3% of men belong to 4 local and 5 national fraternities; 2% of women belong to 3 national sororities. There are 27 groups on campus, including band, cheerleading, choir, chorale, chorus, dance, debate, drama, ethnic, flight team, forensics, honors, international, jazz band, literary magazine, musical theater, newspaper, orchestra, pep band, photography, political, professional, radio and TV, religious, social, social service, student government, symphony, and yearbook. Popular campus events include Fall and Spring Formals, Greek Stock, and International Student Food Festival.

Sports: There are 9 intercollegiate sports for men and 9 for women, and 10 intramural sports for men and 10 for women. Facilities include a recreation center containing a field house with 4 multipurpose courts, a fitness center, an aerobics studio, an 8-lane pool, and an indoor track; a tennis complex; an outdoor track; and baseball, softball, and soccer fields.

Disabled Students: 95% of the campus is accessible. Wheelchair ramps, elevators, special parking, specially equipped rest rooms, special class scheduling, lowered drinking fountains, and lowered telephones are available.

Services: Counseling and information services are available, as is tutoring in most subjects. There is remedial math, reading, and writing. The University Success Program provides assistance to those students who do not meet the outright scholastic requirements.

Campus Safety and Security: Measures include 24-hour foot and vehicle patrol, security escort services, informal discussions, and pamphlets/posters/films. There are emergency telephones and lighted pathways/sidewalks.

Programs of Study: Lewis confers B.A., B.S., B.E.S., and B.S.N. degrees. Associate and master's degrees are also awarded. Bachelor's degrees are awarded in BIOLOGICAL SCIENCE (biochemistry and biology/biological science), BUSINESS (accounting, banking and finance, business administration and management, human resources, management information systems, marketing/retailing/merchandising, and sports management), COMMUNICATIONS AND THE ARTS (broadcasting, communications, communications technology, dramatic arts, drawing, English, illustration, journalism, multimedia, music, music business management, painting, public relations, radio/television technology, and studio art), COMPUTER AND PHYSICAL SCIENCE (atmospheric sciences and meteorology, chemistry, computer science, mathematics, and physics), EDUCATION (athletic training, elementary, secondary, special, and speech correction), ENGINEERING AND ENVIRONMENTAL DESIGN (aircraft mechanics, airline piloting and navigation, aviation administration/management, computer graphics, environmental science, and preengineering), HEALTH PROFESSIONS (community health work, health care administration, nursing, physical therapy, predentistry, premedicine, preoptometry, prepharmacy, and preveterinary science), SOCIAL SCIENCE (Christian studies, criminal justice, economics, history, liberal arts/general studies, philosophy, political science/government, prelaw, psychology, public administration, religion, safety and security technology, social work, and sociology). Aviation, criminal social justice, and nursing education are the strongest academically and have the largest enrollments.

Required: All students must earn 128 credit hours in courses acceptable for graduation, with one third of these courses in the core curriculum. Students must maintain a minimum GPA of 2.0. At least 4 upperdivision courses must be taken in the major. Students must complete the Introduction to the College Experience course and pass a writing proficiency exam.

Special: Lewis offers a general education degree, co-op programs with Chicago College of Pharmacy and Logan Chiropractic College, studentdesigned majors, B.A.-B.S. degrees in nursing, pass/fail options, dual majors, work-study programs, and nondegree study. Internships are required for some majors and optional for all others. There are accelerated-degree programs in business administration, computer network administration, health care leadership, RN-BSN, social and community studies, and nursing. The aviation program permits graduates to qualify for the FAA Airframe and Powerplant certificate. There are 10 national honor societies, a freshman honors program, and 10 departmental honors programs.

Faculty/Classroom: 57% of faculty are male; 43%, female. All teach undergraduates. No introductory courses are taught by graduate students. The average class size in an introductory lecture is 14; in a laboratory, 11; and in a regular course, 13.

Admissions: 66% of the 2003-2004 applicants were accepted. The SAT I scores for the 2003-2004 freshman class were: Verbal--25% below 500, 50% between 500 and 599, and 25% between 600 and 700; Math--25% below 500, 50% between 500 and 599, and 25% between 600

and 700. The ACT scores were 6% below 21, 65% between 21 and 23, 14% between 24 and 26, 14% between 27 and 28, and 4% above 28. 30% of the current freshmen were in the top fifth of their class; 61% were in the top two fifths.

Requirements: The SAT I or ACT is required. In addition, the ACT is preferred, with a minimum composite score of 20. Applicants should be graduates of an accredited secondary school. The GED is accepted. Students should have 18 units consisting of 3 in English and 15 in other college preparatory subjects. A GPA of 2.0 is required. AP and CLEP credits are accepted. Important factors in the admissions decision are advanced placement or honor courses, leadership record, and extracurricular activities record.

Procedure: Freshmen are admitted to all sessions. Entrance exams should be taken prior to enrollment. Application deadlines are open. There is a rolling admissions plan. The fall 2003 application fee was $35. Applications are accepted on-line through College Appply software available through the university's web site.

Transfer: 487 transfer students enrolled in 2002-2003. Applicants must have a 2.0 GPA in transferable course work of at least 12 semester hours, submit official transcripts from all colleges attended, and be in good standing at the previous institution. 32 of 128 credits required for the bachelor's degree must be completed at Lewis.

Visiting: There are regularly scheduled orientations for prospective students, consisting of 1- or 2-day sessions (overnight optional) and parent orientation followed by a welcome weekend before the first class day in the fall. There are guides for informal visits and visitors may sit in on classes and stay overnight. To schedule a visit, contact the Admissions Office at *admissions@lewisu.edu*.

Financial Aid: In a recent year, 67% of all full-time freshmen and 66% of continuing full-time students received some form of financial aid. 55% of full-time freshmen and 48% of continuing full-time students received need-based aid. The average freshman award was $16,125. 12% of undergraduates work part time. Average annual earnings from campus work are $2400. The average financial indebtedness of a recent graduate was $15,621. Lewis is a member of CSS. The FAFSA is required. The deadline for filing freshman financial aid applications for fall entry is May 1.

International Students: There were 73 international students enrolled in a recent year. The school actively recruits these students. They must score 500 on the written TOEFL and also take the SAT I or the ACT.

Computers: The mainframe consists of 3 IBM RS/6000 units. All students may access the system. There are no time limits.

Graduates: In a recent year, 816 bachelor's degrees were awarded. The most popular majors were nursing (12%), criminal and social justice (10%), and business administration (10%). In an average class, 24% graduate in 3 years or less, 42% graduate in 4 years or less, 45% graduate in 5 years or less, and 62% graduate in 6 years or less.

Admissions Contact: Patrick Hughes, Dean of Admission. E-mail: *admissions@lewisu.edu* Web: *www.lewisu.edu*

LOYOLA UNIVERSITY CHICAGO
Chicago, IL 60611

E-2
(312) 915-6500
(800) 262-2373; Fax: (312) 915-7216

Full-time: 2218 men, 4374 women	Faculty: 479; I, -$
Part-time: 466 men, 858 women	Ph.Ds: 98%
Graduate: 2043 men, 3403 women	Student/Faculty: 14 to 1
Year: semesters, summer session	Tuition: $22,340
Application Deadline: April 1	Room & Board: $8824
Freshman Class: 11,979 applied, 9078 accepted, 1915 enrolled	
SAT I Verbal/Math: 580/570	ACT: 25 VERY COMPETITIVE

Loyola University Chicago, founded in 1870, is a private Roman Catholic (Jesuit) university offering undergraduate curricula in the arts and sciences, business, nursing, social work, and education. Some information in the above capsule is approximate. There are 5 undergraduate and 9 graduate schools. In addition to regional accreditation, Loyola has baccalaureate program accreditation with AACSB, CSWE, NCATE, and NLN. The 3 libraries contain 983,023 volumes, 1,625,335 microform items, and 32,777 audio/video tapes/CDs, and subscribe to 110,502 periodicals. Computerized library services include the card catalog, interlibrary loans, and database searching. Special learning facilities include a learning resource center, art gallery, radio station, a nursing resource center, theater, seismograph station, and an electron microscope. The 105-acre campus is in an urban area in Chicago. Including any residence halls, there are 130 buildings.

Student Life: 58% of undergraduates are from Illinois. Students are from 50 states, 78 foreign countries, and Canada. 61% are from public schools. 61% are white. 61% are Catholic; 30% Other: Orthodox (3%), Islam (5%), unknown (11%), other (6%), none (4%); 8% Protestant. The average age of freshmen is 18; all undergraduates, 21. 15% do not continue beyond their first year; 69% remain to graduate.

Housing: 1985 students can be accommodated in college housing, which includes single-sex and coed dorms and on-campus apartments. In addition, there are special-interest houses, a 24-hour quiet center, and a living-learning community. On-campus housing is guaranteed for all 4 years. 79% of students live on campus; of those, 70% remain on campus on weekends. All students may keep cars.

Activities: 3% of men belong to 1 local and 5 national fraternities; 5% of women belong to 8 national sororities. There are 136 groups on campus, including cheerleading, choir, chorus, drama, environmental, ethnic, gay, honors, international, jazz band, literary magazine, musical theater, newspaper, political, professional, radio and TV, religious, social, social service, and student government. Popular campus events include Hunger Week, Harmony Colors Festival, and President's and Valentine's Balls.

Sports: There are 6 intercollegiate sports for men and 7 for women, and 22 intramural sports for men and 22 for women. Facilities include racquetball courts, dance studio, swimming pools, saunas, an elevated jogging track, and weight rooms.

Disabled Students: 95% of the campus is accessible. Wheelchair ramps, elevators, special parking, specially equipped rest rooms, special class scheduling, lowered drinking fountains, and lowered telephones are available.

Services: Counseling and information services are available, as is tutoring in some subjects, including general education courses. There is a reader service for the blind and remedial writing. A writing center is also available for student use.

Campus Safety and Security: Measures include 24-hour foot and vehicle patrol, self-defense education, security escort services, and shuttle buses. There are informal discussions, pamphlets/posters/films, emergency telephones, and lighted pathways/sidewalks.

Programs of Study: Loyola confers B.A., B.S., B.A.Classics, B.B.A., B.S.Ed., and B.S.N. degrees. Master's and doctoral degrees are also awarded. Bachelor's degrees are awarded in BIOLOGICAL SCIENCE (biology/biological science), BUSINESS (accounting, banking and finance, business administration and management, business economics, marketing/retailing/merchandising, and personnel management), COMMUNICATIONS AND THE ARTS (communications, dramatic arts, English, fine arts, French, German, Greek, Italian, Latin, and Spanish), COMPUTER AND PHYSICAL SCIENCE (chemistry, computer science, mathematics, and physics), EDUCATION (elementary and special), HEALTH PROFESSIONS (nursing, predentistry, premedicine, and preveterinary science), SOCIAL SCIENCE (anthropology, classical/ancient civilization, criminal justice, economics, history, philosophy, political science/government, psychology, religion, social work, sociology, and theological studies). Biology, psychology, and nursing are the largest.

Required: To graduate, students must have a total of 128 credit hours with a minimum GPA of 2.0. The number of hours required in the major varies. For the core requirement, all students must take 9 hours each of theology, philosophy, and social sciences, and 6 hours each of English composition and humanities.

Special: Sophomores and juniors may study in 19 countries; 31 different programs. Dual majors, a Washington semester, nondegree study, and pass/fail options are available. The school also offers a B.A.-B.S. degree in chemistry and a 2-3 engineering degree with the University of Illinois at Urbana-Champaign, and Washington University. There is a chapter of Phi Beta Kappa and a freshman honors program.

Faculty/Classroom: 58% of faculty are male; 42%, female. 93% teach undergraduates and all do research. No introductory courses are taught by graduate students. The average class size in an introductory lecture is 25; in a laboratory, 2; and in a regular course, 15.

Admissions: 76% of the 2003-2004 applicants were accepted. The SAT I scores for the 2003-2004 freshman class were: Verbal--15% below 500, 43% between 500 and 599, 35% between 600 and 700, and 7% above 700; Math--21% below 500, 38% between 500 and 599, 36% between 600 and 700, and 5% above 700. The ACT scores were 7% below 21, 19% between 21 and 23, 35% between 24 and 26, 17% between 27 and 28, and 22% above 28. 54% of the current freshmen were in the top fifth of their class; 86% were in the top two fifths. There were 14 National Merit finalists. 12 freshmen graduated first in their class in a recent year.

Requirements: The SAT I or ACT is required. In addition, graduation from an accredited secondary school or satisfactory scores on the GED are required for admission. 15 academic credits are required. Secondary school courses should include 4 credits of English, 2 of math, and 1 each of science and social studies. An interview is recommended but an essay is not required. AP and CLEP credits are accepted. Important factors in the admissions decision are advanced placement or honor courses, evidence of special talent, and leadership record.

Procedure: Freshmen are admitted to all sessions. Entrance exams should be taken as early as possible, normally in the spring of the junior year. There is a rolling admissions plan. Applications should be filed by April 1 for fall entry, along with a $25 fee. Notification is sent on a rolling basis beginning February 15. A waiting list is an active part of the admissions procedure. Applications are accepted on-line (no fee).

Transfer: 591 transfer students enrolled in 2002-2003. Transfer students must have 20 transferable semester hours of credit, with a minimum GPA of 2.0 for the schools of arts and sciences and education. A minimum GPA of 2.5 is required for the schools of nursing and business administration. If transfers have fewer then 20 hours, students must meet the same requirements as entering freshmen. 45 of 128 credits required for the bachelor's degree must be completed at Loyola.

Visiting: There are regularly scheduled orientations for prospective students, including interviews and tours; students may attend classes if previous arrangements have been made. There are guides for informal visits and visitors may sit in on classes and stay overnight. To schedule a visit, contact the Undergraduate Admissions Office at *admission@luc.edu.*

Financial Aid: In 2003-2004, 85% of all full-time freshmen and 96% of continuing full-time students received some form of financial aid. 74% of full-time freshmen and 73% of continuing full-time students received need-based aid. The average freshman award was $14,799. Need-based scholarships or need-based grants averaged $12,032 ($23,000 maximum); need-based self-help aid (loans and jobs) averaged $4965 ($5000 maximum); non-need-based athletic scholarships averaged $19,585 ($30,000 maximum); and other non-need-based awards and non-need-based scholarships averaged $7956. 65% of undergraduates work part time. Average annual earnings from campus work are $1300. The average financial indebtedness of a recent graduate was $16,300. The FAFSA is required. The deadline for filing freshman financial aid applications for fall entry is March 1.

International Students: There are 122 international students enrolled. The school actively recruits these students. They must score 550 on the written TOEFL or 213 on the electronic version.

Computers: More than 190 PCs, networked to commonly used software packages, are available for student use. More than 75 terminals access the mainframe computer for heavy-duty analytical packages. All students may access the system whenever facilities are available. Connection is available from dorm rooms. There are no time limits and no fees.

Graduates: In a recent year, 1318 bachelor's degrees were awarded. The most popular majors were psychology (12%), biology (10%), and nursing (9%). In an average class, 1% graduate in 3 years or less, 46% graduate in 4 years or less, 64% graduate in 5 years or less, and 67% graduate in 6 years or less. 360 companies recruited on campus in a recent year.

Admissions Contact: April Hansen, Director, Undergraduate Admissions. A video is available. E-mail: *admission@luc.edu*
Web: *http://www.luc.edu*

MACMURRAY COLLEGE
Jacksonville, IL 62650

C-3
(217) 479-7056
(800) 252-7485; Fax: (217) 291-0702

Full-time: 264 men, 353 women	**Faculty:** 44; IIB, --$
Part-time: 16 men, 44 women	**Ph.D.s:** 57%
Graduate: none	**Student/Faculty:** 14 to 1
Year: 4-1-4, summer session	**Tuition:** $14,500
Application Deadline: open	**Room & Board:** $5505
Freshman Class: 1104 applied, 700 accepted, 162 enrolled	
SAT I Verbal/Math: 430/500	**ACT:** 20 **LESS COMPETITIVE**

MacMurray College, founded in 1846, is a private liberal arts institution affiliated with the United Methodist Church. In addition to regional accreditation, MacMurray has baccalaureate program accreditation with CCNE and CSWE.The library contains 145,000 volumes, and subscribes to 1500 periodicals. Computerized library services include the card catalog, interlibrary loans, database searching, and Internet access. Special learning facilities include a learning resource center and art gallery. The 60-acre campus is in a small town 30 miles west of Springfield. Including any residence halls, there are 17 buildings.

Student Life: 88% of undergraduates are from Illinois. Students are from 21 states and 6 foreign countries. 90% are from public schools. 82% are white; 11% African American. 46% are Protestant; 31% claim no religious affiliation; 23% Catholic. The average age of freshmen is 18; all undergraduates, 20. 30% do not continue beyond their first year; 46% remain to graduate.

Housing: 725 students can be accommodated in college housing, which includes single-sex and coed dorms. On-campus housing is guaranteed for all 4 years. 54% of students live on campus; of those, 70% remain on campus on weekends. All students may keep cars.

Activities: 18% of men belong to 1 local and 1 national fraternity; 10% of women belong to 2 local sororities. There are 36 groups on campus, including art, bagpipe band, band, cheerleading, choir, chorale, chorus, dance, drama, ethnic, gay, honors, international, literary magazine, musical theater, newspaper, orchestra, pep band, photography, political, professional, religious, social, social service, student government, and yearbook. Popular campus events include Spring formal, Sigma Tau Gamma Day, and midnight breakfasts.

Sports: There are 9 intercollegiate sports for men and 8 for women, and 15 intramural sports for men and 15 for women. Facilities include a gym, 3 basketball courts, tennis and outdoor basketball courts, a competition-size swimming pool, a weight room, a wrestling room, dance studios, a game room and TV lounge, and football, soccer, and baseball fields.

Disabled Students: 90% of the campus is accessible. Wheelchair ramps, elevators, special parking, specially equipped rest rooms, special class scheduling, and special housing are available.

Services: Counseling and information services are available, as is tutoring in every subject. There is remedial math, reading, and writing. The college provides services to visually and hearing impaired students through interpreters, readers, and note takers.

Campus Safety and Security: Measures include security escort services, informal discussions, pamphlets/posters/films, and emergency telephones. There are lighted pathways/sidewalks, evening patrols, and evening sign-in at dorms.

Programs of Study: MacMurray confers B.A., B.S., B.S.N., and B.S.W. degrees. Associate degrees are also awarded. Bachelor's degrees are awarded in BIOLOGICAL SCIENCE (biology/biological science), BUSINESS (accounting, business administration and management, management information systems, marketing/retailing/merchandising, and sports management), COMMUNICATIONS AND THE ARTS (art, dramatic arts, English, journalism, music, and Spanish), COMPUTER AND PHYSICAL SCIENCE (chemistry, computer science, mathematics, and physics), EDUCATION (education of the deaf and hearing impaired, elementary, music, physical, science, secondary, and special), ENGINEERING AND ENVIRONMENTAL DESIGN (preengineering), HEALTH PROFESSIONS (nursing, predentistry, premedicine, and preveterinary science), SOCIAL SCIENCE (criminal justice, history, interpreter for the deaf, liberal arts/general studies, philosophy, political science/government, prelaw, psychology, religion, social work, and youth ministry). Education of the hearing impaired, English, and nursing are the strongest academically. Business, education, and criminal justice are the largest.

Required: To graduate, students must complete 120 semester hours and 2 January term courses, with a minimum GPA of 2.0. All students must take 9 semester hours in rhetorical skills and a 5-course sequence on major ideas in Western civilization and world culture, and satisfy the requirements of the breadth component, a 16-hour distribution of non-major courses. Proficiency exams or equivalent courses in math and composition must be taken by all students before the end of the junior year.

Special: The school has co-op programs in modern languages and international studies and cross-registration with 5 colleges through the West Central Illinois Foreign Language Consortium. A 3-2 engineering degree with Washington and Columbia Universities and the University of Missouri (Rolla), a Washington semester, internships in all majors, work-study programs, dual majors, and pass/fail options are available. Students may study abroad in England, Germany, Japan, or Russia. There are 4 national honor societies, a freshman honors program, and 14 departmental honors programs.

Faculty/Classroom: 47% of faculty are male; 56%, female. All teach undergraduates. The average class size in an introductory lecture is 35; in a laboratory, 16; and in a regular course, 15.

Admissions: 63% of the 2003-2004 applicants were accepted. The SAT I scores for the 2003-2004 freshman class were: Verbal--75% below 500, 17% between 500 and 599, and 8% between 600 and 700. The ACT scores were 63% below 21, 15% between 21 and 23, 15% between 24 and 26, 4% between 27 and 28, and 3% above 28. 28% of the current freshmen were in the top fifth of their class; 50% were in the top two fifths. 3 freshmen graduated first in their class.

Requirements: The SAT I or ACT is required. In addition, applicants must be graduates of an accredited secondary school. The GED is accepted. Secondary school courses should include 4 years of English, 3 years of math, and 2 years each of science, foreign language, and social studies. MacMurray requires applicants to be in the upper 50% of their class. AP and CLEP credits are accepted. Important factors in the admissions decision are advanced placement or honor courses, extracurricular activities record, and leadership record.

Procedure: Freshmen are admitted to all sessions. Entrance exams should be taken in the spring of the junior year. There are early admissions and deferred admissions plans. There is a rolling admissions plan. Application deadlines are open. Notification is sent on a rolling basis. Applications are accepted on-line through Illinois Mentor.

Transfer: 101 transfer students enrolled in 2002-2003. Transfer students must have a minimum GPA of 2.0 in at least 28 transferable semester credits. Nursing applicants must have a GPA of 2.75 and a minimum score of 20 on the ACT. 30 credits of 126 required for the bachelor's degree must be completed at MacMurray.

Visiting: There are regularly scheduled orientations for prospective students, including a financial aid conference, a tour, and faculty appointments. There are guides for informal visits and visitors may sit in on classes and stay overnight. To schedule a visit, contact the Office of Admissions.

Financial Aid: In 2003-2004, 99% of all full-time students received some form of financial aid. 92% of full-time freshmen and 80% of continuing full-time students received need-based aid. The average freshman award was $15,567. Need-based scholarships or need-based grants averaged $4091 ($15,300 maximum); need-based self-help aid (loans and jobs) averaged $3921 ($7625 maximum); and non-need-based awards and non-need-based scholarships averaged $11,279 ($15,300 maximum). 55% of undergraduates work part time. Average annual earnings from campus work are $1134. The average financial indebtedness of the 2003 graduate was $17,477. MacMurray is a member of CSS. The FAFSA is required. The fall application deadline is open.

International Students: There are 10 international students enrolled. They must score 550 on the written TOEFL or 213 on the electronic version.

Computers: The mainframe is a DEC Alpha 2100. There are more than 70 Internet accessible PCs located in student areas in the library or classroom buildings. 24 of these are in a computer classroom in the science building. Additionally, there are 22 PCs in the residence halls. All students may access the system at designated hours throughout the week (8 A.M. to 11 P.M. Monday through Friday) and on weekends. There are no time limits and no fees.

Graduates: From July 1, 2002 to June 30, 2003, 117 bachelor's degrees were awarded. The most popular majors were business administration (16%), nursing (11%), and physical education (11%). In an average class, 42% graduate in 4 years or less, 45% graduate in 5 years or less, and 47% graduate in 6 years or less. 9 companies recruited on campus in 2002-2003. Of the 2002 graduating class, 16% were enrolled in graduate school within 6 months of graduation and 50% were employed.

Admissions Contact: Rhonda Cors, Vice President for Enrollment. A video is available. E-mail: *admiss@mac.edu* Web: *www.mac.edu*

MCKENDREE COLLEGE
Lebanon, IL 62254

C-5
(618) 537-6835
(800) BEARCAT; Fax: (618) 537-6496

Full-time: 652 men, 909 women	**Faculty:** 71; IIB, -$
Part-time: 183 men, 371 women	**Ph.Ds:** 87%
Graduate: none	**Student/Faculty:** 22 to 1
Year: semesters, summer session	**Tuition:** $15,200
Application Deadline: open	**Room & Board:** $5920
Freshman Class: 1190 applied, 870 accepted, 305 enrolled	
ACT: 25	**VERY COMPETITIVE**

McKendree College, founded in 1828, is the oldest college in Illinois. It is a private liberal arts institution affiliated with the United Methodist Church. In addition to regional accreditation, McKendree has baccalaureate program accreditation with CAAHEP, IACBE, and NLN. The library contains 140,000 volumes, 40,000 microform items, and 30,000 audio/video tapes/CDs, and subscribes to 5000 periodicals. Computerized library services include the card catalog, interlibrary loans, database searching, and Internet access. Special learning facilities include a learning resource center, greenhouse, and archives. The 100-acre campus is in a suburban area 23 miles east of St. Louis. Including any residence halls, there are 34 buildings.

Student Life: 69% of undergraduates are from Illinois. Students are from 23 states, 15 foreign countries, and Canada. 92% are from public schools. 82% are white; 11% African American. 38% are Protestant; 32% claim no religious affiliation; 24% Catholic. The average age of freshmen is 18; all undergraduates, 22. 18% do not continue beyond their first year; 64% remain to graduate.

Housing: 690 students can be accommodated in college housing, which includes single-sex and coed dorms, on-campus apartments, and off-campus apartments. On-campus housing is guaranteed for all 4 years. 54% of students live on campus; of those, 75% remain on campus on weekends. Alcohol is not permitted. All students may keep cars.

Activities: 8% of men belong to 1 local and 2 national fraternities; 6% of women belong to 3 local sororities. There are 54 groups on campus, including art, band, cheerleading, choir, chorale, chorus, computers, dance, debate, drama, ethnic, film, forensics, gay, honors, international, jazz band, literary magazine, marching band, musical theater, newspaper, pep band, photography, political, professional, religious, social, social service, student government, and yearbook. Popular campus events include Model United Nations, Family Festival, and Midnight Breakfast.

Sports: There are 9 intercollegiate sports for men and 9 for women, and 13 intramural sports for men and 13 for women. Facilities include a 1600-seat gym, an intramural gym, a fitness center, tennis courts, a student center with table tennis and billiards, an all-weather track, a 3000-seat football stadium, and playing fields.

Disabled Students: 80% of the campus is accessible. Wheelchair ramps, elevators, special parking, specially equipped rest rooms, special class scheduling, and lowered drinking fountains are available.

Services: Counseling and information services are available, as is tutoring in every subject. There is remedial reading and writing.

Campus Safety and Security: Measures include 24-hour foot and vehicle patrol, security escort services, shuttle buses, and informal discussions. There are pamphlets/posters/films, emergency telephones, and lighted pathways/sidewalks.

Programs of Study: McKendree confers B.A., B.S., B.B.A., B.F.A., B.S.Ed., and B.S.N. degrees. Master's degrees are also awarded. Bachelor's degrees are awarded in BIOLOGICAL SCIENCE (biology/biological science), BUSINESS (accounting, banking and finance, business administration and management, and marketing/retailing/merchandising), COMMUNICATIONS AND THE ARTS (art, English, music, music history and appreciation, public relations, and speech/debate/rhetoric), COMPUTER AND PHYSICAL SCIENCE (chemistry, computer science, information sciences and systems, and mathematics), EDUCATION (art, athletic training, business, elementary, and physical), HEALTH PROFESSIONS (medical laboratory technology and nursing), SOCIAL SCIENCE (criminal justice, economics, gerontology, history, international relations, philosophy, political science/government, psychology, religion, religious music, social science, social work, and sociology). Business, mathematics, and computer science are the strongest academically. Business, education, and nursing are the largest.

Required: To graduate, students must complete 128 semester hours, with a minimum GPA of 2.0. The 51- credit-hour core curriculum includes 9 credits of social science, 7 of science, 6 of freshman English, 3 each of speech, math, ethics, philosophy or religion, history, cross-cultural studies, literature, fine or performing arts, and computer competency, and 1 to 2 of phys ed. In addition, 2 writing-intensive courses and a writing proficiency exam must be taken. A thesis is required for biology majors seeking a B.S. degree.

Special: McKendree offers internships, work-study programs, study abroad in England, Ireland, and France, a Washington semester, dual and student-designed majors, and nondegree study, as well as a 3-2 program in occupational therapy with Washington University in St. Louis. There are 10 national honor societies, a freshman honors program, and 1 departmental honors program.

Faculty/Classroom: 55% of faculty are male; 45%, female. All both teach and do research. The average class size in an introductory lecture is 20; in a laboratory, 15; and in a regular course, 12.

Admissions: 73% of the 2003-2004 applicants were accepted. The ACT scores for the 2003-2004 freshman class were: 24% below 21, 27% between 21 and 23, 26% between 24 and 26, 14% between 27 and 28, and 10% above 28. 56% of the current freshmen were in the top fifth of their class; 87% were in the top two fifths. 16 freshmen graduated first in their class.

Requirements: The SAT I or ACT is required. In addition, students must be high school graduates or submit the GED certificate. Completion of at least 15 units of high school work is recommended. A recommendation from the secondary school counselor is required. McKendree requires applicants to be in the upper 50% of their class. A GPA of 2.5 is required. AP and CLEP credits are accepted. Important factors in the admissions decision are advanced placement or honor courses, leadership record, and evidence of special talent.

Procedure: Freshmen are admitted to all sessions. Entrance exams should be taken in the junior year. There is a rolling admissions plan. Application deadlines are open. Application fee is $40. Applications are accepted on-line through the school's web site.

Transfer: 210 transfer students enrolled in 2002-2003. Applicants must have a minimum 2.25 GPA from all colleges previously attended. 64 of 128 credits required for the bachelor's degree must be completed at McKendree.

Visiting: There are regularly scheduled orientations for prospective students, consisting of Preview Days, where faculty members and personnel from several departments answer questions. Student-led tours of the campus and various other events are also available. There are guides for informal visits and visitors may sit in on classes and stay overnight. To schedule a visit, contact Jan Mallich at (800) 232-7228, ext. 6831 or inquiry@mckendree.edu.

Financial Aid: In 2003-2004, 97% of all full-time freshmen and 98% of continuing full-time students received some form of financial aid. 81% of full-time freshmen and 77% of continuing full-time students received need-based aid. The average freshman award was $13,533. Need-based scholarships or need-based grants averaged $11,468 ($15,200 maximum); need-based self-help aid (loans and jobs) averaged $3108 ($6125 maximum); and non-need-based athletic scholarships averaged $4559 ($21,120 maximum). 20% of undergraduates work part time. Average annual earnings from campus work are $930. The average financial indebtedness of the 2003 graduate was $14,592. The FAFSA is required. The priority date for freshman financial aid applications for fall entry is May 15. The deadline for filing freshman financial aid applications for fall entry is August 15.

International Students: There are 23 international students enrolled. The school actively recruits these students. They must score 520 on the written TOEFL or 190 on the electronic version and also take the SAT I or the ACT, scoring 20.

Computers: There are more than 325 terminals on campus and 270 in individual residence rooms. Students may use any of the PCs across 4 labs on campus, another 60 PCs in 3 labs at remote centers, or their own PC in their residence room. All of these computers are networked with access to the Internet. All students may access the system. There are no time limits and no fees.

Graduates: From July 1, 2002 to June 30, 2003, 505 bachelor's degrees were awarded. The most popular majors were business marketing

(28%), education (18%), and health professions (16%). In an average class, 1% graduate in 3 years or less, 40% graduate in 4 years or less, 56% graduate in 5 years or less, and 64% graduate in 6 years or less. 150 companies recruited on campus in 2002-2003. Of the 2002 graduating class, 13% were enrolled in graduate school within 6 months of graduation and 94% were employed.

Admissions Contact: Mark Campbell, Vice President for Admissions and Financial Aid. A video is available.
E-mail: mecampbell@mckendree.edu Web: www.mckendree.edu

MILLIKIN UNIVERSITY
Decatur, IL 62522-2084

D-3
(217) 424-6210
(800) 373-7733; Fax: (217) 425-4669

Full-time: 1100 men, 1412 women	**Faculty:** 154; IIB, -$
Part-time: 34 men, 56 women	**Ph.D.s:** 88%
Graduate: 25 men, 6 women	**Student/Faculty:** 16 to 1
Year: semesters, summer session	**Tuition:** $19,234
Application Deadline: open	**Room & Board:** $6321
Freshman Class: 2823 applied, 2097 accepted, 597 enrolled	
SAT I Verbal/Math: 530/540	**ACT:** 23 COMPETITIVE

Millikin University, founded in 1901, is a private university affiliated with the Presbyterian Church (U.S.A.) offering undergraduate programs in arts and sciences, nursing, fine arts, and business. There are 4 undergraduate schools. In addition to regional accreditation, Millikin has baccalaureate program accreditation with NASM and NLN. The library contains 212,145 volumes, 21,432 microform items, and 2305 audio/video tapes/CDs, and subscribes to 580 periodicals. Computerized library services include the card catalog, interlibrary loans, and database searching. Special learning facilities include a learning resource center, art gallery, radio station, television lab, computer imaging center, audio/video recording studio, and museum of decorative arts. The 70-acre campus is in a suburban area 180 miles southwest of Chicago, 130 miles northeast of St. Louis, Missouri. Including any residence halls, there are 28 buildings.

Student Life: 85% of undergraduates are from Illinois. Students are from 33 states and 13 foreign countries. 85% are from public schools. 84% are white. 53% are Protestant; 24% Catholic; 18% claim no religious affiliation. The average age of freshmen is 18; all undergraduates, 21. 21% do not continue beyond their first year.

Housing: 1425 students can be accommodated in college housing, which includes single-sex and coed dorms, on-campus apartments, off-campus apartments, fraternity houses, and sorority houses. In addition, there are special-interest houses, Greek houses provided by their own organizations, and smoke-free, academic, and freshmen floors in residence halls. On-campus housing is available on a first-come, first-served basis and is available on a lottery system for upperclassmen. 75% of students live on campus; of those, 80% remain on campus on weekends. Upperclassmen may keep cars.

Activities: 16% of men belong to 9 national fraternities; 10% of women belong to 3 national sororities. There are 91 groups on campus, including art, band, cheerleading, chess, choir, chorale, chorus, computers, dance, drama, ethnic, film, gay, honors, international, jazz band, literary magazine, musical theater, newspaper, opera, orchestra, pep band, photography, political, professional, radio and TV, religious, social, social service, student government, symphony, and yearbook. Popular campus events include Springfest, Fall Family Weekend, and Millipalooza.

Sports: There are 10 intercollegiate sports for men and 9 for women, and 12 intramural sports for men and 12 for women. Facilities include a phys ed center with a 6-lane, 25-yard pool, a fitness/wellness center, a sand volleyball court, a playing field for football and track, and an indoor sports center.

Disabled Students: 65% of the campus is accessible. Wheelchair ramps, elevators, special parking, specially equipped rest rooms, special class scheduling, lowered drinking fountains, and lowered telephones are available.

Services: Counseling and information services are available, as is tutoring in most subjects. A writing center and a basic review course in English fundamentals are available.

Campus Safety and Security: Measures include 24-hour foot and vehicle patrol, self-defense education, security escort services, and informal discussions. There are pamphlets/posters/films, emergency telephones, and lighted pathways/sidewalks.

Programs of Study: Millikin confers B.A., B.S., B.F.A., B.M., and B.S.N. degrees. Master's degrees are also awarded. Bachelor's degrees are awarded in BIOLOGICAL SCIENCE (biology/biological science), BUSINESS (accounting, banking and finance, business administration and management, international business management, management information systems, and marketing/retailing/merchandising), COMMUNICATIONS AND THE ARTS (art, arts administration/management, communications, creative writing, dramatic arts, English, French, German, modern language, music, music performance, musical theater, and Spanish), COMPUTER AND PHYSICAL SCIENCE (chemistry, computer science, mathematics, and physics), EDUCATION (art, elementary, foreign languages, middle school, music, physical, science, and secondary), ENGINEERING AND ENVIRONMENTAL DESIGN (commercial art and industrial administration/management), HEALTH PROFESSIONS (art therapy and nursing), SOCIAL SCIENCE (American studies, economics, experimental psychology, history, human services, international studies, philosophy, political science/government, psychology, religion, social science, and sociology). Business, music, and theater are the strongest academically. Accounting, biology, and education are the largest.

Required: Requirements for graduation include courses in critical reading, writing, and research, humanities, fine arts, natural sciences/math, and global and U.S. studies. An off-campus learning experience and a university capstone course are also required. The minimum GPA is 2.0. Students must complete 124 to 136 credit hours, with 33 to 88 in the major.

Special: Millikin offers internships, a Washington semester through American University, study abroad at 22 foreign sites, student-designed majors, a 3-2 engineering degree with Washington University, B.A.-B.S. degrees, credit by exam, and pass/fail options. There are preprofessional programs in engineering, law, optometry, dentistry, medicine, veterinary science, occupational therapy, medical technology, physical therapy, and pharmacy. Students are also offered a United Nations semester at Drew University, affiliate research with the U.S. Department of Energy, affiliate agreements in occupational therapy and medical technology, and an Urban Life Studies Center semester in Chicago. There are 9 national honor societies, a freshman honors program, and 5 departmental honors programs.

Faculty/Classroom: 67% of faculty are male; 33%, female. All both teach and do research. The average class size in an introductory lecture is 25; in a laboratory, 15; and in a regular course, 21.

Admissions: 74% of the 2003-2004 applicants were accepted. The SAT I scores for the 2003-2004 freshman class were: Verbal--33% below 500, 35% between 500 and 599, 26% between 600 and 700, and 6% above 700; Math--34% below 500, 38% between 500 and 599, 26% between 600 and 700, and 2% above 700. The ACT scores were 27% below 21, 27% between 21 and 23, 23% between 24 and 26, 13% between 27 and 28, and 10% above 28. 36% of the current freshmen were in the top fifth of their class; 64% were in the top two fifths. 19 freshmen graduated first in their class in a recent year.

Requirements: The SAT I or ACT is required. In addition, applicants should be graduates of an accredited secondary school or have a GED. They should prepare with 4 units of high school English, 3 each of history, math, and science, and 2 of foreign language. An audition is required for music-theater, music, or theater majors. A portfolio is required for art majors. Millikin requires applicants to be in the upper 50% of their class. AP and CLEP credits are accepted. Important factors in the admissions decision are recommendations by school officials, personality/intangible qualities, and evidence of special talent.

Procedure: Freshmen are admitted to all sessions. Entrance exams should be taken in April. There is a deferred admissions plan and a rolling admissions plan. Application deadlines are open. Notification is sent on a rolling basis beginning October 1. Applications are accepted on-line through the school's web site.

Transfer: 130 transfer students enrolled in 2002-2003. Applicants must provide official transcripts from previous institutions, must be in good standing at the previous institution, and must have earned at least a C average in all college study previously attempted. Submission of official high school transcripts and testing is requested. 33 of 124 credits required for the bachelor's degree must be completed at Millikin.

Visiting: There are regularly scheduled orientations for prospective students, consisting of meetings with faculty and coaches, honors, curriculum, housing, and financial aid presentations, and campus tours. There is also an opportunity for students to audition or have portfolios reviewed. There are guides for informal visits and visitors may sit in on classes and stay overnight. To schedule a visit, contact the Admission Office.

Financial Aid: In 2003-2004, 83% of all full-time freshmen and 61% of continuing full-time students received some form of financial aid. At least 77% of full-time freshmen and 55% of continuing full-time students received need-based aid. The average freshman award was $17,086. Need-based scholarships or need-based grants averaged $11,990; need-based self-help aid (loans and jobs) averaged $1175; and non-need-based awards and non-need-based scholarships averaged $6546. The average financial indebtedness of the 2003 graduate was $17,100. Millikin is a member of CSS. The FAFSA and the college's own financial statement are required. The priority date for freshman financial aid applications for fall entry is April 15. The deadline for filing freshman financial aid applications for fall entry is June 1.

International Students: There are 9 international students enrolled. The school actively recruits these students. They must score 550 on the written TOEFL.

Computers: The mainframe is a DEC MicroVAX 3800. There are approximately 500 PCs available for student use. Through Novell 4.1.1 servers, these provide access to Microsoft Office software, e-mail, and the Internet. All students may access the system. There are no time limits and no fees.

Graduates: From July 1, 2002 to June 30, 2003, 536 bachelor's degrees were awarded. The most popular majors were communications (24%), visual and performing arts (18%), and engineering (15%). In an average class, 60% graduate in 4 years or less, and 61% graduate in 6 years or less. Of a recent graduating class, 14% were enrolled in graduate school within 6 months of graduation and 98% were employed.

Admissions Contact: Lin Stoner, Dean of Admission.
E-mail: *admis@mail.millikin.edu* Web: *www.millikin.edu*

MONMOUTH COLLEGE   C-2
Monmouth, IL 61462   (309) 457-2131
(800) 747-2687; Fax: (309) 457-2141

Full-time: 561 men, 594 women	**Faculty:** 69; IIB, av$
Part-time: 2 men, 5 women	**Ph.D.s:** 83%
Graduate: none	**Student/Faculty:** 17 to 1
Year: semesters	**Tuition:** $18,600
Application Deadline: open	**Room & Board:** $5000
Freshman Class: 1480 applied, 1128 accepted, 353 enrolled	
ACT: 22	**COMPETITIVE**

Monmouth College, founded in 1853, is a private liberal arts institution affiliated with the Presbyterian Church (U.S.A.). The library contains 181,875 volumes, 237,502 microform items, and 7818 audio/video tapes/CDs, and subscribes to 547 periodicals. Computerized library services include the card catalog, interlibrary loans, and database searching. Special learning facilities include a learning resource center, art gallery, radio station, TV station, a biology field station on the Mississippi River, and a prairie plot of native flora. The 70-acre campus is in a small town 45 miles south of Rock Island and Moline. Including any residence halls, there are 26 buildings.

Student Life: 89% of undergraduates are from Illinois. Students are from 20 states, 18 foreign countries, and Canada. 88% are from public schools. 87% are white. 35% are Protestant; 22% Catholic; 20% claim no religious affiliation. The average age of freshmen is 18; all undergraduates, 20. 19% do not continue beyond their first year; 62% remain to graduate.

Housing: 1196 students can be accommodated in college housing, which includes single-sex and coed dorms and fraternity houses. In addition, there are honors houses and special-interest houses. On-campus housing is guaranteed for all 4 years. 96% of students live on campus; of those, 75% remain on campus on weekends. All students may keep cars.

Activities: 22% of men belong to 3 national fraternities; 24% of women belong to 3 national sororities. There are 60 groups on campus, including art, bagpipe band, band, cheerleading, chess, choir, chorale, chorus, computers, dance, debate, drama, ethnic, gay, honors, international, jazz band, literary magazine, musical theater, newspaper, photography, political, professional, radio and TV, religious, social, social service, and student government. Popular campus events include Greek Week, Women's Week, and Family Weekend.

Sports: There are 10 intercollegiate sports for men and 10 for women, and 14 intramural sports for men and 14 for women. Facilities include a track, 2 gyms, weight rooms, a fitness/wellness center, football, baseball, soccer, and softball fields, a climbing wall, a pool and sauna, a putting green, all-purpose indoor courts, and an outdoor tennis stadium.

Disabled Students: 20% of the campus is accessible. Wheelchair ramps, elevators, special parking, specially equipped rest rooms, special class scheduling, lowered drinking fountains, and special housing are available.

Services: Counseling and information services are available, as is tutoring in most subjects. There is remedial math, reading, and writing.

Campus Safety and Security: Measures include self-defense education, security escort services, informal discussions, and pamphlets/posters/films. There are emergency telephones, lighted pathways/sidewalks, and 12-hour foot and vehicle patrols.

Programs of Study: MC confers the B.A. degree. Bachelor's degrees are awarded in BIOLOGICAL SCIENCE (biochemistry and biology/biological science), BUSINESS (accounting, business administration and management, business economics, international business management, and management information systems), COMMUNICATIONS AND THE ARTS (art, classics, communications, dramatic arts, English, French, Greek, Latin, music, and Spanish), COMPUTER AND PHYSICAL SCIENCE (chemistry, computer programming, computer science, mathematics, and physics), EDUCATION (elementary, physical, and secondary), ENGINEERING AND ENVIRONMENTAL DESIGN (environmental science), SOCIAL SCIENCE (anthropology, biopsychology, history, international studies, philosophy, political science/government, psychology, religion, and sociology). Education, sciences, and business are the strongest academically. Business and education are the largest.

Required: To graduate, all students must complete 124 credit hours with a minimum GPA of 2.0. A major program must be completed with a minimum of C in all courses. Students must also fulfill 38 hours of the general education program and pass Introduction to Liberal Arts and a senior seminar.

Special: Monmouth offers 3-2 nursing programs with Rush Hospital, a 3-2 engineering degree with Washington University, Case Western Reserve, and the University of Southern California, and B.A.-B.S. degrees in nursing and engineering. Students have the opportunity to study in more than 15 countries in Europe, Asia, and Africa. Internships, a Washington semester, and dual and student-designed synoptic majors are available. There are 12 national honor societies, a freshman honors program, and 8 departmental honors programs.

Faculty/Classroom: 54% of faculty are male; 46%, female. All teach undergraduates. The average class size in an introductory lecture is 22; in a laboratory, 15; and in a regular course, 20.

Admissions: 76% of the 2003-2004 applicants were accepted. The ACT scores for the 2003-2004 freshman class were: 28% below 21, 32% between 21 and 23, 22% between 24 and 26, 11% between 27 and 28, and 7% above 28. 33% of the current freshmen were in the top fifth of their class; 65% were in the top two fifths. 10 freshmen graduated first in their class.

Requirements: The SAT I or ACT is required, with a recommended minimum composite score of 900 on the SAT I or 19 on the ACT. Applicants must be graduates of accredited high schools and have completed 4 years of English, 3 each of math and social studies, 2 each of science, including 1 of lab, and a foreign language, and 1 of history. A GED is also accepted. MC requires applicants to be in the upper 50% of their class. A GPA of 2.5 is required. AP credits are accepted. Important factors in the admissions decision are advanced placement or honor courses, evidence of special talent, and recommendations by school officials.

Procedure: Freshmen are admitted fall and spring. Entrance exams should be taken by the spring of the junior year. There is a rolling admissions plan. Application deadlines are open. Notification is sent on a rolling basis. Applications are accepted on-line through the college's web site and Illinois Mentor.

Transfer: 54 transfer students enrolled in 2002-2003. Students must have a minimum GPA of 2.5. A minimum composite score of 900 on the SAT I or 19 on the ACT is recommended. 62 credits of 124 required for the bachelor's degree must be completed at MC.

Visiting: There are regularly scheduled orientations for prospective students, including tours, admissions and financial aid discussions, faculty appointments, lunch and entertainment, and a talk with the president. There are guides for informal visits and visitors may sit in on classes and stay overnight. To schedule a visit, contact the Admission Office.

Financial Aid: In 2003-2004, 98% of all full-time freshmen and 94% of continuing full-time students received some form of financial aid. 83% of all full-time students received need-based aid. The average freshman award was $15,772. Need-based scholarships or need-based grants averaged $12,808; and need-based self-help aid (loans and jobs) averaged $4278. 36% of undergraduates work part time. Average annual earnings from campus work are $900. The average financial indebtedness of the 2003 graduate was $18,286. The FAFSA is required. The priority date for freshman financial aid applications for fall entry is March 1. The deadline for filing freshman financial aid applications for fall entry is May 1.

International Students: There are 20 international students enrolled. The school actively recruits these students. They must score 550 on the written TOEFL.

Computers: The mainframe is an HP 9000. There are also more than 250 PCs available, and individual rooms are wired for use. All students may access the system 24 hours a day. There are no time limits and no fees.

Graduates: From July 1, 2002 to June 30, 2003, 224 bachelor's degrees were awarded. The most popular majors were business (29%), education (25%), and communication/theater arts (16%). In an average class, 55% graduate in 4 years or less, 60% graduate in 5 years or less, and 62% graduate in 6 years or less. 59 companies recruited on campus in 2002-2003. Of the 2002 graduating class, 28% were enrolled in graduate school within 6 months of graduation and 99% were employed.

Admissions Contact: John Klockentager, Vice President of Admission. A video is available. E-mail: *admit@monm.edu*
Web: *www.monm.edu*

NAES COLLEGE
Chicago, IL 60659
E-2
(773) 761-5000; Fax: (773) 761-3808

Full-time: 65 men and women	Faculty: 3
Part-time: 15 men and women	Ph.D.s: 20%
Graduate: none	Student/Faculty: 22 to 1
Year: semesters, summer session	Tuition: $5140
Application Deadline: open	Room & Board: n/app
Freshman Class: n/av	
SAT I or ACT: not required	**SPECIAL**

NAES College, founded in 1974, is an independent commuter institution offering a program in community studies for Native Americans employed

in Indian programs and agencies. The multicampus college has evening classes. Figures in the above capsule and in this profile are approximate. There are 4 undergraduate schools. The library contains 13,000 volumes, 5 microform items, and 500 audio/video tapes/CDs, and subscribes to 55 periodicals. Computerized library services include the card catalog. The 1-acre campus is in an urban area in Chicago. There is one building.

Student Life: All are from public schools. 96% are Native American/Eskimo. The average age of freshmen is 34; all undergraduates, 37. 85% of freshmen remain to graduate.

Housing: There are no residence halls. All students commute. Alcohol is not permitted. All students may keep cars.

Activities: There are no fraternities or sororities.

Sports: There is no sports program at NAES.

Disabled Students: All of the campus is accessible. Special class scheduling are available.

Services: Counseling and information services are available, as is tutoring in most subjects.

Campus Safety and Security: Measures include pamphlets/posters/films, emergency telephones, and lighted pathways/sidewalks.

Programs of Study: NAES confers the B.A. degree. Bachelor's degrees are awarded in SOCIAL SCIENCE (community services).

Required: To graduate, students must maintain a 2.0 GPA and complete 120 credit hours, including a core curriculum of 6 6-credit courses, with 57 hours in the major. Students are required to complete courses in art, math, science, English literature, tribal language, composition, and speech, and demonstrate computer competence. A field project in the American Indian community is also required.

Special: Cross-registration with Northeastern Illinois University is available and students may receive credit for prior learning.

Faculty/Classroom: 61% of faculty are male; 39%, female. The average class size in an introductory lecture is 10 and in a regular course, 10.

Requirements: The SAT I or ACT is not required. Applicants must be graduates of an accredited secondary school or have a GED certificate and be employed or a volunteer at an Indian organization or agency that serves Indian people in the community where the campus is located or in which the student lives. Applicants must be at least 24 years old or have an associate of art or science degree, or have completed at least 60 semester hours of transferable credit. CLEP credit is accepted. Important factors in the admissions decision are parents or siblings attending the school, advanced placement or honor courses, and personality/intangible qualities.

Procedure: Freshmen are admitted to all sessions. There is an early admissions plan. There is a rolling admissions plan. Application deadlines are open.

Transfer: Transfer students must satisfy the same requirements as other applicants. 54 of 120 credits required for the bachelor's degree must be completed at NAES.

Visiting: There are regularly scheduled orientations for prospective students. Visitors may sit in on classes. To schedule a visit, contact the campus administrator.

Financial Aid: NAES is a member of CSS. The CSS Profile, FAFSA, FFS, or SFS is required. Check with the school for current deadlines.

Computers: PCs are available in class and for individual use. All students may access the system 9 A.M. to 8 P.M. There are no time limits and no fees.

Admissions Contact: Campus Administrator.
Web: *www.naes.indian.com*

NATIONAL-LOUIS UNIVERSITY
Chicago, IL 60603
E-1
(312) 621-9650; (888) NLU TODAY

Full-time: 584 men, 1335 women	Faculty: 286
Part-time: 107 men, 508 women	Ph.D.s: n/av
Graduate: 1085 men, 4046 women	Student/Faculty: 7 to 1
Year: quarters, summer session	Tuition: $16,240
Application Deadline: open	Room & Board: n/app
Freshman Class: n/av	
SAT I or ACT: required	**LESS COMPETITIVE**

National-Louis University, founded in 1886, is an independent institution offering programs in education, liberal arts, health science, business, and human services for the traditional and the adult student. 4 Chicago-area campuses, in Evanston, Wheaton, Wheeling, and the Chicago Loop, accommodate commuters, and academic centers in Elgin, Illinois, Virginia, Missouri, Georgia, Florida, Wisconsin, and Germany offer selected programs for working adults. Some information in this capsule and profile is approximate. There are 3 undergraduate and 3 graduate schools. In addition to regional accreditation, NLU has baccalaureate program accreditation with CAHEA. The library contains 153,000 volumes, 925,978 microform items, and 5043 audio/video tapes/CDs, and subscribes to 3498 periodicals. Computerized library services include the card catalog, interlibrary loans, and database searching. Special learning facilities include a learning resource center and a pre-K through 8 elementary demonstration school. The 12-acre campus is in a suburban area 12 miles north of Chicago. Including any residence halls, there are 3 buildings.

Student Life: 99% of undergraduates are from Illinois. Students are from 8 states and 16 foreign countries. 27% are white; 25% African American. The average age of freshmen is 25; all undergraduates, 33. 39% do not continue beyond their first year.

Housing: 160 students can be accommodated in college housing, which includes coed dorms. On-campus housing is available on a first-come, first-served basis. Priority is given to out-of-town students. 95% of students commute. Upperclassmen may keep cars.

Activities: There are no fraternities or sororities. There are 30 groups on campus, including chorus, drama, ethnic, honors, musical theater, newspaper, professional, religious, student government, and yearbook. Popular campus events include a ski trip and Valentine's Day Dance.

Sports: There is no sports program at NLU. Facilities include a 300-seat gym, a 700-seat auditorium, and a swimming pool.

Disabled Students: 90% of the campus is accessible. Wheelchair ramps, elevators, and special parking are available.

Services: Counseling and information services are available, as is tutoring in most subjects. There is remedial math, reading, and writing. A center for academic development provides services to academically at-risk students.

Campus Safety and Security: Measures include security escort services, informal discussions, pamphlets/posters/films, and lighted pathways/sidewalks. There are security guards when campus buildings are open.

Programs of Study: NLU confers B.A. and B.S. degrees. Master's and doctoral degrees are also awarded. Bachelor's degrees are awarded in BIOLOGICAL SCIENCE (biology/biological science), BUSINESS (accounting, business administration and management, and management science), COMMUNICATIONS AND THE ARTS (English and fine arts), COMPUTER AND PHYSICAL SCIENCE (information sciences and systems, mathematics, and science), EDUCATION (early childhood and elementary), HEALTH PROFESSIONS (health care administration, medical laboratory technology, radiation therapy, and respiratory therapy), SOCIAL SCIENCE (anthropology, crosscultural studies, human development, human services, psychology, and social science). Education and business are the strongest academically. Management and education are the largest.

Required: Students must take courses in humanities, natural sciences, and behavioral sciences, for a minimum of 50 hours in general education requirements. Other course requirements vary by program. All students must pass an English competency writing exam. A minimum 2.0 GPA and 180 quarter hours, including 45 in the major, are required to graduate. There is a 45 quarter-hour residency requirement.

Special: NLU offers credit by exam and for experiential learning, internships in teaching and human services, and limited nondegree and pass/fail options. There are special completion programs for adults in management, applied behavioral science, and health care leadership. In addition, NLU offers several programs in the field as well as customized programs for working adults. There is 1 national honor society, including Phi Beta Kappa.

Faculty/Classroom: 33% of faculty are male; 67%, female. No introductory courses are taught by graduate students. The average class size in an introductory lecture is 16 and in a regular course, 13.

Requirements: The SAT I or ACT is required for first-time freshmen under 21 years of age. A minimum composite score of 750 on the SAT I or 19 on the ACT is required. Applicants should graduate from an accredited secondary school with 15 academic credits, including 4 in English, 3 in social studies, and 2 each in math and science. The GED is accepted. 2 letters of recommendation, with 1 from the high school counselor recommended, are required; an interview is strongly encouraged. NLU requires applicants to be in the upper 50% of their class. AP and CLEP credits are accepted. Important factors in the admissions decision are recommendations by school officials, leadership record, and evidence of special talent.

Procedure: Freshmen are admitted fall, winter, and spring. Entrance exams should be taken the winter before application. There is a deferred admissions plan. Application deadlines are open. Application fee is $95.

Transfer: 1046 transfer students enrolled in 2002-2003. A minimum GPA of 2.0 is required. Applicants must be in good standing at the college previously attended. Official transcripts from previously attended colleges and letters of recommendation are required. Personal interviews are strongly encouraged. 45 of 180 credits required for the bachelor's degree must be completed at NLU.

Visiting: There are regularly scheduled orientations for prospective students, including campus tours, meeting with students and key administrators, attending typical campus entertainment, and visiting classes. There are guides for informal visits and visitors may sit in on classes. To schedule a visit, contact the Undergraduate Enrollment Office.

Financial Aid: In a recent year, need-based scholarships or need-based grants averaged $9968. The average financial indebtedness of a recent graduate was $8840. NLU is a member of CSS. The FAFSA is required. Check with the school for current deadlines.

International Students: They must take the college's own test.

Computers: The mainframe is an IBM. There are more than 200 Macs and PCs available in computer labs located at the 4 Illinois campuses. Computer access is available at out-of-state campuses. All students may access the system. There are no time limits and no fees. It is recommended that all students have a PC. Discounts are available for IBM, Mac, and Apple computers.

Graduates: From July 1, 2002 to June 30, 2003, 902 bachelor's degrees were awarded. The most popular majors were management (48%), applied behavorial sciences (20%), and elementary education (9%). In an average class, 3% graduate in 3 years or less, 23% graduate in 4 years or less, 32% graduate in 5 years or less, and 44% graduate in 6 years or less.

Admissions Contact: Patricia Petillo, Admissions Director.
E-mail: *nluinfo@nl.edu* Web: *www.nl.edu*

NORTH CENTRAL COLLEGE

E-2

Naperville, IL 60566

(630) 637-5800
(800) 411-1861; Fax: (630) 637-5121

Full-time: 734 men, 1067 women	**Faculty:** 125; IIA, av$
Part-time: 112 men, 173 women	**Ph.D.s:** 86%
Graduate: 182 men, 190 women	**Student/Faculty:** 14 to 1
Year: trimesters, summer session	**Tuition:** $19,281
Application Deadline: open	**Room & Board:** $6375
Freshman Class: 1654 applied, 1171 accepted, 408 enrolled	
SAT I Verbal/Math: 570/580	**ACT:** 24 **VERY COMPETITIVE**

North Central College, founded in 1861, is a private liberal arts institution affiliated with the United Methodist Church. In addition to regional accreditation, North Central has baccalaureate program accreditation with ACS. The library contains 149,181 volumes, 205,396 microform items, and 2212 audio/video tapes/CDs, and subscribes to 648 periodicals. Computerized library services include the card catalog, interlibrary loans, and database searching. Special learning facilities include a learning resource center, art gallery, radio station, an advising center, a foreign language lab, and a writing center. The 54-acre campus is in a suburban area 30 miles west of Chicago. Including any residence halls, there are 24 buildings.

Student Life: 91% of undergraduates are from Illinois. Students are from 23 states and 18 foreign countries. 87% are white. 38% are Protestant; 31% Catholic; 29% claim no religious affiliation. The average age of freshmen is 18; all undergraduates, 23. 23% do not continue beyond their first year; 66% remain to graduate.

Housing: 1021 students can be accommodated in college housing, which includes single-sex and coed dorms and on-campus apartments. There are also learning communities. On-campus housing is available on a lottery system for upperclassmen. 58% of students live on campus; of those, 75% remain on campus on weekends. All students may keep cars.

Activities: There are no fraternities or sororities. There are 35 groups on campus, including art, band, cheerleading, choir, chorale, chorus, dance, drama, ethnic, gay, honors, international, jazz band, literary magazine, musical theater, newspaper, pep band, photography, political, professional, radio and TV, religious, social, social service, student government, and yearbook. Popular campus events include Family Weekend, Winter Carnival, and Arts and Letters Festival.

Sports: There are 10 intercollegiate sports for men and 9 for women, and 4 intramural sports for men and 4 for women. Facilities include indoor and outdoor tracks, a weight room, football and baseball stadiums, soccer fields, a swimming pool, tennis courts, an athletic training facility, and a human performance lab.

Disabled Students: 60% of the campus is accessible. Wheelchair ramps, elevators, special parking, specially equipped rest rooms, special class scheduling, lowered drinking fountains, and lowered telephones are available.

Services: Counseling and information services are available, as is tutoring in most subjects. There is remedial math, reading, and writing.

Campus Safety and Security: Measures include 24-hour foot and vehicle patrol, self-defense education, security escort services, and informal discussions. There are pamphlets/posters/films, emergency telephones, and lighted pathways/sidewalks.

Programs of Study: North Central confers B.A. and B.S. degrees. Master's degrees are also awarded. Bachelor's degrees are awarded in BIOLOGICAL SCIENCE (biochemistry and biology/biological science), BUSINESS (accounting, banking and finance, business administration and management, international business management, and marketing/retailing/merchandising), COMMUNICATIONS AND THE ARTS (broadcasting, communications, English, fine arts, French, German, Japanese, music, Spanish, and speech/debate/rhetoric), COMPUTER AND PHYSICAL SCIENCE (actuarial science, applied mathematics, chemistry, computer science, mathematics, and physics), EDUCATION (elementary and secondary), ENGINEERING AND ENVIRONMENTAL DESIGN (preengineering), HEALTH PROFESSIONS (predentistry, premedicine, and preveterinary science), SOCIAL SCIENCE (anthropology, classical/ancient civilization, economics, history, philosophy, political science/

government, prelaw, psychology, religion, social science, and sociology). Business and education are the largest.

Required: All students must complete a general education core, including 9 hours each in humanities and fine arts, and social sciences, 6.5 hours in life and physical sciences, 3 to 6 hours in composition, and 3 hours each in speech communication and math. A GPA of 2.0 and a total of 120 credit hours are required for graduation, with 24 to 51 credits taken in the major.

Special: North Central offers co-op programs in medical technology, nursing, and physical therapy, cross-registration with Benedictine University, Elmhurst College, and Aurora University, a Washington semester, and study abroad. Internships in most subject areas, work-study programs, a 3-2 engineering degree with Washington and Marquette Universities and the Universities of Minnesota and Illinois at Urbana-Champaign, credit for life experience, and nondegree study are available. Dual majors, a general studies degree, accelerated degree programs, and student-designed majors are also offered. There are 2 national honor societies and a freshman honors program; all departments have honors programs.

Faculty/Classroom: 54% of faculty are male; 46%, female. All teach undergraduates; 40% also do research. No introductory courses are taught by graduate students. The average class size in an introductory lecture is 23; in a laboratory, 17; and in a regular course, 19.

Admissions: 71% of the 2003-2004 applicants were accepted. The SAT I scores for the 2003-2004 freshman class were: Verbal--18% below 500, 39% between 500 and 599, 33% between 600 and 700, and 10% above 700; Math--16% below 500, 37% between 500 and 599, 35% between 600 and 700, and 12% above 700. The ACT scores were 16% below 21, 24% between 21 and 23, 30% between 24 and 26, 16% between 27 and 28, and 13% above 28. 46% of the current freshmen were in the top fifth of their class; 75% were in the top two fifths. 7 freshmen graduated first in their class.

Requirements: The SAT I or ACT is required, with a minimum composite score of 20 on the ACT or 930 on the SAT I. Applicants must be graduates of an accredited secondary school. The GED is accepted. The recommended secondary school courses are 4 years of English, 3 each of math and science, and 2 each of a foreign language, history, and social studies. The school recommends an interview for all applicants. An essay is required. North Central requires applicants to be in the upper 50% of their class. A GPA of 2.0 is required. AP and CLEP credits are accepted. Important factors in the admissions decision are recommendations by school officials, leadership record, and evidence of special talent.

Procedure: Freshmen are admitted fall, winter, and spring. Entrance exams should be taken in the spring of the junior year or the fall of the senior year. There is a deferred admissions plan and a rolling admissions plan. Application deadlines are open. The fall 2003 application fee was $25. Notification is sent on a rolling basis. Applications are accepted on computer disk and on-line.

Transfer: 179 transfer students enrolled in a recent year. Applicants need a 2.25 GPA from the previous school and an interview. 30 credits of 120 required for the bachelor's degree must be completed at North Central.

Visiting: There are regularly scheduled orientations for prospective students, including orientation sessions for all freshmen during the summer. There are guides for informal visits and visitors may sit in on classes and stay overnight. To schedule a visit, contact the Office of Admissions.

Financial Aid: In 2003-2004, 94% of all full-time freshmen and 80% of continuing full-time students received some form of financial aid. 65% of full-time freshmen and 43% of continuing full-time students received need-based aid. The average freshman award was $14,622. 33% of undergraduates work part time. Average annual earnings from campus work are $1150. The average financial indebtedness of the 2003 graduate was $13,195. North Central is a member of CSS. The FAFSA and the college's own financial statement are required. The deadline for filing freshman financial aid applications for fall entry is September 1.

International Students: There are 44 international students enrolled. The school actively recruits these students. They must score 500 on the written TOEFL and also take the SAT I or ACT.

Computers: The mainframe is an HP L2000. Students may use computers located in the on-campus center, computer labs, classrooms, and the library. There are a total of 200 terminals and PCs available to students. All residence halls are connected to the campus network. All students may access the system 7 A.M. to midnight in the computer center or at any time from residence hall rooms and labs. There are no time limits. The fee is $225 per year for residents and $60 per year for commuting students. It is strongly recommended that all students have a personal computer.

Graduates: From July 1, 2002 to June 30, 2003, 515 bachelor's degrees were awarded. The most popular majors were business (23%), social sciences and history (14%), and speech (11%). In an average class, 1% graduate in 3 years or less, 59% graduate in 4 years or less, 67% graduate in 5 years or less, and 68% graduate in 6 years or less. 18 companies recruited on campus in 2002-2003. Of the 2002 graduating class,

17% were enrolled in graduate school within 6 months of graduation and 69% were employed.

Admissions Contact: Marguerite Waters, Dean of Admission. A video is available. E-mail: *ncadm@noctrl.edu* Web: *www.noctrl.edu*

NORTH PARK UNIVERSITY

E-2

Chicago, IL 60625-4987   (312) 583-2700; (800) 888-6728

Full-time: 495 men, 760 women	**Faculty:** 81
Part-time: 105 men, 215 women	**Ph.D.s:** 41%
Graduate: 270 men, 485 women	**Student/Faculty:** 15 to 1
Year: semesters, summer session	**Tuition:** $17,790
Application Deadline: open	**Room & Board:** $6240
Freshman Class: n/av	
SAT I or ACT: recommended	**COMPETITIVE**

North Park University, founded in 1891, is a private liberal arts college affiliated with the Evangelical Covenant Church offering undergraduate programs in the arts and sciences, business, music, and education. There are 5 undergraduate and 3 graduate schools. Figures in the above capsule and in this profile are approximate. In addition to regional accreditation, North Park has baccalaureate program accreditation with NLN. The 2 libraries contain 220,000 volumes, 93,000 microform items, and 6500 audio/video tapes/CDs, and subscribe to 950 periodicals. Computerized library services include the card catalog, interlibrary loans, and database searching. Special learning facilities include a learning resource center, art gallery, and an herbarium. The 30-acre campus is in an urban area 10 miles north of downtown Chicago. Including any residence halls, there are 25 buildings.

Student Life: 68% of undergraduates are from Illinois. Students are from 38 states, 38 foreign countries, and Canada. 55% are white. 57% are Protestant; 16% claim no religious affiliation; 13% Catholic. The average age of freshmen is 18; all undergraduates, 21. 30% do not continue beyond their first year; 65% remain to graduate.

Housing: 943 students can be accommodated in college housing, which includes single-sex dorms, on-campus apartments, off-campus apartments, and married-student housing. In addition, there are honors houses, language houses, special-interest houses, and an international living center. On-campus housing is guaranteed for all 4 years. 60% of students live on campus; of those, 90% remain on campus on weekends. Alcohol is not permitted. All students may keep cars.

Activities: There are no fraternities or sororities. There are 40 groups on campus, including art, band, cheerleading, choir, chorale, chorus, computers, drama, ethnic, honors, international, jazz band, literary magazine, musical theater, newspaper, opera, orchestra, pep band, photography, political, professional, religious, social, social service, student government, symphony, and yearbook. Popular campus events include dances, concerts, and film festivals.

Sports: There are 8 intercollegiate sports for men and 8 for women, and 5 intramural sports for men and 5 for women. Facilities include football, baseball, track, and soccer fields, tennis courts, a weight room, a gym, a fitness center, and a swimming pool.

Disabled Students: 90% of the campus is accessible. Wheelchair ramps, elevators, specially equipped rest rooms, lowered drinking fountains, and lowered telephones are available.

Services: Counseling and information services are available, as is tutoring in every subject. There is a reader service for the blind and remedial math, reading, and writing. An extended orientation program is available.

Campus Safety and Security: Measures include 24-hour foot and vehicle patrol, self-defense education, security escort services, and informal discussions. There are pamphlets/posters/films, emergency telephones, and lighted pathways/sidewalks.

Programs of Study: North Park confers B.A., B.S., B.Mus., and B.S.Med.Tech. degrees. Master's and doctoral degrees are also awarded. Bachelor's degrees are awarded in BIOLOGICAL SCIENCE (biology/biological science), BUSINESS (accounting, banking and finance, business administration and management, international business management, and marketing/retailing/merchandising), COMMUNICATIONS AND THE ARTS (communications, English, music, and Spanish), COMPUTER AND PHYSICAL SCIENCE (chemistry, mathematics, and physics), EDUCATION (early childhood, elementary, and secondary), HEALTH PROFESSIONS (medical laboratory technology, nursing, occupational therapy, physical therapy, predentistry, and premedicine), SOCIAL SCIENCE (anthropology, economics, history, international relations, philosophy, political science/government, prelaw, psychology, religion, and sociology). Music, sciences, and premedicine are the strongest academically. Nursing, education, and psychology are the largest.

Required: Students must successfully complete 120 semester hours with a minimum 2.0 GPA. The required number of hours in the major varies. Students must meet a general requirement of 17 core courses.

Special: Cross-registration with Christian College Coalition schools is possible. Opportunities are provided for a co-op program in occupational therapy, internships, work-study, a Washington semester, 3-2 engineering degrees, accelerated degree programs in organization management and nursing, credit by examination, dual majors, student-designed majors, B.A.-B.S. degrees, pass/fail options, and study abroad. There are 6 national honor societies, a freshman honors program, and 25 departmental honors programs.

Faculty/Classroom: 50% of faculty are male; 50%, female. All teach undergraduates. The average class size in an introductory lecture is 35; in a laboratory, 20; and in a regular course, 25.

Admissions: There was 1 National Merit finalist and 1 semifinalist in a recent year.

Requirements: The SAT I or ACT is recommended. In addition, graduation from an accredited secondary school is required; a GED will be accepted. Students should have completed course work in a foreign language, 4 years of English, and 3 years each of math, science, and social studies. Recommendations from teachers should also be submitted. An essay and an audition are required. An interview is recommended. A GPA of 2.0 is required. AP and CLEP credits are accepted. Important factors in the admissions decision are evidence of special talent, personality/intangible qualities, and parents or siblings attending the school.

Procedure: Freshmen are admitted to all sessions. Entrance exams should be taken during spring of the junior year or fall of the senior year. There is a rolling admissions plan. Application deadlines are open. The fall 2003 application fee was $20.

Transfer: 123 transfer students enrolled in a recent year. To be eligible for transfer admission, students must submit a reference from a faculty member, counselor, or administrator, and official transcripts from the previous college, and must have maintained a minimum GPA of 2.0. An interview is also recommended. 30 of 120 credits required for the bachelor's degree must be completed at North Park.

Visiting: There are regularly scheduled orientations for prospective students. There are guides for informal visits and visitors may sit in on classes and stay overnight. To schedule a visit, contact Campus Visitation Coordinator at (312) 244-5500.

Financial Aid: In a recent year, 98% of all full-time freshmen received some form of financial aid. 77% of full-time freshmen received need-based aid. The average freshman award was $16,100. The average financial indebtedness of a recent graduate was $11,800. The CSS Profile or FFS, the college's own financial statement, and student and parent federal income tax returns are required. Check with the school for current deadlines.

International Students: There were 70 international students enrolled in a recent year. The school actively recruits these students. They must score 550 on the written TOEFL.

Computers: 120 Mac and IBM PCs are in the computer lab. All dorm rooms, public areas, classrooms, and the library are wired or have publicly accessible computers. All students may access the system at any time. There are no time limits and no fees.

Graduates: In a recent year, 311 bachelor's degrees were awarded. The most popular majors were organization management (13%), biology (9%), and business administration (7%). In an average class, 60% graduate in 4 years or less, 65% graduate in 5 years or less, and 65% graduate in 6 years or less. 300 companies recruited on campus in a recent year.

Admissions Contact: John Baworowski, Vice President for Admissions. Web: *http://www.northpark.edu/afao*

NORTHEASTERN ILLINOIS UNIVERSITY   E-2
Chicago, IL 60625   (773) 442-4046; Fax: (773) 442-4020

Full-time: 1810 men, 2910 women	**Faculty:** 346; IIA, -$
Part-time: 1375 men, 2225 women	**Ph.D.s:** 79%
Graduate: 825 men, 1795 women	**Student/Faculty:** 14 to 1
Year: semesters, summer session	**Tuition:** $3166 ($5806)
Application Deadline: see profile	**Room & Board:** n/app
Freshman Class: n/av	
ACT: required	**NONCOMPETITIVE**

Northeastern Illinois University, founded in 1867, is a public liberal arts institution offering degree programs in arts and sciences, business management, and education. There are 4 undergraduate schools and 1 graduate school. Figures in the above capsule and in this profile are approximate. In addition to regional accreditation, Northeastern has baccalaureate program accreditation with NCATE. The library contains 459,191 volumes, 749,370 microform items, and 1001 audio/video tapes/CDs, and subscribes to 73,503 periodicals. Computerized library services include interlibrary loans and database searching. Special learning facilities include a learning resource center, art gallery, and radio station. The 63-acre campus is in an urban area in northwest Chicago. There are 10 buildings.

Student Life: 99% of undergraduates are from Illinois. Students are from 22 states and 9 foreign countries. 55% are from public schools. 44% are white; 27% Hispanic; 14% Asian American; 13% African American. The average age of freshmen is 20; all undergraduates, 28. 45% do not continue beyond their first year; 36% remain to graduate.

Housing: There are no residence halls. All students commute. Alcohol is not permitted. All students may keep cars.

Activities: There is 1 local sorority. There are no fraternities. There are 50 groups on campus, including art, band, cheerleading, chess, choir, chorus, computers, dance, drama, ethnic, film, gay, honors, international, jazz band, literary magazine, musical theater, newspaper, opera, orchestra, photography, political, professional, radio and TV, religious, social, social service, and student government. Popular campus events include International Day, fairs, and the Visiting Lecture Series.

Sports: There are 10 intramural sports for men and 10 for women. Facilities include basketball, tennis, and racquetball courts, indoor and outdoor tracks, a pool, a weight room, and baseball and softball fields.

Disabled Students: 94% of the campus is accessible. Wheelchair ramps, elevators, special parking, specially equipped rest rooms, special class scheduling, lowered drinking fountains, lowered telephones, and a Handicap Education Liaison Program (HELP) that allows priority registration are available.

Services: Counseling and information services are available, as is tutoring in most subjects. There is a reader service for the blind and remedial math, reading, and writing.

Campus Safety and Security: Measures include 24-hour foot and vehicle patrol, security escort services, pamphlets/posters/films, and emergency telephones. There are lighted pathways/sidewalks.

Programs of Study: Northeastern confers B.A. and B.S. degrees. Master's degrees are also awarded. Bachelor's degrees are awarded in AGRICULTURE (environmental studies), BIOLOGICAL SCIENCE (biology/biological science), BUSINESS (accounting, business administration and management, and marketing/retailing/merchandising), COMMUNICATIONS AND THE ARTS (English, fine arts, French, music, Spanish, and speech/debate/rhetoric), COMPUTER AND PHYSICAL SCIENCE (chemistry, computer science, earth science, mathematics, and physics), EDUCATION (bilingual/bicultural, early childhood, elementary, physical, secondary, and special), SOCIAL SCIENCE (anthropology, criminal justice, economics, geography, history, philosophy, political science/government, psychology, social work, and sociology). Education, business, and computer science are the strongest academically. Business and education are the largest.

Required: All students are required to take at least 120 semester hours, including 39 hours of foundational general education, 30 to 60 hours in the major, and 12 hours each in social and natural sciences, 9 in humanities, and 6 in fine arts. A 2.0 overall GPA is required for graduation. An overall GPA and college major GPA of 2.5 are required within the College of Business Management and the College of Education.

Special: Alternative degree and nondegree programs are available, as is cross-registration with Governors State University. Some departments offer internships. A dual major in elementary and early childhood or special education is offered. There are pass/fail options. Honors classes are available. There are 12 national honor societies, a freshman honors program, and 18 departmental honors programs.

Faculty/Classroom: 63% of faculty are male; 37%, female. 90% teach undergraduates. No introductory courses are taught by graduate students. The average class size in an introductory lecture is 80; in a laboratory, 20; and in a regular course, 30.

Requirements: The ACT is required. In addition, for freshmen under 21 years of age. A minimum ACT composite score of 19 is required. Applicants must have graduated from a regionally accredited high school or passed the GED. High school preparation should total at least 12 credits, including 4 years in English, 3 each in math, sciences, and social studies, and 2 in foreign language, music, art, fine arts, or vocational education (only 1 vocational course is accepted). Northeastern requires applicants to be in the upper 50% of their class. AP and CLEP credits are accepted. Important factors in the admissions decision are evidence of special talent, advanced placement or honor courses, and recommendations by school officials.

Procedure: Freshmen are admitted to all sessions. There is a deferred admissions plan. There is a rolling admissions plan. Check with the school for current application deadlines. The college accepts all applicants. Notification is sent on a rolling basis.

Transfer: Applicants are considered if they have completed at least 30 semester hours of study with a C average. Those with fewer than 30 hours of credit must meet freshman admissions requirements. 30 of 120 credits required for the bachelor's degree must be completed at Northeastern.

Visiting: There are guides for informal visits and visitors may sit in on classes. To schedule a visit, contact the School and College Relations Office at (773) 442-4050 or *admrec@neiu.edu*.

Financial Aid: The FAFSA and the college's own financial statement are required. Check with the school for current application deadlines.

International Students: They must score 500 on the written TOEFL or 173 on the electronic version.

Computers: There are 35 IBM terminals in the library and science building, and 100 Macs and IBM PCs in classroom buildings. Those students enrolled in specific courses or doing research may access the system posted times, which vary from 12 to 15 hours daily. There are no time limits and no fees.

Admissions Contact: Miriam Rivera, Director of Admissions and Records. E-mail: *mrivera@neiu.edu* Web: *www.neiu.edu*

NORTHERN ILLINOIS UNIVERSITY
D-2
DeKalb, IL 60115
(815) 753-0446
(800) 892-3050; Fax: (815) 753-1783

Full-time: 7778 men, 8620 women	Faculty: 901; I, --$
Part-time: 871 men, 1006 women	Ph.D.s: 80%
Graduate: 2746 men, 4239 women	Student/Faculty: 18 to 1
Year: semesters, summer session	Tuition: $5974 ($10,052)
Application Deadline: August 1	Room & Board: $5498
Freshman Class: 16,128 applied, 10,028 accepted, 3253 enrolled	
ACT: 22	COMPETITIVE

Northern Illinois University, founded in 1895, is a publicly funded institution offering undergraduate and graduate programs in a comprehensive range of disciplines. There are 6 undergraduate and 2 graduate schools. In addition to regional accreditation, NIU has baccalaureate program accreditation with AACSB, ABET, ACEJMC, APTA, ASLA, CAHEA, NASAD, NASM, NCATE, and NLN. The 3 libraries contain 3,156,871 volumes, 3,009,974 microform items, and 54,783 audio/video tapes/CDs, and subscribe to 18,290 periodicals. Computerized library services include the card catalog, interlibrary loans, and database searching. Special learning facilities include an art gallery, radio station, TV station, and an anthropology museum. The 550-acre campus is in a small town 65 miles west of Chicago. Including any residence halls, there are 55 buildings.

Student Life: 95% of undergraduates are from Illinois. Students are from 50 states, 95 foreign countries, and Canada. 84% are from public schools. 73% are white; 13% African American. 47% are Catholic; 31% Protestant; 14% claim no religious affiliation. The average age of freshmen is 18; all undergraduates, 22. 23% do not continue beyond their first year; 77% remain to graduate.

Housing: 6000 students can be accommodated in college housing, which includes single-sex and coed dorms, on-campus apartments, and married-student housing. In addition, there are honors houses, language houses, and special-interest houses in law, computer science, music, political science, and health professions. On-campus housing is guaranteed for the freshman year only and is available on a first-come, first-served basis. All students may keep cars.

Activities: 15% of men belong to 22 national fraternities; 11% of women belong to 15 national sororities. There are 200 groups on campus, including art, band, cheerleading, chess, choir, chorale, chorus, computers, dance, drama, drill team, ethnic, film, gay, honors, international, jazz band, literary magazine, marching band, musical theater, newspaper, orchestra, pep band, photography, political, professional, radio and TV, religious, social, social service, student government, and symphony. Popular campus events include Unity in Diversity Week, Greek Week, and Springfest.

Sports: There are 8 intercollegiate sports for men and 8 for women, and 15 intramural sports for men and 15 for women. Facilities include a sports stadium, a recreation center and field house with facilities for basketball, volleyball, badminton, table tennis, tennis, racquetball/handball, and weight training, and 2 swimming pools.

Disabled Students: 75% of the campus is accessible. Wheelchair ramps, elevators, special parking, specially equipped rest rooms, special class scheduling, lowered drinking fountains, lowered telephones, special housing, and transportation are available.

Services: Formal tutoring is provided for eligible students.

Campus Safety and Security: Measures include 24-hour foot and vehicle patrol, self-defense education, security escort services, and shuttle buses. There are informal discussions, pamphlets/posters/films, emergency telephones, lighted pathways/sidewalks, and a bicycle patrol.

Programs of Study: NIU confers B.A., B.S., B.F.A., B.G.S., B.M., and B.S.Ed. degrees. Master's and doctoral degrees are also awarded. Bachelor's degrees are awarded in BIOLOGICAL SCIENCE (biology/biological science and nutrition), BUSINESS (accounting, banking and finance, business administration and management, and marketing/retailing/merchandising), COMMUNICATIONS AND THE ARTS (art, art history and appreciation, communications, dramatic arts, English, French, German, journalism, music, Russian, Spanish, and studio art), COMPUTER AND PHYSICAL SCIENCE (atmospheric sciences and meteorology, chemistry, computer science, geology, geoscience, information sciences and systems, mathematics, and physics), EDUCATION (art, early childhood, elementary, health, music, physical, and special), ENGINEERING AND ENVIRONMENTAL DESIGN (electrical/electronics engineering, industrial engineering, mechanical engineering, and technological management), HEALTH PROFESSIONS (clinical science, community health work, health science, nursing, and speech pathology/audiology), SOCIAL SCIENCE (anthropology, child care/child and family studies, dietetics, early childhood studies, economics, geography, history, liberal arts/general studies, philosophy, physical fitness/movement, political science/government, psychology, sociology, and textiles and clothing). Business, engineering, and sciences are the strongest academically. Business, education, and communications are the largest.

Required: To graduate, students must have a minimum of 124 credit hours and a minimum GPA of 2.0. All students must take English 103

and 104 and Communication Studies 100. In addition, they must take Math 101 or obtain at least a C in Math 155, 201, 206, 210, 211, or 229. The school also requires that students complete 29 hours in distributive studies areas, consisting of 9 to 12 hours in the humanities and arts, 7 to 11 hours in science and math, 6 to 9 hours in social science, and 3 to 6 hours in interdisciplinary studies.

Special: NIU offers internships in several areas. Students may study abroad in 30 countries. A physics/engineering degree is offered in cooperation with the University of Illinois. Either a B.A. or a B.S. may be obtained in the social science programs. Work-study programs, a general studies degree, co-op programs, pass/fail options, and student-designed majors are available. There are 5 national honor societies, a freshman honors program, and 18 departmental honors programs.

Faculty/Classroom: 55% of faculty are male; 45%, female. Graduate students teach 20% of introductory courses. The average class size in an introductory lecture is 37; in a laboratory, 17; and in a regular course, 30.

Admissions: 62% of the 2003-2004 applicants were accepted. The ACT scores for the 2003-2004 freshman class were: 37% below 21, 29% between 21 and 23, 21% between 24 and 26, 8% between 27 and 28, and 5% above 28.

Requirements: The ACT is required. In addition, students must have a minimum score of 19 on the ACT and be in the top half of their class, or have an ACT score of 23 and be in the upper two thirds of their class. Graduation from an accredited secondary school or satisfactory scores on the GED are required for admission. Secondary school courses must include 4 years of English and 2 to 3 years each of math, science, and social studies. In addition, students must have completed 1 to 2 years of art, film, foreign language, music, or theater. AP and CLEP credits are accepted.

Procedure: Freshmen are admitted to all sessions. Entrance exams should be taken during the junior year. There is a rolling admissions plan. Applications should be filed by August 1 for fall entry, December 15 for spring entry, and May 15 for summer entry. Notification is sent on a rolling basis. 496 applicants were on the 2003 waiting list. Applications are accepted on-line through the ACT College Connector.

Transfer: 2883 transfer students enrolled in 2002-2003. Transfer students with 24 or more credit hours must have a minimum GPA of 2.0. The core competency requirement in English, math, and speech must be satisfied by all transfer students. 30 of 124 credits required for the bachelor's degree must be completed at NIU.

Visiting: There are regularly scheduled orientations for prospective students, including open house programs, bus tours, faculty meetings, residence hall tours, and department receptions. There are guides for informal visits and visitors may sit in on classes and stay overnight. To schedule a visit, contact the Office of Orientation and Student Assistance at (815) 753-1535.

Financial Aid: 33% of undergraduates work part time. Average annual earnings from campus work are $1200. The FAFSA and the college's own financial statement are required. The deadline for filing freshman financial aid applications for fall entry is March 1.

International Students: There are 179 international students enrolled. They must score 500 on the written TOEFL.

Computers: The mainframe is an Amdahl 5890/300E. PCs and Macs are available throughout the campus. 57 computer labs on campus provide access for particular colleges and departments. Access to the Internet is free to NIU students from any on-campus lab or residence hall, or through modems. E-mail, Phonebook, Web Browser, FTP, and Newreader are available. All students may access the system. Computer labs are open more than 150 hours per week. There are no time limits and no fees.

Graduates: In a recent year, 3416 bachelor's degrees were awarded. The most popular majors were elementary education (8%), communication studies (8%), and marketing (7%). In an average class, 20% graduate in 4 years or less, 43% graduate in 5 years or less, and 49% graduate in 6 years or less. In a recent year, 800 companies recruited on campus in 2002-2003. Of a recent graduating class, 19% were enrolled in graduate school within 6 months of graduation and 89% were employed.

Admissions Contact: Robert Burk, Director of Admissions.
E-mail: *admissions-info@niu.edu* Web: *http://www.niu.edu/*

NORTHWESTERN UNIVERSITY
E-1
Evanston, IL 60208
(847) 491-7271

Full-time: 3694 men, 4103 women	Faculty: 900; I, ++$
Part-time: 86 men, 118 women	Ph.D.s: 100%
Graduate: 3991 men, 2885 women	Student/Faculty: 9 to 1
Year: quarters, summer session	Tuition: $28,524
Application Deadline: January 1	Room & Board: $8967
Freshman Class: 14,137 applied, 4702 accepted, 1941 enrolled	
SAT I Verbal/Math: 695/710	ACT: 31 MOST COMPETITIVE

Northwestern University, founded in 1851, is an independent, nonprofit liberal arts institution offering undergraduate study in the arts and sciences, education and social policy, journalism, music, communication, and engineering and applied science. There are 6 undergraduate and 7 graduate schools. In addition to regional accreditation, Northwestern has baccalaureate program accreditation with AACSB, ABET, ACEJMC, APTA, and NASM. The 3 libraries contain 4,315,314 volumes, 4,225,339 microform items, and 75,358 audio/video tapes/CDs, and subscribe to 39,310 periodicals. Computerized library services include the card catalog, interlibrary loans, database searching, and Internet access. Special learning facilities include an art gallery, radio station, TV station, and an observatory. The 231-acre campus is in a suburban area 12 miles north of Chicago on the shores of Lake Michigan. Including any residence halls, there are 180 buildings.

Student Life: 75% of undergraduates are from out of state, mostly the Midwest. Students are from 50 states, 51 foreign countries, and Canada. 73% are from public schools. 60% are white; 17% Asian American. 33% are Protestant; 25% claim no religious affiliation; 23% Catholic; 16% Jewish. The average age of freshmen is 19; all undergraduates, 20. 3% do not continue beyond their first year; 93% remain to graduate.

Housing: 4250 students can be accommodated in college housing, which includes single-sex and coed dorms, fraternity houses, and sorority houses. In addition, there are special-interest houses. On-campus housing is guaranteed for the freshman year only. 65% of students live on campus; of those, 95% remain on campus on weekends. Upperclassmen may keep cars.

Activities: 30% of men belong to 22 national fraternities; 39% of women belong to 19 national sororities. There are 415 groups on campus, including art, band, cheerleading, chess, choir, chorale, chorus, dance, debate, drama, ethnic, film, gay, honors, international, jazz band, literary magazine, marching band, musical theater, newspaper, opera, orchestra, pep band, photography, political, professional, radio and TV, religious, social, social service, student government, symphony, and yearbook. Popular campus events include Waa-Mu Variety Show, Armadillo Day, and Dance Marathon.

Sports: There are 9 intercollegiate sports for men and 12 for women, and 21 intramural sports for men and 19 for women. Facilities include a stadium, an arena, a gym, lakefront playing fields for soccer, field hockey, and Frisbee, a boat house, and recreation and sports centers housing basketball, volleyball, tennis, racquetball, swimming, badminton, weight training, jogging, squash, fitness facilities, and a golf center.

Disabled Students: All of the campus is accessible. Wheelchair ramps, elevators, special parking, specially equipped rest rooms, special class scheduling, lowered drinking fountains, lowered telephones, and special housing are available.

Services: There is a reader service for the blind and one-on-one compensation, remediation, ADHD coaching, note taking, and real-time captioning.

Campus Safety and Security: Measures include 24-hour foot and vehicle patrol, self-defense education, security escort services, and shuttle buses. There are informal discussions, pamphlets/posters/films, emergency telephones, lighted pathways/sidewalks, and a security keycard system in residence halls.

Programs of Study: Northwestern confers B.A., B.S., B.A.C.M.N., B.A.Mus., B.M.E., B.Mus., B.Ph., B.P.H.C., B.S.A.M., B.S.B.M., B.S.C.H., B.S.C.I., B.S.C.M.N., B.S.C.O., B.S.C.S., B.S.Ed., B.S.E.E., B.S.E.N., B.S.E.S., B.S.G.E., B.S.G.S., B.S.I.E., B.S.J., B.S.M., B.S.M.D., B.S.M.E., B.S.M.F., B.S.M.T., B.S.S.E., and B.S.S.P. degrees. Master's and doctoral degrees are also awarded. Bachelor's degrees are awarded in BIOLOGICAL SCIENCE (biology/biological science, ecology, molecular biology, and neurosciences), BUSINESS (organizational behavior), COMMUNICATIONS AND THE ARTS (art, art history and appreciation, classics, communications, communications technology, comparative literature, dance, dramatic arts, English, fine arts, French, German, Italian, jazz, journalism, linguistics, music, music performance, music technology, music theory and composition, percussion, performing arts, piano/organ, radio/television technology, Slavic languages, Spanish, strings, voice, and winds), COMPUTER AND PHYSICAL SCIENCE (applied mathematics, astronomy, chemistry, computer science, geology, information sciences and systems, mathematics, physics, and statistics), EDUCATION (education, mathematics, music, and secondary), ENGINEERING AND ENVIRONMENTAL DESIGN (biomedical engineering, chemical engineering, civil engineering, computer engineering, electrical/electronics engineering, engineering, environmental engineering, environmental science, industrial engineering, manufacturing engineering, materials engineering, materials science, and mechanical engineering), HEALTH PROFESSIONS (premedicine and speech pathology/audiology), SOCIAL SCIENCE (African American studies, American studies, anthropology, cognitive science, economics, ethics, politics, and social policy, European studies, gender studies, geography, history, human development, international studies, philosophy, political science/government, psychology, religion, science and society, sociology, and urban studies). Journalism, communications, and physical and life sciences are the strongest academically. Economics, political science, and engineering are the largest.

Required: Requirements for graduation vary by school and degree program. Students must maintain a minimum 2.0 GPA and complete a total of 45 to 48 quarter units (courses).

Special: The university offers cooperative engineering programs throughout the country, many off-campus field studies and research opportunities, internships in the arts, journalism, and teaching, study abroad in 46 countries around the world, a Washington semester, and numerous work-study programs both on and off campus. There is an accelerated degree program in medical education, and B.A.-B.S. degrees in liberal arts and engineering, liberal arts and music, and music and engineering. An integrated science program, an interdisciplinary study in mathematical methods in social sciences and numerous other interdisciplinary majors, a variety of dual and student-designed majors, pass/fail options, and a teaching media program are also available. There are 23 national honor societies, including Phi Beta Kappa, a freshman honors program, and 40 departmental honors programs.

Faculty/Classroom: 71% of faculty are male; 29%, female. All both teach and do research. Graduate students teach 3% of introductory courses. The average class size in an introductory lecture is 35; in a laboratory, 14; and in a regular course, 22.

Admissions: 33% of the 2003-2004 applicants were accepted. The SAT I scores for the 2003-2004 freshman class were: Verbal--1% below 500, 8% between 500 and 599, 40% between 600 and 700, and 50% above 700; Math--6% between 500 and 599, 37% between 600 and 700, and 56% above 700. The ACT scores were 1% below 21, 4% between 21 and 23, 7% between 24 and 26, 11% between 27 and 28, and 78% above 28. 95% of the current freshmen were in the top fifth of their class; 99% were in the top two fifths. 187 freshmen graduated first in their class.

Requirements: The SAT I or ACT is required. In addition, applicants must be graduates of an accredited secondary school or have a GED certificate, and have completed a minimum of 16 units, including 4 units of English, 3 of math, 2 or 3 each of a foreign language and history, and 2 of lab sciences. SAT II: Subject tests are required for the accelerated honors program in medical education and the integrated science program. Auditions are required for applicants to the School of Music. AP credits are accepted. Important factors in the admissions decision are advanced placement or honor courses, recommendations by school officials, and extracurricular activities record.

Procedure: Freshmen are admitted to all sessions. Entrance exams should be taken by December of the senior year. There are early decision and deferred admissions plans. Early decision applications should be filed by November 1; regular applications, by January 1 for fall entry, November 1 for winter entry, February 1 for spring entry, and May 1 for summer entry, along with a $65 fee. Notification of early decision is sent December 15; regular decision, April 15. 451 early decision candidates were accepted for the 2003-2004 class. 330 applicants were on the 2003 waiting list; 102 were admitted. Applications are accepted on-line through the school's web site.

Transfer: 129 transfer students enrolled in 2002-2003. Transfer students need a minimum 3.0 GPA, SAT I or ACT scores, high school record, 1 essay, and the dean's reference form. Applicants are required to have a minimum of 1 year of completed college work to apply to Northwestern. 23 of 45 courses required for the bachelor's degree must be completed at Northwestern.

Visiting: There are regularly scheduled orientations for prospective students, including daily information sessions Monday through Friday. There are guides for informal visits and visitors may sit in on classes and stay overnight. To schedule a visit, contact the Admission Office.

Financial Aid: In 2003-2004, 55% of all full-time freshmen and 60% of continuing full-time students received some form of financial aid. 45% of full-time freshmen and 50% of continuing full-time students received need-based aid. The average freshman award was $23,587. 32% of undergraduates work part time. Average annual earnings from campus work are $1842. The average financial indebtedness of the 2003 graduate was $15,136. Northwestern is a member of CSS. The CSS Profile or FAFSA, and tax returns under certain conditions, are required. The deadline for filing freshman financial aid applications for fall entry is February 1.

International Students: There are 415 international students enrolled. The school actively recruits these students. They must score 600 on the written TOEFL or 250 on the electronic version and also take the SAT I or the ACT.

Computers: The mainframe is an IBM 3090/180J. All academic and administrative buildings, as well as student residences, are connected to the campus network, through which students have access to e-mail, the campus bulletin board and calendar, and the Internet, as well as the card catalog of the university library. All students may access the system 24 hours per day. There are no time limits and no fees. It is recommended that students in engineering have personal computers.

Graduates: From July 1, 2002 to June 30, 2003, 2022 bachelor's degrees were awarded. The most popular majors were engineering (15%), economics (11%), and journalism (7%). In an average class, 84% graduate in 4 years or less, 92% graduate in 5 years or less, and 93% graduate in 6 years or less. 350 companies recruited on campus in 2002-2003.

Admissions Contact: Carol Lunkenheimer, Dean of Undergraduate Admission. A video is available.

E-mail: *ug-admission@northwestern.edu*
Web: *www.ugadm.northwestern.edu*

OLIVET NAZARENE UNIVERSITY
Bourbonnais, IL 60914

E-2

(815) 939-5203
(800) 648-1463; Fax: (815) 935-4998

Full-time: 2079 men and women	**Faculty:** 80; IIA, --$
Part-time: 353 men and women	**Ph.Ds:** 72%
Graduate: 1887 men and women	**Student/Faculty:** 26 to 1
Year: semesters, summer session	**Tuition:** $14,980
Application Deadline: see profile	**Room & Board:** $5500
Freshman Class: 1951 applied, 1499 accepted, 594 enrolled	
ACT: 23	**COMPETITIVE**

Olivet Nazarene University, established in 1907, is a private, comprehensive institution affiliated with the Church of the Nazarene. Its undergraduate and graduate programs emphasize the liberal arts, business, communication, health science, art and fine arts, engineering, music, Bible and religious studies, and teacher preparation in an atmosphere of Christian culture. Some information in the above capsule is approximate. In addition to regional accreditation, Olivet has baccalaureate program accreditation with ABET, ADA, CSWE, IACBE, NASM, NCATE, and NLN. The library contains 165,000 volumes, 38,800 microform items, and 4800 audio/video tapes/CDs, and subscribes to 900 periodicals. Computerized library services include the card catalog, interlibrary loans, and database searching. Special learning facilities include a learning resource center, art gallery, natural history museum, planetarium, radio station, and smart board classrooms. The 190-acre campus is in a small town 60 miles south of Chicago. Including any residence halls, there are 34 buildings.

Student Life: 59% of undergraduates are from out of state, mostly the Midwest. Students are from 40 states, 17 foreign countries, and Canada. 88% are white. 87% are Protestant; 6% Catholic. The average age of freshmen is 18; all undergraduates, 20. 32% do not continue beyond their first year; 52% remain to graduate.

Housing: 1550 students can be accommodated in college housing, which includes single-sex dorms, on-campus apartments, and married-student housing. In addition, there are honors houses. On-campus housing is guaranteed for all 4 years. 75% of students live on campus; of those, 80% remain on campus on weekends. Alcohol is not permitted. All students may keep cars.

Activities: There are no fraternities or sororities. There are 32 groups on campus, including art, athletic booster club, band, cheerleading, choir, chorale, chorus, computers, drama, honors, international, jazz band, literary magazine, newspaper, orchestra, pep band, political, professional, radio and TV, religious, social, social service, student government, and yearbook. Popular campus events include Parents Weekend, Halloween Party, and Lipsynch Contest.

Sports: There are 9 intercollegiate sports for men and 9 for women, and 14 intramural sports for men and 14 for women. Facilities include a 3000-seat gym with basketball, volleyball, and racquetball courts, a pool, a weight-lifting room, and an indoor track; a 2500-seat stadium with a track; and an athletic park with softball, baseball, and soccer fields, a jogging track, track and field facilities, an ice rink, and tennis courts.

Disabled Students: 90% of the campus is accessible. Wheelchair ramps, elevators, special parking, specially equipped rest rooms, lowered drinking fountains, and lowered telephones are available.

Services: There is remedial math and writing. In addition to many counseling and information services, tutoring is available in economics, psychology, sociology, chemistry, and Old and New Testament studies. There is a tutoring referral service in all subjects and a learning development center.

Campus Safety and Security: Measures include 24-hour foot and vehicle patrol, self-defense education, security escort services, and informal discussions. There are pamphlets/posters/films, lighted pathways/sidewalks, and an on-campus security service.

Programs of Study: Olivet confers B.A., B.S., B.A.T., and B.S.T. degrees. Associate and master's degrees are also awarded. Bachelor's degrees are awarded in BIOLOGICAL SCIENCE (biology/biological science and zoology), BUSINESS (accounting, business administration and management, and fashion merchandising), COMMUNICATIONS AND THE ARTS (art, English, music, romance languages and literature, and speech/debate/rhetoric), COMPUTER AND PHYSICAL SCIENCE (chemistry, computer science, geology, mathematics, physical sciences, and science technology), EDUCATION (Christian, early childhood, elementary, and physical), ENGINEERING AND ENVIRONMENTAL DESIGN (engineering, environmental design, and environmental science), HEALTH PROFESSIONS (clinical science and nursing), SOCIAL SCIENCE (dietetics, economics, family/consumer studies, history, liberal arts/general studies, philosophy, political science/government, psychology, public affairs, religion, social science, social work, and sociology). Engineering and physical science are the strongest academically. Business administration and education are the largest.

Required: To graduate, students must complete 128 semester hours of credit, with fulfillment of a major and a minimum of 40 hours of credit in upper-division courses, (50 to 64 in the major) and maintain a minimum GPA of 2.0. The required general education studies, 50 to 61 hours, include 12 credit hours of Christianity, 9 to 10 of communication, 7 to 11 of natural science and math, 9 of social sciences, 6 to 8 of international culture, 6 of literature and the arts, and 4 to 5 of personal health. Participation in the Senior Outcomes testing program in general education is required.

Special: Special academic programs include a work-study program, which can be arranged with other institutions, and a general studies degree. A 4-year engineering program (ABET) is available. There are 6 national honor societies and 5 departmental honors programs.

Faculty/Classroom: 66% of faculty are male; 34%, female.

Admissions: 77% of the 2003-2004 applicants were accepted. The ACT scores for the 2003-2004 freshman class were: 25% below 21, 25% between 21 and 23, 25% between 24 and 26, 10% between 27 and 28, and 15% above 28.

Requirements: The ACT is required, with a minimum score of 16. Other admissions requirements include graduation from an accredited secondary school, with 3 units each of English, math, foreign language, and natural science or social science, and an additional 2 of math, foreign language, natural science, or social science. The GED also is accepted. Two certificates of recommendation must be submitted. Olivet requires applicants to be in the upper 50% of their class. A GPA of 2.0 is required. AP and CLEP credits are accepted.

Procedure: Freshmen are admitted to all sessions. Entrance exams should be taken during the spring of the junior year or during the senior year. There is a rolling admissions plan. Notification is sent on a rolling basis. Check with the school for current deadlines. Applications are accepted on-line.

Transfer: 231 transfer students enrolled in a recent year. Transcripts of all college work must be submitted. 30 of 128 credits required for the bachelor's degree must be completed at Olivet.

Visiting: There are regularly scheduled orientations for prospective students, including class visits, financial aid, information tour, lunch, professor meetings, and an optional overnight stay. There are guides for informal visits and visitors may sit in on classes and stay overnight. To schedule a visit, contact Jean Milton, the Campus Visit Coordinator in the Admissions Office at *jmilton@olivet.edu*.

Financial Aid: In a recent year, 95% of all full-time freshmen and 91% of continuing full-time students received some form of financial aid. 54% of full-time freshmen and 58% of continuing full-time students received need-based aid. The average freshman award was $12,834. 50% of undergraduates work part time. The average financial indebtedness of a recent graduate was $13,479. Olivet is a member of CSS. The FAFSA and the college's own financial statement are required. Check with the school for current deadlines.

International Students: There were 15 international students enrolled in a recent year. They must score 500 on the written TOEFL or take the MELAB. They must also take the ACT, scoring 18.

Computers: There are 30 PCs and IBM PS/2 Model 30s available in the computer lab. There is also a Mac lab with 15 machines. 50 PCs are connected to the network with Internet access. All students may access the system. There are no time limits and no fees. It is strongly recommended that all students have a personal computer.

Graduates: In a recent year, 358 bachelor's degrees were awarded. The most popular majors were education (17%), health professions (17%), and business/marketing (15%). In an average class, 52% graduate in 6 years or less.

Admissions Contact: Brian Parker, Director of Admissions.
E-mail: *admissions@olivet.edu* Web: *http://www.olivet.edu*

PRINCIPIA COLLEGE
Elsah, IL 62028

C-4

(618) 374-5181
(800) 277-4648; Fax: (618) 374-4000

Full-time: 243 men, 306 women	**Faculty:** 45; IIB, av$
Part-time: none	**Ph.Ds:** 66%
Graduate: none	**Student/Faculty:** 12 to 1
Year: quarters	**Tuition:** $18,540
Application Deadline: March 1	**Room & Board:** $6504
Freshman Class: 274 applied, 251 accepted, 181 enrolled	
SAT I Verbal/Math: 580/550	**ACT:** 26 **COMPETITIVE+**

Principia College, founded in 1910, is a private liberal arts and sciences college for Christian Scientists. In addition to regional accreditation, Prin has baccalaureate program accreditation with NCATE. The library contains 210,000 volumes, 193,439 microform items, and 7513 audio/video tapes/CDs, and subscribes to more than 12,000 periodicals in multiple databases. Computerized library services include the card catalog, interlibrary loans, database searching, and Internet access. Special learning facilities include a learning resource center, art gallery, planetarium, radio station, and TV station. The 2600-acre campus is in a rural area 30 miles northeast of St. Louis. Including any residence halls, there are 33 buildings.

Student Life: 90% of undergraduates are from out of state, mostly the Midwest. Students are from 38 states, 25 foreign countries, and Canada. 66% are from public schools. 79% are white; 15% foreign nationals. The average age of freshmen is 18; all undergraduates, 20. 12% do not continue beyond their first year; 75% remain to graduate.

Housing: 654 students can be accommodated in college housing, which includes single-sex dorms, on-campus apartments, and married-student housing. In addition, there are language houses and special-interest houses. On-campus housing is guaranteed for all 4 years. 99% of students live on campus; of those, all remain on campus on weekends. Alcohol is not permitted. All students may keep cars.

Activities: There are no fraternities or sororities. There are 34 groups on campus, including art, cheerleading, choir, chorus, computers, dance, drama, ethnic, honors, international, jazz band, literary magazine, musical theater, newspaper, orchestra, photography, political, radio and TV, religious, social, social service, student government, and yearbook. Popular campus events include athletic events, dances, and drama and dance performances.

Sports: There are 10 intercollegiate sports for men and 8 for women, and 3 intramural sports for men and 3 for women. Facilities include 2 gyms, a pool, indoor and outdoor tennis courts, a racquetball court, basketball/volleyball courts, a dance studio, a weight room, baseball, football, soccer, and practice fields, and a 6-lane track.

Disabled Students: 80% of the campus is accessible. Wheelchair ramps, elevators, special parking, specially equipped rest rooms, and lowered drinking fountains are available.

Services: There is remedial reading and writing. Assistance in study skills is available.

Campus Safety and Security: Measures include 24-hour foot and vehicle patrol, informal discussions, emergency telephones, and lighted pathways/sidewalks.

Programs of Study: Prin confers B.A. and B.S. degrees. Bachelor's degrees are awarded in BIOLOGICAL SCIENCE (biology/biological science), BUSINESS (business administration and management and sports management), COMMUNICATIONS AND THE ARTS (communications, dramatic arts, English, fine arts, French, languages, music, Spanish, and studio art), COMPUTER AND PHYSICAL SCIENCE (chemistry, computer science, mathematics, and physics), EDUCATION (elementary), ENGINEERING AND ENVIRONMENTAL DESIGN (environmental science), SOCIAL SCIENCE (economics, German area studies, history, international relations, philosophy, political science/government, religion, and sociology). Education, studio art, and biology are the strongest academically. Business administration, studio art, and education are the largest.

Required: All students must complete a minimum of 180 quarter hours, with 45 to 93 quarter hours in the major (10 to 15 courses) and at least a 2.0 overall GPA. Courses in foreign language, literature, arts, religion and philosophy, history, social science, math, and natural sciences are required. In addition, students must be certified as proficient in written English, pass a moral reasoning seminar, earn 4 credits in individual and team phys ed activities, and pass a survival swim test.

Special: Students may design their own majors, study abroad or in San Francisco, or pursue a B.A.-B.S. degree. Internships, student-planned with a professor, independent study, work-study, and an interdisciplinary major, global studies, are available. A 3-2 engineering program with Washington University in St. Louis, Southern Illinois University at Carbondale, the University of Southern California, or another university with approval is also possible. A San Francisco field program in business administration is offered. There is 1 national honor society, a freshman honors program, and 3 departmental honors programs.

Faculty/Classroom: 57% of faculty are male; 43%, female. All teach undergraduates and 60% do research. The average class size in an introductory lecture is 14; in a laboratory, 13; and in a regular course, 11.

Admissions: 92% of the 2003-2004 applicants were accepted. The SAT I scores for the 2003-2004 freshman class were: Verbal--19% below 500, 32% between 500 and 599, 36% between 600 and 700, and 13% above 700; Math--13% below 500, 42% between 500 and 599, 31% between 600 and 700, and 14% above 700. The ACT scores were 16% below 21, 21% between 21 and 23, 25% between 24 and 26, 18% between 27 and 28, and 21% above 28. 38% of the current freshmen were in the top fifth of their class; 59% were in the top two fifths. There was 1 National Merit finalist and 3 semifinalists. 2 freshmen graduated first in their class.

Requirements: The SAT I or ACT is required; the SAT I is preferred. An essay is required. SAT II: Subject tests in foreign language and math are recommended. High school preparation should include 4 years of English, 3 of math (including algebra II), 2 to 3 of a foreign language, 2 of natural sciences, history or social sciences, and electives. A GPA of 2.3 is required. AP and CLEP credits are accepted. Important factors in the admissions decision are advanced placement or honor courses, recommendations by school officials, and leadership record.

Procedure: Freshmen are admitted fall and winter. Entrance exams should be taken in the spring of the junior year and again in the fall of the senior year. There is a deferred admissions plan and a rolling admissions plan. Early decision applications should be filed by January 15; regular applications, by March 1 for fall entry, November 1 for winter entry, and March 1 for spring entry, along with a $40 fee. Notification of early decision is sent January 20; regular decision, on a rolling basis beginning in November. Applications are accepted on-line through *www.prin.edu/college/admissions*.

Transfer: 24 transfer students enrolled in 2002-2003. Applicants must be in good standing at their previous college or university. 45 credits of 180 required for the bachelor's degree must be completed at Prin.

Visiting: There are regularly scheduled orientations for prospective students, including a visit to classes, meeting professors, living in a dorm, and meeting students (3-day weekend). There are guides for informal visits and visitors may sit in on classes and stay overnight. To schedule a visit, contact Alison Reid at *ajr@prin.edu*.

Financial Aid: In 2003-2004, 86% of all full-time freshmen and 85% of continuing full-time students received some form of financial aid. 63% of full-time freshmen and 62% of continuing full-time students received need-based aid. The average freshman award was $16,467. Need-based scholarships or need-based grants averaged $11,192 ($24,774 maximum); need-based self-help aid (loans and jobs) averaged $4597 ($7625 maximum); and non-need-based awards and non-need-based scholarships averaged $10,477 ($18,270 maximum). 52% of undergraduates work part time. Average annual earnings from campus work are $1368. The average financial indebtedness of the 2003 graduate was $11,314. Prin is a member of CSS. The CSS/Profile and the college's own financial statement are required. The priority date for freshman financial aid applications for fall entry is March 1. The deadline for filing freshman financial aid applications for fall entry is June 1.

International Students: There are 68 international students enrolled. The school actively recruits these students. They must score 550 on the written TOEFL or 213 on the electronic version and also take the SAT I or the ACT, scoring 950 on the SAT I or 19 on the ACT.

Computers: The mainframes are 3 SUN V280R servers running UNIX with Oracle as the database system. About 200 computer workstations are available to students in 5 academic buildings, as PCs or as remote terminals of the college mainframe computer. PCs and Macs are available to all students on a 24-hour basis. All students may access the system 24 hours a day. There are no time limits and no fees.

Graduates: From July 1, 2002 to June 30, 2003, 121 bachelor's degrees were awarded. The most popular majors were business administration (17%), studio art (13%), and mass communication (7%). In an average class, 74% graduate in 4 years or less, 72% graduate in 5 years or less, and 78% graduate in 6 years or less. 20 companies recruited on campus in 2002-2003. Of the 2002 graduating class, 7% were enrolled in graduate school within 6 months of graduation and 92% were employed.

Admissions Contact: Martha Green Quirk, Dean of Admissions. A video is available. E-mail: *collegeadmissions@prin.edu* Web: *www.prin.edu/college/admissions*

QUINCY UNIVERSITY

B-3

Quincy, IL 62301-2699

(217) 228-5210
(800) 688-4295; Fax: (217) 228-5479

Full-time: 441 men, 529 women	**Faculty:** 49; IIB, --$
Part-time: 68 men, 92 women	**Ph.Ds:** 88%
Graduate: 38 men, 101 women	**Student/Faculty:** 20 to 1
Year: semesters, summer session	**Tuition:** $16,850
Application Deadline: open	**Room & Board:** $5480
Freshman Class: 1056 applied, 988 accepted, 223 enrolled	
ACT: 23	**COMPETITIVE**

Quincy University, established in 1860, is a private liberal arts institution conducted by the Franciscan Friars of the Roman Catholic Church. There are 3 undergraduate and 2 graduate schools. In addition to regional accreditation, Quincy has baccalaureate program accreditation with NASM and NLN. The library contains 210,454 volumes, 186,214 microform items, and 6633 audio/video tapes/CDs, and subscribes to 592 periodicals. Computerized library services include the card catalog, interlibrary loans, database searching, and Internet access. Special learning facilities include a learning resource center, art gallery, radio station, and TV station. The 75-acre campus is in a small town 120 miles north of St. Louis. Including any residence halls, there are 41 buildings.

Student Life: 74% of undergraduates are from Illinois. Students are from 21 states, 5 foreign countries, and Canada. 48% are from public schools. 81% are white. 54% are Catholic; 21% claim no religious affiliation; 20% Protestant. The average age of freshmen is 18; all undergraduates, 22. 27% do not continue beyond their first year; 53% remain to graduate.

Housing: 831 students can be accommodated in college housing, which includes single-sex and coed dorms, on-campus apartments, married-student housing, fraternity houses, and sorority houses. In addition, there are special-interest houses. On-campus housing is guaranteed for all 4 years. 70% of students live on campus; of those, 80% remain on campus on weekends. All students may keep cars.

Activities: 14% of men belong to 2 national fraternities; 11% of women belong to 2 national sororities. There are 43 groups on campus, including bagpipe band, band, cheerleading, chess, choir, chorale, chorus, computers, dance, drama, ethnic, honors, international, jazz band, literary magazine, musical theater, newspaper, opera, orchestra, pep band, political, professional, radio and TV, religious, social, social service, student government, symphony, and yearbook. Popular campus events include Fall Fest/Parents Weekend, Hawk Pride Weekend, and Septemberfest.

Sports: There are 9 intercollegiate sports for men and 8 for women, and 11 intramural sports for men and 11 for women. Facilities include a health and fitness center, 2 gyms, a football/baseball stadium, a soccer stadium, a weight room, a college athletic field, and outdoor basketball/volleyball courts.

Disabled Students: 95% of the campus is accessible. Wheelchair ramps, elevators, special parking, specially equipped rest rooms, special class scheduling, lowered drinking fountains, and lowered telephones are available.

Services: Counseling and information services are available, as is tutoring in every subject. There is a reader service for the blind and remedial writing. Skill development and motivation workshops and courses are available.

Campus Safety and Security: Measures include 24-hour foot and vehicle patrol, self-defense education, security escort services, and shuttle buses. There are informal discussions, pamphlets/posters/films, emergency telephones, and lighted pathways/sidewalks.

Programs of Study: Quincy confers B.A., B.S., B.F.A., and B.S.N. degrees. Associate and master's degrees are also awarded. Bachelor's degrees are awarded in BIOLOGICAL SCIENCE (biology/biological science), BUSINESS (accounting, banking and finance, business administration and management, marketing/retailing/merchandising, and sports management), COMMUNICATIONS AND THE ARTS (art, communications, English, music, and music business management), COMPUTER AND PHYSICAL SCIENCE (chemistry, computer science, and information sciences and systems), EDUCATION (elementary, music, physical, science, secondary, and special), ENGINEERING AND ENVIRONMENTAL DESIGN (aviation administration/management), HEALTH PROFESSIONS (medical laboratory technology and nursing), SOCIAL SCIENCE (criminal justice, history, human services, humanities, political science/government, psychology, religious education, social work, and theological studies). Business, education, and science are the strongest academically. Elementary education, nursing, and management are the largest.

Required: Each student is required to complete a minimum of 124 credit hours, with at least 27 in the major and 39 in upper-level courses. In addition, students must complete required courses in rhetoric, science or math, social sciences, humanities, fine arts, theology, and phys ed; complete a senior comprehensive seminar; and maintain a minimum GPA of 2.0.

Special: Dual majors, study abroad in 27 countries, credit by exam, and upper-class and early exploratory internships are available. Pass/fail options, credit for life experience, student-designed majors, and a 3-2 degree with Washington University in St. Louis are also offered. There are 6 national honor societies, and a freshman honors program.

Faculty/Classroom: 64% of faculty are male; 36%, female. All teach undergraduates. No introductory courses are taught by graduate students. The average class size in an introductory lecture is 40; in a laboratory, 20; and in a regular course, 20.

Admissions: 94% of the 2003-2004 applicants were accepted. The ACT scores for the 2003-2004 freshman class were: 19% below 21, 41% between 21 and 23, 27% between 24 and 26, 9% between 27 and 28, and 4% above 28. 23% of the current freshmen were in the top fifth of their class; 55% were in the top two fifths. 2 freshmen graduated first in their class.

Requirements: The SAT I or ACT is required, with a minimum score of 475 verbal and 475 math on the SAT I, or 20 on the ACT. The GED is accepted. College preparatory courses totaling 16 credits should include 4 years of English, 3 each of math and science, and 2 each of a foreign language, history, and social studies. Art students must submit a portfolio, and music students are required to audition. Quincy requires applicants to be in the upper 50% of their class. A GPA of 2.0 is required. AP and CLEP credits are accepted. Important factors in the admissions decision are leadership record, evidence of special talent, and recommendations by school officials.

Procedure: Freshmen are admitted fall and spring. Entrance exams should be taken in October of the senior year. There is a deferred admissions plan and a rolling admissions plan. Application deadlines are open. Application fee is $25. Notification is sent on a rolling basis. Applications are accepted on-line through the university's web site.

Transfer: 100 transfer students enrolled in 2002-2003. Applicants must have a minimum GPA of 2.0. Grades of C or better transfer for credit. 30 credits of 124 required for the bachelor's degree must be completed at Quincy.

Visiting: There are regularly scheduled orientations for prospective students, including weekend advising and registration programs throughout

the summer. There are guides for informal visits and visitors may sit in on classes and stay overnight. To schedule a visit, contact the Admissions Office at *admissions@quincy.edu.*

Financial Aid: In 2003-2004, 99% of all full-time freshmen and 95% of continuing full-time students received some form of financial aid. 82% of full-time freshmen and 89% of continuing full-time students received need-based aid. The average freshman award was $17,635. 43% of undergraduates work part time. Average annual earnings from campus work are $1050. The average financial indebtedness of the 2003 graduate was $15,000. The FAFSA is required. The deadline for filing freshman financial aid applications for fall entry is April 15.

International Students: There were 14 international students enrolled in a recent year. The school actively recruits these students. They must score 500 on the written TOEFL.

Computers: The mainframe is an HP 9000/K460. More than 300 PCs are available throughout campus. The main academic buildings house 5 computer labs, including a 60-station writing lab and classroom. The library, residence halls, and honors houses also have PC labs. The Internet is available in each computer lab, the residence halls, and some classrooms. All students may access the system. There are no time limits and no fees. It is strongly recommended that all students have a personal computer.

Graduates: From July 1, 2002 to June 30, 2003, 255 bachelor's degrees were awarded. The most popular majors were elementary education (14%), nursing (8%), and marketing (6%). In an average class, 41% graduate in 4 years or less, 53% graduate in 5 years or less, and 56% graduate in 6 years or less. Of the 2002 graduating class, 18% were enrolled in graduate school within 6 months of graduation and 79% were employed.

Admissions Contact: Kevin Brown, Director of Admissions.
E-mail: *brownke@quincy.edu* Web: *www.quincy.edu*

ROCKFORD COLLEGE
D-1
Rockford, IL 61108
(815) 226-4140
(800) 892-2984; Fax: (815) 226-4169

Full-time: 287 men, 413 women	**Faculty:** 80
Part-time: 82 men, 118 women	**Ph.D.s:** 45%
Graduate: 210 men, 304 women	**Student/Faculty:** 9 to 1
Year: semesters, summer session	**Tuition:** $20,210
Application Deadline: open	**Room & Board:** $8100
Freshman Class: 610 applied, 350 accepted	
ACT: 23	**VERY COMPETITIVE**

Rockford College, founded in 1847, is a private institution offering undergraduate and graduate instruction in liberal arts and professional programs. Some information in the above capsule is approximate. In addition to regional accreditation, Rockford College has baccalaureate program accreditation with NLN. The library contains 167,983 volumes, 7590 microform items, and 9855 audio/video tapes/CDs, and subscribes to 815 periodicals. Computerized library services include the card catalog, interlibrary loans, and database searching. Special learning facilities include a learning resource center and art gallery. The 130-acre campus is in a suburban area 90 miles west of Chicago. Including any residence halls, there are 26 buildings.

Student Life: 88% of undergraduates are from Illinois. Students are from 9 states and 2 foreign countries. 75% are from public schools. 83% are white. The average age of freshmen is 18; all undergraduates, 23. 36% do not continue beyond their first year.

Housing: 560 students can be accommodated in college housing, which includes single-sex and coed dorms. In addition, there are special-interest houses and intercultural, substance-free, and quiet floors. On-campus housing is guaranteed for all 4 years. 64% of students commute. All students may keep cars.

Activities: There are no fraternities or sororities. There are 28 groups on campus, including art, cheerleading, chorus, computers, dance, drama, ethnic, gay, honors, international, literary magazine, math, musical theater, newspaper, political, professional, religious, scientific, social, social service, society, and student government. Popular campus events include Snowball Dance, Kids and Sibs Weekend, and Family Weekend.

Sports: There are 6 intercollegiate sports for men and 5 for women, and 12 intramural sports for men and 12 for women. Facilities include a swimming pool, athletic fields, tennis courts, and a fitness center with free weights and Nautilus weight rooms.

Disabled Students: 85% of the campus is accessible. Wheelchair ramps, elevators, special parking, specially equipped rest rooms, special class scheduling, lowered drinking fountains, and lowered telephones are available.

Services: Counseling and information services are available, as is tutoring in most subjects. There is a reader service for the blind and remedial math, reading, and writing. Diagnostic testing is available.

Campus Safety and Security: Measures include 24-hour foot and vehicle patrol, security escort services, informal discussions, and pamphlets/posters/films. There are emergency telephones and lighted pathways/sidewalks.

Programs of Study: Rockford College confers B.A., B.S., B.F.A., and B.S.N. degrees. Master's degrees are also awarded. Bachelor's degrees are awarded in BIOLOGICAL SCIENCE (biology/biological science), BUSINESS (accounting and business administration and management), COMMUNICATIONS AND THE ARTS (art, art history and appreciation, classical languages, dramatic arts, English, fine arts, French, German, music, and Spanish), COMPUTER AND PHYSICAL SCIENCE (chemistry, computer science, mathematics, and science), EDUCATION (athletic training, early childhood, elementary, and physical), ENGINEERING AND ENVIRONMENTAL DESIGN (military science and preengineering), HEALTH PROFESSIONS (nursing, predentistry, premedicine, prepharmacy, and preveterinary science), SOCIAL SCIENCE (anthropology, criminal justice, economics, history, human services, humanities, philosophy, political science/government, prelaw, psychology, religion, social science, social work, sociology, and urban studies). Business, education, and psychology are the largest.

Required: To graduate, students must have a total of at least 124 credit hours and a minimum GPA of 2.0 (nursing 2.5). The required hours for each major varies between 28 and 44. Students are required to take 12 hours of social sciences, 8 to 12 of science, math, and computer science, 8 of language and literature, 6 to 9 of freshman English, 6 of art, and 2 hours each of phys ed. Requirements for some degree programs may vary. All students must complete a senior seminar or project and must demonstrate proficiency in writing or public speaking, either by exam or by enrollment in a course that meets the requirement.

Special: The school offers junior and senior year internships, study abroad in 9 countries, a Washington semester at American University, and work-study programs. Dual majors, student-designed majors, nondegree study, and a 3-2 engineering degree with Washington University in St. Louis, the Universities of Southern California and Illinois, and Illinois Institute of Technology also are available. There are 5 national honor societies, including Phi Beta Kappa, and a freshman honors program.

Faculty/Classroom: 57% of faculty are male; 43%, female. All teach undergraduates. No introductory courses are taught by graduate students. The average class size in an introductory lecture is 25; in a laboratory, 12; and in a regular course, 18.

Admissions: 57% of the 2003-2004 applicants were accepted. 4 freshmen graduated first in their class in a recent year.

Requirements: The ACT is required, with a minimum ACT composite score of 18. Applicants must graduate from an accredited secondary school or demonstrate satisfactory scores on the GED. 16 academic credits are required, including 4 years of English, 2 of math, and 1 each of a foreign language, history, and laboratory science. An essay and an interview are recommended. For performing arts students, an audition is recommended. Rockford College requires applicants to be in the upper 50% of their class. A GPA of 2.65 is required. AP and CLEP credits are accepted. Important factors in the admissions decision are advanced placement or honor courses, recommendations by school officials, and leadership record.

Procedure: Freshmen are admitted to all sessions. Entrance exams should be taken by the fall of the senior year. There is a deferred admissions plan. There is a rolling admissions plan. Application deadlines are open. Application fee is $35.

Transfer: 133 transfer students enrolled in a recent year. Applicants must have a minimum GPA of 2.2. Nursing transfer students' minimum GPA is 2.5. 30 of 124 credits required for the bachelor's degree must be completed at Rockford College.

Visiting: There are regularly scheduled orientations for prospective students, consisting of a tour, a meeting with faculty members and other students, class visits, and social/athletic programs. A week-long orientation program is required for all freshmen the week before fall classes begin. There are guides for informal visits and visitors may sit in on classes and stay overnight. To schedule a visit, contact the Admissions Office at *admission@rockford.edu.*

Financial Aid: In 2003-2004, 98% of all full-time students received some form of financial aid. 28% of undergraduates work part time. Average annual earnings from campus work are $1500. The FAFSA is required. Check with the school for current deadlines.

International Students: There were 56 international students enrolled in a recent year. The school actively recruits these students. They must score 525 on the written TOEFL. Students can be conditionally admitted, then tested for English proficiency at the school's English Language Study Center.

Computers: The mainframe is an IBM 4341. All students may use the computer lab located in the science building. All students may access the system. There are no time limits and no fees. It is strongly recommended that all students have a personal computer.

Graduates: In a recent year, 215 bachelor's degrees were awarded. The most popular majors were education (28%), business (26%), and psychology (8%). 69 companies recruited on campus in a recent year.

Admissions Contact: Anna Krug, Assistant Vice President for Public Affairs and Strategic Market. A video is available.
E-mail: *akrug@rockford.edu* Web: *www.rockford.edu*

ROOSEVELT UNIVERSITY
Chicago, IL 60605

E-2
(847) 619-8620
(877) APPLYRU; Fax: (847) 619-8636

Full-time: 677 men, 1178 women	**Faculty:** 190; IIA, +$
Part-time: 744 men, 1691 women	**Ph.D.s:** 85%
Graduate: 1034 men, 2200 women	**Student/Faculty:** 10 to 1
Year: semesters, summer session	**Tuition:** $15,430
Application Deadline: open	**Room & Board:** $7150
Freshman Class: n/av	
ACT: 22	**VERY COMPETITIVE**

Roosevelt University, founded in 1945, an independent, comprehensive university. Some information in the above capsule is approximate. There are 5 undergraduate and 5 graduate schools. In addition to regional accreditation, Roosevelt has baccalaureate program accreditation with AACSB, NASM, and NCATE. The 2 libraries contain 405,022 volumes, 130,233 microform items, and 10,000 audio/video tapes/CDs, and subscribe to 1601 periodicals. Computerized library services include the card catalog, interlibrary loans, and database searching. Special learning facilities include a learning resource center and radio station. The campus is in an urban area downtown Chicago. Including any residence halls, there are 2 buildings.

Student Life: 90% of undergraduates are from Illinois. Students are from 24 states, 70 foreign countries, and Canada. 44% are white; 27% African American; 12% Hispanic; 10% foreign nationals. The average age of freshmen is 21; all undergraduates, 27.

Housing: 300 students can be accommodated in college housing, which includes coed dorms. On-campus housing is available on a first-come, first-served basis. 94% of students commute.

Activities: 1% of men belong to 1 local fraternity; 1% of women belong to 1 local sorority. There are 45 groups on campus, including band, choir, chorale, chorus, computers, cultural, drama, ethnic, honors, international, jazz band, literary magazine, model UN, musical theater, newspaper, opera, orchestra, political, professional, radio and TV, religious, social service, student government, and symphony.

Sports: There is 1 intramural sport for men and 1 for women. Facilities include a fitness center and a recreational gym for basketball, volleyball, soccer, and intramural activities.

Disabled Students: All of the campus is accessible. Wheelchair ramps, elevators, specially equipped rest rooms, special class scheduling, and lowered telephones are available. For special needs, contact the Disabled Student Services Office.

Services: Counseling and information services are available, as is tutoring in most subjects. There is remedial math, reading, and writing, arranged counseling, and testing. Emphasis is placed on individual program planning.

Campus Safety and Security: Measures include shuttle buses and lighted pathways/sidewalks.

Programs of Study: Roosevelt confers B.A., B.S., B.A.Comp.Sci., B.A.Ed., B.F.A.Mus.Theater, B.G.S., B.M., B.S.B.A., B.S. in Hospitality Mgt., and B.S.Telecomm. degrees. Master's and doctoral degrees are also awarded. Bachelor's degrees are awarded in BIOLOGICAL SCIENCE (biology/biological science), BUSINESS (accounting, banking and finance, business administration and management, hotel/motel and restaurant management, insurance, insurance and risk management, management science, marketing/retailing/merchandising, and personnel management), COMMUNICATIONS AND THE ARTS (advertising, art history and appreciation, broadcasting, communications, dramatic arts, English, French, guitar, jazz, journalism, languages, literature, media arts, music, music history and appreciation, music performance, music theory and composition, musical theater, percussion, performing arts, piano/organ, public relations, Spanish, strings, telecommunications, theater design, theater management, voice, and winds), COMPUTER AND PHYSICAL SCIENCE (actuarial science, chemistry, computer science, information sciences and systems, mathematics, and statistics), EDUCATION (early childhood, elementary, music, and secondary), ENGINEERING AND ENVIRONMENTAL DESIGN (electrical/electronics engineering technology and environmental science), HEALTH PROFESSIONS (allied health, medical technology, nuclear medical technology, predentistry, premedicine, prepharmacy, and preveterinary science), SOCIAL SCIENCE (African American studies, American studies, economics, history, international studies, liberal arts/general studies, philosophy, political science/government, prelaw, psychology, public administration, social science, sociology, urban studies, and women's studies). Journalism, accounting, and psychology are the strongest academically.

Required: For graduation, students must complete 120 credit hours, including 54 in the major, with a minimum GPA of 2.0, or 2.5 in the College of Education. The core curriculum consists of courses in the social sciences, natural sciences, and humanities, including English 101 and 102. The last 54 hours must be from a 4-year school.

Special: Roosevelt offers internships in approximately 20 subject areas, on-campus work-study, study abroad in 4 countries, dual and student-designed majors, pass/fail options, and noncredit courses. Adults older than 25 years of age may earn a Bachelor of General Studies through an accelerated degree program. Credit for life, military, and work experience is available in some majors through continuing education. The Roosevelt Scholars Program is offered. There are 4 national honor societies, a freshman honors program, and 20 departmental honors programs.

Faculty/Classroom: All teach undergraduates. No introductory courses are taught by graduate students.

Requirements: The SAT I or ACT is required. In addition, students must have completed 15 academic units, including 4 of English, 3 of math, 2 each of science, social studies, and foreign language, and 1 each of history and electives. An interview is recommended for all applicants, and an audition is required for music and theater candidates. Roosevelt requires applicants to be in the upper 50% of their class. A GPA of 2.3 is required. AP and CLEP credits are accepted. Important factors in the admissions decision are advanced placement or honor courses, evidence of special talent, and extracurricular activities record.

Procedure: Freshmen are admitted to all sessions. There are early decision, early admissions, and deferred admissions plans. There is a rolling admissions plan. Applications should be filed by August 15 for fall entry, January 15 for spring entry, and May 1 for summer entry. The fall 2003 application fee was $25. Notification is sent on a rolling basis. Applications are accepted on-line through the school's web site.

Transfer: 732 transfer students enrolled in a recent year. Applicants must have earned a minimum GPA of 2.0 in all accredited college course work. Offical transcripts must be received from each college where course work was attempted. 30 of 120 credits required for the bachelor's degree must be completed at Roosevelt.

Visiting: There are regularly scheduled orientations for prospective students, including open houses and Transfer Days. There are guides for informal visits and visitors may sit in on classes. To schedule a visit, contact the Undergraduate Admissions Office.

Financial Aid: In 2003-2004, 85% of all full-time freshmen and 65% of continuing full-time students received some form of financial aid. 75% of full-time freshmen and 65% of continuing full-time students received need-based aid. The average freshman award was $10,500. Need-based scholarships or need-based grants averaged $7725; need-based self-help aid (loans and jobs) averaged $7170; and other non-need-based awards and non-need-based scholarships averaged $5220. The FAFSA and the college's own financial statement are required. Check with the school for current deadlines.

International Students: The school actively recruits these students. They must score 550 on the written TOEFL and also take the college's own test.

Computers: The mainframe is an IBM ES/9000 Model 30. PCs and Mac workstations are available for student use. Services include e-mail, Internet access, and computer-aided instruction in open access computer labs. All students may access the system. Students may access the system 1 hour when demand is great. There are no fees.

Admissions Contact: Gwen Kanelos, Assistant Vice President for Enrollment Services. E-mail: *applyru@roosevelt.edu*
Web: *www.roosevelt.edu*

SAINT XAVIER UNIVERSITY
Chicago, IL 60655

E-2

(773) 298-3050
(800) 462-9288; Fax: (773) 298-3076

Full-time: 704 men, 1627 women	**Faculty:** 160; IIA, av$
Part-time: 170 men, 561 women	**Ph.D.s:** 86%
Graduate: 510 men, 1994 women	**Student/Faculty:** 15 to 1
Year: semesters, summer session	**Tuition:** $16,680
Application Deadline: August 15	**Room & Board:** $6464
Freshman Class: 1701 applied, 1159 accepted, 384 enrolled	
ACT: 21	**COMPETITIVE**

Saint Xavier University is a private institution founded by the Sisters of Mercy in 1846 and affiliated with the Roman Catholic Church. There are 4 undergraduate and 4 graduate schools. In addition to regional accreditation, SXU has baccalaureate program accreditation with NASM and NLN. The library contains 172,104 volumes, 10,519 microform items, and 2282 audio/video tapes/CDs, and subscribes to 798 periodicals. Computerized library services include the card catalog, interlibrary loans, database searching, and Internet access. Special learning facilities include a learning resource center, art gallery, and radio station. The 70-acre campus is in an urban area 15 miles southwest of Chicago's loop. Including any residence halls, there are 16 buildings.

Student Life: 96% of undergraduates are from Illinois. Students are from 21 states and 4 foreign countries. 50% are from public schools. 63% are white; 18% African American; 11% Hispanic. 80% are Catholic; 16% Protestant. The average age of freshmen is 18; all undergraduates, 23. 24% do not continue beyond their first year.

Housing: 630 students can be accommodated in college housing, which includes single-sex and coed dorms. On-campus housing is guaranteed for all 4 years. 81% of students commute. Alcohol is not permitted. All students may keep cars.

Activities: There are no fraternities or sororities. There are 37 groups on campus, including art, band, cheerleading, choir, chorus, computers, drama, ethnic, honors, international, jazz band, literary magazine, marching band, musical theater, newspaper, pep band, political, professional, radio and TV, religious, social service, student government, and yearbook. Popular campus events include Xavierfest, Boat Bash, and Octoberfest.

Sports: There are 4 intercollegiate sports for men and 5 for women, and 4 intramural sports for men and 4 for women. Facilities include baseball and softball diamonds, an outdoor sports facility, and a football field. The convocation and athletic center seats 2200 in the main arena with 4 additional competition courts. It also has racquetball courts, an indoor running track, training rooms, and a health and fitness center.

Disabled Students: 98% of the campus is accessible. Wheelchair ramps, elevators, special parking, specially equipped rest rooms, special class scheduling, lowered drinking fountains, and lowered telephones are available.

Services: Counseling and information services are available, as is tutoring in every subject. There are reading and language clinics and a center for learning disabilities.

Campus Safety and Security: Measures include 24-hour foot and vehicle patrol, self-defense education, security escort services, and shuttle buses. There are emergency telephones and lighted pathways/sidewalks.

Programs of Study: SXU confers B.A., B.S., and B.M. degrees. Master's degrees are also awarded. Bachelor's degrees are awarded in BIOLOGICAL SCIENCE (biology/biological science), BUSINESS (accounting, banking and finance, business administration and management, international business management, and marketing/retailing/merchandising), COMMUNICATIONS AND THE ARTS (communications, English, French, music, and Spanish), COMPUTER AND PHYSICAL SCIENCE (chemistry, computer science, and mathematics), EDUCATION (art, early childhood, elementary, foreign languages, middle school, music, science, and secondary), HEALTH PROFESSIONS (nursing, predentistry, premedicine, prepharmacy, and speech pathology/audiology), SOCIAL SCIENCE (criminal justice, history, philosophy, political science/government, prelaw, psychology, religion, social science, and sociology). Business, nursing, and education are the strongest programs academically and have the largest enrollments.

Required: To graduate, the student must complete 120 credit hours, including the school's 57-semester-hour core curriculum, and earn a GPA of 2.0. The credit hours required in the student's major vary by subject.

Special: The university offers internships, and study abroad in England, Ireland, and Italy. There is a freshman honors program.

Faculty/Classroom: 44% of faculty are male; 56%, female. All teach undergraduates. The average class size in an introductory lecture is 20; in a laboratory, 15; and in a regular course, 16.

Admissions: 68% of the 2003-2004 applicants were accepted. The ACT scores for the 2003-2004 freshman class were: 52% below 21, 25% between 21 and 23, 16% between 24 and 26, 3% between 27 and 28, and 3% above 28. 38% of the current freshmen were in the top fifth of their class; 70% were in the top two fifths.

Requirements: The ACT is required. In addition, students must be graduates of an accredited secondary school and have earned 16 specific academic credits, including 4 years each of English and the natural and social sciences, 3 each of math and academic electives, and 2 years of a foreign language. The GED is accepted. AP and CLEP credits are accepted.

Procedure: Freshmen are admitted fall and spring. Entrance exams should be taken during the spring of the junior year. There is a deferred admissions plan. There is a rolling admissions plan. Applications should be filed by August 15 for fall entry and January 15 for spring entry. The fall 2003 application fee was $25. Notification is sent on a rolling basis. Applications are accepted on-line.

Transfer: 471 transfer students enrolled in 2002-2003. Applicants must have completed 12 semester hours with a GPA of 2.25. An interview is recommended. 30 of 120 credits required for the bachelor's degree must be completed at SXU.

Visiting: There are regularly scheduled orientations for prospective students. There are guides for informal visits and visitors may sit in on classes and stay overnight. To schedule a visit, contact the Director of Admissions.

Financial Aid: In 2003-2004, 88% of all full-time freshmen and 82% of continuing full-time students received some form of financial aid. 64% of full-time freshmen and 65% of continuing full-time students received need-based aid. The average freshman award was $15,197. Need-based scholarships or need-based grants averaged $10,123; need-based self-help aid (loans and jobs) averaged $5271; and non-need-based athletic scholarships averaged $4297. 12% of undergraduates work part time. The average financial indebtedness of the 2003 graduate was $19,374. The FAFSA is required. The deadline for filing freshman financial aid applications for fall entry is March 1.

International Students: There were 17 international students enrolled in a recent year. The school actively recruits these students. They must score 550 on the written TOEFL.

Computers: The mainframes are a DEC VAX 11/750 and an Alpha UNIX. Students are assigned e-mail accounts and have access to the Internet. All students may access the system. There are no time limits and no fees.

Graduates: From July 1, 2002 to June 30, 2003, 617 bachelor's degrees were awarded. The most popular majors were education (20%), business (20%), and nursing (17%). In an average class, 30% graduate in 3 years or less, 74% graduate in 4 years or less, 49% graduate in 5 years or less, and 56% graduate in 6 years or less. Of the 2002 graduating class, 23% were enrolled in graduate school within 6 months of graduation and 98% were employed.

Admissions Contact: Beth Gierach, Director of Enrollment Services. E-mail: *admissions@sxu.edu* Web: *www.sxu.edu.admission*

SCHOOL OF THE ART INSTITUTE OF CHICAGO   E-2
Chicago, IL 60603

(312) 899-5219
(800) 232-7242; Fax: (312) 899-1840

Full-time: 635 men, 1030 women	**Faculty:** n/av
Part-time: 40 men, 95 women	**Ph.D.s:** 87%
Graduate: 160 men, 365 women	**Student/Faculty:** 14 to 1
Year: semesters, summer session	**Tuition:** $24,000
Application Deadline: open	**Room & Board:** $7300 (room only)
Freshman Class: n/av	
SAT I or ACT: required	**SPECIAL**

The School of the Art Institute of Chicago, founded in 1866, is a private institution that is affiliated with the museum of the Art Institute of Chicago. The school offers training in the fine arts and design. There is 1 undergraduate and 1 graduate school. Figures in the above capsule and in this profile are approximate. In addition to regional accreditation, SAIC has baccalaureate program accreditation with NASAD. The library contains 7100 volumes, 157 microform items, and 4000 audio/video tapes/CDs, and subscribes to 350 periodicals. Computerized library services include the card catalog, interlibrary loans, and database searching. Special learning facilities include a learning resource center, art gallery, TV station, film center, video data bank, fashion resource center, student galleries, poetry center, web-based radio station, Roger Brown study collection, Joan Flasch artists book collection, Gene Siskel film center, and the Collection of the Art Institute of Chicago. The campus is in an urban area in downtown Chicago. Including any residence halls, there are 5 buildings.

Student Life: 77% of undergraduates are from out of state, mostly the Midwest. Students are from 48 states, 42 foreign countries, and Canada. 67% are white; 12% foreign nationals; 10% Asian American. The average age of freshmen is 19; all undergraduates, 22. 21% do not continue beyond their first year.

Housing: 664 students can be accommodated in college housing, which includes coed dorms. On-campus housing is available on a first-come, first-served basis and is available on a lottery system for upperclassmen. 65% of students commute. Alcohol is not permitted. All students may keep cars.

Activities: There are no fraternities or sororities. There are 24 groups on campus, including art, ethnic, film, gay, international, literary magazine, newspaper, political, professional, radio and TV, religious, social, social service, and student government. Popular campus events include film center screening, visiting artist lectures, and exhibitions/openings at galleries.

Sports: There is no sports program at SAIC.

Disabled Students: 98% of the campus is accessible. Wheelchair ramps, elevators, special parking, specially equipped rest rooms, special class scheduling, lowered drinking fountains, lowered telephones, and assistance in other areas is available on an individual basis are available.

Services: Counseling and information services are available, as is tutoring in every subject. There is remedial reading and writing. Tutoring for students with learning disabilities is provided through the learning center.

Campus Safety and Security: Measures include 24-hour foot and vehicle patrol, self-defense education, shuttle buses, and informal discussions. There are pamphlets/posters/films, emergency telephones, and lighted pathways/sidewalks.

Programs of Study: SAIC confers B.A., B.F.A. and B.Int.Arch. degrees. Master's degrees are also awarded. Bachelor's degrees are awarded in COMMUNICATIONS AND THE ARTS (art history and appreciation, audio technology, ceramic art and design, design, drawing, fiber/textiles/weaving, film arts, painting, photography, printmaking, sculpture, video, and visual and performing arts), COMPUTER AND PHYSICAL SCIENCE (digital arts/technology), EDUCATION (art), ENGINEERING AND ENVIRONMENTAL DESIGN (drafting and design technology and interior design), SOCIAL SCIENCE (fashion design and technology).

Required: All students are required to take 72 credit hours of studio courses, 30 hours of liberal arts, 18 hours of art history, and 12 hours of electives. A total of 132 credit hours must be completed to graduate. All students are required to take English literature and composition, natural science, social science, and humanities courses as well 2-, 3-, and 4-dimensional studio.

Special: The school offers internships, student-designed majors, pass/fail options, visual arts co-op programs, cross-registration with Roosevelt University, and many cooperative work-study opportunities. Dual and student-designed majors, a B.A.-B.S. degree, and study abroad in 20 countries with active exchange programs are possible.

Faculty/Classroom: 60% of faculty are male; 40%, female.

Requirements: The SAT I or ACT is required, with a minimum score of 500 required on the verbal section of the SAT I or an English score of 20 required on the ACT. Applicants must be graduates of an accredited secondary school. The GED is accepted. All students must submit a portfolio and an essay. An interview is recommended. AP and CLEP credits are accepted. Important factors in the admissions decision are evidence of special talent, recommendations by school officials, and personality/intangible qualities.

Procedure: Freshmen are admitted fall and spring. There is a deferred admissions plan. There is a rolling admissions plan. Application deadlines are open. The fall 2003 application fee was $55.

Transfer: 269 transfer students enrolled in a recent year. Transfer students must take the SAT I or ACT. A minimum score of 500 is required on the verbal section of the SAT I and a minimum English score of 20 is required on the ACT. Students must submit a portfolio. 36 of 132 credits required for the bachelor's degree must be completed at SAIC.

Visiting: There are guides for informal visits. To schedule a visit, contact the Office of Admissions.

Financial Aid: In a recent year, 70% of all full-time freshmen and 74% of continuing full-time students received some form of financial aid. 55% of full-time freshmen and 58% of continuing full-time students received need-based aid. The average freshman award was $16,590. 31% of undergraduates work part time. Average annual earnings from campus work are $3420. The average financial indebtedness of a recent graduate was $10,311. The FAFSA and the college's own financial statement are required. Check with the school for current deadlines.

International Students: There were 216 international students enrolled in a recent year. The school actively recruits these students. They must score 527 on the written TOEFL or 197 on the electronic version and also take the college's own test and the SAT I or the ACT.

Computers: Students have access to 40 G3 Macs and 29 Power PC Macs in the computer lab. Additionally, there are 75 G3 Macs and 15 Power PC Macs in computer classrooms; 60 G3 Macs, 25 Power PC Macs, 2 IBM/NT workstations, and 15 SGI workstations in departmental labs; 6 IBM workstations in the library, and 8 Power PC Macs in the residence halls. All students may access the system. There are no time limits and no fees.

Graduates: In a recent year, 302 bachelor's degrees were awarded.

Admissions Contact: Pat Lally, Associate Director of Admissions. A video is available. E-mail: *admiss@artic.edu* Web: *http://www.saic/saichome.html*

SHIMER COLLEGE   C-1
Waukegan, IL 60079

(847) 623-8400
(800) 215-7173; Fax: (847) 249-8798

Full-time: 73 men, 38 women	**Faculty:** 15
Part-time: 6 men, 6 women	**Ph.D.s:** 94%
Graduate: 2 men, 8 women	**Student/Faculty:** 7 to 1
Year: semesters	**Tuition:** $16,875
Application Deadline: March 1	**Room & Board:** $2780
Freshman Class: 64 applied, 61 accepted, 50 enrolled	
SAT I or ACT: recommended	**LESS COMPETITIVE**

Shimer College, founded in 1853, is a private liberal arts institution with a curriculum based on original sources and a Socratic teaching method employing discussion classes of 12 or fewer students. The library contains 200,000 volumes. Computerized library services include the card catalog, interlibrary loans, database searching, and Internet access. The 3-acre campus is in a suburban area 25 miles north of Chicago. Including any residence halls, there are 10 buildings.

Student Life: 58% of undergraduates are from Illinois. Students are from 20 states and 4 foreign countries. 75% are from public schools. 80% are white; 12% African American. The average age of freshmen is 19; all undergraduates, 24. 20% do not continue beyond their first year.

Housing: 65 students can be accommodated in college housing, which includes coed dorms, on-campus apartments, and off-campus apartments. On-campus housing is guaranteed for the freshman year only and is available on a first-come, first-served basis. Priority is given to out-of-town students. 50% of students live on campus; of those, 95% remain on campus on weekends. All students may keep cars.

Activities: There are no fraternities or sororities. There are some groups and organizations on campus, including art, chess, choir, computers, drama, literary magazine, newspaper, photography, and student government. Popular campus events include community lunch and poetry reading.

Sports: There is no sports program at Shimer. Facilities include a gym and a pool.

Disabled Students: 20% of the campus is accessible. Wheelchair ramps are available.

Services: Counseling and information services are available, as is tutoring in every subject.

Campus Safety and Security: Measures include security escort services and informal discussions.

Programs of Study: Shimer confers B.A. and B.S. degrees. Bachelor's degrees are awarded in COMPUTER AND PHYSICAL SCIENCE (natural sciences), SOCIAL SCIENCE (humanities and social science). Humanities and social science are the strongest academically. Humanities is the largest.

Required: To graduate, students must earn 125 credit hours with a GPA of 2.0, complete 2 comprehensive exams, and submit a thesis. The school requires 60 credit hours in the major for the B.S. degree, 40 for the B.A.; 65 in the core curriculum for the B.S., 85 for the B.A.

Special: Shimer offers internships in all areas of study, study abroad at Oxford in England, and Partnerships in Service Learning in 5 other countries. There is an accelerated degree program, a B.A.-B.S. degree, dual majors in all areas, student-designed majors, and a general studies degree. Nondegree study and pass/fail options are possible.

Faculty/Classroom: 67% of faculty are male; 33%, female. All teach undergraduates. No introductory courses are taught by graduate students. The average class size in a regular course is 7.

Admissions: 95% of the 2003-2004 applicants were accepted.

Requirements: The SAT I or ACT is recommended. Requirements are highly individualized. Essays and an interview are required. Important factors in the admissions decision are personality/intangible qualities, recommendations by school officials, and leadership record.

Procedure: Freshmen are admitted fall and spring. There are early decision, early admissions, and deferred admissions plans. There is a rolling admissions plan. Early decision applications should be filed by December 1; regular applications, by March 1 for fall entry and January 1 for spring entry, along with a $25 fee. Notification of early decision is sent December 15; regular decision, on a rolling basis beginning March 15. A waiting list is an active part of the admissions procedure. Applications are accepted on-line through Illinois Mentor.

Transfer: 11 transfer students enrolled in 2002-2003. Applicants are required to have an interview. 60 credits of 125 required for the bachelor's degree must be completed at Shimer.

Visiting: There are regularly scheduled orientations for prospective students, consisting of class visits, lunch, and a financial aid interview. There are guides for informal visits and visitors may sit in on classes and stay overnight. To schedule a visit, contact Bill Paterson at *billp@shimer.edu*.

Financial Aid: 70% of undergraduates work part time. Average annual earnings from campus work are $1800. Shimer is a member of CSS. The CSS/Profile is required. The deadline for filing freshman financial aid applications for fall entry is July 30.

International Students: There are 5 international students enrolled. The school actively recruits these students. They must score 500 on the written TOEFL.

Computers: PCs are available with web and Internet access in the computer lab and college dorm. All students may access the system 24 hours a day. There are no time limits and no fees.

Graduates: From July 1, 2002 to June 30, 2003, 25 bachelor's degrees were awarded. The most popular majors were humanities (55%), social sciences (35%), and natural sciences (10%). In an average class, 7% graduate in 3 years or less, 50% graduate in 4 years or less, 53% graduate in 5 years or less, and 58% graduate in 6 years or less. Of the 2002 graduating class, 20% were enrolled in graduate school within 6 months of graduation and 70% were employed.

Admissions Contact: Bill Paterson, Associate Director of Admissions. E-mail: *admissions@shimer.edu* Web: *www.shimer.edu*

SOUTHERN ILLINOIS UNIVERSITY SYSTEM

The Southern Illinois University System, established in 1965, is 1 of 2 public senior university systems in Illinois. It has two campuses: Southern Illinois University Carbondale, with a School of Medicine in Springfield and a campus in Niigata, Japan, and Southern Illinois University Edwardsville, with a School of Dental Medicine in Alton and a center in East St. Louis. The university offers degree programs from the associate through the doctorate, and professional degrees in law, medicine, dentistry, and pharmacy. The SIU Board of Trustees is the legal entity with overall responsibility for the organization and governance of the university and its constituent institutions. The chief executive officer is the president. Dedicated to the traditional academic pursuits of instruction, scholarship, and public service, the university assigns priority to achieving excellence in undergraduate and graduate education, encourages and supports scholarly research and creative achievement, and strives to achieve and maintain cultural diversity. The recent total enrollment of both campuses was 34,581; there were 1,685 full-time instructional faculty members. Altogether, there are 4 associate, 127 baccalaureate, 117 master's, and 38 doctoral and professional degree programs offered through the Southern Illinois University System. For more information, visit Southern Illinois University on the web at *www.siu.edu*.

SOUTHERN ILLINOIS UNIVERSITY CARBONDALE D-5

Carbondale, IL 62901 (618) 453-2908; Fax: (618) 453-3250

Full-time: 8187 men, 6488 women	Faculty: 907; I, --$
Part-time: 988 men, 703 women	Ph.Ds: 83%
Graduate: 2439 men, 2582 women	Student/Faculty: 16 to 1
Year: semesters, summer session	Tuition: $5521 ($9766)
Application Deadline: open	Room & Board: $4886
Freshman Class: 8538 applied, 6511 accepted, 2505 enrolled	
ACT: 22	COMPETITIVE

Southern Illinois University Carbondale, founded in 1869, is a public institution that is part of the Southern Illinois University system. The multicampus university offers undergraduate programs in the Colleges of Applied Sciences and Arts, Agricultural Sciences, Business and Administration, College of Education and Human Services, Engineering, Liberal Arts, Mass Communication and Media Arts, and Science. There are 8 undergraduate and 3 graduate schools. In addition to regional accreditation, SIUC has baccalaureate program accreditation with AACSB, ABET, ABFSE, ACEJMC, ADA, APTA, CAHEA, CSWE, FIDER, NASAD, NASM, NCATE, NRPA, and SAF. The 2 libraries contain 2,638,512 volumes, 4,502,969 microform items, and 14,229 audio/video tapes/CDs, and subscribe to 25,122 periodicals. Computerized library services include the card catalog, interlibrary loans, and database searching. Special learning facilities include a learning resource center, art gallery, natural history museum, radio station, TV station, student-run newspaper, farms and timberlands, greenhouses, livestock facilities, archeological center, aviation program, crime study center, wildlife lab, international programs and services, a broadcasting division that operates public television and radio stations, a dental lab, and a child development lab. The 1133-acre campus is in a rural area 96 miles southeast of St. Louis. Including any residence halls, there are 256 buildings.

Student Life: 88% of undergraduates are from Illinois. Students are from 50 states, 110 foreign countries, and Canada. 67% are white; 12% African American. The average age of freshmen is 19; all undergraduates, 23. 30% do not continue beyond their first year; 70% remain to graduate.

Housing: 5331 students can be accommodated in college housing, which includes single-sex and coed dorms, on-campus apartments, married-student housing, fraternity houses, and sorority houses. In addition, there are honors houses, special-interest houses, family housing, over-21 residence halls, and residence halls that stay open during breaks. On-campus housing is guaranteed for the freshman year only and is available on a first-come, first-served basis. 73% of students commute. All students may keep cars.

Activities: 5% of men belong to 12 national fraternities; 5% of women belong to 1 local and 4 national sororities. There are 386 groups on campus, including art, band, cheerleading, chess, choir, chorale, chorus, computers, dance, debate, drama, drill team, drum and bugle corps, ethnic, film, forensics, gay, honors, international, jazz band, literary magazine, marching band, musical theater, newspaper, opera, orchestra, pep band, photography, political, professional, radio and TV, religious, social, social service, student government, and symphony. Popular campus events include Cardboard Boat Regatta, International Festival, and Hispanic Month.

Sports: There are 9 intercollegiate sports for men and 9 for women, and 25 intramural sports for men and 25 for women. Facilities include a 17,324-seat stadium, a 10,014-seat arena, a skate park, a women's softball field, a baseball field, a 700-seat gym, a lake and beach with boat docks, tennis courts, and a cross-country course. The 214,000-square-foot student recreation center houses an Olympic-size pool, indoor tracks, racquetball, squash, and tennis courts, aerobics equipment, a weight room, a Nautilus room and numerous exercise stations. The center also offers volleyball, basketball, badminton, handball, indoor soccer, a climbing wall, a dance studio, a boxing practice room, and a martial arts practice room.

Disabled Students: 99% of the campus is accessible. Wheelchair ramps, elevators, special parking, specially equipped rest rooms, special class scheduling, lowered drinking fountains, lowered telephones, special housing, and classroom accommodations are available. Disability support services are available.

Services: Counseling and information services are available, as is tutoring in most subjects. There is a reader service for the blind. There is also new student orientation, a mentoring program, a writing skills lab, premajor advisement, student development programs, and career counseling. Students often are required to pay for tutorial assistance.

Campus Safety and Security: Measures include 24-hour foot and vehicle patrol, self-defense education, security escort services, and shuttle buses. There are informal discussions, pamphlets/posters/films, emergency telephones, and lighted pathways/sidewalks. Campus security is operated by law enforcement officers, supplemented with a student patrol program.

Programs of Study: SIUC confers B.A., B.S., B.F.A., and B.Mus. degrees. Associate, master's, and doctoral degrees are also awarded. Bachelor's degrees are awarded in AGRICULTURE (agricultural economics, agriculture, animal science, forestry and related sciences, and plant science), BIOLOGICAL SCIENCE (avian sciences, biology/biological science, botany, microbiology, physiology, and zoology), BUSINESS (accounting, banking and finance, business administration and management, business economics, business systems analysis, fashion merchandising, funeral home services, management science, marketing/retailing/merchandising, and recreation and leisure services), COMMUNICATIONS AND THE ARTS (art, broadcasting, classics, design, dramatic arts, English, English literature, film arts, fine arts, French, German, journalism, linguistics, music, photography, radio/television technology, Russian, Spanish, and speech/debate/rhetoric), COMPUTER AND PHYSICAL SCIENCE (chemistry, computer science, geology, information sciences and systems, mathematics, physics, and radiological technology), EDUCATION (business, early childhood, elementary, health, physical, special, and vocational), ENGINEERING AND ENVIRONMENTAL DESIGN (architecture, automotive technology, aviation administration/management, aviation computer technology, civil engineering, computer engineering, electrical/electronics engineering, electrical/electronics engineering technology, engineering management, engineering technology, industrial engineering technology, interior design, mechanical engineering, mining and mineral engineering, and technological management), HEALTH PROFESSIONS (dental hygiene, dental laboratory technology, health care administration, physician's assistant, rehabilitation therapy, respiratory therapy, and speech pathology/audiology), SOCIAL SCIENCE (anthropology, clothing and textiles management/production/services, criminal justice, dietetics, economics, family/consumer resource management, fire protection, food science, geography, German area studies, history, international relations, law, liberal arts/general studies, paralegal studies, parks and recreation management, philosophy, political science/government, psychology, social science, social studies, social work, and sociology). Programs in law, education, and medicine and business are the strongest academically. Psychology, radio and television, and workforce education and development are the largest.

Required: To graduate, all students must meet the university and program requirements, maintain a minimum 2.0 GPA, and complete a minimum of 120 semester hours. The total number of hours in the major varies, and students must complete a university core curriculum.

Special: The university offers internships through the Washington center and study abroad in 40 countries, including Europe, Africa, Australia, the British Isles, Latin America, and Spain. Also available are a Washington semester, student-designed majors, work-study programs, accelerated degree programs, dual majors, and B.A.-B.S. degrees in numerous programs. The College of Applied Sciences and Arts offers technically oriented programs, co-op programs, and work-study. Nondegree study is available through the Community Listeners Permit and Elderhostel. A combined total of 40 hours may be earned through proficiency exams and credit for work experience. There are 26 national honor societies, a freshman honors program, and several departmental honors programs.

Faculty/Classroom: 67% of faculty are male; 33%, female. 80% teach undergraduates, 15% do research, and 50% do both. Graduate students teach 30% of introductory courses. The average class size in an introductory lecture is 224; in a laboratory, 23; and in a regular course, 23.

Admissions: 76% of the 2003-2004 applicants were accepted. The SAT I scores for the 2003-2004 freshman class were: Verbal--42% below 500, 34% between 500 and 599, 21% between 600 and 700, and 4% above 700; Math--40% below 500, 32% between 500 and 599, 21% between 600 and 700, and 7% above 700. The ACT scores were 22% below 21, 39% between 21 and 23, 23% between 24 and 26, 8% between 27 and 28, and 7% above 28. 24% of the current freshmen were in the top fifth of their class; 53% were in the top two fifths.

Requirements: The ACT is required. In addition, applicants must be graduates of an accredited secondary high school or have a GED certificate, with 4 years of English, 3 years each of math, lab science, and social science, and 2 years of electives, which may include art, music, foreign language, or vocational education. For general admission, high school transcripts or GED test scores, ACT or SAT I scores, and immunization records are required. Some programs require additional materials and/or screening. AP and CLEP credits are accepted.

Procedure: Freshmen are admitted fall, spring, and summer. Entrance exams should be taken during spring of the junior year. There is a deferred admissions plan and a rolling admissions plan. Application deadlines are open. Application fee is $30. Notification is sent on a rolling basis. Applications are accepted on-line through *http://www.siu.edu/siuc/*.

Transfer: 2842 transfer students enrolled in 2002-2003. All transfer students must have a minimum 2.0 GPA. Students are required to meet freshman admission requirements if they are under 21 years old and have fewer than 26 credit hours of acceptable transfer work. Some academic programs have higher admission requirements. 30 credits of 120 required for the bachelor's degree must be completed at SIUC.

Visiting: There are regularly scheduled orientations for prospective students, including admission counseling, academic program exhibits, student organization exhibits, workshops on financial aid and housing, and tours of the campus and residence halls. There are guides for informal visits and visitors may sit in on classes. To schedule a visit, contact New Student Admission Services at (618) 536-4405 or *admerc@siu.edu*.

Financial Aid: In 2002-2003, 80% of all full-time freshmen and 83% of continuing full-time students received some form of financial aid. 77% of full-time freshmen and 78% of continuing full-time students received need-based aid. The average freshman award was $7329. 54% of undergraduates work part time. Average annual earnings from campus work are $1596. The average financial indebtedness of the 2003 graduate was $12,366. The FAFSA is required. The deadline for filing freshman financial aid applications for fall entry is April 1.

International Students: There were 540 international students enrolled in a recent year. The school actively recruits these students. They must score 520 on the written TOEFL or 190 on the electronic version and also take the SAT I, or ACT, and their own country's standardized college entrance exam.

Computers: The mainframe is an IBM H30. Students may use more than 500 PCs that are networked at 4 computing learning centers. Other departments on campus also have labs connected to the network. All students may access the system all the time, all year. There are no time limits and no fees.

Graduates: From July 1, 2002 to June 30, 2003, 4600 bachelor's degrees were awarded. The most popular majors were workforce education and development (17%), industrial technology (5%), and health care management (5%). In an average class, 17% graduate in 4 years or less, 33% graduate in 5 years or less, and 39% graduate in 6 years or less. 231 companies recruited on campus in 2002-2003.

Admissions Contact: Anne DeLuca, Assistant Vice Chancellor Affairs and Enrollment Management and. A video is available.
E-mail: *adeluca@siu.edu* Web: *www.siuc.edu*

SOUTHERN ILLINOIS UNIVERSITY EDWARDSVILLE C-4
Edwardsville, IL 62026-1600 (618) 650-3705
(800) 447-SIUE; Fax: (618) 650-5013

Full-time: 8359 men and women	**Faculty:** 494; IIA, av$
Part-time: 1655 men and women	**Ph.D.s:** 83%
Graduate: 2502 men and women	**Student/Faculty:** 17 to 1
Year: semesters, summer session	**Tuition:** $3708 ($6678)
Application Deadline: May 31	**Room & Board:** $5016
Freshman Class: 4263 applied, 3371 accepted, 1655 enrolled	
ACT: required	**COMPETITIVE**

Southern Illinois University Edwardsville, founded in 1957, is part of the Southern Illinois University system and offers undergraduate programs in business, education, engineering, arts and sciences, and nursing. Graduate programs also are offered in 34 subject areas, including professional programs in pharmacy and dental medicine. There are 7 undergraduate schools and 1 graduate school. In addition to regional accreditation, SIUE has baccalaureate program accreditation with AACSB, ABET, ACCE, ADA, ASLA, CSWE, NASM, NCATE, and NLN. The library contains 783,050 volumes, 1,658,847 microform items, and 29,183 audio/video tapes/CDs, and subscribes to 14,807 periodicals. Computerized library services include the card catalog, interlibrary loans, database searching, and Internet access. Special learning facilities include a learning resource center, art gallery, radio station, TV station, recording studio, engineering labs, anthropology museum, greenhouse, arboretum, and nursing psychomotor skills lab. The 2660-acre campus is in a suburban area 18 miles northeast of downtown St. Louis, Missouri. Including any residence halls, there are 25 buildings.

Student Life: 86% of undergraduates are from Illinois. Students are from 42 states, 63 foreign countries, and Canada. 83% are white; 10% African American. The average age of all undergraduates is 23. 31% do not continue beyond their first year.

Housing: 3000 students can be accommodated in college housing, which includes coed dorms, on-campus apartments, married-student housing, and fraternity houses. There are alos honors wings and special-interest wings. On-campus housing is available on a first-come, first-served basis. Priority is given to out-of-town students. 72% of students commute. All students may keep cars.

Activities: 5% of men belong to 9 national fraternities; 4% of women belong to 7 national sororities. There are 140 groups on campus, including art, band, cheerleading, choir, chorale, chorus, dance, drama, ethnic, gay, honors, international, jazz band, literary magazine, musical theater, newspaper, opera, orchestra, pep band, photography, political, professional, radio and TV, religious, social, social service, student government, and symphony. Popular campus events include Welcome Week, Arts and Issues Series, and International Week.

Sports: There are 7 intercollegiate sports for men and 8 for women, and 11 intramural sports for men and 11 for women. Facilities include

the Vadalabene Center and Student Fitness Center, which offer racquetball, basketball, aquatics, volleyball, indoor track, exercise, and weight training; the University Center, which features restaurants, a recreation center, billiards, and a bowling alley; an outdoor swimming pool; a lake for canoeing and sailing; an outdoor track and field and soccer stadium; baseball, softball and soccer fields; extensive walking and biking trails; and a frisbee course.

Disabled Students: All of the campus is accessible. Wheelchair ramps, elevators, special parking, specially equipped rest rooms, special class scheduling, lowered drinking fountains, lowered telephones, a Visualtek large-screen TV, Kurzweil readers, test-taking facilities, accessible weight-training equipment, and a swimming pool are available.

Services: Counseling and information services are available, as is tutoring in most subjects. There is a reader service for the blind, and remedial math, reading, and writing.

Campus Safety and Security: Measures include 24-hour foot and vehicle patrol, self-defense education, security escort services, and shuttle buses. There are informal discussions, pamphlets/posters/films, emergency telephones, lighted pathways/sidewalks, and emergency blue lights located throughout campus.

Programs of Study: SIUE confers B.A., B.S., B.F.A., B.L.S., B.M., and B.S.A. degrees. Master's degrees are also awarded. Bachelor's degrees are awarded in BIOLOGICAL SCIENCE (biology/biological science), BUSINESS (accounting, business administration and management, business economics, and management information systems), COMMUNICATIONS AND THE ARTS (art, communications, dance, design, dramatic arts, English, languages, music, and speech/debate/rhetoric), COMPUTER AND PHYSICAL SCIENCE (chemistry, computer science, mathematics, and physics), EDUCATION (early childhood, elementary, health, science, and special), ENGINEERING AND ENVIRONMENTAL DESIGN (civil engineering, computer engineering, construction engineering, electrical/electronics engineering, industrial engineering, manufacturing engineering, and mechanical engineering), HEALTH PROFESSIONS (exercise science, nursing, pharmacy, and speech pathology/audiology), SOCIAL SCIENCE (anthropology, criminal justice, economics, geography, history, liberal arts/general studies, philosophy, political science/government, psychology, social work, and sociology). Business administration, management information systems, and nursing are the largest.

Required: To graduate, students must complete a total of 124 semester hours with a minimum GPA of 2.0. Students must fulfill general education requirements, including 9 hours of math/science, and complete a senior project.

Special: SIUE offers cross-registration with the University of Missouri at St. Louis, co-op programs, internships, which are required by several majors, including mass communications and sociology, work-study programs, dual majors, B.A.-B.S. degrees, student-designed majors (available to specific honors students only), study abroad in 5 countries (England, France, Germany, the Netherlands, and Mexico) by formal exchange agreements, and in a wide variety of others, a liberal studies degree, and a 5-year (3+2) program in dental medicine. There are 12 national honor societies, a freshman honors program, and 15 departmental honors programs.

Faculty/Classroom: 59% of faculty are male; 41%, female. Graduate students teach 2% of introductory courses. The average class size in a regular course is 20.

Admissions: 79% of the 2003-2004 applicants were accepted. The ACT scores for the 2003-2004 freshman class were: 37% below 21, 30% between 21 and 23, 21% between 24 and 26, 7% between 27 and 28, and 5% above 28. 32% of the current freshmen were in the top fifth of their class; 66% were in the top two fifths.

Requirements: The ACT is required. In addition, applicants must be graduates of an accredited secondary school or have a GED certificate. They must have completed 15 academic credits, based on 4 years of English, 3 each of math and lab science, 2 years of any combination of art, foreign language, music, and vocational education, at least 2 years of government and/or history, plus 1 more year of social studies. A GPA of 2.5 is required. AP and CLEP credits are accepted.

Procedure: Freshmen are admitted to all sessions. Entrance exams should be taken before high school graduation. There is a rolling admissions plan. Applications should be filed by May 31 for fall entry, December 15 for spring entry, and May 3 for summer entry, along with a $30 fee. Notification is sent on a rolling basis. Applications are accepted online through *www.siue.edu.*

Transfer: 1283 transfer students enrolled in 2002-2003. Applicants must have a minimum 2.0 GPA in at least 16 semester hours earned. 30 credits of 124 required for the bachelor's degree must be completed at SIUE.

Visiting: There are regularly scheduled orientations for prospective students, including visits before the semester starts. There are guides for informal visits and visitors may sit in on classes. To schedule a visit, contact the Admission Counseling Office.

Financial Aid: In 2003-2004, 49% of all full-time students received some form of financial aid. 38% of all full-time students received need-based aid. The average freshman award was $5304. Need-based scholarships or need-based grants averaged $4211 ($9215 maximum); need-based self-help aid (loans and jobs) averaged $3421 ($5220 maximum); non-need-based athletic scholarships averaged $1986 ($8875 maximum); and other non-need-based awards and non-need-based scholarships averaged $1100 ($2911 maximum). 26% of undergraduates work part time. Average annual earnings from campus work are $1574. The average financial indebtedness of the 2003 graduate was $12,222. The FAFSA is required. The deadline for filing freshman financial aid applications for fall entry is March 1.

International Students: There are 162 international students enrolled. The school actively recruits these students. They must score 550 on the written TOEFL or 213 on the electronic version.

Computers: The mainframe is an IBM 9121/511. There are also 600 PC and Mac workstations located in classrooms and computer labs, including labs at the residence hall and apartment complex. Residence hall rooms and apartments are wired for direct access to the campus network. All students have e-mail accounts and personal web directories. Adaptive equipment is available for students with disabilities. All students may access the system daily at designated hours with some labs open 24 hours. There are no time limits and no fees.

Graduates: From July 1, 2002 to June 30, 2003, 1756 bachelor's degrees were awarded. The most popular majors were business administration (26%), education (23%), and engineering (7%). In an average class, 1% graduate in 3 years or less, 40% graduate in 4 years or less, 33% graduate in 5 years or less, and 10% graduate in 6 years or less. 546 companies recruited on campus in 2002-2003.

Admissions Contact: Admission Counseling. A video is available. E-mail: *admis@siue.edu* Web: *siue.edu*

TRINITY CHRISTIAN COLLEGE
Palos Heights, IL 60463

E-2

(708) 597-3000
(800) 748-0085; Fax: (708) 385-5665

Full-time: 383 men, 649 women	**Faculty:** 65; IIB, -$
Part-time: 86 men, 145 women	**Ph.D.s:** 65%
Graduate: none	**Student/Faculty:** 16 to 1
Year: semesters	**Tuition:** $15,640
Application Deadline: August 15	**Room & Board:** $6000
Freshman Class: 589 applied, 548 accepted, 255 enrolled	
ACT: 23	**VERY COMPETITIVE**

Trinity Christian College, founded in 1959, is a private college offering programs in arts and sciences, business, health science, liberal arts, music, religion, and teacher preparation. In addition to regional accreditation, Trinity has baccalaureate program accreditation with AACSB, CCNE, and NLN. The library contains 75,055 volumes, 34,690 microform items, and 777 audio/video tapes/CDs, and subscribes to 461 periodicals. Computerized library services include the card catalog, interlibrary loans, database searching, and Internet access. Special learning facilities include a learning resource center, art gallery, and a Dutch heritage collection. The 53-acre campus is in a suburban area 20 miles southwest of the Chicago Loop. Including any residence halls, there are 22 buildings.

Student Life: 54% of undergraduates are from Illinois. Students are from 37 states, 10 foreign countries, and Canada. 37% are from public schools. 88% are white. 94% are Protestant. The average age of freshmen is 19; all undergraduates, 33. 27% do not continue beyond their first year; 53% remain to graduate.

Housing: 609 students can be accommodated in college housing, which includes coed dorms, on-campus apartments, and off-campus apartments. On-campus housing is guaranteed for all 4 years. 68% of students live on campus; of those, 45% remain on campus on weekends. Alcohol is not permitted. All students may keep cars.

Activities: There are no fraternities or sororities. There are 21 groups on campus, including art, band, cheerleading, choir, chorale, chorus, drama, ethnic, honors, jazz band, literary magazine, newspaper, pep band, photography, political, professional, religious, social, social service, student government, and yearbook. Popular campus events include the Opus fine arts festival and the Trollstock Concert.

Sports: There are 6 intercollegiate sports for men and 6 for women, and 7 intramural sports for men and 7 for women. Facilities include a gym, a track, a stadium, a baseball diamond, and softball and soccer fields.

Disabled Students: 95% of the campus is accessible. Wheelchair ramps, elevators, special parking, specially equipped rest rooms, and lowered drinking fountains are available.

Services: Counseling and information services are available, as is tutoring in every subject.

Campus Safety and Security: Measures include 24-hour foot and vehicle patrol, self-defense education, security escort services, and informal discussions. There are emergency telephones and lighted pathways/sidewalks.

Programs of Study: Trinity confers B.A., B.S., and B.S.N. degrees. Bachelor's degrees are awarded in BIOLOGICAL SCIENCE (biology/

biological science), BUSINESS (accounting and business administration and management), COMMUNICATIONS AND THE ARTS (applied music, art, communications, English, music, music performance, Spanish, and studio art), COMPUTER AND PHYSICAL SCIENCE (chemistry, computer science, information sciences and systems, and mathematics), EDUCATION (art, education, elementary, music, and special), HEALTH PROFESSIONS (nursing, predentistry, premedicine, and preoptometry), SOCIAL SCIENCE (biblical studies, history, philosophy, prelaw, psychology, social work, sociology, and theological studies). Business, education, and nursing are the strongest academically and have the largest enrollments.

Required: All students must take 9 credits in English, 6 each in philosophy, history, and theology, as well as distribution requirements in cross-cultural studies, natural sciences, social sciences, fine arts, math, and phys ed. Students must complete 125 credit hours and maintain a minimum GPA of 2.0 to graduate.

Special: Students may have various part-time or full-time internships in their major field. There are study-abroad programs in the Netherlands and Spain. Pass/fail options exist. Dual majors are offered. There is 1 national honor society and a freshman honors program.

Faculty/Classroom: 60% of faculty are male; 40%, female. All both teach and do research. The average class size in an introductory lecture is 24; in a laboratory, 17; and in a regular course, 16.

Admissions: 93% of the 2003-2004 applicants were accepted. The ACT scores for the 2003-2004 freshman class were: 30% below 21, 20% between 21 and 23, 26% between 24 and 26, 13% between 27 and 28, and 12% above 28. 22% of the current freshmen were in the top fifth of their class; 48% were in the top two fifths. 11 freshmen graduated first in their class.

Requirements: The ACT is recommended. In addition, applicants should graduate from an accredited high school or have a GED. They should prepare with 3 or 4 years of high school English, 3 years of math, science, and social studies, or 2 years each of a combination of 2 subject areas chosen among foreign language, math, science, or social studies. An interview is required. Trinity requires applicants to be in the upper 60% of their class. A GPA of 2.3 is required. AP and CLEP credits are accepted. Important factors in the admissions decision are advanced placement or honor courses, leadership record, and recommendations by school officials.

Procedure: Freshmen are admitted fall and spring. Entrance exams should be taken during the last semester of the junior year. There is a rolling admissions plan. Applications should be filed by August 15 for fall entry and January 15 for spring entry. The fall 2003 application fee was $20. Notification is sent on a rolling basis.

Transfer: 80 transfer students enrolled in 2002-2003. Applicants must have 24 hours of acceptable credits and a minimum 2.3 GPA. Associate degrees are recognized for transfer. 30 credits of 125 required for the bachelor's degree must be completed at Trinity.

Visiting: There are regularly scheduled orientations for prospective students, including a tour, an interview, a seminar, and class visits. There are guides for informal visits and visitors may sit in on classes and stay overnight. To schedule a visit, contact the Admissions Office at (866) 874-6463 or *admissions@trnty.edu*.

Financial Aid: In 2003-2004, 97% of all full-time freshmen and 92% of continuing full-time students received some form of financial aid. 73% of full-time freshmen and 64% of continuing full-time students received need-based aid. The average freshman award was $8744. 50% of undergraduates work part time. Average annual earnings from campus work are $1300. The average financial indebtedness of the 2003 graduate was $11,625. The FAFSA is required. The deadline for filing freshman financial aid applications for fall entry is February 15.

International Students: There are 22 international students enrolled. They must score 500 on the written TOEFL and also take the SAT I or the ACT, scoring 20 on the ACT.

Computers: There is a PC lab for student use. All students may access the system. There are no time limits and no fees. It is strongly recommended that all students have a personal computer.

Graduates: From July 1, 2002 to June 30, 2003, 186 bachelor's degrees were awarded. The most popular majors were education (29%), business (17%), and organizational management (14%). In an average class, 46% graduate in 4 years or less, 52% graduate in 5 years or less, and 53% graduate in 6 years or less. 10 companies recruited on campus in 2002-2003. Of the 2002 graduating class, 12% were enrolled in graduate school within 6 months of graduation and 93% were employed.

Admissions Contact: Pete Hamstra, Vice President for Admissions and Advancement. E-mail: *admissions@trnty.edu* Web: *www.trnty.edu*

TRINITY COLLEGE OF NURSING AND HEALTH SCIENCES
C-2

Rock Island, IL 61201-5317 (309) 779-7812; Fax: (309) 779-7748

Total Enrollment: 190 men and women	**Faculty:** 14
	Ph.D.s: 20%
Year: semesters, summer session	**Student/Faculty:** n/av
Application Deadline: open	**Tuition:** $4617
	Room & Board: n/app

Freshman Class: n/av

SAT I or ACT: required **SPECIAL**

Trinity College of Nursing and Health Sciences, founded in 1994, is a private institution offering degrees in nursing, radiography, and emergency medical services. The library contains 4200 volumes and subscribes to 64 periodicals. Computerized library services include the card catalog, interlibrary loans, database searching, and Internet access. Special learning facilities include learning lab for all programs. The 2-acre campus is in an urban part of the Illinois/Iowa Quad-Cities on the Mississippi River. There is one building.

Student Life: 82% of undergraduates are from Illinois. Students are from 3 states. 95% are white. The average age of freshmen is 25. 14% do not continue beyond their first year; 86% remain to graduate.

Housing: There are no residence halls. College-sponsored housing is coed. All students commute. Alcohol is not permitted. All students may keep cars.

Activities: There are no fraternities or sororities. There are 5 groups on campus, including honors, social, student government, and Student Nurses' Association. Popular campus events include Visiting Artists cultural presentations.

Sports: There is no sports program at Trinity College.

Disabled Students: 95% of the campus is accessible. Wheelchair ramps, elevators, special parking, specially equipped rest rooms, and special class scheduling are available.

Services: Counseling and information services are available, as is tutoring in every subject. There is remedial math, reading, and writing.

Campus Safety and Security: Measures include informal discussions, pamphlets/posters/films, emergency telephones, and lighted pathways/sidewalks. There is a safety and security overview during orientation, and a foot and vehicle patrol.

Programs of Study: Trinity College confers the B.S.N. degree. Associate degrees are also awarded. Bachelor's degrees are awarded in HEALTH PROFESSIONS (nursing).

Required: Students must complete a minimun of 127 semester hours, including general education courses, and maintain a 2.0 GPA.

Special: There is 1 national honor society and 1 departmental honors program.

Faculty/Classroom: All faculty are female. All teach undergraduates. The average class size in an introductory lecture is 40 and in a laboratory, 25.

Requirements: The SAT I or ACT is required. Applicants should have an ACT composite score of 20 or above or an SAT I score of 800 or above. They should be high school graduates or have the GED. Official transcripts from all high school and postsecondary institutions are required, as is fluency in the English language. Applicants should have the physical ability to provide safe and effective client care and should have CPR certification for health care professionals. A GPA of 2.5 is required. AP and CLEP credits are accepted.

Procedure: Freshmen are admitted in the fall. Entrance exams should be taken in the senior year. There is a rolling admissions plan. Application deadlines are open. Application fee is $50. A waiting list is an active part of the admissions procedure.

Transfer: Applicants should have official transcripts, fluency in the English language, confirmed physical/mental ability to provide safe and effective client care, and CPR certification. They should also complete the nursing transition course with a grade of C or higher. The last 19 of 127 credits required for the bachelor's degree must be completed at Trinity College.

Visiting: There are regularly scheduled orientations for prospective students, consisting of a 2-day orientation 2 weeks prior to the start of the fall term. There are guides for informal visits and visitors may sit in on classes and stay overnight. To schedule a visit, contact Barb Kimpe, Admissions Representative.

Financial Aid: In 2003-2004, 75% of all full-time freshmen and 80% of continuing full-time students received some form of financial aid. 70% of full-time freshmen and 80% of continuing full-time students received need-based aid. The average freshman award was $6375. Need-based scholarships or need-based grants averaged $6000 ($8968 maximum); need-based self-help aid (loans and jobs) averaged $4063 ($10,500 maximum); and non-need-based awards and non-need-based scholarships averaged $500 (maximum). 55% of undergraduates work part time. The average financial indebtedness of the 2003 graduate was $19,125. The FAFSA is required. The priority date for freshman financial aid applications for fall entry is March 1. The deadline for filing freshman financial aid applications for fall entry is June 1.

International Students: International students must score 550 on the written TOEFL.

Computers: There is a computer lab for student use. All students may access the system. There are no time limits and no fees.

Graduates: In a recent year, 8 bachelor's degrees were awarded. One company recruited on campus in a recent year. Of a recent graduating class, all were employed within 6 months of graduation.

Admissions Contact: Barb Kimpe, Admissions Representative. E-mail: *kimpeb@trinityqc.com* Web: *www.trinityqc.edu*

TRINITY INTERNATIONAL UNIVERSITY   E-1
Deerfield, IL 60015   (847) 317-7000
(800) 822-3225; Fax: (847) 317-7081

Full-time: 466 men, 594 women	**Faculty:** 43; IIA, -$
Part-time: 33 men, 50 women	**Ph.D.s:** 81%
Graduate: 710 men, 247 women	**Student/Faculty:** 25 to 1
Year: semesters, summer session	**Tuition:** $17,150
Application Deadline: open	**Room & Board:** $5830
Freshman Class: 498 applied, 412 accepted, 193 enrolled	
SAT I Verbal/Math: 584/567	**ACT:** 23 COMPETITIVE+

Trinity International University, established in 1897 by the Evangelical Free Church, is a Christian, liberal arts institution offering undergraduate, graduate, and doctoral programs. The library contains 240,657 volumes, 110,350 microform items, and 6782 audio/video tapes/CDs, and subscribes to 1371 periodicals. Computerized library services include the card catalog, interlibrary loans, database searching, and Internet access. The 111-acre campus is in a suburban area 25 miles north of Chicago. Including any residence halls, there are 34 buildings.

Student Life: 52% of undergraduates are from out of state, mostly the Midwest. Students are from 33 states, 38 foreign countries, and Canada. 78% are white; 11% African American. Most are Protestant. The average age of freshmen is 18; all undergraduates, 21. 20% do not continue beyond their first year; 50% remain to graduate.

Housing: 700 students can be accommodated in college housing, which includes single-sex dorms, on-campus apartments, off-campus apartments, and married-student housing. On-campus housing is guaranteed for all 4 years. 58% of students live on campus; of those, 75% remain on campus on weekends. Alcohol is not permitted. Upperclassmen may keep cars.

Activities: There are no fraternities or sororities. There are 24 groups on campus, including art, band, cheerleading, choir, chorale, computers, debate, drama, ethnic, gospel choir, handbell choir, honors, international, jazz band, literary magazine, newspaper, orchestra, pep band, political, religious, social service, student government, symphony, and yearbook. Popular campus events include Santa Lucia Festival, Spring Pops Concert, and Fine Arts Series.

Sports: There are 4 intercollegiate sports for men and 4 for women, and 6 intramural sports for men and 6 for women. Facilities include a student center, a sports complex, and football and soccer fields. Students have access to a nearby indoor tennis and racquetball club.

Disabled Students: 75% of the campus is accessible. Wheelchair ramps, elevators, special parking, specially equipped rest rooms, and special class scheduling are available.

Services: Counseling and information services are available, as is tutoring in every subject. There is a reader service for the blind, and remedial math, reading, and writing.

Campus Safety and Security: Measures include 24-hour foot and vehicle patrol, self-defense education, security escort services, and informal discussions. There are emergency telephones and lighted pathways/sidewalks.

Programs of Study: Trinity confers the B.A. degree. Master's and doctoral degrees are also awarded. Bachelor's degrees are awarded in BIOLOGICAL SCIENCE (biology/biological science), BUSINESS (accounting, business administration and management, human resources, international business management, marketing/retailing/merchandising, and sports management), COMMUNICATIONS AND THE ARTS (communications, English, and music), COMPUTER AND PHYSICAL SCIENCE (chemistry and mathematics), EDUCATION (athletic training, elementary, physical, and secondary), HEALTH PROFESSIONS (physical therapy, premedicine, and sports medicine), SOCIAL SCIENCE (biblical studies, Christian studies, history, humanities, liberal arts/general studies, philosophy, psychology, social science, and youth ministry). English, Christian studies, and education are the strongest academically. Business, Christian studies, and education are the largest.

Required: To graduate, all students must complete 126 semester hours, including 58 general education hours and a variable 36 to 54 hours in the major. A GPA of 2.0 is required. Chapel attendance, Christian service, Bible study, and science are also required.

Special: Students can cross-register with the Christian College Consortium and at Trinity Evangelical Divinity School. Trinity offers 3 levels of internships, study abroad in 7 countries, an opportunity through the American Studies Program to spend a semester in Washington, and work-study programs. Dual majors, a general studies degree, and nonde-

gree study are offered. There is 1 national honor society, a freshman honors program, and 15 departmental honors programs.

Faculty/Classroom: 82% of faculty are male; 18%, female. 52% teach undergraduates and 5% do research. No introductory courses are taught by graduate students. The average class size in an introductory lecture is 40; in a laboratory, 20; and in a regular course, 15.

Admissions: 83% of the 2003-2004 applicants were accepted. The SAT I scores for the 2003-2004 freshman class were: Verbal--15% below 500, 46% between 500 and 599, 29% between 600 and 700, and 10% above 700; Math--24% below 500, 32% between 500 and 599, 34% between 600 and 700, and 10% above 700. The ACT scores were 30% below 21, 28% between 21 and 23, 24% between 24 and 26, 9% between 27 and 28, and 9% above 28. 40% of the current freshmen were in the top fifth of their class; 65% were in the top two fifths. 5 freshmen graduated first in their class.

Requirements: The SAT I or ACT is required; the ACT is preferred. A minimum composite score of 890 on the SAT I or 19 on the ACT is required. Applicants should be graduates of an accredited high school and have completed 15 academic credits in art, a foreign language, math, music, science, social studies, and English. A GED is accepted. Recommendations from a pastor must be submitted. Trinity requires applicants to be in the upper 50% of their class. A GPA of 2.5 is required. AP and CLEP credits are accepted. Important factors in the admissions decision are personality/intangible qualities, leadership record, and advanced placement or honor courses.

Procedure: Freshmen are admitted fall and spring. Entrance exams should be taken during spring of the junior year or fall of the senior year. Application deadlines are open. Application fee is $25. Notification is sent on a rolling basis. Applications are accepted on-line through *www.illinoismentor.org*.

Transfer: 77 transfer students enrolled in 2002-2003. Applicants must submit college transcripts and have a cumulative college GPA of 2.0 or higher. 30 of 126 credits required for the bachelor's degree must be completed at Trinity.

Visiting: There are regularly scheduled orientations for prospective students, including class visits, meetings with professors and admission counselors, and a dorm visit. There are guides for informal visits and visitors may sit in on classes and stay overnight. To schedule a visit, contact the Campus Visit Coordinator at *visits@tiu.edu*.

Financial Aid: In 2003-2004, 99% of all full-time freshmen and 98% of continuing full-time students received some form of financial aid. 88% of full-time freshmen and 86% of continuing full-time students received need-based aid. The average freshman award was $16,086. Need-based scholarships or need-based grants averaged $7586 ($12,000 maximum); need-based self-help aid (loans and jobs) averaged $5625 (maximum); non-need-based athletic scholarships averaged $8656 ($22,980 maximum); and other non-need-based awards and non-need-based scholarships averaged $1500 ($4500 maximum). 78% of undergraduates work part time. Average annual earnings from campus work are $1147. The average financial indebtedness of the 2003 graduate was $15,100. Trinity is a member of CSS. The FAFSA is required. The deadline for filing freshman financial aid applications for fall entry is April 15.

International Students: There are 19 international students enrolled. They must score 530 on the written TOEFL or 237 on the electronic version and also take the SAT I or the ACT, scoring 19 on the ACT.

Computers: Trinity provides 100 PCs for academic use. Most dorm rooms have access to the Internet. All students may access the system. There are no time limits and no fees.

Graduates: From July 1, 2002 to June 30, 2003, 158 bachelor's degrees were awarded. The most popular majors were elementary education (10%), youth ministry (9%), and psychology (6%). 20 companies recruited on campus in 2002-2003. Of the 2002 graduating class, 24% were enrolled in graduate school within 6 months of graduation and 50% were employed.

Admissions Contact: Matthew Yoder, Director of Undergraduate Admissions. E-mail: *tcdadm@tiu.edu* Web: *www.tiu.edu*

UNIVERSITY OF CHICAGO   E-2
Chicago, IL 60637   (773) 702-8650; Fax: (773) 702-4199

Full-time: 2005 men, 2045 women	**Faculty:** 927; I, ++$
Part-time: 10 men, 10 women	**Ph.D.s:** 99%
Graduate: 5230 men, 3255 women	**Student/Faculty:** 4 to 1
Year: quarters, summer session	**Tuition:** $28,689
Application Deadline: see profile	**Room & Board:** $9315
Freshman Class: n/av	
SAT I or ACT: required	MOST COMPETITIVE

The University of Chicago, founded in 1891, is a private liberal arts institution offering undergraduate and graduate programs with emphases on the biological and physical sciences, the humanities, and the social sciences. Figures in the above capsule and in this profile are approximate. In addition to regional accreditation, Chicago has baccalaureate program accreditation with NCATE. The 8 libraries contain 5.7 million volumes, 2 million microform items, and 15,000 audio/video tapes/CDs, and subscribe to 47,000 periodicals. Computerized library services include the card catalog, interlibrary loans, and database searching. Special learning facilities include a learning resource center, art gallery, radio station, film studies center, language labs, museum of Near Eastern antiquities, and Renaissance Society (contemporary art). The 190-acre campus is in an urban area in Chicago. Including any residence halls, there are 200 buildings.

Student Life: 79% of undergraduates are from out of state, mostly the Middle Atlantic. Students are from 49 states, 49 foreign countries, and Canada. 70% are from public schools. 65% are white; 16% Asian American. The average age of freshmen is 18; all undergraduates, 20. 5% do not continue beyond their first year.

Housing: 2700 students can be accommodated in college housing, which includes coed dorms, on-campus apartments, and married-student housing. On-campus housing is guaranteed for all 4 years. 66% of students live on campus; of those, 95% remain on campus on weekends. No one may keep cars.

Activities: 12% of men belong to 9 national fraternities; 5% of women belong to 2 national sororities. There are 175 groups on campus, including art, bagpipe band, band, cheerleading, chess, choir, chorale, chorus, college bowl, computers, dance, debate, drama, ethnic, film, gay, honors, international, jazz band, literary magazine, model UN, musical theater, newspaper, orchestra, pep band, photography, political, professional, radio and TV, religious, social, social service, student government, symphony, and yearbook. Popular campus events include Summer Breeze Festival, Kuviasungnerk Winter Festival, and Festival of the Arts.

Sports: There are 10 intercollegiate sports for men and 9 for women, and 18 intramural sports for men and 18 for women. Facilities include a field house, a 1500-seat stadium, a 1500-seat arena, and a student activities center housing a movie theater, TV and pool rooms, and a pub.

Disabled Students: Wheelchair ramps, elevators, special parking, specially equipped rest rooms, special class scheduling, lowered drinking fountains, and lowered telephones are available.

Services: Counseling and information services are available, as is tutoring in some subjects, including math, physics, chemistry, writing, and biology. There is a reader service for the blind.

Campus Safety and Security: Measures include 24-hour foot and vehicle patrol, security escort services, shuttle buses, and informal discussions. There are pamphlets/posters/films, emergency telephones, and lighted pathways/sidewalks.

Programs of Study: Chicago confers B.A. and B.S. degrees. Master's and doctoral degrees are also awarded. Bachelor's degrees are awarded in BIOLOGICAL SCIENCE (biochemistry and biology/biological science), COMMUNICATIONS AND THE ARTS (art history and appreciation, classics, comparative literature, English, film arts, fine arts, German, Japanese, Korean, linguistics, music, romance languages and literature, and Russian), COMPUTER AND PHYSICAL SCIENCE (chemistry, computer science, geoscience, mathematics, physics, and statistics), ENGINEERING AND ENVIRONMENTAL DESIGN (environmental science), SOCIAL SCIENCE (African American studies, anthropology, Asian/Oriental studies, Christian studies, classical/ancient civilization, economics, gender studies, geography, history, humanities, international studies, Judaic studies, Latin American studies, medieval studies, Near Eastern studies, philosophy, political science/government, psychology, public affairs, religion, social science, and sociology). Economics, biology, and political science are the largest.

Required: To graduate, students must complete 42 quarter courses, including 9 to 13 courses in the major, with an overall GPA of 1.75 and 2.0 in the major. The core curriculum includes sequences in humanities, social sciences, biological and physical sciences, civilization, and foreign languages. Also required are 2 quarters of math, 1 of art or music, and 1 year of noncredit phys ed.

Special: Special academic programs include cross-registration through the Committee on Instutional Cooperation, international, national, and local internships in most disciplines as well as a summer internship in Washington, study abroad in 12 countries, and work-study in most departments. There are 3-2 programs available through the schools of law, business, social service administration, and public policy. B.A.-B.S. and general studies degrees are offered, as are student-designed majors. Nondegree study and pass/fail options are possible. There are 2 national honor societies, including Phi Beta Kappa.

Faculty/Classroom: 75% of faculty are male; 25%, female. All both teach and do research.

Admissions: There were 183 National Merit finalists in a recent year.

Requirements: The SAT I or ACT is required. In addition, other admissions criteria include a recommended secondary school curriculum of 4 years of English, 3 to 4 years each of history, social studies, math, and science, and 3 years of a foreign language. The GED is accepted. An essay must be submitted, and an interview is recommended. AP credits are accepted. Important factors in the admissions decision are advanced placement or honor courses, personality/intangible qualities, and extracurricular activities record.

Procedure: Freshmen are admitted in the fall. Entrance exams should be taken during the junior or senior year. There are early decision, early

admissions, and deferred admissions plans. Check with the school for current deadlines and fee. The fall 2003 application fee was $60. Applications are accepted on-line at *uncommonapplication.uchicago.edu*.

Transfer: 72 transfer students were enrolled in a recent year. 18 of 42 credits required for the bachelor's degree must be completed at Chicago.

Visiting: There are regularly scheduled orientations for prospective students, including meeting with an admissions counselor and students, sitting in on classes, visiting faculty, and staying in a residence hall. There are guides for informal visits and visitors may sit in on classes and stay overnight. To schedule a visit, contact College Admissions.

Financial Aid: In a recent year, 65% of all full-time freshmen and 68% of continuing full-time students received some form of financial aid. 55% of full-time freshmen and 56% of continuing full-time students received need-based aid. Chicago is a member of CSS. The CSS Profile or FAFSA and the college's own financial statement are required. Check with the school for current deadlines.

International Students: There were 294 international students enrolled in a recent year. The school actively recruits these students. They must score 600 on the written TOEFL or 250 on the electronic version and also take the SAT I or the ACT.

Computers: The mainframes are a includes an Amdahl 5880, 2 Sun minicomputers, and a Silicon Graphics 4D/240 minicomputer. Students are able to access the Amdahl or the Suns through personal user accounts. In addition, there are 7 public computer clusters with IBM PCs, and Macs as well as computer clusters in many of the residence halls. All residence hall rooms are linked to the campus computer network. All students may access the system any time. There are no time limits and no fees.

Graduates: In a recent year, 989 bachelor's degrees were awarded. The most popular majors were economics (22%), biological science (12%), and political science (8%). In an average class, 85% graduate in 4 years or less, and 90% graduate in 6 years or less.

Admissions Contact: Theodore O'Neill, Dean, College Admissions. Web: *www.uchicago.edu*

UNIVERSITY OF ILLINOIS SYSTEM

The University of Illinois System, established in 1867, is a public system in Illinois. It is governed by a board of trustees, whose chief administrator is the president. The primary goal of the system is to provide undergraduate and graduate education, conduct research, and provide public service. The total enrollment of both campuses is usually about 62,000; there were some 5000 faculty members. Altogether there are some 174 baccalaureate, 164 master's, and 106 doctoral programs offered in University of Illinois System. There is a 4-year campus located in Chicago and Urbana-Champaign. Profiles of the 4-year campuses are included in this section.

UNIVERSITY OF ILLINOIS AT CHICAGO
Chicago, IL 60680   E-2   (312) 996-4350; Fax: (312) 413-7628

Full-time: 6384 men, 7892 women	**Faculty:** 965; I, av$
Part-time: 858 men, 878 women	**Ph.D.s:** 84%
Graduate: 4167 men, 5585 women	**Student/Faculty:** 15 to 1
Year: semesters, summer session	**Tuition:** $6798 ($16,494)
Application Deadline: January 15	**Room & Board:** $6620
Freshman Class: 12,250 applied, 7425 accepted, 2942 enrolled	
ACT: 23	**COMPETITIVE**

The University of Illinois at Chicago, founded in 1946, is a public institution with undergraduate and graduate programs in the liberal arts, art and fine arts, business, engineering, architecture, health sciences, music, teacher preparation, social work, and professional training in dentistry, medicine, and pharmacy. There are 8 undergraduate schools and 1 graduate school. In addition to regional accreditation, UIC has baccalaureate program accreditation with AACSB, ABET, ACPE, ADA, APTA, CCNE, CSAB, CSWE, NAAB, and NASAD. The 5 libraries contain 2,165,704 volumes, 3,791,058 microform items, and 29,105 audio/video tapes/CDs, and subscribe to 25,483 periodicals. Computerized library services include the card catalog, interlibrary loans, and database searching. Special learning facilities include a learning resource center, art gallery, radio station, Jane Addams Hull House, which is a restored settlement house, and the James Woodworth Prairie Reserve. The 240-acre campus is in an urban area just west of downtown Chicago. Including any residence halls, there are 113 buildings.

Student Life: 96% of undergraduates are from Illinois. Students are from 50 states, 102 foreign countries, and Canada. 88% are from public schools. 46% are white; 21% Asian American; 13% Hispanic. The average age of freshmen is 18; all undergraduates, 21. 95% of freshmen remain to graduate.

Housing: 3051 students can be accommodated in college housing, which includes coed dorms and on-campus apartments. In addition, there are honors houses, the President's Award House, and special-interest floors. On-campus housing is available on a first-come, first-served basis. 83% of students commute. All students may keep cars.

Activities: 4% of men belong to 5 local and 6 national fraternities; 3% of women belong to 10 national sororities. There are 233 groups on campus, including art, band, cheerleading, chess, choir, chorus, computers, dance, drama, ethnic, gay, honors, international, jazz band, literary magazine, newspaper, political, professional, religious, social, social service, and student government. Popular campus events include Activities and Services Fair, VIC Fashion Show, and Women's Heritage Month.

Sports: There are 7 intercollegiate sports for men and 7 for women, and 14 intramural sports for men and 14 for women. Facilities include a 12,000-seat sports pavilion, a sports and fitness center, a recreation center, a 1000-seat gym, 3 pools, racquetball and tennis courts, a baseball field, a bowling alley, indoor and outdoor tracks, and weight rooms.

Disabled Students: 80% of the campus is accessible. Wheelchair ramps, elevators, special parking, specially equipped rest rooms, special class scheduling, lowered drinking fountains, and lowered telephones are available.

Services: Counseling and information services are available, as is tutoring in most subjects. There is a reader service for the blind, and remedial math, reading, and writing, a writing center, and academic skills classes.

Campus Safety and Security: Measures include 24-hour foot and vehicle patrol, self-defense education, security escort services, and shuttle buses. There are informal discussions, pamphlets/posters/films, emergency telephones, lighted pathways/sidewalks, and emergency call buttons across campus.

Programs of Study: UIC confers B.A., B.S., B.Arch., B.F.A., B.S.C. and E., B.S.C.E., B.S.Ch.E., B.S.E.E., B.S.E.M., B.S.E.M.A.N., B.S.M.E., B.S.N., and B.S.W. degrees. Master's and doctoral degrees are also awarded. Bachelor's degrees are awarded in BIOLOGICAL SCIENCE (biochemistry, biology/biological science, and nutrition), BUSINESS (accounting, banking and finance, business administration and management, entrepreneurial studies, management science, and marketing/retailing/merchandising), COMMUNICATIONS AND THE ARTS (art history and appreciation, classics, design, dramatic arts, French, graphic design, industrial design, Italian, literature, music, photography, Polish, Russian, Spanish, speech/debate/rhetoric, and studio art), COMPUTER AND PHYSICAL SCIENCE (chemistry, computer science, geology, information sciences and systems, mathematics, physics, and statistics), EDUCATION (art, education, elementary, English, foreign languages, mathematics, physical, science, and secondary), ENGINEERING AND ENVIRONMENTAL DESIGN (architecture, bioengineering, chemical engineering, civil engineering, computer engineering, electrical/electronics engineering, engineering, engineering management, engineering physics, industrial engineering technology, and mechanical engineering), HEALTH PROFESSIONS (medical laboratory science and nursing), SOCIAL SCIENCE (African American studies, anthropology, classical/ancient civilization, criminal justice, economics, German area studies, history, Latin American studies, philosophy, political science/government, psychology, social work, and sociology). Math, nursing, and philosophy are the strongest academically. Accounting, engineering, and psychology are the largest.

Required: Students must demonstrate proficiency in written English through either course work or testing, and complete 24 hours of general education, including 6 hours each of humanities, social sciences, and natural sciences. The remaining 6 hours may be spread across the 3 categories. A minimum overall GPA of 2.0 on a 4.0 scale is required. Total number of hours to graduate varies by major but is always at least 120.

Special: Special academic programs include a wide variety of co-op and program internships, work-study with some 70 on- and off-campus employers, and study abroad opportunities at accredited foreign universities, as well as special programs in France, Italy, Canada, Austria, Spain, and Mexico. There is cross-registration with the City Colleges of Chicago. Interdisciplinary majors are offered in architectural studies, communications and theater, French business studies, math and computer science, bioengineering, and information and decision sciences. Students may pursue a 3-2 engineering degree with Chicago State, Eastern Illinois, Illinois State, Northeastern Illinois, and Western Illinois Universities. Up to 4 semester hours of credit may be granted for military experience. Dual and student-designed majors, nondegree study, and pass/fail options are available. There are 15 national honor societies, including Phi Beta Kappa, and a freshman honors program.

Faculty/Classroom: 64% of faculty are male; 36%, female. 46% teach undergraduates, All do research, and 46% do both. The average class size in an introductory lecture is 116; in a laboratory, 24; and in a regular course, 42.

Admissions: 61% of the 2003-2004 applicants were accepted. The ACT scores for the 2003-2004 freshman class were: 25% below 21, 30% between 21 and 23, 25% between 24 and 26, 10% between 27 and 28, and 10% above 28. 45% of the current freshmen were in the top fifth of their class; 80% were in the top two fifths.

Requirements: The SAT I or ACT is required. In addition, applicants should be graduates of an accredited secondary school; the GED is accepted. The recommended secondary school curriculum varies according to the college program chosen, but 16 high school credits are required. AP and CLEP credits are accepted. Important factors in the admissions decision are recommendations by school officials, evidence of special talent, and advanced placement or honor courses.

Procedure: Freshmen are admitted fall and spring. Entrance exams should be taken in the spring of the junior year or the fall of the senior year. There is a rolling admissions plan. Applications should be filed by January 15 for fall entry and October 1 for spring entry, along with a $40 fee. Notification is sent on a rolling basis. Applications are accepted online through the school's web site.

Transfer: 1973 transfer students enrolled in 2002-2003. Transferable hours and minimum GPA vary according to program. 30 of 120 credits required for the bachelor's degree must be completed at UIC.

Visiting: There are regularly scheduled orientations for prospective students, consisting of a general meeting, a college meeting, and campus tours. There are guides for informal visits and visitors may sit in on classes. To schedule a visit, contact the Office of Undergraduate Admissions.

Financial Aid: The FAFSA is required. The deadline for filing freshman financial aid applications for fall entry is March 1.

International Students: There are 178 international students enrolled. They must score 520 on the written TOEFL or 190 on the electronic version or take the MELAB. Freshmen must also take the SAT I or ACT. Minimum required scores depend on the specific college.

Computers: The mainframe is a several UNIX servers. More than 1100 terminals and PCs are located in labs, classrooms, libraries, and residence halls throughout the campus. All students may access the system 24 hours daily. There are no time limits and no fees.

Graduates: From July 1, 2002 to June 30, 2003, 3174 bachelor's degrees were awarded. The most popular majors were business/marketing (17%), engineering (10%), and psychology (9%). In an average class, 16% graduate in 4 years or less, 37% graduate in 5 years or less, and 44% graduate in 6 years or less. 175 companies recruited on campus in 2002-2003.

Admissions Contact: Thomas E. Glenn, Executive Director of Admissions and Records. E-mail: *uicadmit@uic.edu*
Web: *http://www.uic.edu/depts/oar*

UNIVERSITY OF ILLINOIS AT URBANA-CHAMPAIGN   E-3

Urbana, IL 61801   (217) 333-0302; Fax: (217) 244-0903

Full-time: 14,510 men, 13,110 women	**Faculty:** 1894; I, av$
Part-time: 570 men, 555 women	**Ph.D.s:** 96%
Graduate: 4955 men, 4000 women	**Student/Faculty:** 15 to 1
Year: semesters, summer session	**Tuition:** $7966 ($20,886)
Application Deadline: see profile	**Room & Board:** $6848
Freshman Class: n/av	
SAT I or ACT: not required	**HIGHLY COMPETITIVE+**

The University of Illinois at Urbana-Champaign, founded in 1867, is the oldest and largest campus in the University of Illinois system, offering some 150 undergraduate and more than 100 graduate degree programs. There are 9 undergraduate schools and 1 graduate school. Figures in the above capsule and in this profile are approximate. In addition to regional accreditation, Illinois has baccalaureate program accreditation with AACSB, ABET, ACEJMC, ADA, AHEA, ASLA, CSWE, NAAB, NASAD, NASM, NCATE, NRPA, and SAF. The 42 libraries contain 9,647,652 volumes, 8,976,026 microform items, and 159,365 audio/video tapes/CDs, and subscribe to 91,054 periodicals. Computerized library services include the card catalog, interlibrary loans, and database searching. Special learning facilities include a learning resource center, art gallery, natural history museum, radio station, TV station, language learning lab, performing arts center, and graphic technologies lab. The campus is in a small town 130 miles south of Chicago. Including any residence halls, there are 200 buildings.

Student Life: 93% of undergraduates are from Illinois. Students are from 50 states, 121 foreign countries, and Canada. 67% are white; 12% Asian American. The average age of freshmen is 19; all undergraduates, 21. 7% do not continue beyond their first year; 80% remain to graduate.

Housing: 8374 students can be accommodated in college housing, which includes single-sex and coed dorms, on-campus apartments, and married-student housing. In addition, there are language houses and special-interest houses. On-campus housing is guaranteed for all 4 years. 70% of students commute. All students may keep cars.

Activities: 22% of men belong to 3 local and 52 national fraternities; 22% of women belong to 3 local and 27 national sororities. There are 850 groups on campus, including art, band, cheerleading, choir, chorale, chorus, computers, dance, debate, drama, drill team, ethnic, film, gay, honors, international, jazz band, literary magazine, marching band, musical theater, newspaper, opera, orchestra, pep band, photography, political, professional, radio and TV, religious, social, social service, student government, symphony, and yearbook. Popular campus events include Quad Day to introduce campus organizations, Dad's Weekend, and Mom's Weekend.

Sports: There are 8 intercollegiate sports for men and 9 for women, and 30 intramural sports for men and 30 for women. Facilities include one of the world's largest intramural sports and recreation buildings, numerous student union facilities, and acres of outdoor playing fields. Memorial Football Stadium seats 69,000 and Assembly Hall seats 16,000 for basketball games, concerts, and special events.

Disabled Students: All of the campus is accessible. Wheelchair ramps, elevators, special parking, specially equipped rest rooms, special class scheduling, lowered drinking fountains, lowered telephones, special housing, and fitness equipment are available.

Services: Counseling and information services are available, as is tutoring in every subject. There is a reader service for the blind. Transportation and rehabilitation services are offered, as well as interpreters, note taking, taped lectures, and modified test times or formats.

Campus Safety and Security: Measures include 24-hour foot and vehicle patrol, self-defense education, security escort services, and shuttle buses. There are informal discussions, pamphlets/posters/films, emergency telephones, lighted pathways/sidewalks, and safety presentations and evaluations by campus police.

Programs of Study: Illinois confers A.B., B.S., B.A.U.P., B.F.A., B.Land.Arch., B.Mus., B.S.Ed., B.S.J., B.S.W., and B.V.M. degrees. Master's and doctoral degrees are also awarded. Bachelor's degrees are awarded in AGRICULTURE (agricultural economics, agricultural mechanics, agronomy, animal science, forestry and related sciences, and horticulture), BIOLOGICAL SCIENCE (biochemistry, biology/biological science, biophysics, microbiology, molecular biology, and physiology), BUSINESS (accounting, banking and finance, business administration and management, marketing/retailing/merchandising, and recreation and leisure services), COMMUNICATIONS AND THE ARTS (advertising, art history and appreciation, broadcasting, classics, comparative literature, crafts, dance, dramatic arts, English, French, Germanic languages and literature, graphic design, industrial design, Italian, journalism, linguistics, media arts, music, music history and appreciation, music theory and composition, painting, photography, Portuguese, Russian languages and literature, sculpture, Spanish, speech/debate/rhetoric, and voice), COMPUTER AND PHYSICAL SCIENCE (actuarial science, astronomy, chemistry, computer science, geology, mathematics, physics, and statistics), EDUCATION (agricultural, art, computer, early childhood, elementary, foreign languages, music, physical, secondary, and special), ENGINEERING AND ENVIRONMENTAL DESIGN (aeronautical engineering, agricultural engineering, airline piloting and navigation, architecture, bioengineering, ceramic engineering, chemical engineering, city/community/regional planning, civil engineering, computer engineering, electrical/electronics engineering, engineering, engineering mechanics, engineering physics, environmental science, industrial engineering, landscape architecture/design, materials science, mechanical engineering, metallurgical engineering, and nuclear engineering), HEALTH PROFESSIONS (public health, speech pathology/audiology, and veterinary science), SOCIAL SCIENCE (anthropology, East Asian studies, economics, family/consumer studies, food science, geography, history, human development, humanities, international studies, Latin American studies, liberal arts/general studies, philosophy, political science/government, psychology, religion, Russian and Slavic studies, and sociology). Advertising, engineering and music are the strongest academically. Psychology, accountancy, and electrical and computer engineering are the largest.

Required: All students must demonstrate proficiency in the use of the English language, complete 6 hours each in humanities, social sciences, and natural sciences, and maintain a minimum GPA of 2.0 on a 4.0 scale. Minimum hours needed to graduate range from 120 to 132, depending on the major.

Special: Illinois offers cooperative engineering programs with 30 midwestern liberal arts colleges; 16 summer, semester, and full-year programs abroad and numerous exchange opportunities; and cross-registration with Parkland Community College. Unusual opportunities include a leisure studies semester in Scotland and a summer parliamentary internship in London. A dual degree in liberal arts and engineering is offered, as well as student-designed majors and a 3-2 engineering program with numerous universities. On-campus work-study and pass/fail options are possible. There are 50 national honor societies, including Phi Beta Kappa, and a freshman honors program.

Faculty/Classroom: 77% of faculty are male; 23%, female. 89% teach undergraduates, all do research, and 89% do both. The average class size in an introductory lecture is 124; in a laboratory, 22; and in a regular course, 29.

Requirements: Applicants should be graduates of accredited secondary schools or have the GED. High school preparation must include 4 years of English, 3 or more of math, 2 each of lab science and social studies, and, for most programs, 2 of foreign languages. A personal essay is optional. Visual arts applicants must submit a portfolio; performing arts applicants are required to audition. AP and CLEP credits are accepted. Important factors in the admissions decision are evidence of special talent, advanced placement or honor courses, and geographic diversity.

Procedure: Freshmen are admitted fall and spring. Entrance exams should be taken by spring of the junior year and no later than October of the senior year. There are early admissions and deferred admissions plans. Check with the school for current deadlines and fee. The fall 2003 application fee was $40.

Transfer: 1088 transfer students were enrolled in a recent year. Transfer application requirements differ by degree program. Generally, students transferring should have junior standing of 60 hours; students from other institutions must have at least a C average in previous college work. Admission is also subject to the number of places available. 30 of 120 credits required for the bachelor's degree must be completed at Illinois.

Visiting: There are regularly scheduled orientations for prospective students, consisting of presentations given by the admissions staff at 10 A.M. and 1 P.M. daily on weekdays; a videotape of the campus is shown, and tours are provided. There are guides for informal visits and visitors may sit in on classes. To schedule a visit, contact the Campus Visitors Center at (217) 333-0824 or *visits@oar.vivc.edu.*

Financial Aid: In a recent year, 81% of all full-time freshmen received some form of financial aid. 39% of full-time freshmen and 38% of continuing full-time students received need-based aid. The average freshman award was $5257. 33% of undergraduates work part time. Average annual earnings from campus work are $1594. The average financial indebtedness of a recent graduate was $14,791. The FAFSA and the college's own financial statement are required. Check with the school for current deadlines.

International Students: They must score 550 on the written TOEFL and also take the MELAB.

Computers: The mainframes are an IBM RS/6000/540, an IBM 380, a Sequent Symmetry S81, a Convex C240, and an IBM 3801/KX6. About 3000 computer workstations are located in classrooms, labs, and residence halls across campus. All students may access the system 24 hours a day. Students may access the system 20 hours per week on dial-in access only; there is no limit from networked PCs. There are no fees. It is strongly recommended that all students have a personal computer.

Graduates: In a recent year, 6431 bachelor's degrees were awarded. The most popular majors were finance (7%), biological sciences (7%), and English (7%). In an average class, 2% graduate in 3 years or less, 54% graduate in 4 years or less, 75% graduate in 5 years or less, and 78% graduate in 6 years or less. 999 companies recruited on campus in a recent year. Of a recent graduating class, 40% were enrolled in graduate school within 6 months of graduation and 85% were employed.

Admissions Contact: Tammie Bouseman, Assistant Director, Undergraduate Admissions. A video is available.
E-mail: *admission@oar.uiuc.edu* Web: *www.oar.uiuc.edu*

UNIVERSITY OF SAINT FRANCIS

E-2

Joliet, IL 60435

(815) 740-3400

(800) 735-7500; Fax: (815) 740-5032

Full-time: 354 men, 700 women	**Faculty:** 60; IIA, -$
Part-time: 25 men, 64 women	**Ph.D.s:** 60%
Graduate: 193 men, 652 women	**Student/Faculty:** 18 to 1
Year: semesters, summer session	**Tuition:** $16,820
Application Deadline: September 1	**Room & Board:** $6030
Freshman Class: n/av	
ACT: required	**COMPETITIVE**

The University of Saint Francis, founded as a college in 1920, is a private liberal arts and professional institution affiliated with the Roman Catholic Church. There are 4 undergraduate and 3 graduate schools. In addition to regional accreditation, USF has baccalaureate program accreditation with CSWE, NLN, and NRPA. The library contains 106,346 volumes, 1308 microform items, and 1177 audio/video tapes/CDs, and subscribes to 776 periodicals. Computerized library services include the card catalog, interlibrary loans, and database searching. Special learning facilities include a learning resource center, art gallery, radio station, TV station, greenhouse, and wireless education classroom. The 17-acre campus is in a suburban area 35 miles southwest of Chicago. Including any residence halls, there are 7 buildings.

Student Life: 98% of undergraduates are from Illinois. Students are from 8 states and 2 foreign countries. 77% are from public schools. 79% are white. 57% are Catholic; 23% Protestant. The average age of freshmen is 18; all undergraduates, 23. 28% do not continue beyond their first year; 54% remain to graduate.

Housing: 433 students can be accommodated in college housing, which includes coed dorms and off-campus apartments. There is a learning and living community for the natural sciences and nursing students (special wing in residence hall). On-campus housing is guaranteed for the freshman year only, is available on a first-come, first-served basis, and is available on a lottery system for upperclassmen. Priority is given to out-of-town students. 75% of students commute. All students may keep cars.

Activities: There are no fraternities or sororities. There are 34 groups on campus, including ambassador, art, business, cheerleading, choir, chorale, chorus, drama, education, environmental, ethnic, honors, literary magazine, newspaper, nursing, professional, radio and TV, religious, social, social service, and student government. Popular campus events include artist lecture series, Spring Fling, and Little Sibs Weekend.

Sports: There are 6 intercollegiate sports for men and 8 for women, and 6 intramural sports for men and 6 for women. Facilities include a

10,000-seat lighted football stadium, an indoor arena, a baseball field, a Nautilus center, and basketball, racquetball, volleyball, and badminton courts. A recreation center houses a gym, handball courts, a weight room, a training room, offices, and classrooms; a campus fitness center has facilities for swimming, weight training, aerobic training, and indoor and outdoor tracks. Baseball, softball, football, and golf facilities are available off campus.

Disabled Students: 90% of the campus is accessible. Wheelchair ramps, elevators, special parking, specially equipped rest rooms, special class scheduling, lowered drinking fountains, and lowered telephones are available.

Services: Counseling and information services are available, as is tutoring in most subjects. The writing center provides help with papers. Numerous computerized tutorial programs for courses are also available.

Campus Safety and Security: Measures include 24-hour foot and vehicle patrol, self-defense education, security escort services, and shuttle buses. There are informal discussions, pamphlets/posters/films, emergency telephones, lighted pathways/sidewalks, first-response trained security, sexual assault counseling, and routine fire inspection.

Programs of Study: USF confers B.A., B.S., B.B.A., and B.S.W. degrees. Master's degrees are also awarded. Bachelor's degrees are awarded in BIOLOGICAL SCIENCE (biology/biological science), BUSINESS (accounting, banking and finance, business administration and management, marketing/retailing/merchandising, and recreational facilities management), COMMUNICATIONS AND THE ARTS (communications, English, fine arts, and journalism), COMPUTER AND PHYSICAL SCIENCE (computer programming, computer science, information sciences and systems, and mathematics), EDUCATION (elementary), ENGINEERING AND ENVIRONMENTAL DESIGN (computer technology and environmental science), HEALTH PROFESSIONS (allied health, health, medical technology, nuclear medical technology, nursing, predentistry, premedicine, preveterinary science, radiation therapy, and radiograph medical technology), SOCIAL SCIENCE (history, liberal arts/general studies, political science/government, prelaw, psychology, social work, and theological studies). Biology and education are the strongest academically. Business, nursing, and education are the largest.

Required: To graduate, students are required to complete 128 credit hours with a minimum of 36 hours in the major while maintaining a GPA of 2.0. The required liberal education core includes courses in the following areas: literacy, literary inquiry and aesthetic awareness, numerical understanding and scientific inquiry, historical understanding, social awareness, philosophical inquiry, and religious foundations. A thesis or other senior capstone experience is also required.

Special: Internships, on- and off-campus, paid and unpaid, are available for most majors, in 18 undergraduate programs. Dual and interdisciplinary majors, a pass/fail option, a Washington semester, study abroad through the American Institute of Foreign Study, and credit for life, military, and work experience are available. There are 11 national honor societies.

Faculty/Classroom: 45% of faculty are male; 55%, female. 74% teach undergraduates. No introductory courses are taught by graduate students. The average class size in an introductory lecture is 20; in a laboratory, 16; and in a regular course, 16.

Admissions: 38% of the current freshmen were in the top fifth of their class; 78% were in the top two fifths. 1 freshman graduated first in the class.

Requirements: The ACT is required. In addition, admission requirements also include 4 years of English, 3 of either art, music, foreign language, or computer science, and 2 each of math, including geometry, science (1 lab), and social studies. USF requires applicants to be in the upper 50% of their class. A GPA of 2.0 is required. AP and CLEP credits are accepted. Important factors in the admissions decision are personality/intangible qualities, advanced placement or honor courses, and leadership record.

Procedure: Freshmen are admitted fall and spring. Entrance exams should be taken in the spring of the junior year or the fall of the senior year. There is a deferred admissions plan and a rolling admissions plan. Applications should be filed by September 1 for fall entry. The fall 2003 application fee was $20. Notification is sent on a rolling basis beginning September 1. Applications are accepted on-line through CollegeNET.

Transfer: 278 transfer students enrolled in 2002-2003. Transfer students must have a GPA of 2.0 and must submit transcripts from colleges previously attended; applicants with fewer than 30 semester hours must also submit high school transcripts. Applicants must have taken English at the college level, math at the intermediate algebra level, and present a high school diploma or GED. 32 credits of 128 required for the bachelor's degree must be completed at USF.

Visiting: There are regularly scheduled orientations for prospective students, including orientation, meeting faculty, a tour, and student presentations. There are guides for informal visits and visitors may sit in on classes and stay overnight. To schedule a visit, contact the Admissions Office at admissions@stfrancis.edu.

Financial Aid: In 2003-2004, 99% of all full-time freshmen and 91% of continuing full-time students received some form of financial aid. 71%

of full-time freshmen and 68% of continuing full-time students received need-based aid. The average freshman award was $14,509. Need-based scholarships or need-based grants averaged $8986; need-based self-help aid (loans and jobs) averaged $3753; non-need-based athletic scholarships averaged $8528; and other non-need-based awards and non-need-based scholarships averaged $6010. 73% of undergraduates work part time. Average annual earnings from campus work are $1694. The average financial indebtedness of the 2003 graduate was $16,359. The FAFSA and the college's own financial statement are required. The priority date for freshman financial aid applications for fall entry is May 1.

International Students: There are 2 international students enrolled. They must score 550 on the written TOEFL or 213 on the electronic version and also take the SAT I or the ACT.

Computers: The mainframe is an HP Alpha 4100. There are about 100 terminals and PCs in 3 student labs, network access from dorm rooms, and 24-hour telephone access to the computer network from off campus. All students may access the system 24 hours a day. There are no time limits and no fees.

Graduates: From July 1, 2002 to June 30, 2003, 266 bachelor's degrees were awarded. The most popular majors were education (23%), business (15%), and nursing (12%). In an average class, 49% graduate in 4 years or less, 73% graduate in 5 years or less, and 73% graduate in 6 years or less. 83 companies recruited on campus in 2002-2003. Of the 2002 graduating class, 6% were enrolled in graduate school within 6 months of graduation and 79% were employed.

Admissions Contact: Jean Norris, Vice President, Admissions and Enrollment Services. A video is available.
E-mail: admissions@stfrancis.edu Web: www.stfrancis.edu

VANDERCOOK COLLEGE OF MUSIC   E-2
Chicago, IL 60616-3731   (312) 225-6288
(800) 448-2655; Fax: (312) 225-5211

Full-time: 50 men, 30 women	**Faculty:** 11
Part-time: 5 men and women	**Ph.D.s:** 70%
Graduate: 30 men, 35 women	**Student/Faculty:** 7 to 1
Year: semesters	**Tuition:** $15,290
Application Deadline: see profile	**Room & Board:** $6200
Freshman Class: n/av	
SAT I or ACT: required	**SPECIAL**

VanderCook College of Music, founded in 1909, is devoted solely to the preparation of music educators. There is 1 undergraduate and 1 graduate school. Figures in the above capsule and in this profile are approximate. In addition to regional accreditation, VCM has baccalaureate program accreditation with NASM. The 2 libraries contain 20,000 volumes, 2000 microform items, and 5000 audio/video tapes/CDs, and subscribe to 80 periodicals. Computerized library services include the card catalog, interlibrary loans, and database searching. Special learning facilities include a learning resource center. The 1-acre campus is in an urban area 3 miles from the center of Chicago. Including any residence halls, there is 1 building.

Student Life: 60% of undergraduates are from Illinois. Students are from 11 states, 1 foreign country, and Canada. 80% are from public schools. 63% are white; 32% African American. The average age of freshmen is 19; all undergraduates, 21. 8% do not continue beyond their first year; 80% remain to graduate.

Housing: 100 students can be accommodated in college housing, which includes single-sex and coed dorms, on-campus apartments, married-student housing, and fraternity houses. On-campus housing is guaranteed for all 4 years. 60% of students live on campus; of those, 90% remain on campus on weekends. Alcohol is not permitted. All students may keep cars.

Activities: 50% of men belong to 2 local and 1 national fraternity; 20% of women belong to 2 local and 1 national sorority. There are 9 groups on campus, including band, choir, chorale, chorus, jazz band, musical theater, orchestra, pep band, religious, and student government.

Sports: There is no sports program at VCM. Facilities include a swimming pool, a gym, and tennis courts.

Disabled Students: Special parking and special class scheduling are available.

Campus Safety and Security: Measures include 24-hour foot and vehicle patrol, self-defense education, security escort services, and shuttle buses. There are informal discussions, emergency telephones, and lighted pathways/sidewalks.

Programs of Study: VCM confers the B.M.Ed degree. Master's degrees are also awarded. Bachelor's degrees are awarded in EDUCATION (music).

Required: To graduate, students must complete a total of 134 semester hours distributed in the 5 major categories of general education, professional education, applied music performance, fundamentals and theory, and music education. They must also pass performance proficiency exams on 17 instruments and a vocal proficiency exam.

Faculty/Classroom: 44% of faculty are male; 56%, female. All teach undergraduates. No introductory courses are taught by graduate stu-

dents. The average class size in an introductory lecture is 15; in a laboratory, 15; and in a regular course, 15.

Admissions: There was 1 National Merit semifinalist in a recent year.

Requirements: The SAT I or ACT is required, with a minimum composite score of 900 on the SAT I or 18 on the ACT. Graduation from an accredited secondary school or a satisfactory score on the GED is required for admission. Secondary school courses must include 3 units each of English and science, 2 each of math, social studies, music, and a foreign language, and 1 each of history and art. An audition and an interview are required. VCM requires applicants to be in the upper 75% of their class. A GPA of 2.0 is required. AP and CLEP credits are accepted. Important factors in the admissions decision are evidence of special talent, recommendations by alumni, and extracurricular activities record.

Procedure: Freshmen are admitted fall and spring. Entrance exams should be taken during the junior year. There are early decision, early admissions, and deferred admissions plans. There is a rolling admissions plan. Check with the school for current deadlines and fee. The fall 2003 application fee was $55. The college accepts all applicants. Notification is sent on a rolling basis.

Transfer: 5 transfer students were enrolled in a recent year. Transfer students must have a minimum GPA of 2.5. An audition and an interview are required. Courses taken at other institutions in performance, theory, and history must be validated.

Visiting: There are regularly scheduled orientations for prospective students, including the opportunity to observe a class, meet students and faculty, and tour the campus. There are guides for informal visits and visitors may sit in on classes and stay overnight. To schedule a visit, contact James Malley, Director of Admission.

Financial Aid: In a recent year, 80% of all full-time freshmen and 5% of continuing full-time students received some form of financial aid. 30% of undergraduates work part time. The FAFSA is required. Check with the school for current deadlines.

International Students: There were 3 international students enrolled in a recent year. They must score 500 on the written TOEFL.

Computers: Macs are available. All students may access the system. There are no time limits and no fees.

Graduates: In a recent year, 16 bachelor's degrees were awarded. The most popular major was music education (10%). In an average class, 90% graduate in 4 years or less, and 10% graduate in 5 years or less. Of a recent graduating class, all were employed within 6 months of graduation.

Admissions Contact: James P. Malley, Jr., Director of Admissions. E-mail: *jmalley@vandercook.edu*

WEST SUBURBAN COLLEGE OF NURSING
Oak Park, IL 60302

E-2

(708) 763-6530; Fax: (708) 763-1531

Full-time: 5 men, 125 women	Faculty: 9
Part-time: none	Ph.D.s: 33%
Graduate: none	Student/Faculty: 14 to 1
Year: semesters, summer session	Tuition: $15,180
Application Deadline: open	Room & Board: $4900
Freshman Class: n/av	
ACT: required	SPECIAL

West Suburban College of Nursing, founded in 1982, is a private, nonsectarian college of nursing offering a joint-degree program with Concordia University in River Forest. Figures in the above capsule and in this profile are approximate. In addition to regional accreditation, West Sub has baccalaureate program accreditation with NLN. The library contains 3000 volumes and 1000 audio/video tapes/CDs, and subscribes to 350 periodicals. Computerized library services include the card catalog, interlibrary loans, and database searching. The 20-acre campus is in a suburban area 10 miles west of downtown Chicago. There is 1 building.

Student Life: 95% of undergraduates are from Illinois. Students are from 5 states and 2 foreign countries. 60% are from public schools. 73% are white; 15% African American; 10% Asian American. The average age of freshmen is 18; all undergraduates, 25.

Housing: There are no residence halls. On-campus housing is provided by Concordia University. 60% of students commute. Alcohol is not permitted. All students may keep cars.

Activities: There are no fraternities or sororities.

Sports: There are 4 intercollegiate sports for men and 2 for women, and 1 intramural sport for men. Athletic and recreation facilities are sponsored by Concordia University.

Disabled Students: Lowered drinking fountains are available.

Services: There is remedial math, reading, and writing and tutoring in some subjects, which varies per semester.

Campus Safety and Security: Measures include 24-hour foot and vehicle patrol, security escort services, shuttle buses, and lighted pathways/sidewalks.

Programs of Study: West Sub confers the B.S. degree. Bachelor's degrees are awarded in HEALTH PROFESSIONS (nursing).

Required: To graduate, students must have a minimum of 129 semester hours with a minimum GPA of 2.0. 56 semester hours are required

in nursing. All students must take courses in nursing, psychology, sociology, chemistry, anatomy, physiology, microbiology, statistics, physical education, humanities, communications, and theology.

Faculty/Classroom: All faculty are female. All teach undergraduates. The average class size in an introductory lecture is 20; in a laboratory, 6; and in a regular course, 12.

Requirements: The ACT is required, with a minimum composite score of 20 recommended. Graduation from an accredited secondary school or satisfactory scores on the GED are required for admission. Students should have 16 academic credits, including 4 years of English and 1 unit each in chemistry and biology, as well as courses in math, history, and social studies. A personal recommendation and an essay are required. West Sub requires applicants to be in the upper 33% of their class. A GPA of 2.5 is required. AP and CLEP credits are accepted. Important factors in the admissions decision are recommendations by school officials, advanced placement or honor courses, and personality/intangible qualities.

Procedure: Freshmen are admitted to all sessions. Entrance exams should be taken in the spring of the junior year. There is a rolling admissions plan. Application deadlines are open. The fall 2003 application fee was $25. Applications are accepted on-line at *www.wscn.edu*.

Transfer: 21 transfer students enrolled in a recent year. Transfer students must have a minimum GPA of 2.5 on all college courses completed. A letter of recommendation and an essay are required. 56 of 129 credits required for the bachelor's degree must be completed at West Sub.

Visiting: There are regularly scheduled orientations for prospective students and open houses. There are guides for informal visits and visitors may sit in on classes and stay overnight. To schedule a visit, contact the Admissions Office.

Financial Aid: In a recent year, 90% of all full-time students received some form of financial aid. 90% of all full-time students received need-based aid. The CSS Profile or FAFSA is required.

International Students: They must score 500 on the written TOEFL or take the MELAB. They must also take the ACT, scoring 20.

Computers: PCs are available on the Concordia University campus. There are no fees.

Graduates: In a recent year, 31 bachelor's degrees were awarded.

Admissions Contact: Dara Lawyer, Interim Director of Admissions. Web: *www.wscn.edu*

WESTERN ILLINOIS UNIVERSITY
Macomb, IL 61455-1390

C-3

(309) 298-3157

(877) PICK WIU; Fax: (309) 298-3111

Full-time: 5038 men, 4752 women	Faculty: 609; IIA, av$
Part-time: 542 men, 695 women	Ph.D.s: 70%
Graduate: 930 men, 1512 women	Student/Faculty: 16 to 1
Year: semesters, summer session	Tuition: $4997 ($8912)
Application Deadline: n/av	Room & Board: $5366
Freshman Class: 7612 applied, 5032 accepted, 1970 enrolled	
ACT: 22	COMPETITIVE

Western Illinois University, founded in 1899, is a public institution with 5 colleges, a school of graduate studies, and international studies. There are 5 undergraduate schools and 1 graduate school. In addition to regional accreditation, WIU has baccalaureate program accreditation with AACSB, ADA, ASLA, CAHEA, CSWE, NASM, NCATE, and NRPA. The 5 libraries contain 998,041 volumes, 1,342,620 microform items, and 3445 audio/video tapes/CDs, and subscribe to 3200 periodicals. Computerized library services include the card catalog, interlibrary loans, database searching, and Internet access. Special learning facilities include an art gallery, natural history museum, radio station, and TV station. The 1050-acre campus is in a rural area 76 miles from Peoria and 151 miles from St. Louis. There are 52 buildings.

Student Life: 93% of undergraduates are from Illinois. Students are from 46 states, 44 foreign countries, and Canada. 89% are from public schools. 83% are white. The average age of freshmen is 18; all undergraduates, 22. 24% do not continue beyond their first year; 55% remain to graduate.

Housing: 4960 students can be accommodated in college housing, which includes single-sex and coed dorms, on-campus apartments, and married-student housing. In addition, there are honors houses, special-interest houses, and academic majors, honors, and wellness floors in residence halls. On-campus housing is guaranteed for all 4 years. 52% of students commute. Alcohol is not permitted. All students may keep cars.

Activities: 8% of men belong to 18 national fraternities; 8% of women belong to 10 national sororities. There are 254 groups on campus, including art, band, cheerleading, chess, choir, chorale, chorus, computers, dance, drama, drill team, ethnic, gay, honors, international, jazz band, literary magazine, marching band, musical theater, newspaper, opera, orchestra, pep band, photography, political, professional, radio and TV, religious, social, social service, student government, symphony, and yearbook. Popular campus events include Family Weekend, Summer Music Theater, and International Bazaar.

Sports: There are 10 intercollegiate sports for men and 10 for women, and 25 intramural sports for men and 25 for women. Facilities include an 18-hole golf course, tennis courts, a basketball court, a swimming pool, a recreation center, and softball, soccer, and football fields.

Disabled Students: 95% of the campus is accessible. Wheelchair ramps, elevators, special parking, specially equipped rest rooms, special class scheduling, lowered drinking fountains, and lowered telephones are available.

Services: Counseling and information services are available, as is tutoring in some subjects, including English, math, computer science, science, social sciences, and humanitites. There is a reader service for the blind and remedial math and writing.

Campus Safety and Security: Measures include 24-hour foot and vehicle patrol, self-defense education, security escort services, and shuttle buses. There are informal discussions, pamphlets/posters/films, emergency telephones, lighted pathways/sidewalks, and a beacon system.

Programs of Study: WIU confers B.A., B.S., B.B., B.F.A., B.S.Ed., and B.S.W. degrees. Master's degrees are also awarded. Bachelor's degrees are awarded in AGRICULTURE (agriculture), BIOLOGICAL SCIENCE (biology/biological science), BUSINESS (accounting, banking and finance, business administration and management, management information systems, marketing/retailing/merchandising, and personnel management), COMMUNICATIONS AND THE ARTS (art, communications, dramatic arts, English, French, journalism, media arts, music, and Spanish), COMPUTER AND PHYSICAL SCIENCE (chemistry, computer science, geology, mathematics, and physics), EDUCATION (bilingual/bicultural, elementary, industrial arts, physical, special, and technical), ENGINEERING AND ENVIRONMENTAL DESIGN (industrial engineering technology and manufacturing technology), HEALTH PROFESSIONS (health science, medical technology, and speech pathology/audiology), SOCIAL SCIENCE (economics, family/consumer studies, geography, history, law enforcement and corrections, parks and recreation management, philosophy, political science/government, psychology, social work, and sociology). Accounting, chemistry, and human resource management are the strongest academically. Communication, law enforcement, and justice administration are the largest.

Required: To graduate, all students must complete at least 120 credit hours with 32 hours in the major, and have a minimum 2.0 GPA. Students must take 44 hours in the fields of basic skills, well-being, natural science, math, historical and social foundations, and humanities. A writing exam is also required.

Special: WIU offers internships in business, law enforcement, and physical training, study abroad in 7 countries, and dual programs in engineering, dentistry, medicine, and medical technology. Student-designed majors and independent study are available through the Experimental Studies, Board of Trustees, and Individual Studies programs. The Board of Trustees degree program offers credit for work experience. Also available are a field campus and a life science station on the Mississippi River, a 3-2 engineering program with the University of Illinois, and various preprofessional programs. There are 30 national honor societies, a freshman honors program, and 34 departmental honors programs.

Faculty/Classroom: 62% of faculty are male; 38%, female. 98% teach undergraduates; 90% both teach and do research. Graduate students teach 3% of introductory courses. The average class size in an introductory lecture is 37; in a laboratory, 27; and in a regular course, 25.

Admissions: 66% of the 2003-2004 applicants were accepted. The ACT scores for the 2003-2004 freshman class were: 42% below 21, 33% between 21 and 23, 18% between 24 and 26, 4% between 27 and 28, and 3% above 28. 22% of the current freshmen were in the top fifth of their class; 41% were in the top two fifths. 12 freshmen graduated first in their class.

Requirements: The SAT I or ACT is required, with a minimum composite score of 850 on the SAT I or 18 on the ACT, both for admissions decision and for placement purposes. Students must have 4 years of English, 3 years each of math, science, and social studies, and 2 electives in art, film, foreign language, music, speech, theater, journalism, religion, philosophy, or vocational education. Academic Services is a multicultural recruitment and supportive admissions program for selected students who do not meet freshman or transfer requirements. WIU requires applicants to be in the upper 40% of their class. A GPA of 2.2 is required. AP and CLEP credits are accepted.

Procedure: Freshmen are admitted to all sessions. Entrance exams should be taken by April of the senior year. Check with the school for current application deadlines. There is a deferred admissions plan and a rolling admissions plan. The application fee is $25 (electronic) or $30 (paper). Notification is sent on a rolling basis. Applications are accepted on-line.

Transfer: 1427 transfer students enrolled in 2002-2003. Students transferring fewer than 24 semester credits or 36 quarter credits must submit a high school transcript or GED certificate, have scored at least 22 on the ACT, and be in good standing at their last school. A minimum 2.0 GPA is required. 30 credits of 120 required for the bachelor's degree must be completed at WIU.

Visiting: There are regularly scheduled orientations for prospective students. There are guides for informal visits and visitors may sit in on class-

es and stay overnight. To schedule a visit, contact the Admissions Office at (309) 298-3140.

Financial Aid: In 2003-2004, 79% of all full-time freshmen and 83% of continuing full-time students received some form of financial aid. 49% of full-time freshmen and 53% of continuing full-time students received need-based aid. The average freshman award was $5525 with $2475 from need-based scholarships or need-based grants, $1707 from need-based self-help aid (loans and jobs), $204 from non-need-based athletic scholarships, $509 from other non-need-based awards and non-need-based scholarships, and $630 from non-need-based loans. 21% of undergraduates work part time. Average annual earnings from campus work are $1330. The average financial indebtedness of the 2003 graduate was $13,800. The FAFSA is required. The priority date for freshman financial aid applications for fall entry is February 15. The fall financial aid deadline is open.

International Students: There are 251 international students enrolled. The school actively recruits these students. They must score 550 on the written TOEFL or successfully complete WIU's ESL program.

Computers: The mainframe is an IBM Multiprise 2003 Model 126. Computer access is available through the library, various residence halls, and the computer labs. All students may access the system any time. There are no time limits and no fees.

Graduates: From July 1, 2002 to June 30, 2003, 2416 bachelor's degrees were awarded. The most popular majors were law enforcement and justice administration (12%), elementary education (8%), and communication (6%). In an average class, 32% graduate in 4 years or less, 51% graduate in 5 years or less, and 55% graduate in 6 years or less. 105 companies recruited on campus in 2002-2003. Of the 2002 graduating class, 14% were enrolled in graduate school within 6 months of graduation and 78% were employed.

Admissions Contact: Admissions Office. A video is available. E-mail: *wiuadm@wiu.edu* Web: *www.wiu.edu*

WHEATON COLLEGE   E-2
Wheaton, IL 60187-5593   **(630) 752-5005**
                          (800) 222-2419; Fax: (630) 752-5285

Full-time: 1140 men, 1190 women	**Faculty:** 181; IIA, av$
Part-time: 25 men, 25 women	**Ph.Ds:** 92%
Graduate: 225 men, 235 women	**Student/Faculty:** 13 to 1
Year: semesters, summer session	**Tuition:** $18,500
Application Deadline: see profile	**Room & Board:** $6100
Freshman Class: n/av	
SAT I or ACT: required	**HIGHLY COMPETITIVE**

Wheaton College, founded in 1860, is a nonprofit, private, nondenominational institution committed to providing students with a Christian education. Basically a liberal arts school, it offers undergraduate programs in business, the arts and fine arts, music, teacher preparation, and religious and Bible studies. Figures in the above capsule and in this profile are approximate. In addition to regional accreditation, Wheaton has baccalaureate program accreditation with NASM and NCATE. The 2 libraries contain 342,746 volumes, 674,827 microform items, and 32,761 audio/video tapes/CDs, and subscribe to 3264 periodicals. Computerized library services include the card catalog, interlibrary loans, and database searching. Special learning facilities include a radio station and a communications resource center with TV and audio studios, a special collection of British authors books and papers, an evangelical museum with document archives, and the center for Applied Christian Ethics. The 80-acre campus is in a suburban area 25 miles west of Chicago. Including any residence halls, there are 35 buildings.

Student Life: 77% of undergraduates are from out of state, mostly the Midwest. Students are from 50 states, 13 foreign countries, and Canada. 67% are from public schools. 88% are white. 94% are Protestant; 6% affiliation unknown. The average age of freshmen is 18; all undergraduates, 20. 6% do not continue beyond their first year; 83% remain to graduate.

Housing: 2091 students can be accommodated in college housing, which includes single-sex dorms, on-campus apartments, off-campus apartments, and married-student housing. In addition, the college owns and rents houses to groups of students. On-campus housing is guaranteed for the freshman year only and is available on a lottery system for upperclassmen. 88% of students live on campus; of those, 95% remain on campus on weekends. Alcohol is not permitted. Upperclassmen may keep cars.

Activities: There are no fraternities or sororities. There are 71 groups on campus, including band, cheerleading, chess, choir, chorale, chorus, dance, debate, drama, drill team, ethnic, forensics, international, jazz band, literary magazine, newspaper, orchestra, pep band, radio and TV, religious, social, social service, student government, symphony, and yearbook. Popular campus events include Air Jam and an artist concert series.

Disabled Students: Wheelchair ramps, elevators, special parking, specially equipped rest rooms, special class scheduling, lowered drinking fountains, lowered telephones, and other provisions as needed are available.

Services: There is a reader service for the blind and a writing center. Other services are provided as needed.

Campus Safety and Security: Measures include 24-hour foot and vehicle patrol, self-defense education, security escort services, and informal discussions. There are pamphlets/posters/films, emergency telephones, and lighted pathways/sidewalks.

Programs of Study: Wheaton confers B.A., B.S., B.M., and B.M.E. degrees. Master's and doctoral degrees are also awarded. Bachelor's degrees are awarded in BIOLOGICAL SCIENCE (biology/biological science), BUSINESS (business economics), COMMUNICATIONS AND THE ARTS (art, communications, English, French, German, music, and Spanish), COMPUTER AND PHYSICAL SCIENCE (chemistry, computer science, geology, mathematics, physical sciences, and physics), EDUCATION (elementary, music, science, and secondary), ENGINEERING AND ENVIRONMENTAL DESIGN (environmental science), SOCIAL SCIENCE (anthropology, archeology, biblical studies, economics, history, interdisciplinary studies, philosophy, physical fitness/movement, political science/government, psychology, religion, social science, and sociology).

Required: To graduate, students must complete 124 semester hours, 36 in upper-division courses, with a varying number of hours in a major, and maintain at least a 2.0 GPA. General education requirements include competency in a foreign language, math, speech, writing, and Bible studies; distribution requirements include fine arts, history, literature, sciences, physical sciences, philosophy, social sciences, and sport/fitness.

Special: Special academic programs include internships, study abroad in 8 countries, an urban semester in Chicago and a Washington semester. Dual majors are available in all areas, as are student-designed majors. A 3-2 engineering degree is offered with the Illinois Institute of Technology, University of Illinois, Case Western Reserve University School of Engineering, and Washington University School of Engineering and Applied Science; transfer to other engineering schools is also possible. A 3-2 nursing degree is offered with Emory University, Goshen Nursing School, University of Rochester, and Rush University. Pass/fail options are available. There are 10 national honor societies and 11 departmental honors programs.

Faculty/Classroom: 68% of faculty are male; 32%, female. No introductory courses are taught by graduate students.

Admissions: There were 59 National Merit finalists in a recent year.

Requirements: The SAT I or ACT is required. In addition, a high school diploma is required and the GED is accepted. Wheaton requires a general college preparatory program of 18 units, including 4 of English, 3 to 4 of math, science, and social studies, and 2 to 3 of a foreign language. AP and CLEP credits are accepted. Personality/intangible qualities is an important factor in the admission decision.

Procedure: Freshmen are admitted in the fall. Entrance exams should be taken November of the senior year. There is a deferred admissions plan. Check with the school for current deadlines and fee. The fall 2003 application fee was $35.

Transfer: 75 transfer students enrolled in a recent year. Applicants must have completed 15 semester hours with a 3.0 average and present a high school transcript, college transcript, and an essay or personal statement. An interview is required. 48 of 124 credits required for the bachelor's degree must be completed at Wheaton.

Visiting: There are regularly scheduled orientations for prospective students, consisting of presentations by faculty, administrators, students, and financial aid and admissions staff, as well as social activities. There are guides for informal visits and visitors may sit in on classes and stay overnight. To schedule a visit, contact the Admissions Office at (630) 752-5600.

Financial Aid: In a recent year, 73% of all full-time freshmen and 64% of continuing full-time students received some form of financial aid. The average freshman award was $10,589. The average financial indebtedness of a recent graduate was $14,595. The FAFSA and the college's own financial statement are required. Check with the school for current deadlines.

International Students: The school actively recruits these students. They must score 550 on the written TOEFL or 213 on the electronic version; or take the TSE, with a minimum score of 50; or take the TWE, with a minimum score of 5.0. The ACT or SAT I should be substituted for students who are native speakers of English.

Computers: The mainframes are DEC Alpha and RISC/Ultrix minicomputers. Also available are 95 IBM PCs and Macs located in 5 student labs with networked print services and file servers, all of which have network access, plus 8 dial-up modem lines. There are 31 PCs and 5 printers located in 5 dormitory labs. Students also may access the campus network using their own computers in their dorm rooms. All students may access the system 24 hours a day. Students may access the system 2 hours at one sitting if there is a waiting list; otherwise, there is no limit. There are no fees.

Graduates: In a recent year, 584 bachelor's degrees were awarded. The most popular majors were English (18%), social sciences and history (14%), and philosophy, theology, and religion (14%).

Admissions Contact: Director of Admissions.
E-mail: *admissions@wheaton.edu* Web: *http://www.wheaton.edu*

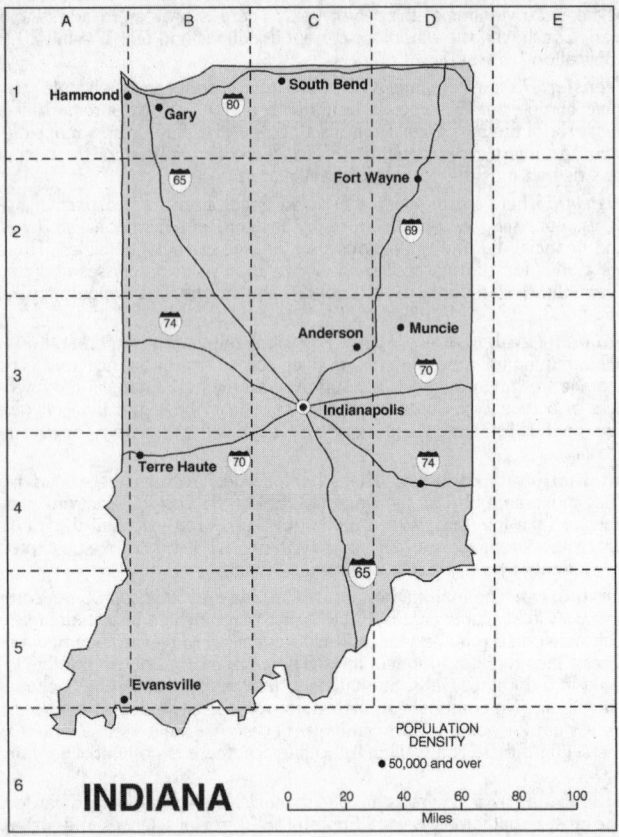

POPULATION
DENSITY

● 50,000 and over

INDIANA

Miles
0   20   40   60   80   100

ethnic, film, honors, international, jazz band, literary magazine, musical theater, newspaper, opera, orchestra, photography, political, professional, radio and TV, religious, social, social service, student government, symphony, and yearbook. Popular campus events include Christmas Carols, Celebration Weekend, and Black Awareness.

Sports: There are 8 intercollegiate sports for men and 8 for women, and 7 intramural sports for men and 6 for women. Facilities include 2 gyms, football, baseball/softball, and soccer fields, an 8-lane all-weather track, tennis courts, a bowling alley, and a game room. The campus stadium seats 4200 and the indoor gym seats 2400.

Disabled Students: 95% of the campus is accessible. Wheelchair ramps, elevators, special parking, specially equipped rest rooms, special class scheduling, lowered drinking fountains, and lowered telephones are available.

Services: Counseling and information services are available, as is tutoring in most subjects. There is a reader service for the blind and remedial math, reading, and writing.

Campus Safety and Security: Measures include 24-hour foot and vehicle patrol, self-defense education, security escort services, and informal discussions. There are pamphlets/posters/films, emergency telephones, lighted pathways/sidewalks, and Indiana State police academy graduates are security officers.

Programs of Study: Anderson confers B.A. and B.S.N. degrees. Associate, master's, and doctoral degrees are also awarded. Bachelor's degrees are awarded in BIOLOGICAL SCIENCE (biology/biological science), BUSINESS (accounting, banking and finance, business administration and management, management science, marketing/retailing/merchandising, and sports management), COMMUNICATIONS AND THE ARTS (communications, dramatic arts, English, fine arts, French, German, graphic design, music business management, music performance, and Spanish), COMPUTER AND PHYSICAL SCIENCE (chemistry, computer science, mathematics, and physics), EDUCATION (art, Christian, elementary, foreign languages, health, music, physical, science, and social studies), HEALTH PROFESSIONS (medical laboratory technology and nursing), SOCIAL SCIENCE (criminal justice, economics, family/consumer studies, history, philosophy, political science/government, psychology, religion, social work, and sociology). Physical sciences is the strongest academically. Business, education, and music are the largest.

Required: Requirements for graduation include the general education core, consisting of 55 hours, a minimum 2.0 GPA overall and in the major, 124 total credit hours, and a minimum of 36 hours in the major. All students must complete a liberal arts seminar. The last 24 credit hours must be taken in residence.

Special: Anderson offers co-op programs with Purdue University, internships through the Center for Public Service, study abroad in 25 countries through the International Studies Program, and a Washington semester. Also available are credit for military experience and pass/fail options. Courses in electronic engineering may be taken through the Purdue Anderson campus. Pre-professional programs are offered in medical, podiatry, dentistry, law, engineering, seminary, and several allied health fields. There are 12 national honor societies, a freshman honors program, and 10 departmental honors programs.

Faculty/Classroom: 57% of faculty are male; 43%, female. 91% teach undergraduates. No introductory courses are taught by graduate students. The average class size in an introductory lecture is 29; in a laboratory, 14; and in a regular course, 17.

Requirements: The SAT I or ACT is required. In addition, applicants must be graduates of an accredited secondary school or have a GED certificate, and submit a photograph, references, and a health form. A GPA of 2.0 is required. AP and CLEP credits are accepted. Important factors in the admissions decision are leadership record, parents or siblings attending the school, and personality/intangible qualities.

Procedure: Freshmen are admitted fall and spring. Entrance exams should be taken in the fall of the junior year. Application deadlines are open. The fall 2003 application fee was $20. Applications are accepted on-line through the school's web site.

Transfer: 104 transfer students enrolled in a recent year. Applicants must have a minimum 2.0 GPA, satisfactory SAT I or ACT scores, and transcripts for all previously attended colleges. 24 of 124 credits required for the bachelor's degree must be completed at Anderson.

Visiting: There are regularly scheduled orientations for prospective students, including a campus tour, an academic overview, a financial aid and athletics overview, and appointments with professors and departmental chairs. There are guides for informal visits and visitors may sit in on classes and stay overnight. To schedule a visit, contact the Admissions Office.

Financial Aid: Anderson is a member of CSS. The FAFSA is required.

International Students: They must score 550 on the written TOEFL and also take the SAT I, scoring 800.

ANDERSON UNIVERSITY
Anderson, IN 46012

C-3

(765) 641-4080
(800) 428-6414; Fax: (765) 641-3851

Full-time: 750 men, 1070 women	**Faculty:** 123; IIB, --$
Part-time: 75 men, 110 women	**Ph.D.s:** 70%
Graduate: 140 men, 110 women	**Student/Faculty:** 14 to 1
Year: semesters, summer session	**Tuition:** $17,990
Application Deadline: open	**Room & Board:** $5820
Freshman Class: n/av	
SAT I or ACT: required	**LESS COMPETITIVE**

Anderson University, founded in 1917, is a private liberal arts institution affiliated with the Church of God. The university offers programs in theoretical and applied science, social and professional studies, and arts, culture, and religion. Figures in the above capsule and in this profile are approximate. There are 3 undergraduate and 3 graduate schools. In addition to regional accreditation, Anderson has baccalaureate program accreditation with ACBSP, CSWE, NASM, NCATE, and NLN. The library contains 264,208 volumes, 89,884 microform items, and 12,000 audio/video tapes/CDs, and subscribes to 947 periodicals. Computerized library services include the card catalog, interlibrary loans, and database searching. Special learning facilities include a learning resource center, art gallery, radio station, and the Museum of the Bible and the Ancient Near East. The 100-acre campus is in a suburban area 40 miles northeast of Indianapolis. Including any residence halls, there are 26 buildings.

Student Life: 61% of undergraduates are from Indiana. Students are from 42 states, 15 foreign countries, and Canada. 97% are from public schools. 93% are white. 83% are Protestant; 13% claim no religious affiliation. The average age of freshmen is 18; all undergraduates, 21. 25% do not continue beyond their first year; 50% remain to graduate.

Housing: 1243 students can be accommodated in college housing, which includes single-sex dorms, on-campus apartments, off-campus apartments, and married-student housing. On-campus housing is guaranteed for all 4 years. 61% of students live on campus; of those, 50% remain on campus on weekends. Alcohol is not permitted. All students may keep cars.

Activities: There are no fraternities or sororities. There are 41 groups on campus, including art, band, cheerleading, choir, chorale, drama,

Computers: The mainframes are an HP 3000/948 and an HP 9000/832. The mainframes are accessible throughout the campus either through a local area network or by modem. All students may access the system. There are no time limits and no fees.

Admissions Contact: Admissions Counselor.
E-mail: *info@anderson.edu* Web: *www.anderson.edu*

BALL STATE UNIVERSITY
B-3
Muncie, IN 47306
(765) 285-8300
(800) 482-4BSU; Fax: (765) 285-1632

Full-time: 6355 men, 7905 women	**Faculty:** 806; I, --$
Part-time: 610 men, 740 women	**Ph.D.s:** 76%
Graduate: 850 men, 1205 women	**Student/Faculty:** 18 to 1
Year: semesters, summer session	**Tuition:** $5532 ($13,950)
Application Deadline: see profile	**Room & Board:** $5880
Freshman Class: n/av	
SAT I or ACT: required	**COMPETITIVE**

Ball State University, founded in 1918, is a public university offering undergraduate and graduate programs through 7 academic colleges in applied sciences and technology; architecture and planning; business; communication, information, and media; fine arts; sciences and humanities; and teacher education. The Honors College and the University College are interdisciplinary colleges. Figures in the above capsule and in this profile are approximate. There are 7 undergraduate schools and 1 graduate school. In addition to regional accreditation, Ball State has baccalaureate program accreditation with AACSB, ACEJMC, ADA, AHEA, CAHEA, CSAB, CSWE, NAAB, NASAD, NASM, NCATE, and NLN. The 3 libraries contain 1,108,532 volumes, 1,012,210 microform items, and 509,899 audio/video tapes/CDs, and subscribe to 3077 periodicals. Computerized library services include interlibrary loans and database searching. Special learning facilities include a learning resource center, art gallery, planetarium, radio station, TV station, and research centers in solar energy, human performance, and international programs. The 955-acre campus is in a suburban area 56 miles northwest of Indianapolis. Including any residence halls, there are 57 buildings.

Student Life: 91% of undergraduates are from Indiana. Students are from 49 states, 86 foreign countries, and Canada. 90% are white. The average age of freshmen is 18; all undergraduates, 21. 23% do not continue beyond their first year.

Housing: 6400 students can be accommodated in college housing, which includes single-sex and coed dorms, on-campus apartments, married-student housing, and fraternity houses. In addition, there are honors houses, special-interest houses, and wellness halls. On-campus housing is guaranteed for the freshman year only. 60% of students commute. Alcohol is not permitted. All students may keep cars.

Activities: 10% of men belong to 19 national fraternities; 10% of women belong to 1 local and 15 national sororities. There are 300 groups on campus, including art, band, cheerleading, chess, choir, chorale, chorus, computers, dance, debate, drama, drill team, ethnic, film, forensics, gay, honors, international, jazz band, literary magazine, marching band, musical theater, newspaper, orchestra, pep band, photography, political, professional, radio and TV, religious, social, social service, student government, symphony, and yearbook. Popular campus events include Watermelon Bust, Unity Week, and Family Weekend.

Sports: There are 9 intercollegiate sports for men and 10 for women, and 43 intramural sports for men and 41 for women. Facilities include an 11,500-seat basketball and volleyball arena, 2 gyms, a field sports building, tennis courts, and an aquatic center. The campus stadium seats 16,320.

Disabled Students: All of the campus is accessible. Wheelchair ramps, elevators, special parking, specially equipped rest rooms, special class scheduling, lowered drinking fountains, and lowered telephones are available. A special resource guide, an accessibility map (including tactile), and text telephones (TDD) in all key offices are also available.

Services: Counseling and information services are available, as is tutoring in most subjects. There is a reader service for the blind.

Campus Safety and Security: Measures include 24-hour foot and vehicle patrol, self-defense education, security escort services, and shuttle buses. There are informal discussions, pamphlets/posters/films, emergency telephones, and lighted pathways/sidewalks.

Programs of Study: Ball State confers B.A., B.S., B.Arch., B.F.A., B.G.S., B.Land.Arch., B.Mus., B.S.W., and B.Urban Planning and Development degrees. Associate, master's, and doctoral degrees are also awarded. Bachelor's degrees are awarded in AGRICULTURE (fishing and fisheries, and natural resource management), BIOLOGICAL SCIENCE (biology/biological science, botany, cell biology, genetics, microbiology, molecular biology, wildlife biology, and zoology), BUSINESS (accounting, banking and finance, business administration and management, business economics, insurance, management science, marketing/retailing/merchandising, personnel management, real estate, and sports management), COMMUNICATIONS AND THE ARTS (art, broadcasting, classical languages, classics, communications, dance, dramatic arts, English, film arts, fine arts, French, German, graphic design,

guitar, journalism, music, music performance, photography, piano/organ, Spanish, speech/debate/rhetoric, telecommunications, and voice), COMPUTER AND PHYSICAL SCIENCE (actuarial science, chemistry, computer science, geology, mathematics, and physics), EDUCATION (art, business, early childhood, education of the deaf and hearing impaired, educational media, elementary, foreign languages, health, home economics, industrial arts, journalism, middle school, music, science, secondary, social studies, special, and technical), ENGINEERING AND ENVIRONMENTAL DESIGN (architecture, environmental design, graphic arts technology, landscape architecture/design, and urban planning technology), HEALTH PROFESSIONS (health science, medical laboratory technology, nursing, predentistry, premedicine, prepharmacy, and speech pathology/audiology), SOCIAL SCIENCE (anthropology, criminal justice, dietetics, economics, food production/management/services, geography, history, home economics, Latin American studies, liberal arts/general studies, paralegal studies, parks and recreation management, philosophy, physical fitness/movement, political science/government, prelaw, psychology, religion, social work, and sociology). Architecture, business, and education are the strongest academically. Elementary education and business are the largest.

Required: All students must take at least 126 credits and maintain a 2.0 GPA for graduation. Required courses are in English composition, math, speech, history, physical sciences, social or behavioral sciences, humanities or fine arts, global studies, and 3 hours of phys ed. In addition, all juniors must pass a writing competency exam.

Special: Nearly all undergraduate disciplines offer internships. Study abroad is possible at the university's London center and in 20 other programs; students may also spend a semester in Washington, D.C., and co-op and work-study programs are available. Most disciplines offer dual majors. There is a 3-2 program in engineering, an award-winning program in entrepreneurship, a general studies degree, nondegree study, and pass/fail options. There are 40 national honor societies and a freshman honors program.

Faculty/Classroom: 63% of faculty are male; 37%, female. 94% teach undergraduates, 75% do research, and 73% do both. No introductory courses are taught by graduate students. The average class size in an introductory lecture is 50; in a laboratory, 18; and in a regular course, 30.

Admissions: In a recent year, there were 7 National Merit finalists and 40 freshmen graduated first in their class.

Requirements: The SAT I or ACT is required. In addition, applicants must be graduates of an accredited high school or have a GED diploma. Admission is based on strength of the applicant's curriculum, grades in English, math, lab sciences, social sciences, and foreign language, curricula patterns and grade trends, and the SAT I or ACT scores. For Indiana applicants, Ball State considers completion of Core 40 as the recommended preparation for college-bound students; completion of the Academic Honors Diploma is encouraged. AP and CLEP credits are accepted. Important factors in the admissions decision are advanced placement or honor courses, recommendations by school officials, and personality/intangible qualities.

Procedure: Freshmen are admitted fall, spring, and summer. Entrance exams should be taken during the spring of the junior year or early in the senior year. There is a deferred admissions plan. There is a rolling admissions plan. Check with the school for current deadlines and fee. The fall 2003 application fee was $25. Notification is sent on a rolling basis.

Transfer: 783 transfer students enrolled in a recent year. Transfer applicants should have earned a 2.0 GPA on a 4.0 scale (as computed by Ball State) to be considered for admission. An official high school transcript or GED score report and official transcripts from each postsecondary institution are required. 63 of 126 credits required for the bachelor's degree must be completed at Ball State.

Visiting: There are regularly scheduled orientations for prospective students. There are guides for informal visits and visitors may sit in on classes and stay overnight. To schedule a visit, contact the University Visitors Center at (765) 285-5683 (out-of-state) or (800) 482-4BSU.

Financial Aid: In a recent year, 85% of all full-time freshmen and 70% of continuing full-time students received some form of financial aid. 49% of full-time freshmen and 47% of continuing full-time students received need-based aid. The average freshman award was $5460. 32% of undergraduates work part time. Average annual earnings from campus work are $1200. The average financial indebtedness of a recent graduate was $15,689. Ball State is a member of CSS. The FAFSA is required. Check with the school for current deadlines.

International Students: The school actively recruits these students. They must score 550 on the written TOEFL.

Computers: The mainframes are an IBM and VAX cluster. The university supports more than 70 computer labs on campus, and there are more than 3000 computer workstations. 2 mainframe computers with about 200 terminals are available to students, as are more than 300 PCs. All students may access the system at any time except Friday from 5 P.M. to 8 A.M. Saturday. There are no time limits and no fees.

Admissions Contact: Lawrence Waters, Dean of Admissions and Enrollment Services. E-mail: *askus@wp.bsu.edu* Web: *www.bsu.edu*

BETHEL COLLEGE
Mishawaka, IN 46545

C-1
(574) 257-3339
(800) 422-4101; Fax: (574) 257-3335

Full-time: 511 men, 778 women	**Faculty:** 59; IIB, --$
Part-time: 125 men, 326 women	**Ph.D.s:** 74%
Graduate: 58 men, 49 women	**Student/Faculty:** 22 to 1
Year: semesters, summer session	**Tuition:** $14,990
Application Deadline: see profile	**Room & Board:** $4680
Freshman Class: 468 applied, 443 accepted, 306 enrolled	
SAT I Verbal/Math: 530/530	**ACT:** 22 COMPETITIVE

Bethel College, founded in 1947, is a private institution affiliated with the Missionary Church, offering a liberal arts education with a Christian perspective. In addition to regional accreditation, Bethel has baccalaureate program accreditation with NCATE and NLN. The library contains 104,076 volumes, 4374 microform items, and 3970 audio/video tapes/CDs, and subscribes to 450 periodicals. Computerized library services include the card catalog, interlibrary loans, database searching, and Internet access. Special learning facilities include a learning resource center, art gallery, and radio station. The 70-acre campus is in a suburban area 90 miles east of Chicago. Including any residence halls, there are 50 buildings.

Student Life: 67% of undergraduates are from Indiana. Students are from 32 states, 13 foreign countries, and Canada. 78% are from public schools. 83% are white; 10% African American. 84% are Protestant; 8% Catholic; 7% claim no religious affiliation. The average age of freshmen is 19; all undergraduates, 26. 13% do not continue beyond their first year; 60% remain to graduate.

Housing: 810 students can be accommodated in college housing, which includes single-sex dorms, on-campus apartments, and married-student housing. In addition, there is a cultural awareness house and a missions house. On-campus housing is guaranteed for all 4 years. 54% of students commute. Alcohol is not permitted. Upperclassmen may keep cars.

Activities: There are no fraternities or sororities. There are 18 groups on campus, including art, band, cheerleading, choir, chorale, chorus, computers, drama, Fellowship of Christian Athletes, Hawaii Fellowship, honors, international, jazz band, literary magazine, musical theater, newspaper, orchestra, pep band, professional, radio and TV, religious, social, social service, student government, and yearbook. Popular campus events include Christmas Banquet, Junior-Senior Banquet, and Spiritual Emphasis Week.

Sports: There are 9 intercollegiate sports for men and 9 for women, and 15 intramural sports for men and 15 for women. Facilities include a gym, a weight room, exercise, baseball and training facilities, baseball, softball, and soccer fields, tennis courts, and a practice track.

Disabled Students: 78% of the campus is accessible. Wheelchair ramps, elevators, special parking, specially equipped rest rooms, lowered drinking fountains, and special housing are available.

Services: Counseling and information services are available, as is tutoring in every subject. There is remedial math, reading, and writing.

Campus Safety and Security: Measures include 24-hour foot and vehicle patrol, security escort services, informal discussions, and pamphlets/posters/films. There are emergency telephones and lighted pathways/sidewalks.

Programs of Study: Bethel confers B.A., B.S., and B.S.N. degrees. Associate and master's degrees are also awarded. Bachelor's degrees are awarded in BIOLOGICAL SCIENCE (biology/biological science and environmental biology), BUSINESS (accounting, business administration and management, and sports management), COMMUNICATIONS AND THE ARTS (art, communications, dramatic arts, English, graphic design, music, music performance, photography, and video), COMPUTER AND PHYSICAL SCIENCE (applied physics, chemistry, computer science, digital arts/technology, mathematics, physics, and web technology), EDUCATION (business, elementary, English, mathematics, music, physical, science, secondary, and social studies), ENGINEERING AND ENVIRONMENTAL DESIGN (aeronautical engineering, chemical engineering, civil engineering, electrical/electronics engineering, interior design, and mechanical engineering), HEALTH PROFESSIONS (exercise science, nursing, predentistry, and premedicine), SOCIAL SCIENCE (biblical studies, criminal justice, history, human services, international studies, interpreter for the deaf, liberal arts/general studies, ministries, missions, philosophy, prelaw, psychology, religion, religious music, social science, sociology, and youth ministry).

Required: To graduate, students must complete 124 credits, including 24 to 52 in the major, with a minimum 2.0 GPA. Also required are 4 semesters of phys ed, 10 credits in Bible and religion, courses in communication skills, social science and history, fine arts and humanities, and natural sciences and math, and a course called Lifelong Physical Awareness. Computer proficiency is also required.

Special: A cooperative program is offered with the University of Notre Dame, and students may cross-register for courses at various local colleges including Northern Indiana Consortium for Education (NICE). Also available are a B.A.-B.S. degree in engineering, a 3-2 engineering de-

gree with the University of Notre Dame and Tri-State University (Angola), a liberal arts degree, and an accelerated degree in organizational management (for students age 25 and over). Bethel also offers nondegree courses, a pass/fail option, student teaching, some business and computer internships, study in Ecuador, China, Russia, New Zealand, Australia, and Jamaica, double majors, and work-study programs. There is a freshman honors program.

Faculty/Classroom: 52% of faculty are male; 48%, female. All teach undergraduates and 10% both teach and do research. No introductory courses are taught by graduate students. The average class size in an introductory lecture is 50; in a laboratory, 15; and in a regular course, 16.

Admissions: 95% of the 2003-2004 applicants were accepted. The SAT I scores for the 2003-2004 freshman class were: Verbal--34% below 500, 42% between 500 and 599, 23% between 600 and 700, and 7% above 700; Math--32% below 500, 45% between 500 and 599, 21% between 600 and 700, and 1% above 700. The ACT scores were 39% below 21, 21% between 21 and 23, 18% between 24 and 26, 10% between 27 and 28, and 11% above 28. 30% of the current freshmen were in the top fifth of their class; 59% were in the top two fifths. There was 1 National Merit semifinalist. 4 freshmen graduated first in their class.

Requirements: The SAT I or ACT is required. In addition, applicants should be graduates of accredited secondary schools or have the GED. Required secondary school credits include 8 units in English, 6 each in math, lab science, and social science, and 4 in a foreign language. Chemistry is required for nursing majors. An interview is recommended. An audition is required of music program applicants. A GPA of 2.0 is required. AP and CLEP credits are accepted.

Procedure: Freshmen are admitted to all sessions. Entrance exams should be taken as early as possible in the junior or senior year. There is a rolling admissions plan. There are early admissions and deferred admissions plans. Check with the school for current application deadlines. Application fee is $25. Applications are accepted on-line through the school's web site.

Transfer: 145 transfer students enrolled in 2002-2003. Grades of C or better are eligible for transfer; students without a minimum GPA of 2.0 may be admitted on probation. Other admission requirements are the same as for entering freshmen. 30 of 124 credits required for the bachelor's degree must be completed at Bethel.

Visiting: There are regularly scheduled orientations for prospective students, including an interview, chapel visit, tour, lunch, and a class or professor visit as requested. There are guides for informal visits and visitors may sit in on classes and stay overnight. To schedule a visit, contact the Office of Admissions at (800) 422-4101 or admissions@bethelcollege.edu.

Financial Aid: In a recent year, 84% of all full-time freshmen and 81% of continuing full-time students received some form of financial aid. 64% of full-time freshmen and 56% of continuing full-time students received need-based aid. The average freshman award was $11,545. 19% of undergraduates work part time. The average financial indebtedness of a recent graduate was $14,330. Bethel is a member of CSS. The FAFSA, the college's own financial statement, and the SAR are required. The deadline for filing freshman financial aid applications for fall entry is March 10.

International Students: There are 34 international students enrolled. They must score 540 on the written TOEFL or 207 on the electronic version.

Computers: The mainframe is a Novell Network. There are 66 IBM and Mac PCs. All students have access to the main computer lab. Residential students have access to the campus network in their residence hall room through their personal computer. Wireless access is also available on campus. All students may access the system Monday through Friday 8 A.M. to midnight and Saturday 8 A.M. to 7 P.M. in the computer labs. There are no time limits and no fees. It is strongly recommended that all students have a personal computer.

Graduates: From July 1, 2002 to June 30, 2003, 307 bachelor's degrees were awarded. The most popular majors were business areas (31%), nursing (17%), and education (16%). In an average class, 2% graduate in 3 years or less, 49% graduate in 4 years or less, 55% graduate in 5 years or less, and 66% graduate in 6 years or less. 68 companies recruited on campus in 2002-2003. Of the 2002 graduating class, 12% were enrolled in graduate school within 6 months of graduation and 70% were employed.

Admissions Contact: Randy Beachy, Assistant Vice President of Enrollment and Marketing. E-mail: beachyr@bethelcollege.edu
Web: www.bethelcollege.edu

BUTLER UNIVERSITY
Indianapolis, IN 46208

C-3

(317) 940-8100
(888) 940-8100; Fax: (317) 940-8150

Full-time: 1367 men, 2378 women	**Faculty:** 249; IIA, av$
Part-time: 30 men, 48 women	**Ph.D.s:** 84%
Graduate: 305 men, 296 women	**Student/Faculty:** 15 to 1
Year: semesters, summer session	**Tuition:** $21,210
Application Deadline: open	**Room & Board:** $7040
Freshman Class: n/av	
SAT I Verbal/Math: 584/597	**ACT:** 26 **VERY COMPETITIVE+**

Butler University, founded in 1855, is an independent, private institution offering programs in liberal arts and sciences, business administration, fine arts, pharmacy, health sciences, and education. There are 5 undergraduate and 5 graduate schools. In addition to regional accreditation, Butler has baccalaureate program accreditation with AACSB, ACPE, NASM, and NCATE. The 2 libraries contain 309,511 volumes, 180,107 microform items, and 14,407 audio/video tapes/CDs, and subscribe to 2126 periodicals. Computerized library services include the card catalog, interlibrary loans, and database searching. Special learning facilities include a learning resource center, planetarium, TV station, and an observatory. The 290-acre campus is in a suburban area 5 miles from downtown Indianapolis. Including any residence halls, there are 19 buildings.

Student Life: 58% of undergraduates are from Indiana. Others are from 41 states, 52 foreign countries, and Canada. 86% are from public schools. 90% are white. 57% are Protestant; 28% Catholic; 11% claim no religious affiliation. The average age of freshmen is 18; all undergraduates, 20. 13% do not continue beyond their first year.

Housing: 1500 students can be accommodated in college housing, which includes single-sex and coed dormitories, on-campus apartments, fraternity houses, and sorority houses. In addition, there are special-interest houses and special-interest units in residence halls. On-campus housing is guaranteed for all 4 years. 63% of students live on campus; of those, 50% remain on campus on weekends. Alcohol is not permitted. All students may keep cars.

Activities: 24% of men belong to 8 national fraternities; 24% of women belong to 8 national sororities. There are 97 groups on campus, including band, cheerleading, choir, chorale, chorus, dance, debate, drama, drill team, ethnic, gay, honors, international, jazz band, literary magazine, marching band, newspaper, opera, orchestra, pep band, photography, political, professional, radio and TV, religious, social, social service, student government, symphony, and yearbook. Popular campus events include Geneva Stunts, Spring Sing, and Spring Sports Spectacular.

Sports: There are 10 intercollegiate sports for men and 9 for women, and 23 intramural sports for men and 23 for women. Facilities include a 10,000-seat field house, a 20,000-seat football stadium, tennis courts, indoor and outdoor tracks, a weight-training room, an aerobics/exercise room, intramural fields, and baseball, softball, and soccer fields.

Disabled Students: 90% of the campus is accessible. Wheelchair ramps, elevators, special parking, specially equipped rest rooms, special class scheduling, and lowered drinking fountains are available.

Services: Counseling and information services are available, as is tutoring in every subject. There is a reader service for the blind. A writer's studio offers assistance in all areas of the writing process.

Campus Safety and Security: Measures include 24-hour foot and vehicle patrol, self-defense education, security escort services, and informal discussions. There are pamphlets/posters/films, emergency telephones, and lighted pathways/sidewalks.

Programs of Study: Butler confers B.A., B.S., B.F.A., B.M., B.S.H.S., and B.S.P. degrees. Master's and doctoral degrees are also awarded. Bachelor's degrees are awarded in BIOLOGICAL SCIENCE (biology/ biological science), BUSINESS (accounting, banking and finance, international business management, and marketing/retailing/merchandising), COMMUNICATIONS AND THE ARTS (arts administration/ management, communications, dance, dramatic arts, English, French, German, Greek, journalism, Latin, music, music business management, music performance, music theory and composition, performing arts, Spanish, speech/debate/rhetoric, and telecommunications), COMPUTER AND PHYSICAL SCIENCE (actuarial science, chemistry, computer science, mathematics, and physics), EDUCATION (elementary, music, and secondary), HEALTH PROFESSIONS (pharmacy, physician's assistant, and speech pathology/audiology), SOCIAL SCIENCE (anthropology, criminal justice, economics, history, international studies, philosophy, political science/government, psychology, religion, and sociology). Pharmacy, chemistry, and biology are the strongest academically. Business, education, and pharmacy are the largest.

Required: The core curriculum includes specific courses in English, speech, computer literacy, phys ed, and interdisciplinary studies, as well as distribution requirements in humanities, fine arts, social science, natural science, and quantitative reasoning. To graduate, students must complete 126 to 166 semester hours with a minimum GPA of 2.0.

Special: Butler offers cross-registration with the 4 other members of the Consortium for Urban Education, co-op programs in business administration, and internships in pharmacy, arts administration, and business

programs. A 3-2 degree program in engineering with Purdue University, extensive study-abroad programs, and work-study programs are available. There are dual majors including French, German, and Spanish combined with business studies, student-designed majors, a general studies degree, pass/fail options, and nondegree study. There are 5 national honor societies and a freshman honors program.

Faculty/Classroom: 58% of faculty are male; 42%, female. 91% teach undergraduates and 75% both teach and do research. No introductory courses are taught by graduate students. The average class size in an introductory lecture is 24; in a laboratory, 18; and in a regular course, 19.

Admissions: The SAT I scores for the 2003-2004 freshman class were: Verbal--13% below 500, 43% between 500 and 599, 37% between 600 and 700, and 7% above 700; Math--12% below 500, 36% between 500 and 599, 43% between 600 and 700, and 9% above 700. The ACT scores were 6% below 21, 15% between 21 and 23, 31% between 24 and 26, 21% between 27 and 28, and 27% above 28. 68% of the current freshmen were in the top fifth of their class; 89% were in the top two fifths. There were 12 National Merit finalists and 26 semifinalists. 60 freshmen graduated first in their class.

Requirements: The SAT I or ACT is required. In addition, applicants should be graduates of an accredited secondary school, but Butler will consider talented or gifted students without a diploma. Students should have earned at least 17 academic units, based on 4 years of English, 3 each of math and lab science, 2 each of a foreign language and history/ social science, and the rest of electives. An audition is required for dance, music, and theater majors, and an interview is required for radio/ TV majors. Butler requires applicants to be in the upper 50% of their class. A GPA of 2.0 is required. AP and CLEP credits are accepted. Important factors in the admissions decision are advanced placement or honor courses, evidence of special talent, and leadership record.

Procedure: Freshmen are admitted to all sessions. Entrance exams should be taken during the junior year. There are early admissions and deferred admissions plans. Application deadlines are open and there is a rolling admissions plan. The application fee is $35. 22 were on the 2003 waiting list; 1 was admitted. Applications are accepted on-line through www.butler.edu.

Transfer: 119 transfer students enrolled in 2003-2004. Applicants who have completed more than 12 hours of college work must present transcripts from all previous colleges attended, indicating good standing and a minimum GPA of 2.0, and an official high school transcript showing a posted date of graduation. Those students with fewer than 12 hours must also submit the SAT I or ACT scores. Students wishing to transfer into pharmacy or physician assistant programs should contact the Office of Admission for requirements and deadlines. 45 of 126 to 166 credits required for the bachelor's degree must be completed at Butler.

Visiting: There are regularly scheduled orientations for prospective students, including a campus tour, faculty visit, and financial aid interview. There are guides for informal visits and visitors may sit in on classes and stay overnight. To schedule a visit, contact the Office of Admission at (888) 940-8100 or admission@butler.edu.

Financial Aid: In 2003-2004, 90% of all full-time freshmen and 86% of continuing full-time students received some form of financial aid. 43% of full-time freshmen and 45% of continuing full-time students received need-based aid. The average freshman award was $13,565. 40% of undergraduates work part time. Average annual earnings from campus work are $1200. The average financial indebtedness of the 2003 graduate was $10,000. Butler is a member of CSS. The FAFSA and the college's own financial statement are required. The deadline for filing freshman financial aid applications for fall entry is March 1.

International Students: There are 81 international students enrolled. The school actively recruits these students. They must score 550 on the written TOEFL or 213 on the electronic version or complete level 5 at the American Language Academy on Butler's campus.

Computers: The mainframe is a DEC VAX 6610. Ethernet fiber-optic technology connects all Macs and PCs (150 in labs for students) to the mainframe. All students may access the system 24 hours a day. There are no time limits and no fees. It is strongly recommended that all students have a personal computer.

Graduates: From July 1, 2002 to June 30, 2003, 833 bachelor's degrees were awarded. The most popular majors were marketing (11%), pharmacy (9%), and elementary education (7%). In an average class, 53% graduate in 4 years or less, 62% graduate in 5 years or less, and 69% graduate in 6 years or less. 300 companies recruited on campus in 2002-2003. Of the 2002 graduating class, 19% were enrolled in graduate school within 6 months of graduation and 74% were employed.

Admissions Contact: Bill Preble, Director of Admission. A video is available. E-mail: admission@butler.edu Web: www.butler.edu

CALUMET COLLEGE OF ST. JOSEPH
Whiting, IN 46394

B-1
(219) 473-4739
(877) 700-9100; Fax: (219) 473-4259

Full-time: 141 men, 301 women	**Faculty:** 23; IIB, --$
Part-time: 338 men, 376 women	**Ph.D.s:** 50%
Graduate: 89 men, 29 women	**Student/Faculty:** 19 to 1
Year: semesters, summer session	**Tuition:** $9000
Application Deadline: open	**Room & Board:** n/app
Freshman Class: 165 applied, 124 accepted, 67 enrolled	
SAT I Math: 584	**ACT:** 17 **LESS COMPETITIVE**

Calumet College of St. Joseph, founded in 1951, is a private, Catholic institution offering commuting students a liberal arts education in a Christian environment. The library contains 93,055 volumes, 3035 microform items, and 6412 audio/video tapes/CDs, and subscribes to 354 periodicals. Computerized library services include interlibrary loans and database searching. Special learning facilities include a learning resource center and art gallery. The 256-acre campus is in an urban area 15 miles southeast of Chicago in northwest Indiana. There is one building.

Student Life: 70% of undergraduates are from Indiana. Others are from 2 states. 65% are from public schools. 46% are white; 33% African American; 19% Hispanic. Most are Catholic. The average age of freshmen is 21; all undergraduates, 35. 42% do not continue beyond their first year; 58% remain to graduate.

Housing: There are no residence halls. All students commute. Alcohol is not permitted. All students may keep cars.

Activities: There are no fraternities or sororities. There are 15 groups on campus, including cheerleading, drama, ethnic, literary magazine, musical theater, newspaper, photography, professional, religious, social, social service, and student government. Popular campus events include Thanksgiving Ethnicfest and Student Appreciation Week.

Sports: There are 3 intercollegiate sports for men and 4 for women, and 1 intramural sport for men.

Disabled Students: All of the campus is accessible. Wheelchair ramps, elevators, special parking, and specially equipped rest rooms are available.

Services: Counseling and information services are available, as is tutoring in most subjects. There is remedial math, reading, and writing.

Campus Safety and Security: Measures include emergency telephones and lighted pathways/sidewalks.

Programs of Study: CCSJ confers B.A., B.S., B.S.Ed., and B.S.M.T. degrees. Associate and master's degrees are also awarded. Bachelor's degrees are awarded in BUSINESS (accounting, business administration and management, and institutional management), COMMUNICATIONS AND THE ARTS (English and media arts), COMPUTER AND PHYSICAL SCIENCE (information sciences and systems), EDUCATION (elementary and secondary), HEALTH PROFESSIONS (health care administration), SOCIAL SCIENCE (criminal justice, human services, law enforcement and corrections, liberal arts/general studies, paralegal studies, psychology, religion, theological studies, and urban studies). Management, accounting, and criminal justice are the strongest academically. Management, human services, and education are the largest.

Required: All students must complete 42 semester hours of general education courses, including English composition, economics, speech, theology, philosophy, communication and fine arts, science and math, and social and behavioral science. A total of 124 semester hours with a minimum GPA of 2.0 is required to graduate.

Special: The college offers a cooperative 3-1 baccalaureate degree in medical technology with the schools of St. Margaret-Mercy Hospital in Indiana, where students complete their study and a clinical internship. Accelerated degree programs in organizational management, health-care mangement, and law enforcement management are possible. The LEAP program offers credit for life experience. Study abroad, internships, work-study programs, a general studies degree, pass/fail options, and nondegree study are possible.

Faculty/Classroom: 75% of faculty are male; 25%, female. All teach undergraduates. The average class size in an introductory lecture is 25; in a laboratory, 20; and in a regular course, 20.

Admissions: 75% of the 2003-2004 applicants were accepted.

Requirements: Applicants should have completed 4 years of high school English, 3 to 4 of math, 2 to 3 of science, and 2 of social studies. The GED is accepted. An essay and an interview are recommended. The Vocabulary and Reading Assessment Test is required. A GPA of 2.0 is required. AP and CLEP credits are accepted. Important factors in the admissions decision are extracurricular activities record, leadership record, and evidence of special talent.

Procedure: Freshmen are admitted to all sessions. There is a deferred admissions plan. Application deadlines are open. There is a rolling admissions plan. Applications are accepted on-line.

Transfer: 382 transfer students enrolled in 2003-2004. A 2.0 GPA is required. An interview is recommended. The Vocabulary and Reading Assessment Test is required. 30 of 124 credits required for the bachelor's degree must be completed at CCSJ.

Visiting: There are regularly scheduled orientations for prospective students. There are guides for informal visits and visitors may sit in on classes. To schedule a visit, contact Chuck Walz, Director of Admissions at (219) 473-4379 or cwalz@ccsj.edu.

Financial Aid: CCSJ is a member of CSS. The FAFSA and the college's own financial statement are required.

International Students: They must score 520 on the written TOEFL or 190 on the electronic version.

Computers: All students may access the system Monday through Friday from 8 A.M. to 10 P.M., except during class lab times. There are no time limits and no fees. It is strongly recommended that all students have a personal computer.

Admissions Contact: Chuck Walz, Director of Admissions. Web: www.ccsj.edu

DEPAUW UNIVERSITY
Greencastle, IN 46135

B-3
(765) 658-4006
(800) 447-2495; Fax: (765) 658-4007

Full-time: 1057 men, 1269 women	**Faculty:** 209; IIB, +$
Part-time: 12 men, 27 women	**Ph.D.s:** 93%
Graduate: none	**Student/Faculty:** 11 to 1
Year: 4-1-4	**Tuition:** $24,450
Application Deadline: February 1	**Room & Board:** $7050
Freshman Class: 3661 applied, 2296 accepted, 581 enrolled	
SAT I Verbal/Math: 600/620	**ACT:** 27 **HIGHLY COMPETITIVE**

DePauw University, founded in 1837, is a private institution affiliated with the United Methodist Church offering programs in the fields of liberal arts and music. There are 2 undergraduate schools. In addition to regional accreditation, DePauw has baccalaureate program accreditation with ACS, CAAHEP, NASM, and NCATE. The 3 libraries contain 283,735 volumes, 371,852 microform items, and 15,659 audio/video tapes/CDs, and subscribe to 4017 periodicals. Computerized library services include the card catalog, interlibrary loans, database searching, and Internet access. Special learning facilities include a learning resource center, art gallery, natural history museum, radio station, TV station, an observatory, an arboretum, a digital video studio, and a digital media lab. The 175-acre campus is in a small town 45 miles west of Indianapolis. Including any residence halls, there are 81 buildings.

Student Life: 50% of undergraduates are from out of state, mostly the Midwest. Students are from 41 states and 19 foreign countries. 88% are from public schools. 85% are white. 45% are Protestant; 22% Catholic. The average age of freshmen is 19; all undergraduates, 20. 7% do not continue beyond their first year; 77% remain to graduate.

Housing: 1275 students can be accommodated in college housing, which includes coed dorms, on-campus apartments, off-campus apartments, fraternity houses, and sorority houses. In addition, there are special-interest houses. On-campus housing is guaranteed for all 4 years. 98% of students live on campus. All students may keep cars.

Activities: 76% of men belong to 12 national fraternities; 70% of women belong to 10 national sororities. There are 80 groups on campus, including art, band, cheerleading, chess, choir, chorale, chorus, computers, dance, debate, drama, ethnic, film, forensics, gay, honors, international, jazz band, literary magazine, musical theater, newspaper, opera, orchestra, pep band, political, professional, radio and TV, religious, social, social service, student government, symphony, and yearbook. Popular campus events include Little 5 track meet, Monon Bell football game, and Old Gold Day.

Sports: There are 17 intercollegiate sports for men and 16 for women, and 14 intramural sports for men and 12 for women. Facilities include a recreation center, a 4000-seat stadium, baseball, soccer, and field hockey fields, 3 basketball courts, indoor/outdoor tennis courts and tracks, a pool, a fitness center, volleyball and badminton courts, and a 3200-seat indoor gym.

Disabled Students: 85% of the campus is accessible. Wheelchair ramps, elevators, special parking, specially equipped rest rooms, special class scheduling, lowered drinking fountains, and lowered telephones are available.

Services: Counseling and information services are available, as is tutoring in most subjects. There is a reader service for the blind.

Campus Safety and Security: Measures include 24-hour foot and vehicle patrol, self-defense education, security escort services, and shuttle buses. There are informal discussions, pamphlets/posters/films, emergency telephones, and lighted pathways/sidewalks.

Programs of Study: DePauw confers B.A., B.M.A., B.M.E., and B.Mu. degrees. Bachelor's degrees are awarded in BIOLOGICAL SCIENCE (biochemistry and biology/biological science), COMMUNICATIONS AND THE ARTS (art history and appreciation, classical languages, communications, English, English literature, French, German, Greek, Latin, music, music business management, music performance, music theory and composition, romance languages and literature, Spanish, and studio art), COMPUTER AND PHYSICAL SCIENCE (chemistry, computer science, earth science, geology, mathematics, and physics), EDUCATION (elementary and music), ENGINEERING AND ENVIRONMENTAL DE-

SIGN (environmental science and preengineering), SOCIAL SCIENCE (African American studies, anthropology, classical/ancient civilization, East Asian studies, economics, geography, history, interdisciplinary studies, peace studies, philosophy, physical fitness/movement, political science/government, psychology, religion, Russian and Slavic studies, sociology, and women's studies). English, economics, and communications are the largest.

Required: Students must demonstrate competence in oral communications, quantitative reasoning, and writing. Successful completion of 124 semester hours, including 32 to 40 in the major, is required for graduation. In addition, students must fulfill distribution requirements in natural sciences and math, social and behavioral sciences, literature and the arts, historical and philosophical understanding, foreign language, and self-expression. A comprehensive exam, thesis, or seminar is required for each major.

Special: DePauw offers dual majors in any 2 disciplines, student-designed majors, internships for honors programs and winter-term projects, unlimited study-abroad options through cooperative arrangements with other universities, a Washington semester, pass/fail options, and credit by departmental exam. Also available are 3-2 engineering degrees with Case Western Reserve, Columbia, and Washington Universities and a 3-2 nursing program with Rush University Hospital in Chicago. The Media Fellows, Management Fellows, and Science Research Fellows programs offer majors in any discipline, plus a semester-long internship. There are 13 national honor societies, including Phi Beta Kappa, a freshman honors program, and 12 departmental honors programs.

Faculty/Classroom: 58% of faculty are male; 42%, female. All teach undergraduates and 82% both teach and do research. The average class size in an introductory lecture is 20; in a laboratory, 14; and in a regular course, 18.

Admissions: 63% of the 2003-2004 applicants were accepted. The SAT I scores for the 2003-2004 freshman class were: Verbal--5% below 500, 41% between 500 and 599, 41% between 600 and 700, and 13% above 700; Math--5% below 500, 33% between 500 and 599, 51% between 600 and 700, and 12% above 700. The ACT scores were 4% below 21, 12% between 21 and 23, 29% between 24 and 26, 22% between 27 and 28, and 32% above 28. 78% of the current freshmen were in the top fifth of their class; 96% were in the top two fifths. There were 11 National Merit finalists and 10 semifinalists. 41 freshmen graduated first in their class.

Requirements: The SAT I or ACT is required. In addition, graduation from an accredited secondary school or a GED is required for admission. Course distribution must include 4 in English, 3 to 4 each in math, social studies, and science (2 or more with lab), and 2 to 4 in a foreign language. An essay is required, and an interview is strongly recommended. Applicants for the School of Music must audition. AP credits are accepted. Important factors in the admissions decision are advanced placement or honor courses, recommendations by school officials, and personality/intangible qualities.

Procedure: Freshmen are admitted fall and spring. Entrance exams should be taken as early as possible. There are early decision, early admissions, and deferred admissions plans. Early decision applications should be filed by November 1; regular applications, by February 1 for fall entry and December 1 for spring entry. Notification of early decision is sent December 1; regular decision, April 1. 49 early decision candidates were accepted for the 2003-2004 class. 181 applicants were on the 2003 waiting list; 12 were admitted. Applications are accepted on-line through the school's web site.

Transfer: 13 transfer students enrolled in 2002-2003. Applicants must submit either the SAT I or ACT scores. High school and college transcripts are required, and a minimum GPA on previous college work of 3.0 is preferred. 60 credits of 124 required for the bachelor's degree must be completed at DePauw.

Visiting: There are regularly scheduled orientations for prospective students, consisting of daylong student/parent programs that include campus tours, faculty viewpoints, conversations with students, admissions information, financial aid and career planning sessions, and a meal in a residence hall. There are guides for informal visits and visitors may sit in on classes and stay overnight. To schedule a visit, contact Anna Logan, Admission Program and Visit Coordinator at *alogan@depauw.edu.*

Financial Aid: In 2003-2004, 94% of all full-time freshmen and 96% of continuing full-time students received some form of financial aid. 56% of full-time freshmen and 51% of continuing full-time students received need-based aid. The average freshman award was $23,343 with $9151 ($25,675 maximum) from need-based scholarships or need-based grants, $4414 ($5825 maximum) from need-based self-help aid (loans and jobs), and $9778 from non-need-based awards and non-need-based scholarships. 39% of undergraduates work part time. Average annual earnings from campus work are $630. The average financial indebtedness of the 2003 graduate was $15,635. DePauw is a member of CSS. The CSS/Profile, FAFSA, and the college's own financial statement are required. The deadline for filing freshman financial aid applications for fall entry is February 15.

International Students: There are 47 international students enrolled. The school actively recruits these students. They must score 560 on the written TOEFL or 225 on the electronic version and also take the SAT I or the ACT.

Computers: The mainframe is a DEC Alpha D520 cluster. 130 PCs are available for student use. Locations include the computer center, library, residence halls, fraternities, sororities, and all academic offices. All public PCs, student rooms, classrooms, and faculty/staff offices are wired for access to the campuswide network and the Internet. Seminars are taught regularly, and all students have a computer account. All students may access the system 24 hours a day.

Graduates: From July 1, 2002 to June 30, 2003, 537 bachelor's degrees were awarded. The most popular majors were communications (16%), creative writing (11%), and economics (10%). In an average class, 73% graduate in 4 years or less, 78% graduate in 5 years or less, and 79% graduate in 6 years or less. 50 companies recruited on campus in 2002-2003. Of the 2002 graduating class, 21% were enrolled in graduate school within 6 months of graduation and 79% were employed.

Admissions Contact: Madeleine R. Eagon, Vice President for Admission and Financial Aid. A video is available.
E-mail: *admissions@depauw.edu* Web: *http://www.depauw.edu*

EARLHAM COLLEGE
Richmond, IN 47374

D-3
(765) 983-1600
(800) 327-5426; Fax: (765) 983-1560

Full-time: 467 men, 592 women	**Faculty:** 92; IIB, +$
Part-time: 6 men, 15 women	**Ph.D.s:** 98%
Graduate: 30 men, 43 women	**Student/Faculty:** 13 to 1
Year: semesters	**Tuition:** $24,560
Application Deadline: February 15	**Room & Board:** $5416
Freshman Class: 1410 applied, 1088 accepted, 351 enrolled	
SAT I Verbal/Math: 630/590	**ACT:** 26 **VERY COMPETITIVE+**

Earlham College, established in 1847 by the Society of Friends, is a private liberal arts college that emphasizes Quaker values. It offers undergraduate programs in humanities, fine arts, social sciences, languages, music, and natural sciences. The 2 libraries contain 392,100 volumes, 235,400 microform items, and 52,997 audio/video tapes/CDs, and subscribe to 1660 periodicals. Computerized library services include the card catalog, interlibrary loans, and database searching. Special learning facilities include a learning resource center, art gallery, natural history museum, planetarium, radio station, observatory, herbarium, and greenhouse. The 800-acre campus is in a small town 70 miles east of Indianapolis and 40 miles west of Dayton, Ohio. Including any residence halls, there are 57 buildings.

Student Life: 68% of undergraduates are from out of state, mostly the Midwest. Students are from 47 states and 28 foreign countries. 75% are from public schools. 73% are white. 33% claim no religious affiliation; 23% Protestant; 13% other non-Protestant (Buddhist, Islamic, etc.). The average age of freshmen is 18; all undergraduates, 20. 15% do not continue beyond their first year.

Housing: 968 students can be accommodated in college housing, which includes single-sex and coed dorms. In addition, there are language houses, special-interest houses, Jewish student and black student cultural centers, on-campus houses, a peace studies house, a Latino and Asian American cultural center, an international cultural center, an interfaith house, and a small working farm. On-campus housing is guaranteed for all 4 years. 87% of students live on campus; of those, 84% remain on campus on weekends. Alcohol is not permitted. All students may keep cars.

Activities: There are no fraternities or sororities. There are 64 groups on campus, including art, cheerleading, choir, chorale, chorus, computers, dance, drama, ethnic, film, gay, international, jazz band, literary magazine, musical theater, newspaper, photography, political, radio and TV, religious, social, social service, student government, symphony, and yearbook. Popular campus events include Reggae Festival, Japanese Spring Festival, and Women's Spring Festival.

Sports: There are 8 intercollegiate sports for men and 9 for women, and 5 intramural sports for men and 5 for women. Facilities include fitness center with cardiovascular equipment and weights, group fitness and dance rooms, a field house with 4 indoor courts for tennis, volleyball, and basketball, 2 racquetball courts, an indoor climbing wall, an indoor running track, a 25-meter pool, a performance gym, and a massage therapist. Outdoor facilities include a natural grass football field, 10 all-weather tennis courts, basketball courts, a trail for cross-country running and skiing, and baseball, softball, soccer, lacrosse, and field hockey fields.

Disabled Students: 90% of the campus is accessible. Wheelchair ramps, elevators, special parking, specially equipped rest rooms, lowered drinking fountains, and special housing are available.

Services: Counseling and information services are available, as is tutoring in some subjects, including humanities, sciences, languages, some math, and other subjects on request. There is a reader service for the blind.

Campus Safety and Security: Measures include 24-hour foot and vehicle patrol, self-defense education, security escort services, and shuttle buses. There are informal discussions, pamphlets/posters/films, and lighted pathways/sidewalks.

Programs of Study: Earlham confers the B.A. degree. Master's degrees are also awarded. Bachelor's degrees are awarded in BIOLOGICAL SCIENCE (biochemistry and biology/biological science), BUSINESS (business administration and management), COMMUNICATIONS AND THE ARTS (art, dramatic arts, English, French, German, Japanese, journalism, languages, music, and Spanish), COMPUTER AND PHYSICAL SCIENCE (astronomy, chemistry, computer science, geoscience, mathematics, and physics), EDUCATION (education, museum studies, and teaching English as a second/foreign language (TESOL/TEFOL)), ENGINEERING AND ENVIRONMENTAL DESIGN (environmental science), SOCIAL SCIENCE (African American studies, anthropology, classical/ancient civilization, economics, Hispanic American studies, history, human development, international studies, Japanese studies, Judaic studies, Latin American studies, law, peace studies, philosophy, physical fitness/movement, political science/government, psychobiology, psychology, religion, sociology, and women's studies). Natural sciences, psychology, and English are the strongest academically. Biology, psychology, and history are the largest.

Required: To graduate, all students must complete courses in humanities, English, history, math, foreign language, fine arts, the natural sciences, social sciences, philosophy, multicultural and intercultural, and phys ed. Students must also maintain a minimum GPA of 2.0 and complete a total of 120 semester hours, including 32 semester hours in the major and at least 36 upper-level semester hours. A comprehensive exam and/or thesis is required, depending on the major.

Special: Opportunities are provided for dual majors, cross-registration with Indiana University East, internships, work-study programs, accelerated degree programs, nondegree study, and student-designed majors. Study abroad is available through 27 foreign and domestic programs. Preprofessional and professional options are offered in law and medicine. There is a 3-2 engineering degree with Case Western Reserve University, Columbia University, University of Rochester, and Rensselaer Polytechnic Institute. There is 1 national honor society, Phi Beta Kappa.

Faculty/Classroom: 62% of faculty are male; 38%, female. All teach undergraduates; 75% both teach and do research. No introductory courses are taught by graduate students. The average class size in an introductory lecture is 25; in a laboratory, 15; and in a regular course, 14.

Admissions: 77% of the 2003-2004 applicants were accepted. The SAT I scores for the 2003-2004 freshman class were: Verbal--10% below 500, 27% between 500 and 599, 38% between 600 and 700, and 25% above 700; Math--11% below 500, 44% between 500 and 599, 31% between 600 and 700, and 14% above 700. The ACT scores were 18% below 21, 15% between 21 and 23, 18% between 24 and 26, 17% between 27 and 28, and 32% above 28. 48% of the current freshmen were in the top fifth of their class; 76% were in the top two fifths. There were 6 National Merit finalists. 7 freshmen graduated first in their class in a recent year.

Requirements: The ACT is required and the SAT I is recommended. In addition, in most cases, graduation from an accredited secondary school is required; a GED will be accepted. Home-schooled students are not required to take the GED or have a high school diploma. Students must have completed at least 15 academic credits, including 4 years of English, 3 of math, and 2 each of science, history or social studies, and a foreign language. Students are required to submit an essay and letters of recommendation from a teacher and guidance counselor. An interview is recommended. AP credits are accepted. Important factors in the admissions decision are advanced placement or honor courses, evidence of special talent, and extracurricular activities record.

Procedure: Freshmen are admitted fall, winter, and spring. Entrance exams should be taken during the spring of the junior year or early fall of the senior year. There are early decision, early admissions, and deferred admissions plans. Early decision applications should be filed by December 1; regular applications, by February 15 for fall entry, and November 15 for winter or spring entry. The fall 2003 application fee was $30. Notification of early decision is sent December 15; regular decision, March 15. 42 early decision candidates were accepted for the 2003-2004 class. 25 applicants were on the 2003 waiting list; 10 were admitted. Applications are accepted on-line through Common App or College-NET.

Transfer: 27 transfer students enrolled in 2002-2003. Applicants must take the SAT I or ACT and have a minimum GPA of 2.3 in college course work. An interview is recommended. High school and college transcripts, an essay, and a statement of good standing from the prior institution are required. 60 credits of 120 required for the bachelor's degree must be completed at Earlham.

Visiting: There are regularly scheduled orientations for prospective students, including class visitation, an admissions interview, a tour, and special appointments with faculty. There are guides for informal visits and visitors may sit in on classes and stay overnight. To schedule a visit, contact the Admissions Office.

Financial Aid: In 2003-2004, 65% of all full-time students received some form of financial aid. At least 62% of all full-time students received need-based aid. The average freshman award was $19,986. Need-based scholarships or need-based grants averaged $12,651; need-based self-help aid (loans and jobs) averaged $4357; and non-need-based awards and non-need-based scholarships averaged $5305. 55% of undergraduates work part time. Average annual earnings from campus work are $790. The average financial indebtedness of the 2003 graduate was $15,444. Earlham is a member of CSS. The FAFSA and the college's own financial statement are required. The deadline for filing freshman financial aid applications for fall entry is March 1.

International Students: There were 52 international students enrolled in a recent year. The school actively recruits these students. They must score 550 on the written TOEFL and also take the SAT I or the ACT.

Computers: The mainframes are a DEC Micro Vax 3100-80, 2 DEC Alpha 1000s, 2 Dell Poweredge 2100/200s, and an Apple Power Mac G3. There are 6 public computer labs containing a total of 120 machines. All lab machines give access to the Internet, the World Wide Web, and e-mail services. In addition, students who have their own computers can connect from dorm rooms to the campus LAN. All students may access the system 24 hours per day. There are no time limits and no fees.

Graduates: From July 1, 2002 to June 30, 2003, 263 bachelor's degrees were awarded. The most popular majors were social sciences and history (14%), interdisciplinary studies (12%), and biology (11%). In an average class, 62% graduate in 4 years or less, 9% graduate in 5 years or less, and 1% graduate in 6 years or less. 86 companies recruited on campus in 2002-2003.

Admissions Contact: Jeff Rickey, Dean of Admissions and Financial Aid. A video is available. E-mail: *admission@earlham.edu* Web: *http://www.earlham.edu*

FRANKLIN COLLEGE
C-4
Franklin, IN 46131
(317) 738-8062
(800) 852-0232; Fax: (317) 738-8274

Full-time: 434 men, 549 women	**Faculty:** 59; IIB, -$
Part-time: 30 men, 25 women	**Ph.D.s:** 92%
Graduate: none	**Student/Faculty:** 17 to 1
Year: 4-1-4, summer session	**Tuition:** ($16,925)
Application Deadline: open	**Room & Board:** $5270
Freshman Class: 681 applied, 587 accepted, 277 enrolled	
SAT I Verbal/Math: 524/530	**ACT:** 23 **COMPETITIVE**

Franklin College, formerly Franklin College of Indiana, founded in 1834, is a private liberal arts college affiliated with the American Baptist Churches, U.S.A. In addition to regional accreditation, Franklin College has baccalaureate program accreditation with NCATE. The library contains 124,661 volumes, 295,251 microform items, and 7432 audio/video tapes/CDs, and subscribes to 806 periodicals. Computerized library services include the card catalog, interlibrary loans, and database searching. Special learning facilities include a learning resource center, radio station, and TV station. The 74-acre campus is in a small town 20 miles south of Indianapolis. Including any residence halls, there are 20 buildings.

Student Life: 94% of undergraduates are from Indiana. Others are from 19 states and 7 foreign countries. 90% are white. 58% are Protestant; 28% claim no religious affiliation; 14% Catholic. The average age of freshmen is 18; all undergraduates, 20. 25% do not continue beyond their first year; 60% remain to graduate.

Housing: 814 students can be accommodated in college housing, which includes single-sex and coed dorms, a substance/alcohol-free residence hall living area, and fraternity houses. On-campus housing is available on a first-come, first-served basis and is available on a lottery system for upperclassmen. 74% of students live on campus. All students may keep cars.

Activities: 49% of men belong to 5 national fraternities; 42% of women belong to 4 national sororities. There are 60 groups on campus, including art, cheerleading, choir, chorus, drama, ethnic, film, honors, international, literary magazine, musical theater, newspaper, photography, political, professional, radio and TV, religious, social, social service, student government, and yearbook. Popular campus events include Grizzly Grand Prix, Annual Kite Carnival, and Greek Week.

Sports: There are 8 intercollegiate sports for men and 8 for women, and 7 intramural sports for men and 6 for women. Facilities include athletic and soccer fields, tennis courts, a phys ed center, and a fitness center.

Disabled Students: All of the campus is accessible. Wheelchair ramps, elevators, special parking, specially equipped rest rooms, special class scheduling, lowered drinking fountains, and special housing are available.

Services: Counseling and information services are available, as is tutoring in most subjects. There is a reader service for the blind, and remedial math, reading, and writing.

Campus Safety and Security: Measures include 24-hour foot and vehicle patrol, security escort services, pamphlets/posters/films, and emergency telephones. There are lighted pathways/sidewalks.

Programs of Study: Franklin College confers the B.A. degree. Bachelor's degrees are awarded in BIOLOGICAL SCIENCE (biology/biological science), BUSINESS (accounting, business administration and management, and recreation and leisure services), COMMUNICATIONS AND THE ARTS (dramatic arts, English, French, journalism, and Spanish), COMPUTER AND PHYSICAL SCIENCE (chemistry, computer science, information sciences and systems, and mathematics), EDUCATION (athletic training, elementary, English, health, journalism, mathematics, physical, science, secondary, and social studies), SOCIAL SCIENCE (American studies, Canadian studies, economics, history, philosophy, political science/government, psychology, religion, and sociology). Journalism, education, and business are the strongest academically and have the largest enrollments.

Required: Requirements for graduation include 96 hours outside the major, including general education; a minimum of 24 hours in the major, and 128 total credit hours. Each student must maintain a minimum GPA of 2.0, and must pass the Senior Competency Test, which is administered by the department in which the student completes a major. All students must complete a leadership winter term course.

Special: Cooperative programs in nursing, political science, Canadian studies, forestry, and engineering are available, as are January and summer internships. Study abroad in 16 countries and cross-registration with 7 Indiana universities and colleges and the Indianapolis Museum of Art are permitted. A 3-2 engineering degree with Washington University at St. Louis is possible. There are 10 national honor societies.

Faculty/Classroom: 59% of faculty are male; 41%, female. All teach undergraduates. The average class size in an introductory lecture is 18; in a laboratory, 15; and in a regular course, 18.

Admissions: 86% of the 2003-2004 applicants were accepted. The SAT I scores for the 2003-2004 freshman class were: Verbal--47% below 500, 39% between 500 and 599, 12% between 600 and 700, and 2% above 700; Math--43% below 500, 45% between 500 and 599, 10% between 600 and 700, and 2% above 700. The ACT scores were 18% below 21, 54% between 21 and 23, 24% between 24 and 26, and 4% above 28. 48% of the current freshmen were in the top fifth of their class; 88% were in the top two fifths. 5 freshmen graduated first in their class.

Requirements: The SAT I or ACT is required. In addition, candidates for admission should have completed 4 years of English, 3 to 4 of math, 2 to 3 of science, 2 each of art and music, social studies, and a foreign language, and typing and basic computing skill courses. The GED is accepted, and an essay is required. AP and CLEP credits are accepted. Important factors in the admissions decision are leadership record, recommendations by school officials, and advanced placement or honor courses.

Procedure: Freshmen are admitted to all sessions. Entrance exams should be taken in spring of the junior year or fall of the senior year. Application deadlines are open and the application fee is $30. Applications are accepted on-line through CollegeNET. Notification is sent on a rolling basis.

Transfer: 59 transfer students enrolled in 2003-2004. Transfer students must have at least a 2.0 cumulative GPA and submit official transcripts from previously attended colleges. 30 of 128 credits required for the bachelor's degree must be completed at Franklin College.

Visiting: There are regularly scheduled orientations for prospective students, including academic presentations, admissions and financial presentations, a student life presentation, campus tours, lunch, and opportunities to talk to professors and sit in on a class. There are guides for informal visits and visitors may stay overnight. To schedule a visit, contact the Admissions Office at admissions@franklincollege.edu.

Financial Aid: The average freshman award was $12,753. Need-based scholarships or need-based grants averaged $2000 ($9100 maximum); and need-based self-help aid (loans and jobs) averaged $4100 ($5500 maximum). 28% of undergraduates work part time. Average annual earnings from campus work are $1500. The average financial indebtedness of the 2003 graduate was $18,054. The FAFSA and the college's own financial statement are required. The deadline for filing freshman financial aid applications for fall entry is March 1.

International Students: There are 7 international students enrolled. The school actively recruits these students. They must score 550 on the written TOEFL. Completion of level 109 in an English language service (ELS) center is necessary.

Computers: There are 105 PCs in labs in the computer center, library, teaching and learning centers, and other campus buildings, and 80 laptops are available for class use. All students may access the system 8 A.M. to midnight (24 hours in one lab). There are no time limits and no fees.

Graduates: From July 1, 2002 to June 30, 2003, 185 bachelor's degrees were awarded. The most popular majors were journalism (16%), elementary education (16%), and sociology (12%). 36 companies recruited on campus in 2002-2003. Of the 2002 graduating class, 10% were enrolled in graduate school within 6 months of graduation and 80% were employed.

Admissions Contact: Alan Hill, VP for Enrollment and Student Affairs. E-mail: admissions@franklincollege.edu
Web: http://www.franklincollege.edu/admissions_index.htm

GOSHEN COLLEGE
C-1
Goshen, IN 46526
(574) 535-7535
(800) 348-7422; Fax: (574) 535-7609

Full-time: 319 men, 468 women	**Faculty:** 72
Part-time: 38 men, 95 women	**Ph.D.s:** 59%
Graduate: none	**Student/Faculty:** 11 to 1
Year: semesters, summer session	**Tuition:** $16,650
Application Deadline: February 15	**Room & Board:** $5800
Freshman Class: 584 applied, 471 accepted, 181 enrolled	
SAT I Verbal/Math: 590/580	**ACT:** 25 **VERY COMPETITIVE**

Goshen College, founded in 1894, is a private liberal arts institution affiliated with the Mennonite Church. In addition to regional accreditation, Goshen has baccalaureate program accreditation with CSWE, NCATE, and NLN. The library contains 120,000 volumes, 140,000 microform items, and 1500 audio/video tapes/CDs, and subscribes to 900 periodicals. Computerized library services include the card catalog, interlibrary loans, and database searching. Special learning facilities include a learning resource center, art gallery, and radio station. The 135-acre campus is in a small town 120 miles east of Chicago. Including any residence halls, there are 25 buildings.

Student Life: 52% of undergraduates are from Indiana. Students are from 29 states, 30 foreign countries, and Canada. 83% are white. Most are Protestant. The average age of freshmen is 18; all undergraduates, 21. 19% do not continue beyond their first year; 66% remain to graduate.

Housing: 696 students can be accommodated in college housing, which includes single-sex and coed dorms, off-campus apartments, and married-student housing. In addition, there are small-group special-interest houses. On-campus housing is guaranteed for all 4 years. 69% of students live on campus; of those, 85% remain on campus on weekends. Alcohol is not permitted. All students may keep cars.

Activities: There are no fraternities or sororities. There are 26 groups on campus, including chess, choir, chorale, chorus, drama, ethnic, honors, international, jazz band, literary magazine, musical theater, newspaper, opera, orchestra, photography, professional, radio and TV, religious, social, social service, student government, and yearbook. Popular campus events include February Fest, Fall Fest, and Celebrate Service Day.

Sports: There are 7 intercollegiate sports for men and 7 for women, and 8 intramural sports for men and 8 for women. Facilities include a fitness center with an indoor track and swimming pool, 3 basketball courts, a soccer field, tennis courts, a sand volleyball court, a 400-meter, all-weather track, and baseball and softball diamonds.

Disabled Students: All of the campus is accessible. Wheelchair ramps, elevators, special parking, specially equipped rest rooms, special class scheduling, lowered drinking fountains, and lowered telephones are available.

Services: Counseling and information services are available, as is tutoring in every subject. There is a reader service for the blind, and remedial math, reading, and writing.

Campus Safety and Security: Measures include 24-hour foot and vehicle patrol, self-defense education, security escort services, and informal discussions. There are pamphlets/posters/films and lighted pathways/sidewalks.

Programs of Study: Goshen confers B.A., B.S., and B.S.N. degrees. Bachelor's degrees are awarded in BIOLOGICAL SCIENCE (biology/biological science and molecular biology), BUSINESS (accounting, business administration and management, institutional management, and management information systems), COMMUNICATIONS AND THE ARTS (American Sign Language, communications, dramatic arts, English, music, and Spanish), COMPUTER AND PHYSICAL SCIENCE (chemistry, computer programming, information sciences and systems, mathematics, and physics), EDUCATION (art, business, elementary, foreign languages, middle school, music, physical, science, and secondary), ENGINEERING AND ENVIRONMENTAL DESIGN (environmental science and preengineering), HEALTH PROFESSIONS (nursing, predentistry, premedicine, prepharmacy, and preveterinary science), SOCIAL SCIENCE (biblical studies, history, peace studies, psychology, religion, social work, and sociology). Nursing, elementary education, and biology are the largest.

Required: All students must complete the general education program, including courses in literature and communication, fine arts, Bible, religion, philosophy, natural science, math, social science, and history, and 12 hours of international education in the Study Service Term and 1 hour of phys ed. A total of 120 credit hours with a minimum GPA of 2.0 is required to graduate.

Special: A semester abroad internship in the required Study Service Term is possible in China, Indonesia, Germany, Ivory Coast, Cuba, and the Dominican Republic. Cross-registration is offered with member colleges of the Northern Indiana Consortium for Education. A Washington semester, dual majors, student-designed majors, and a 3-2 engineering degree with the University of Illinois, Washington University in St. Louis, and Case Western Reserve University are available. Credit for life experience, pass/fail options, and nondegree study are possible. There is 1 national honor society, a freshman honors program, and 1 departmental honors program.

Faculty/Classroom: 56% of faculty are male; 44%, female. All both teach and do research. The average class size in an introductory lecture is 28; in a laboratory, 14; and in a regular course, 22.

Admissions: 81% of the 2003-2004 applicants were accepted. The SAT I scores for the 2003-2004 freshman class were: Verbal--22% below 500, 29% between 500 and 599, 31% between 600 and 700, and 18% above 700; Math--17% below 500, 39% between 500 and 599, 34% between 600 and 700, and 10% above 700. The ACT scores were 20% below 21, 16% between 21 and 23, 26% between 24 and 26, 11% between 27 and 28, and 27% above 28. 53% of the current freshmen were in the top fifth of their class; 73% were in the top two fifths. There were 2 National Merit finalists. 5 freshmen graduated first in their class.

Requirements: The SAT I or ACT is required. In addition, applicants should be graduates of an accredited secondary school or have a GED equivalent, with 4 years of high school English, 2 to 4 years of math, and 2 years each of foreign language, science, history, and social studies. An interview is recommended. AP and CLEP credits are accepted. Important factors in the admissions decision are advanced placement or honor courses, recommendations by school officials, and recommendations by alumni.

Procedure: Freshmen are admitted to all sessions. Entrance exams should be taken by fall of the senior year. There is a deferred admissions plan. Applications should be filed by February 15 for fall entry, December 15 for winter entry, and April 15 for spring entry. The fall 2003 application fee was $25. Notification is sent on a rolling basis. Applications are accepted on-line through the school's web site.

Transfer: 65 transfer students enrolled in 2002-2003. A GPA of 2.0 or higher is required on previous college work. 30 of 120 credits required for the bachelor's degree must be completed at Goshen.

Visiting: There are regularly scheduled orientations for prospective students, consisting of a campus tour, a parents session, talks with professors, a financial aid session, visitation, an overnight stay in the dorms, a student panel, and a campus interview. There are guides for informal visits and visitors may sit in on classes and stay overnight. To schedule a visit, contact the Admissions Office.

Financial Aid: In 2003-2004, 99% of all full-time students received some form of financial aid. 75% of full-time freshmen and 71% of continuing full-time students received need-based aid. The average freshman award was $16,036. Need-based scholarships or need-based grants averaged $11,781 ($23,700 maximum); need-based self-help aid (loans and jobs) averaged $4527 ($16,425 maximum); non-need-based athletic scholarships averaged $2400 ($3000 maximum); and other non-need-based awards and non-need-based scholarships averaged $10,167 ($21,000 maximum). 72% of undergraduates work part time. Average annual earnings from campus work are $1470. The average financial indebtedness of the 2003 graduate was $15,689. Goshen is a member of CSS. The FAFSA and the college's own financial statement are required. The priority date for freshman financial aid applications for fall entry is February 15.

International Students: There are 77 international students enrolled. The school actively recruits these students. They must score 550 on the written TOEFL or 213 on the electronic version and also take the SAT I or the ACT.

Computers: The mainframe is a DEC MicroVAX 3100. There are 2 computer labs available to all students. Each computer lab has 60 computers. All dorm rooms are wired for Ethernet access to the Internet. All students may access the system. There are no time limits and no fees.

Graduates: From July 1, 2002 to June 30, 2003, 229 bachelor's degrees were awarded. The most popular majors were organizational management (10%), elementary education (8%), and nursing (5%). In an average class, 46% graduate in 4 years or less, 65% graduate in 5 years or less, and 66% graduate in 6 years or less. 28 companies recruited on campus in 2002-2003. Of the 2002 graduating class, 30% were enrolled in graduate school within 6 months of graduation and 70% were employed.

Admissions Contact: Karen Lowe Raftus, Director of Admission. A video is available. E-mail: *admission@goshen.edu* Web: *www.goshen.edu*

GRACE COLLEGE C-2
Winona Lake, IN 46590
(574) 372-5100, ext. 6114
(800) 54-GRACE; Fax: (574) 372-5114

Full-time: 312 men, 497 women	**Faculty:** 39; IIA, --$
Part-time: 48 men, 50 women	**Ph.D.s:** 63%
Graduate: 10 men, 16 women	**Student/Faculty:** 21 to 1
Year: semesters, summer session	**Tuition:** $14,070
Application Deadline: August 1	**Room & Board:** $5755
Freshman Class: 616 applied, 446 accepted, 138 enrolled	
SAT I Verbal/Math: 532/579	**ACT:** 23 **VERY COMPETITIVE**

Grace College, founded in 1948, is a Christian liberal arts institution affiliated with the Fellowship of Grace Brethren Churches. In addition to regional accreditation, Grace has baccalaureate program accreditation with CSWE, NASM, and NCATE. The library contains 142,000 volumes, 26,000 microform items, and 2400 audio/video tapes/CDs, and subscribes to 360 periodicals. Computerized library services include the card catalog, interlibrary loans, and database searching. Special learning facilities include an art gallery. The 150-acre campus is in an urban area 40 miles west of Fort Wayne. Including any residence halls, there are 15 buildings.

Student Life: 55% of undergraduates are from Indiana. Others are from 35 states, 8 foreign countries, and Canada. 74% are from public schools. 91% are white. Most are Protestant. The average age of freshmen is 18; all undergraduates, 23. 23% do not continue beyond their first year; 77% remain to graduate.

Housing: 684 students can be accommodated in college housing, which includes single-sex dorms and on-campus apartments. On-campus housing is available on a first-come, first-served basis and is available on a lottery system for upperclassmen. Priority is given to out-of-town students. 74% of students live on campus; of those, 80% remain on campus on weekends. Alcohol is not permitted. All students may keep cars.

Activities: There are no fraternities or sororities. There are 14 groups on campus, including band, cheerleading, choir, drama, honors, international, musical theater, newspaper, orchestra, pep band, religious, social, student government, and yearbook. Popular campus events include Fall Fest, Heart of the Holidays, and VIP Days.

Sports: There are 7 intercollegiate sports for men and 7 for women, and 4 intramural sports for men and 2 for women. Facilities include a gym, soccer fields, tennis courts, softball and baseball diamonds, and a recreation center with basketball courts, indoor track, and weight and exercise rooms.

Disabled Students: 80% of the campus is accessible. Wheelchair ramps, elevators, special parking, and specially equipped rest rooms are available.

Services: Counseling and information services are available, as is tutoring in most subjects. There is remedial math, reading, and writing.

Campus Safety and Security: Measures include 24-hour foot and vehicle patrol, security escort services, and lighted pathways/sidewalks.

Programs of Study: Grace confers B.A., B.S., B.M., and B.S.W. degrees. Associate and master's degrees are also awarded. Bachelor's degrees are awarded in BIOLOGICAL SCIENCE (biology/biological science), BUSINESS (accounting, business administration and management, and management information systems), COMMUNICATIONS AND THE ARTS (art, communications, English, French, German, graphic design, journalism, music, Russian, and Spanish), COMPUTER AND PHYSICAL SCIENCE (mathematics and science), EDUCATION (art, business, elementary, English, foreign languages, journalism, mathematics, music, physical, science, and special), HEALTH PROFESSIONS (predentistry and premedicine), SOCIAL SCIENCE (biblical studies, counseling/psychology, criminal justice, prelaw, psychology, religion, social work, sociology, and youth ministry). Biology, psychology, and business are the strongest academically. Psychology, elementary education, and biblical studies are the largest.

Required: To graduate, students must complete 124 hours, including 36 to 54 in the major, and have a minimum GPA of 2.0. The required core curriculum of 56 hours consists of languages/literature, humanities, religion/philosophy, education, social sciences, and natural sciences.

Special: Students may study abroad in 5 countries. A B.A.-B.S. degree is available in all majors except languages, English, and biblical studies. Dual majors are offered in psychology, sociology, communication, business, accounting, youth ministries, and management information technology. There is 1 national honor society and a freshman honors program.

Faculty/Classroom: 75% of faculty are male; 25%, female. 99% teach undergraduates and 10% both teach and do research. No introductory courses are taught by graduate students. The average class size in an introductory lecture is 48; in a laboratory, 14; and in a regular course, 17.

Admissions: 72% of the 2003-2004 applicants were accepted. The SAT I scores for the 2003-2004 freshman class were: Verbal--32% below 500, 40% between 500 and 599, 26% between 600 and 700, and 2% above 700; Math--32% below 500, 49% between 500 and 599, 18% be-

tween 600 and 700, and 1% above 700. The ACT scores were 29% below 21, 22% between 21 and 23, 23% between 24 and 26, 13% between 27 and 28, and 13% above 28. 41% of the current freshmen were in the top fifth of their class; 69% were in the top two fifths. 10 freshmen graduated first in their class.

Requirements: The SAT I or ACT is recommended with a minimum composite score of 20 on the ACT or 950 on the SAT I. Applicants must have completed 15 Carnegie units, including 4 of English, 3 each of math and science, 2 each of a foreign language and social studies, and 1 of history. A GED is accepted. Grace requires applicants to be in the upper 50% of their class. A GPA of 2.3 is required. AP and CLEP credits are accepted. Important factors in the admissions decision are advanced placement or honor courses, leadership record, and personality/intangible qualities.

Procedure: Freshmen are admitted to all sessions. Entrance exams should be taken in October, December, or February. There is a deferred admissions plan. Applications should be filed by August 1 for fall entry and December 1 for spring entry, along with a $25 fee. There is a rolling admissions plan and notification is sent on a rolling basis. Applications are accepted on-line through the Grace College web site, www.grace.edu.

Transfer: 61 transfer students enrolled in 2003-2004. Transfer applicants should have a minimum 2.0 GPA in addition to fulfilling freshman entrance requirements. 60 of 124 credits required for the bachelor's degree must be completed at Grace.

Visiting: There are regularly scheduled orientations for prospective students, including tours, class visits, and meetings with professors. There are guides for informal visits and visitors may sit in on classes and stay overnight. To schedule a visit, contact the Visitors Center at (574) 372-5100, ext. 6003.

Financial Aid: In 2003-2004, 63% of all full-time freshmen and 84% of continuing full-time students received some form of financial aid. 61% of full-time freshmen and 83% of continuing full-time students received need-based aid. The average freshman award was $13,059. Need-based scholarships or need-based grants averaged $8513 ($13,000 maximum); need-based self-help aid (loans and jobs) averaged $5449 ($9500 maximum); non-need-based athletic scholarships averaged $3165 ($15,500 maximum); and other non-need-based awards and non-need-based scholarships averaged $3670 ($14,070 maximum). 47% of undergraduates work part time. Average annual earnings from campus work are $1300. The average financial indebtedness of the 2003 graduate was $19,709. The FAFSA is required. The deadline for filing freshman financial aid applications for fall entry is March 1.

International Students: There are 15 international students enrolled. They must score 500 on the written TOEFL and also take the SAT I or the ACT, scoring 950 on the SAT I.

Computers: The mainframe is an IBM AS/400. There are 2 classroom labs along with satellite labs located in major dorms. 60 PCs are available to students and all provide access to the Internet. Network and Internet access are also available in campus dorm rooms. All students may access the system when the classrooms and labs are open. There are no time limits and no fees. It is strongly recommended that all students have a personal computer.

Graduates: From July 1, 2002 to June 30, 2003, 216 bachelor's degrees were awarded. The most popular majors were elementary education (16%), psychology (10%), and business administration (7%). In an average class, 48% graduate in 4 years or less, 10% graduate in 5 years or less, and 1% graduate in 6 years or less.

Admissions Contact: Anecia R. Miller, Director of Admissions.
E-mail: millerar@grace.edu Web: http://www.grace.edu

HANOVER COLLEGE

D-5

Hanover, IN 47243

(812) 866-7022
(800) 213-2178; Fax: (812) 866-7098

Full-time: 456 men, 532 women	**Faculty:** 85; IIB, +$
Part-time: 5 men, 4 women	**Ph.D.s:** 99%
Graduate: none	**Student/Faculty:** 12 to 1
Year: 4-1-4	**Tuition:** $19,300
Application Deadline: March 1	**Room & Board:** $5900

Freshman Class: 1364 applied, 1073 accepted, 292 enrolled

SAT I Verbal/Math: 570/580   **ACT:** 23   **VERY COMPETITIVE**

Hanover College, founded in 1827 and the oldest private college in Indiana, is a liberal arts school affiliated with the United Presbyterian Church. In addition to regional accreditation, Hanover has baccalaureate program accreditation with NCATE. The library contains 222,782 volumes, 44,951 microform items, and 10,015 audio/video tapes/CDs, and subscribes to 1667 periodicals. Computerized library services include the card catalog, interlibrary loans, database searching, and Internet access. Special learning facilities include a learning resource center, art gallery, planetarium, TV station, and a geology museum. The 650-acre campus is in a rural area 45 miles north of Louisville, Kentucky. Including any residence halls, there are 35 buildings.

Student Life: 68% of undergraduates are from Indiana. Students are from 33 states and 15 foreign countries. 86% are from public schools.

89% are white. 43% are Protestant; 40% claim no religious affiliation; 16% Catholic. The average age of freshmen is 18; all undergraduates, 19. 25% do not continue beyond their first year; 68% remain to graduate.

Housing: 1050 students can be accommodated in college housing, which includes single-sex and coed dorms, on-campus apartments, fraternity houses, and sorority houses. In addition, there are honors houses, special-interest houses, and a multicultural center. On-campus housing is guaranteed for all 4 years. 95% of students live on campus. Alcohol is not permitted, with the exception of approved functions. Upperclassmen may keep cars.

Activities: 42% of men belong to 4 national fraternities; 59% of women belong to 4 national sororities. There are 44 groups on campus, including band, cheerleading, choir, chorus, computers, dance, debate, drama, ethnic, film, gay, honors, international, jazz band, literary magazine, musical theater, newspaper, orchestra, pep band, photography, political, professional, radio and TV, religious, social, social service, student government, and yearbook. Popular campus events include a community artist series, a foreign film series, and Spring Fling.

Sports: There are 8 intercollegiate sports for men and 8 for women, and 10 intramural sports for men and 10 for women. Facilities include a health and recreation center consisting of a 2000-seat performance gym, a multisports forum, a suspended running track, racquetball and squash courts, a weight room, a training room, and a physiology lab. There also is an outdoor athletic complex consisting of a 5000-seat stadium and performance and practice fields.

Disabled Students: 75% of the campus is accessible. Wheelchair ramps, elevators, special parking, lowered drinking fountains, and lowered telephones are available.

Services: Counseling and information services are available, as is tutoring in most subjects. There is remedial writing.

Campus Safety and Security: Measures include 24-hour foot and vehicle patrol, self-defense education, security escort services, and shuttle buses. There are informal discussions, pamphlets/posters/films, emergency telephones, and lighted pathways/sidewalks.

Programs of Study: Hanover confers the B.A. degree. Bachelor's degrees are awarded in BIOLOGICAL SCIENCE (biology/biological science), BUSINESS (business administration and management), COMMUNICATIONS AND THE ARTS (art, art history and appreciation, classics, communications, dramatic arts, English, French, German, music, and Spanish), COMPUTER AND PHYSICAL SCIENCE (chemistry, computer science, geology, mathematics, and physics), EDUCATION (physical), SOCIAL SCIENCE (anthropology, economics, history, international studies, Latin American studies, medieval studies, philosophy, political science/government, psychology, sociology, and theological studies). Arts and sciences and interdisciplinary studies are the strongest academically. Business administration is the largest.

Required: The required core curriculum includes foreign language, philosophy, phys ed, fine arts, English, 3 physical or life sciences, 2 social sciences, speech, and history. Students must complete 37 units of credit, including 8 to 12 in the major, maintain a GPA of 2.0, pass a comprehensive exam, and participate in a culminating experience in the major.

Special: Internships, study abroad, a Washington semester, and student-designed majors in international studies and Latin American studies are offered. In addition, there is cross-registration with the Spring Term Consortium, the University of Indianapolis, and Alma, Elmira, Northland, Transylvania, Wartburg, and William Woods Colleges. There are 8 national honor societies.

Faculty/Classroom: 64% of faculty are male; 36%, female. All teach undergraduates. The average class size in an introductory lecture is 21; in a laboratory, 16; and in a regular course, 13.

Admissions: 79% of the 2003-2004 applicants were accepted. The SAT I scores for the 2003-2004 freshman class were: Verbal--21% below 500, 40% between 500 and 599, 34% between 600 and 700, and 5% above 700; Math--14% below 500, 44% between 500 and 599, 35% between 600 and 700, and 7% above 700. The ACT scores were 13% below 21, 23% between 21 and 23, 32% between 24 and 26, 18% between 27 and 28, and 14% above 28. 60% of the current freshmen were in the top fifth of their class; 87% were in the top two fifths. 14 freshmen graduated first in their class.

Requirements: The SAT I or ACT is required. Admission is competitive, based on the applicant pool. The college requires 16 academic credits, including 4 years of English and 2 each of a foreign language, math, science, and either history or social studies. The GED is accepted. The college also requires a foreign language achievement test as well as an essay; an interview is recommended. AP credits are accepted. Important factors in the admissions decision are recommendations by school officials, advanced placement or honor courses, and extracurricular activities record.

Procedure: Freshmen are admitted fall and winter. Entrance exams should be taken late in the spring of the junior year. There are early admissions and deferred admissions plans. There is a rolling admissions plan. Applications should be filed by March 1 for fall entry, along with a $30 fee. Notification is sent on a rolling basis beginning January 20.

92 applicants were on the 2003 waiting list; 55 were admitted. Applications are accepted on computer disk and on-line through Common Application and *www.applyweb.com*.

Transfer: 29 transfer students enrolled in 2002-2003. Transfer students must submit transcripts from all colleges attended and must have performed successfully. SAT I or ACT scores and high school record may also be taken into consideration. 17 credits of 37 required for the bachelor's degree must be completed at Hanover.

Visiting: There are regularly scheduled orientations for prospective students. There are guides for informal visits and visitors may sit in on classes and stay overnight. To schedule a visit, contact the Office of Admissions at *admissions@hanover.edu*.

Financial Aid: In 2003-2004, 79% of all full-time freshmen and 86% of continuing full-time students received some form of financial aid. 79% of full-time freshmen and 86% of continuing full-time students received need-based aid. The average freshman award was $15,245. Need-based scholarships or need-based grants averaged $13,764; need-based self-help aid (loans and jobs) averaged $2525; and non-need-based awards and non-need-based scholarships averaged $15,332. 28% of undergraduates work part time. Average annual earnings from campus work are $1300. The average financial indebtedness of the 2003 graduate was $11,583. The FAFSA is required. The deadline for filing freshman financial aid applications for fall entry is March 1.

International Students: There are 37 international students enrolled. The school actively recruits these students. They must score 550 on the written TOEFL or 213 on the electronic version and also take the SAT I or the ACT.

Computers: The mainframe is a DEC Alpha server 2100. Mac and PC networks are available. Students may access the system in computer labs and through ports located in every dorm room. All students may access the system in computer labs, 8 A.M. to 11 P.M. Monday through Thursday and Sunday, and 8 A.M. to 5 P.M. Friday and Saturday. The library has a 24-hour lab. There are no time limits and no fees.

Graduates: From July 1, 2002 to June 30, 2003, 256 bachelor's degrees were awarded. The most popular majors were business administration (12%), elementary education (11%), and history (8%). In an average class, 65% graduate in 4 years or less, 67% graduate in 5 years or less, and 67% graduate in 6 years or less. 57 companies recruited on campus in 2002-2003. Of the 2002 graduating class, 27% were enrolled in graduate school within 6 months of graduation and 72% were employed.

Admissions Contact: Kenneth P. Moyer, Dean of Admissions. A video is available. E-mail: *admission@hanover.edu* Web: *www.hanover.edu*

HUNTINGTON COLLEGE
Huntington, IN 46750

D-2

(260) 358-4000
(800) 642-6493; Fax: (260) 358-3699

Full-time: 373 men, 475 women	**Faculty:** 51; IIB, -$
Part-time: 26 men, 49 women	**Ph.D.s:** 85%
Graduate: 36 men, 17 women	**Student/Faculty:** 17 to 1
Year: 4-1-4, summer session	**Tuition:** $17,700
Application Deadline: August 15	**Room & Board:** $5890
Freshman Class: 702 applied, 641 accepted, 269 enrolled	
SAT I or ACT: required	**COMPETITIVE**

Huntington College, founded in 1897, is a private Christian liberal arts college affiliated with the Church of the United Brethren in Christ. In addition to regional accreditation, Huntington has baccalaureate program accreditation with NASM and NCATE. Computerized library services include the card catalog, interlibrary loans, database searching, and Internet access. Special learning facilities include a learning resource center, art gallery, radio station, TV station, a writing center, and an arboretum. The 170-acre campus is in a small town 20 miles southwest of Fort Wayne. Including any residence halls, there are 25 buildings.

Student Life: 60% of undergraduates are from Indiana. Students are from 27 states, 15 foreign countries, and Canada. 95% are white. 88% are Protestant; 7% of another Christian denomination. The average age of freshmen is 18; all undergraduates, 20. 6% do not continue beyond their first year; 60% remain to graduate.

Housing: 683 students can be accommodated in college housing, which includes single-sex dorms, on-campus apartments, and married-student housing. On-campus housing is guaranteed for all 4 years. 79% of students live on campus; of those, 60% remain on campus on weekends. Alcohol is not permitted. All students may keep cars.

Activities: There are no fraternities or sororities. There are 30 groups on campus, including art, band, cheerleading, choir, chorale, chorus, computers, drama, ethnic, film, honors, international, jazz band, literary magazine, musical theater, newspaper, opera, orchestra, pep band, photography, professional, radio and TV, religious, social, social service, student government, symphony, and yearbook. Popular campus events include Chapel series, Forester Lecture Series, and Service Emphasis Week.

Sports: There are 7 intercollegiate sports for men and 7 for women, and 5 intramural sports for men and 3 for women. Facilities include a field house with an indoor running track, 3 basketball courts, indoor and outdoor tennis courts, a swimming pool, softball and baseball diamonds, an outdoor track, soccer and intramural fields, rollerblading, and a gym.

Disabled Students: 90% of the campus is accessible. Wheelchair ramps, elevators, special parking, specially equipped rest rooms, lowered drinking fountains, and special housing are available.

Services: Counseling and information services are available, as is tutoring in most subjects, including English and math. There is a reader service for the blind and remedial math, reading, and writing.

Campus Safety and Security: Measures include 24-hour foot and vehicle patrol, self-defense education, and lighted pathways/sidewalks.

Programs of Study: Huntington confers B.A., B.S., B.Mus., and B.S.Sc. degrees. Associate and master's degrees are also awarded. Bachelor's degrees are awarded in BIOLOGICAL SCIENCE (biology/biological science), BUSINESS (business administration and management and organizational behavior), COMMUNICATIONS AND THE ARTS (art, communications, English, and music performance), COMPUTER AND PHYSICAL SCIENCE (chemistry, information sciences and systems, and mathematics), EDUCATION (art, education, elementary, English, mathematics, music, physical, science, and social studies), HEALTH PROFESSIONS (medical laboratory technology and premedicine), SOCIAL SCIENCE (biblical studies, history, ministries, parks and recreation management, philosophy, prelaw, psychology, sociology, and youth ministry). Education, youth ministries, and business are the strongest academically. Business and elementary education are the largest.

Required: Students must complete a minimum of 128 credit hours including 24 in the major, and maintain a GPA of 2.0 overall and in the major. Students must pass an English competency exam, complete a program in general education, and take 36 hours in upper-division courses numbered 300 or above, 3 hours of computers, 2 hours of phys ed, and 3 January term courses in at least 2 departments. Courses in Bible are required.

Special: Various companies in the area offer internships in business and youth ministries, and a work-study program is available. Students may study abroad in England, Costa Rica, Jamaica, Israel, Spain, and Africa. A Washington semester, a Hollywood semester, dual majors, correspondence courses with other schools, an accelerated degree program in organizational management, and pass/fail options are available. There is a chapter of Phi Beta Kappa and a freshman honors program.

Faculty/Classroom: 64% of faculty are male; 36%, female. All teach undergraduates, 30% do research, and 30% do both. No introductory courses are taught by graduate students. The average class size in an introductory lecture is 35; in a laboratory, 15; and in a regular course, 25.

Admissions: 91% of the 2003-2004 applicants were accepted. The SAT I scores for the 2003-2004 freshman class were: Verbal--22% below 500, 45% between 500 and 599, 25% between 600 and 700, and 8% above 700; Math--21% below 500, 46% between 500 and 599, 27% between 600 and 700, and 6% above 700. The ACT scores were 8% below 18, 44% between 18 and 23, 39% between 24 and 29, and 9% between 30 and 36. 47% of the current freshmen were in the top fifth of their class; 78% were in the top two fifths. There were 3 National Merit finalists and 9 semifinalists. 23 freshmen graduated first in their class.

Requirements: The SAT I or ACT is required. In addition, secondary school courses should include 4 years of English, 3 of college-preparatory math, and 3 of social studies, including 1 each of American and world history. Huntington requires applicants to be in the upper 50% of their class. A GPA of 2.3 is required. AP and CLEP credits are accepted. Important factors in the admissions decision are recommendations by school officials, recommendations by alumni, and personality/intangible qualities.

Procedure: Freshmen are admitted to all sessions. Entrance exams should be taken before or during the fall semester of the senior year. There are early admissions and deferred admissions plans. There is a rolling admissions plan. Applications should be filed by August 15 for fall entry, along with a $20 fee. Notification is sent on a rolling basis.

Transfer: 31 transfer students enrolled in 2002-2003. Transfer applicants should be in good standing at the college previously attended and have maintained a GPA of 2.0. Courses with a grade of C or better transfer. All transcripts and an essay are required. 30 of 128 credits required for the bachelor's degree must be completed at Huntington.

Visiting: There are regularly scheduled orientations for prospective students, available on 3 days notice. There are guides for informal visits and visitors may sit in on classes and stay overnight. To schedule a visit, contact Carlene Peters at *cpeters@huntington.edu*.

Financial Aid: The FAFSA and the college's own financial statement are required.

International Students: There are 25 international students enrolled. They must score 525 on the written TOEFL.

Computers: There are 150 PCs and Macs in classroom buildings. Internet access is available, with an on-campus network. All students may access the system The mainframe computer system may be used from 9 A.M. to 11 P.M. Monday through Thursday, 9 A.M. to 5 P.M. Friday, and 9 A.M. to 2 P.M. Saturday. There are no time limits and no fees. It is strongly recommended that all students have a personal computer.

Graduates: From July 1, 2002 to June 30, 2003, 199 bachelor's degrees were awarded. The most popular majors were education (29%), business/marketing (19%), and philosophy, religion, theology (16%). In an average class, 2% graduate in 3 years or less, and 55% graduate in 4 years or less. 30 companies recruited on campus in 2002-2003. Of the 2002 graduating class, 10% were enrolled in graduate school within 6 months of graduation.

Admissions Contact: Jeff Berggren, Dean of Enrollment. A video is available. E-mail: *admissions@huntington.edu* Web: *www.huntington.edu*

INDIANA INSTITUTE OF TECHNOLOGY D-2
Fort Wayne, IN 46803-1297 (219) 422-5561, ext. 2205
(800) 937-2448; Fax: (219) 422-7696

Full-time: 724 men, 813 women	**Faculty:** 61
Part-time: 523 men, 808 women	**Ph.D.s:** 50%
Graduate: 208 men, 175 women	**Student/Faculty:** 25 to 1
Year: semesters, summer session	**Tuition:** $15,590
Application Deadline: open	**Room & Board:** $6030
Freshman Class: 3338 applied, 1831 accepted, 245 enrolled	
SAT I Verbal/Math: 480/510	**ACT:** 21 **COMPETITIVE**

Indiana Institute of Technology, established in 1930, is a private institution offering degrees primarily in business, engineering, and computer science. There are 2 undergraduate schools. In addition to regional accreditation, Indiana Tech has baccalaureate program accreditation with ABET. The library contains 33,000 volumes, 1000 microform items, and 150 audio/video tapes/CDs, and subscribes to 160 periodicals. Computerized library services include the card catalog, interlibrary loans, and database searching. Special learning facilities include a learning resource center. The 37-acre campus is in an urban area 150 miles east of Chicago. Including any residence halls, there are 11 buildings.

Student Life: 87% of undergraduates are from Indiana. Students are from 30 states and 8 foreign countries. 95% are from public schools. 69% are white; 21% African American. The average age of freshmen is 18; all undergraduates, 35. 47% do not continue beyond their first year; 27% remain to graduate.

Housing: 272 students can be accommodated in college housing, which includes coed dorms and fraternity houses. On-campus housing is guaranteed for the freshman year only and is available on a first-come, first-served basis. Priority is given to out-of-town students. 60% of students commute. Alcohol is not permitted. All students may keep cars.

Activities: 15% of men belong to 3 national fraternities; 5% of women belong to 2 local sororities. There are 20 groups on campus, including cheerleading, chess, choir, computers, dance, ethnic, honors, international, newspaper, pep band, professional, religious, social, social service, and student government. Popular campus events include Cosmic Bowling.

Sports: There are 3 intercollegiate sports for men and 3 for women, and 6 intramural sports for men and 6 for women. Facilities include basketball, badminton, and volleyball courts, a weight room, and an indoor field house for soccer, softball, and baseball.

Disabled Students: 90% of the campus is accessible. Wheelchair ramps, elevators, special parking, specially equipped rest rooms, lowered drinking fountains, lowered telephones, and special housing are available.

Services: Counseling and information services are available, as is tutoring in most subjects. There is remedial math, reading, and writing.

Campus Safety and Security: Measures include 24-hour foot and vehicle patrol, security escort services, lighted pathways/sidewalks, card access and camera surveillance.

Programs of Study: Indiana Tech confers B.A. and B.S. degrees. Associate and master's degrees are also awarded. Bachelor's degrees are awarded in BUSINESS (accounting, business administration and management, and sports management), COMPUTER AND PHYSICAL SCIENCE (computer science, information sciences and systems, and web services), ENGINEERING AND ENVIRONMENTAL DESIGN (biomedical engineering, civil engineering, computer engineering, electrical/electronics engineering, industrial engineering, manufacturing engineering, and mechanical engineering), HEALTH PROFESSIONS (recreation therapy), SOCIAL SCIENCE (human services, parks and recreation management, and psychology). Engineering and computer science are the strongest academically. Business administration is the largest.

Required: To graduate, students must complete a minimum of 120 credit hours, including at least 35 in the major, with a 2.0 minimum GPA. General education requirements include at least 18 hours in social science/humanities and 9 in English.

Special: The school offers co-op programs in business administration and computer studies, internships, work-study programs, and accelerated degree programs in business administration and human services. Credit for life experience is offered through the Extended Studies Program. Dual majors, nondegree study, and pass/fail options are available. There is 1 national honor society.

Faculty/Classroom: 66% of faculty are male; 34%, female. 98% teach undergraduates. No introductory courses are taught by graduate students. The average class size in an introductory lecture is 30; in a laboratory, 22; and in a regular course, 21.

Admissions: 55% of the 2003-2004 applicants were accepted. The SAT I scores for the 2003-2004 freshman class were: Verbal--52% below 500, 34% between 500 and 599, and 11% between 600 and 700; Math--45% below 500, 33% between 500 and 599, 18% between 600 and 700, and 1% above 700. 2 freshmen graduated first in their class.

Requirements: The SAT I or ACT is required. In addition, applicants must be graduates of an accredited secondary school. The GED is accepted. At least 13 academic credits are required, including 4 to 6 units of social studies, 4 units of English, 3 to 6 units of math, and 2 units of a lab science. An interview is recommended. Indiana Tech requires applicants to be in the upper 50% of their class. A GPA of 2.0 is required. AP and CLEP credits are accepted. Important factors in the admissions decision are leadership record, parents or siblings attending the school, and recommendations by alumni.

Procedure: Freshmen are admitted to all sessions. Entrance exams should be taken by January of the senior year. There are early admissions and deferred admissions plans. Early decision applications should be filed by October 1; regular application deadlines are open. Application fee is $50. Notification of early decision is sent October 15. Applications are accepted on-line through *www.indtech.edu*.

Transfer: 63 transfer students enrolled in 2002-2003. Applicants must be in good standing and have a minimum GPA of 2.0. The SAT I is recommended. 30 credits of 120 required for the bachelor's degree must be completed at Indiana Tech.

Visiting: There are regularly scheduled orientations for prospective students, including a campus tour, classroom visits, and meetings with financial aid personnel, coaches, and current students. There are guides for informal visits and visitors may sit in on classes. To schedule a visit, contact Thomas R. Filus at (800) 937-2448, ext. 2205 or *filus@indtech.edu*.

Financial Aid: In 2003-2004, 94% of all full-time freshmen and 93% of continuing full-time students received some form of financial aid. 77% of full-time freshmen and 80% of continuing full-time students received need-based aid. The average freshman award was $13,922. Need-based scholarships or need-based grants averaged $5763 ($7000 maximum); need-based self-help aid (loans and jobs) averaged $6623 ($8000 maximum); non-need-based athletic scholarships averaged $1163; and other non-need-based awards and non-need-based scholarships averaged $4760 ($7000 maximum). 54% of undergraduates work part time. Average annual earnings from campus work are $1600. The average financial indebtedness of the 2003 graduate was $18,800. Indiana Tech is a member of CSS. The FAFSA and the college's own financial statement are required. The deadline for filing freshman financial aid applications for fall entry is March 10.

International Students: There are 8 international students enrolled. The school actively recruits these students. They must score 500 on the written TOEFL, take the college's own test, and also take the SAT I or the ACT, scoring 700 on the SAT I.

Computers: The mainframes are 20 Windows NT 4.0/2000 servers. All students have access to the Internet and a student server from student housing, labs, and multiple areas. 100 PCs are available in the library and labs on the main campus, and another 80 PCs are available at remote campuses. All students may access the system 7 days a week, 24 hours a day. There are no time limits and no fees. All students are required to have personal computers. A PC-compatible typr is recommended.

Graduates: From July 1, 2002 to June 30, 2003, 363 bachelor's degrees were awarded. The most popular majors were business (79%), accounting (8%), and engineering (7%). In an average class, 8% graduate in 3 years or less, 24% graduate in 4 years or less, 31% graduate in 5 years or less, and 33% graduate in 6 years or less. 2 companies recruited on campus in 2002-2003. Of the 2002 graduating class, 6% were enrolled in graduate school within 6 months of graduation and 90% were employed.

Admissions Contact: Thomas R. Filus, Vice President of Enrollment Management. A video is available. E-mail: *filus@indtech.edu* Web: *http://www.indtech.edu*

INDIANA STATE UNIVERSITY
Terre Haute, IN 47809

B-4

(812) 237-2121
(800) 742-0891; Fax: (812) 237-8023

Full-time: 4132 men, 4285 women	Faculty: 489; I, --$
Part-time: 526 men, 672 women	Ph.D.s: n/av
Graduate: 736 men, 1009 women	Student/Faculty: 17 to 1
Year: semesters, summer session	Tuition: $5422 ($11,890)
Application Deadline: August 1	Room & Board: $5297
Freshman Class: 5573 applied, 4864 accepted, 2016 enrolled	
SAT I Verbal/Math: 475/472	ACT: 19 LESS COMPETITIVE

Indiana State University, founded in 1865, is a publicly supported institution offering undergraduate and graduate study in liberal arts and sciences, business, health, phys ed and recreation, education, nursing, and technology. There are 6 undergraduate schools and 1 graduate school. In addition to regional accreditation, ISU has baccalaureate program accreditation with AACSB, ADA, AHEA, CAHEA, NASAD, NASM, NCATE, NLN, and NRPA. The 3 libraries contain 1,354,000 volumes, 997,000 microform items, and 38,000 audio/video tapes/CDs, and subscribe to 2800 periodicals. Computerized library services include the card catalog, interlibrary loans, database searching, and Internet access. Special learning facilities include a learning resource center, art gallery, planetarium, radio station, and an African American cultural center. The 92-acre campus is in an urban area 75 miles west of Indianapolis. Including any residence halls, there are 55 buildings.

Student Life: 90% of undergraduates are from Indiana. Students are from 50 states, 68 foreign countries, and Canada. 95% are from public schools. 81% are white; 11% African American. The average age of freshmen is 19; all undergraduates, 23. 30% do not continue beyond their first year; 40% remain to graduate.

Housing: 3780 students can be accommodated in college housing, which includes single-sex and coed dorms, married-student housing, fraternity houses, and sorority houses. In addition, there are honors houses, special-interest houses, and special freshman dorms. On-campus housing is guaranteed for all 4 years. 55% of students commute. Alcohol is not permitted. All students may keep cars.

Activities: 12% of men belong to 21 national fraternities; 9% of women belong to 13 national sororities. There are more than 180 groups on campus, including art, band, cheerleading, choir, chorale, chorus, computers, drama, drill team, ethnic, film, gay, honors, international, jazz band, marching band, musical theater, newspaper, opera, orchestra, pep band, political, professional, radio and TV, religious, social, social service, student government, symphony, and yearbook. Popular campus events include a contemporary music festival, Theaterfest, and Black History Month.

Sports: There are 7 intercollegiate sports for men and 8 for women, and 27 intramural sports for men and 25 for women. Facilities include a 20,000-seat football stadium, a 10,000-seat basketball arena, 2 softball diamonds, a baseball field, 2 indoor and outdoor tracks, 2 pools, indoor and outdoor basketball and tennis courts, racquetball, sand volleyball, and volleyball courts, a physical fitness center with weight training facilities, a climbing wall, and 3 fitness and wellness facilities located in 2 residence halls and the student union.

Disabled Students: 98% of the campus is accessible. Wheelchair ramps, elevators, special parking, specially equipped rest rooms, special class scheduling, lowered drinking fountains, lowered telephones, and special dining hall facilities are available.

Services: Counseling and information services are available, as is tutoring in most subjects. There is a reader service for the blind, a learning skills center, an academic advisement center, a counseling center, student support services, a math lab, and a writing lab.

Campus Safety and Security: Measures include 24-hour foot and vehicle patrol, self-defense education, security escort services, and informal discussions. There are pamphlets/posters/films, emergency telephones, lighted pathways/sidewalks, and bicycle and car registration.

Programs of Study: ISU confers B.A., B.S., B.F.A., B.M., B.M.E., and B.S.W. degrees. Associate, master's, and doctoral degrees are also awarded. Bachelor's degrees are awarded in BIOLOGICAL SCIENCE (biology/biological science), BUSINESS (accounting, banking and finance, business administration and management, hotel/motel and restaurant management, insurance, management information systems, marketing and distribution, marketing/retailing/merchandising, office supervision and management, recreation and leisure services, and sports management), COMMUNICATIONS AND THE ARTS (art history and appreciation, broadcasting, communications, dramatic arts, English, film arts, fine arts, French, German, journalism, Latin, music, Russian, Spanish, and studio art), COMPUTER AND PHYSICAL SCIENCE (chemistry, computer science, geology, mathematics, and physics), EDUCATION (art, business, early childhood, educational media, elementary, foreign languages, health, home economics, industrial arts, middle school, music, physical, science, secondary, social studies, and special), ENGINEERING AND ENVIRONMENTAL DESIGN (aeronautical technology, airline piloting and navigation, computer technology, construction technology, electrical/electronics engineering technology, industrial engineer-

ing technology, interior design, manufacturing technology, mechanical engineering technology, and preengineering), HEALTH PROFESSIONS (environmental health science, medical laboratory technology, nursing, predentistry, premedicine, prepharmacy, preveterinary science, and speech pathology/audiology), SOCIAL SCIENCE (African American studies, anthropology, child care/child and family studies, criminology, dietetics, economics, food science, geography, history, home economics, interdisciplinary studies, liberal arts/general studies, parks and recreation management, philosophy, political science/government, prelaw, psychology, religion, safety management, social work, sociology, textiles and clothing, and urban studies). Safety management, criminology, and business are the strongest academically. Criminology, communication, and elementary education are the largest.

Required: All students must complete the general education program, as well as a minimum of 50 hours of upper-division course work. A minimum GPA of 2.0 (2.5 for education majors) and a total of 124 credit hours are required for graduation.

Special: The school has cross-registration with the Rose-Hulman Institute of Technology, Saint Mary-of-the-Woods College, and Ivy Tech State College. Internships are available in athletic training, criminology, environmental health, political science, safety management, and sports studies. There is a co-op program, and summer and winter work-study is available. The school offers a general studies degree, study abroad in 30 countries, credit for life experience, nondegree study, and a 3-2 engineering degree with Purdue University. There is a freshman honors program. All departments have honors programs.

Faculty/Classroom: 59% of faculty are male; 41%, female. 85% of full-time faculty teach undergraduates and 57% do research. Graduate students teach 10% of lower-division courses.

Admissions: 87% of the 2003-2004 applicants were accepted. The SAT I scores for the 2003-2004 freshman class were: Verbal--61% below 500, 31% between 500 and 599, 7% between 600 and 700, and 1% above 700; Math--61% below 500, 32% between 500 and 599, 6% between 600 and 700, and 1% above 700. The ACT scores were 61% below 21, 22% between 21 and 23, 11% between 24 and 26, 3% between 27 and 28, and 2% above 28. 18% of the current freshmen were in the top fifth of their class; 44% were in the top two fifths. 16 freshmen graduated first in their class.

Requirements: The SAT I or ACT is required. In addition, the applicant must be a graduate of an accredited secondary school. The GED is accepted. An essay is not required. Applicants are reviewed based on a combination of class rank, grade point average, strength of curriculum, academic progress, and standardized test scores. Those students who rank in the top 50% of their class are routinely admitted, whereas those in the bottom 50% of their class are reviewed on an individual basis. Routine admission does not guarantee admission to specific majors. A GPA of 2.0 is required. AP and CLEP credits are accepted. Important factors in the admissions decision are advanced placement or honor courses, leadership record, and extracurricular activities record.

Procedure: Freshmen are admitted to all sessions. Entrance exams should be taken before January 1. There is a deferred admissions plan and a rolling admissions plan. Applications should be filed by August 1 for fall entry, December 1 for spring entry, and May 1 for summer entry. The fall 2003 application fee was $25. Notification is sent on a rolling basis. Applications are accepted on-line through the university web site.

Transfer: 707 transfer students enrolled in 2002-2003. Transfer students must have a minimum GPA of 2.0. 30 credits of 124 required for the bachelor's degree must be completed at ISU.

Visiting: There are regularly scheduled orientations for prospective students, consisting of Sycamore Preview Days, which include campus tours, opportunities to meet with academic advisers in the majors students are considering, and formal sessions with representatives from financial aid and the career center. There are guides for informal visits and visitors may sit in on classes and stay overnight. To schedule a visit, contact the Admissions Office at admissions@indstate.edu.

Financial Aid: In 2003-2004, 59% of all full-time freshmen and 52% of continuing full-time students received some form of financial aid. 37% of full-time freshmen and 36% of continuing full-time students received need-based aid. The average freshman award was $5793. Need-based scholarships or need-based grants averaged $4277; need-based self-help aid averaged $2901; non-need-based athletic scholarships averaged $8455; other non-need-based awards and non-need-based scholarships averaged $3326; and need-based loans averaged $2602. The average financial indebtedness of the 2003 graduate was $16,242. The FAFSA is required. The deadline for filing freshman financial aid applications for fall entry is March 1.

International Students: There are 150 international students enrolled. The school actively recruits these students. They must score 550 on the written TOEFL or 213 on the electronic version and also take the SAT I or the ACT.

Computers: The mainframes are SUN devices running Solaris. There are more than 600 computers publicly accessible in labs and kiosks across campus. Residence hall students are provided with a live LAN connection for their PCs. All students may access the system.

Graduates: In an average class, 3% graduate in 3 years or less, 22% graduate in 4 years or less, 37% graduate in 5 years or less, and 41% graduate in 6 years or less.

Admissions Contact: Ron Brown, Director.

E-mail: *admissions@indstate.edu*

Web: *http://web.indstate.edu/admissions/*

INDIANA UNIVERSITY SYSTEM

Indiana University, established in 1820, is a public university governed by a board of trustees. The chief administrator is the president. The primary missions of the university are instruction, research, and service. Total enrollment of all 8 campuses generally exceeds 93,000, with some 6800 faculty members. There are 353 baccalaureate, 228 master's, and 102 doctoral programs offered within the university. Four-year campuses are located in Bloomington, Indianapolis, Kokomo, South Bend, Gary, New Albany, and Richmond. Indiana University manages the Indianapolis campus while Purdue University manages the Fort Wayne campus. Profiles of some of these campuses are included in this section.

INDIANA UNIVERSITY BLOOMINGTON

INDIANA UNIVERSITY BLOOMINGTON	**C-4**
Bloomington, IN 47405-1106	**(812) 855-0661**
	Fax: (812) 855-5102
Full-time: 13,573 men, 14,986 women	**Faculty:** 1432; I, av$
Part-time: 832 men, 928 women	**Ph.D.s:** 80%
Graduate: 4089 men, 4181 women	**Student/Faculty:** 20 to 1
Year: semesters, summer session	**Tuition:** $6517 ($17,552)
Application Deadline: February 1	**Room & Board:** $5872
Freshman Class: n/av	
SAT I Verbal/Math: 550/560	**ACT:** 24 **VERY COMPETITIVE**

Indiana University Bloomington, founded in 1820, is a comprehensive institution that is part of the Indiana University system. The university offers undergraduate programs in arts and sciences, allied health sciences, business, dentistry, education, health, physical education, recreation, journalism, music, nursing, optometry, public and environmental affairs, social work, and informatics. In addition to regional accreditation, IU has baccalaureate program accreditation with AACSB, ACBSP, ACEJMC, ADA, APTA, ASLA, CAHEA, CSWE, FIDER, NASAD, NASM, NCATE, and NLN. The 22 libraries contain 6,647,355 volumes, 4,902,515 microform items, and 252,970 audio/video tapes/CDs, and subscribe to 59,439 periodicals. Computerized library services include the card catalog, interlibrary loans, and database searching. Special learning facilities include a learning resource center, art gallery, natural history museum, radio station, TV station, observatory, arboretum, museum of world cultures, garden and nature center, musical arts center, and more than 70 research centers. The 1931-acre campus is in a small town 50 miles southwest of Indianapolis. Including any residence halls, there are 490 buildings.

Student Life: 67% of undergraduates are from Indiana. Students are from 50 states, more than 150 foreign countries, and Canada. 85% are white. The average age of freshmen is 19; all undergraduates, 21. 12% do not continue beyond their first year.

Housing: More than 12,000 students can be accommodated in college housing, which includes single-sex and coed dorms, off-campus apartments, and married-student housing. In addition, there are honors houses, language houses, special-interest houses, living-learning centers, an international center, a center for women, a wellness center, freshmen interest groups (FIGS), and thematic communities. On-campus housing is guaranteed for all 4 years. 58% of students commute. Alcohol is not permitted. All students may keep cars.

Activities: 16% of men belong to fraternities; 18% of women belong to sororities. There are 400 groups on campus, including art, band, cheerleading, chess, choir, chorale, chorus, computers, dance, debate, drama, drill team, ethnic, film, gay, honors, international, jazz band, literary magazine, marching band, musical theater, newspaper, opera, orchestra, pep band, photography, political, professional, radio and TV, religious, social, social service, student government, symphony, and yearbook. Popular campus events include Little 500 and Founder's Day.

Sports: There are 10 intercollegiate sports for men and 12 for women, and more than 27 intramural sports for men and more than 27 for women. Facilities include a 52,000-seat football stadium, an 18,000-seat soccer/bicycle stadium, an 18,000-seat indoor gym, a 2,300-seat auditorium, an assembly hall, indoor/outdoor swimming pools, a tennis pavilion, an indoor practice facility, a golf driving range, and a student recreation and aquatics center.

Disabled Students: 95% of the campus is accessible. Wheelchair ramps, elevators, special parking, specially equipped rest rooms, special class scheduling, lowered drinking fountains, lowered telephones, and scheduled transportation are available.

Services: Counseling and information services are available, as is tutoring in most subjects. There is a reader service for the blind, and remedial math, reading, and writing. Skills workshops are also offered.

Campus Safety and Security: Measures include 24-hour foot and vehicle patrol, self-defense education, security escort services, and shuttle buses. There are informal discussions, pamphlets/posters/films, emergency telephones, lighted pathways/sidewalks, and safety awareness education.

Programs of Study: IU confers B.A., B.S., B.F.A., B.G.S., B.M., B.S.E., B.S.N., B.S.P.A., B.S.P.H., and B.S.W. degrees. Associate, master's, and doctoral degrees are also awarded. Bachelor's degrees are awarded in AGRICULTURE (environmental studies), BIOLOGICAL SCIENCE (biochemistry, biology/biological science, ecology, microbiology, and nutrition), BUSINESS (accounting, apparel and accessories marketing, banking and finance, business administration and management, business economics, entrepreneurial studies, international business management, labor studies, management information systems, management science, marketing/retailing/merchandising, operations research, real estate, recreation and leisure services, sports management, and tourism), COMMUNICATIONS AND THE ARTS (art history and appreciation, audio technology, ballet, ceramic art and design, classics, communications, comparative literature, creative writing, dramatic arts, Dutch, East Asian languages and literature, English, fine arts, folklore and mythology, French, German, graphic design, Greek, guitar, Italian, jazz, journalism, Latin, linguistics, media arts, metal/jewelry, music, music performance, music theory and composition, opera, painting, photography, piano/organ, Portuguese, printmaking, Spanish, speech/debate/rhetoric, studio art, telecommunications, visual and performing arts, and voice), COMPUTER AND PHYSICAL SCIENCE (astronomy, astrophysics, atmospheric sciences and meteorology, chemistry, computer science, digital arts/technology, geology, hydrology, information sciences and systems, mathematics, physics, and statistics), EDUCATION (athletic training, early childhood, educational media, elementary, health, music, physical, science, social studies, and special), ENGINEERING AND ENVIRONMENTAL DESIGN (aerospace studies, environmental science, geological engineering, interior design, and occupational safety and health), HEALTH PROFESSIONS (exercise science, health care administration, nursing, public health, and speech pathology/audiology), SOCIAL SCIENCE (African American studies, anthropology, classical/ancient civilization, cognitive science, criminal justice, dietetics, East Asian studies, economics, ethics, politics, and social policy, family/consumer studies, gender studies, geography, history, human development, international studies, Judaic studies, law, liberal arts/general studies, Near Eastern studies, parks and recreation management, philosophy, physical fitness/movement, political science/government, psychology, public administration, public affairs, religion, Russian and Slavic studies, social work, sociology, textiles and clothing, and urban studies).

Required: The general requirements for graduation include courses in English and writing, math, foreign language, arts and humanities, social and behavioral sciences, natural sciences, and culture studies. Students must complete 122 credit hours, with approximately 36 hours in the major. Many degrees have intensive writing requirements, and the minimum GPA requirement varies by department. Liberal arts requirements are common throughout all degree programs.

Special: IU offers cooperative programs with universities in many countries, including the People's Republic of China, a variety of internships, and study abroad in more than 25 countries. A Washington semester, work-study programs, B.A.-B.S. degrees in the sciences and liberal arts, dual majors, and nondegree study and the general studies degree through the School of Continuing Studies are available. Student-designed majors through the Individualized Major Program, credit for military experience and pass/fail options are also available. There are 18 national honor societies and a freshman honors program.

Faculty/Classroom: 69% of faculty are male; 31%, female.

Admissions: The SAT I scores for the 2003-2004 freshman class were: Verbal--27% below 500, 45% between 500 and 599, 25% between 600 and 700, and 3% above 700; Math--24% below 500, 41% between 500 and 599, 30% between 600 and 700, and 5% above 700. The ACT scores were 15% below 21, 24% between 21 and 23, 31% between 24 and 26, 16% between 27 and 28, and 14% above 28. 46% of the current freshmen were in the top fifth of their class; 84% were in the top two fifths. There were 26 National Merit finalists in a recent year. 121 freshmen graduated first in their class.

Requirements: The SAT I or ACT is required. In addition, applicants must be graduates of an accredited secondary high school or have a GED certificate. SAT II: Subject tests are recommended for credit and placement. Auditions for music majors are required. An interview is recommended for information purposes. AP and CLEP credits are accepted. Important factors in the admissions decision are advanced placement or honor courses, parents or siblings attending the school, and recommendations by school officials.

Procedure: Freshmen are admitted to all sessions. Entrance exams should be taken in the late junior year or early senior year. There is a deferred admissions plan and a rolling admissions plan. Applications should be filed by February 1 for summer or fall entry, and November 1 for spring entry. The fall 2003 application fee was $45. Notification is sent on a rolling basis. Applications are accepted on-line through the school's web site.

Transfer: 788 transfer students enrolled in 2002-2003. Admission for transfers is selective. Most successful applicants have a 2.5 or higher GPA and no grades below C in recent work. Applicants with less than 1 year of transfer work (fewer than 26 credit hours) must also meet freshman admission standards. 30 credits of 122 required for the bachelor's degree must be completed at IU.

Visiting: There are regularly scheduled orientations for prospective students, including admissions counseling and answers to students' questions about the school. There are guides for informal visits and visitors may sit in on classes and stay overnight. To schedule a visit, contact the scheduling director at (812) 855-3512.

Financial Aid: In 2003-2004, 42% of all full-time freshmen and 37% of continuing full-time students received some form of financial aid. At least 27% of full-time freshmen and at least 21% of continuing full-time students received need-based aid. The average freshman award was $10,512. Need-based scholarships or need-based grants averaged $4964; need-based self-help aid (loans and jobs) averaged $1788; non-need-based athletic scholarships averaged $15,450; and other non-need-based awards and non-need-based scholarships averaged $3721. The average financial indebtedness of the 2003 graduate was $18,423. The FAFSA is required. The deadline for filing freshman financial aid applications for fall entry is March 1.

International Students: There are 1449 international students enrolled. The school actively recruits these students. They must take the TOEFL and the SAT I or ACT.

Computers: More than 1500 Macs and PCs are available in more than 55 computing labs across campus. All dorms are wired to handle student PCs. All students may access the system 24 hours a day. There are no time limits. There is a $400 technology fee. It is strongly recommended that all students have a personal computer, especially students in computer science.

Graduates: From July 1, 2002 to June 30, 2003, 6001 bachelor's degrees were awarded. The most popular majors were business/marketing (21%), education (17%), and communications/communication technologies (10%).

Admissions Contact: Mary Ellen Anderson, Director of Admissions. E-mail: *iuadmit@indiana.edu* Web: *http://www.indiana.edu/~iuadmit*

INDIANA UNIVERSITY EAST
Richmond, IN 47374-1289

D-3

(765) 973-8208
(800) 959-4485; Fax: (765) 973-8288

Full-time: 391 men, 894 women	**Faculty:** 69; IIB, -$
Part-time: 351 men, 869 women	**Ph.D.s:** 51%
Graduate: 16 men, 47 women	**Student/Faculty:** 19 to 1
Year: semesters, summer session	**Tuition:** $4433 ($10,383)
Application Deadline: open	**Room & Board:** n/app
Freshman Class: n/av	
SAT I Verbal/Math: 450/410	**ACT:** 19 **LESS COMPETITIVE**

Indiana University East, established in 1971, is a public institution serving a commuter student body. The university offers undergraduate degree programs in humanities, natural science and math, behavioral and social sciences, education, business and technology, nursing, public and environmental affairs, social work, and continuing studies. In addition to regional accreditation, IU East has baccalaureate program accreditation with NCATE and NLN. The library contains 69,204 volumes, 53,013 microform items, and 2219 audio/video tapes/CDs, and subscribes to 76 periodicals. Computerized library services include the card catalog, interlibrary loans, and database searching. Special learning facilities include an art gallery. The 194-acre campus is in a small town 40 miles west of Dayton, Ohio, and 70 miles east of Indianapolis. There are 10 buildings.

Student Life: 90% of undergraduates are from Indiana. Students are from 10 states, 8 foreign countries, and Canada. 90% are white. The average age of freshmen is 23; all undergraduates, 28. 39% do not continue beyond their first year.

Housing: There are no residence halls. All of students commute. Alcohol is not permitted.

Activities: There is 1 national fraternity and 1 national sorority. There are 20 groups on campus, including art, cheerleading, drama, ethnic, newspaper, photography, political, professional, radio and TV, religious, social, social service, and student government. Popular campus events include fall and spring festivals and a Wednesday lunch program.

Sports: There are 4 intramural sports for men and 4 for women. Facilities include a softball field, tennis courts, a sand volleyball court, and a field house.

Disabled Students: 98% of the campus is accessible. Wheelchair ramps, elevators, special parking, lowered drinking fountains, lowered telephones, note taking, and special testing accommodations, are available.

Services: Counseling and information services are available, as is tutoring in some subjects, for several freshman-level courses. There is a reader service for the blind, and remedial math, reading, and writing.

Campus Safety and Security: Measures include security escort services, informal discussions, pamphlets/posters/films, and emergency telephones. There are lighted pathways/sidewalks and a 14-hour foot and vehicle patrol.

Programs of Study: IU East confers B.A., B.S., B.G.S., and B.S.W. degrees. Associate degrees are also awarded. Bachelor's degrees are awarded in BIOLOGICAL SCIENCE (biology/biological science), BUSINESS (business administration and management), COMMUNICATIONS AND THE ARTS (communications, English, and fine arts), COMPUTER AND PHYSICAL SCIENCE (information sciences and systems, mathematics, and natural sciences), EDUCATION (elementary and secondary), HEALTH PROFESSIONS (nursing), SOCIAL SCIENCE (behavioral science, criminal justice, humanities, liberal arts/general studies, and social work). Nursing, business, and education are the largest.

Required: To graduate, students must satisfactorily complete courses in English composition, humanities, biological or physical science, and social science, as well as demonstrate computer literacy, and complete a minimum of 120 semester hours with a GPA of at least 2.0.

Special: IU East offers a cooperative program in criminal justice with Indiana University-Purdue University and an organizational leadership program through Purdue's Statewide Technology program. IU East also offers cross-registration with Earlham College, dual majors, independent study, an internship in social work, pass/fail options, study abroad through Indiana University Bloomington, and credit for life experience. Nondegree study is possible. There is 1 national honor society.

Faculty/Classroom: 39% of faculty are male; 61%, female.

Admissions: The SAT I scores for the 2003-2004 freshman class were: Verbal--70% below 500, 22% between 500 and 599, 6% between 600 and 700, and 1% above 700; Math--76% below 500, 22% between 500 and 599, and 1% above 700. The ACT scores were 67% below 21, 20% between 21 and 23, 12% between 24 and 26, and 1% above 28. 16% of the current freshmen were in the top fifth of their class; 43% were in the top two fifths.

Requirements: The SAT I or ACT is recommended. In addition, a minimum GPA of 2.0 is required for applicants who have graduated from high school in the preceding 3 years. Applicants must be graduates of accredited secondary schools or have earned a GED. They must have completed 15 academic credits, including 4 in English, 2 each in math, social studies, and foreign language and 1 in science, as well as an additional 4 units of academic study. 4 credits in a foreign language are strongly recommended. AP and CLEP credits are accepted.

Procedure: Freshmen are admitted to all sessions. Entrance exams should be taken during the junior or senior year. There are early admissions, rolling admissions, and deferred admissions plans. Application deadlines are open. The fall 2003 appliction fee was $25.

Transfer: 112 transfer students enrolled in 2002-2003. Applicants must have a GPA of 2.0 (2.5 for out-of-state transfer applicants) and submit college transcripts. Grades of C or better transfer for credit. 30 of 120 credits required for the bachelor's degree must be completed at IU East.

Visiting: There are regularly scheduled orientations for prospective students, including tours, counseling, registration, and financial aid sessions. There are guides for informal visits and visitors may sit in on classes. To schedule a visit, contact the Admissions Office.

Financial Aid: In 2003-2004, 61% of all full-time freshmen and 67% of continuing full-time students received some form of financial aid. At least 46% of full-time freshmen and at least 53% of continuing full-time students received need-based aid. The average freshman award was $4156. Need-based scholarships or need-based grants averaged $4408; need-based self-help aid (loans and jobs) averaged $2635; and non-need-based awards and non-need-based scholarships averaged $1185. The average financial indebtedness of the 2003 graduate was $17,547. The FAFSA and the college's own financial statement are required. The deadline for filing freshman financial aid applications for fall entry is March 1.

Computers: There are 110 networked PCs in 7 public labs connected to the Internet. All students may access the system during the operating hours of the university. There are no time limits. There is a $225 technology fee.

Graduates: From July 1, 2002 to June 30, 2003, 149 bachelor's degrees were awarded. The most popular majors were business (28%), education (17%), and health professions (14%). In an average class, 6% graduate in 4 years or less, 13% graduate in 5 years or less, and 5% graduate in 6 years or less.

Admissions Contact: James Bland, Acting Director of Student Recruitment. E-mail: *admit@indiana.edu*
Web: *http://www.iue.indiana.edu/admissions/*

INDIANA UNIVERSITY KOKOMO
Kokomo, IN 46904-9003

C-2

(765) 455-9216
(888) 875-4485; Fax: (765) 455-9537

Full-time: 435 men, 989 women	**Faculty:** 82; IIB, av$
Part-time: 354 men, 952 women	**Ph.D.s:** 62%
Graduate: 88 men, 125 women	**Student/Faculty:** 17 to 1
Year: semesters, summer session	**Tuition:** $4463 ($10,413)
Application Deadline: August 3	**Room & Board:** n/app
Freshman Class: n/av	
SAT I Verbal/Math: 470/460	**ACT:** 19 **LESS COMPETITIVE**

Indiana University Kokomo, founded in 1945 and part of the Indiana University System, offers a wide range of programs that emphasize liberal arts, business, education, and nursing. In addition to regional accreditation, IUK has baccalaureate program accreditation with ABET, NCATE, and NLN. The library contains 133,433 volumes, 466,693 microform items, and 1445 audio/video tapes/CDs, and subscribes to 1448 periodicals. Computerized library services include interlibrary loans, database searching, and Internet access. Special learning facilities include a learning resource center, art gallery, and an observatory. The 51-acre campus is in a small town 45 miles north of Indianapolis. There are 17 buildings.

Student Life: 99% of undergraduates are from Indiana. Students are from 14 states, 9 foreign countries, and Canada. 92% are white. The average age of freshmen is 21; all undergraduates, 26. 40% do not continue beyond their first year.

Housing: There are no residence halls. All of students commute. Alcohol is not permitted.

Activities: There are no fraternities or sororities. There are 20 groups on campus, including chorale, computers, drama, ethnic, honors, political, religious, social service, student government, and yearbook. Popular campus events include the International Festival.

Sports: There is no sports program at IUK.

Disabled Students: All of the campus is accessible. Wheelchair ramps, elevators, special parking, specially equipped rest rooms, special class scheduling, lowered drinking fountains, and lowered telephones are available.

Services: There is remedial math, reading, and writing. Students who do not meet regular admissions standards can be admitted under the Guided Study Program, which includes courses in basic skills as needed, counseling and tutoring, and a seminar on studying.

Campus Safety and Security: Measures include security escort services, emergency telephones, and lighted pathways/sidewalks. Campus police are on duty from 7 A.M. to 10 P.M.

Programs of Study: IUK confers B.A., B.S., B.G.S., B.S.Bus., B.S.Ed., and B.S.N. degrees. Associate and master's degrees are also awarded. Bachelor's degrees are awarded in BIOLOGICAL SCIENCE (biology/biological science), BUSINESS (accounting, business administration and management, business economics, electronic business, labor studies, and marketing management), COMMUNICATIONS AND THE ARTS (communications and English), COMPUTER AND PHYSICAL SCIENCE (chemistry, information sciences and systems, mathematics, and physical sciences), EDUCATION (elementary), HEALTH PROFESSIONS (cytotechnology, health care administration, medical laboratory technology, nuclear medical technology, nursing, occupational therapy, radiation therapy, radiograph medical technology, radiological science, and respiratory therapy), SOCIAL SCIENCE (behavioral science, criminal justice, gerontology, humanities, liberal arts/general studies, psychology, public affairs, social science, and sociology). Education, business, and nursing are the largest.

Required: All students must maintain a minimum GPA of 2.0 while taking 120 credit hours. All students must complete course work in English, computers, and math.

Special: Student-designed majors, a general studies degree, internships, study abroad, joint programs with other Indiana University campuses and with Purdue University, pass/fail options, nondegree study, and credit for military experience and by exam are available. There is 1 national honor society and a freshman honors program.

Faculty/Classroom: 43% of faculty are male; 57%, female. All teach undergraduates. No introductory courses are taught by graduate students.

Admissions: The SAT I scores for the 2003-2004 freshman class were: Verbal--63% below 500, 32% between 500 and 599, and 5% between 600 and 700; Math--66% below 500, 28% between 500 and 599, and 6% between 600 and 700. The ACT scores were 71% below 21, 20% between 21 and 23, and 9% between 24 and 26. 14% of the current freshmen were in the top fifth of their class; 38% were in the top two fifths.

Requirements: The SAT I or ACT is required. In addition, admissions requirements include 14 academic credits, including 4 units of English, 3 units of math, 2 units of social sciences, and 1 unit of science. In addition, 2 units each of a foreign language and history are recommended. The GED is accepted. In-state students should be in the top half of the graduating class; out-of-state students should be in the top one third. IUK requires applicants to be in the upper 50% of their class. AP and CLEP credits are accepted. Important factors in the admissions decision are recommendations by school officials and advanced placement or honor courses.

Procedure: Freshmen are admitted to all sessions. Entrance exams should be taken prior to registration. There are early admissions, rolling admissions, and deferred admissions plans. Applications should be filed by August 3 for fall entry, December 1 for spring entry, and April 15 for summer entry. The fall 2003 application fee was $30. Notification is sent on a rolling basis.

Transfer: 184 transfer students enrolled in 2002-2003. Transfer applicants must have at least 7 credits with a minimum GPA of 2.0 and clear records of conduct from previously attended colleges. Transcripts are required. Transfers are considered on a case-by-case basis. Contact the Admissions Office for more information. 30 of 120 credits required for the bachelor's degree must be completed at IUK.

Visiting: There are regularly scheduled orientations for prospective students. There are guides for informal visits and visitors may sit in on classes. To schedule a visit, contact the Admissions Office.

Financial Aid: In 2003-2004, 40% of all full-time freshmen and 41% of continuing full-time students received some form of financial aid. At least 29% of full-time freshmen and at least 30% of continuing full-time students received need-based aid. The average freshman award was $5619. Need-based scholarships or need-based grants averaged $4476; need-based self-help aid (loans and jobs) averaged $2319; and non-need-based awards and non-need-based scholarships averaged $1783. The average financial indebtedness of the 2003 graduate was $11,681. The FAFSA and the college's own financial statement are required. The deadline for filing freshman financial aid applications for fall entry is March 1.

International Students: They must score 550 on the written TOEFL.

Computers: There is a is $280 technology fee. There are no time limits. Labs are available when not reserved for classes.

Graduates: From July 1, 2002 to June 30, 2003, 229 bachelor's degrees were awarded. The most popular majors were education (22%), liberal arts (20%), and business/marketing (17%). In an average class, 7% graduate in 4 years or less, 6% graduate in 5 years or less, and 5% graduate in 6 years or less.

Admissions Contact: Jackie Kennedy-Fletcher, Director of Admissions. E-mail: iuadmis@iuk.edu
Web: http://www.iuk.edu/student-services/admissions

INDIANA UNIVERSITY NORTHWEST
Gary, IN 46408-1197

B-1

(219) 980-6991
(888) 968-7486; Fax: (219) 981-4219

Full-time: 754 men, 1617 women	**Faculty:** 168; IIA, -$
Part-time: 407 men, 1163 women	**Ph.D.s:** 48%
Graduate: 108 men, 270 women	**Student/Faculty:** 14 to 1
Year: semesters, summer session	**Tuition:** $4538 ($10,488)
Application Deadline: August 1	**Room & Board:** n/app
Freshman Class: n/av	
SAT I Verbal/Math: 450/440	**ACT:** 20 **LESS COMPETITIVE**

Indiana University Northwest, established in 1948, is one of 8 campuses of the Indiana University system. A public commuter school, it offers liberal arts and professional programs. In addition to regional accreditation, IUN has baccalaureate program accreditation with AACSB, ADA, NCATE, and NLN. The library contains 252,137 volumes, 340,849 microform items, and 331 audio/video tapes/CDs, and subscribes to 1527 periodicals. Computerized library services include interlibrary loans. Special learning facilities include a learning resource center and art gallery. The 38-acre campus is in an urban area 30 miles southeast of Chicago. There are 22 buildings.

Student Life: 99% of undergraduates are from Indiana. Students are from 14 states, 34 foreign countries, and Canada. 57% are white; 18% African American; 10% Hispanic. The average age of freshmen is 29; all undergraduates, 30. 38% do not continue beyond their first year.

Housing: There are no residence halls. All students commute. Alcohol is not permitted. All students may keep cars.

Activities: There are 3 national fraternities and 3 national sororities. There are 70 groups on campus, including chess, chorale, drama, ethnic, honors, literary magazine, musical theater, newspaper, political, professional, social, student government, and yearbook. Popular campus events include Student/Faculty Dinner Dance and Health Fair.

Sports: There are 3 intercollegiate sports for men and 3 for women, and 8 intramural sports for men and 5 for women.

Disabled Students: 90% of the campus is accessible. Wheelchair ramps, elevators, special parking, specially equipped rest rooms, special class scheduling, lowered drinking fountains, and lowered telephones are available.

Services: Counseling and information services are available, as is tutoring in some subjects, including biology, anatomy and physiology, Spanish I, chemistry, sociology, and math. There is a reader service for the blind, and remedial math, reading, and writing.

Campus Safety and Security: Measures include 24-hour foot and vehicle patrol, security escort services, emergency telephones, and lighted pathways/sidewalks.

Programs of Study: IUN confers B.A., B.S., and B.G.S. degrees. Associate and master's degrees are also awarded. Bachelor's degrees are awarded in BIOLOGICAL SCIENCE (biology/biological science), BUSINESS (accounting, business administration and management, and labor studies), COMMUNICATIONS AND THE ARTS (communications, dramatic arts, English, fine arts, French, and Spanish), COMPUTER AND PHYSICAL SCIENCE (actuarial science, chemistry, geology, information sciences and systems, and mathematics), EDUCATION (elementary and secondary), ENGINEERING AND ENVIRONMENTAL DESIGN (engineering technology), HEALTH PROFESSIONS (health care administration, nursing, and radiological science), SOCIAL SCIENCE (African American studies, criminal justice, economics, history, liberal arts/general studies, philosophy, political science/government, psychology, public administration, and sociology). Business and nursing are the strongest academically.

Required: Each division sets its own degree requirements. All students must maintain a minimum GPA of 2.0 and complete at least 120 credit hours to graduate. Students must take courses in computer literacy, English, foreign language, humanities, math, science, and social science.

Special: IUN offers cross-registration with Purdue University, work-study, dual majors, independent study, internships, study abroad in 25 countries, credit for life, military, and work experience, nondegree study, accelerated degree programs, student-designed majors, and pass/fail options. There are 2 national honor societies.

Faculty/Classroom: 48% of faculty are male; 52%, female.

Admissions: The SAT I scores for the 2003-2004 freshman class were: Verbal--66% below 500, 24% between 500 and 599, and 10% between 600 and 700; Math--71% below 500, 22% between 500 and 599, and 6% between 600 and 700. The ACT scores were 64% below 21, 19% between 21 and 23, 8% between 24 and 26, 4% between 27 and 28, and 4% above 28. 16% of the current freshmen were in the top fifth of their class; 39% were in the top two fifths.

Requirements: The SAT I or ACT is required for students who graduated in the last 3 years, with a minimum composite SAT I score of 860. Applicants must be graduates of an accredited secondary school, with 16 academic units, including 4 each in English and academic electives, 3 in math, 2 each in social studies and foreign language (recommended) and 1 in science. The GED is accepted. The university recommends an interview. AP and CLEP credits are accepted. Important factors in the admissions decision are advanced placement or honor courses, leadership record, and recommendations by school officials.

Procedure: Freshmen are admitted fall, spring, and summer. Entrance exams should be taken as early as possible. There are early admissions and deferred admissions plans. There is a rolling admissions plan. Applications should be filed by August 1 for fall entry, December 1 for spring entry, and May 1 for summer entry. Notification is sent on a rolling basis. The fall 2003 application fee was $25.

Transfer: 260 transfer students enrolled in 2002-2003. Residents of Indiana must have a 2.0 GPA. Out-of-state transfers must have a C+ average or higher. The SAT I or ACT is recommended. Grades of C or better transfer for credit. High school and college transcripts are required. 30 of 120 credits required for the bachelor's degree must be completed at IUN.

Visiting: There are regularly scheduled orientations for prospective students. There are guides for informal visits and visitors may sit in on classes. To schedule a visit, contact the Admissions Office.

Financial Aid: In 2003-2004, 35% of all full-time freshmen and 43% of continuing full-time students received some form of financial aid. At least 25% of full-time freshmen and 31% of continuing full-time students received need-based aid. The average freshman award was $6515. Need-based scholarships or need-based grants averaged $4569; need-based self-help aid (loans and jobs) averaged $2842; and non-need-based awards and non-need-based scholarships averaged $2155. The average financial indebtedness of the 2003 graduate was $14,444. The FAFSA and the college's own financial statement are required. The priority date for freshman financial aid applications for fall entry is March 1.

International Students: There are 15 international students enrolled. They must score 550 on the written TOEFL and also take the SAT I or the ACT.

Computers: PCs and Macs are available in labs and offices. All students may access the system any time. There are no time limits. The fee is $320.

Graduates: From July 1, 2002 to June 30, 2003, 339 bachelor's degrees were awarded. The most popular majors were business/marketing (17%), public administration (15%), and health professions (13%). In an average class, 8% graduate in 4 years or less, 13% graduate in 5 years or less, and 4% graduate in 6 years or less.

Admissions Contact: Linda Templeton, Director of Admissions. E-mail: *admit@iun.edu* Web: *www.iun.edu/~admit*

INDIANA UNIVERSITY SOUTH BEND
South Bend, IN 46634-7111

C-1
(574) 237-4839
(877) GO-2-IUSB; Fax: (574) 237-4834

Full-time: 1310 men, 2124 women	**Faculty:** 219; IIA, -$
Part-time: 934 men, 1725 women	**Ph.D.s:** 67%
Graduate: 415 men, 772 women	**Student/Faculty:** 16 to 1
Year: semesters, summer session	**Tuition:** $4571 ($11,163)
Application Deadline: July 1	**Room & Board:** n/app
Freshman Class: n/av	
SAT I Verbal/Math: 480/470	**ACT:** 20 **LESS COMPETITIVE**

Indiana University South Bend, a commuter institution of the state-supported university system, was founded in 1941 and offers undergraduate programs in arts and sciences, business and economics, dental health, education, music, nursing, and public and environmental affairs. In addition to regional accreditation, IUSB has baccalaureate program accreditation with ADA, NCATE, and NLN. The library contains 303,203 volumes, 451,621 microform items, and 7524 audio/video tapes/CDs, and subscribes to 1713 periodicals. Computerized library services include the card catalog, interlibrary loans, and database searching. Special learning facilities include a learning resource center, art gallery, science labs, studios for fine and performing arts, instructional media services, and an academic resource center. The 80-acre campus is in a suburban area 90 miles east of Chicago. There are 57 buildings.

Student Life: 98% of undergraduates are from Indiana. Students are from 31 states, 71 foreign countries, and Canada. 85% are white. The average age of freshmen is 21; all undergraduates, 30. 30% do not continue beyond their first year.

Housing: There are no residence halls. There are on-campus apartments, off-campus apartments, and special housing for international students. All students commute. Alcohol is not permitted. No one may keep cars.

Activities: There are no fraternities. There are 52 groups on campus, including art, cheerleading, chorus, drama, ethnic, film, gay, honors, international, jazz band, literary magazine, musical theater, newspaper, opera, orchestra, pep band, political, professional, religious, social, social service, student government, and symphony. Popular campus events include Job Fair, club days, and new student welcome day.

Sports: There is 1 intercollegiate sport for men and 1 for women, and 7 intramural sports for men and 7 for women. Facilities include a running club for men and women.

Disabled Students: 95% of the campus is accessible. Wheelchair ramps, elevators, special parking, specially equipped rest rooms, special class scheduling, lowered drinking fountains, and lowered telephones are available.

Services: Counseling and information services are available, as is tutoring in every subject. There is remedial math, reading, and writing. Taped texts, note takers, and interpreters or transcription services are available.

Campus Safety and Security: Measures include 24-hour foot and vehicle patrol, security escort services, informal discussions, and pamphlets/posters/films. There are emergency telephones and lighted pathways/sidewalks.

Programs of Study: IUSB confers B.S., B.A., B.M., B.M.E., and B.S.Ed. degrees. Associate and master's degrees are also awarded. Bachelor's degrees are awarded in AGRICULTURE (environmental studies), BIOLOGICAL SCIENCE (biology/biological science), BUSINESS (accounting, banking and finance, business administration and management, human resources, labor studies, marketing/retailing/merchandising, and organizational behavior), COMMUNICATIONS AND THE ARTS (advertising, communications, dramatic arts, English, fine arts, French, German, journalism, music, music theory and composition, performing arts, piano/organ, public relations, Spanish, speech/debate/rhetoric, and voice), COMPUTER AND PHYSICAL SCIENCE (actuarial science, applied mathematics, chemistry, computer science, digital arts/technology, information sciences and systems, mathematics, and physics), EDUCATION (early childhood, elementary, English, mathematics, music, science, secondary, social studies, and special), ENGINEERING AND ENVIRONMENTAL DESIGN (industrial administration/management and preengineering), HEALTH PROFESSIONS (allied health, health care administration, nursing, predentistry, premedicine, preoptometry, prepharmacy, and preveterinary science), SOCIAL SCIENCE (applied psychology, counseling/psychology, criminal justice, economics, history, human services, liberal arts/general studies, philosophy, political science/government, prelaw, psychology, public administration, public affairs, social work, sociology, and women's studies). Accounting, management, and marketing are the strongest academically. Business, education, and liberal arts and sciences are the largest.

Required: All students must complete divisional requirements and general education and concentration courses, including English composition, fine arts, computer literacy, humanities, math, physical or biological science, and social science. A total of 120 to 123 semester hours, with a minimum GPA of 2.0, is required to graduate.

Special: Cross-registration with Northern Indiana Consortium for Education (NICE), internships, study abroad, accelerated degree programs, and dual majors are possible. There is a freshman honors program.

Faculty/Classroom: 53% of faculty are male; 47%, female. No introductory courses are taught by graduate students.

Admissions: The SAT I scores for the 2003-2004 freshman class were: Verbal--57% below 500, 34% between 500 and 599, and 9% between 600 and 700; Math--59% below 500, 34% between 500 and 599, and 7% between 600 and 700. The ACT scores were 54% below 21, 22% between 21 and 23, 11% between 24 and 26, 9% between 27 and 28, and 4% above 28. 16% of the current freshmen were in the top fifth of their class; 45% were in the top two fifths.

Requirements: The SAT I or ACT is required. In addition, applicants should have completed 13 units including 4 units in English, 3 in math, 2 in social sciences, and 1 in science. The GED equivalent with a minimum composite of 52 is accepted. An interview is recommended. CLEP credit is accepted. Important factors in the admissions decision are advanced placement or honor courses, extracurricular activities record, and leadership record.

Procedure: Freshmen are admitted to all sessions. Entrance exams should be taken 1 year to 6 months before entering the university. There is a deferred admissions plan. The deadline for filing freshman applications is July 1. The fall 2003 application fee was $40. Early decision notification is sent on a rolling basis.

Transfer: 398 transfer students enrolled in 2002-2003. A 2.0 GPA is required. College transcripts must be submitted. 30 of 120 credits required for the bachelor's degree must be completed at IUSB.

Visiting: There are regularly scheduled orientations for prospective students, including a visit to the admissions office, a campus tour, professor meetings, and information on financial aid. There are guides for informal visits and visitors may sit in on classes. To schedule a visit, contact the Admissions Office at (219) 237-4839.

Financial Aid: In 2003-2004, 45% of all full-time freshmen and 34% of continuing full-time students received some form of financial aid. At least 31% of full-time freshmen and at least 34% of continuing full-time students received need-based aid. The average freshman award was $4895. Need-based scholarships or need-based grants averaged $3448; need-based self-help aid (loans and jobs) averaged $2539; non-need-based athletic scholarships averaged $4300; and other non-need-based awards and non-need-based scholarships averaged $1298. The average financial indebtedness of the 2003 graduate was $16,334. The FAFSA and the college's own financial statement are required. The deadline for filing freshman financial aid applications for fall entry is March 1.

International Students: The school actively recruits these students. They must score 550 on the written TOEFL.

Computers: The mainframe can be accessed through computer labs and networks. More than 800 Macs and PCs are available for student use. Students have e-mail and web access, and can connect to the Indiana University statewide network, which includes IBM mainframes, VAX clusters, and on-line library services. All students may access the system 7 days a week. There are no time limits. The fee is $300.

Graduates: From July 1, 2002 to June 30, 2003, 542 bachelor's degrees were awarded. The most popular majors were education (24%), business/marketing (19%), and liberal arts/general studies (13%). In an average class, 7% graduate in 4 years or less, 11% graduate in 5 years or less, and 6% graduate in 6 years or less.

Admissions Contact: Jeff Johnston, Director of Admissions.
E-mail: *admissio@iusb.edu* Web: *www.iusb.edu/~admissio/*

INDIANA UNIVERSITY SOUTHEAST
New Albany, IN 47150

C-5
(812) 941-2212
(800) 852-8835; Fax: (812) 941-2595

Full-time: 1168 men, 1942 women	Faculty: 182; IIA, -$
Part-time: 827 men, 1372 women	Ph.D.s: 72%
Graduate: 249 men, 440 women	Student/Faculty: 17 to 1
Year: semesters, summer session	Tuition: $4504 ($10,454)
Application Deadline: July 15	Room & Board: n/app
Freshman Class: n/av	
SAT I Verbal/Math: 470/470	ACT: 19 LESS COMPETITIVE

Indiana University Southeast, established in 1941, is a state-supported institution, part of the Indiana University system, and offers undergraduate and graduate programs in humanities, social sciences, natural sciences, business and economics, education, general studies, and nursing. In addition to regional accreditation, IUS has baccalaureate program accreditation with AACSB, NCATE, and NLN. The library contains 223,181 volumes, 356,077 microform items, and 9497 audio/video tapes/CDs, and subscribes to 951 periodicals. Computerized library services include the card catalog, interlibrary loans, and database searching. Special learning facilities include an art gallery. The 177-acre campus is in a suburban area 7 miles northwest of Louisville, Kentucky, and 114 miles south of Indianapolis. There are 20 buildings.

Student Life: 81% of undergraduates are from Indiana. Students are from 9 states, 26 foreign countries, and Canada. 91% are white. The av-

erage age of freshmen is 29; all undergraduates, 30. 33% do not continue beyond their first year.

Housing: There are no residence halls. All students commute. Alcohol is not permitted.

Activities: There are 2 national fraternities and 4 national sororities. There are 50 groups on campus, including academic, art, band, cheerleading, choir, chorus, computers, drama, ethnic, film, gay, honors, literary magazine, newspaper, orchestra, political, religious, social, special-interest, student government, and yearbook.

Sports: There are 4 intercollegiate sports for men and 4 for women, and 5 intramural sports for men and 5 for women. Facilities include a 1600-seat activities building with a basketball court, facilities for jogging, badminton, volleyball, weightlifting, and gymnastics, 6 tennis courts, baseball and softball fields, and playing fields.

Disabled Students: All of the campus is accessible. Wheelchair ramps, elevators, special parking, specially equipped rest rooms, lowered drinking fountains, lowered telephones, and special accommodations as needed are available.

Services: Counseling and information services are available, as is tutoring in every subject. There is a reader service for the blind, and remedial math, reading, and writing. The coordinator for services to students with disabilities provides information and coordination of needed services.

Campus Safety and Security: Measures include 24-hour foot and vehicle patrol, self-defense education, pamphlets/posters/films, and emergency telephones. There are lighted pathways/sidewalks and a police department on campus.

Programs of Study: IUS confers B.A., B.S., and B.G.S. degrees. Associate and master's degrees are also awarded. Bachelor's degrees are awarded in BIOLOGICAL SCIENCE (biology/biological science), BUSINESS (accounting, banking and finance, business administration and management, business economics, management science, marketing/retailing/merchandising, and organizational behavior), COMMUNICATIONS AND THE ARTS (communications, English, fine arts, French, German, journalism, music, and Spanish), COMPUTER AND PHYSICAL SCIENCE (chemistry, computer science, and mathematics), EDUCATION (elementary, English, mathematics, secondary, social studies, and special), HEALTH PROFESSIONS (clinical science, medical technology, and nursing), SOCIAL SCIENCE (criminal justice, economics, geography, history, liberal arts/general studies, philosophy, political science/government, psychology, and sociology). Education, business, and continuing studies are the largest.

Required: Students must complete 120 credit hours, with 30 in upper-level courses and at least 25 in the major, and must maintain a minimum cumulative GPA of 2.0. In addition, all students must complete a core curriculum that includes courses in English composition, math, computer literacy, arts and humanities, and social and natural sciences.

Special: Cross-registration with Metroversity is possible, and opportunities are provided for study abroad, internships, work-study programs, dual majors, a general studies degree, credit by examination, nondegree study, accelerated degree programs, and pass/fail options.

Faculty/Classroom: 51% of faculty are male; 49%, female.

Admissions: The SAT I scores for the 2003-2004 freshman class were: Verbal--62% below 500, 30% between 500 and 599, and 7% between 600 and 700; Math--6% between 600 and 700. The ACT scores were 66% below 21, 22% between 21 and 23, 9% between 24 and 26, 2% between 27 and 28, and 1% above 28. 17% of the current freshmen were in the top fifth of their class; 49% were in the top two fifths.

Requirements: The SAT I or ACT is required. Minimum composite scores are 400 verbal and 400 math on the SAT I or 19 on the ACT. These requirements are waived if the applicant has been out of high school for 3 or more years. Graduation from an accredited secondary school is required; the GED is accepted. Applicants must have completed 14 academic units, including 4 in English, 3 in math, 2 in social studies, 1 in lab science, and 4 academic electives. 2 units in foreign language are recommended. AP and CLEP credits are accepted.

Procedure: Freshmen are admitted to all sessions. Entrance exams should be taken during high school. There are early admissions and deferred admissions plans. There is a rolling admissions plan. Applications should be filed by July 15 for fall entry, December 1 for spring entry, and April 15 for summer entry. Notification is sent on a rolling basis.

Transfer: 347 transfer students enrolled in 2002-2003. A GPA of 2.0 is required for Indiana residents, 2.5 for out-of-state applicants. If the student has fewer than 26 transferable semester hours, the high school record should reflect compliance with freshman admission requirements. 30 of 120 credits required for the bachelor's degree must be completed at IUS.

Visiting: There are regularly scheduled orientations for prospective students, including an opportunity for students to apply for admission, financial aid, and scholarships, a faculty perspective, a student perspective, and a campus tour. There are guides for informal visits and visitors may sit in on classes. To schedule a visit, contact the Office of Admissions.

Financial Aid: In 2003-2004, 41% of all full-time freshmen and 43% of continuing full-time students received some form of financial aid. At least 29% of full-time freshmen and 31% of continuing full-time students received need-based aid. The average freshman award was $5023. Need-based scholarships or need-based grants averaged $4202; need-based self-help aid (loans and jobs) averaged $2257; non-need-based athletic scholarships averaged $827; and other non-need-based awards and non-need-based scholarships averaged $1744. The average financial indebtedness of the 2003 graduate was $12,973. The FAFSA and the college's own financial statement are required. The deadline for filing freshman financial aid applications for fall entry is March 1.

International Students: There are 32 international students enrolled. They must score 550 on the written TOEFL.

Computers: All students have access to the Indiana University Computing Network, notably, the DEC VAX and IBM 3090 series computers. There is a local area network with several general and specialized computing applications on PCs and Macs. There are no time limits. The fee is $288.

Graduates: From July 1, 2002 to June 30, 2003, 603 bachelor's degrees were awarded. The most popular majors were education (28%), business/marketing (20%), and liberal arts (19%). In an average class, 9% graduate in 4 years or less, 15% graduate in 5 years or less, and 6% graduate in 6 years or less.

Admissions Contact: David B. Campbell, Director of Admissions. E-mail: *admissions@ius.edu* Web: *www.ius.edu/Admissions*

INDIANA UNIVERSITY-PURDUE UNIVERSITY FORT WAYNE
D-2

Fort Wayne, IN 46805-1499

(260) 481-6812
(800) 324-4739; Fax: (260) 481-6880

Full-time: 2719 men, 3605 women	**Faculty:** 360; IIA, -$
Part-time: 1912 men, 2832 women	**Ph.D.s:** 90%
Graduate: 295 men, 443 women	**Student/Faculty:** 18 to 1
Year: semesters, summer session	**Tuition:** $5108 ($11,556)
Application Deadline: August 1	**Room & Board:** n/app
Freshman Class: 2486 applied, 2402 accepted, 1643 enrolled	
SAT I Verbal/Math: 479/482	**ACT:** 20 **LESS COMPETITIVE**

In 1964, Indiana University at Fort Wayne, founded in 1917, joined Purdue University at Fort Wayne, founded in 1944. The combined school, a state-controlled institution, offers programs in liberal arts, science, business, education, health sciences, engineering, technology, and public affairs. There are 9 undergraduate and 5 graduate schools. In addition to regional accreditation, IPFW has baccalaureate program accreditation with AACSB, ABET, NASM, NCATE, and NLN. The library contains 460,988 volumes, 538,169 microform items, and 7449 audio/video tapes/CDs, and subscribes to 2766 periodicals. Computerized library services include the card catalog, interlibrary loans, and database searching. Special learning facilities include a learning resource center, art gallery, and TV station. The 565-acre campus is in a suburban area 113 miles north of Indianapolis. There are 11 buildings.

Student Life: 94% of undergraduates are from Indiana. Others are from 40 states, 73 foreign countries, and Canada. 80% are from public schools. 88% are white. The average age of freshmen is 24; all undergraduates, 25. 34% do not continue beyond their first year.

Housing: There are no residence halls. All students commute. Alcohol is not permitted. No one may keep cars.

Activities: 1% of men belong to 2 local fraternities; 1% of women belong to 2 local sororities. There are 61 groups on campus, including art, ASID, cheerleading, choir, dance, debate, drama, ethnic, forensics, gay, honors, international, literary magazine, musical theater, newspaper, pep band, political, professional, radio and TV, religious, social, social service, Society of Women Engineers, and student government. Popular campus events include Mastodon Stomp and Mastodon Roast.

Sports: There are 7 intercollegiate sports for men and 7 for women, and 11 intramural sports for men and 9 for women. Facilities include a physical fitness center with a gym, 3 basketball courts, an indoor track, a weight room, 4 racquetball courts, 1 Wallyball court, a fencing and dance room, baseball and soccer fields, and an indoor soccer facility.

Disabled Students: All of the campus is accessible. Wheelchair ramps, elevators, special parking, specially equipped rest rooms, lowered drinking fountains, and lowered telephones are available.

Services: Counseling and information services are available, as is tutoring in most subjects. There is a reader service for the blind, and remedial math, reading, and writing.

Campus Safety and Security: Measures include 24-hour foot and vehicle patrol, self-defense education, security escort services, and pamphlets/posters/films. There are emergency telephones and lighted pathways/sidewalks.

Programs of Study: IPFW confers B.A., B.S., B.C.L.S., B.F.A., B.G.S., B.M.T.P., B.Mus., B.Mus.Ed., B.S.B., B.S.C., B.S.E., B.S.Ed., B.S.E.E., B.S.G., B.S.H.M., B.S.L.S., B.S.M.E., and B.S.P.A. degrees. Associate and master's degrees are also awarded. Bachelor's degrees are awarded in BIOLOGICAL SCIENCE (biology/biological science), BUSINESS (accounting, banking and finance, business economics, hospitality manage-

ment services, management science, and marketing/retailing/merchandising), COMMUNICATIONS AND THE ARTS (broadcasting, communications, dramatic arts, English, fine arts, French, German, Spanish, speech/debate/rhetoric, and telecommunications), COMPUTER AND PHYSICAL SCIENCE (chemistry, computer programming, computer science, earth science, geology, information sciences and systems, mathematics, and physics), EDUCATION (art, elementary, foreign languages, music, science, and secondary), ENGINEERING AND ENVIRONMENTAL DESIGN (electrical/electronics engineering, engineering, engineering technology, industrial engineering technology, and mechanical engineering), HEALTH PROFESSIONS (health care administration, music therapy, nursing, predentistry, premedicine, and speech pathology/audiology), SOCIAL SCIENCE (anthropology, criminal justice, economics, history, human services, liberal arts/general studies, philosophy, political science/government, prelaw, psychology, public administration, social science, sociology, and women's studies). Engineering is the strongest academically. Business and education are the largest.

Required: All bachelor's degree students must complete 120 credits, including 36 general education hours, with a GPA of 2.0, and take English composition, speech communication, and math to graduate.

Special: There are continuing education, co-op, and work-study programs, as well as study abroad in France, Spain, Austria, and Germany. An accelerated general studies degree, cross-registration with other Fort Wayne colleges, B.A.-B.S. degrees, dual majors, a Washington semester for Public Affairs students, internships, and credit for military experience are available. Nondegree study and pass/fail options are possible. There are 6 national honor societies and a freshman honors program.

Faculty/Classroom: 63% of faculty are male; 37%, female. All teach undergraduates, 92% do research, and 92% do both. The average class size in an introductory lecture is 28; in a laboratory, 21; and in a regular course, 27.

Admissions: 97% of the 2003-2004 applicants were accepted. The SAT I scores for the 2003-2004 freshman class were: Verbal--60% below 500, 31% between 500 and 599, 8% between 600 and 700, and 1% above 700; Math--58% below 500, 32% between 500 and 599, 9% between 600 and 700, and 1% above 700. The ACT scores were 55% below 21, 24% between 21 and 23, 15% between 24 and 26, 4% between 27 and 28, and 2% above 28. 21% of the current freshmen were in the top fifth of their class; 50% were in the top two fifths. 1 freshman graduated first in the class.

Requirements: The SAT I is required and the ACT is recommended with a minimum composite score of 950 on the SAT I. Applicants should have 20 academic credits, including 4 years of English, 3 years of math, and 3 years combination of science, social studies, and foreign language. The GED is accepted. An interview is recommended. AP and CLEP credits are accepted. Important factors in the admissions decision are recommendations by school officials, evidence of special talent, and advanced placement or honor courses.

Procedure: Freshmen are admitted fall, spring, and summer. Entrance exams should be taken in the senior year of high school. Applications should be filed by August 1 for fall entry, December 15 for spring entry, and May 1 for summer entry, along with a $30 fee. There is a rolling admissions plan and notification is sent on a rolling basis. Applications are accepted on-line through *http://www.ipfw.edu/admiss*.

Transfer: 854 transfer students enrolled in 2003-2004. Transfer applicants must have a minimum GPA of 2.0. Grades of C or better transfer for credit. 32 of 120 credits required for the bachelor's degree must be completed at IPFW.

Visiting: There are regularly scheduled orientations for prospective students. There are guides for informal visits and visitors may sit in on classes. To schedule a visit, contact the Admissions Office.

Financial Aid: In 2003-2004, 47% of all full-time freshmen and 48% of continuing full-time students received some form of financial aid. 29% of full-time freshmen and 32% of continuing full-time students received need-based aid. The average freshman award was $4850. Need-based scholarships or need-based grants averaged $3594 ($9347 maximum); need-based self-help aid (loans and jobs) averaged $2191 ($5239 maximum); non-need-based athletic scholarships averaged $2260 ($7602 maximum); and other non-need-based awards and non-need-based scholarships averaged $986 ($5300 maximum). 2% of undergraduates work part time. Average annual earnings from campus work are $2000. The average financial indebtedness of the 2003 graduate was $15,017. IPFW is a member of CSS. The FAFSA is required. The deadline for filing freshman financial aid applications for fall entry is March 1.

International Students: There are 131 international students enrolled. The school actively recruits these students. They must score 550 on the written TOEFL or 213 on the electronic version or take the MELAB. Students must have an SAT I verbal score of 480 or above (combined score of 750), pass level 109 of an ESL program, or receive a "B" at 0 level of G.C.E. The ACT may be substituted.

Computers: The mainframe is an IBM 9672-R21. 278 networked PCs are available in various labs; 30 e-mail kiosks are in lobbies of various buildings. All students may access the system, but they must activate an account first. There are no time limits and no fees.

Graduates: From July 1, 2002 to June 30, 2003, 854 bachelor's degrees were awarded. The most popular majors were general studies (8%), education (8%), and nursing (7%). In an average class, 5% graduate in 4 years or less, 10% graduate in 5 years or less, and 21% graduate in 6 years or less. 110 companies recruited on campus in 2002-2003.

Admissions Contact: Carol Isaacs, Director of Admissions.
E-mail: *ipfwadms@ipfw.edu* Web: *www.ipfw.edu*

INDIANA UNIVERSITY-PURDUE UNIVERSITY INDIANAPOLIS

C-3

Indianapolis, IN 46202-5143

(317) 274-4591
Fax: (317) 278-1862

Full-time: 5477 men, 7894 women	Faculty: IIA, +$
Part-time: 3307 men, 4710 women	Ph.D.s: 84%
Graduate: 2450 men, 3588 women	Student/Faculty: n/av
Year: semesters, summer session	Tuition: $5703 ($14,886)
Application Deadline: open	Room & Board: $2554
Freshman Class: n/av	
SAT I Verbal/Math: 490/490	ACT: 20 LESS COMPETITIVE

The Indianapolis campus, founded in 1946, has offered undergraduate and graduate instruction under the auspices of both Purdue and Indiana Universities since 1969. The state-controlled institution serves a primarily commuter student body and offers degree programs in the arts and sciences, business, education, engineering and technology, health science, religious studies, and professional training. In addition to regional accreditation, IUPUI has baccalaureate program accreditation with AAC-SB, ABET, ACCE, ACEJMC, ADA, APTA, CAHEA, CSWE, NASAD, NASM, NCATE, and NLN. The 4 libraries contain 1,592,144 volumes, 2,461,513 microform items, and 1591 audio/video tapes/CDs, and subscribe to 10,159 periodicals. Computerized library services include the card catalog and database searching. Special learning facilities include an art gallery, an 85-acre medical center, and an electronic classroom. The 513-acre campus is in an urban area near downtown Indianapolis. Including any residence halls, there are 100 buildings.

Student Life: 97% of undergraduates are from Indiana. Students are from 45 states, 116 foreign countries, and Canada. 82% are white; 10% African American. The average age of freshmen is 21; all undergraduates, 23. 33% do not continue beyond their first year.

Housing: 350 students can be accommodated in college housing, which includes coed dorms, on-campus apartments, off-campus apartments, and married-student housing. In addition, there are special-interest houses. On-campus housing is available on a first-come, first-served basis. 99% of students commute. Alcohol is not permitted. All students may keep cars.

Activities: 1% of men belong to 3 national fraternities; 1% of women belong to 2 national sororities. There are 200 groups on campus, including cheerleading, chorale, chorus, dance, debate, drama, ethnic, gay, honors, international, jazz band, literary magazine, newspaper, opera, pep band, political, professional, radio and TV, religious, social, social service, student government, and yearbook. Popular campus events include Career Day and Activities Fair.

Sports: There are 6 intercollegiate sports for men and 8 for women. Facilities include a 12,000-seat track-and-field stadium, a 3-pool natatorium, softball fields, a tennis center, and the National Institute for Fitness and Sport.

Disabled Students: All of the campus is accessible. Wheelchair ramps, elevators, special parking, specially equipped rest rooms, special class scheduling, lowered drinking fountains, lowered telephones, classroom aids, and sign language interpreters are available.

Services: Counseling and information services are available, as is tutoring in most subjects. There is a reader service for the blind, and remedial math, reading, and writing.

Campus Safety and Security: Measures include 24-hour foot and vehicle patrol, self-defense education, security escort services, and shuttle buses. There are informal discussions, pamphlets/posters/films, emergency telephones, and lighted pathways/sidewalks.

Programs of Study: IUPUI confers B.A., B.S., B.A.E., B.F.A., B.G.S., B.S.E., B.S.E.E., B.S.M.E., and B.S.W. degrees. Associate, master's, and doctoral degrees are also awarded. Bachelor's degrees are awarded in BIOLOGICAL SCIENCE (biology/biological science), BUSINESS (accounting, banking and finance, business administration and management, business economics, human resources, labor studies, marketing and distribution, marketing/retailing/merchandising, office supervision and management, and tourism), COMMUNICATIONS AND THE ARTS (American Sign Language, art history and appreciation, ceramic art and design, communications, English, fine arts, French, German, journalism, media arts, painting, photography, printmaking, sculpture, and Spanish), COMPUTER AND PHYSICAL SCIENCE (chemistry, computer science, geology, information sciences and systems, mathematics, and physics), EDUCATION (art, drama, elementary, English, foreign languages, health, mathematics, physical, science, secondary, and social studies), ENGINEERING AND ENVIRONMENTAL DESIGN (biomedical engineering, computer engineering, computer graphics, computer technolo-

gy, construction technology, electrical/electronics engineering, electrical/electronics engineering technology, engineering, furniture design, manufacturing technology, mechanical engineering, and mechanical engineering technology), HEALTH PROFESSIONS (clinical science, cytotechnology, dental hygiene, health care administration, medical laboratory technology, nuclear medical technology, nursing, physical therapy, predentistry, premedicine, preoptometry, preosteopathy, prepharmacy, preveterinary science, public health, radiation therapy, and respiratory therapy), SOCIAL SCIENCE (anthropology, criminal justice, economics, geography, history, international studies, liberal arts/general studies, philosophy, political science/government, prelaw, psychology, public affairs, religion, social work, and sociology). Engineering and technology, nursing, and education are the largest.

Required: All students must complete courses in computer, humanities, math, science, and social science toward the 122 to 126 credits required for the bachelor's degree.

Special: There is a metropolitan studies program for career work in the city and cross-registration with the Consortium for Urban Education. IUPUI also offers study abroad, combined B.A.-B.S. degree programs, internships, work-study programs, dual majors, student-designed majors, nondegree study, nontraditional programs for adult learners, and interdisciplinary majors such as business economics and public policy, health occupations education, and interdisciplinary engineering. There is a freshman honors program.

Faculty/Classroom: 61% of faculty are male; 39%, female.

Admissions: The SAT I scores for the 2003-2004 freshman class were: Verbal--52% below 500, 38% between 500 and 599, 9% between 600 and 700, and 1% above 700; Math--53% below 500, 35% between 500 and 599, 11% between 600 and 700, and 1% above 700. The ACT scores were 52% below 21, 28% between 21 and 23, 13% between 24 and 26, 4% between 27 and 28, and 3% above 28. 24% of the current freshmen were in the top fifth of their class; 55% were in the top two fifths.

Requirements: The SAT I or ACT is required for recent high school graduates. The SAT I is preferred. Applicants should be graduates of an accredited high school, rank in the upper half of their class, and have completed 14 Carnegie units, including 4 in English, 3 in math, 2 in social studies, and 1 in lab science. 2 units of a foreign language are recommended. The GED is accepted. The university accepts applications on computer disk. AP and CLEP credits are accepted.

Procedure: Freshmen are admitted to all sessions. Entrance exams should be taken by the end of junior year or fall of senior year. There are early admissions and deferred admissions plans. Application deadlines are open. The fall 2003 application fee was $45. Notification is sent on a rolling basis.

Transfer: 1534 transfer students enrolled in 2002-2003. Transfers who are Indiana residents must present a minimum GPA of 2.0 in all previous college work; out-of-state residents need a minimum 2.5. All applicants must be in good standing at their former schools. 30 of 122 credits required for the bachelor's degree must be completed at IUPUI.

Visiting: There are regularly scheduled orientations for prospective students, consisting of a campus tour and talks with students. There are guides for informal visits and visitors may sit in on classes. To schedule a visit, contact the Enrollment Center.

Financial Aid: In 2003-2004, 51% of all full-time freshmen and 52% of continuing full-time students received some form of financial aid. At least 32% of full-time freshmen and at least 35% of continuing full-time students received need-based aid. The average freshman award was $6074. Need-based scholarships or need-based grants averaged $4984; need-based self-help aid (loans and jobs) averaged $2486; non-need-based institutional athletic scholarships averaged $2822; and other institutional non-need-based awards and non-need-based scholarships averaged $2088. The average financial indebtedness of the 2003 graduate was $19,660. The FAFSA is required. The deadline for filing freshman financial aid applications for fall entry is March 1.

International Students: There are 434 international students enrolled. They must score 550 on the written TOEFL.

Computers: PCs are available for all students. All students may access the system up to 24 hours a day in some clusters. There are no time limits. The fee is $354.

Graduates: From July 1, 2002 to June 30, 2003, 2430 bachelor's degrees were awarded. The most popular majors were business/marketing (17%), health professions (16%), and liberal arts (16%). In an average class, 5% graduate in 4 years or less, 10% graduate in 5 years or less, and 6% graduate in 6 years or less.

Admissions Contact: Mike Donahue, Director of Admissions.
E-mail: *apply@iupui.edu* Web: *www.enroll.iupui.edu/*

INDIANA WESLEYAN UNIVERSITY
Marion, IN 46953-4974

C-2

(765) 677-2138
(800) 332-6901; Fax: (765) 677-2333

Full-time: 902 men, 1389 women	Faculty: 113
Part-time: 88 men, 126 women	Ph.Ds: 55%
Graduate: 990 men, 1220 women	Student/Faculty: 20 to 1
Year: semesters, summer session	Tuition: $14,420
Application Deadline: August 1	Room & Board: $5480
Freshman Class: 1540 applied, 1439 accepted, 715 enrolled	
SAT I Verbal/Math: 545/540	ACT: 24	COMPETITIVE+

Indiana Wesleyan University, founded in 1920, is a private institution affiliated with the Methodist Church. The university offers undergraduate programs in the arts and sciences, business, education, fine arts, nursing, professional training, and religious studies. There are 2 undergraduate schools and 1 graduate school. In addition to regional accreditation, IWU has baccalaureate program accreditation with CAHEA, CCNE, CSWE, and NLN. The library contains 118,719 volumes, 184,731 microform items, and 9529 audio/video tapes/CDs, and subscribes to 659 periodicals. Computerized library services include the card catalog, interlibrary loans, database searching, and Internet access. Special learning facilities include a learning resource center, art gallery, radio station, and TV station. The 281-acre campus is in an urban area 60 miles north of Indianapolis. Including any residence halls, there are 29 buildings.

Student Life: 60% of undergraduates are from Indiana. Students are from 43 states, 14 foreign countries, and Canada. 22% are from public schools. 98% are white. Most are Protestant. The average age of freshmen is 18. 21% do not continue beyond their first year; 22% remain to graduate.

Housing: 1919 students can be accommodated in college housing, which includes single-sex dorms and on-campus apartments. On-campus housing is guaranteed for all 4 years. 77% of students live on campus; of those, 50% remain on campus on weekends. Alcohol is not permitted. All students may keep cars.

Activities: There are no fraternities or sororities. There are 31 groups on campus, including art, cheerleading, choir, chorale, chorus, drama, film, honors, international, jazz band, literary magazine, newspaper, orchestra, pep band, photography, political, professional, radio and TV, religious, social service, student government, symphony, and yearbook. Popular campus events include Campus Visit Days and "Friday Night Live" comedy event.

Sports: There are 7 intercollegiate sports for men and 7 for women, and 21 intramural sports for men and 21 for women. Facilities include a gym, racquetball courts, a weight room, and a 65-acre outdoor athletic complex featuring a world-class track.

Disabled Students: All of the campus is accessible. Wheelchair ramps, elevators, special parking, specially equipped rest rooms, special class scheduling, lowered drinking fountains, lowered telephones, special housing, amplified telephones, and TTY are available.

Services: Counseling and information services are available, as is tutoring in most subjects. There is a reader service for the blind, remedial reading and writing, external testing, a note-taker service, and advocacy.

Campus Safety and Security: Measures include 24-hour foot and vehicle patrol, self-defense education, security escort services, and pamphlets/posters/films. There are emergency telephones and lighted pathways/sidewalks.

Programs of Study: IWU confers B.A. and B.S. degrees. Associate, master's, and doctoral degrees are also awarded. Bachelor's degrees are awarded in BIOLOGICAL SCIENCE (biology/biological science), BUSINESS (accounting, business administration and management, marketing/retailing/merchandising, and recreational facilities management), COMMUNICATIONS AND THE ARTS (art, communications, creative writing, English, music, Spanish, and studio art), COMPUTER AND PHYSICAL SCIENCE (chemistry, mathematics, and science), EDUCATION (art, elementary, English, music, nursing, physical, science, and social studies), HEALTH PROFESSIONS (medical laboratory technology and premedicine), SOCIAL SCIENCE (biblical studies, criminal justice, economics, history, ministries, political science/government, psychology, religion, religious music, social studies, social work, and sociology). Nursing, education, and religion are the strongest academically and have the largest enrollments.

Required: Students must attend chapel services 3 times a week. General education requirements include 12 credit hours of humanities, 10 of math and science, 9 each of English and history or social studies, 6 of biblical literature, and 3 each of intercultural experience and phys ed. Foreign language courses are required for the B.A., computer literacy courses for the B.S. To graduate, students must complete at least 124 semester hours, including 40 to 60 in a major field of study, with a minimum GPA of 2.0 overall and 2.25 in the major. A thesis is required for the honors college.

Special: Students may study abroad in 20 countries. IWU also offers business, pastoral, nursing, and social work internships, cross-registration with CCCU, a Washington semester, work-study programs with the Economic Growth Council, pass/fail options, and nondegree study. Accelerated degree programs are available in accounting, business administration, business information, management, and nursing. Students may earn a B.A.-B.S. degree in management, business, and education. Dual majors and student-designed majors are available. Adult learners may earn credit for life experience toward bachelor's degrees in business through the APS program. There are 2 national honor societies, a freshman honors program, and 2 departmental honors programs.

Faculty/Classroom: 64% of faculty are male; 36%, female. 98% teach undergraduates and 2% do research. The average class size in an introductory lecture is 30; in a laboratory, 15; and in a regular course, 22.

Admissions: 93% of the 2003-2004 applicants were accepted. The SAT I scores for the 2003-2004 freshman class were: Verbal--28% below 500, 43% between 500 and 599, 25% between 600 and 700, and 4% above 700; Math--32% below 500, 40% between 500 and 599, 25% between 600 and 700, and 4% above 700. The ACT scores were 13% below 20, 18% between 20 and 22, 30% between 23 and 25, 24% between 26 and 28, and 15% above 28. 25% of the current freshmen were in the top fifth of their class; 50% were in the top two fifths. There were 8 National Merit finalists. 20 freshmen graduated first in their class.

Requirements: The SAT I or ACT is required. In addition, applicants should be graduates of accredited secondary schools or have earned a GED. The university requires 10 units of college preparatory study that includes courses in English, science, social science, math, and foreign language. Recommendations are also required. A GPA of 2.0 is required. AP and CLEP credits are accepted.

Procedure: Freshmen are admitted to all sessions. Entrance exams should be taken in the junior year or early in the senior year. There are early admissions and deferred admissions plans. Applications should be filed by August 1 for fall entry. The fall 2003 application fee was $25. Notification is sent on a rolling basis. 171 applicants were on the 2003 waiting list. Applications are accepted on-line through www.indwes.edu.

Transfer: In addition to standard admissions requirements, transfers must submit transcripts of all previous college work and be in good standing at their former school. 60 of 124 credits required for the bachelor's degree must be completed at IWU.

Visiting: There are regularly scheduled orientations for prospective students, including appointments with admissions counselors and professors, campus tours, classroom visits, and meals. There are guides for informal visits and visitors may sit in on classes and stay overnight. To schedule a visit, contact the Admissions Office.

Financial Aid: In 2003-2004, 96% of all full-time freshmen and 85% of continuing full-time students received some form of financial aid. 66% of full-time freshmen received need-based aid. The FAFSA and the college's own financial statement are required. The deadline for filing freshman financial aid applications for fall entry is March 1.

International Students: There are 26 international students enrolled. The school actively recruits these students. They must score 550 on the written TOEFL and also take the college's own test and the SAT I or the ACT.

Computers: The mainframe is an HPL 2000. Students can access the system through computer labs on campus or from residence hall rooms. There are approximately 26 computer labs (general access and specific) on campus for a total of 380 computers. All students may access the system from 8 A.M. to 10 P.M.

Graduates: From July 1, 2002 to June 30, 2003, 326 bachelor's degrees were awarded. The most popular majors were education (24%), behavorial sciences (14%), and business (11%).

Admissions Contact: Dr. John S. Grady, Vice President for Enrollment Management. A video is available.
E-mail: admissions@indwes.edu Web: www.indwes.edu

MANCHESTER COLLEGE
North Manchester, IN 46962-0365

C-2

(260) 982-5055
(800) 852-3648; Fax: (260) 982-5239

Full-time: 499 men, 598 women	Faculty: 68; IIB, -$
Part-time: 5 men, 12 women	Ph.Ds: 93%
Graduate: 7 men, 10 women	Student/Faculty: 16 to 1
Year: 4-1-4, summer session	Tuition: $17,050
Application Deadline: open	Room & Board: $6340
Freshman Class: 1086 applied, 854 accepted, 335 enrolled	
SAT I Verbal/Math: 504/511	ACT: 22	COMPETITIVE

Manchester College, established in 1889, is a private liberal arts college affiliated with the Church of the Brethren offering undergraduate and graduate major programs in accounting, business and economics, premedicine, education, psychology, the social sciences, and the humanities. In addition to regional accreditation, Manchester has baccalaureate program accreditation with CSWE and NCATE. The library contains 174,078 volumes, 23,014 microform items, and 5258 audio/video tapes/CDs, and subscribes to 973 periodicals. Computerized library services include the card catalog, interlibrary loans, database searching, and Internet access. Special learning facilities include a learning resource center, planetarium, radio station, and a 100-acre nature preserve. The 124-

acre campus is in a small town 35 miles west of Fort Wayne in northeastern Indiana. Including any residence halls, there are 44 buildings.

Student Life: 83% of undergraduates are from Indiana. Students are from 29 states, 33 foreign countries, and Canada. 99% are from public schools. 87% are white. 61% are Protestant; 20% claim no religious affiliation; 12% Catholic; 7% , includes Muslim and unknown. The average age of freshmen is 18; all undergraduates, 20. 25% do not continue beyond their first year; 55% remain to graduate.

Housing: 979 students can be accommodated in college housing, which includes single-sex and coed dorms, on-campus apartments, off-campus apartments, and married-student housing. In addition, there are special-interest houses and theme units for students interested in science, health, and international issues located within the residence hall system. On-campus housing is guaranteed for all 4 years. 77% of students live on campus; of those, 50% remain on campus on weekends. Alcohol is not permitted. All students may keep cars.

Activities: There are no fraternities or sororities. There are 55 groups on campus, including band, cheerleading, choir, chorale, chorus, computers, dance, drama, ethnic, gay, honors, international, jazz band, literary magazine, musical theater, newspaper, orchestra, pep band, photography, political, professional, radio and TV, religious, social, social service, student government, symphony, and yearbook. Popular campus events include Parents Weekend, Sibling Weekend, and International Fair.

Sports: There are 9 intercollegiate sports for men and 8 for women, and 13 intramural sports for men and 12 for women. Facilities include a phys ed and recreation center with an 1800-seat gym, racquetball courts, and a fitness center; tennis courts; a cross-country and an all-weather track; and athletic fields for baseball, softball, soccer, and football.

Disabled Students: 20% of the campus is accessible. Wheelchair ramps, elevators, special parking, specially equipped rest rooms, special class scheduling, lowered drinking fountains, and lowered telephones are available.

Services: Counseling and information services are available, as is tutoring in every subject. There is a reader service for the blind. There is also a learning center with an academic assistance program, and a seminar to enhance study and learning skills and time and project management.

Campus Safety and Security: Measures include 24-hour foot and vehicle patrol, security escort services, informal discussions, and pamphlets/posters/films. There are emergency telephones and lighted pathways/sidewalks.

Programs of Study: Manchester confers B.A. and B.S. degrees. Associate and master's degrees are also awarded. Bachelor's degrees are awarded in BIOLOGICAL SCIENCE (biochemistry and biology/biological science), BUSINESS (accounting, banking and finance, and business administration and management), COMMUNICATIONS AND THE ARTS (art, communications, English, French, German, music, and Spanish), COMPUTER AND PHYSICAL SCIENCE (chemistry, computer science, mathematics, and physics), EDUCATION (art, elementary, health, middle school, and secondary), ENGINEERING AND ENVIRONMENTAL DESIGN (engineering), HEALTH PROFESSIONS (medical laboratory technology), SOCIAL SCIENCE (economics, history, interdisciplinary studies, peace studies, philosophy, political science/government, prelaw, psychology, religion, social work, and sociology). Education, accounting, and biology-chemistry are the strongest academically. Education, accounting, and communication studies are the largest.

Required: Students must complete a general studies curriculum, including requirements in humanities, social sciences, and natural sciences, as well as specific courses in English composition, public communication, Western civilization, and physical fitness. In order to graduate, students must complete a minimum of 128 semester hours, including 26 to 52 hours in a major field, with a GPA of at least 2.0 (2.5 for the education major). A comprehensive exam in the major is also required. A thesis for honors students is optional.

Special: The college offers cooperative programs in nursing and engineering science. The Brethren Colleges Abroad program allows study abroad in 12 countries, including Ecuador, China, England, France, Germany, Japan, Mexico, and Spain. Manchester also offers B.A.-B.S. degrees, internships, work-study programs, dual majors, student-designed majors, a 3-2 engineering program, pass/fail options, and nondegree study. Other special academic features include independent study, required study in non-Western culture, and interdisciplinary programs in both peace studies and environmental studies. A January interterm permits internships, travel abroad, and concentrated classes on campus. There are 6 national honor societies, a freshman honors program, and 5 departmental honors programs.

Faculty/Classroom: 63% of faculty are male; 37%, female. All teach undergraduates. No introductory courses are taught by graduate students. The average class size in an introductory lecture is 30; in a laboratory, 15; and in a regular course, 20.

Admissions: 79% of the 2003-2004 applicants were accepted. The SAT I scores for the 2003-2004 freshman class were: Verbal--44% below 500, 38% between 500 and 599, 16% between 600 and 700, and 2% above 700; Math--49% below 500, 37% between 500 and 599, 13% between 600 and 700, and 1% above 700. The ACT scores were 38% below 21, 23% between 21 and 23, 23% between 24 and 26, 12% between 27 and 28, and 4% above 28. 40% of the current freshmen were in the top fifth of their class; 67% were in the top two fifths. 10 freshmen graduated first in their class.

Requirements: The SAT I or ACT is required, with a minimum SAT I composite of 900, with 450 on each part, or an ACT composite of 18. Each application is reviewed on an individual basis. The GED is accepted. For high school students, the college recommends completion of 28 academic credits, based on 4 years each of English, math, and science, and 2 years each of foreign language, history, and social studies. Manchester requires applicants to be in the upper 50% of their class. A GPA of 2.3 is required. AP and CLEP credits are accepted. Important factors in the admissions decision are advanced placement or honor courses, leadership record, and recommendations by school officials.

Procedure: Freshmen are admitted to all sessions. Entrance exams should be taken by November of the senior year. There are early admissions, rolling admissions, and deferred admissions plans. Application deadlines are open. Application fee is $20. Applications are accepted on computer disk.

Transfer: 31 transfer students enrolled in 2002-2003. Transfer students must present a minimum GPA of 2.0 in all previous college work. 96 of 128 credits required for the bachelor's degree must be completed at Manchester.

Visiting: There are regularly scheduled orientations for prospective students, including meetings about financial aid, with faculty and admissions, and campus tours. Visitors may also eat meals on campus, sit in on classes, and meet with current students. There are guides for informal visits and visitors may sit in on classes and stay overnight. To schedule a visit, contact Jill Biehl, Campus Visit Coordinator at jlb@manchester.edu.

Financial Aid: In a recent year, 100% of all full-time freshmen and 96% of continuing full-time students received some form of financial aid. The average freshman award was $15,678. 40% of undergraduates work part time. The average financial indebtedness of the 2003 graduate was $13,461. The FAFSA is required. Freshman financial aid applications for fall entry are accepted on a rolling basis.

International Students: In a recent year, there were 55 international students enrolled. The school actively recruits these students. They must score 550 on the written TOEFL or 213 on the electronic version.

Computers: The mainframe is an IBM AS/400. PC labs are available in various academic buildings and residence halls; in addition, various departments have computer labs for students. All students may access the system any time. There are no time limits and no fees.

Graduates: In a recent year, 171 bachelor's degrees were awarded. The most popular majors were business (28%), education (21%), and communications (8%). In an average class, 44% graduate in 4 years or less, 50% graduate in 5 years or less, and 51% graduate in 6 years or less. 25 companies recruited on campus in 2002-2003. Of the 2002 graduating class, 24% were enrolled in graduate school within 6 months of graduation and 74% were employed.

Admissions Contact: Jolane Rohr, Director of Admissions.
E-mail: *admitinfo@manchester.edu* Web: *www.manchester.edu*

MARIAN COLLEGE
C-3
Indianapolis, IN 46222
(317) 955-6300
(800) 772-7264; Fax: (317) 955-6401

Full-time: 294 men, 636 women	**Faculty:** 77
Part-time: 55 men, 194 women	**Ph.D.s:** 58%
Graduate: 14 women	**Student/Faculty:** 12 to 1
Year: semesters, summer session	**Tuition:** $17,230
Application Deadline: open	**Room & Board:** $5800
Freshman Class: 850 applied, 650 accepted, 230 enrolled	
SAT I or ACT: required	COMPETITIVE

Marian College, a private institution, was founded in 1851 by the Sisters of St. Francis and is today affiliated with the Roman Catholic Church. The college offers undergraduate programs in the arts and sciences, business, education, fine arts, and the health professions. In addition to regional accreditation, Marian has baccalaureate program accreditation with ADA, AHEA, CAHEA, NCATE, and NLN. The library contains 144,000 volumes and 500 audio/video tapes/CDs, and subscribes to 590 periodicals. Computerized library services include the card catalog, interlibrary loans, database searching, and Internet access. Special learning facilities include a learning resource center, art gallery, and the 35-acre Wetlands Ecology Laboratory. The 114-acre campus is in a suburban area 6 miles from downtown Indianapolis. Including any residence halls, there are 22 buildings.

Student Life: 90% of undergraduates are from Indiana. Others are from 19 states, 17 foreign countries, and Canada. 69% are from public schools. 68% are white; 18% African American. 44% are Catholic; 43% Protestant; 8% claim no religious affiliation. The average age of freshmen is 19; all undergraduates, 24. 30% do not continue beyond their first year; 45% remain to graduate.

Housing: 600 students can be accommodated in college housing, which includes single-sex and coed dorms, on-campus apartments, and married-student housing. On-campus housing is guaranteed for all 4 years. 51% of students commute. Alcohol is not permitted. All students may keep cars.

Activities: There are no fraternities or sororities. There are 33 groups on campus, including art, band, cheerleading, choir, chorale, chorus, computers, departmental, drama, drill team, ethnic, honors, international, jazz band, literary magazine, musical theater, pep band, photography, political, professional, religious, social, social service, student government, and yearbook. Popular campus events include Knightly Music Awards, Mock Rock, and Student Production Theater.

Sports: There are 9 intercollegiate sports for men and 9 for women, and 12 intramural sports for men and 12 for women. Facilities include varsity and intramural gyms, racquetball courts, a weight-training room, and a phys ed assessment lab.

Disabled Students: 90% of the campus is accessible. Wheelchair ramps, elevators, special parking, specially equipped rest rooms, and special class scheduling are available.

Services: Counseling and information services are available, as is tutoring in most subjects. There is a reader service for the blind and remedial math and writing. Study skills training and peer tutoring are available.

Campus Safety and Security: Measures include 24-hour foot and vehicle patrol, security escort services, shuttle buses, and informal discussions. There are pamphlets/posters/films and lighted pathways/sidewalks.

Programs of Study: Marian confers B.A., B.S., and B.S.N. degrees. Associate degrees are also awarded. Bachelor's degrees are awarded in BIOLOGICAL SCIENCE (biology/biological science), BUSINESS (accounting, banking and finance, business administration and management, and sports management), COMMUNICATIONS AND THE ARTS (art history and appreciation, communications, dramatic arts, English, French, graphic design, music, Spanish, and studio art), COMPUTER AND PHYSICAL SCIENCE (chemistry and mathematics), EDUCATION (early childhood, elementary, physical, and special), ENGINEERING AND ENVIRONMENTAL DESIGN (environmental science), HEALTH PROFESSIONS (nursing), SOCIAL SCIENCE (economics, history, pastoral studies, philosophy, political science/government, psychology, religious education, sociology, and theological studies). Accounting, finance, and English are the strongest academically. Nursing, business administration, and education are the largest.

Required: To graduate, students must complete 128 semester hours, including 30 to 40 in the major, with a minimum GPA of 2.0 overall and in the major. General education requirements include 14 semester hours in cultural awareness, 10 to 12 in scientific and quantitative reasoning, 9 to 17 in written and oral communication and foreign language, and 9 each in moral reasoning and individual and social awareness.

Special: Co-op programs in accounting, finance, business administration, chemistry, management information systems, and sociology, and cross-registration through the Consortium for Urban Education are offered. A dual degree program in math and computer science and accelerated degrees in nursing, business administration, and management information systems are also offered. Internships, study abroad, independent study, dual and student-designed majors, and pass/fail options are all available. There are 8 national honor societies and a freshman honors program.

Faculty/Classroom: 52% of faculty are male; 48%, female. All teach undergraduates. No introductory courses are taught by graduate students. The average class size in an introductory lecture is 20; in a laboratory, 15; and in a regular course, 15.

Admissions: 76% of the 2003-2004 applicants were accepted. 4 freshmen graduated first in their class.

Requirements: The SAT I or ACT is required. In addition, applicants must be graduates of an accredited secondary school or have a GED. Marian requires 20 academic units, including 4 units in English, 2 each in a foreign language and math, of which algebra and geometry are recommended, and 2 each in a lab science and social studies. A GPA of 2.0 is required. AP and CLEP credits are accepted. Important factors in the admissions decision are recommendations by school officials, recommendations by alumni, and leadership record.

Procedure: Freshmen are admitted to all sessions. Entrance exams should be taken at the end of the junior year or the beginning of the senior year. There is a rolling admissions plan. Application deadlines are open. The application fee is $20. Applications are accepted on-line.

Transfer: 178 transfer students enrolled in a recent year. In addition to meeting standard admissions requirements, applicants must submit transcripts of all college work and be in good standing at their former school. Students transferring fewer than 30 credit hours must have a 1.75 GPA; those having more than 30 hours must have a 2.0 GPA. 32 of 128 credits required for the bachelor's degree must be completed at Marian.

Visiting: There are regularly scheduled orientations for prospective students, including a campus tour, visits with faculty and coaches, and financial aid information. There are guides for informal visits and visitors

may sit in on classes and stay overnight. To schedule a visit, contact the Admissions Office at *admissions@marian.edu*.

Financial Aid: In 2003-2004, 95% of all full-time freshmen and 90% of continuing full-time students received some form of financial aid. 69% of full-time freshmen and 80% of continuing full-time students received need-based aid. The average freshman award was $17,437. Need-based scholarships or need-based grants averaged $10,706 ($19,258 maximum); need-based self-help aid (loans and jobs) averaged $2388 ($4125 maximum); non-need-based athletic scholarships averaged $5000 ($16,800 maximum); and other non-need-based awards and non-need-based scholarships averaged $9791 ($11,100 maximum). 83% of undergraduates work part time. Average annual earnings from campus work are $1000. The average financial indebtedness of the 2003 graduate was $12,110. Marian is a member of CSS. The FAFSA and the college's own financial statement are required. The deadline for filing freshman financial aid applications for fall entry is March 1.

International Students: The school actively recruits these students. They must score 550 on the written TOEFL or 220 on the electronic version.

Computers: More than 150 PCs and Macs are available for student use in the library, several computer centers, and a variety of special-purpose classrooms. The entire campus, including all residence hall rooms, is wired for network access, including a high-speed Internet/Web connection. All students may access the system 24 hours a day, 7 days a week. There are no time limits. The fee is $50 per semester. It is strongly recommended that all students have a personal computer.

Admissions Contact: Karen Full, Director of Admissions.
E-mail: *admissions@marian.edu* Web: *www.marian.edu*

MARTIN UNIVERSITY C-3
Indianapolis, IN 46218 (317) 543-3237; Fax: (317) 543-4790

Full-time: 43 men, 179 women	**Faculty:** 36
Part-time: 105 men, 259 women	**Ph.D.s:** 36%
Graduate: 28 men, 49 women	**Student/Faculty:** 6 to 1
Year: semesters, summer session	**Tuition:** $10,200
Application Deadline: open	**Room & Board:** n/app
Freshman Class: 166 accepted, 156 enrolled	
SAT I or ACT: not required	**SPECIAL**

Martin University, established in 1977, is a private liberal arts institution offering undergraduate programs primarily to low-income minority-group adults. It also offers graduate degrees in community psychology and urban ministry studies. Computerized library services include interlibrary loans and database searching. Special learning facilities include a learning resource center and English and math labs. The 8-acre campus is in an urban area in Indianapolis. There are 4 buildings.

Student Life: 90% of students are from public schools. 90% are African American. The average age of freshmen is 33; all undergraduates, 38.

Housing: There are no residence halls. All students commute. Alcohol is not permitted. No one may keep cars.

Activities: There are no fraternities or sororities. There are some groups and organizations on campus, including choir, civil rights, computers, drama, newspaper, opera, and social service. Popular campus events include internal and external conferences, St. Martin de Porres Feast Day, and Fine Arts Festival.

Sports: There is no sports program at Martin U.

Disabled Students: 90% of the campus is accessible. Wheelchair ramps, elevators, special parking, specially equipped rest rooms, lowered drinking fountains, and lowered telephones are available.

Services: Counseling and information services are available, as is tutoring in most subjects. There is remedial math, reading, and writing and addiction services.

Campus Safety and Security: Measures include 24-hour foot and vehicle patrol, security escort services, pamphlets/posters/films, and lighted pathways/sidewalks.

Programs of Study: Martin U confers B.A. and B.S. degrees. Master's degrees are also awarded. Bachelor's degrees are awarded in BIOLOGICAL SCIENCE (biology/biological science), BUSINESS (accounting, business administration and management, insurance, and marketing/retailing/merchandising), COMMUNICATIONS AND THE ARTS (communications, fine arts, music, and Spanish), COMPUTER AND PHYSICAL SCIENCE (chemistry and mathematics), EDUCATION (early childhood, education, and vocational), ENGINEERING AND ENVIRONMENTAL DESIGN (computer technology and environmental science), SOCIAL SCIENCE (African American studies, community services, counseling/psychology, criminal justice, history, humanities, political science/government, psychology, religion, and sociology). Humanities and psychology are the strongest academically. Business is the largest.

Required: Students must successfully complete 134 credits, including 36 in the humanities, 12 in English, and 6 each in social science and math, with at least 36 in the major and a minimum GPA of 2.0. Other required courses include computer science and critical thinking, and a foreign language for the B.A. Students must complete a final project in their major.

Special: Cross-registration is permitted with 7 schools in the Consortium of Urban Education in the area. Opportunities are provided for internships, student-designed majors, and credit based on assessment of prior learning.

Faculty/Classroom: 55% of faculty are male; 45%, female. All teach undergraduates and 10% do research. No introductory courses are taught by graduate students. The average class size in an introductory lecture is 13 and in a laboratory, 8.

Requirements: Graduation from an accredited secondary school is required; a GED will be accepted. No specific number of academic credits is required. An essay, an interview, and diagnostic testing are required. CLEP credit is accepted.

Procedure: Freshmen are admitted to all sessions. Entrance exams should be taken at the time of admission. Application deadlines are open. Application fee is $25.

Transfer: 49 transfer students enrolled in 2002-2003. Transfers are accepted from accredited regional schools. 34 of 134 credits required for the bachelor's degree must be completed at Martin U.

Visiting: There are regularly scheduled orientations for prospective students, consisting of 4 3-hour sessions. There are guides for informal visits and visitors may sit in on classes. To schedule a visit, contact the Recruitment Office at (317) 543-3865,

Financial Aid: In 2003-2004, 89% of all full-time freshmen and 94% of continuing full-time students received some form of financial aid. 88% of full-time freshmen and 90% of continuing full-time students received need-based aid. The average freshman award was $9121. Average annual earnings from campus work are $2769. The average financial indebtedness of the 2003 graduate was $29,782. The FAFSA is required. The deadline for filing freshman financial aid applications for fall entry is March 10.

International Students: They must score 550 on the written TOEFL.

Computers: The mainframe is a Dell Poweredge 2500 SCSI. There are also 20 IBM PCs available with an assistant on duty. All students may access the system. There are no time limits and no fees. It is strongly recommended that all students have a personal computer.

Graduates: From July 1, 2002 to June 30, 2003, 55 bachelor's degrees were awarded. The most popular majors were business administration (27%), social sciences (20%), and religious studies (14%).

Admissions Contact: Brenda Shaheed, Director of Admissions. E-mail: *bshaheed@martin.edu* Web: *www.martin.edu*

NOTRE DAME UNIVERSITY
(See University of Notre Dame)

OAKLAND CITY UNIVERSITY
Oakland City, IN 47660

A-5
(812) 749-1217
(800) 737-5125; Fax: (812) 749-1233

Full-time: 564 men, 621 women	Faculty: 31
Part-time: 119 men, 133 women	Ph.D.s: 71%
Graduate: 120 men, 140 women	Student/Faculty: 38 to 1
Year: semesters, summer session	Tuition: $12,420
Application Deadline: open	Room & Board: $4560
Freshman Class: 222 applied, 221 accepted, 187 enrolled	
SAT I Verbal/Math: 450/450	ACT: 21 NONCOMPETITIVE

Oakland City University, founded in 1885, is a private liberal arts institution affiliated with the General Association of General Baptists. There are 6 undergraduate and 2 graduate schools. In addition to regional accreditation, OCU has baccalaureate program accreditation with NCATE. The library contains 83,404 volumes, 100,318 microform items, and 2576 audio/video tapes/CDs, and subscribes to more than 8000 periodicals, including electronic subscriptions. Computerized library services include the card catalog, interlibrary loans, database searching, and Internet access. Special learning facilities include a learning resource center, archives, and a curriculum lab. The 20-acre campus is in a small town 30 miles north of Evansville, Illinois. Including any residence halls, there are 13 buildings.

Student Life: 88% of undergraduates are from Indiana. Students are from 18 states and 14 foreign countries. 90% are from public schools. 96% are white. 76% are Protestant. The average age of freshmen is 19; all undergraduates, 24. 30% do not continue beyond their first year; 70% remain to graduate.

Housing: 246 students can be accommodated in college housing, which includes single-sex dorms and on-campus apartments. In addition, there are honors houses and special-interest houses. On-campus housing is available on a first-come, first-served basis. 57% of students commute. Alcohol is not permitted. All students may keep cars.

Activities: There are no fraternities or sororities. There are 19 groups on campus, including art, cheerleading, choir, chorus, computers, departmental, drama, honors, international, musical theater, newspaper, pep band, photography, professional, religious, social, social service, student government, and yearbook. Popular campus events include Fall Festival Week, Spring Fling, and Fine Arts Festival.

Sports: There are 6 intercollegiate sports for men and 7 for women, and 14 intramural sports for men and 14 for women. Facilities include a gym, a health and phys ed center with a 1600-seat gym, a soccer field, a baseball field, and a tennis complex.

Disabled Students: 99% of the campus is accessible. Wheelchair ramps, elevators, special parking, specially equipped rest rooms, lowered drinking fountains, and special housing are available.

Services: Counseling and information services are available, as is tutoring in every subject. There is a reader service for the blind and remedial math, reading, and writing.

Campus Safety and Security: Measures include self-defense education, security escort services, informal discussions, and pamphlets/posters/films. There are emergency telephones, lighted pathways/sidewalks, and security in the evenings.

Programs of Study: OCU confers B.A. and B.S. degrees. Associate and master's degrees are also awarded. Bachelor's degrees are awarded in BIOLOGICAL SCIENCE (biology/biological science), BUSINESS (accounting and business administration and management), COMMUNICATIONS AND THE ARTS (English, fine arts, and music), COMPUTER AND PHYSICAL SCIENCE (chemistry, computer programming, computer science, and mathematics), EDUCATION (art, business, elementary, middle school, music, science, and secondary), HEALTH PROFESSIONS (premedicine), SOCIAL SCIENCE (prelaw and religion). Education is the strongest academically and has the largest enrollment.

Required: Liberal arts students must take a general studies core, including 1 computer science course and 2 hours of phys ed. A minimum GPA of 2.0 (2.5 in the major) and 120 total semester hours are needed.

Special: OCU offers campus work-study programs, an accelerated business degree program, business and networking internships, a B.A.-B.S. degree, dual majors, credit for significant work or service experience, nondegree study, pass/fail options, and a general studies degree. There are 3 national honor societies.

Faculty/Classroom: 58% of faculty are male; 42%, female. All both teach and do research. No introductory courses are taught by graduate students. The average class size in an introductory lecture is 25; in a laboratory, 16; and in a regular course, 25.

Admissions: 99% of the 2003-2004 applicants were accepted. The SAT I scores for the 2003-2004 freshman class were: Verbal--10% below 500, 60% between 500 and 599, 20% between 600 and 700, and 10% above 700; Math--10% below 500, 60% between 500 and 599, 20% between 600 and 700, and 10% above 700. The ACT scores were 50% below 21, 20% between 21 and 23, 20% between 24 and 26, 6% between 27 and 28, and 4% above 28. 20% of the current freshmen were in the top fifth of their class; 40% were in the top two fifths.

Requirements: The SAT I or ACT is required, with a minimum SAT I composite score of 700 or ACT composite score of 18. Preparatory programs usually include 4 units of English, 3 to 4 of math, 2 to 4 of a foreign language, and 2 each of social science and science. An interview is recommended. The GED is accepted. A GPA of 2.0 is required. AP and CLEP credits are accepted. Important factors in the admissions decision are personality/intangible qualities, evidence of special talent, and extracurricular activities record.

Procedure: Freshmen are admitted to all sessions. Entrance exams should be taken in the fall of the senior year. There is a deferred admissions plan. Application deadlines are open. Application fee is $35. Notification is sent on a rolling basis.

Transfer: Transfer applicants need a minimum GPA of 2.0 and a composite score of 700 on the SAT I or 18 on the ACT. An interview is recommended. 35 of 120 credits required for the bachelor's degree must be completed at OCU.

Visiting: There are regularly scheduled orientations for prospective students. There are guides for informal visits and visitors may sit in on classes and stay overnight. To schedule a visit, contact the Admissions Office.

Financial Aid: In 2003-2004, 92% of all full-time freshmen and 87% of continuing full-time students received some form of financial aid. 62% of full-time freshmen received need-based aid. The average freshman award was $13,500. 32% of undergraduates work part time. Average annual earnings from campus work are $2200. The average financial indebtedness of the 2003 graduate was $11,600. OCU is a member of CSS. The FAFSA and the college's own financial statement are required. The priority date for freshman financial aid applications for fall entry is March 1. The deadline for filing freshman financial aid applications for fall entry is open.

International Students: There are 25 international students enrolled. The school actively recruits these students. They must score 500 on the written TOEFL and also take the SAT I or the ACT.

Computers: All students may access the system. There are no time limits and no fees.

Graduates: The most popular majors among 2003 graduates were education (70%), seminary (15%), and business (10%). In an average class, 1% graduate in 3 years or less, 15% graduate in 4 years or less, 72% graduate in 5 years or less, and 5% graduate in 6 years or less. 12 companies recruited on campus in 2002-2003. Of the 2002 graduating class, 3% were enrolled in graduate school within 6 months of graduation and 71% were employed.

Admissions Contact: Buddy Harris, Director of Admissions.
E-mail: *bharris@oak.edu*

PURDUE UNIVERSITY SYSTEM

Purdue University was founded in 1869 as a land-grant institution in West Lafayette, Indiana. Since opening its doors to 39 students in 1874, Purdue has grown to a statewide system whose priorities are teaching, research, and service. The total enrollment of all 5 campuses is approximately 69,050 students with more than 38,800 at the main campus in West Lafayette. Purdue offers nearly 6100 courses in more than 200 specializations. Graduate students can work toward a master's or doctoral degree in approximately 60 different departmental programs. Among the 25 largest colleges and universities in the nation, Purdue maintains a tradition of providing students with an excellent, affordable education.

PURDUE UNIVERSITY/CALUMET B-1
Hammond, IN 46323

(219) 989-2213
(800) HI PURDUE; Fax: (219) 989-2775

Full-time: 1935 men, 2470 women	**Faculty:** 238; IIA, -$
Part-time: 1625 men, 2055 women	**Ph.D.s:** 56%
Graduate: 315 men, 665 women	**Student/Faculty:** n/av
Year: semesters, summer session	**Tuition:** $3630 ($8255)
Application Deadline: open	**Room & Board:** n/app
Freshman Class: n/av	
SAT I or ACT: required	**NONCOMPETITIVE**

Purdue University/Calumet, established in 1946, is a public commuter institution offering undergraduate degrees in general studies, liberal arts, and professional studies. Figures in the above capsule and in this profile are approximate. There are 2 undergraduate schools and 1 graduate school. In addition to regional accreditation, Purdue Cal has baccalaureate program accreditation with ABET, NCATE, and NLN. The library contains 200,000 volumes, 460,000 microform items, and 227 audio/video tapes/CDs, and subscribes to 1640 periodicals. Computerized library services include the card catalog and database searching. Special learning facilities include an art gallery and a computer education building, and an educational media laboratory. The 130-acre campus is in an urban area 25 miles southeast of Chicago. There are 11 buildings.

Student Life: 91% of undergraduates are from Indiana. Students are from 7 states, 3 foreign countries, and Canada. 90% are from public schools. 82% are white. The average age of freshmen is 20; all undergraduates, 29.

Housing: There are no residence halls. All students commute. Alcohol is not permitted.

Activities: There are 3 national fraternities and 3 national sororities. There are 45 groups on campus, including cheerleading, chorus, computers, drama, ethnic, honors, literary magazine, musical theater, newspaper, political, professional, religious, social service, and student government. Popular campus events include Orientation, Latin Culture Month, and Black History Month.

Sports: There are 2 intercollegiate sports for men and 2 for women, and 4 intramural sports for men and 4 for women. Facilities include a 1500-seat gym, racquetball courts, a baseball field, a running track, a weight room, and a total fitness center.

Disabled Students: 90% of the campus is accessible. Wheelchair ramps, elevators, special parking, specially equipped rest rooms, special class scheduling, lowered drinking fountains, and lowered telephones are available. There are electric door openers on all but one student building.

Services: Counseling and information services are available, as is tutoring in most subjects. There is a reader service for the blind, and remedial math, reading, and writing.

Campus Safety and Security: Measures include 24-hour foot and vehicle patrol, security escort services, informal discussions, and pamphlets/posters/films. There are emergency telephones, lighted pathways/sidewalks, and student patrols.

Programs of Study: Purdue Cal confers B.A., B.S., B.S.Ch., and B.S.E. degrees. Associate and master's degrees are also awarded. Bachelor's degrees are awarded in BIOLOGICAL SCIENCE (biology/biological science, biotechnology, microbiology, and zoology), BUSINESS (accounting, banking and finance, business economics, hotel/motel and restaurant management, and marketing/retailing/merchandising), COMMUNICATIONS AND THE ARTS (broadcasting, communications, English, French, German, and Spanish), COMPUTER AND PHYSICAL SCIENCE (chemistry, computer programming, computer science, information sciences and systems, mathematics, and physics), EDUCATION (early childhood, elementary, foreign languages, science, and secondary), ENGINEERING AND ENVIRONMENTAL DESIGN (computer engineering, computer technology, construction technology, electrical/electronics engineering, electrical/electronics engineering technology, engineering, engineering technology, industrial engineering technology, mechanical engineering, and mechanical engineer-

ing technology), HEALTH PROFESSIONS (medical laboratory technology, nursing, optometry, physical therapy, predentistry, premedicine, prepharmacy, and preveterinary science), SOCIAL SCIENCE (criminal justice, history, international relations, philosophy, political science/government, prelaw, psychology, social work, and sociology). Engineering, nursing, and behavioral sciences are the strongest academically. Engineering, business, and nursing are the largest.

Required: Graduation requirements vary depending on the program. The total number of credit hours required for a degree varies from 126 to 136, with 24 to 73 in the major. All students must take English composition and 36 hours of general education courses and maintain a C average.

Special: Some cooperative programs, internships, and work-study programs are available to students. Purdue Cal offers cross-registration in philosophy, study in Spain, and credit for life, military, and work experience, as well as nondegree study and pass/fail options. There is a freshman honors program.

Faculty/Classroom: The average class size in an introductory lecture is 24; in a laboratory, 24; and in a regular course, 24.

Requirements: The SAT I or ACT is required. In addition, the SAT II: Subject test in mathematics is required. Applicants must be graduates of an accredited secondary school. The GED is acccepted. 33 Carnegie units are required for admission. Required courses vary, depending on the curriculum, and include 3 or 4 years of English, 2 or 3 years of math, 2 years of foreign language, and 1 year of history or social studies. Purdue Cal requires applicants to be in the upper 66% of their class. AP and CLEP credits are accepted. Important factors in the admissions decision are recommendations by school officials, advanced placement or honor courses, and personality/intangible qualities.

Procedure: Freshmen are admitted to all sessions. Entrance exams should be taken between November and March of the senior year. There is a rolling admissions plan. Application deadlines are open. Check with the school for current deadlines and fee.

Transfer: Applicants must have a minimum GPA of 2.0. for transfer credit. 36 of 126 credits required for the bachelor's degree must be completed at Purdue Cal.

Visiting: There are regularly scheduled orientations for prospective students. There are guides for informal visits and visitors may sit in on classes. To schedule a visit, contact the Media Service Office, Admissions or the academic departments at (219) 989-2289.

Financial Aid: Purdue Cal is a member of CSS. The CSS Profile is required. Check with the school for current deadlines.

International Students: They must score 550 on the written TOEFL or 213 on the electronic version and also take the SAT I or the ACT, scoring 500.

Computers: The mainframes are an IBM 4341/LI, 2 DEC VAX 11/780s, and a DEC VAX 8600. Numerous PCs are available. All students may access the system. There are no time limits and no fees.

Admissions Contact: Paul McGuinness, Admissions Director.
E-mail: *adms.@calumet.purdue.edu* Web: *www.calumet.purdue.edu*

PURDUE UNIVERSITY/WEST LAFAYETTE B-3
West Lafayette, IN 47907 (765) 494-1776; Fax: (765) 494-0544

Full-time: 17,281 men, 11,770 women	**Faculty:** I, av$
Part-time: 927 men, 873 women	**Ph.D.s:** 99%
Graduate: 4685 men, 3311 women	**Student/Faculty:** n/av
Year: semesters, summer session	**Tuition:** $5860 ($17,640)
Application Deadline: open	**Room & Board:** $6700
Freshman Class: 22,872 applied, 17,292 accepted, 6323 enrolled	
SAT I Verbal/Math: 560/590	**ACT:** 25 **VERY COMPETITIVE**

Purdue University, founded in 1869, is a publicly supported institution offering degree programs with an emphasis on engineering, business, communications, arts, and social sciences. There are 12 undergraduate schools and 1 graduate school. In addition to regional accreditation, Purdue has baccalaureate program accreditation with AACSB, ABET, ACCE, ACPE, ADA, ASLA, NCATE, NLN, and SAF. The 15 libraries contain 1,200,797 volumes, 2,518,849 microform items, and 12,733 audio/video tapes/CDs, and subscribe to 18,374 periodicals. Computerized library services include the card catalog, interlibrary loans, and database searching. Special learning facilities include a learning resource center, art gallery, and radio station. The 1579-acre campus is in a suburban area 65 miles northwest of Indianapolis. Including any residence halls, there are 145 buildings.

Student Life: 69% of undergraduates are from Indiana. Students are from 50 states, 126 foreign countries, and Canada. 84% are white. 86% are claim no religious affiliation; 7% Protestant; 6% Catholic. The average age of freshmen is 18; all undergraduates, 21. 11% do not continue beyond their first year; 67% remain to graduate.

Housing: 11,689 students can be accommodated in college housing, which includes single-sex and coed dorms, on-campus apartments, married-student housing, fraternity houses, and sorority houses. There are also 3 floors in a women's hall for women in engineering or women in science. On-campus housing is available on a first-come, first-served basis. 61% of students commute. Alcohol is not permitted. Upperclassmen may keep cars.

Activities: 17% of men belong to 48 national fraternities; 17% of women belong to 26 national sororities. There are 654 groups on campus, including band, cheerleading, chess, choir, chorale, chorus, computers, dance, debate, drama, ethnic, gay, honors, international, jazz band, literary magazine, marching band, newspaper, orchestra, pep band, photography, political, professional, radio and TV, religious, social, social service, student government, symphony, and yearbook. Popular campus events include Grand Prix Race, Old Masters, and Gala week.

Sports: There are 10 intercollegiate sports for men and 10 for women, and 27 intramural sports for men and 26 for women. Facilities include a 14,000-seat arena, a 62,000-seat stadium, an intercollegiate athletic facility, a recreational gym, a field house, an athletic center, intramural playing fields, 2 golf courses, and baseball, softball, track, and women's soccer fields.

Disabled Students: 90% of the campus is accessible. Wheelchair ramps, elevators, special parking, specially equipped rest rooms, special class scheduling, lowered drinking fountains, lowered telephones, and a lab with assistive technology and special computers are available.

Services: Counseling and information services are available, as is tutoring in every subject. There is a reader service for the blind and remedial math, reading, and writing.

Campus Safety and Security: Measures include 24-hour foot and vehicle patrol, self-defense education, security escort services, and informal discussions. There are pamphlets/posters/films, emergency telephones, lighted pathways/sidewalks, and public transportation routes throughout campus.

Programs of Study: Purdue confers B.A., B.S., B.P.E, B.S.A.A.E., B.S.A.B.E., B.S.A.G.E., B.S.C.E., B.S.C.E.E., B.S.C.E.M., B.S.Ch., B.S.Ch.E., B.S.C.M.P.E., B.S.E., B.S.E.E., B.S.E.H., B.S.F., B.S.I.E., B.S.I.E.D., B.S.I.M., B.S.L.A., B.S.L.S., B.S.L.S.E., B.S.M.E., B.S.M.S.E., B.S.N.E., and B.S.Pharm. degrees. Associate, master's, and doctoral degrees are also awarded. Bachelor's degrees are awarded in AGRICULTURE (agricultural business management, agricultural economics, agricultural mechanics, agriculture, agronomy, animal science, conservation and regulation, forestry and related sciences, horticulture, natural resource management, plant protection (pest management), and wildlife management), BIOLOGICAL SCIENCE (biochemistry, biology/ biological science, ecology, entomology, and nutrition), BUSINESS (accounting, hotel/motel and restaurant management, management science, marketing management, office supervision and management, recreation and leisure services, and retailing), COMMUNICATIONS AND THE ARTS (apparel design, art history and appreciation, classics, communications, comparative literature, crafts, creative writing, design, dramatic arts, English, film arts, fine arts, French, German, industrial design, Japanese, journalism, languages, Latin, linguistics, media arts, photography, public relations, Russian, Spanish, telecommunications, and theater design), COMPUTER AND PHYSICAL SCIENCE (actuarial science, applied mathematics, applied physics, atmospheric sciences and meteorology, chemistry, computer science, earth science, geology, information sciences and systems, mathematics, physics, science, and statistics), EDUCATION (agricultural, art, athletic training, educational media, elementary, English, foreign languages, health, industrial arts, mathematics, physical, science, secondary, social studies, and special), ENGINEERING AND ENVIRONMENTAL DESIGN (aeronautical engineering, aeronautical technology, agricultural engineering, architectural engineering, biomedical engineering, chemical engineering, civil engineering, computer engineering, computer graphics, computer technology, construction engineering, construction technology, electrical/electronics engineering, electrical/electronics engineering technology, engineering, geological engineering, graphic arts technology, industrial administration/management, industrial engineering, industrial engineering technology, interior design, landscape architecture/design, materials engineering, mechanical engineering, mechanical engineering technology, nuclear engineering, ocean engineering, preengineering, surveying engineering, systems engineering, and transportation engineering), HEALTH PROFESSIONS (community health work, environmental health science, exercise science, health science, medical technology, nursing, pharmacy, predentistry, premedicine, prepharmacy, speech pathology/audiology, and veterinary science), SOCIAL SCIENCE (African American studies, American studies, anthropology, child care/child and family studies, consumer services, dietetics, economics, family and community services, food science, history, Italian studies, Judaic studies, law, liberal arts/ general studies, medieval studies, philosophy, political science/ government, prelaw, psychology, religion, sociology, and urban studies). Engineering, actuarial science, and industrial management are the strongest academically. Management, preengineering, and mechanical engineering are the largest.

Required: To graduate, students must complete approximately 128 hours and earn a minimum GPA of 2.0. In most majors, students must take courses in English, math, science, computer science, and social sciences.

Special: Cooperative programs are available in engineering, technology, agriculture, management, science, and consumer and family sci-

ences. Cross-registration with Purdue's regional campuses, numerous internships, study abroad in 45 countries, dual majors, student-designed majors, nondegree study, and pass/fail options are also offered. There are 14 national honor societies, including Phi Beta Kappa, a freshman honors program, and 10 departmental honors programs.

Faculty/Classroom: 75% of faculty are male; 25%, female. Most teach undergraduates. The average class size in an introductory lecture is 50; in a laboratory, 22; and in a regular course, 30.

Admissions: 76% of the 2003-2004 applicants were accepted. The SAT I scores for the 2003-2004 freshman class were: Verbal--22% below 500, 47% between 500 and 599, 27% between 600 and 700, and 4% above 700; Math--13% below 500, 40% between 500 and 599, 36% between 600 and 700, and 11% above 700. The ACT scores were 11% below 21, 21% between 21 and 23, 29% between 24 and 26, 17% between 27 and 28, and 22% above 28. 53% of the current freshmen were in the top fifth of their class; 97% were in the top two fifths. There were 91 National Merit finalists. 202 freshmen graduated first in their class.

Requirements: The SAT I or ACT is required. In addition, Purdue recommends that most students have 15 semester credits including 4 years of English, 3 to 4 of math, and 2 to 4 of lab science. The GED is accepted. AP and CLEP credits are accepted. Important factors in the admissions decision are advanced placement or honor courses, recommendations by school officials, and parents or siblings attending the school.

Procedure: Freshmen are admitted to all sessions. Entrance exams should be taken at the end of the junior year. There is a rolling admissions plan. Application deadlines are open. Application fee is $30. Applications are accepted on-line.

Transfer: 941 transfer students enrolled in 2002-2003. Transfer students must file a regular application at least 30 days before the start of the semester and submit SAT I/ACT results and high school and college transcripts. Students must be in good academic standing and meet the same subject-matter requirements as a beginning student. A minimum 2.2 GPA is required; many programs require a higher average, and some subject requirements. 32 of 128 credits required for the bachelor's degree must be completed at Purdue.

Visiting: There are regularly scheduled orientations for prospective students, including fall and spring preview days, which consist of admission, financial aid, housing, and school sessions, a campus tour, and dorm visits. The Summer Visit Program consists of a counselors' orientation and campus and residence hall visits. There are guides for informal visits and visitors may sit in on classes. To schedule a visit, contact the Office of Admissions at admissions@purdue.edu.

Financial Aid: In a recent year, 76% of all full-time freshmen and 63% of continuing full-time students received some form of financial aid. 54% of full-time freshmen and 49% of continuing full-time students received need-based aid. The average freshman award for 2002-2003 was $8771. 12% of undergraduates work part time. Average annual earnings from campus work are $859. The average financial indebtedness of the 2002 graduate was $15,677. Purdue is a member of CSS. The FAFSA is required. The deadline for filing freshman financial aid applications for fall entry is March 1.

International Students: There are 2081 international students enrolled. The school actively recruits these students. They must score 550 on the written TOEFL or 213 on the electronic version.

Computers: Central computer services are provided on a variety of servers that include about 20 models of the IBM RS/6000 class, about 15 models of the Sun Enterprise 4000 family, an IBM SP2 machine, and an Intel Paragon. Students may access central computing facilities through approximately 80 lab locations containing about 2100 workstations (Windows, Macs, and UNIX.) Direct network connections are also available in each residence hall room. Students are granted a career account that provides e-mail and Internet services during their entire time at Purdue. All students may access the system 24 hours daily. There are no time limits and no fees.

Graduates: From July 1, 2002 to June 30, 2003, 5999 bachelor's degrees were awarded. The most popular majors were management (6%), mechanical engineering (3%), and organizational leadership (3%). In an average class, 1% graduate in 3 years or less, 33% graduate in 4 years or less, 63% graduate in 5 years or less, and 69% graduate in 6 years or less. 800 companies recruited on campus in 2002-2003.

Admissions Contact: Dr. Douglas L. Christiansen, Director, Admissions. E-mail: *admissions@purdue.edu* Web: *www.purdue.edu/*

ROSE-HULMAN INSTITUTE OF TECHNOLOGY
B-4
Terre Haute, IN 47803 (812) 877-1511
(800) 248-7448; Fax: (812) 877-8941

Full-time: 1409 men, 300 women	**Faculty:** 139; IIB, ++$
Part-time: 10 men, 2 women	**Ph.D.s:** 96%
Graduate: 125 men, 18 women	**Student/Faculty:** 12 to 1
Year: quarters, summer session	**Tuition:** $24,705
Application Deadline: March 1	**Room & Board:** $6720
Freshman Class: 3188 applied, 2261 accepted, 490 enrolled	
SAT I Verbal/Math: 630/690	**ACT:** 29

HIGHLY COMPETITIVE+

Rose-Hulman Institute of Technology, founded in 1874, is a private college emphasizing engineering, science, and math. In addition to regional accreditation, Rose-Hulman has baccalaureate program accreditation with ABET. The library contains 72,741 volumes, 532 microform items, and 633 audio/video tapes/CDs, and subscribes to 724 periodicals. Computerized library services include the card catalog, interlibrary loans, database searching, and Internet access. Special learning facilities include a learning resource center, art gallery, planetarium, and radio station. The 200-acre campus is in a suburban area on the east side of Terre Haute. Including any residence halls, there are 35 buildings.

Student Life: 53% of undergraduates are from out of state, mostly the Midwest. Students are from 47 states, 9 foreign countries, and Canada. 93% are white. The average age of freshmen is 18; all undergraduates, 20. 9% do not continue beyond their first year; 82% remain to graduate.

Housing: 1106 students can be accommodated in college housing, which includes single-sex and coed dorms, on-campus apartments, fraternity houses, and sorority houses. On-campus housing is guaranteed for the freshman year only, is available on a first-come, first-served basis, and is available on a lottery system for upperclassmen. 51% of students live on campus; of those, 60% remain on campus on weekends. All students may keep cars.

Activities: 47% of men belong to 8 national fraternities; 58% of women belong to 2 national sororities. There are 60 groups on campus, including band, cheerleading, chess, chorale, chorus, computers, dance, debate, drama, drill team, ethnic, gay, honors, international, jazz band, literary magazine, musical theater, newspaper, pep band, photography, political, professional, radio and TV, religious, social, social service, student government, and yearbook. Popular campus events include art shows, concerts, and plays.

Sports: There are 10 intercollegiate sports for men and 9 for women, and 12 intramural sports for men and 11 for women. Facilities include a field house, a recreational center, a swimming pool, tennis courts, and intramural fields.

Disabled Students: 95% of the campus is accessible. Wheelchair ramps, elevators, special parking, specially equipped rest rooms, special class scheduling, and lowered drinking fountains are available.

Services: Counseling and information services are available, as is tutoring in most subjects.

Campus Safety and Security: Measures include 24-hour foot and vehicle patrol, security escort services, informal discussions, and pamphlets/posters/films. There are emergency telephones, lighted pathways/sidewalks, medical transports, and free traffic assistance.

Programs of Study: Rose-Hulman confers the B.S. degree. Master's degrees are also awarded. Bachelor's degrees are awarded in BIOLOGICAL SCIENCE (biology/biological science), COMPUTER AND PHYSICAL SCIENCE (chemistry, computer science, mathematics, physics, and software engineering), ENGINEERING AND ENVIRONMENTAL DESIGN (biomedical engineering, chemical engineering, civil engineering, computer engineering, electrical/electronics engineering, engineering physics, mechanical engineering, and optical engineering), SOCIAL SCIENCE (economics). Engineering, science, and mathematics are the strongest academically. Mechanical engineering, electrical engineering, and chemical engineering are the largest.

Required: All students must complete at least 196 quarter hours with a minimum GPA of 2.0 and 36 hours in the humanities and social sciences. Freshmen are required to take math, biology, chemistry, or physics.

Special: The Institute offers co-op programs, independent study, cross-registration with Indiana State University and Saint Mary-of-the-Woods College, summer industrial internships, study abroad in 8 countries, and dual majors. Pass/fail options also are available. There are 10 national honor societies and 6 departmental honors programs.

Faculty/Classroom: 83% of faculty are male; 17%, female. All teach undergraduates and 20% do research. No introductory courses are taught by graduate students. The average class size in an introductory lecture is 19; in a laboratory, 21; and in a regular course, 21.

Admissions: 71% of the 2003-2004 applicants were accepted. The SAT I scores for the 2003-2004 freshman class were: Verbal--2% below 500, 35% between 500 and 599, 44% between 600 and 700, and 19% above 700; Math--11% between 500 and 599, 43% between 600 and 700, and 46% above 700. The ACT scores were 6% between 21 and

23, 15% between 24 and 26, 21% between 27 and 28, and 58% above 28. 88% of the current freshmen were in the top fifth of their class; 99% were in the top two fifths. There were 26 National Merit finalists. 50 freshmen graduated first in their class.

Requirements: The SAT I or ACT is required. In addition, candidates should have at least 16 units of credit, including 4 in English, 2 in social sciences, and 1 each in math, chemistry, physics, and electives. An essay and interview are recommended. Rose-Hulman requires applicants to be in the top 25% of their class. AP credits are accepted. Important factors in the admissions decision are advanced placement or honor courses, recommendations by school officials, and extracurricular activities record.

Procedure: Freshmen are admitted in the fall. Entrance exams should be taken in the fall of the senior year or spring of the junior year. Applications should be filed by March 1 for fall entry, along with a $40 fee. Notification is sent on a rolling basis. Applications are accepted on-line through Princeton Review.

Transfer: 22 transfer students enrolled in 2002-2003. Applicants need 1 year each of calculus, physics, and chemistry and a minimum GPA of 3.0. An interview is recommended. 60 of the 188 to 194 quarter credit hous required for the bachelor's degree must be completed at Rose-Hulman.

Visiting: There are regularly scheduled orientations for prospective students, including interviews, campus tours, and academic meetings. There are guides for informal visits and visitors may sit in on classes and stay overnight. To schedule a visit, contact the Admissions Office at (812) 877-8213 or admis.ofc@rose-hulman.edu.

Financial Aid: In 2003-2004, 99% of all full-time freshmen and 96% of continuing full-time students received some form of financial aid. 71% of full-time freshmen and 72% of continuing full-time students received need-based aid. The average freshman award was $20,305. Need-based scholarships or need-based grants averaged $14,329 ($39,140 maximum); need-based self-help aid (loans and jobs) averaged $10,532 ($37,140 maximum); and non-need-based awards and non-need-based scholarships averaged $12,012 ($37,650 maximum). 95% of undergraduates work part time. Average annual earnings from campus work are $1576. The average financial indebtedness of the 2003 graduate was $27,000. Rose-Hulman is a member of CSS. The FAFSA is required. The deadline for filing freshman financial aid applications for fall entry is March 1.

International Students: There are 16 international students enrolled. They must score 550 on the written TOEFL or 210 on the electronic version.

Computers: The mainframes are a SUN and PC clusters. There are network connections in all residence hall rooms and most classrooms and labs. There are more than 7,000 wired ports on campus, and academic buildings also have complete wireless coverage. All students may access the system. There are no time limits and no fees. All students are required to have personal computers. The Compaq Evo N800W is recommended.

Graduates: From July 1, 2002 to June 30, 2003, 372 bachelor's degrees were awarded. The most popular majors were mechanical engineering (32%), electrical engineering (16%), and computer science (15%). In an average class, 1% graduate in 3 years or less, 66% graduate in 4 years or less, 80% graduate in 5 years or less, and 82% graduate in 6 years or less. 165 companies recruited on campus in 2002-2003. Of the 2002 graduating class, 20% were enrolled in graduate school within 6 months of graduation and 95% were employed.

Admissions Contact: Charles G. Howard, Dean of Admissions. E-mail: admis.ofc@rose-hulman.edu Web: www.rose-hulman.edu

SAINT JOSEPH'S COLLEGE
B-2
Rensselaer, IN 47978 (219) 866-6170
(800) 447-8781; Fax: (219) 866-6122

Full-time: 393 men, 449 women	**Faculty:** 54; IIB, --$
Part-time: 31 men, 125 women	**Ph.D.s:** 78%
Graduate: none	**Student/Faculty:** 16 to 1
Year: semesters, summer session	**Tuition:** $18,060
Application Deadline: open	**Room & Board:** $6190
Freshman Class: 1169 applied, 885 accepted, 259 enrolled	
SAT I Verbal/Math: 508/510	**ACT:** 22

COMPETITIVE

St. Joseph's College, founded in 1889, is a private Catholic institution providing a liberal arts core curriculum with an interdisciplinary approach and practical, career-oriented experiences. In addition to regional accreditation, SJC has baccalaureate program accreditation with NCATE. The library contains 156,931 volumes, 67,904 microform items, and 22,814 audio/video tapes/CDs, and subscribes to 416 periodicals. Computerized library services include the card catalog, interlibrary loans, database searching, and Internet access. Special learning facilities include a learning resource center, radio station, and TV station. The 180-acre campus is in a small town 80 miles south of Chicago and 90 miles north of Indianapolis. Including any residence halls, there are 26 buildings.

Student Life: 70% of undergraduates are from Indiana. Others are from 19 states, 3 foreign countries, and Canada. 88% are white. 51% are Catholic; 35% Protestant; 11% claim no religious affiliation. The average age of freshmen is 19; all undergraduates, 22. 31% do not continue beyond their first year; 55% remain to graduate.

Housing: 849 students can be accommodated in college housing, which includes single-sex and coed dorms, on-campus apartments, housing for nontraditional or adult students, and special-interest floors. On-campus housing is guaranteed for all 4 years. 70% of students live on campus; of those, 60% remain on campus on weekends. All students may keep cars.

Activities: There are no fraternities or sororities. There are 48 groups on campus, including art, band, cheerleading, choir, chorale, chorus, computers, debate, drama, ethnic, forensics, honors, jazz band, literary magazine, marching band, musical theater, newspaper, orchestra, pep band, photography, political, professional, radio and TV, religious, social, social service, and student government. Popular campus events include the Little 500 Go-Kart Race and Little Siblings Weekend.

Sports: There are 8 intercollegiate sports for men and 8 for women, and 5 intramural sports for men and 5 for women. Facilities include a field house, a 2500-seat gym, a recreation center, a baseball complex, a lighted soccer field, a football facility, and a lake with a sand beach.

Disabled Students: 74% of the campus is accessible. Wheelchair ramps, elevators, special parking, specially equipped rest rooms, special class scheduling, lowered drinking fountains, and lowered telephones are available.

Services: Counseling and information services are available, as is tutoring in every subject. There is a reader service for the blind, and remedial math, reading, and writing.

Campus Safety and Security: Measures include 24-hour foot and vehicle patrol, security escort services, informal discussions, and pamphlets/posters/films. There are lighted pathways/sidewalks.

Programs of Study: SJC confers B.A., B.S., and B.S.N. degrees. Associate and master's degrees are also awarded. Bachelor's degrees are awarded in BIOLOGICAL SCIENCE (biology/biological science), BUSINESS (accounting, business administration and management, and management information systems), COMMUNICATIONS AND THE ARTS (art, communications, creative writing, English, music, and music business management), COMPUTER AND PHYSICAL SCIENCE (chemistry, computer science, and mathematics), EDUCATION (art, elementary, middle school, music, physical, and secondary), ENGINEERING AND ENVIRONMENTAL DESIGN (environmental science), HEALTH PROFESSIONS (medical technology, nursing, predentistry, and premedicine), SOCIAL SCIENCE (criminal justice, economics, history, international studies, ministries, philosophy, political science/government, prelaw, psychology, religion, social work, and sociology). Accounting, biology-chemistry, and education are the strongest academically. Business administration, education, and criminal justice are the largest.

Required: Students must complete 45 hours in the general education program and 36 hours in the major. A total of 120 credit hours with a minimum GPA of 2.0 is required to graduate.

Special: Cross-registration with Saint Elizabeth's School of Nursing is offered. Internships in all fields, a Washington semester, and study abroad throughout Europe and Latin America are available. Dual majors are offered in biology/chemistry, management/information systems, and math/computer science. Credit for life, military, and work experience, nondegree study, student-designed majors, and pass/fail options are offered. The core program consists of lectures and discussions over a 4-year period. There are 3 national honor societies and a freshman honors program.

Faculty/Classroom: 60% of faculty are male; 40%, female. All teach undergraduates. The average class size in an introductory lecture is 18; in a laboratory, 20; and in a regular course, 14.

Admissions: 76% of the 2003-2004 applicants were accepted. The SAT I scores for the 2003-2004 freshman class were: Verbal--43% below 500, 48% between 500 and 599, 8% between 600 and 700, and 1% above 700; Math--48% below 500, 35% between 500 and 599, 14% between 600 and 700, and 2% above 700. The ACT scores were 46% below 21, 17% between 21 and 23, 18% between 24 and 26, 9% between 27 and 28, and 10% above 28. 28% of the current freshmen were in the top fifth of their class; 55% were in the top two fifths. 4 freshmen graduated first in their class.

Requirements: The SAT I or ACT is required with recommended minimum scores of 500 verbal and 500 math on the SAT I or 18 on the ACT. Applicants should be graduates of an accredited secondary school or have earned the GED. They should have completed 15 academic credits, 10 of which must be from the following academic fields: English, foreign language, social studies, math, and natural sciences. An interview is recommended. SJC requires applicants to be in the upper 50% of their class. A GPA of 2.0 is required. AP and CLEP credits are accepted. Important factors in the admissions decision are advanced placement or honor courses, recommendations by school officials, and recommendations by alumni.

Procedure: Freshmen are admitted fall and winter. Entrance exams should be taken by January of the senior year. There are early decision

and deferred admissions plans. There is a rolling admissions plan. The application deadlines are open. Application fee is $25. 8 early decision candidates were accepted for the 2003-2004 class. Applications are accepted on-line through CollegeView and *www.Saintjoe.edu*.

Transfer: 32 transfer students enrolled in 2003-2004. Applicants must have a GPA of 2.0. A minimum composite score of 1000 on the SAT I or 19 on the ACT is recommended. Grades of C or better transfer for credit. 30 of 120 credits required for the bachelor's degree must be completed at SJC.

Visiting: There are regularly scheduled orientations for prospective students, consisting of Discover Days, Special Interest Days, and early registration. There are guides for informal visits and visitors may sit in on classes and stay overnight. To schedule a visit, contact the Admissions Office at (800) 447-8781 or *admissions@saintjoe.edu*.

Financial Aid: In 2003-2004, 82% of all full-time freshmen and 80% of continuing full-time students received some form of financial aid. 66% of full-time freshmen and 62% of continuing full-time students received need-based aid. The average freshman award was $14,500. Need-based scholarships or need-based grants averaged $11,500; need-based self-help aid (loans and jobs) averaged $4000; non-need-based athletic scholarships averaged $9000 ($24,090 maximum); and other non-need-based awards and non-need-based scholarships averaged $5500 ($24,090 maximum). 45% of undergraduates work part time. Average annual earnings from campus work are $1200. The average financial indebtedness of the 2003 graduate was $18,566. The FAFSA and combined admission and financial aid application are required. The deadline for filing freshmen financial aid applications for fall entry is March 1.

International Students: There are 3 international students enrolled. They must score 550 on the written TOEFL and also take the SAT I or the ACT.

Computers: There are various makes and models of servers networked together. 4 centrally located labs house PCs with Windows and Linux and laser printers. 69 computers are available for student use. Network access is also available in dorm rooms for students who have their own computers. Wireless access is available in various locations on campus. All students may access the system from 7:30 A.M. to midnight, or by special request. Dorm room access is available at all times. There are no time limits and no fees.

Graduates: From July 1, 2002 to June 30, 2003, 168 bachelor's degrees were awarded. The most popular majors were business (21%), education (10%), and psychology (7%). In an average class, 44% graduate in 4 years or less, 53% graduate in 5 years or less, and 54% graduate in 6 years or less. 31 companies recruited on campus in 2002-2003. Of the 2002 graduating class, 18% were enrolled in graduate school within 6 months of graduation and 84% were employed.

Admissions Contact: Mary Lawman, Assistant Director of Admissions. E-mail: *admissions@saintjoe.edu* Web: *www.saintjoe.edu*

SAINT MARY-OF-THE-WOODS COLLEGE	B-4
St. Mary-of-the-Woods, IN 47876	(812) 535-5106
	(800) 926-SMWC; Fax: (812) 535-4900

Full-time: 441 women	**Faculty:** 61; IIB, --$
Part-time: 21 men, 1103 women	**Ph.Ds:** 70%
Graduate: 16 men, 106 women	**Student/Faculty:** 7 to 1
Year: semesters, summer session	**Tuition:** $17,030
Application Deadline: July 15	**Room & Board:** $6250
Freshman Class: n/av	
SAT I Verbal/Math: 510/490	**ACT:** 22 **COMPETITIVE**

Saint Mary-of-the Woods, founded in 1840, is a private, liberal arts women's college affiliated with the Roman Catholic Church. In addition to regional accreditation, The Woods has baccalaureate program accreditation with NASM and NCATE. The library contains 142,000 volumes and 1676 microform items, and subscribes to 460 periodicals. Computerized library services include the card catalog, interlibrary loans, and database searching. Special learning facilities include a learning resource center and art gallery. The 200-acre campus is in a rural area 5 miles northwest of Terre Haute. Including any residence halls, there are 10 buildings.

Student Life: 80% of undergraduates are from Indiana. Others are from 50 states, 5 foreign countries, and Canada. 70% are from public schools. 92% are white. The average age of freshmen is 18; all undergraduates, 32. 37% do not continue beyond their first year; 61% remain to graduate.

Housing: 500 students can be accommodated in college housing, which includes single-sex dorms. Housing for student mothers with young children is available. On-campus housing is guaranteed for all 4 years. 80% of students live on campus; of those, 75% remain on campus on weekends. Alcohol is not permitted. All students may keep cars.

Activities: There are no fraternities or sororities. There are 30 groups on campus, including band, chorale, chorus, computers, dance, drama, ethnic, honors, international, literary magazine, musical theater, orchestra, professional, religious, social, social service, student government, and yearbook. Popular campus events include Ring Day, Christmas at The Woods, and Pops Concert.

Sports: Facilities include stables, an athletic field, a gym, tennis courts, a pool, a weight room, a fitness course, and a volleyball pit.

Disabled Students: All of the campus is accessible. Wheelchair ramps, elevators, special parking, specially equipped rest rooms, and special class scheduling are available.

Services: Counseling and information services are available, as is tutoring in every subject. There is remedial math and writing.

Campus Safety and Security: Measures include 24-hour foot and vehicle patrol, self-defense education, informal discussions, and pamphlets/posters/films. There are emergency telephones and lighted pathways/sidewalks.

Programs of Study: The Woods confers B.A. and B.S. degrees. Associate and master's degrees are also awarded. Bachelor's degrees are awarded in AGRICULTURE (equine science), BIOLOGICAL SCIENCE (biology/biological science), BUSINESS (accounting, business administration and management, electronic business, human resources, and marketing/retailing/merchandising), COMMUNICATIONS AND THE ARTS (English, fine arts, French, graphic design, journalism, languages, music, photography, and Spanish), COMPUTER AND PHYSICAL SCIENCE (computer science, information sciences and systems, and mathematics), EDUCATION (art, early childhood, elementary, foreign languages, middle school, music, science, secondary, and special), HEALTH PROFESSIONS (medical technology, music therapy, predentistry, premedicine, and preveterinary science), SOCIAL SCIENCE (gerontology, history, human services, humanities, international studies, liberal arts/general studies, paralegal studies, political science/government, prelaw, psychology, religious education, social science, social work, and theological studies). Education, music therapy, and equine studies are the strongest academically. Education and business are the largest.

Required: All students must complete a 61-credit-hour general studies curriculum, which includes a freshman course in lifelong learning; courses in writing, speech, phys ed, computer science, and math; selected courses in religion, fine arts, philosophy, science, and social sciences; and 2 capstone interdisciplinary integrative courses. Completion of 125 credit hours with a minimum GPA of 2.0 is necessary for graduation.

Special: The college offers cross-registration with Indiana State University and Rose-Hulman Institute of Technology, student-designed majors, study abroad in Spain, Taiwan, and the United Kingdom, a B.A.-B.S. degree, dual majors, internships, pass/fail options, on-campus work-study, student-designed majors, and nondegree study. The Women's External Degree program, offering 19 majors, provides educational opportunities to women who study mostly at home.

Faculty/Classroom: 10% of faculty are male; 90%, female. 95% teach undergraduates, 3% do research, and 3% do both. No introductory courses are taught by graduate students. The average class size in an introductory lecture is 15; in a laboratory, 15; and in a regular course, 12.

Requirements: The SAT I or ACT is required. In addition, candidates should be graduates of an accredited secondary school. The GED is accepted. Documents needed for acceptance include an application for admission, letter of recommendation, and a high school transcript. Students should have completed 4 years of English, 3 years each of social sciences, lab science, and math (algebra 1, algebra 2, and geometry), and 2 years of a foreign language. A GPA of 2.0 is required.

Procedure: Freshmen are admitted fall and winter. Entrance exams should be taken in the fall semester of the senior year. Applications should be filed by July 15 for fall entry and December 1 for spring entry. The fall 2003 application fee was $30. There is a rolling admissions plan. Notification is sent on a rolling basis.

Transfer: 9 transfer students enrolled in 2003-2004. Transfer students should be in good academic standing at their most recent institution with a minimum 2.0 GPA. 30 of 125 credits required for the bachelor's degree must be completed at The Woods.

Visiting: There are regularly scheduled orientations for prospective students, including a campus tour, class visit, and meetings with faculty, financial aid, and admissions staff. There are guides for informal visits and visitors may sit in on classes and stay overnight. To schedule a visit, contact the Office of Admissions.

Financial Aid: In 2003-2004, 92% of all full-time freshmen and 75% of continuing full-time students received some form of financial aid. 60% of all full-time students received need-based aid. The average freshman award was $10,000. 70% of undergraduates work part time. The average financial indebtedness of the 2003 graduate was $16,000. The FAFSA is required.

International Students: There are 5 international students enrolled. The school actively recruits these students. They must score 500 on the written TOEFL or 173 on the electronic version. The SAT I or ACT is recommended if English is the student's first language. A minimum composite score of 750 is required on the SAT I.

Computers: The mainframe is a Novell PC network. Students have full access to the World Wide Web from several computer labs across campus. All students may access the system during posted lab hours, or access can be made by PCs at any time. There are no time limits and no fees.

Graduates: From July 1, 2002 to June 30, 2003, 145 bachelor's degrees were awarded. The most popular majors were elementary education (12%), psychology (10%), and business administration (8%). In an average class, 53% graduate in 4 years or less, 60% graduate in 5 years or less, and 61% graduate in 6 years or less.

Admissions Contact: Theresa Denton, Director of Admission. A video is available. E-mail: *smwcadms@smwc.edu* Web: *www.smwc.edu*

SAINT MARY'S COLLEGE
C-1
Notre Dame, IN 46556

(219) 284-4587
(800) 551-7621; Fax: (219) 284-4716

Full-time: 1485 women	**Faculty:** 108; IIB, av$
Part-time: 35 women	**Ph.Ds:** 95%
Graduate: none	**Student/Faculty:** 14 to 1
Year: semesters	**Tuition:** $23,284
Application Deadline: see profile	**Room & Board:** $7663
Freshman Class: n/av	
SAT I or ACT: required	**VERY COMPETITIVE**

Saint Mary's College, established in 1844, was founded and sponsored by the Congregation of the Sisters of the Holy Cross. It is a Catholic comprehensive college for women in the liberal arts tradition. Figures in the above capsule and in this profile are approximate. In addition to regional accreditation, Saint Mary's has baccalaureate program accreditation with CSWE, NASAD, NASM, NCATE, and NLN. The library contains 209,375 volumes, 13,905 microform items, and 3399 audio/video tapes/CDs, and subscribes to 776 periodicals. Computerized library services include the card catalog and database searching. Special learning facilities include an art gallery. The 275-acre campus is in a suburban area 90 miles east of Chicago. Including any residence halls, there are 14 buildings.

Student Life: 72% of undergraduates are from out of state, mostly the Midwest. Students are from 49 states and 5 foreign countries. 45% are from public schools. 91% are white. 88% are Catholic; 10% Protestant. The average age of freshmen is 18; all undergraduates, 20. 16% do not continue beyond their first year.

Housing: 1575 students can be accommodated in college housing, which includes dorms. In addition, there is an independent living residence floor for seniors. On-campus housing is guaranteed for all 4 years and is available on a first-come, first-served basis. 82% of students live on campus; of those, 80% remain on campus on weekends. All students may keep cars.

Activities: There are no sororities. There are 80 groups on campus, including art, band, cheerleading, choir, chorale, chorus, dance, drama, drill team, ethnic, honors, international, jazz band, literary magazine, marching band, musical theater, newspaper, orchestra, pep band, political, professional, radio and TV, religious, social, social service, student government, and yearbook. Popular campus events include Fall Festival, winter carnival, and spring celebration.

Sports: There are 8 intercollegiate sports for women and 15 intramural sports for women. Facilities include an athletic facility, outdoor tennis and volleyball courts, a soccer field, a softball field, and a swimming pool.

Disabled Students: 99% of the campus is accessible. Wheelchair ramps, elevators, special parking, specially equipped rest rooms, and lowered drinking fountains are available.

Services: Counseling and information services are available, as is tutoring in most subjects. A writing center is also available.

Campus Safety and Security: Measures include 24-hour foot and vehicle patrol, self-defense education, security escort services, and shuttle buses. There are informal discussions, pamphlets/posters/films, emergency telephones, lighted pathways/sidewalks, key cards for residence hall entry, and underground tunnels connecting buildings.

Programs of Study: Saint Mary's confers B.A., B.S., B.B.A., B.F.A., and B.Mus. degrees. Bachelor's degrees are awarded in BIOLOGICAL SCIENCE (biology/biological science), BUSINESS (business administration and management), COMMUNICATIONS AND THE ARTS (art, communications, dramatic arts, English, fine arts, French, music, and Spanish), COMPUTER AND PHYSICAL SCIENCE (chemistry and mathematics), EDUCATION (elementary), HEALTH PROFESSIONS (nursing), SOCIAL SCIENCE (economics, history, humanities, philosophy, political science/government, psychology, religion, social work, and sociology). Art, business, and English are the strongest academically. Business, education, and communications are the largest.

Required: Students must successfully complete 128 credits, with at least 24 in the major, and must maintain a minimum GPA of 2.0. Students must also complete distribution requirements in fine arts, history, language, literature, math, philosophy, science, religion, and other selected disciplines. Advanced proficiency in composition within the student's major must also be demonstrated, and a comprehensive exam in the major area is required by the end of the senior year.

Special: Cross-registration is permitted with the University of Notre Dame and a consortium of 6 northern Indiana colleges. Opportunities are provided for internships, a Washington semester, an accelerated degree program in nursing, dual and student-designed majors, a 3-2 engineering degree with the University of Notre Dame, nondegree study, pass/fail options, and study abroad in 18 countries. There are 9 national honor societies and 2 departmental honors programs.

Faculty/Classroom: 39% of faculty are male; 61%, female. All teach undergraduates. The average class size in an introductory lecture is 22; in a laboratory, 15; and in a regular course, 16.

Admissions: In a recent year, there were 2 National Merit finalists and 4 semifinalists and 12 freshmen graduated first in their class.

Requirements: The SAT I or ACT is required. In addition, SAT II: Subject tests are required in writing, math, and foreign languange. Graduation from an accredited secondary school is required; a GED will be accepted. Applicants must have completed 16 academic credits, including 4 in English, 3 in math, 2 in a foreign language, 2 in history or social studies, 1 in science, and the remainder from college preparatory electives in the above areas. An essay is required. AP and CLEP credits are accepted. Important factors in the admissions decision are advanced placement or honor courses, evidence of special talent, and recommendations by school officials.

Procedure: Freshmen are admitted fall and spring. Entrance exams should be taken between March of the junior year and December of the senior year. There are early decision and deferred admissions plans. There is a rolling admissions plan. Check with the school for current deadlines and fee.

Transfer: 52 transfer students enrolled in a recent year. Students must submit a transcript from high achool and each previous college attended, along with an essay, a recommendation from a college adviser, and SAT I or ACT test scores if the student has fewer than 30 semester hours of transferable credit. All transfer applicants must have maintained a minimum GPA of 3.0. An interview is recommended. 60 of 128 credits required for the bachelor's degree must be completed at Saint Mary's.

Visiting: There are regularly scheduled orientations for prospective students, including campus tours and visits with admissions and financial aid counselors and faculty and athletic staff. There are guides for informal visits and visitors may sit in on classes and stay overnight. To schedule a visit, contact the Campus Visit Coordinator.

Financial Aid: In a recent year, 89% of all full-time freshmen and 78% of continuing full-time students received some form of financial aid. 61% of full-time freshmen and 57% of continuing full-time students received need-based aid. 45% of undergraduates work part time. Average annual earnings from campus work are $1239. The average financial indebtedness of a recent graduate was $16,346. Saint Mary's is a member of CSS. The CSS Profile or FAFSA is required. Check with the school for current deadlines.

International Students: There were 9 international students enrolled in a recent year. The school actively recruits these students. They must take the TOEFL and the SAT I or the ACT.

Computers: The mainframe is a Sun Ultra Enterprise 450. 162 PCs and Macs are available for student use in the computer labs and at various other locations around campus. All computers are networked and have Internet access. All students have direct access to the campus network from their dorm rooms. The Internet, on-line instructional materials, and the library catalog are available for college-related work. All students may access the system 24 hours a day, 7 days a week. There are no time limits and no fees. It is strongly recommended that all students have a personal computer.

Graduates: In a recent year, 312 bachelor's degrees were awarded. The most popular majors were elementary education (17%), business administration (14%), and communications (10%). In an average class, 65% graduate in 4 years or less, 68% graduate in 5 years or less, and 70% graduate in 6 years or less. 36 companies recruited on campus in a recent year. Of a recent graduating class, 19% were enrolled in graduate school within 6 months of graduation and 74% were employed.

Admissions Contact: Mary Pat Nolan, Director of Admission. A video is available. E-mail: *admission@saintmarys.edu*
Web: *www.saintmarys.edu*

TAYLOR UNIVERSITY
Upland, IN 46989-1001

D-3
(765) 998-5134
(800) 882-3456; Fax: (765) 998-4925

Full-time: 839 men, 950 women	Faculty: 119; IIB, -$
Part-time: 19 men, 26 women	Ph.D.s: 75%
Graduate: 6 men, 3 women	Student/Faculty: 15 to 1
Year: 4-1-4, summer session	Tuition: $18,528
Application Deadline: January 15	Room & Board: $5292
Freshman Class: 1312 applied, 1100 accepted, 470 enrolled	
SAT I Verbal/Math: 596/586	ACT: 26 VERY COMPETITIVE+

Taylor University, founded in 1846, is a private Christian interdenominational liberal arts institution. In addition to regional accreditation, Taylor has baccalaureate program accreditation with CSWE, NASM, and NCATE. The library contains 186,139 volumes, 10,891 microform items, and 7934 audio/video tapes/CDs, and subscribes to 687 periodicals. Computerized library services include the card catalog, interlibrary loans, database searching, and Internet access. Special learning facilities include a learning resource center, art gallery, radio station, TV station,

a 65-acre arboretum, C.S. Lewis Collection, and an observatory. The 250-acre campus is in a rural area 70 miles north of Indianapolis. Including any residence halls, there are 26 buildings.

Student Life: 67% of undergraduates are from out of state, mostly the Midwest. Others are from 45 states and 25 foreign countries. 79% are from public schools. 93% are white. Most are Protestant. The average age of freshmen is 18; all undergraduates, 20. 13% do not continue beyond their first year; 77% remain to graduate.

Housing: 1532 students can be accommodated in college housing, which includes single-sex dormitories, off-campus apartments, and married-student housing. On-campus housing is guaranteed for all 4 years. 97% of students live on campus; of those, 90% remain on campus on weekends. Alcohol is not permitted. All students may keep cars.

Activities: There are no fraternities or sororities. There are more than 100 groups on campus, including art, band, choir, chorale, chorus, computers, drama, ethnic, film, honors, international, jazz band, literary magazine, musical theater, newspaper, opera, orchestra, pep band, photography, political, professional, radio and TV, religious, social, social service, student government, symphony, and yearbook. Popular campus events include Taylathon, Youth Conference, and Martin Luther King Day observances.

Sports: There are 8 intercollegiate sports for men and 7 for women, and 14 intramural sports for men and 14 for women. Facilities include a gym, a field house, a wellness center, tennis and racquetball courts, a track, and a lake for swimming and ice skating.

Disabled Students: 80% of the campus is accessible. Wheelchair ramps, elevators, special parking, specially equipped rest rooms, special class scheduling, lowered drinking fountains, and lowered telephones are available.

Services: Counseling and information services are available, as is tutoring in most subjects. There is a reader service for the blind, and remedial math, reading, and writing.

Campus Safety and Security: Measures include 24-hour foot and vehicle patrol, self-defense education, security escort services, and pamphlets/posters/films. There are lighted pathways/sidewalks.

Programs of Study: Taylor confers B.A., B.S., and B.Mus. degrees. Associate and master's degrees are also awarded. Bachelor's degrees are awarded in BIOLOGICAL SCIENCE (biology/biological science and environmental biology), BUSINESS (accounting, banking and finance, international business management, management science, marketing and distribution, recreation and leisure services, and sports management), COMMUNICATIONS AND THE ARTS (art, communications, dramatic arts, English, French, journalism, music, and Spanish), COMPUTER AND PHYSICAL SCIENCE (chemistry, computer science, mathematics, natural sciences, and physics), EDUCATION (art, athletic training, Christian, elementary, English, foreign languages, mathematics, music, physical, science, and social studies), ENGINEERING AND ENVIRONMENTAL DESIGN (computer engineering, computer graphics, engineering physics, environmental engineering, and environmental science), HEALTH PROFESSIONS (health science), SOCIAL SCIENCE (biblical studies, economics, geography, history, international studies, philosophy, political science/government, psychology, social work, and sociology). Computer science, environmental science, and engineering physics are the strongest academically. Business, education, and computer science are the largest.

Required: Students must complete 128 credits and maintain a minimum GPA of 2.0 overall and 2.3 in the major. In addition to the requirements of the major, which include a comprehensive exam, each student must complete classes in computer science, fine arts, public speaking, Bible literature, Christian belief, literature, writing, science, history, social science, cross-cultural, phys ed, a senior seminar, fitness for life, and an upper-level philosophy course.

Special: Opportunities are provided for internships, cooperative programs, a Washington semester, study abroad in 12 countries, work-study programs, dual majors, student-designed majors, B.A.-B.S. degrees, and a 3-2 engineering degree. There is cross-registration with the other members of the Council for Christian Colleges and Universities and the Christian College Consortium. There are 7 national honor societies, including Phi Beta Kappa, a freshman honors program, and a liberal arts honors program.

Faculty/Classroom: 71% of faculty are male; 29%, female. All teach undergraduates. The average class size in an introductory lecture is 35; in a laboratory, 11; and in a regular course, 21.

Admissions: 84% of the 2003-2004 applicants were accepted. The SAT I scores for the 2003-2004 freshman class were: Verbal--12% below 500, 36% between 500 and 599, 43% between 600 and 700, and 10% above 700; Math--10% below 500, 40% between 500 and 599, 34% between 600 and 700, and 10% above 700. The ACT scores were 12% below 21, 19% between 21 and 23, 26% between 24 and 26, 20% between 27 and 28, and 24% above 28. 53% of the current freshmen were in the top fifth of their class; 80% were in the top two fifths. 33 freshmen graduated first in their class.

Requirements: The SAT I or ACT is required with composite scores of 1000 on the SAT I and 24 on the ACT recommended. Graduation from an accredited secondary school is required; a GED will be accepted. It is recommended that applicants complete 4 years of English, 3 to 4 each of math and lab science, 2 each of social studies and a foreign language, and course work in computing, typing/keyboarding, and the arts. An interview is recommended for all students, and an audition is required for music majors. Taylor requires applicants to be in the upper 40% of their class. A GPA of 2.8 is required. AP and CLEP credits are accepted. Important factors in the admissions decision are recommendations by school officials, extracurricular activities record, and leadership record.

Procedure: Freshmen are admitted fall and spring. Entrance exams should be taken during the spring of the junior year or fall of the senior year. There are early admissions and deferred admissions plans. Early decision applications should be filed by November 1; regular applications, by January 15 for fall entry, along with a $25 fee. Notification is sent February 5. A waiting list is an active part of the admissions procedure. Applications are accepted on-line through *www.tayloru.edu*.

Transfer: 43 transfer students enrolled in 2003-2004. Applicants must have maintained a minimum GPA of 2.5 and have completed at least 12 credit hours at the previous college. An interview is recommended. 48 of 128 credits required for the bachelor's degree must be completed at Taylor.

Visiting: There are regularly scheduled orientations for prospective students, including a campus tour, lunch, class meetings, faculty meetings, a financial aid session, and an admissions interview. There are guides for informal visits and visitors may sit in on classes and stay overnight. To schedule a visit, contact the Campus Visit Coordinator at (765) 998-5555 or *admissions_u@tayloru.edu*.

Financial Aid: In 2003-2004, 59% of all full-time freshmen and 57% of continuing full-time students received some form of financial aid. 56% of full-time freshmen and 53% of continuing full-time students received need-based aid. The average freshman award was $12,890. Need-based scholarships or need-based grants averaged $9773; need-based self-help aid (loans and jobs) averaged $3952; non-need-based athletic scholarships averaged $4138; and other non-need-based awards and non-need-based scholarships averaged $3183. 50% of undergraduates work part time. Average annual earnings from campus work are $1500. The average financial indebtedness of the 2003 graduate was $15,467. Taylor is a member of CSS. The FAFSA and the college's own financial statement are required. The deadline for filing freshman financial aid applications for fall entry is March 1.

International Students: There are 39 international students enrolled. The school actively recruits these students. They must score 550 on the written TOEFL. The school accepts the TOEFL in lieu of the SAT I.

Computers: The mainframes are a DEC PDP 11/70 and MicroVAX 3600 models. There are PCs at sites throughout the campus in a ratio of 1 for every 8 students. All students may access the system. There are no time limits and no fees. It is strongly recommended that all students have a personal computer.

Graduates: From July 1, 2002 to June 30, 2003, 465 bachelor's degrees were awarded. The most popular majors were business (10%), psychology (7%), and education (6%). In an average class, 2% graduate in 3 years or less, 72% graduate in 4 years or less, 76% graduate in 5 years or less, and 77% graduate in 6 years or less. 123 companies recruited on campus in 2002-2003. Of the 2002 graduating class, 13% were enrolled in graduate school within 6 months of graduation and 78% were employed.

Admissions Contact: Stephen Mortland, Director of Admissions. E-mail: *admissions_u@tayloru.edu* Web: *www.tayloru.edu*

TRI-STATE UNIVERSITY-MAIN CAMPUS
Angola, IN 46703

D-1
(260) 665-4365
(800) 347-4878; Fax: (260) 665-4578

Full-time: 709 men, 325 women	**Faculty:** 65; IIB, --$
Part-time: 61 men, 97 women	**Ph.D.s:** 71%
Graduate: 6 men	**Student/Faculty:** 16 to 1
Year: semesters, summer session	**Tuition:** $18,000
Application Deadline: June 1	**Room & Board:** $5600
Freshman Class: 1852 applied, 1330 accepted, 339 enrolled	
SAT I Verbal/Math: 530/560	**ACT:** 23 COMPETITIVE

Tri-State University, founded in 1884, is a private, independent university with 4 schools: Allen School of Engineering and Technology, Ketner School of Business, School of Education, and School of Arts and Sciences. There are 4 undergraduate schools and 1 graduate school. In addition to regional accreditation, Tri-State has baccalaureate program accreditation with ABET. The library contains 141,543 volumes, 15,439 microform items, and 6087 audio/video tapes/CDs, and subscribes to 162 periodicals. Computerized library services include the card catalog, interlibrary loans, database searching, and Internet access. Special learning facilities include a learning resource center and radio station. The 400-acre campus is in a small town 30 miles north of Ft. Wayne. Including any residence halls, there are 18 buildings.

Student Life: 60% of undergraduates are from Indiana. Students are from 23 states, 15 foreign countries, and Canada. 80% are from public

schools. 87% are white. The average age of freshmen is 19; all undergraduates, 22. 25% do not continue beyond their first year.

Housing: 571 students can be accommodated in college housing, which includes coed dorms. On-campus housing is guaranteed for all 4 years. 53% of students commute. Alcohol is not permitted. All students may keep cars.

Activities: 25% of men belong to 8 national fraternities; 15% of women belong to 6 local sororities. There are 35 groups on campus, including cheerleading, choir, computers, drama, ethnic, honors, international, newspaper, pep band, professional, radio and TV, religious, social service, student government, and yearbook.

Sports: There are 9 intercollegiate sports for men and 9 for women, and 6 intramural sports for men and 5 for women. Facilities include a gym with indoor and outdoor tracks, basketball and racquetball courts, an 18-hole golf course, and a football stadium.

Disabled Students: 98% of the campus is accessible. Wheelchair ramps, elevators, special parking, specially equipped rest rooms, special class scheduling, lowered drinking fountains, and lowered telephones are available.

Services: Counseling and information services are available, as is tutoring in some subjects, including math, business, engineering, accounting, and English. There is remedial math.

Campus Safety and Security: Measures include pamphlets/posters/films and lighted pathways/sidewalks.

Programs of Study: Tri-State confers B.A. and B.S. degrees. Associate and master's degrees are also awarded. Bachelor's degrees are awarded in BIOLOGICAL SCIENCE (biology/biological science), BUSINESS (accounting, banking and finance, business administration and management, management information systems, management science, marketing/retailing/merchandising, recreation and leisure services, recreational facilities management, and sports management), COMMUNICATIONS AND THE ARTS (communications), COMPUTER AND PHYSICAL SCIENCE (chemistry, computer science, information sciences and systems, mathematics, and physical sciences), EDUCATION (elementary, English, mathematics, physical, science, secondary, and social science), ENGINEERING AND ENVIRONMENTAL DESIGN (chemical engineering, civil engineering, computer engineering, drafting and design technology, electrical/electronics engineering, engineering management, environmental science, industrial administration/management, and mechanical engineering), HEALTH PROFESSIONS (premedicine), SOCIAL SCIENCE (criminal justice, forensic studies, psychology, and social science). Engineering, business, and education are the strongest academically and have the largest enrollments.

Required: Candidates for graduation must complete 120 to 132 semester hours, satisfying general education, program, and major requirements and maintaining a minimum overall GPA of 2.0. Required courses vary by degree sought. All students must complete a general education curriculum including science, math, American studies, social science, global studies, English composition, humanistics, computer literacy, and oral communication course work. Some majors have senior design projects.

Special: Cooperative education programs are available in engineering, business, and computer science. Opportunities exist for internships and work-study programs with the university and many companies. There are 12 national honor societies.

Faculty/Classroom: 75% of faculty are male; 25%, female. All teach undergraduates and 10% both teach and do research. No introductory courses are taught by graduate students. The average class size in an introductory lecture is 30; in a laboratory, 16; and in a regular course, 18.

Admissions: 72% of the 2003-2004 applicants were accepted. The SAT I scores for the 2003-2004 freshman class were: Verbal--37% below 500, 43% between 500 and 599, 18% between 600 and 700, and 1% above 700; Math--24% below 500, 38% between 500 and 599, 32% between 600 and 700, and 6% above 700. The ACT scores were 28% below 21, 25% between 21 and 23, 26% between 24 and 26, 13% between 27 and 28, and 9% above 28. 42% of the current freshmen were in the top fifth of their class; 69% were in the top two fifths. 8 freshmen graduated first in their class.

Requirements: The SAT I or ACT is required. In addition, candidates for admission should be graduates of accredited secondary schools. The GED is accepted. Most students should have 4 years of English and 2 years each of science, social studies, and math. Tri-State requires applicants to be in the upper 50% of their class. A GPA of 2.0 is required. AP and CLEP credits are accepted. Important factors in the admissions decision are advanced placement or honor courses, recommendations by school officials, and leadership record.

Procedure: Freshmen are admitted to all sessions. Entrance exams should be taken in the junior or senior year. There is a deferred admissions plan. Early decision applications should be filed by March 1; regular applications, by June 1 for fall entry, along with a $20 fee. Notification is sent on a rolling basis. Applications are accepted on-line through the school's web site.

Transfer: 35 transfer students enrolled in a recent year. In addition to meeting the university's requirements for freshmen, applicants must have satisfactory records from previous institutions. 30 of 120 credits required for the bachelor's degree must be completed at Tri-State.

Visiting: There are regularly scheduled orientations for prospective students, including meetings with faculty, administrators, and financial aid personnel, a campus tour, and a reception. There are guides for informal visits and visitors may sit in on classes. To schedule a visit, contact the Admissions Office at (260) 665-4132.

Financial Aid: In a recent year, 99% of all full-time freshmen and 95% of continuing full-time students received some form of financial aid. 32% of full-time freshmen and 22% of continuing full-time students received need-based aid. The average freshman award was $6035. 48% of undergraduates work part time. Average annual earnings from campus work are $500. The average financial indebtedness of a recent year's graduate was $11,872. The FAFSA is required. Check with the school for current application deadlines.

International Students: There are 19 international students enrolled. The school actively recruits these students. They must score 550 on the written TOEFL or take the MELAB. Applicants not transferring credits in math or English must be tested in those subjects.

Computers: There are about 150 networked PCs in 8 labs and other campus locations. All residence halls are networked to the campus computing system and the Internet. All students may access the system. There are no time limits and no fees.

Graduates: In a recent year, 214 bachelor's degrees were awarded. The most popular majors were engineering (42%), business (26%), and education (11%). In an average class, 26% graduate in 4 years or less, 45% graduate in 5 years or less, and 49% graduate in 6 years or less. 25 companies recruited on campus in a recent year. Of the 2002 graduating class, 20% were enrolled in graduate school within 6 months of graduation and 85% were employed.

Admissions Contact: Sara Yarian, Director of Admission.
E-mail: *admit@tristate.edu* Web: *www.tristate.edu*

UNIVERSITY OF EVANSVILLE
A-5
Evansville, IN 47722-0329

(812) 479-2468
(800) 423-8633; Fax: (812) 474-4076

Full-time: 861 men, 1414 women	**Faculty:** 168; IIA, -$
Part-time: 52 men, 45 women	**Ph.D.s:** 85%
Graduate: 28 men, 56 women	**Student/Faculty:** 14 to 1
Year: semesters, summer session	**Tuition:** $18,230
Application Deadline: open	**Room & Board:** $5960
Freshman Class: 2292 applied, 2017 accepted, 663 enrolled	
SAT I Verbal/Math: 570/560	**ACT:** 25 **VERY COMPETITIVE**

The University of Evansville, founded in 1854, is a private institution affiliated with the United Methodist Church. The university offers undergraduate degree programs in arts and sciences, business administration, education, engineering and computing sciences, fine arts, and nursing and health sciences. There are 4 undergraduate schools and 1 graduate school. In addition to regional accreditation, UE has baccalaureate program accreditation with ABET, APTA, NASM, NCATE, and NLN. The library contains 278,887 volumes, 462,749 microform items, and 11,147 audio/video tapes/CDs, and subscribes to 1200 periodicals. Computerized library services include interlibrary loans, database searching, and Internet access. Special learning facilities include a learning resource center, art gallery, and radio station. The 75-acre campus is in an urban area 120 miles west of Louisville. Including any residence halls, there are 39 buildings.

Student Life: 66% of undergraduates are from Indiana. Students are from 44 states, 38 foreign countries, and Canada. 94% are from public schools. 69% are white. 44% are claim no religious affiliation; 36% Protestant; 18% Catholic. The average age of freshmen is 18; all undergraduates, 20. 20% do not continue beyond their first year; 62% remain to graduate.

Housing: 1765 students can be accommodated in college housing, which includes single-sex and coed dorms, on-campus apartments, off-campus apartments, and fraternity houses. In addition, there are honors houses, special-interest houses, and an international house. On-campus housing is guaranteed for all 4 years. 70% of students live on campus; of those, 65% remain on campus on weekends. Alcohol is not permitted. All students may keep cars.

Activities: 30% of men belong to 6 national fraternities; 19% of women belong to 4 national sororities. There are 140 groups on campus, including art, band, cheerleading, choir, chorale, chorus, computers, dance, drama, drill team, ethnic, film, gay, honors, international, jazz band, literary magazine, marching band, musical theater, newspaper, orchestra, pep band, photography, political, professional, radio and TV, religious, social, social service, student government, and yearbook. Popular campus events include Greek Week, Bike Race, and International Bazaar.

Sports: There are 7 intercollegiate sports for men and 8 for women, and 35 intramural sports for men and 35 for women. Facilities include a 12,000- seat basketball arena, 1500-seat soccer stadium, 600-seat baseball/softball stadium, and 600-seat volleyball arena. The university fitness center includes a 25 meter pool, conditioning room, cardio theater with televisions, basketball courts, an indoor track, and a 1/2 mile security lighted jogging trail.

Disabled Students: 98% of the campus is accessible. Wheelchair ramps, elevators, special parking, and specially equipped rest rooms are available.

Services: Counseling and information services are available, as is tutoring in most subjects. There is a reader service for the blind and remedial writing.

Campus Safety and Security: Measures include 24-hour foot and vehicle patrol, security escort services, informal discussions, and pamphlets/posters/films. There are emergency telephones and lighted pathways/sidewalks.

Programs of Study: UE confers B.A., B.S., B.F.A., B.L.S., B.M., B.M.M.E., and B.M.M.T. degrees. Associate and master's degrees are also awarded. Bachelor's degrees are awarded in BIOLOGICAL SCIENCE (biology/biological science), BUSINESS (accounting, banking and finance, business administration and management, international business management, and marketing/retailing/merchandising), COMMUNICATIONS AND THE ARTS (art, art history and appreciation, communications, creative writing, dramatic arts, English, French, German, graphic design, literature, music, music business management, music performance, Spanish, studio art, theater design, and theater management), COMPUTER AND PHYSICAL SCIENCE (chemistry, computer programming, computer science, mathematics, and physics), EDUCATION (art, athletic training, elementary, English, foreign languages, mathematics, middle school, music, physical, science, secondary, social studies, and special), ENGINEERING AND ENVIRONMENTAL DESIGN (civil engineering, computer engineering, electrical/electronics engineering, engineering management, environmental science, and mechanical engineering), HEALTH PROFESSIONS (exercise science, health care administration, music therapy, nursing, physical therapy, predentistry, premedicine, prepharmacy, and sports medicine), SOCIAL SCIENCE (anthropology, archeology, behavioral science, biblical studies, classical/ancient civilization, criminal justice, economics, gerontology, history, international studies, liberal arts/general studies, paralegal studies, philosophy, physical fitness/movement, political science/government, prelaw, psychobiology, psychology, religion, sociology, and theological studies). Theater, physical therapy, and engineering are the strongest academically. Health sciences and psychology are the largest.

Required: To graduate, students must complete at least 124 semester hours with a minimum 2.0 cumulative and in their major, generally with 36 to 40 hours in the major. All students must take a core of 9 hours of world cultures, 7 of natural sciences, 6 each of humanities/fine arts, foreign language, and social sciences, and 3 each of math and senior seminar. 2 years of foreign language are required for the B.A. A demonstration of writing proficiency, a capstone course in the major, and completion of the fitness/wellness course are required for graduation.

Special: Students may study abroad at the University of Evansville British Campus, Harlaxton College, and more than 100 other sites. There is also an Italian excavation summer program, a British Parliament internship, a U.S. Pentagon internship, an accelerated Bachelor of Liberal Studies degree, B.A.-B.S. degrees in electrical engineering and mechanical engineering, accelerated study for adults, combined bachelor's/graduate degrees, cooperative education, distance learning, dual enrollment of high school students, ESL, teacher certification, as well as exchange student, external degree, honors, and independent study programs, internships, and student-designed majors. There are 18 national honor societies, a freshman honors program, and 20 departmental honors programs.

Faculty/Classroom: 67% of faculty are male; 33%, female. All teach undergraduates. No introductory courses are taught by graduate students. The average class size in an introductory lecture is 20 and in a regular course, 18.

Admissions: 88% of the 2003-2004 applicants were accepted. The SAT I scores for the 2003-2004 freshman class were: Verbal--23% below 500, 40% between 500 and 599, 31% between 600 and 700, and 6% above 700; Math--21% below 500, 42% between 500 and 599, 32% between 600 and 700, and 5% above 700. The ACT scores were 13% below 21, 14% between 21 and 23, 36% between 24 and 26, 16% between 27 and 28, and 21% above 28. 60% of the current freshmen were in the top fifth of their class; 85% were in the top two fifths. There were 9 National Merit finalists. 98 freshmen graduated first in their class.

Requirements: The SAT I or ACT is required. In addition, to be competitive for admission, students should submit a minimum SAT I composite score of 1100 or ACT composite of 24. Applicants must be graduates of accredited secondary schools; applicants who have been homeschooled are also considered. The university recommends completion of 4 years of college-preparatory English, 3 each of math (algebra I and II, geometry) and social science, and 2 of a foreign language. An interview is recommended, but not required. UE requires applicants to be in the upper 50% of their class. A GPA of 2.0 is required. AP and CLEP credits are accepted. Important factors in the admissions decision are advanced placement or honor courses, leadership record, and recommendations by school officials.

Procedure: Freshmen are admitted fall and spring. Entrance exams should be taken by December of the senior year. There are rolling and deferred admissions plans. Early decision applications should be filed by December 1, along with a $35 fee. Notification of early decision is sent December 15; regular decision, on a rolling basis. Applications are accepted on-line through *www.evansville.edu.*

Transfer: 101 transfer students enrolled in 2002-2003. Applicants must have a minimum GPA of 2.0 in all previous college work. 63 of 124 credits required for the bachelor's degree must be completed at UE.

Visiting: There are regularly scheduled orientations for prospective students, including a campus tour, faculty academic sessions, financial aid and admission appointments, and study abroad and honors program sessions. There are guides for informal visits and visitors may sit in on classes and stay overnight. To schedule a visit, contact Office of Admissions at *admission@evansville.edu.*

Financial Aid: In 2003-2004, 99% of all full-time freshmen and 87% of continuing full-time students received some form of financial aid. 76% of full-time freshmen and 67% of continuing full-time students received need-based aid. The average freshman award was $17,147. Need-based scholarships or need-based grants averaged $15,016 ($23,280 maximum); need-based self-help aid (loans and jobs) averaged $4211 ($7925 maximum); and non-need-based athletic scholarships averaged $17,463 ($25,590 maximum). 20% of undergraduates work part time. Average annual earnings from campus work are $1280. The average financial indebtedness of the 2003 graduate was $17,566. UE is a member of CSS. The FAFSA is required. The deadline for filing freshman financial aid applications for fall entry is March 1.

International Students: There are 111 international students enrolled. The school actively recruits these students. They must score 500 on the written TOEFL or 173 on the electronic version and also take a writing placement test and the SAT I or the ACT.

Computers: The mainframe is an IBM Multiprise 2003-206. Students access e-mail, university news, grades, on-line class discussions, and pre-register for classes through a personal account on the university intranet. There are 6 public computer labs, several departmental computer clusters, and a small computer lab in each residence hall connected to a LAN using Windows 2000 and Mac servers. All classrooms are wired for Internet access. Students may connect to the Internet from their rooms in the residence halls for $50 per semester. All students may access the system at any time. There are no time limits and no fees. It is strongly recommended that all students have a personal computer.

Graduates: From July 1, 2002 to June 30, 2003, 503 bachelor's degrees were awarded. The most popular majors were social services (16%), business (13%), and health sciences (12%). In an average class, 45% graduate in 4 years or less, 68% graduate in 5 years or less, and 62% graduate in 6 years or less. 100 companies recruited on campus in 2002-2003. Of the 2002 graduating class, 16% were enrolled in graduate school within 6 months of graduation and 73% were employed.

Admissions Contact: Dr. Tom Bear, Dean of Admission. A video is available. E-mail: *admission@evansville.edu*
Web: *http://www.evansville.edu*

UNIVERSITY OF INDIANAPOLIS
Indianapolis, IN 46227-3697

C-3

(317) 788-3216
(800) 232-8634; Fax: (317) 788-3300

Full-time: 759 men, 1323 women	Faculty: 138; IIA, --$
Part-time: 233 men, 601 women	Ph.D.s: 69%
Graduate: 304 men, 659 women	Student/Faculty: 15 to 1
Year: 4-4-1, summer session	Tuition: $16,620
Application Deadline: open	Room & Board: $5940
Freshman Class: 3259 applied, 2364 accepted, 620 enrolled	
SAT I Verbal/Math: 560/560	ACT: 22 VERY COMPETITIVE

The University of Indianapolis, established in 1902, is a private liberal arts school affiliated with the United Methodist Church. It provides undergraduate and graduate studies with an emphasis on education, business, nursing, and arts and sciences. There are 5 undergraduate and 7 graduate schools. In addition to regional accreditation, U of I has baccalaureate program accreditation with ACBSP, ACEJMC, APTA, CSWE, NASM, NCATE, and NLN. The library contains 171,782 volumes, 15,002 microform items, and 7023 audio/video tapes/CDs, and subscribes to 972 periodicals. Computerized library services include the card catalog, interlibrary loans, and database searching. Special learning facilities include a learning resource center, art gallery, planetarium, radio station, TV station, and an archeology lab. The 60-acre campus is in a suburban area on the south side of Indianapolis. Including any residence halls, there are 13 buildings.

Student Life: 85% of undergraduates are from Indiana. Students are from 24 states, 60 foreign countries, and Canada. 79% are white. 55% are Protestant; 23% claim no religious affiliation; 21% Catholic. The average age of freshmen is 18; all undergraduates, 22. 20% do not continue beyond their first year; 60% remain to graduate.

Housing: 1214 students can be accommodated in college housing, which includes single-sex and coed dorms, on-campus apartments, off-campus apartments, and married-student housing. In addition, there are honors houses. On-campus housing is guaranteed for all 4 years. 58% of students live on campus. Alcohol is not permitted. All students may keep cars.

Activities: There are no fraternities or sororities. There are 45 groups on campus, including academic, art, cheerleading, chess, choir, chorale, chorus, computers, dance, debate, drama, ethnic, forensics, gay, honors, international, jazz band, literary magazine, musical theater, newspaper, orchestra, pep band, photography, political, professional, radio and TV, religious, social, social service, and student government. Popular campus events include Cyclerama, winter and spring formals, and Lil' Sibs Weekend.

Sports: There are 11 intercollegiate sports for men and 10 for women, and 7 intramural sports for men and 7 for women. Facilities include a health and fitness center including a 3500-seat gym, an Olympic-size swimming pool, racquetball courts, a weight room, and a dance studio.

Disabled Students: All of the campus is accessible. Wheelchair ramps, elevators, special parking, specially equipped rest rooms, special class scheduling, lowered drinking fountains, and lowered telephones are available.

Services: Counseling and information services are available, as is tutoring in every subject. There is remedial math and writing. There is a special learning disabled program.

Campus Safety and Security: Measures include 24-hour foot and vehicle patrol, self-defense education, security escort services, and emergency telephones. There are lighted pathways/sidewalks.

Programs of Study: U of I confers B.A., B.S., B.F.A., B.M., B.S.N., and B.S.W. degrees. Associate, master's, and doctoral degrees are also awarded. Bachelor's degrees are awarded in BIOLOGICAL SCIENCE (biology/biological science), BUSINESS (accounting, banking and finance, business administration and management, business communications, business economics, entrepreneurial studies, international business management, management information systems, marketing/retailing/merchandising, and sports management), COMMUNICATIONS AND THE ARTS (art, broadcasting, communications, dramatic arts, English, French, German, journalism, music, music performance, musical theater, public relations, Spanish, speech/debate/rhetoric, and studio art), COMPUTER AND PHYSICAL SCIENCE (chemistry, computer science, earth science, mathematics, and physics), EDUCATION (art, athletic training, business, drama, elementary, English, foreign languages, mathematics, middle school, music, physical, science, secondary, and social studies), ENGINEERING AND ENVIRONMENTAL DESIGN (commercial art, electrical/electronics engineering, environmental science, and mechanical engineering), HEALTH PROFESSIONS (art therapy, exercise science, medical laboratory technology, nursing, and respiratory therapy), SOCIAL SCIENCE (anthropology, archeology, corrections, economics, history, international relations, law enforcement and corrections, philosophy, political science/government, psychology, religion, social science, social work, sociology, and youth ministry). Education, nursing, and science (biology/chemistry) are the strongest academically. Business is the largest.

Required: All undergraduate students must complete at least 124 hours, including 24 hours or more in the major with a GPA of 2.0 or better. Requirements include a core curriculum in which 8 learning goals must be met. Students must also take a health and phys ed course and 1 spring term, and attend lecture/performance events. Specific courses include math, social inquiry, history, and cross-cultural understanding and global awareness.

Special: Cross-registration is offered in conjunction with 6 area colleges. Cooperative programs, internships, various work-study programs, study abroad, dual and student-designed majors, accelerated programs in liberal studies and organizational leadership, pass/fail options, and a 3-2 engineering degree with Indiana University Purdue University at Indianapolis are available. A fleximester, which is a 3-week spring term and 27-week summer sessions, is also offered. There are 11 national honor societies, a freshman honors program, and 5 departmental honors programs.

Faculty/Classroom: 50% of faculty are male; 50%, female. 96% teach undergraduates. No introductory courses are taught by graduate students. The average class size in an introductory lecture is 17; in a laboratory, 13; and in a regular course, 17.

Admissions: 73% of the 2003-2004 applicants were accepted. The SAT I scores for the 2003-2004 freshman class were: Verbal--48% below 500, 40% between 500 and 599, 10% between 600 and 700, and 2% above 700; Math--40% below 500, 44% between 500 and 599, 15% between 600 and 700, and 1% above 700. The ACT scores were 14% below 21, 59% between 21 and 23, 12% between 24 and 26, 13% between 27 and 28, and 2% above 28. 51% of the current freshmen were in the top fifth of their class; 84% were in the top two fifths. In a recent year there were 2 National Merit semifinalists. 15 freshmen graduated first in their class.

Requirements: The SAT I or ACT is required, with a minimum SAT I composite of 920 or ACT composite of 20. Each applicant should have at least 24 academic credits, including at least 12 units total from English and literature (not including speech), history, foreign language, math lab science, and social studies. The GED is accepted. An interview is recommended. U of I requires applicants to be in the upper 50% of their class. A GPA of 2.25 is required. AP and CLEP credits are accepted.

Procedure: Freshmen are admitted to all sessions. There is a rolling admissions plan and a deferred admissions plan. Application deadlines are open. Application fee is $20. Applications are accepted on-line through the school's web site, *www.uindy.ed.*

Transfer: 128 transfer students enrolled in 2002-2003. No ACT or SAT I is needed if applicants have a GPA of C and 20 semester hours of credit. 30 of 124 credits required for the bachelor's degree must be completed at U of I.

Visiting: There are regularly scheduled orientations for prospective students, including campus visits and tours. There are guides for informal visits and visitors may sit in on classes and stay overnight. To schedule a visit, contact the Admissions Office at (800) 232-8634, ext. 3441 or *treinhardt@uindy.edu.*

Financial Aid: In 2003-2004, 82% of all full-time freshmen and 87% of continuing full-time students received some form of financial aid. 73% of full-time freshmen and 78% of continuing full-time students received need-based aid. The average freshman award was $13,356. 50% of undergraduates work part time. Average annual earnings from campus work are $1400. The average financial indebtedness of the 2003 graduate was $16,809. U of I is a member of CSS. The FAFSA, the college's own financial statement, and the parent and student tax returns are required. The deadline for filing freshman financial aid applications for fall entry is March 1.

International Students: There are 152 international students enrolled. The school actively recruits these students. They must score 500 on the written TOEFL or 173 on the electronic version.

Computers: The mainframe is a Compaq Alpha Server 2100 A. Students have access from residence halls. There are also both Macs and PCs available to students in 5 of 7 academic buildings. All students may access the system 7 days per week. There are no time limits and no fees.

Graduates: From July 1, 2002 to June 30, 2003, 433 bachelor's degrees were awarded. The most popular majors were business (27%), education (16%), and biology (8%). In an average class, 4% graduate in 3 years or less, 52% graduate in 4 years or less, 58% graduate in 5 years or less, and 60% graduate in 6 years or less. 136 companies recruited on campus in 2002-2003. Of the 2002 graduating class, 26% were enrolled in graduate school within 6 months of graduation and 70% were employed.

Admissions Contact: Ron Wilks, Director of Admissions. E-mail: *admissions@uindy.edu* Web: *www.uindy.edu*

UNIVERSITY OF NOTRE DAME

C-1

Notre Dame, IN 46556 (574) 631-7505

Full-time: 4429 men, 3864 women	**Faculty:** 760; I,
Part-time: 12 men, 6 women	**Ph.D.s:** 98%
Graduate: 1929 men, 1175 women	**Student/Faculty:** 11 to 1
Year: semesters, summer session	**Tuition:** $27,512
Application Deadline: January 7	**Room & Board:** $6930
Freshman Class: 12,095 applied, 3524 accepted, 1996 enrolled	
SAT I Verbal/Math: 667/693	**ACT:** 31 **MOST COMPETITIVE**

The University of Notre Dame, founded in 1842, is a private institution affiliated with the Roman Catholic Church offering undergraduate programs in architecture, arts and letters, business administration, engineering, and science. There are 5 undergraduate and 6 graduate schools. In addition to regional accreditation, Notre Dame has baccalaureate program accreditation with AACSB, ABET, and NAAB. The 8 libraries contain 2,737,784 volumes, 2,100,425 microform items, and 25,513 audio/video tapes/CDs, and subscribe to 17,239 periodicals. Computerized library services include the card catalog, interlibrary loans, and database searching. Special learning facilities include a learning resource center, art gallery, radio station, and an art museum. The 1250-acre campus is in a suburban area 90 miles east of Chicago. Including any residence halls, there are 175 buildings.

Student Life: 91% of undergraduates are from out of state, mostly the Midwest. Students are from 50 states, 100 foreign countries, and Canada. 48% are from public schools. 76% are white. 9% are Catholic; 9% Eastern religions (Eastern Islam, Eastern Orthodox); 7% Protestant. The average age of freshmen is 18; all undergraduates, 20. 3% do not continue beyond their first year; 95% remain to graduate.

Housing: 6255 students can be accommodated in college housing, which includes single-sex dorms. On-campus housing is guaranteed for the freshman year only and is available on a lottery system for upperclassmen. 75% of students live on campus; of those, 90% remain on campus on weekends. Upperclassmen may keep cars.

Activities: There are no fraternities or sororities. There are 264 groups on campus, including art, bagpipe band, band, cheerleading, chess, choir, chorale, chorus, computers, dance, debate, drama, ethnic, film, forensics, honors, international, jazz band, literary magazine, marching band, musical theater, newspaper, orchestra, pep band, photography, political, professional, radio, religious, social, social service, student gov-

ernment, symphony, and yearbook. Popular campus events include a spring festival, home football weekends, and the Collegiate Jazz Festival.

Sports: There are 13 intercollegiate sports for men and 13 for women, and 22 intramural sports for men and 22 for women. Facilities include an athletic and convocation center with an 11,500-seat basketball arena and a hockey arena, a tennis pavilion, a golf course, an indoor sports center, a recreational sports center, and an aquatic center. The campus football stadium seats 80,225. There are general-purpose playing fields, stadiums for track, lacrosse, and baseball, and soccer and softball fields.

Disabled Students: 85% of the campus is accessible. Wheelchair ramps, elevators, special parking, specially equipped rest rooms, special class scheduling, lowered drinking fountains, and lowered telephones are available.

Services: Counseling and information services are available, as is tutoring in most subjects. There is a reader service for the blind.

Campus Safety and Security: Measures include 24-hour foot and vehicle patrol, self-defense education, security escort services, and shuttle buses. There are informal discussions, pamphlets/posters/films, emergency telephones, and lighted pathways/sidewalks.

Programs of Study: Notre Dame confers B.A., B.S., B.Arch., B.B.A., and B.F.A. degrees. Master's and doctoral degrees are also awarded. Bachelor's degrees are awarded in BIOLOGICAL SCIENCE (biochemistry and biology/biological science), BUSINESS (accounting, banking and finance, management information systems, management science, and marketing/retailing/merchandising), COMMUNICATIONS AND THE ARTS (art history and appreciation, Chinese, English, film arts, French, German, Greek, Italian, Japanese, Latin, music, romance languages and literature, Russian, Spanish, and studio art), COMPUTER AND PHYSICAL SCIENCE (applied physics, chemistry, computer science, mathematics, and physics), EDUCATION (science), ENGINEERING AND ENVIRONMENTAL DESIGN (aeronautical engineering, architecture, chemical engineering, civil engineering, computer engineering, electrical/electronics engineering, environmental engineering, environmental science, and mechanical engineering), HEALTH PROFESSIONS (predentistry and premedicine), SOCIAL SCIENCE (American studies, anthropology, classical/ancient civilization, economics, history, liberal arts/general studies, medieval studies, philosophy, political science/government, psychology, sociology, and theological studies). Engineering, theology, and business are the strongest academically. Political science, finance, and English are the largest.

Required: All students must complete courses in English, philosophy, science, history, theology, math, social science, and phys ed. A total of 125 semester hours with a minimum GPA of 2.0 is required to graduate.

Special: Cross-registration is offered with Saint Mary's College. Study abroad is possible in 20 countries. A 5-year arts and letters/engineering B.A.-B.S. degree is offered. There is a program of liberal studies, centered on the discussion of great books. Internships, an accelerated degree program, a Washington semester, dual majors, 3-2 engineering degrees, and pass/fail options are available. There are 9 national honor societies, including Phi Beta Kappa, and 2 departmental honors programs.

Faculty/Classroom: 77% of faculty are male; 23%, female.

Admissions: 29% of the 2003-2004 applicants were accepted. The SAT I scores for the 2003-2004 freshman class were: Verbal--3% below 500, 13% between 500 and 599, 44% between 600 and 700, and 39% above 700; Math--1% below 500, 9% between 500 and 599, 39% between 600 and 700, and 51% above 700. 95% of the current freshmen were in the top fifth of their class; 99% were in the top two fifths.

Requirements: The SAT I or ACT is required. In addition, applicants should be graduates of an accredited secondary school with 16 Carnegie credits completed, including 4 years of English, 3 of math, and 2 each of science, foreign language, and history. The SAT II: Subject test in a foreign language is recommended. An essay is required. An audition or a portfolio is recommended for some majors. AP credits are accepted.

Procedure: Freshmen are admitted in the fall. Entrance exams should be taken by fall of the senior year. There is a deferred admissions plan. Early decision applications should be filed by November 1; regular applications, by January 7 for fall entry. The fall 2003 application fee was $50. Notification of early decision is sent December 15; regular decision, April 1. 840 applicants were on the 2003 waiting list; 572 were admitted. Applications are accepted on-line through the admissions web site, *http://admissions.nd.edu,* or through EXPAN.

Transfer: 129 transfer students enrolled in 2002-2003. Applicants should have completed at least 27 semester hours of transferable credit and maintained a 3.0 GPA in all courses. Admission depends on openings in each undergraduate college. 60 of 125 credits required for the bachelor's degree must be completed at Notre Dame.

Visiting: There are regularly scheduled orientations for prospective students, including small group sessions for students, larger sessions for parents, and tours for all. Visitors may sit in on classes and stay overnight. To schedule a visit, contact the Admissions telephone receptionist at *admissio.1@nd.edu.*

Financial Aid: In a recent year, 81% of all full-time freshmen and 87% of continuing full-time students received some form of financial aid. 50%

of full-time freshmen and 57% of continuing full-time students received need-based aid. The average freshman award was $19,000. 48% of undergraduates work part time. Average annual earnings from campus work are $900. The average financial indebtedness of a recent graduate was $14,290. Notre Dame is a member of CSS. The CSS Profile or FAFSA and federal income tax return are required. The deadline for filing freshman financial aid applications for fall entry is February 15.

International Students: There are 302 international students enrolled. The school actively recruits these students. They must score 550 on the written TOEFL.

Computers: The mainframes are an HP 3000 and two origen 2000s. There are 600 PCs, Macs, and UNIX computers in open clusters that students can use to complete their course work and access the Internet. All students may access the system 24 hours a day. There are no time limits and no fees. It is strongly recommended that all students have a personal computer.

Graduates: From July 1, 2002 to June 30, 2003, 2094 bachelor's degrees were awarded. The most popular majors were finance (10%), government (9%), and accountancy (9%). In an average class, 88% graduate in 4 years or less, 94% graduate in 5 years or less, and 95% graduate in 6 years or less. 340 companies recruited on campus in 2002-2003. Of the 2002 graduating class, 66% were employed within 6 months of graduation.

Admissions Contact: Daniel J. Saracino, Assistant Provost for Enrollment. E-mail: *admissio.1@nd.edu* Web: *http://admissions.nd.edu*

UNIVERSITY OF SAINT FRANCIS
Fort Wayne, IN 46808

D-2

(260) 434-3178
(800) 729-4732; Fax: (260) 434-7590

Full-time: 414 men, 815 women	**Faculty:** 94
Part-time: 58 men, 321 women	**Ph.D.s:** 46%
Graduate: 58 men, 168 women	**Student/Faculty:** 13 to 1
Year: semesters, summer session	**Tuition:** $15,514
Application Deadline: open	**Room & Board:** $5450
Freshman Class: 934 applied, 694 accepted, 352 enrolled	
SAT I Verbal/Math: 470/480	**ACT:** 20 **COMPETITIVE**

University of Saint Francis is a private Roman Catholic liberal arts college founded in 1890 by the Sisters of Saint Francis. In addition to regional accreditation, USF has baccalaureate program accreditation with CAHEA, CSWE, NCATE, and NLN. The 2 libraries contain 85,544 volumes, 618,843 microform items, and 1487 audio/video tapes/CDs, and subscribe to 520 periodicals. Computerized library services include the card catalog, interlibrary loans, database searching, and Internet access. Special learning facilities include a learning resource center, art gallery, and planetarium. The 75-acre campus is in an urban area on the west side of Fort Wayne. Including any residence halls, there are 21 buildings.

Student Life: 91% of undergraduates are from Indiana. Students are from 8 states and 3 foreign countries. 90% are white. 40% are Protestant; 30% claim no religious affiliation; 28% Catholic. The average age of freshmen is 24; all undergraduates, 25. 33% do not continue beyond their first year; 54% remain to graduate.

Housing: 240 students can be accommodated in college housing, which includes coed dorms. On-campus housing is guaranteed for the freshman year only and is available on a first-come, first-served basis. 84% of students commute. Alcohol is not permitted. All students may keep cars.

Activities: There are no fraternities or sororities. There are 25 groups on campus, including art, cheerleading, choir, dance, drama, ethnic, film, honors, musical theater, newspaper, pep band, professional, radio and TV, religious, social, social service, and student government. Popular campus events include Little Regatta and Spring Fling.

Sports: There are 8 intercollegiate sports for men and 8 for women, and 4 intramural sports for men and 4 for women. Facilities include a gym with 2 basketball courts or 3 volleyball courts, a weight room, a baseball diamond, a beach volleyball pit, a football stadium, and soccer, baseball, and softball fields.

Disabled Students: 85% of the campus is accessible. Wheelchair ramps, elevators, special parking, specially equipped rest rooms, and lowered drinking fountains are available.

Services: Counseling and information services are available, as is tutoring in most subjects. There is remedial math, reading, and writing, help for the learning disabled, individual counseling, and peer tutoring.

Campus Safety and Security: Measures include 24-hour foot and vehicle patrol, security escort services, pamphlets/posters/films, and emergency telephones. There are lighted pathways/sidewalks.

Programs of Study: USF confers B.A., B.S., B.B.A., B.L.S., B.S.Ed., B.S.N., and B.S.W. degrees. Associate and master's degrees are also awarded. Bachelor's degrees are awarded in BIOLOGICAL SCIENCE (biology/biological science), BUSINESS (accounting and business administration and management), COMMUNICATIONS AND THE ARTS (communications, English, and fine arts), COMPUTER AND PHYSICAL SCIENCE (chemistry and science), EDUCATION (art, business, elementary, English, health, science, secondary, social studies, and special), EN-

GINEERING AND ENVIRONMENTAL DESIGN (environmental science), HEALTH PROFESSIONS (medical laboratory technology, nursing, predentistry, and premedicine), SOCIAL SCIENCE (history, liberal arts/general studies, ministries, psychology, religion, and social work). Nursing, education, and history are the strongest academically. Business, art, and nursing are the largest.

Required: All students must complete courses in humanities, social and behavioral science, religious studies, life and physical sciences, oral and written communication, phys ed, computer science, and math. 128 semester hours with a minimum GPA of 2.0 and at least 30 hours in the major are required to graduate. A comprehensive exam is required in biology and business administration, and a thesis is required in history.

Special: Internships in art, business, and communication are available, as well as nondegree study. Students also can receive credit for life experience. Cross-registration with the Fort Wayne Higher Education Consortium is available, as well as dual and student-designed majors. There is 1 national honor society, a freshman honors program, and 1 departmental honors program.

Faculty/Classroom: 39% of faculty are male; 61%, female. 94% teach undergraduates. No introductory courses are taught by graduate students. The average class size in an introductory lecture is 30; in a laboratory, 11; and in a regular course, 20.

Admissions: 74% of the 2003-2004 applicants were accepted. The SAT I scores for the 2003-2004 freshman class were: Verbal--61% below 500, 29% between 500 and 599, and 9% between 600 and 700; Math--55% below 500, 37% between 500 and 599, and 7% between 600 and 700. The ACT scores were 64% below 21, 22% between 21 and 23, 12% between 24 and 26, and 2% between 27 and 28. 20% of the current freshmen were in the top fifth of their class; 52% were in the top two fifths. 2 freshmen graduated first in their class.

Requirements: The SAT I or ACT is required, with a minimum composite score of 920 on the SAT I or 19 on the ACT. USF requires applicants to be in the upper 50% of their class. A GPA of 2.0 is required. AP and CLEP credits are accepted. Important factors in the admissions decision are recommendations by school officials, advanced placement or honor courses, and extracurricular activities record.

Procedure: Freshmen are admitted to all sessions. Entrance exams should be taken in the spring of the junior year or fall of the senior year. There is a deferred admissions plan. Application deadlines are open. Application fee is $20. Notification is sent on a rolling basis.

Transfer: 286 transfer students enrolled in 2002-2003. Applicants need a minimum cumulative GPA of 2.0 and must submit all college transcripts. 32 of 128 credits required for the bachelor's degree must be completed at USF.

Visiting: There are regularly scheduled orientations for prospective students, including meetings with faculty and staff and student tours. There are guides for informal visits and visitors may sit in on classes and stay overnight. To schedule a visit, contact the Admissions Office at (260) 434-3279 or *admis@sf.edu*.

Financial Aid: In 2003-2004, 87% of all full-time freshmen and 94% of continuing full-time students received some form of financial aid, including need-based aid. The average freshman award was $13,228. Need-based scholarships or need-based grants averaged $2163 ($5000 maximum); need-based self-help aid (loans and jobs) averaged $2625 ($3460 maximum); non-need-based athletic scholarships averaged $4401 ($20,938 maximum); and other non-need-based awards and non-need-based scholarships averaged $2613 ($7000 maximum). 9% of undergraduates work part time. Average annual earnings from campus work are $877. USF is a member of CSS. The FAFSA is required. The deadline for filing freshman financial aid applications for fall entry is March 10.

International Students: There are 3 international students enrolled. They must score 500 on the written TOEFL.

Computers: The mainframe is an IBM AS/400. More than 25 PCs with links to the World Wide Web are available in classrooms, the library, computer labs, and residence halls. All students may access the system 7 days a week. There are no time limits and no fees.

Graduates: From July 1, 2002 to June 30, 2003, 192 bachelor's degrees were awarded. The most popular majors were business (15%), education (13%), and nursing (12%). In an average class, 3% graduate in 3 years or less, 33% graduate in 4 years or less, 39% graduate in 5 years or less, and 40% graduate in 6 years or less. Of the 2002 graduating class, 4% were enrolled in graduate school within 6 months of graduation and 95% were employed.

Admissions Contact: Matthew P. Nettleton, Director of Admissions. A video is available. E-mail: *mnettleton@sf.edu* Web: *www.sf.edu*

UNIVERSITY OF SOUTHERN INDIANA
Evansville, IN 47712

A-5

(812) 464-1765
(800) 467-1965; Fax: (812) 465-7154

Full-time: 2982 men, 4310 women	**Faculty:** 297; IIA, --$
Part-time: 697 men, 1165 women	**Ph.Ds:** 64%
Graduate: 192 men, 553 women	**Student/Faculty:** 25 to 1
Year: semesters, summer session	**Tuition:** $3885 ($9188)
Application Deadline: August 15	**Room & Board:** $5140
Freshman Class: 4369 applied, 4049 accepted, 2079 enrolled	
SAT I Verbal/Math: 478/474	**ACT:** 20 **LESS COMPETITIVE**

The University of Southern Indiana, founded in 1965, is a public institution offering undergraduate programs in business, education and human service, liberal arts, nursing and health professions, and science and engineering. There are 5 undergraduate schools and 1 graduate school. In addition to regional accreditation, USI has baccalaureate program accreditation with AACSB, ABET, ADA, CSWE, and NCATE. The library contains 333,155 volumes, 576,908 microform items, and 7924 audio/video tapes/CDs, and subscribes to 6463 periodicals. Computerized library services include the card catalog, interlibrary loans, and database searching. Special learning facilities include a learning resource center, radio station, and TV station. The 300-acre campus is in a suburban area 150 miles south of Indianapolis. Including any residence halls, there are 50 buildings.

Student Life: 90% of undergraduates are from Indiana. Others are from 36 states, 39 foreign countries, and Canada. 94% are white. The average age of freshmen is 19; all undergraduates, 23. 38% do not continue beyond their first year; 31% remain to graduate.

Housing: 2947 students can be accommodated in college housing, which includes single-sex and coed dorms, on-campus apartments, off-campus apartments, married-student housing, fraternity houses, and sorority houses. In addition, there are honors houses and special-interest houses. On-campus housing is available on a first-come, first-served basis. Priority is given to out-of-town students. 68% of students commute. Alcohol is not permitted. All students may keep cars.

Activities: 4% of men belong to 6 national fraternities; 4% of women belong to 4 national sororities. There are 97 groups on campus, including art, cheerleading, chess, choir, chorus, computers, dance, drama, ethnic, film, gay, honors, international, jazz band, literary magazine, musical theater, newspaper, pep band, photography, political, professional, radio and TV, religious, social, social service, student government, and yearbook. Popular campus events include Eagle Gran Prix Bike Race, Spring Fling, and Oksoberfest.

Sports: There are 6 intercollegiate sports for men and 7 for women, and 11 intramural sports for men and 11 for women. Facilities include a physical activities center with a swimming pool, a weight room, 6 tennis courts, and a 3000-seat multipurpose area and a recreation and fitness center with weights, cardiovascular equipment, and exercise programs.

Disabled Students: 90% of the campus is accessible. Wheelchair ramps, elevators, special parking, specially equipped rest rooms, special class scheduling, lowered drinking fountains, lowered telephones, and student assistance through the counseling center are available.

Services: Counseling and information services are available, as is tutoring in most subjects. There is a reader service for the blind, and remedial math, reading, and writing.

Campus Safety and Security: Measures include 24-hour foot and vehicle patrol, self-defense education, security escort services, and shuttle buses. There are pamphlets/posters/films, emergency telephones, and lighted pathways/sidewalks.

Programs of Study: USI confers B.A., B.S., B.G.S., B.S.E., B.S.N., and B.S.W. degrees. Associate and master's degrees are also awarded. Bachelor's degrees are awarded in BIOLOGICAL SCIENCE (biology/biological science and biophysics), BUSINESS (accounting, banking and finance, business administration and management, business economics, electronic business, and marketing/retailing/merchandising), COMMUNICATIONS AND THE ARTS (broadcasting, communications, dramatic arts, English, German, journalism, Spanish, and speech/debate/rhetoric), COMPUTER AND PHYSICAL SCIENCE (chemistry and mathematics), EDUCATION (art, business, elementary, middle school, science, secondary, and special), ENGINEERING AND ENVIRONMENTAL DESIGN (engineering), HEALTH PROFESSIONS (nursing, occupational therapy, predentistry, and premedicine), SOCIAL SCIENCE (economics, history, philosophy, political science/government, prelaw, psychology, social work, and sociology). Math and German are the strongest academically. Business administration, education, and nursing are the largest.

Required: The university core curriculum's goals focus on four areas: The Mind (enhancement of cognitive abilities), The Self (enhancement of individual development), The World (enhancement of cultural and natural awareness), and The Synthesis (the integration and application of knowledge). These are then subdivided into 13 objectives concerned with critical thinking, oral and written communication, math, information processing, ethics, the arts, health and lifestyle, history, individual development and social behavior, science, Western culture, global communi-

ties, and interdisciplinary studies. A total of 50 credit hours is distributed among the objectives with a total of 124 credit hours needed to graduate. A minimum cumulative 2.0 GPA is required.

Special: Students may participate in cooperative programs, internships in business and communications, and work-study programs. Study abroad, dual majors, pass/fail options, and B.A.-B.S. degrees are possible. There are 12 national honor societies and a freshman honors program.

Faculty/Classroom: 50% of faculty are male; 50%, female. All teach undergraduates. No introductory courses are taught by graduate students. The average class size in an introductory lecture is 100; in a laboratory, 25; and in a regular course, 25.

Admissions: 93% of the 2003-2004 applicants were accepted. The SAT I scores for the 2003-2004 freshman class were: Verbal--60% below 500, 30% between 500 and 599, 9% between 600 and 700, and 1% above 700; Math--62% below 500, 29% between 500 and 599, 8% between 600 and 700, and 1% above 700. The ACT scores were 57% below 21, 24% between 21 and 23, 14% between 24 and 26, 3% between 27 and 28, and 2% above 28. 19% of the current freshmen were in the top fifth of their class; 42% were in the top two fifths. 31 freshmen graduated first in their class.

Requirements: The SAT I or ACT is required. In addition, applicants must be graduates of an accredited secondary school, with a minimum GPA of 2.0. The GED is accepted. An interview is recommended if the student is below admissions standards. A GPA of 2.0 is required. AP and CLEP credits are accepted. Important factors in the admissions decision are advanced placement or honor courses, evidence of special talent, and leadership record.

Procedure: Freshmen are admitted fall, spring, and summer. Entrance exams should be taken in the spring term of the junior year. Applications should be filed by August 15 for fall entry, January 1 for spring entry, and June 1 for summer entry, along with a $25 fee. There is a rolling admissions plan. Notification is sent on a rolling basis. Applications are accepted on-line through www.usi.edu/admissn/admit.asp.

Transfer: 667 transfer students enrolled in 2003-2004. Grades of C- and above will transfer for credit. 30 of 124 credits required for the bachelor's degree must be completed at USI.

Visiting: There are regularly scheduled orientations for prospective students, including meetings with counselors and faculty and campus tours. There are guides for informal visits and visitors may sit in on classes and stay overnight. To schedule a visit, contact the Office of Admission at enroll@usi.edu.

Financial Aid: In 2003-2004, 78% of all full-time freshmen and 69% of continuing full-time students received some form of financial aid. 60% of full-time freshmen and 53% of continuing full-time students received need-based aid. The average freshman award was $5070. Need-based scholarships or need-based grants averaged $3953 ($13,925 maximum); need-based self-help aid (loans and jobs) averaged $3206 ($12,500 maximum); non-need-based athletic scholarships averaged $3026 ($15,587 maximum); and other non-need-based awards and non-need-based scholarships averaged $2403 ($17,163 maximum). 65% of undergraduates work part time. Average annual earnings from campus work are $1370. The average financial indebtedness of the 2003 graduate was $13,487. USI is a member of CSS. The FAFSA and the college's own financial statement are required. The deadline for filing freshman financial aid applications for fall entry is March 1.

International Students: There are 71 international students enrolled. They must score 500 on the written TOEFL or 173 on the electronic version and also take the SAT I or the ACT.

Computers: The mainframe is an IBM 3000. There are 778 PCs available for student use. All students may access the system. There are no time limits and no fees.

Graduates: From July 1, 2002 to June 30, 2003, 996 bachelor's degrees were awarded. The most popular majors were elementary education (14%), business administration (8%), and psychology (7%). In an average class, 13% graduate in 4 years or less, 27% graduate in 5 years or less, and 31% graduate in 6 years or less. 230 companies recruited on campus in 2002-2003. Of the 2002 graduating class, 18% were enrolled in graduate school within 6 months of graduation and 93% were employed.

Admissions Contact: Eric Otto, Director of Admission.
E-mail: eotto@usi.edu Web: www.usi.edu

VALPARAISO UNIVERSITY
B-1
Valparaiso, IN 46383

(219) 464-5011
(888) GO-VALPO; Fax: (219) 464-6898

Full-time: 1357 men, 1491 women	**Faculty:** 206; IIA, -$
Part-time: 52 men, 127 women	**Ph.Ds:** 88%
Graduate: 349 men, 475 women	**Student/Faculty:** 14 to 1
Year: semesters, summer session	**Tuition:** $20,638
Application Deadline: August 15	**Room & Board:** $5480
Freshman Class: 3576 applied, 2929 accepted, 795 enrolled	
SAT I Verbal/Math: 570/580	**ACT:** 26 **VERY COMPETITIVE+**

Valparaiso University, founded in 1859, is an independent institution affiliated with the Lutheran Church and offering degree programs in arts and sciences, business administration, engineering, nursing, and law. There are 5 undergraduate and 3 graduate schools. In addition to regional accreditation, Valpo has baccalaureate program accreditation with AACSB, ABET, ACS, CCNE, CSWE, NASM, NCATE, and NLN. The 2 libraries contain 517,489 volumes, 1,880,795 microform items, and 15,814 audio/video tapes/CDs, and subscribe to 4982 periodicals. Computerized library services include the card catalog, interlibrary loans, and database searching. Special learning facilities include a learning resource center, art gallery, planetarium, radio station, TV station, observatory, weather station, center for visual and performing arts, and nuclear physics lab. The 310-acre campus is in a small town 45 miles southeast of Chicago. Including any residence halls, there are 53 buildings.

Student Life: 62% of undergraduates are from out of state, mostly the Midwest. Students are from 47 states, 41 foreign countries, and Canada. 80% are from public schools. 87% are white. 61% are Protestant; 22% Catholic; 12% 1% are Hindu, Islam, or another religion. The average age of freshmen is 19; all undergraduates, 21. 14% do not continue beyond their first year; 73% remain to graduate.

Housing: 1955 students can be accommodated in college housing, which includes single-sex and coed dorms, on-campus apartments, off-campus apartments, fraternity houses, and sorority houses. In addition, there are nonsmoking halls, quiet halls, language houses and special-interest houses. On-campus housing is guaranteed for all 4 years. 71% of students live on campus; of those, 80% remain on campus on weekends. Alcohol is not permitted. Upperclassmen may keep cars.

Activities: 30% of men belong to 9 national fraternities; 30% of women belong to 7 national sororities. There are 100 groups on campus, including art, band, cheerleading, chess, choir, chorale, chorus, computers, dance, drama, ethnic, gay, honors, international, jazz band, literary magazine, musical theater, newspaper, orchestra, pep band, photography, political, professional, radio and TV, religious, social, social service, student government, symphony, and yearbook. Popular campus events include Christmas Concert, Madrigal Dinner, and Jazz Festival.

Sports: There are 8 intercollegiate sports for men and 8 for women, and 20 intramural sports for men and 20 for women. Facilities include an athletics-recreation center that houses a 4800-seat gym, racquetball courts, weight rooms, swimming pools, basketball courts, and an indoor track. Other facilities include a 5000-seat football and soccer stadium, baseball, softball, and track fields, a cross-country course, tennis courts, an outdoor recreation center, and game rooms.

Disabled Students: 55% of the campus is accessible. Wheelchair ramps, elevators, special parking, specially equipped rest rooms, and special class scheduling are available.

Services: Counseling and information services are available, as is tutoring in every subject. There is a reader service for the blind. A writing center provides assistance.

Campus Safety and Security: Measures include 24-hour foot and vehicle patrol, self-defense education, security escort services, and shuttle buses. There are informal discussions, pamphlets/posters/films, emergency telephones, and lighted pathways/sidewalks.

Programs of Study: Valpo confers B.A., B.S., B.Mus., B.Mus.Ed., B.S.Acc., B.S.Bus.Adm., B.S.C.E., B.S.Comp.Eng., B.S.Ed., B.S.E.E., B.S.F.A., B.S.M.E., B.S.N., B.S.P.E., and B.S.W. degrees. Associate, master's, and doctoral degrees are also awarded. Bachelor's degrees are awarded in BIOLOGICAL SCIENCE (biology/biological science), BUSINESS (accounting, banking and finance, business administration and management, international business management, international economics, marketing/retailing/merchandising, and sports management), COMMUNICATIONS AND THE ARTS (art, broadcasting, classics, communications, dramatic arts, English, French, German, journalism, music, music business management, public relations, and Spanish), COMPUTER AND PHYSICAL SCIENCE (actuarial science, atmospheric sciences and meteorology, chemistry, computer science, geology, information sciences and systems, mathematics, and physics), EDUCATION (athletic training, elementary, middle school, music, physical, and secondary), ENGINEERING AND ENVIRONMENTAL DESIGN (civil engineering, computer engineering, electrical/electronics engineering, environmental science, and mechanical engineering), HEALTH PROFESSIONS (exercise science and nursing), SOCIAL SCIENCE (American studies, Asian/Oriental studies, criminology, economics, European studies, geography,

history, international public service, ministries, philosophy, political science/government, psychology, religion, social work, sociology, and theological studies). Biology, engineering, and business are the strongest academically. Business, engineering, and education are the largest.

Required: General education requirements include the 10-credit Valpo core plus 3 courses in math/natural and behavioral sciences, 2 each of theology, literature/fine arts, and social analysis, and 1 each of philosophy/history, global perspectives, U.S. diversity, and phys ed; requirements may vary by degree program. To graduate, students must complete at least 124 credit hours, including a minimum of 24 in the major, with a GPA of at least 2.0.

Special: There is cross-registration with Indiana University Northwest. Valparaiso maintains cooperative programs in most majors, including urban studies with the Association of Midwest Colleges, as well as a United Nations semester with Drew University and a Washington semester with American University. Students may study abroad in 9 countries. Internships, the B.A.-B.S. degree, work-study programs, dual and student-designed majors, an accelerated degree program in numerous majors, pass/fail options, and nondegree study are also available. Other special academic features include Christ College, which is an autonomous honors college. There are 8 national honor societies, including Phi Beta Kappa, a freshman honors program, and 25 departmental honors programs.

Faculty/Classroom: 58% of faculty are male; 42%, female. 89% teach undergraduates. No introductory courses are taught by graduate students. The average class size in an introductory lecture is 27; in a laboratory, 20; and in a regular course, 19.

Admissions: 82% of the 2003-2004 applicants were accepted. The SAT I scores for the 2003-2004 freshman class were: Verbal--16% below 500, 43% between 500 and 599, 33% between 600 and 700, and 8% above 700; Math--16% below 500, 38% between 500 and 599, 34% between 600 and 700, and 11% above 700. The ACT scores were 8% below 21, 20% between 21 and 23, 28% between 24 and 26, 19% between 27 and 28, and 25% above 28. 57% of the current freshmen were in the top fifth of their class; 84% were in the top two fifths. There were 10 National Merit finalists. 42 freshmen graduated first in their class.

Requirements: The SAT I or ACT is required. In addition, applicants must be graduates of accredited secondary schools or have earned a GED. Valpo requires completion of 4 years of English, 3 to 4 of math, 2 to 3 of lab science, 2 each of history and foreign language, and 3 of additional academic courses. An essay and an interview are recommended for all applicants, and an audition is required for music majors. AP and CLEP credits are accepted. Important factors in the admissions decision are advanced placement or honor courses, extracurricular activities record, and evidence of special talent.

Procedure: Freshmen are admitted fall, spring, and summer. Entrance exams should be taken prior to the senior year. There are early admissions and deferred admissions plans. Applications should be filed by August 15 for fall entry. The fall 2003 application fee was $30. Notification is sent on a rolling basis. Applications are accepted on-line through http://www.valpo.edu/admissions or CollegeNET.

Transfer: 104 transfer students enrolled in 2003-2004. Applicants must submit official transcripts from all colleges attended. A minimum GPA of 2.0 (3.0 for nursing majors) is required for all college work. If the applicant has completed fewer than 24 credit hours, entrance exam scores are required. An interview is recommended. 30 of 124 credits required for the bachelor's degree must be completed at Valpo.

Visiting: There are regularly scheduled orientations for prospective students, including a campus tour conducted by a current student, an interview with a counselor, and the option to meet with professors, attend a class, and meet with a coach. There are guides for informal visits and visitors may sit in on classes and stay overnight. To schedule a visit, contact the Admissions Office at undergrad.admissions@valpo.edu.

Financial Aid: In 2003-2004, 97% of all full-time freshmen and 93% of continuing full-time students received some form of financial aid. 71% of full-time freshmen and 66% of continuing full-time students received need-based aid. The average freshman award was $15,731. Need-based scholarships or need-based grants averaged $12,334 ($21,260 maximum); need-based self-help aid (loans and jobs) averaged $6005 ($8625 maximum); non-need-based athletic scholarships averaged $10,665 ($27,160 maximum); and other non-need-based awards and non-need-based scholarships averaged $7085 ($20,000 maximum). 35% of undergraduates work part time. Average annual earnings from campus work are $965. The average financial indebtedness of the 2003 graduate was $20,270. Valpo is a member of CSS. The FAFSA is required. The deadline for filing freshman financial aid applications for fall entry is March 1.

International Students: There are 84 international students enrolled. The school actively recruits these students. They must score 550 on the written TOEFL or 213 on the electronic version or complete Valparaiso's institutional intensive English language program.

Computers: Services available to students include academic applications, the library bibliographic system and periodic indexes, the Internet and World Wide Web, and e-mail. There are 580 student computers, primarily Pentiums, and Power Macs, located throughout the campus. UNIX workstations are available in some departments. All residence halls have 24-hour computer clusters. All students may access the system 7 days a week. There are no time limits and no fees. It is recommended that students in engineering have personal computers. Pentium II (450 MHz) PC is recommended.

Graduates: From July 1, 2002 to June 30, 2003, 630 bachelor's degrees were awarded. The most popular majors were elementary education (6%), nursing (5%), and electrical engineering (5%). In an average class, 1% graduate in 3 years or less, 57% graduate in 4 years or less, 71% graduate in 5 years or less, and 71% graduate in 6 years or less. 46 companies recruited on campus in 2002-2003. Of the 2002 graduating class, 27% were enrolled in graduate school within 6 months of graduation and 66% were employed.

Admissions Contact: Office of Admissions.
E-mail: *undergrad.admissions@valpo.edu* Web: *www.valpo.edu*

WABASH COLLEGE
B-3
Crawfordsville, IN 47933-0352
(765) 361-6253
(800) 345-5385; Fax: (765) 361-6437

Full-time: 859 men	Faculty: 86; IIB, +$
Part-time: 4 men	Ph.D.s: 96%
Graduate: none	Student/Faculty: 10 to 1
Year: semesters	Tuition: $21,215
Application Deadline: February 1	Room & Board: $6717
Freshman Class: 1330 applied, 656 accepted, 245 enrolled	
SAT I Verbal/Math: 576/604	ACT: 26 **VERY COMPETITIVE**

Wabash College, founded in 1832, is a private liberal arts men's college with a strong emphasis on preprofessional programs. In addition to regional accreditation, Wabash has baccalaureate program accreditation with NCATE. The library contains 434,460 volumes, 11,359 microform items, and 11,151 audio/video tapes/CDs, and subscribes to 5530 periodicals. Computerized library services include the card catalog, interlibrary loans, database searching, and Internet access. Special learning facilities include a learning resource center, art gallery, radio station, an archival center, and research centers for the study of theology and religion and inquiry in the liberal arts. The 55-acre campus is in a small town 45 miles northwest of Indianapolis. Including any residence halls, there are 35 buildings.

Student Life: 71% of undergraduates are from Indiana. Others are from 34 states and 12 foreign countries. 94% are from public schools. 78% are white. The average age of freshmen is 19; all undergraduates, 20. 13% do not continue beyond their first year; 70% remain to graduate.

Housing: 840 students can be accommodated in college housing, which includes single-sex dorms, on-campus apartments, off-campus apartments, and fraternity houses. In addition, there are language houses. On-campus housing is guaranteed for all 4 years. 92% of students live on campus; of those, 65% remain on campus on weekends. All students may keep cars.

Activities: 62% of men belong to 10 national fraternities. There are 40 groups on campus, including art, band, cheerleading, chess, choir, chorus, computers, debate, drama, drum corps, ethnic, film, foreign language, forensics, gay, honors, international, jazz band, literary magazine, musical theater, newspaper, orchestra, pep band, photography, political, professional, radio, religious, social, social service, student government, symphony, and yearbook. Popular campus events include Pan-Hel Weekend, Fall Bash, and Chapel Sing.

Sports: Facilities include a 4200-seat stadium, indoor and outdoor tennis courts, football, baseball, and soccer fields, a swimming pool, an indoor track, an all-weather track, wrestling and weight rooms, racquetball and handball courts, a ropes challenge course, an 1800-seat basketball arena, a wellness center, and an aerobics studio.

Disabled Students: 60% of the campus is accessible. Wheelchair ramps, elevators, special parking, specially equipped rest rooms, lowered drinking fountains, lowered telephones, and a counseling service are available.

Services: There is a reader service for the blind and remedial math, reading, and writing. There is a quantitative skills center as well as a writing center where, under professional supervision, students help each other.

Campus Safety and Security: Measures include 24-hour foot and vehicle patrol, security escort services, pamphlets/posters/films, and emergency telephones. There are lighted pathways/sidewalks.

Programs of Study: Wabash confers the A.B. degree. Bachelor's degrees are awarded in BIOLOGICAL SCIENCE (biology/biological science), COMMUNICATIONS AND THE ARTS (art, classics, dramatic arts, English, French, German, Greek, Latin, music, Spanish, and speech/debate/rhetoric), COMPUTER AND PHYSICAL SCIENCE (chemistry, mathematics, and physics), SOCIAL SCIENCE (economics, history, philosophy, political science/government, psychology, and religion). Preprofessional studies, economics, and religion are the strongest academically. History, psychology, and economics are the largest.

Required: All students must complete at least 3 courses each in literature/fine arts, behavioral science, and natural science/math, 2 in history,

philosophy, or religion, and 1 in quantitative skills. To graduate, students must maintain a minimum 2.0 GPA for 136 credit hours (34 courses), which include a freshman tutorial and 2 semesters of cultures and traditions. The student must pass a written exam in the major as well as a senior oral exam and must demonstrate proficiency in English and in a foreign language at a level equivalent to 2 college courses.

Special: Wabash offers internships with off-campus organizations, study abroad in an unlimited number of countries, a Washington semester with American University, dual majors, a B.A.-B.S. degree in engineering, and both a 3-2 engineering program and a 3-3 law program with Columbia University and Washington University in St. Louis. A tuition-free Ninth Semester Teacher Education Program is also available. There are 9 national honor societies and 7 departmental honors programs.

Faculty/Classroom: 80% of faculty are male; 20%, female. All teach undergraduates. The average class size in an introductory lecture is 21; in a laboratory, 15; and in a regular course, 13.

Admissions: 49% of the 2003-2004 applicants were accepted. The SAT I scores for the 2003-2004 freshman class were: Verbal--17% below 500, 44% between 500 and 599, 30% between 600 and 700, and 9% above 700; Math--12% below 500, 32% between 500 and 599, 42% between 600 and 700, and 14% above 700. The ACT scores were 5% below 21, 19% between 21 and 23, 36% between 24 and 26, 22% between 27 and 28, and 18% above 28. 60% of the current freshmen were in the top fifth of their class; 84% were in the top two fifths. There were 6 National Merit finalists and 3 semifinalists. 6 freshmen graduated first in their class.

Requirements: The SAT I or ACT is required. Wabash recommends applicants have 4 high school courses in English, 3 to 4 in math, and 2 each in foreign language, lab science, and social studies. An essay is required and an interview is recommended. AP and CLEP credits are accepted. Important in the admissions decision are advanced placement or honor courses, and leadership and extracurricular activities record.

Procedure: Freshmen are admitted fall and spring. Entrance exams should be taken by the spring of the junior year or fall of the senior year. There are early decision, early admissions, and deferred admissions plans. Early decision applications should be filed by November 15; regular applications, by February 1 for fall entry and December 1 for spring entry, along with a $30 fee. Notification of early decision is sent December 15; regular decision, on a rolling basis. 37 early decision candidates were accepted for the 2003-2004 class. 76 were on the 2003 waiting list; 5 were admitted. Applications are accepted on disk and on-line through CollegeLink, EXPAN, Common App, or the school's web site.

Transfer: 7 transfer students enrolled in 2003-2004. Applicants must submit official transcripts of all college courses. Wabash strongly considers the overall high school and college background of applicants. A minimum GPA of 2.5, recommendations from the college adviser and dean of students at the previous college, and a personal written statement are required, with an interview strongly recommended. 17 of 136 credits required for the bachelor's degree must be completed at Wabash.

Visiting: There are regularly scheduled orientations for prospective students. There are guides for informal visits and visitors may sit in on classes and stay overnight. To schedule a visit, contact Mary Skelton of the Admissions Office at (765) 361-6276 or *skeltonm@wabash.edu*.

Financial Aid: In 2003-2004, 84% of all full-time freshmen and 79% of continuing full-time students received some form of financial aid. 71% of full-time freshmen and 81% of continuing full-time students received need-based aid. The average freshman award was $20,645. Need-based scholarships or need-based grants averaged $16,610; and need-based self-help aid (loans and jobs) averaged $3793. 75% of undergraduates work part time. Average annual earnings from campus work are $1000. The average financial indebtedness of the 2003 graduate was $17,818. Wabash is a member of CSS. The CSS/Profile or FAFSA and federal tax form with W-2 statements are required. The priority date for freshman financial aid applications for fall entry is February 15. The deadline for filing freshman financial aid applications for fall entry is March 1.

International Students: There are 32 international students enrolled. The school actively recruits these students. They must score 550 on the written TOEFL or 213 on the electronic version, or take the MELAB, and also take the SAT I or the ACT.

Computers: The mainframe is a DEC Alpha 2100 server. Every student has an account on a Novell server, with a network connection in each living unit. There are more than 100 Macs and Power PCs in 8 public classrooms. All students may access the system 24 hours/day or at designated times for specific computers. There are no time limits or fees.

Graduates: From July 1, 2002 to June 30, 2003, 211 bachelor's degrees were awarded. The most popular majors were English (17%), history (15%), and psychology (14%). In an average class, 70% graduate in 4 years or less, 73% graduate in 5 years or less, and 75% graduate in 6 years or less. 20 companies recruited on campus in 2002-2003. Of the 2002 graduating class, 37% were enrolled in graduate school within 6 months of graduation and 60% were employed.

Admissions Contact: Steve Klein, Director of Admissions. A video is available. E-mail: *admissions@wabash.edu* Web: *www.wabash.edu*

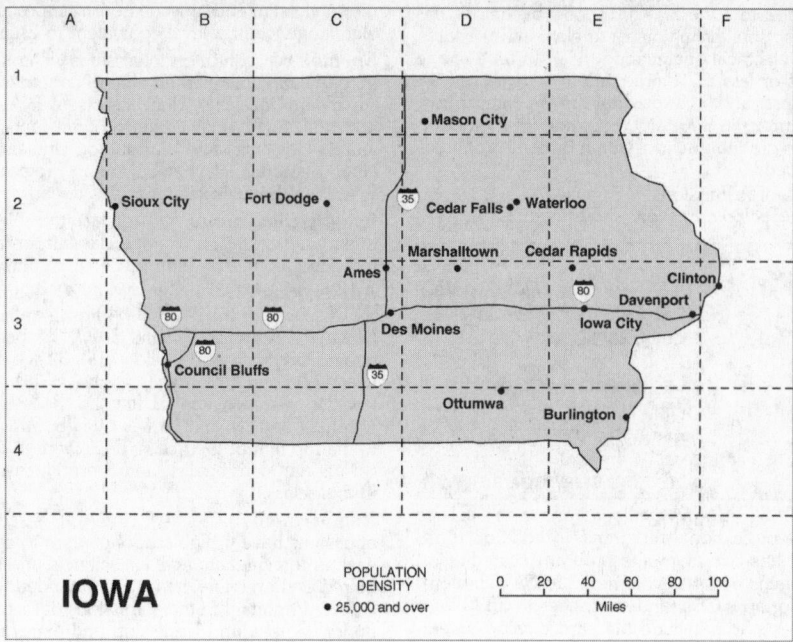

IOWA

POPULATION DENSITY
● 25,000 and over

0 20 40 60 80 100
Miles

ALLEN COLLEGE
Waterloo, IA 50703

D-2

(319) 226-2002; Fax: (319) 226-2051

Full-time: 17 men, 216 women	**Faculty:** 15
Part-time: 2 men, 41 women	**Ph.D.s:** 17%
Graduate: 2 men, 31 women	**Student/Faculty:** 16 to 1
Year: semesters, summer session	**Tuition:** $9591
Application Deadline: open	**Room & Board:** $4930
Freshman Class: 265 applied, 143 accepted, 102 enrolled	
ACT: 20	**SPECIAL**

Allen College, founded in 1989, is a private institution offering a baccalaureate program in nursing and is part of the Iowa Health System. In addition to regional accreditation, Allen College has baccalaureate program accreditation with NLN. The library contains 1603 volumes and 175 audio/video tapes/CDs, and subscribes to 102 periodicals. Computerized library services include the card catalog, interlibrary loans, database searching, and Internet access. The 20-acre campus is in a suburban area in Waterloo. There are 2 buildings.

Student Life: All undergraduates are from Iowa. 95% are white. The average age of freshmen is 18; all undergraduates, 23. 37% do not continue beyond their first year; 63% remain to graduate.

Housing: There are no residence halls. Living facilities are available at cooperative colleges. All of students commute. Alcohol is not permitted. All students may keep cars.

Activities: There are no fraternities or sororities. There are 6 groups on campus, including newspaper, student government, and yearbook. Popular campus events include Fall Fling and Winter Party.

Sports: There is no sports program at Allen College.

Disabled Students: All of the campus is accessible. Wheelchair ramps, elevators, special parking, specially equipped rest rooms, and lowered drinking fountains are available.

Services: Counseling and information services are available, as is tutoring in most subjects.

Campus Safety and Security: Measures include informal discussions, pamphlets/posters/films, and lighted pathways/sidewalks.

Programs of Study: Allen College confers the B.S.N. degree. Associate and master's degrees are also awarded. Bachelor's degrees are awarded in HEALTH PROFESSIONS (nursing).

Required: To graduate, all students must complete general education courses in humanities, social science, natural science, and electives, and maintain a 2.0 GPA; 125 credits are required, with 68 in the major.

Special: Cross-registration is available with the University of Northern Iowa and Wartburg College. Co-op programs in nursing and radiography are also available.

Faculty/Classroom: 4% of faculty are male; 96%, female. 89% teach undergraduates. The average class size in an introductory lecture is 60; in a laboratory, 8; and in a regular course, 30.

Admissions: 54% of the 2003-2004 applicants were accepted. The ACT scores for the 2003-2004 freshman class were: 42% below 21, 45% between 21 and 23, 9% between 24 and 26, and 3% between 27 and 28. 27% of the current freshmen were in the top fifth of their class; 73% were in the top two fifths. 1 freshman graduated first in the class.

Requirements: The ACT is required with a minimum composite score of 18. An essay, a letter of recommendation, and class rank in the upper 50th percentile are required. Core high school courses including 4 years of English, 3 each of math and social studies, and 1 each of chemistry, biology, and 1 other science are required. Students must earn grades of C or better. Allen College requires applicants to be in the upper 50% of their class. AP and CLEP credits are accepted.

Procedure: Freshmen are admitted fall, spring, and summer. Entrance exams should be taken early in the senior year of high school. Application deadlines are open. Notification is sent 1 month after the application process is complete. The application fee is $50. A waiting list is an active part of the admissions procedure. Applications are accepted on-line through *www.allencollege.edu.*

Transfer: 61 transfer students enrolled in 2003-2004. Students must have a college GPA of 2.5 and submit an essay and a letter of recommendation. 30 of 125 credits required for the bachelor's degree must be completed at Allen College.

Visiting: There are regularly scheduled orientations for prospective students, including an opportunity to speak to the Director of Admissions, the Director of Financial Aid, department chairs, and to tour campus. There are guides for informal visits and visitors may sit in on classes. To schedule a visit, contact Lois Hagedorn at (319) 226-2000 or *hagedole@ihs.org.*

Financial Aid: In 2003-2004, 86% of all full-time freshmen and 92% of continuing full-time students received some form of financial aid. 69% of full-time freshmen and 73% of continuing full-time students received need-based aid. The average freshman award was $11,668. Need-based scholarships or need-based grants averaged $4857 ($10,121 maximum); need-based self-help aid (loans and jobs) averaged $2987 ($6312 maximum); and other non-need-based awards and non-need-based scholarships averaged $8012 ($24,852 maximum). 4% of undergraduates work part time. Average annual earnings from campus work are $2000. The average financial indebtedness of the 2003 graduate was $14,138. The FAFSA and the college's own financial statement are required. The priority date for freshman financial aid applications for fall entry is May 1.

International Students: They must score 550 on the written TOEFL and also take the ACT, scoring 18.

Computers: The mainframe is an IBM. A 24-hour computer lab includes 26 computers and Internet access. All students may access the system 24 hours a day. There are no time limits. The fee is $100 per semester. It is strongly recommended that all students have a personal computer.

Graduates: From July 1, 2002 to June 30, 2003, 52 bachelor's degrees were awarded. The most popular major was nursing (100%). In an average class, 57% graduate in 4 years or less, 57% graduate in 5 years or less, and 57% graduate in 6 years or less. 40 companies recruited on campus in 2002-2003. Of the 2002 graduating class, 100% were employed within 6 months of graduation.

Admissions Contact: Barb Seible, Director of Admissions. E-mail: *Seiblebj@ihs.org* Web: *http://www.allencollege.edu*

BRIAR CLIFF UNIVERSITY B-2
Sioux City, IA 51104-0100
(712) 279-5200
(800) 662-3303; Fax: (712) 279-1632

Full-time: 368 men, 516 women	**Faculty:** 47; IIB, --$
Part-time: 54 men, 125 women	**Ph.D.s:** 72%
Graduate: none	**Student/Faculty:** 19 to 1
Year: trimesters, summer session	**Tuition:** $16,350
Application Deadline: open	**Room & Board:** $5310
Freshman Class: 1297 applied, 1040 accepted, 254 enrolled	
SAT I Verbal/Math: 470/500	**ACT:** 21　　**COMPETITIVE**

Briar Cliff University, founded in 1930, is a private Roman Catholic-Franciscan liberal arts institution. In addition to regional accreditation, Briar Cliff has baccalaureate program accreditation with AACSB, CSWE, and NLN. The library contains 83,737 volumes, 21,464 microform items, and 9791 audio/video tapes/CDs, and subscribes to 6366 periodicals. Computerized library services include the card catalog, interlibrary loans, and database searching. Special learning facilities include a learning resource center, art gallery, radio station, TV station, and a cadaver lab. The 70-acre campus is in a suburban area minutes from downtown Sioux City. Including any residence halls, there are 11 buildings.

Student Life: 68% of undergraduates are from Iowa. Others are from 25 states and 1 foreign countries. 91% are white. 40% are Catholic; 40% claim no religious affiliation; 20% Protestant. The average age of freshmen is 18; all undergraduates, 23. 27% do not continue beyond their first year; 44% remain to graduate.

Housing: 577 students can be accommodated in college housing, which includes coed dorms. In addition, there are special-interest houses. 54% of students live on campus. All students may keep cars.

Activities: There are no fraternities or sororities. There are 28 groups on campus, including art, cheerleading, choir, chorus, computers, dance, drama, ethnic, film, international, literary magazine, musical theater, newspaper, pep band, photography, professional, radio and TV, religious, social, social service, student government, and yearbook. Popular campus events include Cliffstock, Family Weekend, and Little Brother Little Sister Weekend.

Sports: There are 8 intercollegiate sports for men and 7 for women, and 15 intramural sports for men and 15 for women. Facilities include baseball, softball, and soccer fields, and a recreation center with 2 racquetball courts, a running track, tennis courts, 2 basketball/volleyball courts, and weight-lifting facilities.

Disabled Students: 90% of the campus is accessible. Wheelchair ramps, elevators, special parking, specially equipped rest rooms, lowered drinking fountains, and lowered telephones are available.

Services: Counseling and information services are available, as is tutoring in most subjects. There is remedial math, reading, and writing.

Campus Safety and Security: Measures include 24-hour foot and vehicle patrol, security escort services, informal discussions, and pamphlets/posters/films. There are emergency telephones and lighted pathways/sidewalks.

Programs of Study: Briar Cliff confers B.A., B.S., B.S.N., and B.S.W. degrees. Associate and master's degrees are also awarded. Bachelor's degrees are awarded in BIOLOGICAL SCIENCE (biology/biological science), BUSINESS (accounting, business administration and management, and human resources), COMMUNICATIONS AND THE ARTS (art, communications, dramatic arts, English, fine arts, graphic design, music, and Spanish), COMPUTER AND PHYSICAL SCIENCE (chemistry, computer science, information sciences and systems, mathematics, and radiological technology), EDUCATION (elementary, health, secondary, and special), ENGINEERING AND ENVIRONMENTAL DESIGN (environmental science), HEALTH PROFESSIONS (medical technology, nursing, predentistry, premedicine, and prepharmacy), SOCIAL SCIENCE (criminal justice, history, political science/government, psychology, social work, sociology, and theological studies). Biology, business administration, and education are the strongest academically. Education, nursing, and business administration are the largest.

Required: To graduate, students must complete a minimum of 120 semester hours with at least 36 in the major. 10 general education foundation courses and 6 1-hour independent research courses are required. A GPA of 2.0 with no more than 1 D in the major must be maintained, and proficiency in standard English expression and oral communication skills must be demonstrated.

Special: Internships in Chicago, study abroad, dual majors, work-study programs, accelerated degree programs in business administration, human resource management, and professional studies, student-designed interdisciplinary majors, and pass/fail options are available. Students may earn a 3-2 engineering degree with Iowa State University.

Faculty/Classroom: 47% of faculty are male; 53%, female. All teach undergraduates. The average class size in an introductory lecture is 20; in a laboratory, 15; and in a regular course, 20.

Admissions: 80% of the 2003-2004 applicants were accepted. The SAT I scores for the 2003-2004 freshman class were: Verbal--77% below 500, and 23% between 500 and 599; Math--44% below 500, and 56% between 500 and 599. The ACT scores were 49% below 21, 28% between 21 and 23, 14% between 24 and 26, 5% between 27 and 28, and 4% above 28. 21% of the current freshmen were in the top fifth of their class; 51% were in the top two fifths.

Requirements: The SAT I or ACT is required. The ACT is preferred, and a score of 18 qualifies for automatic acceptance review. Applicants need not be graduates of an accredited secondary school. The GED is accepted. Admission to freshman standing requires 4 years each of English and math, 3 of science, 2 of history, and 1 of social studies. A GPA of 2.0 is required. AP and CLEP credits are accepted. Important factors in the admissions decision are leadership record, extracurricular activities record, and advanced placement or honor courses.

Procedure: Freshmen are admitted to all sessions. Entrance exams should be taken by October for scholarship consideration, and by April for admission. Application deadlines are open. There is a rolling admissions plan and the application fee is $20. Applications are accepted online through the school's web site.

Transfer: 94 transfer students enrolled in 2003-2004. Applicants must have a minimum GPA of 2.0 with at least 10 credit hours earned and satisfactory dismissal from the previous institution. Grades of D or better transfer for credit. 30 of 120 credits required for the bachelor's degree must be completed at Briar Cliff.

Visiting: There are regularly scheduled orientations for prospective students, including a presidential welcome, a meeting with faculty and student panels, a luncheon, campus tours, a slide show, and financial aid information. There are guides for informal visits and visitors may sit in on classes and stay overnight. To schedule a visit, contact the Admissions Office at (800) 662-3303, ext. 5200 or *admissions@briarcliff.edu*.

Financial Aid: In 2003-2004, all full-time freshmen and 96% of continuing full-time students received some form of financial aid. 74% of full-time freshmen and 71% of continuing full-time students received need-based aid. The average freshman award was $22,500. Need-based scholarships or need-based grants averaged $2724 ($9500 maximum); need-based self-help aid (loans and jobs) averaged $2255 ($11,100 maximum); non-need-based athletic scholarships averaged $3432 ($15,960 maximum); and other non-need-based awards and non-need-based scholarships averaged $3578 ($15,960 maximum). 32% of undergraduates work part time. Average annual earnings from campus work are $684. The average financial indebtedness of the 2003 graduate was $19,794. Briar Cliff is a member of CSS. The FAFSA is required. The priority date for freshman financial aid applications for fall entry is March 1.

International Students: There is 1 international student enrolled. They must score 500 on the written TOEFL or take the MELAB. The TOEFL is preferred.

Computers: The mainframe is a Dell Poweredge 4600. Students use BCU mainframes for Internet and on-line services, including library databases, class schedules, and e-mail. Students have local area network access from their residence hall rooms; there are also student computer labs located on each floor in the residence halls (65 computers total). Other student labs are located in the library and student center. There are 4 computer classrooms with a total of 54 computers. All students may access the system 24 hours each day. There are no time limits. A computer usage fee is part of student fees each term.

Graduates: From July 1, 2002 to June 30, 2003, 162 bachelor's degrees were awarded. The most popular majors were business administration (25%), nursing (10%), human resource management (7%), and education (7%). In an average class, 2% graduate in 3 years or less, 38% graduate in 4 years or less, 45% graduate in 5 years or less, and 46% graduate in 6 years or less.

Admissions Contact: Sharisue Wilcoxon, Vice President/Enrollment Management. E-mail: *wilcoxons@briarcliff.edu* Web: *www.briarcliff.edu*

BUENA VISTA UNIVERSITY B-2
Storm Lake, IA 50588
(712) 749-2235
(800) 383-9600; Fax: (712) 749-2037

Full-time: 596 men, 661 women	**Faculty:** 82; IIB, av$
Part-time: 11 men, 20 women	**Ph.D.s:** 55%
Graduate: 36 men, 40 women	**Student/Faculty:** 15 to 1
Year: 4-1-4, summer session	**Tuition:** $19,862
Application Deadline: open	**Room & Board:** $5544
Freshman Class: n/av	
ACT: 22	**COMPETITIVE**

Buena Vista University, founded in 1891, is a private institution affiliated with the Presbyterian Church (U.S.A.). The university offers undergraduate degree programs in business, education, communication and arts, science, social science, philosophy, and religion, and an accredited master's program in education. Programs emphasize career education with a liberal arts foundation. Some of the information in the above capsule is approximate. There are 5 undergraduate schools and 1 graduate school. In addition to regional accreditation, Buena Vista has baccalaureate program accreditation with CSWE. The library contains 158,070 volumes, 40,657 microform items, and 3920 audio/video tapes/CDs, and subscribes to 675 periodicals. Computerized library services include the card catalog, interlibrary loans, and database searching. Special learning facilities include a learning resource center, art gallery, radio station, TV station, and student newspaper desktop production lab. The 60-acre campus is in a small town 65 miles east of Sioux City. Including any residence halls, there are 16 buildings.

Student Life: 82% of undergraduates are from Iowa. Others are from 16 states and 3 foreign countries. 80% are from public schools. 94% are white. 55% are Protestant; 27% Catholic; 12% claim no religious affiliation. The average age of freshmen is 18; all undergraduates, 20. 25% do not continue beyond their first year; 59% remain to graduate.

Housing: 1136 students can be accommodated in college housing, which includes single-sex and coed dorms and on-campus apartments. In addition, there are honors houses and special-interest houses. On-campus housing is guaranteed for all 4 years. 87% of students live on campus; of those, 60% remain on campus on weekends. All students may keep cars.

Activities: There are no fraternities or sororities. There are 50 groups on campus, including art, band, cheerleading, choir, chorale, chorus, computers, debate, drama, drill team, environmental, ethnic, gay, gender, honors, international, jazz band, literary magazine, musical theater, newspaper, orchestra, pep band, photography, political, professional, radio and TV, religious, social, social service, student government, and yearbook. Popular campus events include Winter Olympics, Academic and Cultural Events Series, and Buenafication Day.

Sports: There are 10 intercollegiate sports for men and 9 for women, and 10 intramural sports for men and 10 for women. Facilities include a 380-seat auditorium, a 1000-seat auditorium, a 4000-seat stadium, a field house with a 4000-seat gym, basketball, volleyball, racquetball, and tennis courts, football, softball, and baseball fields, a track, facilities for weight training and other recreational activities, an Olympic-size indoor pool, and a game room.

Disabled Students: 90% of the campus is accessible. Wheelchair ramps, elevators, special parking, specially equipped rest rooms, special class scheduling, lowered drinking fountains, lowered telephones, and automatic/remote-controlled doors are available.

Services: Counseling and information services are available, as is tutoring in most subjects. There is a reader service for the blind, and remedial math, reading, and writing.

Campus Safety and Security: Measures include 24-hour foot and vehicle patrol, self-defense education, security escort services, and shuttle buses. There are informal discussions, pamphlets/posters/films, emergency telephones, lighted pathways/sidewalks, and an enhanced 911 system on campus.

Programs of Study: Buena Vista confers B.A. and B.S. degrees. Master's degrees are also awarded. Bachelor's degrees are awarded in BIOLOGICAL SCIENCE (biology/biological science), BUSINESS (accounting, banking and finance, business administration and management, business economics, international business management, marketing/retailing/merchandising, and sports management), COMMUNICATIONS AND THE ARTS (art, arts administration/management, communications, English, graphic design, music, Spanish, and speech/debate/rhetoric), COMPUTER AND PHYSICAL SCIENCE (chemistry, computer science, mathematics, physics, and science), EDUCATION (art, business, elementary, middle school, music, science, secondary, and special), SOCIAL SCIENCE (criminal justice, economics, history, philosophy, physical fitness/movement, political science/government, psychology, public administration, religion, social science, and social work). Biology, mass communication, and business are the strongest academically. Education, biology, and management are the largest.

Required: All students must complete 6 semester hours each of natural sciences, humanities, social sciences, communication, and writing, and 3 semester hours of fine arts. In addition, students must successfully complete English 100 and 200, demonstrate proficiency by exam in math and writing, and participate in the Academic and Cultural Events Series, through which they attend lectures and performances by national and world leaders. The bachelor's degree requires a minimum of 128 semester hours, including 30 to 62 hours in the major, with a GPA of at least 2.0, or 2.5 for education majors.

Special: Special academic offerings include a work-study program with Marriott Corporation, and a 3-2 engineering degree program with Washington University in St. Louis. Students may study abroad in Japan, Taiwan, Australia, and Europe. Buena Vista offers dual and student-designed majors, credit for life experience, and pass/fail options in courses outside the major field. Nondegree study is possible. Internships are required in many majors and encouraged in most. The J. Leslie Rollins Fellowship allows 1 or 2 students each year to design an internship anywhere in the world. There is 1 national honor society and a freshman honors program.

Faculty/Classroom: In a recent year, 62% of faculty were male; 38%, female. All taught undergraduates. The average class size in an introductory lecture was 30; in a laboratory, 25; and in a regular course, 18.

Admissions: The ACT scores for the 2003-2004 freshman class were: 32% below 21, 30% between 21 and 23, 24% between 24 and 26, 7% between 27 and 28, and 7% above 28. 33% of the current freshmen were in the top fifth of their class; 63% were in the top two fifths. In a recent year, there were 20 National Merit semifinalists. 22 freshmen graduated first in their class.

Requirements: The ACT is recommended. SAT I scores may be submitted instead. Minimum scores should be 21 on the ACT or 950 on the SAT I, with 475 on each part. Applicants must be graduates of an accredited secondary school or have earned a GED. The college requires 13 academic credits, including 4 of English and 3 each of math, social studies, and science. Campus visits and an interview are recommended. Buena Vista requires applicants to be in the upper 50% of their class. A GPA of 2.75 is required. AP and CLEP credits are accepted. Important factors in the admissions decision are advanced placement or honor courses, leadership record, and recommendations by school officials.

Procedure: Freshmen are admitted fall, winter, and spring. Entrance exams should be taken during the spring of the junior year or October of the senior year. There are early admissions and deferred admissions plans. Application deadlines are open and there is a rolling admissions plan. Applications are accepted on computer disk and on-line through Common App, CollegeNET, Apply, and the school's web site.

Transfer: 61 transfer students enrolled in 2003-2004. A high school diploma and a minimum GPA of 2.5 from the applicant's college are required. 30 of 128 credits required for the bachelor's degree must be completed at Buena Vista.

Visiting: There are regularly scheduled orientations for prospective students, including a campus tour and meetings with an admissions counselor, faculty representatives, coaches, and activity representatives in the student's areas of interest. There are guides for informal visits and visitors may sit in on classes and stay overnight. To schedule a visit, contact the Director of Admissions.

Financial Aid: In a recent year, 99% of all full-time freshmen and 98% of continuing full-time students received some form of financial aid. 89% of full-time freshmen and 90% of continuing full-time students received need-based aid. The average freshman award was $18,184. 60% of undergraduates work part time. Average annual earnings from campus work are $1038. The average financial indebtedness of the 2003 graduate was $20,415. Buena Vista is a member of CSS. The FAFSA and the college's own financial statement are required. The deadline for filing freshman financial aid applications for fall entry is June 1.

International Students: There are 12 international students enrolled. The school actively recruits these students. They must score 500 on the written TOEFL and also take the Comprehensive English Language Test.

Computers: The mainframe is a DEC Alpha AXP. Every student recieves a laptop. Access to the Internet and e-mail is available to all students. All students may access the system. There are no time limits and no fees.

Graduates: From July 1, 2002 to June 30, 2003, 236 bachelor's degrees were awarded. In an average class, 1% graduate in 3 years or less, 50% graduate in 4 years or less, 59% graduate in 5 years or less, and 60% graduate in 6 years or less. 40 companies recruited on campus in 2002-2003. Of a recent year's graduating class, 15% were enrolled in graduate school within 6 months of graduation and 98% were employed.

Admissions Contact: Louise Cummings-Simmons, Director of Admissions. A video is available. E-mail: *admissions@bvu.edu* Web: *www.bvu.edu*

CENTRAL COLLEGE

Pella, IA 50219

D-3

(641) 628-5285
(800) 458-5503; Fax: (641) 628-5316

Full-time: 640 men, 935 women	**Faculty:** 89; IIB, -$
Part-time: 25 men, 25 women	**Ph.D:** 80%
Graduate: none	**Student/Faculty:** 18 to 1
Year: semesters, summer session	**Tuition:** $15,714
Application Deadline: see profile	**Room & Board:** $5492
Freshman Class: n/av	
SAT I or ACT: required	**COMPETITIVE**

Central College, founded in 1853, is a private institution affiliated with the Reformed Church in America. The college offers undergraduate degree programs in applied arts, behavioral sciences, cross-cultural studies, fine arts, humanities, and natural sciences. Figures in the above capsule and in this profile are approximate. In addition to regional accreditation, Central has baccalaureate program accreditation with NASM and NCATE. The 4 libraries contain 195,000 volumes, 55,000 microform items, and 8500 audio/video tapes/CDs, and subscribe to 925 periodicals. Computerized library services include the card catalog, interlibrary loans, and database searching. Special learning facilities include a learning resource center, art gallery, radio station, and fiber-optic classroom.

The 133-acre campus is in a suburban area 45 miles southeast of Des Moines. Including any residence halls, there are 45 buildings.

Student Life: 82% of undergraduates are from Iowa. Students are from 33 states, 13 foreign countries, and Canada. 98% are from public schools. 88% are white. 67% are Protestant; 21% Catholic; 11% claim no religious affiliation. The average age of freshmen is 18; all undergraduates, 20. 20% do not continue beyond their first year.

Housing: 1300 students can be accommodated in college housing, which includes single-sex and coed dorms, on-campus apartments, married-student housing, fraternity houses, and sorority houses. In addition, there are honors houses, language houses, and special-interest houses. On-campus housing is guaranteed for all 4 years. 88% of students live on campus; of those, 70% remain on campus on weekends. Alcohol is not permitted. All students may keep cars.

Activities: 12% of men belong to 4 local fraternities; 5% of women belong to 2 local sororities. There are 71 groups on campus, including art, band, cheerleading, choir, chorus, drama, drill team, ethnic, gay, honors, international, jazz band, literary magazine, marching band, musical theater, newspaper, opera, orchestra, pep band, photography, political, professional, radio and TV, religious, social, social service, student government, symphony, and yearbook. Popular campus events include Career Day, Interdisciplinary Research Symposium, and Academic Seminar.

Sports: There are 9 intercollegiate sports for men and 8 for women, and 12 intramural sports for men and 11 for women. Facilities include an athletic complex with a 7000-seat stadium and 2500-seat gym, a 700-seat auditorium, a golf driving range, several practice and competition fields, tennis courts, and a field house with an indoor track.

Disabled Students: 90% of the campus is accessible. Wheelchair ramps, elevators, special parking, specially equipped rest rooms, special class scheduling, lowered drinking fountains, and lowered telephones are available.

Services: Counseling and information services are available, as is tutoring in every subject. There is a reader service for the blind.

Campus Safety and Security: Measures include 24-hour foot and vehicle patrol, self-defense education, security escort services, and informal discussions. There are pamphlets/posters/films, emergency telephones, and lighted pathways/sidewalks.

Programs of Study: Central confers the B.A. degree. Bachelor's degrees are awarded in BIOLOGICAL SCIENCE (biology/biological science), BUSINESS (accounting, business administration and management, and international business management), COMMUNICATIONS AND THE ARTS (communications, dramatic arts, English, fine arts, French, German, languages, linguistics, music, and Spanish), COMPUTER AND PHYSICAL SCIENCE (chemistry, computer science, mathematics, and physics), EDUCATION (elementary, music, and secondary), ENGINEERING AND ENVIRONMENTAL DESIGN (environmental science), HEALTH PROFESSIONS (exercise science), SOCIAL SCIENCE (anthropology, economics, history, international studies, philosophy, political science/government, psychology, religion, and sociology). Business management, elementary education, and exercise science are the largest.

Required: General education requirements include 44 semester hours, including 11 in cultural awareness, 6 each in central foundations and core focus, and 3 each in art, historical perspectives, mathematical reasoning, religion, scientific inquiry, social and behavioral inquiry, and textual interpretation. Each department also establishes a communication skill requirement, and foreign language proficiency must be demonstrated. To graduate, students must complete a minimum of 120 semester hours with a GPA of at least 2.0.

Special: Nearly half the students participate in study abroad programs in London, Paris, Vienna, Mexico, Spain, Wales, and the Netherlands. Central also offers a Washington semester, a Chicago program, numerous internship opportunities, and work-study. A 3-4 program in architecture and a 3-2 degree program in engineering are offered with Washington University in St. Louis. A general studies degree, student-designed majors, and pass/no credit options are possible. There is 1 national honor society and a freshman honors program.

Faculty/Classroom: 60% of faculty are male; 40%, female. All both teach and do research. The average class size in an introductory lecture is 19; in a laboratory, 15; and in a regular course, 20.

Admissions: 38 freshmen graduated first in their class in a recent year.

Requirements: The SAT I or ACT is required. In addition, applicants must be graduates of an accredited secondary school or have earned a GED. Central requires 16 academic credits and recommends that they include 4 years of English, 3 each of lab science, social studies, and math, including 2 in algebra and 1 in geometry, and 2 of foreign language. An interview is required and an essay is recommended. Central requires applicants to be in the upper 50% of their class. A GPA of 2.7 is required. AP and CLEP credits are accepted. Important factors in the admissions decision are leadership record, recommendations by school officials, and evidence of special talent.

Procedure: Freshmen are admitted to all sessions. Entrance exams should be taken in the spring of the junior year. There is a deferred ad-

missions plan. There is a rolling admissions plan. Check with the school for current deadlines and fee. The fall 2003 application fee was $25. Notification is sent on a rolling basis. Applications are accepted on-line through the school's web site.

Transfer: 48 transfer students enrolled in a recent year. Each tranfer student is considered individually. Interviews are encouraged. 30 of 45 credits required for the bachelor's degree must be completed at Central.

Visiting: There are regularly scheduled orientations for prospective students, including a campus tour, a registration session with academic advisers, and presentations by the academic dean, student life dean, financial aid director, and admissions staff. There are guides for informal visits and visitors may sit in on classes and stay overnight. To schedule a visit, contact the Admissions Office at (641) 628-5286 or *admission@central.edu*.

Financial Aid: In a recent year, all full-time freshmen and 98% of continuing full-time students received some form of financial aid. 82% of all full-time students received need-based aid. The average freshman award was $12,033. 90% of undergraduates work part time. Average annual earnings from campus work are $743. The average financial indebtedness of a recent graduate was $20,499. Central is a member of CSS. The FAFSA is required. Check with the school for current deadlines.

International Students: There were 23 international students enrolled in a recent year. The school actively recruits these students. They must score 530 on the written TOEFL or 197 on the electronic version.

Computers: The mainframes are a DEC VAX 3400 and 5500 and an AT&T 382/4000. There are also 5 VAX 3100 workstations, 63 terminals, and 200 PCs located in 9 labs across campus. Languages supported include Pascal, COBOL, C, PROLOG, LISP, BASIC, FORTRAN, Ada, and Modula-2. Statistical packages available are Minitab and SPSS. Microsoft Word is used for word processing and SuperCalc 4 and EXCEL for spreadsheet. All students may access the system. There are no time limits and no fees.

Graduates: In a recent year, 269 bachelor's degrees were awarded. The most popular majors were business management (14%), elementary education (12%), and exercise science (11%). In an average class, 60% graduate in 4 years or less. 80 companies recruited on campus in a recent year. Of a recent graduating class, 18% were enrolled in graduate school within 6 months of graduation and 90% were employed.

Admissions Contact: Sam Vande Weerd, Director of Admission. E-mail: *admissions@central.edu* Web: *www.central.edu*

CLARKE COLLEGE
Dubuque, IA 52001   E-2
(563) 588-6316
(800) 383-2345; Fax: (563) 588-6789

Full-time: 231 men, 568 women	**Faculty:** 82
Part-time: 66 men, 130 women	**Ph.D.s:** 65%
Graduate: 34 men, 87 women	**Student/Faculty:** 10 to 1
Year: semesters, summer session	**Tuition:** $17,090
Application Deadline: open	**Room & Board:** $6075
Freshman Class: n/av	
SAT I or ACT: required	**COMPETITIVE**

Clarke College, established in 1843 is a private Catholic institution. A strong liberal arts core is integrated into all majors and preprofessional programs. In addition to regional accreditation, Clarke has baccalaureate program accreditation with APTA, CSWE, NASM, NCATE, and NLN. The library contains 116,046 volumes, 8483 microform items, and 1512 audio/video tapes/CDs, and subscribes to 11,102 periodicals. Computerized library services include the card catalog, interlibrary loans, and database searching. Special learning facilities include a learning resource center, art gallery, planetarium, and an art slide library, electronic music studio, and several computer-integrated specialized departmental labs. The 55-acre campus is in an urban area 150 miles west of Chicago. Including any residence halls, there are 13 buildings.

Student Life: 62% of undergraduates are from Iowa. Others are from 29 states, 15 foreign countries, and Canada. 80% are from public schools. 92% are white. 51% are Catholic; 30% claim no religious affiliation; 12% Protestant. The average age of freshmen is 18; all undergraduates, 25. 24% do not continue beyond their first year; 60% remain to graduate.

Housing: 585 students can be accommodated in college housing, which includes single-sex and coed dorms, on-campus apartments, a residence hall reserved for upperclassmen, and an apartment residence building reserved for juniors and seniors. On-campus housing is guaranteed for all 4 years. 64% of students live on campus; of those, 61% remain on campus on weekends. All students may keep cars.

Activities: There are no fraternities or sororities. There are 50 groups on campus, including art, cheerleading, choir, chorus, computers, drama, ethnic, honors, international, jazz band, literary magazine, newspaper, pep band, photography, political, professional, religious, social, social service, and student government. Popular campus events include Family Weekend, New Year's Dance, and Midnight Pancake Breakfast.

Sports: There are 8 intercollegiate sports for men and 8 for women, and 15 intramural sports for men and 13 for women. Facilities include

a 1000-seat gym, a 700-seat arena, an indoor track, a swimming pool, a soccer field, basketball, volleyball, tennis, and racquetball courts, a fitness trail, weight and aerobics rooms, and an indoor batting cage/pitching mound area. There are baseball/softball fields and 2 alpine ski courses nearby, plus a municipal golf course adjacent to the campus.

Disabled Students: 90% of the campus is accessible. Wheelchair ramps, elevators, special parking, specially equipped rest rooms, special class scheduling, lowered drinking fountains, and lowered telephones are available.

Services: Counseling and information services are available, as is tutoring in most subjects. There is remedial math, reading, and writing.

Campus Safety and Security: Measures include 24-hour foot and vehicle patrol, informal discussions, pamphlets/posters/films, and emergency telephones. There are lighted pathways/sidewalks.

Programs of Study: Clarke confers B.A., B.S., and B.F.A. degrees. Associate and master's degrees are also awarded. Bachelor's degrees are awarded in BIOLOGICAL SCIENCE (biology/biological science), BUSINESS (accounting, business administration and management, and marketing management), COMMUNICATIONS AND THE ARTS (advertising, art, art history and appreciation, communications, dramatic arts, English, music, Spanish, and studio art), COMPUTER AND PHYSICAL SCIENCE (chemistry, computer science, information sciences and systems, and mathematics), EDUCATION (art, early childhood, elementary, music, secondary, and special), HEALTH PROFESSIONS (nursing and physical therapy), SOCIAL SCIENCE (history, liberal arts/general studies, philosophy, physical fitness/movement, political science/government, psychology, religion, social work, and sociology). Biology, education, and computer science are the strongest academically. Education, nursing, and computer science are the largest.

Required: To graduate, all students must complete 124 semester hours, with 30 to 70 in the major, and maintain a GPA of 2.0 (2.5 for education majors or 3.25 for physical therapy majors). Students must complete a freshman seminar and courses in logic, composition, speech, research, and thinking skills; demonstrate computer literacy; and take Senior Performance, an integrative studies course in the major. The 51-hour core curriculum also includes 9 hours each of science, social sciences, and humanities and 6 hours each of religious studies, multicultural studies, and philosophy.

Special: There are co-op programs in most majors, cross-registration with Loras College and the University of Dubuque, and study abroad. Clarke also offers internships in chemistry, biology, and communications; an accelerated degree program in many majors for nontraditional, evening students; a B.A.-B.S. degree in biology, chemistry, psychology, business, and computer science; and a B.F.A.-B.A. program in art. There are also on- and off-campus work-study programs, dual majors, student-designed majors, and a freshman-entry 6-year physical therapy program. There are 4 national honor societies, a freshman honors program, and 3 departmental honors programs.

Faculty/Classroom: 37% of faculty are male; 63%, female. All both teach and do research. No introductory courses are taught by graduate students. The average class size in an introductory lecture is 24; in a laboratory, 11; and in a regular course, 14.

Requirements: The SAT I or ACT is required. In addition, the high school transcript should include 4 years of English, 3 each of math, history/social science, and science (4 for human biology and physical therapy majors), 2 of the same foreign language, and 5 of electives. Clarke requires applicants to be in the upper 50% of their class. A GPA of 2.0 is required. AP and CLEP credits are accepted. Advanced placement or honor courses are an important factor in the admission decision.

Procedure: Freshmen are admitted to all sessions. Entrance exams should be taken in the spring of the junior year or the fall of the senior year. There is a deferred admissions plan. Application deadlines are open. Applications are accepted on-line through Clark's web site.

Transfer: 75 transfer students enrolled in a recent year. Applicants must submit a transcript and a recommendation from the dean of students for each college attended. Students with fewer than 24 completed semester hours must also submit a high school transcript and SAT I or ACT scores. 30 of 124 credits required for the bachelor's degree must be completed at Clarke.

Visiting: There are guides for informal visits and visitors may sit in on classes and stay overnight. To schedule a visit, contact the Admissions Office.

Financial Aid: In a recent year, all full-time freshmen and 98% of continuing full-time students received some form of financial aid. 83% of full-time freshmen and 77% of continuing full-time students received need-based aid. The average freshman award was $13,637. 75% of undergraduates work part time. Average annual earnings from campus work were $904. The average financial indebtedness of a recent graduate was $16,778. The FAFSA is required.

International Students: There are 34 international students enrolled in a recent year. The school actively recruits these students. They must score 550 on the written TOEFL. The SAT I or ACT is required. Minimum SAT I score is 1000.

Computers: The mainframes are a 3 IBM RS/6000s model, 43P, 380, and C20. In addition, there are 203 networked PCs located in 17 labs

for student use. All of these have mainframe, Internet, and World Wide Web access. On-campus students have access from residence hall rooms; off-campus students may access a modem pool. All students may access the system at any time. There are no time limits. The fee is $150 per year.

Graduates: In a recent year, 221 bachelor's degrees were awarded. The most popular majors were human health science (34%), communication (25%), and nursing (21%). In an average class, 51% graduate in 4 years or less, 63% graduate in 5 years or less, and 63% graduate in 6 years or less. 50 companies recruited on campus in a recent year. Of a recent graduating class, 32% were enrolled in graduate school within 6 months of graduation and 65% were employed.

Admissions Contact: Omar Correa, Director of Admissions. E-mail: *ocorrea@clarke.edu* Web: *http://www.clarke.edu*

COE COLLEGE   E-3
Cedar Rapids, IA 52402   (319) 399-8500
(877) CALL-COE; Fax: (319) 399-8816

Full-time: 508 men, 669 women	**Faculty:** 74; IIB, av$
Part-time: 54 men, 59 women	**Ph.D.s:** 95%
Graduate: 5 men, 22 women	**Student/Faculty:** 16 to 1
Year: semesters, summer session	**Tuition:** $21,605
Application Deadline: March 1	**Room & Board:** $5780
Freshman Class: 1139 applied, 904 accepted, 309 enrolled	
SAT I Verbal/Math: 560/570	**ACT:** 24 **VERY COMPETITIVE**

Coe College, founded in 1851, is a private liberal arts institution affiliated with the Presbyterian Church (U.S.A.). In addition to regional accreditation, Coe has baccalaureate program accreditation with CAAHEP, NASM, and NLN. The 2 libraries contain 216,699 volumes, 5828 microform items, and 9044 audio/video tapes/CDs, and subscribe to 1380 periodicals. Computerized library services include the card catalog, interlibrary loans, database searching, and Internet access. Special learning facilities include a learning resource center, art gallery, radio station, and an ornithological wing. The 53-acre campus is in an urban area 225 miles west of Chicago. Including any residence halls, there are 22 buildings.

Student Life: 68% of undergraduates are from Iowa. Students are from 34 states and 16 foreign countries. 90% are from public schools. 92% are white. The average age of freshmen is 18; all undergraduates, 22. 19% do not continue beyond their first year; 70% remain to graduate.

Housing: 1036 students can be accommodated in college housing, which includes single-sex and coed dorms and on-campus apartments. In addition, there are special-interest houses and there is a substance-free facility. On-campus housing is guaranteed for all 4 years. 85% of students live on campus; of those, 75% remain on campus on weekends. All students may keep cars.

Activities: 26% of men belong to 5 national fraternities; 19% of women belong to 3 national sororities. There are 60 groups on campus, including art, band, cheerleading, choir, chorale, chorus, computers, dance, drama, ethnic, gay, honors, international, jazz band, literary magazine, newspaper, orchestra, pep band, political, professional, religious, social, social service, student government, and yearbook. Popular campus events include Coe Olympics, International Student Banquet and Cultural Show, and Flunk Day.

Sports: There are 11 intercollegiate sports for men and 10 for women, and 24 intramural sports for men and 24 for women. Facilities include a racquet center with 4 indoor and 6 outdoor tennis courts, 4 racquetball courts, 2 squash courts, and a 200-meter indoor track; and a field house with an indoor natatorium, an indoor track, a wrestling room, a fitness center, a rock climbing wall, courts for basketball and volleyball, and batting cages for baseball and softball. There are also a 400-meter outdoor track, softball diamond, and 1100-seat football/soccer stadium.

Disabled Students: 40% of the campus is accessible. Wheelchair ramps, elevators, special parking, specially equipped rest rooms, and special class scheduling are available.

Services: Counseling and information services are available, as is tutoring in most subjects. There is a reader service for the blind. A writing center and an educational support program is available.

Campus Safety and Security: Measures include 24-hour foot and vehicle patrol, security escort services, informal discussions, and pamphlets/posters/films. There are emergency telephones and lighted pathways/sidewalks.

Programs of Study: Coe confers B.A., B.Mus., and B.S.N. degrees. Master's degrees are also awarded. Bachelor's degrees are awarded in BIOLOGICAL SCIENCE (biochemistry, biology/biological science, and molecular biology), BUSINESS (accounting and business administration and management), COMMUNICATIONS AND THE ARTS (art, dramatic arts, English, French, German, literature, music, public relations, and Spanish), COMPUTER AND PHYSICAL SCIENCE (chemistry, computer science, mathematics, physics, and science), EDUCATION (athletic training, elementary, music, physical, and secondary), ENGINEERING AND ENVIRONMENTAL DESIGN (environmental science and preengineering), HEALTH PROFESSIONS (medical laboratory technology, nursing, physical therapy, predentistry, and premedicine), SOCIAL SCIENCE (African American studies, American studies, Asian/Oriental studies, classical/ancient civilization, economics, history, human services, interdisciplinary studies, philosophy, political science/government, prelaw, psychology, religion, sociology, and women's studies). Chemistry, physics, and psychology are the strongest academically. Business administration, psychology, and biology are the largest.

Required: All students must take 4 writing-emphasis courses, a first-year seminar, and a distribution of courses in fine arts, natural science, social science, and Western and foreign culture. A minimum of 32 course credits, including 9 to 12 in the major, and a 2.0 GPA are required for graduation. Students in an honors program must submit a thesis, and psychology and physics majors must pass a comprehensive examination. All students are required to do an internship, practicum, independent research project, or off-campus study program.

Special: Coe offers cross-registration with nearby Mount Mercy College and the University of Iowa, a cooperative program in architecture, Washington and New York semesters, and study abroad in 17 countries. Nondegree study, and dual and student-designed majors also are possible. Practicum experience is required. Core course instructors serve as students' mentors. There are 8 national honor societies, including Phi Beta Kappa, a freshman honors program, and honors programs in all departments.

Faculty/Classroom: 58% of faculty are male; 42%, female. All teach undergraduates and 95% both teach and do research. No introductory courses are taught by graduate students. The average class size in an introductory lecture is 13; in a laboratory, 14; and in a regular course, 16.

Admissions: 79% of the 2003-2004 applicants were accepted. The SAT I scores for the 2003-2004 freshman class were: Verbal--19% below 500, 39% between 500 and 599, 39% between 600 and 700, and 3% above 700; Math--22% below 500, 37% between 500 and 599, 33% between 600 and 700, and 8% above 700. The ACT scores were 20% below 21, 30% between 21 and 23, 29% between 24 and 26, 11% between 27 and 28, and 10% above 28. 51% of the current freshmen were in the top fifth of their class; 79% were in the top two fifths. 15 freshmen graduated first in their class.

Requirements: The SAT I or ACT is required. In addition, Coe recommends that applicants have 4 years in English, 3 each in math, history, science, and social studies, and 2 in foreign language. All students must submit an essay. In addition, fine arts students need a portfolio or audition. The GED is accepted. Coe requires applicants to be in the upper 60% of their class. A GPA of 2.75 is required. AP and CLEP credits are accepted. Important factors in the admissions decision are advanced placement or honor courses, recommendations by school officials, and extracurricular activities record.

Procedure: Freshmen are admitted fall and spring. Entrance exams should be taken in the spring of the junior year or the fall of the senior year. There is a deferred admissions plan. Early action applications should be filed by December 10; regular applications, by March 1 for fall entry. Notification is sent March 15. Applications are accepted on-line through the school's web site and Common Application.

Transfer: 49 transfer students enrolled in 2002-2003. Applicants must be high school graduates, have a minimum GPA of 2.5, and submit either the SAT I or ACT scores. An associate degree and an interview also are recommended. 8 of 32 course credits required for the bachelor's degree must be completed at Coe.

Visiting: There are regularly scheduled orientations for prospective students, consisting of tours, a luncheon, and informational sessions on admission, financial aid, and student life. There are guides for informal visits and visitors may sit in on classes and stay overnight. To schedule a visit, contact Sharon Fair, Campus Visit Coordinator, at sfair@coe.edu.

Financial Aid: In 2003-2004, 98% of all full-time freshmen and 95% of continuing full-time students received some form of financial aid. 80% of full-time freshmen and 79% of continuing full-time students received need-based aid. The average freshman award was $19,879. Need-based scholarships or need-based grants averaged $14,657 ($21,280 maximum); need-based self-help aid (loans and jobs) averaged $5492 ($8225 maximum); and non-need-based awards and non-need-based scholarships averaged $9396 ($13,000 maximum). 43% of undergraduates work part time. Average annual earnings from campus work are $1400. The average financial indebtedness of the 2003 graduate was $22,157. The FAFSA is required. The priority date for freshman financial aid applications for fall entry is March 1.

International Students: There are 66 international students enrolled. The school actively recruits these students. They must score 500 on the written TOEFL or 173 on the electronic version and also take the SAT I or the ACT.

Computers: The mainframe is a LAN operating under Novell netware. Students may access the campus network from approximately 260 PCs located in 7 labs on campus. All residence hall rooms are networked for student-owned machines. All students may access the system 24 hours a day. There are no time limits and no fees.

Graduates: From July 1, 2002 to June 30, 2003, 307 bachelor's degrees were awarded. The most popular majors were economics and

business administration (16%), psychology (7%), and biology (5%). In an average class, 63% graduate in 4 years or less, and 69% graduate in 5 years or less. 81 companies recruited on campus in 2002-2003. Of the 2002 graduating class, 28% were enrolled in graduate school within 6 months of graduation and 70% were employed.

Admissions Contact: John Sullivan, Executive Director of Admission and Financial Aid. E-mail: jsulliva@coe.edu Web: www.coe.edu

CORNELL COLLEGE   E-3
Mount Vernon, IA 52314-1098   (319) 895-4215
(800) 747-1112; Fax: (319) 895-4451

Full-time: 453 men, 652 women	**Faculty:** 85; IIB, av$
Part-time: 3 men, 9 women	**Ph.Ds:** 85%
Graduate: none	**Student/Faculty:** 13 to 1
Year: terms	**Tuition:** $21,790
Application Deadline: February 1	**Room & Board:** $6035
Freshman Class: 1555 applied, 1067 accepted, 369 enrolled	
SAT I Verbal/Math: 610/600	**ACT:** 26 **VERY COMPETITIVE+**

Cornell College, founded in 1853, is private institution affiliated with the United Methodist Church. Its emphases are on the liberal arts and on student service and leadership. Cornell has a 1-course-at-a-time calendar in which the year is divided into nine 3 1/2 week terms. In addition to regional accreditation, Cornell has baccalaureate program accreditation with NASM. The library contains 176,941 volumes, 235,000 microform items, and 7760 audio/video tapes/CDs, and subscribes to 774 periodicals. Computerized library services include the card catalog, interlibrary loans, and database searching. Special learning facilities include a learning resource center, art gallery, natural history museum, and radio station. The 129-acre campus is in a small town 15 miles east of Cedar Rapids. Including any residence halls, there are 43 buildings.

Student Life: 69% of undergraduates are from out of state, mostly the Midwest. Others are from 42 states, 14 foreign countries, and Canada. 90% are from public schools. 89% are white. 48% are claim no religious affiliation; 31% Protestant; 17% Catholic. The average age of freshmen is 18; all undergraduates, 20. 19% do not continue beyond their first year; 68% remain to graduate.

Housing: 1038 students can be accommodated in college housing, which includes single-sex and coed dorms and on-campus apartments. In addition, there are special-interest houses and living and learning communities. On-campus housing is guaranteed for all 4 years. 92% of students live on campus; of those, 70% remain on campus on weekends. All students may keep cars.

Activities: 30% of men belong to 7 local fraternities; 32% of women belong to 7 local sororities. There are 76 groups on campus, including art, band, cheerleading, chess, choir, chorale, chorus, computers, debate, drama, environmental, ethnic, gay, honors, international, jazz band, leadership development, literary magazine, musical theater, newspaper, opera, orchestra, pep band, performing arts, photography, political, professional, radio and TV, religious, social, social service, student government, and yearbook. Popular campus events include Homecoming and Knock Your Block Off.

Sports: There are 10 intercollegiate sports for men and 9 for women, and 40 intramural sports for men and 40 for women. Facilities include a multisport center, with a 2100-seat basketball and volleyball arena, sports fitness and training facilities, 6-lane track, 4 multipurpose courts for tennis, basketball, and volleyball, batting cages, golf hitting nets; a 2500-seat football and track stadium; and baseball, soccer, softball, and football practice fields, and 6 outdoor tennis courts.

Disabled Students: 43% of the campus is accessible. Wheelchair ramps, elevators, special parking, specially equipped rest rooms, special class scheduling, lowered drinking fountains, and lowered telephones are available.

Services: Counseling and information services are available, as is tutoring in every subject. There is a reader service for the blind.

Campus Safety and Security: Measures include informal discussions, pamphlets/posters/films, emergency telephones, and lighted pathways/sidewalks. A foot and vehicle patrol runs 24 hours on weekends and 4 P.M. to 7 A.M. during weekdays.

Programs of Study: Cornell confers B.A., B.Mus., B.Ph., and B.S.S. degrees. Bachelor's degrees are awarded in BIOLOGICAL SCIENCE (biology/biological science), BUSINESS (international business management), COMMUNICATIONS AND THE ARTS (dramatic arts, English, fine arts, French, German, languages, music, Russian, and Spanish), COMPUTER AND PHYSICAL SCIENCE (chemistry, computer science, geology, mathematics, and physics), EDUCATION (art, elementary, foreign languages, music, science, and secondary), ENGINEERING AND ENVIRONMENTAL DESIGN (environmental science), SOCIAL SCIENCE (anthropology, classical/ancient civilization, economics, history, international relations, Latin American studies, medieval studies, philosophy, political science/government, psychology, religion, sociology, and women's studies). Biology, philosophy, and English are the strongest academically. Psychology, education, and English are the largest.

Required: To graduate, all students must complete 32 course credits (128 semester hours), with 7 to 15 in a faculty-approved major, and maintain at least a 2.0 GPA. B.A. candidates must complete 4 courses in humanities, 2 each in science (1 with a lab) and social science, 1 each in fine arts and math, and 1 to 4 in a foreign language. B.S.S. candidates need not meet all of the above requirements.

Special: Special academic programs include study abroad in 25 countries, internships including a Washington semester, double majors, student-designed majors, and interdisciplinary majors in biochemistry and molecular biology, environmental studies, international relations, and women's studies. A cooperative degree program in nursing and allied health services with Rush University, a 3-2 engineering program and a 3-4 archietecture program with Washington University, and a 3-2 forestry or environmental management program with Duke University are also available. Nondegree study is possible. There are 9 national honor societies, including Phi Beta Kappa.

Faculty/Classroom: 51% of faculty are male; 49%, female. All teach undergraduates, 75% do research, and 75% do both. The average class size in an introductory lecture is 21; in a laboratory, 19; and in a regular course, 15.

Admissions: 69% of the 2003-2004 applicants were accepted. The SAT I scores for the 2003-2004 freshman class were: Verbal--6% below 500, 35% between 500 and 599, 47% between 600 and 700, and 12% above 700; Math--9% below 500, 37% between 500 and 599, 41% between 600 and 700, and 13% above 700. The ACT scores were 6% below 21, 20% between 21 and 23, 26% between 24 and 26, 18% between 27 and 28, and 30% above 28. 50% of the current freshmen were in the top fifth of their class; 79% were in the top two fifths. There were 3 National Merit finalists. 25 freshmen graduated first in their class.

Requirements: The SAT I or ACT is required. In addition, applicants should must be graduates of an accredited secondary school, with a recommended 4 years each of English and history/social studies, 3 each of math and science, 2 to 4 of a foreign language, and 1 each of art and music. The GED is accepted. An essay is required and an interview is advised. Cornell recommends that applicants be in the upper 50% of their class. A GPA of 2.8 is recommended. AP and CLEP credits are accepted. Important factors in the admissions decision are leadership record, evidence of special talent, and advanced placement or honor courses.

Procedure: Freshmen are admitted to all sessions. There are early admissions and deferred admissions plans. Early decision applications should be filed by December 1; regular applications, by February 1 for fall entry. Notification of early decision is sent December 20; regular decision, on a rolling basis. 38 were on the 2003 waiting list; 7 were admitted. Applications are accepted on-line through Common App and Apply Now.

Transfer: 39 transfer students enrolled in 2003-2004. Applicants must submit official college and high school transcripts. 8 of 32 credits required for the bachelor's degree must be completed at Cornell.

Visiting: There are regularly scheduled orientations for prospective students, including campus tours and meetings with an informational panel, a student panel, financial aid staff, and faculty and or coaches as requested. There are guides for informal visits and visitors may sit in on classes and stay overnight. To schedule a visit, contact Judy Penn, Visit Coordinator at (319) 895-4161 or jpenn@cornellcollege.edu.

Financial Aid: In 2003-2004, 94% of all full-time freshmen and 98% of continuing full-time students received some form of financial aid. 79% of full-time freshmen and 75% of continuing full-time students received need-based aid. The average freshman award was $19,460. Need-based scholarships or need-based grants averaged $13,500 ($15,000 maximum); need-based self-help aid (loans and jobs) averaged $4600 ($6125 maximum); and other non-need-based awards and non-need-based scholarships averaged $11,500 ($21,630 maximum). 66% of undergraduates work part time. Average annual earnings from campus work are $1000. The average financial indebtedness of the 2003 graduate was $17,870. The FAFSA and the college's own financial statement are required. The deadline for filing freshman financial aid applications for fall entry is March 1.

International Students: There are 21 international students enrolled. The school actively recruits these students. They must score 500 on the written TOEFL and also take the college's own test.

Computers: The college uses a Windows 2000 servers. There are 120 PCs in all academic labs, the library, and the commons. All academic computer facilities and residence halls have access to the Internet. All students may access the system. There are no time limits and no fees.

Graduates: From July 1, 2002 to June 30, 2003, 197 bachelor's degrees were awarded. The most popular majors were psychology (15%), economics and business (11%), and history (9%). In an average class, 3% graduate in 3 years or less, 62% graduate in 4 years or less, 65% graduate in 5 years or less, and 68% graduate in 6 years or less. 10 companies recruited on campus in 2002-2003. Of the 2002 graduating class, 31% were enrolled in graduate school within 6 months of graduation and 63% were employed.

Admissions Contact: Jonathan Stroud, Vice President of Enrollment and Dean of Admissions. A video is available.

E-mail: *admissions@cornellcollege.edu*
Web: *http://www.cornellcollege.edu/*

DORDT COLLEGE
B-1
Sioux Center, IA 51250
(712) 722-6080
(800) 34-DORDT; Fax: (712) 722-1967

Full-time: 562 men, 671 women	**Faculty:** 75; IIB, av$
Part-time: 27 men, 27 women	**Ph.D.s:** 85%
Graduate: 18 men, 53 women	**Student/Faculty:** 16 to 1
Year: semesters	**Tuition:** $15,770
Application Deadline: n/av	**Room & Board:** $4400
Freshman Class: 780 applied, 717 accepted, 344 enrolled	
SAT I Verbal/Math: 580/586	**ACT:** 24 **VERY COMPETITIVE**

Dordt College, founded in 1955, is a private institution affiliated with the Christian Reformed Church. The curriculum, which is designed to reflect the principles of the Christian faith, leads to degrees in liberal arts, agriculture, art, music, business, engineering, and teaching preparation. In addition to regional accreditation, Dordt has baccalaureate program accreditation with ABET and CSWE. The library contains 185,000 volumes, 14,819 microform items, and 5000 audio/video tapes/CDs, and subscribes to 700 periodicals. Computerized library services include the card catalog and interlibrary loans. Special learning facilities include a learning resource center, planetarium, radio station, and 2 observatories, as well as a 160-acre agriculture stewardship center just north of the campus. The 110-acre campus is in a rural area 42 miles north of Sioux City. Including any residence halls, there are 22 buildings.

Student Life: 58% of undergraduates are from out of state, mostly the Midwest. Others are from 32 states, 12 foreign countries, and Canada. 40% are from public schools. 98% are white. Most are Protestant. The average age of freshmen is 18; all undergraduates, 21. 17% do not continue beyond their first year; 68% remain to graduate.

Housing: 1250 students can be accommodated in college housing, which includes single-sex and coed dorms, on-campus apartments, and off-campus apartments. On-campus housing is guaranteed for all 4 years. 90% of students live on campus; of those, 80% remain on campus on weekends. Alcohol is not permitted. All students may keep cars.

Activities: There are no fraternities or sororities. There are 25 groups on campus, including band, choir, chorale, computers, dance, drama, drill team, forensics, international, jazz band, literary magazine, newspaper, opera, orchestra, pep band, professional, radio and TV, religious, social, social service, student government, symphony, and yearbook. Popular campus events include Parents Day in October.

Sports: There are 7 intercollegiate sports for men and 7 for women, and 10 intramural sports for men and 10 for women. Facilities include a 2500-seat gym with 2 courts; an 85,000-square-foot recreation center, which includes a 200-meter indoor track, 3 courts adaptable for basketball, volleyball, and tennis, 3 racquetball courts, weight lifting and exercise equipment rooms, and a golf simulation room; an outdoor track; tennis courts; soccer, softball, and baseball fields; and an indoor pool and ice arena adjacent to the campus.

Disabled Students: All of the campus is accessible. Wheelchair ramps, elevators, special parking, specially equipped rest rooms, special class scheduling, lowered drinking fountains, lowered telephones, and special housing are available.

Services: Counseling and information services are available, as is tutoring in most subjects. There is a reader service for the blind, and remedial math, reading, and writing.

Campus Safety and Security: Measures include 24-hour foot and vehicle patrol and lighted pathways/sidewalks.

Programs of Study: Dordt confers B.A., B.S., B.S.N., and B.S.W. degrees. Associate and master's degrees are also awarded. Bachelor's degrees are awarded in BIOLOGICAL SCIENCE (biology/biological science), BUSINESS (accounting and business administration and management), COMMUNICATIONS AND THE ARTS (broadcasting, communications, dramatic arts, Dutch, English, fine arts, German, graphic design, journalism, languages, music, Spanish, and speech/debate/rhetoric), COMPUTER AND PHYSICAL SCIENCE (chemistry, computer programming, computer science, information sciences and systems, mathematics, and physics), EDUCATION (art, business, elementary, foreign languages, music, and secondary), ENGINEERING AND ENVIRONMENTAL DESIGN (chemical engineering, electrical/electronics engineering, engineering, environmental science, and mechanical engineering), HEALTH PROFESSIONS (health science, medical laboratory technology, nursing, predentistry, and premedicine), SOCIAL SCIENCE (criminal justice, history, philosophy, political science/government, prelaw, psychology, religion, social science, social work, sociology, and youth ministry). Engineering, business administration, and social work are the strongest academically. Education is the largest.

Required: All students must complete a college introductory course and a distribution of 14 other courses in the various academic disciplines, including General Education 300. Proficiency requirements must be met in English, math, and phys ed. To graduate, students must complete a minimum of 126 credits with a 2.0 GPA.

Special: Students may study abroad in 10 countries. Dordt also offers a Washington semester, a Chicago Metro semester, a joint nursing degree program with St. Luke's School of Nursing, a B.S.N. with Briar Cliff University, B.A.-B.S. degrees in engineering and agriculture, and numerous internships in all majors. Dual majors, student-designed majors, and pass/fail options are available. There is a freshman honors program.

Faculty/Classroom: 85% of faculty are male; 15%, female. All teach undergraduates. The average class size in an introductory lecture is 30; in a laboratory, 20; and in a regular course, 25.

Admissions: 92% of the 2003-2004 applicants were accepted. The SAT I scores for the 2003-2004 freshman class were: Verbal--15% below 500, 38% between 500 and 599, 39% between 600 and 700, and 8% above 700; Math--17% below 500, 38% between 500 and 599, 34% between 600 and 700, and 11% above 700. The ACT scores were 12% below 21, 28% between 21 and 23, 28% between 24 and 26, 18% between 27 and 28, and 14% above 28. 31% of the current freshmen were in the top fifth of their class; 53% were in the top two fifths. There were 3 National Merit finalists and 5 semifinalists. 15 freshmen graduated first in their class.

Requirements: The SAT I or ACT is required. In addition, applicants must be graduates of accredited secondary schools or have earned a GED. The college requires 18 academic credits, including 4 in English and 2 each in foreign language, math, science, and social studies. A GPA of 2.25 is required. AP and CLEP credits are accepted. Important factors in the admissions decision are advanced placement or honor courses, evidence of special talent, and leadership record.

Procedure: Freshmen are admitted fall and spring. Entrance exams should be taken by October of the senior year and no later than April. Notification is sent on a rolling basis. Applications are accepted on-line through *www.dordt.edu*. Check with the school for current deadlines.

Transfer: 47 transfer students enrolled in 2003-2004. Transfer students must have a GPA of 2.0. 62 of 126 credits required for the bachelor's degree must be completed at Dordt.

Visiting: There are regularly scheduled orientations for prospective students, including tours, class visits, personal visits with professors and coaches, and a financial aid session. There are guides for informal visits and visitors may sit in on classes and stay overnight. To schedule a visit, contact the Admissions Office.

Financial Aid: In 2003-2004, 98% of all full-time students received some form of financial aid. 95% of all full-time students received need-based aid. The average freshman award was $13,500. Need-based scholarships or need-based grants averaged $6500; need-based self-help aid (loans and jobs) averaged $6000; non-need-based athletic scholarships averaged $2000; and other non-need-based awards and non-need-based scholarships averaged $3000. 80% of undergraduates work part time. Average annual earnings from campus work are $1300. The average financial indebtedness of the 2003 graduate was $15,100. The FAFSA and the college's own financial statement are required. The deadline for filing freshman financial aid applications for fall entry is April 1.

International Students: There are 139 international students enrolled. The school actively recruits these students. They must score 550 on the written TOEFL or 213 on the electronic version. International students also take the SAT I or the ACT, scoring 19 on the ACT.

Computers: Dordt provides 200 IBM, Mac, and Altos PCs for academic use. All students may access the system. There are no time limits and no fees.

Graduates: From July 1, 2002 to June 30, 2003, 282 bachelor's degrees were awarded. The most popular majors were education (26%), business (18%), and engineering (8%). In an average class, 68% graduate in 4 years or less. 50 companies recruited on campus in 2002-2003. Of the 2002 graduating class, 8% were enrolled in graduate school within 6 months of graduation and 97% were employed.

Admissions Contact: Quentin Van Essen, Executive Director of Admissions. E-mail: *admissions@dordt.edu* Web: *www.dordt.edu*

DRAKE UNIVERSITY
Des Moines, IA 50311

C-3

(515) 271-3181
(800) 44-DRAKE; Fax: (515) 271-2831

Full-time: 1278 men, 1882 women	Faculty: 167; IIA, av$
Part-time: 114 men, 160 women	Ph.D.s: 93%
Graduate: 726 men, 1004 women	Student/Faculty: 19 to 1
Year: semesters, summer session	Tuition: $19,420
Application Deadline: March 1	Room & Board: $5700
Freshman Class: 3174 applied, 2647 accepted, 815 enrolled	
SAT I Verbal/Math: 584/594	ACT: 26 VERY COMPETITIVE+

Drake University, founded in 1881, is a private institution offering undergraduate and graduate programs in arts and sciences, business and public administration, pharmacy and health sciences, journalism and mass communication, education, fine arts, and law. There are 6 undergraduate schools and 1 graduate school. In addition to regional accreditation, Drake has baccalaureate program accreditation with AACSB, ACEJMC, ACPE, NASAD, NASM, NCATE, and NLN. The library contains 480,511 volumes, 875,378 microform items, and 2766 audio/video tapes/CDs, and subscribes to 2000 periodicals. Computerized library services include the card catalog, interlibrary loans, database searching, and Internet access. Special learning facilities include a learning resource center, art gallery, radio station, TV station, observatory, and the Henry G. Harmon Fine Arts Center. The 120-acre campus is in a suburban area in Des Moines. Including any residence halls, there are 48 buildings.

Student Life: 52% of undergraduates are from out of state, mostly the Midwest. Students are from 40 states, 53 foreign countries, and Canada. 89% are from public schools. 85% are white. 23% are Protestant; 17% Catholic; 8% Jewish. The average age of freshmen is 18; all undergraduates, 21. 17% do not continue beyond their first year; 83% remain to graduate.

Housing: 1668 students can be accommodated in college housing, which includes coed dorms, married-student housing, fraternity houses, and sorority houses. On-campus housing is guaranteed for all 4 years, is available on a first-come, first-served basis, and is available on a lottery system for upperclassmen. 57% of students live on campus; of those, 80% remain on campus on weekends. All students may keep cars.

Activities: 30% of men belong to 8 national fraternities; 28% of women belong to 5 national sororities. There are 160 groups on campus, including art, band, cheerleading, chess, choir, chorale, chorus, computers, dance, drama, drill team, ethnic, gay, honors, international, jazz band, literary magazine, marching band, musical theater, newspaper, opera, orchestra, pep band, photography, political, professional, radio and TV, religious, social, social service, student government, and symphony. Popular campus events include Drake Relays, Supreme Court Days, and Parents Weekend.

Sports: There are 8 intercollegiate sports for men and 9 for women, and 24 intramural sports for men and 24 for women. Facilities include a football stadium, an indoor swimming pool, an aerobics room, 2 weight rooms, basketball, volleyball, and badminton courts, 2 indoor tracks and 1 outdoor track, 4 racquetball courts, and 6 indoor and 6 outdoor tennis courts. A recreation and sports facility seats 7000.

Disabled Students: 80% of the campus is accessible. Wheelchair ramps, elevators, special parking, specially equipped rest rooms, special class scheduling, lowered drinking fountains, lowered telephones, an IBM-compatible computer and scanner that includes a voice and screen enlargement program, closed-caption television, and TDD are available.

Services: There is a reader service for the blind. The Student Disability Service works with Recordings for the Blind and the Iowa Department for the Blind to access books on audiotape and to coordinate volunteer readers.

Campus Safety and Security: Measures include 24-hour foot and vehicle patrol, self-defense education, security escort services, and shuttle buses. There are informal discussions, pamphlets/posters/films, emergency telephones, and lighted pathways/sidewalks.

Programs of Study: Drake confers B.A., B.S., B.A.Journ. and Mass Comm., B.Art., B.F.A., B.Mus., B.Mus.Ed., B.S.B.A., B.S.Ed., and B.S.Pharm. degrees. Master's and doctoral degrees are also awarded. Bachelor's degrees are awarded in BIOLOGICAL SCIENCE (biology/biological science and neurosciences), BUSINESS (accounting, banking and finance, business administration and management, insurance and risk management, international business management, management science, marketing management, and marketing/retailing/merchandising), COMMUNICATIONS AND THE ARTS (advertising, art history and appreciation, broadcasting, communications, dramatic arts, English, graphic design, journalism, music, music business management, music performance, printmaking, public relations, speech/debate/rhetoric, and studio art), COMPUTER AND PHYSICAL SCIENCE (actuarial science, chemistry, computer science, information sciences and systems, mathematics, and physics), EDUCATION (elementary, mathematics, music, and secondary), ENGINEERING AND ENVIRONMENTAL DESIGN (environmental science), HEALTH PROFESSIONS (pharmacy), SOCIAL SCIENCE (clinical psychology, economics, ethics, politics, and social policy, history, international relations, law, philosophy, political science/government, psychology, religion, religious music, and sociology). Actuarial science, pharmacy, and physics/astronomy are the strongest academically. Pharmacy, accounting, and music peformance are the largest.

Required: Undergraduates must take a first-year seminar and general education courses, as well as satisfy areas of inquiry requirements that include writing, critical thinking, artistic experience, historical consciousness, information and technical literacy, multicultural experience, scientific and quantitative literacy, values and ethics, and the engaged citizen. A capstone demonstration is required. For graduation, 124 credit hours are required with 27 to 36 hours in the major. The minimum GPA is 2.0.

Special: Study abroad is available in 67 countries and at sea. The university offers cross-registration with Des Moines area Colleges, including Grand View, internships, a Washington semester, a United Nations semester, and work-study programs. Dual majors, B.A.-B.S. degrees, a 3-2 engineering degree with Washington and Cornell Universities, student-designed majors, credit for military and work experience, and nondegree study are possible. Students may take a maximum of 12 hours of course work on a credit/no credit basis. There are 25 national honor societies, including Phi Beta Kappa, a freshman honors program, and 19 departmental honors programs.

Faculty/Classroom: 65% of faculty are male; 32%, female. 70% teach undergraduates and 90% do research. No introductory courses are taught by graduate students. The average class size in an introductory lecture is 31; in a laboratory, 14; and in a regular course, 22.

Admissions: 83% of the 2003-2004 applicants were accepted. The SAT I scores for the 2003-2004 freshman class were: Verbal--13% below 500, 41% between 500 and 599, 39% between 600 and 700, and 7% above 700; Math--13% below 500, 35% between 500 and 599, 40% between 600 and 700, and 12% above 700. The ACT scores were 6% below 21, 20% between 21 and 23, 33% between 24 and 26, 16% between 27 and 28, and 23% above 28. 56% of the current freshmen were in the top fifth of their class; 86% were in the top two fifths. There were 3 National Merit finalists. 20 freshmen graduated first in their class.

Requirements: The SAT I or ACT is required. In addition, applicants must be graduates of an accredited secondary school. The GED is accepted. Students must have completed 4 years of English, 2 years of math, and 10 other units to be selected from English, foreign languages, social studies, math, lab sciences, and others. A portfolio is required for art majors and for those seeking scholarship consideration. An audition is necessary for admission to the music program. Tapes are accepted. Drake requires applicants to be in the upper 60% of their class. A GPA of 2.5 is required. AP and CLEP credits are accepted. Important factors in the admissions decision are advanced placement or honor courses, extracurricular activities record, and leadership record.

Procedure: Freshmen are admitted to all sessions. Entrance exams should be taken during the spring of the junior year or early fall of the senior year. There is a rolling admissions plan and a deferred admissions plan. Early decision applications should be filed by August 1; regular applications, by March 1 for fall entry and December 1 for spring entry, along with a $25 fee. That fee is waived for online applicants. Notification is sent on a rolling basis. Applications are accepted on computer disk and on-line through *www.choose.drake.edu*.

Transfer: 161 transfer students enrolled in 2002-2003. Applicants must have a minimum GPA of 2.0 and have completed 24 credit hours for evaluation. Grades of C or better transfer for credit. There is no assurance that all courses transferred will apply toward the major requirement. The final 30 hours must be completed in residence. Transfer students are admitted in the fall, spring, and summer. 30 of 124 credits required for the bachelor's degree must be completed at Drake.

Visiting: There are regularly scheduled orientations for prospective students, including an opportunity for students and parents to confer with professors, meet with current students, and attend information sessions on academic programs, financial aid, housing, and the Drake campus. Also included are a walking tour and lunch. There are guides for informal visits and visitors may sit in on classes and stay overnight. To schedule a visit, contact the Visit Coordinator in the Office of Admission at *admission@drake.edu*.

Financial Aid: In 2003-2004, 98% of all full-time freshmen and 97% of continuing full-time students received some form of financial aid. 69% of full-time freshmen and 56% of continuing full-time students received need-based aid. The average freshman award was $24,222, with $7595 ($20,800 maximum) from need-based scholarships or need-based grants, $3425 ($11,470 maximum) from need-based self-help aid (loans and jobs), $301 ($19,420 maximum) from non-need-based athletic scholarships, and $12,901 ($19,360 maximum) from other non-need-based awards and non-need-based scholarships. 36% of undergraduates work part time. Average annual earnings from campus work are $1190. The average financial indebtedness of the 2003 graduate was $21,422. The FAFSA is required. The deadline for filing freshman financial aid applications for fall entry is March 1.

International Students: There are 147 international students enrolled. The school actively recruits these students. They must score 530 on the written TOEFL or 197 on the electronic version.

Computers: The mainframes are a several Sun DEC Alpha, and Dell Poweredge servers. Every residence hall room is equipped with a high-speed network connection for each student. The network provides access to the information system, library resourses, course management system, e-mail, and the Internet. All students may access the system. There are no time limits. The fee is $220. It is strongly recommended that all students have a personal computer.

Graduates: From July 1, 2002 to June 30, 2003, 656 bachelor's degrees were awarded. The most popular majors were marketing (7%), biology (6%), and management (5%). In an average class, 56% graduate in 4 years or less, 64% graduate in 5 years or less, and 73% graduate in 6 years or less. 51 companies recruited on campus in 2002-2003. Of the 2002 graduating class, 20% were enrolled in graduate school within 6 months of graduation and 70% were employed.

Admissions Contact: Thomas F. Willoughby, Vice President for Admission and Financial Aid. E-mail: *admission@drake.edu*
Web: *www.choose.drake.edu*

FRANCISCAN UNIVERSITY   F-3
(Formerly Mount St. Clare College)
Clinton, IA 52733-2967

(563) 243-6102
(800) 242-4153; Fax: (563) 242-2003

Full-time: 169 men, 204 women	**Faculty:** 27
Part-time: 17 men, 36 women	**Ph.Ds:** 38%
Graduate: 33 men, 59 women	**Student/Faculty:** 14 to 1
Year: semesters, summer session	**Tuition:** $14,050
Application Deadline: August 15	**Room & Board:** $5250
Freshman Class: n/av	
SAT I: n/av	**ACT:** required **COMPETITIVE**

The Franciscan University, formerly Mount St. Clare College, is a private, Franciscan, liberal arts college founded in 1918 and sponsored by the Sisters of St. Francis. The library contains 80,759 volumes, 73,405 microform items, and 2458 audio/video tapes/CDs, and subscribes to 645 periodicals. Computerized library services include the card catalog, interlibrary loans, and database searching. Special learning facilities include a learning resource center, art gallery, and a living lab adjacent to the campus. The 25-acre campus is in a small town 135 miles west of Chicago. Including any residence halls, there are 6 buildings.

Student Life: 54% of undergraduates are from Iowa. Students are from 10 states, 9 foreign countries, and Canada. 70% are from public schools. 89% are white. 36% claim no religious affiliation; 31% Catholic; 6% Buddhist Christian. The average age of freshmen is 18; all undergraduates, 26. 40% do not continue beyond their first year; 59% remain to graduate.

Housing: 233 students can be accommodated in college housing, which includes single-sex and coed dorms. On-campus housing is guaranteed for all 4 years. 71% of students commute. Alcohol is not permitted. All students may keep cars.

Activities: There are no fraternities or sororities. There are 20 groups on campus, including band, choir, computers, drama, ethnic, gay, honors, international, musical theater, newspaper, professional, religious, SISEA (Iowa State Education Association), social, social service, and student government. Popular campus events include Family Weekend, Matriculation Ceremony, and Earth Day.

Sports: There are 6 intercollegiate sports for men and 6 for women, and 6 intramural sports for men and 6 for women. Facilities include an arena with 2 regulation-size basketball courts, a fitness center, a 4-lane perimeter track, 2 locker rooms plus 2 rooms and 1 training room. St. Francis gym is located on campus. There is a soccer field and an indoor swimming pool.

Disabled Students: 95% of the campus is accessible. Wheelchair ramps, elevators, special parking, specially equipped rest rooms, lowered drinking fountains, and special doors for the disabled are available.

Services: Counseling and information services are available, as is tutoring in most subjects. There is a reader service for the blind, and remedial math, reading, and writing. There is also voice-activated computer software, proctoring exams, and prep courses for the GRE and MCAT.

Campus Safety and Security: Measures include 24-hour foot and vehicle patrol, self-defense education, security escort services, and informal discussions. There are pamphlets/posters/films, emergency telephones, lighted pathways/sidewalks, and a 24-hour campus security department.

Programs of Study: TFU confers B.A., B.S., B.A.S., and B.G.S. degrees. Associate and master's degrees are also awarded. Bachelor's degrees are awarded in BIOLOGICAL SCIENCE (biology/biological science), BUSINESS (accounting, business administration and management, management information systems, marketing management, and sports management), COMMUNICATIONS AND THE ARTS (English and visual and performing arts), COMPUTER AND PHYSICAL SCIENCE (computer mathematics and computer science), EDUCATION (business, elementary, and science), ENGINEERING AND ENVIRONMENTAL DESIGN (computer graphics), HEALTH PROFESSIONS (clinical science, cytotechnology, and nuclear medical technology), SOCIAL SCIENCE (criminal justice, interdisciplinary studies, liberal arts/general studies, psychology, religion, and social science). Accounting, business administration, and elementary education are the strongest academically. Liberal arts, elementary education, and business administration are the largest.

Required: Students must complete 122 semester hours, including 34 semester hours of general education requirements, plus 12 hours of competencies (computer/writing/math), and 30 in a major, with a minimum 2.0 GPA. A final exam, report, or project is required in every course.

Special: Special academic programs include a co-op program in nursing with Clarke College, internships, study abroad in Italy, a dual major in accounting and business, and a general studies program. There are 2 national honor societies, a freshman honors program, and 1 departmental honors program.

Faculty/Classroom: 58% of faculty are male; 42%, female. All teach undergraduates. No introductory courses are taught by graduate students. The average class size in an introductory lecture is 20; in a laboratory, 14; and in a regular course, 19.

Admissions: 16% of the current freshmen were in the top fifth of their class; 45% were in the top two fifths. In a recent year, 2 freshmen graduated first in their class.

Requirements: The ACT is required; the SAT I is accepted. Applicants must be graduates of an accredited secondary school or have earned a GED and must meet 2 of the following requirements: a GPA of 2.0 in college preparatory or regular high school courses, rank in the upper half of the graduating class, and a minimum ACT composite score of 18 or SAT I composite score of 750. TFU requires applicants to be in the upper 50% of their class. A GPA of 2.0 is required. AP and CLEP credits are accepted.

Procedure: Freshmen are admitted to all sessions. Entrance exams should be taken before enrolling. There is a rolling admissions plan. There are early admissions and deferred admissions plans. Applications should be filed by August 15 for fall entry, January 10 for spring entry, and June 1 for summer entry, along with a $20 fee. Notification is sent on a rolling basis. Applications are accepted on-line through the school's web site.

Transfer: 98 transfer students enrolled in 2002-2003. Applicants may have 64 semester hours of 100-level or higher courses from a 2-year school, and up to 90 semester hours maximum. 30 of 122 credits required for the bachelor's degree must be completed at TFU.

Visiting: There are regularly scheduled orientations for prospective students, including 2-day orientation sessions held prior to the first week of classes for students and parents. There are guides for informal visits and visitors may sit in on classes and stay overnight. To schedule a visit, contact the Admissions Office at (563) 242-4023 or admissions@tfu.edu.

Financial Aid: In 2003-2004, 94% of all full-time freshmen and 95% of continuing full-time students received some form of financial aid. 87% of full-time freshmen and 82% of continuing full-time students received need-based aid. The average freshman award was $15,774. 36% of undergraduates work part time. Average annual earnings from campus work in a recent year was $1106. The average financial indebtedness of the 2003 graduate was $15,868. TFU is a member of CSS. The FAFSA and parents' and student's income tax form are required. The deadline for filing freshman financial aid applications for fall entry is June 1.

International Students: There are 13 international students enrolled. The school actively recruits these students. They must score 420 on the written TOEFL.

Computers: TFU provides 56 PCs in 4 locations for student use. All students may access the system daily during scheduled times. There are no time limits and no fees.

Graduates: In a recent year, 124 bachelor's degrees were awarded. The most popular majors were social science (25%), elementary education (20%), and business administration (18%). In an average class, 27% graduate in 4 years or less, 7% graduate in 5 years or less, and 37% graduate in 6 years or less. 26 companies recruited on campus in 2002-2003. Of the 2002 graduating class, 94% were employed within 6 months of graduation.

Admissions Contact: Waunita M. Sullivan, Director of Enrollment. A video is available. E-mail: admissions@tfu.edu
Web: http://www.tfu.edu

GRACELAND UNIVERSITY
Lamoni, IA 50140

C-4
(641) 784-5118
(866) 472-2352; Fax: (641) 784-5480

Full-time: 570 men, 773 women	**Faculty:** 94; IIB, -$
Part-time: 131 men, 559 women	**Ph.D.s:** 47%
Graduate: 70 men, 256 women	**Student/Faculty:** 14 to 1
Year: 4-1-4, summer session	**Tuition:** $14,800
Application Deadline: May 1	**Room & Board:** $4750
Freshman Class: 1016 applied, 585 accepted, 253 enrolled	
SAT I or ACT: required	COMPETITIVE

Graceland University, formerly Graceland College, established in 1895, is a private liberal arts college sponsored by the Community of Christ. Graceland also maintains a campus in Independence, MO. There are 4 undergraduate and 4 graduate schools. In addition to regional accreditation, Graceland has baccalaureate program accreditation with CCNE, NCATE, and NLN. The library contains 199,447 volumes, 914 microform items, and 3658 audio/video tapes/CDs, and subscribes to 624 periodicals. Computerized library services include the card catalog, interlibrary loans, database searching, and Internet access. Special learning facilities include a learning resource center, art gallery, and a center for the study of the Korean War. The 167-acre campus is in a small town 80 miles south of Des Moines. Including any residence halls, there are 28 buildings.

Student Life: 60% of undergraduates are from out of state, mostly the Midwest. Students are from 49 states, 35 foreign countries, and Canada. 64% are white. 16% are Protestant; 6% Catholic. The average age of freshmen is 18; all undergraduates, 20. 30% do not continue beyond their first year; 47% remain to graduate.

Housing: 715 students can be accommodated in college housing, which includes single-sex dorms and married-student housing. On-campus housing is guaranteed for all 4 years. 64% of students live on campus; of those, 68% remain on campus on weekends. Alcohol is not permitted. All students may keep cars.

Activities: There are no fraternities or sororities. There are 54 groups on campus, including art, band, cheerleading, chess, choir, chorale, chorus, computers, dance, drama, drill team, entrepreneurial, environmental, ethnic, gay, honors, international, jazz band, musical theater, newspaper, orchestra, pep band, political, professional, radio and TV, religious, social, social service, student government, symphony, and yearbook. Popular campus events include Renaissance Week, Multi-Cultural Week, and New Year's in November.

Sports: There are 9 intercollegiate sports for men and 8 for women, and 17 intramural sports for men and 17 for women. Facilities include a sports complex with an all-weather track and lighted soccer and football fields; a phys ed center with an indoor junior Olympic-size pool, a 5-court gym, an indoor track, a weight room, and courts for racquetball, basketball, volleyball, and tennis; an intramural sports complex; 8 lighted tennis courts; an 18-hole disc golf course; and 2 small lakes.

Disabled Students: 86% of the campus is accessible. Wheelchair ramps, elevators, special parking, specially equipped rest rooms, special class scheduling, lowered drinking fountains, lowered telephones, and automatic doors are available.

Services: Counseling and information services are available, as is tutoring in most subjects. There is a reader service for the blind, and remedial math, reading, and writing.

Campus Safety and Security: Measures include 24-hour foot and vehicle patrol, security escort services, informal discussions, and pamphlets/posters/films. There are emergency telephones, lighted pathways/sidewalks, and night security personnel.

Programs of Study: Graceland confers B.A., B.S., and B.S.N. degrees. Master's degrees are also awarded. Bachelor's degrees are awarded in BIOLOGICAL SCIENCE (biology/biological science), BUSINESS (accounting, business administration and management, international business management, recreation and leisure services, and recreational facilities management), COMMUNICATIONS AND THE ARTS (communications, dramatic arts, English, German, graphic design, literature, modern language, music, Spanish, speech/debate/rhetoric, and studio art), COMPUTER AND PHYSICAL SCIENCE (chemistry, computer science, information sciences and systems, mathematics, and science), EDUCATION (athletic training, elementary, music, and physical), ENGINEERING AND ENVIRONMENTAL DESIGN (commercial art), HEALTH PROFESSIONS (health, medical laboratory technology, nursing, predentistry, premedicine, and preveterinary science), SOCIAL SCIENCE (addiction studies, criminal justice, economics, history, human services, international studies, liberal arts/general studies, philosophy, psychology, religion, social science, and sociology). Business administration, education, and nursing are the largest.

Required: To graduate, students must complete 128 credit hours, including 39 in upper-division courses and an average of 40 in the major, and maintain a minimum GPA of 2.0 overall and in the major. General education requirements include studies in humanities, social sciences, natural sciences, behavioral sciences, ethics, math, computer science, leadership, thinking skills, human diversity, and the arts.

Special: Internships are required in business, education, recreation, communications, and publication design. Graceland offers study abroad, cross-registration, B.A.-B.S. degrees, work-study, dual and student-designed majors, and a general studies degree. Credit for life, military, or work experience is possible. A pass/fail option is available for 2 courses each semester. The university also offers nondegree study, home study in addiction studies and nursing, a program for students with learning disabilities, an accelerated degree program in nursing, and a 3-2 engineering degree with the University of Iowa and the University of Missouri-Rolla. There are 3 national honor societies, a freshman honors program, and 6 departmental honors programs.

Faculty/Classroom: 47% of faculty are male; 53%, female. 93% teach undergraduates and 10% do research. The average class size in an introductory lecture is 24; in a laboratory, 24; and in a regular course, 11.

Admissions: 58% of the 2003-2004 applicants were accepted.

Requirements: The SAT I or ACT is required. In addition, Graceland requires applicants to meet 2 of these 3 criteria: rank in the upper 50% of their class, a GPA of 2.5, and a minimum composite score of 960 on the SAT I or 21 on the ACT. Applicants must be graduates of an accredited secondary school. The GED is accepted. An interview is recommended. AP and CLEP credits are accepted. Important factors in the admissions decision are advanced placement or honor courses, evidence of special talent, and leadership record.

Procedure: Freshmen are admitted to all sessions. Entrance exams should be taken in the junior or senior year. Applications should be filed by May 1 for fall entry and December 1 for spring entry, along with a $50 fee. Notification is sent on a rolling basis. Applications are accepted on computer disk and on-line through CollegeLink, Apply, College Profile, or the school's web site.

Transfer: 121 transfer students enrolled in 2002-2003. Applicants must submit official transcripts from all colleges attended and from high school. The required GPA varies by the number of hours of college study completed. Transfer students are admitted every term. 32 of 128 credits required for the bachelor's degree must be completed at Graceland.

Visiting: There are regularly scheduled orientations for prospective students, including a campus tour and opportunities to meet students, faculty, and campus personnel. There are guides for informal visits and visitors may sit in on classes and stay overnight. To schedule a visit, contact Helen Caples at (641) 784-5127 or caples@graceland.edu.

Financial Aid: In a recent year, 97% of all full-time freshmen and 88% of continuing full-time students received some form of financial aid. 65% of full-time freshmen and 62% of continuing full-time students received need-based aid. The average freshman award was $14,859. 40% of undergraduates work part time. Average annual earnings from campus work are $1104. The average financial indebtedness of a recent graduate was $8715. The FAFSA is required. The deadline for filing freshman financial aid applications for fall entry is March 1.

International Students: There are 147 international students enrolled. The school actively recruits these students. They must score 450 on the written TOEFL or 133 on the electronic version.

Computers: The mainframe is an HP 9000 Model D330. There are workstations in the computer engineering, computer science, chemistry, physics, and music labs, and in the computer center. There are also 3 PC labs and a Mac lab. All residence hall rooms are PC accessible. All students may access the system any time. There are no time limits and no fees. It is strongly recommended that all students have a personal computer.

Graduates: The most popular majors were elementary education (25%), nursing (24%), and business administration (21%).

Admissions Contact: James R. Simpson, Vice Provost for Enrollment. E-mail: admissions@graceland.edu Web: www.graceland.edu

---

GRAND VIEW COLLEGE
Des Moines, IA 50316-1599

C-3
(515) 263-2810
(800) 444-6083; Fax: (515) 263-2974

Full-time: 346 men, 836 women	**Faculty:** 78
Part-time: 144 men, 304 women	**Ph.D.s:** 37%
Graduate: none	**Student/Faculty:** 15 to 1
Year: semesters, summer session	**Tuition:** $14,740
Application Deadline: open	**Room & Board:** $5008
Freshman Class: 438 applied, 414 accepted, 160 enrolled	
ACT: 20	**LESS COMPETITIVE**

Grand View College, founded in 1896, is a private liberal arts college affiliated with the Evangelical Lutheran Church in America, that focuses on connecting liberal arts with career preparation. In addition to regional accreditation, Grand View has baccalaureate program accreditation with NLN. Computerized library services include interlibrary loans, database searching, and Internet access. Special learning facilities include a learning resource center, radio station, and TV station. The 25-acre campus is in an urban area in a residential area of Des Moines. Including any residence halls, there are 22 buildings.

Student Life: 92% of undergraduates are from Iowa. Students are from 26 states, 13 foreign countries, and Canada. 90% are white. 46% are Protestant; 24% Catholic. The average age of freshmen is 18; all undergraduates, 26. 26% do not continue beyond their first year.

Housing: 381 students can be accommodated in college housing, which includes coed dorms and on-campus apartments. In addition, there are special-interest houses. On-campus housing is guaranteed for the freshman year only and is available on a first-come, first-served basis. 70% of students commute. All students may keep cars.

Activities: There are no fraternities or sororities. There are 19 groups on campus, including art, band, cheerleading, choir, chorale, chorus, dance, departmental, drama, ethnic, honors, international, newspaper, professional, radio and TV, religious, social service, and student government. Popular campus events include Stundenterfest.

Sports: There are 4 intercollegiate sports for men and 6 for women, and 8 intramural sports for men and 8 for women. Facilities include a 1200-seat phys ed building with facilities for varsity athletics and recreation programs, tennis courts, and an athletic field.

Disabled Students: 90% of the campus is accessible. Wheelchair ramps, elevators, special parking, specially equipped rest rooms, special class scheduling, lowered drinking fountains, lowered telephones, and support services for the disabled are available.

Services: Counseling and information services are available, as is tutoring in every subject. Support services for the blind and hearing-impaired also are available.

Campus Safety and Security: Measures include 24-hour foot and vehicle patrol, security escort services, shuttle buses, and informal discussions. There are pamphlets/posters/films, emergency telephones, and lighted pathways/sidewalks.

Programs of Study: Grand View confers B.A. and B.S.N. degrees. Associate degrees are also awarded. Bachelor's degrees are awarded in BIOLOGICAL SCIENCE (biology/biological science), BUSINESS (accounting and business administration and management),

COMMUNICATIONS AND THE ARTS (broadcasting, communications, English, graphic design, journalism, and visual and performing arts), COMPUTER AND PHYSICAL SCIENCE (applied mathematics, computer science, and information sciences and systems), EDUCATION (elementary and secondary), HEALTH PROFESSIONS (nursing), SOCIAL SCIENCE (criminal justice, human services, political science/government, and psychology). Art, nursing, and education are the strongest academically. Business, nursing, and education are the largest.

Required: Students must complete core requirements, including courses in English, public speaking, liberal arts, integrating seminar, other culture encounter, religion or philosophy, history or other humanities, laboratory science, and social science. Students must complete at least 124 hours of work, including 60 hours in courses other than the major and 24 hours in the major. Students must maintain an overall GPA of 2.0 and a 2.2 GPA in the major. Students must also demonstrate computer proficiency.

Special: Co-op programs, cross-registration with Drake University and Des Moines Area Community College, student-designed majors, study abroad, and internships for most majors are available. Dual majors, a B.A.-B.S. degree, a Washington semester, work-study programs, and an accelerated degree program in business administration are offered. Non-degree study, a liberal arts degree, a certificate in art therapy, and pass/fail options are possible. There are 4 national honor societies and a freshman honors program.

Faculty/Classroom: 39% of faculty are male; 61%, female. All teach undergraduates and 40% both teach and do research. The average class size in an introductory lecture is 25; in a laboratory, 15; and in a regular course, 25.

Admissions: 95% of the 2003-2004 applicants were accepted. The ACT scores for the 2003-2004 freshman class were: 56% below 21, 19% between 21 and 23, 17% between 24 and 26, 7% between 27 and 28, and 1% above 28. 25% of the current freshmen were in the top fifth of their class; 50% were in the top two fifths. 9 freshmen graduated first in their class.

Requirements: The ACT is required and the SAT I is recommended, with a minimum recommended score of 18 on the ACT, or the equivalent on the SAT I. Students must be graduates of an accredited secondary school. The GED is also accepted. Grand View recommends that students should have completed 4 courses in English, 3 courses each in math, science, and social science, and 2 courses in a foreign language. A GPA of 2.0 is required. AP and CLEP credits are accepted.

Procedure: Freshmen are admitted fall, spring, and summer. Entrance exams should be taken during the second semester of the junior year. There are deferred and rolling admissions plans. Application deadlines are open. Applications are accepted on-line through the school's web site.

Transfer: 205 transfer students enrolled in 2002-2003. Applicants must submit transcripts from each college attended. 30 of 124 credits required for the bachelor's degree must be completed at Grand View.

Visiting: There are regularly scheduled orientations for prospective students, including placement tests, a financial aid session, lunch, adviser meetings, and a registration session. There are guides for informal visits and visitors may sit in on classes and stay overnight. To schedule a visit, contact the Admissions Office at admiss@gvc.edu.

Financial Aid: In 2003-2004, 99% of all full-time freshmen and 98% of continuing full-time students received some form of financial aid. 90% of full-time freshmen and 80% of continuing full-time students received need-based aid. The average freshman award was $17,330. 95% of undergraduates work part time. Average annual earnings from campus work are $1500. The average financial indebtedness of the 2003 graduate was $18,938. Grand View is a member of CSS. The FAFSA is required. The deadline for filing freshman financial aid applications for fall entry is April 15.

International Students: There were 18 international students enrolled in a recent year. They must score 550 on the written TOEFL or 210 on the electronic version. Or students may take the MELAB and also take the SAT I or the ACT, scoring 18.

Computers: The mainframes are a DEC VAX and a DEC Alpha. There are also more than 150 terminals and 60 PCs available for student use in classrooms, 3 computer labs, and faculty and administrative offices. All students may access the system. There are no time limits and no fees.

Graduates: From July 1, 2002 to June 30, 2003, 268 bachelor's degrees were awarded. The most popular majors were business administration (18%), education (18%), and nursing (16%). In an average class, 25% graduate in 4 years or less, 35% graduate in 5 years or less, and 37% graduate in 6 years or less. 66 companies recruited on campus in 2002-2003. Of the 2002 graduating class, 5% were enrolled in graduate school within 6 months of graduation and 95% were employed.

Admissions Contact: Diane Schafer Johnson, Director of Admissions. E-mail: djohnson@gvc.edu Web: gvc.edu

GRINNELL COLLEGE
Grinnell, IA 50112

D-3

(641) 269-3600
(800) 247-0113; Fax: (641) 269-4937

Full-time: 669 men, 816 women	**Faculty:** 139; IIB, ++$
Part-time: 17 men, 22 women	**Ph.D.s:** 96%
Graduate: none	**Student/Faculty:** 11 to 1
Year: semesters	**Tuition:** $24,490
Application Deadline: January 20	**Room & Board:** $6570
Freshman Class: 2284 applied, 1443 accepted, 405 enrolled	
SAT I Verbal/Math: 680/680	**ACT:** 30

HIGHLY COMPETITIVE+

Grinnell College, founded in 1846, is a private (not for profit) institution that offers undergraduate degree programs in the arts and sciences. The 3 libraries contain 503,356 volumes, 375,336 microform items, and 29,016 audio/video tapes/CDs, and subscribe to 3032 periodicals. Computerized library services include the card catalog, interlibrary loans, database searching, and Internet access. Special learning facilities include a learning resource center, art gallery, and an observatory, physics museum, and print and drawing gallery. The 127-acre campus is in a small town 55 miles east of Des Moines. Including any residence halls, there are 63 buildings.

Student Life: 87% of undergraduates are from out of state, mostly the Midwest. Others are from 50 states, 52 foreign countries, and Canada. 82% are from public schools. 69% are white; 10% foreign nationals. 40% are claim no religious affiliation; 30% Protestant; 10% Catholic; 8% Jewish. The average age of freshmen is 18; all undergraduates, 20. 8% do not continue beyond their first year; 85% remain to graduate.

Housing: 1265 students can be accommodated in college housing, which includes single-sex and coed dorms. In addition, there are language houses and special-interest houses. On-campus housing is guaranteed for all 4 years. 86% of students live on campus; of those, 96% remain on campus on weekends. All students may keep cars.

Activities: There are no fraternities or sororities. There are 168 groups on campus, including art, chess, choir, chorale, chorus, computers, dance, debate, drama, ethnic, film, forensics, gay, honors, international, jazz band, literary magazine, musical theater, newspaper, orchestra, photography, political, radio and TV, religious, social, social service, student government, and yearbook. Popular campus events include Winter Waltz, Spring Waltz, and Disco.

Sports: There are 10 intercollegiate sports for men and 10 for women, and 11 intramural sports for men and 11 for women. Facilities include a phys ed complex, a gym, 5 sports fields, a track, and 3 intramural fields.

Disabled Students: 80% of the campus is accessible. Wheelchair ramps, elevators, special parking, specially equipped rest rooms, special class scheduling, lowered drinking fountains, and lowered telephones are available.

Services: Counseling and information services are available, as is tutoring in every subject. There is a reader service for the blind. There are reading, writing, math, and science labs.

Campus Safety and Security: Measures include 24-hour foot and vehicle patrol, self-defense education, security escort services, and informal discussions. There are pamphlets/posters/films, emergency telephones, lighted pathways/sidewalks, fire drills, and a committee on personal safety education. Security information and reports are released to the entire campus when incidents occur.

Programs of Study: Grinnell confers the B.A. degree. Bachelor's degrees are awarded in BIOLOGICAL SCIENCE (biochemistry and biology/biological science), COMMUNICATIONS AND THE ARTS (art, Chinese, classics, dramatic arts, English, French, German, music, Russian, and Spanish), COMPUTER AND PHYSICAL SCIENCE (chemistry, computer science, mathematics, physics, and science), SOCIAL SCIENCE (anthropology, economics, history, philosophy, political science/government, psychology, religion, and sociology). Math, history, and biology are the largest.

Required: All students are required to take a tutorial in the first semester focusing on writing. All students must also complete a major field, which includes between 32 and 48 credits in most departments. Of the total 124 credits needed for the bachelor's degree, no more than 48 may be earned in any one department or 92 in any one division, and a minimum 2.0 GPA must be maintained.

Special: Students may participate in 63 study-abroad programs in 32 countries or in off-campus study at selected locations in the United States. Grinnell offers cooperative programs in architecture with Washington University in St. Louis and a 3-2 engineering program with California Institute of Technology, Columbia University, and Rensselaer Polytechnic Institute. There is also an extensive internship program, a Washington semester, a general studies degree in science, student-designed majors, and S/D/F grading options in selected courses. Grinnell's special "plus-2" option permits students to add 2 credits to a regular course through independent study. Students may pursue one of 10 interdisciplinary concentrations in addition to their major. Accelerated degree programs of 6 to 7 semesters may be approved on an individual

basis. There are 2 national honor societies, including Phi Beta Kappa, and honors programs in all departments.

Faculty/Classroom: 59% of faculty are male; 41%, female. All both teach and do research. The average class size in an introductory lecture is 19; in a laboratory, 13; and in a regular course, 16.

Admissions: 63% of the 2003-2004 applicants were accepted. The SAT I scores for the 2003-2004 freshman class were: Verbal--5% below 500, 13% between 500 and 599, 40% between 600 and 700, and 42% above 700; Math--3% below 500, 12% between 500 and 599, 42% between 600 and 700, and 43% above 700. The ACT scores were 1% below 21, 7% between 21 and 23, 8% between 24 and 26, 13% between 27 and 28, and 72% above 28. 81% of the current freshmen were in the top fifth of their class; 98% were in the top two fifths. 37 freshmen graduated first in their class.

Requirements: The SAT I or ACT is required. In addition, applicants must be graduates of accredited secondary schools. The college recommends 17 Carnegie units, 4 each in English and math, and 3-4 each in lab science, social studies, and a foreign language. An essay is required and an interview is recommended. AP credits are accepted. Important factors in the admissions decision are advanced placement or honor courses, evidence of special talent, and personality/intangible qualities.

Procedure: Freshmen are admitted in the fall. Entrance exams should be taken during the second semester of the junior year or early in the fall semester of the senior year. There are early decision and deferred admissions plans. Early decision applications should be filed by November 20; regular applications, by January 20 for fall entry. Notification of early decision is sent December 20; regular decision, April 1. 94 early decision candidates were accepted for the 2003-2004 class. 93 were on the 2003 waiting list; 1 was admitted. Applications are accepted on-line through CollegeNET or Common App.

Transfer: 13 transfer students enrolled in 2003-2004. Students must submit all college transcripts and have a 3.0 GPA. 62 of 124 credits required for the bachelor's degree must be completed at Grinnell.

Visiting: There are regularly scheduled orientations for prospective students, including a campus tour, an interview with a member of the admissions staff, an opportunity to attend classes, presentations/discussions with students and faculty from a number of academic departments, overnight accommodations, and complimentary meals. There are guides for informal visits and visitors may sit in on classes and stay overnight. To schedule a visit, contact the Admissions Office at *askgrin@grinnell.edu*.

Financial Aid: In 2003-2004, 88% of all full-time freshmen and 87% of continuing full-time students received some form of financial aid. 64% of full-time freshmen and 58% of continuing full-time students received need-based aid. The average freshman award was $18,450. Need-based scholarships or need-based grants averaged $15,876; need-based self-help aid (loans and jobs) averaged $5215; and other non-need-based awards and non-need-based scholarships averaged $10,370. 64% of undergraduates work part time. Average annual earnings from campus work are $1800. The average financial indebtedness of the 2003 graduate was $16,818. The FAFSA and the college's own financial statement are required. The deadline for filing freshman financial aid applications for fall entry is February 1.

International Students: There are 154 international students enrolled. The school actively recruits these students. They must score 550 on the written TOEFL or 220 on the electronic version and also take the SAT I or the ACT.

Computers: The mainframes are a Hewlett-Packard, DL380, DL580, and D545. There are more than 400 networked computers on campus for the exclusive use of students. All college residences have network connections. All students may access the system 24 hours a day. There are no time limits and no fees.

Graduates: From July 1, 2002 to June 30, 2003, 317 bachelor's degrees were awarded. The most popular majors were biology (11%), English (9%), and sociology (8%). In an average class, 83% graduate in 4 years or less, 84% graduate in 5 years or less, and 85% graduate in 6 years or less. 113 companies recruited on campus in 2002-2003. Of the 2002 graduating class, 30% were enrolled in graduate school within 6 months of graduation and 50% were employed.

Admissions Contact: James Sumner, Dean for Admission and Financial Aid. A video is available. E-mail: *askgrin@grinnell.edu* Web: *http://www.grinnell.edu*

IOWA BOARD OF REGENTS

The Iowa Board of Regents, established in 1905, is a public system in Iowa. It is governed by Iowa State Board of Regents, whose chief administrator is Executive Director. The primary goals of the system are teaching, research, and public service. The main priority is Teaching Research Service. The total enrollment of all 3 campuses is usually about 71,000; there were 6500 faculty members. Altogether there are some 336 baccalaureate, 311 master's, and 189 doctoral programs offered in Iowa Board of Regents. Profiles of the 4-year campuses are included in this section.

IOWA STATE UNIVERSITY
Ames, IA 50011-2011

C-3

(515) 294-5836
(800) 262-3810; Fax: (515) 294-2592

Full-time: 11,600 men, 9082 women	**Faculty:** 1232; I, -$
Part-time: 877 men, 671 women	**Ph.D.s:** 88%
Graduate: 2977 men, 2173 women	**Student/Faculty:** 17 to 1
Year: semesters, summer session	**Tuition:** $5028 ($14,370)
Application Deadline: August 1	**Room & Board:** $5740

Freshman Class: 9035 applied, 8116 accepted, 3847 enrolled
ACT: 24 — **VERY COMPETITIVE**

Iowa State University, established in 1858, is a public land-grant institution offering undergraduate and graduate programs in agriculture, business, design, education, engineering, family and consumer sciences, liberal arts and sciences, and veterinary medicine. There are 8 undergraduate schools and 1 graduate school. In addition to regional accreditation, Iowa State has baccalaureate program accreditation with AACSB, ABET, ACEJMC, ACS, ADA, AHEA, APA, ASLA, CSAB, FIDER, NAAB, NASM, and SAF. The library contains 2,386,906 volumes, 3,412,849 microform items, and 64,524 audio/video tapes/CDs, and subscribes to 28,425 periodicals. Computerized library services include the card catalog, interlibrary loans, and database searching. Special learning facilities include a learning resource center, art gallery, natural history museum, planetarium, radio station, and TV station. The 1788-acre campus is in an urban area 30 miles north of Des Moines. Including any residence halls, there are 284 buildings.

Student Life: 74% of undergraduates are from Iowa. Students are from 50 states, 116 foreign countries, and Canada. 94% are from public schools. 84% are white; 11% foreign nationals. The average age of freshmen is 18; all undergraduates, 21. 16% do not continue beyond their first year.

Housing: Up to 10,000 students can be accommodated in college housing, which includes single-sex and coed dorms, on-campus apartments, married-student housing, fraternity houses, and sorority houses. In addition, there are honors houses, special-interest houses, nonalcoholic houses, cross-cultural houses, no-smoking houses, quiet houses, academic learning communities, and adult undergraduate housing. On-campus housing is guaranteed for all 4 years. 51% of students commute. All students may keep cars.

Activities: 13% of men belong to 1 local and 30 national fraternities; 12% of women belong to 1 local and 17 national sororities. There are 515 groups on campus, including art, band, cheerleading, chess, choir, chorale, chorus, computers, dance, debate, drama, drum and bugle corps, ethnic, film, forensics, gay, honoraries, honors, international, jazz band, literary magazine, marching band, musical theater, newspaper, opera, orchestra, pep band, photography, political, professional, radio and TV, recreation/sports, religious, social, social service, special-interest, student government, and symphony. Popular campus events include VEISHEA, spring festival, and Honors Week.

Sports: There are 7 intercollegiate sports for men and 12 for women, and 43 intramural sports for men and 43 for women. Facilities include a coliseum, a stadium/field, a baseball and softball complex, track and tennis complexes, multipurpose gyms, swimming pools, an ice center, a phys ed building, recreation centers, multipurpose intramural-recreation fields, and a soccer competitive site.

Disabled Students: 95% of the campus is accessible. Wheelchair ramps, elevators, special parking, specially equipped rest rooms, special class scheduling, lowered drinking fountains, lowered telephones, voice-recognition and output computer systems, accessible public transportation, and adaptive recreational equipment are available.

Services: Counseling and information services are available, as is tutoring in most subjects. There is a reader service for the blind and remedial math and writing. A Kurzweil Reader, an Arkenstone Reader, enlargement services, talking and braille text from the Iowa Commission for the Blind, a braille printer, loaner computers, a steno-captioning service, a TTY telecommunications device, FM listeners, and sign interpreters are also available.

Campus Safety and Security: Measures include 24-hour foot and vehicle patrol, self-defense education, security escort services, and shuttle buses. There are informal discussions, pamphlets/posters/films, emergency telephones, lighted pathways/sidewalks, and a Help Van for motorists.

Programs of Study: Iowa State confers B.A., B.S., B.Arch., B.B.A., B.F.A., B.L.A., B.L.S., and B.Mus. degrees. Master's and doctoral degrees are also awarded. Bachelor's degrees are awarded in AGRICULTURE (agricultural business management, agriculture, agronomy, animal science, dairy science, forestry and related sciences, horticulture, international agriculture, plant protection (pest management), and plant science), BIOLOGICAL SCIENCE (biochemistry, biology/biological science, biophysics, botany, entomology, genetics, microbiology, nutrition, plant pathology, and zoology), BUSINESS (accounting, banking and finance, business administration and management, fashion merchandising, hotel/motel and restaurant management, international business management, management science, marketing/retailing/merchandising, and transportation management), COMMUNICATIONS AND THE

ARTS (advertising, communications, design, English, fine arts, French, German, graphic design, journalism, linguistics, music, Russian, Spanish, and speech/debate/rhetoric), COMPUTER AND PHYSICAL SCIENCE (atmospheric sciences and meteorology, chemistry, computer science, earth science, geology, mathematics, physics, and statistics), EDUCATION (agricultural, early childhood, elementary, health, industrial arts, music, physical, and secondary), ENGINEERING AND ENVIRONMENTAL DESIGN (aeronautical engineering, agricultural engineering, architecture, chemical engineering, city/community/regional planning, civil engineering, computer engineering, construction engineering, electrical/electronics engineering, engineering, engineering technology, environmental science, industrial engineering technology, interior design, landscape architecture/design, materials engineering, and mechanical engineering), SOCIAL SCIENCE (anthropology, child care/child and family studies, child psychology/development, dietetics, economics, family/consumer resource management, family/consumer studies, fashion design and technology, food science, history, international relations, liberal arts/general studies, philosophy, political science/government, psychology, religion, sociology, and textiles and clothing). Engineering, agriculture, and statistics are the strongest academically. Engineering, business, and agriculture are the largest.

Required: A minimum of 120 1/2 to 169 1/2 credit hours, depending on the major, and a GPA of 2.0 are required for graduation. The total number of credits required in the major varies. All students must take freshman English, library instruction, and 3 credits each in U.S. diversity and internationalization.

Special: Iowa State offers cooperative programs in engineering, forestry, agronomy, chemistry, computer science, economics, agricultural systems technology, business administration, industrial technology, and performing arts, and cross-registration with the Universities of Iowa and Northern Iowa. Internships, study abroad in more than 100 countries, dual majors, the B.A.-B.S. degree, student-designed majors, and accelerated degree programs are available. Interdisciplinary studies include agricultural biochemistry, agricultural systems technology, animal ecology, public service and administration in agriculture, and engineering operations. There are work-study programs, a Washington semester, nondegree study, and pass/no pass options. There are 15 national honor societies, including Phi Beta Kappa, a freshman honors program, and 7 departmental honors programs.

Faculty/Classroom: 69% of faculty are male; 31%, female. 87% teach undergraduates. Graduate students teach 16% of introductory courses. The average class size in a laboratory is 18 and in a regular course, 32.

Admissions: 90% of the 2003-2004 applicants were accepted. The SAT I scores for the 2003-2004 freshman class were: Verbal--19% below 500, 34% between 500 and 599, 34% between 600 and 700, and 13% above 700; Math--11% below 500, 29% between 500 and 599, 41% between 600 and 700, and 19% above 700. The ACT scores were 16% below 21, 25% between 21 and 23, 26% between 24 and 26, 16% between 27 and 28, and 17% above 28. 57% of the current freshmen were in the top fifth of their class; 91% were in the top two fifths. There were 69 National Merit finalists.

Requirements: The SAT I or ACT is required. In addition, applicants must graduate from an accredited secondary school. The GED is accepted. For admission to freshman standing, students must have completed 4 years of English, 3 each of math and science, and 2 to 3 of social studies. For the College of Liberal Arts and Sciences, 2 years of a single foreign language are also required. Iowa State requires applicants to be in the upper 50% of their class. AP and CLEP credits are accepted.

Procedure: Freshmen are admitted to all sessions. Entrance exams should be taken during the spring of the junior year or the fall of the senior year. There is a deferred admissions plan and a rolling admissions plan. Applications should be filed by August 1 for fall entry and December 1 for spring entry, along with a $30 fee ($50 for international students). Notification is sent on a rolling basis beginning November 1. Applications are accepted on-line through EXPAN, Apply, CollegeView, and the school's web site.

Transfer: 1537 transfer students enrolled in 2002-2003. Applicants must have a minimum GPA of 2.0 and at least 24 semester credits of acceptable transfer course work. They must also submit standardized test scores and provide a statement of good standing from prior institutions. 32 credits of 125 (on average) required for the bachelor's degree must be completed at Iowa State.

Visiting: There are regularly scheduled orientations for prospective students, including presentations on academics, admissions, residence hall living, fraternity and sorority life, and financial aid. There is also a group session with an adviser and a tour of the campus. There are guides for informal visits and visitors may sit in on classes and stay overnight. To schedule a visit, contact Phil Caffrey, Admissions Office at (515) 294-0821.

Financial Aid: In 2003-2004, 63% of all full-time freshmen and 85% of continuing full-time students received some form of financial aid. 27% of undergraduates work part time. Average annual earnings from campus work are $3490. The average financial indebtedness of the 2003 graduate was $26,398. Iowa State is a member of CSS. The FAFSA is required. The deadline for filing freshman financial aid applications for fall entry is March 1.

International Students: There are 871 international students enrolled. The school actively recruits these students. They must score 500 on the written TOEFL and also take the college's own test.

Computers: More than 150 instructional computing labs and classrooms are located in campus buildings and residence halls. These sites contain more than 2700 PCs, Macs, and workstations. Almost all machines are connected to the campus network and the Internet. All enrolled students qualify for a network account, which gives them access to e-mail and the Web. All students may access the system. Residence hall labs, Computation Center labs, and a few other sites are open 24 hours a day. Access to labs in academic buildings is restricted to building hours. There are no time limits and no fees.

Graduates: From July 1, 2002 to June 30, 2003, 4481 bachelor's degrees were awarded. The most popular majors were business (21%), engineering (19%), and agriculture (16%). In an average class, 1% graduate in 3 years or less, 29% graduate in 4 years or less, 60% graduate in 5 years or less, and 66% graduate in 6 years or less. 240 companies recruited on campus in 2002-2003. Of the 2002 graduating class, 19% were enrolled in graduate school within 6 months of graduation and 73% were employed.

Admissions Contact: Phil Caffrey, Associate Director, Admissions. E-mail: *admissions@iastate.edu* Web: *www.iastate.edu*

IOWA WESLEYAN COLLEGE
Mount Pleasant, IA 52641

E-4
(319) 385-6231
(800) 582-2383; Fax: (319) 385-6296

Full-time: 254 men, 277 women	**Faculty:** 43
Part-time: 49 men, 173 women	**Ph.Ds:** n/av
Graduate: none	**Student/Faculty:** 12 to 1
Year: 4-1-4, summer session	**Tuition:** $15,310
Application Deadline: open	**Room & Board:** $4680

Freshman Class: 664 applied, 427 accepted, 116 enrolled
ACT: 19

COMPETITIVE

Iowa Wesleyan College, founded in 1842, is a private institution affiliated with the United Methodist Church. The college offers undergraduate degree programs in business, education, fine arts, human studies, language and literature, nursing, and science. There are 7 undergraduate schools. In addition to regional accreditation, IWC has baccalaureate program accreditation with NLN. The library contains 110,000 volumes, 26,757 microform items, and 3492 audio/video tapes/CDs, and subscribes to 400 periodicals. Computerized library services include the card catalog, interlibrary loans, database searching, and Internet access. Special learning facilities include a learning resource center, art gallery, and radio station. The 60-acre campus is in a small town 45 miles south of Iowa City. Including any residence halls, there are 15 buildings.

Student Life: 55% of undergraduates are from Iowa. Students are from 22 states, 14 foreign countries, and Canada. 65% are white; 19% African American. 76% are claim no religious affiliation; 8% Protestant; 7% Catholic. The average age of freshmen is 19; all undergraduates, 28. 32% do not continue beyond their first year; 42% remain to graduate.

Housing: 455 students can be accommodated in college housing, which includes single-sex dorms. On-campus housing is guaranteed for all 4 years. 60% of students live on campus. All students may keep cars.

Activities: 8% of men belong to 1 national fraternity; 12% of women belong to 2 national sororities. There are 42 groups on campus, including art, band, cheerleading, choir, chorus, dance, drama, ethnic, film, honors, international, jazz band, literary magazine, newspaper, orchestra, pep band, photography, professional, radio and TV, religious, social, student government, symphony, and yearbook. Popular campus events include Forum, Winterfest, and Spring Thing.

Sports: There are 6 intercollegiate sports for men and 6 for women, and 11 intramural sports for men and 11 for women. Facilities include a 32-acre complex with baseball, softball, and football fields and an all-weather quarter-mile track. There is also a gym, a remodeled swimming pool, and a basketball court.

Disabled Students: 15% of the campus is accessible. Wheelchair ramps, elevators, special parking, and special class scheduling are available.

Services: Counseling and information services are available, as is tutoring in every subject. There is remedial math, reading, and writing.

Campus Safety and Security: Measures include 24-hour foot and vehicle patrol, self-defense education, security escort services, and informal discussions. There are pamphlets/posters/films, emergency telephones, and lighted pathways/sidewalks.

Programs of Study: IWC confers B.A., B.S., B.G.S., B.M.E., and B.S.N. degrees. Bachelor's degrees are awarded in BIOLOGICAL SCIENCE (biology/biological science and life science), BUSINESS (accounting, business administration and management, and sports management), COMMUNICATIONS AND THE ARTS (communications, English, fine arts, and music), COMPUTER AND PHYSICAL SCIENCE (chemistry, computer science, and mathematics), EDUCATION (art, early childhood, elementary, music, physical, science, and secondary), ENGINEERING AND ENVIRONMENTAL DESIGN (preengineering), HEALTH PROFESSIONS (environmental health science, nursing, predentistry, premedicine, preoptometry, and preveterinary science), SOCIAL SCIENCE (criminal justice, history, prelaw, psychology, and sociology). English, communications, and art are the strongest academically. Business, elementary education, and nursing are the largest.

Required: General education requirements include English (6 semester hours), computer science (3), math (3), communciation (3), civic issues (3), science (4), fine arts (3), religion (3), English literature (3), global issues (3). Students must complete English 102 with a minimum of C-, satisfy a safety and survival requirement, complete 6 semester hours of service learning, and 6 to 14 semester hours of a field experience in the major. A minimum of 124 semester hours is required for the bachelor's degree.

Special: The college maintains a cooperative program with Southeastern Community College. There are also internships in every major, a study-abroad program in Japan, China, and Mexico, a selective studies option, a general studies degree, credit in nursing through challenge examinations, and satisfactory/unsatisfactory grade options. Cross-registration is available with Southeastern, Muscatine, and Indian Hills Community colleges. There are 6 national honor societies.

Faculty/Classroom: 51% of faculty are male; 49%, female. All teach undergraduates. The average class size in an introductory lecture is 22; in a laboratory, 24; and in a regular course, 14.

Admissions: 64% of the 2003-2004 applicants were accepted. The ACT scores for the 2003-2004 freshman class were: 80% below 21, 11% between 21 and 23, and 9% between 24 and 26. 14% of the current freshmen were in the top fifth of their class; 35% were in the top two fifths.

Requirements: The ACT is required. In addition, applicants must be graduates of accredited secondary schools or have earned a GED. IWC requires applicants to be in the upper 50% of their class. A GPA of 2.0 is required. AP and CLEP credits are accepted. Important factors in the admissions decision are geographic diversity, evidence of special talent, and advanced placement or honor courses.

Procedure: Freshmen are admitted fall, winter, and spring. Entrance exams should be taken in April of the junior year or in June, October, or December of the senior year. There are early admissions and deferred admissions plans. There is a rolling admissions plan. Application deadlines are open. Applications are accepted on-line through at *www.iwc.edu*.

Transfer: 75 transfer students enrolled in 2002-2003. A minimum cumulative college GPA of 2.0 is required. 30 of 124 credits required for the bachelor's degree must be completed at IWC.

Visiting: There are regularly scheduled orientations for prospective students, including meetings with admissions, financial-aid, and academic staff, as well as social activities. There are guides for informal visits and visitors may sit in on classes and stay overnight. To schedule a visit, contact the Admissions Office.

Financial Aid: In 2003-2004, 98% of all full-time freshmen and 96% of continuing full-time students received some form of financial aid. 90% of all full-time students received need-based aid. The average freshman award was $13,218. Need-based scholarships or need-based grants averaged $6180 ($14,350 maximum); need-based self-help aid (loans and jobs) averaged $3583 ($7418 maximum); non-need-based athletic scholarships averaged $4435 ($9000 maximum); and other non-need-based awards and non-need-based scholarships averaged $4682 ($19,990 maximum). 56% of undergraduates work part time. Average annual earnings from campus work are $1000. The average financial indebtedness of the 2003 graduate was $21,766. IWC is a member of CSS. The FAFSA and the college's own financial statement are required. The priority date for freshman financial aid applications for fall entry is April 1. The deadline for filing freshman financial aid applications for fall entry is open.

International Students: The school actively recruits these students. They must score 500 on the written TOEFL or 173 on the electronic version.

Computers: The mainframe is an HP9000/Model E25. There are 48 PCs available in open computer labs for students to complete class assignments. Access to the Internet is available on 5 PCs. All students may access the system 8 A.M. to 10 P.M. There are no time limits and no fees.

Admissions Contact: Cary A. Owens, Associate VP and Dean of Enrollment Management. E-mail: *admit@iwc.edu* Web: *www.iwc.edu*

LORAS COLLEGE
Dubuque, IA 52004-0178

E-2

(563) 588-7236
(800) 245-6727; Fax: (563) 588-7119

Full-time: 752 men, 801 women	**Faculty:** 117; IIB, -$
Part-time: 34 men, 26 women	**Ph.D.s:** 96%
Graduate: 57 men, 94 women	**Student/Faculty:** 13 to 1
Year: semesters, summer session	**Tuition:** $18,338
Application Deadline: open	**Room & Board:** $5895

Freshman Class: 1531 applied, 1227 accepted, 412 enrolled

SAT I Verbal/Math: 510/540   **ACT:** 22   **COMPETITIVE**

Loras College, founded in 1839, is a private Roman Catholic liberal arts institution offering degree programs in humanities, social and behavioral studies, natural sciences, philosophy and religious studies, and professional studies. In addition to regional accreditation, Loras has baccalaureate program accreditation with ACS and NCATE. The library contains 440,000 volumes, 8822 microform items, and 2000 audio/video tapes/CDs, and subscribes to 8000 periodicals. Computerized library services include the card catalog, interlibrary loans, and database searching. Special learning facilities include a learning resource center, art gallery, planetarium, radio station, TV station, and a Center for Dubuque History. The 60-acre campus is in a small town 180 miles west of Chicago and 250 miles south of Minneapolis. Including any residence halls, there are 18 buildings.

Student Life: 55% of undergraduates are from Iowa. Students are from 26 states, 13 foreign countries, and Canada. 58% are from public schools. 90% are white. 62% are Catholic; 31% claim no religious affiliation; 8% Methodist and Lutheran. The average age of freshmen is 18; all undergraduates, 21. 23% do not continue beyond their first year; 65% remain to graduate.

Housing: 1098 students can be accommodated in college housing, which includes single-sex and coed dorms, on-campus apartments, and off-campus apartments. In addition, there are honors houses. On-campus housing is guaranteed for all 4 years. 63% of students live on campus; of those, 65% remain on campus on weekends. All students may keep cars.

Activities: 3% of women belong to sororities. There are no fraternities. There are 59 groups on campus, including band, choir, chorus, computers, dance, debate, drama, ethnic, forensics, gay, honors, international, jazz band, literary magazine, musical theater, newspaper, photography, political, professional, radio and TV, religious, social, social service, student government, and yearbook. Popular campus events include Family Weekend, Tri-College Free Day, and Awareness Week.

Sports: There are 11 intercollegiate sports for men and 10 for women, and 111 intramural sports for men and 111 for women. Facilities include a sports center with 3 gym floors, a swimming pool, 4 racquetball courts, and an 8-lane Olympic indoor/outdoor track. There are also 5 outdoor tennis courts, a field house for basketball games, and a soccer field. The campus stadium seats 3500.

Disabled Students: 40% of the campus is accessible. Wheelchair ramps, elevators, special parking, specially equipped rest rooms, special class scheduling, lowered drinking fountains, and lowered telephones are available.

Services: Counseling and information services are available, as is tutoring in every subject. There is a reader service for the blind and remedial math and writing.

Campus Safety and Security: Measures include 24-hour foot and vehicle patrol, security escort services, informal discussions, and pamphlets/posters/films. There are lighted pathways/sidewalks.

Programs of Study: Loras confers B.A., B.S., and B.M. degrees. Associate and master's degrees are also awarded. Bachelor's degrees are awarded in BIOLOGICAL SCIENCE (biochemistry and biology/biological science), BUSINESS (accounting, banking and finance, business administration and management, international business management, management information systems, marketing/retailing/merchandising, personnel management, and sports management), COMMUNICATIONS AND THE ARTS (broadcasting, creative writing, English literature, French, journalism, music, public relations, Spanish, speech/debate/rhetoric, and studio art), COMPUTER AND PHYSICAL SCIENCE (chemistry, computer science, mathematics, and science), EDUCATION (art, early childhood, elementary, foreign languages, music, physical, science, secondary, and special), ENGINEERING AND ENVIRONMENTAL DESIGN (electrical/electronics engineering), HEALTH PROFESSIONS (exercise science), SOCIAL SCIENCE (classical/ancient civilization, criminal justice, economics, history, international studies, philosophy, political science/government, psychology, religion, social work, and sociology). Accounting and business, communication arts, and education are the largest.

Required: To graduate, students must complete a total of 120 credits with a minimum GPA of 2.0. The required number of credits in the major varies. The required general education program totals 36 to 37 credit hours and includes courses in critical thinking, writing, oral communication, quantitative reasoning, the scientific method, cultural diversity and cultural traditions, religion and religious traditions, values, self and society, and aesthetics. All students must complete and present 2 1-credit student portfolios for review. A comprehensive exam and/or a thesis are required for some majors.

Special: The college offers cross-registration with Clarke College and the University of Dubuque, and study abroad in 9 countries. Also available are various internships, on-campus work-study programs, a 3-2 engineering degree, a Washington semester, pass/fail options, combined liberal arts-preprofessional programs, dual and student-designed majors, and adult degree programs offering a B.A.-B.S. degree. There are 7 national honor societies and a freshman honors program.

Faculty/Classroom: 70% of faculty are male; 30%, female. All teach undergraduates. No introductory courses are taught by graduate students. The average class size in an introductory lecture is 20; in a laboratory, 13; and in a regular course, 15.

Admissions: 80% of the 2003-2004 applicants were accepted. The SAT I scores for the 2003-2004 freshman class were: Verbal--27% below 500, 59% between 500 and 599, 5% between 600 and 700, and 9% above 700; Math--18% below 500, 64% between 500 and 599, 14% between 600 and 700, and 5% above 700. The ACT scores were 33% below 21, 29% between 21 and 23, 22% between 24 and 26, 9% between 27 and 28, and 6% above 28. 22% of the current freshmen were in the top fifth of their class; 51% were in the top two fifths. 4 freshmen graduated first in their class.

Requirements: The SAT I or ACT is required. In addition, applicants must be graduates of an accredited secondary school or have a GED certificate, and have completed 4 units of English and 3 each of math, science, social studies, and history. An essay and an interview are recommended. Loras requires applicants to be in the upper 50% of their class. A GPA of 2.5 is required. AP and CLEP credits are accepted. Important factors in the admissions decision are evidence of special talent, leadership record, and advanced placement or honor courses.

Procedure: Freshmen are admitted fall and spring. Entrance exams should be taken in April or June before the senior year or October of the senior year. Application deadlines are open. Application fee is $25. Notification is sent on a rolling basis. Applications are accepted on-line through the ApplyYourself Application Network and CollegeLink.

Transfer: 288 transfer students enrolled in 2002-2003. Transfer students must have a minimum 2.0 GPA and submit transcripts of previous college work. Other requirements apply. 30 of 120 credits required for the bachelor's degree must be completed at Loras.

Visiting: There are regularly scheduled orientations for prospective students, consisting of 5 fall visitation days for all students and 7 programs for specific geographic locations. There are guides for informal visits and visitors may sit in on classes and stay overnight. To schedule a visit, contact the Office of Admissions.

Financial Aid: In 2003-2004, 93% of all full-time freshmen and 85% of continuing full-time students received some form of financial aid. 58% of full-time freshmen and 47% of continuing full-time students received need-based aid. The average freshman award was $10,619. Need-based scholarships or need-based grants averaged $3072 ($9000 maximum); need-based self-help aid (loans and jobs) averaged $1500 ($4000 maximum); and other non-need-based awards and non-need-based scholarships averaged $6813 ($13,028 maximum). 35% of undergraduates work part time. Average annual earnings from campus work are $750. The average financial indebtedness of the 2003 graduate was $15,269. The FAFSA is required. The deadline for filing freshman financial aid applications for fall entry is April 15.

International Students: There are 19 international students enrolled. The school actively recruits these students. They must score 500 on the written TOEFL.

Computers: The mainframe is an IBM RISC 6000. PCs are available throughout the campus. All students may access the system. All computer equipment is available for student use on most days. There are no time limits and no fees. All students are required to have personal computers.

Graduates: From July 1, 2002 to June 30, 2003, 332 bachelor's degrees were awarded. The most popular majors were business (28%), education (20%), and social science and history (9%). In an average class, 49% graduate in 4 years or less, 62% graduate in 5 years or less, and 64% graduate in 6 years or less. 25 companies recruited on campus in 2002-2003. Of the 2002 graduating class, 16% were enrolled in graduate school within 1 year of graduation and 81% were employed.

Admissions Contact: Tim Hauber, Director of Admissions. A video is available. E-mail: *adms@loras.edu* Web: *www.loras.edu*

LUTHER COLLEGE
Decorah, IA 52101

E-1

(563) 387-1287
(800) 458-8437; Fax: (563) 387-2159

Full-time: 997 men, 1506 women	**Faculty:** 185; IIB, av$
Part-time: 27 men, 35 women	**Ph.D.s:** 80%
Graduate: none	**Student/Faculty:** 14 to 1
Year: 4-1-4, summer session	**Tuition:** $21,600
Application Deadline: March 1	**Room & Board:** $4100
Freshman Class: 1991 applied, 1530 accepted, 668 enrolled	
SAT I Verbal/Math: 580/620	**ACT:** 25 **VERY COMPETITIVE**

Luther College, affiliated with the Evangelical Lutheran Church in America, is a private liberal arts institution founded in 1861. In addition to regional accreditation, Luther has baccalaureate program accreditation with CSWE, NASM, NCATE, and NLN. The library contains 336,605 volumes, 25,000 microform items, and 24,000 audio/video tapes/CDs, and subscribes to 1612 periodicals. Computerized library services include the card catalog, interlibrary loans, and database searching. Special learning facilities include a learning resource center, art gallery, natural history museum, planetarium, and radio station. The 800-acre campus is in a small town 70 miles south of Rochester, Minnesota. Including any residence halls, there are 31 buildings.

Student Life: 64% of undergraduates are from out of state, mostly the Midwest. Students are from 35 states and 33 foreign countries. 90% are from public schools. 89% are white. 69% are Protestant; 15% Catholic; 15% claim no religious affiliation. The average age of freshmen is 18; all undergraduates, 20. 15% do not continue beyond their first year; 79% remain to graduate.

Housing: 2159 students can be accommodated in college housing, which includes coed dorms, on-campus apartments, off-campus apartments, and married-student housing. In addition, there are language houses, dialogue floors, and wellness floors. On-campus housing is guaranteed for all 4 years. 81% of students live on campus; of those, 85% remain on campus on weekends. All students may keep cars.

Activities: 7% of men belong to 4 local fraternities; 9% of women belong to 4 local sororities. There are 139 groups on campus, including art, band, cheerleading, choir, chorale, chorus, computers, dance, drama, ethnic, forensics, gay, honors, international, jazz band, literary magazine, musical theater, newspaper, opera, orchestra, pep band, photography, political, professional, radio and TV, religious, social, social service, student government, symphony, and yearbook. Popular campus events include the Ethnic Arts Fair, Parents Weekend, and Flamingo Bar.

Sports: There are 10 intercollegiate sports for men and 9 for women, and 45 intramural sports for men and 46 for women. Facilities include 5 hardwood basketball courts, an indoor swimming pool, 4 batting cages, a fitness center, a climbing wall, 3 soccer fields, a golf driving range, a dance studio, a 4000-seat stadium and 3500-seat gym, 6 indoor tennis courts, 3 racquetball courts, an indoor 6-lane 200-meter track, an outdoor 8-lane polyurethane 400-meter track, and 9 outdoor tennis courts.

Disabled Students: 95% of the campus is accessible. Wheelchair ramps, elevators, special parking, specially equipped rest rooms, lowered drinking fountains, and lowered telephones are available.

Services: Counseling and information services are available, as is tutoring in every subject. There is a reader service for the blind and remedial reading and writing. Reading machines, tape recorders, note taking, and a learning center are available.

Campus Safety and Security: Measures include 24-hour foot and vehicle patrol, self-defense education, security escort services, and informal discussions. There are pamphlets/posters/films, emergency telephones, and lighted pathways/sidewalks.

Programs of Study: Luther confers the B.A. degree. Bachelor's degrees are awarded in BIOLOGICAL SCIENCE (biology/biological science), BUSINESS (accounting, management information systems, and management science), COMMUNICATIONS AND THE ARTS (art, classical languages, communications, dance, English, French, German, Greek, Latin, music, Spanish, speech/debate/rhetoric, and theater management), COMPUTER AND PHYSICAL SCIENCE (chemistry, computer science, mathematics, physics, and statistics), EDUCATION (elementary and physical), HEALTH PROFESSIONS (health and nursing), SOCIAL SCIENCE (African American studies, anthropology, biblical languages, economics, history, philosophy, political science/government, psychobiology, psychology, religion, Scandinavian studies, social work, and sociology). Biology, music, and English are the strongest academically. Biology, management, and psychology are the largest.

Required: Students must complete 11 hours of interdisciplinary English and history, 9 of religion/philosophy, 6 to 9 of foreign language, 7 each of natural science and social science, 3 each of fine arts, global studies, and quantitative/symbolic reasoning, and 2 of phys ed. The B.A. requires 128 semester hours with a GPA of at least 2.0 in the major. A senior project and writing course are required. Foreign language proficiency must be demonstrated.

Special: Internships in all disciplines, work-study programs, a Washington semester, study-abroad plans in numerous countries, pass/fail op-

tions, student-designed and dual majors, and 3-2 engineering degrees with Washington University in St. Louis and the University of Minnesota are available. There are 10 national honor societies, including Phi Beta Kappa, a freshman honors program, and 2 departmental honors programs.

Faculty/Classroom: 56% of faculty are male; 44%, female. All teach undergraduates. The average class size in an introductory lecture is 30; in a laboratory, 13; and in a regular course, 22.

Admissions: 77% of the 2003-2004 applicants were accepted. The SAT I scores for the 2003-2004 freshman class were: Verbal--14% below 500, 42% between 500 and 599, 32% between 600 and 700, and 12% above 700; Math--12% below 500, 34% between 500 and 599, 44% between 600 and 700, and 10% above 700. The ACT scores were 12% below 21, 22% between 21 and 23, 29% between 24 and 26, 18% between 27 and 28, and 19% above 28. 57% of the current freshmen were in the top fifth of their class; 81% were in the top two fifths. There were 7 National Merit finalists and 7 semifinalists. 51 freshmen graduated first in their class.

Requirements: The SAT I or ACT is required, with a minimum composite SAT I score of 990. High school applicants should have 4 years of English, 3 each of math and social studies, and 2 of science. An essay is required, and an interview is recommended. The GED is accepted. Luther requires applicants to be in the upper 50% of their class. A GPA of 2.5 is required. AP and CLEP credits are accepted. Important factors in the admissions decision are advanced placement or honor courses, evidence of special talent, and extracurricular activities record.

Procedure: Freshmen are admitted to all sessions. Entrance exams should be taken by the fall of the senior year. There are early admissions and deferred admissions plans. Applications should be filed by March 1 for fall entry, December 1 for winter entry, and January 1 for spring entry, along with a $25 fee. Notification is sent November 1. Applications are accepted on computer disk and on-line at the school's web site.

Transfer: 82 transfer students enrolled in 2002-2003. Applicants must meet the same high school standards and SAT I or ACT requirements as entering freshmen, with a minimum GPA of 2.5 in parallel college course work. 32 of 128 credits required for the bachelor's degree must be completed at Luther.

Visiting: There are regularly scheduled orientations for prospective students. There are guides for informal visits and visitors may sit in on classes and stay overnight. To schedule a visit, contact the Admissions Office at visit@luther.edu.

Financial Aid: In 2003-2004, 98% of all full-time freshmen and 97% of continuing full-time students received some form of financial aid. 68% of full-time freshmen and 72% of continuing full-time students received need-based aid. The average freshman award was $16,824, with $5684 ($16,510 maximum) from need-based scholarships or need-based grants, $5010 ($8325 maximum) from need-based self-help aid (loans and jobs), and $6130 ($14,500 maximum) from other non-need-based awards and non-need-based scholarships. 72% of undergraduates work part time. Average annual earnings from campus work are $897. The average financial indebtedness of the 2003 graduate was $17,312. Luther is a member of CSS. The FAFSA, the college's own financial statement, and a family tax return are required. The priority date for freshman financial aid applications for fall entry is March 1.

International Students: There are 119 international students enrolled. The school actively recruits these students. They must score 550 on the written TOEFL or 213 on the electronic version and also take the SAT I or the ACT.

Computers: The mainframes are an HP 3000/957 and an HP 9000. Students have access to computers in several clusters around campus. About 300 computers and 16 terminals are connected to the campus network and to the Internet. All students may access the system 8 A.M. to midnight with provision for extending. There are no time limits and no fees.

Graduates: The most popular majors among 2003 graduates were management (14%), biology (12%), and elementary education (8%). 176 companies recruited on campus in 2002-2003. Of the 2002 graduating class, 22% were enrolled in graduate school within 6 months of graduation and 57% were employed.

Admissions Contact: Jon Lund, Vice President for Enrollment Management. A video is available. E-mail: admissions@luther.edu Web: www.luther.edu

MAHARISHI UNIVERSITY OF MANAGEMENT E-4
Fairfield, IA 52557

(641) 472-1110

(800) 369-6480; Fax: (641) 472-1179

Full-time: 123 men, 116 women	**Faculty:** 53
Part-time: 9 men, 3 women	**Ph.D.s:** 70%
Graduate: 383 men, 156 women	**Student/Faculty:** 5 to 1
Year: semesters	**Tuition:** $24,030
Application Deadline: open	**Room & Board:** $5200
Freshman Class: 132 applied, 98 accepted, 88 enrolled	
SAT I Verbal/Math: 575/577	**ACT:** 24 **VERY COMPETITIVE**

Maharishi University of Management, established in 1971, is a private institution offering undergraduate and graduate programs in a broad range of disciplines. The University provides consciousness-based education and incorporates the group practice of the Maharishi Transcendental Meditation technique into a traditional academic program. There are 5 undergraduate and 5 graduate schools. The 2 libraries contain 148,000 volumes, 59,900 microform items, and 24,114 audio/video tapes/CDs, and subscribe to 14,000 periodicals. Computerized library services include the card catalog, interlibrary loans, database searching, and Internet access. Special learning facilities include a learning resource center, art gallery, radio station, psychophysiology, electronic engineering, visual technology, and physics labs, and a scanning electron microscope. The 272-acre campus is in a small town 114 miles southeast of Des Moines. Including any residence halls, there are 50 buildings.

Student Life: 60% of undergraduates are from out of state, mostly the Middle Atlantic. Students are from 21 states, 29 foreign countries, and Canada. 61% are white; 30% foreign nationals. The average age of freshmen is 20; all undergraduates, 23. 29% do not continue beyond their first year; 37% remain to graduate.

Housing: Housing includes single-sex dorms, on-campus apartments, and married-student housing. In addition, there are special-interest houses, and privately owned on-campus family housing for students with families. On-campus housing is guaranteed for all 4 years. 73% of students live on campus; of those, 93% remain on campus on weekends. Alcohol is not permitted. All students may keep cars.

Activities: There are no fraternities or sororities. There are 15 groups on campus, including art, chess, chorale, dance, drama, ecology, entrepreneurial, ethnic, international, musical theater, newspaper, permaculture, photography, political, professional, radio and TV, religious, social, social service, student government, and yearbook. Popular campus events include sports festivals, seasonal celebrations, and International Cultural Exchange Festival.

Sports: There are 2 intercollegiate sports for men and 1 for women, and 5 intramural sports for men and 5 for women. Facilities include outdoor and indoor tennis, basketball, and volleyball courts, a gym, a weight-training room, a field house, a swimming pool, a table tennis room, baseball batting and golf driving cages, a golf putting range, an indoor 4-lane jogging track, a dance studio, and a rock-climbing wall.

Disabled Students: All of the campus is accessible. Wheelchair ramps, special parking, specially equipped rest rooms, and lowered telephones are available.

Services: Counseling and information services are available, as is tutoring in every subject. There is remedial math, reading, and writing.

Campus Safety and Security: Measures include 24-hour foot and vehicle patrol, security escort services, informal discussions, and emergency telephones. There are lighted pathways/sidewalks.

Programs of Study: Maharishi University of Management confers B.A., B.S., and B.F.A. degrees. Master's and doctoral degrees are also awarded. Bachelor's degrees are awarded in AGRICULTURE (environmental studies), BUSINESS (management science), COMMUNICATIONS AND THE ARTS (dramatic arts, fine arts, and literature), COMPUTER AND PHYSICAL SCIENCE (computer science, mathematics, and web services), EDUCATION (education). Math, computer science, and management science are the strongest academically. Fine arts and management are the largest.

Required: Students must complete 166 credit units with a minimum of 60 credits in the major and must also complete the core curriculum of 18 units as well as 20 units in a distribution of academic fields. All students must maintain a minimum GPA of 2.0. Additional requirements include health and fitness courses, the Science of Creative Intelligence course with its applied aspect, the Transcendental Meditation program, and courses in math and writing. The 42-week school year and block scheduling system allow students to take 1 course at a time.

Special: Opportunities are provided for internships, B.A.-B.S. degrees in environmental sciences and computer science, study abroad, and nondegree study. Systematic programs are offered in the Science of Creative Intelligence, by which students apply knowledge to practical professional values. There are several 1-month blocks a year during which students may study, for example, art in Italy, literature in Switzerland, or business in Japan. There is a freshman honors program.

Faculty/Classroom: 67% of faculty are male; 33%, female. All teach undergraduates, 20% do research, and 20% do both. No introductory courses are taught by graduate students. The average class size in an introductory lecture is 35 and in a regular course, 10.

Admissions: 74% of the 2003-2004 applicants were accepted. The SAT I scores for the 2003-2004 freshman class were: Verbal--12% below 500, 41% between 500 and 599, 35% between 600 and 700, and 12% above 700; Math--15% below 500, 44% between 500 and 599, 38% between 600 and 700, and 3% above 700. The ACT scores were 3% below 18, 39% between 18 and 23, 45% between 24 and 29, and 13% above 29. There was 1 National Merit finalist and 2 semifinalists.

Requirements: The SAT I or ACT is required. In addition, applicants must graduate from an accredited secondary school or have a GED. An essay and 2 personal recommendations are required. An interview is recommended. A GPA of 2.5 is required. AP and CLEP credits are accepted. Important factors in the admissions decision are personality/intangible qualities, recommendations by school officials, and leadership record.

Procedure: Freshmen are admitted fall and spring. Entrance exams should be taken in the fall of the senior year or spring of the junior year. There is a rolling admissions plan. Application deadlines are open. Application fee is $25. Applications are accepted on-line.

Transfer: 24 transfer students enrolled in 2002-2003. Students must have a 2.5 GPA, acceptable recommendations, and meet all standards set by the university. 66 of 166 credits required for the bachelor's degree must be completed at Maharishi University of Management.

Visiting: There are regularly scheduled orientations for prospective students, including campus tours, visits to classes, interviews, student panels, and informal dinners. There are guides for informal visits and visitors may sit in on classes and stay overnight. To schedule a visit, contact Julie Beaufort, Director of Guest Services at jbeaufort@mum.edu.

Financial Aid: In 2003-2004, 95% of all full-time freshmen and 98% of continuing full-time students received some form of financial aid. 87% of full-time freshmen and 90% of continuing full-time students received need-based aid. The average freshman award was $26,577, with $18,657 ($21,000 maximum) from need-based scholarships or grants, $6297 ($20,000 maximum) from need-based self-help aid (loans and jobs), and $1623 ($5000 maximum) from non-need-based awards and non-need-based scholarships. 75% of undergraduates work part time. Average annual earnings from campus work are $1600. The average financial indebtedness of the 2003 graduate was $18,996. The FAFSA is required. The priority date for freshman financial aid applications for fall entry is April 15.

International Students: There are 75 international students enrolled. The school actively recruits these students. They must score 550 on the written TOEFL or 213 on the electronic version and also take the college's own test.

Computers: About 300 PCs are available throughout the campus. All students may access the system daytime and evenings. There are no time limits and no fees. All students are required to have personal computers.

Graduates: From July 1, 2002 to June 30, 2003, 48 bachelor's degrees were awarded. The most popular majors were management (31%), fine arts (25%), and computer science (8%). In an average class, 28% graduate in 4 years or less, and 47% graduate in 6 years or less. Of the 2002 graduating class, 22% were enrolled in graduate school within 6 months of graduation and 75% were employed.

Admissions Contact: Richard Neate, Director of Admissions. A video is available. E-mail: admissions@mum.edu Web: www.mum.edu

MERCY COLLEGE OF HEALTH SCIENCES C-8
Des Moines, IA 50309-1239

(515) 643-6715

(800) 637-2994; Fax: (515) 643-6698

Full-time: 39 men, 326 women	**Faculty:** n/av
Part-time: 21 men, 230 women	**Ph.D.s:** n/av
Graduate: none	**Student/Faculty:** n/av
Year: semesters, summer session	**Tuition:** $10,500
Application Deadline: see profile	**Room & Board:** n/app
Freshman Class: 582 applied, 430 accepted, 315 enrolled	
SAT I: n/av	**ACT:** required **SPECIAL**

Mercy College of Health Sciences was founded in 1995 and is a private school affiliated with the Religious Sisters of Mercy (RSM), a religious order of Roman Catholic women. There are 4 undergraduate schools. The 2 libraries contain 8917 volumes and 1070 audio/video tapes/CDs, and subscribe to 96 periodicals. Computerized library services include the card catalog, interlibrary loans, and database searching. Special learning facilities include clinical labs. The 4-acre campus is in an urban area in Des Moines. There are 3 buildings.

Student Life: 95% of undergraduates are from Iowa. Students are from 3 states. 87% are white. The average age of freshmen is 28; all undergraduates, 28.

Housing: There are no residence halls. All students commute. Alcohol is not permitted. All students may keep cars.

Activities: There are no fraternities or sororities. There are 2 groups on campus, including professional and student government. Popular campus events include Mercy Day and Student Appreciation Day.

Sports: There is no sports program at Mercy College of Health Sciences.

Disabled Students: All of the campus is accessible. Wheelchair ramps, elevators, special parking, specially equipped rest rooms, and lowered drinking fountains are available.

Services: Counseling and information services are available, as is tutoring in most subjects.

Campus Safety and Security: Measures include 24-hour foot and vehicle patrol, security escort services, shuttle buses, and informal discussions. There are pamphlets/posters/films and lighted pathways/sidewalks.

Programs of Study: Mercy College of Health Sciences confers B.S.H.C.M., and B.S.N. degrees. Associate degrees are also awarded. Bachelor's degrees are awarded in HEALTH PROFESSIONS (health care administration and nursing). Radiologic technology and diagnostic sonography are the strongest academically. Nursing is the largest.

Required: There is a community service requirement, and a caring course is also required. Students must complete a communication portfolio, and credit hours must be completed to graduate.

Special: Internships offering clinical experience are available. There are 2 national honor societies.

Admissions: 74% of the 2003-2004 applicants were accepted.

Requirements: The ACT is required. A GPA of 2.5 is required.

Procedure: Freshmen are admitted fall, spring, and summer. Check with the school for current application deadlines. The application fee is $25. 30 were on the 2003 waiting list; 14 were admitted.

Transfer: 200 transfer students enrolled in 2002-2003. Requirements vary by program.

Visiting: There are guides for informal visits. To schedule a visit, contact Sandi Nagel or Sara Pratt at (515) 643-3180 or www.mchs.edu.

Financial Aid: The FAFSA is required. Check with the school for current application deadlines.

Computers: There are no time limits and no fees.

Graduates: From July 1, 2002 to June 30, 2003, 27 bachelor's degrees were awarded. The most popular majors were nursing (49%), surgical technology (15%), and radiologic technology (11%).

Admissions Contact: Admissions Officer.
E-mail: admissions@mchs.edu Web: www.mchs.edu

MORNINGSIDE COLLEGE
Sioux City, IA 51106

B-2

(712) 274-5111
(800) 831-0806; Fax: (712) 274-5101

Full-time: 381 men, 490 women	Faculty: 63; IIB, --$
Part-time: 21 men, 50 women	Ph.D.s: 84%
Graduate: 45 men, 189 women	Student/Faculty: 14 to 1
Year: semesters, summer session	Tuition: $16,350
Application Deadline: open	Room & Board: $5260
Freshman Class: 1119 applied, 841 accepted, 272 enrolled	
ACT: 22	COMPETITIVE

Morningside College, founded in 1894, is a private college affiliated with the United Methodist Church. Its curriculum includes liberal arts and pre-professional and professional programs of study. In addition to regional accreditation, Morningside has baccalaureate program accreditation with NASM, NCATE, and NLN. The library contains 114,861 volumes, 287,113 microform items, and 5513 audio/video tapes/CDs, and subscribes to 543 periodicals. Computerized library services include the card catalog, interlibrary loans, database searching, and Internet access. Special learning facilities include a learning resource center, art gallery, radio station, TV station, an observatory, and a theater. The 41-acre campus is in a suburban area 100 miles north of Omaha on Interstate 29, at the convergence of the states of South Dakota, Iowa, and Nebraska. Including any residence halls, there are 19 buildings.

Student Life: 70% of undergraduates are from Iowa. Students are from 23 states and 8 foreign countries. 92% are from public schools. 90% are white. 49% are Protestant; 30% claim no religious affiliation; 21% Catholic. The average age of freshmen is 18; all undergraduates, 21. 36% do not continue beyond their first year; 59% remain to graduate.

Housing: 720 students can be accommodated in college housing, which includes coed dorms and on-campus apartments. In addition, there are freshman halls. On-campus housing is guaranteed for all 4 years. 70% of students live on campus; of those, 60% remain on campus on weekends. All students may keep cars.

Activities: 12% of men belong to 2 national fraternities; 3% of women belong to 1 national sorority. There are 36 groups on campus, including art, band, cheerleading, choir, chorale, chorus, computers, dance, drama, ethnic, honors, international, jazz band, literary magazine, newspaper, orchestra, pep band, photography, political, professional, radio and TV, religious, social, student government, and yearbook. Popular campus events include Friday is Writing Day, Academic and Cultural Arts Series, and Christmas at Morningside.

Sports: There are 8 intercollegiate sports for men and 9 for women, and 12 intramural sports for men and 12 for women. Facilities include an 8000-seat stadium, a football field, a campus recreation center with

basketball, volleyball, badminton, tennis, and racquetball/handball courts, an elevated track, a weight room, and a 6-lane, 25-meter swimming pool.

Disabled Students: 80% of the campus is accessible. Wheelchair ramps, elevators, special parking, specially equipped rest rooms, special class scheduling, and lowered telephones are available.

Services: Counseling and information services are available, as is tutoring in most subjects. There is a reader service for the blind, and remedial math, reading, and writing.

Campus Safety and Security: Measures include self-defense education, security escort services, informal discussions, and pamphlets/posters/films. There are emergency telephones and lighted pathways/sidewalks. The college is in compliance with the Crime Awareness and Campus Security Act of 1990.

Programs of Study: Morningside confers B.A., B.S., B.Mus., B.Mus.Ed., and B.S.N. degrees. Master's degrees are also awarded. Bachelor's degrees are awarded in BIOLOGICAL SCIENCE (biology/biological science), BUSINESS (accounting and business administration and management), COMMUNICATIONS AND THE ARTS (art, communications, dramatic arts, English, graphic design, music, photography, and Spanish), COMPUTER AND PHYSICAL SCIENCE (chemistry, computer science, mathematics, and physics), EDUCATION (art, business, elementary, English, mathematics, music, science, social studies, and special), HEALTH PROFESSIONS (nursing), SOCIAL SCIENCE (history, philosophy, political science/government, psychology, and religion). Business administration, education, and biology are the largest.

Required: The total number of credit hours required for graduation is 124, with 44 hours of core curriculum in liberal arts and 30 hours minimum in the major. Students must have a minimum GPA of 2.0 to graduate.

Special: There is a co-op program in medical technology. Internships are available in all departments. Study abroad in 3 countries, a Washington semester, work-study programs, both on campus and with 20 non-profit agencies, a dual major in philosophy/religious studies, and student-designed majors are available. There are 15 national honor societies and a freshman honors program.

Faculty/Classroom: 59% of faculty are male; 41%, female. All teach undergraduates and 20% do research. No introductory courses are taught by graduate students. The average class size in an introductory lecture is 24; in a laboratory, 10; and in a regular course, 12.

Admissions: 75% of the 2003-2004 applicants were accepted. The ACT scores for the 2003-2004 freshman class were: 40% below 21, 25% between 21 and 23, 25% between 24 and 26, 7% between 27 and 28, and 4% above 28. 30% of the current freshmen were in the top fifth of their class; 63% were in the top two fifths. 11 freshmen graduated first in their class.

Requirements: The ACT is required. In addition, applicants must also be graduates of an accredited secondary school. The GED is accepted. A portfolio is required for all studio art majors and an audition for performing music majors. Applicants graduating from high school 5 years or more prior to entering college are exempted from submitting ACT scores. Those entering from a homeschooled environment must submit a completed Home School Credit Evaluation form, which may be obtained in the Office of Admissions. Morningside requires applicants to be in the upper 50% of their class. A GPA of 2.5 is required. AP and CLEP credits are accepted. Important factors in the admissions decision are recommendations by school officials, evidence of special talent, and advanced placement or honor courses.

Procedure: Freshmen are admitted to all sessions. Entrance exams should be taken in the junior year. Application deadlines are open. Application fee is $25. Notification is sent on a rolling basis. Applications are accepted on-line.

Transfer: 64 transfer students enrolled in 2002-2003. Transfer applicants must take the ACT and have an interview. They must have 24 semester hours with a 2.0 or above cumulative average. They must present official transcripts of previous collegiate records. 30 of 124 credits required for the bachelor's degree must be completed at Morningside.

Visiting: There are regularly scheduled orientations for prospective students, consisting of a campus tour, appointments with faculty and financial aid, and an interview with an admissions counselor. There are guides for informal visits and visitors may sit in on classes and stay overnight. To schedule a visit, contact the Office of Admissions at (800) 831-0806, ext. 5111.

Financial Aid: In 2003-2004, all full-time freshmen and nearly all continuing full-time students received some form of financial aid. 79% of all full-time students received need-based aid. The average freshman award was $18,916. Need-based scholarships or need-based grants averaged $6305 ($14,050 maximum); need-based self-help aid (loans and jobs) averaged $5515 ($8343 maximum); non-need-based athletic scholarships averaged $2702 ($6700 maximum); and other non-need-based awards and non-need-based scholarships averaged $9428 ($23,735 maximum). Average annual earnings from campus work are $1501. The average financial indebtedness of the 2003 graduate was $18,648. The FAFSA is required. The priority date for freshman financial aid applications for fall entry is March 1.

International Students: There are 22 international students enrolled. They must score 425 on the written TOEFL or 113 on the electronic version.

Computers: All new full-time students are issued Gateway Solo notebook computers. A campuswide network connects residence halls, classrooms, and labs. Students have continuous access to the World Wide Web as well as e-mail and campus library resources. All students may access the system. There are no time limits and no fees. It is strongly recommended that all students have a personal computer.

Graduates: From July 1, 2002 to June 30, 2003, 164 bachelor's degrees were awarded. The most popular majors were education (27%), business (18%), and nursing (6%). In an average class, 1% graduate in 3 years or less, 38% graduate in 4 years or less, 49% graduate in 5 years or less, and 52% graduate in 6 years or less. 19 companies recruited on campus in 2002-2003. Of the 2002 graduating class, 12% were enrolled in graduate school within 6 months of graduation and 81% were employed.

Admissions Contact: Joel Weyand, Director of Admissions.
E-mail: *mscadm@morningside.edu* Web: *www.morningside.edu*

MOUNT MERCY COLLEGE
Cedar Rapids, IA 52402

E-3

(319) 368-6460
(800) 248-4504; Fax: (319) 363-5270

Full-time: 274 men, 701 women	**Faculty:** 72; IIB, --$
Part-time: 168 men, 330 women	**Ph.D.s:** 63%
Graduate: none	**Student/Faculty:** 14 to 1
Year: 4-1-4, summer session	**Tuition:** $16,070
Application Deadline: see profile	**Room & Board:** $5330
Freshman Class: 488 applied, 408 accepted, 196 enrolled	
ACT: 22	**COMPETITIVE**

Mount Mercy College, founded in 1928, is a private liberal arts institution affiliated with the Roman Catholic Church. In addition to regional accreditation, Mount Mercy has baccalaureate program accreditation with CSWE and NLN. The library contains 125,400 volumes, 2249 microform items, and 4073 audio/video tapes/CDs, and subscribes to 715 periodicals. Computerized library services include the card catalog, interlibrary loans, and database searching. Special learning facilities include a learning resource center, art gallery, and a video media room. The 40-acre campus is in an urban area in Cedar Rapids, 230 miles west of Chicago. Including any residence halls, there are 14 buildings.

Student Life: 93% of undergraduates are from Iowa. Students are from 17 states, 8 foreign countries, and Canada. 86% are from public schools. 94% are white. 45% are Catholic; 38% Protestant. The average age of freshmen is 18; all undergraduates, 24. 22% do not continue beyond their first year; 62% remain to graduate.

Housing: 510 students can be accommodated in college housing, which includes coed dorms and on-campus apartments. On-campus housing is guaranteed for all 4 years, is available on a first-come, first-served basis, and is available on a lottery system for upperclassmen. 65% of students commute. All students may keep cars.

Activities: There are no fraternities or sororities. There are 34 groups on campus, including academic, art, cheerleading, choir, chorale, chorus, computers, drama, drill team, film, honors, international, literary magazine, musical theater, newspaper, political, professional, religious, social, social service, and student government. Popular campus events include Hillfest, Spring Fling, and family weekend.

Sports: There are 6 intercollegiate sports for men and 7 for women, and 10 intramural sports for men and 10 for women. Facilities include a recreation center, a 2000-seat stadium, an auditorium-gym, an indoor hitting facility, a weight room, an aerobics area, karate facilities, 2 racquetball courts, and a fitness center.

Disabled Students: 95% of the campus is accessible. Wheelchair ramps, elevators, special parking, specially equipped rest rooms, and lowered drinking fountains are available.

Services: Counseling and information services are available, as is tutoring in most subjects, including all communication skills. There is a reader service for the blind, and remedial math, reading, and writing.

Campus Safety and Security: Measures include 24-hour foot and vehicle patrol, self-defense education, security escort services, and informal discussions. There are pamphlets/posters/films, emergency telephones, lighted pathways/sidewalks, and evening and weekend foot patrol, cameras at residence hall entrances, and a patrolled parking area.

Programs of Study: Mount Mercy confers B.A., B.S., B.A.A., B.A.S., and B.B.A. degrees. Bachelor's degrees are awarded in BIOLOGICAL SCIENCE (biology/biological science), BUSINESS (accounting, business administration and management, and marketing/retailing/merchandising), COMMUNICATIONS AND THE ARTS (art, communications, dramatic arts, English, music, speech/debate/rhetoric, and visual and performing arts), COMPUTER AND PHYSICAL SCIENCE (computer science, information sciences and systems, and mathematics), EDUCATION (elementary and music), HEALTH PROFESSIONS (health care administration, medical laboratory technology, and nursing), SOCIAL SCIENCE (criminal justice, history, international studies, political science/government, psychology, religion, social work, sociology, and urban studies). Nursing, social work, and accounting are the strongest academically. Administrative management, nursing, and education are the largest.

Required: To graduate, students must complete 123 semester hours, with at least 30 hours in the major, and maintain at least a 2.0 GPA. General education requirements include a total of 12 courses in philosophy, religious studies, English, speech, arts, social and natural sciences, history, and multicultural studies.

Special: Mount Mercy offers internships in many majors, study abroad in the Czech Republic, work-study programs on campus, cross-registration with Coe College, a general studies degree, accelerated program in business, accounting, and marketing, and student-designed, interdisciplinary majors. Credit for prior experiential learning may be granted, and pass/fail options are possible. There are 2 national honor societies and a freshman honors program.

Faculty/Classroom: 45% of faculty are male; 55%, female. All teach undergraduates. The average class size in an introductory lecture is 25; in a laboratory, 14; and in a regular course, 25.

Admissions: 84% of the 2003-2004 applicants were accepted. The ACT scores for the 2003-2004 freshman class were: 34% below 21, 33% between 21 and 23, 19% between 24 and 26, 8% between 27 and 28, and 5% above 28. 32% of the current freshmen were in the top fifth of their class; 67% were in the top two fifths. 3 freshmen graduated first in their class.

Requirements: The SAT I or ACT is required, with a minimum score of 840 required on the SAT I or a composite score of 19 on the ACT. Other admissions requirements include graduation from an accredited secondary school, with 16 Carnegie units, including 4 of English, 3 of social studies, and 2 each of math, history, and foreign language. A recommendation from a high school teacher or counselor and an essay or personal statement are also required. Mount Mercy requires applicants to be in the upper 50% of their class. A GPA of 2.5 is required. AP and CLEP credits are accepted. Important factors in the admissions decision are recommendations by school officials, extracurricular activities record, and advanced placement or honor courses.

Procedure: Freshmen are admitted to all sessions. Entrance exams should be taken in the junior year or the fall of the senior year. There is a rolling admissions plan and a deferred admissions plan. Applications should be filed by December 30 for winter entry. Notification is sent on a rolling basis. The fall 2003 application fee was $20. Applications are accepted on-line through *www2.mtmercy.edu/admission/applynow.html*.

Transfer: Applicants must have at least a 2.0 GPA. Associate degree holders must submit transcripts from all previous colleges attended; students with fewer credits earned must also submit a high school transcript. An interview is recommended. 30 of 123 credits required for the bachelor's degree must be completed at Mount Mercy.

Visiting: There are regularly scheduled orientations for prospective students, consisting of a presidential welcome, campus tour, student panel, faculty academic fair, presentations on college selection and admission requirements, and student evaluation. There are guides for informal visits and visitors may sit in on classes and stay overnight. To schedule a visit, contact the Admissions Office at (319) 363-8213, ext. 6460 or *admission@mtmercy.edu*.

Financial Aid: In 2003-2004, all full-time freshmen and 94% of continuing full-time students received some form of financial aid. 87% of full-time freshmen and 78% of continuing full-time students received need-based aid. The average freshman award was $14,631. Need-based scholarships or need-based grants averaged $10,589 ($19,650 maximum); need-based self-help aid (loans and jobs) averaged $4534 ($5125 maximum); and other non-need-based awards and non-need-based scholarships averaged $11,496 ($16,070 maximum). 29% of undergraduates work part time. Average annual earnings from campus work are $1500. The average financial indebtedness of the 2003 graduate was $15,726. The FAFSA is required. The deadline for filing freshman financial aid applications for fall entry is March 1.

International Students: There are 10 international students enrolled. They must score 550 on the written TOEFL or 213 on the electronic version.

Computers: 140 PCs are available. All students may access the system 24 hours a day. There are no time limits and no fees.

Graduates: From July 1, 2002 to June 30, 2003, 333 bachelor's degrees were awarded. The most popular majors were business administrative management (16%), nursing (9%), and elementary education/accounting (9%). In an average class, 1% graduate in 3 years or less, 62% graduate in 4 years or less, 66% graduate in 5 years or less, and 61% graduate in 6 years or less. 32 companies recruited on campus in 2002-2003. Of the 2002 graduating class, 8% were enrolled in graduate school within 6 months of graduation and 95% were employed.

Admissions Contact: Margaret M. Jackson, Dean of Admission.
E-mail: *admission@.mtmercy.edu* Web: *www.mtmercy.edu*

MOUNT ST. CLARE COLLEGE
(See Franciscan University)

NORTHWESTERN COLLEGE OF IOWA
Orange City, IA 51041

B-2
(712) 707-7130
(800) 747-4757; Fax: (712) 707-7164

Full-time: 475 men, 751 women	**Faculty:** 77; IIB, --$
Part-time: 27 men, 32 women	**Ph.D.s:** 81%
Graduate: none	**Student/Faculty:** 16 to 1
Year: semesters, summer session	**Tuition:** $15,290
Application Deadline: open	**Room & Board:** $4350
Freshman Class: 1269 applied, 1062 accepted, 311 enrolled	
ACT: 24	COMPETITIVE+

Northwestern College, founded in 1882, is a private college affiliated with the Reformed Church in America and offers liberal arts and teacher education programs. In addition to regional accreditation, Northwestern has baccalaureate program accreditation with CSWE and NCATE. The library contains 12,863 volumes, 153,000 microform items, and 6484 audio/video tapes/CDs, and subscribes to 650 periodicals. Computerized library services include the card catalog, interlibrary loans, and database searching. Special learning facilities include a learning resource center, art gallery, radio station, and TV station. The 55-acre campus is in a small town 40 miles northeast of Sioux City and 75 miles southeast of Sioux Falls. Including any residence halls, there are 27 buildings.

Student Life: 59% of undergraduates are from Iowa. Students are from 29 states, 12 foreign countries, and Canada. 88% are from public schools. 95% are white. Most are Protestant. The average age of freshmen is 18; all undergraduates, 20. 22% do not continue beyond their first year; 59% remain to graduate.

Housing: 1156 students can be accommodated in college housing, which includes single-sex dorms, on-campus apartments, and married-student housing. In addition, there are language houses and special-interest houses. On-campus housing is guaranteed for all 4 years. 86% of students live on campus; of those, 60% remain on campus on weekends. Alcohol is not permitted. All students may keep cars.

Activities: There are no fraternities or sororities. There are 46 groups on campus, including art, band, cheerleading, choir, chorus, dance, drama, drill team, film, honors, international, jazz band, literary magazine, musical theater, newspaper, orchestra, pep band, photography, political, professional, radio and TV, religious, SIFE (Students in Free Enterprise), social, social service, student government, symphony, and yearbook. Popular campus events include Winter Carnival, Spring Fest, and a Model Arab League.

Sports: There are 9 intercollegiate sports for men and 8 for women, and 11 intramural sports for men and 11 for women. Facilities include an athletic field, a 3000-seat stadium, a 2200-seat arena, a 176-meter indoor track, 4 handball/racquetball courts, 4 basketball/volleyball courts, archery, gymnastics rooms, and an outdoor 8-lane state-of-the-art track.

Disabled Students: 90% of the campus is accessible. Wheelchair ramps, elevators, special parking, specially equipped rest rooms, and lowered drinking fountains are available.

Services: Counseling and information services are available, as is tutoring in most subjects. There is remedial math, reading, and writing.

Campus Safety and Security: Measures include informal discussions, pamphlets/posters/films, and lighted pathways/sidewalks.

Programs of Study: Northwestern confers the B.A. degree. Associate degrees are also awarded. Bachelor's degrees are awarded in AGRICULTURE (agricultural business management), BIOLOGICAL SCIENCE (biology/biological science), BUSINESS (accounting, business administration and management, and business economics), COMMUNICATIONS AND THE ARTS (communications, dramatic arts, English, fine arts, French, music, and Spanish), COMPUTER AND PHYSICAL SCIENCE (actuarial science, chemistry, computer science, and mathematics), EDUCATION (art, athletic training, business, Christian, early childhood, elementary, foreign languages, middle school, music, physical, science, secondary, and special), HEALTH PROFESSIONS (medical laboratory technology, predentistry, and premedicine), SOCIAL SCIENCE (criminal justice, economics, history, philosophy, physical fitness/movement, political science/government, prelaw, psychology, religion, religious music, social work, sociology, and youth ministry). Biology, education, and religion are the strongest academically. Business and education are the largest.

Required: All students are required to take 46 to 63 credits in the core curriculum, including courses in Bible, language, history, math, literature, writing, philosophy, social and natural sciences, fine arts, and phys ed. Students must maintain a 2.0 GPA for 124 total credits, with 36 to 42 in the major, and pass both writing and math competency levels.

Special: Northwestern offers co-op programs in nursing and engineering, cross-registration with Dordt College, numerous internships, a Washington semester, student-designed majors, and study abroad in 15 countries, including Spain, France, and the Netherlands. There is a 3-2 engineering degree with Washington University at St. Louis, and a 2-2 nursing program with Trinity College or Briar Cliff College. There are 2 national honor societies, a freshman honors program, and 30 departmental honors programs.

Faculty/Classroom: 65% of faculty are male; 35%, female. All teach undergraduates, 69% do research, and 69% do both. The average class size in an introductory lecture is 22; in a laboratory, 16; and in a regular course, 21.

Admissions: 84% of the 2003-2004 applicants were accepted. The ACT scores for the 2003-2004 freshman class were: 16% below 21, 28% between 21 and 23, 34% between 24 and 26, 10% between 27 and 28, and 12% above 28. 41% of the current freshmen were in the top fifth of their class; 66% were in the top two fifths. 19 freshmen graduated first in their class.

Requirements: The SAT I or ACT is required. Applicants with a minimum ACT composite of 19, in the top half of their high school class, and with a 2.4 GPA are generally accepted. Applicants should be graduates of an accredited secondary school. The suggested distribution of high school courses is 4 years of English, 3 years each of math and social studies, and 2 of natural science. An interview is recommended. The GED is accepted. Northwestern requires applicants to be in the upper 75% of their class. A GPA of 2.0 is required. AP and CLEP credits are accepted. Important factors in the admissions decision are personality/intangible qualities, leadership record, and evidence of special talent.

Procedure: Freshmen are admitted to all sessions. Entrance exams should be taken in the spring of the junior year. There is a rolling admissions plan. Application deadlines are open. Application fee is $25. Applications are accepted on computer disk and on-line through the school's home page and Apply.

Transfer: 49 transfer students enrolled in 2002-2003. Transfer applicants must submit a transcript and letter of recommendation. A minimum college GPA of 2.0 is required. 30 of 124 credits required for the bachelor's degree must be completed at Northwestern.

Visiting: There are regularly scheduled orientations for prospective students. There are guides for informal visits and visitors may sit in on classes and stay overnight. To schedule a visit, contact Harold Hoftyzer at the Admissions Office at (712) 707-7142 or (800) 747-4757 or *haroldh@nwciowa.edu.*

Financial Aid: In 2003-2004, 99% of all full-time students received some form of financial aid. 93% of all full-time students received need-based aid. The average freshman award was $12,000. 71% of undergraduates work part time. Average annual earnings from campus work are $980. The average financial indebtedness of the 2003 graduate was $16,500. Northwestern is a member of CSS. The FAFSA and the college's own financial statement are required. The deadline for filing freshman financial aid applications for fall entry is April 1.

International Students: There are 35 international students enrolled. The school actively recruits these students. They must score 550 on the written TOEFL.

Computers: The mainframe is an HP9000 Novell Network of servers. There are 250 terminals available in residence halls, the learning resource center, and the education and business facilities. All student rooms are wired for PC connection to the network system. All students have access to the Internet and World Wide Web. All students may access the system 24 hours a day in residence halls; 7 A.M. to 12 P.M. in academic buildings. There are no time limits and no fees.

Graduates: From July 1, 2002 to June 30, 2003, 254 bachelor's degrees were awarded. The most popular majors were business administration (26%), elementary education (21%), and biology (9%). In an average class, 1% graduate in 3 years or less, 49% graduate in 4 years or less, 58% graduate in 5 years or less, and 59% graduate in 6 years or less. 20 companies recruited on campus in 2002-2003. Of the 2002 graduating class, 23% were enrolled in graduate school within 6 months of graduation and 66% were employed.

Admissions Contact: Ronald K. De Jong, Dean of Enrollment Services. A video is available. E-mail: *rondj@nwciowa.edu*
Web: *admissions@nwciowa.edu*

SAINT AMBROSE UNIVERSITY
Davenport, IA 52803

E-3
(563) 333-6311
(800) 383-2627; Fax: (563) 333-6297

Full-time: 847 men, 1136 women	**Faculty:** 155; IIB, -$
Part-time: 175 men, 325 women	**Ph.D.s:** 73%
Graduate: 440 men, 524 women	**Student/Faculty:** 13 to 1
Year: 4-1-4, summer session	**Tuition:** $16,650
Application Deadline: open	**Room & Board:** $6150
Freshman Class: 1380 applied, 1167 accepted, 435 enrolled	
ACT: 22	COMPETITIVE

St. Ambrose University, a private institution founded in 1882 in affiliation with the Roman Catholic Church, offers degree programs through the colleges of arts and sciences, business, education and health sciences, and professional studies. There also is a college-level seminary. There are 4 undergraduate and 15 graduate schools. In addition to regional accreditation, St. Ambrose has baccalaureate program accreditation with ABET, ACBSP, ACOTE, AOTA, APTE/APTA, CCNE, and CSWE. The library contains 112,885 volumes, 6655 microform items, and 3167 audio/video tapes/CDs, and subscribes to 27,279 periodicals.

Computerized library services include the card catalog, interlibrary loans, database searching, and Internet access. Special learning facilities include a learning resource center, art gallery, radio station, TV station, and an observatory. The 48-acre campus is in an urban area 180 miles west of Chicago. Including any residence halls, there are 29 buildings.

Student Life: 63% of undergraduates are from Iowa. Students are from 18 states, 9 foreign countries, and Canada. 67% are from public schools. 90% are white. 65% are Catholic; 35% Protestant. The average age of freshmen is 18; all undergraduates, 24. 25% do not continue beyond their first year; 82% remain to graduate.

Housing: 1150 students can be accommodated in college housing, which includes single-sex and coed dorms, on-campus and off-campus apartments, and townhouse residences for upper-division students. On-campus housing is guaranteed for all 4 years. 55% of students commute. All students may keep cars.

Activities: There are no fraternities or sororities. There are 24 groups on campus, including art, band, cheerleading, choir, chorale, computers, dance, debate, drama, ethnic, gay, honors, international, jazz band, literary magazine, musical theater, opera, orchestra, pep band, photography, political, professional, radio and TV, religious, social, social service, student government, symphony, and yearbook. Popular campus events include Multicultural Weeks, Parents Weekend, and Brother/Sister Weekend.

Sports: There are 9 intercollegiate sports for men and 9 for women, and 10 intramural sports for men and 10 for women. Facilities include tennis, handball/racquetball, and volleyball courts, a swimming pool, a golf room, an archery range, a gym, a weight-lifting room, and a running track.

Disabled Students: 96% of the campus is accessible. Wheelchair ramps, elevators, special parking, specially equipped rest rooms, special class scheduling, lowered drinking fountains, and special housing are available.

Services: Counseling and information services are available, as is tutoring in most subjects. There is a reader service for the blind, and remedial math, reading, and writing.

Campus Safety and Security: Measures include 24-hour foot and vehicle patrol, self-defense education, security escort services, and informal discussions. There are pamphlets/posters/films, emergency telephones, and lighted pathways/sidewalks.

Programs of Study: St. Ambrose confers B.A., B.S., B.A.M.T., B.B.A., B.B.A.A., B.E.D., B.E.S., B.M.E., B.S.I.E., B.S.O.T., and B.S.S. degrees. Master's and doctoral degrees are also awarded. Bachelor's degrees are awarded in BIOLOGICAL SCIENCE (biology/biological science), BUSINESS (accounting, business administration and management, business economics, international business management, management science, marketing/retailing/merchandising, and sports management), COMMUNICATIONS AND THE ARTS (communications, English, fine arts, French, German, graphic design, music, Spanish, and speech/debate/rhetoric), COMPUTER AND PHYSICAL SCIENCE (chemistry, computer science, mathematics, and physics), EDUCATION (art, early childhood, elementary, music, physical, and secondary), ENGINEERING AND ENVIRONMENTAL DESIGN (engineering physics and industrial engineering), HEALTH PROFESSIONS (health science), SOCIAL SCIENCE (criminal justice, criminology, economics, history, philosophy, political science/government, psychology, public administration, sociology, and theological studies). Biology, chemistry, and engineering physics are the strongest academically. Business, psychology, and elementary education are the largest.

Required: To graduate, all students must complete at least 120 credit hours, including 45 outside the major and 30 in upper-level courses. A minimum GPA of 2.0 is required. Students must also complete developmental courses and demonstrate proficiency in English composition, math, public speaking, and library skills, among other requirements.

Special: The university offers co-op and work-study programs, study abroad in England, Ireland, Ecuador, Italy, Spain, Austria, and Germany, internships, a 3-2 engineering degree with the University of Iowa and Iowa State University, accelerated degree programs, combined B.A.-B.S. degrees, dual majors, and student-designed majors. Credit for life, military, and work experience, nondegree study, and pass/fail options also are available. There are 10 national honor societies and 5 departmental honors programs.

Faculty/Classroom: 55% of faculty are male; 45%, female. All both teach and do research. No introductory courses are taught by graduate students. The average class size in an introductory lecture is 21; in a laboratory, 19; and in a regular course, 17.

Admissions: 85% of the 2003-2004 applicants were accepted. The ACT scores for the 2003-2004 freshman class were: 37% below 21, 27% between 21 and 23, 23% between 24 and 26, 7% between 27 and 28, and 6% above 28. 30% of the current freshmen were in the top fifth of their class; 52% were in the top two fifths. 28 freshmen graduated first in their class.

Requirements: The ACT is required. The SAT I, with a minimum composite score of 780, may be substituted. Applicants must be graduates of an accredited secondary school; the GED is accepted. An interview is

recommended. St. Ambrose requires applicants to be in the upper 50% of their class. A GPA of 2.5 is required. AP and CLEP credits are accepted. Important factors in the admissions decision are recommendations by school officials, leadership record, and parents or siblings attending the school.

Procedure: Freshmen are admitted to all sessions. Entrance exams should be taken in the spring of the junior year. There is a rolling admissions plan, as well as early decision and deferred admissions plans. Application deadlines are open. Application fee is $25. 541 early decision candidates were accepted for the 2003-2004 class. Applications are accepted on-line through the school's web site: www.sau.edu.

Transfer: 264 transfer students enrolled in 2003-2004. Applicants must have a college GPA of 2.0. 30 of 120 credits required for the bachelor's degree must be completed at St. Ambrose.

Visiting: There are regularly scheduled orientations for prospective students, including breakfast, welcome, testing, panel given by current students, student and parent meeting with faculty mentor, evening meeting and activity; on the next day, there is advising and registration. Parents follow their own agenda (with panels and tours). There are guides for informal visits, and visitors may sit in on classes and stay overnight. To schedule a visit, contact the Admissions Office at (563) 333-6300 or admit@sau.edu.

Financial Aid: In 2003-2004, 97% of all full-time freshmen and 95% of continuing full-time students received some form of financial aid. 76% of all full-time students received need-based aid. The average freshman award was $13,066. Need-based scholarships or need-based grants averaged $4340 ($16,650 maximum); need-based self-help aid (loans and jobs) averaged $3441 ($10,500 maximum); non-need-based athletic scholarships averaged $2669 ($5000 maximum); and other non-need-based awards and non-need-based scholarships averaged $6251 ($9500 maximum). 95% of undergraduates work part time. Average annual earnings from campus work are $1547. The average financial indebtedness of the 2003 graduate was $20,400. St. Ambrose is a member of CSS. The FAFSA is required. The deadline for filing freshman financial aid applications for fall entry is March 15.

International Students: There are 13 international students enrolled. The school actively recruits these students. They must score 500 on the written TOEFL or 213 on the electronic version.

Computers: The mainframe is a DEC ALPHA. There are 180 PC workstations available for students. All residence halls are wired for network connections. All students may access the system 24 hours a day. There are no time limits and no fees.

Graduates: From July 1, 2002 to June 30, 2003, 493 bachelor's degrees were awarded. The most popular majors were business (22%), psychology (13%), and elementary education (12%). In an average class, 1% graduate in 3 years or less, 48% graduate in 4 years or less, 58% graduate in 5 years or less, and 58% graduate in 6 years or less. 48 companies recruited on campus in 2002-2003. Of the 2002 graduating class, 22% were enrolled in graduate school within 6 months of graduation and 85% were employed.

Admissions Contact: Meg Higgins, Director of Admissions. A video is available. E-mail: higginsmegf@sau.edu
Web: http://www.sau.edu/sau.html

SIMPSON COLLEGE
Indianola, IA 50125

C-3
(515) 961-1624
(800) 362-2454; Fax: (515) 961-1870

Full-time: 615 men, 821 women	Faculty: 84; IIB, av$
Part-time: 183 men, 318 women	Ph.Ds: 90%
Graduate: none	Student/Faculty: 17 to 1
Year: 4-4-1, summer session	Tuition: $18,097
Application Deadline: open	Room & Board: $5561
Freshman Class: 1271 applied, 1097 accepted, 413 enrolled	
ACT: 24	COMPETITIVE+

Simpson College, founded in 1860, is a private liberal arts institution affiliated with the United Methodist Church. In addition to regional accreditation, Simpson has baccalaureate program accreditation with NASM. The 2 libraries contain 155,133 volumes, 12,678 microform items, and 5417 audio/video tapes/CDs, and subscribe to 698 periodicals. Computerized library services include the card catalog, interlibrary loans, database searching, and Internet access. Special learning facilities include a learning resource center, art gallery, radio station, a science reference library, and an extensive collection from the Antebellum era. The 63-acre campus is in a suburban area 12 miles south of Des Moines. Including any residence halls, there are 35 buildings.

Student Life: 90% of undergraduates are from Iowa. Students are from 26 states, 10 foreign countries, and Canada. 96% are from public schools. 91% are white. 23% claim no religious affiliation; 21% Catholic. The average age of freshmen is 18; all undergraduates, 22. 18% do not continue beyond their first year; 68% remain to graduate.

Housing: 1103 students can be accommodated in college housing, which includes single-sex and coed dorms, on-campus apartments, fraternity houses, and sorority houses. In addition, there are honors houses, language houses, special-interest houses, and theme houses. On-campus housing is guaranteed for all 4 years. 82% of students live on campus; of those, 85% remain on campus on weekends. All students may keep cars.

Activities: 27% of men belong to 1 local and 3 national fraternities; 25% of women belong to 4 national sororities. There are 80 groups on campus, including art, band, cheerleading, choir, chorale, chorus, computers, drama, drill team, ethnic, gay, honors, international, jazz band, literary magazine, musical theater, newspaper, opera, pep band, political, professional, radio and TV, religious, social, social service, student government, and yearbook. Popular campus events include Campus Day, Greek Week, and Minority Emphasis Week.

Sports: There are 9 intercollegiate sports for men and 9 for women, and 38 intramural sports for men and 38 for women. Facilities include a gym and an athletic center with a field house containing 2 racquetball courts, a wrestling practice room, a weight room, indoor batting facilities, a training room, a pool and sauna, 3 indoor tennis courts, and 2 running tracks. Outdoor facilities include a football stadium, an 8-lane track, 6 tennis courts, 2 basketball courts, a sand volleyball court, and football, soccer, baseball, and softball fields.

Disabled Students: 85% of the campus is accessible. Wheelchair ramps, elevators, special parking, specially equipped rest rooms, special class scheduling, and lowered drinking fountains are available.

Services: Counseling and information services are available, as is tutoring in every subject. There is a reader service for the blind.

Campus Safety and Security: Measures include self-defense education, security escort services, informal discussions, and pamphlets/posters/films. There are emergency telephones, lighted pathways/sidewalks, and a campus patrol during day and evening hours.

Programs of Study: Simpson confers B.A. and B.Mus. degrees. Bachelor's degrees are awarded in BIOLOGICAL SCIENCE (biochemistry and biology/biological science), BUSINESS (accounting, international business management, marketing/retailing/merchandising, and sports management), COMMUNICATIONS AND THE ARTS (art, communications, dramatic arts, English, French, German, journalism, music, music performance, Spanish, and speech/debate/rhetoric), COMPUTER AND PHYSICAL SCIENCE (chemistry, computer science, information sciences and systems, mathematics, and physics), EDUCATION (athletic training, business, drama, elementary, music, and physical), ENGINEERING AND ENVIRONMENTAL DESIGN (environmental science), SOCIAL SCIENCE (criminal justice, economics, history, international relations, philosophy, political science/government, psychology, religion, and sociology). Natural sciences, management, and visual and performing arts are the strongest academically. Management, education, and biology are the largest.

Required: Graduation requirements include at least 128 credit hours for a B.A. and 132 credit hours for a B.Mus., with a GPA of 2.0. Students must satisfactorily complete the Cornerstone Studies in Liberal Arts, including a senior colloquium; fulfill 84 hours in the major division and 30 to 42 hours in the major department; take a May term course each year; and demonstrate competency in writing, math, and foreign language.

Special: Simpson offers a 3-2 engineering degree with Washington University at St. Louis, cross-registration at American and Drew Universities, internships, a Washington semester, study abroad in 15 to 20 countries, and work-study programs. Also available are dual majors, student-designed majors, nondegree study, credit for life, military, and work experience, and a pass/fail option for 1 course per year. There are pre-professional programs in nursing, optometry, physical therapy, dentistry, medicine, pharmacy, and veterinary medicine. There are 13 national honor societies, a freshman honors program, and 8 departmental honors programs.

Faculty/Classroom: 70% of faculty are male; 30%, female. All teach undergraduates. The average class size in an introductory lecture is 30 and in a laboratory, 12.

Admissions: 86% of the 2003-2004 applicants were accepted. The ACT scores for the 2003-2004 freshman class were: 15% below 21, 28% between 21 and 23, 32% between 24 and 26, 15% between 27 and 28, and 9% above 28. 50% of the current freshmen were in the top fifth of their class; 80% were in the top two fifths. 27 freshmen graduated first in their class.

Requirements: The SAT I or ACT is required. In addition, applicants must be graduates of an accredited secondary school. The GED is accepted. Test scores, counselor recommendations, GPA, college prep course grades, and class rank are all considered in a selective admissions process. The college strongly recommends that applicants complete 4 years of English and 3 each of math, lab science, social science, and a foreign language. The college requires an audition for music and theater scholarships. A portfolio is required for art scholarships. AP and CLEP credits are accepted. Important factors in the admissions decision are advanced placement or honor courses, recommendations by school officials, and leadership record.

Procedure: Freshmen are admitted to all sessions. Entrance exams should be taken in the junior or senior year. There is a rolling admissions plan and a deferred admissions plan. Application deadlines are open. Applications are accepted on-line.

Transfer: 82 transfer students enrolled in 2002-2003. In addition to freshman requirements, transfer applicants are considered on the basis of college work taken and grades received. Applicants must take either the SAT I or ACT. The recommended GPA is 2.5, and grades of 2.0 and above transfer for credit. The school admits transfer students every term. 32 of 128 credits required for the bachelor's degree must be completed at Simpson.

Visiting: There are regularly scheduled orientations for prospective students, including a full-day orientation program scheduled 3 times during the summer, when students meet with an academic adviser, register for classes, and participate in activity information sessions. Parents are encouraged to attend. There are guides for informal visits, and visitors may sit in on classes and stay overnight. To schedule a visit, contact the Office of Admissions at (800) 362-2454, ext. 1660, or *dyerb@simpson.edu*.

Financial Aid: In 2003-2004, all full-time students received some form of financial aid. 88% of full-time freshmen and 87% of continuing full-time students received need-based aid. The average freshman award was $18,123. Need-based scholarships or need-based grants averaged $13,676 ($24,251 maximum); need-based self-help aid (loans and jobs) averaged $4762 ($20,825 maximum); and other non-need-based awards and non-need-based scholarships averaged $7704 ($17,438 maximum). 52% of undergraduates work part time. Average annual earnings from campus work are $1004. The average financial indebtedness of the 2003 graduate was $18,521. Simpson is a member of CSS. The FAFSA is required. The deadline for filing freshman financial aid applications for fall entry is July 1.

International Students: The school actively recruits these students. They must score 550 on the written TOEFL or 213 on the electronic version and also take the SAT I or the ACT.

Computers: The mainframe is a Compax Alpha DSZOE. All campus-owned buildings are connected to the mainframe network and have Internet access. There are 273 PCs available for student use in the library, Carver Science Center, McNeill Computer Lab, and student residences where computer consultants are available to assist students. All students may access the system 24 hours a day. There are no time limits and no fees.

Graduates: From July 1, 2002 to June 30, 2003, 350 bachelor's degrees were awarded. The most popular majors were management (16%), elementary education (9%), and biology (7%). In an average class, 3% graduate in 3 years or less, 54% graduate in 4 years or less, 66% graduate in 5 years or less, and 67% graduate in 6 years or less. 92 companies recruited on campus in 2002-2003. Of the 2002 graduating class, 14% were enrolled in graduate school within 6 months of graduation and 79% were employed.

Admissions Contact: Deb Tierney, Vice President for Enrollment. A video is available. E-mail: *admiss@simpson.edu*
Web: *http://www.simpson.edu*

UNIVERSITY OF DUBUQUE
Dubuque, IA 52001

E-2
(563) 589-3214
(800) 722-5583; Fax: (563) 589-3690

Full-time: 624 men, 312 women	**Faculty:** 45
Part-time: 19 men, 26 women	**Ph.D.s:** 80%
Graduate: 158 men, 90 women	**Student/Faculty:** 21 to 1
Year: semesters, summer session	**Tuition:** $15,700
Application Deadline: May 1	**Room & Board:** $5250
Freshman Class: 746 applied, 609 accepted, 290 enrolled	
SAT I Verbal/Math: 500/500	**ACT:** 23 COMPETITIVE

The University of Dubuque, established in 1852, is a private liberal arts institution affiliated with the Presbyterian Church (U.S.A.). Strengths in the undergraduate curriculum include environmental science, business, aviation, education, and computer graphics/interactive media. There are 3 undergraduate and 2 graduate schools. The library contains 164,859 volumes, 20,739 microform items, and 2180 audio/video tapes/CDs, and subscribes to 801 periodicals. Computerized library services include the card catalog, interlibrary loans, database searching, and Internet access. Special learning facilities include a learning resource center, art gallery, and planetarium. The 56-acre campus is in a suburban area 180 miles northwest of Chicago. Including any residence halls, there are 24 buildings.

Student Life: 57% of undergraduates are from out of state, mostly the Midwest. Students are from 35 states and 21 foreign countries. 90% are from public schools. 73% are white; 10% African American. 40% are Protestant; 35% claim no religious affiliation; 25% Catholic. The average age of freshmen is 18; all undergraduates, 22. 12% do not continue beyond their first year; 75% remain to graduate.

Housing: 500 students can be accommodated in college housing, which includes coed dorms, on-campus apartments, and married-student housing. In addition, there are special-interest houses. On-campus housing is guaranteed for all 4 years. 50% of students live on campus; of those, 75% remain on campus on weekends. Alcohol is not permitted. All students may keep cars.

Activities: 11% of men belong to 5 local fraternities; 10% of women belong to 3 local sororities. There are 50 groups on campus, including art, cheerleading, choir, chorale, chorus, computers, dance, drama, ecology, ethnic, honors, international, musical theater, newspaper, pep band, political, professional, religious, social, social service, student government, and yearbook. Popular campus events include Founder's Day Ball, Annual Gala, and Family Weekend.

Sports: There are 8 intercollegiate sports for men and 7 for women, and 13 intramural sports for men and 13 for women. Facilities include a sports center with basketball and volleyball courts, 2 racquetball courts, a wrestling room, and an athletic training room; a football field and track; baseball and softball fields; a practice football/intramural field; and a cardiovascular workout center.

Disabled Students: 50% of the campus is accessible. Wheelchair ramps, elevators, special parking, specially equipped rest rooms, special class scheduling, and lowered drinking fountains are available.

Services: Counseling and information services are available, as is tutoring in some subjects, including English, math, economics, accounting, and computer literacy. There is remedial math, reading, and writing.

Campus Safety and Security: Measures include 24-hour foot and vehicle patrol, self-defense education, security escort services, and shuttle buses. There are informal discussions, pamphlets/posters/films, emergency telephones, lighted pathways/sidewalks, and security-locked residence halls.

Programs of Study: UD confers B.A., B.S., and B.B.A. degrees. Associate, master's, and doctoral degrees are also awarded. Bachelor's degrees are awarded in BIOLOGICAL SCIENCE (biology/biological science), BUSINESS (accounting and business administration and management), COMMUNICATIONS AND THE ARTS (English and speech/debate/rhetoric), COMPUTER AND PHYSICAL SCIENCE (computer science), EDUCATION (education and physical), ENGINEERING AND ENVIRONMENTAL DESIGN (aviation administration/management, computer graphics, and environmental science), SOCIAL SCIENCE (philosophy, psychology, religion, and sociology). Business, environmental science, and education are the strongest academically. Business, aviation management/flight operations, and computer graphics are the largest.

Required: Students must complete 12 hours each in humanities, natural sciences, and social sciences, must fulfill specific requirements in English, literature, world history, science, math, and computer science, and must complete work in a major. A total of 120 credits must be earned, with a minimum GPA of 2.0 (2.5 for education majors), for graduation.

Special: UD offers cross-registration with Loras and Clarke Colleges, internships, study abroad in Europe and South America, a Washington semester, work-study programs, accelerated degree programs, B.A.-B.S. degrees, dual and student-designed majors, credit for life, military, and work experience, nondegree study, and pass/fail options. B.A.-M.A. programs are offered in conjunction with the university's theological seminary. Adult degree programs and an environmental field trip to Colorado and New Mexico are available. There are 8 national honor societies and 2 departmental honors programs.

Faculty/Classroom: 65% of faculty are male; 35%, female. All teach undergraduates. No introductory courses are taught by graduate students. The average class size in an introductory lecture is 25; in a laboratory, 16; and in a regular course, 17.

Admissions: 82% of the 2003-2004 applicants were accepted. The SAT I scores for the 2003-2004 freshman class were: Verbal--26% below 500, 64% between 500 and 599, 9% between 600 and 700, and 1% above 700; Math--17% below 500, 68% between 500 and 599, and 15% between 600 and 700. 23% of the current freshmen were in the top fifth of their class; 50% were in the top two fifths. 5 freshmen graduated first in their class.

Requirements: The SAT I or ACT is required. In addition, applicants must graduate from an accredited secondary school with a minimum of 4 years in English and 3 each in math, social sciences, and natural sciences. Other academic areas, such as foreign languages, business courses, computer programming, and the fine and performing arts, are also considered. The GED is accepted. Essays and recommendations are encouraged and may be required if the ACT is less than 18 or the SAT I is less than 740. Auditions are required for music scholarship candidates. UD requires applicants to be in the upper 50% of their class. A GPA of 2.0 is required. AP and CLEP credits are accepted. Important factors in the admissions decision are leadership record, recommendations by school officials, and extracurricular activities record.

Procedure: Freshmen are admitted fall and spring. Entrance exams should be taken before the senior year. There is a rolling admissions plan and a deferred admissions plan. Applications should be filed by May 1 for fall entry. Notification is sent on a rolling basis. Applications are accepted on-line through the university's web site.

Transfer: 118 transfer students enrolled in 2002-2003. A minimum GPA of 2.0 is required. The applicant must be in good standing at all previously attended institutions. 30 of 120 credits required for the bachelor's degree must be completed at UD.

Visiting: There are regularly scheduled orientations for prospective students, including a campus tour and visits with coaches, faculty, admissions, and financial aid advisers. There are guides for informal visits, and

visitors may sit in on classes and stay overnight. To schedule a visit, contact Jesse James, Admission Director, at *jjames@dbq.edu*.

Financial Aid: The average freshman award was $17,500, with $5000 from need-based scholarships or grants, $6500 from need-based self-help aid (loans and jobs), and $6000 from other non-need-based awards and non-need-based scholarships. 65% of undergraduates work part time. Average annual earnings from campus work are $1500. The average financial indebtedness of the 2003 graduate was $17,250. The FAFSA is required. The priority date for freshman financial aid applications for fall entry is February 1. The deadline for filing freshman financial aid applications for fall entry is April 1.

International Students: There are 70 international students enrolled. The school actively recruits these students. They must score 500 on the written TOEFL or 270 on the electronic version and also take the college's own test.

Computers: The mainframe is a Compaq Proliant 3000. Students have access to 200 PCs and to Internet, e-mail services, and networked services in the residence halls. All students may access the system 24 hours a day, 7 days a week. There are no time limits and no fees.

Graduates: In a recent year, 139 bachelor's degrees were awarded. The most popular majors were business administration (31%), education (21%), and aviation (10%). In an average class, 2% graduate in 3 years or less, 50% graduate in 4 years or less, 60% graduate in 5 years or less, and 70% graduate in 6 years or less. 50 companies recruited on campus in 2002-2003. Of the 2002 graduating class, 15% were enrolled in graduate school within 6 months of graduation and 85% were employed.

Admissions Contact: Jesse L. James, Admission Director.
E-mail: *jjames@dbq.edu* Web: *www.dbq.edu*

UNIVERSITY OF IOWA
Iowa City, IA 52242-1396

E-3
(319) 335-3847
(800) 553-IOWA; Fax: (319) 335-1535

Full-time: 8196 men, 9578 women	**Faculty:** 1623; I, +$
Part-time: 1033 men, 1426 women	**Ph.D.s:** 99%
Graduate: 4667 men, 4845 women	**Student/Faculty:** 11 to 1
Year: semesters, summer session	**Tuition:** $4993 ($15,285)
Application Deadline: April 1	**Room & Board:** $5930
Freshman Class: 13,337 applied, 10,979 accepted, 4083 enrolled	
SAT I Verbal/Math: 590/605	**ACT:** 24 **VERY COMPETITIVE**

The University of Iowa, founded in 1847, is a comprehensive public institution. Its undergraduate and graduate programs emphasize the liberal and fine arts, business, engineering, health science, and the professions. There are 6 undergraduate and 5 graduate schools. In addition to regional accreditation, Iowa has baccalaureate program accreditation with AACSB, ABET, ACEJMC, ACPE, ADA, AHEA, APTA, CAHEA, CSWE, NASM, NCATE, and NLN. The 13 libraries contain 4,381,918 volumes, 7,084,174 microform items, and 275,567 audio/video tapes/CDs, and subscribe to 49,731 periodicals. Computerized library services include the card catalog, interlibrary loans, database searching, and Internet access. Special learning facilities include an art gallery, natural history museum, radio station, UI hospitals and clinics, the Iowa Center for the Arts, and a driving simulator. The 1900-acre campus is in a small town 110 miles east of Des Moines and 220 miles west of Chicago. Including any residence halls, there are 117 buildings.

Student Life: 68% of undergraduates are from Iowa. Students are from 50 states, 65 foreign countries, and Canada. 89% are from public schools. 86% are white. The average age of freshmen is 18; all undergraduates, 21. 18% do not continue beyond their first year; 65% remain to graduate.

Housing: 5600 students can be accommodated in college housing, which includes coed dorms, on-campus apartments, and married-student housing. In addition, there are honors houses, language houses, special-interest houses, a quiet house, upperclass floors, floors for women in science and engineering, and for men in engineering, health sciences, business, performing arts, honors, and writing. On-campus housing is available on a first-come, first-served basis. Alcohol is not permitted. All students may keep cars.

Activities: 9% of men belong to 21 national fraternities; 13% of women belong to 17 national sororities. There are 408 groups on campus, including art, bagpipe band, band, cheerleading, chess, choir, chorale, chorus, computers, dance, debate, drama, drill team, ethnic, film, forensics, gay, honors, international, jazz band, literary magazine, marching band, musical theater, newspaper, opera, orchestra, pep band, photography, political, professional, radio and TV, religious, social, social service, student government, symphony, and yearbook. Popular campus events include Riverfest, Greek Week, and Weeks of Welcome.

Sports: There are 10 intercollegiate sports for men and 12 for women, and 30 intramural sports for men and 28 for women. Facilities include a 70,397-seat stadium, a 15,500-seat arena, softball and baseball stadiums, an 18-hole golf course, a pool, basketball, racquetball and handball courts, outdoor and indoor tennis courts and running tracks, weight and fitness rooms, a 1000-seat field hockey stadium, a field campus for hiking, cross-country skiing, canoeing, and a soccer field.

Disabled Students: 98% of the campus is accessible. Wheelchair ramps, elevators, special parking, specially equipped rest rooms, special class scheduling, lowered drinking fountains, lowered telephones, and a transportation service are available.

Services: Counseling and information services are available, as is tutoring in most subjects. There is a reader service for the blind and remedial math, reading, and writing.

Campus Safety and Security: Measures include 24-hour foot and vehicle patrol, self-defense education, security escort services, and shuttle buses. There are informal discussions, pamphlets/posters/films, emergency telephones, and lighted pathways/sidewalks.

Programs of Study: Iowa confers B.A., B.S., B.B.A., B.F.A., B.L.S., B.M., B.S.E., B.S.M., and B.S.N. degrees. Master's and doctoral degrees are also awarded. Bachelor's degrees are awarded in BIOLOGICAL SCIENCE (biochemistry, biology/biological science, and microbiology), BUSINESS (accounting, banking and finance, business administration and management, business economics, management science, marketing/retailing/merchandising, and recreation and leisure services), COMMUNICATIONS AND THE ARTS (art, art history and appreciation, broadcasting, classics, communications, comparative literature, dance, dramatic arts, English, film arts, fine arts, French, German, Greek, Italian, journalism, Latin, linguistics, music, Portuguese, Russian, Spanish, and speech/debate/rhetoric), COMPUTER AND PHYSICAL SCIENCE (actuarial science, astronomy, chemistry, computer science, geology, information sciences and systems, mathematics, physics, and statistics), EDUCATION (art, elementary, foreign languages, health, middle school, music, science, and secondary), ENGINEERING AND ENVIRONMENTAL DESIGN (biomedical engineering, chemical engineering, civil engineering, computer engineering, electrical/electronics engineering, engineering, environmental science, industrial administration/management, industrial engineering, and mechanical engineering), HEALTH PROFESSIONS (medical laboratory technology, nuclear medical technology, nursing, pharmacy, predentistry, premedicine, and speech pathology/audiology), SOCIAL SCIENCE (African American studies, American studies, anthropology, Asian/Oriental studies, classical/ancient civilization, economics, geography, history, liberal arts/general studies, parks and recreation management, philosophy, political science/government, prelaw, psychology, religion, Russian and Slavic studies, social science, social work, and sociology). Business, engineering, and psychology are the largest.

Required: To graduate, students must complete at least 120 semester hours, with a GPA of 2.0. The general education program includes rhetoric, historical perspectives, foreign language, quantitative and formal reasoning, humanities, and natural and social sciences. In addition, students choose 2 of the following to satisfy a distributed general education area: cultural diversity, fine arts, foreign civilization and culture, phys ed, social science, humanities, or historical perspectives.

Special: The University of Iowa offers cooperative education programs and internships in more than 70 academic departments, combined degree programs in liberal arts and engineering; liberal arts and business; liberal arts and nursing; and study abroad in more than 46 countries. Dual and student-designed majors, B.A.-B.S. degrees, certificate programs including Native American studies, global studies, international business, and women's studies, credit for military experience, and pass/nonpass options are also available. There are 21 national honor societies, including Phi Beta Kappa, a freshman honors program, and 55 departmental honors programs.

Faculty/Classroom: 73% of faculty are male; 27%, female.

Admissions: 82% of the 2003-2004 applicants were accepted. The SAT I scores for the 2003-2004 freshman class were: Verbal--16% below 500, 38% between 500 and 599, 36% between 600 and 700, and 11% above 700; Math--12% below 500, 35% between 500 and 599, 39% between 600 and 700, and 14% above 700. The ACT scores were 11% below 21, 25% between 21 and 23, 33% between 24 and 26, 16% between 27 and 28, and 13% above 28. 42% of the current freshmen were in the top fifth of their class; 80% were in the top two fifths. There were 23 National Merit finalists. 169 freshmen graduated first in their class.

Requirements: The SAT I or ACT is required. In addition, Iowa residents must rank in the upper 50% of their high school class (nonresidents in the upper 30%) or must meet an acceptable combination of class rank and test scores. All applicants must have completed 4 years of high school English, 3 years each of social studies, science, and math (including 2 years of algebra and 1 of geometry), and 2 years of a single foreign language. Music students must audition. AP and CLEP credits are accepted.

Procedure: Freshmen are admitted to all sessions. Entrance exams should be taken in the junior year. There is a deferred admissions plan and a rolling admissions plan. Applications should be filed by April 1 for fall or summer entry and by November 15 for spring entry. The fall 2003 application fee was $30. Notification is sent on a rolling basis. A waiting list is an active part of the admissions procedure. Applications are accepted on-line through the university's web site.

Transfer: 1188 transfer students enrolled in 2002-2003. For the College of Liberal Arts, a GPA of at least 2.25 is required for applicants with 24 or more semester hours of credit. Those with fewer credits are considered on the same criteria as freshmen. Other colleges have different re-

quirements. 30 credits of 120 required for the bachelor's degree must be completed at Iowa.

Visiting: There are regularly scheduled orientations for prospective students, including information sessions, campus tours, and visits to departments, residence halls, and classrooms. There are guides for informal visits and visitors may sit in on classes. To schedule a visit, contact the Admission Visitors Center at (319) 335-1566 or *admission@uiowa.edu.*

Financial Aid: In 2003-2004, 80% of all full-time freshmen and 83% of continuing full-time students received some form of financial aid. 41% of full-time freshmen and 40% of continuing full-time students received need-based aid. The average freshman award was $5150. Need-based scholarships or need-based grants averaged $2400 ($10,000 maximum); need-based self-help aid (loans and jobs) averaged $2100 ($8500 maximum); non-need-based athletic scholarships averaged $9000 ($10,500 maximum); and other non-need-based awards and non-need-based scholarships averaged $2700 ($12,500 maximum). All undergraduates work part time. Average annual earnings from campus work are $2200. The average financial indebtedness of the 2003 graduate was $16,500. The FAFSA and the college's own financial statement are required. Financial aid deadlines are based on first-come, first-served, after January 1.

International Students: There are 346 international students enrolled. The school actively recruits these students. They must score 530 on the written TOEFL or 197 on the electronic version and also take the SAT I or ACT. International students must submit TOEFL for admission purposes and may be asked to take a proficiency exam after arriving on campus.

Computers: The mainframes are an IBM z800 and an IBM 580. There are 1100 networked PCs at 26 public computer centers on campus. There are an additional 500 PCs in 33 departmental instructional labs on campus. All students may access the system 24 hours a day, 7 days a week. There are no time limits. The fee varies by college.

Graduates: From July 1, 2002 to June 30, 2003, 4086 bachelor's degrees were awarded. The most popular majors were communication studies (8%), English (7%), and nursing (6%). In an average class, 1% graduate in 3 years or less, 38% graduate in 4 years or less, 61% graduate in 5 years or less, and 65% graduate in 6 years or less. 272 companies recruited on campus in 2002-2003.

Admissions Contact: Michael Barron, Director of Admissions. E-mail: *admission@uiowa.edu* Web: *http://www.uiowa.edu*

UNIVERSITY OF NORTHERN IOWA D-2
Cedar Falls, IA 50614-0018
(319) 273-2281
(800) 772-2037; Fax: (319) 273-2885

Full-time: 4424 men, 6086 women	**Faculty:** 596; IIA, av$
Part-time: 583 men, 681 women	**Ph.D.s:** 73%
Graduate: 557 men, 1110 women	**Student/Faculty:** 18 to 1
Year: semesters, summer session	**Tuition:** $4916 ($11,874)
Application Deadline: August 15	**Room & Board:** $4918
Freshman Class: 4350 applied, 3518 accepted, 1785 enrolled	
SAT I Verbal/Math: 536/542	**ACT:** 23 **COMPETITIVE**

The University of Northern Iowa, established in 1876, is a public institution offering degree programs in business administration, education, humanities and fine arts, natural science, and social and behavioral sciences. Some information in the above capsule is approximate. There are 5 undergraduate schools and 1 graduate school. In addition to regional accreditation, UNI has baccalaureate program accreditation with AACSB, ACS, ADA, ASLA, CSWE, NASAD, NASM, and NRPA. The library contains 7424 volumes, 1,059,905 microform items, and 22,467 audio/video tapes/CDs, and subscribes to 6976 periodicals. Computerized library services include the card catalog, interlibrary loans, and database searching. Special learning facilities include a learning resource center, art gallery, natural history museum, planetarium, radio station, and observatory. The university also sponsors a laboratory school, a waste reduction center, and several research institutes. The 788-acre campus is in a small town about 100 miles north of Des Moines. Including any residence halls, there are 64 buildings.

Student Life: 93% of undergraduates are from Iowa. Students are from 46 states, 76 foreign countries, and Canada. 89% are white. The average age of freshmen is 18; all undergraduates, 21. 18% do not continue beyond their first year; 60% remain to graduate.

Housing: 4939 students can be accommodated in college housing, which includes single-sex and coed dorms, on-campus apartments, and married-student housing. In addition, there are special-interest houses. On-campus housing is guaranteed for all 4 years. 64% of students commute. All students may keep cars.

Activities: 3% of men belong to 7 national fraternities; 3% of women belong to 4 national sororities. There are 232 groups on campus, including art, band, cheerleading, choir, chorale, chorus, computers, dance, drama, drill team, ethnic, film, gay, honors, international, jazz band, literary magazine, marching band, musical theater, newspaper, nontraditional students, opera, orchestra, pep band, political, professional, radio and TV, religious, social, social service, student government, symphony, and yearbook. Popular campus events include Winterfest, International Food Fair, and Diversity Week.

Sports: There are 9 intercollegiate sports for men and 9 for women, and 25 intramural sports for men and 24 for women. Facilities include a domed stadium, a field house, a basketball facility, and a wellness and recreation center with an 8-lane swimming pool, 6 handball/racquetball courts, a climbing wall, weight rooms, and basketball courts.

Disabled Students: Wheelchair ramps, elevators, special parking, specially equipped rest rooms, special class scheduling, lowered drinking fountains, lowered telephones, and personal care attendants, and TDDs are available.

Services: Counseling and information services are available, as is tutoring in some subjects, including macroeconomics, accounting, business statistics, biology, physics, physical science, chemistry, and Spanish. There is a reader service for the blind, remedial math and writing, and a note-taking service.

Campus Safety and Security: Measures include 24-hour foot and vehicle patrol, security escort services, informal discussions, and pamphlets/posters/films. There are emergency telephones and lighted pathways/sidewalks.

Programs of Study: UNI confers B.A., B.S., B.F.A., B.L.S., B.Mus., and B.T. degrees. Master's and doctoral degrees are also awarded. Bachelor's degrees are awarded in BIOLOGICAL SCIENCE (biology/biological science, biotechnology, microbiology, and nutrition), BUSINESS (accounting, banking and finance, management information systems, management science, marketing/retailing/merchandising, and recreation and leisure services), COMMUNICATIONS AND THE ARTS (art history and appreciation, broadcasting, communications, dramatic arts, English, fine arts, French, German, graphic design, music, music performance, music theory and composition, public relations, Spanish, speech/debate/rhetoric, studio art, and theater design), COMPUTER AND PHYSICAL SCIENCE (chemistry, computer science, earth science, geology, information sciences and systems, mathematics, physics, and science), EDUCATION (art, athletic training, business, early childhood, elementary, foreign languages, health, middle school, music, physical, science, special, teaching English as a second/foreign language (TESOL/TEFOL), and technical), ENGINEERING AND ENVIRONMENTAL DESIGN (construction management, electromechanical technology, energy management technology, industrial engineering technology, and manufacturing technology), HEALTH PROFESSIONS (speech pathology/audiology), SOCIAL SCIENCE (American studies, anthropology, Asian/Oriental studies, clothing and textiles management/production/services, criminology, dietetics, economics, European studies, family and community services, geography, history, humanities, Latin American studies, liberal arts/general studies, philosophy, political science/government, psychology, public administration, religion, Russian and Slavic studies, social science, social work, and sociology). Accounting, management, and education are the strongest academically. Accounting and elementary education are the largest.

Required: Degree requirements include completion of 124 to 130 credits, with 30 to 60 in the major. Liberal arts majors must maintain a minimum GPA of 2.0 (2.5 for education majors). General education requirements include 11 hours of civilizations and cultures, 9 each of natural science/technology, social science, and communication, 6 of arts/literature/philosophy/religion, and 3 of personal wellness. Students must meet requirements in foreign language and complete a capstone course in environment, technology, and society. Education students must complete a 32-credit professional sequence.

Special: Internships and co-op programs are offered through all colleges of the university. Students may study abroad in 19 countries and may participate in a Washington semester. Interdisciplinary majors include safety education, chemistry/marketing, design/human environment, and natural history interpretation. Cross-registration, work-study programs, a general studies degree, dual and student-designed majors, nondegree study, and pass/fail options are also available. There are 25 national honor societies and a freshman honors program.

Faculty/Classroom: 56% of faculty are male; 44%, female. 97% both teach and do research. Graduate students teach 1% of introductory courses. The average class size in an introductory lecture is 49; in a laboratory, 18; and in a regular course, 26.

Admissions: 81% of the 2003-2004 applicants were accepted. The SAT I scores for the 2003-2004 freshman class were: Verbal--40% below 500, 29% between 500 and 599, 26% between 600 and 700, and 5% above 700; Math--40% below 500, 21% between 500 and 599, 33% between 600 and 700, and 6% above 700. The ACT scores were 26% below 21, 33% between 21 and 23, 26% between 24 and 26, 7% between 27 and 28, and 8% above 28. 39% of the current freshmen were in the top fifth of their class; 75% were in the top two fifths. 80 freshmen graduated first in their class in a recent year.

Requirements: The ACT is required. In addition, applicants must graduate from an approved secondary school. The GED, with a minimum standard score of 57, is accepted. High school requirements include 4 years of English, 3 years each of math, social studies, and science, and 2 years or more of electives, which may include foreign language and fine arts. UNI requires applicants to be in the upper 50% of their class.

AP and CLEP credits are accepted. Important factors in the admissions decision are advanced placement or honor courses, evidence of special talent, and leadership record.

Procedure: Freshmen are admitted to all sessions. Entrance exams should be taken by October of the senior year. There is a rolling admissions plan. Applications should be filed by August 15 for fall entry, December 31 for spring entry, and May 15 for summer entry, along with a $20 fee. Notification is sent on a rolling basis. Applications are accepted on-line through the school's web site.

Transfer: 1221 transfer students enrolled in a recent year. Applicants must have a minimum GPA of 2.0 to 2.5, depending on the number of credits they wish to transfer. Other applicants may be admitted on academic probation. 32 of 124 credits required for the bachelor's degree must be completed at UNI.

Visiting: There are regularly scheduled orientations for prospective students, including a student panel, lunch, a campus tour, and presentations by admissions, financial aid, housing, and academic departments. There are guides for informal visits and visitors may sit in on classes and stay overnight. To schedule a visit, contact the Admissions Office.

Financial Aid: In 2003-2004, 82% of all full-time freshmen and 53% of continuing full-time students received some form of financial aid. 59% of full-time freshmen and 62% of continuing full-time students received need-based aid. The average freshman award was $13,061. Need-based scholarships or need-based grants averaged $2761 ($6902 maximum); need-based self-help aid (loans and jobs) averaged $2910 ($4625 maximum); non-need-based athletic scholarships averaged $3509 ($17,112 maximum); and other non-need-based awards and non-need-based scholarships averaged $1894 ($16,804 maximum). 34% of undergraduates work part time. Average annual earnings from campus work are $1753. The average financial indebtedness of a recent graduate was $12,671. The FAFSA is required. The deadline for filing freshman financial aid applications for fall entry is open.

International Students: There were 191 international students enrolled in a recent year. The school actively recruits these students. They must score 550 on the written TOEFL or 213 on the electronic version.

Computers: The mainframes are a consists of a DEC Alpha 4000-160, a DEC Alpha server 2000 4/200, a Sun SPARC Station 10, and an IBM ES 9121/210. The network is available to students through 800 PCs located in 7 public access labs and through 87 dial-in ports. All students may have accounts on the VMS system and Internet privileges. All students may access the system 24 hours a day. There are no time limits and no fees.

Graduates: In a recent year, 2266 bachelor's degrees were awarded. The most popular majors were elementary education (16%), general studies (5%), and management (4%). In an average class, 1% graduate in 3 years or less, 29% graduate in 4 years or less, 62% graduate in 5 years or less, and 64% graduate in 6 years or less. 150 companies recruited on campus in a recent year.

Admissions Contact: Clark Elmer, Director of Enrollment Management and Admissions. E-mail: admissions@uni.edu Web: www.uni.edu

UPPER IOWA UNIVERSITY
Fayette, IA 52142-1857 E-2
(563) 425-5281
(800) 553-4150; Fax: (563) 425-5323

Full-time: 402 men, 266 women	**Faculty:** 36; IIB, --$
Part-time: 10 men, 15 women	**Ph.D.s:** 75%
Graduate: none	**Student/Faculty:** 19 to 1
Year: 2-2-2-2-1	**Tuition:** $15,056
Application Deadline: open	**Room & Board:** $5020
Freshman Class: 725 applied, 654 accepted, 294 enrolled	
ACT: 19	COMPETITIVE

Upper Iowa University, founded in 1857, is a private institution with a liberal arts focus. The library contains 132,175 volumes, 8895 microform items, and 2040 audio/video tapes/CDs, and subscribes to 287 periodicals. Computerized library services include interlibrary loans and database searching. Special learning facilities include a learning resource center and art gallery. The 100-acre campus is in a rural area 65 miles north of Cedar Rapids. Including any residence halls, there are 14 buildings.

Student Life: 60% of undergraduates are from Iowa. Students are from 14 states, 5 foreign countries, and Canada. 90% are from public schools. 75% are white; 13% African American. The average age of freshmen is 19; all undergraduates, 22. 32% do not continue beyond their first year; 68% remain to graduate.

Housing: 515 students can be accommodated in college housing, which includes single-sex dorms and on-campus apartments. On-campus housing is guaranteed for all 4 years. 70% of students live on campus; of those, 50% remain on campus on weekends. All students may keep cars.

Activities: 19% of men belong to 5 local and 1 national fraternity; 40% of women belong to 5 local sororities. There are 31 groups on campus, including art, cheerleading, computers, drama, environmental, international, newspaper, outdoor, political, religious, social, social service, student government, and yearbook. Popular campus events include Winterfest, Greek Week, and Springfest.

Sports: There are 9 intercollegiate sports for men and 8 for women, and 4 intramural sports for men and 4 for women. Facilities include a recreation center, a golf course, an indoor swimming pool, a rock climbing wall, a weight room, and nearby cross-country skiing areas.

Disabled Students: 70% of the campus is accessible. Wheelchair ramps, elevators, special parking, specially equipped rest rooms, special class scheduling, lowered drinking fountains, and lowered telephones are available. The school will make accommodations when necessary.

Services: Counseling and information services are available, as is tutoring in most subjects. There is remedial math, reading, and writing.

Campus Safety and Security: Measures include security escort services, informal discussions, pamphlets/posters/films, and emergency telephones. There are lighted pathways/sidewalks and a security officer lives in each residence hall.

Programs of Study: Upper Iowa confers B.A. and B.S. degrees. Associate and master's degrees are also awarded. Bachelor's degrees are awarded in AGRICULTURE (conservation and regulation), BIOLOGICAL SCIENCE (biology/biological science), BUSINESS (accounting, banking and finance, business administration and management, management information systems, management science, marketing/retailing/merchandising, and recreation and leisure services), COMMUNICATIONS AND THE ARTS (art, arts administration/management, communications, English, fine arts, and graphic design), COMPUTER AND PHYSICAL SCIENCE (chemistry, mathematics, and science), EDUCATION (athletic training, elementary, and physical), HEALTH PROFESSIONS (health and health care administration), SOCIAL SCIENCE (American studies, criminology, human services, physical fitness/movement, psychology, social science, and sociology). Business, education, and preprofessional science are the strongest academically. Conservation management, education, and management information systems are the largest.

Required: All students must complete at least 120 semester hours with a GPA of 2.0 overall and 2.5 in the major. Distribution requirements include 9 hours each in English and speech, 6 each in arts and humanities, natural sciences, and social science, and 3 each in math, computer skills, and cultures.

Special: Internships, a work-study program, study abroad, a 3-year B.A. degree in any major except education, and student-designed majors are available. There are 3 national honor societies and a freshman honors program.

Faculty/Classroom: 55% of faculty are male; 45%, female. All teach undergraduates, 20% do research, and 20% do both. The average class size in an introductory lecture is 30; in a laboratory, 10; and in a regular course, 15.

Admissions: 90% of the 2003-2004 applicants were accepted. The ACT scores for the 2003-2004 freshman class were: 49% below 21, 23% between 21 and 23, 21% between 24 and 26, 5% between 27 and 28, and 2% above 28. 6 freshmen graduated first in their class.

Requirements: The SAT I or ACT is required. In addition, recommendations from counselors and extracurricular activities in school, church, and community are considered in the admissions process. A GPA of 2.0 is required. AP and CLEP credits are accepted.

Procedure: Freshmen are admitted to all sessions. Entrance exams should be taken in the spring of junior year. There is a rolling admissions plan. Application deadlines are open. Application fee is $15.

Transfer: 128 transfer students enrolled in 2002-2003. The prime consideration for transfer students is continued good standing in an accredited institution. Credit is generally given for all lecture and lab courses. 30 of 120 credits required for the bachelor's degree must be completed at Upper Iowa.

Visiting: There are regularly scheduled orientations for prospective students, including campus tours, meals, and visits with faculty and admissions counselors. There are guides for informal visits and visitors may sit in on classes and stay overnight. To schedule a visit, contact Admissions Administrative Assistant/Office Manager at *admission@uiu.edu.*

Financial Aid: In a recent year, 96% of all full-time freshmen and 92% of continuing full-time students received some form of financial aid. 90% of full-time freshmen received need-based aid. The average freshman award was $9125. 100% of undergraduates work part time. Average annual earnings from campus work are $1650. The average financial indebtedness of the 2003 graduate was $17,125. The FAFSA and the college's own financial statement are required. Freshman financial aid applications for fall entry are processed on a rolling basis.

International Students: In a recent year, 34 international students enrolled. The school actively recruits these students. They must score 450 on the written TOEFL.

Computers: The mainframe is an IBM. Macs are also available. All students may access the system. There are no time limits and no fees.

Graduates: In a recent year, 986 bachelor's degrees were awarded. The most popular majors were management (35%), education (19%), and accounting (14%). In an average class, 90% graduate in 4 years or less, and 10% graduate in 5 years or less. 4 companies recruited on campus in 2002-2003. Of the 2002 graduating class, 94% were employed within 6 months of graduation.

Admissions Contact: Linda Hoopes, Director of Admissions. E-mail: *admissions@uiu.edu* Web: *www.uiu.edu*

WARTBURG COLLEGE   D-2
Waverly, IA 50677-0903   (319) 352-8264
(800) 772-2085; Fax: (319) 352-8579

Full-time: 655 men, 905 women	Faculty: 91; IIB, -$
Part-time: 35 men, 50 women	Ph.D.s: 92%
Graduate: none	Student/Faculty: 17 to 1
Year: 4-4-1, summer session	Tuition: $17,530
Application Deadline: see profile	Room & Board: $4800
Freshman Class: n/av	
SAT I or ACT: required	**VERY COMPETITIVE**

Wartburg College, established in 1852, is a private liberal arts institution affiliated with the Evangelical Lutheran Church in America. Figures in the above capsule and in this profile are approximate. In addition to regional accreditation, Wartburg has baccalaureate program accreditation with CSWE, NASM, and NCATE. The library contains 138,763 volumes, 7411 microform items, and 2963 audio/video tapes/CDs, and subscribes to 829 periodicals. Computerized library services include the card catalog, interlibrary loans, and database searching. Special learning facilities include a learning resource center, art gallery, natural history museum, planetarium, radio station, TV station, business center, classroom technology center, fine arts center, journalism lab, symbolic computation lab, music computer lab, 6 acres of native grasses and prairie plants, and more than 100 acres of native timber used for field trips and research. The 118-acre campus is in a small town 15 miles north of Waterloo/Cedar Falls. Including any residence halls, there are 34 buildings.

Student Life: 76% of undergraduates are from Iowa. Students are from 25 states, 32 foreign countries, and Canada. 95% are from public schools. 89% are white. 73% are Protestant; 23% Catholic. The average age of freshmen is 19; all undergraduates, 20. 25% do not continue beyond their first year; 73% remain to graduate.

Housing: 1286 students can be accommodated in college housing, which includes single-sex and coed dorms and on-campus apartments. In addition, there are special-interest houses. On-campus housing is guaranteed for all 4 years. 82% of students live on campus; of those, 60% remain on campus on weekends. All students may keep cars.

Activities: There are no fraternities or sororities. There are 94 groups on campus, including art, band, cheerleading, choir, chorale, chorus, computers, dance, debate, drama, ethnic, forensics, gay, honors, international, jazz band, literary magazine, musical theater, newspaper, opera, orchestra, pep band, photography, political, professional, radio and TV, religious, social, social service, student government, symphony, and yearbook. Popular campus events include Artist Series, Convocations, and Family Weekend.

Sports: There are 10 intercollegiate sports for men and 9 for women, and 8 intramural sports for men and 8 for women. Facilities include a phys ed center, that includes a field house, handball/racquetball/squash courts, basketball and tennis/badminton/volleyball courts, an indoor track, a weight room, a cardiovascular room, and an aerobics and wrestling room; a 5000-seat stadium with a football field and all-weather track; a 2000-seat gym; a lighted baseball park; football, soccer, and softball fields; and outdoor tennis courts.

Disabled Students: 85% of the campus is accessible. Wheelchair ramps, elevators, special parking, specially equipped rest rooms, special class scheduling, lowered drinking fountains, lowered telephones, and special housing are available.

Services: Counseling and information services are available, as is tutoring in most subjects. There is remedial math, a supplemental instruction program, and assistance with speech writing and delivery. A writing and reading center is also available.

Campus Safety and Security: Measures include 24-hour foot and vehicle patrol, self-defense education, security escort services, and informal discussions. There are pamphlets/posters/films, emergency telephones, lighted pathways/sidewalks, night vehicle patrol, part of 24-hour patrol, and student escort service.

Programs of Study: Wartburg confers B.A., B.A.A., B.A.S., B.M., and B.M.E. degrees. Bachelor's degrees are awarded in BIOLOGICAL SCIENCE (biochemistry and biology/biological science), BUSINESS (accounting, banking and finance, business administration and management, international business management, marketing/retailing/merchandising, and recreation and leisure services), COMMUNICATIONS AND THE ARTS (applied music, art, arts administration/management, broadcasting, communications, creative writing, dramatic arts, English, French, German, graphic design, journalism, music, music performance, music theory and composition, public relations, and Spanish), COMPUTER AND PHYSICAL SCIENCE (chemistry, computer science, information sciences and systems, mathematics, and physics), EDUCATION (art, elementary, English, foreign languages, journalism, mathematics, music, physical, science, secondary, and social studies), ENGINEERING AND ENVIRONMENTAL DESIGN (engineering and applied science), HEALTH PROFESSIONS (medical laboratory technology, music therapy, and occupational therapy), SOCIAL SCIENCE (economics, French studies, German area studies, history, international relations, philosophy, political science/government, psychology, religion, religious music, social work, and sociology). Math, biology, and chemistry are the strongest academically. Biology, education, and business are the largest.

Required: Degree requirements include a minimum cumulative and major GPA of 2.0 and completion of 36 course credits (128 semester hours), including 4 May term course credits. All students must complete the Wartburg Plan of Essential Education, an integrative and interdisciplinary program of study, based on course work in thinking strategies, reasoning skills, faith and reflection, health and wellness, and literacy in writing, diversity, and a foreign language. Students must also demonstrate proficiency in information systems and in oral communication and must complete a capstone project.

Special: Special academic programs at Wartburg include those in leadership education and global and multicultural studies. Internships are available in all majors and there are internship programs in Denver, Washington, D.C., and abroad. Study abroad in 15 countries, on-campus work-study, dual majors in any combination, and individualized majors are possible. A 3-2 engineering degree is offered with Iowa State University, the Universities of Iowa and Illinois, and Washington University in St. Louis. Other 3-2 degrees are possible in medical technology and occupational therapy. A deferred admit program with the University of Iowa College of Dentistry is offered, as is an array of experiential learning opportunities. There are 11 national honor societies.

Faculty/Classroom: 52% of faculty are male; 48%, female. All teach undergraduates and 36% do research. The average class size in an introductory lecture is 38; in a laboratory, 22; and in a regular course, 28.

Admissions: In a recent year, there were 4 National Merit finalists and 43 freshmen graduated first in their class.

Requirements: The SAT I or ACT is required, with a minimum score of 790 on the SAT I or 18 on the ACT expected. Candidates for admission must be graduates of an accredited secondary school, having completed 4 years of English, 3 each of math, and science, 2 each of social studies and foreign language, and 1 of introduction to computers. The GED is accepted, with an average of 50 or above expected. Wartburg requires applicants to be in the upper 50% of their class. A GPA of 2.2 is required. AP and CLEP credits are accepted. Important factors in the admissions decision are advanced placement or honor courses, recommendations by school officials, and leadership record.

Procedure: Freshmen are admitted fall and winter. Entrance exams should be taken before the senior year. There is an early admissions plan. There is a rolling admissions plan. Check with the school for current deadlines and fee. The fall 2003 application fee was $20. Notification of early decision is sent rolling.

Transfer: 51 transfer students enrolled in a recent year. Applicants must have earned an associate degree or have maintained a minimum GPA of 2.0 in previous college work for 1 year. The ACT or the SAT I must be taken; the minimum acceptable ACT score is 19. Students must submit official transcripts from all colleges attended. 7 of 36 credits required for the bachelor's degree must be completed at Wartburg.

Visiting: There are regularly scheduled orientations for prospective students, including an introduction to academic and student life conducted by administrators, faculty, and students, and advising and registration. There are guides for informal visits and visitors may sit in on classes and stay overnight. To schedule a visit, contact the Admissions Office.

Financial Aid: The FAFSA is required. Check with the school for current deadlines.

International Students: There were 69 international students enrolled in a recent year. The school actively recruits these students. They must score 550 on the written TOEFL or take the MELAB.

Computers: The mainframes are a DEC VAX 4000-300, DEC Alpha 2000, DEC VAX Station 3100, DEC VAX 3300 l, and two Alpha 1000As. All students may use the mainframe system, Internet, and World Wide Web. Students are assigned a password and a user ID. More than 200 Macs and PCs are also available. All students may access the system. There are no time limits.

Graduates: In a recent year, 324 bachelor's degrees were awarded. The most popular majors were business administration (20%), elementary education (17%), and biology (13%). In an average class, 1% graduate in 3 years or less, 65% graduate in 4 years or less, 70% graduate in 5 years or less, and 71% graduate in 6 years or less. 50 companies recruited on campus in a recent year. Of a recent graduating class, 20% were enrolled in graduate school within 6 months of graduation and 75% were employed.

Admissions Contact: Doug Bowman, Dean of Admissions and Financial Aid. A video is available. E-mail: *admissions@wartburg.edu* Web: *www.wartburg.edu*

WILLIAM PENN UNIVERSITY
Oskaloosa, IA 52577
D-3
(641) 673-1012
(800) 779-7366; Fax: (641) 673-1396

Full-time: 750 men, 630 women	**Faculty:** 43
Part-time: 65 men, 105 women	**Ph.D.s:** 40%
Graduate: none	**Student/Faculty:** 32 to 1
Year: semesters, summer session	**Tuition:** $14,260
Application Deadline: open	**Room & Board:** $4540
Freshman Class: n/av	
SAT I or ACT: required	**LESS COMPETITIVE**

William Penn University, founded in 1873, is a private liberal arts institution affiliated with the Society of Friends (Quakers). Figures in the above capsule and in this profile are approximate. There are 2 undergraduate schools. In addition to regional accreditation, William Penn has baccalaureate program accreditation with NCATE. The library contains 66,500 volumes, 2879 microform items, and 423 audio/video tapes/CDs, and subscribes to 345 periodicals. Computerized library services include the card catalog, interlibrary loans, and database searching. Special learning facilities include a learning resource center, art gallery, radio station, and Mideast collection. The 40-acre campus is in a rural area 58 miles southeast of Des Moines. Including any residence halls, there are 13 buildings.

Student Life: 73% of undergraduates are from Iowa. Students are from 41 states, 10 foreign countries, and Canada. 90% are from public schools. 83% are white; 10% African American. 44% are Protestant; 39% claim no religious affiliation; 13% Catholic. The average age of freshmen is 19; all undergraduates, 25. 35% do not continue beyond their first year; 40% remain to graduate.

Housing: 500 students can be accommodated in college housing, which includes single-sex and coed dorms. On-campus housing is guaranteed for all 4 years. 60% of students commute. Alcohol is not permitted. All students may keep cars.

Activities: 5% of men belong to 2 local fraternities; 5% of women belong to 3 local sororities. There are 30 groups on campus, including band, cheerleading, choir, chorale, chorus, computers, drama, ethnic, honors, international, jazz band, literary magazine, musical theater, newspaper, pep band, photography, professional, radio, religious, social, social service, student government, and yearbook. Popular campus events include Multicultural Day and Campus Beautification Day.

Sports: There are 8 intercollegiate sports for men and 6 for women, and 6 intramural sports for men and 6 for women. Facilities include a gym with 2 regulation-size basketball courts and wrestling and weight training rooms, baseball and softball fields, 3 tennis courts, and football and soccer practice fields.

Disabled Students: 70% of the campus is accessible. Wheelchair ramps, elevators, special parking, specially equipped rest rooms, and special class scheduling are available.

Services: Counseling and information services are available, as is tutoring in most subjects. There is remedial math, reading, and writing.

Campus Safety and Security: Measures include 24-hour foot and vehicle patrol, informal discussions, emergency telephones, and lighted pathways/sidewalks.

Programs of Study: William Penn confers the B.A. degree. Associate degrees are also awarded. Bachelor's degrees are awarded in BIOLOGICAL SCIENCE (biology/biological science and biotechnology), BUSINESS (accounting, business administration and management, recreation and leisure services, and sports management), COMMUNICATIONS AND THE ARTS (communications, English, fine arts, journalism, and public relations), COMPUTER AND PHYSICAL SCIENCE (computer science), EDUCATION (elementary, health, physical, science, secondary, and special), ENGINEERING AND ENVIRONMENTAL DESIGN (environmental science, industrial administration/management, and industrial engineering technology), SOCIAL SCIENCE (criminology, history, human services, political science/government, psychology, and sociology). Elementary and secondary education, industrial technology, and business are the strongest academically. Education and business are the largest.

Required: To graduate, students must complete 124 hours, with 30 to 75 hours in the major. A GPA of 2.0 overall and in major and minor courses is required. Leadership core requirements total 47 hours in English/communications, math, natural science, social science, religion, fine arts, and philosophy.

Special: William Penn offers internships, work-study programs with local businesses, dual majors, nondegree study, pass/fail options, and 3-2 engineering degree programs with Iowa State and Washington Universities. Preprofessional studies, driver and safety education, and endorsements in numerous secondary education subjects are also offered. There are 2 national honor societies, including Phi Beta Kappa.

Faculty/Classroom: 57% of faculty are male; 43%, female. All teach undergraduates. The average class size in an introductory lecture is 25.

Admissions: 2 freshmen graduated first in their class in a recent year.

Requirements: The SAT I or ACT is required. In addition, applicants must be graduates of an accredited secondary and should have completed 15 high school units. The GED is accepted. A GPA of 2.0 is required. AP and CLEP credits are accepted. Important factors in the admissions decision are evidence of special talent, extracurricular activities record, and leadership record.

Procedure: Freshmen are admitted to all sessions. Entrance exams should be taken late in the junior year or early in the senior year. There are early admissions and deferred admissions plans. There is a rolling admissions plan. Application deadlines are open. Application fee is $20. Applications are accepted on-line.

Transfer: 164 transfer students enrolled in a recent year. Applicants must be in good standing at their previous institution and submit official transcripts from previously attended schools. 30 of 124 credits required for the bachelor's degree must be completed at William Penn.

Visiting: There are regularly scheduled orientations for prospective students, including a 1-day visit comprised of meetings with faculty, student services, financial aid, personnel, and people who share students' interests. There are guides for informal visits and visitors may sit in on classes and stay overnight. To schedule a visit, contact the Director of Admissions.

Financial Aid: In a recent year, 97% of all full-time students received some form of financial aid. 95% of full-time freshmen and 96% of con-tinuing full-time students received need-based aid. The average fresh-man award was $18,373. 70% of undergraduates work part time. Average annual earnings from campus work are $1600. The average financial indebtedness of a recent graduate was $18,600. The FAFSA is required.

International Students: There were 15 international students enrolled in a recent year. The school actively recruits these students. They must score 500 on the written TOEFL.

Computers: The mainframe is an HP 3000. There are more than 70 terminals and PCs in the computer lab and library, with data access in every dorm room. All students may access the system. There are no time limits and no fees.

Graduates: In a recent year, 220 bachelor's degrees were awarded. The most popular majors were business management (61%), elementary education (9%), and psychology (5%). In an average class, 56% graduate in 4 years or less, 90% graduate in 5 years or less, and 98% graduate in 6 years or less. 160 companies recruited on campus in a recent year. Of a recent graduating class, 15% were enrolled in graduate school within 6 months of graduation and 75% were employed.

Admissions Contact: Mary Boyd, Director of Admissions. E-mail: *admissions@wmpenn.edu* Web: *www.wmpenn.edu*

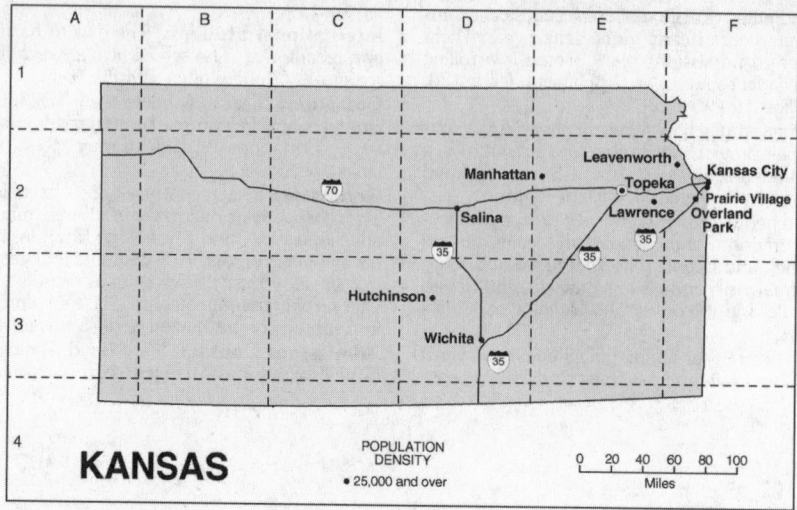

KANSAS

POPULATION
DENSITY
• 25,000 and over

0 20 40 60 80 100
Miles

BAKER UNIVERSITY
Baldwin City, KS 66006

E-2

(785) 594-8386
(800) 873-4282; Fax: (785) 594-8372

Full-time: 418 men, 542 women	**Faculty:** 57; IIB, -$
Part-time: 19 men, 36 women	**Ph.D.s:** 82%
Graduate: none	**Student/Faculty:** 17 to 1
Year: 4-1-4, summer session	**Tuition:** $14,560
Application Deadline: open	**Room & Board:** $5300
Freshman Class: 938 applied, 767 accepted, 225 enrolled	
ACT: 24	**VERY COMPETITIVE**

Baker University, founded in 1858, is a private liberal arts institution operated by the United Methodist Church. There are 2 undergraduate schools and 1 graduate school. In addition to regional accreditation, Baker has baccalaureate program accreditation with ACBSP, NASM, NCATE, and NLN. The library contains 97,000 volumes (including microform items) and 3311 audio/video tapes/CDs, and subscribes to 320 periodicals. Computerized library services include the card catalog, interlibrary loans, and database searching. Special learning facilities include a learning resource center, art gallery, natural history museum, radio station, TV station, greenhouse, and wetlands. The 26-acre campus is in a rural area 35 miles southwest of Kansas City and 15 miles south of Lawrence in a small community. Including any residence halls, there are 26 buildings.

Student Life: 73% of undergraduates are from Kansas. Students are from 21 states and 7 foreign countries. 95% are from public schools. 87% are white. 65% are Protestant; 25% Catholic; 7% claim no religious affiliation. The average age of freshmen is 18; all undergraduates, 20. 26% do not continue beyond their first year; 55% remain to graduate.

Housing: 524 students can be accommodated in college housing, which includes single-sex and coed dorms, on-campus apartments, fraternity houses, and sorority houses. On-campus housing is guaranteed for all 4 years. 83% of students live on campus; of those, 75% remain on campus on weekends. Alcohol is not permitted. All students may keep cars.

Activities: 51% of men belong to 1 local and 3 national fraternities; 52% of women belong to 4 national sororities. There are 70 groups on campus, including art, band, cheerleading, chess, choir, chorale, chorus, dance, debate, drama, drill team, ethnic, forensics, honors, international, jazz band, literary magazine, marching band, musical theater, newspaper, opera, orchestra, pep band, photography, political, professional, radio and TV, religious, social, social service, student government, and yearbook. Popular campus events include Maple Leaf Festival and Alumni Day.

Sports: There are 9 intercollegiate sports for men and 9 for women, and 10 intramural sports for men and 10 for women. Facilities include a 3500-seat stadium, a 2500-seat gym, practice and varsity fields for football, track, soccer, softball and baseball, 3 basketball courts, 4 racquetball courts, a jogging track, 3 tennis courts, a wellness facility, and a weight room.

Disabled Students: 45% of the campus is accessible. Wheelchair ramps, elevators, special parking, specially equipped rest rooms, special class scheduling, lowered drinking fountains, and lowered telephones are available.

Services: Counseling and information services are available, as is tutoring in most subjects. There is a reader service for the blind and remedial math, reading, and writing.

Campus Safety and Security: Measures include 24-hour foot and vehicle patrol, security escort services, informal discussions, and lighted pathways/sidewalks. There is a patrol from 5 P.M. to 6 A.M.

Programs of Study: Baker confers B.A., B.S., B.M., B.M.E., and B.S.N. degrees. Master's degrees are also awarded. Bachelor's degrees are awarded in BIOLOGICAL SCIENCE (biology/biological science and wildlife biology), BUSINESS (accounting, banking and finance, business administration and management, business economics, and international business management), COMMUNICATIONS AND THE ARTS (art history and appreciation, communications, dramatic arts, English, fine arts, French, German, music, Spanish, and studio art), COMPUTER AND PHYSICAL SCIENCE (chemistry, computer science, information sciences and systems, mathematics, and physics), EDUCATION (art, business, elementary, music, and secondary), HEALTH PROFESSIONS (nursing), SOCIAL SCIENCE (economics, history, philosophy, political science/government, psychology, religion, and sociology). Biology, education, and music are the strongest academically. Business, education, and psychology are the largest.

Required: To graduate, all students must complete 132 credit hours, including 24 to 30 hours in the major, a cornerstone liberal arts core, 42 hours in 6 basic areas of study, and a minimal level of proficiency in written and oral communication and math. A minimum GPA of 2.0 is required.

Special: Internships are encouraged for students in most majors during the interterm of the sophomore year. Baker also offers study abroad, B.A.-B.S., dual majors, and pass/fail options. A 3-2 engineering degree may be earned in conjunction with Washington University and the University of Kansas. An interdisciplinary major is offered in molecular bioscience. There are 13 national honor societies, a freshman honors program, and 9 departmental honors programs.

Faculty/Classroom: 55% of faculty are male; 45%, female. All teach undergraduates and 25% both teach and do research. The average class size in an introductory lecture is 35; in a laboratory, 20; and in a regular course, 24.

Admissions: 82% of the 2003-2004 applicants were accepted. The SAT I scores for the 2003-2004 freshman class were: Verbal--39% below 500, 42% between 500 and 599, 17% between 600 and 700, and 2% above 700; Math--33% below 500, 47% between 500 and 599, and 20% between 600 and 700. The ACT scores were 20% below 21, 32% between 21 and 23, 25% between 24 and 26, 13% between 27 and 28, and 10% above 28. In a recent year, there were 6 National Merit semifinalists and 10 freshmen graduated first in their class.

Requirements: The SAT I or ACT is required. In addition, candidates for admission must graduate from an accredited secondary school or earn a GED. High school course work in English, a foreign language, social studies, math, and natural science is recommended. Applications of students not meeting these requirements will be reviewed, and students may be admitted on a probationary basis. Students are required to submit ACT or SAT I scores. A GPA of 3.0 is required. AP and CLEP credits are accepted.

Procedure: Freshmen are admitted fall and spring. Entrance exams should be taken in the fall of the senior year. There is a rolling admissions plan. Application deadlines are open. Application fee is $20. Applications are accepted on-line through CollegeNET and the school's web site.

Transfer: 40 transfer students enrolled in 2002-2003. Transfer applicants must supply a recommendation form, available from the Baker Admissions Office. The ACT or the SAT I score, official high school transcript, and official transcripts of all college courses are required. The minimum GPA is 2.3. 31 of 132 credits required for the bachelor's degree must be completed at Baker.

Visiting: There are regularly scheduled orientations for prospective students. Preview Days are scheduled for freshman in spring and in fall, and for transfers in spring and fall. Individual visits scheduled daily. There are guides for informal visits and visitors may sit in on classes and stay overnight. To schedule a visit, contact Admissions Office at admissions@bakeru.edu.

Financial Aid: In 2003-2004, 98% of all full-time freshmen and 95% of continuing full-time students received some form of financial aid. 59% of full-time freshmen and 69% of continuing full-time students received need-based aid. The average freshman award was $15,298. 38% of undergraduates work part time. Average annual earnings from campus work are $1000. The average financial indebtedness of the 2003 graduate was $18,500. Baker is a member of CSS. The FAFSA, the state aid form, and the college's own financial statement are required. The priority date for freshman financial aid applications for fall entry is March 1. There is no deadline for filing freshman financial aid applications. Applications are processed on a rolling basis.

International Students: There are 9 international students enrolled. The school actively recruits these students. They must score 525 on the written TOEFL.

Computers: The mainframe is an HP Vax. There are 124 PCs available for student use in computer labs. In addition, there are 19 terminals in residence halls for student access, and 32 for use around the library. There are 175 computers total for general access. All students may access the system. There are no time limits and no fees.

Graduates: From July 1, 2002 to June 30, 2003, 161 bachelor's degrees were awarded. The most popular majors were business (25%), phys ed (10%), and psychology (8%). In an average class, 2% graduate in 3 years or less, 64% graduate in 4 years or less, 37% graduate in 5 years or less, and 3% graduate in 6 years or less. Of the 2002 graduating class, 30% were enrolled in graduate school within 6 months of graduation and 72% were employed.

Admissions Contact: Charly Edmonds, Director of Admissions.
E-mail: admissions@bakeru.edu Web: www.bakeru.edu

BENEDICTINE COLLEGE
Atchison, KS 66002
E-1

(913) 367-5340, ext. 2476
(800) 467-5340; Fax: (913) 367-6102

Full-time: 499 men, 478 women	**Faculty:** 54
Part-time: 108 men, 186 women	**Ph.D.s:** 79%
Graduate: 39 men, 20 women	**Student/Faculty:** 18 to 1
Year: semesters, summer session	**Tuition:** $14,613
Application Deadline: open	**Room & Board:** $5990
Freshman Class: 580 applied, 556 accepted, 253 enrolled	
SAT I Verbal/Math: 517/511	**ACT:** 22 **COMPETITIVE**

Benedictine College, established in 1971, is a liberal arts, Catholic, Benedictine institution. In addition to regional accreditation, Benedictine has baccalaureate program accreditation with NASM and NCATE. The library contains 366,936 volumes, 36,440 microform items, and 839 audio/video tapes/CDs, and subscribes to 302 periodicals. Computerized library services include the card catalog, interlibrary loans, and database searching. Special learning facilities include a learning resource center. The 225-acre campus is in a small town 45 miles north of Kansas City. Including any residence halls, there are 18 buildings.

Student Life: 53% of undergraduates are from Kansas. Students are from 38 states and 18 foreign countries. 55% are from public schools. 81% are white. 68% are Catholic; 14% Protestant; 10% claim no religious affiliation. The average age of freshmen is 18; all undergraduates, 23. 30% do not continue beyond their first year.

Housing: 725 students can be accommodated in college housing, which includes single-sex dorms. On-campus housing is guaranteed for all 4 years. 82% of students live on campus. All students may keep cars.

Activities: There are no fraternities or sororities. There are 24 groups on campus, including band, cheerleading, choir, chorale, computers, drama, drill team, ethnic, honors, international, jazz band, literary magazine, musical theater, newspaper, orchestra, pep band, photography, political, professional, religious, social, social service, student government, symphony, and yearbook. Popular campus events include Discovery Week, Parents Weekend, and All School Mass.

Sports: There are 7 intercollegiate sports for men and 8 for women, and 7 intramural sports for men and 7 for women. Facilities include a gym, weight rooms, a football and track stadium, baseball, softball, and track fields, and an isometrics training room.

Disabled Students: 80% of the campus is accessible. Wheelchair ramps, elevators, special parking, specially equipped rest rooms, special class scheduling, and lowered drinking fountains are available.

Services: Counseling and information services are available, as is tutoring in most subjects. There is remedial math, reading, and writing.

Campus Safety and Security: Measures include 24-hour foot and vehicle patrol, informal discussions, pamphlets/posters/films, and lighted pathways/sidewalks.

Programs of Study: Benedictine confers B.A., B.S., and B.Mus.Ed. degrees. Associate and master's degrees are also awarded. Bachelor's degrees are awarded in BIOLOGICAL SCIENCE (biochemistry and biology/biological science), BUSINESS (accounting and business administration and management), COMMUNICATIONS AND THE ARTS (dramatic arts, English, French, journalism, music, Spanish, and theater management), COMPUTER AND PHYSICAL SCIENCE (astronomy, chemistry, computer science, mathematics, natural sciences, and physics), EDUCATION (athletic training, elementary, music, physical, secondary, and special), SOCIAL SCIENCE (economics, history, liberal arts/general studies, philosophy, political science/government, psychology, religion, social science, sociology, and youth ministry). Physical science, biology, and history are the strongest academically. Biology, education, and sociology are the largest.

Required: To graduate, students must complete 128 semester hours, pass a comprehensive exam in their major, and earn a minimum GPA of 2.0 overall and in the major. Curriculum requirements include 9 hours each in philosophy and religious studies, 8 hours each in English, natural science, and foreign language, 6 each in Western civilization and social science, 4 in math, 3 in fine arts, and 2 each in speech communication and phys ed. A dean's colloquium and a comprehensive exam are also required.

Special: Benedictine offers cross-registration with the 14 other members of the Kansas City Regional Council for Higher Education and study abroad in several countries. The school also offers a 3-2 occupational therapy program with Washington University of St. Louis and a 3-2 engineering degree. Internships, work-study programs, dual majors, an interdisciplinary music marketing major, student-designed majors, pass/fail options, and nondegree study are also available. There are 4 national honor societies and 4 departmental honors programs.

Faculty/Classroom: 66% of faculty are male; 34%, female. 96% teach undergraduates. No introductory courses are taught by graduate students. The average class size in an introductory lecture is 25; in a laboratory, 20; and in a regular course, 20.

Admissions: 96% of the 2003-2004 applicants were accepted. The SAT I scores for the 2003-2004 freshman class were: Verbal--34% below 500, 53% between 500 and 599, 12% between 600 and 700, and 3% above 700. 27% of the current freshmen were in the top fifth of their class; 65% were in the top two fifths.

Requirements: The ACT is required. In addition, applicants should graduate in the upper 50% of their class at an accredited secondary school. Students should have 16 academic units, including 4 in English, 3 to 4 in math, 2 to 4 in foreign language and science, 2 in social science, and 1 in history. An interview is recommended. Counselor recommendations are required. A GPA of 2.0 is required. AP and CLEP credits are accepted. Important factors in the admissions decision are advanced placement or honor courses, recommendations by school officials, and recommendations by alumni.

Procedure: Freshmen are admitted to all sessions. Entrance exams should be taken before the July following graduation from high school. There is a rolling admissions plan and a deferred admissions plan. Application deadlines are open. Application fee is $25. Applications are accepted on-line.

Transfer: 99 transfer students enrolled in 2002-2003. Applicants must submit transcripts from all colleges attended, a statement of courses in progress, and, if transferring with less than 60 hours, a high school transcript and ACT score. A minimum GPA of 2.0 is required. 30 of 128 credits required for the bachelor's degree must be completed at Benedictine.

Visiting: There are regularly scheduled orientations for prospective students, consisting of an advanced placement exam, preregistration, meetings with the dean, student affairs, and business office and financial aid representatives, and campus tours. The orientations are scheduled for April, June, and July. There are guides for informal visits, and visitors may sit in on classes and stay overnight. To schedule a visit, contact the Admissions Office at bcadmiss@benedictine.edu.

Financial Aid: In 2003-2004, 98% of all full-time freshmen and 95% of continuing full-time students received some form of financial aid. 74% of full-time freshmen and 75% of continuing full-time students received need-based aid. The average freshman award was $14,395. Need-based scholarships or need-based grants averaged $6480 ($13,500 maximum); need-based self-help aid (loans and jobs) averaged $5425 ($7625 maximum); non-need-based athletic scholarships averaged $6885 ($13,500 maximum); and other non-need-based awards and non-need-based scholarships averaged $2500 ($4000 maximum). 41% of undergraduates work part time. Average annual earnings from campus work are

$900. The average financial indebtedness of the 2003 graduate was $20,822. Benedictine is a member of CSS. The FAFSA and the college's own financial statement are required. The deadline for filing freshman financial aid applications for fall entry is April 1.

International Students: There are 38 international students enrolled. The school actively recruits these students. They must score 535 on the written TOEFL or take the MELAB, and also take the SAT I or the ACT, scoring 18.

Computers: The mainframe is an HP 9000 D 380. There are 2 labs containing 18 Macs and 2 with 20 PCs. Smaller clusters of PCs are available in residence halls and the library building. Each residence hall room has Ethernet access. All students may access the system 24 hours a day in residence halls and 7:45 A.M. to 11 P.M. weekdays, with shorter hours on weekends. There are no time limits and no fees.

Graduates: From July 1, 2002 to June 30, 2003, 174 bachelor's degrees were awarded. The most popular majors were business/marketing (25%), social sciences and history (19%), and education (18%). In an average class, 36% graduate in 4 years or less, 45% graduate in 5 years or less, and 46% graduate in 6 years or less. 26 companies recruited on campus in 2002-2003. Of the 2002 graduating class, 18% were enrolled in graduate school within 6 months of graduation and 63% were employed.

Admissions Contact: Kelly Vowels, Dean of Enrollment Management. E-mail: *kvowels@raven.benedictine.edu* Web: *www.benedictine.edu*

BETHANY COLLEGE
Lindsborg, KS 67456

D-2

(785) 227-3311
(800) 826-2281; Fax: (785) 227-2004

Full-time: 320 men, 259 women	**Faculty:** 42; IIB, --$
Part-time: 31 men, 21 women	**Ph.D.s:** 50%
Graduate: none	**Student/Faculty:** 14 to 1
Year: 4-1-4, summer session	**Tuition:** $14,140
Application Deadline: May 1	**Room & Board:** $4535
Freshman Class: 775 applied, 548 accepted, 172 enrolled	
SAT I Verbal/Math: 450/480	**ACT:** 21 **LESS COMPETITIVE**

Bethany College, founded in 1881, is a private small liberal arts institution affiliated with the Evangelical Lutheran Church in America. There is 1 undergraduate school. In addition to regional accreditation, Bethany has baccalaureate program accreditation with CSWE, NASM, and NCATE. The library contains 110,000 volumes, 59,000 microform items, and 3800 audio/video tapes/CDs, and subscribes to 200 periodicals. Computerized library services include interlibrary loans and database searching. Special learning facilities include a learning resource center and art gallery. The 80-acre campus is in a small town 65 miles north of Wichita and 20 miles south of Salina. Including any residence halls, there are 17 buildings.

Student Life: 59% of undergraduates are from Kansas. Students are from 28 states, 11 foreign countries, and Canada. 98% are from public schools. 81% are white. 61% are Protestant; 13% Catholic. The average age of freshmen is 18; all undergraduates, 20. 22% do not continue beyond their first year; 45% remain to graduate.

Housing: 605 students can be accommodated in college housing, which includes single-sex and coed dorms and on-campus apartments. In addition, there are special-interest houses. On-campus housing is available on a first-come, first-served basis. 72% of students live on campus; of those, 80% remain on campus on weekends. Alcohol is not permitted. All students may keep cars.

Activities: 15% of men belong to 3 local fraternities; 18% of women belong to 3 local sororities. There are 62 groups on campus, including art, band, cheerleading, chess, choir, chorale, chorus, drama, drill team, ethnic, gay, honors, international, jazz band, musical theater, newspaper, orchestra, pep band, photography, professional, religious, social, social service, student government, symphony, and yearbook. Popular campus events include the Messiah Festival of Art and Music Holy Week Festival.

Sports: There are 8 intercollegiate sports for men and 7 for women, and 15 intramural sports for men and 15 for women. Facilities include a 1500-seat gym, a 4000-seat stadium, tennis courts, track and field facilities, handball/racquetball courts, a weight training area, 2 softball and 1 baseball diamond, a soccer field, and a 2-court practice gym.

Disabled Students: 98% of the campus is accessible. Wheelchair ramps, elevators, special parking, specially equipped rest rooms, special class scheduling, and lowered drinking fountains are available.

Services: Counseling and information services are available, as is tutoring in every subject.

Campus Safety and Security: Measures include self-defense education, security escort services, informal discussions, and pamphlets/posters/films. There are emergency telephones, lighted pathways/sidewalks, and a campus patrol at night; residence halls are locked from midnight to 9 A.M.

Programs of Study: Bethany confers the B.A. degree. Bachelor's degrees are awarded in BIOLOGICAL SCIENCE (biology/biological science), BUSINESS (business administration and management and business economics), COMMUNICATIONS AND THE ARTS (art,

communications, English, fine arts, and music), COMPUTER AND PHYSICAL SCIENCE (chemistry and mathematics), EDUCATION (art, athletic training, business, Christian, elementary, English, mathematics, middle school, music, physical, science, and secondary), HEALTH PROFESSIONS (predentistry and premedicine), SOCIAL SCIENCE (criminal justice, economics, history, ministries, parks and recreation management, prelaw, psychology, social science, and social work). Chemistry, English, and history are the strongest academically. Business and education are the largest.

Required: All students must complete 28 to 39 semester hours of general education requirements, including the courses Thinking and Writing and Christianity in the Global Context. A total of 34 semester hours must be in 300-level courses. A total of 128 credit hours with a minimum GPA of 2.0 is required for graduation.

Special: Bethany offers co-op programs and cross-registration through the Associated Colleges of Central Kansas and a 3-2 engineering degree with Wichita State University. Internships, a Chicago semester, a Washington semester, work-study programs, accelerated degree programs in economics/business and pre-engineering, dual majors, including history-political science and religion-philosophy, student-designed majors, and limited pass/fail options are also available. There are 6 national honor societies.

Faculty/Classroom: 53% of faculty are male; 47%, female. All teach undergraduates. The average class size in an introductory lecture is 30; in a laboratory, 8; and in a regular course, 22.

Admissions: The SAT I scores for the 2003-2004 freshman class were: Verbal--68% below 500, 31% between 500 and 599, and 1% between 600 and 700; Math--49% below 500, 42% between 500 and 599, and 9% between 600 and 700. The ACT scores were 45% below 21, 29% between 21 and 23, 19% between 24 and 26, 4% between 27 and 28, and 3% above 28. 26% of the current freshmen were in the top fifth of their class; 54% were in the top two fifths. 6 freshmen graduated first in their class.

Requirements: The ACT is required. In addition, applicants should be graduates of an accredited secondary school, with 4 years of English, 3 of social studies, 2 each of math and science, and 1 each of foreign language and phys ed. The GED is accepted. An interview is recommended, along with a portfolio or an audition for some majors. Bethany requires applicants to be in the upper 50% of their class. A GPA of 2.5 is required. AP and CLEP credits are accepted. Important factors in the admissions decision are advanced placement or honor courses, leadership record, and evidence of special talent.

Procedure: Freshmen are admitted to all sessions. There is a rolling admissions plan. Applications should be filed by May 1 for fall entry, December 15 for winter entry, and January 15 for spring entry, along with a $20 fee. Notification is sent on a rolling basis. Applications are accepted on-line.

Transfer: 66 transfer students enrolled in 2002-2003. A GPA of 2.3 in 24 credit hours is required. 32 of the last 40 credits required for the bachelor's degree must be completed at Bethany.

Visiting: There are regularly scheduled orientations for prospective students, including campus tours, a faculty visit, class enrollment, and a financial aid visit. There are guides for informal visits, and visitors may sit in on classes and stay overnight. To schedule a visit, contact the Office of Admissions at *admissions@bethanylb.edu*.

Financial Aid: In 2003-2004, all full-time freshmen and 98% of continuing full-time students received some form of financial aid. 80% of full-time freshmen and 83% of continuing full-time students received need-based aid. The average freshman award was $15,277. Need-based scholarships or need-based grants averaged $4640 ($9000 maximum); need-based self-help aid (loans and jobs) averaged $5506 ($6625 maximum); non-need-based athletic scholarships averaged $3132 ($4245 maximum); and other non-need-based awards and non-need-based scholarships averaged $4485 ($14,140 maximum). 84% of undergraduates work part time. Average annual earnings from campus work are $987. The average financial indebtedness of the 2003 graduate was $15,167. The priority date for freshman financial aid applications for fall entry is March 15. The deadline for filing freshman financial aid applications for fall entry is May 1.

International Students: There are 14 international students enrolled. The school actively recruits these students. They must score 525 on the written TOEFL and also take the SAT I or the ACT.

Computers: There is a networked computer system with an 8 to 1 student to computer ratio. There are 2 labs with 40 computers. All students may access the system from 6 A.M. to midnight. There are no time limits and no fees.

Graduates: From July 1, 2002 to June 30, 2003, 118 bachelor's degrees were awarded. The most popular majors were economics and business (22%), education (22%), and communication (11%). In an average class, 1% graduate in 3 years or less, 39% graduate in 4 years or less, 45% graduate in 5 years or less, and 47% graduate in 6 years or less. 3 companies recruited on campus in 2002-2003. Of the 2002 graduating class, 23% were enrolled in graduate school within 6 months of graduation and 44% were employed.

Admissions Contact: Thandabantu Maceo, Dean of Enrollment Management. A video is available. E-mail: *maceot@bethanylb.edu*
Web: *www.bethanylb.edu*

BETHEL COLLEGE
North Newton, KS 67117

D-3

(316) 284-5230
(800) 522-1887, ext. 230; Fax: (316) 284-5870

Full-time: 211 men, 224 women	**Faculty:** 45; IIB, --$
Part-time: 11 men, 24 women	**Ph.Ds:** 62%
Graduate: none	**Student/Faculty:** 10 to 1
Year: 4-1-4, summer session	**Tuition:** $13,900
Application Deadline: open	**Room & Board:** $5900
Freshman Class: 527 applied, 378 accepted, 98 enrolled	
SAT I Verbal/Math: 510/540	**ACT:** 24	**COMPETITIVE+**

Bethel College, established in 1887, is a private liberal arts institution affiliated with the Mennonite Church U.S.A. There is 1 undergraduate school. In addition to regional accreditation, Bethel has baccalaureate program accreditation with CSWE and CCNE. The 2 libraries contain 138,741 volumes, 13,792 microform items, and 5832 audio/video tapes/CDs, and subscribe to 571 periodicals. Computerized library services include the card catalog, interlibrary loans, database searching, and Internet access. Special learning facilities include a learning resource center, art gallery, natural history museum, radio station, and an observatory. The 60-acre campus is in a suburban area 25 miles north of Wichita. Including any residence halls, there are 20 buildings.

Student Life: 69% of undergraduates are from Kansas. Students are from 26 states, 15 foreign countries, and Canada. 94% are from public schools. 80% are white. 33% are Protestant; 15% claim no religious affiliation; 7% Catholic. The average age of freshmen is 18; all undergraduates, 22. 25% do not continue beyond their first year; 52% remain to graduate.

Housing: 500 students can be accommodated in college housing, which includes single-sex and coed dorms, off-campus apartments, and married-student housing. On-campus housing is guaranteed for all 4 years. 74% of students live on campus; of those, 80% remain on campus on weekends. Alcohol is not permitted. All students may keep cars.

Activities: There are no fraternities or sororities. There are 40 groups on campus, including art, chess, choir, chorale, chorus, computers, dance, debate, drama, ethnic, forensics, international, jazz band, literary magazine, musical theater, newspaper, opera, orchestra, pep band, radio and TV, religious, social, social service, student government, symphony, and yearbook. Popular campus events include Fall Festival, Winter Frolic, and Spring Fling.

Sports: There are 7 intercollegiate sports for men and 7 for women, and 7 intramural sports for men and 7 for women. Facilities include two gyms, a weight room, an exercise room, tennis courts, a soccer field, an all-weather track, football and baseball fields, an outdoor basketball court, an outdoor sand volleyball court, and a nature trail.

Disabled Students: 70% of the campus is accessible. Wheelchair ramps, elevators, special parking, specially equipped rest rooms, lowered drinking fountains, and special housing are available.

Services: Counseling and information services are available, as is tutoring in most subjects. There is a reader service for the blind, and remedial math, reading, and writing.

Campus Safety and Security: Measures include security escort services, informal discussions, emergency telephones, and lighted pathways/sidewalks.

Programs of Study: Bethel confers B.A., B.S., B.S.N., and B.S.S.W. degrees. Bachelor's degrees are awarded in BIOLOGICAL SCIENCE (biology/biological science), BUSINESS (business administration and management), COMMUNICATIONS AND THE ARTS (art, communications, dramatic arts, English, fine arts, German, music, and Spanish), COMPUTER AND PHYSICAL SCIENCE (chemistry, computer management, computer science, information sciences and systems, mathematics, natural sciences, and physics), EDUCATION (athletic training and elementary), HEALTH PROFESSIONS (health science and nursing), SOCIAL SCIENCE (community services, history, peace studies, psychology, religion, social science, and social work). English, biology, and psychology are the strongest academically. Nursing, elementary education, and business administration are the largest.

Required: To graduate, students must earn a total of 124 credits, including 24 to 50 in the major, 12 to 50 of those in upper-level courses, with a GPA of 2.0. Students must also meet general education requirements that include demonstrating competency in writing, math, speech, computers, and foreign language. Additional distribution requirements include convocation, religious studies, natural sciences, math or philosophy, cross-cultural learning, social sciences, humanities, fine arts, and health management.

Special: Students may cross-register with Associated Colleges of Central Kansas (ACCK) institutions and Hesston College. Internships are required in many majors. Work-study programs, study abroad in 15 countries, dual majors, and a Washington semester are available. The college offers a 3-2 engineering degree with University of Kansas, Kansas State University, and Wichita State University.

Faculty/Classroom: 60% of faculty are male; 40%, female. All teach undergraduates, 50% do research, and 50% do both. The average class size in an introductory lecture is 24; in a laboratory, 12; and in a regular course, 14.

Admissions: 72% of the 2003-2004 applicants were accepted. The SAT I scores for the 2003-2004 freshman class were: Verbal--44% below 500, 33% between 500 and 599, and 22% between 600 and 700; Math--33% below 500, 44% between 500 and 599, and 22% above 700. The ACT scores were 28% below 21, 20% between 21 and 23, 24% between 24 and 26, 13% between 27 and 28, and 15% above 28. 44% of the current freshmen were in the top fifth of their class; 73% were in the top two fifths. There was 1 National Merit semifinalist. 12 freshmen graduated first in their class.

Requirements: The SAT I or ACT is required. Applicants should present a minimum ACT composite of 19 or SAT I total of 890 with a minimum GPA of 2.5 for automatic admission. The GED is accepted. Auditions are required of candidates applying for some scholarships, and interviews are recommended for all applicants. Specific departmental requirements may vary. CLEP, AP, and International Baccalaureate credit may be awarded. A GPA of 2.0 is required. Important factors in the admissions decision are evidence of special talent, recommendations by alumni, and parents or siblings attending the school.

Procedure: Freshmen are admitted to all sessions. Entrance exams should be taken by the fall of the senior year. There is a rolling admissions plan. Application deadlines are open. Application fee is $20. Applications are accepted on-line through the college's web site.

Transfer: 56 transfer students enrolled in 2002-2003. A high school transcript (or GED) or official college transcript (minimum 2.0 GPA), ACT or SAT I scores (waived if the student has more than 24 hours accepted in transfer to Bethel College), and a transfer recommendation are required. Automatic admission requires a cumulative GPA of 2.0 and a 19 ACT or 890 SAT I score. 30 of 124 credits required for the bachelor's degree must be completed at Bethel.

Visiting: There are regularly scheduled orientations for prospective students, including a campus tour, visits with faculty, an interview with an admissions counselor, and lunch. There are guides for informal visits, and visitors may sit in on classes and stay overnight. To schedule a visit, contact the Admissions Office.

Financial Aid: In 2003-2004, 98% of all full-time freshmen and 86% of continuing full-time students received some form of financial aid. 68% of full-time freshmen and 71% of continuing full-time students received need-based aid. The average freshman award was $15,852. Need-based scholarships or need-based grants averaged $4744; need-based self-help aid (loans and jobs) averaged $5396; and non-need-based athletic scholarships averaged $2334. 78% of undergraduates work part time. Average annual earnings from campus work are $823. The average financial indebtedness of the 2003 graduate was $15,927. Bethel is a member of CSS. The FAFSA is required.

International Students: There are 16 international students enrolled. They must score 540 on the written TOEFL or 207 on the electronic version.

Computers: The mainframe consists of IBM PC servers with NT software. 30 IBM and Mac PCs with printers are available in the campus computer center, library, and music and nursing labs. All students may access the system 18 hours a day. There are no time limits and no fees.

Graduates: From July 1, 2002 to June 30, 2003, 97 bachelor's degrees were awarded. The most popular majors were business administration (16%), nursing (11%), and elementary education (10%). In an average class, 40% graduate in 4 years or less, 48% graduate in 5 years or less, and 52% graduate in 6 years or less. Of a recent graduating class, 9% were enrolled in graduate school within 6 months of graduation, and 98% were employed.

Admissions Contact: Allan Bartel, Director of Admissions & Enrollment. A video is available. E-mail: *admissions@bethelks.edu*
Web: *http://www.bethelks.edu*

EMPORIA STATE UNIVERSITY
Emporia, KS 66801-5087

E-2

(620) 341-5465
(877) GO-TO-ESU; Fax: (620) 341-5599

Full-time: 1519 men, 2333 women	**Faculty:** 245; IIA, --$
Part-time: 204 men, 378 women	**Ph.Ds:** 82%
Graduate: 490 men, 1354 women	**Student/Faculty:** 16 to 1
Year: semesters, summer session	**Tuition:** $2776 ($8914)
Application Deadline: open	**Room & Board:** $4222
Freshman Class: 1477 applied, 1090 accepted, 817 enrolled	
ACT: 22	**COMPETITIVE**

Emporia State University, founded in 1863, is a state-supported institution that offers degree programs in liberal arts, business, teacher education, and vocational fields, as well as various graduate programs. There are 3 undergraduate schools and 1 graduate school. In addition to regional accreditation, ESU has baccalaureate program accreditation with AACSB, ACS, CAAHEP, NASM, NCATE, and NLN. The library contains 569,802 volumes, 1,173,546 microform items, and 8180 audio/

video tapes/CDs, and subscribes to 1233 periodicals. Computerized library services include the card catalog, interlibrary loans, and database searching. Special learning facilities include a learning resource center, art gallery, natural history museum, planetarium, a theater, geology museum, and Great Plains study center. The 207-acre campus is in a small town 110 miles from Kansas City in the Bluestem Region of the Flint Hills. Including any residence halls, there are 20 buildings.

Student Life: 94% of undergraduates are from Kansas. Students are from 40 states, 49 foreign countries, and Canada. 97% are from public schools. 82% are white. The average age of freshmen is 20; all undergraduates, 23. 34% do not continue beyond their first year; 66% remain to graduate.

Housing: 1178 students can be accommodated in college housing, which includes single-sex and coed dormitories and on-campus apartments. In addition, there are honors houses, special-interest houses, upperclass houses, and nonsmoking and alcohol-free living areas. On-campus housing is guaranteed for the freshman year only and is available on a first-come, first-served basis. Priority is given to out-of-town students. 74% of students commute. All students may keep cars.

Activities: 8% of men belong to 6 national fraternities; 8% of women belong to 4 national sororities. There are 112 groups on campus, including art, band, cheerleading, choir, chorale, chorus, computers, drama, drill team, ethnic, film, gay, honors, international, jazz band, literary magazine, marching band, musical theater, newspaper, opera, orchestra, pep band, political, professional, religious, social, social service, student government, symphony, and yearbook. Popular campus events include Family Day and Flintstock.

Sports: There are 7 intercollegiate sports for men and 8 for women, and 12 intramural sports for men and 12 for women. Facilities include a 7000-seat stadium, a recreation center, an Olympic-size pool, 5 gyms, 6 handball courts, exercise, physical therapy, and dance rooms, a sports complex with 3 softball fields and 1 baseball diamond, an all-weather 8-lane track, a soccer field, and 3 additional softball fields separate from the sports complex.

Disabled Students: All of the campus is accessible. Wheelchair ramps, elevators, special parking, specially equipped rest rooms, special class scheduling, lowered drinking fountains, lowered telephones, and special housing are available.

Services: There is a reader service for the blind, and remedial math, reading, and writing.

Campus Safety and Security: Measures include 24-hour foot and vehicle patrol, security escort services, informal discussions, and pamphlets/posters/films. There are emergency telephones, lighted pathways/sidewalks, and motorist-assist programs, safety and self-awareness programs for students and parents, 24-hour residence hall monitoring, and smoke detectors in residence halls.

Programs of Study: ESU confers B.A., B.S., B.F.A., B.I.S., B Mus., B.Mus.Ed., B.S.Bus., B.S.Ed., and B.S.N. degrees. Master's and doctoral degrees are also awarded. Bachelor's degrees are awarded in BIOLOGICAL SCIENCE (biology/biological science), BUSINESS (accounting, business administration and management, management information systems, management science, marketing/retailing/merchandising, and recreation and leisure services), COMMUNICATIONS AND THE ARTS (art, communications, dramatic arts, English, and music), COMPUTER AND PHYSICAL SCIENCE (chemistry, computer science, earth science, information sciences and systems, mathematics, physical sciences, and physics), EDUCATION (art, athletic training, business, elementary, foreign languages, health, music, physical, and secondary), HEALTH PROFESSIONS (nursing and rehabilitation therapy), SOCIAL SCIENCE (economics, history, liberal arts/general studies, political science/government, psychology, social science, and sociology). Elementary education is the largest.

Required: To graduate, all students must complete at least 124 credit hours, including 40 in upper-division courses, with a minimum GPA of 2.0. Students must also pass competency exams in reading, math, and writing and complete the general education program for their field of study, which includes courses in math, physical and applied science, humanities, history, speech, cultural diversity, fitness and phys eds.

Special: ESU offers internships in many majors, study abroad in 32 countries, work-study programs, on-campus and on-line general studies degrees, B.A.-B.S. degrees, dual and student-designed majors, 3-2 engineering degrees with Kansas State University, Wichita State University, and the University of Kansas, credit for military experience, nondegree study, independent study, evening and Saturday classes, and pass/no credit options.There is also a law librarian graduate degree program with the University of Kansas. There are 17 national honor societies and a freshman honors program.

Faculty/Classroom: 66% of faculty are male; 34%, female. The average class size in an introductory lecture is 29; in a laboratory, 17; and in a regular course, 22.

Admissions: 74% of the 2003-2004 applicants were accepted.

Requirements: The ACT is required. In addition, applicants must meet 1 of these 3 criteria: an ACT score of 21 or above, class rank in the top third, or a 2.0 GPA in the Kansas core curriculum in-state; 2.5 for out-of-state applicants. Students should have completed 4 units of English, 3 each of natural science, math, and social science, and 1 of computer technology. Applicants may also be admitted through an exceptions window and are encouraged to apply. ESU requires applicants to be in the upper 67% of their class. A GPA of 2.0 is required. AP and CLEP credits are accepted.

Procedure: Freshmen are admitted to all sessions. Entrance exams should be taken in October or December of the senior year. There is a rolling admissions plan, as well as early admissions and deferred admissions plans. Application deadlines are open. A waiting list is an active part of the admissions procedure. Applications are accepted on-line through the school's web site, *www.applyweb.com/apply/emporia/menu.html*.

Transfer: 476 transfer students enrolled in 2002-2003. Applicants must submit official transcripts of all previous college work. The minimum GPA depends on the number of semester hours earned. Physical activity requirements must be met. 30 of 124 credits required for the bachelor's degree must be completed at ESU.

Visiting: There are regularly scheduled orientations for prospective students, including campus and residence hall tours, meetings with admissions and financial aid personnel, and appointments with academic and extracurricular personnel, if desired. There are guides for informal visits, and visitors may sit in on classes and stay overnight. To schedule a visit, contact Laura Eddy, Interim Director of Admissions at *go2esu@emporia.edu*.

Financial Aid: In 2003-2004, 53% of all full-time freshmen and 67% of continuing full-time students received some form of financial aid. 48% of full-time freshmen and 56% of continuing full-time students received need-based aid. The average freshman award was $5145. Need-based scholarships or need-based grants averaged $3315; need-based self-help aid (loans and jobs) averaged $2742; and non-need-based athletic scholarships averaged $2356. 16% of undergraduates work part time. Average annual earnings from campus work are $2178. The average financial indebtedness of the 2003 graduate was $13,036. The FAFSA and the state aid form are required. The priority date for freshman financial aid applications for fall entry is March 15.

International Students: There are 99 international students enrolled. The school actively recruits these students. They must score 450 on the written TOEFL or 133 on the electronic version or take the MELAB or the college's own test. They must also take the ACT, scoring 21.

Computers: The mainframe is an IBM 2003 Model 215. Internet access is available from labs on campus and in the library using Ethernet, in residence halls, or through the purchase of dial-up service. All students may access the system 22 hours per day. There are no time limits. The fee is $70 for a dial-up account.

Graduates: From July 1, 2002 to June 30, 2003, 758 bachelor's degrees were awarded. The most popular majors were elementary education (19%), business administration (7%), and sociology (5%). In an average class, 23% graduate in 4 years or less, 38% graduate in 5 years or less, and 43% graduate in 6 years or less. 238 companies recruited on campus in 2002-2003. Of the 2002 graduating class, 26% were enrolled in graduate school within 6 months of graduation and 70% were employed.

Admissions Contact: Laura Eddy, Interim Director of Admissions. E-mail: *go2esu@emporia.edu* Web: *www.emporia.edu*

FORT HAYS STATE UNIVERSITY
C-2
Hays, KS 67601-4099
(785) 628-5666
(800) 628-FHSU; Fax: (785) 628-4014

Full-time: 1949 men, 2177 women	Faculty: 261; IIA, --$
Part-time: 796 men, 998 women	Ph.D.s: 77%
Graduate: 524 men, 929 women	Student/Faculty: 16 to 1
Year: semesters, summer session	Tuition: $2540 ($8165)
Application Deadline: open	Room & Board: $4823
Freshman Class: 1407 accepted, 882 enrolled	
SAT I: n/av	ACT: recommended
	COMPETITIVE

Fort Hays State University, established in 1902, is a public liberal arts institution offering programs in arts and sciences, business and leadership, education, health and life sciences, and preprofessional study. There are 4 undergraduate schools and 1 graduate school. In addition to regional accreditation, FHSU has baccalaureate program accreditation with AACSB, NASM, NCATE, and NLN. The library contains 300,000 volumes, 500,000 microform items, and 1480 audio/video tapes/CDs, and subscribes to 3100 periodicals. Computerized library services include the card catalog, interlibrary loans, and database searching. Special learning facilities include an art gallery, radio station, TV station, and an English lab. The 200-acre campus is in a small town 180 miles northwest of Wichita. Including any residence halls, there are 44 buildings.

Student Life: 93% of undergraduates are from Kansas. Students are from 36 states, 32 foreign countries, and Canada. 95% are from public schools. 87% are white. The average age of freshmen is 18; all under-

graduates, 23. 61% do not continue beyond their first year; 40% remain to graduate.

Housing: 1000 students can be accommodated in college housing, which includes single-sex and coed dorms, on-campus apartments, married-student housing, fraternity houses, sorority houses, apartments for students with families, and apartments for nontraditional-age students. 82% of students commute. All students may keep cars.

Activities: 1% of men belong to 3 national fraternities; 1% of women belong to 3 national sororities. There are 85 groups on campus, including art, band, cheerleading, choir, chorale, chorus, computers, dance, debate, drama, drill team, ethnic, film, gay, honors, international, jazz band, literary magazine, marching band, musical theater, newspaper, opera, orchestra, pep band, photography, political, professional, radio and TV, religious, social, social service, student government, symphony, and yearbook. Popular campus events include Octoberfest and Parents Day.

Sports: There are 8 intercollegiate sports for men and 7 for women, and 40 intramural sports for men and 40 for women. Facilities include a 6300-seat stadium, tennis courts, and a coliseum containing a 6800-seat basketball arena, a track, and wrestling and training rooms.

Disabled Students: 95% of the campus is accessible. Wheelchair ramps, elevators, special parking, specially equipped rest rooms, special class scheduling, lowered drinking fountains, lowered telephones, and an Arkenstone reader, TDD, and voice dictation programs are available.

Services: Counseling and information services are available, as is tutoring in most subjects. There is remedial math and reading.

Campus Safety and Security: Measures include 24-hour foot and vehicle patrol, security escort services, informal discussions, emergency telephones, and lighted pathways/sidewalks.

Programs of Study: FHSU confers B.A., B.S., B.B.A., B.F.A., B.G.S., B.M., and B.S.W. degrees. Associate and master's degrees are also awarded. Bachelor's degrees are awarded in AGRICULTURE (agricultural business management and agriculture), BIOLOGICAL SCIENCE (biology/biological science), BUSINESS (accounting, banking and finance, business administration and management, management information systems, marketing/retailing/merchandising, and office supervision and management), COMMUNICATIONS AND THE ARTS (art, communications, English, fine arts, French, German, modern language, music, music performance, music theory and composition, Spanish, and telecommunications), COMPUTER AND PHYSICAL SCIENCE (chemistry, computer science, geology, information sciences and systems, mathematics, physical sciences, physics, radiological technology, and science), EDUCATION (art, elementary, music, physical, and technical), HEALTH PROFESSIONS (nursing and speech pathology/audiology), SOCIAL SCIENCE (criminal justice, economics, history, liberal arts/general studies, philosophy, political science/government, psychology, social work, and sociology). Speech pathology is the strongest academically. Interdisciplinary studies, teacher education, and business administration are the largest.

Required: To graduate, students must earn an overall minimum GPA of 2.0 or higher in some departments for 124 credit hours, including 40 hours in upper-level study and 30 hours minimum in the major. The 55-hour liberal arts general education curriculum includes courses addressing personal wellness, analysis and communication, international studies, humanities, math, and natural, social, and behavioral sciences.

Special: Students may, with approval, earn their degrees through a cooperative program with FHSU and another accredited institution, or a correspondence or extension school. Cross-registration with several community colleges, internships, study abroad, work-study programs, a 3-2 engineering degree with Kansas State University, B.A.-B.S. degrees, a general studies degree, and pass/fail options are available. There are 21 national honor societies and a freshman honors program.

Faculty/Classroom: 59% of faculty are male; 41%, female. All teach undergraduates. The average class size in an introductory lecture is 17; in a laboratory, 17; and in a regular course, 18.

Admissions: The ACT scores for the freshman class in a recent year were: 47% below 21, 24% between 21 and 23, 18% between 24 and 26, 6% between 27 and 28, and 5% above 28.

Requirements: The ACT is recommended. In addition, candidates for admission who are residents of Kansas must graduate from an accredited secondary school or earn a GED, with a minimum GPA of 2.0. Nonresidents must have earned better than a 2.0 GPA as well. AP and CLEP credits are accepted.

Procedure: Freshmen are admitted fall, spring, and summer. Entrance exams should be taken in the senior year. There is a rolling admissions plan. Application deadlines are open. Application fee is $30. Applications are accepted on-line through CollegeNET.

Transfer: 567 transfer students enrolled in fall 2003. Applicants must have a minimum college GPA of 2.0 and submit official college transcripts from all institutions previously attended. 30 of 124 credits required for the bachelor's degree must be completed at FHSU.

Visiting: There are regularly scheduled orientations for prospective students. There are guides for informal visits, and visitors may sit in on classes and stay overnight. To schedule a visit, contact the Office of Admissions, Campus Tour Coordinator.

Financial Aid: In a recent year, 78% of all full-time freshmen and 70% of continuing full-time students received some form of financial aid. 60% of undergraduates work part time. Average annual earnings from campus work are $1200. The FFS and the college's own financial statement are required. Check with the school for current application deadlines.

International Students: There are 117 international students enrolled. The school actively recruits these students. They must score 500 on the written TOEFL or 173 on the electronic version.

Computers: The mainframe is an IBM ES/9000 Model 9121. The system may be accessed by modem and by terminals located in dorms and in PC labs in each residence hall and each major academic building. Students can dial into the web using a pool of 48 modems on the campus backbone. There are at least 225 PCs with web access in student labs. All students may access the system The modem pool may be used 24 hours a day, the labs until 11 P.M. There are no time limits and no fees.

Graduates: From July 1, 2002 to June 30, 2003, 936 bachelor's degrees were awarded. The most popular majors were elementary education (12%), nursing (9%), and management (5%). 160 companies recruited on campus in 2002-2003. Of the 2002 graduating class, 16% were enrolled in graduate school within 6 months of graduation and 90% were employed.

Admissions Contact: Roger Schieferecke, Director of Admissions. A video is available. E-mail: *tigers@fhsu.edu* Web: *www.fhsu.edu*

FRIENDS UNIVERSITY
D-3
Wichita, KS 67213

(316) 295-5100
(800) 577-2233; Fax: (316) 295-5101

Full-time: 395 men, 520 women	**Faculty:** IIA, --$
Part-time: 100 men and women	**Ph.D.s:** n/av
Graduate: 275 men, 290 women	**Student/Faculty:** n/av
Year: semesters, summer session	**Tuition:** $13,620
Application Deadline: open	**Room & Board:** $3715
Freshman Class: n/av	
SAT I or ACT: required	**LESS COMPETITIVE**

Friends University, established in 1898, is an interdenominational institution offering undergraduate and graduate degrees through the Colleges of Arts and Sciences, Business and Information Technology, and Adult and Professional Studies. Figures in the above capsule and in this profile are approximate. There are 3 undergraduate and 3 graduate schools. In addition to regional accreditation, Friends has baccalaureate program accreditation with NASM and NCATE. The library contains 75,540 volumes, 319,861 microform items, and 13,135 audio/video tapes/CDs, and subscribes to 321 periodicals. Computerized library services include the card catalog, interlibrary loans, and database searching. Special learning facilities include a learning resource center, art gallery, and observatory. The 54-acre campus is in an urban area 200 miles southwest of Kansas City. Including any residence halls, there are 15 buildings.

Student Life: 71% are white. 86% are Protestant; 10% Catholic. The average age of freshmen is 19; all undergraduates, 21.

Housing: 326 students can be accommodated in college housing, which includes single-sex dorms, on-campus apartments, and off-campus apartments. On-campus housing is available on a first-come, first-served basis. Alcohol is not permitted. All students may keep cars.

Activities: There is 1 local fraternity and 1 national sorority. There are many groups and organizations on campus, including art, band, cheerleading, choir, chorale, chorus, computers, dance, drama, ethnic, honors, international, jazz band, musical theater, orchestra, pep band, photography, political, professional, religious, social, social service, student government, symphony, yearbook, and yell-leading. Popular campus events include Christian Emphasis Week, Cherry Carnival, and Symphony of Spring.

Sports: There are 9 intercollegiate sports for men and 8 for women, and 6 intramural sports for men and 6 for women. Facilities include a 2600-seat stadium and athletic field for football and soccer, a phys ed center with basketball and racquetball courts, an intramural gym, and tennis courts.

Disabled Students: 95% of the campus is accessible. Wheelchair ramps, elevators, special parking, specially equipped rest rooms, special class scheduling, lowered drinking fountains, and lowered telephones are available.

Services: Counseling and information services are available, as is tutoring in most subjects.

Campus Safety and Security: Measures include 24-hour foot and vehicle patrol, pamphlets/posters/films, and lighted pathways/sidewalks.

Programs of Study: Friends confers B.A., B.S., B.B.A., B.F.A., and B.Mus. degrees. Associate and master's degrees are also awarded. Bachelor's degrees are awarded in BIOLOGICAL SCIENCE (biology/biological science and zoology), BUSINESS (accounting, business administration and management, international business management, and management information systems), COMMUNICATIONS AND THE ARTS (art, ballet, English, fine arts, music, musical theater, and Spanish), COMPUTER AND PHYSICAL SCIENCE (chemistry, computer science, information sciences and systems, mathematics, and radiological technology), EDUCATION (art, business, elementary, English, foreign languages, health, music, science, secondary, and social science), ENGINEERING AND ENVIRONMENTAL DESIGN (environmental science), HEALTH PROFESSIONS (premedicine), SOCIAL SCIENCE (history, human services, political science/government, psychology, and religion). Science is the strongest academically. Business and education are the largest.

Required: To graduate, students must complete 124 credit hours, including 33 to 54 in general education (varies by degree sought) and 24 to 45 in the major, with a minimum GPA of 2.0. Distribution requirements include course work in humanities, fine arts, religion and philosophy, behavioral science, and natural science.

Special: Students may cross-register with Newman University, and they can pursue internships in their majors. A study-abroad program is available in Cancun, Mexico, and several Asian countries. Friends offers accelerated degree programs in business management, organizational management and leadership, computer information systems, criminal justice, and electronic commerce management, as well as dual majors in accounting/business administration, and math/computer science. There is a 3-2 engineering degree program with Wichita State University. Friends also offers a general studies degree, credit for life, military, and work experience, nondegree study, and pass/fail options are possible. For working adults, the College of Adult and Professional Studies offers undergraduate degrees and certificate programs. There is 1 national honor society, a freshman honors program, and 1 departmental honors program.

Faculty/Classroom: 92% teach undergraduates. No introductory courses are taught by graduate students. The average class size in an introductory lecture is 35; in a laboratory, 18; and in a regular course, 25.

Requirements: The SAT I or ACT is required. In addition, candidates for admission must graduate from an accredited secondary school or earn a GED, having completed 4 courses in English, 2 each in history and math, and 1 each in science and social studies. The composite ACT score or converted SAT I score is multiplied by the high school GPA. A result of 45 is the minimum for full admission; students scoring lower may be admitted provisionally. Interviews are recommended; portfolios and auditions are advised in appropriate instances. A GPA of 2.0 is required. CLEP credit is accepted.

Procedure: Freshmen are admitted fall and spring. Entrance exams should be taken in the spring of the junior year or fall of the senior year. There is an early admissions plan. There is a rolling admissions plan. Application deadlines are open. The application fee is $15. The application fee for international students is $40.

Transfer: 115 transfer students enrolled in a recent year. Applicants with fewer than 15 semester hours must submit ACT or SAT I scores and high school and college transcripts. 30 of 124 credits required for the bachelor's degree must be completed at Friends.

Visiting: There are regularly scheduled orientations for prospective students, including half-day classroom visits, individual instructor visits, discussion with current students, a tour, lunch, and a financial aid session. There are guides for informal visits and visitors may sit in on classes and stay overnight. To schedule a visit, contact the Admissions Office.

Financial Aid: The FAFSA is required. Check with the school for current deadlines.

International Students: The school actively recruits these students. They must score 500 on the written TOEFL or 118 on the electronic version unless they are either native speakers of English or non-native speakers who attended an English-speaking high school.

Computers: The mainframe is an NCR Tower. 200 Pentium PCs are available for student use. All students may access the system. There are no time limits and no fees. It is strongly recommended that all students have a personal computer.

Graduates: In a recent year, 159 bachelor's degrees were awarded. The most popular majors were business administration (15%), elementary education (12%), and human services/psychology (11%).

Admissions Contact: Tony Myers, Director of Admissions. E-mail: *tmyers@friends.edu* Web: *www.friends.edu*

KANSAS STATE UNIVERSITY
Manhattan, KS 66506   E-2

	(785) 532-6250; Fax: (785) 532-6393
Full-time: 8527 men, 7758 women	Faculty: 1152; I, --$
Part-time: 1334 men, 1464 women	Ph.D.s: 81%
Graduate: 1746 men, 2221 women	Student/Faculty: 14 to 1
Year: semesters, summer session	Tuition: $3358 ($9670)
Application Deadline: open	Room & Board: $5370
Freshman Class: 7952 applied, 4736 accepted, 3439 enrolled	
ACT: required	VERY COMPETITIVE

Kansas State University, established in 1863, is a land-grant institution offering degree programs in agriculture, arts and sciences, business, engineering, human ecology, architecture, education, veterinary medicine, and technology. There are 9 undergraduate schools and 1 graduate school. In addition to regional accreditation, K-State has baccalaureate program accreditation with AACSB, ABET, ACCE, AHEA, CSWE, FIDER, NAAB, NASM, NCATE, and NRPA. The 6 libraries contain 3,478,354 volumes, 2,540,326 microform items, and 6049 audio/video tapes/CDs, and subscribe to 19,444 periodicals. Computerized library services include the card catalog, interlibrary loans, and database searching. Special learning facilities include a learning resource center, art gallery, planetarium, radio station, TV station, nuclear reactor, laser center, cancer research center, and telecommunications satellite teaching. The 668-acre campus is in a suburban area 125 miles west of Kansas City. Including any residence halls, there are 96 buildings.

Student Life: 88% of undergraduates are from Kansas. Students are from 50 states, 100 foreign countries, and Canada. 85% are white. The average age of freshmen is 18; all undergraduates, 21. 21% do not continue beyond their first year; 56% remain to graduate.

Housing: 4300 students can be accommodated in college housing, which includes single-sex and coed dorms, on-campus apartments, off-campus apartments, married-student housing, fraternity houses, and sorority houses. In addition, there are honors houses and special-interest houses. On-campus housing is available on a first-come, first-served basis. 74% of students commute. Alcohol is not permitted. All students may keep cars.

Activities: 20% of men belong to 24 national fraternities; 20% of women belong to 11 national sororities. There are 372 groups on campus, including band, cheerleading, chess, choir, chorale, chorus, computers, dance, drama, drill team, ethnic, film, gay, honors, international, jazz band, literary magazine, marching band, musical theater, newspaper, orchestra, pep band, photography, political, professional, radio and TV, religious, social, social service, student government, symphony, and yearbook. Popular campus events include Family Weekend, K-State Open House, and Winterfest.

Sports: There are 6 intercollegiate sports for men and 8 for women, and 58 intramural sports for men and 58 for women. Facilities include indoor and outdoor tracks, baseball fields, tennis courts, basketball courts, swimming pools, a football stadium, and an indoor practice field. A multipurpose recreation facility is open 16 hours a day.

Disabled Students: 90% of the campus is accessible. Wheelchair ramps, elevators, special parking, specially equipped rest rooms, special class scheduling, lowered drinking fountains, lowered telephones, and a campus shuttle service are available.

Services: Counseling and information services are available, as is tutoring in every subject. There is a reader service for the blind, and remedial math, reading, and writing.

Campus Safety and Security: Measures include 24-hour foot and vehicle patrol, self-defense education, security escort services, and shuttle buses. There are informal discussions, pamphlets/posters/films, emergency telephones, lighted pathways/sidewalks, televised monitors in parking lots, CPR classes, and vehicle assistance devices.

Programs of Study: K-State confers B.A., B.S., B.Arch., B.F.A., B.Int.Arch., B.L.A., B.M., and B.M.E. degrees. Associate, master's, and doctoral degrees are also awarded. Bachelor's degrees are awarded in AGRICULTURE (agricultural business management, agricultural economics, agronomy, animal science, fish and game management, and horticulture), BIOLOGICAL SCIENCE (biochemistry, biology/biological science, entomology, life science, microbiology, nutrition, plant pathology, and wildlife biology), BUSINESS (accounting, apparel and accessories marketing, banking and finance, business administration and management, hotel/motel and restaurant management, management information systems, and marketing/retailing/merchandising), COMMUNICATIONS AND THE ARTS (apparel design, applied music, art, communications, dramatic arts, English, journalism, modern language, and music), COMPUTER AND PHYSICAL SCIENCE (chemistry, computer science, geology, geophysics and seismology, information sciences and systems, mathematics, physical sciences, physics, and statistics), EDUCATION (agricultural, art, athletic training, elementary, music, and secondary), ENGINEERING AND ENVIRONMENTAL DESIGN (aeronautical technology, agricultural engineering, agricultural engineering technology, airline piloting and navigation, architectural engineering, architecture, chemical engineering, civil engineering, computer engineering, construction management, electrical/electronics engineering, electrical/electronics engineering technology, engineering management, industrial engineering, interior design, landscape architecture/design, manufacturing engineering, mechanical engineering, and mechanical engineering technology), HEALTH PROFESSIONS (medical technology), SOCIAL SCIENCE (anthropology, child psychology/development, dietetics, economics, family and community services, family/consumer studies, food science, geography, history, human development, humanities, parks and recreation management, philosophy, physical fitness/movement, political science/government, psychology, social science, social work, sociology, and textiles and clothing). Architecture, engineering, and accounting are the strongest academically. Journalism, animal science, and elementary education are the largest.

Required: To graduate, students must complete 120 to 167 credits with a minimum GPA of 2.0. All students must take expository writing and public speaking. General education requirements vary by major but include at least 18 hours of approved courses.

Special: K-State offers co-op programs, internships, and dual degrees and majors through most of its colleges. Cross-registration is available with Kansas State at Salina and Kansas Wesleyan University, as is study abroad in more than 100 countries. A 3-2 engineering degree program, nondegree study, and pass/fail options are also available. There are 78 national honor societies, including Phi Beta Kappa, a freshman honors program, and 7 departmental honors programs.

Faculty/Classroom: 70% of faculty are male; 30%, female. The average class size in a regular course is 28.

Admissions: 60% of the 2003-2004 applicants were accepted. The ACT scores for the 2003-2004 freshman class were: 23% below 21, 26% between 21 and 23, 26% between 24 and 26, 11% between 27 and 28, and 13% above 28.

Requirements: The ACT is required. In addition, applicants must meet 1 of these 3 criteria: an ACT score of 21 or above, class rank in the top third, or a 2.0 GPA in the Kansas core curriculum. It is recommended that students complete 4 units of English, 3 each of natural science, math, and social studies, and 1 of computer technology. The GED is accepted. AP and CLEP credits are accepted.

Procedure: Freshmen are admitted to all sessions. Entrance exams should be taken in the junior and senior years. Application deadlines are open. The appplication fee is $30. There is a rolling admissions plan. Applications are accepted on-line.

Transfer: 1679 transfer students enrolled in 2002-2003. Applicants must have a minimum of 24 credit hours and a college GPA of 2.0 or otherwise meet freshman requirements. Students must submit official transcripts from previous colleges attended. 30 of 120 credits required for the bachelor's degree must be completed at K-State.

Visiting: There are regularly scheduled orientations for prospective students, including campus tours and visits with academic advisers and admissions representatives. There are guides for informal visits and visitors may sit in on classes and stay overnight. To schedule a visit, contact New Student Services at (785) 532-6318.

Financial Aid: In a recent year, 95% of all full-time freshmen received some form of financial aid. 95% of full-time freshmen and 50% of continuing full-time students received need-based aid. The FAFSA is required. The deadline for filing freshman financial aid applications for fall entry is March 15.

International Students: They must score 550 on the written TOEFL or 213 on the electronic version or present acceptable scores on the SAT I or the ACT and also take an English proficiency test given at the university.

Computers: The mainframe is an IBM 3090/200E. There are 110 PCs in public labs and more than 30 UNIX workstations located at various sites across campus. The Sun UNIX computer has 96 ports. All students may access the system 24 hours a day. There are no time limits. The fee is $11 per credit hour.

Graduates: From July 1, 2002 to June 30, 2003, 3387 bachelor's degrees were awarded. The most popular majors were business (16%), engineering (12%), and agriculture (11%). In an average class, 20% graduate in 4 years or less, 46% graduate in 5 years or less, and 52% graduate in 6 years or less.

Admissions Contact: Larry Moeder, Director of Admissions. A video is available. E-mail: *kstate@ksu.edu* Web: *www.ksu.edu*

KANSAS WESLEYAN UNIVERSITY   D-2
Salina, KS 67401-6196   **(785) 827-5541, ext. 1285**
                         (800) 874-1154, ext. 1285; Fax: (785) 827-0927

Full-time: 259 men, 338 women	**Faculty:** 43; IIB, --$
Part-time: 59 men, 112 women	**Ph.D.s:** 51%
Graduate: 18 men, 19 women	**Student/Faculty:** 14 to 1
Year: semesters, summer session	**Tuition:** $14,200
Application Deadline: open	**Room & Board:** $4700
Freshman Class: 1096 applied, 599 accepted, 317 enrolled	
ACT: 22	**VERY COMPETITIVE**

Kansas Wesleyan, founded in 1886, is affiliated with the United Methodist Church. The college offers undergraduate programs in the arts and sciences, business, and education. In addition to regional accreditation, Kansas Wesleyan has baccalaureate program accreditation with NCATE and NLN. The library contains 82,000 volumes, 33,505 microform items, and 984 audio/video tapes/CDs, and subscribes to 421 periodicals. Computerized library services include the card catalog, interlibrary loans, database searching, and Internet access. Special learning facilities include a learning resource center, art gallery, planetarium, and TV station. The 25-acre campus is in an urban area 90 miles north of Wichita. Including any residence halls, there are 12 buildings.

Student Life: 75% of undergraduates are from Kansas. Students are from 14 states and 3 foreign countries. 92% are from public schools. 85% are white. 48% are Protestant; 39% claim no religious affiliation; 13% Catholic. The average age of freshmen is 22; all undergraduates, 25. 33% do not continue beyond their first year.

Housing: 450 students can be accommodated in college housing, which includes single-sex dorms, on-campus apartments, and married-student housing. On-campus housing is guaranteed for all 4 years. 83% of students commute. Alcohol is not permitted. All students may keep cars.

Activities: 10% of men belong to 1 local and 1 national fraternity; 5% of women belong to 1 local sorority. There are 38 groups on campus, including art, band, cheerleading, choir, chorale, chorus, computers, dance, departmental, drama, ethnic, film, honors, international, literary magazine, musical theater, newspaper, pep band, photography, professional, radio and TV, religious, social, social service, student government, and yearbook. Popular campus events include Spring Fling, Sweetheart Dance, and Family Weekend.

Sports: There are 7 intercollegiate sports for men and 7 for women, and 8 intramural sports for men and 6 for women. Facilities include a gym, a sand volleyball court, football practice and game fields, a multipurpose courtyard, a track, and a weight room.

Disabled Students: 90% of the campus is accessible. Wheelchair ramps, elevators, special parking, specially equipped rest rooms, special class scheduling, lowered drinking fountains, and lowered telephones are available.

Services: Counseling and information services are available, as is tutoring in most subjects. There is remedial reading and writing.

Campus Safety and Security: Measures include self-defense education, security escort services, informal discussions, and pamphlets/posters/films. There are lighted pathways/sidewalks, random security checks, and private service security guards.

Programs of Study: Kansas Wesleyan confers B.A., B.S., and B.S.N. degrees. Associate and master's degrees are also awarded. Bachelor's degrees are awarded in BIOLOGICAL SCIENCE (biology/biological science), BUSINESS (accounting and business economics), COMMUNICATIONS AND THE ARTS (communications, dramatic arts, English, music, Spanish, speech/debate/rhetoric, and studio art), COMPUTER AND PHYSICAL SCIENCE (chemistry, computer science, mathematics, and physics), EDUCATION (art, music, physical, secondary, and special), HEALTH PROFESSIONS (nursing), SOCIAL SCIENCE (addiction studies, criminal justice, history, prelaw, psychology, religion, religious education, and sociology). Premedicine, nursing, and preengineering are the strongest academically. Education, nursing, and business are the largest.

Required: Students must demonstrate proficiency in English and math and must fulfill distribution requirements in 15 liberal arts components, including environmental awareness, biblical heritage, and lifetime recreation. Courses in phys ed and computers are required. To graduate, students must complete at least 126 credit hours, including 30 to 40 in a major field of study, with a minimum GPA of 2.0.

Special: Cross-registration is available with other members of the Associated Colleges of Central Kansas and the Salina College Consortium. Cooperative degree programs are offered in agriculture, cytotechnology, engineering, environmental studies, and medical technology. Kansas Wesleyan also offers January interterm study trips throughout the United States and abroad, Washington, D.C., and UN semesters, internships, dual and student-designed majors, credit for life experience, and nondegree study. A 3-2 engineering degree is offered with Columbia University and Washington University at St. Louis. There are 4 national honor societies.

Faculty/Classroom: 45% of faculty are male; 55%, female. 65% both teach and do research. The average class size in an introductory lecture is 23; in a laboratory, 7; and in a regular course, 13.

Admissions: 55% of the 2003-2004 applicants were accepted. 10 freshmen graduated first in their class.

Requirements: The SAT I or ACT is required, with a minimum composite score of 850 on the SAT I or 18 on the ACT. Applicants must be graduates of accredited secondary schools or have earned a GED. An interview is recommended. A GPA of 2.5 is required. AP and CLEP credits are accepted.

Procedure: Freshmen are admitted to all sessions. Entrance exams should be taken as early as possible. There is a deferred admissions plan. Application deadlines are open. The fall 2003 application fee was $20. Notification is sent on a rolling basis.

Transfer: Transfers must submit transcripts from all colleges previously attended. Those students transferring fewer than 15 credit hours must submit ACT scores and a high school transcript. A minimum GPA of 2.0 is recommended. 63 of 126 credits required for the bachelor's degree must be completed at Kansas Wesleyan.

Visiting: There are regularly scheduled orientations for prospective students. There are guides for informal visits and visitors may sit in on classes and stay overnight. To schedule a visit, contact the Admissions Office.

Financial Aid: In a recent year, 90% of all full-time students received some form of financial aid. Kansas Wesleyan is a member of CSS. The FAFSA and tax forms are required.

International Students: The school actively recruits these students. They must score 500 on the written TOEFL or 173 on the electronic version.

Computers: The mainframe is a Data General MV-8000. PCs are available in the computer science lab and in the library. All students may access the system at any time. There are no time limits and no fees.

Admissions Contact: Admissions Office.
E-mail: *admissions@kwu.edu*

MCPHERSON COLLEGE
McPherson, KS 67460

D-2

(620) 241-0731
(800) 365-7402; Fax: (620) 241-8443

Full-time: 246 men, 137 women	Faculty: 40; IIB, --$
Part-time: 8 men, 21 women	Ph.D.s: 63%
Graduate: none	Student/Faculty: 10 to 1
Year: 4-1-4, summer session	Tuition: $14,645
Application Deadline: open	Room & Board: $5620
Freshman Class: 532 applied, 390 accepted, 133 enrolled	
SAT I or ACT: required	COMPETITIVE

McPherson College, founded in 1887 and affiliated with the Church of the Brethren, is a private, nonprofit institution offering undergraduate programs in the arts and sciences, business, and education. The library contains 89,946 volumes, 60,561 microform items, and 4465 audio/video tapes/CDs, and subscribes to 4056 periodicals. Computerized library services include the card catalog, interlibrary loans, and database searching. Special learning facilities include a learning resource center, art gallery, natural history museum, and an automobile restoration center. The 23-acre campus is in a small town 60 miles north of Wichita. Including any residence halls, there are 15 buildings.

Student Life: 57% of undergraduates are from out of state, mostly the Midwest. Students are from 30 states and 6 foreign countries. 99% are from public schools. 82% are white. 52% are Protestant; 23% Catholic; 6% claim no religious affiliation. The average age of all undergraduates is 20.

Housing: 392 students can be accommodated in college housing, which includes single-sex and coed dorms. On-campus housing is guaranteed for all 4 years. 66% of students live on campus; of those, 65% remain on campus on weekends. Alcohol is not permitted. All students may keep cars.

Activities: There are no fraternities or sororities. There are 26 groups on campus, including art, band, cheerleading, choir, chorus, computers, drama, ethnic, honors, international, musical theater, newspaper, orchestra, pep band, professional, religious, social service, student government, and yearbook. Popular campus events include Family Weekend.

Sports: There are 5 intercollegiate sports for men and 6 for women, and 4 intramural sports for men and 4 for women. Facilities include a sports center with 2 full-size courts, a racquetball court, and a fitness center with an open weight-training room.

Disabled Students: 95% of the campus is accessible. Wheelchair ramps, elevators, special parking, specially equipped rest rooms, special class scheduling, lowered drinking fountains, and special housing are available.

Services: Counseling and information services are available, as is tutoring in most subjects. There is remedial reading and writing.

Campus Safety and Security: Measures include informal discussions, pamphlets/posters/films, emergency telephones, and lighted pathways/sidewalks.

Programs of Study: McPherson confers B.A. and B.S. degrees. Associate degrees are also awarded. Bachelor's degrees are awarded in AGRICULTURE (agricultural economics, agronomy, and animal science), BIOLOGICAL SCIENCE (biology/biological science), BUSINESS (accounting and business administration and management), COMMUNICATIONS AND THE ARTS (art, English, music, Spanish, and speech/debate/rhetoric), COMPUTER AND PHYSICAL SCIENCE (chemistry, computer science, mathematics, and physics), EDUCATION (elementary, physical, secondary, and special), ENGINEERING AND ENVIRONMENTAL DESIGN (industrial engineering technology), SOCIAL SCIENCE (history, philosophy, psychology, religion, and sociology). Natural/physical science, education, and business are the strongest academically. Business and education are the largest.

Required: To graduate, students must complete 124 credits, including 32 in the major, with a GPA of 2.0. All students must fulfill general education requirements in the following areas: written and oral communication, aesthetics, history, society, natural sciences, technology and culture, and religion/beliefs/values. Students must also participate in an integrative seminar and a service experience, and must complete a global/intercultural experience, which may include intercultural studies courses or modern language courses.

Special: Cross-registration with other colleges is available through the Associated Colleges of Central Kansas. McPherson also offers internships, study abroad in 10 countries, credit by exam, a general studies degree, student-designed majors, and pass/fail options. There are preprofessional programs in health, engineering, law, forestry, veterinary medicine, nursing and medicine, optometry, and dentistry. There are 3 national honor societies, including Phi Beta Kappa, and 3 departmental honors programs.

Faculty/Classroom: 67% of faculty are male; 33%, female. All teach undergraduates. The average class size in an introductory lecture is 30; in a laboratory, 12; and in a regular course, 12.

Admissions: 73% of the 2003-2004 applicants were accepted. 2 freshmen graduated first in their class in a recent year.

Requirements: The SAT I or ACT is required. In addition, the GED is accepted. A GPA of 2.0 is required. AP and CLEP credits are accepted. Important factors in the admissions decision are recommendations by school officials, evidence of special talent, and parents or siblings attending the school.

Procedure: Freshmen are admitted fall, winter, and spring. Entrance exams should be taken in the junior year. There is a deferred admissions plan. Application deadlines are open. (The priority date is March 15.) Application fee is $25. Applications are accepted on-line through the school's web site. Notification is sent on a rolling basis.

Transfer: 60 transfer students enrolled in 2003-2004. Applicants must have satisfactorily completed 12 credit hours of college course work covering 3 academic areas with a 2.0 GPA. 32 of 124 credits required for the bachelor's degree must be completed at McPherson.

Visiting: There are regularly scheduled orientations for prospective students, consisting of campus tours, meetings with admissions personnel, and class attendance. There are guides for informal visits and visitors may sit in on classes and stay overnight. To schedule a visit, contact the Admissions Office.

Financial Aid: In 2003-2004, 86% of all full-time freshmen and 84% of continuing full-time students received some form of financial aid. At least 72% of full-time freshmen and 74% of continuing full-time students received need-based aid. The average freshman award was $15,951. Need-based scholarships or need-based grants averaged $5315; need-based self-help aid (loans and jobs) averaged $6002; institutional non-need-based athletic scholarships averaged $4364; and other institutional non-need-based awards and non-need-based scholarships averaged $6273. The average financial indebtedness of the 2003 graduate was $14,450. The FAFSA is required. The priority date for freshman financial aid applications for fall entry is April 1.

International Students: There were 6 international students enrolled in a recent year. They must score 550 on the written TOEFL and also take the ACT, scoring 18.

Computers: The mainframe is an Encore. 2 computer labs provide access to word processing, the Internet, and the Web. Computer hookup is available in dorm rooms as well. All students may access the system. There are no time limits and no fees.

Graduates: From July 1, 2002 to June 30, 2003, 73 bachelor's degrees were awarded. The most popular majors were education (31%), business/marketing (11%), and psychology (9%). In an average class, 17% graduate in 4 years or less, 21% graduate in 5 years or less, and 23% graduate in 6 years or less.

Admissions Contact: Carol Williams, Director of Admissions and Financial Aid. E-mail: *admiss@mcpherson.edu*
Web: *www.mcpherson.edu*

MIDAMERICA NAZARENE UNIVERSITY
Olathe, KS 66062-1899

F-2

(913) 791-3380
(800) 800-8887; Fax: (913) 791-3487

Full-time: 605 men, 673 women	Faculty: 76
Part-time: 51 men, 82 women	Ph.D.s: 44%
Graduate: 132 men, 382 women	Student/Faculty: 17 to 1
Year: semesters, summer session	Tuition: $12,860
Application Deadline: August 1	Room & Board: $5828
Freshman Class: 504 applied, 486 accepted, 260 enrolled	
SAT I Verbal/Math: 519/507	ACT: 22	COMPETITIVE

MidAmerica Nazarene University was founded in 1966 as a private liberal arts institution affiliated with the Church of the Nazarene. In addition to regional accreditation, MNU has baccalaureate program accreditation with ACBSP, NASM, and NLN. The library contains 119,227 volumes, 317,000 microform items, and 3326 audio/video tapes/CDs, and subscribes to 225 periodicals. Computerized library services include the card catalog, interlibrary loans, and database searching. Special learning facilities include a learning resource center and radio station. The 105-acre campus is in a suburban area 19 miles southwest of downtown Kansas City, Missouri. Including any residence halls, there are 21 buildings.

Student Life: 69% of undergraduates are from Kansas. Students are from 33 states, 11 foreign countries, and Canada. 88% are from public schools. 87% are white. 72% are Protestant; 20% claim no religious affiliation; 6% Catholic. The average age of freshmen is 18; all undergraduates, 24. 25% do not continue beyond their first year.

Housing: 704 students can be accommodated in college housing, which includes single-sex dorms, on-campus apartments, and off-campus apartments. On-campus housing is guaranteed for all 4 years. 59% of students live on campus; of those, all remain on campus on weekends. Alcohol is not permitted. All students may keep cars.

Activities: There are no fraternities or sororities. There are 43 groups on campus, including agriculture, cheerleading, choir, chorus, computers, drama, ethnic, honors, international, jazz band, newspaper, orchestra, pep band, political, professional, psychology, radio and TV, religious, student government, writers, and yearbook. Popular campus events include Mr. MNU and Welcome Week.

Sports: There are 6 intercollegiate sports for men and 6 for women, and 6 intramural sports for men and 6 for women. Facilities include a weight room, a football stadium, a gym, a track, tennis and sand volleyball courts, and softball, baseball, and soccer fields.

Disabled Students: 90% of the campus is accessible. Wheelchair ramps, elevators, special parking, specially equipped rest rooms, special class scheduling, and lowered drinking fountains are available.

Services: Counseling and information services are available, as is tutoring in most subjects. There is a reader service for the blind, and remedial math, reading, and writing. There are also test-taking accommodations, interpreters for the hearing impaired, and note takers for the blind, hearing impaired, and learning disabled.

Campus Safety and Security: Measures include 24-hour foot and vehicle patrol, self-defense education, security escort services, and informal discussions. There are pamphlets/posters/films, emergency telephones, and lighted pathways/sidewalks.

Programs of Study: MNU confers B.A., B.M.Ed., and B.S.N. degrees. Associate and master's degrees are also awarded. Bachelor's degrees are awarded in AGRICULTURE (international agriculture), BIOLOGICAL SCIENCE (biology/biological science), BUSINESS (accounting and business administration and management), COMMUNICATIONS AND THE ARTS (communications, dramatic arts, English, modern language, music, and Spanish), COMPUTER AND PHYSICAL SCIENCE (chemistry, computer science, mathematics, and physics), EDUCATION (athletic training, business, Christian, elementary, English, health, mathematics, music, physical, science, social studies, and speech correction), HEALTH PROFESSIONS (nursing), SOCIAL SCIENCE (criminal justice, history, ministries, psychology, and sociology). Management and human relations, elementary education, and business administration are the largest.

Required: All students must meet core curriculum requirements in humanities-communications, natural sciences-math, social sciences, religion-philosophy, and phys ed. Students must maintain a minimum GPA of 2.0 and complete 126 semester hours to graduate.

Special: MNU offers nondegree study, cross-registration with the Christian College Coalition, study abroad in 4 countries, internships, and a Washington semester. There are accelerated degree programs in management and human relations and in nursing. There is 1 national honor society and 4 departmental honors programs.

Faculty/Classroom: 65% of faculty are male; 35%, female. All teach undergraduates. No introductory courses are taught by graduate students. The average class size in an introductory lecture is 27; in a laboratory, 11; and in a regular course, 17.

Admissions: 96% of the 2003-2004 applicants were accepted. The SAT I scores for the 2003-2004 freshman class were: Verbal--48% below 500, 30% between 500 and 599, 19% between 600 and 700, and 3% above 700; Math--41% below 500, 37% between 500 and 599, and 22% between 600 and 700. The ACT scores were 38% below 21, 21% between 21 and 23, 22% between 24 and 26, 11% between 27 and 28, and 8% above 28. 37% of the current freshmen were in the top fifth of their class; 64% were in the top two fifths. 11 freshmen graduated first in their class.

Requirements: The SAT I or ACT is required, with recommended composite scores of 18 on the ACT and 670 on the SAT I. Candidates for admission should be graduates of an accredited secondary school. The GED is accepted. Students should have completed 15 units of study, including 4 units of English and 3 each of natural science, social studies, and math. An essay is optional. A GPA of 2.0 is required. AP and CLEP credits are accepted.

Procedure: Freshmen are admitted to all sessions. Entrance exams should be taken during the senior year. There is a rolling admissions plan and an early admissions plan. Applications should be filed by August 1 for fall entry and December 15 for winter entry. Notification is sent on a rolling basis.

Transfer: 65 transfer students enrolled in a recent year. Transfer applicants should have earned 24 or more hours at an accredited institution and not be on academic or disciplinary probation. ACT or SAT I scores are required. 30 of 126 credits required for the bachelor's degree must be completed at MNU.

Visiting: There are regularly scheduled orientations for prospective students, including an academic fair, advising, class visitation, informational meetings, social activities, and experiencing residential life. There are guides for informal visits, and visitors may sit in on classes and stay overnight. To schedule a visit, contact the Office of Admissions.

Financial Aid: In 2003-2004, 98% of all full-time freshmen and 94% of continuing full-time students received some form of financial aid. 77% of full-time freshmen and 72% of continuing full-time students received need-based aid. The average freshman award was $12,555. Need-based scholarships or need-based grants averaged $6679 ($15,760 maximum); need-based self-help aid (loans and jobs) averaged $4185 ($8075 maximum); non-need-based athletic scholarships averaged $3611 ($11,000 maximum); and other non-need-based awards and non-need-based scholarships averaged $3956 ($11,198 maximum). Average annual earnings from campus work are $1157. The average financial indebtedness of the 2003 graduate was $14,277. The FAFSA and the college's own financial statement are required. The deadline for filing freshman financial aid applications for fall entry is March 1.

International Students: There are 22 international students enrolled. They must score 500 on the written TOEFL. There are placement tests for incoming freshmen and the ACT and/or SAT I is required if from a world area where English is the official first language.

Computers: The mainframes are a DEC Microvax 3100 and DEC Alpha 4000. There are 40 general access PCs in the library, with an additional 35 in the computer lab reserved for business, math, and computer science majors. All students have access to e-mail and the Internet. Dial-up access is available any time from residence halls and off-campus sites. All students may access the system 7:30 A.M. to 11 P.M. Monday to Thursday and to 5 P.M. Friday; 10 A.M. to 5 P.M. Saturday. There are no time limits and no fees. It is recommended that students in OIS and MET have personal computers.

Graduates: From July 1, 2002 to June 30, 2003, 318 bachelor's degrees were awarded. The most popular majors were human resources management (38%), elementary education (8%), and business administration (7%). In an average class, 49% graduate in 6 years or less. 100 companies recruited on campus in 2002-2003.

Admissions Contact: Ann Owens, Applicant Secretary. A video is available. E-mail: *admissions@mnu.edu* Web: *www.mnu.edu*

NEWMAN UNIVERSITY
Wichita, KS 67213

D-3

(316) 942-4291, ext. 144
(877) NEWMANU; Fax: (316) 942-4483

Full-time: 356 men, 730 women	**Faculty:** 67; IIB, --$
Part-time: 272 men, 399 women	**Ph.D.s:** 44%
Graduate: 100 men, 206 women	**Student/Faculty:** 16 to 1
Year: semesters, summer session	**Tuition:** $13,198
Application Deadline: open	**Room & Board:** $4820
Freshman Class: n/av	
SAT I or ACT: required	**COMPETITIVE**

Newman University, established in 1933, is a private, liberal arts institution affiliated with the Roman Catholic Church. There are 5 undergraduate schools and 1 graduate school. In addition to regional accreditation, NU has baccalaureate program accreditation with NLN. The library contains 108,000 volumes, 134,000 microform items, and 2142 audio/video tapes/CDs, and subscribes to 466 periodicals. Computerized library services include the card catalog, interlibrary loans, and database searching. Special learning facilities include a learning resource center, art gallery, planetarium, and allied health and nursing labs. The 61-acre campus is in an urban area west of downtown Wichita. Including any residence halls, there are 13 buildings.

Student Life: 89% of undergraduates are from Kansas. Students are from 30 states and 33 foreign countries. 64% are from public schools. 79% are white. 56% are Protestant; 44% Catholic. The average age of freshmen is 18; all undergraduates, 25. 33% do not continue beyond their first year; 52% remain to graduate.

Housing: 320 students can be accommodated in college housing, which includes single-sex and coed dorms, on-campus apartments, and married-student housing. On-campus housing is guaranteed for all 4 years. 87% of students commute. Alcohol is not permitted. All students may keep cars.

Activities: There are no fraternities or sororities. There are 30 groups on campus, including cheerleading, choir, chorale, computers, dance, drama, ethnic, forensics, honors, international, newspaper, political, professional, religious, social, social service, and student government. Popular campus events include Family Weekend, Take-off Week, and Midnight Madness.

Sports: There are 9 intercollegiate sports for men and 9 for women. Facilities include baseball, softball, and soccer fields, and a sports complex.

Disabled Students: All of the campus is accessible. Wheelchair ramps, elevators, special parking, specially equipped rest rooms, special class scheduling, lowered drinking fountains, and lowered telephones are available.

Services: Counseling and information services are available, as is tutoring in most subjects. There is remedial math and writing.

Campus Safety and Security: Measures include 24-hour foot and vehicle patrol, security escort services, informal discussions, and pamphlets/posters/films. There are emergency telephones and lighted pathways/sidewalks.

Programs of Study: NU confers B.A., B.S., and B.S.N. degrees. Associate and master's degrees are also awarded. Bachelor's degrees are awarded in BIOLOGICAL SCIENCE (biochemistry and biology/biological science), BUSINESS (accounting, business administration and management, management information systems, management science, and marketing and distribution), COMMUNICATIONS AND THE ARTS (art, communications, English, and music), COMPUTER AND PHYSICAL SCIENCE (chemistry, information sciences and systems, and mathematics), EDUCATION (elementary and secondary), ENGINEERING

AND ENVIRONMENTAL DESIGN (preengineering), HEALTH PROFESSIONS (nursing, occupational therapy, physical therapy, predentistry, premedicine, preoptometry, prepharmacy, preveterinary science, and ultrasound technology), SOCIAL SCIENCE (counseling/psychology, criminal justice, history, liberal arts/general studies, pastoral studies, prelaw, psychology, sociology, and theological studies). Nursing, biology, and chemistry are the strongest academically. Nursing, business, and education are the largest.

Required: Degree requirements include completion of 124 credit hours, 30 of which must be upper-division. The number of credits required in the major varies. A minimum GPA of 2.0 is required for graduation, and students must fulfill the college's liberal arts requirement, including courses in philosophy and theology.

Special: NU offers co-op programs in most majors through Friends University, internships, study abroad in Great Britain, the Netherlands, and Ireland, nondegree study, and dual majors. Course requirements for majors in counseling, business management, education, nursing, and liberal studies can be satisfied through evening and weekend classes. There are 3 national honor societies and 1 departmental honors program.

Faculty/Classroom: 49% of faculty are male; 51%, female. 85% teach undergraduates. No introductory courses are taught by graduate students. The average class size in a regular course is 11.

Requirements: The SAT I or ACT is required, with a minimum composite score of 18 on the ACT. Candidates for admission must graduate from an accredited secondary school with 23 high school academic credits, including 4 credits of English, and 3 each of math, science, and social studies. 2 credits of a foreign language are recommended. A GPA of 2.0 is required. AP and CLEP credits are accepted.

Procedure: Freshmen are admitted fall, spring, and summer. Entrance exams should be taken during the spring of the junior year or fall of the senior year. There is a rolling admissions plan and a deferred admissions plan. Application deadlines are open. Application fee is $15.

Transfer: A minimum GPA of 2.0 is required. 30 of 124 credits required for the bachelor's degree must be completed at NU.

Visiting: There are regularly scheduled orientations for prospective students, including a campus tour and meetings with faculty, athletic coaches, co-curricular sponsors, financial aid counselors, and admissions counselors. There are guides for informal visits, and visitors may sit in on classes and stay overnight. To schedule a visit, contact the Admissions Office at (316) 942-4291, ext. 2164 or *admissions@newmanu.edu*.

Financial Aid: In 2003-2004, 97% of all full-time freshmen and 85% of continuing full-time students received some form of financial aid. 65% of full-time freshmen and 64% of continuing full-time students received need-based aid. The average freshman award was $9425. 96% of undergraduates work part time. Average annual earnings from campus work are $1200. The FAFSA and the college's own financial statement are required.

International Students: There are 25 international students enrolled. The school actively recruits these students. They must score 530 on the written TOEFL.

Computers: All students have computer accounts and e-mail. All students may access the system. There are no time limits and no fees.

Graduates: From July 1, 2002 to June 30, 2003, 306 bachelor's degrees were awarded. The most popular majors were elementary education (24%), nursing (15%), and business management (8%). In an average class, 35% graduate in 4 years or less, and 52% graduate in 6 years or less. 20 companies recruited on campus in 2002-2003.

Admissions Contact: Admissions Secretary/Receptionist.
E-mail: *admissions@newmanu.edu* Web: *www.newmanu.edu*

OTTAWA UNIVERSITY
Ottawa, KS 66067-3399

E-2

(785) 242-5200, ext. 5555
(800) 755-5200,; Fax: (785) 229-1008

Full-time: 260 men, 190 women	**Faculty:** 21; IIB, --$
Part-time: 10 men, 15 women	**Ph.D.s:** 54%
Graduate: none	**Student/Faculty:** 20 to 1
Year: semesters, summer session	**Tuition:** $13,060
Application Deadline: open	**Room & Board:** n/app
Freshman Class: n/av	
SAT I: n/av	**ACT:** required

LESS COMPETITIVE

Ottawa University, founded in 1865 and affiliated with the American Baptist Churches, is a private institution offering programs through the divisions of arts and humanities, natural sciences, and social and behavioral sciences. Figures in the above capsule and in this profile are approximate. The library contains 90,000 volumes, and subscribes to 400 periodicals. Computerized library services include interlibrary loans and database searching. Special learning facilities include a learning resource center, art gallery, and radio station. The 64-acre campus is in a small town 45 miles southwest of Kansas City. Including any residence halls, there are 15 buildings.

Student Life: 55% of undergraduates are from Kansas. Students are from 18 states, 5 foreign countries, and Canada. 99% are from public schools. 77% are white; 11% African American. 64% are Protestant; 20% claim no religious affiliation; 13% Catholic. The average age of freshmen is 19; all undergraduates, 22. 25% do not continue beyond their first year; 30% remain to graduate.

Housing: 428 students can be accommodated in college housing, which includes single-sex dorms, on-campus apartments, and married-student housing. On-campus housing is guaranteed for all 4 years. 58% of students live on campus; of those, 65% remain on campus on weekends. Alcohol is not permitted. All students may keep cars.

Activities: There are no fraternities or sororities. There are 35 groups on campus, including cheerleading, choir, chorale, chorus, computers, dance, debate, drama, ethnic, forensics, honors, international, jazz band, musical theater, newspaper, orchestra, pep band, photography, professional, radio and TV, religious, social, social service, student government, and yearbook. Popular campus events include Family Day, Charter Day, and Christmas Feast.

Sports: There are 7 intercollegiate sports for men and 7 for women, and 12 intramural sports for men and 12 for women. Facilities include a field, a sports complex, an athletic center, and a gym with a wellness center.

Disabled Students: 50% of the campus is accessible. Wheelchair ramps, elevators, special parking, specially equipped rest rooms, and special class scheduling are available.

Services: Counseling and information services are available, as is tutoring in most subjects. There is remedial math, reading, and writing.

Campus Safety and Security: Measures include self-defense education, security escort services, pamphlets/posters/films, lighted pathways/sidewalks, and a night security guard. In addition, students are issued individual residence hall security and room keys.

Programs of Study: OU confers the B.A. degree. Bachelor's degrees are awarded in BIOLOGICAL SCIENCE (biology/biological science), BUSINESS (accounting, business administration and management, and management information systems), COMMUNICATIONS AND THE ARTS (art, communications, dramatic arts, English, and music), COMPUTER AND PHYSICAL SCIENCE (chemistry, information sciences and systems, and mathematics), EDUCATION (elementary and physical), SOCIAL SCIENCE (history, human services, political science/government, psychology, religion, and sociology). English, business, and math are the strongest academically. Business, teacher education, and human services are the largest.

Required: To graduate, students must complete 9 courses in 8 academic areas with a minimum GPA of 2.0. The university requires students to complete 124 semester hours, with 24 to 40 in the major. Three interdisciplinary general education seminars must be completed. In addition, students must attend 10 University Program events each semester for 6 semesters.

Special: Internships are available, especially in business, human services, and teacher education. Student-designed majors are an option. 3/2 engineering degrees with Kansas state and the University of Kansas, 3 +1 degree in medical technology, and preprofessional programs in premedicine, predentistry, prelaw, and preministry are available. Work-study programs are also offered. There are 2 national honor societies.

Faculty/Classroom: 60% of faculty are male; 40%, female. All teach undergraduates. The average class size in a laboratory is 12.

Requirements: The ACT is required. In addition, the GED is accepted. There are no specific high school courses required, but a sound college preparatory curriculum is highly recommended. OU requires applicants to be in the upper 50% of their class. A GPA of 2.5 is required. AP and CLEP credits are accepted. Important factors in the admissions decision are parents or siblings attending the school, recommendations by alumni, and recommendations by school officials.

Procedure: Freshmen are admitted to all sessions. Entrance exams should be taken as early as possible. There is a rolling admissions plan. Application deadlines are open. Check with the school for current fees.

Transfer: Transfer applicants must submit transcripts from all colleges attended and must have a 2.0 GPA and 12 hours of college credit, or else they must meet freshman requirements. 30 of 124 credits required for the bachelor's degree must be completed at OU.

Visiting: There are regularly scheduled orientations for prospective students, including Discovery Day in the early spring, which gives prospective students a chance to meet faculty, students, and staff and to learn more about Ottawa University, the admissions process, and financial aid. There are guides for informal visits and visitors may sit in on classes and stay overnight. To schedule a visit, contact the Admissions Office.

Financial Aid: The FAFSA and the college's own financial statement are required. Check with the school for current deadlines.

International Students: The school actively recruits these students. They must score 500 on the written TOEFL or take the MELAB.

Computers: The mainframe is an IBM AS/400. There are 2 computer labs and there is connectivity in every dorm room with Internet access. All students may access the system. There are no time limits and no fees.

Admissions Contact: Tim Albers, Director of Admissions. A video is available. E-mail: *admiss@ottawa.edu* Web: *www.ottawa.edu*

PITTSBURG STATE UNIVERSITY
Pittsburg, KS 66762

F-3

(620) 235-4251
(800) 854-PITT; Fax: (620) 235-6003

Full-time: 2563 men, 2491 women
Part-time: 225 men, 252 women
Graduate: 470 men, 730 women
Year: semesters, summer session
Application Deadline: open
Freshman Class: n/av
ACT: 22

Faculty: IIA, -$
Ph.D.s: 84%
Student/Faculty: n/av
Tuition: $2962 ($8784)
Room & Board: $4166

NONCOMPETITIVE

Pittsburg State University, founded in 1903, is a state-supported institution offering programs in arts and sciences, business, education, and technology. There are 4 undergraduate schools and 1 graduate school. In addition to regional accreditation, Pitt State has baccalaureate program accreditation with AACSB, ABET, CACREP, CSWE, NASM, NCATE, and NLN. The 2 libraries contain 742,735 volumes, 842,616 microform items, and 1712 audio/video tapes/CDs, and subscribe to 7038 periodicals. Computerized library services include the card catalog, interlibrary loans, and database searching. Special learning facilities include a learning resource center, art gallery, planetarium, radio station, TV station, and a dedicated channel on local cable television. The 233-acre campus is in a small town 100 miles south of Kansas City. Including any residence halls, there are 34 buildings.

Student Life: Students are from 40 states, 47 foreign countries, and Canada. 89% are white. The average age of freshmen is 19.

Housing: 1015 students can be accommodated in college housing, which includes coed dorms, fraternity houses, and sorority houses. On-campus housing is guaranteed for all 4 years. Alcohol is not permitted. All students may keep cars.

Activities: There are 7 national fraternities and 3 national sororities. There are 140 groups on campus, including art, band, cheerleading, chess, choir, computers, dance, drama, drill team, ethnic, honors, housing, international, jazz band, literary magazine, marching band, newspaper, pep band, photography, political, professional, radio and TV, recreational, religious, social, social service, student government, and yearbook. Popular campus events include Greek Week, Multicultural Month, and Welcome Week.

Sports: There are 6 intercollegiate sports for men and 5 for women, and 9 intramural sports for men and 9 for women. Facilities include a football stadium, indoor and outdoor tracks, a basketball arena, softball diamonds, a baseball field, a weight room, a dance studio, an Olympic-size pool, volleyball, racquetball, and badminton courts, indoor and outdoor tennis courts, and sand volleyball courts.

Disabled Students: 70% of the campus is accessible. Wheelchair ramps, elevators, special parking, specially equipped rest rooms, special class scheduling, lowered drinking fountains, and lowered telephones are available.

Services: Counseling and information services are available, as is tutoring in some subjects, including accounting, biology, chemistry, foreign language, math, computers, physics, psychology, reading/study, and writing. There is a Student Support Services Office and a counseling center.

Campus Safety and Security: Measures include 24-hour foot and vehicle patrol, security escort services, informal discussions, and pamphlets/posters/films. There are emergency telephones, lighted pathways/sidewalks, crime prevention programs, and engraving of valuables such as bicycles.

Programs of Study: Pitt State confers B.A., B.S., B.B.A., B.F.A., B.Gen.Studies, B.Music, B.M.Ed. B.S. Ed., B.S.E.T., B.S.Med.Tech., B.S.N., B.S.T., and B.Voc.-Tech Ed. degrees. Associate and master's degrees are also awarded. Bachelor's degrees are awarded in BIOLOGICAL SCIENCE (biology/biological science), BUSINESS (accounting, banking and finance, business administration and management, and marketing/retailing/merchandising), COMMUNICATIONS AND THE ARTS (art, communications, English, French, music, and Spanish), COMPUTER AND PHYSICAL SCIENCE (chemistry, computer science, information sciences and systems, mathematics, and physics), EDUCATION (art, elementary, foreign languages, music, and vocational), ENGINEERING AND ENVIRONMENTAL DESIGN (engineering technology and printing technology), HEALTH PROFESSIONS (medical technology and nursing), SOCIAL SCIENCE (criminal justice, economics, family/consumer studies, geography, history, political science/government, psychology, social science, social work, and sociology). Business administration, elementary education, and engineering technology are the largest.

Required: To graduate, students must complete 124 semester hours, including 35 to 60 hours in the major, with a minimum GPA of 2.0. General education requirements total 49 hours (up to 54 for education majors) and include courses in English, speech, math, humanities, social and behavioral sciences, natural and physical sciences, producing and consuming, and lifetime fitness.

Special: Co-op and work-study programs, internships, a general studies degree, B.A.-B.S. degrees, dual majors, a 3-2 engineering degree with the University of Kansas and Kansas State University, credit by exam,

nondegree study, and pass/fail options are available. Pitt State has student exchange programs with 70 countries. There are 19 national honor societies, a freshman honors program, and 23 departmental honors programs.

Faculty/Classroom: The average class size in an introductory lecture is 34; in a laboratory, 14; and in a regular course, 20.

Requirements: The ACT is required. In addition, applicants must meet 1 of these 3 criteria: an ACT score of 21 or above, class rank in the top third, or a 2.0 GPA in the Kansas core curriculum. Candidates may also be accepted through an exceptions window. The GED is accepted. Pitt State requires applicants to be in the upper 50% of their class. A GPA of 2.0 is required. AP and CLEP credits are accepted. Important factors in the admissions decision are advanced placement or honor courses, geographic diversity, and ability to finance college education.

Procedure: Freshmen are admitted to all sessions. Entrance exams should be taken before or during the first semester of the freshman year of college There is a rolling admissions plan. Application deadlines are open. Applications are accepted on-line.

Transfer: Applicants must have 24 credit hours and a college GPA of 2.0 or else meet freshman admissions requirements. 30 of 124 credits required for the bachelor's degree must be completed at Pitt State.

Visiting: There are regularly scheduled orientations for prospective students. There are guides for informal visits, and visitors may sit in on classes. To schedule a visit, contact the Admissions Office.

Financial Aid: The FAFSA is required. The deadline for filing freshman financial aid applications for fall entry is February 15.

International Students: There are 183 international students enrolled. The school actively recruits these students. They must score 520 on the written TOEFL or 190 on the electronic version and also take or submit minimum scores of 980 on the SAT I or 21 on the ACT, or have taken English course work.

Computers: The mainframe is an IBM system. 7 student labs can access the mainframe, e-mail, and university fiber-optic network via PCs. More than 250 workstations and 200 software packages are available. Bitnet and Internet are also available. All students may access the system 8 A.M. to 11:45 P.M. There are no time limits and no fees.

Admissions Contact: Ange Peterson, Director of Admission and Retention. A video is available. E-mail: *psuadmit@pittstate.edu*
Web: *www.pittstate.edu*

SAINT MARY COLLEGE
(See University of Saint Mary)

SOUTHWESTERN COLLEGE
Winfield, KS 67156-2499

D-3

(620) 229-6210
(800) 846-1543; Fax: (620) 229-6344

Full-time: 389 men, 376 women
Part-time: 262 men, 191 women
Graduate: 93 men, 94 women
Year: semesters, summer session
Application Deadline: August 1
Freshman Class: 540 applied, 385 accepted, 177 enrolled
SAT I Verbal/Math: 470/480

Faculty: IIB, --$
Ph.D.s: n/av
Student/Faculty: n/av
Tuition: $14,618
Room & Board: $4942

ACT: 21

COMPETITIVE

Southwestern College, established in 1885, is a private institution affiliated with the Kansas West Conference of the United Methodist Church. In addition to regional accreditation, Southwestern has baccalaureate program accreditation with CSWE, NASM, and NLN. The 2 libraries contain 70,000 volumes, 1000 microform items, and 20 audio/video tapes/CDs, and subscribe to 300 periodicals. Computerized library services include the card catalog, interlibrary loans, and database searching. Special learning facilities include a learning resource center, art gallery, radio station, TV station, and a biological field station. The 82-acre campus is in a small town 45 miles southeast of Wichita. Including any residence halls, there are 20 buildings.

Student Life: 82% of undergraduates are from Kansas. Students are from 18 states and 10 foreign countries. 84% are white. The average age of freshmen is 18; all undergraduates, 29. 33% do not continue beyond their first year; 51% remain to graduate.

Housing: 386 students can be accommodated in college housing, which includes single-sex and coed dorms, on-campus apartments, and married-student housing. In addition, there are honors houses. On-campus housing is guaranteed for the freshman year only and is available on a first-come, first-served basis. 70% of students commute. Alcohol is not permitted. All students may keep cars.

Activities: 15% of men and about 1% of women belong to 1 local and 1 national fraternity; 12% of women belong to 1 local and 1 national sorority. There are 32 groups on campus, including band, cheerleading, choir, chorus, dance, debate, drama, drill team, ethnic, film, forensics, honors, international, jazz band, literary magazine, musical theater, newspaper, orchestra, pep band, photography, political, professional, radio and TV, religious, social, social service, student government, symphony, and yearbook. Popular campus events include Movie Nights, Spring Formal, and Kickback Day.

Sports: There are 7 intercollegiate sports for men and 7 for women, and 2 intramural sports for men and 2 for women. Facilities include a 2400-seat stadium, tennis and basketball courts, playing floors, exercise rooms, a gym, an indoor swimming pool, a running track, a soccer field, a weight room, and a Frisbee golf course.

Disabled Students: 80% of the campus is accessible. Wheelchair ramps, elevators, special parking, specially equipped rest rooms, special class scheduling, lowered drinking fountains, and lowered telephones are available.

Services: Counseling and information services are available, as is tutoring in every subject upon request. There is remedial math, reading, and writing. A reader service is available for dyslexic students.

Campus Safety and Security: Measures include 24-hour foot and vehicle patrol, self-defense education, security escort services, and informal discussions. There are emergency telephones and lighted pathways/sidewalks.

Programs of Study: Southwestern confers B.A., B.S., B.B.A., B.G.S., B.L.S., B.Mus., B.Ph., and B.S.N. degrees. Master's degrees are also awarded. Bachelor's degrees are awarded in BIOLOGICAL SCIENCE (biochemistry, biology/biological science, and marine biology), BUSINESS (business administration and management, human resources, management information systems, management science, purchasing/inventory management, and sports management), COMMUNICATIONS AND THE ARTS (communications, dramatic arts, English, French, music, and Spanish), COMPUTER AND PHYSICAL SCIENCE (chemistry, computer programming, computer science, mathematics, and physics), EDUCATION (drama, early childhood, elementary, English, foreign languages, mathematics, music, physical, and science), ENGINEERING AND ENVIRONMENTAL DESIGN (computer technology and manufacturing technology), HEALTH PROFESSIONS (nursing), SOCIAL SCIENCE (criminal justice, history, liberal arts/general studies, pastoral studies, and psychology). Biology, education, and nursing are the strongest academically and have the largest enrollments.

Required: To graduate, students must earn 124 credits, fulfill all requirements of the major, and maintain a GPA of 2.0. Students must complete the integrative studies requirements.

Special: Southwestern offers internships in industry and social and civic agencies, and study abroad in Japan and Bulgaria. A music and theater dual major is available and other combinations or degrees are possible with approval from the Academic Affairs Committee. There is a 3-2 engineering degree program with Washington University of St. Louis. Work-study programs, an accelerated degree program, credit for life, military, and work experience, nondegree study, and pass/fail options are also available. There are 4 national honor societies, including Phi Beta Kappa, a freshman honors program, and 3 departmental honors programs.

Faculty/Classroom: All teach undergraduates. No introductory courses are taught by graduate students. The average class size in an introductory lecture is 39; in a laboratory, 10; and in a regular course, 13.

Admissions: 71% of the 2003-2004 applicants were accepted. The SAT I scores for the 2003-2004 freshman class were: Verbal--64% below 500, 27% between 500 and 599, 7% between 600 and 700, and 2% above 700; Math--54% below 500, 34% between 500 and 599, 10% between 600 and 700, and 2% above 700. The ACT scores were 43% below 21, 23% between 21 and 23, 24% between 24 and 26, 5% between 27 and 28, and 5% above 28. 32% of the current freshmen were in the top fifth of their class; 33% were in the top two fifths.

Requirements: The ACT is required and the SAT I is recommended. In addition, all candidates for admission must graduate from an accredited secondary school with a specified college-bound curriculum. The GED is accepted and an essay is required. Interviews are recommended. A GPA of 2.5 is required. AP and CLEP credits are accepted.

Procedure: Freshmen are admitted fall, spring, and summer. There is a deferred admissions plan. Applications should be filed by August 1 for fall entry and January 1 for spring entry. The fall 2003 application fee was $20. Notification is sent on a rolling basis. Applications are accepted on-line through *Embark.com*.

Transfer: 72 transfer students enrolled in a recent year. Applicants must have a college GPA of 2.0 and must submit an essay. 30 of 124 credits required for the bachelor's degree must be completed at Southwestern.

Visiting: There are regularly scheduled orientations for prospective students, including 4 Explore More events. There are guides for informal visits and visitors may sit in on classes and stay overnight. To schedule a visit, contact the Admissions Office.

Financial Aid: In 2003-2004, all full-time freshmen and 91% of continuing full-time students received some form of financial aid. 75% of full-time freshmen and 68% of continuing full-time students received need-based aid. The average freshman award was $13,054. Need-based scholarships or need-based grants averaged $3053 ($6550 maximum); need-based self-help aid (loans and jobs) averaged $3952 ($6625 maximum); non-need-based athletic scholarships averaged $2155 ($3000 maximum); other non-need-based awards and non-need-based scholarships averaged $5208 ($14,618 maximum); and outside private scholarships averaged $1486 ($9000 maximum). Average annual earnings from campus work are $700. The average financial indebtedness of a re-

cent year's graduate was $15,206. The FAFSA and the college's own financial statement are required. Check with the school for current deadlines.

International Students: There were 36 international students enrolled in a recent year. The school actively recruits these students. They must score 550 on the written TOEFL or 213 on the electronic version.

Computers: The mainframe is an IBM AS/400. Students have access to Internet connections from all dorm rooms. 5 computer labs with a total of 50 computers that also connect to the World Wide Web are also available. The mainframe is accessed by students with permission from computer lab personnel. IBM ThinkPad laptops are issued to all incoming freshmen. There are no time limits and no fees. All students are required to have personal computers.

Graduates: In a recent year, 389 bachelor's degrees were awarded. The most popular majors were business (54%), nursing (10%), and computer (9%). In an average class, 2% graduate in 3 years or less, 38% graduate in 4 years or less, 46% graduate in 5 years or less, and 48% graduate in 6 years or less. 15 companies recruited on campus in a recent year. Of a recent year's graduating class, 16% were enrolled in graduate school within 6 months of graduation and 90% were employed.

Admissions Contact: Todd Moore, Director of Admission. A video is available. E-mail: *tmoore@sckans.edu* Web: *www.sckans.edu*

STERLING COLLEGE	D-3
Sterling, KS 67579	(316) 278-4275
	(800) 346-1017; Fax: (316) 278-4411

Full-time: 213 men, 220 women	**Faculty:** 39; IIB, --$
Part-time: 29 men, 33 women	**Ph.D.s:** 49%
Graduate: none	**Student/Faculty:** 11 to 1
Year: 4-1-4	**Tuition:** $13,250
Application Deadline: open	**Room & Board:** $5513
Freshman Class: 645 applied, 366 accepted, 126 enrolled	
SAT I Verbal/Math: 430/450	**ACT:** 22	**COMPETITIVE**

Sterling College, established in 1887, is a private liberal arts institution affiliated with the Presbyterian Church (U.S.A.), offering undergraduate curricula in 17 majors plus teacher preparation. The library contains 61,430 volumes, 2120 microform items, and 2125 audio/video tapes/CDs, and subscribes to 846 periodicals. Computerized library services include the card catalog, interlibrary loans, database searching, and Internet access. Special learning facilities include a learning resource center, art gallery, and a museum, and a theater. The 43-acre campus is in a small town 70 miles northwest of Wichita. Including any residence halls, there are 19 buildings.

Student Life: 63% of undergraduates are from Kansas. Students are from 28 states and 15 foreign countries. 85% are from public schools. 82% are white. 74% are Protestant; 20% claim no religious affiliation; 6% Catholic. The average age of freshmen is 18; all undergraduates, 20. 30% do not continue beyond their first year; 40% remain to graduate.

Housing: 525 students can be accommodated in college housing, which includes single-sex dormitories. On-campus housing is guaranteed for all 4 years. 80% of students live on campus; of those, 70% remain on campus on weekends. Alcohol is not permitted. All students may keep cars.

Activities: There are no fraternities or sororities. There are 12 groups on campus, including art, band, cheerleading, choir, chorus, debate, drama, ethnic, forensics, honors, international, jazz band, literary magazine, musical theater, newspaper, pep band, photography, political, professional, religious, social, social service, student government, and yearbook. Popular campus events include Habitat for Humanity Week, community picnic, and Missions and International Peacemaker Convocations/Events.

Sports: There are 6 intercollegiate sports for men and 6 for women, and 6 intramural sports for men and 6 for women. Facilities include a weight-training facility, an exercise deck, a swimming pool, a track and football field and stadium, a baseball diamond, a soccer field, practice fields, and basketball, handball, and tennis courts.

Disabled Students: 88% of the campus is accessible. Wheelchair ramps, elevators, special parking, specially equipped rest rooms, and special class scheduling are available.

Services: Counseling and information services are available, as is tutoring in every subject. There is remedial math, reading, and writing. and special accommodations provided on an as-needed basis.

Campus Safety and Security: Measures include informal discussions, pamphlets/posters/films, lighted pathways/sidewalks, and and evening and nighttime foot and vehicle patrol.

Programs of Study: Sterling confers B.A. and B.S. degrees. Bachelor's degrees are awarded in BIOLOGICAL SCIENCE (biology/biological science), BUSINESS (business administration and management), COMMUNICATIONS AND THE ARTS (art, communications, dramatic arts, English, fine arts, and music), COMPUTER AND PHYSICAL SCIENCE (computer science, and mathematics), EDUCATION (athletic training, elementary, and music), HEALTH PROFESSIONS (exercise science), SO-

CIAL SCIENCE (behavioral science, history, religious education, and theological studies). Biology, behavioral science, and education are the strongest academically. Biology, business administration, and education are the largest.

Required: To graduate, students must complete 52 to 57 credits in a general education curriculum including writing, math, science, social science, philosophy, computers, fine arts, and religion. They must have an overall GPA of 2.0, with 2.5 in the major. A total of 124 credits must be earned, with 39 to 48 in the major. Physical fitness and chapel/convocation requirements must also be met.

Special: Sterling offers cross-registration with the Associated Colleges of Central Kansas and the Council of Christian Colleges and Universities. Internships are available in most majors, as is study abroad in 5 countries. A Washington semester and work-study programs are offered. Student-designed majors are possible. There are 4 national honor societies, and 1 departmental honors program.

Faculty/Classroom: 62% of faculty are male; 38%, female. All teach undergraduates. The average class size in an introductory lecture is 30; in a laboratory, 20; and in a regular course, 15.

Admissions: 57% of the 2003-2004 applicants were accepted. The SAT I scores for the 2003-2004 freshman class were: Verbal--76% below 500, and 24% between 500 and 599; Math--81% below 500, 14% between 500 and 599, and 5% between 600 and 700. The ACT scores were 47% below 21, 14% between 21 and 23, 14% between 24 and 26, 9% between 27 and 28, and 16% above 28. 7 freshmen graduated first in their class.

Requirements: The SAT I or ACT is required. In addition, applicants must graduate from an accredited secondary school or have a GED. An interview is recommended. A GPA of 2.2 is required. AP and CLEP credits are accepted. Important factors in the admissions decision are personality/intangible qualities, extracurricular activities record, and leadership record.

Procedure: Freshmen are admitted fall and spring. Entrance exams should be taken in the spring of the junior year. There is an early admissions plan. Application deadlines are open. Application fee is $25. Applications are accepted on-line through the school's web site.

Transfer: 71 transfer students enrolled in 2002-2003. Transfer students must have a minimum composite ACT score of 18 or a combined SAT I score of 860 if they have fewer than 12 hours of college credit; and a 2.2 GPA. 24 of 124 credits required for the bachelor's degree must be completed at Sterling.

Visiting: There are regularly scheduled orientations for prospective students, including visits with admissions, financial aid, current students, and faculty and campus and housing tours. There are guides for informal visits and visitors may sit in on classes and stay overnight. To schedule a visit, contact the Admissions Office at (620) 278-4314 or *admissions@sterling.edu*.

Financial Aid: In 2003-2004, 100% of all full-time freshmen and 98% of continuing full-time students received some form of financial aid. 92% of all full-time students received need-based aid. The average freshman award was $13,447. Need-based scholarships or need-based grants averaged $3219 ($7383 maximum); need-based self-help aid (loans and jobs) averaged $2010 ($2595 maximum); non-need-based athletic scholarships averaged $4321 ($4515 maximum); and other non-need-based awards and non-need-based scholarships averaged $4743 ($6536 maximum). 60% of undergraduates work part time. Average annual earnings from campus work are $1100. The average financial indebtedness of the 2003 graduate was $16,262. The FAFSA is required. The deadline for filing freshman financial aid applications for fall entry is March 15.

International Students: There are 14 international students enrolled. They must score 520 on the written TOEFL or 190 on the electronic version and also take or ACT or SAT I.

Computers: The mainframe is a Novell Network. There are Internet-connected computer labs in the library, in 3 academic buildings, and in all 4 residence halls. All students may access the system 16 hours per day in the library and academic buildings and 24 hours per day in residence halls. There are no time limits and no fees.

Graduates: From July 1, 2002 to June 30, 2003, 90 bachelor's degrees were awarded. The most popular majors were elementary education (20%), business administration (18%), and biology (11%). In an average class, 68% graduate in 4 years or less, 79% graduate in 5 years or less, and 81% graduate in 6 years or less.

Admissions Contact: Dennis Dutton, VP for Enrollment Services. A video is available. E-mail: *admissions@sterling.edu* Web: *www.sterling.edu*

TABOR COLLEGE   D-2
Hillsboro, KS 67063

(620) 947-3121, ext. 1723
(800) TABOR-99; Fax: (620) 947-6276

Full-time: 229 men, 182 women	**Faculty:** 32; IIB, --$
Part-time: 43 men, 68 women	**Ph.D.s:** 70%
Graduate: 8 men, 13 women	**Student/Faculty:** 13 to 1
Year: 4-1-4	**Tuition:** $14,350
Application Deadline: August 1	**Room & Board:** $5150
Freshman Class: 216 applied, 215 accepted, 86 enrolled	
ACT: 22	NONCOMPETITIVE

Tabor College, established in 1908, is a private liberal arts facility affiliated with the Mennonite Brethren Church. There are 2 undergraduate schools. In addition to regional accreditation, Tabor has baccalaureate program accreditation with CSWE and NASM. The library contains 80,099 volumes, 435 microform items, and 1640 audio/video tapes/CDs, and subscribes to 265 periodicals. Computerized library services include the card catalog, interlibrary loans, database searching, and Internet access. Special learning facilities include a learning resource center and a writing center. The 26-acre campus is in a rural area 50 miles north of Wichita. Including any residence halls, there are 28 buildings.

Student Life: 68% of undergraduates are from Kansas. Students are from 23 states, 5 foreign countries, and Canada. 90% are from public schools. 89% are white. 89% are Protestant; 6% unspecified. The average age of freshmen is 18; all undergraduates, 20. 10% do not continue beyond their first year; 87% remain to graduate.

Housing: 210 students can be accommodated in college housing, which includes single-sex dorms and off-campus apartments. On-campus housing is guaranteed for all 4 years. 78% of students live on campus; of those, 85% remain on campus on weekends. Alcohol is not permitted. All students may keep cars.

Activities: There are no fraternities or sororities. There are 18 groups on campus, including art, band, cheerleading, choir, chorale, chorus, computers, drama, drill team, ethnic, honors, international, jazz band, musical theater, newspaper, pep band, photography, political, religious, social service, student government, and yearbook. Popular campus events include Service Emphasis Week and Mission Emphasis Week.

Sports: There are 8 intercollegiate sports for men and 8 for women, and 10 intramural sports for men and 10 for women. Facilities include 4 lighted tennis courts, 2 racquetball courts, lighted football and baseball fields, several practice fields, a soccer field, a curbed metric all-weather track, a gym with 2 playing floors, a practice/intramural gym, an indoor soccer court, and aerobic exercise, athletic training, and weight rooms.

Disabled Students: 75% of the campus is accessible. Wheelchair ramps, elevators, special parking, specially equipped rest rooms, special class scheduling, lowered drinking fountains, and lowered telephones are available.

Services: Counseling and information services are available, as is tutoring in most subjects. Tutoring is available for most learning disabled students and for those on academic probation.

Campus Safety and Security: Measures include lighted pathways/sidewalks.

Programs of Study: Tabor confers B.A. and B.S. degrees. Associate degrees are also awarded. Bachelor's degrees are awarded in BIOLOGICAL SCIENCE (biology/biological science), BUSINESS (accounting, business administration and management, marketing/retailing/merchandising, and office supervision and management), COMMUNICATIONS AND THE ARTS (applied art, communications, English, graphic design, and music), COMPUTER AND PHYSICAL SCIENCE (chemistry, computer science, mathematics, and natural sciences), EDUCATION (athletic training, business, elementary, health, middle school, music, physical, science, secondary, and special), SOCIAL SCIENCE (biblical studies, history, humanities, international studies, ministries, philosophy, psychology, religion, social science, and sociology). The sciences is the strongest academically. Business and education are the largest.

Required: All students must complete 47 to 59 hours of general education courses including biblical and religious studies, history of diverse cultures, creative expression, natural and mathematical systems, values, social sciences, language, communication, computer literacy, physical fitness, and a college success seminar. A total of 124 credits, 16 of which must be in the major, with a minimum GPA of 2.0, is required in order to graduate.

Special: Cross-registration is offered with the Association of Colleges of Central Kansas. Study abroad in 5 countries is possible. Dual majors, student-designed majors, internships, a Washington semester for juniors or seniors, and pass/fail options are available, as is a 3-2 engineering degree with Wichita State University. An accelerated degree program in management organizational development and preprofessional curricula in allied health, law, and medicine are also offered. There is a freshman honors program.

Faculty/Classroom: 65% of faculty are male; 35%, female. All teach undergraduates. No introductory courses are taught by graduate stu-

dents. The average class size in an introductory lecture is 32; in a laboratory, 12; and in a regular course, 20.

Admissions: All of the 2003-2004 applicants were accepted. The SAT I scores for the 2003-2004 freshman class were: Verbal--38% below 500, 13% between 500 and 599, 25% between 600 and 700, and 25% above 700; Math--50% below 500, 25% between 600 and 599, 25% between 600 and 700, and 25% above 700. The ACT scores were 27% below 21, 31% between 21 and 23, 14% between 24 and 26, 15% between 27 and 28, and 14% above 28. There were 3 National Merit finalists.

Requirements: The ACT is required. In addition, an essay is required and an interview is recommended. A GPA of 2.0 is required. AP and CLEP credits are accepted.

Procedure: Freshmen are admitted to all sessions. Entrance exams should be taken in October of the senior year. There is a rolling admissions plan. Early decision applications should be filed by February 1; regular applications, by August 1 for fall entry, along with a $20 fee. Notification is sent on a rolling basis. Applications are accepted on-line through CollegeLink or the school's web site.

Transfer: 34 transfer students enrolled in 2002-2003. A minimum 2.0 GPA is required and an interview is recommended. 33 of 124 credits required for the bachelor's degree must be completed at Tabor.

Visiting: There are regularly scheduled orientations for prospective students, including a tour, admissions interview, and faculty, class, and financial aid visits. If requested, an audition or tryout will be scheduled. There are guides for informal visits and visitors may sit in on classes and stay overnight. To schedule a visit, contact Admissions Counselors at *campusvisit@tabor.edu.*

Financial Aid: In 2003-2004, 100% of all full-time students received some form of financial aid. 82% of full-time freshmen and 77% of continuing full-time students received need-based aid. The average freshman award was $5022. Need-based scholarships or need-based grants averaged $4488; and non-need-based athletic scholarships averaged $1672. 43% of undergraduates work part time. Average annual earnings from campus work are $1000. The average financial indebtedness of the 2003 graduate was $17,914. The FAFSA, a federal income tax form, and W-2 forms are required. The deadline for filing freshman financial aid applications for fall entry is March 1.

International Students: They must score 525 on the written TOEFL and also take the SAT I or the ACT.

Computers: The mainframe is a Dual 83/80. There are also 60 PCs available in the administration building and labs. All students may access the system. There are no time limits and no fees.

Graduates: From July 1, 2002 to June 30, 2003, 101 bachelor's degrees were awarded. The most popular majors were business marketing (22%), philosophy, religion, theology (21%), and education (14%).

Admissions Contact: Rusty Allen, Director of Admissions.
E-mail: *admissions@.tabor.edu* Web: *www.tabor.edu*

UNIVERSITY OF KANSAS
Lawrence, KS 66045

E-2

(785) 864-3911
(888) 686-7323; Fax: (785) 864-5017

Full-time: 8743 men, 9529 women	**Faculty:** 1168; I, -$
Part-time: 1296 men, 1298 women	**Ph.D.s:** 92%
Graduate: 3416 men, 4333 women	**Student/Faculty:** 16 to 1
Year: semesters, summer session	**Tuition:** $4101 ($11,577)
Application Deadline: April 1	**Room & Board:** $4822
Freshman Class: 9573 applied, 6458 accepted, 4074 enrolled	
ACT: 24	**VERY COMPETITIVE**

The University of Kansas, founded in 1866, is a public, comprehensive institution. Its undergraduate and graduate programs emphasize the liberal arts, business, fine arts, music, teacher preparation, journalism, engineering, architecture, social welfare, law, and health science, including pharmacy. Its medical center campus is located in Kansas City. There are 11 undergraduate and 3 graduate schools. In addition to regional accreditation, KU has baccalaureate program accreditation with AACSB, ABET, ACEJMC, ACPE, AOTA, APTA, CAAHEP, CSWE, NAAB, NAACLS, NASAD, NASM, NCATE, and NLN. The 12 libraries contain 3,980,529 volumes, 3,571,801 microform items, and 52,158 audio/video tapes/CDs, and subscribe to 36,007 periodicals. Computerized library services include the card catalog, interlibrary loans, database searching, and Internet access. Special learning facilities include a learning resource center, art gallery, natural history museum, radio station, TV station, observatory, film studio, space technology center, state-of-the-art performing arts center, art, natural history, classics, anthropology, entomology, and invertebrate paleontology museums, and an organ recital hall. The 1000-acre campus is in a suburban area 40 miles west of Kansas City. Including any residence halls, there are 190 buildings.

Student Life: 73% of undergraduates are from Kansas. Students are from 50 states, 111 foreign countries, and Canada. 84% are white. The average age of freshmen is 18; all undergraduates, 21. 18% do not continue beyond their first year; 57% remain to graduate.

Housing: 5452 students can be accommodated in college housing, which includes single-sex and coed dorms, on-campus apartments, off-

campus apartments, and married-student housing. In addition, there are honors houses, special-interest floors, and 1 residence hall with a fine arts emphasis. On-campus housing is available on a first-come, first-served basis. Alcohol is not permitted. All students may keep cars.

Activities: 14% of men belong to 24 national fraternities; 20% of women belong to 20 national sororities. There are 420 groups on campus, including art, band, cheerleading, chess, choir, chorale, chorus, dance, debate, drama, environmental, ethnic, film, gay, honors, international, jazz band, literary magazine, marching band, musical theater, newspaper, opera, orchestra, pep band, photography, political, professional, radio and TV, religious, social, social service, student government, symphony, and yearbook. Popular campus events include Holiday Vespers, music and theater presentations, and Rock Chalk Revue.

Sports: There are 7 intercollegiate sports for men and 11 for women, and 20 intramural sports for men and 20 for women. Facilities include a field house with an indoor track and basketball and volleyball courts; a 52,000-seat football stadium with an outdoor track; a sports pavilion with an indoor football field; a health and phys ed center housing 2 indoor pools, handball and racquetball courts, and gyms; baseball, lacrosse, ultimate Frisbee, cricket, football, soccer, and rugby fields; tennis courts; a bowling alley; and a student recreation center that contains an indoor climbing wall, a gym, a suspended jogging track, 2 racquetball courts, a free weight/cardiovascular gym area, and aerobic and martial arts rooms.

Disabled Students: 95% of the campus is accessible. Wheelchair ramps, elevators, special parking, specially equipped rest rooms, special class scheduling, lowered drinking fountains, and lowered telephones are available.

Services: Counseling and information services are available, as is tutoring in most subjects. There are how-to sessions on study and organizational skills, and workshops on note-taking. There is a reader service for the blind and remedial math. A writing center is available to students.

Campus Safety and Security: Measures include 24-hour foot and vehicle patrol, shuttle buses, informal discussions, and pamphlets/posters/films. There are emergency telephones and lighted pathways/sidewalks.

Programs of Study: KU confers B.A., B.S., B.A.E., B.Arch., B.F.A., B.G.S., B.M., B.M.E., B.S.B., B.S.E., B.S.J., B.S.N., and B.S.W. degrees. Master's and doctoral degrees are also awarded. Bachelor's degrees are awarded in AGRICULTURE (environmental studies), BIOLOGICAL SCIENCE (biochemistry, biology/biological science, microbiology, and molecular biology), BUSINESS (accounting, business administration and management, and sports management), COMMUNICATIONS AND THE ARTS (art, art history and appreciation, classical languages, dance, design, dramatic arts, East Asian languages and literature, English, French, German, Germanic languages and literature, journalism, linguistics, music history and appreciation, music performance, music theory and composition, painting, printmaking, sculpture, Slavic languages, Spanish, speech/debate/rhetoric, theater design, and voice), COMPUTER AND PHYSICAL SCIENCE (astronomy, atmospheric sciences and meteorology, chemistry, computer science, geology, information sciences and systems, mathematics, and physics), EDUCATION (art, athletic training, elementary, health, middle school, music, physical, and secondary), ENGINEERING AND ENVIRONMENTAL DESIGN (aeronautical engineering, architectural engineering, architecture, chemical engineering, civil engineering, computer engineering, electrical/electronics engineering, engineering physics, mechanical engineering, occupational safety and health, and petroleum/natural gas engineering), HEALTH PROFESSIONS (clinical science, community health work, cytotechnology, music therapy, nursing, pharmacy, respiratory therapy, and speech pathology/audiology), SOCIAL SCIENCE (African American studies, African studies, American studies, anthropology, archeology, behavioral science, economics, European studies, geography, history, humanities, international studies, Latin American studies, philosophy, political science/government, psychology, religion, Russian and Slavic studies, social work, sociology, and women's studies). Business, pharmacy, and engineering are the strongest academically. Engineering, biological sciences, and psychology are the largest.

Required: To graduate with a B.A., B.S., or B.G.S. degree, all students must complete at least 124 credit hours, including 27 to 50 in the major, and maintain a GPA of at least 2.0. These, as well as curricula and distribution requirements, vary according to the school and the major. English composition and literature must be taken.

Special: Special academic programs include internships, study abroad in more than 50 countries, a Washington semester, and work-study programs with the university. A cooperative program in engineering is offered, as are B.A.-B.S. degrees in many combinations, interdisciplinary majors, and dual majors in any approved combination. General studies degrees are available in many areas, and student-designed majors are possible. Nondegree study and pass/fail options are offered. There are 18 national honor societies, including Phi Beta Kappa, a freshman honors program, and a universitywide honors program.

Faculty/Classroom: 63% of faculty are male; 37%, female. 98% teach undergraduates, all do research, and 98% do both. Graduate students teach 12% of introductory courses. The average class size in a laboratory is 20 and in a regular course, 22.

Admissions: 67% of the 2003-2004 applicants were accepted. The ACT scores for the 2003-2004 freshman class were: 18% below 21, 28% between 21 and 23, 27% between 24 and 26, 13% between 27 and 28, and 14% above 28. 56% of the current freshmen were in the top fifth of their class; 87% were in the top two fifths. There were 46 National Merit finalists.

Requirements: The SAT I or ACT is required. Kansas resident applicants must have a minimum 2.0 GPA in the qualified admissions college preparatory curriculum; or have an ACT composite score of 21 or SAT I score of 980; or rank in the top third of their high school class. College preparatory curriculum includes 4 units of English, 3 of college preparatory math, 3 of natural science (1 must be chemistry or physics), 3 of social sciences, and 1 of computer technology. 2 units of foreign language and 1 of fine or performing arts are recommended. Nonresidents have the same curriculum requirements, except they must have a minimum GPA of 2.5; or an ACT composite score of 24 or SAT I score of 1090 with a 2.0 GPA; or be in the top third of their high school class. AP and CLEP credits are accepted. Important factors in the admissions decision are advanced placement or honor courses, evidence of special talent, and recommendations by school officials.

Procedure: Freshmen are admitted to all sessions. Entrance exams should be taken by the end of the junior year. There is a deferred admissions plan and a rolling admissions plan. Applications should be filed by April 1 for fall entry, December 1 for spring entry, and February 1 for summer entry. The fall 2003 application fee was $30. Notification is sent on a rolling basis. 249 applicants were on the 2003 waiting list; 249 were admitted. Applications are accepted on-line through *www.admissions.ku.edu.*

Transfer: 1462 transfer students enrolled in 2002-2003. For entrance to the College of Liberal Arts and Sciences, transfer students must have at least 24 credit hours with a minimum GPA of 2.0 in-state; 2.5 out-of-state. The criteria vary widely within the other KU schools, some of which may also consider the ACT score and course work. 30 credits of 124 required for the bachelor's degree must be completed at KU.

Visiting: There are regularly scheduled orientations for prospective students, consisting of a summer orientation program that includes a 1-day campus visit. There are guides for informal visits and visitors may sit in on classes and stay overnight. To schedule a visit, contact KU Visitor Center at (785) 864-5135 or *visitku@ku.edu.*

Financial Aid: In 2003-2004, 47% of all full-time freshmen and 46% of continuing full-time students received some form of financial aid. 35% of full-time freshmen and 33% of continuing full-time students received need-based aid. The average freshman award was $5540. Need-based scholarships or need-based grants averaged $3228; need-based self-help aid (loans and jobs) averaged $2714; non-need-based athletic scholarships averaged $10,777; and other non-need-based awards and non-need-based scholarships averaged $3007. 16% of undergraduates work part time. Average annual earnings from campus work are $3300. The average financial indebtedness of the 2003 graduate was $18,271. The FAFSA is required. The deadline for filing freshman financial aid applications for fall entry is March 1.

International Students: There are 511 international students enrolled. The school actively recruits these students. They must take the college's own test. Students are tested upon arrival at KU; a high TOEFL score may be accepted in place of the university test.

Computers: The mainframes are multiple servers. There are hundreds of terminals around the campus in labs and at the computer center. Many PCs are also available campuswide. All students may access the system 24 hours a day, 7 days a week. There are no time limits and no fees.

Graduates: From July 1, 2002 to June 30, 2003, 3760 bachelor's degrees were awarded. The most popular majors were business (11%), journalism (10%), and speech (7%). In an average class, 1% graduate in 3 years or less, 26% graduate in 4 years or less, 52% graduate in 5 years or less, and 57% graduate in 6 years or less. 500 companies recruited on campus in 2002-2003. Of the 2002 graduating class, 19% were enrolled in graduate school within 6 months of graduation and 46% were employed.

Admissions Contact: Lisa Pinamonti, Director of Admissions and Scholarships. A video is available. E-mail: *adm@ku.edu* Web: *www.admissions.ku.edu*

UNIVERSITY OF SAINT MARY   F-2
(Formerly Saint Mary College)
Leavenworth, KS 66048   (913) 758-6165
(800) 752-7043; Fax: (913) 758-6140

Full-time: 206 men, 183 women	**Faculty:** 46
Part-time: 58 men, 133 women	**Ph.D.s:** 61%
Graduate: 16 men, 285 women	**Student/Faculty:** 8 to 1
Year: semesters, summer session	**Tuition:** $13,574
Application Deadline: open	**Room & Board:** $5294
Freshman Class: 91 enrolled	
ACT: 21	**COMPETITIVE**

The University of Saint Mary, formerly Saint Mary College, founded in 1923, is a private liberal arts institution affiliated with the Roman Catholic Church and sponsored by the Sisters of Charity of Leavenworth. There is 1 graduate school. In addition to regional accreditation, USM has baccalaureate program accreditation with IACBE and NCATE. The library contains 120,000 volumes and 1675 microform items, and subscribes to 301 periodicals. Computerized library services include the card catalog, interlibrary loans, database searching, and Internet access. Special learning facilities include a learning resource center, art gallery, and several special library collections. The 240-acre campus is in a small town 25 miles northwest of Kansas City, Missouri. Including any residence halls, there are 10 buildings.

Student Life: 75% of undergraduates are from Kansas. Students are from 31 states, 7 foreign countries, and Canada. 73% are white. The average age of freshmen is 18; all undergraduates, 26.

Housing: 333 students can be accommodated in college housing, which includes single-sex and coed dormitories. On-campus housing is guaranteed for all 4 years. 62% of students commute. All students may keep cars.

Activities: There are no fraternities or sororities. There are 25 groups on campus, including art, cheerleading, choir, chorale, chorus, computers, dance, drama, honors, literary magazine, musical theater, newspaper, opera, political, professional, religious, social, social service, and student government. Popular campus events include Fall Convocation, Founders Day, and Family Weekend.

Sports: There are 4 intercollegiate sports for men and 4 for women, and 10 intramural sports for men and 10 for women. Facilities include a 500-seat sports center, soccer and softball fields, a multipurpose field, 3 tennis courts, a sandlot volleyball court, 2 racquetball courts, a weight and exercise room, a swimming pool, a dance and aerobics space, a walking trail, and an indoor jogging track.

Disabled Students: 90% of the campus is accessible. Wheelchair ramps, elevators, special parking, and specially equipped rest rooms are available.

Services: Counseling and information services are available, as is tutoring in most subjects.

Campus Safety and Security: Measures include self-defense education, informal discussions, pamphlets/posters/films, and lighted pathways/sidewalks. There are 14-hour foot and vehicle patrols and controlled access to residence halls.

Programs of Study: USM confers B.A. and B.S. degrees. Associate and master's degrees are also awarded. Bachelor's degrees are awarded in BIOLOGICAL SCIENCE (biology/biological science), BUSINESS (accounting, business administration and management, business systems analysis, and sports management), COMMUNICATIONS AND THE ARTS (art, dramatic arts, and English), COMPUTER AND PHYSICAL SCIENCE (chemistry, information sciences and systems, and mathematics), EDUCATION (elementary), HEALTH PROFESSIONS (medical technology), SOCIAL SCIENCE (applied psychology, child psychology/development, history, interdisciplinary studies, international studies, liberal arts/general studies, pastoral studies, political science/government, psychology, sociology, and theological studies). Elementary education, business administration, and information sciences are the strongest academically.

Required: To graduate, students must complete all general education requirements and earn at least 128 credits, including 30 to 42 in the major, with a minimum GPA of 2.0. The core curriculum includes freshman humanities, colloquium in human communities, introduction to fine arts, and a senior integration project. Distribution requirements include 3 courses each in English, math, and natural science, and social and behavioral sciences, 2 courses each in theology, philosophy, history, and foreign language, plus an additional literature course, a fine arts course, a learning communities course, and an elective in arts. Completion of a writing portfolio is also required. Students must also fulfill cultural literacy and lifetime physical wellness requirements.

Special: The university offers study abroad at various locations in Europe, Latin America, and Australia. Credit for life experience, internships in most major programs, evening and weekend study programs, pass/fail options, and dual majors are also available. There are 2 national honor societies.

Faculty/Classroom: 45% of faculty are male; 55%, female. All teach undergraduates. The average class size in an introductory lecture is 25 and in a laboratory, 12.

Admissions: The ACT scores for the 2003-2004 freshman class were: 43% below 21, 35% between 21 and 23, 16% between 24 and 26, 5% between 27 and 28, and 1% above 28.

Requirements: The SAT I or ACT is required. In addition, applicants should be graduates of an accredited secondary school. The GED is accepted. A GPA of 2.5 is required. AP and CLEP credits are accepted. Important factors in the admissions decision are parents or siblings attending the school, recommendations by alumni, and recommendations by school officials.

Procedure: Freshmen are admitted fall and spring. Entrance exams should be taken in the spring of the junior year and fall of the senior year. There are early decision and early admissions plans. Application deadlines are open. Application fee is $25. Notification is sent on a rolling basis.

Transfer: 54 transfer students enrolled in 2002-2003. A college GPA of 2.0 is required. 30 of 128 credits required for the bachelor's degree must be completed at USM.

Visiting: There are regularly scheduled orientations for prospective students, including interviews with faculty and financial aid representatives and a tour of the campus. There are guides for informal visits and visitors may sit in on classes. To schedule a visit, contact the Admissions Office at (913) 682-5151, ext. 6118.

Financial Aid: In 2003-2004, 95% of all full-time freshmen received some form of financial aid. 85% of full-time freshmen and 65% of continuing full-time students received need-based aid. The average freshman award was $11,100. 27% of undergraduates work part time. Average annual earnings from campus work are $627. The average financial indebtedness of the 2003 graduate was $15,000. USM is a member of CSS. The FAFSA is required. The priority date for freshman financial aid applications for fall entry is April 1.

International Students: There are 11 international students enrolled. The school actively recruits these students. They must score 500 on the written TOEFL or 170 on the electronic version.

Computers: The mainframe is an IBM AS/400. Approximately 40 PCs are available for student use in the library, learning center, and computer labs, and Internet access is available in all residence halls. All students may access the system. There are no time limits and no fees. It is strongly recommended that all students have a personal computer. Incoming freshmen are issued laptops.

Admissions Contact: Judy Weidower, Director of Admissions. A video is available. E-mail: *admiss@stmary.edu* Web: *www.stmary.edu*

WASHBURN UNIVERSITY OF TOPEKA
E-2
Topeka, KS 66621 (785) 231-1010, ext. 1030; (800) 332-0291

Full-time: 1532 men, 2321 women	**Faculty:** 206; IIA, av$
Part-time: 681 men, 1350 women	**Ph.D.s:** 83%
Graduate: 478 men, 640 women	**Student/Faculty:** 19 to 1
Year: semesters, summer session	**Tuition:** $4112 ($9212)
Application Deadline: August 4	**Room & Board:** $4872
Freshman Class: 1705 applied, 1705 accepted, 741 enrolled	
ACT: 21	**NONCOMPETITIVE**

Washburn is a publicly funded, independently governed, state-coordinated university. Established in 1865, the school offers more than 190 programs leading to certification, associate, bachelor, master, and juris doctor degrees through the College of Arts and Sciences and the Schools of Law, Business, Nursing, and Applied Studies. There are 4 undergraduate and 4 graduate schools. In addition to regional accreditation, Washburn has baccalaureate program accreditation with ACS, APTA, CAAHEP, CAHEA, CSWE, NASAD, NASM, and NCATE. The 2 libraries contain 336,973 volumes, 595,244 microform items, and 12,776 audio/video tapes/CDs, and subscribe to 2024 periodicals. Computerized library services include the card catalog, interlibrary loans, database searching, and Internet access. Special learning facilities include a learning resource center, art gallery, planetarium, and TV station. The 160-acre campus is in an urban area 60 miles west of Kansas City. Including any residence halls, there are 25 buildings.

Student Life: 94% of undergraduates are from Kansas. Students are from 40 states, 180 foreign countries, and Canada. 87% are from public schools. 65% are white. The average age of freshmen is 23; all undergraduates, 26. 20% do not continue beyond their first year; 61% remain to graduate.

Housing: 482 students can be accommodated in college housing, which includes coed dorms, fraternity houses, and sorority houses. In addition, there are special-interest houses. On-campus housing is available on a first-come, first-served basis. Priority is given to out-of-town students. 93% of students commute. Alcohol is not permitted. All students may keep cars.

Activities: 12% of men belong to 1 local and 3 national fraternities; 8% of women belong to 4 national sororities. There are 90 groups on campus, including art, band, campus activities board, cheerleading, chess, choir, chorus, computers, dance, debate, drama, drill team, drum and bugle corps, ethnic, forensics, gay, honors, international, jazz band, literary magazine, marching band, musical theater, newspaper, orchestra, pep band, political, professional, radio and TV, religious, social, social service, student government, Washburn University Peer Educators, and yearbook. Popular campus events include Greek Week, Student Activities Fair, and the Annual Music Festival.

Sports: There are 5 intercollegiate sports for men and 5 for women, and 10 intramural sports for men and 10 for women. Facilities include a 2700-seat field house for indoor sports, basketball, volleyball, handball, wrestling, tumbling, and gymnastics, physical education classes, and recreational amd intramural activities; a 7200-seat stadium for intercollegiate football, and a health center with a 6-lane swimming pool, running track, weight training room, and dance studio.

Disabled Students: 95% of the campus is accessible. Wheelchair ramps, elevators, special parking, specially equipped rest rooms, special class scheduling, lowered drinking fountains, lowered telephones, special housing, note takers, readers, library assistance, recorders, reading machines, videotaped classes, oral tests, learning center, tutors, and extended time for tests are also available.

Services: Counseling and information services are available, as is tutoring in most subjects. There is a reader service for the blind and remedial math and writing.

Campus Safety and Security: Measures include 24-hour foot and vehicle patrol, self-defense education, security escort services, and informal discussions. There are pamphlets/posters/films, emergency telephones, lighted pathways/sidewalks, whistle campaign, operation ID, textbook ID program, bicycle patrol, and fire safety programs for residential living facilities.

Programs of Study: Washburn confers B.A., B.S., B.A.S., B.B.A., B.Ed., B.F.A., B.I.S., B.M., B.P.A., B.S.C.J., B.S.N., and B.S.W. degrees. Associate, master's, and doctoral degrees are also awarded. Bachelor's degrees are awarded in BIOLOGICAL SCIENCE (biology/biological science), BUSINESS (accounting, banking and finance, business administration and management, business economics, and marketing/retailing/merchandising), COMMUNICATIONS AND THE ARTS (art, art history and appreciation, communications, dramatic arts, English, French, German, media arts, music, music performance, Spanish, speech/debate/rhetoric, and theater design), COMPUTER AND PHYSICAL SCIENCE (chemistry, computer programming, computer science, information sciences and systems, mathematics, physics, and science), EDUCATION (art, business, early childhood, education, education administration, elementary, music, physical, reading, secondary, and special), ENGINEERING AND ENVIRONMENTAL DESIGN (technological management), HEALTH PROFESSIONS (medical laboratory technology and nursing), SOCIAL SCIENCE (anthropology, corrections, economics, history, human services, law enforcement and corrections, liberal arts/general studies, philosophy, political science/government, psychology, public administration, religion, social work, and sociology). Natural sciences, art, and music are the strongest academically. Business administration, criminal justice, and nursing are the largest.

Required: Students must complete courses in the arts and humanities, English composition, natural sciences, math, social sciences, and phys ed. A minimum GPA of 2.0 is required over 124 credit hours, including 30 to 40 in the major, for graduation.

Special: Washburn offers co-op programs in computer information science, engineering, social/behavorial sciences, education, ad health profession; internships in numerous departments, and study abroad in 12 countries. Dual and student-designed majors, B.A.-B.S. degrees, an integrated studies degree, credit by examination, nondegree study, and pass/fail options are also available. A 3-2 engineering degree is possible in conjunction with the University of Kansas and Kansas State University. There are 9 national honor societies, a freshman honors program, and 22 departmental honors programs.

Faculty/Classroom: 56% of faculty are male; 44%, female. 90% teach undergraduates. No introductory courses are taught by graduate students. The average class size in an introductory lecture is 27; in a laboratory, 16; and in a regular course, 18.

Admissions: 100% of the 2003-2004 applicants were accepted. The ACT scores for the 2003-2004 freshman class were: 44% below 21, 28% between 21 and 23, 17% between 24 and 26, 7% between 27 and 28, and 5% above 28. 31% of the current freshmen were in the top fifth of their class; 60% were in the top two fifths. 30 freshmen graduated first in their class.

Requirements: The ACT is required. In addition, applicants should be graduates of an accredited secondary school or have the GED. AP and CLEP credits are accepted.

Procedure: Freshmen are admitted to all sessions. Entrance exams should be taken during the junior year. Applications should be filed by August 4 for fall entry, January 6 for spring entry, and May 5 for summer entry. There is a $20 application fee. The college accepts all applicants. Notification is sent on a rolling basis. Applications are accepted on-line.

Transfer: 543 transfer students enrolled in 2002-2003. Applicants must meet the same requirements as incoming freshmen. 30 of 124 credits required for the bachelor's degree must be completed at Washburn.

Visiting: There are regularly scheduled orientations for prospective students, consisting of a campus visit program Monday through Friday at 9:30 A.M. or 1:30 P.M. that includes a tour, visits with faculty, financial aid information, and the opportunity to have all questions answered. There are guides for informal visits and visitors may sit in on classes and stay overnight. To schedule a visit, contact Carmen Harness at *admissions@washburn.edu*.

Financial Aid: In 2003-2004, 43% of all full-time freshmen received some form of financial aid. 34% of full-time freshmen received need-based aid. The average freshman award was $2125. Need-based scholarships or need-based grants averaged $1350; need-based self-help aid (loans and jobs) averaged $2812; non-need-based athletic scholarships averaged $4023; and other non-need-based awards and non-need-based scholarships averaged $1551. 8% of undergraduates work part time. Average annual earnings from campus work are $3400. The average financial indebtedness of the 2003 graduate was $11,000. The FAFSA is required. The priority date for freshman financial aid applications for fall entry is March 1. The deadline for filing freshman financial aid applications for fall entry is July 1.

International Students: There are 165 international students enrolled. The school actively recruits these students. They must score 520 on the written TOEFL or 193 on the electronic version.

Computers: The mainframe is an IBM RS 6000. Available computers include Macs, PCs, and Internet stations. All students may access the system 7 A.M. until midnight on campus, by dial-up 24 hours a day. There are no time limits and no fees.

Graduates: From July 1, 2002 to June 30, 2003, 640 bachelor's degrees were awarded. The most popular majors were business (21%), nursing (13%), and criminal justice (12%). In an average class, 42% graduate in 4 years or less, 51% graduate in 5 years or less, and 60% graduate in 6 years or less. 73 companies recruited on campus in 2002-2003. Of the 2002 graduating class, 15% were enrolled in graduate school within 6 months of graduation and 98% were employed.

Admissions Contact: Kirk Haskins, Director of Admissions.
E-mail: *admissions@washburn.edu* Web: *www.washburn.edu*

WICHITA STATE UNIVERSITY
Wichita, KS 67260

D-3

(316) 978-3085
(800) 362-2594; Fax: (316) 978-3174

Full-time: 3264 men, 4113 women	**Faculty:** 460; I, --$
Part-time: 1827 men, 2488 women	**Ph.D.s:** 78%
Graduate: 1467 men, 1737 women	**Student/Faculty:** 16 to 1
Year: semesters, summer session	**Tuition:** $3472 ($10,926)
Application Deadline: open	**Room & Board:** $4620
Freshman Class: 4221 applied, 2625 accepted, 1373 enrolled	
ACT: 21	COMPETITIVE

Wichita State University, established in 1895, is a public institution offering programs in the liberal arts and sciences, business, engineering, education, and health professions. There are 6 undergraduate schools and 1 graduate school. In addition to regional accreditation, WSU has baccalaureate program accreditation with AACSB, ABET, ADA, APTA, CAHEA, CSWE, NASM, NCATE, and NLN. The library contains 1,649,694 volumes, 1,135,688 microform items, and 31,442 audio/video tapes/CDs, and subscribes to 17,545 periodicals. Computerized library services include the card catalog, interlibrary loans, database searching, and Internet access. Special learning facilities include a learning resource center, art gallery, natural history museum, radio station, TV station, electronic classroom, telecourses, the National Institute for Aviation Research, museum of art, and public observatory. The 330-acre campus is in the metropolitan Wichita area. Including any residence halls, there are 61 buildings.

Student Life: 92% of undergraduates are from Kansas. Students are from 46 states, 81 foreign countries, and Canada. 69% are white. The average age of freshmen is 21; all undergraduates, 25. 29% do not continue beyond their first year; 37% remain to graduate.

Housing: 1236 students can be accommodated in college housing, which includes coed dormitories, on-campus apartments, married-student housing, fraternity houses, and sorority houses. In addition, there are honors houses. On-campus housing is available on a first-come, first-served basis. 90% of students commute. All students may keep cars.

Activities: 8% of men belong to 10 national fraternities; 5% of women belong to 8 national sororities. There are 99 groups on campus, including art, band, cheerleading, chess, choir, chorus, computers, dance, debate, drama, ethnic, film, gay, honors, international, jazz band, literary magazine, musical theater, newspaper, opera, orchestra, pep band, photography, political, professional, radio and TV, religious, social, social service, student government, and symphony. Popular campus events include Hippodrome, International Week, and ShocktoberFest.

Sports: There are 7 intercollegiate sports for men and 8 for women, and 24 intramural sports for men and 24 for women. Facilities include a 10,656-seat arena, 2 stadiums, an 18-hole golf course, a baseball field, a tennis complex, and a recreation and sports center.

Disabled Students: 98% of the campus is accessible. Wheelchair ramps, elevators, special parking, specially equipped rest rooms, special class scheduling, lowered drinking fountains, lowered telephones, wheelchairs, and braille typewriters are available. Interpreters for the hearing impaired, note taking, and typing services are also offered.

Services: Counseling and information services are available, as is tutoring in most subjects. There is a reader service for the blind, and remedial math, reading, and writing. Group and individual psychological services are available for students and their families.

Campus Safety and Security: Measures include 24-hour foot and vehicle patrol, self-defense education, security escort services, and shuttle buses. There are informal discussions, pamphlets/posters/films, emergency telephones, lighted pathways/sidewalks, and a bicycle patrol.

Programs of Study: WSU confers B.A., B.S., B.A.E., B.B.A., B.F.A., B.G.S., B.H.S., B.M., B.M.E., B.S.A.E., B.S.E., B.S.E.E., B.S.I.E., B.S.M.E., and B.S.N. degrees. Associate, master's, and doctoral degrees are also awarded. Bachelor's degrees are awarded in BIOLOGICAL SCIENCE (biology/biological science), BUSINESS (accounting, banking and finance, business administration and management, entrepreneurial studies, human resources, international business management, management science, marketing/retailing/merchandising, and sports management), COMMUNICATIONS AND THE ARTS (art, art history and appreciation, communications, English, French, graphic design, Latin, music, Spanish, studio art, and visual and performing arts), COMPUTER AND PHYSICAL SCIENCE (chemistry, computer science, geology, mathematics, and physics), EDUCATION (art, elementary, music, physical, secondary, and special), ENGINEERING AND ENVIRONMENTAL DESIGN (aeronautical engineering, computer engineering, electrical/electronics engineering, industrial engineering, manufacturing engineering, and mechanical engineering), HEALTH PROFESSIONS (health care administration, medical laboratory technology, nursing, physician's assistant, and speech pathology/audiology), SOCIAL SCIENCE (anthropology, criminal justice, economics, ethnic studies, gerontology, history, liberal arts/general studies, philosophy, political science/government, psychology, social work, sociology, and women's studies). Physician assistant, music theater, and speech pathology are the strongest academically. Management, nursing, and elementary education are the largest.

Required: To graduate, students need at least 124 credit hours, with a GPA of 2.0 to 2.5, depending on the major. Specific distribution requirements, as well as department requirements, must also be met. The core curriculum consists of 14 courses (42 hours) in general education.

Special: WSU offers co-op programs, internships, study abroad, work-study programs, and a Washington semester. Dual and student-designed majors, a general studies degree, credit by exam, nondegree study, and pass/fail options are also available. There are 14 national honor societies, and a freshman honors program.

Faculty/Classroom: 63% of faculty are male; 37%, female. 85% both teach and do research. The average class size in an introductory lecture is 20; in a laboratory, 14; and in a regular course, 24.

Admissions: 62% of the 2003-2004 applicants were accepted. The ACT scores for the 2003-2004 freshman class were: 42% below 21, 26% between 21 and 23, 18% between 24 and 26, 8% between 27 and 28, and 6% above 28. 25% of the current freshmen were in the top fifth of their class; 52% were in the top two fifths.

Requirements: The SAT I or ACT is required. Applicants must submit a minimum composite ACT score of 21 or a combined SAT I score of 990, rank in the top one third of their high school graduating class, and have a 2.0 GPA (nonresidents, 2.5). Requirements include 4 years of English, 3 each of math, natural science, and social sciences, and 1 of computer technology. AP and CLEP credits are accepted.

Procedure: Freshmen are admitted to all sessions. There are early admissions and deferred admissions plans. Application deadlines are open. The fall 2003 application fee was $30. Notification is sent on a rolling basis. Applications are accepted on-line through the university's web site.

Transfer: 1304 transfer students enrolled in 2002-2003. Applicants must have a minimum GPA of 2.0 to 2.5, depending on the WSU college they wish to enter. 30 of 124 credits required for the bachelor's degree must be completed at WSU.

Visiting: There are regularly scheduled orientations for prospective students. Students may schedule their visit on-line through the school's web site. There are guides for informal visits and visitors may sit in on classes and stay overnight. To schedule a visit, contact the Admissions Office.

Financial Aid: In a recent year, 26% of full-time freshmen and 51% of continuing full-time students received need-based aid. The average freshman award was $900. Average annual earnings from campus work are $1408. The average financial indebtedness of the 2003 graduate was $17,342. The FAFSA is required. The deadline for filing freshman financial aid applications for fall entry is March 15.

International Students: There are 556 international students enrolled. The school actively recruits these students.

Computers: The mainframes are an IBM ES 9121/440 and a DEC VAX/4000. Computing labs are located throughout the campus. Students have access as needed and required by academic programs and courses. All students may access the system 24 hours a day. There are no fees.

Graduates: From July 1, 2002 to June 30, 2003, 1760 bachelor's degrees were awarded. The most popular majors were elementary education (7%), nursing (5%), and business administration (4%). In an average class, 11% graduate in 4 years or less, 28% graduate in 5 years or less, and 37% graduate in 6 years or less. 58 companies recruited on campus in 2002-2003. Of a recent year's graduating class, 21% were enrolled in graduate school within 6 months of graduation and 96% were employed.

Admissions Contact: Gina Crabtree, Director of Admissions. A video is available. E-mail: *admissions@wichita.edu*
Web: *http://www.wichita.edu*

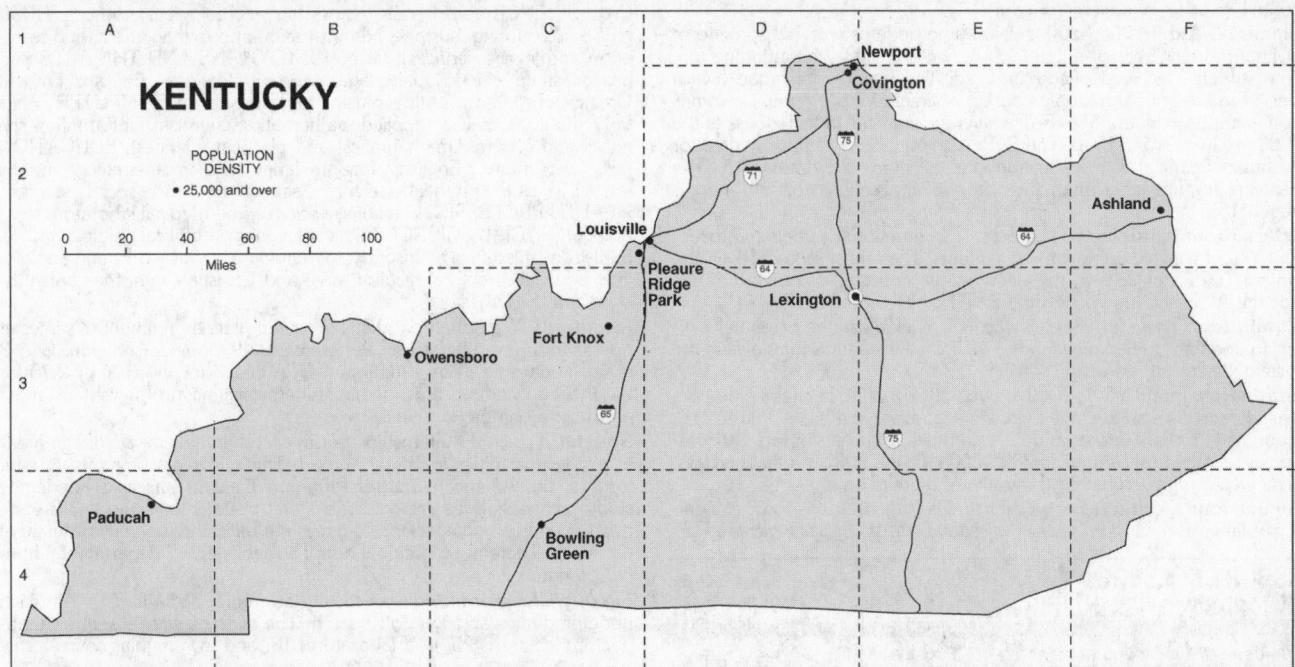

KENTUCKY

POPULATION DENSITY
• 25,000 and over

0   20   40   60   80   100
Miles

ALICE LLOYD COLLEGE
Pippa Passes, KY 41844
E-4

(606) 368-6036, ext. 6134
(888) 280-4252; Fax: (606) 368-6215

Full-time: 275 men, 320 women	**Faculty:** 27
Part-time: 9 men, 13 women	**Ph.Ds:** 65%
Graduate: none	**Student/Faculty:** 22 to 1
Year: semesters	**Tuition:** $860 ($6360)
Application Deadline: July 1	**Room & Board:** $3180
Freshman Class: n/av	
ACT: 20	**COMPETITIVE**

Alice Lloyd College, founded in 1923, is a private liberal arts facility emphasizing Christian values and serving the Appalachian community. Within a 108-county area, which includes most of Eastern Kentucky and parts of Ohio, Tennessee, West Virginia, and Virginia, annual fees are $860; outside of this 108-county area, tuition and fees are $6360 In addition to regional accreditation, ALC has baccalaureate program accreditation with NCATE. The library contains 62,000 volumes, 1500 microform items, and 300 audio/video tapes/CDs, and subscribes to 300 periodicals. Computerized library services include the card catalog, interlibrary loans, and database searching. Special learning facilities include a learning resource center, art gallery, radio station, and a performing arts center. The 225-acre campus is in a rural area in the eastern part of the state. Including any residence halls, there are 35 buildings.

Student Life: 81% of undergraduates are from Kentucky. Students are from 6 states and 3 foreign countries. 95% are from public schools. 97% are white. The average age of freshmen is 18; all undergraduates, 21. 41% do not continue beyond their first year.

Housing: 451 students can be accommodated in college housing, which includes single-sex dorms and Caney Cottage scholarship program housing. On-campus housing is guaranteed for all 4 years. 76% of students live on campus; of those, 35% remain on campus on weekends. Alcohol is not permitted. All students may keep cars.

Activities: There are no fraternities or sororities. There are 16 groups on campus, including art, cheerleading, choir, chorus, computers, drama, honors, newspaper, pep band, photography, professional, radio and TV, religious, social, student government, and yearbook. Popular campus events include Religious Emphasis Week, Alcohol Awareness Week, and Appalachia Day.

Sports: There are 4 intercollegiate sports for men and 3 for women, and 11 intramural sports for men and 11 for women. Facilities include an indoor pool, weight rooms, a 1500-seat gym, recreation areas, 2 tennis courts, a baseball/athletic field, and 2 racquetball courts.

Disabled Students: 95% of the campus is accessible. Wheelchair ramps, elevators, special parking, specially equipped rest rooms, and special class scheduling are available.

Services: Counseling and information services are available, as is tutoring in every subject. There is remedial math, reading, and writing.

Campus Safety and Security: Measures include 24-hour foot and vehicle patrol, self-defense education, security escort services, and informal discussions. There are pamphlets/posters/films, emergency telephones, and lighted pathways/sidewalks.

Programs of Study: ALC confers B.A. and B.S. degrees. Bachelor's degrees are awarded in BIOLOGICAL SCIENCE (biology/biological science), BUSINESS (business administration and management), COMMUNICATIONS AND THE ARTS (English), EDUCATION (elementary, middle school, physical, secondary, and social studies), ENGINEERING AND ENVIRONMENTAL DESIGN (preengineering), HEALTH PROFESSIONS (prepharmacy), SOCIAL SCIENCE (history). Biology, education, and business administration are the strongest academically. Biology is the largest.

Required: To graduate, students must complete a work-study requirement extending through each semester and a 49-semester-hour general education requirement, including phys ed, health, composition, philosophy, and speech. 128 credit hours are required. Students must maintain a 2.0 GPA (2.5 for education majors) to graduate.

Special: Special arrangements include a 2-2 engineering degree with the Universities of Kentucky, Louisville, and West Virginia. Credit by exam is possible. There is 1 national honor society, Phi Beta Kappa.

Faculty/Classroom: 74% of faculty are male; 26%, female. All teach undergraduates and 10% do research. The average class size in an introductory lecture is 30; in a laboratory, 12; and in a regular course, 17.

Admissions: The ACT scores for the 2003-2004 freshman class were: 56% below 21, 26% between 21 and 23, 14% between 24 and 26, 3% between 27 and 28, and 1% above 28. 55% of the current freshmen were in the top fifth of their class; 83% were in the top two fifths. 8 freshmen graduated first in their class.

Requirements: The SAT I or ACT is required. In addition, applicants must be graduates of an accredited secondary school or have a GED, having successfully completed 12 academic credits, including 4 in English, 3 each in math and science, and 2 in social studies. A GPA of 2.25 is required. AP and CLEP credits are accepted. Important factors in the admissions decision, among many others, are leadership record, recommendations by alumni, and recommendations by school officials.

Procedure: Freshmen are admitted fall and spring. Entrance exams should be taken in the fall of the senior year. Applications should be filed by July 1 for fall entry and December 15 for spring entry. Notification is sent on a rolling basis. 35 were on the 2003 waiting list; 10 were admitted. Applications are accepted on-line through the school's web site.

Transfer: 35 transfer students enrolled in 2002-2003. Applicants must have a minimum 2.0 GPA, 2.5 for some majors, be in good standing at their previous school, and have a minimum ACT score of 17. 30 of 128 credits required for the bachelor's degree must be completed at ALC.

Visiting: There are regularly scheduled orientations for prospective students, consisting of summer and fall orientations. There are guides for informal visits and visitors may sit in on classes and stay overnight. To schedule a visit, contact Vikki Hoover, Admissions Assistant at (606) 368-6146 or *vikkihoover@alc.edu.*

Financial Aid: In 2003-2004, all full-time students received some form of financial aid. 57% of full-time freshmen and 60% of continuing full-time students received need-based aid. The average freshman award was $7783. All undergraduates work part time. Average annual earnings from campus work are $1648. The average financial indebtedness of the 2003 graduate was $1060. The FAFSA is required. The priority date for freshman financial aid applications for fall entry is February 15. The deadline for filing freshman financial aid applications for fall entry is March 15.

International Students: There are 3 international students enrolled. The school actively recruits these students. They must score 550 on the written TOEFL or 213 on the electronic version and also take the SAT I or the ACT, scoring 830 on the SAT I or 17 on the ACT.

Computers: There are 70 Gateway PCs available in the computer center. In addition, the science lab has 10 PCs. All students may access the system. There are no fees.

Graduates: From July 1, 2002 to June 30, 2003, 76 bachelor's degrees were awarded. In an average class, 20% graduate in 4 years or less, 21% graduate in 5 years or less, and 22% graduate in 6 years or less. 30 companies recruited on campus in 2002-2003. Of the 2002 graduating class, 96% were employed within 6 months of graduation.

Admissions Contact: Sean Damron, Director of Admissions. A video is available. E-mail: *admissions@alicelloyd.edu* Web: *www.alc.edu*

ASBURY COLLEGE	D-3
Wilmore, KY 40390-1198	(859) 858-3511
	(800) 888-1818; Fax: (859) 858-3921

Full-time: 475 men, 666 women	Faculty: 90; IIB, -$
Part-time: 23 men, 27 women	Ph.D.s: 77%
Graduate: 19 men, 48 women	Student/Faculty: 13 to 1
Year: semesters, summer session	Tuition: $16,500
Application Deadline: open	Room & Board: $4204
Freshman Class: 820 applied, 598 accepted, 258 enrolled	
SAT I Verbal/Math: 588/556	ACT: 24 VERY COMPETITIVE

Asbury College, founded in 1890, is an independent nondenominational liberal arts institution. In addition to regional accreditation, Asbury has baccalaureate program accreditation with NASM. The library contains 143,913 volumes, 22,120 microform items, and 9116 audio/video tapes/CDs, and subscribes to 517 periodicals. Computerized library services include the card catalog, interlibrary loans, and database searching. Special learning facilities include a learning resource center, art gallery, radio station, TV station, and media and fine arts centers. The 65-acre campus is in a rural area 20 miles south of Lexington. Including any residence halls, there are 30 buildings.

Student Life: 75% of undergraduates are from out of state, mostly the South. Students are from 43 states, 10 foreign countries, and Canada. 75% are from public schools. 96% are white. Most are Protestant. The average age of freshmen is 18; all undergraduates, 21. 17% do not continue beyond their first year; 63% remain to graduate.

Housing: 1226 students can be accommodated in college housing, which includes single-sex dorms, on-campus apartments, off-campus apartments, and married-student housing. In addition, there are language houses and leadership development/community service houses. On-campus housing is guaranteed for all 4 years. 90% of students live on campus; of those, 82% remain on campus on weekends. Alcohol is not permitted. Upperclassmen may keep cars.

Activities: There are no fraternities or sororities. There are 50 groups on campus, including art, band, choir, chorale, chorus, computers, debate, drama, ethnic, film, forensics, honors, international, jazz band, literary magazine, missionary, musical theater, newspaper, opera, orchestra, political, radio and TV, religious, social service, student government, and yearbook. Popular campus events include Parents Weekend, Artists Series, and Jym Jamboree.

Sports: There are 7 intercollegiate sports for men and 9 for women, and 9 intramural sports for men and 9 for women. Facilities include a 1500-seat gym, athletic fields, tennis courts, an indoor swimming pool, and indoor/outdoor basketball courts.

Disabled Students: 80% of the campus is accessible. Wheelchair ramps, elevators, special parking, specially equipped rest rooms, special class scheduling, lowered drinking fountains, and lowered telephones are available.

Services: Counseling and information services are available, as is tutoring in most subjects. There is remedial writing. For students on academic probation, there are mentors who provide help in such areas as time management and test-taking skills. There is some help available for the visually impaired, such as tapes and agencies that offer aid.

Campus Safety and Security: Measures include 24-hour foot and vehicle patrol, security escort services, pamphlets/posters/films, and lighted pathways/sidewalks. There are planning forums and a student parking and safety committee.

Programs of Study: Asbury confers B.A. and B.S.Ed. degrees. Master's degrees are also awarded. Bachelor's degrees are awarded in BIOLOGICAL SCIENCE (biochemistry and biology/biological science), BUSINESS (accounting, business administration and management, and recreation and leisure services), COMMUNICATIONS AND THE ARTS (art, broadcasting, classical languages, communications, English, French, Greek, journalism, Latin, music, and Spanish), COMPUTER AND PHYSICAL SCIENCE (applied mathematics, chemistry, information sciences and systems, mathematics, and physical sciences), EDUCATION (art, elementary, English, foreign languages, mathematics, middle school, music, physical, science, secondary, and social studies), HEALTH PROFESSIONS (exercise science and medical laboratory technology), SOCIAL SCIENCE (biblical languages, biblical studies, history, ministries, missions, philosophy, psychology, social work, and sociology). Education, communication arts, and Christian ministries and missions are the largest.

Required: To graduate, students must complete a minimum of semester hours, including liberal arts requirements, 9 hours of religion, and 3 hours of phys ed, with a minimum GPA of 2.0 for the B.A. or 2.75 for the B.S.Ed. Students must demonstrate proficiency in English and math and take a comprehensive exam.

Special: For-credit internships are available in several academic areas as are opportunities for study abroad. There is a Washington semester through the American Studies Program. Dual majors and nondegree study are possible as are credit/no credit options for seniors. 3-2 engineering and computer science degrees are offered with the University of Kentucky. There are 6 national honor societies and 7 departmental honors programs.

Faculty/Classroom: 64% of faculty are male; 36%, female. All teach undergraduates and 1% do research. The average class size in an introductory lecture is 25; in a laboratory, 18; and in a regular course, 15.

Admissions: 73% of the 2003-2004 applicants were accepted. The SAT I scores for the 2003-2004 freshman class were: Verbal--14% below 500, 39% between 500 and 599, 33% between 600 and 700, and 14% above 700; Math--29% below 500, 34% between 500 and 599, 31% between 600 and 700, and 6% above 700. The ACT scores were 19% below 21, 26% between 21 and 23, 24% between 24 and 26, 16% between 27 and 28, and 15% above 28. 60% of the current freshmen were in the top fifth of their class; 85% were in the top two fifths. There were 4 National Merit finalists. 17 freshmen graduated first in their class.

Requirements: The SAT I or ACT is required, with a minimum score of 525 verbal and 505 math on the SAT I or 22 on the ACT. Applicants must be graduates of an accredited secondary school or have the GED. Applicants should complete 15 high school academic credits, including 4 units of English, 3 each of math and social studies, and 2 each of science and a foreign language. Incoming students must take proficiency exams in math and English. A GPA of 2.5 is required. AP and CLEP credits are accepted.

Procedure: Freshmen are admitted to all sessions. Entrance exams should be taken in the junior year or the first semester of the senior year. There is a deferred admissions plan. Application deadlines are open. Application fee is $30. Notification is sent on a rolling basis. A waiting list is an active part of the admissions procedure. Applications are accepted on-line through the school's web site.

Transfer: 62 transfer students enrolled in 2002-2003. Transfer applicants should have completed a minimum of 12 quarter hours or 8 semester hours, have an overall minimum GPA of 2.0, and be in good standing at the previous institutions attended. 49 of 124 credits required for the bachelor's degree must be completed at Asbury.

Visiting: There are regularly scheduled orientations for prospective students, consisting of visitation weekends in which students stay overnight in dorms, visit classes, attend departmental open houses, and participate in meal/question-answer sessions, a financial aid session, chapel, and campus events. There are guides for informal visits and visitors may sit in on classes and stay overnight. To schedule a visit, contact the Admissions Office at (859) 858-3511, ext. 2142.

Financial Aid: In 2003-2004, 72% of all full-time freshmen and 69% of continuing full-time students received some form of financial aid. 72% of full-time freshmen and 61% of continuing full-time students received need-based aid. The average freshman award was $12,565. 44% of undergraduates work part time. Average annual earnings from campus work are $1200. The average financial indebtedness of the 2003 graduate was $18,885. The FAFSA and the college's own financial statement are required. The priority date for freshman financial aid applications for fall entry is March 1. The deadline for filing freshman financial aid applications for fall entry is May 1.

International Students: There are 15 international students enrolled. They must score 550 on the written TOEFL or 213 on the electronic version and also take the SAT I or the ACT.

Computers: There are 185 PCs available in the Microcomputer Resource Center, as well as network connections in each dorm room and throughout the library. All students may access the system. There are no time limits and no fees. It is strongly recommended that all students have a personal computer.

Graduates: From July 1, 2002 to June 30, 2003, 277 bachelor's degrees were awarded. The most popular majors were media communication (14%), elementary education (10%), and Bible/theology (8%). In an average class, 1% graduate in 3 years or less, 41% graduate in 4 years or less, 55% graduate in 5 years or less, and 57% graduate in 6 years or less. 41 companies recruited on campus in 2002-2003.

Admissions Contact: Stan F. Wiggam, Dean of Admissions. A video is available. E-mail: *admissions@asbury.edu* Web: *www.asbury.edu*

BELLARMINE UNIVERSITY
Louisville, KY 40205

D-2

(502) 452-8131
(800) 274-4723; Fax: (502) 452-8002

Full-time: 538 men, 1037 women	**Faculty:** 113
Part-time: 395 men, 562 women	**Ph.D.s:** 92%
Graduate: 161 men, 402 women	**Student/Faculty:** 14 to 1
Year: semesters, summer session	**Tuition:** $18,490
Application Deadline: February 1	**Room & Board:** $5620
Freshman Class: 1494 applied, 1218 accepted, 519 enrolled	
SAT I Verbal/Math: 560/560	**ACT:** 24 **VERY COMPETITIVE**

Bellarmine University, founded in 1950, is a private liberal arts institution affiliated with the Roman Catholic Church. There are 4 undergraduate and 3 graduate schools. In addition to regional accreditation, Bellarmine has baccalaureate program accreditation with NCATE and NLN. The library contains 114,615 volumes, 693,875 microform items, and 4835 audio/video tapes/CDs, and subscribes to 547 periodicals. Computerized library services include the card catalog, interlibrary loans, and database searching. Special learning facilities include a learning resource center, art gallery, and the Thomas Merton Center, a collection of works by and about Thomas Merton. The 120-acre campus is in a suburban area in Louisville. Including any residence halls, there are 28 buildings.

Student Life: 69% of undergraduates are from Kentucky. Students are from 39 states, 11 foreign countries, and Canada. 58% are from public schools. 85% are white. 50% are Catholic; 32% Protestant; 17% Muslim, Hindu, and other denominations. The average age of freshmen is 18; all undergraduates, 22. 22% do not continue beyond their first year; 62% remain to graduate.

Housing: 588 students can be accommodated in college housing, which includes single-sex and coed dorms. There are substance-free floors in 2 residence halls. On-campus housing is guaranteed for all 4 years. 64% of students commute. Alcohol is not permitted. All students may keep cars.

Activities: 2% of men and 3% of women belong to 3 national fraternities; 2% of women belong to 1 national sorority. There are 61 groups on campus, including art, band, cheerleading, choir, chorale, chorus, computers, dance, drama, ethnic, honors, international, jazz band, literary magazine, mock trial team, musical theater, newspaper, opera, pep band, photography, political, professional, religious, social, social service, student government, wind ensemble, and yearbook. Popular campus events include Hillside Concerts, Midnight Breakfast, and Bellarmine Volunteer Days.

Sports: There are 8 intercollegiate sports for men and 9 for women, and 8 intramural sports for men and 8 for women. Facilities include a basketball arena, weight rooms, indoor and outdoor tennis courts, a par 3 golf course, exercise and aerobics rooms in residence halls, a track, and softball, baseball, and soccer fields.

Disabled Students: 85% of the campus is accessible. Wheelchair ramps, elevators, special parking, specially equipped rest rooms, special class scheduling, lowered drinking fountains, lowered telephones, and special housing are available.

Services: Counseling and information services are available, as is tutoring in every subject. The Academic Resource Center provides one-on-one or group tutoring for all 100- and 200-level courses. Disability Services provides notetakers, distraction-reduced testing environments, extended time, books on tape, and scribe services.

Campus Safety and Security: Measures include 24-hour foot and vehicle patrol, self-defense education, security escort services, and shuttle buses. There are informal discussions, pamphlets/posters/films, emergency telephones, lighted pathways/sidewalks, 24-hour locked residence halls, security alert bulletins, CPR-certified security, and security cameras in residence halls and in the parking lot.

Programs of Study: Bellarmine confers B.A., B.S., and B.H.Sc. degrees. Master's degrees are also awarded. Bachelor's degrees are awarded in BIOLOGICAL SCIENCE (biology/biological science), BUSINESS (accounting, business administration and management, and international business management), COMMUNICATIONS AND THE ARTS (art, arts administration/management, communications, English, and music), COMPUTER AND PHYSICAL SCIENCE (actuarial science, chemistry, computer science, information sciences and systems, and mathematics), EDUCATION (elementary, middle school, secondary, and special), ENGINEERING AND ENVIRONMENTAL DESIGN (computer engineering and preengineering), HEALTH PROFESSIONS (cytotechnology, medical technology, nursing, physical therapy, predentistry, premedicine, prepharmacy, preveterinary science, and respiratory therapy), SOCIAL SCIENCE (criminal justice, economics, history, international studies, liberal arts/general studies, philosophy, political science/government, prelaw, psychology, sociology, and theological studies). Premedicine, accounting, and business are the strongest academically. Accounting, business, and nursing are the largest.

Required: In order to graduate, students must complete a minimum of 126 credit hours with a minimum GPA of 2.0. Between 24 and 45 hours are required in the major. All students must fulfill 60 credit hours of core requirements, including English, philosophy, theology, math, social sciences, natural sciences, fine arts, Western civilization, American experience, transcultural experience, and freshman and senior seminars. Students in the honors program must complete a senior honors thesis.

Special: Cross-registration may be arranged through Kentuckiana Metroversity, a consortium of colleges in Kentucky and southern Indiana. Bellarmine also offers study abroad in more than 43 countries, internships in most majors, a Washington semester, a liberal studies degree, dual majors, accelerated degree programs, credit for life experience, pass/fail options during the junior and senior years, and a marine biology program in the Bahamas. There is also an honors program and the Brown Leadership Program. There are 5 national honor societies and a freshman honors program.

Faculty/Classroom: 50% of faculty are male; 50%, female. 98% teach undergraduates, 60% do research, and 60% do both. No introductory courses are taught by graduate students. The average class size in an introductory lecture is 25; in a laboratory, 18; and in a regular course, 19.

Admissions: 82% of the 2003-2004 applicants were accepted. The SAT I scores for the 2003-2004 freshman class were: Verbal--21% below 500, 46% between 500 and 599, 31% between 600 and 700, and 2% above 700; Math--26% below 500, 46% between 500 and 599, 24% between 600 and 700, and 4% above 700. The ACT scores were 14% below 21, 32% between 21 and 23, 33% between 24 and 26, 11% between 27 and 28, and 10% above 28. 51% of the current freshmen were in the top fifth of their class; 83% were in the top two fifths. There was 1 National Merit finalist.

Requirements: The SAT I or ACT is required, with a minimum composite score of 900 on the SAT I or 21 on the ACT. Applicants should have a minimum high school GPA of 2.0. The GED is accepted. High school courses should include 4 years of English, 3 years of math, and 2 years each of science and social studies. An essay is required. AP and CLEP credits are accepted. Important factors in the admissions decision are advanced placement or honor courses, extracurricular activities record, and recommendations by school officials.

Procedure: Freshmen are admitted to all sessions. Entrance exams should be taken by December of the senior year. There are early admissions and deferred admissions plans. Applications should be filed by February 1 for fall entry, along with a $25 fee. Notification is sent on a rolling basis. Applications are accepted on-line through *www.bellarmine.edu.*

Transfer: 80 transfer students enrolled in 2002-2003. Applicants should have a minimum college GPA of 2.0 and must submit transcripts from high school and all postsecondary schools attended. 36 credits of 126 required for the bachelor's degree must be completed at Bellarmine.

Visiting: There are regularly scheduled orientations for prospective students, including an admissions and financial aid session, a campus tour, interviews with faculty, and participation in a student panel. There are guides for informal visits and visitors may sit in on classes and stay overnight. To schedule a visit, contact the Office of Admission at *admissions@bellarmine.edu..*

Financial Aid: In 2003-2004, all full-time freshmen and 85% of continuing full-time students received some form of financial aid. 87% of full-time freshmen and 70% of continuing full-time students received need-based aid. The average freshman award was $14,821. 65% of undergraduates work part time. Average annual earnings from campus work are $1698. The average financial indebtedness of the 2003 graduate was $14,556. Bellarmine is a member of CSS. The FAFSA is required. The priority date for freshman financial aid applications for fall entry is March 1. The deadline for filing freshman financial aid applications for fall entry is May 1.

International Students: There are 16 international students enrolled. They must score 550 on the written TOEFL or 213 on the electronic version or take the MELAB.

Computers: The mainframe is an HP 9000. All computer labs in the academic buildings are on the campus network, with Internet and web access, and are available to all students. Approximately 200 PCs are available to students in locations across campus, including residence halls and 24-hour study rooms. All students may access the system. There are no time limits. The fee is $250 per full-time semester.

Graduates: From July 1, 2002 to June 30, 2003, 400 bachelor's degrees were awarded. The most popular majors were general business (17%), nursing (12%), and economics (11%). In an average class, 1% graduate in 3 years or less, 53% graduate in 4 years or less, 59% graduate in 5 years or less, and 60% graduate in 6 years or less. 35 companies recruited on campus in 2002-2003. Of the 2002 graduating class, 15% were enrolled in graduate school within 6 months of graduation and 90% were employed.

Admissions Contact: Timothy Sturgeon, Dean of Admission.
E-mail: *admissions@bellarmine.edu* Web: *http://www.bellarmine.edu*

BEREA COLLEGE
Berea, KY 40404

D-3

(859) 985-3500
(800) 326-5948; Fax: (859) 985-3512

Full-time: 597 men, 918 women	**Faculty:** 130; IIB, +$
Part-time: 26 men, 19 women	**Ph.D.s:** 91%
Graduate: none	**Student/Faculty:** 12 to 1
Year: 4-1-4, summer session	**Tuition:** $507 (fee)
Application Deadline: open	**Room & Board:** $4523
Freshman Class: 2119 applied, 530 accepted, 396 enrolled	
SAT I Verbal/Math: 545/540	**ACT:** 23 **VERY COMPETITIVE+**

Berea College, founded in 1855, is a private liberal arts institution. Berea combines college, federal, and state grants, as well as outside scholarships earned by students, to provide every admitted student with a 4-year, full-tuition scholarship. Therefore, no student pays tuition at Berea college. The college provides a laptop for every student; students are expected to pay $300 to offset the cost of networking and other related expenses, and the laptop becomes the property of the student at graduation. As part of these scholarship agreements, each student is expected to perform some of the labor required in maintaining the institution while carrying a normal academic load. For participation in the student labor program, each student is credited with a labor grant that is incorporated into the full-tuition scholarship. Room, board, and fees are assessed on a sliding scale according to how much each family can afford. Enrollment figures include both degree- and nondegree-seeking students. In addition to regional accreditation, Berea has baccalaureate program accreditation with ADA, NCATE, and NLN. The library contains 352,210 volumes, 132,336 microform items, and 10,707 audiovisual materials, and subscribes to 2202 periodicals. Computerized library services include the card catalog, interlibrary loans, and database searching. Special learning facilities include a learning resource center, art gallery, planetarium, and a geology museum. The 140-acre campus is in a small town 40 miles south of Lexington. Including any residence halls, there are 58 buildings.

Student Life: 66% of undergraduates are from out of state, mostly the South. Students are from 39 states and 73 foreign countries. 70% are white; 17% African American. The average age of freshmen is 18; all undergraduates, 20. 20% do not continue beyond their first year.

Housing: 1250 students can be accommodated in college housing, which includes single-sex dorms and married-student housing. In addition, there are special-interest houses and a single-parent house. On-campus housing is guaranteed for all 4 years. 81% of students live on campus. Alcohol is not permitted.

Activities: There are no fraternities or sororities. There are 70 groups on campus, including art, band, cheerleading, chess, choir, chorus, dance, debate, drama, ethnic, gay, honors, international, jazz band, literary magazine, newspaper, orchestra, pep band, photography, political, professional, religious, social, social service, student government, and yearbook. Popular campus events include Mountain Day and Labor Day.

Sports: There are 9 intercollegiate sports for men and 8 for women, and 7 intramural sports for men and 7 for women. Facilities include 2 gyms, an indoor swimming pool, 5 racquetball courts, 15 tennis courts, playing fields, a dance studio, a 3-lane indoor walking track, an 8-lane all-weather track, and weight training and cardiovascular exercise rooms.

Disabled Students: 50% of the campus is accessible. Wheelchair ramps, elevators, special parking, specially equipped rest rooms, special class scheduling, lowered drinking fountains, lowered telephones, electronic doors, and a lift chair for the indoor pool are available.

Services: Counseling and information services are available, as is tutoring in some subjects. There is a reader service for the blind, and remedial math, reading, and writing. The Learning Center offers individual consultation in writing, reading, listening, speaking, learning strategies and styles, and study skills. Berea's tutorial labs assist with study skills, project development, homework assignments, clarification of concepts, skill development, and software application.

Campus Safety and Security: Measures include 24-hour foot and vehicle patrol, self-defense education, security escort services, and informal discussions. There are pamphlets/posters/films, emergency telephones, lighted pathways/sidewalks, and Berea has ongoing programs on campus safety, theft prevention, assault and rape prevention, fire prevention, defensive driving, and occupational safety, including work with hazardous materials.

Programs of Study: Berea confers B.A. and B.S. degrees. Bachelor's degrees are awarded in AGRICULTURE (agriculture), BIOLOGICAL SCIENCE (biology/biological science), BUSINESS (business administration and management), COMMUNICATIONS AND THE ARTS (art, classical languages, dramatic arts, English, French, German, industrial

design, music, Spanish, and speech/debate/rhetoric), COMPUTER AND PHYSICAL SCIENCE (chemistry, mathematics, and physics), EDUCATION (art, early childhood, elementary, foreign languages, home economics, middle school, music, physical, and secondary), ENGINEERING AND ENVIRONMENTAL DESIGN (industrial engineering technology), HEALTH PROFESSIONS (nursing), SOCIAL SCIENCE (child care/child and family studies, dietetics, economics, history, philosophy, political science/government, psychology, religion, sociology, and women's studies). Business administration is the largest.

Required: Students must complete a 15-course general education program, including courses in wellness, cultural studies, arts, Western traditions, recent world issues, contemporary Christianity, quantitative reasoning, and natural and social sciences, and courses emphasizing reading and written communication. 3 short-term (January) courses are required. All students will be automatically enrolled in a one-quarter-credit convocation course during each of their regular terms of enrollment, with the exception of the final term of enrollment, for a maximum of 8 such terms. To graduate, students must complete 33 courses, including 8 to 12 in the major, with a minimum GPA of 2.0 overall and in the major. Nursing majors must complete 35 courses.

Special: Students may study abroad in many countries. Internships, work-study programs, dual degrees, independent and team-initiated studies, and dual and student-designed majors are available. A 3-2 engineering degree is offered with Washington University and the University of Kentucky. All students participate in an on-campus work program 10 to 15 hours per week. There are 17 national honor societies.

Faculty/Classroom: 60% of faculty are male; 40%, female. All teach undergraduates. The average class size in a laboratory is 20 and in a regular course, 20.

Admissions: 25% of the 2003-2004 applicants were accepted. The SAT I scores for the 2003-2004 freshman class were: Verbal--30% below 500, 41% between 500 and 599, 24% between 600 and 700, and 6% above 700; Math--28% below 500, 47% between 500 and 599, 24% between 600 and 700, and 1% above 700. The ACT scores were 28% below 21, 31% between 21 and 23, 21% between 24 and 26, 13% between 27 and 28, and 7% above 28. 57% of the current freshmen were in the top fifth of their class; 86% were in the top two fifths. 22 freshmen graduated first in their class.

Requirements: The SAT I or ACT is required. In addition, applicants should be graduates of an accredited secondary school. The GED is accepted. Homeschooled students are also encouraged to apply. Financial need is a requirement for admission. Berea recommends that applicants present as part of their high school record 4 units in English, 3 in math, and 2 each in science and social studies. Work in a foreign language is highly desirable. AP and CLEP credits are accepted. Important factors in the admissions decision are ability to finance college education, geographic diversity, and advanced placement or honor courses.

Procedure: Freshmen are admitted fall and spring. Entrance exams should be taken late in the junior year or early in the senior year. Early review applications are due by November 30; after that date, admissions decisions are made on a monthly basis until spaces are filled. Deadlines are the last day of each month. Applications are accepted on-line through *www.berea.edu/Admissions/apponline.htm.*

Transfer: 47 transfer students enrolled in 2002-2003. Applicants must be in good standing at the last college attended and have a minimum GPA of 2.4. 8 of 33 courses (35 for nursing) required for the bachelor's degree must be completed at Berea.

Visiting: There are regularly scheduled orientations for prospective students, consisting of welcome, admissions, and student and residence life sessions, departmental visits, a campus tour, a musical performance, and lunch. There are guides for informal visits and visitors may sit in on classes and stay overnight. To schedule a visit, contact Nancy Bolin, Campus Visit Coordinator at (800) 326-5948 or (859) 985-3500 or *nancy_bolin@berea.edu.*

Financial Aid: In 2003-2004, all full-time students received some form of financial aid and need-based aid. The average freshman award was $26,605, with $25,485 from need-based scholarships or grants, and $1120 from need-based self-help aid (loans and jobs). All undergraduates work part time. Average annual earnings from campus work are $1317. The average financial indebtedness of the 2003 graduate was $6275. The FAFSA is required. The deadline for filing freshman financial aid applications for fall entry is April 1.

International Students: There are 113 international students enrolled. They must score 500 on the written TOEFL.

Computers: Berea's computing network is linked via category 5 copper wire and fiber-optic cable. Through this network, any computer workstation on campus provides access to an on-line library (BANC); CD-ROM resources; academic software; word procesing, spreadsheet, presentation, and database software; the administrative network; e-mail; and the Internet. Students may access the network from more than 150 PCs found in the computer center, the library, academic department labs, and residence halls. Network link-up ports also enable students to connect their portable computers to the network wherever they happen to be on campus. All students may access the system 24 hours a day, 7 days a week. There are no time limits and no fees.

Graduates: From July 1, 2002 to June 30, 2003, 300 bachelor's degrees were awarded. The most popular majors were business administration (12%), child and family studies (11%), and industrial/manufacturing (10%). In an average class, 36% graduate in 4 years or less, 60% graduate in 5 years or less, and 49% graduate in 6 years or less. 80 companies recruited on campus in 2002-2003.

Admissions Contact: Jamie Ealy, Director of Admissions.
E-mail: *jamie_ealy@berea.edu* Web: *www.berea.edu*

BRESCIA UNIVERSITY B-3
Owensboro, KY 42301 (270) 686-4241; Fax: (270) 686-4314

Full-time: 200 men, 335 women	**Faculty:** 43; IIB, --$
Part-time: 105 men, 165 women	**Ph.D.s:** 70%
Graduate: 15 men, 20 women	**Student/Faculty:** 12 to 1
Year: semesters, summer session	**Tuition:** $10,230
Application Deadline: open	**Room & Board:** $4380
Freshman Class: n/av	
SAT I or ACT: required	**COMPETITIVE**

Brescia University, founded in 1925 as a women's junior college, became a 4-year, coeducational liberal arts institution in 1950. It is a private school affiliated with the Roman Catholic Church. The university offers certificates, associate, baccalaureate, and master's degrees through semester and weekend classes. The figures in the above capsule and in this profile are approximate. The library contains 183,406 volumes, 364,553 microform items, and 6580 audio/video tapes/CDs, and subscribes to 5334 periodicals. Computerized library services include the card catalog, interlibrary loans, and database searching. Special learning facilities include a learning resource center and art gallery. The 6-acre campus is in an urban area 32 miles southeast of Evansville, Indiana, and 125 miles from both Louisville and Nashville. Including any residence halls, there are 14 buildings.

Student Life: 78% of undergraduates are from Kentucky. Students are from 18 states, 18 foreign countries, and Canada. 89% are white. 39% are Catholic; 32% Protestant; 27% claim no religious affiliation. The average age of freshmen is 20; all undergraduates, 30. 33% do not continue beyond their first year.

Housing: 224 students can be accommodated in college housing, which includes single-sex and coed dorms and on-campus apartments. On-campus housing is available on a first-come, first-served basis. 73% of students commute. Alcohol is not permitted. All students may keep cars.

Activities: There are no fraternities or sororities. There are 23 groups on campus, including choir, chorus, computers, creative writing, drama, honors, international, literary magazine, newspaper, philosophy, professional, religious, social, social service, student government, and yearbook. Popular campus events include Family Weekend, Opening Year Mass, and Inaugural Ball.

Sports: There are 4 intercollegiate sports for men and 5 for women, and 11 intramural sports for men and 11 for women. Facilities include 2 tennis courts, a gym, a weight room, a game room, a cardiovascular workout room, a racquetball court, a batting cage, and a baseball field.

Disabled Students: 95% of the campus is accessible. Wheelchair ramps, elevators, special parking, specially equipped rest rooms, lowered drinking fountains, and lowered telephones are available.

Services: Counseling and information services are available, as is tutoring in most subjects. There is remedial math, reading, and writing.

Campus Safety and Security: Measures include security escort services, informal discussions, emergency telephones, and lighted pathways/sidewalks. There are night security.

Programs of Study: Brescia confers B.A., B.S., and B.S.W. degrees. Associate and master's degrees are also awarded. Bachelor's degrees are awarded in BIOLOGICAL SCIENCE (biology/biological science), BUSINESS (accounting, banking and finance, business administration and management, business economics, and human resources), COMMUNICATIONS AND THE ARTS (art, English, and graphic design), COMPUTER AND PHYSICAL SCIENCE (chemistry, computer science, mathematics, and physical sciences), EDUCATION (art, elementary, and special), HEALTH PROFESSIONS (art therapy, medical technology, and speech pathology/audiology), SOCIAL SCIENCE (history, human development, liberal arts/general studies, pastoral studies, psychology, religion, social studies, and social work). Education, business, and English are the strongest academically. Business, social work, and education are the largest.

Required: All students must earn 128 credit hours, including 42 upper-division hours, and 30 or more hours in the major, while maintaining an overall GPA of 2.0 and 2.5 in the major. Distribution requirements include 18 hours in aesthetics, language, and literature, 12 in social science, 9 each in fine arts, science, and math, 6 in religious studies, and 3 in philosophy. Students must also demonstrate computer competency.

Special: Brescia offers a combined engineering degree with the University of Kentucky and the University of Louisville. Work-study programs, student-designed majors, nondegree study, dual majors, study abroad in Mexico, an internship in professional writing, pass/fail options and cross-

registration with Kentucky Wesleyan are available. The Weekend College offers four 9-week modules of study. There are 2 national honor societies and a freshman honors program.

Faculty/Classroom: 47% of faculty are male; 53%, female. All teach undergraduates. No introductory courses are taught by graduate students. The average class size in an introductory lecture is 14; in a laboratory, 10; and in a regular course, 12.

Requirements: The SAT I or ACT is required. In addition, essays and recommendations are helpful. High school units should include 4 of English, 3 of math, and 2 each in social studies, science, foreign language, fine arts, and computer science. Brescia requires applicants to be in the upper 50% of their class. A GPA of 2.5 is required. AP and CLEP credits are accepted. Important factors in the admissions decision are advanced placement or honor courses and recommendations by school officials.

Procedure: Freshmen are admitted to all sessions. Entrance exams should be taken at the end of the junior year. There is a rolling admissions plan. Application deadlines are open. The fall 2003 application fee was $25. Applications are accepted on-line.

Transfer: 80 transfer students enrolled in a recent year. Transfer students must have a minimum GPA of 2.0. 42 of 128 credits required for the bachelor's degree must be completed at Brescia.

Visiting: There are regularly scheduled orientations for prospective students, including spring and fall open houses for freshmen and a spring transfer open house. There are guides for informal visits and visitors may sit in on classes and stay overnight. To schedule a visit, contact the Admissions Director.

Financial Aid: In a recent year, 85% of all full-time freshmen and 80% of continuing full-time students received some form of financial aid. 68% of full-time freshmen and 51% of continuing full-time students received need-based aid. The average freshman award was $9690. All undergraduates work part time. Average annual earnings from campus work are $1236. The average financial indebtedness of a recent graduate was $12,777. Brescia is a member of CSS. The FAFSA is required. Check with the school for current deadlines.

International Students: There were 35 international students enrolled in a recent year. The school actively recruits these students. They must score 550 on the written TOEFL or 213 on the electronic version and also take the SAT I or the ACT.

Computers: 45 PCs are available for student use at various locations on campus. There is a computer lab in each academic building. Student PCs are connected to the campus network, with Internet access. All students may access the system. There are no time limits. The fee is $10 per credit ($40 maximum).

Graduates: In a recent year, 93 bachelor's degrees were awarded. The most popular majors were business (26%), social work (15%), and communication sciences and disorders (10%). In an average class, 2% graduate in 3 years or less, 30% graduate in 4 years or less, 47% graduate in 5 years or less, and 43% graduate in 6 years or less. 21 companies recruited on campus in a recent year. Of a recent graduating class, 19% were enrolled in graduate school within 6 months of graduation and 80% were employed.

Admissions Contact: Sister Mary Austin Blank, Director of Admissions. A video is available. E-mail: *admissions@brescia.edu* Web: *www.brescia.edu*

CAMPBELLSVILLE UNIVERSITY D-3
Campbellsville, KY 42718-2799 (270) 789-5220
(800) 264-6014; Fax: (270) 789-5071

Full-time: 558 men, 618 women	**Faculty:** 73; IIB, --$
Part-time: 183 men, 344 women	**Ph.D.s:** 66%
Graduate: 118 men, 169 women	**Student/Faculty:** 16 to 1
Year: semesters, summer session	**Tuition:** $12,704
Application Deadline: July 1	**Room & Board:** $4976
Freshman Class: 1053 applied, 839 accepted, 363 enrolled	
ACT: 21	**COMPETITIVE**

Campbellsville University, founded in 1906, is a private, comprehensive institution affiliated with the Kentucky Baptist Convention. There are 6 undergraduate and 7 graduate schools. In addition to regional accreditation, Campbellsville has baccalaureate program accreditation with NASM. The 2 libraries contain 108,000 volumes, 24,000 microform items, and 8000 audio/video tapes/CDs, and subscribe to 360 periodicals. Computerized library services include the card catalog, interlibrary loans, and database searching. Special learning facilities include a learning resource center, art gallery, radio station, TV station, a teacher resource center, the Kentuckiana Collection, Clay Hill Memorial Forest, and the American Civil War Institute. The 72-acre campus is in a small town 85 miles southwest of Lexington and 85 miles southeast of Louisville. Including any residence halls, there are 48 buildings.

Student Life: 87% of undergraduates are from Kentucky. Students are from 25 states, 24 foreign countries, and Canada. 95% are from public schools. 86% are white. 60% are Protestant; 12% claim no religious affiliation; 7% Catholic. The average age of freshmen is 19; all undergraduates, 21. 35% do not continue beyond their first year; 40% remain to graduate.

Housing: 750 students can be accommodated in college housing, which includes single-sex dormitories and on-campus apartments. In addition, there are honors houses and special-interest houses. On-campus housing is guaranteed for all 4 years. 64% of students commute. Alcohol is not permitted. All students may keep cars.

Activities: There are no fraternities or sororities. There are 45 groups on campus, including art, band, cheerleading, choir, chorale, chorus, computers, dance, drama, ethnic, honors, international, jazz band, literary magazine, marching band, musical theater, newspaper, opera, orchestra, pep band, photography, political, professional, radio and TV, religious, social, social service, student government, symphony, and yearbook. Popular campus events include Valentine Banquet, a Christmas celebration, and Heritage Day.

Sports: There are 7 intercollegiate sports for men and 7 for women, and 10 intramural sports for men and 10 for women. Facilities include a swimming pool, a 1700-seat gym, a football stadium, a baseball field, an intramural activities center with skating facilities and large game rooms, softball and soccer fields, and an indoor practice field.

Disabled Students: 85% of the campus is accessible. Wheelchair ramps, elevators, special parking, specially equipped rest rooms, special class scheduling, lowered drinking fountains, lowered telephones, and widened doorways are available.

Services: Counseling and information services are available, as is tutoring in most subjects. There is remedial math, reading, and writing. There is also an AIDS education program and a study skills program.

Campus Safety and Security: Measures include 24-hour foot and vehicle patrol, self-defense education, security escort services, and informal discussions. There are pamphlets/posters/films, emergency telephones, and lighted pathways/sidewalks.

Programs of Study: Campbellsville confers B.A., B.S., B.M., B.S.B.A., B.S.Med.Tech, and B.S.W. degrees. Associate and master's degrees are also awarded. Bachelor's degrees are awarded in BIOLOGICAL SCIENCE (biology/biological science), BUSINESS (accounting, business administration and management, and office supervision and management), COMMUNICATIONS AND THE ARTS (art, communications, English, and music), COMPUTER AND PHYSICAL SCIENCE (chemistry, information sciences and systems, and mathematics), EDUCATION (athletic training, elementary, middle school, physical, and recreation), HEALTH PROFESSIONS (medical laboratory technology and sports medicine), SOCIAL SCIENCE (Christian studies, economics, history, political science/government, psychology, religious education, religious music, social work, and sociology). Biology, chemistry, and music are the strongest academically. Elementary education, business administration, and music are the largest.

Required: All candidates must be of good moral character. All students must complete a minimum of 128 semester hours, including 30 in the major, 21 in the minor, and 51 in general education courses. The minimum GPA is 2.5 for education majors, 2.1 for all others. All students must fulfill an English composition requirement.

Special: Legislative and public administration internships, a Washington semester, and federal work-study programs are available. The university also offers a semester in London program, a 3-2 engineering degree with the University of Kentucky, dual majors, credit by exam, credit for life, military, and work experience, nondegree study, and pass/fail options. There is a freshman honors program.

Faculty/Classroom: 56% of faculty are male; 44%, female. All teach undergraduates. No introductory courses are taught by graduate students. The average class size in an introductory lecture is 25; in a laboratory, 13; and in a regular course, 18.

Admissions: 80% of the 2003-2004 applicants were accepted. The ACT scores for the 2003-2004 freshman class were: 47% below 21, 30% between 21 and 23, 17% between 24 and 26, 3% between 27 and 28, and 3% above 28. 45% of the current freshmen were in the top fifth of their class; 75% were in the top two fifths.

Requirements: The ACT is required and the SAT I is recommended; the SAT I may be substituted for the ACT. Applicants must be graduates of an accredited secondary school with a GPA of 2.0. The GED is accepted. An interview is recommended. AP and CLEP credits are accepted. Important factors in the admissions decision are evidence of special talent, leadership record, and advanced placement or honor courses.

Procedure: Freshmen are admitted to all sessions. Entrance exams should be taken no later than February of the senior year. There is a deferred admissions plan. Applications should be filed by July 1 for fall entry and November 1 for spring entry. The fall 2003 application fee was $20. Notification is sent on a rolling basis. Applications are accepted online through the university's web site or CollegeLink.

Transfer: 119 transfer students enrolled in a recent year. Of the 128 credits needed to graduate, all students must complete one third of the credits required for the major and the minor at the university; the last year must be completed in residence. 32 of 128 credits required for the bachelor's degree must be completed at Campbellsville.

Visiting: There are regularly scheduled orientations for prospective students, consisting of visitation days held in October, February, and April.

There are guides for informal visits and visitors may sit in on classes and stay overnight. To schedule a visit, contact the Admissions Office.

Financial Aid: In a recent year, 94% of all full-time students received some form of financial aid. 70% of full-time freshmen and 68% of continuing full-time students received need-based aid. 47% of undergraduates work part time. Average annual earnings from campus work are $1700. Campbellsville is a member of CSS. The FAFSA is required. The priority date for freshman financial aid applications for fall entry is March 15. The deadline for filing freshman financial aid applications for fall entry is April 1.

International Students: There are 91 international students enrolled. The school actively recruits these students. They must score 500 on the written TOEFL or take the MELAB and also take the SAT I or the ACT, scoring 19 on the ACT.

Computers: The mainframe consists of more than 12 client-server systems. There are 4 labs with Pentium-class computers. 125 PCs are available in labs for student use, and 2 residence halls are wired for the Internet from individual rooms. All other students have dial-in access for the Internet both on and off campus. All students may access the system 24 hours a day or during lab hours. Students may access the system 45 hours monthly on dial-in access only. The fee is $200.

Graduates: From July 1, 2002 to June 30, 2003, 183 bachelor's degrees were awarded. In an average class, 38% graduate in 6 years or less.

Admissions Contact: David Walters, Vice President for Admissions. A video is available. E-mail: *admissions@campbellsville.edu* Web: *www.campbellsville.edu*

CENTRE COLLEGE
Danville, KY 40422

D-3
(859) 238-5350
(800) 423-6236; Fax: (859) 238-5373

Full-time: 509 men, 549 women	**Faculty:** 88; IIB, +$
Part-time: 4 women	**Ph.D.s:** 97%
Graduate: none	**Student/Faculty:** 12 to 1
Year: 4-1-4	**Tuition:** $20,400
Application Deadline: February 1	**Room & Board:** $6900
Freshman Class: 1259 applied, 1063 accepted, 272 enrolled	
SAT I Verbal/Math: 622/606	**ACT:** 27 **HIGHLY COMPETITIVE**

Centre College, founded in 1819 by the Presbyterian Church (U.S.A.), is a private liberal arts and sciences institution. The library contains 217,751 volumes, 52,512 microform items, and 3500 audio/video tapes/CDs, and subscribes to 2076 periodicals. Computerized library services include the card catalog, interlibrary loans, database searching, and Internet access. Special learning facilities include an art gallery, natural history museum, and a performing arts center. The 115-acre campus is in a small town 35 miles southwest of Lexington and 80 miles southeast of Louisville. Including any residence halls, there are 60 buildings.

Student Life: 65% of undergraduates are from Kentucky. Students are from 38 states, 7 foreign countries, and Canada. 69% are from public schools. 95% are white. 61% are Protestant; 19% claim no religious affiliation; 18% Catholic. The average age of freshmen is 18; all undergraduates, 20. 10% do not continue beyond their first year; 80% remain to graduate.

Housing: 970 students can be accommodated in college housing, which includes single-sex and coed dorms, on-campus apartments, fraternity houses, and sorority houses. In addition, there is an international student house. On-campus housing is guaranteed for all 4 years. 95% of students live on campus; of those, 90% remain on campus on weekends. All students may keep cars.

Activities: 58% of men belong to 5 national fraternities; 65% of women belong to 4 national sororities. There are 105 groups on campus, including art, band, cheerleading, choir, chorus, computers, dance, debate, drama, ethnic, film, forensics, gay, honors, international, jazz band, literary magazine, musical theater, newspaper, orchestra, pep band, photography, political, professional, religious, social, social service, student government, and yearbook. Popular campus events include Carnival, Honors Convocation, and Honor Walk.

Sports: There are 9 intercollegiate sports for men and 10 for women, and 15 intramural sports for men and 15 for women. Facilities include a complex with a 1500-seat gym, 3 basketball courts, 2 volleyball courts, a training room, a game room, a sauna, a weight room, a fitness center, and racquetball/handball courts. There is also a 2500-seat stadium, tennis courts, and playing fields for football, track, baseball, softball, soccer, field hockey, and other sports. The natatorium has a 25-yard, 6-lane swimming pool. Golf teams compete at the local country club.

Disabled Students: 65% of the campus is accessible. Wheelchair ramps, elevators, special parking, specially equipped rest rooms, special class scheduling, and electronic doors are available.

Services: Counseling and information services are available, as is tutoring in most subjects. There is a reader service for the blind.

Campus Safety and Security: Measures include 24-hour foot and vehicle patrol, self-defense education, security escort services, and informal discussions. There are pamphlets/posters/films, emergency telephones, lighted pathways/sidewalks, and a working relationship with outside agencies.

Programs of Study: Centre confers B.A. and B.S. degrees. Bachelor's degrees are awarded in BIOLOGICAL SCIENCE (biochemistry, biology/biological science, and molecular biology), COMMUNICATIONS AND THE ARTS (dramatic arts, English, fine arts, French, German, music, and Spanish), COMPUTER AND PHYSICAL SCIENCE (chemistry, computer science, mathematics, physical chemistry, and physics), EDUCATION (elementary), SOCIAL SCIENCE (anthropology, classical/ancient civilization, economics, history, international relations, philosophy, political science/government, psychobiology, psychology, religion, and sociology). English, economics, and biology are the strongest academically and have the largest enrollments.

Required: All students must earn an overall GPA of 2.0 and complete a minimum of 111 credit hours. Students also must demonstrate competency in writing, foreign language, and math plus 1 course beyond basic skills in math, foreign language, or computer science. A freshman humanities program and a freshman seminar must be completed. Core curriculum requirements include 2 courses each in the humanities or art from the aesthetic context; the scientific/technological context; the social context; and the fundamental questions context. 2 phys ed courses must be completed by the end of sophomore year.

Special: Centre offers internships, study abroad in 9 countries, a Washington semester through American University, work-study, and a 3-2 engineering degree with Vanderbilt University, Washington University at St. Louis, Columbia University, and the University of Kentucky. Student-designed majors, interdisciplinary majors including chemical physics, secondary education certification, and prelaw, prebusiness, and premedicine programs are available. Pass/fail options also are available. There are 8 national honor societies, including Phi Beta Kappa.

Faculty/Classroom: 58% of faculty are male; 42%, female. All both teach and do research. The average class size in an introductory lecture is 20; in a laboratory, 14; and in a regular course, 17.

Admissions: 84% of the 2003-2004 applicants were accepted. The SAT I scores for the 2003-2004 freshman class were: Verbal--3% below 500, 35% between 500 and 599, 42% between 600 and 700, and 20% above 700; Math--9% below 500, 35% between 500 and 599, 44% between 600 and 700, and 12% above 700. The ACT scores were 2% below 21, 13% between 21 and 23, 33% between 24 and 26, 20% between 27 and 28, and 32% above 28. 72% of the current freshmen were in the top fifth of their class; 97% were in the top two fifths. There was 1 National Merit finalist and 13 semifinalists. 22 freshmen graduated first in their class.

Requirements: The SAT I or ACT is required, but no minimum test scores are required. Students should have completed a minimum of 15 academic credits, including 4 years each in English and math, 3 years each in science and social studies, 2 years in foreign language, and 1 year in an art- or music-related course. An essay is required, and an interview is strongly recommended. AP credits are accepted. Important factors in the admissions decision are recommendations by school officials, extracurricular activities record, and advanced placement or honor courses.

Procedure: Freshmen are admitted in the fall. Entrance exams should be taken by February of the senior year. There are early admissions and deferred admissions plans. Applications should be filed by February 1 for fall entry. The fall 2003 application fee was $40. Notification is sent March 15. 66 were on the 2003 waiting list; 21 were admitted. Applications are accepted on computer disk and on-line through Common Application On-line, Apply!, and the school's web site.

Transfer: 14 transfer students enrolled in 2002-2003. Applicants for transfer must have all previous college transcripts on file and a recommendation from the dean of the most recent college attended. If the student has completed fewer than 2 years of college work, high school records must also be submitted. 45 of 111 credits required for the bachelor's degree must be completed at Centre.

Visiting: There are regularly scheduled orientations for prospective students, including a campus tour, an interview, class visits, faculty appointments, and an overnight stay, if requested. There are guides for informal visits and visitors may sit in on classes and stay overnight. To schedule a visit, contact the Office of Admission.

Financial Aid: In 2003-2004, 90% of all full-time students received some form of financial aid. 70% of full-time freshmen and 66% of continuing full-time students received need-based aid. The average freshman award was $17,922. 49% of undergraduates work part time. Average annual earnings from campus work are $1312. The average financial indebtedness of the 2003 graduate was $14,300. Centre is a member of CSS. The FAFSA and the college's own financial statement are required. The priority date for freshman financial aid applications for fall entry is February 15. The deadline for filing freshman financial aid applications for fall entry is March 1.

International Students: There are 16 international students enrolled. They must score 580 on the written TOEFL or 237 on the electronic version or may submit SAT I or ACT scores.

Computers: There are 150 PCs available for network use in the residence halls, various classroom buildings, and the library. Residence hall rooms are connected to the network. All students may access the system. There are no time limits and no fees.

Graduates: In a recent year, 236 bachelor's degrees were awarded. The most popular majors were history/social science (42%), biology (15%), and English (11%). In an average class, 65% graduate in 4 years or less, and 68% graduate in 6 years or less. 25 companies recruited on campus in a recent year. Of a recent year's graduating class, 35% were enrolled in graduate school within 6 months of graduation and 90% were employed.

Admissions Contact: J. Carey Thompson, Dean of Admission and Student Financial Planning. A video is available.
E-mail: *admission@centre.edu* Web: *www.centre.edu*

CUMBERLAND COLLEGE	E-4
Williamsburg, KY 40769	**(606) 539-4241**
	(800) 343-1609; Fax: (606) 539-4303
Full-time: 647 men, 706 women	**Faculty:** 90
Part-time: 114 men, 134 women	**Ph.Ds:** 68%
Graduate: 28 men, 14 women	**Student/Faculty:** 15 to 1
Year: semesters, summer session	**Tuition:** $11,458
Application Deadline: open	**Room & Board:** $4926
Freshman Class: 1105 applied, 791 accepted, 414 enrolled	
SAT I Verbal/Math: 520/510	**ACT:** 22 COMPETITIVE

Cumberland College, founded in 1889, is a private liberal arts institution affiliated with the Kentucky Baptist Convention. The library contains 190,312 volumes, 770,875 microform items, and 3759 audio/video tapes/CDs, and subscribes to 656 periodicals. Computerized library services include the card catalog, interlibrary loans, and database searching. Special learning facilities include a learning resource center, art gallery, natural history museum, TV station, and a distance learning lab. The 50-acre campus is in a small town 100 miles south of Lexington and 65 miles north of Knoxville. Including any residence halls, there are 30 buildings.

Student Life: 64% of undergraduates are from Kentucky. Others are from 36 states and 21 foreign countries. 94% are from public schools. 89% are white. 24% are Protestant; 16% claim no religious affiliation. The average age of freshmen is 18; all undergraduates, 21. 41% do not continue beyond their first year; 38% remain to graduate.

Housing: 1100 students can be accommodated in college housing, which includes single-sex dorms. On-campus housing is guaranteed for all 4 years. 63% of students live on campus; of those, 60% remain on campus on weekends. Alcohol is not permitted. All students may keep cars.

Activities: There are no fraternities or sororities. There are 45 groups on campus, including art, band, cheerleading, choir, chorale, chorus, dance, debate, drama, drill team, forensics, honors, jazz band, literary magazine, marching band, musical theater, pep band, political, professional, radio and TV, religious, social, social service, student government, and yearbook. Popular campus events include Madrigal Dinner, Hanging of the Greens, and Valentine's Dance.

Sports: There are 12 intercollegiate sports for men and 12 for women, and 6 intramural sports for men and 6 for women. Facilities include a gym, an athletic/convocation complex, a game room, tennis courts, a field house, baseball/softball and practice football fields, a swimming pool, a sauna and weight room located in the housing area, and a football, track, and soccer complex.

Disabled Students: 75% of the campus is accessible. Wheelchair ramps, special parking, specially equipped rest rooms, special class scheduling, and lowered drinking fountains are available.

Services: Counseling and information services are available, as is tutoring in every subject.

Campus Safety and Security: Measures include 24-hour foot and vehicle patrol, self-defense education, security escort services, and informal discussions. There are pamphlets/posters/films and lighted pathways/sidewalks.

Programs of Study: CC confers B.A., B.S., B.G.S., and B.M. degrees. Master's degrees are also awarded. Bachelor's degrees are awarded in BIOLOGICAL SCIENCE (biology/biological science), BUSINESS (accounting, business administration and management, and office supervision and management), COMMUNICATIONS AND THE ARTS (art, communications, dramatic arts, English, and music), COMPUTER AND PHYSICAL SCIENCE (chemistry, information sciences and systems, mathematics, and physics), EDUCATION (art, business, elementary, English, health, mathematics, middle school, music, physical, science, social studies, and special), HEALTH PROFESSIONS (health, medical laboratory technology, and public health), SOCIAL SCIENCE (history, political science/government, psychology, religion, religious music, and social work). Biology, business, and chemistry are the strongest academically. Biology, business, and education are the largest.

Required: All students must complete 128 semester hours, including 49 hours of liberal arts courses and an average of 36 hours in a major, while maintaining an overall GPA of 2.0 (2.5 for those seeking teacher certification). General education requirements include courses from the areas of physical fitness, art, music, theater, speech, religion, English composition, literature, history, math, natural and social sciences, community service, and fine arts or philosophy. A comprehensive exam may be required. Programs presented for graduation must include 2 majors, 1 major and 1 minor, 1 major with 15 hours of restricted electives, or 3 minors.

Special: Internships, study abroad in England and China, a Washington semester, and work-study programs with the college, local businesses, and other educational institutions are available. CC offers B.A.-B.S. degrees in all majors except music, dual majors in all major fields, a general studies degree, and nondegree study. There are 11 national honor societies, a freshman honors program, and 12 departmental honors programs.

Faculty/Classroom: 63% of faculty are male; 37%, female. All teach undergraduates. No introductory courses are taught by graduate students. The average class size in an introductory lecture is 30; in a laboratory, 15; and in a regular course, 21.

Admissions: 72% of the 2003-2004 applicants were accepted. The SAT I scores for the 2003-2004 freshman class were: Verbal--36% below 500, 47% between 500 and 599, 16% between 600 and 700, and 1% above 700; Math--45% below 500, 40% between 500 and 599, 14% between 600 and 700, and 1% above 700. The ACT scores were 38% below 21, 33% between 21 and 23, 16% between 24 and 26, 7% between 27 and 28, and 6% above 28. 33% of the current freshmen were in the top fifth of their class; 61% were in the top two fifths. 13 freshmen graduated first in their class.

Requirements: The SAT I or ACT is required, with composite scores of better than 17 for the ACT or 780 for the SAT I. Consideration is given to those with ACT scores of 16 and 17, provided the high school GPA is 2.5 or above in college prep classes. Although each application is considered individually, students must have fulfilled general high school requirements of 4 years of English, 3 each of math and science, and 2 of social studies. A completed Teacher Recommendation Form from a current teacher, a completed High School Information Form signed by the guidance counselor, and a high school transcript are required. The college also recommends an interview. The GED is accepted. A GPA of 2.0 is required. AP and CLEP credits are accepted. Important factors in the admissions decision are leadership record, recommendations by school officials, and advanced placement or honor courses.

Procedure: Freshmen are admitted to all sessions. Entrance exams should be taken prior to admission consideration. Application deadlines are open. Application fee is $30. Notification is sent on a rolling basis. Applications are accepted on computer disk and on-line.

Transfer: 75 transfer students enrolled in 2002-2003. Applicants must have verification from their previous school that they are eligible to return. Students with fewer than 30 semester or 45 quarter hours must meet freshman admissions requirements. 30 of 128 credits required for the bachelor's degree must be completed at CC.

Visiting: There are regularly scheduled orientations for prospective students, consisting of a tour, a departmental conference, an advising session, adjustment information, and general information. There are guides for informal visits and visitors may sit in on classes and stay overnight. To schedule a visit, contact the Admissions Office at admiss@cumberlandcollege.edu.

Financial Aid: In 2003-2004, 97% of all full-time freshmen and 92% of continuing full-time students received some form of financial aid. 77% of full-time freshmen and 74% of continuing full-time students received need-based aid. The average freshman award was $13,557. Need-based scholarships or need-based grants averaged $4983 ($12,058 maximum); need-based self-help aid (loans and jobs) averaged $3544 ($8325 maximum); non-need-based athletic scholarships averaged $3983 ($16,384 maximum); and other non-need-based awards and non-need-based scholarships averaged $5741 ($16,384 maximum). 62% of undergraduates work part time. Average annual earnings from campus work are $1700. The average financial indebtedness of the 2003 graduate was $12,503. CC is a member of CSS. The FAFSA is required. The priority date for freshman financial aid applications for fall entry is March 1.

International Students: There are 27 international students enrolled. They must score 550 on the written TOEFL or 213 on the electronic version or take the MELAB. They must also take the SAT I, the ACT, or the English Placement Examination, scoring 18 on the ACT.

Computers: The mainframes are a UNIX Sperry UNIVAC and an IBM AS/400. There are more than 300 Pentium, Pentium II, Gateway, and AT&T PCs available throughout the campus, with several dedicated departmental and dorm labs. For those with their own computers, access to the system is available in all dorm rooms. All students may access the system 8 A.M. to 9 P.M. daily for the main lab; hours vary for other labs. There are no time limits. The fee is $260 per year.

Graduates: From July 1, 2002 to June 30, 2003, 244 bachelor's degrees were awarded. The most popular majors were business (15%), elementary education (13%), and biology (10%). In an average class, 1% graduate in 3 years or less, 24% graduate in 4 years or less, 36% graduate in 5 years or less, and 45% graduate in 6 years or less. 10 companies recruited on campus in 2002-2003. Of the 2002 graduating class, 20%

were enrolled in graduate school within 6 months of graduation and 75% were employed.

Admissions Contact: Erica Harris, Director of Admissions. A video is available. E-mail: *admiss@cumberlandcollege.edu*
Web: *www.cumberlandcollege.edu*

EASTERN KENTUCKY UNIVERSITY E-3
Richmond, KY 40475
(859) 622-2106
(800) 465-9191; Fax: (859) 622-3024

Full-time: 3885 men, 5799 women	**Faculty:** 574; IIA, -$
Part-time: 1399 men, 2288 women	**Ph.D.s:** 70%
Graduate: none	**Student/Faculty:** 17 to 1
Year: semesters, summer session	**Tuition:** $3198 ($8790)
Application Deadline: August 1	**Room & Board:** $4510
Freshman Class: 5506 applied, 4208 accepted, 2568 enrolled	
SAT I Verbal/Math: 490/480	**ACT:** 20 **COMPETITIVE**

Eastern Kentucky University, established in 1906, is a public, state-supported institution offering degree programs in the arts and sciences, business, environmental studies, health fields, education, and public service occupations. There are 5 undergraduate schools and 1 graduate school. In addition to regional accreditation, EKU has baccalaureate program accreditation with AACSB, ADA, AHEA, CSWE, FIDER, NASM, NCATE, NLN, and NRPA. The 3 libraries contain 837,945 volumes, 1,410,522 microform items, and 4221 audio/video tapes/CDs, and subscribe to 3565 periodicals. Computerized library services include the card catalog, interlibrary loans, database searching, and Internet access. Special learning facilities include a learning resource center, art gallery, natural history museum, planetarium, radio station, TV station, and law enforcement complex that includes a training tank for underwater rescue and recovery. The 628-acre campus is in a small town 20 miles south of Lexington. Including any residence halls, there are 98 buildings.

Student Life: 90% of undergraduates are from Kentucky. Students are from 45 states, 49 foreign countries, and Canada. 90% are from public schools. 91% are white. The average age of freshmen is 18; all undergraduates, 21. 35% do not continue beyond their first year.

Housing: 5646 students can be accommodated in college housing, which includes single-sex and coed dorms, on-campus apartments, and married-student housing. In addition, there are honors houses, special-interest houses, and special accommodations for senior home economics students. On-campus housing is guaranteed for all 4 years. 67% of students commute. Alcohol is not permitted. All students may keep cars.

Activities: 4% of men belong to 12 national fraternities; 4% of women belong to 10 national sororities. There are 151 groups on campus, including art, band, cheerleading, choir, chorale, chorus, computers, dance, debate, drama, drill team, ethnic, film, gay, honors, international, jazz band, marching band, musical theater, newspaper, orchestra, pep band, photography, political, professional, radio and TV, religious, social service, student government, symphony, and yearbook. Popular campus events include Hanging of the Greens at Christmas, International Month, and fraternity/sorority competitions.

Sports: There are 8 intercollegiate sports for men and 8 for women, and 12 intramural sports for men and 12 for women. Facilities include 5 gyms, 1 outdoor and 2 indoor swimming pools, 19 outdoor hard-court and 4 indoor tennis courts, handball and racquetball courts, training rooms, a dance studio, a martial arts room, a wellness center, a 7000-seat basketball arena, a 20,000-seat stadium, an 8-lane outdoor track, a field hockey area, an 18-hole golf course, fields for baseball, softball and soccer, weight facilities, and a conditioning center.

Disabled Students: 85% of the campus is accessible. Wheelchair ramps, elevators, special parking, specially equipped rest rooms, special class scheduling, lowered drinking fountains, and lowered telephones are available.

Services: Counseling and information services are available, as is tutoring in some subjects, including math, English, and reading. There is a reader service for the blind, and remedial math, reading, and writing. Tutoring is available in other fields upon request.

Campus Safety and Security: Measures include 24-hour foot and vehicle patrol, self-defense education, security escort services, and shuttle buses. There are informal discussions, pamphlets/posters/films, emergency telephones, lighted pathways/sidewalks, and 16 crime-prevention programs.

Programs of Study: EKU confers B.A., B.S., B.B.A., B.F.A., B.I.S., B.M., B.M.Ed., B.S.N., and B.S.W. degrees. Associate and master's degrees are also awarded. Bachelor's degrees are awarded in AGRICULTURE (agriculture, horticulture, and wildlife management), BIOLOGICAL SCIENCE (biology/biological science and microbiology), BUSINESS (accounting, banking and finance, business administration and management, and marketing/retailing/merchandising), COMMUNICATIONS AND THE ARTS (art, broadcasting, dramatic arts, English, French, journalism, music, performing arts, public relations, Spanish, and speech/debate/rhetoric), COMPUTER AND PHYSICAL SCIENCE (chemistry, computer programming, computer science, geology, mathematics, and statistics), EDUCATION (art, business, education of the deaf and hearing impaired, elementary, foreign languages, health, home economics, industrial arts, middle school, music, physical, secondary, special, and technical), ENGINEERING AND ENVIRONMENTAL DESIGN (airline piloting and navigation, construction technology, environmental science, interior design, and manufacturing technology), HEALTH PROFESSIONS (environmental health science, health care administration, nursing, and occupational therapy), SOCIAL SCIENCE (anthropology, child care/child and family studies, corrections, dietetics, economics, fire protection, forensic studies, geography, history, paralegal studies, philosophy, political science/government, psychology, social work, and sociology). Occupational therapy, psychology, and nursing are the strongest academically. Education, nursing, and law enforcement are the largest.

Required: All students must complete 51 credit hours of general education requirements, including courses in phys ed, health, English, natural science, social science, math, and the humanities. Students must complete a total of 128 credit hours, including 45 to 60 credits in the major, with a minimum GPA of 2.0.

Special: EKU offers cooperative programs with all academic colleges, internships, and study abroad in various European countries. Students may opt for credit by exam, nondegree study, pass/fail options, student-designed and dual majors, and a general studies degree. There are 30 national honor societies, including Phi Beta Kappa, a freshman honors program, and 1 departmental honors program.

Faculty/Classroom: 55% of faculty are male; 45%, female. 98% teach undergraduates and 25% both teach and do research. The average class size in an introductory lecture is 30; in a laboratory, 15; and in a regular course, 25.

Admissions: 76% of the 2003-2004 applicants were accepted. The SAT I scores for the 2003-2004 freshman class were: Verbal--94% below 500, 4% between 500 and 599, and 2% between 600 and 700; Math--94% below 500, 4% between 500 and 599, and 2% between 600 and 700. The ACT scores were 59% below 21, 23% between 21 and 23, 13% between 24 and 26, 4% between 27 and 28, and 1% above 28.

Requirements: The ACT is required. A GPA of 2.0 is required. AP and CLEP credits are accepted. Important factors in the admissions decision are evidence of special talent, extracurricular activities record, and leadership record.

Procedure: Freshmen are admitted to all sessions. Entrance exams should be taken prior to enrollment. Applications should be filed by August 1 for fall entry, along with a $25 fee. Notification is sent on a rolling basis. Applications are accepted on-line through the school's web site.

Transfer: Applicants must have a 2.0 cumulative GPA from all accredited institutions previously attended and must not have been dismissed. 30 of 128 credits required for the bachelor's degree must be completed at EKU.

Visiting: There are regularly scheduled orientations for prospective students, consisting of a 1-day program during the summer prior to fall enrollment. There are guides for informal visits and visitors may sit in on classes and stay overnight. To schedule a visit, contact the Admissions Office at admissions@eku.edu.

Financial Aid: EKU is a member of CSS. The CSS/Profile and the college's own financial statement are required. The deadline for filing freshman financial aid applications for fall entry is April 15.

International Students: The school actively recruits these students. They must score 500 on the written TOEFL and also take the ACT or the SAT I for those applicants from states where the SAT I is dominant, scoring 21.

Computers: The mainframe is a DEC VAX. About 300 networked PCs with Internet access are located in various academic buildings, the library, and the student center. Internet service is also available in residence halls. All students may access the system. There are no time limits and no fees.

Admissions Contact: Stephen A. Byrn, Director of Admissions. E-mail: admissions@eku.edu Web: http://www.admissions.eku.edu

---

GEORGETOWN COLLEGE   D-2
Georgetown, KY 40324-1696   (502) 863-8009
                                      (800) 788-9985; Fax: (502) 868-7733

Full-time: 543 men, 700 women	**Faculty:** 90; IIB, -$
Part-time: 28 men, 50 women	**Ph.D.s:** 90%
Graduate: 52 men, 335 women	**Student/Faculty:** 14 to 1
Year: semesters, summer session	**Tuition:** $16,500
Application Deadline: February 15	**Room & Board:** $5500
Freshman Class: 904 applied, 852 accepted, 367 enrolled	
ACT: 25	**VERY COMPETITIVE**

Georgetown College, founded in 1829, is a private liberal arts college affiliated with the Kentucky Baptist Convention. The library contains 152,531 volumes, 177,421 microform items, and 3676 audio/video tapes/CDs, and subscribes to 733 periodicals. Computerized library services include the card catalog, interlibrary loans, and database searching. Special learning facilities include a learning resource center, art gallery, planetarium, and radio station. The 104-acre campus is in a suburban area 12 miles north of Lexington. Including any residence halls, there are 40 buildings.

Student Life: 82% of undergraduates are from Kentucky. Students are from 24 states, 12 foreign countries, and Canada. 90% are from public schools. 94% are white. 78% are Protestant; 12% Catholic; 10% claim no religious affiliation. The average age of freshmen is 18; all undergraduates, 20. 20% do not continue beyond their first year; 60% remain to graduate.

Housing: 1242 students can be accommodated in college housing, which includes single-sex dormitories, on-campus apartments, married-student housing, fraternity houses, and sorority houses. On-campus housing is guaranteed for all 4 years. 92% of students live on campus; of those, 78% remain on campus on weekends. Alcohol is not permitted. All students may keep cars.

Activities: 28% of men belong to 1 local fraternity and 4 national fraternities; 40% of women belong to 4 national sororities. There are 101 groups on campus, including academic team, art, band, cheerleading, choir, chorale, chorus, computers, dance, drama, ethnic, forensics, honors, international, jazz band, literary magazine, musical theater, newspaper, pep band, photography, political, professional, radio and TV, religious, social, social service, student government, and yearbook. Popular campus events include Festival of Song, Parents Day, and Hanging of the Green (Christmas).

Sports: There are 8 intercollegiate sports for men and 8 for women, and 11 intramural sports for men and 11 for women. Facilities include a 3000-seat stadium, 8 tennis courts, soccer, baseball, football, softball, and intramural fields, a 1550-seat gym, racquetball courts, a training room, and a fitness center housing a Nautilus area, weight-lifting area, basketball courts, recreation room, and dressing rooms.

Disabled Students: 70% of the campus is accessible. Wheelchair ramps, elevators, special parking, specially equipped rest rooms, and special class scheduling are available.

Services: Counseling and information services are available, as is tutoring in every subject.

Campus Safety and Security: Measures include 24-hour foot and vehicle patrol, self-defense education, security escort services, and shuttle buses. There are informal discussions, pamphlets/posters/films, emergency telephones, and lighted pathways/sidewalks.

Programs of Study: Georgetown confers B.A., B.S., B.M., and B.M.E. degrees. Master's degrees are also awarded. Bachelor's degrees are awarded in BIOLOGICAL SCIENCE (biology/biological science), BUSINESS (accounting, banking and finance, business economics, international business management, management information systems, management science, marketing/retailing/merchandising, and recreation and leisure services), COMMUNICATIONS AND THE ARTS (art, communications, English, French, German, music, and Spanish), COMPUTER AND PHYSICAL SCIENCE (chemistry, computer science, mathematics, and physics), EDUCATION (elementary, foreign languages, music, and physical), ENGINEERING AND ENVIRONMENTAL DESIGN (environmental science), HEALTH PROFESSIONS (medical laboratory technology and nursing), SOCIAL SCIENCE (American studies, child care/child and family studies, European studies, history, human services, philosophy, political science/government, psychology, religion, religious music, sociology, and youth ministry). Biology and English are the strongest academically. Business and psychology are the largest.

Required: All students are required to complete 56 semester hours of general education courses, including 16 in fine arts and humanities, 9 in foreign language and culture (or otherwise demonstrate proficiency), 8 in communication, 6 each in religion, natural sciences, and social sciences, 3 in math, and 2 in phys ed. A total of 128 semester hours, including 33 to 60 in the major, with a minimum GPA of 2.0, is required to graduate, as is successful completion of a comprehensive exam in the major.

Special: Georgetown offers cross-registration with the University of Kentucky Air Force ROTC for aerospace studies. A 3-2 engineering degree is available with the University of Kentucky and Washington University in St. Louis. Internships, co-op programs in math and computer science, study abroad in 5 countries, work-study programs, dual and student-designed majors, and pass/fail options are available. Interdisciplinary majors include business administration/communication arts and business administration/ethics. A dual degree is offered in liberal studies. Nondegree study is possible. There are 20 national honor societies, and a freshman honors program.

Faculty/Classroom: 68% of faculty are male; 32%, female. All teach undergraduates. No introductory courses are taught by graduate students. The average class size in an introductory lecture is 21 and in a regular course, 18.

Admissions: 94% of the 2003-2004 applicants were accepted. The ACT scores for the 2003-2004 freshman class were: 13% below 21, 32% between 21 and 23, 32% between 24 and 26, 10% between 27 and 28, and 13% above 28. 63% of the current freshmen were in the top fifth of their class; 87% were in the top two fifths. 36 freshmen graduated first in their class.

Requirements: The SAT I or ACT is required. In addition, applicants should have completed 4 high school credits in English, 3 each in math and science, 2 in a foreign language, and 1 each in social studies and history, with additional credits in electives strongly encouraged. A student essay is required; Kentucky high school applicants may substitute a writing portfolio entry. A GPA of 2.0 is required. AP and CLEP credits are accepted. Important factors in the admissions decision are advanced placement or honor courses, evidence of special talent, and leadership record.

Procedure: Freshmen are admitted to all sessions. Entrance exams should be taken from December of the junior year through October of the senior year. Early decision applications should be filed by December 1. For best consideration, students should apply before February 15 of their senior year of high school. The application fee is $30. Notification is sent on a rolling basis. Applications are accepted on-line through the school's web site.

Transfer: 41 transfer students enrolled in 2002-2003. Applicants must be in good standing at the school most recently attended and must submit official college and high school transcripts. 30 of 128 credits required for the bachelor's degree must be completed at Georgetown.

Visiting: There are regularly scheduled orientations for prospective students, consisting of campus tours and information on admissions, financial assistance, student life, and academic programs. There are guides for informal visits and visitors may sit in on classes and stay overnight. To schedule a visit, contact Johnnie Johnson, Director of Admissions at admissions@georgetowncollege.edu.

Financial Aid: In 2003-2004, 98% of all full-time freshmen and 97% of continuing full-time students received some form of financial aid. 76% of all full-time students received need-based aid. The average freshman award was $15,689. $4,747 ($21,785 maximum) from need-based scholarships or need-based grants averaged, $1,785 ($7961 maximum) from need-based self-help aid (loans and jobs), $451 ($16,650 maximum) from non-need-based athletic scholarships, and other $8,705 ($22,550 maximum) from non-need-based awards and non-need-based scholarships. 47% of undergraduates work part time. Average annual earnings from campus work are $1100. The average financial indebtedness of the 2003 graduate was $15,481. The FAFSA is required. The priority date for freshman financial aid applications for fall entry is February 1. The deadline for filing freshman financial aid applications for fall entry is March 1.

International Students: There are 19 international students enrolled. They must score 520 on the written TOEFL or 190 on the electronic version.

Computers: The mainframe is an HP 9000/K2 60 D320. There are about 200 PCs with word processing, statistical analysis, spreadsheets, programming languages, ERIC, and other databases, available in the library and departmental labs. Students may access academic computing via the Ethernet network connection. All students may access the system. There are no time limits and no fees.

Graduates: From July 1, 2002 to June 30, 2003, 260 bachelor's degrees were awarded. The most popular majors were business (27%), communication arts (19%), and psychology (16%). In an average class, 44% graduate in 4 years or less, 59% graduate in 5 years or less, and 61% graduate in 6 years or less. 28 companies recruited on campus in 2002-2003. Of the 2002 graduating class, 45% were enrolled in graduate school within 6 months of graduation and 88% were employed.

Admissions Contact: Johnnie Johnson, Director of Admissions.
E-mail: admissions@georgetowncollege.edu
Web: http://www.georgetowncollege.edu

KENTUCKY CHRISTIAN COLLEGE
Grayson, KY 41143

F-2
(606) 474-6613
(800) KCC-3181; Fax: (606) 474-3155

Full-time: 270 men, 290 women	Faculty: 27; IIB, --$
Part-time: 10 men, 10 women	Ph.D.s: 92%
Graduate: 15 men and women	Student/Faculty: 21 to 1
Year: semesters, summer session	Tuition: $10,560
Application Deadline: open	Room & Board: $4355
Freshman Class: n/av	
SAT I or ACT: required	COMPETITIVE

Kentucky Christian College, established in 1919, is a private Christian college affiliated with the Church of Christ, offering undergraduate programs in Christian ministry, psychology, social work, business administration, teacher education, music, history, and intercultural studies. Figures in the above capsule and in this profile are approximate. In addition to regional accreditation, KCC has baccalaureate program accreditation with CSWE. The library contains 101,859 volumes, 738 microform items, and 3547 audio/video tapes/CDs, and subscribes to 439 periodicals. Computerized library services include interlibrary loans and database searching. Special learning facilities include a learning resource center and radio station. The 121-acre campus is in a small town 20 miles from Ashland and 90 miles east of Lexington. Including any residence halls, there are 16 buildings.

Student Life: 69% of undergraduates are from out of state, mostly the Midwest. Students are from 24 states, 8 foreign countries, and Canada.

94% are white. Most are Protestant. The average age of freshmen is 18; all undergraduates, 20. 34% do not continue beyond their first year.

Housing: 556 students can be accommodated in college housing, which includes single-sex dorms, on-campus apartments, and married-student housing. On-campus housing is guaranteed for all 4 years. 91% of students live on campus. Alcohol is not permitted. All students may keep cars.

Activities: There are no fraternities or sororities. There are 14 groups on campus, including cheerleading, choir, chorale, drama, jazz band, musical theater, newspaper, pep band, professional, radio and TV, religious, social service, student government, and yearbook. Popular campus events include Feast of Christmas, Days of Future Knights, and Summer in the Son.

Sports: There are 4 intercollegiate sports for men and 4 for women, and 16 intramural sports for men and 16 for women. Facilities include a gym, soccer and recreational fields, a baseball diamond, a student life recreational center, and racquetball and tennis courts.

Disabled Students: 95% of the campus is accessible. Wheelchair ramps, elevators, special parking, specially equipped rest rooms, lowered drinking fountains, and lowered telephones are available.

Services: Counseling and information services are available, as is tutoring in some subjects. RAs on campus serve as dorm tutors in various subjects. There is a reader service for the blind, and remedial math, reading, and writing.

Campus Safety and Security: Measures include security escort services, informal discussions, emergency telephones, lighted pathways/sidewalks, and a full-time security guard.

Programs of Study: KCC confers B.A. and B.S. degrees. Associate and master's degrees are also awarded. Bachelor's degrees are awarded in BUSINESS (business administration and management), COMMUNICATIONS AND THE ARTS (literature, music, and music performance), COMPUTER AND PHYSICAL SCIENCE (mathematics and science), EDUCATION (elementary, middle school, and music), SOCIAL SCIENCE (biblical studies, counseling/psychology, history, ministries, philosophy, psychology, religious music, social work, and youth ministry). Teacher education and ministry are the largest.

Required: To graduate, students must complete 132 semester hours with at least 30 hours in the major and a minimum GPA of 2.0. Required courses include freshman orientation, phys ed, English, history, Introduction to Christian Doctrine, and Survey of Biblical Literature. Candidates for the B.A. degree must fulfill a 14-hour language requirement. All students are Bible majors, and most complete the requirements of a second major or a minor. Students must also participate in a Christian service program.

Special: Internships, work-study programs, B.A.-B.S. degrees, and dual majors are offered. Internships are required in business, education, ministry, and social work. Nondegree study is available. There is a chapter of Phi Beta Kappa.

Faculty/Classroom: 81% of faculty are male; 19%, female. All teach undergraduates and 25% both teach and do research. The average class size in an introductory lecture is 30; in a laboratory, 15; and in a regular course, 17.

Admissions: 3 freshmen graduated first in their class in a recent year.

Requirements: The SAT I or ACT is required, with a minimum composite score of 17 on the ACT or 830 on the SAT I. Applicants with lower test scores who have a high school GPA of 2.5 or higher will be considered. Applicants must graduate from an accredited secondary school or have a GED. Essays are required. A GPA of 2.0 is required. AP and CLEP credits are accepted.

Procedure: Freshmen are admitted to all sessions. There are early decision and deferred admissions plans. There is a rolling admissions plan. Application deadlines are open. The fall 2003 application fee was $25. Applications are accepted on-line through the school's web site.

Transfer: 37 transfer students enrolled in a recent year. Applicants must have a cumulative GPA of 2.0. They must submit transcripts from all previous institutions and must be in good standing at the last college attended. 32 of 132 credits required for the bachelor's degree must be completed at KCC.

Visiting: There are regularly scheduled orientations for prospective students, consisting of an interview, a campus tour, lunch, and attending classes. Also, a semester-long orientation class is offered for all first-time freshmen. There are guides for informal visits and visitors may sit in on classes and stay overnight. To schedule a visit, contact Leslie Arnold, Assistant to the Director of Admissions.

Financial Aid: In a recent year, 76% of all full-time freshmen and 71% of continuing full-time students received some form of financial aid. 41% of full-time freshmen and 49% of continuing full-time students received need-based aid. The average freshman award was $6621. 54% of undergraduates work part time. Average annual earnings from campus work are $1586. The average financial indebtedness of a recent graduate was $19,497. The FAFSA and the college's own financial statement are required. Check with the school for current deadlines.

International Students: There were 13 international students enrolled in a recent year. They must score 500 on the written TOEFL and also take the SAT I or the ACT.

Computers: The mainframe is an IBM RS/6000. There is a Novell Network with connections provided in dorm rooms. Computers are located in the library, academic building labs, and student life center. All students may access the system. There are no time limits. The fee is $100.

Graduates: In a recent year, 76 bachelor's degrees were awarded. The most popular majors were Christian ministry (29%), teacher education (24%), and business administration (17%). In an average class, 45% graduate in 4 years or less, and 50% graduate in 6 years or less.

Admissions Contact: Sandra Deakins, Director of Admissions. E-mail: *knights@email.kcc.edu* Web: *www.kcc.edu*

KENTUCKY STATE UNIVERSITY
D-2
Frankfort, KY 40601
(502) 597-6322
1 (800) 325-1716; Fax: (502)597-5814

Full-time: 752 men, 904 women	**Faculty:** n/av
Part-time: 128 men, 353 women	**Ph.D.s:** n/av
Graduate: 82 men, 87 women	**Student/Faculty:** n/av
Year: semesters, summer session	**Tuition:** $3668 ($9582)
Application Deadline: open	**Room & Board:** $5394
Freshman Class: 822 accepted	
SAT I Verbal/Math: 418/426	**ACT:** 17 NONCOMPETITIVE

Kentucky State University, founded in 1886, is a public liberal arts institution that emphasizes student involvement in seminars and course planning. There are 4 undergraduate schools and 1 graduate school. In addition to regional accreditation, KSU has baccalaureate program accreditation with AACSB, ADA, AHEA, CSWE, NASM, NCATE, and NLN. The library contains 437,012 volumes, 323,804 microform items, and 1342 audio/video tapes/CDs, and subscribes to 1009 periodicals. Computerized library services include the card catalog, interlibrary loans, database searching, and Internet access. Special learning facilities include a learning resource center, art gallery, and a 167-acre agricultural research farm. The 308-acre campus is in a small town 25 miles west of Lexington. Including any residence halls, there are 34 buildings.

Student Life: 68% of undergraduates are from Kentucky. Students are from 28 states, 28 foreign countries, and Canada. 99% are from public schools. 62% are African American; 32% white. The average age of all undergraduates is 25. 30% do not continue beyond their first year; 35% remain to graduate.

Housing: 849 students can be accommodated in college housing, which includes single-sex dormitories and on-campus apartments. In addition, there are special-interest houses. On-campus housing is guaranteed for the freshman year only and is available on a first-come, first-served basis. 67% of students commute. Alcohol is not permitted. All students may keep cars.

Activities: 3% of men belong to 6 national fraternities; 4% of women belong to 5 national sororities. There are 70 groups on campus, including art, band, cheerleading, choir, chorale, computers, dance, drama, drill team, honors, international, jazz band, literary magazine, marching band, musical theater, newspaper, opera, orchestra, political, professional, religious, social, social service, student government, symphony, and yearbook. Popular campus events include plays, concerts, and talent shows.

Sports: There are 7 intercollegiate sports for men and 6 for women. Facilities include a 6500-seat football stadium, an indoor swimming pool, tennis courts, a bowling alley, training and weight rooms, a field house, and baseball, track, and field complexes.

Disabled Students: Wheelchair ramps, elevators, special parking, specially equipped rest rooms, lowered drinking fountains, lowered telephones, and electric doors are available.

Services: Counseling and information services are available, as is tutoring in every subject. There is a reader service for the blind, and remedial math, reading, and writing.

Campus Safety and Security: Measures include 24-hour foot and vehicle patrol, self-defense education, and lighted pathways/sidewalks.

Programs of Study: KSU confers B.A. and B.S. degrees. Associate and master's degrees are also awarded. Bachelor's degrees are awarded in BIOLOGICAL SCIENCE (biology/biological science), BUSINESS (apparel and accessories marketing and business administration and management), COMMUNICATIONS AND THE ARTS (art, English, fine arts, music performance, and studio art), COMPUTER AND PHYSICAL SCIENCE (applied mathematics, chemistry, computer science, and mathematics), EDUCATION (art, early childhood, elementary, mathematics, music, physical, secondary, and social studies), SOCIAL SCIENCE (criminal justice, history, liberal arts/general studies, political science/government, psychology, public administration, social work, and sociology).

Required: A total of 128 credits is required to graduate, with 64 in the major and a minimum 2.0 GPA. An assessment may include, but is not limited to, a portfolio, a written exam, a presentation, a recital, and/or a capstone course.

Special: There is 1 national honor society, a freshman honors program, and 10 departmental honors programs.

Faculty/Classroom: 61% of faculty are male; 39%, female. 95% teach undergraduates.

Admissions: The SAT I scores for the 2003-2004 freshman class were: Verbal--87% below 500, 12% between 500 and 599, and 2% between 600 and 700; Math--85% below 500, 10% between 500 and 599, and 5% between 600 and 700. The ACT scores were 86% below 21, 10% between 21 and 23, 3% between 24 and 26, 1% between 27 and 28, and 1% above 28.

Requirements: The ACT is required, with a composite score of 19 in state and 20 out of state needed. Applicants are required to have 4 years in English, 3 in math, 2 each in science and history, and 9 additional precollege curriculum classes. The GED is accepted. A GPA of 2.0 is required. AP and CLEP credits are accepted.

Procedure: Freshmen are admitted to all sessions. Entrance exams should be taken from October to April. There are early admissions and deferred admissions plans. Application deadlines are open. The fall 2003 application fee was $18. Notification is sent on a rolling basis. Applications are accepted on-line through *www.kysu.edu*, "Get Wired."

Transfer: Transfer applicants must have a 2.0 minimum GPA at previous colleges. Only C grades or higher transfer. If fewer than 30 semester credits are transferable, applicants must meet freshman criteria. 45 of 128 credits required for the bachelor's degree must be completed at KSU.

Visiting: There are regularly scheduled orientations for prospective students, including tours and meetings with faculty and financial aid officers. There are guides for informal visits and visitors may sit in on classes. To schedule a visit, contact Admissions at *admission@gwmail.kysu.edu*.

Financial Aid: In 2003-2004, 80% of all full-time freshmen and 85% of continuing full-time students received some form of financial aid. 65% of full-time freshmen and 60% of continuing full-time students received need-based aid. The average freshman award was $6500. Need-based scholarships or need-based grants averaged $500 ($800 maximum); need-based self-help aid (loans and jobs) averaged $2500 ($5500 maximum); non-need-based athletic scholarships averaged $3000 ($14,500 maximum); and other non-need-based awards and non-need-based scholarships averaged $2000 ($14,500 maximum). 55% of undergraduates work part time. Average annual earnings from campus work are $1000. The average financial indebtedness of the 2003 graduate was $12,000. KSU is a member of CSS. The FAFSA and the college's own financial statement are required. The priority date for freshman financial aid applications for fall entry is April 15.

International Students: They must score 525 on the written TOEFL and also take the SAT I or the ACT.

Computers: The mainframe is an IBM 9221 Model 170. Many IBM and Mac PCs are available in departmental computer labs; some are connected to a LAN. A PC lab is in the library for student use. All students may access the system 13 hours a day. There are no time limits and no fees. All students are required to have personal computers.

Graduates: From July 1, 2002 to June 30, 2003, 212 bachelor's degrees were awarded. The most popular majors were business (26%), computer science (12%), and criminal justice (9%).

Admissions Contact: James Burrell, Director of Admissions. A video is available. E-mail: *jburrell@gwmail.kysu.edu* Web: *www.kysu.edu*

KENTUCKY WESLEYAN COLLEGE
B-3
Owensboro, KY 42302-1039
(270) 852-3242
(800) 999-0592; Fax: (270) 926-3196

Full-time: 282 men, 290 women	**Faculty:** 38
Part-time: 20 men, 19 women	**Ph.D.s:** 82%
Graduate: none	**Student/Faculty:** 15 to 1
Year: semesters, summer session	**Tuition:** $11,950
Application Deadline: open	**Room & Board:** $5300
Freshman Class: 813 applied, 611 accepted, 164 enrolled	
SAT I Verbal/Math: 967 (mean)	**ACT:** 21 COMPETITIVE

Kentucky Wesleyan College, founded in 1858, is a private liberal arts institution affiliated with the United Methodist Church. KWC offers undergraduate programs in natural sciences, humanities and fine arts, and social sciences. Additionally, academic programs are offered in criminal justice, nursing, human resources administration, mass communication, and computer science. In addition to regional accreditation, KWC has baccalaureate program accreditation with NLN. The library contains 85,000 volumes, 68,000 microform items, and 3650 audio/video tapes/CDs, and subscribes to 315 periodicals. Computerized library services include the card catalog, interlibrary loans, database searching, and Internet access. Special learning facilities include a learning resource center, art gallery, and radio station. The 55-acre campus is in an urban area 95 miles southwest of Louisville and 120 miles north of Nashville, Tennessee. Including any residence halls, there are 15 buildings.

Student Life: 81% of undergraduates are from Kentucky. Students are from 22 states, 6 foreign countries, and Canada. 93% are from public schools. 86% are white. 48% are Protestant; 26% Catholic; 26% claim no religious affiliation. The average age of freshmen is 18; all undergraduates, 20. 33% do not continue beyond their first year; 44% remain to graduate.

Housing: 392 students can be accommodated in college housing, which includes single-sex and coed dorms, on-campus apartments, fraternity houses, and sorority houses. On-campus housing is guaranteed for all 4 years. 58% of students commute. Alcohol is not permitted. All students may keep cars.

Activities: 19% of men belong to 3 national fraternities; 23% of women belong to 2 national sororities. There are 43 groups on campus, including art, band, cheerleading, choir, chorale, chorus, computers, drama, ethnic, jazz band, literary magazine, marching band, musical theater, newspaper, pep band, political, professional, radio and TV, religious, social, social service, student government, and yearbook. Popular campus events include Family Weekend, Student Appreciation Week, and theater productions.

Sports: There are 6 intercollegiate sports for men and 6 for women, and 7 intramural sports for men and 7 for women. Facilities include a health and recreation center, which houses an 800-seat gym, a fully equipped weight training center, racquetball courts, batting and pitching facilities for softball and baseball, and a multipurpose auxiliary gym. Outdoor facilities include a baseball park, a softball park, a soccer field, and additional practice fields for football and soccer. Varsity basketball games are played in the 5000-seat Owensboro Sports Center.

Disabled Students: 64% of the campus is accessible. Wheelchair ramps, elevators, special parking, specially equipped rest rooms, special class scheduling, and lowered drinking fountains are available.

Services: Counseling and information services are available, as is tutoring in most subjects. There is a reader service for the blind, and remedial math, reading, and writing.

Campus Safety and Security: Measures include 24-hour foot and vehicle patrol, security escort services, informal discussions, and pamphlets/posters/films. There are lighted pathways/sidewalks.

Programs of Study: KWC confers B.A., B.S., B.M., and B.M.E. degrees. Bachelor's degrees are awarded in BIOLOGICAL SCIENCE (biology/biological science), BUSINESS (accounting, business administration and management, business economics, and human resources), COMMUNICATIONS AND THE ARTS (art, communications, dramatic arts, English, and fine arts), COMPUTER AND PHYSICAL SCIENCE (chemistry, computer science, and physics), EDUCATION (art, elementary, middle school, music, physical, and secondary), ENGINEERING AND ENVIRONMENTAL DESIGN (preengineering), HEALTH PROFESSIONS (nursing, predentistry, and premedicine), SOCIAL SCIENCE (criminal justice, early childhood studies, history, political science/government, prelaw, psychology, and sociology). Natural sciences, education, and business are the strongest academically. Business, accounting, and general education are the largest.

Required: All students are required to complete the following general education program of skills and content requirements: 9 hours each in humanities and social sciences, 8 hours in natural science, 6 in history, 3 each in religion, integrated studies, and multicultural studies, and 2 in phys ed. Students must demonstrate proficiency in math, computing, oral and written communication, and foreign language. To graduate, students must complete a total of 128 credits, including 36 in the major, with a 2.0 GPA.

Special: A cooperative program in early childhood development with Brescia University is available. Internships and student-designed majors are available in many programs and are established on an individual basis. A dual degree in engineering is offered with Auburn University and the University of Kentucky. A Washington semester and study abroad in 5 countries are also available. There are 8 national honor societies and 7 departmental honors programs.

Faculty/Classroom: 66% of faculty are male; 34%, female. All teach undergraduates and 30% do research. The average class size in an introductory lecture is 25; in a laboratory, 17; and in a regular course, 15.

Admissions: 75% of the 2003-2004 applicants were accepted. The ACT scores for the 2003-2004 freshman class were: 41% below 21, 23% between 21 and 23, 26% between 24 and 26, 5% between 27 and 28, and 5% above 28. 27 freshmen graduated first in their class.

Requirements: The SAT I or ACT is required if students have been out of high school fewer than 5 years. In addition, applicants should have completed 13 high school units in college preparatory English, math, science, social studies, and a foreign language, or the GED equivalent. Applicants are considered individually. A GPA of 2.25 is required. AP and CLEP credits are accepted. Important factors in the admissions decision are advanced placement or honor courses, evidence of special talent, and leadership record.

Procedure: Freshmen are admitted to all sessions. Entrance exams should be taken during the spring of the junior year or the fall of the senior year. There is a deferred admissions plan. Application deadlines are open. The fall 2003 application fee was $20. Notification is sent on a rolling basis. Applications are accepted on computer disk and on-line through CollegeLink.

Transfer: 40 transfer students enrolled in a recent year. Transfer applicants should have a minimum GPA of 2.0 in all course work and be in good standing at the previously attended institution. 30 of 128 credits required for the bachelor's degree must be completed at KWC.

Visiting: There are regularly scheduled orientations for prospective students, including a campus tour, meetings with faculty and students, and dining on campus. There are guides for informal visits and visitors may sit in on classes and stay overnight. To schedule a visit, contact the Admissions Office at krasp@kwc.edu.

Financial Aid: In a recent year, 93% of all full-time freshmen and 90% of continuing full-time students received some form of financial aid. 84% of full-time freshmen and 77% of continuing full-time students received need-based aid. The average freshman award was $9967. 51% of undergraduates work part time. KWC is a member of CSS. The FAFSA and the college's own financial statement are required. The deadline for filing freshman financial aid applications for fall entry is August 1.

International Students: There are 7 international students enrolled. They must score 500 on the written TOEFL. SAT I or ACT scores are required of international students who do not have a TOEFL score or who want to play NCAA sports.

Computers: The mainframe is an IBM AS/400 minicomputer. The campus computer network links all residential and academic buildings to a central unit. Software includes Harvard Graphics, Lotus 1-2-3, dBASE IV, WordPerfect, e-mail, Pagemaker, Corel Draw, PC Globe, PC USA, and Printshop. The system is available 24 hours a day through in-room network stations or residence hall study rooms. All students may access the system. There are no time limits and no fees.

Graduates: In a recent year, 150 bachelor's degrees were awarded. The most popular majors were accounting (20%), communication arts (16%), and general education (13%). In an average class, 41% graduate in 5 years or less, and 44% graduate in 6 years or less. 17 companies recruited on campus in 2002-2003. Of a recent year's graduating class, 21% were enrolled in graduate school within 6 months of graduation and 84% were employed.

Admissions Contact: Mark Dartt, Director of Institutional Research. A video is available. E-mail: mdartt@kwc.edu Web: www.kwc.edu

---

LINDSEY WILSON COLLEGE
Columbia, KY 42728

D-3
(270) 384-8504
(800) 264-0138; Fax: (270) 384-8591

Full-time: 480 men, 760 women	**Faculty:** 44; IIB, --$
Part-time: 30 men, 110 women	**Ph.D.s:** 57%
Graduate: 10 men, 30 women	**Student/Faculty:** 27 to 1
Year: semesters, summer session	**Tuition:** $11,952
Application Deadline: open	**Room & Board:** $5274
Freshman Class: n/av	
SAT I or ACT: recommended	**LESS COMPETITIVE**

Lindsey Wilson College, founded in 1903, is a private liberal arts college affiliated with the United Methodist Church, offering undergraduate programs in arts and sciences, business administration, education, human services, and pre-health. Some figures in the above capsule and in this profile are approximate. In addition to regional accreditation, Lindsey has baccalaureate program accreditation with NCATE. The library contains 85,000 volumes, 68,000 microform items, and 3650 audio/video tapes/CDs, and subscribes to 35 periodicals. Computerized library services include the card catalog, interlibrary loans, database searching, and Internet access. Special learning facilities include a learning resource center and art gallery. The 40-acre campus is in a small town 100 miles southeast of Louisville. Including any residence halls, there are 35 buildings.

Student Life: 89% of undergraduates are from Kentucky. Students are from 15 states, 23 foreign countries, and Canada. 90% are from public schools. 89% are white. 78% are Protestant; 16% claim no religious affiliation; 6% Catholic. The average age of freshmen is 19; all undergraduates, 24. 46% do not continue beyond their first year.

Housing: 650 students can be accommodated in college housing, which includes single-sex dorms, on-campus apartments, and married-student housing. In addition, there are honors houses. On-campus housing is guaranteed for all 4 years. 51% of students commute. Alcohol is not permitted. All students may keep cars.

Activities: There are no fraternities or sororities. There are 30 groups on campus, including art, cheerleading, choir, chorale, chorus, computers, dance, drama, film, honors, international, literary magazine, musical theater, newspaper, pep band, photography, political, professional, religious, social, social service, student government, and yearbook. Popular campus events include Hanging of the Greens, Parent Day, and Tradition Day.

Sports: There are 8 intercollegiate sports for men and 8 for women, and 15 intramural sports for men and 15 for women. Facilities include a sports center with a 1000-seat gym and a weight-training room, a sand volleyball court, and the student union building.

Disabled Students: 80% of the campus is accessible. Wheelchair ramps, elevators, special parking, specially equipped rest rooms, special class scheduling, and lowered drinking fountains are available.

Services: Counseling and information services are available, as is tutoring in every subject. There is remedial math, reading, and writing.

Campus Safety and Security: Measures include security escort services, informal discussions, pamphlets/posters/films, and lighted pathways/sidewalks. There is a 12-hour foot and vehicle patrol.

Programs of Study: Lindsey confers the B.A. degree. Associate and master's degrees are also awarded. Bachelor's degrees are awarded in BIOLOGICAL SCIENCE (biology/biological science), BUSINESS (accounting and business administration and management), COMMUNICATIONS AND THE ARTS (art, communications, and English), EDUCATION (elementary and secondary), SOCIAL SCIENCE (American studies, criminal justice, history, human services, liberal arts/general studies, and social science). Business, elementary education, and human services are the strongest academically and have the largest enrollments.

Required: All students must complete general education core requirements, including courses in communication of ideas, math, natural science, religion, humanities, fine arts, social behavioral science, and physed, as well as a 1-hour personal development career seminar. A total of 128 semester hours, with a minimum GPA of 2.0, is required to graduate.

Special: Human services majors are offered a social services practicum in their field of study. Internships, work-study programs, a general studies degree, and pass/fail options in some courses are available. Study abroad is possible through Lindsey in London and the Northern Ireland Exchange. There is a freshman honors program.

Faculty/Classroom: 47% of faculty are male; 53%, female. All teach undergraduates. No introductory courses are taught by graduate students. The average class size in an introductory lecture is 26; in a laboratory, 20; and in a regular course, 26.

Requirements: The SAT I or ACT is recommended. In addition, applicants should have completed 20 academic high school credits or the GED equivalent. A GPA of 2.8 is required. AP and CLEP credits are accepted. Important factors in the admissions decision are geographic diversity, recommendations by alumni, and recommendations by school officials.

Procedure: Freshmen are admitted fall and spring. Entrance exams should be taken during the junior year. There is an early decision plan. Application deadlines are open. Notification is sent on a rolling basis.

Transfer: Transfer applicants are required to submit an official transcript from schools previously attended. An interview is recommended. 30 of 128 credits required for the bachelor's degree must be completed at Lindsey.

Visiting: There are regularly scheduled orientations for prospective students. There are guides for informal visits and visitors may sit in on classes and stay overnight. To schedule a visit, contact the Admissions Office.

Financial Aid: Lindsey is a member of CSS. The CSS Profile and the college's own financial statement are required. Check with the school for current deadlines.

International Students: The school actively recruits these students. They must score 490 on the written TOEFL or take the MELAB.

Computers: The mainframe is a Data General MV/15000. There are 40 IBM PC/XT-compatibles in the main computing lab and 40 PCs in the English composition classroom/lab for word processing purposes. Mainly those enrolled in computing courses may access the system. There are no time limits and no fees.

Admissions Contact: David Alls, Director of Admissions.
E-mail: *allsd@lindsey.edu* Web: *www.lindsey.edu*

MIDWAY COLLEGE
Midway, KY 40347-1120

	D-3
	(859) 846-5767
(800) 755-0031; Fax:	(859) 846-5823

Full-time: 90 men, 560 women	**Faculty:** 38; III, --$
Part-time: 30 men, 200 women	**Ph.D.s:** 40%
Graduate: none	**Student/Faculty:** 17 to 1
Year: semesters, summer session	**Tuition:** $11,700
Application Deadline: open	**Room & Board:** $5800
Freshman Class: n/av	
SAT I or ACT: required	**COMPETITIVE**

Midway College, founded in 1847, is a private institution affiliated with the Disciples of Christ. The day college is, for women only and the evening program is an accelerated coed program. Some figures in the above capsule and in this profile are approximate. The library contains 52,000 volumes, 57,000 microform items, and 8900 audio/video tapes/CDs, and subscribes to 450 periodicals. Computerized library services include the card catalog, interlibrary loans, and database searching. Special learning facilities include a learning resource center. The 105-acre campus is in a rural area in Woodford County, 15 minutes from Lexington. Including any residence halls, there are 10 buildings.

Student Life: 88% of undergraduates are from Kentucky. Students are from 31 states, 5 foreign countries, and Canada. 90% are white. 32% are Protestant; 7% Catholic. The average age of freshmen is 26; all undergraduates, 30. 36% do not continue beyond their first year.

Housing: 250 students can be accommodated in college housing, which includes single-sex dorms. On-campus housing is available on a first-come, first-served basis. 79% of students commute. Alcohol is not permitted. All students may keep cars.

Activities: There are no fraternities or sororities. There are 25 groups on campus, including art, choir, chorale, dance, honors, newspaper, professional, religious, social, social service, student government, and yearbook.

Sports: There are 7 intercollegiate sports for women. Facilities include a full-service gym, a weight room, tennis courts, soccer and softball fields, and an equine arena.

Disabled Students: 45% of the campus is accessible. Wheelchair ramps, elevators, special parking, specially equipped rest rooms, special class scheduling, lowered drinking fountains, and lowered telephones are available.

Services: Counseling and information services are available, as is tutoring in every subject. There are writing and math labs.

Campus Safety and Security: Measures include 24-hour foot and vehicle patrol, emergency telephones, and lighted pathways/sidewalks.

Programs of Study: Midway College confers B.A. and B.S. degrees. Associate degrees are also awarded. Bachelor's degrees are awarded in AGRICULTURE (equine science), BIOLOGICAL SCIENCE (biology/biological science), BUSINESS (business administration and management), COMMUNICATIONS AND THE ARTS (English), COMPUTER AND PHYSICAL SCIENCE (chemistry and mathematics), EDUCATION (education), ENGINEERING AND ENVIRONMENTAL DESIGN (environmental science), HEALTH PROFESSIONS (nursing), SOCIAL SCIENCE (liberal arts/general studies and psychology). Biology, nursing, and equine science are the strongest academically. Nursing, equine science, and business are the largest.

Required: All students must complete 130 credits, including 82 to 91 major and elective credits and 39 to 48 general education credits. Core requirements include courses in math, computing, science, communication, and composition. A 2.0 GPA must be maintained.

Special: A cooperative program in teacher education, study abroad in 11 countries, and an accelerated degree program in organizational management are offered. There are 2 national honor societies, including Phi Beta Kappa, and a freshman honors program.

Faculty/Classroom: 29% of faculty are male; 71%, female. All both teach undergraduates and do research. The average class size in an introductory lecture is 16; in a laboratory, 12; and in a regular course, 11.

Admissions: 2 freshmen graduated first in their class in a recent year.

Requirements: The SAT I or ACT is required. A score of 50 or better on the GED is required for acceptance. A GPA of 2.2 is required. AP and CLEP credits are accepted. Important factors in the admissions decision are leadership record, extracurricular activities record, and recommendations by school officials.

Procedure: Freshmen are admitted fall, spring, and summer. SAT I or ACT scores must be received by the school by August 1. Application deadlines are open. The application fee is $25. Notification is sent on a rolling basis.

Transfer: 65 transfer students enrolled in a recent year. Applicants must have a minimum college GPA of 2.0. 39 of 130 credits required for the bachelor's degree must be completed at Midway College.

Visiting: There are regularly scheduled orientations for prospective students, including campus tours, faculty and student conferences, and the president's address. There are guides for informal visits and visitors may sit in on classes. To schedule a visit, contact Lindsay Barnes in Admissions.

Financial Aid: In a recent year, 84% of all full-time freshmen and 73% of continuing full-time students received some form of financial aid. The average freshman award was $10,981. 18% of undergraduates work part time. Average annual earnings from campus work are $1573. The average financial indebtedness of a recent year's graduate was $11,427. Midway College is a member of CSS. The FAFSA is required. Check with the school for current deadlines.

International Students: There were 5 international students enrolled in a recent year. They must score 500 on the written TOEFL and also take the SAT I or the ACT.

Computers: The mainframe is a midrange IBM AS400. Via a Windows network, students have full access to the Internet, e-mail, and Web on 60 PCs located in labs, classrooms, dorms, and the library. All students may access the system. There are no time limits and no fees.

Graduates: In a recent year, 195 bachelor's degrees were awarded. The most popular majors were organizational management and business (32%), nursing (28%), and equine studies/science (9%). In an average class, 22% graduate in 4 years or less, and 32% graduate in 5 years or less. 15 companies recruited on campus in a recent year.

Admissions Contact: Lindsay Barnes, Director of Admissions. A video is available. E-mail: *lbarnes@midway.edu* Web: *www.midway.edu*

MOREHEAD STATE UNIVERSITY

E-2

Morehead, KY 40351

(606) 783-2000

(800) 354-2090; Fax: (606) 783-5038

Full-time: 2863 men, 3764 women	Faculty: 363; IIA, --$
Part-time: 280 men, 1014 women	Ph.D.s: 62%
Graduate: 501 men, 1087 women	Student/Faculty: 18 to 1
Year: semesters, summer session	Tuition: $3364 ($8948)
Application Deadline: open	Room & Board: $4100
Freshman Class: 5187 applied, 3689 accepted, 1520 enrolled	
ACT: 20	COMPETITIVE

Morehead State University, founded in 1922, is a public institution offering degree programs in applied science and technology, humanities, educational and behavioral sciences, and business. There are 4 undergraduate schools and 1 graduate school. In addition to regional accreditation, MSU has baccalaureate program accreditation with ACBSP, CSWE, NASM, NCATE, and NLN. The library contains 333,518 volumes, 781,060 microform items, and 18,808 audio/video tapes/CDs, and subscribes to 13,570 periodicals. Computerized library services include the card catalog, interlibrary loans, database searching, and Internet access. Special learning facilities include a learning resource center, art gallery, planetarium, radio station, TV station, 320-acre farm complex, and a robotics lab. The 1016-acre campus is in a small town 60 miles east of Lexington. Including any residence halls, there are 140 buildings.

Student Life: 84% of undergraduates are from Kentucky. Students are from 38 states, 22 foreign countries, and Canada. 95% are from public schools. 95% are white. The average age of freshmen is 19; all undergraduates, 24. 37% do not continue beyond their first year.

Housing: 3650 students can be accommodated in college housing, which includes single-sex and coed dorms, on-campus apartments, married-student housing, and fraternity houses. In addition, there are honors houses, a cross-cultural house, and housing for farm students, on-campus housing is guaranteed for all 4 years. 57% of students commute. Alcohol is not permitted. All students may keep cars.

Activities: 20% of men belong to 1 local and 13 national fraternities; 20% of women belong to 10 national sororities. There are 95 groups on campus, including art, band, cheerleading, choir, chorale, chorus, computers, dance, drama, drill team, drum and bugle corps, ethnic, honors, international, jazz band, marching band, musical theater, newspaper, orchestra, pep band, photography, political, professional, radio and TV, religious, social, social service, student government, symphony, and yearbook. Popular campus events include Greek Week, Parents Weekend, and Black History Month.

Sports: There are 9 intercollegiate sports for men and 9 for women, and 24 intramural sports for men and 24 for women. Facilities include an athletic complex, a 6500-seat gym, a 10000-seat stadium, a pool, bowling lanes, and a wellness/fitness center.

Disabled Students: 85% of the campus is accessible. Wheelchair ramps, elevators, special parking, specially equipped rest rooms, special class scheduling, lowered drinking fountains, and lowered telephones are available.

Services: Counseling and information services are available, as is tutoring in most subjects. There is a reader service for the blind, and remedial math, reading, and writing.

Campus Safety and Security: Measures include 24-hour foot and vehicle patrol, security escort services, shuttle buses, and informal discussions. There are emergency telephones and lighted pathways/sidewalks.

Programs of Study: MSU confers A.B., B.S., B.B.A., B.M., B.M.Ed., B.S.N., B.S.W., and B.U.S. degrees. Associate and master's degrees are also awarded. Bachelor's degrees are awarded in AGRICULTURE (agriculture), BIOLOGICAL SCIENCE (biology/biological science, ecology, and life science), BUSINESS (accounting, banking and finance, business economics, management science, marketing management, and real estate), COMMUNICATIONS AND THE ARTS (communications, dramatic arts, English, music, and speech/debate/rhetoric), COMPUTER AND PHYSICAL SCIENCE (chemistry, earth science, geology, mathematics, and physics), EDUCATION (agricultural, business, elementary, health, home economics, industrial arts, middle school, music, physical, and special), ENGINEERING AND ENVIRONMENTAL DESIGN (industrial engineering technology), HEALTH PROFESSIONS (medical laboratory technology and nursing), SOCIAL SCIENCE (geography, history, liberal arts/general studies, paralegal studies, philosophy, political science/government, psychology, social science, social work, and sociology). Biological sciences is the strongest academically. Elementary education is the largest.

Required: All students must complete 42 semester hours (45 for teacher certification) of general education courses, including 15 hours in communications and humanities, 12 in natural and mathematical sciences, 12 in social and behavioral sciences, and 3 in health or phys ed. A total of 128 semester hours, with a minimum GPA of 2.0, is required to graduate.

Special: Cross-registration is offered with the University of Kentucky. Students may earn specialist certification in education. Study abroad in 3 countries, a Washington semester, a 3-2 engineering degree, dual and

student-designed majors, a general studies degree, credit for life experience, pass/fail options, and nondegree study are available. There are 9 national honor societies and there is a freshman honors program.

Faculty/Classroom: 55% of faculty are male; 45%, female. All teach undergraduates. No introductory courses are taught by graduate students.

Admissions: 71% of the 2003-2004 applicants were accepted.

Requirements: The SAT I or ACT is required. In addition, applicants should have completed the Kentucky Pre-College Curriculum requirement. An interview is recommended. A GPA of 2.0 is required. AP and CLEP credits are accepted.

Procedure: Freshmen are admitted to all sessions. Entrance exams should be taken in the spring of the junior year. Application deadlines are open. Notification is sent on a rolling basis. Applications are accepted on-line through the school's web site.

Transfer: 466 transfer students enrolled in 2002-2003. Applicants should have a minimum GPA of 2.0 with at least 12 credit hours earned and be in good standing at their previous institution. They must have completed a precollege curriculum or meet any deficiencies. 32 of 128 credits required for the bachelor's degree must be completed at MSU.

Visiting: There are regularly scheduled orientations for prospective students, consisting of registration for classes, advisement, and an overview of MSU. There are guides for informal visits and visitors may sit in on classes. To schedule a visit, contact the Office of Admissions at (800) 585-6781 or admissions@moreheadstate.edu.

Financial Aid: In 2003-2004, 96% of all full-time freshmen received some form of financial aid. 60% of full-time freshmen received need-based aid. The average freshman award was $6375. Need-based scholarships or need-based grants averaged $2182 ($4025 maximum); need-based self-help aid (loans and jobs) averaged $1887 ($2625 maximum); non-need-based athletic scholarships averaged $3318 ($13,404 maximum); and other non-need-based awards and non-need-based scholarships averaged $1762 ($5384 maximum). 12% of undergraduates work part time. Average annual earnings from campus work are $1417. The average financial indebtedness of the 2003 graduate was $14,074. The FAFSA and the college's own financial statement are required. The deadline for filing freshman financial aid applications for fall entry is April 1.

International Students: There are 50 international students enrolled. They must score 500 on the written TOEFL or take the MELAB. They must also take the SAT I or ACT exam, with the ACT preferred.

Computers: The mainframe is an HP 9000. Teaching labs have networked computers. All students may access the system days and evenings. There are no time limits. The fee is $10 per semester.

Graduates: From July 1, 2002 to June 30, 2003, 887 bachelor's degrees were awarded. The most popular majors were elementary education (16%), general studies (9%), and management and marketing (8%). In an average class, 40% graduate in 6 years or less. 500 companies recruited on campus in 2002-2003.

Admissions Contact: Joel Pace, Associate Director, Admissions. E-mail: admissions@morehead-st.edu Web: www.morehead.st.edu

MURRAY STATE UNIVERSITY

B-4

Murray, KY 42071

(270) 762-3741

(800) 272-4678; Fax: (270) 762-3780

Full-time: 2917 men, 3984 women	Faculty: 393; IIA, -$
Part-time: 529 men, 955 women	Ph.D.s: 77%
Graduate: 550 men, 1165 women	Student/Faculty: 18 to 1
Year: semesters, summer session	Tuition: $3436 ($5492)
Application Deadline: August 1	Room & Board: $4380
Freshman Class: 2972 applied, 1873 accepted, 1427 enrolled	
ACT: 23	VERY COMPETITIVE

Murray State University, founded in 1922, is a public institution offering degree programs in business and public affairs, education, health sciences and human services, humanities and fine arts, engineering, technology and science, and agriculture. Some information in this capsule and profile is approximate. There are 6 undergraduate and 6 graduate schools. In addition to regional accreditation, MSU has baccalaureate program accreditation with AACSB, ABET, ACEJMC, ACS, ADA, ASLA, AVMA, CSWE, NASAD, NASM, NCATE, and NLN. The library contains 390,000 volumes, 200,800 microform items, and 10,500 audio/video tapes/CDs, and subscribes to 2043 periodicals. Computerized library services include the card catalog, interlibrary loans, database searching, and Internet access. Special learning facilities include a learning resource center, art gallery, natural history museum, radio station, TV station, biological station, interactive telecommunications network, and web-based courses. The 253-acre campus is in a small town 130 miles northwest of Nashville. Including any residence halls, there are 94 buildings.

Student Life: 71% of undergraduates are from Kentucky. Students are from 43 states, 59 foreign countries, and Canada. 80% are from public schools. 87% are white. The average age of freshmen is 19; all under-

graduates, 24. 32% do not continue beyond their first year; 56% remain to graduate.

Housing: 3000 students can be accommodated in college housing, which includes single-sex and coed dorms, on-campus apartments, married-student housing, residential colleges, and sorority houses. On-campus housing is guaranteed for all 4 years. 62% of students commute. Alcohol is not permitted. All students may keep cars.

Activities: 17% of men belong to 1 local and 14 national fraternities; 10% of women belong to 7 national sororities. There are 210 groups on campus, including art, band, cheerleading, chess, choir, chorale, chorus, computers, dance, debate, drama, drill team, ethnic, forensics, honors, international, jazz band, literary magazine, marching band, musical theater, newspaper, orchestra, pep band, photography, political, professional, radio and TV, religious, social, social service, student government, symphony, and yearbook. Popular campus events include Racer Regatta, Mr. MSU, and Miss MSU.

Sports: There are 10 intercollegiate sports for men and 11 for women, and 20 intramural sports for men and 20 for women. Facilities include a 16,500-seat stadium, 2 gyms seating 6000, gymnastics and weight rooms, an indoor jogging track, racquetball courts, a swimming pool, outdoor tennis, basketball, and volleyball courts, a Parcourse physical fitness trail, and the 8500-seat Regional Special Events Center. A physical fitness center includes 2 pools, 3 gyms, racquetball courts, jogging and walking tracks, cardio and weight areas, an Interent lounge, aerobic studios, and a fitness assessment center.

Disabled Students: 96% of the campus is accessible. Wheelchair ramps, elevators, special parking, specially equipped rest rooms, special class scheduling, lowered drinking fountains, lowered telephones, and special housing are available.

Services: Counseling and information services are available, as is tutoring in most subjects. There is a reader service for the blind and remedial math, reading, and writing.

Campus Safety and Security: Measures include 24-hour foot and vehicle patrol, self-defense education, security escort services, and informal discussions. There are pamphlets/posters/films, emergency telephones, and lighted pathways/sidewalks.

Programs of Study: MSU confers B.A., B.S., B.A.B., B.F.A., B.I.S., B.M., B.M.E., B.S.A., B.S.B., B.S.N., B.S.V.T.E., and B.S.W. degrees. Associate and master's degrees are also awarded. Bachelor's degrees are awarded in AGRICULTURE (agricultural mechanics, agriculture, animal science, fishing and fisheries, and horticulture), BIOLOGICAL SCIENCE (biochemistry, biology/biological science, and wildlife biology), BUSINESS (accounting, banking and finance, business administration and management, business economics, marketing/retailing/merchandising, personnel management, and recreation and leisure services), COMMUNICATIONS AND THE ARTS (advertising, broadcasting, communications, dramatic arts, English, fine arts, French, German, journalism, languages, music, public relations, Spanish, speech/debate/rhetoric, and telecommunications), COMPUTER AND PHYSICAL SCIENCE (chemistry, computer programming, computer science, earth science, geology, information sciences and systems, mathematics, and physics), EDUCATION (agricultural, art, business, early childhood, elementary, foreign languages, health, home economics, industrial arts, middle school, music, secondary, and special), ENGINEERING AND ENVIRONMENTAL DESIGN (civil engineering technology, computer technology, construction technology, electrical/electronics engineering technology, engineering technology, occupational safety and health, and technological management), HEALTH PROFESSIONS (exercise science, nursing, predentistry, premedicine, speech pathology/audiology, and veterinary science), SOCIAL SCIENCE (criminal justice, crosscultural studies, dietetics, economics, geography, history, international studies, liberal arts/general studies, parks and recreation management, philosophy, political science/government, prelaw, psychology, social work, and sociology). Premedicine, engineering, and physics are the strongest academically. Business, nursing, and education are the largest.

Required: All students must complete University Studies requirements, including courses in communications and basic skills, lab sciences and math, humanities and fine arts, social sciences, and foreign language. A total of 128 semester hours, including at least 30 in the major, with a minimum GPA of 2.0 are required to graduate.

Special: MSU offers cooperative programs in all majors, cross-registration through the National Student Exchange, internships, study abroad in 25 countries, work-study, dual majors, B.A.-B.S. degrees, and 3-2 engineering degrees with the University of Louisville and the University of Kentucky. Credit for life experience and a degree in independent studies are also offered. Nondegree study is possible. There are 25 national honor societies, including Phi Beta Kappa, a freshman honors program, and 20 departmental honors programs.

Faculty/Classroom: 60% of faculty are male; 40%, female. All teach undergraduates. The average class size in an introductory lecture is 30 and in a laboratory, 25.

Admissions: 63% of the 2003-2004 applicants were accepted. The ACT scores for the 2003-2004 freshman class were: 20% below 21, 30% between 21 and 23, 30% between 24 and 26, 12% between 27 and 28, and 8% above 28. 60% of the current freshmen were in the top fifth of

their class; 88% were in the top two fifths. 85 freshmen graduated first in their class.

Requirements: The ACT is required, with a minimum score of 18 on the ACT. Applicants must rank in the top half of their class or have a 3.0 GPA. Applicants should have completed 22 high school academic credits, including 4 units in English, 3 in math, 2 each in science and social studies, and 9 in electives; in addition, MSU strongly recommends a fourth year of math, 2 of foreign language, and 1 of fine arts. A portfolio or audition is required for art and music majors. An interview is recommended. MSU requires applicants to be in the upper 50% of their class. A GPA of 3.0 is required. AP and CLEP credits are accepted. Important factors in the admissions decision are advanced placement or honor courses and leadership record.

Procedure: Freshmen are admitted to all sessions. Entrance exams should be taken before January of the enrollment year. There is an early admissions plan. Applications should be filed by August 1 for fall entry, December 1 for spring entry, and May 1 for summer entry, along with a $25 fee. Notification is sent on a rolling basis. Applications are accepted on-line through the school's web site.

Transfer: 813 transfer students enrolled in 2002-2003. Applicants must have a minimum GPA of 2.0 in at least 12 hours of degree credit. 24 of 128 credits required for the bachelor's degree must be completed at MSU.

Visiting: There are regularly scheduled orientations for prospective students, in the fall and spring. There are guides for informal visits and visitors may sit in on classes and stay overnight. To schedule a visit, contact the School Relations Office at (270) 762-2896 or *paul.radke@murraystate.edu.*

Financial Aid: In 2003-2004, 70% of all full-time students received some form of financial aid. 45% of all full-time students received need-based aid. The average freshman award was $4705. Need-based scholarships or need-based grants averaged $1500 ($5950 maximum); need-based self-help aid (loans and jobs) averaged $3300 ($4975 maximum); non-need-based athletic scholarships averaged $6100 ($14,252 maximum); and other non-need-based awards and non-need-based scholarships averaged $3100 ($9804 maximum). 18% of undergraduates work part time. Average annual earnings from campus work are $1532. The average financial indebtedness of the 2003 graduate was $16,146. The FAFSA and the college's own financial statement are required. The deadline for filing freshman financial aid applications for fall entry is April 1.

International Students: There are 196 international students enrolled. The school actively recruits these students. They must score 500 on the written TOEFL or complete level five in MSU's English Language Institute, and also take the ACT.

Computers: The mainframe is an IBM. Students may access the mainframe through computer labs in each of 5 colleges, 1 school, and the student center. PCs are available at these locations and throughout the campus, including the residential colleges and fitness center. All students may access the system. There are no time limits and no fees. It is strongly recommended that all students have a personal computer.

Graduates: From July 1, 2002 to June 30, 2003, 1322 bachelor's degrees were awarded. The most popular majors were early elementary education (10%), agriculture (5%), and business administration (4%). In an average class, 35% graduate in 4 years or less, 52% graduate in 5 years or less, and 56% graduate in 6 years or less. 715 companies recruited on campus in 2002-2003.

Admissions Contact: Mary E. Smith, Director of Admissions Services. E-mail: *mary.smith@murraystate.edu* Web: *http://www.murraystate.edu*

NORTHERN KENTUCKY UNIVERSITY   D-1
Highland Heights, KY 41099

(859) 572-5220
(800) 637-9948; Fax: (859) 572-6665

Full-time: 7700 men and women	**Faculty:** IIA, --$
Part-time: 3200 men and women	**Ph.D.s:** 82%
Graduate: 900 men and women	**Student/Faculty:** n/av
Year: semesters, summer session	**Tuition:** $3744 ($7992)
Application Deadline: August 1	**Room & Board:** $4408
Freshman Class: n/av	
SAT I or ACT: required	**NONCOMPETITIVE**

Northern Kentucky University, founded in 1968, is a publicly controlled institution offering programs in arts and sciences, business, and professional studies. There are 4 undergraduate and 4 graduate schools. In addition to regional accreditation, NKU has baccalaureate program accreditation with CAHEA, CSWE, NASM, and NLN. The 3 libraries contain 267,257 volumes, 135,257 microform items, and 2133 audio/video tapes/CDs, and subscribe to 4423 periodicals. Computerized library services include the card catalog, interlibrary loans, and database searching. Special learning facilities include a learning resource center, art gallery, radio station, TV station, and a biology and geology museum. The 300-acre campus is in a suburban area 7 miles southeast of Cincinnati, Ohio. Including any residence halls, there are 42 buildings.

Student Life: 77% of undergraduates are from Kentucky. Students are from 35 states, 40 foreign countries, and Canada. 80% are white. The average age of freshmen is 20; all undergraduates, 26. 35% do not continue beyond their first year.

Housing: 1140 students can be accommodated in college housing, which includes single-sex and coed dorms and on-campus apartments. On-campus housing is available on a first-come, first-served basis. Priority is given to out-of-town students. 91% of students commute. Alcohol is not permitted. All students may keep cars.

Activities: 4% of men belong to 6 national fraternities; 4% of women belong to 7 national sororities. There are 80 groups on campus, including art, cheerleading, chorale, chorus, computers, dance, drama, drill team, ethnic, film, gay, honors, international, jazz band, literary magazine, musical theater, newspaper, pep band, photography, political, professional, radio and TV, religious, social, social service, and student government. Popular campus events include Northern Noel, Musicfest, and Kentucky Awareness Week.

Sports: There are 6 intercollegiate sports for men and 5 for women, and 15 intramural sports for men and 13 for women. Facilities include a 2000-seat gym, baseball and soccer fields, tennis and racquetball courts, a track, a weight room, and a swimming pool.

Disabled Students: All of the campus is accessible. Elevators, special parking, specially equipped rest rooms, special class scheduling, lowered drinking fountains, and lowered telephones are available.

Services: Counseling and information services are available, as is tutoring in most subjects. There is a reader service for the blind and remedial math, reading, and writing. There are also developmental education courses.

Campus Safety and Security: Measures include 24-hour foot and vehicle patrol, security escort services, informal discussions, and pamphlets/posters/films. There are emergency telephones and lighted pathways/sidewalks.

Programs of Study: NKU confers B.A., B.S., B.Mus., B.Mus.Ed., B.S.N., and B.S.W. degrees. Associate and master's degrees are also awarded. Bachelor's degrees are awarded in BIOLOGICAL SCIENCE (biology/biological science), BUSINESS (accounting, labor studies, management science, marketing/retailing/merchandising, and organizational behavior), COMMUNICATIONS AND THE ARTS (art, dramatic arts, English, French, graphic design, journalism, music, performing arts, radio/television technology, Spanish, and speech/debate/rhetoric), COMPUTER AND PHYSICAL SCIENCE (chemistry, computer science, geology, information sciences and systems, mathematics, and physics), EDUCATION (art, business, elementary, industrial arts, middle school, physical, science, and secondary), ENGINEERING AND ENVIRONMENTAL DESIGN (construction technology, industrial engineering technology, manufacturing engineering, manufacturing technology, and pre-engineering), HEALTH PROFESSIONS (mental health/human services, nursing, predentistry, premedicine, prepharmacy, and preveterinary science), SOCIAL SCIENCE (anthropology, economics, geography, history, international studies, philosophy, physical fitness/movement, political science/government, prelaw, psychology, public administration, social science, social work, and sociology). Education, nursing, and biology are the largest.

Required: All students must complete 54 semester hours of general studies, including English composition and speech, the arts, computer literacy, history, humanities, math, philosophy, sciences, and social sciences, along with major and minor requirements. A total of 128 semester hours, with a minimum GPA of 2.0, is required to graduate.

Special: A 3-2 engineering degree is offered with the University of Kentucky. Cross-registration is possible through the Greater Cincinnati Area Consortium of colleges and universities. Study abroad in 6 countries, a Washington semester, internships for communication majors, on-campus work-study programs, an accelerated degree program, an interdisciplinary honors program, B.A.-B.S. degrees, dual majors, and pass/fail options are offered. There are co-op programs in most majors. Student-designed majors and credit for work experience are available. Nondegree study is possible. There are 8 national honor societies and a freshman honors program.

Faculty/Classroom: 52% of faculty are male; 48%, female. All teach undergraduates. No introductory courses are taught by graduate students. The average class size in a regular course is 26.

Requirements: The SAT I or ACT is required. Students who score at least a 20 on the English and math portions of the ACT and who meet all precollege curriculum requirements, including 4 units of English, 3 of math (algebra I, geometry, algebra II), 2 of U.S. history, world civilization (for Kentucky residents only), and 2 of science (biology and chemistry or physics), are granted regular admission. Others may be admitted with a stipulation or restriction on their admission. A high school diploma is required; the GED is accepted. AP and CLEP credits are accepted.

Procedure: Freshmen are admitted to all sessions. Entrance exams should be taken prior to enrollment. There are early decision, early admissions, and deferred admissions plans. Early decision applications should be filed by February 1; regular applications, by August 1 for fall entry, along with a $25 fee. The college accepts all applicants. Notification is sent on a rolling basis. Applications are accepted on-line.

Transfer: Students must be eligible to return to their previous institution. College transcripts from previous institutions are required. 30 of 128 credits required for the bachelor's degree must be completed at NKU.

Visiting: There are regularly scheduled orientations for prospective students, consisting of a 1-day program with sessions on student services and financial aid, activities, a campus tour, and academic information, advising, and registration. There are guides for informal visits and visitors may sit in on classes and stay overnight. To schedule a visit, contact the Office of Admissions at *admitnku@nku.edu*.

Financial Aid: The average freshman award in a recent year was $4830. 13% of undergraduates work part time. Average annual earnings from campus work are $2423. The average financial indebtedness of a recent year's graduate was $5130. The FAFSA and the college's own financial statement are required. Check with the school for current deadlines.

International Students: The school actively recruits these students. They must score 500 on the written TOEFL or take the MELAB.

Computers: The mainframes are a DEC VAX 4600 and an AXP 4600. Students can access the mainframes via 24 terminals in central computing labs and 10 in specific departments. There are 185 PCs in central labs and 30 dial-in modem lines available. All students may access the system 7 days a week. There are no time limits. The fee is $15 per semester.

Graduates: In a recent year, 1142 bachelor's degrees were awarded. The most popular majors were marketing/business (21%), education (18%), and social science/history (9%). In an average class, 36% graduate in 6 years or less. 102 companies recruited on campus in a recent year.

Admissions Contact: Director of Admissions.
E-mail: *admitnku@nku.edu* Web: *www.nku.edu*

PIKEVILLE COLLEGE   F-3
Pikeville, KY 41501   (606) 218-5251
(866) 232-7700; Fax: (606) 218-5255

Full-time: 321 men, 399 women	**Faculty:** 61; IIB, --$
Part-time: 6 men, 36 women	**Ph.D.s:** 44%
Graduate: 149 men, 102 women	**Student/Faculty:** 12 to 1
Year: semesters, summer session	**Tuition:** $9900
Application Deadline: August 23	**Room & Board:** $5000
Freshman Class: 615 applied, 615 accepted, 149 enrolled	
ACT: 19	**NONCOMPETITIVE**

Pikeville College, founded in 1889 by Prebytery Church, is a private institution that offers a broad liberal arts and sciences education. The 2 libraries contain 72,673 volumes, 39,128 microform items, and 1811 audio/video tapes/CDs, and subscribe to 219 periodicals. Computerized library services include the card catalog, interlibrary loans, database searching, and Internet access. Special learning facilities include a learning resource center and art gallery. The 27-acre campus is in a small town 20 miles from the Virginia border in the eastern Kentucky hills. Including any residence halls, there are 16 buildings.

Student Life: 82% of undergraduates are from Kentucky. Students are from 28 states, 8 foreign countries, and Canada. 99% are from public schools. 91% are white. Most are Protestant. The average age of freshmen is 19; all undergraduates, 22. 45% do not continue beyond their first year; 35% remain to graduate.

Housing: 525 students can be accommodated in college housing, which includes single-sex and coed dorms, on-campus apartments, and married-student housing. On-campus housing is guaranteed for all 4 years. 56% of students commute. Alcohol is not permitted. All students may keep cars.

Activities: There are no fraternities or sororities. There are 22 groups on campus, including band, cheerleading, choir, chorus, computers, dance, debate, drama, honors, jazz band, literary magazine, newspaper, pep band, political, professional, religious, social service, student government, and yearbook. Popular campus events include Founders Day.

Sports: There are 7 intercollegiate sports for men and 7 for women, and 10 intramural sports for men and 10 for women. Facilities include a gym, basketball, volleyball, and tennis courts, softball and baseball fields, and a football stadium.

Disabled Students: 95% of the campus is accessible. Wheelchair ramps, elevators, special parking, specially equipped rest rooms, lowered drinking fountains, and an elevator from the main parking lot to the upper campus are available.

Services: Counseling and information services are available, as is tutoring in most subjects, including math, English, biology, all physical sciences, computers, accounting, and Spanish. There is remedial math, reading, and writing.

Campus Safety and Security: Measures include 24-hour foot and vehicle patrol, self-defense education, security escort services, and shuttle buses. There are informal discussions, pamphlets/posters/films, lighted pathways/sidewalks, and night security guards.

Programs of Study: PC confers B.A., B.S., and B.B.A. degrees. Associate and doctoral degrees are also awarded. Bachelor's degrees are awarded in BIOLOGICAL SCIENCE (biology/biological science), BUSINESS (business administration and management), COMMUNICATIONS AND THE ARTS (art and English), COMPUTER AND PHYSICAL SCIENCE (chemistry, computer science, and mathematics), EDUCATION (elementary, middle school, and secondary), SOCIAL SCIENCE (criminal justice, history, human services, psychology, religion, social science, and sociology). Math, English and chemistry are the strongest academically. Business, psychology, and education are the largest.

Required: All students must complete core courses in humanities, English, social sciences, natural sciences, and math, as well as 2 courses each in religion, phys ed, and history and 1 course in computer science. Additional requirements include 6 hours in a foreign language for the B.A. degree and 2 lab science courses for the B.S. degree. An overall GPA of 2.0 is required. To graduate, students must complete 128 semester hours, with 30 to 60 hours in the major.

Special: Students may earn up to 6 credits at other institutions while enrolled at the college. Internships, B.A.-B.S. degrees, credit for life, military, and work experience, and pass/fail options are offered. Nondegree study is possible. There are 3 national honor societies, and 1 departmental honors program.

Faculty/Classroom: 48% of faculty are male; 52%, female. All teach undergraduates and 10% both teach and do research. No introductory courses are taught by graduate students. The average class size in an introductory lecture is 25; in a laboratory, 20; and in a regular course, 15.

Admissions: All of the 2003-2004 applicants were accepted. The ACT scores for the 2003-2004 freshman class were: 60% below 21, 21% between 21 and 23, 12% between 24 and 26, 6% between 27 and 28, and 1% above 28.

Requirements: The ACT is required. In addition, applicants must graduate from an accredited secondary school or have a GED. An interview is recommended. AP and CLEP credits are accepted.

Procedure: Freshmen are admitted to all sessions. Entrance exams should be taken in October of the year preceding entry. There are early admissions and deferred admissions plans. There is a rolling admissions plan. Applications should be filed by August 23 for fall entry, January 17 for spring entry, and June for summer entry. The college accepts all applicants. Notification is sent on a rolling basis. Applications are accepted on-line through the college's web site.

Transfer: 51 transfer students enrolled in 2002-2003. All college transcripts and a review of students on suspension and probation are required. 30 of 128 credits required for the bachelor's degree must be completed at PC.

Visiting: There are regularly scheduled orientations for prospective students, consisting of a campus tour and lunch. There are guides for informal visits and visitors may sit in on classes and stay overnight. To schedule a visit, contact Missy McCoy.

Financial Aid: In 2003-2004, 95% of all full-time freshmen and 91% of continuing full-time students received some form of financial aid. 85% of full-time freshmen and 67% of continuing full-time students received need-based aid. The average freshman award was $11,278. Need-based scholarships or need-based grants averaged $5904; need-based self-help aid (loans and jobs) averaged $3159; non-need based athletic scholarships averaged $6123; and other non-need based awards and non-need based scholarships averaged $2369. 98% of undergraduates work part time. Average annual earnings from campus work are $1633. The average financial indebtedness of the 2003 graduate was $12,070. The FAFSA and the college's own financial statement are required. The deadline for filing freshman financial aid applications for fall entry is March 15.

International Students: There are 16 international students enrolled. They must score 500 on the written TOEFL and also take the SAT I or ACT for placement purposes only.

Computers: The mainframe is an IBM AS/400. There are 151 PCs available on campus, all with access to the Internet and World Wide Web through a campus network. All students may access the system 8 A.M. to 11 P.M. There are no time limits and no fees.

Graduates: From July 1, 2002 to June 30, 2003, 123 bachelor's degrees were awarded. The most popular majors were business (24%), psychology/human services (21%), and education (10%). In an average class, 2% graduate in 3 years or less, 20% graduate in 4 years or less, 29% graduate in 5 years or less, and 32% graduate in 6 years or less. 112 companies recruited on campus in 2002-2003. Of the 2002 graduating class, 23% were enrolled in graduate school within 6 months of graduation and 83% were employed.

Admissions Contact: Missy McCoy, Director of Admissions.
E-mail: *wewantyou@pc.edu* Web: *http://www.pc.edu*

SPALDING UNIVERSITY

D-2

Louisville, KY 40203-2188

(502) 585-7111
(800) 896-8941, ext. 2111; Fax: (502) 585-7128

Full-time: 194 men, 647 women	**Faculty:** 58
Part-time: none	**Ph.D.s:** 63%
Graduate: 693 men and women	**Student/Faculty:** 15 to 1
Year: terms, summer session	**Tuition:** $13,443
Application Deadline: open	**Room & Board:** $4542
Freshman Class: 333 applied, 208 accepted, 73 enrolled	
ACT: 20	**COMPETITIVE**

Spalding University, established in 1814, is a private (not for profit) institution affiliated with the Roman Catholic Church and offers undergraduate degrees in the social sciences, humanities, health and natural sciences, business, communication studies, and education. There are 4 undergraduate and 4 graduate schools. In addition to regional accreditation, Spalding has baccalaureate program accreditation with CSWE, NCATE, and NLN. The library contains 220,232 volumes, 16,246 microform items, and 8669 audio/video tapes/CDs, and subscribes to 601 periodicals. Computerized library services include the card catalog, interlibrary loans, database searching, and Internet access. Special learning facilities include a learning resource center, art gallery, video production facilities, and a digital media center. The 5-acre campus is in an urban area in downtown Louisville. Including any residence halls, there are 8 buildings.

Student Life: 82% of undergraduates are from Kentucky. Students are from 30 states, 21 foreign countries, and Canada. 85% are from public schools. 69% are white; 15% African American. 40% are claim no religious affiliation; 31% Protestant; 29% Catholic. The average age of freshmen is 21; all undergraduates, 28. 37% do not continue beyond their first year; 57% remain to graduate.

Housing: 276 students can be accommodated in college housing, which includes coed dorms. On-campus housing is guaranteed for all 4 years. 89% of students commute. Alcohol is not permitted. All students may keep cars.

Activities: There are no fraternities or sororities. There are 37 groups on campus, including art, drama, ethnic, gay, international, political, professional, recreational, religious, social, social service, student government, and yearbook. Popular campus events include Annual Running of the Rodents.

Sports: There are 3 intercollegiate sports for men and 4 for women, and 4 intramural sports for men and 4 for women. Facilities include a gym and an exercise room.

Disabled Students: 80% of the campus is accessible. Wheelchair ramps, elevators, special parking, specially equipped rest rooms, special class scheduling, lowered drinking fountains, note takers, extended test taking time, oral testing, and special classroom accommodations are available.

Services: Counseling and information services are available, as is tutoring in every subject.

Campus Safety and Security: Measures include self-defense education, security escort services, informal discussions, and pamphlets/posters/films. There are emergency telephones, lighted pathways/sidewalks, and direct access to campus security from campus phones.

Programs of Study: Spalding confers B.A., B.S., B.S.B.A., B.S.Ed., B.S.N., B.S.O.T., and B.S.S.W. degrees. Associate, master's, and doctoral degrees are also awarded. Bachelor's degrees are awarded in BUSINESS (accounting and business administration and management), COMMUNICATIONS AND THE ARTS (communications), COMPUTER AND PHYSICAL SCIENCE (natural sciences), EDUCATION (education, elementary, and middle school), HEALTH PROFESSIONS (nursing and occupational therapy), SOCIAL SCIENCE (humanities, pastoral studies, psychology, social science, and social work). Nursing, education, and psychology are the strongest academically. Nursing, education, and psychology are the largest.

Required: To graduate, students must earn 125 credits, with a maximum of 40 credits in the major for the B.A. degree and 50 credits for the B.S. degree, and a minimum overall GPA of 2.0. All students must complete a university studies requirement of 15 credits in humanities, 12 credits in social sciences, 12 credits in communication, 9 credits in natural sciences and math, 6 credits in religious studies, and a 1-credit general introduction to the college.

Special: Cross-registration is offered with the Kentuckiana Metroversity Consortium. Internships, study abroad, B.A.-B.S. degrees, dual majors, work-study programs, and accelerated degree programs in business, psychology, and nursing are available. Credit is given for military experience and pass/fail options are available. The SAIL program enables students to earn a bachelor's degree by attending classes only on weekends and evenings. There are 8 national honor societies and 6 departmental honors programs.

Faculty/Classroom: 39% of faculty are male; 61%, female. 83% teach undergraduates. The average class size in an introductory lecture is 20; in a laboratory, 10; and in a regular course, 20.

Admissions: 62% of the 2003-2004 applicants were accepted. 1 freshman graduated first in the class.

Requirements: The SAT I or ACT is required. In addition, applicants must be graduates of an accredited secondary school and should have completed 4 years of high school English and 2 years each of a foreign language, math, science, and social studies. A GED may be substituted for the high school degree. A GPA of 2.5 is required. AP and CLEP credits are accepted. Important factors in the admissions decision are advanced placement or honor courses, recommendations by school officials, and evidence of special talent.

Procedure: Freshmen are admitted to all sessions. Entrance exams should be taken by August 1. There is a rolling admissions plan. Application deadlines are open. Application fee is $20. Applications are accepted on-line through the school's web site.

Transfer: 117 transfer students enrolled in 2002-2003. It is preferred that applicants have a 2.5 GPA. 32 of 125 credits required for the bachelor's degree must be completed at Spalding.

Visiting: There are regularly scheduled orientations for prospective students. There are guides for informal visits and visitors may sit in on classes and stay overnight. To schedule a visit, contact Office of University Admission at *admissions@spalding.edu*.

Financial Aid: In 2003-2004, 74% of all full-time freshmen and 94% of continuing full-time students received some form of financial aid. 67% of full-time freshmen and 83% of continuing full-time students received need-based aid. The average freshman award was $14,513. 13% of undergraduates work part time. Average annual earnings from campus work are $1046. The average financial indebtedness of the 2003 graduate was $15,106. Spalding is a member of CSS. The FAFSA is required. The deadline for filing freshman financial aid applications for fall entry is March 15.

International Students: There are 69 international students enrolled. The school actively recruits these students. They must score 535 on the written TOEFL or 203 on the electronic version and also take the SAT I or the ACT, scoring 20.

Computers: The mainframe is an HP 3000. PCs are available for student use. Spalding maintains computer labs and a digital media center, as well as computer access in the library. Most computers have access to the Internet and a variety of network software applications. All students may access the system. There are no time limits and no fees. It is strongly recommended that all students have a personal computer.

Graduates: From July 1, 2002 to June 30, 2003, 178 bachelor's degrees were awarded. The most popular majors were nursing (23%), business (18%), and education (12%). In an average class, 34% graduate in 4 years or less, 45% graduate in 5 years or less, and 47% graduate in 6 years or less. 10 companies recruited on campus in 2002-2003.

Admissions Contact: Chris J. Houk, Director of Enrollment Management. E-mail: *admissions@spalding.edu* Web: *www.spalding.edu*

THOMAS MORE COLLEGE
D-1
Crestview Hills, KY 41017-3495
(859) 344-3332
(800) 825-4557; Fax: (859) 344-3638

Full-time: 549 men, 500 women	**Faculty:** 71; IIB, --$
Part-time: 129 men, 212 women	**Ph.D.s:** 69%
Graduate: 80 men, 56 women	**Student/Faculty:** 15 to 1
Year: semesters, summer session	**Tuition:** $15,950
Application Deadline: August 15	**Room & Board:** $5400
Freshman Class: n/av	
SAT I or ACT: required	**COMPETITIVE**

Thomas More College, founded in 1921 as Villa Madonna College, is a private Catholic institution offering undergraduate programs in liberal arts and sciences, and an MBA in business administration. In addition to regional accreditation, Thomas More has baccalaureate program accreditation with NLN. The library contains 119,029 volumes, 51,551 microform items, and 2178 audio/video tapes/CDs, and subscribes to 609 periodicals. Computerized library services include the card catalog, interlibrary loans, and database searching. Special learning facilities include a learning resource center, art gallery, an observatory, and biology field station on the Ohio River. The 100-acre campus is in a suburban area 8 miles south of Cincinnati. Including any residence halls, there are 9 buildings.

Student Life: 66% of undergraduates are from Kentucky. Students are from 16 states and 11 foreign countries. 71% are from public schools. 91% are white. 43% are Catholic; 37% unknown; 19% Protestant. The average age of freshmen is 18; all undergraduates, 25. 37% do not continue beyond their first year; 55% remain to graduate.

Housing: 380 students can be accommodated in college housing, which includes single-sex and coed dorms. On-campus housing is available on a first-come, first-served basis. Priority is given to out-of-town students. 80% of students commute. All students may keep cars.

Activities: There are no fraternities or sororities. There are 29 groups on campus, including art, cheerleading, computers, debate, drama, ethnic, honors, international, literary magazine, newspaper, political, professional, religious, social, social service, and student government. Popular campus events include fall and spring formals, Spring Pig Roast, and International Awareness Week.

Sports: There are 6 intercollegiate sports for men and 6 for women, and 6 intramural sports for men and 6 for women. Facilities include an athletic/convocation center with a 1,500-seat indoor gym and a 2,100-seat arena, plus baseball, football, softball, and soccer fields, 16 tennis courts (8 indoor), 4 racquetball courts, an indoor pool, a track, and weight and exercise rooms.

Disabled Students: 99% of the campus is accessible. Wheelchair ramps, elevators, special parking, and specially equipped rest rooms are available.

Services: Counseling and information services are available, as is tutoring in every subject. There is a reader service for the blind, and remedial math, reading, and writing. Signing for the hearing impaired is also available.

Campus Safety and Security: Measures include 24-hour foot and vehicle patrol, self-defense education, security escort services, and informal discussions. There are pamphlets/posters/films and lighted pathways/sidewalks.

Programs of Study: Thomas More confers B.A., B.S., B.B.A., B.E.S., and B.S.N. degrees. Associate and master's degrees are also awarded. Bachelor's degrees are awarded in BIOLOGICAL SCIENCE (biology/biological science), BUSINESS (accounting and business administration and management), COMMUNICATIONS AND THE ARTS (art, communications, dramatic arts, English, fine arts, and speech/debate/rhetoric), COMPUTER AND PHYSICAL SCIENCE (chemistry, computer science, mathematics, and physics), EDUCATION (elementary, middle school, and secondary), HEALTH PROFESSIONS (medical laboratory technology and nursing), SOCIAL SCIENCE (criminal justice, economics, history, international studies, liberal arts/general studies, philosophy, psychology, sociology, and theological studies). Business, biology, and information systems are the largest.

Required: All students must complete 56 to 61 hours of core requirements, including 6 credits each in English, theology, social sciences, global history, fine arts, philosophy, and natural sciences, and 3 each in foreign language, speech, and math. A total of 128 credit hours, including 36 to 76 in the major, with a minimum GPA of 2.0 is required to graduate.

Special: There are co-op programs in all majors except nursing and education, and 3-2 engineering degrees with the universities of Cincinnati, Dayton, Detroit, Kentucky, and Notre Dame. Cross-registration is possible through the Greater Cincinnati Consortium. The college offers dual majors in international studies with a second major of the student's choice. There are also internships, study abroad in 10 countries, B.A.-B.S. degrees, student-designed majors, work-study programs, credit for life experience, and pass/fail options. The Bachelor of Elected Studies degree provides adult learners with an individualized program. Nondegree study is possible. There are 6 national honor societies, a freshman honors program, and honors programs in all departments.

Faculty/Classroom: 57% of faculty are male; 43%, female. All teach undergraduates. No introductory courses are taught by graduate students. The average class size in an introductory lecture is 20; in a laboratory, 10; and in a regular course, 13.

Admissions: 28% of the current freshmen were in the top fifth of their class; 55% were in the top two fifths. 6 freshmen graduated first in their class.

Requirements: The SAT I or ACT is required. The minimum composite score needed is 1010 on the SAT I or 20 on the ACT. Applicants should have completed 16 high school academic credits, including 4 years of English and 2 each of math, science, social studies, and foreign language. Thomas More requires applicants to be in the upper 50% of their class. A GPA of 2.0 is required. AP and CLEP credits are accepted. Important factors in the admissions decision are advanced placement or honor courses, leadership record, and personality/intangible qualities.

Procedure: Freshmen are admitted to all sessions. Entrance exams should be taken in the spring of the junior year or in the fall of the senior year. There are early admissions and deferred admissions plans. There is a rolling admissions plan. Applications should be filed by August 15 for fall entry and January 5 for spring entry, along with a $25 fee. Notification is sent on a rolling basis. The registration fee is waived for students who apply on-line through the school's web site.

Transfer: 33 transfer students enrolled in 2002-2003. Applicants should be in good academic standing and have a minimum GPA of 2.0 in 24 semester hours earned. 38 of 128 credits required for the bachelor's degree must be completed at Thomas More.

Visiting: There are regularly scheduled orientations for prospective students, including a campus tour and meetings with an admissions counselor, a professor in one's major field (if decided), and financial aid staff. There are guides for informal visits and visitors may sit in on classes and stay overnight. To schedule a visit, contact the Admissions Office at *admissions@thomasmore.edu*.

Financial Aid: In 2003-2004, all full-time students received some form of financial aid. 99% of full-time freshmen and 90% of continuing full-time students received need-based aid. The average freshman award was $11,320. Need-based scholarships or need-based grants averaged $1501; need-based self-help aid (loans and jobs) averaged $1734; and other non-need based awards and non-need based scholarships averaged $4783. 95% of undergraduates work part time. The average financial indebtedness of the 2003 graduate was $19,865. Thomas More is a member of CSS. The FAFSA and the college's own financial statement are required. The deadline for filing freshman financial aid applications for fall entry is March 15.

International Students: There were 13 international students enrolled in a recent year. The school actively recruits these students. They must score 515 on the written TOEFL.

Computers: The mainframe is an HP K-9000. There are also 105 PCs available in labs and classrooms, and ports are available in dorms. All students may access the system any time. There are no time limits. The fee is $125 per semester. It is recommended that students in accelerated degree programs for BBA and MBA degrees have personal computers.

Graduates: From July 1, 2002 to June 30, 2003, 214 bachelor's degrees were awarded. The most popular majors were business (54%), social sciences and history (8%), and biology (6%). In an average class, 39% graduate in 4 years or less, 53% graduate in 5 years or less, and 55% graduate in 6 years or less. 84 companies recruited on campus in 2002-2003. Of the 2002 graduating class, 25% were enrolled in graduate school within 6 months of graduation and 75% were employed.

Admissions Contact: James E. Harter, Vice President for Enrollment Management and Marketing. A video is available.
E-mail: *jim.harter@thomasmore.edu* Web: *www.thomasmore.edu*

TRANSYLVANIA UNIVERSITY — D-3
Lexington, KY 40508-1797

(859) 233-8242
(800) 872-6798; Fax: (859) 233-8797

Full-time: 483 men, 640 women	**Faculty:** 76; IIB, av$
Part-time: 5 men, 6 women	**Ph.D.s:** 97%
Graduate: none	**Student/Faculty:** 15 to 1
Year: 4-4-1, summer session	**Tuition:** $17,660
Application Deadline: February 1	**Room & Board:** $6120
Freshman Class: 1156 applied, 993 accepted, 312 enrolled	
SAT I Verbal/Math: 590/590	**ACT:** 26 **VERY COMPETITIVE+**

Transylvania University, founded in 1780, is an independent liberal arts institution affiliated with the Christian Church (Disciples of Christ). In addition to regional accreditation, Transylvania has baccalaureate program accreditation with NCATE. The library contains 120,000 volumes, 57 microform items, and 1632 audio/video tapes/CDs, and subscribes to 540 periodicals. Computerized library services include the card catalog, interlibrary loans, database searching, and Internet access. Special learning facilities include a learning resource center, art gallery, natural history museum, and radio station. The 48-acre campus is in an urban area 80 miles east of Louisville and 80 miles south of Cincinnati, Ohio. Including any residence halls, there are 23 buildings.

Student Life: 79% of undergraduates are from Kentucky. Students are from 3 states and 3 foreign countries. 84% are from public schools. 87% are white. 63% are Protestant; 19% claim no religious affiliation; 17% Catholic. The average age of freshmen is 18; all undergraduates, 20. 16% do not continue beyond their first year; 68% remain to graduate.

Housing: 900 students can be accommodated in college housing, which includes single-sex and coed dorms and on-campus apartments. In addition, there are language houses. On-campus housing is guaranteed for all 4 years. 80% of students live on campus; of those, 85% remain on campus on weekends. All students may keep cars.

Activities: 50% of men belong to 4 national fraternities; 50% of women belong to 4 national sororities. There are 51 groups on campus, including art, band, cheerleading, choir, chorale, chorus, computers, dance, debate, drama, ethnic, forensics, gay, honors, international, jazz band, literary magazine, musical theater, newspaper, opera, orchestra, pep band, political, professional, radio and TV, religious, social, social service, student government, and yearbook. Popular campus events include the Presentation Ball, Madrigal Dinner, and the Kenan Lecture Series.

Sports: There are 7 intercollegiate sports for men and 9 for women, and 10 intramural sports for men and 10 for women. Facilities include a 1300-seat performance gym, 2 recreation gyms, a dance/aerobics room, an indoor jogging track, a swimming pool, basketball and racquetball/handball courts, 6 tennis courts, 3 athletic fields (baseball, men's soccer/field hockey, and women's soccer/softball), and weight and fitness rooms.

Disabled Students: 90% of the campus is accessible. Wheelchair ramps, elevators, special parking, specially equipped rest rooms, special class scheduling, and lowered drinking fountains are available. Arrangements are made according to individual needs.

Services: Counseling and information services are available, as is tutoring in every subject, and a computing center that provides individual help.

Campus Safety and Security: Measures include 24-hour foot and vehicle patrol, self-defense education, security escort services, and shuttle buses. There are informal discussions, pamphlets/posters/films, emergen-

cy telephones, lighted pathways/sidewalks, and a security presentation during freshman orientation.

Programs of Study: Transylvania confers the B.A. degree. Bachelor's degrees are awarded in BIOLOGICAL SCIENCE (biology/biological science), BUSINESS (accounting and business administration and management), COMMUNICATIONS AND THE ARTS (dramatic arts, English, French, music, Spanish, and studio art), COMPUTER AND PHYSICAL SCIENCE (chemistry, computer science, mathematics, and physics), EDUCATION (elementary and middle school), HEALTH PROFESSIONS (exercise science), SOCIAL SCIENCE (anthropology, economics, history, philosophy, political science/government, psychology, religion, and sociology). Business, biology, and psychology are the largest.

Required: All students must complete general education requirements in foundations of the liberal arts, academic career skills, humanities, lifetime fitness, fine arts, natural sciences, math, Western and non-Western cultural traditions, social sciences, and foreign language. 4 upper-level liberal arts classes are also required. Most majors have a capstone course requirement. A total of 36 course units, including 10 to 14 in the major, with a minimum GPA of 2.0, is required to graduate.

Special: 3-2 engineering degrees with the University of Kentucky, Vanderbilt University, and Washington University in St. Louis are offered. Cross-registration with May Term Consortium schools, internships, study abroad in many countries, work-study programs, a Washington semester, dual majors, and student-designed majors are available. There are 9 national honor societies.

Faculty/Classroom: 62% of faculty are male; 38%, female. All teach undergraduates. The average class size in an introductory lecture is 20; in a laboratory, 12; and in a regular course, 18.

Admissions: 86% of the 2003-2004 applicants were accepted. The SAT I scores for the 2003-2004 freshman class were: Verbal--15% below 500, 35% between 500 and 599, 35% between 600 and 700, and 15% above 700; Math--17% below 500, 33% between 500 and 599, 39% between 600 and 700, and 11% above 700. The ACT scores were 6% below 21, 15% between 21 and 23, 27% between 24 and 26, 23% between 27 and 28, and 29% above 28. 76% of the current freshmen were in the top fifth of their class; 94% were in the top two fifths. There were 7 National Merit finalists. 23 freshmen graduated first in their class.

Requirements: The SAT I or ACT is required. In addition, 1 essay and 2 recommendations are required. An interview is strongly recommended. Transylvania requires applicants to be in the upper 50% of their class. A GPA of 2.75 is required. AP credits are accepted. Important factors in the admissions decision are advanced placement or honor courses, recommendations by school officials, and extracurricular activities record.

Procedure: Freshmen are admitted fall and winter. Entrance exams should be taken during the junior year; no later than December of the senior year for scholarship consideration or February for general admission. There are early admissions and deferred admissions plans. There is a rolling admissions plan. Applications should be filed by February 1 for fall entry and December 5 for winter entry, along with a $30 fee. Notification is sent on a rolling basis. A waiting list is an active part of the admissions procedure. Applications are accepted on-line through *www.transy.edu*.

Transfer: 12 transfer students enrolled in 2002-2003. Applicants must have a minimum college GPA of 2.75 and should submit official copies of all college transcripts, 2 recommendations, and 1 essay. A high school transcript or GED is required. 18 of 36 courses required for the bachelor's degree must be completed at Transylvania.

Visiting: There are regularly scheduled orientations for prospective students, consisting of campus open houses in fall and winter for high school juniors and seniors, including a welcome program, an academic information fair, campus tours, a luncheon, a financial aid session, and a faculty session. There are guides for informal visits and visitors may sit in on classes and stay overnight. To schedule a visit, contact Tammie Williams at *twilliams@transy.edy*.

Financial Aid: In 2003-2004, 99% of all full-time freshmen and 98% of continuing full-time students received some form of financial aid. 61% of full-time freshmen and 60% of continuing full-time students received need-based aid. The average freshman award was $15,086. Need-based scholarships or need-based grants averaged $11,736 ($25,780 maximum); need-based self-help aid (loans and jobs) averaged $4288 ($6425 maximum); and non-need based awards and non-need based scholarships averaged $10,073 ($25,780 maximum). 29% of undergraduates work part time. Average annual earnings from campus work are $1080. The average financial indebtedness of the 2003 graduate was $16,005. Transylvania is a member of CSS. The FAFSA is required. The deadline for filing freshman financial aid applications for fall entry is March 1.

International Students: There were 4 international students enrolled in a recent year. They must score 550 on the written TOEFL or 213 on the electronic version and take the TWE. They must also take the SAT I or the ACT, scoring 1030 (SAT I) or 21 (ACT).

Computers: The mainframe is a networked PC system. All students use the network and access e-mail, Internet, and special software for coursework, the on-line library tools, and other features. There are 180 PCs in 8 labs, but most students bring their own PCs to campus. All students may access the system 24 hours a day. There are no time limits and no fees. It is strongly recommended that all students have a personal computer, that is capable of running Microsoft Windows XP.

Graduates: From July 1, 2002 to June 30, 2003, 237 bachelor's degrees were awarded. The most popular majors were business administration (26%), psychology (12%), and biology (10%). In an average class, 1% graduate in 3 years or less, 60% graduate in 4 years or less, 65% graduate in 5 years or less, and 67% graduate in 6 years or less. 13 companies recruited on campus in 2002-2003. Of the 2002 graduating class, 34% were enrolled in graduate school within 6 months of graduation and 65% were employed.

Admissions Contact: Sarah Coen, Director of Admissions. A video is available. E-mail: *admissions@transy.edu* Web: *www.transy.edu*

UNION COLLEGE
Barbourville, KY 40906-9989

E-4

(606) 546-4151, ext. 1229
(800) 489-8646; Fax: (606) 546-1667

Full-time: 260 men, 260 women	**Faculty:** 46
Part-time: 10 men, 40 women	**Ph.D.s:** 63%
Graduate: 110 men, 170 women	**Student/Faculty:** 11 to 1
Year: semesters, summer session	**Tuition:** $13,200
Application Deadline: open	**Room & Board:** $4250
Freshman Class: n/av	
SAT I or ACT: required	**COMPETITIVE**

Union College, founded in 1879, is a private liberal arts institution affiliated with the United Methodist Church. Some figures in the above capsule and in this profile are approximate. The library contains 107,707 volumes, 418,730 microform items, and 5131 audio/video tapes/CDs, and subscribes to 2451 periodicals. Computerized library services include the card catalog, interlibrary loans, and database searching. Special learning facilities include a learning resource center. The 100-acre campus is in a small town 95 miles south of Lexington and 85 miles north of Knoxville, Tennessee. Including any residence halls, there are 20 buildings.

Student Life: 69% of undergraduates are from Kentucky. Students are from 26 states and 12 foreign countries. 93% are from public schools. 80% are white; 13% African American. 65% are Protestant; 11% Catholic; 7% claim no religious affiliation. The average age of freshmen is 19; all undergraduates, 24. 30% do not continue beyond their first year; 47% remain to graduate.

Housing: 415 students can be accommodated in college housing, which includes single-sex and coed dorms, on-campus apartments, and married-student housing. On-campus housing is guaranteed for all 4 years. 53% of students commute. Alcohol is not permitted. All students may keep cars.

Activities: There are no fraternities or sororities. There are 20 groups on campus, including band, cheerleading, chess, choir, chorale, chorus, computers, drama, ethnic, honors, international, literary magazine, newspaper, orchestra, pep band, professional, religious, social, social service, and student government. Popular campus events include Daniel Boone Festival, Halloween and Valentine dances, and Wilson-Gross lecture series.

Sports: There are 6 intercollegiate sports for men and 6 for women, and 5 intramural sports for men and 3 for women. Facilities include a 2800-seat campus stadium, a 3000-seat gym, an indoor pool, tennis courts, a weight training center, an athletic training center, a baseball stadium, and fields for football, soccer, and softball.

Disabled Students: 80% of the campus is accessible. Wheelchair ramps, elevators, special parking, specially equipped rest rooms, special class scheduling, lowered drinking fountains, and lowered telephones are available.

Services: Counseling and information services are available, as is tutoring in most subjects. There is a tutoring lab with computer support.

Campus Safety and Security: Measures include 24-hour foot and vehicle patrol, self-defense education, security escort services, and informal discussions. There are pamphlets/posters/films, emergency telephones, and lighted pathways/sidewalks.

Programs of Study: Union confers B.A., B.S., and B.Mus. degrees. Associate and master's degrees are also awarded. Bachelor's degrees are awarded in BIOLOGICAL SCIENCE (biology/biological science), BUSINESS (accounting, business administration and management, and sports management), COMMUNICATIONS AND THE ARTS (dramatic arts, English, and music), COMPUTER AND PHYSICAL SCIENCE (physics), EDUCATION (business, elementary, middle school, music, secondary, and special), SOCIAL SCIENCE (criminal justice, history, and psychology). Education, sciences, and social sciences are the strongest academically. Education, business, and social sciences are the largest.

Required: All students are required to complete a 46-credit liberal education core, including 12 to 13 hours each in basic competencies and humanities, 9 in history/behavioral sciences, and 7 to 8 in natural sciences. English composition and 3 hours of phys ed also are required. A total of 128 semester hours, including 30 in the major, with a minimum GPA of 2.0 is required to graduate.

Special: A 3-2 engineering degree is offered with the University of Kentucky and Auburn University. Work-study programs, study abroad in 6 countries, and internships in business, sociology, and psychology are available. A 16-credit Appalachian studies semester, dual majors, a general studies degree, and credit for life and work experience are also offered.

Faculty/Classroom: 59% of faculty are male; 41%, female. 94% teach undergraduates and 2% both teach and do research. No introductory courses are taught by graduate students. The average class size in an introductory lecture is 25; in a laboratory, 16; and in a regular course, 15.

Admissions: 3 freshmen graduated first in their class in a recent year.

Requirements: The SAT I or ACT is required. In addition, applicants should present 20 academic credits, including 4 years in English, 3 in math, and 2 each in science, social studies, and history, as well as electives. An interview or audition is recommended. Union requires applicants to be in the upper 50% of their class. A GPA of 2.0 is required. AP and CLEP credits are accepted. Important factors in the admissions decision are evidence of special talent, geographic diversity, and advanced placement or honor courses.

Procedure: Freshmen are admitted to all sessions. Entrance exams should be taken by January of the senior year. There is a deferred admissions plan. Application deadlines are open. The fall 2003 application fee was $20. Notification is sent on a rolling basis. Applications are accepted on-line at the school's web site.

Transfer: 88 transfer students enrolled in a recent year. Applicants should have a minimum GPA of 2.0. 30 of 128 credits required for the bachelor's degree must be completed at Union.

Visiting: There are regularly scheduled orientations for prospective students, consisting of advising and registration, parents sessions, and break-out sessions. There are guides for informal visits and visitors may sit in on classes and stay overnight. To schedule a visit, contact Admissions.

Financial Aid: In a recent year, 95% of all full-time freshmen and 90% of continuing full-time students received some form of financial aid. 90% of full-time freshmen and 81% of continuing full-time students received need-based aid. The average freshman award was $12,061. 45% of undergraduates work part time. Average annual earnings from campus work are $760. The average financial indebtedness of a recent year's graduate was $11,283. Union is a member of CSS. The FAFSA is required. The priority deadline for filing freshman financial aid applications for fall entry is March 15.

International Students: There were 32 international students enrolled in a recent year. The school actively recruits these students. They must score 550 on the written TOEFL or 219 on the electronic version or take the MELAB or the college's own test, and also complete an ELS program at level 109.

Computers: The mainframes are an HP3000, an AT&T, and a UNIX-based super micro. There are 55 terminals in the science center and main classroom buildings, 20 Macs in English writing labs, and 25 Internet workstations in the library. All students may access the system. There are no time limits and no fees.

Graduates: In a recent year, 108 bachelor's degrees were awarded. The most popular majors were education (30%), business (19%), and psychology (10%). In an average class, 16% graduate in 4 years or less, 27% graduate in 5 years or less, and 30% graduate in 6 years or less. 6 companies recruited on campus in a recent year.

Admissions Contact: Andre Washington, Dean of Admissions and Financial Aid. A video is available. E-mail: *contact@unionky.edu* Web: *www.unionky.edu*

UNIVERSITY OF KENTUCKY
Lexington, KY 40506-0032

D-3

(606) 257-2000; Fax: (606) 257-3823

Full-time: 7100 men, 7700 women	**Faculty:** 1239; I, -$
Part-time: 1000 men, 1000 women	**Ph.D.s:** 98%
Graduate: 2900 men, 3400 women	**Student/Faculty:** 12 to 1
Year: semesters, summer session	**Tuition:** $3975 ($10,527)
Application Deadline: February 15	**Room & Board:** $4285
Freshman Class: n/av	
SAT I or ACT: required	**COMPETITIVE**

The University of Kentucky, founded in 1865, is a public land-grant institution offering undergraduate and graduate programs in a variety of areas. Some figures in the above capsule and in this profile are approximate. There are 13 undergraduate schools and 1 graduate school. In addition to regional accreditation, UK has baccalaureate program accreditation with AACSB, ABET, ACEJMC, ACPE, ADA, AHEA, APTA, ASLA, CAHEA, CSWE, FIDER, NAAB, NASAD, NASM, NCATE, NLN, NRPA, and SAF. The 13 libraries contain 2,792,293 volumes, 5,872,795 microform items, and 73,600 audio/video tapes/CDs, and subscribe to 26,539 periodicals. Computerized library services include the card catalog and database searching. Special learning facilities include a learning resource center, art gallery, natural history museum, radio station, and

TV station. The 764-acre campus is in a suburban area 75 miles south of Cincinnati. Including any residence halls, there are 335 buildings.

Student Life: 83% of undergraduates are from Kentucky. Students are from 49 states, 114 foreign countries, and Canada. 85% are from public schools. 87% are white. The average age of freshmen is 18; all undergraduates, 22. 20% do not continue beyond their first year; 50% remain to graduate.

Housing: 6166 students can be accommodated in college housing, which includes single-sex and coed dorms, on-campus apartments, married-student housing, fraternity houses, and sorority houses. In addition, there are honors houses, language houses, and special-interest houses. On-campus housing is available on a first-come, first-served basis. 69% of students commute. Alcohol is not permitted. All students may keep cars.

Activities: 15% of men belong to 22 national fraternities; 17% of women belong to 16 national sororities. There are 272 groups on campus, including band, cheerleading, chess, choir, chorale, chorus, computers, dance, debate, drama, drill team, ethnic, gay, honors, international, jazz band, literary magazine, marching band, musical theater, newspaper, orchestra, pep band, photography, political, professional, radio and TV, religious, social, social service, student government, symphony, and yearbook. Popular campus events include Little Kentucky Derby, Cultural Diversity Week, and Spotlight Jazz Series.

Sports: There are 11 intercollegiate sports for men and 12 for women, and 22 intramural sports for men and 22 for women. Facilities include a 58,000-seat football stadium, a 24,500-seat arena for basketball and other activities, an aquatic center and swimming pool, baseball fields, a training center, indoor tennis courts, and a field house.

Disabled Students: 90% of the campus is accessible. Wheelchair ramps, elevators, special parking, specially equipped rest rooms, special class scheduling, lowered drinking fountains, and lowered telephones are available.

Services: There is a reader service for the blind and remedial math.

Campus Safety and Security: Measures include 24-hour foot and vehicle patrol, self-defense education, security escort services, and shuttle buses. There are informal discussions, pamphlets/posters/films, emergency telephones, and lighted pathways/sidewalks.

Programs of Study: UK confers B.A., B.S., B.Arch., B.B.A., B.F.A., B.H.S., and B.M. degrees. Master's and doctoral degrees are also awarded. Bachelor's degrees are awarded in AGRICULTURE (agricultural economics, agriculture, animal science, and forestry and related sciences), BIOLOGICAL SCIENCE (biology/biological science, botany, and zoology), BUSINESS (accounting, banking and finance, business economics, hotel/motel and restaurant management, and marketing/retailing/merchandising), COMMUNICATIONS AND THE ARTS (advertising, art history and appreciation, arts administration/management, communications, dramatic arts, English, French, German, Italian, journalism, linguistics, music, music performance, Russian, Spanish, and telecommunications), COMPUTER AND PHYSICAL SCIENCE (chemistry, computer science, geology, mathematics, and physics), EDUCATION (agricultural, art, business, early childhood, elementary, foreign languages, health, mathematics, middle school, music, physical, science, secondary, social studies, and special), ENGINEERING AND ENVIRONMENTAL DESIGN (chemical engineering, civil engineering, electrical/electronics engineering, landscape architecture/design, materials engineering, mechanical engineering, and mining and mineral engineering), HEALTH PROFESSIONS (nursing, physical therapy, and physician's assistant), SOCIAL SCIENCE (anthropology, economics, food science, geography, history, Latin American studies, philosophy, political science/government, psychology, social work, sociology, and textiles and clothing). Pharmacy, architecture, and allied health are the strongest academically. Finance, accounting, and marketing are the largest.

Required: All students must maintain a minimum 2.0 GPA and complete at least 120 credit hours. Students must demonstrate competency in math, foreign language, writing, and oral communications. Required studies include courses in basic skills, inference, and communicative skills, along with disciplinary and cross-disciplinary studies.

Special: Co-op programs are offered in engineering, business, computer science, math, and agriculture. The Academic Common Market allows students in 14 southern states to study outside the university. Internships in a variety of fields, study abroad in 36 countries, work-study programs with the university and local businesses, and credit for life experience are also available. An accelerated degree program, B.A.-B.S. degrees, dual and double majors, a general studies degree, student-designed majors, a 3-2 engineering degree with several smaller schools in Kentucky, nondegree study, and pass/fail options are also offered. There are 12 national honor societies, including Phi Beta Kappa, and a freshman honors program.

Faculty/Classroom: 70% of faculty are male; 30%, female. 66% teach undergraduates.

Requirements: The SAT I or ACT is required; minimum scores vary with the GPA. Applicants must complete 20 Carnegie units, including 4 years of English, 3 of math, and 2 each of science and social studies. A fourth year of math, 2 years of foreign language, and 1 year of fine arts

also are recommended. A portfolio is required for art studio courses, and an audition is required for music performance. A GPA of 2.0 is required. AP and CLEP credits are accepted.

Procedure: Freshmen are admitted to all sessions. Entrance exams should be taken before Christmas of the senior year. Applications should be filed by February 15 for fall entry, October 15 for spring entry, and April 15 for summer entry, along with a $30 fee. Notification is sent on a rolling basis.

Transfer: Transfer students need a minimum GPA of 2.0. If they have fewer than 24 credit hours, they must meet freshman admission standards. With 24 credits or more, the SAT I or ACT is not required. 30 of 120 credits required for the bachelor's degree must be completed at UK.

Visiting: There are regularly scheduled orientations for prospective students, including a campus tour and information on admissions, housing, financial aid, and campus activities. There are guides for informal visits and visitors may sit in on classes. To schedule a visit, contact the UK Visitor Center at (859) 257-3595.

Financial Aid: UK is a member of CSS. The FAFSA is required. The deadline for filing freshman financial aid applications for fall entry is February 15.

International Students: The school actively recruits these students. They must score 525 on the written TOEFL.

Computers: The mainframes are an IBM 3090/6055 and a Convex/HP Meta Series System. 21 terminals access the mainframe in the UK computing center. There are 831 PCs in 13 public computer labs, and students may access the university system via phone modem. Several colleges also operate computer labs and classrooms for their students. All students may access the system 24 hours daily in the computing center, and various hours in labs. There are no time limits and no fees.

Admissions Contact: Director of Admissions.
E-mail: *admissio@uky.edu* Web: *www.uky.edu*

UNIVERSITY OF LOUISVILLE
Louisville, KY 40292

D-2
(502) 852-6531
(800) 334-8635; Fax: (502) 852-4476

Full-time: 4968 men, 5708 women	**Faculty:** 720; I, -$
Part-time: 1941 men, 2107 women	**Ph.D.s:** 90%
Graduate: 3074 men, 3666 women	**Student/Faculty:** 15 to 1
Year: semesters, summer session	**Tuition:** $4450 ($12,166)
Application Deadline: open	**Room & Board:** $4312
Freshman Class: n/av	
ACT: 23	**VERY COMPETITIVE**

The University of Louisville, founded in 1798, is a public institution offering a wide range of undergraduate and academic graduate programs. Some information in the above capsule is approximate. There are 8 undergraduate and 4 graduate schools. In addition to regional accreditation, U of L has baccalaureate program accreditation with AACSB, ABET, ACEJMC, ASLA, CAHEA, NAAB, NASM, NCATE, and NLN. The 6 libraries contain 1,700,846 volumes, 1,958,749 microform items, and 24,593 audio/video tapes/CDs, and subscribe to 15,000 periodicals. Computerized library services include the card catalog, interlibrary loans, and database searching. Special learning facilities include a learning resource center, art gallery, planetarium, and radio station. The campus is in an urban area.

Student Life: 87% of undergraduates are from Kentucky. Students are from 50 states, 80 foreign countries, and Canada. 90% are from public schools. 80% are white; 11% African American. The average age of freshmen is 19; all undergraduates, 26. 29% do not continue beyond their first year.

Housing: 2400 students can be accommodated in college housing, which includes coed dorms, on-campus apartments, off-campus apartments, married-student housing, fraternity houses, and sorority houses. In addition, there are honors houses and special-interest houses. On-campus housing is available on a first-come, first-served basis. Priority is given to out-of-town students. 84% of students commute. All students may keep cars.

Activities: 5% of men belong to 14 national fraternities; 3% of women belong to 1 local and 9 national sororities. There are 49 groups on campus, including art, band, cheerleading, chess, choir, chorale, chorus, computers, dance, drama, ethnic, film, gay, honors, international, jazz band, literary magazine, marching band, musical theater, newspaper, opera, orchestra, pep band, photography, political, professional, radio and TV, religious, social, social service, student government, and symphony.

Sports: There are 9 intercollegiate sports for men and 11 for women, and 43 intramural sports for men and 43 for women. Facilities include a 19,400-seat gym and a football stadium.

Disabled Students: 90% of the campus is accessible. Wheelchair ramps, elevators, special parking, specially equipped rest rooms, special class scheduling, lowered drinking fountains, and lowered telephones are available.

Services: Counseling and information services are available, as is tutoring in every subject.

Campus Safety and Security: Measures include 24-hour foot and vehicle patrol, security escort services, shuttle buses, and informal discussions. There are pamphlets/posters/films, emergency telephones, and lighted pathways/sidewalks.

Programs of Study: U of L confers B.A., B.S., and B.F.A. degrees. Associate, master's, and doctoral degrees are also awarded. Bachelor's degrees are awarded in AGRICULTURE (equine science), BIOLOGICAL SCIENCE (biology/biological science), BUSINESS (accounting, banking and finance, business administration and management, business economics, management science, marketing/retailing/merchandising, and sports management), COMMUNICATIONS AND THE ARTS (art, art history and appreciation, communications, dramatic arts, English, French, linguistics, music, and Spanish), COMPUTER AND PHYSICAL SCIENCE (chemistry, computer science, information sciences and systems, mathematics, and physics), EDUCATION (art, business, early childhood, elementary, foreign languages, middle school, music, physical, science, secondary, and teaching English as a second/foreign language (TESOL/TEFOL), ENGINEERING AND ENVIRONMENTAL DESIGN (airline piloting and navigation, chemical engineering, civil engineering, computer engineering, electrical/electronics engineering, engineering, engineering management, industrial engineering, and mechanical engineering), HEALTH PROFESSIONS (health, medical laboratory technology, medical science, and nursing), SOCIAL SCIENCE (African studies, anthropology, criminal justice, geography, history, humanities, liberal arts/general studies, paralegal studies, philosophy, political science/government, psychology, sociology, and women's studies). Engineering, health professional, and business management are the strongest academically. The arts and sciences, business, and education are the largest.

Required: Distribution requirements include at least 6 hours each in social sciences, natural sciences, the history of world civilizations, and humanities. Freshmen are required to take college writing or advanced composition, and 2 phys ed courses. A total of 123 semester hours, including 46 to 60 hours in the major, with a minimum GPA of 2.5 (2.0 in education, 2.75 in engineering) is required in order to graduate.

Special: Cross-registration with other schools, study abroad in 5 countries, work-study programs, and B.A.-B.S. degrees are offered. A general studies degree, nondegree study, and pass/fail options are available. Co-op programs in engineering and business and internships are also possible. There is a freshman honors program.

Faculty/Classroom: 51% of faculty are male; 39%, female. The average class size in an introductory lecture is 31 and in a regular course, 29.

Admissions: The ACT scores for the 2003-2004 freshman class were: 25% below 21, 30% between 21 and 23, 23% between 24 and 26, 11% between 27 and 28, and 11% above 28. There were 4 National Merit finalists and 5 semifinalists in a recent year.

Requirements: The SAT I or ACT is required. In addition, applicants must be graduates from accredited high school or have received a GED and completed pre-college curriculum with a GPA of 2.5 and at least one of the following: Earn a composite ACT score of 20 or SAT I score of 940; have completed U of L enhanced pre-college curriculum (PCC) with a minimum GPA of 2.5; or rank in the top 15% of the high school graduating class. A GPA of 2.5 is required. AP and CLEP credits are accepted.

Procedure: Freshmen are admitted fall, spring, and summer. Entrance exams should be taken in spring or summer of junior year. There are early decision and early admissions plans. There is a rolling admissions plan. Application deadlines are open. The fall 2003 application fee was $25. Applications are accepted on-line through the school's web site.

Transfer: 1053 transfer students enrolled in a recent year. Transfer students must have a minimum GPA of 2.0. 30 of 123 credits required for the bachelor's degree must be completed at U of L.

Visiting: There are regularly scheduled orientations for prospective students. There are guides for informal visits and visitors may sit in on classes. To schedule a visit, contact Admissions.

Financial Aid: In 2003-2004, 90% of all full-time freshmen and 81% of continuing full-time students received some form of financial aid. 50% of full-time freshmen and 44% of continuing full-time students received need-based aid. The average freshman award was $6318. Need-based scholarships or need-based grants averaged $4933 ($19,342 maximum); need-based self-help aid (loans and jobs) averaged $3422 ($22,641 maximum); non-need-based athletic scholarships averaged $12,296 ($22,329 maximum); and other non-need-based awards and non-need-based scholarships averaged $3848 ($23,590 maximum). The CSS Profile or FAFSA and the college's own financial statement are required.

International Students: There were 221 international students enrolled in a recent year. They must score 550 on the written TOEFL.

Computers: All students may access the system. Check with the school for current fees.

Graduates: In a recent year, 1819 bachelor's degrees were awarded. The most popular majors were business (20%), engineering (11%), and social sciences and history (11%).

Admissions Contact: Jenny Sawyer, Director of Admissions. E-mail: admitme@gwise.louisville.edu Web: http://www.louisville.edu

---

WESTERN KENTUCKY UNIVERSITY   C-4
Bowling Green, KY 42101-3576   (270) 745-2551
(800) 495-8463; Fax: (270) 745-6133

Full-time: 4600 men, 6200 women	**Faculty:** 599; IIA, -$
Part-time: 1200 men, 2200 women	**Ph.D.s:** 81%
Graduate: 800 men, 1700 women	**Student/Faculty:** 18 to 1
Year: semesters, summer session	**Tuition:** $4050 ($8898)
Application Deadline: August 1	**Room & Board:** $3990
Freshman Class: n/av	
SAT I or ACT: required	**COMPETITIVE**

Western Kentucky University, founded in 1906, is a public institution with undergraduate and graduate programs in liberal arts, health science, business, agricultural and technical studies, art and fine arts, professional training, music, and teacher preparation. Some figures in the above capsule and in this profile are approximate. There are 6 undergraduate schools and 1 graduate school. In addition to regional accreditation, Western has baccalaureate program accreditation with AACSB, ABET, ACEJMC, ADA, CSAB, CSWE, NASAD, NASM, NCATE, NLN, and NRPA. The 3 libraries contain 591,912 volumes, 2,651,784 microform items, and 93,955 audio/video tapes/CDs, and subscribe to 4564 periodicals. Computerized library services include the card catalog, interlibrary loans, and database searching. Special learning facilities include a learning resource center, art gallery, planetarium, radio station, TV station, and the Kentucky Museum. The 200-acre campus is in a suburban area 65 miles north of Nashville, Tennessee. Including any residence halls, there are 48 buildings.

Student Life: 84% of undergraduates are from Kentucky. Students are from 45 states, 53 foreign countries, and Canada. 88% are white. The average age of freshmen is 19; all undergraduates, 25. 9% do not continue beyond their first year; 41% remain to graduate.

Housing: 4568 students can be accommodated in college housing, which includes single-sex and coed dorms and sorority houses. In addition, there are honors houses. On-campus housing is available on a first-come, first-served basis. Alcohol is not permitted. All students may keep cars.

Activities: 10% of men belong to 14 national fraternities; 10% of women belong to 11 national sororities. There are 215 groups on campus, including band, cheerleading, chess, choir, chorale, chorus, computers, dance, debate, drama, drill team, ethnic, forensics, gay, honors, international, jazz band, literary magazine, marching band, musical theater, newspaper, opera, orchestra, pep band, political, professional, radio and TV, religious, social, social service, student government, symphony, and yearbook. Popular campus events include Spring Tug of War, Spring Sing, and Organizational Fair.

Sports: There are 11 intercollegiate sports for men and 10 for women, and 17 intramural sports for men and 16 for women. Facilities include a 17,500-seat stadium, gyms, a pool, a track, an 11,300-seat arena, basketball and tennis courts, baseball and softball fields, facilities for bowling, billiards, and table tennis, a movie theater, and a night spot. There is also a student health and activities center with an indoor track, a weight room, an aerobics studio, racquetball courts, an Olympic-size pool, and 4 more gyms.

Disabled Students: 60% of the campus is accessible. Wheelchair ramps, elevators, special parking, specially equipped rest rooms, special class scheduling, and lowered telephones are available. Services are available for students with special needs through the Equal Opportunity/504 ADA Compliance Office.

Services: Counseling and information services are available, as is tutoring in some subjects, with both departmental and freelance tutoring offered. The Student Support Services program offers tutoring in general education courses. There is a reader service for the blind and remedial math, reading, and writing.

Campus Safety and Security: Measures include 24-hour foot and vehicle patrol, security escort services, shuttle buses, and informal discussions. There are pamphlets/posters/films, emergency telephones, and lighted pathways/sidewalks.

Programs of Study: Western confers A.B., B.S., B.F.A., B.G.S., B.M., and B.S.N. degrees. Associate and master's degrees are also awarded. Bachelor's degrees are awarded in AGRICULTURE (agriculture), BIOLOGICAL SCIENCE (biochemistry, biology/biological science, and genetics), BUSINESS (accounting, banking and finance, business administration and management, business economics, hotel/motel and restaurant management, marketing/retailing/merchandising, and recreation and leisure services), COMMUNICATIONS AND THE ARTS (advertising, broadcasting, communications, dramatic arts, English, fine arts, French, German, journalism, music, music performance, performing arts, public relations, Spanish, speech/debate/rhetoric, and studio art), COMPUTER AND PHYSICAL SCIENCE (chemistry, computer science, geology, information sciences and systems, mathematics, and physics), EDUCATION (art, business, elementary, health, home economics, library science, middle school, physical, science, special, and trade and industrial), ENGINEERING AND ENVIRONMENTAL DESIGN (civil engineering, civil engineering technology, electrical/electronics engineering, electrical/electronics engineering technology, electromechanical technology, environmental science, industrial engineering technology, interior design, mechanical engineering, and mechanical engineering technology), HEALTH PROFESSIONS (dental hygiene, health care administration, medical technology, nursing, public health, and speech pathology/audiology), SOCIAL SCIENCE (anthropology, dietetics, economics, geography, history, parks and recreation management, philosophy, political science/government, psychology, religion, social studies, social work, sociology, and textiles and clothing). Teacher education, journalism, and biology are the strongest academically. Accounting, elementary education, and psychology are the largest.

Required: To graduate, all students must complete at least 128 semester hours, with a varying number of hours in the major, and maintain a minimum GPA of 2.0. Curricula must include 44 semester hours of general education requirements and 42 semester hours in upper-division courses, and includes 6 semester hours of English composition and 3 semester hours each of Western civilization, foreign language, speech, and literature.

Special: Internships in many areas, study abroad in 20 countries, work-study programs, and cooperative programs with the Universities of Louisville and Kentucky and Eastern Kentucky University are offered. Accelerated degree programs are available in some majors. Dual majors include math and physical science, and physics and engineering. A general studies degree, student-designed majors, a Washington semester, and a 3-2 engineering degree are offered. Credit for life, military, or work experience may be granted, and nondegree study is possible. There are 35 national honor societies and a freshman honors program.

Faculty/Classroom: 57% of faculty are male; 43%, female.

Admissions: There were 4 National Merit semifinalists in a recent year. 86 freshmen graduated first in their class.

Requirements: The SAT I or ACT is required, with a minimum composite ACT score of 20 or SAT I of 930. Other admissions requirements include graduation from an accredited secondary school with 22 academic credits, including 4 years of English, courses in algebra 1 and 2, and geometry, 3 years of social studies, and 3 years of science, including 1 lab. The GED is accepted. A GPA of 2.5 is required. AP and CLEP credits are accepted. Important factors in the admissions decision are advanced placement or honor courses, recommendations by school officials, and recommendations by alumni.

Procedure: Freshmen are admitted to all sessions. Entrance exams should be taken by fall of the senior year. There are early admissions and deferred admissions plans. Applications should be filed by August 1 for fall entry, January 1 for spring entry, and May 1 for summer entry, along with a $30 fee. Notification is sent on a rolling basis. Applications are accepted on-line via CollegeNET.

Transfer: 823 transfer students enrolled in a recent year. Applicants must have a minimum GPA of 2.0, including a 2.0 in the last term before transfer, and be in good standing. 1 official transcript from each college is required. Applicants with fewer than 24 semester hours toward a degree must submit a high school transcript. 32 of 128 credits required for the bachelor's degree must be completed at Western.

Visiting: There are regularly scheduled orientations for prospective students, including campus tours, informational sessions, presentations, and a video. There are guides for informal visits and visitors may sit in on classes and stay overnight. To schedule a visit, contact the Office of Admissions at *tours@wku.edu*.

Financial Aid: In a recent year, 97% of all full-time freshmen and 67% of continuing full-time students received some form of financial aid. 47% of full-time freshmen and 41% of continuing full-time students received need-based aid. The average freshman award was $4412. 8% of undergraduates work part time. Average annual earnings from campus work are $2098. The average financial indebtedness of a recent year's graduate was $14,438. Western is a member of CSS. The FAFSA is required. Check with the school for current deadlines.

International Students: There were 90 international students enrolled in a recent year. They must score 525 on the written TOEFL or 197 on the electronic version or take the MELAB. They must also take the SAT I or the ACT, scoring 20 on the ACT.

Computers: The mainframes are a DEC Alpha 4100 and an IBM 9121-260. Approximately 400 PCs in 7 on-campus and 3 off-campus labs are served by LANs for software and Internet access. All students may use these facilities and have e-mail accounts. In addition, students who live in the residence halls may have their computers connected to the campus LAN for all services available in the computing labs. All students may access the system 8 A.M. to midnight Monday to Thursday, 8 A.M. to 5 P.M. on Saturday, and 1 P.M. to midnight on Sunday. There are no time limits. The fee is $35 per semester.

Graduates: In a recent year, 1695 bachelor's degrees were awarded. The most popular majors were general studies (9%), elementary education (9%), and psychology (4%). 202 companies recruited on campus in a recent year.

Admissions Contact: Director of Admissions. A video is available. E-mail: *admission@wku.edu* Web: *www.wku.edu*

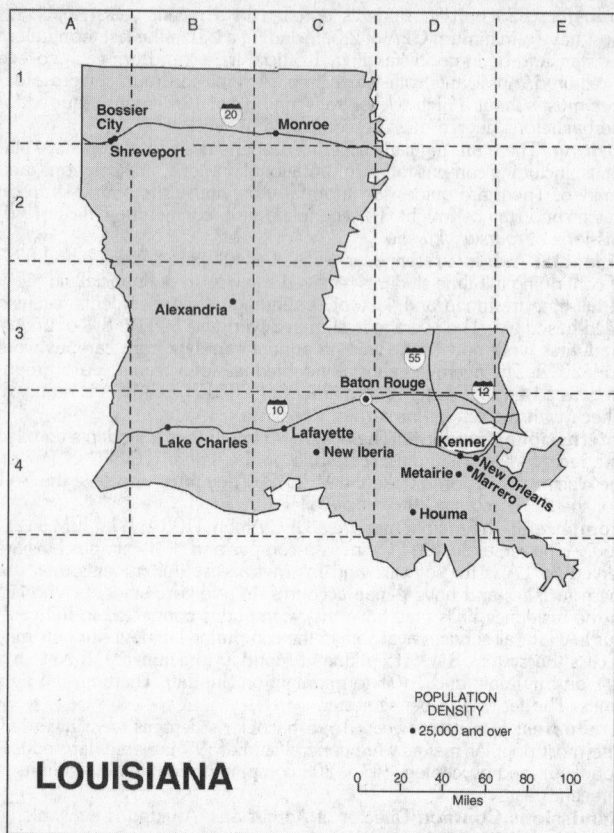

A | B | C | D | E

Bossier
City
Monroe
Shreveport

Alexandria

Baton Rouge

Lake Charles
Lafayette
New Iberia
Kenner
Metairie
New Orleans
Marrero
Houma

POPULATION
DENSITY
• 25,000 and over

LOUISIANA

0   20   40   60   80   100
Miles

CENTENARY COLLEGE OF LOUISIANA   A-1
Shreveport, LA 71104   (318) 869-5131; Fax: (318) 869-5005

Full-time: 332 men, 485 women	**Faculty:** 74; IIB, av$
Part-time: 14 men, 14 women	**Ph.D.s:** 93%
Graduate: 33 men, 119 women	**Student/Faculty:** 11 to 1
Year: semesters, summer session	**Tuition:** $17,250
Application Deadline: February 15	**Room & Board:** $5850
Freshman Class: 802 applied, 594 accepted, 199 enrolled	
SAT I Verbal/Math: 580/570	**ACT:** 26 **VERY COMPETITIVE+**

Centenary College of Louisiana, founded in 1825, is a private institution affiliated with the United Methodist Church, offering degrees in the liberal arts, music, business, sciences, and education. In addition to regional accreditation, Centenary has baccalaureate program accreditation with NASM. The 2 libraries contain 180,000 volumes, 310,671 microform items, and 425 audio/video tapes/CDs, and subscribe to 942 periodicals. Computerized library services include the card catalog, interlibrary loans, and database searching. Special learning facilities include a radio station, a theater, and an art museum. The 65-acre campus is in an urban area in the northwest corner of Louisiana, 180 miles East of Dallas, Texas. Including any residence halls, there are 23 buildings.

Student Life: 62% of undergraduates are from Louisiana. Students are from 37 states, 14 foreign countries, and Canada. 84% are white. 60% are Protestant; 18% Catholic; 15% claim no religious affiliation; 6% Hindu, Unitarian, Mormon, Muslim and Buddhist. The average age of freshmen is 18; all undergraduates, 20. 26% do not continue beyond their first year; 53% remain to graduate.

Housing: 616 students can be accommodated in college housing, which includes single-sex and coed dorms and on-campus apartments. On-campus housing is guaranteed for all 4 years. 70% of students live on campus; of those, 80% remain on campus on weekends. Alcohol is not permitted. All students may keep cars.

Activities: 23% of men belong to 4 national fraternities; 30% of women belong to 2 national sororities. There are 61 groups on campus, including band, cheerleading, choir, chorale, chorus, dance, drama, environmental club, film, forensics, gay, honors, jazz band, literary magazine, musical theater, newspaper, opera, orchestra, pep band, photography, political, professional, radio and TV, religious, social, social service, student government, symphony, and yearbook. Popular campus events include Spring Fling, President's Convocation, and Freak Week.

Sports: There are 7 intercollegiate sports for men and 9 for women, and 16 intramural sports for men and 16 for women. Facilities include a 3000-seat gym, 2 weight rooms, basketball, racquetball, volleyball and tennis courts, baseball, soccer, and softball fields, a fitness center with aerobic exercise and strengthening equipment, and a natatorium.

Disabled Students: 90% of the campus is accessible. Wheelchair ramps, elevators, special parking, specially equipped rest rooms, special class scheduling, lowered drinking fountains, lowered telephones, and lowered security phones are available.

Services: Counseling and information services are available, as is tutoring in most subjects.

Campus Safety and Security: Measures include 24-hour foot and vehicle patrol, security escort services, informal discussions, and pamphlets/posters/films. There are emergency telephones and lighted pathways/sidewalks.

Programs of Study: Centenary confers B.A., B.S., and B.M. degrees. Master's degrees are also awarded. Bachelor's degrees are awarded in BIOLOGICAL SCIENCE (biochemistry, biology/biological science, biophysics, and neurosciences), BUSINESS (accounting, business administration and management, and business economics), COMMUNICATIONS AND THE ARTS (art, communications, dance, English, French, German, Latin, music, music performance, and Spanish), COMPUTER AND PHYSICAL SCIENCE (chemistry, geology, mathematics, and physics), EDUCATION (elementary, foreign languages, music, science, and social studies), ENGINEERING AND ENVIRONMENTAL DESIGN (environmental science), HEALTH PROFESSIONS (health science), SOCIAL SCIENCE (economics, history, liberal arts/general studies, philosophy, political science/government, psychology, religion, religious music, and sociology). Physical sciences, life sciences, and political science are the strongest academically. Business, biology, and psychology are the largest.

Required: To graduate, all students must complete 124 semester hours, with a maximum of 45 in a non-interdisciplinary major and a minimum of 30 at the upper-division level, including a writing and speaking class in the major at the junior level, and maintain a minimum GPA of 2.0. There are 48 to 52 hours of distribution requirements. Core curriculum requirements include courses in the humanities, social sciences, hard sciences, and math. In addition, freshmen must take a liberal arts orientation and seniors must take a seminar. All students must complete a community service project, participate in cultural perspective events, study or live in a different culture, or study abroad, and fulfill career explorations.

Special: Centenary offers study abroad in 7 countries, cross-registration with Associated Colleges of the South, internships in all majors, a Washington semester, and a work-study program within the college. A 3-1 communications disorders degree with Louisiana State University Medical Center is possible, as is a 3-2 engineering degree with Washington University in St. Louis, University of Southern California, and Southern Methodist, Louisiana Tech, and Case Western Reserve Universities. A 3-2 applied science preprofessional degree combines with health administration or medical school. Preveterinary studies, general studies and interdisciplinary degrees, and student-designed majors are available. There are 7 national honor societies and 15 departmental honors programs.

Faculty/Classroom: 63% of faculty are male; 37%, female. 96% teach undergraduates. No introductory courses are taught by graduate students. The average class size in an introductory lecture is 25; in a laboratory, 24; and in a regular course, 25.

Admissions: 74% of the 2003-2004 applicants were accepted. The SAT I scores for the 2003-2004 freshman class were: Verbal--16% below 500, 38% between 500 and 599, 40% between 600 and 700, and 6% above 700; Math--20% below 500, 39% between 500 and 599, 36% between 600 and 700, and 5% above 700. The ACT scores were 10% below 21, 20% between 21 and 23, 24% between 24 and 26, 24% between 27 and 28, and 22% above 28. 68% of the current freshmen were in the top fifth of their class; 88% were in the top two fifths. 11 freshmen graduated first in their class.

Requirements: The SAT I or ACT is required. In addition, applicants should be high school graduates with a minimum composite score of 950 on the SAT I or 20 on the ACT, although accepted students average 1145 and 26 respectively. Secondary school preparation should include 15 academic credits, including 4 of English, 3 each of math and science, 2 each of a foreign language and history, 1 of social studies, and electives. Music students must audition; art students are advised to present a portfolio. A GPA of 2.0 is required. AP credits are accepted. Important factors in the admissions decision are advanced placement or honor courses, extracurricular activities record, and personality/intangible qualities.

Procedure: Freshmen are admitted fall, spring, and summer. Entrance exams should be taken by the fall of the senior year. There are early decision, early admissions, and deferred admissions plans. Early decision applications should be filed by December 1; regular applications, by February 15 for fall entry, December 1 for spring entry, and June 1 for summer entry. Notification of early decision is sent January 1; regular decision, March 15. 48 early decision candidates were accepted for the 2003-2004 class. Applications are accepted on-line through Common App and at the school's web site.

Transfer: 42 transfer students enrolled in 2002-2003. Transfer applicants must have a minimum GPA of 2.0 and demonstrate good performance in a liberal arts curriculum. 45 of 124 credits required for the bachelor's degree must be completed at Centenary.

Visiting: There are regularly scheduled orientations for prospective students, consisting of information sessions with a counselor, a tour of the campus, a visit to a class or with faculty, and lunch. There are guides for informal visits and visitors may sit in on classes and stay overnight. To schedule a visit, contact the Admissions Office at (800) 234-4440 or *tcrowley@centenary.edu*.

Financial Aid: In 2003-2004, 98% of all full-time freshmen and 96% of continuing full-time students received some form of financial aid. 70% of full-time freshmen and 69% of continuing full-time students received need-based aid. The average freshman award was $16,511. Need-based scholarships or need-based grants averaged $10,880 ($21,050 maximum); need-based self-help aid (loans and jobs) averaged $3387 ($7125 maximum); non-need based athletic scholarships averaged $12,049 ($23,928 maximum); other non-need based awards and non-need based scholarships averaged $9395 ($25,100 maximum); and unsubsidized Stafford loans (non-need) averaged $2502 ($6125 maximum). 21% of undergraduates work part time. Average annual earnings from campus work are $1606. The average financial indebtedness of the 2003 graduate was $15,300. Centenary is a member of CSS. The FAFSA is required. The priority date for freshman financial aid applications for fall entry is February 15.

International Students: There are 27 international students enrolled. The school actively recruits these students. They must score 550 on the written TOEFL.

Computers: The mainframe is an IBM RS6000. All students may access the system. There are no time limits. The fee is $50. It is strongly recommended that all students have a personal computer.

Graduates: From July 1, 2002 to June 30, 2003, 191 bachelor's degrees were awarded. The most popular majors were business (30%), biology (16%), and exercise science (16%). In an average class, 38% graduate in 4 years or less, 52% graduate in 5 years or less, and 53% graduate in 6 years or less.

Admissions Contact: Eugene Gregory, Vice President of College Relations. E-mail: *egregory@centenary.edu* Web: *www.centenary.edu*

DILLARD UNIVERSITY
New Orleans, LA 70122-3097

D-4
(504) 816-4670
(800) 216-6637; Fax: (504) 816-4895

Full-time: 2200 men and women	**Faculty:** 143
Part-time: 112 men and women	**Ph.D.s:** 52%
Graduate: none	**Student/Faculty:** 15 to 1
Year: semesters, summer session	**Tuition:** $10,865
Application Deadline: July 1	**Room & Board:** $6460
Freshman Class: 3630 applied, 2155 accepted, 606 enrolled	
SAT I: recommended	**ACT:** required
	VERY COMPETITIVE

Dillard University, established in 1930, is an independent, nonsectarian, liberal arts institution, affiliated with the United Church of Christ and the United Methodist Church. It offers undergraduate programs in business, education, humanities, natural sciences, nursing, and social sciences. There are 6 undergraduate schools. In addition to regional accreditation, Dillard has baccalaureate program accreditation with NLN. The library contains 104,615 volumes, 21,638 microform items, and 426 audio/video tapes/CDs, and subscribes to 295 periodicals. Computerized library services include the card catalog, interlibrary loans, and database searching. Special learning facilities include a learning resource center, art gallery, and radio station. The 55-acre campus is in an urban area in New Orleans. Including any residence halls, there are 21 buildings.

Student Life: 54% of undergraduates are from out of state, mostly the South. Students are from 31 states, 13 foreign countries, and Canada. 98% are African American. 28% do not continue beyond their first year.

Housing: 1058 students can be accommodated in college housing, which includes single-sex dorms, on-campus apartments, and off-campus apartments. On-campus housing is guaranteed for the freshman year only, is available on a first-come, first-served basis, and is available on a lottery system for upperclassmen. Priority is given to out-of-town students. Alcohol is not permitted. All students may keep cars.

Activities: 4% of men belong to 4 national fraternities; 11% of women belong to 4 national sororities. There are 64 groups on campus, including art, cheerleading, chess, choir, chorus, dance, drama, ethnic, honors, professional, religious, social service, student government, and yearbook. Popular campus events include Coronation, Avenue of the Oaks Gala, and Founder's Day.

Sports: There are 3 intercollegiate sports for men and 3 for women. Facilities include a gym, a swimming pool, a Nautilus room, tennis courts, dance facility, and game room.

Disabled Students: 70% of the campus is accessible. Wheelchair ramps, special parking, specially equipped rest rooms, and special class scheduling are available.

Services: Counseling and information services are available, as is tutoring in every subject. There is remedial math, reading, and writing.

Campus Safety and Security: Measures include 24-hour foot and vehicle patrol, shuttle buses, informal discussions, and pamphlets/posters/films. There are lighted pathways/sidewalks.

Programs of Study: Dillard confers B.A., B.S., and B.S.N. degrees. Bachelor's degrees are awarded in BIOLOGICAL SCIENCE (biology/biological science), BUSINESS (accounting and business administration and management), COMMUNICATIONS AND THE ARTS (art, communications, English, French, languages, music, music business management, music performance, and Spanish), COMPUTER AND PHYSICAL SCIENCE (chemistry, computer science, mathematics, and physics), EDUCATION (elementary, secondary, and special), HEALTH PROFESSIONS (nursing and public health), SOCIAL SCIENCE (African studies, economics, history, Japanese studies, political science/government, psychology, sociology, and urban studies). Biological sciences is the largest.

Required: Students must successfully complete 125 semester hours and maintain a minimum overall GPA of 2.0 and a GPA of 2.0 or better in all courses in the major. In addition, all students must complete 35 semester hours in the core curriculum, which includes courses in English composition, world literature, English literature, math, natural sciences, world history, political science, economics, university assembly, phys ed, and academic orientation. Additionally, each student must engage in a minimum of 120 clock hours of volunteer service in the community.

Special: Opportunities are provided for internships, work-study programs, credit by exam, nondegree study, and pass/fail options. All social science majors are encouraged to pursue a double major. There is a 4-year co-op degree in music therapy with Loyola University, a clinical public health curriculum with Howard University, a 5-year joint degree in urban studies with Columbia University, and preengineering dual degree programs with the Georgia Institute of Technology and Auburn and Columbia Universities. There are 3 national honor societies.

Faculty/Classroom: 45% of faculty are male; 55%, female. All teach undergraduates. The average class size in an introductory lecture is 30.

Admissions: 59% of the 2003-2004 applicants were accepted. 18 freshmen graduated first in their class in a recent year.

Requirements: The SAT I or ACT is recommended. In addition, graduation from an accredited secondary school is required; a GED will be accepted. Applicants must submit an academic record of 20 units, distributed as follows: 4 units in English, 3 each in math and natural sciences, 2 in social studies, and 8 in other academic electives. Recommendations from a high school teacher and the principal or a student counselor are required. A GPA of 2.2 is required. AP credits are accepted. Important factors in the admissions decision are recommendations by school officials, leadership record, and personality/intangible qualities.

Procedure: Freshmen are admitted in the spring. Entrance exams should be taken between April of the junior year and December of the senior year. There are early admissions and deferred admissions plans. There is a rolling admissions plan. Applications should be filed by July 1 for fall entry and December 1 for spring entry, along with a $20 fee. Notification is sent on a rolling basis. Applications are accepted on-line through the school's web site.

Transfer: 53 transfer students enrolled in 2002-2003. Applicants for transfer must submit a secondary school record or equivalent, transcripts from previous colleges showing an average grade of C, and personal recommendations. No more than 60 semester hours may be submitted for transfer credit. 65 of 125 credits required for the bachelor's degree must be completed at Dillard.

Visiting: There are regularly scheduled orientations for prospective students, scheduled on an individual basis. There are guides for informal visits and visitors may sit in on classes and stay overnight. To schedule a visit, contact the Campus Visit Coordinator.

Financial Aid: In 2003-2004, 98% of all full-time students received some form of financial aid. 85% of full-time freshmen and 97% of continuing full-time students received need-based aid. The average freshman award was $14,003. Need-based scholarships or need-based grants averaged $3081 ($4050 maximum); need-based self-help aid (loans and jobs) averaged $2458 ($15,000 maximum); and non-need based athletic scholarships averaged $18,585 ($20,025 maximum). 1% of undergraduates work part time. Average annual earnings from campus work are $2000. The average financial indebtedness of the 2003 graduate was $18,000. Dillard is a member of CSS. The FAFSA and the college's own financial statement are required. The deadline for filing freshman financial aid applications for fall entry is March 1.

International Students: There are 42 international students enrolled. They must score 500 on the written TOEFL or 213 on the electronic version and also take the SAT I or the ACT, scoring 18.

Computers: The mainframe is an IBM AS/400. There are no time limits. The fee is $150. It is strongly recommended that all students have a personal computer.

Graduates: From July 1, 2002 to June 30, 2003, 278 bachelor's degrees were awarded. The most popular majors were public health (16%), biology (13%), and mass communications (9%). Of the 2002 graduating class, 45% were enrolled in graduate school within 6 months of graduation and 45% were employed.

Admissions Contact: Linda G. Nash, Director of Admissions.
Web: *www.dillard.edu*

GRAMBLING STATE UNIVERSITY
Grambling, LA 71245

B-1
(318) 274-6423
(888) 863-3655; Fax: (318) 274-3292

Full-time: none	Faculty: 227
Part-time: none	Ph.D.s: 64%
Graduate: none	Student/Faculty: n/av
Year: semesters, summer session	Tuition: $3182 ($3356)
Application Deadline: open	Room & Board: $3356
Freshman Class: n/av	
ACT: 16	NONCOMPETITIVE

Founded in 1901, Grambling State University, a constituent member of the University of Louisiana System, is a historically and predominantly black comprehensive university, offering degrees ranging from associate to doctorate. There are 6 undergraduate schools and 1 graduate school. In addition to regional accreditation, GSU has baccalaureate program accreditation with AACSB, ABET, ACEJMC, ACS, CSAB, CSWE, NASAD, NASM, NASPAA, NCATE, NLN, and NRPA. The library contains 306,990 volumes, 121,954 microform items, and 6282 audio/video tapes/CDs, and subscribes to 109,517 periodicals. Computerized library services include the card catalog, interlibrary loans, database searching, and Internet access. Special learning facilities include a learning resource center, radio station, TV station, and student technology labs. The 383-acre campus is in a small town 60 miles from Shreveport. Including any residence halls, there are 85 buildings.

Student Life: 65% of undergraduates are from Louisiana. Students are from 41 states, 14 foreign countries, and Canada. 95% are African American. 80% are Protestant; 15% Catholic. The average age of freshmen is 18; all undergraduates, 20.

Housing: 2611 students can be accommodated in college housing, which includes single-sex dorms. In addition, there are honors houses and private room floors. On-campus housing is guaranteed for all 4 years. 55% of students commute. Alcohol is not permitted. All students may keep cars.

Activities: 2% of men belong to 4 national fraternities; 7% of women belong to 4 national sororities. There are 81 groups on campus, including art, band, cheerleading, choir, computers, dance, drama, honors, international, jazz band, marching band, newspaper, orchestra, political, professional, radio and TV, religious, social, social service, student government, symphony, and yearbook. Popular campus events include Founders Day, Black History Month, and Springfest.

Sports: There are 8 intercollegiate sports for men and 9 for women, and 6 intramural sports for men and 3 for women. Facilities include a gym, tennis courts, a 20,000-seat football stadium, an intramural center, a baseball field, a softball field, and an 1,850-seat basketball gym.

Disabled Students: 80% of the campus is accessible. Wheelchair ramps, elevators, special parking, specially equipped rest rooms, special class scheduling, lowered drinking fountains, and lowered telephones are available.

Services: Counseling and information services are available, as is tutoring in some subjects, including biology, English, chemistry, history, math, and physics. There is remedial math, reading, and writing.

Campus Safety and Security: Measures include 24-hour foot and vehicle patrol, security escort services, pamphlets/posters/films, and emergency telephones. There are lighted pathways/sidewalks.

Programs of Study: GSU confers B.A., B.S., B.A.S.W., B.P.A., and B.S.N. degrees. Associate, master's, and doctoral degrees are also awarded. Bachelor's degrees are awarded in BIOLOGICAL SCIENCE (biology/biological science), BUSINESS (accounting, business administration and management, business economics, hotel/motel and restaurant management, marketing/retailing/merchandising, and recreation and leisure services), COMMUNICATIONS AND THE ARTS (art, communications, dramatic arts, English, French, music, and Spanish), COMPUTER AND PHYSICAL SCIENCE (chemistry, computer science, information sciences and systems, mathematics, and physics), EDUCATION (art, business, drama, early childhood, elementary, English, foreign languages, home economics, industrial arts, mathematics, music, physical, science, and special), ENGINEERING AND ENVIRONMENTAL DESIGN (engineering technology), HEALTH PROFESSIONS (nursing, premedicine, and speech pathology/audiology), SOCIAL SCIENCE (criminal justice, food production/management/services, history, political science/government, prelaw, psychology, public administration, social

work, and sociology). Nursing, education, and computer science are the strongest academically. Business management is the largest.

Required: To graduate, students must complete a minimum of 125 semester hours, with a minimum GPA of 2.0. Students also must earn a passing grade in each part of the general education integration seminar and pass the senior comprehensive competency exam. An exam is also required in the sophomore year. General education requirements include courses in English, math, computer literacy, natural sciences, arts, humanities, and social studies for a total of 42 semester hours.

Special: B.A.-B.S. degrees in some subjects, work-study programs, nondegree study, and cross-registration with Louisiana Tech University are offered. The university sponsors Project Rescue for disadvantaged students. Internships, study abroad, accelerated degree programs, dual majors, and student-designed majors are also possible. There are 15 national honor societies and a freshman honors program.

Faculty/Classroom: 83% teach undergraduates and 3% do research. The average class size in an introductory lecture is 26; in a laboratory, 20; and in a regular course, 30.

Admissions: The ACT scores for the 2003-2004 freshman class were: 90% below 21, 7% between 21 and 23, and 3% between 24 and 26.

Requirements: The SAT I or ACT is required. In addition, applicants must be graduates of an accredited high school. The GED is accepted. AP and CLEP credits are accepted. Important factors in the admissions decision are ability to finance college education, parents or siblings attending the school, and personality/intangible qualities.

Procedure: Freshmen are admitted fall, spring, and summer. There is an early admissions plan. There is a rolling admissions plan. Application deadlines are open. Application fee is $20. Applications are accepted on-line.

Transfer: 162 transfer students enrolled in a recent year. Applicants must submit official transcripts from all previously attended colleges and be in good standing at the school most recently attended. 30 of 128 credits required for the bachelor's degree must be completed at GSU.

Visiting: There are regularly scheduled orientations for prospective students. There are guides for informal visits and visitors may sit in on classes and stay overnight. To schedule a visit, contact Nora D. Bingaman Taylor.

Financial Aid: In a recent year, 85% of all full-time freshmen received some form of financial aid. 85% of full-time freshmen received need-based aid. The average freshman award was $7405. All of undergraduates work part time. Average annual earnings from campus work are $1030. The average financial indebtedness of a recent graduate was $35,000. The FAFSA, the college's own financial statement, and the Singlefile Form are required. The deadline for filing freshman financial aid applications for fall entry is June 1.

International Students: There were 21 international students enrolled in a recent year. The school actively recruits these students. They must score 450 on the written TOEFL and also take the SAT I or the ACT.

Computers: All students may access the system. There are no time limits and no fees.

Graduates: In a recent year, 663 bachelor's degrees were awarded. The most popular majors were criminal justice (10%), leisure studies (10%), and computer information systems (9%). In an average class, 29% graduate in 6 years or less. 167 companies recruited on campus in a recent year.

Admissions Contact: Nora D. Bingaman Taylor, Director of Admissions. E-mail: *bingnamann@gram.edu* Web: *www.gram.edu*

LOUISIANA COLLEGE
Pineville, LA 71359

B-3
(318) 487-7259
(800) 487-1906; Fax: (318) 487-7550

Full-time: 436 men, 540 women	Faculty: 68; IIB, --$
Part-time: 22 men, 47 women	Ph.D.s: 60%
Graduate: none	Student/Faculty: 14 to 1
Year: semesters, summer session	Tuition: $9750
Application Deadline: open	Room & Board: $3700
Freshman Class: 731 applied, 620 accepted, 266 enrolled	
SAT I Verbal/Math: 490/490	ACT: 23 COMPETITIVE

Louisiana College, founded in 1906, is a private liberal arts college affiliated with the Southern Baptist Churches of Louisiana. In addition to regional accreditation, LC has baccalaureate program accreditation with AACSB, CSWE, NASM, and NLN. The library contains 135,443 volumes, 112,275 microform items, and 2500 audio/video tapes/CDs, and subscribes to 10,235 periodicals. Computerized library services include the card catalog, interlibrary loans, database searching, and Internet access. Special learning facilities include a learning resource center, art gallery, radio station, and a performing arts center. The 81-acre campus is in a small town 1 mile northeast of Alexandria. Including any residence halls, there are 16 buildings.

Student Life: 92% of undergraduates are from Louisiana. Students are from 17 states and 5 foreign countries. 88% are white. 66% are Protestant; 18% claim no religious affiliation; 13% Catholic; 3% other, including nondenominational and Jehovah's Witness. The average age of freshmen is 18; all undergraduates, 22. 36% do not continue beyond their first year; 43% remain to graduate.

Housing: 726 students can be accommodated in college housing, which includes single-sex dorms, on-campus apartments, and married-student housing. On-campus housing is guaranteed for all 4 years. 54% of students live on campus. Alcohol is not permitted. All students may keep cars.

Activities: 5% of men belong to 4 local fraternities; 15% of women belong to 4 local sororities. There are 57 groups on campus, including art, band, campus programming, cheerleading, choir, chorale, chorus, debate, diversity, drama, honors, international, jazz band, literary magazine, musical theater, newspaper, opera, pep band, political, professional, religious, social, social service, student government, symphony, and yearbook. Popular campus events include Gala Christmas, Sanders Lecture Series, and Miss LC Pageant.

Sports: There are 5 intercollegiate sports for men and 5 for women, and 11 intramural sports for men and 11 for women. Facilities include a field house for basketball, a baseball field, a fitness/wellness center, a jogging trail, tennis courts, an intramural/soccer/football field, an outdoor beach volleyball court, softball field, and a practice football field.

Disabled Students: 95% of the campus is accessible. Wheelchair ramps, elevators, special parking, specially equipped rest rooms, and lowered telephones are available.

Services: Counseling and information services are available, as is tutoring in most subjects. There is a reader service for the blind and remedial math and writing. PASS (Program to Assist Student Success) offers services for students with documented learning disabilities.

Campus Safety and Security: Measures include 24-hour foot and vehicle patrol, self-defense education, security escort services, and informal discussions. There are pamphlets/posters/films and lighted pathways/sidewalks.

Programs of Study: LC confers B.A., B.S., B.G.S., B.M., B.S.N., and B.S.W. degrees. Bachelor's degrees are awarded in BIOLOGICAL SCIENCE (biology/biological science), BUSINESS (business administration and management), COMMUNICATIONS AND THE ARTS (communications, dramatic art, English, French, graphic design, journalism, languages, multimedia, music, speech/debate/rhetoric, and studio art), COMPUTER AND PHYSICAL SCIENCE (chemistry and mathematics), EDUCATION (art, athletic training, business, elementary, English, health, mathematics, music, science, secondary, social studies, and special), HEALTH PROFESSIONS (exercise science, medical laboratory technology, music therapy, nursing, predentistry, premedicine, preoptometry, and preveterinary science), SOCIAL SCIENCE (criminal justice, economics, history, philosophy, prelaw, psychology, public administration, religion, religious education, religious music, social work, and sociology). Education, biology, and business are the largest.

Required: To graduate, students must complete 127 total credit hours, 42 of which must be junior-senior level, including a central core of 56 hours in all degree programs, and maintain a minimum GPA of 2.0, 2.25 in the major. They must also complete Cultural/Intellectual and Spiritual Enrichment requirements and earn at least 25% of credit applied toward degree through instruction offered by LC. They must complete the last 30 hours of course work at LC, and take 3 hours each of phys ed and computer applications.

Special: Study abroad in London and Hong Kong, interdisciplinary studies, work-study programs, nondegree study, internships, dual majors, and pass/fail options are offered. There are 13 national honor societies and a freshman honors program.

Faculty/Classroom: 54% of faculty are male; 46%, female. All teach undergraduates. The average class size in an introductory lecture is 30; in a laboratory, 20; and in a regular course, 18.

Admissions: 85% of the 2003-2004 applicants were accepted. The SAT I scores for the 2003-2004 freshman class were: Verbal--55% below 500, 34% between 500 and 599, and 10% between 600 and 700; Math--55% below 500, 17% between 500 and 599, 24% between 600 and 700, and 3% above 700. The ACT scores were 24% below 21, 33% between 21 and 23, 28% between 24 and 26, 2% between 27 and 28, and 12% above 28. 47% of the current freshmen were in the top fifth of their class; 77% were in the top two fifths. There was 1 National Merit finalist and 2 semifinalists. 20 freshmen graduated first in their class.

Requirements: The SAT I or ACT is required. In addition, candidates for admission must have completed 17 units, which must include 4 of English, 3 of math (algebra I, II, and geometry), 3 of social studies, and 3 of science (2 with lab). Graduates of accredited high schools must meet one of the following requirements for unconditional admission: (1) score at least 20 composite on ACT or 930 on the SAT I and possess a GPA of 2.0 on a 4.0 scale; or (2) possess an academic GPA of 2.0 on a 4.0 scale and rank in the upper 50% of their graduating class with an acceptable ACT or SAT I score. LC requires applicants to be in the upper 50% of their class. A GPA of 2.0 is required. AP and CLEP credits are accepted. Important factors in the admissions decision are extracurricular activities record, leadership record, and advanced placement or honor courses.

Procedure: Freshmen are admitted fall, spring, and summer. Entrance exams should be taken during the junior or senior year. There is a rolling admissions plan. Application deadlines are open. Application fee is $25. Applications are accepted on-line through www.lacollege.edu/apply

Transfer: 99 transfer students enrolled in 2002-2003. Applicants must have an overall minimum GPA of 2.0 and finish all remedial course work prior to transfer. 30 of 127 credits required for the bachelor's degree must be completed at LC.

Visiting: There are regularly scheduled orientations for prospective students, consisting of spring and fall campus preview days and a 2-day orientation and pre-registration in June. There are guides for informal visits and visitors may sit in on classes and stay overnight. To schedule a visit, contact the Office of Admissions at admissions@lacollege.edu.

Financial Aid: In 2003-2004, 98% of all full-time freshmen and 95% of continuing full-time students received some form of financial aid. 46% of full-time freshmen and 34% of continuing full-time students received need-based aid. The average freshman award was $6356. Need-based scholarships or need-based grants averaged $2161; need-based self-help aid (loans and jobs) averaged $3869; non-need based awards and non-need based scholarships averaged $2152; and other awards averaged $4162. 19% of undergraduates work part time. The average financial indebtedness of the 2003 graduate was $18,000. The FAFSA or FFS and the college's own financial statement are required. The priority date for freshman financial aid applications for fall entry is March 15. The deadline for filing freshman financial aid applications for fall entry is October 1.

International Students: There are 12 international students enrolled. They must score 550 on the written TOEFL or 213 on the electronic version. The TOEFL is waived for students taking the SAT I who earn 480 on the verbal section. They must also take the SAT I or the ACT, scoring 930 (SAT I) or 20 (ACT).

Computers: The mainframe is a DEC VAX. There are labs for Macs and PCs located in 2 academic buildings, the student center, and the library. All resident halls are wired for Internet access. All students may access the system. There are no time limits and no fees.

Graduates: From July 1, 2002 to June 30, 2003, 158 bachelor's degrees were awarded. The most popular majors were nursing (9%), biology (9%), and social work (8%). In an average class, 24% graduate in 4 years or less, 41% graduate in 5 years or less, and 45% graduate in 6 years or less. 65 companies recruited on campus in 2002-2003.

Admissions Contact: Director of Admissions.
E-mail: admissions@lacollege.edu Web: www.lacollege.edu

LOUISIANA STATE UNIVERSITY SYSTEM

The Louisiana State University System, established in 1860, is a public system governed by a board of supervisors. The chief administrator is the president. The primary goal of the system is to foster excellence in learning (teaching), discovery (research), engagement (service), and health/care (training). The main priority is effectively preparing citizens for an increasingly complex world, using its expertise in the generation, preservation, application, and dissemination of knowledge, healthcare, and the development of new technologies. Each of the ten system campuses, along with its Healthcare Service Division, will serve a vital role by preparing its stakeholders to incorporate new knowledge and technologies into their daily lives, thereby improving their productivity and health while enhancing their quality of life and opportunities for future success. Total enrollment in the LSU System is 62,882 with 3493 faculty, 1556 other academic employees, 3284 professional employees, and 16,774 classified employees. Profiles of the 4-year campuses located in Baton Rouge, Shreveport, and New Orleans are included in this section. For a tour of the Louisiana State University System and its campuses, visit the web site at http://www.lsusystem.lsu.edu/.

LOUISIANA STATE UNIVERSITY AND AGRICULTURAL AND MECHANICAL COLLEGE

C-4

Baton Rouge, LA 70803   (225) 578-1175; Fax: (225) 578-4433

Full-time: 11,331 men, 12,375 women	**Faculty:** 1158; I, --$
Part-time: 1075 men, 1375 women	**Ph.D.s:** 82%
Graduate: 2742 men, 3036 women	**Student/Faculty:** 20 to 1
Year: semesters, summer session	**Tuition:** $3910 ($9210)
Application Deadline: April 15	**Room & Board:** $5216
Freshman Class: 10,147 applied, 8171 accepted, 5428 enrolled	
ACT: 24	**VERY COMPETITIVE**

Louisiana State University and Agricultural and Mechanical College, a public institution founded in 1860, and part of the Louisiana State University System, offers programs in agriculture, arts and sciences, basic sciences, business administration, art and design, education, engineering, music and dramatic arts, and mass communication. There are 12 undergraduate and 4 graduate schools. In addition to regional accreditation, LSU has baccalaureate program accreditation with AACSB, ABET, ACCE, ACEJMC, ADA, ASLA, CSWE, FIDER, NAAB, NASAD, NASM, NCATE, and SAF. The 2 libraries contain 3,213,314 volumes, 6,606,164 microform items, and 24,803 audio/video tapes/CDs, and subscribe to 28,387 periodicals. Computerized library services include the card catalog, interlibrary loans, database searching, and Internet access. Special learning facilities include a learning resource center, art gallery, natural history museum, radio station, TV station, 3 herbaria, and museums of natural science, natural history, geoscience, rural life, and art. The 2000-acre campus is in an urban area in Baton Rouge, Louisiana. Including any residence halls, there are 250 buildings.

Student Life: 88% of undergraduates are from Louisiana. Students are from 47 states, 93 foreign countries, and Canada. 80% are white. 39% are Catholic; 29% claim no religious affiliation; 29% Protestant. The average age of freshmen is 18; all undergraduates, 22. 16% do not continue beyond their first year; 58% remain to graduate.

Housing: 7926 students can be accommodated in college housing, which includes single-sex and coed dorms, on-campus apartments, married-student housing, fraternity houses, and sorority houses. In addition, there are honors houses and special-interest houses. 78% of students commute. All students may keep cars.

Activities: 10% of men belong to 23 national fraternities; 15% of women belong to 15 national sororities. There are 335 groups on campus, including art, band, cheerleading, choir, chorus, computers, dance, debate, drama, ethnic, gay, honors, international, jazz band, literary magazine, marching band, musical theater, newspaper, opera, orchestra, pep band, political, professional, radio and TV, religious, social, social service, student government, symphony, and yearbook. Popular campus events include Rush Week, Martin Luther King Day Celebration, and LSU Union Ice Cream/Watermelon Giveaways.

Sports: There are 8 intercollegiate sports for men and 10 for women, and 7 intramural sports for men and 7 for women. Facilities include a 91,600-sear stadium, a 14,237-seat domed spors center, a 7700- seat baseball stadium, a 400-meter track with seating for 5600, a natatorium with an 8-lane Olympic pool and diving well, an indoor track, and courts for handball, badminton, vollyball, and tennis. The recreational sports facility provides a multifaceted program that includes aquatics, sports clubs, informal recreation, instructional sports, intramural sports, outdoor recreation, special-events activities, and sports medicine. There is also an indoor practice facility for football, a soccer field that seats 1200, and a softball stadium that seats 1500.

Disabled Students: 60% of the campus is accessible. Wheelchair ramps, elevators, special parking, specially equipped rest rooms, special class scheduling, lowered drinking fountains, lowered telephones, and telecommunication devices for the deaf, and power doors are available.

Services: Counseling and information services are available, as is tutoring in some subjects, including English, math, foreign languages, and sciences. There is remedial reading and writing. There are designated sections of math and Latin for students with learning disabilities.

Campus Safety and Security: Measures include 24-hour foot and vehicle patrol, self-defense education, security escort services, and shuttle buses. There are informal discussions, pamphlets/posters/films, emergency telephones, lighted pathways/sidewalks, and specialized crime prevention programs.

Programs of Study: LSU confers B.A., B.S., B.A. in M.C., B.Arch., B.F.A., B.G.S., B.Int.Design, B.Land.Arch., B.M., B.M.Ed., B.S.B.E., B.S.C.E., B.S.Ch.E., B.S.Cons.M., B.S.E.E., B.S.Env.Engineering, B.S.F., B.S.I.E., B.S. in Geol., B.S.M.E., and B.S.P.E. degrees. Master's and doctoral degrees are also awarded. Bachelor's degrees are awarded in AGRICULTURE (agricultural business management, animal science, dairy science, fish and game management, forestry and related sciences, forestry production and processing, plant science, and poultry science), BIOLOGICAL SCIENCE (biochemistry, biology/biological science, and nutrition), BUSINESS (accounting, banking and finance, business administration and management, business economics, international economics, and marketing/retailing/merchandising), COMMUNICATIONS AND THE ARTS (communications, dramatic arts, English, fine arts, French, German, Latin, music, Spanish, and speech/debate/rhetoric), COMPUTER AND PHYSICAL SCIENCE (chemistry, computer science, geology, information sciences and systems, mathematics, and physics), EDUCATION (elementary, music, secondary, and vocational), ENGINEERING AND ENVIRONMENTAL DESIGN (architecture, bioengineering, chemical engineering, civil engineering, computer engineering, construction management, electrical/electronics engineering, environmental engineering, environmental science, industrial engineering, interior design, landscape architecture/design, mechanical engineering, and petroleum/natural gas engineering), HEALTH PROFESSIONS (speech pathology/audiology), SOCIAL SCIENCE (anthropology, clothing and textiles management/production/services, early childhood studies, economics, family/consumer studies, food science, gender studies, geography, history, international studies, liberal arts/general studies, philosophy, physical fitness/movement, political science/government, psychology, Russian and Slavic studies, social science, sociology, textiles and clothing, and women's studies). Biological sciences, chemical engineering, and chemistry are the strongest academically. Biological sciences, mass communication, and general studies are the largest.

Required: To graduate, all students must have a minimum overall 2.0 GPA in 120 to 163 credit hours. They must complete a general educa-

tion component of 38 to 39 semester hours in approved courses in 6 major areas, including 9 hours in humanities, 8 to 9 in natural sciences, 6 each in English composition, analytical reasoning, and social sciences, and 3 in the arts.

Special: Co-op programs in numerous majors, cross-registration with Southern University and Baton Rouge Community College, study abroad, and work-study programs are offered. B.A.-B.S. degrees, dual majors, a general studies degree, nondegree study, an evening school, a program of study for adult learners, and pass/fail options are available. There are 39 national honor societies, including Phi Beta Kappa, a freshman honors program, and 17 departmental honors programs.

Faculty/Classroom: 65% of faculty are male; 35%, female. 85% teach undergraduates, 74% do research, and 70% do both. Graduate students teach 22% of introductory courses. The average class size in an introductory lecture is 44; in a laboratory, 21; and in a regular course, 38.

Admissions: 81% of the 2003-2004 applicants were accepted. The ACT scores for the 2003-2004 freshman class were: 11% below 21, 34% between 21 and 23, 29% between 24 and 26, 15% between 27 and 28, and 12% above 28. 46% of the current freshmen were in the top fifth of their class; 76% were in the top two fifths. There were 45 National Merit finalists and 45 semifinalists. 150 freshmen graduated first in their class.

Requirements: The SAT I or ACT is required. In addition, applicants must be graduates of an accredited secondary school. GED certificates may be accepted in unusual circumstances. Students must have completed 4 credits in English, 3 each in specific math, science, and social studies courses, 2 credits in a foreign language, 1/2 credit in computer skills, and 2 additional credits from the above categories or certain courses in the visual and performing arts. A GPA of 2.8 is required. AP and CLEP credits are accepted. Important factors in the admissions decision are advanced placement or honor courses, evidence of special talent, and recommendations by school officials.

Procedure: Freshmen are admitted to all sessions. Entrance exams should be taken in spring of the junior year or fall of the senior year. There is an early admissions plan. There is a rolling admissions plan. Applications should be filed by April 15 for fall entry, December 1 for spring entry, and April 15 for summer entry, along with a $40 fee. Notification is sent on a rolling basis. Applications are accepted on-line at www.lsu.edu.

Transfer: 939 transfer students enrolled in 2002-2003. Transfer students must submit an official transcript from each previously attended school. Requirements are 30 or more semester hours with a minimum 2.5 GPA, and a college level English and math course. 30 of 120 to 163 credits required for the bachelor's degree must be completed at LSU.

Visiting: There are regularly scheduled orientations for prospective students, including an information session and a tour of campus. Department appointments can be arranged. There are guides for informal visits and visitors may sit in on classes and stay overnight. To schedule a visit, contact the Office of Recruitment and Tours at (225) 578-6652 or pmhowar@lsu.edu.

Financial Aid: In 2002-2003, 95% of all full-time freshmen and 85% of all full-time students received some form of financial aid. 25% of full-time freshmen and 30% of all full-time students received need-based aid. The average freshman award was $5567. Need-based scholarships or need-based grants averaged $2781 ($4000 maximum); need-based self-help aid (loans and jobs) averaged $2332 ($3186 maximum); non-need-based athletic scholarships averaged $10,000 ($13,413 maximum); and other non-need-based awards and non-need-based scholarships averaged $4543 ($16,812 maximum). 26% of undergraduates work part time. Average annual earnings from campus work are $2120. The average financial indebtedness of the 2003 graduate was $17,818. The FAFSA is required. The deadline for filing freshman financial aid applications for fall entry is February 1.

International Students: There are 552 international students enrolled. The school actively recruits these students. They must score 550 on the written TOEFL or 213 on the electronic version and also take the SAT I or the ACT, scoring 20 (ACT) or 940 (SAT I).

Computers: The mainframes are an IBM 2066-002 and an IBM SP. Public labs contain more than 1000 networked PCs. LSU web portal is accessible to all students for registration, grades, and payment. All students may access the system up to 16 hours per day, 7 days per week (public facilities). All web-based resources are available 24 hours a day, 7 days per week. There are no time limits and no fees.

Graduates: From July 1, 2002 to June 30, 2003, 4429 bachelor's degrees were awarded. The most popular majors were general studies (7%), mass communication (6%), and psychology (5%). In an average class, 22% graduate in 4 years or less, 48% graduate in 5 years or less, and 56% graduate in 6 years or less. 513 companies recruited on campus in 2002-2003.

Admissions Contact: Cleve Brooks, Admissions Director. A video is available. E-mail: admissions@lsu.edu Web: www.lsu.edu

LOUISIANA STATE UNIVERSITY IN SHREVEPORT

A-1

Shreveport, LA 71115

(318) 797-5061

(800) 229-5957; Fax: (318) 797-5286

Full-time: 999 men, 1563 women
Part-time: 407 men, 686 women
Graduate: 217 men, 505 women
Year: semesters, summer session
Application Deadline: August 1
Freshman Class: 848 accepted, 579 enrolled
ACT: 20

Faculty: 127; IIA, --$
Ph.D.s: 73%
Student/Faculty: 20 to 1
Tuition: $2884 ($7214)
Room & Board: n/app

NONCOMPETITIVE

Louisiana State University in Shreveport, established in 1965, is a state-supported, primarily commuter institution offering undergraduate and graduate programs through the colleges of liberal arts, business, education, and sciences. There are 4 undergraduate and 4 graduate schools. In addition to regional accreditation, LSUS has baccalaureate program accreditation with AACSB, CSAB, and NCATE. The library contains 279,821 volumes, 364,744 microform items, and 1914 audio/video tapes/CDs, and subscribes to 2000 periodicals. Computerized library services include the card catalog, interlibrary loans, database searching, and Internet access. Special learning facilities include an art gallery, natural history museum, radio station, pioneer heritage center, and museum of life sciences. The 200-acre campus is in an urban area 7 miles south of downtown Shreveport. Including any residence halls, there are 18 buildings.

Student Life: 95% of undergraduates are from Louisiana. Students are from 28 states, 6 foreign countries, and Canada. 95% are from public schools. 65% are white; 21% African American. The average age of freshmen is 19; all undergraduates, 25. 47% do not continue beyond their first year; 23% remain to graduate.

Housing: 480 students can be accommodated in college housing, which includes single-sex and coed on-campus apartments and married-student housing. On-campus housing is available on a first-come, first-served basis. 94% of students commute. All students may keep cars.

Activities: 5% of men belong to 1 national fraternities; 3% of women belong to 3 national sororities. There are 40 groups on campus, including cheerleading, computers, dance, debate, drama, ethnic, film, forensics, honors, international, literary magazine, photography, political, professional, religious, social, social service, student activities board, student government, and yearbook. Popular campus events include Fall Fest, Spring Fling, and Welcome Back Bash.

Sports: There are 2 intercollegiate sports for men and 1 for women. Facilities include tennis and racquetball courts, sand or volleyball courts, a swimming pool, gym, weight room, dance studio, football fields, softball diamonds, and a soccer field.

Disabled Students: All of the campus is accessible. Wheelchair ramps, elevators, special parking, specially equipped rest rooms, special class scheduling, lowered drinking fountains, lowered telephones, special housing, and lowered computer terminals are available.

Services: Counseling and information services are available, as is tutoring in some subjects, including math and English. There is remedial math and writing.

Campus Safety and Security: Measures include 24-hour foot and vehicle patrol, self-defense education, security escort services, and informal discussions. There are emergency telephones, lighted pathways/sidewalks, and commissioned university police officers.

Programs of Study: LSUS confers B.A., B.S., B.C.J., B.G.S. degrees. Master's degrees are also awarded. Bachelor's degrees are awarded in BIOLOGICAL SCIENCE (biochemistry and biology/biological science), BUSINESS (accounting, banking and finance, business administration and management, business economics, management science, and marketing/retailing/merchandising), COMMUNICATIONS AND THE ARTS (communications, English, fine arts, French, journalism, Spanish, and speech/debate/rhetoric), COMPUTER AND PHYSICAL SCIENCE (chemistry, computer science, mathematics, and physics), EDUCATION (art, elementary, and secondary), ENGINEERING AND ENVIRONMENTAL DESIGN (environmental science), SOCIAL SCIENCE (economics, geography, history, liberal arts/general studies, political science/government, psychology, and sociology). Biochemical science and math are the strongest academically. Elementary education, psychology, and biology are the largest.

Required: All students must take a computer course. A minimum of 128 semester hours, with a minimum GPA of 2.0, is required for the bachelor's degree.

Special: Opportunities are provided for cross-registration with Southern University/Shreveport, internships, a Washington semester, a general studies degree, a 3-2 engineering degree with Louisiana Tech University, credit for military service schools, nondegree study, and pass/fail options. There are 5 national honor societies.

Faculty/Classroom: 63% of faculty are male; 37%, female. 80% teach undergraduates, 70% do research, and 70% do both. No introductory courses are taught by graduate students. The average class size in an introductory lecture is 30; in a laboratory, 18; and in a regular course, 19.

Admissions: The ACT scores for the 2003-2004 freshman class were: 51% below 21, 30% between 21 and 23, 14% between 24 and 26, 3% between 27 and 28, and 2% above 28.

Requirements: The ACT is required with a minimum composite score of 18. Graduation from an accredited secondary school is required. The GED will be accepted. Conditional admission is granted to those who do not meet minimum requirements. A GPA of 2.3 is required. AP and CLEP credits are accepted.

Procedure: Freshmen are admitted to all sessions. Entrance exams should be taken at least 2 months before the start of the current semester. There is a rolling admissions plan. Applications should be filed by August 1 for fall entry, December 1 for spring entry, and May 1 for summer entry, along with a $10 fee. Notification is sent on a rolling basis.

Transfer: Transfers must be in good academic standing, with a GPA of 2.0, or they may enter on probation. They must be eligible to continue at the last institution attended. 30 of 128 credits required for the bachelor's degree must be completed at LSUS.

Visiting: There are regularly scheduled orientations for prospective students, including a preview program during the spring semester for high school juniors and seniors. Students may stay overnight for this scheduled visit. There are guides for informal visits. To schedule a visit, contact O.L. Kelly, Lisa Branch, Alison White, or Andranell Watley at (318) 797-5061 or *admissions@pilot.lsus.edu.*

Financial Aid: In 2003-2004, 90% of all full-time freshmen and 80% of continuing full-time students received some form of financial aid. 65% of full-time freshmen and 60% of continuing full-time students received need-based aid. Need-based scholarships or need-based grants averaged $2100 ($4050 maximum); non-need based athletic scholarships averaged $2000 ($5000 maximum); and other non-need based awards and non-need based scholarships averaged $1000 ($3000 maximum). 90% of undergraduates work part time. Average annual earnings from campus work are $3200. The FAFSA is required. The deadline for filing freshman financial aid applications for fall entry is June 1.

International Students: There are 10 international students enrolled. They must score 500 on the written TOEFL and also take the SAT I or the ACT, scoring 18.

Computers: The mainframe is an IBM ES/9000 Model 120. PCs are available for academic use in student labs and faculty offices. PCs with Internet and Web access are located throughout the campus. All students may access the system. There are no time limits.

Admissions Contact: Kelli Stevens, Admission Counselor.
E-mail: *kstevens@pilot.lsus.edu* Web: *www.lsus.edu*

LOUISIANA TECH UNIVERSITY

B-3

Ruston, LA 71272

(318) 257-3036

(800) LATECH-1; Fax: (318) 257-2499

Full-time: 4220 men, 3722 women
Part-time: 801 men, 996 women
Graduate: 815 men, 1406 women
Year: quarters, summer session
Application Deadline: August 4
Freshman Class: 3768 applied, 3454 accepted, 2121 enrolled
SAT I: n/av

Faculty: 397; IIA, -$
Ph.D.s: 80%
Student/Faculty: 20 to 1
Tuition: $3551 ($7346)
Room & Board: $3810

ACT: required **COMPETITIVE**

Louisiana Tech University, founded in 1894, is a public institution offering programs in arts and sciences, business, agriculture, engineering, health science, education, fine and liberal arts, and human ecology. There are 5 undergraduate and 5 graduate schools. In addition to regional accreditation, Tech has baccalaureate program accreditation with AACSB, ABET, ADA, AHEA, ASLA, CAHEA, FIDER, NAAB, NASAD, NASM, NCATE, NLN, and SAF. The library contains 1,131,558 volumes, 2,140,172 microform items, and 511 audio/video tapes/CDs, and subscribes to 2932 periodicals. Computerized library services include the card catalog, interlibrary loans, and database searching. Special learning facilities include a learning resource center, art gallery, natural history museum, planetarium, and radio station. The 235-acre campus is in a small town 30 miles west of Monroe and 90 miles east of Shreveport. Including any residence halls, there are 146 buildings.

Student Life: 85% of undergraduates are from Louisiana. Students are from 48 states, 70 foreign countries, and Canada. 70% are white; 16% African American. 51% are Protestant; 12% Catholic. The average age of freshmen is 19; all undergraduates, 20. 22% do not continue beyond their first year; 49% remain to graduate.

Housing: 3067 students can be accommodated in college housing, which includes single-sex and coed dorms and married-student housing. In addition, there are honors houses. On-campus housing is guaranteed for all 4 years. 74% of students commute. Alcohol is not permitted. All students may keep cars.

Activities: 7% of men belong to 9 national fraternities; 11% of women belong to 5 national sororities. There are 121 groups on campus, including art, band, cheerleading, choir, chorale, chorus, computers, dance, debate, drama, drill team, drum and bugle corps, ethnic, film, honors, international, jazz band, marching band, musical theater, newspaper, opera, orchestra, pep band, photography, political, professional, radio and

TV, religious, social, social service, student government, symphony, and yearbook. Popular campus events include International Student Festival, Spring Fling, and Little Theater concerts.

Sports: There are 5 intercollegiate sports for men and 5 for women, and 10 intramural sports for men and 10 for women. Facilities include a football stadium, a coliseum, an intramural complex, a natatorium, a 9-hole golf course, and 10 lighted tennis courts.

Disabled Students: 95% of the campus is accessible. Wheelchair ramps, elevators, special parking, specially equipped rest rooms, lowered drinking fountains, and lowered telephones are available.

Services: Counseling and information services are available, as is tutoring in some subjects. There is a reader service for the blind and remedial math, reading, and writing.

Campus Safety and Security: Measures include 24-hour foot and vehicle patrol, self-defense education, security escort services, and informal discussions. There are emergency telephones and lighted pathways/sidewalks.

Programs of Study: Tech confers B.A., B.S., B. Arch., B.F.A., and B.G.S. degrees. Associate, master's, and doctoral degrees are also awarded. Bachelor's degrees are awarded in AGRICULTURE (agricultural business management, animal science, forestry and related sciences, and wildlife management), BIOLOGICAL SCIENCE (biology/biological science), BUSINESS (accounting, banking and finance, business administration and management, business economics, business systems analysis, management science, marketing/retailing/merchandising, and personnel management), COMMUNICATIONS AND THE ARTS (English, fine arts, French, journalism, music, music performance, Spanish, and speech/debate/rhetoric), COMPUTER AND PHYSICAL SCIENCE (chemistry, computer science, geology, mathematics, and physics), EDUCATION (art, early childhood, elementary, foreign languages, music, physical, secondary, and special), ENGINEERING AND ENVIRONMENTAL DESIGN (airline piloting and navigation, architecture, aviation administration/management, biomedical engineering, chemical engineering, civil engineering, construction engineering, electrical/electronics engineering technology, environmental science, industrial engineering, and mechanical engineering), HEALTH PROFESSIONS (medical laboratory technology, medical records administration/services, and speech pathology/audiology), SOCIAL SCIENCE (dietetics, geography, history, liberal arts/general studies, political science/government, psychology, and sociology). Business and engineering are the largest and the strongest academically.

Required: All students must complete 45 quarter hours of general education courses, including 12 hours in humanities, 9 each in natural and social sciences, 6 each in English and math, and 3 in arts or computer literacy. A total of 120 to 142 quarter hours, with a minimum GPA of 2.0, is required to graduate.

Special: Co-op programs are available in engineering and applied and natural sciences, and cross-registration with Grambling State University is offered. Internships in agriculture, engineering, dietetics, and human ecology are offered. Study abroad, work-study programs, dual majors, a general studies degree, nondegree study, and pass/fail options are available. There is a chapter of Phi Beta Kappa and a freshman honors program.

Faculty/Classroom: 65% of faculty are male; 35%, female. 95% teach undergraduates and 75% both teach and do research. Graduate students teach 2% of introductory courses. The average class size in an introductory lecture is 40; in a laboratory, 20; and in a regular course, 26.

Admissions: 92% of the 2003-2004 applicants were accepted. The ACT scores for the 2003-2004 freshman class were: 35% below 21, 31% between 21 and 23, 20% between 24 and 26, 8% between 27 and 28, and 6% above 28. There were 5 National Merit finalists.

Requirements: The ACT is required. In addition, applicants must be graduates of an accredited secondary school or have a GED. Tech requires applicants to be in the upper 35% of their class. A GPA of 2.3 is required. AP credits are accepted.

Procedure: Freshmen are admitted to all sessions. Applications should be filed by August 4 for fall entry, October 24 for winter entry, January 30 for spring entry, and May 9 for summer entry. There is a rolling admissions plan. Notification is sent on a rolling basis. The fall 2003 application fee was $20.

Transfer: 526 transfer students enrolled in 2002-2003. Transfer applicants should have a 2.0 GPA and be eligible to enroll in the school from which they are transferring. 30 of 120 credits required for the bachelor's degree must be completed at Tech.

Visiting: There are regularly scheduled orientations for prospective students. There are guides for informal visits and visitors may stay overnight. To schedule a visit, contact the Admissions Office.

Financial Aid: 27% of undergraduates work part time. The FAFSA is required. The deadline for filing freshman financial aid applications for fall entry is July 16.

International Students: There were 139 international students enrolled in a recent year. The school actively recruits these students. They must score 500 on the written TOEFL. A minimum 2.5 GPA is required.

Computers: The mainframe is an IBM 9121-210. Computer labs are located within each college, with PCs and terminals networked to the mainframe, as well as specialized local network workstations. There are also computer labs located in dorms in the central computing center, and in the library. All students may access the system 24 hours a day, 7 days a week. There are no time limits.

Graduates: From July 1, 2002 to June 30, 2003, 1401 bachelor's degrees were awarded. The most popular majors were business (22%), engineering (17%), and education (11%). In an average class, 29% graduate in 4 years or less, 49% graduate in 5 years or less, and 55% graduate in 6 years or less. 632 companies recruited on campus in 2002-2003.

Admissions Contact: Jan Albritton, Admissions Office. A video is available. E-mail: bulldog@latech.edu Web: http://www.latech.edu

---

LOYOLA UNIVERSITY NEW ORLEANS   D-4
New Orleans, LA 70118-6195   **(504) 865-3240**
     (800) 4-LOYOLA; Fax: (504) 865-3383

Full-time: 1260 men, 2023 women	Faculty: 238; IIA, +$
Part-time: 115 men, 251 women	Ph.D.s: 88%
Graduate: 239 men, 591 women	Student/Faculty: 14 to 1
Year: semesters, summer session	Tuition: $23,042
Application Deadline: February 15	Room & Board: $7994
Freshman Class: 3609 applied, 2485 accepted, 861 enrolled	
SAT I or ACT: required	VERY COMPETITIVE+

Loyola University New Orleans, founded in 1912, is a private institution operated by the Society of Jesus and affiliated with the Roman Catholic Church. There are 4 undergraduate schools and 1 graduate school. In addition to regional accreditation, Loyola has baccalaureate program accreditation with AACSB, ACS, NASM, and NLN. The 2 libraries contain 447,380 volumes, 671,775 microform items, and 14,872 audio/video tapes/CDs, and subscribe to 1339 periodicals. Computerized library services include the card catalog, interlibrary loans, database searching, and Internet access. Special learning facilities include a learning resource center, art gallery, TV station, theater, humanities lab with Perseus Project and TLG TV and radio production studios, multimedia classrooms, graphics lab, visual arts lab, ad club/communications lab, computer business lab, audio recording studio, and multimedia training center for nonprofit communication. The 20-acre campus is in an urban area 5 miles from downtown New Orleans. Including any residence halls, there are 24 buildings.

Student Life: 55% of undergraduates are from out of state, mostly the South. Students are from 50 states, 55 foreign countries, and Canada. 40% are from public schools. 66% are white; 11% Hispanic. Most are Catholic. The average age of freshmen is 18; all undergraduates, 20. 20% do not continue beyond their first year; 59% remain to graduate.

Housing: 1381 students can be accommodated in college housing, which includes single-sex and coed dorms and on-campus apartments. In addition, there are special-interest houses. On-campus housing is available on a first-come, first-served basis. Priority is given to out-of-town students. 60% of students commute. Upperclassmen may keep cars.

Activities: 17% of men belong to 2 local and 6 national fraternities; 18% of women belong to 6 national sororities. There are 140 groups on campus, including art, band, cheerleading, choir, chorale, chorus, computers, dance, drama, ethnic, film, gay, honors, international, jazz band, literary magazine, musical theater, newspaper, opera, orchestra, photography, political, professional, radio and TV, religious, social, social service, student government, symphony, and yearbook. Popular campus events include Loyolapalooza Spring Music Festival, Swamp Stomp, and Wolves on the Prowl Community Service Day.

Sports: There are 5 intercollegiate sports for men and 6 for women, and 20 intramural sports for men and 20 for women. Facilities include a sports complex with an arena, 6 multipurpose courts for basketball, tennis, volleyball, badminton, and floor hockey, 3 racquetball courts, an Olympic-style natatorium, a jogging track, and a weight-lifting and conditioning area.

Disabled Students: 99% of the campus is accessible. Wheelchair ramps, elevators, special parking, specially equipped rest rooms, lowered drinking fountains, lowered telephones, special housing, and special class relocation to provide accessibility are available.

Services: Counseling and information services are available, as is tutoring in most subjects. There is remedial math and writing. Peer tutoring is available in all introductory common curriculum courses. A reader service for the blind is provided for all exams and for course work if books on tape are not sufficient.

Campus Safety and Security: Measures include 24-hour foot and vehicle patrol, self-defense education, security escort services, and shuttle buses. There are informal discussions, pamphlets/posters/films, emergency telephones, lighted pathways/sidewalks, and CCTV coverage, card access control, intrusion alarm monitoring, first aid medical assistance, motor vehicle assistance, bicycle registration, finger printing services, and crime prevention services.

Programs of Study: Loyola confers B.A., B.S., B.Acc., B.A.S., B.B.A., B.C.J., B.F.A., B.L.S., B.Mus., B.Mus.Ed., B.Mus.Therapy, and B.S.N. degrees. Master's degrees are also awarded. Bachelor's degrees are awarded in BIOLOGICAL SCIENCE (biology/biological science), BUSINESS (accounting, banking and finance, business administration and management, international business management, management science, marketing/retailing/merchandising, and organizational behavior), COMMUNICATIONS AND THE ARTS (communications, communications technology, creative writing, dramatic arts, English, fine arts, French, German, graphic design, jazz, music business management, music performance, music theory and composition, piano/organ, Russian, Spanish, studio art, and visual and performing arts), COMPUTER AND PHYSICAL SCIENCE (chemistry, computer science, information sciences and systems, mathematics, and physics), EDUCATION (elementary and music), HEALTH PROFESSIONS (music therapy and nursing), SOCIAL SCIENCE (anthropology, classical/ancient civilization, criminal justice, economics, forensic studies, history, philosophy, political science/government, psychology, religion, religious education, social science, and sociology). Biology, chemistry, and English are the strongest academically. Communications, psychology, and biology are the largest.

Required: All students must complete a core curriculum that includes courses in English composition and literature, math, philosophy, science, world civilization, and religious studies; the number of credit hours varies by college. At least 120 credit hours, with at least 30 in the major, and a minimum GPA of 2.0 are required to graduate.

Special: Cross-registration is available with Xavier University, Notre Dame Seminary, the University of New Orleans, Tulane University, and Southern University of New Orleans. Internships with the New Orleans business community are also available. Study abroad in 7 countries, dual and student-designed majors, nondegree studies, and a general studies degree are offered. A Washington semester through American University and a 3-2 engineering degree with Tulane University are also offered. There are 24 national honor societies, a freshman honors program, and 9 departmental honors programs.

Faculty/Classroom: 58% of faculty are male; 42%, female. 89% teach undergraduates and 90% do research. No introductory courses are taught by graduate students. The average class size in an introductory lecture is 26; in a laboratory, 38; and in a regular course, 18.

Admissions: 69% of the 2003-2004 applicants were accepted. 48% of the current freshmen were in the top fifth of their class; 78% were in the top two fifths. 11 freshmen graduated first in their class in a recent year.

Requirements: The SAT I or ACT is required. In addition, candidates for admission must be graduates of an accredited secondary school or have a GED. They should have completed 4 units in high school English and 3 each in math, science, and social sciences, along with 4 academic electives; 2 units in a foreign language are recommended. A portfolio is required for fine arts students; an audition for music majors. An interview is recommended for scholarship consideration. AP and CLEP credits are accepted. Important factors in the admissions decision are advanced placement or honor courses, recommendations by school officials, and evidence of special talent.

Procedure: Freshmen are admitted to all sessions. Entrance exams should be taken during the junior or senior year. There is an early admissions plan. Applications should be filed by February 15 for fall entry and November 1 for spring entry, along with a $20 fee. Notification is sent on a rolling basis. Applications are accepted on computer disk and online through the university's web site or Next Step College, Common App, Catholic Common App, EXPAN, or CollegeLink.

Transfer: 140 transfer students enrolled in 2003-2004. Applicants must have a minimum 2.25 GPA on all attempted college-level work; 12 credit hours are needed for consideration. 30 of 120 credits required for the bachelor's degree must be completed at Loyola.

Visiting: There are regularly scheduled orientations for prospective students, including class and department visits, a student panel, a tour, a financial aid session, a campus support panel, meetings with faculty members, and an overnight stay. There are guides for informal visits and visitors may sit in on classes and stay overnight. To schedule a visit, contact the Admissions Office.

Financial Aid: In 2003-2004, 59% of all full-time freshmen and 55% of continuing full-time students received some form of financial aid. 59% of full-time freshmen and 54% of continuing full-time students received need-based aid. The average freshman award was $18,470. Need-based scholarships or need-based grants averaged $13,693; need-based self-help aid (loans and jobs) averaged $2952; and institutional non-need-based awards and non-need-based scholarships averaged $10,197. The average financial indebtedness of the 2003 graduate was $18,125. The FAFSA is required. The priority date for freshman financial aid applications for fall entry is February 15.

International Students: There are 141 international students enrolled. The school actively recruits these students. They must score 550 on the written TOEFL or 213 on the electronic version and also take the college's own test and the SAT I or the ACT.

Computers: The mainframes are an IBM SP/2, IBM ES/9000, a DEC VAX 3100-80, and 2 DEC Alpha 3000 Model 300s. Students may connect to the system via 2500 campuswide Internet ports, 48 modem lines, 75 public workstations, and Internet-ready residence hall rooms. All students may access the system at any time. There are no time limits. The

fee is a $125 technology fee. It is strongly recommended that all students have a personal computer. An IBM PC is recommended.

Graduates: From July 1, 2002 to June 30, 2003, 815 bachelor's degrees were awarded. The most popular majors were communications (14%), psychology (9%), and biology (5%). In an average class, 49% graduate in 4 years or less, 57% graduate in 5 years or less, and 59% graduate in 6 years or less. 298 companies recruited on campus in 2002-2003. Of the 2002 graduating class, 28% were enrolled in graduate school within 6 months of graduation and 51% were employed.

Admissions Contact: Deborah C. Stieffel, Dean of Admissions and Enrollment Management. A video is available.
E-mail: *admit@loyno.edu* Web: *www.loyno.edu*

MCNEESE STATE UNIVERSITY

Lake Charles, LA 70609-2495

B-4

(337) 475-5148
(800) 622-3352; Fax: (337) 475-5189

Full-time: 2400 men, 3300 women	**Faculty:** 262; IIA, --$
Part-time: 430 men, 720 women	**Ph.D.s:** 64%
Graduate: 280 men, 650 women	**Student/Faculty:** 22 to 1
Year: semesters, summer session	**Tuition:** $2792 ($8858)
Application Deadline: open	**Room & Board:** $4380
Freshman Class: n/av	**ACT:** required

LESS COMPETITIVE

McNeese State University, founded in 1939 and part of the University of Louisiana System, is a public institution offering programs in business, agriculture, engineering, education, film arts, science, liberal arts, and nursing. Some figures in the above capsule and in this profile are approximate. There are 6 undergraduate schools and 1 graduate school. In addition to regional accreditation, MSU has baccalaureate program accreditation with AACSB, AAFCS, ABET, ACS, ADA, CAHEA, CSAB, NAACLS, NASM, NCATE, and NLN. The library contains 546,183 volumes, 1,437,496 microform items, and 1382 audio/video tapes/CDs, and subscribes to 1808 periodicals. Computerized library services include the card catalog, interlibrary loans, and database searching. Special learning facilities include a learning resource center, art gallery, planetarium, a farm, a vertebrate museum, and a community health care clinic. The 580-acre campus is in a suburban area 120 miles west of Baton Rouge and 60 miles east of Beaumont, Texas. Including any residence halls, there are 95 buildings.

Student Life: 92% of undergraduates are from Louisiana. Students are from 33 states, 51 foreign countries, and Canada. 78% are white; 17% African American. The average age of freshmen is 22; all undergraduates, 24. 34% do not continue beyond their first year.

Housing: 850 students can be accommodated in college housing, which includes single-sex and coed dorms, on-campus apartments, and married-student housing. In addition, there are honors houses and a 12-month hall for out-of-state and international students who cannot go home. On-campus housing is guaranteed for all 4 years. 90% of students commute. Alcohol is not permitted. All students may keep cars.

Activities: 5% of men belong to 7 national fraternities; 5% of women belong to 6 national sororities. There are 93 groups on campus, including art, band, cheerleading, choir, chorale, chorus, computers, dance, debate, drama, drill team, ethnic, honors, international, jazz band, marching band, musical theater, newspaper, orchestra, pep band, political, professional, religious, social, social service, student government, symphony, and yearbook. Popular campus events include Spring Fling.

Sports: There are 7 intercollegiate sports for men and 9 for women, and 15 intramural sports for men and 15 for women. Facilities include a football stadium, softball and intramural fields, an indoor/outdoor track, a 50-meter pool, a coliseum, a baseball complex, outdoor tennis courts, an 8000-square-foot weight room, racquetball courts, and 3 regulation basketball courts.

Disabled Students: 94% of the campus is accessible. Wheelchair ramps, elevators, special parking, specially equipped rest rooms, lowered drinking fountains, academic planning and registration assistance, and classroom and testing accommodations are available.

Services: Counseling and information services are available, as is tutoring in some subjects, including English, math, chemistry, physics, and biology. There is remedial math, reading, and writing and a study skills course.

Campus Safety and Security: Measures include 24-hour foot and vehicle patrol, security escort services, informal discussions, and pamphlets/posters/films. There are lighted pathways/sidewalks, security guards posted at the residence halls from 11 P.M. until 7 A.M., and a crime stoppers program.

Programs of Study: MSU confers B.A., B.S., B.Mus., B.Mus.Ed., and B.S.N. degrees. Associate and master's degrees are also awarded. Bachelor's degrees are awarded in AGRICULTURE (agricultural business management, agriculture, animal science, and wildlife management), BIOLOGICAL SCIENCE (biology/biological science), BUSINESS (accounting, banking and finance, business administration and management, and marketing/retailing/merchandising), COMMUNICATIONS AND THE ARTS (broadcasting, communications, dramatic arts, English, fine arts, languages, music, speech/debate/rhetoric, and visual and performing arts), COMPUTER AND PHYSICAL SCIENCE (chemistry, computer science, geology, information sciences and systems, mathematics, physics, and radiological technology), EDUCATION (business, early childhood, elementary, foreign languages, guidance, health, home economics, science, and special), ENGINEERING AND ENVIRONMENTAL DESIGN (chemical engineering, civil engineering, electrical/electronics engineering, environmental science, and mechanical engineering), HEALTH PROFESSIONS (medical laboratory technology and nursing), SOCIAL SCIENCE (criminal justice, economics, family/consumer studies, history, liberal arts/general studies, psychology, and sociology). Education, nursing, and engineering are the largest.

Required: The general requirements for graduation include 9 hours each in the humanities and natural sciences, 6 each in English, math, and social sciences, 3 in arts and computer literacy, and 1 in orientation, for a total of 43 core hours. A total of 120 credit hours with a minimum GPA equivalent of C is needed.

Special: MSU offers co-op programs in engineering, internships in medical technology, radiologic technology, and education, dual majors, a general studies degree, nondegree study, and credit for military experience. There are 13 national honor societies and a freshman honors program.

Faculty/Classroom: 58% of faculty are male; 42%, female. 94% teach undergraduates and 11% both teach and do research. The average class size in an introductory lecture is 38; in a laboratory, 25; and in a regular course, 27.

Requirements: The ACT is required. In addition, applicants must have a high school GPA of at least 3.0 or an ACT score of at least 20 (SAT I, 940). AP and CLEP credits are accepted.

Procedure: Freshmen are admitted to all sessions. Entrance exams should be taken prior to enrolling. There is an early admissions plan. Application deadlines are open. Application fee is $20. Applications are accepted on-line.

Transfer: 355 transfer students enrolled in a recent year. Transferees must be eligible for readmission to the last collegiate institution attended. 30 of 120 credits required for the bachelor's degree must be completed at MSU.

Visiting: There are regularly scheduled orientations for prospective students. There are guides for informal visits and visitors may sit in on classes and stay overnight. To schedule a visit, contact the Enrollment Information Center at (377) 475-5504.

Financial Aid: The FAFSA or FFS and the college's own financial statement are required. Check with the school for current deadlines.

International Students: There were 78 international students enrolled in a recent year. The school actively recruits these students. They must score 525 on the written TOEFL or 195 on the electronic version and also take the SAT I or the ACT.

Computers: The mainframe is an IBM 9121-190. There are numerous Macs and PCs available in labs. The library houses terminals linked to MSU's computing services. The College of Science's academic computer center, the primary facility for computer science students, houses an IBM System/34, a PC lab, and terminals to access the mainframe as well as a VAX 3800-Utrix operating system. All students may access the system during lab operating hours. There are no time limits and no fees.

Graduates: In a recent year, 815 bachelor's degrees were awarded. The most popular majors were education (30%), business (19%), and nursing (6%). 33 companies recruited on campus in a recent year.

Admissions Contact: Director of Admissions.
E-mail: *admissions@mcneese.edu* Web: *www.mcneese.edu*

NICHOLLS STATE UNIVERSITY
Thibodaux, LA 70310

D-4

(504) 448-4507
(877) 642-4655; Fax: (504) 448-4929

Full-time: 2063 men, 3241 women	Faculty: 285
Part-time: 393 men, 827 women	Ph.D.s: 53%
Graduate: 186 men, 552 women	Student/Faculty: 19 to 1
Year: semesters, summer session	Tuition: $2993 ($8441)
Application Deadline: open	Room & Board: $3402
Freshman Class: 2472 applied, 2447 accepted, 1456 enrolled	
SAT I Verbal/Math: 482/483	ACT: 20 NONCOMPETITIVE

Nicholls State University, established in 1948, and part of the University of Louisiana System, is a public liberal arts institution offering instruction in health sciences, fine arts, business, teacher preparation, and agricultural and technical disciplines. There are 6 undergraduate and 4 graduate schools. In addition to regional accreditation, Nicholls has baccalaureate program accreditation with AACSB, AAFCS, ACEJMC, ADA, AHEA, CAAHEB, CSAB, IAME, NASM, NCATE, and NLN. The library contains 436,079 volumes, 340,970 microform items, and 3797 audio/video tapes/CDs, and subscribes to 1281 periodicals. Computerized library services include the card catalog, interlibrary loans, database searching, and Internet access. Special learning facilities include a learning resource center, art gallery, radio station, TV station, culinary institute, rural development institute, and centers for the study of dyslexia,

women and government, and economic education. The 210-acre campus is in a small town 50 miles southwest of New Orleans and 60 miles southeast of Baton Rouge. Including any residence halls, there are 47 buildings.

Student Life: 96% of undergraduates are from Louisiana. Students are from 30 states, 29 foreign countries, and Canada. 76% are white; 17% African American. 62% are claim no religious affiliation; 27% Catholic; 9% Protestant. The average age of freshmen is 19; all undergraduates, 23. 43% do not continue beyond their first year.

Housing: 1056 students can be accommodated in college housing, which includes single-sex and coed dorms and married-student housing. On-campus housing is guaranteed for the freshman year only and is available on a first-come, first-served basis. 85% of students commute. Alcohol is not permitted. All students may keep cars.

Activities: 5% of men belong to 8 national fraternities; 4% of women belong to 7 national sororities. There are 92 groups on campus, including art, band, cheerleading, chess, choir, chorale, chorus, computers, dance, debate, drama, drill team, ethnic, gay, honors, international, jazz band, literary magazine, marching band, musical theater, newspaper, pep band, photography, political, professional, radio and TV, religious, social, social service, student government, symphony, and yearbook. Popular campus events include Midterm Exam Week Breakfast, Family Day, and Crawfish Boil.

Sports: There are 7 intercollegiate sports for men and 8 for women, and 6 intramural sports for men and 4 for women. Facilities include a stadium, 2 gyms, tennis and raquetball courts, a soccer field, a swimming pool, baseball and softball fields, and a weight room.

Disabled Students: Wheelchair ramps, elevators, special parking, specially equipped rest rooms, special class scheduling, lowered drinking fountains, and lowered telephones are available.

Services: Counseling and information services are available, as is tutoring in most subjects. There is a reader service for the blind and remedial math and writing.

Campus Safety and Security: Measures include 24-hour foot and vehicle patrol, self-defense education, security escort services, and informal discussions. There are pamphlets/posters/films, emergency telephones, and lighted pathways/sidewalks.

Programs of Study: Nicholls confers B.A., B.S., B.G.S., B.M.E., and B.S.N. degrees. Associate and master's degrees are also awarded. Bachelor's degrees are awarded in AGRICULTURE (agricultural business management), BIOLOGICAL SCIENCE (biology/biological science), BUSINESS (accounting, banking and finance, business administration and management, marketing/retailing/merchandising, and personnel management), COMMUNICATIONS AND THE ARTS (art, communications, English, French, journalism, and music), COMPUTER AND PHYSICAL SCIENCE (chemistry, computer science, information sciences and systems, and mathematics), EDUCATION (business, elementary, music, secondary, and special), ENGINEERING AND ENVIRONMENTAL DESIGN (manufacturing technology and petroleum/natural gas engineering), HEALTH PROFESSIONS (health science, nursing, and speech pathology/audiology), SOCIAL SCIENCE (dietetics, family/consumer studies, food production/management/services, history, political science/government, psychology, and sociology). Language and literature, art, and economics and finance are the strongest academically. Teacher education, general studies, and nursing are the largest.

Required: All students must complete general education requirements, including 9 hours each in English, natural sciences, and humanities, 6 hours each in social sciences and math, 3 hours each in the arts, and student development, 2 semesters of health and phys ed, and a computer literacy course. At least 125 total credit hours, plus a minimum of 24 hours in the major, with a minimum GPA of 2.0, are required to graduate.

Special: Internships are offered in business areas, government, home economics, computer science, and psychology. A Washington semester congressional internship, dual majors in education, and student-designed majors in general studies are available. Nondegree study and credit for military experience are possible. There is a 7-on/7-off degree program for offshore oil field workers. There are 12 national honor societies, a freshman honors program, and 1 departmental honors program.

Faculty/Classroom: 55% of faculty are male; 45%, female. 98% teach undergraduates, 12% do research, and 12% do both. Graduate students teach 1% of introductory courses. The average class size in an introductory lecture is 38; in a laboratory, 17; and in a regular course, 29.

Admissions: 99% of the 2003-2004 applicants were accepted. The SAT I scores for the 2003-2004 freshman class were: Verbal--64% below 500, 24% between 500 and 599, and 12% between 600 and 700; Math--56% below 500, 41% between 500 and 599, and 3% between 600 and 700. The ACT scores were 62% below 21, 24% between 21 and 23, 10% between 24 and 26, 3% between 27 and 28, and 1% above 28. 28% of the current freshmen were in the top fifth of their class; 51% were in the top two fifths. 9 freshmen graduated first in their class.

Requirements: The ACT is recommended. In addition, applicants must be graduates of an accredited secondary school or have the GED. Institutional placement tests are given for English, math, and reading. Nicholls requires applicants to be in the upper 50% of their class. A GPA of 2.25 is required. AP and CLEP credits are accepted.

Procedure: Freshmen are admitted to all sessions. Entrance exams should be taken as early as possible. There is an early admissions plan and a rolling admissions plan. Application deadlines are open. The fall 2003 application fee was $20. Applications are accepted on-line.

Transfer: 348 transfer students enrolled in 2003. Transfer applicants must be eligible to return to the institution from which they are transferring. 31 of 125 credits required for the bachelor's degree must be completed at Nicholls.

Visiting: There are regularly scheduled orientations for prospective students. There are guides for informal visits and visitors may sit in on classes and stay overnight. To schedule a visit, contact Admissions Information.

Financial Aid: In 2003-2004, 83% of all full-time freshmen and 73% of continuing full-time students received some form of financial aid. 52% of full-time freshmen and 46% of continuing full-time students received need-based aid. The average freshman award was $4223. 9% of undergraduates work part time. Average annual earnings from campus work are $1234. The FAFSA or FFS is required. The deadline for filing freshman financial aid applications for fall entry is April 15.

International Students: In a recent year, there were 44 international students enrolled. The school actively recruits these students. They must score 500 on the written TOEFL or 173 on the electronic version.

Computers: The mainframe is an IBM 9221 Model 170. There are 290 Zenith, Dell, and Mac PCs (386 or above) available in 9 buildings. All students may access the system 24 hours a day. There are no time limits and no fees.

Graduates: From July 1, 2002 to June 30, 2003, 752 bachelor's degrees were awarded. The most popular majors were education (25%), general studies (9%), and nursing (6%). In an average class, 22% graduate in 6 years or less. 134 companies recruited on campus in 2002-2003.

Admissions Contact: Becky L. Durocher, Director of Admissions. E-mail: *esai-bl@nicholls.edu* Web: *www.nicholls.edu*

NORTHWESTERN STATE UNIVERSITY OF LOUISIANA B-2
Natchitoches, LA 71497

(318) 357-4503
(800) 327-1903; Fax: (318) 357-4257

Full-time: 2674 men, 4294 women	Faculty: n/av
Part-time: 540 men, 1843 women	Ph.D.s: 46%
Graduate: 245 men, 909 women	Student/Faculty: n/av
Year: semesters, summer session	Tuition: $3005 ($9083)
Application Deadline: open	Room & Board: $3326
Freshman Class: 4389 applied, 4313 accepted, 2173 enrolled	
SAT I Verbal/Math: 510/490	ACT: 19 NONCOMPETITIVE

Northwestern State University of Louisiana, founded in 1884, offers undergraduate programs in business, education, liberal arts, nursing, and science and technology. There are 7 undergraduate schools and 1 graduate school. In addition to regional accreditation, NSU has baccalaureate program accreditation with AACSB, AAFCS, ABET, ACEJMC, ACS, CACREP, CAHEA, CCNE, CSWE, JRCERT, NASAD, NASM, NCATE, and NLN. The library contains 356,121 volumes, 158,153 microform items, and 7116 audio/video tapes/CDs, and subscribes to 1725 periodicals. Computerized library services include the card catalog, interlibrary loans, database searching, and Internet access. Special learning facilities include an art gallery, natural history museum, radio station, TV station, and Cammie G. Henry Research Center. The 916-acre campus is in a small town in central Louisiana; 60 miles south of Shreveport. Including any residence halls, there are 94 buildings.

Student Life: 94% of undergraduates are from Louisiana. Students are from 40 states, 24 foreign countries, and Canada. 62% are white; 30% African American. The average age of freshmen is 20; all undergraduates, 26. 35% do not continue beyond their first year; 35% remain to graduate.

Housing: 2122 students can be accommodated in college housing, which includes single-sex and coed dorms, on-campus apartments, married-student housing, fraternity houses, and sorority houses. In addition, there are honors houses and CAPA has its own wing in a dorm for music practice. On-campus housing is available on a first-come, first-served basis. 76% of students commute. Alcohol is not permitted. All students may keep cars.

Activities: 12% of men belong to 10 national fraternities; 6% of women belong to 8 national sororities. There are 100 groups on campus, including art, band, cheerleading, chess, choir, chorale, chorus, computers, dance, debate, drama, drill team, ethnic, film, gay, honors, international, jazz band, literary magazine, marching band, musical theater, newspaper, orchestra, pep band, photography, political, professional, radio and TV, religious, social, social service, student government, symphony, and yearbook. Popular campus events include Spring Fling Weeks, Greek Week, and Welcome Week.

Sports: There are 6 intercollegiate sports for men and 7 for women, and 6 intramural sports for men and 6 for women. Facilities include a

16,000-seat football stadium, a 5000-seat indoor gym, sports training and basketball centers, a track, and a coliseum. The largest auditorium/arena seats 1500.

Disabled Students: 91% of the campus is accessible. Wheelchair ramps, elevators, special parking, specially equipped rest rooms, special class scheduling, lowered drinking fountains, and lowered telephones are available.

Services: Counseling and information services are available, as is tutoring in most subjects. There is remedial math, reading, and writing.

Campus Safety and Security: Measures include 24-hour foot and vehicle patrol, security escort services, shuttle buses, and pamphlets/posters/films. There are emergency telephones, lighted pathways/sidewalks, call telephones, and safety entrances.

Programs of Study: NSU confers B.A., B.S., B.G.S., B.M., B.M.Ed., B.S.N., and B.S.W. degrees. Associate and master's degrees are also awarded. Bachelor's degrees are awarded in BIOLOGICAL SCIENCE (biology/biological science), BUSINESS (accounting, business administration and management, and hospitality management services), COMMUNICATIONS AND THE ARTS (dramatic arts, English, fine arts, journalism, and music), COMPUTER AND PHYSICAL SCIENCE (chemistry, information sciences and systems, mathematics, and physics), EDUCATION (early childhood, elementary, health, middle school, music, secondary, and special), ENGINEERING AND ENVIRONMENTAL DESIGN (electrical/electronics engineering technology and industrial engineering technology), HEALTH PROFESSIONS (medical technology, nursing, and radiological science), SOCIAL SCIENCE (anthropology, criminal justice, family/consumer studies, history, liberal arts/general studies, political science/government, psychology, social science, social work, and sociology). Nursing, CAPA, and education are the strongest academically. Elementary education, nursing, and liberal arts/general studies are the largest.

Required: To graduate, all students must complete their senior year in residence, plus an approved curriculum, the university education requirement, and a minimum of 120 semester hours, with at least 30 semester hours in the major field. Distribution requirements include 12 credits each of communications and social sciences, 9 of natural sciences, 6 each of fine arts and math, and 4 of personal fitness. A minimum 2.0 GPA is needed for all hours taken at NSU.

Special: NSU offers cooperative programs with local businesses, internships, study abroad on 5 continents, and work-study programs. A general studies degree, credit for experience, nondegree study, and pass/fail options are available. There are 5 national honor societies, a freshman honors program, and 3 departmental honors programs.

Faculty/Classroom: 46% of faculty are male; 54%, female. 88% teach undergraduates. Graduate students teach 2% of introductory courses.

Admissions: 98% of the 2003-2004 applicants were accepted. The SAT I scores for the 2003-2004 freshman class were: Verbal--43% below 500, 38% between 500 and 599, 18% between 600 and 700, and 1% above 700; Math--52% below 500, 27% between 500 and 599, 20% between 600 and 700, and 1% above 700. The ACT scores were 63% below 21, 21% between 21 and 23, 11% between 24 and 26, 3% between 27 and 28, and 2% above 28.

Requirements: The ACT is required. In addition, applicants must be graduates of an accredited secondary school or have a GED certificate. Students must have completed 4 units of English, 3 units each of science and math, 2 units of social studies, 1 unit each of history and fine arts, and 1/2 unit of computer and foreign language. AP and CLEP credits are accepted.

Procedure: Freshmen are admitted to all sessions. Entrance exams should be taken before the semester begins. There is a deferred admissions plan. Application deadlines are open. There is a rolling admissions plan. Application fee is $20. Applications are accepted on-line through *www.collegenet.com*.

Transfer: 397 transfer students enrolled in 2002-2003. Transfer students must be eligible for readmission to their former university or college in order to enter NSU and submit college transcripts and a statement of good standing. 30 of 120 credits required for the bachelor's degree must be completed at NSU.

Visiting: There are regularly scheduled orientations for prospective students, consisting of a campus tour, with special focus on financial aid, housing and board, academic requirements and selecting a major, registration, campus organizations, and adapting to the college. There are guides for informal visits and visitors may sit in on classes. To schedule a visit, contact Director of University Recruiting at *admissions@nsula.edu*.

Financial Aid: 58% of full-time freshmen and 63% of continuing full-time students received need-based aid. Need-based scholarships or need-based grants averaged $2159; need-based self-help aid (loans and jobs) averaged $1350; non-need-based athletic scholarships averaged $2203; and other non-need-based awards and non-need-based scholarships averaged $1789. The average financial indebtedness of the 2003 graduate was $22,000. NSU is a member of CSS. The FAFSA and the college's own financial statement are required. The priority date for freshman financial aid applications for fall entry is May 1.

International Students: There are 42 international students enrolled. They must score 500 on the written TOEFL or 173 on the electronic version and also take the SAT I or the ACT.

Computers: The mainframes are a DEC VAX 11/785 and 11/750. PCs are available for academic use in the department of business administration, in the computer center, and in the department of math and physical sciences. Numerous labs are located throughout the campus for personal and school-related use. Students can also set up an e-mail account and create their own web page. All students may access the system at all times. There are no time limits and no fees.

Graduates: From July 1, 2002 to June 30, 2003, 1019 bachelor's degrees were awarded. The most popular majors were general studies/liberal arts (19%), business/marketing (17%), and nursing (16%). In an average class, 10% graduate in 4 years or less, 26% graduate in 5 years or less, and 35% graduate in 6 years or less.

Admissions Contact: Jana Lucky, Director of University Recruiting. E-mail: *admissions@nsula.edu*
Web: *http://www.nsula.edu/enrollmentservices/admissions*

OUR LADY OF HOLY CROSS COLLEGE   D-4
New Orleans, LA 70131-7399
(504) 394-7744
(800) 259-7744; Fax: (504) 391-2421

Full-time: 211 men, 655 women	**Faculty:** 20
Part-time: 81 men, 322 women	**Ph.D.s:** 70%
Graduate: 30 men, 134 women	**Student/Faculty:** 43 to 1
Year: semesters, summer session	**Tuition:** $5900
Application Deadline: July 20	**Room & Board:** n/app
Freshman Class: n/av	
ACT: required	**COMPETITIVE**

Our Lady of Holy Cross College, founded in 1916, is a private commuter college affiliated with the Roman Catholic Church. In addition to regional accreditation, OLHCC has baccalaureate program accreditation with NLN. The library contains 56,700 volumes, 136,015 microform items, and 13,598 audio/video tapes/CDs, and subscribes to 601 periodicals. Computerized library services include the card catalog, interlibrary loans, and database searching. The 40-acre campus is in an urban area in New Orleans. There are 2 buildings.

Student Life: 99% of undergraduates are from Louisiana. Students are from 4 states. 39% are from public schools. 74% are white; 15% African American. 74% are Catholic; 14% Protestant; 8% claim no religious affiliation. The average age of freshmen is 18; all undergraduates, 25. 10% do not continue beyond their first year; 70% remain to graduate.

Housing: There are no residence halls. All students commute. Alcohol is not permitted. All students may keep cars.

Activities: There are no fraternities or sororities. There are 13 groups on campus, including choir, chorus, computers, drama, ethnic, honors, international, literary magazine, professional, social, social service, student government, and yearbook. Popular campus events include Fall Fest, Crawfish Boil, and Christmas dances.

Sports: There are 5 intramural sports for men and 4 for women.

Disabled Students: All of the campus is accessible. Wheelchair ramps, elevators, special parking, specially equipped rest rooms, lowered drinking fountains, and lowered telephones are available.

Services: There is remedial math, reading, and writing.

Campus Safety and Security: Measures include self-defense education, security escort services, pamphlets/posters/films, and emergency telephones. There are lighted pathways/sidewalks and a foot patrol inside and outside of the building from 7:30 A.M. to 10 P.M.

Programs of Study: OLHCC confers B.A. and B.S. degrees. Associate and master's degrees are also awarded. Bachelor's degrees are awarded in BIOLOGICAL SCIENCE (biology/biological science), BUSINESS (accounting, business administration and management, and marketing and distribution), COMMUNICATIONS AND THE ARTS (English), EDUCATION (elementary and secondary), HEALTH PROFESSIONS (health science and nursing), SOCIAL SCIENCE (behavioral science, history, liberal arts/general studies, social psychology, and social science). Nursing is the strongest academically. Nursing, business, and education are the largest.

Required: A total of 128 credit hours, with 33 to 36 hours in the major, and a minimum GPA of 2.0 are required to graduate. All students must take courses in theology, philosophy, literature, English composition, math, natural sciences, library orientation, social sciences, speech, fine arts, and computer science.

Special: Co-op programs in business, internships with the Navy Civilian Personnel Office, study abroad in France, and credit for life, military, and work experience are offered.

Faculty/Classroom: 20% of faculty are male; 80%, female. 98% teach undergraduates and 2% do research. The average class size in an introductory lecture is 25; in a laboratory, 24; and in a regular course, 20.

Requirements: The ACT is required. The GED is accepted. A GPA of 2.0 is required. AP and CLEP credits are accepted. Important factors in the admissions decision are leadership record, recommendations by school officials, and recommendations by alumni.

Procedure: Freshmen are admitted to all sessions. Entrance exams should be taken a week before registration. Applications should be filed by July 20 for fall entry, December 20 for spring entry, and May 1 for summer entry. The fall 2003 application fee was $15.

Transfer: Transfer applicants must have an overall 2.0 GPA for unconditional admission. 30 of 128 credits required for the bachelor's degree must be completed at OLHCC.

Visiting: There are regularly scheduled orientations for prospective students. There are guides for informal visits and visitors may sit in on classes. To schedule a visit, contact the Office of Student Affairs and Admissions.

Financial Aid: 3% of undergraduates work part time. Average annual earnings from campus work are $1000. OLHCC is a member of CSS. The FAFSA and the college's own financial statement are required. The deadline for filing freshman financial aid applications for fall entry is April 15.

International Students: They must score 500 on the written TOEFL and also take the SAT I or the ACT.

Computers: There are 30 PCs available in a computer lab and 40 in the academic skills center. All students may access the system. There are no time limits and no fees.

Admissions Contact: Kristine H. Kopecky, Vice President for Student Affairs. A video is available. E-mail: *kkopecky@olhcc.edu*
Web: *www.olhcc.edu*

SOUTHEASTERN LOUISIANA UNIVERSITY   D-3
Hammond, LA 70402
(985) 549-2066
(800) 222-7358; Fax: (985) 549-5632

Full-time: 4512 men, 6908 women	**Faculty:** 456; IIA, --$
Part-time: 681 men, 1528 women	**Ph.D.s:** 57%
Graduate: 418 men, 1615 women	**Student/Faculty:** 25 to 1
Year: semesters, summer session	**Tuition:** $2951 ($8279)
Application Deadline: July 15	**Room & Board:** $3840
Freshman Class: 3488 applied, 3341 accepted, 2700 enrolled	
ACT: 20	**LESS COMPETITIVE**

Southeastern Louisiana University, founded in 1925, is a public university offering courses in liberal arts, fine arts, and professional studies. There are 5 undergraduate schools and 1 graduate school. In addition to regional accreditation, Southeastern has baccalaureate program accreditation with AACSB, ACS, CAAHEP, CSAB, CSWE, NAIT, NASM, NCATE, and NLN. The library contains 375,450 volumes, 780,495 microform items, and 48,979 audio/video tapes/CDs, and subscribes to 2375 periodicals. Computerized library services include the card catalog, interlibrary loans, database searching, and Internet access. Special learning facilities include a learning resource center, art gallery, radio station, and TV station. The 365-acre campus is in a small town 60 miles northwest of New Orleans and 50 miles east of Baton Rouge. Including any residence halls, there are 92 buildings.

Student Life: 97% of undergraduates are from Louisiana. Students are from 45 states, 55 foreign countries, and Canada. 81% are white; 15% African American. The average age of freshmen is 21; all undergraduates, 23. 33% do not continue beyond their first year; 67% remain to graduate.

Housing: 2000 students can be accommodated in college housing, which includes single-sex and coed dorms, on-campus apartments, fraternity houses, and sorority houses. In addition, there are honors houses and special-interest houses. On-campus housing is available on a first-come, first-served basis. Priority is given to out-of-town students. 89% of students commute. Alcohol is not permitted. All students may keep cars.

Activities: 4% of men belong to 7 national fraternities; 4% of women belong to 10 national sororities. There are 94 groups on campus, including art, band, cheerleading, chess, choir, chorale, chorus, computers, dance, debate, drama, drum and bugle corps, ethnic, gay, honors, international, jazz band, literary magazine, marching band, musical theater, newspaper, opera, orchestra, pep band, photography, political, professional, radio and TV, religious, social, social service, student government, symphony, and yearbook. Popular campus events include Fanfare (cultural events month).

Sports: There are 8 intercollegiate sports for men and 8 for women, and 30 intramural sports for men and 30 for women. Facilities include weight, fitness, and aerobics rooms, outdoor elevated track, basketball, volleyball, badminton, tennis, and racquetball courts, multipurpose fields, a pool, gym, a football stadium, and baseball and soccer fields.

Disabled Students: 90% of the campus is accessible. Wheelchair ramps, elevators, special parking, specially equipped rest rooms, special class scheduling, lowered drinking fountains, lowered telephones, and services for the mobility and learning impaired and those with physical disability are available.

Services: Counseling and information services are available, as is tutoring in some subjects, including math, writing, English, and science. There is remedial math, reading, and writing.

Campus Safety and Security: Measures include 24-hour foot and vehicle patrol, self-defense education, security escort services, and informal

discussions. There are pamphlets/posters/films, emergency telephones, lighted pathways/sidewalks, community policing, bicycle patrols, and video cameras.

Programs of Study: Southeastern confers B.A., B.S., B.G.S., B.M., and B.M.E. degrees. Associate and master's degrees are also awarded. Bachelor's degrees are awarded in AGRICULTURE (horticulture), BIOLOGICAL SCIENCE (biology/biological science), BUSINESS (accounting, banking and finance, business administration and management, and marketing/retailing/merchandising), COMMUNICATIONS AND THE ARTS (art, arts administration/management, communications, English, French, music, and Spanish), COMPUTER AND PHYSICAL SCIENCE (chemistry, computer science, mathematics, and physics), EDUCATION (art, elementary, English, foreign languages, mathematics, music, science, social studies, and special), ENGINEERING AND ENVIRONMENTAL DESIGN (industrial engineering technology), HEALTH PROFESSIONS (nursing and speech pathology/audiology), SOCIAL SCIENCE (criminal justice, family/consumer studies, history, liberal arts/general studies, political science/government, psychology, social work, and sociology). Teacher education, nursing, and biological sciences are the largest.

Required: To graduate, students must complete 125 credits in a core curriculum in English composition, literature, math, computer literacy, social, behavioral, and natural sciences, arts, history, and humanities and maintain a 2.0 GPA (2.5 in some majors).

Special: Southeastern offers a general studies degree, co-op programs, study abroad in Costa Rica, France, Germany, Honduras, England, Italy, and Austria, internships, nondegree study, and pass/fail options. Cross-registration is possible with Louisiana State and McNeese State Universities, and the University of Southwestern Louisiana. There are 4 national honor societies, a freshman honors program, and 23 departmental honors programs.

Faculty/Classroom: 43% of faculty are male; 57%, female. 94% teach undergraduates. Graduate students teach 1% of introductory courses. The average class size in an introductory lecture is 40; in a laboratory, 16; and in a regular course, 24.

Admissions: 96% of the 2003-2004 applicants were accepted. The ACT scores for the 2003-2004 freshman class were: 60% below 21, 27% between 21 and 23, 10% between 24 and 26, 2% between 27 and 28, and 1% above 28.

Requirements: The ACT is required. In addition, applicants should have an ACT score of 20 or rank in the uper 50% of their class or have a GPA of 2.0 in a core of courses including English, math, science, and social studies. AP and CLEP credits are accepted.

Procedure: Freshmen are admitted fall, spring, and summer. Entrance exams should be taken prior to registering for classes. There is a deferred admissions plan. There is a rolling admissions plan. Applications should be filed by July 15 for fall entry, December 1 for spring entry, and May 1 for summer entry, along with a $20 fee. Notification is sent on a rolling basis. Applications are accepted on-line through http://www.selu.edu/ProspectiveStudents.html.

Transfer: 773 transfer students enrolled in 2002-2003. Applicants with less than 12 hours must meet freshman entrance requirements. Those with more must have a GPA of 2.0. All must be eligible to attend the last institution. 30 of 125 credits required for the bachelor's degree must be completed at Southeastern.

Visiting: There are regularly scheduled orientations for prospective students, including a 2-day program of credit exams, academic advising, class registration, social programs, and session presentations. There are guides for informal visits and visitors may stay overnight. To schedule a visit, contact the Office of Admission and Financial Aid at admissions@selu.edu.

Financial Aid: In 2003-2004, 74% of all full-time freshmen and 70% of continuing full-time students received some form of financial aid. 47% of full-time freshmen and 48% of continuing full-time students received need-based aid. The average freshman award was $5388. Need-based scholarships or need-based grants averaged $3386 ($4650 maximum); need-based self-help aid (loans and jobs) averaged $3693 ($9825 maximum); non-need based athletic scholarships averaged $1934 ($3660 maximum); and non-need based awards and non-need based scholarships averaged $2712 ($10,884 maximum). 18% of undergraduates work part time. Average annual earnings from campus work are $1244. The average financial indebtedness of the 2003 graduate was $12,025. The FAFSA and the college's own financial statement are required. The deadline for filing freshman financial aid applications for fall entry is May 1.

International Students: There are 96 international students enrolled. They must score 500 on the written TOEFL or 173 on the electronic version and also take the ACT.

Computers: The mainframe consists of 4 IBM RS 6000s. There are PC and mainframe terminals for student use throughout the campus. All students may access the system. There are no time limits and no fees.

Graduates: From July 1, 2002 to June 30, 2003, 1979 bachelor's degrees were awarded. The most popular majors were elementary education (9%), management (8%), and nursing (7%). In an average class, 5%

graduate in 4 years or less, 15% graduate in 5 years or less, and 24% graduate in 6 years or less. 140 companies recruited on campus in 2002-2003.

Admissions Contact: Josie Mercante, Associate Director of Admissions. A video is available. E-mail: admissions@selu.edu
Web: http://www.selu.edu/ProspectiveStudents.html

SOUTHERN UNIVERSITY SYSTEM

The Southern University System, established in 1975, is a public system in Louisiana. It is governed by the Southern University Board of Supervisors and the Louisiana Board of Regents, whose chief administrator is the president. The primary goal of the system is teaching. The main priorities are teaching, public service, and research. The total enrollment of all 3 campuses is usually about 16,000; there were 2400 faculty and staff members. Altogether there are 152 degree programs ranging from certificates to doctorates. There is a 4-year campus located in Baton Rouge and New Orleans. Profiles of the 4-year campuses are included in this section.

SOUTHERN UNIVERSITY AND A&M COLLEGE   C-4
Baton Rouge, LA 70813   (504) 771-2430
                                    (800) 256-1531; Fax: (504) 772-2500

Full-time: 2790 men, 4198 women	**Faculty:** 424; IIA, --$
Part-time: 241 men, 342 women	**Ph.Ds:** 67%
Graduate: 331 men, 982 women	**Student/Faculty:** 16 to 1
Year: semesters, summer session	**Tuition:** $3066 ($8858)
Application Deadline: July 1	**Room & Board:** $4306
Freshman Class: 4265 applied, 2398 accepted, 1298 enrolled	
SAT I Verbal/Math: 425/415	**ACT:** 18 LESS COMPETITIVE

Southern University and A&M College, founded in 1880, is a publicly supported, nonsectarian, land-grant institution offering degree programs in agriculture, family and consumer science, arts and humanities, architecture, business, education, engineering, nursing, public policy and urban affairs, and sciences. There are 9 undergraduate schools and 1 graduate school. In addition to regional accreditation, Southern has baccalaureate program accreditation with AACSB, ABET, ACEJMC, ADA, AHEA, CSAB, CSWE, NAAB, NASM, NCATE, and NLN. The 2 libraries contain 517,711 volumes, 695,571 microform items, and 28,852 audio/video tapes/CDs, and subscribe to 1759 periodicals. Computerized library services include interlibrary loans and database searching. Special learning facilities include a learning resource center, art gallery, Black Heritage Collection, and museum of art. The 884-acre campus is in an urban area of Baton Rouge. Including any residence halls, there are 180 buildings.

Student Life: 83% of undergraduates are from Louisiana. Students are from 42 states, 45 foreign countries, and Canada. 96% are African American. The average age of freshmen is 18; all undergraduates, 22. 28% do not continue beyond their first year; 29% remain to graduate.

Housing: 2945 students can be accommodated in college housing, which includes single-sex dorms. 63% of students commute. Alcohol is not permitted. Upperclassmen may keep cars.

Activities: 2% of men belong to 5 national fraternities; 1% of women belong to 4 national sororities. There are 55 groups on campus, including art, band, cheerleading, chess, choir, chorale, computers, drama, ethnic, honors, international, jazz band, marching band, newspaper, political, professional, religious, social, student government, and yearbook. Popular campus events include Founder's Day and Bayou Classic football game at the New Orleans Super Dome.

Sports: There are 8 intercollegiate sports for men and 10 for women, and 7 intramural sports for men and 7 for women. Facilities include a center around the main activity complex, which accommodates theater, convocations, and athletic contests.

Disabled Students: All of the campus is accessible. Wheelchair ramps, elevators, special parking, specially equipped rest rooms, special class scheduling, and special housing are available.

Services: Counseling and information services are available, as is tutoring in every subject. There is a reader service for the blind, and remedial math, reading, and writing.

Campus Safety and Security: Measures include 24-hour foot and vehicle patrol, informal discussions, pamphlets/posters/films, and emergency telephones. There are lighted pathways/sidewalks.

Programs of Study: Southern confers B.A., B.S., B.Arch., B.Mus., B.Mus.Ed., and B.S.N. degrees. Associate, master's, and doctoral degrees are also awarded. Bachelor's degrees are awarded in AGRICULTURE (agricultural economics, agriculture, and forestry and related sciences), BIOLOGICAL SCIENCE (biology/biological science), BUSINESS (accounting, banking and finance, business administration and management, business economics, and marketing/retailing/merchandising), COMMUNICATIONS AND THE ARTS (communications, dramatic arts, English, fine arts, French, music, and Spanish), COMPUTER AND PHYSICAL SCIENCE (chemistry, computer science, mathematics, and physics), EDUCATION (early childhood, elementary, middle school, music, secondary, and special), ENGINEERING AND ENVIRONMENTAL DESIGN (architecture, civil engineering, electrical/electronics engineering, engineering technology, and mechanical engineering), HEALTH PROFESSIONS (nursing, recreation therapy, rehabilitation therapy, speech pathology/audiology, and speech therapy), SOCIAL SCIENCE (criminal justice, family/consumer studies, history, political science/government, psychology, social work, and sociology). Nursing, engineering and chemistry are the strongest academically. Nursing, business management, and biology are the largest.

Required: All students must pass a general competency exam measuring proficiency in communication, computation, logical thinking, and general knowledge. Courses in English composition and literature, math, natural sciences, arts, humanities, social sciences, health, and phys ed are required, as well as 60 hours of community service and 3 hours of African-American studies. All students also must take the GRE at the end of the junior year. To graduate, they must complete 124 semester hours (at least 31 in the major) with a minimum GPA of 2.0 overall and in the major.

Special: Cross-registration, nondegree study, credit for military experience, accelerated degrees, co-op education, study abroad, internships, work-study, and an exchange program and dual majors in chemistry/chemical engineering with Louisiana State University are available. There are 9 national honor societies, a freshman honors program, and 1 departmental honors program.

Faculty/Classroom: 52% of faculty are male; 48%, female. 95% teach undergraduates. No introductory courses are taught by graduate students. The average class size in a regular course is 30.

Admissions: 56% of the 2003-2004 applicants were accepted. The SAT I scores for the 2003-2004 freshman class were: Verbal--80% below 500, 15% between 500 and 599, and 5% between 600 and 700; Math--80% below 500, 15% between 500 and 599, and 5% between 600 and 700. The ACT scores were 86% below 21, 11% between 21 and 23, and 3% between 24 and 26. 23% of the current freshmen were in the top fifth of their class; 49% were in the top two fifths. 13 freshmen graduated first in their class.

Requirements: The SAT I or ACT is required. In addition, the school recommends that applicants have 15 Carnegie units, including 4 of English, 3 math, biology and 2 other sciences, American history or world history, and 2 other social sciences, 2 foreign languages, 1 computer science, 1 art, and an ACT of 17 or better, SAT I of 830 or better or 2.2 GPA based on 4.0. The GED is accepted. AP and CLEP credits are accepted.

Procedure: Freshmen are admitted to all sessions. Entrance exams should be taken in 11th grade. There is an early admissions plan. There is a rolling admissions plan. The application fee for fall 2003 was $5. Applications should be filed by July 1 for fall entry, December 1 for spring entry, and April 1 for summer entry. Notification is sent on a rolling basis.

Transfer: 225 transfer students enrolled in 2002-2003. Students having less than 24 hours must meet regular admission requirements. If a student has 24 or more hours they must have a 2.0 GPA based on 4.0 scale. All transcripts must be received within 30 days. 31 of 124 credits required for the bachelor's degree must be completed at Southern.

Visiting: There are regularly scheduled orientations for prospective students, consisting of summer and fall orientation programs. There are guides for informal visits. To schedule a visit, contact the Office of Admissions at velva_thomas@cxs.subr.edu.

Financial Aid: In 2003-2004, 76% of all full-time students received some form of financial aid. 75% of full-time freshmen and 76% of continuing full-time students received need-based aid. The average freshman award was $5725. Need-based self-help aid (loans and jobs) averaged $2625 (maximum); non-need based athletic scholarships averaged $3740 (maximum); and other non-need based awards and non-need based scholarships averaged $2625 (maximum). 12% of undergraduates work part time. Average annual earnings from campus work are $1050. The average financial indebtedness of the 2003 graduate was $17,000. The FAFSA is required. The deadline for filing freshman financial aid applications for fall entry is May 31.

International Students: There are 57 international students enrolled. The school actively recruits these students. They must score 500 on the written TOEFL and also take the SAT I or the ACT, scoring 830 (SAT I) or 17 (ACT)..

Computers: The mainframe is an IBM. Students have access to the Internet in departmental labs, the library, and the computer science labs. All students may access the system. There are no time limits and no fees.

Graduates: From July 1, 2002 to June 30, 2003, 907 bachelor's degrees were awarded. The most popular majors were therapeutic recreation and leisure studies (8%), mass communications (5%), and nursing (5%). In an average class, 6% graduate in 4 years or less, 19% graduate in 5 years or less, and 26% graduate in 6 years or less. 198 companies recruited on campus in 2002-2003. Of the 2002 graduating class, 15% were enrolled in graduate school within 6 months of graduation and 33% were employed.

Admissions Contact: Velva Thomas, Director of Admissions.
E-mail: *www.subr.edu/admissions/* Web: *www.subr.edu*

SOUTHERN UNIVERSITY AT NEW ORLEANS
D-4
New Orleans, LA 70126
(504) 286-5314

Total Enrollment: 3600 men and women	Faculty: n/av
	Ph.D.s: n/av
Year: semesters, summer session	Student/Faculty: n/av
Application Deadline: July 1	Tuition: $2114 ($5852)
	Room & Board: n/app
Freshman Class: n/av	ACT: required
	NONCOMPETITIVE

Southern University at New Orleans, established in 1956, is a public commuter institution offering programs in liberal arts and sciences, business, education, and the technologies. Figures given in the above capsule and in this profile are approximate. In addition to regional accreditation, SUNO has baccalaureate program accreditation with CSWE. The library contains 300,000 volumes. The 22-acre campus is in a suburban area. There are 10 buildings.

Programs of Study: Bachelor's degrees are awarded in BIOLOGICAL SCIENCE (biology/biological science), BUSINESS (accounting, business administration and management, secretarial studies/office management, and transportation management), COMMUNICATIONS AND THE ARTS (English, fine arts, journalism, Spanish, and speech/debate/rhetoric), COMPUTER AND PHYSICAL SCIENCE (chemistry, computer science, mathematics, and physics), EDUCATION (art, business, education of the deaf and hearing impaired, elementary, English, foreign languages, mathematics, music, physical, recreation, science, secondary, and social studies), ENGINEERING AND ENVIRONMENTAL DESIGN (technological management), HEALTH PROFESSIONS (health care administration), SOCIAL SCIENCE (addiction studies, criminal justice, economics, history, political science/government, psychology, social work, and sociology).

Requirements: The ACT is required. The GED is accepted.

Procedure: Applications should be filed by July 1 for fall entry, December 1 for spring entry, and May 1 for summer entry, along with a $5 fee. Notification is sent on a rolling basis.

Financial Aid: The FAFSA and the SAR are required. The priority deadline for filing freshman financial aid applications for fall entry is April 15.

International Students: They must score 500 on the written TOEFL.

Computers: All students may access the system. There are no time limits and no fees.

Admissions Contact: Director of Admissions and Registrar. Web: *www.suno.edu*

TULANE UNIVERSITY
D-4
New Orleans, LA 70118
(504) 865-5731
(800) 873-9283; Fax: (504) 862-8715

Full-time: 2961 men, 3028 women	Faculty: I, av$
Part-time: 762 men, 1111 women	Ph.D.s: 90%
Graduate: 1407 men, 1518 women	Student/Faculty: n/av
Year: semesters, summer session	Tuition: $29,810
Application Deadline: January 15	Room & Board: $7641
Freshman Class: 14,111 applied, 7801 accepted, 1684 enrolled	
SAT I Verbal/Math: 659/644	**HIGHLY COMPETITIVE+**

Tulane University, founded in 1834, is a private institution offering degree programs in liberal arts and sciences, business, architecture, and engineering. There are 6 undergraduate and 8 graduate schools. In addition to regional accreditation, Tulane has baccalaureate program accreditation with AACSB, ABET, ACS, CSAB, CSWE, and NAAB. The 9 libraries contain 2,285,029 volumes, 2,534,540 microform items, and 92,904 audio/video tapes/CDs, and subscribe to 14,998 periodicals. Computerized library services include the card catalog, interlibrary loans, and database searching. Special learning facilities include a learning resource center, art gallery, natural history museum, radio station, TV station, an observatory, and a herbarium. The 110-acre campus is in an urban area in uptown New Orleans. Including any residence halls, there are 70 buildings.

Student Life: 62% of undergraduates are from out of state, mostly the Northeast. Students are from 50 states, 100 foreign countries, and Canada. 50% are from public schools. 78% are white; 10% African American. The average age of freshmen is 18; all undergraduates, 20. 13% do not continue beyond their first year; 87% remain to graduate.

Housing: College housing includes single-sex and coed dorms, on-campus apartments, and married-student housing. In addition, there are honors houses and special-interest floors. On-campus housing is guaranteed for the freshman year only and is available on a lottery system for upperclassmen. 60% of students live on campus; of those, 95% remain on campus on weekends. Upperclassmen may keep cars.

Activities: 33% of men belong to 14 national fraternities; 37% of women belong to 9 national sororities. There are 250 groups on campus, including art, band, cheerleading, chess, choir, chorale, chorus, computers, dance, drama, drill team, ethnic, film, gay, honors, international, jazz band, literary magazine, marching band, musical theater, newspaper, opera, orchestra, pep band, photography, political, professional, radio and TV, religious, social, social service, student government, symphony, and yearbook. Popular campus events include Newcomb College Spring Arts Week, International Festival, and Student Activities Expo.

Sports: There are 8 intercollegiate sports for men and 8 for women, and 30 intramural sports for men and 30 for women. Facilities include a baseball diamond, a track complex, a tennis facility, and a recreation center with indoor and outdoor pools, an indoor track, squash and racquetball courts, a gymnastics area, a weight room, and exercise rooms and equipment.

Disabled Students: 60% of the campus is accessible. Wheelchair ramps, elevators, special parking, specially equipped rest rooms, lowered drinking fountains, lowered telephones, and special housing are available.

Services: Counseling and information services are available, as is tutoring in some subjects, including high-demand math and science classes and some languages.

Campus Safety and Security: Measures include 24-hour foot and vehicle patrol, self-defense education, security escort services, and shuttle buses. There are informal discussions, pamphlets/posters/films, emergency telephones, lighted pathways/sidewalks, bike patrols, limited dorm access, smoke detectors, surveillance cameras, trained student patrols, and programs about living safely off campus. Victim resources include academic assistance, legal counseling, emergency housing, and security review of home and personal security habits.

Programs of Study: Tulane confers B.A., B.S., B. Arch., B.B.S., B.F.A., B.G.S., B.S.C., B.S.E., and B.S.M. degrees. Associate, master's, and doctoral degrees are also awarded. Bachelor's degrees are awarded in BIOLOGICAL SCIENCE (biochemistry, cell biology, ecology, and evolutionary biology), BUSINESS (accounting, business administration and management, management science, and marketing management), COMMUNICATIONS AND THE ARTS (art history and appreciation, classics, communications, dance, English, French, German, Italian, linguistics, media arts, music, Portuguese, Russian, Spanish, and studio art), COMPUTER AND PHYSICAL SCIENCE (chemistry, computer science, earth science, geology, information sciences and systems, mathematics, and physics), ENGINEERING AND ENVIRONMENTAL DESIGN (architecture, biomedical engineering, chemical engineering, civil engineering, computer engineering, electrical/electronics engineering, engineering, environmental engineering, environmental science, and mechanical engineering), HEALTH PROFESSIONS (exercise science), SOCIAL SCIENCE (African studies, American studies, anthropology, Asian/Oriental studies, cognitive science, economics, history, Judaic studies, Latin American studies, medieval studies, philosophy, political science/government, psychology, religion, Russian and Slavic studies, sociology, and women's studies). Environmental sciences, political economy, and preprofessional programs are the strongest academically. Business, social sciences, and engineering are the largest.

Required: All students in the liberal arts and sciences must meet proficiency requirements in English, foreign language, and math. They must take a distribution component including courses in humanities and fine arts, social sciences, and sciences and math. A total of 120 credits, including at least 24 in the major, with a minimum cumulative GPA of 2.0, is required to graduate.

Special: Students may pursue cross-registration with Loyola and Xavier Universities, numerous internships, study abroad in 23 countries, work-study programs, a Washington semester, and B.A.-B.S. degrees in liberal arts, engineering, and architecture. Tulane also offers accelerated joint degrees with its schools of medicine, law, business, and public health; student-designed, dual, and interdisciplinary majors, including art and biology, Greek and Latin, mathematical economics, political economy, and cognitive studies; a 3-2 engineering degree with Xavier University of Louisiana, joint graduate/professional programs, and 4+1 programs. There are 32 national honor societies, including Phi Beta Kappa, and a freshman honors program.

Faculty/Classroom: 69% of faculty are male; 31%, female. All both teach and do research. The average class size in an introductory lecture is 30; in a laboratory, 20; and in a regular course, 25.

Admissions: 55% of the 2003-2004 applicants were accepted. The SAT I scores for the 2003-2004 freshman class were: Verbal--3% below 500, 13% between 500 and 599, 52% between 600 and 700, and 32% above 700; Math--2% below 500, 19% between 500 and 599, 54% between 600 and 700, and 25% above 700. 78% of the current freshmen were in the top fifth of their class; 96% were in the top two fifths.

Requirements: The SAT I or ACT is required. In addition, applicants must be graduates of an accredited secondary school or have a GED certificate. It is recommended that students have completed 4 years each of high school English and math, and 3 each of foreign language, social studies, and the sciences. SAT II: Subject tests in writing, math, and foreign language are recommended for placement purposes and are required for home-schooled applicants. An essay is required. A portfolio is recommended for architecture applicants only. AP credits are accepted.

Important factors in the admissions decision are advanced placement or honor courses, recommendations by school officials, and extracurricular activities record.

Procedure: Freshmen are admitted fall and spring. Entrance exams should be taken during the spring of the junior year or the fall of the senior year. There are early decision, early admissions, and deferred admissions plans. Early decision applications should be filed by November 1; regular applications, by January 15 for fall entry and November 1 for spring entry, along with a $55 fee. Notification of early decision is sent December 15; regular decision, by April 1. 98 early decision candidates were accepted for the 2003-2004 class. 485 applicants were on the 2003 waiting list; 6 were admitted. Applications are accepted on-line through Embark, Apply, or CommonApp.

Transfer: 145 transfer students enrolled in 2002-2003. Applicants must submit SAT I or ACT scores, high school transcripts, proof of good standing at previously attended institutions, and transcripts (with course descriptions) from all colleges or universities attended. A minimum 3.0 GPA is recommended. 60 of 120 credits required for the bachelor's degree must be completed at Tulane.

Visiting: There are regularly scheduled orientations for prospective students, including 3 on-campus Saturday programs in the fall, daily information sessions, and tours Monday through Friday and Saturday mornings during the academic year. Also, selected classes are open to visitors. In the spring semester, more structured programs are available daily. There are guides for informal visits and visitors may sit in on classes and stay overnight. To schedule a visit, contact the Office of Undergraduate Admission at *undergrad.admission@tulane.edu.*

Financial Aid: In 2003-2004, 75% of all full-time freshmen received some form of financial aid. 46% of full-time freshmen and 30% of continuing full-time students received need-based aid. The average freshman award was $19,473. 26% of undergraduates work part time. Average annual earnings from campus work are $1090. The average financial indebtedness of the 2003 graduate was $20,983. Tulane is a member of CSS. The CSS Profile or FAFSA is required. In addition, the Noncustodial Parents Statement and the Business/Farm Supplement as applicable are required. The deadline for filing freshman financial aid applications for fall entry is December 15.

International Students: There are 209 international students enrolled. The school actively recruits these students. They must score 550 on the TOEFL and also take the SAT I or the ACT.

Computers: The mainframe is a cluster of 8 IBM RS/6000s. There are 22 computer labs on campus housing more than 250 workstations, all are connected to the university network. Access to the mainframe is possible from any terminal PC/workstation and from residence hall rooms if students have their own PCs. The university network extends to all campus buildings. All students may access the system 24 hours a day. There are no time limits and no fees. It is strongly recommended that all students have a personal computer.

Graduates: From July 1, 2002 to June 30, 2003, 1504 bachelor's degrees were awarded. The most popular majors were business (21%), social sciences (17%), and engineering (9%). 134 companies recruited on campus in 2002-2003.

Admissions Contact: Richard Whiteside, VP for Enrollment Management. A video is available. E-mail: *undergrad.admission@tulane.edu* Web: *www.tulane.edu*

UNIVERSITY OF LOUISIANA AT LAFAYETTE C-4
Lafayette, LA 70504 (337) 482-6473; Fax: (337) 482-6195

Full-time: 5287 men, 6738 women	Faculty: 666; I, --$
Part-time: 919 men, 1641 women	Ph.D.s: 79%
Graduate: 697 men, 926 women	Student/Faculty: 18 to 1
Year: semesters, summer session	Tuition: $2700 ($8960)
Application Deadline: open	Room & Board: $3126
Freshman Class: 4842 applied, 4224 accepted, 2794 enrolled	
ACT: 21	COMPETITIVE

The University of Louisiana at Lafayette, founded in 1898, is a public institution offering degree programs in liberal arts, fine arts, business, agriculture, technical disciplines, health science, engineering, and teacher preparation. There are 9 undergraduate schools and 1 graduate school. In addition to regional accreditation, UL Lafayette has baccalaureate program accreditation with AACSB, ABET, ACEJMC, ADA, AHEA, ASLA, CAHEA, CSAB, FIDER, NAAB, NASM, NCATE, and NLN. The library contains 873,173 volumes, 1,768,368 microform items, and 255,992 audio/video tapes/CDs, and subscribes to 4965 periodicals. Computerized library services include the card catalog, interlibrary loans, and database searching. Special learning facilities include a learning resource center, art gallery, radio station, and numerous research centers for environmental, business, science, computer, and business studies. The 1375-acre campus is in an urban area 129 miles west of New Orleans. Including any residence halls, there are 239 buildings.

Student Life: 95% of undergraduates are from Louisiana. Students are from 48 states, 102 foreign countries, and Canada. 74% are white; 17% African American. 50% are Catholic; 31% claim no religious affiliation;

12% Protestant. The average age of freshmen is 19; all undergraduates, 24. 28% do not continue beyond their first year; 30% remain to graduate.

Housing: 1860 students can be accommodated in college housing, which includes single-sex dormitories, on-campus apartments, and married-student housing. In addition, there are residence halls for athletes and for Pan-Hellenic groups. On-campus housing is guaranteed for all 4 years. 89% of students commute. All students may keep cars.

Activities: 3% of men and about 3% of women belong to 14 national fraternities; 5% of women belong to 8 national sororities. There are 200 groups on campus, including band, cheerleading, choir, chorus, computers, dance, debate, drama, drum and bugle corps, ethnic, forensics, gay, honors, international, jazz band, marching band, musical theater, newspaper, opera, orchestra, photography, political, professional, radio and TV, religious, social, social service, student government, and yearbook. Popular campus events include Rajun Roar, Black Expo Week, and Entertainment Week.

Sports: There are 8 intercollegiate sports for men and 7 for women, and 16 intramural sports for men and 16 for women. Facilities include a 31,000-seat stadium, a 12,000-seat basketball arena, a gym, a track, a softball park, tennis courts, various playing fields, and a health and phys ed complex.

Disabled Students: 90% of the campus is accessible. Wheelchair ramps, elevators, special parking, specially equipped rest rooms, special class scheduling, TDDs, and an adaptive computer lab with voice synthesizer, visual-tech, and brailler are available.

Services: Counseling and information services are available, as is tutoring in most subjects. There is remedial math, reading, and writing. An entering freshman can be in only 1 remedial course.

Campus Safety and Security: Measures include 24-hour foot and vehicle patrol, security escort services, shuttle buses, and informal discussions. There are pamphlets/posters/films, emergency telephones, and lighted pathways/sidewalks.

Programs of Study: UL Lafayette confers B.A., B.S., B.A.M., B.F.A., B.G.S., B.M.E., B.M.P., B.M.P.P., B.S.A., B.S.A.E., B.S.B.A., B.S.C.E., B.S.C.I.E., B.S.E.E., B.S.I.T., B.S.M.E., B.S.N., and B.S.P.E. degrees. Master's and doctoral degrees are also awarded. Bachelor's degrees are awarded in BUSINESS (accounting, banking and finance, business administration and management, fashion merchandising, hotel/motel and restaurant management, management science, marketing/retailing/merchandising, and personnel management), COMMUNICATIONS AND THE ARTS (advertising, broadcasting, communications, dance, dramatic arts, English, fine arts, French, music, public relations, Spanish, and telecommunications), COMPUTER AND PHYSICAL SCIENCE (chemistry, computer science, geology, mathematics, physics, and statistics), EDUCATION (agricultural, art, elementary, English, foreign languages, health, home economics, industrial arts, mathematics, music, science, secondary, social studies, and special), ENGINEERING AND ENVIRONMENTAL DESIGN (chemical engineering, civil engineering, computer engineering, electrical/electronics engineering, industrial engineering, interior design, land use management and reclamation, mechanical engineering, and petroleum/natural gas engineering), HEALTH PROFESSIONS (nursing and speech pathology/audiology), SOCIAL SCIENCE (anthropology, criminal justice, dietetics, economics, history, philosophy, political science/government, psychology, and sociology). Computer science, engineering, and math/statistics/physical sciences are the strongest academically. Nursing, elementary education, and business administration are the largest.

Required: Students are required to complete 42 semester hours of general education courses in the arts, literature, history, math, sciences, behavioral sciences, and composition. Phys ed is required in all but engineering and nursing programs. A minimum of 124 semester hours, with at least 33 in the major, is required for graduation. A minimum GPA of 2.0 is needed; some majors require higher GPAs.

Special: Various internships are available, including a Washington semester. Students may study in France, Canada, Belgium, Japan, and Mexico. UL Lafayette also offers an accelerated degree program in nursing, B.A.-B.S. degrees, and dual majors. There are 6 national honor societies and a freshman honors program.

Faculty/Classroom: 59% of faculty are male; 41%, female.

Admissions: 87% of the 2003-2004 applicants were accepted. The ACT scores for the 2003-2004 freshman class were: 50% below 21, 28% between 21 and 23, 14% between 24 and 26, 5% between 27 and 28, and 3% above 28.

Requirements: The SAT I or ACT is required. Admissions criteria are based on a sliding scale of standardized test scores and GPA. Students should be graduates of accredited secondary schools or have the GED. UL Lafayette requires that students have at least 4 units in English, 3 each in math, science, and social studies, and 4 1/2 in electives, recommended to include 2 in foreign language, 1 each in fine arts and speech, and 1/2 in computer studies. A GPA of 2.0 is required. AP and CLEP credits are accepted.

Procedure: Freshmen are admitted to all sessions. There are early admissions and deferred admissions plans. Application deadlines are open. Application fee is $20. Notification is sent on a rolling basis.

Transfer: 740 transfer students enrolled in 2002-2003. A cumulative GPA of 2.0 is required. 30 of 124 credits required for the bachelor's degree must be completed at UL Lafayette.

Visiting: There are regularly scheduled orientations for prospective students, including campus tours. There are guides for informal visits. To schedule a visit, contact the Secretary of High School Relations at (337) 482-6553 or enroll@louisiana.edu.

Financial Aid: 30% of undergraduates work part time. Average annual earnings from campus work are $1250. UL Lafayette is a member of CSS. The FAFSA is required. The deadline for filing freshman financial aid applications for fall entry is March 1.

International Students: There are 259 international students enrolled. The school actively recruits these students. They must score 450 on the written TOEFL or 133 on the electronic version and also take the SAT I or the ACT, scoring 18 on the ACT. Students must take SAT II: Subject tests in math and English.

Computers: The mainframes are an IBM 9672 and 3 Sun 4/490 servers. About 450 terminals and Sun workstations are located in public terminal rooms and dorms. The Sun facility provides e-mail and various network services. All students may access the system any time. There are no time limits and no fees.

Graduates: From July 1, 2002 to June 30, 2003, 2025 bachelor's degrees were awarded. The most popular majors were business (20%), general studies (14%), and education (14%). In an average class, 7% graduate in 4 years or less, 21% graduate in 5 years or less, and 29% graduate in 6 years or less. 114 companies recruited on campus in 2002-2003.

Admissions Contact: Leroy Broussard, Director of Admissions. A video is available. E-mail: admissions@louisiana.edu Web: www.louisiana.edu

UNIVERSITY OF LOUISIANA AT MONROE
Monroe, LA 71209

C-1
(318) 362-4661
(800) 372-5127; Fax: (318) 342-1049

Total Enrollment: 7,922 men and women	**Faculty:** 467; IIA, --$
	Ph.D.s: 50%
Year: semesters, summer session	**Student/Faculty:** 16 to 1
Application Deadline: open	**Tuition:** $2988 ($8940)
	Room & Board: $2900
Freshman Class: n/av	**ACT:** required
	NONCOMPETITIVE

The University of Louisiana at Monroe, founded in 1931, is a public institution offering programs in business, education, liberal arts, pharmacy and health sciences, and pure and applied science. Some figures in the above capsule and in this profile are approximate. There are 5 undergraduate schools and 1 graduate school. In addition to regional accreditation, ULM has baccalaureate program accreditation with AACSB, ACCE, ACEJMC, ACPE, ADA, AHEA, ASLA, CAHEA, CSAB, CSWE, NASM, NCATE, and NLN. The library contains 605,064 volumes, 550,963 microform items, and 49 audio/video tapes/CDs, and subscribes to 2912 periodicals. Computerized library services include the card catalog, interlibrary loans, and database searching. Special learning facilities include a learning resource center, art gallery, planetarium, radio station, herbarium, state poison control center, and state tumor registry. The 238-acre campus is in an urban area 90 miles east of Shreveport on I-20. Including any residence halls, there are 75 buildings.

Student Life: 93% of undergraduates are from Louisiana. Students are from 42 states, 54 foreign countries, and Canada. 77% are from public schools. 69% are white; 26% African American. The average age of freshmen is 18; all undergraduates, 23. 37% do not continue beyond their first year; 25% remain to graduate.

Housing: 3685 students can be accommodated in college housing, which includes single-sex and coed dorms and a scholastic residence hall. On-campus housing is available on a first-come, first-served basis. 74% of students commute. Alcohol is not permitted. All students may keep cars.

Activities: 3% of men belong to 7 national fraternities; 2% of women belong to 8 national sororities. There are 126 groups on campus, including art, band, cheerleading, choir, chorale, chorus, computers, dance, drama, drill team, ethnic, film, gay, honors, international, jazz band, literary magazine, marching band, musical theater, newspaper, opera, orchestra, pep band, photography, political, professional, radio and TV, religious, social, social service, student government, symphony, and yearbook. Popular campus events include Honors Day Assembly, "Miss Northeast" Pageant, and Spring Fever.

Sports: There are 9 intercollegiate sports for men and 9 for women, and 44 intramural sports for men and 31 for women. Facilities include 2 stadiums, a natatorium, a coliseum, tennis courts, a softball complex, an activity center, a baseball complex, an archery range, bowling lanes, and a bayou.

Disabled Students: 98% of the campus is accessible. Wheelchair ramps, elevators, special parking, specially equipped rest rooms, special

class scheduling, lowered drinking fountains, and specially equipped dorm rooms are available.

Services: Counseling and information services are available, as is tutoring in most subjects. There is remedial math, reading, and writing.

Campus Safety and Security: Measures include 24-hour foot and vehicle patrol, security escort services, shuttle buses, and lighted pathways/sidewalks.

Programs of Study: ULM confers B.A., B.S., B.B.A., B.F.A., B.G.S., B.M., and B.M.E. degrees. Associate, master's, and doctoral degrees are also awarded. Bachelor's degrees are awarded in AGRICULTURE (agricultural business management), BIOLOGICAL SCIENCE (biology/biological science and toxicology), BUSINESS (accounting, banking and finance, business administration and management, insurance, management information systems, management science, and marketing/retailing/merchandising), COMMUNICATIONS AND THE ARTS (art, English, film arts, French, journalism, music, photography, radio/television technology, Spanish, and speech/debate/rhetoric), COMPUTER AND PHYSICAL SCIENCE (atmospheric sciences and meteorology, chemistry, computer science, geology, mathematics, physics, and radiological technology), EDUCATION (art, early childhood, elementary, English, foreign languages, mathematics, music, physical, science, social studies, and special), ENGINEERING AND ENVIRONMENTAL DESIGN (aviation administration/management and construction engineering), HEALTH PROFESSIONS (clinical science, dental hygiene, health, nursing, occupational therapy, pharmacy, premedicine, and speech pathology/audiology), SOCIAL SCIENCE (child care/child and family studies, criminal justice, economics, family/consumer studies, geography, history, liberal arts/general studies, political science/government, prelaw, psychology, social work, and sociology). Pharmacy, occupational therapy, and dental hygiene are the strongest academically. Pharmacy, nursing, and general studies are the largest.

Required: Students are required to take 9 hours each of natural sciences and humanities, 6 each of English, social sciences, and math, and 3 of the arts. An overall minimum GPA of 2.0 is required for graduation along with a total number of credits that varies by degree.

Special: A co-op program in business, an internship in pharmacy, a general studies degree, nondegree study, and credit for life, military, and work experience are offered. There are 22 national honor societies, a freshman honors program, and 2 departmental honors programs.

Faculty/Classroom: 58% of faculty are male; 42%, female. The average class size in a laboratory is 24.

Requirements: The ACT is required. In addition, applicants must be graduates of an accredited high school or have a GED. CLEP credit is accepted.

Procedure: Freshmen are admitted to all sessions. Entrance exams should be taken by April 1. Application deadlines are open. The fall 2003 application fee was $20. Notification is sent on a rolling basis.

Transfer: 673 transfer students enrolled in a recent year. Applicants must submit transcripts from previously attended institutions and should be eligible to return to the school from which they are transferring. 30 credits required for the bachelor's degree must be completed at ULM.

Visiting: There are regularly scheduled orientations for prospective students, consisting of the mandatory PREP program, which includes campus tours, meetings with deans/advisers, class registration, and placement exams. There are guides for informal visits and visitors may sit in on classes. To schedule a visit, contact the Office of Recruitment and Admissions.

Financial Aid: The FAFSA is required. Check with the school for current deadlines.

International Students: The school actively recruits these students. They must score 600 on the written TOEFL and also take the ACT.

Computers: The mainframes are an IBM system/390 multipurpose 2003/105, a DEC Alpha 2100, and a Sunspace Server 1000. The DEC Alpha serves as the primary mail server on the campus academic network that connects 17 academic buildings and supports 150 terminals and 1400 PCs. The IBM system supports the Business Affairs and Enrollment Management Divisions. The Sunspace supports the school's web server. There are 27 computer labs on campus. All students may access the system 24 hours a day. There are no time limits.

Graduates: 392 companies recruited on campus in a recent year.

Admissions Contact: Frances Self, Assistant Director of Admissions. E-mail: *self@ulm.edu* Web: *www.ulm.edu*

UNIVERSITY OF NEW ORLEANS   D-4
New Orleans, LA 70148

(504) 280-6595
(800) 256-5866; Fax: (504) 280-5522

Full-time: 4267 men, 5331 women | **Faculty:** 557; I, --$
Part-time: 1566 men, 2174 women | **Ph.D.s:** 87%
Graduate: 1636 men, 2386 women | **Student/Faculty:** 17 to 1
Year: semesters, summer session | **Tuition:** $3234 ($10,278)
Application Deadline: July 1 | **Room & Board:** $4122
Freshman Class: 5467 applied, 3810 accepted, 2284 enrolled
SAT I Verbal/Math: 540/520 | **ACT:** 21 | **COMPETITIVE**

University of New Orleans, founded in 1958, is a public liberal arts institution. There are 7 undergraduate schools and 1 graduate school. In addition to regional accreditation, UNO has baccalaureate program accreditation with AACSB, ABET, ABFSE, ACS, CACREP, NASM, NAST, and NCATE. The library contains 896,000 volumes, 2,385,500 microform items, and 125,600 audio/video tapes/CDs, and subscribes to 4950 periodicals. Computerized library services include interlibrary loans and database searching. Special learning facilities include a learning resource center, art gallery, and radio station. The 395-acre campus is in an urban area in a residential area of New Orleans. Including any residence halls, there are 30 buildings.

Student Life: 72% of undergraduates are from Louisiana. Students are from 50 states, 95 foreign countries, and Canada. 62% are from public schools. 56% are white; 23% African American. 65% are claim no religious affiliation; 22% Catholic; 10% Protestant. The average age of freshmen is 19; all undergraduates, 24. 33% do not continue beyond their first year.

Housing: 1425 students can be accommodated in college housing, which includes coed dorms and married-student housing. On-campus housing is available on a first-come, first-served basis. 91% of students commute. All students may keep cars.

Activities: 1% of men belong to 7 national fraternities; 1% of women belong to 7 national sororities. There are 125 groups on campus, including art, band, cheerleading, chess, choir, chorale, chorus, computers, dance, drama, ethnic, film, gay, honors, international, jazz band, literary magazine, newspaper, opera, orchestra, pep band, photography, political, professional, radio and TV, religious, social, social service, student government, and yearbook. Popular campus events include Fall Fest, April Fest, and Ambassadors Fishing Rodeo.

Sports: There are 5 intercollegiate sports for men and 5 for women, and 7 intramural sports for men and 7 for women. Facilities include the UNO Lakefront Arena, Privateer Park, 12 tennis courts, a swimming pool, and a health and phys ed center. A recreation and fitness center has free weights, cardiovascular equipment, an indoor track, exercise classes, 2 dry saunas, racquetball courts, basketball courts, a lap pool (indoor), an outdoor pool, and equipment accessible to the disabled.

Disabled Students: 96% of the campus is accessible. Wheelchair ramps, elevators, special parking, specially equipped rest rooms, special class scheduling, lowered drinking fountains, and lowered telephones are available.

Services: Counseling and information services are available, as is tutoring in most subjects. There is a reader service for the blind, and remedial math, reading, and writing.

Campus Safety and Security: Measures include 24-hour foot and vehicle patrol, security escort services, informal discussions, and pamphlets/posters/films. There are emergency telephones, lighted pathways/sidewalks, and monitored parking.

Programs of Study: UNO confers B.A., B.S., and B.G.S. degrees. Master's and doctoral degrees are also awarded. Bachelor's degrees are awarded in BIOLOGICAL SCIENCE (biology/biological science), BUSINESS (accounting, banking and finance, business administration and management, business economics, hotel/motel and restaurant management, marketing/retailing/merchandising, and tourism), COMMUNICATIONS AND THE ARTS (art, communications, dramatic arts, English, fine arts, French, music, and Spanish), COMPUTER AND PHYSICAL SCIENCE (chemistry, computer science, geology, geophysics and seismology, mathematics, and physics), EDUCATION (business, elementary, English, foreign languages, mathematics, music, physical, science, and secondary), ENGINEERING AND ENVIRONMENTAL DESIGN (civil engineering, electrical/electronics engineering, marine engineering, mechanical engineering, and naval architecture and marine engineering), HEALTH PROFESSIONS (medical technology, premedicine, and preveterinary science), SOCIAL SCIENCE (anthropology, economics, geography, history, philosophy, political science/government, psychology, sociology, and urban studies). Business administration, drama, and communications are the largest.

Required: Requirements for graduation include 12 hours in social science and the humanities, 11 hours in science, and 6 each in English composition and literature, and in math. To graduate, students must complete 128 hours with a minimum GPA of 2.0.

Special: Students may participate in co-op programs with LSU Medical Center and may cross-register with Southern University in New Orleans, Elaine P. Nunez Community College, and Delgado Community College.

Internships are required in most professional programs, and work-study programs are available with various federal agencies and private companies. Students may study abroad in 7 countries or participate in a Washington semester. UNO also offers dual and student-designed majors, B.A.-B.S. degrees, preprofessional programs in nursing and physical therapy, and nondegree study. Pass/fail options and limited credit for life, military, and work experience are available. There are 5 national honor societies, a freshman honors program, and 28 departmental honors programs.

Faculty/Classroom: 61% of faculty are male; 39%, female. 96% teach undergraduates and 87% do research. Graduate students teach 16% of introductory courses. The average class size in an introductory lecture is 35; in a laboratory, 23; and in a regular course, 24.

Admissions: 70% of the 2003-2004 applicants were accepted. The SAT I scores for the 2003-2004 freshman class were: Verbal--35% below 500, 35% between 500 and 599, 25% between 600 and 700, and 5% above 700; Math--42% below 500, 34% between 500 and 599, 20% between 600 and 700, and 4% above 700. The ACT scores were 50% below 21, 28% between 21 and 23, 14% between 24 and 26, 5% between 27 and 28, and 4% above 28. 30% of the current freshmen were in the top fifth of their class; 65% were in the top two fifths.

Requirements: The SAT I or ACT is required. In addition, applicants must be high school graduates with a college preparatory program of 4 units in English, 3 each in math and science, 2 each in foreign language, history, and academic social studies, and 1/2 in computer science. A GPA of 2.0 is required. AP and CLEP credits are accepted. Important factors in the admissions decision are advanced placement or honor courses, recommendations by school officials, and evidence of special talent.

Procedure: Freshmen are admitted to all sessions. Entrance exams should be taken at least 6 months prior to enrollment. There is an early admissions plan. Applications should be filed by July 1 for fall entry, November 15 for spring entry, and May 1 for summer entry. The fall 2003 application fee was $20. Notification is sent on a rolling basis.

Transfer: A minimum college GPA of 2.0 is required. Applicants with fewer than 24 semester hours of credit must take the SAT I or the ACT. 30 of 128 credits required for the bachelor's degree must be completed at UNO.

Visiting: There are guides for informal visits and visitors may sit in on classes and stay overnight. To schedule a visit, contact the Office of Admissions.

Financial Aid: In 2003-2004, 75% of all full-time freshmen and 61% of continuing full-time students received some form of financial aid. 37% of full-time freshmen and 36% of continuing full-time students received need-based aid. The average freshman award was $5166. 2% of undergraduates work part time. Average annual earnings from campus work are $2009. UNO is a member of CSS. The FAFSA is required. The deadline for filing freshman financial aid applications for fall entry is May 15.

International Students: There are 316 international students enrolled. The school actively recruits these students. They must score 550 on the written TOEFL or 213 on the electronic version and also take the college's own test and the SAT I or the ACT.

Computers: The mainframes are a DEC VAX 7620, an IBM 9672, and a Cray-YMP. There are 850 PCs connected to the mainframe via the Ethernet network that provide access to word processing, spreadsheets, and database systems. All students may access the system for class assignments and course research. There are no time limits and no fees.

Graduates: From July 1, 2002 to June 30, 2003, 1579 bachelor's degrees were awarded. The most popular majors were business (16%), general studies (13%), and elementary education (6%). In an average class, 4% graduate in 4 years or less, 16% graduate in 5 years or less, and 22% graduate in 6 years or less. 200 companies recruited on campus in 2002-2003.

Admissions Contact: Office of Admissions.
E-mail: *admissions@uno.edu* Web: *http://www.uno.edu*

XAVIER UNIVERSITY OF LOUISIANA

	D-4
New Orleans, LA 70125	**(504) 520-7388; Fax: (504) 520-7941**
Full-time: 730 men, 2270 women	**Faculty:** n/av
Part-time: 42 men, 103 women	**Ph.D.s:** 90%
Graduate: 35 men, 212 women	**Student/Faculty:** n/av
Year: semesters, summer session	**Tuition:** $11,400
Application Deadline: March 1	**Room & Board:** $6200
Freshman Class: 4172 applied, 3508 accepted, 917 enrolled	
SAT I or ACT: required	**COMPETITIVE**

Xavier University of Louisiana, founded in 1925, is a private, historically black liberal arts university affiliated with the Roman Catholic Church. In addition to regional accreditation, Xavier has baccalaureate program accreditation with ACPE, NASM, and NCATE. The library contains 230,548 volumes, 776,442 microform items, and 5893 audio/video tapes/CDs, and subscribes to 1825 periodicals. Computerized library services include the card catalog, interlibrary loans, and database searching.

Special learning facilities include a learning resource center, TV station, and electronic classrooms. The 29-acre campus is in an urban area 2 miles from downtown New Orleans. Including any residence halls, there are 38 buildings.

Student Life: 51% of undergraduates are from Louisiana. 80% are from public schools. 83% are African American. 31% are Baptist; 27% Catholic; 15% claim no religious affiliation. The average age of freshmen is 18; all undergraduates, 20. 27% do not continue beyond their first year.

Housing: 1071 students can be accommodated in college housing, which includes single-sex and coed dorms and on-campus apartments. In addition, there are honors houses. On-campus housing is available on a first-come, first-served basis. Priority is given to out-of-town students. 73% of students commute. Alcohol is not permitted. All students may keep cars.

Activities: 2% of men belong to 4 national fraternities; 6% of women belong to 4 national sororities. There are 80 groups on campus, including art, band, cheerleading, chess, choir, chorus, computers, dance, drill team, ethnic, honors, international, jazz band, literary magazine, newspaper, opera, pep band, political, professional, religious, social, social service, student government, symphony, TV station, and yearbook. Popular campus events include Wellness Week, Octoberfest, and Culturefest.

Sports: There are 3 intercollegiate sports for men and 3 for women, and 22 intramural sports for men and 22 for women. Facilities include a gym, a swimming pool, tennis courts, and a recreation room.

Disabled Students: 99% of the campus is accessible. Wheelchair ramps, elevators, special parking, specially equipped rest rooms, special class scheduling, lowered drinking fountains, and lowered telephones are available.

Services: Counseling and information services are available, as is tutoring in every subject. There is a reader service for the blind, and remedial math, reading, and writing.

Campus Safety and Security: Measures include 24-hour foot and vehicle patrol, security escort services, shuttle buses, and informal discussions. There are pamphlets/posters/films, emergency telephones, and lighted pathways/sidewalks.

Programs of Study: Xavier confers B.A., B.S., and B.M. degrees. Master's and doctoral degrees are also awarded. Bachelor's degrees are awarded in BIOLOGICAL SCIENCE (biochemistry, biology/biological science, microbiology, and toxicology), BUSINESS (accounting, banking and finance, business administration and management, business economics, marketing/retailing/merchandising, and personnel management), COMMUNICATIONS AND THE ARTS (communications, English, fine arts, French, music, and Spanish), COMPUTER AND PHYSICAL SCIENCE (chemistry, computer science, mathematics, physics, and statistics), EDUCATION (art, early childhood, elementary, English, mathematics, music, physical, science, secondary, and social studies), HEALTH PROFESSIONS (predentistry, premedicine, and speech pathology/audiology), SOCIAL SCIENCE (history, philosophy, political science/government, prelaw, psychology, sociology, and theological studies). Science, education, and English are the strongest academically. Pharmacy, biology, and business are the largest.

Required: Requirements for graduation include 9 semester hours in English, 6 each in history, social science, language, theology, philosophy, and natural sciences, 3 each in speech, math, and the arts, and 1 in health and phys ed. Students must complete 128 to 132 total credit hours, including 24 to 54 hours in the major. Students must maintain a minimum GPA of 2.0, take Introduction to African American History/Culture, pass a comprehensive exam, and by the beginning of the junior year declare a minor in an academic discipline other than the major.

Special: The university offers cooperative programs in any major and 3-2 engineering degrees with Tulane, Louisiana State, Morgan State, and Southern Universities as well as the Universities of Wisconsin, Maryland, New Orleans, and Detroit, and Georgia Institute of Technology. In addition, students may cross-register at colleges of the New Orleans Consortium. Internships are available in legal, political, and pharmaceutical areas. Students may earn an accelerated degree in biology, chemistry, psychology, or political science, pursue dual majors in engineering and biostatistics, opt for nondegree study, and earn a B.A.-B.S. degree in almost any combination. Students may study abroad in 6 countries or participate in an exchange program with Notre Dame University. There are 7 national honor societies, a freshman honors program, and 7 departmental honors programs.

Faculty/Classroom: 57% of faculty are male; 43%, female. No introductory courses are taught by graduate students. The average class size in an introductory lecture is 25; in a laboratory, 21; and in a regular course, 21.

Admissions: 84% of the 2003-2004 applicants were accepted. 35% of the current freshmen were in the top quarter of their class; 51% were in the top half.

Requirements: The SAT I or ACT is required. In addition, candidates for admission must have completed 4 units of English, 2 of math, 1 each of science and social studies, and 8 of academic electives. The GED is accepted. A GPA of 2.0 is required. AP and CLEP credits are accepted.

Important factors in the admissions decision are advanced placement or honor courses, recommendations by school officials, and evidence of special talent.

Procedure: Freshmen are admitted fall, spring, and summer. Entrance exams should be taken in the spring of the junior year or the fall of the senior year. There is an early action plan. Early action applications should be filed by January 15; regular applications, by March 1 for fall entry, December 1 for spring entry, and April 15 for summer entry, along with a $25 fee. Notification of early action is sent February 1; regular decision, April 15. 187 applicants were on the 2003 waiting list; 52 were admitted. Applications are accepted on-line through the university's web site.

Transfer: 159 transfer students enrolled in 2002-2003. Applicants must submit college transcripts; high school transcripts are required of applicants with fewer than 30 transferable credits. 30 of 128 to 132 credits required for the bachelor's degree must be completed at Xavier.

Visiting: There are guides for informal visits and visitors may sit in on classes and stay overnight. To schedule a visit, contact the Admissions Office at (504) 520-7578.

Financial Aid: In 2003-2004, 83% of all full-time freshmen and 80% of continuing full-time students received some form of financial aid. 8% of full-time freshmen and 54% of continuing full-time students received need-based aid. The average freshman award was $4438. Need-based self-help aid (loans and jobs) averaged $1406; institutional non-need-based athletic scholarships averaged $6983; and other institutional non-need-based awards and non-need-based scholarships averaged $2988. The average financial indebtedness of the 2003 graduate was $15,292. Xavier is a member of CSS. The FAFSA is required. The priority date for freshman financial aid applications for fall entry is January 1.

International Students: They must score 550 on the written TOEFL and also take the SAT I or the ACT.

Computers: The mainframe is an IBM RS/6000. 2 open labs in the science building have 25 terminals each from which students can log on to the mainframe. In addition, computer labs in other buildings contain PCs for student use. All students may access the system. There are no time limits and no fees.

Graduates: From July 1, 2002 to June 30, 2003, 458 bachelor's degrees were awarded. The most popular majors were biology (40%), psychology (14%), and physical sciences (11%). In an average class, 38% graduate in 4 years or less, 48% graduate in 5 years or less, and 50% graduate in 6 years or less.

Admissions Contact: Winston D. Brown, Dean of Admissions. E-mail: *apply@xula.edu* Web: *www.xula.edu*

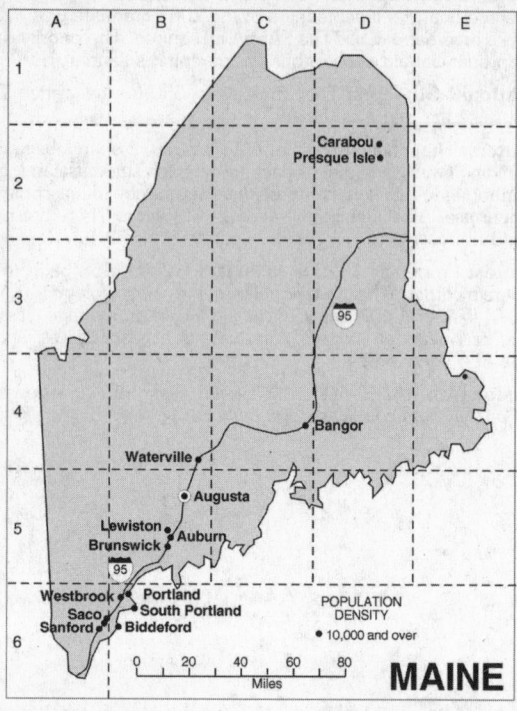

POPULATION DENSITY

● 10,000 and over

0 20 40 60 80
Miles

MAINE

BATES COLLEGE
Lewiston, ME 04240

B-5

(207) 786-6000; Fax: (207) 786-6025

Full-time: 837 men, 909 women	Faculty: 163; IIB, ++$
Part-time: none	Ph.D.s: 99%
Graduate: none	Student/Faculty: 11 to 1
Year: 4-1-4	Tuition: $37,500
Application Deadline: January 15	Room & Board: n/app

Freshman Class: 4089 applied, 1254 accepted, 487 enrolled

SAT I Verbal/Math: 670/670 **MOST COMPETITIVE**

Bates College, founded in 1855, is a private liberal arts institution offering undergraduate and graduate programs in humanities, social sciences, and natural sciences. The library contains 590,299 volumes, 305,911 microform items, and 30,470 audio/video tapes/CDs, and subscribes to 2508 periodicals. Computerized library services include the card catalog, interlibrary loans, database searching, and Internet access. Special learning facilities include a learning resource center, art gallery, planetarium, radio station, TV station, a 654-acre mountain conservation area, an observatory, a language resource center, and the Edmund S. Muskie archives. The 109-acre campus is in a small town 140 miles north of Boston. Including any residence halls, there are 70 buildings.

Student Life: 88% of undergraduates are from out of state, mostly the Northeast. Students are from 44 states, 68 foreign countries, and Canada. 57% are from public schools. 83% are white. The average age of freshmen is 18; all undergraduates, 20. 7% do not continue beyond their first year; 88% remain to graduate.

Housing: 1604 students can be accommodated in college housing, which includes single-sex and coed dorms. In addition, there are special-interest houses, chemical-free housing, and quiet/study housing. On-campus housing is guaranteed for all 4 years. 91% of students live on campus; of those, 95% remain on campus on weekends. All students may keep cars.

Activities: There are no fraternities or sororities. There are 92 groups on campus, including art, chess, choir, chorale, chorus, computers, dance, debate, drama, ethnic, film, gay, honors, international, jazz band, literary magazine, musical theater, newspaper, orchestra, outdoor recreation, pep band, photography, political, professional, radio and TV, religious, social, social service, student government, and yearbook. Popular campus events include Winter Carnival, international dinners, and ocean clambakes.

Sports: There are 15 intercollegiate sports for men and 16 for women, and 8 intramural sports for men and 8 for women. Facilities include a pool, a field house, indoor and outdoor tracks, indoor and outdoor tennis courts, 3 basketball courts, 3 volleyball courts, dance and fencing space, squash and racquetball courts, training rooms, a rock-climbing

wall, a boat house, a winter sports arena, a weight room, and football, soccer, baseball, softball, and lacrosse fields.

Disabled Students: 60% of the campus is accessible. Wheelchair ramps, elevators, special parking, specially equipped rest rooms, special class scheduling, and lowered telephones are available.

Services: Counseling and information services are available, as is tutoring in every subject. There is a reader service for the blind and remedial math and writing.

Campus Safety and Security: Measures include 24-hour foot and vehicle patrol, self-defense education, security escort services, and shuttle buses. There are informal discussions, pamphlets/posters/films, emergency telephones, and lighted pathways/sidewalks.

Programs of Study: Bates confers B.A. and B.S. degrees. Bachelor's degrees are awarded in BIOLOGICAL SCIENCE (biochemistry, biology/biological science, and neurosciences), COMMUNICATIONS AND THE ARTS (art, Chinese, dramatic arts, East Asian languages and literature, English, French, German, Japanese, music, Russian, Spanish, and speech/debate/rhetoric), COMPUTER AND PHYSICAL SCIENCE (chemistry, geology, mathematics, and physics), ENGINEERING AND ENVIRONMENTAL DESIGN (environmental science), SOCIAL SCIENCE (African American studies, American studies, anthropology, classical/ancient civilization, economics, history, philosophy, political science/government, psychology, religion, sociology, and women's studies). Psychology, economics, and political science are the largest.

Required: Requirements for graduation include 5 courses in humanities, 3 each in natural science and social science, and 1 each in quantitative techniques and phys ed. The total number of hours in the major varies by department, but students should take at least 32 courses, plus 2 short terms, and maintain a minimum GPA of 2.0. A senior thesis is required.

Special: Internships, research apprenticeships, work-study programs, study abroad, and a Washington semester are possible. Dual, student-designed, and interdisciplinary majors, and a 3-2 engineering degree with Columbia University, Dartmouth College, Case Western Reserve University, Rensselaer Polytechnic Institute, and Washington University in St. Louis are available. Students in any major may graduate in 3 years, and a B.A.-B.S. is possible in all majors. Students may also participate in the Williams-Mystic Seaport program in marine biology and maritime history, and exchanges with Spelman College, Morehouse College, Washington and Lee University, and McGill University are possible. There are 2 national honor societies, including Phi Beta Kappa. All departments have honors programs.

Faculty/Classroom: 55% of faculty are male; 45%, female. All both teach and do research. The average class size in an introductory lecture is 23; in a laboratory, 20; and in a regular course, 21.

Admissions: 31% of the 2003-2004 applicants were accepted. The SAT I scores for the 2003-2004 freshman class were: Verbal--1% below 500, 7% between 500 and 599, 63% between 600 and 700, and 29% above 700; Math--6% between 500 and 599, 59% between 600 and 700, and 34% above 700. 88% of the current freshmen were in the top fifth of their class; 99% were in the top two fifths.

Requirements: The submission of test scores is optional. Candidates for admission should have completed 4 years of English, 3 each of math, social science, and a foreign language, and 2 of lab science. Essays are required, and an interview on or off campus is strongly recommended. AP credits are accepted. Important factors in the admissions decision are advanced placement or honor courses, evidence of special talent, and leadership record.

Procedure: Freshmen are admitted fall and winter. There are early decision and deferred admissions plans. Early decision applications should be filed by November 15; regular applications, by January 15 for fall entry and November 1 for winter entry, along with a $60 fee. Notification of early decision is sent December 16; regular decision, by March 31. 208 early decision candidates were accepted for the 2003-2004 class. A waiting list is an active part of the admissions procedure. Applications are accepted on-line through Common App.

Transfer: 5 transfer students enrolled in 2002-2003. More weight is given to the student's college record than to high school credentials. Applicants must submit official college and high school transcripts, a statement of good standing, 3 letters of recommendation, and an essay. An interview is strongly recommended. 16 of 32 courses required for the bachelor's degree must be completed at Bates.

Visiting: There are guides for informal visits and visitors may sit in on classes and stay overnight. To schedule a visit, contact the Admissions Office at admissions@bates.edu.

Financial Aid: In 2002-2003, 54% of all full-time freshmen and 47% of continuing full-time students received some form of financial aid, including need-based aid. The average freshman award was $22,850. 50% of undergraduates work part time. Average annual earnings from campus work in a recent year were $1400. The average financial indebtedness of the 2003 graduate was $14,401. Bates is a member of CSS.

The CSS/Profile or FAFSA and parent and student tax returns and W-2 forms are required. The deadline for filing freshman financial aid applications for fall entry is January 15.

International Students: There are 101 international students enrolled. The school actively recruits these students. The TOEFL is preferred, but Bates will consider other parallel forms of exams.

Computers: The mainframes are a DEC Alpha 2100, a Dual Processor RISC, and a DEC 1000 RISC. All students are assigned a user ID, which provides access to academic software, e-mail, and the Internet. There are 785 college desktop computers and workstations. More than 1300 computers were recently hooked up to the system in dorm rooms. All students may access the system. There are no time limits and no fees.

Graduates: From July 1, 2002 to June 30, 2003, 443 bachelor's degrees were awarded. The most popular majors were psychology (11%), English (10%), and biology and political science (9%). In an average class, 1% graduate in 3 years or less, 84% graduate in 4 years or less, 84% graduate in 5 years or less, and 89% graduate in 6 years or less. 70 companies recruited on campus in a recent year.

Admissions Contact: Wylie L. Mitchell, Dean of Admissions. E-mail: *admissions@bates.edu* Web: *www.bates.edu*

BOWDOIN COLLEGE
Brunswick, ME 04011   (207) 725-3100; Fax: (207) 725-3101

B-5

Full-time: 829 men, 811 women	Faculty: 154; IIB, ++$
Part-time: 3 men, 4 women	Ph.D.s: 97%
Graduate: none	Student/Faculty: 11 to 1
Year: semesters	Tuition: $30,120
Application Deadline: January 1	Room & Board: $7670
Freshman Class: 4719 applied, 1154 accepted, 467 enrolled	
SAT I Verbal/Math: 690/680	**MOST COMPETITIVE**

Bowdoin College, established in 1794, is a private liberal arts institution. In addition to regional accreditation, Bowdoin has baccalaureate program accreditation with ASC. The 8 libraries contain 962,255 volumes, 108,444 microform items, and 20,990 audio/video tapes/CDs, and subscribe to 3813 periodicals. Computerized library services include the card catalog, interlibrary loans, database searching, and Internet access. Special learning facilities include a learning resource center, art gallery, radio station, TV station, a museum of art, arctic museum, language media center, women's resource center, electronic classroom, coastal studies center, the John Brown Russwurm African American Center, the Craft Center ceramics studio, and photography darkroom. The Bowdoin Scientific Station, located in the Bay of Fundy, New Brunswick, Canada, is a 200-acre island for scientific study by Bowdoin students. The 200-acre campus is in a small town 25 miles northeast of Portland. Including any residence halls, there are 117 buildings.

Student Life: 87% of undergraduates are from out of state, mostly the Northeast. Students are from 49 states, 29 foreign countries, and Canada. 57% are from public schools. 74% are white; 10% Asian American. The average age of freshmen is 18; all undergraduates, 20. 6% do not continue beyond their first year; 90% remain to graduate.

Housing: 1563 students can be accommodated in college housing, which includes single-sex and coed dorms, on-campus apartments, and off-campus apartments. In addition, there are special-interest houses. All first-year students participate in the College House system; their residence hall is associated with 1 of 6 campus houses. All upperclass students are also eligible to participate. All first-year students and sophomores are required to live on campus. On-campus housing is available on a lottery system for upperclassmen. 92% of students live on campus; of those, 99% remain on campus on weekends. All students may keep cars.

Activities: There are no fraternities or sororities. There are 109 groups on campus, including a cappella singing, art, choir, chorale, chorus, computers, dance, debate, drama, ethnic, film, gay, honors, improvisational comedy, international, intramural sports, jazz band, literary magazine, musical theater, newspaper, orchestra, outing, photography, political, professional, radio and TV, religious, social, social service, student government, symphony, volunteer, and yearbook. Popular campus events include Sara and James Bowdoin Day, Parents Weekend, and Ivies Weekend.

Sports: There are 13 intercollegiate sports for men and 14 for women, and 12 intramural sports for men and 11 for women. Facilities include an ice arena, a field house, a swimming pool, 2 gyms, indoor and outdoor track facilities, tennis and squash courts, a climbing wall, a boathouse, outdoor leadership center, and cross-country ski trails. There are also weight and aerobics rooms and 60 acres of playing fields for football, baseball, softball, lacrosse, field hockey, and soccer. The fitness center includes Cybex ergonometric equipment, free weights, and various fitness machines.

Disabled Students: 60% of the campus is accessible. Wheelchair ramps, elevators, special parking, specially equipped rest rooms, lowered drinking fountains, lowered telephones, and special housing are available. All new buildings and renovations to old buildings are built to ADA compliance standards.

MAINE 697

Services: Counseling and information services are available, as is tutoring in most subjects. There is a reader service for the blind. A counselor is available to assist students with accommodations as needed. Tutoring is available through the Quantitative Skills Program and the Writing Skills Project.

Campus Safety and Security: Measures include 24-hour foot and vehicle patrol, self-defense education, security escort services, and shuttle buses. There are informal discussions, pamphlets/posters/films, emergency telephones, lighted pathways/sidewalks, and emergency warning whistles. Residences are locked 24 hours a day, and a staffed communications center is available around the clock.

Programs of Study: Bowdoin confers the A.B. degree. Bachelor's degrees are awarded in BIOLOGICAL SCIENCE (biochemistry, biology/biological science, and neurosciences), COMMUNICATIONS AND THE ARTS (art history and appreciation, classics, dramatic arts, English, French, German, music, romance languages and literature, Russian, Spanish, studio art, and visual and performing arts), COMPUTER AND PHYSICAL SCIENCE (chemical physics, chemistry, computer science, geology, mathematics, and physics), ENGINEERING AND ENVIRONMENTAL DESIGN (environmental science), SOCIAL SCIENCE (African studies, anthropology, archeology, Asian/Oriental studies, classical/ancient civilization, economics, European studies, history, Latin American studies, philosophy, political science/government, psychology, religion, sociology, and women's studies). Biology, economics, government and legal studies are the strongest academically. Government and legal studies, economics, and history are the largest.

Required: Degree requirements include 32 courses, with at least 2 semesters in natural science and math, social and behavioral sciences, humanities and fine arts, and non-Eurocentric studies, and completion of major requirements.

Special: Students may take advantage of about 100 approved programs all over the world, including Intercollegiate Center for Classical Studies in Rome, Intercollegiate Sri Lanka Education (ISLE), South India Term Abroad (SITA), The Swedish Program, Semester in Environmental Science at the Marine Biological Laboratory, Woods Hole, and the Twelve College Exchange (including Williams College-Mystic Seaport and National Theater Institute). Dual majors in any combination, internships, interdisciplinary majors, student-designed majors, B.A.-B.S. degrees, and pass/fail options are available. The college offers a 3-2 engineering degree with the California Institute of Technology and Columbia University, and 3-3 legal studies with Columbia University Law School. There is 1 national honor society, including Phi Beta Kappa, and all departments have honors programs.

Faculty/Classroom: 58% of faculty are male; 42%, female. All both teach and do research. The average class size in an introductory lecture is 25; in a laboratory, 12; and in a regular course, 16.

Admissions: 24% of the 2003-2004 applicants were accepted. The SAT I scores for the 2003-2004 freshman class were: Verbal--1% below 500, 7% between 500 and 599, 45% between 600 and 700, and 47% above 700; Math--1% below 500, 8% between 500 and 599, 51% between 600 and 700, and 40% above 700. 88% of the current freshmen were in the top fifth of their class; 98% were in the top two fifths. There were 20 National Merit finalists and 3 semifinalists. 31 freshmen graduated first in their class.

Requirements: There are no specific academic requirements, but typical applicants for admission will have 4 years each of English, social studies, foreign language, and math, 3 1/2 years of science, and 1 course each in art, music, and history. A high school record, 2 teacher recommendations, and an essay are required. AP credits are accepted.

Procedure: Freshmen are admitted in the fall. Entrance exams are required for counseling and placement only and should be submitted by the late summer before the freshman year. There are early decision and deferred admissions plans. Early decision applications should be filed by November 15 or January 1; regular applications, by January 1 for fall entry, along with a $60 fee. Notification of early decision is sent December 15; regular decision, April 15. 167 early decision candidates were accepted for the 2003-2004 class. A waiting list is an active part of the admissions procedure. Applications are accepted on-line through the school's web site.

Transfer: 5 transfer students enrolled in 2002-2003. College grades of B or better are required to transfer. Applicants should submit high school and college transcripts, a dean's or adviser's statement from the most recent college attended, and 2 recommendations from recent professors. 16 credits of 32 required for the bachelor's degree must be completed at Bowdoin.

Visiting: There are regularly scheduled orientations for prospective students, in which students should be prepared to talk informally about their academic record, interests, talents, and goals. There are guides for informal visits and visitors may sit in on classes and stay overnight. To schedule a visit, contact the Admissions Office at *admissions@bowdoin.edu*.

Financial Aid: In 2003-2004, 47% of all full-time freshmen and 46% of continuing full-time students received some form of financial aid. 44% of full-time freshmen and 45% of continuing full-time students received need-based aid. The average freshman award was $27,162. Need-based

scholarships or need-based grants averaged $23,916 ($40,250 maximum); need-based self-help aid (loans and jobs) averaged $4148 ($24,688 maximum); and non-need-based awards and non-need-based scholarships averaged $1000 ($2000 maximum). 65% of undergraduates work part time. Average annual earnings from campus work are $1075. The average financial indebtedness of the 2003 graduate was $14,830. Bowdoin is a member of CSS. The CSS/Profile or FAFSA and the college's own financial statement are required. The deadline for filing freshman financial aid applications for fall entry is February 15.

International Students: There are 52 international students enrolled. The school actively recruits these students. They must score 600 on the written TOEFL or 250 on the electronic version. SAT I scores must be submitted at matriculation for counseling and placement.

Computers: The mainframes are a Linux, Mac OS, Unix, and Windows NT. Students access servers from 310 public PCs and terminals. Network access, including the Internet and the Web, is available from all dorm rooms. More than 1000 students access the network from their dorm rooms. Almost all students use e-mail. All students may access the system 24 hours a day. There are no time limits and no fees. It is strongly recommended that all students have a personal computer.

Graduates: From July 1, 2002 to June 30, 2003, 453 bachelor's degrees were awarded. The most popular majors were government and legal studies (17%), English (10%), and economics (10%). In an average class, 84% graduate in 4 years or less, 88% graduate in 5 years or less, and 90% graduate in 6 years or less. 350 companies recruited on campus in 2002-2003. Of the 2002 graduating class, 14% were enrolled in graduate school within 6 months of graduation and 71% were employed.

Admissions Contact: James Miller, Dean of Admissions/Student Aid. A video is available. E-mail: *admissions@bowdoin.edu* Web: *www.bowdoin.edu*

COLBY COLLEGE
Waterville, ME 04901-8841

B-4
(207) 872-3168
(800) 723-3032; Fax: (207) 872-3474

Full-time: 817 men, 951 women	**Faculty:** 158; IIB, ++$
Part-time: none	**Ph.Ds:** 97%
Graduate: none	**Student/Faculty:** 11 to 1
Year: 4-1-4	**Tuition:** $37,570
Application Deadline: January 1	**Room & Board:** 0
Freshman Class: 4126 applied, 1388 accepted, 474 enrolled	
SAT I Verbal/Math: 670/680	**ACT:** 28 MOST COMPETITIVE

Colby College, founded in 1813, is a private liberal arts college. Students are charged a comprehensive fee of $37,570 annually, which includes tuition, room and board, and required fees. In addition to regional accreditation, Colby has baccalaureate program accreditation with ACS. The 3 libraries contain 953,160 volumes, 303,050 microform items, and 21,915 audio/video tapes/CDs, and subscribe to 2230 periodicals. Computerized library services include the card catalog, interlibrary loans, database searching, and Internet access. Special learning facilities include a learning resource center, art gallery, radio station, observatory, astronomy classroom, arboretum, state wildlife management area, and electronic-research classroom. The 714-acre campus is in a small town 75 miles north of Portland. Including any residence halls, there are 58 buildings.

Student Life: 88% of undergraduates are from out of state, mostly the Northeast. Students are from 48 states, 69 foreign countries, and Canada. 56% are from public schools. 83% are white. The average age of freshmen is 18; all undergraduates, 20. 7% do not continue beyond their first year; 88% remain to graduate.

Housing: 1703 students can be accommodated in college housing, which includes coed dorms and on-campus apartments. In addition, there are substance-free halls, quiet halls, and apartments for seniors. On-campus housing is guaranteed for all 4 years. 94% of students live on campus. All students may keep cars.

Activities: There are no fraternities or sororities. There are 114 groups on campus, including art, band, choir, chorale, chorus, coed woodsmen's team, computers, dance, debate, drama, environmental, ethnic, film, gay, honors, human rights, international, jazz band, literary magazine, musical theater, newspaper, orchestra, outdoor, photography, political, professional, radio and TV, religious, social, social service, student government, symphony, women's and yearbook. Popular campus events include Family Weekend, Foss Arts Festival, and International Extravaganza.

Sports: There are 16 intercollegiate sports for men and 17 for women, and 8 intramural sports for men and 8 for women. Facilities include an athletic center with fitness, weight training, and exercise areas; a gym with badminton, volleyball, and basketball courts; a hockey and skating rink; a field house for track and field, soccer, baseball, softball, tennis, lacrosse, and golf; a swimming pool and saunas; and squash and handball courts. There are also outdoor playing fields, tennis courts, an all-weather track, a climbing wall, cross-country skiing, and running trails.

Disabled Students: 90% of the campus is accessible. Wheelchair ramps, elevators, special parking, specially equipped rest rooms, special class scheduling, lowered drinking fountains, and lowered telephones are available.

Services: Counseling and information services are available, as is tutoring in every subject. There is a reader service for the blind. There is also a writing center and a support program for learning-disabled students.

Campus Safety and Security: Measures include 24-hour foot and vehicle patrol, self-defense education, security escort services, and shuttle buses. There are informal discussions, pamphlets/posters/films, emergency telephones, lighted pathways/sidewalks, a women's safety program, a property identification program, party monitors (security officers), a student emergency response team, courtesy rides, and keycard dorm access.

Programs of Study: Colby confers the B.A. degree. Bachelor's degrees are awarded in BIOLOGICAL SCIENCE (biology/biological science), COMMUNICATIONS AND THE ARTS (art, classics, creative writing, English, German, Germanic languages and literature, music, performing arts, and Spanish), COMPUTER AND PHYSICAL SCIENCE (applied mathematics, chemistry, computer science, geology, mathematics, physics, and science technology), ENGINEERING AND ENVIRONMENTAL DESIGN (environmental science), SOCIAL SCIENCE (American studies, anthropology, classical/ancient civilization, East Asian studies, economics, French studies, history, international studies, Latin American studies, philosophy, political science/government, psychology, religion, sociology, and women's studies). Biology, chemistry, and physics are the strongest academically. Biology, English, and government are the largest.

Required: To graduate, all students must take English composition and fulfill a foreign language requirement. They must also take 2 courses in the natural sciences and 1 course each in the arts, historical studies, literature, quantitative reasoning, the social sciences, and human or cultural diversity, and meet Colby's wellness requirement by attending 8 lectures. Students must complete a total of 128 credit hours, including 3 January term courses, and maintain a GPA of 2.0.

Special: Colby offers study abroad in numerous countries, and the Colby-Bates-Bowdoin consortium has centers in London; Quito, Ecuador; and CapeTown, South Africa. Colby also offers Washington semester programs through American University and the Washington Center, on-campus work-study, exchange programs with various colleges and universities, a 3-2 engineering degree with Dartmouth College, and maritime and oceanographic studies programs. Dual and student-designed majors are possible. There are 9 national honor societies, including Phi Beta Kappa, and 22 departmental honors programs.

Faculty/Classroom: 56% of faculty are male; 44%, female. All both teach and do research. The average class size in a regular course is 17.

Admissions: 34% of the 2003-2004 applicants were accepted. The SAT I scores for the 2003-2004 freshman class were: Verbal--2% below 500, 9% between 500 and 599, 64% between 600 and 700, and 26% above 700; Math--1% below 500, 11% between 500 and 599, 59% between 600 and 700, and 29% above 700. The ACT scores were 4% between 21 and 23, 18% between 24 and 26, 28% between 27 and 28, and 50% above 28. 83% of the current freshmen were in the top fifth of their class; 93% were in the top two fifths. 21 freshmen graduated first in their class.

Requirements: The SAT I or ACT is required. In addition, candidates should be high school graduates with a recommended academic program of 4 years of English, 3 each of foreign language and math, and 2 each of science (including lab work), social studies/history, and other college-preparatory courses. AP credits are accepted. Important factors in the admissions decision are leadership record, advanced placement or honor courses, and extracurricular activities record.

Procedure: Freshmen are admitted fall and winter. Entrance exams should be taken by January of the senior year. There are early decision, early admissions, and deferred admissions plans. Applications should be filed by January 1 for fall entry. Notification is sent April 1. 201 early decision candidates were accepted for a recent class. Applications are accepted on-line through Common App (with a Colby supplement), Apply, and the web site at *www.colby.edu/admissions.*

Transfer: 7 transfer students enrolled in 2002-2003. Applicants must have a minimum GPA of 3.0 and, as a rule, have earned enough credit hours to qualify for at least sophomore standing. They must be in good academic and social standing and should submit references from a faculty member and a dean of their current school. If the SAT I or ACT has been taken, the results must be submitted as well. 64 of 128 credits required for the bachelor's degree must be completed at Colby.

Visiting: There are regularly scheduled orientations for prospective students, including panel discussions, tours, class visits, complimentary meals, interviews, and information sessions. There are guides for informal visits and visitors may sit in on classes and stay overnight. To schedule a visit, contact the Overnight Host Hotline at (207) 872-3377 or *admvol@colby.edu.*

Financial Aid: 45% of full-time freshmen and 38% of continuing full-time students received need-based aid. The average freshman award was $25,468. Need-based scholarships or need-based grants averaged $25,937; and need-based self-help aid (loans and jobs) averaged $3302. 67% of undergraduates work part time. Average annual earnings from campus work are $905. The average financial indebtedness of the 2003 graduate was $17,809. The CSS Profile or FAFSA and the college's own financial statement are required. The deadline for filing freshman financial aid applications for fall entry is February 1.

International Students: There are 174 international students enrolled. The school actively recruits these students. They must score 600 on the written TOEFL or 240 on the electronic version.

Computers: The mainframes are 3 HP806/E25, an HP820/D280, HP871/D270, HP770/J210, and an HP867/G40. Access to the campus network, local resources, and the Internet is available in all classrooms, labs, offices, and library study areas, as well as from each residence hall, where there is a port for every student and additional ports in lounges. 300 computers are available for student use in open clusters, departmental clusters, and labs. All students may access the system 24 hours a day. There are no time limits and no fees. It is strongly recommended that all students have a personal computer. A Dell Optiplex/Latitude is recommeded.

Graduates: From July 1, 2002 to June 30, 2003, 499 bachelor's degrees were awarded. The most popular majors were biology (11%), English (11%), and economics (11%). In an average class, 85% graduate in 4 years or less, 87% graduate in 5 years or less, and 88% graduate in 6 years or less. 96 companies recruited on campus in 2002-2003. Of the 2002 graduating class, 19% were enrolled in graduate school within 6 months of graduation and 80% were employed.

Admissions Contact: Parker J. Beverage, Dean of Admissions and Financial Aid. E-mail: *admissions@colby.edu* Web: *www.colby.edu*

COLLEGE OF THE ATLANTIC
Bar Harbor, ME 04609

D-5

(207) 288-5015
(800) 528-0025; Fax: (207) 288-4126

Full-time: 117 men, 148 women	**Faculty:** 18
Part-time: 6 men, 7 women	**Ph.D.s:** 68%
Graduate: 1 man, 4 women	**Student/Faculty:** 15 to 1
Year: trimesters	**Tuition:** $23,961
Application Deadline: February 15	**Room & Board:** $6543
Freshman Class: 252 applied, 187 accepted, 67 enrolled	
SAT I Verbal/Math: 628/593	**ACT:** 26 **VERY COMPETITIVE+**

College of the Atlantic, founded in 1969, is a private liberal arts college dedicated to the study of human ecology. The library contains 38,500 volumes, 274 microform items, and 1950 audio/video tapes/CDs, and subscribes to 400 periodicals. Computerized library services include the card catalog, interlibrary loans, and database searching. Special learning facilities include a learning resource center, art gallery, natural history museum, writing center, taxidermy lab, photography lab, marine mammal research center, 2 greenhouses, 80-acre organic farm, and 2 offshore research stations. The 34-acre campus is in a small town 45 miles southeast of Bangor, along the Atlantic Ocean shoreline. Including any residence halls, there are 13 buildings.

Student Life: 75% of undergraduates are from out of state, mostly the Northeast. Students are from 34 states, 33 foreign countries, and Canada. 74% are from public schools. The average age of freshmen is 18; all undergraduates, 20. 1% do not continue beyond their first year; 62% remain to graduate.

Housing: 100 students can be accommodated in college housing, which includes coed dorms. In addition, there are substance-free houses. On-campus housing is guaranteed for the freshman year only, is available on a first-come, first-served basis, and is available on a lottery system for upperclassmen. Priority is given to out-of-town students. 60% of students commute. Alcohol is not permitted. All students may keep cars.

Activities: There are no fraternities or sororities. There are 21 groups on campus, including art, chess, chorus, computers, dance, drama, environmental, film, gay, international, jazz band, literary magazine, musical theater, newspaper, orchestra, photography, political, social, social service, and student government. Popular campus events include the annual Bar Island swim, contra dances, and Winter Carnival.

Sports: There are 3 intramural sports for men and 3 for women. All students are members of the local YMCA and may use its pool, Nautilus equipment, and volleyball and basketball facilities, as well as nearby tennis courts. Acadia National Park offers seasonal outdoor activities. The college has camping and outdoor equipment and canoes, a sea kayaks, and sailboats for student use, and offers a sailing class, a sea kayaking class, and a wilderness first responder class.

Disabled Students: 80% of the campus is accessible. Wheelchair ramps, elevators, special parking, specially equipped rest rooms, lowered drinking fountains, lowered telephones, and specially equipped residence hall rooms are available.

Services: Counseling and information services are available, as is tutoring in some subjects, including writing, math, language, photography, and computer use. There is remedial math and writing.

Campus Safety and Security: Measures include 24-hour foot and vehicle patrol, security escort services, shuttle buses, and informal discussions. There are pamphlets/posters/films, emergency telephones, and lighted pathways/sidewalks.

Programs of Study: COA confers the B.A. degree. Master's degrees are also awarded. Bachelor's degrees are awarded in SOCIAL SCIENCE (human ecology).

Required: Students design their own program. They must complete a total of 36 COA credits, including 2 interdisciplinary core courses and 2 courses each in environmental science, human studies, and arts and design. Also required are group study, a 3-credit internship, a human ecology essay, participation in a 3-credit senior project, and community service.

Special: Teacher certification is offered in elementary, and secondary, science, English, and social studies education. Students may cross-register with the University of Maine and other local nautical schools. Study abroad is available in Uruguay, Mexico, and the Czech Republic. Students arrange internships with a broad range of employers. Pass/ fail grading options are available.

Faculty/Classroom: 64% of faculty are male; 36%, female. All teach undergraduates, and 60% both teach and do research. The average class size in an introductory lecture is 20; in a laboratory, 14; and in a regular course, 14.

Admissions: 74% of the 2003-2004 applicants were accepted. The SAT I scores for the 2003-2004 freshman class were: Verbal--7% below 500, 27% between 500 and 599, 55% between 600 and 700, and 11% above 700; Math--18% below 500, 34% between 500 and 599, and 48% between 600 and 700. The ACT scores were 38% between 24 and 26, 25% between 27 and 28, and 38% above 28. 45% of the current freshmen were in the top fifth of their class; 80% were in the top two fifths. There were 2 National Merit finalists and 7 semifinalists in a recent year.

Requirements: Candidates for admission must be high school graduates who have completed 4 years of English, 3 to 4 of math, 2 to 3 of science, 2 of a foreign language, and 1 of history. AP and CLEP credits are accepted. Important factors in the admissions decision are advanced placement or honor courses, leadership record, and personality/ intangible qualities.

Procedure: Freshmen are admitted fall, winter, and spring. Entrance exams should be taken in the junior or senior year. There are early decision and deferred admissions plans. Early decision applications should be filed by December 1; regular applications, by February 15 for fall entry, November 15 for winter entry, and February 15 for spring entry, along with a $45 fee. Notification of early decision is sent December 15; regular decision, April 1. 35 early decision candidates were accepted for the 2003-2004 class. A waiting list is an active part of the admissions procedure. Applications are accepted on-line through Common Application.

Transfer: 32 transfer students enrolled in 2002-2003. 18 of 36 credits required for the bachelor's degree must be completed at COA.

Visiting: There are regularly scheduled orientations for prospective students, including an annual fall tour for high school seniors on Columbus Day. There are guides for informal visits and visitors may sit in on classes and stay overnight. To schedule a visit, contact Donna McFarland at *dlm@coa.edu*.

Financial Aid: The average freshman award for 2003-2004 was $19,800. 60% of undergraduates work part time. Average annual earnings from campus work are $1000. COA is a member of CSS. The FAFSA and the college's own financial statement are required. The deadline for filing freshman financial aid applications for fall entry is February 15.

International Students: There are 51 international students enrolled. The school actively recruits these students. They must score 550 on the written TOEFL or 217 on the electronic version and also take IB English exam.

Computers: More than 40 PCs, including Dell System 220/325, IBM XT and AT, and Mac, are available in 2 computer centers and a science lab. The graphics lab contains 7 workstations and peripherals. There is Internet access in each dorm room. All students may access the system 24 hours a day. There are no time limits and no fees. It is strongly recommended that all students have a personal computer, specifically a Dell Optiplex for desktop, a Toshiba Satellite for notebooks, or MACS.

Graduates: From July 1, 2002 to June 30, 2003, 54 bachelor's degrees were awarded. In an average class, 34% graduate in 4 years or less, 59% graduate in 5 years or less, and 62% graduate in 6 years or less. Of the 2002 graduating class, 99% were employed within 6 months of graduation.

Admissions Contact: Sarah G. Baker, Director of Admission. E-mail: *inquiry@coa.edu* Web: *www.coa.edu*

HUSSON COLLEGE
Bangor, ME 04401-2999

C-4

(207) 941-7100
(800) 448-7766; Fax: (207) 941-7935

Full-time: 476 men, 657 women	**Faculty:** 50
Part-time: 223 men, 411 women	**Ph.Ds:** 56%
Graduate: 92 men, 179 women	**Student/Faculty:** 23 to 1
Year: semesters, summer session	**Tuition:** $10,620
Application Deadline: open	**Room & Board:** $5680
Freshman Class: 975 applied, 943 accepted, 510 enrolled	
SAT I Verbal/Math: 459/468	**ACT:** 22 **LESS COMPETITIVE**

Husson College, founded in 1898, is a private institution offering business, health careers, teaching, and other professional training. There are 4 undergraduate and 2 graduate schools. In addition to regional accreditation, Husson has baccalaureate program accreditation with CAPTE and CCNE. The library contains 36,704 volumes, 11,074 microform items, and 174 audio/video tapes/CDs, and subscribes to 500 periodicals. Computerized library services include the card catalog, interlibrary loans, database searching, and Internet access. Special learning facilities include a learning resource center, art gallery, and radio station. The 200-acre campus is in an urban area in the city of Bangor. Including any residence halls, there are 8 buildings.

Student Life: 85% of undergraduates are from Maine. Students are from 22 states, 12 foreign countries, and Canada. 90% are from public schools. 92% are white. The average age of freshmen is 20; all undergraduates, 21. 32% do not continue beyond their first year.

Housing: 800 students can be accommodated in college housing, which includes coed dorms. In addition, there are honors houses. On-campus housing is guaranteed for all 4 years. 52% of students live on campus; of those, 40% remain on campus on weekends. All students may keep cars.

Activities: 2% of men belong to 1 local and 2 national fraternities; 4% of women belong to 3 local sororities. There are 29 groups on campus, including cheerleading, choir, computers, drama, ethnic, international, literary magazine, newspaper, pep band, professional, radio and TV, religious, social, social service, student government, and yearbook. Popular campus events include Spring Fling, Winter Carnival, and Greek Alumni Weekend.

Sports: There are 6 intercollegiate sports for men and 6 for women, and 8 intramural sports for men and 8 for women. Facilities include a gym, an Olympic-size swimming pool, weight training and mat rooms, a health and fitness center, basketball and tennis courts, a baseball complex, and a soccer field.

Disabled Students: 80% of the campus is accessible. Wheelchair ramps, elevators, special parking, specially equipped rest rooms, lowered drinking fountains, and lowered telephones are available.

Services: Counseling and information services are available, as is tutoring in most subjects. There is remedial math and writing.

Campus Safety and Security: Measures include security escort services, informal discussions, pamphlets/posters/films, and lighted pathways/sidewalks.

Programs of Study: Husson confers the B.S. degree. Associate and master's degrees are also awarded. Bachelor's degrees are awarded in BIOLOGICAL SCIENCE (biology/biological science), BUSINESS (accounting, banking and finance, business administration and management, business systems analysis, hospitality management services, marketing/retailing/merchandising, and sports management), COMPUTER AND PHYSICAL SCIENCE (computer programming), EDUCATION (physical), HEALTH PROFESSIONS (nursing), SOCIAL SCIENCE (criminal justice, paralegal studies, and psychology). Accounting, nursing, and physical therapy are the strongest academically. Business administration is the largest.

Required: Requirements for graduation vary by program, but a total of 120 credit hours with a minimum GPA of 2.0 is necessary. A course in computer information systems is required in the first year for most programs.

Special: Experiential learning is part of the core curriculum in all majors. Internships are incorporated in accounting, computer information systems, sports management, hospitality management, nursing, physical therapy, occupational therapy, international business, and family business. Co-op programs, externships, and clinicals are included in the curriculum in all other majors. Students can go a fifth year and obtain a master's in business in accounting, business administration, or CIS, and in phys ed with a concentration in sports management. An accelerated degree program, dual majors, and student-designed majors are also available.

Faculty/Classroom: 50% of faculty are male; 50%, female. All teach undergraduates. No introductory courses are taught by graduate students. The average class size in an introductory lecture is 20; in a laboratory, 16; and in a regular course, 19.

Admissions: 97% of the 2003-2004 applicants were accepted. The SAT I scores for the 2003-2004 freshman class were: Verbal--68% below 500, 28% between 500 and 599, and 4% between 600 and 700; Math--66% below 500, 27% between 500 and 599, 6% between 600 and 700, and 1% above 700. 17% of the current freshmen were in the top fifth of their class; 45% were in the top two fifths. 4 freshmen graduated first in their class.

Requirements: The SAT I is required. In addition, applicants must be graduates of an accredited secondary school or have earned a GED. A recommendation from a high school counselor is required. Husson requires applicants to be in the upper 50% of their class. A GPA of 2.0 is required. AP and CLEP credits are accepted. Important factors in the admissions decision are advanced placement or honor courses, recommendations by school officials, and leadership record.

Procedure: Freshmen are admitted to all sessions. Entrance exams should be taken prior to enrollment. There are early admissions and deferred admissions plans. Application deadlines are open. There is a rolling admissions plan. Notification is sent on a rolling basis. Application fee is $25. 12 applicants were on the 2003 waiting list; 7 were admitted. Applications are accepted on computer disk and on-line through the school's web site.

Transfer: 103 transfer students enrolled in 2002-2003. Applicants must have a 2.0 GPA. Courses with a C grade or better transfer. 30 credits of 120 required for the bachelor's degree must be completed at Husson.

Visiting: There are regularly scheduled orientations for prospective students, including an interview and campus tour. There are guides for informal visits and visitors may sit in on classes and stay overnight. To schedule a visit, contact the Admissions Office at *admit@husson.edu*.

Financial Aid: In a recent year, 92% of all full-time freshmen and 83% of continuing full-time students received some form of financial aid. 92% of full-time freshmen and 86% of continuing full-time students received need-based aid. The average freshman award was $12,400. 80% of undergraduates work part time. Average annual earnings from campus work are $1505. The average financial indebtedness of the 2003 graduate was $17,025. Husson is a member of CSS. The FAFSA is required. The fall deadline for filing freshman financial aid applications is open.

International Students: There are 43 international students enrolled. The school actively recruits these students. They must score 500 on the written TOEFL or 173 on the electronic version and also take the SAT I or ACT. Students who score less than 500 on the TOEFL may be accepted conditionally and must enroll in a full-time intensive English program.

Computers: The mainframe is a CAMS-Microsoft 2000. Computer labs with a total of 120 workstations are available exclusively for student use. There is a Fractional DS3-6 megabyte pipe hookup. All students may access the system 24 hours a day. There are no time limits and no fees.

Graduates: From July 1, 2002 to June 30, 2003, 286 bachelor's degrees were awarded. The most popular majors were business administration (35%), nursing (10%), and accounting (10%). In an average class, 62% graduate in 4 years or less, 43% graduate in 5 years or less, and 45% graduate in 6 years or less. 50 companies recruited on campus in 2002-2003. Of the 2002 graduating class, 2% were enrolled in graduate school within 6 months of graduation and 95% were employed.

Admissions Contact: Jane Goodwin, Director of Admissions. A video is available. E-mail: *admit@husson.edu* Web: *http://www.husson.edu*

MAINE COLLEGE OF ART
Portland, ME 04101

B-6

(207) 775-5157, ext. 254
(800) 639-4808; Fax: (207) 772-5069

Full-time: 126 men, 216 women	**Faculty:** 30
Part-time: 16 men, 26 women	**Ph.Ds:** 93%
Graduate: 13 men, 17 women	**Student/Faculty:** 11 to 1
Year: semesters	**Tuition:** $21,132
Application Deadline: open	**Room & Board:** $7680
Freshman Class: 368 applied, 319 accepted, 141 enrolled	
SAT I Verbal/Math: 540/505	**ACT:** 20 **SPECIAL**

Maine College of Art, established in 1882, is a private, independent visual art college. In addition to regional accreditation, MECA has baccalaureate program accreditation with NASAD. The library contains 18,500 volumes and 150 audio/video tapes/CDs, and subscribes to 100 periodicals. Computerized library services include the card catalog, interlibrary loans, and database searching. Special learning facilities include an art gallery. The campus is in an urban area 100 miles north of Boston in downtown Portland. Including any residence halls, there are 6 buildings.

Student Life: 65% of undergraduates are from out of state, mostly the Northeast. Students are from 29 states and 6 foreign countries. 94% are white. The average age of freshmen is 20; all undergraduates, 22. 30% do not continue beyond their first year.

Housing: 100 students can be accommodated in college housing, which includes coed dorms and on-campus apartments. On-campus housing is available on a first-come, first-served basis. 75% of students commute. Alcohol is not permitted. All students may keep cars.

Activities: There are no fraternities or sororities. There are 10 groups on campus, including art, computers, dance, drama, gay, international, newspaper, photography, social, and student government. Popular campus events include annual art sale, art auction, and Earth Day celebration.

Sports: There is no sports program at MECA.

Disabled Students: 65% of the campus is accessible. Wheelchair ramps, elevators, specially equipped rest rooms, and lowered drinking fountains are available.

Services: Counseling and information services are available, as is tutoring in every subject. There is remedial math, reading, and writing. Academic support for writing papers, study skills, and time management is available, as is help for students with learning disabilities.

Campus Safety and Security: Measures include self-defense education, informal discussions, pamphlets/posters/films, emergency telephones, and safety training by local police.

Programs of Study: MECA confers the B.F.A. degree. Master's degrees are also awarded. Bachelor's degrees are awarded in COMMUNICATIONS AND THE ARTS (graphic design, media arts, metal/jewelry, painting, photography, printmaking, and sculpture), ENGINEERING AND ENVIRONMENTAL DESIGN (ceramic science). Painting, photography, and ceramics are the largest.

Required: All students must take 2 years of studio foundation courses and 2 years in the studio major, as well as 5 semesters of art history, 3 of humanities or social science, 2 each of English composition, natural science, and Western civilization, and 1 of critical issues. 129 total credit hours are necessary, with 36 in the major. Students must maintain a minimum GPA of 2.0. A senior thesis is required.

Special: Cross-registration with Bowdoin College, the Greater Portland Alliance of Colleges and Universities, and AICAD Mobility is available, as are internships utilizing professional artists and design and photography studios. An internship coordinator supervises the formal program for elective credit. There are also Art in Service internships. The continuing studies program provides for nondegree study. Minors in art history, drawing, and illustration are also offered, as are dual and student-designed majors.

Faculty/Classroom: 50% of faculty are male; 50%, female. All teach undergraduates. No introductory courses are taught by graduate students. The average class size in an introductory lecture is 136; in a laboratory, 18; and in a regular course, 20.

Admissions: 87% of the 2003-2004 applicants were accepted. The SAT I scores for the 2003-2004 freshman class were: Verbal--29% below 500, 45% between 500 and 599, 22% between 600 and 700, and 4% above 700; Math--49% below 500, 36% between 500 and 599, 14% between 600 and 700, and 1% above 700. The ACT scores were 67% below 21, 17% between 21 and 23, and 17% between 24 and 26. 31% of the current freshmen were in the top fifth of their class; 57% were in the top two fifths.

Requirements: The SAT I or ACT is required. In addition, it is recommended that candidates for admission complete 4 years of English, 3 years each of art and math, and 2 years each of foreign language, science, and social studies. AP credits are accepted. Important factors in the admissions decision are personality/intangible qualities, advanced placement or honor courses, and evidence of special talent.

Procedure: Freshmen are admitted fall and spring. Entrance exams should be taken in the fall of the senior year. There is a deferred and a rolling admissions plan. Application deadlines are open. Application fee is $40.

Transfer: 46 transfer students enrolled in 2002-2003. Transfers must submit an official copy of their college transcripts. 65 of 129 credits required for the bachelor's degree must be completed at MECA.

Visiting: There are regularly scheduled orientations for prospective students, including a tour, a portfolio review, and a faculty-student panel, and opportunities to observe classes and meet with an admissions counselor or other staff. There are guides for informal visits and visitors may sit in on classes. To schedule a visit, contact Kate Quin-Easter in the Admissions Office at (800) 639-4808 or (207) 775-5157, ext. 226 or *kquin-easter@meca.edu.*

Financial Aid: In a recent year, 78% of all full-time freshmen and 99% of continuing full-time students received some form of financial aid. 78% of full-time freshmen and 99% of continuing full-time students received need-based aid. The average freshman award was $14,464. 21% of undergraduates work part time. Average annual earnings from campus work are $1341. The average financial indebtedness of a recent graduate was $23,634. MECA is a member of CSS. The FAFSA is required. The deadline for filing freshman financial aid applications for fall entry is March 1.

International Students: There are 12 international students enrolled. The school actively recruits these students. They must score 500 on the written TOEFL or 173 on the electronic version and also take the SAT I or the ACT.

Computers: Technology allowing digital imaging, animation, web site design, and Internet access is available to students through the Imaging Center. General computer access is available in the student center, and the computer lab. All students may access the system. Time is scheduled around classroom use. There are no time limits and no fees.

Graduates: From July 1, 2002 to June 30, 2003, 60 bachelor's degrees were awarded. The most popular majors were graphic design (21%), painting (18%), and sculpture (17%). In an average class, 33% graduate

in 4 years or less, 38% graduate in 5 years or less, and 48% graduate in 6 years or less.

Admissions Contact: Joshua Bergey, Dean of Admissions. A video is available. E-mail: *admissions@meca.edu* Web: *www.meca.edu*

MAINE MARITIME ACADEMY C-5
Castine, ME 04420 (207) 326-2206
(800) 227-8465; Fax: (207) 326-2515

Full-time: 587 men, 160 women	**Faculty:** 65
Part-time: 12 men, 1 woman	**Ph.D.s:** 37%
Graduate: 12 men, 2 women	**Student/Faculty:** 12 to 1
Year: semesters	**Tuition:** $6560 ($11,610)
Application Deadline: July 1	**Room & Board:** $5820
Freshman Class: 652 applied, 443 accepted, 244 enrolled	
SAT I Verbal/Math: 510/540	**ACT:** 21 COMPETITIVE

Maine Maritime Academy, founded in 1941, is a public institution offering degree programs in ocean and marine-oriented studies with emphasis on engineering, transportation, business management, and ocean sciences, as well as preparing graduates for the merchant marine and uniformed services of the United States. The academic calendar consists of 2 semesters plus a 2- to 3-month annual training cruise. There are 4 undergraduate schools and 1 graduate school. In addition to regional accreditation, MMA has baccalaureate program accreditation with ABET. The library contains 75,381 volumes and 600 audio/video tapes/CDs, and subscribes to 950 periodicals. Computerized library services include the card catalog, interlibrary loans, and database searching. Special learning facilities include a planetarium, more than 60 vessels, and bridge, radar, power plant, and cargo system simulators. The 50-acre campus is in a small town 38 miles south of Bangor on the east coast of Penobscot Bay. Including any residence halls, there are 14 buildings.

Student Life: 65% of undergraduates are from Maine. Students are from 35 states, 7 foreign countries, and Canada. 90% are from public schools. 97% are white. The average age of freshmen is 19; all undergraduates, 24. 12% do not continue beyond their first year; 75% remain to graduate.

Housing: 600 students can be accommodated in college housing, which includes coed dorms and on-campus apartments. On-campus housing is guaranteed for all 4 years. 85% of students live on campus; of those, 30% remain on campus on weekends. Alcohol is not permitted. All students may keep cars.

Activities: 6% of men and about 25% of women belong to 1 national fraternity. There are no sororities. There are 30 groups on campus, including amateur radio, bagpipe band, band, chess, drama, drill team, engineering, ethnic, international, marching band, newspaper, outing, pep band, photography, professional, rugby, social, social service, student government, and yearbook. Popular campus events include Daisy Day, Klondike Derby, and Family Weekend.

Sports: There are 6 intercollegiate sports for men and 6 for women, and 10 intramural sports for men and 10 for women. Facilities include 2 weight rooms, an Olympic pool, a field house, a gym, racquetball and squash courts, an aerobics room, and a multisports athletic field.

Disabled Students: All of the campus is accessible. Wheelchair ramps, elevators, special parking, and specially equipped rest rooms are available.

Services: Counseling and information services are available, as is tutoring in most subjects. There is remedial math, reading, and writing.

Campus Safety and Security: Measures include 24-hour foot and vehicle patrol, informal discussions, pamphlets/posters/films, and lighted pathways/sidewalks. There are medical and counseling services.

Programs of Study: MMA confers the B.S. degree. Associate and master's degrees are also awarded. Bachelor's degrees are awarded in BUSINESS (international business management), COMPUTER AND PHYSICAL SCIENCE (oceanography), ENGINEERING AND ENVIRONMENTAL DESIGN (engineering, engineering technology, marine engineering, maritime science, and transportation technology). Marine systems engineering is the strongest academically. Marine engineering technology is the largest.

Required: A minimum GPA of 2.0 in an average of 140 total credit hours is required for graduation. A comprehensive exam is required for USCG license candidates.

Special: The annual training cruise gives students practical experience aboard the academy's 500-foot ship or on assigned merchant ships. Co-op programs and internships are offered, as is study abroad through special agreements with other maritime colleges worldwide. Dual and student-designed majors are possible.

Faculty/Classroom: 76% of faculty are male; 24%, female. All teach undergraduates. No introductory courses are taught by graduate students. The average class size in an introductory lecture is 30; in a laboratory, 15; and in a regular course, 25.

Admissions: 68% of the 2003-2004 applicants were accepted.

Requirements: The SAT I or ACT is required. In addition, candidates for admission must have completed 4 years of English, 3 of math, and

2 of lab science. Courses must include algebra I, algebra II or trigonometry, geometry, and either chemistry or physics with a lab. A GPA of 2.0 is required. AP and CLEP credits are accepted. Important factors in the admissions decision are advanced placement or honor courses, evidence of special talent, and leadership record.

Procedure: Freshmen are admitted fall and spring. Entrance exams should be taken as early as possible in the senior year. There are early decision and deferred admissions plans. Early decision applications should be filed by December 20; regular applications, by July 1 for fall entry and November 1 for spring entry. The fall 2003 application fee was $15. Notification is sent on a rolling basis. 25 early decision candidates were accepted for the 2003-2004 class. Applications are accepted on-line through the academy's web site and CollegeLink.

Transfer: 16 transfer students enrolled in 2002-2003. Applicants must have a minimum 2.0 GPA in previous college work and meet the same prerequisites as entering freshmen.

Visiting: There are regularly scheduled orientations for prospective students, consisting of 3 open houses per year; campus visits are available weekdays throughout the year. There are guides for informal visits and visitors may sit in on classes and stay overnight. To schedule a visit, contact the Admissions Office at (207) 326-4311 or *admissions@mma.edu*.

Financial Aid: In a recent year, 74% of all full-time freshmen and 76% of continuing full-time students received some form of financial aid. The average freshman award was $8100. 38% of undergraduates work part time. Average annual earnings from campus work are $460. The average financial indebtedness of a recent year's graduate was $15,650. MMA is a member of CSS. The FAFSA, student and parent tax returns, and a verification worksheet are required. The deadline for filing freshman financial aid applications for fall entry is March 1.

International Students: There were 30 international students enrolled in a recent year. They must score 550 on the written TOEFL and also take the SAT I or the ACT.

Computers: Some PCs are available. Internet access is available campuswide and on the training ship. All students may access the system. There are no time limits. The fee is $100. All students are required to have laptops.

Graduates: From July 1, 2002 to June 30, 2003, 130 bachelor's degrees were awarded. The most popular majors were marine engineering (42%), marine transportation (20%), and power engineering (12%). In an average class, 75% graduate in 4 years or less, and 4% graduate in 5 years or less. 60 companies recruited on campus in a recent year. Of a recent graduating class, 4% were enrolled in graduate school within 6 months of graduation and 95% were employed.

Admissions Contact: Jeff Wright, Director of Admissions. A video is available. E-mail: *admissions@mma.edu*
Web: *www.mainemaritime.edu*

SAINT JOSEPH'S COLLEGE OF MAINE A-6
Standish, ME 04084-5263 (207) 893-7746
(800) 338-7057; Fax: (207) 893-7862

Full-time: 313 men, 616 women	**Faculty:** 57; IIB, --$
Part-time: 10 men, 14 women	**Ph.D.s:** 98%
Graduate: none	**Student/Faculty:** 16 to 1
Year: semesters, summer session	**Tuition:** $18,070
Application Deadline: open	**Room & Board:** $7530
Freshman Class: 962 applied, 763 accepted, 245 enrolled	
SAT I Verbal/Math: 500/490	**COMPETITIVE**

Saint Joseph's College of Maine, founded in 1912, is a private, Roman Catholic institution offering liberal arts and preprofessional programs. In addition to regional accreditation, Saint Joseph's College of Maine has baccalaureate program accreditation with CCNE. The library contains 96,900 volumes, 6710 microform items, and 1240 audio/video tapes/CDs, and subscribes to 407 periodicals. Computerized library services include interlibrary loans, database searching, and Internet access. Special learning facilities include a learning resource center, radio station, and telescope observatory. The 331-acre campus is in a rural area 18 miles west of Portland. Including any residence halls, there are 20 buildings.

Student Life: 65% of undergraduates are from Maine. Students are from 17 states, 3 foreign countries, and Canada. 86% are white. The average age of freshmen is 18; all undergraduates, 20. 23% do not continue beyond their first year; 56% remain to graduate.

Housing: 829 students can be accommodated in college housing, which includes single-sex and coed dorms. In addition, there is substance-free housing. On-campus housing is guaranteed for all 4 years. 85% of students live on campus; of those, 70% remain on campus on weekends. All students may keep cars.

Activities: There are no fraternities or sororities. There are 30 groups on campus, including Americorp for Literacy, cheerleading, choir, chorale, computers, drama, ethnic, Habitat for Humanity, high adventure club, honors, ice hockey, international, literary magazine, musical theater, newspaper, photography, political, professional, radio and TV, religious, social, social service, student government, SuperKids, and yearbook. Popular campus events include Family Weekend, Christmas Benefit Concert, and Spring Fling.

Sports: There are 5 intercollegiate sports for men and 6 for women, and 12 intramural sports for men and 12 for women. Facilities include a multipurpose facility housing a gym, a workout room with free weights, Nautilus and other weight-training equipment, a cardiovascular workout room, dance aerobics rooms, a climbing wall, a 25-meter pool, saunas, and an elevated jogging track. There are also soccer and field hockey fields, a private beach on a lake, lighted athletic fields for baseball and softball, cross-country running and ski trails, and a low ropes course.

Disabled Students: 40% of the campus is accessible. Wheelchair ramps, elevators, special parking, specially equipped rest rooms, special class scheduling, and lowered drinking fountains are available.

Services: Counseling and information services are available, as is tutoring in most subjects. There is a reader service for the blind.

Campus Safety and Security: Measures include 24-hour foot and vehicle patrol, self-defense education, security escort services, and informal discussions. There are pamphlets/posters/films, emergency telephones, lighted pathways/sidewalks, and round-the-clock security officers.

Programs of Study: Saint Joseph's College of Maine confers B.A., B.S., B.S.B.A., and B.S.N. degrees. Associate and master's degrees are also awarded. Bachelor's degrees are awarded in BIOLOGICAL SCIENCE (biology/biological science), BUSINESS (business administration and management), COMMUNICATIONS AND THE ARTS (communications and English), COMPUTER AND PHYSICAL SCIENCE (chemistry and mathematics), EDUCATION (elementary and physical), ENGINEERING AND ENVIRONMENTAL DESIGN (environmental science), HEALTH PROFESSIONS (nursing and prepharmacy), SOCIAL SCIENCE (criminal justice, history, philosophy, psychology, sociology, and theological studies). Business, nursing, and biology are the strongest academically. Elementary education, business, and nursing are the largest.

Required: To graduate, students must complete 128 credit hours with a minimum GPA of 2.0, including 8 hours of English, history, theology, and a foreign language, 4 each of science and math, and 8 of electives.

Special: Saint Joseph's offers internships, cross-registration with 4 southern Maine colleges, study abroad in Nova Scotia and Ireland, a semester at sea, dual majors, work-study programs, and non-degree study. There are 2 national honor societies, a freshman honors program, and 6 departmental honors programs.

Faculty/Classroom: 50% of faculty are male; 50%, female. All teach undergraduates. The average class size in an introductory lecture is 25; in a laboratory, 12; and in a regular course, 18.

Admissions: 79% of the 2003-2004 applicants were accepted. The SAT I scores for the 2003-2004 freshman class were: Verbal--50% below 500, 38% between 500 and 599, and 12% between 600 and 700; Math--53% below 500, 36% between 500 and 599, and 11% between 600 and 700. 2 freshmen graduated first in their class.

Requirements: The SAT I or ACT is required. In addition, candidates for admission must be high school graduates who have completed a college preparatory curriculum with a recommended 4 units in English, 3 to 4 in math, 2 in foreign language, and 1 to 3 each in history, science, and social studies. A GPA of 2.0 is required. AP and CLEP credits are accepted. Important factors in the admissions decision are advanced placement or honor courses, recommendations by school officials, and extracurricular activities record.

Procedure: Freshmen are admitted fall and spring. Entrance exams should be taken by January of the senior year. There are early admissions and deferred admissions plans. Application deadlines are open. The fall 2003 application fee was $35. Notification is sent beginning December 15. 45 applicants were on the 2003 waiting list; 25 were admitted. Applications are accepted on-line at *www.sjcme.edu/application*.

Transfer: 40 transfer students enrolled in 2002-2003. Transfer students should have a minimum GPA of 2.0. 32 of 128 credits required for the bachelor's degree must be completed at Saint Joseph's College of Maine.

Visiting: There are regularly scheduled orientations for prospective students, including Application and Acceptance Day programs, visits on 5 fall Saturdays, and summer visits. There are guides for informal visits and visitors may sit in on classes and stay overnight. To schedule a visit, contact the Office of Admission.

Financial Aid: In 2003-2004, 99% of all full-time freshmen and 92% of continuing full-time students received some form of financial aid. 85% of all full-time students received need-based aid. The average freshman award was $15,722. Need-based scholarships or need-based grants averaged $10,737 ($17,500 maximum); need-based self-help aid (loans and jobs) averaged $5578 ($11,700 maximum); and non-need-based awards and non-need-based scholarships averaged $9787 ($17,430 maximum). 35% of undergraduates work part time. Average annual earnings from campus work are $835. The average financial indebtedness of the 2003 graduate was $17,177. Saint Joseph's College of Maine is a member of CSS. The FAFSA is required. The priority date for freshman financial aid applications for fall entry is March 1.

International Students: There are 3 international students enrolled. They must take the TOEFL, scoring in the 50th percentile, and also take the SAT I.

Computers: The mainframes are an AT&T 3430 Server and a Pyramid Mis-Z. There are 71 PCs available to students in the computer room, the library, the resource center, and most academic departments. All students may access the system 24 hours a day in all labs and until 10 P.M. in the library. There are no time limits and no fees. It is strongly recommended that all students have a personal computer.

Graduates: From July 1, 2002 to June 30, 2003, 148 bachelor's degrees were awarded. The most popular majors were education (20%), business (20%), and nursing (12%). In an average class, 51% graduate in 4 years or less, 55% graduate in 5 years or less, and 56% graduate in 6 years or less. 18 companies recruited on campus in 2002-2003. Of the 2002 graduating class, 15% were enrolled in graduate school within 6 months of graduation and 92% were employed.

Admissions Contact: Alexander Popovics, Vice President for Enrollment Management. E-mail: *admission@sjcme.edu*
Web: *http://www.sjcme.edu*

THOMAS COLLEGE
Waterville, ME 04901

B-4
(207) 877-0101
(800) 339-7001; Fax: (207) 877-0114

Full-time: 293 men, 249 women	**Faculty:** 23; IIB, --$
Part-time: 40 men, 116 women	**Ph.D.s:** 50%
Graduate: 62 men, 72 women	**Student/Faculty:** 24 to 1
Year: semesters, summer session	**Tuition:** $13,890
Application Deadline: open	**Room & Board:** $6070
Freshman Class: 588 applied, 428 accepted, 179 enrolled	
SAT I Verbal/Math: 439/451	**LESS COMPETITIVE**

Thomas College, founded in 1894, is a private institution that provides a supportive learning environment that values the needs and goals of individual students and prepares them for success in their personal and professional lives. Each program at the college promotes professional excellence, informed by ethics and integrity. The library contains 24,800 volumes and 600 audio/video tapes/CDs, and subscribes to 10,000 periodicals. Computerized library services include the card catalog, interlibrary loans, database searching, and Internet access. Special learning facilities include a learning resource center and art gallery. The 70-acre campus is in a rural area 75 miles north of Portland. Including any residence halls, there are 9 buildings.

Student Life: 81% of undergraduates are from Maine. Students are from 8 states and 1 foreign countries. 85% are from public schools. 96% are white. The average age of freshmen is 23; all undergraduates, 25.

Housing: 375 students can be accommodated in college housing, which includes coed dorms and off-campus apartments. On-campus housing is guaranteed for the freshman year only, is available on a first-come, first-served basis, and is available on a lottery system for upperclassmen. 67% of students live on campus; of those, 55% remain on campus on weekends. All students may keep cars.

Activities: 3% of men belong to 1 local and 1 national fraternity; 5% of women belong to 2 local and 1 national sorority. There are 30 groups on campus, including cheerleading, computers, drama, honors, international, newspaper, professional, religious, social, social service, student government, and yearbook. Popular campus events include Winter Carnival, Spring Fling, and Olympic Day.

Sports: There are 6 intercollegiate sports for men and 6 for women, and 6 intramural sports for men and 6 for women. Facilities include a gym, a basketball court, a weight, fitness, and aerobics room, soccer and softball fields, a training area, a baseball field, a field hockey field, an intramural field, and cross-country skiing and snowshoe trails. Facilities for swimming, indoor tennis, racquetball, and hockey are available locally.

Disabled Students: 80% of the campus is accessible. Wheelchair ramps, special parking, specially equipped rest rooms, and special class scheduling are available.

Services: Counseling and information services are available, as is tutoring in most subjects. There is remedial math, reading, and writing.

Campus Safety and Security: Measures include 24-hour foot and vehicle patrol, informal discussions, pamphlets/posters/films, and lighted pathways/sidewalks.

Programs of Study: Thomas confers the B.S. degree. Associate and master's degrees are also awarded. Bachelor's degrees are awarded in BUSINESS (accounting, business administration and management, business economics, management information systems, management science, marketing management, and sports management), COMMUNICATIONS AND THE ARTS (communications), COMPUTER AND PHYSICAL SCIENCE (information sciences and systems), EDUCATION (business and elementary), SOCIAL SCIENCE (criminal justice, international studies, and psychology). Accounting and management information systems are the strongest academically. Accounting, management, and computer information systems are the largest.

Required: To graduate, students must achieve a minimum GPA of 2.0, fulfill all course requirements, and complete a minimum of 120 total credit hours of study including 30 hours in the major.

Special: Students may cross-register with Colby College and Kennebec Valley Community College. There are co-op programs and internships available in most majors. The college also offers study in Canada through the New England - Quebec Exchange and in France and Austra-

lia. 5-year degrees are offered in most majors where a B.S. is available. There are 2 national honor societies.

Faculty/Classroom: 60% of faculty are male; 40%, female. All teach undergraduates. The average class size in an introductory lecture is 22 and in a regular course, 14.

Admissions: 73% of the 2003-2004 applicants were accepted. 13% of the current freshmen were in the top fifth of their class; 30% were in the top two fifths.

Requirements: The SAT I is required. In addition, candidates for admission must be high school graduates with an academic program that includes 4 years of English, 3 of math, 3 of sciences, 2 of social studies, 2 of foreign language, and 2 other. A letter of recommendation from a secondary school counselor is required. An interview is highly recommended. A GPA of 2.0 is required. AP and CLEP credits are accepted. Important factors in the admissions decision are advanced placement or honor courses, recommendations by school officials, and personality/intangible qualities.

Procedure: Freshmen are admitted to all sessions. Entrance exams should be taken by the fall of the senior year. There are early admissions and deferred admissions plans. There is a rolling admissions plan. Application deadlines are open. Application fee is $35. Applications are accepted on-line at *www.thomas.edu*.

Transfer: Applicants should have a minimum college GPA of 2.0. The school recommends the SAT I (with a minimum score of 860) as well as an interview. Official transcripts from all previously attended postsecondary institutions are required. 60 of 120 credits required for the bachelor's degree must be completed at Thomas.

Visiting: There are regularly scheduled orientations for prospective students, includes 3 to 4 open houses and 1 new student orientation/preregistration. There are guides for informal visits and visitors may sit in on classes. To schedule a visit, contact the Admissions Office.

Financial Aid: The FAFSA is required. The deadline for filing freshman financial aid applications for fall entry is open.

International Students: The school actively recruits these students. They must score 530 on the written TOEFL and also take the SAT I.

Computers: 75 networked PCs are available to students at various locations. Internet access is available from all computers. Desktop publishing, spreadsheet, database, word processing, graphics, presentation, web browsing, and e-mail software are also available on all computers. All students may access the system 24 hours a day. There are no time limits and no fees. It is strongly recommended that all students have a personal computer.

Graduates: From July 1, 2002 to June 30, 2003, 176 bachelor's degrees were awarded. The most popular majors were accounting (28%), computer information systems (20%), and sports management (14%). In an average class, 41% graduate in 4 years or less, and 9% graduate in 5 years or less. 58 companies recruited on campus in 2002-2003.

Admissions Contact: Robert Callahan, Vice President for Enrollment Management. E-mail: *admiss@thomas.edu* Web: *www.thomas.edu*

UNITY COLLEGE
Unity, ME 04988-0532

C-4
(207) 948-3131; Fax: (207) 948-6277

Full-time: 330 men, 160 women	**Faculty:** 34
Part-time: 10 men, 10 women	**Ph.D.s:** 61%
Graduate: none	**Student/Faculty:** 16 to 1
Year: semesters, summer session	**Tuition:** $14,420
Application Deadline: open	**Room & Board:** $5900
Freshman Class: n/av	
SAT I: not required	**LESS COMPETITIVE**

Unity College, founded in 1965, is a private, independent institution offering undergraduate programs in environmental science, natural resource management, and wilderness-based outdoor recreation. Some information in the above capsule and in this profile is approximate. In addition to regional accreditation, Unity has baccalaureate program accreditation with SAF. The library contains 46,000 volumes and 750 audio/video tapes/CDs, and subscribes to 651 periodicals. Computerized library services include the card catalog, interlibrary loans, and database searching. Special learning facilities include a learning resource center and art gallery. The 205-acre campus is in a rural area 18 miles east of Waterville. Including any residence halls, there are 18 buildings.

Student Life: 72% of undergraduates are from out of state, mostly the Northeast. Students are from 23 states and 2 foreign countries. 97% are from public schools. 99% are white. 57% are Catholic; 30% Protestant. The average age of freshmen is 18; all undergraduates, 20. 18% do not continue beyond their first year; 82% remain to graduate.

Housing: 306 students can be accommodated in college housing, which includes coed dorms and off-campus apartments. On-campus housing is guaranteed for all 4 years. 80% of students live on campus; of those, 80% remain on campus on weekends. All students may keep cars.

Activities: There are no fraternities or sororities. There are 34 groups on campus, including art, drama, literary magazine, newspaper, photography, student government, and yearbook. Popular campus events include Regional Woodsman's Meet in October.

Sports: There are 3 intercollegiate sports for men and 2 for women, and 10 intramural sports for men and 8 for women. Facilities include a gym, a weight training room, playing fields, a nature trail, and game rooms.

Disabled Students: 80% of the campus is accessible. Wheelchair ramps, special parking, and special class scheduling are available.

Services: Counseling and information services are available, as is tutoring in every subject. There is remedial math, reading, and writing. A full-time learning disability specialist is on staff.

Campus Safety and Security: Measures include 24-hour foot and vehicle patrol, informal discussions, and emergency telephones.

Programs of Study: Unity confers B.A. and B.S. degrees. Associate degrees are also awarded. Bachelor's degrees are awarded in AGRICULTURE (conservation and regulation and fishing and fisheries), BIOLOGICAL SCIENCE (ecology, environmental biology, and wildlife biology), EDUCATION (environmental), ENGINEERING AND ENVIRONMENTAL DESIGN (environmental science), HEALTH PROFESSIONS (environmental health science), SOCIAL SCIENCE (human ecology, interdisciplinary studies, and parks and recreation management). Aquaculture, fisheries, and ecology are the strongest academically. Conservation law enforcement, wilderness-based recreation, and wildlife are the largest.

Required: General education requirements include 38 credits in English composition, oral communication, math, computer science, life science, physical science, and electives, as well as 9 credits in a specialization outside the major field. Students must complete at least 120 credit hours with a minimum GPA of 2.0. An internship, thesis, or seminar is required in all bachelor's degree programs.

Special: The college offers co-op programs, credit-bearing internships, study abroad, a Washington semester, work-study programs, accelerated degree programs, dual and student-designed majors, and credit for life experience. A mentor program, in which a faculty member assists a student with research, is available to those students who earn a minimum GPA of 3.33 in their first 30 credit hours. There is 1 national honor society and a freshman honors program.

Faculty/Classroom: 66% of faculty are male; 33%, female. All teach undergraduates.

Requirements: SAT I or ACT scores, though not required, should be submitted, if available, for placement purposes. Applicants must be graduates of an accredited secondary school with a minimum GPA of 2.0. The GED is accepted. An essay is required, and an interview is recommended. AP and CLEP credits are accepted. Important factors in the admissions decision are advanced placement or honor courses, recommendations by alumni, and leadership record.

Procedure: Freshmen are admitted fall and spring. Entrance exams should be taken in the junior or senior year. There are early admissions and deferred admissions plans. Application deadlines are open. Application fee is $25. Notification is sent within 1 month after receipt of all required materials. A waiting list is an active part of the admissions procedure.

Transfer: Applicants must present a minimum college GPA of 2.0 and are encouraged to submit SAT I scores. 60 of 120 credits required for the bachelor's degree must be completed at Unity.

Visiting: There are regularly scheduled orientations for prospective students. There are guides for informal visits and visitors may sit in on classes and stay overnight. To schedule a visit, contact the Admissions Office.

Financial Aid: Unity is a member of CSS. The CSS Profile or FAFSA and the college's own financial statement are required. Check with the school for current deadlines.

International Students: The school actively recruits these students. They must score 500 on the written TOEFL.

Computers: A network of IBM-compatible PCs is available in the environmental science building. Macs are available in a number of locations on campus. All residence hall systems are hard-wired for Internet access. All students may access the system. There are no time limits and no fees.

Admissions Contact: Kay Fiedler, Director of Admissions.
E-mail: *admissions@unity.edu* Web: *www.unity.edu*

UNIVERSITY OF MAINE SYSTEM

Established in 1968, the University of Maine System is the state's largest educational institution with more than 34,400 students currently enrolled and nearly 1500 faculty members. It features seven universites across the state, as well as 10 University College outreach centers and 100 interactive distance education sites. Each of the universities profiled in this section has a distinct mission and serves as the educational and cultural center of its community. The University of Maine, located in Orono, and the University of Southern Maine, located in Portland and Gorham, offer graduate and undergraduate degrees, while the system's universities in Augusta, Farmington, Fort Kent, Machias, and Presque Isle offer undergraduate degrees. Governed by a board of trustees, which appoints a system chancellor as chief administrator, the University of Maine System offers 34 associate, 220 baccalaureate, 79 master's, and 29 doctoral programs. Log onto *www.maine.edu* for more information.

UNIVERSITY OF MAINE
Orono, ME 04469-5713

C-4
(207) 581-1561
(877) 4UM-ADMIT; Fax: (207) 581-1213

Full-time: 3729 men, 3605 women	**Faculty:** I, --$
Part-time: 572 men, 1066 women	**Ph.D.s:** 86%
Graduate: 766 men, 1484 women	**Student/Faculty:** n/av
Year: semesters, summer session	**Tuition:** $5914 ($14,614)
Application Deadline: open	**Room & Board:** $6166
Freshman Class: 5540 applied, 4204 accepted, 1698 enrolled	
SAT I Verbal/Math: 530/540	**ACT:** 24 COMPETITIVE+

The University of Maine, established in 1865, is a publicly funded, land-grant institution in the University of Maine system. The university offers degree programs in the arts and sciences, business, public policy, health fields, engineering, education, forestry, and agriculture. There are 5 undergraduate schools and 1 graduate school. In addition to regional accreditation, U Maine has baccalaureate program accreditation with AACSB, ABET, ACS, ADA, AHEA, ASLHA, CSAB, CSWE, NASM, NASPAA, NCATE, NLN, and SAF. The library contains 1,261,243 volumes, 2,441,201 microform items, and 26,647 audio/video tapes/CDs, and subscribes to 13,041 periodicals. Computerized library services include the card catalog, interlibrary loans, database searching, and Internet access. Special learning facilities include an art gallery, natural history museum, planetarium, radio station, concert hall, other music facilities, 2 theaters, a digital media lab, and an anthropology museum. The 3300-acre campus is in a small town 8 miles north of Bangor. Including any residence halls, there are 158 buildings.

Student Life: 85% of undergraduates are from Maine. Students are from 47 states, 71 foreign countries, and Canada. 93% are white. The average age of freshmen is 18; all undergraduates, 22. 22% do not continue beyond their first year; 60% remain to graduate.

Housing: 3500 students can be accommodated in college housing, which includes coed dorms, on-campus apartments, off-campus apartments, and married-student housing. In addition, there are honors houses, language houses, special-interest houses, substance-free housing, quiet sections, graduate family, and academic wings. On-campus housing is guaranteed for the freshman year only and is available on a first-come, first-served basis. 57% of students live on campus; of those, 80% remain on campus on weekends. All students may keep cars.

Activities: There are 1 local and 12 national fraternities and 6 national sororities. There are 234 groups on campus, including art, band, cheerleading, chess, choir, chorale, chorus, computers, dance, drama, drill team, ethnic, film, gay, honors, international, jazz band, literary magazine, marching band, musical theater, newspaper, opera, orchestra, pep band, photography, political, professional, radio and TV, religious, social, social service, student government, symphony, and yearbook. Popular campus events include Maine Day, Family and Friends Weekend, and International Week.

Sports: There are 9 intercollegiate sports for men and 10 for women, and 53 intramural sports for men and 53 for women. Facilities include a sports arena for hockey and basketball, a field house, an indoor climbing center, a fitness center, a swimming pool, a weight room, an indoor track, a dance studio, basketball, volleyball, badminton, squash, tennis, and racquetball courts, and baseball, softball, soccer, field hockey, and football fields.

Disabled Students: 90% of the campus is accessible. Wheelchair ramps, elevators, special parking, specially equipped rest rooms, special class scheduling, lowered drinking fountains, lowered telephones, and a transport van are available.

Services: Counseling and information services are available, as is tutoring in some subjects, including 100- and 200-level courses. There is a reader service for the blind. Developmental courses are offered in remedial math, reading, and writing.

Campus Safety and Security: Measures include 24-hour foot and vehicle patrol, self-defense education, security escort services, and informal discussions. There are pamphlets/posters/films, emergency telephones, and lighted pathways/sidewalks.

Programs of Study: U Maine confers B.A., B.S., B.F.A., B.M.E., and B.U.S. degrees. Master's and doctoral degrees are also awarded. Bachelor's degrees are awarded in AGRICULTURE (agriculture, animal science, fishing and fisheries, forest engineering, forestry and related sciences, horticulture, natural resource management, wildlife management, and wood science), BIOLOGICAL SCIENCE (biochemistry, biology/biological science, biotechnology, botany, cell biology, marine biology, marine science, microbiology, molecular biology, nutrition, and zoology), BUSINESS (business administration and management and business economics), COMMUNICATIONS AND THE ARTS (art, communications, dramatic arts, English, French, German, journalism, Latin, media arts, modern language, music, music performance, romance languages and literature, Spanish, speech/debate/rhetoric, and studio art), COMPUTER AND PHYSICAL SCIENCE (chemistry, computer science, geology, information sciences and systems, mathematics, and physics), EDUCATION (art, elementary, health, music, physical, recreation, and secondary), ENGINEERING AND ENVIRONMENTAL DESIGN (bioengineering, chemical engineering, civil engineering, computer engineering, construction technology, electrical/electronics engineering, electrical/electronics engineering technology, engineering physics, environmental science, mechanical engineering, mechanical engineering technology, paper and pulp science, and surveying engineering), HEALTH PROFESSIONS (clinical science, medical laboratory technology, nursing, and speech pathology/audiology), SOCIAL SCIENCE (anthropology, child care/child and family studies, economics, food science, history, interdisciplinary studies, international studies, parks and recreation management, philosophy, political science/government, psychology, public administration, social work, sociology, and women's studies). Engineering and technology, business administration, and forest resources are the strongest academically. Education, business administration, and psychology are the largest.

Required: To graduate, students must complete a minimum of 120 credit hours, including a minimum of 48 in the major, with a minimum GPA of 2.0. 40 credits in approved courses must be taken. General education requirements include 18 credits in human values and social context, 6 credits in math/statistics/computer science, 2 courses in science, and at least 1 course in ethics. English composition is required. Students must demonstrate writing competency, and complete a capstone.

Special: A Professional Preparation Team program is offered by the College of Education. Cross-registration through the National Student Exchange and at other University of Maine campuses, internships at the upper level, a Washington semester, work-study programs both on- and off-campus, a B.A.-B.S. degree, dual majors, a general studies degree, and pass/fail options are available. Students may study abroad in more than 40 countries. Cooperative programs are available in most majors, and accelerated degrees may be arranged. There are 43 national honor societies, including Phi Beta Kappa, and a freshman honors program.

Faculty/Classroom: 62% of faculty are male; 38%, female. 4% teach undergraduates. Graduate students teach 6% of introductory courses. The average class size in an introductory lecture is 24; in a laboratory, 16; and in a regular course, 21.

Admissions: 76% of the 2003-2004 applicants were accepted. The SAT I scores for the 2003-2004 freshman class were: Verbal--31% below 500, 45% between 500 and 599, 21% between 600 and 700, and 3% above 700; Math--28% below 500, 44% between 500 and 599, 24% between 600 and 700, and 4% above 700. The ACT scores were 28% below 21, 20% between 21 and 23, 23% between 24 and 26, 15% between 27 and 28, and 14% above 28. 44% of the current freshmen were in the top fifth of their class; 78% were in the top two fifths. There were 3 National Merit finalists. 87 freshmen graduated first in their class.

Requirements: The SAT I or ACT is required. The GED is accepted. The number of academic or Carnegie credits required varies according to the program. The required secondary school courses also vary with each program but should include 4 credits of English, 3 of math, 2 each of lab science, social studies, and a foreign language, and 3 of electives. Guidance counselor recommendation is required for high school students. The school recommends that students submit an essay. An audition is required for music majors. AP and CLEP credits are accepted. Important factors in the admissions decision are advanced placement or honor courses, recommendations by school officials, and evidence of special talent.

Procedure: Freshmen are admitted fall and spring. Entrance exams should be taken by January of the senior year. There is a deferred admissions plan and a rolling admissions plan. Application deadlines are open. The application fee is $40. Applications are accepted on-line through *apply.maine.edu, commonapp.org,* and *collegeboard.com.*

Transfer: 494 transfer students enrolled in 2002-2003. Applicants must submit transcripts of all college and high school records. A minimum GPA of 2.0 is required. 30 of 120 credits required for the bachelor's degree must be completed at U Maine.

Visiting: There are regularly scheduled orientations for prospective students, including an opening welcome, campus tours, registration, department tours, student panel, admissions, financial aid, student life sessions, performing arts presentation, and music auditions. There are guides for informal visits and visitors may sit in on classes. To schedule a visit, contact the Visitors' Center at (207) 581-3740.

Financial Aid: In 2003-2004, 82% of all full-time freshmen and 83% of continuing full-time students received some form of financial aid. 59% of full-time freshmen and 51% of continuing full-time students received need-based aid. The average freshman award was $9047. Need-based scholarships or need-based grants averaged $5667; need-based self-help aid (loans and jobs) averaged $3875; non-need-based athletic scholarships averaged $11,005; and other non-need-based awards and non-need-based scholarships averaged $3882. 60% of undergraduates work part time. Average annual earnings from campus work are $2000. The average financial indebtedness of the 2003 graduate was $18,922. The FAFSA is required. The deadline for filing freshman financial aid applications for fall entry is March 1.

International Students: There are 146 international students enrolled. The school actively recruits these students. They must score 530 on the written TOEFL or 197 on the electronic version and also take the SAT I or the ACT. The SAT I is preferred.

Computers: The mainframe is an IBM S/390 parallel enterprise server. There are 12 public computer clusters on campus, 11 private clusters, numerous department clusters, and connectivity available in the residence halls. All students may access the system 24 hours a day. There are no time limits and no fees.

Graduates: From July 1, 2002 to June 30, 2003, 1422 bachelor's degrees were awarded. The most popular majors were education (16%), engineering (13%), and business (11%). In an average class, 30% graduate in 4 years or less, 54% graduate in 5 years or less, and 60% graduate in 6 years or less. 178 companies recruited on campus in 2002-2003. Of the 2002 graduating class, 25% were enrolled in graduate school within 6 months of graduation and 89% were employed.

Admissions Contact: Jonathan H. Henry, Director of Admissions. A video is available. E-mail: *um-admit@maine.edu*
Web: *www.umaine.edu*

UNIVERSITY OF MAINE AT AUGUSTA
Augusta, ME 04430

B-5
(207) 621-3390
(877) UMA-1234; Fax: (207) 621-3116

Full-time: 536 men, 1155 women	**Faculty:** 93; IIB, -$
Part-time: 969 men, 3283 women	**Ph.D.s:** 41%
Graduate: none	**Student/Faculty:** 18 to 1
Year: semesters, summer session	**Tuition:** $4065 ($9315)
Application Deadline: June 15	**Room & Board:** n/app
Freshman Class: 2294 applied, 2000 accepted, 1544 enrolled	
SAT I or ACT: not required	**COMPETITIVE**

The University of Maine at Augusta, founded in 1965, offers both associate and baccalaureate degrees and is part of the University of Maine System. There are 3 undergraduate schools. In addition to regional accreditation, UMA has baccalaureate program accreditation with ADA, NEASC, and NLN. The 2 libraries contain 77,398 volumes, 7084 microform items, and 3473 audio/video tapes/CDs, and subscribe to 637 periodicals. Computerized library services include the card catalog, interlibrary loans, and database searching. Special learning facilities include a learning resource center, art gallery, and an interactive television system. The 159-acre campus is in a small town 50 miles north of Portland. There are 14 buildings.

Student Life: 97% of undergraduates are from Maine. Students are from 16 states, 4 foreign countries, and Canada. 99% are from public schools. 96% are white. The average age of freshmen is 27; all undergraduates, 33. 40% do not continue beyond their first year; 30% remain to graduate.

Housing: There are no residence halls. All students commute. Alcohol is not permitted. All students may keep cars.

Activities: There are no fraternities or sororities. There are 8 groups on campus, including art, gay, honors, international, jazz band, pep band, professional, and student government. Popular campus events include UMA Day, Mile of Art, and Jazz Week.

Sports: There is 1 intercollegiate sport for men and 1 for women, and 2 intramural sports for men and 2 for women. Facilities include the UMA Community Outdoor Leisure Center, which is also open to the public. Facilities provide for seasonal activities and feature a running and cross-country skiing trail, tennis courts, a soccer field, and a softball field. Indoor facilities include a small gym, a racquetball court, and a small fitness center.

Disabled Students: 95% of the campus is accessible. Wheelchair ramps, elevators, special parking, specially equipped rest rooms, lowered drinking fountains, and lowered telephones are available.

Services: Counseling and information services are available, as is tutoring in some subjects, including developmental and introductory level courses. There is a reader service for the blind, and remedial math, reading, and writing. There are workshops on a variety of student success skills, such as effective learning and reducing test anxiety.

Campus Safety and Security: Measures include pamphlets/posters/films, lighted pathways/sidewalks, a late-night transport/escort service, student patrols, and security personnel.

Programs of Study: UMA confers B.A., B.S., and B.Mus. degrees. Associate degrees are also awarded. Bachelor's degrees are awarded in BIOLOGICAL SCIENCE (biology/biological science), BUSINESS (accounting and business administration and management), COMMUNICATIONS AND THE ARTS (art, English, and jazz), COMPUTER AND PHYSICAL SCIENCE (information sciences and systems), EDUCATION (library science), HEALTH PROFESSIONS (dental hygiene and mental health/human services), SOCIAL SCIENCE (interdisciplinary studies, law enforcement and corrections, public administration, and social science). Mental health and human services is the largest.

Required: All students must complete at least 120 hours, including 30 to 40 in the major, with a minimum GPA of 2.0. All degree programs require courses in English and communications, humanities, math and computer sciences, social sciences, fine arts, and college writing. Specific course requirements differ by degree program.

Special: Work-study and internship programs with local employers, study abroad, a general studies degree, nondegree study, and pass/fail options are available. UMA administers a displaced homemakers project, offering personal and professional development training and counseling. Cross-registration is offered with University of Maine System campuses. There is 1 national honor society.

Faculty/Classroom: 49% of faculty are male; 51%, female. All teach undergraduates. The average class size in an introductory lecture is 19; in a laboratory, 14; and in a regular course, 19.

Admissions: 87% of the 2003-2004 applicants were accepted. 12% of the current freshmen were in the top fifth of their class; 63% were in the top two fifths.

Requirements: Students are encouraged to submit SAT I scores for placement only. Applicants should have a high school diploma or the GED. Recommended secondary preparation varies according to the degree program. Applicants for the B.M. program must audition. UMA requires applicants to be in the upper 25% of their class. A GPA of 2.0 is required. AP and CLEP credits are accepted.

Procedure: Freshmen are admitted fall and spring. Entrance exams should be taken in November or January of the senior year. There are early decision, early admissions, and deferred admissions plans. Early decision applications should be filed by November 1; regular applications, by June 15 for fall entry and October 15 for spring entry, along with a $25 fee. Notification of early decision is sent December 1; regular decision, on a rolling basis. A waiting list is an active part of the admissions procedure. Applications are accepted on computer disk and on-line through the university's web site.

Transfer: 506 transfer students enrolled in 2002-2003. High school/college transcripts and a statement of good standing from prior institutions are required. Standardized test scores are required for some students, and an interview is recommended. 30 of 120 credits required for the bachelor's degree must be completed at UMA.

Visiting: There are regularly scheduled orientations for prospective students during the month before the beginning of a semester. There are guides for informal visits and visitors may sit in on classes. To schedule a visit, contact the Admissions Office at (207) 621-3185 or umaar@maine.edu.

Financial Aid: In 2003-2004, 50% of all full-time freshmen and 68% of continuing full-time students received some form of financial aid. 46% of full-time freshmen and 64% of continuing full-time students received need-based aid. The average freshman award was $5124. Need-based scholarships or need-based grants averaged $4264 ($6500 maximum); need-based self-help aid (loans and jobs) averaged $2582 ($6625 maximum); and other non-need-based awards and non-need-based scholarships averaged $3168 ($4000 maximum). 3% of undergraduates work part time. Average annual earnings from campus work are $3930. The average financial indebtedness of the 2003 graduate was $11,993. The FAFSA is required. The priority date for freshman financial aid applications for fall entry is March 1.

International Students: There are 11 international students enrolled. They must score 500 on the written TOEFL.

Computers: The mainframes are an IBM 3033 and an IBM 4381. Computers are available at the Student Computer Center on the main campus and at off-campus locations. All students may access the system 24 hours a day at home, 8 A.M. to 9 P.M. in a shared lab. There are no time limits and no fees.

Graduates: From July 1, 2002 to June 30, 2003, 202 bachelor's degrees were awarded. The most popular majors were mental health/human services (40%), business administration (12%), and social sciences (11%). In an average class, 20% graduate in 4 years or less, 13% graduate in 5 years or less, and 13% graduate in 6 years or less. More than 10 companies recruited on campus in 2002-2003.

Admissions Contact: Sheri Fraser, Interim Director of Admissions. A video is available. E-mail: fraser@maine.edu
Web: www.uma.maine.edu

UNIVERSITY OF MAINE AT FARMINGTON
Farmington, ME 04938-1990
B-4
(207) 778-7050
Fax: (207) 778-8182

Full-time: 711 men, 1389 women	**Faculty:** 119; IIB, --$
Part-time: 77 men, 245 women	**Ph.D.s:** 90%
Graduate: none	**Student/Faculty:** 18 to 1
Year: semesters, summer session	**Tuition:** $4790 ($10,920)
Application Deadline: open	**Room & Board:** $5318
Freshman Class: 1521 applied, 1095 accepted, 631 enrolled	
SAT I Verbal/Math: 535/520	**COMPETITIVE**

The University of Maine at Farmington, part of the University of Maine System, is a public liberal arts institution offering programs in arts and sciences, teacher education, and human services. There are 2 undergraduate schools. In addition to regional accreditation, UMF has baccalaureate program accreditation with NCATE. The library contains 98,248 volumes, 82,773 microform items, and 7663 audio/video tapes/CDs, and subscribes to 1581 periodicals. Computerized library services include the card catalog, interlibrary loans, database searching, and Internet access. Special learning facilities include a learning resource cen-

ter, art gallery, radio station, instructional media center, archeology research center, 20-workstation electronic classroom, and an observatory. The 50-acre campus is in a small town 38 miles northwest of Augusta. Including any residence halls, there are 35 buildings.

Student Life: 82% of undergraduates are from Maine. Students are from 32 states, 6 foreign countries, and Canada. 88% are from public schools. 95% are white. The average age of all undergraduates is 23. 21% do not continue beyond their first year; 54% remain to graduate.

Housing: 1030 students can be accommodated in college housing, which includes single-sex and coed dorms and on-campus apartments. In addition, there is an international guest house and wellness floors. On-campus housing is guaranteed for all 4 years. 60% of students commute. All students may keep cars.

Activities: There are no fraternities or sororities. There are 51 groups on campus, including band, chamber choir, cheerleading, choir, chorus, commuter, computers, dance, drama, environmental, film, gay, honors, international, language, literary magazine, musical theater, newspaper, orchestra, outing, pep band, photography, political, professional, radio and TV, religious, social, social service, student government, and yearbook. Popular campus events include Parents and Alumni weekends, Winter Carnival Weekend, and Student Symposium Day.

Sports: There are 5 intercollegiate sports for men and 6 for women, and 12 intramural sports for men and 12 for women. Facilities include a 500-seat gym, baseball, softball, and soccer fields, a field house with an indoor jogging track, 4 multipurpose courts, a swimming pool, and a weight-training center. A ski area and mountain climbing, canoeing, fishing, white water rafting, and mountain biking opportunities are nearby.

Disabled Students: 55% of the campus is accessible. Wheelchair ramps, elevators, special parking, specially equipped rest rooms, special class scheduling, lowered drinking fountains, lowered telephones, an accessible van, a swimming pool, and TDD are available.

Services: Counseling and information services are available, as is tutoring in every subject. There is a reader service for the blind, and remedial math, reading, and writing.

Campus Safety and Security: Measures include 24-hour foot and vehicle patrol, self-defense education, security escort services, and informal discussions. There are pamphlets/posters/films, emergency telephones, lighted pathways/sidewalks, and safety whistles.

Programs of Study: UMF confers B.A., B.S., B.F.A., and B.G.S. degrees. Bachelor's degrees are awarded in BIOLOGICAL SCIENCE (biology/biological science), BUSINESS (business economics), COMMUNICATIONS AND THE ARTS (art, creative writing, English, language arts, music, and visual and performing arts), COMPUTER AND PHYSICAL SCIENCE (computer science, geochemistry, geology, and mathematics), EDUCATION (early childhood, elementary, health, secondary, and special), ENGINEERING AND ENVIRONMENTAL DESIGN (environmental science), HEALTH PROFESSIONS (community health work and rehabilitation therapy), SOCIAL SCIENCE (geography, history, interdisciplinary studies, international studies, liberal arts/general studies, philosophy, political science/government, psychology, sociology, and women's studies). Education, environmental science, and creative writing are the strongest academically. Elementary education, psychology, and interdisciplinary studies are the largest.

Required: All students must maintain a minimum GPA of 2.0 while earning 120 semester hours, including 30 in their major. Core requirements include 9 hours each in social and behavioral sciences and the humanities, 8 in natural science, 4 in English composition, 3 each in math, health, and phys ed, and a foreign language.

Special: Study abroad in 4 countries, as well as numerous opportunities through the National Student Exchange program, work-study with UMF, and student-designed majors are available. Study abroad is possible through other universities as well. Internships are required in rehabilitation and health and are available in all disciplines. Student teaching is required of all education majors. Also possible is interdisciplinary field study in many disciplines, a ski industry certificate, nondegree study, and pass/fail options. There are 2 national honor societies, a freshman honors program, and 10 departmental honors programs.

Faculty/Classroom: 47% of faculty are male; 53%, female. All teach undergraduates. The average class size in an introductory lecture is 45; in a laboratory, 20; and in a regular course, 19.

Admissions: 72% of the 2003-2004 applicants were accepted. The SAT I scores for the 2003-2004 freshman class were: Verbal--35% below 500, 42% between 500 and 599, 20% between 600 and 700, and 3% above 700; Math--38% below 500, 46% between 500 and 599, 14% between 600 and 700, and 2% above 700. 14% of the current freshmen were in the top tenth of their class; 73% were in the top half. 3 freshmen graduated first in their class.

Requirements: Applicants are required to have 16 to 19 college preparatory courses, including 4 in English, 3 to 5 in math, 3 electives, 2 to 3 in lab science, and 2 each in social science and foreign language. An essay and a counselor recommendation are required, and an interview is recommended. The GED is accepted for older, highly motivated students. AP and CLEP credits are accepted. Important factors in the admissions decision are advanced placement or honor courses, recommendations by school officials, and leadership record.

Procedure: Freshmen are admitted fall and spring. There are early admissions and deferred admissions plans. Application deadlines are open.The fall 2003 applicationi fee was $40. Notification of early decision is sent December 15; regular decision, on a rolling basis. Applications are accepted on-line through Apply and CollegeLink.

Transfer: 153 transfer students enrolled in 2002-2003. Applicants must have a minimum GPA of 2.0 (2.5 for some majors). 30 of 120 credits required for the bachelor's degree must be completed at UMF.

Visiting: There are regularly scheduled orientations for prospective students, including sessions on financial aid, majors, student life, the admissions process, and special opportunities such as study abroad, and tours of the campus. There are guides for informal visits and visitors may sit in on classes. To schedule a visit, contact the Admissions Office.

Financial Aid: In 2003-2004, 91% of all full-time freshmen and 67% of continuing full-time students received some form of financial aid. 81% of full-time freshmen and 63% of continuing full-time students received need-based aid. The average freshman award was $8497. Need-based scholarships or need-based grants averaged $4189 ($14,100 maximum); need-based self-help aid (loans and jobs) averaged $3556 ($6325 maximum); non-need-based scholarships averaged $2718 ($10,841 maximum); and non-need-based self-help aid averaged $3187 ($9625 maximum). 45% of undergraduates work part time. Average annual earnings from campus work are $1631. The average financial indebtedness of the 2003 graduate was $14,435. UMF is a member of CSS. The FAFSA is required. The deadline for filing freshman financial aid applications for fall entry is March 1.

International Students: There are 9 international students enrolled. The school actively recruits these students. They must score 530 on the written TOEFL or 190 on the electronic version.

Computers: The mainframes are Novell and Linux servers. There are 38 Pentium PCs and 30 Macs for general student use at the Computer Center. There are 10 departmental student labs housing 52 PCs and 10 Macs. All have Internet and Web access through the campus 10 Mbps ATM link. All students have network access to Microsoft Office and other networked applications, networked disk and web publishing space, access to the campuswide wireless network, and 50 hours per month of dial-in access. All resident students have wired network access in their rooms. All students may access the system. 128 stations are available 24 hours a day; the rest, 80 hours per week. There are no time limits. The fee is $65 per semester.

Graduates: From July 1, 2002 to June 30, 2003, 428 bachelor's degrees were awarded. The most popular majors were interdisciplinary (33%), elementary education (30%), and rehabilitation services (11%). In an average class, 33% graduate in 4 years or less, 47% graduate in 5 years or less, and 54% graduate in 6 years or less. 31 companies recruited on campus in 2002-2003. Of the 2002 graduating class, 18% were enrolled in graduate school within 6 months of graduation and 92% were employed.

Admissions Contact: Sharon Oliver, Director of Admissions.
E-mail: *umfadmit@maine.edu* Web: *www.umf.maine.edu*

UNIVERSITY OF MAINE AT FORT KENT   D-1
Fort Kent, ME 04743

(207) 834-7600
(888) TRY-UMFK; Fax: (207) 834-7609

Full-time: 271 men, 397 women	**Faculty:** 38; IIB, -$
Part-time: 53 men, 203 women	**Ph.D.s:** 70%
Graduate: none	**Student/Faculty:** 18 to 1
Year: semesters, summer session	**Tuition:** $4890 ($10,140)
Application Deadline: open	**Room & Board:** $4880
Freshman Class: 774 applied, 618 accepted, 431 enrolled	
SAT I Verbal/Math: 440/440	**LESS COMPETITIVE**

The University of Maine at Fort Kent, founded in 1878, is a publicly funded liberal arts institution within the University of Maine system. There are 7 undergraduate schools. In addition to regional accreditation, UMFK has baccalaureate program accreditation with NLN and SAF. The library contains 65,000 volumes and 1300 audio/video tapes/CDs, and subscribes to 360 periodicals. Computerized library services include the card catalog, interlibrary loans, database searching, and Internet access. Special learning facilities include a learning resource center, radio station, a greenhouse, and biological park. The 52-acre campus is in a small town 200 miles north of Bangor. Including any residence halls, there are 15 buildings.

Student Life: 63% of undergraduates are from Maine. Students are from 15 states, 2 foreign countries, and Canada. 96% are from public schools. 63% are white; 32% foreign nationals. The average age of freshmen is 20; all undergraduates, 26. 30% do not continue beyond their first year; 40% remain to graduate.

Housing: 175 students can be accommodated in college housing, which includes coed dorms. On-campus housing is guaranteed for all 4 years. 87% of students commute. Alcohol is not permitted. All students may keep cars.

Activities: 5% of men belong to 1 national fraternity; 2% of women belong to 1 national sorority. There are 25 groups on campus, including

cheerleading, chorale, chorus, computers, dance, drama, environmental, international, literary magazine, literature, musical theater, newspaper, outing, professional, radio and TV, religious, and student government. Popular campus events include French Heritage Festival, Spring Meltdown, and Winter Carnival.

Sports: There are 4 intercollegiate sports for men and 4 for women, and 10 intramural sports for men and 10 for women. Facilities include an 11,500-square-foot gym, racquetball courts, soccer field, weight room, cardiovascular room, intramural fields, and game rooms in the residence halls.

Disabled Students: 80% of the campus is accessible. Wheelchair ramps, elevators, special parking, specially equipped rest rooms, special class scheduling, lowered drinking fountains, lowered telephones, and special housing are available.

Services: Counseling and information services are available, as is tutoring in every subject. There is a reader service for the blind and remedial math, reading, and writing.

Campus Safety and Security: Measures include informal discussions, pamphlets/posters/films, lighted pathways/sidewalks, and night watchmen from 11 P.M. to 7 A.M.

Programs of Study: UMFK confers B.A., B.S., B.S.E.S, B.S.N., and B.U.S. degrees. Associate degrees are also awarded. Bachelor's degrees are awarded in BIOLOGICAL SCIENCE (biology/biological science), BUSINESS (business administration and management), COMMUNICATIONS AND THE ARTS (English and French), COMPUTER AND PHYSICAL SCIENCE (computer science), EDUCATION (elementary), ENGINEERING AND ENVIRONMENTAL DESIGN (environmental science), HEALTH PROFESSIONS (nursing), SOCIAL SCIENCE (behavioral science, liberal arts/general studies, and social science). Environmental studies, nursing, and biology are the strongest academically. Education, nursing, and behavioral science are the largest.

Required: A minimum GPA of 2.0 and a total of 120 credit hours (2.5 GPA and 127 credit hours for nursing, 128 credit hours for business management) are required for graduation. Curricula and distribution requirements vary by major.

Special: Internships are required for business majors, nursing (clinicals), and education (student teaching). A general studies degree, a B.A.-B.S. degree in bilingual-bicultural studies, credit for life experience, nondegree study, and an accelerated nursing program are available. Students may cross-register with the College Universitaire St. Louis Maillet in New Brunswick. Study abroad may be arranged in Canada, France, and Mexico through the University of Maine at Farmington. Interactive TV courses broadcast from other universities are available on campus. There is 1 national honor society.

Faculty/Classroom: All teach undergraduates. The average class size in an introductory lecture is 20; in a laboratory, 15; and in a regular course, 25.

Admissions: 80% of the 2003-2004 applicants were accepted.

Requirements: The SAT I is required for some programs. In addition, applicants should be graduates of an accredited secondary school. The GED is accepted. Required secondary school courses include 4 years of English and 2 each of social studies, math, and lab science. A foreign language is suggested. An essay and an interview are recommended. A GPA of 2.0 is required. AP and CLEP credits are accepted. Important factors in the admissions decision are recommendations by school officials, advanced placement or honor courses, and evidence of special talent.

Procedure: Freshmen are admitted fall and spring. Entrance exams should be taken before March of the senior year. There are early decision, early admissions, and deferred admissions plans. Application deadlines are open. Application fee is $25. Applications are accepted on-line.

Transfer: 196 transfer students enrolled in 2002-2003. Applicants must submit transcripts from each college and secondary school attended. The SAT I and an interview are recommended. 30 of 120 credits required for the bachelor's degree must be completed at UMFK.

Visiting: There are regularly scheduled orientations for prospective students, including placement testing, meetings with advisers, campus tours, and get-acquainted activities. There are guides for informal visits and visitors may sit in on classes and stay overnight. To schedule a visit, contact the Admissions Office at (888) 879-8635 or *umfkadm@maine.edu*.

Financial Aid: 54% of undergraduates work part time. Average annual earnings from campus work are $1500. UMFK is a member of CSS. The FAFSA and income tax forms are required. The deadline for filing freshman financial aid applications for fall entry is March 1.

International Students: The school actively recruits these students. They must score 500 on the written TOEFL and also take the college's own test. SAT I scores may be submitted in place of the TOEFL.

Computers: The mainframes include a Novell 311 and Novell 3.12 serving a Dell 2100/200 Poweredge CPU and Dell Poweredge 4100. PCs are available in the dorms, the library, and 2 computer centers. All students may access the system from 8 A.M. to 11 P.M. in the library and computer centers, and 24 hours a day in the dorms. There are no time limits. The fee is $5.

Graduates: From July 1, 2002 to June 30, 2003, 203 bachelor's degrees were awarded. The most popular majors were education (43%), nursing (10%), and business (8%). In an average class, 28% graduate in 4 years or less, 8% graduate in 5 years or less, and 3% graduate in 6 years or less. 2 companies recruited on campus in 2002-2003. Of the 2002 graduating class, 5% were enrolled in graduate school within 6 months of graduation and 90% were employed.

Admissions Contact: Melik P. Khoury, Director of Admissions. A video is available. E-mail: *umfkadm@maine.edu*
Web: *www.umfk.maine.edu*

UNIVERSITY OF MAINE AT MACHIAS
E-4
Machias, ME 04654

(207) 255-1318
(888) 468-6866; Fax: (207) 255-1363

Full-time: 216 men, 361 women	**Faculty:** 31; IIB, --$
Part-time: 154 men, 582 women	**Ph.D.s:** 71%
Graduate: none	**Student/Faculty:** 19 to 1
Year: semesters, summer session	**Tuition:** $4121 ($10,115)
Application Deadline: open	**Room & Board:** $5150
Freshman Class: 510 applied, 416 accepted, 160 enrolled	
SAT I Verbal/Math: 460/460	**ACT:** 21 **LESS COMPETITIVE**

The University of Maine at Machias, founded in 1909, is a publicly funded liberal arts institution in the University of Maine system. In addition to regional accreditation, UMM has baccalaureate program accreditation with NRPA. The library contains 81,287 volumes, 4765 microform items, and 3178 audio/video tapes/CDs, and subscribes to 318 periodicals. Computerized library services include the card catalog, interlibrary loans, database searching, and Internet access. Special learning facilities include a learning resource center, art gallery, radio station, and aquariums for marine and aquaculture studies. The 42-acre campus is in a rural area 85 miles east of Bangor. Including any residence halls, there are 8 buildings.

Student Life: 82% of undergraduates are from Maine. Students are from 26 states, 16 foreign countries, and Canada. 98% are from public schools. 90% are white. The average age of freshmen is 20; all undergraduates, 29. 28% do not continue beyond their first year; 45% remain to graduate.

Housing: 353 students can be accommodated in college housing, which includes single-sex and coed dorms. On-campus housing is guaranteed for all 4 years. 76% of students commute. All students may keep cars.

Activities: 7% of men belong to 2 local and 2 national fraternities; 3% of women belong to 1 local sorority and 3 national sororities. There are 34 groups on campus, including art, cheerleading, chorale, chorus, computers, dance, drama, gay, honors, international, literary magazine, musical theater, outing club, pep band, photography, pop band, professional, radio, religious, social service, and student government. Popular campus events include Winter Carnival, Spring Weekend, and Family Weekend.

Sports: There are 3 intercollegiate sports for men and 4 for women, and 10 intramural sports for men and 10 for women. Facilities include 2 gyms, weight/exercise rooms, handball/racquetball courts, a pool, and a 64-acre recreational center with a lodge and cabins on the lake.

Disabled Students: 85% of the campus is accessible. Wheelchair ramps, elevators, special parking, specially equipped rest rooms, lowered drinking fountains, and automatic doors are available.

Services: Counseling and information services are available, as is tutoring in every subject. There is remedial math, reading, and writing. The Student Resource Coordinator provides one-on-one services, including learning strategies, study skills, and assistance with papers and learning styles.

Campus Safety and Security: Measures include self-defense education, security escort services, informal discussions, and pamphlets/posters/films. There are lighted pathways/sidewalks, a keyless entry system for residence halls, and a security patrol from 5 P.M. to 5 A.M. daily.

Programs of Study: UMM confers B.A., B.S., and B.C.S. degrees. Bachelor's degrees are awarded in BIOLOGICAL SCIENCE (biology/biological science and marine biology), BUSINESS (accounting, business administration and management, marketing/retailing/merchandising, and recreation and leisure services), COMMUNICATIONS AND THE ARTS (English and fine arts), EDUCATION (business and elementary), ENGINEERING AND ENVIRONMENTAL DESIGN (environmental science), SOCIAL SCIENCE (behavioral science, history, human services, and liberal arts/general studies). Elementary education, marine biology, and environmental studies are the strongest academically. Elementary education, business administration, and behavioral science are the largest.

Required: To graduate, students must complete a minimum of 120 credit hours with a GPA of 2.0. The core curriculum consists of 40 to 43 hours in the areas of communication skills, science and math, humans in social context, fine arts, historical and cultural perspectives, and lifetime fitness.

Special: Co-op programs in all majors except education, cross-registration, internships, work-study programs, a B.A.-B.S. degree, study abroad in England and Wales, and a student-designed concentration in

environmental science are available. UMM also offers a Bachelor of College Studies program, credit for prior learning, nondegree study, and a pass/fail option in certain courses. There is a freshman honors program.

Faculty/Classroom: 54% of faculty are male; 46%, female. All teach undergraduates. The average class size in an introductory lecture is 21; in a laboratory, 16; and in a regular course, 17.

Admissions: 82% of the 2003-2004 applicants were accepted. The SAT I scores for the 2003-2004 freshman class were: Verbal--65% below 500, 25% between 500 and 599, 9% between 600 and 700, and 1% above 700; Math--66% below 500, 29% between 500 and 599, and 5% between 600 and 700. The ACT scores were 44% below 21, 33% between 21 and 23, 11% between 24 and 26, and 11% between 27 and 28.

Requirements: The SAT I or ACT is required. In addition, all candidates must be graduates of an accredited secondary school, although the GED is accepted. UMM recommends that students place in the top half of their graduating class and that composite SAT I scores be at least 1000. UMM also recommends completion of 4 units of English, 3 of math, 2 each of lab science, social science/history, and fine arts or foreign language, and 3 of electives. An essay is required, and an interview is strongly recommended. A GPA of 2.0 is required. AP and CLEP credits are accepted. Important factors in the admissions decision are extracurricular activities record, leadership record, and recommendations by school officials.

Procedure: Freshmen are admitted fall, spring, and summer. There are early admissions and deferred admissions plans. Application deadlines are open; August 15 is recommended for fall entry. Application fee is $25. Notification is sent on a rolling basis. Applications are accepted online through *http://apply.maine.edu*.

Transfer: 55 transfer students enrolled in 2002-2003. A minimum college GPA of 2.0 and evidence of good standing are required of transfer applicants. 30 of 120 credits required for the bachelor's degree must be completed at UMM.

Visiting: There are regularly scheduled orientations for prospective students, consisting of traditional orientations prior to the fall and spring semesters, which include programming to guide students in all aspects of starting college—academic, student services and activities, and administrative. UMM also offers 2 summer student orientations, which include aspects of the fall orientations plus a parent orientation. There are guides for informal visits and visitors may sit in on classes. To schedule a visit, contact the Admissions Office.

Financial Aid: In 2002-2003, 71% of all full-time freshmen and 77% of continuing full-time students received some form of financial aid. 61% of full-time freshmen and 66% of continuing full-time students received need-based aid. The average freshman award was $7088. Need-based scholarships or need-based grants averaged $5099; need-based self-help aid (loans and jobs) averaged $2924; and other non-need-based awards and non-need-based scholarships averaged $3654. 70% of undergraduates work part time. Average annual earnings from campus work are $1000. The average financial indebtedness of the 2002 graduate was $14,873. The FAFSA is required. The deadline for filing freshman financial aid applications for fall entry is March 1.

International Students: There are 50 international students enrolled. The school actively recruits these students. They must score 500 on the written TOEFL or 173 on the electronic version and also take the SAT I or the ACT.

Computers: The mainframe consists of Novell servers. Students have unrestricted access to the Internet and courseware from residence hall rooms and wireless access points all across campus. There are 5 computer labs with high-speed Internet access. All students may access the system 24 hours a day, 7 days a week in dorms and the 24-hour room. Other computer labs are open during library hours. There is no set time limit, but students must yield a machine for academic priorities. There are no fees.

Graduates: From July 1, 2002 to June 30, 2003, 100 bachelor's degrees were awarded. The most popular majors were behavioral science (15%), business administration (13%), and recreation management (13%). In an average class, 19% graduate in 4 years or less, 42% graduate in 5 years or less, and 46% graduate in 6 years or less. 10 companies recruited on campus in 2002-2003.

Admissions Contact: Jennifer L. Farrell, Assistant Director of Admissions. A video is available. E-mail: *ummadmissions@maine.edu*
Web: *www.umm.maine.edu*

UNIVERSITY OF MAINE AT PRESQUE ISLE
Presque Isle, ME 04769-2888

D-2
(207) 768-9536
Fax: (207) 768-9777

Full-time: 400 men, 679 women	**Faculty:** 56; IIB, --$
Part-time: 116 men, 351 women	**Ph.D.s:** 56%
Graduate: none	**Student/Faculty:** 19 to 1
Year: semesters, summer session	**Tuition:** $4190 ($9740)
Application Deadline: open	**Room & Board:** $4965
Freshman Class: 520 applied, 454 accepted, 236 enrolled	
SAT I or ACT: not required	**LESS COMPETITIVE**

The University of Maine at Presque Isle, founded in 1903, is a public institution within the University of Maine system offering liberal arts, teacher education, and professional programs leading to post-secondary certificates, associate, and bachelor's degrees. There are 2 undergraduate schools. In addition to regional accreditation, UM-Presque Isle has baccalaureate program accreditation with CAAHEP, CSWE, and NAACLS. The library contains 75,000 volumes, 750,000 microform items, and 1400 audio/video tapes/CDs, and subscribes to 2000 periodicals. Computerized library services include the card catalog, interlibrary loans, database searching, and Internet access. Special learning facilities include a learning resource center, art gallery, natural history museum, radio station, and a theater. The 150-acre campus is in a rural area 150 miles north of Bangor. Including any residence halls, there are 11 buildings.

Student Life: 76% of undergraduates are from Maine. Students are from 20 states, 6 foreign countries, and Canada. 67% are white; 10% foreign nationals. The average age of freshmen is 20; all undergraduates, 26. 34% do not continue beyond their first year; 41% remain to graduate.

Housing: 359 students can be accommodated in college housing, which includes coed dorms, off-campus apartments, and married-student housing. On-campus housing is guaranteed for all 4 years. 72% of students commute. All students may keep cars.

Activities: 2% of men belong to 1 national fraternity; 1% of women belong to 1 national sorority. There are 25 groups on campus, including a cappella, activities board, band, chess, chorale, debate, diversity, drama, ethnic, gay, honors, international, newspaper, nontraditional students, professional, radio and TV, religious, social, social service, and student government. Popular campus events include Spring Ball, Winter Blast, and Spring Fest.

Sports: There are 5 intercollegiate sports for men and 5 for women, and 15 intramural sports for men and 15 for women. Facilities include a multifunctional structure that houses a gym, a weight room, phys ed labs, a sports medicine facility, Athletic Hall of Fame, and an auditorium. A large playing field contains baseball, soccer, and tennis courts. There are also hiking trails, a bike path, and a ropes course.

Disabled Students: All of the campus is accessible. Wheelchair ramps, elevators, special parking, specially equipped rest rooms, special class scheduling, lowered drinking fountains, and lowered telephones are available.

Services: Counseling and information services are available, as is tutoring in most subjects. There is remedial math, reading, and writing.

Campus Safety and Security: Measures include security escort services, informal discussions, pamphlets/posters/films, and lighted pathways/sidewalks.

Programs of Study: UM-Presque Isle confers B.A., B.S., B.A.A.E., B.F.A., B.L.S., and B.S.W. degrees. Associate degrees are also awarded. Bachelor's degrees are awarded in BIOLOGICAL SCIENCE (biology/biological science), BUSINESS (accounting, business administration and management, and recreation and leisure services), COMMUNICATIONS AND THE ARTS (art and English), EDUCATION (elementary, health, physical, and secondary), ENGINEERING AND ENVIRONMENTAL DESIGN (environmental science), SOCIAL SCIENCE (behavioral science, criminal justice, international studies, liberal arts/general studies, and social work). Education, social work, and criminal justice are the largest.

Required: Core requirements for the B.A. degree include 18 credits in humanities, 12 in social science, 11 in math/science, and 4 in phys ed/health. The student must complete a minimum number of credits, which varies according to major, with a cumulative GPA of 2.0 in 120 to 133 credit hours. Requirements for the B.S. and other degrees vary considerably with each major.

Special: The university participates in transfer programs in agriculture, nutrition science, and animal and veterinary science. There is a nursing program with the University of Maine at Fort Kent. There are study-abroad programs in France, Ireland, Canada (other countries are available), and internships in many majors. UM-Presque Isle offers work-study programs, dual and student-designed majors, a B.A.-B.S. degree, and nondegree study. Students can apply for credit by exam and credit for life, military, and work experience. A credit/no credit option is available. There is 1 national honor society, a freshman honors program, and 5 departmental honors programs.

Faculty/Classroom: 50% of faculty are male; 50%, female. All teach undergraduates. The average class size in an introductory lecture is 20; in a laboratory, 12; and in a regular course, 15.

Admissions: 87% of the 2003-2004 applicants were accepted. 17% of the current freshmen were in the top fifth of their class; 44% were in the top two fifths. 2 freshmen graduated first in their class.

Requirements: Applicants should have completed 16 academic credits at an accredited secondary school, including 4 in English, 3 each in math and social studies, and 2 each in science with a lab, foreign language, and electives. A GED certificate may be substituted. The university recommends an essay and an interview for all candidates. Art majors must submit a portfolio. AP and CLEP credits are accepted. Important factors in the admissions decision are advanced placement or honor courses, recommendations by school officials, and extracurricular activities record.

Procedure: Freshmen are admitted fall, spring, and summer. Entrance exams should be taken by January 1. There are early decision and deferred admissions plans. There is a rolling admissions plan. Application deadlines are open. Notification is sent on a rolling basis. Applications are accepted on computer disk and on-line through the school's web site.

Transfer: 223 transfer students enrolled in 2002-2003. A GPA of 2.0 from an accredited college or university is required. It is recommended that applicants submit SAT I scores and arrange an interview. Transfer applicants must also submit official transcripts from all colleges attended along with an official high school transcript. 30 credits of 120 to 133 required for the bachelor's degree must be completed at UM-Presque Isle.

Visiting: There are regularly scheduled orientations for prospective students, including advisement, a campus tour, and meetings with faculty and coaches. There are guides for informal visits and visitors may sit in on classes and stay overnight. To schedule a visit, contact Beverly A. McAvaddy at (207) 768-9532 or mcavaddy@umpi.maine.edu.

Financial Aid: In a recent year, 91% of full-time freshmen and 88% of continuing full-time students received need-based aid. The average freshman award was $6758. The average financial indebtedness of the 2003 graduate was $5193. The FAFSA is required. The deadline for filing freshman financial aid applications for fall entry is April 1.

International Students: There are 308 international students enrolled. The school actively recruits these students. They must score 550 on the written TOEFL or 230 on the electronic version.

Computers: Macs and PCs are available in the computer lab. 90 stations are available for student access. All students may access the system. There are no time limits. The fee is nominal.

Graduates: In a recent year, 240 bachelor's degrees were awarded. The most popular majors were liberal arts/general studies (39%), education (15%), and interdisciplinary studies (11%). In an average class, 10% graduate in 4 years or less, 19% graduate in 5 years or less, and 5% graduate in 6 years or less. 35 companies recruited on campus in 2002-2003. Of the 2002 graduating class, 7% were enrolled in graduate school within 6 months of graduation.

Admissions Contact: Brian M. Manter, Director of Admissions. A video is available. E-mail: adventure@umpi.maine.edu
Web: www.umpi.maine.edu

UNIVERSITY OF NEW ENGLAND
Biddeford, ME 04005

A-6
(207) 283-0171
(800) 477-4863; Fax: (207) 286-3678

Full-time: 297 men, 961 women	**Faculty:** 94; IIA, --$
Part-time: 71 men, 212 women	**Ph.D.s:** n/av
Graduate: 512 men, 1139 women	**Student/Faculty:** 13 to 1
Year: semesters, summer session	**Tuition:** $19,640
Application Deadline: open	**Room & Board:** $7560
Freshman Class: 1878 applied, 1706 accepted, 522 enrolled	
SAT I Verbal/Math: 510/510	**LESS COMPETITIVE**

University of New England, founded in 1831, offers undergraduate degrees in the health sciences, natural sciences, social sciences, liberal arts, education, and management; graduate degrees in professional and occupational programs; teacher education; doctor of osteopathic medicine; and continuing education. There are 2 undergraduate and 6 graduate schools. In addition to regional accreditation, UNE has baccalaureate program accreditation with APTA and NLN. The 2 libraries contain 139,783 volumes, 7416 microform items, and 9674 audio/video tapes/CDs, and subscribe to 1032 periodicals. Computerized library services include the card catalog, interlibrary loans, database searching, and Internet access. Special learning facilities include a learning resource center and art gallery. The 550-acre campus is in a rural area. Including any residence halls, there are 38 buildings.

Student Life: 53% of undergraduates are from out of state, mostly the Northeast. Students are from 35 states, 5 foreign countries, and Canada. 98% are white. The average age of freshmen is 22; all undergraduates, 21.6. 29% do not continue beyond their first year; 71% remain to graduate.

Housing: 840 students can be accommodated in college housing, which includes single-sex and coed dorms and on-campus apartments. On-campus housing is guaranteed for the freshman year only. 60% of students live on campus; of those, 50% remain on campus on weekends. Upperclassmen may keep cars.

Activities: There are no fraternities or sororities. There are 44 groups on campus, including environmental, gay, honors, international, literary magazine, newspaper, professional, religious, sailing, social, social service, student government, and yearbook. Popular campus events include Welcome Back Week, Family and Friends Weekend, and a leadership retreat.

Sports: There are 5 intercollegiate sports for men and 7 for women, and 15 intramural sports for men and 15 for women. Facilities include a 1500-seat gym, a fitness center, a pool, racquetball courts, soccer and softball fields, outdoor volleyball facilities, and a multipurpose recreational field.

Disabled Students: 85% of the campus is accessible. Wheelchair ramps, elevators, special parking, specially equipped rest rooms, special class scheduling, lowered drinking fountains, lowered telephones, and stair climbers are available.

Services: Counseling and information services are available, as is tutoring in most subjects. There is a reader service for the blind, and remedial math, reading, and writing.

Campus Safety and Security: Measures include 24-hour foot and vehicle patrol, self-defense education, security escort services, and informal discussions. There are pamphlets/posters/films, emergency telephones, and lighted pathways/sidewalks. A safe-ride program provides drivers for students.

Programs of Study: UNE confers B.A., B.S., and B.S.N. degrees. Associate, master's, and doctoral degrees are also awarded. Bachelor's degrees are awarded in BIOLOGICAL SCIENCE (biology/biological science, environmental biology, and marine biology), BUSINESS (business administration and management and sports management), COMMUNICATIONS AND THE ARTS (English), EDUCATION (elementary and secondary), ENGINEERING AND ENVIRONMENTAL DESIGN (environmental science), HEALTH PROFESSIONS (biomedical science, dental hygiene, health care administration, and nursing), SOCIAL SCIENCE (American studies, psychology, and sociology).

Required: A total of 120 credits with a minimum GPA of 2.0 is required for graduation. Some programs require more than 120 credits. Students must take 43 credits in a liberal arts core curriculum of humanities, sciences, and social sciences. Most majors require 1-semester internships. Courses in English composition, Western traditions, human development, and math are required.

Special: UNE offers cross-registration with the Greater Portland Alliance of Colleges and Universities, internships in all majors, work-study programs, study abroad, student-designed and dual majors in all departments, a 3-4 medical program, and a 3-2 pre-physician assistant program. The Freshmen Biology Learning Community provides combined studies in English and life sciences. There is 1 national honor society.

Faculty/Classroom: 49% of faculty are male; 51% female. 67% teach undergraduates. No introductory courses are taught by graduate students.

Admissions: 91% of the 2003-2004 applicants were accepted. The SAT I scores for the 2003-2004 freshman class were: Verbal--43% below 500, 42% between 500 and 599, and 16% between 600 and 700; Math--43% below 500, 41% between 500 and 599, and 16% between 600 and 700. 37% of the current freshmen were in the top fifth of their class; 69% were in the top two fifths. 3 freshmen graduated first in their class.

Requirements: The SAT I or ACT is required. In addition, applicants should be high school graduates with 4 years of English, 3 each of math and science, and 2 each of history and social studies. The GED is accepted. A personal interview is recommended. AP and CLEP credits are accepted. Important factors in the admissions decision are advanced placement or honor courses, recommendations by school officials, and leadership record.

Procedure: Freshmen are admitted fall and spring. Entrance exams should be taken in the spring of the junior year or the fall of the senior year. There are early decision, early admissions, and deferred admissions plans. Early decision applications should be filed by November 15; regular application deadlines are open. The fee is $40. Notification of early decision is sent December 15; regular decision, on a rolling basis. Applications are accepted on-line through the school's web site.

Transfer: 152 transfer students enrolled in 2002-2003. Transfer applicants should present a GPA of at least 2.5 in college work. An interview is recommended. 30 of 120 credits required for the bachelor's degree must be completed at UNE.

Visiting: There are regularly scheduled orientations for prospective students, including a tour and information session, and an interview if the student has formally applied. There are guides for informal visits and visitors may sit in on classes. To schedule a visit, contact the Admissions Office.

Financial Aid: In 2003-2004, 85% of all full-time freshmen and 84% of continuing full-time students received some form of financial aid. 85%

of full-time freshmen and 82% of continuing full-time students received need-based aid. The average freshman award was $16,048. Need-based scholarships or need-based grants averaged $8759; need-based self-help aid (loans and jobs) averaged $7860; and non-need-based awards and non-need-based scholarships averaged $5509. The average financial indebtedness of the 2003 graduate was $28,421. The FAFSA is required. The deadline for filing freshman financial aid applications for fall entry is May 1.

International Students: There are 6 international students enrolled. They must score 550 on the written TOEFL.

Computers: The mainframe is a Novell network. There are 95 PCs available in the main academic building and the libraries and 20 kiosks. All students may access the system. There are no time limits and no fees.

Graduates: From July 1, 2002 to June 30, 2003, 218 bachelor's degrees were awarded. The most popular majors were health science (30%), medical biology (22%), and education (9%).

Admissions Contact: Robert Pecchia, Associate Dean of Admissions. E-mail: admissions@une.edu Web: www.une.edu

UNIVERSITY OF SOUTHERN MAINE   B-6
Gorham, ME 04038-1088

(207) 780-5670
(800) 800-4876; Fax: (207) 780-5640

Full-time: 1897 men, 2771 women	**Faculty:** 378; IIA, av$
Part-time: 1455 men, 2490 women	**Ph.Ds:** 75%
Graduate: 768 men, 1626 women	**Student/Faculty:** 12 to 1
Year: semesters, summer session	**Tuition:** $5198 ($12,878)
Application Deadline: February 15	**Room & Board:** $6014
Freshman Class: 3346 applied, 2588 accepted, 959 enrolled	
SAT I Verbal/Math: 515/510	**COMPETITIVE**

The University of Southern Maine, founded in 1878, is a publicly funded, multicampus, comprehensive, residential, liberal arts institution serving the University of Maine system. There are 5 undergraduate and 8 graduate schools. In addition to regional accreditation, USM has baccalaureate program accreditation with AACSB, ABET, CSAB, CSWE, NASM, NCATE, NLN, and NRPA. The 3 libraries contain 569,698 volumes, 1,031,195 microform items, and 2688 audio/video tapes/CDs, and subscribe to 3001 periodicals. Computerized library services include the card catalog, interlibrary loans, and database searching. Special learning facilities include a learning resource center, art gallery, planetarium, radio station, TV station, and cartography collections. The 144-acre campus is in an urban area 110 miles north of Boston and 10 miles west of the urban Portland campus. Including any residence halls, there are 66 buildings.

Student Life: 91% of undergraduates are from Maine. Students are from 30 states, 20 foreign countries, and Canada. 97% are white. The average age of freshmen is 22; all undergraduates, 26. 28% do not continue beyond their first year.

Housing: 1500 students can be accommodated in college housing, which includes coed dorms, on-campus apartments, and married-student housing. In addition, there are honors houses, special-interest houses, and a fine arts house. The Russell Scholors program is a selected small community in which students live and attend classes together. A chemical-free floor and a 24 hour quiet floor are also available. On-campus housing is guaranteed for all 4 years. 82% of students commute. All students may keep cars.

Activities: 4% of men belong to 1 local fraternity and 3 national fraternities; 4% of women belong to 2 local and 2 national sororities. There are 100 groups on campus, including art, band, cheerleading, chess, choir, chorale, chorus, commuter, computers, dance, drama, environmental, ethnic, film, gay, honors, international, jazz band, literary magazine, musical theater, newspaper, opera, orchestra, outing, photography, political, professional, radio and TV, religious, ski, social, social service, student government, and yearbook. Popular campus events include Winter Weekend, Spring Fling, and comedy nights.

Sports: There are 11 intercollegiate sports for men and 12 for women, and 19 intramural sports for men and 19 for women. Facilities include gyms, tennis courts, athletic fields, racquetball and squash courts, cross-country ski trails, 2 weight-training and fitness facilities, an ice arena, a field house, and an indoor track.

Disabled Students: All of the campus is accessible. Wheelchair ramps, elevators, special parking, specially equipped rest rooms, special class scheduling, lowered drinking fountains, and lowered telephones are available.

Services: Counseling and information services are available, as is tutoring in most subjects. There is a reader service for the blind, and remedial math, reading, and writing.

Campus Safety and Security: Measures include 24-hour foot and vehicle patrol, self-defense education, security escort services, and shuttle buses. There are informal discussions, pamphlets/posters/films, emergency telephones, lighted pathways/sidewalks, and preventive programs within residence halls.

Programs of Study: USM confers B.A., B.S., and B.F.A. degrees. Associate, master's, and doctoral degrees are also awarded. Bachelor's degrees are awarded in BIOLOGICAL SCIENCE (biology/biological science), BUSINESS (accounting and business administration and management), COMMUNICATIONS AND THE ARTS (communications, dramatic arts, English, fine arts, French, music, and music performance), COMPUTER AND PHYSICAL SCIENCE (chemistry, computer science, geology, geoscience, mathematics, and physics), EDUCATION (music and technical), ENGINEERING AND ENVIRONMENTAL DESIGN (electrical/electronics engineering, environmental science, and industrial engineering technology), HEALTH PROFESSIONS (environmental health science, health science, nursing, recreation therapy, and sports medicine), SOCIAL SCIENCE (anthropology, economics, geography, history, philosophy, political science/government, psychology, social work, sociology, and women's studies). Electrical engineering, computer science, and nursing are the strongest academically. Business administration, nursing, and psychology are the largest.

Required: A total of 120 hours, of which 36 to 94 are in the major, and a minimum GPA of 2.0 are required for graduation. All students must fulfill the distribution requirements of the 3-part core curriculum: basic competence, methods of inquiry/ways of knowing, and interdisciplinary studies.

Special: Cross-registration within the University of Maine system and 4 Greater Portland colleges, a Washington semester, and study abroad in more than 12 countries are offered. Internships, co-op and work-study programs, a B.A.-B.S. degree, dual and student-designed majors, a 2-2 engineering program with the University of Maine, credit for life experience, nondegree study, and pass/fail options are also available. There is a January intersession. There are 2 national honor societies, a freshman honors program, and 1 departmental honors program.

Faculty/Classroom: 49% of faculty are male; 51%, female. 80% teach undergraduates and all do research. No introductory courses are taught by graduate students. The average class size in an introductory lecture is 50; in a laboratory, 20; and in a regular course, 22.

Admissions: 77% of the 2003-2004 applicants were accepted. The SAT I scores for the 2003-2004 freshman class were: Verbal--38% below 500, 44% between 500 and 599, 17% between 600 and 700, and 1% above 700; Math--42% below 500, 46% between 500 and 599, 11% between 600 and 700, and 1% above 700. The ACT scores were 46% below 21, 23% between 21 and 23, 26% between 24 and 26, and 5% between 27 and 28. 23% of the current freshmen were in the top fifth of their class; 59% were in the top two fifths. 2 freshmen graduated first in their class.

Requirements: The SAT I or ACT is required. In addition, applicants must be graduates of an accredited secondary school. The GED is accepted. Either 41 academic credits or 20 1/2 Carnegie units are required. Secondary school courses should include 4 years of English, 3 of math, 2 each of a foreign language and lab science, and 1 each of history and social studies. An essay is required, as are auditions for music applicants and interviews for applicants to the School of Applied Science. Guidance counselor recommendations are required for those students applying during their senior year. USM requires applicants to be in the upper 50% of their class. A GPA of 2.0 is required. AP and CLEP credits are accepted. Important factors in the admissions decision are advanced placement or honor courses, recommendations by school officials, and extracurricular activities record.

Procedure: Freshmen are admitted fall and spring. Entrance exams should be taken between May of the junior year and January of the senior year. There is a deferred admissions plan. Applications should be filed by February 15 for fall entry and December 1 for spring entry. The fall 2003 application fee was $40. Notification is sent on a rolling basis. Applications are accepted on computer disk and on-line through *http:// apply.maine.edu*, the Common Application, Apply/Peterson's, Next Step College, The Princeton Review, and CollegeLink.

Transfer: 704 transfer students enrolled in 2002-2003. Applicants must have a minimum GPA of 2.0 or 2.75 for those from nonregionally accredited institutions. Students who have been out of high school for less than 3 years must submit SAT I scores. 30 of 120 credits required for the bachelor's degree must be completed at USM.

Visiting: There are regularly scheduled orientations for prospective students, including regularly scheduled campus tours and group information sessions, as well as special events such as fall open houses. Interviews are also available on request. There are guides for informal visits and visitors may sit in on classes. To schedule a visit, contact the Office of Admission.

Financial Aid: In 2003-2004, 75% of all full-time freshmen and 81% of continuing full-time students received some form of financial aid. 64% of full-time freshmen and 73% of continuing full-time students received need-based aid. The average freshman award was $7460. Need-based scholarships or need-based grants averaged $4078; need-based self-help aid (loans and jobs) averaged $4686; and other non-need-based awards and non-need-based scholarships averaged $3000. 80% of undergraduates work part time. Average annual earnings from campus work are $1500. The average financial indebtedness of the 2003 graduate was $21,720. USM is a member of CSS. The FAFSA is required. The deadline for filing freshman financial aid applications for fall entry is February 15.

International Students: There are 37 international students enrolled. They must score 500 on the written TOEFL or 175 on the electronic version and also take the SAT I or the ACT.

Computers: The mainframe is an IBM 4341. The mainframe is linked to the Bitnet, Internet, and Gopher networks. There are about 1000 terminals and computer workstations, of which 550 are available for student use. Most residence hall rooms have computer hookups. All students may access the system 16 hours per day. There are no time limits and no fees.

Graduates: From July 1, 2002 to June 30, 2003, 1022 bachelor's degrees were awarded. The most popular majors were social science and history (23%), business (13%), and nursing (11%). In an average class, 1% graduate in 3 years or less, 11% graduate in 4 years or less, 22% graduate in 5 years or less, and 27% graduate in 6 years or less. 50 companies recruited on campus in 2002-2003.

Admissions Contact: David M. Pirani, Director of Admission.
E-mail: *usmadm@maine.maine.edu* Web: *http://www.usm.maine.edu*

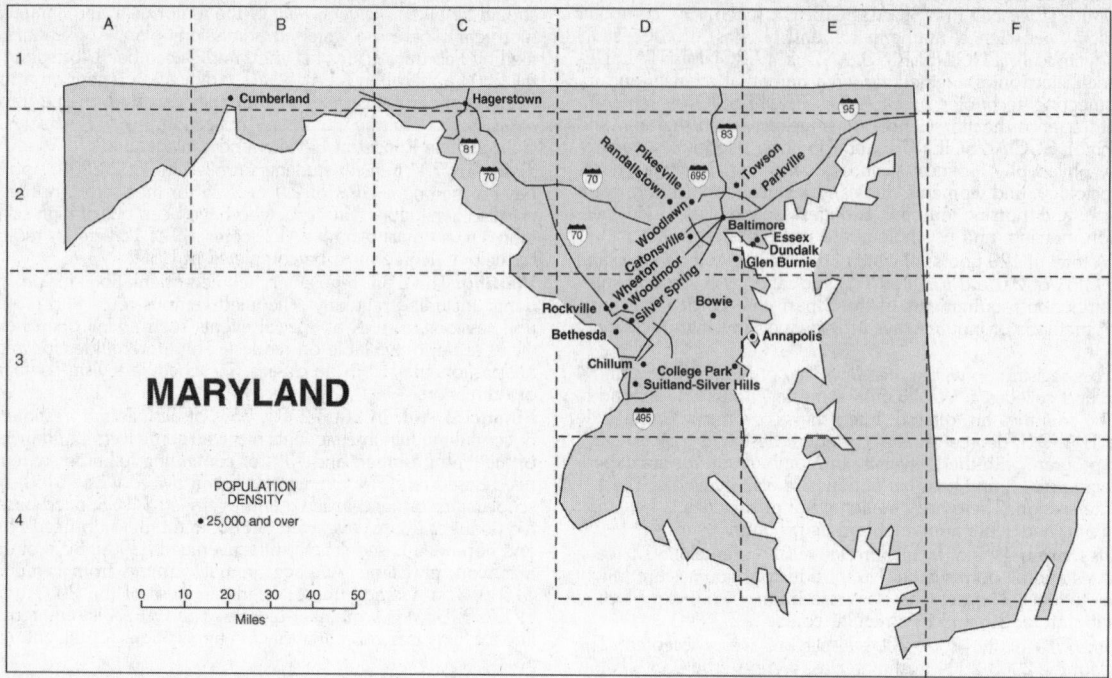

MARYLAND

POPULATION
DENSITY
• 25,000 and over

0 10 20 30 40 50
Miles

BALTIMORE HEBREW UNIVERSITY
Baltimore, MD 21215-3996

D-2

(410) 578-6903
(888) 248-7420; Fax: (410) 578-6940

Full-time: 10 men, 16 women	**Faculty:** 8
Part-time: 10 men, 42 women	**Ph.D.s:** 90%
Graduate: 16 men, 57 women	**Student/Faculty:** 3 to 1
Year: semesters, summer session	**Tuition:** $8900
Application Deadline: August 15	**Room & Board:** n/app
Freshman Class: 71 applied, 57 accepted, 47 enrolled	
SAT I or ACT: not required	**SPECIAL**

Baltimore Hebrew University, founded in 1919, is a private nonsectarian institution of Jewish higher education and a major center of advanced Jewish study in the United States. There is 1 graduate school. The library contains 100,000 volumes, 7500 microform items, and 1100 audio/video tapes/CDs, and subscribes to 225 periodicals. Computerized library services include the card catalog, interlibrary loans, database searching, and Internet access. Special learning facilities include a language lab. The 2-acre campus is in an urban area in residential northwest Baltimore. There is 1 building.

Student Life: 96% of undergraduates are from Maryland. Students are from 8 states, 4 foreign countries, and Canada. 98% are white. Most are Jewish. The average age of all undergraduates is 44.

Housing: There are no residence halls. All students commute. Alcohol is not permitted. All students may keep cars.

Activities: There are no fraternities or sororities. Popular campus events include film series, singles brunches, and concerts.

Sports: There is no sports program at BHU.

Disabled Students: Wheelchair ramps and special parking are available.

Services: Counseling and information services are available, as is tutoring in some subjects, including Hebrew, Yiddish, and Russian.

Campus Safety and Security: Measures include security escort services, pamphlets/posters/films, lighted pathways/sidewalks, a lighted parking lot, and guards during open building hours.

Programs of Study: BHU confers the B.A. degree. Master's and doctoral degrees are also awarded. Bachelor's degrees are awarded in SOCIAL SCIENCE (Judaic studies).

Required: To graduate, students must earn a minimum GPA of 2.0 in a total of 120 credits, including 60 of Jewish studies in literature, philosophy, and history and 60 of general studies in social and behavioral sciences, arts and humanities, literature, physical or biological science, math, and English composition.

Special: BHU offers study abroad in Israel, cross-registration with Johns Hopkins and Towson Universities and Goucher College, and co-op programs with Johns Hopkins University, University of Maryland/Baltimore County, and University of Maryland School of Social Work.

Faculty/Classroom: 50% of faculty are male; 50%, female. 85% teach undergraduates and 90% do research. No introductory courses are taught by graduate students. The average class size in an introductory lecture is 10 and in a regular course, 10.

Admissions: 80% of the 2003-2004 applicants were accepted.

Requirements: A candidate's high school record is reviewed by the dean, who also conducts a personal interview. A GPA of 3.0 is required. AP and CLEP credits are accepted. Important factors in the admissions decision are recommendations by school officials, personality/intangible qualities, and evidence of special talent.

Procedure: Freshmen are admitted fall and spring. Applications should be filed by August 15 for fall entry and December 15 for spring entry, along with a $50 fee. Notification is sent on a rolling basis.

Transfer: Applicants must meet freshman requirements. 30 of 120 credits required for the bachelor's degree must be completed at BHU.

Visiting: There are regularly scheduled orientations for prospective students. There are guides for informal visits and visitors may sit in on classes. To schedule a visit, contact the Director of Admissions.

Financial Aid: 80% of full-time freshmen received need-based aid. The FAFSA and the college's own financial statement are required.

International Students: They must score 213 on the electronic TOEFL and also take the college's own test.

Computers: PCs in the computer room and library with Hebrew language software are available for word processing and computer course assignments. All students may access the system. There are no time limits and no fees.

Admissions Contact: Director of Admissions. E-mail: *bhu@bhu.edu* Web: *www.bhu.edu*

BOWIE STATE UNIVERSITY
Bowie, MD 20715

D-3

(301) 860-3421; Fax: (301)860-3438

Full-time: 1186 men, 1936 women	**Faculty:** 158; IIA, av$
Part-time: 287 men, 579 women	**Ph.D.s:** n/av
Graduate: 377 men, 1089 women	**Student/Faculty:** 20 to 1
Year: semesters, summer session	**Tuition:** $4853 ($12,465)
Application Deadline: April 1	**Room & Board:** $6020
Freshman Class: 3543 applied, 1711 accepted, 768 enrolled	
SAT I Verbal/Math: 448/439	**COMPETITIVE+**

Bowie State University, founded in 1865, is a historically black, publicly supported comprehensive liberal arts institution within the University System of Maryland. There are 3 undergraduate schools and 1 graduate school. In addition to regional accreditation, BSU has baccalaureate program accreditation with ACBSP, CSAB, CSWE, NCATE, and NLN. The library contains 242,907 volumes, 424,056 microform items, and 6104 audio/video tapes/CDs, and subscribes to 748 periodicals. Computerized library services include the card catalog, interlibrary loans, database searching, and Internet access. Special learning facilities include a learning resource center, art gallery, radio station, TV station, media center, and satellite operations and control center. The 312-acre campus is in a suburban area 18 miles north of Washington, D.C. Including any residence halls, there are 26 buildings.

Student Life: 89% of undergraduates are from Maryland. Students are from 31 states, 39 foreign countries, and Canada. 95% are from public schools. 90% are African American. The average age of all undergraduates is 24. 30% do not continue beyond their first year; 70% remain to graduate.

Housing: 890 students can be accommodated in college housing, which includes single-sex and coed dorms and off-campus apartments. In addition, there are honors houses. On-campus housing is available on a first-come, first-served basis. Priority is given to out-of-town students. 78% of students commute. Alcohol is not permitted. All students may keep cars.

Activities: 2% of men belong to 6 national fraternities; 2% of women belong to 4 national sororities. There are 52 groups on campus, including art, band, cheerleading, choir, chorale, commuter, computers, dance, drama, drill team, honors, international, jazz band, literary magazine, marching band, musical theater, NAACP, pep band, political, professional, radio and TV, religious, social, social service, student government, Urban League, and yearbook. Popular campus events include Black History Month Convocation, Parents/Founders Day, and Honors Convocation.

Sports: There are 4 intercollegiate sports for men and 6 for women. Facilities include an athletic complex with a basketball arena, an Olympic-size pool, 8 handball/racquetball courts, a wrestling room, weight training rooms, a dance studio, a gymnastics room, a 4500-seat football/soccer stadium, a baseball diamond, 6 outdoor tennis courts, 4 outdoor basketball courts, and a track-and-field facility with a walking/jogging lane.

Disabled Students: All of the campus is accessible. Wheelchair ramps, elevators, special parking, specially equipped rest rooms, lowered drinking fountains, lowered telephones, and wide doors are available.

Services: Counseling and information services are available, as is tutoring in most subjects. There is a reader service for the blind, and remedial math, reading, and writing.

Campus Safety and Security: Measures include 24-hour foot and vehicle patrol, self-defense education, security escort services, and shuttle buses. There are informal discussions, pamphlets/posters/films, emergency telephones, and lighted pathways/sidewalks.

Programs of Study: BSU confers B.A.and B.S. degrees. Master's and doctoral degrees are also awarded. Bachelor's degrees are awarded in BIOLOGICAL SCIENCE (biology/biological science), BUSINESS (business administration and management), COMMUNICATIONS AND THE ARTS (broadcasting, English, and fine arts), COMPUTER AND PHYSICAL SCIENCE (computer science and mathematics), EDUCATION (early childhood, elementary, English, and science), ENGINEERING AND ENVIRONMENTAL DESIGN (computer technology), HEALTH PROFESSIONS (nursing), SOCIAL SCIENCE (criminal justice, history, interdisciplinary studies, political science/government, psychology, social work, and sociology). Business administration, computer science, and elementary education are the largest.

Required: A total of 120 credit hours with a minimum GPA of 2.0 is required for graduation. The number of hours that must be taken in a student's major varies. General education requirements include 12 credits in social science, 9 in arts and humanities, 7 to 8 in sciences, 6 in English composition, and 3 each in math, computer literacy, health and wellness, and freshman seminar.

Special: BSU offers cooperative programs, internships in communications and practice teaching, work-study programs, B.A.-B.S. degrees, dual majors, credit for life experience, and a 3-2 engineering degree. Dual-degree programs in engineering and dentistry are available at the University of Maryland. Cross-registration is offered with other members of the University System of Maryland. There are 16 national honor societies and a freshman honors program.

Faculty/Classroom: 57% of faculty are male; 43%, female. 23% do research and 23% both teach and do research. No introductory courses are taught by graduate students. The average class size in an introductory lecture is 30; in a laboratory, 20; and in a regular course, 25.

Admissions: 48% of the 2003-2004 applicants were accepted. The SAT I scores for the 2003-2004 freshman class were: Verbal--81% below 500, 17% between 500 and 599, and 3% between 600 and 700; Math--82% below 500, 15% between 500 and 599, and 3% between 600 and 700.

Requirements: The SAT I or ACT is required. In addition, applicants should be graduates of an accredited secondary school. The GED is accepted. Students should have completed 15 academic units, including 4 of English, 3 each of math, sciences, and social science/history, and 2 of a foreign language or advanced technology. A GPA of 2.0 is required. AP and CLEP credits are accepted. Important factors in the admissions decision are advanced placement or honor courses, extracurricular activities record, and leadership record.

Procedure: Freshmen are admitted fall and spring. Entrance exams should be taken before the end of January. There is a deferred admissions plan. Applications should be filed by April 1 for fall entry and November 1 for spring entry, along with a $40 fee. Notification is sent on a rolling basis. Applications are accepted on-line through the school's web site.

Transfer: 394 transfer students enrolled in 2002-2003. Applicants must have a minimum GPA of 2.0. The SAT I is required if fewer than 24 credit hours are being transferred. 30 of 120 credits required for the bachelor's degree must be completed at BSU.

Visiting: There are regularly scheduled orientations for prospective students. There are guides for informal visits. To schedule a visit, contact Vonetta Rector at (301) 860-3428 or ugradadmissions@bowiestate.edu.

Financial Aid: In 2003-2004, 58% of all full-time freshmen received some form of financial aid. 52% of full-time freshmen and 50% of continuing full-time students received need-based aid. The average freshman award was $5846. Need-based scholarships or need-based grants averaged $1200 ($4890 maximum); need-based self-help aid (loans and jobs) averaged $5125 ($6530 maximum); non-need-based athletic scholarships averaged $3289 ($5000 maximum); and other non-need-based awards and non-need-based scholarships averaged $2000 ($2999 maximum). 3% of undergraduates work part time. Average annual earnings from campus work are $2500. The FAFSA and the college's own financial statement are required. The deadline for filing freshman financial aid applications for fall entry is March 1.

International Students: There are 41 international students enrolled. The school actively recruits these students. They must score 500 on the written TOEFL and also take the SAT I, ACT, or the college's own entrance exam, scoring 900 on the SAT I or 19 on the ACT.

Computers: E-mail and computer accounts are available to all students. There is a laptop program for freshmen, and the library distributes laptops to students with financial need. Wired and wireless network access is also available. All students may access the system 24 hours a day. There are no time limits. The fee is $120.

Graduates: From July 1, 2002 to June 30, 2003, 540 bachelor's degrees were awarded. The most popular major was psychology (10%). In an average class, 2% graduate in 3 years or less, 12% graduate in 4 years or less, 30% graduate in 5 years or less, and 38% graduate in 6 years or less. Of the 2002 graduating class, 46% were enrolled in graduate school within 6 months of graduation and 68% were employed.

Admissions Contact: Shingiral Chanaiwa, Director of Admissions. E-mail: schanaiwa@bowiestate.edu Web: www.bowiestate.edu

CAPITOL COLLEGE
Laurel, MD 20708

D-3
(301) 953-3200
(800) 950-1992; Fax: (301) 953-1442

Full-time: 105 men, 37 women	**Faculty:** n/av
Part-time: 124 men, 22 women	**Ph.D.s:** n/av
Graduate: 336 men, 123 women	**Student/Faculty:** n/av
Year: semesters, summer session	**Tuition:** $17,400
Application Deadline: open	**Room & Board:** $3850
Freshman Class: 175 applied, 120 accepted	
SAT I Verbal/Math: 500/540	**COMPETITIVE**

Capitol College was founded in 1927 as the Capitol Radio Engineering Institute, a correspondence school. Today it is a private college offering undergraduate programs in engineering and computer technology, as well as graduate programs in management and electronic commerce. In addition to regional accreditation, Capitol has baccalaureate program accreditation with ABET. The library contains 10,000 volumes and subscribes to 100 periodicals. Computerized library services include the card catalog, interlibrary loans, and database searching. Special learning facilities include a learning resource center and state-of-the-art labs. The 52-acre campus is in a rural area 19 miles north of Washington, D.C. Including any residence halls, there are 9 buildings.

Student Life: 72% of undergraduates are from Maryland. Students are from 16 states and 21 foreign countries. 43% are white; 39% African American. The average age of freshmen is 23; all undergraduates, 28. 41% do not continue beyond their first year.

Housing: 100 students can be accommodated in college housing, which includes coed on-campus apartments. On-campus housing is available on a first-come, first-served basis. Priority is given to out-of-town students. 87% of students commute. All students may keep cars.

Activities: There are no fraternities or sororities. There are 17 groups on campus, including chess, computers, literary magazine, newspaper, professional, and student government. Popular campus events include Octoberfest and Spring Bash.

Sports: Facilities include an off-campus gym, a basketball court, a student center, and an athletic field.

Disabled Students: All of the campus is accessible. Wheelchair ramps, elevators, special parking, specially equipped rest rooms, and lowered drinking fountains are available.

Services: Counseling and information services are available, as is tutoring in most subjects, including math, electronics, English, and developmental English.

Campus Safety and Security: Measures include lighted pathways/ sidewalks.

Programs of Study: Capitol confers the B.S. degree. Associate and master's degrees are also awarded. Bachelor's degrees are awarded in COMMUNICATIONS AND THE ARTS (telecommunications), COMPUTER AND PHYSICAL SCIENCE (optics), ENGINEERING AND ENVIRONMENTAL DESIGN (computer engineering, electrical/electronics engineering, and engineering technology). Electrical/electronics engineering is the strongest academically and has the largest enrollment.

Required: A minimum GPA of 2.0 and 130 to 137 credit hours are required for graduation. Additional curriculum requirements vary with the major.

Special: Internships and work-study programs are offered through the school's cooperative education program. There are 2 national honor societies.

Faculty/Classroom: All teach undergraduates. No introductory courses are taught by graduate students. The average class size in an introductory lecture is 20 and in a regular course, 22.

Admissions: 69% of the 2003-2004 applicants were accepted. The SAT I scores for the 2003-2004 freshman class were: Verbal--5% below 500, 83% between 500 and 599, 10% between 600 and 700, and 2% above 700; Math--7% below 500, 75% between 500 and 599, 15% between 600 and 700, and 3% above 700.

Requirements: The SAT I is required, with a minimum composite score of 860. Applicants should be graduates of an accredited secondary school. The GED is accepted. 20 academic credits or 20 Carnegie units are required. Secondary school courses must include 4 units of English, 3 of math, and 2 each of science and social studies. An essay and an interview are recommended. Capitol requires applicants to be in the upper 50% of their class. A GPA of 2.8 is required. AP and CLEP credits are accepted. Important factors in the admissions decision are advanced placement or honor courses, recommendations by school officials, and extracurricular activities record.

Procedure: Freshmen are admitted to all sessions. Entrance exams should be taken by March 1. There is a rolling admissions plan. Application deadlines are open. Application fee is $25. Applications are accepted on-line through the school's web site.

Transfer: Transfer students must have earned 15 college credits and a minimum GPA of 2.0. 40 of 130 to 137 credits required for the bachelor's degree must be completed at Capitol.

Visiting: There are regularly scheduled orientations for prospective students. There are guides for informal visits and visitors may sit in on classes and stay overnight. To schedule a visit, contact the Admissions Office.

Financial Aid: Capitol is a member of CSS. The CSS Profile is required. Check with the school for current deadlines.

International Students: The school actively recruits international students. They must score 500 on the written TOEFL.

Computers: The mainframe is a DEC VAX 11/750. There are also 25 PCs available in labs. All students may access the system. There are no time limits and no fees.

Admissions Contact: Darnell Edwards, Director of Admissions.
E-mail: *admissions@capitol-college.edu* Web: *www.capitol-college.edu*

COLLEGE OF NOTRE DAME OF MARYLAND
Baltimore, MD 21210

D-2

(410) 532-5330
(800) 435-0300; Fax: (410) 532-6287

Full-time: 1 man, 621 women	Faculty: 74; IIB, av$
Part-time: 87 men, 873 women	Ph.D.s: 65%
Graduate: 265 men, 1183 women	Student/Faculty: 8 to 1
Year: 4-1-4, summer session	Tuition: $20,300
Application Deadline: open	Room & Board: $7400
Freshman Class: 341 applied, 288 accepted, 123 enrolled	
SAT I Verbal/Math: 530/510	COMPETITIVE

The College of Notre Dame of Maryland, founded in 1873, is a private liberal arts institution primarily for women and affiliated with the Catholic Church. Some figures in the above capsule are approximate. In addition to regional accreditation, Notre Dame has baccalaureate program accreditation with NLN. The library contains 290,000 volumes, 378,138 microform items, and 24,000 audio/video tapes/CDs, and subscribes to 2000 periodicals. Computerized library services include the card catalog and database searching. Special learning facilities include a learning resource center, art gallery, planetarium, radio station, TV station, graphic arts studio, roof-top greenhouse, and cultural center. The 58-acre campus is in a suburban area 10 miles north of Baltimore. Including any residence halls, there are 11 buildings.

Student Life: 70% of undergraduates are from Maryland. Students are from 21 states.

Housing: 450 students can be accommodated in college housing, which includes single-sex dorms. On-campus housing is guaranteed for

all 4 years. 65% of students live on campus; of those, 60% remain on campus on weekends. Alcohol is not permitted. All students may keep cars.

Activities: There are no fraternities or sororities. There are 24 groups on campus, including art, choir, dance, drama, ethnic, honors, international, literary magazine, newspaper, political, professional, radio and TV, religious, social, social service, student government, and yearbook. Popular campus events include Honors Convocation, Antostal Day, and Multicultural Awareness Week.

Sports: Facilities include a sports/activities complex that houses racquetball courts, a dance studio, a fitness center, an indoor walking track, a game room, an activities resource center, and a basketball court.

Disabled Students: 98% of the campus is accessible. Wheelchair ramps, elevators, special parking, specially equipped rest rooms, and lowered drinking fountains are available.

Services: Counseling and information services are available, as is tutoring in most subjects.

Campus Safety and Security: Measures include 24-hour foot and vehicle patrol, self-defense education, security escort services, and informal discussions. There are pamphlets/posters/films and lighted pathways/ sidewalks.

Programs of Study: Notre Dame confers B.A. and B.S. degrees. Master's degrees are also awarded. Bachelor's degrees are awarded in BIOLOGICAL SCIENCE (biology/biological science), BUSINESS (accounting, banking and finance, business administration and management, international business management, and marketing/retailing/ merchandising), COMMUNICATIONS AND THE ARTS (art history and appreciation, classics, communications, English, graphic design, modern language, music, photography, and studio art), COMPUTER AND PHYSICAL SCIENCE (chemistry, computer science, information sciences and systems, mathematics, and physics), EDUCATION (art, early childhood, elementary, foreign languages, music, science, secondary, and special), ENGINEERING AND ENVIRONMENTAL DESIGN (preengineering), HEALTH PROFESSIONS (nursing, predentistry, premedicine, and prepharmacy), SOCIAL SCIENCE (economics, history, interdisciplinary studies, international relations, liberal arts/general studies, political science/government, prelaw, psychology, and religion). Business, education, and communication arts are the strongest academically.

Required: To graduate, students must complete a total of 128 credit hours with a minimum GPA of 2.0 (2.5 in many majors). All students must fulfill the distribution requirements in the general education core, the major, and electives, and must demonstrate proficiency in writing, public speaking, computer literacy, and library research. In most majors, a minimum of 42 hours is required. All students must take a speech course and 2 courses in phys ed, and some majors require senior practicums.

Special: The college offers cross-registration with Johns Hopkins, Towson State, and Morgan State Universities; Coppin State, Goucher, and Loyola Colleges; and the Maryland Institute College of Art. Study abroad, internships, dual bachelor's degrees in nursing and engineering, 3-2 engineering degrees with Johns Hopkins University and the University of Maryland, and pass/fail options are available. Notre Dame's Weekend College offers bachelor's degree programs for employed adults. There are 8 national honor societies, a freshman honors program, and 4 departmental honors programs.

Faculty/Classroom: 30% of faculty are male; 70%, female. All teach undergraduates. The average class size in an introductory lecture is 30; in a laboratory, 20; and in a regular course, 20.

Admissions: 84% of the 2003-2004 applicants were accepted. The SAT I scores for the 2003-2004 freshman class were: Verbal--42% below 500, 40% between 500 and 599, 14% between 600 and 700, and 4% above 700; Math--46% below 500, 39% between 500 and 599, 14% between 600 and 700, and 1% above 700. 39% of freshmen were in the upper 25% of their class; 79% were in the upper half.

Requirements: The SAT I or ACT is required for scholarship purposes. In addition, applicants should be graduates of an accredited secondary school. 18 academic credits are required, including 4 units of English, 3 each of math and a foreign language, and 2 each of history and science, plus 4 electives. An essay is required and an interview is recommended. A GPA of 2.5 is required. AP credits are accepted. Important factors in the admissions decision are recommendations by school officials, advanced placement or honor courses, and leadership record.

Procedure: Freshmen are admitted fall and spring. Entrance exams should be taken no later than January of the senior year. There are early decision, early admissions, and deferred admissions plans. The priority is February 15. Regular application deadlines are open. Applications are accepted on-line through *www.ndm.edu*. Notification is sent on a rolling basis beginning in October.

Transfer: Notre Dame requires a minimum GPA of 2.5 for transfer students but recommends a GPA of 3.0. A combined score of 800 is required for the SAT I and 18 for the ACT. Students must also submit a letter of recommendation and an essay. 60 of 128 credits required for the bachelor's degree must be completed at Notre Dame.

Visiting: There are regularly scheduled orientations for prospective students, consisting of programs in June and January, each of which includes a stay in the dorm, registration, and advisement. There are guides for informal visits and visitors may sit in on classes. To schedule a visit, contact the Office of Admissions.

Financial Aid: In 2003-2004, 85% of all full-time freshmen and 89% of continuing full-time students received some form of financial aid. 80% of full-time freshmen and 75% of continuing full-time students received need-based aid. The average freshman award was $20,796. Need-based scholarships or need-based grants averaged $15,600 ($22,750 maximum); need-based self-help aid (loans and jobs) averaged $4011 ($6125 maximum); and other non-need-based awards and non-need-based scholarships averaged $9202 ($18,700 maximum). Notre Dame is a member of CSS. The CSS Profile or FAFSA is required.

International Students: The school actively recruits these students. They must take the TOEFL and the college's own entrance exam for placement purposes.

Computers: The mainframe is a DEC MicroVAX II. There are 80 PC and Mac workstations located in academic and administrative buildings. Access to the Internet is possible. All students may access the system 7 days a week. There are no time limits and no fees.

Admissions Contact: Sharon Bogdan, Director of Admissions.
E-mail: *admiss@ndm.edu* Web: *www.ndm.edu*

COLUMBIA UNION COLLEGE
Takoma Park, MD 20912

D-3
(301) 891-4080
(800) 835-4212; Fax: (301) 891-4230

Full-time: 292 men, 470 women	**Faculty:** 53; IIB, --$
Part-time: 130 men, 267 women	**Ph.D.s:** 42%
Graduate: 5 men, 19 women	**Student/Faculty:** 14 to 1
Year: semesters, summer session	**Tuition:** $15,248
Application Deadline: May 1	**Room & Board:** $5295
Freshman Class: 851 applied, 460 accepted, 187 enrolled	
SAT I Verbal/Math: 445/427	**ACT:** 18 COMPETITIVE

Columbia Union College, founded in 1904, is a private liberal arts institution affiliated with the Seventh-day Adventist Church. In addition to regional accreditation, CUC has baccalaureate program accreditation with CAHEA and NLN. The library contains 131,617 volumes and 7500 audio/video tapes/CDs, and subscribes to 5356 periodicals. Computerized library services include the card catalog, interlibrary loans, database searching, and Internet access. Special learning facilities include a learning resource center and radio station. The 19-acre campus is in a suburban area 7 miles north of Washington, D.C. Including any residence halls, there are 17 buildings.

Student Life: 59% of undergraduates are from Maryland. Students are from 36 states, 3 foreign countries, and Canada. 49% are from public schools. 52% are African American; 20% white; 10% Hispanic. The average age of freshmen is 18; all undergraduates, 28. 36% do not continue beyond their first year; 64% remain to graduate.

Housing: 440 students can be accommodated in college housing, which includes single-sex dorms and married-student housing. On-campus housing is guaranteed for all 4 years. 62% of students commute. Alcohol is not permitted. All students may keep cars.

Activities: There are no fraternities or sororities. There are 11 groups on campus, including band, choir, chorale, ethnic, honors, newspaper, orchestra, radio and TV, religious, student government, and yearbook.

Sports: There are 6 intercollegiate sports for men and 5 for women, and 5 intramural sports for men and 4 for women. Facilities include a swimming pool, a gym, racquetball and tennis courts, a sports field, a student lounge, and a weight room.

Disabled Students: 1% of the campus is accessible. Elevators and specially equipped rest rooms are available.

Services: Counseling and information services are available, as is tutoring in some subjects, including all English, math, accounting, and chemistry courses. There is a reader service for the blind and remedial math and writing.

Campus Safety and Security: Measures include 24-hour foot and vehicle patrol, security escort services, informal discussions, and pamphlets/posters/films. There are lighted pathways/sidewalks.

Programs of Study: CUC confers B.A., B.S., and B.M. degrees. Associate and master's degrees are also awarded. Bachelor's degrees are awarded in BIOLOGICAL SCIENCE (biochemistry), BUSINESS (accounting, business administration and management, management science, and personnel management), COMMUNICATIONS AND THE ARTS (communications, English, journalism, and music), COMPUTER AND PHYSICAL SCIENCE (chemistry, computer science, information sciences and systems, and mathematics), EDUCATION (elementary, English, and mathematics), HEALTH PROFESSIONS (health care administration, nursing, predentistry, premedicine, and respiratory therapy), SOCIAL SCIENCE (history, liberal arts/general studies, prelaw, psychology, and religion). Nursing, business, and music are the strongest academically. Communications, business, and nursing are the largest.

Required: To graduate, students must earn 120 to 128 credit hours, including 36 upper division, with a minimum GPA of 2.0 overall and 2.5 in the major. Students must take 12 hours of religion, 9 of social sci-

ences, 8 of physical sciences, natural sciences, and math, 6 of humanities and practical and applied arts, and 3 of phys ed and health. Courses in English, communication, and computer science are also required.

Special: CUC offers co-op programs in business communication, computer science, English, biochemistry, and math, internships in counseling psychology, work-study programs, a general studies degree, student-designed majors, credit for life experience, nondegree study, and pass/fail options. Dual majors are available in engineering/chemistry, and math with the University of Maryland. Students may study abroad in France, Spain, Austria, and Germany. There is an adult evening program for degree completion as well as an external (correspondence) degree. There are 6 national honor societies.

Faculty/Classroom: 55% of faculty are male; 45%, female. All teach undergraduates and 10% both teach and do research. No introductory courses are taught by graduate students. The average class size in an introductory lecture is 30; in a laboratory, 16; and in a regular course, 12.

Admissions: 54% of the 2003-2004 applicants were accepted. The SAT I scores for the 2003-2004 freshman class were: Verbal--70% below 500, 21% between 500 and 599, 7% between 600 and 700, and 1% above 700.

Requirements: The SAT I or ACT is required, with a minimum composite score of 800, or at least 400 in each section, on the SAT I or 18 on the ACT. Applicants must be graduates of an accredited secondary school. The GED is accepted. 21 Carnegie units are required, including 4 years of high school English and 2 years each of history, math, and lab science. An essay is recommended. A GPA of 2.5 is required. AP and CLEP credits are accepted. Important factors in the admissions decision are advanced placement or honor courses, leadership record, and recommendations by school officials.

Procedure: Freshmen are admitted to all sessions. Entrance exams should be taken in the fall semester of the senior year. There is a deferred admissions plan. Applications should be filed by May 1 for fall entry and December 1 for spring entry, along with a $25 fee. Notification is sent on a rolling basis. Applications are accepted on-line.

Transfer: Transfer students must have at least 12 hours of college credit and a minimum GPA of 2.0. 30 of 120 to 128 credits required for the bachelor's degree must be completed at CUC.

Visiting: There are regularly scheduled orientations for prospective students. There are guides for informal visits and visitors may sit in on classes and stay overnight. To schedule a visit, contact the Office of Enrollment Services.

Financial Aid: The FAFSA is required. The deadline for filing freshman financial aid applications for fall entry is March 1.

International Students: There are 28 international students enrolled. They must score 550 on the written TOEFL or 213 on the electronic version or take the MELAB or the college's own test.

Computers: The mainframes are an AT&T 3B2/400 and an HP 932. There are 40 PCs available in the computer lab and in academic departments. All dorm rooms have Internet access. All students may access the system. It is strongly recommended that all students have a personal computer.

Graduates: From July 1, 2002 to June 30, 2003, 244 bachelor's degrees were awarded. The most popular majors were business/marketing (26%), psychology (21%), and computer and information sciences (17%). In an average class, 28% graduate in 6 years or less.

Admissions Contact: Emile John, Director of Admissions.
E-mail: *enroll@cuc.edu* Web: *www.cuc.edu*

COPPIN STATE COLLEGE
Baltimore, MD 21216

D-2
(410) 951-3600
(800) 635-3674; Fax: (410) 523-7351

Full-time: 632 men, 1786 women	**Faculty:** 110; IIB, av$
Part-time: 169 men, 686 women	**Ph.D.s:** 64%
Graduate: 158 men, 665 women	**Student/Faculty:** 22 to 1
Year: semesters, summer session	**Tuition:** $4239 ($10,061)
Application Deadline: July 15	**Room & Board:** $5952
Freshman Class: n/av	
SAT I or ACT: required	LESS COMPETITIVE

Coppin State College, founded in 1900 and part of the University System of Maryland, offers undergraduate programs in liberal arts, teacher education, and nursing. There are 3 undergraduate schools and 1 graduate school. In addition to regional accreditation, Coppin has baccalaureate program accreditation with NCATE and NLN. The library contains 200,000 volumes and 233,000 microform items, and subscribes to 715 periodicals. Computerized library services include the card catalog, interlibrary loans, and Internet access. Special learning facilities include a learning resource center, art gallery, radio station, TV station, and an on-campus video production company. The 45-acre campus is in an urban area in Baltimore. Including any residence halls, there are 9 buildings.

Student Life: 90% of undergraduates are from Maryland. Others are from 10 states and 5 foreign countries. 90% are from public schools. 80% are African American; 10% white. The average age of freshmen is 19; all undergraduates, 23.

Housing: 690 students can be accommodated in college housing, which includes coed dorms. The housing office maintains lists of community housing available. On-campus housing is guaranteed for all 4 years. 93% of students commute. Alcohol is not permitted. All students may keep cars.

Activities: 20% of men and about 30% of women belong to 5 national fraternities; 27% of women belong to 4 national sororities. There are 40 groups on campus, including art, cheerleading, choir, chorus, computers, dance, drama, ethnic, film, honors, international, musical theater, newspaper, political, professional, radio and TV, religious, social, social service, student government, and yearbook. Popular campus events include the Lyceum Series, the Honors Program, and Black History Month.

Sports: There are 7 intercollegiate sports for men and 7 for women, and 5 intramural sports for men and 5 for women. Facilities include a 2500-seat gym, an indoor swimming pool, handball and racquetball courts, a soccer field, a dance studio, a weight room, a track, and a baseball field.

Disabled Students: 95% of the campus is accessible. Wheelchair ramps, elevators, special parking, specially equipped rest rooms, lowered drinking fountains, lowered telephones, and individual attention for students requiring specialized materials, equipment, or instructional style accommodation are available.

Services: Counseling and information services are available, as is tutoring in every subject. There is remedial math, reading, and writing.

Campus Safety and Security: Measures include 24-hour foot and vehicle patrol, security escort services, shuttle buses, and pamphlets/posters/films. There are emergency telephones and lighted pathways/sidewalks.

Programs of Study: Coppin confers B.A., B.S., and B.S.N. degrees. Master's degrees are also awarded. Bachelor's degrees are awarded in BIOLOGICAL SCIENCE (biology/biological science), BUSINESS (business administration and management, marketing management, and sports management), COMMUNICATIONS AND THE ARTS (English), COMPUTER AND PHYSICAL SCIENCE (chemistry, computer science, and mathematics), EDUCATION (elementary and special), ENGINEERING AND ENVIRONMENTAL DESIGN (preengineering), HEALTH PROFESSIONS (nursing, predentistry, and prepharmacy), SOCIAL SCIENCE (criminal justice, history, liberal arts/general studies, psychology, social science, and social work). Management science, education, and nursing are the strongest academically. Management science, education, and criminal justice are the largest.

Required: To graduate, all students must have a minimum 2.0 GPA and a minimum of 120 credit hours, with 36 to 40 hours in the major. Students must complete about 50 hours of liberal arts courses in English, math, speech, history, health, phys ed, natural and social sciences, and philosophy. All seniors must take a standardized exit exam relevant to their major.

Special: The college offers co-op programs with Dundalk Community College and Morgan University, internships in criminal justice, management science, and sociology, dual majors in engineering, pharmacy, physical therapy, and dentistry, study abroad, and B.A.-B.S. degrees in all majors. Work-study is also available. There are 3 national honor societies, including Phi Beta Kappa, and a freshman honors program.

Faculty/Classroom: 54% of faculty are male; 46%, female. The average class size in a regular course is 25.

Requirements: The SAT I or ACT is required. In addition, applicants must be graduates of an accredited secondary school with a minimum GPA of 2.0, or have a GED certificate. Students must have completed 4 courses in English, 2 courses each in history, math, science, and social studies, and 1 course in foreign language. Up to 15% of a freshman class may be admitted conditionally without these requirements, and those students who graduated high school more than 5 years ago will be reviewed individually. A GPA of 2.5 is required. CLEP credit is accepted. Important factors in the admissions decision are advanced placement or honor courses, extracurricular activities record, and evidence of special talent.

Procedure: Freshmen are admitted to all sessions. There are early decision and early admissions plans. Applications should be filed by July 15 for fall entry and December 15 for spring entry, along with a $35 fee. Notification is sent on a rolling basis. Applications are accepted on-line through the college's web site.

Transfer: Transfer students must have a minimum 2.0 GPA and be in good academic standing at the former institution. Applicants with fewer than 25 credits must meet freshman requirements. 30 of 120 credits required for the bachelor's degree must be completed at Coppin.

Visiting: There are regularly scheduled orientations for prospective students, consisting of open houses. There are guides for informal visits and visitors may sit in on classes. To schedule a visit, contact Admissions.

Financial Aid: Coppin is a member of CSS. The FAFSA and the college's own financial statement are required. The deadline for filing freshman financial aid applications for fall entry is July 15.

International Students: They must score 500 on the written TOEFL or 173 on the electronic version.

Computers: The mainframe is a DEC VAX 11/780. There are more than 200 PCs available for students. All students may access the system. There are no time limits and no fees.

Admissions Contact: Michelle Gross, Director of Admissions. E-mail: *admissions@coppin.edu* Web: *http://www.coppin.edu/*

FROSTBURG STATE UNIVERSITY
B-1

Frostburg, MD 21532   (301) 687-4201; Fax: (301) 687-7074

Full-time: 2132 men, 2132 women	Faculty: 239; IIA, av$
Part-time: 123 men, 201 women	Ph.D.s: 85%
Graduate: 327 men, 554 women	Student/Faculty: 18 to 1
Year: semesters, summer session	Tuition: $5342 ($12,242)
Application Deadline: open	Room & Board: $5772
Freshman Class: 3905 applied, 3068 accepted, 1000 enrolled	
SAT I: required	COMPETITIVE

Frostburg State University, founded in 1898, is a part of the University System of Maryland. The university offers programs through the colleges of liberal arts and sciences, business, and education. There are 3 undergraduate and 10 graduate schools. In addition to regional accreditation, FSU has baccalaureate program accreditation with CSWE and NRPA. The library contains 356,200 volumes, 300,203 microform items, and 71,985 audio/video tapes/CDs, and subscribes to 3390 periodicals. Computerized library services include the card catalog, interlibrary loans, and database searching. Special learning facilities include a learning resource center, art gallery, planetarium, radio station, TV station, environmental lab, and distance education labs. The 260-acre campus is in a small town about 150 miles west of Baltimore and northwest of Washington, D.C. Including any residence halls, there are 32 buildings.

Student Life: 88% of undergraduates are from Maryland. Students are from 27 states, 20 foreign countries, and Canada. 81% are white; 12% African American. The average age of freshmen is 19; all undergraduates, 22. 30% do not continue beyond their first year; 52% remain to graduate.

Housing: 1700 students can be accommodated in college housing, which includes single-sex and coed dorms. In addition, there are honors houses, special-interest houses, and international houses. On-campus housing is guaranteed for all 4 years. 66% of students commute. All students may keep cars.

Activities: 10% of men belong to 5 national fraternities; 10% of women belong to 5 national sororities. There are 150 groups on campus, including art, band, cheerleading, choir, chorale, chorus, computers, dance, drama, drill team, ethnic, gay, honors, international, jazz band, literary magazine, marching band, musical theater, newspaper, orchestra, pep band, photography, political, professional, radio and TV, religious, social, social service, student government, symphony, and yearbook. Popular campus events include Parents Weekend, cultural events series, and Welcome Week.

Sports: There are 9 intercollegiate sports for men and 11 for women, and 5 intramural sports for men and 4 for women. Facilities include a game room, a 3600-seat main arena, a practice gym, 5 athletic fields, 2 intramural fields, an indoor swimming pool, a dance studio, a wellness room, 6 lighted tennis courts, weight rooms, a dance lab, a football stadium, an 8-lane, 400-meter track, training rooms, team rooms, and baseball, racquetball, squash, and archery rooms.

Disabled Students: All of the campus is accessible. Wheelchair ramps, elevators, special parking, specially equipped rest rooms, special class scheduling, lowered drinking fountains, lowered telephones, and special housing are available.

Services: Counseling and information services are available, as is tutoring in every subject. There is a reader service for the blind and remedial math, reading, and writing.

Campus Safety and Security: Measures include 24-hour foot and vehicle patrol, self-defense education, security escort services, and shuttle buses. There are informal discussions, pamphlets/posters/films, emergency telephones, lighted pathways/sidewalks, and a bicycle patrol.

Programs of Study: FSU confers B.A., B.S., B.F.A., B.T.P., and B.U.R. degrees. Master's degrees are also awarded. Bachelor's degrees are awarded in AGRICULTURE (fish and game management and wildlife management), BIOLOGICAL SCIENCE (biology/biological science), BUSINESS (accounting, business administration and management, and recreation and leisure services), COMMUNICATIONS AND THE ARTS (communications, design, dramatic arts, English, languages, and music), COMPUTER AND PHYSICAL SCIENCE (actuarial science, chemistry, computer science, mathematics, physics, and science), EDUCATION (business, early childhood, elementary, middle school, and physical), ENGINEERING AND ENVIRONMENTAL DESIGN (environmental science), SOCIAL SCIENCE (criminal justice, economics, geography, history, international studies, law enforcement and corrections, liberal arts/general studies, philosophy, political science/government, psychology, social science, social work, and sociology). Business, education, and the natural sciences are the strongest academically. Education, business, and computer science are the largest.

Required: A minimum GPA of 2.0 and 120 credit hours are required to graduate. All students must complete 7 to 14 credits in natural science,

6 to 9 credits in humanities and social sciences, and 3 to 6 credits in creative and performing arts. Courses in computer science, speech and composition, personalized health fitness, and math are also required.

Special: FSU offers co-op programs in applied physics, electrical engineering, and mechanical engineering with the University of Maryland, internships through individual departments, study abroad in Ireland, England, Germany, Denmark, and Ecuador through the International Student Exchange Program, work-study and accelerated degree programs, B.A.-B.S. degrees in all majors, and a dual major in engineering. The 3-2 engineering degree is coordinated with the University of Maryland at College Park. Cross-registration, nondegree study, and pass/fail options are also available. Distance learning and an advanced degree program are available. There are 18 national honor societies, a freshman honors program, and 15 departmental honors programs.

Faculty/Classroom: 58% of faculty are male; 42%, female. All teach undergraduates. No introductory courses are taught by graduate students. The average class size in an introductory lecture is 25; in a laboratory, 13; and in a regular course, 20.

Admissions: 79% of the 2003-2004 applicants were accepted. The SAT I scores for the 2003-2004 freshman class were: Verbal--45% below 500, 42% between 500 and 599, 12% between 600 and 700, and 1% above 700; Math--41% below 500, 43% between 500 and 599, 14% between 600 and 700, and 1% above 700. The ACT scores were 63% below 21, 19% between 21 and 23, 17% between 24 and 26, and 1% above 28. 24% of the current freshmen were in the top fifth of their class; 54% were in the top two fifths.

Requirements: The SAT I is required. In addition, applicants must be graduates of an accredited secondary school or have the GED. Secondary preparation should include 4 units of English, 3 each of math and social studies, and 2 of a foreign language and science. An interview is recommended. A GPA of 2.0 is required. AP and CLEP credits are accepted. Important factors in the admissions decision are recommendations by school officials, extracurricular activities record, and advanced placement or honor courses.

Procedure: Freshmen are admitted to all sessions. Entrance exams should be taken in the junior or senior year. There is an early admissions plan. Application deadlines are open. Application fee is $30. Notification is sent on a rolling basis. Applications are accepted on-line through *http://www.frostburg.edu/ungrad/admiss/onlineappproc.htm*.

Transfer: 370 transfer students enrolled in 2002-2003. Transfer students with 12 to 23 credits must have a minimum GPA of 2.5 and provide an official high school transcript and SAT I scores. Students with 24 or more credits must have a minimum GPA of 2.0. 30 of 120 credits required for the bachelor's degree must be completed at FSU.

Visiting: There are regularly scheduled orientations for prospective students, including tours Monday through Friday at 11 A.M. and 2 P.M. There are guides for informal visits and visitors may sit in on classes. To schedule a visit, contact the Office of Admissions.

Financial Aid: In 2003-2004, 75% of all full-time freshmen and 59% of continuing full-time students received some form of financial aid. 46% of full-time freshmen and 45% of continuing full-time students received need-based aid. The average freshman award was $7715. Need-based scholarships or need-based grants averaged $4423 ($8000 maximum); need-based self-help aid (loans and jobs) averaged $2448 ($2625 maximum); and non-need-based awards and non-need-based scholarships averaged $5731 ($17,618 maximum). 35% of undergraduates work part time. Average annual earnings from campus work are $750. The average financial indebtedness of the 2003 graduate was $15,174. The FAFSA and the college's own financial statement are required. The deadline for filing freshman financial aid applications for fall entry is March 1.

International Students: There are 28 international students enrolled. The school actively recruits these students. They must score 560 on the written TOEFL or 220 on the electronic version and also take the SAT I or the ACT, scoring 850 on the SAT I.

Computers: The mainframe is a VAX/VMS 4300. There are 668 computers in open and specialized labs throughout the campus. All students may access the system 8 A.M. to midnight. There are no time limits and no fees. It is strongly recommended that all students have a personal computer.

Graduates: From July 1, 2002 to June 30, 2003, 812 bachelor's degrees were awarded. The most popular majors were business administration (15%), education (10%), and psychology (9%). In an average class, 27% graduate in 4 years or less, 49% graduate in 5 years or less, and 52% graduate in 6 years or less. 61 companies recruited on campus in 2002-2003.

Admissions Contact: Trisha Gregory, Associate Director of Admissions. E-mail: *fsuadmissions@frostburg.edu* Web: *www.frostburg.edu*

GOUCHER COLLEGE
Baltimore, MD 21204

D-2
(410) 337-6100
(800) 468-2437; Fax: (410) 337-6354

Full-time: 398 men, 870 women	**Faculty:** 98; IIB, +$
Part-time: 20 men, 22 women	**Ph.D.s:** 90%
Graduate: 202 men, 799 women	**Student/Faculty:** 13 to 1
Year: semesters	**Tuition:** $24,450
Application Deadline: February 1	**Room & Board:** $8200
Freshman Class: 2746 applied, 1771 accepted, 350 enrolled	
SAT I Verbal/Math: 618/594	**HIGHLY COMPETITIVE**

Goucher College, founded in 1885, is a private liberal arts college. In addition to regional accreditation, Goucher has baccalaureate program accreditation with NCATE. The library contains 308,031 volumes, 24,836 microform items, and 3757 audio/video tapes/CDs, and subscribes to 2574 periodicals. Computerized library services include the card catalog, interlibrary loans, database searching, and Internet access. Special learning facilities include a learning resource center, art gallery, radio station, TV station, TV studio, theater, technology/learning center, international technology and media center, and centers for writing, math, and politics. The 287-acre campus is in a suburban area 8 miles north of Baltimore. Including any residence halls, there are 18 buildings.

Student Life: 60% of undergraduates are from out of state, mostly the Middle Atlantic. 70% are from public schools. 63% are white. The average age of freshmen is 19; all undergraduates, 22. 20% do not continue beyond their first year; 69% remain to graduate.

Housing: 875 students can be accommodated in college housing, which includes single-sex and coed dorms and on-campus apartments. In addition, there are language houses and special-interest houses. On-campus housing is guaranteed for all 4 years. 74% of students live on campus. All students may keep cars.

Activities: There are no fraternities or sororities. There are 40 groups on campus, including art, chorale, chorus, dance, drama, environmental, ethnic, film, gay, honors, international, jazz band, literary magazine, martial arts, newspaper, orchestra, political, professional, religious, social, social service, student government, symphony, and yearbook. Popular campus events include Get into Goucher Day, Spring Gala, and Blind Date Ball.

Sports: There are 7 intercollegiate sports for men and 9 for women, and 12 intramural sports for men and 12 for women. Facilities include 2 gyms, an indoor swimming pool, a weight room, a dance studio, a training room, racquetball and squash courts, tennis courts, and indoor and outdoor equestrian facilities.

Disabled Students: All of the campus is accessible. Wheelchair ramps, elevators, special parking, specially equipped rest rooms, special class scheduling, and an auditorium loop for the hearing impaired are available.

Services: Counseling and information services are available, as is tutoring in most subjects. There is a reader service for the blind. Many academic support options are available through the college's Academic Center for Excellence (ACE).

Campus Safety and Security: Measures include 24-hour foot and vehicle patrol, self-defense education, security escort services, and shuttle buses. There are informal discussions, pamphlets/posters/films, emergency telephones, lighted pathways/sidewalks, a whistle-alert program, a student safety and security committee, and a manned guard/gatehouse during evening hours.

Programs of Study: Goucher confers the B.A. degree. Master's degrees are also awarded. Bachelor's degrees are awarded in BIOLOGICAL SCIENCE (biology/biological science), BUSINESS (management science), COMMUNICATIONS AND THE ARTS (art history and appreciation, arts administration/management, communications, dance, dramatic arts, English, French, historic preservation, music, Russian, Spanish, and studio art), COMPUTER AND PHYSICAL SCIENCE (applied physics, chemistry, computer science, mathematics, and physics), EDUCATION (elementary and special), SOCIAL SCIENCE (American studies, economics, history, interdisciplinary studies, international relations, international studies, philosophy, political science/government, psychology, social science, sociology, and women's studies). Biology, chemistry, and history are the strongest academically. English, management, and psychology are the largest.

Required: To graduate, all students must complete 120 hours, with a minimum GPA of 2.0. Requirements include 1 lab-related course in the natural sciences, 1 course each in the humanities, social sciences, math, and the arts, and the first-year colloquium course for freshmen. Students are also required to demonstrate proficiency in computers, writing, and a foreign language. Other requirements include a 4-class distribution requirement in phys ed and at least 3 semester hours of an off-campus experience.

Special: Goucher offers internships, study abroad in 11 countries, and other off-campus experiences. The college also collaborates with many of the 22 other colleges in the Baltimore Collegetown Network (*www.colltown.org*). Students may cross-register with Johns Hopkins University, Towson University, Loyola College, Morgan State University,

College of Notre Dame, Baltimore Hebrew University, and Maryland Institute, College of Art. An advanced degree program with the Monterey Institute for International Studies, and a 3-2 engineering degree with Johns Hopkins University are offered. Dual majors are an option, and student-designed majors and pass/no pass options are also available. There is 1 national honor society, including Phi Beta Kappa, a freshman honors program, and 18 departmental honors programs.

Faculty/Classroom: 38% of faculty are male; 62%, female. All teach undergraduates.

Admissions: 64% of the 2003-2004 applicants were accepted. The SAT I scores for the 2003-2004 freshman class were: Verbal--7% below 500, 33% between 500 and 599, 45% between 600 and 700, and 15% above 700; Math--10% below 500, 38% between 500 and 599, 44% between 600 and 700, and 8% above 700. 61% of the current freshmen were in the top fifth of their class; 88% were in the top two fifths.

Requirements: The SAT I or ACT is required. In addition, applicants should be graduates of an accredited high school or have earned the GED. Secondary preparation should include at least 14 academic units, preferably 4 in English, 3 in math (algebra I and II and geometry), 2 each in the same foreign language and in lab science, and 2 or 3 in social studies. A personal essay is required, and an interview is recommended. Prospective arts majors are urged to seek an audition or submit a portfolio. AP credits are accepted. Important factors in the admissions decision are extracurricular activities record, recommendations by school officials, and advanced placement or honor courses.

Procedure: Freshmen are admitted fall and spring. Entrance exams should be taken in spring of the junior year or fall of the senior year. There are early admissions and deferred admissions plans. Applications should be filed by February 1 for fall entry and December 1 for spring entry, along with a $40 application fee. Notification of early decision is sent January 15; regular decision, April 1. 367 applicants were on the 2003 waiting list; 26 were admitted. Applications are accepted on computer disk.

Transfer: 39 transfer students enrolled in 2002-2003. Applicants must present a GPA of at least 2.5 in 30 hours of college work. An interview, a personal essay, and recommendations from college teachers or counselors are also required, as is a graded paper. 60 of 120 credits required for the bachelor's degree must be completed at Goucher.

Visiting: There are regularly scheduled orientations for prospective students, including an academic presentation, student panel, discussions, a campus tour, an interview, and an opportunity to meet with faculty, coaches, and other staff. There are guides for informal visits and visitors may sit in on classes and stay overnight. To schedule a visit, contact the Office of Admissions at *admissions@goucher.edu.*

Financial Aid: In 2003-2004, 56% of all full-time freshmen and 58% of continuing full-time students received some form of financial aid. 54% of full-time freshmen and 56% of continuing full-time students received need-based aid. The average freshman award was $18,565. 46% of undergraduates work part time. Average annual earnings from campus work are $1200. The average financial indebtedness of the 2003 graduate was $16,062. Goucher is a member of CSS. The CSS Profile or FAFSA and the college's own financial statement are required. The deadline for filing freshman financial aid applications for fall entry is February 15.

International Students: There are 14 international students enrolled. The school actively recruits these students. They must score 550 on the written TOEFL and also take the SAT I or the ACT.

Computers: The mainframes are an HP 9000, Series 800. PCs are available in academic labs, dorms, and the library. All dorm rooms are wired for direct access to the Internet and the Web. An intracampus network is in place. All students may access the system. Some facilities are available around the clock. There are no time limits and no fees.

Graduates: From July 1, 2002 to June 30, 2003, 235 bachelor's degrees were awarded. The most popular majors were psychology (14%), communication (12%), and biological science (8%). 38 companies recruited on campus in 2002-2003.

Admissions Contact: Carlton E. Surbeck, Director of Admissions. A video is available. E-mail: *admission@goucher.edu*
Web: *www.goucher.edu*

HOOD COLLEGE
Frederick, MD 21701-8575

C-2

(301) 696-3400
(800) 922-1599; Fax: (301) 696-3819

Full-time: 80 men, 607 women	**Faculty:** 76; IIA, --$
Part-time: 48 men, 129 women	**Ph.D.s:** 95%
Graduate: 301 men, 628 women	**Student/Faculty:** 9 to 1
Year: semesters, summer session	**Tuition:** $20,275
Application Deadline: February 15	**Room & Board:** $7520
Freshman Class: 1001 applied, 546 accepted, 181 enrolled	
SAT I Verbal/Math: 550/543	**ACT:** 22 **VERY COMPETITIVE**

Hood College, founded in 1893, is an independent, comprehensive college that offers an integration of the liberal arts and professional preparation, as well as undergraduate majors in the natural sciences. In addition to regional accreditation, Hood has baccalaureate program accreditation with ADA and CSWE. The library contains 206,608 volumes, 565,981 microform items, and 4041 audio/video tapes/CDs, and subscribes to 909 periodicals. Computerized library services include the card catalog, interlibrary loans, and database searching. Special learning facilities include a learning resource center, art gallery, an aquatic center, a child development lab, an observatory, and Whitaker Campus Center, a library and information technology center that forms the hub of the campus computing network. The 50-acre campus is in a suburban area 45 miles northwest of Washington, D.C., and 45 miles west of Baltimore. Including any residence halls, there are 31 buildings.

Student Life: 79% of undergraduates are from Maryland. Students are from 27 states, 22 foreign countries, and Canada. 66% are white; 13% African American. The average age of freshmen is 18; all undergraduates, 24. 25% do not continue beyond their first year; 75% remain to graduate.

Housing: 640 students can be accommodated in college housing, which includes single-sex and coed dorms. In addition, there are language houses. Special -interest floors in the residence halls include a living/learning floor and a community service floor. On-campus housing is guaranteed for all 4 years. 54% of students live on campus; of those, 60% remain on campus on weekends. All students may keep cars.

Activities: There are no fraternities or sororities. There are 59 groups on campus, including art, choir, chorale, chorus, computers, dance, drama, environmental, ethnic, gay, honors, international, literary magazine, musical theater, newspaper, opera, political, professional, religious, social, social service, student government, and yearbook. Popular campus events include Ring Formal, performance of "The Messiah" with the U.S. Naval Academy, and Spirit Week.

Sports: There are 5 intercollegiate sports for men and 10 for women and 1 intramural sport for women. Facilities include a gym with regulation basketball and volleyball courts, a weight room, an aerobics room, indoor and outdoor swimming pools, a 1-mile par course, a softball diamond, 6 tennis courts, an outdoor volleyball court, and 3 multiuse fields (field hockey, soccer, and lacrosse).

Disabled Students: 37% of the campus is accessible. Wheelchair ramps, elevators, special parking, specially equipped rest rooms, and special class scheduling are available.

Services: Counseling and information services are available, as is tutoring in some subjects. There are readers for the blind, interpreters for the hearing impaired, services for students with learning disabilities, a writing lab, a language lab, and courses in time management and study skills.

Campus Safety and Security: Measures include 24-hour foot and vehicle patrol, self-defense education, security escort services, and informal discussions. There are pamphlets/posters/films, emergency telephones, lighted pathways/sidewalks, and an electronic access control system with 24-hour monitoring in all residence halls.

Programs of Study: Hood confers B.A. and B.S. degrees. Master's degrees are also awarded. Bachelor's degrees are awarded in BIOLOGICAL SCIENCE (biochemistry and biology/biological science), BUSINESS (business administration and management and management science), COMMUNICATIONS AND THE ARTS (art, communications, English, French, German, music, and Spanish), COMPUTER AND PHYSICAL SCIENCE (chemistry, computer science, information sciences and systems, and mathematics), EDUCATION (early childhood, English, foreign languages, mathematics, science, secondary, and special), ENGINEERING AND ENVIRONMENTAL DESIGN (environmental science), SOCIAL SCIENCE (economics, history, Latin American studies, law, philosophy, political science/government, psychology, religion, social work, and sociology). Biology, math, and computer science are the strongest academically. Early childhood education, biology, and psychology are the largest.

Required: To graduate, students must complete a total of 124 credit hours, with a minimum GPA of 2.0, and a 2.0 GPA in the major. 24 to 57 credits are required in a student's major. All students must complete 32 to 41 credits in the core curriculum, which includes English, math, and language courses, courses in methods of inquiry, and interdisciplinary courses in Western civilization, non-Western civilization and society, science, and technology. Phys ed courses are also required. Enrollment in the final 30 credits must be on the Hood campus as a degree candidate.

Special: The college offers a Washington semester with American University, dual majors, student-designed majors, a B.A.-B.S. degree in engineering/math, credit for life experience, nondegree study, an accelerated degree program, pass/fail options, and cross-registration with area colleges and the Duke University Marine Sciences Education Consortium. Internships of up to 15 credits are available in all majors at more than 100 sites throughout the United States and abroad. Students may study abroad in the Dominican Republic, Japan, Spain, France, and other countries. There is a 4-year honors program featuring 1 interdisciplinary course per semester and special cocurricular activities. There are 11 national honor societies and a freshman honors program.

Faculty/Classroom: 49% of faculty are male; 51%, female. All both teach and do research. The average class size in an introductory lecture is 16; in a laboratory, 10; and in a regular course, 15.

Admissions: 55% of the 2003-2004 applicants were accepted. The SAT I scores for the 2003-2004 freshman class were: Verbal--29% below 500, 40% between 500 and 599, 26% between 600 and 700, and 5% above 700; Math--29% below 500, 45% between 500 and 599, 24% between 600 and 700, and 2% above 700. The ACT scores were 44% below 21, 26% between 21 and 23, 15% between 24 and 26, 8% between 27 and 28, and 8% above 28. 47% of the current freshmen were in the top fifth of their class; 82% were in the top two fifths. 9 freshmen graduated first in their class.

Requirements: The SAT I or ACT is required. In addition, applicants should be graduates of an accredited secondary school. The GED is accepted. Hood recommends the completion of at least 16 academic credits in high school, including courses in English, social sciences, natural sciences, foreign languages, and math. An essay is required, and an interview is recommended. A GPA of 2.5 is required. AP and CLEP credits are accepted. Important factors in the admissions decision are advanced placement or honor courses, leadership record, and extracurricular activities record.

Procedure: Freshmen are admitted fall and spring. Entrance exams should be taken in spring of the junior year or fall of the senior year. There are early admissions and deferred admissions plans. Applications should be filed by February 15 for fall entry and December 31 for spring entry. The fall 2003 application fee was $35. Notification is sent March 15. Applications are accepted on-line through either the Common Application or the Hood College on-line application.

Transfer: 109 transfer students enrolled in 2002-2003. Applicants must have at least 12 college credits and a minimum GPA of 2.5. A total of 70 credits may be transferred. 30 of 124 credits required for the bachelor's degree must be completed at Hood.

Visiting: There are regularly scheduled orientations for prospective students, including tours and meetings with faculty, students, and administrators and admissions interviews. There are guides for informal visits and visitors may sit in on classes and stay overnight. To schedule a visit, contact the Admissions Office.

Financial Aid: In 2003-2004, all full-time freshmen and 99% of continuing full-time students received some form of financial aid. 78% of full-time freshmen and 77% of continuing full-time students received need-based aid. The average freshman award was $19,565. Need-based scholarships or need-based grants averaged $15,974 ($26,000 maximum); and need-based self-help aid (loans and jobs) averaged $4678 ($7237 maximum). 26% of undergraduates work part time. Average annual earnings from campus work are $1700. The average financial indebtedness of the 2003 graduate was $17,392. The FAFSA is required. The deadline for filing freshman financial aid applications for fall entry is February 15.

International Students: There are 42 international students enrolled. The school actively recruits these students. They must score 550 on the written TOEFL or 215 on the electronic version and also take the Comprehensive English Language Test or the college's own test. SAT I scores may be substituted for the TOEFL.

Computers: The mainframes include 35 Dell Poweredge, Sun Solaris, and Compaq multiprocessor servers. All students have access to computing resources and the Internet, including residential access for student-owned computers. Students may use a 10 PC 24-hour computing lab or any of 240 PCs in 21 student labs throughout campus. Off-campus students can dial in to computing facilities. All residence halls have 3 to 4 public computers. All students may access the system 24 hours per day, 7 days a week. There are no time limits and no fees. It is strongly recommended that all students have a personal computer. A Pentium 4 class machine with WinXP Pro, 256 MB memory, Ethernet, and 7200 RPM hard drive is recommended.

Graduates: From July 1, 2002 to June 30, 2003, 226 bachelor's degrees were awarded. The most popular majors were psychology (13%), management (12%), and early childhood education (12%). In an average class, 4% graduate in 3 years or less, 63% graduate in 4 years or less, 70% graduate in 5 years or less, and 75% graduate in 6 years or less. 58 companies recruited on campus in 2002-2003. Of the 2002 graduating class, 22% were enrolled in graduate school within 6 months of graduation and 76% were employed.

Admissions Contact: Dr. Susan Hallenbeck, Dean of Admissions. E-mail: *admissions@hood.edu* Web: *www.hood.edu*

JOHNS HOPKINS UNIVERSITY **D-2**
Baltimore, MD 21218   (410) 516-8341; Fax: (410) 516-6025

Full-time: 2361 men, 1775 women	Faculty: 455
Part-time: 25 men, 16 women	Ph.D.s: 96%
Graduate: 968 men, 608 women	Student/Faculty: 9 to 1
Year: 4-1-4, summer session	Tuition: $29,230
Application Deadline: January 1	Room & Board: $9142
Freshman Class: 3052 applied, 1022 accepted, 1048 enrolled	
SAT I Verbal/Math: 675/705	ACT: 30 MOST COMPETITIVE

The Johns Hopkins University, founded in 1876, is a private multicampus institution offering undergraduate degrees at the Homewood campus through the Zanvyl Krieger School of Arts and Sciences, the Whiting School of Engineering, and the Peabody Institute (music). There are 5 undergraduate and 8 graduate schools. In addition to regional accreditation, Johns Hopkins has baccalaureate program accreditation with ABET. The 4 libraries contain 3,380,206 volumes, 3,990,862 microform items, and 95,952 audio/video tapes/CDs, and subscribe to 23,043 periodicals. Computerized library services include the card catalog, interlibrary loans, database searching, and Internet access. Special learning facilities include an art gallery and radio station. The 140-acre campus is in a suburban area in a residential setting in northern Baltimore. Including any residence halls, there are 36 buildings.

Student Life: 80% of undergraduates are from out of state, mostly the Middle Atlantic. Students are from 49 states, 50 foreign countries, and Canada. 60% are from public schools. 64% are white; 21% Asian American. The average age of freshmen is 18; all undergraduates, 20. 5% do not continue beyond their first year; 88% remain to graduate.

Housing: 2200 students can be accommodated in college housing, which includes single-sex and coed dorms, on-campus apartments, off-campus apartments, and married-student housing. In addition, there are special-interest houses and non-university-sponsored fraternity and sorority houses. On-campus housing is available on a lottery system for upperclassmen. 50% of students live on campus; of those, 90% remain on campus on weekends. Upperclassmen may keep cars.

Activities: 23% of men belong to 11 national fraternities; 22% of women belong to 7 national sororities. There are 180 groups on campus, including art, band, cheerleading, chess, choir, chorale, chorus, computers, dance, debate, drama, ethnic, film, forensics, gay, honors, international, jazz band, literary magazine, marching band, musical theater, newspaper, opera, orchestra, pep band, photography, political, professional, radio and TV, religious, social, social service, student government, symphony, volunteer, and yearbook. Popular campus events include Culturefest, Spring Fair, and Milton E. Eisenhower Symposium.

Sports: There are 14 intercollegiate sports for men and 12 for women, and 20 intramural sports for men and 20 for women. Facilities include a recreation center that includes a swimming pool and diving board, wrestling and fencing roooms, a weight room, saunas, a climbing wall, and courts for basketball, badminton, squash, and handball. There is also a 4000-seat stadium, outdoor playing fields, and tennis courts.

Disabled Students: Wheelchair ramps, elevators, special parking, specially equipped rest rooms, special class scheduling, lowered drinking fountains, and lowered telephones are available. JHU works with all individuals to ensure access to all programs and services.

Services: Counseling and information services are available, as is tutoring in most subjects. There is a reader service for the blind.

Campus Safety and Security: Measures include 24-hour foot and vehicle patrol, self-defense education, security escort services, and shuttle buses. There are informal discussions, pamphlets/posters/films, emergency telephones, and lighted pathways/sidewalks.

Programs of Study: Johns Hopkins confers B.A. and B.S. degrees. Master's and doctoral degrees are also awarded. Bachelor's degrees are awarded in BIOLOGICAL SCIENCE (biology/biological science, biophysics, cell biology, ecology, life science, molecular biology, and neurosciences), BUSINESS (banking and finance, business administration and management, human resources, management science, and marketing management), COMMUNICATIONS AND THE ARTS (art history and appreciation, classics, English, French, German, Italian, media arts, music, music performance, music theory and composition, performing arts, romance languages and literature, and Spanish), COMPUTER AND PHYSICAL SCIENCE (applied mathematics, chemistry, computer science, earth science, geology, geophysics and seismology, information sciences and systems, mathematics, natural sciences, oceanography, physics, and quantitative methods), EDUCATION (music), ENGINEERING AND ENVIRONMENTAL DESIGN (biomedical engineering, chemical engineering, civil engineering, computer engineering, electrical/electronics engineering, engineering, engineering mechanics, environmental engineering, environmental science, industrial engineering, materials engineering, materials science, and mechanical engineering), HEALTH PROFESSIONS (nursing, premedicine, and public health), SOCIAL SCIENCE (American studies, anthropology, cognitive science, crosscultural studies, East Asian studies, economics, geography, history, history of science, humanities, interdisciplinary studies, international studies, Latin American studies, Near Eastern studies, philosophy, political science/government, prelaw, psychology, public affairs, social science, sociology, and urban studies). Biology, international studies, and biomedical engineering are the largest.

Required: Although there is no required core curriculum, all students must take 40 hours in the major and 30 hours outside their major field. The B.A. requires a total of 120 hours; the B.S. in engineering requires 120 to 128 hours, depending on the major. A GPA of at least 2.0 is required for graduation. All students must take at least 4 courses (2 for engineers) with a writing-intensive component to graduate.

Special: Internships, dual majors in music and arts and sciences and engineering, cross-registration with all Baltimore-area colleges and all Johns Hopkins divisions, a cooperative 5-year civil engineering program, a student-designed semester at the Johns Hopkins School of International al Studies in Washington, D.C., and various multidisciplinary programs are offered. Students may enroll at Johns Hopkins in Bologna, Italy, or Nanjing, China, or arrange programs in Europe, South America, the Far East, or Australia. Accelerated degrees are available in 21 fields of study. Students may earn combined B.A.-B.S. degrees in biomedical, computer, and mathematical engineering or a combined B.A.-B.M. through the Peabody Institute. Pass/fail options are available in nonmajor courses. There are 4 national honor societies, including Phi Beta Kappa, and 25 departmental honors programs.

Faculty/Classroom: 77% of faculty are male; 23%, female.

Admissions: 30% of the 2003-2004 applicants were accepted. The SAT I scores for the 2003-2004 freshman class were: Verbal--1% below 500, 11% between 500 and 599, 50% between 600 and 700, and 38% above 700; Math--6% between 500 and 599, 35% between 600 and 700, and 59% above 700. The ACT scores were 2% between 18 and 23, 39% between 24 and 29, and 59% 30 and above. 76% of the current students were in the top tenth of their class; 95% were in the top quarter. There were 32 National Merit finalists. 91 freshmen graduated first in their class.

Requirements: The SAT I or ACT is required. In addition, all freshman applicants must take either the SAT I and 3 SAT II: Subject Tests (one of which must be writing) or the ACT. In addition, applicants should be graduates of an accredited secondary school or have the GED. The university recommends that secondary preparation include 4 years each of English and math, 2 (prefer 3) of social science or history and lab science, and 3 to 4 of a foreign language (2 for engineering majors). 2 personal essays are required, and an interview is recommended. AP credits are accepted. Important factors in the admissions decision are advanced placement or honor courses, leadership record, and evidence of special talent.

Procedure: Freshmen are admitted in the fall. Entrance exams should be taken by January for regular decision, or November for early decision. There are early decision and deferred admissions plans. Early decision applications should be filed by November 15; regular applications, by January 1 for fall entry. Notification of early decision is sent December 15; regular decision, by April 1. 349 early decision candidates were accepted for the 2003-2004 class. The fall 2003 application fee was $60. 675 applicants were on the 2003 waiting list; 84 were admitted. Applications are accepted on-line at *http://apply.jhu.edu.*

Transfer: 22 transfer students enrolled in 2002-2003. Applicants should have sophomore or junior standing and at least a B average in previous college work. Applications must include a written essay and at least 1 letter of recommendation. High school records and standardized test scores are also required. 60 of 120 credits required for the bachelor's degree must be completed at Johns Hopkins.

Visiting: There are regularly scheduled orientations for prospective students, including scheduled open house programs, campus tours and group information sessions offered weekday mornings and afternoons, and individual day visits with a current student. A schedule of events and a virtual tour is available at *http://apply.jhu.edu.* There are guides for informal visits and visitors may sit in on classes and stay overnight. To schedule a visit, contact the Office of Undergraduate Admissions at (410) 516-8171 or *gotojhu@jhu.edu.*

Financial Aid: In 2003-2004, 42% of all full-time freshmen and 40% of continuing full-time students received some form of financial aid. 42% of full-time freshmen and 30% of continuing full-time students received need-based aid. The average freshman award was $26,850. Need-based scholarships or need-based grants averaged $22,893; and need-based self-help aid (loans and jobs) averaged $4002. 50% of undergraduates work part time. Average annual earnings from campus work are $1000. The average financial indebtedness of the 2003 graduate was $13,300. The FAFSA and the college's own financial statement are required. The deadline for filing freshman financial aid applications for fall entry is February 15.

International Students: There are 311 international students enrolled. The school actively recruits these students. They must score 600 on the written TOEFL or 250 on the electronic version and also take the SAT I or the ACT. Students must take 3 SAT II: Subject tests; one must be writing.

Computers: Students living in university dorms and apartments can connect directly to the Internet and the JHU network via a high-speed data jack. Wireless network coverage is available throughout a number of areas of campus with the use of a supported wireless LAN card. The Academic Computing Lab, which has more than 115 PCs, as well as student consultants, is open 24 hours per day, Sunday through Friday. The Brown Foundation Digital Media Center features 12 high-end computers that enable digital and audio composition and editing, animation, virtual painting, and 3-D modeling. All students may access the system 24 hours a day, 7 days a week. There are no time limits. The fee is $112 per semester.

Graduates: From July 1, 2002 to June 30, 2003, 953 bachelor's degrees were awarded. The most popular majors were biomedical engineering (13%), international studies (10%), and economics (6%). In an average class, 5% graduate in 3 years or less, 80% graduate in 4 years

or less, 85% graduate in 5 years or less, and 87% graduate in 6 years or less. More than 200 companies recruited on campus in 2002-2003. Of the 2002 graduating class, 42% were enrolled in graduate school within 6 months of graduation and 40% were employed.

Admissions Contact: John Latting, Director of Undergraduate Admissions. E-mail: *gotojhu@jhu.edu* Web: *http://apply.jhu.edu*

LOYOLA COLLEGE IN MARYLAND
Baltimore, MD 21210

D-2
(410) 617-5012
(800) 221-9107; Fax: (410) 617-2176

Full-time: 1417 men, 1933 women	Faculty: 230; IIA, +$
Part-time: 30 men, 33 women	Ph.D.s: 85%
Graduate: 1015 men, 1605 women	Student/Faculty: 15 to 1
Year: semesters, summer session	Tuition: $26,610
Application Deadline: January 15	Room & Board: $7950
Freshman Class: 6621 applied, 4675 accepted, 921 enrolled	
SAT I Verbal/Math: 606/617	HIGHLY COMPETITIVE

Loyola College, founded in 1852, is a private liberal arts college affiliated with the Roman Catholic Church and the Jesuit tradition. It offers degree programs in arts and sciences, business, and management. There are 2 undergraduate and 2 graduate schools. In addition to regional accreditation, Loyola College has baccalaureate program accreditation with AACSB, ABET, CSAB, NASDTEC, and NCATE. The library contains 437,571 volumes, 338,337 microform items, and 39,422 audio/video tapes/CDs, and subscribes to 14,901 periodicals. Computerized library services include the card catalog, interlibrary loans, and database searching. Special learning facilities include an art gallery and radio station. The 89-acre campus is in an urban area 3 miles from downtown Baltimore. Including any residence halls, there are 29 buildings.

Student Life: 80% of undergraduates are from out of state, mostly the Middle Atlantic. Students are from 38 states, 15 foreign countries, and Canada. 88% are white. 78% are Catholic. The average age of freshmen is 18; all undergraduates, 20. 82% of freshmen remain to graduate.

Housing: 2798 students can be accommodated in college housing, which includes coed dorms and on-campus apartments. In addition, there are honors houses and special-interest houses. On-campus housing is guaranteed for the freshman year only and is available on a first-come, first-served basis. 79% of students live on campus. Alcohol is not permitted. Upperclassmen may keep cars.

Activities: There are no fraternities or sororities. There are 101 groups on campus, including art, band, cheerleading, chess, choir, chorale, chorus, computers, dance, drama, ethnic, honors, international, jazz band, literary magazine, musical theater, newspaper, orchestra, pep band, photography, political, professional, radio and TV, religious, social, social service, student government, symphony, and yearbook.

Sports: There are 7 intercollegiate sports for men and 8 for women, and 15 intramural sports for men. Facilities include a pool, a sauna, a weight room, racquetball, tennis, and squash courts, a 3000-seat arena, a 2000-seat multipurpose outdoor facility, and a fitness center.

Disabled Students: 99% of the campus is accessible. Wheelchair ramps, elevators, special parking, specially equipped rest rooms, special class scheduling, lowered drinking fountains, and lowered telephones are available.

Services: Counseling and information services are available, as is tutoring in most subjects. There is a reader service for the blind and remedial math.

Campus Safety and Security: Measures include 24-hour foot and vehicle patrol, self-defense education, security escort services, and shuttle buses. There are informal discussions, pamphlets/posters/films, emergency telephones, and lighted pathways/sidewalks.

Programs of Study: Loyola College confers B.A., B.S., B.B.A., B.S.E.E., and B.S.E.S. degrees. Master's and doctoral degrees are also awarded. Bachelor's degrees are awarded in BIOLOGICAL SCIENCE (biology/biological science), BUSINESS (accounting and business administration and management), COMMUNICATIONS AND THE ARTS (communications, creative writing, English, fine arts, French, German, Latin, and Spanish), COMPUTER AND PHYSICAL SCIENCE (chemistry, computer science, mathematics, and physics), EDUCATION (elementary), ENGINEERING AND ENVIRONMENTAL DESIGN (electrical/ electronics engineering and engineering), HEALTH PROFESSIONS (speech pathology/audiology), SOCIAL SCIENCE (classical/ancient civilization, economics, history, philosophy, political science/government, psychology, sociology, and theological studies). General business, psychology, and communication are the largest.

Required: All students must complete 120 hours, including 36 in the major, with at least a 2.0 GPA. The required core curriculum includes 2 courses each in history, language (at the second-year level), literature, philosophy, social sciences, and theology; 1 course each in composition, ethics, fine arts, math, and natural sciences; and 1 additional course in math, natural science, or computer science.

Special: Loyola offers cross-registration with Johns Hopkins, Towson, and Morgan State Universities, Goucher College, the College of Notre Dame, Maryland Art Institute, and Peabody Conservatory. Credit-bearing internships are available in most majors and study abroad is possible in 36 countries. Work-study programs and dual majors are also offered. There are 23 national honor societies, including Phi Beta Kappa, a freshman honors program, and 1 departmental honors program.

Faculty/Classroom: 55% of faculty are male; 45%, female. 90% teach undergraduates, 98% do research, and 87% do both. No introductory courses are taught by graduate students. The average class size in an introductory lecture is 25; in a laboratory, 16; and in a regular course, 21.

Admissions: 71% of the 2003-2004 applicants were accepted. The SAT I scores for the 2003-2004 freshman class were: Verbal--4% below 500, 44% between 500 and 599, 44% between 600 and 700, and 8% above 700; Math--3% below 500, 35% between 500 and 599, 53% between 600 and 700, and 9% above 700. 61% of the current freshmen were in the top fifth of their class; 89% were in the top two fifths. 10 freshmen graduated first in their class.

Requirements: The SAT I or ACT is required. In addition, applicants should have graduated from an accredited secondary school or have earned the GED. Secondary preparation should include 4 years of English, 3 to 4 each of math, foreign language, natural science, and classical or modern foreign language, and 2 to 3 of history. A personal essay is required; an interview is recommended. AP and CLEP credits are accepted. Important factors in the admissions decision are advanced placement or honor courses, recommendations by school officials, and extracurricular activities record.

Procedure: Freshmen are admitted fall, spring, and summer. Entrance exams should be taken by December of the senior year. There are early admissions and deferred admissions plans. Applications should be filed by January 15 for fall entry and December 15 for spring entry, along with a $30 fee. Notification is sent April 15. A waiting list is an active part of the admissions procedure.

Transfer: 41 transfer students enrolled in 2002-2003. Transfer applicants should have at least a 2.5 GPA in previous college work and should submit SAT I scores. Other factors considered include types of college courses taken and the secondary school record. 60 credits of 120 required for the bachelor's degree must be completed at Loyola College.

Visiting: There are regularly scheduled orientations for prospective students, including a general information session, an interview, and a campus tour. There are guides for informal visits and visitors may sit in on classes. To schedule a visit, contact the Admissions Office.

Financial Aid: In 2003-2004, 51% of all full-time freshmen and 47% of continuing full-time students received some form of financial aid. 32% of full-time freshmen and 41% of continuing full-time students received need-based aid. The average freshman award was $18,700. Need-based scholarships or need-based grants averaged $11,215 ($26,010 maximum); need-based self-help aid (loans and jobs) averaged $7485 ($7950 maximum); and non-need-based athletic scholarships averaged $24,930 ($36,985 maximum). 15% of undergraduates work part time. Average annual earnings from campus work are $1380. The average financial indebtedness of the 2003 graduate was $15,870. Loyola College is a member of CSS. The CSS Profile, FAFSA, and, if applicable, a non-custodial parent's statement and business/farm supplement are required. The deadline for filing freshman financial aid applications for fall entry is February 15.

International Students: There are 30 international students enrolled. The school actively recruits these students. They must score 550 on the written TOEFL and also take the SAT I.

Computers: The mainframes are 2 DEC VAX 11/785 computers. There are more than 200 PCs and Macs available. All students may access the system. There are no time limits and no fees.

Graduates: From July 1, 2002 to June 30, 2003, 854 bachelor's degrees were awarded. The most popular majors were general business (29%), communication (13%), and psychology (8%). In an average class, 78% graduate in 4 years or less, and 82% graduate in 6 years or less.

Admissions Contact: William Bossemeyer, Dean of Admissions. A video is available. Web: *www.loyola.edu*

MARYLAND INSTITUTE COLLEGE OF ART	D-2
Baltimore, MD 21217	(410) 225-2222; Fax: (410) 225-2337
Full-time: 465 men, 788 women	**Faculty:** 113
Part-time: 19 men, 24 women	**Ph.D.s:** 77%
Graduate: 58 men, 127 women	**Student/Faculty:** 11 to 1
Year: semesters, summer session	**Tuition:** $23,710
Application Deadline: February 15	**Room & Board:** $7180
Freshman Class: 1944 applied, 971 accepted, 386 enrolled	
SAT I Verbal/Math: 600/560	SPECIAL

Maryland Institute College of Art, founded in 1826, is a private accredited institution offering undergraduate and graduate degrees in the fine arts. There are 7 graduate schools. In addition to regional accreditation, MICA has baccalaureate program accreditation with NASAD. The library contains 53,000 volumes and 4600 audio/video tapes/CDs, and subscribes to 305 periodicals. Computerized library services include the card catalog, interlibrary loans, database searching, and Internet access. Spe-

cial learning facilities include a learning resource center, 7 large art galleries open to the public year-round and featuring work by MICA faculty, students, and nationally and internationally known artists, and a slide library containing 200,000 slides, 4 guest-curated major art galleries, and 5 other galleries for undergraduate and graduate exhibitions. The 12-acre campus is in an urban area in the Mt. Royal cultural center of Baltimore. Including any residence halls, there are 25 buildings.

Student Life: 79% of undergraduates are from out of state, mostly the Northeast. Students are from 45 states, 47 foreign countries, and Canada. 76% are from public schools. 67% are white. The average age of freshmen is 18; all undergraduates, 20. 13% do not continue beyond their first year; 66% remain to graduate.

Housing: 605 students can be accommodated in college housing, which includes coed dorms, on-campus apartments, and off-campus apartments. Residence halls include project rooms where students can do artwork 24 hours a day. On-campus housing is guaranteed for the freshman year only, is available on a first-come, first-served basis, and is available on a lottery system for upperclassmen. 88% of students live on campus; of those, 95% remain on campus on weekends. Alcohol is not permitted. All students may keep cars.

Activities: There are no fraternities or sororities. There are 22 groups on campus, including art, choir, computers, dance, drama, ethnic, film, gay, international, literary magazine, outdoor (camping, skiing, biking), photography, playwriting, political, professional, religious, social, social service, and student government. Popular campus events include regular bus trips to galleries and museums in New York and Washington, D.C., dances, and exhibition openings.

Sports: There is 1 intramural sport for men and 1 for women. Facilities include an outdoor volleyball court and a fitness center for weight lifting and aerobics on campus. There is also a recreation center 5 blocks from campus with a basketball court and other fitness equipment.

Disabled Students: 85% of the campus is accessible. Wheelchair ramps, elevators, special parking, specially equipped rest rooms, special class scheduling, lowered drinking fountains, lowered telephones, and lowered fire extinguishers are available.

Services: Counseling and information services are available, as is tutoring in some subjects, including writing and study skills. There is remedial writing.

Campus Safety and Security: Measures include 24-hour foot and vehicle patrol, self-defense education, security escort services, and shuttle buses. There are informal discussions, pamphlets/posters/films, emergency telephones, lighted pathways/sidewalks, building monitors in most buildings, and periodic discussions and seminars on safety.

Programs of Study: MICA confers the B.F.A. degree. Master's degrees are also awarded. Bachelor's degrees are awarded in COMMUNICATIONS AND THE ARTS (animation, ceramic art and design, drawing, fiber/textiles/weaving, fine arts, graphic design, illustration, media arts, painting, photography, printmaking, sculpture, and video), ENGINEERING AND ENVIRONMENTAL DESIGN (environmental design and interior design). Fine arts, painting, and graphic design are the strongest academically and have the largest enrollments.

Required: All students complete a foundation program in their first year, including courses in painting, drawing, 2- and 3-dimensional design, liberal arts, and electronic arts. Of a total 126 credits, students must take one third of the courses in liberal arts and two thirds in studio arts, with 60 credits in the major and a minimum 2.0 GPA. Seniors must complete a focused, professionally oriented body of work.

Special: Exchange programs are offered with Goucher College, Loyola and Notre Dame Colleges, Johns Hopkins University, the Peabody Conservatory of Music, the University of Baltimore, University of Maryland Baltimore County, Towson University, Morgan State University, and Baltimore Hebrew College. Cross-registration is possible with any member schools in the Alliance of Independent Colleges of Art and the East Coast Art Schools Consortium. A New York studio semester is available. Study abroad is possible in the junior year in any of 12 countries including MICA's Center for Advanced Art and Culture in Aix-en-Provence, France. Dual and student-designed majors are available, and there are work-study programs. Juniors and seniors who meet prerequisites are eligible for credit-earning internships locally and nationally.

Faculty/Classroom: 47% of faculty are male; 53%, female. 95% teach undergraduates. No introductory courses are taught by graduate students. The average class size in an introductory lecture is 25 and in a regular course, 18.

Admissions: 50% of the 2003-2004 applicants were accepted. The SAT I scores for the 2003-2004 freshman class were: Verbal--13% below 500, 36% between 500 and 599, 41% between 600 and 700, and 10% above 700; Math--20% below 500, 45% between 500 and 599, 31% between 600 and 700, and 4% above 700. 39% of the current freshmen were in the top fifth of their class; 68% were in the top two fifths. There were 3 National Merit finalists and 2 semifinalists. 2 freshmen graduated first in their class.

Requirements: The SAT I is required. Emphasis is primarily on the applicant's portfolio, which is reviewed as part of the admissions process. Applicants submit 12 to 20 pieces of their best current work in and out of school, including samples of drawing from observation. Academic history, including grades and course level, is also seriously considered. AP credits are accepted. Important factors in the admissions decision are extracurricular activities record, advanced placement or honor courses, and evidence of special talent.

Procedure: Freshmen are admitted fall and spring. Entrance exams should be taken in the spring of the junior year. There are early decision, early admissions, and deferred admissions plans. Early decision applications should be filed by November 15; regular applications, by February 15 for fall entry and December 1 for spring entry, along with a $50 fee. Notification of early decision is sent December 15; regular decision, March 1. 22 early decision candidates were accepted for the 2003-2004 class.

Transfer: 76 transfer students enrolled in 2002-2003. Transfer applicants must submit high school and college transcripts, a personal essay, a portfolio of artwork, and letters of recommendation. 62 of 126 credits required for the bachelor's degree must be completed at MICA.

Visiting: There are regularly scheduled orientations for prospective students, including campus tours, portfolio reviews, personal interviews, discussions about careers in art and financing one's education, and opportunities to sit in on classes. There are guides for informal visits and visitors may sit in on classes. To schedule a visit, contact the Office of Undergraduate Admission.

Financial Aid: In 2003-2004, 81% of all full-time freshmen and 74% of continuing full-time students received some form of financial aid. 62% of full-time freshmen and 60% of continuing full-time students received need-based aid. The average freshman award was $11,675. 60% of undergraduates work part time. Average annual earnings from campus work are $1100. The average financial indebtedness of the 2003 graduate was $12,500. MICA is a member of CSS. The FAFSA and the college's own financial statement are required. The deadline for filing freshman financial aid applications for fall entry is March 1.

International Students: There are 60 international students enrolled. The school actively recruits these students. They must score 550 on the written TOEFL or 213 on the electronic version and also take the college's own test. The SAT I or the Cambridge Exam may also be considered as a test of English proficiency.

Computers: The mainframes are an IBM AS/400, an IBM Netfinity 7000, and an IBM Netfinity 5500 M10. There are 250 IBM PCs and Macs available for student use, throughout the campus with Internet access. Every student has an e-mail address, and residence halls are wired for Internet access. Also available are high-end peripherals such as scanners, digital video editing equipment, and state-of-the-art software for 2-D and 3-D applications. All students may access the system 14 hours a day. There are no time limits and no fees.

Graduates: From July 1, 2002 to June 30, 2003, 263 bachelor's degrees were awarded. The most popular majors were general fine arts (27%), graphic design (19%), and painting (18%). In an average class, 1% graduate in 3 years or less, 58% graduate in 4 years or less, 66% graduate in 5 years or less, and 67% graduate in 6 years or less. 30 companies recruited on campus in 2002-2003. Of the 2002 graduating class, 26% were enrolled in graduate school within 6 months of graduation and 75% were employed.

Admissions Contact: Theresa Lynch Bedoya, Vice President and Dean of Admission. E-mail: *admissions@mica.edu*
Web: *www.mica.edu*

MCDANIEL COLLEGE   D-1
(Formerly Western Maryland College)
Westminster, MD 21157-4390

(410) 857-2230
(800) 638-5005; Fax: (410) 857-2757

Full-time: 726 men, 958 women	**Faculty:** 125; IIB, +$
Part-time: 24 men, 34 women	**Ph.D.s:** 97%
Graduate: 351 men, 1199 women	**Student/Faculty:** 17 to 1
Year: 4-1-4	**Tuition:** $23,160
Application Deadline: February 1	**Room & Board:** $5280
Freshman Class: 2008 applied, 1676 accepted, 451 enrolled	
SAT I Verbal/Math: 550/560	**VERY COMPETITIVE**

McDaniel College, formerly Western Maryland College and founded in 1867, is a private college offering programs in the liberal arts. In addition to regional accreditation, McDaniel has baccalaureate program accreditation with ACS and CSWE. The library contains 197,286 volumes, 1,444,720 microform items, and 162,540 audio/video tapes/CDs, and subscribes to 4342 periodicals. Computerized library services include the card catalog, interlibrary loans, database searching, and Internet access. Special learning facilities include an art gallery, radio station, TV station, physics observatory, and student research science labs. The 160-acre campus is in a suburban area 30 miles northwest of Baltimore. Including any residence halls, there are 62 buildings.

Student Life: 74% of undergraduates are from Maryland. Students are from 27 states and 23 foreign countries. 80% are white; 10% African American. Most claim no religious affiliation. The average age of fresh-

men is 18; all undergraduates, 20. 17% do not continue beyond their first year; 73% remain to graduate.

Housing: 1314 students can be accommodated in college housing, which includes single-sex and coed dorms and on-campus apartments. In addition, there are honors houses, language houses, special-interest houses, fraternity and sorority floors, academic clusters, and substance-free floors. On-campus housing is guaranteed for all 4 years. 77% of students live on campus; of those, 85% remain on campus on weekends. Upperclassmen may keep cars.

Activities: 16% of men belong to 2 local and 3 national fraternities; 12% of women belong to 2 local and 2 national sororities. There are 128 groups on campus, including art, band, cheerleading, choir, chorale, chorus, computers, drama, ethnic, film, forensics, gay, honors, international, jazz band, literary magazine, musical theater, newspaper, orchestra, pep band, photography, political, professional, radio and TV, religious, social, social service, student government, Ultimate Frisbee, and yearbook. Popular campus events include Spring Fling, Senior Week, and Families Weekend.

Sports: There are 11 intercollegiate sports for men and 11 for women, and 13 intramural sports for men and 12 for women. Facilities include a 9-hole golf course, tennis courts, a swimming pool, a football stadium with a track, a squash/racquetball court, a weight training center, basketball and volleyball courts, and soccer, softball, and lacrosse fields.

Disabled Students: 85% of the campus is accessible. There are wheelchair ramps, elevators, special parking, specially equipped rest rooms, special class scheduling, lowered drinking fountains, lowered telephones, interpreting, and TTY availability.

Services: Counseling and information services are available, as is tutoring in most subjects. There is a reader service for the blind and remedial math and writing.

Campus Safety and Security: Measures include 24-hour foot and vehicle patrol, security escort services, informal discussions, and pamphlets/posters/films. There are emergency telephones and lighted pathways/sidewalks.

Programs of Study: McDaniel College confers the B.A. degree. Master's degrees are also awarded. Bachelor's degrees are awarded in BIOLOGICAL SCIENCE (biology/biological science), BUSINESS (business administration and management), COMMUNICATIONS AND THE ARTS (art history and appreciation, communications, dramatic arts, English, fine arts, French, German, music, and Spanish), COMPUTER AND PHYSICAL SCIENCE (chemistry, computer science, mathematics, and physics), EDUCATION (physical), SOCIAL SCIENCE (economics, history, philosophy, political science/government, psychology, religion, social work, and sociology). Business administration, psychology, and biology are the largest.

Required: Distribution requirements for all students include cross-cultural studies, literature and fine arts, humanities, natural sciences, quantitative analysis, and social sciences. All students must take English composition, foreign language, and phys ed (4 courses) and pass a math proficiency exam. A total of 128 credit hours is required for graduation, including 38 to 50 in the major. The college uses a 4-course system, with most courses 4 credits. The minimum GPA for graduation is 2.0.

Special: Internships are available in all majors. Study abroad is available around the world including McDaniel's program in Budapest. There is a Washington semester in conjunction with American University and 3-2 engineering programs with Washington University and the University of Maryland. The college offers work-study programs, dual and student-designed majors, credit by exam (in foreign languages), and pass/fail options. McDaniel College has a 5-year deaf education program and offers certification in elementary and secondary education. The college also offers advanced standing for international baccalaureate recipients. There are 20 national honor societies, including Phi Beta Kappa, a freshman honors program, and 24 departmental honors programs.

Faculty/Classroom: 58% of faculty are male; 42%, female. All teach undergraduates. No introductory courses are taught by graduate students. The average class size in an introductory lecture is 18; in a laboratory, 17; and in a regular course, 18.

Admissions: 83% of the 2003-2004 applicants were accepted. The SAT I scores for the 2003-2004 freshman class were: Verbal--26% below 500, 46% between 500 and 599, 23% between 600 and 700, and 5% above 700; Math--22% below 500, 50% between 500 and 599, 25% between 600 and 700, and 2% above 700. 52% of the current freshmen were in the top quarter of their class; 87% were in the top half. 27 freshmen graduated first in their class.

Requirements: The SAT I is required, with a minimum composite score of 900. Applicants must be graduates of an accredited secondary school or have a GED. 16 academic credits are required, including 4 years of English, 3 each of foreign language, math, and social studies, and 2 of a lab science. SAT II: Subject tests and an interview are recommended. An essay is required. McDaniel requires applicants to be in the upper 50% of their class. A GPA of 2.5 is required. AP and CLEP credits are accepted. Important factors in the admissions decision are advanced placement or honor courses, leadership record, and evidence of special talent.

Procedure: Freshmen are admitted fall and spring. Entrance exams should be taken at the end of the junior year. There is a deferred admissions plan. Applications should be filed by February 1 for fall entry and January 15 for spring entry, along with a $50 fee. Notification is sent April 1. 70 were on the 2003 waiting list; 29 were admitted. Applications are accepted on computer disk and on-line through CollegeLink and Common App.

Transfer: 73 transfer students enrolled in 2002-2003. A minimum college GPA of 2.5 is required. 30 of 128 credits required for the bachelor's degree must be completed at McDaniel.

Visiting: There are regularly scheduled orientations for prospective students, including meeting the president, a panel of faculty, and a panel of students. Tours of the campus for parents are conducted by faculty members; students tour with current students. There are guides for informal visits and visitors may sit in on classes and stay overnight. To schedule a visit, contact the Admissions Office at *admissions@mcdaniel.edu.*

Financial Aid: In 2003-2004, 67% of all full-time freshmen and 63% of continuing full-time students received some form of financial aid. 67% of full-time freshmen and 62% of continuing full-time students received need-based aid. The average freshman award was $18,574. Need-based scholarships or need-based grants averaged $8023 ($21,700 maximum); need-based self-help aid (loans and jobs) averaged $4792 ($5520 maximum); and other non-need-based awards and non-need-based scholarships averaged $7640 ($22,860 maximum). 15% of undergraduates work part time. Average annual earnings from campus work are $652. The average financial indebtedness of the 2003 graduate was $17,784. The CSS Profile, FAFSA, FFS, or SFS and the college's own financial statement are required. The deadline for filing freshman financial aid applications for fall entry is March 1.

International Students: There are 40 international students enrolled. The school actively recruits these students. They must score 213 on the electronic TOEFL.

Computers: The mainframe is an IBM RISC 6000. 7 labs provide access to 132 PCs, all with access to the Internet and the World Wide Web. All students may access the system. One lab is open 24 hours per day; other labs are open 8:30 A.M. to midnight daily. The network is available 24 hours per day. There are no time limits and no fees.

Graduates: From July 1, 2002 to June 30, 2003, 366 bachelor's degrees were awarded. The most popular majors were sociology (16%), economics and business administration (13%), and communication (10%). In an average class, 2% graduate in 3 years or less, 66% graduate in 4 years or less, 72% graduate in 5 years or less, and 73% graduate in 6 years or less. 49 companies recruited on campus in 2002-2003. Of the 2002 graduating class, 43% were enrolled in graduate school within 6 months of graduation and 74% were employed.

Admissions Contact: Martha O'Connell, Dean of Admissions. E-mail: *admissions@mcdaniel.edu* Web: *www.mcdaniel.edu*

MORGAN STATE UNIVERSITY
Baltimore, MD 21251

D-2

(443) 885-3000
(800) 332-6674; Fax: (443) 319-3684

Full-time: 2070 men, 2940 women	**Faculty:** 243
Part-time: 350 men, 440 women	**Ph.D.s:** 80%
Graduate: 200 men, 290 women	**Student/Faculty:** 21 to 1
Year: semesters, summer session	**Tuition:** $5076 ($12,076)
Application Deadline: April 15	**Room & Board:** $6394
Freshman Class: 7347 applied, 4345 accepted, 1850 enrolled	
SAT I Verbal/Math: 470/490	**ACT:** 21 **COMPETITIVE**

Morgan State University, founded in 1867, is a comprehensive public institution offering undergraduate and graduate programs leading to liberal arts, preprofessional, and professional degrees. There are 6 undergraduate and 4 graduate schools. In addition to regional accreditation, Morgan State has baccalaureate program accreditation with AACSB, ABET, ADA, ASLA, CSWE, NAAB, NASAD, NASM, and NCATE. The library contains 389,516 volumes, 738,311 microform items, and 45,855 audio/video tapes/CDs, and subscribes to 3011 periodicals. Computerized library services include the card catalog, interlibrary loans, and database searching. Special learning facilities include a learning resource center, art gallery, radio station, and TV station. The 140-acre campus is in a suburban area in the northeast corner of Baltimore. Including any residence halls, there are 41 buildings.

Student Life: 60% of undergraduates are from Maryland. Students are from 40 states, 20 foreign countries, and Canada. 91% are from public schools. 92% are African American. The average age of freshmen is 18; all undergraduates, 21. 24% do not continue beyond their first year; 45% remain to graduate.

Housing: 1800 students can be accommodated in college housing, which includes single-sex dorms and on-campus apartments. In addition, there are honors houses. On-campus housing is guaranteed for the freshman year only and is available on a first-come, first-served basis. 70% of students commute. Alcohol is not permitted. All students may keep cars.

Activities: 4% of men belong to 2 local and 4 national fraternities; 3% of women belong to 3 local and 4 national sororities. There are 132 groups on campus, including art, band, cheerleading, chess, choir, chorale, chorus, computers, dance, debate, drama, drill team, drum and bugle corps, ethnic, film, forensics, gay, honors, international, jazz band, literary magazine, marching band, musical theater, newspaper, opera, orchestra, pep band, photography, political, professional, radio and TV, religious, social, social service, student government, symphony, and yearbook. Popular campus events include Kwanzaa and I Love Morgan Day.

Sports: There are 6 intercollegiate sports for men and 6 for women, and 17 intramural sports for men and 16 for women. Facilities include a field house, a gym, a weight room, a swimming pool, tennis and racquetball courts, and various playing fields.

Disabled Students: 90% of the campus is accessible. Wheelchair ramps, elevators, special parking, specially equipped rest rooms, special class scheduling, and lowered drinking fountains are available.

Services: Counseling and information services are available, as is tutoring in every subject. There is a reader service for the blind and remedial math, reading, and writing. There are also note takers and sign language interpreters for disabled students.

Campus Safety and Security: Measures include 24-hour foot and vehicle patrol, self-defense education, security escort services, and shuttle buses. There are informal discussions, pamphlets/posters/films, emergency telephones, and lighted pathways/sidewalks.

Programs of Study: Morgan State confers B.A., B.S., A.B., and B.S.Ed. degrees. Master's and doctoral degrees are also awarded. Bachelor's degrees are awarded in BIOLOGICAL SCIENCE (biology/biological science), BUSINESS (accounting, business administration and management, hospitality management services, and marketing/retailing/merchandising), COMMUNICATIONS AND THE ARTS (dramatic arts, English, fine arts, music, speech/debate/rhetoric, and telecommunications), COMPUTER AND PHYSICAL SCIENCE (chemistry, computer science, information sciences and systems, mathematics, and physics), EDUCATION (elementary, health, and physical), ENGINEERING AND ENVIRONMENTAL DESIGN (civil engineering, electrical/electronics engineering, engineering physics, and industrial engineering technology), HEALTH PROFESSIONS (medical laboratory technology and mental health/human services), SOCIAL SCIENCE (African American studies, economics, history, home economics, philosophy, political science/government, psychology, religion, social work, and sociology). Engineering, chemistry, and social work are the strongest academically. Business administration, accounting, and electrical engineering are the largest.

Required: To graduate, students must complete at least 120 credit hours, including 74 in the major, with a 2.0 GPA. All students must pass speech and writing proficiency exams prior to their senior year. The 46-credit general education requirement includes courses in English, humanities, logic, history, behavioral science, science, math, African American history, and health and phys ed. Seniors must pass a proficiency exam in their major.

Special: Co-op programs in public and private institutions may be arranged for pharmacy honors, predentistry, premedicine, and special education students. The university also offers internships for juniors and seniors, study abroad in 3 countries, work-study programs, and preprofessional physical therapy and prelaw programs. Dual majors may be pursued, but do not lead to a dual degree. There are 28 national honor societies, including Phi Beta Kappa, and a freshman honors program.

Faculty/Classroom: 67% of faculty are male; 33%, female. All teach undergraduates and 76% do research. No introductory courses are taught by graduate students. The average class size in an introductory lecture is 25; in a laboratory, 26; and in a regular course, 21.

Admissions: 59% of the 2003-2004 applicants were accepted.

Requirements: The SAT I or ACT is required, with a minimum composite score of 900 on the SAT I. In addition, applicants should be high school graduates, or have earned the GED, and are encouraged to have 4 years of English, 3 of math, 2 each of science, social studies, and history, and 1 of a foreign language. A personal essay is recommended and, when appropriate, an audition. A GPA of 2.5 is required. AP and CLEP credits are accepted. Important factors in the admissions decision are recommendations by school officials, evidence of special talent, and parents or siblings attending the school.

Procedure: Freshmen are admitted fall and spring. Entrance exams should be taken during the fall semester of the junior or senior year. There is an early admissions plan and a rolling admissions plan. Applications should be filed by April 15 for fall entry and November 15 for spring entry. Notification is sent within 2 weeks after a decision is made. The fall 2003 application fee was $25.

Transfer: 411 transfer students enrolled in 2002-2003. Applicants with fewer than 24 credits must submit high school transcripts; those with fewer than 12 credits must also submit SAT I scores. Applicants are expected to have at least a 2.0 GPA in all college work attempted and be in good standing at the last institution attended. 30 of 120 credits required for the bachelor's degree must be completed at Morgan State.

Visiting: There are regularly scheduled orientations for prospective students, including placement testing and academic advising. There are guides for informal visits and visitors may sit in on classes and stay overnight. To schedule a visit, contact Cheryl Hopson at (443) 885-1922.

Financial Aid: In 2003-2004, 87% of all full-time freshmen and 85% of continuing full-time students received some form of financial aid. 74% of full-time freshmen and 75% of continuing full-time students received need-based aid. Morgan State is a member of CSS. The FAFSA and the college's own financial statement are required.

International Students: They must score 550 on the written TOEFL or take the ALIGU and also take the SAT I or ACT. Students who have not attended any school during the preceding 3 years are not required to submit standardized test scores.

Computers: The mainframes are a DEC VAX 11/780 and an 8300. There are also IBMs and Macs available. All students may access the system. There are no time limits and no fees.

Graduates: From July 1, 2002 to June 30, 2003, 818 bachelor's degrees were awarded. In an average class, 12% graduate in 4 years or less, and 12% graduate in 5 years or less. 79 companies recruited on campus in 2002-2003.

Admissions Contact: Edwin T. Johnson, Director of Admission and Recruitment. A video is available. E-mail: *Admissions@morgan.edu* Web: *www.morgan.edu*

MOUNT SAINT MARY'S COLLEGE
Emmitsburg, MD 21727

D-1

(301) 447-5214
(800) 448-4347; Fax: (301) 447-5860

Full-time: 603 men, 769 women	**Faculty:** 90; II A, --$
Part-time: 75 men, 147 women	**Ph.Ds:** 89%
Graduate: 293 men, 202 women	**Student/Faculty:** 15 to 1
Year: semesters, summer session	**Tuition:** $21,000
Application Deadline: March 1	**Room & Board:** $7400
Freshman Class: 1894 applied, 1624 accepted, 397 enrolled	
SAT I Verbal/Math: 540/540	**COMPETITIVE**

Mount Saint Mary's College, founded in 1808, is a private liberal arts institution affiliated with the Roman Catholic Church. In addition to regional accreditation, the Mount has baccalaureate program accreditation with NASDTEC. The library contains 211,158 volumes, 17,885 microform items, and 4825 audio/video tapes/CDs, and subscribes to 905 periodicals. Computerized library services include the card catalog, interlibrary loans, and database searching. Special learning facilities include a learning resource center, art gallery, radio station, TV station, and archives. The 1400-acre campus is in a rural area 60 miles northwest of Washington, D.C., and 50 miles west of Baltimore. Including any residence halls, there are 25 buildings.

Student Life: 56% of undergraduates are from Maryland. Others are from 24 states and 5 foreign countries. 55% are from public schools. 88% are white. 82% are Catholic; 17% Protestant. The average age of freshmen is 18; all undergraduates, 20. 20% do not continue beyond their first year; 71% remain to graduate.

Housing: 1205 students can be accommodated in college housing, which includes coed dormitories and on-campus apartments. In addition, there are special-interest houses, wellness floors, and quiet floors. On-campus housing is guaranteed for all 4 years. 83% of students live on campus; of those, 80% remain on campus on weekends. All students may keep cars.

Activities: There are no fraternities or sororities. There are 65 groups on campus, including art, band, cheerleading, chess, choir, chorale, dance, drama, ethnic, honors, international, literary magazine, musical theater, newspaper, photography, political, professional, radio and TV, religious, social, social service, student government, and yearbook. Popular campus events include Spring Fling, Founders Day, and Mountapalooza.

Sports: There are 9 intercollegiate sports for men and 9 for women, and 20 intramural sports for men and 20 for women. Facilities include multipurpose indoor courts, a track, a pool, aerobics facilities, a sauna, a weight room, a basketball arena, lighted tennis courts, and playing fields.

Disabled Students: 60% of the campus is accessible. Wheelchair ramps, elevators, special parking, specially equipped rest rooms, special class scheduling, lowered drinking fountains, and lowered telephones are available.

Services: Counseling and information services are available, as is tutoring in every subject. There is a reader service for the blind and remedial math. There is a study skills and language lab and a writing center. Closed-caption TV and software for sight-impaired students are also available.

Campus Safety and Security: Measures include 24-hour foot and vehicle patrol, security escort services, informal discussions, and pamphlets/posters/films. There are emergency telephones, lighted pathways/sidewalks, and access control.

Programs of Study: The Mount confers B.A. and B.S. degrees. Master's degrees are also awarded. Bachelor's degrees are awarded in BIOLOGICAL SCIENCE (biochemistry and biology/biological science), BUSINESS (accounting and business administration and management),

COMMUNICATIONS AND THE ARTS (communications, English, fine arts, French, German, and Spanish), COMPUTER AND PHYSICAL SCIENCE (chemistry, computer science, information sciences and systems, and mathematics), EDUCATION (elementary and secondary), SOCIAL SCIENCE (criminal justice, economics, history, interdisciplinary studies, international studies, philosophy, political science/government, psychology, social studies, sociology, and theological studies). Business and finance, sociology, and elementary education are the largest.

Required: Students are required to take a 4-year, 52-credit core curriculum (with an additional foreign language proficiency requirement) in liberal arts, which includes a freshman seminar, a 4-course Western civilization sequence including art and literature, and courses in science and math, American culture, philosophy, theology, non-Western culture, and ethics. Graduation requirements include 120 credits, with most majors requiring 36 credits (30 to 36 in the major) and a minimum GPA of 2.0.

Special: Mount Saint Mary's offers cross-registration with an area community college, study abroad in the U.K., Europe, and South America, and secondary teacher certification in biology, business education, English, foreign languages, math, and social science. Dual majors, interdisciplinary majors in biopsychology, American culture, and classical studies, a general studies degree, a 3-2 nursing degree, and nondegree and accelerated study are possible. A number of independently designed internships, work-study programs, and pass/fail options are available. There also is an integrated freshman-year program. There are 16 national honor societies, a freshman honors program, and 14 departmental honors programs.

Faculty/Classroom: 62% of faculty are male; 38%, female. 90% teach undergraduates, and 87% both teach and do research. No introductory courses are taught by graduate students. The average class size in an introductory lecture is 24; in a laboratory, 18; and in a regular course, 20.

Admissions: 86% of the 2003-2004 applicants were accepted. The SAT I scores for the 2003-2004 freshman class were: Verbal--29% below 500, 44% between 500 and 599, 23% between 600 and 700, and 4% above 700; Math--30% below 500, 44% between 500 and 599, 23% between 600 and 700, and 3% above 700. 36% of the current freshmen were in the top fifth of their class; 68% were in the top two fifths. 6 freshmen graduated first in their class.

Requirements: The SAT I is required. In addition, applicants should be graduates of an accredited secondary school or hold the GED. Secondary preparation should include 4 years of English, 3 each of math, history, natural science, and social sciences, and 2 of a foreign language. An interview is recommended. AP and CLEP credits are accepted. Important factors in the admissions decision are recommendations by school officials, advanced placement or honor courses, and extracurricular activities record.

Procedure: Freshmen are admitted fall and spring. Entrance exams should be taken by January of the senior year. There are early admissions and deferred admissions plans. Applications should be filed by March 1 for fall entry and December 1 for spring entry; the fall 2003 application fee was $35. Notification is sent on a rolling basis. Applications are accepted on-line through the school's web site.

Transfer: 44 transfer students enrolled in 2003-2004. Transfer applicants should have at least a 2.0 GPA in previous college work, be in good academic and disciplinary standing, and account for all time elapsed since graduation from high school. 30 of 120 credits required for the bachelor's degree must be completed at the Mount.

Visiting: There are regularly scheduled orientations for prospective students, including campus tours and information sessions on academic programs, community life, admissions, and financial aid. There are guides for informal visits and visitors may sit in on classes and stay overnight. To schedule a visit, contact the Admissions Office at *admissions@msmary.edu*.

Financial Aid: In a recent year, 97% of all full-time freshmen and 92% of continuing full-time students received some form of financial aid. 66% of all full-time students received need-based aid. The average freshman award was $16,090; need-based scholarships or need-based grants averaged $4101 ($12,000 maximum); need-based self-help aid (loans and jobs) averaged $3958 ($5625 maximum); non-need-based athletic scholarships averaged $7554 ($28,800 maximum); and other non-need-based awards and non-need-based scholarships averaged $9800 ($20,400 maximum). 35% of undergraduates work part time. Average annual earnings from campus work are $1200. The average financial indebtedness of the 2003 graduate was $8553. The Mount is a member of CSS. The FAFSA and the college's own financial statement are required. The deadline for filing freshman financial aid applications for fall entry is March 15.

International Students: There are 9 international students enrolled. They must score 550 on the written TOEFL or 213 on the electronic version and also take the SAT I or the ACT.

Computers: Computer facilities include Dell servers. There are 135 PCs located in 7 computer labs across campus; students have access to the SPARC Server via Telnet. All students may access the system 24 hours per day. There are no time limits and no fees. It is strongly recommended that all students have a personal computer.

Graduates: From July 1, 2002 to June 30, 2003, 334 bachelor's degrees were awarded. The most popular majors were business (30%), elementary education (15%), and sociology (8%). In an average class, 1% graduate in 3 years or less, 67% graduate in 4 years or less, 70% graduate in 5 years or less, and 71% graduate in 6 years or less. 100 companies recruited on campus in 2002-2003. Of the 2002 graduating class, 36% were enrolled in graduate school within 6 months of graduation and 92% were employed.

Admissions Contact: Stephen Neitz, Executive Director of Admissions and Financial Aid. A video is available.
E-mail: *admissions@msmary.edu* Web: *http://www.msmary.edu*

SAINT JOHN'S COLLEGE   E-3
Annapolis, MD 21404
(410) 626-2523
(800) 727-9238; Fax: (410) 269-7916

Full-time: 258 men, 220 women	**Faculty:** 70; IIB, +$
Part-time: 1 man, 1 woman	**Ph.D.s:** 70%
Graduate: 53 men, 35 women	**Student/Faculty:** 7 to 1
Year: semesters, summer session	**Tuition:** $29,040
Application Deadline: open	**Room & Board:** $7320
Freshman Class: 531 applied, 389 accepted, 142 enrolled	
SAT I Verbal/Math: 700/640	**HIGHLY COMPETITIVE+**

St. John's College, founded as King William's School in 1696 and chartered as St. John's in 1784, is a private institution that offers a single all-required curriculum sometimes called the Great Books Program. Students and faculty work together in small discussion classes without lecture courses, written finals, or emphasis on grades. The program is a rigorous interdisciplinary curriculum based on the great works of literature, math, philosophy, theology, sciences, political theory, music, history, and economics. There is also a campus in Santa Fe, New Mexico. The 2 libraries contain 102,000 volumes, 412 microform items, and 1873 audio/video tapes/CDs, and subscribe to 123 periodicals. Computerized library services include the card catalog, interlibrary loans, database searching, and Internet access. Special learning facilities include an art gallery and planetarium. The 36-acre campus is in a small town 35 miles east of Washington, D.C., and 32 miles south of Baltimore. Including any residence halls, there are 16 buildings.

Student Life: 87% of undergraduates are from out of state, mostly the Middle Atlantic. Students are from 47 states, 5 foreign countries, and Canada. 65% are from public schools. 90% are white. The average age of freshmen is 19; all undergraduates, 20. 20% do not continue beyond their first year; 17% remain to graduate.

Housing: 307 students can be accommodated in college housing, which includes coed dormitories. In addition, there are special-interest houses. On-campus housing is guaranteed for the freshman year only and is available on a lottery system for upperclassmen. 65% of students live on campus; of those, 95% remain on campus on weekends. Upperclassmen may keep cars.

Activities: There are no fraternities or sororities. There are 49 groups on campus, including art, chess, chorus, community garden, computers, dance, drama, film, gay, international, literary magazine, newspaper, photography, poetry, political, religious, social, social service, student government, vegetarian, and yearbook. Popular campus events include Reality Weekend, Senior Prank, and College Navy Croquet Match.

Sports: There are 2 intercollegiate sports for men and 2 for women, and 19 intramural sports for men and 19 for women. Facilities include a gym with a weight room, cardio room, and indoor running track, tennis courts, a boathouse for sailing and crew, and playing fields.

Disabled Students: 70% of the campus is accessible. Wheelchair ramps, elevators, special parking, specially equipped rest rooms, special class scheduling, lowered drinking fountains, lowered telephones, and ground floor dorm rooms are available.

Services: Counseling and information services are available, as is tutoring in most subjects. There is remedial math and writing.

Campus Safety and Security: Measures include 24-hour foot and vehicle patrol, informal discussions, pamphlets/posters/films, and emergency telephones. There are lighted pathways/sidewalks and a 24-hour security escort service.

Programs of Study: St. John's confers the B.A. degree. Master's degrees are also awarded. Bachelor's degrees are awarded in SOCIAL SCIENCE (liberal arts/general studies, Western civilization/culture, and Western European studies).

Required: The common curriculum, equivalent to 132 credits, covers a range of classic to modern works. Students attend small seminars; 9-week preceptorials on specific works or topics; language, music, and math tutorials; and a 3-year natural sciences lab. Active learning occurs through discussion, translations, writing, experiment, mathematical demonstration, and musical analysis. Students take oral exams each semester and submit annual essays. Sophomores also take a math exam and seniors an oral exam that admits them to degree candidacy. Seniors also present a final essay to the faculty and take a 1-hour public oral exam.

Faculty/Classroom: 74% of faculty are male; 26%, female. All teach undergraduates. No introductory courses are taught by graduate stu-

dents. The average class size in a laboratory is 15 and in a regular course, 15.

Admissions: 73% of the 2003-2004 applicants were accepted. 67% of the current freshmen were in the top fifth of their class; 89% were in the top two fifths. There were 7 National Merit finalists and 11 semifinalists.

Requirements: Test scores may be submitted but are not required. In addition, applicants need not be high school graduates; some students are admitted before they complete high school. Secondary preparation should include 4 years of English, 3 years of math, and 2 years each of foreign language, science, and history. Applicants must submit written essays; which are critical to the admissions decision, and are strongly urged to schedule an interview. Important factors in the admissions decision are recommendations by school officials, advanced placement or honor courses, and personality/intangible qualities.

Procedure: Freshmen are admitted fall and spring. There are early admissions and deferred admissions plans. Recommended application deadlines are March 1 for fall entry and December 15 for spring entry. Notification is sent on a rolling basis.

Transfer: 14 transfer students enrolled in 2003-2004. Transfer students may enter only as freshmen and must complete the entire program at St. John's. The admissions criteria are the same as for regular students. Students in good academic standing may transfer to the Santa Fe campus at the beginning of any academic year. 132 of 132 credits required for the bachelor's degree must be completed at St. John's.

Visiting: There are regularly scheduled orientations for prospective students, consisting of an overnight stay on campus, class visits, and a tour. There are guides for informal visits and visitors may sit in on classes and stay overnight. To schedule a visit, contact the Admission Office at (410) 626-2522.

Financial Aid: In 2003-2004, 54% of all full-time freshmen and 58% of continuing full-time students received some form of financial aid. 54% of full-time freshmen and 55% of continuing full-time students received need-based aid. The average freshman award was $22,220. Need-based scholarships or need-based grants averaged $16,510; and need-based self-help aid (loans and jobs) averaged $5710. 75% of undergraduates work part time. Average annual earnings from campus work are $2410. The average financial indebtedness of the 2003 graduate was $18,125. The CSS/Profile or FAFSA is required. The deadline for filing freshman financial aid applications for fall entry is February 15.

International Students: There were 11 international students enrolled in a recent year. The school actively recruits these students. They must take the SAT I.

Computers: The mainframe is an IBM AS/400. There is a network of 8 Macs available for student use in a computer room, as well as 1 Mac and 10 PCs in the library. They are equipped with word-processing programs and a variety of other software. All student dorms are connected to the network. All students may access the system 24 hours a day. There are no time limits and no fees.

Graduates: From July 1, 2002 to June 30, 2003, 127 bachelor's degrees were awarded. The most popular major was liberal arts (100%). In an average class, 59% graduate in 4 years or less, 67% graduate in 5 years or less, and 69% graduate in 6 years or less. 5 companies recruited on campus in 2002-2003. Of the 2002 graduating class, 19% were enrolled in graduate school within 6 months of graduation and 40% were employed.

Admissions Contact: John Christensen, Director of Admissions.
E-mail: *admissions@sjca.edu* Web: *http://www.sjca.edu*

SAINT MARY'S COLLEGE OF MARYLAND   E-4
St. Marys City, MD 20686
(240) 895-5000
(800) 492-7181; Fax: (240) 895-5001

Full-time: 714 men, 1092 women	**Faculty:** 117
Part-time: 49 men, 67 women	**Ph.D.s:** 97%
Graduate: none	**Student/Faculty:** 15 to 1
Year: semesters, summer session	**Tuition:** $8740 ($15,060)
Application Deadline: January 15	**Room & Board:** $7168
Freshman Class: 2262 applied, 1243 accepted, 421 enrolled	
SAT I Verbal/Math: 640/630	**VERY COMPETITIVE+**

St. Mary's College of Maryland, founded in 1840, is a small public liberal arts college in the Maryland State College and University System. In addition to regional accreditation, St. Mary's has baccalaureate program accreditation with NASM. The library contains 183,958 volumes, 45,449 microform items, and 10,772 audio/video tapes/CDs, and subscribes to 2106 periodicals. Computerized library services include the card catalog, interlibrary loans, database searching, and Internet access. Special learning facilities include a learning resource center, art gallery, radio station, TV station, historic archeological site, and estuarine research facilities. The 319-acre campus is in a rural area 70 miles south of Washington, D.C. Including any residence halls, there are 47 buildings.

Student Life: 83% of undergraduates are from Maryland. Students are from 36 states, 28 foreign countries, and Canada. 82% are from public schools. 85% are white. 40% are Protestant; 28% claim no religious affiliation; 22% Catholic; 8% Islam, Buddhist, and other. The average age of freshmen is 18; all undergraduates, 21. 15% do not continue beyond their first year; 75% remain to graduate.

Housing: 1488 students can be accommodated in college housing, which includes single-sex and coed dorms and on-campus apartments. In addition, there are language houses and special-interest houses. On-campus housing is guaranteed for all 4 years. 77% of students live on campus; of those, 75% remain on campus on weekends. All students may keep cars.

Activities: There are no fraternities or sororities. There are many groups and organizations on campus, including academic, art, band, cheerleading, chess, choir, chorale, chorus, computers, dance, drama, ethnic, film, gay, honors, international, jazz band, literary magazine, musical theater, newspaper, orchestra, outdoor, photography, political, professional, radio and TV, religious, social, social service, student government, symphony, and yearbook. Popular campus events include Parents Weekend, World Carnival, and concerts.

Sports: There are 7 intercollegiate sports for men and 8 for women, and 12 intramural sports for men and 12 for women. Facilities include an athletic track, a pool, basketball, volleyball, and tennis courts, training, weight, and exercise rooms, a boat house, pier, and sailing fleet, and baseball, soccer, and lacrosse fields.

Disabled Students: 86% of the campus is accessible. Wheelchair ramps, elevators, special parking, specially equipped rest rooms, special class scheduling, lowered drinking fountains, lowered telephones, and living suites that meet ADA standards are available.

Services: Counseling and information services are available, as is tutoring in some subjects, including math, writing, physics, foreign languages, chemistry, economics, English, psychology, history, sociology, and anthropology. There is a reader service for the blind.

Campus Safety and Security: Measures include 24-hour foot and vehicle patrol, self-defense education, security escort services, and informal discussions. There are pamphlets/posters/films, emergency telephones, lighted pathways/sidewalks, and student security-assistant foot patrols.

Programs of Study: St. Mary's confers the B.A. degree. Bachelor's degrees are awarded in BIOLOGICAL SCIENCE (biochemistry and biology/biological science), COMMUNICATIONS AND THE ARTS (dramatic arts, English, fine arts, languages, and music), COMPUTER AND PHYSICAL SCIENCE (chemistry, computer science, mathematics, natural sciences, and physics), SOCIAL SCIENCE (anthropology, economics, history, human development, philosophy, political science/government, psychology, public affairs, religion, and sociology). Economics, psychology, and English are the largest.

Required: Students must complete general education requirements in writing, math, foreign language, history, the arts, literature, physical, biological, behavioral, and policy sciences, philosophy, and an interdisciplinary seminar. There is a senior project. Students must meet additional requirements in their major fields and complete 128 semester hours with at least a 2.0 GPA.

Special: St. Mary's offers a co-op program in computer science, internships, study abroad, national and international exchange programs, and work-study. Dual and student-designed majors and a 3-2 engineering degree with the University of Maryland, College Park, also are offered. Nondegree study and pass/fail options are possible. There are 8 national honor societies, including Phi Beta Kappa, a freshman honors program, and 6 departmental honors programs.

Faculty/Classroom: 56% of faculty are male; 44%, female. All both teach and do research.

Admissions: 55% of the 2003-2004 applicants were accepted. The SAT I scores for the 2003-2004 freshman class were: Verbal--4% below 500, 23% between 500 and 599, 52% between 600 and 700, and 20% above 700; Math--4% below 500, 29% between 500 and 599, 51% between 600 and 700, and 15% above 700. 71% of the current freshmen were in the top fifth of their class; 90% were in the top two fifths.

Requirements: The SAT I or ACT is required. In addition, applicants should have graduated from an accredited secondary school or earned the GED. Minimum high school preparation should include 4 units of English, 3 each of math, social studies, and science, and 7 electives. An essay, a resume of cocurricular activities, and 2 letters of recommendation are required. A GPA of 2.0 is required. AP and CLEP credits are accepted. Important factors in the admissions decision are advanced placement or honor courses, recommendations by school officials, and extracurricular activities record.

Procedure: Freshmen are admitted fall and spring. Entrance exams should be taken in May of the junior year or November of the senior year. There is an early decision plan. Early decision applications should be filed by December 1; regular applications, by January 15 for fall entry and October 15 for spring entry, along with a $40 fee. Notification of early decision is sent January 1; regular decision, April 1. 182 early decision candidates were accepted for the 2003-2004 class. 443 applicants were on the 2003 waiting list; 83 were admitted. Applications are accepted on-line through the college's web site.

Transfer: 80 transfer students enrolled in 2002-2003. Transfer applicants with a minimum of 24 credits should have at least a 2.0 GPA. Those with fewer credits should have at least a 2.5 GPA. 38 of 128 credits required for the bachelor's degree must be completed at St. Mary's.

Visiting: There are regularly scheduled orientations for prospective students, including group presentations, interaction with faculty and students, and campus tours. There are guides for informal visits and visitors may sit in on classes and stay overnight. To schedule a visit, contact the Admissions Office.

Financial Aid: In 2003-2004, 78% of all full-time freshmen and 72% of continuing full-time students received some form of financial aid. 30% of full-time freshmen and 42% of continuing full-time students received need-based aid. The average freshman award was $5020, with $1320 ($5800 maximum) from need-based scholarships or need-based grants, $1000 ($1500 maximum) from need-based self-help aid (loans and jobs), and $2700 ($6625 maximum) from other non-need-based awards and non-need-based scholarships. 25% of undergraduates work part time. Average annual earnings from campus work are $1000. The average financial indebtedness of the 2003 graduate was $17,700. St. Mary's is a member of CSS. The FAFSA is required. The deadline for filing freshman financial aid applications for fall entry is March 1.

International Students: There are 40 international students enrolled. They must score 550 on the written TOEFL and also take the SAT I or the ACT.

Computers: Students can use any of the 140 Pentium systems, 3 Mac workstations, or multimedia stand-alone workstations. Access to the Internet and e-mail is available. There are several computer labs on campus. All students may access the system during all lab hours. There are no time limits and no fees.

Graduates: From July 1, 2002 to June 30, 2003, 288 bachelor's degrees were awarded. The most popular majors were psychology (14%), economics (12%), and political science (10%). In an average class, 1% graduate in 3 years or less, 67% graduate in 4 years or less, 74% graduate in 5 years or less, and 75% graduate in 6 years or less. 78 companies recruited on campus in 2002-2003. Of the 2002 graduating class, 44% were enrolled in graduate school within 1 year of graduation and 95% were employed.

Admissions Contact: Richard Edgar, Director of Admissions. A video is available. E-mail: *admissions@smcm.edu*
Web: *http://www.smcm.edu*

SALISBURY UNIVERSITY
F-4
Salisbury, MD 21801   (410) 543-6161; Fax: (410) 546-6016

Full-time: 2332 men, 3102 women	**Faculty:** 301
Part-time: 311 men, 454 women	**Ph.D.s:** 78%
Graduate: 171 men, 446 women	**Student/Faculty:** 18 to 1
Year: 4-1-4, summer session	**Tuition:** $5564 ($12,452)
Application Deadline: January 15	**Room & Board:** $7100
Freshman Class: 5550 applied, 2882 accepted, 951 enrolled	
SAT I Verbal/Math: 556/578	**VERY COMPETITIVE**

Salisbury University, founded in 1925, is a public comprehensive university providing undergraduate programs in the liberal arts, sciences, pre-professional and professional programs, and select, mostly applied, graduate programs in business, education, nursing, psychology, English, and history. There are 4 undergraduate schools and 1 graduate school. In addition to regional accreditation, SU has baccalaureate program accreditation with AACSB, ACS, CAAHEP, CSWE, NAACLS, NCATE, NEHSPAC, and NLN. The library contains 253,168 volumes, 752,088 microform items, and 4535 audio/video tapes/CDs, and subscribes to 1711 periodicals. Computerized library services include the card catalog, interlibrary loans, database searching, and Internet access. Special learning facilities include a learning resource center, art gallery, radio station, TV station, Research Center for Delmarva History and Culture, Enterprise Development Group, Shorecan Small Business Resources Center, and Scarborough Leadership Center. The 144-acre campus is in a small town 110 miles southeast of Baltimore and 100 miles east of Washington, D.C. Including any residence halls, there are 45 buildings.

Student Life: 82% of undergraduates are from Maryland. Students are from 27 states, 36 foreign countries, and Canada. 85% are from public schools. 85% are white. The average age of freshmen is 18; all undergraduates, 22. 19% do not continue beyond their first year; 71% remain to graduate.

Housing: 1701 students can be accommodated in college housing, which includes single-sex and coed dorms and off-campus apartments. On-campus housing is available on a first-come, first-served basis and is available on a lottery system for upperclassmen. 68% of students commute. Upperclassmen may keep cars.

Activities: 5% of men belong to 4 national fraternities; 6% of women belong to 4 national sororities. There are 104 groups on campus, including art, band, cheerleading, chess, choir, chorale, chorus, computers, dance, drama, ethnic, film, gay, honors, international, jazz band, literary magazine, musical theater, newspaper, orchestra, pep band, political, professional, radio and TV, religious, social, social service, student government, symphony, and yearbook. Popular campus events include October Fest, Spring Fling, and Festival of Culture.

Sports: There are 10 intercollegiate sports for men and 11 for women, and 20 intramural sports for men and 20 for women. Facilities include

a 3000-seat stadium, a 2000-seat gym, a multipurpose gym, a 25-meter, 6-lane swimming pool, indoor climbing walls, a dance studio, racquetball and indoor and outdoor tennis courts, a baseball diamond, varsity and practice fields, an all-weather track, a fitness center, a strength room, lighted intramural fields, and outdoor sand volleyball courts.

Disabled Students: 90% of the campus is accessible. Wheelchair ramps, elevators, special parking, specially equipped rest rooms, special class scheduling, lowered drinking fountains, and lowered telephones are available. All emergency phones meet ADA standards.

Services: Counseling and information services are available, as is tutoring in some subjects. There is a reader service for the blind, remedial math, reading, and writing, and extended test-taking time.

Campus Safety and Security: Measures include 24-hour foot and vehicle patrol, self-defense education, security escort services, and shuttle buses. There are informal discussions, pamphlets/posters/films, emergency telephones, and lighted pathways/sidewalks.

Programs of Study: SU confers B.A., B.S., B.A.S.W., and B.F.A. degrees. Master's degrees are also awarded. Bachelor's degrees are awarded in AGRICULTURE (environmental studies), BIOLOGICAL SCIENCE (biology/biological science), BUSINESS (accounting, banking and finance, business administration and management, management information systems, and marketing/retailing/merchandising), COMMUNICATIONS AND THE ARTS (art, communications, English, fine arts, French, music, Spanish, and theater management), COMPUTER AND PHYSICAL SCIENCE (chemistry, computer science, mathematics, and physics), EDUCATION (athletic training, elementary, health, and physical), HEALTH PROFESSIONS (environmental health science, exercise science, medical technology, nursing, and respiratory therapy), SOCIAL SCIENCE (economics, geography, history, interdisciplinary studies, international studies, peace studies, philosophy, political science/government, psychology, social work, and sociology). Chemistry, business, and education are the strongest academically. Business administration, elementary education, and biology are the largest.

Required: Students must complete 45 semester hours of general education requirements, including specific courses in English composition and literature, world civilization, humanities, social studies, math, and phys ed. The bachelor's degree requires completion of at least 120 semester hours, including 30 or more in the major field, with a minimum GPA of 2.0. Some majors may have higher requirements. 30 of the last 37 credit hours must be completed at SU, except for special co-op programs.

Special: Cross-registration with schools in the University System of Maryland, and study abroad in numerous countries are offered. SU also offers an Annapolis semester, a Washington semester, internships, work-study programs, accelerated degree programs in dentistry, optometry, podiatric medicine, and pharmacy, dual majors in biology/environmental marine science, social work/sociology, and physical engineering, interdisciplinary and student-designed majors including physics/microelectronics, a 3-2 engineering degree with the University of Maryland at College Park, Old Dominion University, and Widener University, a co-op program in electrical engineering, and pass/fail options. There are 20 national honor societies, a freshman honors program, and 15 departmental honors programs.

Faculty/Classroom: 58% of faculty are male; 42%, female. All teach undergraduates and 16% both teach and do research. No introductory courses are taught by graduate students. The average class size in an introductory lecture is 30; in a laboratory, 25; and in a regular course, 25.

Admissions: 52% of the 2003-2004 applicants were accepted. The SAT I scores for the 2003-2004 freshman class were: Verbal--15% below 500, 59% between 500 and 599, 23% between 600 and 700, and 2% above 700; Math--10% below 500, 52% between 500 and 599, 35% between 600 and 700, and 4% above 700. 52% of the current freshmen were in the top fifth of their class; 89% were in the top two fifths. There were 3 National Merit finalists. 10 freshmen graduated first in their class.

Requirements: The SAT I is required. In addition, applicants must be graduates of accredited secondary schools or have earned a GED. The university requires 14 academic credits or 20 Carnegie units, including 4 in English, 3 each in math and social studies, 3 in science (2 with labs), and 2 in foreign language. Auditions are required for admission into the music and B.F.A. programs once admission to the university is granted. Essays are recommended but are not required. A campus visit is recommended for all students. A GPA of 2.0 is required. AP and CLEP credits are accepted. Important factors in the admissions decision are advanced placement or honor courses, leadership record, and extracurricular activities record.

Procedure: Freshmen are admitted to all sessions. Entrance exams should be taken by December of the senior year. There is an early admissions plan. Early decision applications should be filed by December 15; regular applications, by January 15 for fall entry and January 1 for spring entry. The fall 2003 application fee was $45. Applicants must submit applications on-line. Notification of early decision is sent January 15; regular decision, March 15. 1251 were on the 2003 waiting list; 32 were admitted. Applications are accepted on-line through the school's web site at *http://www.salisbury.edu/apply/*.

Transfer: 676 transfer students enrolled in 2002-2003. Applicants must present a minimum GPA of 2.0 in at least 24 transferable credit hours

earned. Students with fewer than 24 credit hours must be eligible for freshman admission in addition to maintaining at least a 2.0 GPA in college courses. 30 of 120 credits required for the bachelor's degree must be completed at SU.

Visiting: There are regularly scheduled orientations for prospective students, including presentations, tours, meetings with faculty and staff, and Saturday open house programs. There are guides for informal visits and visitors may sit in on classes. To schedule a visit, contact the Admissions Office at (888) 543-0148.

Financial Aid: In 2003-2004, 75% of all full-time freshmen and 67% of continuing full-time students received some form of financial aid. 58% of full-time freshmen and 54% of continuing full-time students received need-based aid. The average freshman award was $4205. Need-based scholarships or need-based grants averaged $5379 ($5629 maximum); need-based self-help aid (loans and jobs) averaged $2332 ($3481 maximum); and other non-need-based awards and non-need-based scholarships averaged $3126 ($3129 maximum). 30% of undergraduates work part time. Average annual earnings from campus work are $1500. The average financial indebtedness of the 2003 graduate was $14,759. SU is a member of CSS. The FAFSA is required. The priority date for freshman financial aid applications for fall entry is February 1. The deadline for filing freshman financial aid applications for fall entry is March 1.

International Students: There are 42 international students enrolled. They must score 550 on the written TOEFL or 213 on the electronic version and also take the SAT I.

Computers: SU runs the PeopleSoft suite of applications on Intel-based servers from Dell and Compaq. The university's labs are connected to the campus network, which provides Internet access. SU has 7 PC (30 units or more) computer labs as well as a 19-station Mac lab. Scanning and printing stations are available for student use in the main labs. The campus network extends to all residence halls through the RESNET program. There are 2350 ports in residence halls. Each room has 2 connections, 1 for each student. All students may access the system 24 hours daily via modem or in residence halls. There are no time limits. The fee is $120. It is strongly recommended that all students have a personal computer.

Graduates: From July 1, 2002 to June 30, 2003, 1364 bachelor's degrees were awarded. The most popular majors were elementary education (14%), business administration (12%), and communication arts (10%). In an average class, 46% graduate in 4 years or less, 67% graduate in 5 years or less, and 71% graduate in 6 years or less. 250 companies recruited on campus in 2002-2003. Of the 2002 graduating class, 27% were enrolled in graduate school within 6 months of graduation and 96% were employed.

Admissions Contact: Jane H. Dane, Dean of Enrollment Management. E-mail: *admissions@salisbury.edu*
Web: *http://www.salisbury.edu/admissions*

SOJOURNER-DOUGLASS COLLEGE

D-2

Baltimore, MD 21201   (410) 276-0306; Fax: (410) 675-1810

Total enrollment: n/av	Faculty: 14
Year: trimesters	Ph.Ds: 18%
Application Deadline: open	Student/Faculty: 13 to 1
	Tuition: $5590
	Room & Board: n/app
Freshman Class: n/av	
SAT I or ACT: not required	LESS COMPETITIVE

Sojourner-Douglass College, established in 1980, is a private institution offering undergraduate programs in administration, human and social resources, and human growth and development to a predominantly black student body. Some figures given in the above capsule and in this profile are approximate. The library contains 20,000 volumes. Special learning facilities include a learning resource center. The campus is in an urban area in Baltimore.

Housing: There are no residence halls. All students commute. Alcohol is not permitted.

Activities: There are no fraternities or sororities. There are 5 groups on campus, including student government and yearbook.

Sports: There is no sports program at Sojourner-Douglass.

Disabled Students: Wheelchair ramps, elevators, and special parking are available.

Services: Counseling and information services are available, as is tutoring in some subjects, including reading, writing, math, and study skills.

Programs of Study: Sojourner-Douglass confers the B.A. degree. Bachelor's degrees are awarded in BUSINESS (business administration and management and tourism), COMMUNICATIONS AND THE ARTS (broadcasting), EDUCATION (early childhood), HEALTH PROFESSIONS (health care administration), SOCIAL SCIENCE (criminal justice, gerontology, psychology, public administration, and social work).

Required: To graduate, students must earn 63 to 66 general education credits, with 15 credits in English literature and composition; 15 credits in political science, history, economics, sociology, geography, psychology, and anthropology; 12 credits in the humanities; 9 credits in natural science and math; and 3 credits each in career planning and personal development, psychology of the black family in America, and psychology of racism. 12 credits must be earned in a project that demonstrates competence in the major. 6 credits must be earned in the sociology of work. There is also a 3-credit education seminar requirement. A total of 132 credits is needed to graduate, with 54 to 69 in the major.

Special: Credit may be granted for life, military and work experience. Faculty-supervised independent study is possible for adult students.

Requirements: The SAT I or ACT is not required. Applicants must be graduates of an accredited secondary school or have a GED certificate. They must have completed 4 years of English and 2 years each of math, history, and social studies. Autobiographical essays, resumes, and interviews are required.

Procedure: Freshmen are admitted to all sessions. Application deadlines are open.

Transfer: Transfer criteria are the same as for entering freshmen; however, transfers are not accepted to all classes.

Visiting: There are regularly scheduled orientations for prospective students. To schedule a visit, contact the Office of Admissions.

Financial Aid: The CSS Profile, FAFSA, FFS, or SFS and federal income tax form are required. Check with the school for current deadlines.

Computers: There are no time limits and no fees.

Admissions Contact: Director of Admissions. Web: *www.sdc.edu*

TOWSON UNIVERSITY
Towson, MD 21252-0001

D-2

(410) 704-2113
(888) 4-TOWSON; Fax: (410) 704-3030

Full-time: 4656 men, 7396 women	**Faculty:** 585; IIA, av$
Part-time: 822 men, 1108 women	**Ph.D.s:** n/av
Graduate: 801 men, 2407 women	**Student/Faculty:** 21 to 1
Year: semesters, summer session	**Tuition:** $6226 ($14,298)
Application Deadline: May 2	**Room & Board:** $6468
Freshman Class: 11,568 applied, 5971 accepted, 1754 enrolled	
SAT I Verbal/Math: 540/550	**VERY COMPETITIVE**

Towson University, founded in 1866, is part of the University System of Maryland and offers undergraduate and graduate programs in liberal arts and sciences, allied health sciences, education, fine arts, communication, and business and economics. There are 6 undergraduate schools and 1 graduate school. In addition to regional accreditation, Towson has baccalaureate program accreditation with AACSB, CAHEA, NASDTEC, NASM, and NLN. The library contains 364,468 volumes, 830,286 microform items, and 14,174 audio/video tapes/CDs, and subscribes to 2164 periodicals. Computerized library services include the card catalog, interlibrary loans, database searching, and Internet access. Special learning facilities include a learning resource center, art gallery, planetarium, radio station, TV station, a curriculum center, an herbarium, an animal museum, an observatory, and a greenhouse. The 321-acre campus is in a suburban area 2 miles north of Baltimore.

Student Life: 81% of undergraduates are from Maryland. 87% are white; 11% African American. The average age of all undergraduates is 21. 14% do not continue beyond their first year.

Housing: 3310 students can be accommodated in college housing, which includes coed dorms, on-campus apartments, and married-student housing. In addition, there are honors houses, separate floors that are alcohol-free, smoke-free, substance-free leadership, quiet, or coed, and an international house. On-campus housing is available on a first-come, first-served basis and is available on a lottery system for upperclassmen. Priority is given to out-of-town students. 75% of students commute. Upperclassmen may keep cars.

Activities: 8% of men belong to fraternities; 7% of women belong to sororities. There are many groups and organizations on campus, including art, band, cheerleading, choir, chorale, chorus, computers, dance, debate, drama, drill team, ethnic, film, forensics, honors, international, jazz band, literary magazine, marching band, musical theater, newspaper, opera, orchestra, pep band, photography, political, radio and TV, religious, social, student government, symphony, and yearbook. Popular campus events include fraternity and sorority dances, Ethics Forum, and Tiger Fest.

Sports: Facilities include an athletic center, a stadium with artificial turf, baseball and softball fields, tennis courts, a pool, a soccer field, and 3 practice fields. Recreation facilities include 3 gyms, a weight room, a pool, lighted playing fields, and an indoor climbing wall.

Disabled Students: 85% of the campus is accessible. Wheelchair ramps, elevators, special parking, specially equipped rest rooms, special class scheduling, lowered drinking fountains, lowered telephones, special housing, automatic doors, assistive listening devices in theaters and concert halls, and interior and exterior signage are available.

Services: Counseling and information services are available, as is tutoring in most subjects. There is a reader service for the blind, and remedial math, reading, and writing. There are also note takers, English language and tutorial services centers, a writing lab, and signers for the hearing impaired.

Campus Safety and Security: Measures include 24-hour foot and vehicle patrol, self-defense education, security escort services, and shuttle buses. There are informal discussions, pamphlets/posters/films, emergency telephones, lighted pathways/sidewalks, Operation ID, and a police dog on campus.

Programs of Study: Towson confers B.A., B.S., B.F.A., and B.M. degrees. Master's and doctoral degrees are also awarded. Bachelor's degrees are awarded in BIOLOGICAL SCIENCE (biology/biological science and molecular biology), BUSINESS (accounting, business administration and management, and sports management), COMMUNICATIONS AND THE ARTS (art, communications, dance, English, French, German, media arts, music, Spanish, and theater design), COMPUTER AND PHYSICAL SCIENCE (chemistry, computer science, earth science, geology, geoscience, information sciences and systems, mathematics, and physics), EDUCATION (art, athletic training, dance, early childhood, education, education of the deaf and hearing impaired, elementary, music, physical, and special), ENGINEERING AND ENVIRONMENTAL DESIGN (environmental science), HEALTH PROFESSIONS (exercise science, health care administration, health science, medical laboratory technology, nursing, occupational therapy, speech pathology/audiology, and sports medicine), SOCIAL SCIENCE (anthropology, crosscultural studies, economics, family/consumer studies, geography, gerontology, history, interdisciplinary studies, international studies, law, philosophy, political science/government, psychology, religion, social science, sociology, and women's studies). Fine arts, business, and education are the strongest academically. Business disciplines, mass communications, and psychology are the largest.

Required: Students must complete course work in the arts, English, humanities, math, biological or physical science, social science, information technology, and global awareness.

Special: Towson University offers cooperative programs with other institutions in the University System of Maryland and at Loyola College, the College of Notre Dame, or Johns Hopkins University, cross-registration at more than 80 colleges through the National Student Exchange, and study abroad. Students may pursue a dual major in physics and engineering, an interdisciplinary studies degree, which allows them to design their own majors, a 3-2 engineering program with the University of Maryland at College Park, or nondegree study. There are pass/fail options, extensive evening offerings, and opportunities to earn credits between semesters. Internships are available in most majors, and work-study programs are offered both on and off campus. There are 20 national honor societies, a freshman honors program, and 12 departmental honors programs.

Faculty/Classroom: 53% of faculty are male; 47%, female. The average class size in an introductory lecture is 25; in a laboratory, 24; and in a regular course, 25.

Admissions: 52% of the 2003-2004 applicants were accepted. The SAT I scores for the 2003-2004 freshman class were: Verbal--25% below 500, 54% between 500 and 599, 20% between 600 and 700, and 2% above 700; Math--20% below 500, 53% between 500 and 599, 24% between 600 and 700, and 2% above 700. 41% of the current freshmen were in the top fifth of their class; 78% were in the top two fifths.

Requirements: The SAT I or ACT is required, generally with a composite score of 1100 on the SAT I. Applicants should have graduated from an accredited secondary school or earned the GED. Secondary preparation should include 4 years of English, 3 each of math, lab science, and social studies, and 2 of foreign language. Prospective music and dance majors must audition. A GPA of 3.11 is required. AP and CLEP credits are accepted. Important factors in the admissions decision are advanced placement or honor courses, recommendations by school officials, and leadership record.

Procedure: Freshmen are admitted in the fall. Entrance exams should be taken in the junior and senior year. There is a deferred admissions plan. Applications should be filed by May 2 for fall entry and December 1 for spring entry. The fall 2003 application fee was $35. Notification is sent on a rolling basis. 540 applicants were on the 2003 waiting list; 186 were admitted. Applications are accepted on-line through the school's web site.

Transfer: 1141 transfer students enrolled in 2002-2003. Transfer applicants should have earned at least 30 academic credits. For those with less than 30 attempted, freshman requirements must be met. Minimum GPA requirements range from 2.0 to 2.5, depending on the number of credits completed. Transcripts are required, and a personal statement and interview are recommended. 30 of 120 credits required for the bachelor's degree must be completed at Towson.

Visiting: There are regularly scheduled orientations for prospective students, including campus tours, a session for parents, a session on the admissions process for transfers and freshmen, and a roundtable discussion. There are guides for informal visits. To schedule a visit, contact the Admissions Office.

Financial Aid: In 2003-2004, 45% of all full-time freshmen and 38% of continuing full-time students received some form of financial aid. 55% of full-time freshmen and 51% of continuing full-time students received need-based aid. The average freshman award was $7260. Need-based scholarships or need-based grants averaged $4393; need-based self-help aid (loans and jobs) averaged $3211; institutional non-need-based athletic scholarships averaged $8467; and other institutional non-need-based awards and non-need-based scholarships averaged $4237. 72% of undergraduates work part time. Average annual earnings from campus work are $1185. The average financial indebtedness of the 2003 graduate was $15,530. Towson is a member of CSS. The FAFSA is required. The priority date for freshman financial aid applications for fall entry is March 1.

International Students: There were 430 international students enrolled in a recent year. The school actively recruits these students. The TOEFL is required at preadmission, with a minimum score of 500; a college test is required at postadmission. The SAT I or ACT is also required, but the school accepts the TOEFL as a substitute for the verbal SAT I. Graduates of the campus English language center are not required to take the TOEFL.

Computers: The mainframes are 3 SGI Challenge/IRIX systems, 2 DEC VAX/VMS systems, and 2 DEC 5200/Ultrix systems. Each student receives a computer account that provides e-mail, personal web pages, and access to UNIX System software. There are 65 labs on campus with 1208 total workstations, including 1009 PCs, 133 Macs, and 22 UNIX workstations. Systems are accessible 24 hours daily except 5 P.M. to 9 P.M. Fridays. There are no time limits and no fees.

Graduates: From July 1, 2002 to June 30, 2003, 2561 bachelor's degrees were awarded. The most popular majors were business administration (19%), education (12%), and social sciences/history (11%). In an average class, 30% graduate in 4 years or less, 22% graduate in 5 years or less, and 4% graduate in 6 years or less. 115 companies recruited on campus in 2002-2003.

Admissions Contact: Louise Shulack, Director of Admissions. A video is available. E-mail: *admissions@towson.edu* Web: *www.towson.edu*

UNITED STATES NAVAL ACADEMY
Annapolis, MD 21402-5018

E-3

(410) 293-4361
(800) 638-9156; Fax: (410) 293-4348

Full-time: 3600 men, 600 women	**Faculty:** 600; IIB, ++$
Part-time: none	**Ph.D.s:** 90%
Graduate: none	**Student/Faculty:** 7 to 1
Year: semesters, summer session	**Tuition:** 0
Application Deadline: open	**Room & Board:** n/app
Freshman Class: 1450 accepted, 1245 enrolled	
SAT I Verbal/Math: 650/670	**ACT:** 29 **MOST COMPETITIVE**

The United States Naval Academy, founded in 1845, is a national military service college offering undergraduate degree programs and professional training in aviation, surface ships, submarines, and various military, maritime, and technical fields. The U.S. Navy pays tuition, room and board, medical and dental care, and a monthly stipend to all Naval Academy students. Figures in the above capsule are approximate. In addition to regional accreditation, Annapolis has baccalaureate program accreditation with ABET and CSAB. The library contains 530,000 volumes, and subscribes to 2000 periodicals. Computerized library services include the card catalog, interlibrary loans, and database searching. Special learning facilities include a learning resource center, art gallery, planetarium, radio station, TV station, a propulsion laboratory, a nuclear reactor, an oceanographic research vessel, towing tanks, a flight simulator, and a naval history museum. The 329-acre campus is in a small town 30 miles southeast of Baltimore and 35 miles east of Washington, D.C. Including any residence halls, there are 25 buildings.

Student Life: 97% of undergraduates are from out of state, mostly the Northeast. Students are from 50 states and 21 foreign countries. 80% are white. 50% are Protestant; 49% Catholic. The average age of freshmen is 18; all undergraduates, 20. 11% do not continue beyond their first year; 77% remain to graduate.

Housing: 4200 students can be accommodated in college housing, which includes coed dorms. On-campus housing is guaranteed for all 4 years. All students live on campus; of those, 75% remain on campus on weekends. Alcohol is not permitted. Upperclassmen may keep cars.

Activities: There are no fraternities or sororities. There are 75 groups on campus, including bagpipe band, cheerleading, chess, choir, chorus, computers, debate, drama, drill team, drum and bugle corps, ethnic, honors, international, jazz band, literary magazine, musical theater, pep band, photography, professional, radio and TV, religious, social, social service, student government, and yearbook. Popular campus events include Commissioning Week, which includes the Plebe Recognition Ceremony, Ring Dance, and graduation.

Sports: There are 20 intercollegiate sports for men and 9 for women, and 23 intramural sports for men and 10 for women. Facilities include a 30,000-seat stadium, a 5000-seat basketball arena, an Olympic pool with a diving well for 10-meter diving boards, a wrestling arena, a 200-meter indoor track, a 400-meter outdoor track, an indoor ice rink, 6 Nautilus and weight rooms, and facilities for gymnastics, boxing, fencing, and other sports.

Disabled Students: All of the campus is accessible. Wheelchair ramps, elevators, special parking, and specially equipped rest rooms are available.

Services: Counseling and information services are available, as is tutoring in most subjects. There is remedial math, reading, and writing.

Campus Safety and Security: Measures include 24-hour foot and vehicle patrol, self-defense education, shuttle buses, and emergency telephones. There are lighted pathways/sidewalks and gate guards.

Programs of Study: Annapolis confers the B.S. degree. Bachelor's degrees are awarded in COMMUNICATIONS AND THE ARTS (English), COMPUTER AND PHYSICAL SCIENCE (chemistry, computer science, mathematics, oceanography, physics, and science), ENGINEERING AND ENVIRONMENTAL DESIGN (aeronautical engineering, electrical/electronics engineering, engineering, marine engineering, mechanical engineering, naval architecture and marine engineering, ocean engineering, and systems engineering), SOCIAL SCIENCE (economics, history, and political science/government). Chemistry, aeronautical engineering, and systems engineering are the strongest academically. Mechanical engineering, math, and oceanography are the largest.

Required: Students must complete 140 semester hours, including core requirements in engineering, natural sciences, humanities, and social sciences. Phys ed is required during all 4 years. Physical readiness testing must be passed. During required summer training sessions, students train aboard U.S. ships, submarines, and aircraft. Graduates serve at least 5 years on active duty as commissioned officers of the Navy or Marine Corps.

Special: Study in Washington, D.C., is available during 1 semester of the senior year. A voluntary graduate program is available for those who complete requirements early and wish to begin master's work at nearby institutions, such as Georgetown or Johns Hopkins Universities. Trident Scholars may spend their senior year in independent research. There are 10 national honor societies and 5 departmental honors programs.

Faculty/Classroom: 80% of faculty are male; 20%, female. All teach undergraduates. The average class size in an introductory lecture is 23; in a laboratory, 10; and in a regular course, 15.

Requirements: The SAT I or ACT is required. In addition, candidates must be unmarried with no dependents, U.S. citizens of good moral character, and between 17 and 23 years of age. Candidates should have a sound secondary school background, including 4 years each of English and math, 2 years of a foreign language, and 1 year each of U.S. history, world or European history, chemistry, physics, and computer literacy. Candidates must obtain an official nomination from congressional or military sources. An interview is conducted, and medical and physical exams must be passed to qualify for admission. AP credits are accepted. Important factors in the admissions decision are advanced placement or honor courses, recommendations by school officials, and leadership record.

Procedure: Freshmen are admitted in the summer. Entrance exams should be taken after December of the junior year. Application deadlines are open. Notification is sent on a rolling basis.

Transfer: All students enter as freshmen. 140 of 140 credits required for the bachelor's degree must be completed at Annapolis.

Visiting: There are regularly scheduled orientations for prospective students, including visitation weekends for candidates likely to be accepted, summer seminars, and Admissions Day. Visitors may sit in on classes.

International Students: International students must take the TOEFL and the SAT I or the ACT.

Computers: The mainframe is a Honeywell DPS8. There are also 1500 PCs available in the dorm, library, computer center, and computer lab. All students may access the system. There are no time limits and no fees. Each student is issued a personal computer.

Admissions Contact: Candidate Guidance Office.
Web: *www.usna.edu*

UNIVERSITY OF MARYLAND/BALTIMORE COUNTY
Baltimore, MD 21250

D-2

(410) 455-2291
UMBC-4U2; Fax: (410) 455-1094

Full-time: 4236 men, 3788 women	**Faculty:** 464; I, -$
Part-time: 831 men, 791 women	**Ph.D.s:** 85%
Graduate: 1023 men, 1203 women	**Student/Faculty:** 17 to 1
Year: 4-1-4, summer session	**Tuition:** $7388 ($14,290)
Application Deadline: February 1	**Room & Board:** $7280
Freshman Class: 5501 applied, 3167 accepted, 1507 enrolled	
SAT I Verbal/Math: 590/630	**ACT:** 25 **VERY COMPETITIVE+**

University of Maryland/Baltimore County, founded in 1966, is a public research university offering programs in liberal arts and sciences and engineering. There are 3 undergraduate and 2 graduate schools. In addition to regional accreditation, UMBC has baccalaureate program accreditation with ABET, CSWE, and NCATE. The library contains 938,653 volumes, 1,078,767 microform items, and 1,925,000 audio/video tapes/CDs, and subscribes to 4302 periodicals. Computerized library services include the card catalog, interlibrary loans, database searching, and Internet access. Special learning facilities include a learning resource cen-

ter, art gallery, radio station, centers for imaging research, earth systems technology, and telecommunications research, and institutes for medicine and policy analysis and research. The 530-acre campus is in a suburban area 5 miles southwest of Baltimore and 35 miles north of Washington, D.C. Including any residence halls, there are 50 buildings.
Student Life: 88% of undergraduates are from Maryland. Students are from 48 states, 108 foreign countries, and Canada. 84% of freshmen are from public schools. 55% are white; 17% Asian American; 14% African American. The average age of freshmen is 18; all undergraduates, 23. 18% do not continue beyond their first year; 53% remain to graduate.
Housing: 3432 students can be accommodated in college housing, which includes single-sex and coed dorms and on-campus apartments. In addition, there are honors houses, language houses, special-interest houses, wellness and quiet-study floors, and same-sex floors. On-campus housing is guaranteed for the freshman year only and is available on a first-come, first-served basis. 67% of students commute. Alcohol is not permitted. All students may keep cars.
Activities: 3% of men belong to 11 national fraternities; 3% of women belong to 8 national sororities. There are 180 groups on campus, including band, cheerleading, chess, choir, chorus, computers, Council of Majors, dance, debate, drama, ethnic, film, gay, honors, Intellectual Sports Council, international, jazz band, literary magazine, Model United Nations, musical theater, newspaper, opera, orchestra, pep band, political, professional, radio and TV, religious, social, social service, student government, symphony, and yearbook. Popular campus events include Quadmania, Welcome Week, and Family Weekend.
Sports: There are 8 intercollegiate sports for men and 10 for women, and 16 intramural sports for men and 16 for women. Facilities include a multipurpose arena, an aquatic center, a fitness center, tennis courts, a 4500-seat stadium, playing and practice fields, an indoor track, an outdoor cross-country course, a golf driving range, a track and field complex, and a soccer stadium.
Disabled Students: 95% of the campus is accessible. Wheelchair ramps, elevators, special parking, specially equipped rest rooms, special class scheduling, lowered drinking fountains, lowered telephones, a Braille writer, tape recorders, talking book machines, TTY, talking calculators, Optacon, and information on the talking computer are available.
Services: Counseling and information services are available, as is tutoring in most subjects. There is a reader service for the blind and remedial math, reading, and writing. Other services include notetakers, readers, mobility training, American Sign Language interpreters, and scribes for students who have a need based on a manual or learning disability.
Campus Safety and Security: Measures include self-defense education, security escort services, shuttle buses, and pamphlets/posters/films. There are emergency telephones, lighted pathways/sidewalks, a 24-hour police department, and a campus risk management department.
Programs of Study: UMBC confers B.A., B.S., B.F.A., and B.S.E. degrees. Master's and doctoral degrees are also awarded. Bachelor's degrees are awarded in AGRICULTURE (environmental studies), BIOLOGICAL SCIENCE (biochemistry and biology/biological science), COMMUNICATIONS AND THE ARTS (dance, dramatic arts, English, fine arts, French, German, linguistics, modern language, music, Russian, Spanish, theater design, and visual and performing arts), COMPUTER AND PHYSICAL SCIENCE (chemistry, computer science, information sciences and systems, mathematics, physics, and statistics), ENGINEERING AND ENVIRONMENTAL DESIGN (chemical engineering, computer engineering, environmental science, and mechanical engineering), HEALTH PROFESSIONS (emergency medical technologies and health science), SOCIAL SCIENCE (African American studies, American studies, anthropology, classical/ancient civilization, economics, geography, history, interdisciplinary studies, philosophy, political science/government, psychology, social work, and sociology). Information systems, computer science, and biological sciences are the largest.
Required: To graduate, students are required to complete at least 120 credits, including 45 at the upper-division level, with a minimum GPA of 2.0. The core curriculum includes courses in arts and humanities, social sciences, math and natural sciences, phys ed, and modern or classical language and culture. Students must pass an English composition course with a C or better.
Special: Dual and student-designed majors, cooperative education programs in all majors, a Washington semester, the Sondheim Public Affairs Scholars Program, cross-registration with University of Maryland schools and Johns Hopkins University, internships, both paid and nonpaid, in public, private, and nonprofit organizations, study abroad in 19 countries, work-study programs, B.A.-B.S. degrees, pass/fail options, and nondegree study are available. UMBC also offers various opportunities in interdisciplinary studies and in such fields as artificial intelligence and optical communications. There are 15 national honor societies, including Phi Beta Kappa, a freshman honors program, and 17 departmental honors programs.
Faculty/Classroom: 66% of faculty are male; 34%, female. All both teach and do research. The average class size in an introductory lecture is 36; in a laboratory, 19; and in a regular course, 27.
Admissions: 58% of the 2003-2004 applicants were accepted. The SAT I scores for the 2003-2004 freshman class were: Verbal--9% below

500, 44% between 500 and 599, 38% between 600 and 700, and 9% above 700; Math--3% below 500, 32% between 500 and 599, 48% between 600 and 700, and 17% above 700. The ACT scores were 13% below 21, 23% between 21 and 23, 32% between 24 and 26, 12% between 27 and 28, and 20% above 28. 53% of the current freshmen were in the top fifth of their class; 78% were in the top two fifths. There were 4 National Merit finalists. 120 freshmen graduated first in their class.
Requirements: The SAT I or ACT is required. In addition, minimum high school preparation should include 4 years of English, 3 years each of social science/history and math, including algebra I and II and geometry, 3 years of lab sciences, and 2 of a foreign language. An essay is required of all freshman applicants. A GPA of 3.0 is required. AP and CLEP credits are accepted. Important factors in the admissions decision are advanced placement or honor courses, recommendations by school officials, and leadership record.
Procedure: Freshmen are admitted to all sessions. Entrance exams should be taken by fall of the senior year. There is an early decision plan. Early decision applications should be filed by November 1; regular applications, by February 1 for fall entry, December 1 for winter entry, December 15 for spring entry, and May 15 for summer entry, along with a $50 fee. Notification is sent in February. Applications are accepted online at the school's web site through CollegeNET.
Transfer: 1133 transfer students enrolled in 2002-2003. A 2.5 cumulative GPA for all previous college work is recommended. Applicants with fewer than 30 semester hours should submit SAT I scores and the high school transcript; they must also meet freshman admission requirements. 30 of 120 credits required for the bachelor's degree must be completed at UMBC.
Visiting: There are regularly scheduled orientations for prospective students, including a group information session with an admissions counselor or followed by a student-guided walking tour of campus. Saturday information sessions and 4 campus open houses are also scheduled each fall. Summer preview days are available for incoming freshmen. There are guides for informal visits and visitors may sit in on classes and stay overnight. To schedule a visit, contact the Office of Undergraduate Admissions.
Financial Aid: Average annual earnings from campus work are $1335. The FAFSA is required. The priority date for freshman financial aid applications for fall entry is February 15.
International Students: There are 466 international students enrolled. They must score 213 on the electronic TOEFL.
Computers: Multiple Linux, Silicon Graphics, and Sun servers are available for general purpose use. UMBC has approximately 3500 computers on campus, all of which have access to the Internet via I1 and I2 connections. Some 1100 of these are available for student use in various labs throughout the campus. These include 800 dual host Windows-Linux machines and 300 Macs running OSX. The campus also has 400 modems for off-campus dial-up access. All students may access the system. There is a 200 hour per month limit for modem dial-up access. All other access is unlimited. There are no fees. It is strongly recommended that all students have a personal computer.
Graduates: From July 1, 2002 to June 30, 2003, 1729 bachelor's degrees were awarded. The most popular majors were information systems (22%), psychology (10%), and computer science (8%). In an average class, 1% graduate in 3 years or less, 28% graduate in 4 years or less, 48% graduate in 5 years or less, and 53% graduate in 6 years or less. 997 companies recruited on campus in 2002-2003. Of the 2001 graduating class, 39% were enrolled in graduate school within 12 months of graduation and 93% were employed.
Admissions Contact: Yvette Mozie-Ross, Director of Admissions. E-mail: *admissions@umbc.edu* Web: *http://www.umbc.edu*

UNIVERSITY OF MARYLAND/COLLEGE PARK
College Park, MD 20742
D-3
(301) 314-8385
(800) 422-5867; Fax: (301) 314-9693

Full-time: 11,591 men, 11,425 women	**Faculty:** 1580; I, +$
Part-time: 1343 men, 1087 women	**Ph.D.s:** n/av
Graduate: 5060 men, 4803 women	**Student/Faculty:** 15 to 1
Year: semesters, summer session	**Tuition:** $6759 ($17,433)
Application Deadline: January 20	**Room & Board:** $7468
Freshman Class: 25,053 applied, 10,702 accepted, 4066 enrolled	
SAT I or ACT: required	**HIGHLY COMPETITIVE**

University of Maryland/College Park, founded in 1856, is a land-grant institution, the flagship campus of the state's university system, offering undergraduate and graduate degrees. There are 11 undergraduate and 13 graduate schools. In addition to regional accreditation, Maryland has baccalaureate program accreditation with AACSB, ABET, ACEJMC, ASLA, ASLHA, CACREP, CADE, NAAB, NASM, NAST, and NCATE. The 7 libraries contain 3,016,940 volumes, 5,541,175 microform items, and 244,911 audio/video tapes/CDs, and subscribe to 34,091 periodicals. Computerized library services include the card catalog, interlibrary loans, and database searching. Special learning facilities include a learning resource center, art gallery, radio station, TV station, and an observatory. The 1250-acre campus is in a suburban area 3 miles northeast of Washington, D.C., and 35 miles south of Baltimore. Including any residence halls, there are 268 buildings.

Student Life: 75% of undergraduates are from Maryland. Students are from 50 states and U.S. territories, 159 foreign countries, and Canada. 59% are white; 14% Asian American; 12% African American. 26% are Catholic; 23% claim no religious affiliation; 22% Protestant; 16% Jewish. The average age of freshmen is 18; all undergraduates, 21. 7% do not continue beyond their first year; 70% remain to graduate.

Housing: 8394 students can be accommodated in college housing, which includes single-sex and coed dorms, on-campus apartments, fraternity houses, and sorority houses. In addition, there are honors houses, language houses, and special-interest houses. On-campus housing is guaranteed for first-time fresmen only and is available on a lottery system for upperclassmen. 64% of students commute. Alcohol is not permitted. Upperclassmen may keep cars.

Activities: 9% of men belong to 27 national fraternities; 9% of women belong to 19 national sororities. There are 515 groups on campus, including art, band, cheerleading, chess, choir, chorale, chorus, computers, dance, debate, drama, drill team, ethnic, film, forensics, gay, honors, international, jazz band, literary magazine, marching band, musical theater, newspaper, opera, orchestra, pep band, photography, political, professional, radio and TV, religious, social, social service, student government, symphony, and yearbook. Popular campus events include Art Attack, Union All-Niter, and Pride Days.

Sports: There are 12 intercollegiate sports for men and 15 for women, and 15 intramural sports for men and 15 for women. Facilities include 2 indoor and 2 outdoor swimming pools, intramural fields, tennis, squash, racquetball, volleyball, and basketball courts, a fitness center including weight rooms, aerobic rooms, martial arts rooms, saunas, and an indoor track, a bowling alley, a golf course, and an outdoor artificial turf field. Athletics facilities include a 51,000-seat stadium, a 17,950-seat gym, and indoor and outdoor artificial turf practice fields.

Disabled Students: 95% of the campus is accessible. Wheelchair ramps, elevators, special parking, specially equipped rest rooms, special class scheduling, lowered drinking fountains, lowered telephones, a special shuttle service, and electronic doors are available.

Services: Counseling and information services are available, as is tutoring in most subjects, including all 100- and 200-level courses. There is a reader service for the blind and remedial math.

Campus Safety and Security: Measures include 24-hour foot and vehicle patrol, self-defense education, security escort services, and shuttle buses. There are informal discussions, pamphlets/posters/films, emergency telephones, lighted pathways/sidewalks, and video surveillance.

Programs of Study: Maryland confers B.A., B.S., B.L.A., B.M., and B.M.E. degrees. Master's and doctoral degrees are also awarded. Bachelor's degrees are awarded in AGRICULTURE (agricultural business management, agricultural economics, agriculture, agronomy, animal science, horticulture, natural resource management, and plant science), BIOLOGICAL SCIENCE (biochemistry, biology/biological science, marine biology, microbiology, nutrition, and zoology), BUSINESS (accounting, banking and finance, business administration and management, human resources, management information systems, and marketing management), COMMUNICATIONS AND THE ARTS (art history and appreciation, Chinese, classics, communications, dance, dramatic arts, English, French, Germanic languages and literature, Japanese, journalism, linguistics, music, music performance, romance languages and literature, Russian, Spanish, and studio art), COMPUTER AND PHYSICAL SCIENCE (astronomy, chemistry, computer science, geology, information sciences and systems, mathematics, physical sciences, and physics), EDUCATION (art, drama, early childhood, elementary, English, mathematics, music, physical, science, secondary, and special), ENGINEERING AND ENVIRONMENTAL DESIGN (aeronautical engineering, architecture, bioengineering, chemical engineering, civil engineering, computer engineering, electrical/electronics engineering, engineering, environmental science, fire protection engineering, landscape architecture/design, materials engineering, mechanical engineering, and nuclear engineering), SOCIAL SCIENCE (African American studies, American studies, anthropology, criminal justice, criminology, dietetics, economics, family/consumer studies, food science, geography, history, Italian studies, Judaic studies, philosophy, political science/government, psychology, Russian and Slavic studies, sociology, and women's studies). Engineering, computer science, and business are the strongest academically. Criminology and criminal justice, computer science, and psychology are the largest.

Required: Most programs require a minimum of 120 credits for graduation; the number of hours required in the major varies. All students must take 43 to 46 credits in a multidisciplinary core curriculum, including 10 in math and science, 9 each in social sciences, and humanities and the arts, 6 in advanced studies, and 3 diversity credits. Freshman and junior composition are also required, and students must maintain a 2.0 GPA.

Special: Each of the 11 undergraduate schools offers special programs, and there is a campuswide co-op education program offering engineering and other majors. In addition, the university offers cross-registration with other colleges in the Consortium of Universities of the Washington Metropolitan Area, several Living-Learning programs for undergradu-

ates, the B.A./B.S. degree in most majors, dual and student-designed majors, nondegree study, an accelerated veterinary medicine program, varied study-abroad opportunities, work-study programs with government and nonprofit organizations, and internship opportunities with federal and state legislators, the local media, and various federal agencies. There are 51 national honor societies, including Phi Beta Kappa, a freshman honors program, and 39 departmental honors programs.

Faculty/Classroom: 63% of faculty are male; 37%, female. 58% teach undergraduates and 42% do research. Graduate students teach 20% of introductory courses. The average class size in an introductory lecture is 42; in a laboratory, 21; and in a regular course, 36.

Admissions: 43% of the 2003-2004 applicants were accepted. The SAT I scores for the 2003-2004 freshman class were: Verbal--7% below 500, 29% between 500 and 599, 49% between 600 and 700, and 15% above 700; Math--5% below 500, 18% between 500 and 599, 51% between 600 and 700, and 26% above 700. 89% of the current freshmen were in the top quarter of their class.

Requirements: The SAT I or ACT is required. The university evaluates exam scores along with GPA, curriculum, and other criteria. Applicants should be graduates of accredited secondary schools or have the GED. Secondary preparation should include 4 years of English, 3 of history or social sciences, 2 of algebra and 1 of plane geometry, and 2 of lab sciences. An essay and counselor recommendation are required. Music majors must also audition. AP and CLEP credits are accepted. Important factors in the admissions decision are advanced placement or honor courses, recommendations by school officials, and evidence of special talent.

Procedure: Freshmen are admitted fall, spring, and summer. Entrance exams should be taken at the end of the junior year or the beginning of the senior year. There is an early admissions plan. Early decision applications should be filed by December 1; regular applications, by January 20 for fall entry and December 15 for spring entry. The fall 2003 application fee was $50. Notification of early decision is sent February 1; regular decision, April 1. 2614 were on the 2003 waiting list; 173 were admitted. Applications are accepted on-line through the university's web site.

Transfer: 2978 transfer students enrolled in 2002-2003. Transfer applicants from regionally accredited institutions should have attempted at least 12 credits and have earned at least a 2.5 GPA, although this requirement varies depending on space available. Applicants from Maryland community colleges may be given special consideration. 30 of 120 credits required for the bachelor's degree must be completed at Maryland.

Visiting: There are regularly scheduled orientations for prospective students, consisting of 3 fall and 4 spring open house programs for admitted students, as well as regularly scheduled information sessions followed by a campus tour. There are guides for informal visits and visitors may sit in on classes and stay overnight. To schedule a visit, contact Office of Undergraduate Admissions at (800) 422-5867 or *www.uga.umd.edu/visit*.

Financial Aid: In a recent year, 73% of all full-time freshmen and 66% of continuing full-time students received some form of financial aid. 35% of full-time freshmen and 40% of continuing full-time students received need-based aid. The average freshman award was $7016. 5% of undergraduates work part time. Average annual earnings from campus work are $1280. The average financial indebtedness of a recent year's graduate was $14,076. The FAFSA is required. The deadline for filing freshman financial aid applications for fall entry is February 15.

International Students: There are 562 international students enrolled. They must score 575 on the written TOEFL or take the APIEL or ELPT. They must also take the SAT I or the ACT.

Computers: The mainframe is an IBM 9672/RB6. There are approximately 800 PCs available for student use, both day and evening, in computer labs supported by the Office of Information Technology, as well as approximately that number of computers in labs supported by individual colleges and in libraries. All residence halls are wired for PCs. IBM and Mac word processing programs are available to all registered students. All students may access the system 24 hours a day, 7 days a week. There are no time limits and no fees.

Graduates: From July 1, 2002 to June 30, 2003, 5681 bachelor's degrees were awarded. The most popular majors were criminology and criminal justice (7%), communication (6%), and computer science (5%). In an average class, 43% graduate in 4 years or less, 66% graduate in 5 years or less, and 70% graduate in 6 years or less. 331 companies recruited on campus in 2002-2003.

Admissions Contact: Admissions Officer. A video is available. E-mail: *um-admit@uga.umd.edu* Web: *www.maryland.edu*

UNIVERSITY OF MARYLAND/EASTERN SHORE F-4
Princess Anne, MD 21853   (410) 651-6410; Fax: (410) 651-7922

Full-time: 1222 men, 1809 women	Faculty: 90
Part-time: 124 men, 171 women	Ph.D.s: 80%
Graduate: 185 men, 251 women	Student/Faculty: 34 to 1
Year: semesters, summer session	Tuition: $4334 ($9669)
Application Deadline: July 15	Room & Board: $5630
Freshman Class: 3500 applied, 2200 accepted, 1053 enrolled	
SAT I Verbal/Math: 450/400	ACT: 18 COMPETITIVE

University of Maryland/Eastern Shore, founded in 1886, is a public university, part of the University of Maryland System, offering undergraduate and graduate programs in the arts and sciences, professional studies, and agricultural sciences. There are 3 undergraduate schools and 1 graduate school. The library contains 150,000 volumes. Computerized library services include the card catalog, interlibrary loans, and database searching. Special learning facilities include a learning resource center, art gallery, and radio station. The 700-acre campus is in a rural area 15 miles south of Salisbury. Including any residence halls, there are 40 buildings.

Student Life: 71% of undergraduates are from Maryland. Students are from 32 states, 48 foreign countries, and Canada. 85% are from public schools. 76% are African American; 18% white. 90% are Protestant; 10% claim no religious affiliation. The average age of freshmen is 18; all undergraduates, 24. 25% do not continue beyond their first year; 36% remain to graduate.

Housing: 1530 students can be accommodated in college housing, which includes single-sex dorms, on-campus apartments, and off-campus apartments. In addition, there are honors houses and a residential complex. On-campus housing is available on a first-come, first-served basis and is available on a lottery system for upperclassmen. 50% of students live on campus; of those, 30% remain on campus on weekends. All students may keep cars.

Activities: 20% of men belong to 4 national fraternities; 20% of women belong to 4 national sororities. There are 25 groups on campus, including art, band, cheerleading, choir, chorale, chorus, computers, dance, drama, drill team, ethnic, honors, international, jazz band, literary magazine, musical theater, newspaper, pep band, photography, political, professional, radio and TV, religious, social, social service, student government, and yearbook. Popular campus events include Parents Day, Spring Festival, and Ethnic Festival.

Sports: There are 5 intercollegiate sports for men and 5 for women, and 4 intramural sports for men and 4 for women. Facilities include an indoor swimming pool and a 3000-seat stadium.

Disabled Students: 20% of the campus is accessible. Wheelchair ramps, elevators, special parking, specially equipped rest rooms, special class scheduling, lowered drinking fountains, and lowered telephones are available.

Services: Counseling and information services are available, as is tutoring in every subject. There is remedial math, reading, and writing.

Campus Safety and Security: Measures include 24-hour foot and vehicle patrol, security escort services, shuttle buses, and informal discussions. There are pamphlets/posters/films, emergency telephones, lighted pathways/sidewalks, and a student security team.

Programs of Study: UMES confers B.A., B.S., B.G.S., and B.M. degrees. Master's and doctoral degrees are also awarded. Bachelor's degrees are awarded in AGRICULTURE (agriculture and poultry science), BIOLOGICAL SCIENCE (biology/biological science), BUSINESS (accounting, business administration and management, and hotel/motel and restaurant management), COMMUNICATIONS AND THE ARTS (English), COMPUTER AND PHYSICAL SCIENCE (chemistry, computer science, and mathematics), EDUCATION (agricultural, art, business, elementary, health, home economics, industrial arts, mathematics, music, physical, science, secondary, and social science), ENGINEERING AND ENVIRONMENTAL DESIGN (aeronautical science, construction technology, engineering technology, and environmental science), HEALTH PROFESSIONS (physical therapy and rehabilitation therapy), SOCIAL SCIENCE (criminal justice, history, home economics, liberal arts/general studies, and sociology). Physical therapy, engineering, and environmental science are the strongest academically. Business, hotel and restaurant management, and biology are the largest.

Required: Students must complete 122 hours, including 36 hours in the major, 15 in communicative and quantitative skills, 9 in humanities, 7 in natural sciences, 6 in social sciences, and 4 in health and phys ed. A minimum 2.0 overall GPA is required.

Special: Students may cross-register at Salisbury State University. A cooperative education program, internships, a winter term, work-study programs, a general studies degree, and dual and student-designed majors are offered. Also available are an accelerated degree program and a 3-2 engineering degree with the University of Maryland/College Park. There are pass/fail options. There is 1 national honor society, a freshman honors program, and 10 departmental honors programs.

Faculty/Classroom: 45% of faculty are male; 55%, female. 85% teach undergraduates and 15% do research. Graduate students teach 1% of

introductory courses. The average class size in an introductory lecture is 75; in a laboratory, 18; and in a regular course, 30.

Admissions: 63% of the 2003-2004 applicants were accepted.

Requirements: The SAT I is required. In addition, applicants should be graduates of accredited secondary schools or have the GED. High school preparation should include 4 years of English, 3 each of social science or history and math, including 2 of algebra and 1 of geometry, and 2 of lab science. An essay and interview are recommended. UMES recommends that prospective art education majors submit a portfolio. Students may earn credit by exam. A GPA of 2.5 is required. AP and CLEP credits are accepted. Important factors in the admissions decision are advanced placement or honor courses, leadership record, and recommendations by school officials.

Procedure: Freshmen are admitted to all sessions. Entrance exams should be taken by April. There are early decision, early admissions, and deferred admissions plans. Applications should be filed by July 15 for fall entry and December 1 for spring entry, along with a $25 fee. Notification is sent on a rolling basis.

Transfer: 129 transfer students enrolled in 2002-2003. Transfer applicants must have attempted at least 9 credits at another institution and have a cumulative GPA of at least 2.0, or have earned an associate degree or completed 56 hours of community college work. 75 of 122 credits required for the bachelor's degree must be completed at UMES.

Visiting: There are regularly scheduled orientations for prospective students, including 2 formal orientation sessions and 9 visitation/open house days. There are guides for informal visits and visitors may sit in on classes. To schedule a visit, contact the Office of Recruitment at (410) 651-6178 or *recruitment@mail.umes.edu*.

Financial Aid: In a recent year, 85% of all full-time freshmen received some form of financial aid. UMES is a member of CSS. The college's own financial statement is required.

International Students: There were 122 international students enrolled in a recent year. They must score 500 on the written TOEFL and also take the SAT I, scoring 800.

Computers: The mainframe is an IBM 4341. About 80 PCs are available in the library and various departments. There are no fees. It is strongly recommended that all students have a personal computer.

Graduates: In a recent year, 347 bachelor's degrees were awarded. The most popular majors were business administration (16%), hotel and restaurant management (10%), and physical therapy (10%). In an average class, 25% graduate in 6 years or less. 120 companies recruited on campus in 2002-2003.

Admissions Contact: Cheryll Collier-Mills, Director of Admissions and Recruitment. E-mail: *ccmills@mail.umes.edu* Web: *www.umes.edu*

UNIVERSITY OF MARYLAND/UNIVERSITY COLLEGE D-3
Adelphi, MD 20783   (301) 985-7000
(800) 285-6832; Fax: (301) 985-7364

Full-time: 850 men, 1350 women	Faculty: 77
Part-time: 5900 men, 8000 women	Ph.D.s: 81%
Graduate: 3100 men, 3100 women	Student/Faculty: 28 to 1
Year: semesters, summer session	Tuition: $6510 ($11,970)
Application Deadline: open	Room & Board: n/app
Freshman Class: n/av	
SAT I or ACT: not required	SPECIAL

University of Maryland/University College was founded in 1947 to serve the needs of the adult continuing education student. It offers evening and weekend courses in the liberal arts and sciences and in business at more than 20 locations throughout the Washington, D.C.-Baltimore area and the state of Maryland. Some figures in the above capsule and in this profile are approximate. The library subscribes to 22 periodicals. Computerized library services include the card catalog, interlibrary loans, and database searching. Special learning facilities include an art gallery and TV station. The campus is in an urban area.

Student Life: 83% of undergraduates are from Maryland. Students are from 49 states, 65 foreign countries, and Canada. 48% are white; 31% African American. The average age of all undergraduates is 34.

Housing: There are no residence halls. All students commute. Alcohol is not permitted. All students may keep cars.

Activities: There are no fraternities or sororities.

Sports: There is no sports program at UMUC.

Services: Counseling and information services are available, as is tutoring in some subjects, including math, writing, accounting, and computing. Referrals are available for tutoring in other subjects. There are fees for tutoring. There is a reader service for the blind.

Campus Safety and Security: Measures include 24-hour foot and vehicle patrol and emergency telephones.

Programs of Study: UMUC confers B.A. and B.S. degrees. Associate and master's degrees are also awarded. Bachelor's degrees are awarded in BUSINESS (accounting, business administration and management, human resources, management science, and marketing management), COMMUNICATIONS AND THE ARTS (communications and English),

COMPUTER AND PHYSICAL SCIENCE (computer science and information sciences and systems), ENGINEERING AND ENVIRONMENTAL DESIGN (computer technology and environmental science), SOCIAL SCIENCE (criminal justice, fire science, history, humanities, liberal arts/general studies, paralegal studies, psychology, and social science). Business has the largest enrollment.

Required: A general education requirement of 30 semester hours includes courses in communications, humanities, social sciences, and math/science. The B.A. degree requires 12 semester hours of a foreign language. A minimum 2.0 GPA and 120 credit hours are required to graduate.

Special: UMUC offers cooperative programs in interdisciplinary studies. There are a number of work-study programs with local employers. Credit by exam, credit for life/work experience, nondegree study, and pass/fail options are available. Through UMUC's open learning program, a number of independent learning courses, including telecourses, are available. There are 4 national honor societies.

Faculty/Classroom: 67% of faculty are male; 33%, female. All teach undergraduates. The average class size in a regular course is 24.

Requirements: Students should be graduates of an accredited secondary school or have a GED equivalent. AP and CLEP credits are accepted.

Procedure: Freshmen are admitted to all sessions. Application deadlines are open. Application fee is $30. Notification is sent on a rolling basis. Applications are accepted on-line via the school's web site.

Transfer: 2562 transfer students enrolled in a recent year. 30 of 120 credits required for the bachelor's degree must be completed at UMUC.

Financial Aid: The average financial indebtedness of a recent year's graduate was $1846. The FAFSA and SAR (for Pell grants) are required. Check with the school for current deadlines.

International Students: There were 92 international students enrolled in a recent year. They must score 550 on the written TOEFL or 213 on the electronic version and also take the college's own test.

Computers: All students may access the system. There are no time limits and no fees.

Graduates: In a recent year, 2157 bachelor's degrees were awarded. The most popular majors were business and management (21%), information systems management (14%), and computer and information science (13%).

Admissions Contact: Technical Director, Admission and Information. E-mail: *umucinfo@nova.umuc.edu* Web: *www.umuc.edu*

UNIVERSITY SYSTEM OF MARYLAND

The University System of Maryland, established in 1807, is a public system in Maryland. It is governed by a Board of Regents, whose chief administrator is chancellor. The primary goals of the system are research, teaching, and public service. The total enrollment of all 13 campuses is usually about 128,000; there were about 10,000 faculty members. Altogether more than 600 academic programs are offered in University System of Maryland. Profiles of the 4-year campuses are included in this section.

VILLA JULIE COLLEGE
Stevenson, MD 21153

D-2

(410) 486-7001
(877) 468-6852; Fax: (410) 602-6600

Full-time: 597 men, 1463 women	**Faculty:** 85
Part-time: 127 men, 469 women	**Ph.D.s:** 66%
Graduate: 32 men, 22 women	**Student/Faculty:** 24 to 1
Year: semesters, summer session	**Tuition:** $13,693
Application Deadline: open	**Room & Board:** $4700
Freshman Class: 2195 applied, 1382 accepted, 539 enrolled	
SAT I Verbal/Math: 519/521	COMPETITIVE

Villa Julie College, founded in 1947, is an independent, comprehensive college offering a liberal arts education combined with career preparation. In addition to regional accreditation, VJC has baccalaureate program accreditation with ABA, CAHEA, NAACLS, and NLN. The library contains 70,201 volumes, 141,886 microform items, and 2408 audio/video tapes/CDs, and subscribes to 689 periodicals. Computerized library services include the card catalog, interlibrary loans, database searching, and Internet access. Special learning facilities include a learning resource center, art gallery, a theater, and a video studio. The 60-acre campus is in a suburban area 10 miles northwest of Baltimore. Including any residence halls, there are 15 buildings.

Student Life: 96% of undergraduates are from Maryland. Students are from 14 states and 6 foreign countries. 76% are from public schools. 79% are white; 13% African American. 41% are claim no religious affiliation; 29% Catholic; 25% Protestant. The average age of freshmen is 18; all undergraduates, 24. 16% do not continue beyond their first year.

Housing: 372 students can be accommodated in college housing, which includes coed off-campus apartments. On-campus housing is available on a first-come, first-served basis. Priority is given to out-of-town students. 82% of students commute. Alcohol is not permitted. All students may keep cars.

Activities: 22% of women belong to 1 national sorority. There are no fraternities. There are 30 groups on campus, including academic, art, band, cheerleading, chess, chorus, computers, dance, drama, environmental, ethnic, film, gay, honors, jazz band, literary magazine, newspaper, orchestra, pep band, photography, political, professional, religious, service learning, social, social service, student government, and wilderness. Popular campus events include Welcome Picnic, art receptions, and BSU Latin Dance.

Sports: There are 9 intercollegiate sports for men and 10 for women, and 8 intramural sports for men and 8 for women. Facilities include tennis courts and an athletic field, a 1000-seat gym, a fitness center, a NATA-certified training room, and an aerobics room.

Disabled Students: 95% of the campus is accessible. Wheelchair ramps, elevators, special parking, specially equipped rest rooms, special class scheduling, lowered drinking fountains, lowered telephones, and special housing are available.

Services: Counseling and information services are available, as is tutoring in most subjects. There is remedial math, reading, and writing. Free individual tutoring as well as study groups led by a tutor, peer tutoring, paraprofessional tutoring, and faculty tutoring is available.

Campus Safety and Security: Measures include self-defense education, security escort services, shuttle buses, and informal discussions. There are pamphlets/posters/films, emergency telephones, lighted pathways/sidewalks, and 15-hour foot and vehicle patrols during VJC's operating hours.

Programs of Study: VJC confers B.A., B.S. degrees. Associate and master's degrees are also awarded. Bachelor's degrees are awarded in BIOLOGICAL SCIENCE (biology/biological science and biotechnology), BUSINESS (business administration and management and business systems analysis), COMMUNICATIONS AND THE ARTS (design and English), COMPUTER AND PHYSICAL SCIENCE (chemistry and information sciences and systems), HEALTH PROFESSIONS (nursing), SOCIAL SCIENCE (family/consumer studies, interdisciplinary studies, liberal arts/general studies, paralegal studies, and psychology). Education, nursing, and paralegal are the strongest academically. Paralegal, nursing, and business are the largest.

Required: The core curriculum includes courses in writing, communication, fine arts, social sciences, math, natural science, humanities, and phys ed. Students must complete a minimum of 120 hours, including 45 hours in upper-level courses, with at least a 2.0 overall GPA. The number of hours required per major varies. Many majors require a capstone course and an internship.

Special: VJC offers co-op programs in several majors as well as cross-registration through the Baltimore Student Exchange Program. Also offered are supervised internships for second-year students in several majors, which require a minimum of 120 hours per semester, and Washington Center internships. There are work-study programs, and study abroad is possible in 4 countries through programs offered at other colleges. There also are accelerated degree programs in nursing, paralegal studies, and business administration. Student-designed majors are possible, as are interdisciplinary majors, including liberal arts and technology, computer acccounting, and business information systems. Education courses for state cerification are available, and students may earn credit by exam. There are 6 national honor societies, a freshman honors program, and 7 departmental honors programs.

Faculty/Classroom: 45% of faculty are male; 55%, female. 99% teach undergraduates. No introductory courses are taught by graduate students. The average class size in an introductory lecture is 18; in a laboratory, 14; and in a regular course, 18.

Admissions: 63% of the 2003-2004 applicants were accepted. The SAT I scores for the 2003-2004 freshman class were: Verbal--41% below 500, 43% between 500 and 599, 15% between 600 and 700, and 1% above 700; Math--38% below 500, 41% between 500 and 599, 20% between 600 and 700, and 1% above 700. 41% of the current freshmen were in the top fifth of their class; 72% were in the top two fifths. 7 freshmen graduated first in their class.

Requirements: The SAT I or ACT is required. In addition, applicants must be graduates of an accredited secondary school. Although a secondary transcript is required, particular secondary preparation is not stipulated for all programs. Some degree programs do require specific high school courses, however. An essay is required and an interview is recommended. AP and CLEP credits are accepted. Important factors in the admissions decision are advanced placement or honor courses, recommendations by school officials, and leadership record.

Procedure: Freshmen are admitted fall, spring, and summer. Entrance exams should be taken between September and November of the senior year. There is a deferred and a rolling admissions plan. Application deadlines are open. Notification is sent on a rolling basis beginning December 1. The fall 2003 application fee was $25. Applications are accepted on-line.

Transfer: 221 transfer students enrolled in 2002-2003. Transfer applicants must provide both college and secondary school transcripts and have a minimum 2.5 GPA. Grades earned at other institutions are not included in calculating the GPA required for graduation. Transfer students with a 2.0 cumulative GPA and other accomplishments or experience may be granted conditional admission to the college. 30 of 120 credits required for the bachelor's degree must be completed at VJC.

Visiting: There are regularly scheduled orientations for prospective students, including a general overview, information on how to apply and how to finance a college education, special academic presentations, tours, meetings with faculty and students, and lunch. There are guides for informal visits and visitors may sit in on classes. To schedule a visit, contact the Admissions Office.

Financial Aid: In 2003-2004, 61% of all full-time freshmen and 59% of continuing full-time students received some form of financial aid. 53% of full-time freshmen and 52% of continuing full-time students received need-based aid. The average freshman award was $9016. 5% of undergraduates work part time. Average annual earnings from campus work are $1400. The average financial indebtedness of the 2003 graduate was $16,832. VJC is a member of CSS. The FAFSA is required. The priority date for freshman financial aid applications for fall entry is February 15. The deadline for filing freshman financial aid applications for fall entry is March 1.

International Students: There are 6 international students enrolled. They must score 550 on the written TOEFL.

Computers: The mainframe is an IBM. More than 250 networked PCs are available for student use in classrooms and labs. The campuswide fiber-optic backbone provides an SNA gateway to the IBM mainframe, library card catalog access via a CD-ROM server, remote access from home, Mac connectivity, e-mail, and hundreds of software applications in all disciplines. All students may access the system at all times. There are no time limits and no fees.

Graduates: From July 1, 2002 to June 30, 2003, 465 bachelor's degrees were awarded. The most popular majors were computer and information systems (23%), business (16%), and nursing (15%). In an average class, 31% graduate in 4 years or less, 45% graduate in 5 years or less, and 46% graduate in 6 years or less. 60 companies recruited on campus in 2002-2003. Of the 2002 graduating class, 11% were enrolled in graduate school within 6 months of graduation and 96% were employed.

Admissions Contact: Mark J. Hergan, Dean of Admissions. A video is available. E-mail: *admissions@vjc.edu* Web: *www.vjc.edu*

WASHINGTON COLLEGE
Chestertown, MD 21620-1197

E-2

(410) 778-7700
(800) 422-1782; Fax: (410) 778-7287

Full-time: 505 men, 844 women	Faculty: 86; IIB, +$
Part-time: 15 men, 35 women	Ph.D.s: 92%
Graduate: 37 men, 46 women	Student/Faculty: 16 to 1
Year: semesters	Tuition: $24,800
Application Deadline: March 15	Room & Board: $5740
Freshman Class: 2114 applied, 1290 accepted, 358 enrolled	
SAT I Verbal/Math: 578/567	ACT: 23 VERY COMPETITIVE

Washington College, founded in 1782, is an independent college offering programs in the liberal arts and sciences, business management, and teacher preparation. The library contains 243,952 volumes, 250,567 microform items, and 6342 audio/video tapes/CDs, and subscribes to 863 periodicals. Computerized library services include the card catalog, interlibrary loans, database searching, and Internet access. Special learning facilities include a learning resource center and the Center for the American Experience and the Center for Environment and Society. The 112-acre campus is in a small town 75 miles from Baltimore. Including any residence halls, there are 52 buildings.

Student Life: 53% of undergraduates are from Maryland. Students are from 37 states, 36 foreign countries, and Canada. 66% are from public schools. 82% are white. The average age of freshmen is 19; all undergraduates, 21. 16% do not continue beyond their first year; 66% remain to graduate.

Housing: 1130 students can be accommodated in college housing, which includes single-sex and coed dorms and on-campus apartments. In addition, there are special-interest houses, an international house, a science house, and substance-free housing. On-campus housing is guaranteed for the freshman year only and is available on a lottery system for upperclassmen. 78% of students live on campus; of those, 65% remain on campus on weekends. All students may keep cars.

Activities: 20% of men belong to 3 national fraternities; 20% of women belong to 3 national sororities. There are 52 groups on campus, including cheerleading, chorale, chorus, dance, debate, drama, education and leadership, ethnic, gay, honors, international, jazz band, literary magazine, minority and human rights, newspaper, opera, orchestra, photography, political, professional, religious, social, social service, student government, and yearbook. Popular campus events include fall and spring convocations, George Washington Birthday Ball, and May Day.

Sports: There are 15 intercollegiate sports for men and 15 for women, and 12 intramural sports for men and 11 for women. Facilities include

a swim center, a gym, a field house, squash and racquetball courts, a fitness center, playing and practice fields, and a boat house. There are riding facilities nearby.

Disabled Students: 80% of the campus is accessible. Wheelchair ramps, elevators, special parking, specially equipped rest rooms, special class scheduling, lowered drinking fountains, lowered telephones, motorized carts, and curb cuts are available.

Services: Counseling and information services are available, as is tutoring in every subject. There is remedial math and writing, a writing center, a math lab, a study skills tutor, and peer tutors.

Campus Safety and Security: Measures include 24-hour foot and vehicle patrol, security escort services, informal discussions, and pamphlets/posters/films. There are emergency telephones, lighted pathways/sidewalks, and peer education through student groups.

Programs of Study: WC confers B.A. and B.S. degrees. Master's degrees are also awarded. Bachelor's degrees are awarded in BIOLOGICAL SCIENCE (biology/biological science), BUSINESS (business administration and management), COMMUNICATIONS AND THE ARTS (art, dramatic arts, English, fine arts, French, German, music, and Spanish), COMPUTER AND PHYSICAL SCIENCE (chemistry, computer science, mathematics, and physics), ENGINEERING AND ENVIRONMENTAL DESIGN (environmental science), SOCIAL SCIENCE (American studies, anthropology, economics, history, humanities, international studies, philosophy, political science/government, psychology, and sociology). English, psychology, and business management are the strongest academically and are the largest.

Required: All students are required to take 2 freshman seminars, and 11 courses distributed among the social sciences, natural sciences, humanities, quantitative studies, foreign langauges, and a writing requirement. The senior obligation consists of a comprehensive exam, thesis, or independent project. Students must complete 128 credit hours, including at least 32 in the major, to graduate. A minimum GPA of 2.0 is required.

Special: Internships are available in all majors. There is study abroad in 20 countries and a Washington semester at American University. The college offers a 3-2 engineering degree with the University of Maryland at College Park, as well as a 3-2 nursing program with John Hopkins University, credit by exam, pass/fail options, and student-designed majors. There are 7 national honor societies.

Faculty/Classroom: 56% of faculty are male; 44%, female. 97% teach undergraduates. No introductory courses are taught by graduate students. The average class size in an introductory lecture is 24; in a laboratory, 16; and in a regular course, 16.

Admissions: 61% of the 2003-2004 applicants were accepted. The SAT I scores for the 2003-2004 freshman class were: Verbal--10% below 500, 46% between 500 and 599, 37% between 600 and 700, and 7% above 700; Math--14% below 500, 53% between 500 and 599, 29% between 600 and 700, and 4% above 700. 10 freshmen graduated first in their class.

Requirements: The SAT I or ACT is required. In addition, applicants must be graduates of an accredited secondary school or have a GED. 16 Carnegie units are required. Applicants should take high school courses in English, foreign language, history, math, science, and social studies. An essay is required, and an interview is recommended. A GPA of 2.5 is required. AP and CLEP credits are accepted. Important factors in the admissions decision are advanced placement or honor courses, recommendations by school officials, and leadership record.

Procedure: Freshmen are admitted fall and spring. Entrance exams should be taken in the spring of the junior year or fall of the senior year. There is an early decision plan. Early decision applications should be filed by November 15; regular applications, by March 15 for fall entry and December 1 for spring entry, along with a $40 fee. Notification is sent on a rolling basis. 36 early decision candidates were accepted for the 2003-2004 class. 67 applicants were on the 2003 waiting list. Applications are accepted on-line through Common Application.

Transfer: 46 transfer students enrolled in a recent year. A minimum GPA of 2.5 is required. An associate degree and interview are recommended. 56 of 128 credits required for the bachelor's degree must be completed at WC.

Visiting: There are regularly scheduled orientations for prospective students, consisting of weekday visits. There are guides for informal visits and visitors may sit in on classes and stay overnight. To schedule a visit, contact the Admissions Office.

Financial Aid: In 2003-2004, 89% of all full-time freshmen and 88% of continuing full-time students received some form of financial aid. The average freshman award was $18,223. 50% of undergraduates work part time. Average annual earnings from campus work are $760. The average financial indebtedness of a recent graduate was $17,711. WC is a member of CSS. The FAFSA, the college's own financial statement, and the parents' and students' federal income tax returns are required. The deadline for filing freshman financial aid applications for fall entry is February 15.

International Students: The school actively recruits these students. They must score 550 on the written TOEFL and also take the SAT I or the ACT.

Computers: Students may access the mainframe, the library collection, and the Internet via a campus network of more than 130 Macs in the library, academic buildings, and dorms. All students may access the system. There are no time limits and no fees. It is strongly recommended that all students have a Mac or a PowerBook personal computer.

Graduates: From July 1, 2002 to June 30, 2003, 227 bachelor's degrees were awarded. The most popular majors were psychology (13%), business management (12%), and English (11%). In an average class, 2% graduate in 3 years or less, 63% graduate in 4 years or less, 65% graduate in 5 years or less, and 66% graduate in 6 years or less. 35 companies recruited on campus in 2002-2003. Of the 2002 graduating class, 38% were enrolled in graduate school within 6 months of graduation and 84% were employed.

Admissions Contact: Kevin Coveney, Vice President of Admissions. A video is available. E-mail: *adm-off@washcoll.edu*
Web: *www.washcoll.edu*

WESTERN MARYLAND COLLEGE
(See McDaniel College)

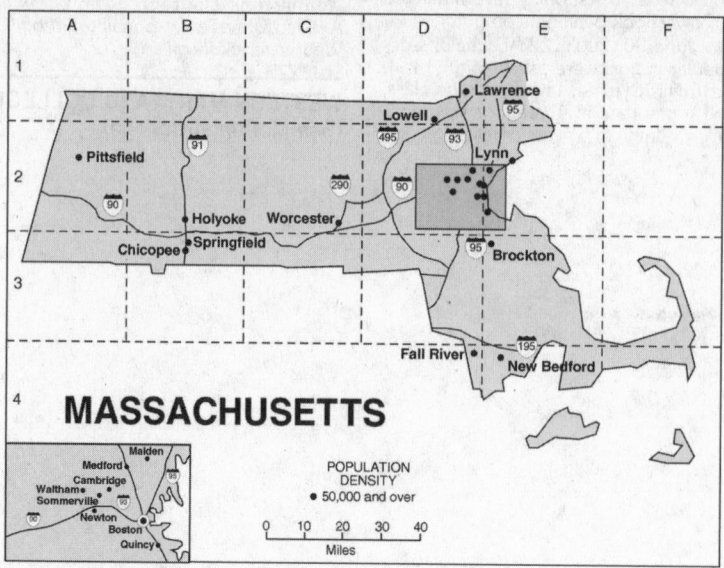

AMERICAN INTERNATIONAL COLLEGE   B-3
Springfield, MA 01109   **(413) 205-3201**
                           (800) 242-3142; Fax: (413) 205-3051

Full-time: 487 men, 526 women	**Faculty:** 70
Part-time: 72 men, 103 women	**Ph.D.s:** 70%
Graduate: 141 men, 266 women	**Student/Faculty:** 14 to 1
Year: semesters, summer session	**Tuition:** $16,700
Application Deadline: open	**Room & Board:** $7990
Freshman Class: 1347 applied, 1031 accepted, 331 enrolled	
SAT I Verbal/Math: 465/455	**LESS COMPETITIVE**

American International College, founded in 1885, is an independent institution offering programs in liberal arts, business, health science, and teacher preparation. There are 4 undergraduate and 3 graduate schools. In addition to regional accreditation, AIC has baccalaureate program accreditation with ACOTE, APTA, IACBE, NASDTEC, and NLN. The library contains 118,000 volumes, 450,000 microform items, and 1380 audio/video tapes/CDs, and subscribes to 425 periodicals. Computerized library services include the card catalog, interlibrary loans, database searching, and Internet access. Special learning facilities include a learning resource center, art gallery, radio station, TV station, and an anatomical lab for health sciences. The 58-acre campus is in an urban area 75 miles west of Boston. Including any residence halls, there are 22 buildings.

Student Life: 60% of undergraduates are from Massachusetts. Students are from 30 states, 15 foreign countries, and Canada. 85% are from public schools. 66% are white; 25% African American. 66% are Catholic; 26% Protestant; 6% Jewish. The average age of freshmen is 19; all undergraduates, 23. 56% of freshmen remain to graduate.

Housing: 680 students can be accommodated in college housing, which includes single-sex and coed dorms. On-campus housing is guaranteed for all 4 years. 60% of students live on campus; of those, 65% remain on campus on weekends. Alcohol is not permitted. All students may keep cars.

Activities: There are no fraternities or sororities. There are 40 groups on campus, including cheerleading, chorale, computers, dance, drama, ethnic, honors, international, literary magazine, musical theater, newspaper, political, professional, radio and TV, religious, social, social service, student government, women's, and yearbook. Popular campus events include holiday semi-formals and international festival.

Sports: There are 9 intercollegiate sports for men and 7 for women, and 9 intramural sports for men and 8 for women. Facilities include 2 gyms, a football stadium, tennis courts, playing fields, and a health and fitness center.

Disabled Students: 75% of the campus is accessible. Wheelchair ramps, elevators, special parking, specially equipped rest rooms, special class scheduling, and lowered drinking fountains are available.

Services: Counseling and information services are available, as is tutoring in every subject. There is remedial math and writing.

Campus Safety and Security: Measures include 24-hour foot and vehicle patrol, self-defense education, security escort services, and shuttle buses. There are informal discussions, pamphlets/posters/films, and lighted pathways/sidewalks.

Programs of Study: AIC confers B.A., B.S., B.B.A., B.S.B.A., B.S.N., and B.S.O.T. degrees. Associate, master's, and doctoral degrees are also awarded. Bachelor's degrees are awarded in BIOLOGICAL SCIENCE (biochemistry and biology/biological science), BUSINESS (accounting, business administration and management, business economics, entrepreneurial studies, human resources, international business management, and marketing/retailing/merchandising), COMMUNICATIONS AND THE ARTS (advertising, communications, English, and Spanish), COMPUTER AND PHYSICAL SCIENCE (chemistry, mathematics, and science), EDUCATION (early childhood, elementary, foreign languages, middle school, science, secondary, and special), HEALTH PROFESSIONS (medical laboratory technology, nursing, occupational therapy, physical therapy, predentistry, and premedicine), SOCIAL SCIENCE (criminal justice, economics, history, international relations, liberal arts/general studies, philosophy, political science/government, prelaw, psychology, public administration, and sociology). Psychology, preprofessional, and health sciences are the strongest academically. Criminal justice, physical therapy, and nursing are the largest.

Required: Distribution requirements include 12 credits of social sciences, 9 of English, 8 of lab science, 6 of humanities, and 3 each of math and computer-oriented courses. A total of 120 credit hours is required for graduation, with 30 to 36 hours in the major. A minimum 2.0 GPA is required for graduation. Students must take 4 credits of phys ed.

Special: Cross-registration with the Cooperative Colleges of Greater Springfield is permitted. Internships are available in all programs, for up to 6 credits in every major, and study abroad is offered, as is a Washington semester. AIC also offers dual majors, credit by exam, credit for life/military/work experience, nondegree study, and for lower-division students, pass/fail options. There are 2 national honor societies, a freshman honors program, and 9 departmental honors programs.

Faculty/Classroom: 48% of faculty are male; 52%, female. All teach undergraduates, 15% do research, and 15% do both. No introductory courses are taught by graduate students. The average class size in an introductory lecture is 27; in a laboratory, 16; and in a regular course, 19.

Admissions: 77% of the 2003-2004 applicants were accepted. The SAT I scores for the 2003-2004 freshman class were: Verbal--62% below 500, 35% between 500 and 599, and 3% between 600 and 700; Math--65% below 500, 33% between 500 and 599, and 2% between 600 and 700. 20% of the current freshmen were in the top fifth of their class; 45% were in the top two fifths. 3 freshmen graduated first in their class.

Requirements: The SAT I is required. In addition, students must be graduates of an accredited secondary school or have a GED. They must have completed 16 academic credits of secondary school work with a minimum of 4 years of English, 2 each of history, math, and science, and 1 of social studies. An interview is recommended. A GPA of 2.0 is required. AP and CLEP credits are accepted. Important factors in the admissions decision are recommendations by school officials, recommendations by alumni, and advanced placement or honor courses.

Procedure: Freshmen are admitted to all sessions. Entrance exams should be taken by March of the senior year. There are early decision and deferred admissions plans. There is a rolling admissions plan. Application deadlines are open. Application fee is $20. Applications are accepted on-line.

Transfer: 159 transfer students enrolled in 2002-2003. Transfer applicants must have at least a 2.0 GPA. 45 of 120 credits required for the bachelor's degree must be completed at AIC.

Visiting: There are regularly scheduled orientations for prospective students, including open houses with faculty, a student life panel, departmental faculty presentations, a financial aid presentation, a tour, and brunch. There are guides for informal visits and visitors may sit in on classes and stay overnight. To schedule a visit, contact the Admissions Office at *ccote@acad.aic.edu*.

Financial Aid: In 2003-2004, 89% of all full-time freshmen and 85% of continuing full-time students received some form of financial aid. 70% of full-time freshmen and 73% of continuing full-time students received need-based aid. The average freshman award was $17,500. 62% of undergraduates work part time. Average annual earnings from campus work are $2000. The average financial indebtedness of the 2003 graduate was $19,425. The FAFSA is required. The deadline for filing freshman financial aid applications for fall entry is May 1.

International Students: There are 50 international students enrolled. The school actively recruits these students. They must score 500 on the written TOEFL or 173 on the electronic version and also take the SAT I or the ACT.

Computers: The mainframe is an IBM Alpha. The college network is accessible by PCs located in computer labs throughout campus, all with Internet access. Free Internet access is also provided in all residence hall rooms. In addition, dorms have a wireless capability network. All students may access the system 7 days per week for a total of 80 hours. There are no time limits and no fees.

Graduates: From July 1, 2002 to June 30, 2003, 226 bachelor's degrees were awarded. The most popular majors were business (22%), health professions (22%), and criminal justice (15%). In an average class, 40% graduate in 4 years or less, 45% graduate in 5 years or less, and 50% graduate in 6 years or less. 50 companies recruited on campus in 2002-2003. Of the 2002 graduating class, 21% were enrolled in graduate school within 6 months of graduation and 81% were employed.

Admissions Contact: Peter Miller, Dean of Admissions. A video is available. E-mail: *inquiry@www.aic.edu* Web: *www.aic.edu*

AMHERST COLLEGE
Amherst, MA 01002-5000

	B-2
Full-time: 833 men, 785 women	(413) 542-2328; Fax: (413) 542-2040
Part-time: 1 man, 4 women	Faculty: 182; IIB, ++$
Graduate: none	Ph.D.s: 93%
Year: semesters	Student/Faculty: 9 to 1
Application Deadline: December 31	Tuition: $29,730
Freshman Class: 5631 applied, 1001 accepted, 413 enrolled	Room & Board: $7740
SAT I Verbal/Math: 720/720	ACT: 32 MOST COMPETITIVE

Amherst College, founded in 1821, is a private liberal arts institution. The 5 libraries contain 1,001,981 volumes, 248,100 microform items, and 60,826 audio/video tapes/CDs, and subscribe to 5563 periodicals. Computerized library services include the card catalog, interlibrary loans, database searching, and Internet access. Special learning facilities include a learning resource center, art gallery, natural history museum, planetarium, radio station, observatory, the Emily Dickinson Museum, and the Amherst Center for Russian Culture. The 999-acre campus is in a small town 90 miles west of Boston. Including any residence halls, there are 75 buildings.

Student Life: 81% of undergraduates are from out of state, mostly the Middle Atlantic. Students are from 49 states, 30 foreign countries, and Canada. 56% are from public schools. 45% are white; 12% Asian American; 10% African American. The average age of freshmen is 18; all undergraduates, 19. 4% do not continue beyond their first year; 97% remain to graduate.

Housing: 1630 students can be accommodated in college housing, which includes single-sex and coed dorms. In addition, there are language houses, special-interest houses, and 1 cooperative house. On-campus housing is guaranteed for all 4 years. 98% of students live on campus; of those, 95% remain on campus on weekends. Upperclassmen may keep cars.

Activities: There are no fraternities or sororities. There are more than 100 groups on campus, including art, band, chess, choir, chorale, chorus, computers, dance, debate, drama, ethnic, film, gay, honors, international, jazz band, literary magazine, mock trial, musical theater, newspaper, opera, orchestra, photography, political, professional, radio and TV, religious, social, social service, student government, symphony, and yearbook. Popular campus events include Newport Jazz, Harlem Renaissance, and Casino Night.

Sports: There are 13 intercollegiate sports for men and 14 for women, and 6 intramural sports for men and 6 for women. Facilities include 2 gyms, a pool, a field house, a hockey rink, an outdoor track, a fitness center, 10 international squash courts, an indoor jogging track, 3 indoor and 30 outdoor tennis courts, baseball and softball diamonds, a 9-hole golf course, and playing fields.

Disabled Students: Wheelchair ramps, elevators, special parking, specially equipped rest rooms, special class scheduling, lowered drinking fountains, and lowered telephones are available.

Services: Counseling and information services are available, as is tutoring in every subject. There is a reader service for the blind. A quantitative skills center and a writing center are also available.

Campus Safety and Security: Measures include 24-hour foot and vehicle patrol, self-defense education, security escort services, and shuttle buses. There are informal discussions, pamphlets/posters/films, emergency telephones, lighted pathways/sidewalks, ACEMS (Amherst College Emergency Medical Service), and access code pad security to dorms, plus "blue light" emergency telephones placed in 19 locations around campus.

Programs of Study: Amherst confers the B.A. degree. Bachelor's degrees are awarded in BIOLOGICAL SCIENCE (biology/biological science and neurosciences), COMMUNICATIONS AND THE ARTS (classics, dance, dramatic arts, English, fine arts, French, German, Greek, Latin, music, Russian, and Spanish), COMPUTER AND PHYSICAL SCIENCE (astronomy, chemistry, computer science, geology, mathematics, and physics), SOCIAL SCIENCE (African American studies, American studies, anthropology, Asian/Oriental studies, economics, European studies, history, interdisciplinary studies, law, philosophy, political science/government, psychology, religion, sociology, and women's studies). English, psychology, and biology are the largest.

Required: To earn the B.A., all students must complete 32 courses, equivalent to 128 credits, 8 to 14 of which are in the major, with at least a C average. Other than a 1-semester freshman seminar in liberal studies, there are no specific course requirements. A thesis or comparable work is required for honors candidates.

Special: Students may cross-register through the Five College Consortium, the other members of which are all within 10 miles of Amherst, or through the Twelve College Exchange Program. A number of interterm and summer internships are available, as is study abroad in 36 countries. Dual majors, student-designed interdisciplinary majors based on independent study as of the junior or senior year, and work-study programs are possible. There are limited pass/fail options. There are 2 national honor societies, including Phi Beta Kappa, and 10 departmental honors programs.

Faculty/Classroom: 62% of faculty are male; 38%, female. All both teach and do research. The average class size in a laboratory is 20 and in a regular course, 15.

Admissions: 18% of the 2003-2004 applicants were accepted. The SAT I scores for the 2003-2004 freshman class were: Verbal--7% between 500 and 599, 29% between 600 and 700, and 64% above 700; Math--7% between 500 and 599, 28% between 600 and 700, and 65% above 700. The ACT scores were 4% below 21, 1% between 21 and 23, 10% between 24 and 26, 10% between 27 and 28, and 78% above 28. 95% of the current freshmen were in the top fifth of their class; 98% were in the top two fifths. There were 84 National Merit semifinalists. 34 freshmen graduated first in their class.

Requirements: The SAT I or ACT is required. In addition, 3 SAT II: Subject tests are required for admission. Amherst strongly recommends that applicants take 4 years of English, math through calculus, 3 or 4 years of a foreign language, 2 years of history and social science, and at least 2 years of natural science, including a lab science. 2 essays are required. Important factors in the admissions decision are advanced placement or honor courses, recommendations by school officials, and evidence of special talent.

Procedure: Freshmen are admitted in the fall. Entrance exams should be taken no later than December of the senior year. There are early decision and deferred admissions plans. Early decision applications should be filed by November 15; regular applications, by December 31 for fall entry. The fall 2003 application fee was $55. Notification of early decision is sent December 15; regular decision, April 1. 130 early decision candidates were accepted for the 2003-2004 class. 411 applicants were on the 2003 waiting list; 72 were admitted. Applications are accepted on-line through *www.embark.com*, *www.commonapp.org*, or the school's web site.

Transfer: 10 transfer students enrolled in 2002-2003. Applicants must have full sophomore standing prior to applying and a minimum 3.0 GPA in previous college work. Transfers are accepted for the sophomore and junior classes only, and Amherst recommends that they submit SAT I or ACT scores, plus high school and college transcripts, and seek a personal interview. 64 of 128 credits required for the bachelor's degree must be completed at Amherst.

Visiting: There are regularly scheduled orientations for prospective students, consisting of information sessions led by a dean and student-led tours. There are guides for informal visits and visitors may sit in on classes and stay overnight. To schedule a visit, contact the Admission Office.

Financial Aid: In 2003-2004, 46% of all full-time freshmen and 48% of continuing full-time students received some form of financial aid. 44% of full-time freshmen and 47% of continuing full-time students received need-based aid. The average freshman award was $23,487, with $21,798 ($40,342 maximum) from need-based scholarships or need-based grants and $1689 ($5050 maximum) from need-based self-help aid (loans and jobs). 60% of undergraduates work part time. Average annual earnings from campus work are $1150. The average financial indebtedness of the 2003 graduate was $10,787. Amherst is a member of CSS. The CSS Profile or FAFSA is required. The deadline for filing freshman financial aid applications for fall entry is February 1.

International Students: There are 95 international students enrolled. The school actively recruits these students. They must score 600 on the written TOEFL or 250 on the electronic version or take the MELAB or the SAT II: ELAP if English is not the applicant's first language. They must also take the SAT I or the ACT and any 3 SAT II: Subject tests.

Computers: The main configuration includes more than 30 Windows 2000 and Windows 2003 Linux systems. There are more than 160 PCs around campus. Most are located in the computer center, library, campus center, and labs. In addition, each student has a hard-wired point of access from each dorm room with Ethernet, Internet, and e-mail accounts. All students may access the system 24 hours a day. There are no time limits and no fees.

Graduates: From July 1, 2002 to June 30, 2003, 415 bachelor's degrees were awarded. The most popular majors were English (13%), psychology (12%), and law, jurisprudence, and social thought (12%). In an average class, 89% graduate in 4 years or less, 95% graduate in 5 years or less, and 97% graduate in 6 years or less. 38 companies recruited on campus in 2002-2003. Of the 2002 graduating class, 29% were enrolled in graduate school within 6 months of graduation and 60% were employed.

Admissions Contact: Katherine L. Fretwell, Director of Admission. E-mail: *admission@amherst.edu* Web: *http://www.amherst.edu*

ANNA MARIA COLLEGE
Paxton, MA 01612-1198

C-2

(508) 849-3360
(800) 344-4586; Fax: (508) 849-3362

Full-time: 178 men, 369 women	**Faculty:** 37; IIB, --$
Part-time: 67 men, 117 women	**Ph.D.s:** 43%
Graduate: 145 men, 271 women	**Student/Faculty:** 15 to 1
Year: semesters, summer session	**Tuition:** $19,145
Application Deadline: March 1	**Room & Board:** $6995
Freshman Class: 568 applied, 500 accepted, 154 enrolled	
SAT I Verbal/Math: 460/450	**ACT:** 14 **LESS COMPETITIVE**

Anna Maria College, founded in 1946, is a small, comprehensive Catholic college offering career-oriented programs in liberal and fine arts, business, and teacher preparation. There is 1 graduate school. In addition to regional accreditation, AMC has baccalaureate program accreditation with CSWE and NLN. The library contains 81,010 volumes, 1702 microform items, and 6095 audio/video tapes/CDs, and subscribes to 277 periodicals. Computerized library services include the card catalog and database searching. Special learning facilities include a learning resource center, art gallery, and , an audiovisual center, and nature trail. The 180-acre campus is in a rural area 8 miles northwest of Worcester. Including any residence halls, there are 13 buildings.

Student Life: 77% of undergraduates are from Massachusetts. Students are from 11 states, 7 foreign countries, and Canada. 70% are from public schools. 86% are white. The average age of freshmen is 18; all undergraduates, 21. 31% do not continue beyond their first year; 54% remain to graduate.

Housing: 394 students can be accommodated in college housing, which includes coed dorms. On-campus housing is guaranteed for the freshman year only, is available on a first-come, first-served basis, and is available on a lottery system for upperclassmen. Priority is given to out-of-town students. 60% of students live on campus. All students may keep cars.

Activities: There are no fraternities or sororities. There are 25 groups on campus, including art, cheerleading, choir, chorus, computers, drama, ethnic, gay, honors, international, jazz band, musical theater, political, professional, religious, social, social service, student government, and yearbook. Popular campus events include Harvest Weekend, Winter Semi-Formal, and Spring Weekend.

Sports: There are 5 intercollegiate sports for men and 6 for women, and 2 intramural sports for men and 2 for women. Facilities include an activities center with a basketball court, locker rooms, and weight and fitness equipment; soccer, baseball, and softball fields; an outdoor basketball court; and a fitness trail.

Disabled Students: 93% of the campus is accessible. Wheelchair ramps, elevators, special parking, specially equipped rest rooms, and special class scheduling are available.

Services: Counseling and information services are available, as is tutoring in every subject through a tutoring lab. There is a reader service for the blind, and remedial math, reading, and writing.

Campus Safety and Security: Measures include 24-hour foot and vehicle patrol, security escort services, shuttle buses, and informal discussions. There are pamphlets/posters/films, emergency telephones, and lighted pathways/sidewalks.

Programs of Study: AMC confers B.A., B.S., B.B.A., B.F.A., B.M., and B.S.N. degrees. Associate and master's degrees are also awarded. Bachelor's degrees are awarded in BIOLOGICAL SCIENCE (biology/biological science), BUSINESS (business administration and management), COMMUNICATIONS AND THE ARTS (art, English, music, music performance, and studio art), EDUCATION (art, early childhood, elementary, and music), HEALTH PROFESSIONS (art therapy, music therapy, and nursing), SOCIAL SCIENCE (criminal justice, fire science, history, human development, liberal arts/general studies, paralegal studies, political science/government, psychology, social science, and social work). Criminal justice, education, and business are the largest.

Required: The 60-credit core curriculum consists of classes in English, literature, math, computers, natural science, foreign language, fine arts, history, philosophy, social/behavioral sciences, and religious studies. A total of 120 credits is required for graduation, with a minimum of 30 in the major, and a 2.0 GPA.

Special: Cross-registration with the colleges of the Worcester Consortium, internships in all majors, and a 3-2 engineering degree in conjunction with the Worcester Polytechnic Institute are available. The art and business major results in a B.F.A. degree. There are preprofessional concentrations in law, dentistry, medicine, and veterinary science. The college offers study abroad, a Washington semester, accelerated degree programs, a general studies degree, credit by exam, work-study programs, and 5-year advanced degree programs in business, counseling psychology, and criminal justice. There are 5 national honor societies and 2 departmental honors programs.

Faculty/Classroom: 32% of faculty are male; 68%, female. All teach undergraduates. No introductory courses are taught by graduate students. The average class size in an introductory lecture is 20; in a laboratory, 20; and in a regular course, 13.

Admissions: 88% of the 2003-2004 applicants were accepted. The SAT I scores for the 2003-2004 freshman class were: Verbal--63% below 500, 31% between 500 and 599, and 6% between 600 and 700; Math--69% below 500, 23% between 500 and 599, and 8% between 600 and 700. The ACT scores were all below 21. 17% of the current freshmen were in the top fifth of their class; 50% were in the top two fifths.

Requirements: The SAT I or ACT is required. In addition, 16 academic units are recommended, including 4 years of English, 2 years each of foreign language, history, math, and sciences, and 1 year of social studies. A GED is accepted. When applicable, an audition or portfolio are required. Students who have been out of high school for 3 or more years, or transfer students with 10 or more college-level courses, do not need to submit standardized test scores. An essay is required. An interview is recommended. A GPA of 2.0 is required. AP and CLEP credits are accepted. Important factors in the admissions decision are advanced placement or honor courses, evidence of special talent, and leadership record.

Procedure: Freshmen are admitted fall and spring. Entrance exams should be taken in the spring of the junior year and in the fall of the senior year. There is a deferred admissions plan. For priority consideration, applications should be filed by March 1 for fall entry and January 1 for spring entry, along with a $40 fee. Notification is sent on a rolling basis beginning January 15. Applications are accepted on computer disk and on-line through massmentor.org and the college's web site.

Transfer: 16 transfer students enrolled in 2002-2003. Transfers with a minimum GPA of 2.0 are accepted for upper-division work. 45 of 120 credits required for the bachelor's degree must be completed at AMC.

Visiting: There are regularly scheduled orientations for prospective students, including on-campus interviews, campus tours, a day visitation program by appointment, and a fall open house. There are guides for informal visits and visitors may sit in on classes and stay overnight. To schedule a visit, contact the Undergraduate Admission Office at *admission@annamaria.edu*.

Financial Aid: In 2003-2004, 88% of all full-time freshmen and 80% of continuing full-time students received some form of financial aid. 87% of full-time freshmen and 78% of continuing full-time students received need-based aid. The average freshman award was $15,423. Need-based scholarships or need-based grants averaged $10,252; need-based self-help aid (loans and jobs) averaged $6046; and non-need-based awards and non-need-based scholarships averaged $10,385. The average financial indebtedness of the 2003 graduate was $18,869. The FAFSA is required. The priority date for freshman financial aid applications for fall entry is February 1.

International Students: There are 8 international students enrolled. The school actively recruits these students. They must score 470 on the written TOEFL or 150 on the electronic version. Students who score below 500 on the TOEFL may be admitted to the college's ESL program.

Computers: There is a main computer lab in the library with more than 21 computers, a minilab in the learning center, and access to the network in every dorm room along with a minilab in the dorm. Available programs include e-mail, the Internet, MS Office, CD-ROM, accounting software, and an on-line legal database.

Graduates: From July 1, 2002 to June 30, 2003, 196 bachelor's degrees were awarded. The most popular majors were criminal justice

(38%), business (12%), and fire science (11%). In an average class, 54% graduate in 6 years or less.

Admissions Contact: Wylie Culhane, Director of Admission.
E-mail: *admission@annamaria.edu* Web: *www.annamaria.edu*

ART INSTITUTE OF BOSTON AT LESLEY UNIVERSITY
Boston, MA 02215-2598

E-2

(617) 585-6710
(800) 773-0494; Fax: (617) 585-6720

Full-time: 198 men, 260 women	**Faculty:** 24
Part-time: 26 men, 32 women	**Ph.Ds:** 79%
Graduate: none	**Student/Faculty:** 19 to 1
Year: semesters, summer session	**Tuition:** $18,710
Application Deadline: February 15	**Room & Board:** $9370
Freshman Class: 489 applied, 375 accepted, 95 enrolled	
SAT I Verbal/Math: 531/512	SPECIAL

The Art Institute of Boston at Lesley University, founded in 1912, is a private institution offering undergraduate visual art programs leading to the baccalaureate degree, 3-year diplomas, and Advanced Professional Certificates, as well as continuing and professional education, intensive workshops, and precollege courses. There is 1 graduate school. In addition to regional accreditation, AIB has baccalaureate program accreditation with NASAD. The 2 libraries contain 120,254 volumes, 878,187 microform items, and 55,799 audio/video tapes/CDs, and subscribe to 684 periodicals. Computerized library services include the card catalog, interlibrary loans, database searching, and Internet access. Special learning facilities include a learning resource center, art gallery, computer labs, state-of-the-art animation lab, printmaking studio, clay studio, woodworking studio, photo lab, and digital-printing lab. The 2-acre campus is in an urban area in the Kenmore Square area of Boston. Including any residence halls, there are 2 buildings.

Student Life: 57% of undergraduates are from Massachusetts. Students are from 35 states, 23 foreign countries, and Canada. 78% are white; 10% foreign nationals. The average age of freshmen is 19; all undergraduates, 21. 33% do not continue beyond their first year; 72% remain to graduate.

Housing: 142 students can be accommodated in college housing, which includes single-sex and coed dorms. On-campus housing is available on a first-come, first-served basis. 73% of students commute. Alcohol is not permitted. No one may keep cars.

Activities: There are no fraternities or sororities. There are 12 groups on campus, including art, chorale, chorus, drama, ethnic, gay, international, literary magazine, musical theater, religious, social service, and student government. Popular campus events include student lunches, student and faculty coffee hours, and Edible Art.

Sports: There are 5 intercollegiate sports for women and 3 intramural sports for women. Facilities include an outdoor tennis court, a fitness center with Nautilus circuit, free weights, and cardiovascular equipment on the main campus. In addition, students may also use an Olympic-size swimming pool at a nearby school and local playing field facilities.

Disabled Students: 75% of the campus is accessible. Wheelchair ramps, elevators, specially equipped rest rooms, special class scheduling, and lowered drinking fountains are available.

Services: Counseling and information services are available, as is tutoring in some subjects. There is a reader service for the blind and remedial math and writing.

Campus Safety and Security: Measures include 24-hour foot and vehicle patrol, security escort services, shuttle buses, and informal discussions. There are pamphlets/posters/films, emergency telephones, lighted pathways/sidewalks, alarms, and electronically operated entrances in some buildings.

Programs of Study: AIB confers the B.F.A. degree. Master's degrees are also awarded. Bachelor's degrees are awarded in COMMUNICATIONS AND THE ARTS (design, fine arts, illustration, and photography). Design and photography are the strongest academically. Illustration/animation is the largest.

Required: All students must complete 124 to 128 credits, including 31 credits in the foundation program and 82 or more in the major. Juniors and seniors must maintain a minimum GPA of 2.3; freshmen and sophomores, 2.0. Senior juries are required.

Special: There is cross-registration with Lesley University. Internships are required for design majors and encouraged for all other majors. Accelerated degree programs in all majors, study abroad in Italy and Ireland, and dual majors in fine art/illustration, design/illustration, illustration/animation, and art education are offered. There is a freshman honors program.

Faculty/Classroom: 58% of faculty are male; 42%, female. All teach undergraduates. The average class size in an introductory lecture is 25; in a laboratory, 12; and in a regular course, 15.

Admissions: 77% of the 2003-2004 applicants were accepted. The SAT I scores for the 2003-2004 freshman class were: Verbal--32% below 500, 47% between 500 and 599, 17% between 600 and 700, and 4%

above 700; Math--46% below 500, 41% between 500 and 599, and 13% between 600 and 700.

Requirements: The SAT I or ACT is required for some programs. In addition, applicants must submit an official high school transcript, and an essay and do a portfolio review. Letters of recommendation and a campus tour are encouraged. A GPA of 2.0 is required. AP and CLEP credits are accepted. Important factors in the admissions decision are evidence of special talent, personality/intangible qualities, and advanced placement or honor courses.

Procedure: Freshmen are admitted fall and spring. Entrance exams should be taken by February 15. There is a deferred admissions plan. Applications should be filed by February 15 for fall entry and November 15 for spring entry. The fall 2003 application fee was $40. A waiting list is an active part of the admissions procedure. Applications are accepted on-line.

Transfer: 52 transfer students enrolled in 2002-2003. High school and college transcripts, a portfolio review, an essay, and SAT I/ACT scores (if graduated since 1995) are required. 45 of 124 credits required for the bachelor's degree must be completed at AIB.

Visiting: There are regularly scheduled orientations for prospective students, including meetings with faculty and students. There are guides for informal visits and visitors may sit in on classes. To schedule a visit, contact the Office of Admissions.

Financial Aid: In 2003-2004, 68% of all full-time freshmen and 55% of continuing full-time students received some form of financial aid. 51% of full-time freshmen and 34% of continuing full-time students received need-based aid. The average freshman award was $7753. Need-based scholarships or need-based grants averaged $4283; and need-based self-help aid (loans and jobs) averaged $4523. 18% of undergraduates work part time. Average annual earnings from campus work are $2000. The average financial indebtedness of the 2003 graduate was $14,110. The FAFSA and the college's own financial statement are required. The priority date for freshman financial aid applications for fall entry is March 15.

International Students: There are 63 international students enrolled. The school actively recruits these students. They must score 500 on the written TOEFL or 173 on the electronic version.

Computers: The mainframe is an IBM AIX RS6000 H70. AIB has 80 computers for student use. Wireless access enables students with laptops to access AIB's academic network. All of the networks have Internet access. Students can access the administrative database via LOIS (Lesley Online Information System) to review their own academic information. Via LOIS, students can review their course schedule, available courses, financial aid, and grades and register on-line. All students may access the system. There are no time limits and no fees.

Graduates: From July 1, 2002 to June 30, 2003, 100 bachelor's degrees were awarded. The most popular majors were illustration (33%), design (24%), and photography (21%). In an average class, 19% graduate in 4 years or less, 34% graduate in 5 years or less, and 36% graduate in 6 years or less. Of the 2002 graduating class, 8% were enrolled in graduate school within 6 months of graduation and 79% were employed.

Admissions Contact: Bradford White, Director of Admissions.
E-mail: *admissions@aiboston.edu* Web: *www.aiboston.edu*

ASSUMPTION COLLEGE
Worcester, MA 01609-1296

C-2

(508) 767-7285
(888) 882-7786; Fax: (508) 799-4412

Full-time: 795 men, 1321 women	**Faculty:** 128; IIB, av$
Part-time: 6 men, 1 woman	**Ph.Ds:** 94%
Graduate: 66 men, 175 women	**Student/Faculty:** 17 to 1
Year: semesters, summer session	**Tuition:** $21,165
Application Deadline: March 1	**Room & Board:** $8210
Freshman Class: 2901 applied, 2279 accepted, 640 enrolled	
SAT I Verbal/Math: 580/540	**ACT:** 21 COMPETITIVE

Assumption College, founded in 1904 by Augustinians of the Assumption, offers a Catholic, liberal arts and sciences education to undergraduates, along with programs for graduate and continuing education students. The library contains 198,300 volumes, 18,564 microform items, and 1778 audio/video tapes/CDs, and subscribes to 1136 periodicals. Computerized library services include the card catalog, interlibrary loans, database searching, and Internet access. Special learning facilities include a learning resource center and TV station. The 150-acre campus is in a suburban area 45 miles west of Boston. Including any residence halls, there are 46 buildings.

Student Life: 68% of undergraduates are from Massachusetts. Students are from 23 states, 10 foreign countries, and Canada. 68% are from public schools. 83% are white. The average age of freshmen is 18; all undergraduates, 20. 14% do not continue beyond their first year; 76% remain to graduate.

Housing: 1918 students can be accommodated in college housing, which includes single-sex dorms and on-campus apartments. In addition, there are special-interest houses. On-campus housing is guaranteed for all 4 years. 89% of students live on campus; of those, 75% remain on campus on weekends. Upperclassmen may keep cars.

Activities: There are no fraternities or sororities. There are 40 groups on campus, including art, band, cheerleading, choir, chorale, chorus, computers, dance, drama, ethnic, film, honors, international, literary magazine, musical theater, newspaper, pep band, photography, political, professional, radio and TV, religious, social, social service, student government, and yearbook. Popular campus events include Sibling Weekend, Holiday Ball, and Family Weekend.

Sports: There are 11 intercollegiate sports for men and 10 for women, and 16 intramural sports for men and 16 for women. Facilities include a 3000-seat gym, baseball and softball diamonds, a field hockey area, a soccer field, and tennis courts. A recreation center houses a 6-lane swimming pool, a jogging/walking track, 4 racquetball courts, an aerobics/dance studio, fully equipped Bodymaster and free-weight rooms, a fitness center, and a field house with 3 multipurpose courts for basketball, volleyball, and floor hockey.

Disabled Students: 71% of the campus is accessible. Wheelchair ramps, elevators, special parking, specially equipped rest rooms, special class scheduling, lowered drinking fountains, lowered telephones, and special housing are available.

Services: Counseling and information services are available, as is tutoring in most subjects, including math, reading, and writing. There is a reader service for the blind, signing for the deaf, and technology services for the disabled.

Campus Safety and Security: Measures include 24-hour foot and vehicle patrol, self-defense education, security escort services, and shuttle buses. There are informal discussions, pamphlets/posters/films, emergency telephones, and lighted pathways/sidewalks.

Programs of Study: Assumption confers the B.A. degree. Master's degrees are also awarded. Bachelor's degrees are awarded in BIOLOGICAL SCIENCE (biology/biological science), BUSINESS (accounting, business administration and management, institutional management, international business management, international economics, and marketing management), COMMUNICATIONS AND THE ARTS (classics, English, French, languages, Spanish, and visual and performing arts), COMPUTER AND PHYSICAL SCIENCE (chemistry, computer science, and mathematics), ENGINEERING AND ENVIRONMENTAL DESIGN (environmental science), HEALTH PROFESSIONS (rehabilitation therapy), SOCIAL SCIENCE (economics, French studies, history, international studies, Latin American studies, philosophy, political science/government, psychology, sociology, Spanish studies, and theological studies). Natural sciences, political science, and psychology are the strongest academically. English, business studies, and math and computer science are the largest.

Required: Students must complete a core curriculum of 3 courses from different disciplines in social science: 2 courses in 1 and 1 course in another of the 3 areas of math, natural science, and foreign languages; 2 courses each of English composition, philosophy, and theology; 1 each of literature, history, and either art, music, or theater arts, and 1 additional course in 2 of the 3 areas of philosophy and theology, literature, and history. A minimum of 120 semester credit hours, with a minimum of 38 semester courses, must be completed; 9 to 12 courses must be in the upper division of the major. A minimum 2.0 GPA is required.

Special: There are co-op programs in gerontology studies and marine studies. Cross-registration with the Worcester Consortium and a 3-2 engineering program with Worcester Polytechnic Institute are offered. The college offers internships, study abroad, a Washington semester, student-designed and dual majors, credit by exam, and credit for military experience. There are 9 national honor societies and a freshman honors program.

Faculty/Classroom: 61% of faculty are male; 39%, female. All teach undergraduates. No introductory courses are taught by graduate students. The average class size in an introductory lecture is 24; in a laboratory, 17; and in a regular course, 23.

Admissions: 79% of the 2003-2004 applicants were accepted. The SAT I scores for the 2003-2004 freshman class were: Verbal--26% below 500, 53% between 500 and 599, 20% between 600 and 700, and 1% above 700; Math--26% below 500, 52% between 500 and 599, 21% between 600 and 700, and 1% above 700. The ACT scores were 40% below 21, 30% between 21 and 23, 21% between 24 and 26, 8% between 27 and 28, and 1% above 28. 34% of the current freshmen were in the top fifth of their class; 67% were in the top two fifths. 1 freshman graduated first in the class.

Requirements: The SAT I is required. In addition, all applicants must graduate from an accredited secondary school or have a GED. 18 academic units are required, including 4 years of English, 3 of math, and 2 each of history, science, and foreign language. An essay and an interview are recommended. AP and CLEP credits are accepted. Important factors in the admissions decision are advanced placement or honor courses, recommendations by school officials, and leadership record.

Procedure: Freshmen are admitted fall and spring. Entrance exams should be taken in May of the junior year or November of the senior year. There are early decision and deferred admissions plans. Early deci-

sion applications should be filed by November 15; regular applications, by March 1 for fall entry and December 1 for spring entry, along with a $50 fee. Notification of early decision is sent December 15; regular decision, on a rolling basis. 27 early decision candidates were accepted for the 2003-2004 class. 108 applicants were on the 2003 waiting list; 42 were admitted. Applications are accepted on-line through EXPAN, Apply, MassMentor, CollegeLink, and Common App.

Transfer: 52 transfer students enrolled in 2002-2003. Transfer students must have maintained a minimum 2.5 GPA at their previous college. SAT I scores and high school and college transcripts are required. 60 of 120 credits required for the bachelor's degree must be completed at Assumption.

Visiting: There are regularly scheduled orientations for prospective students, consisting of new student orientation, meetings with future classmates, choosing roommates, registration, testing, conferences with academic advisers, and discussions of aspects of college life. There are guides for informal visits and visitors may sit in on classes. To schedule a visit, contact the Admissions Office.

Financial Aid: In 2003-2004, 94% of all full-time freshmen and 92% of continuing full-time students received some form of financial aid. 72% of full-time freshmen and 67% of continuing full-time students received need-based aid. The average freshman award was $13,899. Need-based scholarships or need-based grants averaged $6213 ($14,280 maximum); need-based self-help aid (loans and jobs) averaged $3299 ($5625 maximum); non-need-based athletic scholarships averaged $1853 ($5500 maximum); and other non-need-based awards and non-need-based scholarships averaged $9297 ($15,000 maximum). 78% of undergraduates work part time. Average annual earnings from campus work are $1108. The average financial indebtedness of the 2003 graduate was $22,825. The FAFSA is required. The priority date for freshman financial aid applications for fall entry is February 1. The deadline for filing freshman financial aid applications for fall entry is March 1.

International Students: There are 17 international students enrolled. The school actively recruits these students. They must take the TOEFL. Students may be requested to submit SAT I or ACT scores as well.

Computers: There are 38 servers, most powerful of which is a DEC 4100, Dell Quad. Students have full Ethernet access to the Internet and campus networked information systems in all classrooms, dorm rooms, the computer center, the library, and other areas. There are some 1700 computers connected to the network. Roughly 160 of these are public cluster machines spread throughout the campus. All access the Web and e-mail as well as a full suite of applications. All students may access the system. There are no time limits and no fees.

Graduates: From July 1, 2002 to June 30, 2003, 481 bachelor's degrees were awarded. The most popular majors were communications (11%), English (10%), and social and rehabilitation services (10%). In an average class, 75% graduate in 4 years or less, 76% graduate in 5 years or less, and 76% graduate in 6 years or less. Of the 2002 graduating class, 22% were enrolled in graduate school within 6 months of graduation and 89% were employed.

Admissions Contact: Kathleen Murphy, Dean of Enrollment. A video is available. E-mail: *admiss@assumption.edu* Web: *www.assumption.edu*

ATLANTIC UNION COLLEGE
South Lancaster, MA 01561

C-2
(978) 368-2235
(800) 282-2030; Fax: (978) 368-2517

Full-time: 125 men, 236 women	**Faculty:** 46
Part-time: 23 men, 59 women	**Ph.D.s:** 61%
Graduate: 1 man, 16 women	**Student/Faculty:** 8 to 1
Year: semesters, summer session	**Tuition:** $13,780
Application Deadline: August 1	**Room & Board:** $5088
Freshman Class: 303 applied, 281 accepted, 105 enrolled	
SAT I Verbal/Math: 430/400	**ACT:** 17 COMPETITIVE

Atlantic Union College, established in 1882, is a private liberal arts institution associated with the Seventh-day Adventist Church, offering professional and preprofessional programs. In addition to regional accreditation, AUC has baccalaureate program accreditation with CSWE, NASM, and NLN. The library contains 135,215 volumes, 14,871 microform items, and 4474 audio/video tapes/CDs, and subscribes to 583 periodicals. Computerized library services include the card catalog, interlibrary loans, and database searching. Special learning facilities include a learning resource center, art gallery, model elementary and secondary schools, and a music conservatory. The 135-acre campus is in a small town 50 miles west of Boston. Including any residence halls, there are 54 buildings.

Student Life: 56% of undergraduates are from out of state, mostly the Northeast. Students are from 16 states, 11 foreign countries, and Canada. 53% are African American; 22% Hispanic; 15% white; 11% foreign nationals. Most claim no religious affiliation. 29% do not continue beyond their first year.

Housing: 469 students can be accommodated in college housing, which includes single-sex dormitories, on-campus apartments, and married-student housing. On-campus housing is guaranteed for all 4 years. 58% of students live on campus; of those, 80% remain on campus on weekends. Alcohol is not permitted. All students may keep cars.

Activities: There are no fraternities or sororities. There are 13 groups on campus, including art, band, choir, chorale, drama, ethnic, honors, newspaper, orchestra, religious, student government, and yearbook. Popular campus events include Fall Picnic, Cultural Heritage Weeks, and Fine Arts Week.

Sports: There are 7 intramural sports for men and 7 for women. Facilities include a gym and field house with a weight room and tennis/volleyball/badminton, racquetball/handball, and basketball courts, a swimming pool, and athletic fields for flag football, soccer, softball, and baseball.

Disabled Students: 73% of the campus is accessible. Wheelchair ramps, elevators, special parking, and specially equipped rest rooms are available.

Services: Counseling and information services are available, as is tutoring in most subjects. There is remedial math, reading, and writing. Additional services are provided upon request.

Campus Safety and Security: Measures include self-defense education, security escort services, informal discussions, and lighted pathways/sidewalks.

Programs of Study: AUC confers B.A., B.S., and B.M. degrees. Associate and master's degrees are also awarded. Bachelor's degrees are awarded in BIOLOGICAL SCIENCE (biology/biological science and life science), BUSINESS (accounting and business administration and management), COMMUNICATIONS AND THE ARTS (art, English, and music), COMPUTER AND PHYSICAL SCIENCE (computer science, information sciences and systems, and mathematics), EDUCATION (early childhood, elementary, and music), HEALTH PROFESSIONS (nursing), SOCIAL SCIENCE (history, liberal arts/general studies, ministries, psychology, religion, social work, and theological studies). Nursing, English, and business are the strongest academically. Business, education, and nursing are the largest.

Required: Students must complete 12 hours in religion/ethics and 9 hours each in humanities, science, and social science. Foreign language proficiency, a phys ed requirement, 40 hours of community service, and a course in college writing must also be completed. AUC requires 128 to 143 credit hours for the bachelor's degree, with 30 to 60 in the major, and a 2.0 GPA.

Special: There is cross-registration with Mount Wachusett Community College and the Colleges of Worcester Consortium. Students may study abroad in 6 countries. AUC also offers newspaper and biology research internships, cooperative programs in several majors, pass/fail options, and nondegree study. The Summer Advantage in New England program offers precollege credit to high school honor students. There is also an adult degree program, in which most study is done at home and in which student-designed majors are permitted. Dual majors, an accelerated degree in management and professional studies, a 1-3 engineering degree with Walla Walla College, and preprofessional curricula in dentistry, dental hygiene, medicine, respiratory therapy, radiologic technology, and veterinary medicine in conjunction with Loma Linda University are offered. There are 3 national honor societies, a freshman honors program, and 3 departmental honors programs.

Faculty/Classroom: 50% of faculty are male; 50%, female. All teach undergraduates and 10% both teach and do research. No introductory courses are taught by graduate students. The average class size in an introductory lecture is 16; in a laboratory, 14; and in a regular course, 16.

Admissions: 93% of the 2003-2004 applicants were accepted.

Requirements: The SAT I or ACT is required. In addition, applicants should be graduates of an accredited secondary school. The GED is accepted with a minimum score of 250. Required academic credits include 4 years of high school English and 2 years each of a foreign language, math, history, and science. A GPA of 2.0 is required. AP and CLEP credits are accepted. Important factors in the admissions decision are recommendations by school officials, recommendations by alumni, and personality/intangible qualities.

Procedure: Freshmen are admitted fall and spring. Entrance exams should be taken during the senior year of high school. Applications should be filed by August 1 for fall entry and January 2 for spring entry, along with a $25 fee. Notification is sent on a rolling basis. Applications are accepted on-line through CollegeNET, CollegeLink, and the college's web site.

Transfer: 35 transfer students enrolled in a recent year. Applicants who have completed at least 24 semester hours are not required to submit SAT I or ACT scores. Applicants from junior colleges may receive credit for up to 72 semester hours. Only a grade of C or better transfers for credit. 30 of 128 credits required for the bachelor's degree must be completed at AUC.

Visiting: There are regularly scheduled orientations for prospective students, including campus tours, class visits, and financial aid and admissions information sessions. There are guides for informal visits and visitors may sit in on classes and stay overnight. To schedule a visit, contact Maureen Moncrieffe at (978) 368-2556 or *mhmoncrieffe@atlanticuc.edu*.

Financial Aid: In 2003-2004, 88% of all full-time freshmen and 84% of continuing full-time students received some form of financial aid. 75% of full-time freshmen and 77% of continuing full-time students received need-based aid. The average freshman award was $12,823. Need-based scholarships or need-based grants averaged $7635; need-based self-help aid (loans and jobs) averaged $6050; and other non-need based awards and non-need based scholarships averaged $6347. 60% of undergraduates work part time. Average annual earnings from campus work are $2210. The average financial indebtedness of the 2003 graduate was $16,398. The FAFSA is required. The deadline for filing freshman financial aid applications for fall entry is May 1.

International Students: There are 49 international students enrolled. The school actively recruits these students. They must score 525 on the written TOEFL or 195 on the electronic version and also take the SAT I or the ACT, scoring 830 on the SAT I or 17 on the ACT.

Computers: The mainframe is a DEC MicroVAX II on a Novell Network. 40 PCs and terminals are available for student use in the computer lab. All students may access the system. There are no time limits and no fees. It is strongly recommended that all students have a personal computer.

Graduates: From July 1, 2002 to June 30, 2003, 150 bachelor's degrees were awarded. The most popular majors were business administration (16%), psychology (14%), and social work (13%). In an average class, 29% graduate in 3 years or less, 56% graduate in 4 years or less, 81% graduate in 5 years or less, and 91% graduate in 6 years or less. Of the 2002 graduating class, 10% were enrolled in graduate school within 6 months of graduation and 93% were employed.

Admissions Contact: Rosita Lashley, Director of Admissions. A video is available. E-mail: *enroll@atlanticuc.edu* Web: *www.atlanticuc.edu*

BABSON COLLEGE

Babson Park, MA 02457

D-2

(781) 239-5522

(800) 488-3696; Fax: (781) 239-4135

Full-time: 1028 men, 689 women	**Faculty:** IIB, ++$
Part-time: none	**Ph.D.s:** 91%
Graduate: 1158 men, 467 women	**Student/Faculty:** n/av
Year: semesters, summer session	**Tuition:** $27,248
Application Deadline: February 1	**Room & Board:** $9978
Freshman Class: 2991 applied, 1110 accepted, 398 enrolled	
SAT I Verbal/Math: 604/648	**HIGHLY COMPETITIVE**

Babson College, founded in 1919, is a private business school. All students start their own businesses during their freshman year with money loaned by the college. In addition to regional accreditation, Babson has baccalaureate program accreditation with AACSB. The library contains 132,024 volumes, 346,941 microform items, and 4645 audio/video tapes/CDs, and subscribes to 511 periodicals. Computerized library services include the card catalog, interlibrary loans, database searching, and Internet access. Special learning facilities include a learning resource center, art gallery, radio station, performing arts theater, center for entrepreneurial studies, management center, language and culture center, writing center, math center, visual arts center, center for executive education, and center for women's leadership. The 370-acre campus is in a suburban area 14 miles west of Boston. Including any residence halls, there are 53 buildings.

Student Life: 65% of undergraduates are from out of state, mostly the Northeast. Students are from 46 states, 62 foreign countries, and Canada. 55% are from public schools. 44% are white; 19% foreign nationals. The average age of freshmen is 18; all undergraduates, 20. 7% do not continue beyond their first year; 81% remain to graduate.

Housing: 1418 students can be accommodated in college housing, which includes single-sex and coed dorms, on-campus apartments, and married-student housing. In addition, there are special-interest houses, substance-free living, fraternity and sorority towers, and a cultural house. On-campus housing is guaranteed for all 4 years. 85% of students live on campus; of those, 70% remain on campus on weekends. All students may keep cars.

Activities: 9% of men belong to 3 national fraternities; 9% of women belong to 2 national sororities. There are 60 groups on campus, including a cappella group, art, band, cheerleading, choir, chorus, dance, drama, ethnic, gay, honors, international, jazz band, literary magazine, musical theater, newspaper, photography, political, professional, radio and TV, religious, social, social service, student government, and yearbook. Popular campus events include Family Weekend, Founders Day, and Multicultural Week.

Sports: There are 11 intercollegiate sports for men and 11 for women, and 11 intramural sports for men and 11 for women. Facilities include a sports complex with an indoor pool, a 200-meter, 6-lane indoor track, a 1500-square-foot field house, a 600-seat gym with 3 basketball courts, 5 squash and 2 racquetball courts, a fitness center, a dance aerobics studio, locker rooms with saunas, and a sports medicine facility.

Disabled Students: 75% of the campus is accessible. Wheelchair ramps, elevators, special parking, specially equipped rest rooms, special class scheduling, and lowered drinking fountains are available.

Services: Counseling and information services are available, as is tutoring in most subjects. There are writing/speech skills and math/science skills centers.

Campus Safety and Security: Measures include 24-hour foot and vehicle patrol, self-defense education, security escort services, and shuttle buses. There are informal discussions, pamphlets/posters/films, emergency telephones, lighted pathways/sidewalks, a motorist assist program, a transportation service for the cross-registration program, vans available to students for school activities, and crime prevention programs.

Programs of Study: Babson confers the B.S.M. degree. Master's degrees are also awarded. Bachelor's degrees are awarded in BUSINESS (business administration and management).

Required: Students must complete a curriculum of general management and liberal arts, with 50% in management and 50% in liberal arts. A total of 128 semester hours is required for graduation. A minimum GPA of 2.0 is required. The curriculum focuses on rhetoric, numeracy, ethics/social responsibility, international/multicultural perspectives, and leadership/teamwork/creativity competencies. Students specialize in certain aspects of business.

Special: There is cross-registration with Brandeis University, Pine Manor, Wellesley, and Regis Colleges, and F.W. Olin College of Engineering. Internships and study abroad in 20 countries are available. All concentrations are self-designed. There is a freshman honors program.

Faculty/Classroom: 68% of faculty are male; 32%, female. No introductory courses are taught by graduate students. The average class size in an introductory lecture is 34; in a laboratory, 20; and in a regular course, 27.

Admissions: 37% of the 2003-2004 applicants were accepted. The SAT I scores for the 2003-2004 freshman class were: Verbal--2% below 500, 43% between 500 and 599, 47% between 600 and 700, and 7% above 700; Math--17% between 500 and 599, 64% between 600 and 700, and 19% above 700. 80% of the current freshmen were in the top fifth of their class.

Requirements: The SAT I or ACT is required. In addition, applicants must be graduates of an accredited secondary school or have a GED. 16 academic courses are required, including 4 credits of English, 3 of math, 2 of social studies, and 1 of science. A fourth year of math is strongly recommended. Essays are required. An interview is recommended. SAT II: Subject tests in writing and math (either IC or IIC) are recommended. AP and CLEP credits are accepted. Important factors in the admissions decision are advanced placement or honor courses, evidence of special talent, and leadership record.

Procedure: Freshmen are admitted in the fall. Entrance exams should be taken prior to application (SAT I or ACT). There are early decision, early admissions, and deferred admissions plans. Early decision and early action applications should be filed by November 15; regular applications, by February 1 for fall entry. The fall 2003 application fee was $60. Notification of early decision is sent December 15 (early action, January 1); regular decision, April 1. 100 early decision candidates were accepted for the 2003-2004 class. 529 were on the 2003 waiting list; 56 were admitted. Applications are accepted on computer disk and on-line through CollegeLink, EXPAN, CollegeView, and CollegeEdge.

Transfer: 51 transfer students enrolled in 2002-2003. Transfer applicants are expected to demonstrate solid academic performance at their prior institution and must submit 1 essay and 1 recommendation from a college teacher or administrator, in addition to a high school transcript and SAT I scores. They must also submit course descriptions and syllabi for any courses they have taken. 64 of 128 credits required for the bachelor's degree must be completed at Babson.

Visiting: There are regularly scheduled orientations for prospective students, including an open house each year, personal interviews, campus tours, group information sessions, and Fall Preview Days (select Saturdays—"mini Open House"). There are guides for informal visits. To schedule a visit, contact the Admission Office at least 2 weeks in advance.

Financial Aid: In 2003-2004, 45% of all full-time freshmen and 44% of continuing full-time students received some form of financial aid. 41% of all full-time students received need-based aid. The average freshman award was $22,477, with $18,147 from need-based scholarships or need-based grants and $4330 from need-based self-help aid (loans and jobs). 42% of undergraduates work part time. Average annual earnings from campus work are $1580. The average financial indebtedness of the 2003 graduate was $20,531. Babson is a member of CSS. The CSS Profile or FAFSA and tax returns are required. The priority date for filing the CSS Profile for fall entry is December 1. The deadline for filing freshman financial aid applications for fall entry is February 15.

International Students: There are 318 international students enrolled. The school actively recruits these students. They must score 550 on the written TOEFL or 213 on the electronic version or take English Language Proficiency Test. They must also take the SAT I or the ACT. SAT II: Subject tests in math (IC or IIC) and writing are recommended.

Computers: Residence hall rooms have access to GlobeNet through a 10-Base-T Ethernet connection. Access to the Internet, including Netscape for browsing the World Wide Web, and e-mail are also provided.

3500 students access the network and the Internet. There are 300 computers in labs across the campus. Every undergraduate student has a college-provided laptop. All students may access the system. There are no time limits and no fees. It is strongly recommended that all students have a personal computer, specifically an IBM ThinkPad.

Graduates: From July 1, 2002 to June 30, 2003, 439 bachelor's degrees were awarded. In an average class, 81% graduate in 4 years or less, 84% graduate in 5 years or less, and 85% graduate in 6 years or less. 301 companies recruited on campus in 2002-2003. Of the 2002 graduating class, 3% were enrolled in graduate school within 6 months of graduation and 92% were employed.

Admissions Contact: Monica Inzer, Dean of Undergraduate Admission and Financial Services. A video is available.
E-mail: *ugradadmission@babson.edu* Web: *www.babson.edu*

BAY PATH COLLEGE
Longmeadow, MA 01106

(413) 565-1331
(800) 782-7284; Fax: (413) 565-1105

Full-time: 1016 women	Faculty: n/av
Part-time: 226 women	Ph.D.s: 54%
Graduate: 18 men, 54 women	Student/Faculty: n/av
Year: semesters	Tuition: $16,890
Application Deadline: open	Room & Board: $8020
Freshman Class: 476 applied, 389 accepted, 156 enrolled	
SAT I Verbal/Math: 510/490	COMPETITIVE

Bay Path College, founded in 1897, is a private liberal arts institution offering innovative undergraduate programs for women only and graduate programs for men and women. In addition to regional accreditation, Bay Path has baccalaureate program accreditation with AOTA. The library contains 47,933 volumes, 4225 microform items, and 3121 audio/video tapes/CDs, and subscribes to 151 periodicals. Computerized library services include the card catalog, interlibrary loans, and database searching. Special learning facilities include a learning resource center. The 48-acre campus is in a suburban area 3 miles south of Springfield. Including any residence halls, there are 17 buildings.

Student Life: 59% of undergraduates are from Massachusetts. Students are from 15 states and 10 foreign countries. 93% are from public schools. 79% are white; 11% African American. The average age of freshmen is 18; all undergraduates, 35. 30% do not continue beyond their first year; 50% remain to graduate.

Housing: 376 students can be accommodated in college housing, which includes single-sex dorms. On-campus housing is guaranteed for all 4 years. 65% of students commute. Alcohol is not permitted. All students may keep cars.

Activities: There are no sororities. There are 35 groups on campus, including cheerleading, chorale, computers, dance, ethnic, honors, international, literary magazine, musical theater, newspaper, professional, radio and TV, religious, social, social service, student government, and yearbook. Popular campus events include Fall and Spring Campus Days and Six Flags New England Day.

Sports: Facilities include a fitness center that houses a weight training room, a dance studio, and an aerobics room and a nearby 12-acre playing field with soccer and softball fields, a walking/jogging track, and a field house.

Disabled Students: 50% of the campus is accessible. Wheelchair ramps, elevators, special parking, and specially equipped rest rooms are available.

Services: Counseling and information services are available, as is tutoring in every subject.

Campus Safety and Security: Measures include 24-hour foot and vehicle patrol, self-defense education, security escort services, and informal discussions. There are pamphlets/posters/films, emergency telephones, lighted pathways/sidewalks, and fire, vehicle, and driving safety education programs.

Programs of Study: Bay Path confers B.A. and B.S. degrees. Associate and master's degrees are also awarded. Bachelor's degrees are awarded in BIOLOGICAL SCIENCE (biology/biological science), BUSINESS (business administration and management, international business management, management information systems, and marketing/retailing/merchandising), COMMUNICATIONS AND THE ARTS (communications and graphic design), COMPUTER AND PHYSICAL SCIENCE (information sciences and systems), EDUCATION (early childhood and elementary), ENGINEERING AND ENVIRONMENTAL DESIGN (interior design), HEALTH PROFESSIONS (occupational therapy), SOCIAL SCIENCE (child psychology/development, criminal justice, forensic studies, law, liberal arts/general studies, and psychology).

Required: To graduate, students must complete at least 120 credits with a minimum GPA of 2.0. The 46-hour core curriculum includes course work in communication, science, social science, math, and fine and performing arts.

Special: Cross-registration is possible with other member schools of the Cooperating Colleges of Greater Springfield Consortium. Bay Path's capital of the world program allows students to visit a different world center during each spring break.

Faculty/Classroom: 44% of faculty are male; 56%, female. All teach undergraduates. No introductory courses are taught by graduate students.

Admissions: 82% of the 2003-2004 applicants were accepted. The SAT I scores for the 2003-2004 freshman class were: Verbal--43% below 500, 46% between 500 and 599, and 11% between 600 and 700; Math--55% below 500, 38% between 500 and 599, and 8% between 600 and 700.

Requirements: The SAT I or ACT is required. In addition, applicants should have completed at least 4 academic courses each year, including 4 years of English, 3 of math, at least 2 each of social studies and lab sciences, and 2 of a foreign language. An essay is required, as are letters of recommendation from a guidance counselor and a teacher. An interview is strongly recommended. A GPA of 2.0 is required. AP and CLEP credits are accepted.

Procedure: Freshmen are admitted fall and spring. Entrance exams should be taken in the spring of the junior year or by December of the senior year. There are early admissions and deferred admissions plans. Application deadlines are open. Application fee is $25. Notification is sent on a rolling basis. Applications are accepted on-line.

Transfer: 34 transfer students enrolled in 2002-2003. Applicants must be in good standing at their previous school and are encouraged to arrange for an interview at Bay Path. Students who have earned fewer than 12 credits must submit SAT I or ACT scores. 30 of 120 credits required for the bachelor's degree must be completed at Bay Path.

Visiting: There are regularly scheduled orientations for prospective students. There are guides for informal visits and visitors may sit in on classes. To schedule a visit, contact Brenda Wishart, Director of Admissions.

Financial Aid: In 2003-2004, 93% of all full-time freshmen and 94% of continuing full-time students received some form of financial aid. The average freshman award was $12,570. Need-based scholarships or need-based grants averaged $8591 ($12,125 maximum); need-based self-help aid (loans and jobs) averaged $4320 ($7625 maximum); and other non-need-based awards and non-need-based scholarships averaged $11,498 ($13,550 maximum). 39% of undergraduates work part time. Average annual earnings from campus work are $1285. The average financial indebtedness of the 2003 graduate was $18,250. The FAFSA, the college's own financial statement, and parent and student income tax forms are required. The priority date for freshman financial aid applications for fall entry is May 1.

International Students: There are 23 international students enrolled. The school actively recruits these students. They must score 500 on the written TOEFL and also take the SAT I, scoring 800.

Computers: The mainframe is an IBM AS/400. There are 200 PCs distributed throughout the campus. All provide Internet and e-mail access. All students may access the system. There are no time limits and no fees.

Graduates: From July 1, 2002 to June 30, 2003, 180 bachelor's degrees were awarded. The most popular majors were business (32%), liberal studies (20%), and psychology (5%). In an average class, 40% graduate in 4 years or less, 44% graduate in 5 years or less, and 45% graduate in 6 years or less.

Admissions Contact: Brenda Wishart, Director of Admissions.
E-mail: *admiss@baypath.edu* Web: *www.baypath.edu*

BECKER COLLEGE C-2
Worcester, MA 01615-0071
(508) 791-9241, ext. 245
(877) 523-2537; Fax: (508) 890-1500

Full-time: 185 men, 623 women	**Faculty:** 40
Part-time: 120 men, 546 women	**Ph.D.s:** 33%
Graduate: none	**Student/Faculty:** 19 to 1
Year: semesters, summer session	**Tuition:** $16,010
Application Deadline: open	**Room & Board:** $7700
Freshman Class: 1503 applied, 1163 accepted, 442 enrolled	
SAT I Verbal/Math: 443/433	**LESS COMPETITIVE**

Becker College, founded in 1887, is an independent undergraduate liberal arts and sciences institution offering baccalaureate degrees in various programs. In addition to regional accreditation, Becker College has baccalaureate program accreditation with NLN. The 2 libraries contain 75,000 volumes, and subscribe to 253 periodicals. Computerized library services include the card catalog, interlibrary loans, database searching, and Internet access. Special learning facilities include a learning resource center, a day care center, a veterinary clinic, and a preschool facility. The Worcester campus is in an urban area 40 miles west of Boston. The Leicester campus is in a small town 45 miles west of Boston. Including any residence halls, there are 27 buildings.

Student Life: 68% of undergraduates are from Massachusetts. Students are from 18 states and 6 foreign countries. 52% are white. The average age of all undergraduates is 22. 36% do not continue beyond their first year; 30% remain to graduate.

Housing: 200 students can be accommodated in college housing, which includes single-sex and coed dorms. In addition, there is 21 and

over housing. On-campus housing is guaranteed for all 4 years. 60% of students commute. All students may keep cars.

Activities: There are no fraternities or sororities. There are 22 groups on campus, including animal club, art, chorus, dance, drama, ethnic, gay, honors, international, newspaper, outdoors, photography, professional, social, social service, student government, and yearbook. Popular campus events include Family Day, Class Day, and Spree Day.

Sports: There are 6 intercollegiate sports for men and 8 for women, and 5 intramural sports for men and 5 for women. Facilities include a gym, on-campus field hockey and soccer fields, and tennis courts.

Disabled Students: 80% of the campus is accessible. Wheelchair ramps, elevators, special parking, specially equipped rest rooms, lowered drinking fountains, lowered telephones, and special housing are available. All classes are accessible.

Services: Counseling and information services are available, as is tutoring in most subjects. There is remedial math and writing. There is also an academic support center for students.

Campus Safety and Security: Measures include 24-hour foot and vehicle patrol, self-defense education, security escort services, and shuttle buses. There are informal discussions, pamphlets/posters/films, emergency telephones, and lighted pathways/sidewalks.

Programs of Study: Becker College confers B.A. and B.S. degrees. Associate degrees are also awarded. Bachelor's degrees are awarded in BUSINESS (accounting, banking and finance, business administration and management, hospitality management services, human resources, marketing and distribution, and sports management), COMMUNICATIONS AND THE ARTS (communications, design, and graphic design), EDUCATION (early childhood and elementary), ENGINEERING AND ENVIRONMENTAL DESIGN (interior design), HEALTH PROFESSIONS (exercise science, health, and veterinary science), SOCIAL SCIENCE (criminal justice, human development, law, and psychology). Nursing and veterinary science are the strongest academically. Business administration is the largest.

Required: To graduate, baccalaureate students must complete 122 semester hours and maintain a 2.0 minimum GPA. Distribution requirements vary with the program of study.

Special: Cross-registration is offered through the Worcester Consortium of Higher Education. There are co-op programs, internships, study abroad, student-designed majors, work-study programs, and B.A.-B.S. degrees. There is 1 national honor society and a freshman honors program.

Faculty/Classroom: 31% of faculty are male; 69%, female. All teach undergraduates. The average class size in an introductory lecture is 20; in a laboratory, 15; and in a regular course, 25.

Admissions: 77% of the 2003-2004 applicants were accepted. The SAT I scores for the 2003-2004 freshman class were: Verbal--76% below 500, 22% between 500 and 599, and 2% between 600 and 700; Math--81% below 500, 18% between 500 and 599, and 1% between 600 and 700. The ACT scores were 86% below 21, and 14% between 24 and 26.

Requirements: The SAT I is required and the ACT is recommended. In addition, a high school transcript is required. A GPA of 2.0 is required. AP and CLEP credits are accepted.

Procedure: Freshmen are admitted to all sessions. Entrance exams should be taken before submitting the application. Application deadlines are open. The fall 2003 application fee was $30. Notification is sent on a rolling basis. Applications are accepted on-line through Common App and the school's web site.

Transfer: 150 transfer students enrolled in 2002-2003. Requirements for transfer students depend on the program. 62 of 122 credits required for the bachelor's degree must be completed at Becker College.

Visiting: There are regularly scheduled orientations for prospective students, consisting of 2 open houses each year and group tours. There are guides for informal visits and visitors may sit in on classes. To schedule a visit, contact the Admissions Receptionist at *admissions@beckercollege.edu*.

Financial Aid: In 2003-2004, 82% of all full-time freshmen and 80% of continuing full-time students received some form of financial aid. 78% of full-time freshmen and 76% of continuing full-time students received need-based aid. The average freshman award was $6054. Need-based scholarships or need-based grants averaged $2868 ($4500 maximum); need-based self-help aid (loans and jobs) averaged $5381 ($10,500 maximum); and private loans and private alternative loans averaged $12,381. 40% of undergraduates work part time. Average annual earnings from campus work are $1000. The average financial indebtedness of the 2003 graduate was $17,125. The FAFSA is required. The priority date for freshman financial aid applications for fall entry is March 1.

International Students: There are 6 international students enrolled. The school actively recruits these students. They must score 500 on the written TOEFL or 173 on the electronic version. The ELPT is also accepted. The SAT I or the ACT is also required.

Computers: Any vacant computer is available for student use. Internet access is available in libraries. All residence halls are wired for Internet access. All students may access the system. There are no time limits and no fees.

Graduates: From July 1, 2002 to June 30, 2003, 101 bachelor's degrees were awarded. The most popular major was business administration (31%). In an average class, 40% graduate in 3 years or less, 8% graduate in 4 years or less, 3% graduate in 5 years or less, and 1% graduate in 6 years or less. 45 companies recruited on campus in 2002-2003. Of the 2002 graduating class, 43% were enrolled in graduate school within 6 months of graduation and 67% were employed.

Admissions Contact: Karen Schedin, Director of Recruitment and Admissions. E-mail: *admissions@beckercollege.edu*
Web: *www.beckercollege.edu*

BENJAMIN FRANKLIN INSTITUTE OF TECHNOLOGY   E-2
Boston, MA 02116   (617) 423-4630; Fax: (617) 482-3706

Full-time: 388 men and women	**Faculty:** 32
Part-time: none	**Ph.D.s:** 3%
Graduate: none	**Student/Faculty:** 12 to 1
Year: semesters, summer session	**Tuition:** $12,839
Application Deadline: August 15	**Room & Board:** $9000
Freshman Class: n/av	
SAT I or ACT: recommended	**SPECIAL**

Benjamin Franklin Institute of Technology, founded in 1908, is a private technical college offering degree programs in industrial and engineering technologies. Some information in this capsule and profile is approximate. In addition to regional accreditation, BFIT has baccalaureate program accreditation with ABET. The library contains 10,000 volumes, and subscribes to 70 periodicals. Computerized library services include the card catalog, interlibrary loans, database searching, and Internet access. Special learning facilities include a learning resource center. The 3-acre campus is in an urban area. Including any residence halls, there are 3 buildings.

Student Life: 95% of undergraduates are from Massachusetts. Students are from 7 states and 7 foreign countries. 35% are African American; 35% white; 14% Hispanic; 12% Asian American. The average age of freshmen is 22; all undergraduates, 22.

Housing: 20 students can be accommodated in college housing, which includes single-sex dorms. On-campus housing is available on a first-come, first-served basis. Priority is given to out-of-town students. Almost all students commute. Alcohol is not permitted. No one may keep cars.

Activities: There are no fraternities or sororities. There are 2 groups on campus, including student government and women's. Popular campus events include Technology Olympics and International Culture Day.

Sports: There are 2 intercollegiate sports for men, and 2 intramural sports for men.

Disabled Students: 50% of the campus is accessible. Elevators and specially equipped rest rooms are available.

Services: Counseling and information services are available, as is tutoring in every subject. There is remedial math, reading, and writing.

Programs of Study: BFIT confers the B.S. degree. Associate degrees are also awarded. Bachelor's degrees are awarded in ENGINEERING AND ENVIRONMENTAL DESIGN (automotive technology). Mechanical and electrical engineering technology are the strongest academically. Automotive and computers are the largest.

Required: To graduate, students must earn a minimum cumulative GPA of 2.0. 2 college English courses are required.

Special: If qualified, 2-year BFIT graduates may transfer to Northeastern University. Automotive technology management students have access to Northeastern's facilities and resources.

Faculty/Classroom: 74% of faculty are male; 26%, female. All teach undergraduates. The average class size in an introductory lecture is 30; in a laboratory, 12; and in a regular course, 25.

Requirements: The SAT I or ACT is recommended. In addition, applicants should be high school graduates or have the GED. A GPA of 2.0 is required.

Procedure: Freshmen are admitted fall and spring. Applications should be filed by August 15 for fall entry and January 1 for spring entry, along with a $25 fee. Notification is sent on a rolling basis.

Visiting: Visitors may sit in on classes. To schedule a visit, contact the Office of Admission at (617) 423-4630, ext. 121.

Financial Aid: In 2003-2004, 94% of all full-time freshmen and 90% of continuing full-time students received some form of financial aid. BFIT is a member of CSS. The FAFSA and federal tax returns are required. The priority date for freshman financial aid applications for fall entry is April 15.

International Students: They must score 500 on the written TOEFL or 173 on the electronic version and also take the college's own test. Applicants may satisfactorily complete Franklin's or another recognized ESL program and also take the college's own entrance exam.

Computers: There are more than 130 networked computers in labs, the library, and electronic classrooms. All have access to the Internet via a T-1 line. All students may access the system. There are no time limits and no fees. It is strongly recommended that all students have a personal computer.

Graduates: 34 companies recruited on campus in a recent year. Of the 2002 graduating class, 98% were employed within 6 months of graduation.

Admissions Contact: Will Arvelo, Dean of Enrollment Services. E-mail: *warvelo@bfit.edu* Web: *www.bfit.edu*

BENTLEY COLLEGE   D-2
Waltham, MA 02452-4705   (781) 891-2244
(800) 523-2354; Fax: (781) 891-3414

Full-time: 2268 men, 1624 women	**Faculty:** 250; IIA, ++$
Part-time: 218 men, 194 women	**Ph.D.s:** 83%
Graduate: 755 men, 574 women	**Student/Faculty:** 16 to 1
Year: semesters, summer session	**Tuition:** $24,324
Application Deadline: February 1	**Room & Board:** $9580
Freshman Class: 5474 applied, 2529 accepted, 941 enrolled	
SAT I Verbal/Math: 560/600	**VERY COMPETITIVE**

Bentley College is a private institution that offers advanced business education along with a strong foundation in the arts and sciences. In addition to regional accreditation, Bentley has baccalaureate program accreditation with AACSB. The library contains 212,573 volumes, 1320 microform items, and 4705 audio/video tapes/CDs, and subscribes to 650 periodicals. Computerized library services include the card catalog, interlibrary loans, database searching, and Internet access. Special learning facilities include a learning resource center, art gallery, planetarium, radio station, the Accounting Center for Electronic Learning and Business Management, the Center for Languages and International Collaboration, the Center for Marketing Technology, the Design and Usability Testing Center, an academic technology center, and a trading room. The 163-acre campus is in a suburban area 10 miles west of Boston. Including any residence halls, there are 43 buildings.

Student Life: 53% of undergraduates are from Massachusetts. Others are from 41 states, 70 foreign countries, and Canada. 75% are from public schools. 71% are white. The average age of freshmen is 18; all undergraduates, 21. 7% do not continue beyond their first year; 77% remain to graduate.

Housing: 3187 students can be accommodated in college housing, which includes single-sex and coed dormitories, on-campus apartments, and off-campus apartments. In addition, there are special-interest houses and substance-free, intensive study, and smoke-free housing. On-campus housing is guaranteed for all 4 years. 80% of students live on campus. Upperclassmen may keep cars.

Activities: 12% of men belong to 4 local and 2 national fraternities; 12% of women belong to 5 national sororities. There are 90 groups on campus, including alcohol awareness, art, band, cheerleading, choir, chorale, computers, dance, debate, drama, ethnic, film, forensics, gay, honors, international, jazz band, literary magazine, musical theater, newspaper, pep band, photography, political, professional, radio and TV, religious, social, social service, student government, and yearbook. Popular campus events include Monte Carlo Night, a film series, and Spring Weekend.

Sports: There are 11 intercollegiate sports for men and 10 for women, and 8 intramural sports for men and 8 for women. Facilities include a basketball court; a competition-size swimming pool with a diving tank; saunas and a steam bath; volleyball courts; baseball batting and golf cages; racquetball/handball courts; an indoor track; a dance studio; a 7000-square-foot exercise room with fitness equipment that includes treadmills, stationary bikes, StairMaster and Nautilis equipment, and free weights; 2 lighted playing fields, one natural grass and one synthetic, for football, soccer, lacrosse and other sports; 6 lighted tennis courts; a baseball field with seating for 1700; and an outdoor track.

Disabled Students: 95% of the campus is accessible. Wheelchair ramps, elevators, special parking, specially equipped rest rooms, and lowered telephones are available.

Services: Counseling and information services are available, as is tutoring in most subjects. There is remedial math, reading, and writing. A Kurzweil reading machine is available.

Campus Safety and Security: Measures include 24-hour foot and vehicle patrol, self-defense education, security escort services, and shuttle buses. There are informal discussions, pamphlets/posters/films, emergency telephones, and lighted pathways/sidewalks.

Programs of Study: Bentley confers B.A. and B.S. degrees. Associate and master's degrees are also awarded. Bachelor's degrees are awarded in BUSINESS (accounting, banking and finance, business administration and management, business economics, management information systems, and marketing management), COMMUNICATIONS AND THE ARTS (communications and English), COMPUTER AND PHYSICAL SCIENCE (mathematics), SOCIAL SCIENCE (history, interdisciplinary studies, international studies, liberal arts/general studies, paralegal studies, philosophy, and public affairs). Accountancy and finance are the strongest academically. Management and finance are the largest.

Required: All undergraduate students complete general education courses in areas such as expository writing, mathematical sciences, natural sciences, humanities, behavioral sciences, information technology, political science, history, philosophy, and economics. Students in B.S. programs take a common core of 10 courses covering major business areas such as accounting, business law, and marketing. All students take elective courses that fulfill a diversity, international, and communication-intensive requirement. A total of 120 to 122 credit hours is required for graduation, with a minimum GPA of 2.0. All students must take phys ed, and first-year students complete a first-year seminar course.

Special: There is cross-registration with Regis College and Brandeis University, and internships are available in business and public service. The college offers study abroad in 11 countries, a Washington semester, work-study programs, accelerated degree programs, student-designed majors, credit by exam, and nondegree study. There is also a minor concentration program through which business majors can broaden their exposure to the arts and sciences, and arts and science majors can minor in business or interdisciplinary topics. There is 1 national honor society, a freshman honors program, and 17 departmental honors programs.

Faculty/Classroom: 63% of faculty are male; 37%, female. All teach undergraduates. No introductory courses are taught by graduate students. The average class size in a regular course is 30.

Admissions: 46% of the 2003-2004 applicants were accepted. The SAT I scores for the 2003-2004 freshman class were: Verbal--13% below 500, 52% between 500 and 599, 34% between 600 and 700, and 1% above 700; Math--3% below 500, 35% between 500 and 599, 54% between 600 and 700, and 9% above 700. 61% of the current freshmen were in the top fifth of their class; 91% were in the top two fifths. 19 freshmen graduated first in their class.

Requirements: The SAT I or ACT is required. In addition, applicants must be graduates of an accredited high school or have a GED. Recommended high school preparation is 4 units each in English and math, including algebra I and II, geometry, and a senior-year math course; 3 units in lab science; 2 to 3 units in a foreign language; 2 units in social science; and 2 additional units in English, math, social science or lab science, foreign language, or speech. AP and CLEP credits are accepted. Important factors in the admissions decision are advanced placement or honor courses and recommendations by school officials.

Procedure: Freshmen are admitted fall and spring. Entrance exams should be taken before the January test date. There are early decision, early admissions, and deferred admissions plans. Early decision applications should be filed by December 1; regular applications, by February 1 for fall entry and November 15 for spring entry, along with a $50 fee. Notification of early decision is sent December 28; regular decision, April 1. 124 early decision candidates were accepted for the 2003-2004 class. 952 applications were on the 2003 waiting list; 60 were admitted. Applications are accepted on computer disk and on-line through CollegeNET, Common App, MassMentor, NextStop College, and College Quest.

Transfer: 154 transfer students enrolled in 2003-2004. The SAT I or the ACT is required of all applicants who have completed fewer than 30 college credits. All official college transcripts must be submitted. 45 of 120 credits required for the bachelor's degree must be completed at Bentley.

Visiting: There are regularly scheduled orientations for prospective students, including fall, spring, and summer open house programs. Interviews are arranged by appointment; campus tours take place at regularly scheduled times each weekday. There are fall Fridays information sessions. There are guides for informal visits and visitors may sit in on classes. To schedule a visit, contact the Office of Undergraduate Admission at (781) 891-2455.

Financial Aid: In 2003-2004, 72% of all full-time freshmen and 79% of continuing full-time students received some form of financial aid. 62% of full-time freshmen and 73% of continuing full-time students received need-based aid. The average freshman award was $22,260. 26% of undergraduates work part time. Average annual earnings from campus work are $1330. The average financial indebtedness of the 2003 graduate was $19,560. Bentley is a member of CSS. The CSS/Profile or FAFSA is required. The deadline for filing freshman financial aid applications for fall entry is February 1.

International Students: There are 353 international students enrolled. The school actively recruits these students. They must score 551 on the written TOEFL and also take the SAT I or the ACT.

Computers: The mainframes are a DEC VAX 6620 and a DEC VAX 6510. With one "port-per-pillow" in residence halls, students have individual access from their dorm room to the campus computing system and the Internet. A growing number of Bentley classrooms feature port-per-seat network connections as well. The college also provides more than 100 PCs and Macs in centralized labs. All have network access. All students may access the system during lab hours, 7 days a week. There are no time limits and no fees. All undergraduate students are required to have laptop computers. The IBM ThinkPad T40 is recommended.

Graduates: From July 1, 2002 to June 30, 2003, 985 bachelor's degrees were awarded. The most popular majors were finance (20%), accountancy (18%), and marketing (18%). In an average class, 71% graduate in 4 years or less, 76% graduate in 5 years or less, and 77% graduate in 6 years or less. 250 companies recruited on campus in 2002-2003. Of the 2002 graduating class, 16% were enrolled in graduate school within 6 months of graduation and 81% were employed.

Admissions Contact: Office of Undergraduate Admissions.
E-mail: *ugadmission@bentley.edu* Web: *www.bentley.edu*

BERKLEE COLLEGE OF MUSIC   E-2
Boston, MA 02215-3693   (617) 266-1400, ext. 2222
(800) BERKLEE; Fax: (617) 747-2047

Full-time: 2880 men, 919 women	**Faculty:** 193; IIB, +$
Part-time: none	**Ph.D.s:** n/av
Graduate: none	**Student/Faculty:** 20 to 1
Year: semesters, summer session	**Tuition:** $22,167
Application Deadline: open	**Room & Board:** $10,280
Freshman Class: 2954 applied, 1811 accepted, 916 enrolled	
SAT I or ACT: required	**SPECIAL**

Berklee College of Music, founded in 1945, is a private institution offering programs in music production and engineering, film scoring, music business/management, composition, music synthesis, music education, music therapy, performance, contemporary writing and production, jazz composition, songwriting, and professional music. The library contains 31,274 volumes and 22,974 audio/video tapes/CDs, and subscribes to 122 periodicals. Computerized library services include the card catalog, database searching, and Internet access. Special learning facilities include a learning resource center, 12 recording studios, 5 performance venues, and film scoring, music synthesis, and songwriting labs. The campus is in an urban area in the Fenway Cultural District, Back Bay, Boston. Including any residence halls, there are 16 buildings.

Student Life: 82% of undergraduates are from out of state, mostly the Northeast. Students are from 50 states, 73 foreign countries, and Canada. 73% are white; 25% foreign nationals. The average age of all undergraduates is 22. 20% do not continue beyond their first year; 60% remain to graduate.

Housing: 840 students can be accommodated in college housing, which includes coed dorms. On-campus housing is available on a first-come, first-served basis and is available on a lottery system for upperclassmen. 88% of students commute. Alcohol is not permitted. No one may keep cars.

Activities: There are no fraternities or sororities. There are 62 groups on campus, including art, band, choir, chorale, chorus, computers, ethnic, gay, international, jazz band, musical theater, newspaper, orchestra, professional, religious, social, social service, and student government. Popular campus events include International Night, daily recitals and concerts, and Singer Showcase.

Sports: There are 4 intramural sports for men and 4 for women. Discount memberships at the YMCA, a student rate at the Massachusetts College of Art fitness room, and membership at the Sheraton Fitness Center and the Tennis and Racquet Club of Boston are available.

Disabled Students: All of the campus is accessible. Wheelchair ramps, elevators, special class scheduling, lowered drinking fountains, and lowered telephones are available.

Services: Counseling and information services are available, as is tutoring in every subject. There is a reader service for the blind, tape recorders, untimed testing, and learning center resources.

Campus Safety and Security: Measures include 24-hour foot and vehicle patrol, security escort services, informal discussions, and pamphlets/posters/films. There are emergency telephones and lighted pathways/sidewalks.

Programs of Study: Berklee confers the B.M. degree. Master's degrees are also awarded. Bachelor's degrees are awarded in COMMUNICATIONS AND THE ARTS (audio technology, jazz, music, music business management, music performance, and music theory and composition), EDUCATION (music), HEALTH PROFESSIONS (music therapy). Performance, professional music, and music production and engineering are the largest.

Required: Students working toward a degree must take general education courses in English composition/literature, history, physical science, and social sciences. Music course programs vary by specialization. A total of 120 credits must be completed with a minimum GPA of 2.0.

Special: Berklee offers cross-registration with the Pro-Arts Consortium, study abroad in the Netherlands, internships in music education and music production and engineering, 5-year dual majors, and a 4-year professional (nondegree) diploma program. Work-study programs, an accelerated degree program, student-designed majors, and credit by exam are available.

Faculty/Classroom: 82% of faculty are male; 18%, female. All teach undergraduates. The average class size in an introductory lecture is 30; in a laboratory, 8; and in a regular course, 14.

Admissions: 61% of the 2003-2004 applicants were accepted.

Requirements: The SAT I or ACT is required. In addition, applicants must be graduates of an accredited secondary school that has a college preparatory program or have their GED. An audition and interview are recommended. Applicants must also submit a detailed reference letter regarding their training and experience in music, a letter from a private instructor, school music director, or professional musician. A GPA of 2.0 is required. AP credits are accepted. Important factors in the admissions decision are evidence of special talent, extracurricular activities record, and recommendations by alumni.

Procedure: Freshmen are admitted to all sessions. Entrance exams should be taken in the fall of the senior year of high school. There are early admissions and deferred admissions plans. Application deadlines are open. Application fee is $75. Notification is sent on a rolling basis. A waiting list is an active part of the admissions procedure. Applications are accepted on-line through *www.Embark.com*.

Transfer: 268 transfer students enrolled in a recent year. Applicants must go through the same application procedures as entering freshmen, as well as submit all previous college records. 60 of 120 credits required for the bachelor's degree must be completed at Berklee.

Visiting: There are regularly scheduled orientations for prospective students, consisting of 2 tours scheduled daily during semesters, with the morning tour followed by an information session given by an admissions counselor. There are guides for informal visits. To schedule a visit, contact the Admissions Office.

Financial Aid: The CSS/Profile or FFS and the college's own financial statement are required. The priority date for freshman financial aid applications for fall entry is February 14.

International Students: There are 955 international students enrolled. The school actively recruits these students. They must take the college's own test and also take the SAT I or the ACT.

Computers: There are more than 50 networked Macs in the learning center. Entering students also purchase laptops with all appropriate software and Internet access. All students may access the system. There are no time limits and no fees. It is strongly recommended that all students have a personal computer.

Graduates: From July 1, 2002 to June 30, 2003, 650 bachelor's degrees were awarded.

Admissions Contact: Damien Bracken, Director of Admissions. A video is available. E-mail: *admissions@berklee.edu*
Web: *www.berklee.edu*

BOSTON ARCHITECTURAL CENTER

E-2
Boston, MA 02115 — (617) 262-5000; Fax: (617) 585-0121

Full-time: 310 men, 115 women	**Faculty:** n/av
Part-time: 60 men, 15 women	**Ph.Ds:** 80%
Graduate: 110 men, 80 women	**Student/Faculty:** n/av
Year: semesters, summer session	**Tuition:** $10,464
Application Deadline: open	**Room & Board:** n/app
Freshman Class: n/av	
SAT I or ACT: not required	**SPECIAL**

Boston Architectural Center, founded in 1889 as the Boston Architectural Club, is an independent, commuter institution offering professional programs in architecture and interior design. Students work in architectural and interior design offices during the day and attend classes at night. Some figures in the above capsule and in this profile are approximate. There are 2 undergraduate and 2 graduate schools. In addition to regional accreditation, BAC has baccalaureate program accreditation with NAAB. The library contains 25,000 volumes, and subscribes to 140 periodicals. Computerized library services include the card catalog and database searching. Special learning facilities include an art gallery. The campus is in an urban area in Boston. There are 2 buildings.

Student Life: 53% of undergraduates are from Massachusetts. Students are from 43 states and 1 foreign country. 88% are white. The average age of freshmen is 26; all undergraduates, 26. 47% do not continue beyond their first year; 25% remain to graduate.

Housing: There are no residence halls. All students commute. Alcohol is not permitted.

Activities: There are no fraternities or sororities. There are 4 groups on campus, including newspaper, professional, student government, and yearbook.

Sports: There is no sports program at BAC.

Disabled Students: All of the campus is accessible. Wheelchair ramps, elevators, special parking, and specially equipped rest rooms are available.

Services: Counseling and information services are available, as is tutoring in most subjects. The writing center provides one-on-one writing assistance and special services for ESL students.

Campus Safety and Security: Measures include pamphlets/posters/films, lighted pathways/sidewalks, and full-time building security during operating hours.

Programs of Study: BAC confers B.Arch. and B.Int.Design. degrees. Master's degrees are also awarded. Bachelor's degrees are awarded in ENGINEERING AND ENVIRONMENTAL DESIGN (architecture and interior design).

Required: To graduate, all students must complete 123 academic credits, 93 of which must be in professional subjects and 30 in general education courses; 21 credits must be earned in liberal arts courses. Students must earn 54 additional credits by working in architectural or interior-design offices or related fields. Academic study is divided into 3 seg-

ments, the final segment being the thesis year, which consists of 2 semesters of student-designed study under the guidance of a faculty adviser. A minimum 2.5 GPA is required.

Special: BAC offers study abroad and cross-registration with schools in the Professional Arts Consortium in Boston and with the Art Institute of Boston for studio and professional courses. The participating schools are BAC, Berklee College of Music, Boston Conservatory, Emerson College, Massachusetts College of Art, and School of the MFA.

Faculty/Classroom: 86% of faculty are male; 14%, female. All teach undergraduates. The average class size in an introductory lecture is 33 and in a laboratory, 8.

Requirements: All applicants who have graduated from high school or have a college degree are admitted on a first-come, first-served basis. Official transcripts from previously attended secondary schools and colleges must be submitted to determine qualification for admission and advanced placement. AP credits are accepted.

Procedure: Freshmen are admitted fall and spring. There is a deferred admissions plan. Application deadlines are open. The fall 2003 application fee was $50. Notification is sent on a rolling basis.

Transfer: Applicants for transfer must have a 2.0 GPA to receive transfer credit in most courses; 3.0 in math and physics. 47 of 123 credits required for the bachelor's degree must be completed at BAC.

Visiting: There are regularly scheduled orientations for prospective students, consisting of monthly presentations. There are guides for informal visits and visitors may sit in on classes. To schedule a visit, contact the Admissions Office at (617) 585-0123.

Financial Aid: BAC is a member of CSS. The FAFSA and the college's own financial statement are required. Check with the school for current deadlines.

International Students: They must score 550 on the written TOEFL.

Computers: There are 50 Macs and IBM PCs available for student use, all with Internet access. All students may access the system. There are no time limits.

Admissions Contact: Director of Admissions.
E-mail: *admissions@the-bac.edu* Web: *www.the-bac.edu*

BOSTON COLLEGE

E-2
Chestnut Hill, MA 02467 — (617) 552-3100
(800) 360-2522; Fax: (617) 552-0798

Full-time: 4450 men, 4450 women	**Faculty:** 645; I, ++$
Part-time: none	**Ph.Ds:** 98%
Graduate: 2350 men, 2350 women	**Student/Faculty:** 14 to 1
Year: semesters, summer session	**Tuition:** $27,847
Application Deadline: January 2	**Room & Board:** $9300
Freshman Class: n/av	
SAT I or ACT: required	**MOST COMPETITIVE**

Boston College, founded in 1863, is an independent institution affiliated with the Roman Catholic Church and the Jesuit Order. It offers undergraduate programs in the arts and sciences, business, nursing, and education, and graduate and professional programs. Some information in this profile is approximate. There are 4 undergraduate and 7 graduate schools. In addition to regional accreditation, BC has baccalaureate program accreditation with AACSB, CSWE, NCATE, and NLN. The 6 libraries contain 1,737,880 volumes, 3,249,601 microform items, and 118,054 audio/video tapes/CDs, and subscribe to 20,910 periodicals. Computerized library services include the card catalog, interlibrary loans, and database searching. Special learning facilities include a learning resource center, art gallery, radio station, and TV station. The 240-acre campus is in a suburban area 6 miles west of Boston. Including any residence halls, there are 90 buildings.

Student Life: 73% of undergraduates are from out of state, mostly the Northeast. Students are from 50 states, 99 foreign countries, and Canada. 61% are from public schools. 75% are white. 76% are Catholic; 11% claim no religious affiliation; 11% Protestant. The average age of freshmen is 19; all undergraduates, 20. 6% do not continue beyond their first year; 85% remain to graduate.

Housing: 6475 students can be accommodated in college housing, which includes single-sex and coed dorms and on-campus apartments. In addition, there are honors houses, language houses, special-interest houses, community and multicultural housing, quiet residences, single-sex freshman halls, perspectives academic program housing, and a substance-free floor. On-campus housing is guaranteed for the freshman year only and is available on a lottery system for upperclassmen. 74% of students live on campus; of those, 75% remain on campus on weekends. Upperclassmen may keep cars.

Activities: There are no fraternities or sororities. There are 100 groups on campus, including art, band, cheerleading, chess, choir, chorale, chorus, computers, dance, debate, drama, ethnic, film, honors, international, jazz band, literary magazine, marching band, musical theater, newspaper, orchestra, pep band, photography, political, professional, radio and TV, religious, social, social service, student government, symphony, and yearbook. Popular campus events include Middlemarch Ball, Christmas Chorale, and Senior Week.

Sports: There are 17 intercollegiate sports for men and 16 for women, and 8 intramural sports for men and 7 for women. Facilities include a 44,500-seat stadium, a forum that seats 8500 for basketball and 7600 for ice hockey, a field, a track, and a student recreation complex.

Disabled Students: All of the campus is accessible. Wheelchair ramps, elevators, special parking, specially equipped rest rooms, special class scheduling, lowered drinking fountains, and lowered telephones are available.

Services: Counseling and information services are available, as is tutoring in most subjects. There is a reader service for the blind and an academic development center that serves all students.

Campus Safety and Security: Measures include 24-hour foot and vehicle patrol, self-defense education, security escort services, and shuttle buses. There are informal discussions, pamphlets/posters/films, emergency telephones, lighted pathways/sidewalks, safety seminars and safety walking tours, and whistles distributed to incoming students.

Programs of Study: BC confers B.A. and B.S. degrees. Master's and doctoral degrees are also awarded. Bachelor's degrees are awarded in BIOLOGICAL SCIENCE (biochemistry and biology/biological science), BUSINESS (accounting, banking and finance, business administration and management, business economics, human resources, management science, marketing/retailing/merchandising, and operations research), COMMUNICATIONS AND THE ARTS (art history and appreciation, classics, communications, dramatic arts, English, film arts, French, Italian, linguistics, music, romance languages and literature, and studio art), COMPUTER AND PHYSICAL SCIENCE (chemistry, computer science, geology, geophysics and seismology, information sciences and systems, mathematics, and physics), EDUCATION (early childhood, elementary, secondary, and special), ENGINEERING AND ENVIRONMENTAL DESIGN (environmental science), HEALTH PROFESSIONS (nursing), SOCIAL SCIENCE (classical/ancient civilization, economics, German area studies, Hispanic American studies, history, human development, philosophy, political science/government, psychology, Russian and Slavic studies, sociology, and theological studies). Humanities and social sciences are the strongest academically. English, finance, and psychology are the largest.

Required: Core requirements include 2 courses each in natural science, social science, history, philosophy, and theology, and 1 course each in literature, writing, math, cultural diversity, and the arts. To graduate, students must complete 114 credits (121 in nursing), including at least 30 in the major, with a minimum 1.667 GPA (1.5 in management). Computer science is required for management majors, intermediate-level foreign language proficiency for arts and sciences and management students, and a freshman writing seminar for all students except Honors and AP students.

Special: There are internship programs in arts and sciences. Students may cross-register with Boston, Brandeis, and Tufts Universities, and Hebrew, Pine Manor, Regis Colleges. BC also offers a Washington semester with American University, work-study programs with nonprofit agencies, study abroad, dual and student-designed majors, credit by exam, and pass/fail options. Students may pursue a 3-2 engineering program with Boston University and accelerated programs in business, social work, and education. There are also special programs in social work and philosophy/theology, in language immersion, capstone courses, and in exploring fundamental questions of faith, peace, and justice. There are 12 national honor societies, including Phi Beta Kappa, a freshman honors program, and 8 departmental honors programs.

Faculty/Classroom: 67% of faculty are male; 33%, female. All both teach and do research. Graduate students teach 12% of introductory courses. The average class size in a laboratory is 15 and in a regular course, 30.

Requirements: The SAT I or ACT is required. In addition, students must also take SAT II: Subject tests in writing, math level I or II, and any third test. Applicants must be graduates of an accredited high school completing 4 units each of English, foreign language, and math, and 4 units of science. Those students applying to the School of Nursing must complete at least 2 years of a lab science, including 1 unit of chemistry. Applicants to the School of Management are strongly encouraged to take 4 years of college preparatory math. An essay is required. AP credits are accepted. Important factors in the admissions decision are evidence of special talent, leadership record, and advanced placement or honor courses.

Procedure: Freshmen are admitted fall and spring. Entrance exams should be taken no later than January of the senior year. There are early admissions and deferred admissions plans. Early decision applications should be filed by November 1; regular applications, by January 2 for fall entry and November 1 for spring entry along with a $60 fee. Notification of early decision is sent December 25; regular decision, April 15. A waiting list is an active part of the admissions procedure. Applications are accepted on-line through *www.apply.embark.com/ugrad/bc*, *www.commonapp.org*, and *www.nextstopcollege.*

Transfer: Applicants must have a current GPA of at least 2.5 and must have earned a minimum of 9 semester hours. High school transcripts, letters of recommendation, and SAT I or ACT scores are required. 54

credits of 114 required for the bachelor's degree must be completed at BC.

Visiting: There are regularly scheduled orientations for prospective students, consisting of group information sessions and campus tours Monday through Friday. There are guides for informal visits and visitors may sit in on classes. To schedule a visit, contact the Office of Undergraduate Admission.

Financial Aid: BC is a member of CSS. The CSS Profile, FAFSA, the federal IRS income tax form, W-2s, and a noncustodial parent's statement (when applicable) are required. The deadline for filing freshman financial aid applications for fall entry is February 1.

International Students: International students must score 600 on the written TOEFL or 250 on the electronic version and also take the SAT I or the ACT. Students must take SAT II: Subject tests in writing, math level I or II, and any third test.

Computers: The mainframes are an IBM 3270 and DEC VAX 11/785 and 8700 units. More than 200 PCs are available, providing database searches, optical disk references, and on-line access to catalog services. Software includes word processing, programming languages, statistical analysis, graphics production, and database management packages. Printers include high-speed line printers, high-resolution dot-matrix printers, and laser printers. All students may access the system at all times. There are no time limits and no fees.

Admissions Contact: John L. Mahoney Jr., Dir, Undergraduate Admission. A video is available.
E-mail: *undergraduate.admission@bc.edu* Web: *www.bc.edu*

BOSTON CONSERVATORY E-2
Boston, MA 02215 (617) 536-6340; Fax: (617) 536-3176

Total enrollment: n/av	**Faculty:** 17
Year: semesters, summer session	**Ph.D.s:** 1%
Application Deadline: open	**Student/Faculty:** 15 to 1
	Tuition: $20,500
	Room & Board: $7000

Freshman Class: n/av
SAT I or ACT: recommended   SPECIAL

The Boston Conservatory, founded in 1867, is a private college providing degree programs in music, musical theater, and dance. Figures in the above capsule and in this profile are approximate. In addition to regional accreditation, the conservatory has baccalaureate program accreditation with NASM. The library contains 40,000 volumes, and subscribes to 120 periodicals. Computerized library services include interlibrary loans and database searching. The campus is in an urban area in Boston's Back Bay. Including any residence halls, there are 7 buildings.

Student Life: 20% of undergraduates are from Massachusetts. Students are from 36 states, 29 foreign countries, and Canada. 90% are white. The average age of freshmen is 18. 23% do not continue beyond their first year; 44% remain to graduate.

Housing: 164 students can be accommodated in college housing, which includes single-sex and coed dorms. In addition, there are special-interest houses and international housing. On-campus housing is guaranteed for all 4 years. 67% of students commute. Alcohol is not permitted. All students may keep cars.

Activities: There is 1 national fraternity and 2 national sororities. There are 19 groups on campus, including band, choir, chorale, chorus, dance, drama, ethnic, gay, international, musical theater, newspaper, opera, orchestra, political, professional, religious, social service, student government, and yearbook. Popular campus events include Parents Weekend.

Sports: There is no sports program at the conservatory.

Disabled Students: 20% of the campus is accessible. Elevators are available.

Services: Counseling and information services are available, as is tutoring in every subject. A fee is required.

Campus Safety and Security: Measures include 24-hour foot and vehicle patrol, self-defense education, and informal discussions.

Programs of Study: The conservatory confers B.F.A. and B.Mus. degrees. Bachelor's degrees are awarded in COMMUNICATIONS AND THE ARTS (dance, guitar, music, music performance, music theory and composition, musical theater, opera, and piano/organ), EDUCATION (music). Music is the largest.

Required: All students must successfully complete the curriculum with no more than 12 credit hours of D-grade work. In addition, music performance majors must present recitals, music education majors must present a recital from memory, and composition majors must pass an exam on their primary instrument, present a portfolio of original composition, and perform a recital.

Special: There are 3 national honor societies, and 1 departmental honors program.

Faculty/Classroom: All teach undergraduates. No introductory courses are taught by graduate students. The average class size in an introductory lecture is 15; in a laboratory, 5; and in a regular course, 15.

Requirements: The SAT I or ACT is recommended and scores are reviewed. An audition is required. An academic high school diploma or

GED also is required. A GPA of 2.0 is required. AP and CLEP credits are accepted. Important factors in the admissions decision are evidence of special talent, extracurricular activities record, and personality/intangible qualities.

Procedure: Freshmen are admitted in the fall. Entrance exams should be taken as early as possible. There is a deferred admissions plan. Application deadlines are open.

Transfer: A successful audition and a 2.0 GPA are required. Transfer credits are determined by exam or review by the division head and the dean. The high school transcript is required if fewer than 30 college credits have been earned.

Visiting: Visitors may sit in on classes. To schedule a visit, contact the Admissions Office.

Financial Aid: The conservatory is a member of CSS. The CSS Profile and the college's own financial statement are required. Check with the school for current deadlines.

International Students: The school actively recruits these students. They must take the TOEFL or the MELAB or the college's own test, or the SAT I, scoring 950. An audition also is required.

Computers: Macs are available to all students when the library is open. There are no time limits and no fees.

Admissions Contact: Halley Shefler, Director of Enrollment Management.

BOSTON UNIVERSITY
Boston, MA 02215　　　　　　E-2

Full-time: 6492 men, 9756 women	**Faculty:** 1283; I, +$
Part-time: 779 men, 656 women	**Ph.D.s:** 82%
Graduate: 5424 men, 5944 women	**Student/Faculty:** 13 to 1
Year: semesters, summer session	**Tuition:** $28,906
Application Deadline: January 1	**Room & Board:** $9288
Freshman Class: 29,356 applied, 15,191 accepted, 3961 enrolled	
SAT I Verbal/Math: 640/650	**ACT:** 28

(617) 353-2300; Fax: (617) 353-9695

HIGHLY COMPETITIVE+

Boston University, founded in 1839, is a private institution offering undergraduate and graduate programs in basic studies, liberal arts, communication, hotel and food administration, allied health education management, and fine arts. There are 11 undergraduate and 15 graduate schools. In addition to regional accreditation, BU has baccalaureate program accreditation with ABET and NASM. The 23 libraries contain 1,749,000 volumes, 2,701,000 microform items, and 51,214 audio/video tapes/CDs, and subscribe to 21,400 periodicals. Computerized library services include the card catalog, interlibrary loans, and database searching. Special learning facilities include a learning resource center, art gallery, planetarium, radio station, TV station, an astronomy observatory, 20th century archives, a theater and theater company in residence, a scientific computing and visualization lab, the Geddes language lab, a speech, language, and hearing clinic, a hotel/food administration culinary center, a performance center, a multimedia center, a center for photonics research, a center for remote sensing, and the Metcalf Center for Science and Engineering. The 132-acre campus is in an urban area on the Charles River in Boston's Back Bay. Including any residence halls, there are 348 buildings.

Student Life: 78% of undergraduates are from out of state, mostly the Middle Atlantic. Students are from 50 states, 135 foreign countries, and Canada. 72% are from public schools. 60% are white; 13% Asian American. 34% are Catholic; 23% Protestant; 20% claim no religious affiliation; 13% Jewish; 10% Buddhist, Hindu, Islamic, and Eastern Rite Orthodox. The average age of freshmen is 19; all undergraduates, 21. 10% do not continue beyond their first year.

Housing: 10,872 students can be accommodated in college housing, which includes single-sex and coed dorms, on-campus apartments, off-campus apartments, and married-student housing. In addition, there are honors houses, language houses, special-interest houses, and international floors and houses. On-campus housing is guaranteed for all 4 years. 74% of students live on campus; of those, 80% remain on campus on weekends. All students may keep cars.

Activities: 4% of men belong to 8 national fraternities; 6% of women belong to 10 national sororities. There are 40 groups on campus, including art, band, cheerleading, chess, choir, chorale, chorus, computers, dance, drama, ethnic, film, gay, honors, international, jazz band, literary magazine, marching band, multicultural, musical theater, newspaper, opera, orchestra, pep band, photography, political, professional, radio and TV, religious, social, social service, student government, symphony, and yearbook. Popular campus events include World Fair, Head of the Charles River Regatta, and the Boston Marathon.

Sports: There are 12 intercollegiate sports for men and 13 for women, and 16 intramural sports for men and 15 for women. Facilities include 2 gyms, an ice-skating rink, saunas, a pool, a dance studio, a crew tank, a weight room, indoor and outdoor tracks, tennis and volleyball courts, multipurpose playing fields, and a boat house.

Disabled Students: 90% of the campus is accessible. Wheelchair ramps, elevators, special parking, specially equipped rest rooms, special class scheduling, lowered drinking fountains, lowered telephones, tactile and access maps, visual fire alarms for the deaf, adaptive computers, and ASL interpreters are available.

Services: Counseling and information services are available, as is tutoring in most subjects, including liberal arts, science, engineering, and management. There is a reader service for the blind. Comprehensive learning strategy for the learning disabled is available.

Campus Safety and Security: Measures include 24-hour foot and vehicle patrol, security escort services, shuttle buses, and informal discussions. There are pamphlets/posters/films, emergency telephones, lighted pathways/sidewalks, and a mountain bicycle patrol system. There is a uniformed safety/security assistant on duty 24 hours a day in large residence halls, and there are 60 academy-trained officers in the university police department.

Programs of Study: BU confers B.A., B.S., B.F.A., B.L.S., B.Mus., and B.S.B.A. degrees. Master's and doctoral degrees are also awarded. Bachelor's degrees are awarded in AGRICULTURE (environmental studies), BIOLOGICAL SCIENCE (biochemistry, biology/biological science, ecology, environmental biology, neurosciences, nutrition, and physiology), BUSINESS (accounting, banking and finance, business administration and management, entrepreneurial studies, hotel/motel and restaurant management, international business management, management information systems, management science, marketing/retailing/merchandising, operations research, and organizational behavior), COMMUNICATIONS AND THE ARTS (apparel design, classics, communications, dramatic arts, East Asian languages and literature, English, film arts, French, German, Germanic languages and literature, graphic design, Greek (classical), Greek (modern), Italian, journalism, Latin, linguistics, music, music history and appreciation, music performance, music theory and composition, painting, performing arts, public relations, sculpture, Spanish, theater design, and theater management), COMPUTER AND PHYSICAL SCIENCE (astronomy, astrophysics, chemistry, computer science, earth science, geophysics and seismology, mathematics, physics, and planetary and space science), EDUCATION (art, athletic training, bilingual/bicultural, drama, early childhood, education, education of the deaf and hearing impaired, elementary, English, foreign languages, mathematics, music, physical, science, social studies, and special), ENGINEERING AND ENVIRONMENTAL DESIGN (aeronautical engineering, biomedical engineering, computer engineering, electrical/electronics engineering, engineering, environmental science, manufacturing engineering, and mechanical engineering), HEALTH PROFESSIONS (exercise science, health, health science, physical therapy, rehabilitation therapy, and speech pathology/audiology), SOCIAL SCIENCE (American studies, anthropology, archeology, Asian/Oriental studies, classical/ancient civilization, East Asian studies, Eastern European studies, economics, French studies, geography, Hispanic American studies, history, interdisciplinary studies, international relations, Italian studies, Japanese studies, Latin American studies, philosophy, physical fitness/movement, political science/government, psychology, religion, sociology, and urban studies). The University Professors Program, accelerated medical and dental programs, and the management honors program are the strongest academically.

Required: Most students are required to complete 128 credit hours to qualify for graduation. Hours in the major, specific disciplines, curricula, distribution requirements, and minimum GPA vary, depending on the school or college of BU attended. In addition, students in the College of Arts and Sciences must complete the College Writing Program.

Special: Cross-registration is permitted with Brandeis University, Tufts University, Boston College, and Hebrew College in Massachusetts. Opportunities are provided for internships, co-op programs in engineering, a Washington semester, on- and off-campus work-study, accelerated degrees in medicine and dentistry, B.A.-B.S. degrees, dual majors, student-designed majors, credit by exam, nondegree studies, pass/fail options, and study abroad in 14 countries. A 3-2 engineering degree is offered with 16 schools, and 2-2 engineering agreements with 6 schools, plus 107 other 2-2 agreements. The University Professors Program offers a creative cross-disciplinary approach, and the College of Basic Studies offers team teaching. There are 11 national honor societies, including Phi Beta Kappa, and a freshman honors program.

Faculty/Classroom: 64% of faculty are male; 36%, female. 57% teach undergraduates. The average class size in an introductory lecture is 58; in a laboratory, 18; and in a regular course, 19.

Admissions: 52% of the 2003-2004 applicants were accepted. The SAT I scores for the 2003-2004 freshman class were: Verbal--22% between 500 and 599, 62% between 600 and 700, and 16% above 700; Math--15% between 500 and 599, 64% between 600 and 700, and 21% above 700. The ACT scores were 3% between 21 and 23, 23% between 24 and 26, 28% between 27 and 28, and 46% above 28. 86% of the current freshmen were in the top fifth of their class; 99% were in the top two fifths. There were 41 National Merit finalists. 117 freshmen graduated first in their class.

Requirements: The SAT I or ACT is required. Applicants are evaluated on an individual basis. Evidence of strong academic performance in a college prep curriculum, including 4 years of English, math, science, and social studies/history with at least 2 years of a foreign language, will be the most important aspect of a student's application review. SAT II: Subject tests are required for the accelerated medical and dental programs and recommended for the College of Communication, The University Professors, and the College of Arts and Sciences. Candidates for the School for the Arts must present a portfolio or participate in an audition. AP and CLEP credits are accepted.

Procedure: Freshmen are admitted fall and spring. Entrance exams should be taken in the junior year or early in the senior year. There are early decision, early admissions, and deferred admissions plans. Early decision applications should be filed by November 1; regular applications, by January 1 for fall entry. The fall 2003 application fee was $60. Notification of early decision is sent December 15. 249 early decision candidates were accepted for the 2003-2004 class. 2871 were on the 2003 waiting list; 1214 were admitted. Applications are accepted on-line through CollegeView, EXPAN, and the school's web site.

Transfer: 241 transfer students enrolled in 2002-2003. College transcripts, SAT I or ACT scores, and a complete high school transcript (or GED) should be submitted. Recommendations and an essay are also recommended.

Visiting: There are regularly scheduled orientations for prospective students, consisting of personal interviews, class visits, lunch with current students, campus tours, and information sessions. Appointments must be made in advance. There are guides for informal visits and visitors may sit in on classes and stay overnight. To schedule a visit, contact the Admissions Reception Center at (617) 353-2318.

Financial Aid: In 2003-2004, 73% of all full-time freshmen and 66% of continuing full-time students received some form of financial aid. 55% of full-time freshmen and 50% of continuing full-time students received need-based aid. The average freshman award was $24,669. Need-based scholarships or need-based grants averaged $17,289 ($34,300 maximum); need-based self-help aid (loans and jobs) averaged $4468 ($7000 maximum); non-need-based athletic scholarships averaged $27,699 ($40,400 maximum); and other non-need-based awards and non-need-based scholarships averaged $11,902 ($29,000 maximum). 74% of undergraduates work part time. Average annual earnings from campus work are $1647. The average financial indebtedness of the 2003 graduate was $17,535. BU is a member of CSS. The CSS Profile or FAFSA is required. The priority date for freshman financial aid applications for fall entry is February 15.

International Students: There are 1434 international students enrolled. The school actively recruits these students. They must score 550 on the written TOEFL or 213 on the electronic version and also take the SAT I or the ACT.

Computers: The mainframe is an IBM RS/6000 cluster. The campus network provides the entire university community with high-speed access to e-mail, the Internet, the World Wide Web, and other resources. Facilities include a supercomputer cluster of SGI/Cray Origin 2000 systems, an SGI Power Challenge Array, several SGI workstations, and a computer graphics lab. All students may access the system 24 hours a day.

Graduates: From July 1, 2002 to June 30, 2003, 3765 bachelor's degrees were awarded. The most popular majors were business and management (17%), social sciences (16%), and communications (15%). In an average class, 2% graduate in 3 years or less, 62% graduate in 4 years or less, 12% graduate in 5 years or less, and 2% graduate in 6 years or less. 325 companies recruited on campus in 2002-2003.

Admissions Contact: Kelly Walter, Director, Undergraduate Admissions. A video is available. E-mail: *admissions@bu.edu* or *intadmis@bu.edu* Web: *www.bu.edu*

BRANDEIS UNIVERSITY
Waltham, MA 02454

D-2

(781) 736-3500
(800) 622-0622; Fax: (781) 736-3536

Full-time: 1373 men, 1764 women	**Faculty:** 335; I, av$
Part-time: 18 men, 20 women	**Ph.D.s:** 94%
Graduate: 867 men, 943 women	**Student/Faculty:** 9 to 1
Year: semesters, summer session	**Tuition:** $29,875
Application Deadline: January 31	**Room & Board:** $8323
Freshman Class: 5770 applied, 2524 accepted, 823 enrolled	
SAT I Verbal/Math: 670/675	**MOST COMPETITIVE**

Brandeis University, founded in 1948, is a private liberal arts institution. There are 4 graduate schools. The 3 libraries contain 918,385 volumes, 900,009 microform items, and 34,404 audio/video tapes/CDs, and subscribe to 21,857 periodicals. Computerized library services include the card catalog, interlibrary loans, and database searching. Special learning facilities include a learning resource center, an art gallery, a radio station, a TV station, an astronomical observatory, a cultural center, a treasure hall, an art museum, and an audiovisual center. The 235-acre campus is in a suburban area 10 miles west of Boston. Including any residence halls, there are 98 buildings.

Student Life: 75% of undergraduates are from out of state, mostly the Northeast. Students are from 50 states, 54 foreign countries, and Canada. 70% are from public schools. 68% are white. The average age of

freshmen is 18; all undergraduates, 20. 7% do not continue beyond their first year; 78% remain to graduate.

Housing: 2542 students can be accommodated in college housing, which includes coed dorms, on-campus apartments, and off-campus apartments. In addition, there are special-interest houses. On-campus housing is guaranteed for the freshman year only, is available on a first-come, first-served basis, and is available on a lottery system for upperclassmen. 82% of students live on campus; of those, 90% remain on campus on weekends. All students may keep cars.

Activities: There are no fraternities or sororities. There are 184 groups on campus, including art, cheerleading, chess, choir, chorale, chorus, computers, dance, debate, drama, ethnic, film, gay, honors, international, jazz band, literary magazine, musical theater, newspaper, orchestra, pep band, photography, political, professional, radio and TV, religious, social, social service, student government, symphony, and yearbook. Popular campus events include Community Service Day, Intercultural Center Open House, and Midnight Madness.

Sports: There are 11 intercollegiate sports for men and 11 for women, and 6 intramural sports for men and 5 for women. Facilities include a 7000-seat field house, a basketball arena, an indoor swimming pool, 3 indoor tennis courts, 10 squash and racquetball courts, an indoor track, several multipurpose rooms for fencing, aerobics, dance, and wrestling, sauna and steam rooms, Nautilus and free weight rooms, soccer and practice fields, baseball and softball diamonds, a cross-country and fitness trail, and 10 outdoor tennis courts.

Disabled Students: 78% of the campus is accessible. Wheelchair ramps, elevators, special parking, specially equipped rest rooms, special class scheduling, lowered drinking fountains, and lowered telephones are available. Libraries, student centers, several other buildings, sports facilities, and the majority of residence halls are fully accessible.

Services: Counseling and information services are available, as is tutoring in most subjects.

Campus Safety and Security: Measures include 24-hour foot and vehicle patrol, self-defense education, security escort services, and shuttle buses. There are informal discussions, pamphlets/posters/films, emergency telephones, and lighted pathways/sidewalks.

Programs of Study: Brandeis confers B.A. and B.S. degrees. Master's and doctoral degrees are also awarded. Bachelor's degrees are awarded in BIOLOGICAL SCIENCE (biochemistry, biology/biological science, and neurosciences), COMMUNICATIONS AND THE ARTS (American literature, art history and appreciation, classics, comparative literature, dramatic arts, English, English literature, fine arts, French, German, linguistics, music, performing arts, Russian, and Spanish), COMPUTER AND PHYSICAL SCIENCE (chemistry, computer science, mathematics, physics, and science), SOCIAL SCIENCE (African American studies, African studies, American studies, anthropology, economics, European studies, history, Islamic studies, Judaic studies, Latin American studies, Middle Eastern studies, Near Eastern studies, philosophy, political science/government, psychology, and sociology). Sciences, history, and English are the strongest academically. Economics, biology, and politics are the largest.

Required: For the bachelor's degree, all students must complete 3 interrelated semester courses from an approved cluster, including selections from at least 2 different schools of the university. They must also complete 1 course from the University Seminar in Humanistic Inquiries and 1 in non-Western or cross-cultural studies, as well as a 1-semester course in each of the university's schools of creative arts, humanities, science, and social science. Writing, quantitative reasoning, and foreign language requirements also must be met. A total of 32 semester courses must be completed to graduate.

Special: Students may pursue interdepartmental programs in 18 different fields. Students may cross-register with Boston, Wellesley, Babson, and Bentley Colleges, and Boston and Tufts Universities. Study abroad is possible in 48 countries. Internships are available in virtually every field, and a work-study program is also provided. Dual and student-designed majors can be arranged. The university also offers credit by exam, nondegree study, and pass/fail options. Opportunities for early acceptance to area medical schools are offered to Brandeis students. There are 4 national honor societies, including Phi Beta Kappa, a freshman honors program, and 99 departmental honors programs.

Faculty/Classroom: 61% of faculty are male; 39%, female. All both teach and do research. Graduate students teach 10% of introductory courses. The average class size in a regular course is 21.

Admissions: 44% of the 2003-2004 applicants were accepted. The SAT I scores for the 2003-2004 freshman class were: Verbal--1% below 500, 13% between 500 and 599, 54% between 600 and 700, and 33% above 700; Math--2% below 500, 15% between 500 and 599, 52% between 600 and 700, and 30% above 700. 86% of the current freshmen were in the top fifth of their class; 99% were in the top two fifths.

Requirements: The SAT I or ACT is required. In addition, students submitting the SAT I score must also take 3 SAT II: Subject tests, including writing. The ACT may be submitted instead of the SAT I and II. Applicants should prepare with 4 years of high school English, 3 each of foreign language and math, and at least 1 each of science and social studies. An essay is required, and an interview is recommended. AP credits are accepted. Important factors in the admissions decision are advanced placement or honor courses, recommendations by school officials, and extracurricular activities record.

Procedure: Freshmen are admitted fall and spring. Entrance exams should be taken by the fall of the senior year. There are early decision and deferred admissions plans. Early decision applications should be filed by January 1; regular applications, by January 31 for fall entry and December 1 for spring entry. The fall 2003 application fee was $55. Notification of regular decision is sent April 15. A waiting list is an active part of the admissions procedure. Applications are accepted on computer disk and on-line through Common App, CollegeLink, Apply, and the school's web site.

Transfer: 43 transfer students enrolled in 2002-2003. Major consideration is given to the quality of college-level work completed, the secondary school record, testing, professors' and deans' evaluations, and the impression made by the candidate. Because there is a 2-year residence requirement, students should apply before entering their junior year. 16 of 32 courses required for the bachelor's degree must be completed at Brandeis.

Visiting: There are regularly scheduled orientations for prospective students, including year-round student-led campus tours and, in the summer, information sessions given by the admissions staff. There are guides for informal visits and visitors may sit in on classes and stay overnight. To schedule a visit, contact the Office of Admissions.

Financial Aid: In 2003-2004, 42% of all full-time freshmen and 45% of continuing full-time students received some form of financial aid. 37% of full-time freshmen and 40% of continuing full-time students received need-based aid. The average freshman award was $25,856. 42% of undergraduates work part time. Average annual earnings from campus work are $1326. Brandeis is a member of CSS. The CSS/Profile or FAFSA and copies of student and parent income tax returns for matriculating students are required. The deadline for filing freshman financial aid applications for fall entry is January 31.

International Students: In a recent year, there were 188 international students enrolled. The school actively recruits these students. They must score 600 on the written TOEFL or 250 on the electronic version. Applicants whose native language is English must take the SAT I and SAT II: Subject tests.

Computers: The mainframe is a DEC VAX cluster for undergraduate network services. There are 3 clusters located throughout the campus containing more than 100 Macs and PCs and printers for both. All Macs and some PCs are connected to the campus network via an Ethernet gateway, giving students access to Student Network Services accounts. Access to the mainframe is also available from students' rooms. All students may access the system. There are no time limits and no fees.

Graduates: In a recent year, 753 bachelor's degrees were awarded. The most popular majors were social science and history (38%), biological/life sciences (15%), and psychology (11%). In an average class, 80% graduate in 4 years or less, 83% graduate in 5 years or less, and 84% graduate in 6 years or less. 60 companies recruited on campus in a recent year.

Admissions Contact: Deena Whitfield, Director of Enrollment. E-mail: *sendinfo@brandeis.edu* Web: *http://www.brandeis.edu*

BRIDGEWATER STATE COLLEGE
Bridgewater, MA 02325

	E-3
	(508) 531-1237; Fax: (508) 531-1746
Full-time: 2456 men, 3791 women	**Faculty:** 261; IIA, av$
Part-time: 524 men, 826 women	**Ph.D.s:** 51%
Graduate: 258 men, 808 women	**Student/Faculty:** 24 to 1
Year: semesters, summer session	**Tuition:** $4560 ($10,700)
Application Deadline: February 15	**Room & Board:** $5922
Freshman Class: 5540 applied, 4005 accepted, 1304 enrolled	
SAT I Verbal/Math: 520/520	**ACT:** 21 **COMPETITIVE**

Bridgewater State College, founded in 1840, is a state-supported college offering undergraduate and graduate programs in liberal arts, education, business, aviation science, and preprofessional studies. There are 3 undergraduate schools and 1 graduate school. In addition to regional accreditation, the college has baccalaureate program accreditation with ACS, CAAHEP, CSWE, IACBE, and NCATE. The library contains 290,426 volumes, 3949 microform items, and 10,923 audio/video tapes/CDs, and subscribes to 1064 periodicals. Computerized library services include the card catalog, interlibrary loans, and database searching. Special learning facilities include a learning resource center, art gallery, radio station, an astronomical observatory, a human performance lab and flight simulators, electronic classrooms, a teleconferencing facility with a satellite dish, and a children's developmental clinic. The 235-acre campus is in a suburban area 28 miles south of Boston. Including any residence halls, there are 41 buildings.

Student Life: 97% of undergraduates are from Massachusetts. Students are from 22 states, 13 foreign countries, and Canada. 77% are white. The average age of freshmen is 19; all undergraduates, 23. 23% do not continue beyond their first year.

Housing: 1745 students can be accommodated in college housing, which includes single-sex and coed dorms and on-campus apartments. On-campus housing is guaranteed for all 4 years. 69% of students commute. All students may keep cars.

Activities: 2% of men and about 2% of women belong to 2 local and 3 national fraternities; 2% of women belong to 3 national sororities. There are 74 groups on campus, including adult student, band, cheerleading, choir, chorale, computers, dance, drama, ethnic, gay, honors, interfraternal, international, jazz band, literary magazine, musical theater, newspaper, pep band, photography, political, professional, radio, religious, social, social service, student government, women's, and yearbook. Popular campus events include Convocation, Multiculture Day, and Christmas and Spring balls.

Sports: There are 10 intercollegiate sports for men and 11 for women, and 6 intramural sports for men and 4 for women. Facilities include 2 gyms, an Olympic-size swimming pool, tennis courts, a football stadium, a 9-lane track, soccer, lacrosse, and field hockey fields, and a baseball and softball complex.

Disabled Students: 95% of the campus is accessible. Wheelchair ramps, elevators, special parking, specially equipped rest rooms, special class scheduling, lowered drinking fountains, lowered telephones, special housing, a handicapped van service, and a college-operated transit system are available.

Services: Counseling and information services are available, as is tutoring in most subjects. There is a reader service for the blind, and remedial math, reading, and writing. There are taped texts, classroom interpreters, scribes and note takers, testing accommodations, and a speech/hearing/language center.

Campus Safety and Security: Measures include 24-hour foot and vehicle patrol, self-defense education, security escort services, and shuttle buses. There are informal discussions, pamphlets/posters/films, emergency telephones, lighted pathways/sidewalks, a college-operated transit system that runs from 7 A.M. to midnight Monday through Friday, and a safety-escort van that runs from 6 P.M. to 3 A.M.

Programs of Study: The college confers B.A., B.S., and B.S.Ed. degrees. Master's degrees are also awarded. Bachelor's degrees are awarded in BIOLOGICAL SCIENCE (biology/biological science), BUSINESS (accounting and management science), COMMUNICATIONS AND THE ARTS (art, communications, English, music, and Spanish), COMPUTER AND PHYSICAL SCIENCE (chemistry, computer science, earth science, geology, mathematics, and physics), EDUCATION (early childhood, elementary, health, physical, and special), ENGINEERING AND ENVIRONMENTAL DESIGN (aviation administration/management), SOCIAL SCIENCE (anthropology, criminal justice, economics, geography, history, philosophy, political science/government, psychology, social work, and sociology). Management science, aviation science, and education are the strongest academically. Management science, psychology, and education are the largest.

Required: Students are required to complete a minimum of 120 semester hours, with 30 to 36 hours in the major and 52 to 55 hours in general education courses. Students must maintain a minimum GPA of 2.0 and must complete an introduction to information resources course.

Special: Opportunities are provided for cross-registration with other Massachusetts schools, internships in most majors, dual majors in any 2 subjects, core requirement credit for military service and work experience, nondegree study, and study abroad in England and Canada. A Washington semester offers possible internship experience in political science. There are 11 national honor societies, a freshman honors program, and 14 departmental honors programs.

Faculty/Classroom: 54% of faculty are male; 46%, female. All teach undergraduates. No introductory courses are taught by graduate students. The average class size in an introductory lecture is 32; in a laboratory, 18; and in a regular course, 24.

Admissions: 72% of the 2003-2004 applicants were accepted. The SAT I scores for the 2003-2004 freshman class were: Verbal--37% below 500, 52% between 500 and 599, 10% between 600 and 700, and 1% above 700; Math--36% below 500, 51% between 500 and 599, 12% between 600 and 700, and 1% above 700. The ACT scores were 44% below 21, 38% between 21 and 23, 14% between 24 and 26, and 4% above 28. 16% of the current freshmen were in the top fifth of their class; 42% were in the top two fifths.

Requirements: The SAT I or ACT is required. In addition, graduation from an accredited secondary school is required; a GED will be accepted. Applicants must have successfully completed 16 Carnegie units, including 4 years of English, 3 of math, 3 of science with 2 lab sciences, 2 of a foreign language, 1 each of history and social studies, and 2 in other college preparatory electives. An essay is recommended. A GPA of 2.0 is required. AP and CLEP credits are accepted. Important factors in the admissions decision are advanced placement or honor courses, leadership record, and extracurricular activities record.

Procedure: Freshmen are admitted fall and spring. Entrance exams should be taken no later than January. There are early action and deferred admissions plans. Early action applications should be filed by November 16; regular applications, by February 15 for fall entry and December 1 for spring entry. The fall 2003 application fee was $25. Notification of early action is sent December 15; regular decision, by April 1. Applications are accepted on-line through the college's web site at *www.bridgew@edu/admission/applybsc.cfm*, or through CollegeLink or EXPAN.

Transfer: 691 transfer students enrolled in 2002-2003. Transfer students must have maintained a minimum GPA of 2.0 at the previous college, although this alone does not guarantee admission. Priority is given to community college graduates. 30 of 120 credits required for the bachelor's degree must be completed at Bridgewater State.

Visiting: There are regularly scheduled orientations for prospective students, including tours Monday through Friday at 11 A.M. and 3 P.M. and information sessions on Fridays at 10 A.M. when college is in session. Visitations are available on a limited basis Saturdays during the fall. Campus tours are available year round. There are guides for informal visits and visitors may sit in on classes. To schedule a visit, contact the Office of Admissions.

Financial Aid: In 2003-2004, 45% of all full-time freshmen and 30% of continuing full-time students received some form of financial aid. 43% of full-time freshmen and 27% of continuing full-time students received need-based aid. The average freshman award was $6230. Need-based scholarships or need-based grants averaged $3396; need-based self-help aid (loans and jobs) averaged $2651; and other non-need-based awards and non-need-based scholarships averaged $3876. 22% of undergraduates work part time. Average annual earnings from campus work are $4000. The average financial indebtedness of the 2003 graduate was $9243. The college is a member of CSS. The FAFSA and parents' tax returns are required. The priority date for freshman financial aid applications for fall entry is March 1.

International Students: There were 157 international students enrolled in a recent year. They must score 500 on the written TOEFL.

Computers: The mainframes are a DEC 3000-300LX, a DEC Alpha server 1000 4/200, a DEC 300-600, an Alpha server 4000 5/400, a VAX 4000-300, a DEC Alpha server 2100 4/233, and a DEC VAXstation 4000/600. In addition to the computer facilities for instructional purposes, the college provides general access to about 400 PCs. The college also provides connectivity to hosts and the home page via SLIP/PPP connection from off-campus using a modem. Residential students' PCs may be connected to the campus network and the Internet. All students may access the system 7 days a week. There are no time limits and no fees.

Graduates: From July 1, 2002 to June 30, 2003, 1185 bachelor's degrees were awarded. The most popular majors were education (14%), management (14%), and psychology (13%). In an average class, 1% graduate in 3 years or less, 18% graduate in 4 years or less, 41% graduate in 5 years or less, and 46% graduate in 6 years or less. 83 companies recruited on campus in a recent year. Of a recent year's graduating class, 16% were enrolled in graduate school within 6 months of graduation and 92% were employed.

Admissions Contact: Gregg Meyer, Director of Admissions. E-mail: *admission@bridgew.edu* Web: *www.bridgew.edu*

CAMBRIDGE COLLEGE
Cambridge, MA 02138

D-2
(617) 868-1000
(800) 877-4723; Fax: (617) 868-1124

Full-time: none	**Faculty:** n/av
Part-time: 893 men and women	**Ph.D.s:** n/av
Graduate: 4580 men and women	**Student/Faculty:** n/av
Year: semesters, summer session	**Tuition:** $10,800
Application Deadline: open	**Room & Board:** n/app
Freshman Class: n/av	
SAT I or ACT: not required	SPECIAL

Cambridge College is a private college with 1 undergraduate school and 3 graduate schools. There is an on-line library. Students have access to museums at Harvard University and in the Boston area. The school is located in an urban area of Cambridge. There are 2 buildings.

Housing: There are no residence halls.

Activities: There are no fraternities or sororities.

Disabled Students: All of the campus is accessible. Elevators, specially equipped rest rooms, and special class scheduling are available.

Services: There is remedial math and writing.

Programs of Study: Cambridge College confers B.A. and B.S. degrees. Master's degrees are also awarded. Bachelor's degrees are awarded in BUSINESS (management science), SOCIAL SCIENCE (human services, interdisciplinary studies, and psychology).

Required: Students must complete 120 credit hours with 36 in the major to graduate. They also must complete 9 hours each in arts and humanities, natural and physical sciences, and social sciences, and complete a capstone course.

Faculty/Classroom: All teach undergraduates. No introductory courses are taught by graduate students.

Admissions: All of the 2003-2004 applicants were accepted. There is an open admissions policy.

Requirements: CLEP credit is accepted.

Procedure: Application deadlines are open. The application fee is $30.

Transfer: 30 of 120 credits required for the bachelor's degree must be completed at Cambridge College.

Financial Aid: In 2003-2004, 77% of all full-time freshmen received some form of financial aid.

International Students: They must score 550 on the written TOEFL or 213 on the electronic version.

Computers: There are computer facilities for student use.

Admissions Contact: Dr. Ezat Parnia, Vice President for Enrollment and Marketing. Web: *www.cambridgecollege.edu*

CLARK UNIVERSITY
Worcester, MA 01610-1477

C-2
(508) 793-7431
(800) 462-5275; Fax: (508) 793-8821

Full-time: 787 men, 1215 women	**Faculty:** 171; IIA, ++$
Part-time: 76 men, 112 women	**Ph.D.s:** 98%
Graduate: 412 men, 482 women	**Student/Faculty:** 12 to 1
Year: semesters, summer session	**Tuition:** $26,965
Application Deadline: February 1	**Room & Board:** $5150
Freshman Class: 3950 applied, 2488 accepted, 541 enrolled	
SAT I Verbal/Math: 600/590	**ACT:** 25 VERY COMPETITIVE

Clark University, founded in 1887, is an independent liberal arts and research institution. There are 2 undergraduate and 3 graduate schools. In addition to regional accreditation, Clark has baccalaureate program accreditation with AACSB and NASDTEC. The 4 libraries contain 592,159 volumes, 59,953 microform items, and 984 audio/video tapes/CDs, and subscribe to 1303 periodicals. Computerized library services include the card catalog, interlibrary loans, and database searching. Special learning facilities include a learning resource center, art gallery, radio station, TV studio, campus cable network, center for music with 2 studios for electronic music, 2 theaters, magnetic resonance imaging facility, and arboretum. The 50-acre campus is in an urban area 50 miles west of Boston. Including any residence halls, there are 56 buildings.

Student Life: 63% of undergraduates are from out of state, mostly the Northeast. Students are from 44 states, 56 foreign countries, and Canada. 73% are from public schools. 65% are white. 34% claim no religious affiliation; 20% Protestant; 19% Catholic; 17% Jewish. The average age of freshmen is 19; all undergraduates, 20. 14% do not continue beyond their first year; 68% remain to graduate.

Housing: 1588 students can be accommodated in college housing, which includes single-sex and coed dorms and on-campus apartments. In addition, there are special-interest houses, and nonsmoking, quiet, substance awareness, and year-round houses. On-campus housing is guaranteed for the freshman year only and is available on a lottery system for upperclassmen. 77% of students live on campus. All students may keep cars.

Activities: There are no fraternities or sororities. There are 74 groups on campus, including art, band, chess, choir, chorale, chorus, dance, debate, drama, ethnic, film, gay, honors, international, jazz band, literary magazine, musical theater, newspaper, pep band, photography, political, professional, radio and TV, religious, social, social service, student government, and yearbook. Popular campus events include Gryphon & Pleiades Honor Society Variety Show, International Gala, and Speaker's Forum.

Sports: There are 8 intercollegiate sports for men and 9 for women, and 14 intramural sports for men and 14 for women. Facilities include an athletic center with a 2000-seat gym, a pool, a fitness center, tennis courts, outdoor fields, baseball and softball diamonds, and a boat house.

Disabled Students: 90% of the campus is accessible. Wheelchair ramps, elevators, special parking, specially equipped rest rooms, special class scheduling, lowered drinking fountains, lowered telephones, and special housing are available.

Services: Counseling and information services are available, as is tutoring in some subjects, including math, biology, chemistry, economics, and psychology. For learning-disabled students, the university provides early orientation, alternative test-taking accommodations, a learning specialist, and compensatory skill training in written expression, math application, and learning strategies. A writing center provides assistance to all students.

Campus Safety and Security: Measures include 24-hour foot and vehicle patrol, self-defense education, security escort services, and shuttle buses. There are informal discussions, pamphlets/posters/films, emergency telephones, and lighted pathways/sidewalks.

Programs of Study: Clark confers the B.A. degree. Master's and doctoral degrees are also awarded. Bachelor's degrees are awarded in BIOLOGICAL SCIENCE (biochemistry and biology/biological science), BUSINESS (business administration and management), COMMUNICATIONS AND THE ARTS (art history and appreciation, communications, comparative literature, dramatic arts, English, film arts, fine arts, French, languages, music, romance languages and literature, Spanish, studio art, and visual and performing arts), COMPUTER AND PHYSICAL SCIENCE (chemistry, computer science, mathematics, and physics), ENGINEERING AND ENVIRONMENTAL DESIGN (environmental science),

HEALTH PROFESSIONS (predentistry and premedicine), SOCIAL SCIENCE (classical/ancient civilization, economics, geography, history, international relations, international studies, philosophy, political science/government, prelaw, psychology, and sociology). Psychology, biology, and government and international relations are the strongest academically. Psychology, government and international relations, and business management are the largest.

Required: Each student is required to complete 2 critical thinking courses in 2 categories of verbal expression and formal analysis, and 6 perspectives courses, representing the categories of aesthetics, comparative, historical, language and culture, science, and values. A student must receive passing grades in a minimum of 32 full courses, with a C- or better in at least 24 of these courses, and maintain a minimum 2.0 GPA to graduate.

Special: For-credit internships are available in all disciplines with private corporations and small businesses, medical centers, and government agencies. There is cross-registration with members of the Worcester Consortium, including Holy Cross and Worcester Polytechnic Institute. Clark also offers study abroad in 11 countries, a Washington semester with American University, work-study programs, dual and student-designed majors, pass/no record options, and a 3-2 engineering degree with Columbia University, Washington University, and Worcester Polytechnic Institute. A gerontology certificate is offered with the Worcester Consortium for Higher Education. There are 7 national honor societies, including Phi Beta Kappa, and 17 departmental honors programs.

Faculty/Classroom: 65% of faculty are male; 35%, female. All both teach and do research. No introductory courses are taught by graduate students. The average class size in an introductory lecture is 34; in a laboratory, 14; and in a regular course, 21.

Admissions: 63% of the 2003-2004 applicants were accepted. The SAT I scores for the 2003-2004 freshman class were: Verbal--10% below 500, 36% between 500 and 599, 44% between 600 and 700, and 10% above 700; Math--12% below 500, 39% between 500 and 599, 40% between 600 and 700, and 9% above 700. The ACT scores were 20% below 21, 18% between 21 and 23, 30% between 24 and 26, 15% between 27 and 28, and 17% above 28. 60% of the current freshmen were in the top fifth of their class; 89% were in the top two fifths. 7 freshmen graduated first in their class.

Requirements: The SAT I or ACT is required. The SAT II: Writing test is also recommended. Applicants must graduate from an accredited secondary school or have a GED. 16 Carnegie units are required, including 4 years of English, 3 each of math and science, and 2 each of foreign language and social studies, including history. An interview is recommended. AP credits are accepted. Important factors in the admissions decision are advanced placement or honor courses, recommendations by alumni, and recommendations by school officials.

Procedure: Freshmen are admitted fall and spring. Entrance exams should be taken by November of the senior year. There are early decision and deferred admissions plans. Early decision applications should be filed by November 15; regular applications, by February 1 for fall entry and November 15 for spring entry, along with a $50 fee. Notification of early decision is sent January 1; regular decision, April 1. 58 early decision candidates were accepted for the 2003-2004 class. 60 applicants were on the 2003 waiting list; 8 were admitted. Applications are accepted on-line through the school's web site and Common Application.

Transfer: 37 transfer students enrolled in 2003-2004. Applicants should have a minimum GPA of about 2.8. At least 1 full semester of college course work is required. High school and college transcripts, recent SAT I or ACT test scores, a staement of good standing from previous institutions attended, and a transfer statement are required. Grades of C or better in comparable course work transfer for credit. 16 of 32 courses required for the bachelor's degree must be completed at Clark.

Visiting: There are regularly scheduled orientations for prospective students, consisting of open houses during fall and spring semesters, that include tours, information sessions, and talks with faculty, administration, and coaches. There are guides for informal visits and visitors may sit in on classes. To schedule a visit, contact the Admissions Office.

Financial Aid: In 2003-2004, 83% of all full-time freshmen and 86% of continuing full-time students received some form of financial aid. 63% of all full-time students received need-based aid. The average freshman award was $18,843. 70% of undergraduates work part time. Average annual earnings from campus work are $1700. The average financial indebtedness of the 2003 graduate was $18,375. Clark is a member of CSS. The CSS/Profile or FAFSA is required. The deadline for filing freshman financial aid applications for fall entry is February 1.

International Students: There are 137 international students enrolled. The school actively recruits these students. They must score 550 on the written TOEFL or 213 on the electronic version and also take the SAT I or the ACT, scoring 400 on the verbal section of the SAT I and 400 on the math section..

Computers: The mainframes are a network including Dell Poweredge servers, HP Net Servers, and Compaq Proliants. Students can access the Internet via the wireless campus network, networked computers in all campus buildings, Windows and Mac computers in computer labs, "Network Express Station" kiosks in the library and student union area, and

residence hall rooms, which all have active network ports. All students may access the system 7 days per week. There are no time limits and no fees. It is strongly recommended that all students have a personal computer.

Graduates: From July 1, 2002 to June 30, 2003, 416 bachelor's degrees were awarded. The most popular majors were psychology (18%), government and international relations (12%), and management (10%). In an average class, 1% graduate in 3 years or less, 63% graduate in 4 years or less, 66% graduate in 5 years or less, and 68% graduate in 6 years or less. 100 companies recruited on campus in 2002-2003. Of the 2002 graduating class, 30% were enrolled in graduate school within 6 months of graduation.

Admissions Contact: Harold M. Wingood, Dean of Admissions. E-mail: *admissions@clarku.edu*

COLLEGE OF OUR LADY OF THE ELMS
Chicopee, MA 01013

B-3
(413) 592-3189
(800) 255-ELMS; Fax: (413) 594-2781

Full-time: 60 men, 350 women	**Faculty:** 38
Part-time: 25 men, 190 women	**Ph.D.s:** 76%
Graduate: 10 men, 80 women	**Student/Faculty:** 11 to 1
Year: semesters	**Tuition:** $15,000
Application Deadline: open	**Room & Board:** $6000
Freshman Class: n/av	
SAT I or ACT: required	**COMPETITIVE**

College of Our Lady of the Elms, founded in 1928, is a Roman Catholic institution offering undergraduate degrees in liberal arts and sciences and graduate degrees in liberal arts, education, and theology. Figures in the above capsule are approximate. In addition to regional accreditation, Elms College has baccalaureate program accreditation with CSWE and NLN. The library contains 103,136 volumes, 77,784 microform items, and 2208 audio/video tapes/CDs, and subscribes to 695 periodicals. Computerized library services include the card catalog, interlibrary loans, and database searching. Special learning facilities include a learning resource center, art gallery, radio station, TV station, and rare books collection. The 32-acre campus is in a suburban area 2 miles north of Springfield and 90 miles west of Boston. Including any residence halls, there are 11 buildings.

Student Life: 85% of undergraduates are from Massachusetts. Students are from 9 states and 10 foreign countries. 74% are from public schools. 80% are white. 60% are Catholic. The average age of freshmen is 20; all undergraduates, 22. 11% do not continue beyond their first year.

Housing: 315 students can be accommodated in college housing, which includes single-sex and coed dorms. On-campus housing is guaranteed for all 4 years. 60% of students commute. All students may keep cars.

Activities: There are no fraternities or sororities. There are 41 groups on campus, including art, choir, chorale, chorus, computers, dance, drama, ethnic, honors, international, literary magazine, musical theater, newspaper, photography, professional, radio and TV, religious, social, social service, student government, and yearbook. Popular campus events include Soph Show, Cap and Gown, and Ring Ceremony.

Sports: There are 6 intercollegiate sports for men and 9 for women, and 6 intramural sports for men and 6 for women. Facilities include a fitness and athletic center housing a suspended indoor track, a 25-meter, 6-lane pool, a weight and aerobics room, a multipurpose arena, and basketball and volleyball courts.

Disabled Students: 40% of the campus is accessible. Wheelchair ramps, elevators, special parking, specially equipped rest rooms, special class scheduling, lowered drinking fountains, lowered telephones, and automated doors are available.

Services: Counseling and information services are available, as is tutoring in every subject. There is a reader service for the blind, and remedial math, reading, and writing. There also is an academic advising and resource center, a counseling service office, career services, wellness services, student activities, a campus ministry office, and resident advisers.

Campus Safety and Security: Measures include 24-hour foot and vehicle patrol, self-defense education, security escort services, and informal discussions. There are pamphlets/posters/films, emergency telephones, and lighted pathways/sidewalks. A safety and security manual is published each year, and there is a safety and security committee of administrators, students, faculty, and staff.

Programs of Study: Elms College confers B.A. and B.S. degrees. Associate and master's degrees are also awarded. Bachelor's degrees are awarded in BIOLOGICAL SCIENCE (biology/biological science), BUSINESS (accounting, business administration and management, international business management, and marketing/retailing/merchandising), COMMUNICATIONS AND THE ARTS (English, fine arts, and Spanish), COMPUTER AND PHYSICAL SCIENCE (chemistry, computer science, mathematics, and natural sciences), EDUCATION (bilingual/bicultural, early childhood, elementary, foreign languages, middle school, science, secondary, special, and teaching English as a second/foreign language (TESOL/TEFOL)), HEALTH PROFESSIONS (health science, medical laboratory technology, nursing, predentistry, premedicine, and speech pathology/audiology), SOCIAL SCIENCE (American studies, international studies, paralegal studies, prelaw, psychology, religion, social work, and sociology). Nursing, education, and biology are the strongest academically. Education, business, and nursing are the largest.

Required: To graduate, all students must complete 120 hours with a 2.0 GPA. 54 hours are required in courses in rhetoric, computer science, history, religion, phys ed, philosophy, sociology, fine arts, humanities, foreign language, math, senior seminar, and service learning experience.

Special: Students may cross-register at any of the Cooperating Colleges of Greater Springfield or Consortium of Sisters of St. Joseph Colleges. Internships are available with local hospitals, businesses, and schools. Study abroad, student-designed interdepartmental majors, accelerated degree programs, work-study, dual majors, nondegree study, and pass/fail options are offered. There are 5 national honor societies, including Phi Beta Kappa, and a freshman honors program.

Faculty/Classroom: 35% of faculty are male; 65%, female. 90% teach undergraduates, 93% do research, and 92% do both. No introductory courses are taught by graduate students. The average class size in an introductory lecture is 13; in a laboratory, 8; and in a regular course, 11.

Requirements: The SAT I or ACT is required. The college prefers SAT I composite scores of at least 900. Applicants should be graduates of accredited high schools or have earned the GED. Secondary preparation should include 4 units of English, 3 each of math and science, and 2 each of foreign language, history, and social studies. A personal essay is required; an interview is recommended. Elms College requires applicants to be in the upper 50% of their class. A GPA of 2.5 is required. AP and CLEP credits are accepted. Important factors in the admissions decision are advanced placement or honor courses, recommendations by school officials, and extracurricular activities record.

Procedure: Freshmen are admitted fall and spring. Entrance exams should be taken no later than November of the senior year. There are early admissions and deferred admissions plans. There is a rolling admissions plan. Application deadlines are open. The fall 2003 application fee was $30. Notification is sent on a rolling basis. Applications are accepted on-line through CollegeLink, Common App, and National Catholic College Common Application.

Transfer: Applicants must have a minimum 2.0 GPA. 45 credits of 120 required for the bachelor's degree must be completed at Elms College.

Visiting: There are regularly scheduled orientations for prospective students, including tours and interviews scheduled weekdays between 9 A.M. and 4 P.M. as well as 2 open houses in the fall and 1 in the spring. There are guides for informal visits and visitors may sit in on classes and stay overnight. To schedule a visit, contact the Admission Office.

Financial Aid: In a recent year, 75% of all full-time freshmen and 89% of continuing full-time students received some form of financial aid. 75% of full-time freshmen and 88% of continuing full-time students received need-based aid. The average freshman award was $11,618. 30% of undergraduates work part time. Average annual earnings from campus work are $1200. The average financial indebtedness of a recent graduate was $18,600. Elms College is a member of CSS. The FAFSA and the college's own financial statement are required. Check with the school for current deadlines.

International Students: The school actively recruits these students. The college requires either the TOEFL, with a minimum score of 500, or the SAT I.

Computers: The mainframe is a DEC Alpha 2100 4/275. Computer labs consist of 1 in the library, 3 in the main building, 2 in residence halls, and 1 in the college center. 4 of the labs offer web access, 6 offer Internet access. All students have e-mail accounts. All students may access the system 8 A.M. to 10 P.M. Monday through Friday, 12 noon to 9 P.M. Saturday and Sunday; residence hall labs are open 24 hours. There are no time limits and no fees.

Graduates: In a recent year, 134 bachelor's degrees were awarded. The most popular majors were nursing (17%), social work (13%), and education (10%). In an average class, 1% graduate in 3 years or less, 54% graduate in 4 years or less, and 56% graduate in 5 years or less.

Admissions Contact: Joseph P. Wagner, Director of Admission. E-mail: *admissions@elms.edu* Web: *www.elms.edu*

COLLEGE OF THE HOLY CROSS
Worcester, MA 01610

C-2
(508) 793-2443
(800) 442-2421; Fax: (508) 793-3888

Full-time: 1276 men, 1472 women	**Faculty:** 228; IIB, ++$
Part-time: 9 men, 16 women	**Ph.D.s:** 95%
Graduate: none	**Student/Faculty:** 12 to 1
Year: semesters	**Tuition:** $28,011
Application Deadline: January 15	**Room & Board:** $8440
Freshman Class: 5035 applied, 2131 accepted, 704 enrolled	
SAT I Verbal/Math: 633/637	**MOST COMPETITIVE**

College of the Holy Cross, founded in 1843, is a private liberal arts college affiliated with the Jesuit order of the Roman Catholic Church. In addition to regional accreditation, Holy Cross has baccalaureate program accreditation with NAST. The 4 libraries contain 593,561 volumes, 15,691 microform items, and 25,636 audio/video tapes/CDs, and subscribe to 1808 periodicals. Computerized library services include the card catalog, interlibrary loans, and database searching. Special learning facilities include an art gallery, radio station, greenhouses, facilities for aquatic research, and a multimedia resource center. The 174-acre campus is in a suburban area 45 miles west of Boston. Including any residence halls, there are 30 buildings.

Student Life: 66% of undergraduates are from out of state, mostly the Northeast. Students are from 46 states, 18 foreign countries, and Canada. 53% are from public schools. 77% are white. 77% are Catholic; 10% Protestant. The average age of freshmen is 18; all undergraduates, 20. 2% do not continue beyond their first year; 98% remain to graduate.

Housing: 2344 students can be accommodated in college housing, which includes coed dorms. In addition, there are special-interest houses, a substance-free house, and a first-year living and learning house. On-campus housing is guaranteed for all 4 years. 87% of students live on campus; of those, 90% remain on campus on weekends. Upperclassmen may keep cars.

Activities: There are no fraternities or sororities. There are 85 groups on campus, including art, band, cheerleading, choir, chorale, chorus, computers, dance, debate, drama, drill team, ethnic, film, gay, honors, international, jazz band, literary magazine, marching band, musical theater, newspaper, orchestra, pep band, photography, political, professional, religious, social, social service, student government, and yearbook. Popular campus events include Spring Weekend, Family Weekend, and Senior Weekend.

Sports: There are 13 intercollegiate sports for men and 14 for women, and 6 intramural sports for men and 5 for women. Facilities include an Astroturf playing field, baseball and football fields, indoor and outdoor running tracks, a swimming pool, an ice rink, indoor crew tanks, a basketball arena, weight and exercise rooms, a wellness center, and tennis, squash, and racquetball courts.

Disabled Students: 85% of the campus is accessible. Wheelchair ramps, elevators, special parking, specially equipped rest rooms, special class scheduling, lowered drinking fountains, and lowered telephones are available.

Services: Counseling and information services are available, as is tutoring in some subjects, including math, science, economics, and language.

Campus Safety and Security: Measures include 24-hour foot and vehicle patrol, self-defense education, security escort services, and shuttle buses. There are informal discussions, pamphlets/posters/films, emergency telephones, and lighted pathways/sidewalks.

Programs of Study: Holy Cross confers the A.B. degree. Bachelor's degrees are awarded in AGRICULTURE (environmental studies), BIOLOGICAL SCIENCE (biology/biological science), COMMUNICATIONS AND THE ARTS (art history and appreciation, classics, dramatic arts, English, film arts, French, German, Italian, literature, music, Russian, Spanish, and studio art), COMPUTER AND PHYSICAL SCIENCE (chemistry, mathematics, and physics), SOCIAL SCIENCE (African studies, anthropology, Asian/Oriental studies, economics, German area studies, history, medieval studies, Middle Eastern studies, philosophy, political science/government, psychology, religion, Russian and Slavic studies, and sociology). Economics, psychology, and political science are the largest.

Required: Distribution requirements include social science, natural and mathematical science, cross-cultural studies, religious and philosophical studies, historical studies and the arts, and literature. In addition, students must demonstrate competence in a classical or modern language or American sign language. A total of 32 courses worth at least 1 unit each is required for graduation, with 10 to 14 courses in the major. The minimum GPA for graduation is 2.0.

Special: Local academic internships are available through the Center for Interdisciplinary and Special Studies in health and education, law and business, journalism, social service, state and local government, scientific research, and cultural affairs. Student-designed majors, dual majors including economics-accounting, a Washington semester, and study abroad are possible. There is a 3-2 engineering program with Columbia University or Dartmouth College, and premedicine and predentistry programs are available. Students may cross-register with other universities in the Colleges of Worcester Consortium. Nondegree study is possible. There are 15 national honor societies, including Phi Beta Kappa, and 2 departmental honors programs. In addition, the college has a multidisciplinary honors program available to students on a highly selective basis.

Faculty/Classroom: 57% of faculty are male; 43%, female. All both teach and do research. The average class size in an introductory lecture is 23; in a laboratory, 20; and in a regular course, 17.

Admissions: 42% of the 2003-2004 applicants were accepted. The SAT I scores for the 2003-2004 freshman class were: Verbal--2% below 500, 27% between 500 and 599, 52% between 600 and 700, and 19% above 700; Math--2% below 500, 19% between 500 and 599, 65% between 600 and 700, and 14% above 700. 88% of the current freshmen were in the top fifth of their class; 99% were in the top two fifths. There were 2 National Merit finalists. 19 freshmen graduated first in their class.

Requirements: The SAT I or ACT is required. In addition, applicants should be graduates of an accredited secondary school or hold the GED. Recommended preparatory courses include English, foreign language, history, math, and science. An essay and the SAT II: Subject tests in writing and 2 other areas are required. An interview is recommended. AP credits are accepted. Important factors in the admissions decision are advanced placement or honor courses, recommendations by school officials, and evidence of special talent.

Procedure: Freshmen are admitted in the fall. Entrance exams should be taken by December of the senior year. There are early decision, early admissions, and deferred admissions plans. Early decision applications should be filed by December 15; regular applications, by January 15 for fall entry. The fall 2003 application fee was $50. Notification of early decision is sent on a rolling basis; regular decision, April 1. 221 early decision candidates were accepted for the 2003-2004 class. 374 were on the 2003 waiting list; 88 were admitted. Applications are accepted on-line through the college's web site.

Transfer: 20 transfer students enrolled in 2002-2003. Transfer students must have a minimum GPA of 3.2. The SAT I is required, as are transcripts and 2 teacher recommendations. Personal interviews are highly recommended. 16 of 32 credits required for the bachelor's degree must be completed at Holy Cross.

Visiting: There are regularly scheduled orientations for prospective students, including fall open houses in October and November consisting of informational panels on academics, admissions, financial aid, and student life, as well as tours of the facilities. There are guides for informal visits and visitors may sit in on classes and stay overnight. To schedule a visit, contact the Admissions Office at (800) 442-2421 or *admissions@holycross.edu*.

Financial Aid: In 2003-2004, 56% of all full-time freshmen and 55% of continuing full-time students received some form of financial aid. 45% of full-time freshmen and 42% of continuing full-time students received need-based aid. The average freshman award was $16,812. Need-based scholarships or need-based grants averaged $14,237 ($36,000 maximum); need-based self-help aid (loans and jobs) averaged $6564 ($7025 maximum); non-need-based athletic scholarships averaged $36,451 (maximum); and other non-need-based awards and non-need-based scholarships averaged $15,308 ($27,560 maximum). 32% of undergraduates work part time. Average annual earnings from campus work are $1471. The average financial indebtedness of the 2003 graduate was $17,253. Holy Cross is a member of CSS. The CSS Profile or FAFSA is required. The deadline for filing freshman financial aid applications for fall entry is February 1.

International Students: There are 44 international students enrolled. The school actively recruits these students. They must score 550 on the written TOEFL or 213 on the electronic version and also take the SAT I or the ACT. Students must take SAT II: Subject tests in writing and 2 other areas of the student's choice.

Computers: The mainframe is a DEC Alpha 3100. There are 4 public labs and a dozen departmental labs on campus housing more than 463 Intel PCs. Every residence hall room has access to the college computer network. All students may access the system 24 hours per day.

Graduates: From July 1, 2002 to June 30, 2003, 700 bachelor's degrees were awarded. The most popular majors were economics (17%), psychology (13%), and political science (12%). In an average class, 89% graduate in 4 years or less, 90% graduate in 5 years or less, and 89% graduate in 6 years or less. 42 companies recruited on campus in 2002-2003. Of the 2002 graduating class, 24% were enrolled in graduate school within 6 months of graduation and 61% were employed.

Admissions Contact: Admissions Office. A video is available.
E-mail: *admissions@holycross.edu* Web: *www.holycross.edu*

CURRY COLLEGE
Milton, MA 02186-9984

E-2

(617) 333-2210
(800) 669-0686; Fax: (617) 333-2114

Full-time: 620 men, 610 women	**Faculty:** 80; IIB, av$
Part-time: 500 men, 600 women	**Ph.Ds:** 53%
Graduate: 70 men, 60 women	**Student/Faculty:** 15 to 1
Year: semesters, summer session	**Tuition:** $19,000
Application Deadline: see profile	**Room & Board:** $7500
Freshman Class: n/av	
SAT I or ACT: required	**LESS COMPETITIVE**

Curry College, founded in 1879, is a private liberal arts institution. Figures in the above capsule and in this profile are approximate. In addition to regional accreditation, Curry has baccalaureate program accreditation with NLN. The library contains 90,000 volumes, 14,000 microform items, and 190 audio/video tapes/CDs, and subscribes to 625 periodicals. Computerized library services include the card catalog, interlibrary loans, and database searching. Special learning facilities include a learning resource center and radio station. The 131-acre campus is in a suburban area 7 miles southwest of Boston. Including any residence halls, there are 36 buildings.

Student Life: 79% of undergraduates are from Massachusetts. Students are from 31 states, 12 foreign countries, and Canada. 68% are from public schools. 71% are white. The average age of freshmen is 18; all undergraduates, 20. 30% do not continue beyond their first year; 51% remain to graduate.

Housing: 826 students can be accommodated in college housing, which includes single-sex and coed dorms. In addition, there are honors houses, special-interest houses, and a 9-month house for international students. On-campus housing is available on a first-come, first-served basis and is available on a lottery system for upperclassmen. 66% of students live on campus; of those, 80% remain on campus on weekends. All students may keep cars.

Activities: There are no fraternities or sororities. There are 20 groups on campus, including cheerleading, chorale, dance, drama, ethnic, film, honors, international, literary magazine, musical theater, newspaper, photography, political, professional, radio and TV, religious, social, social service, student government, and yearbook. Popular campus events include formal dances, a concert series, and Career Day.

Sports: There are 7 intercollegiate sports for men and 6 for women, and 5 intramural sports for men and 5 for women. Facilities include a 500-seat gym, a dance studio, 13 outdoor tennis courts, an outdoor pool, 5 athletic fields, a 1000-seat stadium, a 500-seat auditorium, and a 5000-meter cross-country trail.

Disabled Students: 60% of the campus is accessible. Wheelchair ramps, elevators, special parking, specially equipped rest rooms, and special class scheduling are available.

Services: Counseling and information services are available, as is tutoring in most subjects. There is a reader service for the blind, and remedial math, reading, and writing. General development courses in writing, reading, and math are designed to develop the student's basic skills. LD tutoring, an Essential Skills Center, and the Program for Advancement of Learning are also available.

Campus Safety and Security: Measures include 24-hour foot and vehicle patrol, security escort services, shuttle buses, and informal discussions. There are pamphlets/posters/films, emergency telephones, and lighted pathways/sidewalks. A campus safety office offers security services.

Programs of Study: Curry confers B.A. and B.S.N. degrees. Master's degrees are also awarded. Bachelor's degrees are awarded in BIOLOGICAL SCIENCE (biology/biological science), BUSINESS (business administration and management), COMMUNICATIONS AND THE ARTS (communications, English, and visual and performing arts), COMPUTER AND PHYSICAL SCIENCE (chemistry and physics), EDUCATION (early childhood, elementary, health, and special), ENGINEERING AND ENVIRONMENTAL DESIGN (environmental science), HEALTH PROFESSIONS (nursing), SOCIAL SCIENCE (criminal justice, history, philosophy, psychology, and sociology). Nursing is the strongest academically. Business, communications, and criminal justice are the largest.

Required: Successful completion of the liberal arts core curriculum and a total of 120 semester hours (121 for nursing), with at least 30 in the major, and a minimum 2.0 GPA, are required for graduation. Nursing students must pass a comprehensive exam.

Special: Curry offers internships in all majors, an accelerated degree with approval of the dean, study abroad, work-study programs, dual and student-designed majors, credit by exam and for life, work, and military experience, nondegree study, and pass/fail options. There are 2 national honor societies.

Faculty/Classroom: 43% of faculty are male; 57%, female. All teach undergraduates. No introductory courses are taught by graduate students. The average class size in an introductory lecture is 20; in a laboratory, 12; and in a regular course, 20.

Requirements: The SAT I or ACT is required, with average scores of 450 verbal and 430 math on the SAT I. Applicants must be graduates of an accredited secondary school or have a GED. 16 credits are required, including 4 years of English, 3 of math, and 2 each of foreign language, history, science, and social studies. An essay is required, and an interview recommended. A portfolio where appropriate is also advised. A GPA of 2.0 is required. AP and CLEP credits are accepted. Important factors in the admissions decision are recommendations by school officials, extracurricular activities record, and evidence of special talent.

Procedure: Freshmen are admitted fall and spring. Entrance exams should be taken in the junior year or in November of the senior year. There are early decision, early admissions, and deferred admissions plans. There is a rolling admissions plan. Notification is sent on a rolling basis. Check with the school for current deadlines. The fee is $40. Applications are accepted on-line at the Curry web site.

Transfer: 81 transfer students enrolled in a recent year. Transfer applicants must be in good academic standing at their previous college with a minimum GPA of 2.0. An interview is recommended. 30 credits of 120 required for the bachelor's degree must be completed at Curry.

Visiting: There are regularly scheduled orientations for prospective students, consisting of interviews with an admissions counselor and tours with a student. There are guides for informal visits and visitors may sit in on classes and stay overnight. To schedule a visit, contact the Admissions Office.

Financial Aid: Curry is a member of CSS. The FAFSA and the college's own financial statement are required. The deadline for filing freshman financial aid applications for fall entry is March 1.

International Students: The school actively recruits these students. They must score 500 on the written TOEFL and also take the SAT I or the ACT.

Computers: The mainframe is a DEC 2100/400 AXP. All students have access to the Internet from residence hall rooms. More than 100 PCs are available for student use in various campus locations. All students may access the system. There are no time limits and no fees. It is strongly recommended that all students have a personal computer.

Admissions Contact: Michael Poll, Dean of Admissions and Financial Aid. E-mail: *curryadm@curry.edu* Web: *www.curry.edu*

EASTERN NAZARENE COLLEGE
Quincy, MA 02170

E-2

(617) 745-3711
(800) 883-6288; Fax: (617) 745-3980

Full-time: 250 men, 350 women	**Faculty:** 52
Part-time: 15 men, 25 women	**Ph.D.s:** 57%
Graduate: 30 men, 150 women	**Student/Faculty:** 13 to 1
Year: 4-1-4, summer session	**Tuition:** $16,608
Application Deadline: see profile	**Room & Board:** $5638
Freshman Class: n/av	
SAT I or ACT: required	**LESS COMPETITIVE**

Eastern Nazarene College, founded in 1918, is a private college affiliated with the Church of the Nazarene. It offers a program in the liberal arts. Figures in the above capsule and in this profile are approximate. In addition to regional accreditation, ENC has baccalaureate program accreditation with CSWE. The library contains 115,000 volumes, and subscribes to 600 periodicals. Computerized library services include interlibrary loans and database searching. Special learning facilities include a learning resource center and radio station. The 15-acre campus is in a suburban area 6 miles south of Boston. Including any residence halls, there are 16 buildings.

Student Life: 55% of undergraduates are from out of state, mostly the Northeast. Students are from 27 states, 24 foreign countries, and Canada. 88% are white. 88% are Protestant. The average age of freshmen is 18; all undergraduates, 20. 25% do not continue beyond their first year; 60% remain to graduate.

Housing: 638 students can be accommodated in college housing, which includes single-sex dorms and married-student housing. On-campus housing is guaranteed for all 4 years. 75% of students live on campus; of those, 75% remain on campus on weekends. Alcohol is not permitted. All students may keep cars.

Activities: There are no fraternities or sororities. There are 34 groups on campus, including band, cheerleading, choir, chorale, chorus, drama, jazz band, literary magazine, musical theater, newspaper, pep band, photography, professional, radio and TV, religious, social service, student government, and yearbook. Popular campus events include Freshmen Breakout, All-School Outing, and Junior/Senior Banquet.

Sports: There are 5 intercollegiate sports for men and 5 for women, and 4 intramural sports for men and 5 for women. Facilities include a phys ed center equipped with a basketball area, batting cage, and playing courts.

Disabled Students: 65% of the campus is accessible. Wheelchair ramps, elevators, special parking, and specially equipped rest rooms are available.

Services: Counseling and information services are available, as is tutoring in most subjects. There is remedial math, reading, and writing.

Campus Safety and Security: Measures include 24-hour foot and vehicle patrol, self-defense education, security escort services, and informal discussions. There are pamphlets/posters/films, emergency telephones, and lighted pathways/sidewalks.

Programs of Study: ENC confers B.A. and B.S. degrees. Associate and master's degrees are also awarded. Bachelor's degrees are awarded in BIOLOGICAL SCIENCE (biology/biological science and marine biology), BUSINESS (accounting and business administration and management), COMMUNICATIONS AND THE ARTS (advertising, broadcasting, communications, dramatic arts, English, French, journalism, literature, music, music performance, Spanish, and speech/debate/rhetoric), COMPUTER AND PHYSICAL SCIENCE (chemistry, computer science, mathematics, physics, and science), EDUCATION (athletic training, education, elementary, music, science, and social science), ENGINEERING AND ENVIRONMENTAL DESIGN (computer engineering, engineering physics, and environmental science), HEALTH PROFESSIONS (sports medicine), SOCIAL SCIENCE (child psychology/development, Christian studies, clinical psychology, history, ministries, physical fitness/movement, psychology, religion, religious music, social studies, social work, and sociology). Chemistry, physics, and history are the strongest academically. Education, business, and psychology are the largest.

Required: All students must complete the core curriculum of writing and rhetoric, biblical history, social science, science or math, symbolic

systems and intercultural awareness, philosophy and religion, and phys ed. A total of 130 credits is required for the B.A. or B.S., with 32 to 40 in the major. Minimum GPA for graduation is 2.0.

Special: Internships are available in the metropolitan Boston area. Study abroad in Costa Rica, a Washington semester, a 3-2 engineering degree with Boston University, and a cooperative program with the Massachusetts College of Pharmacy are offered. Work-study programs, dual majors, credit for life/military/work experience, and pass/fail options are available. An off-campus degree-completion program for adults in business administration is offered. There is 1 national honor society.

Faculty/Classroom: 72% of faculty are male; 28%, female. 83% teach undergraduates. No introductory courses are taught by graduate students. The average class size in an introductory lecture is 75; in a laboratory, 20; and in a regular course, 22.

Requirements: The SAT I or ACT is required. In addition, applicants must be graduates of an accredited secondary school or have a GED. They must have a minimum of 16 academic credits, including 4 of English, 2 to 4 each of math and foreign language, 1 to 4 of science, and 1 to 2 each of history and social studies. Music students must audition. An essay and interview are recommended. A GPA of 2.3 is required. AP and CLEP credits are accepted. Important factors in the admissions decision are advanced placement or honor courses, recommendations by school officials, and leadership record.

Procedure: Freshmen are admitted to all sessions. Entrance exams should be taken in the spring of the junior year. There is a deferred admissions plan and a rolling admissions plan. The fall 2003 application fee was $25. Notification is sent on a rolling basis. Check with the school for current deadlines.

Transfer: A minimum 2.0 GPA is required. An interview is recommended. 60 credits of 130 required for the bachelor's degree must be completed at ENC.

Visiting: There are regularly scheduled orientations for prospective students. There are guides for informal visits and visitors may sit in on classes and stay overnight. To schedule a visit, contact the Office of Admissions.

Financial Aid: ENC is a member of CSS. The FAFSA and the college's own financial statement are required. Check with the school for current deadlines.

International Students: They must score 500 on the written TOEFL.

Computers: The mainframes are a DEC VAX 11/750 and a Plexus P/60. There are more than 30 PCs available for student use in the library. Access to the mainframe computers is gained by assigned password, and terminals are plentiful. All students may access the system. There are no time limits. The fee is $5.

Graduates: In an average class, 44% graduate in 4 years or less, and 51% graduate in 5 years or less.

Admissions Contact: James Heyward, Director of Admissions. E-mail: *admissio@enc.edu* Web: *www.enc.edu*

EMERSON COLLEGE
Boston, MA 02116-4624

E-2

(617) 824-8600; Fax: (617) 824-8609

Full-time: 1186 men, 1761 women	**Faculty:** 136; IIA, +$
Part-time: 131 men, 323 women	**Ph.D.s:** 79%
Graduate: 250 men, 734 women	**Student/Faculty:** 22 to 1
Year: semesters, summer session	**Tuition:** $22,663
Application Deadline: January 15	**Room & Board:** $9542
Freshman Class: 4321 applied, 2090 accepted, 700 enrolled	
SAT I Verbal/Math: 621/592	**ACT: 26 HIGHLY COMPETITIVE**

Emerson College, founded in 1880, is a private, independent college for the study of commmunication and performing arts. There are 2 undergraduate and 2 graduate schools. The library contains 165,000 volumes, 8713 microform items, and 9278 audio/video tapes/CDs, and subscribes to 13,972 periodicals. Computerized library services include the card catalog, interlibrary loans, and database searching. Special learning facilities include a learning resource center, radio station, TV station, film production facilities, DVD authoring and digital production labs, speech-language-hearing clinics, and a proscenium stage theater. The campus is in an urban area in the Theater District on Boston Common. Including any residence halls, there are 11 buildings.

Student Life: 65% of undergraduates are from out of state, mostly the Middle Atlantic. Students are from 45 states, 35 foreign countries, and Canada. 76% are from public schools. 85% are white. The average age of freshmen is 18; all undergraduates, 20. 17% do not continue beyond their first year.

Housing: 1207 students can be accommodated in college housing, which includes coed dorms. In addition, there are living and learning communities such as writer's block and digital culture floors. On-campus housing is available on a first-come, first-served basis and is available on a lottery system for upperclassmen. No one may keep cars.

Activities: 5% of men belong to 2 local fraternities and 1 national fraternity; 4% of women belong to 2 local sororities and 1 national sorority. There are 60 groups on campus, including computers, dance, debate, drama, ethnic, film, forensics, gay, honors, international, literary magazine, musical theater, newspaper, photography, political, professional, radio and TV, religious, social, social service, student government, and yearbook. Popular campus events include Live Music Week, Cultural Awareness and Holiday Celebration, and Hand Me Down Night.

Sports: There are 6 intercollegiate sports for men and 7 for women. Facilities include a 10,000-square-foot fitness center.

Disabled Students: 50% of the campus is accessible. Wheelchair ramps, elevators, specially equipped rest rooms, special class scheduling, and special housing are available.

Services: Counseling and information services are available, as is tutoring in most subjects. There is remedial math, reading, and writing.

Campus Safety and Security: Measures include 24-hour foot and vehicle patrol, self-defense education, security escort services, and shuttle buses. There are informal discussions, pamphlets/posters/films, emergency telephones, and lighted pathways/sidewalks.

Programs of Study: Emerson confers B.A., B.S., B.F.A., and B.S.Sp. degrees. Master's and doctoral degrees are also awarded. Bachelor's degrees are awarded in BUSINESS (marketing management), COMMUNICATIONS AND THE ARTS (advertising, broadcasting, communications, creative writing, dramatic arts, film arts, journalism, media arts, musical theater, performing arts, public relations, publishing, radio/television technology, speech/debate/rhetoric, theater design, and theater management), HEALTH PROFESSIONS (speech pathology/audiology), SOCIAL SCIENCE (interdisciplinary studies). Visual and media arts, writing, and literature and publishing are the strongest academically. Visual and media arts, performing arts, and communication are the largest.

Required: All students must complete 128 credit hours, with 40 to 64 in their major and a minimum GPA of 2.0. The required general education curriculum consists of communications, liberal arts, and global multicultural perspectives course work, for a total of 56 credits. A course in voice and articulation is required.

Special: Student-designed, interdisciplinary, and dual majors are available. Cross-registration is offered with the 6-member Boston ProArts consortium, Suffolk University, and Wheelock College. 700 internships are possible in Boston and 250 in Los Angeles. Internships bear credit and are graded. Emerson has nondegree study and pass/fail options, as well as study abroad in the Netherlands and a summer film program in Prague. There is 1 national honor society, a freshman honors program, and 6 departmental honors programs.

Faculty/Classroom: 57% of faculty are male; 43%, female. All teach undergraduates. Graduate students teach 4% of introductory courses. The average class size in an introductory lecture is 35; in a laboratory, 19; and in a regular course, 20.

Admissions: 48% of the 2003-2004 applicants were accepted. The SAT I scores for the 2003-2004 freshman class were: Verbal--2% below 500, 34% between 500 and 599, 51% between 600 and 700, and 13% above 700; Math--6% below 500, 48% between 500 and 599, 40% between 600 and 700, and 6% above 700. The ACT scores were 3% below 21, 18% between 21 and 23, 31% between 24 and 26, 28% between 27 and 28, and 20% above 28. 70% of the current freshmen were in the top fifth of their class; 85% were in the top two fifths. 5 freshmen graduated first in their class.

Requirements: The SAT I or ACT is required. In addition, candidates must be graduates of an accredited secondary school or hold a GED certificate. They must have completed 16 Carnegie units, including 4 in English and 3 each in science, social studies, foreign language, and math. An essay is required. Candidates for performing arts programs may be required to audition or interview, or submit a portfolio, resume, or essay. AP and CLEP credits are accepted. Important factors in the admissions decision are advanced placement or honor courses, evidence of special talent, and recommendations by school officials.

Procedure: Freshmen are admitted fall and spring. Entrance exams should be taken before January of the senior year. There are early action, early admissions, and deferred admissions plans. Early action applications should be filed by November 1; regular applications, by January 15 for fall entry and November 1 for spring entry. The fall 2003 application fee was $55. Notification of early action is sent December 15; regular decision, April 1. 1045 early action candidates were accepted for the 2003-2004 class. 314 applicants were on the 2003 waiting list; none were admitted. Applications are accepted on-line through the school's web site and Apply Yourself.

Transfer: 215 transfer students enrolled in 2002-2003. Official transcripts from high school (or a GED), all college course work, plus 2 letters of recommendation are required. SAT I or ACT scores must be submitted, unless the candidate possesses an associate degree or has been out of school 3 or more years. 32 of 128 credits required for the bachelor's degree must be completed at Emerson.

Visiting: There are regularly scheduled orientations for prospective students, including an information session with an admissions representative and a tour lead by a currently enrolled student. There are guides for informal visits and visitors may sit in on classes. Visits may be scheduled on-line.

Financial Aid: In 2003-2004, 59% of all full-time freshmen and 52% of continuing full-time students received some form of financial aid. 57%

of full-time freshmen and 51% of continuing full-time students received need-based aid. The average freshman award was $13,000. Need-based scholarships or need-based grants averaged $11,000; need-based self-help aid (loans and jobs) averaged $7000; and non-need-based awards and non-need-based scholarships averaged $11,000. 56% of undergraduates work part time. Average annual earnings from campus work are $1600. The average financial indebtedness of the 2003 graduate was $17,125. The CSS/Profile or FAFSA and the college's own financial statement are required. The deadline for filing freshman financial aid applications for fall entry is March 1.

International Students: There are 112 international students enrolled. The school actively recruits these students. They must score 550 on the written TOEFL or 213 on the electronic version or take the IELTS. They must also take the SAT I or the ACT.

Computers: The mainframe is a DEC VAX 4500. Many PCs are available in the academic computing center and the media center. All campus buildings, including residence halls, are networked and have direct access to the college server. All students may access the system 24 hours a day. There are no time limits and no fees. It is strongly recommended that all students have a personal computer.

Graduates: From July 1, 2002 to June 30, 2003, 769 bachelor's degrees were awarded. The most popular majors were visual and media arts (30%), communication (25%), and performing arts (25%). In an average class, 1% graduate in 3 years or less, 58% graduate in 4 years or less, 61% graduate in 5 years or less, and 63% graduate in 6 years or less. 100 companies recruited on campus in a recent year. Of a recent graduating class, 3% were enrolled in graduate school within 6 months of graduation and 87% were employed.

Admissions Contact: Sara S. Ramirez, Director of Undergraduate Admission. E-mail: *admission@emerson.edu* Web: *www.emerson.edu*

EMMANUEL COLLEGE   E-2
Boston, MA 02115   **(617) 735-9715; Fax: (617) 735-9801**

Full-time: 273 men, 877 women	**Faculty:** 48; IIB, av$
Part-time: 95 men, 347 women	**Ph.Ds:** 77%
Graduate: 55 men, 173 women	**Student/Faculty:** 24 to 1
Year: semesters, summer session	**Tuition:** $19,200
Application Deadline: rolling	**Room & Board:** $8400
Freshman Class: 2621 applied, 1569 accepted, 449 enrolled	
SAT I Verbal/Math: 510/490	**ACT:** 24 **COMPETITIVE+**

Emmanuel College, founded in 1919 by the Sisters of Notre Dame de Namar, is a Catholic college offering a liberal arts and sciences curriculum that emphasizes career development. In addition to regional accreditation, Emmanuel College has baccalaureate program accreditation with ACPE and NLN. The library contains 97,000 volumes, 2005 microform items, and 531 audio/video tapes/CDs, and subscribes to 414 periodicals. Computerized library services include the card catalog, interlibrary loans, database searching, and Internet access. Special learning facilities include a learning resource center and art gallery. The 17-acre campus is in an urban area in Boston. Including any residence halls, there are 12 buildings.

Student Life: 64% of undergraduates are from Massachusetts. Others are from 33 states and 32 foreign countries. 72% are from public schools. 62% are white. 46% are Catholic; 34% claim no religious affiliation. The average age of freshmen is 18; all undergraduates, 20. 20% do not continue beyond their first year; 60% remain to graduate.

Housing: 879 students can be accommodated in college housing, which includes single-sex and coed dormitories. On-campus housing is guaranteed for all 4 years. 83% of students live on campus; of those, 70% remain on campus on weekends. Alcohol is not permitted. Upperclassmen may keep cars.

Activities: There are no fraternities or sororities. There are 26 groups on campus, including art, chorus, dance, drama, ethnic, honors, international, literary magazine, musical theater, newspaper, orchestra, political, professional, religious, social, social service, student government, and yearbook. Popular campus events include Spring Weekend, Clam Bake, and Tap Off Tournament.

Sports: There are 6 intercollegiate sports for men and 8 for women, and 2 intramural sports for men and 2 for women. Facilities include a 500-seat gym, a training room/locker room, a fitness center, and a 500-seat auditorium. Students have access to a swimming pool, aerobic facilities, and 2 tennis courts.

Disabled Students: 75% of the campus is accessible. Wheelchair ramps, elevators, special parking, specially equipped rest rooms, special class scheduling, and lowered telephones are available.

Services: Counseling and information services are available, as is tutoring in every subject. There is remedial math, reading, and writing.

Campus Safety and Security: Measures include 24-hour foot and vehicle patrol, self-defense education, shuttle buses, and informal discussions. There are pamphlets/posters/films, emergency telephones, lighted pathways/sidewalks, and 24-hour staffed residence hall desks.

Programs of Study: Emmanuel College confers B.A., B.S., and B.F.A. degrees. Master's degrees are also awarded. Bachelor's degrees are awarded in BIOLOGICAL SCIENCE (biochemistry and biology/biological science), BUSINESS (business administration and management), COMMUNICATIONS AND THE ARTS (art history and appreciation, communications, English, fine arts, Spanish, and studio art), COMPUTER AND PHYSICAL SCIENCE (chemistry and mathematics), EDUCATION (art, elementary, and secondary), HEALTH PROFESSIONS (art therapy, health care administration, medical laboratory technology, nursing, predentistry, premedicine, and preveterinary science), SOCIAL SCIENCE (interdisciplinary studies, international studies, liberal arts/general studies, political science/government, prelaw, psychology, and sociology). Biology is the strongest academically. Business administration, psychology, and biology are the largest.

Required: Students must complete a broad range of distribution requirements, including fine arts, math, writing, humanities, foreign language, philosophy, science, social science, and religious studies. Computer literacy is required. The core curriculum includes 2 interdisciplinary courses. A total of 128 credit hours is required, with 10 to 17 courses in the major, 15 general requirements, 5 to 7 elective or minor courses, and a minimum GPA of 2.0 for graduation.

Special: There is cross-registration with Wheelock College, Simmons College, Massachusetts College of Art, Massachusetts College of Pharmacy, Wentworth Institute of Technology, and Andover-Newton Theological School. The college offers internships, study abroad, a Washington semester, work-study programs on campus and in Boston-area organizations, an accelerated degree program in business administration, a B.A.-B.S. degree in biology, dual and student-designed majors, a general studies degree, a 3-2 engineering degree with Wentworth Institute of Technology, and pass/fail options. The adult learner degree program offers learning opportunities at off-campus sites for men and women age 23 and older. There are 4 national honor societies and a freshman honors program. All departments have honors programs.

Faculty/Classroom: 29% of faculty are male; 71%, female. All both teach and do research. No introductory courses are taught by graduate students. The average class size in an introductory lecture is 18 and in a laboratory, 11.

Admissions: 60% of the 2003-2004 applicants were accepted. The SAT I scores for the 2003-2004 freshman class were: Verbal--32% below 500, 46% between 500 and 599, 20% between 600 and 700, and 2% above 700; Math--43% below 500, 40% between 500 and 599, 16% between 600 and 700, and 1% above 700.

Requirements: The SAT I or ACT is required. In addition, applicants must be graduates of an accredited secondary school or have a GED. 16 academic credits are required, including 4 years of English, 3 years of math, and 2 years each of foreign language, lab science, and social studies. An essay and an interview are required. AP and CLEP credits are accepted. Important factors in the admissions decision are advanced placement or honor courses, evidence of special talent, and parents or siblings attending the school.

Procedure: Freshmen are admitted fall and spring. Entrance exams should be taken by November of the senior year. There are early decision, early admissions, and deferred admissions plans. Early decision applications should be filed by November 1; regular application deadlines are rolling. The fee is $40. Notification of early decision is sent December 1; regular decision, on a rolling basis. Applications are accepted on computer disk and on-line through the school's web site.

Transfer: 65 transfer students enrolled in 2003-2004. Students must submit essays, college and high school transcripts, and 2 letters of recommendation. They must be financially and academically eligible to return to the previously attended institution. 64 of 128 credits required for the bachelor's degree must be completed at Emmanuel College.

Visiting: There are regularly scheduled orientations for prospective students. There are guides for informal visits and visitors may sit in on classes and stay overnight. To schedule a visit, contact the Admissions Office.

Financial Aid: In 2003-2004, 87% of all full-time freshmen and 93% of continuing full-time students received some form of financial aid. 71% of full-time freshmen and 86% of continuing full-time students received need-based aid. The average freshman award was $14,452. 39% of undergraduates work part time. Average annual earnings from campus work are $1226. The average financial indebtedness of the 2003 graduate was $15,325. The FAFSA, the college's own financial statement, and parents' and students' income tax forms are required. The deadline for filing freshman financial aid applications for fall entry is April 1.

International Students: There were 69 international students enrolled in a recent year. The school actively recruits these students. They must score 500 on the written TOEFL or take ELS level 109 or the equivalent, and also take the SAT I or the ACT.

Computers: The mainframe is an IBM RS/6000 Model 390. IBM PCs and Macs are available in the computer and academic resource centers. A campuswide network permits access to the Internet and other services from the library, dorm rooms, and other locations. All students may access the system. There are no time limits and no fees.

Graduates: From July 1, 2002 to June 30, 2003, 345 bachelor's degrees were awarded. The most popular majors were business management (25%), English (12%), and psychology (12%). In an average class,

1% graduate in 3 years or less, 52% graduate in 4 years or less, 54% graduate in 5 years or less, and 60% graduate in 6 years or less.

Admissions Contact: Sandra Robbins, Dean of Admissions.
E-mail: *enroll@emmanuel.edu* Web: *www.emmanuel.edu*

ENDICOTT COLLEGE

E-2
Beverly, MA 01915
(978) 921-1000
(800) 325-1114; Fax: (978) 232-2520

Full-time: 577 men, 982 women	**Faculty:** 57; IIB, av$
Part-time: 150 men and women	**Ph.D.s:** 40%
Graduate: 860 men and women	**Student/Faculty:** 27 to 1
Year: semesters, summer session	**Tuition:** $17,408
Application Deadline: February 15	**Room & Board:** $7858
Freshman Class: 2661 applied, 1271 accepted, 506 enrolled	
SAT I Verbal/Math: 519/527	**COMPETITIVE+**

Endicott College, founded in 1939, is a private institution offering programs in arts and sciences, business and communications, health sciences, sports science and hospitality, education, art and design, criminal justice, and computer and information technology. In addition to regional accreditation, Endicott College has baccalaureate program accreditation with FIDER and NLN. The library contains 114,000 volumes, 23,500 microform items, and 475 audio/video tapes/CDs, and subscribes to 4000 periodicals. Computerized library services include the card catalog, interlibrary loans, database searching, and Internet access. Special learning facilities include a learning resource center, art gallery, radio station, TV station, and an archives museum. The 240-acre campus is in a suburban area 20 miles north of Boston. Including any residence halls, there are 36 buildings.

Student Life: 60% of undergraduates are from out of state, mostly the Northeast. Students are from 30 states, 32 foreign countries, and Canada. 81% are white. The average age of freshmen is 18; all undergraduates, 20. 20% do not continue beyond their first year; 50% remain to graduate.

Housing: 1368 students can be accommodated in college housing, which includes single-sex and coed dormitories, on-campus apartments, and off-campus apartments. In addition, there is substance-free housing. On-campus housing is guaranteed for the freshman year only, is available on a first-come, first-served basis, and is available on a lottery system for upperclassmen. 88% of students live on campus. All students may keep cars.

Activities: There are no fraternities or sororities. There are 30 groups on campus, including adventure, art, campus activities board, cheerleading, chorus, computers, dance, drama, ethnic, film, fitness, honors, international, literary magazine, newspaper, professional, radio and TV, religious, sailing, social, social service, student government, and yearbook. Popular campus events include hypnotist and comedian acts, performing arts events, and Founders Day.

Sports: There are 10 intercollegiate sports for men and 10 for women, and 6 intramural sports for men and 6 for women. Facilities include a 1400-seat gym with a racquetball and basketball courts, weight, fitness, and aerobics rooms, an indoor track, and a field house. Outdoor facilities include 6 tennis courts, field hockey, softball, lighted baseball, lacrosse, and soccer fields, and a 2200-seat multipurpose football stadium.

Disabled Students: 90% of the campus is accessible. Wheelchair ramps, elevators, special parking, specially equipped rest rooms, special class scheduling, and lowered drinking fountains are available.

Services: Counseling and information services are available, as is tutoring in every subject. There is a reader service for the blind, and remedial math, reading, and writing. An interpreter service for hearing-impaired students is available.

Campus Safety and Security: Measures include 24-hour foot and vehicle patrol, self-defense education, security escort services, and shuttle buses. There are informal discussions, pamphlets/posters/films, emergency telephones, and lighted pathways/sidewalks.

Programs of Study: Endicott College confers B.A., B.S., and B.F.A. degrees. Associate and master's degrees are also awarded. Bachelor's degrees are awarded in AGRICULTURE (environmental studies), BUSINESS (business administration and management, hotel/motel and restaurant management, and sports management), COMMUNICATIONS AND THE ARTS (communications, English, and fine arts), EDUCATION (athletic training, education, and physical), ENGINEERING AND ENVIRONMENTAL DESIGN (computer technology and interior design), HEALTH PROFESSIONS (nursing), SOCIAL SCIENCE (criminal justice, international studies, liberal arts/general studies, and psychology). Business is the largest.

Required: To graduate, students must complete 128 credit hours with a minimum GPA of 2.0 (2.5 in education and nursing). Core requirements include 9 credits in science, humanities, social sciences, math, and writing courses, 12 upper-division electives and 3 credits each in first-year seminar, senior seminar, and capstone.

Special: Cross-registration is available with NECCUM, and internships are required in every major. Students may study abroad, and there are accelerated degree programs in business administration and psychology.

Student-designed majors are available in liberal studies. There are 4 national honor societies, a freshman honors program, and 3 departmental honors programs.

Faculty/Classroom: 48% of faculty are male; 52%, female. All teach undergraduates. No introductory courses are taught by graduate students. The average class size in an introductory lecture is 19; in a laboratory, 19; and in a regular course, 19.

Admissions: 48% of the 2003-2004 applicants were accepted. The SAT I scores for the 2003-2004 freshman class were: Verbal--37% below 500, 54% between 500 and 599, and 9% between 600 and 700; Math--29% below 500, 59% between 500 and 599, and 12% between 600 and 700. 25% of the current freshmen were in the top fifth of their class; 58% were in the top two fifths.

Requirements: The SAT I is required. In addition, essays and 2 science and math recommendations are required for nursing (including chemistry) and athletic training majors. Endicott College requires applicants to be in the upper 50% of their class. A GPA of 2.9 is required. AP and CLEP credits are accepted. Important factors in the admissions decision are leadership record, recommendations by school officials, and extracurricular activities record.

Procedure: Freshmen are admitted fall and spring. Entrance exams should be taken in fall of the senior year. There is a deferred admissions plan. Applications should be filed by February 15 for fall entry and December 15 for spring entry, along with a $40 fee. Notification is sent on a rolling basis. 61 were on the 2003 waiting list. Applications are accepted on-line through the college's web site.

Transfer: 49 transfer students enrolled in 2003-2004. The SAT I or ACT is required, as are official high school and college transcripts, and a letter of recommendation. 24 of 128 credits required for the bachelor's degree must be completed at Endicott College.

Visiting: There are regularly scheduled orientations for prospective students, including testing, preregistration, and an introduction to general student life. There are guides for informal visits and visitors may sit in on classes and stay overnight. To schedule a visit, contact the Admission Office.

Financial Aid: In 2003-2004, 84% of all full-time freshmen and 77% of continuing full-time students received some form of financial aid. 66% of full-time freshmen and 60% of continuing full-time students received need-based aid. The average freshman award was $11,668. 25% of undergraduates work part time. Average annual earnings from campus work are $1500. The average financial indebtedness of the 2003 graduate was $17,125. Endicott College is a member of CSS. The FAFSA and the college's own financial statement are required. The priority date for freshman financial aid applications for fall entry is March 15.

International Students: There are 110 international students enrolled. The school actively recruits these students. They must score 525 on the written TOEFL.

Computers: There are 5 academic computer labs that house Mac computers. Students have access to the Internet, e-mail, and a 24/7 cyber PC café. All students may access the system 24 hours a day, 7 days a week. There are no time limits. The fee is $350. It is strongly recommended that all students have a personal computer. It is recommended that students in business have personal computers.

Graduates: From July 1, 2002 to June 30, 2003, 316 bachelor's degrees were awarded. The most popular majors were business administration (25%), art and design (22%), and communications (12%). In an average class, 50% graduate in 6 years or less. 50 companies recruited on campus in 2002-2003. Of the 2002 graduating class, 9% were enrolled in graduate school within 6 months of graduation and 87% were employed.

Admissions Contact: Thomas J. Redman, Vice President, Admissions. A video is available. E-mail: *admissio@endicott.edu* Web: *www.endicott.edu*

FISHER COLLEGE
Boston, MA 02116-1500

D-13

(617) 236-8818
(800) 446-1226; Fax: (617) 236-5473

Full-time: 160 men, 370 women	**Faculty:** 28
Part-time: 10 men and women	**Ph.D.s:** 22%
Graduate: none	**Student/Faculty:** 19 to 1
Year: semesters, summer session	**Tuition:** $16,950
Application Deadline: open	**Room & Board:** $8975
Freshman Class: n/av	
ACT: n/av	**COMPETITIVE**

Fisher College, founded in 1903, is an independent institution offering a bachelor's degree in management. Figures in the above capsule and in this profile are approximate. The 2 libraries contain 32,000 volumes and 1500 audio/video tapes/CDs, and subscribe to 150 periodicals. Computerized library services include the card catalog, interlibrary loans, and database searching. Special learning facilities include a learning resource center. The 1-acre campus is in an urban area in Boston. Including any residence halls, there are 12 buildings.

Student Life: 60% of undergraduates are from Massachusetts. Students are from 15 states, 87 foreign countries, and Canada. 80% are from

public schools. 37% are white; 21% African American; 10% Hispanic. The average age of freshmen is 17; all undergraduates, 17.

Housing: 292 students can be accommodated in college housing, which includes single-sex and coed dorms. On-campus housing is available on a first-come, first-served basis and is available on a lottery system for upperclassmen. Priority is given to out-of-town students. 50% of students live on campus. Alcohol is not permitted. No one may keep cars.

Activities: There are no fraternities or sororities. There are 15 groups on campus, including cheerleading, chess, computers, ethnic, gay, honors, international, photography, political, professional, religious, social, social service, student government, and yearbook. Popular campus events include ski trips, dances, and horseback riding.

Sports: There are 2 intercollegiate sports for men and 2 for women.

Disabled Students: 85% of the campus is accessible. Wheelchair ramps, elevators, special parking, and specially equipped rest rooms are available.

Services: Counseling and information services are available, as is tutoring in every subject. There is remedial math, reading, and writing.

Campus Safety and Security: Measures include 24-hour foot and vehicle patrol, shuttle buses, pamphlets/posters/films, and lighted pathways/sidewalks.

Programs of Study: Fisher College confers B.S. and B.S.M. degrees. Associate degrees are also awarded. Bachelor's degrees are awarded in BUSINESS (business administration and management). Management is the largest.

Required: Students must complete a minimum of 120 hours, with at least 36 in the major and a minimum GPA of 2.0. Students must also take English I, English II, and a freshman seminar. Distribution requirements include 6 hours each in humanities, social science, and math/science.

Special: Internships, work-study, and dual majors are available. There is 1 national honor society, including Phi Beta Kappa, a freshman honors program, and 1 departmental honors program.

Faculty/Classroom: 45% of faculty are male; 55%, female. All teach undergraduates; 10% both teach and do research. The average class size in an introductory lecture is 17; in a laboratory, 12; and in a regular course, 19.

Requirements: AP and CLEP credits are accepted. Important factors in the admissions decision are recommendations by school officials, leadership record, and advanced placement or honor courses.

Procedure: Freshmen are admitted fall and spring. There is a rolling admissions plan. Application deadlines are open. Application fee is $25. Notification is sent on a rolling basis. Applications are accepted on-line at the college's web site.

Transfer: 60 transfer students enrolled in a recent year. Transfer requirements are the same as for all students, including submission of college transcript. 30 credits of 120 required for the bachelor's degree must be completed at Fisher College.

Visiting: There are regularly scheduled orientations for prospective students. There are guides for informal visits and visitors may sit in on classes. To schedule a visit, contact the Office of Admissions at *admissions@fisher.edu*.

Financial Aid: In a recent year, 83% of all full-time freshmen and 51% of continuing full-time students received some form of financial aid. 75% of full-time freshmen received need-based aid. The average freshman award was $10,611. 38% of undergraduates work part time. Average annual earnings from campus work are $479. The average financial indebtedness of a recent graduate was $14,125. The FAFSA is required. Check with the school for current deadlines.

International Students: There were 87 international students enrolled in a recent year. The school actively recruits these students. They must score 450 on the written TOEFL or 133 on the electronic version and also take the college's own test.

Computers: All students may access the system. There are no time limits and no fees.

Graduates: In a recent year, 5 bachelor's degrees were awarded.

Admissions Contact: Marietta Baier, Associate Director Admissions. E-mail: *admissions@fisher.edu* Web: *www.fisher.edu*

FITCHBURG STATE COLLEGE
Fitchburg, MA 01420-2697

C-2

(978) 665-3144
(800) 705-9692; Fax: (978) 665-4540

Full-time: 1017 men, 1419 women	**Faculty:** 180; IIA, av$
Part-time: 430 men, 513 women	**Ph.D.s:** 75%
Graduate: 413 men, 1257 women	**Student/Faculty:** 14 to 1
Year: semesters	**Tuition:** $4186 ($10,266)
Application Deadline: April 1	**Room & Board:** $5436
Freshman Class: 2718 applied, 1644 accepted, 520 enrolled	
SAT I Verbal/Math: 490/490	**COMPETITIVE**

Fitchburg State College, founded in 1894, is a public college offering programs in liberal arts, business, communications, health sciences, and education. In addition to regional accreditation, Fitchburg State has baccalaureate program accreditation with CCNE, IACBE, NAACLS, and NCATE. The library contains 235,669 volumes and 454,817 microform items, and subscribes to 2100 periodicals. Computerized library services include the card catalog, interlibrary loans, database searching, and Internet access. Special learning facilities include a learning resource center, art gallery, radio station, a campus school, a graphics center, and a TV studio. The 45-acre campus is in a suburban area 45 miles west of Boston. Including any residence halls, there are 33 buildings.

Student Life: 93% of undergraduates are from Massachusetts. Others are from 14 states and 8 foreign countries. 80% are from public schools. 91% are white. The average age of freshmen is 18; all undergraduates, 20. 29% do not continue beyond their first year; 44% remain to graduate.

Housing: 1337 students can be accommodated in college housing, which includes coed dormitories and on-campus apartments. In addition, there are special-interest houses. 55% of students commute. All students may keep cars.

Activities: 3% of men belong to 4 national fraternities; 3% of women belong to 1 local sorority and 2 national sororities. There are 65 groups on campus, including band, cheerleading, choir, computers, dance, drama, ethnic, film, gay, honors, international, jazz band, literary magazine, newspaper, photography, political, professional, radio and TV, religious, social, social service, student government, and yearbook. Popular campus events include Falcon Fest and Center Stage Performing Arts Series.

Sports: There are 8 intercollegiate sports for men and 8 for women, and 8 intramural sports for men and 8 for women. Facilities include a 1000-seat gym, an indoor/outdoor track, a weight room, varsity and intramural fields, the student union, volleyball, basketball, racquetball, and tennis courts, a swimming pool, and a dance studio.

Disabled Students: 80% of the campus is accessible. Wheelchair ramps, elevators, special parking, specially equipped rest rooms, special class scheduling, lowered drinking fountains, lowered telephones, special housing, and an adaptive computer lab are available.

Services: Counseling and information services are available, as is tutoring in most subjects. There is a reader service for the blind, and remedial math, reading, and writing.

Campus Safety and Security: Measures include 24-hour foot and vehicle patrol, self-defense education, security escort services, and shuttle buses. There are informal discussions, pamphlets/posters/films, emergency telephones, and lighted pathways/sidewalks.

Programs of Study: Fitchburg State confers B.A., B.S., and B.S.Ed. degrees. Master's degrees are also awarded. Bachelor's degrees are awarded in BIOLOGICAL SCIENCE (biology/biological science), BUSINESS (business administration and management), COMMUNICATIONS AND THE ARTS (communications and English), COMPUTER AND PHYSICAL SCIENCE (computer science, earth science, and mathematics), EDUCATION (early childhood, elementary, industrial arts, middle school, secondary, and special), ENGINEERING AND ENVIRONMENTAL DESIGN (industrial engineering technology), HEALTH PROFESSIONS (nursing), SOCIAL SCIENCE (criminal justice, economics, geography, history, human services, liberal arts/general studies, political science/government, psychology, and sociology). Computer science and nursing are the strongest academically. Business administration, communications, and nursing are the largest.

Required: All students must complete a minimum of 120 credit hours with a GPA of at least 2.0 overall and in the major. Distribution requirements include courses from the categories of ideas and events, human behavior, literature/language/arts, and the quantitative/scientific area. 2 introductory semesters of writing plus junior/senior writing in the major, 1 semester of health and fitness, and a computer literacy course are also required.

Special: Students may cross-register at any other Massachusetts state college. Internships in a variety of fields, study abroad in 11 countries, accelerated degree programs, B.A.-B.S. degrees, dual majors, and a student-designed general studies major are offered. There are 6 national honor societies, a freshman honors program, and 7 departmental honors programs.

Faculty/Classroom: 55% of faculty are male; 45%, female. All teach undergraduates. No introductory courses are taught by graduate students. The average class size in an introductory lecture is 20; in a laboratory, 15; and in a regular course, 20.

Admissions: 60% of the 2003-2004 applicants were accepted. The SAT I scores for the 2003-2004 freshman class were: Verbal--48% below 500, 44% between 500 and 599, 7% between 600 and 700, and 1% above 700; Math--52% below 500, 38% between 500 and 599, and 10% between 600 and 700.

Requirements: The SAT I is required. In addition, applicants should be graduates of accredited high schools or have the GED. Secondary preparation should include 4 years of English, 3 years each of math and liberal arts or phys ed, and 2 years each of a foreign language, social studies including U.S. history, and science. A GPA of 2.0 is required. AP and CLEP credits are accepted. Important factors in the admissions decision are advanced placement or honor courses, leadership record, and extracurricular activities record.

Procedure: Freshmen are admitted fall and spring. Entrance exams should be taken in the junior or senior year. There are early admissions and deferred admissions plans. Applications should be filed by April 1 for fall entry and December 1 for spring entry, along with a $10 fee. Notification is sent on a rolling basis. Applications are accepted on-line through *www.fsc.edu/admissions.*

Transfer: 364 transfer students enrolled in 2003-2004. Applicants should present a minimum GPA of 2.0 in at least 12 credits of transferable college work. 45 of 120 credits required for the bachelor's degree must be completed at Fitchburg State.

Visiting: There are regularly scheduled orientations for prospective students, including tours of the campus and residence halls, admissions/financial aid information, and academic program advising. There are guides for informal visits and visitors may sit in on classes. To schedule a visit, contact the Admissions Office.

Financial Aid: The FAFSA and the college's own financial statement are required. The deadline for filing freshman financial aid applications for fall entry is March 1.

International Students: There are 20 international students enrolled. The school actively recruits these students. They must score 550 on the written TOEFL or 213 on the electronic version.

Computers: The mainframe is a Tricord ES8000. Some 250 PCs are available for student use in the residence halls and in various labs throughout the campus. All residence hall rooms have full Internet access. All students may access the system 24 hours per day. There are no time limits and no fees.

Graduates: From July 1, 2002 to June 30, 2003, 467 bachelor's degrees were awarded. The most popular majors were business administration (15%), communications (15%), and nursing (13%). In an average class, 21% graduate in 4 years or less, 40% graduate in 5 years or less, and 44% graduate in 6 years or less. 30 companies recruited on campus in 2002-2003. Of a recent graduating class, 10% were enrolled in graduate school within 6 months of graduation and 94% were employed.

Admissions Contact: Lynn Petricco, Director of Admissions. A video is available. E-mail: *admissions@fsc.edu* Web: *www.fsc.edu*

FRAMINGHAM STATE COLLEGE   D-2
Framingham, MA 01701-9101   (508) 626-4500
                                          Fax: (508) 626-4017

Full-time: 1026 men, 2106 women	**Faculty:** 168
Part-time: 298 men, 462 women	**Ph.D.s:** 73%
Graduate: 510 men, 1754 women	**Student/Faculty:** 19 to 1
Year: semesters, summer session	**Tuition:** $4324 ($10,404)
Application Deadline: February 15	**Room & Board:** $5057
Freshman Class: 4214 applied, 2319 accepted, 625 enrolled	
SAT I Verbal/Math: 533/525	**COMPETITIVE**

Framingham State College, founded in 1839, is a comprehensive public institution offering degree programs based on a liberal arts foundation that includes distinctive career opportunities. There is 1 undergraduate and 1 graduate school. In addition to regional accreditation, FSC has baccalaureate program accreditation with ADA, AHEA, and NLN. The library contains 202,452 volumes, 658,830 microform items, and 3313 audio/video tapes/CDs, and subscribes to 409 periodicals. Computerized library services include the card catalog, interlibrary loans, database searching, and Internet access. Special learning facilities include a learning resource center, art gallery, planetarium, radio station, and greenhouse, TV studio, early childhood demonstration lab, and education and teaching center. The 73-acre campus is in a suburban area 20 miles west of Boston. Including any residence halls, there are 19 buildings.

Student Life: 92% of undergraduates are from Massachusetts. Students are from 15 states, 25 foreign countries, and Canada. 80% are from public schools. 90% are white. The average age of freshmen is 19; all undergraduates, 21. 27% do not continue beyond their first year; 42% remain to graduate.

Housing: 1450 students can be accommodated in college housing, which includes single-sex and coed dorms. 55% of students commute. Alcohol is not permitted. Upperclassmen may keep cars.

Activities: There are no fraternities or sororities. There are 35 groups on campus, including art, cheerleading, chorale, chorus, computers, dance, drama, ethnic, gay, honors, international, literary magazine, newspaper, political, professional, radio and TV, religious, social, social service, student government, and yearbook. Popular campus events include the Sandbox Festival and performances by the Hilltop Players.

Sports: There are 6 intercollegiate sports for men and 6 for women, and 10 intramural sports for men and 9 for women. Facilities include an athletic and recreation center, a gym, and a student center. A field for soccer, football, field hockey, and intramural sports is available on lower campus fields.

Disabled Students: 95% of the campus is accessible. Wheelchair ramps, elevators, special parking, specially equipped rest rooms, special class scheduling, lowered drinking fountains, and lowered telephones are available.

Services: Counseling and information services are available, as is tutoring in most subjects. There is a reader service for the blind and remedial math, reading, and writing. The College Skills Center offers free tutoring in writing, math, and reading. Subject tutoring may be arranged for an hourly fee.

Campus Safety and Security: Measures include 24-hour foot and vehicle patrol, self-defense education, security escort services, and shuttle buses. There are informal discussions, pamphlets/posters/films, emergency telephones, and lighted pathways/sidewalks.

Programs of Study: FSC confers B.A. and B.S. degrees. Master's degrees are also awarded. Bachelor's degrees are awarded in BIOLOGICAL SCIENCE (biology/biological science and nutrition), BUSINESS (business administration and management and fashion merchandising), COMMUNICATIONS AND THE ARTS (art history and appreciation, communications, English, French, Spanish, and studio art), COMPUTER AND PHYSICAL SCIENCE (chemistry, computer science, and mathematics), EDUCATION (early childhood and elementary), HEALTH PROFESSIONS (nursing), SOCIAL SCIENCE (consumer services, economics, family/consumer studies, fashion design and technology, food science, geography, history, interdisciplinary studies, political science/government, psychology, sociology, and textiles and clothing). Business administration, elementary/early childhood education, and food and nutrition are the largest.

Required: The college's goal-based general education model includes: writing; math; language; literature or philosophy; visual or performing arts; physical science; life science; historical studies; social and behavioral sciences; forces in the United States; study of Constitutions; gender, class, and race; and non-Western studies. Every student must take 12 general education courses and fulfill all required goals. A total of 128 credits (32 courses), including 40 to 68 credits in the major, and a 2.0 GPA is required to graduate.

Special: The college offers a 2-3 preengineering program in cooperation with the University of Massachusetts at Amherst, Lowell, and Dartmouth. Cross-registration is possible at any of the state colleges. Study abroad in 7 countries, a Washington semester, and various internships are available. Pass/fail options are limited to 2 courses. There are 6 national honor societies, a freshman honors program, and 6 departmental honors programs.

Faculty/Classroom: 55% of faculty are male; 45%, female. All teach undergraduates. No introductory courses are taught by graduate students. The average class size in an introductory lecture is 25 and in a laboratory, 25.

Admissions: 55% of the 2003-2004 applicants were accepted. The SAT I scores for the 2003-2004 freshman class were: Verbal--31% were 500, 53% between 500 and 599, 15% between 600 and 700, and 1% above 700; Math--33% below 500, 52% between 500 and 599, 14% between 600 and 700, and 1% above 700. 28% of the current freshmen were in the top fifth of their class; 64% were in the top two fifths. 2 freshmen graduated first in their class in a recent year.

Requirements: The SAT I is required. In addition, applicants must have a high school diploma or the GED. Secondary preparation must total 16 college-preparatory credits, including 4 years of English, 3 each of math and science (2 with lab), and 2 each of foreign language and social science. The required 2 years of electives may include additional academic subjects or art, music, or computer courses. Prospective art majors must submit a portfolio. A GPA of 3.0 is required. AP and CLEP credits are accepted. Important factors in the admissions decision are advanced placement or honor courses, leadership record, and recommendations by school officials.

Procedure: Freshmen are admitted fall and spring. Entrance exams should be taken in the spring of the junior year or fall of the senior year. There are early admissions and deferred admissions plans. There is a rolling admissions plan. Applications should be filed by February 15 for fall entry and December 1 for spring entry, along with a $25 fee (in-state) or $40 (out-of-state). Notification is sent on a rolling basis. Applications are accepted on-line at *www.framingham.ma.edu.*

Transfer: 518 transfer students enrolled in 2002-2003. Applicants with more than 24 college credits must present a college GPA of at least 2.5; those with fewer than 24 credits must also meet freshman admission requirements. Official transcripts must be submitted from all colleges previously attended at the time of application. 32 of 128 credits required for the bachelor's degree must be completed at FSC.

Visiting: There are regularly scheduled orientations for prospective students, including campus tours and information sessions. There are guides for informal visits and visitors may sit in on classes and stay overnight by arrangement. To schedule a visit, contact the Admissions Office.

Financial Aid: In 2003-2004, 46% of all full-time freshmen and 50% of continuing full-time students received some form of financial aid. 56% of full-time freshmen and 62% of continuing full-time students received need-based aid. The average freshman award was $5580. Need-based scholarships or need-based grants averaged $3380; need-based self-help aid (loans and jobs) averaged $2730; and non-need-based awards and non-need-based scholarships averaged $1500. 45% of undergraduates work part time. Average annual earnings from campus work are $1000. The average financial indebtedness of the 2003 graduate was $10,875.

FSC is a member of CSS. The FAFSA is required. The priority date for freshman financial aid applications for fall entry is March 1.

International Students: There are 72 international students enrolled. They must score 550 on the written TOEFL or 213 on the electronic version.

Computers: The college computers have been upgraded to the Microsoft Windows 2000 operating system. FSC provides wireless access to students throughout the campus. There are a total of 185 PCs and 28 Macs in 11 labs across campus as well as 24 PCs in 7 residence halls. There is 1 port per student in the residence halls. All students may access the system at any time. There are no time limits and no fees. All students are required to have personal computers. Dell, Gateway, or a compatible is recommended.

Graduates: From July 1, 2002 to June 30, 2003, 630 bachelor's degrees were awarded. The most popular majors were business and management (13%), psychology (12%), and sociology (12%). In an average class, 40% graduate in 4 years or less, 41% graduate in 5 years or less, and 42% graduate in 6 years or less. Of the 2002 graduating class, 15% were enrolled in graduate school within 6 months of graduation and 85% were employed.

Admissions Contact: Dr. Phillip M. Dooher, Vice President, Enrollment Management and Dean of Admissions.
E-mail: *admiss@frc.mass.edu* Web: *http://www.framingham.edu*

GORDON COLLEGE
E-2
Wenham, MA 01984
(978) 867-4217
(800) 343-1379; Fax: (978) 867-4657

Full-time: 560 men, 1037 women	**Faculty:** 87; IIB, +$
Part-time: 20 men, 23 women	**Ph.D.s:** 89%
Graduate: 6 men, 35 women	**Student/Faculty:** 18 to 1
Year: semesters	**Tuition:** $20,234
Application Deadline: March 1	**Room & Board:** $5748
Freshman Class: 1080 applied, 845 accepted, 428 enrolled	
SAT I Verbal/Math: 610/600	**ACT:** 27 **VERY COMPETITIVE+**

Gordon College, founded in 1889, is a private Christian college emphasizing a Christian approach to the liberal arts and sciences. In addition to regional accreditation, Gordon has baccalaureate program accreditation with CSWE, NASDTEC, and NASM. The library contains 186,224 volumes, 31,491 microform items, and 4543 audio/video tapes/CDs, and subscribes to 536 periodicals. Computerized library services include the card catalog, interlibrary loans, database searching, and Internet access. Special learning facilities include a learning resource center and art gallery. The 500-acre campus is in a small town 25 miles north of Boston. Including any residence halls, there are 30 buildings.

Student Life: 74% of undergraduates are from out of state, mostly the Northeast. Students are from 45 states, 24 foreign countries, and Canada. 91% are white. Most are Protestant. The average age of freshmen is 18; all undergraduates, 20. 13% do not continue beyond their first year; 65% remain to graduate.

Housing: 1400 students can be accommodated in college housing, which includes single-sex and coed dormitories, on-campus apartments, and married-student housing. In addition, there are special-interest houses. On-campus housing is available on a lottery system for upperclassmen. 87% of students live on campus; of those, 70% remain on campus on weekends. Alcohol is not permitted. All students may keep cars.

Activities: There are no fraternities or sororities. There are 35 groups on campus, including art, band, cheerleading, chess, choir, chorale, chorus, computers, dance, drama, ethnic, honors, international, jazz band, literary magazine, musical theater, newspaper, off-campus ministries, orchestra, pep band, photography, political, professional, religious, social, social service, student government, student outreach, symphony, and yearbook. Popular campus events include Genesis Week, International Week, and an artist series.

Sports: There are 7 intercollegiate sports for men and 9 for women, and 12 intramural sports for men and 12 for women. Facilities include a gym, weight rooms, tennis courts, athletic fields, a training room, a swimming pool, a climbing wall, racquetball courts, an aerobics room, ski/running trails, an outdoor ropes course, a sauna, and a walking track.

Disabled Students: 90% of the campus is accessible. Wheelchair ramps, elevators, special parking, specially equipped rest rooms, special class scheduling, lowered drinking fountains, lowered telephones, special housing, and electric doors are available.

Services: Counseling and information services are available, as is tutoring in some subjects, including math, writing, and core science. There is a reader service for the blind, and remedial math, reading, and writing. There are writing and academic support centers. Gordon also provides special advising, study skills help, support groups for some liberal arts core courses, walk-in help, and assistance finding volunteer note takers.

Campus Safety and Security: Measures include 24-hour foot and vehicle patrol, security escort services, informal discussions, and pamphlets/posters/films. There are emergency telephones and lighted pathways/sidewalks.

Programs of Study: Gordon confers B.A., B.S., and B.Mu. degrees. Master's degrees are also awarded. Bachelor's degrees are awarded in BIOLOGICAL SCIENCE (biology/biological science), BUSINESS (accounting, banking and finance, business administration and management, and recreation and leisure services), COMMUNICATIONS AND THE ARTS (art, communications, dramatic arts, English, French, German, languages, music, music performance, and Spanish), COMPUTER AND PHYSICAL SCIENCE (chemistry, computer science, mathematics, and physics), EDUCATION (early childhood, elementary, middle school, music, secondary, and special), SOCIAL SCIENCE (biblical studies, economics, history, international studies, philosophy, physical fitness/movement, political science/government, psychology, social work, sociology, and youth ministry). English, biology, and psychology are the strongest academically. English, business administration, and communications are the largest.

Required: All students must demonstrate competency in writing, speech, and foreign language. The core curriculum consists of 8 credits in biblical studies, 8 in social and behavioral sciences, 8 in natural sciences, math, and computer science, 6 in humanities, and 4 each in fine arts and freshman seminar. A total of 124 credits is required for graduation, with 18 or more in the major and a minimum GPA of 2.0.

Special: Gordon offers cooperative education, internships, and cross-registration with other institutions in the Northeast Consortium of Colleges and Universities in Massachusetts. There is a 3-2 engineering program with the University of Massachusetts at Lowell and a 2-2 program in allied health with the Thomas Jefferson College of Allied Health Science in Philadelphia. B.A.-B.S. degrees, dual majors, student-designed majors, nondegree study, and pass/fail options are all available. Off-campus study opportunities include a Washington semester, the Christian College Consortium Visitor Program, the LaVida Wilderness Expedition, the Nova Scotia Student Exchange Program, and study abroad in Europe, the Middle East, China, the Philippines, and Latin America. There are 2 national honor societies and 12 departmental honors programs.

Faculty/Classroom: 71% of faculty are male; 29%, female. All teach undergraduates. No introductory courses are taught by graduate students. The average class size in an introductory lecture is 26; in a laboratory, 14; and in a regular course, 21.

Admissions: 78% of the 2003-2004 applicants were accepted. The SAT I scores for the 2003-2004 freshman class were: Verbal--4% below 500, 36% between 500 and 599, 48% between 600 and 700, and 12% above 700. 49% of the current freshmen were in the top fifth of their class; 70% were in the top two fifths. There were 17 National Merit finalists and 1 semifinalist.

Requirements: The SAT I or ACT is required. In addition, applicants must graduate from an accredited secondary school or have a GED. A minimum of 17 Carnegie units is required, including 4 English courses and 2 courses each in math, science, and social studies. Foreign language is a recommended elective. An essay, a personal reference, and an interview are required. Music majors must audition. AP and CLEP credits are accepted. Important factors in the admissions decision are advanced placement or honor courses, leadership record, and personality/intangible qualities.

Procedure: Freshmen are admitted fall and spring. Entrance exams should be taken in the spring of the junior year and the fall of the senior year. There are early decision and deferred admissions plans. Early decision applications should be filed by December 1; regular applications, by March 1 for fall entry and October 15 for spring entry, along with a $40 fee. Notification of early decision is sent January 1; regular decision, March 15. 91 early decision candidates were accepted for the 2003-2004 class. 42 applicants were on the 2003 waiting list; 4 were admitted. Applications are accepted on-line through the school's web site at *www.gordon.edu/admissions/apply/onlineapplication.htm.*

Transfer: 70 transfer students enrolled in 2003-2004. Applicants must have a minimum GPA of 2.5. College transcripts, high school transcripts, and SAT I or ACT scores if the applicant has completed less than 1 year of full-time study, an essay, an interview, and personal and academic references are required. 32 of 124 credits required for the bachelor's degree must be completed at Gordon.

Visiting: There are regularly scheduled orientations for prospective students, consisting of 5 open house programs throughout the fall, winter, and spring. There are guides for informal visits and visitors may sit in on classes and stay overnight. To schedule a visit, contact Sasha Moen, Visitation Coordinator.

Financial Aid: In 2003-2004, 78% of all full-time freshmen and 70% of continuing full-time students received some form of financial aid. 63% of full-time freshmen and 66% of continuing full-time students received need-based aid. The average freshman award was $13,852; need-based scholarships or need-based grants averaged $10,443; and need-based self-help aid (loans and jobs) averaged $4120. 90% of undergraduates work part time. Average annual earnings from campus work are $1200. The average financial indebtedness of the 2003 graduate was $7413. Gordon is a member of CSS. The CSS/Profile or FAFSA is required. The deadline for filing freshman financial aid applications for fall entry is March 1.

International Students: There were 53 international students enrolled in a recent year. The school actively recruits these students. They must score 550 on the written TOEFL or 213 on the electronic version and also take or take the SAT I or ACT.

Computers: The mainframe is a 4 DEC/Compaq Alpha. There are also 125 Macs and IBM PCs available in student labs, kiosks, and the computer center. The campus network may be accessed from residence halls, and there is access to the Internet and the World Wide Web. All students may access the system at any time. There are no time limits and no fees.

Graduates: From July 1, 2002 to June 30, 2003, 404 bachelor's degrees were awarded. The most popular majors were economics and business (11%), biblical studies (9%), and English (8%). In an average class, 53% graduate in 4 years or less, 66% graduate in 5 years or less, and 68% graduate in 6 years or less.

Admissions Contact: Nancy Mering, Dean of Admissions.
E-mail: *mering@hope.gordon.edu* Web: *www.gordon.edu*

HAMPSHIRE COLLEGE B-2

Amherst, MA 01002 (413) 559-5471; Fax: (413) 559-5631

Full-time: 558 men, 774 women	**Faculty:** 115; IIB,
Part-time: none	**Ph.D.s:** 90%
Graduate: none	**Student/Faculty:** 12 to 1
Year: 4-1-4	**Tuition:** $29,348
Application Deadline: February 1	**Room & Board:** $7689
Freshman Class: 2271 applied, 1248 accepted, 425 enrolled	
SAT I Verbal/Math: 650/600	**ACT:** 27 HIGHLY COMPETITIVE

Hampshire College, founded in 1965, is a private institution offering a liberal arts education with an emphasis on independent research, creative work, and multidisciplinary study. The library contains 124,710 volumes, 4534 microform items, and 8727 audio/video tapes/CDs, and subscribes to 731 periodicals. Computerized library services include the card catalog, interlibrary loans, and database searching. Special learning facilities include an art gallery, multimedia center, farm center, music and dance studios, optics lab, electronics shop, integrated greenhouse and aquaculture facility, fabrication shop, and performing arts center. The 800-acre campus is in a rural area 20 miles north of Springfield. Including any residence halls, there are 28 buildings.

Student Life: 86% of undergraduates are from out of state, mostly the Northeast. Students are from 46 states, 25 foreign countries, and Canada. 76% are white. The average age of freshmen is 18; all undergraduates, 20. 21% do not continue beyond their first year.

Housing: 1100 students can be accommodated in college housing, which includes single-sex and coed dorms and on-campus apartments. In addition, there are special-interest houses. On-campus housing is guaranteed for all 4 years. 92% of students live on campus. All students may keep cars.

Activities: There are no fraternities or sororities. There are 80 groups on campus, including art, chorus, computers, dance, drama, ethnic, film, gay, international, literary magazine, musical theater, orchestra, photography, political, radio and TV, religious, social, social service, and student government. Popular campus events include Southern Exposure, Spring Jam, and Casino Night.

Sports: There are 3 intercollegiate sports for men and 2 for women, and 18 intramural sports for men and 18 for women. Facilities include 2 multipurpose sports centers housing a glass-enclosed swimming pool, a 12,000-square-foot playing floor, a 30-foot climbing wall, a weight lifting area, 4 indoor tennis courts, and a jogging track. Other facilities include soccer fields, 10 outdoor tennis courts, 2 softball diamonds, and a 2-mile nature trail.

Disabled Students: 90% of the campus is accessible. Wheelchair ramps, elevators, special parking, specially equipped rest rooms, special class scheduling, lowered drinking fountains, lowered telephones are available. The college provides a variety of support services to meet individual special needs.

Services: Counseling and information services are available, as is tutoring in most subjects. There is a reader service for the blind, an advising center, a writing and reading program, and a lab quantitative skills program.

Campus Safety and Security: Measures include 24-hour foot and vehicle patrol, security escort services, informal discussions, and pamphlets/posters/films. There are lighted pathways/sidewalks, an EMT on-call program, and dorm doors accessible by students only.

Programs of Study: Hampshire confers the B.A. degree. Bachelor's degrees are awarded in AGRICULTURE (agriculture and animal science), BIOLOGICAL SCIENCE (biology/biological science, botany, ecology, marine biology, nutrition, and physiology), COMMUNICATIONS AND THE ARTS (art history and appreciation, communications, comparative literature, creative writing, dance, dramatic arts, film arts, fine arts, journalism, linguistics, literature, media arts, music, performing arts, photography, and video), COMPUTER AND PHYSICAL SCIENCE (chemistry, computer science, geology, mathematics, physics, and science), EDUCATION (education), ENGINEERING AND ENVIRONMENTAL DESIGN (architecture, environmental design, and environmental science), HEALTH PROFESSIONS (health science and premedicine), SOCIAL SCIENCE (African American studies, African studies, American studies, anthropology, Asian/Oriental studies, cognitive science, crosscultural studies, economics, family/consumer studies, geography, history, humanities, international relations, international studies, Judaic studies, Latin American studies, law, Middle Eastern studies, peace studies, philosophy, political science/government, psychology, religion, sociology, urban studies, and women's studies). Film/photography/video is the strongest academically. Social sciences is the largest.

Required: All students must complete 3 divisions of study. In Division I, Basic Studies, students work in each of Hampshire's 5 schools: Cognitive Science; Humanities, Arts and Cultural studies; Natural Science; Interdisciplinary Arts; and Social Science, and must complete 2 courses or the Division I exam project. In Division II, the Concentration, students explore their field or fields of emphasis through individually designed internships or field studies. In Division III, Advanced Studies, students complete a major independent study project, centered on a specific topic, question, or idea. Students must also include service to the college or the surrounding community and consider some aspect of their work from a non-Western perspective.

Special: Cross-registration is possible with other members of the Five-College Consortium (Amherst College, the University of Massachusetts, Smith College, and Mount Holyoke). Internships, multidisciplinary dual majors, and study abroad (in the ISEP program, Tibetan Center, or a Costa Rica semester) are offered. All majors are student-designed. Students may complete their programs in fewer than 4 years.

Faculty/Classroom: 50% of faculty are male; 50%, female. All teach undergraduates. The average class size in a regular course is 17.

Admissions: 55% of the 2003-2004 applicants were accepted. The SAT I scores for the 2003-2004 freshman class were: Verbal--2% below 500, 20% between 500 and 599, 50% between 600 and 700, and 28% above 700; Math--8% below 500, 36% between 500 and 599, 45% between 600 and 700, and 11% above 700. The ACT scores were 2% below 21, 10% between 21 and 23, 31% between 24 and 26, 24% between 27 and 28, and 33% above 28. 57% of the current freshmen were in the top fifth of their class; 86% were in the top two fifths. There were 6 National Merit semifinalists. 7 freshmen graduated first in their class.

Requirements: Applicants must submit all transcripts from 9th grade on or GED/state equivalency exam results. Students are required to submit a personal statement and an analytic essay or academic paper. An interview is recommended. AP credits are accepted. Important factors in the admissions decision are personality/intangible qualities, evidence of special talent, and extracurricular activities record.

Procedure: Freshmen are admitted fall and spring. There are early decision, early admissions, and deferred admissions plans. Early decision applications should be filed by November 15; regular applications, by February 1 for fall entry and November 15 for spring entry. Notification of early decision is sent December 15; regular decision, April 1. 62 early decision candidates were accepted for the 2003-2004 class. 389 applicants were on the 2003 waiting list. Applications are accepted on-line through CommonApp.

Transfer: 33 transfer students enrolled in 2002-2003. A proposed program of study, high school and college transcripts, and 1 recommendation must be submitted.

Visiting: There are regularly scheduled orientations for prospective students, including interviews, information sessions, campus tours, Discover Hampshire Days, Campus Visitation Days, and an overnight program. There are guides for informal visits and visitors may sit in on classes and stay overnight. To schedule a visit, contact the Admissions Office at *admissions@hampshire.edu.*

Financial Aid: In 2003-2004, 60% of all full-time freshmen and 54% of continuing full-time students received some form of financial aid. 60% of full-time freshmen and 54% of continuing full-time students received need-based aid. The average freshman award was $26,700. Average annual earnings from campus work are $2300. The average financial indebtedness of the 2003 graduate was $16,975. Hampshire is a member of CSS. The CSS Profile or FAFSA, the college's own financial statement, and the non-custodial parent statement are required. The deadline for filing freshman financial aid applications for fall entry is February 1.

International Students: There are 43 international students enrolled. The school actively recruits these students. They must score 577 on the written TOEFL or 233 on the electronic version.

Computers: The mainframe is a Sun SPARC Station 20 model 50. Hampshire uses a variety of computers as file servers. Several computing labs on campus allow students access to PCs and networked systems. In addition, all student rooms are networked and many students own PCs. All students may access the system 24 hours per day via their own PCs or at designated hours in the labs, generally 8 A.M. to midnight, but up to 24 hours at semester's end. There are no time limits and no fees.

Graduates: From July 1, 2002 to June 30, 2003, 273 bachelor's degrees were awarded. The most popular majors were art (9%), film/photo (9%), and theater (6%).

Admissions Contact: Karen S. Parker, Director of Admissions. E-mail: *admissions@hampshire.edu* Web: *www.hampshire.edu*

HARVARD UNIVERSITY/HARVARD COLLEGE D-2
Cambridge, MA 02138 (617) 495-1551; Fax: (617) 495-8821

Full-time: 3502 men, 3133 women	**Faculty:** 837; I, ++$
Part-time: 6 men, 6 women	**Ph.D.s:** 99%
Graduate: 5547 men, 4804 women	**Student/Faculty:** 8 to 1
Year: semesters, summer session	**Tuition:** $29,060
Application Deadline: January 1	**Room & Board:** $8868
Freshman Class: 20,987 applied, 2095 accepted, 1635 enrolled	
SAT I or ACT: required	**MOST COMPETITIVE**

Harvard College is the undergraduate college of Harvard University. Harvard College was founded in 1636. Harvard University also has 10 graduate schools. In addition to regional accreditation, Harvard has baccalaureate program accreditation with ABET. The 97 libraries contain 13 million volumes, and subscribe to 100,000 periodicals. Computerized library services include the card catalog, interlibrary loans, and database searching. Special learning facilities include a learning resource center, art gallery, natural history museum, planetarium, and radio station. The 380-acre campus is in an urban area across the Charles River from Boston. Including any residence halls, there are 400 buildings.

Student Life: 81% of undergraduates are from out of state, mostly the Middle Atlantic. Students are from 50 states, 118 foreign countries, and Canada. 67% are from public schools. 43% are white; 17% Asian American. The average age of freshmen is 18; all undergraduates, 20. 96% of freshmen remain to graduate.

Housing: 6325 students can be accommodated in college housing, which includes coed dorms and on-campus apartments. On-campus housing is guaranteed for all 4 years. 97% of students live on campus. All students may keep cars.

Activities: There are no fraternities or sororities. There are 250 groups on campus, including art, band, cheerleading, chess, choir, chorale, chorus, computers, dance, debate, drama, ethnic, film, gay, honors, international, jazz band, literary magazine, marching band, musical theater, newspaper, opera, orchestra, pep band, photography, political, professional, radio and TV, religious, social, social service, student government, symphony, and yearbook. Popular campus events include Harvard/Yale football, Head of the Charles crew regatta, and Cultural Rhythms Festival.

Sports: There are 21 intercollegiate sports for men and 20 for women, and 16 intramural sports for men and 16 for women. Facilities include several gyms and athletic centers, pools, a track, boat houses, a sailing center, a hockey rink, and various courts and playing fields.

Disabled Students: Wheelchair ramps, elevators, special parking, specially equipped rest rooms, special class scheduling, lowered drinking fountains, lowered telephones, tutors, adaptive equipment in the field of information technology, TDD/TTY, shuttle van service, a student support organization called ABLE, and an adaptive technology lab are available.

Services: Counseling and information services are available, as is tutoring in every subject. There is a reader service for the blind.

Campus Safety and Security: Measures include 24-hour foot and vehicle patrol, self-defense education, security escort services, and shuttle buses. There are informal discussions, pamphlets/posters/films, emergency telephones, and lighted pathways/sidewalks.

Programs of Study: Harvard confers A.B. and S.B. degrees. Master's and doctoral degrees are also awarded. Bachelor's degrees are awarded in BIOLOGICAL SCIENCE (biochemistry, biology/biological science, and biophysics), COMMUNICATIONS AND THE ARTS (art history and appreciation, Chinese, classics, creative writing, English, fine arts, folklore and mythology, French, German, Greek, Hebrew, Italian, Japanese, Latin, linguistics, literature, music, Portuguese, Russian, and Spanish), COMPUTER AND PHYSICAL SCIENCE (applied mathematics, astronomy, chemistry, computer science, geology, geophysics and seismology, mathematics, physical sciences, physics, and statistics), ENGINEERING AND ENVIRONMENTAL DESIGN (engineering, environmental design, environmental science, and preengineering), SOCIAL SCIENCE (African American studies, American studies, anthropology, Asian/Oriental studies, economics, European studies, history, humanities, Middle Eastern studies, philosophy, political science/government, psychology, religion, Russian and Slavic studies, Sanskrit and Indian studies, social science, social studies, sociology, and women's studies). Economics, government, and biology are the largest.

Required: In 8 semesters, students must pass a minimum of 32 1-semester courses. The average course load is 4 courses per semester, but the course rate may be varied for special reasons. A typical balanced program devotes about one fourth of its courses to core curriculum requirements, one half to the concentration (or major field), and the remaining one fourth to electives.

Special: Students may cross-register with MIT and with other schools within the university, and may design their own concentrations or enroll for nondegree study. Internships and study abroad may be arranged. Accelerated degree programs, dual majors, a 3-2 engineering degree, and a combined A.B.-S.B. in engineering are offered. There are pass/fail options. There is a chapter of Phi Beta Kappa.

Faculty/Classroom: 98% teach undergraduates, 97% do research, and 95% do both. No introductory courses are taught by graduate students. The average class size in a regular course is 25.

Admissions: 10% of the 2003-2004 applicants were accepted. 98% of the current freshmen were in the top fifth of their class; all were in the top two fifths.

Requirements: The SAT I or ACT is required, as well as 3 SAT II: Subject tests. Applicants need not be high school graduates but are expected to be well prepared academically. An essay and an interview are required, in addition to a transcript, a counselor report, and 2 teacher recommendations from academic disciplines. AP credits are accepted. Important factors in the admissions decision are evidence of special talent, personality/intangible qualities, and recommendations by school officials.

Procedure: Freshmen are admitted in the fall. Entrance exams should be taken by January of the senior year. There are early action, early admissions, and deferred admissions plans. Early action applications should be filed by November 1; regular applications, by January 1 for fall entry. The fall 2003 application fee was $60. Notification of early action is sent December 12; regular decision, April 1. A waiting list is an active part of the admissions procedure.

Transfer: Transfer applicants must have completed at least 1 full year of daytime study in a degree-granting program at 1 institution. Students are required to submit the SAT I or ACT, 2 letters of recommendation, high school and college transcripts with a dean's report, and several essays. 16 courses of 32 required for the bachelor's degree must be completed at Harvard.

Visiting: There are regularly scheduled orientations for prospective students, consisting of group information sessions and tours. There are guides for informal visits and visitors may sit in on classes and stay overnight. To schedule a visit, contact the Undergraduate Admissions Office.

Financial Aid: In 2003-2004, 80% of all full-time freshmen and 69% of continuing full-time students received some form of financial aid. 51% of full-time freshmen and 46% of continuing full-time students received need-based aid. The average freshman award was $26,465, with $24,904 from need-based scholarships or need-based grants and $1561 from need-based self-help aid (loans and jobs). 70% of undergraduates work part time. Harvard is a member of CSS. The CSS Profile or FAFSA, the college's own financial statement, and federal tax forms are required. Check with the school for current deadlines.

International Students: The school actively recruits these students. They must take the TOEFL and either the SAT I or the ACT. Students must take SAT II: Subject tests in any 3 subjects.

Computers: All residences have Internet access. There are also PCs available for use in the science center and all residence halls. All students may access the system 24 hours per day. There are no time limits and no fees.

Admissions Contact: Marlyn McGrath Lewis, Director of Admissions. A video is available. E-mail: *college@harvard.edu* Web: *www.college.harvard.edu*

HELLENIC COLLEGE/HOLY CROSS GREEK ORTHODOX SCHOOL OF THEOLOGY

D-2

Brookline, MA 02445

(617) 731-3500, ext.1260
Fax: (617) 850-1460

Full-time: 53 men, 37 women	Faculty: 8
Part-time: 2 men	Ph.D.s: 100%
Graduate: 116 men, 15 women	Student/Faculty: 11 to 1
Year: semesters	Tuition: $14,415
Application Deadline: May 1	Room & Board: $8400
Freshman Class: 56 applied, 42 accepted, 30 enrolled	
SAT I or ACT: required	COMPETITIVE

Hellenic College, founded in 1937, is a private college affiliated with the Greek Orthodox Church. It offers programs in the classics, elementary education, religious studies, human development, and management and leadership. In addition to regional accreditation, Hellenic College/Holy Cross Greek Orthodox School of Theology has baccalaureate program accreditation with NASDTEC. The library contains 117,000 volumes, 863 microform items, and 3204 audio/video tapes/CDs, and subscribes to 754 periodicals. Computerized library services include the card catalog, interlibrary loans, database searching, and Internet access. Special learning facilities include archives, rare books, a Greek cultural center, and a language lab. The 52-acre campus is in an urban area 4 miles southwest of Boston. Including any residence halls, there are 7 buildings.

Student Life: 95% of undergraduates are from out of state, mostly the Midwest. Students are from 29 states, 8 foreign countries, and Canada. 98% are from public schools. 98% are white; 10% foreign nationals. Most are Greek or Eastern Orthodox. The average age of freshmen is 20; all undergraduates, 25. 3% do not continue beyond their first year; 93% remain to graduate.

Housing: 220 students can be accommodated in college housing, which includes coed dormitories, on-campus apartments, and married-student housing. On-campus housing is guaranteed for all 4 years. 95% of students live on campus; of those, 95% remain on campus on weekends. Alcohol is not permitted. All students may keep cars.

Activities: There are 9 groups on campus, including choir, ethnic, photography, religious, social, social service, student government, and yearbook. Popular campus events include Feast of the Holy Cross, Matriculation Day, and Campus Christmas Party.

Sports: Facilities include a gym, tennis, basketball, and racquetball courts, and a soccer field.

Disabled Students: 10% of the campus is accessible. Wheelchair ramps, elevators, special parking, specially equipped rest rooms, and lowered drinking fountains are available.

Services: Counseling and information services are available, as is tutoring in some subjects, including Greek and music writing and composition. There is remedial math, reading, and writing.

Campus Safety and Security: Measures include shuttle buses, informal discussions, pamphlets/posters/films, lighted pathways/sidewalks, and a 16-hour security patrol.

Programs of Study: Hellenic College/Holy Cross Greek Orthodox School of Theology confers the B.A. degree. Master's degrees are also awarded. Bachelor's degrees are awarded in BUSINESS (management information systems), COMMUNICATIONS AND THE ARTS (classics), EDUCATION (elementary), SOCIAL SCIENCE (human development and religion). Religious studies and classics are the strongest academically. Religious studies and human development are the largest.

Required: To graduate, students must complete 129 credits, with 39 in the major, and maintain a minimum overall GPA of 2.0. General education requirements include 72 credits, with courses in English language and literature, music, history, science, philosophy, and social science.

Special: The college offers cross-registration with Boston Theological Institute and with Newbury College, credit by exam, and study abroad in Greece.

Faculty/Classroom: 80% of faculty are male; 20%, female. All teach undergraduates. No introductory courses are taught by graduate students. The average class size in an introductory lecture is 20; in a laboratory, 20; and in a regular course, 15.

Admissions: 75% of the 2003-2004 applicants were accepted. There were 2 National Merit finalists.

Requirements: The SAT I or ACT is required. In addition, applicants should graduate from an accredited secondary school or have a GED. 15 academic credits are required, including 4 units of English, 2 each of math, foreign language, and social studies, and 1 of science. An essay is required. A GPA of 2.5 is required. AP and CLEP credits are accepted. Important factors in the admissions decision are recommendations by school officials, advanced placement or honor courses, and recommendations by alumni.

Procedure: Freshmen are admitted fall and spring. There are early decision and deferred admissions plans. Early decision applications should be filed by December 1; regular applications, by May 1 for fall entry and December 1 for spring entry. The fall 2003 application fee was $50. Notification of early decision is sent February 1; regular decision, June 15. 12 early decision candidates were accepted for the 2003-2004 class.

Transfer: 11 transfer students enrolled in a recent year. The SAT I, an essay, recommendation letters, high school transcripts, an interview, and a health certificate are required. 60 of 129 credits required for the bachelor's degree must be completed at Hellenic College/Holy Cross Greek Orthodox School of Theology.

Visiting: There are regularly scheduled orientations for prospective students, including observation of classroom and student life. There are guides for informal visits and visitors may sit in on classes and stay overnight. To schedule a visit, contact Agnes Desses, Office of Admissions at (617) 850-1260.

Financial Aid: In 2003-2004, 95% of all full-time students received some form of financial aid. The FAFSA and the college's own financial statement are required. The priority date for freshman financial aid applications for fall entry is April 15. The deadline for filing freshman financial aid applications for fall entry is July 1.

International Students: There are 28 international students enrolled. They must score 500 on the written TOEFL or 173 on the electronic version and also take the SAT I or the ACT.

Computers: The mainframe is an IBM AS/400 Model F20. 10 PCs are available for student use in the computer lab, and Internet access is provided through the library computers. The library is on an integrated network with 13 other libraries. All students may access the system. There are no time limits and no fees.

Graduates: In a recent year, 10 bachelor's degrees were awarded. The most popular majors were religious studies (60%), elementary education (30%), and human development (10%). In an average class, 97% graduate in 4 years or less, and 100% graduate in 5 years or less.

Admissions Contact: Agnes Desses, Assistant Director, Admissions. A video is available. E-mail: *admissions@hchc.edu* Web: *www.hchc.edu*

HOLY CROSS
(See College of the Holy Cross)

LASELL COLLEGE
D-2
Newton, MA 02466
(617) 243-2225
(888) LASELL-4; Fax: (617) 243-2380

Full-time: 282 men, 772 women	**Faculty:** 46; IIB, -$
Part-time: 11 men, 18 women	**Ph.D.s:** 38%
Graduate: 18 men and women	**Student/Faculty:** 23 to 1
Year: semesters	**Tuition:** $17,500
Application Deadline: open	**Room & Board:** $8500
Freshman Class: 2064 applied, 1558 accepted, 368 enrolled	
SAT I Verbal/Math: 480/470	**ACT:** 20 COMPETITIVE

Lasell College, founded in 1851, is a private nonsecular institution whose curriculum combines classroom study with practical experience in the sciences, business, education, and health fields. There are 3 undergraduate schools and 1 graduate school. In addition to regional accreditation, Lasell has baccalaureate program accreditation with CAAHEP and NAEYC. The library contains 55,335 volumes, 48,197 microform items, and 2560 audio/video tapes/CDs, and subscribes to 494 periodicals. Computerized library services include the card catalog, interlibrary loans, database searching, and Internet access. Special learning facilities include a learning resource center, art gallery, an early childhood curriculum library, Lasell Village (retirement community), a nursery school, and a day care center. The 50-acre campus is in a suburban area 8 miles west of Boston. Including any residence halls, there are 42 buildings.

Student Life: 56% of undergraduates are from Massachusetts. Students are from 20 states, 8 foreign countries, and Canada. 95% are from public schools. 73% are white. 39% are Catholic; 30% Protestant; 25% claim no religious affiliation. The average age of freshmen is 18; all undergraduates, 21. 32% do not continue beyond their first year; 55% remain to graduate.

Housing: 850 students can be accommodated in college housing, which includes single-sex and coed dorms and on-campus apartments. In addition, there are special-interest houses. On-campus housing is guaranteed for all 4 years. 80% of students live on campus; of those, 80% remain on campus on weekends. All students may keep cars.

Activities: There are no fraternities or sororities. There are 30 groups on campus, including cheerleading, chorale, chorus, dance, drama, ethnic, gay, honors, international, literary magazine, newspaper, political, professional, social, social service, student government, and yearbook. Popular campus events include River Day, Torchlight Parade, and Awards Night.

Sports: There are 5 intercollegiate sports for men and 7 for women, and 3 intramural sports for men and 3 for women. Facilities include an athletic center with a basketball court, a volleyball court, an indoor track, a dance studio, an exercise room, and locker rooms, plus 2 athletic fields.

Disabled Students: 50% of the campus is accessible. Wheelchair ramps, elevators, special parking, specially equipped rest rooms, lowered drinking fountains, and lowered telephones are available.

Services: Counseling and information services are available, as is tutoring in most subjects. There is remedial math and writing and books on tape.

Campus Safety and Security: Measures include 24-hour foot and vehicle patrol, self-defense education, shuttle buses, and informal discussions. There are pamphlets/posters/films, emergency telephones, and lighted pathways/sidewalks.

Programs of Study: Lasell confers B.A. and B.S. degrees. Master's degrees are also awarded. Bachelor's degrees are awarded in BUSINESS (accounting, banking and finance, business administration and management, fashion merchandising, hospitality management services, hotel/motel and restaurant management, international business management, management information systems, marketing/retailing/merchandising, sports management, and tourism), COMPUTER AND PHYSICAL SCIENCE (computer science), EDUCATION (athletic training, early childhood, elementary, and secondary), HEALTH PROFESSIONS (exercise science and health care administration), SOCIAL SCIENCE (child care/child and family studies, criminal justice, fashion design and technology, human services, law, liberal arts/general studies, paralegal studies, physical fitness/movement, psychology, and sociology). Allied health is the strongest academically. Business, education, and criminal justice are the largest.

Required: To graduate, students must complete 124 credit hours with a minimum GPA of 2.0. Requirements include 2 courses each in writing and math, 1 course in literature, art, music, or drama, 1 in history, philosophy, or language, 1 each in social science, and science, and a computer literacy course. An internship is also required.

Special: Internships are built into the curriculum, and work-study programs are available on campus. Student-designed majors and student-arranged study-abroad programs are possible. All programs feature connected learning, which is an ongoing practical application of classroom theory. There is a freshman honors program.

Faculty/Classroom: 33% of faculty are male; 67%, female. All teach undergraduates. No introductory courses are taught by graduate students. The average class size in an introductory lecture is 20; in a laboratory, 11; and in a regular course, 15.

Admissions: 75% of the 2003-2004 applicants were accepted. The SAT I scores for the 2003-2004 freshman class were: Verbal--57% below 500, 36% between 500 and 599, and 7% between 600 and 700; Math--58% below 500, 35% between 500 and 599, and 7% between 600 and 700.

Requirements: The SAT I is required. In addition, applicants should have completed 16 Carnegie units of high school study. The GED is accepted. A letter of recommendation is required, and an interview is recommended. A GPA of 2.0 is required. AP and CLEP credits are accepted. Important factors in the admissions decision are advanced placement or honor courses, personality/intangible qualities, and leadership record.

Procedure: Freshmen are admitted fall and spring. Application deadlines are open. Application fee is $40. Notification is sent on a rolling basis beginning December 15. Applications are accepted on-line.

Transfer: 73 transfer students enrolled in 2002-2003. Applicants must have a minimum 2.0 GPA. 45 of 124 credits required for the bachelor's degree must be completed at Lasell.

Visiting: There are regularly scheduled orientations for prospective students, consisting of the president's welcome, faculty presentations, tours, and student panels. There are guides for informal visits and visitors may sit in on classes and stay overnight. To schedule a visit, contact the Office of Admission at info@lasell.edu.

Financial Aid: In 2003-2004, 89% of all full-time freshmen and 88% of continuing full-time students received some form of financial aid. 82% of full-time freshmen and 86% of continuing full-time students received need-based aid. The average freshman award was $15,800. 32% of undergraduates work part time. Lasell is a member of CSS. The FAFSA and the college's own financial statement are required. The deadline for filing freshman financial aid applications for fall entry is March 1.

International Students: There are 30 international students enrolled. They must score 530 on the written TOEFL or 173 on the electronic version.

Computers: The mainframe is a Windows NT network. The college is served by a local area network, with computer equipment available in 6 labs. There are 125 units in class and lab space. Residence halls are wired and additional PCs are available in study areas within residence halls and public spaces. All students may access the system 24 hours per day 7 days per week. There are no time limits and no fees.

Graduates: From July 1, 2002 to June 30, 2003, 67 bachelor's degrees were awarded. The most popular majors were business (26%), education (21%), and fashion (18%). In an average class, 55% graduate in 4 years or less. Of the 2002 graduating class, 20% were enrolled in graduate school within 6 months of graduation and 90% were employed.

Admissions Contact: James M. Tweed, Director of Admission. E-mail: info@lasell.edu Web: www.lasell.edu

LESLEY UNIVERSITY
D-2
Cambridge, MA 02138-2790
(617) 349-8800
(800) 999-1959 ext. 8800; Fax: (617) 349-8810

Full-time: 498 women	**Faculty:** 34
Part-time: 18 women	**Ph.D.s:** 100%
Graduate: 789 men, 5028 women	**Student/Faculty:** 15 to 1
Year: semesters, summer session	**Tuition:** $21,275
Application Deadline: March 1	**Room & Board:** $9370
Freshman Class: 365 applied, 281 accepted, 102 enrolled	
SAT I Verbal/Math: 520/520	COMPETITIVE

Lesley University, founded in 1909, is a private, primarily women's institution, offering degree programs in education, human services, and the arts. Expanded resources, course work, and opportunities are available to students through the larger coeducational Lesley University system, including cross-registration with the Art Institute of Boston. There are 3 undergraduate and 2 graduate schools. In addition to regional accreditation, Lesley has baccalaureate program accreditation with AACTE, CACREP, NASAD, and TEAC. The 2 libraries contain 120,254 volumes, 878,187 microform items, and 55,799 audio/video tapes/CDs, and subscribe to 684 periodicals. Computerized library services include the card catalog, interlibrary loans, database searching, and Internet access. Special learning facilities include a learning resource center, art gallery, center for teaching resources, media production facility, and instructional computing. The 5-acre campus is in an urban area just outside of Harvard Square in Cambridge. Including any residence halls, there are 45 buildings.

Student Life: 64% of undergraduates are from Massachusetts. Students are from 21 states, 8 foreign countries, and Canada. 77% are white. The average age of freshmen is 19; all undergraduates, 21. 20% do not continue beyond their first year; 74% remain to graduate.

Housing: 425 students can be accommodated in college housing, which includes single-sex dorms. In addition, there are special-interest houses, a wellness floor, a substance-free floor, and a mind, body, and spirit house. On-campus housing is guaranteed for all 4 years. 86% of students live on campus. No one may keep cars.

Activities: There are no fraternities or sororities. There are 21 groups on campus, including choir, chorus, dance, drama, ethnic, gay, international, literary magazine, musical theater, political, professional, religious, social, social service, student government, women's group, and yearbook. Popular campus events include Family and Friends Weekend, Quad Fest, and World Fest.

Sports: There are 5 intercollegiate sports for women and 3 intramural sports for women. Facilities include outdoor tennis courts, and a fitness center with Nautilus circuit, free weights, and cardiovascular equipment. Students may also use an Olympic-size swimming pool at a nearby school and local playing field facilities.

Disabled Students: 80% of the campus is accessible. Wheelchair ramps, elevators, special parking, specially equipped rest rooms, special class scheduling, and lowered drinking fountains are available. The Disability Services Office provides document review and arranges for reasonable accommodations for special needs students.

Services: Counseling and information services are available, as is tutoring in most subjects. There is a reader service for the blind, remedial math, and study skills and interpreter services.

Campus Safety and Security: Measures include 24-hour foot and vehicle patrol, self-defense education, security escort services, and shuttle buses. There are informal discussions, pamphlets/posters/films, emergency telephones, lighted pathways/sidewalks, and watch tours.

Programs of Study: Lesley confers the B.S. degree. Associate, master's, and doctoral degrees are also awarded. Bachelor's degrees are awarded in BUSINESS (management science), COMPUTER AND PHYSICAL SCIENCE (natural sciences), EDUCATION (early childhood, elementary, middle school, and special), SOCIAL SCIENCE (human services, humanities, and social science). Education, counseling, and art therapy are the largest.

Required: Students must complete 45 hours of general education requirements, including 15 of humanities, 12 of natural science, 9 of social science, 6 of multicultural perspectives, and 3 of first-year seminar; emphasis is given to cross-curriculum components in writing, critical and quantitative reasoning, global perspectives, and leadership and ethics. To graduate, students need 128 total credit hours, including 30 to 33 in the liberal arts majors or 41 to 43 in professional majors, with a minimum 2.0 GPA.

Special: Study abroad in Cuba, England, and Sweden, a Washington Justice semester, and on-campus work-study programs are offered. All students participate in at least 3 field placement experiences, beginning in their freshman year. There are combined accelerated degree programs in management, counseling, and education majors. Accelerated and weekend course programs as well as cross-registration with AIB are offered for Adult Baccalaureate College and School of Management degree programs.

Faculty/Classroom: 29% of faculty are male; 71%, female. All both teach and do research. No introductory courses are taught by graduate students. The average class size in an introductory lecture is 25 and in a regular course, 14.

Admissions: 77% of the 2003-2004 applicants were accepted. The SAT I scores for the 2003-2004 freshman class were: Verbal--29% below 500, 54% between 500 and 599, 14% between 600 and 700, and 3% above 700; Math--42% below 500, 47% between 500 and 599, and 11% between 600 and 700. 33% of the current freshmen were in the top fifth of their class; 66% were in the top two fifths.

Requirements: The SAT I or ACT is required. In addition, it is recommended that students complete 20 academic units in high school, including 4 in English, 3 each in science and math, and 2 in U.S. history. A writing sample and 2 recommendations are also required as part of the application; a personal interview is recommended. Applicants must have a high school diploma from an accredited secondary school or a GED. AP and CLEP credits are accepted. Important factors in the admissions decision are extracurricular activities record, recommendations by school officials, and advanced placement or honor courses.

Procedure: Freshmen are admitted fall and spring. Entrance exams should be taken by March 1. There is a deferred admissions plan. Applications should be filed by March 1 for fall entry and December 15 for spring entry, along with a $35 fee. Notification is sent on a rolling basis. Applications are accepted on computer disk and on-line through Apply and CollegeLink.

Transfer: 48 transfer students enrolled in 2002-2003. Applicants must have a minimum 2.5 GPA. Recommendations are required, and an interview is recommended. 68 of 128 credits required for the bachelor's degree must be completed at Lesley.

Visiting: There are regularly scheduled orientations for prospective students, including personal interviews with professional staff, student campus tours, information sessions, class visits, and meetings with financial aid. There are guides for informal visits and visitors may sit in on classes and stay overnight. To schedule a visit, contact Lesley University Office of Admissions.

Financial Aid: In 2003-2004, 86% of all full-time freshmen and 81% of continuing full-time students received some form of financial aid. 84% of full-time freshmen and 81% of continuing full-time students received need-based aid. The average freshman award was $16,152. Need-based scholarships or need-based grants averaged $10,049; need-based self-help aid (loans and jobs) averaged $5512; and non-need-based awards and non-need-based scholarships averaged $10,981. 30% of undergraduates work part time. Average annual earnings from campus work are $2000. The average financial indebtedness of the 2003 graduate was $13,125. The FAFSA, the college's own financial statement, and parent and student federal tax returns are required. The priority date for freshman financial aid applications for fall entry is February 1.

International Students: There are 18 international students enrolled. The school actively recruits these students. They must score 500 on the written TOEFL or 173 on the electronic version.

Computers: The mainframe is an IBM AIX RS6000 H70. Students can access the administrative database via LOIS (Lesley Online Information System) to review their own academic information. Via LOIS, students can review their course schedule, available courses, financial aid, and grades and register on-line. Students can also access the Internet and have e-mail. In addition, local networks provide access to faculty folders and printing. All students may access the system during library hours primarily; the word processing center is available 24 hours a day. There are no time limits and no fees.

Graduates: From July 1, 2002 to June 30, 2003, 105 bachelor's degrees were awarded. The most popular majors were education (40%), psychology (24%), and liberal arts (12%). In an average class, 58% graduate in 4 years or less, 71% graduate in 5 years or less, and 74% graduate in 6 years or less. 25 companies recruited on campus in 2002-2003. Of the 2002 graduating class, 29% were enrolled in graduate school within 6 months of graduation and 87% were employed.

Admissions Contact: Jane A. Raley, Director, Women's College Admissions. E-mail: *ugadm@mail.lesley.edu* Web: *http://www.lesley.edu*

MASSACHUSETTS BOARD OF HIGHER EDUCATION

The Massachusetts Board of Higher Education, established in 1991, is a public system in Massachusetts. It is governed by an 11-member Board of Regents appointed by the governor, whose chief administrator is chancellor. The board is the central governing authority for the state's public higher education system. The total enrollment of all 29 campuses is usually about 177,000. Profiles of the 4-year campuses are included in this section.

MASSACHUSETTS COLLEGE OF ART   E-2
Boston, MA 02115   (617) 879-7222; Fax: (617) 879-7250

Full-time: 453 men, 813 women	**Faculty:** 73
Part-time: 65 men, 142 women	**Ph.D.s:** 71%
Graduate: 40 men, 91 women	**Student/Faculty:** 17 to 1
Year: semesters, summer session	**Tuition:** $5768 ($16,478)
Application Deadline: February 15	**Room & Board:** $9800
Freshman Class: 1149 applied, 608 accepted, 239 enrolled	
SAT I Verbal/Math: 560/530	**SPECIAL**

Massachusetts College of Art, founded in 1873, is a public institution offering undergraduate and graduate programs in art, design, and education. In addition to regional accreditation, MassArt has baccalaureate program accreditation with NASAD. The library contains 231,586 volumes and 8700 microform items, and subscribes to 757 periodicals. Computerized library services include the card catalog and interlibrary loans. Special learning facilities include an art gallery and a computer arts center, performance spaces, and film viewing rooms. The 5-acre campus is in an urban area in Boston. Including any residence halls, there are 6 buildings.

Student Life: 77% of undergraduates are from Massachusetts. Students are from 25 states, 51 foreign countries, and Canada. 85% are from public schools. 70% are white. The average age of freshmen is 18; all undergraduates, 23. 10% do not continue beyond their first year; 60% remain to graduate.

Housing: 356 students can be accommodated in college housing, which includes single-sex and coed dorms and on-campus apartments. In addition, there is a visual art college residence hall with ventilated workrooms, a visiting artist suite, and gallery space. On-campus housing is guaranteed for the freshman year only (for students who meet deadline), is available on a first-come, first-served basis, and is available on a lottery system for upperclassmen. Priority is given to out-of-town students. 74% of students commute. Alcohol is not permitted. No one may keep cars.

Activities: There are no fraternities or sororities. There are 30 groups on campus, including art, computers, ethnic, film, gay, international, literary magazine, newspaper, photography, political, professional, radio and TV, social, social service, student government, and yearbook. Popular campus events include Eventworks, First Night Ice Sculpture, and gallery exhibitions and openings.

Sports: There are 7 intercollegiate sports for men and 6 for women, and 8 intramural sports for men and 6 for women. Facilities include a gym, a fitness center, and courts for squash, volleyball, and basketball.

Disabled Students: 95% of the campus is accessible. Wheelchair ramps, elevators, special parking, specially equipped rest rooms, special class scheduling, lowered drinking fountains, and lowered telephones are available.

Services: There is remedial reading and writing.

Campus Safety and Security: Measures include 24-hour foot and vehicle patrol, self-defense education, security escort services, and shuttle buses. There are informal discussions, pamphlets/posters/films, emergency telephones, and lighted pathways/sidewalks.

Programs of Study: MassArt confers the B.F.A. degree. Master's degrees are also awarded. Bachelor's degrees are awarded in COMMUNICATIONS AND THE ARTS (art history and appreciation, ceramic art and design, fiber/textiles/weaving, film arts, fine arts, glass, graphic design, illustration, industrial design, media arts, metal/jewelry, painting, photography, printmaking, sculpture, and studio art), EDUCATION (art), ENGINEERING AND ENVIRONMENTAL DESIGN (architecture), SOCIAL SCIENCE (fashion design and technology). Painting, illustration, and graphic design are the largest.

Required: A total of 120 semester credits is required for graduation; the minimum GPA varies by major. Typically, students take 42 credits in liberal arts, 18 in studio foundations, 36 in the major, and 24 in electives. Beginning in the sophomore year, the student's work is reviewed by panels of faculty and visiting artists.

Special: MassArt offers cross-registration with several consortiums, internships for advanced students, on- and off-campus work-study programs, study-abroad and foreign-exchange programs, an open major for exceptional students, and dual majors in most combinations of concentrations.

Faculty/Classroom: 51% of faculty are male; 49%, female. All teach undergraduates. No introductory courses are taught by graduate students. The average class size in an introductory lecture is 23; in a laboratory, 12; and in a regular course, 14.

Admissions: 53% of the 2003-2004 applicants were accepted. The SAT I scores for the 2003-2004 freshman class were: Verbal--19% below 500, 50% between 500 and 599, 26% between 600 and 700, and 5% above 700; Math--29% below 500, 50% between 500 and 599, 19% between 600 and 700, and 2% above 700. 41% of the current freshmen were in the top fifth of their class; 86% were in the top two fifths.

Requirements: The SAT I is required. In addition, applicants should be graduates of an accredited secondary school or have earned the GED. College preparatory studies should include as a minimum 4 years of English, 2 each of social studies, math, and science; plus 2 academic electives, 1 each of math or science and 1 art elective; and a foreign language. A personal essay and portfolio are required, and an interview and letters of reference are recommended. A GPA of 3.0 is required. AP and CLEP credits are accepted. Important factors in the admissions decision are evidence of special talent, recommendations by school officials, and personality/intangible qualities.

Procedure: Freshmen are admitted fall and spring. Entrance exams should be taken in the early fall of the senior year. There are early decision and deferred admissions plans. There is a rolling admissions plan. Early decision applications should be filed by December 1; regular applications, by February 15 for fall entry and November 1 for spring entry, along with a $30 (in-state) or $65 (out-of-state) fee. Notification of early decision is sent December 20; regular decision, on a rolling basis by April 1. 13 early decision candidates were accepted for the 2003-2004 class. A waiting list is an active part of the admissions procedure. Applications are accepted on-line through CollegeNET.

Transfer: 123 transfer students enrolled in 2002-2003. Applicants must submit secondary school and postsecondary school transcripts, a statement of purpose, and a portfolio of at least 15 pieces, preferably in slides. An interview is recommended. 60 of 120 credits required for the bachelor's degree must be completed at MassArt.

Visiting: There are regularly scheduled orientations for prospective students, including an information session and a campus tour. There are guides for informal visits and visitors may sit in on classes. To schedule a visit, contact the Admissions Office at admissions@massart.edu.

Financial Aid: In 2002-2003, 75% of all full-time freshmen and 65% of continuing full-time students received some form of financial aid. 60% of full-time freshmen and 68% of continuing full-time students received need-based aid. The average freshman award was $9741. Need-based scholarships or need-based grants averaged $3603; need-based self-help aid (loans and jobs) averaged $3194; and other non-need-based awards and non-need-based scholarships averaged $3083. 84% of undergraduates work part time. Average annual earnings from campus work are $1000. The average financial indebtedness of the 2003 graduate was $18,337. The CSS Profile, FAFSA, FFS, or SFS is required. The deadline for filing freshman financial aid applications for fall entry is May 1.

International Students: There are 62 international students enrolled. They must score 530 on the written TOEFL.

Computers: The mainframe is an IBM. MassArt provides Amiga and Mac PCs for academic use. They are located in the computer center. All students may access the system. There are no time limits. The fee is $100 for students using the computer arts center who are not enrolled in a computer design course.

Graduates: From July 1, 2002 to June 30, 2003, 260 bachelor's degrees were awarded. The most popular majors were painting (16%), graphic design (14%), and photography (10%). In an average class, 1% graduate in 3 years or less, 25% graduate in 4 years or less, 45% graduate in 5 years or less, and 53% graduate in 6 years or less. 8 companies recruited on campus in 2002-2003. Of the 2002 graduating class, 2% were enrolled in graduate school within 6 months of graduation and 87% were employed.

Admissions Contact: Kay Ransdell, Dean of Admissions. A video is available. E-mail: admissions@massart.edu
Web: http://www.massart.edu

MASSACHUSETTS COLLEGE OF LIBERAL ARTS   A-1
North Adams, MA 01247-4100   **(413) 662-5410**
(800) 292-6632; Fax: (413) 662-5179

Full-time: 450 men, 650 women	**Faculty:** 84
Part-time: 100 men, 200 women	**Ph.D.s:** 73%
Graduate: 50 men, 80 women	**Student/Faculty:** 13 to 1
Year: semesters, summer session	**Tuition:** $5396 ($14,341)
Application Deadline: open	**Room & Board:** $5620
Freshman Class: n/av	
SAT I or ACT: required	**LESS COMPETITIVE**

Massachusetts College of Liberal Arts, founded in 1894, is a liberal arts institution emphasizing business and education courses. Figures in the above capsule and in this profile are approximate. In addition to regional accreditation, MCLA has baccalaureate program accreditation with NCATE. The library contains 168,225 volumes, 312,298 microform items, and 6645 audio/video tapes/CDs, and subscribes to 583 periodicals. Computerized library services include the card catalog, interlibrary loans, and database searching. Special learning facilities include a learning resource center, art gallery, radio station, and TV station. The 80-acre campus is in a rural area 45 miles east of Albany. Including any residence halls, there are 19 buildings.

Student Life: 84% of undergraduates are from Massachusetts. Students are from 20 states, 5 foreign countries, and Canada. 80% are from public schools. 91% are white. The average age of freshmen is 19; all undergraduates, 24. 28% do not continue beyond their first year; 35% remain to graduate.

Housing: 1100 students can be accommodated in college housing, which includes single-sex and coed dorms and on-campus apartments. On-campus housing is guaranteed for all 4 years. Upperclassmen may keep cars.

Activities: 4% of men belong to 2 local and 1 national fraternity; 9% of women belong to 2 local and 3 national sororities. There are 50 groups on campus, including band, cheerleading, choir, chorus, computers, dance, drama, ethnic, gay, honors, international, jazz band, literary magazine, musical theater, newspaper, photography, political, professional, radio and TV, religious, social, social service, student government, and yearbook. Popular campus events include Parents Weekend and Winter Carnival.

Sports: There are 6 intercollegiate sports for men and 6 for women, and 10 intramural sports for men and 10 for women. Facilities include a campus center with a swimming pool, weight rooms, a fitness center, and handball, squash, and racquetball courts; an outdoor complex with tennis courts and soccer, baseball, and softball fields; a 1750-seat gym; and a 5-mile cross-country running trail.

Disabled Students: 80% of the campus is accessible. Wheelchair ramps, elevators, special parking, specially equipped rest rooms, and special class scheduling are available.

Services: Counseling and information services are available, as is tutoring in some subjects, including most general education requirements. There is remedial math, reading, and writing. The Tutoring Exchange Network has qualified peers tutoring small groups.

Campus Safety and Security: Measures include 24-hour foot and vehicle patrol, self-defense education, security escort services, and informal discussions. There are pamphlets/posters/films, emergency telephones, and lighted pathways/sidewalks.

Programs of Study: MCLA confers B.A. and B.S. degrees. Master's degrees are also awarded. Bachelor's degrees are awarded in BIOLOGICAL SCIENCE (biology/biological science), BUSINESS (business administration and management), COMMUNICATIONS AND THE ARTS (English and fine arts), COMPUTER AND PHYSICAL SCIENCE (computer science, mathematics, and physics), EDUCATION (education), SOCIAL SCIENCE (history, interdisciplinary studies, philosophy, psychology, and sociology). English, education, and biology are the strongest academically. Business and education are the largest.

Required: All students must complete at least 120 credits, including 50 in a core curriculum, and maintain a GPA of at least 2.0. Phys ed and computer science courses are required.

Special: MCLA offers cross-registration with Williams College and Berkshire Community College, dual majors, internships in all majors, and study abroad in many countries within the International College Program. Student-designed majors, pass/fail options, nondegree study, and independent study also are available. There are 8 national honor societies, a freshman honors program, and 6 departmental honors programs.

Faculty/Classroom: 69% of faculty are male; 31%, female. All teach undergraduates. No introductory courses are taught by graduate students. The average class size in an introductory lecture is 20; in a laboratory, 9; and in a regular course, 19.

Requirements: The SAT I or ACT is required. An eligibility index is used to determine a minimum SAT I score. Applicants should have completed 16 Carnegie units, including 4 courses in English, 3 each in science and math, and 2 each in foreign language, history/social science, and electives. The GED is accepted. A GPA of 2.0 is required. AP and CLEP credits are accepted. Important factors in the admissions decision are advanced placement or honor courses, evidence of special talent, and parents or siblings attending the school.

Procedure: Freshmen are admitted fall and spring. There is a rolling admissions plan. Entrance exams should be taken by January of the senior year. There are early decision and deferred admissions plans. Early decision applications should be filed by December 1; regular application deadlines are open. Application fee is $25. Notification is sent on a rolling basis.

Transfer: Applicants who have a minimum of 12 semester hours from an accredited college are eligible. Students are evaluated on the basis of past college records, which must include a GPA of at least 2.5 with fewer than 25 credits or a 2.0 with 25 credits or more. 30 credits of 120 required for the bachelor's degree must be completed at MCLA.

Visiting: There are regularly scheduled orientations for prospective students, including a 2-day, overnight program for students who have been accepted. There are guides for informal visits and visitors may sit in on classes. To schedule a visit, contact the Admissions Office.

Financial Aid: MCLA is a member of CSS. The FAFSA and the college's own financial statement are required. Check with the school for current deadlines.

International Students: The school actively recruits international students. They must score 550 on the written TOEFL and also take the SAT I.

Computers: The mainframes are a CDC CYBER 815 and a DEC VAX 1850. There are 5 general-use computer labs, 3 with Gateway PCs and 2 with Apple G3 computers. All are connected to the campus network, the e-mail server, and the Internet. Special-purpose labs are available in the sciences, social sciences, and computer science. Limits on student access to the system vary with the time of year. The fee is $25 per year.

Admissions Contact: Denise C. Richardello, Dean of Enrollment Management. A video is available. E-mail: *admissions@mcla.mass.edu* Web: *www.mcla.mass.edu*

MASSACHUSETTS COLLEGE OF PHARMACY AND HEALTH SCIENCES
E-2

Boston, MA 02115

(617) 732-2850
(800) 225-5506; Fax: (617) 732-2118

Full-time: 424 men, 993 women	**Faculty:** 104
Part-time: 41 men, 65 women	**Ph.D.s:** 72%
Graduate: 294 men, 639 women	**Student/Faculty:** 14 to 1
Year: semesters, summer session	**Tuition:** $18,600
Application Deadline: February 1	**Room & Board:** $10,170
Freshman Class: 651 applied, 312 accepted, 201 enrolled	
SAT I Verbal/Math: 496/545	**ACT:** 21 SPECIAL

The Massachusetts College of Pharmacy and Health Sciences, established in 1823, is a private institution offering undergraduate and graduate programs in chemistry, pharmacy, dental hygiene, and health sciences. There are 3 undergraduate schools and 1 graduate school. In addition to regional accreditation, MCPHS has baccalaureate program accreditation with ACPE, ADA, and ARC-PA. The library contains 40,000 volumes and 750 audio/video tapes/CDs, and subscribes to 700 periodicals. Computerized library services include the card catalog, interlibrary loans, and database searching. Special learning facilities include a learning resource center and a pharmacy lab. The 2-acre campus is in an urban area 1 mile from Boston's center. Including any residence halls, there are 3 buildings.

Student Life: Undergraduates are from 32 states, 31 foreign countries, and Canada. 44% are white; 36% Asian American. The average age of freshmen is 18; all undergraduates, 21. 10% do not continue beyond their first year; 84% remain to graduate.

Housing: 293 students can be accommodated in college housing, which includes single-sex and coed dorms. On-campus housing is guaranteed for the freshman year only, is available on a first-come, first-

served basis, and is available on a lottery system for upperclassmen. 85% of students commute. Alcohol is not permitted. No one may keep cars.

Activities: 5% of men belong to 6 national fraternities; 5% of women belong to 2 national sororities. There are 40 groups on campus, including academic, dance, drama, ethnic, gay, international, newspaper, professional, religious, social service, student government, and yearbook. Popular campus events include International Fair and Mission Hill Walk for Health.

Sports: There are 6 intramural sports for men and 6 for women. MCPHS shares facilities with the Massachusetts College of Art, which include a wellness center with weight training equipment and a gym with court space for basketball, volleyball, and badminton.

Disabled Students: 90% of the campus is accessible. Wheelchair ramps, elevators, special parking, specially equipped rest rooms, and lowered drinking fountains are available. All dorm rooms have elevator access and meet handicapped access requirements.

Services: Counseling and information services are available, as is tutoring in some subjects. Tutoring is free of charge and includes both group and individual peer tutoring.

Campus Safety and Security: Measures include security escort services, shuttle buses, informal discussions, and pamphlets/posters/films. There are lighted pathways/sidewalks, security guards at all entrances, and admission to all buildings by means of a security pass worn by all students, faculty, and staff.

Programs of Study: MCPHS confers B.S., B.S.Ch., B.S.H., B.S.Nuc.T., B.S.P., and B.S.Rad.Tech. degrees. Associate, master's, and doctoral degrees are also awarded. Bachelor's degrees are awarded in COMPUTER AND PHYSICAL SCIENCE (chemistry and radiological technology), HEALTH PROFESSIONS (allied health, dental hygiene, health, nuclear medical technology, pharmacy, and premedicine), SOCIAL SCIENCE (psychology). Pharmacy is the largest.

Required: Graduation requirements vary by program. Students must complete course work in expository writing, history and politics, psychology, sociology, interpersonal communications in the health professions, evolution of the health professions, biomedical ethics, and humanities. Quarter hours required for graduation range from 190 to 274, depending on the degree. Students must maintain a minimum GPA of 2.0 overall and a professional GPA that varies by program.

Special: MCPHS offers cross-registration with the other colleges of the Fenway Consortium, cooperative programs with Simmons College and Western New England College, an externship program in radiopharmacy in conjunction with Massachusetts General Hospital, internships, and work-study programs. Accelerated degrees and dual majors are available in some programs. There are 2 national honor societies.

Faculty/Classroom: 39% of faculty are male; 61%, female. All both teach and do research. No introductory courses are taught by graduate students. The average class size in a regular course is 14.

Admissions: 48% of the 2003-2004 applicants were accepted. The SAT I scores for the 2003-2004 freshman class were: Verbal--52% below 500, 38% between 500 and 599, and 10% between 600 and 700; Math--21% below 500, 55% between 500 and 599, 21% between 600 and 700, and 3% above 700. The ACT scores were 10% below 21, 75% between 21 and 23, and 15% between 24 and 26. 30% of the current freshmen were in the top fifth of their class; 85% were in the top two fifths. 3 freshmen graduated first in their class.

Requirements: The SAT I is required. In addition, applicants must graduate from an accredited secondary school with 16 units, including 4 of English, 3 of math, 2 of lab science, 1 of history, and 6 of other college-preparatory subjects. The college also advises advanced chemistry or physics with lab and an extra unit of math. Interviews are recommended. Letters of reference from a guidance counselor and a science or math teacher and 2 student essays are required. A GPA of 3.0 is required. AP and CLEP credits are accepted. Important factors in the admissions decision are evidence of special talent, recommendations by school officials, and advanced placement or honor courses.

Procedure: Freshmen are admitted in the fall. Entrance exams should be taken by December of the senior year. There are early decision and deferred admissions plans. Early decision applications should be filed by November 1; regular applications, by February 1 for fall entry. The fall 2003 application fee was $70. Notification of early decision is sent December 1; regular decision, April 1. 21 early decision candidates were accepted for the 2003-2004 class. Applications are accepted on-line through the school's web site.

Transfer: 340 transfer students enrolled in 2003-2004. Applicants must have a minimum GPA of 2.5. Those with 1 year or less of college credit must submit secondary school transcripts.

Visiting: There are regularly scheduled orientations for prospective students, including a campus tour and information sessions. There are guides for informal visits and visitors may sit in on classes. To schedule a visit, contact the Admissions Office.

Financial Aid: In a recent year, 90% of all full-time students received some form of financial aid. 85% of all full-time students received need-based aid. The average freshman award in 2003-2004 was $15,485.

20% of undergraduates work part time. Average annual earnings from campus work are $1200. The average financial indebtedness of the 2003 graduate was $43,300. The FAFSA is required. The deadline for filing freshman financial aid applications for fall entry is March 15.

International Students: The school actively recruits these students. They must score 550 on the written TOEFL or 213 on the electronic version and also take the college's own test and the SAT I or the ACT.

Computers: The college provides PCs for academic use by all students. They are available in the library, the lab, and the research facility. All students may access the system. There are no time limits and no fees. It is strongly recommended that all students have a personal computer.

Graduates: From July 1, 2002 to June 30, 2003, 68 bachelor's degrees were awarded. In an average class, 32% graduate in 4 years or less, 45% graduate in 5 years or less, and 82% graduate in 6 years or less.

Admissions Contact: Julie Donlon, Director of Admissions. A video is available. E-mail: *admissions@mcp.edu* Web: *www.mcp.edu*

MASSACHUSETTS INSTITUTE OF TECHNOLOGY
Cambridge, MA 02139   D-2
(617) 253-4791; Fax: (617) 258-8304

Full-time: 2345 men, 1725 women	**Faculty:** 960; I, ++$
Part-time: 28 men, 14 women	**Ph.D.s:** 97%
Graduate: 4430 men, 1798 women	**Student/Faculty:** 4 to 1
Year: 4-1-4	**Tuition:** $29,600
Application Deadline: January 1	**Room & Board:** $8710
Freshman Class: 10,549 applied, 1735 accepted, 1019 enrolled	
SAT I Verbal/Math: 710/770	**ACT:** 32 **MOST COMPETITIVE**

Massachusetts Institute of Technology, founded in 1861, is a private, independent, land-grant institution offering programs in architecture and planning, engineering, humanities and social science, science, health sciences, technology, and management. Tuition figures in the above capsule do not include a $1440 required hospital and accident insurance fee, which can be waived for those with existing comparable coverage. There are 5 undergraduate and 6 graduate schools. In addition to regional accreditation, MIT has baccalaureate program accreditation with AACSB, ABET, and CSAB. The 10 libraries contain 2,707,849 volumes, 2,367,273 microform items, and 596,928 audio/video tapes/CDs, and subscribe to 22,597 periodicals. Computerized library services include the card catalog, interlibrary loans, database searching, and Internet access. Special learning facilities include an art gallery, radio station, TV station, and numerous labs and centers. The 154-acre campus is in an urban area 1 mile north of Boston. Including any residence halls, there are 159 buildings.

Student Life: 91% of undergraduates are from out of state, mostly the Northeast. Students are from 50 states, 79 foreign countries, and Canada. 35% are white; 28% Asian American; 12% Hispanic. The average age of freshmen is 18; all undergraduates, 20. 2% do not continue beyond their first year; 92% remain to graduate.

Housing: 4500 students can be accommodated in college housing, which includes single-sex and coed dorms, on-campus apartments, married-student housing, fraternity houses, and sorority houses. In addition, there are language houses, special-interest houses, off-campus independent living groups, and non-Greek cooperative houses. On-campus housing is guaranteed for all 4 years. 94% of students live on campus. Upperclassmen may keep cars.

Activities: 40% of men belong to 2 local and 25 national fraternities; 26% of women belong to 5 national sororities. There are 330 groups on campus, including art, band, cheerleading, chess, choir, chorale, chorus, computers, dance, debate, drama, ethnic, film, gay, honors, international, jazz band, literary magazine, marching band, musical theater, newspaper, orchestra, photography, political, professional, radio and TV, religious, social, social service, student government, symphony, and yearbook. Popular campus events include Rush/Orientation Week, Senior Week, and Spring Weekend.

Sports: There are 23 intercollegiate sports for men and 19 for women, and 23 intramural sports for men and 24 for women. Facilities include an athletic complex consisting of 10 buildings and 26 acres of playing fields.

Disabled Students: Wheelchair ramps, elevators, special parking, specially equipped rest rooms, special class scheduling, lowered drinking fountains, lowered telephones, wheelchair lifts, and automatic doors are available. An adaptive technology lab and special library services are also in place.

Services: Counseling and information services are available, as is tutoring in every subject, including . There is a reader service for the blind. Accommodations for students with documented disabilities include exam time extensions, exams on tape, readers, scribes, textbooks on tape, enlarged materials, braille materials, and notetakers.

Campus Safety and Security: Measures include 24-hour foot and vehicle patrol, self-defense education, security escort services, and shuttle buses. There are informal discussions, pamphlets/posters/films, emergency telephones, and lighted pathways/sidewalks.

Programs of Study: MIT confers the B.S. degree. Master's and doctoral degrees are also awarded. Bachelor's degrees are awarded in BIOLOGI-CAL SCIENCE (biology/biological science), BUSINESS (management science), COMMUNICATIONS AND THE ARTS (creative writing, dramatic arts, German, literature, media arts, and music), COMPUTER AND PHYSICAL SCIENCE (chemistry, computer science, earth science, mathematics, and physics), ENGINEERING AND ENVIRONMENTAL DESIGN (aeronautical engineering, aerospace studies, chemical engineering, civil engineering, computer engineering, electrical/electronics engineering, environmental engineering, materials engineering, materials science, mechanical engineering, nuclear engineering, ocean engineering, and urban planning technology), SOCIAL SCIENCE (American studies, anthropology, archeology, cognitive science, East Asian studies, economics, history, Latin American studies, medieval studies, philosophy, political science/government, psychology, Russian and Slavic studies, and women's studies). Engineering, science, and management are the strongest academically. Engineering is the largest.

Required: To graduate, students must fulfill the General Institute Requirements, as well as writing and phys ed requirements, and earn an additional 180 to 198 credit units, while fulfilling departmental program requirements. A GPA of 3.0 on a scale of 5.0 should be maintained. The General Institute Requirements consist of 8 courses in humanities, arts, and social sciences, 6 in science, including chemistry, physics, calculus, and biology, 2 in restricted science and technology electives, and 1 lab, for a total of 17 courses.

Special: MIT offers cross-registration with Harvard, Wellesley, the Massachusetts College of Art, and the School of the Museum of Fine Arts. Internships are offered including a summer freshman/alumni program, an engineering internship and an electrical engineering and computer science internship. Study abroad is offered in the Cambridge-MIT Institute in England, departmental exchange programs in Europe and the Netherlands, and through programs administered by other schools. A Washington semester, on- and off-campus work-study, and accelerated degree and dual major programs in all majors are offered. There is also the Undergraduate Research Opportunities Program (UROP), offering students research work with faculty, the undergraduate Practice Opportunities Program (UPOP), real-world, for-credit placements in industry or government for sophomores, and the Second Summer Program, which places minority students in paid engineering-aide jobs the summer before their sophomore year. There are 12 national honor societies, including Phi Beta Kappa, and 9 departmental honors programs.

Faculty/Classroom: 83% of faculty are male; 17%, female. All both teach and do research. No introductory courses are taught by graduate students.

Admissions: 16% of the 2003-2004 applicants were accepted. The SAT I scores for the 2003-2004 freshman class were: Verbal--1% below 500, 4% between 500 and 599, 32% between 600 and 700, and 63% above 700; Math--11% between 600 and 700, and 89% above 700. The ACT scores were 1% below 21, 1% between 21 and 23, 8% between 24 and 26, 8% between 27 and 28, and 82% above 28. All of the current freshmen were in the top fifth of their class. 241 freshmen graduated first in their class.

Requirements: The SAT I or ACT is required. In addition, 3 SAT II: Subject tests, including math, a science, and an English or history are required. 14 academic units are recommended, including 4 each of English, math, and science, 2 of social studies and a foreign language. The GED is accepted. Essays, 2 teacher evaluations, an official transcript, and a guidance counselor report are required. An interview is strongly recommended. AP credits are accepted. Important factors in the admissions decision are evidence of special talent, extracurricular activities record, and leadership record.

Procedure: Freshmen are admitted in the fall. Entrance exams should be taken by the January test date. There are early action and deferred admissions plans. Applications should be filed by January 1 for fall entry, along with a $65 fee. Notification is sent March 25. 491 applicants were on the 2003 waiting list. Applications are accepted on-line through *http://web.mit.edu/admissions/www/applications*.

Transfer: 5 transfer students enrolled in 2002-2003. Transfer applicants must have completed 2 or more terms at an accredited college, university, technical institute, military academy, or community college and be in good standing there. They must have taken 1 year of college-level calculus and calculus-based physics, and 1 semester each of biology and chemistry. They must also submit scores for 3 SAT II: Subject tests in a math, a science, and an English or history. Nonnative English speakers may substitute the TOEFL for the SAT II: Subject test in English or history. Competitive applicants should have a 3.5 GPA or above. 3 semesters must be completed at MIT.

Visiting: There are regularly scheduled orientations for prospective students, including information sessions and tours. Overnight visits may be scheduled for nonvacation periods from October through March. Visitors may sit in on classes. To schedule a visit, contact the Admissions office at (617) 258-5515.

Financial Aid: In 2003-2004, 80% of all full-time freshmen and 78% of continuing full-time students received some form of financial aid. 67% of full-time freshmen and 64% of continuing full-time students received need-based aid. The average freshman award was $24,357. Need-based scholarships or need-based grants averaged $20,799 ($35,530 maximum); and need-based self-help aid (loans and jobs) averaged $4177 ($5500 maximum). 58% of undergraduates work part time. Average annual earnings from campus work are $1869. The average financial indebtedness of the 2003 graduate was $19,824. MIT is a member of CSS. The CSS Profile or FAFSA, parent W2s, 1040s, and business tax form are required. The deadline for filing freshman financial aid applications for fall entry is February 1.

International Students: There are 330 international students enrolled. They must take the SAT I or the ACT. Students must take SAT II: Subject tests in a math, a science, and an English or history. Students may opt to take the TOEFL and 2 SAT II: Subject tests in math and sciences. Applicants who have been using English less than 5 years or who not speak it at home are encouraged to take the TOEFL as a supplement to the required tests.

Computers: The mainframe is an IBM 7060-H30. An Athena Computing Environment provides approximately 700 public workstations distributed across campus. Specialized departmental computing facilities are also available. Digital-network connections are provided to dorm rooms and living groups. All students may access the system at all times. There are no time limits and no fees. It is strongly recommended that all students have a personal computer.

Graduates: From July 1, 2002 to June 30, 2003, 1281 bachelor's degrees were awarded. The most popular majors were computer science and engineering (13%), electrical engineering and computer scie (11%), and management science (9%). In an average class, 4% graduate in 3 years or less, 81% graduate in 4 years or less, 90% graduate in 5 years or less, and 92% graduate in 6 years or less. Of the 2002 graduating class, 55% were enrolled in graduate school within 1 year of graduation.

Admissions Contact: Admissions Officers.
Web: *http://web.mit.edu/admissions/www/*

MASSACHUSETTS MARITIME ACADEMY　　E-4
Buzzards Bay, MA 02532-1803　　(508) 830-5000; (800) 544-3411

Full-time: 758 men, 116 women	Faculty: 60; IIB, +$
Part-time: 25 men, 5 women	Ph.D.s: 70%
Graduate: none	Student/Faculty: 15 to 1
Year: semesters	Tuition: $4663 ($15,143)
Application Deadline: open	Room & Board: $5809
Freshman Class: 650 applied, 435 accepted, 261 enrolled	
SAT I Verbal/Math: 510/540	COMPETITIVE

Massachusetts Maritime Academy, founded in 1891, is the oldest continuously operating maritime academy in the country. Cooperative educational learning and leadership training opportunities prepare graduates for professional positions within private industry or, if opted, military commissions. In addition to the tuition stated in the above capsule, all freshmen are required to participate in a winter sea term at the cost of $2563. The library contains 40,171 volumes, 11,674 microform items, and 1113 audio/video tapes/CDs, and subscribes to 505 periodicals. Computerized library services include the card catalog, interlibrary loans, database searching, and Internet access. Special learning facilities include a learning resource center, planetarium, a full bridge-training simulator, an oil-spill management simulator, a liquid cargo-handling simulator, and a computer-aided design lab. The 55-acre campus is in a small town 60 miles south of Boston. Including any residence halls, there are 9 buildings.

Student Life: 70% of undergraduates are from Massachusetts. Students are from 26 states and 11 foreign countries. 73% are from public schools. 90% are white. The average age of freshmen is 18; all undergraduates, 21. 15% do not continue beyond their first year; 70% remain to graduate.

Housing: 800 students can be accommodated in college housing, which includes coed dorms. On-campus housing is guaranteed for all 4 years. 97% of students live on campus; of those, 35% remain on campus on weekends. Alcohol is not permitted. All students may keep cars.

Activities: There are no fraternities or sororities. There are 15 groups on campus, including band, choir, chorus, computers, drill team, jazz band, marching band, newspaper, photography, professional, religious, scuba, social service, student government, and yearbook. Popular campus events include Ring Dance, Emory Rice Day, and Recognition.

Sports: There are 8 intercollegiate sports for men and 6 for women, and 13 intramural sports for men and 5 for women. Facilities include football and baseball fields, a pistol range, outdoor tennis and basketball courts, a sailing center, an Olympic-size swimming pool, 2 weight rooms, 3 multipurpose handball courts, and wrestling courts and fitness rooms. An indoor gym/auditorium seats 2500.

Disabled Students: 90% of the campus is accessible. Wheelchair ramps, elevators, special parking, and specially equipped rest rooms are available.

Services: Counseling and information services are available, as is tutoring in most subjects.

Campus Safety and Security: Measures include 24-hour foot and vehicle patrol and lighted pathways/sidewalks.

Programs of Study: MMA confers the B.S. degree. Master's degrees are also awarded. Bachelor's degrees are awarded in BUSINESS (international business management and transportation management), ENGINEERING AND ENVIRONMENTAL DESIGN (environmental engineering, industrial engineering, and marine engineering). Marine engineering is the strongest academically and has the largest enrollment.

Required: All students must complete 164 credit hours with a minimum of 60 hours in the major and a GPA of 2.0. Requirements include 4 courses in phys ed, 2 each in chemistry and naval science, and 1 each in algebra/trigonometry, introduction to computers, English composition, American literature, Western civilization, economics, analysis, American government, first aid, admiralty law, introduction to marine transportation, introduction to marine engineering, sea term/deck, sea term/engine, and calculus.

Special: MMA offers a junior-year internship in a commercial shipping program. Educational experience includes a minimum of 120 days aboard a training ship, with visits to foreign ports. There are cooperative programs in facilities and environmental engineering and in marine safety and environmental protection. A dual major is available in marine engineering and marine transportaton. A concentration is available in emergency management.

Faculty/Classroom: 96% of faculty are male; 4%, female. All teach undergraduates and 3% do research. The average class size in an introductory lecture is 25; in a laboratory, 12; and in a regular course, 22.

Admissions: 67% of the 2003-2004 applicants were accepted. The SAT I scores for the 2003-2004 freshman class were: Verbal--48% below 500, 42% between 500 and 599, 9% between 600 and 700, and 1% above 700; Math--36% below 500, 47% between 500 and 599, 16% between 600 and 700, and 1% above 700. 15% of the current freshmen were in the top fifth of their class; 70% were in the top two fifths.

Requirements: The SAT I or ACT is required. In addition, applicants must have graduated from an accredited secondary school or hold a GED certificate. They should have completed 16 Carnegie units, including 4 in English, 3 in math, and 2 each in a foreign language, science, and social science. An essay is required, and an interview is strongly recommended. A GPA of 2.0 is required. AP and CLEP credits are accepted. Important factors in the admissions decision are advanced placement or honor courses, leadership record, and extracurricular activities record.

Procedure: Freshmen are admitted in the fall. There are early decision and deferred admissions plans. Early decision applications should be filed by November 1; regular applications by July 15, along with a $50 fee. Notification of early decision is sent December 15.

Transfer: Students must have a minimum GPA of 2.0. 30 of 164 credits required for the bachelor's degree must be completed at MMA.

Visiting: There are regularly scheduled orientations for prospective students, including a campus tour and an admissions interview. An optional overnight visit can arranged. There are guides for informal visits and visitors may sit in on classes and stay overnight. To schedule a visit, contact Anne Ford at (800) 544-3400 or *admissions@maritime.edu*.

Financial Aid: 16% of undergraduates work part time. Average annual earnings from campus work are $1000. MMA is a member of CSS. The CSS Profile or FAFSA and the college's own financial statement are required. The deadline for filing freshman financial aid applications for fall entry is March 1.

International Students: They must score 500 on the written TOEFL and also take the SAT I or the ACT.

Computers: The mainframe is a CDC Cyber 172. PCs are provided for student use in the computer lab and dorm. All students may access the system 8 A.M. to 11 P.M. There are no time limits and no fees. All students are required to have personal computers.

Graduates: From July 1, 2002 to June 30, 2003, 180 bachelor's degrees were awarded. The most popular majors were marine engineering (45%), marine safety environmental protection (20%), and marine transportation (10%). In an average class, 70% graduate in 4 years or less. 60 companies recruited on campus in 2002-2003. Of the 2002 graduating class, all were employed within 6 months of graduation.

Admissions Contact: Francis McDonald, Dean of Enrollment Services. A video is available. E-mail: *admissions@mma.mass.edu*
Web: *www.maritime.edu*

MERRIMACK COLLEGE　　E-2
North Andover, MA 01845　　(978) 837-5100; Fax: (978) 837-5133

Full-time: 925 men, 1121 women	Faculty: 142; IIB, +$
Part-time: 153 men, 190 women	Ph.D.s: 80%
Graduate: 4 men, 11 women	Student/Faculty: 14 to 1
Year: semesters, summer session	Tuition: $20,875
Application Deadline: February 1	Room & Board: $8750
Freshman Class: 3353 applied, 2000 accepted, 593 enrolled	
SAT I Verbal/Math: 540/540	ACT: 21　　COMPETITIVE

Merrimack College, founded in 1947 by the Augustinian clergy of the Roman Catholic Church, is a private institution that offers undergraduate programs in science, engineering, business administration, and liberal arts. In addition to regional accreditation, Merrimack has baccalaureate program accreditation with ABET and CAAHEP. The library contains 116,054 volumes, 11,759 microform items, and 1796 audio/video tapes/CDs, and subscribes to 700 periodicals. Computerized library services include the card catalog, interlibrary loans, and database searching. Special learning facilities include a learning resource center, art gallery, planetarium, TV station, a chemistry center, an urban resource institute, and a center for the arts. The 220-acre campus is in a suburban area 25 miles north of Boston. Including any residence halls, there are 34 buildings.

Student Life: 71% of undergraduates are from Massachusetts. Students are from 29 states, 16 foreign countries, and Canada. 60% are from public schools. 95% are white. 75% are Catholic; 12% Protestant. The average age of freshmen is 18; all undergraduates, 20. 14% do not continue beyond their first year; 69% remain to graduate.

Housing: 1590 students can be accommodated in college housing, which includes coed dorms and on-campus apartments. In addition, there are special-interest houses and international, wellness, engineering, and theme housing. On-campus housing is guaranteed for all 4 years. 72% of students live on campus; of those, 90% remain on campus on weekends. Upperclassmen may keep cars.

Activities: 3% of men belong to 3 national fraternities; 5% of women belong to 3 national sororities. There are 48 groups on campus, including art, cheerleading, choir, chorale, chorus, computers, dance, drama, ethnic, gay, honors, international, literary magazine, musical theater, newspaper, pep band, photography, political, professional, radio and TV, religious, social, social service, student government, and yearbook. Popular campus events include Springfest, Peace and Social Justice Awareness Week, and Family Weekend.

Sports: There are 8 intercollegiate sports for men and 8 for women, and 3 intramural sports for men and 3 for women. Facilities include an athletic complex including an ice rink, basketball, an aerobics studio, and a well-equipped exercise room, and outdoor facilities including 2 sets of tennis courts and baseball, football, softball, soccer, lacrosse, and field hockey fields.

Disabled Students: All of the campus is accessible. Wheelchair ramps, elevators, special parking, specially equipped rest rooms, special class scheduling, lowered drinking fountains, and lowered telephones are available.

Services: Counseling and information services are available, as is tutoring in every subject. Math, science, and writing resource centers are available to all students.

Campus Safety and Security: Measures include 24-hour foot and vehicle patrol, security escort services, shuttle buses, and informal discussions. There are pamphlets/posters/films, emergency telephones, and lighted pathways/sidewalks. Rape Aggressive Defense is available through police services.

Programs of Study: Merrimack confers B.A. and B.S. degrees. Associate and master's degrees are also awarded. Bachelor's degrees are awarded in BIOLOGICAL SCIENCE (biochemistry and biology/biological science), BUSINESS (accounting, business administration and management, business economics, international business management, and marketing/retailing/merchandising), COMMUNICATIONS AND THE ARTS (communications, English, and modern language), COMPUTER AND PHYSICAL SCIENCE (chemistry, computer science, mathematics, and physics), EDUCATION (elementary and secondary), ENGINEERING AND ENVIRONMENTAL DESIGN (civil engineering, electrical/electronics engineering, and environmental science), HEALTH PROFESSIONS (allied health, predentistry, premedicine, and sports medicine), SOCIAL SCIENCE (economics, history, philosophy, political science/government, prelaw, psychology, religion, and sociology). Science, engineering, and business are the strongest academically. Business, psychology, and liberal arts are the largest.

Required: All students are required to emphasize liberal arts with a variety of courses that must include 3 each in humanities, social science, and math and science, 2 each in theology and philosophy, and 1 each in English composition and freshman seminar. Students also must maintain a minimum GPA of 2.0 while taking a total of 120 credit hours, including 30 in the major.

Special: Merrimack offers cooperative programs in business, engineering, liberal arts, and computer science, cross-registration through the Northeast Consortium, internships in all arts and science programs, study abroad in 15 countries, and a Washington semester at American University. Work-study programs, a 5-year combined B.A.-B.S. degree in many major fields, and dual and self-designed majors are available. General studies, nondegree study, and pass/fail options are possible. There are 7 national honor societies, and 2 departmental honors programs.

Faculty/Classroom: 56% of faculty are male; 44%, female. All teach undergraduates, and 60% both teach and do research. No introductory courses are taught by graduate students. The average class size in an introductory lecture is 28; in a laboratory, 15; and in a regular course, 15.

Admissions: 60% of the 2003-2004 applicants were accepted. The SAT I scores for the 2003-2004 freshman class were: Verbal--20% below 500, 64% between 500 and 599, and 16% between 600 and 700; Math--10% below 500, 69% between 500 and 599, 19% between 600 and 700, and 2% above 700. The ACT scores were 38% below 21, 34% be-

tween 21 and 23, 22% between 24 and 26, 4% between 27 and 28, and 2% above 28. 30% of the current freshmen were in the top fifth of their class; 72% were in the top two fifths. 4 freshmen graduated first in their class in a recent year.

Requirements: The SAT I or ACT is required. In addition, for business administration, humanities, and social science majors, Merrimack recommends that applicants complete 4 units of English, 3 each of math and science, 2 of social studies, and a foreign language. For other majors, an additional math course and 1 additional course in science are needed. An essay is required, and an interview is recommended. Applicants should have completed 16 Carnegie units. Merrimack requires applicants to be in the upper 50% of their class. A GPA of 2.7 is required. AP and CLEP credits are accepted. Important factors in the admissions decision are advanced placement or honor courses, recommendations by school officials, and leadership record.

Procedure: Freshmen are admitted fall and spring. Entrance exams should be taken during the spring of the junior year and the fall of the senior year. There are early admissions and deferred admissions plans. Early decision applications should be filed by November 30; regular applications, by February 1 for fall entry and December 15 for spring entry, along with a $50 fee. Notification of early decision is sent December 15; regular decision, March 15. 367 applicants were on the 2003 waiting list. Applications are accepted on-line through Apply and CollegeLink.

Transfer: 123 transfer students enrolled in 20032-2003. Applicants must have maintained a minimum 2.0 GPA while accumulating 30 credits. The SAT I, an interview, and a letter of recommendation are recommended. 45 of 120 credits required for the bachelor's degree must be completed at Merrimack.

Visiting: There are regularly scheduled orientations for prospective students, including 10 information sessions on Saturdays in the fall and 4 financial aid information sessions throughout the year. There are guides for informal visits and visitors may sit in on classes and stay overnight. To schedule a visit, contact the Office of Admissions.

Financial Aid: In 2003-2004, 75% of all full-time freshmen and 70% of continuing full-time students received some form of financial aid. 70% of full-time freshmen and 52% of continuing full-time students received need-based aid. The average freshman award was $15,125, with $10,000 ($20,000 maximum) from need-based scholarships or need-based grants and $5125 (maximum) from need-based self-help aid (loans and jobs). 80% of undergraduates work part time. Average annual earnings from campus work are $2000. The average financial indebtedness of the 2003 graduate was $21,125. The FAFSA is required. The deadline for filing freshman financial aid applications for fall entry is February 1.

International Students: There are 35 international students enrolled. The school actively recruits these students. They must score 600 on the written TOEFL or 250 on the electronic version and also take the Comprehensive English Language Test.

Computers: The mainframe is a DEC VAX 11/785. PCs for academic use are available in the library, classrooms, residence halls, and the campus center. All students may access the system. There are no time limits and no fees. It is strongly recommended that all students have a personal computer. Students in the Business School, which provides a laptop rental program, must have personal computers. An IBM or Gateway is recommended.

Graduates: In a recent year, 472 bachelor's degrees were awarded. The most popular majors were management (15%), accounting (12%), and psychology (7%). In an average class, 49% graduate in 4 years or less, 65% graduate in 5 years or less, and 67% graduate in 6 years or less. 154 companies recruited on campus in 2002-2003. Of the 2002 graduating class, 9% were enrolled in graduate school within 6 months of graduation and 90% were employed.

Admissions Contact: Mary Lou Retelle, Vice President for Enrollment Management. E-mail: *admissions@merrimack.edu* Web: *www.merrimack.edu*

MONTSERRAT COLLEGE OF ART
Beverly, MA 01915

E-2
(978) 921-4242
(800) 836-0487; Fax: (978) 921-4241

Full-time: 148 men, 213 women	**Faculty:** 25
Part-time: 8 men, 14 women	**Ph.Ds:** 64%
Graduate: none	**Student/Faculty:** 14 to 1
Year: semesters	**Tuition:** $17,840
Application Deadline: open	**Room & Board:** $4950
Freshman Class: n/av	
SAT I or ACT: required	**SPECIAL**

Montserrat College of Art, founded in 1970, is a private, residential, professional institution offering degrees in painting and drawing, fine arts, printmaking, graphic design, illustration, photography, and sculpture, with a complementary program in art education. In addition to regional accreditation, Montserrat has baccalaureate program accreditation with ACBSP and NASAD. The library contains 12,000 volumes and 450 audio/video tapes/CDs, and subscribes to 70 periodicals. Computerized library services include the card catalog, interlibrary loans, and database searching. Special learning facilities include a learning resource center and art gallery. The 10-acre campus is in a suburban area 26 miles north of Boston. Including any residence halls, there are 12 buildings.

Student Life: 52% of undergraduates are from out of state, mostly the Northeast. Students are from 22 states and 4 foreign countries. 77% are white. The average age of freshmen is 18; all undergraduates, 20. 38% do not continue beyond their first year; 48% remain to graduate.

Housing: 247 students can be accommodated in college housing, which includes single-sex and coed on-campus apartments and quiet housing. All housing is smoke free. On-campus housing is available on a first-come, first-served basis and is available on a lottery system for upperclassmen. 63% of students live on campus. Alcohol is not permitted. All students may keep cars.

Activities: There are no fraternities or sororities. There are 9 groups on campus, including art, international, literary magazine, newspaper, radio and TV, social, and student government. Popular campus events include Forum Days, Halloween and holiday parties, and gallery openings.

Sports: There are 4 intramural sports for men and 4 for women. Montserrat uses the facilities of the local YMCA.

Disabled Students: 50% of the campus is accessible. Wheelchair ramps, elevators, special parking, specially equipped rest rooms, and special class scheduling are available.

Services: Counseling and information services are available, as is tutoring in some subjects, including art history. There is remedial writing and a reader service for students with dyslexia.

Campus Safety and Security: Measures include informal discussions, pamphlets/posters/films, emergency telephones, and lighted pathways/sidewalks. In addition, there is a security guard in the main building and resident assistants trained in first aid and CPR who patrol the buildings.

Programs of Study: Montserrat confers the B.F.A. degree. Bachelor's degrees are awarded in COMMUNICATIONS AND THE ARTS (fine arts, graphic design, illustration, painting, photography, printmaking, and sculpture), EDUCATION (art).

Required: To graduate, all students are required to complete 120 credits, including 78 in studio courses and 42 in liberal arts courses. To enter the senior program, Montserrat students must have a portfolio. During semester-end evaluations, each student displays work from all courses and is evaluated by a faculty panel.

Special: Montserrat is a member of the Northeast Consortium of Colleges and Universities in Massachusetts, which allows students to take classes at any member college for the same cost. Credit study is available through the continuing education department. Montserrat also offers internships, summer study in New York City or Italy, dual and student-designed majors in fine arts and in art education, and a mobility program that allows students to spend a semester at another school within the Association of Independent Colleges of Art and Design.

Faculty/Classroom: 48% of faculty are male; 52%, female. All teach undergraduates. The average class size in an introductory lecture is 20 and in a regular course, 18.

Requirements: The SAT I or ACT is required. In addition, students must submit an artist's statement, a portfolio, 2 letters of recommendation, and a high school transcript, although no specific program of study is required. A portfolio interview is strongly recommended. A GPA of 2.25 is required. AP and CLEP credits are accepted. Important factors in the admissions decision are evidence of special talent, advanced placement or honor courses, and personality/intangible qualities.

Procedure: Freshmen are admitted fall and spring. There is a deferred admissions plan. Application deadlines are open. Application fee is $40. Notification is sent December 20.

Transfer: 25 transfer students enrolled in 2002-2003. Applicants are required to submit a portfolio, transcripts from a previous college, and an artist's statement. They should also be interviewed. 60 of 120 credits required for the bachelor's degree must be completed at Montserrat.

Visiting: There are regularly scheduled orientations for prospective students, including tours of college studios, observation of classes, and portfolio consultations. There are guides for informal visits and visitors may sit in on classes. To schedule a visit, contact the Admissions Coordinator.

Financial Aid: In 2003-2004, 72% of all full-time freshmen and 74% of continuing full-time students received some form of financial aid. 64% of full-time freshmen and 70% of continuing full-time students received need-based aid. The average freshman award was $9536. Need-based scholarships or need-based grants averaged $2822 ($6000 maximum); need-based self-help aid (loans and jobs) averaged $2777 ($5500 maximum); and non-need-based awards and non-need-based scholarships averaged $3689 ($12,000 maximum). 15% of undergraduates work part time. Average annual earnings from campus work are $1500. The average financial indebtedness of the 2003 graduate was $12,500. Montserrat is a member of CSS. The FAFSA is required. The priority date for freshman financial aid applications for fall entry is March 1. The deadline for filing freshman financial aid applications for fall entry is June 1.

International Students: There are 5 international students enrolled. The school actively recruits these students. They must score 550 on the written TOEFL or 213 on the electronic version and also take the SAT I or the ACT.

Computers: The graphic design department provides 27 Macs, digital photography capabilities, and CD-ROM. Access to the Internet and the World Wide Web is available in the library. All students may access the system 8 A.M. to 11 P.M. daily. There are no time limits and no fees.

Graduates: From July 1, 2002 to June 30, 2003, 81 bachelor's degrees were awarded. The most popular majors were fine arts (56%), graphic design (23%), and illustration (21%). In an average class, 84% graduate in 4 years or less, 99% graduate in 5 years or less, and all graduate in 6 years or less.

Admissions Contact: Stephen M. Negron, Dean of Enrollment Management and Admissions. E-mail: *admiss@montserrat.edu* Web: *www.montserrat.edu*

MOUNT HOLYOKE COLLEGE
South Hadley, MA 01075   B-3
(413) 538-2023; Fax: (413) 538-2409

Full-time: 2 men, 2087 women	Faculty: 211; IIB, ++$
Part-time: 1 man, 58 women	Ph.D.s: 96%
Graduate: 4 women	Student/Faculty: 10 to 1
Year: semesters	Tuition: $29,338
Application Deadline: January 15	Room & Board: $8580
Freshman Class: 2845 applied, 1477 accepted, 518 enrolled	
SAT I Verbal/Math: 660/630	ACT: 29

HIGHLY COMPETITIVE+

Mount Holyoke, founded in 1837, is the oldest institution of higher learning for women in the United States. An independent, liberal arts college, it affords students great freedom in selecting course studies. The 3 libraries contain 709,613 volumes, 26,000 microform items, and 5788 audio/video tapes/CDs, and subscribe to 3564 periodicals. Computerized library services include the card catalog, interlibrary loans, database searching, and Internet access. Special learning facilities include a learning resource center, art gallery, radio station, an observatory, child study center, a center for foreign languages, a center for leadership, a botanical garden and greenhouse, and an equestrian center. The 800-acre campus is in a small town 90 miles west of Boston and 160 miles north of New York City. Including any residence halls, there are 62 buildings.

Student Life: 78% of undergraduates are from out of state, mostly the Northeast. Students are from 48 states, 79 foreign countries, and Canada. 62% are from public schools. 55% are white; 16% foreign nationals; 10% Asian American. The average age of freshmen is 18; all undergraduates, 20. 8% do not continue beyond their first year; 92% remain to graduate.

Housing: 2031 students can be accommodated in college housing, which includes single-sex dorms and on-campus apartments. On-campus housing is guaranteed for all 4 years. Special accommodations are available by need. 95% of students live on campus. All students may keep cars.

Activities: There are no fraternities or sororities. There are 145 groups on campus, including art, band, cheerleading, choir, chorale, chorus, computers, dance, debate, drama, ethnic, film, gay, honors, international, jazz band, literary magazine, musical theater, newspaper, orchestra, photography, political, radio and TV, religious, social, social service, student government, symphony, and yearbook. Popular campus events include Festival of Diversity, Glascock Intercollegiate Poetry Contest, and the Founders Day Ceremony.

Sports: Facilities include a sports and dance complex that houses 2 rehearsal dance studios, a performance dance studio, and a classroom; gym with basketball, volleyball, and badminton courts; 8-lane, 25-meter pool and separate diving tank; 3,100-square-foot weight room; and field house with 1/8 mile 4-lane track, indoor pole vault pit, indoor long jump pit, 6 tennis courts, cardiovascular area, 5 international squash courts, and 2 racquetball courts. Outdoor facilities include 12 tennis courts, 1/4 mile 6-lane track, field hockey, soccer, lacrosse, rugby, and softball fields, rowing tank, a cross-country course, an equestrian center with 2 indoor arenas, and a golf course.

Disabled Students: 90% of the campus is accessible. Wheelchair ramps, elevators, special parking, specially equipped rest rooms, and special class scheduling are available.

Services: Counseling and information services are available, as is tutoring in every subject. The writing center is available to all students at all levels. There is a reader service for the blind. Special testing accommodations, diagnostic testing services, note-taking services, as well as readers and tutors, are available. There is also an adaptive technology lab.

Campus Safety and Security: Measures include 24-hour foot and vehicle patrol, self-defense education, security escort services, and shuttle buses. There are pamphlets/posters/films, emergency telephones, and lighted pathways/sidewalks.

Programs of Study: Mount Holyoke confers the A.B. degree. Master's degrees are also awarded. Bachelor's degrees are awarded in AGRICULTURE (environmental studies), BIOLOGICAL SCIENCE (biochemistry, biology/biological science, and neurosciences), COMMUNICATIONS AND THE ARTS (art history and appreciation, classics, dance, dramatic arts, English, film arts, French, Greek, Italian, Latin, music, romance languages and literature, Russian, Spanish, and studio art), COMPUTER

AND PHYSICAL SCIENCE (astronomy, chemistry, computer science, geology, mathematics, physics, and statistics), EDUCATION (early childhood, elementary, mathematics, psychology, science, and social science), ENGINEERING AND ENVIRONMENTAL DESIGN (engineering), SOCIAL SCIENCE (African American studies, American studies, anthropology, Asian/Oriental studies, classical/ancient civilization, economics, ethics, politics, and social policy, European studies, geography, German area studies, history, international relations, Judaic studies, Latin American studies, medieval studies, philosophy, political science/government, psychobiology, religion, sociology, and women's studies). Sciences, mathematics, and international relations are the strongest academically. English, politics, and biology are the largest.

Required: Students must maintain a minimum GPA of 2.0 while taking 128 total credits, with 32 to 56 in the major. Students must complete 3 courses in the humanities, 2 courses each in science/math and social studies, a foreign language, a multicultural perspective course, and 6 credits in phys ed. A minor field of study is necessary for those not pursuing a double major, or an interdisciplinary major.

Special: Mount Holyoke offers students cross-registration through the Five-College Consortium. The college also offers dual-degree opportunities, including a 3-2 engineering program and a 3-2 program in public health, both with the University of Massachusetts at Amherst, and 3-2 programs in engineering with Dartmouth College and Caltech. Other opportunities include the 12-College Exchange Program, science and international studies internships, study-abroad programs (semester or full-year), a Washington semester, work-study, student-designed majors, dual majors, a January program, accelerated degrees, nondegree study, and pass/fail options. A B.A.-B.S. degree in nursing at Johns Hopkins and a teacher licensure program are available. There are 2 national honor societies, including Phi Beta Kappa; all departments have honors programs.

Faculty/Classroom: 46% of faculty are male; 54%, female. All both teach and do research. No introductory courses are taught by graduate students. The average class size in an introductory lecture is 15; in a laboratory, 12; and in a regular course, 15.

Admissions: 52% of the 2003-2004 applicants were accepted. The SAT I scores for the 2003-2004 freshman class were: Verbal--1% below 500, 13% between 500 and 599, 58% between 600 and 700, and 28% above 700; Math--1% below 500, 25% between 500 and 599, 60% between 600 and 700, and 14% above 700. The ACT scores were 5% between 21 and 23, 17% between 24 and 26, 26% between 27 and 28, and 52% above 28. 82% of the current freshmen were in the top fifth of their class; 98% were in the top two fifths. There were 10 National Merit semifinalists. 18 freshmen graduated first in their class.

Requirements: The SAT I/ACT is not required. The school recommends that applicants have 4 years each of English and foreign language, 3 each of math and science, and 2 of social studies. An essay is required and an interview is strongly recommended. AP credits are accepted. Important factors in the admissions decision are recommendations by school officials, leadership record, and advanced placement or honor courses.

Procedure: Freshmen are admitted in the fall. Entrance exams should be taken before the application deadline. There are early decision, early admissions, and deferred admissions plans. Early decision applications should be filed by November 15; regular applications, by January 15 for fall entry. The fall 2003 application fee was $55. Notification of early decision is sent December 31; regular decision, April 1. 180 early decision candidates were accepted for the 2003-2004 class. 157 applicants were on the 2003 waiting list; 33 were admitted. Applications are accepted on-line through Embark.com and the school's web site.

Transfer: 67 transfer students enrolled in 2002-2003. A statement of good standing, transcripts of secondary school or college-level work, and an essay are required of transfer applicants. An interview is recommended. SAT I scores will be considered if submitted, but are not required. 64 credits of 128 required for the bachelor's degree must be completed at Mount Holyoke.

Visiting: There are regularly scheduled orientations for prospective students, including tours, on-campus interviews, overnight stays, and meetings with professors and coaches. There are guides for informal visits and visitors may sit in on classes and stay overnight. To schedule a visit, contact the Admission Office at *admission@mtholyoke.edu.*

Financial Aid: In 2003-2004, 67% of all full-time freshmen and 75% of continuing full-time students received some form of financial aid. 60% of full-time freshmen and 70% of continuing full-time students received need-based aid. The average freshman award was $23,887. Need-based scholarships or need-based grants averaged $20,042, and need-based self-help aid (loans and jobs) averaged $4252. 55% of undergraduates work part time. Average annual earnings from campus work are $1800. The average financial indebtedness of the 2003 graduate was $17,000. The CSS/Profile, FAFSA, and parent and student tax returns are required. The deadline for filing freshman financial aid applications for fall entry is January 15.

International Students: There are 335 international students enrolled. The school actively recruits these students. They must score 600 on the written TOEFL or 250 on the electronic version if English is not their first language.

Computers: The mainframe is a Compaq/Digital Alpha DS20. A computer center houses several labs containing various PCs and workstations. There are 4 other labs distributed elsewhere. Most residence halls contain word-processing facilities with 3 to 6 computers. The mainframes may be accessed via PCs connected to Ethernet or by modem. Network connections beyond the campus are through a T1 line. There is an Information Commons in the library to provide a specific location designated to deliver electronic resources for research. All students may access the system. There are no time limits and no fees.

Graduates: From July 1, 2002 to June 30, 2003, 570 bachelor's degrees were awarded. The most popular majors were social sciences and history (32%), biological sciences (10%), and interdisciplinary studies (10%). In an average class, 72% graduate in 4 years or less, 77% graduate in 5 years or less, and 79% graduate in 6 years or less. 47 companies recruited on campus in 2002-2003. Of the 2002 graduating class, 18% were enrolled in graduate school within 6 months of graduation and 89% were employed.

Admissions Contact: Diane C. Anci, Dean of Admission. A video is available. E-mail: *admission@mtholyoke.edu* Web: *mtholyoke.edu*

MOUNT IDA COLLEGE

Newton, MA 02459 — D-2

(617) 928-4553; Fax: (617) 928-4507

Full-time: 389 men, 655 women	Faculty: 56; IIB, -$
Part-time: 10 men, 22 women	Ph.D.s: 61%
Graduate: none	Student/Faculty: 19 to 1
Year: semesters, summer session	Tuition: $16,596
Application Deadline: open	Room & Board: $9000
Freshman Class: n/av	
SAT I or ACT: required	**LESS COMPETITIVE**

Mount Ida College, founded in 1899, is an independent baccalaureate college that prepares students for a profession through a curriculum that emphasizes career studies integrated with liberal learning. There are 5 undergraduate schools. In addition to regional accreditation, Mount Ida has baccalaureate program accreditation with ABFSE, ADA, FIDER, and NASAD. The library contains 62,500 volumes, 68 microform items, and 2000 audio/video tapes/CDs, and subscribes to 530 periodicals. Computerized library services include the card catalog, interlibrary loans, database searching, and Internet access. Special learning facilities include a learning resource center, art gallery, radio station, TV station, communication lab, darkroom, sewing rooms, blueprint-making facility, and dental labs. The 72-acre campus is in a suburban area 8 miles west of downtown Boston. Including any residence halls, there are 18 buildings.

Student Life: 54% of undergraduates are from Massachusetts. Students are from 23 states, 33 foreign countries, and Canada. 80% are from public schools. 63% are white; 16% African American; 10% foreign nationals. The average age of freshmen is 19; all undergraduates, 21.

Housing: 803 students can be accommodated in college housing, which includes single-sex and coed dorms. In addition, there are honors houses and housing for students over age 21. On-campus housing is guaranteed for all 4 years. 60% of students live on campus. Upperclassmen may keep cars.

Activities: There are no fraternities or sororities. There are 25 groups on campus, including AIGA, art, cheerleading, chess, choir, commuter, dance, drama, equestrian, ethnic, fashion, gay, honors, international, literary magazine, newspaper, photography, professional, radio and TV, religious, social, social service, student government, travel, vet technology, and yearbook. Popular campus events include Welcome Week, Spring Fling, and Senior Week.

Sports: There are 7 intercollegiate sports for men and 6 for women, and 8 intramural sports for men and 10 for women. Facilities include a gym, playing fields, a fitness center, tennis courts, an outdoor swimming pool, athletic fields, and an athletic center.

Disabled Students: 75% of the campus is accessible. Wheelchair ramps, elevators, special parking, specially equipped rest rooms, special class scheduling, lowered drinking fountains, lowered telephones, and special housing are available.

Services: Counseling and information services are available, as is tutoring in most subjects. There is remedial math, reading, and writing. There is a program for learning disabled students, for which a fee is charged. Studies skills courses are also available. The Learning Circle is another innovative campuswide initiative that provides a professional learning specialist to assist students and monitor their academic progress.

Campus Safety and Security: Measures include 24-hour foot and vehicle patrol, self-defense education, security escort services, and shuttle buses. There are informal discussions, pamphlets/posters/films, emergency telephones, and lighted pathways/sidewalks.

Programs of Study: Mount Ida confers B.A., B.S., and B.L.S. degrees. Associate degrees are also awarded. Bachelor's degrees are awarded in AGRICULTURE (equine science), BUSINESS (business administration and management, fashion merchandising, funeral home services, hospitality management services, marketing/retailing/merchandising, retailing, and small business management), COMMUNICATIONS AND THE ARTS (communications, graphic design, journalism, media arts, and radio/television technology), EDUCATION (early childhood), ENGINEERING AND ENVIRONMENTAL DESIGN (interior design), HEALTH PROFESSIONS (veterinary science), SOCIAL SCIENCE (child psychology/development, criminal justice, fashion design and technology, law, and liberal arts/general studies). Veterinary technology, dental hygiene, and funeral service are the strongest academically. Business and veterinary technology are the largest.

Required: Candidates for a bachelor's degree require 128 credits with a 2.0 GPA. The distribution requirement varies for each major. 1 phys ed course is required. The all-college curriculum includes these common experiences for all students: a college success course, a junior year interdisciplinary seminar, and a senior capstone project.

Special: Internships in the form of work experience are available in each department. Work-study provided by the college, student-designed majors, study abroad in 14 countries, exchange program with Strasbourg, France, a general studies degree, an interdisciplinary major in legal studies, nondegree study, and an accelerated degree program in funeral service are also available. There are 4 national honor societies, a freshman honors program, and 4 departmental honors programs.

Faculty/Classroom: 46% of faculty are male; 54%, female. All teach undergraduates. The average class size in an introductory lecture is 25; in a laboratory, 16; and in a regular course, 20.

Requirements: The SAT I or ACT is required. In addition, applicants are required to have 4 units of English, 2 of social studies, and 3 each of math and science. A portfolio is recommended for certain programs, while an interview is recommended for all applicants. The GED is accepted. A GPA of 2.0 is required. AP and CLEP credits are accepted. Important factors in the admissions decision are advanced placement or honor courses, evidence of special talent, and recommendations by school officials.

Procedure: Freshmen are admitted fall and spring. Entrance exams should be taken as early as possible by the junior year. There are early admissions and deferred admissions plans. There is a rolling admissions plan. Application deadlines are open. Application fee is $35. Applications are accepted on-line through *www.mountida.edu.*

Transfer: 144 transfer students enrolled in 2002-2003. Applicants need a minimum grade average of C and must submit college and high school transcripts. 32 of 120 credits required (with some exceptions) for the bachelor's degree must be completed at Mount Ida.

Visiting: There are regularly scheduled orientations for prospective students, consisting of fall and spring open houses, Saturday sessions, and weekday appointments. There are guides for informal visits and visitors may sit in on classes and stay overnight. To schedule a visit, contact the Admissions Office at *admissions@mountida.edu.*

Financial Aid: 70% of undergraduates work part time. Average annual earnings from campus work are $1500. The average financial indebtedness of the 2003 graduate was $19,268. Mount Ida is a member of CSS. The FAFSA is required. The priority date for freshman financial aid applications for fall entry is May 1.

International Students: There are 93 international students enrolled. The school actively recruits these students. They must score 425 on the written TOEFL or 113 on the electronic version and also take the SAT I or the ACT.

Computers: The mainframe is an IBM AS/400. There are 80 computers for student use, including IBM and Mac. Web access is available. In addition, there are 20 Mac G5 computers in the School of Design. All students may access the system. There are no time limits and no fees. It is strongly recommended that all students have a personal computer. Macs are recommended for graphic design majors.

Graduates: From July 1, 2002 to June 30, 2003, 128 bachelor's degrees were awarded. The most popular majors were criminal justice (16%), graphic design (13%), and management (11%).

Admissions Contact: Judith A. Kaufman.
E-mail: *admissions@mountida.edu* Web: *www.mountida.edu*

NEW ENGLAND CONSERVATORY OF MUSIC   E-2
Boston, MA 02115   (617) 585-1101; Fax: (617) 585-1115

Full-time: 199 men, 175 women	**Faculty:** 84; IIA, --$
Part-time: 9 men, 12 women	**Ph.Ds:** 22%
Graduate: 159 men, 222 women	**Student/Faculty:** 4 to 1
Year: semesters	**Tuition:** $24,750
Application Deadline: December 1	**Room & Board:** $10,250
Freshman Class: 943 applied, 344 accepted, 118 enrolled	
SAT I or ACT: required	SPECIAL

The New England Conservatory of Music, founded in 1867, is the oldest private school of its kind in the United States. It combines classroom study of music with an emphasis on performance for talented young musicians. In addition to regional accreditation, NEC has baccalaureate program accreditation with NASM. The 3 libraries contain 80,000 volumes, 500 microform items, and 50,000 audio/video tapes/CDs, and

subscribe to 275 periodicals. Computerized library services include the card catalog and interlibrary loans. Special learning facilities include an electronic music studio. The 8-acre campus is in an urban area 2 miles south of downtown Boston. Including any residence halls, there are 4 buildings.

Student Life: 71% of undergraduates are from out of state, mostly the Northeast. Students are from 47 states, 39 foreign countries, and Canada. 75% are from public schools. 57% are white; 24% foreign nationals. The average age of freshmen is 18; all undergraduates, 21.

Housing: 169 students can be accommodated in college housing, which includes coed dorms. On-campus housing is guaranteed for the freshman year only. 79% of students commute. Alcohol is not permitted. No one may keep cars.

Activities: There are no fraternities or sororities. There are 14 groups on campus, including band, choir, chorale, chorus, computers, gay, international, jazz band, opera, orchestra, political, religious, student government, and symphony. Popular campus events include visits by guest performers and 600 NEC concerts per year.

Sports: There is no sports program at NEC.

Disabled Students: All of the campus is accessible. Elevators, special parking, specially equipped rest rooms, and lowered drinking fountains are available.

Services: Counseling and information services are available, as is tutoring in most subjects. There is remedial writing.

Campus Safety and Security: Measures include security escort services, informal discussions, pamphlets/posters/films, and 24-hour security at the residence hall.

Programs of Study: NEC confers the B.Mus. degree. Master's and doctoral degrees are also awarded. Bachelor's degrees are awarded in COMMUNICATIONS AND THE ARTS (applied music, jazz, music, music history and appreciation, music performance, music theory and composition, and visual and performing arts).

Required: Requirements for graduation include a minimum 2.0 GPA, an average of 120 total credits, and a senior recital.

Special: NEC offers cross-registration with Northeastern and Tufts Universities and Simmons College, as well as a 5-year double major degree program with Tufts University. There is a freshman honors program.

Faculty/Classroom: 64% of faculty are male; 36%, female. All teach undergraduates. The average class size in an introductory lecture is 30 and in a regular course, 15.

Admissions: 36% of the 2003-2004 applicants were accepted.

Requirements: The SAT I or ACT is required. In addition, the applicant must be a graduate of an accredited secondary school or have a GED. An essay is required, as is an audition after submitting the formal application. In some cases, taped auditions are accepted; these must be submitted with the admissions application. Applicants are expected to have reached an advanced level of performance accomplishment. A GPA of 2.75 is required. AP and CLEP credits are accepted. Important factors in the admissions decision are evidence of special talent, recommendations by school officials, and parents or siblings attending the school.

Procedure: Freshmen are admitted fall and spring. Entrance exams should be taken by March 1. There is a deferred admissions plan. Applications should be filed by December 1 for fall entry and November 1 for spring entry, along with a $100 fee. Notification is sent by April 1. 254 applicants were on the 2003 waiting list; 21 were admitted. Applications are accepted on-line through *www.unifiedapps.org.*

Transfer: 14 transfer students enrolled in 2002-2003. Transfer students must audition and submit all college-level transcripts and a transfer statement. 60 of 120 credits required for the bachelor's degree must be completed at NEC.

Visiting: There are regularly scheduled orientations for prospective students, consisting of tours offered regularly during the week. Visitors may sit in on classes. To schedule a visit, contact the Admissions Office.

Financial Aid: In 2003-2004, 88% of all full-time freshmen and 87% of continuing full-time students received some form of financial aid. 84% of full-time freshmen and 87% of continuing full-time students received need-based aid. The average freshman award was $9640. Need-based scholarships or need-based grants averaged $9640 ($24,500 maximum); and need-based self-help aid (loans and jobs) averaged $2625 (maximum). 55% of undergraduates work part time. Average annual earnings from campus work are $1120. The average financial indebtedness of the 2003 graduate was $36,040. NEC is a member of CSS. The FAFSA and the college's own financial statement are required. The deadline for filing freshman financial aid applications for fall entry is December 1.

International Students: There are 45 international students enrolled. The school actively recruits these students. They must score 500 on the written TOEFL or 173 on the electronic version and also take the SAT I or the ACT, scoring 1000 on the SAT I.

Computers: Macs, PCs, and a library of music software and synthesizers are available in the computer studio. There are 6 terminals in the dorm, and 3 terminals in the other campus buildings for public use. All students may access the system. There are no time limits and no fees.

Graduates: From July 1, 2002 to June 30, 2003, 76 bachelor's degrees were awarded. The most popular majors were performance (72%) and composition (4%). In an average class, all graduate in 5 years or less. 50 companies recruited on campus in 2002-2003. Of the 2002 graduating class, 85% were enrolled in graduate school within 6 months of graduation.

Admissions Contact: Thomas Novak, Dean of Admissions and Financial Aid. E-mail: *admissions@newenglandconservatory.edu* Web: *www.newenglandconservatory.edu*

NEWBURY COLLEGE
D-2
Brookline, MA 02445-5796
(617) 730-7007
(800) NEWBURY; Fax: (617) 731-9618

Full-time: 390 men, 410 women	**Faculty:** 54
Part-time: 1200 men and women	**Ph.D.s:** 20%
Graduate: none	**Student/Faculty:** 15 to 1
Year: semesters, summer session	**Tuition:** $15,875
Application Deadline: March 1	**Room & Board:** $7575
Freshman Class: 1300 applied, 1008 accepted, 304 enrolled	
ACT: 20	**COMPETITIVE**

Newbury College, founded in 1962, is a private institution offering career-relevant degree programs in business, graphic design, legal studies, computer science, interior design, communication, culinary arts, hotel and restaurant management, and psychology. There are 3 undergraduate schools. In addition to regional accreditation, Newbury has baccalaureate program accreditation with FIDER. The library contains 32,459 volumes, 74,000 microform items, and 1900 audio/video tapes/CDs, and subscribes to 127,000 periodicals. Computerized library services include the card catalog, interlibrary loans, and database searching. Special learning facilities include a learning resource center, art gallery, radio station, and TV station. The 10-acre campus is in a suburban area 3 miles west of Boston. Including any residence halls, there are 10 buildings.

Student Life: 64% of undergraduates are from Massachusetts. Students are from 20 states, 42 foreign countries, and Canada. 60% are from public schools. 52% are white; 24% foreign nationals; 14% African American. The average age of freshmen is 19; all undergraduates, 21. 15% do not continue beyond their first year; 80% remain to graduate.

Housing: 202 students can be accommodated in college housing, which includes single-sex and coed dorms. In addition, there are special-interest houses. On-campus housing is available on a lottery system for upperclassmen. Priority is given to out-of-town students. 65% of students commute. Alcohol is not permitted. Upperclassmen may keep cars.

Activities: There are no fraternities or sororities. There are 20 groups on campus, including debate, drama, ethnic, gay, honors, international, jazz band, literary magazine, professional, radio and TV, social, social service, student government, and yearbook. Popular campus events include Multicultural Week, Spring Fling, and Fall Fest.

Sports: There are 6 intercollegiate sports for men and 6 for women, and 9 intramural sports for men and 9 for women. Facilities include an off-site gym and a cardiovascular/weight room.

Disabled Students: 71% of the campus is accessible. Wheelchair ramps, elevators, special parking, and specially equipped rest rooms are available.

Services: Counseling and information services are available, as is tutoring in every subject. There is a reader service for the blind and remedial math, reading, and writing.

Campus Safety and Security: Measures include 24-hour foot and vehicle patrol, security escort services, shuttle buses, and pamphlets/posters/films. There are lighted pathways/sidewalks.

Programs of Study: Newbury confers the B.S. degree. Associate degrees are also awarded. Bachelor's degrees are awarded in BUSINESS (accounting, business administration and management, hotel/motel and restaurant management, and international business management), COMMUNICATIONS AND THE ARTS (communications and graphic design), COMPUTER AND PHYSICAL SCIENCE (computer science), ENGINEERING AND ENVIRONMENTAL DESIGN (interior design), HEALTH PROFESSIONS (health care administration), SOCIAL SCIENCE (criminal justice, food production/management/services, paralegal studies, prelaw, and psychology). Legal studies and hotel and restaurant management are the strongest academically. Business administration, culinary arts, and interior design are the largest.

Required: Candidates for a bachelor's degree must earn 120 credits or 60 credits beyond the associate degree, with a 2.0 GPA. Distribution requirements include courses in math, lab science, literature, and social science, as well as 3 additional credits in arts and sciences.

Special: Internships are part of the bachelor's degree program. Dual majors are available. Credits earned for associate degrees in professional areas can be applied toward the college's bachelor's degree programs. There is a 3-3 law program with Massachusetts School of Law and study abroad in many countries. There is a freshman honors program.

Faculty/Classroom: 51% of faculty are male; 49%, female. All teach undergraduates. The average class size in an introductory lecture is 20; in a laboratory, 10; and in a regular course, 16.

Admissions: 78% of the 2003-2004 applicants were accepted.

Requirements: The SAT I or ACT is recommended. In addition, applicants must submit 2 letters of recommendation and high school transcripts. A personal interview is strongly recommended. A GPA of 2.0 is required. AP and CLEP credits are accepted. Important factors in the admissions decision are leadership record, recommendations by alumni, and extracurricular activities record.

Procedure: Freshmen are admitted fall and spring. Entrance exams should be taken following acceptance. There is a deferred admissions plan. Early decision applications should be filed by December 1; regular applications, by March 1 for fall entry and November 1 for spring entry, along with a $50 fee. Notification of early decision is sent January 1; regular decision, on a rolling basis. Applications are accepted on-line through *www.newbury.edu* and *Embark.com*.

Transfer: 35 transfer students enrolled in a recent year. Transfer students must submit 2 recommendations and high school and college transcripts. 30 of 120 credits required for the bachelor's degree must be completed at Newbury.

Visiting: There are regularly scheduled orientations for prospective students, including fall and spring open houses, daily interviews, and campus tours. There are guides for informal visits and visitors may sit in on classes. To schedule a visit, contact the Office of Admission.

Financial Aid: In 2003-2004, 80% of all full-time freshmen and 78% of continuing full-time students received some form of financial aid. 75% of all full-time students received need-based aid. 58% of undergraduates work part time. Average annual earnings from campus work are $1250. The FAFSA and the college's own financial statement are required. The priority date for freshman financial aid applications for fall entry is November 1. The deadline for filing freshman financial aid applications for fall entry is March 1.

International Students: There are 230 international students enrolled. The school actively recruits these students. They must score 500 on the written TOEFL or 167 on the electronic version and also take the college's own test.

Computers: The mainframes are a DEC VAX 4000-100 and 3600. Students have access to Macs and PCs in the computer labs, all with Internet access. All students may access the system. There are no time limits and no fees.

Graduates: In a recent year, 115 bachelor's degrees were awarded. The most popular majors were hotel and restaurant management (25%), business management (18%), and computer science (10%). 60 companies recruited on campus in a recent year. Of a recent year's graduating class, 12% were enrolled in graduate school within 6 months of graduation and 96% were employed.

Admissions Contact: Jacqueline Giordano, Vice President. E-mail: *info@newbury.edu* Web: *www.newbury.edu*

NICHOLS COLLEGE
C-3
Dudley, MA 01571
(508) 943-2055
(800) 470-3379; Fax: (508) 943-9885

Full-time: 555 men, 270 women	**Faculty:** 33
Part-time: 232 men, 270 women	**Ph.D.s:** 61%
Graduate: 197 men, 148 women	**Student/Faculty:** 25 to 1
Year: semesters, summer session	**Tuition:** $19,650
Application Deadline: open	**Room & Board:** $7912
Freshman Class: 1045 applied, 912 accepted, 291 enrolled	
SAT I Verbal/Math: 460/450	**LESS COMPETITIVE**

Nichols College, founded in 1931, is a private institution emphasizing business and liberal arts. There are campuses in Dudley, Auburn, and Marlborough. The library contains 43,989 volumes, 3808 microform items, and 1711 audio/video tapes/CDs, and subscribes to 211 periodicals. Computerized library services include the card catalog, interlibrary loans, database searching, and Internet access. Special learning facilities include a learning resource center, radio station, and the Robert C. Fischer Policy and Cultural Institute. The 200-acre campus is in a rural area 20 miles south of Worcester. Including any residence halls, there are 27 buildings.

Student Life: 70% of undergraduates are from Massachusetts. Students are from 20 states and 3 foreign countries. 91% are white. The average age of freshmen is 18; all undergraduates, 21. 36% do not continue beyond their first year; 45% remain to graduate.

Housing: 737 students can be accommodated in college housing, which includes coed dorms. There is substance-free housing. On-campus housing is guaranteed for all 4 years. 80% of students live on campus; of those, 65% remain on campus on weekends. All students may keep cars.

Activities: There are no fraternities or sororities. There are 32 groups on campus, including cheerleading, chess, computers, departmental, drama, ethnic, honors, international, literary magazine, newspaper, political, professional, radio and TV, religious, student government, and yearbook. Popular campus events include Spring Weekend and 100 Days Social.

Sports: There are 8 intercollegiate sports for men and 7 for women, and 5 intramural sports for men and 4 for women. Facilities include a

field house with basketball courts, a sauna, aerobics and weight training rooms, and athletic training facilities. There is also an athletic complex with a gym, a suspended jogging track, 2 racquetball courts, a squash court, an indoor climbing wall, and 2 fitness rooms. Outdoor facilities include 6 tennis courts, a volleyball court, and a basketball court.

Disabled Students: 67% of the campus is accessible. Wheelchair ramps, elevators, special parking, specially equipped rest rooms, special class scheduling, lowered drinking fountains, and special housing are available. The college makes every effort to accommodate students with special needs.

Services: Counseling and information services are available, as is tutoring in most subjects. There is remedial math and writing and ESL assistance by appointment.

Campus Safety and Security: Measures include 24-hour foot and vehicle patrol, self-defense education, security escort services, and informal discussions. There are pamphlets/posters/films and lighted pathways/sidewalks.

Programs of Study: Nichols confers B.A. and B.S.B.A. degrees. Associate and master's degrees are also awarded. Bachelor's degrees are awarded in BUSINESS (accounting, banking and finance, business administration and management, management information systems, marketing/retailing/merchandising, personnel management, and sports management), COMMUNICATIONS AND THE ARTS (English), COMPUTER AND PHYSICAL SCIENCE (mathematics), SOCIAL SCIENCE (economics, history, and psychology). Accounting, management, and marketing are the strongest academically. Sports management and accounting are the largest.

Required: All students must complete a program of study within 10 semesters and maintain a GPA of 2.0 overall and in their major. Business students need 33 hours of business core classes out of the total 122 hours required of all students for graduation. Students must complete 2 writing-intensive upper-level courses, and they must attend 28 events within the Cultural Experience: The Arts, Sciences, and Public Policy Program.

Special: Nichols offers cross-registration with the Worcester Consortium of Colleges, internships designed with departmental approval, study abroad at Regents College in London and at the University of Nova Scotia, a Washington semester, a general business degree, a teacher certification program, an accelerated degree program in business administration, and nondegree study. There are 5 national honor societies and 8 departmental honors programs.

Faculty/Classroom: 62% of faculty are male; 38%, female. All teach undergraduates, and 45% both teach and do research. No introductory courses are taught by graduate students. The average class size in an introductory lecture is 21; in a laboratory, 18; and in a regular course, 23.

Admissions: 87% of the 2003-2004 applicants were accepted. The SAT I scores for the 2003-2004 freshman class were: Verbal--76% below 500, 23% between 500 and 599, and 1% between 600 and 700; Math--70% below 500, 27% between 500 and 599, and 3% between 600 and 700. 5% of the current freshmen were in the top fifth of their class; 24% were in the top two fifths.

Requirements: The SAT I or ACT is required. In addition, applicants must be graduates of accredited secondary schools or have earned a GED. Recommended preparation includes 4 years of high school English, 3 of math, 2 each of science and social studies, and 5 of academic electives. A GPA of 2.0 is required. AP and CLEP credits are accepted. Important factors in the admissions decision are advanced placement or honor courses, recommendations by school officials, and personality/intangible qualities.

Procedure: Freshmen are admitted fall and spring. Entrance exams should be taken by November of the senior year. There is a deferred admissions plan. Application deadlines are open. Application fee is $25 (on-line application fee is $10). Notification is sent on a rolling basis. Applications are accepted on-line through the school's web site.

Transfer: 30 transfer students enrolled in 2002-2003. Applicants need a minimum GPA of 2.0 in courses to be transferred and must submit official transcripts of all previous college study. 30 of 122 credits required for the bachelor's degree must be completed at Nichols.

Visiting: There are regularly scheduled orientations for prospective students, including meetings with faculty members and preregistration; separate orientation programs are tailored for transfers only. There are guides for informal visits and visitors may sit in on classes and stay overnight. To schedule a visit, contact the Admissions Office.

Financial Aid: In 2003-2004, 91% of all full-time freshmen and 96% of continuing full-time students received some form of financial aid. 80% of full-time freshmen and 77% of continuing full-time students received need-based aid. The average freshman award was $14,718. Need-based scholarships or need-based grants averaged $9561 ($21,476 maximum); need-based self-help aid (loans and jobs) averaged $5555 ($12,000 maximum); and non-need-based awards and non-need-based scholarships averaged $10,860 ($19,400 maximum). 27% of undergraduates work part time. Average annual earnings from campus work are $828. The average financial indebtedness of the 2003 graduate was $21,996. The FAFSA is required. The deadline for filing freshman financial aid applications for fall entry is March 1.

International Students: There are 6 international students enrolled. The school actively recruits these students. They must score 500 on the written TOEFL or 173 on the electronic version or have acceptable scores on the SAT I or ACT.

Computers: There are 246 connections to the central network in the academic center and 1 or 2 connections in every dorm room. A laptop PC with printer, software, and hardware is included in the tuition for each incoming student. All students may access the system 24 hours a day. There are no time limits and no fees. All students are required to have personal computers.

Graduates: In a recent year, 142 bachelor's degrees were awarded. The most popular majors were general business (25%), general management (16%), and marketing (11%). In an average class, 1% graduate in 3 years or less, 33% graduate in 4 years or less, 41% graduate in 5 years or less, and 43% graduate in 6 years or less. Of the 2002 graduating class, 1% were enrolled in graduate school within 6 months of graduation and 91% were employed.

Admissions Contact: R. Joseph Bellavance, Dean of Admissions and Financial Aid. E-mail: *admissions@nichols.edu* Web: *www.nichols.edu*

NORTHEASTERN UNIVERSITY E-2
Boston, MA 02115 (617) 373-2200; Fax: (617) 373-8780

Full-time: 7219 men, 7273 women	**Faculty:** 830; I, av$
Part-time: none	**Ph.D.s:** 80%
Graduate: 1876 men, 1799 women	**Student/Faculty:** 17 to 1
Year: semesters, summer session	**Tuition:** $25,840
Application Deadline: February 15	**Room & Board:** $9810
Freshman Class: 21,484 applied, 10,200 accepted, 3194 enrolled	
SAT I Verbal/Math: 590/611	**HIGHLY COMPETITIVE**

Northeastern University, founded in 1898, is a private, nonsectarian institution offering programs that include an experiential learning component and that integrate professional work experience with classroom study. The academic program usually requires 5 years to complete. There are 6 undergraduate and 8 graduate schools. In addition to regional accreditation, Northeastern has baccalaureate program accreditation with AACSB, ABET, ACPE, ADA, APTA, CAHEA, CSAB, and NLN. The 4 libraries contain 984,443 volumes, 2,260,556 microform items, and 17,970 audio/video tapes/CDs, and subscribe to 7654 periodicals. Computerized library services include the card catalog, interlibrary loans, database searching, and Internet access. Special learning facilities include a learning resource center, art gallery, and radio station. The 67-acre campus is in an urban area in the heart of the Back Bay section of Boston. Including any residence halls, there are 69 buildings.

Student Life: 64% of undergraduates are from out of state, mostly the Northeast. Students are from 50 states, 125 foreign countries, and Canada. 74% are white. The average age of freshmen is 18; all undergraduates, 21. 12% do not continue beyond their first year.

Housing: 6864 students can be accommodated in college housing, which includes single-sex and coed dorms, on-campus apartments, and fraternity houses. In addition, there are honors houses, special-interest houses, and quiet, engineering, living and learning, international, and wellness halls. On-campus housing is guaranteed for the freshman year only, is available on a first-come, first-served basis, and is available on a lottery system for upperclassmen. 93% of freshmen live on campus. Upperclassmen may keep cars.

Activities: 4% of men belong to 4 local and 10 national fraternities; 4% of women belong to 8 national sororities. There are 200 groups on campus, including art, band, cheerleading, chess, chorale, chorus, computers, dance, debate, disabled students, drama, ethnic, gay, honors, international, jazz band, literary magazine, musical theater, newspaper, orchestra, outing, pep band, photography, political, professional, radio and TV, religious, social, social service, student government, symphony, and yearbook. Popular campus events include SpringFest, International Carnevale, and Nataraj.

Sports: There are 9 intercollegiate sports for men and 11 for women, and 14 intramural sports for men and 14 for women. Facilities include outdoor and indoor tracks and tennis courts, a football stadium, an indoor hockey arena, a swimming pool, racquetball, squash, volleyball, and basketball courts, and exercise and weight machines.

Disabled Students: More than 95% of the campus is accessible. Wheelchair ramps, elevators, special parking, specially equipped rest rooms, special class scheduling, lowered drinking fountains, lowered telephones, and special housing are available.

Services: Counseling and information services are available, as is tutoring in most subjects. The Academic Assistance Center offers tutoring services in reading, language, vocabulary, note taking, test preparation, and related study skills. Individualized computer instruction is provided through the Computer-Aided Instruction Lab. There is a reader service for the blind, and remedial math, reading, and writing.

Campus Safety and Security: Measures include 24-hour foot and vehicle patrol, self-defense education, security escort services, and pamphlets/posters/films. There are emergency telephones, lighted pathways/sidewalks, and awareness programs on rape prevention, alcohol abuse, personal safety, and crime prevention. A fire and security alarm center monitors residence halls, academic buildings, and athletic facilities.

Programs of Study: Northeastern confers B.A. and B.S. degrees. Associate, master's, and doctoral degrees are also awarded. Bachelor's degrees are awarded in BIOLOGICAL SCIENCE (biochemistry, biology/biological science, neurosciences, and toxicology), BUSINESS (accounting, business administration and management, human resources, international business management, management information systems, and marketing/retailing/merchandising), COMMUNICATIONS AND THE ARTS (advertising, art, communications, dramatic arts, English, French, journalism, languages, linguistics, music, performing arts, public relations, and Spanish), COMPUTER AND PHYSICAL SCIENCE (applied physics, chemistry, computer programming, computer science, geology, information sciences and systems, mathematics, and physics), EDUCATION (athletic training, early childhood, and elementary), ENGINEERING AND ENVIRONMENTAL DESIGN (architecture, chemical engineering, civil engineering, computer engineering, computer technology, electrical/electronics engineering, electrical/electronics engineering technology, engineering, engineering technology, industrial engineering, mechanical engineering, and mechanical engineering technology), HEALTH PROFESSIONS (health science, medical laboratory science, nursing, pharmacy, physical therapy, rehabilitation therapy, and speech pathology/audiology), SOCIAL SCIENCE (African American studies, anthropology, criminal justice, economics, history, human services, interdisciplinary studies, international relations, interpreter for the deaf, philosophy, physical fitness/movement, political science/government, psychology, and sociology). Engineering, computer science, and business administration are the strongest academically. Arts and sciences and business administration are the largest.

Required: Although each college has its own requirements, students must generally complete an upper-division writing proficiency requirement in addition to at least 132 semester hours with a minimum GPA of 2.0. Students must also fulfill a diversity requirement.

Special: Northeastern offers paid professional internships with area companies in Boston, around the country, and throughout the world to integrate classroom instruction with professional experience. Cross-registration with the New England Conservatory of Music and Hebrew College, among other universities and colleges, study abroad in dozens of countries, a Washington semester, work-study through the university and in neighboring public and private agencies, dual majors, and student-designed majors in the arts and sciences are also offered. Nondegree adult and continuing education are available, as are programs and scholarships for racial minorities and women, and accelerated degrees in engineering, nursing, the arts and sciences, pharmacy, and business. There are 26 national honor societies, a freshman honors program, and 10 departmental honors programs.

Faculty/Classroom: 64% of faculty are male; 36%, female.

Admissions: 47% of the 2003-2004 applicants were accepted. The SAT I scores for the 2003-2004 freshman class were: Verbal--9% below 500, 41% between 500 and 599, 43% between 600 and 700, and 6% above 700; Math--6% below 500, 31% between 500 and 599, 52% between 600 and 700, and 11% above 700. 61% of the current freshmen were in the top fifth of their class; 89% were in the top two fifths.

Requirements: The SAT I is required and the ACT is recommended. In addition, Northeastern recommends that applicants have 17 academic units, including 4 in English, 3 each in math, science, and social studies, and 2 each in foreign language and history. An essay is required. AP credits are accepted. Important factors in the admissions decision are advanced placement or honor courses, leadership record, and recommendations by school officials.

Procedure: Freshmen are admitted fall and spring. Entrance exams should be taken from October of the junior year through December of the senior year. There is a deferred admissions plan. Early decision applications should be filed by January 1; regular applications, by February 15 for fall entry. The fall 2003 application fee was $50. Notification is sent between March 1 and April 1. 801 applicants were on the 2003 waiting list. Applications are accepted on-line through Common App and the school's web site.

Transfer: 540 transfer students enrolled in 2002-2003. The most successful transfer students have earned a cumulative GPA of 3.0. Students have also completed the introductory level courses for their intended major. Transfer students with fewer than 27 semester hours of college-level credit must also submit their high school transcript and SAT I or ACT scores. 32 of the last 40 semester hours of 132 required for the bachelor's degree must be completed at Northeastern.

Visiting: There are regularly scheduled orientations for prospective students. There are guides for informal visits. To schedule a visit, contact the Office of Undergraduate Admissions at (617) 373-2211 or *admissions@neu.edu.*

Financial Aid: In 2003-2004, 86% of all full-time freshmen and 72% of continuing full-time students received some form of financial aid. 78% of full-time freshmen and 71% of continuing full-time students received need-based aid. The average freshman award was $17,334. Need-based scholarships or need-based grants averaged $13,515 ($25,600 maximum); need-based self-help aid (loans and jobs) averaged $4252

($5102 maximum); non-need-based athletic scholarships averaged $25,395 ($36,840 maximum); and other non-need-based awards and non-need-based scholarships averaged $10,438 ($36,840 maximum). 38% of undergraduates work part time. Average annual earnings from campus work are $1806. Northeastern is a member of CSS. The CSS Profile and FAFSA are required. The deadline for filing freshman financial aid applications for fall entry is February 15.

International Students: There are 758 international students enrolled. The school actively recruits these students. They must score 550 on the written TOEFL and also take the SAT I or ACT. Minimum scores vary by and within programs.

Computers: The mainframe is a Super-miniVAX cluster consisting of 2 DEC VAX 6000-440 computers. Students may gain access to the mainframe systems from on-campus computer labs or off-campus dial-in modems. The computers accessed are utilized for various computer courses, e-mail, computer conferencing, and bulletin board purposes. All students may access the system 24 hours daily. There are no time limits and no fees.

Graduates: From July 1, 2002 to June 30, 2003, 2393 bachelor's degrees were awarded. The most popular majors were business (29%), engineering (14%), and health sciences (9%). In an average class, 56% graduate in 6 years or less. 48 companies recruited on campus in 2002-2003. Of the 2002 graduating class, 18% were enrolled in graduate school within 9 months of graduation and 92% were employed.

Admissions Contact: Ronne A. Patrick, Director of Admissions. A video is available. E-mail: *admissions@neu.edu* Web: *www.northeastern.edu*

PINE MANOR COLLEGE
Chestnut Hill, MA 02467

E-2
(617) 731-7104
(800) 762-1357; Fax: (617) 731-7102

Full-time: 475 women	**Faculty:** 31; IIB, -$
Part-time: 12 women	**Ph.D.s:** 84%
Graduate: none	**Student/Faculty:** 15 to 1
Year: semesters, summer session	**Tuition:** $13,612
Application Deadline: open	**Room & Board:** $8526
Freshman Class: 461 applied, 427 accepted, 159 enrolled	
SAT I or ACT: required	**LESS COMPETITIVE**

Pine Manor College, established in 1911, is a private liberal arts college for women. The library contains 64,799 volumes, 57,289 microform items, and 1836 audio/video tapes/CDs, and subscribes to 273 periodicals. Computerized library services include the card catalog, interlibrary loans, database searching, and Internet access. Special learning facilities include a learning resource center, art gallery, radio station, TV station, and a language lab. The 60-acre campus is in a suburban area 5 miles west of Boston. Including any residence halls, there are 28 buildings.

Student Life: 67% of undergraduates are from Massachusetts. Students are from 26 states and 27 foreign countries. 30% are African American; 29% white; 17% Hispanic; 11% foreign nationals. The average age of freshmen is 19; all undergraduates, 20. 30% do not continue beyond their first year.

Housing: 481 students can be accommodated in college housing, which includes single-sex dorms. In addition, there are special-interest houses, nonsmoking dorms, and a wellness floor (no alcohol allowed). On-campus housing is guaranteed for all 4 years. 71% of students live on campus; of those, 80% remain on campus on weekends. All students may keep cars.

Activities: There are no sororities. There are 25 groups on campus, including chorus, dance, diversity, drama, ethnic, gay, honors, interior design (ASID), international, literary magazine, minority (ALANA), musical theater, newspaper, political, professional, psychology, radio and TV, religious, social, social service, student government, student health, and yearbook. Popular campus events include Late Night Breakfast during finals, Stressbusters, and Halloween Party.

Sports: Facilities include a modern gym, softball and soccer fields, cross-country trails, tennis courts, a dance studio, and a weight room.

Disabled Students: 40% of the campus is accessible. Wheelchair ramps, elevators, special parking, specially equipped rest rooms, and lowered drinking fountains are available.

Services: Counseling and information services are available, as is tutoring in every subject. There is remedial math, reading, and writing. The learning resource center has professional and peer tutoring and workshops.

Campus Safety and Security: Measures include 24-hour foot and vehicle patrol, self-defense education, security escort services, and shuttle buses. There are informal discussions, pamphlets/posters/films, emergency telephones, and lighted pathways/sidewalks.

Programs of Study: PMC confers the B.A. degree. Associate degrees are also awarded. Bachelor's degrees are awarded in BIOLOGICAL SCIENCE (biology/biological science), BUSINESS (business administration and management), COMMUNICATIONS AND THE ARTS (art, communications, and English), SOCIAL SCIENCE (ethics, politics, and social policy, history, liberal arts/general studies, and psychology). Psychology, visual arts, and business administration are the largest.

Required: An outcomes-based general education program, with portfolio assessment, is a college requirement. A 4-year leadership program complements the portfolio program. This assists students in exploring inclusive and socially responsible leadership. In addition, students must maintain a minimum GPA of 2.0 and take a total of 132 semester hours.

Special: Pine Manor offers cross-registration with area colleges, internships at more than 1000 sites, and study abroad throughout the world, and at sea. A Washington semester, work-study programs, dual majors, student-designed majors, a B.A.-B.S. degree, nondegree study within continuing education, and pass/fail options for 1 course each semester also are available as is the English Language Institute for students whose native language is not English. There is 1 national honor society and a freshman honors program.

Faculty/Classroom: 28% of faculty are male; 72%, female. All teach undergraduates. The average class size in an introductory lecture is 16; in a laboratory, 16; and in a regular course, 13.

Admissions: 93% of the 2003-2004 applicants were accepted. 3% of the current freshmen were in the top fifth of their class; 8% were in the top two fifths.

Requirements: The SAT I or ACT is required. In addition, applicants are required to have taken 4 courses in English and 2 in math. Additional courses in foreign language, social science, natural science, and elective areas are recommended. An essay is also required. An interview is recommended. The GED is accepted, and the number of Carnegie units required is 16. AP and CLEP credits are accepted. Important factors in the admissions decision are recommendations by school officials, leadership record, and advanced placement or honor courses.

Procedure: Freshmen are admitted fall and spring. There is a deferred admissions plan. Application deadlines are open. Application fee is $25. Notification is sent on a rolling basis. Applications are accepted on computer disk and on-line through the school's web site and via Next Stop College.

Transfer: 25 transfer students enrolled in 2002-2003. Pine Manor requires transfer students to submit 2 letters of recommendation (1 from a professor) and college and high school transcripts. The SAT I or ACT also is recommended. 32 of 132 credits required for the bachelor's degree must be completed at PMC.

Visiting: There are regularly scheduled orientations for prospective students, including a campus tour and interview. There are guides for informal visits and visitors may sit in on classes and stay overnight. To schedule a visit, contact the Admissions Office.

Financial Aid: In 2003-2004, 86% of all full-time students received some form of financial aid. The average freshman award was $14,840. Average annual earnings from campus work are $1500. The average financial indebtedness of the 2003 graduate is $16,554. PMC is a member of CSS. The FAFSA is required. The priority date for freshman financial aid applications for fall entry is March 15.

International Students: There are 51 international students enrolled. The school actively recruits these students. They must score 475 on the written TOEFL or 153 on the electronic version.

Computers: PCs and Macs are available for student use in computer centers in the library and in the science, management, and art buildings. The communications center houses a computerized print media room. All students may access the system. There are no time limits and no fees.

Graduates: From July 1, 2002 to June 30, 2003, 54 bachelor's degrees were awarded. The most popular majors were psychology (20%), business administration (20%), and biology (19%). In an average class, 50% graduate in 5 years or less.

Admissions Contact: Bill Nichols, Dean of Admissions.
E-mail: *admissions@pmc.edu* Web: *www.pmc.edu*

REGIS COLLEGE
Weston, MA 02493-1571

D-2
(781) 768-7100
(866) 438-7344; Fax: (781) 768-7071

Full-time: 2 men, 587 women	Faculty: 47
Part-time: 15 men, 196 women	Ph.D.s: 86%
Graduate: 22 men, 261 women	Student/Faculty: 13 to 1
Year: semesters, summer session	Tuition: $19,910
Application Deadline: open	Room & Board: $9090
Freshman Class: 569 applied, 497 accepted, 156 enrolled	
SAT I Verbal/Math: 500/480	COMPETITIVE

Regis College, founded in 1927, is a private liberal arts institution for women, affiliated with the Roman Catholic Church. In addition to regional accreditation, Regis has baccalaureate program accreditation with CSWE, NASDTEC, and NLN. The library contains 137,955 volumes, 9468 microform items, and 5624 audio/video tapes/CDs, and subscribes to 805 periodicals. Computerized library services include the card catalog, interlibrary loans, database searching, and Internet access. Special learning facilities include a learning resource center, art gallery, radio station, museum of stamps and postal history, and fine arts center. The 140-acre campus is in a suburban area 12 miles west of Boston. Including any residence halls, there are 15 buildings.

Student Life: 87% of undergraduates are from Massachusetts. Students are from 16 states and 7 foreign countries. 73% are from public schools. 42% are white. The average age of freshmen is 18; all undergraduates, 22. 24% do not continue beyond their first year; 65% remain to graduate.

Housing: 619 students can be accommodated in college housing, which includes single-sex dorms. There are quiet housing floors. On-campus housing is guaranteed for all 4 years. 71% of students live on campus; of those, 50% remain on campus on weekends. All students may keep cars.

Activities: There are no sororities. There are 30 groups on campus, including art, choir, chorale, chorus, commuter association, computers, dance, drama, ethnic, honors, international, literary magazine, musical theater, newspaper, photography, political, professional, radio and TV, religious, social, social service, student government, and yearbook. Popular campus events include Father/Daughter Dance, Mother/Daughter Brunch, and Family Weekend.

Sports: Facilities include a softball diamond, a soccer field, 4 tennis courts, and an athletic facility with a gym, an aerobics and dance studio, squash courts, a pool, and a sauna and Jacuzzi. A fitness center provides a full range of cardiovascular machines as well as free weights and Nautilus equipment.

Disabled Students: 87% of the campus is accessible. Wheelchair ramps, elevators, special parking, specially equipped rest rooms, special class scheduling, lowered drinking fountains, lowered telephones, and special housing are available.

Services: Counseling and information services are available, as is tutoring in every subject. There is a reader service for the blind and remedial math and writing. There are academic support services for learning-disabled students.

Campus Safety and Security: Measures include 24-hour foot and vehicle patrol, self-defense education, security escort services, and shuttle buses. There are informal discussions, pamphlets/posters/films, emergency telephones, and lighted pathways/sidewalks.

Programs of Study: Regis confers B.A., B.S.N., and B.S.W. degrees. Associate and master's degrees are also awarded. Bachelor's degrees are awarded in BIOLOGICAL SCIENCE (biochemistry and biology/biological science), BUSINESS (management science), COMMUNICATIONS AND THE ARTS (art, communications, dramatic arts, English, and Spanish), COMPUTER AND PHYSICAL SCIENCE (computer science), EDUCATION (museum studies), HEALTH PROFESSIONS (nursing), SOCIAL SCIENCE (history, political science/government, psychology, social work, and sociology). Communication, English, and biology are the largest.

Required: To graduate, students must complete a total of 38 4-credit courses (152 credits), including 8 to 12 in the major, with a minimum GPA of 2.0.

Special: Cross-registration with Boston, Babson, and Bentley Colleges and through the Sisters of St. Joseph Consortium is offered. Students may study abroad at Regis affiliates in London, Ireland, and Kyoto, Japan, or through programs of other American colleges. Regis also offers internships, a Washington semester at American University, dual and self-designed majors, work-study, nondegree study, and pass/fail options. There are special programs in American studies, communication, computer science, graphics, Greek, international, legal, and women's studies, and teacher training. A 3-2 engineering degree is available with Worcester Polytechnic Institute. There are 8 national honor societies, a freshman honors program, and 17 departmental honors programs.

Faculty/Classroom: 21% of faculty are male; 79%, female. 83% teach undergraduates. No introductory courses are taught by graduate students. The average class size in an introductory lecture is 21; in a laboratory, 15; and in a regular course, 15.

Admissions: 87% of the 2003-2004 applicants were accepted. The SAT I scores for the 2003-2004 freshman class were: Verbal--50% below 500, 39% between 500 and 599, 10% between 600 and 700, and 1% above 700; Math--55% below 500, 35% between 500 and 599, and 10% between 600 and 700. 38% of the current freshmen were in the top fifth of their class; 60% were in the top two fifths.

Requirements: The SAT I is required. In addition, applicants should have 4 years of English, 3 or 4 of electives, 3 of math, and 2 each of foreign language, social studies, and natural science, including a lab science. An essay and 2 letters of recommendation are required. An interview is strongly encouraged. The GED is accepted. On-line applications must be accompanied by a transcript, letters of recommendation, and official SAT I or ACT scores. Regis requires applicants to be in the upper 50% of their class. A GPA of 2.5 is required. AP and CLEP credits are accepted. Important factors in the admissions decision are recommendations by school officials, extracurricular activities record, and ability to finance college education.

Procedure: Freshmen are admitted fall and spring. Entrance exams should be taken during the fall before enrollment. There is a deferred admissions plan. Application deadlines are open. The fall 2003 application fee was $30. Notification is sent within 2 weeks after receipt of the complete application. Applications are accepted on-line through CollegeLink, MassMentor, and the Common Application.

Transfer: 45 transfer students enrolled in 2002-2003. Transfer students need an admission application and fee; an official high school transcript if fewer than 9 college courses have been completed; an official college transcript; 1 letter of recommendation from a professor at the previous college attended; the academic catalog of the previous college; an essay; SAT I scores if fewer than 16 courses have been completed; and health records. 72 of 152 credits required for the bachelor's degree must be completed at Regis.

Visiting: There are regularly scheduled orientations for prospective students, including a welcome tour, lunch, speaker panels, and overnight programs offering class participation. There are guides for informal visits and visitors may sit in on classes and stay overnight. To schedule a visit, contact the Admissions Office.

Financial Aid: In 2003-2004, 93% of all full-time freshmen and 79% of continuing full-time students received some form of financial aid. 83% of full-time freshmen and 77% of continuing full-time students received need-based aid. The average freshman award was $17,827. Need-based scholarships or need-based grants averaged $8585 ($27,830 maximum); need-based self-help aid (loans and jobs) averaged $6625 ($8625 maximum); non-need-based awards and non-need-based scholarships averaged $8333 ($14,000 maximum); and a sibling discount of 25% between both students averaged $4977 (maximum). 46% of undergraduates work part time. Average annual earnings from campus work are $1234. The average financial indebtedness of the 2003 graduate was $26,758. The FAFSA and the college's own financial statement are required. The deadline for filing freshman financial aid applications for fall entry is March 1.

International Students: There are 10 international students enrolled. The school actively recruits these students. They must score 500 on the written TOEFL or 173 on the electronic version and also take the SAT I or the ACT.

Computers: The mainframe is an HP 9000/K360. There are 155 PCs and Macs available in the academic computer center and in various departments. All computers have access to the Internet and Web. Students have access to a web server, NT servers for printing, and AppleShare servers for file sharing. All students may access the system daily at posted hours in the academic computing center or by permission in the individual departments. There are no time limits and no fees.

Graduates: From July 1, 2002 to June 30, 2003, 193 bachelor's degrees were awarded. The most popular majors were nursing (17%), communications (14%), and English and social work (10%). In an average class, 63% graduate in 4 years or less, 65% graduate in 5 years or less, and 66% graduate in 6 years or less. 10 companies recruited on campus in 2002-2003.

Admissions Contact: Office of Admission.
E-mail: *admission@regiscollege.edu* Web: *www.regiscollege.edu*

SALEM STATE COLLEGE
Salem, MA 01970

E-2

(978) 542-6200; Fax: (978) 542-6893

Full-time: 1734 men, 2962 women	**Faculty:** 320
Part-time: 627 men, 1185 women	**Ph.D.s:** 77%
Graduate: 598 men, 2014 women	**Student/Faculty:** 15 to 1
Year: semesters, summer session	**Tuition:** $5038 ($11,178)
Application Deadline: open	**Room & Board:** $3554
Freshman Class: 4018 applied, 3313 accepted, 1017 enrolled	
SAT I or ACT: required	**COMPETITIVE**

Salem State College, founded in 1854, is a public institution offering programs in liberal arts, business, education, and nursing. There are 5 undergraduate schools and 1 graduate school. In addition to regional accreditation, Salem State has baccalaureate program accreditation with CSWE, NASAD, NCATE, and NLN. The library contains 301,876 volumes and 566,592 microform items, and subscribes to 1145 periodicals. Computerized library services include the card catalog, interlibrary loans, database searching, and Internet access. Special learning facilities include a learning resource center, art gallery, radio station, TV station, and observatory. The 62-acre campus is in an urban area 18 miles northeast of Boston. Including any residence halls, there are 19 buildings.

Student Life: 93% of undergraduates are from Massachusetts. Students are from 21 states, 40 foreign countries, and Canada. 98% are from public schools. 80% are white. The average age of freshmen is 19; all undergraduates, 24. 28% do not continue beyond their first year; 29% remain to graduate.

Housing: 950 students can be accommodated in college housing, which includes single-sex and coed dorms and on-campus apartments. On-campus housing is available on a first-come, first-served basis. Priority is given to out-of-town students. 79% of students commute. Upperclassmen may keep cars.

Activities: There are no fraternities or sororities. There are 44 groups on campus, including art, band, cheerleading, choir, chorale, chorus, computers, dance, drama, ethnic, gay, honors, international, jazz band, literary magazine, musical theater, newspaper, photography, political, radio and TV, religious, social, social service, student government, and yearbook. Popular campus events include Welcome Week, Arts Festival, and Senior Week.

Sports: There are 10 intercollegiate sports for men and 10 for women, and 15 intramural sports for men and 15 for women. Facilities include an athletic center with 27 facilities, including a 1600-seat gym, a 2800-seat ice rink, an 8-lane swimming pool, 4 tennis courts, a weight room, a dance studio, and a wellness fitness center.

Disabled Students: 90% of the campus is accessible. Wheelchair ramps, elevators, special parking, specially equipped rest rooms, lowered drinking fountains, and lowered telephones are available.

Services: Counseling and information services are available, as is tutoring in every subject. There is a reader service for the blind and remedial math, reading, and writing.

Campus Safety and Security: Measures include 24-hour foot and vehicle patrol, self-defense education, security escort services, and shuttle buses. There are informal discussions, pamphlets/posters/films, emergency telephones, and lighted pathways/sidewalks.

Programs of Study: Salem State confers B.A., B.S., B.F.A., B.G.S., B.S.B.A., B.S.Ed., B.S.N., and B.S.W. degrees. Master's degrees are also awarded. Bachelor's degrees are awarded in BIOLOGICAL SCIENCE (biology/biological science), BUSINESS (accounting, banking and finance, business administration and management, and marketing/retailing/merchandising), COMMUNICATIONS AND THE ARTS (advertising, communications, design, dramatic arts, English, fine arts, and photography), COMPUTER AND PHYSICAL SCIENCE (chemistry, computer programming, earth science, geology, and mathematics), EDUCATION (art, business, education, science, and secondary), ENGINEERING AND ENVIRONMENTAL DESIGN (cartography), HEALTH PROFESSIONS (medical laboratory technology and nursing), SOCIAL SCIENCE (criminal justice, economics, geography, history, psychology, social work, and sociology). Sciences are the strongest academically. Business administration is the largest.

Required: All students must demonstrate basic competence in reading, math, and computer literacy, and are required to take a distribution of classes that includes 36 to 38 credits in humanities, sciences, and social sciences. Specific courses required are English composition, speech, phys ed, and the first-year seminar. All core and distribution requirements may be waived if the student passes a departmentally prescribed exemption exam. A minimum GPA of 2.0 and a total of 127 credits, with 36 in the major, are needed to graduate.

Special: Study abroad is available in 3 countries. Cross-registration through a consortium, internships, work-study programs, student-designed and dual majors, B.A.-B.S. degrees, and a general studies degree are offered. Life experience credit, nondegree study, and pass/fail options also are possible. There are 13 national honor societies, a freshman honors program, and 9 departmental honors programs.

Faculty/Classroom: All teach undergraduates. The average class size in an introductory lecture is 22; in a laboratory, 12; and in a regular course, 17.

Admissions: 82% of the 2003-2004 applicants were accepted.

Requirements: The SAT I or ACT is required. In addition, Salem State requires that applicants earn 16 credits, including 4 years of English, 3 years each of math and science, and 2 years each of foreign language and history. Courses in music, art, drama, computer science, and psychology are suggested. Art majors must provide a portfolio. A GED is acceptable. Students with a GED, those out of school more than 3 years, and the learning disabled do not need the SAT I. A GPA of 2.9 is required. AP and CLEP credits are accepted. Important factors in the admissions decision are advanced placement or honors courses, evidence of special talent, and recommendations by school officials.

Procedure: Freshmen are admitted in the fall. Entrance exams should be taken November and December of the senior year. There are rolling and deferred admissions plans. Application deadlines are open. Application fee is $25. A waiting list is an active part of the admissions procedure. Applications are accepted on-line through *www.salemstate.edu/admissions*.

Transfer: 739 transfer students enrolled in 2002-2003. Transfer students are required to have a minimum GPA of 2.0 with more than 24 credits; 2.5 with fewer than 24 credits. 30 of 127 credits required for the bachelor's degree must be completed at Salem State.

Visiting: There are regularly scheduled orientations for prospective students. There are guides for informal visits and visitors may sit in on classes. To schedule a visit, contact the Admissions Office.

Financial Aid: 86% of undergraduates work part time. Average annual earnings from campus work are $1600. Salem State is a member of CSS. The FAFSA is required.

International Students: There are 260 international students enrolled. The school actively recruits these students. They must score 500 on the written TOEFL.

Computers: The mainframe is a SUN 3500 with an Enterprise server. More than 500 networked PCs are available throughout the campus. All students may access the system 7 days a week. There are no time limits and no fees.

Graduates: From July 1, 2002 to June 30, 2003, 919 bachelor's degrees were awarded. The most popular majors were education (19%), nursing (8%), and criminal justice (7%).

Admissions Contact: Nate Bryant, Director of Admissions.
E-mail: *nate.bryant@salem.mass.edu* Web: *www.salem.mass.edu*

SIMMONS COLLEGE
Boston, MA 02115

E-2
(617) 521-2051
(800) 345-8468; Fax: (617) 521-3190

Full-time: 1385 women	**Faculty:** 130; IIA, +$
Part-time: 170 women	**Ph.Ds:** 65%
Graduate: 343 men, 2187 women	**Student/Faculty:** 11 to 1
Year: semesters, summer session	**Tuition:** $23,550
Application Deadline: February 1	**Room & Board:** $9450
Freshman Class: 1895 applied, 1291 accepted, 355 enrolled	
SAT I Verbal/Math: 558/539	**ACT:** 24 **VERY COMPETITIVE**

Simmons College, founded in 1899, is a private institution primarily for women that offers a comprehensive education combining the arts, sciences, and humanities with preprofessional training. Most graduate programs are co-ed. There are 3 undergraduate and 5 graduate schools. In addition to regional accreditation, Simmons has baccalaureate program accreditation with ADA, APTA, CSWE, and NLN. The library contains 235,431 volumes, 9599 microform items, and 2873 audio/video tapes/CDs, and subscribes to 1675 periodicals. Computerized library services include the card catalog, interlibrary loans, database searching, and Internet access. Special learning facilities include an art gallery and TV studio, modern language lab, physical therapy motion lab, nursing lab, and library science technology center. The 12-acre campus is in an urban area in Boston. Including any residence halls, there are 26 buildings.

Student Life: 60% of undergraduates are from Massachusetts. Students are from 38 states and 26 foreign countries. 78% are from public schools. 70% are white. The average age of freshmen is 18; all undergraduates, 23. 13% do not continue beyond their first year; 72% remain to graduate.

Housing: 1049 students can be accommodated in college housing, which includes single-sex and coed dorms and off-campus apartments. In addition, there are special-interest houses. On-campus housing is guaranteed for all 4 years. 70% of students live on campus; of those, 75% remain on campus on weekends. No one may keep cars.

Activities: There are no fraternities or sororities. There are 70 groups on campus, including chorale, dance, debate, drama, ethnic, film, gay, honors, international, literary magazine, newspaper, political, professional, religious, social, social service, student government, and yearbook. Popular campus events include Spring Spree, May Day Breakfast, and Culture Shock.

Sports: There are 8 intercollegiate sports for women and 4 intramural sports for women. Facilities include an 8-lane pool, a spa and sauna, 2 racquetball and 2 squash courts, 2 rowing tanks, 3 fitness rooms, a dance studio, an indoor track, and a gym with 3 badminton courts, 2 volleyball courts, and a basketball court.

Disabled Students: All of the campus is accessible. Wheelchair ramps, elevators, special parking, specially equipped rest rooms, special class scheduling, lowered drinking fountains, and lowered telephones are available.

Services: Counseling and information services are available, as is tutoring in some subjects, including basic freshman courses, languages, biology, chemistry, psychology, and math. There is a reader service for the blind and remedial math and writing. The school also provides study groups, individual tutoring, help with study skills and time management, and assistance for students with learning disabilities and special needs.

Campus Safety and Security: Measures include 24-hour foot and vehicle patrol, self-defense education, security escort services, and shuttle buses. There are informal discussions, pamphlets/posters/films, emergency telephones, lighted pathways/sidewalks, closed-circuit TV, ID card access, and security training in first response and crisis intervention.

Programs of Study: Simmons confers B.A. and B.S. degrees. Master's and doctoral degrees are also awarded. Bachelor's degrees are awarded in BIOLOGICAL SCIENCE (biochemistry, biology/biological science, and nutrition), BUSINESS (banking and finance, management information systems, and marketing/retailing/merchandising), COMMUNICATIONS AND THE ARTS (advertising, art, arts administration/management, communications, English, English as a second/foreign language, French, music, and Spanish), COMPUTER AND PHYSICAL SCIENCE (chemistry, computer science, and mathematics), EDUCATION (early childhood, elementary, secondary, and special), ENGINEERING AND ENVIRONMENTAL DESIGN (environmental science), HEALTH PROFESSIONS (nursing, physical therapy, and premedicine), SOCIAL SCIENCE (African American studies, dietetics, East Asian studies, economics, food science, history, human services, international relations, philosophy, political science/government, prelaw, psychobiology, psychology, sociology, and women's studies). Physical therapy, biology, and communication are the strongest academically. Physical therapy, psychology, and communication are the largest.

Required: To graduate, students must complete 128 semester hours, including 24 to 48 in the major, and maintain a minimum GPA of 2.0. 8 semester hours in a supervised independent learning experience or an internship are also required. 6 modes of inquiry courses are required. They must also fulfill foreign language and math competency requirements. In addition to completing the multidisciplinary core course, students must complete 1 course from each of the following categories: creative and performing arts; language, literature, and culture; quantitative analysis and reasoning; social and historical perspectives; and psychological and ethical development. A thesis is optional.

Special: Cross-registration is available with the New England Conservatory of Music, Hebrew, Emmanuel, and Wheelock Colleges, Massachusetts College of Art, Massachusetts College of Pharmacy and Health Sciences, and Wentworth Institute of Technology. Simmons offers study abroad in Europe through the Institute of European studies. A Washington semester at American University, accelerated degree programs, profit and nonprofit internship programs, a B.A.-B.S. degree, dual majors, interdisciplinary majors, student-designed majors, work-study programs, and pass/fail options are also offered. There is a dual-degree program in chemistry, pharmacy, and physician's assistant with Massachusetts College of Pharmacy and Health Sciences. There is a freshman honors program.

Faculty/Classroom: 25% of faculty are male; 75%, female. All both teach and do research. No introductory courses are taught by graduate students. The average class size in an introductory lecture is 50; in a laboratory, 12; and in a regular course, 16.

Admissions: 68% of the 2003-2004 applicants were accepted. The SAT I scores for the 2003-2004 freshman class were: Verbal--21% below 500, 47% between 500 and 599, 26% between 600 and 700, and 5% above 700; Math--26% below 500, 55% between 500 and 599, 18% between 600 and 700, and 1% above 700. 49% of the current freshmen were in the top fifth of their class; 78% were in the top two fifths. There were 7 National Merit semifinalists.

Requirements: The SAT I or ACT is required. In addition, simmons recommends that applicants have 4 years of English, 3 each of math, science, and social studies, and 2 of foreign language. An essay is required, and an interview is strongly recommended. A GPA of 3.0 is required. AP and CLEP credits are accepted. Important factors in the admissions decision are advanced placement or honor courses, recommendations by school officials, and extracurricular activities record.

Procedure: Freshmen are admitted fall and spring. Entrance exams should be taken by February 1 of the senior year. There are early admissions and deferred admissions plans. Early decision applications should be filed by December 1; regular applications, by February 1 for fall entry and December 1 for spring entry, along with a $35 fee. Notification of early decision is sent January 20; regular decision, April 15. 11 applicants were on the 2003 waiting list; 4 were admitted. Applications are accepted on computer disk and on-line through the school's web site and Common App.

Transfer: 39 transfer students enrolled in a recent year. Applicants should have a GPA of 2.8, at least 9 college-level credit hours, official transcripts from all colleges attended, and a faculty recommendation and dean's report from the previous college attended. 48 of 128 credits required for the bachelor's degree must be completed at Simmons.

Visiting: There are regularly scheduled orientations for prospective students, including a campus tour, class attendance, an interview, and meetings with faculty and students. There are guides for informal visits and visitors may sit in on classes and stay overnight. To schedule a visit, contact the Admissions Office.

Financial Aid: In 2003-2004, 87% of all full-time freshmen and 80% of continuing full-time students received some form of financial aid. 74% of full-time freshmen and 73% of continuing full-time students received need-based aid. The average freshman award was $20,400. Need-based scholarships or need-based grants averaged $6800 ($20,000 maximum); need-based self-help aid (loans and jobs) averaged $5400 ($8625 maximum); and non-need-based awards and non-need-based scholarships averaged $10,700 ($22,860 maximum). 75% of undergraduates work part time. Average annual earnings from campus work are $4800. The average financial indebtedness of the 2003 graduate was $21,125. Simmons is a member of CSS. The FAFSA and federal tax returns or W2 forms are required. The priority date for freshman financial aid applications for fall entry is April 1.

International Students: The school actively recruits these students. They must score 560 on the written TOEFL or 220 on the electronic version and also take the SAT I or the ACT.

Computers: The mainframe is a Dell Poweredge 2400/Enterprise Linux 2.1. There are more than 300 Macs and PCs on the academic network, including public-access machines in the library and residence halls. These are available for course-related web access, general web access and e-mail, with Minitab and SAS statistics packages and personal productivity and design applications. All students may access the system. There are no time limits and no fees. It is strongly recommended that all students have a personal computer.

Graduates: From July 1, 2002 to June 30, 2003, 290 bachelor's degrees were awarded. The most popular majors were nursing (12%), sociology (9%), and psychology (7%). In an average class, 61% graduate in 4 years or less, 65% graduate in 5 years or less, and 66% graduate in 6 years or less. 25 companies recruited on campus in 2002-2003. Of the 2002 graduating class, 75% were employed within 6 months of graduation.

Admissions Contact: Jennifer O'Loughlin Hieber, Director of Undergraduate Admission. E-mail: *ugadm@simmons.edu*
Web: *www.simmons.edu*

SIMON'S ROCK COLLEGE OF BARD
Great Barrington, MA 01230-9702

A-2

(413) 528-7313
(800) 235-7186; Fax: (413) 528-7334

Full-time: 162 men, 224 women	**Faculty:** 37
Part-time: 7 men, 6 women	**Ph.D.s:** 89%
Graduate: none	**Student/Faculty:** 10 to 1
Year: semesters	**Tuition:** $28,950
Application Deadline: open	**Room & Board:** $7630
Freshman Class: 404 applied, 184 accepted, 144 enrolled	
SAT I Verbal/Math: 650/620	**ACT:** 27 **HIGHLY COMPETITIVE**

Simon's Rock College of Bard, founded in 1964, is a private liberal arts school especially designed to permit students who have completed the 10th or 11th grades to enroll for collegiate studies in 8 interdisciplinary majors. The library contains 70,791 volumes, 7550 microform items, and 4382 audio/video tapes/CDs, and subscribes to 437 periodicals. Computerized library services include the card catalog, interlibrary loans, database searching, and Internet access. Special learning facilities include a learning resource center, art gallery, radio station, TV station, language lab, greenhouse, and community garden. The 275-acre campus is in a small town 50 miles west of Springfield. Including any residence halls, there are 47 buildings.

Student Life: 80% of undergraduates are from out of state, mostly the Middle Atlantic. Students are from 44 states and 4 foreign countries. 67% are from public schools. 74% are white. The average age of freshmen is 17; all undergraduates, 18. 22% do not continue beyond their first year.

Housing: 356 students can be accommodated in college housing, which includes single-sex and coed dorms and on-campus apartments. In addition, there are special-interest houses. On-campus housing is guaranteed for all 4 years. 85% of students live on campus; of those, 85% remain on campus on weekends. Alcohol is not permitted. Upperclassmen may keep cars.

Activities: There are no fraternities or sororities. There are 25 groups on campus, including art, chorus, computers, dance, debate, drama, ethnic, film, gay, jazz band, labor coalition, literary magazine, math, multicultural, newspaper, orchestra, photography, political, radio and TV, religious, social, social service, student government, women's center, and yearbook. Popular campus events include Winter Solstice, May Fest, and Prom nite.

Sports: There are 3 intercollegiate sports for men and 3 for women, and 7 intramural sports for men and 7 for women. Facilities include an 8-lane swimming pool, a multicourt gym, 3 racquetball courts, an elevated running track, a fitness and weight-training center, a rock-climbing wall, a soccer field, 4 tennis courts, and hiking trails.

Disabled Students: 80% of the campus is accessible. Wheelchair ramps, elevators, special parking, specially equipped rest rooms, special class scheduling, and lowered drinking fountains are available.

Services: Counseling and information services are available, as is tutoring in most subjects. Study skills instruction is available.

Campus Safety and Security: Measures include self-defense education, security escort services, informal discussions, and pamphlets/posters/films. There are emergency telephones, lighted pathways/sidewalks, and security officers from 4 P.M. to 8 P.M. weekdays and 24 hours a day on weekends.

Programs of Study: Simon's Rock confers the B.A. degree. Associate degrees are also available. Bachelor's degrees are awarded in BIOLOGICAL SCIENCE (biology/biological science and ecology), COMMUNICATIONS AND THE ARTS (art, art history and appreciation, creative writing, dance, dramatic arts, drawing, English literature, fine arts, French, German, Germanic languages and literature, literature, modern language, music history and appreciation, music performance, music theory and composition, painting, performing arts, photography, Spanish, studio art, and visual and performing arts), COMPUTER AND PHYSICAL SCIENCE (applied mathematics, chemistry, mathematics, natural sciences, physics, quantitative methods, and science), HEALTH PROFESSIONS (premedicine), SOCIAL SCIENCE (African American studies, American studies, Asian/Oriental studies, crosscultural studies, East Asian studies, Eastern European studies, ethics, politics, and social policy, European studies, French studies, German area studies, interdisciplinary studies, Latin American studies, philosophy, political science/government, psychology, and Russian and Slavic studies). Cross-cultural relations, psychology, and music are the strongest academically. Politics, law, and society; cross-cultural relations; and theater are the largest.

Required: All students must complete a writing and thinking workshop, a 2-semester freshman seminar, a sophomore seminar, and a cultural

perspectives seminar. The core curriculum also includes distribution requirements in the arts, math, natural sciences, and foreign languages, and phys ed. A total of 120 credits, including at least 32 in the major, plus an interdisciplinary B.A. seminar, an 8-credit senior thesis, and a minimum 2.0 GPA are needed for the B.A. in liberal arts.

Special: A major consists of selecting 2 concentrations from the 36 available; 1 concentration may be self-designed. Independent study internships in many fields, study abroad, a cooperative program with Bard College, and a 3-2 engineering degree with Columbia University, Dartmouth College, or Washington University in St. Louis are available.

Faculty/Classroom: 63% of faculty are male; 37%, female. All both teach and do research. The average class size in an introductory lecture is 14; in a laboratory, 10; and in a regular course, 10.

Admissions: 46% of the 2003-2004 applicants were accepted. The SAT I scores for the 2003-2004 freshman class were: Verbal--5% below 500, 20% between 500 and 599, 50% between 600 and 700, and 25% above 700; Math--14% below 500, 30% between 500 and 599, 33% between 600 and 700, and 23% above 700. The ACT scores were 30% between 21 and 23, 50% between 24 and 28, and 20% above 28.

Requirements: The SAT I is required and the ACT is recommended. The admissions committee looks more toward the required interview, essay, recommendations, and special talent. The school recommends that prospective students finish 2 years each of English, foreign languages, history, math, science, and social studies. A GPA of 2.0 is required. AP credits are accepted. Important factors in the admissions decision are advanced placement or honor courses, recommendations by school officials, and evidence of special talent.

Procedure: Freshmen are admitted fall and spring. Entrance exams should be taken prior to June 10. There are early admissions and deferred admissions plans. Application deadlines are open. Application fee is $40. Notification is sent on a rolling basis. A waiting list is an active part of the admissions procedure.

Transfer: Transfer students must be evaluated by the dean of academic affairs and registrar. 72 of 120 credits required for the bachelor's degree must be completed at Simon's Rock.

Visiting: There are regularly scheduled orientations for prospective students, including attending a class, a campus tour, and an interview. There are guides for informal visits and visitors may sit in on classes. To schedule a visit, contact Barbara Shultis, Receptionist, Office of Admission, at (413) 528-7312 or (800) 235-7186.

Financial Aid: In 2003-2004, 85% of all full-time students received some form of financial aid. 59% of full-time freshmen and 60% of continuing full-time students received need-based aid. The average freshman award was $18,021, with $14,472 from need-based scholarships and need-based grants, $2625 from need-based self-help aid (loans and jobs), and $924 from work contracts. 40% of undergraduates work part time. Average annual earnings from campus work are $1500. The average financial indebtedness of the 2003 graduate was $13,525. Simon's Rock is a member of CSS. The CSS Profile or FAFSA is required. The deadline for filing freshman financial aid applications for fall entry is June 15.

International Students: There are 4 international students enrolled. They must score 500 on the written TOEFL.

Computers: Students may access the central servers from PCs in their dorm rooms or from 2 computer labs. A network connection is available in each dorm room. All students may access the system. There are no time limits and no fees. It is strongly recommended that all students have a personal computer.

Graduates: From July 1, 2002 to June 30, 2003, 45 bachelor's degrees were awarded. The most popular majors were politics, law, and society (13%), cross-cultural relations (13%), and theater (9%). In an average class, 77% graduate in 4 years or less, 86% graduate in 5 years or less, and 91% graduate in 6 years or less.

Admissions Contact: Mary-King Austin, Dean of Admission. A video is available. Web: *http://www.simons-rock.edu/*

SMITH COLLEGE
Northampton, MA 01063

B-2

(413) 585-2500; Fax: (413) 585-2527

Full-time: 2625 women	**Faculty:** 287; IIA, ++$
Part-time: 40 women	**Ph.D.s:** 98%
Graduate: 50 men, 400 women	**Student/Faculty:** 9 to 1
Year: semesters	**Tuition:** $27,544
Application Deadline: January 15	**Room & Board:** $9490
Freshman Class: 2869 applied, 1634 accepted, 635 enrolled	
SAT I Verbal/Math: 660/640	**ACT:** 28
	HIGHLY COMPETITIVE+

Smith College, founded in 1871, is the largest independent women's college in the United States and offers a liberal arts education. Enrollment figures in the above capsule are approximate. The 4 libraries contain 1,268,443 volumes, 139,674 microform items, and 64,126 audio/video tapes/CDs, and subscribe to 2775 periodicals. Computerized library services include the card catalog, interlibrary loans, and database searching. Special learning facilities include a learning resource center, art gallery, radio station, TV station, astronomy observatories, center for foreign languages and culture, digital design studio, plant and horticultural labs, art studios with casting, printmaking, and darkroom facilities, and specialized libraries for science, music, and art. The 125-acre campus is in a small town 90 miles west of Boston. Including any residence halls, there are 105 buildings.

Student Life: 77% of undergraduates are from out of state, mostly the Middle Atlantic. Students are from 50 states, 53 foreign countries, and Canada. 65% are from public schools. 71% are white. 21% claim no religious affiliation; 17% Protestant; 14% Catholic; 13% including Bahai, Buddhist, Eastern Orthodox, Hindu, Mormon, and Muslim; 10% Jewish. The average age of freshmen is 18; all undergraduates, 21. 8% do not continue beyond their first year; 83% remain to graduate.

Housing: 2453 students can be accommodated in college housing, which includes single-sex dorms and on-campus apartments. In addition, there are language houses, nonsmoking houses, 2 cooperative houses, housing for nontraditional-age students, an apartment complex for a limited number of juniors and seniors, a senior house, a French-speaking house, and special-interest houses. On-campus housing is guaranteed for all 4 years. 96% of students live on campus. Upperclassmen may keep cars.

Activities: There are no fraternities. There are 102 groups on campus, including art, chess, choir, chorale, chorus, computers, dance, debate, drama, ethnic, film, gay, honors, international, literary magazine, musical theater, newspaper, orchestra, photography, political, professional, radio and TV, religious, social, social service, student government, symphony, and yearbook. Popular campus events include International Student Day, Spring and Winter Weekends, and Rally Day.

Sports: Facilities include indoor and outdoor tracks and tennis courts, riding rings, 2 gyms, a climbing wall, an indoor swimming pool with 1- and 3-meter diving boards, 2 weight-training rooms, a dance studio, 2 athletic training rooms, a human performance lab, squash courts, and field hockey, soccer, lacrosse, and softball fields. There is a performing arts center and a concert hall.

Disabled Students: 75% of the campus is accessible. Wheelchair ramps, elevators, special parking, specially equipped rest rooms, special class scheduling, lowered drinking fountains, lowered telephones, communications-accessible rooms, and accessible van service are available.

Services: Counseling and information services are available, as is tutoring in every subject. There is a reader service for the blind. Numerous services are provided for learning-disabled students, including note taking, oral tests, readers, tutors, books on tape, reading software, voice recognition, tape recorders, extended-timed tests, and writing counselors.

Campus Safety and Security: Measures include 24-hour foot and vehicle patrol, self-defense education, security escort services, and shuttle buses. There are informal discussions, pamphlets/posters/films, emergency telephones, and lighted pathways/sidewalks. First-year students are required to attend panel discussions on campus safety. Specialized personal safety presentations, including self defense and sexual assault information, are provided to various houses and organizations. There is also bicycle registration.

Programs of Study: Smith confers A.B. and B.S.E.S degrees. Master's and doctoral degrees are also awarded. Bachelor's degrees are awarded in BIOLOGICAL SCIENCE (biochemistry, biology/biological science, and neurosciences), COMMUNICATIONS AND THE ARTS (art history and appreciation, classics, comparative literature, dance, dramatic arts, East Asian languages and literature, English, French, Germanic languages and literature, Greek, Italian, Latin, music, Russian, Spanish, and studio art), COMPUTER AND PHYSICAL SCIENCE (astronomy, chemistry, computer science, geology, mathematics, and physics), EDUCATION (early childhood, education, and elementary), ENGINEERING AND ENVIRONMENTAL DESIGN (architecture and engineering), SOCIAL SCIENCE (African American studies, American studies, anthropology, classical/ancient civilization, economics, French studies, history, Latin American studies, Luso-Brazilian studies, medieval studies, philosophy, political science/government, psychology, religion, Russian and Slavic studies, sociology, and women's studies). Government, psychology, and art are the largest.

Required: All students plan individual programs in consultation with faculty advisers and take 64 credits outside their major and 36 to 64 credits in the major. Students must maintain a minimum 2.0 GPA in all academic work and during the senior year. A total of 128 credits is needed to graduate.

Special: Smith offers study abroad in more than 50 countries including the Smith College programs in Italy, France, Germany, and Switzerland, affiliated programs in India, Japan, Russia, China, South Africa, Peru, Brazil, and Spain, and many others. Other opportunities include cross-registration with 5 area colleges, a Washington semester, Smithsonian internships, exchanges with historically Black colleges and other liberal arts colleges, and at BioSphere2. Support for non-traditional-age students and for international students is provided, and funding for a summer internship is available for every undergraduate. Accelerated degree programs, student-designed majors, dual majors, and non-degree study are offered. There are 3 national honor societies, including Phi Beta Kappa.

Faculty/Classroom: 54% of faculty are male; 46%, female. All both teach and do research. No introductory courses are taught by graduate students. The average class size in an introductory lecture is 23; in a laboratory, 15; and in a regular course, 17.

Admissions: 57% of the 2003-2004 applicants were accepted. The ACT scores for the 2003-2004 freshman class were: 7% below 21, 9% between 21 and 23, 21% between 24 and 26, 21% between 27 and 28, and 41% above 28. 81% of the current freshmen were in the top fifth of their class; 97% were in the top two fifths. 19 freshmen graduated first in their class in a recent year.

Requirements: The SAT I or ACT is required. In addition, Smith highly recommends that applicants have 4 years of English, 3 years each of math, science, and a foreign language, and 2 years of history. SAT II: Subject tests, especially in writing, are strongly recommended, as are personal interviews. The GED is accepted. AP credits are accepted. Important factors in the admissions decision are advanced placement or honor courses, recommendations by school officials, and leadership record.

Procedure: Freshmen are admitted in the fall. Entrance exams should be taken before January of the senior year. There are early decision, early admissions, and deferred admissions plans. Early decision applications should be filed by November 15; regular applications, by January 15 for fall entry, along with a $60 fee. Notification of early decision is sent December 15; regular decision, April 1. 152 early decision candidates were accepted for the 2003-2004 class. 380 applicants were on the 2003 waiting list; 42 were admitted. Applications are accepted on-line through CollegeNET and Common App.

Transfer: 93 transfer students enrolled in a recent year. Criteria for transfer students are similar to those for entering freshmen, with more emphasis on the college record. 64 of 128 credits required for the bachelor's degree must be completed at Smith.

Visiting: There are regularly scheduled orientations for prospective students, including student-guided tours available 4 times a day, Monday through Friday, when school is in full session and on Saturday mornings from September to January. Interviews may also be scheduled during these times. Information sessions are offered twice daily most of the year. There are guides for informal visits and visitors may sit in on classes and stay overnight. To schedule a visit, contact the Office of Admissions receptionist.

Financial Aid: In 2003-2004, 59% of all full-time freshmen and 64% of continuing full-time students received some form of financial aid. 59% of full-time freshmen and 64% of continuing full-time students received need-based aid. The average freshman award was $25,521. Need-based scholarships or need-based grants averaged $21,627 ($38,334 maximum); need-based self-help aid (loans and jobs) averaged $8898 ($40,986 maximum); and non-need-based awards and non-need-based scholarships averaged $4627 ($27,330 maximum). 60% of undergraduates work part time. Average annual earnings from campus work are $2039. The average financial indebtedness of the 2003 graduate was $20,570. Smith is a member of CSS. The CSS Profile or FAFSA is required. The deadline for filing freshman financial aid applications for fall entry is February 1.

International Students: There are 185 international students enrolled. The school actively recruits these students. They must take the TOEFL and the SAT I if the language of instruction is English.

Computers: The mainframe consists of 1 DEC VAX, 5 DEC Alphas, 4 Sun, 11 other UNIX systems, and more than 40 Novell and NT servers. Computing facilities include more than 550 PCs and Mac computers in public labs, classrooms, the libraries, and the foreign language center. All dorm rooms have high-speed Ethernet connections and offer unlimited Internet access at no cost. Computing resources are connected by a campuswide fiber-optic network. All students may access the system. There are no time limits and no fees.

Graduates: From July 1, 2002 to June 30, 2003, 722 bachelor's degrees were awarded. The most popular majors were government (16%), psychology (15%), and art (12%). In an average class, 1% graduate in 3 years or less, 82% graduate in 4 years or less, 83% graduate in 5 years or less, and 86% graduate in 6 years or less. 58 companies recruited on campus in 2002-2003. Of the 2002 graduating class, 16% were enrolled in graduate school within 6 months of graduation and 68% were employed.

Admissions Contact: Debra Shaver, Director of Admission. E-mail: *admission@smith.edu* Web: *smith.edu*

SPRINGFIELD COLLEGE
Springfield, MA 01109

B-3

(413) 748-3136
(800) 343-1257; Fax: (413) 748-3694

Full-time: 3800 men and women	**Faculty:** 210; IIA, --$
Part-time: 200 men and women	**Ph.D.s:** 62%
Graduate: 1000 men and women	**Student/Faculty:** 10 to 1
Year: semesters, summer session	**Tuition:** $19,410
Application Deadline: April 1	**Room & Board:** $7520
Freshman Class: n/av	
SAT I or ACT: required	**COMPETITIVE**

Springfield College, established in 1885, is a private liberal arts and sciences institution. There are 3 undergraduate schools and 1 graduate school. Figures in the above capsule and in this profile are approximate. In addition to regional accreditation, S.C. has baccalaureate program accreditation with APTA, CAHEA, and NRPA. The library contains 168,332 volumes, 736,056 microform items, and 3200 audio/video tapes/CDs, and subscribes to 831 periodicals. Computerized library services include the card catalog, interlibrary loans, and database searching. Special learning facilities include an art gallery, radio station, and an outdoor center. The 160-acre campus is in a suburban area 26 miles north of Hartford, Connecticut. Including any residence halls, there are 38 buildings.

Student Life: Students are from 30 states, 12 foreign countries, and Canada. 83% are from public schools. 93% are white. The average age of freshmen is 18; all undergraduates, 21. 12% do not continue beyond their first year.

Housing: 1980 students can be accommodated in college housing, which includes single-sex and coed dorms, on-campus apartments, off-campus apartments, and married-student housing. In addition, there are special-interest houses and a wellness dorm. On-campus housing is guaranteed for all 4 years. 85% of students live on campus; of those, 70% remain on campus on weekends. Alcohol is not permitted. Upperclassmen may keep cars.

Activities: There are no fraternities or sororities. There are 58 groups on campus, including art, band, cheerleading, choir, chorus, club sports, computers, dance, drama, ethnic, film, gay, honors, international, jazz band, literary magazine, musical theater, newspaper, pep band, professional, radio and TV, religious, social, social service, student government, and yearbook. Popular campus events include Parents Weekend and Stepping Up Day.

Sports: There are 13 intercollegiate sports for men and 11 for women, and 10 intramural sports for men and 10 for women. Facilities include a 2000-seat stadium, a 2000-seat gym, a superturf football/soccer/lacrosse/field hockey field, 8 tennis courts, baseball and softball fields, and free weight and Nautilus rooms.

Disabled Students: 75% of the campus is accessible. Wheelchair ramps, elevators, special parking, specially equipped rest rooms, special class scheduling, and lowered drinking fountains are available.

Services: Counseling and information services are available, as is tutoring in every subject. There is remedial math and writing.

Campus Safety and Security: Measures include 24-hour foot and vehicle patrol, self-defense education, security escort services, and shuttle buses. There are informal discussions, pamphlets/posters/films, emergency telephones, and lighted pathways/sidewalks.

Programs of Study: S.C. confers B.A. and B.S. degrees. Master's and doctoral degrees are also awarded. Bachelor's degrees are awarded in BIOLOGICAL SCIENCE (biochemistry, biology/biological science, and biotechnology), BUSINESS (business administration and management and sports management), COMMUNICATIONS AND THE ARTS (English and fine arts), COMPUTER AND PHYSICAL SCIENCE (chemistry, information sciences and systems, and mathematics), EDUCATION (early childhood, elementary, health, middle school, physical, science, and secondary), ENGINEERING AND ENVIRONMENTAL DESIGN (computer graphics), HEALTH PROFESSIONS (art therapy, emergency medical technologies, environmental health science, health care administration, predentistry, premedicine, recreation therapy, and rehabilitation therapy), SOCIAL SCIENCE (gerontology, history, human services, parks and recreation management, physical fitness/movement, political science/government, prelaw, psychology, and sociology). Physical therapy and athletic training are the strongest academically. Physical education is the largest.

Required: To graduate, students must complete a total of 130 credits with a 2.0 GPA. Core requirements include 50 semester hours in English, social and natural sciences, health, religion, philosophy, and art, and 4 credits in phys ed.

Special: There is a co-op program and cross-registration with cooperating colleges in the greater Springfield area. Internships are required in most majors, and there is limited study abroad. There are 2 national honor societies.

Faculty/Classroom: 52% of faculty are male; 48%, female. No introductory courses are taught by graduate students. The average class size in an introductory lecture is 125; in a laboratory, 20; and in a regular course, 30.

Requirements: The SAT I or ACT is required. In addition, applicants must be graduates of an accredited secondary school and have completed 4 years of English and 3 years each of history, math, and science. The school accepts the GED. An essay is required and an interview is recommended. AP and CLEP credits are accepted. Important factors in the admissions decision are advanced placement or honor courses, leadership record, and extracurricular activities record.

Procedure: Freshmen are admitted fall and spring. Entrance exams should be taken by November of the senior year. There are early decision, early admissions, and deferred admissions plans. There is a rolling admissions plan. Early decision applications should be filed by December 1; regular applications, by April 1 for fall entry and December 1 for spring entry, along with a $40 fee. Notification of early decision is sent February 1; regular decision, on a rolling basis. A waiting list is an active part of the admissions procedure. Applications are accepted on-line.

Transfer: Grades of 2.0 transfer for credit. Transfer students are admitted in the fall and spring.

Visiting: There are guides for informal visits and visitors may sit in on classes and stay overnight. To schedule a visit, contact the Admissions Office.

Financial Aid: The CSS Profile or FAFSA, and tax returns for parents and the student are required. The deadline for filing freshman financial aid applications for fall entry is March 15.

International Students: There were 20 international students enrolled in a recent year. The school actively recruits these students. They must score 525 on the written TOEFL and also take the SAT I or the ACT.

Computers: The mainframe is an IBM AS/400. There are also 30 PCs and Apple IIe computers available for academic use. All students may access the system. There are no time limits and no fees.

Graduates: Of a recent graduating class, 19% were enrolled in graduate school within 6 months of graduation and 78% were employed.

Admissions Contact: Mary N. DeAngelo, Director of Admissions. A video is available. E-mail: *admissions@spfldcol.edu* Web: *www.springfieldcollege.edu*

STONEHILL COLLEGE
Easton, MA 02357

E-3

(508) 565-1373; Fax: (508) 565-1545

Full-time: 952 men, 1273 women	**Faculty:** 130; IIB, +$
Part-time: 107 men, 235 women	**Ph.D.s:** 82%
Graduate: 8 men, 7 women	**Student/Faculty:** 17 to 1
Year: semesters, summer session	**Tuition:** $21,302
Application Deadline: January 15	**Room & Board:** $9450
Freshman Class: 4806 applied, 2364 accepted, 566 enrolled	
SAT I Verbal/Math: 590/600	**ACT: 25 HIGHLY COMPETITIVE**

Stonehill College, founded in 1948 by the Holy Cross Fathers, is a private Roman Catholic college offering undergraduate degrees in business administration, liberal arts, and the sciences. The library contains 205,600 volumes, 350,500 microform items, and 3262 audio/video tapes/CDs, and subscribes to 2271 periodicals. Computerized library services include the card catalog, interlibrary loans, database searching, and Internet access. Special learning facilities include a learning resource center, art gallery, radio station, an observatory, and an institute for the study of law and society. The 375-acre campus is in a suburban area 20 miles south of Boston. Including any residence halls, there are 26 buildings.

Student Life: 62% of undergraduates are from Massachusetts. Students are from 29 states, 10 foreign countries, and Canada. 73% are from public schools. 86% are white. 69% are Catholic; 16% claim no religious affiliation; 10% Protestant. The average age of freshmen is 18; all undergraduates, 21. 11% do not continue beyond their first year; 85% remain to graduate.

Housing: 1825 students can be accommodated in college housing, which includes single-sex and coed dorms. In addition, there are special-interest houses, substance-free/wellness housing, and community service housing. On-campus housing is guaranteed for all 4 years. 76% of students live on campus; of those, 75% remain on campus on weekends. Upperclassmen may keep cars.

Activities: There are no fraternities or sororities. There are 65 groups on campus, including academic, ACES (Active, Concerned and Educated Students), band, cheerleading, chess, choir, chorus, computers, dance, drama, environmental, ethnic, gay, honors, international, literary magazine, musical theater, newspaper, pep band, political, professional, radio and TV, religious, social, social service, student government, and yearbook. Popular campus events include Fall Concert, Spring Weekend, and Halloween Mixer.

Sports: There are 9 intercollegiate sports for men and 11 for women, and 17 intramural sports for men and 17 for women. Facilities include a 2000-seat stadium for football, soccer, and lacrosse, a gym with basketball and volleyball courts, a recreational and intramural sports complex, tennis courts, baseball, softball, and field hockey fields, and 3 recreational fields for intramural and club sports.

Disabled Students: 85% of the campus is accessible. Wheelchair ramps, elevators, special parking, specially equipped rest rooms, special

class scheduling, lowered drinking fountains, lowered telephones, tele-communication devices for the deaf, and 10 dorm rooms designed specifically for disabled students are available.

Services: Counseling and information services are available, as is tutoring in most subjects, an LD specialist, and free diagnostic testing. There is a reader service for the blind and remedial writing.

Campus Safety and Security: Measures include 24-hour foot and vehicle patrol, self-defense education, security escort services, and informal discussions. There are pamphlets/posters/films, emergency telephones, lighted pathways/sidewalks, bicycle patrols, and a weekend guest sign-in policy.

Programs of Study: Stonehill confers B.A., B.S., and B.S.B.A. degrees. Master's degrees are also awarded. Bachelor's degrees are awarded in BIOLOGICAL SCIENCE (biochemistry and biology/biological science), BUSINESS (accounting, banking and finance, business administration and management, business economics, and marketing/retailing/merchandising), COMMUNICATIONS AND THE ARTS (communications, English, fine arts, and languages), COMPUTER AND PHYSICAL SCIENCE (chemistry, computer science, and mathematics), EDUCATION (education), ENGINEERING AND ENVIRONMENTAL DESIGN (computer engineering), HEALTH PROFESSIONS (health care administration and medical technology), SOCIAL SCIENCE (American studies, criminal justice, economics, history, interdisciplinary studies, international studies, philosophy, political science/government, psychology, public administration, religion, and sociology). Biology, English, and accounting are the strongest academically. Business, psychology, and education are the largest.

Required: All students must complete a cornerstone program, which consists of 4 common courses within history/literature and philosophy/religious studies; a learning community consisting of 2 linked courses and a third tutorial course; a moral reasoning course; and a senior capstone experience. Distribution requirements include 1 course each in natural science, social science, and statistical reasoning and 1 year of a foreign language. Students must complete 120 hours (40 3- to 4-credit courses) while maintaining a minimum GPA of 2.0.

Special: On-campus work-study, international and domestic internships, and a Washington semester through the Washington Center are available. Cross-registration with 8 other Massachusetts schools in the SACHEM consortium is also available. A 3-2 computer engineering degree is offered with the University of Notre Dame. Opportunities for study abroad include a Stonehill-Quebec Exchange and a worldwide Foreign Studies Program. Nondegree, directed, and field study are available as well as a pass/fail option for upperclassmen. Programs in early childhood, elementary, and secondary education lead to the state's provisional teacher certification. Stonehill is also a member of the Marine Studies Consortium. Preprofessional preparation is available in medicine, dentistry, law, and theology. There are 13 national honor societies, a freshman honors program, and 7 departmental honors programs.

Faculty/Classroom: 61% of faculty are male; 39%, female. All full-time faculty both teach and do research. No introductory courses are taught by graduate students. The average class size in an introductory lecture is 21; in a laboratory, 17; and in a regular course, 20.

Admissions: 49% of the 2003-2004 applicants were accepted. The SAT I scores for the 2003-2004 freshman class were: Verbal--6% below 500, 45% between 500 and 599, 45% between 600 and 700, and 3% above 700; Math--4% below 500, 42% between 500 and 599, 50% between 600 and 700, and 4% above 700. 75% of the current freshmen were in the top fifth of their class; 98% were in the top two fifths. 3 freshmen graduated first in their class.

Requirements: The SAT I or ACT is required. In addition, applicants should be graduates of an accredited high school or have earned the GED. Secondary preparation should include 4 units of English, 2 units of the same foreign language, 2 units of algebra, 1 unit of a lab science, 1 unit of geometry, and 3 combined units of history, political science, and social sciences. To these units elective subjects are to be added. Additional units in math are generally suggested, especially for business and science majors. An essay, a school report, and teacher evaluations are also required. AP and CLEP credits are accepted. Important factors in the admissions decision are advanced placement or honor courses, leadership record, and extracurricular activities record.

Procedure: Freshmen are admitted fall and spring. Entrance exams should be taken in October. There are early decision and deferred admissions plans. Early decision applications should be filed by November 1; regular applications, by January 15 for fall entry and November 1 for spring entry, along with a $50 fee. Notification of early decision is sent December 15; regular decision, by April 1. 50 early decision candidates were accepted for the 2003-2004 class. 723 applicants were on the 2003 waiting list; 53 were admitted. Applications are accepted on-line through *princetonreview.com* and Common App.

Transfer: 49 transfer students enrolled in 2002-2003. Applicants must have a minimum GPA of 2.0, with 3.0 to 4.0 recommended. Official high school transcripts and college transcripts, along with catalogs with course descriptions from all colleges attended, are required. SAT I or ACT scores are required, and an interview is recommended. 60 of 120

credits required for the bachelor's degree must be completed at Stonehill.

Visiting: There are regularly scheduled orientations for prospective students, consisting of group information sessions and guided campus tours available by appointment throughout the year. Visitors may sit in on classes. To schedule a visit, contact the Admissions Office.

Financial Aid: In 2003-2004, 91% of all full-time freshmen and 89% of continuing full-time students received some form of financial aid. 65% of full-time freshmen and 62% of continuing full-time students received need-based aid. The average freshman award was $15,425. Need-based scholarships or need-based grants averaged $6823 ($31,104 maximum); need-based self-help aid (loans and jobs) averaged $6340 ($8625 maximum); non-need-based athletic scholarships averaged $7309 ($31,152 maximum); and other non-need-based awards and non-need-based scholarships averaged $4965 ($30,752 maximum). 39% of undergraduates work part time. Average annual earnings from campus work are $852. The average financial indebtedness of the 2003 graduate was $11,893. Stonehill is a member of CSS. The CSS Profile or FAFSA is required. The deadline for filing freshman financial aid applications for fall entry is February 1.

International Students: There are 18 international students enrolled. The school actively recruits these students. They must score 550 on the written TOEFL or 213 on the electronic version and also take the SAT I or the ACT.

Computers: The mainframe is an IBM AS/400. More than 250 PCs are available in public labs throughout the campus. Available software includes instructional packages, web page development tools, graphics tools, programming languages, and database tools for student use. Every resident has a direct network connection, and laptop connections are available in many common areas and the library. Students are provided e-mail accounts, personal web pages, and central data storage. Nearly all of the administrative systems are available to students through the Internet. All students may access the system 7 days a week, 24 hours a day. There are no time limits and no fees. It is strongly recommended that all students have a personal computer.

Graduates: From July 1, 2002 to June 30, 2003, 559 bachelor's degrees were awarded. The most popular majors were business (30%), education (11%), and communication (10%). In an average class, 81% graduate in 4 years or less, 83% graduate in 5 years or less, and 85% graduate in 6 years or less. 75 companies recruited on campus in 2002-2003. Of the 2002 graduating class, 16% were enrolled in graduate school within 6 months of graduation and 79% were employed.

Admissions Contact: Brian P. Murphy, Dean of Admissions and Enrollment. E-mail: *admissions@stonehill.edu* Web: *www.stonehill.edu*

SUFFOLK UNIVERSITY
Boston, MA 02108-2770

E-2
(617) 573-8460
(800) 6SUFFOL; Fax: (617) 742-4291

Full-time: 1496 men, 1982 women	**Faculty:** 251; IIA, ++$
Part-time: 284 men, 310 women	**Ph.D.s:** 92%
Graduate: 866 men, 1089 women	**Student/Faculty:** 14 to 1
Year: semesters, summer session	**Tuition:** $18,750
Application Deadline: open	**Room & Board:** $10,450
Freshman Class: 4464 applied, 3658 accepted, 925 enrolled	
SAT I Verbal/Math: 570/500	**ACT:** 20 **COMPETITIVE**

Suffolk University, founded in 1906, is a private institution offering undergraduate and graduate degrees in the arts and sciences, business, and law. There are 2 undergraduate and 3 graduate schools. In addition to regional accreditation, Suffolk has baccalaureate program accreditation with AACSB, FIDER, and NASAD. The 3 libraries contain 300,894 volumes, 262,078 microform items, and 319 audio/video tapes/CDs, and subscribe to 6528 periodicals. Computerized library services include the card catalog, interlibrary loans, database searching, and Internet access. Special learning facilities include a learning resource center, art gallery, radio station, and TV station. The 2-acre campus is in an urban area in the Beacon Hill area of downtown Boston. Including any residence halls, there are 17 buildings.

Student Life: 71% of undergraduates are from Massachusetts. Students are from 37 states, 96 foreign countries, and Canada. 69% are from public schools. 60% are white; 14% foreign nationals. The average age of freshmen is 18; all undergraduates, 22. 25% do not continue beyond their first year; 55% remain to graduate.

Housing: 506 students can be accommodated in college housing, which includes coed dorms. On-campus housing is available on a first-come, first-served basis and is available on a lottery system for upperclassmen. 78% of students commute. Alcohol is not permitted. No one may keep cars.

Activities: There are no fraternities or sororities. There are 75 groups on campus, including art, choir, chorale, chorus, computers, dance, debate, drama, ethnic, film, forensics, gay, honors, international, jazz band, literary magazine, musical theater, newspaper, photography, political, professional, radio and TV, religious, social, social service, student government, and yearbook. Popular campus events include Hispanic Fiesta, Fallfest Talent Show, and Temple Street Fair.

Sports: There are 7 intercollegiate sports for men and 6 for women, and 3 intramural sports for men and 1 for women. A gym for basketball, volleyball, aerobics, intramurals, and indoor baseball/softball practice, and a fully equipped fitness center are available to the university community.

Disabled Students: 95% of the campus is accessible. Wheelchair ramps, elevators, specially equipped rest rooms, special class scheduling, lowered drinking fountains, and lowered telephones are available.

Services: Counseling and information services are available, as is tutoring in every subject. There is a reader service for the blind and remedial math, reading, and writing.

Campus Safety and Security: Measures include 24-hour foot and vehicle patrol, self-defense education, security escort services, and informal discussions. There are pamphlets/posters/films, emergency telephones, and lighted pathways/sidewalks.

Programs of Study: Suffolk confers B.A., B.S., B.F.A., B.S.B.A., B.S.G.S., and B.S.J. degrees. Associate, master's, and doctoral degrees are also awarded. Bachelor's degrees are awarded in BIOLOGICAL SCIENCE (biochemistry, biology/biological science, and marine science), BUSINESS (accounting, banking and finance, entrepreneurial studies, international business management, international economics, management science, and marketing/retailing/merchandising), COMMUNICATIONS AND THE ARTS (broadcasting, communications, dramatic arts, English, fine arts, French, graphic design, journalism, performing arts, public relations, Spanish, and speech/debate/rhetoric), COMPUTER AND PHYSICAL SCIENCE (chemistry, computer programming, computer science, information sciences and systems, mathematics, and physics), EDUCATION (business and elementary), ENGINEERING AND ENVIRONMENTAL DESIGN (computer engineering, electrical/electronics engineering, environmental engineering, environmental engineering technology, environmental science, and interior design), HEALTH PROFESSIONS (cytotechnology, medical laboratory technology, medical science, and radiological science), SOCIAL SCIENCE (criminal justice, economics, history, human development, human services, humanities, industrial and organizational psychology, paralegal studies, philosophy, political science/government, psychology, public administration, social science, and sociology). Business, sociology, and criminal justice are the strongest academically. Business subjects, sociology, and communications are the largest.

Required: All students must complete 122 semester hours with at least a 2.0 GPA. Distribution requirements vary by degree program.

Special: Numerous cooperative education and work-study programs are available in the Boston area. Cross-registration is offered with Emerson College. Study abroad in 25 countries and a semester internship in Washington, D.C., as well as local and international internships, are possible. Majors in medical biophysics and radiation biology taught in collaboration with Massachusetts General Hospital, dual and student-designed majors, and a lawyer's assistant certificate program are also available. Also, Suffolk has opened campuses in Spain and Senegal. There are 19 national honor societies, including Phi Beta Kappa, a freshman honors program, and 12 departmental honors programs.

Faculty/Classroom: 57% of faculty are male; 43%, female. 95% teach undergraduates, and 90% both teach and do research. The average class size in an introductory lecture is 20; in a laboratory, 12; and in a regular course, 17.

Admissions: 82% of the 2003-2004 applicants were accepted. The SAT I scores for the 2003-2004 freshman class were: Verbal--44% below 500, 42% between 500 and 599, 14% between 600 and 700, and 1% above 700; Math--46% below 500, 41% between 500 and 599, 12% between 600 and 700, and 1% above 700. The ACT scores were 51% below 21, 30% between 21 and 23, 15% between 24 and 26, and 4% between 27 and 28. 20% of the current freshmen were in the top fifth of their class; 51% were in the top two fifths.

Requirements: The SAT I is required. In addition, applicants should have a high school diploma or the GED. Recommended secondary preparation includes 4 years of English, 3 of math, 2 each of a foreign language and science, and 1 of American history. Exact requirements differ by degree program. A personal essay is required, and an interview is recommended. A GPA of 2.0 is required. AP and CLEP credits are accepted. Important factors in the admissions decision are advanced placement or honor courses, recommendations by school officials, and leadership record.

Procedure: Freshmen are admitted to all sessions. Entrance exams should be taken by December of the senior year. There are early admissions and deferred admissions plans. Application deadlines are open. Application fee is $50. Applications are accepted on-line through Common App and CollegeNET.

Transfer: 303 transfer students enrolled in 2002-2003. Applicants should have a minimum 2.5 GPA from an accredited college. Those with fewer than 15 college credits must submit a high school transcript. 30 of 122 credits required for the bachelor's degree must be completed at Suffolk.

Visiting: There are regularly scheduled orientations for prospective students, including a general presentation and an overview panel presentation of student life, career and co-op opportunities, learning center services, and athletics, academic department meetings, and campus tours. There are guides for informal visits and visitors may sit in on classes. To schedule a visit, contact the Admissions Office.

Financial Aid: In 2003-2004, 79% of all full-time freshmen and 73% of continuing full-time students received some form of financial aid. 63% of full-time freshmen and 57% of continuing full-time students received need-based aid. The average freshman award was $16,549. Need-based scholarships or need-based grants averaged $6011 ($24,050 maximum); need-based self-help aid (loans and jobs) averaged $5286 ($18,125 maximum); and non-need-based awards and non-need-based scholarships averaged $4327 ($19,170 maximum). 56% of undergraduates work part time. Average annual earnings from campus work are $1500. Suffolk is a member of CSS. The FAFSA, the college's own financial statement, and verification of income are required. The deadline for filing freshman financial aid applications for fall entry is March 1.

International Students: There are 499 international students enrolled. The school actively recruits these students. They must score 525 on the written TOEFL or 197 on the electronic version and also take the college's own test and the SAT I or the ACT.

Computers: The mainframe is an IBM RS/6000. Various computer labs on campus house more than 200 PCs with access to the mainframe. Students have access to the Internet, Lexis/Nexis database, the Suffolk online library system, CD-ROM library and information systems, as well as Sun and DEC UNIX workstations. All students may access the system. There are no time limits and no fees.

Graduates: From July 1, 2002 to June 30, 2003, 689 bachelor's degrees were awarded. The most popular majors were communications (14%), finance (9%), and sociology (9%). In an average class, 3% graduate in 3 years or less, 40% graduate in 4 years or less, 52% graduate in 5 years or less, and 54% graduate in 6 years or less. 43 companies recruited on campus in 2002-2003. Of the 2002 graduating class, 27% were enrolled in graduate school within 6 months of graduation and 80% were employed.

Admissions Contact: John Hamel, Director of Undergraduate Admissions. A video is available. E-mail: *admission@suffolk.edu* Web: *www.suffolk.edu*

TUFFS UNIVERSITY

TUFTS UNIVERSITY D-2
Medford, MA 02155 (617) 627-3170; Fax: (617) 627-3860

Full-time: 2201 men, 2599 women	**Faculty:** 583; I, av$
Part-time: 40 men, 52 women	**Ph.D.s:** 99%
Graduate: 1975 men, 2642 women	**Student/Faculty:** 8 to 1
Year: semesters, summer session	**Tuition:** $29,593
Application Deadline: January 1	**Room & Board:** $8640
Freshman Class: 14,528 applied, 3830 accepted, 1282 enrolled	
SAT I or ACT: n/av	**MOST COMPETITIVE**

Tufts University, founded in 1852, is a private institution offering undergraduate programs in liberal arts and sciences and engineering. There are 2 undergraduate and 8 graduate schools. In addition to regional accreditation, Tufts has baccalaureate program accreditation with ABET, ADA, and CAHEA. The 2 libraries contain 1,079,000 volumes, 1,180,000 microform items, and 33,800 audio/video tapes/CDs, and subscribe to 5204 periodicals. Computerized library services include the card catalog, interlibrary loans, database searching, and Internet access. Special learning facilities include a learning resource center, art gallery, radio station, TV station, and theater. The 140-acre campus is in a suburban area 5 miles northwest of Boston. Including any residence halls, there are 167 buildings.

Student Life: 75% of undergraduates are from out of state, mostly the Middle Atlantic. Students are from 50 states, 67 foreign countries, and Canada. 60% are from public schools. 55% are white; 14% Asian American. The average age of freshmen is 18; all undergraduates, 20. 4% do not continue beyond their first year.

Housing: 3550 students can be accommodated in college housing, which includes single-sex and coed dorms, on-campus apartments, fraternity houses, and sorority houses. In addition, there are language houses, cooperative houses, and special-interest houses. On-campus housing is available on a lottery system for upperclassmen. 75% of students live on campus. Upperclassmen may keep cars.

Activities: 15% of men belong to 10 national fraternities; 3% of women belong to 3 national sororities. There are 160 groups on campus, including art, band, cheerleading, chess, choir, chorale, chorus, computers, dance, debate, drama, environmental, ethnic, forensics, gay, honors, international, jazz band, literary magazine, marching band, musical theater, newspaper, orchestra, outdoors, pep band, photography, political, professional, radio and TV, religious, social, social service, student government, symphony, and yearbook. Popular campus events include a dramatic arts series, national and international forums, and an international affairs symposium.

Sports: There are 17 intercollegiate sports for men and 16 for women, and 10 intramural sports for men and 6 for women. Facilities include a football stadium, 2 gyms, an 8-lane all-weather track, 9 tennis courts, a field house, an indoor cage, an indoor track, 7 squash courts, a swimming pool, a dance room, a weight room, a sauna, a sailing center, an exercise center, and baseball, softball, and playing fields.

Disabled Students: 90% of the campus is accessible. Wheelchair ramps, elevators, special parking, specially equipped rest rooms, special class scheduling, lowered drinking fountains, lowered telephones, and other special services as needed are available.

Services: Counseling and information services are available, as is tutoring in some subjects, as needed, through the Academic Resources Center. There is a reader service for the blind. Services are also available through women's, African American, Hispanic American, Asian American, international, and lesbian-gay-bisexual centers, and through the Counseling Center and Career Planning Center.

Campus Safety and Security: Measures include 24-hour foot and vehicle patrol, security escort services, shuttle buses, and informal discussions. There are pamphlets/posters/films, emergency telephones, and lighted pathways/sidewalks.

Programs of Study: Tufts confers B.A., B.S., B.S.C.E., B.S.Ch.E., B.S. Comp. Eng., B.S.E., B.S.E.E., B.S.E.S., B.S. Environmental Eng., and B.S.M.E. degrees. Master's and doctoral degrees are also awarded. Bachelor's degrees are awarded in BIOLOGICAL SCIENCE (biochemistry, biology/biological science, and biotechnology), COMMUNICATIONS AND THE ARTS (art history and appreciation, Chinese, classics, dramatic arts, English, French, German, Greek, Japanese, Latin, music, Russian, and Spanish), COMPUTER AND PHYSICAL SCIENCE (applied physics, astrophysics, chemistry, computer science, geology, mathematics, and physics), EDUCATION (early childhood), ENGINEERING AND ENVIRONMENTAL DESIGN (architecture, biomedical engineering, chemical engineering, civil engineering, computer engineering, electrical/electronics engineering, engineering, engineering and applied science, engineering physics, environmental science, and mechanical engineering), SOCIAL SCIENCE (American studies, anthropology, archeology, Asian/Oriental studies, biopsychology, child psychology/development, clinical psychology, economics, experimental psychology, German area studies, history, international relations, Judaic studies, Middle Eastern studies, peace studies, philosophy, political science/government, psychology, religion, Russian and Slavic studies, sociology, and women's studies). International relations and biology are the largest.

Required: Liberal arts students must complete 34 courses, 10 of them in the area of concentration. Requirements include foundation courses in writing and foreign language or culture and courses in humanities, arts, social sciences, math, and natural sciences. Requirements for engineering students include a total of 38 courses, 12 of them in the area of concentration, and distribution requirements in English, math and science, humanities, and social sciences.

Special: The university offers cross-registration at Swarthmore College, Boston University, Boston College, and Brandeis University, a Washington semester, and study abroad in England, Spain, France, Chile, Japan, Ghana, and Germany. Many internships are available. Double majors in the liberal arts are common; student-designed majors are possible. There is a 5-year B.A./M.A. or B.S./M.S. program in engineering or liberal arts, a B.A.-B.F.A. program with the Museum School of Fine Arts, and a B.A.-B.M. program with the New England Conservatory of Music. Pass/fail options are offered. There are 4 national honor societies, including Phi Beta Kappa.

Faculty/Classroom: 60% of faculty are male; 40%, female. All both teach and do research. No introductory courses are taught by graduate students. The average class size in a regular course is 20.

Admissions: 26% of the 2003-2004 applicants were accepted. 89% of the current freshmen were in the top fifth of their class; 98% were in the top two fifths. There were 41 National Merit finalists.

Requirements: The university accepts either the SAT I and the results of 3 SAT II: Subject tests, or the ACT. Liberal arts applicants should take the SAT II: Subject test in writing and 2 others; engineering applicants should take writing, math level I or II, and either physics or chemistry. In addition, all applicants should be high school graduates or hold the GED. Academic preparation is expected to include 4 years of English, 3 years each of humanities and a foreign language, 2 years each of social and natural sciences, and 1 year of history. A personal essay is required. AP credits are accepted. Important factors in the admissions decision are advanced placement or honor courses, recommendations by school officials, and extracurricular activities record.

Procedure: Freshmen are admitted in the fall. Entrance exams should be taken by January of the senior year. There are early decision, early admissions, and deferred admissions plans. Early decision applications should be filed by November 15; regular applications, by January 1 for fall entry, along with a $60 fee. Notification of early decision is sent December 15; regular decision, April 1. 508 early decision candidates were accepted for the 2003-2004 class. A waiting list is an active part of the admissions procedure. Applications are accepted on-line through Embark.com and CommonApp.

Transfer: 107 transfer students enrolled in 2002-2003. Admission is competitive. Primary consideration is given to college and secondary school achievement and record of personal involvement. 17 of 34 courses required for the bachelor's degree must be completed at Tufts.

Visiting: There are regularly scheduled orientations for prospective students, including orientation sessions twice a day, Monday through Friday, April 1 to early December, followed by campus tours. There are additional orientation sessions and tours on selected Saturday mornings during the fall. There are guides for informal visits and visitors may sit in on classes and stay overnight. To schedule a visit, contact the Admissions Office.

Financial Aid: In 2003-2004, 40% of all full-time freshmen and 41% of continuing full-time students received some form of financial aid. 37% of all full-time students received need-based aid. The average freshman award was $24,483. 40% of undergraduates work part time. The average financial indebtedness of the 2003 graduate was $14,925. Tufts is a member of CSS. The CSS Profile or FAFSA and parent and student federal income tax forms are required. The deadline for filing freshman financial aid applications for fall entry is February 15.

International Students: There are 306 international students enrolled. The school actively recruits these students. Students must take the TOEFL if English is not their first language. Students must also take the ACT, or the SAT I and 3 SAT II: Subject tests, including writing.

Computers: The mainframes are a DEC Alpha Server 8200 with 4 Alpha processors and a DEC MicroVAX with 3600 processors; the machines operate on VMS and UNIX. Mainframes and PC labs are networked on a universitywide computer network called Jumbonet. There are 254 terminals and PCs in 5 locations across campus, supported by 45 printers in various locations. A special computer-aided design (CAD) lab is available to undergraduates. All campus residence rooms are hardwired for access to the university computer. All students may access the system 24 hours a day. There are no time limits and no fees.

Graduates: From July 1, 2002 to June 30, 2003, 1355 bachelor's degrees were awarded. The most popular majors were international relations (12%), economics (11%), and biology (7%). In an average class, 90% graduate in 6 years or less. 150 companies recruited on campus in 2002-2003.

Admissions Contact: Lee A. Coffin, Dean of Admissions.
E-mail: *admissions.inquiry@ase.tufts.edu* Web: *www.tufts.edu*

UNIVERSITY OF MASSACHUSETTS AMHERST B-2
Amherst, MA 01003 (413) 545-0222; Fax: (413) 545-4312

Full-time: 8588 men, 8637 women	Faculty: 1077; I, av$
Part-time: 678 men, 815 women	Ph.D.s: 94%
Graduate: 2754 men, 2838 women	Student/Faculty: 16 to 1
Year: semesters, summer session	Tuition: $8232 ($16,455)
Application Deadline: January 15	Room & Board: $5748
Freshman Class: 16,427 applied, 13,461 accepted, 4077 enrolled	
SAT I Verbal/Math: 560/570	COMPETITIVE+

Established in 1863, University of Massachusetts Amherst is a major public, research land-grant institution offering nearly 100 academic majors. There are 9 undergraduate and 9 graduate schools. In addition to regional accreditation, UMass has baccalaureate program accreditation with AACSB, ABET, ASLA, FIDER, NASM, NCATE, NLN, and SAF. The 3 libraries contain 3,444,741 volumes, 2,517,808 microform items, and 21,934 audio/video tapes/CDs, and subscribe to 15,427 periodicals. Computerized library services include the card catalog, interlibrary loans, database searching, and Internet access. Special learning facilities include a learning resource center, art gallery, radio station, TV station, and botanical gardens. The 1463-acre campus is in a small town 90 miles west of Boston and 60 miles north of Hartford, Connecticut. Including any residence halls, there are 200 buildings.

Student Life: 83% of undergraduates are from Massachusetts. Students are from 49 states, 37 foreign countries, and Canada. 76% are white. The average age of freshmen is 18; all undergraduates, 21. 16% do not continue beyond their first year; 98% remain to graduate.

Housing: 11,000 students can be accommodated in college housing, which includes single-sex and coed dorms, on-campus apartments, married-student housing, fraternity houses, and sorority houses. In addition, there are honors houses, language houses, special-interest houses, international student housing, and first-year experience housing. On-campus housing is guaranteed for the freshman year only and is available on a lottery system for upperclassmen. 59% of students live on campus. All students may keep cars.

Activities: 3% of men belong to 2 local and 15 national fraternities; 7% of women belong to 1 local and 14 national sororities. There are 200 groups on campus, including art, band, cheerleading, chess, choir, chorale, chorus, computers, dance, debate, drama, ethnic, film, gay, honors, international, jazz band, literary magazine, marching band, musical theater, newspaper, opera, orchestra, pep band, photography, political, professional, radio and TV, religious, social, social service, student government, student-owned business, symphony, and yearbook. Popular campus events include First Week, Family Day, and Oozefest (annual mud volleyball tournament).

Sports: There are 10 intercollegiate sports for men and 11 for women, and 12 intramural sports for men and 14 for women. Facilities include 120 acres of multipurpose fields, football stadium, a track, and 22 tennis courts. Indoor facilities include 3 pools, 3 handball/squash courts, weight rooms, fitness centers, basketball/volleyball/badminton courts, and a track.

Disabled Students: Wheelchair ramps, elevators, special parking, specially equipped rest rooms, special class scheduling, lowered drinking fountains, lowered telephones, and special housing. All programs are made accessible through accommodations.

Services: Counseling and information services are available, as is tutoring in most subjects. There is a reader service for the blind and remedial math and reading.

Campus Safety and Security: Measures include 24-hour foot and vehicle patrol, self-defense education, shuttle buses, and informal discussions. There are pamphlets/posters/films, emergency telephones, lighted pathways/sidewalks, and tight restrictions on residence hall access.

Programs of Study: UMass confers B.A., B.S., B.B.A., B.F.A., B.G.S., and B.Mus. degrees. Associate, master's, and doctoral degrees are also awarded. Bachelor's degrees are awarded in AGRICULTURE (animal science, forestry and related sciences, natural resource management, plant science, soil science, and wildlife management), BIOLOGICAL SCIENCE (biochemistry, biology/biological science, microbiology, and nutrition), BUSINESS (accounting, banking and finance, business administration and management, hotel/motel and restaurant management, marketing management, and sports management), COMMUNICATIONS AND THE ARTS (art history and appreciation, Chinese, classics, communications, comparative literature, dance, design, dramatic arts, English, French, German, Japanese, journalism, linguistics, music, Portuguese, Spanish, and studio art), COMPUTER AND PHYSICAL SCIENCE (astronomy, chemistry, computer science, earth science, geology, mathematics, physics, and science), EDUCATION (early childhood, elementary, and secondary), ENGINEERING AND ENVIRONMENTAL DESIGN (chemical engineering, civil engineering, computer engineering, construction technology, electrical/electronics engineering, environmental design, environmental science, industrial engineering, landscape architecture/design, and mechanical engineering), HEALTH PROFESSIONS (exercise science, medical laboratory technology, nursing, predentistry, premedicine, preveterinary science, and speech pathology/audiology), SOCIAL SCIENCE (African American studies, anthropology, economics, ethics, politics, and social policy, food science, geography, history, interdisciplinary studies, Italian studies, Judaic studies, law, liberal arts/general studies, Middle Eastern studies, philosophy, political science/government, prelaw, psychology, Russian and Slavic studies, sociology, and women's studies). Engineering, computer science, and management are the strongest academically. Psychology, communication, and biology are the largest.

Required: For graduation, students must complete 120 credit hours and maintain a minimum GPA of 2.0 overall and in the major, with at least 2 courses fulfilling a diversity requirement. The general education requirements for all students include courses in writing, the social world, the biological and physical world, math, and analytic reasoning.

Special: Cross-registration is possible with Smith, Mt. Holyoke, Hampshire, and Amherst Colleges. Co-op programs, internships in every major, study abroad in more than 30 countries, a Washington semester, work-study programs, dual majors, and B.A.-B.S. degrees are available. The Bachelor's Degree with Individual Concentration (BDIC) is also available. The Commonwealth College welcomes honor students. There are 25 national honor societies, including Phi Beta Kappa, a freshman honors program, and 70 departmental honors programs.

Faculty/Classroom: 68% of faculty are male; 32%, female. All both teach and do research.

Admissions: 82% of the 2003-2004 applicants were accepted. The SAT I scores for the 2003-2004 freshman class were: Verbal--20% below 500, 47% between 500 and 599, 28% between 600 and 700, and 5% above 700; Math--15% below 500, 46% between 500 and 599, 32% between 600 and 700, and 7% above 700. 34% of the current freshmen were in the top fifth of their class; 72% were in the top two fifths. 52 freshmen graduated first in their class in a recent year.

Requirements: The SAT I or ACT is required. In addition, applicants must be graduates of an accredited secondary school, or have the GED. The university recommends that students complete 16 Carnegie units, including 4 years of English, 3 years of math, 3 years of natural sciences (including 2 years lab), 2 years of electives, 2 years of foreign language, and 2 years of social sciences. 4 years of math are required for business, computer science, and engineering majors. Students must present a portfolio for admission to the art program and must audition for admission to music and dance. A GPA of 2.0 is required. AP and CLEP credits are accepted. Important factors in the admissions decision are extracurricular activities record, evidence of special talent, and personality/intangible qualities.

Procedure: Freshmen are admitted fall and spring. Entrance exams should be taken before February 1. There is a deferred admissions plan. There is a rolling admissions plan. Applications should be filed by January 15 for fall entry and October 15 for spring entry, along with a $40 fee (in-state), $50 (out-of-state), or $60 (international). Notification is sent on a rolling basis. Applications are accepted on-line through *www.umass.edu/home/admissions.*

Transfer: 1153 transfer students enrolled in 2002-2003. Transfer applicants must submit transcripts from all colleges or universities attended and an essay. Those with fewer than 30 credits must submit high school transcripts and SAT I scores. Priority is given to students with an associate degree. Grades of C- or better transfer for credit. 45 of 120 credits required for the bachelor's degree must be completed at UMass.

Visiting: There are regularly scheduled orientations for prospective students, including twice-daily guided tours and daily information sessions. There are guides for informal visits and visitors may sit in on classes and stay overnight. To schedule a visit, contact the University Tour Service at (413) 545-4237.

Financial Aid: In 2003-2004, 47% of all full-time freshmen and 46% of continuing full-time students received some form of financial aid. At least 42% of all full-time students received need-based aid. The average freshman award was $8084. Need-based scholarships or need-based grants averaged $5557; need-based self-help aid (loans and jobs) averaged $3443; non-need-based athletic scholarships averaged $11,307; and other non-need-based awards and non-need-based scholarships averaged $4708. The average financial indebtedness of the 2003 graduate was $15,374. UMass is a member of CSS. The FAFSA is required. The priority date for freshman financial aid applications for fall entry is March 1.

International Students: There are 310 international students enrolled. They must score 550 on the written TOEFL or 213 on the electronic version.

Computers: There are approximately 450 computers, both PCs and Macs, in 11 computer labs and classrooms throughout the campus. Nearly all residence hall rooms have direct, high-speed connections to the campus network. Students have access to e-mail, the Internet, and the Web. All students may access the system. There are no time limits and no fees. It is strongly recommended that all students have a personal computer.

Graduates: From July 1, 2002 to June 30, 2003, 3988 bachelor's degrees were awarded. The most popular majors were psychology (6%), biology (4%), and communciation (4%). In an average class, 44% graduate in 4 years or less, 17% graduate in 5 years or less, and 4% graduate in 6 years or less.

Admissions Contact: Michael Gargano, Vice Chancellor for Student Affairs. A video is available. E-mail: *mail@admissions.umass.edu* Web: *www.umass.edu*

UNIVERSITY OF MASSACHUSETTS BOSTON   E-2
Boston, MA 02125-3393   (617) 287-6100; Fax: (617) 287-6242

Full-time: 2382 men, 3257 women	**Faculty:** 427; I, -$
Part-time: 1954 men, 2478 women	**Ph.D.s:** 93%
Graduate: 827 men, 1821 women	**Student/Faculty:** 13 to 1
Year: semesters, summer session	**Tuition:** $6227 ($16,887)
Application Deadline: January 1	**Room & Board:** n/app
Freshman Class: 2704 applied, 1478 accepted, 576 enrolled	
SAT I Verbal/Math: 520/520	**COMPETITIVE**

The University of Massachusetts Boston, established in 1964, is a public commuter institution offering undergraduate studies in arts and sciences and in preprofessional training. There are 5 undergraduate and 6 graduate schools. In addition to regional accreditation, UMass Boston has baccalaureate program accreditation with AACSB and NLN. The library contains 463,385 volumes, 827,171 microform items, and 1902 audio/video tapes/CDs, and subscribes to 2779 periodicals. Computerized library services include the card catalog, interlibrary loans, and database searching. Special learning facilities include a learning resource center, art gallery, radio station, tropical greenhouse, observatory, adaptive computer lab, languages lab, and applied language and math center. The 177-acre campus is in an urban area 5 miles south of downtown Boston. There are 10 buildings.

Student Life: 92% of undergraduates are from Massachusetts. Students are from 35 states, 89 foreign countries, and Canada. 48% are white; 11% African American. The average age of freshmen is 19; all undergraduates, 27. 30% do not continue beyond their first year; 34% remain to graduate.

Housing: There are no residence halls. All students commute. Alcohol is not permitted. All students may keep cars.

Activities: There are no fraternities or sororities. There are 72 groups on campus, including art, band, cheerleading, chess, choir, chorale, chorus, computers, dance, drama, ethnic, film, gay, honors, international, jazz band, literary magazine, musical theater, newspaper, orchestra, photography, political, professional, radio and TV, religious, social, social service, student government, and yearbook. Popular campus events include Convocation Day, seasonal festivals, and lecture series.

Sports: There are 7 intercollegiate sports for men and 7 for women, and 16 intramural sports for men and 16 for women. Facilities include an athletic center with a 3500-seat gym with 4 basketball and 2 volleyball courts, an ice rink that seats 1000, an Olympic-size swimming pool with high-dive area, a multipurpose weight room, and a sports medicine area; an 8-lane, 400-meter track; 8 tennis courts; a softball diamond, 3 multipurpose fields primarily used for soccer and lacrosse, and several other recreational fields; a boat house, dock, and fleet of sailboats and rowing dories; and a fitness center with strength-training equipment, cardiovascular machines, and racquetball and squash courts.

Disabled Students: All of the campus is accessible. Wheelchair ramps, elevators, special parking, specially equipped rest rooms, special class scheduling, lowered drinking fountains, lowered telephones, amplified phones, powered doors, indoor-connected building access, an accessible shuttle bus, an adaptive computer lab, and a center for students with disabilities are available.

Services: Counseling and information services are available, as is tutoring in every subject. There is a reader service for the blind, and remedial math, reading, and writing. There are also reading study skills workshops and a math resource center available.

Campus Safety and Security: Measures include 24-hour foot and vehicle patrol, self-defense education, security escort services, and shuttle buses. There are informal discussions, pamphlets/posters/films, emergency telephones, lighted pathways/sidewalks, Operation ID, motorist assistance, and crime prevention programs.

Programs of Study: UMass Boston confers B.A. and B.S. degrees. Master's and doctoral degrees are also awarded. Bachelor's degrees are awarded in BIOLOGICAL SCIENCE (biochemistry and biology/ biological science), BUSINESS (labor studies and management science), COMMUNICATIONS AND THE ARTS (art, classical languages, classics, dramatic arts, English, French, Greek (classical), Italian, Latin, music, Russian, and Spanish), COMPUTER AND PHYSICAL SCIENCE (applied mathematics, chemistry, computer science, earth science, mathematics, and physics), EDUCATION (physical), ENGINEERING AND ENVIRONMENTAL DESIGN (engineering and engineering physics), HEALTH PROFESSIONS (medical technology and nursing), SOCIAL SCIENCE (African American studies, American studies, anthropology, community services, criminal justice, economics, ethics, politics, and social policy, geography, German area studies, gerontology, Hispanic American studies, history, human services, paralegal studies, philosophy, political science/government, psychology, sociology, and women's studies). Management, nursing, and psychology are the largest.

Required: For graduation, students must complete 120 credit hours (123 hours in the College of Nursing) and maintain a minimum GPA of 2.0. Distribution requirements vary by college. All students must demonstrate writing proficiency.

Special: Students may cross-register with Massachusetts College of Art, Bunker Hill Community College, Roxbury Community College, and Hebrew College. UMass Boston also offers cooperative programs, internships, study abroad, work-study programs, student-designed majors, B.A.-B.S. degrees, nondegree study, pass/fail options, and dual and interdisciplinary majors, including anthropology/history, biology/medical technology, philosophy/public policy, and psychology/sociology. Also available are 3-1 and 2-2 engineering programs with various area institutions. The College of Public and Community Service provides social-oriented education, generally to older students. There are 3 national honor societies and a freshman honors program.

Faculty/Classroom: 52% of faculty are male; 48%, female. All both teach and do research. No introductory courses are taught by graduate students. The average class size in an introductory lecture is 19; in a laboratory, 14; and in a regular course, 20.

Admissions: 55% of the 2003-2004 applicants were accepted. The SAT I scores for the 2003-2004 freshman class were: Verbal--48% below 500, 35% between 500 and 599, 15% between 600 and 700, and 2% above 700; Math--43% below 500, 38% between 500 and 599, 16% between 600 and 700, and 3% above 700. 22% of the current freshmen were in the top fifth of their class; 62% were in the top two fifths.

Requirements: The SAT I or ACT is required with a minimum composite score of 900 on the SAT I. Test scores are not required of students who have been out of high school for 3 or more years. Applicants should be graduates of an accredited secondary school. The GED is accepted. The university requires the completion of 16 Carnegie units, including 4 years of English, 3 of college preparatory math and science, 2 each of a foreign language and social studies, and 2 electives in the above academic areas or in humanities, arts, or computer science. An essay is recommended. A GPA of 3.0 is required. AP and CLEP credits are accepted. Important factors in the admissions decision are advanced placement or honor courses, evidence of special talent, and recommendations by school officials.

Procedure: Freshmen are admitted fall and spring. Entrance exams should be taken by the fall of the senior year. There is a deferred admissions plan and a rolling admissions plan. Applications should be filed by January 1 for fall entry and July 1 for spring entry, along with a $40 fee. Notification is sent on a rolling basis. Applications are accepted on-line through EXPAN.

Transfer: 1382 transfer students enrolled in 2002-2003. Applicants with fewer than 24 credits must meet freshman requirements. To transfer, students must have a minimum GPA of 2.5 (2.75 for management, nursing, and engineering). Grades of C- or better transfer for credit. 30 of 120 credits required for the bachelor's degree must be completed at UMass Boston.

Visiting: There are regularly scheduled orientations for prospective students, including general information sessions about the university and the admissions process and a tour of the campus. There are guides for informal visits and visitors may sit in on classes. To schedule a visit, contact Marketing and Information Services at (617) 287-6000.

Financial Aid: In 2003-2004, 67% of all full-time freshmen and 56% of continuing full-time students received some form of financial aid. 51% of full-time freshmen and 48% of continuing full-time students received need-based aid. The average freshman award was $9100. Need-based scholarships or need-based grants averaged $4800 ($9200 maximum); need-based self-help aid (loans and jobs) averaged $3300 ($9100 maximum); and non-need-based awards and non-need-based scholarships averaged $3200 ($5000 maximum). 13% of undergraduates work part time. Average annual earnings from campus work are $2406. The average financial indebtedness of the 2003 graduate was $9600. UMass Boston is a member of CSS. The FAFSA is required.

International Students: There are 430 international students enrolled. The school actively recruits these students. They must score 550 on the written TOEFL or 213 on the electronic version and also take the SAT I if the language of instruction is English. A score of 900 is required.

Computers: There are a number of labs containing Macs and other PCs. Most of the PCs are located in the library, with the remainder in classroom buildings. All students may access the system 24 hours a day. There are no time limits and no fees.

Graduates: From July 1, 2002 to June 30, 2003, 1586 bachelor's degrees were awarded. The most popular majors were management (20%), social science (10%), and psychology (9%). In an average class, 1% graduate in 3 years or less, 8% graduate in 4 years or less, 28% graduate in 5 years or less, and 35% graduate in 6 years or less. 110 companies recruited on campus in 2002-2003.

Admissions Contact: Liliana Mickle, Director, Undergraduate Admissions. E-mail: *undergrad@umb.edu* Web: *www.umb.edu*

UNIVERSITY OF MASSACHUSETTS DARTMOUTH   E-4
North Dartmouth, MA 02747-2300
(508) 999-8605
Fax: (508) 999-8755

Full-time: 2969 men, 2943 women	**Faculty:** 330; IIA, +$
Part-time: 537 men, 910 women	**Ph.Ds:** 88%
Graduate: 433 men, 492 women	**Student/Faculty:** 18 to 1
Year: semesters, summer session	**Tuition:** $6129 ($15,629)
Application Deadline: open	**Room & Board:** $6706
Freshman Class: 6049 applied, 4268 accepted, 1392 enrolled	
SAT I Verbal/Math: 530/540	**COMPETITIVE**

University of Massachusetts Dartmouth, founded in 1895, is a public institution that provides undergraduate and graduate programs in the liberal and creative arts and sciences and in professional training. There are 5 undergraduate schools and 1 graduate school. In addition to regional accreditation, UMass Dartmouth has baccalaureate program accreditation with AACSB, ABET, ACS, CSAB, NAACLS, NASAD, NASDTEC, and NLN. The library contains 455,323 volumes, 810,127 microform items, and 12,980 audio/video tapes/CDs, and subscribes to 2925 periodicals. Computerized library services include the card catalog, interlibrary loans, database searching, and Internet access. Special learning facilities include a learning resource center, art gallery, radio station, an observatory, marine research vessels, and a number of cultural and research centers. The 710-acre campus is in a suburban area approximately 60 miles south of Boston, 35 miles east of Providence, Rhode Island, and 3 miles west of Cape Cod. Including any residence halls, there are 22 buildings.

Student Life: 94% of undergraduates are from Massachusetts. Students are from 32 states, 30 foreign countries, and Canada. 85% are from public schools. 87% are white. The average age of freshmen is 19; all undergraduates, 23. 21% do not continue beyond their first year; 52% remain to graduate.

Housing: 3230 students can be accommodated in college housing, which includes coed dorms and on-campus apartments. In addition, there are honors houses a quiet house, and apartments for upperclassmen. On-campus housing is guaranteed for the freshman year only, is available on a first-come, first-served basis, and is available on a lottery system for upperclassmen. Priority is given to out-of-town students. 52% of students commute. All students may keep cars.

Activities: 1% of men belong to 1 local and 2 national fraternities; 1% of women belong to 1 national sorority. There are 90 groups on campus, including art, band, cheerleading, choir, chorale, chorus, computers, drama, ethnic, film, gay, honors, international, jazz band, literary magazine, musical theater, newspaper, orchestra, pep band, political, professional, radio and TV, religious, social, social service, student government, symphony, and yearbook. Popular campus events include Welcome Back Week, Winterfest, and Spring Fling Week.

Sports: There are 11 intercollegiate sports for men and 12 for women, and 10 intramural sports for men and 10 for women. Facilities include a 3000-seat gym, an 1850-seat football stadium, an aquatic sports center, 13 tennis courts, a weight room, a running track, and soccer, softball, and intramural fields.

Disabled Students: 92% of the campus is accessible. Wheelchair ramps, elevators, special parking, specially equipped rest rooms, special class scheduling, lowered drinking fountains, lowered telephones, limited special housing, mobility assistance, note takers/readers, alternative testing, and an office of disabled student services are available.

Services: Counseling and information services are available, as is tutoring in most subjects, including through the writing/reading, science/engineering, math/business, and academic resource centers. There is a reader service for the blind, and remedial math, reading, and writing.

Campus Safety and Security: Measures include 24-hour foot and vehicle patrol, self-defense education, security escort services, and shuttle buses. There are pamphlets/posters/films, emergency telephones, lighted pathways/sidewalks, and a bicycle patrol.

Programs of Study: UMass Dartmouth confers B.A., B.S., and B.F.A. degrees. Master's and doctoral degrees are also awarded. Bachelor's degrees are awarded in BIOLOGICAL SCIENCE (biochemistry, biology/biological science, and marine biology), BUSINESS (accounting, banking and finance, business administration and management, management information systems, and marketing/retailing/merchandising), COMMUNICATIONS AND THE ARTS (art history and appreciation, ceramic art and design, design, English, fiber/textiles/weaving, French, graphic design, illustration, metal/jewelry, music, painting, photography, Portuguese, sculpture, Spanish, and technical and business writing), COMPUTER AND PHYSICAL SCIENCE (chemistry, computer science, mathematics, and physics), EDUCATION (art), ENGINEERING AND ENVIRONMENTAL DESIGN (civil engineering, computer engineering, electrical/electronics engineering, materials science, mechanical engineering, and textile technology), HEALTH PROFESSIONS (medical laboratory science and nursing), SOCIAL SCIENCE (anthropology, criminal justice, economics, history, humanities and social science, interdisciplinary studies, philosophy, political science/government, psychology, and sociology). Engineering, physical/life sciences, and design/fine arts are the strongest academically. Design, psychology, and nursing are the largest.

Required: The core curriculum requires 9 credits each of communication skills, cultural and artistic literacy, and math/science/technology, 6 each of global awareness and information/computer literacy, and 3 of ethics. Colleges set some additional distribution course requirements. The B.A. requires foreign language study. To graduate, students must complete 120 to 132 credit hours and maintain a 2.0 GPA.

Special: The university permits cross-registration through the SACHEM Consortium of 9 schools in Massachusetts. Study abroad in 9 countries, an engineering or business co-op program, a Washington semester, internships, numerous work-study programs, dual majors, and student-designed majors are available. Teacher certification in elementary and secondary education is available. Nondegree study, pass/fail options, B.S.-M.S. degrees in chemistry and nursing, and credit for life experience are possible. There are 5 national honor societies and a freshman honors program.

Faculty/Classroom: 65% of faculty are male; 35%, female. All teach undergraduates and 60% do research. Graduate students teach 3% of introductory courses. The average class size in an introductory lecture is 28; in a laboratory, 11; and in a regular course, 20.

Admissions: 71% of the 2003-2004 applicants were accepted. The SAT I scores for the 2003-2004 freshman class were: Verbal--30% below 500, 52% between 500 and 599, 17% between 600 and 700, and 1% above 700; Math--27% below 500, 54% between 500 and 599, 17% between 600 and 700, and 2% above 700. 3 freshmen graduated first in their class.

Requirements: The SAT I is required. In addition, applicants should have 4 years of English, 3 each of science and math, 2 of the same foreign language, 1 each of social studies and U.S. history, and 2 of college-preparatory electives. The GED is accepted. An audition is necessary for music majors, and a portfolio is recommended for studio arts and design applicants. All applicants must submit an essay. A GPA of 3.0 is required. AP and CLEP credits are accepted. Important factors in the admissions decision are recommendations by school officials, advanced placement or honor courses, and evidence of special talent.

Procedure: Freshmen are admitted fall and spring. Entrance exams should be taken during the spring of the junior year or early fall of the senior year. There are early decision, early admissions, a rolling admissions, and deferred admissions plans. Application deadlines are open. Application fee is $35 for in-state applicants and $55 for out-of-state applicants. In a recent year, 43 early decision candidates were accepted. Applications are accepted on-line through *www.umassd.edu/admissions/applyonline.cfm.*

Transfer: 447 transfer students enrolled in 2002-2003. Applicants must submit all official college transcripts and must take the SAT I unless they graduated from high school more than 3 years prior to applying. Those with fewer than 30 transferable credits must submit high school records. 45 of 120 credits required for the bachelor's degree must be completed at UMass Dartmouth.

Visiting: There are regularly scheduled orientations for prospective students, including scheduled campus tours Monday through Friday and most Saturdays. There are guides for informal visits and visitors may sit in on classes. To schedule a visit, contact the Admissions Office, or sign up through the school's web site at *www.umassd.edu/admissions/toursignup2.cfm.*

Financial Aid: The FAFSA is required. The priority date for freshman financial aid applications for fall entry is March 1.

International Students: There are 56 international students enrolled. They must score 500 on the written TOEFL and also take the SAT I.

Computers: The mainframe is a DEC Alpha 2100 cluster. There are several computer labs on campus that have more than 368 PCs available, and computer ports are in every dorm room for students with their own terminal to hook into the university mainframe. All students may access the system during the day and evening as well as on weekends. There are no time limits and no fees. It is strongly recommended that all students have a personal computer.

Graduates: From July 1, 2002 to June 30, 2003, 1016 bachelor's degrees were awarded. The most popular majors were psychology (10%), visual design (9%), and marketing (8%). In an average class, 29% graduate in 4 years or less, 49% graduate in 5 years or less, and 53% graduate in 6 years or less. 400 companies recruited on campus in 2002-2003.

Admissions Contact: Steve Briggs, Director of Admissions.
E-mail: *admissions@umassd.edu* Web: *www.umassd.edu/admissions*

UNIVERSITY OF MASSACHUSETTS LOWELL D-1
Lowell, MA 01854

(978) 934-3931 or (978) 934-3931
(800) 410-4607; Fax: (978) 934-3086

Full-time: 3335 men, 2505 women	**Faculty:** 359; I, +$
Part-time: 1953 men, 1213 women	**Ph.D.s:** 94%
Graduate: 1470 men, 1230 women	**Student/Faculty:** 16 to 1
Year: semesters, summer session	**Tuition:** $6213 ($16,651)
Application Deadline: open	**Room & Board:** $5724
Freshman Class: 4233 applied, 2630 accepted, 1020 enrolled	
SAT I Verbal/Math: 537/556	**VERY COMPETITIVE**

The University of Massachussets Lowell, founded in 1895, is a public institution offering undergraduate programs through the schools of arts and sciences, engineering, health professions, management science, and music, and graduate programs in education. There are 5 undergraduate schools and 1 graduate school. In addition to regional accreditation, UMass Lowell has baccalaureate program accreditation with AACSB, ABET, APTA, CAHEA, CSAB, NASAD, NASM, NCATE, and NLN. The 3 libraries contain 810,849 volumes, 1,701,316 microform items, and 7205 audio/video tapes/CDs, and subscribe to 1865 periodicals. Computerized library services include the card catalog, interlibrary loans, and database searching. Special learning facilities include a learning resource center, art gallery, radio station, many experimental and investigative labs, and the Research Foundation, which includes a materials testing division and centers for atmospheric research and tropical disease. The 100-acre campus is in an urban area 30 miles northwest of Boston. Including any residence halls, there are 37 buildings.

Student Life: 89% of undergraduates are from Massachusetts. Students are from 41 states, 68 foreign countries, and Canada. 62% are white. The average age of freshmen is 18; all undergraduates, 23. 26% do not continue beyond their first year; 44% remain to graduate.

Housing: 2536 students can be accommodated in college housing, which includes single-sex and coed dorms, off-campus apartments, and married-student housing. In addition, there are special-interest houses. On-campus housing is available on a first-come, first-served basis. 68% of students commute. All students may keep cars.

Activities: There are no fraternities or sororities. There are 100 groups on campus, including art, band, cheerleading, computers, drama, ethnic, gay, honors, international, marching band, newspaper, pep band, photography, political, professional, radio and TV, religious, social, social service, student government, and yearbook.

Sports: There are 15 intercollegiate sports for men and 10 for women, and 34 intramural sports for men and 34 for women. Facilities include a 2000-seat gym, a pool, weight-training facilities, and areas for gymnastics, wrestling, and judo. There are also courts for handball, squash, and tennis and various playing fields.

Disabled Students: 70% of the campus is accessible. Wheelchair ramps, elevators, special parking, specially equipped rest rooms, special class scheduling, lowered drinking fountains, and lowered telephones are available.

Services: Counseling and information services are available, as is tutoring in most subjects. There is a reader service for the blind and remedial writing.

Campus Safety and Security: Measures include 24-hour foot and vehicle patrol, security escort services, shuttle buses, and informal discussions. There are pamphlets/posters/films, emergency telephones, and lighted pathways/sidewalks.

Programs of Study: UMass Lowell confers B.A., B.S., B.F.A., B.L.A., B.M., B.S.B.A., B.S.E., B.S.E.T., B.S.I.M., and B.S.I.T. degrees. Associate, master's, and doctoral degrees are also awarded. Bachelor's degrees are awarded in BIOLOGICAL SCIENCE (biology/biological science), BUSINESS (business administration and management), COMMUNICATIONS AND THE ARTS (English, fine arts, modern language, and music performance), COMPUTER AND PHYSICAL SCIENCE (applied mathematics, chemistry, computer science, information sciences and systems, mathematics, and physics), ENGINEERING AND ENVIRONMENTAL DESIGN (chemical engineering, civil engineering, electrical/electronics engineering, engineering technology, environmental science, industrial administration/management, industrial engineering technology, mechanical engineering, and plastics engineering), HEALTH PROFESSIONS (clinical science, community health work, exercise science, and nursing), SOCIAL SCIENCE (American studies, criminal justice, economics, history, liberal arts/general studies, philosophy, political science/government, psychology, and sociology). Engineering and management are the largest.

Required: All students must complete a minimum of 120 credits with a 2.0 GPA. Core requirements include 6 credits of English composition, 3 credits of human values, and an area distribution requirement of 27 to 29 credits outside the major in behavioral and social science, fine arts and the humanities, and math and the sciences.

Special: Cross-registration, co-op, and work-study programs are available, as are opportunities for study abroad. The university offers a combined B.A.-B.S. degree in engineering, dual majors, nondegree study, and pass/fail options. There are 2 national honor societies and a freshman honors program.

Faculty/Classroom: 68% of faculty are male; 32%, female. All teach undergraduates.

Admissions: 62% of the 2003-2004 applicants were accepted. The SAT I scores for the 2003-2004 freshman class were: Verbal--29% below 500, 50% between 500 and 599, 18% between 600 and 700, and 3% above 700; Math--18% below 500, 53% between 500 and 599, 26% between 600 and 700, and 3% above 700. 28% of the current freshmen were in the top fifth of their class; 61% were in the top two fifths. 6 freshmen graduated first in their class.

Requirements: The SAT I or ACT is required; the SAT I is preferred. In addition, applicants should have a high school diploma or the GED. The university recommends that secondary school preparation include 4 courses in English, 3 each in social science/history and math, 2 each in science and a foreign language, and 2 academic electives. Prospective music majors must audition, and an interview is recommended for all students. A GPA of 3.0 is required. AP and CLEP credits are accepted.

Procedure: Freshmen are admitted fall and spring. Entrance exams should be taken by January of the senior year. There is a deferred admissions plan. Applications should be filed by July 1 for fall entry. Application fee is $20. Notification sent on a rolling basis. Applications are accepted on-line.

Transfer: 767 transfer students enrolled in 2002-2003. Transfer applicants must present at least a 2.0 GPA in previous college work. Those with fewer than 30 credits must meet freshman admission requirements. 30 of 120 credits required for the bachelor's degree must be completed at UMass Lowell.

Visiting: There are regularly scheduled orientations for prospective students. To schedule a visit, contact the Office of Student Services at (978) 934-2105.

Financial Aid: In 2003-2004, 63% of all full-time freshmen received some form of financial aid. 39% of full-time freshmen received need-based aid. The average freshman award was $7015. Need-based scholarships or need-based grants averaged $3580; need-based self-help aid (loans and jobs) averaged $3054; non-need-based athletic scholarships averaged $6958; other non-need-based awards and non-need-based scholarships averaged $3221; and other awards averaged $2117. 16% of undergraduates work part time. Average annual earnings from campus work are $3084. The average financial indebtedness of the 2003 graduate was $15,258. The FAFSA is required. The priority date for freshman financial aid applications for fall entry is March 1.

International Students: There are 153 international students enrolled. They must score 500 on the written TOEFL or 178 on the electronic version and also take the SAT I or the ACT. The minimum score required on the SAT I or ACT varies according to GPA.

Computers: The mainframes are a cluster of DEC VAX 6420s, 8700s, and 8800s. 2500 terminals, PCs, and workstations are linked to more than 150 multiuser systems in a campuswide communications network. All students may access the system. There are no time limits and no fees.

Graduates: From July 1, 2002 to June 30, 2003, 1096 bachelor's degrees were awarded. The most popular majors were business administration (21%), criminal justice (11%), and psychology (8%). In an average class, 22% graduate in 4 years or less, 39% graduate in 5 years or less, and 44% graduate in 6 years or less.

Admissions Contact: Lisa Johnson, Director, Admissions.
Web: *admissions@uml.edu*

WELLESLEY COLLEGE   D-2
Wellesley, MA 02481   (781) 283-2270; Fax: (781) 283-3678

Full- and part-time: 2300 students	**Faculty:** IIB, ++$
Graduate: none	**Ph.D.s:** n/av
Year: semesters	**Student/Faculty:** n/av
Application Deadline: January 15	**Tuition:** $27,904
	Room & Board: $8612

Freshman Class: 3434 applied, 1394 accepted, 591 enrolled
SAT I Verbal/Math: 678/673   **ACT:** 29   **MOST COMPETITIVE**

Wellesley College, established in 1870, is a small, private, diverse liberal arts and sciences college for women. The 5 libraries contain 1.3 million volumes, and subscribe to 2500 periodicals. Computerized library services include the card catalog, interlibrary loans, and database searching. Special learning facilities include a learning resource center, art gallery, radio station, a science center, a botanic greenhouse, an observatory, a center for developmental studies and services, centers for research on women and child study, and a media and technology center. The 500-acre campus is in a suburban area 12 miles west of Boston. Including any residence halls, there are 64 buildings.

Student Life: 80% of undergraduates are from out of state, mostly the Middle Atlantic. Students are from 50 states, 52 foreign countries, and Canada. 63% are from public schools. 48% are white; 25% Asian American. The average age of freshmen is 18; all undergraduates, 20. 5% do not continue beyond their first year; 87% remain to graduate.

Housing: 2120 students can be accommodated in college housing, which includes single-sex dorms. In addition, there are language houses, special-interest houses, language corridors, and co-ops. On-campus housing is guaranteed for all 4 years. 97% of students live on campus. Upperclassmen may keep cars.

Activities: There are no sororities. There are more than 160 groups on campus, including art, choir, chorus, computers, dance, debate, drama, ethnic, film, gay, honors, international, jazz band, literary magazine, musical theater, newspaper, orchestra, photography, political, professional, radio and TV, religious, social, social service, student government, symphony, and yearbook. Popular campus events include Parent and Family Weekend, Spring Weekend, and International Week.

Sports: Facilities include an indoor pool, dance studios, a weight room, an indoor track, a golf course, and courts for racquetball, squash, tennis, and volleyball.

Disabled Students: All of the campus is accessible. Wheelchair ramps, elevators, special parking, specially equipped rest rooms, special class scheduling, lowered drinking fountains, lowered telephones, special housing, and signage in braille are available.

Services: Counseling and information services are available, as is tutoring in every subject. There is a reader service for the blind.

Campus Safety and Security: Measures include 24-hour foot and vehicle patrol, self-defense education, security escort services, and shuttle buses. There are informal discussions, pamphlets/posters/films, emergency telephones, and lighted pathways/sidewalks.

Programs of Study: Wellesley confers the B.A. degree. Bachelor's degrees are awarded in AGRICULTURE (environmental studies), BIOLOGICAL SCIENCE (biochemistry, biology/biological science, and neurosciences), COMMUNICATIONS AND THE ARTS (art history and appreciation, Chinese, comparative literature, dramatic arts, English, film arts, French, German, Greek, Japanese, Latin, music, Russian, Russian languages and literature, Spanish, and studio art), COMPUTER AND PHYSICAL SCIENCE (astronomy, astrophysics, chemistry, computer science, geology, mathematics, and physics), ENGINEERING AND ENVIRONMENTAL DESIGN (architecture), SOCIAL SCIENCE (African American studies, American studies, anthropology, archeology, Asian/Oriental studies, classical/ancient civilization, cognitive science, economics, French studies, German area studies, history, international relations, Italian studies, Japanese studies, Judaic studies, Latin American studies, medieval studies, Middle Eastern studies, peace studies, philosophy, political science/government, psychology, religion, sociology, and women's studies). Psychology, English, and economics are the largest.

Required: All students must complete 32 units, at least 8 of which are in the major field, with a minimum 2.0 GPA. Requirements include 3 courses each in humanities, social science, and natural science and math; 1 multicultural course; 1 semester of expository writing in any department; and 8 credits in phys ed. Students must also possess proficiency in a modern or ancient foreign language. A thesis is required for departmental honors. A quantitative reasoning requirement must be satisfied by all students.

Special: Students may cross-register at MIT, Brandeis University, or Babson College. Exchange programs are available with Spelman College in Georgia and Mills College in California, with members of the Twelve College Exchange Program, with Williams College's maritime studies program, and with Connecticut College's National Theater Institute. Study abroad is possible through Wellesley-administered programs in France and Austria, exchange programs in Argentina, Japan, Korea, and the United Kingdom, and other programs in Italy, Japan, Spain, South Africa, and China. There are summer internship programs in Boston and

Washington, D.C. Dual majors, student-designed majors, nondegree study, and pass/fail options are possible. A 3-2 program with MIT awards a B.A.-B.S. degree. There are 2 national honor societies, including Phi Beta Kappa, and 51 departmental honors programs.

Admissions: 41% of the 2003-2004 applicants were accepted. The SAT I scores for the 2003-2004 freshman class were: Verbal--1% below 500, 11% between 500 and 599, 43% between 600 and 700, and 45% above 700; Math--1% below 500, 12% between 500 and 599, 46% between 600 and 700, and 41% above 700. The ACT scores were 6% between 18 and 23; 39% between 24 and 29; and 55% between 30 and 36. 95% of the current freshmen were in the top quarter of their class; all were in the top half.

Requirements: The SAT I and 3 SAT II: Subject tests (including the writing test), or the ACT, are required. Wellesley College does not require a fixed plan of secondary school course preparation. Entering students normally have completed 4 years of college preparatory studies in secondary school that include training in clear and coherent writing and interpreting literature; history; principles of math (typically 4 years); competence in at least 1 foreign language, ancient or modern (usually 4 years of study); and experience in at least 2 lab sciences. An essay is required, and an interview is recommended. AP credits are accepted. Important factors in the admissions decision are advanced placement or honor courses, extracurricular activities record, and recommendations by school officials.

Procedure: Freshmen are admitted in the fall. Entrance exams should be taken during the spring of the junior year or fall of the senior year (no later than December). There are early decision, early admissions, and deferred admissions plans. Early decision applications should be filed by November 1; regular applications, by January 15 for fall entry. The fall 2003 application fee was $50. Notification of early decision is sent December 15; regular decision, by April 1. 123 early decision candidates were accepted for the 2003-2004 class. 708 applicants were on the 2003 waiting list; 93 were admitted. Applications are accepted on-line through the college's web site or Common App.

Transfer: 12 transfer students enrolled in 2002-2003. Applicants must provide high school and college transcripts, SAT I and II or ACT scores, a personal statement, and a statement of good standing from institutions previously attended. An interview is required. 16 of 32 units required for the bachelor's degree must be completed at Wellesley.

Visiting: There are guides for informal visits and visitors may sit in on classes and stay overnight. To schedule a visit, contact the Admissions Office.

Financial Aid: In 2003-2004, 56% of all full-time freshmen and 54% of continuing full-time students received some form of financial aid, including need-based aid. The average freshman award was $22,614. Average annual earnings from campus work are $2000. Wellesley is a member of CSS. The CSS/Profile or FAFSA, the college's own financial statement and the most recent income tax returns of parents and student are required. The deadline for filing freshman financial aid applications for fall entry is January 15.

International Students: There were 162 international students enrolled in a recent year. The school actively recruits these students. They must score 600 on the written TOEFL or 250 on the electronic version or take the ELPT or the APIEL. They must also take the SAT I and SAT II: Subject tests in writing and 2 others areas, or the ACT.

Computers: The mainframes are a DEC VAX 8550 and a Digital AXP. Students may access the mainframe through more than 200 PCs located in the science center, library, and dorms. All students may access the system. There are no time limits and no fees.

Graduates: In a recent year, 601 bachelor's degrees were awarded. The most popular majors were economics (9%), psychology (9%), and English (9%). In an average class, 86% graduate in 4 years or less, 89% graduate in 5 years or less, and 90% graduate in 6 years or less. 124 companies recruited on campus in a recent year. Of a recent graduating class, 19% were enrolled in graduate school within 6 months of graduation and 77% were employed.

Admissions Contact: Dean of Admission. A video is available. E-mail: *admission@wellesley.edu* Web: *www.wellesley.edu*

WENTWORTH INSTITUTE OF TECHNOLOGY E-2
Boston, MA 02115 (617) 989-4000
(800) 556-0610; Fax: (617) 989-4010

Full-time: 2147 men, 500 women	**Faculty:** 122
Part-time: 499 men, 89 women	**Ph.D.s:** 30%
Graduate: none	**Student/Faculty:** 22 to 1
Year: semesters, summer session	**Tuition:** $15,000
Application Deadline: May 1	**Room & Board:** $8000
Freshman Class: 3719 applied, 2427 accepted, 978 enrolled	
SAT I Verbal/Math: 514/553	**COMPETITIVE**

Wentworth Institute of Technology, founded in 1904, is a private college specializing in architecture, design, engineering, technology, and management. In addition to regional accreditation, Wentworth has baccalaureate program accreditation with ABET, ACCE, FIDER, IACBE, and

NAAB. The library contains 77,000 volumes, 90 microform items, and 750 audio/video tapes/CDs, and subscribes to 500 periodicals. Computerized library services include the card catalog, interlibrary loans, database searching, and Internet access. Special learning facilities include a learning resource center, radio station, printed-circuit lab, CAD/CAM/CAE labs, design studios, and numerically controlled manufacturing systems. The 35-acre campus is in an urban area in Boston. Including any residence halls, there are 27 buildings.

Student Life: 65% of students are white. The average age of freshmen is 20; all undergraduates, 22. 31% do not continue beyond their first year; 52% remain to graduate.

Housing: 1665 students can be accommodated in college housing, which includes coed dorms and on-campus apartments. On-campus housing is available on a first-come, first-served basis and is available on a lottery system for upperclassmen. Priority is given to out-of-town students. 60% of students live on campus. Alcohol is not permitted. Upperclassmen may keep cars.

Activities: There are no fraternities or sororities. There are 40 groups on campus, including computers, dance, drama, ethnic, gay, honors, international, literary magazine, musical theater, newspaper, orchestra, professional, radio and TV, religious, social, social service, student government, and yearbook. Popular campus events include Design Lecture Series, Beaux Arts Ball, and Women's History Month.

Sports: There are 9 intercollegiate sports for men and 6 for women, and 5 intramural sports for men and 5 for women. Facilities include gyms, tennis courts, a riflery range, a fitness center, an outdoor basketball court, and softball, soccer, and lacrosse playing fields.

Disabled Students: 30% of the campus is accessible. Wheelchair ramps, elevators, special parking, specially equipped rest rooms, special class scheduling, lowered drinking fountains, and lowered telephones are available.

Services: Counseling and information services are available, as is tutoring in every subject. There is remedial math and writing. Free tutoring is available to all students through the learning center.

Campus Safety and Security: Measures include 24-hour foot and vehicle patrol, self-defense education, security escort services, and shuttle buses. There are pamphlets/posters/films, emergency telephones, and lighted pathways/sidewalks. All campus police officers have emergency medical training.

Programs of Study: Wentworth confers B.S. and B.Arch. degrees. Associate degrees are also awarded. Bachelor's degrees are awarded in COMMUNICATIONS AND THE ARTS (industrial design), COMPUTER AND PHYSICAL SCIENCE (computer science and information sciences and systems), ENGINEERING AND ENVIRONMENTAL DESIGN (architectural technology, architecture, civil engineering technology, computer technology, construction management, construction technology, electrical/electronics engineering technology, electromechanical technology, environmental engineering, industrial administration/management, interior design, mechanical engineering technology, and technological management). Architectural engineering technology, computer science, and electronic engineering technology are the largest.

Required: For a bachelor's degree, students must complete a total of 136 to 176 hours, depending on the major, with a minimum GPA of 2.0 overall and 2.5 in the major. An introductory computer course is required of all students. All full-time bachelor's degree candidates must complete 2 semesters of co-op, beginning after the first 2 years of study. A writing competency assessment is required at the end of the sophomore year.

Special: Wentworth offers extensive cooperative programs; cross-registration with other members of the Colleges of the Fenway Consortium; study abroad, including study in France for third-year architecture students; interdisciplinary majors, including engineering technology and facilities planning and management; a dual major in technical management; and nondegree study. Most students at the bachelor's level attend school in the summer, as most cooperative work occurs during the academic year. There is 1 national honor society.

Faculty/Classroom: 76% of faculty are male; 24%, female. All teach undergraduates. The average class size in an introductory lecture is 25; in a laboratory, 25; and in a regular course, 22.

Admissions: 65% of the 2003-2004 applicants were accepted. The SAT I scores for the 2003-2004 freshman class were: Verbal--41% below 500, 44% between 500 and 599, 14% between 600 and 700, and 1% above 700; Math--22% below 500, 50% between 500 and 599, 25% between 600 and 700, and 3% above 700.

Requirements: The SAT I or ACT is required. In addition, applicants must be graduates of an accredited secondary school or have the GED. High school course requirements vary by major. AP and CLEP credits are accepted. Important factors in the admissions decision are advanced placement or honor courses, leadership record, and extracurricular activities record.

Procedure: Freshmen are admitted fall and spring. Entrance exams should be taken in the spring of the junior year or the fall of the senior year. There is a rolling admissions plan and a deferred admissions plan. Applications should be filed by May 1 for fall entry and December 1 for spring entry, along with a $30 fee (waived for on-line applications). Notification is sent on a rolling basis. Applications are accepted on-line through the school's web site.

Transfer: 144 transfer students enrolled in a recent year. Requirements for transfer students vary by program. All applicants must submit official college and high school transcripts. Portfolios and faculty reviews are recommended of applicants to industrial design, interior design, and architecture programs. Grades of C or better transfer for credit. Transfer students must take 50% of the course work in their degree program at Wentworth to graduate.

Visiting: There are regularly scheduled orientations for prospective students, including a 2-day orientation with an optional overnight stay. There are guides for informal visits and visitors may sit in on classes and stay overnight. To schedule a visit, contact the Admissions Office.

Financial Aid: In a recent year, 76% of all full-time freshmen and 43% of continuing full-time students received some form of financial aid. 57% of full-time freshmen and 43% of continuing full-time students received need-based aid. The average freshman award was $6725. 29% of undergraduates work part time. Average annual earnings from campus work are $1600. The average financial indebtedness of a recent graduate was $10,199. The FAFSA is required. The priority date for freshman financial aid applications for fall entry is March 1. The deadline for filing freshman financial aid applications for fall entry is rolling.

International Students: There were 225 international students enrolled in a recent year. The school actively recruits these students. They must score 525 on the written TOEFL or 197 on the electronic version or take the MELAB, the Comprehensive English Language Test, or the college's own test, and also take the SAT I or ACT, with the SAT I recommended.

Computers: The mainframe is a DEC VAX 400/300. The academic VAX may be accessed via 30 terminals and several modems, as well as from 115 networked PCs in various student labs. In addition, 122 Pentium systems and 47 Mac and Power Mac systems, all networked, are available in student labs throughout the institute. All residence hall rooms have Internet access. All students have "LConnect" web portal and e-mail accounts. All students may access the system. There are no time limits and no fees. It is strongly recommended that all students have a personal computer.

Admissions Contact: Kathleen Lynch, Director of Admissions. E-mail: *admissions@wit.edu* Web: *www.wit.edu*

WESTERN NEW ENGLAND COLLEGE

Springfield, MA 01119

B-3
(413) 782-1321
(800) 325-1122 ext. 1321; Fax: (413) 782-1777

Full-time: 1263 men, 974 women	**Faculty:** 127; IIA, ++$
Part-time: 925 men, 206 women	**Ph.D.s:** 92%
Graduate: 501 men, 226 women	**Student/Faculty:** 18 to 1
Year: semesters, summer session	**Tuition:** $20,824
Application Deadline: open	**Room & Board:** $8100
Freshman Class: n/av	
SAT I Verbal/Math: 520/540	**COMPETITIVE**

Western New England College, founded in 1919, is a private institution offering undergraduate programs in business, engineering, and liberal arts. There are 3 undergraduate and 2 graduate schools. In addition to regional accreditation, WNEC has baccalaureate program accreditation with AACSB, ABET, and CSWE. The library contains 123,475 volumes and 364,075 microform items, and subscribes to 176 periodicals. Computerized library services include the card catalog, interlibrary loans, database searching, and Internet access. Special learning facilities include an art gallery and radio station. The 215-acre campus is in a suburban area 90 miles west of Boston. Including any residence halls, there are 21 buildings.

Student Life: 58% of undergraduates are from out of state, mostly the Northeast. Students are from 29 states and 4 foreign countries. 86% are white. 81% are claim no religious affiliation; 14% Catholic. The average age of freshmen is 18; all undergraduates, 20. 25% do not continue beyond their first year; 54% remain to graduate.

Housing: 1680 students can be accommodated in college housing, which includes single-sex and coed dorms and on-campus apartments. Students are often grouped by academic interest areas or theme housing. On-campus housing is guaranteed for all 4 years. 79% of students live on campus. All students may keep cars.

Activities: There are no fraternities or sororities. There are 60 groups on campus, including art, cheerleading, chorus, computers, dance, drama, ethnic, gay, honors, international, jazz band, literary magazine, newspaper, pep band, photography, political, professional, radio and TV, religious, social, social service, student government, and yearbook. Popular campus events include Spring Week, Family and Friends Weekend, and Winter Week.

Sports: There are 10 intercollegiate sports for men and 9 for women, and 9 intramural sports for men and 9 for women. Facilities include a healthful living center equipped for basketball (2000 seats), wrestling, racquetball, squash, aerobics, fitness, and volleyball, as well as a weight room, an 8-lane pool, and a track. There is also a 1200-seat football stadium.

Disabled Students: 90% of the campus is accessible. Wheelchair ramps, elevators, special parking, specially equipped rest rooms, special class scheduling, lowered drinking fountains, and lowered telephones are available.

Services: Counseling and information services are available, as is tutoring in most subjects.

Campus Safety and Security: Measures include 24-hour foot and vehicle patrol, self-defense education, security escort services, and informal discussions. There are pamphlets/posters/films, emergency telephones, lighted pathways/sidewalks, security cameras, medical response, fire response, and a comprehensive public safety awareness program.

Programs of Study: WNEC confers B.A., B.S., B.S.B.A., B.S.E., B.S.E.E., B.S.I.E., B.S.L.E., B.S.M.E., and B.S.W. degrees. Associate and master's degrees are also awarded. Bachelor's degrees are awarded in BIOLOGICAL SCIENCE (biology/biological science), BUSINESS (accounting, banking and finance, business administration and management, management science, marketing/retailing/merchandising, and sports management), COMMUNICATIONS AND THE ARTS (advertising, communications, and English), COMPUTER AND PHYSICAL SCIENCE (chemistry, computer science, information sciences and systems, and mathematics), EDUCATION (elementary and secondary), ENGINEERING AND ENVIRONMENTAL DESIGN (bioengineering, biomedical engineering, computer engineering, electrical/electronics engineering, industrial engineering, and mechanical engineering), SOCIAL SCIENCE (criminal justice, economics, history, international studies, law enforcement and corrections, liberal arts/general studies, political science/government, psychology, social work, and sociology). Criminal justice, management, and psychology are the largest.

Required: To graduate, students must complete 122 credit hours, with a minimum GPA of 2.0. Requirements include 2 courses each in English, math, lab science, and phys ed and 1 course each in history, culture, and computers. A first-year seminar is also required for freshmen. Other requirements vary according to the major.

Special: Students may cross-register with cooperating colleges of Greater Springfield. The college offers internships, study abroad, a Washington semester, work-study programs, B.A.-B.S. degrees, an accelerated degree program, and dual and student-designed majors. The 3+3 law program offers qualified students the opportunity to earn a J.D. in 6 years. Pharmacy and physician assistant programs are offered in association with the Massachusetts College of Pharmacy and Health Sciences. There are 6 national honor societies, and a freshman honors program.

Faculty/Classroom: 68% of faculty are male; 32%, female. No introductory courses are taught by graduate students. The average class size in an introductory lecture is 23; in a laboratory, 20; and in a regular course, 20.

Admissions: The SAT I scores for the 2003-2004 freshman class were: Verbal--36% below 500, 49% between 500 and 599, 14% between 600 and 700, and 1% above 700; Math--30% below 500, 46% between 500 and 599, 22% between 600 and 700, and 2% above 700. 24% of the current freshmen were in the top fifth of their class; 53% were in the top two fifths.

Requirements: The SAT I or ACT is required. In addition, applicants must be graduates of an approved secondary school and must have completed 4 years of high school English, 2 or more years of math, 1 or more years of science, and 1 year of history and social science. An interview is recommended. A GPA of 2.2 is required. AP and CLEP credits are accepted. Important factors in the admissions decision are advanced placement or honor courses, extracurricular activities record, and recommendations by school officials.

Procedure: Freshmen are admitted fall and spring. Entrance exams should be taken in the spring of the junior year or fall of the senior year. There are early admissions and deferred admissions plans. Application deadlines are open. The priority date is March 1. The fall 2003 application fee was $50. Notification is sent on a rolling basis. Applications are accepted on-line.

Transfer: 108 transfer students enrolled in 2002-2003. Applicants must have a minimum GPA of 2.3. Grades of C or better transfer for credit. The college admits transfer students in the fall and spring. 30 of 122 credits required for the bachelor's degree must be completed at WNEC.

Visiting: There are regularly scheduled orientations for prospective students, including multiple open houses. There are guides for informal visits and visitors may sit in on classes and stay overnight. To schedule a visit, contact the Undergraduate Admissions Office.

Financial Aid: In 2003-2004, 93% of all full-time freshmen received some form of financial aid. 77% of full-time freshmen received need-based aid. The average freshman award was $12,483. WNEC is a member of CSS. The FAFSA and federal tax returns are required. The priority date for freshman financial aid applications for fall entry is April 1. The deadline for filing freshman financial aid applications for fall entry is rolling.

International Students: There are 8 international students enrolled. They must score 500 on the written TOEFL or 173 on the electronic version.

Computers: There are 489 PCs/terminals in labs in various locations on campus. All students have e-mail and Internet access from residence hall rooms. All students may access the system at varying hours from campus labs; 24 hours a day from residence halls. There are no time limits and no fees.

Graduates: From July 1, 2002 to June 30, 2003, 674 bachelor's degrees were awarded. The most popular majors were accounting (7%), criminal justice (7%), and psychology (7%). In an average class, 42% graduate in 4 years or less, 52% graduate in 5 years or less, and 54% graduate in 6 years or less. Of the 2002 graduating class, 26% were enrolled in graduate school within 6 months of graduation and 85% were employed.

Admissions Contact: Dr. Charles R. Pollock, Vice President for Enrollment Management. A video is available. E-mail: *ugradmis@wnec.edu* Web: *www.wnec.edu*

WESTFIELD STATE COLLEGE
Westfield, MA 01086-1630   B-3
(413) 572-5218
(800) 322-8401; Fax: (413) 572-0520

Full-time: 1648 men, 2066 women	Faculty: 171; IIA, av$
Part-time: 255 men, 323 women	Ph.D.s: 85%
Graduate: 197 men, 448 women	Student/Faculty: 22 to 1
Year: semesters, summer session	Tuition: $4857 ($10,937)
Application Deadline: March 1	Room & Board: $5290
Freshman Class: 3838 applied, 2521 accepted, 852 enrolled	
SAT I Verbal/Math: 520/510	COMPETITIVE

Westfield State College, founded in 1838, is a public college with liberal arts and teacher preparation programs and professional training. There is 1 undergraduate and 1 graduate school. In addition to regional accreditation, Westfield State has baccalaureate program accreditation with CAAHEP and CSWE. The library contains 124,363 volumes, 547,002 microform items, and 2379 audio/video tapes/CDs, and subscribes to 819 periodicals. Computerized library services include the card catalog, interlibrary loans, and database searching. Special learning facilities include a learning resource center, art gallery, radio station, TV station, and a geology museum. The 257-acre campus is in a rural area 15 miles west of Springfield. Including any residence halls, there are 14 buildings.
Student Life: 93% of undergraduates are from Massachusetts. Students are from 20 states, 1 foreign country, and Canada. 78% are white. The average age of freshmen is 18; all undergraduates, 20. 26% do not continue beyond their first year.
Housing: 2114 students can be accommodated in college housing, which includes coed dorms and on-campus apartments. In addition, there is a living/learning unit and special housing for international students. On-campus housing is guaranteed for all 4 years. 59% of students live on campus; of those, 70% remain on campus on weekends. Upperclassmen may keep cars.
Activities: There are no fraternities or sororities. There are 50 groups on campus, including art, band, chess, choir, chorale, chorus, drama, ethnic, gay, honors, jazz band, literary magazine, musical theater, newspaper, orchestra, pep band, photography, political, professional, radio and TV, religious, social service, student government, and yearbook. Popular campus events include Halloween Dance, Spring Weekend, and Comedy Night.
Sports: There are 6 intercollegiate sports for men and 8 for women, and 11 intramural sports for men and 11 for women. Facilities include a track, baseball and softball fields, tennis courts, a 400-seat gym, and a 5000-seat stadium.
Disabled Students: 60% of the campus is accessible. Wheelchair ramps, elevators, special parking, specially equipped rest rooms, special class scheduling, lowered telephones, and special housing are available.
Services: Counseling and information services are available, as is tutoring in every subject. There is a reader service for the blind and remedial math, reading, and writing.
Campus Safety and Security: Measures include 24-hour foot and vehicle patrol, security escort services, shuttle buses, and pamphlets/posters/films. There are emergency telephones and lighted pathways/sidewalks.
Programs of Study: Westfield State confers B.A., B.S., and B.S.E. degrees. Master's degrees are also awarded. Bachelor's degrees are awarded in BIOLOGICAL SCIENCE (biology/biological science), BUSINESS (business administration and management), COMMUNICATIONS AND THE ARTS (communications, dramatic arts, English, fine arts, and music), COMPUTER AND PHYSICAL SCIENCE (computer science, information sciences and systems, and mathematics), EDUCATION (art, business, early childhood, elementary, middle school, music, science, secondary, and special), ENGINEERING AND ENVIRONMENTAL DESIGN (environmental science), SOCIAL SCIENCE (criminal justice, economics, history, interdisciplinary studies, physical fitness/movement, political science/government, psychology, social work, sociology, and urban studies). Computer science, English, and psychology are the strongest academically. Criminal justice, education, and business are the largest.

Required: Students must complete a total of 120 credit hours, with 43 or more credits in 8 specified areas and 30 to 40 hours in the major. The college requires a 2.0 GPA overall and 2.0 in major courses. U.S. history or government and diversity awareness courses are required.
Special: Students may cross-register through College Academic Program Sharing, National Student Exchange, and Cooperating Colleges of Greater Springfield. Internships are for credit only in conjunction with all major programs. The college offers study abroad in 36 countries, a Washington semester for political science, criminal justice, and psychology majors, dual majors, student-designed majors, and some credit for military experience. There are 8 national honor societies and a freshman honors program.
Faculty/Classroom: 63% of faculty are male; 37%, female. All teach undergraduates. No introductory courses are taught by graduate students. The average class size in an introductory lecture is 28; in a laboratory, 15; and in a regular course, 25.
Admissions: 66% of the 2003-2004 applicants were accepted. The SAT I scores for the 2003-2004 freshman class were: Verbal--40% below 500, 50% between 500 and 599, 9% between 600 and 700, and 1% above 700; Math--42% below 500, 50% between 500 and 599, and 9% between 600 and 700.
Requirements: The SAT I is required. In addition, applicants must achieve between a 2.0 and 3.0 cumulative average in academic subjects, contingent upon the SAT I scores. They must be graduates of an accredited secondary school and must have completed 4 years of college preparatory level English, 3 years of math (algebra I and II and geometry), 2 years of social sciences (including 1 year of U.S history), 3 sciences, including 2 with lab, 2 foreign language, and 2 years of electives. The GED is accepted. A portfolio is required for admission to the art program, and an audition is necessary for admission to the music program. A GPA of 2.0 is required. AP and CLEP credits are accepted. Important factors in the admissions decision are advanced placement or honor courses, leadership record, and evidence of special talent.
Procedure: Freshmen are admitted fall and spring. Entrance exams should be taken in the spring of the junior year and fall of the senior year. There is a deferred admissions plan. Applications should be filed by March 1 for fall entry and November 15 for spring entry along with a $25 application fee (in-state) or $40 (if out-of-state). Notification is sent on a rolling basis between January 1 and April 15. Applications are accepted on-line through *http://infowise.wsc.ma.edu*.
Transfer: 284 transfer students enrolled in 2002-2003. Transfer students must have 24 transferable credits with a minimum cumulative GPA of 2.0 (higher for some majors). A grade of C- or better with a 2.0 GPA will transfer for credit. Of the 120 credits required for a bachelor's degree, a minimum of 30 credits must be completed at the college. Transfer students are admitted in the fall and spring. 30 of 120 credits required for the bachelor's degree must be completed at Westfield State.
Visiting: There are regularly scheduled orientations for prospective students, including a campus tour, classroom observation, academic department presentations, lunch with faculty, staff, and students, and a question-and-answer session moderated by a panel of administrators. There are guides for informal visits. To schedule a visit, contact the Admission Office.
Financial Aid: In 2003-2004, 58% of all full-time freshmen and 62% of continuing full-time students received some form of financial aid. At least 44% of full-time freshmen and 45% of continuing full-time students received need-based aid. The average freshman award was $4878. Need-based scholarships or need-based grants averaged $3764; and need-based self-help aid (loans and jobs) averaged $2330. 21% of undergraduates work part time. The average financial indebtedness of the 2003 graduate was $12,347. Westfield State is a member of CSS. The FAFSA is required. The deadline for filing freshman financial aid applications for fall entry is March 1.
International Students: They must score 550 on the written TOEFL and also take the SAT I.
Computers: The mainframe is a DEC Alpha. There are 200 public access PCs in 9 campus labs supporting both Mac and PC platforms. The campus network has 650 nodes. Residence halls are fully wired for Internet access and about a quarter of resident students are connected. All students may access the system. There are no time limits and no fees.
Graduates: In a recent year, 840 bachelor's degrees were awarded. The most popular majors were criminal justice (20%), elementary education (15%), and business management (13%). In an average class, 37% graduate in 4 years or less, 52% graduate in 5 years or less, and 53% graduate in 6 years or less. 80 companies recruited on campus in a recent year.

Admissions Contact: Michelle Mattie, Director of Student Administration Service Center. A video is available.
E-mail: *admission@wsc.ma.edu* Web: *www.wsc.ma.edu*

WHEATON COLLEGE
D-3
Norton, MA 02766
(508) 286-8251
(800) 394-6003; Fax: (508) 286-8271

Full-time: 564 men, 981 women	**Faculty:** 121; IIB, ++$
Part-time: 5 men, 15 women	**Ph.D.s:** 97%
Graduate: none	**Student/Faculty:** 13 to 1
Year: semesters	**Tuition:** $28,900
Application Deadline: January 15	**Room & Board:** $7430
Freshman Class: 3465 applied, 1492 accepted, 445 enrolled	
SAT I Verbal/Math: 620/610	**ACT:** 25 **HIGHLY COMPETITIVE**

Wheaton College, established in 1834, is an independent liberal arts institution. The library contains 373,659 volumes, 84,124 microform items, and 13,306 audio/video tapes/CDs, and subscribes to 3186 periodicals. Computerized library services include the card catalog, interlibrary loans, database searching, and Internet access. Special learning facilities include a learning resource center, art gallery, planetarium, radio station, and TV station. The 385-acre campus is in a suburban area 35 miles southeast of Boston and 15 miles north of Providence. Including any residence halls, there are 87 buildings.

Student Life: 67% of undergraduates are from out of state, mostly the Northeast and Middle Atlantic. Students are from 42 states, 32 foreign countries, and Canada. 63% are from public schools. 80% are white. The average age of freshmen is 18; all undergraduates, 20. 11% do not continue beyond their first year; 78% remain to graduate.

Housing: 1565 students can be accommodated in college housing, which includes single-sex and coed dormitories. In addition, there are language houses and special-interest houses; special-interest houses include, among others, Center for Religious Diversity, Women Empowering Women, Global Awareness, and Outdoor Education. On-campus housing is guaranteed for all 4 years. 97% of students live on campus; of those, 68% remain on campus on weekends. All students may keep cars. Parking space is available on a first-come, first-served basis, with priority given to upperclassmen and all students with special circumstances.

Activities: There are no fraternities or sororities. There are 65 groups on campus, including art, BACCHUS, band, choir, chorale, chorus, dance, drama, ethnic, film, gay, Habitat for Humanity, honors, international, jazz band, literary magazine, musical theater, newspaper, photography, political, radio and TV, religious, social, social service, student government, symphony, and yearbook. Popular campus events include Otis Social Justice Symposium and Award and Spring Weekend.

Sports: There are 9 intercollegiate sports for men and 12 for women, and 2 intramural sports for men and 2 for women; most intramural sports are coed. Facilities include an 8-lane stretch pool, a field house with 5 tennis courts, 1 outdoor and 3 indoor basketball courts, a 200-meter track, a golf/archery range and batting cage, an 850-seat gym, 7 lighted outdoor tennis courts, a running course, a baseball stadium, 2 athletic fields, an aerobics/dance studio, and a fitness center.

Disabled Students: 50% of the campus is accessible. Wheelchair ramps, elevators, special parking, specially equipped rest rooms, special class scheduling, and lowered telephones are available.

Services: Counseling and information services are available, as is tutoring in most subjects. There is a reader service for the blind and remedial writing. Peer tutoring and note takers for hearing-impaired students are available.

Campus Safety and Security: Measures include 24-hour foot and vehicle patrol, self-defense education, security escort services, and informal discussions. There are pamphlets/posters/films, emergency telephones, and lighted pathways/sidewalks.

Programs of Study: Wheaton confers the A.B. degree. Bachelor's degrees are awarded in BIOLOGICAL SCIENCE (biochemistry and biology/biological science), COMMUNICATIONS AND THE ARTS (art history and appreciation, classics, creative writing, dramatic arts, English, fine arts, French, German, Greek, Latin, literature, music, Russian, and studio art), COMPUTER AND PHYSICAL SCIENCE (astronomy, chemistry, computer mathematics, computer science, mathematics, and physics), ENGINEERING AND ENVIRONMENTAL DESIGN (environmental science), SOCIAL SCIENCE (American studies, anthropology, Asian/Oriental studies, classical/ancient civilization, economics, German area studies, Hispanic American studies, history, international relations, Italian studies, philosophy, political science/government, psychobiology, psychology, religion, Russian and Slavic studies, social psychology, sociology, and women's studies). Arts and sciences are the strongest academically. Psychology, English, and economics are the largest.

Required: Among the requirements for graduation are 32 course credits (4 semester hours each), with a minimum of 9 courses in the major, at least 3 of which are at the 300 level or above. The core classes consist of English, quantitative skills, foreign language, natural science, and non-Western history. Students must maintain a minimum GPA of 2.0 (C-) in all courses to remain in good academic standing.

Special: Students may cross-register with Brown University as well as with colleges in the Southeastern Association for Cooperation in Higher Education in Massachusetts and with schools participating in the 12 College Exchange Program. Wheaton offers study abroad in 20 countries, internship programs, nondegree study, dual majors, student-designed majors, a Washington semester at American University, and interdisciplinary majors, including math and economics, math and computer science, physics and astronomy, and theater and English dramatic literature. A 3-2 engineering degree is offered with George Washington University, Dartmouth College, and Worcester Polytechnic Institute. Pass/fail options are possible. There are 8 national honor societies, including Phi Beta Kappa, and a freshman honors program. All departments have honors programs.

Faculty/Classroom: 50% of faculty are male; 50%, female. All both teach and do research. The average class size in an introductory lecture is 40; in a laboratory, 20; and in a regular course, 19.

Admissions: 43% of the 2003-2004 applicants were accepted. The SAT I scores for the 2003-2004 freshman class were: Verbal--3% below 500, 34% between 500 and 599, 52% between 600 and 700, and 11% above 700; Math--3% below 500, 41% between 500 and 599, 50% between 600 and 700, and 6% above 700. The ACT scores were 9% between 21 and 23, 44% between 24 and 26, 22% between 27 and 28, and 25% above 28. 65% of the current freshmen were in the top fifth of their class; 89% were in the top two fifths. There were 10 National Merit semifinalists. 7 freshmen graduated first in their class.

Requirements: Submission of SAT I or ACT scores is optional. Applicants must be graduates of an accredited secondary school. Recommended courses include English with emphasis on composition skills, 4 years; foreign language and math, 3 to 4 years each; social studies, 3 years; and lab science, 2 to 3 years. Wheaton requires an essay and a graded writing sample and strongly recommends an interview. AP credits are accepted. Important factors in the admissions decision are advanced placement or honor courses, extracurricular activities record, and leadership record.

Procedure: Freshmen are admitted fall and spring. Entrance exams should be taken in October and/or November. There are early decision, early admissions, and deferred admissions plans. Early decision 1 applications should be filed by November 15 (early decision 2, January 15) regular applications, by January 15 for fall entry. The fall 2003 application fee was $55. Notification of early decision 1 is sent December 15 (early decision 2, February 15); regular decision, April 1. 209 early decision candidates were accepted for the 2003-2004 class. 1059 applicants were on the 2003 waiting list; 69 were admitted. Applications are accepted on-line.

Transfer: 18 transfer students enrolled in 2002-2003. Transfer students are encouraged to present a strong B average in their college work to date. Preference will be given to college over high school work. The college transcript is evaluated individually for transfer of credit. 16 of 32 credits required for the bachelor's degree must be completed at Wheaton.

Visiting: There are regularly scheduled orientations for prospective students, including class visits, tours, panels on financial aid, student life, and athletics, lunch with faculty, and department open houses. There are guides for informal visits and visitors may sit in on classes and stay overnight. To schedule a visit, contact the Admissions Office.

Financial Aid: In 2003-2004, 64% of all full-time freshmen and 71% of continuing full-time students received some form of financial aid. 58% of full-time freshmen and 60% of continuing full-time students received need-based aid. The average freshman award was $18,149. 45% of undergraduates work part time. Average annual earnings from campus work are $800. The average financial indebtedness of the 2003 graduate was $20,188. Wheaton is a member of CSS. The CSS/Profile or FAFSA, parents' and student's federal tax returns, and if applicable, noncustodial parent's statement and business/farm supplement are required. The deadline for filing freshman financial aid applications for fall entry is February 1.

International Students: There are 37 international students enrolled. The school actively recruits these students. They must score 550 on the written TOEFL or 213 on the electronic version.

Computers: The networked campus provides students with the ability to do course work in a web-based course management system; electronic access to college data such as the library catalog and campus news; and access to e-mail and all other aspects of the Internet, all from their residence hall. Web-based self-service applications, including registration, grades, and student bills, are available. All students may access the system 24 hours a day, 7 days a week. There are no time limits and no fees. It is strongly recommended that all students have a personal computer.

Graduates: From July 1, 2002 to June 30, 2003, 362 bachelor's degrees were awarded. The most popular majors were psychology (19%), English (10%), and economics (9%). In an average class, 68% graduate in 4 years or less, 73% graduate in 5 years or less, and 75% graduate in 6 years or less. 24 companies recruited on campus in 2002-2003. Of the 2002 graduating class, 27% were enrolled in graduate school within 6 months of graduation and 58% were employed.

Admissions Contact: Gail Berson, Vice President for Enrollment and Dean of Admission and Student Aid.

E-mail: *admission@wheatoncollege.edu*
Web: *www.wheatoncollege.edu*

WHEELOCK COLLEGE
Boston, MA 02215-4176

E-2

(617) 879-2206
(800) 734-5212; Fax: (617) 879-2449

Full-time: 35 men, 542 women	**Faculty:** 56; IIA, av$
Part-time: 10 women	**Ph.D.s:** 84%
Graduate: 23 men, 332 women	**Student/Faculty:** 10 to 1
Year: semesters	**Tuition:** $20,400
Application Deadline: March 1	**Room & Board:** $8600
Freshman Class: 609 applied, 407 accepted, 140 enrolled	
SAT I Verbal/Math: 523/483	**COMPETITIVE**

Wheelock College, established in 1888, is a private institution with programs in education, child life and family studies, social work, and human services. In addition to regional accreditation, Wheelock College has baccalaureate program accreditation with CSWE and NCATE. The library contains 92,199 volumes, 477,771 microform items, and 2487 audio/video tapes/CDs, and subscribes to 539 periodicals. Computerized library services include the card catalog, interlibrary loans, and database searching. Special learning facilities include a learning resource center, art gallery, and the Wheelock Family Theater. The 7-acre campus is in an urban area in Boston. Including any residence halls, there are 12 buildings.

Student Life: 54% of undergraduates are from Massachusetts. Students are from 17 states, 4 foreign countries, and Canada. 90% are from public schools. 84% are white. The average age of freshmen is 18; all undergraduates, 20. 29% do not continue beyond their first year; 73% remain to graduate.

Housing: 500 students can be accommodated in college housing, which includes single-sex and coed dorms. In addition, there is a cooperative living house, nonsmoking floors, and a wellness floor. On-campus housing is guaranteed for all 4 years. 73% of students live on campus; of those, 50% remain on campus on weekends. Upperclassmen may keep cars.

Activities: There are no fraternities or sororities. There are 25 groups on campus, including Best Buddies, choir, chorale, drama, ethnic, gay, honors, international, newspaper, professional, religious, social, social service, student government, and women's center. Popular campus events include Kids Day, Family Weekend, and Senior/Sophomore Banquet.

Sports: There are 5 intercollegiate sports for women, and 9 intramural sports for men and 9 for women. Facilities include a sports complex at a neighboring college with a pool and diving board, racquetball courts, a weight room, an indoor track, a basketball court, crew tanks, and cardiovascular equipment.

Disabled Students: 67% of the campus is accessible. Wheelchair ramps, elevators, special parking, specially equipped rest rooms, special class scheduling, lowered drinking fountains, lowered telephones, and assistive technology in the learning center are available.

Services: Counseling and information services are available, as is tutoring in every subject. There is a reader service for the blind and remedial math, reading, and writing. Academic support services provide individualized assistance upon request.

Campus Safety and Security: Measures include 24-hour foot and vehicle patrol, security escort services, informal discussions, and emergency telephones. There are lighted pathways/sidewalks.

Programs of Study: Wheelock College confers B.A., B.S., and B.S.W. degrees. Associate and master's degrees are also awarded. Bachelor's degrees are awarded in EDUCATION (early childhood, elementary, and special), SOCIAL SCIENCE (child care/child and family studies, human development, and social work). Teaching, social work, and child life are the strongest academically and have the largest enrollments.

Required: To graduate, students must complete between 134 and 140 credit hours, with a minimum GPA of 2.0. Wheelock requires at least a 32-credit major combined with a 36-credit professional studies program. Students must earn 26 credits in English composition, math, human growth and development, children and their environments, first-year seminar, visual and performing arts, and 1 course in first aid.

Special: Wheelock offers cross-registration with all colleges in the Colleges of the Fenway and internships that include student teaching and social work practice. Dual majors, study-abroad programs, and pass/fail options are available. Students may receive credit for life and work experience. Students begin practical field work their freshman year and continue for all 4 years. There is 1 national honor society.

Faculty/Classroom: 19% of faculty are male; 81%, female. 61% teach undergraduates. No introductory courses are taught by graduate students. The average class size in an introductory lecture is 20; in a laboratory, 17; and in a regular course, 15.

Admissions: 67% of the 2003-2004 applicants were accepted. The SAT I scores for the 2003-2004 freshman class were: Verbal--37% below 500, 45% between 500 and 599, 14% between 600 and 700, and 4% above 700; Math--42% below 500, 42% between 500 and 599, and 15% between 600 and 700. 24% of the current freshmen were in the top fifth of their class; 55% were in the top two fifths. 1 freshman graduated first in the class in a recent year.

Requirements: The SAT I is required. In addition, applicants must be graduates of an accredited secondary school and must have completed 4 years of English, 3 years of math, and 2 years each of science and history. The GED is accepted. The college requires an essay and recommends an interview. A GPA of 2.0 is required. AP and CLEP credits are accepted. Important factors in the admissions decision are advanced placement or honor courses, evidence of special talent, and personality/intangible qualities.

Procedure: Freshmen are admitted fall and spring. Entrance exams should be taken in the spring of the junior year and/or fall of the senior year. There are early decision and deferred admissions plans. Early decision applications should be filed by December 1; regular applications, by March 1 for fall entry and December 1 for spring entry, along with a $35 fee. Notification of early decision is sent January 1; regular decision, on a rolling basis. 44 early decision candidates were accepted for the 2003-2004 class. Applications are accepted on-line through CollegeLink, CollegeView, and other electronic application services, but hard copies of all applications are required.

Transfer: 57 transfer students enrolled in 2002-2003. Transfer students must have a minimum GPA of 2.0 and must present 2 letters of recommendation. Grades of C- or better transfer for credit. 67 of 134 credits required for the bachelor's degree must be completed at Wheelock College.

Visiting: There are regularly scheduled orientations for prospective students. Information sessions are held on select Saturdays in the fall and spring. Students hear a presentation from a counselor, have a tour, and may speak to a counselor individually. There are guides for informal visits and visitors may sit in on classes and stay overnight. To schedule a visit, contact the Undergraduate Admissions Office at *undergrad@wheelock.edu*.

Financial Aid: In 2003-2004, 94% of all full-time freshmen and 82% of continuing full-time students received some form of financial aid. 83% of full-time freshmen and 70% of continuing full-time students received need-based aid. The average freshman award was $21,244. Need-based scholarships or need-based grants averaged $4267 ($6145 maximum); need-based self-help aid (loans and jobs) averaged $8214 ($12,194 maximum); and non-need-based awards and non-need-based scholarships averaged $18,828 ($20,477 maximum). 33% of undergraduates work part time. Average annual earnings from campus work are $900. The average financial indebtedness of the 2003 graduate was $19,445. The FAFSA and the college's own financial statement are required. The priority date for freshman financial aid applications for fall entry is March 1.

International Students: There are 5 international students enrolled. They must score 500 on the written TOEFL or 173 on the electronic version and also take the SAT I or the ACT.

Computers: The mainframe is an HP Alpha Server ES20. Students have port-per-pillow access to the Internet through 4 1 gigabit campus-wide backbone network. All classrooms are equipped with dataports integrating technology into the curriculum. All students may access the system 24 hours a day any time school is in session. There are no time limits and no fees.

Graduates: From July 1, 2002 to June 30, 2003, 109 bachelor's degrees were awarded. The most popular majors were teacher education (68%), child life (16%), and social work (16%). In an average class, 50% graduate in 4 years or less, 54% graduate in 5 years or less, and 59% graduate in 6 years or less. 35 companies recruited on campus in 2002-2003. Of the 2002 graduating class, 22% were enrolled in graduate school within 6 months of graduation and 95% were employed.

Admissions Contact: Lynne E. Harding, Dean of Admissions.
E-mail: *undergrad@wheelock.edu* Web: *www.wheelock.edu*

WILLIAMS COLLEGE
Williamstown, MA 01267

A-1

(413) 597-2211

Full-time: 985 men, 984 women	**Faculty:** 267; IIB, ++$
Graduate: 28 men, 29 women	**Ph.D.s:** 96%
Year: 4-1-4	**Student/Faculty:** 8 to 1
Application Deadline: January 1	**Tuition:** $27,890
	Room & Board: $7860
Freshman Class: 5341 applied, 1122 accepted, 533 enrolled	
SAT I or ACT: required	**MOST COMPETITIVE**

Williams College, founded in 1793, is a private institution offering undergraduate degrees in liberal arts and graduate degrees in art history and development economics. Figures in the above capsule and in this profile are approximate. The 11 libraries contain 850,114 volumes, 491,466 microform items, and 37,103 audio/video tapes/CDs, and subscribe to 4789 paper and electronic periodicals. Computerized library services include the card catalog, interlibrary loans, and database searching. Special learning facilities include a learning resource center, art gallery, planetarium, radio station, a 2500-acre experimental forest, an environmental studies center, a center for foreign languages, literatures, and cultures, a rare book library, and a studio art center. The 450-acre campus is in a small town 150 miles north of New York City and west of Boston. Including any residence halls, there are 112 buildings.

Student Life: 86% of undergraduates are from out of state, mostly the Northeast. Students are from 48 states, 37 foreign countries, and Canada. 55% are from public schools. 75% are white. 31% are Protestant; 28% claim no religious affiliation; 22% Catholic; 10% Jewish. The average age of freshmen is 18; all undergraduates, 20. 3% do not continue beyond their first year; 94% remain to graduate.

Housing: 2001 students can be accommodated in college housing, which includes single-sex and coed dorms and on-campus apartments. In addition, there is cooperative housing, in which students prepare their own meals. On-campus housing is guaranteed for all 4 years. 96% of students live on campus. Upperclassmen may keep cars.

Activities: There are no fraternities or sororities. There are more than 160 groups on campus, including a cappella singing, art, band, chess, choir, chorale, chorus, comedy, computers, dance, debate, drama, ethnic, film, gay, handbell choirs, honors, international, jazz band, literary magazine, marching band, musical theater, newspaper, orchestra, pep band, photography, political, radio and TV, religious, social service, student government, symphony, and yearbook. Popular campus events include Winter Carnival, Mountain Day, and Multicultural Center-sponsored activities.

Sports: There are 16 intercollegiate sports for men and 15 for women, and 11 intramural sports for men and 11 for women. Facilities include 2 gyms, a 50-meter pool, a dance studio, a weight room, rowing tanks, a boat house, a golf course, playing fields, and courts for tennis, squash, and paddle tennis. The campus stadium seats 6795.

Disabled Students: Wheelchair ramps, elevators, special parking, specially equipped rest rooms, special class scheduling, lowered drinking fountains, lowered telephones, wheelchair lifts, and special laundry and kitchen facilities are available.

Services: Counseling and information services are available, as is tutoring in every subject. There is a reader service for the blind and remedial math, reading, and writing. Other services include a peer health program, a rape and sexual assault hotline, and 10-1 counseling service.

Campus Safety and Security: Measures include 24-hour foot and vehicle patrol, self-defense education, security escort services, and informal discussions. There are pamphlets/posters/films, emergency telephones, and lighted pathways/sidewalks.

Programs of Study: Williams confers the B.A. degree. Master's degrees are also awarded. Bachelor's degrees are awarded in BIOLOGICAL SCIENCE (biology/biological science), COMMUNICATIONS AND THE ARTS (art, art history and appreciation, classics, dramatic arts, English, fine arts, French, German, Japanese, literature, music, Russian, and Spanish), COMPUTER AND PHYSICAL SCIENCE (astronomy, astrophysics, chemistry, computer science, geology, mathematics, and physics), SOCIAL SCIENCE (American studies, anthropology, Asian/Oriental studies, economics, history, philosophy, political science/government, psychology, religion, sociology, and women's studies). English, psychology, and economics are the largest.

Required: All students must complete 4 winter studies and 32 courses, 9 of which are in the major field, with a C- or higher. Requirements include 3 semester-long courses in each of 3 academic divisions: languages and arts, social sciences, and science and math. Also required are 1 course in cultural pluralism and 4 semesters of phys ed.

Special: Students may cross-register at Bennington or Massachusetts College of Liberal Arts and study abroad in Madrid, Oxford, Cairo, Beijing, and Kyoto, or any approved program with another college or university. Teaching and medical field experiences, dual and student-designed majors, internships, and a 3-2 engineering program with Columbia and Washington Universities are offered. There are pass/fail options during the winter term. Each department offers at least one Oxford-model tutorial every year. There are 2 national honor societies, including Phi Beta Kappa.

Faculty/Classroom: 60% of faculty are male; 40%, female. All both teach and do research. No introductory courses are taught by graduate students. The average class size in an introductory lecture is 31; in a laboratory, 14; and in a regular course, 22.

Admissions: 21% of the 2003-2004 applicants were accepted.

Requirements: The SAT I or ACT is required. In addition, SAT II: Subject tests in 3 subjects are required. Secondary preparation should include 4 years each of English and math, 3 to 4 years of foreign language, and at least 2 years each of science and social studies. A personal essay must be submitted. AP credits are accepted. Important factors in the admissions decision are advanced placement or honor courses, recommendations by school officials, and evidence of special talent.

Procedure: Freshmen are admitted in the fall. There are early decision and deferred admissions plans. Early decision applications should be filed by November 15; regular applications, by January 1, along with a $50 fee. Notification of early decision is sent December 15; regular decision, the first week in April. A waiting list is an active part of the admissions procedure. Applications are accepted on-line via the Common Application, EXPAN, Apply, and College Link.

Transfer: Transfer applicants should present a 3.5 GPA in previous college work and must submit either the SAT I or ACT scores. 2 years must be completed at Williams.

Visiting: There are regularly scheduled orientations for prospective students, consisting of panels, forums, class visits, and campus tours. There are guides for informal visits and visitors may sit in on classes and stay overnight. To schedule a visit, contact the Purple Key Society office at (413) 597-3148.

Financial Aid: In 2003-2004, 44% of all full-time freshmen and 40% of continuing full-time students received some form of financial aid. 58% of all full-time students received some form of financial aid. The average freshman award was $24,500. 60% of undergraduates work part time. Average annual earnings from campus work are $800. The average financial indebtedness of a recent graduate was $15,625. Williams is a member of CSS. The CSS Profile, FAFSA, the college's own financial statement, income tax returns, noncustodial parent's statement, and business/farm supplements, if applicable, are required. The deadline for filing freshman financial aid applications for fall entry is February 1.

International Students: The school actively recruits these students. They must score 600 on the written TOEFL if English is not the applicant's first language, and also take the SAT I or the ACT. Students must take SAT II: Subject tests in English and 2 other subjects.

Computers: The mainframe is a DEC VAX 11/785. The Computer Center houses the mainframe, which has 40 ports, as well as 7 Sun Microsystems workstations and 100 assorted PCs, Macs, and graphics terminals. Additional PCs are located in the library and other academic buildings. All public-access DEC terminals and PCs are networked. All students may access the system. There are no time limits and no fees.

Graduates: In an average class, 92% graduate in 4 years or less and 96% graduate in 6 years or less.

Admissions Contact: Richard Nesbitt, Director of Admission.
E-mail: *admission@williams.edu* Web: *www.williams.edu/admissions/*

WORCESTER POLYTECHNIC INSTITUTE   C-2
Worcester, MA 01609-2280   (508) 831-5286; Fax: (508) 831-5875

Full-time: 2066 men, 644 women	**Faculty:** 212; IIA, ++$
Part-time: 53 men, 10 women	**Ph.Ds:** 98%
Graduate: 759 men, 258 women	**Student/Faculty:** 13 to 1
Year: quarters, summer session	**Tuition:** $28,420
Application Deadline: February 1	**Room & Board:** $8984
Freshman Class: 3373 applied, 2548 accepted, 640 enrolled	
SAT I Verbal/Math: 610/660	**ACT:** 27 HIGHLY COMPETITIVE

Worcester Polytechnic Institute, founded in 1865, is a private institution with a unique, project-oriented program of study primarily in engineering and other technical fields. In addition to regional accreditation, WPI has baccalaureate program accreditation with ABET. The library contains 277,844 volumes, 109,648 microform items, and 2500 audio/video tapes/CDs, and subscribes to 4698 periodicals. Computerized library services include the card catalog, interlibrary loans, and database searching. Special learning facilities include a learning resource center, radio station, TV station, a robotics lab, a wind tunnel, and a greenhouse. The 80-acre campus is in a suburban area 40 miles west of Boston. Including any residence halls, there are 30 buildings.

Student Life: 50% of undergraduates are from out of state, mostly the Northeast. Students are from 42 states, 70 foreign countries, and Canada. 74% are from public schools. 82% are white. The average age of freshmen is 18; all undergraduates, 20. 6% do not continue beyond their first year; 80% remain to graduate.

Housing: 1247 students can be accommodated in college housing, which includes coed dorms, on-campus apartments, off-campus apartments, and fraternity houses. In addition, there are special-interest houses. On-campus housing is guaranteed for the freshman year only and is available on a lottery system for upperclassmen. Upperclassmen may keep cars.

Activities: 32% of men belong to 12 national fraternities; 34% of women belong to 2 national sororities. There are more than 100 groups on campus, including art, band, cheerleading, chess, choir, chorale, chorus, computers, dance, drama, ethnic, gay, honors, international, jazz band, literary magazine, musical theater, newspaper, orchestra, pep band, photography, political, professional, radio and TV, religious, social, social service, student government, symphony, and yearbook. Popular campus events include Traditions Day, New Voices Festival, and Winter Carnival.

Sports: There are 11 intercollegiate sports for men and 10 for women, and 12 intramural sports for men and 12 for women. Facilities include an aerobics area, baseball and softball fields, bowling alleys, an 8-lane synthetic surface track, a fitness center, a crew center, a playing field with artificial turf, a pool, basketball, tennis, racquetball and squash courts, and a 2,800-seat gym.

Disabled Students: 90% of the campus is accessible. Wheelchair ramps, elevators, special parking, specially equipped rest rooms, special class scheduling, and lowered drinking fountains are available.

Services: Counseling and information services are available, as is tutoring in every subject.

Campus Safety and Security: Measures include 24-hour foot and vehicle patrol, self-defense education, security escort services, and shuttle buses. There are informal discussions, pamphlets/posters/films, emergency telephones, lighted pathways/sidewalks, and a student-run emergency medical service supervised by the campus police department.

Programs of Study: WPI confers the B.S. degree. Master's and doctoral degrees are also awarded. Bachelor's degrees are awarded in BIOLOGICAL SCIENCE (biochemistry, biology/biological science, and biotechnology), BUSINESS (management engineering, management information systems, and management science), COMPUTER AND PHYSICAL SCIENCE (chemistry, computer science, mathematics, and physics), ENGINEERING AND ENVIRONMENTAL DESIGN (biomedical engineering, chemical engineering, civil engineering, electrical/electronics engineering, engineering physics, industrial engineering, manufacturing engineering, and mechanical engineering), SOCIAL SCIENCE (economics, humanities, interdisciplinary studies, and social science). Engineering and computer science are the largest.

Required: For a B.S. degree, WPI requires that students in science and engineering complete an individual project in the humanities. Students must also complete 2 major team projects. Distribution requirements vary according to the major, and all students must take courses in social sciences and phys ed.

Special: Students may cross-register with 9 other colleges in the Colleges of Worcester Consortium. Co-op programs in all majors, internships, work-study programs, dual majors in every subject, student-designed majors, 3-2 engineering degrees, nondegree study, and pass/fail options are all available. There is an accelerated degree program in fire protection engineering. There are special project centers in Europe, Latin America, Asia, Australia, Africa, and the U.S. There are 10 national honor societies.

Faculty/Classroom: 82% of faculty are male; 18%, female. 96% teach undergraduates and 50% do research. No introductory courses are taught by graduate students. The average class size in an introductory lecture is 35; in a laboratory, 20; and in a regular course, 25.

Admissions: 76% of the 2003-2004 applicants were accepted. The SAT I scores for the 2003-2004 freshman class were: Verbal--4% below 500, 35% between 500 and 599, 49% between 600 and 700, and 11% above 700; Math--13% between 500 and 599, 58% between 600 and 700, and 28% above 700. The ACT scores were 3% below 21, 13% between 21 and 23, 30% between 24 and 26, 22% between 27 and 28, and 32% above 28. 78% of the current freshmen were in the top fifth of their class; 98% were in the top two fifths. There were 13 National Merit finalists. 15 freshmen graduated first in their class.

Requirements: The SAT I or ACT is required. In addition, SAT II: Subject tests in writing, math I or II, and a science are also required. Applicants must have completed 4 years of math precalculus and 2 lab sciences. An essay is optional. AP credits are accepted. Important factors in the admissions decision are advanced placement or honor courses, recommendations by school officials, and extracurricular activities record.

Procedure: Freshmen are admitted fall and spring. Entrance exams should be taken between April and December. There are early decision, early admissions, and deferred admissions plans. Early decision applications should be filed by November 15; regular applications, by February 1 for fall entry and November 15 for spring entry. The fall 2003 application fee was $63. Notification of early decision is sent December 15; regular decision, April 1. 152 early decision candidates were accepted for the 2003-2004 class. 160 applicants were on the 2003 waiting list; 25 were admitted. Applications are accepted on-line through EXPAN or CollegeLink.

Transfer: 63 transfer students enrolled in 2002-2003. Grades of C or better transfer for credit. A high school transcript or GED, is requried. Students who have been out of school for a year or more must present a resume or personal biography, and a professional recommendation. 25 of 45 credits required for the bachelor's degree must be completed at WPI.

Visiting: There are regularly scheduled orientations for prospective students, consisting of meetings and presentations from various academic and extracurricular groups. There are guides for informal visits and visitors may sit in on classes and stay overnight. To schedule a visit, contact the Admissions Office.

Financial Aid: In 2003-2004, 89% of all full-time freshmen and 86% of continuing full-time students received some form of financial aid. 73% of full-time freshmen and 70% of continuing full-time students received need-based aid. The average freshman award was $24,956. 59% of undergraduates work part time. Average annual earnings from campus work are $1200. The average financial indebtedness of the 2003 graduate was $25,251. WPI is a member of CSS. The CSS/Profile or FAFSA and CSS Non Custodial Parent Statement are required. The deadline for filing freshman financial aid applications for fall entry is March 1.

International Students: There are 166 international students enrolled. The school actively recruits these students. They must score 550 on the written TOEFL or the ELPT test and also take the SAT I or the ACT. Students must take SAT II: Subject tests in math, and science (and writing, if not taking TOEFL or ELPT).

Computers: The UNIX-based mainframe is accessible via 8 parallel processors and a campuswide data network available in many locations, including the College Computer Center. The center also features 56 X terminals. More than 1,000 IBM PC-6300 computers are available throughout the campus in general-access and specialized labs and computer classrooms. All students may access the system 24 hours daily. There are no time limits and no fees.

Graduates: In a recent year, 586 bachelor's degrees were awarded. The most popular majors were mechanical engineering (20%), electrical engineering (17%), and computer science (16%). In an average class, 1% graduated in 3 years or less, 66% graduated in 4 years or less, 75% graduated in 5 years or less, and 80% graduated in 6 years or less. 200 companies recruited on campus in a recent year.

Admissions Contact: Kristin R. Tichenor, Director of Admissions. E-mail: *admissions@wpi.edu* Web: *www.wpi.edu*

WORCESTER STATE COLLEGE
C-2
Worcester, MA 01602-2597   **(508) 929-8040; Fax: (508) 929-8131**

Full-time: 1275 men, 1826 women	**Faculty:** 162
Part-time: 577 men, 991 women	**Ph.D.s:** n/av
Graduate: 191 men, 610 women	**Student/Faculty:** 19 to 1
Year: semesters, summer session	**Tuition:** $4123 ($10,203)
Application Deadline: open	**Room & Board:** $5882
Freshman Class: n/av	
SAT I: required	**COMPETITIVE**

Worcester State College, established in 1874, is part of the Massachusetts public higher education system and offers undergraduate and graduate programs. A liberal arts core is emphasized, as are selected areas of science, the health professions, education, business and management. In addition to regional accreditation, WSC has baccalaureate program accreditation with ASLA, NLN, and ACOTE, JRCERT. The library contains 193,112 volumes, 16,159 microform items, and 5017 audio/video tapes/CDs, and subscribes to 1982 periodicals. Computerized library services include the card catalog, interlibrary loans, database searching, and Internet access. Special learning facilities include a learning resource center, radio station, TV station, and photographic labs, audiovisual center, multimedia classrooms with satellite connectivity, discipline-specific computer labs, and a speech, language, and hearing clinic. The 53-acre campus is in an urban area 40 miles west of Boston. Including any residence halls, there are 8 buildings.

Student Life: 97% of undergraduates are from Massachusetts. Others are from 19 states, 42 foreign countries, and Canada. 78% are white. The average age of freshmen is 23; all undergraduates, 25.

Housing: 693 students can be accommodated in college housing, which includes coed dormitories and on-campus apartments. On-campus housing is available on a first-come, first-served basis. Priority is given to out-of-town students. 85% of students commute. Alcohol is not permitted. Upperclassmen may keep cars.

Activities: There are no fraternities or sororities. There are 52 groups on campus, including cheerleading, chorale, drama, ethnic, gay, honors, international, jazz band, newspaper, professional, radio and TV, religious, social, social service, student government, and yearbook. Popular campus events include Winter Carnival, Senior Week, and a lecture series.

Sports: There are 9 intercollegiate sports for men and 10 for women, and 13 intramural sports for men and 13 for women. Facilities include an auditorium, a gym, a fitness center, tennis courts, a track, baseball and softball diamonds, and football, field hockey, and all-purpose fields.

Disabled Students: All of the campus is accessible. Wheelchair ramps, elevators, special parking, specially equipped rest rooms, lowered drinking fountains, lowered telephones, special housing, and priority registration are available.

Services: Counseling and information services are available, as is tutoring in most subjects. There is a reader service for the blind. in conjunction with Quinsigamond Community College courses and WSC instructors.

Campus Safety and Security: Measures include 24-hour foot and vehicle patrol, self-defense education, informal discussions, and pamphlets/posters/films. There are emergency telephones, lighted pathways/sidewalks, and The dormitory is protected by a security system. An escort service is available on request.

Programs of Study: WSC confers B.A. and B.S. degrees. Master's degrees are also awarded. Bachelor's degrees are awarded in BIOLOGICAL SCIENCE (biology/biological science, and biotechnology), BUSINESS (business administration and management), COMMUNICATIONS AND THE ARTS (communications, English, and Spanish), COMPUTER AND PHYSICAL SCIENCE (chemistry, computer science, mathematics, and natural sciences), EDUCATION (early childhood, and elementary), HEALTH PROFESSIONS (health, health science, nursing, occupational therapy, and speech pathology/audiology), SOCIAL SCIENCE (criminal justice, economics, geography, history, psychology, sociology, and urban studies). Occupational therapy and nursing are the strongest academically. Business administration, psychology, and communications are the largest.

Required: To graduate, students must complete a foundation requirement, including English composition, math, and the study of the U.S. and Massachusetts constitutions. Distribution requirements include 12 credits each in humanities, behavioral and social sciences, and natural sciences and math; 9 in fine arts; and 3 in health or phys ed. Students must complete 120 credits, 30 to 48 in the major, with a minimum 2.0 GPA overall and in the major.

Special: Cross-registration with the Worcester Consortium for Higher Education is availlable, as are co-op programs, internships, study abroad, a Washington semester, work-study, B.A.-B.S. degrees, dual majors, a 3-2 engineering degree with Worcester Polytechnic Institute and the Universities of Massachusetts at Dartmouth and Lowell, nondegree study, and a pass/fail option. There are 17 national honor societies, a freshman honors program, and 15 departmental honors programs.

Faculty/Classroom: 50% of faculty are male; 50%, female. All teach undergraduates. No introductory courses are taught by graduate students.

Requirements: The SAT I is required. In addition, for students with a GPA of 2.9 or above, a minimum SAT I or ACT score may be required. For students whose GPA is below 2.9, a minimum SAT I or ACT score is applied according to a scale established by WSC. Applicants must graduate from an accredited secondary school. They should have completed 4 years of English, 3 of math, 2 each of a foreign language, a lab science, and social studies, including 1 year of U.S. history and government, and 2 electives. The College Board Student Descriptive questionnaire must be submitted. A GPA of 2.0 is required. AP and CLEP credits are accepted.

Procedure: Freshmen are admitted fall, spring, and summer. Entrance exams should be taken in spring of the junior year or fall of the senior year. There is a deferred admissions plan. Application deadlines are open. Application fee is $20. Applications are accepted on-line through CollegeNET.

Transfer: 384 transfer students enrolled in 2002-2003. Transfer applicants must have earned a minimum of 12 college credits with a minimum 2.5 GPA or 13 to 23 credits with a minimum 2.0 GPA. Students with fewer than 23 transfer credits may be admitted under the same criteria as first-time freshmen. 30 of 120 credits required for the bachelor's degree must be completed at WSC.

Visiting: There are regularly scheduled orientations for prospective students, including a campus tour and review of campus life and organizations, success in college, special opportunities, and available services. There are guides for informal visits and visitors may sit in on classes and stay overnight. To schedule a visit, contact Dean of Enrollment Management.

Financial Aid: In 2003-2004, 86% of all full-time freshmen and 58% of continuing full-time students received some form of financial aid. 60% of full-time freshmen and 38% of continuing full-time students received need-based aid. The average freshman award was $6539. The average financial indebtedness of the 2003 graduate was $11,843. WSC is a member of CSS. The FAFSA is required. The deadline for filing freshman financial aid applications for fall entry is March 1.

International Students: There are 81 international students enrolled. They must score 550 on the written TOEFL and also take the SAT I or the ACT.

Computers: The mainframe is a Digital ALPHA 4100. Students apply for a user ID or enroll in courses requiring use of discipline-specific labs. Students work at PC workstations on the collegewide network. There are 449 PC workstations at various campus locations. Students with user IDs may access e-mail and the Internet. All students may access the system. There are no time limits and no fees.

Graduates: From July 1, 2002 to June 30, 2003, 728 bachelor's degrees were awarded. The most popular majors were business administration (15%), psychology (10%), and communications (8%).

Admissions Contact: Alan Kines, Dean of Enrollment Management. A video is available. E-mail: *admissions@worcester.edu* Web: *http://www.worcester.edu/*

MICHIGAN

POPULATION
DENSITY

● 50,000 and over

0   20   40   60   80   100
Miles

a sport and fitness center featuring a multipurpose forum with 3 courts for basketball, volleyball, and tennis, and an indoor track, racquetball courts, a weight room, and a 1350-seat performance gym; a 5000-seat football stadium; baseball and softball fields; 2 soccer fields; 6 tennis courts; a 400-meter track; and numerous intramural fields.

Disabled Students: 80% of the campus is accessible. Wheelchair ramps, elevators, special parking, specially equipped rest rooms, lowered drinking fountains, lowered telephones, special housing, readers, note takers, and test accommodations are available.

Services: Counseling and information services are available, as is tutoring in most subjects. There is a reader service for the blind, and remedial math, reading, and writing. There are scribes and note takers available.

Campus Safety and Security: Measures include 24-hour foot and vehicle patrol, self-defense education, security escort services, and informal discussions. There are pamphlets/posters/films, emergency telephones, and lighted pathways/sidewalks.

Programs of Study: Adrian confers B.A., B.S., B.B.A., B.F.A., B.M., and B.M.E. degrees. Associate degrees are also awarded. Bachelor's degrees are awarded in BIOLOGICAL SCIENCE (biology/biological science), BUSINESS (accounting, business administration and management, and international business management), COMMUNICATIONS AND THE ARTS (art, arts administration/management, communications, dramatic arts, English, French, German, music, musical theater, and Spanish), COMPUTER AND PHYSICAL SCIENCE (chemistry, earth science, mathematics, and physics), EDUCATION (elementary, physical, and secondary), ENGINEERING AND ENVIRONMENTAL DESIGN (environmental science and interior design), SOCIAL SCIENCE (criminal justice, economics, history, human services, international studies, philosophy, political science/government, psychology, religion, and sociology). Social sciences, art and design, and teacher education are the largest.

Required: To graduate, students must maintain a 2.0 average over 124 credit hours, 30 of which must be in upper-division courses. 19 hours of distribution requirements and 25 of basic educational proficiency are required, including 2 semesters of foreign language and 1 each of communication, English, fine arts, fitness, humanities, math, natural or physical science, religion or philosophy, and social science.

Special: Adrian offers preprofessional programs in engineering, health sciences, law, ministry, and art therapy; study abroad in 16 countries and a Washington semester; student-designed majors and a dual philosophy/religion program; internships in more than 650 locations, and a 3-2 engineering degree with Washington University in St. Louis and the University of Detroit Mercy. There are 14 national honor societies and a freshman honors program.

Faculty/Classroom: 65% of faculty are male; 35%, female. All teach undergraduates. The average class size in an introductory lecture is 20; in a laboratory, 13; and in a regular course, 15.

Admissions: 88% of the 2003-2004 applicants were accepted. The ACT scores for the 2003-2004 freshman class were: 46% below 21, 25% between 21 and 23, 20% between 24 and 26, 7% between 27 and 28, and 2% above 28. 41% of the current freshmen were in the top fifth of their class; 72% were in the top two fifths.

Requirements: The SAT I or ACT is required. In addition, applicants must be graduates of an accredited secondary school. The GED is accepted. Each student is reviewed individually based on several criteria. An interview is recommended. Adrian requires applicants to be in the upper 50% of their class. A GPA of 2.5 is required. AP and CLEP credits are accepted. Important factors in the admissions decision are advanced placement or honor courses, leadership record, and extracurricular activities record.

Procedure: Freshmen are admitted in the fall. Entrance exams should be taken during the spring of the junior year or fall of the senior year. There is a deferred admissions plan and a rolling admissions plan. Applications should be filed by March 15 for fall entry. Notification is sent on a rolling basis. Applications are accepted on-line through the college's web site.

Transfer: 38 transfer students enrolled in 2002-2003. Applicants must have an above-average GPA and provide final high school transcripts. If the student has completed fewer than 24 semester hours, ACT or SAT I test scores are also required. Grades of 2.0 and above transfer for credit. The college admits transfer students every semester. 34 of 124 credits required for the bachelor's degree must be completed at Adrian.

Visiting: There are regularly scheduled orientations for prospective students, including a student-guided campus tour and visits with an admissions counselor, professors from the student's area of interest, and an athletics coach, if applicable. Visitors may sit in on classes and stay overnight. To schedule a visit, contact the Admissions Office at *admissions@adrian.edu*.

Financial Aid: In 2003-2004, 79% of all full-time freshmen and 71% of continuing full-time students received some form of financial aid. 79% of full-time freshmen and 75% of continuing full-time students received

---

ADRIAN COLLEGE
Adrian, MI 49221-2575   E-5

(517) 265-5161, ext. 4326
(800) 877-2246; Fax: (517) 264-3331

Full-time: 439 men, 547 women	**Faculty:** 65
Part-time: 16 men, 26 women	**Ph.D.s:** 85%
Graduate: none	**Student/Faculty:** 15 to 1
Year: semesters, summer session	**Tuition:** $16,570
Application Deadline: March 15	**Room & Board:** $5380
Freshman Class: 1300 applied, 1143 accepted, 307 enrolled	
ACT: 22	**COMPETITIVE**

Adrian College, founded in 1859, is a private liberal arts institution affiliated with the United Methodist Church. The library contains 146,194 volumes, 47,520 microform items, and 1480 audio/video tapes/CDs, and subscribes to 596 periodicals. Computerized library services include the card catalog, interlibrary loans, database searching, and Internet access. Special learning facilities include a learning resource center, art gallery, planetarium, radio station, a solar greenhouse, and an observatory. The 100-acre campus is in a suburban area 35 miles southwest of Ann Arbor. Including any residence halls, there are 30 buildings.

Student Life: 80% of undergraduates are from Michigan. Students are from 14 states and 7 foreign countries. 76% are white; 40% claim no religious affiliation; 20% Catholic; 18% Protestant. The average age of freshmen is 18; all undergraduates, 19. 28% do not continue beyond their first year; 49% remain to graduate.

Housing: 1117 students can be accommodated in college housing, which includes single-sex and coed dorms, fraternity houses, sorority houses, substance-free, smoking-free, extended quiet hours, and upper classmen only residence halls. On-campus housing is guaranteed for all 4 years. 75% of students live on campus. All students may keep cars.

Activities: 30% of men belong to 4 national fraternities; 30% of women belong to 3 national sororities. There are 60 groups on campus, including art, band, cheerleading, choir, chorale, chorus, computers, dance, drama, ethnic, gay, honors, international, jazz band, literary magazine, musical theater, orchestra, photography, political, professional, radio and TV, religious, social, social service, student government, symphony, and yearbook. Popular campus events include Greek Week, Family Weekend, and International Week.

Sports: There are 8 intercollegiate sports for men and 8 for women, and 10 intramural sports for men and 10 for women. Facilities include

need-based aid. The average freshman award was $16,684. Need-based scholarships or need-based grants averaged $10,344; and need-based self-help aid (loans and jobs) averaged $4786. 50% of undergraduates work part time. Average annual earnings from campus work are $757. The average financial indebtedness of the 2003 graduate was $13,970. The FAFSA is required. The deadline for filing freshman financial aid applications for fall entry is March 15.

International Students: There are 20 international students enrolled. The school actively recruits these students. They must score 500 on the written TOEFL or 173 on the electronic version and also take the SAT I or the ACT.

Computers: The mainframes are 3 micro vaxes and 3 super micro Dual Xcon servers. Networked labs with 100 PCs are located in academic buildings. Every residence hall room has a network connection. Workstations are 17-inch monitors with Pentium 4.1 GHz processors with 256 Megs of RAM and 20 gig hard drives. All students may access the system 24 hours a day. There are no time limits and no fees. It is strongly recommended that all students have a personal computer.

Graduates: From July 1, 2002 to June 30, 2003, 192 bachelor's degrees were awarded. The most popular majors were social sciences/history (20%), business (17%), and visual and performing arts (14%). In an average class, 28% graduate in 4 years or less, 39% graduate in 5 years or less, and 41% graduate in 6 years or less. 22 companies recruited on campus in 2002-2003.

Admissions Contact: Janel Sutkus, Director of Admissions.
E-mail: *admissions@adrian.edu* Web: *www.adrian.edu*

ALBION COLLEGE

Albion, MI 49224

D-5

(517) 629-0321
(800) 858-6770; Fax: (517) 629-0569

Full-time: 750 men, 900 women	**Faculty:** 121; IIB, av$
Part-time: 1 man, 5 women	**Ph.D.s:** 92%
Graduate: none	**Student/Faculty:** 13 to 1
Year: semesters, summer session	**Tuition:** $22,048
Application Deadline: March 1	**Room & Board:** $6262
Freshman Class: n/av	
SAT I or ACT: required	**VERY COMPETITIVE**

Albion College, established in 1835, is a private institution affiliated with the United Methodist Church and offering undergraduate degrees in liberal arts curricula. Figures in the above capsule and in this profile are approximate. In addition to regional accreditation, Albion has baccalaureate program accreditation with NASM. The library contains 355,040 volumes, 67,188 microform items, and 6040 audio/video tapes/CDs, and subscribes to 986 periodicals. Computerized library services include the card catalog, interlibrary loans, and database searching. Special learning facilities include a learning resource center, art gallery, radio station, nature center, women's center, observatory, and honors program center. The 225-acre campus is in a small town 90 miles west of Detroit and 175 miles east of Chicago. Including any residence halls, there are 30 buildings.

Student Life: 89% of undergraduates are from Michigan. Students are from 28 states, 19 foreign countries, and Canada. 84% are from public schools. 86% are white. 28% are Catholic; 26% claim no religious affiliation. The average age of freshmen is 18; all undergraduates, 20. 15% do not continue beyond their first year.

Housing: 1600 students can be accommodated in college housing, which includes single-sex and coed dorms, on-campus apartments, off-campus apartments, married-student housing, and fraternity houses. In addition, there are language houses, special-interest houses, and special-interest annexes. On-campus housing is guaranteed for all 4 years. 99% of students live on campus; of those, 70% remain on campus on weekends. All students may keep cars.

Activities: 40% of men belong to 5 national fraternities; 40% of women belong to 6 national sororities. There are 122 groups on campus, including art, band, cheerleading, chess, choir, chorale, chorus, computers, dance, drama, ethnic, film, gay, honors, international, jazz band, literary magazine, marching band, medieval society, musical theater, newspaper, opera, orchestra, pep band, political, professional, radio and TV, religious, social, social service, a sports club association, student government, symphony, and yearbook. Popular campus events include International Week, Briton Bash, and Albion Performing Arts and Lecture Series.

Sports: There are 9 intercollegiate sports for men and 9 for women, and 19 intramural sports for men and 18 for women. Facilities include a stadium, an aquatic center, a gym, baseball, soccer, and football fields, tennis courts, an archery range, a surfaced track, a field events area, outdoor basketball courts, practice fields, and a canoeing facility. There is also a recreation and wellness center with intramural basketball, volleyball, badminton, racquetball, and tennis courts, a track, a weight training room, a human performance lab, and a training/rehabilitation unit.

Disabled Students: 90% of the campus is accessible. Wheelchair ramps, elevators, special parking, specially equipped rest rooms, special

class scheduling, lowered drinking fountains, and lowered telephones are available.

Services: Counseling and information services are available, as is tutoring in most subjects, and assistance for the deaf. There is a reader service for the blind. The Developing Skills Center offers individual assistance to students for study skills enhancement.

Campus Safety and Security: Measures include 24-hour foot and vehicle patrol, self-defense education, security escort services, and shuttle buses. There are informal discussions, pamphlets/posters/films, emergency telephones, and lighted pathways/sidewalks.

Programs of Study: Albion confers B.A. and B.F.A. degrees. Bachelor's degrees are awarded in BIOLOGICAL SCIENCE (biology/biological science), COMMUNICATIONS AND THE ARTS (art, art history and appreciation, English, French, German, music, Spanish, speech/debate/rhetoric, and visual and performing arts), COMPUTER AND PHYSICAL SCIENCE (chemistry, computer science, earth science, geoscience, mathematics, and physics), EDUCATION (physical), HEALTH PROFESSIONS (predentistry and premedicine), SOCIAL SCIENCE (American studies, anthropology, economics, history, international studies, philosophy, political science/government, psychology, public affairs, religion, and sociology). English, economics, and biology are the strongest academically. Economics, English, and psychology are the largest.

Required: To graduate, students must complete 2 units each in social science, humanities, and math and science, and 1 each in fine arts, environmental studies, gender studies, and ethnic studies. Students must maintain a minimum GPA of 2.0 and complete 124 semester hours with 32 hours in the major. All students must pass a writing competence exam.

Special: Albion offers work-study and internship programs, study abroad in 19 countries, an accelerated degree program, a Washington semester, and study in New York City, Philadelphia, Oak Ridge, Chicago, and the Virgin Islands. Students may earn a 3-2 engineering degree in conjunction with Columbia, Case Western, or Michigan Technological Universities, or the University of Michigan. Student-designed majors, dual and interdisciplinary majors, including computational math, speech communication and theater, math/physics, and math/economics, and pass/fail grading are possible. There are 4 national honor societies, including Phi Beta Kappa, a freshman honors program, and 18 departmental honors programs.

Faculty/Classroom: 70% of faculty are male; 30%, female. All teach undergraduates and 94% do research. The average class size in an introductory lecture is 27; in a laboratory, 16; and in a regular course, 17.

Requirements: The SAT I or ACT is required. In addition, applicants must graduate from an accredited secondary school or earn a GED. Completion of 15 Carnegie credits is required. A strong background in English, math, and lab and social sciences is recommended. Albion requires applicants to be in the upper 50% of their class. A GPA of 2.5 is required. AP and CLEP credits are accepted. Important factors in the admissions decision are advanced placement or honor courses, extracurricular activities record, and personality/intangible qualities.

Procedure: Freshmen are admitted fall and spring. Entrance exams should be taken in April and June of the junior year. There are early decision, early admissions, and deferred admissions plans. There is a rolling admissions plan. Early decision applications should be filed by November 15; regular applications, by March 1 for fall entry, along with a $20 fee. Notification of early decision is sent December 15; regular decision, on a rolling basis. 35 early decision candidates were accepted for a recent class. Applications are accepted on-line at the Albion web site via CollegeNET and through CommonApp.

Transfer: 24 transfer students enrolled in a recent year. Transfer applicants must submit official college transcripts. Grades of 2.0 or better are considered for transfer credit. Albion evaluates the applicant's course work before conferring transfer credit. 12 credits of 124 required for the bachelor's degree must be completed at Albion.

Visiting: There are regularly scheduled orientations for prospective students, consisting of 5 SOAR programs for students and parents: 1 1/2-day events held from early May to late August. There are guides for informal visits and visitors may sit in on classes and stay overnight. To schedule a visit, contact the Admissions Office.

Financial Aid: In a recent year, 98% of all full-time freshmen and 96% of continuing full-time students received some form of financial aid. 66% of full-time freshmen and 60% of continuing full-time students received need-based aid. The average freshman award was $16,823. 57% of undergraduates work part time. Average annual earnings from campus work are $989. The average financial indebtedness of a recent graduate was $16,244. Albion is a member of CSS. The FAFSA is required. The deadline for filing freshman financial aid applications for fall entry is February 1.

International Students: There were 23 international students enrolled in a recent year. The school actively recruits these students. They must score 550 on the written TOEFL and also take the SAT I or the ACT.

Computers: The mainframe is a DEC Alpha 2100/400. Suites of Macs and PCs are available in locations across campus. They operate as on-line terminals and are connected to the campus network. All students may access the system most days and during evening hours. There are no time limits and no fees. It is strongly recommended that all students have a personal computer.

Graduates: In a recent year, 334 bachelor's degrees were awarded. The most popular majors were economics/management (32%), English (14%), and biology (10%). In an average class, 1% graduate in 3 years or less, 71% graduate in 4 years or less, 74% graduate in 5 years or less, and 77% graduate in 6 years or less. 205 companies recruited on campus in a recent year. Of a recent graduating class, 38% were enrolled in graduate school within 6 months of graduation and 92% were employed.

Admissions Contact: Doug Kellar, Associate Vice President for Enrollment. A video is available. E-mail: *dkellar@albion.edu* Web: *www.albion.edu*

ALMA COLLEGE
Alma, MI 48801-1599 **D-4**

(989) 463-7139
(800) 321-ALMA; Fax: (989) 463-7057

Full-time: 523 men, 726 women	**Faculty:** 84; IIB, +$
Part-time: 13 men, 29 women	**Ph.D.s:** 88%
Graduate: none	**Student/Faculty:** 15 to 1
Year: 4-4-1	**Tuition:** $18,854
Application Deadline: open	**Room & Board:** $6712
Freshman Class: 1497 applied, 1155 accepted, 322 enrolled	
ACT: 25	**VERY COMPETITIVE**

Alma College, established in 1886, is a private, liberal arts and sciences institution affiliated with the Presbyterian Church (U.S.A.). In addition to regional accreditation, Alma has baccalaureate program accreditation with ACS and NASM. The library contains 251,641 volumes, 243,334 microform items, and 8377 audio/video tapes/CDs, and subscribes to 1175 periodicals. Computerized library services include the card catalog, interlibrary loans, database searching, and Internet access. Special learning facilities include a learning resource center, art gallery, planetarium, radio station, audio-visual center, and language lab. The 125-acre campus is in a small town 50 miles north of Lansing. Including any residence halls, there are 25 buildings.

Student Life: 95% of undergraduates are from Michigan. Students are from 20 states, 10 foreign countries, and Canada. 93% are from public schools. 93% are white. 30% claim no religious affiliation; 28% are Protestant; 23% Catholic; 17% more than 15 other denominations. The average age of freshmen is 18; all undergraduates, 20. 15% do not continue beyond their first year; 72% remain to graduate.

Housing: 1155 students can be accommodated in college housing, which includes single-sex and coed dorms, on-campus apartments, fraternity houses, and sorority houses. In addition, there are special-interest houses and an international house for students who live or have traveled overseas. On-campus housing is available on a first-come, first-served basis. 86% of students live on campus; of those, 65% remain on campus on weekends. All students may keep cars.

Activities: 17% of men belong to 1 local and 4 national fraternities; 39% of women belong to 1 local and 4 national sororities. There are 96 groups on campus, including art, bagpipe band, band, cheerleading, chess, choir, chorale, chorus, computers, dance, drama, ethnic, gay, honors, international, jazz band, literary magazine, marching band, newspaper, orchestra, photography, political, professional, radio and TV, religious, social, social service, student government, symphony, and yearbook. Popular campus events include All Nighter and Song Fest.

Sports: There are 9 intercollegiate sports for men and 9 for women, and 15 intramural sports for men and 15 for women. Facilities include a recreation center with a climbing wall, fitness center, 4 courts and suspended 3-lane track; an indoor gym and pool; an outdoor sports complex with an artificial turf playing field, an 8-lane track, baseball, soccer and softball fields; a weight training room; and racquetball and tennis courts.

Disabled Students: 90% of the campus is accessible. Wheelchair ramps, elevators, special parking, specially equipped rest rooms, special class scheduling, lowered drinking fountains, 2 residence halls with private baths, and several small housing units are available.

Services: Counseling and information services are available, as is tutoring in every subject. Both individual and group tutoring are available. There is remedial math, reading, and writing.

Campus Safety and Security: Measures include informal discussions, pamphlets/posters/films, emergency telephones, lighted pathways/sidewalks, and 24-hour foot patrol.

Programs of Study: Alma confers B.A., B.S., B.M., and B.F.A. degrees. Bachelor's degrees are awarded in BIOLOGICAL SCIENCE (biochemistry, and biology/biological science), BUSINESS (business administration and management and international business management), COMMUNICATIONS AND THE ARTS (art, communications, design, dramatic arts, English, French, German, music, and Spanish), COMPUTER AND PHYSICAL SCIENCE (chemistry, computer science, mathematics, and physics), EDUCATION (elementary and secondary), HEALTH PROFESSIONS (health science), SOCIAL SCIENCE (anthro-

pology, economics, history, philosophy, political science/government, psychology, religion, and sociology). Education, business administration, and biology are the strongest academically and are the largest.

Required: Degree requirements include completion of a minimum of 136 credit hours; 148 hours are required for the B.F.A. degree, 136 to 156 for the B.M. degree. Students must attain a minimum GPA of 2.0, or 3.0 for fine arts majors. All students must demonstrate proficiency in English, communication, and computation, and they must complete distribution requirements, which include 16 fine arts and humanities credits (4 credits in each of creative or performing arts, literature, philosophy, or religious studies, and humanities), and 16 each of social science and life and physical science credits. The total number of program credits is 36 for a departmental major, 56 for an interdepartmental major, and 56 to 58 for self-designed majors.

Special: Alma offers internships in many fields, study abroad in 15 countries, experiential learning program at the Philadelphia Center, and a Washington semester at American University. There are work-study programs, dual majors, B.A.-B.S. degrees, and student-designed majors in a wide variety of subjects. The college confers 3-2 engineering degrees in conjunction with the University of Michigan, Michigan Technological University, and Washington University in St. Louis. Nondegree study may be pursued, and students have a pass/fail grading option. A 4-week spring term provides intensive study in 1 course, often combined with travel. There are 4 national honor societies, including Phi Beta Kappa, a freshman honors program, and 16 departmental honors programs.

Faculty/Classroom: 63% of faculty are male; 37%, female. All teach undergraduates and 73% do research. The average class size in an introductory lecture is 22; in a laboratory, 15; and in a regular course, 20.

Admissions: 77% of the 2003-2004 applicants were accepted. The ACT scores for the 2003-2004 freshman class were: 15% below 21, 25% between 21 and 23, 29% between 24 and 26, 14% between 27 and 28, and 17% above 28. 61% of the current freshmen were in the top fifth of their class; 87% were in the top two fifths. There were 7 National Merit finalists. 25 freshmen graduated first in their class.

Requirements: The SAT I or ACT is required; the ACT is preferred. Applicants must have graduated from an accredited secondary school and have earned 16 Carnegie units, including 4 years of English and 3 each of math, science, and social studies, with 2 of a foreign language recommended. Alma prefers applicants in the upper 25% of their class. An essay is recommended and a portfolio and audition are required for performing arts scholarships. A GPA of 3.0 is required. AP credits are accepted. Important factors in the admissions decision are advanced placement or honor courses, leadership record, and recommendations by school officials.

Procedure: Freshmen are admitted fall, winter, and spring. Entrance exams should be taken in the spring of the junior year or as late as the winter of the senior year. There is a rolling admissions plan. There are early admissions and deferred admissions plans. Early decision applications should be filed by November 1; regular applications are open for fall entry. Application fee is $25. Notification of early decision is sent November 15; regular decision, on a rolling basis. Applications are accepted on-line through *www.alma.edu/admissions/application.htm*.

Transfer: 29 transfer students enrolled in 2002-2003. Students wishing to transfer to Alma must have a minimum GPA of 2.0 from other colleges attended. 34 of 136 credits required for the bachelor's degree must be completed at Alma.

Visiting: There are regularly scheduled orientations for prospective students, consisting of faculty talks, tours, a meal on campus, financial aid information, and admissions sessions. There are guides for informal visits and visitors may sit in on classes and stay overnight. To schedule a visit, contact the Admissions Office at *admissions@alma.edu*.

Financial Aid: In 2003-2004, 98% of all full-time freshmen and 99% of continuing full-time students received some form of financial aid. 45% of full-time freshmen and 77% of continuing full-time students received need-based aid. The average freshman award was $17,417. Need-based scholarships or need-based grants averaged $17,417 ($18,684 maximum); need-based self-help aid (loans and jobs) averaged $4301 ($5625 maximum); and non-need-based awards and non-need-based scholarships averaged $2850. Other aid includes external and restricted awards, plus employee dependent tuition grants. 45% of undergraduates work part time. Average annual earnings from campus work are $900. The average financial indebtedness of the 2003 graduate was $19,235. Alma is a member of CSS. The FAFSA is required. The priority date for freshman financial aid applications for fall entry is February 21. The deadline for filing freshman financial aid applications for fall entry is March 1.

International Students: There are 16 international students enrolled. The school actively recruits these students. They must score 525 on the written TOEFL or 195 on the electronic version. The SAT I or ACT is required if the TOEFL is not submitted.

Computers: The on-campus network links 694 terminals, printers, and PCs across campus. Macs are available in 6 residence halls, department labs, the Colina Library classroom, and the Academic Center. All residence halls are wired for Internet access. All students may access the system all hours. There are no time limits and no fees. It is strongly recommended that all students have a personal computer.

Graduates: From July 1, 2002 to June 30, 2003, 281 bachelor's degrees were awarded. The most popular majors were business administration (20%), education (13%), and biology (9%). In an average class, 1% graduate in 3 years or less, 54% graduate in 4 years or less, 69% graduate in 5 years or less, and 72% graduate in 6 years or less. 28 companies recruited on campus in 2002-2003. Of the 2002 graduating class, 30% were enrolled in graduate school within 6 months of graduation and 93% were employed.

Admissions Contact: Paul Pollatz, Director of Admissions.
E-mail: *admissions@alma.edu* Web: *www.alma.edu*

ANDREWS UNIVERSITY
Berrien Springs, MI 49104-0740

C-5
(616) 471-6343
(800) 253-2874; Fax: (616) 471-3228

Full-time: 674 men, 781 women	**Faculty:** 112
Part-time: 113 men, 119 women	**Ph.D.s:** 71%
Graduate: 805 men, 503 women	**Student/Faculty:** 13 to 1
Year: semesters	**Tuition:** $14,570
Application Deadline: open	**Room & Board:** $4980
Freshman Class: n/av	
SAT I Verbal/Math: 530/530	**ACT:** 23 **COMPETITIVE**

Andrews University, established in 1874, is a private institution affiliated with the Seventh-day Adventist Church that offers undergraduate degrees in business, education, arts and sciences, and technology. There are 5 undergraduate and 6 graduate schools. In addition to regional accreditation, Andrews has baccalaureate program accreditation with ADA, AHEA, APTA, CAHEA, NAAB, NASM, NCATE, and NLN. The library contains 750,000 volumes, 1,110,000 microform items, and 1025 audio/video tapes/CDs, and subscribes to 2200 periodicals. Computerized library services include the card catalog, interlibrary loans, database searching, and Internet access. Special learning facilities include an art gallery, natural history museum, radio station, and an archeological museum. The 1600-acre campus is in a rural area 15 miles south of Benton Harbor. Including any residence halls, there are 57 buildings.

Student Life: 58% of undergraduates are from out of state, mostly the Midwest. Students are from 47 states, 49 foreign countries, and Canada. 19% are from public schools. 46% are white; 19% African American; 18% foreign nationals; 10% Hispanic. 86% are Protestant; 14% unknown. The average age of freshmen is 19; all undergraduates, 22. 24% do not continue beyond their first year; 48% remain to graduate.

Housing: 1500 students can be accommodated in college housing, which includes single-sex dorms, on-campus apartments, and married-student housing. On-campus housing is available on a first-come, first-served basis. 58% of students live on campus. Alcohol is not permitted. All students may keep cars.

Activities: There is 1 national fraternity and 1 national sorority. There are 30 groups on campus, including band, choir, chorale, chorus, computers, drama, ethnic, honors, international, newspaper, professional, religious, social, social service, student government, and yearbook. Popular campus events include Alumni Weekend and International Food Fair.

Sports: There are 6 intramural sports for men and 4 for women. Facilities include a gym, a pool, racquetball courts, and health clubs in 2 of 3 dorms.

Disabled Students: 70% of the campus is accessible. Wheelchair ramps, elevators, special parking, specially equipped rest rooms, special class scheduling, lowered drinking fountains, lowered telephones, and special housing are available. A special committee deals with needs as they arise.

Services: Counseling and information services are available, as is tutoring in most subjects. There are math, writing, and reading learning and assessment centers.

Campus Safety and Security: Measures include 24-hour foot and vehicle patrol, security escort services, informal discussions, and pamphlets/posters/films. There are lighted pathways/sidewalks and CPR training.

Programs of Study: Andrews confers B.A., B.S., B.B.A., B.F.A., B.Mus., B.S.D., B.S.Educ., B.S.El.Ed., B.S.W., and B.T. degrees. Associate, master's, and doctoral degrees are also awarded. Bachelor's degrees are awarded in AGRICULTURE (agriculture, animal science, and horticulture), BIOLOGICAL SCIENCE (anatomy, biochemistry, biology/biological science, biophysics, botany, molecular biology, nutrition, physiology, and zoology), BUSINESS (accounting, banking and finance, business administration and management, business economics, management information systems, and marketing/retailing/merchandising), COMMUNICATIONS AND THE ARTS (art, ceramic art and design, communications, creative writing, design, English, French, graphic design, journalism, literature, music, music performance, painting, photography, public relations, Spanish, and visual and performing arts), COMPUTER AND PHYSICAL SCIENCE (applied mathematics, chemistry, computer science, information sciences and systems, mathematics, and physics), EDUCATION (art, elementary, English, mathematics, music,

physical, science, secondary, social studies, teaching English as a second/foreign language (TESOL/TEFOL), and technical), ENGINEERING AND ENVIRONMENTAL DESIGN (aeronautical technology, aircraft mechanics, architecture, automotive technology, aviation administration/management, aviation computer technology, biomedical equipment technology, computer graphics, computer technology, construction management, electrical/electronics engineering, electrical/electronics engineering technology, engineering, environmental science, graphic arts technology, industrial engineering, landscape architecture/design, and mechanical engineering technology), HEALTH PROFESSIONS (allied health, art therapy, biomedical science, exercise science, medical laboratory technology, nursing, preveterinary science, public health, and speech pathology/audiology), SOCIAL SCIENCE (anthropology, behavioral science, crosscultural studies, dietetics, economics, family/consumer studies, history, human development, interdisciplinary studies, pastoral studies, political science/government, psychology, religion, religious education, social studies, social work, sociology, theological studies, and youth ministry). Health sciences, business, and biology are the largest.

Required: Students must complete a minimum of 124 semester credits. Specific course requirements include religion, English, behavioral sciences, fine arts, and phys ed.

Special: Students may pursue a second major in business administration. Study abroad, student-designed majors, nondegree study, and pass/fail options are available. There is a freshman honors program.

Faculty/Classroom: 68% of faculty are male; 32%, female. The average class size in a laboratory is 16 and in a regular course, 18.

Admissions: The SAT I scores for the 2003-2004 freshman class were: Verbal--37% below 500, 36% between 500 and 599, 20% between 600 and 700, and 7% above 700; Math--48% below 500, 34% between 500 and 599, 11% between 600 and 700, and 7% above 700. The ACT scores were 24% below 21, 23% between 21 and 23, 23% between 24 and 26, 9% between 27 and 28, and 11% above 28. 31% of the current freshmen were in the top fifth of their class; 54% were in the top two fifths. There were 5 National Merit finalists.

Requirements: The SAT I or ACT is required, with the ACT preferred. Candidates for admission must graduate from an accredited secondary school or earn a GED. Ten Carnegie units are required, and students must have completed 4 courses in English and 2 courses each in history, math, and science. Interviews are recommended for all applicants. A GPA of 2.25 is required. CLEP credit is accepted. Important factors in the admissions decision are advanced placement or honor courses, recommendations by school officials, and evidence of special talent.

Procedure: Freshmen are admitted fall, spring, and summer. Entrance exams should be taken as early as possible. There is a deferred and a rolling admissions plan. Application deadlines are open. Application fee is $30.

Transfer: 134 transfer students enrolled in 2002-2003. Transfer applicants must submit a high school transcript and transcripts from all colleges attended. A maximum of 70 semester credits from a 2-year school or 90 semester credits from a 4-year school may be transferred toward a bachelor's degree. Credits should be relevant to the students major at Andrews University. The minimum GPA is 2.25, and the ACT is preferred. Students must meet freshman entrance requirements if they are transferring with less than sophomore standing from an accredited college. 30 of a minimum of 124 credits must be completed at Andrews.

Visiting: There are regularly scheduled orientations for prospective students, tours, meetings with faculty, and social activities. There are guides for informal visits and visitors may sit in on classes and stay overnight. To schedule a visit, contact the Admissions Office at (800) 253-2874 or *visit@andrews.edu*.

Financial Aid: Andrews is a member of CSS. The FAFSA is required. The deadline for freshman financial aid applications for fall entry is open.

International Students: There are 170 international students enrolled. The school actively recruits these students. They must score 550 on the written TOEFL or 213 on the electronic version.

Computers: Internet access is available in all dorm rooms and computer labs. All students may access the system. There are no time limits and no fees. It is strongly recommended that all students have a personal computer, and students in architecture are required to have them. A Dell is recommended.

Graduates: From July 1, 2002 to June 30, 2003, 303 bachelor's degrees were awarded. The most popular majors were health professions (21%), biology and life sciences (10%), and visual and performing arts (10%). In an average class, 28% graduate in 4 years or less, 42% graduate in 5 years or less, and 48% graduate in 6 years or less.

Admissions Contact: Charlotte Coy, Undergraduate Admissions Supervisor. E-mail: *undergraduate@andrews.edu*
Web: *www.andrews.edu*

AQUINAS COLLEGE

D-4

Grand Rapids, MI 49506-1799

(616) 732-4460

(800) 678-9593; Fax: (616) 732-4469

Full-time: 502 men, 980 women	**Faculty:** 99; IIB, --$
Part-time: 121 men, 225 women	**Ph.D.s:** 65%
Graduate: 175 men, 355 women	**Student/Faculty:** 15 to 1
Year: semesters, summer session	**Tuition:** $16,400
Application Deadline: open	**Room & Board:** $5494
Freshman Class: 1361 applied, 1078 accepted, 284 enrolled	
ACT: 23	**COMPETITIVE**

Aquinas College, established in 1866, is a private liberal arts institution affiliated with the Roman Catholic Church that offers undergraduate and graduate degrees through day and evening programs. There are 3 undergraduate and 2 graduate schools. The library contains 112,252 volumes, 227,444 microform items, and 5890 audio/video tapes/CDs, and subscribes to 792 periodicals. Computerized library services include the card catalog, interlibrary loans, database searching, and Internet access. Special learning facilities include a learning resource center, art gallery, radio station, greenhouses, and an observatory. The 107-acre campus is in a suburban area in Grand Rapids. Including any residence halls, there are 30 buildings.

Student Life: 94% of undergraduates are from Michigan. Students are from 21 states, 11 foreign countries, and Canada. 80% are from public schools. 93% are white. 59% are Catholic; 12% Protestant; 19% unknown. The average age of freshmen is 18; all undergraduates, 20. 25% do not continue beyond their first year; 51% remain to graduate.

Housing: 700 students can be accommodated in college housing, which includes single-sex and coed dorms and on-campus apartments. In addition, there are special-interest houses and service learning houses. On-campus housing is guaranteed for all 4 years. 51% of students live on campus; of those, 35% remain on campus on weekends. All students may keep cars.

Activities: There are no fraternities or sororities. There are 45 groups on campus, including cheerleading, choir, chorus, computers, dance, drama, ethnic, honors, international, jazz band, literary magazine, newspaper, photography, political, radio and TV, religious, social, social service, student government, and yearbook. Popular campus events include Spring Fling, Activities @ Moose Cafe, and a jazz festival.

Sports: There are 9 intercollegiate sports for men and 10 for women, and 13 intramural sports for men and 13 for women. Facilities include a gym, a weight room, a recreation room, an indoor track, softball and soccer fields, and indoor tennis courts.

Disabled Students: 95% of the campus is accessible. Wheelchair ramps, elevators, special parking, specially equipped rest rooms, special class scheduling, lowered drinking fountains, and lowered telephones are available.

Services: Counseling and information services are available, as is tutoring in most subjects. There is a reader service for the blind, and remedial math, reading, and writing.

Campus Safety and Security: Measures include 24-hour foot and vehicle patrol, security escort services, informal discussions, and pamphlets/posters/films. There are emergency telephones and lighted pathways/sidewalks.

Programs of Study: Aquinas confers B.A., B.S., B.A.G.E., B.F.A., B.S.B.A., and B.S.I.B. degrees. Associate and master's degrees are also awarded. Bachelor's degrees are awarded in BIOLOGICAL SCIENCE (biology/biological science), BUSINESS (business administration and management, business economics, and international business management), COMMUNICATIONS AND THE ARTS (art, art history and appreciation, communications, drawing, English, fine arts, French, German, language arts, music, painting, photography, printmaking, sculpture, and Spanish), COMPUTER AND PHYSICAL SCIENCE (chemistry, information sciences and systems, and mathematics), EDUCATION (education, physical, and special), ENGINEERING AND ENVIRONMENTAL DESIGN (environmental science), HEALTH PROFESSIONS (health, medical technology, and nuclear medical technology), SOCIAL SCIENCE (community services, economics, geography, history, interdisciplinary studies, international studies, philosophy, political science/government, psychology, sociology, and theological studies). Business administration and education are the strongest academically and have the largest enrollments.

Required: To graduate, students must complete 124 semester hours, with 30 to 48 in the major, and maintain a minimum GPA of 2.0. The general education program consists of a core of 18 to 30 hours, which includes, from the first to the fourth year, foreign language and a year-long integrated skills course, and courses in the humanities, religion, and global perspectives; and distribution requirements of 30 to 33 hours, which include courses in cultural diversity, mythology and spirituality, natural sciences, the fine arts, and quantitative reasoning and technology.

Special: Students may cross-register with the Dominican Consortium and may study abroad in Ireland, Germany, France, Spain, Costa Rica, Peru, or Japan. Co-op programs and internships are available in all majors, and work-study programs are also available. Students may pursue dual majors in business administration and accounting, sports management, communication arts, or art, and B.A.-B.S. degrees in business, geography, or psychology. Student-designed majors can be arranged. There is a 3-1 program in nuclear medicine technology with St. Louis University, as well as preengineering, prehealth, and teacher certification programs. Aquinas offers a general studies degree and may confer credit for life, military, and work experience. A pass/fail grading option is available. There are 5 national honor societies, a freshman honors program, and 5 departmental honors programs.

Faculty/Classroom: 52% of faculty are male; 48%, female. All teach undergraduates. No introductory courses are taught by graduate students. The average class size in an introductory lecture is 20; in a laboratory, 20; and in a regular course, 16.

Admissions: 79% of the 2003-2004 applicants were accepted. The ACT scores for the 2003-2004 freshman class were: 31% below 21, 23% between 21 and 23, 27% between 24 and 26, 10% between 27 and 28, and 9% above 28. 30% of the current freshmen were in the top fifth of their class; 52% were in the top two fifths. 10 freshmen graduated first in their class.

Requirements: The SAT I or ACT is recommended; the minimum acceptable composite ACT score is 18. Candidates for admission must graduate from an accredited secondary school. Students must have completed 15 Carnegie units, 4 years of English and social studies, and 3 to 4 years each of math and science. Interviews are recommended for all applicants, and auditions are recommended in appropriate instances. A GPA of 2.5 is required. AP and CLEP credits are accepted. Important factors in the admissions decision are advanced placement or honor courses, leadership record, and extracurricular activities record.

Procedure: Freshmen are admitted fall and winter. Entrance exams should be taken during the spring of the junior year. Application deadlines are open. There is a rolling admissions plan. Notification is sent on a rolling basis. Applications are accepted on-line through the school's web site.

Transfer: 67 transfer students enrolled in 2002-2003. Transfer applicants must have earned at least 12 credits in academic course work from an accredited junior or 4-year college with a minimum GPA of 2.0. Interviews are recommended. 30 credits of 124 required for the bachelor's degree must be completed at Aquinas.

Visiting: There are regularly scheduled orientations for prospective students, consisting of a tour of the campus and presentations by financial aid personnel, program directors, coaches, and faculty. There are guides for informal visits and visitors may sit in on classes and stay overnight. To schedule a visit, contact Thomas Mikowski, Director of Admissions at (616) 459-8281, ext. 2853 or admissions@aquinas.edu.

Financial Aid: In 2003-2004, all full-time freshmen and 76% of continuing full-time students received some form of financial aid. 79% of full-time freshmen and 72% of continuing full-time students received need-based aid. The average freshman award was $16,001. Need-based scholarships or need-based grants averaged $12,661; need-based self-help aid (loans and jobs) averaged $2800; non-need-based athletic scholarships averaged $2200; and other non-need-based awards and non-need-based scholarships averaged $9767. 22% of undergraduates work part time. Average annual earnings from campus work are $2767. The average financial indebtedness of the 2003 graduate was $13,638. The FAFSA is required. The deadline for filing freshman financial aid applications for fall entry is June 1.

International Students: There are 13 international students enrolled. They must score 550 on the written TOEFL or take the MELAB.

Computers: The mainframe is Digital Alpha 2100. There are 85 terminals available in classrooms, computer labs, dorms, and the residence halls. All students may access the system 91 hours per week during open lab times. There are no time limits and no fees. It is strongly recommended that all students have a personal computer.

Graduates: From July 1, 2002 to June 30, 2003, 359 bachelor's degrees were awarded. The most popular majors were education (20%), business administration (18%), and social science (12%). In an average class, 33% graduate in 4 years or less, 49% graduate in 5 years or less, and 52% graduate in 6 years or less. 30 companies recruited on campus in 2002-2003. Of the 2002 graduating class, 30% were enrolled in graduate school within 6 months of graduation and 70% were employed.

Admissions Contact: Thomas Mikowski, Director of Admissions. A video is available. E-mail: mikowtho@aquinas.edu Web: www.aquinas.edu/admissions

BAKER COLLEGE OF FLINT
Flint, MI 48507-5508

E-4
(810) 766-4000
(800) 822-2537; Fax: (810) 766-4049

Full-time: 780 men, 1600 women	Faculty: 23
Part-time: 650 men, 1400 women	Ph.D.s: 13%
Graduate: none	Student/Faculty: 41 to 1
Year: quarters, summer session	Tuition: $7000
Application Deadline: open	Room & Board: $800
Freshman Class: n/av	
SAT I or ACT: not required	NONCOMPETITIVE

Baker College, established in 1911, is an independent institution offering undergraduate degrees in business, health science, and technical curricula. It is part of the Baker College System. Figures in the above capsule and in this profile are approximate. In addition to regional accreditation, Baker has baccalaureate program accreditation with CAHEA. The library contains 60,000 volumes, 1200 microform items, and 475 audio/video tapes/CDs, and subscribes to 190 periodicals. Computerized library services include the card catalog, interlibrary loans, and database searching. Special learning facilities include a learning resource center. The 30-acre campus is in an urban area 60 miles northwest of Detroit. Including any residence halls, there are 6 buildings.

Student Life: 92% of undergraduates are from Michigan. Students are from 4 foreign countries and Canada. 72% are white; 22% African American. The average age of all undergraduates is 28.

Housing: 189 students can be accommodated in college housing, which includes single-sex and coed dorms, on-campus apartments, and off-campus apartments. On-campus housing is available on a first-come, first-served basis. Priority is given to out-of-town students. 98% of students commute. Alcohol is not permitted. All students may keep cars.

Activities: There are no fraternities or sororities. There are 15 groups on campus, including computers, literary magazine, professional, and social. Popular campus events include Baker College Spirit Day and Martin Luther King, Jr. Day.

Sports: There is no sports program at Baker. Facilities include a gym and a weight room.

Disabled Students: All of the campus is accessible. Wheelchair ramps, elevators, special parking, specially equipped rest rooms, lowered drinking fountains, and lowered telephones are available.

Services: Counseling and information services are available, as is tutoring in most subjects.

Campus Safety and Security: Measures include 24-hour foot and vehicle patrol, self-defense education, security escort services, and informal discussions. There are pamphlets/posters/films, and lighted pathways/sidewalks. High-traffic areas of the college are monitored by video camera.

Programs of Study: Baker confers B.B.A., B.B.L., and B.I.M. degrees. Associate degrees are also awarded. Bachelor's degrees are awarded in BUSINESS (accounting, business administration and management, marketing management, and office supervision and management), COMPUTER AND PHYSICAL SCIENCE (computer programming), ENGINEERING AND ENVIRONMENTAL DESIGN (aviation administration/management, drafting and design technology, electrical/electronics engineering technology, and interior design), HEALTH PROFESSIONS (health care administration and occupational therapy). Business administration and health information management are the largest.

Required: Degree requirements include completion of 180 to 208 quarter hours with a minimum GPA of 2.0. All students must complete math and computer courses and an employment course.

Special: Co-op programs, work-study, internships, and dual and interdisciplinary majors are available. An accelerated degree program is possible in business administration.

Faculty/Classroom: 46% of faculty are male; 54%, female. All teach undergraduates.

Requirements: There are no entrance requirements to Baker College. Students without either a high school diploma or a GED may still be admitted on the basis of Baker College test results.

Procedure: Freshmen are admitted to all sessions. There is a rolling admissions plan. Application deadlines are open. The fall 2003 application fee was $20. Notification is sent on a rolling basis.

Transfer: 527 transfer students enrolled in a recent year. Transcripts from all previous colleges must be submitted. Grades of C or better are eligible for transfer credit. 48 quarter hours of 180 to 208 required for the bachelor's degree must be completed at Baker.

Visiting: There are regularly scheduled orientations for prospective students, including orientation and testing. There are guides for informal visits and visitors may sit in on classes. To schedule a visit, contact the Admissions Office.

Financial Aid: The FAFSA and the college's own financial statement are required. Check with the school for current deadlines.

Computers: The mainframe is an IBM System 36 Model B24. There are 220 networked PCs available for student use. All students may access the system during school hours. There are no time limits and no fees.

Graduates: In a recent year, 227 bachelor's degrees were awarded. The most popular majors were business/marketing (63%), health (23%), and information science (6%).
Admissions Contact: Mark Heaton, Vice President of Admissions.
E-mail: *heaton_m@flint.baker.edu*

CALVIN COLLEGE
Grand Rapids, MI 49546

D-4
(616) 526-6106
(800) 688-0122; Fax: (616) 526-6777

Full-time: 1812 men, 2273 women	Faculty: 305; IIB, av$
Part-time: 86 men, 111 women	Ph.D.s: 95%
Graduate: 6 men, 28 women	Student/Faculty: 13 to 1
Year: 4-1-4, summer session	Tuition: $16,775
Application Deadline: August 15	Room & Board: $5840
Freshman Class: 1933 applied, 1906 accepted, 1042 enrolled	
SAT I Verbal/Math: 610/610	ACT: 26 NONCOMPETITIVE

Calvin College, established in 1876, is a private institution affiliated with the Christian Reformed Church, offering undergraduate and graduate degrees in liberal arts. In addition to regional accreditation, Calvin has baccalaureate program accreditation with ABET, ACCE, CSWE, NASM, NCATE, and NLN. The library contains 802,000 volumes, 785,000 microform items, and 22,400 audio/video tapes/CDs, and subscribes to 2700 periodicals. Computerized library services include the card catalog, interlibrary loans, database searching, and Internet access. Special learning facilities include a learning resource center, art gallery, ecosystem preserve, electron microscope lab, an observatory with a 16-inch telescope, and a greenhouse. The 370-acre campus is in a suburban area 7 miles southeast of downtown Grand Rapids. Including any residence halls, there are 40 buildings.

Student Life: 53% of undergraduates are from Michigan. Students are from 47 states, 40 foreign countries, and Canada. 43% are from public schools. 84% are white. Most are Protestant. The average age of freshmen is 19; all undergraduates, 20. 13% do not continue beyond their first year; 74% remain to graduate.

Housing: 2397 students can be accommodated in college housing, which includes single-sex dorms and on-campus apartments. In addition, there are language houses, a residence hall wing designated as a multicultural community, and 3 urban houses designated as residential living with a community/urban focus. On-campus housing is guaranteed for freshman and sophomore years. 56% of students live on campus; of those, 90% remain on campus on weekends. Alcohol is not permitted. All students may keep cars.

Activities: There are no fraternities or sororities. There are 40 groups on campus, including art, band, cheerleading, chess, choir, chorale, chorus, computers, dance, drama, ethnic, film, honors, international, jazz band, literary magazine, musical theater, newspaper, orchestra, pep band, political, professional, radio and TV, religious, social, social service, student government, symphony, and yearbook. Popular campus events include Family Weekend, the spring and fall music and art festivals, and the January lecture series.

Sports: There are 8 intercollegiate sports for men and 9 for women, and 18 intramural sports for men and 14 for women. Facilities include a 4500-seat field house, a soccer facility, baseball and softball diamonds, an 8-lane, 400-meter polyurethane track, a weight-training/exercise room, a natatorium that contains a diving pool, 6 tennis courts, 2 sand beach volleyball courts, a paved recreational trail around campus, and multiple playing/practice fields.

Disabled Students: 85% of the campus is accessible. Wheelchair ramps, elevators, special parking, specially equipped rest rooms, special class scheduling, lowered drinking fountains, lowered telephones, special housing, electric door openers, and reserved classroom seating are available.

Services: Counseling and information services are available, as is tutoring in most subjects. There is a reader service for the blind, and remedial math, reading, and writing. There is a Braille print service for the blind, books on tape, note taking, interpreting, diagnostic testing, special advising, and early registration.

Campus Safety and Security: Measures include 24-hour foot and vehicle patrol, self-defense education, security escort services, and informal discussions. There are pamphlets/posters/films, emergency telephones, lighted pathways/sidewalks, a crime alert bulletin, and reports in the school newspaper.

Programs of Study: Calvin confers B.A., B.S., B.C.S., B.F.A., B.M.E., B.S.A., B.S.C.D., B.S.E., B.S.N., B.S.P.A., B.S.R., and B.S.W. degrees. Master's degrees are also awarded. Bachelor's degrees are awarded in BIOLOGICAL SCIENCE (biochemistry, biology/biological science, and biotechnology), BUSINESS (accounting, business administration and management, and recreation and leisure services), COMMUNICATIONS AND THE ARTS (art history and appreciation, classical languages, classics, communications, dramatic arts, Dutch, English, film arts, French, German, Greek, Latin, media arts, music, and Spanish), COMPUTER AND PHYSICAL SCIENCE (chemistry, computer science, digital arts/technology, geology, information sciences and systems, mathematics, and physics), EDUCATION (art, elementary, physical, secondary, and special), ENGINEERING AND ENVIRONMENTAL DESIGN (chemical engineering, civil engineering, electrical/electronics engineering, engineering, environmental science, and mechanical engineering), HEALTH PROFESSIONS (nursing, predentistry, and speech pathology/audiology), SOCIAL SCIENCE (American studies, criminal justice, economics, European studies, geography, history, international studies, philosophy, political science/government, prelaw, psychology, religion, social work, and sociology). Natural sciences, history, and English are the strongest academically. Education, engineering, and business are the largest.

Required: Degree requirements include completion of 124 credit hours, with 28 credits in the major. All students must complete specific course work in English, religion, history, science, math, communication, fine arts, psychology or sociology, economics or political science, philosophy, phys ed, information technology, and cross-cultural engagement. A minimum GPA of 2.0 is required.

Special: A variety of dual majors and student-designed majors is available, as well as combined curriculum programs in occupational therapy, and speech pathology. Students may study abroad in 16 countries and enroll in a Washington semester. Cooperative programs include Los Angeles film studies, the Au Sable Institute, the Chicago Metropolitan program, Oregon extension, Latin American, Middle East, Chinese, and Russian studies, and in business. Internships, work-study programs, and cross-registration at Grand Valley State University in special education, at Michigan State in communications disorders, in occupational therapy at Washington University, and in religion at Reformed Bible College are also available. There are 6 national honor societies, a freshman honors program, and 25 departmental honors programs.

Faculty/Classroom: 65% of faculty are male; 35%, female. All both teach and do research. No introductory courses are taught by graduate students. The average class size in an introductory lecture is 26; in a laboratory, 17; and in a regular course, 20.

Admissions: 99% of the 2003-2004 applicants were accepted. The SAT I scores for the 2003-2004 freshman class were: Verbal--8% below 500, 34% between 500 and 599, 40% between 600 and 700, and 18% above 700; Math--8% below 500, 38% between 500 and 599, 41% between 600 and 700, and 13% above 700. The ACT scores were 6% below 21, 21% between 21 and 23, 30% between 24 and 26, 18% between 27 and 28, and 25% above 28. 49% of the current freshmen were in the top fifth of their class; 75% were in the top two fifths. There were 25 National Merit finalists and 25 semifinalists. 41 freshmen graduated first in their class.

Requirements: The ACT is required. In addition, in selecting students for admission, Calvin College looks for evidence of Christian commitment and for the capacity and desire to learn. Students who are interested in the Christian perspective and curriculum of Calvin, and who show interest in its aims, are eligible for consideration. Although the prospect of academic success is of primary consideration, the aspirations of the applicant, the recommendation of a high school counselor, teacher, or principal, and the ability of Calvin to be of service, will also be considered in admission decisions. A GPA of 2.5 is required. AP and CLEP credits are accepted. Important factors in the admissions decision are recommendations by school officials, leadership record, and extracurricular activities record.

Procedure: Freshmen are admitted to all sessions. Entrance exams should be taken during the spring of the junior year or fall of the senior year. There is a deferred admissions plan and a rolling admissions plan. Applications should be filed by August 15 for fall entry, January 15 for spring entry, and open for summer entry. The fall 2003 application fee was $35 for on-line application and $50 for paper application. Notification is sent on a rolling basis. Applications are accepted on-line through the school's web site and through applyweb.com.

Transfer: 124 transfer students enrolled in 2002-2003. Applicants from 4-year colleges are required to have a minimum GPA of 2.0; from 2-year colleges, 2.5. The SAT I minimum requirements are 390 on the verbal section and 420 on the math section. A minimum score of 20 is required on the ACT. 31 of 124 credits required for the bachelor's degree must be completed at Calvin.

Visiting: There are regularly scheduled orientations for prospective students. Prospective students and their families are invited to explore Calvin firsthand by scheduling an individual visit or through the "Fridays at Calvin" campus visitation program, which offers sectionals, class visits, lunch with professors, campus tours, and an overnight stay at the residence halls. There are guides for informal visits and visitors may sit in on classes and stay overnight. To schedule a visit, contact the Admissions Office.

Financial Aid: In 2003-2004, 94% of all full-time freshmen and 91% of continuing full-time students received some form of financial aid. 63% of full-time freshmen and 64% of continuing full-time students received need-based aid. The average freshman award was $12,583. Need-based scholarships or need-based grants averaged $8912; need-based self-help aid (loans and jobs) averaged $5832; and other non-need-based awards and non-need-based scholarships averaged $4389. 80% of undergraduates work part time. Average annual earnings from campus work are

$1200. The average financial indebtedness of the 2003 graduate was $17,000. The FAFSA and the college's own financial statement are required. The priority date for freshman financial aid applications for fall entry is February 15. The deadline for filing freshman financial aid applications for fall entry is August 1.

International Students: There are 340 international students enrolled. The school actively recruits these students. They must score 550 on the written TOEFL or take the MELAB if the student scored low on the TOEFL. They must also take the SAT I or ACT. Exceptions are made for strong students without access to standardized exams.

Computers: The mainframe is an IBM RS/6000. There are 1500 PCs on campus with access to the network/Internet, and more than 900 are available to students. All students may access the system at any time. There are no time limits and no fees.

Graduates: From July 1, 2002 to June 30, 2003, 894 bachelor's degrees were awarded. The most popular majors were business (10%), English (8%), and elementary education (7%). In an average class, 1% graduate in 3 years or less, 56% graduate in 4 years or less, 72% graduate in 5 years or less, and 74% graduate in 6 years or less. 36 companies recruited on campus in 2002-2003. Of the 2002 graduating class, 19% were enrolled in graduate school within 6 months of graduation and 80% were employed.

Admissions Contact: Dale D. Kuiper, Director of Admissions. E-mail: *admissions@calvin.edu* Web: *www.calvin.edu*

CENTRAL MICHIGAN UNIVERSITY D-4
Mount Pleasant, MI 48859 (989) 774-3076; Fax: (989) 774-7267

Full-time: 7035 men, 10,055 women	**Faculty:** 806; IIA, av$
Part-time: 1080 men, 1472 women	**Ph.D.s:** 80%
Graduate: 3169 men, 5192 women	**Student/Faculty:** 21 to 1
Year: semesters, summer session	**Tuition:** $5218 ($11,140)
Application Deadline: open	**Room & Board:** $5924
Freshman Class: 13,520 applied, 9519 accepted, 3623 enrolled	
SAT I Verbal/Math: 524/525	**ACT:** 22 COMPETITIVE

Central Michigan University, founded in 1892, is a public university offering programs in liberal arts, business, and health, education, and human services. There are 6 undergraduate schools and 1 graduate school. In addition to regional accreditation, CMU has baccalaureate program accreditation with AACSB, ACCE, ACEJMC, NASM, NCATE, and NRPA. The library contains 998,460 volumes, 1,331,385 microform items, and 17,286 audio/video tapes/CDs, and subscribes to 4600 periodicals. Computerized library services include the card catalog, interlibrary loans, database searching, and Internet access. Special learning facilities include a learning resource center, art gallery, natural history museum, radio station, TV station, an observatory, and a student newspaper. The 837-acre campus is in a small town 70 miles north of Lansing. Including any residence halls, there are 96 buildings.

Student Life: 97% of undergraduates are from Michigan. Students are from 50 states, 69 foreign countries, and Canada. 89% are from public schools. 87% are white. The average age of freshmen is 18; all undergraduates, 21. 23% do not continue beyond their first year; 49% remain to graduate.

Housing: 6635 students can be accommodated in college housing, which includes single-sex and coed dorms, on-campus apartments, and married-student housing. In addition, there are honors houses. On-campus housing is guaranteed for all 4 years. 67% of students commute. Alcohol is not permitted. All students may keep cars.

Activities: 5% of men belong to 13 national fraternities; 6% of women belong to 11 national sororities. There are 35 groups on campus, including art, cheerleading, choir, chorus, computers, dance, drama, ethnic, gay, honors, international, jazz band, literary magazine, marching band, musical theater, newspaper, orchestra, pep band, photography, political, professional, radio and TV, religious, social, social service, student government, symphony, and yearbook. Popular campus events include Student Activities Fair, CMU and You Day, and Big/Little Sister/Brother Weekend.

Sports: There are 6 intercollegiate sports for men and 8 for women, and 27 intramural sports for men and 27 for women. Facilities include 9 flag football/soccer and 4 lighted softball fields; 6 outdoor tennis, 12 racquetball, 11 basketball, 10 volleyball, and 16 badminton courts; 3 swimming pools; 2 saunas; an indoor track; indoor turf and tennis courts, weight rooms, an aerobics area, 2 auxiliary gyms for floor hockey, basketball, and indoor soccer; a 12-lane bowling alley; and 8 pool/billiard tables. The campus football stadium seats 20,086, the baseball stadium 4200, and the basketball gym 6050.

Disabled Students: 95% of the campus is accessible. Wheelchair ramps, elevators, special parking, specially equipped rest rooms, special class scheduling, lowered drinking fountains, and lowered telephones are available.

Services: Counseling and information services are available, as is tutoring in most subjects. There is a reader service for the blind, and remedial math, reading, and writing. Tutoring is provided free of charge to students with a GPA below 2.0.

Campus Safety and Security: Measures include security escort services, shuttle buses, informal discussions, and pamphlets/posters/films. There are emergency telephones and lighted pathways/sidewalks.

Programs of Study: CMU confers B.A., B.S., B.A.A., B.F.A., B.Indiv.S., B.Mus., B.S.B.A., B.S.E., and B.S.E.T. degrees. Master's and doctoral degrees are also awarded. Bachelor's degrees are awarded in BIOLOGICAL SCIENCE (biology/biological science), BUSINESS (accounting, banking and finance, business administration and management, court reporting, management science, marketing/retailing/merchandising, and retailing), COMMUNICATIONS AND THE ARTS (broadcasting, communications, dramatic arts, English, fine arts, French, German, journalism, languages, music, and Spanish), COMPUTER AND PHYSICAL SCIENCE (actuarial science, chemistry, computer science, earth science, geology, mathematics, physical sciences, physics, and statistics), EDUCATION (art, bilingual/bicultural, business, early childhood, education, elementary, foreign languages, guidance, health, home economics, industrial arts, middle school, music, science, secondary, and special), ENGINEERING AND ENVIRONMENTAL DESIGN (engineering technology and industrial administration/management), HEALTH PROFESSIONS (speech pathology/audiology and sports medicine), SOCIAL SCIENCE (anthropology, economics, geography, history, parks and recreation management, philosophy, political science/government, psychology, religion, and sociology). Physical therapy and education are the strongest academically. Science and technology, humanities and social and behavioral sciences, and business administration are the largest.

Required: To graduate, students must complete 124 credit hours, including 30 in the major, with a GPA of 2.0. They must fulfill the university's distribution requirements in humanities, natural science, and social science, earn 30 hours in interpretive and area studies, and demonstrate written, oral, and math competency. A course in advanced English composition is required.

Special: CMU offers internships in business administration, study abroad in 11 countries, and dual majors in chemistry/physics and computer science/math. Student-designed majors are available for a B.A. in individual studies, and there is credit for life, military, and work experience. Students may take up to 25 hours for pass/fail grades. The Institute for Personal and Career Development offers external degree programs in which students can get degrees without attending classes on campus. There are 33 national honor societies, a freshman honors program, and 21 departmental honors programs.

Faculty/Classroom: 60% of faculty are male; 40%, female. Graduate students teach 2% of introductory courses. The average class size in an introductory lecture is 34; in a laboratory, 26; and in a regular course, 23.

Admissions: 70% of the 2003-2004 applicants were accepted. The SAT I scores for the 2003-2004 freshman class were: Verbal--41% below 500, 34% between 500 and 599, 22% between 600 and 700, and 3% above 700; Math--33% below 500, 43% between 500 and 599, 21% between 600 and 700, and 3% above 700. The ACT scores were 36% below 21, 31% between 21 and 23, 22% between 24 and 26, 7% between 27 and 28, and 4% above 28.

Requirements: The ACT is recommended. In addition, applicants must be high school graduates or hold a GED. The university strongly recommends 4 years each of English and math, 3 each of science and social studies, and 2 of foreign language, as well as 1 course each in computer science and fine arts. AP and CLEP credits are accepted.

Procedure: Freshmen are admitted to all sessions. Entrance exams should be taken during the junior or senior year of high school. There is a deferred admissions plan and a rolling admissions plan. Application deadlines are open. A waiting list is an active part of the admissions procedure. The fall 2003 application fee was $35. Applications are accepted on-line through the school's web site at *http://eweb.cmich.edu/apptype.htm*.

Transfer: 1079 transfer students enrolled in 2002-2003. Transfer students must have a GPA of 2.5. 30 of 124 credits required for the bachelor's degree must be completed at CMU.

Visiting: There are guides for informal visits and visitors may sit in on classes and stay overnight. To schedule a visit, contact Admissions at *cmuadmit@cmich.edu*.

Financial Aid: In a recent year, 94% of all full-time freshmen and 76% of continuing full-time students received some form of financial aid. 69% of full-time freshmen and 45% of continuing full-time students received need-based aid. The average freshman award was $7247. 22% of undergraduates work part time. Average annual earnings from campus work were $1584. The average financial indebtedness of a recent graduate was $14,898. The FAFSA is required. The priority date for freshman financial aid applications for fall entry is March 15.

International Students: There are 105 international students enrolled. The school actively recruits these students. They must score 520 on the written TOEFL.

Computers: The mainframe is an IBM 9672 model R32. There are 273 Mac and IBM PCs available for student use throughout the campus and in the dorms; 21 languages and software packages are available. All students may access the system at any time. There are no time limits and no fees.

Graduates: From July 1, 2002 to June 30, 2003, 2981 bachelor's degrees were awarded. The most popular majors were psychology (6%), and marketing (5%). In an average class, 1% graduate in 3 years or less, 17% graduate in 4 years or less, 42% graduate in 5 years or less, and 51% graduate in 6 years or less. 619 companies recruited on campus in 2002-2003.

Admissions Contact: Betty Wagner, Director of Admissions.
E-mail: *cmuadmit@cmuvm.csv.cmich.edu* Web: *www.cmich.edu*

CLEARY COLLEGE
E-5
Ann Arbor, MI 48197
(517) 548-3670 (Howell)
(800) 589-1979; Fax: (517) 548-2170

Full-time: 150 men, 250 women	**Faculty:** 11; III, --$
Part-time: 70 men, 200 women	**Ph.D.s:** 12%
Graduate: none	**Student/Faculty:** 35 to 1
Year: quarters, summer session	**Tuition:** $10,500
Application Deadline: open	**Room & Board:** n/app
Freshman Class: n/av	
SAT I: n/av	**ACT:** recommended

LESS COMPETITIVE

Cleary College, founded in 1883, is a private college of business offering bachelor's and associate degrees in business. Figures in the above capsule and in this profile are approximate. The college serves an entirely commuter student body. A second campus, similar in size and programs, is located in Howell, and there are extension sites throughout southeastern Michigan. The library contains 7877 volumes and 175 audio/video tapes/CDs, and subscribes to 30 periodicals. Computerized library services include the card catalog, interlibrary loans, and database searching. Special learning facilities include a learning resource center. The 27-acre campus is in a suburban area 25 miles east of Lansing and 40 miles west of Detroit. There is 1 building.

Student Life: 99% of undergraduates are from Michigan. Students are from 2 states, 1 foreign country, and Canada. 90% are from public schools. 91% are white. The average age of all undergraduates is 36.

Housing: There are no residence halls. All students commute. Alcohol is not permitted. All students may keep cars.

Activities: There are no fraternities or sororities. Popular campus events include picnics.

Sports: There is no sports program at Cleary.

Disabled Students: All of the campus is accessible. Wheelchair ramps, special parking, specially equipped rest rooms, lowered drinking fountains, and lowered telephones are available.

Services: Counseling and information services are available, as is tutoring in some subjects, including English, math, and computers. There is remedial math and writing.

Campus Safety and Security: Measures include informal discussions, pamphlets/posters/films, and lighted pathways/sidewalks.

Programs of Study: Cleary confers the B.B.A. degree. Associate degrees are also awarded. Bachelor's degrees are awarded in BUSINESS (accounting, banking and finance, business administration and management, human resources, and marketing management), COMPUTER AND PHYSICAL SCIENCE (information sciences and systems), HEALTH PROFESSIONS (health care administration). Accounting is the strongest academically. Business administration is the largest.

Required: Core requirements include 90 quarter credits of business courses in economics, management, basic accounting, communication, and ethics. To graduate, students must complete a senior project and at least 180 quarter credit hours with a minimum GPA of 2.5.

Special: Cleary offers internships, work-study, co-op programs in all majors, and accelerated degree programs in accounting, marketing, finance, management information technology, quality management, human resource management, health services management, corporate and public accounting, and business management. Cleary also offers credit for prior learning experiences and opportunities for individualized study. Nondegree study is possible.

Faculty/Classroom: 45% of faculty are male; 55%, female. All teach undergraduates. The average class size in an introductory lecture is 15; in a laboratory, 12; and in a regular course, 12.

Requirements: The ACT is recommended. In addition, applicants must be graduates of an accredited secondary school or have earned a GED, and have a minimum GPA of 2.5. AP and CLEP credits are accepted.

Procedure: Freshmen are admitted to all sessions. There are early decision, early admissions, and deferred admissions plans. There is a rolling admissions plan. Application deadlines are open. The application fee is $25. Notification is sent on a rolling basis.

Transfer: Applicants must submit official transcripts from all institutions previously attended and have a minimum GPA of 2.5. 45 quarter credits of 180 required for the bachelor's degree must be completed at Cleary.

Visiting: There are regularly scheduled orientations for prospective students. There are guides for informal visits and visitors may sit in on classes. To schedule a visit, contact Admissions.

Financial Aid: 1% of undergraduates work part time. Average annual earnings from campus work are $2500. Cleary is a member of CSS. The FAFSA is required. Check with the school for current deadlines.

International Students: They must score 600 on the written TOEFL or take the MELAB.

Computers: The mainframe consists of several Windows NT servers. Each campus has 2 computer labs equipped with PCs for academic use. The Internet is available for distance learning classes. All students may access the system. There are no time limits and no fees. All students are required to have personal computers.

Admissions Contact: Carrie Bonofiglio, Director of Admissions.
Web: www.cleary.edu

COLLEGE FOR CREATIVE STUDIES
Detroit, MI 48202-4034

E-5
(313) 664-7425
(800) 952-ARTS; Fax: (313) 872-2739

Full-time: 621 men, 431 women	**Faculty:** 43
Part-time: 89 men, 77 women	**Ph.D.s:** 78%
Graduate: none	**Student/Faculty:** 24 to 1
Year: semesters, summer session	**Tuition:** $19,798
Application Deadline: August 1	**Room & Board:** $3500
Freshman Class: 751 applied, 575 accepted, 347 enrolled	
ACT: 21	**SPECIAL**

The College for Creative Studies, established in 1906, is a private, independent institution offering comprehensive 4-year B.F.A programs in animation and digital media, crafts, fine arts, communication design, industrial design, interior design, and photography, as well as teacher certification in art education. In addition to regional accreditation, CCS has baccalaureate program accreditation with NASAD. The library contains 21,000 volumes, and subscribes to 100 periodicals. Special learning facilities include a learning resource center and art gallery. The 11-acre campus is in an urban area 3 miles from downtown Detroit in the University Cultural Center, which includes the Detroit Institute of Art. Including any residence halls, there are 6 buildings.

Student Life: 83% of undergraduates are from Michigan. Students are from 35 states, 18 foreign countries, and Canada. 66% are white. The average age of freshmen is 18; all undergraduates, 23. 26% do not continue beyond their first year; 56% remain to graduate.

Housing: 263 students can be accommodated in college housing, which includes coed on-campus apartments. On-campus housing is available on a first-come, first-served basis. Priority is given to out-of-town students. 79% of students commute. Alcohol is not permitted. All students may keep cars.

Activities: There are no fraternities or sororities. There are 6 groups on campus, including ethnic, professional, and student government. Popular campus events include an annual student exhibition, Noel Night, and Detroit Festival of the Arts.

Sports: There is no sports program at CCS.

Disabled Students: All of the campus is accessible. Wheelchair ramps, elevators, special parking, specially equipped rest rooms, and lowered telephones are available.

Services: Counseling and information services are available, as is tutoring in every subject. There is remedial reading and writing.

Campus Safety and Security: Measures include 24-hour foot and vehicle patrol, security escort services, informal discussions, and pamphlets/posters/films. There are lighted pathways/sidewalks.

Programs of Study: CCS confers the B.F.A. degree. Bachelor's degrees are awarded in COMMUNICATIONS AND THE ARTS (advertising, animation, ceramic art and design, fine arts, glass, graphic design, illustration, industrial design, metal/jewelry, painting, photography, printmaking, and sculpture), COMPUTER AND PHYSICAL SCIENCE (digital arts/technology), EDUCATION (art), ENGINEERING AND ENVIRONMENTAL DESIGN (interior design), SOCIAL SCIENCE (textiles and clothing). Industrial design and communication design are the strongest academically. Animation and digital media are the largest.

Required: Degree requirements include work in English, behavioral science, art, history, history, speech, philosophy, and art and design. Students must complete 42 credits in liberal arts. A minimum GPA of 2.0 is required, and students must complete 126 credits with 63 in the major, to graduate.

Special: Internships are available within the student's departmental major. Credit for internships and dual majors are available. Study abroad is possible.

Faculty/Classroom: 62% of faculty are male; 38%, female. All teach undergraduates. The average class size in an introductory lecture is 20; in a laboratory, 15; and in a regular course, 18.

Admissions: 77% of the 2003-2004 applicants were accepted.

Requirements: The SAT I or ACT is required. In addition, applicants must graduate from an accredited secondary school or earn a GED. A portfolio of representative work and an essay are required. A GPA of 2.5 is required. AP and CLEP credits are accepted. Important factors in the admissions decision are evidence of special talent and advanced placement or honor courses.

Procedure: Freshmen are admitted fall and winter. There is a deferred admissions plan and a rolling admissions plan. Applications should be filed by August 1 for fall entry and December 1 for spring entry, along with a $35 fee. Notification is sent on a rolling basis. Applications are accepted on-line through the school's web site and CollegeNET.

Transfer: 155 transfer students enrolled in 2002-2003. Transfer applicants should submit a portfolio that includes artwork done at the previous college. Transcripts and portfolio review will determine how many credits may transfer. The approval of the chairperson of the department to which the student is applying is required for transfer of studio credit. The minimum GPA is 2.0. 33 of 126 credits required for the bachelor's degree must be completed at CCS.

Visiting: There are regularly scheduled orientations for prospective students, including an introduction to the college by an admission professional, a digital presentation of student work, application/financial aid information, and a campus tour. The orientations are scheduled every other week from September through April. There are guides for informal visits and visitors may sit in on classes. To schedule a visit, contact the Admission Office at admissions@ccscad.edu.

Financial Aid: In a recent year, 99% of all full-time freshmen and 95% of continuing full-time students received some form of financial aid. 14% of undergraduates work part time. Average annual earnings from campus work were $1200. The average financial indebtedness of the 2003 graduate was $21,000. The FAFSA is required. The deadline for filing freshman financial aid applications for fall entry is February 21.

International Students: In a recent year there were 68 international students enrolled. The school actively recruits these students. They must score 527 on the written TOEFL or 197 on the electronic version and also take the SAT I or the ACT.

Computers: All students may access the system. There are no time limits and no fees. It is strongly recommended that all students have a personal computer.

Graduates: From July 1, 2002 to June 30, 2003, 190 bachelor's degrees were awarded. The most popular majors were industrial design (28%), animation and digital media (16%), and communication design (15%). In an average class, 56% graduate in 6 years or less. 35 companies recruited on campus in 2002-2003.

Admissions Contact: Admissions Officer.
E-mail: admissions@ccscad.edu Web: www.ccscad.edu

CONCORDIA UNIVERSITY
Ann Arbor, MI 48105

E-5
(734) 995-7311
(800) 253-0680; Fax: (734) 995-4610

Full-time: 161 men, 215 women	**Faculty:** 40
Part-time: 27 men, 35 women	**Ph.D.s:** 68%
Graduate: 15 men, 24 women	**Student/Faculty:** 9 to 1
Year: semesters, summer session	**Tuition:** $17,350
Application Deadline: open	**Room & Board:** $6745
Freshman Class: 320 applied, 241 accepted, 74 enrolled	
SAT I Verbal/Math: 550/530	**ACT:** 22 **COMPETITIVE**

Concordia University, established in 1963, is a private institution affiliated with Missouri Synod of the Lutheran Church, offering undergraduate and graduate degrees in the arts and sciences, business, education, and human services. There are 4 undergraduate schools and 1 graduate school. In addition to regional accreditation, Concordia has baccalaureate program accreditation with NCATE. The library contains 112,000 volumes, 36,000 microform items, and 6550 audio/video tapes/CDs, and subscribes to 1320 periodicals. Computerized library services include the card catalog, interlibrary loans, database searching, and Internet access. Special learning facilities include a learning resource center and art gallery. The 234-acre campus is in a suburban area 40 miles west of Detroit. Including any residence halls, there are 30 buildings.

Student Life: 77% of undergraduates are from Michigan. Students are from 12 states, 3 foreign countries, and Canada. 62% are from public schools. 86% are white. 80% are Protestant; 10% Catholic; 8% claim no religious affiliation. The average age of freshmen is 18; all undergraduates, 21. 35% do not continue beyond their first year.

Housing: 448 students can be accommodated in college housing, which includes single-sex dorms and married-student housing. On-campus housing is guaranteed for all 4 years. 65% of students live on campus; of those, 55% remain on campus on weekends. Alcohol is not permitted. All students may keep cars.

Activities: There are no fraternities or sororities. There are 21 groups on campus, including band, choir, chorale, chorus, computers, debate, drama, ethnic, jazz band, musical theater, pep band, religious, social, social service, student government, and yearbook. Popular campus events include Boar's Head Festival, Servant Events, and a Fall carnival.

Sports: There are 3 intercollegiate sports for men and 4 for women, and 7 intramural sports for men and 7 for women. Facilities include a soccer field, baseball and softball diamonds, sand volleyball courts, a phys ed building (gymnasium), and an open field for intramurals.

Disabled Students: 90% of the campus is accessible. Wheelchair ramps, elevators, special parking, specially equipped rest rooms, and lowered drinking fountains are available.

Services: Counseling and information services are available, as is tutoring in every subject. There is remedial math, reading, and writing.

Campus Safety and Security: Measures include 24-hour foot and vehicle patrol, security escort services, informal discussions, and pamphlets/posters/films. There are lighted pathways/sidewalks.

Programs of Study: Concordia confers the B.A. degree. Associate and master's degrees are also awarded. Bachelor's degrees are awarded in BIOLOGICAL SCIENCE (biology/biological science), BUSINESS (business administration and management), COMMUNICATIONS AND THE ARTS (art, communications, English, and music), COMPUTER AND PHYSICAL SCIENCE (information sciences and systems, mathematics, and science), EDUCATION (elementary, physical, and secondary), SOCIAL SCIENCE (biblical languages, criminal justice, family/consumer studies, history, psychology, religion, and social studies). Education is the strongest academically. Business administration and teacher education are the largest.

Required: Degree requirements include completion of 128 credit hours, with 30 to 36 in the major, 33 credit hours of integrated studies, and a minimum GPA of 2.0. The student must also demonstrate proficiency in foreign language, writing, speech, and math. Required courses include upper-level general studies, writing-intensive, physical activities, and computer applications. A senior project is required.

Special: Internships are available in most academic majors. Students may study abroad in 7 countries. Accelerated degree programs are available in business administration and criminal justice administration. The college confers credit for life, military, and work experience through the School of Adult and Continuing Education. Nondegree study, dual majors in many combinations, and a pass/fail grading option are available.

Faculty/Classroom: 55% of faculty are male; 45%, female. All teach undergraduates. No introductory courses are taught by graduate students. The average class size in an introductory lecture is 25; in a laboratory, 10; and in a regular course, 15.

Admissions: 75% of the 2003-2004 applicants were accepted. The SAT I scores for the 2003-2004 freshman class were: Verbal--24% below 500, 38% between 500 and 599, and 38% between 600 and 700; Math--31% below 500, 54% between 500 and 599, and 15% between 600 and 700. The ACT scores were 33% below 21, 26% between 21 and 23, 4% between 24 and 26, 10% between 27 and 28, and 10% above 28.

Requirements: The SAT I or ACT is required; the ACT is preferred, with a minimum score of 18. Applicants must graduate from an accredited secondary school or have the GED. 20 Carnegie units are required, including 4 units in English and 3 each in math, science, and social studies. AP and CLEP credits are accepted. Important factors in the admissions decision are evidence of special talent, advanced placement or honor courses, and leadership record.

Procedure: Freshmen are admitted fall and winter. There is a deferred admissions plan and a rolling admissions plan. Application deadlines are open. The fall 2003 application fee was $25. Applications are accepted on-line through Apply Web and the school's web site.

Transfer: 60 transfer students enrolled in 2002-2003. A GPA of 2.0 is required for transfer students; a GPA of 2.5 is required for admittance to the teacher education program. Transfer students who have earned 12 or more credits are not required to take the ACT. Interviews are recommended. 30 of 128 credits required for the bachelor's degree must be completed at Concordia.

Visiting: There are regularly scheduled orientations for prospective students, including 3 Discover Concordia days, Teacher Education Information Day, Senior Day, Junior Day, Art Day, Music Day, and Theatre Day. There are guides for informal visits and visitors may sit in on classes and stay overnight. To schedule a visit, contact the Admissions Office.

Financial Aid: In 2003-2004, 99% of all full-time students received some form of financial aid. 79% of full-time freshmen and 85% of continuing full-time students received need-based aid. The average freshman award was $17,022, with $5018 ($14,002 maximum) from need-based scholarships or need-based grants, $3920 ($8175 maximum) from need-based self-help aid (loans and jobs), $1075 ($6000 maximum) from non-need-based athletic scholarships, $4833 ($17,250 maximum) from other non-need-based awards and non-need-based scholarships, and $2176 (13,000 maximum) from non-need-based loans. 46% of undergraduates work part time. Average annual earnings from campus work are $1122. The average financial indebtedness of the 2003 graduate was $15,938. The FAFSA and the college's own financial statement are required. The deadline for filing freshman financial aid applications for fall entry is May 1.

International Students: There are 4 international students enrolled. They must score 520 on the written TOEFL or 180 on the electronic version or take the MELAB and also take the SAT I or the ACT.

Computers: More than 55 PCs are available for student use in the library and in clusters around the campus. All students may access the system 8 A.M. to midnight, with 24-hour access from dorm rooms. There are no time limits and no fees.

Graduates: From July 1, 2002 to June 30, 2003, 125 bachelor's degrees were awarded. The most popular majors were teacher education (33%), business (16%), and English (11%). In an average class, 1% graduate in 3 years or less, 15% graduate in 4 years or less, 27% graduate in 5 years or less, and 28% graduate in 6 years or less.

Admissions Contact: Catherine Wolf, Director of Admissions.
E-mail: *www.cuaa.edu*

CORNERSTONE UNIVERSITY AND GRAND RAPIDS THEOLOGICAL SEMINARY   D-4
Grand Rapids, MI 49525

(616) 222-1426
(800) 787-9778; Fax: (616) 222-1418

Full-time: 587 men, 989 women	**Faculty:** 69; IIB, --$
Part-time: 210 men, 285 women	**Ph.D.s:** 60%
Graduate: 180 men, 94 women	**Student/Faculty:** 23 to 1
Year: semesters, summer session	**Tuition:** $14,420
Application Deadline: open	**Room & Board:** $5426
Freshman Class: 824 applied, 798 accepted, 332 enrolled	
SAT I Verbal/Math: 540/520	**ACT:** 23 COMPETITIVE

Cornerstone University and Grand RapidsTheological Seminary founded in 1941, is a private liberal arts college and graduate seminary educating students from a Christian perspective. Major undergraduate programs include business, teacher education, music, and ministry. There are 3 graduate schools. In addition to regional accreditation, Cornerstone has baccalaureate program accreditation with NASM. The library contains 144,556 volumes, 288,342 microform items, and 4109 audio/video tapes/CDs, and subscribes to 1060 periodicals. Computerized library services include the card catalog, interlibrary loans, database searching, and Internet access. Special learning facilities include a learning resource center and radio station. The 132-acre campus is in a suburban area on the northeast side of Grand Rapids. Including any residence halls, there are 25 buildings.

Student Life: 79% of undergraduates are from Michigan. Students are from 31 states, 12 foreign countries, and Canada. 62% are from public schools. 81% are white; 14% African American. 53% are Protestant; 17% claim no religious affiliation. The average age of freshmen is 18; all undergraduates, 22. 27% do not continue beyond their first year; 42% remain to graduate.

Housing: 852 students can be accommodated in college housing, which includes single-sex dorms, on-campus apartments, and married-student housing. In addition, there are honors houses. On-campus housing is guaranteed for all 4 years. 56% of students live on campus; of those, 50% remain on campus on weekends. Alcohol is not permitted. All students may keep cars.

Activities: There are no fraternities or sororities. There are 22 groups on campus, including band, cheerleading, choir, chorale, chorus, drama, ethnic, honors, jazz band, musical theater, pep band, photography, political, professional, religious, social, social service, student government, symphony, and yearbook. Popular campus events include Sibling Weekends, Friends Weekend, and Variety Show.

Sports: There are 6 intercollegiate sports for men and 7 for women, and 6 intramural sports for men and 6 for women. Facilities include a 2700-seat basketball/volleyball arena, field house servicing tennis, volleyball, basketball, soccer, and softball, a baseball diamond, 2 soccer fields/intramural fields, a softball field, sand volleyball court, fitness center, human performance labs, 6 locker rooms, training room, and raquetball courts.

Disabled Students: All of the campus is accessible. Wheelchair ramps, elevators, special parking, specially equipped rest rooms, special class scheduling, special housing, and large computer monitors for the visually impaired, and soundproof rooms for using tape recorders that read books-on-tape are available.

Services: Counseling and information services are available, as is tutoring in every subject. There is a Learning Center with a computer lab and special adaptive software, tutoring by appointment in the residence halls, test-taking assistance, and readers and typists as needed. There is a reader service for the blind and remedial math and writing.

Campus Safety and Security: Measures include 24-hour foot and vehicle patrol, security escort services, informal discussions, and pamphlets/posters/films. There are emergency telephones and lighted pathways/sidewalks.

Programs of Study: Cornerstone confers B.A., B.S., and B.Mus. degrees. Associate and master's degrees are also awarded. Bachelor's degrees are awarded in BIOLOGICAL SCIENCE (biology/biological science), BUSINESS (accounting, business administration and management, international business management, and marketing/retailing/merchandising), COMMUNICATIONS AND THE ARTS (communications, English, fine arts, music, music performance, music theory and composition, and speech/debate/rhetoric), COMPUTER AND PHYSICAL SCIENCE (computer science), EDUCATION (elementary, middle school, music, physical, science, and secondary), HEALTH PROFESSIONS (predentistry, premedicine, and preveterinary science), SOCIAL SCIENCE (biblical languages, biblical studies, family/consumer studies, history, interdisciplinary studies, philosophy, political science/government, prelaw, psychology, religion, religious education, social work, sociology, and youth ministry). English, music, and education are the strongest academically. Education, business, and youth ministry are the largest.

Required: To graduate, the student must complete 120 to 129 credit hours depending on degree, including 58 in the liberal arts core consisting of the humanities, math, social sciences, science, Bible/religion, foreign language, and phys ed. Specific courses include 2 phys ed courses, freshman rhetoric, biology, math, psychology or sociology, world civilization, fine arts, philosophy, Old Testament, and inductive Bible study. The number of hours in the major varies. The student must have an overall GPA of 2.0, 2.5 in the major, 2.0 in the minor, and pass a comprehensive exam.

Special: All students choose a student-ministries assignment each semester. Cornerstone requires internships in all areas of study. Study abroad in 8 countries, a co-op program in political science, cross-registration with Calvin College, an accelerated degree program in organizational leadership, a Washington semester, and an interdisciplinary major in missionary aviation, are available. There is 1 national honor society and a freshman honors program.

Faculty/Classroom: 73% of faculty are male; 27%, female. 88% teach undergraduates. The average class size in an introductory lecture is 75; in a laboratory, 30; and in a regular course, 21.

Admissions: 97% of the 2003-2004 applicants were accepted. The SAT I scores for the 2003-2004 freshman class were: Verbal--33% below 500, 44% between 500 and 599, 16% between 600 and 700, and 7% above 700; Math--44% below 500, 33% between 500 and 599, 16% between 600 and 700, and 7% above 700. The ACT scores were 30% below 21, 29% between 21 and 23, 20% between 24 and 26, 11% between 27 and 28, and 10% above 28. 34% of the current freshmen were in the top fifth of their class; 56% were in the top two fifths. There was 1 National Merit finalist. 17 freshmen graduated first in their class.

Requirements: The ACT is required, with a minimum score of 19, or 900 on the SAT I. The college requires a high school transcript or GED certificate, and recommends 15 Carnegie units, including 4 years of English, 3 each of math and social sciences, 2 of science, as well as 10 semesters of electives. The college recommends that the student appear for an interview, and requires auditions for music scholarships. A pastoral reference is required. A GPA of 2.5 is required. AP and CLEP credits are accepted. Important factors in the admissions decision are personality/intangible qualities, extracurricular activities record, and leadership record.

Procedure: Freshmen are admitted to all sessions. Entrance exams should be taken during the junior or senior year. There is a deferred admissions plan and a rolling admissions plan. Application deadlines are open. Application fee is $25. Applications are accepted on-line through the school's web site.

Transfer: 104 transfer students enrolled in 2002-2003. The college requires high school and college transcripts from students, as well as a pastor's reference. The applicant must have taken the ACT if under 25 years of age with fewer than 30 hours of college credit. 32 of 129 credits required for the bachelor's degree must be completed at Cornerstone.

Visiting: There are regularly scheduled orientations for prospective students, including admissions and financial aid presentations, class visits, and course preregistration. There are guides for informal visits and visitors may sit in on classes and stay overnight. To schedule a visit, contact the Admissions Office.

Financial Aid: In 2003-2004, 98% of all full-time freshmen and 97% of continuing full-time students received some form of financial aid. 78% of full-time freshmen and 76% of continuing full-time students received need-based aid. The average freshman award was $12,763. Need-based scholarships or need-based grants averaged $7562 ($20,646 maximum); need-based self-help aid (loans and jobs) averaged $6106 ($19,169 maximum); non-need-based athletic scholarships averaged $4115 ($14,369 maximum); and other non-need-based awards and non-need-based scholarships averaged $4376 ($17,977 maximum). 34% of undergraduates work part time. Average annual earnings from campus work are $938. The average financial indebtedness of the 2003 graduate was $19,173. The FAFSA is required. The priority date for freshman financial aid applications for fall entry is February 20.

International Students: There are 22 international students enrolled. They must score 500 on the written TOEFL or 173 on the electronic version and also take the SAT I or the ACT, scoring 900.

Computers: The mainframes are a Windows 2000 network and services. Undergraduate students are issued laptops. All laptops have integrated network cards for accessing the university LAN and the Internet. Additionally, several PCs are located throughout campus. All students may access the system year-round; 24 hours a day. There are no time limits and no fees. All students are required to have personal computers. All traditional undergrads are in the laptop program. The school chooses a new model each year.

Graduates: From July 1, 2002 to June 30, 2003, 333 bachelor's degrees were awarded. The most popular majors were business (16%), ed-ucation (15%), and English (15%). In an average class, 1% graduate in 3 years or less, 30% graduate in 4 years or less, 35% graduate in 5 years or less, and 42% graduate in 6 years or less.

Admissions Contact: Brent Rudin, Director of Undergraduate Admissions. E-mail: *admissions@cornerstone.edu*
Web: *www.cornerstone.edu*

DAVENPORT UNIVERSITY
Grand Rapids, MI 49503   **D-4**
(616) 732-1200
(800) 632-9569; Fax: (616) 732-1185

Full-time: 1140 men, 2827 women	**Faculty:** 133
Part-time: 2083 men, 6666 women	**Ph.D.s:** 24%
Graduate: 325 men, 486 women	**Student/Faculty:** 30 to 1
Year: semesters, summer session	**Tuition:** $8236
Application Deadline: September	**Room & Board:** $3400
Freshman Class: 4291 applied, 4291 accepted, 2742 enrolled	
SAT I or ACT: not required	**NONCOMPETITIVE**

Davenport University, founded in 1866, is a private, independent institution specializing in business education. It serves 13,500 students at 24 campuses throughout Michigan and northern Indiana. Davenport offers business-focused degrees. The university also offers online courses. There are 4 undergraduate schools and 1 graduate school. In addition to regional accreditation, Davenport has baccalaureate program accreditation with CAAHEP. The library contains 127,424 volumes, 346 microform items, and 13,695 audio/video tapes/CDs, and subscribes to 1914 periodicals. Computerized library services include interlibrary loans, database searching, and Internet access. Special learning facilities include a learning resource center. The 10-acre campus is in an urban area in Grand Rapids. Including any residence halls, there are 7 buildings.

Student Life: 97% of undergraduates are from Michigan. Students are from 11 states, 39 foreign countries, and Canada. 97% are from public schools. 64% are white; 30% African American. The average age of freshmen is 29; all undergraduates, 31.

Housing: 50 students can be accommodated in college housing, which includes coed dorms. Almost all students commute. Alcohol is not permitted. All students may keep cars.

Activities: There are no fraternities or sororities. There are 5 groups on campus, including ethnic, professional, religious, student government, and yearbook. Popular campus events include Diversity Book Club.

Sports: There are 4 intercollegiate sports for men and 3 for women.

Disabled Students: All of the campus is accessible. Wheelchair ramps, elevators, special parking, specially equipped rest rooms, special class scheduling, lowered drinking fountains, and lowered telephones are available.

Services: Counseling and information services are available, as is tutoring in most subjects. There are tutoring labs for math, English, and computers, and there is a learning assistance center. There is remedial math, reading, and writing.

Campus Safety and Security: Measures include security escort services, emergency telephones, lighted pathways/sidewalks, and 24-hour foot patrols.

Programs of Study: Davenport confers the B.B.A. degree. Associate and master's degrees are also awarded. Bachelor's degrees are awarded in BUSINESS (accounting, banking and finance, electronic business, entrepreneurial studies, human resources, international business management, management science, and marketing management), COMMUNICATIONS AND THE ARTS (advertising), COMPUTER AND PHYSICAL SCIENCE (information sciences and systems and web technology), HEALTH PROFESSIONS (medical records administration/services and nursing), SOCIAL SCIENCE (paralegal studies). Business is the strongest academically. Accounting and management are the largest.

Required: Davenport requires all students to complete 120 credit hours, 37 in the major, with a minimum GPA of 2.0 overall and in career courses. The general education core consists of 42 credits, and the business core of 26 credits. At least 18 credits must be completed on campus in the classroom.

Special: Davenport offers co-op programs in administrative services, sales and marketing, and paralegal studies. There are internships in most disciplines. Study abroad is available through C.I.E.E. and A.I.F.S.

Faculty/Classroom: 50% of faculty are male; 50%, female. 99% teach undergraduates. The average class size in an introductory lecture is 13 and in a regular course, 13.

Admissions: All of the 2003-2004 applicants were accepted.

Requirements: Graduation from an accredited secondary school or a GED is accepted. An interview is recommended. CLEP credit is accepted. Important factors in the admissions decision are ability to finance college education, recommendations by school officials, and personality/intangible qualities.

Procedure: Freshmen are admitted to all sessions. There is a rolling admissions plan. There is an early decision plan. Early decision applications should be filed by August; regular applications, by September for fall entry, January for winter entry, March for spring entry, and June for summer entry, along with a $25 fee. The college accepts all applicants. Notification is sent on a rolling basis. Applications are accepted on-line.

Transfer: 1240 transfer students enrolled in 2002-2003. C is the minimum grade accepted for transfer. There is a 75% maximum credit transfer for the bachelor's degree. 30 of 120 credits required for the bachelor's degree must be completed at Davenport.

Visiting: There are regularly scheduled orientations for prospective students, consisting of an appointment, set up in advance. There are guides for informal visits and visitors may sit in on classes and stay overnight. To schedule a visit, contact Admissions at *gr_admiss@davenport.edu*.

Financial Aid: The FAFSA is required.

International Students: There are 181 international students enrolled. The school actively recruits these students. They must score 500 on the written TOEFL.

Computers: The mainframe is an HP 3000/Series 58. A complete lab with PCs is available. All students may access the system 8 A.M. to midnight on weekdays, and noon to 6 P.M. on weekends. There are no time limits and no fees.

Graduates: From July 1, 2002 to June 30, 2003, 1015 bachelor's degrees were awarded. The most popular majors were management (30%), applied business (11%), and accounting (10%).

Admissions Contact: Karen Gooley-Ripple, Admissions Representative. E-mail: *karen.gooley-ripple@davenport.edu*
Web: *www.davenport.edu*

DETROIT COLLEGE OF BUSINESS
(See Davenport University)

EASTERN MICHIGAN UNIVERSITY
E-5
Ypsilanti, MI 48197
(734) 487-0193
(800) GO TO EMU; Fax: (734) 487-1484

Full-time: 5348 men, 8225 women	**Faculty:** 773; IIA, +$
Part-time: 2356 men, 3648 women	**Ph.D.s:** 80%
Graduate: 1598 men, 2954 women	**Student/Faculty:** 18 to 1
Year: semesters, summer session	**Tuition:** $5628 ($15,046)
Application Deadline: July 31	**Room & Board:** $5850
Freshman Class: 9044 applied, 7139 accepted, 2577 enrolled	
SAT I Verbal/Math: 510/510	**ACT:** 20　　**COMPETITIVE**

Eastern Michigan University, founded in 1849, is a public institution offering programs in arts and sciences, business, education, health and human services, and technology. There are 5 undergraduate schools and 1 graduate school. In addition to regional accreditation, EMU has baccalaureate program accreditation with AACN, AACSB, ABET, ACCE, ACS, ADA, AHEA, AOTA, ASLA, ASLHA, CACREP, CAHEA, CCNE, CED, CSWE, FIDER, NAACLS, NASM, NCATE, NLN, and NRPA. The library contains 1,040,897 volumes, 975,709 microform items, and 12,026 audio/video tapes/CDs, and subscribes to 4439 periodicals. Computerized library services include the card catalog, interlibrary loans, and database searching. Special learning facilities include a learning resource center, art gallery, and radio station. The 460-acre campus is in a suburban area 8 miles east of Ann Arbor. Including any residence halls, there are 112 buildings.

Student Life: 92% of undergraduates are from Michigan. Students are from 43 states, 67 foreign countries, and Canada. 90% are from public schools. 75% are white; 18% African American. The average age of freshmen is 18; all undergraduates, 22. 29% do not continue beyond their first year; 38% remain to graduate.

Housing: 3760 students can be accommodated in college housing, which includes single-sex and coed dorms, on-campus apartments, married-student housing, and sorority houses. In addition, there are honors houses, special-interest houses, upper-class halls, a first-year center, and special housing known as Community of Scholars. On-campus housing is available on a first-come, first-served basis and is available on a lottery system for upperclassmen. 83% of students commute. All students may keep cars.

Activities: 4% of men belong to 2 local and 13 national fraternities; 4% of women belong to 1 local and 14 national sororities. There are 190 groups on campus, including art, band, cheerleading, chess, choir, chorale, chorus, computers, dance, debate, drama, drill team, ethnic, film, forensics, gay, honors, international, jazz band, literary magazine, marching band, musical theater, opera, orchestra, pep band, photography, political, professional, radio and TV, religious, social, social service, student government, symphony, and yearbook. Popular campus events include Martin Luther King Birthday Celebration and Family Weekend.

Sports: There are 9 intercollegiate sports for men and 12 for women, and 25 intramural sports for men and 25 for women. Facilities include a 30,000-seat stadium, outdoor playing fields, a field house, a student recreation and intramural center, and an outdoor park including a lake, amphitheater, lighted basketball courts, volleyball courts, and lake house. There are 2 pools, a whirlpool/sauna, softball and soccer fields, 4 weight rooms, an aerobic studio, and a pro shop.

Disabled Students: 93% of the campus is accessible. Wheelchair ramps, elevators, special parking, specially equipped rest rooms, special

class scheduling, lowered drinking fountains, lowered telephones, and special housing are available.

Services: Counseling and information services are available, as is tutoring in every subject. There is a reader service for the blind and remedial math, reading, and writing. Notetakers and interpreters are provided for the handicapped.

Campus Safety and Security: Measures include 24-hour foot and vehicle patrol, self-defense education, security escort services, and shuttle buses. There are informal discussions, pamphlets/posters/films, emergency telephones, lighted pathways/sidewalks, bicycle patrols, a crime prevention officer, area police officers in dorms, an anonymous tip line, Operation Identification, vehicle glass etching, a bike lock lease program, and surveillance cameras.

Programs of Study: EMU confers B.A., B.S., B.A.E., B.A. in Language and World Business, B.B.A., B.B.E., B.F.A., B.M.E., B.M.P., B.M.T., and B.S.N. degrees. Master's and doctoral degrees are also awarded. Bachelor's degrees are awarded in AGRICULTURE (forestry and related sciences), BIOLOGICAL SCIENCE (biochemistry, biology/biological science, botany, microbiology, and zoology), BUSINESS (accounting, banking and finance, business administration and management, business data processing, business economics, business systems analysis, fashion merchandising, hospitality management services, insurance and risk management, international business management, labor studies, management information systems, management science, marketing/retailing/merchandising, office supervision and management, personnel management, real estate, recreation and leisure services, secretarial studies/office management, and tourism), COMMUNICATIONS AND THE ARTS (advertising, American literature, applied music, art, arts administration/management, classical languages, communications, communications technology, dance, design, dramatic arts, English, English as a second/foreign language, English literature, film arts, fine arts, French, German, graphic design, historic preservation, Japanese, journalism, linguistics, literature, music, music performance, performing arts, piano/organ, Spanish, speech/debate/rhetoric, and telecommunications), COMPUTER AND PHYSICAL SCIENCE (actuarial science, applied mathematics, astronomy, chemistry, computer programming, computer science, earth science, geology, information sciences and systems, mathematics, physics, polymer science, and statistics), EDUCATION (art, bilingual/bicultural, business, computer, drama, early childhood, education, education of the deaf and hearing impaired, education of the emotionally handicapped, education of the mentally handicapped, education of the multiply handicapped, education of the physically handicapped, education of the visually handicapped, educational media, elementary, English, foreign languages, health, industrial arts, mathematics, middle school, music, physical, psychology, reading, school psychology, science, secondary, social foundations, social science, special, and teaching English as a second/foreign language (TESOL/TEFOL)), ENGINEERING AND ENVIRONMENTAL DESIGN (aviation administration/management, city/community/regional planning, computer graphics, computer technology, construction management, interior design, land use management and reclamation, manufacturing technology, military science, plastics technology, preengineering, and urban planning technology), HEALTH PROFESSIONS (allied health, health care administration, medical laboratory technology, music therapy, nursing, occupational therapy, predentistry, premedicine, preoptometry, prepharmacy, recreation therapy, speech pathology/audiology, and sports medicine), SOCIAL SCIENCE (African American studies, anthropology, area studies, clothing and textiles management/production/services, counseling/psychology, criminal justice, dietetics, economics, family/consumer studies, geography, gerontology, history, interdisciplinary studies, international relations, liberal arts/general studies, paralegal studies, parks and recreation management, philosophy, political science/government, prelaw, psychology, public administration, social science, social work, sociology, and women's studies). Education, business, and health/nursing are the strongest academically. Elementary education, arts/sciences, and business are the largest.

Required: To graduate, students must have a GPA of 2.0, and complete a minimum of 124 semester hours, including usually 30 in the major, and 40 or more of basic studies. Required courses include English composition, political science, computer literacy, and phys ed.

Special: EMU offers internships, work-study programs, a Washington semester in public administration, and co-op programs and cross-registration with the University of Michigan at Ann Arbor, Concordia College, and Washtenaw Community College. Students may study abroad in more than 23 countries. EMU allows dual majors, nondegree study, B.A.-B.S. degrees in all majors and student-designed majors, accelerated degree programs, and confers a general studies degree, as well as a B.A.-B.B.A. degree in language and world business. Students may receive credit for life, military, and work experience, and pass/fail options are open. There are 9 national honor societies, a freshman honors program, and 36 departmental honors programs.

Faculty/Classroom: 56% of faculty are male; 44%, female. 70% teach undergraduates. Graduate students teach 2% of introductory courses. The average class size in a laboratory is 15 and in a regular course, 27.

Admissions: 79% of the 2003-2004 applicants were accepted. The SAT I scores for the 2003-2004 freshman class were: Math--45% below 500, 35% between 500 and 599, 16% between 600 and 700, and 3% above 700. The ACT scores were 52% below 21, 24% between 21 and 23, 16% between 24 and 26, 4% between 27 and 28, and 3% above 28. 28% of the current freshmen were in the top fifth of their class; 55% were in the top two fifths. 13 freshmen graduated first in their class.

Requirements: The SAT I or ACT is required with a minimum composite of 17 on the ACT or 789 on the SAT I. Applicants should be high school graduates or hold a GED. The university recommends that students complete 19 academic credits in high school, consisting of 4 in English, 3 each in math, science, and social studies, 2 each in foreign language and history, and 2 to 3 in other traditional college-preparatory courses. A portfolio is required for applicants to the art program, and an audition is required for music students. A GPA of 2.0 is required. AP and CLEP credits are accepted.

Procedure: Freshmen are admitted to all sessions. Entrance exams should be taken by November of the senior year of high school. There is a rolling admissions plan. Applications should be filed by July 31 for fall entry, December 9 for winter entry, April 15 for spring entry, and June 6 for summer entry. Notification is sent on a rolling basis. The fall 2003 application fee was $20 (on-line) and $35 (paper). Applications are accepted on-line.

Transfer: 1770 transfer students enrolled in 2002-2003. Transfer students must have at least 12 semester hours of college credit, with a GPA of 2.0. 30 of 124 credits required for the bachelor's degree must be completed at EMU.

Visiting: There are regularly scheduled orientations for prospective students, including tours scheduled every morning and afternoon, as well as Saturday morning, with trained student tour guides. There are guides for informal visits and visitors may sit in on classes and stay overnight. To schedule a visit, contact the admissions On-Campus Programs at (734) 487-1111.

Financial Aid: In 2003-2004, 59% of all full-time students received some form of financial aid. 29% of all full-time students received need-based aid. The average freshman award was $13,379. Need-based scholarships or need-based grants averaged $4103 ($6525 maximum); need-based self-help aid (loans and jobs) averaged $4300 ($6925 maximum); non-need-based athletic scholarships averaged $10,553 ($20,667 maximum); and other non-need-based awards and non-need-based scholarships averaged $2050 ($20,895 maximum). 20% of undergraduates work part time. Average annual earnings from campus work are $2700. The average financial indebtedness of a recent graduate was $12,018. The FAFSA is required. The deadline for filing freshman financial aid applications for fall entry is December 21.

International Students: There are 258 international students enrolled. The school actively recruits these students. They must score 500 on the written TOEFL or 173 on the electronic version or take the MELAB.

Computers: Computer labs and stations are available throughout the campus, and residence halls are 75% networked. All workstations have Internet access. All students may access the system at all times. Dial-in access is limited to 1 to 2 hours per session if using a modem. On campus there is no limit. There is network connection.

Graduates: From July 1, 2002 to June 30, 2003, 2862 bachelor's degrees were awarded. The most popular majors were elementary education (9%), psychology (5%), and special education (5%). In an average class, 8% graduate in 4 years or less, 24% graduate in 5 years or less, and 35% graduate in 6 years or less. 840 companies recruited on campus in 2002-2003. Of the 2002 graduating class, 12% were enrolled in graduate school within 6 months of graduation and 93% were employed.

Admissions Contact: Judy Benfield-Tatum, Director of Admissions. Web: *www.emich.edu/public/admissions/admissions.html*

FERRIS STATE UNIVERSITY
Big Rapids, MI 49307

D-4

(231) 591-2100
(800) 433-7747; Fax: (231) 591-3944

Full-time: 4707 men, 3774 women	**Faculty:** 484; IIA, av$
Part-time: 1048 men, 1239 women	**Ph.D.s:** 60%
Graduate: 435 men, 619 women	**Student/Faculty:** 18 to 1
Year: semesters, summer session	**Tuition:** $6186 ($12,230)
Application Deadline: August 1	**Room & Board:** $6326
Freshman Class: 12,184 applied, 8951 accepted, 2366 enrolled	
ACT: 21	**COMPETITIVE**

Ferris State University, established in 1884, is a public institution offering day and evening courses through its Schools of Arts and Sciences, Education, Allied Health, Technology, Business, and Pharmacy, College of Optometry, University College, and Kendall College of Art and Design. There are 9 undergraduate and 3 graduate schools. In addition to regional accreditation, Ferris State has baccalaureate program accreditation with ABET, ACPE, ADA, AHEA, CAHEA, CSWE, and NLN. The library contains 339,891 volumes, 3,630,677 microform items, and 4125 audio/video tapes/CDs, and subscribes to 3294 periodicals. Computer-

ized library services include the card catalog, interlibrary loans, database searching, and Internet access. Special learning facilities include a learning resource center, art gallery, natural history museum, planetarium, and TV station. The 880-acre campus is in a small town 55 miles north of Grand Rapids. Including any residence halls, there are 98 buildings.

Student Life: 96% of undergraduates are from Michigan. Students are from 43 states, 55 foreign countries, and Canada. 79% are white. The average age of freshmen is 19; all undergraduates, 23. 35% do not continue beyond their first year.

Housing: 4333 students can be accommodated in college housing, which includes single-sex and coed dorms, on-campus apartments, and married-student housing. In addition, there are honors houses. On-campus housing is guaranteed for all 4 years. All students may keep cars.

Activities: 6% of men belong to 30 national fraternities; 4% of women belong to 8 national sororities. There are 220 groups on campus, including art, band, cheerleading, chess, choir, chorale, chorus, computers, dance, drama, drill team, drum and bugle corps, ethnic, film, gay, honors, international, jazz band, newspaper, orchestra, pep band, photography, political, professional, radio and TV, religious, social, social service, student government, and symphony. Popular campus events include January Jams Concert, Ferris Fest, and Autumn aLIVE Concert.

Sports: There are 7 intercollegiate sports for men and 8 for women, and 21 intramural sports for men and 19 for women. Facilities include a golf course, a racquetball and fitness club, an ice arena, a 10,000-seat stadium, a student recreation center with a pool, and tennis courts.

Disabled Students: All of the campus is accessible. Wheelchair ramps, elevators, special parking, specially equipped rest rooms, special class scheduling, lowered drinking fountains, and lowered telephones are available.

Services: Counseling and information services are available, as is tutoring in most subjects. There is a reader service for the blind, and remedial math, reading, and writing.

Campus Safety and Security: Measures include 24-hour foot and vehicle patrol, self-defense education, security escort services, and informal discussions. There are pamphlets/posters/films, emergency telephones, and lighted pathways/sidewalks.

Programs of Study: Ferris State confers B.A., B.S., B.F.A, B.S.N, and B.S.W. degrees. Associate and master's degrees are also awarded. Bachelor's degrees are awarded in BIOLOGICAL SCIENCE (biology/biological science), BUSINESS (accounting, banking and finance, business administration and management, hospitality management services, human resources, insurance, international business management, marketing/retailing/merchandising, and small business management), COMMUNICATIONS AND THE ARTS (advertising and public relations), COMPUTER AND PHYSICAL SCIENCE (applied mathematics and computer programming), EDUCATION (business, mathematics, and technical), ENGINEERING AND ENVIRONMENTAL DESIGN (construction management, engineering technology, plastics engineering, and surveying engineering), HEALTH PROFESSIONS (health care administration, nuclear medical technology, nursing, optometry, and pharmacy), SOCIAL SCIENCE (criminal justice and social work). Pharmacy and optometry are the strongest academically. Business administration and marketing are the largest.

Required: Degree requirements include a minimum 2.0 GPA, 12 semester credit hours in English and speech communications, 9 each in the humanities and social sciences, and 7 to 8 in natural sciences. The number of credits students must earn in the major and the total required for graduation vary by course of study.

Special: Ferris State offers co-op programs in automotive service technology with GM, Chrysler, and Ford, internships, study abroad, work-study programs, accelerated degrees, dual and student-designed majors, credit for life, military, and work experience, and a pass/fail grading option. There are 8 national honor societies and a freshman honors program.

Faculty/Classroom: 60% of faculty are male; 40%, female. All teach undergraduates. No introductory courses are taught by graduate students. The average class size in an introductory lecture is 23; in a laboratory, 17; and in a regular course, 21.

Admissions: 73% of the 2003-2004 applicants were accepted. The ACT scores for the 2003-2004 freshman class were: 53% below 21, 24% between 21 and 23, 15% between 24 and 26, 5% between 27 and 28, and 3% above 28.

Requirements: The SAT I or ACT is required. In addition, applicants must graduate from an accredited secondary school or earn a GED. Four years each of English and math, 3 years each of biophysical/physical sciences and history, 2 years each of a foreign language and fine arts, and 1 year of computer literacy are advised. Interviews are recommended. A GPA of 2.25 is required. AP and CLEP credits are accepted. Important factors in the admissions decision are recommendations by school officials, evidence of special talent, and advanced placement or honor courses.

Procedure: Freshmen are admitted to all sessions. Entrance exams should be taken before course registration. There is a deferred admissions plan and a rolling admissions plan. Applications should be filed by

August 1 for fall entry. The fall 2003 application fee was $30. Notification is sent on a rolling basis.

Transfer: 1145 transfer students enrolled in 2002-2003. A GPA of at least 2.0 is required. 30 credits required for the bachelor's degree must be completed at Ferris State.

Visiting: There are regularly scheduled orientations for prospective students. There are guides for informal visits and visitors may sit in on classes and stay overnight. To schedule a visit, contact the Admissions Office at (231) 433-7747 or *ferris_talk@hotmail.com* between 3 P.M. and 5 P.M. or *http://ferris.edu/admissions*.

Financial Aid: In 2003-2004, 62% of all full-time freshmen and 66% of continuing full-time students received some form of financial aid. 34% of full-time freshmen and 33% of continuing full-time students received need-based aid. The average freshman award was $7050. Need-based scholarships or need-based grants averaged $3000; need-based self-help aid (loans and jobs) averaged $2315; non-need-based athletic scholarships averaged $3900; and other non-need-based awards and non-need-based scholarships averaged $2000. 49% of undergraduates work part time. Average annual earnings from campus work are $1654. The average financial indebtedness of the 2003 graduate was $14,500. Ferris State is a member of CSS. The FAFSA is required. The deadline for filing freshman financial aid applications for fall entry is March 15.

International Students: There are 274 international students enrolled. The school actively recruits these students. They must score 500 on the written TOEFL and also take the SAT I or ACT with a score of 15 or a supplemental math exam.

Computers: The mainframe is an IBM S/390. Residence hall rooms and apartments have access to local and worldwide computer networks. Computer labs are available in every residence hall and at various locations on campus. All students may access the system at any time; labs are open 16 hours daily. Students may access the system 6 A.M. to 10 P.M. There are no fees.

Graduates: From July 1, 2002 to June 30, 2003, 1312 bachelor's degrees were awarded. The most popular majors were automotive service technology (9%), business administration (9%), and criminal justice (8%). 378 companies recruited on campus in 2002-2003.

Admissions Contact: Admissions Officer. A video is available. Web: *www.ferris.edu/admissions/appprocess.htm*

GMI INSTITUTE
(See Kettering University)

GRACE BIBLE COLLEGE
Grand Rapids, MI 49509   **D-4**
(616) 538-2330
(800) 968-1887; Fax: (616) 538-2330

Full-time: 71 men, 74 women	**Faculty:** 29
Part-time: 4 men, 4 women	**Ph.D.s:** 22%
Graduate: none	**Student/Faculty:** 5 to 1
Year: semesters	**Tuition:** $9730
Application Deadline: open	**Room & Board:** $6160
Freshman Class: 188 applied, 90 accepted, 32 enrolled	
SAT I Verbal/Math: 555/522	**ACT:** 21 **COMPETITIVE**

Grace Bible College, founded in 1939, is a private institution affiliated with the Grace Gospel Fellowship. Its mission is to provide a curriculum that integrates general education and biblical studies and prepares students for service in their career, church, and society. In addition to regional accreditation, GBC has baccalaureate program accreditation with AABC. The library contains 41,700 volumes and 2316 audio/video tapes/CDs, and subscribes to 192 periodicals. Computerized library services include the card catalog, database searching, and Internet access. Special learning facilities include a recording studio. The 16-acre campus is in a suburban area on the southwest side of Grand Rapids. Including any residence halls, there are 11 buildings.

Student Life: 69% of undergraduates are from Michigan. Students are from 17 states and 7 foreign countries. 95% are white. All are Protestant. The average age of freshmen is 18; all undergraduates, 21. 70% do not continue beyond their first year; 37% remain to graduate.

Housing: 80 students can be accommodated in college housing, which includes single-sex dorms, on-campus apartments, off-campus apartments, and married-student housing. On-campus housing is guaranteed for all 4 years. 58% of students live on campus; of those, 60% remain on campus on weekends. Alcohol is not permitted. All students may keep cars.

Activities: There are no fraternities or sororities. There are some groups and organizations on campus, including drama, musical theater, newspaper, religious, and student government. Popular campus events include Opera Dinner Theater, Winter Formal, and Missions Conference.

Sports: There are 2 intercollegiate sports for men and 2 for women. Facilities include a 500-seat soccer field and an athletic center with a 500-seat gym for basketball and volleyball, a racquetball court, and an exercise and weight room.

Disabled Students: 85% of the campus is accessible. Wheelchair ramps, elevators, special parking, specially equipped rest rooms, and lowered drinking fountains are available.

Services: Counseling and information services are available, as is tutoring in most subjects. There is remedial writing.

Campus Safety and Security: Measures include informal discussions, pamphlets/posters/films, lighted pathways/sidewalks, and evening and overnight foot patrol.

Programs of Study: GBC confers B.S., B.Mus., B.R.E., and B.Th. degrees. Associate degrees are also awarded. Bachelor's degrees are awarded in BUSINESS (business administration and management), COMMUNICATIONS AND THE ARTS (music and music performance), COMPUTER AND PHYSICAL SCIENCE (digital arts/technology), EDUCATION (elementary and secondary), SOCIAL SCIENCE (early childhood studies, human services, interdisciplinary studies, missions, pastoral studies, religion, religious education, and youth ministry). Elementary/secondary education, digital communication/media/multimedia, and human services are the largest.

Required: To graduate, students must complete 126 to 158 credits, depending on the major, with a minimum GPA of 2.0 and must be considered worthy in character and conduct by the faculty. Course work is required in arts and sciences, ministry studies, Bible/theology, math/computer science, lab science, and phys ed. Attendance is expected at worship services twice a week.

Special: Cross-registration is available with Cornerstone and Davenport Universities. GBC offers 6-month internships for theology majors.

Faculty/Classroom: 69% of faculty are male; 31%, female. All teach undergraduates. The average class size in an introductory lecture is 30 and in a regular course, 25.

Admissions: 48% of the 2003-2004 applicants were accepted. The SAT I scores for the 2003-2004 freshman class were: Verbal--25% below 500, 25% between 500 and 599, and 50% between 600 and 700; Math--50% below 500, and 50% between 600 and 700. The ACT scores were 43% below 21, 29% between 21 and 23, 16% between 24 and 26, 4% between 27 and 28, and 8% above 28. 20% of the current freshmen were in the top fifth of their class; 45% were in the top two fifths.

Requirements: The ACT is required. In addition, applicants must be graduates of accredited secondary schools or have earned a GED. The application must show involvement in Christian activities and personal salvation through Jesus Christ. GBC requires applicants to be in the upper 50% of their class. A GPA of 2.5 is required. AP and CLEP credits are accepted.

Procedure: Freshmen are admitted fall and spring. Application deadlines are open. There is a rolling admissions plan.

Transfer: 18 transfer students enrolled in 2002-2003. Applicants must present a GPA of 2.0 and be in good standing at their previous school. Those with fewer than 24 college credit hours must submit high school records. 63 to 79 of the 126 to 158 credits required for the bachelor's degree must be completed at GBC.

Visiting: There are regularly scheduled orientations for prospective students, consisting of 7 Friday programs a year that include workshops, class visits, and campus tours. There are guides for informal visits and visitors may sit in on classes and stay overnight. To schedule a visit, contact Kevin Gilliam, Director of Enrollment, at *enrollment@gbcol.edu*.

Financial Aid: In 2003-2004, 99% of all full-time freshmen and 98% of continuing full-time students received some form of financial aid. 72% of full-time freshmen and 85% of continuing full-time students received need-based aid. The average freshman award was $3625, with $500 ($1200 maximum) from need-based scholarships or grants, $2625 (maximum) from need-based self-help aid (loans and jobs), $500 ($1000 maximum) from non-need-based awards and non-need-based scholarships. 40% of undergraduates work part time. Average annual earnings from campus work are $1900. The average financial indebtedness of the 2003 graduate was $3239. The FAFSA is required. The deadline for filing freshman financial aid applications for fall entry is March 1.

International Students: There are 4 international students enrolled. They must score 500 on the written TOEFL or 173 on the electronic version.

Computers: GBC operates a LAN system with a Windows NT 4.0 server. Internet and library collection searches are available on 6 PCs in the library. Students who bring a PC to school need a Windows-based system to interface with GBC's network.

Graduates: From July 1, 2002 to June 30, 2003, 27 bachelor's degrees were awarded. The most popular majors were liberal arts/biblical (60%), philosophy, religion, theology (35%), and visual performing arts (30%). In an average class, 37% graduate in 4 years or less.

Admissions Contact: Kevin Gilliam, Director of Enrollment. E-mail: *enrollment@gbcol.edu* Web: *www.gbcol.edu*

GRAND VALLEY STATE UNIVERSITY
Allendale, MI 49401-9403

D-4

(616) 331-2025
(800) 331-0246; Fax: (616) 895-2000

Full-time: 6005 men, 8997 women	**Faculty:** 839; IIA, av$
Part-time: 1075 men, 1730 women	**Ph.D.s:** 80%
Graduate: 1231 men, 2391 women	**Student/Faculty:** 18 to 1
Year: semesters, summer session	**Tuition:** $5254 ($12,216)
Application Deadline: July 31	**Room & Board:** $5768
Freshman Class: 12,145 applied, 8861 accepted, 3384 enrolled	
ACT: 23	**VERY COMPETITIVE**

Grand Valley State University, founded in 1960, is a comprehensive public institution offering graduate and undergraduate liberal arts and professional education. There are 12 undergraduate and 9 graduate schools. In addition to regional accreditation, Grand Valley has baccalaureate program accreditation with AACSB, ABET, APTA, CSWE, NASAD, NASM, NCATE, and NLN. The 2 libraries contain 672,000 volumes, 577,780 microform items, and 9816 audio/video tapes/CDs, and subscribe to 3690 periodicals. Computerized library services include the card catalog, interlibrary loans, database searching, and Internet access. Special learning facilities include a learning resource center, art gallery, radio station, TV station, cadaver lab, 2 Great Lakes research vessels, a performance auditorium, and dance studios. The 900-acre campus is in a small town 12 miles west of Grand Rapids. Including any residence halls, there are 64 buildings.

Student Life: 96% of undergraduates are from Michigan. Students are from 43 states, 52 foreign countries, and Canada. 75% are from public schools. 88% are white. The average age of freshmen is 18; all undergraduates, 22. 22% do not continue beyond their first year; 48% remain to graduate.

Housing: 4832 students can be accommodated in college housing, which includes coed dorms, on-campus apartments, off-campus apartments, and married-student housing. In addition, there are honors houses, language houses, and special-interest houses. On-campus housing is guaranteed for the freshman year only, is available on a first-come, first-served basis, and is available on a lottery system for upperclassmen. Priority is given to out-of-town students. 71% of students commute. Alcohol is not permitted. All students may keep cars.

Activities: 3% of men belong to 2 local and 8 national fraternities; 3% of women belong to 2 local and 9 national sororities. There are 130 groups on campus, including art, band, cheerleading, chess, choir, chorale, chorus, computers, dance, drama, ethnic, film, gay, honors, international, jazz band, literary magazine, marching band, newspaper, orchestra, pep band, photography, political, professional, radio and TV, religious, social, social service, student government, and symphony. Popular campus events include Family Day, Hispanic Awareness Week, and Black History Month.

Sports: There are 9 intercollegiate sports for men and 10 for women, and 22 intramural sports for men and 21 for women. Facilities include a football stadium, a baseball field, a basketball arena, swimming and diving pools, an indoor track, a weight room, a fitness building/intramural center, and an outdoor cross-country track.

Disabled Students: 98% of the campus is accessible. Wheelchair ramps, elevators, special parking, specially equipped rest rooms, special class scheduling, lowered drinking fountains, and lowered telephones are available.

Services: Counseling and information services are available, as is tutoring in most subjects. There is a reader service for the blind, and remedial math, reading, and writing.

Campus Safety and Security: Measures include 24-hour foot and vehicle patrol, self-defense education, security escort services, and shuttle buses. There are informal discussions, pamphlets/posters/films, emergency telephones, and lighted pathways/sidewalks.

Programs of Study: Grand Valley confers B.A., B.S., B.B.A., B.F.A., B.M., B.M.E., B.S.E., B.S.N., and B.S.W. degrees. Master's degrees are also awarded. Bachelor's degrees are awarded in BIOLOGICAL SCIENCE (biology/biological science), BUSINESS (accounting, banking and finance, business administration and management, business economics, hotel/motel and restaurant management, international business management, management science, marketing/retailing/merchandising, and personnel management), COMMUNICATIONS AND THE ARTS (advertising, broadcasting, communications, design, dramatic arts, English, film arts, fine arts, journalism, languages, music, and photography), COMPUTER AND PHYSICAL SCIENCE (chemistry, computer science, geology, mathematics, and physics), EDUCATION (art, elementary, foreign languages, middle school, music, science, and secondary), ENGINEERING AND ENVIRONMENTAL DESIGN (engineering and industrial engineering technology), HEALTH PROFESSIONS (health science, medical laboratory technology, nursing, physical therapy, physician's assistant, predentistry, and premedicine), SOCIAL SCIENCE (anthropology, criminal justice, economics, geography, history, international relations, philosophy, political science/government, prelaw, psychology, public administration, social science, social work, and sociology). Health sciences, English, and psychology are the largest.

Required: To graduate, students must have earned 30 credits in general education, comprised of 10 courses selected from specific groups, and have completed the university's required courses in English and math, as well as the upper-division writing course. A total of 120 credits, with 36 to 60 in the major, and a GPA of 2.0, are required to graduate.

Special: Many programs offer dual majors and internships, and most majors qualify for B.A.-B.S. degrees. There is an engineering cooperative program, a student-designed major in liberal studies, and many work-study programs. Outside opportunities include study abroad in 10 countries and a Washington semester. There are 14 national honor societies, a freshman honors program, and 12 departmental honors programs.

Faculty/Classroom: 56% of faculty are male; 44%, female. 94% teach undergraduates. No introductory courses are taught by graduate students. The average class size in an introductory lecture is 47; in a laboratory, 18; and in a regular course, 27.

Admissions: 73% of the 2003-2004 applicants were accepted. The ACT scores for the 2003-2004 freshman class were: 19% below 21, 34% between 21 and 23, 28% between 24 and 26, 10% between 27 and 28, and 9% above 28. 41% of the current freshmen were in the top fifth of their class; 74% were in the top two fifths. 10 freshmen graduated first in their class.

Requirements: The ACT is required. In addition, Michigan residents must submit ACT test scores, nonresidents either ACT or SAT I scores. In addition, high school transcripts should indicate 4 years of English with 1 composition course, 2 of a foreign language, and 3 each of history, math (including 2 years of algebra), science, and social studies. Applicants who graduated from high school more than 3 years ago need not show test results. The GED is accepted. A GPA of 3.0 is required. AP and CLEP credits are accepted.

Procedure: Freshmen are admitted to all sessions. Entrance exams should be taken during the junior year. Applications should be filed by July 31 for fall entry, November 15 for winter entry, April 10 for spring entry, and May 10 for summer entry, along with a $30 fee. There is a rolling admissions plan. Notification is sent on a rolling basis. A waiting list is an active part of the admissions procedure. Applications are accepted on computer disk and on-line through the university's web site.

Transfer: 1772 transfer students enrolled in 2002-2003. Transfer students must have a minimum of 30 college credits with a 2.0 GPA. 30 of 120 credits required for the bachelor's degree must be completed at Grand Valley.

Visiting: There are regularly scheduled orientations for prospective students, including registration activities. There are guides for informal visits and visitors may sit in on classes and stay overnight. To schedule a visit, contact the Admissions Office.

Financial Aid: In 2003-2004, 81% of all full-time freshmen and 69% of continuing full-time students received some form of financial aid. 54% of full-time freshmen and 51% of continuing full-time students received need-based aid. The average freshman award was $6614, with $2645 ($6725 maximum) from need-based scholarships or need-based grants, $2941 ($6825 maximum) from need-based self-help aid (loans and jobs), $120 ($10,521 maximum) from non-need-based athletic scholarships, and $908 ($9200 maximum) from other non-need-based awards and non-need-based scholarships. 72% of undergraduates work part time. Average annual earnings from campus work are $1800. The average financial indebtedness of the 2003 graduate was $8928. Grand Valley is a member of CSS. The FAFSA is required. The deadline for filing freshman financial aid applications for fall entry is February 15.

International Students: There are 98 international students enrolled. The school actively recruits these students. They must score 550 on the written TOEFL or take the MELAB or the Comprehensive English Language Test.

Computers: The mainframe is an IBM 9672-R12 system 390 parallel server. There is a 5-to-1 student/computer ratio with computers spread throughout the campus. LANs and computing labs are open 7 days a week, and PCs are connected to LAN and mainframe networks. All students have e-mail and access to the Internet. All students may access the system. There are no time limits and no fees. It is strongly recommended that all students have a personal computer.

Graduates: In a recent year, 2024 bachelor's degrees were awarded. The most popular majors were business (20%), health sciences (18%), and psychology (10%). In an average class, 48% graduated in 6 years or less. 133 companies recruited on campus in a recent year. In a recent graduating class, 87% were employed within 6 months of graduation.

Admissions Contact: Jodi Chycinski, Director of Admissions. A video is available. E-mail: go2gvsu@gvsu.edu Web: www.gvsu.edu

HILLSDALE COLLEGE

D-5

Hillsdale, MI 49242   (517) 607-2327; Fax: (517) 607-2298

Full-time: 565 men, 630 women	**Faculty:** 89
Part-time: 11 men, 24 women	**Ph.D.s:** 90%
Graduate: none	**Student/Faculty:** 12 to 1
Year: semesters, summer session	**Tuition:** $16,150
Application Deadline: June 15	**Room & Board:** $6300
Freshman Class: 1150 applied, 880 accepted, 389 enrolled	
SAT I Verbal/Math: 640/610	**ACT:** 27 **HIGHLY COMPETITIVE**

Hillsdale College, founded in 1844, is a private liberal arts college emphasizing preprofessional, business, and education programs. The 3 libraries contain 300,000 volumes, 61,000 microform items, and 8000 audio/video tapes/CDs, and subscribe to 1600 periodicals. Computerized library services include the card catalog, interlibrary loans, database searching, and Internet access. Special learning facilities include a learning resource center, a media center, an early childhood education lab, an arboretum, a 3000-book economics library, and a rare books room. The 250-acre campus is in a small town 120 miles southwest of Detroit. Including any residence halls, there are 55 buildings.

Student Life: 51% of undergraduates are from out of state, mostly the Midwest. Students are from 47 states, 14 foreign countries, and Canada. 40% are from public schools. 96% are white. 47% are claim no religious affiliation; 35% Protestant; 17% Catholic. The average age of freshmen is 18; all undergraduates, 20. 13% do not continue beyond their first year; 72% remain to graduate.

Housing: 950 students can be accommodated in college housing, which includes single-sex dorms, on-campus apartments, fraternity houses, and sorority houses. In addition, there are honors houses and special-interest houses. On-campus housing is guaranteed for all 4 years. 80% of students live on campus; of those, 85% remain on campus on weekends. Alcohol is not permitted. All students may keep cars.

Activities: 35% of men belong to 4 national fraternities; 45% of women belong to 4 national sororities. There are 60 groups on campus, including art, bagpipe band, cheerleading, choir, chorale, chorus, computers, dance, debate, drama, drill team, drum and bagpipes corps, ethnic, forensics, honors, international, jazz band, literary magazine, musical theater, newspaper, orchestra, pep band, photography, political, professional, radio and TV, religious, social, student government, and yearbook. Popular campus events include Parents Weekend, President's Ball, and Greek Week.

Sports: There are 9 intercollegiate sports for men and 9 for women, and 7 intramural sports for men and 7 for women. Facilities include an athletic complex with a prescription turf football field, a swimming pool, a 200-meter indoor track, a basketball arena, a weight room, an outdoor Olympic track, an exercise/physiology room, and volleyball, handball, racquetball, wallyball, and indoor tennis courts. The campus stadium seats 8000; the gym, 2600.

Disabled Students: 85% of the campus is accessible. Wheelchair ramps, elevators, special parking, specially equipped rest rooms, and lowered drinking fountains are available.

Services: Counseling and information services are available, as is tutoring in every subject. A writing center on campus and a peer tutoring program are administered by current students.

Campus Safety and Security: Measures include 24-hour foot and vehicle patrol, informal discussions, pamphlets/posters/films, and emergency telephones. There are lighted pathways/sidewalks.

Programs of Study: Hillsdale confers B.A. and B.S. degrees. Bachelor's degrees are awarded in BIOLOGICAL SCIENCE (biology/biological science), BUSINESS (accounting, banking and finance, business administration and management, international business management, and marketing/retailing/merchandising), COMMUNICATIONS AND THE ARTS (classics, comparative literature, dramatic arts, English, fine arts, French, German, music, Spanish, and speech/debate/rhetoric), COMPUTER AND PHYSICAL SCIENCE (chemistry, mathematics, and physics), EDUCATION (art, early childhood, elementary, foreign languages, middle school, music, physical, science, and secondary), HEALTH PROFESSIONS (predentistry, premedicine, and preveterinary science), SOCIAL SCIENCE (American studies, Christian studies, economics, European studies, history, political science/government, prelaw, psychology, religion, social science, and sociology). History, economics, and biology are the strongest academically. Business, history, and English are the largest.

Required: To graduate, the student must complete 124 semester hours with a GPA of 2.0. Required courses include 1 year of English, 1 year of science, 1 semester of Western Heritage and 1 semester of American Heritage, 9 hours of the humanities, 8 of the natural sciences and math, 6 of the social sciences, and 2 of phys ed. Students must also enroll in 2 seminars at the school's Center for Constructive Alternatives. 12 credit hours in a foreign language for a B.A. degree and 36 credit hours in math and science for a B.S. degree are also required.

Special: Special academic programs include the Washington Journalism Internship at the National Journalism Center and the Washington-Hillsdale Intern Program (WHIP), which places students in congressional or government offices. Students may study abroad in France, Germany, or Spain, and qualified students are chosen to attend Oxford University for a year. A business internship is offered in London at Regents College. The Thomas Professional Sales Intern program is also available. The college offers an accelerated degree; interdisciplinary majors, including political economy combining economics, history, and political science; 3-2 and 2-2 engineering degrees; and work-study programs at the city radio station WCSR and the city newspaper, the Hillsdale Daily News. There are 20 national honor societies and a freshman honors program.

Faculty/Classroom: 75% of faculty are male; 25%, female. All teach undergraduates and 1% both teach and do research. The average class size in an introductory lecture is 24; in a laboratory, 7; and in a regular course, 21.

Admissions: 77% of the 2003-2004 applicants were accepted. The SAT I scores for the 2003-2004 freshman class were: Verbal--3% below 500, 26% between 500 and 599, 46% between 600 and 700, and 25% above 700; Math--7% below 500, 31% between 500 and 599, 48% between 600 and 700, and 14% above 700. The ACT scores were 4% below 21, 18% between 21 and 23, 28% between 24 and 26, 19% between 27 and 28, and 31% above 28. 74% of the current freshmen were in the top fifth of their class; 96% were in the top two fifths. There were 12 National Merit finalists and 68 semifinalists. 20 freshmen graduated first in their class.

Requirements: The SAT I or ACT is required. In addition, the student must be a high school graduate or have earned a GED, and must have completed 4 years of English, 3 each of math and science, and 2 each of history, social studies, and foreign language. The college requires a letter of recommendation and an essay. An interview is also recommended. For music majors, an audition is required. The school recommends taking SAT II: Subject tests. Hillsdale requires applicants to be in the upper 50% of their class. A GPA of 3.1 is required. AP and CLEP credits are accepted. Important factors in the admissions decision are advanced placement or honor courses, leadership record, and extracurricular activities record.

Procedure: Freshmen are admitted to all sessions. Entrance exams should be taken in the spring of the junior year and/or the fall of the senior year. There is a rolling admissions plan. Applications should be filed by June 15 for fall entry, December 15 for spring entry, and May 1 for summer entry, along with a $15 fee. Notification is sent on a rolling basis. Applications are accepted on-line through a hot link from the school's web site to *embark.com*.

Transfer: 43 transfer students enrolled in 2002-2003. Transfer students must have a GPA of 3.0, and have a transfer evaluation form completed by the dean of students of their school. Hillsdale also requires high school and college transcripts. 24 of 124 credits required for the bachelor's degree must be completed at Hillsdale.

Visiting: There are regularly scheduled orientations for prospective students, including a spring orientation and a formal junior and senior visitation program. There are guides for informal visits and visitors may sit in on classes and stay overnight. To schedule a visit, contact Mary Ewers at the Admissions Office at (517) 607-2327 or *admissions@hillsdale.edu*.

Financial Aid: In 2003-2004, 83% of all full-time freshmen and 87% of continuing full-time students received some form of financial aid. 77% of full-time freshmen and 80% of continuing full-time students received need-based aid. The average freshman award was $10,500. 65% of undergraduates work part time. Average annual earnings from campus work are $1300. The average financial indebtedness of the 2003 graduate was $13,000. Hillsdale is a member of CSS. The CSS/Profile or FAFSA and the college's own financial statement are required. The priority date for freshman financial aid applications for fall entry is February 1. The deadline for filing freshman financial aid applications for fall entry is April 15.

International Students: There are 26 international students enrolled. They must score 530 on the written TOEFL or 190 on the electronic version and also take the Comprehensive English Language Test, or the college's own test. Applicants can also complete ESL level 108, with a minimum score of 15 in the motivational and proficiency categories.

Computers: The mainframe is an IBM AS/400. There are 5 computer labs on campus with more than 250 PCs including a graphics lab. All students may access the system at any time. There are no time limits and no fees.

Graduates: From July 1, 2002 to June 30, 2003, 242 bachelor's degrees were awarded. The most popular majors were business (26%), biology (14%), and history (13%). In an average class, 1% graduate in 3 years or less, 68% graduate in 4 years or less, 71% graduate in 5 years or less, and 72% graduate in 6 years or less. 50 companies recruited on campus in 2002-2003. Of the 2002 graduating class, 20% were enrolled in graduate school within 6 months of graduation and 78% were employed.

Admissions Contact: Jeffrey S. Lantis, Director of Admissions. A video is available. E-mail: *jeff.lantis@hillsdale.edu*
Web: *http://www.hillsdale.edu*

HOPE COLLEGE

Holland, MI 49423

C-4

(616) 395-7850
(800) 968-7850; Fax: (616) 395-7130

Full-time: 1110 men, 1848 women	**Faculty:** 203; IIB, +$
Part-time: 52 men, 58 women	**Ph.D.s:** 78%
Graduate: none	**Student/Faculty:** 15 to 1
Year: semesters, summer session	**Tuition:** $19,322
Application Deadline: open	**Room & Board:** $6018
Freshman Class: 2481 applied, 2056 accepted, 793 enrolled	
SAT I Verbal/Math: 588/597	**ACT:** 25 **VERY COMPETITIVE**

Hope College, founded by Dutch pioneers in 1866, is a private liberal arts institution affiliated with the Reformed Church in America. In addition to regional accreditation, Hope has baccalaureate program accreditation with ABET, ACS, CSWE, NASAD, NASD, NASM, NAST, NCATE, and NLN. The 2 libraries contain 336,755 volumes, 340,419 microform items, and 11,173 audio/video tapes/CDs, and subscribe to 1959 periodicals. Computerized library services include the card catalog, interlibrary loans, and database searching. Special learning facilities include a learning resource center, art gallery, planetarium, radio station, TV station, an academic support center, and a modern and classical language lab. The 45-acre campus is in a suburban area 26 miles southwest of Grand Rapids and 5 miles east of Lake Michigan. Including any residence halls, there are 105 buildings.

Student Life: 76% of undergraduates are from Michigan. Students are from 45 states, 32 foreign countries, and Canada. 86% are from public schools. 93% are white. 67% are Protestant; 11% Catholic. The average age of freshmen is 18; all undergraduates, 20. 13% do not continue beyond their first year; 75% remain to graduate.

Housing: 2200 students can be accommodated in college housing, which includes single-sex and coed dorms, on-campus apartments, married-student housing, fraternity houses, and sorority houses. In addition, there are language houses and student cottages. On-campus housing is guaranteed for all 4 years. 81% of students live on campus; of those, 75% remain on campus on weekends. Alcohol is not permitted. All students may keep cars.

Activities: 6% of men belong to 6 local fraternities; 15% of women belong to 6 local sororities. There are 67 groups on campus, including art, band, cheerleading, choir, chorale, chorus, computers, dance, drama, ethnic, film, honors, international, jazz band, literary magazine, musical theater, newspaper, orchestra, pep band, photography, political, professional, radio and TV, religious, social, social service, student government, and yearbook. Popular campus events include Winter Fantasia, Spring Festival, and Nykerk Cup Competition.

Sports: There are 9 intercollegiate sports for men and 9 for women, and 16 intramural sports for men and 13 for women. Facilities include athletic fields, a field house, a tennis center, and a health and phys ed center that contains gyms, a running track, a swimming and diving pool, exercise rooms, a dance studio, racquetball courts, gymnastics rooms, and health-fitness equipment.

Disabled Students: 95% of the campus is accessible. Wheelchair ramps, elevators, special parking, specially equipped rest rooms, special class scheduling, and lowered drinking fountains are available.

Services: Counseling and information services are available, as is tutoring in every subject. There is a reader service for the blind.

Campus Safety and Security: Measures include 24-hour foot and vehicle patrol, security escort services, shuttle buses, and informal discussions. There are pamphlets/posters/films, emergency telephones, and lighted pathways/sidewalks.

Programs of Study: Hope confers B.A., B.S., B.Mus., and B.S.N. degrees. Bachelor's degrees are awarded in BIOLOGICAL SCIENCE (biochemistry and biology/biological science), BUSINESS (accounting and business administration and management), COMMUNICATIONS AND THE ARTS (communications, dance, dramatic arts, English, fine arts, French, German, Latin, music, and Spanish), COMPUTER AND PHYSICAL SCIENCE (chemistry, computer science, geology, mathematics, and physics), EDUCATION (art, business, elementary, foreign languages, music, science, secondary, and special), ENGINEERING AND ENVIRONMENTAL DESIGN (engineering), HEALTH PROFESSIONS (nursing, predentistry, and premedicine), SOCIAL SCIENCE (economics, history, international relations, philosophy, physical fitness/movement, political science/government, prelaw, psychology, religion, social work, and sociology). Chemistry, biological sciences, and psychology are the strongest academically. Business, biology, and English are the largest.

Required: To graduate, students must complete 126 semester hours with a 2.0 GPA. All students must take 51 hours of the general education program, including a first-year seminar, 10 hours of math and natural science, 8 of cultural heritage, 6 each of social science, performing and fine arts, and religion, 4 each of a language and writing, 3 in a senior seminar, 2 of health dynamics, and a cultural diversity course.

Special: The college offers internships in all academic areas as well as on-campus work-study programs, study abroad in more than 40 countries, and Washington, Chicago, New York, and Philadelphia semesters.

Students may take dual majors. There are 20 national honor societies, including Phi Beta Kappa, and 1 departmental honors program.

Faculty/Classroom: 54% of faculty are male; 46%, female. All teach undergraduates. The average class size in an introductory lecture is 25; in a laboratory, 25; and in a regular course, 25.

Admissions: 83% of the 2003-2004 applicants were accepted. The SAT I scores for the 2003-2004 freshman class were: Verbal--12% below 500, 39% between 500 and 599, 35% between 600 and 700, and 13% above 700; Math--11% below 500, 37% between 500 and 599, 38% between 600 and 700, and 13% above 700. The ACT scores were 2% between 12 and 17, 31% between 18 and 23, 50% between 24 and 29, and 17% above 30. 52% of the current freshmen were in the top fifth of their class; 75% were in the top two fifths. There were 14 National Merit finalists.

Requirements: The SAT I or ACT is required. In addition, the college requires a high school transcript, which must include 4 years of English, 2 each of math, a foreign language, and social science, and 1 year of a lab science, as well as 5 other academic courses. The college requires submission of an essay and recommends an interview. A portfolio or audition is required for certain majors. The GED is considered. AP and CLEP credits are accepted. Important factors in the admissions decision are advanced placement or honor courses, leadership record, and evidence of special talent.

Procedure: Freshmen are admitted fall, winter, and spring. Entrance exams should be taken during spring of the junior year or fall of the senior year. There are early admissions, deferred admissions plans, and a rolling admissions plan. Application deadlines are open. The fall 2003 application fee was $35. Applications are accepted on-line through CollegeNET.

Transfer: 53 transfer students enrolled in 2002-2003. Transfer students must have a GPA of 2.0 in at least 1 year of liberal arts courses. 32 of 126 credits required for the bachelor's degree must be completed at Hope.

Visiting: There are regularly scheduled orientations for prospective students, including tours, classes, lunch with a current student, and appointments with professors. There are guides for informal visits and visitors may sit in on classes and stay overnight. To schedule a visit, contact the Admissions Office at (800) 968-7850 or admissions@hope.edu.

Financial Aid: In 2003-2004, 95% of all full-time freshmen and 90% of continuing full-time students received some form of financial aid. 64% of full-time freshmen and 59% of continuing full-time students received need-based aid. The average freshman award was $17,221. Need-based scholarships or need-based grants averaged $12,885; need-based self-help aid (loans and jobs) averaged $4336; and non-need-based awards and non-need-based scholarships averaged $5808. 40% of undergraduates work part time. Average annual earnings from campus work are $1515. The average financial indebtedness of the 2003 graduate was $18,316. Hope is a member of CSS. The FAFSA and the college's own financial statement are required. The priority date for freshman financial aid applications for fall entry is February 15.

International Students: There are 47 international students enrolled. The school actively recruits these students. They must score 550 on the written TOEFL and also take the SAT I or the ACT.

Computers: The mainframe is a DEC VAX 4200. Terminals and PCs are located in most dorms and in academic buildings, the library, and the student center. All students may access the system 24 hours a day. There are no time limits and no fees.

Graduates: From July 1, 2002 to June 30, 2003, 679 bachelor's degrees were awarded. The most popular majors were business administration (12%), psychology (8%), and biology (6%). In an average class, 1% graduate in 3 years or less, 64% graduate in 4 years or less, 73% graduate in 5 years or less, and 75% graduate in 6 years or less. 37 companies recruited on campus in 2002-2003. Of the 2002 graduating class, 24% were enrolled in graduate school within 6 months of graduation and 71% were employed.

Admissions Contact: James R. Bekkering, Vice President for Admissions. E-mail: admissions@hope.edu Web: www.hope.edu

KALAMAZOO COLLEGE

Kalamazoo, MI 49006-3295

D-5

(616) 337-7166
(800) 253-3602; Fax: (616) 337-7390

Full-time: 600 men, 700 women	**Faculty:** 97; IIB, av$
Part-time: none	**Ph.D.s:** 90%
Graduate: none	**Student/Faculty:** 13 to 1
Year: quarters	**Tuition:** $22,908
Application Deadline: February 15	**Room & Board:** $6480
Freshman Class: 1603 applied, 1127 accepted, 383 enrolled	
SAT I or ACT: required	**HIGHLY COMPETITIVE+**

Kalamazoo College is a liberal arts and sciences institution founded in 1833. Figures in the above capsule and in this profile are approximate. The library contains 346,648 volumes, 54,055 microform items, and 8938 audio/video tapes/CDs, and subscribes to 1250 periodicals. Computerized library services include the card catalog, interlibrary loans, and database searching. Special learning facilities include a learning resource center, art gallery, and radio station. The 60-acre campus is in a suburban area 140 miles from Detroit and Chicago. Including any residence halls, there are 30 buildings.

Student Life: 76% of undergraduates are from Michigan. Students are from 42 states, 16 foreign countries, and Canada. 85% are from public schools. 83% are white. 40% claim no religious affiliation; 34% Protestant; 22% Catholic. The average age of freshmen is 18; all undergraduates, 20. 12% do not continue beyond their first year; 71% remain to graduate.

Housing: 868 students can be accommodated in college housing, which includes coed dorms. In addition, there are special-interest houses and a wellness house. On-campus housing is guaranteed for all 4 years. 75% of students live on campus; of those, 85% remain on campus on weekends. Upperclassmen may keep cars.

Activities: There are no fraternities or sororities. There are more than 50 groups on campus, including art, band, cheerleading, choir, chorale, chorus, computers, dance, drama, environmental, ethnic, film, gay, honors, international, jazz band, literary magazine, musical theater, newspaper, orchestra, photography, political, professional, radio and TV, religious, social, social service, student government, symphony, and yearbook. Popular campus events include Monte Carlo Night, Quadstock, and Day of Gracious Living.

Sports: There are 8 intercollegiate sports for men and 8 for women, and 12 intramural sports for men and 11 for women. Facilities include a field house that houses a 2000-seat gym, basketball and volleyball courts, weight-training rooms, and a dance studio; a 1500-seat, 11-court tennis stadium; a racquet center with 4 tennis courts, 3 racquetball courts, and a squash court; a natatorium; a 4000-seat football stadium; and soccer and baseball fields.

Disabled Students: 25% of the campus is accessible. Wheelchair ramps, elevators, special parking, specially equipped rest rooms, and special class scheduling are available.

Services: Counseling and information services are available, as is tutoring in most subjects. A writing center, language labs, and supplemental instruction are also provided.

Campus Safety and Security: Measures include 24-hour foot and vehicle patrol, self-defense education, security escort services, and informal discussions. There are pamphlets/posters/films, emergency telephones, lighted pathways/sidewalks, and secured residence halls with an electronic entry system.

Programs of Study: Kalamazoo confers the B.A. degree. Bachelor's degrees are awarded in BIOLOGICAL SCIENCE (biology/biological science), BUSINESS (business economics), COMMUNICATIONS AND THE ARTS (art, art history and appreciation, dramatic arts, English, French, German, music, and Spanish), COMPUTER AND PHYSICAL SCIENCE (chemistry, computer science, mathematics, and physics), HEALTH PROFESSIONS (health science), SOCIAL SCIENCE (anthropology, classical/ancient civilization, history, human development, interdisciplinary studies, international relations, international studies, philosophy, political science/government, psychology, religion, and sociology). Foreign languages, international studies and commerce, and health sciences are the strongest academically. Economics, English, and political science are the largest.

Required: To graduate, students must complete 38 academic units, including 8 units in the major, with a minimum 2.0 GPA. Required courses include 4 units in social science, 3 in natural science, computer science, or math, 2 each in literature and philosophy/religion, and 1 in fine arts. The college further requires completion of a senior individualized project, a credit from the liberal arts colloquium, and a passing grade on a comprehensive exam in the major. The student must also take 5 non-credit courses in phys ed and show proficiency in writing as well as in a foreign language.

Special: Students may study abroad in more than 12 countries and choose from among 900 career internships in the United States, Europe, Asia, and Africa. The school offers a Washington semester, allows dual and interdisciplinary majors, and has cross-registration with Western Michigan University. A 3-2 engineering degree is offered with Washington University and the University of Michigan. There are accelerated 3-year programs in predentistry, premedicine, and preveterinary medicine. There are 3 national honor societies, including Phi Beta Kappa.

Faculty/Classroom: 52% of faculty are male; 48%, female. All teach undergraduates. The average class size in an introductory lecture is 18; in a laboratory, 24; and in a regular course, 18.

Admissions: 70% of the 2003-2004 applicants were accepted. There were 11 National Merit finalists in a recent year. 21 freshmen graduated first in their class.

Requirements: The SAT I or ACT is required. In addition, the college also requires a high school transcript, an essay, and teacher and counselor recommendations; an interview is recommended. AP credits are accepted. Important factors in the admissions decision are advanced placement or honor courses, evidence of special talent, and leadership record.

Procedure: Freshmen are admitted fall and winter. Entrance exams should be taken by December of the senior year. There are early decision, early admissions, and deferred admissions plans. Early decision applications should be filed by November 15; regular applications, by February 15 for fall entry. The fall 2003 application fee was $25. Notification of early decision is sent December 1; regular decision, April 1. 21 early decision candidates were admitted for the 2003-2004 class. Applications are accepted on computer disk.

Transfer: 15 transfer students enrolled in a recent year. A 3.0 GPA from previous institution(s) is required. 18 credits of 38 required for the bachelor's degree must be completed at Kalamazoo.

Visiting: There are regularly scheduled orientations for prospective students, including interviews, tours, and class visits as requested. Special preview events include formal presentation of the unique curriculum and financial aid seminars. There are guides for informal visits and visitors may sit in on classes and stay overnight. To schedule a visit, contact the visit coordinator, Ms. Pat Marcinkowski.

Financial Aid: In a recent year, 98% of all full-time freshmen and 96% of continuing full-time students received some form of financial aid. 46% of all full-time students received need-based aid. The average freshman award was $17,130. 40% of undergraduates work part time. Average annual earnings from campus work are $1045. The average financial indebtedness of the 2003 graduate was $17,400. The CSS Profile, FAFSA, and a supplemental aid form are required. The deadline for filing freshman financial aid applications for fall entry is February 15.

International Students: There were 31 international students enrolled in a recent year. The school actively recruits these students. They must score 550 on the written TOEFL or take the MELAB, and also take the SAT I or ACT.

Computers: The mainframe is a Sun Ultra 2. There are 130 PCs available for student use, 10 of which are limited to physics students. All PCs and Macs are networked on the Internet. All rooms in the residence halls are wired for network access. All students may access the system. There are no time limits and no fees. It is strongly recommended that all students have a personal computer.

Graduates: In a recent year, 214 bachelor's degrees were awarded. The most popular majors were economics (14%), English (14%), and biology (12%). In an average class, 65% graduate in 4 years or less, 71% graduate in 5 years or less, and 73% graduate in 6 years or less. 35 companies recruited on campus in a recent year. Of a recent graduating class, 30% were enrolled in graduate school within 6 months of graduation and 60% were employed.

Admissions Contact: John M. Carroll, Director of Admission. A video is available. E-mail: *admissions@kzoo.edu* Web: *www.kzoo.edu*

KENDALL COLLEGE OF ART AND DESIGN OF FERRIS STATE UNIVERSITY
D-4

Grand Rapids, MI 49503-3102
(616) 451-2787
(800) 676-2787; Fax: (616) 831-9689

Full-time: 688 men and women	**Faculty:** 36
Part-time: 218 men and women	**Ph.D.s:** 89%
Graduate: 18 men and women	**Student/Faculty:** 19 to 1
Year: semesters, summer session	**Tuition:** $10,784 ($15,544)
Application Deadline: open	**Room & Board:** n/app
Freshman Class: n/av	
SAT I or ACT: required	**SPECIAL**

The Kendall College of Art and Design of Ferris State University, founded in 1928, is a commuter institution specializing in design studies and the fine arts. In addition to regional accreditation, Kendall has baccalaureate program accreditation with FIDER and NASAD. The library contains 23,000 volumes, 1000 microform items, and 3500 audio/video tapes/CDs, and subscribes to 150 periodicals. Computerized library services include the card catalog. Special learning facilities include a learning resource center, art gallery, a model and wood shop, a photography lab, a printmaking lab, fine art studios, and a student gallery. The 1-acre campus is in an urban area in downtown Grand Rapids. There are 2 buildings.

Student Life: 91% of undergraduates are from Michigan. 90% are from public schools. 81% are white. The average age of all undergraduates is 24.

Housing: There are no residence halls. All students commute. Alcohol is not permitted.

Activities: There are no fraternities or sororities. There are 11 groups on campus, including art, ethnic, film, gay, international, literary magazine, newspaper, photography, professional, religious, and student government. Popular campus events include Advising Day, pancake supper, and all-campus picnic.

Sports: There is no sports program at Kendall. Facilities include Grand Rapids Community College's pool, track, and sports facilities, which students may use upon payment of an annual fee.

Disabled Students: All of the campus is accessible. Wheelchair ramps, elevators, special parking, specially equipped rest rooms, lowered drinking fountains, lowered telephones, and special drawing tables are available.

Services: Counseling and information services are available, as is tutoring in every subject. There is a reader service for the blind.

Campus Safety and Security: Measures include security escort services, informal discussions, pamphlets/posters/films, and emergency telephones. There are lighted pathways/sidewalks.

Programs of Study: Kendall confers B.S. and B.F.A. degrees. Bachelor's degrees are awarded in COMMUNICATIONS AND THE ARTS (art history and appreciation, drawing, graphic design, illustration, industrial design, media arts, metal/jewelry, multimedia, photography, printmaking, and sculpture), COMPUTER AND PHYSICAL SCIENCE (digital arts/technology), EDUCATION (art), ENGINEERING AND ENVIRONMENTAL DESIGN (furniture design, interior design, and woodworking). Illustration and visual communication are the largest.

Required: To graduate, students must complete 120 credit hours, including 45 to 69 in the major, 30 to 45 of liberal arts and sciences, 12 to 18 of a foundation studio core, 12 to 15 of art history, and 12 to 15 of studio electives. All students must complete a graduation portfolio. A minimum GPA of 2.0 is required, with a minimum GPA of 2.25 in the student's major studio core courses.

Special: Cross-registration is offered through a consortium of schools. Internships are available in all majors. Study abroad may be arranged by the student and approved by the college; trips to Perugia, Italy, and London, England, are offered each year. Dual majors are possible.

Faculty/Classroom: 56% of faculty are male; 44%, female. All teach undergraduates. No introductory courses are taught by graduate students. The average class size in an introductory lecture is 35; in a laboratory, 15; and in a regular course, 20.

Requirements: The SAT I or ACT is required; ACT or SAT I scores are not required of applicants who are 23 years old or older. In addition, a high school transcript is required. The GED certificate is accepted. Students must submit an essay with their application, and most majors require a portfolio review. An interview is recommended. Prospective students are encouraged to take courses in drawing, painting, and design in high school. A GPA of 2.25 is required. AP and CLEP credits are accepted. Important factors in the admissions decision are leadership record, personality/intangible qualities, and evidence of special talent.

Procedure: Freshmen are admitted to all sessions. There are early decision, early admissions, and deferred admissions plans. Application deadlines are open. Application fee is $30. Notification is sent on a rolling basis. 18 early decision candidates were accepted for the 2003-2004 class.

Transfer: 167 transfer students enrolled in 2002-2003. Applicants must have a GPA of 2.25 and pass a portfolio review. An interview is recommended. 30 of 120 to 134 credits required for the bachelor's degree must be completed at Kendall.

Visiting: There are regularly scheduled orientations for prospective students, consisting of Explore Art Today days several times a year, during which prospective students may see student work, visit studios and classrooms, and talk with staff, faculty, and students. There are guides for informal visits and visitors may sit in on classes. To schedule a visit, contact the Admissions Office at (616) 451-2787 or (800) 676-2787 or *jonesp@ferris.edu.*

Financial Aid: In 2003-2004, 76% of all full-time freshmen and 79% of continuing full-time students received some form of financial aid. 70% of full-time freshmen and 71% of continuing full-time students received need-based aid. The average freshman award was $7491. Need-based scholarships or need-based grants averaged $3089 ($9344 maximum); need-based self-help aid (loans and jobs) averaged $5091 ($22,744 maximum); and non-need-based awards and non-need-based scholarships averaged $3456 ($15,596 maximum). 6% of undergraduates work part time. Average annual earnings from campus work are $2000. The average financial indebtedness of the 2003 graduate was $18,000. The FAFSA is required. The priority date for freshman financial aid applications for fall entry is February 15.

International Students: There are 10 international students enrolled. They must score 500 on the written TOEFL or 173 on the electronic version and also take the SAT I or the ACT.

Computers: The college provides Macs for student use in classroom work and design. Library computers provide Internet access. Students may use the computer labs from 8 A.M. to 12 P.M. There are no time limits. The fee is $200.

Graduates: In an average class, 20% graduate in 4 years or less, 33% graduate in 5 years or less, and 37% graduate in 6 years or less.

Admissions Contact: Sandy Britton, Director of Enrollment Management. E-mail: *brittons@ferris.edu* Web: *www.kcad.edu*

KETTERING UNIVERSITY
Flint, MI 48504-4898

E-4

(810) 762-7865
(800) 955-4464; Fax: (810) 762-9837

Full-time: 2086 men, 439 women	Faculty: 139
Part-time: none	Ph.D.s: 89%
Graduate: 504 men, 189 women	Student/Faculty: 18 to 1
Year: semesters, summer session	Tuition: $21,554
Application Deadline: open	Room & Board: $4924
Freshman Class: 2365 applied, 1669 accepted, 561 enrolled	
SAT I Verbal/Math: 590/640	ACT: 26 HIGHLY COMPETITIVE

Kettering University is a private college founded in 1919. In the 5-year undergraduate program students alternate 11-week terms of full-time classes with 12-week terms of full-time paid professional cooperative education (co-op) work experience in industry. Students typically begin co-op during their freshman year and co-op in 43 states and several countries. There are 3 undergraduate schools and 1 graduate school. In addition to regional accreditation, Kettering has baccalaureate program accreditation with ABET and ACBSP. The library contains 120,000 volumes, 8100 microform items, and 300 audio/video tapes/CDs, and subscribes to 555 periodicals. Computerized library services include interlibrary loans, database searching, and Internet access. Special learning facilities include a learning resource center, art gallery, radio station, and Industrial History Archives. The 85-acre campus is in a suburban area 60 miles north of Detroit. Including any residence halls, there are 10 buildings.

Student Life: 63% of undergraduates are from Michigan. Students are from 50 states, 24 foreign countries, and Canada. 85% are from public schools. 74% are white. The average age of freshmen is 18; all undergraduates, 20. 12% do not continue beyond their first year; 65% remain to graduate.

Housing: 623 students can be accommodated in college housing, which includes single-sex and coed dorms, on-campus apartments, fraternity houses, and sorority houses. On-campus housing is guaranteed for the freshman year only and is available on a lottery system for upperclassmen. Priority is given to out-of-town students. Alcohol is not permitted. All students may keep cars.

Activities: 40% of men belong to 12 national fraternities; 33% of women belong to 6 national sororities. There are 40 groups on campus, including art, chorus, computers, drama, ethnic, honors, international, jazz band, literary magazine, newspaper, pep band, photography, political, professional, radio and TV, religious, social, social service, student government, and yearbook. Popular campus events include Greek Week, Diversity Week, and Student and Alumni Industry Speaker Series.

Sports: There are 2 intercollegiate sports for men, and 22 intramural sports for men and 22 for women. Facilities include a recreation center with 2 basketball and 2 tennis/basketball courts; 4 racquetball and squash courts; a one-eighth mile track; an Olympic-size pool; and free weight, Nautilus, and aerobic rooms. A 25-acre sports and recreation complex includes 4 softball and 2 soccer fields, outdoor tennis courts, a sand volleyball court, a golf green, and a picnic pavilion.

Disabled Students: All of the campus is accessible. Wheelchair ramps, elevators, special parking, specially equipped rest rooms, special class scheduling, lowered drinking fountains, and lowered telephones are available.

Services: Counseling and information services are available, as is tutoring in most subjects. Tutoring is routinely available for most subjects in the Academic Support Center, in the residence hall, and with faculty. Supplemental tutoring is coordinated through the Academic Services Department. Math and writing labs are available. A Strategies for Academic Success program is available.

Campus Safety and Security: Measures include 24-hour foot and vehicle patrol, self-defense education, security escort services, and informal discussions. There are pamphlets/posters/films, emergency telephones, and lighted pathways/sidewalks. After-hours access (e.g., to the academic building) is secure via the tunnel from the residence hall and campus center.

Programs of Study: Kettering confers B.S.A.M., B.S.A.P., B.S.C.E., B.S.C.S., B.S.E.C., B.S.E.E., B.S.I.E., B.S.M., and B.S.M.E. degrees. Master's degrees are also awarded. Bachelor's degrees are awarded in BUSINESS (business administration and management), COMPUTER AND PHYSICAL SCIENCE (applied mathematics, applied physics, and computer science), ENGINEERING AND ENVIRONMENTAL DESIGN (computer engineering, electrical/electronics engineering, environmental science, industrial engineering, and mechanical engineering). Mechanical engineering, electrical engineering, and computer engineering are the largest.

Required: Degree requirements include completion of 160 credit hours, with 60 in the major. All students must take specific courses in math, chemistry, physics, written and oral communication, computers, history, humanities, and economics, and complete at least 5 terms of co-op experience in industry plus 2 work terms designated for a senior thesis project. A minimum grade average of 80 on a scale of 100 is required for graduation. The GPA is determined by a formula combining the numerical grades achieved and the number of credits attempted. Students must complete a fifth-year thesis project.

Special: All undergraduate students participate in paid professional co-operative education work experience. Students may pursue a dual major in electrical and mechanical engineering. Accelerated degree programs in engineering are available in most majors, as is study abroad in 6 countries. There are 9 national honor societies.

Faculty/Classroom: 82% of faculty are male; 18%, female. All teach undergraduates and 55% both teach and do research. No introductory courses are taught by graduate students. The average class size in an introductory lecture is 39; in a laboratory, 14; and in a regular course, 25.

Admissions: 71% of the 2003-2004 applicants were accepted. The SAT I scores for the 2003-2004 freshman class were: Verbal--10% below 500, 43% between 500 and 599, 39% between 600 and 700, and 8% above 700; Math--22% between 500 and 599, 56% between 600 and 700, and 22% above 700. The ACT scores were 7% below 21, 19% between 21 and 23, 30% between 24 and 26, 22% between 27 and 28, and 22% above 28. 53% of the current freshmen were in the top fifth of their class; 86% were in the top two fifths. 19 freshmen graduated first in their class.

Requirements: The SAT I or ACT is required. In addition, applicants must graduate from an accredited secondary school with a minimum of 16 academic credits. Applicants must have completed 3 years of English, 3 1/2 years of math, including trigonometry, and 2 years of lab science, 1 of which must be chemistry or physics (both are strongly recommended). AP credits are accepted. Important factors in the admissions decision are leadership record, advanced placement or honor courses, and extracurricular activities record.

Procedure: Freshmen are admitted fall, winter, and summer. Entrance exams should be taken during the spring of the junior year and fall of the senior year. There is a rolling admissions plan and a deferred admissions plan. Application deadlines are open. Application fee is $35. Applications are accepted on-line through the university's web site.

Transfer: 80 transfer students enrolled in 2002-2003. Transfer applicants must present the same minimum preparation as freshmen in math and science and must submit both high school and college transcripts and SAT I or ACT scores. Required courses can be taken in high school or college. A minimum GPA of 3.0 in English, math, and science is expected. Transfers who present less than 30 credits of full-time study will be judged on both their college and high school record and test scores. 85 of 160 credits required for the bachelor's degree must be completed at Kettering.

Visiting: There are regularly scheduled orientations for prospective students, including 3 open house programs for prospective students. There are guides for informal visits and visitors may sit in on classes and stay overnight. To schedule a visit, contact the Admissions Office at (800) 955-4464, ext. 7865 or *admissions@kettering.edu*.

Financial Aid: In 2003-2004, 88% of all full-time freshmen and 84% of continuing full-time students received some form of financial aid. 72% of full-time freshmen and 58% of continuing full-time students received need-based aid. The average freshman award was $12,652. Need-based scholarships or need-based grants averaged $4352; need-based self-help aid (loans and jobs) averaged $2141 ($3845 maximum); and non-need-based awards and non-need-based scholarships averaged $6453. 13% of undergraduates work part time. Average annual earnings from campus work are $532. The FAFSA and the college's own financial statement are required. The priority date for freshman financial aid applications for fall entry is February 14.

International Students: There are 57 international students enrolled. The school actively recruits these students. They must score 550 on the written TOEFL or 213 on the electronic version or take the MELAB.

Computers: The mainframe consists of Sun Enterprise servers. All campus buildings and residence hall rooms are fully networked. Telephone and web access is available from off campus. There are more than 450 workstations, networked PCs, and CAD/CAE workstations for general student use. Stand-alone and dedicated PCs are available for each engineering lab. All students may access the system 24 hours per day, 7 days per week. There are no time limits and no fees. It is strongly recommended that all students have a personal computer.

Graduates: From July 1, 2002 to June 30, 2003, 394 bachelor's degrees were awarded. The most popular majors were mechanical engineering (56%), electrical engineering (18%), and industrial and manufacturing (8%). In an average class, 3% graduate in 4 years or less, 54% graduate in 5 years or less, and 65% graduate in 6 years or less. 100 companies recruited on campus in 2002-2003. Of the 2002 graduating class, 20% were enrolled in graduate school within 6 months of graduation and 94% were employed.

Admissions Contact: Barbara Sosin, Director of Admissions.
E-mail: *admissions@kettering.edu* Web: *www.kettering.edu*

LAKE SUPERIOR STATE UNIVERSITY D-2
Sault Sainte Marie, MI 49783-1699

(906) 635-2231
(888) 800-5778; Fax: (906) 635-6669

Full-time: 1300 men, 1150 women	**Faculty:** 114; IIA, --$
Part-time: 300 men, 450 women	**Ph.D.s:** 56%
Graduate: 85 men, 65 women	**Student/Faculty:** 22 to 1
Year: semesters, summer session	**Tuition:** $4500 ($8500)
Application Deadline: open	**Room & Board:** $5000
Freshman Class: n/av	
ACT: required	**LESS COMPETITIVE**

Lake Superior State University, founded in 1946, is a business, technical, and liberal arts institution. There are 3 undergraduate schools and 1 graduate school. Figures in the above capsule and in this profile are approximate. In addition to regional accreditation, LSSU has baccalaureate program accreditation with ABET and NLN. The library contains 100,000 volumes and 1000 audio/video tapes/CDs, and subscribes to 950 periodicals. Computerized library services include the card catalog, interlibrary loans, and database searching. Special learning facilities include a learning resource center, natural history museum, planetarium, radio station, fish hatchery and aquatics lab, and interactive television for distance education. The 121-acre campus is in a small town 280 miles north of Lansing. Including any residence halls, there are 36 buildings.

Student Life: 75% of undergraduates are from Michigan. Students are from 20 states, 7 foreign countries, and Canada. 94% are from public schools. 76% are white; 17% foreign nationals. The average age of all undergraduates is 23. 33% do not continue beyond their first year; 45% remain to graduate.

Housing: 1198 students can be accommodated in college housing, which includes single-sex and coed dorms, on-campus apartments, married-student housing, and fraternity houses. On-campus housing is guaranteed for the freshman year only, is available on a first-come, first-served basis, and is available on a lottery system for upperclassmen. 73% of students commute. All students may keep cars.

Activities: There are 1 local and 4 national fraternities; 10% of women belong to 5 national sororities. There are 44 groups on campus, including band, cheerleading, chess, chorale, computers, drama, ethnic, film, honors, jazz band, literary magazine, musical theater, newspaper, orchestra, pep band, political, professional, radio and TV, religious, social, social service, student government, and symphony. Popular campus events include Winter Carnival, Spring Fling, and Beach Party.

Sports: There are 5 intercollegiate sports for men and 5 for women, and 17 intramural sports for men and 15 for women. Facilities include a 2800-seat gym, 4100-seat ice arena, basketball courts, indoor and outdoor tennis courts, racquetball courts, an indoor pool, weight rooms, a dance studio, and a quarter-mile all-weather track.

Disabled Students: 90% of the campus is accessible. Wheelchair ramps, elevators, special parking, specially equipped rest rooms, special class scheduling, lowered drinking fountains, and lowered telephones are available.

Services: Counseling and information services are available, as is tutoring in most subjects, on request and free of charge. There is a reader service for the blind and remedial math, reading, and writing. There are also math, reading, and writing labs.

Campus Safety and Security: Measures include 24-hour foot and vehicle patrol, self-defense education, security escort services, and informal discussions. There are pamphlets/posters/films and lighted pathways/sidewalks.

Programs of Study: LSSU confers B.A. and B.S. degrees. Associate and master's degrees are also awarded. Bachelor's degrees are awarded in AGRICULTURE (fish and game management and wildlife management), BIOLOGICAL SCIENCE (biology/biological science), BUSINESS (accounting, business administration and management, and marketing/retailing/merchandising), COMMUNICATIONS AND THE ARTS (English and fine arts), COMPUTER AND PHYSICAL SCIENCE (computer science, geology, and mathematics), EDUCATION (athletic training, early childhood, elementary, and secondary), ENGINEERING AND ENVIRONMENTAL DESIGN (electrical/electronics engineering, engineering, engineering management, engineering technology, environmental engineering technology, environmental science, manufacturing technology, and mechanical engineering), HEALTH PROFESSIONS (exercise science, medical laboratory technology, nursing, predentistry, premedicine, and recreation therapy), SOCIAL SCIENCE (criminal justice, economics, fire science, history, human services, paralegal studies, parks and recreation management, political science/government, prelaw, psychology, social science, and sociology). Engineering technology, nursing, and biology are the strongest academically. Business and criminal justice are the largest.

Required: To graduate, students must complete 124 semester hours with a GPA of 2.0. The core curriculum includes course work in computer literacy, English, oral communications, aesthetics, critical thinking, humanities, math, science, social science, ethics, and cultural diversity. At least 32 of the final credits, and 50% of all upper-level courses, must be taken in residence at Lake State. Math and English competency must be met.

Special: Lake State offers internships in criminal justice, medical technology, human services, legal assistance studies, and natural resources technology, work-study programs, co-op programs in engineering technology, and cross-registration with the Canadian Colleges of Sault and Algoma and Bridge International Consortium. Study abroad, a Washington semester, and student-designed majors are available. Distance learning and weekend college study formats are offered. There is a freshman honors program.

Faculty/Classroom: 71% of faculty are male; 29%, female. All teach undergraduates. No introductory courses are taught by graduate students. The average class size in a laboratory is 14 and in a regular course, 30.

Requirements: The ACT is required. In addition, applicants should be high school graduates with 3 years of English, 2 each of math and social studies, and 1 of history, and should have a GPA of 2.0. The GED is accepted. An interview is recommended. AP and CLEP credits are accepted. Important factors in the admissions decision are advanced placement or honor courses, recommendations by school officials, and recommendations by alumni.

Procedure: Freshmen are admitted to all sessions. There is a deferred admissions plan. Application deadlines are open. Check with the school for current application fee.

Transfer: Applicants must be eligible to return to the last institution attended, and must have an overall college GPA of 2.0. An interview is recommended. ACT scores are required if high school graduation was within 26 months of the semester of entry. High school transcripts and GED scores are required if transferring with fewer than 19 semester hours of credit. 32 of 124 credits required for the bachelor's degree must be completed at LSSU.

Visiting: There are regularly scheduled orientations for prospective students. There are guides for informal visits and visitors may sit in on classes. To schedule a visit, contact the Admissions Office.

Financial Aid: The FAFSA is required. Check with the school for current deadlines.

International Students: The school actively recruits these students. They must score 550 on the written TOEFL.

Computers: The mainframe is a DEC Alpha. Students have access to a DEC MicroVAX 3400 through terminals located in the computer lab. There are more than 190 PCs for student use in a number of locations across campus. All students may access the system during lab hours. There are no time limits and no fees.

Admissions Contact: Kevin Pollock, Director of Admissions.
E-mail: *admissions@lakers.lssu.edu* Web: *www.lssu.edu*

LAWRENCE TECHNOLOGICAL UNIVERSITY E-5
Southfield, MI 48075

(248) 204-3160
(800) CALL-LTU; Fax: (248) 204-3188

Full-time: 1247 men, 417 women	**Faculty:** 115
Part-time: 1061 men, 228 women	**Ph.D.s:** 79%
Graduate: 841 men, 447 women	**Student/Faculty:** 14 to 1
Year: semesters, summer session	**Tuition:** $14,362
Application Deadline: open	**Room & Board:** $6125
Freshman Class: 1417 applied, 1081 accepted, 470 enrolled	
SAT I Verbal/Math: 500/580	**ACT:** 23 COMPETITIVE

Lawrence Technological University, founded in 1932 as the Lawrence Institute of Technology, is a private institution housing colleges of engineering, management, arts and sciences, and architecture and design. There are 4 undergraduate and 4 graduate schools. In addition to regional accreditation, Lawrence Tech has baccalaureate program accreditation with ABET, ACBSP, FIDER, NAAB, and NASAD. The library contains 114,263 volumes, 28,100 microform items, and 423 audio/video tapes/CDs, and subscribes to 725 periodicals. Computerized library services include the card catalog, interlibrary loans, database searching, and Internet access. Special learning facilities include a learning resource center, a Frank Lloyd Wright-designed home, used as an academic resource, and the personal library of the late architect Albert Kahn. The 115-acre campus is in a suburban area 30 minutes north of downtown Detroit. Including any residence halls, there are 10 buildings.

Student Life: 92% of undergraduates are from Michigan. Students are from 16 states, 16 foreign countries, and Canada. 61% are white; 14% Asian American; 10% African American. The average age of freshmen is 19; all undergraduates, 23. 29% do not continue beyond their first year; 44% remain to graduate.

Housing: 547 students can be accommodated in college housing, which includes coed on-campus apartments. On-campus housing is available on a first-come, first-served basis. 90% of students commute. All students may keep cars.

Activities: 5% of men belong to 1 local fraternity and 4 national fraternities; 9% of women belong to 2 local and 2 national sororities. There are 40 groups on campus, including art, chess, computers, ethnic, honors, newspaper, political, professional, religious, social, and student gov-

ernment. Popular campus events include Open House, Reunion Weekend, and Greek Week.

Sports: There are 10 intramural sports for men and 10 for women. Facilities include a field house with 4 racquetball courts, a weight room, a track, a sauna, and a gym. The gym seats 1500; an arena, 350.

Disabled Students: 97% of the campus is accessible. Wheelchair ramps, elevators, special parking, specially equipped rest rooms, special class scheduling, lowered drinking fountains, and lowered telephones are available.

Services: Counseling and information services are available, as is tutoring in some subjects, including math, computers, science, engineering, and English. There is a reader service for the blind and remedial math, reading, and writing. There is also a learning center.

Campus Safety and Security: Measures include 24-hour foot and vehicle patrol, security escort services, pamphlets/posters/films, and emergency telephones. There are lighted pathways/sidewalks and closed-circuit camera monitoring.

Programs of Study: Lawrence Tech confers B.S., B.Admin., and B.F.A. degrees. Associate and master's degrees are also awarded. Bachelor's degrees are awarded in BUSINESS (business administration and management and small business management), COMMUNICATIONS AND THE ARTS (illustration and technical and business writing), COMPUTER AND PHYSICAL SCIENCE (chemistry, computer science, information sciences and systems, mathematics, and physics), ENGINEERING AND ENVIRONMENTAL DESIGN (architecture, civil engineering, computer engineering, construction management, electrical/electronics engineering, engineering technology, environmental science, industrial administration/management, interior design, mechanical engineering, and technological management), SOCIAL SCIENCE (humanities and psychology). Mathematics, computer science, and engineering are the strongest academically. Engineering and architecture are the largest.

Required: To graduate, students must have completed, depending on the major, 120 to 131 semester credit hours, with a GPA no lower than 2.0. Senior projects are required in most degree programs.

Special: There are co-op programs in a number of majors, internships, dual majors, and work-study programs. There are 7 national honor societies, and 6 departmental honors programs.

Faculty/Classroom: 75% of faculty are male; 25%, female. No introductory courses are taught by graduate students. The average class size in an introductory lecture is 19; in a laboratory, 18; and in a regular course, 19.

Admissions: 76% of the 2003-2004 applicants were accepted. The SAT I scores for the 2003-2004 freshman class were: Verbal--45% below 500, 27% between 500 and 599, 21% between 600 and 700, and 7% above 700; Math--25% below 500, 34% between 500 and 599, 25% between 600 and 700, and 16% above 700. The ACT scores were 29% below 21, 23% between 21 and 23, 27% between 24 and 26, 12% between 27 and 28, and 9% above 28. 41% of the current freshmen were in the top fifth of their class; 73% were in the top two fifths. 9 freshmen graduated first in their class.

Requirements: The ACT is required and the SAT I is recommended. In addition, students must have a high school diploma and a GPA of no lower than 2.5, at least 2.0 in each subject area pertaining to their major. Applicants should have taken 4 years each of math, science, and English and 3 years of social science. The GED is accepted. An interview is recommended. AP and CLEP credits are accepted. Important factors in the admissions decision are advanced placement or honor courses, personality/intangible qualities, and leadership record.

Procedure: Freshmen are admitted to all sessions. Entrance exams should be taken in the semester preceding entry. There are early admissions and deferred admissions plans. Application deadlines are open. The fall 2003 application fee was $30. Notification is sent on a rolling basis. Applications are accepted on-line through *www.ltu.edu*.

Transfer: 256 transfer students enrolled in 2002-2003. Admission is based on the college GPA, which must be 2.0 or higher, with 30 or more semester hours. If fewer than 30 hours have been completed, admission is based on high school transcripts. 28 of 120 to 131 credits required for the bachelor's degree must be completed at Lawrence Tech.

Visiting: There are regularly scheduled orientations for prospective students. There are guides for informal visits and visitors may sit in on classes and stay overnight. To schedule a visit, contact the Admissions Office.

Financial Aid: In 2003-2004, 94% of all full-time freshmen and 96% of continuing full-time students received some form of financial aid. 58% of full-time freshmen and 55% of continuing full-time students received need-based aid. The average freshman award was $11,573. Need-based scholarships or need-based grants averaged $3909 ($9050 maximum); need-based self-help aid (loans and jobs) averaged $3920 ($8625 maximum); and other non-need-based awards and non-need-based scholarships averaged $8011 ($21,000 maximum). All of undergraduates work part time. Average annual earnings from campus work are $1833. The average financial indebtedness of the 2003 graduate was $18,000. The FAFSA is required. The deadline for filing freshman financial aid applications for fall entry is April 1.

International Students: There are 282 international students enrolled. The school actively recruits these students. They must score 550 on the written TOEFL or 213 on the electronic version or take the MELAB or the Comprehensive English Language Test. The SAT I or ACT is required for incoming freshmen only.

Computers: The mainframe is 10 Compaq Alpha systems operated as 2 computing clusters. All student computing takes place on their laptops or dedicated UNIX workstations. There are 9 open computer labs with 200 PC systems connected to the Internet. All students may access the system 24 hours daily. There are no time limits and no fees. Laptops are provided to all undergraduates. Students are provided with systems that have software images appropriate to their major.

Graduates: From July 1, 2002 to June 30, 2003, 439 bachelor's degrees were awarded. The most popular majors were mechanical engineering (26%), architecture (20%), and engineering technology (18%). In an average class, 6% graduate in 4 years or less, 21% graduate in 5 years or less, and 44% graduate in 6 years or less. 175 companies recruited on campus in 2002-2003.

Admissions Contact: Jane Rohrback, Admissions Director. A video is available. E-mail: *admissions@ltu.edu* Web: *http://www.ltu.edu*

MADONNA UNIVERSITY
Livonia, MI 48150-1173

E-5
(734) 432-5317
(800) 852-4951; Fax: (734) 432-5424

Full-time: 300 men, 1100 women	**Faculty:** 114; IIB, av$
Part-time: 370 men, 1300 women	**Ph.Ds:** 55%
Graduate: 225 men, 550 women	**Student/Faculty:** 12 to 1
Year: semesters, summer session	**Tuition:** $7000
Application Deadline: open	**Room & Board:** $5000
Freshman Class: n/av	**ACT:** required
	VERY COMPETITIVE

Madonna University, founded in 1947, is a liberal arts institution affiliated with the Roman Catholic Church. There are 6 undergraduate schools and 1 graduate school. Figures in the above capsule and in this profile are approximate. In addition to regional accreditation, MU has baccalaureate program accreditation with ADA, CSWE, NCATE, and NLN. The 2 libraries contain 170,000 volumes, 450,000 microform items, and 6540 audio/video tapes/CDs, and subscribe to 3600 periodicals. Computerized library services include interlibrary loans and database searching. Special learning facilities include a learning resource center, art gallery, radio station, TV station, computerized writing lab, and the Center for Personalized Instruction. The 48-acre campus is in a suburban area 20 miles west of Detroit. Including any residence halls, there are 4 buildings.

Student Life: 96% of undergraduates are from Michigan. Students are from 13 states, 6 foreign countries, and Canada. 85% are from public schools. 77% are white; 12% African American. 41% are Catholic; 18% Protestant. The average age of freshmen is 29; all undergraduates, 30. 22% do not continue beyond their first year.

Housing: 180 students can be accommodated in college housing, which includes single-sex dorms. On-campus housing is guaranteed for all 4 years. 96% of students commute. Alcohol is not permitted. All students may keep cars.

Activities: There are no fraternities or sororities. There are 22 groups on campus, including art, chorale, computers, ethnic, honors, newspaper, orchestra, photography, political, professional, radio and TV, religious, social, social service, and student government. Popular campus events include Founders Day, Halloween Magic, and Christmas for Kids.

Sports: There are 3 intercollegiate sports for men and 4 for women. Facilities include an activities center, a weight training room, a 700-seat gym, and an outdoor softball arena.

Disabled Students: All of the campus is accessible. Wheelchair ramps, elevators, special parking, specially equipped rest rooms, special class scheduling, lowered drinking fountains, lowered telephones, telecommunication devices, and visible fire alarms for hearing-impaired students are available.

Services: Counseling and information services are available, as is tutoring in most subjects. There is a reader service for the blind; remedial math, reading, and writing; and interpreters and note takers for hearing-impaired and visually impaired students.

Campus Safety and Security: Measures include 24-hour foot and vehicle patrol, security escort services, informal discussions, and pamphlets/posters/films. There are emergency telephones, lighted pathways/sidewalks, and an emergency car service.

Programs of Study: MU confers B.A., B.S., B.A.S., B.S.M.T., B.S.N., and B.S.W. degrees. Associate and master's degrees are also awarded. Bachelor's degrees are awarded in BIOLOGICAL SCIENCE (biochemistry, biology/biological science, and nutrition), BUSINESS (accounting, business administration and management, hospitality management services, international business management, management science, and marketing/retailing/merchandising), COMMUNICATIONS AND THE ARTS (art, English, fine arts, graphic design, journalism, music, Spanish, technical and business writing, and video), COMPUTER AND PHYSICAL SCIENCE (chemistry, computer science, information sciences and systems, mathematics, natural sciences, and science), EDUCATION (mu-

sic and secondary), ENGINEERING AND ENVIRONMENTAL DESIGN (commercial art and occupational safety and health), HEALTH PROFESSIONS (allied health, hospice care, medical laboratory technology, and nursing), SOCIAL SCIENCE (child psychology/development, criminal justice, dietetics, family/consumer studies, fire science, food science, gerontology, history, interpreter for the deaf, liberal arts/general studies, pastoral studies, psychology, religion, religious music, safety and security technology, social science, social work, and sociology). Nursing is the strongest academically. Nursing and business administration are the largest.

Required: To graduate, students must complete at least 120 semester hours with a 2.0 GPA; required hours in the major vary from 30 to 62. A minimum of 52 hours of general education courses are required, including 25 hours in humanities, 15 in social science, and 12 in math and science. All students are required to take English 101 and 102 and a senior seminar, which includes a comprehensive exam.

Special: MU offers cross-registration with Marygrove and St. Mary of Orchard Lake Colleges, Sacred Heart Seminary, and the University of Detroit Mercy. Students may pursue co-op programs in 43 majors, internships, and a B.A.-B.S. degree in gerontology, and may receive credit for life, military, or work experience. MU also has affiliations with universities in Argentina, Belgium, Great Britain, Japan, Poland, and Taiwan. There are 7 national honor societies, including Phi Beta Kappa, and 7 departmental honors programs.

Faculty/Classroom: 46% of faculty are male; 54%, female. All both teach and do research. No introductory courses are taught by graduate students. The average class size in an introductory lecture is 22; in a laboratory, 13; and in a regular course, 17.

Requirements: The ACT is required. In addition, students should have completed 4 years of English, 3 of math, 2 of science, and 1 of history. The school accepts the GED. An essay is required. For some majors, students are asked to submit a portfolio or to appear for an interview or audition. A GPA of 2.75 is required. AP and CLEP credits are accepted. Important factors in the admissions decision are advanced placement or honor courses, recommendations by school officials, and leadership record.

Procedure: Freshmen are admitted to all sessions. Entrance exams should be taken during either the junior or senior year. Application deadlines are open. Check with the school for current fee. Applications are accepted on-line via the school's web site.

Transfer: 529 transfer students enrolled in a recent year. Applicants must be in good academic and personal standing at their previous colleges and must submit official transcripts of college and high school work. Courses completed at an accredited institution with a grade of C or better will be considered for transfer credit. 30 of 120 credits required for the bachelor's degree must be completed at MU.

Visiting: There are regularly scheduled orientations for prospective students, including an interview and a tour of the campus. There are guides for informal visits and visitors may sit in on classes and stay overnight. To schedule a visit, contact the Office of Undergraduate Admissions at (734) 432-5339 or *admis@madonna.edu*.

Financial Aid: The FAFSA is required. Check with the school for current deadlines.

International Students: There were 43 international students enrolled in a recent year. The school actively recruits these students. They must score 540 on the written TOEFL or take the MELAB or an equivalent English proficiency test, and also take the ACT.

Computers: The mainframe is an IBM AS/400, networked with 20 PCs that can be used for class assignments. 80 PCs are networked via a Novell LAN in the computer lab and in the library. Decentralized labs are found in the Health Instruction Center, the tutoring center, and the physics lab. All students may access the system 9 A.M. to 10 P.M. daily, 9 A.M. to 5 P.M. Saturday, and 1 P.M. to 5 P.M. Sunday. Students may access the system 3 hours per day if others are waiting. There are no fees.

Graduates: 536 bachelor's degrees were awarded in a recent year. The most popular majors were nursing (10%), business (5%), and criminal justice (4%). In an average class, 22% graduate in 4 years or less, 65% graduate in 5 years or less, and 81% graduate in 6 years or less.

Admissions Contact: Frank Hribar, Director for Enrollment Management. A video is available. E-mail: *fhribar@madonna.edu* Web: *www.madonna.edu*

MARYGROVE COLLEGE
Detroit, MI 48221-2599

E-5

(313) 927-1240
1 (866) 313-1927; Fax: (313) 927-1345

Full-time: 91 men, 330 women   **Faculty:** 67; IIA, --$
Part-time: 79 men, 358 women   **Ph.D.s:** 75%
Graduate: 1135 men, 3649 women   **Student/Faculty:** 6 to 1
Year: semesters, summer session   **Tuition:** $11,750
Application Deadline: August 15   **Room & Board:** $5800
Freshman Class: 117 applied, 70 accepted, 60 enrolled
ACT: 19   **COMPETITIVE**

Founded in 1927 and grounded in the liberal arts, Marygrove College is a private comprehensive institution affiliated with the Catholic Church. In addition to regional accreditation, Marygrove College has baccalaureate program accreditation with ADA, CAHEA, CSWE, and NCATE. The library contains 76,292 volumes, 65,650 microform items, and 2132 audio/video tapes/CDs, and subscribes to 487 periodicals. Computerized library services include the card catalog, interlibrary loans, and database searching. Special learning facilities include a learning resource center, art gallery, a writing center, a learning clinic, and a theater. The 50-acre campus is in an urban area 11 miles from downtown Detroit. Including any residence halls, there are 4 buildings.

Student Life: 99% of undergraduates are from Michigan. Students are from 3 states, 2 foreign countries, and Canada. 72% are African American. The average age of freshmen is 21; all undergraduates, 33. 33% do not continue beyond their first year; 35% remain to graduate.

Housing: 70 students can be accommodated in college housing, which includes coed dorms. 92% of students commute. Alcohol is not permitted. All students may keep cars.

Activities: There are no fraternities or sororities. There are 17 groups on campus, including art, choir, chorale, computers, honors, religious, social service, and student government. Popular campus events include Honors Day, Martin Luther King Day, and contemporary American authors lecture series.

Sports: There is 1 intercollegiate sport for men and 1 for women. Facilities include a fitness center and a gym.

Disabled Students: 90% of the campus is accessible. Wheelchair ramps, elevators, special parking, specially equipped rest rooms, lowered drinking fountains, and portable wheelchair ramps are available.

Services: Counseling and information services are available, as is tutoring in most subjects. There is remedial math, reading, and writing.

Campus Safety and Security: Measures include 24-hour foot and vehicle patrol, self-defense education, security escort services, and informal discussions. There are pamphlets/posters/films, emergency telephones, and lighted pathways/sidewalks.

Programs of Study: Marygrove College confers B.A., B.S., B.A.S., B.B.A., B.F.A., B.M., and B.S.W. degrees. Associate and master's degrees are also awarded. Bachelor's degrees are awarded in BIOLOGICAL SCIENCE (biology/biological science and nutrition), BUSINESS (business administration and management), COMMUNICATIONS AND THE ARTS (art, dance, English, language arts, and music), COMPUTER AND PHYSICAL SCIENCE (chemistry, information sciences and systems, mathematics, and science), EDUCATION (early childhood, social studies, and special), ENGINEERING AND ENVIRONMENTAL DESIGN (environmental science), HEALTH PROFESSIONS (art therapy), SOCIAL SCIENCE (child psychology/development, history, home economics, political science/government, psychology, religion, social science, and social work). English, education, and social work are the strongest academically. Business, computer science, and education are the largest.

Required: To graduate, students must complete 128 semester hours with a minimum GPA of 2.0. The required core program includes a first-year seminar, 18 hours in arts and letters, 12 in social sciences, 8 in math and natural science (including 1 lab science), and courses in communications (composition, oral communication, and computer literacy). The required number of hours in the major varies.

Special: A consortium program is offered with the University of Detroit Mercy, Saint Mary's College, Sacred Heart Seminary, and Madonna University. Also available are nondegree study, student-designed and dual majors, study abroad in 5 countries, internships, pass/fail options, and work-study programs. Students may acquire credit for life experience by documenting their achievements in a portfolio. There are 4 national honor societies, a freshman honors program, and 1 departmental honors program.

Faculty/Classroom: 37% of faculty are male; 63%, female. All teach undergraduates. No introductory courses are taught by graduate students. The average class size in an introductory lecture is 17 and in a laboratory, 10.

Admissions: 60% of the 2003-2004 applicants were accepted. The ACT scores for the 2003-2004 freshman class were: 95% below 21, and 5% between 21 and 23.

Requirements: The ACT is required. In addition, the applicant must be a graduate of an accredited high school. An interview is recommended.

The student's average, class rank, recommendations, and special talents are important factors in admission. Entering students must take the College Placement Examinations. A GPA of 2.0 is required. AP and CLEP credits are accepted. Important factors in the admissions decision are recommendations by school officials, evidence of special talent, and advanced placement or honor courses.

Procedure: Freshmen are admitted to all sessions. There is a deferred admissions plan. Applications should be filed by August 15 for fall entry. Notification of early decision and regular decision is sent on a rolling basis.

Transfer: 102 transfer students enrolled in 2002-2003. Transfer students must have a minimum 2.0 GPA. An associate degree or 24 completed credit hours and an interview are recommended. 30 of 128 credits required for the bachelor's degree must be completed at Marygrove College.

Visiting: There are regularly scheduled orientations for prospective students, including a tour of the campus followed by college workshops, first-year-student panels, and a college financial planning seminar. There are guides for informal visits and visitors may sit in on classes. To schedule a visit, contact the Admissions Office at info@marygrove.edu.

Financial Aid: In 2003-2004, 80% of all full-time freshmen and 85% of continuing full-time students received some form of financial aid. 85% of all full-time students received need-based aid. The average freshman award was $9200. 14% of undergraduates work part time. Average annual earnings from campus work are $2700. The average financial indebtedness of the 2003 graduate was $25,000. Marygrove College is a member of CSS. The CSS Profile or FAFSA and the college's own financial statement are required. The deadline for filing freshman financial aid applications for fall entry is March 15.

International Students: There are 18 international students enrolled. They must score 520 on the written TOEFL and also take a placement test in reading, writing, and math after admission.

Computers: The mainframes are a Burroughs B1000 and a Unisys AY. There is a computer center and lab in the liberal arts building and a computer-aided instruction lab. All students may access the system. There are no time limits and no fees.

Graduates: From July 1, 2002 to June 30, 2003, 90 bachelor's degrees were awarded. The most popular majors were social work (29%), business and management (25%), and education (10%). In an average class, 5% graduate in 4 years or less, 13% graduate in 5 years or less, and 30% graduate in 6 years or less. 20 companies recruited on campus in 2002-2003. Of the 2002 graduating class, 35% were enrolled in graduate school within 6 months of graduation.

Admissions Contact: Sally Janecek, Director of Admission. A video is available. E-mail: sjanecek@marygrove.edu Web: www.marygrove.edu

MICHIGAN STATE UNIVERSITY
East Lansing, MI 48824

D-4

(517) 355-8332; Fax: (517) 353-1647

Full-time: 14,349 men, 16,766 women   **Faculty:** I, +$
Part-time: 1840 men, 1898 women   **Ph.D.s:** 95%
Graduate: 4204 men, 5485 women   **Student/Faculty:** 13 to 1
Year: semesters, summer session   **Tuition:** $6703 ($16,663)
Application Deadline: July 25   **Room & Board:** $5230
Freshman Class: 24,973 applied, 17,690 accepted, 6849 enrolled
SAT I Verbal/Math: 560/580   **ACT:** 24   **VERY COMPETITIVE**

Michigan State University, a pioneer land-grant institution, was founded in 1855. Its 14 colleges and more than 100 departments offer 200 undergraduate and 250 graduate fields of study. The university's Honors College offers students an alternative education program. There are 12 undergraduate and 13 graduate schools. In addition to regional accreditation, MSU has baccalaureate program accreditation with AACSB, ABET, ACEJMC, ADA, ASLA, CAHEA, CSWE, FIDER, NASM, NCATE, NLN, and SAF. The 10 libraries contain 4,503,950 volumes, 5,601,101 microform items, and 299,287 audio/video tapes/CDs, and subscribe to 33,760 periodicals. Computerized library services include the card catalog, interlibrary loans, database searching, and Internet access. Special learning facilities include a learning resource center, art gallery, natural history museum, planetarium, radio station, TV station, a botanical garden, a superconducting cyclotron lab, an environmental toxicology center, a pesticide research center, and a center for computer-aided engineering and manufacturing. The 5239-acre campus is in a suburban area 80 miles northwest of Detroit. Including any residence halls, there are 564 buildings.

Student Life: 93% of undergraduates are from Michigan. Students are from 50 states, 120 foreign countries, and Canada. 79% are white. The average age of freshmen is 18; all undergraduates, 20. 15% do not continue beyond their first year; 70% remain to graduate.

Housing: 17,000 students can be accommodated in college housing, which includes coed dorms, on-campus apartments, and married-student housing. In addition, there are honors houses, special-interest houses, 2 residential colleges, an international hall, 9 living-learning communities, quiet floors, and substance-free environments. On-campus housing is guaranteed for all 4 years. 58% of students commute. Upperclassmen may keep cars.

Activities: There are 33 national fraternities and 16 national sororities. There are 525 groups on campus, including art, band, cheerleading, chess, choir, chorale, chorus, computers, dance, debate, drama, ethnic, film, gay, honors, international, jazz band, marching band, musical theater, newspaper, opera, orchestra, pep band, photography, political, professional, radio and TV, religious, social, social service, student government, symphony, and yearbook. Popular campus events include home football games and Welcome Days.

Sports: There are 12 intercollegiate sports for men and 13 for women, and 22 intramural sports for men and 22 for women. Facilities include a 76,000-seat stadium, a 4000-seat gym and field house, an ice arena, and a multipurpose 15,500-seat student events center. The university also has an indoor football practice facility, 3 intramural facilities, indoor and outdoor tennis courts, ball fields, a running track, 2 golf courses, and 4 swimming pools, including 1 Olympic-size outdoor pool.

Disabled Students: 75% of the campus is accessible. Wheelchair ramps, elevators, special parking, specially equipped rest rooms, special class scheduling, lowered drinking fountains, lowered telephones, tape recorders, videotaped classes, reading machines, readers, and note takers are available.

Services: Counseling and information services are available, as is tutoring in most subjects. There is a reader service for the blind and remedial math and writing.

Campus Safety and Security: Measures include 24-hour foot and vehicle patrol, self-defense education, security escort services, and shuttle buses. There are informal discussions, pamphlets/posters/films, emergency telephones, lighted pathways/sidewalks, and a regional/campus bus service.

Programs of Study: MSU confers B.A., B.S., B.F.A., B.Land.Arch., B.Mus., and B.S. in Nursing degrees. Master's and doctoral degrees are also awarded. Bachelor's degrees are awarded in AGRICULTURE (agriculture, animal science, environmental studies, fishing and fisheries, forestry and related sciences, horticulture, natural resource management, soil science, and wildlife management), BIOLOGICAL SCIENCE (biochemistry, bioinformatics, biology/biological science, biotechnology, botany, entomology, environmental biology, microbiology, nutrition, physiology, plant pathology, and zoology), BUSINESS (accounting, banking and finance, business administration and management, hospitality management services, human resources, marketing management, marketing/retailing/merchandising, personnel management, and tourism), COMMUNICATIONS AND THE ARTS (advertising, art history and appreciation, communications, dramatic arts, East Asian languages and literature, English, French, German, jazz, journalism, Latin, linguistics, music, music performance, music theory and composition, Russian, Spanish, studio art, and telecommunications), COMPUTER AND PHYSICAL SCIENCE (astrophysics, chemical physics, chemistry, computer science, earth science, geology, geophysics and seismology, geoscience, information sciences and systems, mathematics, physical sciences, physics, and statistics), EDUCATION (agricultural, art, education, music, physical, and special), ENGINEERING AND ENVIRONMENTAL DESIGN (chemical engineering, city/community/regional planning, civil engineering, computational sciences, computer engineering, construction management, electrical/electronics engineering, engineering, engineering mechanics, interior design, landscape architecture/design, manufacturing engineering, materials engineering, mechanical engineering, textile technology, and urban planning technology), HEALTH PROFESSIONS (clinical science, medical laboratory technology, music therapy, nursing, speech pathology/audiology, and veterinary science), SOCIAL SCIENCE (American studies, anthropology, child psychology/development, classical/ancient civilization, criminal justice, dietetics, economics, family and community services, family/consumer resource management, family/consumer studies, food production/management/services, food science, geography, history, humanities, interdisciplinary studies, parks and recreation management, philosophy, political science/government, prelaw, psychology, public administration, religion, social science, social work, sociology, and women's studies). Engineering, education, and business are the strongest academically. Business, communications, and social science are the largest.

Required: To graduate, students must complete a freshman writing course and a writing course specified by the major and degree program. Students must complete the 26-credit University Integrative Studies requirement consisting of 8 credits each of arts and humanities, social, behavioral, economic, and general sciences, and 3 of a transcollegiate course. Students must also complete a math requirement determined by each undergraduate college (a minimum of college algebra plus trigonometry/finite math/statistics.) A minimum 2.0 GPA and 120 semester hours are required.

Special: Special academic programs include an engineering co-op program with business and industry; internships in business, education, political science, agriculture, and communication arts; study abroad in more than 62 countries; on-campus work-study programs; and a sea semester. An accelerated degree program in all majors and student-designed majors are offered at the Honors College. Nondegree study,

pass/fail options in some courses, and dual majors are possible. Educationally disadvantaged students may avail themselves of the College Achievement Admissions Program (CAAP). Cross-registration with the Committee on Institutional Cooperation schools is available. There are 48 national honor societies, including Phi Beta Kappa, and a freshman honors program.

Faculty/Classroom: 65% of faculty are male; 35%, female. The average class size in an introductory lecture is 100; in a laboratory, 30; and in a regular course, 30.

Admissions: 71% of the 2003-2004 applicants were accepted. The SAT I scores for the 2003-2004 freshman class were: Verbal--24% below 500, 40% between 500 and 599, 30% between 600 and 700, and 6% above 700; Math--17% below 500, 37% between 500 and 599, 37% between 600 and 700, and 9% above 700. The ACT scores were 14% below 21, 26% between 21 and 23, 32% between 24 and 26, 14% between 27 and 28, and 14% above 28. 56% of the current freshmen were in the top fifth of their class; 89% were in the top two fifths.

Requirements: The SAT I or ACT is required. In addition, applicants must be graduates of an accredited secondary school and have completed 4 years of English, 3 years each of math and social studies, and 2 years each of science and a single foreign language. A personal statement is strongly recommended. The GED is accepted. Music majors must audition. AP and CLEP credits are accepted. Important factors in the admissions decision are advanced placement or honor courses, recommendations by school officials, and evidence of special talent.

Procedure: Freshmen are admitted fall, spring, and summer. Entrance exams should be taken during the junior year of high school. There is a deferred admissions plan and a rolling admissions plan. Applications should be filed by July 25 for fall entry, December 1 for spring entry, and April 15 for summer entry. The fall 2003 application fee was $35. Notification is sent on a rolling basis. 1524 applicants were on the 2003 waiting list; 228 were admitted. Applications are accepted on-line through *www.admissions.msu.edu.*

Transfer: 2150 transfer students enrolled in 2002-2003. To transfer, a minimum GPA of 2.0 is required, although a 3.0 is preferred. The MSU Integrative Studies requirement should be fulfilled (28 general graduation credits), and college algebra completed. 30 credits of 120 required for the bachelor's degree must be completed at MSU.

Visiting: There are regularly scheduled orientations for prospective students, including a presentation and a tour of the campus. There are guides for informal visits and visitors may sit in on classes and stay overnight. To schedule a visit, contact the Admissions office.

Financial Aid: In 2002-2003, 93% of all full-time freshmen and 68% of continuing full-time students received some form of financial aid. 28% of full-time freshmen and 22% of continuing full-time students received need-based aid. The average freshman award was $7148. The average financial indebtedness of the 2003 graduate was $18,121. MSU is a member of CSS. The FAFSA is required. The priority date for freshman financial aid applications for fall entry is March 1. The deadline for filing freshman financial aid applications for fall entry is June 30.

International Students: There are 1046 international students enrolled. The school actively recruits these students. They must score 550 on the written TOEFL or 213 on the electronic version or take the MELAB. They must also take the Comprehensive English Language Test or the college's own test.

Computers: The mainframes are an IBM 3090, a CONVEX 220, and a 96 Node GP1000. There are more than 5000 networked PCs from various vendors located in 25 public microlabs and numerous restricted micro-facilities. 7 residence halls have public labs with computers that are on the Internet. All residence hall rooms are hardwired with 2 jacks for students to access the Ethernet. All students may access the system 24 hours per day; 7 days per week. There are no time limits and no fees. All students are required to have personal computers.

Graduates: The most popular majors were business (19%), communications (14%), and social science (10%). In an average class, 36% graduate in 4 years or less, 64% graduate in 5 years or less, and 69% graduate in 6 years or less.

Admissions Contact: Pamela T. Horne, Director of Admissions and Scholarships. A video is available. E-mail: *admis@msu.edu* Web: *admissions.msu.edu*

MICHIGAN TECHNOLOGICAL UNIVERSITY B-1
Houghton, MI 49931-1295
(906) 487-2335
(888) MTU-1885; Fax: (906) 487-2125

Full-time: 3766 men, 1182 women	**Faculty:** 351; I, -$
Part-time: 627 men, 190 women	**Ph.D.s:** 83%
Graduate: 534 men, 266 women	**Student/Faculty:** 14 to 1
Year: semesters, summer session	**Tuition:** $7440 ($18,330)
Application Deadline: open	**Room & Board:** $5795
Freshman Class: 3080 applied, 2861 accepted, 1187 enrolled	
SAT I Verbal/Math: 575/615	**ACT:** 25 **VERY COMPETITIVE**

Michigan Technological University, founded in 1885, is a state-supported institution offering degrees in engineering, liberal arts, sciences, forestry, business, and technology. There are 5 undergraduate schools and 1 graduate school. In addition to regional accreditation, Michigan Tech has baccalaureate program accreditation with AACSB, ABET, and SAF. The library contains 825,000 volumes, 542,162 microform items, and 4391 audio/video tapes/CDs, and subscribes to 10,281 periodicals. Computerized library services include the card catalog, interlibrary loans, and database searching. Special learning facilities include a learning resource center, radio station, a mineral museum, an observatory, a forestry center, and a performing arts center. The 143-acre campus is in a small town 325 miles northwest of Milwaukee, Wisconsin. Including any residence halls, there are 42 buildings.

Student Life: 74% of undergraduates are from Michigan. Students are from 45 states, 78 foreign countries, and Canada. 81% are white; 10% foreign nationals. The average age of freshmen is 19; all undergraduates, 21. 19% do not continue beyond their first year; 68% remain to graduate.

Housing: 2734 students can be accommodated in college housing, which includes coed dorms, on-campus apartments, and married-student housing. In addition, a floor in 1 dorm is for seniors and graduate students. Also, each dorm has chemical-free floors where tobacco and alcohol are not allowed. Plus, there are separate areas for international students and the first-year experience program. On-campus housing is guaranteed for the freshman year only and is available on a first-come, first-served basis. 60% of students commute. All students may keep cars.

Activities: 7% of men belong to 4 local and 10 national fraternities; 11% of women belong to 4 local and 4 national sororities. There are 180 groups on campus, including art, band, cheerleading, chess, choir, chorale, chorus, computers, dance, drama, drill team, ethnic, film, gay, honors, international, jazz band, literary magazine, musical theater, newspaper, orchestra, pep band, photography, political, professional, radio and TV, religious, social, social service, student government, and symphony. Popular campus events include Winter Carnival, K-Day, and Spring Fling.

Sports: There are 7 intercollegiate sports for men and 6 for women, and 38 intramural sports for men and 37 for women. Facilities include a complex with a 4200-seat ice arena and a 3200-seat gym, a lakeside golf course, football and softball fields, a tennis center, Mont Ripley Ski Hill and a cross-country ski trail, a multipurpose room, a pool, a fitness center, racquetball/squash courts, a dance room, and a gymnastics room.

Disabled Students: 90% of the campus is accessible. Wheelchair ramps, elevators, special parking, specially equipped rest rooms, special class scheduling, and lowered drinking fountains are available.

Services: Counseling and information services are available, as is tutoring in some subjects. There is remedial math, reading, and writing. Learning centers for English, math, chemistry, and physics are available.

Campus Safety and Security: Measures include 24-hour foot and vehicle patrol, self-defense education, security escort services, and shuttle buses. There are informal discussions, pamphlets/posters/films, emergency telephones, and lighted pathways/sidewalks.

Programs of Study: Michigan Tech confers B.A. and B.S. degrees. Associate, master's, and doctoral degrees are also awarded. Bachelor's degrees are awarded in AGRICULTURE (forestry and related sciences), BIOLOGICAL SCIENCE (biology/biological science and ecology), BUSINESS (business administration and management and business economics), COMMUNICATIONS AND THE ARTS (technical and business writing), COMPUTER AND PHYSICAL SCIENCE (chemistry, computer science, geology, geophysics and seismology, mathematics, and physics), ENGINEERING AND ENVIRONMENTAL DESIGN (biomedical engineering, chemical engineering, civil engineering, computer engineering, electrical/electronics engineering, engineering, engineering technology, environmental engineering, geological engineering, mechanical engineering, mining and mineral engineering, and surveying engineering), HEALTH PROFESSIONS (medical laboratory technology), SOCIAL SCIENCE (liberal arts/general studies and social science). Engineering, forestry, and physical science are the strongest academically. Mechanical, electrical, and civil engineering are the largest.

Required: To graduate, students must complete 120 to 146 credit hours, maintain a minimum GPA of 2.0, and fulfill basic general education requirements. The basic general education curriculum consists of 4 core courses to be taken by every baccalaureate student, a 5-course distribution requirement, physical education, and a science/math requirement. In general, 30 of the last 36 credit hours and 30 hours of advanced-level courses must be completed at MTU.

Special: Michigan Tech offers co-op programs in almost all majors, internships in medical technology and secondary teacher education, work-study programs, study abroad in more than 20 countries, dual majors, and a B.A.-B.S. degree in scientific and technical communication. There are interinstitutional programs with Northwestern Michigan, Gogebic Community, Lansing Community, and Delta Colleges. A 3-2 engineering degree is possible in conjunction with the University of Wisconsin/Superior, the College of St. Scholastica, and Adrian, Albion, Augsburg, Northland, Olivet, and Mount Senario Colleges. There are 16 national honor societies.

Faculty/Classroom: 76% of faculty are male; 24%, female. All teach undergraduates and 73% do research. Graduate students teach 6% of introductory courses. The average class size in an introductory lecture is 60; in a laboratory, 20; and in a regular course, 28.

Admissions: 93% of the 2003-2004 applicants were accepted. The SAT I scores for the 2003-2004 freshman class were: Verbal--16% below 500, 42% between 500 and 599, 33% between 600 and 700, and 9% above 700; Math--8% below 500, 30% between 500 and 599, 50% between 600 and 700, and 12% above 700. The ACT scores were 11% below 21, 20% between 21 and 23, 31% between 24 and 26, 18% between 27 and 28, and 20% above 28. 52% of the current freshmen were in the top fifth of their class; 80% were in the top two fifths. There were 5 National Merit finalists. 60 freshmen graduated first in their class.

Requirements: The SAT I or ACT is required. Scores are used for admission and placement. Admissions requirements include graduation from an accredited secondary school, with 15 academic credits. These must include 3 credits in English, 1 credit of chemistry or physics, and 3 credits in math for engineering and science curricula; credits in social studies and foreign language are recommended. The GED is accepted. AP and CLEP credits are accepted. Important factors in the admissions decision are advanced placement or honor courses, leadership record, and recommendations by school officials.

Procedure: Freshmen are admitted to all sessions. Entrance exams should be taken in the junior year. There is a deferred and a rolling admissions plan. Application deadlines are open. The fall 2003 application fee was $30. Applications are accepted on-line through the university's web site.

Transfer: 181 transfer students enrolled in 2002-2003. Transfer students must have a minimum GPA of 2.5 on a 4.0 scale; grades of B or better are expected in math and science courses. 30 of 120 to 146 credits required for the bachelor's degree must be completed at Michigan Tech.

Visiting: There are regularly scheduled orientations for prospective students, including campus tours at 10 A.M. and 2 P.M. Monday through Friday. Separate interviews are available with academic department personnel and admissions representatives. There are guides for informal visits and visitors may sit in on classes and stay overnight. To schedule a visit, contact the Admissions Office.

Financial Aid: In 2003-2004, 89% of all full-time freshmen and 83% of continuing full-time students received some form of financial aid. 53% of all full-time students received need-based aid. The average freshman award was $8495. Need-based scholarships or need-based grants averaged $3731 ($17,700 maximum); need-based self-help aid (loans and jobs) averaged $8495 ($10,645 maximum); non-need-based athletic scholarships averaged $9511 ($17,700 maximum); and other non-need-based awards and non-need-based scholarships averaged $5465 ($17,700 maximum). 39% of undergraduates work part time. Average annual earnings from campus work are $4500. The average financial indebtedness of the 2003 graduate was $12,789. Michigan Tech is a member of CSS. The FAFSA is required. The priority date for freshman financial aid applications for fall entry is February 21.

International Students: There are 285 international students enrolled. The school actively recruits these students. They must score 500 on the written TOEFL or 173 on the electronic version.

Computers: Almost every department has 1 or more student computing labs. Equipment varies but includes PCs, Macs, Sun workstations, laser printers, electrostatic plotters, and scanners. Software includes general productivity packages, such as word processing and spreadsheets, and specialized applications, such as CAD/CAM, GIS, and publishing. All students may access the system 24 hours a day. There are no time limits. The fee varies with major.

Graduates: From July 1, 2002 to June 30, 2003, 975 bachelor's degrees were awarded. The most popular majors were mechanical engineering (22%), electrical engineering (10%), and civil engineering (9%). In an average class, 29% graduate in 4 years or less, 58% graduate in 5 years or less, and 64% graduate in 6 years or less. 280 companies recruited on campus in a recent year. Of a recent graduating class, 15% were enrolled in graduate school within 6 months of graduation and 95% were employed.

Admissions Contact: Nancy Rehling, Director of Undergraduate Admissions. E-mail: *mtu4u@mtu.edu* Web: *www.mtu.edu/apply/*

NORTHERN MICHIGAN UNIVERSITY
Marquette, MI 49855

C-2

(906) 227-2650
(800) 682-9797; Fax: (906) 227-1747

Full-time: 3152 men, 3400 women	**Faculty:** 294; IIA, av$
Part-time: 395 men, 536 women	**Ph.D.s:** 80%
Graduate: 276 men, 428 women	**Student/Faculty:** 22 to 1
Year: semesters, summer session	**Tuition:** $5110 ($8278)
Application Deadline: open	**Room & Board:** $5724
Freshman Class: 4461 applied, 3762 accepted, 1302 enrolled	
ACT: 23	**COMPETITIVE**

Northern Michigan University, founded in 1899, is a public institution offering undergraduate programs in the arts and sciences, business, education, health science, human services, nursing, and technology. There are 4 undergraduate schools and 1 graduate school. In addition to regional accreditation, NMU has baccalaureate program accreditation with AACSB, ADA, CSWE, NASM, NCATE, and NLN. The library contains 592,689 volumes, 830,197 microform items, and 7369 audio/video tapes/CDs, and subscribes to 1,437,492 periodicals. Computerized library services include the card catalog, interlibrary loans, database searching, and Internet access. Special learning facilities include a learning resource center, art gallery, radio station, TV station, and an observatory. The 320-acre campus is in an urban area on the southern shores of Lake Superior. Including any residence halls, there are 55 buildings.

Student Life: 84% of undergraduates are from Michigan. Students are from 49 states, 36 foreign countries, and Canada. 91% are white. The average age of freshmen is 20; all undergraduates, 24. 31% do not continue beyond their first year.

Housing: 2500 students can be accommodated in college housing, which includes coed dorms, on-campus apartments, and married-student housing. In addition, there are honors houses, special-interest houses, and smoke-free and chemical-free houses. On-campus housing is guaranteed for all 4 years. 70% of students commute. All students may keep cars.

Activities: 1% of men and about 1% of women belong to 2 national fraternities; 1% of women belong to 3 national sororities. There are 200 groups on campus, including art, band, cheerleading, chess, choir, chorale, chorus, computers, dance, drama, drill team, ethnic, film, gay, health, honors, international, international dance, jazz band, literary magazine, marching band, musical theater, newspaper, orchestra, pep band, philosophy, photography, political, professional, radio and TV, religious, social, social service, student government, and symphony. Popular campus events include Winterfest, Be a Part from the Start, and U.P. 200 Dog Sled Race.

Sports: There are 5 intercollegiate sports for men and 7 for women, and 11 intramural sports for men and 11 for women. Facilities include indoor and outdoor playing fields, an aerobic and fitness training area, an ice rink, a swimming pool, a diving tank, a field house, an 8000-seat stadium, a 4000-seat basketball and hockey arena, a rock-climbing wall, racquetball courts, the neighboring forests and rivers, and Lake Superior.

Disabled Students: 90% of the campus is accessible. Wheelchair ramps, elevators, special parking, specially equipped rest rooms, lowered drinking fountains, lowered telephones, and special housing are available.

Services: Counseling and information services are available, as is tutoring in every subject. There is a reader service for the blind and remedial math, reading, and writing.

Campus Safety and Security: Measures include 24-hour foot and vehicle patrol, self-defense education, security escort services, and shuttle buses. There are informal discussions, pamphlets/posters/films, emergency telephones, lighted pathways/sidewalks, and a crime prevention program with a full-time staff.

Programs of Study: NMU confers B.A., B.S., B.F.A., B.M.Ed., B.S.N., and B.S.W. degrees. Associate and master's degrees are also awarded. Bachelor's degrees are awarded in BIOLOGICAL SCIENCE (biochemistry, biology/biological science, botany, ecology, microbiology, physiology, and zoology), BUSINESS (accounting, banking and finance, business administration and management, entrepreneurial studies, and marketing/retailing/merchandising), COMMUNICATIONS AND THE ARTS (broadcasting, communications, design, dramatic arts, English, fine arts, French, music, public relations, Spanish, and speech/debate/rhetoric), COMPUTER AND PHYSICAL SCIENCE (chemistry, computer programming, computer science, earth science, information sciences and systems, mathematics, and physics), EDUCATION (art, business, computer, education of the mentally handicapped, elementary, health, industrial arts, music, physical, science, and secondary), ENGINEERING AND ENVIRONMENTAL DESIGN (construction management, electrical/electronics engineering technology, industrial engineering technology, and manufacturing technology), HEALTH PROFESSIONS (clinical science, cytotechnology, medical laboratory technology, nursing, predentistry, premedicine, preveterinary science, and speech pathology/audiology), SOCIAL SCIENCE (criminal justice, economics, geography, history, international studies, parks and recreation management, philosophy, physical fitness/movement, political science/government, prelaw,

psychology, public administration, social work, sociology, and water resources). Biology, chemistry, and education are the strongest academically. Business, education, and biology are the largest.

Required: Students must earn 40 semester credits in liberal studies requirements, including courses in humanities, composition, natural sciences/math, social sciences, communications, and visual and performing arts. Graduation requirements vary by degree program; at the minimum, students must earn 124 semester credits, including 32 in a major field, with a GPA of 2.0. Courses in phys ed/health and world culture and a writing proficiency exam are also required.

Special: Cross-registration is available with other Michigan universities and colleges. Students may study abroad in Europe, Latin America, and Japan. NMU also offers internships, a co-op program in business, accelerated degree programs, a combined accounting/computer information systems major, dual and student-designed majors, limited pass/fail options, and nondegree study. There are 9 national honor societies, a freshman honors program, and 5 departmental honors programs.

Faculty/Classroom: 63% of faculty are male; 37%, female. All teach undergraduates. Graduate students teach 1% of introductory courses. The average class size in an introductory lecture is 23; in a laboratory, 16; and in a regular course, 23.

Admissions: 84% of the 2003-2004 applicants were accepted. The ACT scores for the 2003-2004 freshman class were: 38% below 21, 21% between 21 and 23, 19% between 24 and 26, 7% between 27 and 28, and 5% above 28. 16 freshmen graduated first in their class.

Requirements: The SAT I or ACT is required, with a minimum composite score of 900 for the SAT I and 19 for the ACT. Applicants must be graduates of accredited secondary schools or have earned a GED. NMU requires 12 to 16 Carnegie units; recommended secondary school preparation includes 4 years of English, 3 each of math, history, social studies, foreign language, and science, 2 of fine arts or performing arts, and 1 of computer instruction. Students seeking art scholarships must submit a portfolio; those seeking music and theater scholarships must audition. A GPA of 2.25 is required. AP and CLEP credits are accepted. Important factors in the admissions decision are advanced placement or honor courses, evidence of special talent, and recommendations by school officials.

Procedure: Freshmen are admitted to all sessions. Entrance exams should be taken during the year prior to enrollment. There is a deferred admissions plan. Application deadlines are open. Application fee is $25. Notification is sent on a rolling basis. Applications are accepted on-line.

Transfer: Applicants must present a minimum GPA of 2.0 in at least 12 semester credits of college-level work. 32 of 124 credits required for the bachelor's degree must be completed at NMU.

Visiting: There are regularly scheduled orientations for prospective students, including an admissions interview, a tour, and a faculty visit. Visitors may sit in on classes and stay overnight. To schedule a visit, contact the Campus Visit Office at (906) 227-1709.

Financial Aid: The FAFSA is required. The priority date for freshman financial aid applications for fall entry is February 1.

International Students: There are 107 international students enrolled. The school actively recruits these students. They must score 500 on the written TOEFL or 173 on the electronic version. Canadian students must take the SAT I or ACT, scoring 19 on the ACT.

Computers: The mainframe is an IBM 9672-R11. Those students who use the computer for instruction or research may access the mainframe from 7 A.M. to midnight daily. There are no time limits and no fees. All students are required to have personal computers. An IBM ThinkPad or iBook is provided as part of tuition and fees.

Admissions Contact: Gerri Daniels, Director of Admissions. A video is available. E-mail: admiss@nmu.edu Web: www.nmu.edu

NORTHWOOD UNIVERSITY
Midland, MI 48640

D-4

(989) 837-4273
(800) 457-7878; Fax: (989) 837-4104

Full-time: 1077 men, 626 women	**Faculty:** 44
Part-time: 23 men, 31 women	**Ph.D.s:** 23%
Graduate: 191 men, 107 women	**Student/Faculty:** 39 to 1
Year: quarters, summer session	**Tuition:** $13,995
Application Deadline: August 1	**Room & Board:** $6270
Freshman Class: 1387 applied, 1200 accepted, 400 enrolled	
SAT I Verbal/Math: 470/480	**ACT:** 20 **LESS COMPETITIVE**

Northwood University, founded in 1959, is a private, nonprofit college offering undergraduate and graduate programs in business management. Campuses are located in Florida, Michigan, and Texas. The library contains 40,935 volumes, 46,540 microform items, and 65 audio/video tapes/CDs, and subscribes to 334 periodicals. Computerized library services include the card catalog, interlibrary loans, and database searching. Special learning facilities include a learning resource center, art gallery, and a creativity center. The 270-acre campus is in a suburban area 135 miles north of Detroit. Including any residence halls, there are 29 buildings.

Student Life: 75% of undergraduates are from Michigan. Students are from 35 states, 27 foreign countries, and Canada. 70% are from public schools. 71% are white; 15% African American; 10% foreign nationals. The average age of freshmen is 19; all undergraduates, 21. 28% do not continue beyond their first year; 56% remain to graduate.

Housing: 868 students can be accommodated in college housing, which includes single-sex dorms and on-campus apartments. On-campus housing is guaranteed for the freshman year only and is available on a first-come, first-served basis. 63% of students commute. All students may keep cars.

Activities: 30% of men belong to 3 local and 4 national fraternities; 20% of women belong to 1 local sorority and 3 national sororities. There are 35 groups on campus, including cheerleading, chorale, computers, dance, drama, ethnic, forensics, honors, international, investment, newspaper, pep band, political, professional, religious, social, social service, student government, and yearbook. Popular campus events include Auto Show Weekend, Greek Week, and Values Emphasis Week.

Sports: There are 8 intercollegiate sports for men and 9 for women, and 10 intramural sports for men and 10 for women. Facilities include a 1500-seat indoor gym, a 3500-seat stadium, 3 multipurpose courts, a 4-lane track, and a fitness center.

Disabled Students: 95% of the campus is accessible. Wheelchair ramps, elevators, special parking, specially equipped rest rooms, special class scheduling, and lowered drinking fountains are available.

Services: Counseling and information services are available, as is tutoring in most subjects. There is remedial math, reading, and writing.

Campus Safety and Security: Measures include 24-hour foot and vehicle patrol, informal discussions, pamphlets/posters/films, lighted pathways/sidewalks, and a professional security force.

Programs of Study: Northwood confers the B.B.A. degree. Associate and master's degrees are also awarded. Bachelor's degrees are awarded in BUSINESS (accounting, banking and finance, business administration and management, business economics, fashion merchandising, hotel/motel and restaurant management, international business management, management information systems, marketing management, sports management, and transportation and travel marketing), COMMUNICATIONS AND THE ARTS (advertising), COMPUTER AND PHYSICAL SCIENCE (computer management). Accounting is the strongest academically. Marketing/management is the largest.

Required: To graduate, all students must complete a minimum of 180 credit hours, with 36 credit hours in the major. A minimum GPA of 2.0 must be maintained, and 6 credits of computer science management and 2 credits of executive fitness must be completed. Internships for 1 to 6 credits are required in some majors.

Special: Northwood offers on- and off-campus work-study and a competitive study-abroad program in 20 countries. Dual majors with management are available in all majors. Credit for life and military work experience is possible through a plan of study. Nondegree study, accelerated degree programs, externships in most majors, and pass/fail options are offered. There is a freshman honors program.

Faculty/Classroom: 59% of faculty are male; 41%, female. All teach undergraduates. No introductory courses are taught by graduate students. The average class size in an introductory lecture is 21; in a laboratory, 14; and in a regular course, 22.

Admissions: 87% of the 2003-2004 applicants were accepted. The SAT I scores for the 2003-2004 freshman class were: Verbal--81% below 500, 15% between 500 and 599, and 4% between 600 and 700; Math--57% below 500, 32% between 500 and 599, and 11% between 600 and 700. The ACT scores were 55% below 21, 23% between 21 and 23, 16% between 24 and 26, 4% between 27 and 28, and 2% above 28. 24% of the current freshmen were in the top fifth of their class; 45% were in the top two fifths. 3 freshmen graduated first in their class.

Requirements: The SAT I or ACT is required. In addition, graduation from an accredited secondary school is required. The GED is accepted. A GPA of 2.0 is required. AP and CLEP credits are accepted. Important factors in the admissions decision are advanced placement or honor courses, evidence of special talent, and leadership record.

Procedure: Freshmen are admitted to all sessions. Entrance exams should be taken in the spring of the junior year. There are early admissions and deferred admissions plans. Applications should be filed by August 1 for fall entry, November 15 for winter entry, February 15 for spring entry, and June 1 for summer entry, along with a $25 fee. Notification is sent on a rolling basis. Applications are accepted on-line.

Transfer: 217 transfer students enrolled in 2002-2003. Transfer students must have a minimum of 12 credit hours and a minimum GPA of 2.0. An associate's degree and an interview are recommended. 45 of 180 credits required for the bachelor's degree must be completed at Northwood.

Visiting: There are regularly scheduled orientations for prospective students, including academic and social seminars and presentations. There are guides for informal visits and visitors may sit in on classes and stay overnight. To schedule a visit, contact the Admissions Department.

Financial Aid: In 2003-2004, 93% of all full-time freshmen and 94% of continuing full-time students received some form of financial aid. 68%

of full-time freshmen and 74% of continuing full-time students received need-based aid. The average freshman award was $12,757. Need-based scholarships or need-based grants averaged $7607 ($11,640 maximum); need-based self-help aid (loans and jobs) averaged $4296 ($10,724 maximum); non-need-based athletic scholarships averaged $4567 ($20,565 maximum); and other non-need-based awards and non-need-based scholarships averaged $5036 ($14,495 maximum). 16% of undergraduates work part time. Average annual earnings from campus work are $1715. The average financial indebtedness of the 2003 graduate was $10,770. The FAFSA is required. The deadline for filing freshman financial aid applications for fall entry is rolling.

International Students: There are 160 international students enrolled. The school actively recruits these students. They must score 500 on the written TOEFL or 173 on the electronic version.

Computers: The mainframe is an IBM RS/6000. All students may access the system any time.

Graduates: From July 1, 2002 to June 30, 2003, 787 bachelor's degrees were awarded. The most popular majors were management (29%), marketing management (24%), and international business (11%). In an average class, 41% graduate in 4 years or less, and 56% graduate in 6 years or less. 33 companies recruited on campus in 2002-2003. Of the 2002 graduating class, 3% were enrolled in graduate school within 6 months of graduation and 84% were employed.

Admissions Contact: Dan Toland, Director of Admissions. A video is available. E-mail: *admissions@northwood.edu*
Web: *www.northwood.edu*

OAKLAND UNIVERSITY
Rochester, MI 48309-4401

E-4

(248) 370-3360; Fax: (800) OAK-UNIV

Full-time: 3423 men, 5856 women	**Faculty:** IIA, +$
Part-time: 1441 men, 2239 women	**Ph.D.s:** n/av
Graduate: 1375 men, 2242 women	**Student/Faculty:** n/av
Year: semesters, summer session	**Tuition:** $5260 ($11,954)
Application Deadline: open	**Room & Board:** $5540
Freshman Class: 6321 applied, 5079 accepted, 2101 enrolled	
ACT: 21	**COMPETITIVE**

Oakland University, established in 1957, is a comprehensive state-supported institution serving a primarily commuter student body. There are 6 undergraduate schools and 1 graduate school. In addition to regional accreditation, Oakland has baccalaureate program accreditation with AACSB, ABET, ACS, APTA, CCNE, CSAB, NASD, NASM, NASPAA, NAST, NCATE, and NLN. The 2 libraries contain 819,979 volumes, 1,172,386 microform items, and 16,508 audio/video tapes/CDs, and subscribe to 2995 periodicals. Computerized library services include the card catalog, interlibrary loans, and database searching. Special learning facilities include a learning resource center, art gallery, radio station, the Product Development and Manufacturing Center, and the Historical House Museum. The 1444-acre campus is in a suburban area 25 miles north of Detroit. Including any residence halls, there are 46 buildings.

Student Life: 97% of undergraduates are from Michigan. Students are from 35 states, 34 foreign countries, and Canada. 84% are white. The average age of freshmen is 19; all undergraduates, 23. 27% do not continue beyond their first year.

Housing: 1870 students can be accommodated in college housing, which includes single-sex and coed dorms, on-campus apartments, married-student housing, and sorority houses. In addition, there are honors houses, special-interest houses, and a wellness dorm. On-campus housing is guaranteed for all 4 years. All students may keep cars.

Activities: 3% of men belong to 6 national fraternities; 2% of women belong to 7 national sororities. There are 114 groups on campus, including art, band, cheerleading, choir, chorale, chorus, computers, dance, drama, ethnic, forensics, gay, honors, international, jazz band, musical theater, newspaper, orchestra, pep band, political, professional, radio and TV, religious, social, social service, student government, and symphony. Popular campus events include Pig Roast, African-American celebration month, and Midnight Madness.

Sports: There are 6 intercollegiate sports for men and 8 for women, and 8 intramural sports for men and 8 for women. Facilities include a 250,000-square-foot student recreation and athletic center that includes softball and baseball diamonds, an indoor track, soccer and touch football fields, and facilities for swimming, basketball, weight training, dance, fencing, handball, squash, racquetball, and golf.

Disabled Students: 90% of the campus is accessible. Wheelchair ramps, elevators, special parking, specially equipped rest rooms, special class scheduling, lowered drinking fountains, lowered telephones, special housing, and automatic door openers are available.

Services: Counseling and information services are available, as is tutoring in every subject. There is a reader service for the blind, remedial math and writing, and a mentorship program.

Campus Safety and Security: Measures include 24-hour foot and vehicle patrol, self-defense education, security escort services, and informal discussions. There are pamphlets/posters/films, emergency telephones, and lighted pathways/sidewalks.

Programs of Study: Oakland confers B.A., B.S., B.G.S., B.Mus., B.S.E., and B.S.N. degrees. Master's and doctoral degrees are also awarded. Bachelor's degrees are awarded in BIOLOGICAL SCIENCE (biochemistry and biology/biological science), BUSINESS (accounting, banking and finance, business administration and management, human resources, management information systems, marketing/retailing/merchandising, and personnel management), COMMUNICATIONS AND THE ARTS (art history and appreciation, Chinese, communications, English, fine arts, French, German, Japanese, journalism, linguistics, music, performing arts, Russian, Spanish, and studio art), COMPUTER AND PHYSICAL SCIENCE (chemistry, computer science, information sciences and systems, mathematics, medical physics, physics, and statistics), EDUCATION (elementary and music), ENGINEERING AND ENVIRONMENTAL DESIGN (chemical engineering, computer engineering, electrical/electronics engineering, engineering chemistry, engineering physics, mechanical engineering, and systems engineering), HEALTH PROFESSIONS (environmental health science, health science, industrial hygiene, medical laboratory science, nursing, physical therapy, and preventive/wellness health care), SOCIAL SCIENCE (African American studies, anthropology, Asian/Oriental studies, East Asian studies, economics, history, Latin American studies, liberal arts/general studies, philosophy, political science/government, psychology, public administration, Russian and Slavic studies, sociology, South Asian studies, and women's studies). Physical sciences, biological sciences, and engineering are the strongest academically. Psychology, elementary education, and communications are the largest.

Required: To graduate, students must complete 124 credit hours for a B.A. (128 for a B.Mus. or a B.S. in environmental health), including 32 to 36 in the major. A minimum GPA of 2.0 is required. The core curriculum must include 1 course each in arts, literature, social science, natural science, language, math/logic, international studies, and Western civilization, and completion of 1 course that meets the ethnic diversity requirement; writing proficiency must be demonstrated as well.

Special: Special academic programs include internships, cooperative programs for most disciplines, and many work-study opportunities. There are organized programs for study abroad in 7 countries; independent programs can be arranged. Oakland also offers a B.A.-B.S. degree in biology and economics, a general studies program, dual majors, and preprofessional studies in medicine, dentistry, optometry, and veterinary medicine. There are 6 national honor societies, a freshman honors program, and 39 departmental honors programs.

Faculty/Classroom: No introductory courses are taught by graduate students. The average class size in an introductory lecture is 40; in a laboratory, 16; and in a regular course, 31.

Admissions: 80% of the 2003-2004 applicants were accepted. The ACT scores for the 2003-2004 freshman class were: 44% below 21, 27% between 21 and 23, 18% between 24 and 26, 7% between 27 and 28, and 4% above 28.

Requirements: The ACT is required. In addition, admissions requirements include graduation from an accredited secondary school and high school level college preparatory work including 4 years of English and 3 years each of math, science, and social studies. 2 years of foreign language and 1 semester of computer science are recommended as well. Music and dance majors must audition. A GPA of 2.5 is required. AP and CLEP credits are accepted. Important factors in the admissions decision are advanced placement or honor courses, leadership record, and evidence of special talent.

Procedure: Freshmen are admitted to all sessions. Entrance exams should be taken during the spring of the junior year or early fall of the senior year. There is a deferred admissions plan. Application deadlines are open. The fall 2003 application fee was $35. Notification is sent on a rolling basis.

Transfer: 1294 transfer students enrolled in 2002-2003. Applicants must have at least a 2.5 GPA; a higher GPA is required in some majors. 32 of 124 to 128 credits required for the bachelor's degree must be completed at Oakland.

Visiting: There are regularly scheduled orientations for prospective students, including a review of services, academic advising, and course registration. There are guides for informal visits and visitors may sit in on classes and stay overnight. To schedule a visit, contact the Admissions Office.

Financial Aid: Oakland is a member of CSS. The FAFSA and the college's own financial statement are required. The deadline for filing freshman financial aid applications for fall entry is April 1.

International Students: There are 89 international students enrolled. They must score 550 on the written TOEFL or 213 on the electronic version and also take the ACT.

Computers: There are 39 networked labs with 558 stations, and 9 nonnetworked labs with 55 stations. All students may access the system. There are no time limits and no fees.

Graduates: From July 1, 2002 to June 30, 2003, 1794 bachelor's degrees were awarded. The most popular majors were elementary education (13%), communications (8%), and management information systems (7%). In an average class, 11% graduate in 4 years or less, 32% graduate in 5 years or less, and 41% graduate in 6 years or less.

Admissions Contact: Peter Nacy, Director of Admissions. A video is available. E-mail: *ouinfo@oakland.edu* Web: *www.oakland.edu*

OLIVET COLLEGE
Olivet, MI 49076

D-4

(800) 456-7189; Fax: (616) 749-3821

Full-time: 533 men, 407 women	**Faculty:** 55; IIB, --$
Part-time: 58 men, 44 women	**Ph.Ds:** 36%
Graduate: 10 men, 18 women	**Student/Faculty:** 17 to 1
Year: semesters, summer session	**Tuition:** $15,182
Application Deadline: open	**Room & Board:** $4802
Freshman Class: 1200 applied, 545 accepted, 285 enrolled	
ACT: 19	**COMPETITIVE+**

Olivet College, founded in 1844, is a private liberal arts institution affiliated with both the United Church of Christ and the Congregational Christian Churches. There is 1 graduate school. The library contains 85,000 volumes and 117 microform items, and subscribes to 450 periodicals. Computerized library services include the card catalog, interlibrary loans, database searching, and Internet access. Special learning facilities include a learning resource center, art gallery, planetarium, radio station, an observatory, and a nature preserve. The 92-acre campus is in a small town 30 miles south of Lansing and 120 miles west of Detroit. Including any residence halls, there are 24 buildings.

Student Life: 82% of undergraduates are from Michigan. Students are from 15 states, 12 foreign countries, and Canada. 92% are from public schools. 72% are white; 16% African American. 21% are Catholic; 18% claim no religious affiliation; 6% Protestant. The average age of freshmen is 19; all undergraduates, 23. 35% do not continue beyond their first year; 40% remain to graduate.

Housing: 700 students can be accommodated in college housing, which includes single-sex and coed dorms, fraternity houses, and sorority houses. In addition, there are honors houses, special-interest houses, a global cultural center, and an African American cultural center. On-campus housing is guaranteed for all 4 years. 72% of students live on campus; of those, 45% remain on campus on weekends. All students may keep cars.

Activities: 9% of men and about 2% of women belong to 6 local fraternities; 7% of women belong to 4 local sororities. There are 27 groups on campus, including art, band, cheerleading, choir, chorale, chorus, computers, drama, drill team, drum and bugle corps, ethnic, gay, honors, international, literary magazine, musical theater, newspaper, pep band, photography, professional, radio and TV, religious, social, social service, student government, and yearbook. Popular campus events include Diversity Week, Community Service Week, and Honors Convocation.

Sports: There are 9 intercollegiate sports for men and 9 for women, and 6 intramural sports for men and 6 for women. Facilities include an athletic center, a football field, a gym, a fitness center, soccer fields, softball and baseball fields, tennis courts, a student center, and a pool.

Disabled Students: 25% of the campus is accessible. Wheelchair ramps, elevators, special parking, and specially equipped rest rooms are available.

Services: Counseling and information services are available, as is tutoring in most subjects. There is a reader service for the blind and remedial math, reading, and writing.

Campus Safety and Security: Measures include 24-hour foot and vehicle patrol, self-defense education, security escort services, and informal discussions. There are pamphlets/posters/films, emergency telephones, and lighted pathways/sidewalks.

Programs of Study: Olivet confers the B.A. degree. Master's degrees are also awarded. Bachelor's degrees are awarded in BIOLOGICAL SCIENCE (biochemistry and biology/biological science), BUSINESS (accounting, business administration and management, insurance, international business management, and marketing management), COMMUNICATIONS AND THE ARTS (communications, design, English, fine arts, illustration, and journalism), COMPUTER AND PHYSICAL SCIENCE (chemistry, computer science, and mathematics), EDUCATION (athletic training, elementary, physical, and secondary), ENGINEERING AND ENVIRONMENTAL DESIGN (environmental science), HEALTH PROFESSIONS (health, predentistry, premedicine, and preveterinary science), SOCIAL SCIENCE (anthropology, criminal justice, economics, history, prelaw, psychology, social studies, and sociology). Business administration, teacher education, and criminal justice are the strongest academically.

Required: To graduate, students must complete 120 semester hours, 36 to 60 in the major. Their minimum GPA must be 2.0; those seeking certification must maintain a minimum 2.5 GPA in all education courses and in all courses in their major and minor fields. Students must demonstrate competency in 16 areas and complete a 33-hour general education program. In addition, a 40-hour service learning course and senior experience class are required.

Special: Olivet offers internships, cooperative education opportunities, and both student-designed and dual majors. There are 2 national honor societies, a freshman honors program, and 4 departmental honors programs.

Faculty/Classroom: 55% of faculty are male; 45%, female. All teach undergraduates. No introductory courses are taught by graduate students. The average class size in an introductory lecture is 20; in a laboratory, 14; and in a regular course, 16.

Admissions: 45% of the 2003-2004 applicants were accepted. The ACT scores for the 2003-2004 freshman class were: 25% below 21, 40% between 21 and 23, 15% between 24 and 26, 15% between 27 and 28, and 5% above 28. 25% of the current freshmen were in the top fifth of their class; 50% were in the top two fifths. 6 freshmen graduated first in their class.

Requirements: The SAT I or ACT is recommended; the minimum score considered on the ACT is 13. Students must be graduates of an accredited secondary school, with a scholastic GPA of at least 2.6 and completion of college-preparatory courses. The GED is accepted. Individual consideration is given to applicants not meeting these criteria but demonstrating other potential. AP and CLEP credits are accepted. Important factors in the admissions decision are evidence of special talent, extracurricular activities record, and recommendations by school officials.

Procedure: Freshmen are admitted fall, spring, and summer. There is a deferred admissions plan. Application deadlines are open. Application fee is $25. Notification is sent on a rolling basis. Applications are accepted on-line through the school's web site.

Transfer: 105 transfer students enrolled in 2002-2003. Transcripts of college work completed elsewhere must show a 2.0 GPA. Transfer applicants must be high school graduates or the equivalent. 30 of 120 credits required for the bachelor's degree must be completed at Olivet.

Visiting: There are regularly scheduled orientations for prospective students, consisting of a day and a half of orientation. There are guides for informal visits and visitors may sit in on classes and stay overnight. To schedule a visit, contact the Admissions Office.

Financial Aid: In 2003-2004, 94% of all full-time freshmen and 95% of continuing full-time students received some form of financial aid. 88% of full-time freshmen and 92% of continuing full-time students received need-based aid. The average freshman award was $6500. 45% of undergraduates work part time. Average annual earnings from campus work are $1200. The average financial indebtedness of the 2003 graduate was $18,000. Olivet is a member of CSS. The FAFSA is required. The priority date for freshman financial aid applications for fall entry is March 1. The deadline for filing freshman financial aid applications for fall entry is June 15.

International Students: There are 42 international students enrolled. The school actively recruits these students. They must score 500 on the written TOEFL.

Computers: The mainframe is a DEC Alpha 1000. There are 65 PCs available to all students, which are networked and provide access to the Web. All students may access the system 24 hours a day, 7 days per week during the academic year. There are no time limits and no fees.

Graduates: From July 1, 2002 to June 30, 2003, 147 bachelor's degrees were awarded. The most popular majors were business administration (17%), psychology (11%), and biology (11%). 9 companies recruited on campus in 2002-2003.

Admissions Contact: Bernie McConnel, Assistant Vice President for Enrollment Management. E-mail: *admissions@olivetcollege.edu* Web: *olivetcollege.edu*

ROCHESTER COLLEGE
Rochester Hills, MI 48307

E-4

(248) 218-2031
(800) 521-6010; Fax: (248) 218-2035

Full-time: 290 men, 350 women	**Faculty:** 32
Part-time: 118 men, 243 women	**Ph.D.s:** 28%
Graduate: none	**Student/Faculty:** 20 to 1
Year: semesters	**Tuition:** $11,040
Application Deadline: open	**Room & Board:** $5678
Freshman Class: 358 applied, 272 accepted, 152 enrolled	
SAT I Verbal/Math: 500/510	**ACT:** 21 **COMPETITIVE**

Rochester College, founded in 1959, is a private institution affiliated with the Churches of Christ. It offers undergraduate programs in business, behavioral sciences, Christian services, English, interdisciplinary studies, history, music, communication, and general science. Some information in the above capsule is approximate. The library contains 68,922 volumes, 16,725 microform items, and 956 audio/video tapes/CDs, and subscribes to 642 periodicals. Computerized library services include interlibrary loans and database searching. The 83-acre campus is in a suburban area 25 miles north of Detroit. Including any residence halls, there are 12 buildings.

Student Life: 82% of undergraduates are from Michigan. Students are from 19 states, 10 foreign countries, and Canada. 83% are white; 11% African American. 84% are Protestant; 15% Catholic. The average age of freshmen is 20; all undergraduates, 21.

Housing: 366 students can be accommodated in college housing, which includes single-sex dorms and married-student housing. On-campus housing is available on a first-come, first-served basis. 50% of students live on campus. Alcohol is not permitted. All students may keep cars.

Activities: There are no fraternities or sororities. There are 22 groups on campus, including cheerleading, chorale, chorus, drama, jazz band, newspaper, professional, religious, social, social service, student government, and yearbook. Popular campus events include Celebration.

Sports: There are 5 intercollegiate sports for men and 5 for women, and 9 intramural sports for men and 9 for women. Facilities include a gym, plus soccer, baseball, and softball fields.

Disabled Students: 75% of the campus is accessible. Wheelchair ramps, elevators, special parking, specially equipped rest rooms, and special class scheduling are available.

Services: Counseling and information services are available, as is tutoring in some subjects, including Bible. There is remedial math, reading, and writing.

Campus Safety and Security: Measures include lighted pathways/sidewalks and evening security guards.

Programs of Study: RC confers B.S., B.B.A., and B.R.E. degrees. Associate degrees are also awarded. Bachelor's degrees are awarded in BUSINESS (accounting, business administration and management, and marketing management), COMMUNICATIONS AND THE ARTS (communications, English, and music), COMPUTER AND PHYSICAL SCIENCE (computer management and science), SOCIAL SCIENCE (behavioral science, biblical studies, Christian studies, history, interdisciplinary studies, ministries, and psychology). Management, interdisciplinary studies, and psychology are the largest.

Required: All students must follow a core curriculum that includes courses in religion, communication, humanities, phys ed, science, math, and social science. To graduate, students must complete 128 credits with a minimum GPA of 2.0.

Special: A co-op program in education is available. Cross-registration with Oakland University, Madonna University, Oakland Community College, and Macomb Community College is offered. Internships, which are required for many majors, study abroad, and work-study programs are also offered. There are 2 national honor societies and 1 departmental honors program.

Faculty/Classroom: 65% of faculty are male; 35%, female. All teach undergraduates. The average class size in an introductory lecture is 40; in a laboratory, 10; and in a regular course, 23.

Admissions: 76% of the 2003-2004 applicants were accepted. The SAT I scores for the 2003-2004 freshman class were: Verbal--50% below 500, 25% between 500 and 599, and 25% between 600 and 700; Math--50% below 500, 33% between 500 and 599, and 17% between 600 and 700. The ACT scores were 48% below 21, 27% between 21 and 23, 14% between 24 and 26, 4% between 27 and 28, and 7% above 28. 16% of the current freshmen were in the top fifth of their class; 39% were in the top two fifths.

Requirements: The SAT I or ACT is required. A GPA of 2.25 is required. AP and CLEP credits are accepted.

Procedure: Freshmen are admitted to all sessions. Entrance exams should be taken as early as possible. There are early admissions and deferred admissions plans. There is a rolling admissions plan. Application deadlines are open. Application fee is $25. Applications are accepted on-line through *www.rc.edu*.

Transfer: 54 transfer students enrolled in a recent year. A 2.0 college GPA is required. 32 of 128 credits required for the bachelor's degree must be completed at RC.

Visiting: There are regularly scheduled orientations for prospective students, including several College Life Preview Days in fall and winter and Celebration Saturday in March. There are guides for informal visits and visitors may sit in on classes and stay overnight. To schedule a visit, contact Enrollment Services Office.

Financial Aid: In 2003-2004, 98% of all full-time freshmen and 96% of continuing full-time students received some form of financial aid. 69% of full-time freshmen and 79% of continuing full-time students received need-based aid. The average freshman award was $7747. Need-based scholarships or need-based grants averaged $3343 ($7250 maximum); need-based self-help aid (loans and jobs) averaged $1550 ($8125 maximum); non-need-based athletic scholarships averaged $2000 ($3500 maximum); and other non-need-based awards and non-need-based scholarships averaged $3278 ($8217 maximum). 25% of undergraduates work part time. Average annual earnings from campus work are $994. The average financial indebtedness of a recent graduate was $10,416. The CSS Profile, FAFSA, FFS, or SFS and the college's own financial statement are required. Check with the school for current deadlines.

International Students: There were 29 international students enrolled in a recent year. The school actively recruits these students. They must score 500 on the written TOEFL or 173 on the electronic version.

Computers: Students may use Pentium 200 MXX workstations in the student computer lab, IBM workstations in the learning lab or library, or dial-up access from the residence halls. Internet access is available. All students may access the system. Schedules for computer use vary. There are no time limits and no fees.

MICHIGAN 827

Graduates: In a recent year, 136 bachelor's degrees were awarded. The most popular majors were management (28%), early childhood education (8%), and business communication (5%). In an average class, 8% graduate in 4 years or less, 10% graduate in 5 years or less, and 12% graduate in 6 years or less.

Admissions Contact: Toby Osbum, Vice President for Enrollment Service and Dean of Admissions. E-mail: *admissions@rc.edu* Web: *www.rc.edu*

SAGINAW VALLEY STATE UNIVERSITY
University Center, MI 48710-0001

D-4
(989) 964-4200
(800) 968-9500; Fax: (989) 790-0180

Full-time: 2183 men, 3322 women
Part-time: 832 men, 1243 women
Graduate: 436 men, 1152 women
Year: semesters, summer session
Application Deadline: open
Freshman Class: 3328 applied, 2987 accepted, 1181 enrolled
ACT: 21

Faculty: 244
Ph.Ds: n/av
Student/Faculty: 23 to 1
Tuition: $5410 ($11,009)
Room & Board: $5645

COMPETITIVE

Saginaw Valley State University, founded in 1963, is a state-supported institution offering undergraduate and graduate degrees in arts and behavioral sciences, business and management, education, nursing and health sciences, and science, engineering, and technology. There are 5 undergraduate and 6 graduate schools. In addition to regional accreditation, SVSU has baccalaureate program accreditation with ABET, CSWE, NCATE, and NLN. The library contains 217,336 volumes, 356,088 microform items, and 23,366 audio/video tapes/CDs, and subscribes to 2344 periodicals. Computerized library services include the card catalog, interlibrary loans, database searching, and Internet access. Special learning facilities include a learning resource center, art gallery, and an observatory. The 782-acre campus is in a suburban area 5 miles north of Saginaw.

Student Life: 99% of undergraduates are from Michigan. Others are from 18 states, 52 foreign countries, and Canada. 97% are from public schools. 68% are white. The average age of freshmen is 18; all undergraduates, 25. 30% do not continue beyond their first year.

Housing: 1600 students can be accommodated in college housing, which includes coed dorms, on-campus apartments, and married-student housing. In addition, there are healthy lifestyle floors and buildings, and first-year suites. On-campus housing is guaranteed for all 4 years. 62% of students commute. Alcohol is not permitted. All students may keep cars.

Activities: 8% of men and about 2% of women belong to 13 national fraternities; 5% of women belong to 5 national sororities. There are 75 groups on campus, including art, band, cheerleading, choir, chorus, computers, dance, drama, ethnic, film, gay, honors, international, jazz band, literary magazine, marching band, musical theater, newspaper, orchestra, pep band, photography, political, professional, religious, social, social service, and student government. Popular campus events include Comedy Night, Family Festival Day, and Cards Party.

Sports: There are 9 intercollegiate sports for men and 8 for women, and 26 intramural sports for men and 22 for women. Facilities include a health and phys ed complex with an Olympic-size pool, indoor track, and racquetball courts; tennis courts; intramural, baseball, softball, and soccer fields; archery; a fitness trail; a football stadium; a golf and tee range; and horseshoe pits.

Disabled Students: 99% of the campus is accessible. Wheelchair ramps, elevators, special parking, specially equipped rest rooms, special class scheduling, lowered drinking fountains, lowered telephones, special housing, electronically opened doors, and special access to the library. All buildings are interconnected on the second floor.

Services: Counseling and information services are available, as is tutoring in most subjects, including most 100- and 200-level classes. There is a reader service for the blind, and remedial math, reading, and writing.

Campus Safety and Security: Measures include 24-hour foot and vehicle patrol, self-defense education, security escort services, and informal discussions. There are pamphlets/posters/films, emergency telephones, lighted pathways/sidewalks, and the SVSU public safety department has commissioned police officers providing police services.

Programs of Study: SVSU confers B.A., B.S., B.A.S., B.B.A., B.F.A., B.P.A., B.S.E.E., B.S.M.E., B.S.N., and B.S.W. degrees. Master's degrees are also awarded. Bachelor's degrees are awarded in BIOLOGICAL SCIENCE (biochemistry and biology/biological science), BUSINESS (accounting, banking and finance, business administration and management, business economics, business law, and marketing management), COMMUNICATIONS AND THE ARTS (art, communications, design, dramatic arts, English, fine arts, French, music, and Spanish), COMPUTER AND PHYSICAL SCIENCE (applied physics, chemistry, computer mathematics, computer science, mathematics, optics, and physics), EDUCATION (art, elementary, English, foreign languages, mathematics, music, physical, and special), ENGINEERING AND ENVIRONMENTAL DESIGN (electrical/electronics engineering, environmental science, industrial administration/management, and mechanical engi-

neering), HEALTH PROFESSIONS (allied health, nursing, and occupational therapy), SOCIAL SCIENCE (criminal justice, economics, history, interdisciplinary studies, international studies, political science/government, psychology, public administration, social work, and sociology). Preelementary education, criminal justice, and elementary education are the largest.

Required: Students must complete a minimum of 124 credits, satisfy basic skills and general education requirements, maintain a minimum GPA of 2.0, complete at least 31 credits at SVSU, and be enrolled on campus the last semester.

Special: Opportunities are provided for student-designed majors, work-study, internships, co-op education, credit by exam, nondegree study, pass/fail options, and study abroad in 7 countries. There are 3 national honor societies.

Faculty/Classroom: All teach undergraduates. No introductory courses are taught by graduate students.

Admissions: 90% of the 2003-2004 applicants were accepted.

Requirements: The ACT is required. In addition, graduation from an accredited secondary school or a GED is required. Applicants should submit records of successful completion of 4 years each of English and math, 3 each of social science and science, 2 each of a foreign language and fine arts, and 1 course in computer literacy. A GPA of 2.5 is required. AP and CLEP credits are accepted.

Procedure: Freshmen are admitted to all sessions. Application deadlines are open. There is a rolling admissions plan. Application fee is $25. Applications are accepted on-line.

Transfer: 572 transfer students enrolled in 2002-2003. Transfer students with fewer than 45 credits from a previous college must submit high school and college transcripts. A minimum GPA of 2.0 is needed. An interview may be required. 31 of 124 credits required for the bachelor's degree must be completed at SVSU.

Visiting: There are regularly scheduled orientations for prospective students, including tours, help with schedules, basic information, and counseling. There are guides for informal visits. To schedule a visit, contact the Office of Admissions.

Financial Aid: In 2003-2004, 54% of all full-time freshmen and 51% of continuing full-time students received some form of financial aid. 75% of full-time freshmen and 74% of continuing full-time students received need-based aid. Average annual earnings from campus work are $1500. The average financial indebtedness of the 2003 graduate was $10,501. The FAFSA is required. The priority date for freshman financial aid applications for fall entry is February. The deadline for filing freshman financial aid applications for fall entry is March.

International Students: There are 195 international students enrolled. The school actively recruits these students. They must score 525 on the written TOEFL or 197 on the electronic version and also take the college's own entrance exam.

Computers: The mainframe is a DEC Alpha 1000. The mainframe is accessible from any of 300 Macs or PCs available in networked student computer labs or via Internet dial-in. All stations have access to the Internet and the Web. All students may access the system. There are no time limits and no fees.

Graduates: From July 1, 2002 to June 30, 2003, 941 bachelor's degrees were awarded. The most popular majors were elementary education (21%), criminal justice (7%), and nursing (5%). 167 companies recruited on campus in 2002-2003.

Admissions Contact: James Dwyer, Director of Admissions. E-mail: *admissions@svsu.edu* Web: *www.svsu.edu*

SAINT MARY'S COLLEGE
Orchard Lake, MI 48324

E-4
(248) 683-0528; Fax: (248) 683-0402

Full-time: 120 men, 70 women
Part-time: 70 men, 85 women
Graduate: none
Year: semesters, summer session
Application Deadline: see profile
Freshman Class: n/av
ACT: required

Faculty: 19
Ph.Ds: 80%
Student/Faculty: 10 to 1
Tuition: $9000
Room & Board: $5000

LESS COMPETITIVE

Saint Mary's College, founded in 1885, is an independent institution affiliated with the Roman Catholic Church. Figures in the above capsule and in this profile are approximate. The library contains 75,000 volumes and 6200 microform items, and subscribes to 450 periodicals. Computerized library services include the card catalog, interlibrary loans, and database searching. Special learning facilities include a learning resource center and art gallery. The 122-acre campus is in a suburban area 17 miles from Detroit. Including any residence halls, there are 13 buildings.

Student Life: 95% of undergraduates are from Michigan. Students are from 11 states, 16 foreign countries, and Canada. 70% are from public schools. 91% are white. 60% are Catholic; 34% Protestant. The average age of freshmen is 19; all undergraduates, 29. 31% do not continue beyond their first year; 20% remain to graduate.

Housing: 150 students can be accommodated in college housing, which includes single-sex dorms. On-campus housing is guaranteed for all 4 years. 74% of students commute. Alcohol is not permitted. All students may keep cars.

Activities: There are no fraternities or sororities. There are 12 groups on campus, including dance, drama, ethnic, honors, international, literary magazine, newspaper, religious, social, social service, student government, and yearbook.

Sports: There are 3 intercollegiate sports for men and 1 for women, and 5 intramural sports for men and 5 for women. Facilities include a stadium, 2 gyms, a weight room, an outdoor track, and baseball, football, and soccer fields.

Disabled Students: 80% of the campus is accessible. Wheelchair ramps, special parking, and specially equipped rest rooms are available.

Services: Counseling and information services are available, as is tutoring in most subjects. There is remedial math, reading, and writing.

Campus Safety and Security: Measures include informal discussions, pamphlets/posters/films, emergency telephones, and lighted pathways/sidewalks. There is evening security in dorms.

Programs of Study: Saint Mary's confers B.A., B.S., B.G.S., and B.H.S. degrees. Bachelor's degrees are awarded in BIOLOGICAL SCIENCE (biology/biological science), BUSINESS (business administration and management), COMMUNICATIONS AND THE ARTS (communications, English, and modern language), COMPUTER AND PHYSICAL SCIENCE (chemistry, computer science, and radiological technology), EDUCATION (education), HEALTH PROFESSIONS (health science and premedicine), SOCIAL SCIENCE (community services, human services, philosophy, prelaw, psychology, religious education, social science, sociology, and theological studies). Premedicine, communication arts, and theology are the strongest academically. Business, communication arts, and psychology are the largest.

Required: To graduate, students must complete 120 credit hours, with 30 to 36 hours in the major and a minimum GPA of 2.0. All students must take 60 hours of core curriculum courses in the following areas: communications, ultimate meaning and value, interpretation and analysis of the arts, historical consciousness, foreign language, social science, natural science, and math. The college requires that students demonstrate writing proficiency.

Special: The college offers co-op programs with colleges in the Detroit Area Consortium of Catholic Colleges. Internships, study abroad, an accelerated degree program in organizational management, dual majors, a general studies degree, directed study, and nondegree study are available. A program in Polish studies is offered at the school's Center of Polish Studies and Culture.

Faculty/Classroom: 60% of faculty are male; 40%, female. All teach undergraduates.

Requirements: The ACT is required, with a minimum composite score of 19. Applicants must be graduates of an accredited secondary school. The GED is accepted. Students must complete 16 high school academic credits. Students may submit applications on-line. A GPA of 2.5 is required. CLEP credit is accepted. Important factors in the admissions decision are evidence of special talent, advanced placement or honor courses, and leadership record.

Procedure: Freshmen are admitted fall, winter, and spring. There are early decision and early admissions plans. Notification is sent on a rolling basis. Applications are accepted on-line. Check with the school for current application deadlines and fee.

Transfer: Applicants must have a minimum GPA of 2.0. The ACT is required unless the student is classified as a nontraditional student or has 12 or more semester hours of college credit. 30 of 120 credits required for the bachelor's degree must be completed at Saint Mary's.

Visiting: There are regularly scheduled orientations for prospective students, Transfer students may attend a day or evening orientation prior to the fall semester. There are guides for informal visits and visitors may sit in on classes and stay overnight. To schedule a visit, contact the Admissions Office at (248) 683-1757.

Financial Aid: Saint Mary's is a member of CSS. The CSS Profile and the college's own financial statement are required. Check with the school for current deadlines.

International Students: The school actively recruits these students. They must score 500 on the written TOEFL or take the MELAB.

Computers: The mainframe is an IBM/36. The college makes available a substantial number of PCs for students. There are no time limits and no fees. It is strongly recommended that all students have a personal computer.

Admissions Contact: David Sichterman, Assistant Director of Admissions. E-mail: stmcoll@aol.com Web: www.stmarys-orchardlake.edu

---

SIENA HEIGHTS UNIVERSITY
(Formerly Siena Height College)
Adrian, MI 49221

E-5

(517) 264-7183
(800) 521-0009; Fax: (517) 264-7745

Full-time: 270 men, 480 women	**Faculty:** 53; IIB, -$
Part-time: 70 men, 155 women	**Ph.D.s:** 64%
Graduate: 45 men, 110 women	**Student/Faculty:** 14 to 1
Year: semesters, summer session	**Tuition:** $12,000
Application Deadline: open	**Room & Board:** $4500
Freshman Class: n/av	
ACT: required	**LESS COMPETITIVE**

Siena Heights University, founded in 1919, is a private liberal arts institution affiliated with the Roman Catholic Church. There is 1 graduate school. Figures in the above capsule and in this profile are approximate. In addition to regional accreditation, Siena has baccalaureate program accreditation with NASAD. The library contains 112,000 volumes, 24,000 microform items, and 4800 audio/video tapes/CDs, and subscribes to 450 periodicals. Computerized library services include the card catalog, interlibrary loans, and database searching. Special learning facilities include an art gallery. The 140-acre campus is in a small town 75 miles southwest of Detroit. Including any residence halls, there are 12 buildings.

Student Life: 80% are from public schools. 84% are white. The average age of freshmen is 18; all undergraduates, 25. 45% do not continue beyond their first year.

Housing: 450 students can be accommodated in college housing, which includes coed dorms. On-campus housing is available on a first-come, first-served basis and is available on a lottery system for upperclassmen. Priority is given to out-of-town students. 69% of students commute. All students may keep cars.

Activities: 10% of men belong to 2 national fraternities; 10% of women belong to 2 national sororities. There are 30 groups on campus, including art, cheerleading, choir, chorale, chorus, computers, drama, ethnic, international, jazz band, literary magazine, musical theater, newspaper, professional, religious, social, social service, student government, and symphony. Popular campus events include Alumni/Family Weekend, International Dinner, and athletic banquets.

Sports: There are 6 intercollegiate sports for men and 6 for women, and 6 intramural sports for men and 6 for women. Facilities include a 57000-square-foot student activity center, which houses 5 basketball, 4 volleyball, and 2 tennis courts, a 200-meter, 4-lane track, a baseball batting cage, training and exercise rooms, ballrooms, and the Sage Union. The indoor gym seats 4000. There is also a soccer field and a sand volleyball pit.

Disabled Students: 70% of the campus is accessible. Wheelchair ramps, elevators, special parking, specially equipped rest rooms, and lowered drinking fountains are available.

Services: Counseling and information services are available, as is tutoring in most subjects. There is remedial math, reading, and writing.

Campus Safety and Security: Measures include 24-hour foot and vehicle patrol, self-defense education, security escort services, and informal discussions. There are pamphlets/posters/films and lighted pathways/sidewalks.

Programs of Study: Siena confers B.A., B.S., B.A.S., and B.F.A. degrees. Associate and master's degrees are also awarded. Bachelor's degrees are awarded in BIOLOGICAL SCIENCE (biology/biological science), BUSINESS (accounting, business administration and management, hotel/motel and restaurant management, and retailing), COMMUNICATIONS AND THE ARTS (art history and appreciation, communications, English, fine arts, music, and Spanish), COMPUTER AND PHYSICAL SCIENCE (chemistry, information sciences and systems, mathematics, and natural sciences), EDUCATION (business, elementary, and music), HEALTH PROFESSIONS (premedicine), SOCIAL SCIENCE (American studies, child psychology/development, criminal justice, history, human services, humanities, liberal arts/general studies, philosophy, psychology, public administration, religion, social science, and social work). Art, business, and biology are the strongest academically. Business, art, and education are the largest.

Required: To graduate, students must complete 120 semester hours, including 30 hours in the major, and maintain at least a 2.0 GPA. A core curriculum of 33 to 35 semester hours is required, including 2 courses in English composition and 1 each in literature, math, science, fine/performing arts, social science, history, philosophy, and religious studies. A seminar in education is also required.

Special: Special academic programs include 2-2 engineering co-op programs with the University of Detroit and the University of Michigan, a 2-2 business administration program at Lake Michigan College, internships in a student's major, study abroad in Mexico for various majors and Siena, Italy, for art students, and on- and off-campus work-study. Also offered are dual and inverted majors, B.A.-B.S. degrees, a general studies degree, and student-designed majors. 3-year bachelor's degrees may be earned, and a directed student-teaching program is available for education majors. Flexible learning formats include weekend and evening courses. There is 1 national honor society.

Faculty/Classroom: 52% of faculty are male; 48%, female. 95% teach undergraduates. No introductory courses are taught by graduate students. The average class size in a regular course is 15.

Requirements: The ACT is required, with a minimum score of 17. Admissions requirements include graduation from an accredited secondary school. The GED is accepted. A GPA of 2.3 is required. AP and CLEP credits are accepted. Important factors in the admissions decision are recommendations by school officials, parents or siblings attending the school, and recommendations by alumni.

Procedure: Freshmen are admitted to all sessions. SAT I or ACT scores should be available when the application is filed. There is a deferred admissions plan. Application deadlines are open. Check with the school for current fee.

Transfer: Applicants must have a 2.0 GPA. High school and college transcripts must be submitted. 30 of 120 credits required for the bachelor's degree must be completed at Siena.

Visiting: There are regularly scheduled orientations for prospective students. There are guides for informal visits and visitors may sit in on classes and stay overnight. To schedule a visit, contact the Admissions Office at (517) 264-7180 or (800) 521-0009, ext. 7180.

Financial Aid: Siena is a member of CSS. The FAFSA is required. Check with the school for current deadlines.

International Students: The school actively recruits these students. They must score 500 on the written TOEFL and also take the ACT, scoring 17.

Computers: The mainframe is an IBM RS/6000 320H. The PC lab has Mac and IBM computers for student use, with access to the Internet and the Web. All students may access the system from 8 A.M. to 11 P.M., except when classes are in session. There are no time limits and no fees.

Admissions Contact: Kevin C. Kucera, Dean of Admissions and Enrollment Services. E-mail: *admissions@sienahts.edu*

SPRING ARBOR UNIVERSITY
Spring Arbor, MI 49283-9799

D-5

(517) 750-6468
(800) 968-0011; Fax: (517) 750-6620

Full-time: 454 men, 775 women	Faculty: 73; IIB, --$
Part-time: 65 men, 159 women	Ph.Ds: 56%
Graduate: 244 men, 664 women	Student/Faculty: 17 to 1
Year: semesters, summer session	Tuition: $14,916
Application Deadline: open	Room & Board: $5290
Freshman Class: n/av	
ACT: recommended	COMPETITIVE

Spring Arbor University, founded in 1873, is a private institution affiliated with the Free Methodist Church. It offers undergraduate programs in fine arts, humanities, philosophy, religion, natural science, social science, and education. Graduate programs in business and education are also offered. There are 3 undergraduate and 5 graduate schools. In addition to regional accreditation, SAU has baccalaureate program accreditation with CSWE and NCATE. The library contains 97,831 volumes, 333,051 microform items, and 6042 audio/video tapes/CDs, and subscribes to 665 periodicals. Computerized library services include the card catalog, interlibrary loans, database searching, and Internet access. Special learning facilities include a learning resource center, radio station, and TV production facilities and equipment. The 123-acre campus is in a small town 8 miles west of Jackson. Including any residence halls, there are 36 buildings.

Student Life: 87% of undergraduates are from Michigan. Students are from 27 states, 11 foreign countries, and Canada. 87% are white. 69% are Protestant; 23% claim no religious affiliation; 6% miscellaneous denominations. 20% do not continue beyond their first year; 57% remain to graduate.

Housing: 850 students can be accommodated in college housing, which includes single-sex dorms, on-campus apartments, and married-student housing. On-campus housing is guaranteed for all 4 years. 60% of students live on campus; of those, 50% remain on campus on weekends. Alcohol is not permitted. All students may keep cars.

Activities: There are no fraternities or sororities. There are 34 groups on campus, including band, cheerleading, choir, chorale, drama, ethnic, honors, international, jazz band, newspaper, radio and TV, religious, social, social service, student government, and yearbook. Popular campus events include Arbor Games, Midnight Breakfast, and Spring Banquet.

Sports: There are 7 intercollegiate sports for men and 7 for women, and 8 intramural sports for men and 4 for women. Facilities include a 500-seat stadium, a 2600-seat gym, all-weather and indoor tracks, tennis courts, a basketball court, an Olympic pool, a weight-training room with cardiovascular equipment, and baseball, softball, and soccer fields.

Disabled Students: 80% of the campus is accessible. Wheelchair ramps, elevators, special parking, specially equipped rest rooms, lowered drinking fountains, and lowered telephones are available.

Services: Counseling and information services are available, as is tutoring in most subjects. There is a reader service for the blind and remedial

math, reading, and writing. Religious counseling and health services are also available.

Campus Safety and Security: Measures include self-defense education, security escort services, informal discussions, and lighted pathways/sidewalks. There is a night security guard and a bike patrol.

Programs of Study: SAU confers B.A. and B.S.W. degrees. Associate and master's degrees are also awarded. Bachelor's degrees are awarded in BIOLOGICAL SCIENCE (biochemistry and biology/biological science), BUSINESS (accounting, business administration and management, institutional management, management information systems, and personnel management), COMMUNICATIONS AND THE ARTS (art, communications, English, film arts, language arts, music, Spanish, and speech/debate/rhetoric), COMPUTER AND PHYSICAL SCIENCE (chemistry, computer science, mathematics, and physics), EDUCATION (Christian, music, and special), HEALTH PROFESSIONS (exercise science, health care administration, and nursing), SOCIAL SCIENCE (history, ministries, philosophy, physical fitness/movement, psychology, social science, social studies, social work, sociology, and youth ministry). Business, teacher education, and social science are the strongest academically. English, business, and special education are the largest.

Required: Students must complete 4 Christian perspective courses, cross-cultural studies, writing skills, speech, and physical fitness. Liberal arts requirements are in fine arts, humanities, natural science/math, philosophy/religion, and social science. To graduate, at least 124 semester hours, 30 to 60 in the major, with a minimum GPA of 2.0 overall and 2.2 in the major, are needed.

Special: Each student participates in a cross-cultural experience, which includes travel to a foreign country or to an urban center in the United States. Additional study-abroad opportunities can be arranged. A Washington semester is available through the American Studies Program. The university also offers cross-registration with Jackson Community College, work-study, a dual major in physics/math, student-designed majors, pass/fail options, and nondegree study. Alternative programs for adult learners provide field-based study and assign credit for life experience. An accelerated B.A. program for such students is also offered. A 3-2 engineering degree is offered with the University of Michigan and Michigan State, Western Michigan, and Tri-State Universities. There are 3 national honor societies and a freshman honors program.

Faculty/Classroom: 59% of faculty are male; 41%, female. All teach undergraduates. No introductory courses are taught by graduate students.

Admissions: 42% of the current freshmen were in the top fifth of their class; 67% were in the top two fifths. 13 freshmen graduated first in their class.

Requirements: The ACT is recommended, with a composite score of 20 recommended. Applicants must be graduates of accredited secondary schools or have a GED. An interview is advised for those who do not meet the requirements. Homeschooled applicants must take the ACT or the SAT I, provide transcripts of course work, and submit a 2- to 3-page paper. A GPA of 2.6 is required. AP and CLEP credits are accepted. Important factors in the admissions decision are personality/intangible qualities, parents or siblings attending the school, and leadership record.

Procedure: Freshmen are admitted to all sessions. Entrance exams should be taken in the spring of the junior year or fall of the senior year. There are early admissions and deferred admissions plans. Application deadlines are open. The fall 2003 application fee was $30. Notification is sent on a rolling basis.

Transfer: 129 transfer students enrolled in 2002-2003. Applicants should have a minimum GPA of 2.0 and are encouraged to arrange an interview. A release of information form is required from the previous college attended. 30 of 124 credits required for the bachelor's degree must be completed at SAU.

Visiting: There are regularly scheduled orientations for prospective students, including a tour, class and chapel attendance, lunch, and a student panel discussion. There are guides for informal visits and visitors may sit in on classes and stay overnight. To schedule a visit, contact the Admissions Office.

Financial Aid: 30% of undergraduates work part time. Average annual earnings from campus work are $1000. SAU is a member of CSS. The FAFSA is required. The deadline for filing freshman financial aid applications for fall entry is May 1.

International Students: There are 27 international students enrolled. They must score 525 on the written TOEFL or take the MELAB. They must also take the ACT.

Computers: Computer labs in the science building, art building, student center, and Lowell lounge are open to all students. A lab in the learning center is for the special needs population. All students may access the system. There are no time limits and no fees. It is strongly recommended that all students have a personal computer.

Graduates: From July 1, 2002 to June 30, 2003, 638 bachelor's degrees were awarded. The most popular majors were business (32%), family life (16%), and education (8%). In an average class, 29% graduate in 4 years or less, 53% graduate in 5 years or less, and 57% graduate in 6 years or less. Of the 2002 graduating class, 20% were enrolled in graduate school within 6 months of graduation.

Admissions Contact: Randy Comfort, Director of Admissions. A video is available. E-mail: *admissions@arbor.edu* Web: *www.arbor.edu*

UNIVERSITY OF DETROIT MERCY
Detroit, MI 48219-0900

E-5

(313) 993-1245
(800) 635-5020; Fax: (313) 993-3317

Full-time: 754 men, 1132 women	**Faculty:** n/av
Part-time: 386 men, 1111 women	**Ph.D.s:** 85%
Graduate: 1054 men, 1134 women	**Student/Faculty:** n/av
Year: semesters, summer session	**Tuition:** $19,200
Application Deadline: see profile	**Room & Board:** $6382
Freshman Class: 2181 applied, 1498 accepted, 486 enrolled	
ACT: 21	**COMPETITIVE**

University of Detroit Mercy, founded in 1877, is a private, independent institution affiliated with the Jesuits and Sisters of Mercy. It offers undergraduate programs in liberal arts, education and human services, business administration, engineering and science, architecture, and nursing and health sciences. There are 7 undergraduate and 5 graduate schools. In addition to regional accreditation, U of DM has baccalaureate program accreditation with AACSB, ABET, ADA, CSWE, NAAB, and NLN. The 3 libraries contain 733,000 volumes, 1,007,505 microform items, and 33,153 audio/video tapes/CDs, and subscribe to 4049 periodicals. Computerized library services include the card catalog, interlibrary loans, database searching, and Internet access. Special learning facilities include a learning resource center and radio station. The 70-acre campus is in an urban area 7 miles north of downtown Detroit.

Student Life: 93% of undergraduates are from Michigan. Students are from 27 states, 19 foreign countries, and Canada. 50% are white; 33% African American. 32% are Catholic; 32% a variety of denominations and religions; 26% claim no religious affiliation; 11% Protestant. The average age of freshmen is 18; all undergraduates, 29. 12% do not continue beyond their first year.

Housing: 955 students can be accommodated in college housing, which includes coed dorms and married-student housing. In addition, there are honors floors, a peace and justice floor, and a freshman residence program. On-campus housing is guaranteed for all 4 years. 79% of students commute. All students may keep cars.

Activities: There are 3 national fraternities and 3 national sororities. There are 50 groups on campus, including cheerleading, chorale, computers, drama, ethnic, honors, international, literary magazine, newspaper, pep band, political, professional, radio and TV, religious, social, social service, and student government. Popular campus events include Engineering and Architecture Week, Ethics Bowl, and Alternative Spring Break.

Sports: There are 7 intercollegiate sports for men and 8 for women, and 7 intramural sports for men and 7 for women. Facilities include a fitness center, a gym, racquetball/handball courts, an indoor track, a game room in the Student Union, and soccer, softball, and baseball fields.

Disabled Students: 80% of the campus is accessible. Wheelchair ramps, elevators, special parking, and special class scheduling are available.

Services: Counseling and information services are available, as is tutoring in most subjects, including all freshman courses and many other courses. There is remedial math, reading, and writing.

Campus Safety and Security: Measures include 24-hour foot and vehicle patrol, self-defense education, security escort services, and informal discussions. There are pamphlets/posters/films, emergency telephones, and lighted pathways/sidewalks.

Programs of Study: U of DM confers B.A., B.S., B.Arch., B.B.A., B.C.E., B.E.E., B.En., B.F.A., B.M.E., B.S.C.S., B.S.Ed., B.S.N., and B.S.W. degrees. Associate, master's, and doctoral degrees are also awarded. Bachelor's degrees are awarded in BIOLOGICAL SCIENCE (biochemistry and biology/biological science), BUSINESS (accounting and business administration and management), COMMUNICATIONS AND THE ARTS (communications, dramatic arts, and English), COMPUTER AND PHYSICAL SCIENCE (chemistry, computer science, information sciences and systems, and mathematics), EDUCATION (early childhood, elementary, middle school, secondary, and special), ENGINEERING AND ENVIRONMENTAL DESIGN (architecture, civil engineering, electrical/electronics engineering, engineering, manufacturing engineering, and mechanical engineering), HEALTH PROFESSIONS (dental hygiene, health care administration, nursing, predentistry, premedicine, and sports medicine), SOCIAL SCIENCE (addiction studies, criminal justice, economics, history, human services, liberal arts/general studies, paralegal studies, philosophy, political science/government, prelaw, psychology, religion, social work, and sociology). Engineering, nursing, and business administration are the strongest academically. Business administration, nursing, and mechanical engineering are the largest.

Required: Students must successfully complete at least 126 credit hours, including a core curriculum, and maintain a minimum GPA of 2.0. Required courses include English composition, religion, philosophy, speech fundamentals, math, and a computer course.

Special: Cooperative education is mandatory for engineering, architecture, and nursing majors and is optional for others. Cross-registration is available with a consortium of Catholic colleges in the Detroit area. There are internships, and a B.A.-B.S. degree is available for math, chemistry, and biology majors. An accelerated 6-year degree program in dentistry is provided. Study abroad is available in England, China, Canada, Mexico, Italy, Poland, Israel, and Greece. Academic exploration courses are provided to help students who are undecided about a future vocation. There are 3 national honor societies and a freshman honors program.

Admissions: 69% of the 2003-2004 applicants were accepted. The ACT scores for the 2003-2004 freshman class were: 37% below 21, 29% between 21 and 23, 18% between 24 and 26, 11% between 27 and 28, and 5% above 28. 22% of the current freshmen were in the top fifth of their class; 33% were in the top two fifths.

Requirements: The SAT I or ACT is required. In addition, graduation from an accredited secondary school is required; a GED will be accepted. Students must submit 16 academic credits, which should include, as a minimum, 4 units of English, 3 of math, and 2 each of history or social studies and natural science, including a lab course. Remaining credits should be distributed in a foreign language, speech, music, art, and other college preparatory electives. An interview is recommended. A GPA of 2.5 is required. AP and CLEP credits are accepted. Advanced placement or honor courses are an important factor in the admission decision.

Procedure: Freshmen are admitted to all sessions. Entrance exams should be taken during the junior or senior year. There is a rolling admissions plan and an early admissions plan. Preferential consideration is given to applications completed before March 1 for the fall or summer terms, and before December 1 for the term beginning in January. Notification is sent on a rolling basis. Applications are accepted on-line.

Transfer: Transfer applicants with fewer than 24 semester hours of credit at an accredited institution must submit SAT I or ACT scores and have maintained a minimum GPA of 2.0. If the student is older than 23 years of age, SAT I/ACT scores need not be submitted. 32 of 126 credits required for the bachelor's degree must be completed at U of DM.

Visiting: There are regularly scheduled orientations for prospective students, including a look at student life, testing and advising, and registration. There are guides for informal visits and visitors may sit in on classes and stay overnight. To schedule a visit, contact the Admissions Office.

Financial Aid: In 2003-2004, all full-time students received some form of financial aid. 81% of full-time freshmen and 65% of continuing full-time students received need-based aid. The average freshman award was $22,851. Need-based scholarships or need-based grants averaged $5711 ($7650 maximum); need-based self-help aid (loans and jobs) averaged $6308 ($10,025 maximum); non-need-based athletic scholarships averaged $8323 ($26,182 maximum); and other non-need-based awards and non-need-based scholarships averaged $12,017 ($19,590 maximum). 22% of undergraduates work part time. Average annual earnings from campus work are $2500. U of DM is a member of CSS. The FAFSA is required. The priority date for freshman financial aid applications for fall entry is March 1. The deadline for filing freshman financial aid applications for fall entry is August 1.

International Students: There are 79 international students enrolled. The school actively recruits these students. They must take the college's own test.

Computers: The mainframe is a Unisys A3K. PCs are available throughout the campus. All students may access the system. There are no time limits and no fees.

Admissions Contact: Admissions Counselors.
E-mail: *admissions@udmercy.edu* Web: *www.udmercy.edu*

UNIVERSITY OF MICHIGAN/ANN ARBOR
Ann Arbor, MI 48109

E-5

(734) 764-7433; Fax: (734) 936-0740

Full-time: 11,340 men, 11,972 women	**Faculty:** I, +$
Part-time: 615 men, 590 women	**Ph.D.s:** 88%
Graduate: 8171 men, 6343 women	**Student/Faculty:** n/av
Year: trimesters, summer session	**Tuition:** $7160 ($23,377)
Application Deadline: February 1	**Room & Board:** $6704
Freshman Class: 25,943 applied, 13,814 accepted, 5553 enrolled	
SAT I Verbal/Math: 630/670	**ACT:** 28
	HIGHLY COMPETITIVE+

The University of Michigan/Ann Arbor, founded in 1817, is the main campus of the University of Michigan. The public institution offers undergraduate programs in the arts and sciences, architecture, business administration, education, engineering, fine arts, kinesiology, natural resources, nursing, and professional studies, as well as a wide range of graduate and professional programs. There are 12 undergraduate and 19 graduate schools. In addition to regional accreditation, UM has baccalaureate program accreditation with AACSB, ABET, ACEJMC, ACPE, ADA, ASLA, CSWE, NAAB, NASAD, NASM, NCATE, NLN, and SAF. The 24 libraries contain 7,348,460 volumes, 6,037,194 microform items, and 56,512 audio/video tapes/CDs, and subscribe to 68,798 periodicals. Computerized library services include the card catalog, interlibrary loans, database searching, and Internet access. Special learning facilities include a learning resource center, art gallery, natural history museum, planetarium, radio station, TV station, archeology museum, botanical gardens, and 2 historical museums. The 3114-acre campus is in a suburban area 38 miles west of Detroit. Including any residence halls, there are 211 buildings.

Student Life: 69% of undergraduates are from Michigan. Students are from 50 states, 90 foreign countries, and Canada. 64% are white; 13% Asian American. The average age of freshmen is 18; all undergraduates, 20. 5% do not continue beyond their first year.

Housing: 11,102 students can be accommodated in college housing, which includes single-sex and coed dorms, on-campus apartments, married-student housing, fraternity houses, and sorority houses. In addition, there are honors houses, language houses, special-interest houses, substance-free dorms, women-in-science housing, and cooperative housing. On-campus housing is guaranteed for the freshman year only, is available on a first-come, first-served basis, and is available on a lottery system for upperclassmen. 63% of students commute to campus. All students may keep cars.

Activities: 17% of men belong to 1 local and 37 national fraternities; 17% of women belong to 24 national sororities. There are 900 groups on campus, including art, band, cheerleading, chess, choir, chorale, chorus, computers, dance, debate, drama, ethnic, film, forensics, gay, honors, international, jazz band, literary magazine, marching band, musical theater, newspaper, opera, orchestra, pep band, photography, political, professional, radio and TV, religious, social, social service, student government, symphony, and yearbook. Popular campus events include Martin Luther King Day, Native American Powwow, and Holocaust conference.

Sports: There are 12 intercollegiate sports for men and 13 for women, and 25 intramural sports for men and 25 for women. Facilities include a 107,501-seat stadium, a 1000-seat gym, an indoor track and tennis complex, an indoor practice center, 3 recreational buildings, 2 golf courses, a natatorium and separate swimming pools, an ice arena, and several other athletic arenas, the largest of which seats 13,000.

Disabled Students: 97% of the campus is accessible. Wheelchair ramps, elevators, special parking, specially equipped rest rooms, special class scheduling, lowered drinking fountains, lowered telephones, special housing, and para-transit service, specially equipped vans, talking calculators, telecommunication devices for the deaf, and an adaptive technology computing site that includes a high-speed scanner, voice input and voice output, braille display and large-print screens, and a braille printer are available.

Services: Counseling and information services are available, as is tutoring in some subjects, including introductory English and math. There is a reader service for the blind.

Campus Safety and Security: Measures include 24-hour foot and vehicle patrol, self-defense education, security escort services, and shuttle buses. There are informal discussions, pamphlets/posters/films, emergency telephones, lighted pathways/sidewalks, a nite-owl bus service, officer bicycle patrols, and a taxi service.

Programs of Study: UM confers A.B., B.S., A.B.E.D., B.B.A., B.D.A., B.F.A., B.F.A.D., B.F.A.M.T., B.F.A.(T), B.G.S., B.Mus., B.Mus.A., B.S.A.O.S., B.S.Chem., B.S.D.Hyg., B.S.E.AET., B.S.E.C.E., B.S.E.Ch., B.S.E.Civ., B.S.E.Comp., B.S.Ed., B.S.E.E.E., B.S.E.E.P., B.S.E.E.S., B.S.E.I.O., B.S.E.I.S., B.S.E.M.A., B.S.E.M.E., B.S.E.Met., B.S.E.M.S., B.S.Eng., B.S.M.C., B.S.MET., B.S.N., B.S.(NRE), B.S.P.O., and B.S.P.S. degrees. Master's and doctoral degrees are also awarded. Bachelor's degrees are awarded in AGRICULTURE (natural resource management), BIOLOGICAL SCIENCE (biochemistry, biology/biological science, biophysics, botany, cell biology, ecology, microbiology, nutrition, wildlife biology, and zoology), BUSINESS (business administration and management, recreation and leisure services, and sports management), COMMUNICATIONS AND THE ARTS (applied music, Arabic, art history and appreciation, ceramic art and design, Chinese, classical languages, communications, comparative literature, creative writing, dance, design, dramatic arts, English, fiber/textiles/weaving, film arts, French, German, graphic design, Greek, Hebrew, industrial design, Italian, Japanese, jazz, journalism, Latin, linguistics, literature, media arts, metal/jewelry, music, music history and appreciation, music performance, music theory and composition, musical theater, painting, percussion, performing arts, photography, piano/organ, printmaking, romance languages and literature, Russian, sculpture, Spanish, speech/debate/rhetoric, strings, voice, and winds), COMPUTER AND PHYSICAL SCIENCE (applied mathematics, astronomy, astrophysics, atmospheric sciences and meteorology, chemistry, computer science, geoscience, mathematics, oceanography, physics, and statistics), EDUCATION (art, elementary, music, physical, and secondary), ENGINEERING AND ENVIRONMENTAL DESIGN (aeronautical engineering, architecture, chemical engineering, civil engineering, computer engineering, electrical/electronics engineering, engineering, engineering and applied science, engineering physics, environmental engineering, environmental science, industrial engineering, interior design, landscape architecture/design, materials engineering, materials science, mechanical engineering, naval architecture and marine engineering, and nuclear engineering),

HEALTH PROFESSIONS (biomedical science, dental hygiene, medical technology, nursing, and pharmacy), SOCIAL SCIENCE (African American studies, African studies, American studies, anthropology, archeology, Asian/Oriental studies, biblical languages, biblical studies, biopsychology, classical/ancient civilization, economics, geography, Hispanic American studies, history, humanities, Islamic studies, Judaic studies, Latin American studies, liberal arts/general studies, medieval studies, Middle Eastern studies, Near Eastern studies, philosophy, physical fitness/movement, political science/government, psychology, religion, Russian and Slavic studies, Scandinavian studies, social science, sociology, Western European studies, and women's studies). Classics, English, and political science are the strongest academically. Psychology, engineering, and business administration are the largest.

Required: Academic requirements vary by program. For the College of Literature, Science, and the Arts, most students must fulfill requirements in English (including composition), race and ethnicity (1 course), and foreign language, and must complete 9 semester hours each of humanities, social science, and natural science/math. Students must also meet the quantitative reasoning requirement, designed to ensure proficiency in using and analyzing quantitative information. To graduate, students must complete 120 to 128 semester hours, including 24 to 30 in a major field, with a minimum GPA of 2.0.

Special: A co-op program in engineering and cross-registration with Big Ten institutions and the University of Chicago are available, as are internships, study abroad in some 35 countries, and a Washington semester. B.A.-B.S. degrees, dual and student-designed majors, and a 3-2 engineering degree with several colleges and universities are possible. Interdisciplinary majors are offered in anthropology and zoology, music and technology, natural resources and biometry, materials and metallurgical engineering, materials science and engineering, biopsychology and cognitive science, and social anthropology. Interdisciplinary liberal arts programs offering small group living/learning environments are available in the Residential College and the Lloyd Scholars Program. Also available are Honors College preferred admission to professional programs and a Women in Science Program. There are 21 national honor societies, including Phi Beta Kappa, and a freshman honors program.

Faculty/Classroom: 63% of faculty are male; 37%, female. All both teach and do research. The average class size in a regular course is 29.

Admissions: 53% of the 2003-2004 applicants were accepted. The SAT I scores for the 2003-2004 freshman class were: Verbal--5% below 500, 25% between 500 and 599, 50% between 600 and 700, and 20% above 700; Math--3% below 500, 13% between 500 and 599, 45% between 600 and 700, and 39% above 700. The ACT scores were 3% below 21, 1% between 12 and 17, 9% between 18 and 23, 56% between 24 and 29, and 34% between 30 and 36. 88% of the current freshmen were in the top fifth of their class; 98% were in the top two fifths. There were 76 National Merit finalists in a recent year.

Requirements: The SAT I or ACT is required. In addition, applicants must be graduates of accredited secondary schools or have earned a GED. The university requires 15 academic credits or 20 Carnegie units, including 4 in English, 3 in math (4 for engineering majors), 3 in history and social studies, 2 in foreign language, and 2 in science. The following are recommended electives: 1 unit of hands-on computer study and 1 unit of fine or performing arts. An essay is required for all applicants. Students applying to the School of Art must submit a portfolio; those applying to the School of Music must present an audition. AP and CLEP credits are accepted.

Procedure: Freshmen are admitted to all sessions. Entrance exams should be taken at the end of the junior year or the beginning of the senior year. There is a deferred admissions plan. There is a rolling admissions plan. Applications should be filed by February 1 for fall entry, November 1 for winter entry, February 1 for spring entry, and February 1 for summer entry. Notification is sent on a rolling basis. 4100 applicants were on the 2003 waiting list; none were admitted. The fall 2003 application fee was $40. Applications are accepted on-line through CD-ROM at www.weapply.com, or a PDF application can be downloaded from www.umich.edu/~info/admissions, or on-line at embark.edu.

Transfer: 836 transfer students enrolled in 2002-2003. A minimum college GPA of 3.0 is required for junior-level transfers. 60 of 120 credits required for the bachelor's degree must be completed at UM.

Visiting: There are regularly scheduled orientations for prospective students, including placement testing, academic counseling, course registration, social activities, and informational programs on student life, computing resources, campus safety, and career planning. There are guides for informal visits and visitors may sit in on classes.

Financial Aid: In fall 2002, 69% of all full-time freshmen and 62% of continuing full-time students received some form of financial aid. 43% of full-time freshmen and 40% of continuing full-time students received need-based aid. The average freshman award was $10,461. Need-based scholarships or need-based grants averaged $7324; need-based self-help aid (loans and jobs) averaged $4756; non-need-based athletic scholarships averaged $21,547; and other non-need-based awards and non-need-based scholarships averaged $4728. 42% of undergraduates work part time. Average annual earnings from campus work are $1205. The average financial indebtedness of the 2003 graduate was $19,407. The

FAFSA and tax returns are required. The deadline for filing freshman financial aid applications for fall entry is September 30.

International Students: There are 1058 international students enrolled. They must score 570 on the written TOEFL or 230 on the electronic version or take the MELAB. They must also take the SAT I or the ACT.

Computers: The mainframes are comprised of an IBM system 390 Multiprise 2000 Series Processor, CMOS, Model 2003-135. 2500 PCs are available to members of the university community. The 15 campus computing sites provide networked computers, laser printers, and hundreds of software programs. There are also 15 residence hall sites, 10 computer-equipped classrooms, special multimedia labs, and an adaptive technology computing site for users with disabilities. All resident hall rooms are wired with Ethernet for Internet connectivity. All students may access the system at any time. There are no time limits and no fees.

Graduates: From July 1, 2002 to June 30, 2003, 5939 bachelor's degrees were awarded. The most popular majors were engineering (17%), psychology (10%), and English (6%). In an average class, 2% graduate in 3 years or less, 62% graduate in 4 years or less, 80% graduate in 5 years or less, and 82% graduate in 6 years or less. 999 companies recruited on campus in 2002-2003.

Admissions Contact: Theodore L. Spencer, Director of Admissions. A video is available. E-mail: *ugadmiss@umich.edu*
Web: *www.admissions.umich.edu*

UNIVERSITY OF MICHIGAN/DEARBORN
E-5
Dearborn, MI 48128-1491   (313) 593-5100; Fax: (313) 436-9167

Full-time: 1812 men, 1862 women	**Faculty:** IIA, +$
Part-time: 1184 men, 1501 women	**Ph.D.s:** 88%
Graduate: 1233 men, 987 women	**Student/Faculty:** n/av
Year: semesters, summer session	**Tuition:** $6843 ($15,643)
Application Deadline: open	**Room & Board:** n/app
Freshman Class: 2679 applied, 1785 accepted, 704 enrolled	
SAT I or ACT: required	**VERY COMPETITIVE**

The University of Michigan/Dearborn, founded in 1959, is a public, comprehensive commuter institution that is part of the University of Michigan system. The emphasis of its degree programs is on the liberal arts, management, engineering, and education. There are 4 undergraduate and 4 graduate schools. In addition to regional accreditation, University of Michigan/Dearborn has baccalaureate program accreditation with ABET and NCATE. The library contains 334,620 volumes, 548,011 microform items, and 4593 audio/video tapes/CDs, and subscribes to 1097 periodicals. Computerized library services include the card catalog, interlibrary loans, and database searching. Special learning facilities include a learning resource center, art gallery, natural history museum, radio station, TV station, and a nature preserve, an Armenian research center, a child development center, an engineering education and practice center, and the Henry Ford Estate, a National Historic Landmark. The 196-acre campus is in a suburban area 10 miles from Detroit. There are 20 buildings.

Student Life: 96% of undergraduates are from Michigan. Students are from 16 states, 22 foreign countries, and Canada. 77% are from public schools. 73% are white. The average age of freshmen is 18; all undergraduates, 22.

Housing: There are no residence halls. All students commute. Alcohol is not permitted. All students may keep cars.

Activities: 2% of men and about 1% of women belong to 7 national fraternities; 2% of women belong to 4 national sororities. There are 92 groups on campus, including art, cheerleading, chess, choir, computers, debate, drama, ethnic, film, gay, honors, international, literary magazine, newspaper, pep band, photography, political, professional, radio and TV, religious, social, social service, and student government. Popular campus events include Martin Luther King Diversity Celebration, Native American Pow Wow, and Fallfest.

Sports: There is 1 intercollegiate sport for men and 2 for women, and 21 intramural sports for men and 20 for women. Facilities include a 1200-seat gym, an ice rink, an indoor/outdoor track, a playing field, sand volleyball courts, weight and exercise rooms, and outdoor tennis courts.

Disabled Students: All of the campus is accessible. Wheelchair ramps, elevators, special parking, specially equipped rest rooms, lowered drinking fountains, and lowered telephones are available.

Services: Counseling and information services are available, as is tutoring in most subjects, including science, computer classes, composition, and math. There is a reader service for the blind and remedial math, reading, and writing.

Campus Safety and Security: Measures include 24-hour foot and vehicle patrol, self-defense education, security escort services, and informal discussions. There are pamphlets/posters/films, emergency telephones, lighted pathways/sidewalks, and vehicle etching, Crime Prevention Day, CPR training, and a rape awareness seminar.

Programs of Study: University of Michigan/Dearborn confers B.A., B.S., B.B.A., B.G.S., B.S.A., and B.S.E. degrees. Master's degrees are also awarded. Bachelor's degrees are awarded in BIOLOGICAL SCIENCE (biochemistry, biology/biological science, and microbiology), BUSINESS (business administration and management), COMMUNICATIONS AND THE ARTS (art history and appreciation, arts administration/management, English, languages, and music history and appreciation), COMPUTER AND PHYSICAL SCIENCE (chemistry, computer science, mathematics, physics, and science), EDUCATION (early childhood, elementary, science, secondary, and social studies), ENGINEERING AND ENVIRONMENTAL DESIGN (computer engineering, electrical/electronics engineering, environmental science, industrial engineering, manufacturing engineering, and mechanical engineering), SOCIAL SCIENCE (American studies, anthropology, behavioral science, economics, history, humanities, international studies, liberal arts/general studies, philosophy, political science/government, psychology, social science, and sociology). Electrical engineering and business administration are the strongest academically. Mechanical engineering, prebusiness, and business administration are the largest.

Required: Each college within the university has its own unique requirements. To graduate, students must complete 120 to 128 credit hours.

Special: UMD offers internships, study abroad, work-study and accelerated degree programs, a general studies degree, a dual major in engineering mathematics, student-designed majors, and co-op programs in engineering, business administration, and arts and sciences. Nondegree study and pass/fail options are possible. There is a freshman honors program.

Faculty/Classroom: 68% of faculty are male; 32%, female. The average class size in an introductory lecture is 43 and in a regular course, 28.

Admissions: 67% of the 2003-2004 applicants were accepted. 12 freshmen graduated first in their class in a recent year.

Requirements: The SAT I or ACT is required, with a minimum composite score of 1030 on the SAT I or 22 on the ACT. Other admissions requirements normally include graduation from an accredited secondary school; recommended high school units include 4 years each in math, English, and history, 3 each in science and foreign language, and 1 each in art and information technology. The GED is accepted with a minimum score of 55. An essay and interview are recommended. A GPA of 3.0 is required. AP credits are accepted. Important factors in the admissions decision are advanced placement or honor courses, recommendations by school officials, and leadership record.

Procedure: Freshmen are admitted to all sessions. Entrance exams should be taken in the spring of the junior year or the fall of the senior year. There is a deferred admissions plan. Application deadlines are open, but the priority date is May 1. Notification is sent on a rolling basis beginning September 1.

Transfer: 721 transfer students enrolled in 2003-2004. Applicants are required to have 25 to 30 transferable semester/credit hours; if they have fewer than 25, the SAT I or ACT is mandatory. The required minimum GPA ranges from 2.5 to 3.0, depending on the intended major. 60 of 120 credits required for the bachelor's degree must be completed at University of Michigan/Dearborn.

Visiting: There are regularly scheduled orientations for prospective students, consisting of a tour, a student panel, academic unit introduction, and campus life sessions. There are guides for informal visits and visitors may sit in on classes. To schedule a visit, contact the Admissions Office.

Financial Aid: In 2002-2003, 38% of all full-time freshmen and 39% of continuing full-time students received some form of financial aid. At least 24% of full-time freshmen and at least 35% of continuing full-time students received need-based aid. The average freshman award was $6173. Need-based scholarships or need-based grants averaged $3604; need-based self-help aid (loans and jobs) averaged $2104; non-need-based institutional athletic scholarships averaged $1133; and other non-need-based institutional awards and non-need-based scholarships averaged $2014. 85% of undergraduates work part time. Average annual earnings from campus work are $2000. The average financial indebtedness of the 2003 graduate was $23,753. The FAFSA is required. The priority date for freshman financial aid applications for fall entry is April 1.

International Students: There were 100 international students enrolled in a recent year. They must score 550 on the written TOEFL or 213 on the electronic version, or take the MELAB, or the APIEL exam. The SAT I or ACT is also required.

Computers: There is a minicomputer with 400 networked PCs for students, including IBM PCs, Macs, and Sun models. All students may access the system. There are no time limits and no fees.

Graduates: From July 1, 2002 to June 30, 2003, 1141 bachelor's degrees were awarded. The most popular majors were business/marketing (21%), engineering/engineering technologies (20%), and education (11%). In an average class, 14% graduate in 4 years or less, 42% graduate in 5 years or less, and 54% graduate in 6 years or less.

Admissions Contact: Gabrielle Williams, Assistant Director of Admissions and Orientation. E-mail: *admissions@umd.umich.edu*
Web: *www.umd.umich.edu*

UNIVERSITY OF MICHIGAN/FLINT
Flint, MI 48502-1950

E-4

(810) 762-3300; Fax: (810) 762-3272

Full-time: 1226 men, 2166 women
Part-time: 780 men, 1406 women
Graduate: 234 men, 340 women
Year: semesters, summer session
Application Deadline: September 15
Freshman Class: 1113 applied, 902 accepted, 474 enrolled
ACT: 21

Faculty: 214; IIA, -$
Ph.Ds: 79%
Student/Faculty: 16 to 1
Tuition: $5548 ($10,548)
Room & Board: n/app

COMPETITIVE

The University of Michigan/Flint, established in 1956, is a public institution offering programs in the liberal arts and sciences. There are 4 undergraduate and 5 graduate schools. In addition to regional accreditation, UM-Flint has baccalaureate program accreditation with AACN, AACSB, ACS, CAPTE, CCNE, CSWE, JRCERT, NASM, and NLN. The library contains 304,747 volumes, 668,934 microform items, and 18,063 audio/video tapes/CDs, and subscribes to 1111 periodicals. Computerized library services include the card catalog, interlibrary loans, and database searching. Special learning facilities include a learning resource center, art gallery, and TV station. The 72-acre campus is in an urban area 60 miles northwest of Detroit, 50 miles east of Lansing, and 55 miles north of Ann Arbor. There are 9 buildings.

Student Life: 99% of undergraduates are from Michigan. Students are from 22 states, 18 foreign countries, and Canada. 96% are from public schools. 78% are white; 10% African American. The average age of freshmen is 18; all undergraduates, 26. 44% do not continue beyond their first year; 38% remain to graduate.

Housing: There are no residence halls. There are off-campus apartments. All students commute. Alcohol is not permitted. All students may keep cars.

Activities: 1% of men belong to 1 local and 2 national fraternities; 1% of women belong to 1 local and 4 national sororities. There are 54 groups on campus, including art, band, choir, chorale, chorus, computers, dance, drama, ethnic, gay, honors, jazz band, literary magazine, musical theater, newspaper, political, professional, radio and TV, religious, social, social service, and student government. Popular campus events include Welcome Back Picnic and Wacky Wednesday.

Sports: There are 10 intramural sports for men and 10 for women. Facilities include a recreation building housing a multipurpose gym, racquetball courts, a weight training area, and a swimming pool.

Disabled Students: 97% of the campus is accessible. Wheelchair ramps, elevators, special parking, specially equipped rest rooms, special class scheduling, lowered drinking fountains, lowered telephones, and telephones for the hearing impaired are available. Reasonable accommodations may be made for students with documented disabilities.

Services: Counseling and information services are available, as is tutoring in every subject. There is a reader service for the blind and remedial math, reading, and writing.

Campus Safety and Security: Measures include 24-hour foot and vehicle patrol, self-defense education, security escort services, and informal discussions. There are pamphlets/posters/films, emergency telephones, and lighted pathways/sidewalks.

Programs of Study: UM-Flint confers B.A., B.S., B.A.S., B.B.A., B.F.A., B.G.S., B.Mus.Ed., and B.S.N. degrees. Master's degrees are also awarded. Bachelor's degrees are awarded in BIOLOGICAL SCIENCE (biology/biological science and ecology), BUSINESS (accounting, banking and finance, business administration and management, human resources, and marketing/retailing/merchandising), COMMUNICATIONS AND THE ARTS (communications, dramatic arts, English, French, music, and Spanish), COMPUTER AND PHYSICAL SCIENCE (chemistry, computer science, mathematics, physical sciences, and physics), EDUCATION (early childhood, elementary, foreign languages, music, and secondary), ENGINEERING AND ENVIRONMENTAL DESIGN (engineering), HEALTH PROFESSIONS (environmental health science, health care administration, health science, medical laboratory technology, nursing, physical therapy, and radiation therapy), SOCIAL SCIENCE (anthropology, community psychology, criminal justice, economics, geography, history, philosophy, political science/government, psychology, public administration, social science, social work, sociology, and urban studies). Business and nursing are the strongest academically. Business, education, and health sciences are the largest.

Required: To graduate, all students must complete at least 120 credits, including 30 to 70 in the major along with satisfying all major requirements, and maintain a GPA of 2.0. Distribution requirements total 50 credits in English composition, humanities, fine arts, social science, and natural science.

Special: Special arrangements include co-op programs and dual majors, student-designed majors, cross-registration with Mott Community College, internships, study abroad, work-study, a 3-2 engineering program, an accelerated business degree, a general studies degree, nondegree study, and pass/fail options. There is a chapter of Phi Beta Kappa and a freshman honors program.

Faculty/Classroom: 51% of faculty are male; 49%, female. All both teach and do research. No introductory courses are taught by graduate students. The average class size in an introductory lecture is 25; in a laboratory, 20; and in a regular course, 22.

Admissions: 81% of the 2003-2004 applicants were accepted. The SAT I scores for the 2003-2004 freshman class were: Verbal--22% below 500, 45% between 500 and 599, and 33% between 600 and 700; Math--22% below 500, 33% between 500 and 599, and 45% between 600 and 700. The ACT scores were 42% below 21, 29% between 21 and 23, 18% between 24 and 26, 7% between 27 and 28, and 4% above 28. 42% of the current freshmen were in the top fifth of their class; 71% were in the top two fifths. 2 freshmen graduated first in their class.

Requirements: The SAT I or ACT is required. In addition, with the ACT preferred. Graduation from secondary school is required, with 4 years of English, 3 each of math and social studies, and 2 of science. The GED is accepted. SAT II: Subject tests and an interview are recommended. Applied music students must audition. A GPA of 2.0 is required. AP and CLEP credits are accepted. Important factors in the admissions decision are advanced placement or honors courses, evidence of special talent, and leadership record.

Procedure: Freshmen are admitted to all sessions. Entrance exams should be taken in the spring of the junior year or fall of the senior year. There is a deferred admissions plan. Applications should be filed by September 15 for fall entry and December 15 for winter entry. Notification is sent on a rolling basis. The fall 2003 application fee was $30. Applications are accepted on-line through www.umflint.edu.

Transfer: 1149 transfer students enrolled in 2002-2003. Applicants must have at least 12 college credits and a minimum GPA of 2.0 in transferable courses. An associate degree and an interview are recommended. 45 of 120 credits required for the bachelor's degree must be completed at UM-Flint.

Visiting: There are regularly scheduled orientations for prospective students. There are guides for informal visits and visitors may sit in on classes. To schedule a visit, contact the Admissions Office at admissions@umflint.edu.

Financial Aid: In 2003-2004, 46% of all full-time freshmen and 54% of continuing full-time students received some form of financial aid. 26% of full-time freshmen and 34% of continuing full-time students received need-based aid. The average freshman award was $6325. The FAFSA is required. The deadline for filing freshman financial aid applications for fall entry is March 1.

International Students: There are 21 international students enrolled. They must score 550 on the written TOEFL or 213 on the electronic version or take the MELAB.

Computers: PCs are available with e-mail capabilities. All students may access the system. There are no fees.

Graduates: In a recent year, 892 bachelor's degrees were awarded. The most popular majors were elementary education (21%), business (16%), and health professions (12%). In an average class, 1% graduate in 3 years or less, 10% graduate in 4 years or less, 29% graduate in 5 years or less, and 38% graduate in 6 years or less. 125 companies recruited on campus in 2002-2003. Of the 2002 graduating class, 9% were enrolled in graduate school within 6 months of graduation.

Admissions Contact: Mary Jo Sekelsky, Interim Director of Admissions. E-mail: admissions@list.umich.edu Web: www.flint.umich.edu

WAYNE STATE UNIVERSITY
Detroit, MI 48202

E-5

(313) 577-3577; Fax: (313) 577-7536

Full-time: 11,005 men and women
Part-time: 9143 men and women
Graduate: 12,943 men and women
Year: semesters, summer session
Application Deadline: August 1
Freshman Class: 8477 applied, 5764 accepted, 2866 enrolled
ACT: 20

Faculty: 1689; I, av$
Ph.Ds: 85%
Student/Faculty: 7 to 1
Tuition: $5274 ($11,295)
Room & Board: $6500

COMPETITIVE

Wayne State University, founded in 1868, is a state-supported, nonprofit institution. Primarily a commuter college, it offers a variety of academic and professional programs. Some information in this profile and capsule is approximate. There are 11 undergraduate and 13 graduate schools. In addition to regional accreditation, Wayne State has baccalaureate program accreditation with AACSB, ABET, ABFSE, ACPE, ACS, ADA, AOTA, APTA, ASHLA, CAHEA, CCNE, CSWE, NAACLS, NASM, NCATE, and NLN. The 6 libraries contain 3,323,580 volumes, 3,816,051 microform items, and 71,715 audio/video tapes/CDs, and subscribe to 18,643 periodicals. Computerized library services include the card catalog, database searching, and Internet access. Special learning facilities include a learning resource center, art gallery, natural history museum, planetarium, and TV station. The 203-acre campus is in an urban area 2 miles north of downtown Detroit in the New Center area. There are 97 buildings.

Student Life: 89% of undergraduates are from Michigan. Students are from 42 states, 107 foreign countries, and Canada. 87% are from public schools. 50% are white; 26% African American; 10% foreign nationals. The average age of freshmen is 22; all undergraduates, 26.

Housing: There are no residence halls, but there are coed on-campus apartments. On-campus housing is available on a first-come, first-served basis. 95% of students commute. All students may keep cars.

Activities: 2% of men belong to 8 national fraternities; 2% of women belong to 10 national sororities. There are 114 groups on campus, including band, chess, choir, computers, dance, ethnic, film, forensics, gay, honors, international, jazz band, marching band, newspaper, orchestra, pep band, political, professional, radio and TV, religious, social, social service, student government, symphony, and yearbook. Popular campus events include Student Organization Day, the International Fair, and Detroit Festival of the Arts.

Sports: There are 9 intercollegiate sports for men and 8 for women, and 6 intramural sports for men and 6 for women. Facilities include a phys ed building, a recreation and fitness center, various swimming pools, courts, and soccer and softball fields.

Disabled Students: All of the campus is accessible. Wheelchair ramps, elevators, special parking, specially equipped rest rooms, lowered drinking fountains, lowered telephones, and educational accessibility services are available.

Services: Counseling and information services are available, as is tutoring in every subject. There is a reader service for the blind and remedial math, reading, and writing. Tutorial services are available through centralized counseling or academic departments.

Campus Safety and Security: Measures include 24-hour foot and vehicle patrol, self-defense education, security escort services, and informal discussions. There are pamphlets/posters/films, emergency telephones, and lighted pathways/sidewalks.

Programs of Study: Wayne State confers B.A., B.S., B.A.S., B.F.A., B.I.S., B.Mus., B.P.A., B.S.A.H.S., B.S.C.T., B.S.E.T., B.S.M.S., B.S.N., B.S.W., and B.T.I.S. degrees. Master's and doctoral degrees are also awarded. Bachelor's degrees are awarded in BIOLOGICAL SCIENCE (biology/biological science), BUSINESS (accounting, banking and finance, business economics, funeral home services, labor studies, management information systems, management science, and marketing/retailing/merchandising), COMMUNICATIONS AND THE ARTS (Arabic, art, art history and appreciation, broadcasting, classics, communications, dance, design, dramatic arts, English, film arts, fine arts, German, Italian, journalism, linguistics, music, public relations, Russian, Slavic languages, and Spanish), COMPUTER AND PHYSICAL SCIENCE (chemistry, computer science, geology, information sciences and systems, mathematics, and physics), EDUCATION (art, business, elementary, mathematics, physical, science, special, and technical), ENGINEERING AND ENVIRONMENTAL DESIGN (chemical engineering, civil engineering, computer technology, electrical/electronics engineering, industrial engineering technology, manufacturing technology, mechanical engineering, and mechanical engineering technology), HEALTH PROFESSIONS (nursing, occupational therapy, pharmacy, radiation therapy, and speech pathology/audiology), SOCIAL SCIENCE (African studies, American studies, anthropology, criminal justice, dietetics, economics, food science, French studies, geography, history, international studies, liberal arts/general studies, Mexican-American/Chicano studies, Near Eastern studies, parks and recreation management, peace studies, philosophy, political science/government, psychology, public affairs, social work, sociology, urban studies, and women's studies). Chemistry, biology, and pharmacy are the strongest academically. Elementary education, art, and psychology are the largest.

Required: To graduate, students must complete at least 120 credit hours and have a minimum GPA of 2.0. General Education has 2 components. Students must complete competencies in written communication, math, oral communication, and computer literacy. In addition, students must complete group requirements in natural science, social science, American society and institutions, foreign culture, humanities, and the university and its libraries.

Special: Special academic programs include cross-registration with Macomb University Center, the University of Michigan, and the University of Windsor; internships in business, industry, or communications; study abroad in Germany, Japan, or England; on-campus work-study programs; accelerated degree programs in liberal arts, science, engineering, and nursing; a general studies degree; co-op programs; nondegree study; and limited pass/fail options. The College of Lifelong Learning offers televised, weekend, and evening courses. There is 1 national honor society, including Phi Beta Kappa, a freshman honors program, and 23 departmental honors programs.

Faculty/Classroom: 61% of faculty are male; 39%, female. 62% teach undergraduates, 92% do research, and 54% do both. Graduate students teach 13% of introductory courses. The average class size in an introductory lecture is 100; in a laboratory, 20; and in a regular course, 30.

Admissions: 68% of the 2003-2004 applicants were accepted. 40% of the current freshmen were in the top fifth of their class.

Requirements: The SAT I or ACT is required, with the ACT preferred. If the GPA is below 2.75, the applicant must have composite SAT I scores totaling at least 990 or an ACT score of 21. Admissions requirements include graduation from an accredited secondary school; the GED with an acceptable SAT I or ACT score is also allowable. A GPA of 2.75 is required. AP and CLEP credits are accepted.

Procedure: Freshmen are admitted to all sessions. If necessary, the ACT should be taken in the junior year or the SAT I in the senior year. There is a deferred admissions plan. Applications should be filed by August 1 for fall entry, December 1 for winter entry, April 1 for spring entry, and April 1 for summer entry, along with a $30 fee. Notification is sent on a rolling basis. Applications are accepted on-line through *www.apply.wayne.edu.*

Transfer: 2551 transfer students enrolled in 2002-2003. Applicants must have 30 transferable credit hours with a 3.0 GPA, and an overall minimum GPA of 2.0. 30 of 120 credits required for the bachelor's degree must be completed at Wayne State.

Visiting: There are guides for informal visits and visitors may sit in on classes. To schedule a visit, contact the Office of Admissions.

Financial Aid: In 2003-2004, 58% of all full-time freshmen and 49% of continuing full-time students received some form of financial aid. 40% of full-time freshmen and 34% of continuing full-time students received need-based aid. The average freshman award was $6473. Need-based scholarships or need-based grants averaged $3833; need-based self-help aid (loans and jobs) averaged $2993; non-need-based athletic scholarships averaged $4659; and other non-need-based awards and non-need-based scholarships averaged $4720. 11% of undergraduates work part time. Average annual earnings from campus work are $2786. The average financial indebtedness of the 2003 graduate was $15,457. Wayne State is a member of CSS. The FAFSA, federal tax returns, and W-2s are required. The deadline for filing freshman financial aid applications for fall entry is March 1.

International Students: There are 1074 international students enrolled. The school actively recruits these students. They must score 550 on the written TOEFL or 213 on the electronic version or take the MELAB.

Computers: There are 1000 PCs and Macs available in the libraries, the student union, and academic departments. All students may access the system 24 hours a day. There are no time limits and no fees.

Graduates: From July 1, 2002 to June 30, 2003, 2249 bachelor's degrees were awarded. The most popular majors were elementary education (9%), psychology (7%), and nursing (6%). In an average class, 12% graduate in 3 years or less, 27% graduate in 4 years or less, 37% graduate in 5 years or less, and 42% graduate in 6 years or less. 93 companies recruited on campus in 2002-2003. Of the 2002 graduating class, 36% were enrolled in graduate school within 6 months of graduation and 98% were employed.

Admissions Contact: Susan A. Zwieg, Director of Admissions. E-mail: *admissions@wayne.edu* Web: *www.wayne.edu*

WESTERN MICHIGAN UNIVERSITY   D-5
Kalamazoo, MI 49008

(269) 387-2000
(800) 400-4968; Fax: (269) 387-2096

Full-time: 9892 men, 10,356 women	**Faculty:** I, -$
Part-time: 1453 men, 1608 women	**Ph.D.s:** n/av
Graduate: 2387 men, 3482 women	**Student/Faculty:** 21 to 1
Year: semesters, summer session	**Tuition:** $5535 ($13,048)
Application Deadline: open	**Room & Board:** $6496
Freshman Class: 15,219 applied, 12,532 accepted, 4333 enrolled	
ACT: 22	**COMPETITIVE**

Western Michigan University, founded in 1903, is a public institution offering 254 degree programs in the liberal arts and sciences, aviation, business, education, engineering, fine arts, health and human services, and preprofessional studies. There are 7 undergraduate schools and 1 graduate school. In addition to regional accreditation, WMU has baccalaureate program accreditation with AACSB, ABET, ACOTE, ACS, ADA, ARC-PA, CAA, CSAB, CSWE, FIDER, NASAD, NASM, NASPE, NCATE, and NLN. The 5 libraries contain 2,043,852 volumes, 1,879,076 microform items, and 25,706 audio/video tapes/CDs, and subscribe to 9145 periodicals. Computerized library services include the card catalog, interlibrary loans, and database searching. Special learning facilities include a learning resource center, art gallery, radio station, aviation flight simulators, an electron microscope, a particle accelerator, a paper manufacturing and fiber recovery pilot plant, and a business technology park. The 1200-acre campus is in an urban area 140 miles west of Detroit and 140 miles east of Chicago. Including any residence halls, there are 136 buildings.

Student Life: 76% of undergraduates are from Michigan. Students are from 49 states, 110 foreign countries, and Canada. 85% are white. The average age of freshmen is 18; all undergraduates, 21. 24% do not continue beyond their first year; 53% remain to graduate.

Housing: 6200 students can be accommodated in college housing, which includes single-sex and coed dorms, on-campus apartments, off-campus apartments, married-student housing, fraternity houses, and sorority houses. In addition, there are honors houses, special-interest houses, a health and wellness house, and an international house.. On-campus housing is guaranteed for the freshman year only and is available on a first-come, first-served basis. 77% of students commute. Alcohol is not permitted. All students may keep cars.

Activities: 8% of men belong to 2 local and 17 national fraternities; 8% of women belong to 1 local and 12 national sororities. There are 300 groups on campus, including art, band, cheerleading, chess, choir, chorale, chorus, computers, dance, drama, ethnic, film, gay, honors, international, jazz band, literary magazine, marching band, musical theater, orchestra, pep band, photography, political, professional, radio and TV, religious, social, social service, student government, symphony, and yearbook. Popular campus events include Family Weekend, Into the Streets, and Campus Classic races.

Sports: There are 9 intercollegiate sports for men and 11 for women, and 24 intramural sports for men and 24 for women. Facilities include a recreation center designed as a sports village, which includes a recreational swimming pool, a swirl pool, a weight and fitness room with more than 100 stations, facilities for basketball, floor hockey, and indoor soccer, a climbing wall, baseball/softball infields, a golf driving range, an elevated track for jogging, and facilities for aerobics, archery, badminton, tennis, and volleyball. The field house includes a 5800-seat arena for basketball and volleyball competition and facilities for gymnasts. There is also a 400-meter Olympic model Martin-surface track, a cross-country course, bowling lanes, a video game area, tennis courts, a 30,000-seat stadium, a competition swimming pool, an ice arena, and outdoor baseball, softball, touch football, and soccer fields.

Disabled Students: 85% of the campus is accessible. Wheelchair ramps, elevators, special parking, specially equipped rest rooms, special class scheduling, lowered drinking fountains, lowered telephones, and special housing. A lift-equipped van to take disabled students to classes and adaptive computer equipment are also available.

Services: Counseling and information services are available, as is tutoring in most subjects. There is a reader service for the blind, and remedial math, reading, and writing.

Campus Safety and Security: Measures include 24-hour foot and vehicle patrol, self-defense education, security escort services, and shuttle buses. There are informal discussions, pamphlets/posters/films, emergency telephones, and lighted pathways/sidewalks. There is also a student watch program, Operation Identification, an enhanced telephone system, and a residence hall security system.

Programs of Study: WMU confers B.A., B.S., B.B.A., B.F.A., B.Mus., B.S., B.S.E., B.S.N., and B.S.W. degrees. Master's and doctoral degrees are also awarded. Bachelor's degrees are awarded in AGRICULTURE (environmental studies), BIOLOGICAL SCIENCE (biochemistry and biology/biological science), BUSINESS (accounting, banking and finance, business administration and management, business communications, business economics, human resources, logistics, management information systems, management science, marketing/retailing/merchandising, recreation and leisure services, and tourism), COMMUNICATIONS AND THE ARTS (advertising, art, art history and appreciation, broadcasting, communications, dance, dramatic arts, English, French, German, graphic design, industrial design, jazz, journalism, Latin, media arts, music, music history and appreciation, music performance, music theory and composition, musical theater, public relations, Spanish, telecommunications, and theater design), COMPUTER AND PHYSICAL SCIENCE (chemistry, computer science, digital arts/technology, earth science, geochemistry, geology, geophysics and seismology, hydrology, information sciences and systems, mathematics, physics, and statistics), EDUCATION (art, athletic training, business, elementary, health, home economics, marketing and distribution, music, physical, secondary, special, and vocational), ENGINEERING AND ENVIRONMENTAL DESIGN (aeronautical engineering, aeronautical science, aircraft mechanics, airline piloting and navigation, aviation administration/management, chemical engineering, civil engineering, computer engineering, construction engineering, drafting and design technology, electrical/electronics engineering, engineering management, graphic arts technology, industrial engineering, industrial engineering technology, interior design, manufacturing engineering, manufacturing technology, mechanical engineering, paper and pulp science, and paper engineering), HEALTH PROFESSIONS (biomedical science, community health work, exercise science, health, music therapy, nursing, occupational therapy, predentistry, premedicine, and speech pathology/audiology), SOCIAL SCIENCE (African studies, American studies, anthropology, criminal justice, dietetics, economics, family/consumer studies, food production/management/services, geography, gerontology, history, interdisciplinary studies, international studies, philosophy, political science/government, prelaw, psychology, public administration, religion, social work, sociology, textiles and clothing, and women's studies). Marketing, finance and commercial law, and education are the largest.

Required: Students must complete 122 semester hours, including 35 of general education courses and a minimum of 24 in the major. A minimum GPA of 2.0 is required. Students must complete courses in science, social science, humanities, and fine arts, and 1 course in non-Western world study. Comprehensive exams are required in some departments. All students must complete 2 semester hours of phys ed and demonstrate computer literacy.

Special: Cross-registration is available through the Kalamazoo Consortium. Opportunities are provided for internships in occupational and music therapy, teaching, business, history, and engineering. Also available

are work-study programs, student-designed majors, pass/fail options, and credit by exam. Students may study abroad in more than 65 countries on 4 continents. There are 29 national honor societies, including Phi Beta Kappa, a freshman honors program, and 6 departmental honors programs.

Faculty/Classroom: 57% of faculty are male; 43%, female.

Admissions: 82% of the 2003-2004 applicants were accepted. The ACT scores for the 2003-2004 freshman class were: 36% below 21, 31% between 21 and 23, 21% between 24 and 26, 8% between 27 and 28, and 5% above 28. 35% of the current freshmen were in the top fifth of their class; 73% were in the top two fifths.

Requirements: The ACT is required. In addition, applicants must submit an official high school transcript. An audition is required for music majors. An interview may be recommended. The College of Fine Arts requires an audition, portfolio, or interview of all applicants. A GPA of 2.0 is required. AP and CLEP credits are accepted. Important factors in the admissions decision are advanced placement or honor courses, extracurricular activities record, and recommendations by school officials.

Procedure: Freshmen are admitted to all sessions. Entrance exams should be taken late in the junior year or early in the senior year. There is a deferred and a rolling admissions plan. Application deadlines are open. Application fee is $25. Applications are accepted on-line through the university's web site.

Transfer: 1734 transfer students enrolled in 2002-2003. Applicants must have a minimum GPA of 2.0 in transferable college courses. Consideration will also be given to the trend of grades and recent course work. 30 of 122 credits required for the bachelor's degree must be completed at WMU.

Visiting: There are regularly scheduled orientations for prospective students, including an admission presentation, departmental advising, lunch, and a campus tour. Visitors may sit in on classes and stay overnight. To schedule a visit, contact the campus visit coordinator at (616) 387-2289.

Financial Aid: In 2003-2004, 68% of all full-time freshmen and 69% of continuing full-time students received some form of financial aid. 78% of full-time freshmen and 66% of continuing full-time students received need-based aid. The average freshman award was $14,500. Need-based scholarships or need-based grants averaged $4300 ($8300 maximum); need-based self-help aid (loans and jobs) averaged $2480 ($6425 maximum); non-need-based athletic scholarships averaged $6400 ($14,500 maximum); and other non-need-based awards and non-need-based scholarships averaged $7300 ($14,500 maximum). 27% of undergraduates work part time. Average annual earnings from campus work are $4211. The average financial indebtedness of the 2003 graduate is $16,100. The FAFSA is required. The priority date for freshman financial aid applications for fall entry is February 15. The deadline for filing freshman financial aid applications for fall entry is April 1.

International Students: There are 633 international students enrolled. The school actively recruits these students. They must score 550 on the written TOEFL or take the MELAB.

Computers: The mainframes are a DEC VAX 7620 and an IBM 3090/300J. The mainframe is used for institutional and research purposes as well as for course work. About 2000 workstations are available in classroom buildings, dorms, and the student center. A Sun operating system is networked in labs for student use. All students may access the system 24 hours a day. Time limits are set individually by class. There are no fees.

Graduates: From July 1, 2002 to June 30, 2003, 4208 bachelor's degrees were awarded. The most popular majors were education (20%), marketing (10%), and finance (5%). In an average class, 18% graduate in 4 years or less, 45% graduate in 5 years or less, and 53% graduate in 6 years or less. 351 companies recruited on campus in 2002-2003.

Admissions Contact: John Fraire, Dean, Admissions and Orientation. E-mail: *ask-wmu@wmich.edu* Web: *http://www.wmich.edu/*

WILLIAM TYNDALE COLLEGE   E-5
Farmington Hills, MI 48331-3147   (248) 553-7200
(800) 483-0707; Fax: (248) 553-5963

Full-time: 62 men, 59 women	**Faculty:** 6
Part-time: 94 men, 75 women	**Ph.D.s:** 40%
Graduate: none	**Student/Faculty:** 20 to 1
Year: semesters, summer session	**Tuition:** $8650
Application Deadline: open	**Room & Board:** $3520
Freshman Class: 19 applied, 19 accepted, 19 enrolled	
ACT: 23	**NONCOMPETITIVE**

William Tyndale College, established in 1945, is a Christian liberal arts college offering undergraduate degrees in Christian studies, humanities and social sciences, math and natural sciences, and professional studies. The library contains 50,000 volumes and 300 audio/video tapes/CDs, and subscribes to 230 periodicals. Computerized library services include the card catalog, interlibrary loans, database searching, and Internet access. The 28-acre campus is in a suburban area 15 miles west of Detroit. Including any residence halls, there are 2 buildings.

Student Life: 96% of undergraduates are from Michigan. Students are from 5 states, 10 foreign countries, and Canada. 73% are from public schools. 64% are white; 32% African American. 76% are Protestant; 22% claim no religious affiliation. The average age of freshmen is 28; all undergraduates, 32. 34% do not continue beyond their first year.

Housing: 54 students can be accommodated in college housing, which includes coed dorms. On-campus housing is available on a first-come, first-served basis. Priority is given to out-of-town students. 85% of students commute. Alcohol is not permitted. All students may keep cars.

Activities: There are no fraternities or sororities. There are 9 groups on campus, including choir, drama, honors, international, newspaper, religious, social, social service, and student government. Popular campus events include New Student Retreat, Senior Banquet, and Billy T's Coffee House.

Sports: There is 1 intramural sport for men and 1 for women. Facilities include a soccer field and access to local school gyms.

Disabled Students: All of the campus is accessible. Wheelchair ramps, elevators, special parking, specially equipped rest rooms, lowered drinking fountains, and lowered telephones are available.

Services: Counseling and information services are available, as is tutoring in every subject. There is remedial math, reading, and writing.

Campus Safety and Security: Measures include lighted pathways/sidewalks.

Programs of Study: Tyndale confers B.A., B.B.A., B.Mus., and B.R.E. degrees. Associate degrees are also awarded. Bachelor's degrees are awarded in BUSINESS (business administration and management), COMMUNICATIONS AND THE ARTS (communications, English, music, and music performance), SOCIAL SCIENCE (biblical studies, Christian studies, history, pastoral studies, psychology, religious music, social science, theological studies, and youth ministry). Business administration, Christian thought, and psychology are the largest.

Required: Students must complete 120 credits, with at least 30 in the major, and maintain a minimum GPA of 2.0. Special curriculum requirements include 28 hours of social and natural sciences, 27 hours of humanities, and 24 of Christian thought.

Special: Internships in youth studies and pastoral studies majors are available. An accelerated degree program in business administration allows students to complete a B.B.A. degree in 19 months attending class once a week. Dual majors in music/youth are offered. There are 2 national honor societies.

Faculty/Classroom: 59% of faculty are male; 41%, female. All teach undergraduates. The average class size in an introductory lecture is 18.

Admissions: All of the 2003-2004 applicants were accepted. The ACT scores for the 2003-2004 freshman class were: 33% below 21, 33% between 21 and 23, 17% between 24 and 26, and 17% above 28. 60% of the current freshmen were in the top fifth of their class; 80% were in the top two fifths.

Requirements: The ACT is required with a minimum composite score of 18. Graduation from an accredited secondary school is required; the GED is accepted. Music majors must audition. In addition, home-schooled students must provide writing samples, a recommendation, and an interview; business administration students must submit an essay. A GPA of 2.0 is required. AP and CLEP credits are accepted. Important factors in the admissions decision are advanced placement or honor courses, leadership record, and parents or siblings attending the school.

Procedure: Freshmen are admitted to all sessions. Entrance exams should be taken in the senior year. There is a deferred admissions plan. Application deadlines are open. Applications are accepted on-line.

Transfer: 110 transfer students enrolled in a recent year. Transfer students must have a GPA of 2.0 for college work. A high school transcript is required if they have fewer than 30 college credits. 45 of 120 credits required for the bachelor's degree must be completed at Tyndale.

Visiting: There are regularly scheduled orientations for prospective students, including an overview of academic programs, student life, campus activities, financial aid, registration, and advising. There are guides for informal visits and visitors may sit in on classes and stay overnight. To schedule a visit, contact the Admissions Counselor, Office of Admissions at admissions@williamtyndale.edu.

Financial Aid: In 2003-2004, 83% of all full-time freshmen and 80% of continuing full-time students received some form of financial aid. 63% of full-time freshmen and 60% of continuing full-time students received need-based aid. The average freshman award was $5177. Need-based scholarships or need-based grants averaged $3941 ($8196 maximum); need-based self-help aid (loans and jobs) averaged $3905 ($6939 maximum); and non-need-based awards and non-need-based scholarships averaged $2794 ($6000 maximum). 5% of undergraduates work part time. Average annual earnings from campus work are $1963. Tyndale is a member of CSS. The FAFSA and the college's own financial statement are required. The priority date for freshman financial aid applications for fall entry is February 21. The deadline for filing freshman financial aid applications for fall entry is May 1.

International Students: The school actively recruits these students. They must score 525 on the written TOEFL.

Computers: The mainframes are a Novell server and an NT 4.0 server. There is a computer lab for students and faculty. All students may access the system 7 A.M. to 10 P.M. Monday through Saturday. There are no time limits and no fees. It is strongly recommended that all students have a personal computer. A Dell Optiplex desktop or Dell Dimension laptop is recommended.

Graduates: From July 1, 2002 to June 30, 2003, 151 bachelor's degrees were awarded.

Admissions Contact: Fred A. Schebor, Vice President for Enrollment Management. E-mail: faschebor@williamtyndale.edu
Web: www.williamtyndale.edu

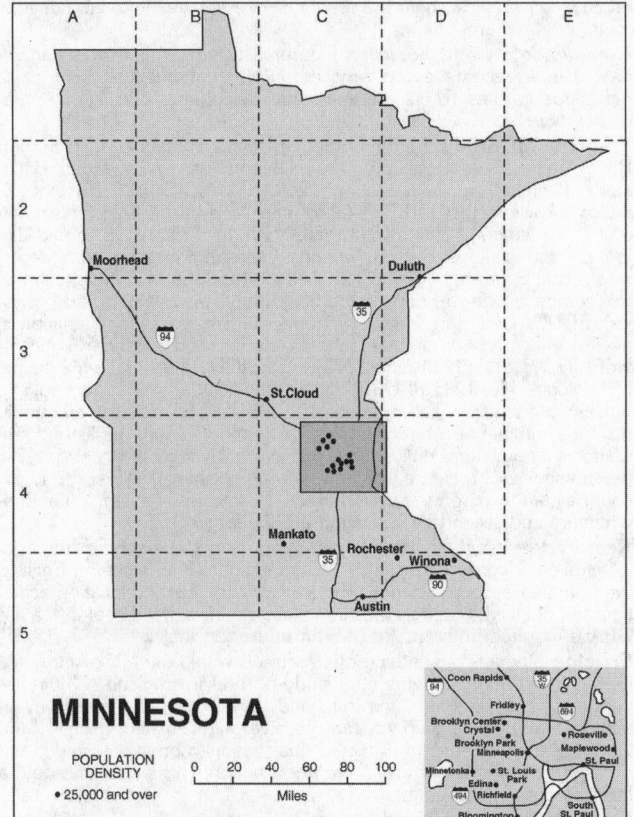

MINNESOTA

POPULATION
DENSITY
• 25,000 and over

0 20 40 60 80 100
Miles

AUGSBURG COLLEGE

Minneapolis, MN 55454

C-4

(612) 330-1001
(800) 788-5678; Fax: (612) 330-1590

Full-time: 1001 men, 1325 women	**Faculty:** 156; IIB, -$
Part-time: 194 men, 341 women	**Ph.D.s:** n/av
Graduate: 74 men, 237 women	**Student/Faculty:** 15 to 1
Year: semesters, summer session	**Tuition:** $19,398
Application Deadline: May 1	**Room & Board:** $5900
Freshman Class: 883 applied, 723 accepted, 348 enrolled	
SAT I Verbal/Math: 541/542	**ACT:** 23 **COMPETITIVE**

Augsburg College, established in 1869, is a private liberal arts institution affiliated with the Evangelical Lutheran Church in America. In addition to regional accreditation, Augsburg has baccalaureate program accreditation with CSWE, NASM, NCATE, and NLN. The library contains 182,289 volumes, 21,355 microform items, and 3477 audio/video tapes/CDs, and subscribes to 686 periodicals. Computerized library services include the card catalog, interlibrary loans, and database searching. Special learning facilities include a learning resource center, art gallery, radio station, and TV station. The 23-acre campus is in an urban area in Minneapolis. Including any residence halls, there are 25 buildings.

Student Life: 87% of undergraduates are from Minnesota. Students are from 44 states, 29 foreign countries, and Canada. 65% are white. 50% are Protestant; 30% claim no religious affiliation; 17% Catholic. The average age of freshmen is 19; all undergraduates, 26. 20% do not continue beyond their first year.

Housing: 949 students can be accommodated in college housing, which includes coed dorms, on-campus apartments, and married-student housing. In addition, there are special-interest houses. On-campus housing is available on a first-come, first-served basis and is available on a lottery system for upperclassmen. Priority is given to out-of-town students. 55% of students live on campus; of those, 60% remain on campus on weekends. All students may keep cars.

Activities: There are no fraternities or sororities. There are 40 groups on campus, including art, band, cheerleading, choir, chorus, dance, drama, ethnic, gay, honors, international, jazz band, literary magazine, newspaper, orchestra, pep band, political, professional, radio and TV, religious, social, social service, student government, and yearbook. Popular campus events include Days in May, Spring Affair, and Advent Vespers.

Sports: There are 9 intercollegiate sports for men and 7 for women, and 4 intramural sports for men and 4 for women. Facilities include a 1500-seat sports field, a 2800-seat gym, tennis courts, a double-rink ice arena, and a domed field facility for winter.

Disabled Students: 92% of the campus is accessible. Wheelchair ramps, elevators, special parking, specially equipped rest rooms, special class scheduling, lowered drinking fountains, and lowered telephones are available.

Services: Counseling and information services are available, as is tutoring in every subject. There is a reader service for the blind, remedial math and writing, taped textbooks, and adaptive computer technology, including a text scanner, speaking software, a touch tablet, and text magnification software.

Campus Safety and Security: Measures include 24-hour foot and vehicle patrol, self-defense education, security escort services, and informal discussions. There are pamphlets/posters/films, emergency telephones, and lighted pathways/sidewalks.

Programs of Study: Augsburg confers B.A., B.S., and B.M. degrees. Master's degrees are also awarded. Bachelor's degrees are awarded in BIOLOGICAL SCIENCE (biology/biological science), BUSINESS (accounting, business administration and management, international business management, management information systems, and marketing/retailing/merchandising), COMMUNICATIONS AND THE ARTS (art history and appreciation, communications, dramatic arts, English, French, German, music, Scandinavian languages, Spanish, speech/debate/rhetoric, and studio art), COMPUTER AND PHYSICAL SCIENCE (chemistry, computer science, mathematics, and physics), EDUCATION (elementary, health, music, physical, and secondary), HEALTH PROFESSIONS (music therapy), SOCIAL SCIENCE (East Asian studies, economics, history, international relations, philosophy, political science/government, psychology, religion, Russian and Slavic studies, Scandinavian studies, social work, sociology, urban studies, and women's studies). Physics, chemistry, and English are the strongest academically. Business, communication, and education are the largest.

Required: To graduate, all students must have a minimum GPA of 2.0 and a total of 32 course credits, with 10 to 15 in the major. They must complete 15 courses from 8 Perspective areas, and first-year fall orientation and seminar. Students must also satisfy entry-level and graduation skills requirements in writing, critical thinking, math, quantitative reasoning, and speaking and demonstrate proficiency in 2 sports.

Special: Special academic programs include internships and co-op programs in business, government, and nonprofit and community-based organizations, a Washington semester, and study abroad in Europe, Latin America, and Africa. There are student-designed majors, cross-registration through the Associated Colleges of the Twin Cities (ACTC), dual and 3-2 engineering degrees with Washington University, Michigan Technological University, and the University of Minnesota, and pre-professional programs in dentistry, law, medicine, physical therapy, pharmacy, theology, and veterinary medicine. Credit for previous learning experience may be granted, and pass/fail options are possible. There is 1 national honor society and a freshman honors program.

Faculty/Classroom: 50% of faculty are male; 50%, female. 99% teach undergraduates. No introductory courses are taught by graduate students. The average class size in an introductory lecture is 20; in a laboratory, 16; and in a regular course, 16.

Admissions: 82% of the 2003-2004 applicants were accepted. The SAT I scores for the 2003-2004 freshman class were: Verbal--18% below 500, 42% between 500 and 599, 35% between 600 and 700, and 5% above 700; Math--15% below 500, 55% between 500 and 599, 25% between 600 and 700, and 5% above 700. The ACT scores were 27% below 21, 30% between 21 and 23, 24% between 24 and 26, 10% between 27 and 28, and 9% above 28. 30% of the current freshmen were in the top fifth of their class; 61% were in the top two fifths. 8 freshmen graduated first in their class.

Requirements: The SAT I or ACT is required, with minimum scores of 430 (verbal) and 430 (math) on the SAT I or 20 on the ACT. Admissions requirements include graduation from an accredited secondary school, with 4 years of English. The GED is also accepted. An essay is required, and an interview is recommended. Augsburg requires applicants to be in the upper 50% of their class. A GPA of 2.5 is required. AP and CLEP credits are accepted. Important factors in the admissions decision are advanced placement or honor courses, leadership record, and recommendations by school officials.

Procedure: Freshmen are admitted fall and spring. Entrance exams should be taken during the fall of the senior year in high school. There is a deferred admissions plan. Early decision applications should be filed by December 15; regular applications, by May 1 for fall entry and December 1 for spring entry. The fall 2003 application fee was $25. Notification is sent on a rolling basis.

Transfer: 345 transfer students enrolled in 2002-2003. Applicants must have a minimum GPA of 2.2 in college course work. 9 of 32 credits required for the bachelor's degree must be completed at Augsburg.

Visiting: There are regularly scheduled orientations for prospective students, including admissions interviews and campus tours. Students may also arrange to meet with professors and coaches and to attend lectures. There are guides for informal visits and visitors may sit in on classes and stay overnight. To schedule a visit, contact the Admissions Office at admissions@augsburg.edu.

Financial Aid: In 2003-2004, 88% of all full-time freshmen and 79% of continuing full-time students received some form of financial aid. 72% of full-time freshmen and 65% of continuing full-time students received need-based aid. The average freshman award was $24,150. 44% of undergraduates work part time. Average annual earnings from campus work are $1710. The average financial indebtedness of the 2003 graduate was $24,546. Augsburg is a member of CSS. The FAFSA and the college's own financial statement are required. The priority date for freshman financial aid applications for fall entry is April 15.

International Students: There are 62 international students enrolled. The school actively recruits these students. They must score 550 on the written TOEFL or 213 on the electronic version or take the MELAB.

Computers: The mainframe is an IBM AS400. All residential students have Internet access in their rooms via one of the 1320 network jacks located in the residence halls. There are 3792 jacks total all over campus, and there are more than 260 public computers in classrooms and labs available for all students. All students may access the system. There are no time limits and no fees.

Graduates: From July 1, 2002 to June 30, 2003, 453 bachelor's degrees were awarded. The most popular majors were business/marketing (28%), education (14%), and social sciences and history (11%). In an average class, 1% graduate in 3 years or less, 35% graduate in 4 years or less, 49% graduate in 5 years or less, and 51% graduate in 6 years or less. 65 companies recruited on campus in 2002-2003. Of the 2002 graduating class, 13% were enrolled in graduate school within 6 months of graduation and 85% were employed.

Admissions Contact: Sally Daniels, Director of Admissions.
E-mail: *daniels@augsburg.edu* Web: *www.augsburg.edu*

BEMIDJI STATE UNIVERSITY
Bemidji, MN 56601-2699

B-2

(218) 755-2040
(800) 475-2001; Fax: (218) 755-2074

Full-time: 1718 men, 1735 women	**Faculty:** IIB, +$
Part-time: 477 men, 742 women	**Ph.D.s:** n/av
Graduate: 136 men, 211 women	**Student/Faculty:** n/av
Year: semesters, summer session	**Tuition:** $5049 ($9911)
Application Deadline: open	**Room & Board:** $4054

Freshman Class: 1542 applied, 1134 accepted, 677 enrolled
ACT: 22
COMPETITIVE

Bemidji State University, founded in 1919, is a public liberal arts university. There are 3 undergraduate schools and 1 graduate school. In addition to regional accreditation, Bemidji State University has baccalaureate program accreditation with CSWE, NASM, and NLN. The library contains 190,000 volumes, 721,255 microform items, and 2500 audio/video tapes/CDs, and subscribes to 907 periodicals. Computerized library services include the card catalog, interlibrary loans, and database searching. Special learning facilities include a learning resource center, art gallery, radio station, and TV station. The 89-acre campus is in a small town 220 miles northwest of Minneapolis. Including any residence halls, there are 21 buildings.

Student Life: 88% of undergraduates are from Minnesota. Students are from 46 states, 34 foreign countries, and Canada. 95% are from public schools. 89% are white. The average age of freshmen is 20; all undergraduates, 25. 29% do not continue beyond their first year; 43% remain to graduate.

Housing: 1700 students can be accommodated in college housing, which includes single-sex and coed dorms and on-campus apartments. In addition, there are special-interest houses and single-parent apartments. On-campus housing is available on a first-come, first-served basis. 68% of students commute. Alcohol is not permitted. All students may keep cars.

Activities: 2% of men belong to 2 national fraternities; 1% of women belong to 1 national sorority. There are 80 groups on campus, including art, band, cheerleading, choir, chorus, computers, dance, drama, ethnic, gay, honors, international, jazz band, literary magazine, musical theater, newspaper, opera, orchestra, pep band, political, professional, radio and TV, religious, social, social service, and student government. Popular campus events include Funtastic Dance Follies, madrigal music, and plays and concerts.

Sports: There are 7 intercollegiate sports for men and 7 for women, and 7 intramural sports for men and 4 for women. Facilities include a basketball gym, an Olympic-size pool, a hockey arena, a football stadium, indoor and outdoor tracks, baseball and softball fields, tennis, racquetball, and handball courts, weight rooms, and a dance studio.

Disabled Students: 95% of the campus is accessible. Wheelchair ramps, elevators, special parking, specially equipped rest rooms, lowered drinking fountains, and lowered telephones are available.

Services: Counseling and information services are available, as is tutoring in every subject. There is a reader service for the blind and remedial math, reading, and writing.

Campus Safety and Security: Measures include 24-hour foot and vehicle patrol, security escort services, informal discussions, and pamphlets/posters/films. There are emergency telephones and lighted pathways/sidewalks.

Programs of Study: Bemidji State University confers B.A., B.S., and B.F.A. degrees. Associate and master's degrees are also awarded. Bachelor's degrees are awarded in BIOLOGICAL SCIENCE (biology/biological science), BUSINESS (accounting and business administration and management), COMMUNICATIONS AND THE ARTS (broadcasting, communications, English, fine arts, German, journalism, languages, music, and Spanish), COMPUTER AND PHYSICAL SCIENCE (chemistry, computer science, earth science, geology, mathematics, and physics), EDUCATION (art, early childhood, elementary, foreign languages, health, industrial arts, middle school, science, and secondary), ENGINEERING AND ENVIRONMENTAL DESIGN (industrial engineering technology), HEALTH PROFESSIONS (medical laboratory technology, nursing, predentistry, and premedicine), SOCIAL SCIENCE (community services, criminal justice, economics, geography, history, parks and recreation management, philosophy, political science/government, prelaw, psychology, social science, social work, and sociology). Nursing and accounting are the strongest academically. Business administration and elementary and secondary education are the largest.

Required: All students must complete at least 128 semester hours, of which 42 are general education, including courses in freshman English, the humanities, social science, physical science, liberal education activities, and phys ed. Students must maintain a minimum GPA of 2.0; a 2.3 GPA is required in the major (2.5 for education majors).

Special: Students may attend other schools within the Minnesota State University system. Students may study abroad in England, China, Japan, and Malaysia. Paid internships and work-study programs are available in many fields. Students may receive credit for life, military, and work experience. Student-designed dual majors, nondegree study, and pass/fail options are offered. There are 2 national honor societies and a freshman honors program.

Faculty/Classroom: Graduate students teach 1% of introductory courses. The average class size in an introductory lecture is 35; in a laboratory, 20; and in a regular course, 23.

Admissions: 74% of the 2003-2004 applicants were accepted. The ACT scores for the 2003-2004 freshman class were: 27% below 21, 47% between 21 and 23, 20% between 24 and 26, and 6% between 27 and 28. 31% of the current freshmen were in the top fifth of their class; 64% were in the top two fifths.

Requirements: The ACT is required. In addition, applicants must have a minimum high school rank of 50% or a composite score of 21 on the ACT. They should have had 4 years of English and 3 years each of math, science, and social studies. AP and CLEP credits are accepted. Important factors in the admissions decision are recommendations by school officials, advanced placement or honor courses, and extracurricular activities record.

Procedure: Freshmen are admitted to all sessions. Entrance exams should be taken during the junior year. There is a deferred admissions plan. Application deadlines are open. Application fee is $20. Notification is sent on a rolling basis.

Transfer: 450 transfer students enrolled in 2002-2003. Applicants must have a minimum GPA of 2.0. 32 of 128 credits required for the bachelor's degree must be completed at Bemidji State University.

Visiting: There are regularly scheduled orientations for prospective students, including an interview with an admissions counselor, a tour of the campus, and visits with faculty. There are guides for informal visits and visitors may sit in on classes and stay overnight. To schedule a visit, contact the Admissions Office at (888) 345-1721.

Financial Aid: In 2003-2004, 78% of all full-time freshmen and 79% of continuing full-time students received some form of financial aid. 68% of full-time freshmen and 72% of continuing full-time students received need-based aid. The average freshman award was $5120. 35% of undergraduates work part time. Average annual earnings from campus work are $1950. The average financial indebtedness of the 2003 graduate was $12,400. The FAFSA and the college's own financial statement are required. The priority date for freshman financial aid applications for fall entry is May 15. The deadline for filing freshman financial aid applications is no later than 2 months prior to the start of the term.

International Students: There are 150 international students enrolled. The school actively recruits these students. They must score 550 on the written TOEFL.

Computers: The mainframes are a DEC VAX 785 and a Sperry UNIVAC 1180. There are PC labs and 135 terminals in various campus locations. There are approximately 35 mainframe access terminals in 4 locations. All residence hall rooms are connected to the network. All students may access the system 24 hours a day on campus; 18 hours a day in other locations. There are no time limits. The fee is $1 per credit.

Graduates: From July 1, 2002 to June 30, 2003, 741 bachelor's degrees were awarded. 45 companies recruited on campus in 2002-2003.

Admissions Contact: Paul Muller, Associate Director, Admissions. A video is available. E-mail: *admissions@bemidjistate.edu* Web: *www.bemidjistate.edu*

BETHEL COLLEGE
C-4
St. Paul, MN 55112
(651) 638-6242
(800) 255-8706; Fax: (651) 635-1490

Full-time: 1019 men, 1572 women	**Faculty:** 165; IIB, av$
Part-time: 112 men, 208 women	**Ph.D.s:** 72%
Graduate: 101 men, 291 women	**Student/Faculty:** 16 to 1
Year: 4-1-4, summer session	**Tuition:** $18,800
Application Deadline: December 1	**Room & Board:** $6,380
Freshman Class: 1631 applied, 1370 accepted, 691 enrolled	
SAT I Verbal/Math: 585/585	**ACT:** 24 **VERY COMPETITIVE**

Bethel College, established in 1871, is a private liberal arts college affiliated with the Baptist General Conference. In addition to regional accreditation, Bethel has baccalaureate program accreditation with CSWE, NCATE, and NLN. The library contains 158,886 volumes, 178,650 microform items, and 12,204 audio/video tapes/CDs, and subscribes to 970 periodicals. Computerized library services include the card catalog, interlibrary loans, database searching, and Internet access. Special learning facilities include a learning resource center, art gallery, radio station, and TV station. The 231-acre campus is in a suburban area 10 miles north of Minneapolis/St. Paul. Including any residence halls, there are 14 buildings.

Student Life: 73% of undergraduates are from Minnesota. Students are from 40 states, 17 foreign countries, and Canada. 94% are white. Most are Protestant. The average age of freshmen is 18; all undergraduates, 21. 18% do not continue beyond their first year; 70% remain to graduate.

Housing: 1982 students can be accommodated in college housing, which includes single-sex dorms, on-campus apartments, and off-campus apartments. In addition, there are townhouses. On-campus housing is available on a first-come, first-served basis and is available on a lottery system for upperclassmen. 71% of students live on campus. Alcohol is not permitted. Upperclassmen may keep cars.

Activities: There are no fraternities or sororities. There are 37 groups on campus, including art, band, cheerleading, choir, chorale, chorus, debate, drama, ethnic, film, forensics, honors, international, jazz band, literary magazine, musical theater, newspaper, orchestra, pep band, political, professional, radio and TV, religious, social, social service, and student government. Popular campus events include Snow Daze, Royal Cup Competition, and Spring Festival.

Sports: There are 9 intercollegiate sports for men and 8 for women, and 12 intramural sports for men and 12 for women. Facilities include a gym, an indoor recreation center, with 1/8-mile track and 4 multipurpose courts, weight room, racquetball courts, soccer fields, tennis courts, and a football, baseball, and softball stadium.

Disabled Students: 99% of the campus is accessible. Wheelchair ramps, elevators, special parking, specially equipped rest rooms, special class scheduling, lowered drinking fountains, and lowered telephones are available.

Services: Counseling and information services are available, as is tutoring in most subjects. There is a reader service for the blind. An academic enrichment and support center offers tutoring, a writing lab, and time management and study skills workshops.

Campus Safety and Security: Measures include 24-hour foot and vehicle patrol, security escort services, shuttle buses, and pamphlets/posters/films. There are emergency telephones and lighted pathways/sidewalks.

Programs of Study: Bethel confers B.A., B.S., B.Mus., B.Mus.Ed., and B.S.N. degrees. Associate and master's degrees are also awarded. Bachelor's degrees are awarded in BIOLOGICAL SCIENCE (biochemistry and biology/biological science), BUSINESS (accounting, banking and finance, business administration and management, and marketing/retailing/merchandising), COMMUNICATIONS AND THE ARTS (communications, dramatic arts, English, fine arts, multimedia, music, Spanish, and speech/debate/rhetoric), COMPUTER AND PHYSICAL SCIENCE (chemistry, computer science, mathematics, and physics), EDUCATION (art, athletic training, business, early childhood, elementary, foreign languages, health, mathematics, music, physical, science, and secondary), ENGINEERING AND ENVIRONMENTAL DESIGN (engineering and applied science and environmental science), HEALTH PROFESSIONS (nursing), SOCIAL SCIENCE (economics, ethnic studies, history, international relations, philosophy, political science/government, psychology, religion, social work, and youth ministry). Physical sciences, life sciences, and computer science are the strongest academically. Education, business, and biology are the largest.

Required: Students must complete a minimum of 122 semester credit hours, with 30 to 60 in the major and 50 to 51 in general education. Specific general education courses include introduction to the Bible, Christianity and Western culture, college writing, creativity in fine arts, and physical wellness. An overall GPA of 2.0 and a GPA of 2.25 in the major are needed.

Special: Students may arrange internships, study abroad in various countries, participate in a Washington semester with the Christian College Coalition, and select various work-study programs. Dual majors in cross-cultural studies are available. Students may design their own majors, earn a 3-2 engineering degree, and select limited pass/fail options. An adult degree completion program is offered. There are 2 national honor societies and a freshman honors program. All departments have honors programs.

Faculty/Classroom: 57% of faculty are male; 43%, female. All teach undergraduates. No introductory courses are taught by graduate students. The average class size in an introductory lecture is 40; in a laboratory, 20; and in a regular course, 35.

Admissions: 84% of the 2003-2004 applicants were accepted. The SAT I scores for the 2003-2004 freshman class were: Verbal--20% below 500, 37% between 500 and 599, 26% between 600 and 700, and 17% above 700; Math--16% below 500, 35% between 500 and 599, 38% between 600 and 700, and 11% above 700. The ACT scores were 18% below 21, 28% between 21 and 23, 24% between 24 and 26, 15% between 27 and 28, and 15% above 28. 50% of the current freshmen were in the top fifth of their class; 78% were in the top two fifths. There were 9 National Merit finalists and 3 semifinalists. 30 freshmen graduated first in their class.

Requirements: The SAT I or ACT is required. The PSAT is accepted. In addition, applicants must be graduates of an accredited secondary school or have a GED. An interview is recommended. Bethel requires applicants to be in the upper 50% of their class. AP and CLEP credits are accepted. Important factors in the admissions decision are advanced placement or honor courses, extracurricular activities record, and personality/intangible qualities.

Procedure: Freshmen are admitted fall, winter, and spring. Entrance exams should be taken in the spring of the junior year. There is an early admissions plan. Applications should be filed by December 1 for fall entry, November 1 for winter entry, and December 1 for spring entry, along with a $25 fee. Notification is sent January 15. 275 applicants were on the 2003 waiting list. Applications are accepted on-line through College-NET and at *www.bethel.edu/college/admissions*.

Transfer: 150 transfer students enrolled in 2002-2003. Applicants must have a minimum GPA of 2.5 and must submit all college transcripts. 28 of 122 credits required for the bachelor's degree must be completed at Bethel.

Visiting: There are regularly scheduled orientations throughout the school year for prospective students. There are guides for informal visits and visitors may sit in on classes and stay overnight. To schedule a visit, contact the Admissions Office.

Financial Aid: In 2003-2004, 95% of all full-time freshmen and 96% of continuing full-time students received some form of financial aid. 65% of full-time freshmen and 70% of continuing full-time students received need-based aid. The average freshman award was $13,500. Need-based scholarships or need-based grants averaged $5000 ($18,000 maximum); need-based self-help aid (loans and jobs) averaged $6000 ($7225 maximum); and non-need-based awards and non-need-based scholarships averaged $4130 ($12,000 maximum). 55% of undergraduates work part time. Average annual earnings from campus work are $1202. The average financial indebtedness of the 2003 graduate was $21,000. Bethel is a member of CSS. The FAFSA, the college's own financial statement, and students' and parents' most recent federal tax returns are required. The deadline for filing freshman financial aid applications for fall entry is April 15.

International Students: There are 16 international students enrolled. They must score 525 on the written TOEFL or 195 on the electronic version and also take the SAT I or the ACT.

Computers: The mainframes are a Dell system PC and an 850 workgroup server for Macs. The computer labs have more than 300 Macs and PCs; the on-campus housing options are fully wired, allowing for 2 mainframe connections per room. All students may access the system 24 hours a day. There are no time limits and no fees.

Graduates: From July 1, 2002 to June 30, 2003, 638 bachelor's degrees were awarded. The most popular majors were business (17%), nursing (13%), and elementary education (9%). In an average class, 64% graduate in 4 years or less, 71% graduate in 5 years or less, and 72% graduate in 6 years or less.

Admissions Contact: Jay T. Fedje, Director of Admissions. E-mail: *bcoll-admit@bethel.edu* Web: *http://www.bethel.edu*

CARLETON COLLEGE
Northfield, MN 55057

C-4

(507) 646-4190
(800) 995-CARL; Fax: (507) 646-4526

Full-time: 927 men, 1003 women	Faculty: 196; IIB, ++$
Part-time: 8 men, 8 women	Ph.D.s: 95%
Graduate: none	Student/Faculty: 10 to 1
Year: trimesters	Tuition: $28,527
Application Deadline: January 15	Room & Board: $5868
Freshman Class: 4737 applied, 1414 accepted, 498 enrolled	
SAT I or ACT: required	MOST COMPETITIVE

Carleton College, founded in 1866, is a private liberal arts college. The library contains 851,434 volumes, 203,313 microform items, and 794 audio/video tapes/CDs, and subscribes to 1553 periodicals. Computerized library services include the card catalog, interlibrary loans, database searching, and Internet access. Special learning facilities include a learning resource center, art gallery, radio station, an observatory, and an 850-acre arboretum. The 945-acre campus is in a small town 35 miles south of Minneapolis-St. Paul. Including any residence halls, there are 45 buildings.

Student Life: 76% of undergraduates are from out of state, mostly the Midwest. Students are from 49 states, 30 foreign countries, and Canada. 74% are from public schools. 77% are white. The average age of freshmen is 18; all undergraduates, 20. 3% do not continue beyond their first year; 86% remain to graduate.

Housing: 1627 students can be accommodated in college housing, which includes single-sex and coed dorms, on-campus apartments, and off-campus apartments. In addition, there are language houses and special-interest houses. On-campus housing is guaranteed for all 4 years. 82% of students live on campus; of those, 97% remain on campus on weekends. No one may keep cars.

Activities: There are no fraternities or sororities. There are 132 groups on campus, including art, band, chess, choir, chorale, chorus, computers, dance, debate, drama, ethnic, film, gay, honors, international, jazz band, literary magazine, musical theater, newspaper, orchestra, photography, political, professional, radio and TV, religious, social, social service, student government, symphony, and yearbook. Popular campus events include Mai Fete, spring concert, and Winter Ball.

Sports: There are 10 intercollegiate sports for men and 10 for women, and 8 intramural sports for men and 8 for women. Facilities include a gym with a 1220-seat arena, 6-lane swimming pool, and wrestling room; a recreation center with a gym, dance studio, indoor tennis court, sauna, and 5-lane swimming pool; a 7000-seat stadium complex with handball and racquetball courts; a 200-meter indoor track, a baseball batting cage, and a weight room; an additional recreation center with a 200-meter indoor track, sport courts, weight room, dance studio, and climbing wall. In addition, there are fields for baseball, softball, soccer, ultimate Frisbee, lacrosse, rugby, and field hockey; 12 outdoor tennis courts; and 16 miles of running, biking, hiking, and cross-country skiing trails in Carleton's 800-acre arboretum.

Disabled Students: 28% of the campus is accessible. Wheelchair ramps, elevators, special parking, specially equipped rest rooms, special class scheduling, lowered drinking fountains, and lowered telephones are available.

Services: Counseling and information services are available, as is tutoring in every subject. There are also writing and math skills assistance centers. There is a reader service for the blind.

Campus Safety and Security: Measures include 24-hour foot and vehicle patrol, self-defense education, security escort services, and informal discussions. There are pamphlets/posters/films, emergency telephones, lighted pathways/sidewalks, and nighttime transport service.

Programs of Study: Carleton confers the B.A. degree. Bachelor's degrees are awarded in BIOLOGICAL SCIENCE (biology/biological science), COMMUNICATIONS AND THE ARTS (art history and appreciation, classics, English, French, German, Greek, Latin, music, romance languages and literature, Russian, Spanish, and studio art), COMPUTER AND PHYSICAL SCIENCE (chemistry, computer science, geology, mathematics, and physics), SOCIAL SCIENCE (African American studies, African studies, American studies, anthropology, Asian/Oriental studies, classical/ancient civilization, economics, history, international relations, Latin American studies, philosophy, political science/government, psychology, religion, sociology, and women's studies). Social sciences and history, physical sciences, and biological life sciences are the largest.

Required: Students are required to demonstrate proficiency in English composition and in a foreign language, and to take 1 course centrally concerned with another culture. 4 terms of phys ed are required. Students must complete 210 credits, or 117 semester hours, including 12 credits each from arts and literature and humanities, and 18 credits each from social sciences and math and science. Students must maintain a minimum GPA of 2.0. The total number of hours required for the major varies by department (72 is the norm). All seniors must complete a senior integrative exercise in their major, which may consist of a compre-

hensive exam, an extensive research project or paper, a public lecture, or a combination of these.

Special: Students may cross-register with Saint Olaf College and pursue a variety of internships. The college offers study abroad in 44 countries. Dual majors in all areas and student-designed majors are available. Students may earn a 3-2 engineering degree with Washington or Columbia Universities, a 3-2 degree in nursing, and a 3-3 degree in law. Pass/fail options are offered. There is a chapter of Phi Beta Kappa.

Faculty/Classroom: 58% of faculty are male; 42%, female. All both teach and do research. The average class size in an introductory lecture is 21; in a laboratory, 14; and in a regular course, 15.

Admissions: 30% of the 2003-2004 applicants were accepted. The SAT I scores for the 2003-2004 freshman class were: Verbal--1% below 500, 9% between 500 and 599, 39% between 600 and 700, and 52% above 700; Math--8% between 500 and 599, 48% between 600 and 700, and 43% above 700. The ACT scores were 6% between 18 and 23, 36% between 24 and 29, and 58% 30 and above. 90% of the current freshmen were in the top quarter of their class; 99% were in the top half. There were 83 National Merit finalists. 68 freshmen graduated first in their class.

Requirements: The SAT I or ACT is required. There are no secondary school requirements, but it is recommended that applicants have completed 4 years of English, 3 years each of math and a foreign language, 2 years each of history and science, and 1 year of social studies. An essay and 2 teacher recommendations are required. AP credits are accepted. Important factors in the admissions decision are advanced placement or honor courses, personality/intangible qualities, and evidence of special talent.

Procedure: Freshmen are admitted in the fall. Entrance exams should be taken before March 1. There are early decision and deferred admissions plans. Early decision applications should be filed by November 15; regular applications, by January 15 for fall entry, along with a $30 fee. Notification of early decision is sent December 15; regular decision, by April 15. 200 early decision candidates were accepted for the 2003-2004 class. 272 applicants were on the 2003 waiting list; 8 were admitted. Applications are accepted on-line through ApplyYourself and Common App.

Transfer: 1 transfer student enrolled in 2002-2003. Transfers are usually accepted for sophomore and junior classes. A 3.0 GPA is recommended. 108 of 210 credits required for the bachelor's degree must be completed at Carleton.

Visiting: There are regularly scheduled orientations for prospective students, including an open house in October. There are guides for informal visits and visitors may sit in on classes and stay overnight. To schedule a visit, contact the Admissions Office.

Financial Aid: In 2003-2004, 55% of full-time freshmen and 54% of continuing full-time students received need-based aid. The average freshman award was $22,267. 86% of undergraduates work part time. Average annual earnings from campus work are $1920. The average financial indebtedness of the 2003 graduate was $15,689. Carleton is a member of CSS. The CSS/Profile or FAFSA is required. The deadline for filing freshman financial aid applications for fall entry is February 15.

International Students: There are 89 international students enrolled. The school actively recruits these students. They must take the TOEFL or take the SAT I or the ACT.

Computers: There are 221 terminals in 31 labs, including 12 general-purpose labs. Internet access, e-mail, and on-line registration are available. All students may access the system 24 hours a day. There are no time limits and no fees.

Graduates: From July 1, 2002 to June 30, 2003, 436 bachelor's degrees were awarded. The most popular majors were social science and history (28%), biological and life sciences (13%), and physical sciences (9%). In an average class, 85% graduate in 4 years or less, and 89% graduate in 5 years or less. 27 companies recruited on campus in 2002-2003. Of the 2002 graduating class, 20% were enrolled in graduate school within 6 months of graduation and 54% were employed.

Admissions Contact: Paul Thiboutot, Dean of Admissions. A video is available. E-mail: *admissions@acs.carleton.edu*
Web: *www.carleton.edu*

COLLEGE OF SAINT BENEDICT
St. Joseph, MN 56374-2099

C-3

(320) 363-2196
(800) 544-1489; Fax: (320) 363-2750

Full-time: 1998 women	Faculty: 148; IIB, av$
Part-time: 56 women	Ph.D.s: 81%
Graduate: none	Student/Faculty: 13 to 1
Year: semesters	Tuition: $20,685
Application Deadline: open	Room & Board: $5987
Freshman Class: 1174 applied, 1057 accepted, 502 enrolled	
SAT I Verbal/Math: 560/570	ACT: 25 VERY COMPETITIVE

The College of Saint Benedict, established in 1887, is a private, Benedictine Catholic institution offering undergraduate liberal arts study for women in conjunction with St. John's University, a Benedictine Catholic institution for men. The coordinate institutions share an academic calendar, academic curriculum, and many combined extracurricular activities. In addition to regional accreditation, St. Benedict has baccalaureate program accreditation with ACS, ADA, CCNE, CSWE, NASM, and NCATE. The 3 libraries contain 680,888 volumes, 119,665 microform items, and 33,471 audio/video tapes/CDs, and subscribe to 11,364 periodicals. Computerized library services include the card catalog, interlibrary loans, and database searching. Special learning facilities include a learning resource center, art gallery, radio station, a pottery studio, an arboretum, an observatory, a greenhouse, and Hill Monastic Manuscript library and natural history museum at St. John's University. The 315-acre campus is in a small town 70 miles northwest of Minneapolis and 10 miles west of St. Cloud. Including any residence halls, there are 33 buildings.

Student Life: 82% of undergraduates are from Minnesota. Students are from 31 states, 24 foreign countries, and Canada. 73% are from public schools. 92% are white. 68% are Catholic; 25% Protestant; 6% claim no religious affiliation. The average age of freshmen is 18; all undergraduates, 20. 12% do not continue beyond their first year; 81% remain to graduate.

Housing: 1536 students can be accommodated in college housing, which includes single-sex dorms, on-campus apartments, and off-campus apartments. In addition, there is a health and wellness floor, a service learning/social justice floor, a global initiative group, the Explore program, and an environmental living group. On-campus housing is guaranteed for the freshman and sophomore years only, is available on a first-come, first-served basis, and is available on a lottery system for upperclassmen. 80% of students live on campus. All students may keep cars.

Activities: There are no sororities. There are 90 groups on campus, including academic, art, band, choir, chorale, chorus, computers, dance, drama, ethnic, gay, honors, international, jazz band, literary magazine, musical theater, opera, orchestra, outdoor leadership, political, professional, radio and TV, religious, social, social service, student government, symphony, and yearbook. Popular campus events include Festival of Cultures, Asian New Year, and Stella Maris Ball.

Sports: There are 11 intercollegiate sports and 10 to 15 intramural sports. Facilities include a 1000-seat volleyball and basketball arena, racquetball and indoor and outdoor tennis courts, a weight room, an indoor pool, a field house with indoor running track, an aerobics studio, a fitness center with exercise and weight-training equipment, a softball diamond, soccer fields, and 30 miles of cross-country ski trails. Students have access to St. John's University facilities as well, including a 4-story climbing wall and a fitness center.

Disabled Students: 90% of the campus is accessible. Wheelchair ramps, elevators, special parking, specially equipped rest rooms, special class scheduling, lowered drinking fountains, lowered telephones, and special housing are available.

Services: Counseling and information services are available, as is tutoring in most subjects, a writing center, a math skills center, test-taking skills instruction, reading machines, and note-taking services.

Campus Safety and Security: Measures include 24-hour foot and vehicle patrol, self-defense education, security escort services, and shuttle buses. There are informal discussions, pamphlets/posters/films, emergency telephones, and lighted pathways/sidewalks.

Programs of Study: St. Benedict confers B.A. and B.S.N. degrees. Bachelor's degrees are awarded in AGRICULTURE (environmental studies and forestry and related sciences), BIOLOGICAL SCIENCE (biochemistry, biology/biological science, and nutrition), BUSINESS (accounting and management science), COMMUNICATIONS AND THE ARTS (art, classics, communications, dramatic arts, English, fine arts, French, German, music, and Spanish), COMPUTER AND PHYSICAL SCIENCE (chemistry, computer science, mathematics, natural sciences, and physics), EDUCATION (elementary), ENGINEERING AND ENVIRONMENTAL DESIGN (preengineering), HEALTH PROFESSIONS (nursing, occupational therapy, physical therapy, predentistry, premedicine, prepharmacy, and preveterinary science), SOCIAL SCIENCE (dietetics, economics, history, humanities, liberal arts/general studies, ministries, pastoral studies, peace studies, philosophy, political science/government, prelaw, psychology, social science, social work, sociology, and theological studies). The humanities, biology, and chemistry are the strongest academically. Nursing, psychology, and communication are the largest.

Required: To graduate, students must complete the core curriculum of writing, discussion, quantitative reasoning, and gender and global perspectives. Distribution requirements include 6 credits in fine arts, 5 in humanities, 2 each in natural science and social science, and 1 in math. All students must prove math and foreign language proficiency. A total of 124 credits must be earned, with 40 credits in upper-division courses and an overall GPA of 2.0. Students must complete a first-year symposium and a senior seminar.

Special: Students may cross-register with St. John's University and St. Cloud State University. There are study-abroad programs in Ireland, China, Central America, Japan, South Africa, Australia, and European cities. Internships, student-designed majors, preprofessional programs,

and liberal studies degrees may be pursued. A 3-2 engineering program is offered with the University of Minnesota. Nondegree study and a pass/fail grading option are also available. There is 1 national honor society and a freshman honors program.

Faculty/Classroom: 41% of faculty are male; 59%, female. All both teach and do research. The average class size in an introductory lecture is 25; in a laboratory, 18; and in a regular course, 22.

Admissions: 90% of the 2003-2004 applicants were accepted. The SAT I scores for the 2003-2004 freshman class were: Verbal--23% below 500, 39% between 500 and 599, 34% between 600 and 700, and 4% above 700; Math--20% below 500, 41% between 500 and 599, 36% between 600 and 700, and 3% above 700. The ACT scores were 11% below 21, 26% between 21 and 23, 35% between 24 and 26, 13% between 27 and 28, and 15% above 28. 60% of the current freshmen were in the top fifth of their class; 90% were in the top two fifths. There were 5 National Merit finalists. 28 freshmen graduated first in their class.

Requirements: The SAT I or ACT is required. In addition, students should be graduates of an accredited secondary school. Academic preparation should include 17 units, including 4 of English, 3 of math, 2 each of science and social studies, and 6 electives. A foreign language is recommended. The GED is accepted. An essay is required. Homeschooled applicants are not required to have a high school diploma but are required to provide appropriate documentation of college preparatory curriculum. St. Benedict requires applicants to be in the upper 50% of their class. A GPA of 3.0 is required. AP and CLEP credits are accepted. Important factors in the admissions decision are advanced placement or honor courses, evidence of special talent, and extracurricular activities record.

Procedure: Freshmen are admitted fall and spring. Entrance exams should be taken during the spring of the junior year or fall of the senior year. There are early admissions and deferred admissions plans. Application deadlines are open, but the priority filing date for fall entry is January 15 and early action is December 1. The fall 2003 application fee was $30. Notification is sent on a rolling basis beginning January 15. 15 applicants were on the 2003 waiting list; 3 were admitted. Applications are accepted on computer disk and on-line through CollegeNET, Common App, and the school's web site at *www.csbsju.edu*.

Transfer: 38 transfer students enrolled in 2002-2003. Transfer applicants must have a minimum college GPA of 2.75. An essay or personal statement, high school and college transcripts, and a transfer student evaluation form are required. Standardized test scores may be required of some. 45 of 124 credits required for the bachelor's degree must be completed at St. Benedict.

Visiting: There are regularly scheduled orientations for prospective students, programs that vary with student interest. Information can be found at the college's web site. There are guides for informal visits and visitors may sit in on classes and stay overnight. To schedule a visit, contact the Admissions Office.

Financial Aid: In 2003-2004, 97% of all full-time freshmen and 94% of continuing full-time students received some form of financial aid. 73% of full-time freshmen and 67% of continuing full-time students received need-based aid. The average freshman award was $17,823. Need-based scholarships or need-based grants averaged $12,163; and need-based self-help aid (loans and jobs) averaged $5532. 45% of undergraduates work part time. Average annual earnings from campus work are $2100. The average financial indebtedness of the 2003 graduate was $22,688. The FAFSA and the college's own financial statement are required. The priority date for freshman financial aid applications for fall entry is March 15. The deadline for filing freshman financial aid applications for fall entry is May 1.

International Students: There are 79 international students enrolled. The school actively recruits these students. They must score 500 on the written TOEFL or 173 on the electronic version or take the MELAB. The SAT I or the ACT is recommended.

Computers: The mainframe is a Windows 2000 network. Students have free 24-hour access to computers in each college residence, in numerous departments, and in 4 public access areas. Most residence halls and apartments are computer-wired. All students may access the system 24 hours per day. There are no time limits and no fees.

Graduates: From July 1, 2002 to June 30, 2003, 458 bachelor's degrees were awarded. The most popular majors were communication (12%), nursing (11%), and management (11%). In an average class, 1% graduate in 3 years or less, 72% graduate in 4 years or less, 78% graduate in 5 years or less, and 79% graduate in 6 years or less. 22 companies recruited on campus in 2002-2003. Of the 2002 graduating class, 13% were enrolled in graduate school within 6 months of graduation and 82% were employed.

Admissions Contact: Mary Milbert, Dean of Admission. A video is available. E-mail: *admissions@csbsju.edu* Web: *www.csbsju.edu*

COLLEGE OF SAINT CATHERINE
C-4
St. Paul, MN 55105
(651) 690-8850
(800) 656-KATE; Fax: (651) 690-8824

Full-time: 28 men, 2365 women	**Faculty:** 224; IIA, --$
Part-time: 72 men, 1216 women	**Ph.D.s:** 61%
Graduate: 143 men, 983 women	**Student/Faculty:** 11 to 1
Year: 4-1-4, summer session	**Tuition:** $18,550
Application Deadline: open	**Room & Board:** $5460
Freshman Class: 1170 applied, 904 accepted, 407 enrolled	
SAT I Verbal/Math: 605/590	**ACT:** 23 **VERY COMPETITIVE**

The College of Saint Catherine, founded in 1905, is a private, comprehensive, women's college affiliated with the Roman Catholic Church. In addition to regional accreditation, CSC has baccalaureate program accreditation with ADA, APTA, NASM, and NLN. The 2 libraries contain 390,613 volumes, 169,236 microform items, and 13,627 audio/video tapes/CDs, and subscribe to 2166 periodicals. Computerized library services include the card catalog, interlibrary loans, and database searching. Special learning facilities include a learning resource center, art gallery, and observatory. The 110-acre campus is in an urban area 6 miles southwest of downtown St. Paul. Including any residence halls, there are 19 buildings.

Student Life: 86% of undergraduates are from Minnesota. Students are from 29 states, 30 foreign countries, and Canada. 80% are from public schools. 75% are white. 50% are Catholic; 20% Protestant. The average age of freshmen is 18; all undergraduates, 22. 19% do not continue beyond their first year; 60% remain to graduate.

Housing: 700 students can be accommodated in college housing, which includes single-sex dorms and on-campus apartments. On-campus housing is guaranteed for all 4 years. 63% of students commute. All students may keep cars.

Activities: There are 2 local sororities. There are no fraternities. There are 42 groups on campus, including art, band, choir, chorale, chorus, dance, drama, ethnic, gay, honors, international, jazz band, literary magazine, musical theater, newspaper, orchestra, photography, political, professional, religious, social, social service, and student government. Popular campus events include Student Life Week, Dew Drop Bop, and opening convocation and picnic.

Sports: Facilities include a fitness facility, a gym, a weight room, a swimming pool, an outdoor fitness course, tennis courts, a soccer field, and a softball field.

Disabled Students: 90% of the campus is accessible. Wheelchair ramps, elevators, special parking, specially equipped rest rooms, special class scheduling, lowered drinking fountains, and lowered telephones are available.

Services: Counseling and information services are available, as is tutoring in most subjects. There is a reader service for the blind and remedial math, reading, and writing.

Campus Safety and Security: Measures include 24-hour foot and vehicle patrol, self-defense education, security escort services, and informal discussions. There are pamphlets/posters/films, emergency telephones, and lighted pathways/sidewalks.

Programs of Study: CSC confers B.A. and B.S. degrees. Associate and master's degrees are also awarded. Bachelor's degrees are awarded in BIOLOGICAL SCIENCE (biochemistry, biology/biological science, and nutrition), BUSINESS (accounting, business administration and management, fashion merchandising, international economics, management information systems, and marketing/retailing/merchandising), COMMUNICATIONS AND THE ARTS (American Sign Language, art, communications, dramatic arts, English, fine arts, French, media arts, music, Spanish, and speech/debate/rhetoric), COMPUTER AND PHYSICAL SCIENCE (chemistry, information sciences and systems, and mathematics), EDUCATION (art, early childhood, elementary, home economics, music, and physical), HEALTH PROFESSIONS (health care administration, medical records administration/services, nursing, occupational therapy, rehabilitation therapy, and respiratory therapy), SOCIAL SCIENCE (dietetics, economics, ethnic studies, family/consumer studies, fashion design and technology, history, international relations, philosophy, physical fitness/movement, political science/government, psychology, social studies, social work, sociology, theological studies, and women's studies). Nursing, business administration, and elementary education are the largest.

Required: To graduate, students must complete 130 semester credits, including a liberal arts core with courses in history, foreign language, philosophy, math, fine arts, literature, and theology, and 80 credits outside the major. Required courses are The Reflective Woman and The Global Search for Justice. At least 36 hours are required in the major. Students must have a minimum 2.0 GPA and demonstrate proficiency in composition, math, and computer literacy.

Special: CSC offers co-op programs with Carondolet College, the University of Minnesota, and George Washington University, and cross-registration with the Associated Colleges of the Twin Cities and other colleges sponsored by the Sisters of St. Joseph. Students may arrange internships, a Washington semester, and study abroad. Dual majors are

available in the sciences and engineering. Students may receive credit for life, military, or work experience. Student-designed majors, nondegree study, and pass/fail options are available. The Weekend College offers a B.A. degree. There are 24 national honor societies, including Phi Beta Kappa, and a freshman honors program.

Faculty/Classroom: 18% of faculty are male; 82%, female. All teach undergraduates. No introductory courses are taught by graduate students. The average class size in an introductory lecture is 16; in a laboratory, 14; and in a regular course, 13.

Admissions: 77% of the 2003-2004 applicants were accepted. The SAT I scores for the 2003-2004 freshman class were: Verbal--13% below 500, 28% between 500 and 599, 50% between 600 and 700, and 9% above 700; Math--25% below 500, 28% between 500 and 599, 25% between 600 and 700, and 22% above 700. The ACT scores were 23% below 21, 30% between 21 and 23, 26% between 24 and 26, 13% between 27 and 28, and 8% above 28. 47% of the current freshmen were in the top fifth of their class; 80% were in the top two fifths. There were 4 National Merit semifinalists. 8 freshmen graduated first in their class.

Requirements: The SAT I or ACT is required. In addition, applicants must have completed a college preparatory program including 4 courses in English, 3 in math, and 2 each in a foreign language, science, and social studies. CSC requires applicants to be in the upper 50% of their class. A GPA of 2.5 is required. AP and CLEP credits are accepted. Important factors in the admissions decision are advanced placement or honor courses, recommendations by school officials, and extracurricular activities record.

Procedure: Freshmen are admitted to all sessions. Entrance exams should be taken during the senior year. There is a rolling admissions plan and a deferred admissions plan. Application deadlines are open. Application fee is $20. Applications are accepted on-line through the Catholic College Admission Application, EXPAN, and Apply.

Transfer: 793 transfer students enrolled in 2002-2003. Transfer applicants must submit high school and college transcripts. 48 of 130 credits required for the bachelor's degree must be completed at CSC.

Visiting: There are regularly scheduled orientations for prospective students, including a tour, an admissions interview, and an appointment with a faculty member. There are guides for informal visits and visitors may sit in on classes and stay overnight. To schedule a visit, contact the Admissions Office.

Financial Aid: In 2003-2004, 98% of all full-time freshmen and 90% of continuing full-time students received some form of financial aid. 73% of full-time freshmen and 71% of continuing full-time students received need-based aid. The average freshman award was $19,926. Need-based scholarships or need-based grants averaged $7658; and need-based self-help aid (loans and jobs) averaged $4451. 93% of undergraduates work part time. Average annual earnings from campus work are $1800. The average financial indebtedness of the 2003 graduate was $24,537. CSC is a member of CSS. The FAFSA and the college's own financial statement are required. The deadline for filing freshman financial aid applications for fall entry is April 1.

International Students: There are 85 international students enrolled. The school actively recruits these students. They must score 500 on the written TOEFL or take the MELAB or the college's own test. The SAT I is required only if the student attended a U.S. high school, whether in this country or overseas.

Computers: The mainframe is an HP 9000/826. More than 350 PCs are available throughout campus for students to access the Internet and work on class assignments. All students may access the system 24 hours a day. There are no time limits and no fees.

Graduates: From July 1, 2002 to June 30, 2003, 506 bachelor's degrees were awarded. The most popular majors were nursing (17%), occupational therapy (10%), and elementary education (9%). In an average class, 3% graduate in 3 years or less, 40% graduate in 4 years or less, 57% graduate in 5 years or less, and 60% graduate in 6 years or less. 9 companies recruited on campus in 2002-2003. Of the 2002 graduating class, 12% were enrolled in graduate school within 6 months of graduation and 90% were employed.

Admissions Contact: Marlene Mohs, Senior Associate Director of Admission. E-mail: admissions@stkate.edu Web: www.stkate.edu

COLLEGE OF SAINT SCHOLASTICA
D-3
Duluth, MN 55811
(218) 723-6046
(800) 447-5444; Fax: (218) 723-5991

Full-time: 591 men, 1461 women	**Faculty:** 123; IIB, -$
Part-time: 91 men, 165 women	**Ph.D.s:** 60%
Graduate: 142 men, 388 women	**Student/Faculty:** 17 to 1
Year: semesters, summer session	**Tuition:** $19,302
Application Deadline: open	**Room & Board:** $5668
Freshman Class: 1206 applied, 1062 accepted, 437 enrolled	
SAT I Verbal/Math: 560/560	**ACT:** 24 **COMPETITIVE+**

The College of St. Scholastica, founded in 1912, is a private liberal arts college affiliated with the Roman Catholic Church. In addition to regional accreditation, Saints has baccalaureate program accreditation with

APTA, CAHEA, CSWE, and NLN. The library contains 126,835 volumes, 1810 microform items, and 13,754 audio/video tapes/CDs, and subscribes to 628 periodicals. Computerized library services include the card catalog, interlibrary loans, database searching, and Internet access. Special learning facilities include a learning resource center and music library. The 186-acre campus is in a suburban area 150 miles north of Minneapolis and St. Paul. Including any residence halls, there are 14 buildings.

Student Life: 89% of undergraduates are from Minnesota. Students are from 26 states, 15 foreign countries, and Canada. 87% are white. 32% are Catholic; 30% claim no religious affiliation; 30% Protestant. The average age of freshmen is 22; all undergraduates, 24. 18% do not continue beyond their first year; 54% remain to graduate.

Housing: 742 students can be accommodated in college housing, which includes coed dorms and on-campus apartments. On-campus housing is available on a first-come, first-served basis and is available on a lottery system for upperclassmen. 65% of students commute. All students may keep cars.

Activities: There are no fraternities or sororities. There are 54 groups on campus, including band, cheerleading, choir, chorale, chorus, computers, dance, drama, ethnic, gay, honors, international, jazz band, literary magazine, newspaper, pep band, photography, political, professional, religious, social, social service, student government, and yearbook. Popular campus events include Mayfest Week, Fall Fest, and Welcome Back Week.

Sports: There are 6 intercollegiate sports for men and 7 for women, and 6 intramural sports for men and 6 for women. Facilities include a recreation center.

Disabled Students: 95% of the campus is accessible. Wheelchair ramps, elevators, special parking, specially equipped rest rooms, special class scheduling, lowered drinking fountains, lowered telephones, and special housing are available.

Services: Counseling and information services are available, as is tutoring in most subjects. There is a reader service for the blind and remedial math and writing. Sign language interpreters, a note-taking service, tape recorders, voice input computers, and remedial study skills are also available.

Campus Safety and Security: Measures include 24-hour foot and vehicle patrol, self-defense education, security escort services, and informal discussions. There are pamphlets/posters/films, emergency telephones, lighted pathways/sidewalks, electronically operated dorm entrances, and student door monitors in the evening and night.

Programs of Study: Saints confers the B.A. degree. Master's degrees are also awarded. Bachelor's degrees are awarded in BIOLOGICAL SCIENCE (biochemistry and biology/biological science), BUSINESS (accounting, business administration and management, marketing management, and organizational behavior), COMMUNICATIONS AND THE ARTS (communications, English, languages, and music), COMPUTER AND PHYSICAL SCIENCE (chemistry, computer science, information sciences and systems, mathematics, and natural sciences), EDUCATION (education, educational media, elementary, and social science), HEALTH PROFESSIONS (exercise science, health care administration, health science, and nursing), SOCIAL SCIENCE (behavioral science, economics, history, humanities, Native American studies, psychology, religion, and social work). Education, nursing, and computer science/information systems are the largest.

Required: To graduate, students must complete 128 semester credits, with a 2.0 GPA. 44 credits of general education courses are required, including 4 credits each of English composition, social science, natural science, oral communication, literature, history, fine arts, philosophy, religious studies, math, and cultural diversity and 2 to 8 credits in a foreign language. The hours required in the major vary. Computer literacy is required of all students. Most majors require an internship for graduation. A senior project may be required.

Special: Students may cross-register with the University of Minnesota at Duluth and the University of Wisconsin at Superior. Self-designed majors, a Washington semester with American University, internships, study abroad in 5 countries, accelerated degrees, nondegree study, pass/fail options, and credit for life, military, or work experience are available. There is a 3-2 engineering degree with the Institute of Technology of the University of Minnesota. A service learning program is offered in Tanzania and Cameroon. There are 2 national honor societies and a freshman honors program.

Faculty/Classroom: 38% of faculty are male; 62%, female. 95% teach undergraduates and 13% both teach and do research. No introductory courses are taught by graduate students. The average class size in an introductory lecture is 24; in a laboratory, 20; and in a regular course, 21.

Admissions: 88% of the 2003-2004 applicants were accepted. The SAT I scores for the 2003-2004 freshman class were: Verbal--21% below 500, 46% between 500 and 599, 29% between 600 and 700, and 4% above 700; Math--29% below 500, 42% between 500 and 599, 25% between 600 and 700, and 4% above 700. 51% of the current freshmen were in the top fifth of their class; 78% were in the top two fifths. 12 freshmen graduated first in their class.

Requirements: The SAT I or ACT is required; PSAT scores may also be submitted. Students are also required to send official high school transcripts. AP and CLEP credits are accepted. Important factors in the admissions decision are personality/intangible qualities, advanced placement or honor courses, and recommendations by school officials.

Procedure: Freshmen are admitted to all sessions. Entrance exams should be taken by January of the senior year of high school. There are early admissions and deferred admissions plans. There is a rolling admissions plan. Application deadlines are open. Application fee is $25. Applications are accepted on-line through Peterson's, Apply, and ACT College Connector.

Transfer: 171 transfer students enrolled in 2002-2003. Applicants must have a GPA of 2.0 or a college aptitude rating score of 50 or higher. 32 of 128 credits required for the bachelor's degree must be completed at Saints.

Visiting: There are regularly scheduled orientations for prospective students, including a class placement survey, peer and academic advisement, and registration. There are guides for informal visits and visitors may sit in on classes and stay overnight. To schedule a visit, contact the Admissions Office at admissions@css.edu.

Financial Aid: In 2003-2004, 98% of all full-time freshmen and 96% of continuing full-time students received some form of financial aid. 83% of full-time freshmen and 85% of continuing full-time students received need-based aid. The average freshman award was $16,351. 32% of undergraduates work part time. Average annual earnings from campus work are $1845. The average financial indebtedness of the 2003 graduate was $25,474. Saints is a member of CSS. The FAFSA, and the college's own financial statement are required. The deadline for filing freshman financial aid applications for fall entry is March 15.

International Students: There are 17 international students enrolled. The school actively recruits these students. They must score 550 on the written TOEFL or 213 on the electronic version or take the MELAB.

Computers: The mainframe is a Sun Fire V880. There are 145 PCs on a network in labs throughout the campus. Web access will allow students to see accounts, grades, schedules, financial aid, and transcripts. All students may access the system 7 A.M. to midnight Monday through Thursday, 7 A.M. to 5 P.M. on Friday, noon to 6 P.M. on Saturday, and noon to midnight on Sunday. There are no time limits and no fees.

Graduates: From July 1, 2002 to June 30, 2003, 418 bachelor's degrees were awarded. The most popular majors were health professions and related sciences (31%), management (29%), and computer science/computer information systems (7%). In an average class, 55% graduate in 4 years or less, 64% graduate in 5 years or less, and 65% graduate in 6 years or less. One company recruited on campus in 2002-2003. Of the 2002 graduating class, 31% were enrolled in graduate school within 6 months of graduation and 60% were employed.

Admissions Contact: Brian Dalton, Vice President for Enrollment Management. A video is available. E-mail: bdalton@css.edu Web: www.css.edu

COLLEGE OF ST. BENEDICT
(See Saint John's University)

COLLEGE OF VISUAL ARTS
St. Paul, MN 55102

C-4
(651) 224-3416
(800) 224-1536; Fax: (651) 224-8854

Full-time: 84 men, 102 women	**Faculty:** 9
Part-time: 14 men, 18 women	**Ph.D.s:** 58%
Graduate: none	**Student/Faculty:** 21 to 1
Year: semesters, summer session	**Tuition:** $16,106
Application Deadline: May 1	**Room & Board:** n/app
Freshman Class: 142 applied, 52 enrolled	
SAT I or ACT: recommended	**SPECIAL**

Founded in 1924, the College of Visual Arts is a fully accredited private college of art and design, offering degrees in communication design, photography, illustration, and fine arts (painting, drawing, sculpture, and printmaking). The library contains 6700 volumes, 220 audio/video tapes/CDs, and 30,500 slides, and subscribes to 38 periodicals. Computerized library services include the card catalog, interlibrary loans, database searching, and Internet access. Special learning facilities include a learning resource center and art gallery. The 3-acre campus is in an urban area in a historic residential area near downtown St. Paul. There are 5 buildings.

Student Life: 88% of undergraduates are from Minnesota. Students are from 13 states and 5 foreign countries. 89% are white. Most claim no religious affiliation. The average age of freshmen is 19. 57% do not continue beyond their first year; 43% remain to graduate.

Housing: There are no residence halls. College-sponsored living facilities include off-campus apartments. Housing assistance is offered. All students commute. Alcohol is not permitted. All students may keep cars.

Activities: There are no fraternities or sororities. There are some groups and organizations on campus, including professional. Popular campus events include an annual lecture series and exhibit openings.

Sports: There is no sports program at CVA.

Disabled Students: 30% of the campus is accessible. Special parking, specially equipped rest rooms, and lowered drinking fountains are available.

Services: Counseling and information services are available, as is tutoring in most subjects. There is remedial math, reading, and writing.

Campus Safety and Security: Measures include security escort services and a security guard for evenings and weekends.

Programs of Study: CVA confers the B.F.A. degree. Bachelor's degrees are awarded in COMMUNICATIONS AND THE ARTS (drawing, fine arts, graphic design, illustration, painting, photography, printmaking, sculpture, and visual and performing arts).

Required: All students must complete 126 semester hours, including an 18-credit first-year foundation program, 48 hours of liberal arts requirements, 33 to 39 hours in the major, 9 to 12 hours of supportive art/design requirements, and 18 hours of studio electives. A minimum GPA of 2.0 is needed, and projects in art and design must be completed.

Special: Juniors and seniors are encouraged to take internships with various area organizations and businesses. CVA also offers study abroad in France, Italy, and England and a German exchange program.

Faculty/Classroom: 51% of faculty are male; 49%, female. All teach undergraduates. The average class size in an introductory lecture is 24 and in a laboratory, 15.

Requirements: The SAT I or ACT is recommended. In addition, applicants must submit a personal statement of interest and a portfolio. An interview and a visit to the college are highly recommended. A GPA of 2.7 is required. Important factors in the admissions decision are personality/intangible qualities, evidence of special talent, and recommendations by school officials.

Procedure: Freshmen are admitted fall and spring. Entrance exams should be taken in fall or spring of the junior year or fall of the senior year. There are early admissions and deferred admissions plans. Priority application dates are May 1 for fall entry and December 1 for spring entry. The fee is $40. Notification is sent on a rolling basis.

Transfer: 35 transfer students enrolled in a recent year. Required are a personal statement, an interview, transcripts from all postsecondary institutions attended, and a faculty review of work done in studio art classes at other postsecondary institutions. 66 of 126 credits required for the bachelor's degree must be completed at CVA.

Visiting: There are regularly scheduled orientations for prospective students, consisting of annual open house events, including slide presentations of student artwork, a financial aid discussion, a tour of facilities, and a student panel discussion. There are guides for informal visits and visitors may sit in on classes. To schedule a visit, contact the Admissions Office.

Financial Aid: In 2003-2004, 90% of all full-time freshmen and 88% of continuing full-time students received some form of financial aid. 73% of full-time freshmen and 75% of continuing full-time students received need-based aid. The average freshman award was $14,188. 20% of undergraduates work part time. Average annual earnings from campus work are $3000. The average financial indebtedness of the 2003 graduate was $30,000. CVA is a member of CSS. The FAFSA and the college's own financial statement are required.

International Students: They must score 500 on the written TOEFL or 273 on the electronic version and also take the ACT or the college's own entrance exam, scoring 17 on the ACT.

Computers: Student computer labs are networked to allow classes to share and transfer graphics files. All students may access the system. There are no time limits. The fee is $75. It is strongly recommended that all students have a personal computer.

Graduates: From July 1, 2002 to June 30, 2003, 48 bachelor's degrees were awarded. The most popular majors were communication design (42%), photography (19%), and fine arts (8%). In an average class, 50% graduate in 4 years or less, 83% graduate in 5 years or less, and all graduate in 6 years or less. Of the 2002 graduating class, 75% were employed within 6 months of graduation.

Admissions Contact: Lynn E. Tanaka, Director of Admissions. A video is available. E-mail: *info@cva.edu* Web: *www.cva.edu*

CONCORDIA COLLEGE
(See Concordia University/St.Paul)

CONCORDIA COLLEGE: MOORHEAD	A-2
Moorhead, MN 56562	(218) 299-3004 (collect)
	(800) 699-9897; Fax: (218) 299-3947

Full-time: 1010 men, 1756 women	**Faculty:** 183; IIB, av$
Part-time: 40 men, 50 women	**Ph.D.s:** 72%
Graduate: none	**Student/Faculty:** 15 to 1
Year: semesters, summer session	**Tuition:** $17,770
Application Deadline: open	**Room & Board:** $4690
Freshman Class: 2444 applied, 2098 accepted, 775 enrolled	
SAT I Verbal/Math: 580/660	**ACT:** 24 VERY COMPETITIVE+

Concordia College, founded in 1891, is a private, liberal arts institution affiliated with the Evangelical Lutheran Church in America. Some information in this capsule and profile is approximate. In addition to regional accreditation, Concordia has baccalaureate program accreditation with ADA, CSWE, NASM, NCATE, and NLN. The library contains 300,000 volumes, 43,296 microform items, and 11,048 audio/video tapes/CDs, and subscribes to 1463 periodicals. Computerized library services include the card catalog, interlibrary loans, and database searching. Special learning facilities include a learning resource center, art gallery, radio station, TV station, and observatory. The 120-acre campus is in an urban area 240 miles northwest of Minneapolis and St. Paul. Including any residence halls, there are 36 buildings.

Student Life: 61% of undergraduates are from Minnesota. Students are from 37 states, 34 foreign countries, and Canada. 96% are from public schools. 93% are white. 81% are Protestant; 13% Catholic. The average age of freshmen is 18; all undergraduates, 20. 21% do not continue beyond their first year; 70% remain to graduate.

Housing: 1850 students can be accommodated in college housing, which includes single-sex dorms and on-campus apartments. In addition, there are language houses. On-campus housing is guaranteed for the freshman year only, is available on a first-come, first-served basis, and is available on a lottery system for upperclassmen. Priority is given to out-of-town students. 56% of students live on campus; of those, 75% remain on campus on weekends. Alcohol is not permitted. All students may keep cars.

Activities: There are no fraternities or sororities. There are 150 groups on campus, including art, band, cheerleading, choir, chorale, chorus, dance, debate, drama, drill team, ethnic, film, forensics, gay, honors, international, jazz band, literary magazine, musical theater, newspaper, orchestra, pep band, photography, political, professional, radio and TV, religious, social, social service, student government, symphony, and yearbook. Popular campus events include Family Weekend, Winter Meltdown, and Black History Week.

Sports: There are 10 intercollegiate sports for men and 10 for women, and 9 intramural sports for men and 10 for women. Facilities include a health club, a 200-meter indoor track with 4 multipurpose basketball/tennis courts, an indoor swimming pool and sauna, a 7000-seat stadium with an all-weather track, a field house with a 4500-seat auditorium, 2 more basketball courts, 2 auxiliary gyms and a weight room, 6 outdoor tennis courts, softball and soccer competition fields, a baseball complex, and soccer practice fields.

Disabled Students: 95% of the campus is accessible. Wheelchair ramps, elevators, special parking, specially equipped rest rooms, special class scheduling, lowered drinking fountains, and automatic doors are available.

Services: Counseling and information services are available, as is tutoring in most subjects. There is a reader service for the blind and an interpreter service for the deaf.

Campus Safety and Security: Measures include 24-hour foot and vehicle patrol, security escort services, informal discussions, and pamphlets/posters/films. There are lighted pathways/sidewalks.

Programs of Study: Concordia confers B.A. and B.M. degrees. Bachelor's degrees are awarded in BIOLOGICAL SCIENCE (biology/biological science), BUSINESS (accounting, business administration and management, international business management, and office supervision and management), COMMUNICATIONS AND THE ARTS (advertising, apparel design, art history and appreciation, classical languages, communications, creative writing, dramatic arts, English, French, German, journalism, Latin, literature, music, music performance, public relations, Spanish, speech/debate/rhetoric, and studio art), COMPUTER AND PHYSICAL SCIENCE (chemistry, computer science, mathematics, and physics), EDUCATION (art, business, elementary, foreign languages, health, home economics, middle school, music, physical, science, secondary, and social studies), ENGINEERING AND ENVIRONMENTAL DESIGN (environmental science and preengineering), HEALTH PROFESSIONS (health, health care administration, medical laboratory technology, nursing, predentistry, premedicine, and preveterinary science), SOCIAL SCIENCE (dietetics, economics, family/consumer studies, history, humanities, international relations, ministries, philosophy, political science/government, prelaw, psychology, religion, Russian and Slavic studies, Scandinavian studies, social work, and sociology). Premedicine, prelaw, and math are the strongest academically. Business administration, communications, and biology are the largest.

Required: All students must maintain a minimum GPA of 2.0 while taking 126 semester hours, including at least 32 in the major. Required courses include freshman English, an introduction to liberal arts, an integration course, and 2 courses each in phys ed and religion. Distribution requirements include 7 courses taken from 5 areas: science and math, social science, foreign language, foundation/premises of civilization, and literature/fine arts.

Special: Cross-registration is offered through the Tri-College University Consortium. Co-op programs and internships are available in most majors, and accelerated degree programs and dual majors are available in all majors. There is a Washington semester and an urban studies semester in Chicago. Study abroad in more than 30 countries, on- and off-campus work-study, a B.A.-B.M. degree in music, and 3-2 and 2-2 engineering degrees with Washington and North Dakota State Universities and the University of Minnesota are possible. Nondegree study for special students and pass/fail options are also available. There are 10 national honor societies, a freshman honors program, and 11 departmental honors programs.

Faculty/Classroom: 60% of faculty are male; 40%, female. All teach undergraduates. The average class size in an introductory lecture is 25; in a laboratory, 18; and in a regular course, 19.

Admissions: 86% of the 2003-2004 applicants were accepted. The SAT I scores for the 2003-2004 freshman class were: Verbal--16% below 500, 42% between 500 and 599, 36% between 600 and 700, and 5% above 700; Math--19% below 500, 45% between 500 and 599, 33% between 600 and 700, and 4% above 700. The ACT scores were 21% below 21, 25% between 21 and 23, 28% between 24 and 26, 13% between 27 and 28, and 12% above 28. 50% of the current freshmen were in the top fifth of their class; 79% were in the top two fifths.

Requirements: The SAT I or ACT is required. In addition, 2 character references are required, and an interview is recommended. The GED is accepted. Academic performance and preparation, as evidenced in a high school transcript, is the single most important factor in the admissions decision. AP and CLEP credits are accepted. Important factors in the admissions decision are recommendations by school officials, advanced placement or honor courses, and personality/intangible qualities.

Procedure: Freshmen are admitted to all sessions. Entrance exams should be taken by the first semester of the senior year. There are early admissions and deferred admissions plans. There is a rolling admissions plan. Application deadlines are open. The fall 2003 application fee was $20. Notification is sent on a rolling basis. A waiting list is an active part of the admissions procedure. Applications are accepted on computer disk and on-line through the school's web site or CollegeLink.

Transfer: Transfer applicants must have a minimum 2.0 GPA, and provide official transcripts from previously attended schools. 32 credits of 126 required for the bachelor's degree must be completed at Concordia.

Visiting: There are regularly scheduled orientations for prospective students, including an extensive campus tour and meetings with admissions counselors and faculty members. There are guides for informal visits and visitors may sit in on classes and stay overnight. To schedule a visit, contact the Office of Admissions.

Financial Aid: In 2002-2003, 90% of all full-time freshmen and 78% of continuing full-time students received some form of financial aid. 57% of full-time freshmen and 53% of continuing full-time students received need-based aid. Need-based scholarships or need-based grants averaged $4998 ($15,635 maximum); need-based self-help aid (loans and jobs) averaged $4612 ($11,834 maximum); and non-need-based awards and non-need-based scholarships averaged $8160 ($21,640 maximum). 52% of undergraduates work part time. Average annual earnings from campus work are $1058. Concordia is a member of CSS. The FAFSA and the college's own financial statement are required. Check with the school for current deadlines.

International Students: The school actively recruits these students. They must score 500 on the written TOEFL.

Computers: The mainframe is a Unisys A2400 Model 311. Macs and PCs are available in 16 computer labs on campus and in each residence hall. All students are assigned an e-mail account and have access to about 265 computers, all of which have Internet access. All students may access the system 20 to 24 hours per day. There are no time limits and no fees.

Graduates: In an average class, 59% graduate in 4 years or less, 67% graduate in 5 years or less, and 68% graduate in 6 years or less.

Admissions Contact: Office of Admissions, Concordia College: Moorhead. E-mail: *admissions@gloria.cord.edu* Web: *www.cord.edu*

CONCORDIA UNIVERSITY/ST.PAUL   C-4
St. Paul, MN 55104-5494   (651) 641-8230
(800) 333-4705; Fax: (651)603-6320

Full-time: 631 men, 874 women   **Faculty:** 85
Part-time: 77 men, 159 women   **Ph.D.s:** 81%
Graduate: 93 men, 217 women   **Student/Faculty:** 18 to 1
Year: semesters, summer session   **Tuition:** $18,624
Application Deadline: August 1   **Room & Board:** $5862
Freshman Class: 729 applied, 467 accepted, 167 enrolled
ACT: 21   **COMPETITIVE**

Concordia University/St.Paul, founded in 1893 and a unit of the Concordia University system, is a private institution affiliated with the Lutheran Church – Missouri Synod and offering programs in teacher education, business, church vocations, and the liberal arts. Programs are also available for adult learners seeking to complete bachelor's degrees. There are 3 undergraduate schools and 1 graduate school. In addition to regional accreditation, CSP has baccalaureate program accreditation with NCATE. The library contains 131,242 volumes, 13,284 microform items, and 6843 audio/video tapes/CDs, and subscribes to 501 periodicals. Computerized library services include the card catalog, interlibrary loans, and database searching. Special learning facilities include a learning resource center, art gallery, and natural history museum. The 37-acre campus is in an urban area in the Midway area of St. Paul. Including any residence halls, there are 28 buildings.

Student Life: 79% of undergraduates are from Minnesota. Students are from 40 states, 9 foreign countries, and Canada. 64% are white. 47% are Protestant; 16% Catholic. The average age of freshmen is 18; all undergraduates, 25. 29% do not continue beyond their first year.

Housing: 481 students can be accommodated in college housing, which includes single-sex dorms, on-campus apartments, and married-student housing. On-campus housing is guaranteed for the freshman year only and is available on a first-come, first-served basis. Priority is given to out-of-town students. 50% of students live on campus. Alcohol is not permitted. All students may keep cars.

Activities: There are no fraternities or sororities. There are 40 groups on campus, including art, band, cheerleading, choir, drama, ethnic, jazz band, musical theater, newspaper, pep band, religious, social, student government, and yearbook.

Sports: There are 5 intercollegiate sports for men and 7 for women, and 5 intramural sports for men and 5 for women. Facilities include a 4500-seat stadium, a 1200-seat gym, a health and wellness center, a rock climbing wall, a 200-meter track, and several playing fields for various sports.

Disabled Students: 95% of the campus is accessible. Wheelchair ramps, elevators, special parking, specially equipped rest rooms, special class scheduling, lowered drinking fountains, lowered telephones, and touch-pad doors are available.

Services: Counseling and information services are available, as is tutoring in every subject. There is remedial math, reading, and writing.

Campus Safety and Security: Measures include 24-hour foot and vehicle patrol, self-defense education, security escort services, and informal discussions. There are pamphlets/posters/films, emergency telephones, and lighted pathways/sidewalks.

Programs of Study: CSP confers B.A. and B.B.A. degrees. Associate and master's degrees are also awarded. Bachelor's degrees are awarded in BIOLOGICAL SCIENCE (biology/biological science), BUSINESS (accounting, banking and finance, business administration and management, management information systems, marketing management, and organizational behavior), COMMUNICATIONS AND THE ARTS (art, communications, dramatic arts, English, music, and studio art), COMPUTER AND PHYSICAL SCIENCE (natural sciences), EDUCATION (early childhood, elementary, English, mathematics, middle school, music, physical, science, secondary, and social studies), ENGINEERING AND ENVIRONMENTAL DESIGN (environmental science), SOCIAL SCIENCE (child care/child and family studies, criminal justice, history, psychology, religion, religious education, religious music, sociology, and theological studies). Business, education, and psychology are the largest.

Required: To graduate, students must complete 128 credit hours in the form of 1 major or 2 minors. GPA varies from 2.0 to 2.75 and required hours in the major vary from 32 to 44, depending on the program. The core curriculum consists of 48 hours of liberal arts courses.

Special: CSP offers cross-registration with other area colleges and other members of the Concordia University system, internships in most programs, and study abroad in England, India, and Mexico. Accelerated degree programs, B.A. degrees, and interdisciplinary majors are also available. Credit for life experience, nondegree study, and pass/fail options are possible. In lieu of a major, 2 minors may be chosen.

Faculty/Classroom: 66% of faculty are male; 34%, female. 85% teach undergraduates. No introductory courses are taught by graduate students. The average class size in an introductory lecture is 20; in a laboratory, 20; and in a regular course, 15.

Admissions: 64% of the 2003-2004 applicants were accepted. The ACT scores for the 2003-2004 freshman class were: 47% below 21, 23%

between 21 and 23, 17% between 24 and 26, 6% between 27 and 28, and 7% above 28. 23% of the current freshmen were in the top fifth of their class; 52% were in the top two fifths.

Requirements: The ACT is recommended. In addition, applicants are required to have 4 years of English, 2 each of math, science, fine arts, and history/social studies, and 1 of health or phys ed. An interview and essay are recommended. 2 letters of recommendation are required. The GED is accepted. CSP requires applicants to be in the upper 50% of their class. A GPA of 2.0 is required. AP and CLEP credits are accepted.

Procedure: Freshmen are admitted to all sessions. Entrance exams should be taken during the senior year. There is a deferred admissions plan. Applications should be filed by August 1 for fall entry and December 1 for spring entry. The fall 2003 application fee was $30. Notification is sent on a rolling basis. Applications are accepted on-line through CollegeNET, CollegeLink, or the school's web site.

Transfer: 97 transfer students enrolled in 2002-2003. Applicants must have a 2.0 GPA and submit 2 letters of recommendation. Students with fewer than 1 year of college credits must also submit ACT scores and an official high school transcript. 32 of 128 credits required for the bachelor's degree must be completed at CSP.

Visiting: There are regularly scheduled orientations for prospective students, including a 3-day program before classes begin, with class visits, lunch, and meetings with professors. There are guides for informal visits and visitors may sit in on classes and stay overnight. To schedule a visit, contact the Director of Undergraduate Admission.

Financial Aid: In 2003-2004, 96% of all full-time freshmen and 64% of continuing full-time students (includes students in adult degree completion programs) received some form of financial aid. 86% of full-time freshmen and 54% of continuing full-time students (includes students in adult degree completion programs) received need-based aid. The average freshman award was $20,604. The FAFSA, the college's own financial statement, and a federal tax return are required. The deadline for filing freshman financial aid applications for fall entry is March 1.

International Students: There are 12 international students enrolled. The school actively recruits these students. They must score 500 on the written TOEFL or 173 on the electronic version or take the MELAB or Level 109 of ELS.

Computers: The mainframe is a DEC Alpha 2100 200. Full-time undergraduates in traditional programs are issued IBM ThinkPad computers. All students may access the system during the hours the media center and science building are open. There are no time limits and no fees. All students are required to have personal computers.

Graduates: From July 1, 2002 to June 30, 2003, 494 bachelor's degrees were awarded. The most popular majors were organizational management (29%), marketing (19%), and teacher education (13%). In an average class, 47% graduate in 6 years or less. 25 companies recruited on campus in 2002-2003.

Admissions Contact: Director of Undergraduate Admission.
E-mail: *admiss@csp.edu* Web: *www.csp.edu*

GUSTAVUS ADOLPHUS COLLEGE   C-4
St. Peter, MN 56082-1498   (507) 933-7676
                            (800) GUSTAVU; Fax: (507) 933-6270

Full-time: 1080 men, 1453 women	**Faculty:** 178; IIB, +$
Part-time: 19 men, 22 women	**Ph.D.s:** 87%
Graduate: none	**Student/Faculty:** 14 to 1
Year: 4-1-4	**Tuition:** $21,660
Application Deadline: April 1	**Room & Board:** $5460
Freshman Class: 2317 applied, 1790 accepted, 688 enrolled	
SAT I Verbal/Math: 610/620	**ACT:** 25 **VERY COMPETITIVE+**

Gustavus Adolphus College, founded in 1862, is a private liberal arts college affiliated with the Lutheran Church. In addition to regional accreditation, Gustavus has baccalaureate program accreditation with NASM, NCATE, and NLN. The library contains 287,243 volumes, 35,797 microform items, and 18,203 audio/video tapes/CDs, and subscribes to 999 periodicals. Computerized library services include the card catalog, interlibrary loans, database searching, and Internet access. Special learning facilities include an art gallery, radio station, and an arboretum. The 340-acre campus is in a small town 65 miles southwest of Minneapolis. Including any residence halls, there are 55 buildings.

Student Life: 81% of undergraduates are from Minnesota. Students are from 41 states, 18 foreign countries, and Canada. 93% are from public schools. 92% are white. 74% are Protestant; 18% Catholic. The average age of freshmen is 18; all undergraduates, 20. 11% do not continue beyond their first year; 79% remain to graduate.

Housing: 1960 students can be accommodated in college housing, which includes coed dorms and on-campus apartments. In addition, there are language houses and special-interest houses. On-campus housing is guaranteed for all 4 years. 80% of students live on campus; of those, 80% remain on campus on weekends. Upperclassmen may keep cars.

Activities: 20% of men belong to 6 local fraternities; 17% of women belong to 4 local sororities and 1 national sorority. There are 85 groups

on campus, including band, cheerleading, choir, chorus, dance, debate, drama, ethnic, forensics, gay, honors, international, jazz band, literary magazine, newspaper, orchestra, pep band, political, professional, radio and TV, religious, social, social service, student government, and yearbook. Popular campus events include Christmas in Christ Chapel and Frost Week.

Sports: There are 12 intercollegiate sports for men and 13 for women, and 17 intramural sports for men and 10 for women. Facilities include an ice arena, an Olympic-size pool, a gymnastics area, an indoor tennis center, an arena, playing fields, racquetball and tennis courts, a weight room, an indoor and an outdoor running track, and varsity and intramural fields for soccer, softball, baseball, lacrosse, rugby, and Ultimate Frisbee.

Disabled Students: 90% of the campus is accessible. Wheelchair ramps, elevators, special parking, specially equipped rest rooms, special class scheduling, and lowered drinking fountains are available.

Services: Counseling and information services are available, as is tutoring in most subjects. A writing lab is available.

Campus Safety and Security: Measures include 24-hour foot and vehicle patrol, security escort services, shuttle buses, and informal discussions. There are pamphlets/posters/films, emergency telephones, and lighted pathways/sidewalks.

Programs of Study: Gustavus confers the B.A. degree. Bachelor's degrees are awarded in AGRICULTURE (environmental studies), BIOLOGICAL SCIENCE (biochemistry and biology/biological science), BUSINESS (accounting, business administration and management, business economics, and international business management), COMMUNICATIONS AND THE ARTS (classics, communications, dance, dramatic arts, English, fine arts, French, German, music, Russian, Scandinavian languages, Spanish, and speech/debate/rhetoric), COMPUTER AND PHYSICAL SCIENCE (chemistry, computer science, geology, mathematics, and physics), EDUCATION (art, business, elementary, foreign languages, health, middle school, music, science, and secondary), HEALTH PROFESSIONS (nursing, physical therapy, predentistry, and premedicine), SOCIAL SCIENCE (anthropology, criminal justice, economics, geography, history, philosophy, political science/government, prelaw, psychology, religion, social science, sociology, and women's studies). Physical science and social science are the strongest academically. Business, biology, and social science are the largest.

Required: All students are required to complete 35 courses totaling 140 semester hours, including 3 January-term courses and 1 course in phys ed. Core and distribution requirements include a first-term seminar and 2 additional writing classes, 4 courses in language and humanities, 2 each in fine arts, math/science, social science, and foreign culture, and 1 in religion. A minimum GPA of 2.0 is necessary for graduation. A total of 7 to 11 courses is required in the major.

Special: Co-op programs in nursing with St. Olaf College and cross-registration with Minnesota State University are available. The college offers internships, a Washington semester, study abroad in 22 countries, student-designed majors, nondegree study, and pass/fail options for some courses. A 3-2 engineering degree program with the University of Minnesota and Minnesota State University, Mankato is offered. The Curriculum II core offers a 12-course interdisciplinary program. There are 16 national honor societies, including Phi Beta Kappa, and 12 departmental honors programs.

Faculty/Classroom: 62% of faculty are male; 38%, female. 97% both teach and do research. The average class size in an introductory lecture is 25; in a laboratory, 15; and in a regular course, 15.

Admissions: 77% of the 2003-2004 applicants were accepted. The SAT I scores for the 2003-2004 freshman class were: Verbal--10% below 500, 32% between 500 and 599, 41% between 600 and 700, and 17% above 700; Math--6% below 500, 31% between 500 and 599, 49% between 600 and 700, and 14% above 700. The ACT scores were 16% below 21, 21% between 21 and 23, 26% between 24 and 26, 13% between 27 and 28, and 24% above 28. 60% of the current freshmen were in the top fifth of their class; 87% were in the top two fifths. There were 12 National Merit finalists. 57 freshmen graduated first in their class.

Requirements: The SAT I or ACT is required. In addition, applicants must have completed 4 years of English, 3 each of math and science, and 2 each of a foreign language, history, and social studies. AP credits are accepted. Important factors in the admissions decision are advanced placement or honor courses, evidence of special talent, and parents or siblings attending the school.

Procedure: Freshmen are admitted fall, winter, and spring. Entrance exams should be taken in the fall of the senior year. There are early admissions and deferred admissions plans. Applications should be filed by April 1 for fall entry, December 15 for winter entry, and January 15 for spring entry. Notification is sent on a rolling basis. 125 applicants were on the 2003 waiting list; 11 were admitted. Applications are accepted on-line through CollegeNET and the school's web site.

Transfer: 27 transfer students enrolled in 2002-2003. Transfer applicants must have earned a 2.4 GPA at their previous college. 72 of 140 credits required for the bachelor's degree must be completed at Gustavus.

Visiting: There are regularly scheduled orientations for prospective students, consisting of an interview, a tour, and meetings with faculty and students. There are guides for informal visits and visitors may sit in on classes and stay overnight. To schedule a visit, contact the Admissions Office at *admission@gustavus.edu.*

Financial Aid: In 2003-2004, 93% of all full-time freshmen and 92% of continuing full-time students received some form of financial aid. 68% of full-time freshmen and 65% of continuing full-time students received need-based aid. The average freshman award was $14,363. Need-based scholarships or need-based grants averaged $8063 ($28,355 maximum); and need-based self-help aid (loans and jobs) averaged $5200 ($6800 maximum). 71% of undergraduates work part time. Average annual earnings from campus work are $1600. The average financial indebtedness of the 2003 graduate was $16,900. Gustavus is a member of CSS. The FAFSA, the college's own financial statement, and the the CSS Profile for early aid decisions are required. The priority date for freshman financial aid applications for fall entry is December 1. The deadline for filing freshman financial aid applications for fall entry is April 1.

International Students: There are 31 international students enrolled. The school actively recruits these students. They must score 550 on the written TOEFL or 213 on the electronic version or take the MELAB.

Computers: The mainframes are a DEC MicroVAX 3600 and a MicroVAX II. Students have access to 6 computer networks, some of which are connected with the Minnesota State University System. These include 55 Mac, 50 IBM, and 27 NeXT PCs located in the library and various academic buildings. There is also an electronic music lab. All students may access the system. There are no time limits and no fees. It is strongly recommended that all students have a personal computer.

Graduates: From July 1, 2002 to June 30, 2003, 591 bachelor's degrees were awarded. The most popular majors were management (9%), biology (8%), and communications (8%). In an average class, 2% graduate in 3 years or less, 79% graduate in 4 years or less, 82% graduate in 5 years or less, and 82% graduate in 6 years or less. 40 companies recruited on campus in a recent year. Of a recent graduating class, 30% were enrolled in graduate school within 6 months of graduation and 65% were employed.

Admissions Contact: Mark H. Anderson, Dean of Admission. A video is available. E-mail: *markande@gustavus.edu* Web: *www.gustavus.edu*

HAMLINE UNIVERSITY
St. Paul, MN 55104-1284

C-4

(651) 523-2207
(800) 753-9753; Fax: (651) 523-2458

Full-time: 707 men, 1165 women	Faculty: 104; IIA, -$
Part-time: 32 men, 76 women	Ph.D.s: 100%
Graduate: 788 men, 1701 women	Student/Faculty: 18 to 1
Year: 4-1-4, summer session	Tuition: $20,832
Application Deadline: May 1	Room & Board: $6220
Freshman Class: 1813 applied, 1348 accepted, 456 enrolled	
SAT I Verbal/Math: 598/589	ACT: 24 VERY COMPETITIVE

Hamline University, founded in 1854, is a private liberal arts and sciences university affiliated with the United Methodist Church. Graduate enrollment figures in the above capsule include the law school. In addition to regional accreditation, Hamline has baccalaureate program accreditation with NASM and NCATE. The 2 libraries contain 292,178 volumes, 931,602 microform items, and 2642 audio/video tapes/CDs, and subscribe to 4041 periodicals. Computerized library services include the card catalog, interlibrary loans, database searching, and Internet access. Special learning facilities include a learning resource center, art gallery, radio station, centers for environmental education and applied research, the Jewish History Society Archives, and the Center for Excellence in Urban Teaching. The 57-acre campus is in an urban area between the downtowns of Minneapolis and St. Paul. Including any residence halls, there are 27 buildings.

Student Life: 21% of students are Catholic; 10% claim no religious affiliation. The average age of freshmen is 18; all undergraduates, 21. 16% do not continue beyond their first year; 67% remain to graduate.

Housing: 922 students can be accommodated in college housing, which includes coed dorms and on-campus apartments. In addition, there are language houses, special-interest houses, and smoke-free, substance-free, and living/learning floors. On-campus housing is guaranteed for all 4 years. 53% of students live on campus; of those, 90% remain on campus on weekends. All students may keep cars.

Activities: 55% of women belong to 1 local sorority. There are no fraternities. There are 80 groups on campus, including art, band, cheerleading, chess, choir, chorale, chorus, computers, dance, drama, ethnic, film, gay, honors, international, jazz band, literary magazine, marching band, musical theater, newspaper, orchestra, pep band, political, professional, radio and TV, religious, social, social service, student government, symphony, and yearbook. Popular campus events include World Fest, Community Service Week, and Fall Fair.

Sports: There are 9 intercollegiate sports for men and 9 for women, and 8 intramural sports for men and 10 for women. Facilities include a stadium, a field house and swimming pool, a playing field, and an athletic center.

Disabled Students: 75% of the campus is accessible. Wheelchair ramps, elevators, special parking, specially equipped rest rooms, special class scheduling, lowered drinking fountains, and lowered telephones are available.

Services: Counseling and information services are available, as is tutoring in every subject. There is a reader service for the blind, and remedial math, reading, and writing.

Campus Safety and Security: Measures include 24-hour foot and vehicle patrol, self-defense education, security escort services, and informal discussions. There are pamphlets/posters/films, emergency telephones, and lighted pathways/sidewalks.

Programs of Study: Hamline confers the B.A. degree. Master's and doctoral degrees are also awarded. Bachelor's degrees are awarded in BIOLOGICAL SCIENCE (biology/biological science), BUSINESS (business administration and management and international business management), COMMUNICATIONS AND THE ARTS (art, art history and appreciation, communications, dramatic arts, English, fine arts, French, German, music, and Spanish), COMPUTER AND PHYSICAL SCIENCE (chemistry, mathematics, and physics), EDUCATION (athletic training, elementary, foreign languages, physical, science, and secondary), ENGINEERING AND ENVIRONMENTAL DESIGN (environmental science), HEALTH PROFESSIONS (predentistry and premedicine), SOCIAL SCIENCE (anthropology, criminal justice, East Asian studies, economics, European studies, history, international relations, Latin American studies, paralegal studies, peace studies, philosophy, political science/government, prelaw, psychology, religion, social science, sociology, urban studies, and women's studies). Prelaw, premedicine, and international relations are the strongest academically. Psychology, English, and political science are the largest.

Required: To graduate, students must complete 32 course credits (128 semester hours) with a minimum overall GPA of 2.0. 63 course credits must be outside the major. In their first year, all students are required to take a freshman seminar and freshman English, and demonstrate computer literacy. All students must also take 3 writing-intensive courses, 1 each year following, and 3 courses on human or cultural diversity; 2 speaking-intensive courses and 2 courses each in fine arts, humanities, natural sciences, and social sciences; and 1 course each in computer utilization and formal reasoning. An independent study project and an internship are also required.

Special: Cross-registration with Augsburg, Macalester, and Saint Catherine Colleges and the University of Saint Thomas is possible. Students may select cooperative programs, study abroad, a Washington semester with American University, dual majors, student-designed majors, and pass/fail options. Students may earn a 3-2 or 4-2 engineering degree at the University of Minnesota or Washington University. On-campus work-study is available, as are extensive internship opportunities on and off campus. There are 18 national honor societies, including Phi Beta Kappa, a freshman honors program, and 10 departmental honors programs.

Faculty/Classroom: 50% of faculty are male; 50%, female. All teach undergraduates. No introductory courses are taught by graduate students. The average class size in an introductory lecture is 27; in a laboratory, 14; and in a regular course, 19.

Admissions: 74% of the 2003-2004 applicants were accepted. 58% of the current freshmen were in the top fifth of their class; 79% were in the top two fifths. There were 3 National Merit finalists and 7 semifinalists. 22 freshmen graduated first in their class.

Requirements: The ACT is required and the SAT I is recommended. In addition, it is recommended that candidates for admission complete 4 years of English with 1 year of college preparatory writing, 3 years each of math, lab science, and social science, and 2 years of a foreign language. AP and CLEP credits are accepted. Important factors in the admissions decision are advanced placement or honor courses, recommendations by school officials, and leadership record.

Procedure: Freshmen are admitted in the fall. Entrance exams should be taken by February of the senior year. There are early admissions and deferred admissions plans. Applications should be filed by May 1 for fall entry. Notification of early decision is sent December 15; regular decision, on a rolling basis. Applications are accepted on-line through *www.hamline.edu/cla/admission/applyonline/index.html.*

Transfer: 131 transfer students enrolled in 2002-2003. Transfer applicants must submit the application form, transcript copies, a teacher/adviser recommendation, and a secondary school transcript, if fewer than 32 semester hours have been completed. 42 of 128 credits required for the bachelor's degree must be completed at Hamline.

Visiting: There are guides for informal visits and visitors may sit in on classes and stay overnight. To schedule a visit, contact the Admissions Office.

Financial Aid: In 2003-2004, 84% of full-time freshmen and 83% of continuing full-time students received need-based aid. Need-based scholarships or need-based grants averaged $14,783; need-based self-help aid (loans and jobs) averaged $1738; and other non-need-based awards and non-need-based scholarships averaged $4552. All undergraduates work part time. Average annual earnings from campus work are $2100. The average financial indebtedness of the 2003 graduate was $21,156. The FAFSA and the college's own financial statement are required. The deadline for filing freshman financial aid applications for fall entry is March 15.

International Students: There are 71 international students enrolled. The school actively recruits these students. They must score 550 on the written TOEFL or take the MELAB.

Computers: The mainframe is a Sequent NUMA-Q 2000 high-end Enterprise Server. There are 360 PCs available for student use in the computer center, the library, and classrooms. All students may access the system 24 hours a day, year-round. There are no time limits and no fees. It is strongly recommended that all students have a personal computer.

Graduates: From July 1, 2002 to June 30, 2003, 419 bachelor's degrees were awarded. The most popular majors were psychology (14%), management (12%), and English (10%). In an average class, 1% graduate in 3 years or less, 61% graduate in 4 years or less, 64% graduate in 5 years or less, and 67% graduate in 6 years or less. 18 companies recruited on campus in 2002-2003. Of the 2002 graduating class, 35% were enrolled in graduate school within 6 months of graduation and 91% were employed.

Admissions Contact: Steven Bjork, Director of Admissions.
E-mail: *cla-admis@gw.hamline.edu* Web: *www.hamline.edu*

MACALESTER COLLEGE
C-4

St. Paul, MN 55105

(651) 696-6357

(800) 231-7974; Fax: (651) 696-6724

Full-time: 780 men, 1055 women	**Faculty:** 149; IIB, ++$
Part-time: 20 men, 29 women	**Ph.D.s:** 95%
Graduate: none	**Student/Faculty:** 11 to 1
Year: semesters	**Tuition:** $25,070
Application Deadline: January 15	**Room & Board:** $6874
Freshman Class: 4341 applied, 1920 accepted, 513 enrolled	
SAT I Verbal/Math: 687/662	**ACT:** 30 **MOST COMPETITIVE**

Macalester College, founded in 1874, is a nonsectarian liberal arts and sciences institution affiliated with the United Presbyterian Church. In addition to regional accreditation, Macalester has baccalaureate program accreditation with NASM. The library contains 439,568 volumes, 76,762 microform items, and 9753 audio/video tapes/CDs, and subscribes to 2493 periodicals. Computerized library services include the card catalog, interlibrary loans, database searching, and Internet access. Special learning facilities include a learning resource center, art gallery, radio station, and a 280-acre natural history study area 25 miles from campus. The 53-acre campus is in an urban area midway between downtown St. Paul and Minneapolis. Including any residence halls, there are 36 buildings.

Student Life: 65% of undergraduates are from out of state, mostly the Midwest. Students are from 50 states, 74 foreign countries, and Canada. 67% are from public schools. 74% are white; 14% foreign nationals. The average age of freshmen is 18; all undergraduates, 20. 8% do not continue beyond their first year; 80% remain to graduate.

Housing: 1280 students can be accommodated in college housing, which includes single-sex and coed dorms and on-campus apartments. In addition, there are language houses, special-interest houses, a vegetarian co-op, and a Hebrew house. On-campus housing is available on a lottery system for upperclassmen. 69% of students live on campus; of those, 99% remain on campus on weekends. Upperclassmen may keep cars.

Activities: There are no fraternities or sororities. There are 70 groups on campus, including art, bagpipe band, band, chess, choir, chorale, chorus, computers, dance, debate, drama, ethnic, forensics, gay, honors, international, jazz band, literary magazine, newspaper, orchestra, photography, political, professional, radio and TV, religious, social, social service, student government, and symphony. Popular campus events include Volunteer Service Week, Fall Festival, and Midnight Breakfast.

Sports: There are 10 intercollegiate sports for men and 11 for women, and 20 intramural sports for men and 20 for women. Facilities include a field house, a 650-seat gym, a 4000-seat stadium, a swimming pool, 2 racquetball courts, 6 tennis courts, a dance studio, a track, 2 weight rooms, and baseball and softball diamonds.

Disabled Students: 80% of the campus is accessible. Wheelchair ramps, elevators, special parking, specially equipped rest rooms, special class scheduling, lowered drinking fountains, and lowered telephones are available.

Services: Counseling and information services are available, as is tutoring in most subjects. There is a reader service for the blind and remedial math, reading, and writing.

Campus Safety and Security: Measures include 24-hour foot and vehicle patrol, self-defense education, security escort services, and informal discussions. There are pamphlets/posters/films, emergency telephones, lighted pathways/sidewalks, and a security site on the school's web site.

Programs of Study: Macalester confers the B.A. degree. Bachelor's degrees are awarded in BIOLOGICAL SCIENCE (biology/biological science and neurosciences), COMMUNICATIONS AND THE ARTS (art,

classics, dramatic arts, English, French, Japanese, linguistics, music, Russian, and Spanish), COMPUTER AND PHYSICAL SCIENCE (chemistry, computer science, geology, mathematics, and physics), ENGINEERING AND ENVIRONMENTAL DESIGN (environmental science), SOCIAL SCIENCE (American studies, anthropology, Asian/Oriental studies, economics, geography, German area studies, history, international relations, Latin American studies, philosophy, political science/government, psychology, religion, Russian and Slavic studies, sociology, urban studies, and women's studies). International studies, economics, and biology are the strongest academically. Economics, political science, and English are the largest.

Required: All students are required to complete 128 semester hours, with 32 to 44 in the major, and an overall minimum GPA of 2.0. Required courses include 12 hours in humanities and fine arts, 8 hours in natural science and/or math, 8 hours in social science, 4 hours each in domestic diversity and international diversity, and a first-year course. Second language proficiency equivalent to 2 years of college-level language must be shown, and every major requires a capstone experience.

Special: Cross-registration at Minneapolis College of Art and Design is offered; in addition, the college belongs to several consortiums, including the Associated Colleges of the Twin Cities. There also are cooperative programs in liberal arts and architecture with Washington University in St. Louis, engineering with the same school and the University of Minnesota, and nursing with Rush-Presbyterian-St. Luke's Medical Center in Chicago. Internships are available in government, financial services, law, medicine, research, the arts, and other fields. Students may study abroad in more than 40 countries. Credit by exam under supervision of individual instructors, nondegree study, student-designed majors, and pass/fail options for no more than 1 course per semester also are available. There are 14 national honor societies, including Phi Beta Kappa, and 30 departmental honors programs.

Faculty/Classroom: 53% of faculty are male; 47%, female. All teach undergraduates and 90% both teach and do research. The average class size in an introductory lecture is 19; in a laboratory, 11; and in a regular course, 14.

Admissions: 44% of the 2003-2004 applicants were accepted. The SAT I scores for the 2003-2004 freshman class were: Verbal--9% between 500 and 599, 40% between 600 and 700, and 51% above 700; Math--13% between 500 and 599, 57% between 600 and 700, and 30% above 700. The ACT scores were 1% between 21 and 23, 13% between 24 and 26, 23% between 27 and 28, and 62% above 28. 88% of the current freshmen were in the top fifth of their class; all were in the top two fifths. There were 50 National Merit finalists. 32 freshmen graduated first in their class.

Requirements: The SAT I or ACT is required. In addition, applicants should have earned at least 16 academic credits, including 4 years of English and 3 each in math, laboratory science, foreign language, and social studies/history. The college also expects applicants to have taken honors, AP, or IB courses where available. An essay is required, and an interview is recommended. AP credits are accepted. Important factors in the admissions decision are advanced placement or honor courses, extracurricular activities record, and recommendations by school officials.

Procedure: Freshmen are admitted in the fall. Entrance exams should be taken in the fall of the senior year. There are early decision and deferred admissions plans. Early decision applications should be filed by November 15; regular applications, by January 15 for fall entry, along with a $40 fee. Notification of early decision is sent December 15; regular decision, April 1. 105 early decision candidates were accepted for the 2003-2004 class. 104 applicants were on the 2003 waiting list; none were admitted. Applications are accepted on-line through Next Stop College, Common App, and CollegeNET.

Transfer: 24 transfer students enrolled in 2002-2003. Transfer students usually must present a GPA of 3.33 (B+), a secondary school transcript, and recommendations from 2 teachers and from the dean of students. In addition, the SAT I or ACT is required, and an interview is recommended. Transferable grades are evaluated on the basis of the nature and quality of work. Generally, a grade of C or better is accepted. 64 of 128 credits required for the bachelor's degree must be completed at Macalester.

Visiting: There are regularly scheduled orientations for prospective students, including interviews, information sessions, a class visit, and a tour of campus. There are guides for informal visits and visitors may sit in on classes and stay overnight. To schedule a visit, contact the Admissions Office at *admissions@macalester.edu*.

Financial Aid: In 2003-2004, 74% of all full-time freshmen and 76% of continuing full-time students received some form of financial aid. 70% of full-time freshmen and 68% of continuing full-time students received need-based aid. The average freshman award was $20,302. Need-based scholarships or need-based grants averaged $16,568; and need-based self-help aid (loans and jobs) averaged $3734. 65% of undergraduates work part time. Average annual earnings from campus work are $1450. The average financial indebtedness of the 2003 graduate was $15,000. Macalester is a member of CSS. The CSS Profile or FAFSA, parent's W-2 and tax forms, and student tax forms are required. The deadline for filing freshman financial aid applications for fall entry is February 8.

International Students: There are 264 international students enrolled. The school actively recruits these students. They must score 573 on the written TOEFL or 230 on the electronic version or take the MELAB.

Computers: The central computer provides access to the Internet and to e-mail. There are approximately 300 PCs and Macs available for general student use. All students may access the system 24 hours a day. There are no time limits and no fees.

Graduates: From July 1, 2002 to June 30, 2003, 403 bachelor's degrees were awarded. The most popular majors were economics (10%), political science (10%), and English (9%). In an average class, 75% graduate in 4 years or less, 81% graduate in 5 years or less, and 81% graduate in 6 years or less. 54 companies recruited on campus in 2002-2003. Of the 2002 graduating class, 29% were enrolled in graduate school within 6 months of graduation and 67% were employed.

Admissions Contact: Lorne T. Robinson, Dean of Admissions and Financial Aid. E-mail: *admissions@macalester.edu*
Web: *www.macalester.edu*

METROPOLITAN STATE UNIVERSITY

St. Paul, MN 55106   (651) 793-1305; Fax: (651) 793-1310   C-4

Full-time: 835 men, 1099 women	**Faculty:** 103; IIA, av$
Part-time: 1586 men, 2420 women	**Ph.D.s:** 73%
Graduate: 231 men, 296 women	**Student/Faculty:** 19 to 1
Year: semesters, summer session	**Tuition:** $3852 ($8232)
Application Deadline: July 23	**Room & Board:** n/app
Freshman Class: n/av	
SAT I or ACT: recommended	**SPECIAL**

Metropolitan State University, founded in 1971, is a public institution primarily serving working adults through a variety of majors and individually designed degree programs. There are 6 undergraduate and 2 graduate schools. In addition to regional accreditation, Metro State has baccalaureate program accreditation with NLN. The 2 libraries contain 9500 volumes and 1500 audio/video tapes/CDs, and subscribe to 230 periodicals. Computerized library services include the card catalog, interlibrary loans, database searching, and Internet access. Special learning facilities include a learning resource center. The campus is composed of several small dispersed sites throughout the Twin Cities Metro area. There are 7 buildings.

Student Life: 98% of undergraduates are from Minnesota. Students are from 14 states, 53 foreign countries, and Canada. 95% are from public schools. 41% are white. The average age of freshmen is 28; all undergraduates, 32.

Housing: There are no residence halls. All students commute. Alcohol is not permitted.

Activities: There are no fraternities or sororities. There are 18 groups on campus, including drama, ethnic, gay, honors, international, literary magazine, newspaper, professional, religious, social, and student government.

Sports: There is no sports program at Metro State.

Disabled Students: All of the campus is accessible. Elevators, special parking, specially equipped rest rooms, lowered drinking fountains, and lowered telephones are available.

Services: Counseling and information services are available, as is tutoring in some subjects, including accounting, finance, economics, writing, math, and ESL.

Campus Safety and Security: Measures include security escort services, pamphlets/posters/films, and surveillance cameras.

Programs of Study: Metro State confers B.A., B.S., B.A.S., and B.S.N. degrees. Master's degrees are also awarded. Bachelor's degrees are awarded in BIOLOGICAL SCIENCE (biology/biological science), BUSINESS (accounting, banking and finance, business administration and management, hospitality management services, human resources, international business management, management information systems, marketing management, and trade and industrial supervision and management), COMMUNICATIONS AND THE ARTS (advertising, dramatic arts, English, playwriting/screenwriting, and technical and business writing), COMPUTER AND PHYSICAL SCIENCE (applied mathematics, computer science, and information sciences and systems), EDUCATION (early childhood), HEALTH PROFESSIONS (nursing), SOCIAL SCIENCE (addiction studies, criminal justice, culinary arts, early childhood studies, economics, ethnic studies, food production/management/services, history, human services, law enforcement and corrections, liberal arts/general studies, philosophy, psychology, public administration, social science, social work, and women's studies). Nursing is the strongest academically. Accounting and business administration are the largest.

Required: To graduate, all students must complete 120 to 124 semester credits, with a varying number of hours required in the major, 48 credits in a core curriculum, and a 2.0 GPA. Other requirements include natural/physical science, math/logic, global awareness, humanities and fine arts.

Special: Internships, co-op programs in many areas, study abroad, dual majors, and student-designed programs are offered.

Faculty/Classroom: 55% of faculty are male; 45%, female. All teach undergraduates. The average class size in an introductory lecture is 24; in a laboratory, 24; and in a regular course, 19.

Requirements: The SAT I or ACT is recommended. In addition, Metro State requires applicants to be in the upper 50% of their class or have ACT, PSAT, or SAT I scores at or above the national median. Applicants not meeting these requirements will be considered in the alternative admissions process. The GED is accepted. CLEP credit is accepted.

Procedure: Freshmen are admitted to all sessions. There is a deferred admissions plan. Applications should be filed by July 23 for fall entry, December 15 for spring entry, and April 10 for summer entry, along with a $20 fee. Notification is sent on a rolling basis. Applications are accepted on-line.

Transfer: 3738 transfer students enrolled in 2002-2003. Applicants must have at least a C average. 30 of 120 to 124 credits required for the bachelor's degree must be completed at Metro State.

Visiting: There are regularly scheduled orientations for prospective students, including a campus tour, meetings with a financial adviser, faculty, and students, and a general information session. To schedule a visit, contact the Admissions Office at (651) 793-1300.

Financial Aid: In 2003-2004, 63% of all full-time freshmen and 71% of continuing full-time students received some form of financial aid, including need-based aid. The average freshman award was $3000. Need-based scholarships or need-based grants averaged $1500 ($4050 maximum); need-based self-help aid (loans and jobs) averaged $4000 ($10,500 maximum); and non-need-based awards and non-need-based scholarships averaged $500 ($3000 maximum). 94% of undergraduates work part time. Average annual earnings from campus work are $3000. The average financial indebtedness of the 2003 graduate was $12,125. Metro State is a member of CSS. The FAFSA is required. The deadline for filing freshman financial aid applications for fall entry is August 1.

International Students: There are 182 international students enrolled. They must score 500 on the written TOEFL or take the MELAB.

Computers: There are 3 student computer centers with a total of 230 Mac and IBM PCs. Software is accessed through servers. All students may access the system Monday through Thursday 8:30 A.M. to 10 P.M. and Friday and Saturday 8:30 A.M. to 5 P.M. There are no time limits. The fee is $5 per credit hour.

Graduates: From July 1, 2002 to June 30, 2003, 912 bachelor's degrees were awarded. The most popular majors were individualized (20%), business (15%), and psychology (7%). In an average class, 22% graduate in 4 years or less. 30 companies recruited on campus in 2002-2003.

Admissions Contact: Bruce Holzschuh, Admissions Counselor. E-mail: *bruce.holzschuh@metrostate.edu*

MINNEAPOLIS COLLEGE OF ART AND DESIGN

Minneapolis, MN 55404   (612) 874-3760   C-4
(800) 874-6223; Fax: (612) 874-3701

Full-time: 324 men, 273 women	**Faculty:** 39; IIB, -$
Part-time: 3 men, 1 woman	**Ph.D.s:** 67%
Graduate: 26 men, 32 women	**Student/Faculty:** 15 to 1
Year: semesters, summer session	**Tuition:** $22,950
Application Deadline: February 15	**Room & Board:** $6000
Freshman Class: 429 applied, 300 accepted, 198 enrolled	
SAT I Verbal/Math: 550/525	**ACT:** 23 **SPECIAL**

The Minneapolis College of Art and Design, founded in 1886, is a private college of art. In addition to regional accreditation, MCAD has baccalaureate program accreditation with NASAD. The library contains 60,000 volumes, 9 microform items, and 2103 audio/video tapes/CDs, and subscribes to 180 periodicals. Computerized library services include interlibrary loans, database searching, and Internet access. Special learning facilities include a learning resource center, art gallery, and on-line radio. The 7-acre campus is in an urban area 1 mile south of downtown Minneapolis. Including any residence halls, there are 9 buildings.

Student Life: 64% of undergraduates are from Minnesota. Students are from 36 states, 21 foreign countries, and Canada. 90% are from public schools. 80% are white. The average age of freshmen is 19; all undergraduates, 22. 18% do not continue beyond their first year; 33% remain to graduate.

Housing: 285 students can be accommodated in college housing, which includes coed on-campus apartments. On-campus housing is available on a first-come, first-served basis and is available on a lottery system for upperclassmen. Priority is given to out-of-town students. 53% of students commute. All students may keep cars.

Activities: There are no fraternities or sororities. There are 9 groups on campus, including art, computers, drama, film, gay, photography, professional, and student government. Popular campus events include Senior Show, Thanksgiving Dinner, and Art Sale.

Sports: There are 2 intramural sports for men and 2 for women. Students have use of off-campus facilities.

Disabled Students: 95% of the campus is accessible. Wheelchair ramps, elevators, special parking, specially equipped rest rooms, and special class scheduling are available.

Services: Counseling and information services are available, as is tutoring in most subjects. There is remedial reading and writing.

Campus Safety and Security: Measures include 24-hour foot and vehicle patrol, self-defense education, security escort services, and informal discussions. There are pamphlets/posters/films, emergency telephones, lighted pathways/sidewalks, and a taxi service.

Programs of Study: MCAD confers B.S. and B.F.A. degrees. Master's degrees are also awarded. Bachelor's degrees are awarded in COMMUNICATIONS AND THE ARTS (advertising, animation, design, drawing, film arts, graphic design, illustration, painting, photography, printmaking, sculpture, studio art, and video), COMPUTER AND PHYSICAL SCIENCE (digital arts/technology), ENGINEERING AND ENVIRONMENTAL DESIGN (furniture design). Graphic design, illustration, and photography are the largest.

Required: All B.F.A. students must satisfactorily complete 120 semester credits, including 38 in foundation studies and 27 to 42 in the major. A 2.0 minimum GPA must be maintained. A senior project is required.

Special: MCAD offers cross-registration with Macalester College, internships, study abroad in Italy, Japan, Germany, England, and Ireland, and work-study programs.

Faculty/Classroom: 55% of faculty are male; 45%, female. All teach undergraduates. No introductory courses are taught by graduate students. The average class size in an introductory lecture is 25; in a laboratory, 18; and in a regular course, 18.

Admissions: 70% of the 2003-2004 applicants were accepted. The SAT I scores for the 2003-2004 freshman class were: Verbal--20% below 500, 40% between 500 and 599, 30% between 600 and 700, and 10% above 700; Math--30% below 500, 35% between 500 and 599, 25% between 600 and 700, and 10% above 700. The ACT scores were 20% below 21, 40% between 21 and 23, 30% between 24 and 26, 7% between 27 and 28, and 3% above 28. 40% of the current freshmen were in the top fifth of their class; 70% were in the top two fifths.

Requirements: The SAT I or ACT is required. In addition, applicants must submit a personal statement of interest, an essay, a letter of recommendation, transcripts, and a portfolio (B.F.A.). An interview is strongly encouraged. The GED is accepted. A GPA of 2.5 is required. AP credits are accepted. Important factors in the admissions decision are evidence of special talent, personality/intangible qualities, and recommendations by school officials.

Procedure: Freshmen are admitted fall and spring. Entrance exams should be taken in the spring of the junior year in high school. There is a deferred admissions plan. For priority consideration, applications should be filed by February 15 for fall entry and October 1 for spring entry. The fall 2003 application fee was $35. Notification is sent on a rolling basis.

Transfer: B.F.A. applicants must submit a portfolio for the transfer of studio credit and an official transcript from all postsecondary schools. 45 of 120 credits required for the bachelor's degree must be completed at MCAD.

Visiting: There are regularly scheduled orientations for prospective students, consisting of tours, a program about putting a portfolio together, career information, and financial aid information. There are guides for informal visits and visitors may sit in on classes and stay overnight. To schedule a visit, contact the Admissions Office.

Financial Aid: MCAD is a member of CSS. The FAFSA and parent and student federal income tax forms are required. Check with the school for current application deadlines.

International Students: They must score 550 on the written TOEFL or 213 on the electronic version or take ESL level 109.

Computers: The Computer Center services more than 118 workstations in 7 locations. There is software for word processing, painting, drawing, 2- and 3-dimensional design, programming, electronic imaging (digitizing), scanning, image processing, page layout prepress color separation, 2- and 3-dimensional animation, and modeling. All students may access the system. There are no time limits.

Graduates: In an average class, 29% graduate in 4 years or less, 34% graduate in 5 years or less, and 35% graduate in 6 years or less.

Admissions Contact: William Mullen, Director of Admissions and Recruitment. E-mail: *admissions@mcad.edu* Web: *www.mcad.edu*

MINNESOTA STATE UNIVERSITY, MANKATO   C-4
Mankato, MN 56001   (507) 389-1822
(800) 722-0544; Fax: (507) 389-1511

Full-time: 5328 men, 5857 women	**Faculty:** 467; IIA, av$
Part-time: 540 men, 663 women	**Ph.D.s:** 78%
Graduate: 611 men, 1038 women	**Student/Faculty:** 24 to 1
Year: semesters, summer session	**Tuition:** $4506 ($8775)
Application Deadline: open	**Room & Board:** $4297
Freshman Class: 5661 applied, 4956 accepted, 2288 enrolled	
ACT: 21	**LESS COMPETITIVE**

Minnesota State University, Mankato, founded in 1868 and a unit of Minnesota State Colleges and Universities, offers programs in the liberal arts and sciences, as well as business, education, engineering and technology, and nursing. There are 6 undergraduate schools and 1 graduate school. In addition to regional accreditation, Minnesota State has baccalaureate program accreditation with AACSB, ABET, ADA, CSWE, NASAD, NASM, NCATE, NLN, and NRPA. The library contains 1,107,354 volumes, 253,560 microform items, and 30,686 audio/video tapes/CDs, and subscribes to 3126 periodicals. Computerized library services include the card catalog, interlibrary loans, database searching, and Internet access. Special learning facilities include a learning resource center, art gallery, radio station, and 2 observatories. The 354-acre campus is in a rural area 85 miles southwest of Minneapolis-St. Paul. Including any residence halls, there are 18 buildings.

Student Life: 84% of undergraduates are from Minnesota. Students are from 49 states, 70 foreign countries, and Canada. 94% are from public schools. 62% are white. The average age of freshmen is 19; all undergraduates, 22. 22% do not continue beyond their first year; 49% remain to graduate.

Housing: 3100 students can be accommodated in college housing, which includes coed dorms. There are special-interest floors, including freshman quiet-study floors, engineering floors, and computer science floors. On-campus housing is guaranteed for the freshman year only, is available on a first-come, first-served basis, and is available on a lottery system for upperclassmen. 75% of students commute. Alcohol is not permitted. All students may keep cars.

Activities: 1% of men belong to 7 national fraternities; 1% of women belong to 4 national sororities. There are 114 groups on campus, including art, band, cheerleading, choir, chorale, chorus, computers, dance, debate, drama, ethnic, film, forensics, gay, honors, international, jazz band, literary magazine, marching band, musical theater, newspaper, opera, orchestra, pep band, photography, political, professional, radio and TV, religious, social, social service, and student government. Popular campus events include Greek Week and multicultural activities and celebrations.

Sports: There are 10 intercollegiate sports for men and 10 for women, and 35 intramural sports for men and 35 for women. Facilities include a 7000-seat stadium, 2 gyms, a field house, indoor tracks, tennis and racquetball courts, an indoor swimming pool, and a 5000-seat ice hockey arena (city-owned).

Disabled Students: 90% of the campus is accessible. Wheelchair ramps, elevators, special parking, specially equipped rest rooms, special class scheduling, lowered drinking fountains, lowered telephones, and assistive technology are available.

Services: Counseling and information services are available, as is tutoring in most subjects. There is a reader service for the blind, and remedial math, reading, and writing. Also available are alternative testing accommodations, note taking, sign language interpreting, and taped texts.

Campus Safety and Security: Measures include 24-hour foot and vehicle patrol, self-defense education, security escort services, and shuttle buses. There are informal discussions, pamphlets/posters/films, emergency telephones, lighted pathways/sidewalks, closed-circuit parking lot cameras, and motion-sensitive lights in low traffic areas.

Programs of Study: Minnesota State confers B.A., B.S., B.F.A., B.Mus., B.S.E.E., and B.S.M.E. degrees. Associate and master's degrees are also awarded. Bachelor's degrees are awarded in BIOLOGICAL SCIENCE (avian sciences, biochemistry, biology/biological science, and biotechnology), BUSINESS (accounting, banking and finance, business administration and management, international business management, management science, and marketing/retailing/merchandising), COMMUNICATIONS AND THE ARTS (applied art, art, communications, dance, dramatic arts, English, French, German, journalism, music, music business management, Spanish, and speech/debate/rhetoric), COMPUTER AND PHYSICAL SCIENCE (astronomy, chemistry, earth science, information sciences and systems, mathematics, and physics), EDUCATION (art, athletic training, elementary, foreign languages, health, industrial arts, music, physical, science, and secondary), ENGINEERING AND ENVIRONMENTAL DESIGN (automotive technology, aviation administration/management, construction management, electrical/electronics engineering, electrical/electronics engineering technology, engineering technology, environmental science, interior design, manufacturing technology, mechanical engineering, and preengineering), HEALTH PROFESSIONS (dental hygiene, health science, medical laboratory technology, nursing, predentistry, premedicine, preosteopathy, prepharmacy, prepodiatry, preveterinary science, public health, and speech pathology/audiology), SOCIAL SCIENCE (anthropology, corrections, dietetics, economics, ethnic studies, family/consumer studies, food science, geography, history, humanities, law enforcement and corrections, parks and recreation management, philosophy, political science/government, prelaw, psychology, social studies, social work, sociology, urban studies, and women's studies). Engineering, nursing, and sciences are the strongest academically. Business, social work, and psychology are the largest.

Required: To graduate, students must complete 128 semester hours of credit, with a minimum GPA of 2.0 and at least 45 hours in the major. Most programs require 44 hours of general education, including courses in English, speech, science, math, social/behavioral science, arts and humanities, cultural diversity, global perspective, ethnic/civic responsibility, and people and the environment.

Special: The university offers cross-registration within the Minnesota State University System and with Gustavus Adolphus College. Students may serve internships, study abroad, or participate in an accelerated degree program. B.A.-B.S. degrees, dual and student-designed majors, nondegree study, and pass/fail options also are available. There are 11 national honor societies, a freshman honors program, and 1 departmental honors program.

Faculty/Classroom: 58% of faculty are male; 42%, female. 96% teach undergraduates and 51% do research. Graduate students teach 4% of introductory courses. The average class size in an introductory lecture is 43; in a laboratory, 11; and in a regular course, 21.

Admissions: 88% of the 2003-2004 applicants were accepted. The ACT scores for the 2003-2004 freshman class were: 40% below 21, 36% between 21 and 23, 18% between 24 and 26, 5% between 27 and 28, and 2% above 28. 21% of the current freshmen were in the top fifth of their class; 54% were in the top two fifths. 20 freshmen graduated first in their class.

Requirements: The ACT is required. In addition, applicants must be graduates of an accredited secondary school and rank in the top 50% of their high school class or have an ACT composite score of 21 or higher along with a satisfactory class rank. AP and CLEP credits are accepted.

Procedure: Freshmen are admitted to all sessions. Entrance exams should be taken in the spring of the junior year or the fall of the senior year. There is a deferred admissions plan. Application deadlines are open. The fall 2003 application fee was $20. Notification is sent on a rolling basis. Applications are accepted on-line through *mnsu.edu*.

Transfer: 1341 transfer students enrolled in 2002-2003. Transfer applicants must have a minimum GPA of 2.0 and have completed at least 75% of all college-level courses attempted. 30 of 128 credits required for the bachelor's degree must be completed at Minnesota State.

Visiting: There are regularly scheduled orientations for prospective students, consisting of overview presentations, campus tours, and academic information fairs. Visitors may sit in on classes. To schedule a visit, contact the Admissions Office.

Financial Aid: In a recent year, 45% of all full-time freshmen and 46% of continuing full-time students received some form of financial aid. 32% of full-time freshmen and 33% of continuing full-time students received need-based aid. The average freshman award was $4977. 21% of undergraduates work part time. Average annual earnings from campus work are $1960. The FAFSA is required. The deadline for filing freshman financial aid applications for fall entry is March 15.

International Students: There are 460 international students enrolled. They must score 500 on the written TOEFL or 173 on the electronic version and also take an English placement test at matriculation.

Computers: Mac and PCs are available at several campus locations, including a centralized lab with 475 computers and 6 computerized classrooms. All students may access the system. There are no time limits. The fee is $3.11 per semester credit. For the College of Business, a laptop PC is required.

Graduates: From July 1, 2002 to June 30, 2003, 1819 bachelor's degrees were awarded. The most popular majors were elementary education (11%), management (8%), and computer and information sciences (6%). In an average class, 2% graduate in 3 years or less, 21% graduate in 4 years or less, 43% graduate in 5 years or less, and 49% graduate in 6 years or less. 260 companies recruited on campus in 2002-2003.

Admissions Contact: Walt Wolff, Director of Admissions.
E-mail: *admissions@mankato.msus.edu* Web: *www.mankato.msus.edu*

MINNESOTA STATE UNIVERSITY, MOORHEAD A-2
Moorhead, MN 56563 (218) 236-2161
(800) 593-7246; Fax: (218) 236-2168

Full-time: 6321 men and women	Faculty: 255
Part-time: 1417 men and women	Ph.D.s: 75%
Graduate: 300 men and women	Student/Faculty: 19 to 1
Year: semesters, summer session	Tuition: $4254 ($7884)
Application Deadline: August 1	Room & Board: $4340
Freshman Class: n/av	
SAT I or ACT: required	LESS COMPETITIVE

Minnesota State University, Moorhead, founded in 1885, is a public liberal arts institution. In addition to regional accreditation, Moorhead State has baccalaureate program accreditation with AACN, ACS, ASLHA, CACREP, CSWE, NAIT, NASAD, NASM, and NCATE. The library contains 570,000 volumes, 45,000 microform items, and 7000 audio/video tapes/CDs, and subscribes to 4000 periodicals. Computerized library services include the card catalog, interlibrary loans, and database searching. Special learning facilities include an art gallery, planetarium, radio station, TV station, and a science center. The 119-acre campus is in a suburban area 240 miles northwest of Minneapolis-St. Paul and across the river from Fargo, North Dakota. Including any residence halls, there are 26 buildings.

Student Life: 96% are white. The average age of freshmen is 18; all undergraduates, 24.

Housing: 1824 students can be accommodated in college housing, which includes single-sex and coed dorms and on-campus apartments. On-campus housing is available on a first-come, first-served basis. 67% of students commute. Alcohol is not permitted. All students may keep cars.

Activities: 2% of men belong to 1 local and 1 national fraternity; 1% of women belong to 3 national sororities. There are 150 groups on campus, including art, band, cheerleading, choir, chorus, computers, dance, drama, drill team, ethnic, film, gay, honors, international, jazz band, literary magazine, musical theater, newspaper, orchestra, pep band, photography, political, professional, radio and TV, religious, social, social service, and student government. Popular campus events include Parents Day, Straw Hat Summer Theatre, and Meltdown Concert.

Sports: There are 5 intercollegiate sports for men and 9 for women, and 14 intramural sports for men and 14 for women. Facilities include 4 gyms, racquetball and volleyball courts, 2 swimming pools, indoor and outdoor tennis courts, weight and wrestling rooms, a running track, and 3 softball diamonds.

Disabled Students: Wheelchair ramps, elevators, special parking, specially equipped rest rooms, lowered drinking fountains, and lowered telephones are available.

Services: Counseling and information services are available, as is tutoring in every subject. There is a reader service for the blind and remedial math, reading, and writing.

Campus Safety and Security: Measures include 24-hour foot and vehicle patrol, self-defense education, security escort services, and informal discussions. There are pamphlets/posters/films, emergency telephones, and lighted pathways/sidewalks.

Programs of Study: Moorhead State confers B.A., B.S., B.F.A., B.M., B.S.N., and B.S.W. degrees. Associate and master's degrees are also awarded. Bachelor's degrees are awarded in BIOLOGICAL SCIENCE (biology/biological science), BUSINESS (accounting, banking and finance, business administration and management, hotel/motel and restaurant management, international business management, marketing/retailing/merchandising, and trade and industrial supervision and management), COMMUNICATIONS AND THE ARTS (advertising, broadcasting, communications, dramatic arts, English, fine arts, French, German, journalism, music, public relations, Spanish, and speech/debate/rhetoric), COMPUTER AND PHYSICAL SCIENCE (chemistry, computer science, mathematics, and physics), EDUCATION (art, early childhood, elementary, foreign languages, health, industrial arts, music, science, secondary, social studies, and special), ENGINEERING AND ENVIRONMENTAL DESIGN (construction engineering), HEALTH PROFESSIONS (medical laboratory technology, nursing, predentistry, premedicine, prepharmacy, preveterinary science, and speech pathology/audiology), SOCIAL SCIENCE (American studies, anthropology, criminal justice, economics, history, paralegal studies, philosophy, political science/government, prelaw, psychology, social science, social work, and sociology). Music and speech/theater are the strongest academically. Business, education, and mass communications are the largest.

Required: To graduate students must have a 2.0 GPA and complete 128 semester hours, including a liberal arts core of 45 credits and 43 semester hours in upper-division courses. Required courses include 6 hours each of natural science, social science, humanities, and communications, language, or symbolic systems, and 5 credits in cultural diversity. All students must complete an upper-level writing requirement.

Special: Internships are available in most disciplines. The university offers cross-registration with North Dakota State University and Concordia College, and is a member of the National Student Exchange. Students may study abroad in more than 60 countries. Student-designed and dual majors, credit for military experience, nondegree study, and pass/fail options are possible. There are 7 national honor societies, a freshman honors program, and 1 departmental honors program.

Requirements: A high school diploma is required, and the GED is accepted. An SAT I combined score of 1000 or ACT of 21 is required. Moorhead State requires applicants to be in the upper 50% of their class. AP and CLEP credits are accepted.

Procedure: Freshmen are admitted to all sessions. Entrance exams should be taken in the junior or senior year of high school. Applications should be filed by August 1 for fall entry, along with a $20 fee. Notification is sent on a rolling basis.

Transfer: 690 transfer students enrolled in 2002-2003.

Visiting: There are regularly scheduled orientations for prospective students, including a campus tour, lunch, and meetings with faculty and an admissions officer. There are guides for informal visits. To schedule a visit, contact the Admissions Office.

Financial Aid: 80% of undergraduates work part time. The FAFSA is required. The priority date for freshman financial aid applications for fall entry is March 1.

International Students: The school actively recruits these students. They must score 500 on the written TOEFL.

Computers: The mainframe is a DEC 4000/700A. There are 450 PCs available for student use, as well as 7 DEC and Data General minicomputers with more than 200 terminals. All students may access the system 24 hours a day, 7 days a week. There are no time limits.

Admissions Contact: Director of Admissions.

NORTH CENTRAL UNIVERSITY
C-4

Minneapolis, MN 55404

(612) 343-4460

(800) 289-6222; Fax: (612) 343-4778

Full-time: 530 men, 700 women	**Faculty:** 40
Part-time: none	**Ph.D.s:** 50%
Graduate: none	**Student/Faculty:** 31 to 1
Year: semesters, summer session	**Tuition:** $10,594
Application Deadline: June 1	**Room & Board:** $4310
Freshman Class: 800 applied, 770 accepted, 500 enrolled	
SAT I Verbal/Math: 500/500	**ACT:** 22 **COMPETITIVE**

North Central University, founded in 1930 and affiliated with the Assemblies of God, is a Christian University that emphasizes rigorous academic training and spiritual passion. The library contains 70,041 volumes, 29 microform items, and 200 audio/video tapes/CDs, and subscribes to 325 periodicals. Computerized library services include the card catalog, interlibrary loans, database searching, and Internet access. Special learning facilities include a learning resource center, radio station, and TV station. The 8-acre campus is in an urban area in downtown Minneapolis. Including any residence halls, there are 12 buildings.

Student Life: 65% of undergraduates are from out of state, mostly the Midwest. Students are from 42 states, 7 foreign countries, and Canada. 88% are from public schools. 94% are white. Most are Protestant. The average age of freshmen is 18; all undergraduates, 20. 25% do not continue beyond their first year; 50% remain to graduate.

Housing: 950 students can be accommodated in college housing, which includes single-sex dorms and on-campus apartments. In addition, there are honors houses. 78% of students live on campus. Alcohol is not permitted. Upperclassmen may keep cars.

Activities: There are no fraternities or sororities. There are 28 groups on campus, including art, band, choir, chorale, chorus, drama, jazz band, literary magazine, musical theater, newspaper, orchestra, photography, political, radio and TV, religious, social, student government, and yearbook. Popular campus events include All-College Picnic, Community Outreach Day, and Spring Banquet.

Sports: There are 6 intercollegiate sports for men and 6 for women, and 4 intramural sports for men and 4 for women. Facilities include Elliot Park, the Clark-Danielson College Life Center gym, and the National Sports Complex.

Disabled Students: All of the campus is accessible. Wheelchair ramps, elevators, special parking, specially equipped rest rooms, special class scheduling, lowered drinking fountains, and lowered telephones are available.

Services: Counseling and information services are available, as is tutoring in every subject.

Campus Safety and Security: Measures include 24-hour foot and vehicle patrol, security escort services, pamphlets/posters/films, and lighted pathways/sidewalks.

Programs of Study: NCU confers B.A. and B.S. degrees. Associate degrees are also awarded. Bachelor's degrees are awarded in COMMUNICATIONS AND THE ARTS (communications), EDUCATION (elementary), SOCIAL SCIENCE (behavioral science, biblical languages, ministries, pastoral studies, religion, religious education, and religious music). Elementary education, English, and business are the strongest academically. Music, elementary education, and youth ministries are the largest.

Required: Students must complete 129 to 144 credits for their particular bachelor's degree. Each program has specific requirements, including general education and biblical studies core classes. Internships are required for all programs. Students must take 60 or more total hours in their major, with a minimum overall GPA of 2.0 (2.2 for teacher education).

Special: Students may pursue co-op programs in nursing or secondary education, study abroad in 6 countries, or nondegree study, or receive credit for life, military, or work experience. Work-study, dual majors, and student-designed majors are available.

Faculty/Classroom: 63% of faculty are male; 37%, female. All teach undergraduates. The average class size in an introductory lecture is 80; in a laboratory, 15; and in a regular course, 25.

Admissions: 96% of the 2003-2004 applicants were accepted. The SAT I scores for the 2003-2004 freshman class were: Verbal--25% below 500, 50% between 500 and 599, and 25% between 600 and 700; Math--25% below 500, 50% between 500 and 599, and 25% between 600 and 700. The ACT scores were 25% below 21, 50% between 21 and 23, 10% between 24 and 26, 10% between 27 and 28, and 5% above 28.

Requirements: The ACT or SAT I is required, with a minimum ACT score of 18 or a total SAT I score of 850 or above. In addition, high school transcripts and academic and pastoral references are required. A GPA of 2.2 is required. AP and CLEP credits are accepted.

Procedure: Freshmen are admitted fall and spring. Entrance exams should be taken during the junior or senior year of high school. There is an early admissions plan. Applications should be filed by June 1 for fall entry and December 31 for spring entry, along with a $25 fee. Notification is sent on a rolling basis.

Transfer: 146 transfer students enrolled in 2002-2003. Transfer applicants must submit a completed application, a pastor's reference, a high school transcript or the GED, and college transcripts. Applicants with less than a year of college credit must also submit ACT or SAT I scores and academic references. 27 of 129 to 144 credits required for the bachelor's degree must be completed at NCU.

Visiting: There are regularly scheduled orientations for prospective students. There are guides for informal visits and visitors may sit in on classes and stay overnight. To schedule a visit, contact the Admissions Office at (800) 289-6222 or admissions@northcentral.edu.

Financial Aid: In 2003-2004, 90% of all full-time students received some form of financial aid, including need-based aid. The average freshman award was $6000. All undergraduates work part time. Average annual earnings from campus work are $3500. The average financial indebtedness of the 2003 graduate was $13,369. The FAFSA or FFS and the college's own financial statement are required. The deadline for filing freshman financial aid applications for fall entry is May 1.

International Students: There are 18 international students enrolled. They must score 500 on the written TOEFL and also take the SAT I or the ACT, scoring 850 combined on the SAT I or 18 on the ACT.

Computers: The mainframe is a Hewlett Packard 5500. PCs are available in the library and in the computer lab. All students may access the system. There are no time limits. The fee is $42.

Graduates: The most popular majors among 2003 graduates were music (10%), elementary education (10%), and youth ministries (10%). In an average class, 40% graduate in 4 years or less, 50% graduate in 5 years or less, and 10% graduate in 6 years or less. Of the 2002 graduating class, 10% were enrolled in graduate school within 6 months of graduation and 90% were employed.

Admissions Contact: Jim Hubert, Admissions Director.
E-mail: jghubert@northcentral.edu Web: www.northcentral.edu

NORTHWESTERN COLLEGE
C-4

St. Paul, MN 55113-1598

(651) 631-5209

(800) 827-6827; Fax: (651) 631-5680

Full-time: 611 men, 1053 women	**Faculty:** 68; IIB, -$
Part-time: 23 men, 28 women	**Ph.D.s:** 76%
Graduate: none	**Student/Faculty:** 24 to 1
Year: quarters, summer session	**Tuition:** $17,400
Application Deadline: August 1	**Room & Board:** $5420
Freshman Class: 959 applied, 919 accepted, 432 enrolled	
SAT I Verbal/Math: 575/560	**ACT:** 23 **COMPETITIVE+**

Northwestern College, founded in 1902, is a Christian college offering traditional undergraduate programs in Bible, liberal arts, and professional studies and providing nontraditional educational opportunities through its degree completion and distance education divisions. Some information in this capsule and profile is approximate. In addition to regional accreditation, Northwestern has baccalaureate program accreditation with NASM. The library contains 92,410 volumes, 281 microform items, and 5785 audio/video tapes/CDs, and subscribes to 1989 periodicals. Computerized library services include the card catalog, interlibrary loans, and database searching. Special learning facilities include a learning resource center, art gallery, radio station, and language labs. The 100-acre campus is in a suburban area 7 miles north of downtown St. Paul. Including any residence halls, there are 12 buildings.

Student Life: 62% of undergraduates are from Minnesota. Students are from 32 states, 27 foreign countries, and Canada. 81% are from public schools. 94% are white. Most are Protestant. The average age of freshmen is 18; all undergraduates, 20. 22% do not continue beyond their first year.

Housing: 978 students can be accommodated in college housing, which includes single-sex dorms and on-campus apartments. On-campus housing is guaranteed for the freshman year only and is available on a first-come, first-served basis. Priority is given to out-of-town students. 61% of students live on campus; of those, 70% remain on campus on weekends. Alcohol is not permitted. All students may keep cars.

Activities: There are no fraternities or sororities. There are 26 groups on campus, including art, band, cheerleading, choir, chorale, chorus, drama, ethnic, forensics, international, jazz band, literary magazine, musical theater, newspaper, opera, orchestra, pep band, photography, political, professional, radio and TV, religious, social, social service, student government, and yearbook. Popular campus events include Spiritual Emphasis Week, Parents Weekend, and residence hall open house.

Sports: There are 8 intercollegiate sports for men and 8 for women, and 15 intramural sports for men and 15 for women. Facilities include softball, baseball, and football/soccer fields, outdoor tennis courts, and a waterfront for aquatic sports in summer and broomball in winter. There is a health and phys ed center, with a full basketball court, 2 racquetball courts, an elevated jogging surface, a fitness center, and an athletic training room. The student center has a small swimming pool.

Disabled Students: 70% of the campus is accessible. Wheelchair ramps, elevators, special parking, specially equipped rest rooms, special class scheduling, lowered drinking fountains, and lowered telephones are available.

Services: Counseling and information services are available, as is tutoring in some subjects, including math, English, Bible, Greek, biology, and accounting. There is remedial math, reading, and writing.

Campus Safety and Security: Measures include 24-hour foot and vehicle patrol, self-defense education, security escort services, and shuttle buses. There are informal discussions, pamphlets/posters/films, emergency telephones, and lighted pathways/sidewalks.

Programs of Study: Northwestern confers B.A., B.S., B.M.E. (music education), and B.Mus. degrees. Associate degrees are also awarded. Bachelor's degrees are awarded in BIOLOGICAL SCIENCE (biology/biological science), BUSINESS (accounting, banking and finance, business administration and management, international business management, management information systems, marketing management, and sports management), COMMUNICATIONS AND THE ARTS (broadcasting, communications, dramatic arts, English, graphic design, journalism, music, music performance, Spanish, and studio art), COMPUTER AND PHYSICAL SCIENCE (mathematics), EDUCATION (art, Christian, early childhood, elementary, English, mathematics, music, physical, social studies, and teaching English as a second/foreign language (TESOL/TEFOL)), HEALTH PROFESSIONS (sports medicine), SOCIAL SCIENCE (biblical studies, criminal justice, history, ministries, missions, pastoral studies, psychology, social science, and youth ministry). Elementary/secondary education, business, and music are the strongest academically. Education, business, and psychology are the largest.

Required: To graduate, students must complete 124 semester credits with a 2.0 GPA. The number of credits required in the major varies from 36 to 102 (average of 58). Core courses include 30 credits of Bible, 10 credits of composition/speech/computer literacy, 7 to 8 credits of Western civilization, social science, and foreign language/cross-cultural courses, 6 to 8 credits of math and science, 6 credits each of fine arts/literature/philosophy, and 1 credit of phys ed.

Special: The college offers 5 study-abroad programs and 4 U.S. off-campus programs through the Council for Christian Colleges and Universities. International business majors are placed in 6-month internships in Japan. There are also co-op programs in engineering, environmental studies, law, and ROTC training. A 3-2 engineering degree with the University of Minnesota-Twin Cities is offered. There are 2 national honor societies and a freshman honors program.

Faculty/Classroom: 56% of faculty are male; 44%, female. All teach undergraduates. The average class size in an introductory lecture is 33; in a laboratory, 14; and in a regular course, 24.

Admissions: 96% of the 2003-2004 applicants were accepted. The SAT I scores for the 2003-2004 freshman class were: Verbal--26% below 500, 26% between 500 and 599, 29% between 600 and 700, and 19% above 700; Math--24% below 500, 38% between 500 and 599, 36% between 600 and 700, and 2% above 700. The ACT scores were 23% below 21, 28% between 21 and 23, 26% between 24 and 26, 13% between 27 and 28, and 10% above 28. 46% of the current freshmen were in the top fifth of their class; 75% were in the top two fifths. There were 5 National Merit semifinalists in a recent year. 9 freshmen graduated first in their class.

Requirements: The ACT is required and the SAT I is recommended, with the ACT preferred. A high school diploma is required; the GED is accepted. The minimum high school GPA is 2.0, but a 3.0 or higher is

recommended. Applicants are expected to have completed the following Carnegie units: 4 in English, 3 each in math, science, and social studies, and 2 in foreign language. A statement of Christian faith and an assent to a lifestyle agreement are required. 2 letters of reference must be submitted, 1 from the applicant's pastor. A personal interview is required for some applicants. AP and CLEP credits are accepted. Important factors in the admissions decision are personality/intangible qualities, recommendations by school officials, and extracurricular activities record.

Procedure: Freshmen are admitted to all sessions. Entrance exams should be taken no later than June of the year of intended fall entry. There are early admissions and deferred admissions plans. There is a rolling admissions plan. Applications should be filed by August 1 for fall entry, December 15 for spring entry, and May 1 for summer entry, along with a $25 fee. Notification is sent on a rolling basis.

Transfer: 97 transfer students enrolled in a recent year. Applicants must have an average of C or better from an accredited institution. 30 credits of 124 required for the bachelor's degree must be completed at Northwestern.

Visiting: There are regularly scheduled orientations for prospective students. There are guides for informal visits and visitors may sit in on classes and stay overnight. To schedule a visit, contact the Admissions Office at (651) 631-5111 or *admissions@bwc.edu*.

Financial Aid: In 2003-2004, 98% of all full-time freshmen and 99% of continuing full-time students received some form of financial aid. 82% of full-time freshmen and 83% of continuing full-time students received need-based aid. The average freshman award was $12,879. Need-based scholarships or need-based grants averaged $9904; need-based self-help aid (loans and jobs) averaged $3556; and non-need-based awards and non-need-based scholarships averaged $4442. 71% of undergraduates work part time. Average annual earnings from campus work are $1750. The average financial indebtedness of a recent graduate was $15,500. The FAFSA and the college's own financial statement are required. Check with the school for current deadlines.

International Students: There were 11 international students enrolled in a recent year. They must score 530 on the written TOEFL or 197 on the electronic version or take the MELAB and also take the SAT I or the ACT.

Computers: The mainframe is an IBM RS/6000, for administrative use only. 100 PCs are available for student use in 5 computer labs, including 1 in the student center/residence hall complex. 85 are IBMs with Internet access; the other 15 are Macs for education majors. All students may access the system. There are no time limits and no fees.

Graduates: In a recent year, 259 bachelor's degrees were awarded. The most popular majors were elementary and secondary education (25%), business administration (11%), and psychology (7%). In an average class, 2% graduate in 3 years or less, 44% graduate in 4 years or less, 53% graduate in 5 years or less, and 54% graduate in 6 years or less. 144 companies recruited on campus in a recent year. Of a recent graduating class, 4% were enrolled in graduate school within 6 months of graduation and 74% were employed.

Admissions Contact: Kenneth K. Faffler, Director of Admissions. A video is available. E-mail: *kkfaffler@nwc.edu* Web: *www.nwc.edu*

SAINT CLOUD STATE UNIVERSITY
C-3
St. Cloud, MN 56301-4498
(320) 308-2244
(800)369-4260; Fax: (320) 308-2243

Full-time: 5421 men, 6369 women	Faculty: 629; IIA, av$
Part-time: 1159 men, 1534 women	Ph.D.s: 69%
Graduate: 509 men, 933 women	Student/Faculty: 20 to 1
Year: semesters, summer session	Tuition: $4550 ($9209)
Application Deadline: open	Room & Board: $3812
Freshman Class: 6011 applied, 4581 accepted, 2298 enrolled	
ACT: 21	COMPETITIVE

Saint Cloud State University, founded in 1869, is a comprehensive university with 5 colleges plus 5 graduate schools offering programs that include the liberal arts and career preparation with emphasis on diversity, hands-on learning, and service to the community. In addition to regional accreditation, SCSU has baccalaureate program accreditation with AACSB, ABET, ACEJMC, ASLA, CSWE, NASAD, NASM, and NCATE. The library contains 887,462 volumes, 1,810,866 microform items, and 24,244 audio/video tapes/CDs, and subscribes to 1762 periodicals. Computerized library services include the card catalog, interlibrary loans, database searching, and Internet access. Special learning facilities include a learning resource center, art gallery, natural history museum, planetarium, radio station, TV station, and a National Hockey Center. The 922-acre campus is in a suburban area 60 miles northwest of Minneapolis. Including any residence halls, there are 35 buildings.

Student Life: 91% of undergraduates are from Minnesota. Students are from 50 states, 85 foreign countries, and Canada. 99% are from public schools. 74% are white. The average age of freshmen is 19; all undergraduates, 21. 27% do not continue beyond their first year.

Housing: 3000 students can be accommodated in college housing, which includes single-sex and coed dorms. In addition, there are honors houses and a nontraditional student floor. On-campus housing is guaranteed for all 4 years. 79% of students commute. Alcohol is not permitted. All students may keep cars.

Activities: There are 5 national fraternities and 4 national sororities. There are 240 groups on campus, including art, band, cheerleading, chess, choir, chorale, chorus, computers, dance, drama, entrepreneurial, ethnic, film, gay, hobby, honors, international, jazz band, literary magazine, marching band, musical theater, opera, orchestra, pep band, photography, political, professional, radio and TV, religious, social, social service, student government, symphony, travel, and yearbook. Popular campus events include Music Festival, Ethnic Awareness Week, and major speakers and workshops.

Sports: There are 18 intercollegiate sports for men and 16 for women, and 19 intramural sports for men and 18 for women. Facilities include a wrestling room, a weight room, a dance studio, a racquetball court, gyms, swimming and diving pools, indoor and outdoor tracks, and baseball and football fields.

Disabled Students: 86% of the campus is accessible. Wheelchair ramps, elevators, special parking, specially equipped rest rooms, special class scheduling, lowered drinking fountains, and lowered telephones are available.

Services: Counseling and information services are available, as is tutoring in every subject. There is a reader service for the blind, and remedial math, reading, and writing.

Campus Safety and Security: Measures include 24-hour foot and vehicle patrol, self-defense education, security escort services, and shuttle buses. There are informal discussions, pamphlets/posters/films, emergency telephones, lighted pathways/sidewalks, and a required short safety course.

Programs of Study: SCSU confers B.A., B.S., B.E.S., B.F.A., and B.Mus. degrees. Associate, master's, and doctoral degrees are also awarded. Bachelor's degrees are awarded in BIOLOGICAL SCIENCE (biology/biological science), BUSINESS (accounting, banking and finance, business administration and management, business economics, international business management, marketing/retailing/merchandising, and personnel management), COMMUNICATIONS AND THE ARTS (advertising, broadcasting, communications, dramatic arts, English, fine arts, journalism, languages, music, and speech/debate/rhetoric), COMPUTER AND PHYSICAL SCIENCE (atmospheric sciences and meteorology, chemistry, computer science, earth science, geology, mathematics, physics, and statistics), EDUCATION (art, early childhood, elementary, foreign languages, guidance, health, industrial arts, music, science, and secondary), ENGINEERING AND ENVIRONMENTAL DESIGN (aviation administration/management, electrical/electronics engineering, engineering technology, and manufacturing engineering), HEALTH PROFESSIONS (predentistry, premedicine, public health, and speech pathology/audiology), SOCIAL SCIENCE (anthropology, criminal justice, economics, geography, history, international relations, philosophy, political science/government, prelaw, psychology, public administration, social science, social work, sociology, and urban studies). Business, education, and social sciences are the largest.

Required: Students must complete a minimum of 120 semester credit hours, including 40 hours of general education requirements, and 60 to 180 hours in the major, and must maintain at least a 2.0 GPA, higher for many majors. Students must complete English 191, English 192, Speech 192, 2 credits in phys ed, and 24 credits in philosophy/humanities/fine arts, natural science and math, social and behavioral science, and diversity courses.

Special: The university offers cross-registration, internships in almost all majors, work-study programs, and study abroad in 15 countries. Students may take dual majors, design their own majors for a Bachelor of Elective Studies degree, and earn a general degree or a B.A.-B.S. degree in all majors, including meteorology and photographic technology. The university gives credit for military experience and allows nondegree study and pass/fail options. There are 4 national honor societies, and a freshman honors program.

Faculty/Classroom: 59% of faculty are male; 41%, female. All teach undergraduates. The average class size in an introductory lecture is 36; in a laboratory, 20; and in a regular course, 25.

Admissions: 76% of the 2003-2004 applicants were accepted. The ACT scores for the 2003-2004 freshman class were: 43% below 21, 29% between 21 and 23, 19% between 24 and 26, 6% between 27 and 28, and 3% above 28. 21% of the current freshmen were in the top fifth of their class; 57% were in the top two fifths. There were 3 National Merit finalists.

Requirements: The ACT is required. SCSU requires applicants to be in the upper 50% of their class. AP and CLEP credits are accepted.

Procedure: Freshmen are admitted fall, spring, and summer. Entrance exams should be taken in the junior or senior year. Application deadlines are open. The fall 2003 application fee was $20.

Transfer: 1287 transfer students enrolled in 2002-2003. Applicants must have a minimum 2.0 GPA from their previous college if they transfer with 12 or more credits. If they have fewer than 12 credits, they are treated as entering freshmen. 30 of 120 credits required for the bachelor's degree must be completed at SCSU.

Visiting: There are regularly scheduled orientations for prospective students. There are guides for informal visits and visitors may sit in on classes. To schedule a visit, contact the Admissions Office.

Financial Aid: The FAFSA and the college's own financial statement are required. The deadline for filing freshman financial aid applications for fall entry is open.

International Students: There are 646 international students enrolled. The school actively recruits these students. They must score 500 on the written TOEFL or take the MELAB or the Comprehensive English Language Test, plus the college's own test.

Computers: There are 16 computer labs and 650 PCs for student use; 175 are networked to share printers and 60 are networked to the mainframes for disk sharing and file server capabilities. All students may access the system any time. There are no time limits and no fees.

Graduates: In a recent year, 2350 bachelor's degrees were awarded. The most popular majors were business marketing (26%), education (20%), and social science and history (9%). In an average class, 17% graduate in 4 years or less, 35% graduate in 5 years or less, and 41% graduate in 6 years or less.

Admissions Contact: Pat Krueger, Associate Director of Admissions. A video is available. E-mail: *scsu4u@stcloudstate.edu*
Web: *www.stcloudstate.edu*

SAINT JOHN'S UNIVERSITY
B-3
Collegeville, MN 56321-7155 (320) 363-2196
(800) 544-1489; Fax: (320) 363-2750

Full-time: 1896 men	Faculty: 149; IIB, +$
Part-time: 44 men	Ph.D.s: 83%
Graduate: 57 men, 70 women	Student/Faculty: 13 to 1
Year: semesters	Tuition: $20,685
Application Deadline: open	Room & Board: $5788
Freshman Class: 1049 applied, 932 accepted, 490 enrolled	
SAT I Verbal/Math: 585/605	ACT: 25 VERY COMPETITIVE

St. John's University (for men) and the College of Saint Benedict (for women) are 2 Catholic liberal arts colleges that share a unique partnership featuring 2 campuses, 1 academic calendar, a joint academic curriculum, and many combined extracurricular activities. There is 1 graduate school. In addition to regional accreditation, St. John's has baccalaureate program accreditation with ACS, ADA, ATS, CCNE, CSWE, NASM, and NCATE. The 3 libraries contain 680,888 volumes, 119,665 microform items, and 33,471 audio/video tapes/CDs, and subscribe to 11,364 periodicals. Computerized library services include the card catalog, interlibrary loans, and database searching. Special learning facilities include a learning resource center, art gallery, natural history museum, radio station, an observatory, a greenhouse, an arboretum, an herbarium, a pottery studio, and Hill Monastic Manuscript Library. The 2400-acre campus is in a rural area 15 miles west of St. Cloud and 70 miles northwest of Minneapolis and St. Paul. Including any residence halls, there are 35 buildings.

Student Life: 82% of undergraduates are from Minnesota. Others are from 34 states, 27 foreign countries, and Canada. 73% are from public schools. 92% are white. 68% are Catholic; 22% Protestant; 8% claim no religious affiliation. The average age of freshmen is 19; all undergraduates, 20. 10% do not continue beyond their first year; 83% remain to graduate.

Housing: 1500 students can be accommodated in college housing, which includes single-sex dorms and on-campus apartments. In addition, there are special-interest houses. On-campus housing is available on a first-come, first-served basis and is available on a lottery system for upperclassmen. 82% of students live on campus. All students may keep cars.

Activities: There are 90 groups on campus, including academic, art, band, choir, chorale, chorus, computers, dance, debate, drama, ethnic, gay, honors, international, jazz band, literary magazine, musical theater, newspaper, opera, orchestra, outdoor leadership center, political, professional, radio and TV, religious, social, social service, student government, symphony, and yearbook. Popular campus events include Pinestock, Asian New Year, and Battle of the Bands.

Sports: Facilities include basketball and racquetball courts, soccer, baseball, and rugby fields, indoor and outdoor tennis courts, indoor and sand volleyball courts, indoor and outdoor tracks, an aerobics studio, a fitness center, a swimming pool, a 4-story climbing wall, 5 lakes for canoeing, fishing, swimming, rowing, and wind sailing, and access to facilities at the College of Saint Benedict.

Disabled Students: 90% of the campus is accessible. Wheelchair ramps, elevators, special parking, specially equipped rest rooms, special class scheduling, lowered drinking fountains, lowered telephones, and special housing are available.

Services: Counseling and information services are available, as is tutoring in every subject. There is a reader service for the blind. There is a skills center, study and test-taking skills instruction, limited note-taking services, reading machines, a writing center, and a math skills study center. Special needs will be met as required.

Campus Safety and Security: Measures include 24-hour foot and vehicle patrol, self-defense education, security escort services, and shuttle buses. There are informal discussions, pamphlets/posters/films, emergency telephones, and lighted pathways/sidewalks.

Programs of Study: St. John's confers B.A. and B.S.N. degrees. Master's degrees are also awarded. Bachelor's degrees are awarded in AGRICULTURE (environmental studies and forestry and related sciences), BIOLOGICAL SCIENCE (biochemistry, biology/biological science, and nutrition), BUSINESS (accounting and management science), COMMUNICATIONS AND THE ARTS (art, classics, communications, dramatic arts, English, fine arts, French, German, music, and Spanish), COMPUTER AND PHYSICAL SCIENCE (chemistry, computer science, mathematics, natural sciences, and physics), EDUCATION (elementary), ENGINEERING AND ENVIRONMENTAL DESIGN (preengineering), HEALTH PROFESSIONS (nursing, occupational therapy, physical therapy, predentistry, premedicine, prepharmacy, and preveterinary science), SOCIAL SCIENCE (dietetics, economics, history, humanities, liberal arts/general studies, pastoral studies, peace studies, philosophy, political science/government, prelaw, psychology, social science, social work, sociology, and theological studies). The humanities, biology, and political science are the strongest academically. Management, biology, and economics are the largest.

Required: To graduate, students must complete the core curriculum of writing, discussion, quantitative reasoning, and gender and global perspectives. Distribution requirements include 6 credits in fine arts, 5 in humanities, 2 each in natural science and social science, and 1 in math. All students must prove proficiency in math and foreign language. A total of 124 credits must be earned, with 40 credits in upper-division courses and an overall GPA of 2.0. Students must complete a first-year symposium and senior seminar.

Special: Students may cross-register with the College of Saint Benedict and Saint Cloud State University. There are study-abroad programs in Ireland, China, Central America, Japan, South Africa, Chile, Australia, and European cities. Internships, student-designed majors, preprofessional programs, and liberal studies degrees may be pursued. A 3-2 engineering program is offered with the University of Minnesota. Nondegree study and a pass/fail grading option are also available. There is 1 national honor society, and a freshman honors program.

Faculty/Classroom: 72% of faculty are male; 28%, female. All both teach and do research. No introductory courses are taught by graduate students. The average class size in an introductory lecture is 25; in a laboratory, 18; and in a regular course, 22.

Admissions: 89% of the 2003-2004 applicants were accepted. The SAT I scores for the 2003-2004 freshman class were: Verbal--10% below 500, 45% between 500 and 599, 40% between 600 and 700, and 5% above 700; Math--11% below 500, 36% between 500 and 599, 43% between 600 and 700, and 10% above 700. The ACT scores were 9% below 21, 27% between 21 and 23, 33% between 24 and 26, 11% between 27 and 28, and 20% above 28. 39% of the current freshmen were in the top fifth of their class; 72% were in the top two fifths. There were 5 National Merit finalists. 28 freshmen graduated first in their class.

Requirements: The SAT I or ACT is required. In addition, students should be graduates of an accredited secondary school. Academic preparation should include 17 units, including 4 of English, 3 of math, 2 each of science and social studies, and 6 electives. A foreign language is recommended. The GED is accepted. An essay is required. Home-schooled applicants are not required to have a high school diploma but are required to provide appropriate documentation of college preparatory curriculum. St. John's requires applicants to be in the upper 50% of their class. A GPA of 3.0 is required. AP and CLEP credits are accepted. Important factors in the admissions decision are advanced placement or honor courses, evidence of special talent, and extracurricular activities record.

Procedure: Freshmen are admitted fall and spring. Entrance exams should be taken by the fall of the senior year. There are early admissions and deferred admissions plans. Application deadlines are open. The priority application date for fall entry is January 15. The fall 2003 application fee was $30. Notification is sent on a rolling basis beginning January 15. 10 to 15 were on the 2003 waiting list; 2 to 3 were admitted. Applications are accepted on computer disk and on-line through Common App and CollegeNET and at www.csbsju.edu.

Transfer: 43 transfer students enrolled in 2002-2003. Transfer applicants must have a minimum college GPA of 2.75. An essay or personal statement, high school and college transcripts, and a transfer student evaluation form are also required. Standardized test scores may be required and of some value. 45 of 124 credits required for the bachelor's degree must be completed at St. John's.

Visiting: There are regularly scheduled orientations for prospective students, including programs that vary according to student interest. Information can be found at the school's web site. There are guides for informal visits and visitors may sit in on classes and stay overnight. To schedule a visit, contact the Admissions Office.

Financial Aid: In 2003-2004, 93% of all full-time freshmen and 89% of continuing full-time students received some form of financial aid. 67% of full-time freshmen and 61% of continuing full-time students received

need-based aid. The average freshman award was $18,050. Need-based scholarships or need-based grants averaged $12,781; and need-based self-help aid (loans and jobs) averaged $5155. 63% of undergraduates work part time. Average annual earnings from campus work are $2100. The average financial indebtedness of the 2003 graduate was $21,000. The FAFSA, the college's own financial statement, and federal tax returns and W-2s are required. The priority date for freshman financial aid applications for fall entry is March 15. The deadline for filing freshman financial aid applications for fall entry is May 1.

International Students: There are 71 international students enrolled. The school actively recruits these students. They must score 500 on the written TOEFL or 173 on the electronic version or take the MELAB.

Computers: The mainframe is a Windows 2000 network. Students have free access 24 hours a day to computers in each college residence, in numerous departments, and in 4 public access areas. There are no time limits. The fee is $170.

Graduates: From July 1, 2002 to June 30, 2003, 393 bachelor's degrees were awarded. The most popular majors were business and management (17%), biology (8%), and political science and economics (7%). In an average class, 1% graduate in 3 years or less, 73% graduate in 4 years or less, 82% graduate in 5 years or less, and 83% graduate in 6 years or less. 20 companies recruited on campus in 2002-2003. Of the 2002 graduating class, 16% were enrolled in graduate school within 6 months of graduation and 81% were employed.

Admissions Contact: Mary Milbert, Dean of Admissions.
E-mail: *admissions@csbsju.edu* Web: *www.csbsju.edu*

SAINT MARY'S UNIVERSITY OF MINNESOTA D-5
Winona, MN 55987-1399

(507) 457-1700
(800) 635-5987; Fax: (507) 457-1722

Full-time: 576 men, 722 women	**Faculty:** 99; IIA, --$
Part-time: 15 men, 44 women	**Ph.D.s:** 72%
Graduate: 3292 men and women	**Student/Faculty:** 13 to 1
Year: semesters	**Tuition:** $16,335
Application Deadline: May 1	**Room & Board:** $5200
Freshman Class: 1312 applied, 981 accepted, 365 enrolled	
SAT I Verbal/Math: 549/557	**ACT:** 23 COMPETITIVE

Saint Mary's University of Minnesota, founded in 1912, is a private liberal arts college affiliated with the Roman Catholic Church, offering a traditional liberal arts and sciences curriculum combined with career preparation. There are 4 undergraduate schools and 1 graduate school. The library contains 151,643 volumes, 129,075 microform items, and 7485 audio/video tapes/CDs, and subscribes to 699 periodicals. Computerized library services include the card catalog, interlibrary loans, database searching, and Internet access. Special learning facilities include a learning resource center, art gallery, radio station, observatory, and natural resource center. The 400-acre campus is in a small town 110 miles southeast of the Twin Cities, and 275 miles northwest of Chicago. Including any residence halls, there are 48 buildings.

Student Life: 61% of undergraduates are from Minnesota. Students are from 25 states and 13 foreign countries. 67% are from public schools. 84% are white. 60% are Catholic; 27% claim no religious affiliation; 12% Protestant. The average age of freshmen is 18; all undergraduates, 20. 25% do not continue beyond their first year; 60% remain to graduate.

Housing: 1103 students can be accommodated in college housing, which includes single-sex and coed dorms and on-campus apartments. There are first-year and substance-free residence halls. On-campus housing is guaranteed for all 4 years. 78% of students live on campus. All students may keep cars.

Activities: 2% of men belong to 2 national fraternities; 1% of women belong to 1 national sorority. There are 84 groups on campus, including art, band, cheerleading, choir, chorale, chorus, dance, drama, ethnic, gay, honors, international, jazz band, literary magazine, musical theater, newspaper, political, professional, radio and TV, religious, social, social service, student government, and yearbook. Popular campus events include Cardinal Days, Family Weekend, and Taylor Richmond Benefit Dance.

Sports: There are 9 intercollegiate sports for men and 10 for women, and 15 intramural sports for men and 15 for women. Facilities include 7 basketball courts, indoor tennis courts, an indoor ice arena, 4 racquetball courts, exercise and weight rooms, baseball, softball, and soccer fields, Nordic ski trails, running trails, and an indoor track.

Disabled Students: 75% of the campus is accessible. Wheelchair ramps, elevators, special parking, specially equipped rest rooms, lowered drinking fountains, special housing, and TDD phones are available.

Services: Counseling and information services are available, as is tutoring in most subjects. There is a reader service for the blind, and remedial math, reading, and writing.

Campus Safety and Security: Measures include 24-hour foot and vehicle patrol, self-defense education, security escort services, and shuttle buses. There are informal discussions, pamphlets/posters/films, emergency telephones, and lighted pathways/sidewalks.

Programs of Study: SMU confers the B.A. degree. Master's and doctoral degrees are also awarded. Bachelor's degrees are awarded in BIOLOGICAL SCIENCE (biology/biological science, biophysics, and environmental biology), BUSINESS (accounting, business administration and management, international business management, and marketing/retailing/merchandising), COMMUNICATIONS AND THE ARTS (creative writing, dramatic arts, French, graphic design, literature, music business management, music performance, public relations, publishing, Spanish, and studio art), COMPUTER AND PHYSICAL SCIENCE (chemistry, computer science, mathematics, physical chemistry, and physics), EDUCATION (elementary, English, foreign languages, middle school, music, science, and social science), HEALTH PROFESSIONS (cytotechnology, medical laboratory technology, nuclear medical technology, physical therapy, predentistry, premedicine, and preveterinary science), SOCIAL SCIENCE (criminal justice, history, human services, philosophy, political science/government, prelaw, psychology, public administration, social science, sociology, theological studies, and youth ministry). Biology, accounting, and chemistry are the strongest academically. Marketing, biology, and psychology are the largest.

Required: Students must have a 2.0 cumulative major GPA and complete a minimum of 122 semester credits, including at least 45 at the upper-division level. Students must complete 32 to 59 credits in the major and courses in English composition or Argumentative and Research Writing, intermediate algebra (or pass a placement test or take Elementary Mathematical Ideas), and phys ed. Students must spend their final year in academic residence.

Special: Students may cross-register with Winona State University. Internships, co-op programs, student teaching and study abroad, work-study programs, and a Washington semester are available. The university also offers dual and student-designed majors, a 3-2 engineering degree, nondegree study, pass/fail options, credit for life, military, and work experience, and an honors program that also serves as an alternative general education program. There are 13 national honor societies.

Faculty/Classroom: 61% of faculty are male; 39%, female. All teach undergraduates and 5% both teach and do research. No introductory courses are taught by graduate students. The average class size in an introductory lecture is 22; in a laboratory, 20; and in a regular course, 13.

Admissions: 75% of the 2003-2004 applicants were accepted. The SAT I scores for the 2003-2004 freshman class were: Verbal--22% below 500, 49% between 500 and 599, 24% between 600 and 700, and 5% above 700; Math--27% below 500, 41% between 500 and 599, 29% between 600 and 700, and 2% above 700. The ACT scores were 25% below 21, 29% between 21 and 23, 28% between 24 and 26, 11% between 27 and 28, and 7% above 28. 37% of the current freshmen were in the top fifth of their class; 62% were in the top two fifths. 6 freshmen graduated first in their class.

Requirements: The ACT is required. In addition, candidates for admission should have completed 4 units of English, 3 each of natural science, math, social studies, and academic electives, and 2 of foreign language. SMU requires applicants to be in the upper 50% of their class. A GPA of 2.5 is required. AP and CLEP credits are accepted. Important factors in the admissions decision are advanced placement or honor courses, leadership record, and extracurricular activities record.

Procedure: Freshmen are admitted fall and spring. Entrance exams should be taken by the fall of the senior year. There is a deferred admissions plan. Applications should be filed by May 1 for fall entry and December 1 for spring entry, along with a $25 fee. Notification is sent on a rolling basis. Applications are accepted on-line through *smumn.edu.*

Transfer: 43 transfer students enrolled in 2002-2003. Applicants must have a 2.0 GPA with at least 12 credits. 60 of 122 credits required for the bachelor's degree must be completed at SMU.

Visiting: There are regularly scheduled orientations for prospective students, including an interview, a tour, class visits, and lunch. There are guides for informal visits and visitors may sit in on classes and stay overnight. To schedule a visit, contact the Office of Admissions at (800) 635-8987, ext. 1700 or *admissions@smumn.edu.*

Financial Aid: In 2003-2004, 95% of all full-time freshmen and 85% of continuing full-time students received some form of financial aid. 62% of full-time freshmen and 61% of continuing full-time students received need-based aid. The average freshman award was $15,623. Need-based scholarships or need-based grants averaged $6918 ($16,662 maximum); need-based self-help aid (loans and jobs) averaged $2971 ($7825 maximum); and non-need-based awards and non-need-based scholarships averaged $4827 ($15,500 maximum). 47% of undergraduates work part time. Average annual earnings from campus work are $1022. The average financial indebtedness of the 2003 graduate was $21,915. The FAFSA and the college's own financial statement are required. The priority date for freshman financial aid applications for fall entry is March 15. The deadline for filing freshman financial aid applications for fall entry is open.

International Students: There are 16 international students enrolled. The school actively recruits these students. They must score 520 on the written TOEFL.

Computers: The mainframe is a VAX. 395 Macs and PCs are available in computer labs, departmental areas, residence halls, and classrooms. All students may access the system any time. There are no time limits and no fees.

Graduates: From July 1, 2002 to June 30, 2003, 268 bachelor's degrees were awarded. The most popular majors were biology (9%), childhood/early adolescent education (8%), and accounting (7%). In an average class, 1% graduate in 3 years or less, 52% graduate in 4 years or less, 58% graduate in 5 years or less, and 60% graduate in 6 years or less. 108 companies recruited on campus in 2002-2003. Of the 2002 graduating class, 31% were enrolled in graduate school within 6 months of graduation and 65% were employed.

Admissions Contact: Anthony M. Piscitiello, Vice President for Admission. A video is available. E-mail: *admissions@smumn.edu* Web: *http://www.smumn.edu*

SAINT OLAF COLLEGE   C-4
Northfield, MN 55057-1098   (507) 646-3025
                                   (800) 800-3025; Fax: (507) 646-3832

Full-time: 1200 men, 1729 women	**Faculty:** 206; IIB, +$
Part-time: 32 men, 33 women	**Ph.D.s:** 91%
Graduate: none	**Student/Faculty:** 14 to 1
Year: 4-1-4, summer session	**Tuition:** $23,650
Application Deadline: February 1	**Room & Board:** $4850
Freshman Class: 2807 applied, 1894 accepted, 720 enrolled	
SAT I Verbal/Math: 636/635	**ACT:** 27 HIGHLY COMPETITIVE

St. Olaf College, founded in 1874, is a private liberal arts institution affiliated with the Evangelical Lutheran Church in America. In addition to regional accreditation, St. Olaf has baccalaureate program accreditation with CSWE, NASD, NASM, NCATE, and NLN. The 4 libraries contain 654,950 volumes, 6567 microform items, and 16,824 audio/video tapes/CDs, and subscribe to 1743 periodicals. Computerized library services include the card catalog, interlibrary loans, database searching, and Internet access. Special learning facilities include a learning resource center, art gallery, radio station, and 700 acres of land dedicated to natural habitat, sustainable agriculture, and conventional agriculture. The 300-acre campus is in a small town 35 miles south of Minneapolis. Including any residence halls, there are 57 buildings.

Student Life: 54% of undergraduates are from Minnesota. Students are from 48 states and 22 foreign countries. 88% are from public schools. 86% are white. 67% are Protestant; 17% various and unknown; 14% Catholic. The average age of freshmen is 18; all undergraduates, 20. 8% do not continue beyond their first year; 81% remain to graduate.

Housing: 2703 students can be accommodated in college housing, which includes coed dorms. In addition, there are honors houses, language houses, and special-interest houses. On-campus housing is guaranteed for all 4 years. 96% of students live on campus; of those, 80% remain on campus on weekends. Alcohol is not permitted. No one may keep cars, but a limited number of permits may be issued in special circumstances.

Activities: There are no fraternities or sororities. There are 114 groups on campus, including art, band, chess, choir, chorus, computers, dance, drama, ethnic, film, gay, honors, international, jazz band, literary magazine, musical theater, newspaper, opera, orchestra, pep band, photography, political, professional, radio and TV, religious, social, social service, student government, symphony, and yearbook. Popular campus events include Christmas Festival, Wellstock, and President's Ball.

Sports: There are 14 intercollegiate sports for men and 13 for women, and 16 intramural sports for men and 16 for women. Facilities include 2 athletic complexes, a field house with batting cages, a long jump pit, 5 indoor tennis courts, and a 6-lane indoor track plus an upper-level walking/running track, a fitness center, a 45-foot climbing wall, a soccer pitch, baseball diamonds, 2 weight rooms, a football field, an 8-lane all-weather track and field, a 9-hole Frisbee golf course, a 6-lane swimming pool, and practice and recreation space.

Disabled Students: 75% of the campus is accessible. Wheelchair ramps, elevators, special parking, specially equipped rest rooms, special class scheduling, lowered drinking fountains, lowered telephones, special housing, electric door openers, and curb cuts are available.

Services: Counseling and information services are available, as is tutoring in every subject. There is a reader service for the blind. Study sessions are available.

Campus Safety and Security: Measures include 24-hour foot and vehicle patrol, self-defense education, security escort services, and informal discussions. There are pamphlets/posters/films, emergency telephones, and lighted pathways/sidewalks. All residence halls are card access.

Programs of Study: St. Olaf confers B.A. and B.Mus. degrees. Bachelor's degrees are awarded in AGRICULTURE (environmental studies), BIOLOGICAL SCIENCE (biology/biological science), COMMUNICATIONS AND THE ARTS (art, art history and appreciation, classics, dance, dramatic arts, English, French, German, Greek, Latin, music, music performance, music theory and composition, Russian, Slavic languages, Spanish, and studio art), COMPUTER AND PHYSICAL SCI-

ENCE (chemistry, computer science, mathematics, and physics), EDUCATION (music and social studies), HEALTH PROFESSIONS (exercise science and nursing), SOCIAL SCIENCE (American studies, Asian/American studies, classical/ancient civilization, economics, ethnic studies, family/consumer studies, Hispanic American studies, history, interdisciplinary studies, medieval studies, philosophy, political science/government, psychology, religion, religious music, Russian and Slavic studies, social work, sociology, and women's studies). Biology, English, and economics are the largest.

Required: In addition to the distribution requirements, students are required to demonstrate skills at an intermediate level in a foreign language and proficiency in English composition, to complete the phys ed requirement, and to have taken a 1/4-credit oral communication course and a 1-credit mathematical reasoning course. A minimum of 24 full-course credits out of 35 must be graded. A minimum of 8 full-credit courses in a disciplinary or interdisciplinary major are required. All majors include writing requirements. Students must complete 35 credits and maintain a minimum GPA of 2.0.

Special: St. Olaf offers cross-registration with Carleton College, study abroad in 42 countries, a Washington semester, preprofessional programs, internships, and a 3-2 B.A.-B.S.E. degree in engineering with Washington University in St. Louis. There are dual majors, nondegree study, and pass/fail options. The Center for Integrative Studies allows students to design individual majors with an emphasis on tutorials and seminars. There are 18 national honor societies, including Phi Beta Kappa.

Faculty/Classroom: 55% of faculty are male; 45%, female. All both teach and do research. The average class size in an introductory lecture is 28; in a laboratory, 18; and in a regular course, 23.

Admissions: 67% of the 2003-2004 applicants were accepted. The SAT I scores for the 2003-2004 freshman class were: Verbal--5% below 500, 25% between 500 and 599, 44% between 600 and 700, and 26% above 700; Math--5% below 500, 23% between 500 and 599, 51% between 600 and 700, and 21% above 700. The ACT scores were 2% below 18, 13% between 18 and 23, 57% between 24 and 29, and 28% above 29. 70% of the current freshmen were in the top fifth of their class; 93% were in the top two fifths. There were 39 National Merit finalists. 64 freshmen graduated first in their class.

Requirements: The SAT I or ACT is required. In addition, applicants should have completed 4 years of English, 3 to 4 each of math and social studies, and 2 to 3 each of science and a foreign language. A GPA of 3.0 is required. AP credits are accepted.

Procedure: Freshmen are admitted fall, winter, and spring. Entrance exams should be taken in the spring of the junior year or the fall of the senior year. There are early decision and deferred admissions plans. Early decision applications should be filed by November 15; regular applications, by February 1 for fall entry, along with a $35 fee. Notification of early decision is sent December 1; regular decision, on a rolling basis beginning March 1. 115 early decision candidates were accepted for the 2003-2004 class. 252 applicants were on the 2003 waiting list; 53 were admitted. Applications are accepted on-line through Apply, Common App, and the school's web site.

Transfer: 33 transfer students enrolled in 2002-2003. Applicants must have a 3.0 GPA at their previous institution. 17 of 35 course credits required for the bachelor's degree must be completed at St. Olaf.

Visiting: There are regularly scheduled orientations for prospective students, consisting of information sessions in an open house format. There are guides for informal visits and visitors may sit in on classes and stay overnight. To schedule a visit, contact Anne Donahue, Visit Coordinator, at *admissions@stolaf.edu.*

Financial Aid: In 2003-2004, 85% of all full-time freshmen and 82% of continuing full-time students received some form of financial aid. 67% of full-time freshmen and 62% of continuing full-time students received need-based aid. The average freshman award was $12,834. Need-based scholarships or need-based grants averaged $12,834 ($25,662 maximum); and need-based self-help aid (loans and jobs) averaged $4450 ($9500 maximum). 65% of undergraduates work part time. Average annual earnings from campus work are $1474. The average financial indebtedness of the 2003 graduate was $18,024. St. Olaf is a member of CSS. The CSS/Profile or FAFSA and noncustodial parent's statement are required. The priority date for freshman financial aid applications for fall entry is December 15. The deadline for filing freshman financial aid applications for fall entry is February 1.

International Students: There are 40 international students enrolled. The school actively recruits these students. They must score 550 on the written TOEFL or 213 on the electronic version.

Computers: The mainframes are Suns, DECs, Gateways, and IBMs. 783 institutionally owned computers and/or workstations are available for student use. All students may access the system. There are no time limits and no fees.

Graduates: From July 1, 2002 to June 30, 2003, 690 bachelor's degrees were awarded. The most popular majors were biology (12%), psychology (9%), and English (9%). In an average class, 75% graduate in 4 years or less, 80% graduate in 5 years or less, and 81% graduate in

6 years or less. 104 companies recruited on campus in 2002-2003. Of the 2002 graduating class, 27% were enrolled in graduate school within 6 months of graduation and 61% were employed.

Admissions Contact: Jeff McLaughlin, Director of Admissions. E-mail: *admissions@stolaf.edu* Web: *http://www.stolaf.edu/admissions/*

SOUTHWEST MINNESOTA STATE UNIVERSITY B-4
Marshall, MN 56258
(507) 537-6286
(800) 642-0684; Fax: (507) 537-7154

Full-time: 1000 men, 1300 women	**Faculty:** IIB, +$
Part-time: 700 men, 1200 women	**Ph.D.s:** n/av
Graduate: 196 men, 402 women	**Student/Faculty:** n/av
Year: semesters, summer session	**Tuition:** $4615
Application Deadline: August 15	**Room & Board:** $4491
Freshman Class: 1337 applied, 629 accepted, 537 enrolled	
ACT: 22	**VERY COMPETITIVE**

Southwest Minnesota State University, formerly Southwest State University and founded in 1963, is a public institution offering programs in liberal arts, technology, and preprofessional training. The library contains 165,000 volumes, 37,000 microform items, and 12,000 audio/video tapes/CDs, and subscribes to 800 periodicals. Computerized library services include the card catalog, interlibrary loans, and database searching. Special learning facilities include an art gallery, natural history museum, planetarium, radio station, and TV station. The 216-acre campus is in a rural area 150 miles southwest of Minneapolis. Including any residence halls, there are 51 buildings.

Student Life: 77% of undergraduates are from Minnesota. Students are from 27 states and 23 foreign countries. 95% are from public schools. 91% are white. The average age of all undergraduates is 22. 20% do not continue beyond their first year; 35% remain to graduate.

Housing: 1250 students can be accommodated in college housing, which includes single-sex and coed dorms. In addition, there are special-interest houses and a quiet house. On-campus housing is guaranteed for the freshman year only. 61% of students live on campus. Alcohol is not permitted. All students may keep cars.

Activities: There are no fraternities or sororities. There are 60 groups on campus, including art, band, cheerleading, chess, choir, chorus, computers, dance, drama, ethnic, honors, international, jazz band, literary magazine, marching band, newspaper, pep band, political, radio and TV, religious, student government, and symphony. Popular campus events include Prairie Festival and Rural Writer's Conference.

Sports: There are 5 intercollegiate sports for men and 4 for women. Facilities include a gym, baseball and softball facilities, handball and squash courts, a track, a football field, tennis courts, wrestling rooms, a weight room, an Olympic-size pool, and a 5000-seat stadium.

Disabled Students: 95% of the campus is accessible. Wheelchair ramps, elevators, special parking, specially equipped rest rooms, special class scheduling, lowered drinking fountains, and lowered telephones are available.

Services: Counseling and information services are available, as is tutoring in most subjects. There is a reader service for the blind and remedial math, reading, and writing.

Campus Safety and Security: Measures include 24-hour foot and vehicle patrol, security escort services, informal discussions, and pamphlets/posters/films. There are emergency telephones and lighted pathways/sidewalks.

Programs of Study: SMSU confers B.A. and B.S. degrees. Associate and master's degrees are also awarded. Bachelor's degrees are awarded in AGRICULTURE (agricultural business management), BIOLOGICAL SCIENCE (biology/biological science), BUSINESS (accounting, business administration and management, marketing/retailing/merchandising, and office supervision and management), COMMUNICATIONS AND THE ARTS (art, communications, creative writing, literature, music, and Spanish), COMPUTER AND PHYSICAL SCIENCE (chemistry, computer science, and mathematics), EDUCATION (art, business, early childhood, elementary, health, mathematics, music, and physical), HEALTH PROFESSIONS (medical technology), SOCIAL SCIENCE (history, interdisciplinary studies, political science/government, psychology, social work, and sociology). Education, business administration, and accounting are the largest.

Required: To graduate, students must complete at least 128 semester credit hours, a minimum of 27 of which must be the 300 or 400 level, and a liberal arts core curriculum, with a minimum GPA of 2.0.

Special: SMSU has cooperative programs with various local colleges, cross-registration with several state universities, and an accelerated degree in business administration. SMSU also offers internships in every discipline, work-study programs, study abroad in Japan, student-designed and interdisciplinary majors including speech communication and theater arts, nondegree study, pass/fail options, and credit for life, military, and work experience. There are 2 national honor societies and a freshman honors program.

Faculty/Classroom: 95% teach undergraduates.

Admissions: 47% of the 2003-2004 applicants were accepted. The ACT scores for the 2003-2004 freshman class were: 41% below 21, 29% between 21 and 23, 18% between 24 and 26, 5% between 27 and 28, and 4% above 28.

Requirements: The ACT is required and the SAT I is recommended; the ACT is preferred, with a composite score of 21, or a combined verbal and math score of 970 on the SAT I. Students should be graduates of an accredited secondary school or have a GED certificate. An interview is recommended. SMSU requires applicants to be in the upper 50% of their class. AP and CLEP credits are accepted. Important factors in the admissions decision are recommendations by school officials, leadership record, and personality/intangible qualities.

Procedure: Freshmen are admitted to all sessions. Entrance exams should be taken during the junior or senior year. There are early decision, early admissions, and deferred admissions plans. Applications are accepted on a rolling basis until August 15 for fall entry and January 10 for spring entry. The fall 2003 application fee was $20. Notification is sent on a rolling basis.

Transfer: Applicants need a minimum GPA of 2.0 in previous college-level work at an accredited institution. High school transcripts are required if students are transferring with fewer than 24 semester credits. 48 of 128 credits required for the bachelor's degree must be completed at SMSU.

Visiting: There are regularly scheduled orientations for prospective students. There are guides for informal visits and visitors may sit in on classes and stay overnight. To schedule a visit, contact the Admissions Office.

Financial Aid: The FAFSA is required. Check with the school for current deadlines.

International Students: The school actively recruits these students. They must score 500 on the written TOEFL.

Computers: The mainframes are a DEC Alpha system 2100 VMS and a DEC Alpha server 1000 UNIX system. There are Mac and IBM PCs available. All students may access the system 24 hours per day. There are no time limits.

Admissions Contact: Richard Shearer, Director of Enrollment. E-mail: *shearerr@southwestmsu.edu* Web: *www.southwestmsu.edu*

UNIVERSITY OF MINNESOTA SYSTEM

The University of Minnesota System, established in 1851, is a public system governed by a Board of Regents. The chief administrator is the president. The primary goal of the system is teaching, research, and public service. The total enrollment of all four campuses is 63,769, with 3136 faculty members. There are 336 baccalaureate, 232 master's, and 129 doctoral degree programs offered through the system. The U of M four-year campuses are located in Crookston, Duluth, Morris, and Twin Cities.

UNIVERSITY OF MINNESOTA/CROOKSTON
Crookston, MN 56716-5001

A-2
(218) 281-8569
(800) 232-6466; Fax: (218) 281-8050

Full-time: 1200 men and women	**Faculty:** IIB, av$
Part-time: n/av	**Ph.D.s:** n/av
Graduate: none	**Student/Faculty:** n/av
Year: semesters, summer session	**Tuition:** $6098
Application Deadline: open	**Room & Board:** $4464
Freshman Class: n/av	**ACT:** required
	NONCOMPETITIVE

University of Minnesota/Crookston, founded in 1965, is a public institution offering undergraduate degrees in agriculture, business, and hotel, restaurant, and institutional management. Figures in this profile are approximate. In addition to regional accreditation, UMC has baccalaureate program accreditation with AACSB and ADA. The library contains 30,000 volumes, 300 microform items, and 2300 audio/video tapes/CDs, and subscribes to 770 periodicals. Computerized library services include the card catalog, interlibrary loans, and database searching. Special learning facilities include a learning resource center. The 237-acre campus is in a rural area 25 miles from Grand Forks, North Dakota. Including any residence halls, there are 28 buildings.

Student Life: 75% of undergraduates are from Minnesota. 94% are white. The average age of freshmen is 18; all undergraduates, 26. 45% do not continue beyond their first year.

Housing: 500 students can be accommodated in college housing, which includes coed dorms and on-campus apartments. On-campus housing is available on a first-come, first-served basis. Priority is given to out-of-town students. 55% of students commute. Alcohol is not permitted. All students may keep cars.

Activities: There are no fraternities or sororities. There are more than 30 groups on campus, including cheerleading, choir, computers, drama, ethnic, newspaper, pep band, student government, and yearbook. Popular campus events include Agriculture Activities Day and Business Activities Day.

Sports: There are 5 intercollegiate sports for men and 6 for women, and 6 intramural sports for men and 6 for women. Facilities include a large indoor and outdoor sports complex.

Disabled Students: 95% of the campus is accessible. Wheelchair ramps, elevators, special parking, specially equipped rest rooms, special class scheduling, lowered drinking fountains, and lowered telephones are available.

Services: Counseling and information services are available, as is tutoring in most subjects. There is a reader service for the blind and remedial math, reading, and writing. An academic assistance center is also available.

Campus Safety and Security: Measures include pamphlets/posters/films and lighted pathways/sidewalks.

Programs of Study: Bachelor's degrees are awarded in AGRICULTURE (agricultural business management, agronomy, animal science, equine science, horticulture, and natural resource management), BUSINESS (accounting, business administration and management, hotel/motel and restaurant management, management science, and sports management), COMPUTER AND PHYSICAL SCIENCE (information sciences and systems), EDUCATION (early childhood education), ENGINEERING AND ENVIRONMENTAL DESIGN (environmental engineering technology and technological management), HEALTH PROFESSIONS (health care administration), SOCIAL SCIENCE (food production/management/services).

Requirements: The ACT is required. In addition, students with a high school diploma or equivalent are eligible for admission. AP and CLEP credits are accepted.

Procedure: Freshmen are admitted fall and spring. There are early admissions and deferred admissions plans. Application deadlines are open. The fall 2003 application fee was $25. Applications are accepted on-line at the school's web site.

Transfer: 30 of 120 credits required for the bachelor's degree must be completed at UMC.

Visiting: There are guides for informal visits and visitors may sit in on classes and stay overnight. To schedule a visit, contact the Admissions Office.

Financial Aid: Average annual earnings from campus work in a recent year were $900. UMC is a member of CSS. The FAFSA is required. The priority date for freshman financial aid applications is March 31.

International Students: The school actively recruits these students. They must score 500 on the written TOEFL.

Computers: All full-time students pay an access fee to the local area network and are issued a notebook computer. All students may access the system. There are no time limits and no fees.

Admissions Contact: Russell L. Kreager, Director of Enrollment Management. E-mail: *infor@crk.umn.edu* Web: *www.crk.umn.edu/people/admissions*

UNIVERSITY OF MINNESOTA/DULUTH
Duluth, MN 55812-2496

D-3
(218) 726-7171
(800) 232-1339; Fax: (218) 726-6394

Full-time: 4243 men, 4076 women	**Faculty:** 363; IIA, +$
Part-time: 541 men, 520 women	**Ph.D.s:** 76%
Graduate: 383 men, 368 women	**Student/Faculty:** 23 to 1
Year: semesters, summer session	**Tuition:** $7370 ($17,735)
Application Deadline: August 1	**Room & Board:** $5100
Freshman Class: 6900 applied, 5133 accepted, 2194 enrolled	
ACT: 23	**COMPETITIVE**

The University of Minnesota Duluth, founded in 1947, is a liberal arts institution offering undergraduate and graduate programs as a campus of the University of Minnesota. There are 5 undergraduate and 2 graduate schools. In addition to regional accreditation, UMD has baccalaureate program accreditation with ABET, ASLA, CSAB, CSWE, NASM, and NCATE. The library contains 705,000 volumes, 750,000 microform items, and 14,000 audio/video tapes/CDs, and subscribes to 2737 periodicals. Computerized library services include the card catalog, interlibrary loans, and database searching. Special learning facilities include a learning resource center, art gallery, planetarium, radio station, TV station, and a performing arts center. The 244-acre campus is in a suburban area 150 miles north of Minneapolis and St. Paul. Including any residence halls, there are 52 buildings.

Student Life: 87% of undergraduates are from Minnesota. Students are from 28 states, 31 foreign countries, and Canada. 95% are from public schools. 89% are white. The average age of freshmen is 18; all undergraduates, 22. 25% do not continue beyond their first year; 38% remain to graduate.

Housing: 3081 students can be accommodated in college housing, which includes single-sex and coed dorms and on-campus apartments. On-campus housing is available on a first-come, first-served basis and is available on a lottery system for upperclassmen. 70% of students commute. Alcohol is not permitted. All students may keep cars.

Activities: 1% of men belong to 2 local and 2 national fraternities; 1% of women belong to 2 local sororities and 1 national sorority. There are

120 groups on campus, including band, chamber orchestra, cheerleading, chess, choir, chorale, chorus, dance, drama, ethnic, gay, honors, international, jazz band, jazz choir, musical theater, newspaper, opera, orchestra, pep band, political, professional, radio and TV, religious, social, social service, student government, and wind ensemble. Popular campus events include Winter Festival, Black History Month, and Hispanic Heritage Month.

Sports: There are 7 intercollegiate sports for men and 8 for women, and 16 intramural sports for men and 16 for women. Facilities include a multipurpose ice center, a football and track-and-field stadium, a baseball park, softball and soccer fields, a field house for track and tennis, and a gym for basketball and volleyball, as well as a nearby country club for cross-country and golf.

Disabled Students: All of the campus is accessible. Wheelchair ramps, elevators, special parking, specially equipped rest rooms, lowered drinking fountains, lowered telephones, and special housing are available.

Services: Counseling and information services are available, as is tutoring in some subjects, including math, business, economics, sciences, accounting, computer science, and writing. There is a reader service for the blind and remedial math and writing. Workshops and seminars are also offered on study skills, note taking, time management, test-taking strategies, and goal setting.

Campus Safety and Security: Measures include 24-hour foot and vehicle patrol, self-defense education, security escort services, and pamphlets/posters/films. There are emergency telephones and lighted pathways/sidewalks.

Programs of Study: UMD confers B.A., B.S., B.A.A., B.Ac., B.A.S., B.B.A., B.Ch.E., B.E.C.E., B.F.A., B.I.E., B.M., B.S.CH.E., B.S.E.C.E., and B.S.I.E. degrees. Master's degrees are also awarded. Bachelor's degrees are awarded in BIOLOGICAL SCIENCE (biology/biological science), BUSINESS (business administration and management), COMMUNICATIONS AND THE ARTS (art, communications, dramatic arts, English, graphic design, jazz, music, music performance, and Spanish), COMPUTER AND PHYSICAL SCIENCE (chemistry, computer science, earth science, geology, mathematics, and physics), EDUCATION (art, athletic training, elementary, English, foreign languages, health, mathematics, music, physical, recreation, science, and social studies), ENGINEERING AND ENVIRONMENTAL DESIGN (chemical engineering, computer engineering, electrical/electronics engineering, environmental science, and industrial engineering), HEALTH PROFESSIONS (speech pathology/audiology), SOCIAL SCIENCE (anthropology, criminology, early childhood studies, economics, geography, history, interdisciplinary studies, international studies, Native American studies, philosophy, political science/government, psychology, sociology, urban studies, and women's studies). Business, sciences, and engineering are the strongest academically. Business administration, communication, and biology are the largest.

Required: To graduate, students must complete 120 to 136 semester credits, including 2 courses in college writing and a liberal education distribution of at least 35 credits in 10 academic areas. At least 4 credits of course work must emphasize cultural diversity, and 4 should emphasize an international perspective.

Special: Students may study abroad in England, Sweden, and Finland. UMD also offers a 3-2 engineering degree with the University of Minnesota Twin Cities, cross-registration with the College of St. Scholastica and the University of Wisconsin/Superior, internships, work-study programs, a B.A.-B.S. degree in several fields, dual degrees such as biochemistry and molecular biology, student-designed majors, and nondegree study. There are 6 national honor societies, including Phi Beta Kappa, a freshman honors program, and 17 departmental honors programs.

Faculty/Classroom: 57% of faculty are male; 43%, female. All teach undergraduates. No introductory courses are taught by graduate students.

Admissions: 74% of the 2003-2004 applicants were accepted. The ACT scores for the 2003-2004 freshman class were: 15% below 21, 45% between 21 and 23, 24% between 24 and 26, 13% between 27 and 28, and 3% above 28. 31% of the current freshmen were in the top fifth of their class; 66% were in the top two fifths. 70 freshmen graduated first in their class.

Requirements: The ACT is required and the SAT I is recommended. In addition, applicants must have completed 4 years in English, 3 each in math and sciences, and 2 each in a single second language and social studies. Course work in the visual and performing arts and computer skills is recommended. Students with a GED certificate will be admitted selectively as space permits. UMD requires applicants to be in the upper 60% of their class. AP and CLEP credits are accepted. Important factors in the admissions decision are advanced placement or honor courses, recommendations by school officials, and evidence of special talent.

Procedure: Freshmen are admitted to all sessions. Entrance exams should be taken at the end of the junior year or the beginning of the senior year. Applications should be filed by August 1 for fall entry and November 15 for spring entry. The fall 2003 application fee was $35. Notification is sent on a rolling basis.

Transfer: 409 transfer students enrolled in 2002-2003. Applicants who have completed 26 or more semester credits must have a minimum 2.0 GPA and a 75% completion ratio; applicants who have attempted fewer than 26 semester credits must have a high school rank at or above the 50th percentile, a 1.8 GPA in their previous college work, and a 75% completion ratio. 30 of 120 credits required for the bachelor's degree must be completed at UMD.

Visiting: There are regularly scheduled orientations for prospective students, including a campus tour and an appointment with admissions counselors, faculty, or coaches, if requested. There are guides for informal visits and visitors may sit in on classes. To schedule a visit, contact the Admissions Office.

Financial Aid: In 2003-2004, 85% of all full-time freshmen received some form of financial aid. 7% of undergraduates work part time. The FAFSA is required. The deadline for filing freshman financial aid applications for fall entry is March 31.

International Students: There are 88 international students enrolled. The school actively recruits these students. They must score 550 on the written TOEFL.

Computers: The mainframe is a UNIX operating system with Novell servers. Mainframe access is available through 6 computer labs across campus. Students may also open an account for personal use on the central UNIX system. All students may access the system 8 A.M. to 12 P.M. weekdays; Saturday and Sunday hours are also available. There are no time limits. The fee is $2 per credit.

Graduates: In a recent year, 1164 bachelor's degrees were awarded. The most popular majors were business administration (18%), communication (18%), and criminology (10%). In an average class, 5% graduate in 3 years or less, 19% graduate in 4 years or less, 17% graduate in 5 years or less, and 5% graduate in 6 years or less. 58 companies recruited on campus in 2002-2003.

Admissions Contact: Beth Esselstrom, Director of Admissions. E-mail: *umdadmis@d.umn.edu* Web: *http://www.d.umn.edu*

UNIVERSITY OF MINNESOTA/MORRIS B-3
Morris, MN 56267-2199 (320) 589-6035
(800) 992-8863; Fax: (320) 589-1673

Full-time: 707 men, 1020 women	**Faculty:** 128; IIB, av$
Part-time: 38 men, 96 women	**Ph.D.s:** 90%
Graduate: none	**Student/Faculty:** 13 to 1
Year: semesters, summer session	**Tuition:** $8096
Application Deadline: February 1	**Room & Board:** $4800
Freshman Class: 1120 applied, 925 accepted, 412 enrolled	
SAT I Verbal/Math: 600/600	**ACT:** 25 VERY COMPETITIVE

The University of Minnesota/Morris, founded in 1959, is a public liberal arts institution within the University of Minnesota system. In addition to regional accreditation, UMM has baccalaureate program accreditation with NCATE. The library contains 197,220 volumes, 221,216 microform items, and 2140 audio/video tapes/CDs, and subscribes to 885 paper and 12,200 electronic periodicals. Computerized library services include the card catalog, interlibrary loans, and database searching. Special learning facilities include a learning resource center, art gallery, radio station, TV station, language lab, observatory, and agricultural experiment station. The 130-acre campus is in a small town 150 miles northwest of Minneapolis. Including any residence halls, there are 36 buildings.

Student Life: 79% of undergraduates are from Minnesota. Students are from 32 states, 15 foreign countries, and Canada. 95% are from public schools. 84% are white. The average age of freshmen is 18; all undergraduates, 21. 18% do not continue beyond their first year; 60% remain to graduate.

Housing: 1032 students can be accommodated in college housing, which includes coed dorms and on-campus apartments. On-campus housing is guaranteed for all 4 years. 51% of students live on campus; of those, 80% remain on campus on weekends. All students may keep cars.

Activities: There are no fraternities or sororities. There are 90 groups on campus, including art, band, cheerleading, chess, choir, chorus, computers, dance, debate, drama, ethnic, forensics, gay, honors, international, jazz band, literary magazine, mentoring, musical theater, newspaper, orchestra, photography, political, professional, radio and TV, religious, riding, social, social service, student government, swing dancing, and yearbook. Popular campus events include Cultural Heritage Week, Diversity Jam, and Jazz Fest.

Sports: There are 6 intercollegiate sports for men and 9 for women, and 12 intramural sports for men and 12 for women. Facilities include a 4500-seat stadium, a phys ed center, 5 gyms, wrestling, exercise, and weight rooms, an Olympic-size pool, handball and racquetball courts, a track, fields for softball, baseball, soccer, and football, a diving well, a warm-water pool and slide, an indoor track, and a cardiovascular fitness room.

Disabled Students: 70% of the campus is accessible. Wheelchair ramps, elevators, special parking, specially equipped rest rooms, special class scheduling, lowered drinking fountains, and a disability services coordinator are available. Special learning equipment and services are available through the academic assistance center.

Services: Counseling and information services are available, as is tutoring in every subject. There is a reader service for the blind, and remedial math, reading, and writing.

Campus Safety and Security: Measures include 24-hour foot and vehicle patrol, self-defense education, security escort services, and shuttle buses. There are informal discussions, pamphlets/posters/films, emergency telephones, and lighted pathways/sidewalks.

Programs of Study: UMM confers the B.A. degree. Bachelor's degrees are awarded in BIOLOGICAL SCIENCE (biology/biological science), BUSINESS (management science), COMMUNICATIONS AND THE ARTS (art history and appreciation, dramatic arts, English, French, German, music, Spanish, speech/debate/rhetoric, and studio art), COMPUTER AND PHYSICAL SCIENCE (chemistry, computer science, geology, mathematics, physics, and statistics), EDUCATION (elementary and secondary), HEALTH PROFESSIONS (premedicine), SOCIAL SCIENCE (anthropology, economics, European studies, history, Latin American studies, liberal arts/general studies, philosophy, political science/government, prelaw, psychology, social science, sociology, and women's studies). Psychology and sciences are the strongest academically. Education, English, and biology are the largest.

Required: In addition to 40 semester hours in the major, students are required to complete 60 credits of a general education curriculum, including courses in writing, computing, foreign language or equivalent, and advanced study, as well as courses focusing on the arts, the physical and abstract worlds, and the self and others. All first-year students participate in a freshman seminar and the cumulative of their major work is presented in the senior seminar, which is a requirement for all seniors.

Special: UMM offers work-study programs, internships, study abroad, dual majors, student-designed majors, nondegree study, pass/fail options, and credit for life, military, and work experience. There is a 3-2 engineering degree with the University of Minnesota at Twin Cities. A competitive, merit-based program that pairs students and professors in order to undertake creative projects is available. There is a freshman honors program. All departments have honors programs.

Faculty/Classroom: 58% of faculty are male; 42%, female. All teach undergraduates and 89% both teach and do research. The average class size in an introductory lecture is 25; in a laboratory, 20; and in a regular course, 18.

Admissions: 83% of the 2003-2004 applicants were accepted. The SAT I scores for the 2003-2004 freshman class were: Verbal--15% below 500, 35% between 500 and 599, 35% between 600 and 700, and 15% above 700; Math--12% below 500, 35% between 500 and 599, 40% between 600 and 700, and 13% above 700. The ACT scores were 10% below 21, 25% between 21 and 23, 36% between 24 and 26, 15% between 27 and 28, and 14% above 28. 74% of the current freshmen were in the top fifth of their class; 92% were in the top two fifths. There were 2 National Merit finalists and 7 semifinalists. 29 freshmen graduated first in their class.

Requirements: The SAT I or ACT is required. In addition, applicants should be graduates of an accredited secondary school or have a GED certificate. They must have completed 4 years of English, 3 each of math and science, 2 of a single foreign language, and 1 each of social studies and American history. A GPA of 3.0 is required. AP and CLEP credits are accepted. Important factors in the admissions decision are leadership record, extracurricular activities record, and advanced placement or honor courses.

Procedure: Freshmen are admitted fall and spring. Entrance exams should be taken before December 1 of the senior year. There are early admissions and deferred admissions plans. Early action applications should be filed by December 1; regular applications, by February 1 for fall entry and March 15 for winter entry, along with a $35 fee. Notification of early decision is sent December 15; regular decision, April 1. Applications are accepted on-line through *www.mrs.umn.edu/admissions*.

Transfer: 82 transfer students enrolled in 2002-2003. Applicants must complete the application for admission, submit all college transcripts, and have maintained a minimum GPA of 2.5. 30 of 120 credits required for the bachelor's degree must be completed at UMM.

Visiting: There are regularly scheduled orientations for prospective students, including a campus tour, lunch with faculty, a session with admissions staff, and a student panel. There are guides for informal visits and visitors may sit in on classes and stay overnight. To schedule a visit, contact the Admissions Office.

Financial Aid: In 2003-2004, 61% of all full-time freshmen and 74% of continuing full-time students received some form of financial aid. 59% of full-time freshmen and 61% of continuing full-time students received need-based aid. The average freshman award was $9477. Need-based scholarships or need-based grants averaged $5669; need-based self-help aid (loans and jobs) averaged $4853; and non-need based-awards and non-need-based scholarships averaged $2719. 78% of undergraduates work part time. Average annual earnings from campus work are $1065. The average financial indebtedness of the 2003 graduate was $15,194. The FAFSA is required. The priority date for freshman financial aid applications for fall entry is March 1.

International Students: There are 23 international students enrolled. They must score 550 on the written TOEFL or 213 on the electronic version and also take the SAT I or the ACT.

Computers: The mainframes are a cluster of HP and Sun computers and shared mainframe resources with the University of Minnesota/Twin Cities. There are 7 PC and Mac public computer labs on campus. All residence hall rooms have high-speed access to the Internet and U of M servers. All students may access the system 24 hours per day. There are no time limits and no fees.

Graduates: From July 1, 2002 to June 30, 2003, 339 bachelor's degrees were awarded. The most popular majors were biology (12%), English (12%), and elementary education (10%). In an average class, 44% graduate in 4 years or less, 60% graduate in 5 years or less, and 67% graduate in 6 years or less. 72 companies recruited on campus in 2002-2003. Of the 2002 graduating class, 29% were enrolled in graduate school within 6 months of graduation and 71% were employed.

Admissions Contact: James Mootz, Associate Vice Chancellor for Enrollment. E-mail: *admissions@mrs.umn.edu*
Web: *http://www.mrs.umn.edu*

UNIVERSITY OF MINNESOTA/TWIN CITIES C-4
Minneapolis, MN 55455

(612) 625-2008
(800) 752-1000; Fax: (612) 625-1693

Full-time: 12,440 men, 13,733 women	**Faculty:** 2463; I, +$
Part-time: 2877 men, 3424 women	**Ph.D.s:** 91%
Graduate: 8056 men, 8944 women	**Student/Faculty:** 11 to 1
Year: semesters, summer session	**Tuition:** $7116 ($18,746)
Application Deadline: December 15	**Room & Board:** $6044
Freshman Class: 17,311 applied, 13,106 accepted, 5180 enrolled	
SAT I Verbal/Math: 596/616	**ACT:** 25 **VERY COMPETITIVE**

University of Minnesota/Twin Cities, founded in 1851, is a land-grant institution offering programs in liberal and fine arts, physical and biological sciences, health sciences, education, natural resources, human ecology, business, agriculture, engineering, and professional training in law, medicine, dentistry, pharmacy, and veterinary medicine. Some information in the above capsule is approximate. There are 18 undergraduate schools and 1 graduate school. In addition to regional accreditation, the university has baccalaureate program accreditation with AACSB, ABET, ABFSE, ACEJMC, ADA, APTA, ASLA, CSWE, FIDER, NAAB, NASM, NCATE, NLN, and SAF. The 17 libraries contain 5,600,000 volumes, 5,400,000 microform items, and 500,000 audio/video tapes/CDs, and subscribe to 48,105 periodicals. Computerized library services include the card catalog, interlibrary loans, and database searching. Special learning facilities include a learning resource center, art gallery, natural history museum, planetarium, radio station, and TV station. The 2000-acre campus is in an urban area within both Minneapolis and St. Paul. Including any residence halls, there are 205 buildings.

Student Life: 72% of undergraduates are from Minnesota. Students are from 50 states, 110 foreign countries, and Canada. 85% are from public schools. 83% are white. The average age of freshmen is 18; all undergraduates, 22. 17% do not continue beyond their first year; 56% remain to graduate.

Housing: 5636 students can be accommodated in college housing, which includes single-sex and coed dorms, on-campus apartments, off-campus apartments, married-student housing, fraternity houses, and sorority houses. In addition, there are honors houses and special-interest houses. On-campus housing is guaranteed for the freshman year only, is available on a first-come, first-served basis, and is available on a lottery system for upperclassmen. 88% of students commute. Alcohol is not permitted on campus. All students may keep cars on campus.

Activities: There are 33 local fraternities and 18 local sororities. There are 525 groups on campus, including art, band, cheerleading, chess, choir, chorale, chorus, computers, dance, debate, drama, ethnic, film, gay, honors, international, jazz band, literary magazine, marching band, musical theater, newspaper, orchestra, pep band, photography, political, professional, radio and TV, religious, social, social service, student government, symphony, and yearbook. Popular campus events include Campus Carnival.

Sports: There are 12 intercollegiate sports for men and 11 for women, and 16 intramural sports for men and 16 for women. Facilities include a domed stadium, 3 gyms, 2 field houses, a hockey rink, an Olympic-size aquatic center, and a student recreation center.

Disabled Students: 75% of the campus is accessible. Wheelchair ramps, elevators, special parking, specially equipped rest rooms, special class scheduling, lowered drinking fountains, lowered telephones, listening devices, TTY and volume-control phones, print enlargers, and adaptive computers are available. In addition, support groups and counselors provide assistance with all areas of university life and career planning.

Services: Counseling and information services are available, as is tutoring in every subject. There is a reader service for the blind and remedial math, reading, and writing. In addition there is test proctoring and sign language interpreters.

Campus Safety and Security: Measures include 24-hour foot and vehicle patrol, self-defense education, security escort services, and shuttle buses. There are informal discussions, pamphlets/posters/films, emergency telephones, lighted pathways/sidewalks, a 20-member university police force, and blue light phone centers.

Programs of Study: the university confers B.A., B.S., B.Aerospace Eng., B.Agr.Eng., B.C.E., B.Ch., B.Ch.E., B.Comp.Sci., B.E.E., B.F.A., B.G.E., B.I.S., B.M., B.Materials Sci., B.Mathematics, B.M.E., B.Pcs., B.S.Bus., B.S.G., B.S. in Astrophysics, B.S. in Geophysics, B.S.N., and B.Statistics. degrees. Master's and doctoral degrees are also awarded. Bachelor's degrees are awarded in AGRICULTURE (agricultural business management, agricultural economics, fishing and fisheries, forestry and related sciences, forestry production and processing, and natural resource management), BIOLOGICAL SCIENCE (biochemistry, biology/biological science, botany, cell biology, ecology, evolutionary biology, genetics, microbiology, nutrition, physiology, and wildlife biology), BUSINESS (accounting, business administration and management, management science, marketing/retailing/merchandising, recreation and leisure services, recreational facilities management, and retailing), COMMUNICATIONS AND THE ARTS (art history and appreciation, Chinese, classical languages, dance, English, film arts, French, German, Greek, Hebrew, Italian, Japanese, languages, Latin, linguistics, music, Russian, Scandinavian languages, Spanish, speech/debate/rhetoric, and studio art), COMPUTER AND PHYSICAL SCIENCE (actuarial science, astronomy, astrophysics, chemistry, computer science, geology, geophysics and seismology, mathematics, physics, and statistics), EDUCATION (agricultural, art, bilingual/bicultural, business, early childhood, elementary, English, home economics, industrial arts, mathematics, music, physical, science, social studies, and teaching English as a second/foreign language (TESOL/TEFOL), ENGINEERING AND ENVIRONMENTAL DESIGN (aeronautical engineering, agricultural engineering, architecture, chemical engineering, civil engineering, electrical/electronics engineering, environmental design, geological engineering, industrial engineering, interior design, landscape architecture/design, materials engineering, materials science, mechanical engineering, and metallurgical engineering), HEALTH PROFESSIONS (dental hygiene, medical laboratory technology, music therapy, nursing, occupational therapy, pharmacy, physical therapy, predentistry, premedicine, prepharmacy, preveterinary science, and speech pathology/audiology), SOCIAL SCIENCE (African American studies, African studies, American Indian studies, American studies, anthropology, child psychology/development, East Asian studies, economics, food science, geography, history, humanities, international relations, Mexican-American/Chicano studies, Middle Eastern studies, philosophy, political science/government, prelaw, psychology, Russian and Slavic studies, sociology, South Asian studies, textiles and clothing, urban studies, and women's studies). Chemical engineering, psychology, and economics are the strongest academically. Mechanical engineering, psychology, and electrical engineering are the largest.

Required: To graduate, students must complete 120 to 130 semester credits, including 45 in the major, with a minimum GPA of 2.0. Distribution requirements include course work in the 4 areas of communication, language, and symbolic systems, physical and biological sciences, the individual and society, and artistic expression. Other requirements vary by program.

Special: The university offers cooperative programs, cross-registration with the Minnesota Community College system, internships, study abroad in 65 countries, work-study programs both on and off campus, a B.A.-B.S. degree in all majors, a general studies degree, and dual and student-designed majors. Pass/fail options and credit for life, military, or work experience are available. There are 21 national honor societies, including Phi Beta Kappa, a freshman honors program, and 8 departmental honors programs.

Faculty/Classroom: 75% of faculty are male; 25%, female. All both teach and do research. The average class size in an introductory lecture is 29.

Admissions: 76% of the 2003-2004 applicants were accepted. The SAT I scores for the 2003-2004 freshman class were: Verbal--14% below 500, 30% between 500 and 599, 44% between 600 and 699, and 12% 700 and above. Math--12% below 500, 28% between 500 and 599, 44% between 600 and 699, and 19% 700 and above. The ACT scores were 15% below 21, 19% between 21 and 23, 29% between 24 and 26, 17% between 27 and 28, and 20% above 28. 61% of the current freshmen were in the top fifth of their class; 88% were in the top two fifths.

Requirements: The ACT is recommended. In addition, the university uses a formula index in evaluating high school rank and ACT test scores. A portfolio is required for studio arts and architecture, an audition for music, and an interview for architecture and education. AP and CLEP credits are accepted. Important factors in the admissions decision are advanced placement or honor courses, evidence of special talent, and leadership record.

Procedure: Freshmen are admitted to all sessions. Entrance exams should be taken by the end of the junior year or October/November/December of the senior year. There is an early admissions plan. There is a rolling admissions plan. Applications should be filed by December 15 (priority) for fall entry and October 15 (priority) for spring entry. The fall

2003 application fee was $25. Notification is sent on a rolling basis. Applications are accepted on-line through the university's web site.

Transfer: Admission requirements vary by major/program, with a minimum 2.2 GPA needed for consideration. 30 of 120 credits required for the bachelor's degree must be completed at the university.

Visiting: There are regularly scheduled orientations for prospective students. There are guides for informal visits and visitors may sit in on classes and stay overnight. To schedule a visit, contact The Visit Line at (612) 625-0000.

Financial Aid: In 2003-2004, 66% of all full-time freshmen and 57% of continuing full-time students received some form of financial aid. 52% of full-time freshmen and 78% of continuing full-time students received need-based aid. The average freshman award was $9377. Need-based scholarships or need-based grants averaged $6463; and need-based self-help aid (loans and jobs) averaged $5553. The FAFSA is required. There is no deadline for filing freshman financial aid applications for fall entry.

International Students: They must score 550 on the written TOEFL or take the MELAB, the college's own test, or Minnesota Battery and the Institutional TOEFL. The ACTis required for residents of Minnesota and neighboring states, and SAT I for residents of other states.

Computers: The mainframes are an IBM/CMS, CDC CYBER NOSNE, NOS, EP/IX, and DEC VMS. There are about 250 terminals and 1000 PCs for public use. All the PCs are networked. All students may access the system 24 hours a day, 7 days a week. Students may access the system 2 hours per session if there are others waiting or signed on. The fee is $45 per quarter. It is strongly recommended that all students have a personal computer.

Admissions Contact: Dr. Wayne Sigler, Ph.D., Director of Admissions. A video is available. E-mail: *admissions@tc.umn.edu.* Web: *www.umn.edu*

UNIVERSITY OF SAINT THOMAS C-4
St. Paul, MN 55105 (651) 962-6150
(800) 328-6819, ext. 2-6150; Fax: (651) 962-6160

Full-time: 2285 men, 2338 women	**Faculty:** 243; I, --$
Part-time: 302 men, 318 women	**Ph.D.s:** 84%
Graduate: 2813 men, 2953 women	**Student/Faculty:** 19 to 1
Year: 4-1-4, summer session	**Tuition:** $20,608
Application Deadline: open	**Room & Board:** $6310
Freshman Class: 2980 applied, 2583 accepted, 1039 enrolled	
SAT I Verbal/Math: 570/580	**ACT:** 24 **VERY COMPETITIVE**

The University of Saint Thomas, founded in 1885, is a private liberal arts institution affiliated with the Roman Catholic Church. There are 4 undergraduate and 9 graduate schools. In addition to regional accreditation, Saint Thomas has baccalaureate program accreditation with ABET, ACS, CSWE, NASM, and NCATE. The 3 libraries contain 541,588 volumes, 980,795 microform items, and 5108 audio/video tapes/CDs, and subscribe to 4753 periodicals. Computerized library services include the card catalog, interlibrary loans, and database searching. Special learning facilities include a learning resource center. The 78-acre campus is in an urban area 5 miles west of St. Paul and 5 miles east of Minneapolis. Including any residence halls, there are 74 buildings.

Student Life: 82% of undergraduates are from Minnesota. Students are from 44 states, 54 foreign countries, and Canada. 73% are from public schools. 89% are white. 53% are Catholic; 23% Protestant; 16% Muslim, Orthodox, Buddhist, Hindu, and other denominations; 8% claim no religious affiliation. The average age of freshmen is 18; all undergraduates, 21. 15% do not continue beyond their first year; 85% remain to graduate.

Housing: 2000 students can be accommodated in college housing, which includes single-sex dorms, on-campus apartments, and off-campus apartments. In addition, there are special-interest houses, chemical-free lifestyle, first-year experience, and women in science housing. On-campus housing is available on a first-come, first-served basis and is available on a lottery system for upperclassmen. 60% of students commute. All students may keep cars.

Activities: There are no fraternities or sororities. There are 94 groups on campus, including art, band, cheerleading, chess, choir, chorus, computers, dance, debate, drama, drill team, ethnic, gay, honors, international, jazz band, lecture committee, literary magazine, musical theater, newspaper, pep band, photography, political, professional, radio and TV, religious, social, social service, student government, student programming board, and yearbook. Popular campus events include Spring Fling, Taste of St. Thomas, and Senior Send-off.

Sports: There are 10 intercollegiate sports for men and 10 for women, and 10 intramural sports for men and 10 for women. Facilities include a field house with a 1/10-mile track, 5 volleyball courts, a 2000-seat gym, 4 basketball courts, 4 tennis courts, 6 racquetball courts, a fitness center, weight training and aerobics rooms, 2 swimming pools, 2 squash courts, a 5000-seat football and track stadium that includes an 8-lane Olympic caliber track, a baseball diamond, soccer, softball, and other playing fields, and 6 outdoor tennis courts.

Disabled Students: 80% of the campus is accessible. Wheelchair ramps, elevators, special parking, specially equipped rest rooms, special class scheduling, lowered drinking fountains, and lowered telephones are available.

Services: Counseling and information services are available, as is tutoring in most subjects. There is a reader service for the blind.

Campus Safety and Security: Measures include 24-hour foot and vehicle patrol, security escort services, shuttle buses, and informal discussions. There are pamphlets/posters/films, emergency telephones, and lighted pathways/sidewalks.

Programs of Study: Saint Thomas confers B.A., B.S., B.S.E., and B.S.M.E. degrees. Master's and doctoral degrees are also awarded. Bachelor's degrees are awarded in AGRICULTURE (environmental studies), BIOLOGICAL SCIENCE (biochemistry, biology/biological science, and neurosciences), BUSINESS (accounting, banking and finance, business administration and management, entrepreneurial studies, international business management, marketing management, personnel management, and real estate), COMMUNICATIONS AND THE ARTS (art history and appreciation, classical languages, communications, dramatic arts, English, French, German, journalism, Latin, literature, music, music business management, Russian, and Spanish), COMPUTER AND PHYSICAL SCIENCE (actuarial science, chemistry, computer science, geology, mathematics, and physics), EDUCATION (elementary, health, music, physical, science, and secondary), ENGINEERING AND ENVIRONMENTAL DESIGN (electrical/electronics engineering, environmental science, and mechanical engineering), HEALTH PROFESSIONS (community health work), SOCIAL SCIENCE (Christian studies, classical/ancient civilization, criminal justice, East Asian studies, economics, geography, history, international studies, peace studies, philosophy, political science/government, psychology, Russian and Slavic studies, social science, social studies, social work, sociology, theological studies, and women's studies). Business is the largest.

Required: All students must maintain a minimum GPA of 2.0 and complete at least 33 courses, or 132 semester credits, plus 1 in phys ed for no credit. Core curriculum requirements include 3 courses each in language and culture, faith and Catholic tradition, and natural science and mathematical and quantitative reasoning, 2 courses each in moral and philosophical reasoning and literature and writing, and 1 course each in fine arts, historical studies, social analysis, and human diversity. Students must complete 84 credits outside their major and demonstrate proficiency in operating a computer.

Special: Students may cross-register with Augsburg and Macalester Colleges, the College of Saint Catherine, and Hamline University. Study abroad is available in more than 40 countries, and there are several work-study programs. There are formal 3-2 engineering degree arrangements with Washington and Notre Dame Universities and the University of Minnesota, and 3-2 engineering degrees can also be arranged with many other accredited engineering programs. Nondegree study and pass/fail options also are available. There are 14 national honor societies and a freshman honors program.

Faculty/Classroom: 64% of faculty are male; 36%, female. 80% teach undergraduates and 20% do research. No introductory courses are taught by graduate students. The average class size in an introductory lecture is 24; in a laboratory, 15; and in a regular course, 21.

Admissions: 87% of the 2003-2004 applicants were accepted. The SAT I scores for the 2003-2004 freshman class were: Verbal--15% below 500, 47% between 500 and 599, 27% between 600 and 700, and 10% above 700; Math--11% below 500, 46% between 500 and 599, 34% between 600 and 700, and 9% above 700. The ACT scores were 12% below 21, 32% between 21 and 23, 32% between 24 and 26, 12% between 27 and 28, and 12% above 28. 55% of the current freshmen were in the top fifth of their class; 75% were in the top two fifths. There were 11 National Merit finalists. 41 freshmen graduated first in their class.

Requirements: The SAT I or ACT is required. In addition, Saint Thomas recommends 4 units each of English, math (3 units of math required), and foreign language and 2 each of science and history or social sciences. An essay is required. The GED is accepted. AP and CLEP credits are accepted. Important factors in the admissions decision are recommendations by school officials, geographic diversity, and parents or siblings attending the school.

Procedure: Freshmen are admitted fall and spring. Entrance exams should be taken by the fall of the senior year. There is a deferred admissions and a rolling admissions plan. Application deadlines are open. The fall 2003 application fee was $30. Applications are accepted on computer disk and on-line through the school's web site.

Transfer: 246 transfer students enrolled in 2002-2003. Transfer applicants must have a minimum GPA of 2.3 in transferable college credits. 32 of 132 credits required for the bachelor's degree must be completed at Saint Thomas.

Visiting: There are regularly scheduled orientations for prospective students, consisting of an open house in fall and spring that includes an admissions counselor presentation, a tour, a faculty fair, lunch, and a financial aid presentation. Other smaller orientations are also available. There are guides for informal visits and visitors may sit in on classes and stay overnight. To schedule a visit, contact the Visit Coordinator at (651) 962-6154 or *admvisit@stthomas.edu*.

Financial Aid: In 2003-2004, 95% of all full-time freshmen and 87% of continuing full-time students received some form of financial aid. 48% of full-time freshmen and 49% of continuing full-time students received need-based aid. The average freshman award was $13,963. Need-based scholarships or need-based grants averaged $5527 ($30,698 maximum); need-based self-help aid (loans and jobs) averaged $2538 ($12,925 maximum); and non-need-based awards and non-need-based scholarships averaged $2729 ($29,625 maximum). 53% of undergraduates work part time. Average annual earnings from campus work are $2460. The average financial indebtedness of the 2003 graduate was $23,084. The FAFSA is required. The deadline for filing freshman financial aid applications for fall entry is April 1.

International Students: There were 63 international students enrolled in a recent year. They must score 550 on the written TOEFL or take the MELAB.

Computers: The mainframes are a VMS cluster, composed of a Compaq ES (Enterprise Server) 40 and an AXP4100. Connection to the network is via fastnet, with full access from all resident hall rooms. Students are given access to the Internet via the school's network, a personal e-mail account, personal web page space, and NT storage space. All computers in all labs have Internet access. There are 7 public labs, 7 resident hall labs, and 58 discipline-specific labs with a total of 570 PCs. All students may access the system any time. There are no time limits and no fees.

Graduates: From July 1, 2002 to June 30, 2003, 1151 bachelor's degrees were awarded. The most popular majors were business administration/marketing (43%), journalism/communications (9%), and social science/history (9%). In an average class, 1% graduate in 3 years or less, 62% graduate in 4 years or less, 74% graduate in 5 years or less, and 76% graduate in 6 years or less. 70 companies recruited on campus in 2002-2003. Of the 2002 graduating class, 20% were enrolled in graduate school within 6 months of graduation and 92% were employed.

Admissions Contact: Marla Friederichs, Associate Vice President for Enrollment Management. E-mail: *admissions@stthomas.edu* Web: *www.stthomas.edu*

WINONA STATE UNIVERSITY　　　　　D-5
Winona, MN 55987-5838　　　　　　**(507) 457-5100**
　　　　　　　　　　　　(800) DIAL-WSU; Fax: (507) 457-5620

Full-time: 7536 men and women	**Faculty:** 305; IIB, +$
Part-time: none	**Ph.D.s:** 80%
Graduate: 625 men and women	**Student/Faculty:** n/av
Year: semesters, summer session	**Tuition:** $4800 ($9260)
Application Deadline: December 1	**Room & Board:** $4640
Freshman Class: 4519 applied, 3798 accepted, 1648 enrolled	
ACT: 23	**COMPETITIVE**

Winona State University, founded in 1858, is a public liberal arts institution and part of the Minnesota State Colleges and Universities system. There are 5 undergraduate schools and 1 graduate school. In addition to regional accreditation, WSU has baccalaureate program accreditation with ABET, ACCE, CSWE, NCATE, and NLN. The library contains 245,000 volumes and 831,000 microform items, and subscribes to 1400 periodicals. Computerized library services include interlibrary loans and database searching. Special learning facilities include a learning resource center, art gallery, and radio station. The 47-acre campus is in a small town 100 miles southeast of Minneapolis and St. Paul. Including any residence halls, there are 29 buildings.

Student Life: 55% of undergraduates are from Minnesota. Students are from 40 states, 51 foreign countries, and Canada. 80% are from public schools. 94% are white. 40% are Catholic; 40% Protestant. The average age of freshmen is 18; all undergraduates, 23. 25% do not continue beyond their first year; 55% remain to graduate.

Housing: 2500 students can be accommodated in college housing, which includes single-sex and coed dorms and on-campus apartments. In addition, there are honors houses. On-campus housing is guaranteed for the freshman year only, is available on a first-come, first-served basis, and is available on a lottery system for upperclassmen. Alcohol is not permitted. All students may keep cars.

Activities: 3% of men belong to 3 national fraternities; 3% of women belong to 3 national sororities. There are 155 groups on campus, including art, band, cheerleading, chess, choir, chorale, chorus, computers, dance, debate, drama, ethnic, forensics, gay, honors, international, jazz band, literary magazine, musical theater, newspaper, orchestra, pep band, photography, political, professional, radio and TV, religious, social, social service, student government, and symphony.

Sports: There are 6 intercollegiate sports for men and 9 for women, and 15 intramural sports for men and 15 for women. Facilities include a 4000-seat stadium, 8 outdoor tennis courts, and a field house with 10 gyms, 3 weight rooms, a swimming pool, indoor track and tennis facilities, handball/racquetball courts, and a wellness center.

Disabled Students: Wheelchair ramps, elevators, special parking, specially equipped rest rooms, special class scheduling, lowered drinking fountains, lowered telephones, and special housing are available.

Services: Counseling and information services are available, as is tutoring in most subjects.

Campus Safety and Security: Measures include 24-hour foot and vehicle patrol, self-defense education, security escort services, and shuttle buses. There are informal discussions, pamphlets/posters/films, emergency telephones, and lighted pathways/sidewalks.

Programs of Study: WSU confers B.A., B.S., B.S.E., and B.S.N. degrees. Associate and master's degrees are also awarded. Bachelor's degrees are awarded in BIOLOGICAL SCIENCE (biology/biological science), BUSINESS (accounting, banking and finance, business administration and management, business economics, human resources, management information systems, marketing/retailing/merchandising, personnel management, and recreation and leisure services), COMMUNICATIONS AND THE ARTS (advertising, broadcasting, communications, dramatic arts, English, fine arts, French, German, graphic design, journalism, music, Spanish, and speech/debate/rhetoric), COMPUTER AND PHYSICAL SCIENCE (chemistry, computer science, earth science, geology, mathematics, physics, and statistics), EDUCATION (art, business, early childhood, elementary, foreign languages, health, music, physical, science, secondary, and special), ENGINEERING AND ENVIRONMENTAL DESIGN (materials engineering), HEALTH PROFESSIONS (cytotechnology, exercise science, medical laboratory technology, nursing, physical therapy, predentistry, premedicine, preveterinary science, and public health), SOCIAL SCIENCE (community services, criminal justice, economics, history, international relations, liberal arts/general studies, paralegal studies, parks and recreation management, physical fitness/movement, political science/government, prelaw, psychology, public administration, social science, social work, and sociology). Engineering, nursing, and education are the strongest academically. Business administration, mass communication, and education are the largest.

Required: To graduate, students must complete 128 credit hours with a minimum GPA of 2.5 in most majors. General education requirements include 6 credits each in humanities, science/math, social science, and a different culture, 4 in English, 3 each in speech and math, and 2 in phys ed. Majors average 46 credits and some require a capstone experience.

Special: WSU offers cross-registration with St. Mary's University, study abroad in 25 countries, internships, work-study programs, student-designed majors, dual majors, pass/fail options, and credit for life, military, and work experience. Students may earn accelerated degrees in all majors and a general studies degree. There are 12 national honor societies, including Phi Beta Kappa, and 8 departmental honors programs.

Faculty/Classroom: 60% of faculty are male; 40%, female. 90% teach undergraduates, 10% do research, and 25% do both. No introductory courses are taught by graduate students. The average class size in an introductory lecture is 40; in a laboratory, 20; and in a regular course, 30.

Admissions: 84% of the 2003-2004 applicants were accepted. 40% of the current freshmen were in the top fifth of their class; 75% were in the top two fifths. There were 4 National Merit finalists and 48 semifinalists. 48 freshmen graduated first in their class.

Requirements: The ACT is required. In addition, candidates should have completed 4 units of English, 1 of which may be speech; 3 each of math, social studies, and science; 2 of a world language; and 1 elective, preferably in world culture, the arts, or computer science. WSU requires applicants to be in the upper 50% of their class. AP and CLEP credits are accepted. Important factors in the admissions decision are advanced placement or honor courses, leadership record, and evidence of special talent.

Procedure: Freshmen are admitted fall, spring, and summer. Entrance exams should be taken in the junior year. There are early admissions and deferred admissions plans. Applications should be filed by December 1 for fall entry and are open for spring entry. The application fee is $20 . Notification is sent on a rolling basis. 190 applicants were on the 2003 waiting list. Applications are accepted on-line.

Transfer: 564 transfer students enrolled in 2002-2003. Applicants must have completed 24 semester hours of credit with a minimum GPA of 2.4. 32 of 128 credits required for the bachelor's degree must be completed at WSU.

Visiting: There are regularly scheduled orientations for prospective students, including daily tours and admissions visits from October through January on select Saturday mornings. There are guides for informal visits and visitors may sit in on classes. To schedule a visit, contact the Office of Admissions.

Financial Aid: In 2003-2004, 73% of all full-time freshmen and 70% of continuing full-time students received some form of financial aid. 50% of full-time freshmen received need-based aid. The average freshman award was $3700. 40% of undergraduates work part time. Average annual earnings from campus work are $1800. The average financial indebtedness of the 2003 graduate was $7500. The FAFSA is required. The priority date for freshman financial aid applications for fall entry is February 1. The deadline for filing freshman financial aid applications for fall entry is April 1.

International Students: There are 325 international students enrolled. The school actively recruits these students. They must score 500 on the written TOEFL or 173 on the electronic version or take the MELAB.

Computers: The mainframes are a Unisys, DEC VAX, IBM AS/400, and other models. All students must lease laptops through WSU. The campus is completely wired. All students may access the system 24 hours a day. There are no time limits. The fee is $1000 for the laptop lease program and includes hardware, software, and network access. Models vary from year to year.

Admissions Contact: Douglas R. Schacke, Director of Admissions. A video is available. E-mail: admissions@winona.edu
Web: www.winona.edu

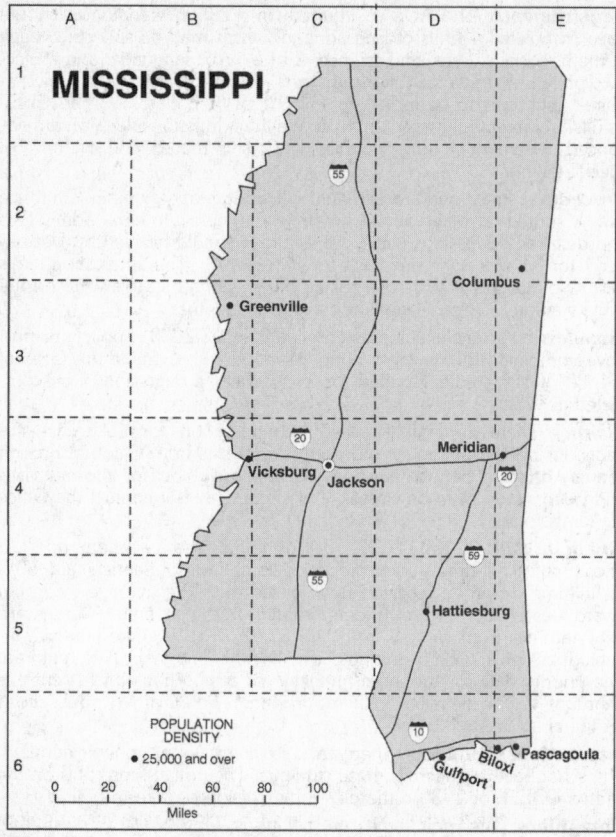

MISSISSIPPI

Columbus
● Greenville
Vicksburg ● Jackson
Meridian
Hattiesburg
Biloxi ● Pascagoula
Gulfport

POPULATION
DENSITY
● 25,000 and over

0 20 40 60 80 100
Miles

ALCORN STATE UNIVERSITY
Alcorn State, MS 39096-7500

B-4
(601) 877-6147
(800) 222-6790; Fax: (601) 877-6347

Full-time: 952 men, 1406 women	**Faculty:** 200; IIB, --$
Part-time: 85 men, 219 women	**Ph.D.s:** 48%
Graduate: 172 men, 475 women	**Student/Faculty:** 12 to 1
Year: semesters, summer session	**Tuition:** $3459 ($7965)
Application Deadline: open	**Room & Board:** $3831
Freshman Class: 1630 applied, 1008 accepted, 483 enrolled	
SAT I or ACT: required	**COMPETITIVE**

Alcorn State University, founded in 1871, is a public institution offering programs in agriculture, the arts and sciences, business, engineering, and nursing. There are 6 undergraduate schools and 1 graduate school. In addition to regional accreditation, Alcorn State University has baccalaureate program accreditation with AACSB, AAFCS, ADA, AHEA, NAIT, NASM, NCATE, and NLN. The library contains 205,582 volumes, 544,356 microform items, and 6276 audio/video tapes/CDs, and subscribes to 1046 periodicals. Computerized library services include the card catalog, interlibrary loans, and database searching. Special learning facilities include a learning resource center and radio station. The 1756-acre campus is in a rural area 45 miles south of Vicksburg and 7 miles west of Lorman. Including any residence halls, there are 127 buildings.

Student Life: 82% of undergraduates are from Mississippi. Students are from 27 states, 11 foreign countries, and Canada. 95% are from public schools. 92% are African American. The average age of freshmen is 21; all undergraduates, 23. 29% do not continue beyond their first year; 48% remain to graduate.

Housing: 2417 students can be accommodated in college housing, which includes single-sex dorms. In addition, there are honors houses. On-campus housing is guaranteed for all 4 years. 55% of students live on campus; of those, 45% remain on campus on weekends. Alcohol is not permitted. All students may keep cars.

Activities: 8% of men belong to 5 local and 4 national fraternities; 10% of women belong to 4 local and 4 national sororities. There are 83 groups on campus, including band, cheerleading, choir, chorus, drama, honors, jazz band, marching band, newspaper, photography, religious, student government, and yearbook. Popular campus events include High School Day and Career Development Day.

Sports: There are 7 intercollegiate sports for men and 8 for women, and 8 intramural sports for men and 9 for women. Facilities include a 10,000-seat stadium and a 5000-seat gym.

Disabled Students: 15% of the campus is accessible. Wheelchair ramps, elevators, special parking, specially equipped rest rooms, and lowered drinking fountains are available.

Services: Counseling and information services are available, as is tutoring in most subjects. There is remedial math, reading, writing, and English.

Campus Safety and Security: Measures include 24-hour foot and vehicle patrol, pamphlets/posters/films, and lighted pathways/sidewalks.

Programs of Study: Alcorn State University confers B.A., B.S., B.M., B.M.E., and B.S.N. degrees. Associate and master's degrees are also awarded. Bachelor's degrees are awarded in AGRICULTURE (agricultural economics, agriculture, animal science, and plant science), BIOLOGICAL SCIENCE (biology/biological science and nutrition), BUSINESS (accounting, business administration and management, and office supervision and management), COMMUNICATIONS AND THE ARTS (communications and English), COMPUTER AND PHYSICAL SCIENCE (chemistry, computer science, and mathematics), EDUCATION (elementary, industrial arts, music, physical, recreation, science, and special), ENGINEERING AND ENVIRONMENTAL DESIGN (industrial administration/management), HEALTH PROFESSIONS (health science and nursing), SOCIAL SCIENCE (child care/child and family studies, criminal justice, economics, family/consumer studies, history, liberal arts/general studies, political science/government, psychology, and sociology). General studies and industrial technologies are the largest.

Required: To graduate, students must complete at least 128 semester hours with a minimum GPA of 2.0. Core requirements include 12 hours of social science, 9 each of natural science and creative arts, 6 of English, 4 of phys ed or military science, and 3 each of math and oral communications, as well as 1 of student adjustment.

Special: The university offers cooperative programs in medical technology and physical therapy, internships, and work-study programs. There is 1 national honor society, including Phi Beta Kappa, a freshman honors program, and 5 departmental honors programs.

Faculty/Classroom: 51% of faculty are male; 49%, female. 95% teach undergraduates and 1% do research. The average class size in a laboratory is 16 and in a regular course, 17.

Admissions: 62% of the 2003-2004 applicants were accepted. The ACT scores for the 2003-2004 freshman class were: 79% below 21, 15% between 21 and 23, 5% between 24 and 26, and 1% between 27 and 28.

Requirements: The SAT I or ACT is required. In addition, students must have graduated from an accredited high school with at least a C average and have completed 15 1/2 units of a college prep curriculum. A GPA of 2.0 is required. AP and CLEP credits are accepted.

Procedure: Freshmen are admitted to all sessions. Entrance exams should be taken so that scores may be submitted at the time application is made. There are early decision, early admissions, rolling, and deferred admissions plans. Application deadlines are open.

Transfer: 201 transfer students enrolled in 2002-2003. Applicants must have at least 6 hours each of composition and laboratory sciences, 3 hours of college algebra or above, and 9 other transferable elective hours, and have maintained an overall minimum GPA of 2.0. 104 of 128 credits required for the bachelor's degree must be completed at Alcorn State University.

Visiting: There are regularly scheduled orientations for prospective students. There are guides for informal visits and visitors may sit in on classes and stay overnight. To schedule a visit, contact Emanuel F. Barnes.

Financial Aid: In 2003-2004, 70% of all full-time freshmen and 74% of continuing full-time students received some form of financial aid. 36% of full-time freshmen received need-based aid. The average freshman award was $6600. Need-based scholarships or need-based grants averaged $1200 ($2400 maximum); need-based self-help aid (loans and jobs) averaged $2578 ($4685 maximum); and non-need-based athletic scholarships averaged $7280 ($11,786 maximum). 65% of undergraduates work part time. Average annual earnings from campus work are $2060. The average financial indebtedness of the 2003 graduate was $6500. Alcorn State University is a member of CSS. The CSS Profile or FAFSA is required.

International Students: There are 30 international students enrolled. The school actively recruits these students. They must score 525 on the written TOEFL, take the college's own test, and also take the SAT I or the ACT, scoring 21.

Computers: The mainframe is an IBM 4361/PO2. All students may access the system. There are no time limits and no fees.

Graduates: From July 1, 2002 to June 30, 2003, 371 bachelor's degrees were awarded. The most popular majors were general studies (73%), industrial technology (40%), and biology (38%). 253 companies recruited on campus in 2002-2003.

Admissions Contact: Emanuel F. Barnes, Director of Admissions.
E-mail: *ebarnes@lorman.alcorn.edu* Web: *www.alcorn.edu*

BELHAVEN COLLEGE
Jackson, MS 39202

C-4

(601) 968-5940
(800) 960-5940; Fax: (601) 968-8946

Full-time: 565 men, 945 women	**Faculty:** 51
Part-time: 60 men, 100 women	**Ph.D.s:** 79%
Graduate: 75 men, 140 women	**Student/Faculty:** 30 to 1
Year: semesters, summer session	**Tuition:** $12,000
Application Deadline: open	**Room & Board:** $4500
Freshman Class: n/av	
SAT I or ACT: required	**COMPETITIVE+**

Belhaven College, founded in 1883, is a private liberal arts institution with a Presbyterian heritage. There is 1 graduate school. Figures in the above capsule and in this profile are approximate. In addition to regional accreditation, Belhaven has baccalaureate program accreditation with NASAD and NASM. The library contains 115,000 volumes, 9000 microform items, and 16,000 audio/video tapes/CDs, and subscribes to 560 periodicals. Computerized library services include the card catalog, interlibrary loans, and database searching. Special learning facilities include an art gallery. The 42-acre campus is in an urban area in Jackson. Including any residence halls, there are 13 buildings.

Student Life: 69% of undergraduates are from Mississippi. Students are from 35 states, 11 foreign countries, and Canada. 61% are white; 35% African American. Most are Protestant. The average age of freshmen is 18; all undergraduates, 29. 38% do not continue beyond their first year; 43% remain to graduate.

Housing: 540 students can be accommodated in college housing, which includes single-sex dorms. On-campus housing is guaranteed for all 4 years. 73% of students commute. Alcohol is not permitted. All students may keep cars.

Activities: There are no fraternities or sororities. There are 22 groups on campus, including art, cheerleading, choir, chorus, dance, drama, ethnic, honors, literary magazine, musical theater, newspaper, political, professional, religious, social service, student government, and yearbook. Popular campus events include Singing Christmas Tree, concert and lecture series, and Lake Day.

Sports: There are 7 intercollegiate sports for men and 7 for women, and 4 intramural sports for men and 4 for women. Facilities include a gym, 5 tennis courts, a lake, an intramural and soccer field, a baseball field, a football/soccer practice field, an athletic training facility, and an exercise, weight, and conditioning complex.

Disabled Students: 25% of the campus is accessible. Wheelchair ramps, elevators, special parking, specially equipped rest rooms, special class scheduling, and lowered drinking fountains are available.

Services: There is remedial math and writing and study halls for athletes.

Campus Safety and Security: Measures include 24-hour foot and vehicle patrol, security escort services, informal discussions, and lighted pathways/sidewalks.

Programs of Study: Belhaven confers B.A., B.S., B.A.A., B.B.A., B.F.A., and B.S.M. degrees. Associate and master's degrees are also awarded. Bachelor's degrees are awarded in BIOLOGICAL SCIENCE (biology/biological science), BUSINESS (accounting and business administration and management), COMMUNICATIONS AND THE ARTS (art, ballet, communications, dance, dramatic arts, English, and music), COMPUTER AND PHYSICAL SCIENCE (chemistry, computer science, information sciences and systems, and mathematics), EDUCATION (athletic training and elementary), HEALTH PROFESSIONS (exercise science), SOCIAL SCIENCE (biblical studies, history, humanities, philosophy, political science/government, psychology, religious music, and social work). Biology and chemistry are the strongest academically. Business administration and education are the largest.

Required: Requirements for graduation vary by degree, but students must complete at least 124 semester hours, including 25 hours of World View Curriculum courses, with a minimum 2.0 GPA.

Special: Students may participate in various internships, including one in Washington, D.C., or in 6 countries through the study-travel program. Belhaven also offers, dual majors, nondegree study, pass/fail options, a 3-2 engineering degree with Mississippi State University, and work-study. 2 1-month summer sessions and 2 2-week minisessions offer additional opportunities for credit. There are 3 national honor societies, a freshman honors program, and 1 departmental honors program.

Faculty/Classroom: 66% of faculty are male; 34%, female. 90% teach undergraduates. No introductory courses are taught by graduate students. The average class size in an introductory lecture is 24; in a laboratory, 16; and in a regular course, 18.

Requirements: The SAT I or ACT is required; the ACT is preferred. Applicants should be graduates of an accredited secondary school, with 16 academic units, including 4 of English, 2 of math, 1 each of history and natural science, a recommended 2 of a foreign language, and 6 of electives. A personal recommendation is also required. A GPA of 2.0 is

required. AP and CLEP credits are accepted. Important factors in the admissions decision are advanced placement or honor courses, evidence of special talent, and extracurricular activities record.

Procedure: Freshmen are admitted to all sessions. Entrance exams should be taken in the junior year. There is an early admissions plan. Application deadlines are open. Check with the school for current application fee.

Transfer: 318 transfer students enrolled in a recent year. Transfer applicants must have a minimum 2.0 GPA and submit all college transcripts. 31 of 124 credits required for the bachelor's degree must be completed at Belhaven.

Visiting: There are guides for informal visits and visitors may sit in on classes and stay overnight. To schedule a visit, contact the Admissions Office.

Financial Aid: The FAFSA and the college's own financial statement are required. Check with the school for current deadlines.

International Students: The school actively recruits these students. They must score 500 on the written TOEFL or 173 on the electronic version.

Computers: More than 30 PCs are available for academic use in the library and computer lab. All are wired to the campus fiber-optic network, the Internet, and the World Wide Web. All students may access the system. There are no time limits and no fees.

Graduates: In a recent year, 299 bachelor's degrees were awarded. The most popular majors were business administration (52%), psychology (8%), and elementary education (7%). In an average class, 34% graduate in 4 years or less, 43% graduate in 5 years or less, and 44% graduate in 6 years or less.

Admissions Contact: Dr. Stephen D. Livesay, Vice President for Advancement. E-mail: *admissions@belhaven.edu* Web: *www.belhaven.edu*

BLUE MOUNTAIN COLLEGE
Blue Mountain, MS 38610-0160

D-1

(662) 685-4161
(800) 235-0136; Fax: (662) 685-4776

Full-time: 68 men, 266 women	**Faculty:** 22
Part-time: 11 men, 86 women	**Ph.D.s:** 54%
Graduate: none	**Student/Faculty:** 15 to 1
Year: semesters, summer session	**Tuition:** $6700
Application Deadline: open	**Room & Board:** $3526
Freshman Class: 128 applied, 82 accepted, 61 enrolled	
ACT: 21	**COMPETITIVE**

Blue Mountain College, founded in 1873 and affiliated with the Southern Baptist Church, is a private liberal arts college for women that also admits men who are preparing for a church-related vocation. The 2 libraries contain 51,089 volumes, 375 microform items, and 4457 audio/video tapes/CDs, and subscribe to 200 periodicals. Computerized library services include the card catalog, database searching, and Internet access. The 44-acre campus is in a rural area 65 miles southeast of Memphis. Including any residence halls, there are 14 buildings.

Student Life: 88% of undergraduates are from Mississippi. Students are from 6 states and 1 foreign country. 82% are from public schools. 87% are white; 10% African American. Most are Protestant. The average age of freshmen is 20; all undergraduates, 26. 29% do not continue beyond their first year; 46% remain to graduate.

Housing: 252 students can be accommodated in college housing, which includes single-sex dorms. In addition, there are special-interest houses. On-campus housing is guaranteed for all 4 years. 68% of students commute. Alcohol is not permitted. All students may keep cars.

Activities: There are no fraternities or sororities. There are 30 groups on campus, including art, choir, chorale, chorus, drama, honors, literary magazine, musical theater, professional, religious, social, student government, and yearbook. Popular campus events include High School Weekend, Field Day, and formal dinners and plays.

Sports: There are 2 intercollegiate sports for women, and 3 intramural sports for men and 7 for women. Facilities include a gym, a swimming pool, and a softball field.

Disabled Students: 25% of the campus is accessible. Wheelchair ramps, elevators, special parking, specially equipped rest rooms, special class scheduling, and lowered drinking fountains are available.

Services: There is remedial math, reading, and writing.

Campus Safety and Security: Measures include self-defense education, informal discussions, and lighted pathways/sidewalks.

Programs of Study: BMC confers B.A., B.S., and B.S.Ed. degrees. Bachelor's degrees are awarded in BIOLOGICAL SCIENCE (biology/biological science), BUSINESS (business administration and management), COMMUNICATIONS AND THE ARTS (dramatic arts, English, music, piano/organ, Spanish, and speech/debate/rhetoric), COMPUTER AND PHYSICAL SCIENCE (chemistry and mathematics), EDUCATION (business, elementary, English, foreign languages, mathematics, music, physical, science, secondary, and social science), HEALTH PROFESSIONS (medical technology), SOCIAL SCIENCE (biblical studies, history, psychology, and social science). Education is the strongest academically. Elementary education is the largest.

Required: All students must take 120 semester hours, including 6 hours each of English composition, literature, history, and Bible, 3 hours of psychology, 2 semesters of phys ed, and a computer course. Students must maintain a minimum GPA of 2.5 for the teaching degree and 2.0 for other degrees. Majors require 30 or more hours.

Special: Students may take summer business internships. The college offers pass/fail options and dual majors. There is 1 national honor society and 6 departmental honors programs.

Faculty/Classroom: 38% of faculty are male; 62%, female. 87% teach undergraduates. The average class size in an introductory lecture is 21; in a laboratory, 16; and in a regular course, 15.

Admissions: 64% of the 2003-2004 applicants were accepted. The ACT scores for the 2003-2004 freshman class were: 58% below 21, 21% between 21 and 23, 13% between 24 and 26, 2% between 27 and 28, and 6% above 28. 25% of the current freshmen were in the top fifth of their class; 48% were in the top two fifths. 1 freshman graduated first in the class.

Requirements: The SAT I or ACT is required. In addition, BMC recommends that applicants for admission have completed 4 units of English, 3 each of math, science, and social studies, and 2 of a foreign language. A GPA of 2.0 is required. AP and CLEP credits are accepted. Important factors in the admissions decision are ability to finance college education, extracurricular activities record, and geographic diversity.

Procedure: Freshmen are admitted fall, spring, and summer. Entrance exams should be taken starting in the junior year. There is an early admissions plan and a rolling admissions plan. Application deadlines are open. The application fee is $10.

Transfer: 112 transfer students enrolled in 2002-2003. 30 of 120 credits required for the bachelor's degree must be completed at BMC.

Visiting: There are regularly scheduled orientations for prospective students. There are guides for informal visits and visitors may sit in on classes and stay overnight. To schedule a visit, contact the Office of Admissions.

Financial Aid: In 2003-2004, 95% of all full-time freshmen and 96% of continuing full-time students received some form of financial aid. 56% of full-time freshmen and 63% of continuing full-time students received need-based aid. The average freshman award was $7589. Need-based scholarships or need-based grants averaged $1431 ($5650 maximum); need-based self-help aid (loans and jobs) averaged $1319 ($4025 maximum); non-need-based athletic scholarships averaged $312 ($10,246 maximum); and other non-need-based awards and non-need-based scholarships averaged $3962 ($6300 maximum). 22% of undergraduates work part time. Average annual earnings from campus work are $1400. The average financial indebtedness of the 2003 graduate was $9000. BMC is a member of CSS. The FAFSA and the college's own financial statement are required. The priority date for freshman financial aid applications for fall entry is March 1. The deadline for filing freshman financial aid applications for fall entry is July 15.

International Students: There is 1 international student enrolled. They must score 500 on the written TOEFL or 173 on the electronic version and also take the SAT I or the ACT.

Computers: There are 10 PCs with Internet access available to all students in the library and computer hook-ups are available in 2 of 3 dorms. All students may access the system during regular library hours. There are no time limits and no fees. It is strongly recommended that all students have a personal computer.

Graduates: From July 1, 2002 to June 30, 2003, 67 bachelor's degrees were awarded. The most popular majors were elementary education (45%), biblical studies (13%), and English (10%). In an average class, 1% graduate in 3 years or less, 32% graduate in 4 years or less, 43% graduate in 5 years or less, and 46% graduate in 6 years or less. Of the 2002 graduating class, 9% were enrolled in graduate school within 6 months of graduation and 73% were employed.

Admissions Contact: Tina Barkley, Director of Admissions.
E-mail: tbarkley@bmc.edu Web: www.bmc.edu

DELTA STATE UNIVERSITY
Cleveland, MS 38733

C-2

(662) 846-4655
(800) 468-6378; Fax: (662) 846-4683

Full-time: 1018 men, 1532 women	**Faculty:** IIA, --$
Part-time: 191 men, 415 women	**Ph.D.s:** 55%
Graduate: 191 men, 438 women	**Student/Faculty:** n/av
Year: semesters, summer session	**Tuition:** $3348 ($7965)
Application Deadline: August 1	**Room & Board:** $3270
Freshman Class: 358 enrolled	
ACT: 20	**COMPETITIVE**

Delta State University, founded in 1924, is a public liberal arts institution offering degrees in arts and sciences, business, education, health science, and nursing. There are 4 undergraduate and 4 graduate schools. In addition to regional accreditation, DSU has baccalaureate program accreditation with AAFCS, ACBSP, ACEJMC, ACS, AHEA, CAAHEP, CSWE,

NASAD, NASM, NCATE, and NLN. The library contains 331,251 volumes, 795,827 microform items, and 16,975 audio/video tapes/CDs, and subscribes to 1330 periodicals. Computerized library services include the card catalog, interlibrary loans, and database searching. Special learning facilities include a learning resource center, art gallery, natural history museum, planetarium, and a performing arts center. The 332-acre campus is in a small town 110 miles south of Memphis, and 130 miles north of Jackson. Including any residence halls, there are 46 buildings.

Student Life: 90% of undergraduates are from Mississippi. Students are from 30 states, 15 foreign countries, and Canada. 63% are white; 35% African American. The average age of freshmen is 18; all undergraduates, 26. 32% do not continue beyond their first year; 47% remain to graduate.

Housing: 1587 students can be accommodated in college housing, which includes single-sex dorms and married-student housing. On-campus housing is guaranteed for all 4 years. 71% of students commute. Alcohol is not permitted. All students may keep cars.

Activities: 14% of men belong to 8 national fraternities; 14% of women belong to 6 national sororities. There are 116 groups on campus, including art, band, cheerleading, choir, chorale, chorus, computers, dance, drama, drill team, ethnic, honors, jazz band, literary magazine, marching band, musical theater, newspaper, opera, orchestra, pep band, photography, political, professional, religious, social, social service, student government, and yearbook. Popular campus events include Springfest and Christmas Madrigal Feast.

Sports: There are 7 intercollegiate sports for men and 6 for women, and 16 intramural sports for men and 16 for women. Facilities include a coliseum, an indoor pool, a gym, a baseball field, a softball field, a football stadium, a 9-hole golf course, outdoor tennis courts, 2 intramural fields, an outdoor walking facility, and a fitness center.

Disabled Students: 90% of the campus is accessible. Wheelchair ramps, elevators, special parking, specially equipped rest rooms, special class scheduling, lowered drinking fountains, and lowered telephones are available.

Services: Counseling and information services are available, as is tutoring in every subject. There is remedial math, reading, and writing.

Campus Safety and Security: Measures include 24-hour foot and vehicle patrol, self-defense education, security escort services, and informal discussions. There are pamphlets/posters/films, emergency telephones, and lighted pathways/sidewalks.

Programs of Study: DSU confers B.A., B.S., B.B.A., B.C.A., B.F.A., B.M., B.M.E., B.S.C.J., B.S.E., B.S.G.S., B.S.N., and B.S.W. degrees. Master's and doctoral degrees are also awarded. Bachelor's degrees are awarded in BIOLOGICAL SCIENCE (biology/biological science), BUSINESS (accounting, business administration and management, fashion merchandising, hospitality management services, insurance, management science, marketing/retailing/merchandising, and secretarial studies/office management), COMMUNICATIONS AND THE ARTS (art, English, journalism, music, and music performance), COMPUTER AND PHYSICAL SCIENCE (chemistry, information sciences and systems, and mathematics), EDUCATION (athletic training, business, elementary, English, foreign languages, health, mathematics, music, science, secondary, social science, social studies, and special), ENGINEERING AND ENVIRONMENTAL DESIGN (aviation administration/management and environmental science), HEALTH PROFESSIONS (nursing, predentistry, premedicine, and speech pathology/audiology), SOCIAL SCIENCE (criminal justice, family/consumer studies, history, political science/government, psychology, social science, social work, and sociology). Elementary education, biology, and computer information systems are the largest.

Required: To graduate, students must complete 128 semester hours, including 30 to 54 in the major, with a minimum GPA of 2.0. General education requirements include 6 hours each of English composition, English literature, history, lab science, and social science; 3 hours each of fine arts, math, psychology, and speech; and 2 hours of phys ed.

Special: DSU offers internships in several majors. A general studies degree and nondegree study are also available. There are 16 national honor societies, a freshman honors program, and 7 departmental honors programs.

Faculty/Classroom: 56% of faculty are male; 44%, female. No introductory courses are taught by graduate students.

Admissions: The ACT scores for the 2003-2004 freshman class were: 63% below 21, 21% between 21 and 23, 8% between 24 and 26, 4% between 27 and 28, and 4% above 28. 34% of the current freshmen were in the top fifth of their class; 63% were in the top two fifths.

Requirements: The SAT I or ACT is required. In addition, students may gain admission by completing the college prep curriculum with a minimum of 3.2 GPA; by completing the college prep curriculum with a minimum of 2.5 GPA and scoring at least 16 on the ACT (at least 650 on the SAT I); by ranking in the upper 50% of the class and scoring at least 16 on the ACT (at least 650 on the SAT I); or by completing the college prep curriculum with a minimum 2.0 GPA and scoring 18 or higher on the ACT (at least 740 on the SAT I). The Nelson Denny Reading Test and Math Placement Test must also be taken. Applicants must be graduates of an accredited secondary school or have the GED. They should have completed 4 courses in English; 3 each in math, science, and social studies; 2 in a foreign language, world geography, or additional science/math; and 1/2 in computer applications. A GPA of 2.0 is required. AP credits are accepted.

Procedure: Freshmen are admitted to all sessions. Entrance exams should be taken as early as possible. There is a rolling admissions plan. Applications should be filed by August 1 for fall entry and January 1 for spring entry. Notification is sent on a rolling basis. Applications are accepted on-line through the school's web site.

Transfer: 469 transfer students enrolled in 2002-2003. A minimum GPA of 2.0 is required, and an associate degree and ACT or SAT I scores are recommended. 30 of 128 credits required for the bachelor's degree must be completed at DSU.

Visiting: There are regularly scheduled orientations for prospective students, including campus tours and introduction to faculty and staff. There are guides for informal visits and visitors may sit in on classes and stay overnight. To schedule a visit, contact School Relations and Recruitment at (662) 846-4018.

Financial Aid: In 2003-2004, 82% of all full-time freshmen and 80% of continuing full-time students received some form of financial aid. 10% of undergraduates work part time. The average financial indebtedness of the 2003 graduate was $17,000. The FAFSA is required. The deadline for filing freshman financial aid applications for fall entry is June 1.

International Students: There are 33 international students enrolled. They must score 525 on the written TOEFL or 196 on the electronic version and also take the SAT I or the ACT.

Computers: The mainframe is an IBM RS/6000 Model 570. There are 257 PCs available in various locations. Students have access to the Internet and web from computer labs, dorm rooms, and the library. All students may access the system from 8 A.M. to 11 P.M. daily. There are no time limits and no fees. It is recommended that students in the executive MBA program have personal computers.

Graduates: From July 1, 2002 to June 30, 2003, 596 bachelor's degrees were awarded. The most popular majors were elementary education (11%), computer information systems (7%), and management (6%). In an average class, 1% graduate in 3 years or less, 21% graduate in 4 years or less, 39% graduate in 5 years or less, and 45% graduate in 6 years or less. 130 companies recruited on campus in 2002-2003.

Admissions Contact: Debbie Heslep, Associate Dean of Enrollment Services. E-mail: dheslep@deltastate.edu Web: http://deltastate.edu

---

JACKSON STATE UNIVERSITY
Jackson, MS 39217

C-4

(601) 979-2100
(800) 848-6817; Fax: (601) 973-3445

Full-time: 2197 men, 3241 women	**Faculty:** 356; IIA, --$
Part-time: 257 men, 597 women	**Ph.D.s:** 70%
Graduate: 432 men, 1091 women	**Student/Faculty:** 15 to 1
Year: semesters, summer session	**Tuition:** $3612 ($8116)
Application Deadline: open	**Room & Board:** $4770
Freshman Class: 5937 applied, 2542 accepted, 955 enrolled	
ACT: 18	**COMPETITIVE**

Jackson State University, founded in 1877, is a public institution with an emphasis on liberal arts, business, music, and teacher preparation. There are 5 undergraduate schools and 1 graduate school. In addition to regional accreditation, JSU has baccalaureate program accreditation with AACSB, CSWE, NASAD, NASM, and NCATE. The library contains 486,478 volumes, 675,035 microform items, and 2104 audio/video tapes/CDs, and subscribes to 1736 periodicals. Computerized library services include the card catalog, interlibrary loans, database searching, and Internet access. Special learning facilities include a learning resource center and radio station. The 150-acre campus is in an urban area 190 miles north of New Orleans. Including any residence halls, there are 40 buildings.

Student Life: 80% of undergraduates are from Mississippi. Students are from 40 states and 38 foreign countries. 94% are African American. The average age of freshmen is 21; all undergraduates, 23. 24% do not continue beyond their first year; 37% remain to graduate.

Housing: 2454 students can be accommodated in college housing, which includes single-sex dorms. In addition, there are honors houses. On-campus housing is available on a first-come, first-served basis. 53% of students commute. Alcohol is not permitted. All students may keep cars.

Activities: 5% of men belong to 4 national fraternities; 5% of women belong to 4 national sororities. There are many groups and organizations on campus, including art, band, cheerleading, choir, dance, drama, drill team, ethnic, honors, jazz band, marching band, musical theater, newspaper, opera, orchestra, pep band, photography, political, radio and TV, religious, social service, student government, symphony, and yearbook.

Sports: There are 7 intercollegiate sports for men and 4 for women, and 2 intramural sports for men and 2 for women. Facilities include an Olympic-size swimming pool, a gym with 2 basketball courts, indoor and outdoor tennis courts, badminton and volleyball courts, a dance studio, a baseball diamond, soccer and athletic fields, an archery range, a track, and a bowling alley.

Disabled Students: All of the campus is accessible. Wheelchair ramps, elevators, special parking, specially equipped rest rooms, lowered drinking fountains, and lowered telephones are available.

Services: Counseling and information services are available, as is tutoring in every subject. There is remedial math, reading, and writing.

Campus Safety and Security: Measures include 24-hour foot and vehicle patrol, self-defense education, shuttle buses, and informal discussions. There are pamphlets/posters/films and emergency telephones.

Programs of Study: JSU confers B.A., B.S., B.B.A., B.M., B.M.E., B.S.Ed., and B.S.W. degrees. Master's and doctoral degrees are also awarded. Bachelor's degrees are awarded in BIOLOGICAL SCIENCE (biology/biological science), BUSINESS (accounting, banking and finance, business administration and management, marketing/retailing/merchandising, and office supervision and management), COMMUNICATIONS AND THE ARTS (art, communications, English, languages, piano/organ, and speech/debate/rhetoric), COMPUTER AND PHYSICAL SCIENCE (atmospheric sciences and meteorology, chemistry, computer science, mathematics, and physics), EDUCATION (business, elementary, health, industrial arts, mathematics, music, social science, and special), HEALTH PROFESSIONS (premedicine), SOCIAL SCIENCE (child care/child and family studies, corrections, criminal justice, economics, history, political science/government, psychology, social work, sociology, and urban studies). Computer science, biology, and accounting are the strongest academically. Biology, elementary education, and business administration are the largest.

Required: To graduate, students must complete at least 128 semester hours with a minimum GPA of 2.0. At least 30 upper-division hours must be earned in the major. Distribution requirements include a total of 49 to 59 hours in communications, humanities and fine arts, social and behavioral sciences, natural sciences, health and physical education, and concepts for success in college.

Special: Internships with various corporations, nondegree study, work-study programs, a cooperative education program, accelerated degrees, combined B.A.-B.S. degrees, and a student-exchange program are available. There are 4 national honor societies, a freshman honors program, and 14 departmental honors programs.

Faculty/Classroom: 55% of faculty are male; 45%, female.

Admissions: 43% of the 2003-2004 applicants were accepted. The ACT scores for the 2003-2004 freshman class were: 78% below 21, 14% between 21 and 23, 7% between 24 and 26, and 1% between 27 and 28. 40% of the current freshmen were in the top fifth of their class; 74% were in the top two fifths.

Requirements: The SAT I or ACT is required. In addition, applicants must be graduates of an accredited secondary school or have a GED certificate. They must have earned 15½ Carnegie units, including 4 of English, 3 each of math, social studies, and sciences, 2 of advanced electives, and ½ of computer applications. A composite ACT score of 20 or above, or an SAT I score of 800 or above exempts students from the specific high school unit requirements. An interview is recommended. A GPA of 2.0 is required. AP and CLEP credits are accepted. Important factors in the admissions decision are recommendations by school officials, leadership record, and extracurricular activities record.

Procedure: Freshmen are admitted to all sessions. Entrance exams should be taken during the first semester of the senior year. There are early admissions and deferred admissions plans. There is a rolling admissions plan. Application deadlines are open. Notificationis sent on a rolling basis. Applications are accepted on computer disk and on-line through www.jsums.edu.

Transfer: 379 transfer students enrolled in 2002-2003. Applicants should submit an official transcript from each institution attended, be in good standing at the last college or university attended, and have a minimum cumulative GPA of 2.0. 30 credits of 128 required for the bachelor's degree must be completed at JSU.

Visiting: There are regularly scheduled orientations for prospective students. There are guides for informal visits and visitors may sit in on classes and stay overnight. To schedule a visit, contact the Office of Marketing and Recruitment at (601) 979-2911 or www.recruitment@jsums.edu.

Financial Aid: In 2003-2004, 97% of all full-time freshmen and 93% of continuing full-time students received some form of financial aid. 84% of full-time freshmen and 83% of continuing full-time students received need-based aid. The average freshman award was $8812. Need-based scholarships or need-based grants averaged $2866 ($4050 maximum); need-based self-help aid (loans and jobs) averaged $3906 ($8500 maximum); non-need-based athletic scholarships averaged $5561 ($8308 maximum); other non-need-based awards and non-need-based scholarships averaged $2662 ($16,552 maximum); and other awards averaged $3768 ($17,824 maximum). Average annual earnings from campus work are $2200. The average financial indebtedness of the 2003 graduate was $18,000. JSU is a member of CSS. The FAFSA is required.

International Students: The school actively recruits these students. They must score 525 on the written TOEFL and also take a placement test and the SAT I or the ACT, scoring 20 on the ACT.

Computers: The mainframes are 2 DEC VAX 11/780s. There are also PCs available throughout the campus. All students may access the system 7 A.M. to 12 A.M., with access to PCs during business hours. There are no time limits and no fees.

Graduates: From July 1, 2002 to June 30, 2003, 760 bachelor's degrees were awarded. The most popular majors were biology (8%), child care and family education (8%), and business administration (7%). In an average class, 37% graduate in 6 years or less.

Admissions Contact: Stephanie Chatman, Associate Director of Admissions. E-mail: *schatman@ccaix.jsums.edu* Web: *www.jsums.edu*

MILLSAPS COLLEGE
Jackson, MS 39210

C-4
(601) 974-1050
(800) 352-1050; Fax: (601) 974-1059

Full-time: 501 men, 582 women	Faculty: 93; IIB, av$
Part-time: 14 men, 26 women	Ph.D.s: 95%
Graduate: 36 men, 41 women	Student/Faculty: 12 to 1
Year: semesters, summer session	Tuition: $18,414
Application Deadline: June 1	Room & Board: $6768
Freshman Class: 1045 applied, 880 accepted, 260 enrolled	
SAT I Verbal/Math: 590/570	ACT: 25 VERY COMPETITIVE

Millsaps College, founded in 1890, is an independent liberal arts institution affiliated with the United Methodist Church. There is 1 graduate school. In addition to regional accreditation, Millsaps has baccalaureate program accreditation with AACSB, ACS, and NCATE.The library contains 188,423 volumes, 84,388 microform items, and 8174 audio/video tapes/CDs, and subscribes to 10,566 periodicals. Computerized library services include the card catalog, interlibrary loans, database searching, and Internet access. Special learning facilities include an art gallery and an observatory. The 100-acre campus is in an urban area in the capital city of Jackson. Including any residence halls, there are 36 buildings.

Student Life: 56% of undergraduates are from Mississippi. Students are from 30 states and 5 foreign countries. 61% are from public schools. 84% are white; 10% African American. 54% are Protestant; 23% claim no religious affiliation; 18% Catholic. The average age of freshmen is 18; all undergraduates, 21. 17% do not continue beyond their first year.

Housing: 961 students can be accommodated in college housing, which includes single-sex and coed dorms and fraternity houses. In addition, there are special-interest houses and designated housing for freshmen. On-campus housing is guaranteed for the freshman year only, is available on a first-come, first-served basis, and is available on a lottery system for upperclassmen. 75% of students live on campus; of those, 75% remain on campus on weekends. All students may keep cars.

Activities: 55% of men belong to 6 national fraternities; 56% of women belong to 6 national sororities. There are 72 groups on campus, including art, band, cheerleading, choir, chorale, chorus, computers, dance team, debate, drama, ethnic, gay, honors, international, literary magazine, musical theater, newspaper, pep band, photography, political, professional, religious, social, social service, student government, and yearbook. Popular campus events include Major Madness, Family Weekend, and Crawfish Boil.

Sports: There are 7 intercollegiate sports for men and 7 for women, and 21 intramural sports for men and 21 for women. Facilities include a 63,300-sq.ft. activities center containing a fitness center with basketball and volleyball courts, a cardio theater, an aerobics room, fitness and weight training equipment, a free weight room, an outdoor pool, racquetball and handball courts, and a squash court. Outdoor areas include 6 tennis courts, a sand volleyball court, and softball, baseball, football, soccer and multipurpose fields.

Disabled Students: 90% of the campus is accessible. Wheelchair ramps, elevators, special parking, specially equipped rest rooms, special class scheduling, lowered drinking fountains, and lowered telephones are available. Other needs can be addressed through the ADA coordinator on an individual basis.

Services: Counseling and information services are available, as is tutoring in most subjects, by request, as needed. A writing center, a language lab, and a math lab are available for assistance.

Campus Safety and Security: Measures include 24-hour foot and vehicle patrol, self-defense education, security escort services, and informal discussions. There are pamphlets/posters/films, emergency telephones, lighted pathways/sidewalks, and key card access to buildings. Entrances to campus are staffed at night.

Programs of Study: Millsaps confers B.A., B.S., and B.B.A. degrees. Master's degrees are also awarded. Bachelor's degrees are awarded in BIOLOGICAL SCIENCE (biology/biological science), BUSINESS (accounting and business administration and management), COMMUNICATIONS AND THE ARTS (art, classics, dramatic arts, English, French, German, music, and Spanish), COMPUTER AND PHYSICAL SCIENCE (chemistry, computer science, geology, mathematics, and physics), EDUCATION (elementary), SOCIAL SCIENCE (anthropology, economics,

European studies, history, philosophy, political science/government, psychology, religion, and sociology). Chemistry, geology, and sociology/anthropolgy are the strongest academically. Business administration, English, and psychology are the largest.

Required: To graduate, students must complete 128 credit hours with 32 to 48 hours in the major and a minimum GPA of 2.0. The core curriculum includes 2 courses in liberal studies, 4 interdisciplinary courses in humanities, and 4 in the sciences and math. Students must also take introduction to liberal studies during the freshman year and reflections in liberal studies during the senior year. Other requirements include satisfactory completion of a 7-paper writing proficiency portfolio and a comprehensive exam in the specific field of study.

Special: Millsaps offers study abroad in England, Germany, Italy, France, Costa Rica, Mexico, China, and Greece, a Washington semester, internships, dual majors, a B.A.-B.S. degree in most majors, 3-2 degree programs in engineering with Washington, Auburn, Vanderbilt, and Columbia Universities and a 3-2 degree in business administration. There are 25 national honor societies, including Phi Beta Kappa, and 25 departmental honors programs.

Faculty/Classroom: 59% of faculty are male; 41%, female. All teach undergraduates and 90% both teach and do research. No introductory courses are taught by graduate students. The average class size in an introductory lecture is 19; in a laboratory, 16; and in a regular course, 15.

Admissions: 84% of the 2003-2004 applicants were accepted. The SAT I scores for the 2003-2004 freshman class were: Verbal--7% below 500, 45% between 500 and 599, 38% between 600 and 700, and 10% above 700; Math--20% below 500, 42% between 500 and 599, 28% between 600 and 700, and 10% above 700. The ACT scores were 7% below 21, 25% between 21 and 23, 31% between 24 and 26, 16% between 27 and 28, and 23% above 28. 59% of the current freshmen were in the top fifth of their class; 86% were in the top two fifths. 18 freshmen graduated first in their class.

Requirements: The SAT I or ACT is required. In addition, applicants should be graduates of an accredited secondary school or have a GED certificate, and have completed at least 14 academic units of English, math, social studies, natural sciences, or foreign languages (4 units of English should be included). An essay is required. Millsaps requires applicants to be in the upper 50% of their class. A GPA of 2.5 is required. AP and CLEP credits are accepted. Important factors in the admissions decision are advanced placement or honor courses, extracurricular activities record, and recommendations by school officials.

Procedure: Freshmen are admitted fall, winter, and spring. Entrance exams should be taken in the spring of the junior year or fall of the senior year. There are early admissions, deferred admissions, and rolling admissions plans. Early decision applications should be filed by February 1; regular applications, by June 1 for fall entry and December 1 for spring entry, along with a $25 fee. Notification is sent on a rolling basis. Applications are accepted on computer disk and on-line through Common App or the school's web site.

Transfer: 58 transfer students enrolled in 2003-2004. Applicants must have a minimum GPA of 2.75 and be in good standing at their previous school. Requirements include high school and college transcripts, an essay or personal statement, and standardized test scores. 32 of 128 credits required for the bachelor's degree must be completed at Millsaps.

Visiting: There are regularly scheduled orientations for prospective students, including meetings with faculty and student services personnel. There are guides for informal visits and visitors may sit in on classes and stay overnight. To schedule a visit, contact Admissions Office at *admissions@millsaps.edu*.

Financial Aid: In 2003-2004, 96% of all full-time freshmen and 92% of continuing full-time students received some form of financial aid. 61% of full-time freshmen and 56% of continuing full-time students received need-based aid. The average freshman award was $17,152. Need-based scholarships or need-based grants averaged $13,656 ($24,000 maximum); need-based self-help aid (loans and jobs) averaged $4646 ($2625 maximum); and other non-need-based awards and non-need-based scholarships averaged $11,516 ($24,000 maximum). 54% of undergraduates work part time. Average annual earnings from campus work are $852. The average financial indebtedness of the 2003 graduate was $15,942. Millsaps is a member of CSS. The FAFSA and the college's own financial statement are required. The priority date for freshman financial aid applications for fall entry is March 1.

International Students: There are 5 international students enrolled. They must score 550 on the written TOEFL.

Computers: The mainframes are an Alpha 4100 (UNIX) and Dell Linux and Microsoft servers. There are 130 PCs in 5 academic labs. All residence halls and fraternity houses are Internet accessible with 2 ports per room. All students may access the system at any time. There are no time limits and no fees. It is strongly recommended that all students have a personal computer.

Graduates: From July 1, 2002 to June 30, 2003, 261 bachelor's degrees were awarded. The most popular majors were business administration (21%), biology (13%), and psychology (11%). In an average class, 62% graduate in 4 years or less, 69% graduate in 5 years or less, and

74% graduate in 6 years or less. 28 companies recruited on campus in 2002-2003. Of the 2002 graduating class, 43% were enrolled in graduate school within 6 months of graduation and 90% were employed.

Admissions Contact: Ann Hendrick, Dean of Admissons and Financial Aid. E-mail: *admissions@millsaps.edu*
Web: *http://www.gomillsaps.edu* or *http://millsaps.edu*

MISSISSIPPI COLLEGE
Clinton, MS 39058

C-4
(601) 925-3800
(800) 738-1236; Fax: (601) 925-3950

Full-time: 840 men, 1200 women	**Faculty:** 143
Part-time: 100 men, 170 women	**Ph.Ds:** 67%
Graduate: 400 men, 530 women	**Student/Faculty:** 14 to 1
Year: semesters, summer session	**Tuition:** $10,500
Application Deadline: open	**Room & Board:** $4500
Freshman Class: n/av	
SAT I or ACT: required	**COMPETITIVE**

Mississippi College, founded in 1826 and affiliated with the Southern Baptist Church, is a private institution offering degrees in liberal arts, business, education, and health sciences. There are 4 undergraduate and 2 graduate schools. Figures in the above capsule and in this profile are approximate. In addition to regional accreditation, MC has baccalaureate program accreditation with ACBSP, CSWE, NASM, NCATE, and NLN. The 2 libraries contain 235,000 volumes, 265,000 microform items, and 13,000 audio/video tapes/CDs, and subscribe to 750 periodicals. Computerized library services include the card catalog, interlibrary loans, and database searching. Special learning facilities include a learning resource center, art gallery, radio station, and TV station. The 320-acre campus is in a suburban area 5 miles west of Jackson. Including any residence halls, there are 30 buildings.

Student Life: 82% of undergraduates are from Mississippi. 87% are white; 11% African American. Most are Protestant. The average age of freshmen is 18; all undergraduates, 22.

Housing: 1599 students can be accommodated in college housing, which includes single-sex dorms and married-student housing. On-campus housing is available on a first-come, first-served basis. 61% of students live on campus. Alcohol is not permitted. All students may keep cars.

Activities: There are no fraternities or sororities. There are 55 groups on campus, including art, band, cheerleading, choir, chorale, chorus, computers, debate, drama, ethnic, forensics, honors, international, jazz band, literary magazine, marching band, musical theater, newspaper, opera, pep band, political, professional, radio and TV, religious, social, social service, student government, and yearbook. Popular campus events include I Love America Day, Derby Day, and Spring Fever Week.

Sports: There are 6 intercollegiate sports for men and 6 for women, and 6 intramural sports for men and 6 for women. Facilities include a coliseum, an 8300-seat stadium, tennis courts, soccer and softball fields, a swimming pool, a 4000-seat gym, a fitness facility, and a campus weight traning facility.

Disabled Students: 95% of the campus is accessible. Wheelchair ramps, elevators, special parking, specially equipped rest rooms, special class scheduling, lowered drinking fountains, lowered telephones, wide doors, and special dorm rooms equipped for the physically disabled are available.

Services: Counseling and information services are available, as is tutoring in most subjects, and study skills classes. There is remedial math, reading, and writing.

Campus Safety and Security: Measures include 24-hour foot and vehicle patrol, security escort services, informal discussions, and emergency telephones. There are lighted pathways/sidewalks.

Programs of Study: MC confers B.A., B.S., B.M., B.M.Ed., B.S.B.A., B.S.Ed., B.S.N., and B.S.W. degrees. Master's degrees are also awarded. Bachelor's degrees are awarded in BIOLOGICAL SCIENCE (biochemistry and biology/biological science), BUSINESS (accounting, business administration and management, and marketing/retailing/merchandising), COMMUNICATIONS AND THE ARTS (applied music, art, communications, English, French, graphic design, languages, modern language, music, music theory and composition, piano/organ, Spanish, voice, and winds), COMPUTER AND PHYSICAL SCIENCE (chemistry, computer science, mathematics, and physics), EDUCATION (art, business, elementary, music, and special), ENGINEERING AND ENVIRONMENTAL DESIGN (engineering physics and interior design), HEALTH PROFESSIONS (nursing), SOCIAL SCIENCE (American studies, Christian studies, criminal justice, family/consumer studies, history, paralegal studies, political science/government, psychology, religious music, social studies, social work, and sociology). Premedicine, nursing, and business are the strongest academically. Business, education, and biology are the largest.

Required: To graduate, students must complete 130 credit hours, with an average of C or better in the major. The core curriculum includes English, history, economics, computer science, religion, math, art, social science, phys ed, and chapel. 30 hours are usually required in the major;

some majors require 36 to 45. Students must pass a writing proficiency exam. B.A. candidates and English majors must take 12 hours of a foreign language.

Special: Cooperative programs, including a 3-2 engineering degree and a program in agriculture, are offered with the University of Mississippi, Mississippi State University, and Auburn University. MC also offers study abroad in up to 10 countries, a 3-3 law school program with the School of Law, work-study programs, internships, B.A.-B.S. degrees, and credit for military experience and by exam. There are 18 national honor societies and a freshman honors program.

Faculty/Classroom: 62% of faculty are male; 38%, female. 82% teach undergraduates. Graduate students teach 19% of introductory courses. The average class size in an introductory lecture is 30; in a laboratory, 25; and in a regular course, 25.

Requirements: In addition to the application for admission, students must submit a 250-word essay, at least one letter of recommendation (3 are recommended for scholarship consideration), and a transcript from all schools previously attended. For freshmen, SAT I or ACT scores must be submitted (ACT is preferred). A minimum ACT score of 18, or SAT I composite score of 870 is required for regular admission. Students scoring below these levels may be considered for acceptance into the developmental program. A well-rounded high school program is advisable. An interview is recommended, as is a portfolio or audition for some majors. A GPA of 2.0 is required. AP and CLEP credits are accepted. Important factors in the admissions decision are personality/intangible qualities, extracurricular activities record, and leadership record.

Procedure: Freshmen are admitted fall, spring, and summer. Entrance exams should be taken by December of the senior year. Application deadlines are open. The fall 2003 application fee was $25.

Transfer: 324 transfer students enrolled in a recent year. Applicants must be junior college graduates or students in good academic standing with the college they last attended. They must have a minimum GPA of 2.0. Transfer students will be considered as freshmen if fewer than 12 semester hours or 16 quarter hours have been completed. Applicants must submit transcripts from all schools previously attended. 33 of 130 credits required for the bachelor's degree must be completed at MC.

Visiting: There are regularly scheduled orientations for prospective students, including attending classes, touring the campus, and meeting with administrators and departmental representatives. There are guides for informal visits and visitors may sit in on classes and stay overnight. To schedule a visit, contact Director of Admissions.

Financial Aid: In a recent year, 83% of all full-time freshmen and 86% of continuing full-time students received some form of financial aid. 41% of full-time freshmen and 52% of continuing full-time students received need-based aid. The average freshman award was $9821. 19% of undergraduates work part time. Average annual earnings from campus work were $1052. The average financial indebtedness of a recent graduate was $20,570. The FAFSA is required. Check with the school for current application deadlines.

International Students: They must score 550 on the written TOEFL or 213 on the electronic version.

Computers: The mainframe is an HP 3000/Series III. Students may access the college-wide network through various points on campus. The academic computer labs consist of some 200 workstations that are attached to Novell servers and connected to the Internet. Students who have been assigned an account may access the system from 8 A.M. to midnight Monday through Thursday, from 8 A.M. to 11 P.M. Friday, from 8 A.M. to 6 P.M. Saturday, and from 1 P.M. to 11 P.M. Sunday. There are no time limits and no fees.

Graduates: In a recent year, 442 bachelor's degrees were awarded. The most popular majors were business administration (10%), nursing (9%), and biology (9%). 83 companies recruited on campus.

Admissions Contact: Mr. Chad Phillips, Director of Admissions.
E-mail: *enrollment-services@mc.edu* Web: *www.mc.edu*

MISSISSIPPI STATE UNIVERSITY
Mississippi State, MS 39762

E-3
(662) 325-2224
Fax: (662) 325-7360

Full-time: 5950 men, 5258 women	**Faculty:** 1043; I, --$
Part-time: 805 men, 845 women	**Ph.Ds:** 80%
Graduate: 1662 men, 1706 women	**Student/Faculty:** 11 to 1
Year: semesters, summer session	**Tuition:** $3874 ($8780)
Application Deadline: August 1	**Room & Board:** $5265
Freshman Class: 4646 applied, 3492 accepted, 1688 enrolled	
ACT: 22	**COMPETITIVE**

Mississippi State University, founded in 1878 as a land-grant institution, offers degree programs in the arts and sciences, agriculture, business and industry, education, engineering, forest resources, architecture, accounting, and professional training in veterinary medicine. There are 9 undergraduate schools and 1 graduate school. In addition to regional accreditation, State has baccalaureate program accreditation with AACSB, ABET, ACCE, ACS, ADA, AHEA, APA, ASLA, CACREP, CSWE, FIDER, NAAB, NASAD, NASM, NASPAA, NCATE, and SAF. The 3 libraries contain 2,051,388 volumes, 2,903,393 microform items, and 19,456 audio/video tapes/CDs, and subscribe to 18,104 periodicals. Computerized library services include the card catalog, interlibrary loans, database searching, and Internet access. Special learning facilities include a learning resource center, art gallery, natural history museum, planetarium, radio station, TV station, music museum, archeology museum, and entomology museum. The 4200-acre campus is in a small town 125 miles northeast of Jackson. Including any residence halls, there are 164 buildings.

Student Life: 80% of undergraduates are from Mississippi. Students are from 50 states, 66 foreign countries, and Canada. 75% are white; 18% African American. The average age of freshmen is 21; all undergraduates, 23. 19% do not continue beyond their first year; 81% remain to graduate.

Housing: 4000 students can be accommodated in college housing, which includes single-sex and coed dorms, on-campus apartments, married-student housing, fraternity houses, and sorority houses. In addition, there are honors houses. On-campus housing is available on a first-come, first-served basis. 80% of students commute. Alcohol is not permitted. All students may keep cars.

Activities: 17% of men belong to 17 national fraternities; 18% of women belong to 1 local and 11 national sororities. There are 302 groups on campus, including art, band, cheerleading, chess, choir, chorale, chorus, computers, dance, drama, drill team, ethnic, gay, honors, international, jazz band, literary magazine, marching band, musical theater, newspaper, orchestra, pep band, political, professional, radio and TV, religious, social, social service, student government, symphony, and yearbook. Popular campus events include pep rallies, concerts, and Lyceum Series.

Sports: There are 7 intercollegiate sports for men and 9 for women, and 16 intramural sports for men and 16 for women. Facilities include a 52,000-seat football stadium, a 6,700-seat baseball park, a 9,200-seat multipurpose coliseum, a physical fitness complex, an all-weather track, 4 practice football fields, a 6-court tennis complex, an 18-hole golf course, 5 lighted tennis courts, the Sanderson Center, which consists of 7 basketball courts, 6 volleyball courts, 8 racquetball courts, 10,000 square feet for strength and aerobic conditioning, 3 full size dance studios, an indoor rock climbing wall, a 1/8 mile walking track, and Rec-Plex, which is a multipurpose field complex with 4 softball, 2 soccer, and 6 flag football fields.

Disabled Students: 90% of the campus is accessible. Wheelchair ramps, elevators, special parking, specially equipped rest rooms, special class scheduling, lowered drinking fountains, lowered telephones, special housing, and phones equipped with TTY in the union and library are available.

Services: Counseling and information services are available, as is tutoring in some subjects, including math, English, chemistry, physics, and study skills. There is a reader service for the blind, and remedial math, reading, and writing. Writing effectiveness, study assistance, preparation for professional exams, and credit courses in reading and study skills are also available.

Campus Safety and Security: Measures include 24-hour foot and vehicle patrol, self-defense education, security escort services, and shuttle buses. There are informal discussions, pamphlets/posters/films, emergency telephones, lighted pathways/sidewalks, and a bicycle patrol.

Programs of Study: State confers B.A., B.S., B.Accy., B.Arch., B.B.A., B.F.A., B.G.S., B.Land.Arch., B.Mus.Ed., and B.S.W. degrees. Master's and doctoral degrees are also awarded. Bachelor's degrees are awarded in AGRICULTURE (agricultural business management, agricultural economics, agriculture, agronomy, animal science, fishing and fisheries, forestry production and processing, horticulture, plant protection (pest management), poultry science, and wildlife management), BIOLOGICAL SCIENCE (biochemistry, biology/biological science, and microbiology), BUSINESS (accounting, banking and finance, business administration and management, insurance, marketing/retailing/merchandising, real estate, and trade and industrial supervision and management), COMMUNICATIONS AND THE ARTS (art, communications, English, and languages), COMPUTER AND PHYSICAL SCIENCE (chemistry, computer science, geoscience, information sciences and systems, mathematics, physics, and science), EDUCATION (agricultural, business, education, elementary, music, physical, secondary, special, and technical), ENGINEERING AND ENVIRONMENTAL DESIGN (aerospace studies, agricultural engineering technology, architecture, bioengineering, chemical engineering, civil engineering, computer engineering, electrical/electronics engineering, industrial engineering, industrial engineering technology, landscape architecture/design, and mechanical engineering), HEALTH PROFESSIONS (medical technology), SOCIAL SCIENCE (anthropology, economics, food science, history, interdisciplinary studies, liberal arts/general studies, philosophy, political science/government, psychology, social work, and sociology). Accounting, biochemistry, and physics are the strongest academically. General business administration, elementary education, and biology are the largest.

Required: The core curriculum includes 6 to 9 hours of math and natural science, 6 each of humanities, English composition, and social behavior, and 3 each of public speaking, computer literacy, and fine arts, and junior/senior-level writing. The total number of hours required for graduation and in the major varies. A minimum GPA of 2.0 must be maintained.

Special: Cooperative education, cross-registration with the Academic Common Market, internships, and study abroad in 15 countries are offered. Work-study programs, a Washington semester, accelerated degree programs, a general studies degree, nondegree study, student-designed majors, B.A.-B.S. degrees, and pass/fail options for some courses are available. There are 40 national honor societies, a freshman honors program, and 14 departmental honors programs.

Faculty/Classroom: 68% of faculty are male; 32%, female.

Admissions: 75% of the 2003-2004 applicants were accepted. The ACT scores for the 2003-2004 freshman class were: 37% below 21, 22% between 21 and 23, 17% between 24 and 26, 10% between 27 and 28, and 14% above 28. 30% of the current freshmen were in the top fifth of their class; 50% were in the top two fifths. There were 22 National Merit finalists. 51 freshmen graduated first in their class.

Requirements: The SAT I or ACT is required. In addition, applicants should have completed 15 1/2 high school academic credits, including 4 in English, 3 each in math, science, and social science, 2 advanced electives (foreign language, world geography, 4th year lab-based science, or 4th year math), and 1/2 credit in the computer as a productivity tool (not keyboarding). Full admission is granted with all of the above and one of the following: minimum 3.2 GPA on required high school courses; 2.5 GPA on required high school classes or class standing in top 50% with ACT score of 16 or higher/SAT I combined score of 750 or higher; 2.0 GPA on required high school classes with ACT score of 18 or higher/SAT I combined 840 or higher; or satisfy National Collegiate Athletic Association standards for student-athletes who are full qualifiers under Division I guidelines. Students with a GED are accepted with the required ACT/SAT I score. A GPA of 2.0 is required. AP and CLEP credits are accepted.

Procedure: Freshmen are admitted fall, spring, and summer. Entrance exams should be taken in the spring semester of junior year or fall semester of senior year. There are early admissions, deferred admissions, and rolling admissions plans. Applications should be filed by August 1 for fall entry, November 15 for spring entry, and May 15 for summer entry. Notification is sent on a rolling basis. Applications are accepted online through MSU's web site *www.msstate.edu* (link to Prospective Student).

Transfer: 1593 transfer students enrolled in 2002-2003. Applicants must submit an official college transcript from each college attended, indicating a minimum GPA of 2.0 (some departments require 2.5), and must be in good standing at their previous school. 32 of 136 credits required for the bachelor's degree must be completed at State.

Visiting: There are regularly scheduled orientations for prospective students, including 2-day sessions for freshmen, and 1-day session for transfers. There are guides for informal visits and visitors may sit in on classes and stay overnight. To schedule a visit, contact John Dickerson, Director of Enrollment Services at (662) 325-3076 or *lead@msstate.edu*.

Financial Aid: In 2003-2004, 75% of all full-time freshmen and 76% of continuing full-time students received some form of financial aid. 35% of full-time freshmen and 40% of continuing full-time students received need-based aid. The average freshman award was $5230. Need-based scholarships or need-based grants averaged $3505 ($5550 maximum); need-based self-help aid (loans and jobs) averaged $3022 ($5785 maximum); non-need-based athletic scholarships averaged $3611 ($6855 maximum); and other non-need-based awards and non-need-based scholarships averaged $3506 ($17,970 maximum). 39% of undergraduates work part time. Average annual earnings from campus work are $1996. The average financial indebtedness of the 2003 graduate was $16,996. The FAFSA is required. The deadline for filing freshman financial aid applications for fall entry is April 1.

International Students: There are 126 international students enrolled. They must score 525 on the written TOEFL or 197 on the electronic version and also take the SAT I or the ACT.

Computers: The mainframes are a Sun E10000, a Sun Enterprise Server 6000, and a Sun Enterprise Server 2000. Mainframes, servers, and PCs are connected to a campus ATM/Ethernet network. 2 public labs and several departmental labs provide 2000 PCs for student use. All have access to the Internet. All students may access the system 24 hours a day. There are no time limits and no fees.

Graduates: From July 1, 2002 to June 30, 2003, 2698 bachelor's degrees were awarded. The most popular majors were elementary education (9%), marketing (8%), and business administration (6%). In an average class, 25% graduate in 4 years or less, 48% graduate in 5 years or less, and 56% graduate in 6 years or less. 285 companies recruited on campus in 2002-2003.

Admissions Contact: Diane Wolfe, Director of Admissions.
E-mail: *admit@admissions.msstate.edu*
Web: *http://www.msstate.edu/dept/admissions*

MISSISSIPPI UNIVERSITY FOR WOMEN
Columbus, MS 39701

E-2

(662) 329-7106
(877) 462-8439; Fax: (662) 241-7481

Full-time: 300 men, 1600 women	**Faculty:** 116; IIB, --$
Part-time: 300 men, 1000 women	**Ph.D.s:** 68%
Graduate: 20 men, 120 women	**Student/Faculty:** 16 to 1
Year: semesters, summer session	**Tuition:** $2800 ($7000)
Application Deadline: open	**Room & Board:** $3000
Freshman Class: n/av	
SAT I or ACT: recommended	**LESS COMPETITIVE**

Mississippi University for Women, founded in 1884, is a public institution offering degrees in liberal arts, education, business and communications, nursing, human sciences, science and math, health and kinesiology, and culinary arts. There are 8 undergraduate and 2 graduate schools. Figures given in above capsule and in this profile are approximate. In addition to regional accreditation, MUW has baccalaureate program accreditation with AHEA, NASAD, NASM, NCATE, and NLN. The library contains 235,000 volumes, 570,000 microform items, and 100 audio/video tapes/CDs, and subscribes to 1620 periodicals. Computerized library services include the card catalog, interlibrary loans, and database searching. Special learning facilities include a learning resource center, art gallery, radio station, TV station, and distance learning studio. The 110-acre campus is in a small town 120 miles west of Birmingham, Alabama. Including any residence halls, there are 53 buildings.

Student Life: 89% of undergraduates are from Mississippi. 84% are from public schools. 70% are white; 27% African American. The average age of freshmen is 19; all undergraduates, 29. 30% do not continue beyond their first year; 43% remain to graduate.

Housing: 1100 students can be accommodated in college housing, which includes single-sex dorms, on-campus apartments, and married-student housing. On-campus housing is available on a first-come, first-served basis. 77% of students commute. Alcohol is not permitted. All students may keep cars.

Activities: 10% of men belong to 2 local and 1 national fraternity; 20% of women belong to 12 local and 3 national sororities. There are 84 groups on campus, including art, band, choir, chorale, chorus, computers, dance, drama, ethnic, film, honors, international, jazz band, literary magazine, musical theater, newspaper, orchestra, photography, political, professional, radio and TV, religious, social, social service, student government, and yearbook. Popular campus events include Mardi Gras, Oktoberfest, and Nutcracker.

Sports: There are 4 intercollegiate sports for women, and 5 intramural sports for men and 5 for women. Facilities include 3 gyms, a softball field, tennis and racquetball courts, indoor and outdoor swimming pools, a gymnastics room, a weight room, a dance studio, a 3-hole pitch-and-putt golf course, a soccer and flag football field, and a Vita course.

Disabled Students: 95% of the campus is accessible. Wheelchair ramps, elevators, special parking, specially equipped rest rooms, special class scheduling, lowered drinking fountains, and lowered telephones are available.

Services: Counseling and information services are available, as is tutoring in most subjects. There is remedial math, reading, and writing.

Campus Safety and Security: Measures include 24-hour foot and vehicle patrol, security escort services, informal discussions, and pamphlets/posters/films. There are lighted pathways/sidewalks and guard gates, and freshman orientation class.

Programs of Study: MUW confers B.A., B.S., B.F.A., B.M., and B.S.N. degrees. Associate and master's degrees are also awarded. Bachelor's degrees are awarded in BIOLOGICAL SCIENCE (biology/biological science and microbiology), BUSINESS (accounting, business administration and management, fashion merchandising, and sports management), COMMUNICATIONS AND THE ARTS (communications, English, fine arts, music, and Spanish), COMPUTER AND PHYSICAL SCIENCE (chemistry, mathematics, and physical sciences), EDUCATION (art, elementary, and music), HEALTH PROFESSIONS (nursing and speech pathology/audiology), SOCIAL SCIENCE (clothing and textiles management/production/services, food production/management/services, history, human development, paralegal studies, physical fitness/movement, political science/government, psychology, and social science). Biology, chemistry, and English are the strongest academically. Business, nursing, and elementary education are the largest.

Required: To graduate, students must complete 128 credit hours, including 30 to 39 in a major, with a minimum GPA of 2.0. The core curriculum requires 12 hours of English, 8 of lab-based science, 6 each of history and social sciences, 3 each of speech or philosophy, fine arts, and math, 2 of phys ed, and 1 of a freshman seminar. Students must also pass a comprehensive exam.

Special: Cross-registration and a 3-2 engineering degree are available with Mississippi State University. MUW also offers internships in all divisions, co-op and work-study programs, several combinations of dual majors, study abroad in 5 countries, credit for experience, nondegree study, and a pass/fail option. There are 15 national honor societies, a freshman honors program, and 3 departmental honors programs.

Faculty/Classroom: 39% of faculty are male; 61%, female. 94% teach undergraduates. No introductory courses are taught by graduate students. The average class size in an introductory lecture is 35; in a laboratory, 23; and in a regular course, 25.

Requirements: The SAT I or ACT is recommended. In addition, prospective students should have completed 4 units of English; 3 each of math, science, and social studies courses in U.S. history, world history, government, and economics or geography; 2 of advanced electives, including foreign language or geography, and a course in computer applications. A GPA of 2.0 is required. AP and CLEP credits are accepted. Important factors in the admissions decision are recommendations by school officials, leadership record, and advanced placement or honor courses.

Procedure: Freshmen are admitted to all sessions. Entrance exams should be taken as early as possible. There are early decision and early admissions plans. Application deadlines are open. Check with the school for current application fee.

Transfer: Applicants must have a GPA of 2.0 in 6 semester hours of both English composition and a lab science, 3 of college algebra or above, and 9 of transferable electives. High school and college transcripts are required. 32 of 128 credits required for the bachelor's degree must be completed at MUW.

Visiting: There are regularly scheduled orientations for prospective students, including talks with various student services officers and pre-registering. There are guides for informal visits and visitors may sit in on classes and stay overnight. To schedule a visit, contact the Director of Admissions.

Financial Aid: MUW is a member of CSS. The FAFSA is required. Check with the school for current deadlines.

International Students: The school actively recruits these students. They must score 525 on the written TOEFL and also take the SAT I or the ACT, scoring 16.

Computers: The mainframe is an IBM ES9000. The academic computing center offers access to mainframe terminals and more than 100 networked PCs. Computer labs on campus house additional networked PCs. Internet access is available to all students. All students may access the system 8 A.M. to 12 A.M. Monday through Friday. There are no time limits and no fees. It is strongly recommended that all students have a personal computer.

Admissions Contact: Melanie Freeman, Director of Admissions.
E-mail: *mfreeman@muw.edu* Web: *www.muw.edu*

MISSISSIPPI VALLEY STATE UNIVERSITY
Itta Bena, MS 38941-1400

C-2

(662) 254-3347; Fax: (662) 254-7900

Full-time: 856 men, 2046 women	**Faculty:** 122
Part-time: 62 men, 325 women	**Ph.D.s:** 62%
Graduate: 131 men, 590 women	**Student/Faculty:** 24 to 1
Year: semesters, summer session	**Tuition:** $3411 ($7965)
Application Deadline: August 10	**Room & Board:** $3354
Freshman Class: n/av	
SAT I: recommended	**ACT:** required
	NONCOMPETITIVE

Mississippi Valley State University, founded in 1946, offers programs in the arts and sciences, business, and education. There are 5 undergraduate schools and 1 graduate school. In addition to regional accreditation, MVSU has baccalaureate program accreditation with NASAD, NASM, and NCATE. The library contains 127,109 volumes, 295,500 microform items, and 853 audio/video tapes/CDs, and subscribes to 350 periodicals. Computerized library services include the card catalog, interlibrary loans, database searching, and Internet access. Special learning facilities include a learning resource center, art gallery, radio station, TV station, and a campus nursery/preschool. The 450-acre campus is in a small town 8 miles from Greenwood and 100 miles north of Jackson. Including any residence halls, there are 35 buildings.

Student Life: 97% of undergraduates are from Mississippi. Students are from 17 states, 3 foreign countries, and Canada. 92% are from public schools. 94% are African American. The average age of freshmen is 18; all undergraduates, 20.

Housing: 1914 students can be accommodated in college housing, which includes single-sex dorms. In addition, there are honors houses. On-campus housing is available on a first-come, first-served basis. 66% of students commute. Alcohol is not permitted. All students may keep cars.

Activities: There are 5 local and 4 national fraternities and 5 local and 4 national sororities. There are 44 groups on campus, including art, band, cheerleading, choir, chorale, chorus, computers, dance, drama, drill team, honors, jazz band, literary magazine, marching band, newspaper, performing, political, professional, radio and TV, religious, social, social service, student government, and yearbook. Popular campus events include Founders Day, Pride Day, and Black History Month.

Sports: There are 8 intercollegiate sports for men and 6 for women, and 10 intramural sports for men and 9 for women. Facilities include a stadium for football and track, a gymnastics room, a dance studio, an indoor pool, a 2200-seat gym, basketball arena, a weight-training room, and handball, squash, and paddleball courts.

Disabled Students: 99% of the campus is accessible. Wheelchair ramps, elevators, special parking, specially equipped rest rooms, and lowered drinking fountains are available.

Services: Counseling and information services are available, as is tutoring in most subjects. There is remedial math, reading, and writing.

Campus Safety and Security: Measures include 24-hour foot and vehicle patrol, informal discussions, pamphlets/posters/films, and emergency telephones. There are lighted pathways/sidewalks.

Programs of Study: MVSU confers B.A., B.S., B.M.E., B.S.E, and B.S.W. degrees. Master's degrees are also awarded. Bachelor's degrees are awarded in BIOLOGICAL SCIENCE (biology/biological science), BUSINESS (accounting, business administration and management, and office supervision and management), COMMUNICATIONS AND THE ARTS (art, communications, English, fine arts, and speech/debate/rhetoric), COMPUTER AND PHYSICAL SCIENCE (chemistry, computer science, and mathematics), EDUCATION (early childhood, elementary, English, mathematics, music, physical, science, and social science), ENGINEERING AND ENVIRONMENTAL DESIGN (industrial engineering technology), HEALTH PROFESSIONS (environmental health science), SOCIAL SCIENCE (criminal justice, history, political science/government, public administration, social work, and sociology). Education, business, and social work are the largest.

Required: General education requirements include 12 semester hours in English, 6 each in social studies and lab science, 3 each in college algebra, speech, fine arts, psychology, and health ed, and 2 in phys ed. To graduate, students must complete at least 124 credit hours with a minimum GPA of 2.0 overall and in the major.

Special: MVSU offers a special cooperative education program, B.A.-B.S. degree, internships in social work and environmental health, an accelerated degree program, work-study, and nondegree study. Credit may be granted for military experience. A pass/fail option is possible. There are 4 national honor societies, a freshman honors program, and 2 departmental honors programs.

Faculty/Classroom: 60% of faculty are male; 40%, female. All teach undergraduates. No introductory courses are taught by graduate students. The average class size in an introductory lecture is 30; in a laboratory, 25; and in a regular course, 30.

Admissions: The ACT scores for the 2003-2004 freshman class were: 88% below 21, 11% between 21 and 23, and 1% between 24 and 26.

Requirements: The ACT is required for Mississippi residents. Out-of-state students may submit SAT I scores. Applicants must be graduates of a secondary school or have a GED and have completed 4 credits in English, 3 each in math and natural sciences, 2 1/2 in social sciences, and 1 in a foreign language. Recommendations are considered important. A GPA of 2.0 is required. AP and CLEP credits are accepted. Important factors in the admissions decision are evidence of special talent, leadership record, and advanced placement or honor courses.

Procedure: Freshmen are admitted fall, spring, and summer. There is an early admissions plan and a rolling admissions plan. Applications should be filed by August 10 for fall entry, January for spring entry, and May for summer entry. Notification is sent on a rolling basis. Applications are accepted on-line through the school's web site.

Transfer: 249 transfer students enrolled in fall 2003. Transfers must have a minimum 2.0 GPA in at least 24 specified credit hours. 30 of 124 credits required for the bachelor's degree must be completed at MVSU.

Visiting: There are regularly scheduled orientations for prospective students, including campus tours with a student guide. Visitors may sit in on classes. To schedule a visit, contact the Dean of Students at (601) 254-3637.

Financial Aid: The CSS Profile or FAFSA and the college's own financial statement are required. The deadline for filing freshman financial aid applications for fall entry is June 1.

International Students: There are 13 international students enrolled. The school actively recruits these students. They must score 400 on the written TOEFL and also take the SAT I or the ACT, scoring 16.

Computers: The mainframe is an IBM 4331. PCs are available in various computer labs, the library, and dorms offering Internet and e-mail access. All students may access the system at various times depending on location. There are no time limits and no fees. It is strongly recommended that all students have a personal computer.

Graduates: From July 1, 2002 to June 30, 2003, 334 bachelor's degrees were awarded. The most popular majors were business administration (12%), social work (10%), and biology (10%). 30 companies recruited on campus in 2002-2003.

Admissions Contact: Mr. Wilson Lee, Acting Director.
E-mail: *admsn@mvsu.edu*

RUST COLLEGE
D-1
Holly Springs, MS 38635
(662) 252-8000, ext. 4059
(888) 886-8492, ext. 4059; Fax: (662) 252-8895

Full-time: 295 men, 498 women
Part-time: 57 men, 138 women
Graduate: none
Year: semesters, summer session
Application Deadline: July 15
Freshman Class: 3720 applied, 1816 accepted, 348 enrolled
ACT: 16

Faculty: 43
Ph.D.s: 46%
Student/Faculty: 18 to 1
Tuition: $5600
Room & Board: $2600

COMPETITIVE+

Rust College, founded in 1866, is a private liberal arts college affiliated with the United Methodist Church. The academic year consists of semesters, each divided into two 8-week modules, plus a summer term. The library contains 126,353 volumes, 9158 microform items, and 940 audio/video tapes/CDs, and subscribes to 322 periodicals. Computerized library services include the card catalog, interlibrary loans, and Internet access. Special learning facilities include a learning resource center, radio station, TV station, and Dr. Ron Trojak collection of African tribal art. The 126-acre campus is in a small town 35 miles southeast of Memphis, Tennessee. Including any residence halls, there are 23 buildings.

Student Life: 55% of undergraduates are from Mississippi. Students are from 22 states and 7 foreign countries. 90% are from public schools. 88% are African American; 10% foreign nationals. 67% are Protestant; 29% claim no religious affiliation. The average age of freshmen is 19; all undergraduates, 22. 52% do not continue beyond their first year.

Housing: 856 students can be accommodated in college housing, which includes single-sex dorms. In addition, there are honors houses. On-campus housing is guaranteed for all 4 years. 56% of students live on campus; of those, 50% remain on campus on weekends. Alcohol is not permitted. All students may keep cars.

Activities: 10% of men belong to 3 local and 3 national fraternities; 14% of women belong to 4 local and 4 national sororities. There are 32 groups on campus, including band, cheerleading, choir, chorale, computers, drama, ethnic, honors, international, marching band, newspaper, political, radio and TV, religious, social, social service, student government, and yearbook. Popular campus events include Career Day, Founders Day, and Religious Emphasis Week.

Sports: There are 7 intercollegiate sports for men and 7 for women. Facilities include a 2500-seat gym, a swimming pool, tennis courts, a track, a 2000-seat stadium, a bowling alley, pool tables, and the Magic Johnson Sports Arena.

Disabled Students: All of the campus is accessible. Wheelchair ramps, elevators, special parking, specially equipped rest rooms, and lowered drinking fountains are available.

Services: Counseling and information services are available, as is tutoring in most subjects. There is remedial math, reading, and writing.

Campus Safety and Security: Measures include 24-hour foot and vehicle patrol, security escort services, informal discussions, and pamphlets/posters/films. There are lighted pathways/sidewalks.

Programs of Study: Rust confers B.A., B.S., and B.S.W. degrees. Associate degrees are also awarded. Bachelor's degrees are awarded in BIOLOGICAL SCIENCE (biology/biological science), BUSINESS (business administration and management), COMMUNICATIONS AND THE ARTS (communications, English, journalism, and music), COMPUTER AND PHYSICAL SCIENCE (chemistry, computer science, and mathematics), EDUCATION (business, elementary, English, mathematics, science, secondary, and social science), HEALTH PROFESSIONS (health), SOCIAL SCIENCE (political science/government, social work, and sociology). Business administration and management are the strongest academically. Biology, computer science, and social work are the largest.

Required: All students must earn a minimum of 124 semester hours while maintaining a cumulative GPA of 2.0. Distribution requirements include 59 1/2 general education credits in the fields of education, humanities, science, and math, and a required freshman program. A minimum of 50 credits constitutes a major, and comprehensive exams are given in all programs. Required courses in addition to the freshmen program include math, biology, physical science, computer science, English, foreign language, literature, speech, social science, and history.

Special: Internships are available in all areas and may be required for some majors. On-campus work-study, study abroad, credit by examination, independent study, B.A.-B.S. degrees, and dual majors in a variety of programs are available. There are 3-2 degrees in preprofessional programs and medical technology, and a 3-2 engineering degree with the student's school of choice. There are 3 national honor societies, a freshman honors program, and 5 departmental honors programs.

Faculty/Classroom: 67% of faculty are male; 33%, female. All teach undergraduates. The average class size in an introductory lecture is 10; in a laboratory, 10; in a regular course, 25.

Admissions: 49% of the 2003-2004 applicants were accepted. The ACT scores for the 2003-2004 freshman class were: 81% below 21, 18% between 21 and 23, and 1% between 24 and 26.

Requirements: The ACT is required. In addition, students must submit 19 academic credits, including 4 in English, 3 each in math, science, and social studies, and 6 electives. An audition, an interview, and 2 letters of recommendation are required. The GED is accepted. An essay and portfolio are recommended. A GPA of 2.0 is required. AP and CLEP credits are accepted. Important factors in the admissions decision are evidence of special talent, extracurricular activities record, and recommendations by school officials.

Procedure: Freshmen are admitted fall, spring, and summer. Entrance exams should be taken prior to the first semester of the freshman year. There is a rolling admissions plan. Applications should be filed by July 15 for fall entry and December 15 for spring entry, along with a $10 fee. Notification is sent on a rolling basis.

Transfer: 43 transfer students enrolled in 2003-2004. Transfer applicants with at least 15 semester hours of credit need not take the ACT or SAT I. Only C grades or better transfer. 30 of 124 credits required for the bachelor's degree must be completed at Rust.

Visiting: There are regularly scheduled orientations for prospective students, including a campus tour, departmental visits, introduction to the application process, financial aid orientation, and question-and-answer session. There are guides for informal visits and visitors may sit in on classes and stay overnight. To schedule a visit, contact Johnny McDonald, Enrollment Services at jbmcdonald@rustcollege.edu.

Financial Aid: In 2003-2004, 96% of all full-time students received some form of financial aid. 82% of full-time freshmen and 68% of continuing full-time students received need-based aid. The average freshman award was $7848. Need-based scholarships or need-based grants averaged $4056 ($6550 maximum); need-based self-help aid (loans and jobs) averaged $2613 ($3625 maximum); non-need-based awards and non-need-based scholarships averaged $2064 ($8400 maximum); and non-need-based jobs averaged $650 ($1100 maximum). 64% of undergraduates work part time. Average annual earnings from campus work are $1100. The average financial indebtedness of the 2003 graduate was $8434. The FFS and the college's own financial statement are required. The deadline for filing freshman financial aid applications for fall entry is July 15.

International Students: There are 74 international students enrolled. They must score 540 on the written TOEFL.

Computers: The mainframe is an IBM AS/400. Computer labs are located in all academic divisions. 18 PC labs exist for academic programs. Internet access is available at the library. All students may access the system. There are no time limits and no fees.

Graduates: From July 1, 2002 to June 30, 2003, 106 bachelor's degrees were awarded. The most popular majors were computer science (17%), biology (14%), and business administration (12%). In an average class, 14% graduate in 4 years or less, 12% graduate in 5 years or less, and 3% graduate in 6 years or less. 42 companies recruited on campus in 2002-2003. Of the 2002 graduating class, 19% were enrolled in graduate school within 6 months of graduation and 52% were employed.

Admissions Contact: Johnny McDonald, Director Enrollment Services. E-mail: jbmcdonald@rustcollege.edu Web: rustcollege.edu

---

TOUGALOO COLLEGE
Tougaloo, MS 39174

C-4
(601) 977-7764
(888) 424-2566; Fax: (601) 977-6185

Full-time: 270 men, 600 women	Faculty: 66
Part-time: 20 men, 50 women	Ph.D.s: 52%
Graduate: none	Student/Faculty: 13 to 1
Year: semesters	Tuition: $6500
Application Deadline: open	Room & Board: $3000
Freshman Class: n/av	
SAT I or ACT: required	NONCOMPETITIVE

Tougaloo College, founded in 1869, is a private liberal arts institution affiliated with the United Church of Christ. Figures given in above capsule and in this profile are approximate. The library contains 117,000 volumes, 7200 microform items, and 4300 audio/video tapes/CDs, and subscribes to 370 periodicals. Computerized library services include the card catalog, interlibrary loans, and database searching. Special learning facilities include a learning resource center and art gallery. The 500-acre campus is in a suburban area 1 mile north of Jackson. Including any residence halls, there are 18 buildings.

Student Life: 87% of undergraduates are from Mississippi. Students are from 23 states and 2 foreign countries. 98% are from public schools. 98% are African American. Most are Baptist. The average age of freshmen is 18; all undergraduates, 20. 18% do not continue beyond their first year; 42% remain to graduate.

Housing: 632 students can be accommodated in college housing, which includes single-sex dorms. On-campus housing is available on a first-come, first-served basis. 60% of students live on campus; of those, 80% remain on campus on weekends. Alcohol is not permitted. All students may keep cars.

Activities: 35% of men belong to 4 national fraternities; 40% of women belong to 4 national sororities. There are many groups and organizations on campus, including art, cheerleading, choir, chorus, computers, honors, international, newspaper, photography, political, professional, religious, social, social service, student government, and yearbook. Popular campus events include Founders Day.

Sports: There are 2 intercollegiate sports for men and 1 for women. Facilities include a gym, a tennis court, and access to a bowling alley and a golf course.

Disabled Students: 20% of the campus is accessible. Wheelchair ramps, elevators, and specially equipped rest rooms are available.

Services: Counseling and information services are available, as is tutoring in every subject. There is remedial math, reading, and writing.

Campus Safety and Security: Measures include 24-hour foot and vehicle patrol, self-defense education, informal discussions, and pamphlets/posters/films. There are emergency telephones and lighted pathways/sidewalks.

Programs of Study: Tougaloo confers B.A. and B.S. degrees. Associate degrees are also awarded. Bachelor's degrees are awarded in BIOLOGICAL SCIENCE (biology/biological science), BUSINESS (recreation and leisure services), COMMUNICATIONS AND THE ARTS (art, English, and music), COMPUTER AND PHYSICAL SCIENCE (chemistry, mathematics, and physics), EDUCATION (elementary, health, and physical), SOCIAL SCIENCE (economics, history, political science/government, psychology, and sociology). Physical sciences is the strongest academically. Biology and economics are the largest.

Required: To graduate, students must complete 124 credit hours, including 27 to 48 in the major, with a minimum GPA of 2.0. Students must fulfill about 56 hours of general education requirements, take computer science and phys ed courses, and complete a senior paper.

Special: Tougaloo offers cooperative programs with Brown and Boston Universities, study abroad in Africa, a Washington semester in conjunction with American University, internships, work-study programs, credit for military service, pass/fail options, and a 3-2 engineering degree with Georgia Tech, the University of Wisconsin at Madison, and Brown, Mississippi, Tuskegee, and Howard Universities. There are 3 national honor societies and a freshman honors program.

Faculty/Classroom: 55% of faculty are male; 45%, female. All teach undergraduates.

Requirements: The SAT I or ACT is required. In addition, candidates should be graduates of an accredited secondary school or have a GED certificate. They should have completed 3 credits of English, 2 each of math and science, and 1 each of history and social studies. An interview is recommended. A GPA of 2.0 is required. AP and CLEP credits are accepted. Important factors in the admissions decision are advanced placement or honor courses, evidence of special talent, and extracurricular activities record.

Procedure: Freshmen are admitted in the fall. Entrance exams should be taken by March of the senior year. There is an early admissions plan. Application deadlines are open. Check with the school for current fee.

Transfer: Applicants must submit transcripts of all college course work and have a minimum GPA of 2.0. 30 of 124 credits required for the bachelor's degree must be completed at Tougaloo.

Visiting: Visitors may sit in on classes and stay overnight. To schedule a visit, contact the Office of Student Enrollment at (601) 977-7765.

Financial Aid: Tougaloo is a member of CSS. The CSS Profile, FAFSA, FFS, or SFS is required.

International Students: They must score 500 on the written TOEFL and also take the SAT I or the ACT.

Computers: The mainframe is a DEC. Macs and PCs are available in the Academic Computing Center. There are no time limits and no fees.

Admissions Contact: Carolyn L. Evans, Enrollment Services. A video is available.

UNIVERSITY OF MISSISSIPPI
University, MS 38677

D-2
(662) 915-7226
(800) OLE-MISS; Fax: (662) 915-5869

Full-time: 4530 men, 4750 women	Faculty: 495; I, --$
Part-time: 280 men, 330 women	Ph.D.s: 83%
Graduate: 1000 men, 985 women	Student/Faculty: 17 to 1
Year: semesters, summer session	Tuition: $3800 ($8200)
Application Deadline: see profile	Room & Board: $4100
Freshman Class: n/av	
SAT I or ACT: required	COMPETITIVE

The University of Mississippi, founded in 1844, is a public institution offering undergraduate and graduate programs in the liberal arts, business, pharmacy, engineering, accountancy, and education. There are 6 undergraduate and 2 graduate schools. Figures in the above capsule and in this profile are approximate. In addition to regional accreditation, Ole Miss has baccalaureate program accreditation with AACSB, ABET, ACE-JMC, CSAB, CSWE, NASAD, NASM, and NCATE. The 3 libraries contain 1 million volumes and 42,000 audio/video tapes/CDs, and subscribe to 6400 periodicals. Computerized library services include the card catalog, interlibrary loans, and database searching. Special learning facilities include a learning resource center, art gallery, radio station, TV station, a museum, the Center for the Study of Southern Culture, the National

Center for Physical Acoustics, Rowan Oak, the home of William Faulkner, the National Center for Development of Natural Products, National Food Service Management Institute, and the Croft Institute for International Studies. The 2000-acre campus is in a small town 70 miles southeast of Memphis, Tennessee. Including any residence halls, there are 193 buildings.

Student Life: 65% of undergraduates are from Mississippi. Students are from 47 states, 70 foreign countries, and Canada. 70% are from public schools. 82% are white; 12% African American. The average age of all undergraduates is 21. 26% do not continue beyond their first year; 54% remain to graduate.

Housing: 4513 students can be accommodated in college housing, which includes single-sex dorms, on-campus apartments, married-student housing, fraternity houses, and sorority houses. On-campus housing is guaranteed for the freshman year only, is available on a first-come, first-served basis, and is available on a lottery system for upperclassmen. Alcohol is not permitted. All students may keep cars.

Activities: 35% of men belong to 19 national fraternities; 40% of women belong to 13 national sororities. There are 200 groups on campus, including art, band, cheerleading, chess, choir, chorale, chorus, computers, dance, drama, drill team, ethnic, gay, honors, international, jazz band, literary magazine, marching band, musical theater, newspaper, orchestra, pep band, political, professional, radio and TV, religious, social, social service, student government, symphony, and yearbook. Popular campus events include Faulkner and Yoknapatawpha Conference, Red and Blue Week, and Oxford Conference for the Book.

Sports: There are 8 intercollegiate sports for men and 10 for women, and 35 intramural sports for men and 35 for women. Facilities include a 50,577-seat football stadium, an 8800-seat gym, a baseball diamond, an indoor pool, 10 racquetball courts, 23 outdoor tennis courts, 3 playing fields, women's soccer and softball fields, volleyball, an indoor tennis facility, and a fitness center.

Disabled Students: 25% of the campus is accessible. Wheelchair ramps, elevators, special parking, specially equipped rest rooms, special class scheduling, lowered drinking fountains, and lowered telephones are available.

Services: Counseling and information services are available, as is tutoring in every subject. There is a reader service for the blind and remedial math and reading.

Campus Safety and Security: Measures include 24-hour foot and vehicle patrol, self-defense education, security escort services, and informal discussions. There are pamphlets/posters/films, emergency telephones, lighted pathways/sidewalks, and a full-time campus safety officer.

Programs of Study: Ole Miss confers B.A., B.S., B.Ac., B.A.E., B.A.Ed., B.A.L.M., B.B.A., B.C.R., B.E., B.F.A., B.Mus., B.P.A., B.S.C.E., B.S.Ch.E., B.S.C.S., B.S.E.E., B.S.E.S., B.S.F.C.S., B.S.G.E., B.S.J., B.S.M.E., B.S.Pharm., and B.S.W. degrees. Master's and doctoral degrees are also awarded. Bachelor's degrees are awarded in BIOLOGICAL SCIENCE (biology/biological science), BUSINESS (accounting, banking and finance, business administration and management, business economics, court reporting, insurance, international business management, investments and securities, management information systems, management science, marketing/retailing/merchandising, real estate, recreation and leisure services, and recreational facilities management), COMMUNICATIONS AND THE ARTS (advertising, art, art history and appreciation, broadcasting, design, dramatic arts, English, French, German, journalism, linguistics, music, radio/television technology, and Spanish), COMPUTER AND PHYSICAL SCIENCE (chemistry, computer science, geology, and physics), EDUCATION (elementary, English, foreign languages, home economics, mathematics, science, social science, and special), ENGINEERING AND ENVIRONMENTAL DESIGN (chemical engineering, civil engineering, electrical/electronics engineering, engineering, geological engineering, and mechanical engineering), HEALTH PROFESSIONS (biomedical science, exercise science, medical laboratory technology, medical technology, pharmacy, speech pathology/audiology, and speech therapy), SOCIAL SCIENCE (anthropology, area studies, classical/ancient civilization, economics, family/consumer studies, forensic studies, history, international studies, liberal arts/general studies, philosophy, political science/government, psychology, public administration, social work, and sociology). General business, accountancy, and biological sciences are the largest.

Required: Students must maintain a minimum GPA of 2.0 (2.5 in teacher education) while taking 126 to 139 semester hours, including 24 to 42 in the major. Other requirements include 6 hours each of English composition and lab science and 3 each of college algebra and humanities and fine arts.

Special: Internships in journalism, accounting, and engineering, study abroad in numerous countries, and work-study programs within the college are offered. Dual majors, a general studies degree, credit by exam, special testing in music and languages, credit for military experience, and limited pass/fail options also are available. There are 24 national honor societies and a freshman honors program.

Faculty/Classroom: 69% of faculty are male; 31%, female.

Requirements: The SAT I or ACT is required, with a minimum composite score of 840 on the SAT I or 18 on the ACT. Applicants need 15 academic credits, including 4 units in English, 3 each in math, science lab courses, and social studies, 2 in foreign language or world geography, and 1/2 in computer applications. A portfolio for art majors and an audition for theater and music majors are required. The GED is not accepted. A GPA of 2.0 is required. AP and CLEP credits are accepted.

Procedure: Freshmen are admitted to all sessions. Entrance exams should be taken. There are early admissions and deferred admissions plans. Check with the school for current application deadlines and fee. Notification is sent on a rolling basis.

Transfer: Transfer students must have earned a minimum 2.0 GPA on previous college work. The SAT I or ACT may be required depending on credits earned. 30 of 126 credits required for the bachelor's degree must be completed at Ole Miss.

Visiting: There are regularly scheduled orientations for prospective students, including academic information/student life discussions and tours. Class attendance and academic appointments can be arranged. There are guides for informal visits and visitors may sit in on classes and stay overnight. To schedule a visit, contact the Office of Admissions.

Financial Aid: In a recent year, 75% of all full-time freshmen and 74% of continuing full-time students received some form of financial aid. 28% of full-time freshmen and 32% of continuing full-time students received need-based aid. The average freshman award was $5351. Ole Miss is a member of CSS. The FAFSA is required. Check with the school for current deadlines.

International Students: The school actively recruits these students. They must score 550 on the written TOEFL or 213 on the electronic version and also take the university's own test, and the SAT I or the ACT.

Computers: The mainframes are an IBM ES 9000, an SGI Challenge L, an SGI Power Challenge L, a CRAY Y-MP83, and a CRAY J916. The computer center runs a 120-unit general-access lab housing Novell networked PCs with mainframe connection via the campus fiber optic network. Various academic departments operate their own PC labs, some of which are networked and connected to the campus backbone fiber. All students may access the system 24 hours daily. There are no time limits and no fees. It is strongly recommended that all students have a personal computer.

Admissions Contact: Beckett Howorth, Director of Admissions and Records. A video is available. E-mail: admissions@olemiss.edu Web: www.olemiss.edu

UNIVERSITY OF SOUTHERN MISSISSIPPI   D-5
Hattiesburg, MS 39406-1000
(601) 266-5000
Fax: (601) 266-5148

Full-time: 3950 men, 6038 women	**Faculty:** n/av
Part-time: 977 men, 1406 women	**Ph.D.s:** 69%
Graduate: 1031 men, 1648 women	**Student/Faculty:** n/av
Year: semesters, summer session	**Tuition:** $3874 ($8752)
Application Deadline: see profile	**Room & Board:** $4450
Freshman Class: 3555 applied, 2631 accepted, 1872 enrolled	
SAT I: n/av	**ACT:** required
	LESS COMPETITIVE

The University of Southern Mississippi, founded in 1910, is a public institution offering comprehensive undergraduate and graduate programs. There are 5 undergraduate schools and 1 graduate school. In addition to regional accreditation, Southern Miss has baccalaureate program accreditation with AACSB, ABET, ACEJMC, ADA, AHEA, ASLA, CAHEA, CSAB, CSWE, FIDER, NASAD, NASM, NCATE, NLN, and NRPA. The 2 libraries contain 1,319,836 volumes, 4,813,531 microform items, and 19,082 audio/video tapes/CDs, and subscribe to 19,759 (5759 print, 14,000 electronic) periodicals. Computerized library services include the card catalog, interlibrary loans, database searching, and Internet access. Special learning facilities include a learning resource center, art gallery, natural history museum, radio station, TV station, TV production studios, the Museum of Natural Science, and music resource center. The 1090-acre campus is in a suburban area 90 miles southeast of Jackson and 105 miles north of New Orleans. Including any residence halls, there are 185 buildings.

Student Life: 90% of undergraduates are from Mississippi. Students are from 47 states, 41 foreign countries, and Canada. 72% are white; 24% African American. The average age of freshmen is 20; all undergraduates, 24. 27% do not continue beyond their first year; 47% remain to graduate.

Housing: 3488 students can be accommodated in college housing, which includes single-sex dorms, married-student housing, and fraternity houses. In addition, there are special-interest houses. A section in 1 dorm is reserved for honor students. Freshmen are housed together. On-campus housing is available on a first-come, first-served basis. 70% of students commute. Alcohol is not permitted. All students may keep cars.

Activities: 16% of men belong to 16 local and 16 national fraternities; 15% of women belong to 12 local and 12 national sororities. There are 239 groups on campus, including art, band, cheerleading, choir, chorale, chorus, computers, dance, drama, drum and bugle corps, ethnic, gay, honors, international, jazz band, marching band, musical theater, newspaper, opera, orchestra, pep band, photography, political, professional, radio and TV, religious, social, social service, student government, symphony, and yearbook.

Sports: There are 7 intercollegiate sports for men and 9 for women, and 41 intramural sports for men and 41 for women. Facilities include a recreational lake, a football stadium, a basketball coliseum, a baseball park, a golf course, a softball stadium, a track and field stadium, a fitness institute, a natatorium, and playing fields for softball, flag football, and soccer.

Disabled Students: 80% of the campus is accessible. Wheelchair ramps, elevators, special parking, specially equipped rest rooms, special class scheduling, lowered drinking fountains, lowered telephones, and an Office of Support Services for students with disabilities are available.

Services: Counseling and information services are available, as is tutoring in most subjects. There is a reader service for the blind and remedial math, reading, and writing.

Campus Safety and Security: Measures include 24-hour foot and vehicle patrol, self-defense education, security escort services, and shuttle buses. There are informal discussions, pamphlets/posters/films, emergency telephones, and lighted pathways/sidewalks.

Programs of Study: Southern Miss confers B.A., B.S., B.F.A., B.M., B.M.E., and B.S.B.A degrees. Master's and doctoral degrees are also awarded. Bachelor's degrees are awarded in BIOLOGICAL SCIENCE (biology/biological science), BUSINESS (accounting, banking and finance, business administration and management, business economics, hotel/motel and restaurant management, international business management, marketing/retailing/merchandising, and personnel management), COMMUNICATIONS AND THE ARTS (advertising, communications, dance, design, dramatic arts, English, fine arts, journalism, languages, music, radio/television technology, and speech/debate/rhetoric), COMPUTER AND PHYSICAL SCIENCE (chemistry, computer science, geology, information sciences and systems, mathematics, physics, polymer science, and statistics), EDUCATION (art, business, early childhood, elementary, foreign languages, guidance, health, home economics, industrial arts, middle school, music, science, and secondary), ENGINEERING AND ENVIRONMENTAL DESIGN (architectural technology, computer technology, construction technology, electrical/electronics engineering technology, engineering technology, and mechanical engineering technology), HEALTH PROFESSIONS (medical laboratory technology, nursing, predentistry, premedicine, and speech pathology/audiology), SOCIAL SCIENCE (anthropology, criminal justice, economics, geography, history, international studies, parks and recreation management, philosophy, political science/government, prelaw, psychology, social science, social work, and sociology). Polymer science and accounting are the strongest academically. Accounting is the largest.

Required: To graduate, students must complete at least 128 semester hours, including 64 at the senior college level, with a minimum GPA of 2.0. Core requirements include courses in reasoning and communication skills, humanities and fine arts, social and behavioral sciences, human wellness, and natural and applied sciences.

Special: Southern Miss offers many cooperative programs, internships, dual majors, nondegree study, limited pass/fail options, credit for life experience, and study abroad in England, Germany, Austria, and Italy. The university also participates in the Title IV College Work-Study Program. There are 27 national honor societies and a freshman honors program.

Faculty/Classroom: 60% of faculty are male; 40%, female. 91% teach undergraduates and 75% do research. The average class size in an introductory lecture is 37; in a laboratory, 32; and in a regular course, 29.

Admissions: 74% of the 2003-2004 applicants were accepted. There were 3 National Merit semifinalists.

Requirements: The ACT is required, with a minimum score of 15. Applicants must be graduates of an accredited secondary school or have a GED certificate. They should have completed 4 units of English, 3 each of math, science, and social studies, 2 of advanced electives, and 1/2 of computer applications. A GPA of 2.0 is required. AP and CLEP credits are accepted.

Procedure: Freshmen are admitted to all sessions. Entrance exams should be taken in the fall of the senior year. There are early decision and early admissions plans. Check with the school for current application deadlines. Applications are accepted on-line through *www.usm.edu/admissions.*

Transfer: 1793 transfer students enrolled in 2002-2003. Applicants must be eligible to return to their previous institution. 32 of 128 credits required for the bachelor's degree must be completed at Southern Miss.

Visiting: There are regularly scheduled orientations for prospective students, including campus tours and general session orientations. There are guides for informal visits and visitors may sit in on classes. To schedule a visit, contact the Office of Admission.

Financial Aid: In a recent, 56% of all full-time freshmen and 61% of continuing full-time students received some form of financial aid. 44% of full-time freshmen and 50% of continuing full-time students received need-based aid. The average freshman award was $6266. Need-based scholarships or need-based grants averaged $3258; need-based self-help

aid (loans and jobs) averaged $3168; non-need-based athletic scholarships averaged $5943; and other non-need-based awards and non-need-based scholarships averaged $2062. The average financial indebtedness of the 2002 graduate was $11,202. The FAFSA and the college's own financial statement are required. The priority date for freshman financial aid applications for fall entry is March 15.

International Students: There are 114 international students enrolled. The school actively recruits these students. They must score 525 on the written TOEFL and also take the ACT, scoring 18.

Computers: There are approximately 450 PCS and 60 Macs available on campus. All students may access the system at any time labs are open (departmental labs are for the department only). There are no time limits and no fees.

Graduates: From July 1, 2002 to June 30, 2003, 2587 bachelor's degrees were awarded. The most popular majors were business (23%), education (13%), and psychology (5%). In an average class, 20% graduate in 4 years or less, 38% graduate in 5 years or less, and 46% graduate in 6 years or less. 918 companies recruited on campus in 2002-2003.

Admissions Contact: Matthew Cox, Admissions Office. A video is available. E-mail: *admissions@usm.edu* Web: *www.usm.edu*

WILLIAM CAREY COLLEGE

D-5
Hattiesburg, MS 39401-5499
(601) 582-6103
(800) 962-5991; Fax: (601) 582-6454

Full-time: 500 men, 900 women	**Faculty:** 80
Part-time: 150 men, 300 women	**Ph.D.s:** 57%
Graduate: none	**Student/Faculty:** 17 to 1
Year: trimesters, summer session	**Tuition:** $7150
Application Deadline: see profile	**Room & Board:** $3000
Freshman Class: n/av	
ACT: required	**LESS COMPETITIVE**

William Carey College, founded in 1906, is a private liberal arts college affiliated with the Mississippi Baptist Convention. There are 4 undergraduate and 2 graduate schools. Figures in the above capsule and in this profile are approximate. In addition to regional accreditation, Carey has baccalaureate program accreditation with NASDTEC, NASM, and NLN. The 4 libraries contain 135,000 volumes, 30,000 microform items, and 3000 audio/video tapes/CDs, and subscribe to 600 periodicals. Computerized library services include the card catalog, interlibrary loans, and database searching. Special learning facilities include a learning resource center and art gallery. The 120-acre campus is in a small town 100 miles from New Orleans, Louisiana. Including any residence halls, there are 15 buildings.

Student Life: The average age of freshmen is 18.

Housing: 428 students can be accommodated in college housing, which includes single-sex dorms and on-campus apartments. 50% of students live on campus. Alcohol is not permitted. All students may keep cars.

Activities: There is 1 national fraternity and 2 local and 1 national sorority. There are 20 groups on campus, including art, cheerleading, choir, chorale, drama, ethnic, honors, international, literary magazine, newspaper, pep band, professional, religious, social, social service, student government, and yearbook. Popular campus events include Hydromania and Mudbowl, Spring Fling Week, and Crawfish Boil.

Sports: There are 4 intercollegiate sports for men and 4 for women, and 3 intramural sports for men and 3 for women. Facilities include a gym, a baseball field, an intramural field, and tennis courts.

Disabled Students: 80% of the campus is accessible. Wheelchair ramps, special parking, specially equipped rest rooms, and special class scheduling are available.

Services: Counseling and information services are available, as is tutoring in every subject. There is remedial math, reading, and writing.

Campus Safety and Security: Measures include 24-hour foot and vehicle patrol, security escort services, informal discussions, and pamphlets/posters/films. There are emergency telephones and lighted pathways/sidewalks. Campus security personnel are on duty 24 hours a day.

Programs of Study: Carey confers B.A., B.S., B.F.A., B.G.S., B.L.S., B.M., B.S.B., and B.S.N. degrees. Master's degrees are also awarded. Bachelor's degrees are awarded in BIOLOGICAL SCIENCE (biology/biological science), BUSINESS (business administration and management), COMMUNICATIONS AND THE ARTS (art, communications, dramatic arts, English, music, music performance, and Spanish), COMPUTER AND PHYSICAL SCIENCE (chemistry, mathematics, and radiological technology), EDUCATION (elementary, music, and physical), HEALTH PROFESSIONS (medical laboratory technology, music therapy, and nursing), SOCIAL SCIENCE (history, liberal arts/general studies, psychology, religion, religious music, and social science). Education, music, and nursing are the strongest academically. Education and nursing are the largest.

Required: Students must complete a core curriculum, including 6 credits each in religion, English, history, and social and behavioral science; 4 in lab science; 3 each in math, fine arts, communication, and literature;

and 2 in phys ed. A total of 128 trimester hours, with a minimum 2.0 GPA overall and in the major, is needed to graduate.

Special: Internships are available in some disciplines, and nondegree study, a 3-2 program in forestry, and a 3-1 program in medical technology are also available. 2-year professional programs are possible in engineering, physical therapy, medical records administration, radiological technology, optometry, and pharmacy. Upperclassmen may choose 1 pass/fail option per trimester. There are 7 national honor societies and a freshman honors program.

Requirements: The ACT is required. In addition, applicants must have earned 16 Carnegie units, including courses in English, foreign language, social studies, science, and math. The admissions committee also considers special skills or aptitudes and other evidence of academic potential. Recommendations from high school officials and college alumni, extracurricular activities, honors courses, leadership potential, and ability to pay also are considered. Carey requires applicants to be in the upper 50% of their class. A GPA of 2.0 is required. AP and CLEP credits are accepted.

Procedure: Freshmen are admitted to all sessions. There are early admissions and deferred admissions plans. Notification is sent on a rolling basis. Check with the school for current application deadlines and fee.

Transfer: Transfer students must have a minimum GPA of 1.4 for freshmen, 1.7 for sophomores, and 2.0 for juniors. 30 of 128 credits required for the bachelor's degree must be completed at Carey.

Visiting: There are regularly scheduled orientations for prospective students, including panel discussions, campus tours, faculty advising, and financial aid seminars. There are guides for informal visits and visitors may sit in on classes and stay overnight. To schedule a visit, contact the Admissions Office.

Financial Aid: The FAFSA is required. Check with the school for current deadlines.

International Students: They must score 525 on the written TOEFL or take the MELAB or the college's own test and the SAT I or the ACT.

Computers: The computer lab is located in the learning resource center. All students may access the system. There are no time limits and no fees.

Admissions Contact: Thomas Huebner, Jr., Director of Admissions. E-mail: *admiss@wmcarey.edu* Web: *www.wmcarey.edu*

MISSOURI

POPULATION DENSITY

● 25,000 and over

0   20   40   60   80   100
Miles

AVILA UNIVERSITY
Kansas City, MO 64145

A-2

(816) 501-2400
(800) GO-AVILA; Fax: (816) 501-2453

Full-time: 344 men, 540 women	**Faculty:** 59; IIB, --$
Part-time: 100 men, 276 women	**Ph.D.s:** 77%
Graduate: 166 men, 357 women	**Student/Faculty:** 15 to 1
Year: semesters, summer session	**Tuition:** $15,000
Application Deadline: open	**Room & Board:** $5300
Freshman Class: 1163 applied, 645 accepted, 152 enrolled	
SAT I Verbal/Math: 530/530	**ACT:** 21 **COMPETITIVE**

Avila University, formerly Avila College, founded in 1916, is a comprehensive liberal arts institution sponsored by the Sisters of St. Joseph of Carondelet. Some information in the above capsule is approximate. In addition to regional accreditation, Avila has baccalaureate program accreditation with CAHEA, CCNE, and CSWE. The library contains 70,935 volumes, 480,000 microform items, and 3094 audio/video tapes/CDs, and subscribes to 551 periodicals. Computerized library services include the card catalog, interlibrary loans, and database searching. Special learning facilities include a learning resource center, art gallery, TV station, a 500-seat theater, an interactive video library, and video production facilities. The 48-acre campus is in a suburban area in Kansas City, Missouri. Including any residence halls, there are 11 buildings.

Student Life: 70% of undergraduates are from Missouri. Students are from 16 states, 20 foreign countries, and Canada. 90% are from public schools. 74% are white; 13% African American. Most are Catholic. The average age of freshmen is 18; all undergraduates, 27. 30% do not continue beyond their first year.

Housing: 230 students can be accommodated in college housing, which includes coed dorms. On-campus housing is guaranteed for all 4 years. 82% of students commute. Alcohol is not permitted. All students may keep cars.

Activities: There are no fraternities or sororities. There are 23 groups on campus, including cheerleading, choir, chorus, computers, dance, debate, drama, ethnic, film, forensics, honors, international, literary magazine, musical theater, photography, political, professional, radio and TV, religious, social, social service, student government, and yearbook. Popular campus events include sports and theatrical events, Family Day, and International Festival.

Sports: There are 4 intercollegiate sports for men and 4 for women, and 8 intramural sports for men and 8 for women. Facilities include a field house with basketball and volleyball courts, a training room, and weight and fitness equipment. There is also an athletic complex with baseball, softball, and soccer fields, tennis courts, and practice fields.

Disabled Students: 80% of the campus is accessible. Wheelchair ramps, elevators, special parking, specially equipped rest rooms, special class scheduling, lowered drinking fountains, and lowered telephones are available.

Services: Counseling and information services are available, as is tutoring in most subjects. There is a reader service for the blind and remedial math, reading, and writing.

Campus Safety and Security: Measures include self-defense education, security escort services, informal discussions, and pamphlets/posters/films. There are lighted pathways/sidewalks, evening and night security patrols, and 24-hour closed-circuit television in residence hall entryways.

Programs of Study: Avila confers B.A., B.S., B.F.A., B.S.B.A., B.S.N., and B.S.W. degrees. Master's degrees are also awarded. Bachelor's degrees are awarded in BIOLOGICAL SCIENCE (biology/biological science), BUSINESS (accounting, banking and finance, business administration and management, international business management, management science, and marketing/retailing/merchandising), COMMUNICATIONS AND THE ARTS (art, communications, dramatic arts, English, and music), COMPUTER AND PHYSICAL SCIENCE (chemistry, computer science, information sciences and systems, mathematics, natural sciences, and radiological technology), EDUCATION (business, elementary, middle school, and special), HEALTH PROFESSIONS (medical laboratory technology, nursing, premedicine, and sports medicine), SOCIAL SCIENCE (history, liberal arts/general studies, paralegal studies, political science/government, psychology, social work, sociology, and theological studies). Nursing, education, and communications are the strongest academically. Nursing, education, and radiologic technology are the largest.

Required: To graduate, students must complete at least 128 semester hours with a minimum 2.0 GPA. The 42- to 47-hour core curriculum consists of courses in composition, communication, math, history, literature, theology, philosophy, the arts, the sciences, and social institutions.

Special: Students may cross-register with the Kansas City Area Student Exchange, the Sisters of Saint Joseph College Consortium, and the Council of Independent Colleges Student Exchange. Avila also offers internships, work-study, a Washington center program, dual majors in science, math, and health professions, and accelerated degree programs in business administration, and psychology. There are 6 national honor societies.

Faculty/Classroom: 42% of faculty are male; 58%, female. All both teach and do research. No introductory courses are taught by graduate students. The average class size in an introductory lecture is 22; in a laboratory, 16; and in a regular course, 16.

Admissions: 55% of the 2003-2004 applicants were accepted. 1 freshman graduated first in their class in a recent year.

Requirements: The SAT I or ACT is required; a minimum ACT score of 20 or SAT I composite score of 900 is recommended. Applicants must be graduates of an accredited secondary school or have a GED certificate. They should have completed 16 academic units, including 4 in English, 3 in math, 2 to 4 in foreign language, 2 to 3 in natural and social sciences, and 1 to 2 in fine arts is advised. A GPA of 2.5 is required. AP and CLEP credits are accepted. Important factors in the admissions decision are recommendations by school officials, extracurricular activities record, and leadership record.

Procedure: Freshmen are admitted to all sessions. Entrance exams should be taken in the spring or summer of the junior year. There is a rolling admissions plan. Application deadlines are open.

Transfer: 185 transfer students enrolled in a recent year. Applicants must have a minimum GPA of 2.0. 30 of 128 credits required for the bachelor's degree must be completed at Avila.

Visiting: There are regularly scheduled orientations for prospective students, including a visit with admissions and a faculty member and a campus tour. There are guides for informal visits and visitors may sit in on classes and stay overnight. To schedule a visit, contact the Director of Admissions.

Financial Aid: In a recent year, 97% of all full-time freshmen and 87% of continuing full-time students received some form of financial aid. 76% of full-time freshmen and 74% of continuing full-time students received need-based aid. The average freshman award was $8550. 92% of undergraduates work part time. Average annual earnings from campus work are $1200. The average financial indebtedness of a recent graduate was $11,000. The FAFSA is required.

International Students: There were 73 international students enrolled in a recent year. The school actively recruits these students. They must score 550 on the written TOEFL.

Computers: The mainframe is a Compaq DEC Alpha 2100 4/233. There are 60 IBM PCs and 27 Macs located in computer labs, residence halls, and the library. All students may access the system. There are no time limits and no fees.

Graduates: In a recent year, 170 bachelor's degrees were awarded. The most popular majors were business (25%), education (14%), and radiological technology (10%). In an average class, 31% graduate in 4 years or less, 43% graduate in 5 years or less, and 44% graduate in 6 years or less. Of a recent graduating class, 18% were enrolled in graduate school within 6 months of graduation and 97% were employed.

Admissions Contact: Paige Illum, Assistant Vice President for Undergraduate Admissions. E-mail: *admissions1@mail.avila.edu* Web: *www.avila.edu*

CENTRAL METHODIST COLLEGE
C-2
Fayette, MO 65248

(660) 248-6247
(888) CMC-1854; Fax: (660) 248-1872

Full-time: 545 men, 743 women	**Faculty:** 64
Part-time: 20 men, 25 women	**Ph.Ds:** 50%
Graduate: 10 men, 45 women	**Student/Faculty:** 12 to 1
Year: semesters, summer session	**Tuition:** $13,760
Application Deadline: open	**Room & Board:** $4920
Freshman Class: n/av	
SAT I: n/av	**ACT:** required **COMPETITIVE**

Central Methodist College, founded in 1854, is a private liberal arts institution affiliated with the Methodist Church. Figures in the above capsule and in this profile are approximate. In addition to regional accreditation, CMC has baccalaureate program accreditation with NASM. The library contains 102,695 volumes, 140,812 microform items, and 3736 audio/video tapes/CDs, and subscribes to 447 periodicals. Computerized library services include the card catalog, interlibrary loans, and database searching. Special learning facilities include a learning resource center, art gallery, natural history museum, radio station, TV station, and observatory. The 52-acre campus is in a small town 30 miles northwest of Columbia. Including any residence halls, there are 22 buildings.

Student Life: 90% of undergraduates are from Missouri. Students are from 20 states, 8 foreign countries, and Canada. 96% are from public schools. 87% are white. 77% are Protestant; 20% Catholic. The average age of freshmen is 18; all undergraduates, 21. 39% do not continue beyond their first year.

Housing: 667 students can be accommodated in college housing, which includes single-sex and coed dorms, off-campus apartments, and married-student housing. On-campus housing is guaranteed for all 4 years. 70% of students live on campus; of those, 60% remain on campus on weekends. Alcohol is not permitted. All students may keep cars.

Activities: 40% of men belong to 6 local fraternities; 40% of women belong to 5 local sororities. There are 30 groups on campus, including band, cheerleading, choir, chorale, chorus, computers, debate, drama, drill team, honors, jazz band, literary magazine, marching band, newspaper, pep band, photography, political, professional, radio and TV, religious, social, social service, student government, and yearbook. Popular campus events include the Music Festival.

Sports: There are 7 intercollegiate sports for men and 7 for women, and 10 intramural sports for men and 10 for women. Facilities include a field house with a 2000-seat gym, playing fields, and a recreation center.

Disabled Students: 65% of the campus is accessible. Wheelchair ramps, elevators, special parking, specially equipped rest rooms, special class scheduling, and lowered drinking fountains are available.

Services: Counseling and information services are available, as is tutoring in some subjects. There is remedial math, reading, and writing.

Campus Safety and Security: Measures include 24-hour foot and vehicle patrol, security escort services, informal discussions, and pamphlets/posters/films. There are emergency telephones and lighted pathways/sidewalks.

Programs of Study: CMC confers B.A., B.S., B.M., B.M.E., B.S.E., and B.S.N. degrees. Associate degrees are also awarded. Bachelor's degrees are awarded in BIOLOGICAL SCIENCE (biology/biological science), BUSINESS (accounting, business administration and management, and recreational facilities management), COMMUNICATIONS AND THE ARTS (broadcasting, communications, dramatic arts, English, French, music, and Spanish), COMPUTER AND PHYSICAL SCIENCE (chemistry, computer science, mathematics, and physics), EDUCATION (athletic training, early childhood, elementary, foreign languages, music, physical, science, and social science), ENGINEERING AND ENVIRONMENTAL DESIGN (environmental science), HEALTH PROFESSIONS (nursing), SOCIAL SCIENCE (criminal justice, economics, history, interdisciplinary studies, philosophy, political science/government, psychology, public administration, religion, and sociology). Sciences, music, and preprofessional programs are the strongest academically. Business and education are the largest.

Required: To graduate, students must complete 124 to 131 credit hours, including at least 24 in the major, depending on the degree

---

sought. A minimum GPA of 2.0 is required for all but the athletic training and education programs, which require a 2.5. Students must complete 53 hours of a distribution curriculum, including computer literacy, phys ed or a competency exam, religion, philosophy, freshman orientation to college life and a senior capstone.

Special: CMC offers cooperative programs in medical technology and physical therapy, and 3-2 engineering degrees with the University of Missouri at Rolla, the University of Evansville, Stanford University, and Washington University at St. Louis. Work-study programs, internships, study abroad in France, Germany, and Spain, dual majors, a general studies degree, and nondegree study are also available. There are 10 national honor societies and a freshman honors program.

Faculty/Classroom: 60% of faculty are male; 40%, female. All teach undergraduates. No introductory courses are taught by graduate students. The average class size in a laboratory is 9 and in a regular course, 14.

Requirements: The ACT is required, with a minimum score of 18. Those students with a GPA lower than 2.0 may write a letter of appeal and have an interview. Applicants should be graduates of an accredited secondary school or have a GED certificate. Recommended preparatory courses include 4 units of English, 3 of math, and 2 each of science, social studies, and humanities. A GPA of 2.0 is required. AP and CLEP credits are accepted. Important factors in the admissions decision are advanced placement or honor courses, evidence of special talent, and extracurricular activities record.

Procedure: Freshmen are admitted fall, winter, and summer. There is a rolling admissions plan. There are early decision and early admissions plans. Application deadlines are open. The fall 2003 application fee was $20. Applications are accepted on-line through the school's web site (no fee).

Transfer: 158 transfer students enrolled in a recent year. Transfer applicants must be in good academic standing at their previous college. 30 of 124 credits required for the bachelor's degree must be completed at CMC.

Visiting: There are regularly scheduled orientations for prospective students, including a campus tour and visits with faculty members. There are guides for informal visits and visitors may sit in on classes and stay overnight. To schedule a visit, contact Admissions/Student Affairs at (660) 248-2242.

Financial Aid: In a recent year, all full-time freshmen and 96% of continuing full-time students received some form of financial aid. 87% of full-time freshmen and 81% of continuing full-time students received need-based aid. The average freshman award was $12,144. 35% of undergraduates work part time. Average annual earnings from campus work are $700. The average financial indebtedness of a recent graduate was $17,617. The FAFSA is required. Check with the school for current deadlines.

International Students: There were 15 international students enrolled in a recent year. The school actively recruits these students. They must score 500 on the written TOEFL or take the MELAB.

Computers: The mainframes are a DEC VAX 3100 and an IBM 80. There are also 24 terminals and 50 PCs available throughout the campus. All students may access the system during lab hours for up to an hour at a time. The fee is $100 per year.

Graduates: In a recent year, 287 bachelor's degrees were awarded. The most popular majors were elementary education (30%), nursing (11%), and biology (6%).

Admissions Contact: Office of Admissions. A video is available. E-mail: *admissions@cmu.edu* Web: *www.cmc.edu*

CENTRAL MISSOURI STATE UNIVERSITY
B-2
Warrensburg, MO 64093

(660) 543-4290
(800) 956-0177; Fax: (660) 543-8517

Full-time: 3315 men, 3813 women	**Faculty:** 428; IIA, --$
Part-time: 667 men, 912 women	**Ph.Ds:** 67%
Graduate: 650 men, 994 women	**Student/Faculty:** 17 to 1
Year: semesters, summer session	**Tuition:** $4980 ($9600)
Application Deadline: open	**Room & Board:** $4796
Freshman Class: 3544 applied, 2709 accepted, 1438 enrolled	
ACT: 22	**COMPETITIVE**

Central Missouri State University, founded in 1871, is a public liberal arts institution offering a comprehensive range of degree programs. There are 5 undergraduate schools and 1 graduate school. In addition to regional accreditation, Central has baccalaureate program accreditation with AACSB, ABET, ACCE, ACS, ADA, ADDA, ASLA, CAA, CSWE, NAIT, NASAD, NASM, NASPE, NCATE, NLN, and SOA. The library contains 2,502,944 volumes, 1,601,691 microform items, and 23,871 audio/video tapes/CDs, and subscribes to 3541 periodicals. Computerized library services include the card catalog, interlibrary loans, and database searching. Special learning facilities include a learning resource center, art gallery, natural history museum, radio station, TV station, instructional airport, 200-acre farm, driving/safety range, speech and hearing clinic, a child development lab, and English Language Center.

The 1561-acre campus is in a small town 50 miles southeast of Kansas City. Including any residence halls, there are 50 buildings.

Student Life: 90% of undergraduates are from Missouri. Students are from 43 states, 59 foreign countries, and Canada. 92% are from public schools. 88% are white. 62% are Protestant; 23% Catholic; 8% claim no religious affiliation. The average age of freshmen is 18; all undergraduates, 21. 28% do not continue beyond their first year; 46% remain to graduate.

Housing: 3545 students can be accommodated in college housing, which includes single-sex and coed dorms, on-campus apartments, off-campus apartments, married-student housing, fraternity houses, and sorority houses. In addition, there are honors houses, special-interest houses, and quiet dorms. On-campus housing is available on a first-come, first-served basis. 68% of students commute. All students may keep cars.

Activities: 12% of men belong to 13 national fraternities; 10% of women belong to 10 national sororities. There are 200 groups on campus, including art, band, cheerleading, chess, choir, chorale, chorus, computers, dance, debate, drama, drill team, ethnic, film, forensics, gay, honors, international, jazz band, literary magazine, marching band, musical theater, newspaper, opera, orchestra, pep band, photography, political, professional, radio and TV, religious, social, social service, student government, symphony, and yearbook. Popular campus events include Performing Arts Series, Technology Fair, and Repertory Theater.

Sports: There are 7 intercollegiate sports for men and 7 for women, and 45 intramural sports for men and 45 for women. Facilities include a stadium seating more than 12,000, 3 gyms, baseball, softball, women's soccer, and practice fields, a bowling alley, tennis courts, and a multipurpose building that contains a swimming pool, weight rooms, and courts for basketball, racquetball, and volleyball. A nearby outdoor recreation area has an 18-hole golf course and facilities for swimming and other activities.

Disabled Students: 95% of the campus is accessible. Wheelchair ramps, elevators, special parking, specially equipped rest rooms, special class scheduling, lowered drinking fountains, lowered telephones, and special housing are available.

Services: Counseling and information services are available, as is tutoring in some subjects, including, for a fee, math, chemistry, physics, biology, accounting, economics, and business. There is a reader service for the blind and remedial math. Writing and learning labs are available for all students. Tutoring is available through TRIO Student Support Services.

Campus Safety and Security: Measures include 24-hour foot and vehicle patrol, self-defense education, security escort services, and informal discussions. There are pamphlets/posters/films, emergency telephones, lighted pathways/sidewalks, a bike patrol, and canine patrol.

Programs of Study: Central confers B.A., B.S., B.F.A., B.M., B.M.E., B.S.B.A., B.S.Ed., and B.S.W. degrees. Associate and master's degrees are also awarded. Bachelor's degrees are awarded in AGRICULTURE (agricultural business management, agricultural economics, and conservation and regulation), BIOLOGICAL SCIENCE (biology/biological science), BUSINESS (accounting, banking and finance, business administration and management, hotel/motel and restaurant management, human resources, management science, marketing/retailing/merchandising, organizational behavior, recreation and leisure services, and tourism), COMMUNICATIONS AND THE ARTS (broadcasting, communications, English, French, German, journalism, music, photography, public relations, Spanish, speech/debate/rhetoric, studio art, and theater design), COMPUTER AND PHYSICAL SCIENCE (actuarial science, chemistry, computer science, earth science, geology, information sciences and systems, mathematics, and physics), EDUCATION (agricultural, art, business, early childhood, elementary, English, foreign languages, home economics, industrial arts, mathematics, middle school, music, physical, science, secondary, social studies, and special), ENGINEERING AND ENVIRONMENTAL DESIGN (agricultural engineering technology, automotive technology, aviation computer technology, commercial art, construction management, drafting and design technology, electrical/electronics engineering, electrical/electronics engineering technology, engineering, engineering technology, graphic arts technology, industrial engineering technology, interior design, manufacturing technology, and occupational safety and health), HEALTH PROFESSIONS (medical laboratory technology, nursing, predentistry, premedicine, and speech pathology/audiology), SOCIAL SCIENCE (child care/child and family studies, criminal justice, dietetics, economics, geography, history, political science/government, prelaw, psychology, safety management, social work, sociology, and textiles and clothing). Curriculum and instruction, criminal justice, and business management are the largest.

Required: To graduate, students must complete a minimum of 124 hours, including 35 to 64 in the major, and have a minimum GPA of 2.0; several majors require a higher cumulative GPA. General education requirements include a total of 39 to 45 hours in humanities, social sciences, multicultural studies, technology, English and oral communications, math, science, and individual development. A comprehensive exam may be part of the exit assessment in selected majors.

Special: Central offers cross-registration with the Midwest Student Exchange Program, credit and noncredit internships, study abroad in more than 15 countries, a B.A.-B.S. degree, dual and student-designed majors, credit for military service, pass/fail options, nondegree study, and a 3-2 engineering degree with the University of Missouri at Columbia and at Rolla and with the University of Indiana. There are 25 national honor societies and a freshman honors program.

Faculty/Classroom: 62% of faculty are male; 38%, female. The average class size in an introductory lecture is 30.

Admissions: 76% of the 2003-2004 applicants were accepted. The ACT scores for the 2003-2004 freshman class were: 41% below 21, 31% between 21 and 23, 15% between 24 and 26, 7% between 27 and 28, and 6% above 28. 32% of the current freshmen were in the top fifth of their class; 58% were in the top two fifths. There was 1 National Merit finalist. 32 freshmen graduated first in their class.

Requirements: The ACT is required. In addition, applicants must have completed 16 academic credits, including 4 in English with a writing emphasis, and 3 each in math (algebra and beyond) and social science, 2 in natural sciences, and 1 in fine or performing arts, as well as 3 in academic electives. A foreign language is recommended. The GED is accepted. Central requires applicants to be in the upper 50% of their class. AP and CLEP credits are accepted.

Procedure: Freshmen are admitted to all sessions. Entrance exams should be taken in the junior year. The application deadline for fall entry is open. The application fee is $25. Notification is sent on a rolling basis. Applications are accepted on-line through the college's web site.

Transfer: 752 transfer students enrolled in 2003-2004. Applicants must have a minimum GPA of 2.0, as indicated by an official college transcript. 30 of 124 credits required for the bachelor's degree must be completed at Central.

Visiting: There are regularly scheduled orientations for prospective students, including orientation sessions on housing, general education requirements, and enrollment for fall classes. There are guides for informal visits and visitors may sit in on classes and stay overnight. To schedule a visit, contact the Office of Admissions at admit@cmsuvmb.cmsu.edu.

Financial Aid: In 2003-2004, 82% of all full-time freshmen and 81% of continuing full-time students received some form of financial aid. 75% of all full-time students received need-based aid. The average freshman award was $6752. Need-based scholarships or need-based grants averaged $3754 ($7350 maximum); need-based self-help aid (loans and jobs) averaged $2308 ($3597 maximum); non-need-based athletic scholarships averaged $3616 ($12,975 maximum); and other non-need-based awards and non-need-based scholarships averaged $2643 ($19,491 maximum). 39% of undergraduates work part time. Average annual earnings from campus work are $1900. The average financial indebtedness of the 2003 graduate was $9300. Central is a member of CSS. The FAFSA is required. The deadline for filing freshman financial aid applications for fall entry is March 1.

International Students: There are 309 international students enrolled. The school actively recruits these students. They must score 500 on the written TOEFL and also take participate in institutional assessment.

Computers: The mainframes are an IBM 4381 and an ES 9000 9121 Model 210. There are 350 terminals in the 2 mainframe labs, as well as 1300 lab/classroom PCs in various buildings, and 8 open labs for student use. All students may access the system 24 hours a day. There are no time limits and no fees.

Graduates: From July 1, 2002 to June 30, 2003, 1643 bachelor's degrees were awarded. The most popular majors were curriculum and instruction (66%), criminal justice (37%), and computer information systems and business (34%). In an average class, 1% graduate in 3 years or less, 20% graduate in 4 years or less, 39% graduate in 5 years or less, and 49% graduate in 6 years or less. 322 companies recruited on campus in 2002-2003. Of the 2002 graduating class, 12% were enrolled in graduate school within 6 months of graduation and 94% were employed.

Admissions Contact: Dr. Matt Melvin, Assistant Provost of Enrollment Management. A video is available. E-mail: admit@cmsuvmb.cmsu.edu Web: cmsu.edu

COLLEGE OF THE OZARKS
B-4
Point Lookout, MO 65726

(417) 334-6411, ext. 4219
(800) 222-0525; Fax: (417) 335-2618

Full-time: 561 men, 717 women	Faculty: 89; IIB, -$
Part-time: 32 men, 38 women	Ph.D.s: 56%
Graduate: none	Student/Faculty: 14 to 1
Year: semesters	Tuition: $250
Application Deadline: February 1	Room & Board: $3250
Freshman Class: 2137 applied, 290 accepted, 254 enrolled	
ACT: 22	VERY COMPETITIVE+

College of the Ozarks, founded in 1906, is a private liberal arts college affiliated with the Presbyterian Church (U.S.A.). Instead of paying tuition, students work a total of 560 hours in campus jobs and are responsible only for room and board, books, personal expenses, and an incidental fee of $250. Students may also elect to work in a summer program, which will cover their room and board costs as well. The library contains 120,632 volumes, 30,960 microform items, and 5476 audio/video tapes/CDs, and subscribes to 522 periodicals. Computerized library services include the card catalog, interlibrary loans, and database searching. Special learning facilities include a learning resource center, art gallery, radio station, museum, grist mill, weaving studio, airport, firehouse, print shop, orchid greenhouses, fruitcake/jelly kitchens, day care center, and 3 farm operations. The 1000-acre campus is in a small town 40 miles south of Springfield, adjacent to the resort town of Branson. Including any residence halls, there are 82 buildings.

Student Life: 62% of undergraduates are from Missouri. Students are from 40 states and 15 foreign countries. 85% are from public schools. 86% are white; 10% foreign nationals. 74% are Protestant; 20% claim no religious affiliation; 6% Catholic. The average age of freshmen is 19; all undergraduates, 21. 24% do not continue beyond their first year; 70% remain to graduate.

Housing: 1031 students can be accommodated in college housing, which includes single-sex dorms. Student members of the volunteer fire department have living facilities in the campus fire station. On-campus housing is guaranteed for all 4 years. 68% of students live on campus; of those, 80% remain on campus on weekends. Alcohol is not permitted. All students may keep cars.

Activities: There are no fraternities or sororities. There are 49 groups on campus, including art, band, cheerleading, choir, chorale, computers, dance, departmental academic major clubs, drama, film, international, jazz band, literary magazine, musical theater, newspaper, orchestra, pep band, photography, political, professional, radio and TV, religious, social service, student government, and yearbook. Popular campus events include Fourth of July, lectures, and concerts.

Sports: There are 2 intercollegiate sports for men and 2 for women, and 12 intramural sports for men and 12 for women. Facilities include an all-weather track, an indoor walking track, horseshoe pit, softball and baseball fields, tennis courts, handball courts, volleyball and sand volleyball, badminton and table tennis facilities, an aerobics room and rehabilitation training room, and a field house with a 4500-seat gym, 3 basketball courts, an Olympic-size pool, a weight training room, racquetball courts, and a dance studio.

Disabled Students: 95% of the campus is accessible. Wheelchair ramps, elevators, special parking, and specially equipped rest rooms are available.

Services: Counseling and information services are available, as is tutoring in some subjects, including math and foreign language. There is also a center for writing and thinking. There is remedial math.

Campus Safety and Security: Measures include 24-hour foot and vehicle patrol, informal discussions, pamphlets/posters/films, and emergency telephones. There are lighted pathways/sidewalks, a parking lot security system, and a 24-hour paramedic service on campus. The front gate is locked at 1 P.M. daily and women's dorms are locked at closing hours.

Programs of Study: C of O confers B.A. and B.S. degrees. Bachelor's degrees are awarded in AGRICULTURE (agricultural business management, agriculture, agronomy, animal science, conservation and regulation, horticulture, and poultry science), BIOLOGICAL SCIENCE (biology/biological science), BUSINESS (accounting, business administration and management, business economics, hotel/motel and restaurant management, international business management, and marketing management), COMMUNICATIONS AND THE ARTS (art, broadcasting, communications, dramatic arts, English, French, German, journalism, media arts, music, music business management, musical theater, performing arts, public relations, Spanish, studio art, and theater design), COMPUTER AND PHYSICAL SCIENCE (chemistry, computer science, information sciences and systems, and mathematics), EDUCATION (agricultural, art, business, early childhood, elementary, English, foreign languages, industrial arts, mathematics, middle school, music, physical, recreation, secondary, social studies, technical, and vocational), ENGINEERING AND ENVIRONMENTAL DESIGN (agricultural engineering technology, aviation computer technology, graphic arts technology, industrial engineering technology, and preengineering), HEALTH PROFESSIONS (health, medical technology, premedicine, prepharmacy, preveterinary science, and speech pathology/audiology), SOCIAL SCIENCE (child psychology/development, clothing and textiles management/production/services, corrections, criminal justice, criminology, dietetics, family/consumer studies, food science, forensic studies, gerontology, history, home economics, interdisciplinary studies, law enforcement and corrections, philosophy, political science/government, prelaw, psychology, religion, religious music, safety management, social work, and sociology). Business administration, sciences, and history are the strongest academically. Business administration is the largest.

Required: 55 to 58 hours of general education requirements include specific courses in English, speech, religion, history and political science, math, and phys ed. Students must also select courses from an arts and letters, social science, and physical science distribution. B.A. candidates must complete 8 credit hours of foreign language, and B.S. candidates must complete 6 to 8 credit hours of additional physical science, biology, or math. To graduate, all students must complete at least 124 credit hours, including 36 upper level and 30 in a major field, with a minimum

GPA of 2.0 in the major as well as overall. A portfolio is required. A comprehensive exam in psychology is required.

Special: The college offers co-op programs, study abroad in the Netherlands, Korea, Bali, Indonesia, and Thailand, internships through numerous departments, preprofessional programs in nursing, medical technology, and engineering, a 3-2 engineering degree program, independent study/practicum courses, student-designed interdisciplinary majors, and credit for military experience. Pass/fail grading is allowed for proficiency exams. There are 4 national honor societies and 4 departmental honors programs.

Faculty/Classroom: 68% of faculty are male; 32%, female. All teach undergraduates. The average class size in an introductory lecture is 40; in a laboratory, 16; and in a regular course, 21.

Admissions: 14% of the 2003-2004 applicants were accepted. The ACT scores for the 2003-2004 freshman class were: 37% below 21, 29% between 21 and 23, 19% between 24 and 26, 10% between 27 and 28, and 4% above 28. 33% of the current freshmen were in the top fifth of their class; 61% were in the top two fifths. 10 freshmen graduated first in their class.

Requirements: The ACT is required. In addition, applicants must be graduates of accredited secondary schools or have earned a GED or have an ACT score of 19 or better. A physical exam, financial aid application, 2 recommendations (preferably from school personnel) and an interview are required. C of O requires applicants to be in the upper 3% of their class. A GPA of 3.0 is required. AP and CLEP credits are accepted. Important factors in the admissions decision are leadership record, extracurricular activities record, and advanced placement or honor courses.

Procedure: Freshmen are admitted fall and spring. Entrance exams should be taken in October or December of the senior year. There is a rolling admissions plan. Early decision application should be filed by February 15; regular applications, by March 15 for fall entry. Notification of early decision is sent February 15; regular decision, March 15. A waiting list is an active part of the admissions procedure. Applications are accepted on-line through *www.cofo.edu*, the school's web site.

Transfer: 56 transfer students enrolled in 2002-2003. Transfer applicants must present a minimum GPA of 2.0 and may not have a previous disciplinary or loan default record. The ACT or the SAT I is required if the applicant has completed fewer than 48 credit hours. An interview is required. The dean of students at the transfer college must complete a form attesting to the positive character of the applicant. All transfer students must submit a financial aid transcript. 45 of 125 credits required for the bachelor's degree must be completed at C of O.

Visiting: There are regularly scheduled orientations for prospective students, Mondays through Fridays. There are guides for informal visits and visitors may sit in on classes. To schedule a visit, contact the Admissions Office at (417) 334-6411 or *admiss4@cofo.edu*.

Financial Aid: In 2003-2004, all full-time students received some form of financial aid. 90% of all full-time students received need-based aid. The average freshman award was $12,018. Need-based scholarships or need-based grants averaged $11,937 ($14,450 maximum); need-based self-help aid (loans and jobs) averaged $2884 (maximum); and non-need-based athletic scholarships averaged $2659 ($3250 maximum). All undergraduates work part time. Average annual earnings from campus work are $2884. The average financial indebtedness of the 2003 graduate was $6060. The FAFSA and student and parent federal tax returns are required. The priority date for freshman financial aid applications for fall entry is February 15. The deadline for filing freshman financial aid applications for fall entry is March 15.

International Students: There are 27 international students enrolled. They must score 550 on the written TOEFL and it is recommended that they also take the ACT or the SAT I.

Computers: There are 136 PCs. Various other campus departments have computers for classroom instruction and use. The students have access from labs, work offices, dorm lobbies, and dorm rooms. All students may access the system from 8 A.M. to 11 P.M. There are no time limits and no fees.

Graduates: From July 1, 2002 to June 30, 2003, 258 bachelor's degrees were awarded. The most popular majors were education (16%), business (14%), and psychology (1%). In an average class, 21% graduate in 4 years or less, 39% graduate in 5 years or less, and 44% graduate in 6 years or less. 172 companies recruited on campus in 2002-2003.

Admissions Contact: Marci Linson, Dean of Admissions.
E-mail: *admiss4@cofo.edu* Web: *http://www.cofo.edu*

COLUMBIA COLLEGE
C-2
Columbia, MO 65216

(573) 875-7352
(800) 231-2391; Fax: (573) 875-7506

Full-time: 261 men, 425 women
Part-time: 93 men, 143 women
Graduate: 44 men, 108 women
Year: semesters, summer session
Application Deadline: open
Freshman Class: 891 applied, 524 accepted, 157 enrolled
ACT: 22

Faculty: 59; IIB, --$
Ph.Ds: 90%
Student/Faculty: 12 to 1
Tuition: $11,362
Room & Board: $4777

COMPETITIVE

Columbia College, founded in 1851, is a private liberal arts institution affiliated with the Disciples of Christ. In addition to regional accreditation, Columbia has baccalaureate program accreditation with CSWE. The library contains 80,000 volumes, 18,000 microform items, and 3000 audio/video tapes/CDs, and subscribes to 600 periodicals. Computerized library services include the card catalog, interlibrary loans, and database searching. Special learning facilities include a learning resource center and art gallery. The 39-acre campus is in a small town 120 miles east of Kansas City and 120 miles west of St. Louis. Including any residence halls, there are 13 buildings.

Student Life: 92% of undergraduates are from Missouri. Students are from 15 states, 34 foreign countries, and Canada. 79% are white. 57% claim no religious affiliation; 28% Protestant; 13% Catholic. The average age of freshmen is 19; all undergraduates, 23. 30% do not continue beyond their first year; 45% remain to graduate.

Housing: 303 students can be accommodated in college housing, which includes single-sex and coed dorms. In addition, there is a wellness floor. On-campus housing is guaranteed for all 4 years. 68% of students commute. Alcohol is not permitted. All students may keep cars.

Activities: There are no fraternities or sororities. There are 37 groups on campus, including art, cheerleading, choir, chorale, computers, ethnic, honors, international, literary magazine, pep band, photography, political, professional, religious, social, social service, student government, and yearbook. Popular campus events include International Student Festival, Black History Convocation, and Women's History Convocation.

Sports: There are 3 intercollegiate sports for men and 2 for women, and 16 intramural sports for men and 16 for women. Facilities include softball and soccer fields, a dance studio, indoor tennis courts, an exercise/weight room, and a gym and sports complex.

Disabled Students: 97% of the campus is accessible. Wheelchair ramps, elevators, special parking, specially equipped rest rooms, special class scheduling, lowered drinking fountains, and lowered telephones are available.

Services: Counseling and information services are available, as is tutoring in most subjects, including accounting, English composition, geography, math, history, and psychology, as well as in study skills. There is remedial math and writing.

Campus Safety and Security: Measures include 24-hour foot and vehicle patrol, security escort services, informal discussions, and pamphlets/posters/films. There are emergency telephones and lighted pathways/sidewalks.

Programs of Study: Columbia confers B.A., B.S., B.A.G.S., B.F.A., and B.S.W. degrees. Associate and master's degrees are also awarded. Bachelor's degrees are awarded in AGRICULTURE (environmental studies), BIOLOGICAL SCIENCE (biology/biological science), BUSINESS (accounting, banking and finance, business administration and management, and marketing/retailing/merchandising), COMMUNICATIONS AND THE ARTS (art, English, and fine arts), COMPUTER AND PHYSICAL SCIENCE (chemistry, computer science, information sciences and systems, and natural sciences), EDUCATION (elementary and secondary), SOCIAL SCIENCE (criminal justice, forensic studies, history, interdisciplinary studies, philosophy, political science/government, psychology, social work, and sociology). Art, history/government, and education are the strongest academically. Business administration is the largest.

Required: To graduate, students must complete 120 semester hours, including 39 to 72 in the major, with a minimum GPA of 2.0. Distribution requirements include 18 hours in humanities, 9 in basic skills such as English composition and computers, 9 in social science, and 8 in math and science. All majors require students to complete a capstone course.

Special: Columbia offers cross-registration with the University of Missouri/Columbia and Stephens College, internships, study abroad in more than 20 countries, B.A.-B.S. degrees in most disciplines, an individual studies degree, student-designed and dual majors, nondegree study, and pass/fail options. Select students who complete a special 2-semester project earn a bachelor's degree with distinction (B.A.D.). There are 8 national honor societies, a freshman honors program, and honors programs in all departments.

Faculty/Classroom: 55% of faculty are male; 45%, female. All teach undergraduates and 50% do research. No introductory courses are taught by graduate students. The average class size in an introductory lecture is 23; in a laboratory, 22; and in a regular course, 15.

Admissions: 59% of the 2003-2004 applicants were accepted. The ACT scores for the 2003-2004 freshman class were: 37% below 21, 25% between 21 and 23, 20% between 24 and 26, 10% between 27 and 28, and 8% above 28. 32% of the current freshmen were in the top fifth of their class; 48% were in the top two fifths. 8 freshmen graduated first in their class.

Requirements: The ACT is required. In addition, applicants must be graduates of an accredited secondary school or have a GED certificate. Students should have completed 4 units of English, 3 of math including 2 of algebra and 1 of geometry, and 2 each of natural science and social studies. Columbia requires applicants to be in the upper 50% of their class. A GPA of 2.0 is required. AP and CLEP credits are accepted. Important factors in the admissions decision are advanced placement or honor courses, leadership record, and evidence of special talent.

Procedure: Freshmen are admitted to all sessions. Entrance exams should be taken in spring of the junior year or fall of the senior year. There is a rolling admissions plan and a deferred admissions plan. Application deadlines are open. Applications are accepted on-line through the school's web site.

Transfer: 125 transfer students enrolled in a recent year. Applicants must have a minimum GPA of 2.0 overall and in the last semester attended and must submit a high school transcript and SAT I or ACT scores. 24 of 120 credits required for the bachelor's degree must be completed at Columbia.

Visiting: There are regularly scheduled orientations for prospective students, including a campus tour, a workshop in financial aid, an academic/organization fair, and a luncheon. There are guides for informal visits and visitors may sit in on classes and stay overnight. To schedule a visit, contact the Admissions Office at (800) 231-2391, ext. 7352 or *admissions@ccis.edu*.

Financial Aid: In 2003-2004, 83% of all full-time freshmen and 78% of continuing full-time students received some form of financial aid. 55% of full-time freshmen and 56% of continuing full-time students received need-based aid. The average freshman award was $10,485. 64% of undergraduates work part time. Average annual earnings from campus work are $2400. Columbia is a member of CSS. The FAFSA and the college's own financial statement are required. The deadline for filing freshman financial aid applications for fall entry is April 30.

International Students: There were 51 international students enrolled in a recent year. The school actively recruits these students. They must score 500 on the written TOEFL or 173 on the electronic version.

Computers: The mainframe is an HP 9000/Model K370. There are terminals located in the computer lab, library, and residence halls. All students may access the system from 8 A.M. to 10 P.M. in the computer lab. There are no time limits and no fees. It is strongly recommended that all students have a personal computer.

Graduates: From July 1, 2002 to June 30, 2003, 166 bachelor's degrees were awarded. The most popular majors were business administration (28%), education (14%), and criminal justice (10%). In an average class, 35% graduate in 4 years or less, 40% graduate in 5 years or less, and 45% graduate in 6 years or less.

Admissions Contact: Regina Morin, Director of Admissions.
E-mail: *admissions@ccis.edu* Web: *www.ccis.edu*

CULVER-STOCKTON COLLEGE
C-1
Canton, MO 63435-1299

(217) 231-6331
(800) 537-1883; Fax: (217) 231-6618

Full-time: 334 men, 433 women
Part-time: 22 men, 46 women
Graduate: none
Year: semesters, summer session
Application Deadline: open
Freshman Class: 1018 applied, 729 accepted, 219 enrolled
ACT: 21

Faculty: 57
Ph.Ds: 63%
Student/Faculty: 14 to 1
Tuition: $12,400
Room & Board: $5450

COMPETITIVE

Culver-Stockton College, established in 1853, is a private liberal arts institution affiliated with the Disciples of Christ. In addition to regional accreditation, C-SC has baccalaureate program accreditation with NLN. The library contains 162,790 volumes, 5211 microform items, and 4485 audio/video tapes/CDs, and subscribes to 10,257 periodicals. Computerized library services include the card catalog, interlibrary loans, and database searching. Special learning facilities include a learning resource center, art gallery, radio station, rare books collection, performing arts center, publications lab, and tutorial center. The 143-acre campus is in a rural area 125 miles north of St. Louis. Including any residence halls, there are 19 buildings.

Student Life: 54% of undergraduates are from Missouri. 90% are white. The average age of freshmen is 18; all undergraduates, 19. 30% do not continue beyond their first year.

Housing: 650 students can be accommodated in college housing, which includes single-sex and coed dorms, fraternity houses, and sorority houses. On-campus housing is guaranteed for all 4 years. 71% of students live on campus; of those, 50% remain on campus on weekends. Alcohol is not permitted. All students may keep cars.

Activities: 44% of men belong to 4 national fraternities; 38% of women belong to 3 national sororities. There are 37 groups on campus, including art, band, cheerleading, choir, chorus, dance, drama, ethnic, forensics, honors, international, jazz band, literary magazine, musical theater, newspaper, opera, pep band, photography, political, professional, radio, religious, social, social service, and student government. Popular campus events include National Collegiate Alcohol Awareness Week, Spring Fling, and Family Weekend.

Sports: There are 5 intercollegiate sports for men and 5 for women, and 9 intramural sports for men and 9 for women. Facilities include a 2000-seat football stadium, a soccer field, a baseball field, intramural fields, a swimming pool, a dance studio, a weight room, and a field house with basketball, volleyball, tennis, and racquetball courts.

Disabled Students: 40% of the campus is accessible. Wheelchair ramps, elevators, special parking, and specially equipped rest rooms are available.

Services: Counseling and information services are available, as is tutoring in most subjects. There is remedial math and writing.

Campus Safety and Security: Measures include self-defense education, security escort services, informal discussions, and pamphlets/posters/films. There are emergency telephones, lighted pathways/sidewalks, and a nighttime security patrol.

Programs of Study: C-SC confers B.A., B.S., B.F.A., B.M.E., and B.S.N. degrees. Bachelor's degrees are awarded in BIOLOGICAL SCIENCE (biology/biological science), BUSINESS (accounting, banking and finance, business administration and management, management science, and recreational facilities management), COMMUNICATIONS AND THE ARTS (art, arts administration/management, communications, dramatic arts, English, and music), COMPUTER AND PHYSICAL SCIENCE (chemistry, information sciences and systems, and mathematics), EDUCATION (art, athletic training, drama, elementary, music, and physical), HEALTH PROFESSIONS (medical laboratory science and nursing), SOCIAL SCIENCE (criminal justice, history, psychology, religion, and sociology). Education and nursing are the strongest academically. Education, business, and nursing are the largest.

Required: To graduate, students must complete 124 credit hours, including 24 to 64 in the major, with a minimum GPA of 2.0. Distribution requirements include 5 to 9 hours in social science, 4 to 9 in humanities, 3 to 9 in natural science, 3 to 6 in fine arts, 3 to 6 in math, and 2 to 3 in computer science. English composition, speech, phys ed, introductory computer, and Christian heritage courses are required.

Special: Culver-Stockton offers a joint-degree program in nursing in conjunction with Blessing-Rieman College of Nursing, a 2-2 degree in engineering with the University of Missouri-Rolla, and a 3-2 degree in occupational therapy with Washington University at St. Louis. Study abroad, internships, and dual and individualized majors are also available. A course entitled Decades of Destiny is presented in nontraditional 5-week modules. There are 8 national honor societies, a freshman honors program, and 18 departmental honors programs.

Faculty/Classroom: 64% of faculty are male; 36%, female. All teach undergraduates. The average class size in an introductory lecture is 22; in a laboratory, 15; and in a regular course, 16.

Admissions: 72% of the 2003-2004 applicants were accepted. The ACT scores for the 2003-2004 freshman class were: 44% below 21, 25% between 21 and 23, 22% between 24 and 26, 4% between 27 and 28, and 4% above 28. 26% of the current freshmen were in the top fifth of their class; 56% were in the top two fifths. 7 freshmen graduated first in their class in a recent year.

Requirements: The SAT I or ACT is required, with the ACT preferred. Secondary school preparation should include 4 years of English, 2 to 4 of science, and 2 of math. The GED is accepted. C-SC requires applicants to be in the upper 50% of their class. A GPA of 2.0 is required. AP and CLEP credits are accepted. Important factors in the admissions decision are advanced placement or honor courses, recommendations by school officials, and evidence of special talent.

Procedure: Freshmen are admitted fall and spring. Entrance exams should be taken by April of the entering school year. There is a deferred admissions plan and a rolling admissions plan. Application deadlines are open. The application fee is $25. Applications are accepted on-line through the college's web site.

Transfer: 50 transfer students enrolled in 2003–2004. Transfer applicants must submit college transcripts and must have a minimum college GPA of 2.0. 30 of 124 credits required for the bachelor's degree must be completed at C-SC.

Visiting: There are regularly scheduled orientations for prospective students, including meetings with professors, students, coaches, and extracurricular advisers, and financial aid information, a student life panel, and campus tours. There are guides for informal visits and visitors may sit in on classes and stay overnight. To schedule a visit, contact Enrollment Services.

Financial Aid: In 2003-2004, 91% of all full-time freshmen and 85% of continuing full-time students received some form of financial aid. 91% of full-time freshmen and 85% of continuing full-time students received need-based aid. The average freshman award was $11,637. Need-based

scholarships or need-based grants averaged $8922; need-based self-help aid (loans and jobs) averaged $3122; non-need-based athletic scholarships averaged $2533; and other non-need-based awards and non-need-based scholarships averaged $8562. The average financial indebtedness of the 2003 graduate was $14,438. C-SC is a member of CSS. The FAFSA is required. The deadline for filing freshman financial aid applications for fall entry is June 15.

International Students: There are 18 international students enrolled. The school actively recruits these students. They must score 500 on the written TOEFL or 173 on the electronic version. International students are not required to take the TOEFL if they have resided in this country for 1 semester or submit SAT I or ACT scores.

Computers: The mainframe is an HP Netserver LC IV. There are 70 IBM PCs available in the library, the computer lab, various classroom buildings, and residence halls. Mainframe access is also available from student rooms through student-owned PCs. All students may access the system days, evenings, and weekends. There are no time limits and no fees.

Graduates: From July 1, 2002 to June 30, 2003, 150 bachelor's degrees were awarded. The most popular majors were business administration (25%), education (14%), and nursing (13%). In an average class, 40% graduate in 4 years or less, 47% graduate in 5 years or less, and 48% graduate in 6 years or less. 50 companies recruited on campus in a recent year. Of the 2002 graduating class, 96% were enrolled in graduate school or employed within 6 months of graduation.

Admissions Contact: Ron Cronacher, Director of Enrollment Services. A video is available. E-mail: *enrollment@culver.edu*
Web: *www.culver.edu*

DEACONESS COLLEGE OF NURSING   D-2
St. Louis, MO 63139

(314) 768-3179
(800) 942-4310; Fax: (314) 768-5673

Full- and part-time: 440 men and women	**Faculty:** 16
	Ph.Ds: 15%
Graduate: none	**Student/Faculty:** n/av
Year: semesters, summer session	**Tuition:** $11,341
Application Deadline: open	**Room & Board:** $4600
Freshman Class: 162 applied, 115 accepted, 100 enrolled	
ACT: 21	**SPECIAL**

Deaconess College of Nursing, established in 1889 and affiliated with the United Church of Christ, is a private college offering undergraduate programs in nursing. In addition to regional accreditation, Deaconess has baccalaureate program accreditation with NLN. The library contains 8000 volumes and 130 audio/video tapes/CDs, and subscribes to 230 periodicals. Computerized library services include interlibrary loans and database searching. Special learning facilities include a learning resource center, nursing archives, and a nursing arts lab. The 15-acre campus is in an urban area 4 miles west of downtown St. Louis. Including any residence halls, there are 10 buildings.

Student Life: 72% of undergraduates are from Missouri. Students are from 6 states and 2 foreign countries. 78% are from public schools. 87% are white; 10% African American. 46% are Catholic; 40% Protestant; 14% claim no religious affiliation. The average age of freshmen is 21; all undergraduates, 23. 13% do not continue beyond their first year; 65% remain to graduate.

Housing: 98 students can be accommodated in college housing, which includes coed dorms. On-campus housing is available on a first-come, first-served basis. Priority is given to out-of-town students. 72% of students commute. Alcohol is not permitted. Upperclassmen may keep cars.

Activities: There are no fraternities or sororities. There are 7 groups on campus, including newspaper, professional, religious, social, and student government. Popular campus events include Dedication Ceremony, Christmas Tea, and Welcome Week.

Sports: There is no sports program at Deaconess. Facilities include a weight room.

Disabled Students: 90% of the campus is accessible. Wheelchair ramps, elevators, special parking, and specially equipped rest rooms are available.

Services: Counseling and information services are available, as is tutoring in some subjects, including sciences and statistics. There is remedial math, reading, and writing. Each student is assigned an academic adviser.

Campus Safety and Security: Measures include 24-hour foot and vehicle patrol, self-defense education, security escort services, and shuttle buses. There are informal discussions, pamphlets/posters/films, emergency telephones, lighted pathways/sidewalks, and a card reader security system.

Programs of Study: Deaconess confers the B.S.N. degree. Associate degrees are also awarded. Bachelor's degrees are awarded in HEALTH PROFESSIONS (nursing).

Required: To graduate, students must complete 128 credit hours, including 62 in nursing courses, with a minimum GPA of 2.0. General education requirements include 30 hours of math and science, 24 of liberal arts and humanities, and 12 of social science.

Special: Students may opt for credit by exam. A work-study program with Deaconess Hospital and cross-registration with Fontbonne University are available.

Faculty/Classroom: All faculty are female. All teach undergraduates and 2% both teach and do research. The average class size in an introductory lecture is 30; in a laboratory, 20; and in a regular course, 25.

Admissions: 71% of the 2003-2004 applicants were accepted. The ACT scores for the 2003-2004 freshman class were: 70% between 21 and 23, and 30% between 24 and 26. All of the current freshmen were in the top two fifths of their class.

Requirements: The SAT I or ACT is required; the ACT is preferred. Applicants must be graduates of an accredited secondary school or have a GED certificate. They should have completed 4 years of English and 3 years each of math and science. An essay must be submitted. Deaconess requires applicants to be in the upper 30% of their class. A GPA of 3.5 is required. AP and CLEP credits are accepted. Important factors in the admissions decision are advanced placement or honor courses, recommendations by school officials, and recommendations by alumni.

Procedure: Freshmen are admitted in the fall. Entrance exams should be taken by December of the senior year. Application deadlines are open. The fall 2003 application fee was $30. Notification is sent on a rolling basis. Applications are accepted on-line through the college's web site.

Transfer: Academic ranking in the top third of the high school graduating class is preferred. Applicants should have a cumulative GPA of 2.5 in postsecondary work. 44 of 128 credits required for the bachelor's degree must be completed at Deaconess.

Visiting: There are regularly scheduled orientations for prospective students, consisting of an introduction to the school and its program, a review of the curriculum, admissions procedures, and financial aid, and tours. There are guides for informal visits and visitors may sit in on classes and stay overnight. To schedule a visit, contact the Admissions Office.

Financial Aid: The FAFSA is required.

International Students: They must score 500 on the written TOEFL.

Computers: There are 7 stand-alone PCs in the library and 13 networked PCs in the computer lab. All students may access the system. There are no time limits and no fees.

Graduates: In an average class, 65% graduate in 4 years or less, and 70% graduate in 5 years or less.

Admissions Contact: Michelle McGrail, Dean of Enrollment. Web: *www.deaconess.edu*

DEVRY UNIVERSITY/KANSAS CITY
Kansas City, MO 64131-3626

A-2

(816) 941-2810
(800) 821-3766; Fax: (816) 941-0896

Full-time: 1005 men, 270 women	**Faculty:** n/av
Part-time: 429 men, 223 women	**Ph.D.s:** n/av
Graduate: none	**Student/Faculty:** n/av
Year: semesters, summer session	**Tuition:** $10,670
Application Deadline: open	**Room & Board:** n/app
Freshman Class: n/av	
SAT I or ACT: n/av	**LESS COMPETITIVE**

DeVry University/Kansas City, a private institution founded in 1931, joined the DeVry schools in 1969. 1 of 67 DeVry University locations in the United States and Canada, the school offers undergraduate programs in business administration, electronics, engineering, telecommunications, computer information systems, technical management, information technology, and computer engineering technology. In addition to regional accreditation, DeVry has baccalaureate program accreditation with ABET. The library contains 16,837 volumes, 28,684 microform items, and 514 audio/video tapes/CDs, and subscribes to 68 periodicals. Computerized library services include the card catalog, interlibrary loans, and database searching. Special learning facilities include a learning resource center and electronics and other labs. The 11-acre campus is in an urban area. There is one building.

Student Life: 76% of students are white; 16% African American. The average age of all undergraduates is 28.

Housing: There are no residence halls. Housing referrals may be obtained through the Student Housing Office. There are private apartments, student-plan housing, and private rooms. All students commute. Alcohol is not permitted. All students may keep cars.

Activities: There are no fraternities or sororities. There are 9 groups on campus, including ethnic, honors, international, newspaper, paintball, professional, religious, social, and student government. Popular campus events include Try-Athalon, Student Picnic, and Casino Night.

Sports: There are 3 intramural sports for men and 3 for women.

Disabled Students: All of the campus is accessible. Wheelchair ramps, elevators, special parking, specially equipped rest rooms, special class scheduling, lowered drinking fountains, and lowered telephones are available.

Services: Counseling and information services are available, as is tutoring in every subject.

Campus Safety and Security: Measures include 24-hour foot and vehicle patrol and lighted pathways/sidewalks. A security detection system is deployed when the facility is closed.

Programs of Study: DeVry confers the B.S. degree. Associate degrees are also awarded. Bachelor's degrees are awarded in BIOLOGICAL SCIENCE (bioinformatics), BUSINESS (business administration and management), COMMUNICATIONS AND THE ARTS (telecommunications), COMPUTER AND PHYSICAL SCIENCE (information sciences and systems), ENGINEERING AND ENVIRONMENTAL DESIGN (biomedical engineering, computer engineering, electrical/electronics engineering technology, and technological management). Telecommunications and computer information systems are the largest.

Required: To graduate, students must achieve a GPA of at least 2.0 and satisfactorily complete all curriculum requirements. Course requirements vary according to program. All first-semester students take courses in business organization, computer applications, algebra, psychology, and student success strategies.

Special: Nondegree study, co-op programs, accelerated degree programs, distance learning, and evening and weekend classes are possible. There are 2 national honor societies.

Faculty/Classroom: All teach undergraduates.

Requirements: Admissions requirements include graduation from a secondary school; the GED is also accepted. Applicants must pass the DeVry entrance exam or present satisfactory ACT or SAT I scores. An interview is required. CLEP credit is accepted.

Procedure: Freshmen are admitted fall, spring, and summer. There is a rolling admissions plan. There are early admissions and deferred admissions plans. Application deadlines are open. Application fee is $50. Applications are accepted on-line through *https://apply.embark.com/UGrad/DeVry/21.*

Transfer: 465 transfer students enrolled in a recent year. Applicants must present passing grades in all completed college course work, demonstrate language skills proficiency with at least 24 completed semester credits, and present evidence of math proficiency by appropriate college-level credits. A minimum GPA of 2.0 is required. 25% of 48 to 154 credits required for the bachelor's degree must be completed at DeVry.

Visiting: There are regularly scheduled orientations for prospective students. There are guides for informal visits. To schedule a visit, contact the New Student Coordinator at (816) 941-0430.

Financial Aid: In 2002-2003, 50% of all full-time freshmen and 73% of continuing full-time students received some form of financial aid. At least 49% of full-time freshmen and at least 72% of continuing full-time students received need-based aid. The average freshman award was $6588. Need-based scholarships or need-based grants averaged $3801; need-based self-help aid (loans and jobs) averaged $4220; and institutional non-need-based awards and non-need-based scholarships averaged $7554. The FAFSA is required. The deadline for filing freshman financial aid applications is rolling.

International Students: There were 19 international students enrolled in a recent year. They must score 500 on the written TOEFL or 173 on the electronic version.

Computers: The mainframe is an IBM 3081K. Lab facilities include PCs in stand-alone and network configurations, with access to the mainframe. LANs provide access to a wide range of applications software. Hard copy from the mainframe is provided through a local minicomputer and medium- and high-speed printers. Students in the computer information systems program may access the system during published lab hours. There are no fees.

Graduates: From July 1, 2002 to June 30, 2003, 471 bachelor's degrees were awarded. The most popular majors were computer information systems (78%), business (14%), and electronics engineering technology (8%). 40 companies recruited on campus in a recent year.

Admissions Contact: Shane Smeed, Director of Admissions. E-mail: *ssmeed@kc.devry.edu* Web: *www.kc.devry.edu*

DRURY UNIVERSITY
Springfield, MO 65802

B-3

(417) 873-7205
(800) 922-2274; Fax: (417) 866-3873

Full-time: 650 men, 852 women	**Faculty:** 114; II B, -$
Part-time: 39 men, 25 women	**Ph.D.s:** 95%
Graduate: 105 men, 287 women	**Student/Faculty:** 13 to 1
Year: semesters, summer session	**Tuition:** $13,200
Application Deadline: August 1	**Room & Board:** $4885
Freshman Class: 1128 applied, 865 accepted, 366 enrolled	
SAT I Verbal/Math: 591/614	**ACT:** 26 **VERY COMPETITIVE+**

Drury University, founded in 1873, is a private university with degree programs emphasizing the liberal arts, architecture, business, communications, economics, education, and health sciences. There are 3 undergraduate and 5 graduate schools. In addition to regional accreditation, Drury has baccalaureate program accreditation with ACBSP, NAAB, NASM, and NCATE. The 2 libraries contain 177,794 volumes, 119,683 microform items, and 60,098 audio/video tapes/CDs, and subscribe to 868 periodicals. Computerized library services include the card catalog, interlibrary loans, and database searching. Special learning facilities include an art gallery, radio station, TV station, teleconference facility, art and architecture slide collection, speech communication center, and writing center. The 80-acre campus is in an urban area 200 miles southwest of St. Louis and 150 miles southeast of Kansas City. Including any residence halls, there are 38 buildings.

Student Life: 77% of undergraduates are from Missouri. Students are from 35 states, 45 foreign countries, and Canada. 85% are from public schools. 91% are white. The average age of freshmen is 18; all undergraduates, 20. 17% do not continue beyond their first year; 65% remain to graduate.

Housing: 830 students can be accommodated in college housing, which includes single-sex and coed dorms, on-campus apartments, off-campus apartments, married-student housing, and fraternity houses. There are also leadership, community service, and living-learning communities. On-campus housing is guaranteed for all 4 years. 52% of students live on campus; of those, 80% remain on campus on weekends. All students may keep cars.

Activities: 39% of men belong to 4 national fraternities; 42% of women belong to 4 national sororities. There are 50 groups on campus, including academic interests, art, band, cheerleading, chess, choir, chorale, chorus, computers, dance, debate, drama, environmental, ethnic, film, gay, honors, international, jazz band, leadership, literary magazine, musical theater, newspaper, opera, orchestra, pep band, photography, political, professional, radio and TV, religious, social, social service, student government, student life, symphony, and yearbook. Popular campus events include men's and women's basketball, fall festival, and Christmas vespers.

Sports: There are 6 intercollegiate sports for men and 7 for women, and 10 intramural sports for men and 10 for women. Facilities include a gym, lighted tennis and racquetball courts, playing fields, an Olympic-size pool, a fitness center, a running track, a lighted soccer field, and a 2200-seat indoor stadium for basketball and volleyball.

Disabled Students: 90% of the campus is accessible. Wheelchair ramps, elevators, special parking, specially equipped rest rooms, special class scheduling, lowered drinking fountains, and lowered telephones are available.

Services: Counseling and information services are available, as is tutoring in every subject. There is a reader service for the blind. There is a math and reading learning center, a writing center, and a communications center.

Campus Safety and Security: Measures include 24-hour foot and vehicle patrol, self-defense education, security escort services, and informal discussions. There are pamphlets/posters/films, emergency telephones, lighted pathways/sidewalks, and lighted parking lots with security cameras monitored 24 hours a day.

Programs of Study: Drury confers B.A., B.Arch., and B.M. degrees. Master's degrees are also awarded. Bachelor's degrees are awarded in BIOLOGICAL SCIENCE (biology/biological science), BUSINESS (accounting, business administration and management, international business management, and sports management), COMMUNICATIONS AND THE ARTS (advertising, art history and appreciation, arts administration/management, broadcasting, communications, dramatic arts, English, fine arts, French, German, journalism, music, public relations, Spanish, and speech/debate/rhetoric), COMPUTER AND PHYSICAL SCIENCE (chemistry, computer science, information sciences and systems, mathematics, and physics), EDUCATION (elementary, music, physical, and secondary), ENGINEERING AND ENVIRONMENTAL DESIGN (architecture and environmental science), HEALTH PROFESSIONS (exercise science, predentistry, premedicine, and preveterinary science), SOCIAL SCIENCE (criminology, economics, history, international studies, philosophy, political science/government, prelaw, psychology, and sociology). Premedicine, education, and preprofessional programs are the strongest academically. Business administration, biology, and architecture are the largest.

Required: To graduate, students must complete 124 credit hours (150 for accounting and 170 for B.Arch.). They must also maintain a minimum GPA of 2.0 and complete 26 to 32 credit hours in the major (99 for architecture). Students pursue a broad curriculum called Global Perspectives that includes requirements in science, math, humanities, fine arts, fitness, foreign language, and social science, with specific classes in Alpha Seminar, Math and Science Inquiry, Global Awareness, Global Futures, and Values Analysis. All students who complete the curriculum are awarded a minor in global studies.

Special: Drury offers work-study, cross-registration with Colleges in London, Germany, Spain, and Australia, co-op programs in international business, computer information systems, and arts administration, study abroad in 8 countries, internships, a Washington semester, credit by exam, nondegree study, dual majors in most majors, satisfactory/unsatisfactory options, and a 3-2 engineering degree in conjunction with the University of Missouri and Washington University in St. Louis, as well as a premedical early admission arrangement with St. Louis University

and the University of Missouri-Columbia. There are 17 national honor societies, a freshman honors program, and 19 departmental honors programs.

Faculty/Classroom: 67% of faculty are male; 33%, female. All teach undergraduates and 40% both teach and do research. No introductory courses are taught by graduate students. The average class size in an introductory lecture is 23; in a laboratory, 16; and in a regular course, 16.

Admissions: 77% of the 2003-2004 applicants were accepted. The SAT I scores for the 2003-2004 freshman class were: Verbal--12% below 500, 43% between 500 and 599, 26% between 600 and 700, and 19% above 700; Math--5% below 500, 29% between 500 and 599, 52% between 600 and 700, and 14% above 700. The ACT scores were 9% below 21, 24% between 21 and 23, 28% between 24 and 26, 13% between 27 and 28, and 25% above 28. 61% of the current freshmen were in the top fifth of their class; 84% were in the top two fifths. There were 2 National Merit finalists and 4 semifinalists.

Requirements: The SAT I or ACT is required. In addition, applicants must be graduates of an accredited secondary school or have a GED certificate. Recommended high school credits include 4 units of English and at least 3 each of math through algebra II, natural science, and social studies. An essay and a reference from the high school counselor or principal are required. Drury requires applicants to be in the upper 50% of their class. A GPA of 2.7 is required. AP and CLEP credits are accepted. Important factors in the admissions decision are advanced placement or honor courses, extracurricular activities record, and leadership record.

Procedure: Freshmen are admitted to all sessions. Entrance exams should be taken in the spring of the junior year or fall of the senior year. There is a deferred admissions plan and a rolling admissions plan. Applications should be filed by August 1 for fall entry and December 1 for spring entry, along with a $20 fee. Notification is sent on a rolling basis. Applications are accepted on computer disk and on-line through the school's web site.

Transfer: 111 transfer students enrolled in 2002-2003. Applicants must have a minimum GPA of 2.0 in all college work completed, and supply an essay or writing sample. 30 of 124 credits required for the bachelor's degree must be completed at Drury.

Visiting: There are regularly scheduled orientations for prospective students, consisting of special visit days for pre-med, architecture, pre-engineering, math, physics, computer sciences, arts and sciences, and social sciences. There are guides for informal visits and visitors may sit in on classes and stay overnight. To schedule a visit, contact the Admissions Office at *druryad@drury.edu*.

Financial Aid: In 2003-2004, 94% of all full-time freshmen and 86% of continuing full-time students received some form of financial aid. 79% of full-time freshmen and 72% of continuing full-time students received need-based aid. The average freshman award was $7445. Need-based scholarships or need-based grants averaged $4100 ($12,995 maximum); need-based self-help aid (loans and jobs) averaged $2200 ($12,000 maximum); non-need-based athletic scholarships averaged $5250 ($12,995 maximum); and other non-need-based awards and non-need-based scholarships averaged $2500 ($13,411 maximum). 87% of undergraduates work part time. Average annual earnings from campus work are $2250. The average financial indebtedness of the 2003 graduate was $14,200. Drury is a member of CSS. The FAFSA and the college's own financial statement are required. The deadline for filing freshman financial aid applications for fall entry is March 15.

International Students: There are 70 international students enrolled. The school actively recruits these students. They must score 530 on the written TOEFL or 197 on the electronic version and also take the college's own test and the SAT I (scoring 500 verbal) or the ACT (scoring 21).

Computers: The mainframes are an IBM AS/400, available only to office employees. 325 computers are available to students 24 hours a day in several campus technology centers. Facilities include color and large-format printing and video conferencing. All university-owned computers are connected to the Internet. Network ports are available in student housing (1 port per occupant), many classrooms, and common areas, including the library. Wireless networks cover 40% of the campus. All students may access the system 24 hours a day, 7 days a week in technology centers. There are no time limits and no fees.

Graduates: From July 1, 2002 to June 30, 2003, 290 bachelor's degrees were awarded. The most popular majors were business administration (15%), biology (12%), and communication (10%). In an average class, 1% graduate in 3 years or less, 47% graduate in 4 years or less, 63% graduate in 5 years or less, and 63% graduate in 6 years or less. 15 companies recruited on campus in 2002-2003. Of the 2002 graduating class, 36% were enrolled in graduate school within 6 months of graduation and 59% were employed.

Admissions Contact: Chip Parker, Director of Admission. E-mail: *druryad@drury.edu* Web: *www.drury.edu*

EVANGEL UNIVERSITY
Springfield, MO 65802

B-3
(417) 865-2811
(800) EVANGEL; Fax: (417) 865-9599

Full-time: 646 men, 969 women
Part-time: 34 men, 40 women
Graduate: 12 men, 29 women
Year: semesters, summer session
Application Deadline: see profile
Freshman Class: 862 applied, 696 accepted, 442 enrolled
ACT: 21

Faculty: n/av
Ph.D.s: n/av
Student/Faculty: n/av
Tuition: $11,305
Room & Board: $4130

COMPETITIVE

Evangel University, established in 1955, is a private facility affiliated with the Assemblies of God. In addition to regional accreditation, Evangel has baccalaureate program accreditation with CSWE, NASM, and NCATE. The library contains 96,487 volumes, 11,386 microform items, and 6801 audio/video tapes/CDs, and subscribes to 748 periodicals. Computerized library services include interlibrary loans. Special learning facilities include a learning resource center, radio station, and TV station. The 80-acre campus is in an urban area 225 miles west of St. Louis. Including any residence halls, there are 14 buildings.

Student Life: 56% of undergraduates are from out of state, mostly the Midwest. Students are from 47 states, 9 foreign countries, and Canada. 81% are from public schools. 91% are white. Most are Protestant. The average age of freshmen is 18; all undergraduates, 20. 26% do not continue beyond their first year; 74% remain to graduate.

Housing: 1460 students can be accommodated in college housing, which includes single-sex and coed dorms and married-student housing. There are also honors floors. On-campus housing is guaranteed for all 4 years. 78% of students live on campus; of those, all remain on campus on weekends. Alcohol is not permitted. All students may keep cars.

Activities: There are no fraternities or sororities. There are 16 groups on campus, including band, cheerleading, choir, chorale, chorus, drama, forensics, honors, jazz band, musical theater, newspaper, orchestra, pep band, photography, political, professional, radio and TV, religious, student government, and yearbook. Popular campus events include College Weekend and performances of the Springfield Symphony.

Sports: There are 5 intercollegiate sports for men and 6 for women, and 4 intramural sports for men and 4 for women. Facilities include a student activities center and a 2000-seat gym.

Disabled Students: All of the campus is accessible. Wheelchair ramps, elevators, special parking, specially equipped rest rooms, lowered drinking fountains, and lowered telephones are available.

Services: Counseling and information services are available, as is tutoring in every subject. There is a reader service for the blind and remedial math, reading, and writing.

Campus Safety and Security: Measures include 24-hour foot and vehicle patrol, security escort services, emergency telephones, and lighted pathways/sidewalks.

Programs of Study: Evangel confers B.A., B.S., B.B.A., B.F.A., B.M., and B.S.W. degrees. Associate and master's degrees are also awarded. Bachelor's degrees are awarded in BIOLOGICAL SCIENCE (biology/ biological science), BUSINESS (accounting, management science, and marketing/retailing/merchandising), COMMUNICATIONS AND THE ARTS (art, broadcasting, communications, design, dramatic arts, English, journalism, music, music performance, Spanish, and speech/ debate/rhetoric), COMPUTER AND PHYSICAL SCIENCE (chemistry, computer science, and mathematics), EDUCATION (business, early childhood, elementary, foreign languages, music, physical, science, secondary, and special), HEALTH PROFESSIONS (medical laboratory technology), SOCIAL SCIENCE (biblical studies, criminal justice, history, international studies, missions, parks and recreation management, political science/government, psychology, public administration, religion, religious music, social science, social work, and sociology). Business, education, and music are the strongest academically. Business and education are the largest.

Required: All students must complete 50 to 53 general education hours, including courses in phys ed, computer literacy, English composition, English literature, and Bible study. A minimum GPA of 2.0 is required for graduation. Students must complete 124 credit hours, 36 of which are upper division level, with approximately 30 credit hours in the major.

Special: There are 3-2 engineering degrees available in conjunction with Washington University and University of Missouri at Columbia. Other options include work-study, credit by exam, and a Washington semester. There are 9 national honor societies, and 7 departmental honors programs.

Faculty/Classroom: 62% of faculty are male; 38%, female. All teach undergraduates. No introductory courses are taught by graduate students. The average class size in an introductory lecture is 40 and in a regular course, 20.

Admissions: 81% of the 2003-2004 applicants were accepted. The ACT scores for the 2003-2004 freshman class were: 3% below 21, 51% between 21 and 23, 24% between 24 and 26, 17% between 27 and 28, and 5% above 28.

Requirements: The SAT I or ACT is recommended. In addition, the recommended preparatory curriculum includes 3 credits in English, 2 each in math and social studies, and 1 in lab science. The GED is accepted. A GPA of 2.0 is required. AP and CLEP credits are accepted.

Procedure: Freshmen are admitted to all sessions. Entrance exams should be taken before high school graduation. There is a rolling admissions plan. Contact the school for current application deadlines. The application fee is $25. Notification is sent on a rolling basis. Applications are accepted on-line.

Transfer: 110 transfer students enrolled in a recent year. Transfer applicants must be in good standing with their previous institutions and have a cumulative GPA of 2.0. 30 of 124 credits required for the bachelor's degree must be completed at Evangel.

Visiting: There are regularly scheduled orientations for prospective students, consisting of scheduled visits every Friday and by appointment. There are guides for informal visits and visitors may sit in on classes and stay overnight. To schedule a visit, contact Office of Admissions at *waltnerc@evangel.edu*.

Financial Aid: In 2003-2004, 91% of all full-time freshmen and 94% of continuing full-time students received some form of financial aid. 78% of full-time freshmen and 77% of continuing full-time students received need-based aid. The average freshman award was $5847. 26% of undergraduates work part time. Average annual earnings from campus work are $1875. Evangel is a member of CSS. The FAFSA is required. The deadline for filing freshman financial aid applications for fall entry is August 1.

International Students: There are 17 international students enrolled. They must score 490 on the written TOEFL and also take the SAT I or the ACT.

Computers: The mainframes are a DEC VAX II/750 and a DEC MicroVAX II. There are 3 computer labs with PCs available for student use. Computers are also located in each residence hall. All students may access the system during hours of operation. There are no time limits and no fees. It is strongly recommended that all students have a personal computer.

Graduates: From July 1, 2002 to June 30, 2003, 362 bachelor's degrees were awarded. The most popular majors were education (21%), behavioral science (15%), and business (13%). In an average class, 96% graduate in 4 years or less, and 4% graduate in 5 years or less. 69 companies recruited on campus in 2002-2003.

Admissions Contact: Charity Waltner, Director of Admissions. A video is available. E-mail: *admissions@evangel.edu*
Web: *http://www.evangel.edu/*

FONTBONNE UNIVERSITY
St. Louis, MO 63105

D-2
(314) 889-1413; Fax: (314) 889-1451

Full-time: 303 men, 997 women
Part-time: 112 men, 355 women
Graduate: 191 men, 584 women
Year: semesters, summer session
Application Deadline: August 1
Freshman Class: 495 applied, 409 accepted, 205 enrolled
ACT: 21

Faculty: 60; IIA, --$
Ph.D.s: 62%
Student/Faculty: 22 to 1
Tuition: $14,520
Room & Board: $6988

COMPETITIVE

Fontbonne University, founded in 1917, is a private institution affiliated with the Catholic Church. It offers undergraduate degree programs in education, natural sciences, human environmental sciences, business, communication, and fine arts. In addition to regional accreditation, Fontbonne has baccalaureate program accreditation with ADA and ASLA. The library contains 90,000 volumes and 4141 audio/video tapes/CDs, and subscribes to 310 periodicals. Computerized library services include the card catalog, interlibrary loans, and database searching. Special learning facilities include a learning resource center, art gallery, radio station, a biological field station, a broadcast center, and a communication disorders clinic. The 13-acre campus is in a suburban area 1 mile west of St. Louis. Including any residence halls, there are 10 buildings.

Student Life: 90% of undergraduates are from Missouri. Students are from 22 states and 19 foreign countries. 55% are from public schools. 64% are white; 30% African American. 55% are Catholic; 23% Protestant; 10% claim no religious affiliation. The average age of freshmen is 18; all undergraduates, 30. 26% do not continue beyond their first year; 54% remain to graduate.

Housing: 270 students can be accommodated in college housing, which includes single-sex and coed dorms and on-campus apartments. On-campus housing is guaranteed for the freshman year only and is available on a first-come, first-served basis. Priority is given to out-of-town students. 86% of students commute. All students may keep cars.

Activities: There is 1 local fraternity. There are no sororities. There are 24 groups on campus, including cheerleading, choir, chorus, computers, drama, drill team, ethnic, gay, honors, international, literary magazine, musical theater, photography, political, professional, radio and TV, religious, social, social service, student government, and yearbook. Popular campus events include Spring Fest, art shows, and musical performances.

Sports: There are 7 intercollegiate sports for men and 8 for women, and 4 intramural sports for men and 7 for women. Facilities include a student activity center that houses a 2000-seat gym, a weight room, a track, an aerobics room, and a cafe.

Disabled Students: 70% of the campus is accessible. Wheelchair ramps, elevators, special parking, specially equipped rest rooms, lowered drinking fountains, lowered telephones, and special class scheduling when possible are available.

Services: Counseling and information services are available, as is tutoring in most subjects. There is remedial math, reading, and writing.

Campus Safety and Security: Measures include self-defense education, informal discussions, pamphlets/posters/films, and emergency telephones. There are lighted pathways/sidewalks and security personnel as needed.

Programs of Study: Fontbonne confers B.A., B.S., and B.F.A. degrees. Master's degrees are also awarded. Bachelor's degrees are awarded in BIOLOGICAL SCIENCE (biology/biological science and biotechnology), BUSINESS (business administration and management, fashion merchandising, and sports management), COMMUNICATIONS AND THE ARTS (advertising, art, broadcasting, communications, English, fine arts, and performing arts), COMPUTER AND PHYSICAL SCIENCE (computer science, information sciences and systems, and mathematics), EDUCATION (art, early childhood, education of the deaf and hearing impaired, elementary, middle school, and special), HEALTH PROFESSIONS (speech pathology/audiology), SOCIAL SCIENCE (dietetics, family/consumer studies, history, human services, liberal arts/general studies, and prelaw). Education, computer science, and math are the strongest academically. Business, communication studies, and education are the largest.

Required: To graduate, students must complete 128 credit hours, including 44 in general education requirements, with a minimum GPA of 2.0. The number of hours required for the major varies.

Special: Fontbonne offers cross-registration with several area colleges and a student exchange program with the Sisters of St. Joseph Consortium. There are also cooperative programs in all majors except education, internships with major companies, study abroad in 2 countries, work-study programs, student-designed and dual majors, credit by exam, nondegree study, pass/fail options, and B.A.-B.S. degrees. In addition, an accelerated degree program in business is available, as are 3-2 degrees in engineering and social work with Washington University. There are 4 national honor societies and a freshman honors program.

Faculty/Classroom: 46% of faculty are male; 54%, female. 91% teach undergraduates, 2% do research, and 2% do both. The average class size in an introductory lecture is 21; in a laboratory, 8; and in a regular course, 15.

Admissions: 83% of the 2003-2004 applicants were accepted. The ACT scores for the 2003-2004 freshman class were: 51% below 21, 27% between 21 and 23, 14% between 24 and 26, 5% between 27 and 28, and 3% above 28. 46% of the current freshmen were in the top fifth of their class; 71% were in the top two fifths.

Requirements: The SAT I or ACT is required, with a minimum SAT I composite score of 900 or ACT score of 20 recommended. Applicants must be graduates of an accredited secondary school or have a GED certificate. They must have completed 16 academic credits, including 4 in English, 3 in math, 2 each in science and social studies, and 1 in history. An audition or portfolio may be required. Fontbonne requires applicants to be in the upper 50% of their class. A GPA of 2.5 is required. AP and CLEP credits are accepted. Important factors in the admissions decision are advanced placement or honor courses, extracurricular activities record, and leadership record.

Procedure: Freshmen are admitted to all sessions. Entrance exams should be taken prior to registration. There are early admissions and deferred admissions plans. There is a rolling admissions plan. Applications should be filed by August 1 for fall entry and January 1 for spring entry. The fall 2003 application fee was $25. Notification is sent on a rolling basis. Applications are accepted on computer disk and on-line.

Transfer: 136 transfer students enrolled in a recent year. Applicants must have a minimum GPA of 2.0 and either submit ACT or SAT I scores or take a placement test. Students with fewer than 30 credits must submit a high school transcript. An interview is recommended. 32 credits of 128 required for the bachelor's degree must be completed at Fontbonne.

Visiting: There are regularly scheduled orientations for prospective students, including a campus tour, a financial aid presentation, and visits with faculty and current students. There are guides for informal visits and visitors may sit in on classes and stay overnight. To schedule a visit, contact the Admissions Office.

Financial Aid: In a recent year, 92% of all full-time freshmen and 99% of continuing full-time students received some form of financial aid. 62% of full-time freshmen and 79% of continuing full-time students received need-based aid. The average freshman award was $11,830. 22% of undergraduates work part time. Average annual earnings from campus work are $1243. The average financial indebtedness of a recent graduate was $22,000. The CSS Profile, FAFSA, FFS, and the college's own

financial statement are required. The deadline for filing freshman financial aid applications for fall entry is April 1.

International Students: There are 13 international students enrolled. The school actively recruits these students. They must score 500 on the written TOEFL.

Computers: The mainframe is an HP9000 D350. More than 40 Macs and PCs are available, as is Internet access. All students may access the system during regular hours. There are no time limits. The fee is $35.

Graduates: From July 1, 2002 to June 30, 2003, 303 bachelor's degrees were awarded. The most popular majors were business (47%), elementary education (7%), and special education (5%). In an average class, 33% graduate in 4 years or less, 54% graduate in 5 years or less, and 50% graduate in 6 years or less. 25 companies recruited on campus in 2002-2003.

Admissions Contact: Ketih Quigley, Director of Freshman Recruitment. E-mail: *kquigley@fontbonne.edu* Web: *www.fontbonne.edu*

HANNIBAL-LAGRANGE COLLEGE
Hannibal, MO 63401

D-2

(573) 221-3113
(800) HLG-1119; Fax: (573) 221-6594

Full-time: 278 men, 453 women	**Faculty:** 53
Part-time: 152 men, 250 women	**Ph.D.s:** 34%
Graduate: none	**Student/Faculty:** 14 to 1
Year: semesters, summer session	**Tuition:** $10,160
Application Deadline: August 29	**Room & Board:** $3780
Freshman Class: 362 applied, 350 accepted, 161 enrolled	
SAT I or ACT: required	**COMPETITIVE**

Hannibal-LaGrange College, founded in 1858, is a private facility affiliated with the Southern Baptist Church. The library contains 91,785 volumes, 21,163 microform items, and 6764 audio/video tapes/CDs, and subscribes to 475 periodicals. Computerized library services include the card catalog, interlibrary loans, database searching, and Internet access. Special learning facilities include an art gallery and a nature trail. The 110-acre campus is in a small town 100 miles north of St. Louis. Including any residence halls, there are 17 buildings.

Student Life: 80% of undergraduates are from Missouri. Students are from 24 states and 10 foreign countries. 98% are from public schools. 97% are white. The average age of freshmen is 18; all undergraduates, 23. 28% do not continue beyond their first year.

Housing: 457 students can be accommodated in college housing, which includes single-sex dorms and on-campus apartments. In addition, there are honors houses. On-campus housing is guaranteed for all 4 years. 60% of students live on campus; of those, 70% remain on campus on weekends. Alcohol is not permitted. All students may keep cars.

Activities: There are no fraternities or sororities. There are 27 groups on campus, including art, band, cheerleading, choir, chorus, drama, honors, jazz band, musical theater, newspaper, pep band, photography, political, professional, religious, science, social, social service, student government, women's studies, and yearbook. Popular campus events include Campus Visitation Days, Encounter Visitation Days, and Springfest.

Sports: There are 4 intercollegiate sports for men and 5 for women, and 6 intramural sports for men and 6 for women. Facilities include baseball, softball, and soccer fields and a 41,000-square foot sports complex that contains a gym, weight and aerobics rooms, and volleyball, tennis, and racquetball courts.

Disabled Students: 65% of the campus is accessible. Wheelchair ramps, elevators, special parking, specially equipped rest rooms, special class scheduling, lowered drinking fountains, and special housing are available.

Services: Counseling and information services are available, as is tutoring in some subjects, including math and business/accounting. There is a reader service for the blind, remedial math, reading, and writing, and sign language for hearing-impaired students.

Campus Safety and Security: Measures include 24-hour foot and vehicle patrol, security escort services, pamphlets/posters/films, and emergency telephones. There are lighted pathways/sidewalks.

Programs of Study: HLG confers B.A., B.S., B.A.S., B.S.E., and B.S.N. degrees. Associate degrees are also awarded. Bachelor's degrees are awarded in BIOLOGICAL SCIENCE (biology/biological science), BUSINESS (accounting, business administration and management, organizational behavior, and recreation and leisure services), COMMUNICATIONS AND THE ARTS (art, communications, dramatic arts, English, music, music performance, piano/organ, and speech/debate/rhetoric), COMPUTER AND PHYSICAL SCIENCE (computer programming, information sciences and systems, and mathematics), EDUCATION (Christian, early childhood, elementary, music, and secondary), HEALTH PROFESSIONS (nursing), SOCIAL SCIENCE (biblical studies, criminal justice, history, human services, liberal arts/general studies, psychology, religious music, and sociology). Accounting and business administration are the strongest academically. Education, business, and organizational management are the largest.

Required: All students must complete 124 credit hours with a 2.0 GPA to graduate. The major usually requires 36 or more credit hours of study.

General education requirements include 8 hours in natural science; 6 hours each in Bible, composition, literature, foreign language, history, fine arts, and social science; 3 hours each in speech and algebra; 2 hours in phys ed; and 1 hour in Success in Education. Different core requirements pertain to education and nursing students.

Special: Internships are available for students taking courses in human services, data processing, criminal justice, and Bible studies. Study abroad in England is also available. There are accelerated-degree programs in administration of justice and organizational management, and a 3-2 engineering degree with the University of Missouri/Rolla. Student-designed majors, credit by examination, and nondegree study are possible. There is 1 national honor society, Phi Beta Kappa, and a freshman honors program.

Faculty/Classroom: 55% of faculty are male; 45%, female. All teach undergraduates. The average class size in an introductory lecture is 17; in a laboratory, 18; and in a regular course, 16.

Admissions: 97% of the 2003-2004 applicants were accepted. The ACT scores for the 2003-2004 freshman class were: 22% below 21, 45% between 21 and 23, 21% between 24 and 26, 5% between 27 and 28, and 7% above 28. 28% of the current freshmen were in the top fifth of their class; 75% were in the top two fifths. 5 freshmen graduated first in their class.

Requirements: The SAT I or ACT is required. In addition, applicants must be graduates of an accredited secondary school or have the GED. An interview is required. A GPA of 2.0 is required. AP and CLEP credits are accepted.

Procedure: Freshmen are admitted to all sessions. Entrance exams should be taken before registration. There is a rolling admissions plan. Applications should be filed by August 29 for fall entry and January 8 for spring entry, along with a $25 fee. Notification is sent on a rolling basis. Applications are accepted on-line through www.hlg.edu.

Transfer: 81 transfer students enrolled in 2002-2003. Applicants must submit transcripts from all colleges attended. Students applying with fewer than 30 credit hours must also submit a high school transcript along with ACT or SAT I scores. 32 of 124 credits required for the bachelor's degree must be completed at HLG.

Visiting: There are regularly scheduled orientations for prospective students, consisting of Encounter Days, which are organized tours of the campus covering financial aid, student affairs, and academic areas, which includes lunch in the cafeteria. There are guides for informal visits and visitors may sit in on classes and stay overnight. To schedule a visit, contact the Admissions Office at (800) HLG-1119 or jjohnson@hlg.edu.

Financial Aid: In 2003-2004, 98% of all full-time freshmen and 93% of continuing full-time students received some form of financial aid. 68% of full-time freshmen and 61% of continuing full-time students received need-based aid. The average freshman award was $10,968. 68% of undergraduates work part time. Average annual earnings from campus work are $1100. The average financial indebtedness of the 2003 graduate was $14,719. The FAFSA is required. The deadline for filing freshman financial aid applications for fall entry is July 1.

International Students: There are 13 international students enrolled. The school actively recruits these students. They must score 520 on the written TOEFL or 190 on the electronic version and also take the ACT.

Computers: 30 PCs are available in the technical center, library, and snack shack for all students, 34 in classrooms, and 22 in 6 departmental labs, all with network and Internet access. All students may access the system. There are no time limits and no fees.

Graduates: 135 bachelor's degrees were awarded in a recent year. The most popular majors were education (29%), organizational management (13%), and administration of justice (11%). In an average class, 60% graduate in 4 years or less, and 64% graduate in 6 years or less. 24 companies recruited on campus in a recent year. Of the 2002 graduating class, 5% were enrolled in graduate school within 6 months of graduation.

Admissions Contact: Ray Carty, Vice President of Enrollment Management. E-mail: rcarty@hlg.edu Web: www.hlg.edu

HARRIS-STOWE STATE COLLEGE	D-2
St. Louis, MO 63103	(314) 340-3300; Fax: (314) 340-3555
Full-time: 189 men, 380 women	Faculty: 55
Part-time: 120 men, 558 women	Ph.D.s: 65%
Graduate: none	Student/Faculty: 10 to 1
Year: semesters, summer session	Tuition: $3200 ($6226)
Application Deadline: open	Room & Board: n/app
Freshman Class: 898 applied, 659 accepted, 441 enrolled	
ACT: 18	SPECIAL

Harris-Stowe State College, founded in 1857, is a state-supported, commuter institution offering undergraduate programs in business administration, teacher, and urban education. In addition to regional accreditation, Harris-Stowe has baccalaureate program accreditation with ACBSP, IACBE, and NCATE. The library contains 99,000 volumes and 32,124 microform items, and subscribes to 352 periodicals. Computerized library services include the card catalog, interlibrary loans, database searching, and Internet access. Special learning facilities include a learning resource center and Jazz Institute. The 22-acre campus is in an urban area in metropolitan St. Louis. There are 3 buildings.

Student Life: 99% of undergraduates are from Missouri. Students are from 3 states, 13 foreign countries, and Canada. 84% are African American; 13% white. The average age of freshmen is 24; all undergraduates, 28. 38% do not continue beyond their first year; 62% remain to graduate.

Housing: There are no residence halls. All students commute. Alcohol is not permitted. All students may keep cars.

Activities: 1% of men belong to 5 local and 5 national fraternities; 1% of women belong to 4 local and 4 national sororities. There are 43 groups on campus, including art, cheerleading, choir, chorale, dance, drama, ethnic, honors, international, literary magazine, newspaper, professional, religious, social, student government, and yearbook. Popular campus events include President's Tailgate Party.

Sports: There are 3 intercollegiate sports for men and 4 for women.

Disabled Students: All of the campus is accessible. Wheelchair ramps, elevators, special parking, specially equipped rest rooms, special class scheduling, lowered drinking fountains, and lowered telephones are available.

Services: Counseling and information services are available, as is tutoring in most subjects. There is remedial math, reading, and writing.

Campus Safety and Security: Measures include 24-hour foot and vehicle patrol, security escort services, shuttle buses, and pamphlets/posters/films. There are lighted pathways/sidewalks.

Programs of Study: Harris-Stowe confers B.S.B.A., B.S.T.E., and B.S.U.E. degrees. Bachelor's degrees are awarded in BUSINESS (business administration and management), EDUCATION (early childhood, education, elementary, and middle school). Teacher education is the strongest academically. Teacher education and business administration are the largest.

Required: Students are required to complete 120 to 149 semester hours, including a 42-hour core curriculum of general education courses, and must maintain a minimum GPA of 2.5 (2.0 for nonteaching majors).

Special: Opportunities are provided for internships as part of the degree in urban education, credit by examination, and pass/fail options in developmental courses. Cross-registration with the University of Missouri-St. Louis and St. Louis University and student-designed majors are possible. There are 3 national honor societies.

Faculty/Classroom: 52% of faculty are male; 48%, female. All teach undergraduates. The average class size in an introductory lecture is 30; in a laboratory, 25; and in a regular course, 30.

Admissions: 73% of the 2003-2004 applicants were accepted. The ACT scores for the 2003-2004 freshman class were: 76% below 21, 22% between 21 and 23, and 2% between 27 and 28. 22% of the current freshmen were in the top fifth of their class; 41% were in the top two fifths.

Requirements: The SAT I or ACT is required. In addition, applicants should have completed 16 academic units at an accredited secondary school or hold a GED. A GPA of 2.0 is required. AP and CLEP credits are accepted.

Procedure: Freshmen are admitted to all sessions. Entrance exams should be taken before the close of registration. There is a deferred admissions plan and a rolling admissions plan. Application deadlines are open. The application fee is $15. Notification is sent on a rolling basis.

Transfer: 206 transfer students enrolled in 2002-2003. Students must have completed 24 college-level credit hours. 30 of 120 to 149 credits required for the bachelor's degree must be completed at Harris-Stowe.

Visiting: There are guides for informal visits and visitors may sit in on classes. To schedule a visit, contact the Director of Admissions/Academic Advisement at admissions@hssc.edu.

Financial Aid: In 2003-2004, 88% of all full-time freshmen and 81% of continuing full-time students received some form of financial aid. 86% of full-time freshmen and 65% of continuing full-time students received need-based aid. Need-based scholarships or need-based grants averaged $2890 ($3120 maximum); need-based self-help aid (loans and jobs) averaged $1779 ($3120 maximum); and non-need-based athletic scholarships averaged $1782 ($3120 maximum). Average annual earnings from campus work are $3000. The average financial indebtedness of the 2003 graduate was $14,000. The FAFSA and the college's own financial statement are required. The deadline for filing freshman financial aid applications for fall entry is April 1.

International Students: There are 18 international students enrolled. They must score 500 on the written TOEFL or 173 on the electronic version and also take the SAT I, ACT, or Harris-Stowe's own examination if ACT/SAT I scores are not high enough.

Computers: The mainframe is an IBM RS6000 H50. PCs are available for student use in the academic support center, the PC lab, and the library. There are no time limits and no fees.

Graduates: From July 1, 2002 to June 30, 2003, 147 bachelor's degrees were awarded. The most popular majors were professional interdisciplinary studies (21%), elementary education (20%), and information science and computer technology (8%). 80 companies recruited on campus in 2002-2003.

Admissions Contact: LaShanda Boone, Director of Admissions. A video is available. E-mail: *boonel@hssc.edu* Web: *www.hssc.edu*

JEWISH HOSPITAL COLLEGE OF NURSING AND ALLIED HEALTH
D-2

St. Louis, MO 63110-1091

(314) 454-7057
(800) 832-9009; Fax: (314) 454-5239

Full-time: 24 men, 176 women	**Faculty:** n/av
Part-time: 51 men, 435 women	**Ph.D.s:** n/av
Graduate: 7 men, 88 women	**Student/Faculty:** 9 to 1
Year: 8-week terms, summer session	**Tuition:** $8700
Application Deadline: open	**Room & Board:** $2500
Freshman Class: 59 applied, 59 accepted	
SAT I or ACT: required	SPECIAL

Jewish Hospital College of Nursing and Allied Health, founded in 1993, is a small private college located within the Washington University Medical Center. In addition to regional accreditation, Jewish Hospital College has baccalaureate program accreditation with NLN. The library contains 3200 volumes and 450 audio/video tapes/CDs, and subscribes to 123 periodicals. Computerized library services include the card catalog, interlibrary loans, database searching, and Internet access. The 4-acre campus is in an urban area in the central west end of the city of St. Louis. Including any residence halls, there is 1 building.

Student Life: 60% of undergraduates are from Missouri. Students are from 10 states. 68% are white; 20% African American. The average age of freshmen is 26; all undergraduates, 29. 10% do not continue beyond their first year; 85% remain to graduate.

Housing: 82 students can be accommodated in college housing, which includes coed dorms. On-campus housing is available on a first-come, first-served basis. 92% of students commute. All students may keep cars.

Activities: There are no fraternities or sororities. There are 3 groups on campus, including computers, professional, and student government. Popular campus events include Holiday Party, Lobby Day, and walkathons.

Sports: There is no sports program at Jewish Hospital College.

Disabled Students: 60% of the campus is accessible. Wheelchair ramps, elevators, special parking, specially equipped rest rooms, and lowered drinking fountains are available.

Services: Counseling and information services are available, as is tutoring in most subjects.

Campus Safety and Security: Measures include 24-hour foot and vehicle patrol, security escort services, shuttle buses, and informal discussions. There are pamphlets/posters/films and lighted pathways/sidewalks.

Programs of Study: Jewish Hospital College confers B.S. and B.S.N. degrees. Associate and master's degrees are also awarded. Bachelor's degrees are awarded in HEALTH PROFESSIONS (clinical science, cytotechnology, nursing, and radiological science). Nursing is the largest.

Required: To graduate, 121 credit hours are required with a minimum GPA of 2.0.

Special: Study abroad in 1 country is offered.

Admissions: All of the 2003-2004 applicants were accepted.

Requirements: The SAT I or ACT is required. Jewish Hospital College requires applicants to be in the upper 50% of their class. A GPA of 2.5 is required. CLEP credit is accepted. Advanced placement or honor courses is an important factor in the admission decision.

Procedure: Freshmen are admitted fall and spring. There are early decision, deferred admissions, and rolling admissions plans. Application deadlines are open. The application fee is $25. A waiting list is an active part of the admissions procedure.

Transfer: Applicants should be high school graduates in the upper half of their class, with a 2.5 GPA in high school and college and with a composite score of 21 on the ACT or 1000 on the SAT I. 30 of 121 credits required for the bachelor's degree must be completed at Jewish Hospital College.

Visiting: There are regularly scheduled orientations for prospective students, including an overview of the college and programs offered, tours given by current students, and a question-and-answer period. There are guides for informal visits and visitors may sit in on classes. To schedule a visit, contact the recruiter.

Financial Aid: In 2003-2004, 75% of all full-time students received need-based aid. The average freshman award was $7000. Need-based scholarships or need-based grants averaged $2000 ($8500 maximum); need-based self-help aid (loans and jobs) averaged $2625 ($10,000 maximum); and non-need-based awards and non-need-based scholarships averaged $500 ($1200 maximum). 88% of undergraduates work part time. Average annual earnings from campus work are $1000. The average financial indebtedness of the 2003 graduate was $15,000. The FAFSA and the college's own financial statement are required. The priority date for freshman financial aid applications for fall entry is April 1. The deadline for filing freshman financial aid applications for fall entry is December 1.

International Students: There are 10 international students enrolled. They must score 550 on the written TOEFL and also take the SAT I or the ACT, scoring 21.

Computers: All students may access the system. There are no time limits and no fees.

Graduates: From July 1, 2002 to June 30, 2003, 34 bachelor's degrees were awarded. The most popular majors were nursing (97%), cytotechnology (2%), and allied health (1%). In an average class, 85% graduate in 3 years or less, and 5% graduate in 4 years or less. 5 companies recruited on campus in 2002-2003. Of the 2002 graduating class, 10% were enrolled in graduate school within 6 months of graduation and 96% were employed.

Admissions Contact: Christie Schneider, Chief Admissions Officer. E-mail: *jhcollegeinquiry@bjc.org* Web: *www.jhconah.edu*

KANSAS CITY ART INSTITUTE
A-2

Kansas City, MO 64111

(816) 474-5224
(800) 522-5224; Fax: (816) 802-3309

Full-time: 265 men, 300 women	**Faculty:** 42; IIB, --$
Part-time: 5 men, 2 women	**Ph.D.s:** 88%
Graduate: none	**Student/Faculty:** 13 to 1
Year: semesters, summer session	**Tuition:** $20,310
Application Deadline: rolling	**Room & Board:** $6540
Freshman Class: 538 applied, 472 accepted, 178 enrolled	
SAT I Verbal/Math: 547/516	**ACT:** 22 SPECIAL

The Kansas City Art Institute, founded in 1885, is an independent professional college of art and design. In addition to regional accreditation, KCAI has baccalaureate program accreditation with NASAD. The library contains 30,000 volumes and 22 audio/video tapes/CDs, and subscribes to 125 periodicals. Computerized library services include the card catalog, interlibrary loans, and database searching. Special learning facilities include a learning resource center and art gallery. The 17-acre campus is in an urban area. Including any residence halls, there are 14 buildings.

Student Life: 61% of undergraduates are from out of state, mostly the Midwest. Students are from 37 states and 11 foreign countries. 90% are from public schools. 82% are white. The average age of freshmen is 18; all undergraduates, 21. 26% do not continue beyond their first year; 43% remain to graduate.

Housing: 180 students can be accommodated in college housing, which includes single-sex and coed dorms and off-campus apartments. On-campus housing is guaranteed for the freshman year only. The Student Affairs Office offers assistance finding off-campus housing. 75% of students commute. Alcohol is not permitted. All students may keep cars.

Activities: There are no fraternities or sororities. There are 2 groups on campus, including literary magazine and newspaper. Popular campus events include dances, film series, and poetry readings.

Sports: There is no sports program at KCAI.

Disabled Students: 50% of the campus is accessible. Wheelchair ramps, specially equipped rest rooms, and sign language interpreters are available.

Services: Counseling and information services are available, as is tutoring in every subject. There is remedial reading and writing.

Campus Safety and Security: Measures include 24-hour foot and vehicle patrol, security escort services, informal discussions, and pamphlets/posters/films. There are emergency telephones, lighted pathways/sidewalks, and a free taxi service.

Programs of Study: KCAI confers the B.F.A. degree. Bachelor's degrees are awarded in COMMUNICATIONS AND THE ARTS (art history and appreciation, ceramic art and design, creative writing, design, fiber/textiles/weaving, illustration, painting, photography, printmaking, sculpture, and video). Painting, printmaking, and sculpture are the strongest academically. Painting, design, and fiber are the largest.

Required: Students must maintain a minimum GPA of 2.0 overall and within their studio major. A total of 129 credit hours is needed, including 81 in studio classes; 45 distributed among courses in history of Western thought, art history, literature, humanities, and other liberal arts; and 3 in electives.

Special: KCAI offers internships with major corporations such as Hallmark and Disney, independent study, work-study programs, study abroad in 7 countries, cross-registration, intermedia majors, an exchange program, and nondegree study.

Faculty/Classroom: 59% of faculty are male; 41%, female. All teach undergraduates. The average class size in an introductory lecture is 34; in a laboratory, 14; and in a regular course, 22.

Admissions: 88% of the 2003-2004 applicants were accepted. The SAT I scores for the 2003-2004 freshman class were: Verbal--30% below 500, 38% between 500 and 599, 25% between 600 and 700, and 7% above 700; Math--40% below 500, 39% between 500 and 599, 18% between 600 and 700, and 3% above 700. The ACT scores were 34% below 21, 34% between 21 and 23, 17% between 24 and 26, 8% between 27 and 28, and 7% above 28. 20% of the current freshmen were in the top fifth of their class; 51% were in the top two fifths.

Requirements: The SAT I or ACT is required. In addition, applicants must submit a portfolio consisting of 10 to 20 pieces of artwork, 2 letters of recommendation, and high school transcripts. The GED is accepted. A statement of purpose and an interview are required. A GPA of 2.5 is required. AP and CLEP credits are accepted. Important factors in the admissions decision are evidence of special talent, advanced placement or honor courses, and recommendations by school officials.

Procedure: Freshmen are admitted fall and spring. Entrance exams should be taken in spring of the junior year or fall of the senior year. There is a deferred admissions plan and a rolling admissions plan. Application deadlines for fall entry are rolling. The application fee is $25. Notification is sent on a rolling basis.

Transfer: 65 transfer students enrolled in 2002-2003. Transfer applicants must submit official transcripts and a portfolio. A minimum GPA of 2.0 is required. 72 of 129 credits required for the bachelor's degree must be completed at KCAI.

Visiting: There are regularly scheduled orientations for prospective students, consisting of information sessions offered every other Friday. There are guides for informal visits and visitors may sit in on classes and stay overnight. To schedule a visit, contact the Admissions Office at (816) 802-3300 or *admiss@kcai.edu*.

Financial Aid: In 2003-2004, 95% of all full-time freshmen and 80% of continuing full-time students received some form of financial aid. 79% of full-time freshmen and 84% of continuing full-time students received need-based aid. The average freshman award was $16,477. Need-based scholarships or need-based grants averaged $11,134 ($19,274 maximum); need-based self-help aid (loans and jobs) averaged $5180 ($9625 maximum); and non-need-based awards and non-need-based scholarships averaged $13,915 ($19,274 maximum). 67% of undergraduates work part time. Average annual earnings from campus work are $1500. The average financial indebtedness of the 2003 graduate was $17,125. The FAFSA, the college's own financial statement, and student and parent IRS tax forms, if requested, are required. The deadline for filing freshman financial aid applications for fall entry is March 1.

International Students: There are 14 international students enrolled. They must score 500 on the written TOEFL or 213 on the electronic version.

Computers: The mainframe is an Apple CSX. There is a computer graphics center with software for computer-generated art and design, including digital painting, image processing and composing, layout and illustration, and 3-D modeling and animation. All students may access the system. There are no time limits and no fees. It is strongly recommended that all students have a personal computer.

Graduates: From July 1, 2002 to June 30, 2003, 108 bachelor's degrees were awarded. The most popular majors were painting (16%), sculpture (16%), and illustration and ceramics (16%). In an average class, 43% graduate in 4 years or less, 52% graduate in 5 years or less, and 52% graduate in 6 years or less. Of the 2002 graduating class, 11% were enrolled in graduate school within 6 months of graduation and 50% were employed.

Admissions Contact: Larry Stone, Vice President for Enrollment Management. E-mail: *admiss@kcai.edu* Web: *www.kcai.edu*

LESTER L. COX COLLEGE OF NURSING AND HEALTH SCIENCES

B-3

Springfield, MO 65802

(417) 269-3069
(866) 898-5355; Fax: (417) 269-3581

Full-time: 164 women	**Faculty:** 21
Part-time: 128 women	**Ph.D.s:** 24%
Graduate: none	**Student/Faculty:** 12 to 1
Year: semesters, summer session	**Tuition:** $7642
Application Deadline: February 1	**Room & Board:** $1650
Freshman Class: n/av	
ACT: recommended	**SPECIAL**

Lester L. Cox College of Nursing and Health Sciences, founded in 1994, is a private institution providing comprehensive educational programs that prepare graduates for a changing health care environment. In addition to regional accreditation, Cox College has baccalaureate program accreditation with CCNE and NLN. The library contains 6988 volumes, and subscribes to 441 periodicals. Computerized library services include the card catalog, interlibrary loans, database searching, and Internet access. Special learning facilities include a learning resource center, a nursing skills lab, and an audiovisual learning center. The campus is in an urban area adjacent to the Cox Health North Campus. Including any residence halls, there is 1 building.

Student Life: 99% of undergraduates are from Missouri. 96% are white. The average age of all undergraduates is 27.

Housing: 60 students can be accommodated in college housing. On-campus housing is available on a first-come, first-served basis. 90% of students commute. Alcohol is not permitted. All students may keep cars.

Activities: There are no fraternities or sororities. There are 3 groups on campus, including professional, religious, and student government. Popular campus events include Fall Fling, Wellness Days, and Diversity Day.

Sports: There is no sports program at Cox College.

Disabled Students: Wheelchair ramps, elevators, and special parking are available.

Services: Counseling and information services are available, as is tutoring in some subjects, including math and writing. There is remedial math, reading, and writing. Peer tutoring is available for most science courses.

Campus Safety and Security: Measures include 24-hour foot and vehicle patrol, security escort services, pamphlets/posters/films, and emergency telephones. There are lighted pathways/sidewalks.

Programs of Study: Cox College confers the B.S.N. degree. Associate degrees are also awarded. Bachelor's degrees are awarded in HEALTH PROFESSIONS (nursing).

Required: A total of 122 credit hours is required for the B.S.N.

Special: Cox College offers cross-registration with Evangel University, work-study programs, and an accelerated degree program in nursing.

Faculty/Classroom: 32% of faculty are male; 68%, female. All teach undergraduates. The average class size in an introductory lecture is 25; in a laboratory, 33; and in a regular course, 25.

Admissions: The ACT scores for the 2003-2004 freshman class were: 94% between 21 and 23, 5% between 24 and 26, and 1% above 28.

Requirements: The ACT is recommended. A GPA of 2.5 is required. AP and CLEP credits are accepted.

Procedure: Freshmen are admitted fall, spring, and summer. Entrance exams should be taken after admission, prior to registration. There is an early decision plan. Early decision applications should be filed by November 1; regular applications, by February 1 for fall entry, September 1 for spring entry, and February 1 for summer entry, along with a $30 fee. The college accepts all applicants. Notification of early decision is sent December 1; regular decision, March 1. 10 early decision candidates were accepted for the 2003-2004 class.

Transfer: 59 transfer students enrolled in a recent year. A GPA of 2.5 or better is required, with 12 or more hours of credit. Only courses with a grade of C or better will be considered for transfer. Transfer applicants are not required to submit an ACT score. 30 of 122 credits required for the bachelor's degree must be completed at Cox College.

Visiting: There are guides for informal visits and visitors may sit in on classes. To schedule a visit, contact Julie Nelson.

Financial Aid: In a recent year, 92% of all full-time freshmen and 90% of continuing full-time students received some form of financial aid. 71% of full-time freshmen and 77% of continuing full-time students received need-based aid. The average freshman award was $7254. 4% of undergraduates work part time. Average annual earnings from campus work are $960. The average financial indebtedness of a recent graduate was $13,480. The FAFSA is required. The priority date for freshman financial aid applications for fall entry is April 1.

International Students: They must score 500 on the written TOEFL or 173 on the electronic version and also take the ACT or ASSET, scoring 22 on the ACT.

Computers: There are 2 computer labs with 34 workstations, 2 programatic labs with 17 workstations, and 2 resident pool labs with 6 workstations, all with Internet access; 1 audiovisual lab has 4 workstations, not accessible to the Internet. There are no time limits and no fees.

Graduates: The most popular major was nursing (100%). Of the 2002 graduating class, all were employed within 6 months of graduation.

Admissions Contact: Julie Nelson, Admissions Counselor/Recruiter. A video is available. E-mail: *admissions@coxcollege.edu* Web: *coxcollege.edu*

LINCOLN UNIVERSITY

C-2

Jefferson City, MO 65102-0029

(573) 681-5599
(800) 521-5052; Fax: (573) 681-5889

Full-time: 925 men, 1100 women	**Faculty:** 141; IIA, --$
Part-time: 350 men, 700 women	**Ph.D.s:** 30%
Graduate: 70 men, 185 women	**Student/Faculty:** 14 to 1
Year: semesters, summer session	**Tuition:** $3618 ($6940)
Application Deadline: July 15	**Room & Board:** $3790
Freshman Class: n/av	
SAT I: n/av	**ACT:** required
	NONCOMPETITIVE

Lincoln University, established in 1866, is a land-grant institution offering degree programs in agriculture, arts and sciences, business, applied technology, and education. Figures in the above capsule and in this profile are approximate. There are 3 undergraduate schools and 1 graduate school. In addition to regional accreditation, LU has baccalaureate program accreditation with NASM and NCATE. The library contains 340,000 volumes, 100,000 microform items, and 3000 audio/video tapes/CDs, and subscribes to 1000 periodicals. Computerized library services include the card catalog, interlibrary loans, and database searching. Special learning facilities include a learning resource center, radio station, TV station, and ethnic studies center. The 155-acre campus is in a small town 130 miles west of St. Louis. Including any residence halls, there are 36 buildings.

Student Life: 89% of undergraduates are from Missouri. Students are from 28 states, 29 foreign countries, and Canada. 63% are white; 30% African American. The average age of freshmen is 18; all undergraduates, 22.

Housing: 630 students can be accommodated in college housing, which includes single-sex dorms. On-campus housing is available on a first-come, first-served basis. 82% of students commute. Alcohol is not permitted. All students may keep cars.

Activities: 3% of men belong to 4 national fraternities and 4 national sororities. There are 28 groups on campus, including art, band, cheerleading, choir, dance, drama, honors, international, jazz band, marching band, newspaper, opera, professional, radio and TV, religious, student government, and yearbook. Popular campus events include Black History Week and Unity Awards in Media.

Sports: There are 6 intercollegiate sports for men and 4 for women, and 2 intramural sports for men. Facilities include a 5600-seat stadium and a 2500-seat gym.

Disabled Students: Wheelchair ramps, elevators, special parking, specially equipped rest rooms, special class scheduling, lowered drinking fountains, and lowered telephones are available.

Services: Counseling and information services are available, as is tutoring in most subjects. There is a reader service for the blind and remedial math, reading, and writing.

Campus Safety and Security: Measures include 24-hour foot and vehicle patrol, self-defense education, security escort services, and informal discussions. There are pamphlets/posters/films, emergency telephones, and lighted sidewalks.

Programs of Study: LU confers B.A., B.S., B.M.E., and B.S.Ed. degrees. Associate and master's degrees are also awarded. Bachelor's degrees are awarded in AGRICULTURE (agriculture), BIOLOGICAL SCIENCE (biology/biological science), BUSINESS (accounting, business administration and management, marketing/retailing/merchandising, and office supervision and management), COMMUNICATIONS AND THE ARTS (art, English, French, journalism, and Spanish), COMPUTER AND PHYSICAL SCIENCE (chemistry, information sciences and systems, mathematics, and physics), EDUCATION (art, business, elementary, home economics, music, physical, social science, and special), ENGINEERING AND ENVIRONMENTAL DESIGN (civil engineering technology, engineering, and mechanical design technology), HEALTH PROFESSIONS (medical technology and nursing), SOCIAL SCIENCE (criminal justice, economics, history, liberal arts/general studies, philosophy, political science/government, psychology, public administration, and sociology). Business administration, nursing, and education are the largest.

Required: To graduate, students must complete 121 semester hours including at least 30 in the major, with 18 hours in upper-division courses. Students must maintain a minimum GPA of 2.0. Course work is required in math, English, speech, humanities, history, social science, cultural diversity, and phys ed. Seniors must pass a major field exit exam.

Special: LU offers cross-registration with the University of Missouri/Columbia and William Woods, Westminster, and Columbia Colleges; federal, state, local, and private internships; co-op programs, and a 3-2 engineering degree with the University of Missouri Rolla. Credit by exam, student-designed majors, and a continuing education program are available. There is a freshman honors program.

Faculty/Classroom: 61% of faculty are male; 39%, female. All teach undergraduates and 14% do research. No introductory courses are taught by graduate students. The average class size in an introductory lecture is 50; in a laboratory, 13; and in a regular course, 25.

Requirements: The ACT is required. In addition, students must be graduates of an accredited secondary school or have the GED. A GPA of 2.0 is required. CLEP credit is accepted.

Procedure: Freshmen are admitted to all sessions. Entrance exams should be taken prior to registration. There is a rolling admissions plan and an early admissions plan. Applications should be filed by July 15 for fall entry and November 20 for spring entry, along with a $17 fee. The college accepts all in-state residents. Notification is sent on a rolling basis.

Transfer: All applicants must submit a college transcript from each institution previously attended; those students transferring fewer than 30 hours must also submit the high school transcript and ACT scores. 30 of 121 credits required for the bachelor's degree must be completed at LU.

Visiting: There are regularly scheduled orientations for prospective students, consisting of a freshman orientation held each July. There are guides for informal visits and visitors may sit in on classes and stay overnight. To schedule a visit, contact the Enrollment Services Office at (573) 681-5022.

Financial Aid: LU is a member of CSS. The FAFSA is required. Check with the school for current deadlines.

International Students: International students must score 500 on the written TOEFL or take the MELAB and also take the ACT and placement tests.

Computers: The mainframes are a Unisys B5935, AL-FS, and A6-KX. The mainframes are networked with the Internet. There are also 5 PC labs with a total of 150 computers for student use. All students may access the system 8 A.M. to 10 P.M. Monday through Friday, 8 A.M. to 7 P.M. Saturday, and 9 A.M. to 2 P.M. Sunday. There are no time limits and no fees.

Admissions Contact: Constance Williams, Vice President, Student Affairs. Web: www.lincolnu.edu

LINDENWOOD UNIVERSITY
St. Charles, MO 63301-1695

D-2
(636) 949-4949
Fax: (636) 949-4989

Full-time: 1912 men, 2453 women	**Faculty:** 175
Part-time: 266 men, 292 women	**Ph.D.s:** 60%
Graduate: 880 men, 2035 women	**Student/Faculty:** 25 to 1
Year: 4-1-4, summer session	**Tuition:** $11,650
Application Deadline: open	**Room & Board:** $5400
Freshman Class: 2428 applied, 1112 accepted, 784 enrolled	
ACT: 23	**VERY COMPETITIVE**

Lindenwood University, founded in 1827, is a private institution offering undergraduate and graduate degree programs in the arts and sciences, business, education, and preprofessional fields. There are 6 undergraduate and 5 graduate schools. In addition to regional accreditation, Lindenwood has baccalaureate program accreditation with CAAHEP. The library contains 170,928 volumes, 26,128 microform items, and 1739 audio/video tapes/CDs, and subscribes to 598 periodicals. Computerized library services include the card catalog, interlibrary loans, and database searching. Special learning facilities include a learning resource center, art gallery, radio station, TV station, a greenhouse, and wetlands program facility. The 420-acre campus is in a suburban area 25 miles west of St. Louis. Including any residence halls, there are 30 buildings.

Student Life: 82% of undergraduates are from Missouri. Students are from 48 states, 65 foreign countries, and Canada. 79% are white; 12% African American. 49% are Catholic; 45% Protestant. The average age of freshmen is 19; all undergraduates, 25. 36% do not continue beyond their first year; 40% remain to graduate.

Housing: 2553 students can be accommodated in college housing, which includes single-sex dorms, on-campus apartments, married-student housing, and sorority houses. In addition, there are honors houses. On-campus housing is guaranteed for all 4 years. 70% of students live on campus; of those, 67% remain on campus on weekends. Alcohol is not permitted. All students may keep cars.

Activities: 6% of men belong to 1 national fraternity; 10% of women belong to 1 national sorority. There are 65 groups on campus, including art, band, cheerleading, chess, choir, chorale, chorus, computers, dance, drama, drill team, film, honors, international, jazz band, literary magazine, marching band, musical theater, newspaper, pep band, photography, political, professional, radio and TV, religious, social, social service, student government, and yearbook. Popular campus events include Spring Fling, Alumni Weekend, and Christmas Walk.

Sports: There are 20 intercollegiate sports for men and 18 for women, and 6 intramural sports for men and 6 for women. Facilities include an indoor pool, a gym, weight rooms, a 5000-seat stadium, a 3000-seat performance arena, a sand volleyball court, tennis courts, softball, baseball, and soccer fields, and a state-of-the art all-weather track. Students may use the local golf course and bowling alley for a discounted fee.

Disabled Students: 50% of the campus is accessible. Wheelchair ramps, elevators, special parking, specially equipped rest rooms, special class scheduling, lowered drinking fountains, lowered telephones, and curb cuts are available.

Services: Counseling and information services are available, as is tutoring in every subject. There is a reader service for the blind and remedial math, reading, and writing.

Campus Safety and Security: Measures include 24-hour foot and vehicle patrol, self-defense education, security escort services, and informal discussions. There are pamphlets/posters/films, emergency telephones, and lighted pathways/sidewalks.

Programs of Study: Lindenwood confers B.A., B.S., and B.F.A. degrees. Master's degrees are also awarded. Bachelor's degrees are awarded in AGRICULTURE (agricultural business management), BIOLOGICAL SCIENCE (biology/biological science), BUSINESS (accounting, banking and finance, business administration and management, human resources, management information systems, marketing/retailing/merchandising, and sports management), COMMUNICATIONS AND THE ARTS (art history and appreciation, communications, creative writing, dance, dramatic arts, English, French, music, performing arts, Spanish, and studio art), COMPUTER AND PHYSICAL SCIENCE (chemistry, computer science, and mathematics), EDUCATION (art, athletic training, business, early childhood, elementary, music, physical, science, and secondary), ENGINEERING AND ENVIRONMENTAL DESIGN (engineering), HEALTH PROFESSIONS (medical technology), SOCIAL SCIENCE (criminal justice, fashion design and technology, history, human services, international studies, liberal arts/general studies, ministries, political science/government, prelaw, psychology, public administration, religion, social work, and sociology). Biology, education, and mass communications are the strongest academically. Business, education, and mass communications are the largest.

Required: In order to graduate, students must complete a minimum of 128 credit hours, including at least 36 in the major and 42 in upper-division courses, with a minimum GPA of 2.0. Core curriculum courses include 10 hours of math and science, 9 each of social sciences, humanities, and civilization, 6 of English, and 3 each of fine arts and communications.

Special: The university offers internships in most majors, a co-op program in computer science, study abroad and a Washington semester for juniors, and cross-registration through a consortium of Greater St. Louis Colleges and Universities. Dual and student-designed majors, accelerated degree programs, 3-2 degrees in engineering with Washington University in St. Louis and the University of Missouri-Columbia, work-study programs, and nondegree study are also available. Lindenwood is also designed to meet the needs of working adults; there are evening and weekend classes and 5-year bachelor's programs. There are 9 national honor societies, a freshman honors program, and 6 departmental honors programs.

Faculty/Classroom: 57% of faculty are male; 43%, female. 68% teach undergraduates. No introductory courses are taught by graduate students. The average class size in an introductory lecture is 30; in a laboratory, 25; and in a regular course, 25.

Admissions: 46% of the 2003-2004 applicants were accepted. The ACT scores for the 2003-2004 freshman class were: 22% below 21, 49% between 21 and 23, 15% between 24 and 26, 9% between 27 and 28, and 5% above 28. 27% of the current freshmen were in the top fifth of their class; 60% were in the top two fifths. 11 freshmen graduated first in their class.

Requirements: The SAT I or ACT is required; the minimum required score on the ACT is 18. Applicants must be graduates of an accredited secondary school or have a GED. High school preparation should include at least 16 academic units, including 4 years of English, 2 to 3 each of math, science, and social studies, 2 of a foreign language, and some study of fine or performing arts. An essay and an interview are recommended. Lindenwood requires applicants to be in the upper 50% of their class. A GPA of 2.5 is required. AP and CLEP credits are accepted. Important factors in the admissions decision are leadership record, evidence of special talent, and advanced placement or honor courses.

Procedure: Freshmen are admitted to all sessions. There are early admissions, deferred admissions, and rolling admissions plans. Application deadlines are open. The application fee is $25.

Transfer: 676 transfer students enrolled in 2002-2003. Applicants must have a minimum GPA of 2.0 and should submit official college transcripts in order to transfer credits. 38 of 128 credits required for the bachelor's degree must be completed at Lindenwood.

Visiting: There are regularly scheduled orientations for prospective students, including an admissions interview, a campus tour, and advising. There are guides for informal visits and visitors may sit in on classes and stay overnight. To schedule a visit, contact the Office of Undergraduate Admissions.

Financial Aid: 91% of undergraduates work part time. Average annual earnings from campus work are $1800. Lindenwood is a member of CSS. The FAFSA is required. The priority date for freshman financial aid applications for fall entry is April 1.

International Students: There are 350 international students enrolled. The school actively recruits these students. They must score 500 on the written TOEFL or 173 on the electronic version.

Computers: The mainframe is a DEC VAX 11/750. There are 126 PCs, all of which are networked, in the library, classroom buildings, and campus center. All students may access the system 8 A.M. to 11 P.M. There are no time limits and no fees.

Graduates: From July 1, 2002 to June 30, 2003, 652 bachelor's degrees were awarded. The most popular majors were business administration (26%), education (8%), and information technology (5%). In an average class, 5% graduate in 3 years or less, 25% graduate in 4 years or less, 37% graduate in 5 years or less, and 77% graduate in 6 years or less. 77 companies recruited on campus in 2002-2003. Of the 2002 graduating class, 14% were enrolled in graduate school within 6 months of graduation and 94% were employed.

Admissions Contact: John Guffey, Dean of Admissions. A video is available. E-mail: *admissions@lindenwood.edu* Web: *www.lindenwood.edu*

MARYVILLE UNIVERSITY OF SAINT LOUIS   D-2
St. Louis, MO 63141-7299   (314) 529-9350
1-(800) 627-9855, ext.9350; Fax: (314) 529-9927

Full-time: 387 men, 1131 women	**Faculty:** 82; IIA, --$
Part-time: 271 men, 916 women	**Ph.D.s:** 90%
Graduate: 143 men, 453 women	**Student/Faculty:** 19 to 1
Year: semesters, summer session	**Tuition:** $15,440
Application Deadline: open	**Room & Board:** $6650
Freshman Class: n/av	
ACT: 24	**VERY COMPETITIVE**

Maryville University of Saint Louis, established in 1872, is an independent institution offering undergraduate programs in arts, sciences, business, education, and health-related fields and graduate programs in business administration, education, health administration, nursing, occupational therapy, physical therapy, and rehabilitation counseling. There are 4 undergraduate and 3 graduate schools. In addition to regional accreditation, Maryville has baccalaureate program accreditation with ACBSP, AOTA, APTA, CCNE, CORE, FIDER, NASAD, NASM, NCATE, and NLN. The library contains 205,512 volumes, 487,824 microform items, and 10,933 audio/video tapes/CDs, and subscribes to 9004 periodicals. Computerized library services include the card catalog, interlibrary loans, database searching, and Internet access. Special learning facilities include a learning resource center, art gallery, observatory, teaching lab, art and design labs, clinical labs for nursing, occupational therapy, and physical therapy, a communications lab, video conferencing facilities on all campuses, 4 multimedia-ready classrooms, and residence hall computer labs. The 130-acre campus is in a suburban area 20 miles west of downtown St. Louis. Including any residence halls, there are 18 buildings.

Student Life: 92% of undergraduates are from Missouri. Students are from 18 states, 23 foreign countries, and Canada. 80% are from public schools. 72% are white. 62% claim no religious affiliation; 16% Catholic; 7% Protestant. The average age of freshmen is 18; all undergraduates, 27. 26% do not continue beyond their first year; 69% remain to graduate.

Housing: 450 students can be accommodated in college housing, which includes single-sex and coed dorms and on-campus apartments. On-campus housing is available on a first-come, first-served basis. 70% of students commute. All students may keep cars.

Activities: There are no fraternities or sororities. There are 33 groups on campus, including art, band, cheerleading, chorale, dance, departmental, drama, ethnic, honors, international, jazz band, literary magazine, newspaper, political, professional, religious, social, social service, and student government. Popular campus events include Christmas tree-lighting ceremony, Fall Festival, and Cram Jam.

Sports: There are 6 intercollegiate sports for men and 6 for women, and 8 intramural sports for men and 8 for women. Facilities include an outdoor swimming pool, tennis courts, soccer, softball, and baseball fields, a gym, outdoor and indoor basketball hoops, an expanded fitness center, a student center with table tennis and billiards, a sand volleyball court, and outdoor walking and hiking trails.

Disabled Students: 90% of the campus is accessible. Wheelchair ramps, elevators, special parking, specially equipped rest rooms, special class scheduling, lowered drinking fountains, lowered telephones, electronic doors, note takers, and interpreters for the hearing impaired are available.

Services: Counseling and information services are available, as is tutoring in every subject. There is a reader service for the blind. There also is a writing center, learning styles inventorying, and help with time management and test-taking skills, and there are study skills materials, workshops, and individual consultations.

Campus Safety and Security: Measures include 24-hour foot and vehicle patrol, self-defense education, security escort services, and pamphlets/posters/films. There are emergency telephones, lighted pathways/sidewalks, video security systems in residence halls, and security key operated dorm entrances.

Programs of Study: Maryville confers B.A., B.S., B.F.A., B.S.C.L.S., B.S.M.T., and B.S.N. degrees. Master's degrees are also awarded. Bachelor's degrees are awarded in AGRICULTURE (environmental studies), BIOLOGICAL SCIENCE (biology/biological science), BUSINESS (accounting, business administration and management, electronic business, marketing/retailing/merchandising, and organizational behavior), COMMUNICATIONS AND THE ARTS (communications, English, graphic design, and studio art), COMPUTER AND PHYSICAL SCIENCE (actuarial science, chemistry, computer science, information sciences and systems, mathematics, and science), EDUCATION (art, early childhood, elementary, middle school, and secondary), ENGINEERING AND ENVIRONMENTAL DESIGN (environmental science and interior design), HEALTH PROFESSIONS (clinical science, health care administration, health science, music therapy, and nursing), SOCIAL SCIENCE (criminology, history, liberal arts/general studies, paralegal studies, psychology, and sociology). Actuarial science, education, and physical therapy are the strongest academically. Nursing, business administration, and accounting are the largest.

Required: To graduate, all students must complete a minimum of 128 credit hours, with a minimum GPA of 2.0. The core curriculum consists of 12 credit hours each of humanities, math and science, and social and behavioral science, and 8 credit hours each of communication skills and fine arts. 48 upper-division credits must be completed.

Special: There is cross-registration with Missouri Baptist College and Fontbonne, Webster, and Lindenwood Universities. Students may choose internships in various fields, and cooperative programs are available with such employers as Edward Jones, Daimler Chrysler, Smith Barney, Verizon Wireless, Gateway, the U.S. Army Corps of Engineers, IBM, Citimortgage, Northwestern Mutual, and Walgreens. Other options include dual and student-designed majors, study abroad in England, Japan, Korea, China, and other countries, a Washington semester, nondegree study, and pass-fail grading. A 3-2 engineering degree is available in conjunction with Washington University. There are 8 national honor societies and a freshman honors program.

Faculty/Classroom: 37% of faculty are male; 63%, female. 71% teach undergraduates. No introductory courses are taught by graduate students. The average class size in an introductory lecture is 17; in a laboratory, 15; and in a regular course, 16.

Admissions: The ACT scores for the 2003-2004 freshman class were: 22% below 21, 28% between 21 and 23, 31% between 24 and 26, 10% between 27 and 28, and 9% above 28. 49% of the current freshmen were in the top fifth of their class; 76% were in the top two fifths. 4 freshmen graduated first in their class.

Requirements: The SAT I or ACT is required. In addition, students must have graduated from an accredited secondary school with 22 academic credits or have the GED. Expected preparatory courses include 4 units of English, 3 of math, and 2 each of science and social studies, plus 3 additional units in any of the perceding areas or in a foreign language. Some majors have additional admission requirements. A GPA of 2.5 is required. AP and CLEP credits are accepted. Important factors in the admissions decision are recommendations by school officials, advanced placement or honor courses, and leadership record.

Procedure: Freshmen are admitted to all sessions. Entrance exams should be taken during the junior year. There is a rolling admissions plan. Application deadlines are open. The application fee is $25. Notification is sent on a rolling basis. Applications are accepted on computer disk and on-line through the university's web site.

Transfer: 403 transfer students enrolled in 2002-2003. A minimum GPA of 2.0, or higher for some majors, is required. Some majors may require ACT or SAT I scores. 30 of 128 credits required for the bachelor's degree must be completed at Maryville.

Visiting: There are regularly scheduled orientations for prospective students, including visiting the campus and arranging a personal interview with an admissions counselor. There are guides for informal visits and visitors may sit in on classes and stay overnight. To schedule a visit, contact the Admissions Office.

Financial Aid: In 2003-2004, 98% of all full-time freshmen and 76% of continuing full-time students received some form of financial aid. 76% of full-time freshmen and 68% of continuing full-time students received need-based aid. The average freshman award was $12,409. Need-based scholarships or need-based grants averaged $12,106 ($18,800 maximum); need-based self-help aid (loans and jobs) averaged $8489 ($21,960 maximum); non-need-based awards and non-need-based scholarships averaged $5549 ($21,850 maximum); and parental loans averaged $17,085 ($20,400 maximum). 17% of undergraduates work part time. Average annual earnings from campus work are $1655. The average financial indebtedness of the 2003 graduate was $11,167. Maryville is a member of CSS. The FAFSA is required. The priority date for freshman financial aid applications for fall entry is March 1. The deadline for filing freshman financial aid applications for fall entry is April 1.

International Students: There are 45 international students enrolled. The school actively recruits these students. They must score 500 on the written TOEFL or 173 on the electronic version.

Computers: The mainframe is an HP 9000K210. There are more than 400 IBM and Mac PCs available for academic use at several computer centers, residence halls, and the library. All students may access the system in the computer center lab from 8 A.M. to 10 P.M.; 24-hour access is available from 2 residence halls. There are no time limits and no fees.

Graduates: From July 1, 2002 to June 30, 2003, 558 bachelor's degrees were awarded. The most popular majors were information systems (10%), business administration (8%), and nursing (8%). In an average class, 55% graduate in 4 years or less, 67% graduate in 5 years or less, and 69% graduate in 6 years or less. 62 companies recruited on campus in 2002-2003.

Admissions Contact: Lynn Jackson, Director of Admissions. A video is available. E-mail: admissions@maryville.edu Web: www.maryville.edu

MISSOURI BAPTIST UNIVERSITY — D-2
St. Louis, MO 63141-8660

(314) 392-2296
(877) 434-1115; Fax: (314) 434-7596

Full-time: 452 men, 568 women	Faculty: 46; IIB, --$
Part-time: 709 men, 1218 women	Ph.D.s: 56%
Graduate: 131 men, 578 women	Student/Faculty: 22 to 1
Year: semesters, summer session	Tuition: $12,210
Application Deadline: open	Room & Board: $5800
Freshman Class: 712 applied, 507 accepted, 210 enrolled	
ACT: 21	COMPETITIVE

Missouri Baptist University, formerly Missouri Baptist College and established in 1964, is a private liberal arts institution affiliated with the Missouri Baptist Convention. There are 6 undergraduate schools and 1 graduate school. The library contains 103,747 volumes, 52,216 microform items, and 4327 audio/video tapes/CDs, and subscribes to 446 periodicals. Computerized library services include the card catalog, interlibrary loans, and database searching. Special learning facilities include an audiovisual production lab. The 63-acre campus is in a suburban area 15 miles west of St. Louis. Including any residence halls, there are 6 buildings.

Student Life: 94% of undergraduates are from Missouri. Students are from 19 states, 22 foreign countries, and Canada. 71% are from public schools. 88% are white. 46% are Protestant; 31% claim no religious affiliation; 16% are Catholic. The average age of freshmen is 19; all undergraduates, 22. 36% do not continue beyond their first year.

Housing: 260 students can be accommodated in college housing, which includes single-sex dorms and off-campus apartments. In addition, there are honors houses. On-campus housing is available on a first-come, first-served basis. 70% of students commute. Alcohol is not permitted. All students may keep cars.

Activities: There are no fraternities or sororities. There are 31 groups on campus, including band, business, cheerleading, choir, chorale, chorus, computers, drama, film, honors, international, jazz band, literary magazine, musical theater, opera, political, professional, religious, student government, and yearbook. Popular campus events include Spring Musical, Christmas Concert, and Hanging of the Green.

Sports: There are 7 intercollegiate sports for men and 5 for women, and 4 intramural sports for men and 4 for women. Facilities include a gym, weight training rooms, a game room, and baseball, softball, and soccer fields.

Disabled Students: 64% of the campus is accessible. Wheelchair ramps, elevators, special parking, specially equipped rest rooms, and lowered drinking fountains are available.

Services: Counseling and information services are available, as is tutoring in some subjects, by arrangement. There is a reader service for the blind, remedial math and writing, and a writing lab.

Campus Safety and Security: Measures include 24-hour foot and vehicle patrol, self-defense education, and lighted pathways/sidewalks.

Programs of Study: MBU confers B.A., B.S., B.M., B.P.S., B.S.E., and B.S.N. degrees. Associate and master's degrees are also awarded. Bachelor's degrees are awarded in BIOLOGICAL SCIENCE (biology/biological science), BUSINESS (accounting, business administration and management, management science, and sports management), COMMUNICATIONS AND THE ARTS (communications, English, and music performance), COMPUTER AND PHYSICAL SCIENCE (chemistry, information sciences and systems, mathematics, and science), EDUCATION (athletic training, early childhood, elementary, middle school, and music), HEALTH PROFESSIONS (health science, nursing, and sports medicine), SOCIAL SCIENCE (behavioral science, child psychology/development, criminal justice, history, human services, ministries, physical fitness/movement, psychology, religion, religious education, religious music, and social science). Education, business, and religion are the strongest academically. Education, business, and communications are the largest.

Required: All students must take courses in the humanities/fine arts, social and behavorial sciences, natural sciences, phys ed, computer literacy, and Old and New Testament history. A minimum GPA of 2.0 is required (some majors require a GPA of 2.5 or better). To graduate, students must complete at least 128 credit hours, with a minimum of 30 hours in the major and 45 hours of upper-division courses; pass a general education exam and an exit exam or other assessment in the major; and complete a capstone project.

Special: There is cross-registration with Fontbonne College and Maryville, Lindenwood, and Webster Universities. Students may opt for credit by examination, nondegree study, and student-designed majors. A 3-2 engineering degree with the University of Missouri/Columbia or a 2-2 engineering degree with the University of Missouri/Rolla is available. Study abroad is possible at Harlaxton College in England and at Hong Kong Baptist University. MBU also offers internships in various disciplines and dual majors in some business and education fields. There are 5 national honor societies.

Faculty/Classroom: 60% of faculty are male; 40%, female. 94% teach undergraduates. No introductory courses are taught by graduate stu-

dents. The average class size in an introductory lecture is 22; in a laboratory, 10; and in a regular course, 13.

Admissions: 71% of the 2003-2004 applicants were accepted. The ACT scores for the 2003-2004 freshman class were: 46% below 21, 20% between 21 and 23, 21% between 24 and 26, 8% between 27 and 28, and 5% above 28. 26% of the current freshmen were in the top fifth of their class; 55% were in the top two fifths. In a recent year, 4 freshmen graduated first in their class.

Requirements: The ACT or SAT I is required, with a minimum score of 18 on the ACT or 800 on the SAT I. In addition, applicants must be graduates of an accredited secondary school. GED and home-schooled students are accepted. MBU requires applicants to be in the upper 50% of their class. A GPA of 2.0 is required. AP and CLEP credits are accepted. Important factors in the admissions decision are advanced placement or honor courses, leadership record, and evidence of special talent.

Procedure: Freshmen are admitted to all sessions. Entrance exams should be taken in the junior year. Application deadlines are open. The application fee is $25. There is a rolling admissions plan. Applications are accepted on-line through the school's web site.

Transfer: 235 transfer students enrolled in a recent year. Applicants must have a 2.0 GPA, with some programs requiring 2.5 or better. Students must submit official transcripts from all previous colleges attended, along with a character reference. 24 of 128 credits required for the bachelor's degree must be completed at MBU.

Visiting: There are regularly scheduled orientations for prospective students, consisting of Welcome Weekend, open houses, and campus tours. There are guides for informal visits and visitors may sit in on classes and stay overnight. To schedule a visit, contact the Admissions Office at *admissions@mobap.edu.*

Financial Aid: In 2003-2004, 88% of all full-time freshmen and 83% of continuing full-time students received some form of financial aid. 50% of full-time freshmen and 67% of continuing full-time students received need-based aid. The average freshman award was $5634. 6% of undergraduates work part time. Average annual earnings from campus work are $1133. The FAFSA and the college's own financial statement are required. Check with the school for current deadlines.

International Students: In a recent year, there were 35 international students enrolled. They must score 500 on the written TOEFL or 173 on the electronic version and also take the ACT or the SAT I, scoring 18 on the ACT. Those with a TOEFL between 430 and 499 (paper) or 117 and 172 (electronic) are eligible for provisional admission and must take the Intensive English sequence.

Computers: On the main campus there are 30 PCs available for academic use in the computer lab, 2 labs with 5 PCs each in the residence halls, a music lab with Macs, an education lab with Macs, a math/science lab with 5 PCs, and an additional 14 PCs in the library. All are networked and have access to the Internet and the Web. All residence hall rooms are networked and Internet-ready for students who bring their own PCs to campus. All students may access the system. There are no time limits. The fee is $4 per credit hour.

Graduates: In a recent year, 170 bachelor's degrees were awarded. The most popular majors were elementary education (21%), business administration (12%), and psychology (8%). In an average class, 42% graduate in 6 years or less. 63 companies recruited on campus in a recent year.

Admissions Contact: Jon Hessel, Director of Admissions.
E-mail: *admissions@mobap.edu* Web: *www.mobap.edu*

MISSOURI SOUTHERN STATE UNIVERSITY	A-4
Joplin, MO 64801-1595	(417) 782-6772
	(866) 818-6778; Fax: (417) 659-4429

Full-time: 1494 men, 2037 women	**Faculty:** 198; IIB, -$
Part-time: 698 men, 1181 women	**Ph.D.s:** n/av
Graduate: none	**Student/Faculty:** 18 to 1
Year: semesters, summer session	**Tuition:** $3976 ($7786)
Application Deadline: August 21	**Room & Board:** $4340
Freshman Class: 1771 applied, 1317 accepted, 692 enrolled	
ACT: 22	**COMPETITIVE**

Missouri Southern State University, formerly Missouri Southern State College and founded in 1937, is a public, primarily commuter institution offering undergraduate degree programs in the arts and sciences, business, education, psychology, and technology. International or global education is a distinctive theme of the college mission. There are 4 undergraduate schools. In addition to regional accreditation, Missouri Southern has baccalaureate program accreditation with ABET, ACBSP, ADA, NAACLS, NCATE, and NLN. Computerized library services include the card catalog, interlibrary loans, database searching, and Internet access. Special learning facilities include a learning resource center, art gallery, radio station, TV station, a biology pond, a child development center, a crime lab, a small business development center, a performing arts center, a greenhouse, and an international trade and quality center. The 334-acre campus is in a small town in the southwest corner

of the state, 138 miles south of Kansas City. Including any residence halls, there are 40 buildings.

Student Life: 87% of undergraduates are from Missouri. Students are from 50 states. 90% are white. The average age of freshmen is 21; all undergraduates, 27. 29% of freshmen remain to graduate.

Housing: 750 students can be accommodated in college housing, which includes single-sex dorms and on-campus apartments. On-campus housing is available on a first-come, first-served basis. 92% of students commute. Alcohol is not permitted. All students may keep cars.

Activities: 1% of men belong to 2 national fraternities; 1% of women belong to 2 national sororities. There are many groups and organizations on campus, including art, band, cheerleading, chess, choir, chorale, chorus, computers, dance, debate, drama, ethnic, film, forensics, honors, international, jazz band, literary magazine, marching band, musical theater, newspaper, orchestra, pep band, photography, political, professional, radio and TV, religious, social, social service, student government, and symphony. Popular campus events include Spring Fling, Natural High, and Welcome Week.

Sports: Facilities include a 10,000-seat Astroturf football stadium, a 4000-seat gym, a 4000-seat auditorium, a natatorium, a student life center, a black-box theater, a 3240-seat gym with a basketball court, a 6-lane 200-meter indoor track, a training and weight room, a cross-country course, and soccer, softball, and baseball fields.

Disabled Students: 99% of the campus is accessible. Wheelchair ramps, elevators, special parking, specially equipped rest rooms, special class scheduling, lowered drinking fountains, lowered telephones, and special housing are available.

Services: There is a reader service for the blind, and remedial math, reading, and writing. Assistance is also provided for improving time management and test-taking skills.

Campus Safety and Security: Measures include 24-hour foot and vehicle patrol, security escort services, informal discussions, and pamphlets/posters/films. There are lighted pathways/sidewalks.

Programs of Study: Missouri Southern confers B.A., B.S., B.G.S., B.S.B.A., and B.S.E. degrees. Associate degrees are also awarded. Bachelor's degrees are awarded in BIOLOGICAL SCIENCE (biology/biological science, biotechnology, ecology, genetics, marine biology, and microbiology), BUSINESS (accounting, banking and finance, business administration and management, business economics, international business management, management information systems, management science, and marketing/retailing/merchandising), COMMUNICATIONS AND THE ARTS (art, communications, dramatic arts, English, fine arts, French, German, graphic design, music, Spanish, and speech/debate/rhetoric), COMPUTER AND PHYSICAL SCIENCE (chemistry, computer mathematics, computer science, information sciences and systems, mathematics, and physics), EDUCATION (art, business, drama, early childhood, elementary, English, foreign languages, health, mathematics, middle school, music, physical, reading, science, secondary, social science, social studies, and special), ENGINEERING AND ENVIRONMENTAL DESIGN (computer technology and manufacturing technology), HEALTH PROFESSIONS (environmental health science, medical laboratory technology, nursing, physical therapy, predentistry, premedicine, preoptometry, prepharmacy, and preveterinary science), SOCIAL SCIENCE (criminal justice, economics, history, international studies, liberal arts/general studies, political science/government, psychology, social science, social studies, and sociology). Preengineering and physical science are the strongest academically. Business, education, and criminal justice are the largest.

Required: General education requirements include a total of 51 credit hours, with 15 in basic studies, 12 each in science and cultural studies, 9 in humanities, and 3 in international studies. Students must also demonstrate proficiency in computer skills and writing. To graduate, students must complete at least 124 credit hours, including a minimum of 40 in the major, and present a minimum GPA of 2.0, 2.75 for the B.S.E.

Special: There are co-op programs in radiological and medical technology, respiratory therapy, paramedical studies, aviation, and engineering. Students may study abroad at Oxford or Cambridge and in 100 countries through ISEP. Missouri Southern also offers internships in many majors, accelerated degree programs in all majors, a 3-2 engineering degree with the University of Missouri-Rolla, a general studies degree, and credit for life experience. Nondegree study is possible. There are 13 national honor societies, a freshman honors program, and 1 departmental honors program.

Faculty/Classroom: 60% of faculty are male; 40%, female. All teach undergraduates.

Admissions: 74% of the 2003-2004 applicants were accepted. The ACT scores for the 2003-2004 freshman class were: 50% below 21, 18% between 21 and 23, 18% between 24 and 26, 7% between 27 and 28, and 7% above 28. 25% of the current freshmen were in the top fifth of their class; 50% were in the top two fifths. 14 freshmen graduated first in their class.

Requirements: The ACT is required, with a minimum composite score of 18. Applicants must be graduates of accredited secondary schools or have earned a GED. The college requires completion of 16 Carnegie units in core courses for high school graduates. AP and CLEP credits are accepted. Advanced placement or honor courses is an important factor in the admission decision.

Procedure: Freshmen are admitted to all sessions. Entrance exams should be taken during the junior or senior year of high school. There is a deferred admissions plan. Applications should be filed by August 21 for fall entry, January 15 for spring entry, and June 5 for summer entry. The fall 2003 application fee was $15. Notification is sent on a rolling basis. Applications are accepted on computer disk and on-line through the university's web site.

Transfer: 407 transfer students enrolled in 2002-2003. Applicants must have a GPA of 2.0. They must be able to return to their previous college. 30 of 124 credits required for the bachelor's degree must be completed at Missouri Southern.

Visiting: There are regularly scheduled orientations for prospective students, including a preenrollment tour during the summer. There are guides for informal visits and visitors may sit in on classes and stay overnight. To schedule a visit, contact the Admissions Office.

Financial Aid: The FAFSA is required. The deadline for filing freshman financial aid applications for fall entry is August 1.

International Students: There are 114 international students enrolled. The school actively recruits these students. They must score 535 on the written TOEFL or take the MELAB. They must also take the ACT, scoring 18.

Computers: The mainframe is an ES/9000 with USE/ESA. There are 455 Windows-based PCs in open student labs equipped with Internet and productivity software. Also available are some 25 Macs equipped with productivity software, some with Internet capability. All students may access the system. There are no time limits. The fee is $20.

Graduates: From July 1, 2002 to June 30, 2003, 679 bachelor's degrees were awarded. The most popular majors were business (21%), education (16%), and criminal justice (14%). In an average class, 10% graduate in 4 years or less, 25% graduate in 5 years or less, and 29% graduate in 6 years or less.

Admissions Contact: Derek S. Skaggs, Director of Enrollment Services. E-mail: *admissions@mssu.edu* Web: *http://www.mssu.edu*

MISSOURI VALLEY COLLEGE
Marshall, MO 65340

B-2

(660) 831-4157; Fax: (660) 831-4039

Full-time: 790 men, 515 women	**Faculty:** 57
Part-time: 100 men, 160 women	**Ph.D.s:** 58%
Graduate: none	**Student/Faculty:** 23 to 1
Year: 4-1-4, summer session	**Tuition:** $13,300
Application Deadline: open	**Room & Board:** $5200
Freshman Class: 1363 applied, 898 accepted, 625 enrolled	
ACT: 20	**COMPETITIVE**

Missouri Valley College, founded in 1889, is a private liberal arts college, affiliated with the Presbyterian Church (U.S.A.), offering 25 majors. Some figures in the above capsule and in this profile are approximate. The library contains 71,000 volumes, 1700 microform items, and 1100 audio/video tapes/CDs, and subscribes to 400 periodicals. Computerized library services include interlibrary loans and database searching. Special learning facilities include a learning resource center, radio station, and TV station. The 140-acre campus is in a small town 80 miles from Kansas City and 150 miles from St. Louis. Including any residence halls, there are 17 buildings.

Student Life: 66% of undergraduates are from Missouri. Students are from 43 states, 9 foreign countries, and Canada. 75% are from public schools. 79% are white; 13% African American. 73% are Protestant; 20% Catholic. The average age of freshmen is 19; all undergraduates, 21. 25% do not continue beyond their first year; 20% remain to graduate.

Housing: 1100 students can be accommodated in college housing, which includes single-sex dorms, on-campus apartments, married-student housing, fraternity houses, and sorority houses. In addition, there are honors houses and special-interest houses. On-campus housing is guaranteed for all 4 years. 81% of students live on campus; of those, 50% remain on campus on weekends. Alcohol is not permitted. All students may keep cars.

Activities: 30% of men belong to 4 national fraternities; 20% of women belong to 3 national sororities. There are 40 groups on campus, including art, band, cheerleading, choir, chorale, chorus, computers, dance, drama, drill team, ethnic, film, honors, international, jazz band, literary magazine, musical theater, newspaper, orchestra, pep band, photography, radio and TV, religious, SADD, social, social service, student government, symphony, and yearbook. Popular campus events include Springfest and Parents Weekend.

Sports: There are 8 intercollegiate sports for men and 7 for women, and 7 intramural sports for men and 7 for women. Facilities include a 2000-seat gym, tennis and basketball courts, football and soccer fields, a 1000-seat stadium, and horse stables.

Disabled Students: 20% of the campus is accessible. Wheelchair ramps, elevators, special parking, specially equipped rest rooms, special class scheduling, and lowered drinking fountains are available.

Services: Counseling and information services are available, as is tutoring in most subjects. There is remedial math, reading, and writing.

Campus Safety and Security: Measures include security escort services, informal discussions, pamphlets/posters/films, and emergency telephones. There are lighted pathways/sidewalks and a 5 P.M. to 3 A.M. foot and vehicle patrol.

Programs of Study: MVC confers B.A. and B.S. degrees. Associate degrees are also awarded. Bachelor's degrees are awarded in AGRICULTURE (agricultural business management), BIOLOGICAL SCIENCE (biology/biological science), BUSINESS (accounting, business administration and management, and recreational facilities management), COMMUNICATIONS AND THE ARTS (art, communications, dramatic arts, English, and speech/debate/rhetoric), COMPUTER AND PHYSICAL SCIENCE (actuarial science, information sciences and systems, and mathematics), EDUCATION (elementary, physical, and social studies), HEALTH PROFESSIONS (exercise science), SOCIAL SCIENCE (addiction studies, criminal justice, economics, history, human services, liberal arts/general studies, philosophy, political science/government, psychology, public administration, religion, and sociology). Education is the strongest academically. Business administration, phys ed, and psychology are the largest.

Required: All students must complete 128 credit hours, including 35 to 40 hours in their major, with a GPA of at least 2.0. Distribution requirements include the 40-hour core curriculum of English, phys ed, math, fine arts, and science. A computer course is strongly recommended. All students must complete a senior assessment.

Special: Accelerated degree programs, internships, work-study, co-op programs, nondegree study, and pass/fail options are available. There are 3 national honor societies and 3 departmental honors programs.

Faculty/Classroom: 73% of faculty are male; 27%, female. All teach undergraduates. The average class size in an introductory lecture is 30; in a laboratory, 25; and in a regular course, 28.

Admissions: 66% of the 2003-2004 applicants were accepted. There were 5 National Merit semifinalists.

Requirements: The SAT I or ACT is required. In addition, students must have graduated from an accredited secondary school or have the GED. A GPA of 2.0 is required. AP and CLEP credits are accepted. Important factors in the admissions decision are advanced placement or honor courses, evidence of special talent, and extracurricular activities record.

Procedure: Freshmen are admitted to all sessions. Entrance exams should be taken as early as possible. Application deadlines are open. Application fee is $15. Applications are accepted on-line.

Transfer: A minimum GPA of 2.0 is recommended; D grades do not transfer. 30 of 128 credits required for the bachelor's degree must be completed at MVC.

Visiting: There are regularly scheduled orientations for prospective students, including jump-start days in the summer and registration days during the school year. There are guides for informal visits and visitors may sit in on classes and stay overnight. To schedule a visit, contact the Admission Coordinator at (660) 831-4114.

Financial Aid: MVC is a member of CSS. The FAFSA is required. Check with the school for current application deadlines.

International Students: The school actively recruits these students. They must take the TOEFL and also the SAT I or the ACT.

Computers: 150 PCs and Macs are available on campus. Free access to the Internet is available to students on 25 computers in the library. All students may access the system. There are no time limits and no fees. It is strongly recommended that all students have a personal computer. An IBM is recommended.

Admissions Contact: Jamie L. Gold-Naylor, Director of Student Affairs. E-mail: *naylorj@moval.edu* Web: *www.moval.edu*

MISSOURI WESTERN STATE COLLEGE
St. Joseph, MO 64507

A-2

(816) 271-4266
(800) 662-7041; Fax: (816) 271-5833

Full-time: 1526 men, 2178 women	**Faculty:** 180; IIB, -$
Part-time: 435 men, 789 women	**Ph.D.s:** 81%
Graduate: none	**Student/Faculty:** 21 to 1
Year: semesters, summer session	**Tuition:** $4464 ($8040)
Application Deadline: July 25	**Room & Board:** $4058
Freshman Class: 2789 applied, 2789 accepted, 1234 enrolled	
ACT: 19	**NONCOMPETITIVE**

Missouri Western State College, founded in 1915, is a public institution offering undergraduate degrees in the arts and sciences, business administration, education, nursing, technology, and social work. There are 2 undergraduate schools. In addition to regional accreditation, Western has baccalaureate program accreditation with ABET, CSWE, NASM, NCATE, and NLN. The library contains 207,383 volumes, 111,544 microform items, and 16,024 audio/video tapes/CDs, and subscribes to 1504 periodicals. Computerized library services include the card catalog, interlibrary loans, and database searching. Special learning facilities include a learning resource center, planetarium, and a biology nature study area. The 740-acre campus is in a suburban area 50 miles north of Kansas City. Including any residence halls, there are 15 buildings.

Student Life: 91% of undergraduates are from Missouri. Students are from 35 states, 10 foreign countries, and Canada. 86% are white; 11% African American. The average age of freshmen is 20; all undergraduates, 24. 44% do not continue beyond their first year; 29% remain to graduate.

Housing: 1050 students can be accommodated in college housing, which includes single-sex and coed dorms and on-campus apartments. On-campus housing is available on a first-come, first-served basis. 80% of students commute. Alcohol is not permitted. All students may keep cars.

Activities: 7% of men belong to 5 national fraternities; 3% of women belong to 7 national sororities. There are 51 groups on campus, including art, band, cheerleading, choir, dance, drama, drill team, ethnic, honors, international, jazz band, marching band, musical theater, newspaper, pep band, political, professional, religious, social, social service, student government, symphony, and yearbook. Popular campus events include Spring Fest, Fall Convocation, and Family Day.

Sports: There are 4 intercollegiate sports for men and 5 for women, and 20 intramural sports for men and 20 for women. Facilities include tennis and racquetball courts, a 6000-seat football stadium, a 468-seat auditorium, a swimming pool, a jogging/walking trail, a fitness center, baseball and softball fields, a trapshooting range, a volleyball area, a track, and 2 gyms, the larger seating 4000.

Disabled Students: 99% of the campus is accessible. Wheelchair ramps, elevators, special parking, specially equipped rest rooms, lowered drinking fountains, and lowered telephones are available.

Services: Counseling and information services are available, as is tutoring in some subjects. There is a reader service for the blind and remedial math, reading, and writing.

Campus Safety and Security: Measures include 24-hour foot and vehicle patrol, self-defense education, security escort services, and informal discussions. There are pamphlets/posters/films, emergency telephones, and lighted pathways/sidewalks.

Programs of Study: Western confers B.A., B.S., B.I.S., B.S.B.A., B.S.E., B.S.N., B.S.T., and B.S.W. degrees. Associate degrees are also awarded. Bachelor's degrees are awarded in BIOLOGICAL SCIENCE (biology/biological science), BUSINESS (accounting, business administration and management, and marketing/retailing/merchandising), COMMUNICATIONS AND THE ARTS (communications, English, fine arts, French, graphic design, music, Spanish, and speech/debate/rhetoric), COMPUTER AND PHYSICAL SCIENCE (chemistry, computer programming, computer science, information sciences and systems, mathematics, and natural sciences), EDUCATION (art, early childhood, elementary, foreign languages, middle school, music, and secondary), ENGINEERING AND ENVIRONMENTAL DESIGN (engineering technology), HEALTH PROFESSIONS (medical laboratory technology and nursing), SOCIAL SCIENCE (criminal justice, economics, history, parks and recreation management, political science/government, psychology, and social work). Physical sciences is the strongest academically. Education, nursing, and criminal justice are the largest.

Required: The core curriculum consists of 12 credit hours of basic skills (English composition, algebra, and speech), 9 to 10 of humanities, 9 of social sciences, 8 to 10 of natural sciences, and 4 of physical health. To graduate, students must complete at least 124 credit hours, including 45 to 71 in the major, with a minimum GPA of 2.0.

Special: MWSC offers internships, work-study programs with local employers, dual majors, a 3-2 engineering degree program with the University of Missouri/Rolla, credit for life experience, pass/fail options, and nondegree study. There are 6 national honor societies, a freshman honors program, and 12 departmental honors programs.

Faculty/Classroom: 59% of faculty are male; 41%, female. All teach undergraduates. The average class size in an introductory lecture is 35; in a laboratory, 25; and in a regular course, 25.

Admissions: All of the 2003-2004 applicants were accepted. There is an open admissions policy. The ACT scores for the 2003-2004 freshman class were: 65% below 21, 21% between 21 and 23, 9% between 24 and 26, 4% between 27 and 28, and 1% above 28. 18% of the current freshmen were in the top fifth of their class; 44% were in the top two fifths. 14 freshmen graduated first in their class.

Requirements: The ACT is required. In addition, applicants must be graduates of an accredited secondary school or have earned a GED. AP and CLEP credits are accepted.

Procedure: Freshmen are admitted to all sessions. Entrance exams should be taken at least 6 months prior to enrollment. Applications should be filed by July 25 for fall entry, December 20 for spring entry, and May 15 for summer entry, along with a $15 fee. The college accepts all applicants.

Transfer: 269 transfer students enrolled in 2002-2003. The required GPA depends on the number of credit hours completed, but a minimum of 2.0 is standard. 30 of 124 credits required for the bachelor's degree must be completed at Western.

Visiting: There are regularly scheduled orientations for prospective students. There are guides for informal visits. To schedule a visit, contact the Admissions Office at admissn@mwsc.edu.

Financial Aid: In 2003-2004, 80% of all full-time freshmen and 85% of continuing full-time students received some form of financial aid. 70% of full-time freshmen and 80% of continuing full-time students received need-based aid. 69% of undergraduates work part time. Average annual earnings from campus work are $1900. The FAFSA is required. The deadline for filing freshman financial aid applications for fall entry is March 1.

International Students: There are 17 international students enrolled. They must score 500 on the written TOEFL and also take the ACT.

Computers: The mainframes are an HP 3000/ Models 58 and 42/ and an IBM RISC/6000 UNIX system. About 300 PCs are available, most in departmental labs and nearly 50 in other areas for general student access. About 30 terminals are also available. Students have access to e-mail and to the Internet. A PC lab is located in the residence complex. All students may access the system. There are no time limits. The fee is $4 per credit hour. This fee is included in the required fees.

Graduates: From July 1, 2002 to June 30, 2003, 758 bachelor's degrees were awarded. The most popular majors were management (15%), criminal justice (15%), and elementary education (7%). In an average class, 12% graduate in 4 years or less, 24% graduate in 5 years or less, and 29% graduate in 6 years or less. Of the 2002 graduating class, 20% were enrolled in graduate school within 6 months of graduation and 90% were employed.

Admissions Contact: Howard McCauley, Director of Admissions. A video is available. E-mail: admissn@mwsc.edu Web: www.mwsc.edu

---

NORTHWEST MISSOURI STATE UNIVERSITY A-1
Maryville, MO 64468
(660) 562-1722
(800) 633-1175; Fax: (660) 562-1121

Full-time: 2200 men, 2800 women	Faculty: 244; IIA, --$
Part-time: 300 men, 350 women	Ph.Ds: 71%
Graduate: 290 men, 740 women	Student/Faculty: 20 to 1
Year: trimesters, summer session	Tuition: $4522 ($7798)
Application Deadline: open	Room & Board: $4812
Freshman Class: 2700 applied, 2400 accepted, 1215 enrolled	
SAT I or ACT: required	COMPETITIVE

Northwest Missouri State University, founded in 1905, is a public institution offering undergraduate courses in agriculture, science, arts and humanities, business, government, computer science, and education. Some information in the above capsule is approximate. There are 3 undergraduate schools and 1 graduate school. In addition to regional accreditation, Northwest has baccalaureate program accreditation with ADA, AHEA, NASM, and NCATE. The library contains 286,302 volumes, 15,864 microform items, and 1937 audio/video tapes/CDs, and subscribes to 3411 periodicals. Computerized library services include the card catalog, interlibrary loans, and database searching. Special learning facilities include a learning resource center, art gallery, radio station, TV station, and a model elementary library collection with curriculum materials for grades K-6. The 240-acre campus is in a rural area 90 miles north of Kansas City. Including any residence halls, there are 33 buildings.

Student Life: 66% of undergraduates are from Missouri. Students are from 41 states, 23 foreign countries, and Canada. 95% are from public schools. 93% are white. The average age of freshmen is 19; all undergraduates, 21. 35% do not continue beyond their first year; 40% remain to graduate.

Housing: 2800 students can be accommodated in college housing, which includes single-sex and coed dorms and sorority houses. On-campus housing is guaranteed for all 4 years. 51% of students live on campus; of those, 65% remain on campus on weekends. Alcohol is not permitted. All students may keep cars.

Activities: 10% of men belong to 9 national fraternities; 10% of women belong to 5 national sororities. There are 162 groups on campus, including band, cheerleading, choir, chorale, chorus, computers, drama, drill team, drum and bugle corps, ethnic, international, jazz band, literary magazine, marching band, newspaper, pep band, photography, political, professional, radio and TV, religious, social, student government, and yearbook. Popular campus events include Tower Dance, Black Awareness Week, and Greek Week.

Sports: There are 6 intercollegiate sports for men and 5 for women, and 35 intramural sports for men and 35 for women. Facilities include a 7000-seat stadium, a 3000-seat basketball arena, 3 gyms, 4 racquetball courts, a weight-lifting area, volleyball and tennis courts, dance areas, and an aquatic center with 2 pools.

Disabled Students: 90% of the campus is accessible. Wheelchair ramps, elevators, special parking, specially equipped rest rooms, special class scheduling, lowered drinking fountains, and lowered telephones are available.

Services: Counseling and information services are available, as is tutoring in most subjects. There is a reader service for the blind and remedial math, reading, and writing.

Campus Safety and Security: Measures include 24-hour foot and vehicle patrol, security escort services, informal discussions, and pamphlets/posters/films. There are lighted pathways/sidewalks.

Programs of Study: Northwest confers B.A., B.S., B.F.A., B.S.Ed., B.S.Med.Tech., and B.Tech. degrees. Master's degrees are also awarded. Bachelor's degrees are awarded in AGRICULTURE (agricultural business management, agricultural mechanics, agriculture, agronomy, animal science, conservation and regulation, forestry and related sciences, horticulture, and wildlife management), BIOLOGICAL SCIENCE (biology/biological science, botany, and zoology), BUSINESS (accounting, banking and finance, business administration and management, business economics, international business management, marketing/retailing/merchandising, personnel management, and recreation and leisure services), COMMUNICATIONS AND THE ARTS (advertising, art, broadcasting, communications, dramatic arts, English, fine arts, French, journalism, music, public relations, Spanish, and speech/debate/rhetoric), COMPUTER AND PHYSICAL SCIENCE (chemistry, computer management, computer science, earth science, geology, information sciences and systems, mathematics, physics, science, and statistics), EDUCATION (agricultural, art, business, early childhood, education of the mentally handicapped, elementary, mathematics, middle school, music, physical, recreation, science, secondary, special, and specific learning disabilities), ENGINEERING AND ENVIRONMENTAL DESIGN (preengineering), HEALTH PROFESSIONS (predentistry, premedicine, prepharmacy, and preveterinary science), SOCIAL SCIENCE (child care/child and family studies, clothing and textiles management/production/services, economics, family/consumer resource management, food science, geography, history, home economics, humanities, industrial and organizational psychology, philosophy, political science/government, prelaw, psychology, public administration, social science, sociology, and textiles and clothing). Education, mass communications, and agriculture are the strongest academically.

Required: All students must maintain a minimum GPA of 2.0 while taking at least 124 credit hours. Distribution requirements include 9 hours each in social science and humanities, 8 in natural science, 6 in composition, 4 each in math and phys ed, 3 each in oral communications and behavioral sciences, and 1 in freshman seminar.

Special: Co-op programs with the University of Missouri/Rolla, cross-registration with Missouri Western State College, campuswide internships, study abroad in England and Mexico, and a Washington semester are available. Work-study programs, student-designed majors, a 3-2 engineering degree with the University of Missouri/Rolla, credit for military experience, nondegree study, and pass/fail options are possible. There are 3 national honor societies.

Faculty/Classroom: 61% of faculty are male; 39%, female. All teach undergraduates. No introductory courses are taught by graduate students. The average class size in an introductory lecture is 40; in a laboratory, 20; and in a regular course, 24.

Admissions: 89% of the 2003-2004 applicants were accepted. 43% of the current freshmen were in the top fifth of their class; 78% were in the top two fifths.

Requirements: The SAT I or ACT is required, with a minimum composite score of 970 on the SAT I or 21 on the ACT; if scores are below those levels, a combined percentile index obtained from the SAT I or ACT score and high school rank will be used. Northwest requires applicants to be in the upper 50% of their class. A GPA of 2.0 is required. AP and CLEP credits are accepted. Important factors in the admissions decision are evidence of special talent, leadership record, and recommendations by alumni.

Procedure: Freshmen are admitted fall, spring, and summer. Entrance exams should be taken in the fall of the senior year. Application deadlines are open. The fall 2003 application fee was $15. Notification is sent on a rolling basis. Applications are accepted on-line through CollegeLink.

Transfer: 360 transfer students enrolled in a recent year. Applicants must present a minimum GPA of 2.0. 30 of 124 credits required for the bachelor's degree must be completed at Northwest.

Visiting: There are regularly scheduled orientations for prospective students. There are guides for informal visits and visitors may sit in on classes and stay overnight. To schedule a visit, contact the Mable Cook Admissions and Visitors Center at (660) 562-1562.

Financial Aid: In a recent year, 81% of all full-time freshmen and 69% of continuing full-time students received some form of financial aid. 56% of full-time freshmen and 63% of continuing full-time students received need-based aid. The average freshman award was $5234. 50% of undergraduates work part time. Average annual earnings from campus work are $1138. The average financial indebtedness of a recent year's graduate was $15,144. The FAFSA is required.

International Students: There were 196 international students enrolled in a recent year. They must score 500 on the written TOEFL.

Computers: The mainframe is 10 clustered DEC VAX computers. Students may access the mainframe from more than 3400 PCs and note-book computers located in residence halls, the library, and labs. Students may also use the networks available to access libraries, campuses, and computers located around the country. All students may access the system 24 hours daily. There are no time limits and no fees. It is strongly recommended that all students have a personal computer.

Graduates: In a recent year, 977 bachelor's degrees were awarded. The most popular majors were education (24%), business marketing (21%), and social science history (10%).

Admissions Contact: Jeremy Waldeier, Associate Director, Admissions. A video is available. E-mail: *jeremyw@mail.nwmissouri.edu* Web: *www.nwmissouri.edu*

PARK UNIVERSITY
A-2
Parkville, MO 64152-9974
(816) 584-6215
(800) 745-7275; Fax: (816) 741-4462

Full-time: 428 men, 754 women	**Faculty:** 101
Part-time: 11,521 men and women	**Ph.D.s:** 54%
Graduate: 136 men, 212 women	**Student/Faculty:** 12 to 1
Year: semesters, summer session	**Tuition:** $5600
Application Deadline: August 15	**Room & Board:** $5180
Freshman Class: 676 applied, 172 accepted, 100 enrolled	
ACT: 20	**COMPETITIVE+**

Park University, founded in 1875, is a private institution offering degree programs in the humanities, performing arts, natural and life sciences, and social and administrative sciences. There are 2 undergraduate and 3 graduate schools. In addition to regional accreditation, Park has baccalaureate program accreditation with NLN. The library contains 141,870 volumes, 195,530 microform items, and 670 audio/video tapes/CDs, and subscribes to 775 periodicals. Computerized library services include the card catalog, interlibrary loans, and database searching. Special learning facilities include a learning resource center, art gallery, radio station, and TV station. The 800-acre campus is in a suburban area 12 miles north of Kansas City. Including any residence halls, there are 17 buildings.

Student Life: 80% of undergraduates are from Missouri. Students are from 49 states, 90 foreign countries, and Canada. 80% are from public schools. 59% are white; 21% African American; 15% Hispanic. 88% claim no religious affiliation; 6% Protestant. The average age of freshmen is 18; all undergraduates, 31. 26% do not continue beyond their first year; 37% remain to graduate.

Housing: 226 students can be accommodated in college housing, which includes coed dorms and on-campus apartments. In addition, there are honors houses. On-campus housing is guaranteed for all 4 years. 98% of students commute. Alcohol is not permitted. All students may keep cars.

Activities: There are no fraternities or sororities. There are 30 groups on campus, including cheerleading, computers, drama, ethnic, honors, international, literary magazine, newspaper, outdoor, photography, political, professional, radio and TV, religious, social, social service, student government, and yearbook. Popular campus events include Fall Harvest Festival, Spring Fling, and International Week.

Sports: There are 6 intercollegiate sports for men and 7 for women, and 3 intramural sports for men and 3 for women. Facilities include an 800-seat indoor gym with basketball and volleyball courts, 350-seat indoor gym with basketball and volleyball courts, an all-weather outdoor track, soccer and softball fields, a sports medicine room, 4 tennis courts, and an outdoor sand volleyball and basketball court.

Disabled Students: 95% of the campus is accessible. Wheelchair ramps, elevators, special parking, specially equipped rest rooms, special class scheduling, and lowered drinking fountains are available.

Services: Counseling and information services are available, as is tutoring in most subjects. There is a reader service for the blind and remedial math, reading, and writing.

Campus Safety and Security: Measures include 24-hour foot and vehicle patrol, security escort services, informal discussions, and pamphlets/posters/films. There are lighted pathways/sidewalks.

Programs of Study: Park confers B.A., B.S., and B.P.A. degrees. Associate and master's degrees are also awarded. Bachelor's degrees are awarded in BIOLOGICAL SCIENCE (biology/biological science), BUSINESS (accounting, business administration and management, business economics, human resources, management information systems, and marketing management), COMMUNICATIONS AND THE ARTS (communications, English, fine arts, graphic design, public relations, and Spanish), COMPUTER AND PHYSICAL SCIENCE (chemistry, computer science, information sciences and systems, mathematics, and natural sciences), EDUCATION (athletic training, early childhood, and elementary), ENGINEERING AND ENVIRONMENTAL DESIGN (aviation administration/management, computational sciences, engineering management, and interior design), HEALTH PROFESSIONS (health care administration), SOCIAL SCIENCE (child care/child and family studies, criminal justice, economics, fire protection, fire services administration, history, human services, law, liberal arts/general studies, political science/government, psychology, public administration, social psychology, social work, and sociology). Management information systems and management and human resources are the largest.

Required: All students must complete core requirements, including 3 semesters of English composition, and 1 of algebra, as well as 1 science course. They must also complete 24 to 27 hours of general education courses and 9 hours of Liberal Learning courses. Of the 120 credit hours needed for the bachelor's degree, 45 must be completed in upper-division work and 30 to 60 in the major, with a minimum GPA of 2.0.

Special: Cross-registration is available through a Kansas City consortium, and study abroad is possible through other schools. The college also offers internships in most majors, work-study programs with local companies, a Washington semester, credit for life and military experience, pass/fail options, and nondegree study. An accelerated degree program is offered in some majors. There are 2 national honor societies and a freshman honors program.

Faculty/Classroom: 72% of faculty are male; 28%, female. All teach undergraduates and 80% do research. No introductory courses are taught by graduate students. The average class size in an introductory lecture is 20; in a laboratory, 10; and in a regular course, 15.

Admissions: 25% of the 2003-2004 applicants were accepted. The ACT scores for the 2003-2004 freshman class were: 52% below 21, 26% between 21 and 23, 12% between 24 and 26, 7% between 27 and 28, and 2% above 28. 20% of the current freshmen were in the top fifth of their class; 51% were in the top two fifths. 3 freshmen graduated first in their class.

Requirements: The SAT I or ACT is required. In addition, the GED is accepted with a minimum total score of 225 and no area less than 35. Park requires applicants to be in the upper 50% of their class. A GPA of 2.0 is required. AP and CLEP credits are accepted. Important factors in the admissions decision are advanced placement or honor courses, leadership record, and extracurricular activities record.

Procedure: Freshmen are admitted fall, spring, and summer. Entrance exams should be taken during the junior year or early in the senior year. There is an early admissions plan and a rolling admissions plan. Applications should be filed by August 15 for fall entry and December 15 for spring entry. The fall 2003 application fee was $25. Notification is sent on a rolling basis. Applications are accepted on-line through the school's web site.

Transfer: 2052 transfer students enrolled in a recent year. The college requires a GPA of at least 2.0. A minimum ACT composite score of 20 is recommended, but is waived for students age 25 or older. 24 of 120 credits required for the bachelor's degree must be completed at Park.

Visiting: There are regularly scheduled orientations for prospective students, including a campus tour, lunch, an information session with a student panel, sessions on admissions, scholarships, and financial aid, and a chance to attend a class and meet with a faculty member. There are guides for informal visits and visitors may sit in on classes and stay overnight. To schedule a visit, contact Jo Henderson, Director of Admissions at *admissions@park.edu*.

Financial Aid: In a recent year, the average freshman award was $5130. 85% of undergraduates work part time. Average annual earnings from campus work are $1000. The average financial indebtedness of the 2003 graduate was $10,000. The FAFSA and the college's own financial statement are required. The deadline for filing freshman financial aid applications for fall entry is April 1.

International Students: The school actively recruits these students. They must score 500 on the written TOEFL.

Computers: The mainframe is an HP 9000/Series 857. There are also 135 PCs available for student use with access to the Internet mostly in academic buildings, dorms, the library, and computer labs; 80 are in a lab environment with access to the Internet. All students may access the system Monday through Thursday, 8 A.M. to 11 P.M.; Friday, 8 A.M. to 5 p.m; Saturday, 10 A.M. to 5 P.M.; Sunday, 12 noon to 5 P.M. There are no time limits and no fees.

Graduates: From July 1, 2002 to June 30, 2003, 2970 bachelor's degrees were awarded. The most popular majors were management (19%), human resources (15%), and management information systems (13%). In an average class, 2% graduate in 3 years or less, 20% graduate in 4 years or less, and 36% graduate in 5 years or less. 15 companies recruited on campus in 2002-2003. Of the 2002 graduating class, 9% were enrolled in graduate school within 6 months of graduation and 94% were employed.

Admissions Contact: Jo Henderson, Director of Admissions.
E-mail: *admissions@park.edu* Web: *www.park.edu*

RESEARCH COLLEGE OF NURSING
Kansas City, MO 64132

A-2

(816) 501-4000
(800) 842-6776; Fax: (816) 501-4241

Full-time: 22 men, 153 women	**Faculty:** 33
Part-time: 1 man, 1 woman	**Ph.D.s:** 23%
Graduate: 4 men, 18 women	**Student/Faculty:** 5 to 1
Year: semesters, summer session	**Tuition:** $17,410
Application Deadline: June 30	**Room & Board:** $5550
Freshman Class: 94 applied, 72 accepted, 29 enrolled	
ACT: 22	**SPECIAL**

Research College of Nursing, founded in 1980, is a private college of nursing affiliated with Rockhurst University of Kansas City, a Jesuit-run, 25-acre liberal arts college with an enrollment of about 1500 undergraduates. Located on the campus of the Research Medical Center, the Research College of Nursing offers classes on its home campus, on the Rockhurst campus, and in a variety of health-related settings in the Kansas City area. In addition to regional accreditation, Research College has baccalaureate program accreditation with CCNE and NLN. The library contains 109,000 volumes, 150,000 microform items, and 1100 audio/video tapes/CDs, and subscribes to 700 periodicals. Computerized library services include the card catalog, interlibrary loans, database searching, and Internet access. Special learning facilities include a learning resource center, art gallery, and radio station. The campus is in an urban area in Kansas City. Including any residence halls, there are 3 buildings.

Student Life: 90% of undergraduates are from Missouri. Students are from 6 states and 1 foreign country. 55% are from public schools. 79% are white. 45% are Catholic; 17% Protestant. The average age of freshmen is 18; all undergraduates, 22. 30% do not continue beyond their first year; 63% remain to graduate.

Housing: 815 students can be accommodated in college housing, which includes single-sex and coed dorms, on-campus apartments, married-student housing, and fraternity houses. In addition, there are special-interest houses. On-campus housing is guaranteed for all 4 years. 65% of students live on campus; of those, 60% remain on campus on weekends. All students may keep cars.

Activities: 27% of men belong to 4 national fraternities; 12% of women belong to 3 national sororities. There are 35 groups on campus, including art, cheerleading, chess, choir, chorus, computers, drama, drill team, ethnic, honors, international, literary magazine, musical theater, newspaper, political, professional, radio and TV, religious, social, social service, student government, and yearbook. Popular campus events include the Mass of the Holy Spirit.

Sports: There are 6 intercollegiate sports for men and 5 for women, and 30 intramural sports for men and 30 for women. Facilities include a gym, an exercise facility, a fitness center, and racquetball courts.

Disabled Students: 80% of the campus is accessible. Wheelchair ramps, elevators, special parking, specially equipped rest rooms, lowered drinking fountains, and lowered telephones are available.

Services: Counseling and information services are available, as is tutoring in some subjects, including primarily freshman- and sophomore-level courses. There is remedial writing. The learning center offers assistance with college writing tasks and study strategies.

Campus Safety and Security: Measures include 24-hour foot and vehicle patrol, security escort services, informal discussions, and emergency telephones. There are lighted pathways/sidewalks.

Programs of Study: Research College confers the B.S.N. degree. Master's degrees are also awarded. Bachelor's degrees are awarded in HEALTH PROFESSIONS (nursing).

Required: To earn the B.S.N., students must complete a total of 128 semester hours, with 66 in liberal arts and sciences and 62 in the nursing major. A 2.0 GPA overall and in all nursing course work is required to graduate.

Special: Work-study, co-op, and accelerated degree programs, study abroad in 7 countries, and a Washington semester are available. There is a chapter of Phi Beta Kappa and a freshman honors program.

Faculty/Classroom: All faculty are female. All teach undergraduates. No introductory courses are taught by graduate students. The average class size in an introductory lecture is 55 and in a laboratory, 8.

Admissions: 77% of the 2003-2004 applicants were accepted. The ACT scores for the 2003-2004 freshman class were: 23% below 21, 46% between 21 and 23, and 31% between 24 and 26. 33% of the current freshmen were in the top fifth of their class; 67% were in the top two fifths.

Requirements: The ACT is required, with a minimum composite score of 20 on each area. A minimum score of 960 on the SAT I may be substituted. Applicants should graduate from an accredited secondary school or have the GED. An interview is recommended. Applicants should have completed 3 years of high school math, including algebra II, 3 years of English, and 2 years of science, including chemistry. Research College requires applicants to be in the upper 50% of their class. A GPA of 2.0 is required. AP and CLEP credits are accepted. Important factors in the admissions decision are advanced placement or honor courses, recommendations by school officials, and leadership record.

Procedure: Freshmen are admitted to all sessions. Entrance exams should be taken during the junior or senior year of high school. There is a deferred admissions plan and a rolling admissions plan. Applications should be filed by June 30 for fall entry, along with a $25 fee. Notification is sent on a rolling basis.

Transfer: 18 transfer students enrolled in 2002-2003. A minimum GPA of 2.5 is required to interview for the Research/Rockhurst Joint B.S.N. Program. Students must complete the sophomore-level nursing course before entering the junior-level clinical; this course is offered only in the spring. Admission requires an interview along with all official transcripts. Admission for transfers is very limited. 30 of 128 credits required for the bachelor's degree must be completed at Research College.

Visiting: There are regularly scheduled orientations for prospective students, consisting of 5 weekend programs for students and their parents. There are guides for informal visits and visitors may sit in on classes and stay overnight. To schedule a visit, contact the Admission and Financial Aid Office at (816) 502-4100 or *amy.johnson@rockhurst.edu.*

Financial Aid: In a recent year, 29% of undergraduates worked part time. Average annual earnings from campus work were $1500. Research College is a member of CSS. The FAFSA is required. Check with the school for current deadlines.

International Students: There was 1 international student enrolled in a recent year. They must score 550 on the written TOEFL and also take the ACT or SAT I. The school will accept the SAT I but prefers the ACT, scoring 20.

Computers: The mainframe is a DEC VAX 8530. Computers are available for student use in all academic buildings and the library. All students may access the system. There are no time limits and no fees.

Graduates: From July 1, 2002 to June 30, 2003, 40 bachelor's degrees were awarded. The most popular major was nursing (100%). Of the 2002 graduating class, 95% were employed within 6 months of graduation.

Admissions Contact: Amy Johnson, Admission Counselor.
E-mail: *amy.johnson@rockhurst.edu* Web: *www.researchcollege.edu*

ROCKHURST UNIVERSITY
A-2
Kansas City, MO 64110-2561

(816) 501-4100
(800) 842-6776; Fax: (816) 501-4241

Full-time: 499 men, 584 women	**Faculty:** 119; IIB, --$
Part-time: 349 men, 526 women	**Ph.D.s:** 84%
Graduate: 377 men, 430 women	**Student/Faculty:** 9 to 1
Year: semesters, summer session	**Tuition:** $17,410
Application Deadline: June 30	**Room & Board:** $5550
Freshman Class: 956 applied, 766 accepted, 244 enrolled	
SAT I Verbal/Math: 580/580	**ACT:** 24 COMPETITIVE+

Rockhurst University, founded in 1910, is a private comprehensive, Catholic Jesuit institution that offers undergraduate programs in the arts and sciences, education, nursing, and business. There are 4 undergraduate and 2 graduate schools. In addition to regional accreditation, Rockhurst has baccalaureate program accreditation with AACTE, APTA, CAHEA, NLN, and TEAC. The library contains 375,000 volumes, 250,000 microform items, and 4000 audio/video tapes/CDs, and subscribes to 6000 periodicals (electronic databases). Computerized library services include the card catalog, interlibrary loans, and database searching. Special learning facilities include a learning resource center, art gallery, radio station, and multimedia classrooms. The 55-acre campus is in an urban area in Kansas City. Including any residence halls, there are 19 buildings.

Student Life: 68% of undergraduates are from Missouri. Students are from 24 states and 10 foreign countries. 58% are from public schools. 75% are white. 53% are Catholic; 38% Protestant; 8% claim no religious affiliation. The average age of freshmen is 18; all undergraduates, 22. 18% do not continue beyond their first year; 66% remain to graduate.

Housing: 815 students can be accommodated in college housing, which includes single-sex and coed dorms and on-campus apartments. In addition, there are honors houses and special-interest houses. On-campus housing is available on a first-come, first-served basis. Priority is given to out-of-town students. 55% of students live on campus; of those, 45% remain on campus on weekends. All students may keep cars.

Activities: 19% of men belong to 3 national fraternities; 21% of women belong to 3 national sororities. There are 55 groups on campus, including art, cheerleading, choir, chorale, chorus, computers, drama, ethnic, honors, international, literary magazine, musical theater, newspaper, photography, political, professional, radio and TV, religious, social, social service, student government, and yearbook. Popular campus events include fraternity socials, coffee house events, and Rockstock (live bands).

Sports: There are 5 intercollegiate sports for men and 5 for women, and 12 intramural sports for men and 12 for women. Facilities include athletic and soccer fields; tennis, handball, racquetball, badminton, basketball, and volleyball courts; a weight and exercise room, gymnastics facilities, and an NCAA baseball field.

Disabled Students: 90% of the campus is accessible. Wheelchair ramps, elevators, special parking, specially equipped rest rooms, lowered drinking fountains, and lowered telephones are available.

Services: Counseling and information services are available, as is tutoring in some subjects, including primarily freshman- and sophomore-level courses. The Learning Center offers tutoring in many subjects, assistance with any college writing task, and study strategies.

Campus Safety and Security: Measures include 24-hour foot and vehicle patrol, self-defense education, security escort services, and shuttle buses. There are informal discussions, pamphlets/posters/films, emergency telephones, lighted pathways/sidewalks, formal presentations, and a full in-house security program geared toward integration of security into the overall campus operation.

Programs of Study: Rockhurst confers B.A., B.S., B.S.B.A., and B.S.N. degrees. Master's and doctoral degrees are also awarded. Bachelor's degrees are awarded in BIOLOGICAL SCIENCE (biology/biological science), BUSINESS (accounting, banking and finance, business administration and management, business economics, human resources, institutional management, management information systems, management science, marketing/retailing/merchandising, and personnel management), COMMUNICATIONS AND THE ARTS (communications, dramatic arts, English, French, and Spanish), COMPUTER AND PHYSICAL SCIENCE (chemistry, computer science, information sciences and systems, mathematics, and physics), EDUCATION (elementary, foreign languages, and secondary), ENGINEERING AND ENVIRONMENTAL DESIGN (computer technology and industrial administration/management), HEALTH PROFESSIONS (clinical science, nursing, and speech pathology/audiology), SOCIAL SCIENCE (economics, history, international relations, philosophy, political science/government, psychology, sociology, and theological studies). Chemistry, psychology, and philosophy are the strongest academically. Biology, nursing, and psychology are the largest.

Required: Students must complete 128 credit hours with a minimum of 18 in the major, with at least a 2.0 GPA. 52 prescribed semester hours in philosophy, theology, history, literature, science, social studies, and the arts are required. Students must also demonstrate proficiency in oral and written communication and math.

Special: Students may obtain career-related work experience through the Cooperative Education Program. Internships for credit and salary are available. Students are encouraged to study abroad in 1 of 5 countries for a semester, to take a semester in New York at Fordham University, or to participate in a congressional intern/study program in Washington, D.C., through Marquette University. B.A.-B.S. degrees are available in finance economics, management, marketing, international business, finance/accounting, information systems, and knowledge management. Work-study and an accelerated degree in nursing are also available. Students may pursue a 3-2 engineering degree and interdisciplinary majors. There are 6 national honor societies, including Phi Beta Kappa, a freshman honors program, and 11 departmental honors programs.

Faculty/Classroom: 57% of faculty are male; 43%, female. 89% teach undergraduates. No introductory courses are taught by graduate students. The average class size in an introductory lecture is 20; in a laboratory, 14; and in a regular course, 21.

Admissions: 80% of the 2003-2004 applicants were accepted. The SAT I scores for the 2003-2004 freshman class were: Verbal--20% below 500, 33% between 500 and 599, 33% between 600 and 700, and 14% above 700; Math--20% below 500, 42% between 500 and 599, 24% between 600 and 700, and 14% above 700. The ACT scores were 21% below 21, 23% between 21 and 23, 25% between 24 and 26, 15% between 27 and 28, and 16% above 28. 39% of the current freshmen were in the top fifth of their class; 71% were in the top two fifths. 11 freshmen graduated first in their class.

Requirements: The SAT I or ACT is required. In addition, minimum composite scores of 960 (480 on each part) on the SAT I, or 20 on the ACT are required. In addition, the applicant must be a graduate of an accredited secondary school or have earned a GED. The university requires completion of 15 academic credits, including 4 years of English, 3 to 4 of history/social science, 3 of math, 2 to 4 of a foreign language, and 1 of visual or performing arts. An interview is recommended, and a recommendation is required. Rockhurst requires applicants to be in the upper 50% of their class. A GPA of 2.0 is required. AP and CLEP credits are accepted. Important factors in the admissions decision are advanced placement or honor courses, recommendations by school officials, and leadership record.

Procedure: Freshmen are admitted to all sessions. Entrance exams should be taken in April or June of the junior year or October, December, or February of the senior year. There are early decision, deferred, and rolling admissions plans. Early decision applications should be filed by May 1; regular applications, by June 30 for fall entry. The fall 2003 application fee was $25. Notification of early decision is sent July 1; regular decision, on a rolling basis. 50 early decision candidates were accepted for the 2003-2004 class. Applications are accepted on computer disk and on-line through *www.rockhurst.edu* and *Embark.com.*

Transfer: 127 transfer students enrolled in 2003-2004. Transfer applicants must have a GPA of at least 2.25. An interview is recommended. All college transcripts must be submitted; a high school transcript and test scores are required if the applicant has completed fewer than 24 college semester hours. 30 of 128 credits required for the bachelor's degree must be completed at Rockhurst.

Visiting: There are regularly scheduled orientations for prospective students, including a campus tour, an interview with an admissions counselor, and a classroom visit or meeting with a faculty member. There are guides for informal visits and visitors may sit in on classes and stay overnight. To schedule a visit, contact Tiffany Pearson in Admissions at (816) 501-4542 or *www.rockhurst.edu/admissionevents/smartstart.*

Financial Aid: In 2003-2004, 93% of all full-time freshmen and 85% of continuing full-time students received some form of financial aid. 76% of full-time freshmen and 67% of continuing full-time students received need-based aid. The average freshman award was $17,169. Need-based scholarships or need-based grants averaged $4946 ($25,966 maximum); need-based self-help aid (loans and jobs) averaged $3129 ($5975 maximum); non-need-based athletic scholarships averaged $10,242 ($23,930 maximum); and other non-need-based awards and non-need-based scholarships averaged $9202 ($16,950 maximum). 22% of undergraduates work part time. Average annual earnings from campus work are $1500. The average financial indebtedness of the 2003 graduate was $14,556. The FAFSA is required. The priority date for freshman financial aid applications for fall entry is March 1. The deadline for filing freshman financial aid applications for fall entry is June 1.

International Students: There are 10 international students enrolled. The school actively recruits these students. They must score 550 on the written TOEFL and also take the SAT I or the ACT, scoring 20 on the ACT.

Computers: The mainframe is a Hewlett-Packard ES 45. There are approximately 500 PCs and Macs available in computer labs, classrooms, the library, and residence halls. All students can connect to the Internet. All students may access the system 24 hours a day. There are no time limits. The fee is $50 per semester.

Graduates: From July 1, 2002 to June 30, 2003, 339 bachelor's degrees were awarded. The most popular majors were business/marketing (19%), nursing/health professions (14%), and psychology/social science/history (14%). In an average class, 51% graduate in 4 years or less, 63% graduate in 5 years or less, and 66% graduate in 6 years or less. 63 companies recruited on campus in 2002-2003.

Admissions Contact: Phil Gebauer, Director of Undergraduate Admission. E-mail: *admission@rockhurst.edu* Web: *rockhurst.edu*

SAINT LOUIS UNIVERSITY
St. Louis, MO 63103-2097

	D-2
	(314) 977-2500
	(800) SLUFORU; Fax: (314) 977-7136

Full-time: 2988 men, 3473 women	Faculty: 422; I, -$
Part-time: 223 men, 407 women	Ph.D.s: 96%
Graduate: 1744 men, 2382 women	Student/Faculty: 15 to 1
Year: semesters, summer session	Tuition: $22,210
Application Deadline: December 1	Room & Board: $7570
Freshman Class: 6405 applied, 4500 accepted, 1377 enrolled	
ACT: 26	VERY COMPETITIVE+

Saint Louis University, founded in 1818, is a private (not for profit) institution affiliated with the Jesuit Order of the Roman Catholic Church. There are 9 undergraduate schools and 1 graduate school. In addition to regional accreditation, SLU has baccalaureate program accreditation with AACSB, ABET, ACOTE, ACS, APTA, ASLHA, CAA, CAAHEP, CADE, CAPTE, CCNE, CSWE, JRCNMT, NAACLS, NCATE, and NLN. The 3 libraries contain 1,846,912 volumes, 2,591,741 microform items, and 196,377 audio/video tapes/CDs, and subscribe to 12,027 periodicals. Computerized library services include the card catalog, interlibrary loans, database searching, and Internet access. Special learning facilities include a learning resource center, art gallery, radio station, and TV station. The 373-acre campus is in an urban area in the Midtown Arts District of St. Louis. Including any residence halls, there are 151 buildings.

Student Life: 53% of undergraduates are from Missouri. Students are from 48 states, 78 foreign countries, and Canada. 76% are white. 56% are Catholic; 17% Protestant; 11% claim no religious affiliation. The average age of freshmen is 19; all undergraduates, 22. 12% do not continue beyond their first year; 71% remain to graduate.

Housing: 3376 students can be accommodated in college housing, which includes single-sex and coed dorms, on-campus apartments, and married-student housing. In addition, there are honors houses, language houses, and special-interest houses. 54% of students commute. All students may keep cars.

Activities: 21% of men belong to 12 national fraternities; 18% of women belong to 5 national sororities. There are 100 groups on campus, including band, cheerleading, choir, chorale, chorus, computers, dance, debate, drama, drill team, ethnic, film, gay, honors, international, musical theater, newspaper, pep band, political, professional, radio and TV, religious, social, social service, student government, and yearbook. Popular campus events include Student Activities Fair, Spring Fever, and Billiken World Festival.

Sports: There are 9 intercollegiate sports for men and 10 for women, and 27 intramural sports for men and 27 for women. Facilities include a 2000-seat gym, a 6050-seat outdoor sports center, a 19,000-seat off-campus arena, a recreation center with multipurpose courts, a swimming pool, a diving well, track facilities, a weight-training room, and a natural grass soccer facility.

Disabled Students: 90% of the campus is accessible. Wheelchair ramps, elevators, special parking, specially equipped rest rooms, special class scheduling, lowered drinking fountains, lowered telephones, tutoring, writing, and assistance in finding student services, and a reader/scanner are available.

Services: Counseling and information services are available, as is tutoring in most subjects, including math, English, history, economics, and natural sciences. There is a reader service for the blind and remedial math, reading, and writing. There are also books on tape, academic success seminars, time management help, and test-taking techniques dealing with test anxiety and study skills.

Campus Safety and Security: Measures include 24-hour foot and vehicle patrol, self-defense education, security escort services, and shuttle buses. There are informal discussions, pamphlets/posters/films, emergency telephones, lighted pathways/sidewalks, metrolink field trips, residence hall presentations, community building programs, 24-hour emergency telephone/alarm devices, and electronically operated dorm entrances.

Programs of Study: SLU confers B.A. and B.S. degrees. Associate, master's, and doctoral degrees are also awarded. Bachelor's degrees are awarded in BIOLOGICAL SCIENCE (biology/biological science and nutrition), BUSINESS (accounting, banking and finance, business administration and management, human resources, international business management, management science, marketing/retailing/merchandising, and organizational behavior), COMMUNICATIONS AND THE ARTS (art history and appreciation, communications, dramatic arts, English, French, German, Greek, Latin, music, Russian, Spanish, and studio art), COMPUTER AND PHYSICAL SCIENCE (atmospheric sciences and meteorology, chemistry, computer science, earth science, geology, geophysics and seismology, information sciences and systems, mathematics, and physics), EDUCATION (education), ENGINEERING AND ENVIRONMENTAL DESIGN (aeronautical engineering, aeronautical technology, aircraft mechanics, airline piloting and navigation, aviation administration/management, biomedical engineering, computer technology, electrical/electronics engineering, engineering management, environmental science, and mechanical engineering), HEALTH PROFESSIONS (clinical science, exercise science, health care administration, nuclear medical technology, nursing, occupational therapy, and speech pathology/audiology), SOCIAL SCIENCE (American studies, classical/ancient civilization, criminal justice, economics, history, humanities, international studies, philosophy, political science/government, psychology, social science, social work, sociology, theological studies, urban studies, and women's studies). Aerospace engineering, psychology, and philosophy are the strongest academically. Finance, psychology, and marketing are the largest.

Required: Students must maintain a 2.0 GPA while completing a minimum of 120 credit hours. The core curriculum includes courses in philosophy, theology, math, English, science, and social/behavioral science.

Special: Students may study abroad in Spain, France, Germany, and Belgium. Cross-registration with Washington University and the University of Missouri at St. Louis, internships with local financial institutions, work-study programs on campus, an accelerated degree program in nursing, a 3-2 engineering degree program with Washington University in St. Louis, dual majors, student-designed majors, and pass/fail options are also possible. Students may also participate in university-sponsored mission trips. There are 18 national honor societies, including Phi Beta Kappa, and a freshman honors program.

Faculty/Classroom: 68% of faculty are male; 32%, female. 73% teach undergraduates. All do research, and 73% both teach and do research. The average class size in an introductory lecture is 27; in a laboratory, 15; and in a regular course, 22.

Admissions: 70% of the 2003-2004 applicants were accepted. The ACT scores for the 2003-2004 freshman class were: 7% below 21, 17% between 21 and 23, 29% between 24 and 26, 20% between 27 and 28, and 27% above 28. 54% of the current freshmen were in the top fifth of their class; 81% were in the top two fifths. There were 18 National Merit finalists.

Requirements: The ACT is required. In addition, applicants must be graduates of accredited secondary schools or have earned a GED. Students are encouraged to take 4 or more academic courses each semester of high school including 4 years of English, 3 each of math, academic electives, and sciences, and 2 of social sciences and foreign language. Other requirements include courses in biology and chemistry for the School of Nursing and the School of Allied Health Professions; physics, an additional year of natural science, and 4 years of math for the physical therapy program; a third year of natural science (preferably physics) for admission to the occupational therapy and nutrition and dietetics programs; and a fourth year of math for the Parks College engineering or aviation programs. A GPA of 2.0 is required. AP and CLEP credits are accepted. Important factors in the admissions decision are leadership record, extracurricular activities record, and personality/intangible qualities.

Procedure: Freshmen are admitted fall, spring, and summer. Entrance exams should be taken during spring of junior year and fall of senior year. There is a deferred admissions plan and a rolling admissions plan. Applications should be filed by December 1 (priority scholarship deadline) for fall entry, along with a $25 fee. Notification is sent on a rolling basis within 2 to 3 weeks of receipt of a complete file. Applications are accepted on computer disk and on-line through *www.slu.edu* and *www.collegeboard.com*.

Transfer: 323 transfer students enrolled in 2002-2003. The university recommends that transfer applicants present an associate degree or a minimum of 12 credit hours with a GPA of at least 2.0. 30 of 120 credits required for the bachelor's degree must be completed at SLU.

Visiting: There are regularly scheduled orientations for prospective students, consisting of a campus tour, individual and group visits to a class or an academic department, and admissions and financial aid counseling. There are guides for informal visits and visitors may sit in on classes and stay overnight. To schedule a visit, contact Admissions at *admitme@slu.edu*.

Financial Aid: In 2003-2004, 96% of all full-time freshmen and 92% of continuing full-time students received some form of financial aid. 63% of full-time freshmen and 60% of continuing full-time students received need-based aid. The average freshman award was $19,376. Need-based scholarships or need-based grants averaged $12,492; need-based self-help aid (loans and jobs) averaged $10,267; and non-need-based awards and non-need-based scholarships averaged $18,595. 17% of undergraduates work part time. Average annual earnings from campus work are $1376. The average financial indebtedness of the 2003 graduate was $16,150. The FAFSA is required. The priority date for freshman financial aid applications for fall entry is December 1. The deadline for filing freshman financial aid applications for fall entry is July 1.

International Students: There are 164 international students enrolled. The school actively recruits these students. They must score 500 on the written TOEFL or 193 on the electronic version or take the MELAB writing test.

Computers: The mainframe is a DEC Alpha 2000 cluster. There are more than 1200 PCs available for student use in various labs, which have Internet access. All students may access the system. There are no time limits and no fees. It is strongly recommended that all students have a personal computer.

Graduates: From July 1, 2002 to June 30, 2003, 1703 bachelor's degrees were awarded. The most popular majors were finance (7%), psychology (6%), and marketing (6%). In an average class, 54% graduate in 4 years or less, 68% graduate in 5 years or less, and 71% graduate in 6 years or less. 216 companies recruited on campus in 2002-2003. Of the 2002 graduating class, 28% were enrolled in graduate school within 6 months of graduation and 64% were employed.

Admissions Contact: Shani Lenore, Director of Undergraduate Admissions. A video is available. E-mail: *admitme@slu.edu*
Web: *imagine.slu.edu*

SOUTHEAST MISSOURI STATE UNIVERSITY E-3
Cape Girardeau, MO 63701   (573) 651-2590; Fax: (573) 651-5936

Full-time: 2796 men, 3808 women	**Faculty:** 389; IIA, --$
Part-time: 775 men, 1104 women	**Ph.D.s:** 81%
Graduate: 265 men, 822 women	**Student/Faculty:** 17 to 1
Year: semesters, summer session	**Tuition:** $4254 ($7839)
Application Deadline: open	**Room & Board:** $5450
Freshman Class: 3910 applied, 3238 accepted, 1495 enrolled	
ACT: 22	**COMPETITIVE**

Southeast Missouri State University, founded in 1873, is a public institution offering undergraduate and graduate programs in arts and sciences, business, agriculture, education, and health. It includes a school of polytechnic studies. There are 7 undergraduate schools and 1 graduate school. In addition to regional accreditation, Southeast has baccalaureate program accreditation with AACSB, ACS, ADA, ASLA, CSWE, NASM, NCATE, NLN, and NRPA. The library contains 419,987 volumes, 1,280,202 microform items, and 8835 audio/video tapes/CDs, and subscribes to 2081 periodicals. Computerized library services include the card catalog, interlibrary loans, database searching, and Internet access. Special learning facilities include a learning resource center, radio station, and a museum of archeological items and artworks. The 693-acre campus is in a small town 120 miles south of St. Louis. Including any residence halls, there are 73 buildings.

Student Life: 85% of undergraduates are from Missouri. Students are from 41 states, 37 foreign countries, and Canada. 81% are from public schools. 89% are white. 53% are Protestant; 32% Catholic; 11% claim no religious affiliation. The average age of freshmen is 19; all undergraduates, 23. 30% do not continue beyond their first year; 46% remain to graduate.

Housing: 2484 students can be accommodated in college housing, which includes single-sex and coed dorms, on-campus apartments, fraternity houses, and sorority houses. In addition, there are honors houses and special-interest houses. On-campus housing is guaranteed for the freshman year only and is available on a first-come, first-served basis. 71% of students commute. Alcohol is not permitted. All students may keep cars.

Activities: 16% of men belong to 10 national fraternities; 18% of women belong to 8 national sororities. There are 132 groups on campus, including art, band, cheerleading, choir, chorus, dance, drama, drill team, ethnic, honors, international, jazz band, literary magazine, marching band, musical theater, orchestra, pep band, political, professional, radio and TV, religious, social, social service, student government, symphony, and yearbook. Popular campus events include Family Weekends, Spring Fling, and International Week.

Sports: There are 7 intercollegiate sports for men and 9 for women, and 28 intramural sports for men and 28 for women. Facilities include a student recreation center housing an indoor track, a climbing wall, 6 racquetball courts, 3 indoor basketball courts, a weight room, volleyball courts, and bicycle and rowing machines.

Disabled Students: All of the campus is accessible. Wheelchair ramps, elevators, special parking, specially equipped rest rooms, special class scheduling, lowered drinking fountains, lowered telephones, and priority enrollment are available.

Services: Counseling and information services are available, as is tutoring in most subjects. There is a reader service for the blind, and remedial math, reading, and writing.

Campus Safety and Security: Measures include 24-hour foot and vehicle patrol, self-defense education, security escort services, and shuttle buses. There are informal discussions, pamphlets/posters/films, emergency telephones, and lighted pathways/sidewalks.

Programs of Study: Southeast confers B.A., B.S., B.F.A., B.F.C.S.Ed., B.G.S., B.S.B.A., B.S.Ed., B.S.M., B.S.Mus.Ed., and B.S.N. degrees. Associate and master's degrees are also awarded. Bachelor's degrees are awarded in AGRICULTURE (agricultural business management, agriculture, agronomy, animal science, and horticulture), BIOLOGICAL SCIENCE (biology/biological science), BUSINESS (accounting, banking and finance, business economics, fashion merchandising, marketing/retailing/merchandising, and office supervision and management), COMMUNICATIONS AND THE ARTS (advertising, art, communications, dramatic arts, English, French, German, journalism, music, music performance, music theory and composition, public relations, radio/television technology, and Spanish), COMPUTER AND PHYSICAL SCIENCE (chemistry, computer science, earth science, geoscience, mathematics, and physics), EDUCATION (art, athletic training, business, early childhood, elementary, English, foreign languages, industrial arts, mathematics, music, physical, science, secondary, social studies, and special), ENGINEERING AND ENVIRONMENTAL DESIGN (engineering technology, environmental science, industrial engineering technology, and interior design), HEALTH PROFESSIONS (nursing, speech pathology/audiology, and sports medicine), SOCIAL SCIENCE (anthropology, corrections, criminal justice, economics, family/consumer studies, food science, geography, history, law enforcement and corrections, liberal arts/general studies, philosophy, political science/government, psychology, social work, and sociology). Teacher education is the strongest academically. Elementary education is the largest.

Required: Students must complete 124 credit hours, up to 64 in the major. The core curriculum includes 48 credit hours in the University Studies program, as well as interdisciplinary studies, English, and math. Minimum GPAs (at least 2.0) and other graduation requirements vary by program. A writing exam must also be passed.

Special: Southeast offers co-op programs in education and cross-registration with Southern Illinois University. Opportunities are provided for individually arranged internships and work-study, study abroad in 48 countries, a general studies degree, dual and student-designed majors (interdisciplinary studies), credit by exam, nondegree study, and pass/fail options. A 3-2 engineering degree is possible in conjunction with the University of Missouri at Rolla or at Columbia. There are 8 national honor societies and a freshman honors program.

Faculty/Classroom: 53% of faculty are male; 47%, female. All teach undergraduates.

Admissions: 83% of the 2003-2004 applicants were accepted. The ACT scores for the 2003-2004 freshman class were: 36% below 21, 29% between 21 and 23, 21% between 24 and 26, 9% between 27 and 28, and 6% above 28. 29% of the current freshmen were in the top fifth of their class; 58% were in the top two fifths. There was 1 National Merit finalist. 27 freshmen graduated first in their class.

Requirements: The ACT is required. In addition, graduation from an accredited secondary school is required; the GED is accepted. Applicants should submit an academic record with 4 credits in English, 3 in social studies, 3 in algebra or higher math, 3 in science, 3 additional credits in English, math, science, social studies, speech, or a foreign language, and 1 unit in visual/performing arts. A GPA of 2.0 is required. AP and CLEP credits are accepted.

Procedure: Freshmen are admitted fall, spring, and summer. Entrance exams should be taken in the spring of the junior year or fall of the senior year. Application deadlines are open. The fall 2003 application fee was $20. Notification is sent on a rolling basis. Applications are accepted on-line.

Transfer: 602 transfer students enrolled in 2002-2003. Transcripts from the student's previous college must be submitted, listing at least 24 credits earned and a minimum GPA of 2.0. The ACT is required for those students who have less than 24 credit hours. 30 of 124 credits required for the bachelor's degree must be completed at Southeast.

Visiting: There are regularly scheduled orientations for prospective students, including academic advising and other university information. There are guides for informal visits and visitors may sit in on classes and stay overnight. To schedule a visit, contact the Admissions Office at *admissions@semovm.semo.edu.*

Financial Aid: In 2003-2004, 85% of all full-time freshmen and 75% of continuing full-time students received some form of financial aid. 53% of full-time freshmen and 50% of continuing full-time students received need-based aid. The average freshman award was $8269. Need-based scholarships or need-based grants averaged $3368 ($6350 maximum); need-based self-help aid (loans and jobs) averaged $3234 ($8649 maximum); non-need-based athletic scholarships averaged $7260 ($14,505 maximum); other non-need-based awards and non-need-based scholarships averaged $6101 ($19,190 maximum); and fee waivers averaged $1145 ($1268 maximum). 29% of undergraduates work part time. Average annual earnings from campus work are $1500. The average financial indebtedness of the 2003 graduate was $13,480. The FAFSA is required. The priority date for freshman financial aid applications for fall entry is March 1.

International Students: There are 150 international students enrolled. The school actively recruits these students. They must score 550 on the written TOEFL or 213 on the electronic version and also take the ACT, scoring 18.

Computers: The mainframe is an IBM 4381. There are 650 terminals and PCs in various campus locations, including the dorms. All students may access the system. There are no time limits and no fees.

Graduates: From July 1, 2002 to June 30, 2003, 1290 bachelor's degrees were awarded. The most popular majors were elementary education (12%), business administration and management (7%), and communications (7%). In an average class, 23% graduate in 4 years or less, 41% graduate in 5 years or less, and 43% graduate in 6 years or less.

Admissions Contact: Deborah Below, Director of Admissions. A video is available. E-mail: *admissions@semo.edu*
Web: *www.semo.edu/admissions/index.htm*

SOUTHWEST BAPTIST UNIVERSITY
Bolivar, MO 65613

B-3

(417) 328-1810
(800) 526-5859; Fax: (417) 328-1514

Full-time: 681 men, 1145 women	Faculty: 87
Part-time: 252 men, 668 women	Ph.D.s: 70%
Graduate: 178 men, 639 women	Student/Faculty: 21 to 1
Year: 4-1-4, summer session	Tuition: $11,591
Application Deadline: open	Room & Board: $3780
Freshman Class: 814 applied, 702 accepted, 397 enrolled	
SAT I Verbal/Math: 520/540	ACT: 23	COMPETITIVE

Southwest Baptist University, founded in 1878, is a private liberal arts institution affiliated with the Southern Baptist Convention. There are 5 undergraduate and 3 graduate schools. In addition to regional accreditation, SBU has baccalaureate program accreditation with ACBSP, ADA, CAPTE, NASM, and NLN. The library contains 165,000 volumes, 429,626 microform items, and 10,576 audio/video tapes/CDs, and subscribes to 1973 periodicals. Computerized library services include the card catalog, interlibrary loans, and database searching. Special learning facilities include a learning resource center and a child study center. The 152-acre campus is in a rural area 28 miles north of Springfield. Including any residence halls, there are 37 buildings.

Student Life: 72% of undergraduates are from Missouri. Students are from 41 states, 10 foreign countries, and Canada. 94% are white. Most are Protestant. The average age of freshmen is 20; all undergraduates, 21. 25% do not continue beyond their first year; 57% remain to graduate.

Housing: 1110 students can be accommodated in college housing, which includes single-sex dorms and on-campus apartments. On-campus housing is guaranteed for all 4 years. 63% of students commute. Alcohol is not permitted. All students may keep cars.

Activities: There are no fraternities or sororities. There are many groups and organizations on campus, including art, band, cheerleading, choir, chorale, chorus, computers, debate, drama, forensics, honors, international, jazz band, musical theater, newspaper, opera, orchestra, pep band, photography, political, professional, radio and TV, religious, social service, student government, and yearbook. Popular campus events include fall and spring visitation days and Parents Day.

Sports: There are 7 intercollegiate sports for men and 6 for women, and 12 intramural sports for men and 12 for women. Facilities include a 2500-seat field house and a 1260-seat gym, weight rooms, training facilities, a baseball diamond, a football stadium, an outdoor track, and 5 tennis courts. There are also fields for flag football, soccer, and softball and a natatorium with a 25-meter swimming pool.

Disabled Students: 75% of the campus is accessible. Wheelchair ramps, elevators, special parking, specially equipped rest rooms, special class scheduling, and lowered drinking fountains are available.

Services: Counseling and information services are available, as is tutoring in every subject. There is remedial math, reading, and writing.

Campus Safety and Security: Measures include 24-hour foot and vehicle patrol, informal discussions, emergency telephones, and lighted pathways/sidewalks.

Programs of Study: SBU confers B.A., B.S., B.A.S., B.M., and B.S.N. degrees. Associate and master's degrees are also awarded. Bachelor's degrees are awarded in BIOLOGICAL SCIENCE (biology/biological science), BUSINESS (accounting, business administration and management, recreation and leisure services, and sports management), COMMUNICATIONS AND THE ARTS (art, communications, dramatic arts, English, music, and Spanish), COMPUTER AND PHYSICAL SCIENCE (chemistry, computer science, information sciences and systems, and mathematics), EDUCATION (art, athletic training, early childhood, elementary, middle school, music, physical, and social science), ENGINEERING AND ENVIRONMENTAL DESIGN (commercial art and occupational safety and health), HEALTH PROFESSIONS (medical technology and nursing), SOCIAL SCIENCE (biblical studies, criminal justice, history, human services, ministries, political science/government, psychology, religion, religious education, religious music, and sociology). Education, nursing, and business administration are the largest.

Required: To graduate, students must complete 128 credit hours, with 40 in upper-division courses, and maintain a 2.0 GPA. Distribution requirements for most bachelor's degrees include 10 to 11 hours in science and math, 9 to 12 in humanities, 9 in communications, 8 in religion, 6 in business and community leadership, 5 in personal and family development, and 3 in computer literacy. B.A. students must demonstrate foreign language proficiency. All students must also fulfill the chapel attendance requirement.

Special: SBU offers internships, study abroad, and Washington, Russian, Latin American, Middle Eastern, and Hollywood semester programs. 3-2 engineering degrees with the University of Missouri-Rolla and Washington University are also offered. On-campus work-study, dual majors, pass-fail options, correspondence courses, and nondegree study are available. There are 2 national honor societies and 5 departmental honors programs.

Faculty/Classroom: 66% of faculty are male; 34%, female. All teach undergraduates. No introductory courses are taught by graduate students. The average class size in an introductory lecture is 35; in a laboratory, 60; and in a regular course, 20.

Admissions: 86% of the 2003-2004 applicants were accepted. The SAT I scores for the 2003-2004 freshman class were: Verbal--33% below 500, 50% between 500 and 599, 14% between 600 and 700, and 3% above 700; Math--40% below 500, 38% between 500 and 599, 17% between 600 and 700, and 5% above 700. The ACT scores were 30% below 21, 20% between 21 and 23, 18% between 24 and 26, 12% between 27 and 28, and 20% above 28. 42% of the current freshmen were in the top fifth of their class; 56% were in the top two fifths.

Requirements: The SAT I or ACT is required, with a minimum composite score of 890 on the SAT I or 19 on the ACT for unconditional admission. Students must be graduates of an accredited secondary school or have earned a GED. Applicants are required to have 13 academic credits, including a recommended 4 credits in English, 3 in math, 2 each in natural science and history or social science, and 2 in English, math, foreign language, computer science, social studies, and natural science electives. An interview and, where applicable, an audition are recommended. AP and CLEP credits are accepted.

Procedure: Freshmen are admitted to all sessions. Entrance exams should be taken at any time prior to admission. There are early decision, deferred, and rolling admissions plans. Application deadlines are open. The fall 2003 application fee was $25.

Transfer: 117 transfer students enrolled in a recent year. Applicants must submit official college and high school transcripts and have a minimum GPA of 2.0. An interview is encouraged. Students who have not yet met SBU's English and math requirements must present scores from the ACT, SAT I, or other approved placement test. Only 6 hours of D credit will be accepted. 30 of 128 credits required for the bachelor's degree must be completed at SBU.

Visiting: There are regularly scheduled orientations for prospective students, including fall and spring visitation days. There are guides for informal visits and visitors may sit in on classes and stay overnight. To schedule a visit, contact Rob Harris, Director of Admissions.

Financial Aid: In a recent year, 95% of all full-time freshmen and 76% of continuing full-time students received some form of financial aid. 75% of full-time freshmen and 83% of continuing full-time students received need-based aid. The average freshman award was $6354. 28% of undergraduates work part time. Average annual earnings from campus work are $822. The average financial indebtedness of a recent year's graduate was $15,417. The FAFSA and the college's own financial statement are required. Check with the school for current application deadlines.

International Students: There were 10 international students enrolled in a recent year. They must score 550 on the written TOEFL and also take the SAT I or the ACT.

Computers: The mainframe is an HP 9000-D330 midrange system for administrative records systems. There are 220 terminals or PCs located in the computer center, the library, and classrooms and available for student use. 7 dorms are wired for connection to the campus network and for e-mail and Internet access. There are also 48 dial-up lines for access from off campus or from unwired residence halls. All students may access the system from 8 A.M. to 1:30 A.M. daily. There are no time limits. The fee is $35.

Graduates: In a recent year, 377 bachelor's degrees were awarded. The most popular majors were education (31%), nursing (14%), and business (11%). In an average class, 12% graduate in 3 years or less, 55% graduate in 4 years or less, 68% graduate in 5 years or less, and 70% graduate in 6 years or less. 74 companies recruited on campus in a recent year.

Admissions Contact: Rob Harris, Director of Admissions. A video is available. E-mail: *rharris@sbuniv.edu* Web: *www.sbuniv.edu*

SOUTHWEST MISSOURI STATE UNIVERSITY

B-3

Springfield, MO 65804

(417) 836-5521
(800) 492-7900; Fax: (417) 836-6334

Full-time: 5400 men, 6400 women	**Faculty:** 668; IIA, -$
Part-time: 1200 men, 1550 women	**Ph.D.s:** 81%
Graduate: 990 men, 1875 women	**Student/Faculty:** 17 to 1
Year: semesters, summer session	**Tuition:** $4636 ($8776)
Application Deadline: open	**Room & Board:** $4282
Freshman Class: 6316 applied, 5446 accepted, 2695 enrolled	
ACT: 23	**COMPETITIVE**

Southwest Missouri State University, founded in 1905, is a public institution offering undergraduate programs in arts and letters, business administration, humanities and social sciences, education and psychology, health and applied sciences, and science and math. Figures in above capsule are approximate. There are 7 undergraduate schools and 1 graduate school. In addition to regional accreditation, SMSU has baccalaureate program accreditation with AACSB, ADA, AHEA, ASLA, CSAB, CSWE, NASM, NCATE, NLN, and NRPA. The library contains 675,000 volumes, 900,000 microform items, and 30,000 audio/video tapes/CDs, and subscribes to 5000 periodicals. Computerized library services include the card catalog, interlibrary loans, and database searching. Special learning facilities include a learning resource center, art gallery, and radio station. The 225-acre campus is in a suburban area 220 miles southwest of St. Louis. Including any residence halls, there are 60 buildings.

Student Life: 92% of undergraduates are from Missouri. Students are from 47 states, 66 foreign countries, and Canada. 90% are from public schools. 89% are white. The average age of freshmen is 18; all undergraduates, 21. 32% do not continue beyond their first year.

Housing: 4170 students can be accommodated in college housing, which includes single-sex and coed dorms, on-campus apartments, married-student housing, fraternity houses, and sorority houses. In addition, there are honors houses. On-campus housing is guaranteed for all 4 years. Alcohol is not permitted. All students may keep cars.

Activities: 14% of men and about 9% of women belong to 15 national fraternities; 10% of women belong to 10 national sororities. There are 252 groups on campus, including art, band, cheerleading, chess, choir, chorale, chorus, computers, dance, drama, drill team, ethnic, gay, honors, international, jazz band, literary magazine, marching band, musical theater, newspaper, orchestra, pep band, political, professional, radio and TV, religious, social, social service, student government, symphony, and yearbook. Popular campus events include Tent Theater, Spring Fling, and Leadership Conference.

Sports: There are 10 intercollegiate sports for men and 9 for women, and 19 intramural sports for men and 19 for women. Facilities include a 16,600-seat stadium, a 9000-seat arena, a 9000-seat gym, a student center, an athletic center, a swimming pool, softball and practice fields, tennis courts, and bowling lanes.

Disabled Students: 95% of the campus is accessible. Wheelchair ramps, elevators, special parking, specially equipped rest rooms, special class scheduling, lowered drinking fountains, lowered telephones, special housing, TDD terminals, and automatic door openers are available.

Services: Counseling and information services are available, as is tutoring in some subjects. There is a reader service for the blind, and remedial math, reading, and writing. A math center and a writing center are available for student use. Proctors are available for tests given to those with disabilities.

Campus Safety and Security: Measures include 24-hour foot and vehicle patrol, self-defense education, security escort services, and shuttle buses. There are informal discussions, pamphlets/posters/films, emergency telephones, and lighted pathways/sidewalks.

Programs of Study: SMSU confers B.A., B.S., B.F.A., B.M., B.S.E., B.S.N., and B.S.W. degrees. Master's degrees are also awarded. Bachelor's degrees are awarded in AGRICULTURE (agriculture, agronomy, animal science, conservation and regulation, horticulture, and wildlife management), BIOLOGICAL SCIENCE (biology/biological science, cell biology, and nutrition), BUSINESS (accounting, banking and finance, business administration and management, hotel/motel and restaurant management, institutional management, insurance, marketing/retailing/merchandising, and recreation and leisure services), COMMUNICATIONS AND THE ARTS (art, broadcasting, communications, dance, design, dramatic arts, English, film arts, French, German, Latin, music, music performance, Spanish, speech/debate/rhetoric, and technical and business writing), COMPUTER AND PHYSICAL SCIENCE (chemistry, computer science, earth science, geology, information sciences and systems, mathematics, and physics), EDUCATION (agricultural, art, athletic training, business, early childhood, elementary, foreign languages, health, home economics, industrial arts, middle school, music, physical, science, secondary, and special), ENGINEERING AND ENVIRONMENTAL DESIGN (cartography, construction management, drafting and design, electrical/electronics engineering technology, engineering physics, industrial administration/management, interior design, manufacturing technology, mechanical design technology, printing technology, and urban planning technology), HEALTH PROFESSIONS (medical laboratory technology, nursing, predentistry, radiograph medical technology, respiratory therapy, and speech pathology/audiology), SOCIAL SCIENCE (anthropology, child care/child and family studies, clothing and textiles management/production/services, dietetics, economics, geography, gerontology, history, parks and recreation management, philosophy, political science/government, psychology, public administration, religion, social science, social work, and sociology). Education and business are the largest.

Required: A total of 125 to 130 semester hours, including 30 to 60 in the major, and a minimum GPA of 2.0 are required. 45 general education semester hours are required, to include 8 in natural sciences, 6 to 9 each in social sciences and humanities, 6 in American studies, 4 in phys ed, 3 to 6 in English composition, 3 each in math and speech, and 1 in freshman orientation.

Special: Southwest Missouri offers co-op programs, internships, study abroad in 40 countries, and work-study programs. Also available are B.A.-B.S. degrees in 12 majors, preprofessional programs in law and medicine, and student-designed and interdisciplinary majors, including antiquities, agriculture business and agriculture education, chemistry/biochemistry, communication management, and finance/real estate. A 3-2 engineering degree is available through the University of Missouri-Rolla. Credit for military experience and pass/not-pass options are offered. There are 31 national honor societies and a freshman honors program.

Faculty/Classroom: 70% of faculty are male; 30%, female. 97% teach undergraduates. Graduate students teach 4% of introductory courses. The average class size in a regular course is 23.

Admissions: 86% of the 2003-2004 applicants were accepted. The ACT scores for the 2003-2004 freshman class were: 23% below 21, 31% between 21 and 23, 24% between 24 and 26, 10% between 27 and 28, and 13% above 28. 40% of the current freshmen were in the top fifth of their class; 70% were in the top two fifths.

Requirements: The SAT I or ACT is required; the ACT is preferred. Admission is based on a sliding scale of rank or GPA and test score. Freshmen must also have a 16-unit high school core curriculum, including 4 in English, 3 each in math and social studies, 2 in science, 1 in visual and performing arts, and 3 electives. AP and CLEP credits are accepted.

Procedure: Freshmen are admitted to all sessions. Entrance exams should be taken as early as possible. The 2003 application fee was $30. Notification is sent on a rolling basis.

Transfer: Applicants must present a minimum GPA of 2.0 on transferable courses. If they have completed less than 24 semester hours, they are also required to meet freshman admission requirements. 30 to 60 of 125 to 130 credits required for the bachelor's degree must be completed at SMSU.

Visiting: There are regularly scheduled orientations for prospective students, including academic advising and enrollment for classes. There are guides for informal visits. To schedule a visit, contact the Admissions Office.

Financial Aid: 51% of undergraduates work part time. Average annual earnings from campus work are $1500. SMSU is a member of CSS. The FAFSA is required.

International Students: The school actively recruits these students. They must score 500 on the written TOEFL.

Computers: The mainframes are a UNIX processors and Novell servers. 3 computer labs contain approximately 300 PCs, most of which are connected to the campus network. Access to the campus network is available through the residence halls and through dial-in services. All students may access the system. There are no time limits and no fees.

Graduates: From July 1, 2002 to June 30, 2003, 1139 bachelor's degrees were awarded.

Admissions Contact: Donald E. Simpson, Director of Admissions. A video is available. E-mail: *smsuinfo@mail.smsu.edu* Web: *www.smsu.edu*

STEPHENS COLLEGE
Columbia, MO 65215

C-2

(573) 876-7207
(800) 876-7207; Fax: (573) 876-7237

Full-time: 11 men, 436 women	**Faculty:** 47
Part-time: 7 men, 123 women	**Ph.Ds:** 83%
Graduate: 10 men, 60 women	**Student/Faculty:** 10 to 1
Year: semesters	**Tuition:** $17,360
Application Deadline: open	**Room & Board:** $6900
Freshman Class: n/av	
SAT I Verbal/Math: 580/530	**ACT:** 24 **COMPETITIVE+**

Stephens College, founded in 1833, is a private college for women, offering undergraduate programs in the arts and sciences, business, education, and fine arts. There are 6 undergraduate and 2 graduate schools. The library contains 119,695 volumes, 11,322 microform items, and 4430 audio/video tapes/CDs, and subscribes to 202 periodicals. Computerized library services include interlibrary loans, database searching, and Internet access. Special learning facilities include a learning resource center, art gallery, radio station, and TV station. The 86-acre campus is in an urban area 120 miles west of St. Louis. Including any residence halls, there are 35 buildings.

Student Life: 54% of undergraduates are from Missouri. Students are from 42 states and 3 foreign countries. 80% are from public schools. 87% are white. The average age of freshmen is 18; all undergraduates, 20. 34% do not continue beyond their first year; 50% remain to graduate.

Housing: 775 students can be accommodated in college housing, which includes single-sex dorms and on-campus apartments. In addition, there are honors houses, special-interest houses for intercultural scholars and fine arts majors, and houses with designated academic floors or nonsmoking floors. On-campus housing is guaranteed for all 4 years. 75% of students live on campus; of those, 90% remain on campus on weekends. All students may keep cars.

Activities: 88% of women belong to 2 national sororities. There are no fraternities. There are 45 groups on campus, including art, choir, chorale, chorus, dance, drama, ethnic, gay, honors, international, literary magazine, musical theater, newspaper, photography, political, professional, radio and TV, religious, social, social service, student government, and yearbook. Popular campus events include the opening convocation, Honors Convocation, and performing arts events.

Sports: Facilities include a 300-seat gym, an Olympic-size pool, and tennis courts.

Disabled Students: 80% of the campus is accessible. Wheelchair ramps, elevators, special parking, specially equipped rest rooms, special class scheduling, lowered drinking fountains, and special housing are available.

Services: Counseling and information services are available, as is tutoring in most subjects, including English and courses with written expectations. There is remedial writing.

Campus Safety and Security: Measures include 24-hour foot and vehicle patrol, self-defense education, security escort services, and informal discussions. There are pamphlets/posters/films, emergency telephones, and lighted pathways/sidewalks.

Programs of Study: Stephens confers B.A., B.S., and B.F.A. degrees. Associate and master's degrees are also awarded. Bachelor's degrees are awarded in AGRICULTURE (equine science), BIOLOGICAL SCIENCE (biology/biological science), BUSINESS (accounting, business administration and management, and fashion merchandising), COMMUNICATIONS AND THE ARTS (creative writing, dance, dramatic arts, English, graphic design, public relations, and Spanish), COMPUTER AND PHYSICAL SCIENCE (mathematics), EDUCATION (early childhood and elementary), ENGINEERING AND ENVIRONMENTAL DESIGN (environmental science), SOCIAL SCIENCE (fashion design and technology, international studies, liberal arts/general studies, philosophy, political science/government, prelaw, and social science). Psychology and education are the strongest academically. Performing arts, fashion, and psychology are the largest.

Required: All students must complete English 101 and 102, a math course, and a distribution of 9 courses in lower-division work. The bachelor's degree requires completion of at least 120 semester hours, including 30 to 72 in a major field, with a minimum GPA of 2.0.

Special: Students may study abroad in England, Canada, Mexico, and Spain. Stephens also offers cross-registration with the Mid-Missouri Association of Colleges and Universities, many internships, a Washington semester, dual and student-designed majors, a 3-2 occupational therapy

degree program with Washington University, and pass/fail options for electives. There are 8 national honor societies, and 8 departmental honors programs.

Faculty/Classroom: 45% of faculty are male; 55%, female. All both teach and do research.

Admissions: The SAT I scores for the 2003-2004 freshman class were: Verbal--12% below 500, 54% between 500 and 599, 32% between 600 and 700, and 2% above 700; Math--29% below 500, 49% between 500 and 599, 22% between 600 and 700, and 2% above 700. The ACT scores were 16% below 21, 31% between 21 and 23, 37% between 24 and 26, 10% between 27 and 28, and 6% above 28. 43% of the current freshmen were in the top fifth of their class; 74% were in the top two fifths. 3 freshmen graduated first in their class.

Requirements: The SAT I or ACT is required. In addition, applicants must be graduates of accredited secondary schools or have earned a GED. An essay is also required, and an interview is recommended. A GPA of 2.5 is required. AP and CLEP credits are accepted. Important factors in the admissions decision are advanced placement or honor courses, leadership record, and recommendations by school officials.

Procedure: Freshmen are admitted fall and spring. There is a deferred admissions plan. Application deadlines are open. Application fee is $25. Applications are accepted on-line through the school's web site.

Transfer: 26 transfer students enrolled in 2002-2003. Applicants must submit official transcripts from all college work attempted or completed as well as a recommendation from an academic college instructor. Transfers must submit an official high school transcript. 36 of 120 credits required for the bachelor's degree must be completed at Stephens.

Visiting: There are regularly scheduled orientations for prospective students, consisting of attendance at classes, a campus tour, an appointment with instructors, and an interview. There are guides for informal visits and visitors may sit in on classes and stay overnight. To schedule a visit, contact the campus visit coordinator at *apply@stephens.edu*.

Financial Aid: In 2003-2004, 85% of all full-time students received some form of financial aid. 85% of all full-time students received need-based aid. The average freshman award was $14,000. 55% of undergraduates work part time. Average annual earnings from campus work are $800. The average financial indebtedness of the 2003 graduate was $14,080. The FAFSA is required. The priority date for freshman financial aid applications for fall entry is March 15.

International Students: There are 3 international students enrolled. The school actively recruits these students. They must score 550 on the written TOEFL or 213 on the electronic version.

Computers: The mainframe is a DEC Alpha 2000. There is an academic lab with 30 computers with access to the Internet and the Web. Departmental labs have 3 to 10 computers each. Each residence hall has a lab with 4 to 8 computers, all with Internet access. All students may access the system. There are no time limits and no fees. It is strongly recommended that all students have a personal computer.

Graduates: From July 1, 2002 to June 30, 2003, 119 bachelor's degrees were awarded. The most popular majors were theater arts (29%), fashion marketing (8%), and psychology (8%). In an average class, 30% graduate in 3 years or less, 72% graduate in 4 years or less, 91% graduate in 5 years or less, and 94% graduate in 6 years or less. 15 companies recruited on campus in 2002-2003.

Admissions Contact: Amy Shaver, Director of Enrollment. E-mail: *ashaver@stephens.edu* Web: *www.stephens.edu*

TRUMAN STATE UNIVERSITY
Kirksville, MO 63501

C-1

(660) 785-4114
(800) 892-7792; Fax: (660) 785-7456

Full-time: 2190 men, 3148 women	**Faculty:** 349; IIA, --$
Part-time: 73 men, 68 women	**Ph.Ds:** 85%
Graduate: 63 men, 170 women	**Student/Faculty:** 15 to 1
Year: semesters, summer session	**Tuition:** $4656 ($8456)
Application Deadline: March 1	**Room & Board:** $5072
Freshman Class: 4334 applied, 3622 accepted, 1317 enrolled	
SAT I Verbal/Math: 670/650	**ACT:** 27
	HIGHLY COMPETITIVE+

Truman State University, founded in 1867, and formerly known as Northeast Missouri State University, is a public liberal arts institution offering undergraduate and graduate degree programs in business and accountancy, education, fine arts, human potential and performance, language and literature, mathematics and computer science, science, and social science. There are 7 undergraduate and 7 graduate schools. In addition to regional accreditation, Truman has baccalaureate program accreditation with AACSB, ASLA, NASM, NCATE, and NLN. The library contains 449,275 volumes, 1,524,690 microform items, and 37,896 audio/video tapes/CDs, and subscribes to 3476 periodicals. Computerized library services include the card catalog, interlibrary loans, database searching, and Internet access. Special learning facilities include a learning resource center, art gallery, radio station, TV studio, a biofeedback lab, an independent learning center for nursing students, an observatory, a greenhouse chamber, and a speech and hearing clinic. The 140-acre campus is in a small town 170 miles northeast of Kansas City and 200 miles north of St. Louis. Including any residence halls, there are 39 buildings.

Student Life: 72% of undergraduates are from Missouri. Students are from 43 states and 48 foreign countries. 80% are from public schools. 84% are white. 52% are Protestant; 28% Catholic; 19% no affiliation, unknown affiliation, or other religious affiliation. The average age of freshmen is 18; all undergraduates, 20. 16% do not continue beyond their first year; 64% remain to graduate.

Housing: 2929 students can be accommodated in college housing, which includes single-sex and coed dorms, on-campus apartments, married-student housing, and sorority houses. All residence halls are designated residential colleges that provide professional advisers to all freshmen, classrooms, and academic centers within the colleges, a low student-to-adviser ratio, and an integrative living-learning environment. On-campus housing is guaranteed for the freshman year only, is available on a first-come, first-served basis, and is available on a lottery system for upperclassmen. 54% of students commute. Alcohol is not permitted. All students may keep cars.

Activities: 31% of men belong to 17 national fraternities; 22% of women belong to 1 local and 9 national sororities. There are 210 groups on campus, including art, band, cheerleading, chess, choir, chorale, chorus, computers, dance, debate, drama, drill team, ethnic, film, gay, honors, international, jazz band, literary magazine, marching band, musical theater, newspaper, orchestra, pep band, political, professional, radio and TV, religious, social, social service, student government, and yearbook. Popular campus events include Dog Days (Spring Carnival), Family Day, and International Week.

Sports: There are 11 intercollegiate sports for men and 10 for women, and 19 intramural sports for men and 19 for women. Facilities include a 5000-seat football stadium, a soccer field, tennis and racquetball courts, a softball diamond, a baseball diamond, a 3000-seat arena with 3 basketball courts, an Olympic-size pool, weight training rooms, indoor and outdoor track facilities, and a 60,000-square-foot student recreation center.

Disabled Students: 90% of the campus is accessible. Wheelchair ramps, elevators, special parking, specially equipped rest rooms, special class scheduling, lowered drinking fountains, lowered telephones, and special housing are available. The swimming pool is equipped with a lift to assist physically disabled swimmers.

Services: Counseling and information services are available, as is tutoring in most subjects. Services for the hearing impaired, a braille scanner, and a printer are also available. There is a reader service for the blind. Services for Individuals with Disabilities provides recording, note-taking, test-taking, and advising services.

Campus Safety and Security: Measures include 24-hour foot and vehicle patrol, self-defense education, security escort services, and informal discussions. There are pamphlets/posters/films, emergency telephones, and lighted pathways/sidewalks, and personal body alarms, available on a limited basis.

Programs of Study: Truman confers B.A., B.S., B.F.A., B.M., and B.S.N. degrees. Master's degrees are also awarded. Bachelor's degrees are awarded in AGRICULTURE (agricultural economics, agriculture, agronomy, animal science, and equine science), BIOLOGICAL SCIENCE (biology/biological science), BUSINESS (accounting and business administration and management), COMMUNICATIONS AND THE ARTS (art, art history and appreciation, classics, communications, dramatic arts, English, fine arts, French, German, journalism, music, music performance, Russian, Spanish, and speech/debate/rhetoric), COMPUTER AND PHYSICAL SCIENCE (chemistry, computer science, mathematics, and physics), ENGINEERING AND ENVIRONMENTAL DESIGN (preengineering), HEALTH PROFESSIONS (health science, medical technology, nursing, physical therapy, predentistry, premedicine, preoptometry, prepharmacy, preveterinary science, and speech pathology/audiology), SOCIAL SCIENCE (criminal justice, economics, history, philosophy, physical fitness/movement, political science/government, prelaw, psychology, religion, and sociology). Chemistry, political science, and business are the strongest academically. Business administration, biology, and English are the largest.

Required: All students must complete 63 hours of course work in the liberal arts, 16 of which must be in written and oral communication, math and statistics, computer literacy, and personal well-being, and 23 of which must be in history, science, social science, philosophy/religion, and aesthetics. The B.A., B.F.A., and B.M. degree require intermediate proficiency in one foreign language, and the B.S. and B.S.N. require additional course work in science, math, statistics, computer science, social sciences, or logic. Skills such as writing, quantitative analysis, problem solving, and critical thinking are reinforced throughout the curriculum, and all seniors end their studies with a capstone, or culminating experience, in their majors. Students must also complete a nationally normed exam in their subject area as part of Truman's assessment program.

Special: Study abroad in 39 countries is offered through Truman's own programs and those of the College Consortium for International Studies, the Council on International Educational Exchange, and the International Student Exchange Program. The university requires internships in education and health and exercise science. Voluntary legislative internships are offered to all students at the state capitol, and internships through the Washington Center. There is a 3-2 engineering program with the University of Missouri-Rolla. Work-study programs, B.A.-B.S. degrees, dual majors, student-designed majors in health and exercise science, biology, history, and agricultural science, credit for military experience, pass/fail options for internships, and nondegree study are available. There are 13 national honor societies, including Phi Beta Kappa, a freshman honors program, and 15 departmental honors programs.

Faculty/Classroom: 56% of faculty are male; 44%, female. 98% teach undergraduates. Graduate students teach 4% of introductory courses. The average class size in an introductory lecture is 28; in a laboratory, 17; and in a regular course, 22.

Admissions: 84% of the 2003-2004 applicants were accepted. The SAT I scores for the 2003-2004 freshman class were: Verbal--5% below 500, 36% between 500 and 599, 41% between 600 and 700, and 18% above 700; Math--7% below 500, 34% between 500 and 599, 47% between 600 and 700, and 12% above 700. The ACT scores were 4% below 21, 11% between 21 and 23, 29% between 24 and 26, 19% between 27 and 28, and 39% above 28. 75% of the current freshmen were in the top fifth of their class; 96% were in the top two fifths. There were 16 National Merit finalists. 144 freshmen graduated first in their class.

Requirements: The SAT I or ACT is required. The University prefers the ACT, with a recommended minimum score of 22. Recommended minimum composite score on the SAT I is 1010, or 550 on each part. Applicants should have completed 4 units of English, 3 each of science and social studies, 2 of foreign language, and 1 of art or music. 4 units of math are strongly recommended. An essay is required and an interview or visit is recommended. AP and CLEP credits are accepted. Important factors in the admissions decision are leadership record, advanced placement or honor courses, and extracurricular activities record.

Procedure: Freshmen are admitted to all sessions. Entrance exams should be taken during the spring or summer following the junior year. There are early admissions and deferred admissions plans. Early admission applications should be filed by November 15; regular applications, by March 1 for fall entry. Notification of early admission is sent December 15; regular decision, on a rolling basis. Applications are accepted online through Apply, Next Stop College, CollegeLink, or the school's web site.

Transfer: 100 transfer students enrolled in 2002-2003. Transfer applicants should present a minimum 2.75 GPA on transferable hours and must meet minimum criteria for entering freshmen. 45 of 124 credits required for the bachelor's degree must be completed at Truman.

Visiting: There are regularly scheduled orientations for prospective students, including an interview with an admission counselor, a student-led campus tour, an appointment with a faculty member in the student's major, appointments in any areas of special interest, and the opportunity to observe a class. There are guides for informal visits and visitors may sit in on classes and stay overnight. To schedule a visit, contact the Admissions Office at (660) 785-4135 or admissions@truman.edu.

Financial Aid: In 2003-2004, 98% of all full-time freshmen and 92% of continuing full-time students received some form of financial aid. 32% of full-time freshmen and 30% of continuing full-time students received need-based aid. The average freshman award was $6872. Need-based scholarships or need-based grants averaged $3188 ($4600 maximum); need-based self-help aid (loans and jobs) averaged $2875 ($10,500 maximum); non-need-based athletic scholarships averaged $3523 ($12,622 maximum); and other non-need-based awards and non-need-based scholarships averaged $3326 ($16,946 maximum). 39% of undergraduates work part time. Average annual earnings from campus work are $899. The average financial indebtedness of the 2003 graduate was $15,655. Truman is a member of CSS. The FAFSA and the university's own financial statement are required. The deadline for filing freshman financial aid applications for fall entry is April 1.

International Students: There are 268 international students enrolled. The school actively recruits these students. They must score 550 on the written TOEFL or 213 on the electronic version and also take the Comprehensive English Language Test.

Computers: Students have access to the university's PC-based network. All students receive free computer accounts for e-mail, printing, and saving files. Approximately 745 workstations are available for student use; PCs are located in 8 residence halls and most academic buildings. All residence hall rooms are wired with network connections. All students may access the system. Labs are open until 1 A.M. in the academic buildings, and 7:30 A.M. to 1 A.M. in the library. Residence hall labs are always open. An individual time limit of 30 minutes is imposed only when other students are waiting. There are no fees.

Graduates: From July 1, 2002 to June 30, 2003, 1227 bachelor's degrees were awarded. The most popular majors were business administration (18%), English (10%), and biology (9%). In an average class, 2% graduate in 3 years or less, 40% graduate in 4 years or less, 64% graduate in 5 years or less, and 66% graduate in 6 years or less. Of the 2002 graduating class, 40% were enrolled in graduate school within 6 months of graduation and 57% were employed.

Admissions Contact: Brad Chambers, Co-Director of Admission.
E-mail: *admissions@truman.edu* Web: *admissions.truman.edu*

UNIVERSITY OF MISSOURI SYSTEM

The University of Missouri System, established in 1966, is a public system in Missouri. It is governed by a board of curators, whose chief administrator is the president. The primary goal of the system is teaching, research, extension, and other public service. The main priorities are to provide the highest quality of instructional and research programs, to provide educational access to qualified students who demonstrate likelihood of academic success, and to operate in an effective and cost-efficient manner. The total enrollment of all 4 campuses is usually about 55,000; there were approximately 9500 faculty members. Altogether there are 224 baccalaureate, 202 master's, and 117 doctoral programs offered in University of Missouri System. 4-year campuses are located in Columbia, Kansas City, Rolla, and St. Louis. Profiles of the 4-year campuses are included in this section.

UNIVERSITY OF MISSOURI/COLUMBIA   C-2
Columbia, MO 65211

(573) 882-7786
(800) 225-6075; Fax: (573) 882-7887

Full-time: 9228 men, 9805 women	**Faculty:** 1487; I, --$
Part-time: 660 men, 748 women	**Ph.D.s:** 94%
Graduate: 2868 men, 3496 women	**Student/Faculty:** 13 to 1
Year: semesters, summer session	**Tuition:** $6558 ($16,005)
Application Deadline: May 1	**Room & Board:** $7224
Freshman Class: 10,449 applied, 9327 accepted, 4669 enrolled	
ACT: 25	**VERY COMPETITIVE**

The University of Missouri/Columbia, established in 1839, offers a comprehensive array of undergraduate and graduate programs as well as professional training in law, medicine, and veterinary medicine. There are 10 undergraduate and 20 graduate schools. In addition to regional accreditation, Mizzou has baccalaureate program accreditation with AACSB, ABET, ACEJMC, ADA, APTA, CAHEA, CSWE, FIDER, NASAD, NASM, NRPA, and SAF. The 11 libraries contain 3,149,211 volumes and 6,833,496 microform items, and subscribe to 26,886 periodicals. Computerized library services include the card catalog, interlibrary loans, and database searching. Special learning facilities include a learning resource center, art gallery, natural history museum, radio station, TV station, astronomy observatory, freedom of information center, herbarium, and anthropology, fishery, and wildlife collections. The 1358-acre campus is in a small town 120 miles west of St. Louis and 120 miles east of Kansas City. Including any residence halls, there are 355 buildings.

Student Life: 87% of undergraduates are from Missouri. Students are from 50 states, 99 foreign countries, and Canada. 81% are white. The average age of freshmen is 18; all undergraduates, 20. 16% do not continue beyond their first year; 67% remain to graduate.

Housing: 9032 students can be accommodated in college housing, which includes single-sex and coed dorms, off-campus apartments, married-student housing, fraternity houses, and sorority houses. In addition, there are honors houses, language houses, special-interest houses, international houses, quiet houses, and graduate/professional houses. On-campus housing is guaranteed for all 4 years. 58% of students commute. Alcohol is not permitted. All students may keep cars.

Activities: 20% of men belong to 32 national fraternities; 25% of women belong to 25 national sororities. There are 442 groups on campus, including art, band, cheerleading, choir, chorale, chorus, computers, dance, debate, drama, drill team, drum and bugle corps, ethnic, gay, honors, international, jazz band, literary magazine, marching band, musical theater, newspaper, orchestra, pep band, photography, political, professional, radio and TV, religious, social, social service, student government, symphony, and yearbook. Popular campus events include Big Twelve athletics, academic weeks, and Meet Mizzou Day.

Sports: There are 7 intercollegiate sports for men and 9 for women, and 20 intramural sports for men and 20 for women. Facilities include a recreation center with more than 10 multicourts, 21 racquetball courts, a natatorium, an indoor running track, and 2 weight rooms. There is a 62,000-seat stadium, a 1300-seat indoor gym, and an 18,000-seat auditorium.

Disabled Students: All of the campus is accessible. Wheelchair ramps, elevators, special parking, specially equipped rest rooms, special class scheduling, lowered drinking fountains, and lowered telephones are available.

Services: Counseling and information services are available, as is tutoring in some subjects. There is a reader service for the blind.

Campus Safety and Security: Measures include 24-hour foot and vehicle patrol, self-defense education, security escort services, and shuttle buses. There are informal discussions, pamphlets/posters/films, emergency telephones, lighted pathways/sidewalks, and a 24-hour bicycle patrol.

Programs of Study: Mizzou confers B.A., B.S., B.E.S., B.F.A., B.G.S., B.H.S., B.J., B.M., B.S.Acc., B.S.B.A., B.S.B.E., B.S.C.E., B.S.ChE., B.S.CiE., B.S.CoE, B.S.Ed., B.S.E.E., B.S.F., B.S.F.W., B.S.H.E.S., B.S.I.E., B.S.M.E., B.S.N., and B.S.W. degrees. Master's and doctoral degrees are also awarded. Bachelor's degrees are awarded in AGRICULTURE (agricultural business management, agricultural economics, agriculture, animal science, plant science, and soil science), BIOLOGICAL SCIENCE (biochemistry, biology/biological science, microbiology, and nutrition), BUSINESS (accounting, banking and finance, business administration and management, business economics, hotel/motel and restaurant management, marketing/retailing/merchandising, real estate, and tourism), COMMUNICATIONS AND THE ARTS (advertising, art history and appreciation, broadcasting, classics, communications, design, dramatic arts, English, French, German, journalism, linguistics, music, Russian, and Spanish), COMPUTER AND PHYSICAL SCIENCE (atmospheric sciences and meteorology, chemistry, computer science, geology, mathematics, physics, and statistics), EDUCATION (art, early childhood, education, elementary, middle school, music, and secondary), ENGINEERING AND ENVIRONMENTAL DESIGN (biomedical engineering, chemical engineering, civil engineering, computer engineering, electrical/electronics engineering, industrial engineering, and mechanical engineering), HEALTH PROFESSIONS (nursing, occupational therapy, physical therapy, radiological science, and respiratory therapy), SOCIAL SCIENCE (anthropology, archeology, economics, family/consumer resource management, food science, geography, history, human development, international studies, liberal arts/general studies, parks and recreation management, philosophy, political science/government, psychology, religion, social science, social work, sociology, and textiles and clothing). Biological sciences, business administration, and psychology are the strongest academically. Business, journalism, and engineering are the largest.

Required: To graduate, students must maintain a minimum 2.0 GPA and complete at least 120 credits, of which at least 30 must be in their major, although credit requirements can vary by degree program. All students must take English, plus 2 additional writing-intensive courses, demonstrate competency in college algebra, take 1 additional course in development math and reasoning skills, and complete a course in American history or government. Students must complete 9 hours each in social and behavioral sciences, physical and biological sciences (including 1 lab course), and humanities and fine arts. A capstone experience is also required.

Special: Available academic programs include co-op programs and cross-registration with other schools, internships, study abroad, a Washington semester, and work-study programs. Special degrees or studies include an accelerated degree, dual majors, a general studies degree, and student-designed majors. For highly motivated students there is an honors college and the possibility of early admission to the schools of law and medicine. There are 24 national honor societies, including Phi Beta Kappa, and a freshman honors program.

Faculty/Classroom: 69% of faculty are male; 31%, female.

Admissions: 89% of the 2003-2004 applicants were accepted. The ACT scores for the 2003-2004 freshman class were: 8% below 21, 25% between 21 and 23, 30% between 24 and 26, 17% between 27 and 28, and 21% above 28. 49% of the current freshmen were in the top fifth of their class; 79% were in the top two fifths. There were 19 National Merit finalists. 86 freshmen graduated first in their class.

Requirements: The ACT is required. Students may gain probationary admission with sufficient GED scores. The usual requirements are completion of 17 Carnegie units, including 4 each in English and math, 3 each in social studies and science, 2 in a foreign language, and 1 in fine arts. Admission is determined by these units and a combination of class rank and ACT score. AP and CLEP credits are accepted. Important factors in the admissions decision are advanced placement or honor courses and evidence of special talent.

Procedure: Freshmen are admitted to all sessions. Entrance exams should be taken late in the junior year or in the senior year. There is a deferred admissions plan and a rolling admissions plan. Applications should be filed by May 1 for fall entry, along with a $35 fee. Notification is sent on a rolling basis. Applications are accepted on-line through *http://admissions.missouri.edu/applying/index.php*.

Transfer: 1235 transfer students enrolled in 2002-2003. Transfer students must present 24 hours of completed college-level course work with a minimum 2.0 GPA, and show a C average in all course work attempted. An interview is recommended. The number of credits required for the bachelor's degree varies by division.

Visiting: There are regularly scheduled orientations for prospective students, consisting of a campus tour, a visit with an admissions representative, and a visit with an academic representative on request. There are guides for informal visits and visitors may sit in on classes. To schedule a visit, contact High School and Transfer Relations at (573) 882-2456.

Financial Aid: In 2003-2004, 80% of all full-time freshmen and 75% of continuing full-time students received some form of financial aid. 41% of full-time freshmen and 40% of continuing full-time students received need-based aid. Need-based scholarships or need-based grants averaged $5721; need-based self-help aid (loans and jobs) averaged $3813; and non-need-based athletic scholarships averaged $9384. 6% of undergraduates work part time. The average financial indebtedness of the

2003 graduate was $20,428. The FAFSA is required. The deadline for filing freshman financial aid applications for fall entry is March 1.

International Students: There are 260 international students enrolled. They must score 500 on the written TOEFL.

Computers: The mainframes are a UMMVSB and UMMVSG. There are 41 general access computing sites with more than 1400 workstations equipped with Macs, Windows, and Silicon Graphics, and laser printers for output from the mainframe or PCs. 30 sites house more than 150 Windows and Mac workstations for students in residence halls. All students may access the system 24 hours daily by modem; lab hours vary, but they are open 7 days a week and 3 are open 21 hours. There are no time limits. The fee is $10 per credit hour.

Graduates: From July 1, 2002 to June 30, 2003, 3848 bachelor's degrees were awarded. The most popular majors were business (15%), journalism (12%), and sociology (9%). In an average class, 1% graduate in 3 years or less, 37% graduate in 4 years or less, 63% graduate in 5 years or less, and 67% graduate in 6 years or less. 1500 companies recruited on campus in 2002-2003.

Admissions Contact: Georgeanne Porter, Director Undergraduate Admissions. E-mail: MU4U@missouri.edu Web: www.missouri.edu

---

UNIVERSITY OF MISSOURI/KANSAS CITY   A-2
Kansas City, MO 64110   (816) 235-1111; Fax: (816) 235-5544

Full-time: 1973 men, 3076 women	Faculty: 615; 1, --$
Part-time: 1678 men, 2440 women	Ph.D.s: 84%
Graduate: 2085 men, 2974 women	Student/Faculty: 8 to 1
Year: semesters, summer session	Tuition: $6146 ($14,964)
Application Deadline: open	Room & Board: $7270
Freshman Class: 1884 applied, 1746 accepted, 785 enrolled	
ACT: 24	VERY COMPETITIVE

The University of Missouri/Kansas City, which opened in 1933, is a public institution offering undergraduate and graduate programs in the arts and sciences, engineering, business, education, health fields, preprofessional, and professional studies. There are 9 undergraduate and 13 graduate schools. In addition to regional accreditation, UMKC has baccalaureate program accreditation with AACSB, ABET, ACPE, ADA, NASM, NCATE, and NLN. The 4 libraries contain 1,265,118 volumes, 2,377,482 microform items, and 451,563 audio/video tapes/CDs, and subscribe to 7222 periodicals. Computerized library services include the card catalog, interlibrary loans, and database searching. Special learning facilities include a learning resource center, art gallery, natural history museum, planetarium, and radio station. The 262-acre campus is in an urban area in Kansas City. Including any residence halls, there are 42 buildings.

Student Life: 79% of undergraduates are from Missouri. Students are from 42 states, 81 foreign countries, and Canada. 63% are white; 14% African American. The average age of freshmen is 19; all undergraduates, 23. 28% do not continue beyond their first year; 76% remain to graduate.

Housing: 1300 students can be accommodated in college housing, which includes coed dorms and on-campus apartments. On-campus housing is available on a first-come, first-served basis. 90% of students commute. Alcohol is not permitted. All students may keep cars.

Activities: 3% of men belong to 6 national fraternities; 5% of women belong to 2 local and 7 national sororities. There are 202 groups on campus, including art, band, cheerleading, chess, choir, chorale, chorus, computers, dance, debate, drama, ethnic, gay, honors, international, jazz band, literary magazine, newspaper, opera, orchestra, photography, political, professional, radio and TV, religious, social, social service, student government, and yearbook. Popular campus events include International Food and Culture Night, Welcome Back Week, and Spring Fling.

Sports: There are 6 intercollegiate sports for men and 7 for women, and 13 intramural sports for men and 13 for women. Facilities include a recreation center with 5 gyms, an indoor/outdoor pool, indoor and outdoor tracks, a fitness center, and handball, racquetball, and squash courts. There are also recreation facilities at the University Center.

Disabled Students: 95% of the campus is accessible. Wheelchair ramps, elevators, special parking, specially equipped rest rooms, special class scheduling, lowered drinking fountains, and lowered telephones are available.

Services: There is a reader service for the blind.

Campus Safety and Security: Measures include 24-hour foot and vehicle patrol, self-defense education, security escort services, and shuttle buses. There are informal discussions, pamphlets/posters/films, emergency telephones, and lighted pathways/sidewalks.

Programs of Study: UMKC confers B.A., B.S., B.B.A., B.F.A., B.I.T., B.L.A., B.M., B.M.E., B.S.C.I.E., B.S.D.H., B.S.E.E., B.S.M.E., and B.S.N. degrees. Master's and doctoral degrees are also awarded. Bachelor's degrees are awarded in BIOLOGICAL SCIENCE (biology/biological science), BUSINESS (accounting and business administration and management), COMMUNICATIONS AND THE ARTS (art, art history and appreciation, communications, dance, dramatic arts, English, fine arts, French, German, music, music performance, music theory and composi-

tion, performing arts, Spanish, speech/debate/rhetoric, and studio art), COMPUTER AND PHYSICAL SCIENCE (chemistry, computer science, geology, information sciences and systems, mathematics, and physics), EDUCATION (elementary, health, music, physical, and secondary), ENGINEERING AND ENVIRONMENTAL DESIGN (civil engineering, electrical/electronics engineering, environmental science, and mechanical engineering), HEALTH PROFESSIONS (dental hygiene, medical technology, music therapy, and nursing), SOCIAL SCIENCE (American studies, criminal justice, economics, geography, history, Judaic studies, liberal arts/general studies, philosophy, political science/government, psychology, sociology, and urban studies). Health sciences and performing arts are the strongest academically. Liberal arts is the largest.

Required: Most candidates for the B.A. and B.S. degrees must complete a core curriculum that consists of courses in English, a foreign language, math, philosophy, fine arts, history, literature, natural sciences, and social sciences. They must complete 120 credit hours, including 36 in their major, with a 2.0 GPA.

Special: Special academic programs include co-op programs and internships in several majors, study abroad in 8 countries, an accelerated degree program, dual majors, and numerous work-study opportunities in the Kansas City area. Special degrees include a B.A.-B.S. degree in the computer science program and a liberal arts degree offered by the adult program. The pass/fail option is available in some courses. Freshmen may enter 6-year medical and dental programs. There are 4 national honor societies, a freshman honors program, and 1 departmental honors program.

Faculty/Classroom: 57% of faculty are male; 43%, female. The average class size in an introductory lecture is 30; in a laboratory, 16; and in a regular course, 24.

Admissions: 93% of the 2003-2004 applicants were accepted. The SAT I scores for the 2003-2004 freshman class were: Verbal--19% below 500, 29% between 500 and 599, 40% between 600 and 700, and 11% above 700; Math--11% below 500, 38% between 500 and 599, 36% between 600 and 700, and 15% above 700. The ACT scores were 25% below 21, 22% between 21 and 23, 24% between 24 and 26, 12% between 27 and 28, and 16% above 28. 60% of the current freshmen were in the top fifth of their class; 85% were in the top two fifths.

Requirements: The ACT is required. A combination of the student's test score and class rank determines admissibility; if the rank is 47 or below, the ACT score must be 24 or higher. Graduation from an accredited secondary school is a requirement for admission; the GED is also accepted. Required high school subjects include 4 units of English, 3 each of math and social studies, 2 of science, 1 of arts, and 3 more units selected from the above subjects or from a foreign language. A portfolio is required for art majors, an audition for music majors, and an interview for only those students applying for the pharmacy degree or the 6-year medical and dental programs. AP and CLEP credits are accepted.

Procedure: Freshmen are admitted to all sessions. Entrance exams should be taken by March of the senior year. There is a rolling admissions plan. Application deadlines are open. The fall 2003 application fee was $35.

Transfer: 1477 transfer students enrolled in 2002-2003. A maximum of 60 semester hours from community colleges or 30 hours earned within the University of Missouri System will be accepted. Transfer students must have maintained a 2.0 GPA. The SAT I or ACT is recommended. 30 of 120 credits required for the bachelor's degree must be completed at UMKC.

Visiting: There are regularly scheduled orientations for prospective students, consisting of a 1-day program for new freshmen or a half-day optional program for transfer students. There are guides for informal visits. To schedule a visit, contact the UMKC Welcome Center at (816) 235-8652.

Financial Aid: In 2003-2004, 61% of all full-time students received some form of financial aid. 50% of full-time freshmen and 40% of continuing full-time students received need-based aid. The average freshman award was $16,206. Need-based scholarships or need-based grants averaged $4597; need-based self-help aid (loans and jobs) averaged $6195; non-need-based athletic scholarships averaged $11,577; and other non-need-based awards and non-need-based scholarships averaged $4989. 6% of undergraduates work part time. Average annual earnings from campus work are $2930. The average financial indebtedness of the 2003 graduate was $15,714. The FAFSA is required. The deadline for filing freshman financial aid applications for fall entry is March 1.

International Students: There are 290 international students enrolled. The school actively recruits these students. They must score 500 on the written TOEFL.

Computers: The mainframe is a 5 Compaq Alpha 2100 minicomputers. There are more than 400 PCs available at various student computer labs. All students may access the system 24 hours, 7 days a week. There is a dial-up limit of 15 hours; no limit for lab use. The fee is $9.90 per credit hour.

Graduates: From July 1, 2002 to June 30, 2003, 1138 bachelor's degrees were awarded. The most popular majors were liberal arts (21%), business/marketing (11%), and education, social sciences, history (8%). In an average class, 11% graduate in 4 years or less, 24% graduate in 5 years or less, and 42% graduate in 6 years or less. 475 companies recruited on campus in 2002-2003.

Admissions Contact: Jennifer DeHaemers, Director of Admissions. E-mail: *admit@umkc.edu* Web: *http://www.umkc.edu*

UNIVERSITY OF MISSOURI/ROLLA
Rolla, MO 65409-

C-3
(573) 341-4164
(800) 522-0938; Fax: (573) 341-4082

Full-time: 2850 men, 827 women	**Faculty:** 275; I, -$
Part-time: 279 men, 133 women	**Ph.D.s:** 91%
Graduate: 1082 men, 288 women	**Student/Faculty:** 13 to 1
Year: semesters, summer session	**Tuition:** $6839 ($16,286)
Application Deadline: July 1	**Room & Board:** $5453
Freshman Class: 1887 applied, 1488 accepted, 878 enrolled	
ACT: 27	**HIGHLY COMPETITIVE**

The University of Missouri/Rolla, founded in 1870, is part of the University of Missouri system. A public institution, it offers comprehensive undergraduate and graduate programs and confers degrees in arts and sciences, engineering, mines and metallurgy, and management and information systems. There are 4 undergraduate and 4 graduate schools. In addition to regional accreditation, UMR has baccalaureate program accreditation with ABET and CSAB. The library contains 435,008 volumes, 51,443 microform items, and 6268 audio/video tapes/CDs, and subscribes to 1580 periodicals. Computerized library services include the card catalog, interlibrary loans, database searching, and Internet access. Special learning facilities include a learning resource center, radio station, a writing center, student design center, nuclear reactor, observatory, explosives testing labs, and underground mine. The 284-acre campus is in a small town 90 miles southwest of St. Louis. Including any residence halls, there are 71 buildings.

Student Life: 78% of undergraduates are from Missouri. Others are from 43 states, 34 foreign countries, and Canada. 85% are from public schools. 83% are white. 37% are Protestant; 34% claim no religious affiliation; 22% Catholic. The average age of freshmen is 18; all undergraduates, 21. 17% do not continue beyond their first year; 60% remain to graduate.

Housing: 1365 students can be accommodated in college housing, which includes single-sex and coed dorms, on-campus apartments, married-student housing, fraternity houses, and sorority houses. In addition, there is the Voyageur Program, and community learning centers. On-campus housing is guaranteed for the freshman year only and is available on a first-come, first-served basis. 53% of students live on campus; of those, 65% remain on campus on weekends. Alcohol is not permitted. All students may keep cars.

Activities: 27% of men belong to 20 national fraternities; 24% of women belong to 1 local and 5 national sororities. There are more than 200 groups on campus, including bagpipe band, band, cheerleading, chess, choir, chorale, chorus, computers, drama, drill team, ethnic, gay, honors, international, jazz band, literary magazine, marching band, musical theater, newspaper, orchestra, pep band, political, professional, radio and TV, religious, social, social service, student government, and yearbook. Popular campus events include St. Patrick's Day, Black Culture Month, and Hispanic Culture Month.

Sports: There are 7 intercollegiate sports for men and 5 for women, and 19 intramural sports for men and 19 for women. Facilities include a gym, a weight room, a pool, a golf course, a track, racquetball and tennis courts, ball and soccer fields, and a 5000-seat stadium.

Disabled Students: 95% of the campus is accessible. Wheelchair ramps, elevators, special parking, specially equipped rest rooms, special class scheduling, lowered drinking fountains, lowered telephones, special housing, assistive listening devices, closed-circuit TV, wheelchairs, signers, aides, and specialized testing accommodations are available.

Services: Counseling and information services are available, as is tutoring in 24 subjects. There is a reader service for the blind.

Campus Safety and Security: Measures include 24-hour foot and vehicle patrol, self-defense education, security escort services, and informal discussions. There are pamphlets/posters/films, emergency telephones, lighted pathways/sidewalks, and crime prevention and rape/sexual assault programs.

Programs of Study: UMR confers B.A. and B.S. degrees. Master's and doctoral degrees are also awarded. Bachelor's degrees are awarded in BIOLOGICAL SCIENCE (biology/biological science, environmental biology, and life science), BUSINESS (business administration and management, electronic business, and management information systems), COMMUNICATIONS AND THE ARTS (English and technical and business writing), COMPUTER AND PHYSICAL SCIENCE (applied mathematics, chemistry, computer science, geology, geophysics and seismology, information sciences and systems, mathematics, physics, polymer science, and statistics), EDUCATION (secondary), ENGINEERING AND ENVIRONMENTAL DESIGN (aeronautical engineering, architectural engineering, ceramic engineering, chemical engineering, civil engineering,

computer engineering, electrical/electronics engineering, engineering, engineering management, engineering mechanics, environmental engineering, geological engineering, industrial engineering, manufacturing engineering, materials engineering, mechanical engineering, metallurgical engineering, mining and mineral engineering, nuclear engineering, petroleum/natural gas engineering, plastics engineering, and systems engineering), HEALTH PROFESSIONS (environmental health science, predentistry, and premedicine), SOCIAL SCIENCE (economics, history, philosophy, prelaw, and psychology). Engineering, science, and technology are the strongest academically. Engineering, arts, sciences and mines, and metallurgy are the largest.

Required: Candidates for graduation must maintain at least a 2.0 GPA. A total of 120 to 132 credits, depending on the degree, is required. An assessment exam is required.

Special: UMR offers internships in business and government, co-op programs in which students work and attend school on alternating schedules, and study abroad in 20 countries. Accelerated degrees in science and engineering, dual majors, B.A.-B.S. degrees, a 3-2 engineering degree, work-study programs, a 5-year master's degree program, credit for life/military/work experience, and pass/fail options in certain courses are also available. There are 23 national honor societies, a freshman honors program, and 24 departmental honors programs.

Faculty/Classroom: 86% of faculty are male; 14%, female. 88% teach undergraduates. Graduate students teach 25% of introductory courses. The average class size in an introductory lecture is 36; in a laboratory, 18; and in a regular course, 25.

Admissions: 79% of the 2003-2004 applicants were accepted. The ACT scores for the 2003-2004 freshman class were: 5% below 21, 11% between 21 and 23, 25% between 24 and 26, 20% between 27 and 28, and 39% above 28. 61% of the current freshmen were in the top fifth of their class; 88% were in the top two fifths. There were 44 National Merit finalists in a recent year. 26 freshmen graduated first in their class.

Requirements: The SAT I or ACT is required. In addition, the sum of the high school student's class rank percentile and aptitude exam percentile must be 120 or higher. Candidates must be graduates of an accredited secondary school or have the GED. The applicant must have completed 16 academic credit units, including 4 each in English and math, 3 each in science and social studies, and 2 in a foreign language. AP and CLEP credits are accepted. Important factors in the admissions decision are leadership record, extracurricular activities record, and advanced placement or honor courses.

Procedure: Freshmen are admitted fall, winter, and summer. Entrance exams should be taken late in the junior year or early in the senior year. There is a rolling admissions plan. Applications should be filed by July 1 for fall entry, December 1 for spring entry, and May 1 for summer entry, along with a $50 fee. Notification is sent on a rolling basis beginning October 1. A waiting list is an active part of the admissions procedure. Applications are accepted on-line through the school's web site at *www.umr.edu/enrol*.

Transfer: 254 transfer students enrolled in 2002-2003. Applicants with fewer than 24 semester hours of college-level work must apply as freshmen; those with 24 or more must have attained at least a 2.0 GPA in all college-level courses. 60 credits of 120 to 132 required for the bachelor's degree must be completed at UMR.

Visiting: There are regularly scheduled orientations for prospective students, including a tour with a student, admissions and financial aid counseling, special interest contact, and a departmental visit with a faculty member. There are guides for informal visits and visitors may sit in on classes and stay overnight. To schedule a visit, contact UMR Visitor's Center at (573) 341-4165.

Financial Aid: In a recent year, 92% of all full-time freshmen and 84% of continuing full-time students received some form of financial aid. 50% of all full-time students received need-based aid. The average freshman award was $8652. 38% of undergraduates work part time. Average annual earnings from campus work are $1080. The average financial indebtedness of a recent graduate was $16,850. UMR is a member of CSS. The FAFSA is required. The deadline for filing freshman financial aid applications for fall entry is March 1.

International Students: There are 107 international students enrolled. They must score 550 on the written TOEFL or 213 on the electronic version or take the MELAB, the Comprehensive English Language Test, or the college's own test.

Computers: The mainframe consists of UNIX Servers. All students have free access to campus servers and to 700 networked PCs and Macs at 40 locations. Also available are 100 UNIX workstations (HP and Sun). A complete array of software is provided on all platforms, and 24-hour service is offered. All students may access the system. There are no time limits and no fees.

Graduates: From July 1, 2002 to June 30, 2003, 743 bachelor's degrees were awarded. The most popular majors were mechanical engineering (17%), electrical engineering (11%), and civil engineering (10%). In an average class, 14% graduate in 4 years or less, 43% graduate in 5 years or less, and 57% graduate in 6 years or less. 561 companies recruited on campus in 2002-2003. Of the 2002 graduating class,

17% were enrolled in graduate school within 6 months of graduation and 79% were employed.

Admissions Contact: Lynn Stichnote, Director of Admissions. A video is available. E-mail: *umrolla@umr.edu* Web: *http://www.umr.edu/admissions*

UNIVERSITY OF MISSOURI/ST. LOUIS
D-2
St. Louis, MO 63121-4499
(314) 516-5451
888 GO-2-UMSL; Fax: (314) 516-5310

Full-time: 2291 men, 3340 women	**Faculty:** 364; I, --$
Part-time: 2677 men, 4322 women	**Ph.D.s:** 57%
Graduate: 929 men, 1887 women	**Student/Faculty:** 15 to 1
Year: semesters, summer session	**Tuition:** $6056 ($15,503)
Application Deadline: July 1	**Room & Board:** $5600
Freshman Class: 2433 applied, 1178 accepted, 534 enrolled	
ACT: required	**VERY COMPETITIVE**

The University of Missouri/St. Louis, founded in 1963, is a public institution offering undergraduate and graduate programs and conferring degrees in arts and sciences, business, nursing, education, and engineering. There are 6 undergraduate and 2 graduate schools. In addition to regional accreditation, UM-St. Louis has baccalaureate program accreditation with AACSB, ABET, CSWE, NASM, NCATE, and NLN. The 3 libraries contain 778,867 volumes, 1,255,484 microform items, and 3871 audio/video tapes/CDs, and subscribe to 3596 periodicals. Computerized library services include interlibrary loans and database searching. Special learning facilities include a learning resource center, art gallery, planetarium, and radio station. The Mercantile Library Collection is housed in the Thomas Jefferson Library. The 275-acre campus is in an urban area 10 miles north of downtown St. Louis. Including any residence halls, there are 44 buildings.

Student Life: 92% of undergraduates are from Missouri. Others are from 40 states, 60 foreign countries, and Canada. 72% are white; 14% African American. The average age of freshmen is 18; all undergraduates, 22. 26% do not continue beyond their first year; 74% remain to graduate.

Housing: 1100 students can be accommodated in college housing, which includes coed dorms, on-campus apartments, and married-student housing. In addition, there are honors houses. On-campus housing is available on a first-come, first-served basis. Priority is given to out-of-town students. 92% of students commute. Alcohol is not permitted. All students may keep cars.

Activities: 1% of men belong to 2 national fraternities; 1% of women belong to 2 national sororities. There are 200 groups on campus, including art, band, cheerleading, chess, choir, chorale, chorus, computers, dance, debate, drama, ethnic, forensics, gay, honors, international, jazz band, literary magazine, newspaper, pep band, photography, political, professional, radio and TV, religious, social, social service, and student government. Popular campus events include Mirthday, Expo, and Welcome Week.

Sports: There are 5 intercollegiate sports for men and 6 for women, and 12 intramural sports for men and 12 for women. Facilities include indoor handball/racquetball, basketball, volleyball, and badminton courts, wrestling, dance, and conditioning rooms, and a swimming pool; outdoors, there are intramural fields and facilities for baseball, soccer, handball, racquetball, and tennis.

Disabled Students: All of the campus is accessible. Wheelchair ramps, elevators, special parking, specially equipped rest rooms, special class scheduling, lowered drinking fountains, and lowered telephones are available.

Services: Counseling and information services are available, as is tutoring in most subjects. There is a reader service for the blind, and remedial math, reading, and writing.

Campus Safety and Security: Measures include 24-hour foot and vehicle patrol, self-defense education, security escort services, and shuttle buses. There are informal discussions, pamphlets/posters/films, emergency telephones, and lighted pathways/sidewalks.

Programs of Study: UM-St. Louis confers B.A., B.S., B.F.A., B.G.S., B.H.S., B.M., B.ME., B.S.Acc., B.S.B.A., B.S.C.E., B.S.Ed., B.S.E.E., B.S.M.E., B.S.MIS., B.S.N., B.S.P.A., and B.S.W. degrees. Master's and doctoral degrees are also awarded. Bachelor's degrees are awarded in BIOLOGICAL SCIENCE (biology/biological science), BUSINESS (accounting, business administration and management, and management information systems), COMMUNICATIONS AND THE ARTS (art history and appreciation, communications, English, fine arts, French, music, and Spanish), COMPUTER AND PHYSICAL SCIENCE (applied mathematics, chemistry, computer science, mathematics, and physics), EDUCATION (early childhood, elementary, music, physical, secondary, and special), ENGINEERING AND ENVIRONMENTAL DESIGN (civil engineering, electrical/electronics engineering, engineering, and mechanical engineering), HEALTH PROFESSIONS (health science and nursing), SOCIAL SCIENCE (anthropology, criminal justice, economics, history, philosophy, political science/government, psychology, social work,

and sociology). Business, chemistry, and education are the strongest academically. Business, education, and nursing are the largest.

Required: To graduate, students must complete 120 credit hours, 42 of which must be in the area of general education. They must maintain a 2.0 GPA.

Special: Cross-registration with Washington University, St. Louis University, and St. Louis Community College and cooperative programs in all majors are offered. Study abroad in 30 countries, including England, France, and Germany, and a general studies degree in which credit can be earned for life, military, or work experience are available. Almost all the degree programs are available through the Evening College. Some work-study is available. There is an accelerated nursing degree program and student-designed majors for the B.G.S. There are 18 national honor societies, a freshman honors program, and 16 departmental honors programs.

Faculty/Classroom: 53% of faculty are male; 46%, female.

Admissions: 48% of the 2003-2004 applicants were accepted. The SAT I scores for the 2003-2004 freshman class were: Verbal--33% below 500, 36% between 500 and 599, 26% between 600 and 700, and 5% above 700; Math--31% below 500, 40% between 500 and 599, 24% between 600 and 700, and 5% above 700. The ACT scores were 4% below 21, 52% between 21 and 23, 35% between 24 and 26, 3% between 27 and 28, and 6% above 28. 47% of the current freshmen were in the top fifth of their class; 79% were in the top two fifths.

Requirements: The ACT is required. In addition, applicants are required to have a total of 17 units, including 4 each in English and math, 3 each in social studies and science, 2 in the same foreign language, and 1 in fine arts. Class rank and test scores are used to determine eligibility for admission. AP and CLEP credits are accepted.

Procedure: Freshmen are admitted fall, spring, and summer. Applications should be filed by July 1 for fall entry, December 1 for winter entry, and May 1 for summer entry, along with a $35 fee. Notification is sent on a rolling basis. Applications are accepted on-line.

Transfer: 1787 transfer students enrolled in 2002-2003. Transfer students must have earned a minimum of 24 credit hours and maintained a minimum 2.0 GPA. 30 of 120 credits required for the bachelor's degree must be completed at UM-St. Louis.

Visiting: There are regularly scheduled orientations for prospective students. There are guides for informal visits and visitors may sit in on classes and stay overnight. To schedule a visit, contact Yolanda Weathersby at (314) 516-5460 or *hawkinsy@msx.umsl.edu.*

Financial Aid: In a recent year, 66% of all full-time freshmen received some form of financial aid. The average freshman award was $2500. The FAFSA is required. Check with the school for current application deadlines.

International Students: The school actively recruits these students. They must score 500 on the written TOEFL or 173 on the electronic version and also take the college's own test.

Computers: The mainframe is a Sun Microsystems Enterprise 4000. Students may access 7 instructional computing labs with 700 computers, and dial-up access is available 24 hours a day, 7 days a week. All students may access the system. There are no time limits. The fee is $9.90 per credit hour. It is strongly recommended that all students have a personal computer.

Graduates: From July 1, 2002 to June 30, 2003, 1853 bachelor's degrees were awarded. The most popular majors were business (31%), education (15%), and social science/history (10%). In an average class, 12% graduate in 4 years or less, 28% graduate in 5 years or less, and 36% graduate in 6 years or less. Of the 2002 graduating class, 93% were employed within 6 months of graduation.

Admissions Contact: Melissa Hattman, Director of Undergraduate Admissions. E-mail: *admissionsu@msx.umsl.edu* Web: *www.umsl.edu*

WASHINGTON UNIVERSITY IN ST. LOUIS
D-2
St. Louis, MO 63130-4899
(314) 935-6000
(800) 638-0700; Fax: (314) 935-4290

Full-time: 2850 men, 3062 women	**Faculty:** 757; I, ++$
Part-time: 497 men, 779 women	**Ph.D.s:** 99%
Graduate: 3120 men, 2712 women	**Student/Faculty:** 8 to 1
Year: semesters, summer session	**Tuition:** $29,053
Application Deadline: January 15	**Room & Board:** $9240
Freshman Class: 20,378 applied, 4080 accepted, 1367 enrolled	
SAT I or ACT: required	**MOST COMPETITIVE**

Washington University, founded in 1853, is a private, independent institution offering undergraduate and graduate programs in arts and sciences, business, architecture, engineering, art, and professional programs in law, medicine (including physical therapy and occupational therapy), and social work. There are 5 undergraduate and 8 graduate schools. In addition to regional accreditation, Washington U. has baccalaureate program accreditation with AACSB, ABET, and NASAD. The 14 libraries contain 3,608,538 volumes, 3,274,165 microform items, and 71,085 audio/video tapes/CDs, and subscribe to 43,453 periodicals. Computerized library services include the card catalog, interlibrary loans, database searching, and Internet access. Special learning facilities include a learning resource center, art gallery, planetarium, radio station, TV station, dance studio, professional theater, observatory, and studio theater. The 169-acre campus is in a suburban area 7 miles west of downtown St. Louis. Including any residence halls, there are 105 buildings.

Student Life: 89% of undergraduates are from out of state, mostly the Midwest. Students are from 50 states, 88 foreign countries, and Canada. 61% are from public schools. 66% are white. 25% are claim no religious affiliation; 20% Catholic; 20% Jewish. The average age of freshmen is 18; all undergraduates, 20. 3% do not continue beyond their first year; 89% remain to graduate.

Housing: 4430 students can be accommodated in college housing, which includes single-sex and coed dorms, on-campus apartments, off-campus apartments, married-student housing, and fraternity houses. In addition, there are special-interest houses, language and special-interest suites within residence halls, upper-class housing, single-sex floors in coed buildings, and small group housing for students who share common interests and goals. On-campus housing is guaranteed for the freshman year only and is available on a lottery system for upperclassmen. 65% of students live on campus; of those, 97% remain on campus on weekends. Upperclassmen may keep cars.

Activities: 28% of men belong to 12 national fraternities; 24% of women belong to 6 national sororities. There are 200 groups on campus, including art, band, cheerleading, chess, choir, chorale, chorus, computers, dance, debate, drama, ethnic, film, forensics, gay, honors, international, jazz band, literary magazine, musical theater, newspaper, opera, orchestra, pep band, photography, political, professional, radio and TV, religious, social, social service, student government, symphony, and yearbook. Popular campus events include multicultural celebrations, College Bowl, and all-student theater.

Sports: There are 9 intercollegiate sports for men and 9 for women, and 30 intramural sports for men and 30 for women. Facilities include gyms, a swimming pool, tracks, a weight room, saunas, recreational playing fields, a football stadium, a fitness center, and racquetball, tennis, handball, wallyball, and squash courts.

Disabled Students: 95% of the campus is accessible. Wheelchair ramps, elevators, special parking, specially equipped rest rooms, special class scheduling, lowered drinking fountains, lowered telephones, magnification devices, and hearing-assist devices are available.

Services: Counseling and information services are available, as is tutoring in every subject. There is a reader service for the blind.

Campus Safety and Security: Measures include 24-hour foot and vehicle patrol, self-defense education, security escort services, and shuttle buses. There are informal discussions, pamphlets/posters/films, emergency telephones, and lighted pathways/sidewalks.

Programs of Study: Washington U. confers B.A., B.S., B.F.A., B.M., B.S.B.A., B.S.B.M.E., B.S.C.E., B.S.Ch.E., B.S.C.S., B.S.Co.E., B.S.E.E., B.S.I.M., B.S.M.E., and B.S.S.S.E. degrees. Master's and doctoral degrees are also awarded. Bachelor's degrees are awarded in AGRICULTURE (environmental studies and plant science), BIOLOGICAL SCIENCE (biochemistry, biology/biological science, biophysics, and neurosciences), BUSINESS (accounting, banking and finance, business administration and management, business economics, entrepreneurial studies, human resources, international business management, international economics, marketing management, marketing/retailing/merchandising, and trade and industrial supervision and management), COMMUNICATIONS AND THE ARTS (advertising, American literature, Arabic, art history and appreciation, ceramic art and design, Chinese, classical languages, classics, communications, comparative literature, creative writing, dance, design, dramatic arts, drawing, East Asian languages and literature, English, English literature, film arts, fine arts, French, German, Germanic languages and literature, graphic design, Greek (classical), Hebrew, illustration, Italian, Japanese, journalism, languages, Latin, literature, music, music theory and composition, painting, performing arts, photography, printmaking, romance languages and literature, Russian, sculpture, Spanish, studio art, and visual and performing arts), COMPUTER AND PHYSICAL SCIENCE (applied mathematics, chemistry, computer programming, computer science, earth science, geology, information sciences and systems, mathematics, physical sciences, physics, and statistics), EDUCATION (art, education, elementary, foreign languages, mathematics, middle school, science, secondary, social science, and social studies), ENGINEERING AND ENVIRONMENTAL DESIGN (aerospace studies, architectural technology, architecture, bioengineering, biomedical engineering, chemical engineering, civil engineering, commercial art, computer engineering, electrical/electronics engineering, engineering, engineering mechanics, engineering physics, environmental science, geological engineering, mechanical engineering, systems engineering, and technology and public affairs), HEALTH PROFESSIONS (pharmacy, predentistry, premedicine, prepharmacy, and preveterinary science), SOCIAL SCIENCE (African American studies, African studies, American studies, anthropology, archeology, area studies, Asian/Oriental studies, biopsychology, East Asian studies, Eastern European studies, economics, ethnic studies, European studies, fashion design and technology, history, humanities, industrial and organizational

psychology, interdisciplinary studies, international relations, international studies, Islamic studies, Judaic studies, Latin American studies, medieval studies, Middle Eastern studies, Near Eastern studies, philosophy, political science/government, psychology, religion, Russian and Slavic studies, social science, South Asian studies, systems science, urban studies, Western European studies, and women's studies). Natural sciences and engineering are the strongest academically. Natural sciences, engineering, and business are the largest.

Required: Students must complete 120 credits and maintain a minimum GPA of 2.0. In addition, all students must complete a course in English composition and 3 courses in the major liberal arts disciplines.

Special: Opportunities are provided for cooperative programs with other schools, internships, work-study programs, study abroad, a Washington (D.C.) semester, accelerated degree programs, a B.A.-B.S. engineering degree, credit by examination, nondegree study, pass/fail options, and dual and student-designed majors. There are 18 national honor societies, including Phi Beta Kappa.

Faculty/Classroom: 69% of faculty are male; 31%, female. The average class size in an introductory lecture is 24; in a laboratory, 16; and in a regular course, 20.

Admissions: 20% of the 2003-2004 applicants were accepted. The SAT I scores for the 2003-2004 freshman class were: Verbal--6% between 500 and 599, 47% between 600 and 700, and 47% above 700; Math--2% between 500 and 599, 38% between 600 and 700, and 60% above 700. The ACT scores were 1% between 21 and 23, 5% between 24 and 26, 11% between 27 and 28, and 83% above 28. There were 210 National Merit finalists. 136 freshmen graduated first in their class.

Requirements: The SAT I or ACT is required. In addition, an essay is required from all applicants. Fine arts students may submit portfolios. 4 years of English, math, science, and social science/history, and 2 of a foreign language are recommended. Also required are recommendations from a teacher and a counselor. AP credits are accepted. Important factors in the admissions decision are advanced placement or honor courses, evidence of special talent, and extracurricular activities record.

Procedure: Freshmen are admitted in the fall. Entrance exams should be taken by December of the senior year. There are early decision and deferred admissions plans. Early decision applications should be filed by November 15; regular applications, by January 15 for fall entry, along with a $55 fee. Notification of early decision is sent December 15; regular decision, April 1. A waiting list is an active part of the admissions procedure. 29 wait-listed applicants were admitted. Applications are accepted on-line through http://admissions.wustl.edu.

Transfer: 181 transfer students enrolled in 2002-2003. Students less than 5 years out of high school must also submit an offical transcript from secondary schools previously attended. A minimum GPA of 3.0 is required. An interview is recommended. If the student has taken the SAT I or the ACT in the last 5 years, results must be submitted. College transcript(s) and recommendations from a professor and dean/adviser are required. 36 of 120 credits required for the bachelor's degree must be completed at Washington U.

Visiting: There are regularly scheduled orientations for prospective students, consisting of group presentations followed by a campus tour, as well as visits to classes and meetings with current students and faculty. There are guides for informal visits and visitors may sit in on classes and stay overnight. To schedule a visit, contact the Office of Undergraduate Admissions at admissions@wustl.edu.

Financial Aid: In 2003-2004, 58% of all full-time freshmen and 60% of continuing full-time students received some form of financial aid. 42% of full-time freshmen and 46% of continuing full-time students received need-based aid. 50% of undergraduates work part time. Average annual earnings from campus work are $2000. Washington U. is a member of CSS. The CSS Profile or FAFSA and noncustodial parent's statement; student and parent 1040 tax return, or signed wavier if there is no tax return, are required. The deadline for filing freshman financial aid applications for fall entry is February 15.

International Students: There are 271 international students enrolled. The school actively recruits these students. They must score 550 on the written TOEFL or 213 on the electronic version and also take the SAT I or the ACT.

Computers: The mainframes are an IBM 7060-H55 and IBM 9121-621. Specialized computing resources are available to students. The Center for Engineering Computing provides access to about 100 computing stations from the campus-wide network. The School of Business provides a student lab with more than 65 computers. In addition, Residential Technology Services provides 11 computer clusters throughout the residence halls that are available 24 hours a day. All rooms in residence halls have Internet connections. The Olin Library provides access to the Internet, e-mail, and a variety of other specialized software. All students may access the system 24 hours per day, 7 days per week. There are no time limits and no fees.

Graduates: From July 1, 2002 to June 30, 2003, 1581 bachelor's degrees were awarded. The most popular majors were biology and psychology (19%), business (14%), and engineering (13%). In an average class, 1% graduate in 3 years or less, 79% graduate in 4 years or less,

88% graduate in 5 years or less, and 89% graduate in 6 years or less. 250 companies recruited on campus in 2002-2003. Of the 2002 graduating class, 33% were enrolled in graduate school within 6 months of graduation and 62% were employed.

Admissions Contact: Office of Undergraduate Admissions. A video is available. E-mail: *admissions@wustl.edu*
Web: *http://admissions.wustl.edu*

WEBSTER UNIVERSITY   D-2
St. Louis, MO 63119-3194

(314) 968-6991
(800) 75-ENROL; Fax: (314) 968-7115

Full-time: 1295 men, 1925 women	**Faculty:** 170; IIA, av$
Part-time: 734 men, 1118 women	**Ph.D.s:** 75%
Graduate: 7171 men, 8601 women	**Student/Faculty:** 19 to 1
Year: semesters, summer session	**Tuition:** $15,480
Application Deadline: March 1	**Room & Board:** $6368
Freshman Class: 1148 applied, 738 accepted, 437 enrolled	
SAT I Verbal/Math: 610/560	**ACT:** 24 **VERY COMPETITIVE**

Webster University, founded in 1915, is an independent institution with programs in fine and performing arts, liberal arts and sciences, education, nursing, and business. There are 5 undergraduate and 5 graduate schools. In addition to regional accreditation, Webster has baccalaureate program accreditation with NASM and NLN. The library contains 267,988 volumes, 136,888 microform items, and 14,795 audio/video tapes/CDs, and subscribes to 14,480 periodicals. Computerized library services include the card catalog, interlibrary loans, database searching, and Internet access. Special learning facilities include a learning resource center, art gallery, radio station, media center, writing center, and a theater. The 47-acre campus is in a suburban area 12 miles southwest of St. Louis. Including any residence halls, there are 44 buildings.

Student Life: 56% of undergraduates are from Missouri. Students are from 44 states, 85 foreign countries, and Canada. 67% are from public schools. 56% are white; 22% foreign nationals; 11% African American. The average age of freshmen is 19; all undergraduates, 25. 20% do not continue beyond their first year; 57% remain to graduate.

Housing: 500 students can be accommodated in college housing, which includes single-sex and coed dorms and on-campus apartments. In addition, there are special-interest houses, on-campus houses, and substance-free housing. On-campus housing is guaranteed for the freshman year only, is available on a first-come, first-served basis, and is available on a lottery system for upperclassmen. Priority is given to out-of-town students. 80% of students commute. Upperclassmen may keep cars.

Activities: There are no fraternities or sororities. There are 48 groups on campus, including amnesty, art, band, cheerleading, chess, choir, chorale, chorus, computers, dance, debate, departmental, drama, ethnic, film, forensics, gay, honors, international, jazz band, literary magazine, musical theater, newspaper, opera, orchestra, outdoor, photography, political, professional, radio and TV, religious, social, social service, student government, symphony, and women. Popular campus events include Spring Fest, Back-to-School Dance, and Multicultural Week.

Sports: There are 6 intercollegiate sports for men and 7 for women, and 4 intramural sports for men and 4 for women. Facilities include a gym, an athletic training center, a sauna, a fitness center, a 25-yard, 6-lane indoor swiming pool, and a chipping and putting green.

Disabled Students: 75% of the campus is accessible. Wheelchair ramps, elevators, special parking, specially equipped rest rooms, special class scheduling, lowered drinking fountains, lowered telephones, special housing, telephones for the hearing impaired, automatic door openers, a reading machine, computer for paraplegic students, reading and writing software, deaf interpreters, note takers, and textbooks on tape are availble. All TV monitors in classrooms have closed caption capabilities.

Services: Counseling and information services are available, as is tutoring in most subjects. There is a reader service for the blind, peer tutoring, and study skills training.

Campus Safety and Security: Measures include 24-hour foot and vehicle patrol, self-defense education, security escort services, and informal discussions. There are pamphlets/posters/films, emergency telephones, and lighted pathways/sidewalks.

Programs of Study: Webster confers B.A., B.S., B.B.A., B.F.A., B.M., B.M.Ed., and B.S.N. degrees. Master's and doctoral degrees are also awarded. Bachelor's degrees are awarded in BIOLOGICAL SCIENCE (biology/biological science), BUSINESS (accounting, business administration and management, and management science), COMMUNICATIONS AND THE ARTS (advertising, art, audio technology, broadcasting, communications, dance, dramatic arts, English, film arts, French, German, journalism, literature, media arts, music, musical theater, photography, public relations, Spanish, theater design, and video), COMPUTER AND PHYSICAL SCIENCE (computer science, information sciences and systems, and mathematics), EDUCATION (education and music), ENGINEERING AND ENVIRONMENTAL DESIGN (environmental science), HEALTH PROFESSIONS (nursing), SOCIAL SCIENCE (anthropology, economics, history, international relations, international

studies, law, philosophy, political science/government, psychology, religion, social science, and sociology). Liberal arts is the strongest academically. Business and communications are the largest.

Required: To graduate, students must complete at least 128 semester hours, with a minimum GPA of 2.0. A freshman seminar is required; otherwise, the curriculum requires specific courses within the major field of study only, as well as successful completion of an approved major, and successful completion of 9 general education goals, usually by taking a 3-credit course in each area. At least 30 semester credits of a student's final 36 credits must be earned at Webster.

Special: Students may cross-register with Washington University and the University of Missouri/Columbia, and with Fontbonne, Maryville, Lindenwood, and Missouri Baptist Colleges and Eden Seminary. The university offers co-op programs, work-study programs, internships, dual majors, student-designed majors, B.A.-B.S. degrees, a 3-2 engineering degree with the University of Missouri/Columbia and Washington University, and a 3-4 architecture program with Washington University. Study abroad, nondegree study, pass/fail options, and credit for life, military, and work experience are available. There is 1 national honor society.

Faculty/Classroom: 60% of faculty are male; 40%, female. No introductory courses are taught by graduate students. The average class size in an introductory lecture is 15; in a laboratory, 10; and in a regular course, 15.

Admissions: 64% of the 2003-2004 applicants were accepted. The SAT I scores for the 2003-2004 freshman class were: Verbal--11% below 500, 35% between 500 and 599, 45% between 600 and 700, and 9% above 700; Math--25% below 500, 40% between 500 and 599, 28% between 600 and 700, and 7% above 700. The ACT scores were 21% below 21, 28% between 21 and 23, 23% between 24 and 26, 15% between 27 and 28, and 13% above 28. 45% of the current freshmen were in the top fifth of their class; 73% were in the top two fifths. There were 2 National Merit semifinalists. 6 freshmen graduated first in their class.

Requirements: The SAT I or ACT is required. In addition, applicants must be graduates of an accredited secondary school. The GED is accepted. Webster recommends that students complete 16 high school academic units, including 4 units of English, 3 each of social studies/history and math, and 2 each of foreign language, science, and electives. An essay is required of all students, and a portfolio or audition is required for art, dance, music, musical theater, theater, and film applicants. Webster requires applicants to be in the upper 50% of their class. A GPA of 2.5 is required. AP and CLEP credits are accepted. Important factors in the admissions decision are advanced placement or honor courses, leadership record, and recommendations by school officials.

Procedure: Freshmen are admitted fall and spring. Entrance exams should be taken in the spring of the junior year. There are early admissions and deferred admissions plans. Applications should be filed by March 1 for fall entry and December 1 for spring entry, along with a $25 fee. Notification is sent on a rolling basis. Applications are accepted on computer disk and on-line through Common App.

Transfer: 518 transfer students enrolled in 2002-2003. Applicants for transfer must have a minimum GPA of 2.5. for college credit completed. If they have fewer than 30 transferable hours, they must submit high school transcripts. 30 of 128 credits required for the bachelor's degree must be completed at Webster.

Visiting: There are regularly scheduled orientations for prospective students, consisting of an open house, which includes classes, meetings with faculty, a financial aid workshop, a tour of the university, and a student activities overview. There are guides for informal visits and visitors may sit in on classes and stay overnight. To schedule a visit, contact the Visit Coordinator at (800) 753-6765 or *admit@webster.edu*.

Financial Aid: In 2003-2004, 82% of all full-time freshmen and 67% of continuing full-time students received some form of financial aid. 68% of full-time freshmen and 54% of continuing full-time students received need-based aid. The average freshman award was $14,561, with $5126 from need-based scholarships or grants, $3879 ($4625 maximum) from need-based self-help aid (loans and jobs), and $5556 from non-need-based awards and non-need-based scholarships. 24% of undergraduates work part time. Average annual earnings from campus work are $2175. The average financial indebtedness of the 2003 graduate was $17,823. The FAFSA and the university's own financial statement are required. The deadline for filing freshman financial aid applications for fall entry is April 1.

International Students: There are 110 international students enrolled. The school actively recruits these students. They must score 490 on the written TOEFL or 163 on the electronic version. They also take written and oral/listening tests. The SAT I or ACT is required if they are graduates of U.S. high schools or international secondary schools that use English as the language of instruction.

Computers: The mainframe is an HP 9000. Student dorms use the mainframe. In addition, there are 350 Pentium PCs and Macs available in the library, the central labs, student lounges, and distributed departments. 10 e-mail stations are located in dorms and classroom buildings. All computers access the Internet and Web. . There are no time limits and no fees.

Graduates: From July 1, 2002 to June 30, 2003, 1183 bachelor's degrees were awarded. The most popular majors were management (21%), computer science (12%), and business (9%). In an average class, 1% graduate in 3 years or less, 39% graduate in 4 years or less, 51% graduate in 5 years or less, and 55% graduate in 6 years or less. 60 companies recruited on campus in 2002-2003. Of the 2002 graduating class, 17% were enrolled in graduate school within 6 months of graduation and 95% were employed.

Admissions Contact: Niel DeVasto, Director, Freshman Admissions. A video is available. E-mail: *admit@websteruniv.edu* Web: *www.webster.edu*

WESTMINSTER COLLEGE   C-2
Fulton, MO 65251

(573) 592-5251
(800) 475-3361; Fax: (573) 592-5255

Full-time: 476 men, 327 women	**Faculty:** 58; IIB, -$
Part-time: 8 men, 12 women	**Ph.D.s:** 80%
Graduate: none	**Student/Faculty:** 14 to 1
Year: semesters, summer session	**Tuition:** $12,720
Application Deadline: open	**Room & Board:** $5430
Freshman Class: 944 applied, 705 accepted, 240 enrolled	
SAT I Verbal/Math: 530/530	**ACT:** 24 **COMPETITIVE+**

Westminster College, founded in 1851, is a private liberal arts and sciences college affiliated with the Presbyterian Church (U.S.A.). The 2 libraries contain 93,705 volumes, 16,282 microform items, and 6914 audio/video tapes/CDs, and subscribe to 409 periodicals. Computerized library services include the card catalog, interlibrary loans, and database searching. Special learning facilities include a learning resource center and a photospectrometer lab, a multimedia language and learning lab, a multimedia classroom, and Winston Churchill Memorial Museum. The 65-acre campus is in a small town 20 miles east of Columbia. Including any residence halls, there are 26 buildings.

Student Life: 73% of undergraduates are from Missouri. Students are from 23 states and 8 foreign countries. 70% are from public schools. 84% are white. 47% are Protestant; 25% Catholic; 20% claim no religious affiliation. The average age of freshmen is 18; all undergraduates, 20. 24% do not continue beyond their first year; 52% remain to graduate.

Housing: 442 students can be accommodated in college housing, which includes single-sex and coed dorms, off-campus apartments, and fraternity houses. In addition, there are special-interest houses. On-campus housing is guaranteed for all 4 years. 85% of students live on campus; of those, 95% remain on campus on weekends. All students may keep cars.

Activities: 66% of men belong to 6 national fraternities; 65% of women belong to 3 national sororities. There are 56 groups on campus, including art, cheerleading, choir, chorale, chorus, drama, ethnic, honors, international, investment, literary magazine, multicultural, musical theater, newspaper, pep band, photography, political, professional, religious, social, social service, student government, and yearbook. Popular campus events include Alumni Weekend, College Bowl, and Fulton Jazz Festival.

Sports: There are 6 intercollegiate sports for men and 6 for women, and 16 intramural sports for men and 10 for women. Facilities include an 800-seat gym, an aerobic training center, weight room and a training room, football, baseball, softball, and soccer fields, a field sports area, tennis, racquetball, and sand volleyball courts, a swimming pool, an indoor rifle range, and a 1500-seat auditorium/arena.

Disabled Students: 50% of the campus is accessible. Wheelchair ramps, elevators, special parking, specially equipped rest rooms, special class scheduling, lowered drinking fountains, and lowered telephones are available.

Services: Counseling and information services are available, as is tutoring in most subjects. There is remedial math and reading.

Campus Safety and Security: Measures include 24-hour foot and vehicle patrol, self-defense education, security escort services, and informal discussions. There are pamphlets/posters/films, emergency telephones, and lighted pathways/sidewalks.

Programs of Study: Westminster confers the B.A. degree. Bachelor's degrees are awarded in BIOLOGICAL SCIENCE (biology/biological science), BUSINESS (accounting, business administration and management, international business management, and management information systems), COMMUNICATIONS AND THE ARTS (English, French, and Spanish), COMPUTER AND PHYSICAL SCIENCE (chemistry, computer science, mathematics, and physics), EDUCATION (elementary, middle school, physical, and secondary), ENGINEERING AND ENVIRONMENTAL DESIGN (environmental science), SOCIAL SCIENCE (anthropology, economics, history, international studies, philosophy, political science/government, psychology, religion, and sociology). English, biology, and psychology are the strongest academically. Business administration, biology, and psychology are the largest.

Required: To graduate, students must complete 122 credit hours, including a maximum of 40 hours in their major, with a minimum GPA of 2.0. All students are required to take Westminster seminar, academic writing, statistics or calculus, 4 hours of foreign language, and 1 hour of phys ed. Students must also take 6 to 10 hours (37 to 42 total) in scientific inquiry, historical awareness, fundamental questions, artistic expression, human behaviors and institutions, cultural diversity, and global interdependence. In addition, an integrative upper-level course, 2 writing intensive courses, and an upper-level course from a non-major academic division are required.

Special: Westminster offers co-op programs with colleges of the Mid-Missouri Associated Colleges and Universities, cross-registration with William Woods University, internships in all areas, study abroad in 15 countries, a Washington semester, a United Nations semester, and an urban studies program in Chicago. Student-designed majors are available as well as a 3-2 engineering degree with Washington University in St. Louis. The pass/fail option and dual majors are available. There are 15 national honor societies, a freshman honors program, and 8 departmental honors programs.

Faculty/Classroom: 64% of faculty are male; 36%, female. All teach undergraduates, 75% do research, and 75% do both. The average class size in an introductory lecture is 19; in a laboratory, 20; and in a regular course, 15.

Admissions: 75% of the 2003-2004 applicants were accepted. The SAT I scores for the 2003-2004 freshman class were: Verbal--30% below 500, 34% between 500 and 599, 32% between 600 and 700, and 5% above 700; Math--30% below 500, 41% between 500 and 599, 23% between 600 and 700, and 7% above 700. The ACT scores were 19% below 21, 32% between 21 and 23, 30% between 24 and 26, 9% between 27 and 28, and 10% above 28. 40% of the current freshmen were in the top fifth of their class; 65% were in the top two fifths. There were 2 National Merit finalists and 3 semifinalists. 6 freshmen graduated first in their class.

Requirements: The SAT I or ACT is required. In addition, applicants must be graduates of an accredited secondary school. The GED is also accepted. Students must have completed 4 years each of social studies and English, 3 years each of math and science, and 2 years each of a foreign language and history. An essay is required and an interview is recommended. Westminster requires applicants to be in the upper 50% of their class. A GPA of 2.5 is required. AP and CLEP credits are accepted. Important factors in the admissions decision are advanced placement or honor courses, leadership record, and extracurricular activities record.

Procedure: Freshmen are admitted to all sessions. Entrance exams should be taken in the junior year of high school. There are early decision and deferred admissions plans. Application deadlines are open. Thee is a rolling admissions plan. Applications are accepted on-line through the school's web site at *http://www.wcmo.edu*.

Transfer: 29 transfer students enrolled in 2002-2003. Applicants must have taken either the ACT or the SAT I and must complete at least 4 semesters at Westminster as full-time students. 60 of 122 credits required for the bachelor's degree must be completed at Westminster.

Visiting: There are regularly scheduled orientations for prospective students, including 1-day summer programs with a general orientation and class registration. There are guides for informal visits and visitors may sit in on classes and stay overnight. To schedule a visit, contact Barbara McGee, Office of Enrollment Services at (573) 592-5251.

Financial Aid: In 2003-2004, 99% of all full-time students received some form of financial aid. 51% of full-time freshmen and 49% of continuing full-time students received need-based aid. The average freshman award was $11,700, with $2700 ($8000 maximum) from need-based scholarships or grants, $1600 ($2625 maximum) from need-based self-help aid (loans and jobs), and $7400 (12,300 maximum) from non-need-based awards and non-need-based scholarships. 35% of undergraduates work part time. Average annual earnings from campus work are $774. The average financial indebtedness of the 2003 graduate was $9100. Westminster is a member of CSS. The FAFSA is required. The priority date for freshman financial aid applications for fall entry is February 15.

International Students: There are 34 international students enrolled. The school actively recruits these students. They must score 550 on the written TOEFL or 213 on the electronic version.

Computers: The mainframes are 2 Dell Poweredge 2600s, a Dell Poweredge 5500, and 2 Compaq 3550s. There are 250 PCs and Macs available for student use. All residential halls, fraternities, and office areas are wired to a campus network and the Internet. All students may access the system. There are no time limits and no fees.

Graduates: The most popular majors were business administration (20%), management information systems (11%), and biology (9%). In an average class, 47% graduate in 4 years or less, 51% graduate in 5 years or less, and 52% graduate in 6 years or less. 71 companies recruited on campus in 2002-2003. Of the 2002 graduating class, 20% were enrolled in graduate school within 6 months of graduation and 94% were employed.

Admissions Contact: Patrick Kirby, Dean of Enrollment Services. E-mail: *kirbypt@jaynet.wcmo.edu* Web: *http://www.wcmo.edu*

WILLIAM JEWELL COLLEGE
Liberty, MO 64068

B-2

(816) 781-7700, ext. 5137
(800) 753-7009; Fax: (816) 415-5027

Full-time: 525 men, 749 women	**Faculty:** 75; IIB, av$
Part-time: 17 men, 22 women	**Ph.D.s:** 84%
Graduate: none	**Student/Faculty:** 17 to 1
Year: semesters, summer session	**Tuition:** $16,500
Application Deadline: March 15	**Room & Board:** $4820
Freshman Class: n/av	
SAT I Verbal/Math: 580/580	**ACT:** 25 **VERY COMPETITIVE**

William Jewell College, founded in 1849, is an academically selective Christian liberal arts college and offers undergraduate programs in the arts and sciences, business, education, and health fields. In addition to regional accreditation, Jewell has baccalaureate program accreditation with CCNE and NASM. The library contains 271,275 volumes, 219,574 microform items, and 29,437 audio/video tapes/CDs, and subscribes to 780 periodicals. Computerized library services include the card catalog, interlibrary loans, database searching, and Internet access. Special learning facilities include a learning resource center, art gallery, planetarium, and radio station. The 200-acre campus is in a suburban area 15 miles northeast of Kansas City. Including any residence halls, there are 23 buildings.

Student Life: 75% of undergraduates are from Missouri. Students are from 28 states, 12 foreign countries, and Canada. 90% are from public schools. 90% are white. 75% are Protestant; 20% Catholic. The average age of freshmen is 18; all undergraduates, 19. 10% do not continue beyond their first year; 62% remain to graduate.

Housing: 906 students can be accommodated in college housing, which includes single-sex and coed dorms, fraternity houses, and sorority houses. In addition, there are honors houses and language houses. On-campus housing is guaranteed for all 4 years. 63% of students live on campus; of those, 60% remain on campus on weekends. Alcohol is not permitted. All students may keep cars.

Activities: 32% of men belong to 3 national fraternities; 34% of women belong to 4 national sororities. There are 47 groups on campus, including cheerleading, choir, chorale, chorus, computers, dance, debate, drama, drill team, ethnic, honors, international, jazz band, ministries, musical theater, newspaper, orchestra, pep band, photography, political, professional, radio and TV, religious, social, social service, student government, symphony, and yearbook. Popular campus events include Parents/Grandparents Day, Hanging of the Green/Lighting of the Quad, and Undergraduate Research Colloquium.

Sports: There are 9 intercollegiate sports for men and 9 for women, and 12 intramural sports for men and 12 for women. Facilities include a football and soccer stadium, a complex for baseball and softball, and a phys ed center with an indoor track, a dance room, and facilities for basketball, racquetball, swimming, indoor tennis, volleyball, and weight lifting. The total seating capacity of the stadium is 3200 and that of the indoor gym is 1000.

Disabled Students: 30% of the campus is accessible. Wheelchair ramps, elevators, special parking, specially equipped rest rooms, special class scheduling, and lowered drinking fountains are available.

Services: Counseling and information services are available, as is tutoring in most subjects.

Campus Safety and Security: Measures include 24-hour foot and vehicle patrol, self-defense education, informal discussions, and pamphlets/posters/films. There are emergency telephones and lighted pathways/sidewalks.

Programs of Study: Jewell confers B.A. and B.S. degrees. Bachelor's degrees are awarded in BIOLOGICAL SCIENCE (biochemistry and biology/biological science), BUSINESS (accounting, business administration and management, business economics, and international business management), COMMUNICATIONS AND THE ARTS (art, communications, dramatic arts, English, French, music, and Spanish), COMPUTER AND PHYSICAL SCIENCE (chemistry, computer science, information sciences and systems, mathematics, and physics), EDUCATION (elementary, music, and secondary), HEALTH PROFESSIONS (medical laboratory technology and nursing), SOCIAL SCIENCE (history, international relations, Japanese studies, philosophy, political science/government, psychology, and religion). Business is the largest.

Required: To graduate, students must complete a minimum of 124 credits with a minimum 2.0 GPA, fulfilling the proper core requirements for their major and degree. All students must take The Responsible Self in their first semester, and must also take courses in oral and written communication, phys ed, math, foreign language, interdisciplinary courses in 4 categories, and a general education capstone course. Comprehensive exams in most majors are required.

Special: Internships for juniors or seniors, study abroad in Europe, Japan, Mexico, Australia, and Hong Kong, and a Washington semester are offered. B.A.-B.S. degrees, dual majors of any combination, student-designed majors, and 3-2 engineering degrees with Washington University and the Universities of Missouri and Kansas are available. The Oxbridge Honors Program for major study is patterned after the teaching methods of Oxford and Cambridge and includes a year at either Oxford or Cambridge. Leadership and service learning programs are offered. There are 13 national honor societies, a freshman honors program, and 13 departmental honors programs.

Faculty/Classroom: 56% of faculty are male; 44%, female. All teach undergraduates. The average class size in an introductory lecture is 30; in a laboratory, 20; and in a regular course, 15.

Admissions: The SAT I scores for the 2003-2004 freshman class were: Verbal--20% below 500, 33% between 500 and 599, 37% between 600 and 700, and 10% above 700; Math--10% below 500, 40% between 500 and 599, 35% between 600 and 700, and 15% above 700. The ACT scores were 2% below 21, 45% between 21 and 23, 43% between 24 and 26, and 12% above 28. 47% of the current freshmen were in the top fifth of their class; 84% were in the top two fifths. There were 3 National Merit finalists and 6 semifinalists. 18 freshmen graduated first in their class.

Requirements: The SAT I or ACT is required. In addition, students must be graduates of an accredited secondary school; the GED is also accepted. The college recommends that applicants have taken 4 English courses, 3 courses each in math, social studies, and science, and 2 in foreign language. An interview is recommended. An audition is advised for music applicants. AP and CLEP credits are accepted. Important factors in the admissions decision are advanced placement or honor courses, extracurricular activities record, and leadership record.

Procedure: Freshmen are admitted fall, spring, and summer. Entrance exams should be taken in the junior year. There are early admissions and deferred admissions plans. Applications should be filed by March 15 for fall entry, along with a $25 fee. Notification is sent on a rolling basis. Applications are accepted on-line through the college's web site.

Transfer: 90 transfer students enrolled in 2002-2003. Transfer students must have maintained a 2.0 GPA and be in good academic standing with their former schools. Education majors must take the ACT, achieving a minimum score of 20. An interview is recommended for all students. 30 of 124 credits required for the bachelor's degree must be completed at Jewell.

Visiting: There are regularly scheduled orientations for prospective students, and personalized visits can be arranged upon request. There are guides for informal visits and visitors may sit in on classes and stay overnight. To schedule a visit, contact the Admission Office.

Financial Aid: In a recent year, 68% of all full-time freshmen and 60% of continuing full-time students received some form of financial aid. 68% of full-time freshmen and 60% of continuing full-time students received need-based aid. The average freshman award was $9229. The average financial indebtedness of a recent graduate was $17,500. Jewell is a member of CSS. The FAFSA and the college's own financial statement are required. The deadline for filing freshman financial aid applications for fall entry is March 1.

International Students: There are 13 international students enrolled. The school actively recruits these students. They must score 550 on the written TOEFL or 213 on the electronic version or take the MELAB.

Computers: The mainframe consists of Compaq servers. The college provides approximately 120 PCs for academic use. All students may access the system. There are no time limits and no fees. It is strongly recommended that all students have a personal computer.

Graduates: From July 1, 2002 to June 30, 2003, 247 bachelor's degrees were awarded. The most popular majors were business (25%), psychology (12%), and communication and history (9%). In an average class, 56% graduate in 6 years or less. 36 companies recruited on campus in 2002-2003. Of the 2002 graduating class, 32% were enrolled in graduate school within 6 months of graduation and 77% were employed.

Admissions Contact: Chad Jolly, Dean of Enrollment Development. E-mail: *admission@william.jewell.edu* Web: *www.jewell.edu*

WILLIAM WOODS UNIVERSITY
Fulton, MO 65251

C-2

(573) 592-4221
(800) 995-3159; Fax: (573) 592-1146

Full-time: 220 men, 565 women	**Faculty:** 56
Part-time: 61 men, 145 women	**Ph.D.s:** 66%
Graduate: 462 men, 713 women	**Student/Faculty:** 14 to 1
Year: semesters, summer session	**Tuition:** $14,420
Application Deadline: open	**Room & Board:** $5700
Freshman Class: 612 applied, 492 accepted, 196 enrolled	
SAT I Verbal/Math: 508/483	**ACT:** 22 **COMPETITIVE**

William Woods University, founded in 1870, is an independent professions-oriented, liberal arts institution affiliated with the Christian Church (Disciples of Christ). Unique programs of study include an equestrian studies program and a four-year American Sign Language Interpreting program. There is 1 graduate school. In addition to regional accreditation, William Woods has baccalaureate program accreditation with ABA and CSWE. The library contains 131,820 volumes, 11,060 microform items, and 28,443 audio/video tapes/CDs, and subscribes to 2380 periodicals. Computerized library services include the card catalog, interlibrary loans, database searching, and Internet access. Special learning facilities include a learning resource center, art gallery, radio station, and labs for photography, foreign languages, and art; equestrian studies stables, a model courtroom, an American Sign Language interpreting lab, and an observatory. The 170-acre campus is in a small town 100 miles west of St. Louis. Including any residence halls, there are 35 buildings.

Student Life: 71% of undergraduates are from Missouri. Students are from 40 states, 14 foreign countries, and Canada. 83% are white. 37% are Protestant; 22% Catholic. The average age of freshmen is 18; all undergraduates, 21. 19% do not continue beyond their first year; 52% remain to graduate.

Housing: 750 students can be accommodated in college housing, which includes single-sex and coed dorms, on-campus apartments, fraternity houses, and sorority houses. In addition, there are special-interest houses and nonsmoking and independent housing. On-campus housing is guaranteed for all 4 years. 80% of students live on campus; of those, 50% remain on campus on weekends. All students may keep cars.

Activities: 36% of men belong to 2 national fraternities; 38% of women belong to 4 national sororities. There are 42 groups on campus, including art, choir, drama, honors, international, musical theater, professional, radio and TV, religious, social, social service, student government, and yearbook. Popular campus events include Salute to the Arts, Campus Involvement and Activities Fair.

Sports: There are 5 intercollegiate sports for men and 6 for women, and 7 intramural sports for men and 7 for women. Facilities include a gym, a fitness center, a sand volleyball court, tennis courts, soccer, baseball, and softball fields, a weight room, a lake with a sand beach, table tennis and pool tables, and a sauna.

Disabled Students: 66% of the campus is accessible. Wheelchair ramps, elevators, special parking, specially equipped rest rooms, special class scheduling, lowered telephones, and campus access to TTY phones are available.

Services: Counseling and information services are available, as is tutoring in most subjects. There is a reader service for the blind and remedial math and writing. Interpreting is provided for the deaf upon request and receipt of supporting documentation. Study skills improvement courses are available.

Campus Safety and Security: Measures include 24-hour foot and vehicle patrol, self-defense education, security escort services, and informal discussions. There are pamphlets/posters/films and lighted pathways/sidewalks.

Programs of Study: William Woods confers B.A., B.S., B.F.A., and B.S.W. degrees. Associate and master's degrees are also awarded. Bachelor's degrees are awarded in AGRICULTURE (equine science), BIOLOGICAL SCIENCE (biology/biological science), BUSINESS (accounting and business administration and management), COMMUNICATIONS AND THE ARTS (art, communications, dramatic arts, English, graphic design, journalism, and studio art), COMPUTER AND PHYSICAL SCIENCE (computer science, information sciences and systems, mathematics, and science), EDUCATION (athletic training, early childhood, elementary, middle school, physical, and special), SOCIAL SCIENCE (family/juvenile justice, history, interdisciplinary studies, international studies, interpreter for the deaf, paralegal studies, political science/government, psychology, and social work). Business, equestrian studies, and political/legal studies are the strongest academically. Business, equestrian studies, and ASL/English interpreting are the largest.

Required: Students must complete a minimum of 122 credits to graduate, including at least 30 in the major and 52 in Common Studies, with 7 in the natural sciences, 6 each in English, the humanities, and behavioral and social sciences, 3 each in oral communication, math, and fine or performing arts, and 2 in freshman seminar. They must have maintained a minimum GPA of 2.0.

Special: William Woods University offers cross-registration with schools in the Mid-Missouri Association of Colleges and Universities, internships in various fields, including equestrian studies and computer information systems, study abroad, a Washington semester, and work-study. An accelerated degree program in most majors, B.A.-B.S. degrees, and student-designed and dual majors are possible. Credit for life, military, and work experience and pass/fail are available.The LEAD (Leading , Edu-

cating, Achieving, and Developing) program provides awards ($5000 to residential students) to any incoming student who makes a commitment to campus and community involvement. There are 12 national honor societies and a freshman honors program.

Faculty/Classroom: 50% of faculty are male; 50%, female. All teach undergraduates. No introductory courses are taught by graduate students. The average class size in an introductory lecture is 25; in a laboratory, 15; and in a regular course, 25.

Admissions: 80% of the 2003-2004 applicants were accepted. 5% of the current freshmen were in the top fifth of their class; 24% were in the top two fifths. 2 freshmen graduated first in their class.

Requirements: The SAT I or ACT is required, with a recommended composite SAT I score of 900 and ACT score of 21. To be admitted to the university, applicants must be graduates of an accredited secondary school; the GED is also accepted. They must have completed 16 course units, 11 of which must be distributed among English, a foreign language, math, natural sciences, and social sciences. 2 references and an interview are recommended. William Woods requires applicants to be in the upper 50% of their class. A GPA of 2.5 is required. AP and CLEP credits are accepted. Important factors in the admissions decision are personality/intangible qualities, leadership record, and recommendations by school officials.

Procedure: Freshmen are admitted to all sessions. Entrance exams should be taken in the spring of the junior year or the fall of the senior year. There is an early admissions plan. Application deadlines are open. There is a rolling admissions plan. Application fee is $25. Applications are accepted on-line through the university's web site.

Transfer: 59 transfer students enrolled in 2002-2003. Transfer students must submit high school transcripts or GED and all college transcripts. They must also provide 2 references and be in good standing with their previous institution. 30 of 122 credits required for the bachelor's degree must be completed at William Woods.

Visiting: There are regularly scheduled orientations for prospective students, including the opportunity to talk with an academic adviser and an extensive student development-directed orientation to campus life. There are guides for informal visits and visitors may sit in on classes and stay overnight. To schedule a visit, contact the Office of Enrollment Services at (800) 995-3159, ext. 4221.

Financial Aid: In a recent year, 100% of all full-time freshmen and 95% of continuing full-time students received some form of financial aid. 56% of full-time freshmen and 51% of continuing full-time students received need-based aid. The average freshman award was $10,732. Need-based scholarships or need-based grants averaged $1771 ($15,120 maximum); need-based self-help aid (loans and jobs) averaged $2747 ($15,000 maximum); non-need-based athletic scholarships averaged $6102 ($9000 maximum); and other non-need-based awards and non-need-based scholarships averaged $3244 ($14,000 maximum). 52% of undergraduates work part time. Average annual earnings from campus work are $840. The average financial indebtedness of a recent graduate was $20,290. The FAFSA is required. The priority date for freshman financial aid applications for fall entry is March 1. The deadline for filing freshman financial aid applications for fall entry is March 1.

International Students: There are 58 international students enrolled. The school actively recruits these students. They must score 550 on the written TOEFL.

Computers: The university provides 175 PCs and Macs for academic use. These can be found in classrooms, dorms, computer labs, and the library. E-mail and connections to the Internet are also available. Students have access to the campus network from all residence hall rooms. All students may access the system 7 days a week. There are no time limits. The fee is $70 per semester.

Graduates: From July 1, 2002 to June 30, 2003, 222 bachelor's degrees were awarded. The most popular majors were business administration/business management (15%), equestrian studies/equestrian administration (12%), and computer information science (7%). In an average class, 42% graduate in 4 years or less, and 52% graduate in 6 years or less.

Admissions Contact: Jimmy Clay, Executive Director of Enrollment Services. E-mail: *admissions@williamwoods.edu* Web: *www.williamwoods.edu*

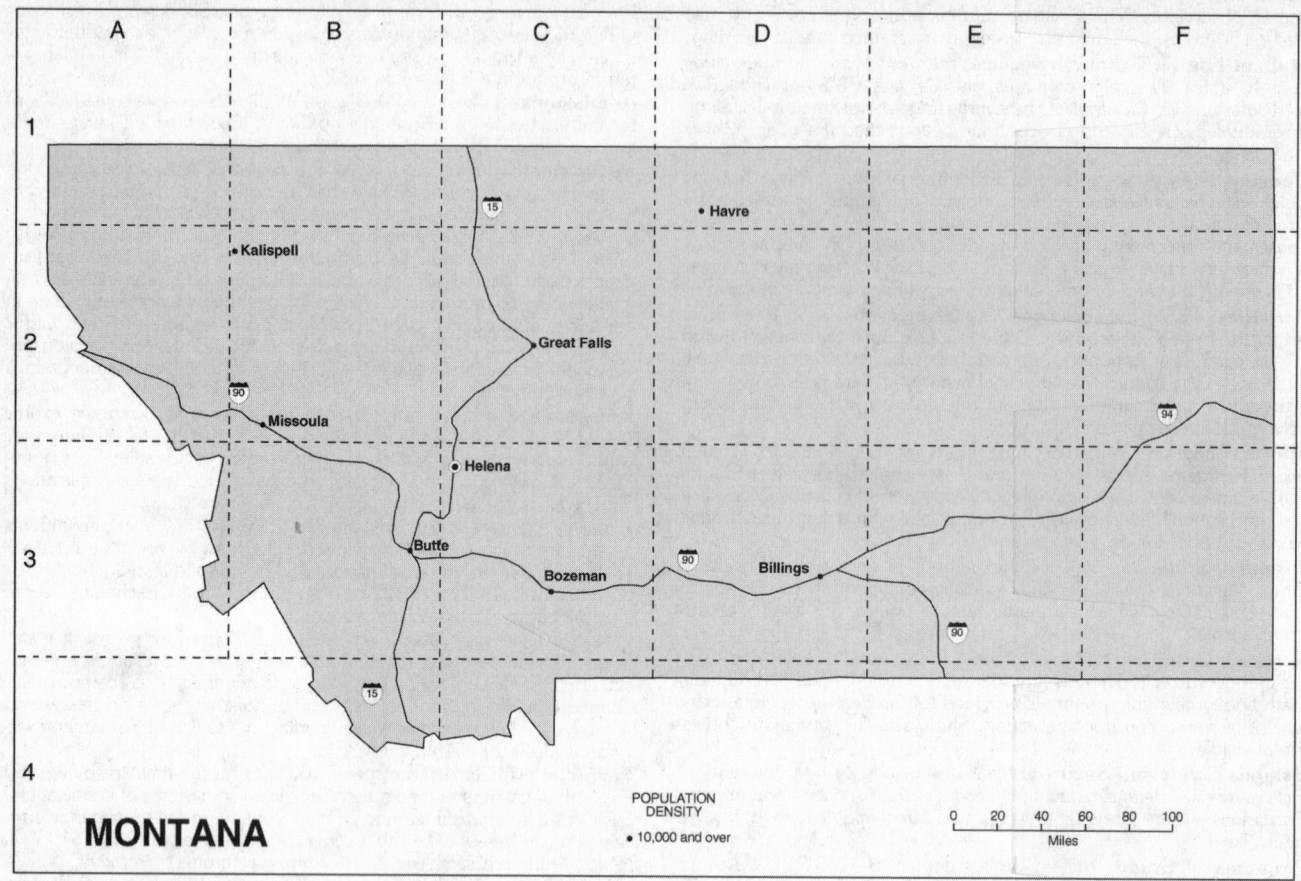

MONTANA

POPULATION
DENSITY

• 10,000 and over

0 20 40 60 80 100
Miles

CARROLL COLLEGE
Helena, MT 59625-0002

C-2

(406) 447-4384
(800) 992-3648; Fax: (406) 447-4533

Full-time: 523 men, 738 women	**Faculty:** 79
Part-time: 80 men, 128 women	**Ph.D.s:** 67%
Graduate: none	**Student/Faculty:** 16 to 1
Year: semesters, summer session	**Tuition:** $14,766
Application Deadline: June 1	**Room & Board:** $5810
Freshman Class: 854 applied, 718 accepted, 295 enrolled	
SAT I or ACT: required	**VERY COMPETITIVE**

Carroll College, founded in 1909, is a small liberal arts college affiliated with the Roman Catholic Church. It offers undergraduate programs in arts and sciences, business, engineering, education, religion, and selected preprofessional training. In addition to regional accreditation, Carroll has baccalaureate program accreditation with CAHEA, CSWE, NLN, and NRPA. The library contains 89,003 volumes, 64,500 microform items, and 3890 audio/video tapes/CDs, and subscribes to 504 periodicals. Computerized library services include the card catalog, interlibrary loans, and database searching. Special learning facilities include a learning resource center, radio station, and civil engineering lab. The 64-acre campus is in a small town 110 miles east of Missoula and 100 miles west of Bozeman. Including any residence halls, there are 12 buildings.

Student Life: 68% of undergraduates are from Montana. Students are from 21 states, 10 foreign countries, and Canada. 82% are from public schools. 73% are white. 41% are Catholic; 41% unknown. The average age of freshmen is 19; all undergraduates, 22. 19% do not continue beyond their first year.

Housing: 830 students can be accommodated in college housing, which includes single-sex and coed dorms and on-campus apartments. There is also a freshman dorm. On-campus housing is guaranteed for all 4 years. 50% of students live on campus; of those, 95% remain on campus on weekends. All students may keep cars.

Activities: There are no fraternities or sororities. There are 35 groups on campus, including cheerleading, choir, drama, ethnic, film, forensics, honors, international, jazz band, literary magazine, musical theater, newspaper, pep band, political, professional, radio and TV, religious, so-

cial, social service, student government, and yearbook. Popular campus events include theme dances, casino night, and softball tournament.

Sports: There are 3 intercollegiate sports for men and 5 for women, and 10 intramural sports for men and 10 for women. Facilities include basketball, tennis, and racquetball courts, weight-lifting, aerobics, and dance rooms, a swimming pool, and a 4200-seat gym.

Disabled Students: 75% of the campus is accessible. Wheelchair ramps, elevators, special parking, specially equipped rest rooms, special class scheduling, and lowered drinking fountains are available.

Services: Counseling and information services are available, as is tutoring in most subjects, including writing, math, statistics, economics, chemistry, accounting, and anatomy and physiology. There is remedial math, reading, and writing.

Campus Safety and Security: Measures include security escort services, informal discussions, and lighted pathways/sidewalks.

Programs of Study: Carroll confers the B.A. degree. Associate degrees are also awarded. Bachelor's degrees are awarded in BIOLOGICAL SCIENCE (biology/biological science), BUSINESS (accounting and business administration and management), COMMUNICATIONS AND THE ARTS (classical languages, communications, creative writing, dramatic arts, English, French, performing arts, public relations, and Spanish), COMPUTER AND PHYSICAL SCIENCE (chemistry, computer science, and mathematics), EDUCATION (elementary, foreign languages, physical, secondary, and teaching English as a second/foreign language (TESOL/TEFOL)), ENGINEERING AND ENVIRONMENTAL DESIGN (civil engineering and environmental science), HEALTH PROFESSIONS (clinical science, health care administration, nursing, predentistry, premedicine, preoptometry, prepharmacy, and preveterinary science), SOCIAL SCIENCE (history, international relations, philosophy, political science/government, prelaw, psychology, public administration, religion, social science, social work, and sociology). Business, nursing, and biology are the largest.

Required: To graduate, students must complete 122 semester hours and maintain the specific GPA and credit concentration required by their major. The college's general liberal arts requirements include courses in writing, communications, history, math, natural and social sciences, philosophy, theology, and fine arts.

Special: Carroll College offers a 3-2 engineering program leading to acceptance to any of 6 cooperating universities. In addition, internships, study abroad in Paris, Japan, Spain, Gemany, Korea, and many other countries through a consortium for international studies, and work-study programs in certain fields are available. Students may take a dual major in any two fields of study, select an interdisciplinary major such as health information management, earn credit for life, military, and work experience, or pursue nondegree study. The pass/fail option is available. There are 6 national honor societies, including Phi Beta Kappa, a freshman honors program, and 5 departmental honors programs.

Faculty/Classroom: 56% of faculty are male; 44%, female. All teach undergraduates. The average class size in an introductory lecture is 22; in a laboratory, 13; and in a regular course, 17.

Admissions: 84% of the 2003-2004 applicants were accepted. The SAT I scores for the 2003-2004 freshman class were: Verbal--26% below 500, 47% between 500 and 599, 20% between 600 and 700, and 7% above 700; Math--24% below 500, 53% between 500 and 599, 19% between 600 and 700, and 4% above 700. The ACT scores were 2% below 21, 43% between 21 and 23, 46% between 24 and 26, and 9% above 28. 57% of the current freshmen were in the top fifth of their class; 85% were in the top two fifths. 25 freshmen graduated first in their class.

Requirements: The SAT I or ACT is required. Composite scores of 1000 on the SAT I or 21 on the ACT are recommended. Students must be graduates of an accredited secondary school or have a GED. An essay is required. A GPA of 2.5 is required. AP and CLEP credits are accepted. Important factors in the admissions decision are advanced placement or honor courses, recommendations by school officials, and leadership record.

Procedure: Freshmen are admitted fall and spring. Entrance exams should be taken in the fall of the senior year. There is a deferred admissions plan and a rolling admissions plan. Applications should be filed by June 1 for fall entry, along with a $35 fee. Notification is sent on a rolling basis. Applications are accepted on-line through Carroll College's web site or CollegeLink.

Transfer: 64 transfer students enrolled in a recent year. Transfer students need a 2.5 GPA and must submit ACT or SAT I scores if fewer than 30 college credits have been completed. Letters of recommendation are required. 30 of 122 credits required for the bachelor's degree must be completed at Carroll.

Visiting: There are regularly scheduled orientations for prospective students, including of 3 visiting sessions in the summer that include a tour of the campus, overnight housing, social activities, and preregistration for classes. Orientation takes place Thursday through Monday before the start of fall classes. There are guides for informal visits and visitors may sit in on classes and stay overnight. To schedule a visit, contact the Admissions Office.

Financial Aid: In 2003-2004, 71% of all full-time freshmen and 68% of continuing full-time students received some form of financial aid. 61% of full-time freshmen and 60% of continuing full-time students received need-based aid. The average freshman award was $14,377. The average financial indebtedness of the 2003 graduate was $22,868. Carroll is a member of CSS. The FAFSA is required. The deadline for filing freshman financial aid applications for fall entry is March 1.

International Students: The school actively recruits these students. They must score 550 on the written TOEFL and also take the college's own test. English-speaking students must submit SAT I or ACT scores.

Computers: The mainframe is an IBM AS/400. All residence hall rooms are wired for access to the network, with access also available in computer labs and the library. Internet access is available. There are 100 computers available for student use in various locations around campus. All students may access the system. There are no time limits and no fees.

Graduates: In a recent year, 203 bachelor's degrees were awarded. The most popular majors were business (19%), biology (13%), and education (13%). In an average class, 39% graduate in 4 years or less, 49% graduate in 5 years or less, and 50% graduate in 6 years or less.

Admissions Contact: Candace Cain, Director of Admissions. A video is available. E-mail: *enroll@caroll.edu* Web: *www.carroll.edu*

MONTANA STATE UNIVERSITY-BILLINGS
Billings, MT 59101-0298

D-3

(406) 657-2158

(800) 565-MSUB; Fax: (406) 657-2302

Full-time: 1203 men, 1975 women	Faculty: 156; IIA, --$
Part-time: 314 men, 647 women	Ph.D.s: 87%
Graduate: 147 men, 384 women	Student/Faculty: 20 to 1
Year: semesters, summer session	Tuition: $4180 ($11,540)
Application Deadline: open	Room & Board: $5310
Freshman Class: 996 applied, 966 accepted, 649 enrolled	
SAT I Verbal/Math: 505/514	ACT: 21 COMPETITIVE

Montana State University-Billings, founded in 1927, is a comprehensive, regional, public university offering instructional and learning opportunities in the arts and sciences as well as professional programs in business, technology, human services, rehabilitation, and education. There are 6 undergraduate schools and 1 graduate school. In addition to regional accreditation, MSU-Billings has baccalaureate program accreditation with CORE, NASAD, NASM, and NCATE. The 2 libraries contain 294,562 volumes, 530,891 microform items, and 3667 audio/video tapes/CDs, and subscribe to 790 periodicals. Computerized library services include the card catalog, interlibrary loans, and database searching. Special learning facilities include a learning resource center, art gallery, radio station, scientific field station, a small business institute, an urban institute, a special education learning center, a disabilities center, a center for business enterprise, and a center for applied economic research. The 92-acre campus is in an urban area in Billings. Including any residence halls, there are 21 buildings.

Student Life: 93% of undergraduates are from Montana. Students are from 34 states, 13 foreign countries, and Canada. 97% are from public schools. 85% are white. The average age of freshmen is 21; all undergraduates, 26. 46% do not continue beyond their first year; 27% remain to graduate.

Housing: 558 students can be accommodated in college housing, which includes single-sex and coed dorms and married-student housing. On-campus housing is available on a first-come, first-served basis. 90% of students commute. All students may keep cars.

Activities: There are no fraternities or sororities. There are 53 groups on campus, including art, band, cheerleading, choir, chorale, chorus, computers, drama, ethnic, honors, international, jazz band, literary magazine, newspaper, orchestra, pep band, political, professional, radio and TV, religious, social, social service, and student government. Popular campus events include Powwow and Native American Day.

Sports: There are 4 intercollegiate sports for men and 6 for women, and 7 intramural sports for men and 7 for women. Facilities include a phys ed building with an Olympic-size pool, 2 gyms, a running track, weight-training equipment, 6 racquetball courts, and a soccer/softball field.

Disabled Students: All of the campus is accessible. Wheelchair ramps, elevators, special parking, specially equipped rest rooms, special class scheduling, lowered drinking fountains, lowered telephones, and a Disability Support Services Office are available.

Services: Counseling and information services are available, as is tutoring in most subjects. There is a reader service for the blind, and remedial math, reading, and writing. There is an academic support center.

Campus Safety and Security: Measures include 24-hour foot and vehicle patrol, security escort services, informal discussions, and pamphlets/posters/films. There are emergency telephones and lighted pathways/sidewalks.

Programs of Study: MSU-Billings confers B.A., B.S., B.A. or B.S. in Business Administration, B.A.S., B.S.Ed., B.S.H.S., B.S.L.S., and B.S. in Rehabilitation and Related Services degrees. Associate and master's degrees are also awarded. Bachelor's degrees are awarded in BIOLOGICAL SCIENCE (biology/biological science), BUSINESS (business administration and management), COMMUNICATIONS AND THE ARTS (art, communications, dramatic arts, English, music, music performance, and public relations), COMPUTER AND PHYSICAL SCIENCE (chemistry, information sciences and systems, and mathematics), EDUCATION (art, early childhood, education, elementary, health, mathematics, middle school, music, physical, science, secondary, social science, social studies, and special), ENGINEERING AND ENVIRONMENTAL DESIGN (environmental science), HEALTH PROFESSIONS (health care administration and rehabilitation therapy), SOCIAL SCIENCE (history, liberal arts/general studies, psychology, sociology, and Spanish studies). The sciences, business, and education are the strongest academically. Education and business are the largest.

Required: To graduate, students must have earned a minimum of 120 semester credits, including 30 in their major. They must maintain a minimum 2.0 GPA; education and human services majors must maintain a minimum 2.7 GPA. General education requirements must also be fulfilled.

Special: MSU-Billings offers co-op programs in business, human services, and liberal arts, internships, work-study programs, B.A.-B.S. degrees, dual majors, nondegree study, and pass/fail options. There are 10 national honor societies, a freshman honors program, and 1 departmental honors program.

Faculty/Classroom: 59% of faculty are male; 41%, female. All teach undergraduates. Graduate students teach 1% of introductory courses. The average class size in an introductory lecture is 30 and in a laboratory, 20.

Admissions: 97% of the 2003-2004 applicants were accepted. The SAT I scores for the 2003-2004 freshman class were: Verbal--43% below 500, 42% between 500 and 599, 11% between 600 and 700, and 4% above 700; Math--44% below 500, 35% between 500 and 599, 15% between 600 and 700, and 6% above 700. The ACT scores were 57% below 21, 20% between 21 and 23, 15% between 24 and 26, 5% between 27 and 28, and 3% above 28. 21% of the current freshmen were in the top fifth of their class; 51% were in the top two fifths. 10 freshmen graduated first in their class.

Requirements: The SAT I or ACT is required. In addition, applicants must be graduates of an accredited secondary school; the GED is also accepted. The applicant must have taken 4 years of English, 3 each of social science and math, and 2 each of science, foreign languages, or humanities. Students need to meet 1 of 3 criteria: be in the upper 50% of their class; have a GPA of 2.0 or better; or have minimum composite scores of 22 on the ACT or 1030 on the SAT I. AP and CLEP credits are accepted. Important factors in the admissions decision are advanced placement or honor courses, geographic diversity, and evidence of special talent.

Procedure: Freshmen are admitted to all sessions. Entrance exams should be taken in the senior year of high school. There is a deferred admissions plan. The fall 2003 application fee was $30. Application deadlines are open. There is a rolling admissions plan. Applications are accepted on-line through CollegeNET.

Transfer: 381 transfer students enrolled in 2002-2003. Out-of-state transfer students must have earned a 2.0 GPA; in-state transfer students must be in good academic standing. 32 of 120 credits required for the bachelor's degree must be completed at MSU-Billings.

Visiting: There are regularly scheduled orientations for prospective students. There are guides for informal visits and visitors may sit in on classes and stay overnight. To schedule a visit, contact Shelly Andersen at *sandersen@msubillings.edu*.

Financial Aid: In 2003-2004, 58% of all full-time freshmen and 61% of continuing full-time students received some form of financial aid. 46% of full-time freshmen and 56% of continuing full-time students received need-based aid. The average freshman award was $4325. Average annual earnings from campus work are $1600. The average financial indebtedness of the 2003 graduate was $16,000. The FAFSA and the university's own financial statement are required. The priority date for freshman financial aid applications for fall entry is March 1.

International Students: There are 21 international students enrolled. The school actively recruits these students. They must score 525 on the written TOEFL and also take the SAT I or the ACT.

Computers: The mainframe is a DEC 8100. There are also 550 PCs available at various campus locations. All have access to e-mail, the web, and on-line library resources, course registration, and courses. All students may access the system 24 hours a day. There are no time limits. The fee is $2.65 per credit hour. It is strongly recommended that all students have a personal computer.

Graduates: From July 1, 2002 to June 30, 2003, 519 bachelor's degrees were awarded. The most popular majors were arts and sciences (44%), education (33%), and business (23%). In an average class, 7% graduate in 4 years or less, 24% graduate in 5 years or less, and 28% graduate in 6 years or less. 100 companies recruited on campus in 2002-2003. Of the 2002 graduating class, 7% were enrolled in graduate school within 6 months of graduation and 90% were employed.

Admissions Contact: Karen Everett, Director of Admissions and Records and Registrar. E-mail: *keverett@msubillings.edu*
Web: *www.msubillings.edu*

MONTANA STATE UNIVERSITY-BOZEMAN   C-3
Bozeman, MT 59717   (406) 994-2452; Fax: (406) 994-1923

Full-time: 5056 men, 4228 women	**Faculty:** 545; I, --$
Part-time: 748 men, 718 women	**Ph.D.s:** 83%
Graduate: 743 men, 642 women	**Student/Faculty:** 17 to 1
Year: semesters, summer session	**Tuition:** $4145 ($12,707)
Application Deadline: open	**Room & Board:** $5370
Freshman Class: 4380 applied, 3547 accepted, 2165 enrolled	
SAT I Verbal/Math: 544/559	**ACT:** 23 COMPETITIVE

Montana State University-Bozeman, founded in 1893, is a public, land-grant institution offering programs in agriculture, business, arts and architecture, education, engineering, health and human development, nursing, and letters and science. There are 7 undergraduate schools and 1 graduate school. In addition to regional accreditation, MSU-Bozeman has baccalaureate program accreditation with AACSB, AAFCS, ABET, ADA, CACREP, CCNE, CSAB, NAAB, NASAD, NASM, NCATE, and NLN. The 2 libraries contain 670,407 volumes, 2,107,544 microform items, and 5386 audio/video tapes/CDs, and subscribe to 6643 periodicals. Computerized library services include the card catalog, interlibrary loans, and database searching. Special learning facilities include a learning resource center, art gallery, natural history museum, planetarium, radio station, TV station, Center for Biofilm Engineering, Burns Telecommunication Center, and a geographic information and analysis center. The 1170-acre campus is in a small town 140 miles west of Billings and 90 miles north of Yellowstone National Park. Including any residence halls, there are 83 buildings.

Student Life: 69% of undergraduates are from Montana. Students are from 49 states, 59 foreign countries, and Canada. 87% are white. The average age of freshmen is 19; all undergraduates, 22. 30% do not continue beyond their first year; 42% remain to graduate.

Housing: 5400 students can be accommodated in college housing, which includes coed dorms and married-student housing. In addition, there are honors houses, international houses, houses for older students, non-smoking floors, and wellness floors. On-campus housing is guaranteed for the freshman year only and is available on a first-come, first-served basis. 78% of students commute. All students may keep cars.

Activities: 2% of men belong to 9 national fraternities and 4 national sororities. There are 150 groups on campus, including art, band, cheerleading, chess, choir, chorale, chorus, computers, dance, drama, drill team, ethnic, film, gay, honors, international, jazz band, marching band, musical theater, newspaper, orchestra, pep band, photography, political, professional, radio and TV, religious, social, social service, student government, and symphony. Popular campus events include International Food Bazaar and Native American Pow-Wow.

Sports: There are 6 intercollegiate sports for men and 8 for women, and 38 intramural sports for men and 40 for women. Facilities include a 10,000-seat stadium, numerous gyms, handball courts, weight rooms, and 2 pools.

Disabled Students: 90% of the campus is accessible. Wheelchair ramps, elevators, special parking, specially equipped rest rooms, special class scheduling, lowered drinking fountains, lowered telephones, services through the resource center, and a taping service for the blind are available.

Services: Counseling and information services are available, as is tutoring in most subjects. There is a reader service for the blind and remedial math, reading, and writing.

Campus Safety and Security: Measures include 24-hour foot and vehicle patrol, self-defense education, security escort services, and informal discussions. There are pamphlets/posters/films, emergency telephones, and lighted pathways/sidewalks.

Programs of Study: MSU-Bozeman confers B.A., B.S., B.F.A., and B.Mus.Ed. degrees. Master's and doctoral degrees are also awarded. Bachelor's degrees are awarded in AGRICULTURE (agricultural business management, animal science, horticulture, natural resource management, plant science, and range/farm management), BIOLOGICAL SCIENCE (biology/biological science, biotechnology, cell biology, microbiology, and neurosciences), BUSINESS (business administration and management), COMMUNICATIONS AND THE ARTS (art, English, fine arts, media arts, modern language, and music), COMPUTER AND PHYSICAL SCIENCE (chemistry, computer science, earth science, mathematics, and physics), EDUCATION (agricultural, elementary, music, secondary, and technical), ENGINEERING AND ENVIRONMENTAL DESIGN (agricultural engineering technology, chemical engineering, civil engineering, computer engineering, construction engineering, electrical/electronics engineering, environmental design, environmental science, industrial engineering, land use management and reclamation, mechanical engineering, and mechanical engineering technology), HEALTH PROFESSIONS (health and nursing), SOCIAL SCIENCE (anthropology, economics, history, human development, philosophy, political science/government, psychology, and sociology). Engineering, physical science, and architecture are the strongest academically. Business, education, and nursing are the largest.

Required: To graduate, students must complete a core curriculum of 8 credits of natural sciences, 6 credits each of multicultural studies, humanities, social science, and communications, and 3 credits each of fine arts and math. The total number of credits required varies by program, with 120 being the minimum; at least one third must be in upper-division courses. A minimum 2.0 GPA is needed. Students must be officially registered in their chosen curriculum for at least 2 semesters before graduation.

Special: MSU-Bozeman offers internships in selected majors, study in 40 countries, cross-registration in selected programs, B.A.-B.S. degrees, dual and interdisciplinary majors, nondegree study, and pass/fail options. There are 23 national honor societies and a freshman honors program.

Faculty/Classroom: 60% of faculty are male; 40%, female. All both teach and do research. Graduate students teach 21% of introductory courses. The average class size in an introductory lecture is 66; in a laboratory, 18; and in a regular course, 22.

Admissions: 81% of the 2003-2004 applicants were accepted. The SAT I scores for the 2003-2004 freshman class were: Verbal--31% below 500, 45% between 500 and 599, 22% between 600 and 700, and 2% above 700; Math--24% below 500, 42% between 500 and 599, 28% between 600 and 700, and 6% above 700. The ACT scores were 28% below 21, 26% between 21 and 23, 26% between 24 and 26, 12% between 27 and 28, and 8% above 28. 38% of the current freshmen were in the top fifth of their class; 45% were in the top two fifths. There were 17 National Merit finalists and 3 semifinalists. 94 freshmen graduated first in their class.

Requirements: The SAT I or ACT is required. In addition, MSU-Bozeman requires applicants to have a minimum GPA of 2.5, rank in the upper 50% of their graduating class, or have minimum composite scores of 22 on the ACT or 1030 on the SAT I. They must be graduates of an accredited secondary school. The GED is accepted. Students should have completed 4 years of English, 3 years each of social studies and math, 2 years of lab science, and 2 years of language, computer science, visual and performing arts, or vocational education. MSU-Bozeman requires applicants to be in the upper 50% of their class. A GPA of 2.5 is required. AP and CLEP credits are accepted.

Procedure: Freshmen are admitted fall, spring, and summer. Entrance exams should be taken in the fall of the senior year. There are early admissions, deferred admissions, and rolling admissions plans. Application deadlines are open. The fall 2003 application fee was $30. Applications are accepted on-line through Embark.com and *www.montana.edu/wwwcat/appopts.html*.

Transfer: 774 transfer students enrolled in 2002-2003. Applicants must have a minimum GPA of 2.0; grades of D or better transfer for credit. 30 of 120 credits required for the bachelor's degree must be completed at MSU-Bozeman.

Visiting: There are regularly scheduled orientations for prospective students, including program overviews, a tour, and meetings with assistant deans. There are guides for informal visits and visitors may sit in on classes and stay overnight. To schedule a visit, contact the Office of New Student Services at (888) MSU-CATS or *admissions@montana.edu*.

Financial Aid: In 2003-2004, 50% of all full-time freshmen and 52% of continuing full-time students received some form of financial aid. At least 40% of full-time freshmen and at least 45% of continuing full-time students received need-based aid. The average freshman award was $6400. Need-based scholarships or need-based grants averaged $3625; need-based self-help aid (loans and jobs) averaged $3467; non-need-based athletic scholarships averaged $5814; and other non-need-based awards and non-need-based scholarships averaged $2455. 20% of undergraduates work part time. Average annual earnings from campus work are $3000. The average financial indebtedness of the 2003 graduate was $15,385. The FAFSA is required. The deadline for filing freshman financial aid applications for fall entry is March 1.

International Students: There are 164 international students enrolled. The school actively recruits these students. They must score 525 on the written TOEFL or 195 on the electronic version and also submit proof of American Cultural Exchange Language Institute Level 6 (available at MSU).

Computers: The mainframes are a two-node Hewlett-Packard ES-47 cluster and storage area network. Labs, residence halls, the library, and departments have 850 computers available for student use. All students may access the system. There are no time limits. The fee is included in mandatory fees. It is recommended that students in environmental design have personal computers.

Graduates: From July 1, 2002 to June 30, 2003, 1831 bachelor's degrees were awarded. The most popular majors were business (12%), health and human development (7%), and biological sciences (6%). In an average class, 14% graduate in 4 years or less, 49% graduate in 5 years or less, and 93% graduate in 6 years or less. 127 companies recruited on campus in 2002-2003. Of the 2002 graduating class, 7% were enrolled in graduate school within 6 months of graduation and 93% were employed.

Admissions Contact: Ronda Russell, Director, Office of New Student Services. A video is available. E-mail: *admissions@montana.edu* Web: *http://www.montana.edu/wwwnss/*

MONTANA STATE UNIVERSITY-NORTHERN D-1
Havre, MT 59501-7751

(406) 265-3704
(800) 662-6132; Fax: (406) 265-3792

Full-time: 640 men, 540 women	**Faculty:** 71; IIA, --$
Part-time: 100 men, 210 women	**Ph.D.s:** 47%
Graduate: 40 men, 70 women	**Student/Faculty:** 16 to 1
Year: semesters, summer session	**Tuition:** $3494 ($8600)
Application Deadline: open	**Room & Board:** $5500
Freshman Class: n/av	
SAT I or ACT: required	**NONCOMPETITIVE**

Montana State University-Northern, founded in 1929, is part of the Montana University System and offers programs in the liberal arts, teacher education, business, and technology. Figures in the above capsule and in this profile are approximate. There is 1 graduate school. In addition to regional accreditation, MSU-Northern has baccalaureate program accreditation with NLN. The library contains 100,000 volumes and 600,000 microform items, and subscribes to 650 periodicals. Computerized library services include the card catalog, interlibrary loans, and database searching. Special learning facilities include a learning resource center and radio station. The 105-acre campus is in a small town 115 miles north of Great Falls. Including any residence halls, there are 21 buildings.

Student Life: The average age of freshmen is 21; all undergraduates, 28.

Housing: 450 students can be accommodated in college housing, which includes single-sex and coed dorms, on-campus apartments, and married-student housing. On-campus housing is guaranteed for all 4 years. 60% of students live on campus. All students may keep cars.

Activities: There are no fraternities or sororities. There are 30 groups on campus, including dance, ethnic, musical theater, newspaper, pep band, religious, social service, student government, and yearbook. Popular campus events include concerts, dances, and theatrical productions.

Sports: There are 3 intercollegiate sports for men and 3 for women, and 11 intramural sports for men and 9 for women. Facilities include tennis courts, a swimming pool, weight and wrestling rooms, and 2 gyms, the larger seating 2500. Nearby Glacier National Park offers outdoor facilities.

Disabled Students: Wheelchair ramps, elevators, special parking, and specially equipped rest rooms are available.

Services: Counseling and information services are available, as is tutoring in every subject. There is remedial math, reading, and writing.

Campus Safety and Security: Measures include lighted pathways/sidewalks.

Programs of Study: MSU-Northern confers B.A., B.S., B.S.Ed., and B.T. degrees. Associate and master's degrees are also awarded. Bachelor's degrees are awarded in AGRICULTURE (agricultural mechanics), BIOLOGICAL SCIENCE (biology/biological science and ecology), COMMUNICATIONS AND THE ARTS (communications, dramatic arts, English, fine arts, French, and music), COMPUTER AND PHYSICAL SCIENCE (chemistry), EDUCATION (business, elementary, industrial arts, physical, science, secondary, and social science), ENGINEERING AND ENVIRONMENTAL DESIGN (automotive technology, civil engineering technology, construction technology, drafting and design technology, electrical/electronics engineering technology, engineering technology, environmental science, and manufacturing technology), HEALTH PROFESSIONS (nursing), SOCIAL SCIENCE (history, humanities, interdisciplinary studies, Native American studies, and social science). Business technology, nursing, and education are the largest.

Required: To graduate, students must complete at least 128 credits with a minimum GPA of 2.0 overall and 2.25 in their major and minor. Distribution requirements include 12 credits each of humanities, social science, math/science, and technology/applied arts. Students also must demonstrate proficiency in computing and in written and oral communication.

Special: B.A.-B.S. and other dual-degree programs, pass/fail options, cooperative programs in most disciplines, independent study, dual majors, and work-study programs are available.

Faculty/Classroom: All teach undergraduates. No introductory courses are taught by graduate students.

Requirements: The SAT I or ACT is required, with a minimum composite score of 20 on the ACT. Applicants must be graduates of an accredited high school or have a GED certificate. They should have completed 4 years of English, 3 each of math, social science, and history, including global studies and U.S. history, and 2 each of lab science and electives. MSU-Northern requires applicants to be in the upper 50% of their class. A GPA of 2.5 is required. CLEP credit is accepted.

Procedure: Freshmen are admitted to all sessions. There is a rolling admissions plan and an early admissions plan. Application deadlines are open. Application fee is $30.

Transfer: Nonresidents must have a minimum GPA of 2.0. Any applicant with fewer than 12 transfer credits must submit a transcript of college work completed and meet standard freshman requirements. 36 of 128 credits required for the bachelor's degree must be completed at MSU-Northern.

Visiting: There are regularly scheduled orientations for prospective students. There are guides for informal visits and visitors may sit in on classes and stay overnight. To schedule a visit, contact the Admissions Office.

Financial Aid: The college's own financial statement is required.

International Students: The school actively recruits international students. They must score 500 on the written TOEFL.

Computers: There are Apple computers available in various locations. All students may access the system when the buildings are open. There are no time limits.

Admissions Contact: Stacey Gonsalez, Admissions Counselor. E-mail: *msunadmit@msun.edu* Web: *www.msun.edu*

MONTANA TECH OF THE UNIVERSITY OF MONTANA C-3
Butte, MT 59701-8997

(406) 496-4178
(800) 445-TECH; Fax: (406) 496-4710

Full-time: 1022 men, 752 women	**Faculty:** 107; IIB, av$
Part-time: 143 men, 225 women	**Ph.D.s:** 75%
Graduate: 51 men, 39 women	**Student/Faculty:** 17 to 1
Year: semesters, summer session	**Tuition:** $4208 ($12,076)
Application Deadline: open	**Room & Board:** $5106
Freshman Class: 404 applied, 395 accepted, 393 enrolled	
SAT I Verbal/Math: 530/549	**ACT:** 22 **NONCOMPETITIVE**

Founded in 1893 as the Montana School of Mines, Montana Tech still focuses on its original programs in minerals and energy engineering and has expanded its offerings to include science, engineering, business, computer science, technical communications, health care, and related programs. There are 4 undergraduate schools and 1 graduate school. In addition to regional accreditation, Montana Tech has baccalaureate program accreditation with ABET and ACS. The library contains 167,262 volumes, 259,581 microform items, and 2947 audio/video tapes/CDs, and subscribes to 394 periodicals. Computerized library services include the card catalog, interlibrary loans, and database searching. Special learning facilities include a learning resource center, radio station, mineral museum, and METNET 2-way interactive communication studio. The 56-acre campus is in a small town. Including any residence halls, there are 19 buildings.

Student Life: 86% of undergraduates are from Montana. Students are from 33 states, 17 foreign countries, and Canada. 90% are from public schools. 92% are white. The average age of freshmen is 19; all undergraduates, 22. 39% do not continue beyond their first year; 58% remain to graduate.

Housing: 426 students can be accommodated in college housing, which includes coed dorms, off-campus apartments, and married-student housing. On-campus housing is guaranteed for the freshman year only and is available on a first-come, first-served basis. Priority is given to out-of-town students. 87% of students commute. All students may keep cars.

Activities: There are no fraternities or sororities. There are 33 groups on campus, including band, cheerleading, choir, chorale, computers, ethnic, international, newspaper, pep band, photography, professional, radio and TV, religious, social, social service, student government, and symphony. Popular campus events include M-Day, International Dinner, and Comedy Night.

Sports: There are 3 intercollegiate sports for men and 3 for women, and 10 intramural sports for men and 10 for women. Facilities include an athletic/recreational complex housing 4 basketball courts, a 25-meter swimming pool, volleyball courts, a weight-lifting room, 6 handball/racquetball courts, tennis courts, a stadium with skybox seating, 3 classrooms, 2 practice fields, and a baseball facility.

Disabled Students: 75% of the campus is accessible. Wheelchair ramps, elevators, special parking, specially equipped rest rooms, special class scheduling, lowered drinking fountains, and lowered telephones are available.

Services: Counseling and information services are available, as is tutoring in most subjects, including math, physics, chemistry, biology, engineering science, business, and computer science. Tutoring in additional subject areas is available upon request. There is a reader service for the blind and remedial math.

Campus Safety and Security: Measures include 24-hour foot and vehicle patrol, self-defense education, informal discussions, and pamphlets/posters/films. There are emergency telephones and lighted pathways/sidewalks.

Programs of Study: Montana Tech confers B.S. and B.A.S degrees. Associate and master's degrees are also awarded. Bachelor's degrees are awarded in BIOLOGICAL SCIENCE (biology/biological science), BUSINESS (business systems analysis), COMMUNICATIONS AND THE ARTS (communications and communications technology), COMPUTER AND PHYSICAL SCIENCE (chemistry, computer programming, computer science, mathematics, and science), ENGINEERING AND ENVIRONMENTAL DESIGN (computer engineering, engineering, environmental engineering, geological engineering, geophysical engineering, metallurgical engineering, mining and mineral engineering, occupational safety and health, and petroleum/natural gas engineering), SOCIAL SCIENCE (humanities and social science and liberal arts/general studies). Engineering and science are the strongest programs academically and have the largest enrollments.

Required: For graduation, students must complete at least 120 semester credits (more for engineering degrees) and maintain a minimum 2.0 GPA. Requirements include 6 hours each of communications, humanities, mathematical sciences, and social sciences, and 6 to 7 hours of physical and life sciences. Engineering students must satisfy specific requirements within the individual curriculum.

Special: Montana Tech has cooperative programs in all areas with 7 other institutions and cross-registration with Flathead Valley Community College, Montana State University, and the University of Montana. Internships are available, and there is a student-faculty exchange program with the People's Republic of China and a mining exchange program with Peru. Work-study, accelerated degree programs, 3-2 engineering degrees, student-designed majors, nondegree study, and credit for military experience are available. There are 3 national honor societies.

Faculty/Classroom: 80% of faculty are male; 20%, female. All teach undergraduates and 25% do research. The average class size in an introductory lecture is 34; in a laboratory, 15; and in a regular course, 21.

Admissions: 98% of the 2003-2004 applicants were accepted. The SAT I scores for the 2003-2004 freshman class were: Verbal--34% below 500, 46% between 500 and 599, 19% between 600 and 700, and 1% above 700; Math--26% below 500, 46% between 500 and 599, 23% between 600 and 700, and 6% above 700. The ACT scores were 33% below 21, 30% between 21 and 23, 18% between 24 and 26, 14% between 27 and 28, and 4% above 28. 35% of the current freshmen were in the top fifth of their class; 66% were in the top two fifths. In a recent year, 19 freshmen graduated first in their class.

Requirements: The SAT I or ACT is required. In addition, applicants must be graduates of an accredited secondary school. The GED is accepted. 14 academic credits are required, including English, 4 years;

math and social studies, 3 years each; science, 2 years; plus 2 years chosen from foreign language, computer science, visual and performing arts, or vocational education. Applicants must have minimum composite scores of 22 on the ACT or 1030 on the SAT I or a 2.5 GPA, or be in the top half of their graduating class. Other factors regarding admissions are considered only if the preceding standards are not met. AP and CLEP credits are accepted.

Procedure: Freshmen are admitted to all sessions. Entrance exams should be taken in the senior year. There is a deferred admissions plan. Early decision applications should be filed by March 1; application deadlines are open for regular applications The application fee is $30. There is a rolling admissions plan. Applications are accepted on computer disk and on-line through CollegeNET.

Transfer: 123 transfer students enrolled in a recent year. Transfer applicants must have a minimum GPA of 2.0. Grades of C and above transfer for credit. 30 of 120 credits required for the bachelor's degree must be completed at Montana Tech.

Visiting: There are regularly scheduled orientations for prospective students, including an official fall orientation, though visits are welcome any time. There are guides for informal visits and visitors may sit in on classes and stay overnight. To schedule a visit, contact the Admissions Office at *admissions@mtech.edu.*

Financial Aid: In 2003-2004, 75% of all full-time freshmen and 80% of continuing full-time students received some form of financial aid. 60% of full-time freshmen and 70% of continuing full-time students received need-based aid. The average freshman award was $5000. Need-based scholarships or need-based grants averaged $2000 ($4050 maximum); need-based self-help aid (loans and jobs) averaged $4000 ($4625 maximum); non-need-based athletic scholarships averaged $3236 (maximum); and other non-need-based awards and non-need-based scholarships averaged $2000 ($6000 maximum). 63% of undergraduates work part time. Average annual earnings from campus work are $1800. The average financial indebtedness of a recent year's graduate was $11,500. Montana Tech is a member of CSS. The FAFSA is required. Check with the school for current deadlines.

International Students: In a recent year, there were 56 international students enrolled. The school actively recruits these students. They must score 525 on the written TOEFL or 195 on the electronic version and also take the SAT I or the ACT, scoring 22 on the ACT.

Computers: The mainframe is a series of Compaq servers. There are some 1500 PCs connected to the campus LAN. All have access to both the Internet and campus intranet resources. Many PCs on both campuses are designated as "general use" for all students. Additionally, departments provide PCs configured for the requirements of their individual programs. All students may access the system any time. There are no time limits. The fee is $36 per semester.

Graduates: In a recent year, 243 bachelor's degrees were awarded. The most popular majors were general engineering (17%), petroleum engineering (14%), and business and information technology (12%). In an average class, 1% graduate in 3 years or less, 40% graduate in 4 years or less, 60% graduate in 5 years or less, and 67% graduate in 6 years or less. 153 companies recruited on campus in a recent year. Of a recent graduating class, 10% were enrolled in graduate school within 6 months of graduation and 95% were employed.

Admissions Contact: Ray Rogers, Director of College Relations and Marketing. A video is available. E-mail: *admissions@mtech.edu* Web: *www.mtech.edu*

MONTANA UNIVERSITY SYSTEM

The Montana University System, established in 1972, is a public system. It is governed by a Board of Regents whose chief administrator is the Commissioner of Higher Education. The primary goal of the system is teaching first, then research and public service. The main priorities are funding, system structure, and transfer articulation. The total enrollment of all six 4-year campuses is approximately 32,059, with about 1100 faculty members. There are 148 baccalaureate, 107 master's, and 33 doctoral programs offered in the system. Profiles of the 4-year campuses are included in this section.

ROCKY MOUNTAIN COLLEGE	D-3
Billings, MT 59102	**(406) 657-1000 or 657-1026**
	(800) 877-6259; Fax: (406) 259-9751
Full-time: 386 men, 475 women	**Faculty:** 45; IIB, --$
Part-time: 19 men, 39 women	**Ph.Ds:** 67%
Graduate: 8 men, 11 women	**Student/Faculty:** 19 to 1
Year: semesters, summer session	**Tuition:** $14,115
Application Deadline: August 1	**Room & Board:** $4900
Freshman Class: 720 applied, 611 accepted, 233 enrolled	
SAT I Verbal/Math: 539/525	**ACT:** 22 COMPETITIVE

Rocky Mountain College, established in 1878, is a private (not for profit) liberal arts institution affiliated with the United Church of Christ, the United Methodist Church, and the Presbyterian Church (U.S.A.). In addition to regional accreditation, Rocky has baccalaureate program accreditation with ARC-PA, CAAHEP, and IACBE. The library contains 97,094 volumes and 799 audio/video tapes/CDs, and subscribes to 376 periodicals. Computerized library services include the card catalog, interlibrary loans, database searching, and Internet access. Special learning facilities include a learning resource center, art gallery, flight school, and equestrian facilities. The 60-acre campus is in a small town 550 miles north of Denver, Colorado, in south-central Montana. Including any residence halls, there are 16 buildings.

Student Life: 62% of undergraduates are from Montana. Students are from 39 states, 23 foreign countries, and Canada. 80% are white. 46% are Protestant; 31% claim no religious affiliation; 20% Catholic. The average age of freshmen is 19; all undergraduates, 23. 33% do not continue beyond their first year; 33% remain to graduate.

Housing: 303 students can be accommodated in college housing, which includes coed dorms, on-campus apartments, and married-student housing. On-campus housing is guaranteed for the freshman year only and is available on a first-come, first-served basis. 62% of students commute. All students may keep cars.

Activities: There are no fraternities or sororities. There are 25 groups on campus, including aviation, band, choir, chorale, chorus, computers, drama, equestrian, forensics, honors, international, jazz band, literary magazine, marching band, musical theater, newspaper, pep band, photography, professional, religious, social, social service, student government, and yearbook. Popular campus events include Convocations, intercollegiate athletics, and Woodrow Wilson Visiting Fellow.

Sports: There are 4 intercollegiate sports for men and 4 for women, and 12 intramural sports for men and 12 for women. Activities include backpacking in Glacier National Park, white-water river rafting in the Tetons, and climbing at Beartooth Mountain.

Disabled Students: 60% of the campus is accessible. Wheelchair ramps, elevators, special parking, specially equipped rest rooms, special class scheduling, lowered drinking fountains, and special housing are available.

Services: Counseling and information services are available, as is tutoring in most subjects. There is a reader service for the blind and remedial math, reading, and writing.

Campus Safety and Security: Measures include self-defense education, security escort services, informal discussions, and pamphlets/posters/films. There are lighted pathways/sidewalks and security cameras.

Programs of Study: Rocky confers B.A. and B.S. degrees. Associate and master's degrees are also awarded. Bachelor's degrees are awarded in AGRICULTURE (equine science), BIOLOGICAL SCIENCE (biology/biological science), BUSINESS (accounting, business administration and management, and business economics), COMMUNICATIONS AND THE ARTS (art, communications, dramatic arts, literature, and music performance), COMPUTER AND PHYSICAL SCIENCE (chemistry, computer science, earth science, information sciences and systems, mathematics, and natural sciences), EDUCATION (art, education, elementary, English, mathematics, music, physical, psychology, science, social science, and social studies), ENGINEERING AND ENVIRONMENTAL DESIGN (aeronautical science and aviation administration/management), SOCIAL SCIENCE (anthropology, economics, history, philosophy, political science/government, psychology, religion, and sociology). Education, business and economics, and aviation are the largest.

Required: To graduate, students must complete 124 credit hours, 24 in a major and 18 in a minor, with a minimum overall GPA of 2.0 and 2.25 in the major. There are general education requirements in humanities, the natural and social sciences, fine arts, and religious thought, as well as writing, speech, math, experiential learning, and health requirements.

Special: The college offers internships, study abroad in 32 countries, work-study, dual majors, individualized programs of study, and credit for life, military, and work experience. Juniors and seniors may elect to take 1 course on a pass/fail basis each semester. There is a freshman honors program.

Faculty/Classroom: 56% of faculty are male; 44%, female. All teach undergraduates and 15% do research. No introductory courses are taught by graduate students. The average class size in an introductory lecture is 19; in a laboratory, 14; and in a regular course, 15.

Admissions: 85% of the 2003-2004 applicants were accepted. The SAT I scores for the 2003-2004 freshman class were: Verbal--27% below 500, 51% between 500 and 599, 18% between 600 and 700, and 4% above 700; Math--30% below 500, 55% between 500 and 599, 14% between 600 and 700, and 1% above 700. The ACT scores were 36% below 21, 29% between 21 and 23, 20% between 24 and 26, 9% between 27 and 28, and 5% above 28. 35% of the current freshmen were in the top fifth of their class; 63% were in the top two fifths. 9 freshmen graduated first in their class.

Requirements: The SAT I or ACT is required. In addition, applicants must be graduates of an accredited secondary school; the GED is accepted. Students must have completed 4 units of English, 1 unit of history, and 2 units each in 3 of the following: foreign language, math, natural sciences, and social sciences. The school recommends a portfolio for ad-

mission to the art program, an audition for admission to the music program, and an interview for academically weak students. A GPA of 2.5 is required. AP and CLEP credits are accepted.

Procedure: Freshmen are admitted fall, spring, and summer. There are early admissions, deferred admissions, and rolling admissions plans. Applications should be filed by August 1 for fall entry, along with a $25 fee. Notification is sent on October 1. Applications are accepted on-line through *www.rocky.edu/admissions/whichone.shtml*.

Transfer: 101 transfer students enrolled in 2003-2004. Transfer students must have a minimum GPA of 2.0; grades of 2.0 and higher transfer for credit. Transfers are admitted every term. 24 of 124 credits required for the bachelor's degree must be completed at Rocky.

Visiting: There are regularly scheduled orientations for prospective students, in late spring and summer. There are guides for informal visits and visitors may sit in on classes and stay overnight. To schedule a visit, contact the Director of Admissions at (406) 657-1026 or *hendersl@rocky.edu*.

Financial Aid: In 2003-2004, 95% of all full-time freshmen and 97% of continuing full-time students received some form of financial aid. 74% of full-time freshmen and 81% of continuing full-time students received need-based aid. The average freshman award was $12,949. Need-based scholarships or need-based grants averaged $8739; need-based self-help aid (loans and jobs) averaged $3995; non-need-based athletic scholarships averaged $8388; and other non-need-based awards and non-need-based scholarships averaged $5871. Average annual earnings from campus work are $1000. The average financial indebtedness of the 2003 graduate was $20,571. The FAFSA and the college's own financial statement are required. The deadline for filing freshman financial aid applications for fall entry is April 1.

International Students: There are 60 international students enrolled. The school actively recruits these students. They must score 525 on the written TOEFL or 197 on the electronic version.

Computers: 11 student computer labs housing 193 PCs are available. All students may access the system. There are no time limits and no fees.

Graduates: From July 1, 2002 to June 30, 2003, 172 bachelor's degrees were awarded. The most popular majors were business/marketing (25%), education (14%), and physician assistant (12%). In an average class, 27% graduate in 4 years or less, 44% graduate in 5 years or less, and 50% graduate in 6 years or less. 75 companies recruited on campus in 2002-2003. Of the 2002 graduating class, 12% were enrolled in graduate school within 6 months of graduation and all were employed.

Admissions Contact: LynAnn Henderson, Director of Admissions. A video is available. E-mail: *admissions@rocky.edu* Web: *www.rocky.edu*

UNIVERSITY OF GREAT FALLS
Great Falls, MT 59405
C-2
(406) 791-5200
(800) 856-9544; Fax: (406) 791-5209

Full-time: 160 men, 330 women	**Faculty:** 41
Part-time: 80 men, 190 women	**Ph.D.s:** 54%
Graduate: 30 men, 95 women	**Student/Faculty:** 12 to 1
Year: semesters, summer session	**Tuition:** $11,600
Application Deadline: August 1	**Room & Board:** $5100
Freshman Class: n/av	
SAT I or ACT: recommended	**COMPETITIVE**

The University of Great Falls, established in 1932, is a private, liberal arts institution affiliated with the Roman Catholic Church. There are 2 undergraduate schools and 1 graduate school. Figures in the above capsule and in this profile are approximate. The library contains 106,135 volumes, 124,608 microform items, and 3894 audio/video tapes/CDs, and subscribes to 587 periodicals. Computerized library services include the card catalog, interlibrary loans, and database searching. Special learning facilities include a learning resource center and art gallery. The 40-acre campus is in an urban area. Including any residence halls, there are 13 buildings.

Student Life: 93% of undergraduates are from Montana. Students are from 20 states and Canada. 99% are from public schools. 80% are white. 28% are Catholic; 22% claim no religious affiliation; 19% Protestant. The average age of freshmen is 26; all undergraduates, 33. 46% do not continue beyond their first year; 20% remain to graduate.

Housing: 189 students can be accommodated in college housing, which includes single-sex and coed dorms, off-campus apartments, and married-student housing. On-campus housing is guaranteed for the freshman year only and is available on a first-come, first-served basis. Priority is given to out-of-town students. 88% of students commute. Alcohol is not permitted. All students may keep cars.

Activities: There are no fraternities or sororities. There are 15 groups on campus, including art, cheerleading, chess, choir, chorus, computers, drama, ethnic, forensics, honors, literary magazine, musical theater, newspaper, orchestra, photography, professional, religious, social, social service, student government, Students in Free Enterprise (SIFE), and symphony. Popular campus events include Orientation Barbecue, Halloween Dance, and Intramural Festival.

Sports: There is 1 intercollegiate sport for men and 2 for women, and 7 intramural sports for men and 7 for women. Facilities include a gym, Olympic-size pool, game room, and workout room.

Disabled Students: All of the campus is accessible. Wheelchair ramps, elevators, special parking, specially equipped rest rooms, special class scheduling, and lowered drinking fountains are available.

Services: Counseling and information services are available, as is tutoring in some subjects, including 100-level courses, 200-level courses, and selected 300-level courses. There is a reader service for the blind, remedial math, reading, and writing, and tutoring in basic skills.

Campus Safety and Security: Measures include 24-hour foot and vehicle patrol, self-defense education, security escort services, and informal discussions. There are pamphlets/posters/films, emergency telephones, and lighted pathways/sidewalks.

Programs of Study: UGF confers B.A. and B.S. degrees. Associate and master's degrees are also awarded. Bachelor's degrees are awarded in BIOLOGICAL SCIENCE (biology/biological science, botany, microbiology, molecular biology, and physiology), BUSINESS (accounting, business administration and management, management science, and marketing/retailing/merchandising), COMMUNICATIONS AND THE ARTS (art, English, and fine arts), COMPUTER AND PHYSICAL SCIENCE (computer management, computer programming, computer science, mathematics, physical sciences, and science), EDUCATION (education of the exceptional child, elementary, health, mathematics, middle school, physical, reading, science, secondary, social studies, and special), ENGINEERING AND ENVIRONMENTAL DESIGN (computer graphics), HEALTH PROFESSIONS (health care administration, predentistry, and premedicine), SOCIAL SCIENCE (counseling/psychology, criminal justice, history, human services, law enforcement and corrections, paralegal studies, political science/government, prelaw, psychology, religion, social science, sociology, and theological studies). Biology, paralegal studies, and computer science are the strongest academically. Education, criminal justice, and business are the largest.

Required: Students must complete 128 credit hours, including 30 to 65 in the major, plus 15 to 21 minor credits, maintaining a minimum GPA of 2.0. The 52-credit-hour core curriculum includes math, computer science, art, behavioral science, history, literature, philosophy, science, writing, theology, and religion. Specific disciplines required include human nature, intellectual inquiry, and religious dimension.

Special: Internships are offered in sociology, criminal justice, paralegal studies, health care administration, and chemical-dependency counseling. Opportunities are provided for work-study programs, B.A.-B.S. degrees in most majors, dual majors, a general studies degree, credit by exam or for military service, and nondegree study. A 3-2 engineering degree for applied computer science and applied math majors is offered with Montana State University-Bozeman. Specialized instruction is available through the use of videotape and telephone discussions in 14 locations throughout Montana and Canada. There is 1 national honor society.

Faculty/Classroom: 59% of faculty are male; 42%, female. All teach undergraduates. No introductory courses are taught by graduate students. The average class size in an introductory lecture is 15; in a laboratory, 10; and in a regular course, 14.

Requirements: The SAT I or ACT is recommended. In addition, graduation from an accredited secondary school is required; the GED is accepted. Applicants should have 4 years of English, 3 of math, and 2 each of social studies, science, and electives, including foreign language, art, music, and vocational education. An interview is recommended. A GPA of 2.0 is required. AP and CLEP credits are accepted.

Procedure: Freshmen are admitted fall, spring, and summer. Entrance exams should be taken prior to registration. There is a rolling admissions plan. Applications should be filed by August 1 for fall entry, along with a $35 fee. Notification is sent on a rolling basis.

Transfer: 98 transfer students enrolled in a recent year. Transfer applicants must be in good academic standing from another accredited college or university, and must submit official transcripts from all colleges or universities attended. Those without a bachelor's degree must also submit an official high school transcript. 30 of 128 credits required for the bachelor's degree must be completed at UGF.

Visiting: There are regularly scheduled orientations for prospective students, including meeting with prospective advisers and staff, financial aid presentation, campus tour, and lunch. There are guides for informal visits and visitors may sit in on classes and stay overnight. To schedule a visit, contact the Office of Admissions.

Financial Aid: In a recent year, 81% of all full-time freshmen and 83% of continuing full-time students received some form of financial aid. 82% of full-time freshmen and 61% of continuing full-time students received need-based aid. The average freshman award was $9578. 39% of undergraduates work part time. Average annual earnings from campus work are $3000. The average financial indebtedness of a recent graduate was $20,470. UGF is a member of CSS. The FAFSA is required.

International Students: There were 19 international students enrolled in a recent year. The school actively recruits these students. They must score 550 on the written TOEFL.

Computers: There are 250 Pentium PCs with full Internet access via a T1 line. All students may access the system 7 days a week. There are no time limits and no fees. It is strongly recommended that all students have a personal computer.

Graduates: In a recent year, 180 bachelor's degrees were awarded. The most popular majors were education (29%), criminal justice (13%), and business (11%). In an average class, 6% graduate in 3 years or less, 6% graduate in 4 years or less, 14% graduate in 5 years or less, and 20% graduate in 6 years or less. 70 companies recruited on campus in 2002-2003.

Admissions Contact: Cathy Day, Director of Admissions.
E-mail: *adminrec@ugf.edu* Web: *www.ugf.edu*

UNIVERSITY OF MONTANA
Missoula, MT 59812

B-2
(406) 243-6266
(800) 462-8636; Fax: (406) 243-5711

Full-time: 4421 men, 4896 women	**Faculty:** 439; I, --$
Part-time: 758 men, 784 women	**Ph.D.s:** 86%
Graduate: 696 men, 841 women	**Student/Faculty:** 21 to 1
Year: semesters, summer session	**Tuition:** $4103 ($11,474)
Application Deadline: July 1	**Room & Board:** $5292

Freshman Class: 3719 applied, 3071 accepted, 1792 enrolled
SAT I or ACT: required   **COMPETITIVE**

The University of Montana, founded in 1893, is a public institution with programs in arts and sciences, business administration, fine arts, education, forestry, journalism, and pharmacy and allied health sciences. It is part of the Montana University System. There are 8 undergraduate and 2 graduate schools. In addition to regional accreditation, U of M has baccalaureate program accreditation with AACSB, ACCE, ACPE, APTA, CAHEA, CSAB, CSWE, NASAD, NASDTEC, NASM, NCATE, and SAF. The 4 libraries contain 913,000 volumes, 1,991,267 microform items, and 27,600 audio/video tapes/CDs, and subscribe to 4700 periodicals. Computerized library services include the card catalog, interlibrary loans, and database searching. Special learning facilities include an art gallery, radio station, TV station, experimental forest, biological station, ranch, Center for People and Forests, geology field camp, international language lab, wilderness institute, observatory, and freshwater research center. The 220-acre campus is in an urban area 200 miles east of Spokane. Including any residence halls, there are 57 buildings.

Student Life: 70% of undergraduates are from Montana. Students are from 50 states, 67 foreign countries, and Canada. 80% are from public schools. 93% are white. The average age of freshmen is 19; all undergraduates, 25. 22% do not continue beyond their first year; 39% remain to graduate.

Housing: 2600 students can be accommodated in college housing, which includes single-sex and coed dorms, off-campus apartments, and married-student housing. In addition, there are honors houses, special-interest houses, an international house, and nontraditional houses. On-campus housing is guaranteed for the freshman year only. 75% of students commute. All students may keep cars.

Activities: 10% of men belong to 9 national fraternities; 8% of women belong to 4 national sororities. There are 130 groups on campus, including academic, art, band, cheerleading, chess, choir, chorale, chorus, computers, creative writing, dance, drill team, ethnic, forestry, gay, honors, international, jazz band, literary magazine, marching band, newspaper, opera, orchestra, pep band, political, professional, radio and TV, religious, social, social service, student government, and symphony. Popular campus events include Foresters Day, Founders Day, and International Week.

Sports: There are 6 intercollegiate sports for men and 8 for women, and 16 intramural sports for men and 12 for women. Facilities include a field house, a 10,000-seat gym, an 18,000-seat stadium, a fitness center, a golf course, soccer and rugby fields, an Olympic-size pool, a game room, a climbing wall, weight rooms, and mountain trails.

Disabled Students: 75% of the campus is accessible. Wheelchair ramps, elevators, special parking, specially equipped rest rooms, special class scheduling, lowered drinking fountains, lowered telephones, special housing, and stadium access are available.

Services: Counseling and information services are available, as is tutoring in every subject. There is a reader service for the blind and remedial math, reading, and writing. Mentors and note takers are available, as are books on tape for LD students.

Campus Safety and Security: Measures include 24-hour foot and vehicle patrol, self-defense education, security escort services, and informal discussions. There are pamphlets/posters/films, emergency telephones, and lighted pathways/sidewalks.

Programs of Study: U of M confers B.A., B.S., B.A.E., B.S.H.P.E., and B.S.M. degrees. Associate, master's, and doctoral degrees are also awarded. Bachelor's degrees are awarded in AGRICULTURE (environmental studies and forestry and related sciences), BIOLOGICAL SCIENCE (biology/biological science, botany, microbiology, wildlife biology, and zoology), BUSINESS (accounting, banking and finance, business administration and management, marketing/retailing/merchandising, personnel management, and small business management), COMMUNICATIONS AND THE ARTS (classics, communications, dramatic arts, English, fine arts, French, German, Japanese, journalism, music, music performance, radio/television technology, Russian, and Spanish), COMPUTER AND PHYSICAL SCIENCE (chemistry, computer science, geology, mathematics, and physics), EDUCATION (elementary, music, physical, science, and secondary), HEALTH PROFESSIONS (medical technology and pharmacy), SOCIAL SCIENCE (anthropology, economics, geography, history, liberal arts/general studies, Native American studies, philosophy, political science/government, psychology, social work, sociology, and women's studies). Journalism, forestry, and liberal arts are the strongest academically. Business, forestry, and education are the largest.

Required: A total of 120 credits is required for graduation in most majors. The number of hours in the major varies; some majors require a thesis. There are competency requirements in writing, math, and foreign language or symbolic systems. Juniors must pass writing exams. Distribution requirements include courses in expressive arts, literary and artistic studies, historical and cultural studies, social sciences, ethical and human values, and natural sciences. A minimum GPA of 2.0 must be maintained.

Special: Students may cross-register with Montana Tech and Western Montana College. Co-op programs exist in business, communications, economics, management, and liberal studies; internships in most majors, work-study programs with nonprofit organizations, and study abroad in 12 countries are available. The school offers a B.A.-B.S. degree in chemistry, pass/fail options in classes other than major requirements, and dual majors in physics and computer science as well as history and political science. There are 7 national honor societies, including Phi Beta Kappa, a freshman honors program, and 5 departmental honors programs.

Faculty/Classroom: 67% of faculty are male; 33%, female. All both teach and do research. Graduate students teach 2% of introductory courses. The average class size in an introductory lecture is 35; in a laboratory, 25; and in a regular course, 35.

Admissions: 83% of the 2003-2004 applicants were accepted. 30% of the current freshmen were in the top fifth of their class; 62% were in the top two fifths.

Requirements: The SAT I or ACT is required, with a minimum composite ACT score of 22 or a minimum SAT I composite score of 1030. Applicants must be graduates of an accredited secondary school. The GED is accepted. Students should have completed 4 years of English, 3 each of math and social studies, 2 of lab science, and 2 elective credits (foreign language recommended). U of M requires applicants to be in the upper 50% of their class. A GPA of 2.5 is required. AP and CLEP credits are accepted. Important factors in the admissions decision are advanced placement or honor courses, evidence of special talent, and geographic diversity.

Procedure: Freshmen are admitted to all sessions. There is a deferred admissions plan. Applications should be filed by July 1 for fall entry and November 15 for spring entry. The fall 2003 application fee was $30. Notification is sent on a rolling basis. Applications are accepted on computer disk and on-line through the school's web site, CollegeNET, Apply, or Education Connect.

Transfer: Applicants must have a minimum GPA of 2.0. Grades of 2.0 or better transfer for credit. 30 of 120 credits required for the bachelor's degree must be completed at U of M.

Visiting: There are regularly scheduled orientations for prospective students, including placement testing, advising, workshops, and social events. There are guides for informal visits and visitors may sit in on classes. To schedule a visit, contact the Office of Admissions and New Student Services.

Financial Aid: In 2003-2004, 79% of all full-time freshmen and 83% of continuing full-time students received some form of financial aid, including need-based aid. The average freshman award was $8000. Need-based scholarships or need-based grants averaged $3069; need-based self-help aid (loans and jobs) averaged $7961; non-need-based athletic scholarships averaged $2297; and other non-need-based awards and non-need-based scholarships averaged $3000. U of M is a member of CSS. The FAFSA is required. The deadline for filing freshman financial aid applications for fall entry is March 1.

International Students: The school actively recruits these students. They must score 500 on the written TOEFL.

Computers: The mainframe is 2 DEC Alpha 8200 servers. Terminal rooms are located campuswide, including in dorms. Several academic departments have their own terminal rooms. Off-campus services have access through Interact. All students may access the system any time. There are no time limits. The fee is $3 per credit. It is strongly recommended that all students have a personal computer.

Admissions Contact: Frank Matule, Director of Admissions and New Student Services. A video is available. E-mail: admiss@selway.umt.edu Web: www.umt.edu/nss

UNIVERSITY OF MONTANA--WESTERN
Dillon, MT 59725
B-3
(406) 683-7331
(866) UMW-MONT; Fax: (406) 683-7493

Full-time: 416 men, 432 women	**Faculty:** 47; IIB, --$
Part-time: 32 men, 166 women	**Ph.D.s:** 75%
Graduate: none	**Student/Faculty:** 18 to 1
Year: semesters, summer session	**Tuition:** $3473 ($10,690)
Application Deadline: July 1	**Room & Board:** $4600
Freshman Class: 293 applied, 293 accepted, 147 enrolled	
SAT I Verbal/Math: 470/472	**ACT:** 19 NONCOMPETITIVE

The University of Montana-Western College, established in 1893, is a public institution, part of the University of Montana system. The college emphasizes teacher education and liberal studies. There are 2 undergraduate schools. In addition to regional accreditation, Western has baccalaureate program accreditation with NCATE. The library contains 90,431 volumes, 5792 microform items, and 3718 audio/video tapes/CDs, and subscribes to 7127 periodicals. Computerized library services include the card catalog, interlibrary loans, database searching, and Internet access. Special learning facilities include a learning resource center, art gallery, radio station, and a humanities resource center. The 34-acre campus is in a small town 60 miles south of Butte and 150 miles from Yellowstone National Park. Including any residence halls, there are 29 buildings.

Student Life: 86% of undergraduates are from Montana. Students are from 12 states, 2 foreign countries, and Canada. 90% are from public schools. 76% are white. The average age of freshmen is 22; all undergraduates, 22. 30% do not continue beyond their first year.

Housing: 485 students can be accommodated in college housing, which includes single-sex and coed dorms, on-campus apartments, and married-student housing. On-campus housing is guaranteed for all 4 years. All students may keep cars.

Activities: There are no fraternities or sororities. There are 18 groups on campus, including art, band, cheerleading, choir, chorale, drama, ethnic, honors, musical theater, newspaper, pep band, political, radio and TV, religious, social, social service, student government, and yearbook. Popular campus events include Alumni Weekend and International Week.

Sports: There are 4 intercollegiate sports for men and 4 for women, and 7 intramural sports for men and 7 for women. Facilities include a 5000-seat gym, 3 basketball and 4 racquetball courts, a dance floor, tennis courts, 2 weight rooms, an aerobics room, circuit training, an indoor arena, and a 3000-seat stadium.

Disabled Students: 98% of the campus is accessible. Wheelchair ramps, elevators, special parking, specially equipped rest rooms, special class scheduling, lowered drinking fountains, and lowered telephones are available.

Services: Counseling and information services are available, as is tutoring in most subjects. There is a reader service for the blind and remedial math.

Campus Safety and Security: Measures include 24-hour foot and vehicle patrol, security escort services, informal discussions, and pamphlets/posters/films. There are emergency telephones and lighted pathways/sidewalks.

Programs of Study: Western confers B.A., B.S. Business, B.Applied Sc., and B.S.Ed. degrees. Associate degrees are also awarded. Bachelor's degrees are awarded in COMMUNICATIONS AND THE ARTS (art, communications, creative writing, English literature, and technical and business writing), EDUCATION (art, business, elementary, industrial arts, middle school, music, science, and secondary), ENGINEERING AND ENVIRONMENTAL DESIGN (environmental science), SOCIAL SCIENCE (liberal arts/general studies and social science). Elementary education is the largest.

Required: For graduation, students must complete 120 credit hours (128 for education) and maintain a minimum GPA of 2.0. Other requirements vary by major.

Special: The college offers co-op programs, work-study programs, B.A.-B.S. degrees, dual majors, and pass/fail options. The Rural Education Program is designed to prepare students for teaching in smaller rural school settings. There are 2 national honor societies, and a freshman honors program.

Faculty/Classroom: 56% of faculty are male; 44%, female. All teach undergraduates. The average class size in an introductory lecture is 35; in a laboratory, 20; and in a regular course, 19.

Admissions: 100% of the 2003-2004 applicants were accepted. The SAT I scores for the 2003-2004 freshman class were: Verbal--59% below 500, 39% between 500 and 599, and 2% between 600 and 700; Math--66% below 500, 32% between 500 and 599, and 2% between 600 and 700. The ACT scores were 68% below 21, 24% between 21 and 23, 6% between 24 and 26, 1% between 27 and 28, and 1% above 28. 13% of the current freshmen were in the top fifth of their class; 45% were in the top two fifths. 3 freshmen graduated first in their class.

Requirements: The SAT I or ACT is required. New students who have not taken the ACT or SAT I must complete it during their first semester of attendance. Applicants must be graduates of an accredited secondary school. The GED is accepted. Students should have completed 4 years of English, 3 each of social studies and math, 2 years of lab science, and 2 years of electives. Western requires applicants to be in the upper 50% of their class. A GPA of 2.5 is required. AP and CLEP credits are accepted.

Procedure: Freshmen are admitted to all sessions. There is a deferred admissions plan and a rolling admissions plan. Applications should be filed by July 1 for fall entry, December 1 for spring entry, and May 1 for summer entry, along with a $30 fee. The college accepts all applicants. Notification is sent on a rolling basis. Applications are accepted on-line through CollegeNET, available on Western's web site.

Transfer: 124 transfer students enrolled in 2002-2003. Transfers must have attempted a minimum of 12 credit hours and have a cumulative GPA of 2.0. Credits earned at any accredited college can be used to satisfy curriculum or degree requirements only after evaluation. 30 of 120 credits required for the bachelor's degree must be completed at Western.

Visiting: There are regularly scheduled orientations for prospective students, including Sunday through Monday overnight stays. There are guides for informal visits and visitors may sit in on classes and stay overnight. To schedule a visit, contact the Admissions Office.

Financial Aid: In 2003-2004, 68% of all full-time freshmen and 75% of continuing full-time students received some form of financial aid. 74% of full-time freshmen and 51% of continuing full-time students received need-based aid. The average freshman award was $4743. 99% of undergraduates work part time. Average annual earnings from campus work are $1500. The average financial indebtedness of the 2003 graduate was $13,510. Western is a member of CSS. The FAFSA is required. The deadline for filing freshman financial aid applications for fall entry is March 1.

International Students: There are 3 international students enrolled. They must score 500 on the written TOEFL or 173 on the electronic version. The ACT or SAT I is required for Canadian high school students.

Computers: The mainframe is a DEC PDP 11/60. PCs are available in the computer learning center/office simulation center, with access to the Internet. All students may access the system from 8 A.M. to 10 P.M. There are no time limits. The fee is $36.

Graduates: From July 1, 2002 to June 30, 2003, 164 bachelor's degrees were awarded. The most popular majors were elementary education (36%), liberal arts and sciences (35%), and secondary education (28%). Of the 2002 graduating class, 94% were employed within 6 months of graduation.

Admissions Contact: Arlene Williams, Dean of Enrollment Management. E-mail: *admissions@umwestern.edu* Web: *www.umwestern.edu*

WESTERN MONTANA COLLEGE OF THE UNIVERSITY OF MONTANA
(See University of Montana--Western)

NEBRASKA

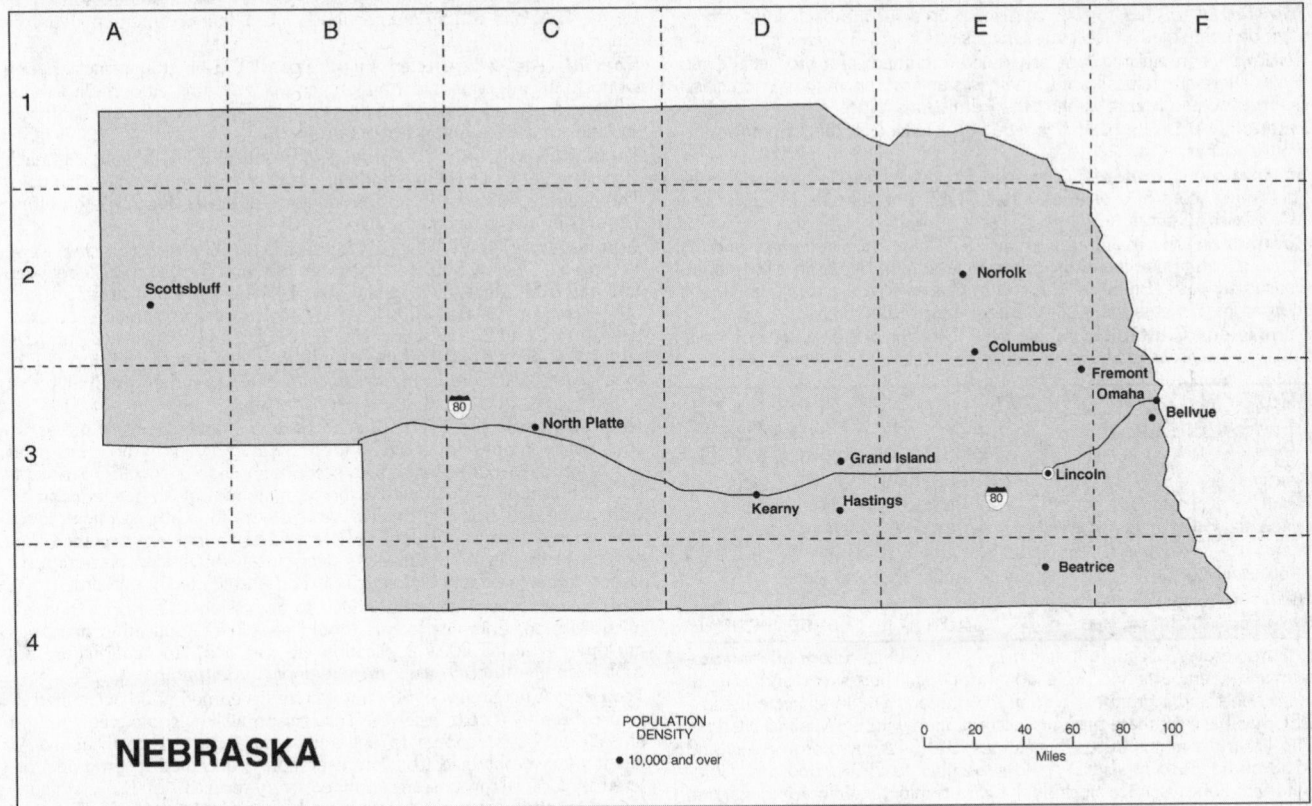

NEBRASKA

POPULATION DENSITY
● 10,000 and over

0 20 40 60 80 100
Miles

BELLEVUE UNIVERSITY
Bellevue, NE 68005

F-3

(402) 293-3702
(800) 756-7920; Fax: (402) 293-3730

Full-time: 1282 men, 1140 women	**Faculty:** 48; IIA, --$
Part-time: 590 men, 654 women	**Ph.D.s:** 56%
Graduate: 534 men, 643 women	**Student/Faculty:** 50 to 1
Year: semesters, summer session	**Tuition:** $4440
Application Deadline: open	**Room & Board:** n/app
Freshman Class: n/av	
SAT I: n/av	**ACT:** required

NONCOMPETITIVE

Bellevue University, established in 1966, is a private commuter institution offering undergraduate degrees in arts and sciences, professional studies, and business. Some information in this capsule and profile is approximate. There are 3 undergraduate schools and 1 graduate school. The library contains 122,000 volumes and 6700 microform items, and subscribes to 507 periodicals. Computerized library services include the card catalog, interlibrary loans, and database searching. Special learning facilities include a learning resource center and art gallery. The 19-acre campus is in a suburban area 5 miles south of Omaha. There are 6 buildings.

Student Life: 95% of undergraduates are from Nebraska. Students are from 66 foreign countries. 90% are from public schools. 86% are white. The average age of all undergraduates is 25. 12% do not continue beyond their first year; 40% remain to graduate.

Housing: There are no residence halls, but there are on-campus apartments. Most students commute. Alcohol is not permitted.

Activities: There are no fraternities or sororities. There are 3 groups on campus, including cheerleading, newspaper, and professional. Popular campus events include Halloween and Christmas parties, Black History Month, and Spring Bash.

Sports: There are 2 intercollegiate sports for men and 1 for women. Facilities include racquetball, basketball, and volleyball courts, and weightlifting equipment.

Disabled Students: All of the campus is accessible. Wheelchair ramps, special parking, specially equipped rest rooms, and lowered drinking fountains are available.

Services: Counseling and information services are available, as is tutoring in most subjects.

Campus Safety and Security: Measures include self-defense education, informal discussions, pamphlets/posters/films, and lighted pathways/sidewalks.

Programs of Study: Bellevue University confers B.A., B.S., and B.F.A. degrees. Master's degrees are also awarded. Bachelor's degrees are awarded in BUSINESS (accounting, business administration and management, and personnel management), COMMUNICATIONS AND THE ARTS (communications, English, fine arts, and photography), COMPUTER AND PHYSICAL SCIENCE (information sciences and systems), EDUCATION (physical), SOCIAL SCIENCE (criminal justice, geography, history, philosophy, political science/government, psychology, social science, sociology, and urban studies). Business administration is the strongest academically.

Required: To graduate, students must complete the core curriculum, with course work in communicative arts, a foreign language, art, English literature, foreign language literature, culture, civilization, music, philosophy, biology, chemistry, geology, math, geography, physics, psychology, sociology, economics, history, and political science. The required distribution of core credits varies by degree program from 63 to 66, and the total number of hours in the major varies by major. Students must earn 127 to 132 credits, depending on the degree. The minimum required GPA is 2.0 overall and 2.5 in the major.

Special: Bellevue University offers co-op programs with Buena Vista Colleges and Grace College of the Bible, internships, and work-study. Students may earn B.A.-B.S. degrees, and an accelerated degree program is possible in professional studies. The college permits dual majors, and composite, interdisciplinary majors are available in the social sciences and urban studies. Credit may be conferred for military experience. Nondegree study is possible. The Lockstep Degree Competition Program offers an alternative to the traditional academic structure. The School of Arts and Sciences operates on a 4-day academic week to provide flexibility. There is 1 national honor society.

Faculty/Classroom: 91% teach undergraduates. No introductory courses are taught by graduate students. The average class size in an introductory lecture is 35; in a laboratory, 25; and in a regular course, 25.

Requirements: The ACT, with a recommended minimum score of 19, or the SAT I is required for those entering college within 2 years after high school graduation; submission of ACT/SAT I scores is recommended for all others. Applicants must be graduates of an accredited secondary school or have a GED. Interviews are recommended. AP and CLEP credits are accepted.

Procedure: Freshmen are admitted to all sessions. Entrance exams should be taken in April. There are early decision and early admissions plans. Application deadlines are open. The fall 2003 application fee was $10. Notification is sent on a rolling basis.

Transfer: 30 of 127 to 132 credits required for the bachelor's degree must be completed at Bellevue University.

Visiting: There are regularly scheduled orientations for prospective students. There are guides for informal visits and visitors may sit in on classes. To schedule a visit, contact the Admissions Office.

Financial Aid: The FAFSA is required. Check with the school for current deadlines.

International Students: The school actively recruits these students. They must score 500 on the written TOEFL or take the MELAB. The ACT is also required.

Computers: The mainframe is an HP. There are 8 terminals and 25 PCs in the computer lab and computer classroom. Use is on a first-come, first-served basis. Students enrolled in classes where a computer fee is charged may access the system. There are no time limits.

Admissions Contact: Elizabeth Wall, Director of Admissions.
E-mail: *eaw@scholars.bellevue.edu* Web: *http://www.bellevue.edu*

CHADRON STATE COLLEGE
B-1
Chadron, NE 69337

(308) 432-6263
(800) CHADRON; Fax: (308) 432-6229

Full-time: 754 men, 1013 women	Faculty: 98; IIA, --$
Part-time: 170 men, 357 women	Ph.D.s: 74%
Graduate: 115 men, 302 women	Student/Faculty: 18 to 1
Year: semesters, summer session	Tuition: $2424 ($4512)
Application Deadline: open	Room & Board: $3862
Freshman Class: n/av	
SAT I Verbal/Math: 440/480	ACT: 21 NONCOMPETITIVE

Chadron State College, founded in 1911, is a public college offering programs in liberal arts and professional training. There are 2 undergraduate schools and 1 graduate school. In addition to regional accreditation, CSC has baccalaureate program accreditation with CSWE and NCATE. The library contains 205,398 volumes, 361,342 microform items, and 4160 audio/video tapes/CDs, and subscribes to 720 periodicals. Computerized library services include the card catalog, interlibrary loans, and database searching. Special learning facilities include a learning resource center, natural history museum, planetarium, and radio station. The 281-acre campus is in a small town 100 miles south of Rapid City, South Dakota. Including any residence halls, there are 27 buildings.

Student Life: 72% of undergraduates are from Nebraska. Students are from 6 foreign countries and Canada. 97% are from public schools. 90% are white. 45% are Protestant; 40% Catholic; 13% claim no religious affiliation. The average age of freshmen is 18; all undergraduates, 22. 35% do not continue beyond their first year; 33% remain to graduate.

Housing: 1200 students can be accommodated in college housing, which includes single-sex and coed dorms and married-student housing. In addition, there are honors houses. On-campus housing is guaranteed for all 4 years. 65% of students commute. Alcohol is not permitted. All students may keep cars.

Activities: There are no fraternities or sororities. There are 71 groups on campus, including art, band, cheerleading, choir, dance, ethnic, gay, honors, international, jazz band, musical theater, newspaper, orchestra, pep band, photography, political, radio and TV, science fiction, student government, symphony, and video. Popular campus events include Spring Daze.

Sports: There are 5 intercollegiate sports for men and 5 for women, and 46 intramural sports for men and 46 for women. Facilities include a 3000-seat stadium, a gym, a swimming pool, and an activity center.

Disabled Students: All of the campus is accessible. Wheelchair ramps, elevators, special parking, specially equipped rest rooms, special class scheduling, lowered drinking fountains, and special housing are available.

Services: Counseling and information services are available, as is tutoring in most subjects. There is a reader service for the blind, and remedial math, reading, and writing.

Campus Safety and Security: Measures include 24-hour foot and vehicle patrol, self-defense education, informal discussions, and pamphlets/posters/films. There are emergency telephones and lighted pathways/sidewalks.

Programs of Study: CSC confers B.A., B.S., and B.S.E. degrees. Master's degrees are also awarded. Bachelor's degrees are awarded in BIOLOGICAL SCIENCE (biology/biological science), BUSINESS (business administration and management), COMMUNICATIONS AND THE ARTS (art, dramatic arts, English, music, and speech/debate/rhetoric), COMPUTER AND PHYSICAL SCIENCE (chemistry, mathematics, and physics), EDUCATION (early childhood, elementary, health, science, and secondary), ENGINEERING AND ENVIRONMENTAL DESIGN (industrial engineering technology), HEALTH PROFESSIONS (predentistry and premedicine), SOCIAL SCIENCE (criminal justice, history, political science/government, prelaw, psychology, social science, social work, and

sociology). Education, business, and health professions are the strongest academically. Education, business, and justice studies are the largest.

Required: For graduation, students must complete 125 credit hours, including 47 hours of general education courses, and maintain a 2.0 GPA for the B.A. and a 2.5 GPA for the B.S.E. Other requirements vary by major.

Special: The college offers internships, a Washington semester, and work-study programs. Dual majors, co-op programs, and credit for life, military, and work experience are possible. There are 12 national honor societies and a freshman honors program.

Faculty/Classroom: 72% of faculty are male; 28%, female. All teach undergraduates. Graduate students teach 2% of introductory courses. The average class size in an introductory lecture is 36; in a laboratory, 19; and in a regular course, 25.

Admissions: The SAT I scores for the 2003-2004 freshman class were: Verbal--57% below 500, 14% between 500 and 599, and 29% between 600 and 700; Math--57% below 500, 14% between 500 and 599, and 29% between 600 and 700. The ACT scores were 46% below 21, 25% between 21 and 23, 17% between 24 and 26, 11% between 27 and 28, and 1% above 28. 20% of the current freshmen were in the top fifth of their class; 41% were in the top two fifths. 12 freshmen graduated first in their class.

Requirements: The SAT I or ACT is recommended, unless the applicant has been out of high school for more than 5 years. Applicants need not be graduates of an accredited secondary school. The GED is accepted. High school work should include a minimum of 15 academic units, with at least 3 units in English, and others in math, science, social studies, and foreign language. AP and CLEP credits are accepted. Important factors in the admissions decision are advanced placement or honor courses, evidence of special talent, and leadership record.

Procedure: Freshmen are admitted to all sessions. There is rolling admissions plan. Entrance exams should be taken. Application deadlines are open. The fall 2003 application fee was $15. Applications are accepted on-line through *www.csc.edu/apply/undergrad.htm.*

Transfer: A maximum of 66 semester credits earned at an accredited 2-year college may be transferred. The registrar will evaluate credit earned at a 3- or 4-year college to determine the student's classification. All passing credit obtained from an institution is accepted in programs offered by CSC. Transfers are admitted every term. 30 of 125 credits required for the bachelor's degree must be completed at CSC.

Visiting: There are regularly scheduled orientations for prospective students, including visits with faculty, tours of the campus, meetings with financial aid and housing advisers, and complimentary meals. There are guides for informal visits and visitors may sit in on classes and stay overnight. To schedule a visit, contact the Admissions Office at *inquire@csc.edu.*

Financial Aid: In a recent year, 78% of all full-time freshmen and 73% of continuing full-time students received some form of financial aid. 54% of full-time freshmen received need-based aid. The average freshman award was $2168. Average annual earnings from campus work are $1000. The FAFSA is required. The deadline for filing freshman financial aid applications for fall entry is June 1.

International Students: There were 17 international students enrolled in a recent year. They must score 550 on the written TOEFL and also take the SAT I or the ACT.

Computers: The mainframe is a DEC Alpha 3800. There are 3 networked labs with 12 PCs, 10 Macs, and 8 digital terminals. All students may access the system 7:30 A.M. to 10:30 P.M.

Graduates: From July 1, 2002 to June 30, 2003, 499 bachelor's degrees were awarded. The most popular majors were education (27%), business (25%), and justice studies (15%). In an average class, 1% graduate in 3 years or less, 12% graduate in 4 years or less, 30% graduate in 5 years or less, and 34% graduate in 6 years or less. 7 companies recruited on campus in 2002-2003.

Admissions Contact: Tena Cook Gould, Director of Admissions.
E-mail: *tgould@csc.edu* Web: *www.csc.edu*

CLARKSON COLLEGE
F-3
Omaha, NE 68131

(402) 552-3041
(800) 647-5500; Fax: (402) 552-6057

Full-time: 10 men, 190 women	Faculty: 43; IIB, --$
Part-time: 15 men, 140 women	Ph.D.s: 36%
Graduate: 5 men, 90 women	Student/Faculty: 4 to 1
Year: semesters, summer session	Tuition: $9400
Application Deadline: open	Room & Board: $3590
Freshman Class: n/av	
SAT I or ACT: required	COMPETITIVE

Clarkson College, established in 1888 and affiliated with the Episcopal Church, offers undergraduate and graduate degrees in the health care professions and business. There are 3 undergraduate and 2 graduate schools. Figures in the above capsule and in this profile are approximate. In addition to regional accreditation, Clarkson has baccalaureate program accreditation with NLN. The library contains 8097 volumes, 115 microform items, and 559 audio/video tapes/CDs, and subscribes to 299 periodicals. Computerized library services include the card catalog, interlibrary loans, and database searching. Special learning facilities include a learning resource center, art gallery, and regional medical center. The 29-acre campus is in an urban area in Omaha. Including any residence halls, there are 13 buildings.

Student Life: 61% of undergraduates are from Nebraska. Students are from 13 states and 1 foreign country. 90% are from public schools. 90% are white. 50% are Catholic; 45% Protestant. The average age of freshmen is 23; all undergraduates, 27. 10% do not continue beyond their first year; 87% remain to graduate.

Housing: 54 students can be accommodated in college housing, which includes coed on-campus apartments. On-campus housing is available on a first-come, first-served basis. Priority is given to out-of-town students. 90% of students commute. Alcohol is not permitted. All students may keep cars.

Activities: There are no fraternities or sororities. There are 12 groups on campus, including chorus, newspaper, professional, social, social service, and student government. Popular campus events include holiday dances and parties.

Sports: There is no sports program at Clarkson. Facilities are available at the adjacent University of Nebraska Medical Center and include basketball and volleyball courts, exercise equipment, and a weight room.

Disabled Students: 95% of the campus is accessible. Wheelchair ramps, elevators, special parking, specially equipped rest rooms, special class scheduling, lowered drinking fountains, and lowered telephones are available.

Services: Counseling and information services are available, as is tutoring in every subject.

Campus Safety and Security: Measures include 24-hour foot and vehicle patrol, self-defense education, security escort services, and informal discussions. There are pamphlets/posters/films, emergency telephones, and lighted pathways/sidewalks.

Programs of Study: Clarkson confers B.S. and B.S.N. degrees. Associate and master's degrees are also awarded. Bachelor's degrees are awarded in BUSINESS (business administration and management), COMPUTER AND PHYSICAL SCIENCE (radiological technology), HEALTH PROFESSIONS (nursing and radiograph medical technology). Radiological technology and nursing are the strongest academically. Nursing is the largest.

Required: To graduate, students must complete 128 credit hours, including 68 in the major, and maintain a minimum GPA of 2.0. General education requirements include courses in the humanities, English, behavioral and social sciences, science and math, and phys ed. A 9-hour core curriculum is also required.

Special: A co-op program in nursing, study abroad in England, work-study programs, and dual majors are available. Credit is given for military experience, and nondegree study is possible. The distance education option allows advanced placement students living a distance from the campus to complete their studies at home. There is 1 national honor society.

Faculty/Classroom: 21% of faculty are male; 79%, female. All teach undergraduates. No introductory courses are taught by graduate students. The average class size in an introductory lecture is 45; in a laboratory, 10; and in a regular course, 35.

Requirements: The SAT I or ACT is required, with a minimum composite score of 20 on the ACT or 850 on the SAT I. The ACT is preferred. Tests are not required for applicants more than 2 years out of high school. Applicants must be graduates of an accredited secondary school, with 3 years of English and 2 each of social science, algebra, and science (including lab science). The GED is accepted. Clarkson requires applicants to be in the upper 50% of their class. A GPA of 2.0 is required. AP and CLEP credits are accepted. Important factors in the admissions decision are advanced placement or honor courses, extracurricular activities record, and evidence of special talent.

Procedure: Freshmen are admitted to all sessions. Entrance exams should be taken during the junior year or first semester of the senior year. There is a deferred admissions plan. Application deadlines are open. The application fee is $15. A waiting list is an active part of the admissions procedure.

Transfer: Transfer students must have a minimum GPA of 2.5. Grades of C or better transfer for credit. Transfers are admitted for fall and spring. An interview is sometimes required. 64 of 128 credits required for the bachelor's degree must be completed at Clarkson.

Visiting: There are regularly scheduled orientations for prospective students. There are guides for informal visits and visitors may sit in on classes. To schedule a visit, contact the Admissions Office.

Financial Aid: Clarkson is a member of CSS. The FAFSA and the college's own financial statement are required. Check with the school for current application deadlines.

International Students: International students must score 600 on the written TOEFL or 85 on the MELAB and 5 on the TWE, and also take the SAT I or the ACT.

Computers: The mainframe is a DEC VAX 4400. There are IBM and Mac systems available for student use. 20 IBM and Mac PCs, with 10 mainframe terminals, are housed in special labs for their instruction and use. In addition, there are 10 terminals in the residence hall computer lab. All students may access the system 7 A.M. to 8:30 P.M. There are no time limits and no fees.

Admissions Contact: Tami Bartunek, Director of Admissions.
E-mail: *bartunek@clarksoncollege.edu* Web: *www.clarksoncollege.edu*

COLLEGE OF SAINT MARY
F-2
Omaha, NE 68124
(402) 399-2425
(800) 926-5534; Fax: (402) 399-2412

Full-time: 595 women	**Faculty:** 43
Part-time: 1 man, 296 women	**Ph.D.s:** 44%
Graduate: none	**Student/Faculty:** 14 to 1
Year: semesters, summer session	**Tuition:** $16,010
Application Deadline: open	**Room & Board:** $5500
Freshman Class: 218 applied, 153 accepted, 58 enrolled	
ACT: 22	**COMPETITIVE**

College of Saint Mary, founded in 1923, is a private Roman Catholic women's college offering a program that combines training for professional careers with a liberal arts component. In addition to regional accreditation, CSM has baccalaureate program accreditation with ACOTE, AHIMA, CAHEA, and NLN. The library contains 94,000 volumes and 1360 audio/video tapes/CDs, and subscribes to 375 periodicals. Computerized library services include the card catalog, interlibrary loans, database searching, and Internet access. Special learning facilities include a learning resource center and art gallery. The 25-acre campus is in a suburban area 5 miles west of downtown Omaha. Including any residence halls, there are 8 buildings.

Student Life: 87% of undergraduates are from Nebraska. Students are from 14 states and 8 foreign countries. 82% are from public schools. 89% are white. Most are Catholic. The average age of freshmen is 20; all undergraduates, 29. 33% do not continue beyond their first year; 49% remain to graduate.

Housing: 257 students can be accommodated in college housing, which includes single-sex dorms. On-campus housing is available on a first-come, first-served basis. 82% of students commute. All students may keep cars.

Activities: There are no sororities. There are 18 groups on campus, including ethnic, honors, international, professional, religious, social, social service, and student government. Popular campus events include Fine Arts Festival, the Queen of Hearts Dance, and Casino Nite.

Sports: There are 6 intercollegiate sports for women. Facilities include a gym, a 6-lane swimming pool, a weight room, an elevated running track, 2 racquetball courts, an exercise room, a training room, 4 outdoor tennis courts, 2 soccer fields, and 2 softball fields.

Disabled Students: 85% of the campus is accessible. Wheelchair ramps, elevators, special parking, specially equipped rest rooms, special class scheduling, lowered drinking fountains, and electric door openers are available.

Services: Counseling and information services are available, as is tutoring in most subjects. There is a reader service for the blind, and remedial math, reading, and writing. There are also study groups.

Campus Safety and Security: Measures include 24-hour foot and vehicle patrol, self-defense education, security escort services, and informal discussions. There are pamphlets/posters/films, lighted pathways/sidewalks, and camera-monitored and coded entrances to residence halls.

Programs of Study: CSM confers B.A., B.S., B.B.L., and B.G.S. degrees. Associate degrees are also awarded. Bachelor's degrees are awarded in BIOLOGICAL SCIENCE (biology/biological science), BUSINESS (business administration and management), COMMUNICATIONS AND THE ARTS (art and English), COMPUTER AND PHYSICAL SCIENCE (chemistry, computer management, mathematics, and natural sciences), EDUCATION (early childhood, education, elementary, and special), HEALTH PROFESSIONS (medical laboratory technology, nursing, and occupational therapy), SOCIAL SCIENCE (human services, humanities, liberal arts/general studies, paralegal studies, and psychology). Pre-professional studies and occupational therapy are the strongest academically. Nursing, business, and education are the largest.

Required: To graduate, students must complete 128 semester hours, with a minimum of 30 hours in the major and a 2.0 GPA in the major and overall. Required core education courses total 47 hours, with 9 in math and science, 6 in English, 3 each in communications, computer, ethics, fine arts, liberal arts, history, philosophy, social science, and theology, and 1 each in phys ed and a core seminar. Students must demonstrate competency in math and English.

Special: Students may pursue internships in any major, including research courses in the sciences. CSM also offers dual majors, study abroad in 11 countries, nondegree study, pass/fail options, an accelerated degree program in business leadership, and credit for life, military, and work experience. There are 2 national honor societies.

Faculty/Classroom: 25% of faculty are male; 75%, female. All teach undergraduates. The average class size in an introductory lecture is 19; in a laboratory, 20; and in a regular course, 11.

Admissions: 70% of the 2003-2004 applicants were accepted. 2 freshmen graduated first in their class.

Requirements: The SAT I or ACT is required. In addition, students must meet 2 out of 3 criteria: a minimum composite score of 19 on the ACT, a GPA of at least 2.0, and rank in the upper 50% of their class. Applicants must be graduates of an accredited secondary school. The GED is accepted. Students should have completed 16 academic units, including 4 years of English and 2 each of math, social studies and science, with biology and chemistry required for the various health profession majors. An interview is recommended. CSM requires applicants to be in the upper 50% of their class. A GPA of 2.0 is required. AP and CLEP credits are accepted.

Procedure: Freshmen are admitted to all sessions. Entrance exams should be taken in the junior or senior year. There is a deferred admissions plan and a rolling admissions plan. Application deadlines are open. Application fee is $30. Regular decision notification is sent within 2 weeks of receipt of application. Applications are accepted on-line through the school's web site.

Transfer: 192 transfer students enrolled in 2002-2003. Applicants should have a minimum GPA of 2.0 and submit official transcripts from previous colleges attended. Students with fewer than 12 credit hours must also submit ACT or SAT I scores. Grades of C or better transfer for credit. Students are admitted every term. 30 of 128 credits required for the bachelor's degree must be completed at CSM.

Visiting: There are regularly scheduled orientations for prospective students, consisting of touring the campus, attending financial aid and student-life presentations, and sitting in on classes of a student's choice. Visitors are CSM's guests for lunch or overnight. There are guides for informal visits and visitors may sit in on classes and stay overnight. To schedule a visit, contact the Office of Enrollment Services at (402) 399-2405 or enroll@csm.edu.

Financial Aid: In 2003-2004, 98% of all full-time freshmen and 65% of continuing full-time students received some form of financial aid. 59% of full-time freshmen and 74% of continuing full-time students received need-based aid. The average freshman award was $13,037. Need-based scholarships or need-based grants averaged $8974; need-based self-help aid (loans and jobs) averaged $4903; non-need-based athletic scholarships averaged $4701; and other non-need-based awards and non-need-based scholarships averaged $6999. 12% of undergraduates work part time. Average annual earnings from campus work are $1250. The average financial indebtedness of the 2003 graduate was $16,000. The FAFSA is required. The priority date for freshman financial aid applications for fall entry is March 1. The deadline for filing freshman financial aid applications for fall entry is April 1.

International Students: There are 9 international students enrolled. The school actively recruits these students. They must score 550 on the written TOEFL.

Computers: The mainframes are a Compaq client/server network and a Dell computer. Students may access the campus network and the Internet via 154 PCs in various locations. All students may access the system 8 A.M. to midnight Monday through Thursday, 8 A.M. to 5 P.M. Friday, 10 A.M. to 5 P.M. Saturday, and 1 P.M. to midnight Sunday. There are no time limits and no fees.

Graduates: From July 1, 2002 to June 30, 2003, 177 bachelor's degrees were awarded. The most popular majors were nursing (32%), business (20%), and health information management (10%). In an average class, 39% graduate in 4 years or less, 46% graduate in 5 years or less, and 49% graduate in 6 years or less. 86 companies recruited on campus in 2002-2003. Of the 2002 graduating class, 3% were enrolled in graduate school within 6 months of graduation and 98% were employed.

Admissions Contact: Sue Kropf, Enrollment Director.
E-mail: enroll@csm.edu Web: www.csm.edu

CONCORDIA UNIVERSITY NEBRASKA
Seward, NE 68434

E-3

(402) 643-7233
(800) 535-5494; Fax: (402) 643-4073

Full-time: 493 men, 629 women	**Faculty:** 66; IIB, --$
Part-time: 29 men, 51 women	**Ph.D.s:** 85%
Graduate: 39 men, 76 women	**Student/Faculty:** 17 to 1
Year: semesters, summer session	**Tuition:** $16,000
Application Deadline: August 1	**Room & Board:** $4302
Freshman Class: 728 applied, 646 accepted, 221 enrolled	
SAT I Verbal/Math: 543/541	**ACT:** 24 COMPETITIVE+

Concordia University Nebraska, founded in 1894, is a private university owned and operated by the Lutheran Church-Missouri Synod, with degree programs in professional education and liberal arts. Among Concordia's major programs are those for professional work in the Lutheran Church: teacher education, director of Christian education, preseminary pastoral training, and church music. In addition to regional accreditation, Concordia has baccalaureate program accreditation with NCATE. The 3

libraries contain 177,683 volumes, 10,719 microform items, and 13,214 audio/video tapes/CDs, and subscribe to 545 periodicals. Computerized library services include the card catalog and database searching. Special learning facilities include a learning resource center, art gallery, natural history museum, and observatory. The 120-acre campus is in a small town 25 miles west of Lincoln. Including any residence halls, there are 25 buildings.

Student Life: 59% of undergraduates are from out of state, mostly the Midwest. Students are from 37 states and 9 foreign countries. 95% are white. Most are Protestant. The average age of freshmen is 18; all undergraduates, 21. 48% of freshmen remain to graduate.

Housing: 815 students can be accommodated in college housing, which includes single-sex dorms, off-campus apartments, and married-student housing. On-campus housing is guaranteed for all 4 years. 90% of students live on campus; of those, 90% remain on campus on weekends. Alcohol is not permitted. All students may keep cars.

Activities: There are no fraternities or sororities. There are 35 groups on campus, including band, cheerleading, choir, chorale, chorus, computers, dance, debate, drama, drill team, ethnic, forensics, honors, international, jazz band, literary magazine, musical theater, newspaper, orchestra, pep band, photography, professional, religious, social, social service, student government, and yearbook. Popular campus events include Spring Weekend and Multicultural Awareness Week.

Sports: There are 8 intercollegiate sports for men and 8 for women, and 7 intramural sports for men and 7 for women. Facilities include a gym, a weight-training room, an indoor pool, football, baseball, and soccer fields, and a track-and-field stadium.

Disabled Students: 35% of the campus is accessible. Wheelchair ramps, elevators, special parking, specially equipped rest rooms, lowered drinking fountains, and lowered telephones are available.

Services: Counseling and information services are available, as is tutoring in every subject. There is a reader service for the blind, talking books, and tape recorders.

Campus Safety and Security: Measures include 24-hour foot and vehicle patrol, self-defense education, security escort services, and informal discussions. There are pamphlets/posters/films, emergency telephones, lighted pathways/sidewalks, vehicle and bicycle registration, and a possession ID engraving program.

Programs of Study: Concordia confers B.A., B.S., B.F.A., B.S.Med.Tech., B.Mus., and B.Sacred Music degrees. Master's degrees are also awarded. Bachelor's degrees are awarded in BIOLOGICAL SCIENCE (biology/biological science), BUSINESS (accounting, business administration and management, and sports management), COMMUNICATIONS AND THE ARTS (communications, dramatic arts, English, fine arts, music, speech/debate/rhetoric, and studio art), COMPUTER AND PHYSICAL SCIENCE (chemistry, computer science, mathematics, natural sciences, and physical sciences), EDUCATION (business, Christian, early childhood, elementary, home economics, industrial arts, middle school, music, physical, science, secondary, and special), HEALTH PROFESSIONS (exercise science, health, medical laboratory technology, predentistry, and premedicine), SOCIAL SCIENCE (behavioral science, geography, history, physical fitness/movement, prelaw, psychology, and theological studies). Education, business, and art are the strongest academically. Education is the largest.

Required: To graduate, students must complete a minimum of 128 credits with a GPA of at least 2.0. Required general education courses include 12 hours of theology, 9 hours each of English/speech, social science, and science, 6 of fine arts, 3 each of math and health and phys ed, 2 to 3 of electives, and 1 hour minimum of computer literacy.

Special: Concordia offers cross-registration with the University of Nebraska in Lincoln. Internships are available in education, business, and Christian education. B.A.-B.S. degrees, student-designed majors, dual majors, study abroad in England and China, nondegree studies, and pass/fail options are available. There is an accelerated degree program in organizational management. There is a freshman honors program and 3 departmental honors programs.

Faculty/Classroom: 71% of faculty are male; 29%, female. All teach undergraduates. Graduate students teach 1% of introductory courses. The average class size in an introductory lecture is 20; in a laboratory, 15; and in a regular course, 15.

Admissions: 89% of the 2003-2004 applicants were accepted. The SAT I scores for the 2003-2004 freshman class were: Verbal--29% below 500, 48% between 500 and 599, 14% between 600 and 700, and 10% above 700; Math--36% below 500, 33% between 500 and 599, 21% between 600 and 700, and 10% above 700. 43% of the current freshmen were in the top fifth of their class.

Requirements: The SAT I or ACT is required, with a minimum composite score of 18 recommended for the ACT. Applicants need not be graduates of an accredited secondary school. The GED is accepted. The school strongly encourages high school courses in art, English, foreign language, history, math, music, phys ed, science, and social studies. An interview is recommended. Concordia requires applicants to be in the upper 50% of their class. A GPA of 2.0 is required. AP and CLEP credits are accepted. Important factors in the admissions decision are ability to finance college education, leadership record, and recommendations by alumni.

Procedure: Freshmen are admitted to all sessions. Entrance exams should be taken in the junior or senior year. There is a rolling admissions plan. Applications should be filed by August 1 for fall entry and January 1 for spring entry. The fall 2003 application fee was $15. Notification is sent on a rolling basis. Applications are accepted on-line through *www.applyweb.com.*

Transfer: 74 transfer students enrolled in a recent year. Applicants should have a minimum GPA of 2.0 and a minimum ACT score of 18. An interview is recommended. Passing grades transfer for credit. Transfers are admitted every term. 30 credits of 128 required for the bachelor's degree must be completed at Concordia.

Visiting: There are regularly scheduled orientations for prospective students, including a campus tour, sitting in on classes, visits with professors/coaches, and an admission interview. There are guides for informal visits and visitors may stay overnight. To schedule a visit, contact the Office of Admission.

Financial Aid: The FAFSA and the college's own financial statement are required. The deadline for filing freshman financial aid applications for fall entry is August 15.

International Students: There were 15 international students enrolled in a recent year. The school actively recruits these students. They must score 500 on the written TOEFL and also take the SAT I or the ACT.

Computers: The mainframe is a DEC VAX 4105A. More than 150 PCs are available across campus, with Internet and web access on all. All students may access the system. There are no time limits and no fees.

Graduates: The most popular majors in a recent year were teacher education (75%), business/marketing (10%), and social science/history (4%). In an average class, 57% graduate in 6 years or less.

Admissions Contact: Office of Admission. A video is available. E-mail: *admiss@seward.cune.edu* Web: *www.cune.edu/*

CREIGHTON UNIVERSITY
Omaha, NE 68178-0001

F-3
(402) 280-2703
(800) 282-5835; Fax: (402) 280-2685

Full-time: 1373 men, 2071 women	**Faculty:** 252; IIA, av$
Part-time: 91 men, 201 women	**Ph.D.s:** 92%
Graduate: 1350 men, 1451 women	**Student/Faculty:** 14 to 1
Year: semesters, summer session	**Tuition:** $19,922
Application Deadline: August 1	**Room & Board:** $6826
Freshman Class: 3200 applied, 2814 accepted, 936 enrolled	
SAT I Verbal/Math: 590/600	**ACT:** 26 VERY COMPETITIVE+

Creighton University, founded in 1878, is a private Jesuit Catholic institution offering undergraduate programs in arts and sciences, business administration, dentistry, medicine, law, nursing, pharmacy, and health professions. It also offers graduate, continuing education, and noncredit programs. There are 4 undergraduate and 5 graduate schools. In addition to regional accreditation, Creighton has baccalaureate program accreditation with AACSB, ACPE, NCATE, and NLN. The 3 libraries contain 945,525 volumes, 1,743,254 microform items, and 64,878 audio/video tapes/CDs, and subscribe to 24,379 periodicals. Computerized library services include the card catalog, interlibrary loans, and database searching. Special learning facilities include a learning resource center and art gallery. The 110-acre campus is in an urban area near downtown Omaha. Including any residence halls, there are 46 buildings.

Student Life: 50% of undergraduates are from out of state, mostly the Midwest. Students are from 43 states, 52 foreign countries, and Canada. 60% are from public schools. 82% are white. 61% are Catholic; 20% Protestant; 16% claim no religious affiliation. The average age of freshmen is 18; all undergraduates, 20. 15% do not continue beyond their first year; 71% remain to graduate.

Housing: 1727 students can be accommodated in college housing, which includes single-sex and coed dorms, on-campus apartments, and married-student housing. In addition, there are special-interest houses, Cortina Community, Freshman Leadership, Links Program, and Loyola House. On-campus housing is guaranteed for all 4 years. 51% of students live on campus; of those, 95% remain on campus on weekends. All students may keep cars.

Activities: 21% of men belong to 5 national fraternities; 28% of women belong to 5 national sororities. There are 171 groups on campus, including art, band, cheerleading, chess, choir, chorale, chorus, computers, dance, debate, drama, drill team, ethnic, film, forensics, honors, international, jazz band, literary magazine, musical theater, newspaper, orchestra, pep band, photography, political, professional, radio and TV, religious, social, social service, student government, and yearbook. Popular campus events include Diversity Week, JayJam and Carnival, and Spring Fling Week.

Sports: There are 6 intercollegiate sports for men and 8 for women, and 24 intramural sports for men and 24 for women. Facilities include a sports complex, an outdoor artificial turf area with baseball, softball, and soccer fields, a natural grass intercollegiate soccer facility, and a physical fitness center with courts for basketball, volleyball, badminton,

or gymnastics, a pool, a weight room, and a jogging track; another center offers practice courts and training rooms for all intercollegiate sports.

Disabled Students: 80% of the campus is accessible. Wheelchair ramps, elevators, special parking, specially equipped rest rooms, special class scheduling, lowered drinking fountains, lowered telephones, and special housing are available.

Services: Counseling and information services are available, as is tutoring in most subjects. There is a reader service for the blind, and remedial math, reading, and writing.

Campus Safety and Security: Measures include 24-hour foot and vehicle patrol, self-defense education, security escort services, and shuttle buses. There are informal discussions, pamphlets/posters/films, emergency telephones, and lighted pathways/sidewalks.

Programs of Study: Creighton confers B.A., B.S., B.F.A., B.S. Atmospheric Science, B.S.B.A., B.S.Chem., B.S. Computer Science, B.S. Environmental Science, B.S. Mathematics, B.S.N., B.S. Physics, B.S.Soc., and B.S.W. degrees. Associate, master's, and doctoral degrees are also awarded. Bachelor's degrees are awarded in BIOLOGICAL SCIENCE (biology/biological science), BUSINESS (accounting, banking and finance, business administration and management, international business management, management information systems, and marketing/retailing/merchandising), COMMUNICATIONS AND THE ARTS (art, communications, dramatic arts, English, fine arts, French, German, Greek, journalism, Latin, music, Spanish, and speech/debate/rhetoric), COMPUTER AND PHYSICAL SCIENCE (atmospheric sciences and meteorology, chemistry, computer science, mathematics, and physics), EDUCATION (elementary, secondary, and special), ENGINEERING AND ENVIRONMENTAL DESIGN (environmental science), HEALTH PROFESSIONS (emergency medical technologies and nursing), SOCIAL SCIENCE (American studies, classical/ancient civilization, economics, history, ministries, philosophy, political science/government, prelaw, psychology, social work, sociology, and theological studies). Nursing, biology, and psychology are the largest.

Required: For graduation, students must complete a minimum of 128 credit hours and maintain a GPA of 2.0. Each school has general education requirements. Total number of hours required in major varies by major.

Special: The university offers study abroad at more than 110 partner institutions in 40 countries, a Washington semester, internships, and work-study programs. Nursing students may take an accelerated degree program, and B.A.-B.S. degrees are possible. Dual majors, nondegree study, pass/fail options, and credit for life, military, and work experience are available. There are 13 national honor societies, a freshman honors program, and 1 departmental honors program.

Faculty/Classroom: 68% of faculty are male; 32%, female. No introductory courses are taught by graduate students. The average class size in an introductory lecture is 29; in a laboratory, 22; and in a regular course, 25.

Admissions: 88% of the 2003-2004 applicants were accepted. The SAT I scores for the 2003-2004 freshman class were: Verbal--15% below 500, 38% between 500 and 599, 37% between 600 and 700, and 10% above 700; Math--11% below 500, 37% between 500 and 599, 42% between 600 and 700, and 10% above 700. The ACT scores were 8% below 21, 22% between 21 and 23, 26% between 24 and 26, 20% between 27 and 28, and 24% above 28. 62% of the current freshmen were in the top fifth of their class; 82% were in the top two fifths. 80 freshmen graduated first in their class.

Requirements: The SAT I or ACT is required. In addition, applicants must be graduates of an accredited secondary school. The GED is accepted. Students should have completed 16 credits, including 4 credits in English, 3 each in math and electives, and 2 each in foreign language, science, and social studies. Home-schooled students are welcome. Creighton requires applicants to be in the upper 50% of their class. A GPA of 2.5 is required. AP and CLEP credits are accepted. Important factors in the admissions decision are recommendations by school officials, advanced placement or honor courses, and leadership record.

Procedure: Freshmen are admitted to all sessions. Entrance exams should be taken prior to May 1 of the senior year. There is a rolling admissions plan. Applications should be filed by August 1 for fall entry and January 1 for spring entry, along with a $40 fee. Notification is sent on a rolling basis. Applications are accepted on-line through the school's web site.

Transfer: 98 transfer students enrolled in 2002-2003. Applicants must have a 2.0 minimum GPA in a regionally accredited school. A minimum score of 21 on the ACT or 990 on the SAT I is recommended. Grades of C or better transfer for credit. Transfers are admitted every semester. 48 of 128 credits required for the bachelor's degree must be completed at Creighton.

Visiting: There are regularly scheduled orientations for prospective students, consisting of an open house program with various presentations and campus tours. There are guides for informal visits and visitors may sit in on classes and stay overnight. To schedule a visit, contact the Admissions Office at *admission@creighton.edu.*

Financial Aid: In 2003-2004, 93% of all full-time freshmen and 88% of continuing full-time students received some form of financial aid. 59%

of full-time freshmen and 58% of continuing full-time students received need-based aid. The average freshman award was $15,699. Need-based scholarships or need-based grants averaged $4700; need-based self-help aid (loans and jobs) averaged $5760; non-need-based athletic scholarships averaged $11,750; and other non-need-based awards and non-need-based scholarships averaged $6200. 42% of undergraduates work part time. Average annual earnings from campus work are $1357. The average financial indebtedness of the 2003 graduate was $20,517. The FAFSA and the college's own financial statement are required. The deadline for filing freshman financial aid applications for fall entry is April 1.

International Students: There are 48 international students enrolled. The school actively recruits these students. They must score 550 on the written TOEFL or 213 on the electronic version.

Computers: The mainframes are HP 9000s and numerous network servers. There are more than 500 PCs available throughout the campus and in computer labs. Students have access to e-mail and personal web pages. All students may access the system any time. There are no time limits and no fees. It is strongly recommended that all students have a personal computer.

Graduates: From July 1, 2002 to June 30, 2003, 776 bachelor's degrees were awarded. The most popular majors were nursing (18%), biology (9%), and psychology (8%). In an average class, 1% graduate in 3 years or less, 57% graduate in 4 years or less, 69% graduate in 5 years or less, and 71% graduate in 6 years or less. 102 companies recruited on campus in 2002-2003.

Admissions Contact: Mary Chase, Director of Admissions. A video is available. E-mail: *admissions@creighton.edu* Web: *admission@creighton.edu*

DANA COLLEGE
Blair, NE 68008-1099

F-2

(402) 426-7222
(800) 444-3262; Fax: (402) 426-7386

Full-time: 333 men, 230 women	**Faculty:** 44
Part-time: 8 men, 10 women	**Ph.D's:** 59%
Graduate: none	**Student/Faculty:** 13 to 1
Year: 4-1-4, summer session	**Tuition:** $15,750
Application Deadline: August 1	**Room & Board:** $4530
Freshman Class: 760 applied, 562 accepted, 164 enrolled	
SAT I Verbal/Math: 490/505	**ACT:** 22 COMPETITIVE

Dana College, established in 1884, is a private liberal arts institution affiliated with the Evangelical Lutheran Church in America. In addition to regional accreditation, Dana has baccalaureate program accreditation with ACBSP, CSWE, and NCATE. The library contains 198,863 volumes, 15,627 microform items, and 4451 audio/video tapes/CDs, and subscribes to 537 periodicals. Computerized library services include the card catalog, interlibrary loans, database searching, and Internet access. Special learning facilities include a learning resource center, art gallery, radio station, TV station, a theater, and Danish immigrant archives. The 150-acre campus is in a small town 20 miles north of Omaha. Including any residence halls, there are 17 buildings.

Student Life: 51% of undergraduates are from Nebraska. Students are from 32 states and 2 foreign countries. 87% are white. 25% are Protestant; 24% claim no religious affiliation; 20% Catholic. The average age of freshmen is 19; all undergraduates, 21. 39% do not continue beyond their first year; 53% remain to graduate.

Housing: 617 students can be accommodated in college housing, which includes single-sex and coed dorms, on-campus apartments, married-student housing, and a residence hall for upperclassmen. On-campus housing is guaranteed for all 4 years. 63% of students live on campus; of those, 50% remain on campus on weekends. Alcohol is not permitted. All students may keep cars.

Activities: There are no fraternities or sororities. There are 35 groups on campus, including art, band, cheerleading, choir, chorale, chorus, computers, dance, drama, drill team, environmental, ethnic, honors, international, jazz band, literary magazine, musical theater, newspaper, orchestra, pep band, photography, political, professional, radio and TV, religious, social, social service, student government, and yearbook. Popular campus events include Sights and Sounds of Christmas, Spring Fling, and Winterfest.

Sports: There are 8 intercollegiate sports for men and 7 for women, and 14 intramural sports for men and 14 for women. Facilities include fields for soccer, cross-country, football/track, softball, and baseball, and a coliseum for basketball, swimming, tennis, racquetball, volleyball, wrestling, and weight training.

Disabled Students: 70% of the campus is accessible. Wheelchair ramps, elevators, special parking, specially equipped rest rooms, special class scheduling, and lowered drinking fountains are available.

Services: Counseling and information services are available, as is tutoring in some subjects, including most 100- and 200-level general education courses. There is a reader service for the blind and remedial math and writing. A study skills course and study sessions for individual courses are available.

Campus Safety and Security: Measures include 24-hour foot and vehicle patrol, self-defense education, security escort services, and informal discussions. There are pamphlets/posters/films, emergency telephones, and lighted pathways/sidewalks.

Programs of Study: Dana confers the B.A. degree. Bachelor's degrees are awarded in BIOLOGICAL SCIENCE (biology/biological science), BUSINESS (accounting, and business administration and management), COMMUNICATIONS AND THE ARTS (art, communications, English, German, music, and Spanish), COMPUTER AND PHYSICAL SCIENCE (chemistry, computer science, and mathematics), EDUCATION (art, business, drama, elementary, English, foreign languages, mathematics, music, physical, science, secondary, social science, social studies, and special), ENGINEERING AND ENVIRONMENTAL DESIGN (environmental science), SOCIAL SCIENCE (history, interdisciplinary studies, international relations, liberal arts/general studies, psychology, religion, social science, social work, and sociology). Social work, education, and business are the strongest academically. Elementary education, biology, and business administration are the largest.

Required: To graduate, students must complete 128 credit hours, including at least 30 in the major and 40 at the 300 or 400 level, with a minimum GPA of 2.0. Other requirements include demonstrated competency in verbal and written communication skills, 15 core hours in liberal arts, 2 credits in wellness, and 1 religion course. Also required are 18 distributive hours in 3 of 4 areas of study: human culture, human scientific inquiry, human development and organizations, and human aesthetic expression.

Special: Dana offers cross-registration with Midland Lutheran College, internships in most majors, study abroad, and work-study programs. Integrated studies, credit for life, military, and work experience, nondegree study, and pass/fail options are available. There are preprofessional programs in prechiropractic, preoccupational therapy, prephysician's assistant, preseminary, and prelaw. Students in the medical arts major, leading to a degree or certification in a medical technology field, spend the senior year in a hospital-based program. There are 3 national honor societies, a freshman honors program, and 1 departmental honors program.

Faculty/Classroom: 53% of faculty are male; 46%, female. All teach undergraduates and 60% do research. The average class size in an introductory lecture is 35; in a laboratory, 10; and in a regular course, 24.

Admissions: 74% of the 2003-2004 applicants were accepted. The SAT I scores for the 2003-2004 freshman class were: Verbal--28% below 500, 41% between 500 and 599, 18% between 600 and 700, and 12% above 700; Math--40% below 500, 41% between 500 and 599, and 18% between 600 and 700. The ACT scores were 51% below 21, 25% between 21 and 23, 21% between 24 and 26, 3% between 27 and 28, and 2% above 28. 33% of the current freshmen were in the top fifth of their class; 64% were in the top two fifths. 9 freshmen graduated first in their class.

Requirements: The SAT I or ACT is required, with a recommended minimum composite score of 19 on the ACT or 890 on the SAT I. Applicants must be graduates of an accredited secondary school. The GED is accepted. Prospective students are encouraged to take college-preparatory courses, including 4 years each of English and social science, 3 each of science and math, and 2 of a foreign language. An interview is recommended. A GPA of 2.0 is required. AP and CLEP credits are accepted. Important factors in the admissions decision are advanced placement or honor courses, recommendations by school officials, and leadership record.

Procedure: Freshmen are admitted to all sessions. Entrance exams should be taken in the spring of the junior year or fall of the senior year. There are early admissions, deferred admissions and rolling admissions plans. Applications should be filed by August 1 for fall entry and January 10 for spring entry. Notification is sent on a rolling basis. Applications are accepted on computer disk and on-line through the school's web site.

Transfer: 30 transfer students enrolled in 2002-2003. Applicants with an associate degree and a minimum college GPA of 2.0 will be considered, those with less than a 2.0 GPA will be evaluated on the basis of high school performance and an interview with the admissions committee. Grades of C or better transfer for credit. Students are admitted every term. 32 of 128 credits required for the bachelor's degree must be completed at Dana.

Visiting: There are regularly scheduled orientations for prospective students, including appointments with faculty, coaches, and activity directors, a campus tour, a financial-aid session, an admissions session, and lunch. Overnight lodging is available at no charge. There are guides for informal visits and visitors may sit in on classes and stay overnight. To schedule a visit, contact the Admissions Office at *bsprau@fs1.dana.edu*.

Financial Aid: The average freshman award was $15,100. Need-based scholarships or need-based grants averaged $4141; need-based self-help aid (loans and jobs) averaged $4862; and non-need-based athletic scholarships averaged $7000. 53% of undergraduates work part time. Average annual earnings from campus work are $760. The average financial indebtedness of the 2003 graduate was $16,182. The FAFSA and the college's own financial statement are required. The priority date for freshman financial aid applications for fall entry is March 15. The deadline for filing freshman financial aid applications for fall entry is April 1.

International Students: In a recent year, there were 12 international students enrolled. The school actively recruits these students. They must score 500 on the written TOEFL. Applicants with TOEFL scores of at least 460 may be accepted into a program supported by ESL courses.

Computers: The campus is fully networked. Approximately 250 PCs are distributed among the 7 computer labs and 5 residence halls. Internet access is available without charge. Access is available in all resident hall rooms, and wireless access is available throughout the campus. All students may access the system 24 hours a day. There are no time limits and no fees. It is recommended that students in interactive media major by junior year have personal computers.

Graduates: From July 1, 2002 to June 30, 2003, 98 bachelor's degrees were awarded. The most popular majors were education (29%), business (17%), and social work (17%). In an average class, 1% graduate in 3 years or less, 74% graduate in 4 years or less, and 99% graduate in 5 years or less. 19 companies recruited on campus in 2002-2003. Of the 2002 graduating class, 7% were enrolled in graduate school within 6 months of graduation and 96% were employed.

Admissions Contact: James Lynes, Director of Admissions.
E-mail: *admissions@fs1.dana.edu* Web: *www.dana.edu*

DOANE COLLEGE
Crete, NE 68333

E-3

(402) 826-8222
(800) 333-6263; Fax: (402) 826-8600

Full-time: 998 men and women	**Faculty:** 79; IIA, --$
Part-time: 19 men and women	**Ph.D.s:** 63%
Graduate: none	**Student/Faculty:** 13 to 1
Year: 4-1-4, summer session	**Tuition:** $15,400
Application Deadline: August 15	**Room & Board:** $4600
Freshman Class: n/av	
ACT: 23	**COMPETITIVE**

Doane College, founded in 1872 and the oldest liberal arts college in Nebraska, is a private, independent, comprehensive college that maintains historic ties with the United Church of Christ. In addition to regional accreditation, Doane has baccalaureate program accreditation with NCATE. The library contains 296,024 volumes and 3754 audio/video tapes/CDs. Computerized library services include the card catalog, interlibrary loans, database searching, and Internet access. Special learning facilities include a learning resource center, art gallery, radio station, TV station, and an observatory. The 300-acre campus is in a small town 25 miles southwest of Lincoln. Including any residence halls, there are 27 buildings.

Student Life: 82% of undergraduates are from Nebraska. Students are from 23 states and 1 foreign country. 80% are from public schools. 94% are white. 34% are Protestant; 23% Catholic. The average age of freshmen is 18; all undergraduates, 21. 18% do not continue beyond their first year; 62% remain to graduate.

Housing: 875 students can be accommodated in college housing, which includes single-sex and coed dorms, on-campus apartments, and married-student housing. In addition, there are honors houses and special-interest houses. On-campus housing is guaranteed for all 4 years. 74% of students live on campus. All students may keep cars.

Activities: 48% of men belong to 5 local fraternities; 40% of women belong to 4 local sororities. There are 50 groups on campus, including alternative spring break, art, band, cheerleading, choir, chorale, chorus, computers, dance, drama, ethnic, forensics, gay, Hanson Leadership Program, honors, international, investment, jazz band, literary magazine, marching band, musical theater, newspaper, pep band, photography, political, professional, radio and TV, religious, social, social service, speech team, student government, wildlife/conservation, and yearbook. Popular campus events include Parents Day, Stop Day, and Christmas festival and concert.

Sports: There are 8 intercollegiate sports for men and 8 for women, and 4 intramural sports for men and 4 for women. Facilities include a phys ed building, field house, sports field, fitness center, gym, pool, nature and cross-country trails, challenge course, and indoor and outdoor tracks.

Disabled Students: 60% of the campus is accessible. Wheelchair ramps, elevators, special parking, specially equipped rest rooms, and special class scheduling are available.

Services: Counseling and information services are available, as is tutoring in every subject. There is remedial math, reading, and writing.

Campus Safety and Security: Measures include security escort services, informal discussions, pamphlets/posters/films, and emergency telephones. There are lighted pathways/sidewalks and evening patrols by trained security personnel.

Programs of Study: Doane confers B.A. and B.S. degrees. Master's degrees are also awarded. Bachelor's degrees are awarded in BIOLOGICAL SCIENCE (biology/biological science), BUSINESS (accounting and business administration and management), COMMUNICATIONS AND THE ARTS (art, communications, dramatic arts, English, English as a second/foreign language, French, German, language arts, music, Spanish, speech/debate/rhetoric, and technical and business writing), COMPUTER AND PHYSICAL SCIENCE (chemistry, computer science, mathematics, physical sciences, and physics), EDUCATION (business, elementary, physical, science, social science, and special), ENGINEERING AND ENVIRONMENTAL DESIGN (environmental science), HEALTH PROFESSIONS (industrial hygiene), SOCIAL SCIENCE (economics, history, international studies, philosophy, political science/government, psychology, public administration, religion, and sociology). Education is the strongest academically. Education and business administration are the largest.

Required: The Doane Plan requires students to complete 60 to 70 credits in heritage studies, contemporary issues, international/multicultural perspective, natural science, quantitative reasoning, communication, aesthetic perspective, health and well-being, and community and leadership. Students are also required to complete 2 hours of phys ed, demonstrate computer skills in word processing, and in most disciplines, complete a senior seminar. Students must complete 132 credit hours and have a minimum GPA of 2.0 in the major to graduate.

Special: Internships for sophomores through seniors, a Washington semester, and study abroad in numerous countries are possible. A 3-2 engineering program in conjunction with Washington at St. Louis and Columbia Universities, work-study, student-designed and interdisciplinary majors, dual majors and accelerated degrees in all areas, credit by exam, nondegree study, and pass/fail options are available. Doane also offers the HELPS program, designed for Doane College graduates who wish to return as full-time students to seek further education in preparation for career advancement. Students may pursue a 3-2 environmental studies/forestry degree in conjunction with Duke University. Doane's Lincoln campus, designed for adults, offers intensive 8-week classes in the evening and on weekends in both undergraduate and graduate programs. Doane offers an honors program, leadership development program, and the opportunity to conduct summer research projects with faculty. There are 7 national honor societies, a freshman honors program, and 2 departmental honors programs.

Faculty/Classroom: 61% of faculty are male; 39%, female. All teach undergraduates. The average class size in an introductory lecture is 24; in a laboratory, 16; and in a regular course, 18.

Admissions: 45% of the current freshmen were in the top fifth of their class; 80% were in the top two fifths.

Requirements: The SAT I or ACT is required; the ACT is preferred. Applicants must be graduates of an accredited secondary school. The GED is accepted. It is recommended that 4 units of English and 3 units each of math, science, and the social sciences be completed. An interview is recommended. Art students must submit a portfolio, and music and drama students must audition. AP and CLEP credits are accepted. Important factors in the admissions decision are advanced placement or honor courses, recommendations by school officials, and ability to finance college education.

Procedure: Freshmen are admitted fall, winter, and spring. Entrance exams should be taken by spring of junior year or early senior year. There is a deferred admissions plan and a rolling admissions plan. Applications should be filed by August 15 for fall entry. The fall 2003 application fee was $15. Notification is sent on a rolling basis. Applications are accepted on-line through the school's web site at *www.doane.edu*.

Transfer: Transfer students must submit a transcript from previously attended colleges and have been in good standing. The SAT I or ACT is usually required. Grades of 2.0 or higher generally transfer for credit. 30 credits of 132 required for the bachelor's degree must be completed at Doane.

Visiting: There are regularly scheduled orientations for prospective students, including 4 scheduled half-day visits that incorporate a parents program. There are guides for informal visits and visitors may sit in on classes and stay overnight. To schedule a visit, contact the Admissions Office at *dkunzman@doane.edu*.

Financial Aid: In a recent year, 80% of all full-time freshmen and 75% of continuing full-time students received some form of financial aid. 81% of full-time freshmen and 70% of continuing full-time students received need-based aid. The average freshman award was $11,913. 48% of undergraduates work part time. Average annual earnings from campus work are $766. The average financial indebtedness of a recent graduate was $14,009. The FAFSA is required. The deadline for filing freshman financial aid applications for fall entry is March 1.

International Students: There were 5 international students enrolled in a recent year. The school actively recruits these students. They must score 550 on the written TOEFL.

Computers: The mainframe is a Compaq DS-20. Every residence hall has a PC lab networked to the server and Internet. Several large labs are available 73 hours a week. All students have e-mail, Internet services, and web access. All residence rooms have unlimited access. All students may access the system any time. There are no time limits and no fees.

Graduates: In a recent year, 171 bachelor's degrees were awarded. The most popular majors were elementary education (14%), business administration (11%), and biology (10%). In an average class, 1% graduate in 3 years or less, 85% graduate in 4 years or less, 99% graduate in 5 years or less, and 100% graduate in 6 years or less. 45 companies recruited on campus in a recent year. Of a recent graduating class, 37% were enrolled in graduate school within 6 months of graduation and 83% were employed.

Admissions Contact: Dan Kunzman, Dean of Admissions. A video is available. E-mail: *admissions@doane.edu* Web: *www.doane.edu*

HASTINGS COLLEGE
Hastings, NE 68901   **D-3**

(402) 461-7315
(800) 532-7642; Fax: (402) 461-7490

Full-time: 549 men, 505 women	**Faculty:** 80; IIB, -$
Part-time: 7 men, 13 women	**Ph.Ds:** 71%
Graduate: 17 men, 22 women	**Student/Faculty:** 13 to 1
Year: 4-1-4, summer session	**Tuition:** $15,398
Application Deadline: August 1	**Room & Board:** $4530
Freshman Class: 1553 applied, 1236 accepted, 386 enrolled	
ACT: 23	**VERY COMPETITIVE**

Hastings College, founded in 1882 and affiliated with the Presbyterian Church (U.S.A.) offers programs in the liberal arts and sciences, education, business, and pre-health professions. In addition to regional accreditation, Hastings College has baccalaureate program accreditation with NASM and NCATE. The library contains 135,975 volumes, 117,490 microform items, and 1600 audio/video tapes/CDs, and subscribes to 935 periodicals. Computerized library services include the card catalog, interlibrary loans, database searching, and Internet access. Special learning facilities include a learning resource center, art gallery, radio station, TV station, an observatory, and a glass blowing studio. The 190-acre campus is in a rural area 150 miles west of Omaha. Including any residence halls, there are 33 buildings.

Student Life: 76% of undergraduates are from Nebraska. Students are from 25 states, 10 foreign countries, and Canada. 86% are from public schools. 92% are white. 41% are Protestant; 23% Catholic. The average age of freshmen is 18; all undergraduates, 21. 23% do not continue beyond their first year; 61% remain to graduate.

Housing: 619 students can be accommodated in college housing, which includes single-sex and coed dorms and on-campus apartments. In addition, there are honors houses and off-campus apartments. On-campus housing is guaranteed for the freshman year only and is available on a first-come, first-served basis. Priority is given to out-of-town students. 50% of students live on campus; of those, 60% remain on campus on weekends. Alcohol is not permitted. All students may keep cars.

Activities: 20% of men belong to 4 local fraternities; 30% of women belong to 4 local sororities. There are 84 groups on campus, including art, band, cheerleading, choir, chorus, dance, debate, drama, ethnic, flag team, forensics, gay, health advisory council, honors, jazz band, literary magazine, marching band, musical theater, newspaper, nontraditional students, opera, orchestra, peer educators, pep band, photography, political, professional, public relations, radio and TV, religious, social, social service, student government, symphony, and yearbook. Popular campus events include May Fete, Festival of Lessons and Carols, and Artist Lecture Series.

Sports: There are 9 intercollegiate sports for men and 9 for women, and 9 intramural sports for men and 9 for women. Facilities include a physical fitness center, a pool, a weight room, indoor and outdoor tennis courts, a 3000-seat stadium, a 2500-seat gym, and an all-weather track.

Disabled Students: 90% of the campus is accessible. Wheelchair ramps, elevators, special parking, specially equipped rest rooms, special class scheduling, lowered drinking fountains, and lowered telephones are available.

Services: Counseling and information services are available, as is tutoring in most subjects, including all core subjects and most lower-division courses.

Campus Safety and Security: Measures include security escort services, pamphlets/posters/films, emergency telephones, and lighted pathways/sidewalks. There is a night security patrol.

Programs of Study: Hastings College confers B.A. and B.M. degrees. Master's degrees are also awarded. Bachelor's degrees are awarded in BIOLOGICAL SCIENCE (biology/biological science), BUSINESS (accounting and business administration and management), COMMUNICATIONS AND THE ARTS (broadcasting, communications, dramatic arts, English, fine arts, German, music, Spanish, and speech/debate/rhetoric), COMPUTER AND PHYSICAL SCIENCE (chemistry, computer science, mathematics, and physics), EDUCATION (art, business, elementary, foreign languages, music, science, secondary, and special), HEALTH PROFESSIONS (health care administration), SOCIAL SCIENCE (economics, history, human services, philosophy, political science/government, psychology, religion, social science, and sociology). Physics is the strongest academically. Business administration and education are the largest.

Required: Students are required to take courses in written and oral communication, physical and life science, foreign language, history, so-

cial and political science, literature, philosophy, religion, health/wellness, computer science, the fine arts, and phys ed. A minimum 2.0 GPA and 127 credit hours, with 30 to 36 in the major, are required to graduate.

Special: There is a co-op nursing program with Creighton University, a 3-2 engineering program with Columbia and Washington Universities and Georgia Institute of Technology, and a 3-2 degree in occupational therapy with Boston and Washington Universities. Internships, study abroad in England, Spain, Russia, Ireland, Holland, and Germany, work-study, dual majors in all areas, and student-designed majors are possible. Credit by exam, credit for military experience, and pass/fail options are available. There are 12 national honor societies.

Faculty/Classroom: 67% of faculty are male; 33%, female. All teach undergraduates and 25% both teach and do research. No introductory courses are taught by graduate students. The average class size in an introductory lecture is 25; in a laboratory, 25; and in a regular course, 18.

Admissions: 80% of the 2003-2004 applicants were accepted. The SAT I scores for the 2003-2004 freshman class were: Verbal--15% below 500, 40% between 500 and 599, 25% between 600 and 700, and 18% above 700; Math--19% below 500, 37% between 500 and 599, 24% between 600 and 700, and 20% above 700. The ACT scores were 13% below 21, 29% between 21 and 23, 26% between 24 and 26, 18% between 27 and 28, and 14% above 28. 52% of the current freshmen were in the top fifth of their class; 85% were in the top two fifths. 19 freshmen graduated first in their class.

Requirements: The SAT I or ACT is required. In addition, applicants should graduate from an accredited secondary school with a minimum of 4 academic credits in English and 2 each in math, science, social studies, and a foreign language. Generally, placement in the upper half of the graduating class, a minimum GPA of 2.0, or a composite score of 20 on the enhanced ACT, is a minimal requirement for consideration for admission. Hastings College requires applicants to be in the upper 50% of their class. A GPA of 2.0 is required. AP and CLEP credits are accepted. Important factors in the admissions decision are advanced placement or honor courses, leadership record, and personality/intangible qualities.

Procedure: Freshmen are admitted to all sessions. Entrance exams should be taken before November. There is a rolling admissions plan. Applications should be filed by August 1 for fall entry, December 1 for winter entry, January 1 for spring entry, and May 15 for summer entry. Notification of both early and regular decision is sent on a rolling basis. The fall 2003 application fee was $20. Applications are accepted on computer disk and on-line.

Transfer: 26 transfer students enrolled in 2002-2003. Transfer students must have completed course work equivalent by description to that of Hastings and have earned grades of C or better. 30 of 127 credits required for the bachelor's degree must be completed at Hastings College.

Visiting: There are regularly scheduled orientations for prospective students, including academic department presentations, a financial aid session, a student panel discussion, a student guided tour, and an activities fair. There are guides for informal visits and visitors may sit in on classes and stay overnight. To schedule a visit, contact the Admissions Office.

Financial Aid: In 2003-2004, 99% of all full-time freshmen and 98% of continuing full-time students received some form of financial aid. 79% of full-time freshmen and 71% of continuing full-time students received need-based aid. The average freshman award was $12,066. Need-based scholarships or need-based grants averaged $9072; need-based self-help aid (loans and jobs) averaged $3613; and non-need-based athletic scholarships averaged $3896. 54% of undergraduates work part time. Average annual earnings from campus work are $775. The average financial indebtedness of the 2003 graduate was $15,778. Hastings College is a member of CSS. The FAFSA is required. The deadline for filing freshman financial aid applications for fall entry is May 1.

International Students: There are 15 international students enrolled. The school actively recruits these students. They must score 600 on the written TOEFL or 250 on the electronic version. International athletes should take a standardized test for athletic eligibility.

Computers: The mainframes are multiple servers, including Compaq, Dell and Hewlett-Packard. 160 Windows-based PCs and 28 Macs are available for academic use in several computer labs across campus. All students can connect their computers to the campus network to access the Internet. All library resources are available and each student has an e-mail address. All students may access the system. There are no time limits and no fees.

Graduates: From July 1, 2002 to June 30, 2003, 220 bachelor's degrees were awarded. The most popular majors were education (22%), business administration (20%), and biology (12%). In an average class, 51% graduate in 4 years or less, 60% graduate in 5 years or less, and 62% graduate in 6 years or less. 35 companies recruited on campus in 2002-2003. Of a recent graduating class, 19% were enrolled in graduate school within 6 months of graduation and 66% were employed.

Admissions Contact: Mary Molliconi, Director of Admissions. A video is available. E-mail: *mmolliconi@hastings.edu* Web: *www.hastings.edu*

MIDLAND LUTHERAN COLLEGE
Fremont, NE 68025

E-2
(402) 941-6501
(800) 642-8382; Fax: (402)-721-2050

Full-time: 410 men, 530 women	Faculty: 69; IIB, --$
Part-time: 20 men, 35 women	Ph.Ds: 45%
Graduate: none	Student/Faculty: 14 to 1
Year: 4-1-4, summer session	Tuition: $16,310
Application Deadline: see profile	Room & Board: $4420
Freshman Class: n/av	
SAT I or ACT: recommended	**COMPETITIVE**

Midland Lutheran College, established in 1883, is a private liberal arts institution affiliated with the Evangelical Lutheran Church in America. Figures in the above capsule and in this profile are approximate. In addition to regional accreditation, Midland has baccalaureate program accreditation with NLN. The library contains 105,000 volumes and 1000 audio/video tapes/CDs, and subscribes to 900 periodicals. Computerized library services include interlibrary loans and database searching. Special learning facilities include a learning resource center and planetarium. The 27-acre campus is in a small town 30 miles northwest of Omaha. Including any residence halls, there are 18 buildings.

Student Life: 75% of undergraduates are from Nebraska. Students are from 23 states, 10 foreign countries, and Canada. 94% are from public schools. 91% are white. 57% are Protestant; 32% Catholic; 10% claim no religious affiliation. The average age of freshmen is 18; all undergraduates, 20. 16% do not continue beyond their first year; 56% remain to graduate.

Housing: 575 students can be accommodated in college housing, which includes single-sex and coed dorms and off-campus apartments. On-campus housing is guaranteed for all 4 years, is available on a first-come, first-served basis, and is available on a lottery system for upperclassmen. 52% of students live on campus; of those, 50% remain on campus on weekends. Alcohol is not permitted. All students may keep cars.

Activities: 20% of men belong to 4 local fraternities; 20% of women belong to 4 local sororities. There are 36 groups on campus, including art, band, cheerleading, choir, chorale, chorus, computers, drama, drill team, ethnic, film, forensics, honors, jazz band, literary magazine, musical theater, newspaper, pep band, photography, political, professional, radio and TV, religious, social, social service, student government, and yearbook. Popular campus events include Greek Games, Snow Week, and Martin Luther King Day.

Sports: There are 9 intercollegiate sports for men and 9 for women, and 6 intramural sports for men and 6 for women. Facilities include a phys ed center, an athletic practice field, an indoor pool, an indoor track, and a weight room.

Disabled Students: 90% of the campus is accessible. Wheelchair ramps, elevators, special parking, specially equipped rest rooms, special class scheduling, lowered drinking fountains, and lowered telephones are available.

Services: Counseling and information services are available, as is tutoring in every subject. There is remedial reading and writing.

Campus Safety and Security: Measures include 24-hour foot and vehicle patrol, security escort services, informal discussions, pamphlets/posters/films, and lighted pathways/sidewalks.

Programs of Study: Midland confers B.A., B.S., B.S.B.A., and B.S.N. degrees. Associate degrees are also awarded. Bachelor's degrees are awarded in BIOLOGICAL SCIENCE (biology/biological science), BUSINESS (accounting, business administration and management, business economics, management information systems, and marketing/retailing/merchandising), COMMUNICATIONS AND THE ARTS (advertising, communications, English, fine arts, journalism, and music), COMPUTER AND PHYSICAL SCIENCE (chemistry, computer programming, computer science, and mathematics), EDUCATION (art, business, early childhood, elementary, middle school, music, science, and secondary), HEALTH PROFESSIONS (nursing, predentistry, and premedicine), SOCIAL SCIENCE (community services, economics, history, parks and recreation management, prelaw, psychology, religion, social science, and sociology). Business, journalism, and education are the strongest academically. Business, education, and nursing are the largest.

Required: To graduate, students need a total of 128 credit hours, with 33 of these in distribution requirements of the student's selection. 1 course in English, speech, and math is required, as well as 1 year of foreign language on the high school or college level. The total number of hours in the major varies from 34 to 48, and students must maintain a GPA of at least 2.0 overall and 2.25 in the major, with some departments requiring a higher minimum GPA.

Special: There is cross-registration with Dana College in Blair, internships in business, public relations, journalism, and art, study abroad in 3 countries, student-designed majors, work-study programs, and a 3-2 engineering degree with Washington University. Other options include dual majors, independent study, directed study, and the pass/no credit grading system. There are 2 national honor societies.

Faculty/Classroom: 60% of faculty are male; 40%, female. All teach undergraduates. The average class size in a laboratory is 20 and in a regular course, 20.

Requirements: The SAT I or ACT is recommended. In addition, applicants should be graduates of an accredited secondary school. The GED is accepted. Recommended preparation includes 3 units of English, 2 each of math, and foreign language, and 10 of electives. An interview is recommended. Midland requires applicants to be in the upper 50% of their class. AP and CLEP credits are accepted. Important factors in the admissions decision are leadership record, extracurricular activities record, and evidence of special talent.

Procedure: Freshmen are admitted fall and winter. Entrance exams should be taken during the fall of the senior year. There is a rolling admissions plan. There are early decision, early admissions, and deferred admissions plans. Applications should be filed early in the senior year, along with a $30 fee (waived for on-line applications). Notification is sent on a rolling basis. 25 early decision candidates were accepted for a recent class. Applications are accepted on computer disk and on-line.

Transfer: 60 transfer students enrolled in a recent year. Applicants must be in good standing at their previous college and generally have a 2.0 minimum GPA. Grades of C or higher transfer for credit. 30 of 128 credits required for the bachelor's degree must be completed at Midland.

Visiting: There are regularly scheduled orientations for prospective students, Campus visits are scheduled on an individual basis and as much as possible include visits with faculty, students, and financial aid counselors. There are guides for informal visits and visitors may sit in on classes and stay overnight. To schedule a visit, contact the Admissions Office at *admissions@admin.mlc.edu*.

Financial Aid: In a recent year, 93% of all full-time freshmen and 90% of continuing full-time students received some form of financial aid. 75% of full-time freshmen and 80% of continuing full-time students received need-based aid. The average freshman award was $12,400. 80% of undergraduates work part time. Average annual earnings from campus work are $800. The average financial indebtedness of a recent graduate was $18,200. Midland is a member of CSS. The FAFSA or FFS is required. Check with the school for current application deadlines.

International Students: There were 16 international students enrolled in a recent year. The school actively recruits these students. They must score 500 on the written TOEFL.

Computers: The mainframes are a DEC Vax VMS 4400 and 4106 models. 65 Mac and IBM computers are available with complete access to the Web and Internet. All students have e-mail accounts. All students may access the system. There are no time limits and no fees. It is recommended that students in business and education have personal computers.

Graduates: In a recent year, 170 bachelor's degrees were awarded. The most popular majors were business (30%), education (25%), and nursing (20%). In an average class, 1% graduate in 3 years or less, 52% graduate in 4 years or less, 55% graduate in 5 years or less, and 56% graduate in 6 years or less. 38 companies recruited on campus in a recent year. Of a recent graduating class, 11% were enrolled in graduate school within 6 months of graduation and 86% were employed.

Admissions Contact: John Klockentager, Vice President for Enrollment Services. E-mail: *klock@admin.mlc.edu* Web: *www.mlc.edu*

NEBRASKA METHODIST COLLEGE OF NURSING AND ALLIED HEALTH
Omaha, NE 68114

F-3
(402) 354-4879
(800) 335-5510; Fax: (402) 354-8875

Full-time: 50 men, 340 women	Faculty: 28
Part-time: none	Ph.Ds: 10%
Graduate: 1 man, 31 women	Student/Faculty: 14 to 1
Year: semesters, summer session	Tuition: $10,200
Application Deadline: March 1	Room & Board: $1700
Freshman Class: 85 applied, 69 accepted, 47 enrolled	
ACT: 20	**SPECIAL**

Nebraska Methodist College of Nursing and Allied Health, founded in 1891 as the Methodist School of Nursing and chartered in the state of Nebraska in 1985 with its present name, is part of the Nebraska Methodist Health Systems. The college is a private, primarily commuter institution offering career training in the health sciences. In addition to regional accreditation, Nebraska Methodist College has baccalaureate program accreditation with CAHEA and CCNE. The library contains 13,059 volumes, 1722 microform items, and 500 audio/video tapes/CDs, and subscribes to 598 periodicals. Computerized library services include the card catalog, interlibrary loans, and database searching. Special learning facilities include a learning resource center, an assessment lab for nursing and respiratory care studies, and a human cadaver lab. The 5-acre campus is in an urban area in the center of Omaha. Including any residence halls, there are 3 buildings.

Student Life: 95% of undergraduates are from Nebraska. Students are from 10 states, 2 foreign countries, and Canada. 95% are from public schools. 89% are white. The average age of freshmen is 18; all under-

graduates, 27. 10% do not continue beyond their first year; 74% remain to graduate.

Housing: 80 students can be accommodated in college housing, which includes coed dorms. On-campus housing is available on a first-come, first-served basis. Priority is given to out-of-town students. 80% of students commute. Alcohol is not permitted. All students may keep cars.

Activities: There are no fraternities or sororities. There are 10 groups on campus, including ethnic, professional, social, social service, and student government. Popular campus events include Honors Convocation and pledging ceremonies.

Sports: There is no sports program at Nebraska Methodist College. Facilities include a fitness center.

Disabled Students: 75% of the campus is accessible. Elevators, special parking, and specially equipped rest rooms are available.

Services: Counseling and information services are available, as is tutoring in most subjects. There is remedial math, reading, and writing. A reader service for the blind is available in the metropolitan area.

Campus Safety and Security: Measures include self-defense education, informal discussions, pamphlets/posters/films, and lighted pathways/sidewalks.

Programs of Study: Nebraska Methodist College confers B.S. and B.S.N. degrees. Associate and master's degrees are also awarded. Bachelor's degrees are awarded in HEALTH PROFESSIONS (nursing, respiratory therapy, and ultrasound technology). Nursing is the strongest program academically and has the largest enrollment.

Required: All students must complete 45 credit hours of core curriculum courses in the humanities, social and behavioral sciences, and natural and applied sciences. A total of 127 credit hours is required, 55 of these in the major. Students must maintain a minimum GPA of 2.0.

Special: There is nondegree study and credit by exam. Credit by correspondence may be considered. An accelerated degree in nursing is offered. There is 1 national honor society and 2 departmental honors programs.

Faculty/Classroom: 15% of faculty are male; 85%, female. All teach undergraduates. No introductory courses are taught by graduate students. The average class size in an introductory lecture is 35; in a laboratory, 10; and in a regular course, 20.

Admissions: 81% of the 2003-2004 applicants were accepted. The ACT scores for the 2003-2004 freshman class were: 50% below 21, 35% between 21 and 23, 10% between 24 and 26, and 5% between 27 and 28. 30% of the current freshmen were in the top fifth of their class; 70% were in the top two fifths. 1 freshman graduated first in the class.

Requirements: The ACT is required, with a minimum acceptable score of 18. Students must be graduates of an accredited secondary school with the number of academic credits required under Nebraska state law. The GED is accepted. Students should have completed 4 years of English and 2 years each of math, science, and social studies. An essay and an interview are required. Nebraska Methodist College requires applicants to be in the upper 75% of their class. A GPA of 2.0 is required. AP and CLEP credits are accepted. Important factors in the admissions decision are personality/intangible qualities, advanced placement or honor courses, and leadership record.

Procedure: Freshmen are admitted fall and spring. Entrance exams should be taken as early as possible. There is a rolling admissions plan. Applications should be filed by March 1 for fall entry and October 1 for spring entry, along with a $25 fee. Notification is sent on a rolling basis. Applications are accepted on-line through the school's web site.

Transfer: 151 transfer students enrolled in 2002-2003. Applicants must have a GPA above 2.0. Grades of C and above can be transferred for credit. An interview is required. 30 of 127 credits required for the bachelor's degree must be completed at Nebraska Methodist College.

Visiting: There are regularly scheduled orientations for prospective students. There are guides for informal visits and visitors may sit in on classes. To schedule a visit, contact the Admissions Office at admissions@methodistcollege.edu.

Financial Aid: 66% of undergraduates work part time. The FAFSA and the college's own financial statement are required. The deadline for filing freshman financial aid applications for fall entry is May 1.

International Students: There are 2 international students enrolled. They must score 550 on the written TOEFL or 213 on the electronic version and also take the ACT, scoring 20.

Computers: The mainframe is an IBM. 60 PCs are available in labs on each campus. Students have access to e-mail and the Internet. All students may access the system. There are no time limits and no fees.

Graduates: From July 1, 2002 to June 30, 2003, 74 bachelor's degrees were awarded. The most popular majors were nursing (85%), sonography (10%), and respiratory care (5%). In an average class, 72% graduate in 4 years or less. 4 companies recruited on campus in 2002-2003. Of the 2002 graduating class, 90% were employed within 6 months of graduation.

Admissions Contact: Admissions Officer.
E-mail: admissions@methodistcollege.edu
Web: www.methodistcollege.edu

NEBRASKA WESLEYAN UNIVERSITY
Lincoln, NE 68504

E-3
(402) 465-2218
(800) 541-3818; Fax: (402) 465-2179

Full-time: 692 men, 838 women	**Faculty:** 101; IIB, av$
Part-time: 55 men, 102 women	**Ph.Ds:** 86%
Graduate: 29 men, 124 women	**Student/Faculty:** 15 to 1
Year: semesters, summer session	**Tuition:** $16,430
Application Deadline: May 1	**Room & Board:** $4767
Freshman Class: 1312 applied, 1214 accepted, 420 enrolled	
ACT: 24	**COMPETITIVE+**

Nebraska Wesleyan University, founded in 1887, is a private liberal arts institution affiliated with the United Methodist Church. In addition to regional accreditation, NWU has baccalaureate program accreditation with ACBSP, CSWE, NASM, NCATE, and NLN. The library contains 203,303 volumes, 4606 microform items, and 6527 audio/video tapes/CDs, and subscribes to 667 periodicals. Computerized library services include the card catalog, interlibrary loans, and database searching. Special learning facilities include a learning resource center, art gallery, planetarium, and , laboratory theater, sleep lab, greenhouse, herbarium, and nuclear magnetic resonance lab. The 50-acre campus is in a suburban area 50 miles west of Omaha. Including any residence halls, there are 23 buildings.

Student Life: 94% of undergraduates are from Nebraska. Students are from 25 states and 8 foreign countries. 95% are white. 61% are Protestant; 24% Catholic; 9% claim no religious affiliation. The average age of freshmen is 18; all undergraduates, 21. 18% do not continue beyond their first year; 63% remain to graduate in 6 years.

Housing: 1006 students can be accommodated in college housing, which includes single-sex and coed dorms, on-campus apartments, off-campus apartments, fraternity houses, and sorority houses. In addition, there are special-interest houses. Housing costs vary according to type. On-campus housing is guaranteed for all 4 years. 61% of students live on campus; of those, 70% remain on campus on weekends. All students may keep cars.

Activities: 26% of men belong to 1 local fraternity and 3 national fraternities; 27% of women belong to 2 local and 2 national sororities. There are 80 groups on campus, including art, band, cheerleading, choir, chorus, computers, debate, drama, drill team, ethnic, forensics, gay, honors, international, jazz band, literary magazine, musical theater, newspaper, opera, orchestra, pep band, political, professional, religious, social, social service, student government, and yearbook. Popular campus events include international dinners, Mosaic Week (week emphasizing multicultural activities), and Visions and Ventures Symposium.

Sports: There are 8 intercollegiate sports for men and 8 for women, and 10 intramural sports for men and 10 for women. Facilities include a recreation and fitness center, a field house and gym, a football/soccer stadium, a swimming pool, an outdoor track, football and baseball fields, and tennis courts.

Disabled Students: 85% of the campus is accessible. Wheelchair ramps, elevators, special parking, specially equipped rest rooms, special class scheduling, lowered drinking fountains, lowered telephones, and special housing are available. All academic programs can be moved or adapted as needed to accommodate students.

Services: Counseling and information services are available, as is tutoring in some subjects, including sciences, social sciences, humanities, and math.

Campus Safety and Security: Measures include security escort services, informal discussions, emergency telephones, lighted pathways/sidewalks, and nighttime foot patrol.

Programs of Study: NWU confers B.A., B.S., B.F.A., B.M., and B.S.N. degrees. Master's degrees are also awarded. Bachelor's degrees are awarded in BIOLOGICAL SCIENCE (biochemistry, biology/biological science, and molecular biology), BUSINESS (accounting, business administration and management, international business management, and sports management), COMMUNICATIONS AND THE ARTS (applied music, art, communications, dramatic arts, English, French, German, language arts, music, Spanish, and studio art), COMPUTER AND PHYSICAL SCIENCE (chemistry, computer programming, computer science, information sciences and systems, mathematics, and physics), EDUCATION (athletic training, elementary, English, middle school, music, physical, science, social science, and special), HEALTH PROFESSIONS (exercise science, health, and nursing), SOCIAL SCIENCE (anthropology, biopsychology, economics, history, international studies, paralegal studies, philosophy, political science/government, psychology, religion, social work, sociology, and women's studies). Business administration, biology, and psychology are the largest.

Required: To graduate, students must complete approximately 42 to 48 hours of general education requirements, including 9 hours in First-year Experience, 8 in Developing Foundations courses, 7 in Scientific Inquiry, 6 in U.S. Culture and Society, 3 to 11 in Global Perspectives, 3 in Western Intellectual and Religious Traditions, and 3 in Fine Arts. At least 126 credit hours, including 30 in the major, must be completed with a minimum GPA of 2.0. A senior comprehensive is also needed, consisting of a comprehensive exam in the major discipline, a thesis or independent study, or an internship, presentation, or performance.

Special: NWU offers the Capitol Hill Internship Program, study abroad in 35 countries, a global studies major, and a department of interdisciplinary studies. Internships are available in most departments and required in many. Natural sciences majors can complete summer research fellowships at labs, universities, and agencies nationwide and internationally. Other options include pass/fail options, dual majors, credit by exam, and a 3-2 engineering degree in conjunction with Washington and Columbia Universities. There are 20 national honor societies.

Faculty/Classroom: 44% of faculty are male; 56%, female. 98% teach undergraduates. No introductory courses are taught by graduate students. The average class size in an introductory lecture is 20; in a laboratory, 15; and in a regular course, 20.

Admissions: 93% of the 2003-2004 applicants were accepted. The ACT scores for the 2003-2004 freshman class were: 15% below 21, 27% between 21 and 23, 32% between 24 and 26, 15% between 27 and 28, and 11% above 28. 47% of the current freshmen were in the top fifth of their class; 80% were in the top two fifths. 30 freshmen graduated first in their class.

Requirements: The SAT I or ACT is required, with a minimum composite score of 950 on the SAT I or 20 on the ACT. Freshmen must be graduates of an accredited secondary school or submit the GED. A campus visit is recommended. NWU requires applicants to be in the upper 50% of their class. AP and CLEP credits are accepted.

Procedure: Freshmen are admitted fall and spring. Entrance exams should be taken no later than December of the senior year. There are early decision and deferred admissions plans. Early decision applications should be filed by November 15; regular applications, by May 1 for fall entry, December 15 for spring entry, and April 15 for summer entry. The fall 2003 application fee was $20. Notification of early decision is sent December 15; regular decision, January 15. 309 early decision candidates were accepted for the 2003-2004 class. Applications are accepted on-line through the school's web site.

Transfer: 77 transfer students enrolled in 2002-2003. Applicants must be in good standing at their previous school and have a 2.0 GPA or higher. A minimum of 950 on the SAT I or 20 on the ACT is recommended. Grades of C- or better transfer for credit. 30 of 126 credits required for the bachelor's degree must be completed at NWU.

Visiting: There are regularly scheduled orientations for prospective students, consisting of a tour, classroom visits, and meetings with faculty, financial aid and admissions personnel, and current students. There are guides for informal visits and visitors may sit in on classes and stay overnight. To schedule a visit, contact the Admissions Office at *admissions@nebrwesleyan.edu.*

Financial Aid: In 2003-2004, 97% of all full-time freshmen and 95% of continuing full-time students received some form of financial aid. 70% of full-time freshmen and 69% of continuing full-time students received need-based aid. The average freshman award was $10,833, with $3576 ($11,900 maximum) from need-based scholarships or need-based grants, $2218 ($4125 maximum) from need-based self-help aid (loans and jobs), and $5039 ($11,500 maximum) from other non-need-based awards and non-need-based scholarships. 91% of undergraduates work part time. Average annual earnings from campus work are $1100. The average financial indebtedness of the 2003 graduate was $16,698. The FAFSA is required. The deadline for filing freshman financial aid applications for fall entry is August 15.

International Students: There are 15 international students enrolled. The school actively recruits these students. They must score 525 on the written TOEFL or 195 on the electronic version. The SAT I or ACT is recommended.

Computers: 35 computer labs—11 general-use labs (including 7 in residence halls) and 24 departmental labs—containing a total of 343 computers are available for student use. All computer labs, classrooms, offices, and residence hall rooms are wired and networked for campus and Internet access. All students may access the system 24 hours a day, 7 days a week. There is no fee.

Graduates: In a recent year, 334 bachelor's degrees were awarded. The most popular majors were business administration (22%), psychology (9%), and elementary education (7%). In an average class, 46% graduate in 4 years or less, 60% graduate in 5 years or less, and 62% graduate in 6 years or less. 83 companies recruited on campus in 2002-2003.

Admissions Contact: Patty Karthauser, Vice President for Enrollment and Marketing. A video is available.
E-mail: *admissions@nebrwesleyan.edu*
Web: *http://www.nebrwesleyan.edu*

NEBRASKA 933

PERU STATE COLLEGE
Peru, NE 68421-0010

F-3
(402) 872-2221
(800) 742-4412; Fax: (402) 872-2296

Full-time: 420 men, 460 women	**Faculty:** 39; IIB, --$
Part-time: 240 men, 330 women	**Ph.D.s:** 64%
Graduate: 45 men, 135 women	**Student/Faculty:** 23 to 1
Year: semesters, summer session	**Tuition:** $2600 ($4700)
Application Deadline: open	**Room & Board:** $3800
Freshman Class: n/av	
ACT: recommended	**NONCOMPETITIVE**

Peru State College, established in 1867 and a part of the Nebraska State College System, is a public institution offering curricula in the arts, business, military studies, teacher preparation, and technical studies. Figures in the above capsule and in this profile are approximate. In addition to regional accreditation, PSC has baccalaureate program accreditation with NCATE. The library contains 102,432 volumes, 494,101 microform items, and 10,403 audio/video tapes/CDs, and subscribes to 313 periodicals. Computerized library services include the card catalog, interlibrary loans, and database searching. Special learning facilities include a learning resource center and art gallery. The 103-acre campus is in a rural area 60 miles south of Omaha. Including any residence halls, there are 21 buildings.

Student Life: Students are from 12 states, 8 foreign countries, and Canada. 98% are from public schools. 87% are white. The average age of freshmen is 18; all undergraduates, 22. 28% do not continue beyond their first year; 35% remain to graduate.

Housing: 590 students can be accommodated in college housing, which includes single-sex dorms, on-campus apartments, and married-student housing. In addition, there are substance-free facilities. On-campus housing is guaranteed for all 4 years. 65% of students live on campus; of those, 27% remain on campus on weekends. Alcohol is not permitted. All students may keep cars.

Activities: There are no fraternities or sororities. There are 27 groups on campus, including art, band, cheerleading, choir, chorus, computers, drama, ethnic, gay, honors, jazz band, pep band, photography, professional, religious, social, social service, student government, and yearbook. Popular campus events include Spring Break Trip.

Sports: There are 3 intercollegiate sports for men and 3 for women, and 7 intramural sports for men and 7 for women. Facilities include a playing field, an activity trail, a 2500-seat stadium, and a health and recreation complex containing basketball and tennis courts, an indoor track, and an Olympic-sized swimming pool.

Disabled Students: 80% of the campus is accessible. Wheelchair ramps, elevators, special parking, specially equipped rest rooms, special class scheduling, lowered drinking fountains, and lowered telephones are available.

Services: Counseling and information services are available, as is tutoring in most subjects. There is a reader service for the blind and remedial math, reading, and writing. Tutoring is available in writing and other subjects.

Campus Safety and Security: Measures include 24-hour foot and vehicle patrol, security escort services, informal discussions, pamphlets/posters/films, and lighted pathways/sidewalks.

Programs of Study: Bobcats confers B.A., B.S., and B.T. degrees. Master's degrees are also awarded. Bachelor's degrees are awarded in AGRICULTURE (wildlife management), BIOLOGICAL SCIENCE (biology/biological science), BUSINESS (accounting, business administration and management, marketing/retailing/merchandising, and sports management), COMMUNICATIONS AND THE ARTS (English, music, and music business management), COMPUTER AND PHYSICAL SCIENCE (computer management, computer programming, computer science, mathematics, nuclear technology, and physical sciences), EDUCATION (art, elementary, music, physical, science, secondary, and special), ENGINEERING AND ENVIRONMENTAL DESIGN (preengineering), HEALTH PROFESSIONS (premedicine, prepharmacy, and preveterinary science), SOCIAL SCIENCE (history, prelaw, psychology, social science, and sociology).

Required: To graduate, students must complete 45 to 53 hours of general education requirements in literature, communications, fine arts, social and behavioral sciences, health and hygiene, computer science, and natural sciences, as well as a phys ed requirement. Teacher education majors must have a GPA of 2.5; all others must have a GPA of 2.0. The college requires 125 credit hours for graduation.

Special: The college offers cooperative programs, internships, B.A.-B.S. degrees, dual majors, work-study programs, and nondegree study. Credit may be granted for military experience. There are 2 national honor societies and a freshman honors program.

Faculty/Classroom: 79% of faculty are male; 21%, female. All teach undergraduates. No introductory courses are taught by graduate students. The average class size in an introductory lecture is 40; in a laboratory, 25; and in a regular course, 25.

Requirements: The ACT is recommended. Applicants who have graduated from an accredited Nebraska secondary school will be admitted;

holders of the GED will be considered. Out-of-state applicants should have earned 16 Carnegie units. A GPA of 2.0 is required. AP and CLEP credits are accepted.

Procedure: Freshmen are admitted to all sessions. There is a rolling admissions plan and a deferred admissions plan. Application deadlines are open. The fall 2003 application fee was $10. Applications are accepted on-line at *www.peru.edu/admissions/application.html.*

Transfer: 149 transfer students enrolled in a recent year. Transfer students must be in good standing with the previously attended institution. 30 of 125 credits required for the bachelor's degree must be completed at PSC.

Visiting: There are regularly scheduled orientations for prospective students. There are guides for informal visits and visitors may sit in on classes and stay overnight. To schedule a visit, contact the Admissions Office.

Financial Aid: In a recent year, 73% of all full-time freshmen received some form of financial aid. 40% of undergraduates work part time. Average annual earnings from campus work are $800. The average financial indebtedness of a recent graduate was $14,000. The FAFSA is required. Check with the school for current deadlines.

International Students: There were 12 international students enrolled in a recent year. They must score 550 on the written TOEFL or 230 on the electronic version.

Computers: Peru State provides 48 Macs in labs for students enrolled in computer courses. There are no time limits and no fees.

Graduates: In a recent year, 229 bachelor's degrees were awarded. The most popular majors were education (38%) and business administration (38%). In an average class, 11% graduate in 4 years or less, 20% graduate in 5 years or less, and 30% graduate in 6 years or less. 10 companies recruited on campus in a recent year. Of a recent graduating class, 10% were enrolled in graduate school within 6 months of graduation and 93% were employed.

Admissions Contact: Janelle Moran, Director of Admission and Recruitment. E-mail: *jmoran@oakmail.peru.edu*
Web: *http://www.peru.edu*

UNION COLLEGE
Lincoln, NE 68506

E-3

(402) 486-2504
(800) 228-4600; Fax: (402) 486-2895

Full-time: 311 men, 447 women	**Faculty:** 52
Part-time: 58 men, 87 women	**Ph.D.s:** 44%
Graduate: none	**Student/Faculty:** 15 to 1
Year: semesters, summer session	**Tuition:** $12,920
Application Deadline: open	**Room & Board:** $4210
Freshman Class: 165 enrolled	
ACT: 21	**COMPETITIVE**

Union College, established in 1891, is a nonprofit, private, liberal arts institution affiliated with the Seventh-day Adventist Church. In addition to regional accreditation, Union College has baccalaureate program accreditation with CSWE and NCATE. The library contains 109,026 volumes, 1026 microform items, and 2971 audio/video tapes/CDs, and subscribes to 515 periodicals. Computerized library services include the card catalog, interlibrary loans, and database searching. Special learning facilities include a learning resource center, art gallery, and a state-run natural arboretum. The 26-acre campus is in a suburban area in southeast Lincoln. Including any residence halls, there are 11 buildings.

Student Life: 82% of undergraduates are from out of state, mostly the Midwest. Students are from 42 states, 29 foreign countries, and Canada. 17% are from public schools. 77% are white; 14% foreign nationals. The average age of freshmen is 18; all undergraduates, 22. 28% do not continue beyond their first year; 45% remain to graduate.

Housing: 635 students can be accommodated in college housing, which includes single-sex dorms, on-campus apartments, and married-student housing. On-campus housing is guaranteed for the freshman year only and is available on a first-come, first-served basis. 58% of students live on campus; of those, 67% remain on campus on weekends. Alcohol is not permitted. All students may keep cars.

Activities: There are no fraternities or sororities. There are 16 groups on campus, including art, band, choir, chorale, computers, drama, ethnic, honors, international, literary magazine, newspaper, orchestra, photography, religious, student government, and yearbook.

Sports: There are 2 intercollegiate sports for men and 3 for women, and 8 intramural sports for men and 8 for women. Facilities include an Olympic-size indoor swimming pool, a weight room, tennis courts, and a sandlot volleyball court.

Disabled Students: 75% of the campus is accessible. Wheelchair ramps, elevators, special parking, specially equipped rest rooms, and lowered telephones are available.

Services: Counseling and information services are available, as is tutoring in most subjects. There is remedial math, reading, and writing. Tutoring is available upon request.

Campus Safety and Security: Measures include security escort services and lighted pathways/sidewalks.

Programs of Study: Union College confers B.A., B.S., B.A.T., B.Ed., B.M., B.S.W., and B.T. degrees. Associate degrees are also awarded. Bachelor's degrees are awarded in BIOLOGICAL SCIENCE (biology/biological science), BUSINESS (accounting, banking and finance, business administration and management, management science, marketing and distribution, and small business management), COMMUNICATIONS AND THE ARTS (communications, English, French, German, graphic design, journalism, literature, music, music performance, public relations, Spanish, and studio art), COMPUTER AND PHYSICAL SCIENCE (chemistry, computer science, mathematics, physics, and science), EDUCATION (art, business, computer, elementary, English, mathematics, music, physical, secondary, and social science), HEALTH PROFESSIONS (medical laboratory technology, nursing, and physician's assistant), SOCIAL SCIENCE (history, international studies, pastoral studies, physical fitness/movement, psychology, religion, religious education, social science, social work, and theological studies). Physician's assistant and physical science are the strongest academically. Business administration and nursing are the largest.

Required: Students must complete 128 semester hours, with fulfillment of a major, and maintain a minimum GPA of 2.0. There are 39 hours of core classes, including those in art/fine arts, computer science, English, history, math, science, and philosophy/religion.

Special: Special academic programs include study abroad in 4 countries, co-op programs with 9 Adventist institutions abroad, and cross-registration with the University of Nebraska, Nebraska Wesleyan University, and Southeast Community College. Student-designed majors are available through the Personalized Bachelor's Degree Program. There are pass/fail options in electives for upperclassmen with a minimum cumulative GPA of 2.0. Some internships are available. There is a freshman honors program.

Faculty/Classroom: 56% of faculty are male; 44%, female. The average class size in an introductory lecture is 21 and in a regular course, 18.

Admissions: The ACT scores for the 2003-2004 freshman class were: 40% below 21, 30% between 21 and 23, 17% between 24 and 26, 8% between 27 and 28, and 5% above 28. 28% of the current freshmen were in the top fifth of their class; 55% were in the top two fifths.

Requirements: The ACT is required. Freshmen with a high school GPA below 2.5 and/or an ACT composite score below the 20th percentile will be enrolled in the freshman development program. Applicants must have graduated from an accredited secondary school with 18 academic credits, including 3 units of English and 1 unit each of math, science, and history. For math and science programs, 2 units of algebra and 1 unit each of geometry and trigonometry are recommended. For majors in nursing, biology, chemistry, physics, or engineering, applicants should complete physics and chemistry courses. The GED is also accepted. An essay and interview are advised, and music students should audition. A GPA of 2.5 is required. AP and CLEP credits are accepted.

Procedure: Freshmen are admitted fall and spring. Entrance exams should be taken by fall of the senior year. Application deadlines are open. Notification is sent on a rolling basis.

Transfer: 74 transfer students enrolled in a recent year. Transfer students must have a minimum GPA of 2.0. The ACT is required, and high school and college transcripts must be submitted. 30 of 128 credits required for the bachelor's degree must be completed at Union College.

Visiting: There are regularly scheduled orientations for prospective students. There are guides for informal visits and visitors may sit in on classes and stay overnight. To schedule a visit, contact the Admissions Office Campus Hostess.

Financial Aid: In a recent year, all full-time freshmen and 95% of continuing full-time students received some form of financial aid. 55% of full-time freshmen and 54% of continuing full-time students received need-based aid. The average freshman award was $7152. 48% of undergraduates work part time. Average annual earnings from campus work are $1960. The average financial indebtedness of a recent year's graduate was $17,913. Union College is a member of CSS. The FAFSA is required. Check with the school for current application deadlines.

International Students: There are 87 international students enrolled. The school actively recruits these students. They must score 550 on the written TOEFL.

Computers: The mainframes are an HP 3000 and an HP 9000. There are also 65 computers in labs and Ethernet for student-owned PCs. All students may access the system. There are no time limits and no fees. It is strongly recommended that all students have a personal computer.

Graduates: From July 1, 2002 to June 30, 2003, 152 bachelor's degrees were awarded. The most popular majors were physician's assistant (16%), business administration (13%), and nursing (11%). In an average class, 23% graduate in 4 years or less, and 40% graduate in 6 years or less. 32 companies recruited on campus in 2002-2003. Of the 2002 graduating class, 13% were enrolled in graduate school within 6 months of graduation and 69% were employed.

Admissions Contact: Buell Fogg, Vice President of Enrollment Services. E-mail: *ucenrol@ucollege.edu* Web: *www.ucollege.edu*

UNIVERSITY OF NEBRASKA SYSTEM

The University of Nebraska System, established in 1869, is a public system. It is governed by a Board of Regents and a central administration, whose chief administrator is the president. The primary mission and priorities of the system are teaching, research, and service. The total enrollment of all campuses is nearly 46,000, with more than 2600 faculty members. Altogether, there are 330 baccalaureate, 160 master's, and 45 doctoral programs offered. There are 4-year campuses located in Kearney, Lincoln, and Omaha. Profiles of these campuses are included in this section.

UNIVERSITY OF NEBRASKA AT KEARNEY
Kearney, NE 68849

D-3

(308) 865-8526
(800) KEARNEY; Fax: (308) 865-8987

Full-time: 2409 men, 2964 women	**Faculty:** 305; IIA, -$
Part-time: 300 men, 440 women	**Ph.D.s:** 74%
Graduate: 608 men, 1198 women	**Student/Faculty:** 18 to 1
Year: semesters, summer session	**Tuition:** $3884 ($7146)
Application Deadline: open	**Room & Board:** $4402
Freshman Class: n/av	
SAT I or ACT: required	**NONCOMPETITIVE**

The University of Nebraska at Kearney, founded in 1903, is a public facility. Some enrollment figures in above capsule are approximate. There are 4 undergraduate schools and 1 graduate school. In addition to regional accreditation, UNK has baccalaureate program accreditation with ADA, CSWE, NASM, NCATE, and NLN. The library contains 287,000 volumes, 985,000 microform items, and 1300 audio/video tapes/CDs, and subscribes to 1650 periodicals. Computerized library services include the card catalog, interlibrary loans, database searching, and Internet access. Special learning facilities include a learning resource center, art gallery, planetarium, radio station, TV station, and writing center. The 235-acre campus is in a small town 180 miles west of Omaha. Including any residence halls, there are 36 buildings.

Student Life: 91% of undergraduates are from Nebraska. Students are from 39 states, 46 foreign countries, and Canada. 93% are white. The average age of freshmen is 19; all undergraduates, 21. 20% do not continue beyond their first year; 47% remain to graduate.

Housing: 2600 students can be accommodated in college housing, which includes single-sex and coed dorms, off-campus apartments, married-student housing, fraternity houses, and sorority houses. In addition, there are honors houses and special-interest houses. On-campus housing is guaranteed for the freshman year only and is available on a first-come, first-served basis. 60% of students commute. Alcohol is not permitted. All students may keep cars.

Activities: 11% of men belong to 16 national fraternities; 10% of women belong to 4 national sororities. There are 160 groups on campus, including art, band, cheerleading, choir, chorale, chorus, computers, dance, debate, drama, drill team, ethnic, forensics, gay, honors, international, jazz band, marching band, musical theater, newspaper, opera, orchestra, pep band, photography, political, professional, radio and TV, religious, social, social service, student government, symphony, and yearbook. Popular campus events include Welcome Week, Bike Bowl, and the Midwest Conference on World Affairs.

Sports: There are 8 intercollegiate sports for men and 8 for women, and 14 intramural sports for men and 14 for women. Facilities include a field, tennis courts, and a health and sports facility.

Disabled Students: Wheelchair ramps, elevators, special parking, specially equipped rest rooms, and lowered drinking fountains are available.

Services: Counseling and information services are available, as is tutoring in most subjects. There is a reader service for the blind and remedial math, reading, and writing.

Campus Safety and Security: Measures include 24-hour foot and vehicle patrol, security escort services, informal discussions, and pamphlets/posters/films. There are also emergency telephones and lighted pathways/sidewalks.

Programs of Study: UNK confers B.A., B.S., B.A.Ed., B.F.A., B.G.S., and B.S.Ed. degrees. Master's degrees are also awarded. Bachelor's degrees are awarded in BIOLOGICAL SCIENCE (biology/biological science), BUSINESS (accounting, banking and finance, business administration and management, business economics, marketing/retailing/merchandising, personnel management, and tourism), COMMUNICATIONS AND THE ARTS (advertising, broadcasting, communications, dramatic arts, English, fine arts, French, German, journalism, music, Spanish, speech/debate/rhetoric, and telecommunications), COMPUTER AND PHYSICAL SCIENCE (chemistry, computer programming, computer science, information sciences and systems, mathematics, physics, and statistics), EDUCATION (art, business, early childhood, elementary, foreign languages, health, middle school, music, physical, science, secondary, special, and teaching English as a second/foreign language (TESOL/TEFOL)), HEALTH PROFESSIONS (nursing, predentistry, and premedicine), SOCIAL SCIENCE (criminal justice,

economics, family/consumer studies, geography, history, human development, international studies, political science/government, prelaw, psychology, social science, social work, and sociology). Business, communication, and psychology are the strongest academically. Business administration, elementary education, and special education are the largest.

Required: To graduate, all students must complete courses in humanities, communications, civilization, math, natural sciences, and social and behavioral sciences. A minimum of 125 credit hours is required, with approximately 60 in the major. Students must maintain a GPA of 2.0 or higher.

Special: Special arrangements include internships, work-study programs, study at other U.S. colleges and universities under the auspices of the National Student Exchange Program, and study abroad in more than 40 countries through the International Student Exchange Program. Cooperative programs in some health science majors, an international studies degree, and a credit/no credit grading option are available. There is a chapter of Phi Beta Kappa and a freshman honors program.

Faculty/Classroom: 66% of faculty are male; 34%, female. 99% teach undergraduates. The average class size in an introductory lecture is 32; in a laboratory, 25; and in a regular course, 20.

Requirements: The SAT I or ACT is required. In addition, applicants must be graduates of an accredited secondary school. The GED is accepted. They should have completed 4 years of high school English, 3 years each of math, science, and social studies, 2 years of the same foreign language, and 1 year of an academic elective. They should score 20 or above on the ACT or 950 on the SAT I, or be in the top half of their graduating class. UNK requires applicants to be in the upper 50% of their class. AP and CLEP credits are accepted. Important factors in the admissions decision are recommendations by school officials, evidence of special talent, and advanced placement or honor courses.

Procedure: Freshmen are admitted fall, spring, and summer. Entrance exams should be taken at the end of the junior year or beginning of the senior year. Application deadlines are open. Application fee is $45. Applications are accepted on-line through *www.unk.edu*. Notification is sent on a rolling basis.

Transfer: Transfer students must supply transcripts from previous institutions. If the GPA from the previous school is lower than 2.0, students will be evaluated by the Admissions Director. Transfers must show proof of honorable dismissal from the last institution attended. Grades of C and above transfer for credit. 45 of 125 credits required for the bachelor's degree must be completed at UNK.

Visiting: There are regularly scheduled orientations for prospective students, including registration for classes and campus orientation. There are guides for informal visits and visitors may sit in on classes and stay overnight. To schedule a visit, contact the Admissions Office.

Financial Aid: 80% of undergraduates work part time. The FAFSA and the college's own financial statement are required. Check with the school for current deadlines.

International Students: There are 295 international students enrolled. The school actively recruits these students. They must score 500 on the written TOEFL or 173 on the electronic version. Submitting ACT scores is recommended.

Computers: The mainframe is an Alpha 1000A. There are 700 Macs and PCs available. All students may access the system. There are no time limits. It is strongly recommended that all students have a personal computer.

Graduates: From July 1, 2002 to June 30, 2003, 1058 bachelor's degrees were awarded.

Admissions Contact: John Kundel, Director of Admissions. E-mail: *admissionsug@unk.edu* Web: *www.unk.edu*

UNIVERSITY OF NEBRASKA AT LINCOLN
Lincoln, NE 68588-0417

E-3

(402) 472-2023
(800) 742-8800; Fax: (402) 472-0670

Full-time: 8456 men, 7763 women	**Faculty:** I, av$
Part-time: 915 men, 717 women	**Ph.D.s:** 93%
Graduate: 2287 men, 2421 women	**Student/Faculty:** n/av
Year: semesters, summer session	**Tuition:** $4771 ($12,353)
Application Deadline: June 30	**Room & Board:** $5204
Freshman Class: 7375 applied, 5586 accepted, 3679 enrolled	
SAT I Verbal/Math: 583/596	**ACT:** 24 **COMPETITIVE+**

University of Nebraska-Lincoln, part of the University of Nebraska system, was founded in 1869 as a land-grant facility. There are 8 undergraduate schools and 1 graduate school. In addition to regional accreditation, UNL has baccalaureate program accreditation with ABET, ACCE, ACEJMC, ADA, FIDER, and NCATE. The 12 libraries contain 2,404,351 volumes, 117,588 microform items, and 33,675 audio/video tapes/CDs, and subscribe to 30,659 periodicals. Computerized library services include the card catalog, interlibrary loans, and database searching. Special learning facilities include a learning resource center, art gallery, natural history museum, planetarium, radio station, TV station, a center for mass spectrometry, an observatory, the Buros Institute of Mental Measurements, an animal sciences complex, and a center for performing arts. The 628-acre campus is in an urban area 55 miles southwest of Omaha. Including any residence halls, there are 238 buildings.

Student Life: 85% of undergraduates are from Nebraska. Students are from 50 states, 113 foreign countries, and Canada. 89% are from public schools. 85% are white. The average age of freshmen is 18; all undergraduates, 21. 20% do not continue beyond their first year; 59% remain to graduate.

Housing: 5561 students can be accommodated in college housing, which includes single-sex and coed dorms, on-campus apartments, off-campus apartments, married-student housing, fraternity houses, and sorority houses. In addition, there are honors houses, language houses, special-interest houses, floors for modern languages, scholars, engineering, business, and journalism, and an International House. On-campus housing is guaranteed for the freshman year only and is available on a first-come, first-served basis. 74% of students commute. Alcohol is not permitted. All students may keep cars.

Activities: 15% of men belong to 1 local and 20 national fraternities; 18% of women belong to 14 national sororities. There are 335 groups on campus, including art, band, cheerleading, chess, choir, chorale, chorus, computers, dance, debate, drama, ethnic, film, forensics, gay, honors, international, jazz band, literary magazine, marching band, musical theater, newspaper, opera, orchestra, pep band, photography, political, professional, radio and TV, religious, social, social service, student government, symphony, and yearbook. Popular campus events include Cornstock, Parents Weekend, and Freshmen Friday.

Sports: There are 9 intercollegiate sports for men and 12 for women, and 65 intramural sports for men and 45 for women. Facilities include a recreation center and 34 acres of outdoor recreational space.

Disabled Students: 80% of the campus is accessible. Wheelchair ramps, elevators, special parking, specially equipped rest rooms, special class scheduling, lowered drinking fountains, lowered telephones, and assistance from the Office of Handicapped Services are available.

Services: Counseling and information services are available, as is tutoring in most subjects. There is a reader service for the blind.

Campus Safety and Security: Measures include 24-hour foot and vehicle patrol, self-defense education, security escort services, and shuttle buses. There are informal discussions, pamphlets/posters/films, emergency telephones, and lighted pathways/sidewalks.

Programs of Study: UNL confers B.A., B.S., B.A.Ed., B.B.A., B.F.A., B.F.A.Ed., B.J., B.M., B.M.Ed., B.S.A.E., B.S.Agr., B.S.Arch., B.S.B.A., B.S.B.S.E., B.S.C., B.S.C.E., B.S.C.M., B.S.C.S., B.S.Ch.E., B.S.E.E., B.S.E.T., B.S.Ed., B.S.H.E., B.S.H.R.E.S., B.S.I.C.E., B.S.I.E., B.S.I.T., B.S.M.E., and B.S.N.R. degrees. Associate, master's, and doctoral degrees are also awarded. Bachelor's degrees are awarded in AGRICULTURE (agricultural business management, agricultural economics, agricultural mechanics, agriculture, agronomy, animal science, environmental studies, fish and game management, horticulture, natural resource management, plant protection (pest management), range/farm management, and soil science), BIOLOGICAL SCIENCE (biochemistry and biology/biological science), BUSINESS (accounting, banking and finance, business administration and management, business economics, international business management, management science, and marketing/retailing/merchandising), COMMUNICATIONS AND THE ARTS (advertising, art, art history and appreciation, broadcasting, classics, communications, dance, design, dramatic arts, English, English as a second/foreign language, film arts, fine arts, French, German, Greek, journalism, languages, Latin, music, Russian, Spanish, and speech/debate/rhetoric), COMPUTER AND PHYSICAL SCIENCE (actuarial science, atmospheric sciences and meteorology, chemistry, computer science, geology, mathematics, and physics), EDUCATION (agricultural, art, athletic training, business, early childhood, education, elementary, foreign languages, guidance, health, home economics, industrial arts, middle school, music, science, secondary, and special), ENGINEERING AND ENVIRONMENTAL DESIGN (agricultural engineering, architectural engineering, architecture, bioengineering, chemical engineering, civil engineering, computer engineering, construction management, construction technology, drafting and design technology, electrical/electronics engineering, electrical/electronics engineering technology, environmental science, fire protection engineering, industrial engineering, industrial engineering technology, manufacturing technology, and mechanical engineering), HEALTH PROFESSIONS (dental hygiene, exercise science, medical laboratory technology, predentistry, premedicine, prepharmacy, public health, speech pathology/audiology, and veterinary science), SOCIAL SCIENCE (anthropology, dietetics, economics, family/consumer studies, food science, geography, history, human development, international relations, Latin American studies, law, medieval studies, parks and recreation management, philosophy, political science/government, psychology, sociology, textiles and clothing, water resources, Western European studies, and women's studies). Biochemistry, engineering, and journalism are the strongest academically. Psychology, business administration, and education are the largest.

Required: Distribution requirements include 9 courses across 8 areas of essential studies and 10 courses from the integrative studies area. A minimum GPA of 2.0 is required. Each college and major has its own requirements; there are few graduation requirements that apply to all students.

Special: There is cross-registration with many schools, and co-op programs are available in the Colleges of Engineering and Technology and Agriculture. Through membership in the International Student Exchange Program, the university can place students in more than 90 universities around the world. Internship opportunities abound, as do work-study programs. Accelerated degree programs, a Washington semester, B.A.-B.S. degrees, dual majors, combined pre-professional programs, student-designed majors, credit by exam, nondegree study, and pass/fail options are also available. There are 51 national honor societies, including Phi Beta Kappa, a freshman honors program, and 18 departmental honors programs.

Faculty/Classroom: 75% of faculty are male; 25%, female. Graduate students teach 30% of introductory courses. The average class size in an introductory lecture is 43; in a laboratory, 16; and in a regular course, 29.

Admissions: 76% of the 2003-2004 applicants were accepted. The SAT I scores for the 2003-2004 freshman class were: Verbal--18% below 500, 38% between 500 and 599, 31% between 600 and 700, and 13% above 700; Math--16% below 500, 33% between 500 and 599, 35% between 600 and 700, and 16% above 700. The ACT scores were 19% below 21, 44% between 21 and 25, 25% between 26 and 29, and 13% above 30. 43% of the current freshmen were in the top fifth of their class; 71% were in the top two fifths. There were 29 National Merit finalists and 122 semifinalists.

Requirements: The SAT I or ACT is recommended. In addition, applicants must be graduates of an accredited secondary school. The GED is accepted. Students must have completed 3 years of English, 2 years each of math, science, and social studies, and an additional year of language arts. UNL requires applicants to be in the upper 50% of their class. AP and CLEP credits are accepted. Important factors in the admissions decision are advanced placement or honor courses, recommendations by school officials, and evidence of special talent.

Procedure: Freshmen are admitted to all sessions. Entrance exams should be taken in April of the junior year. There is a rolling admissions plan. Applications should be filed by June 30 for fall entry and December 15 for spring entry, along with a $25 fee. Notification is sent on a rolling basis. Applications are accepted on-line.

Transfer: 803 transfer students enrolled in 2002-2003. Transfer students must have a 2.0 GPA for both the cumulative average of all postsecondary facilities attended and for the most recent term of attendance. In certain majors, a higher GPA and/or extra course work may be required. 30 credits required for the bachelor's degree must be completed at UNL.

Visiting: There are regularly scheduled orientations for prospective students, including an information session, a campus tour, a visit to areas of academic interest, and a meeting with a department representative. There are guides for informal visits and visitors may sit in on classes and stay overnight. To schedule a visit, contact High School and College Relations at (402) 472-4887.

Financial Aid: In 2003-2004, 77% of all full-time freshmen and 67% of continuing full-time students received some form of financial aid. 42% of full-time freshmen and 38% of continuing full-time students received need-based aid. The average freshman award was $6184. Need-based scholarships or need-based grants averaged $3716; need-based self-help aid (loans and jobs) averaged $2869; non-need-based athletic scholarships averaged $4153; and other non-need-based awards and non-need-based- scholarships averaged $2849. All undergraduates work part time. Average annual earnings from campus work are $1200. The average financial indebtedness of the 2003 graduate was $15,682. The FAFSA is required. The deadline for filing freshman financial aid applications for fall entry is March 1.

International Students: There are 417 international students enrolled. The school actively recruits these students. They must score 500 on the written TOEFL.

Computers: The mainframes are an IBM RS/6000/F50, several DEC Alpha server 2100s, and a cluster of Sun Systems. There are 500 PCs in public facilities located throughout both city and east campuses. Colleges and departments have additional facilities for their own students. PC facilities are in all residence complexes. All facilities are part of the campus network. All students may access the system 24 hours a day, 7 days per week. There are no time limits and no fees. It is recommended that students in architecture and community and regional planning have personal computers.

Graduates: From July 1, 2002 to June 30, 2003, 2980 bachelor's degrees were awarded. The most popular majors were business/marketing (21%), engineering/engineering technologies (13%), and communications/communications technologies (9%). In an average class, 22% graduate in 4 years or less, 54% graduate in 5 years or less, and 59% graduate in 6 years or less. 261 companies recruited on campus in 2002-2003.

Admissions Contact: Alan Cervaney, Dean of Admissions.
E-mail: *nuhusker@unl.edu* Web: *http://www.unl.edu*

UNIVERSITY OF NEBRASKA AT OMAHA
F-3
Omaha, NE 68182
(402) 554-2393
(800) 858-8648; Fax: (402) 554-3472

Full-time: 3765 men, 4355 women	**Faculty:** 492; IIA, av$
Part-time: 1458 men, 1524 women	**Ph.D.s:** 81%
Graduate: 1114 men, 1781 women	**Student/Faculty:** 17 to 1
Year: semesters, summer session	**Tuition:** $4082 ($10,932)
Application Deadline: August 1	**Room & Board:** $3998
Freshman Class: 3994 applied, 3383 accepted, 1543 enrolled	
ACT: 23	**COMPETITIVE**

The University of Nebraska at Omaha, established in 1908, is a public institution and part of the University of Nebraska system. There are 9 undergraduate schools and 1 graduate school. In addition to regional accreditation, UNOmaha has baccalaureate program accreditation with AACSB, AHEA, CSWE, and NCATE. The library contains 750,000 volumes, 2 million microform items, and 7000 audio/video tapes/CDs, and subscribes to 3000 periodicals. Computerized library services include the card catalog, interlibrary loans, and database searching. Special learning facilities include an art gallery, radio station, and TV station. The 158-acre campus is in a suburban area within the Omaha city limits. Including any residence halls, there are 36 buildings.

Student Life: 89% of undergraduates are from Nebraska. Students are from 47 states, 71 foreign countries, and Canada. 84% are from public schools. 82% are white. The average age of freshmen is 20; all undergraduates, 23. 32% do not continue beyond their first year; 47% remain to graduate.

Housing: 1212 students can be accommodated in college housing, which includes single-sex and coed dorms and on-campus apartments. In addition, there are honors houses. On-campus housing is available on a first-come, first-served basis. 90% of students commute. Alcohol is not permitted. All students may keep cars.

Activities: 7% of men belong to 7 national fraternities; 4% of women belong to 8 national sororities. There are 126 groups on campus, including band, cheerleading, choir, chorale, chorus, dance, drama, drill team, ethnic, gay, honors, international, jazz band, marching band, newspaper, pep band, political, professional, radio and TV, religious, social, social service, and student government. Popular campus events include Celebrate UNO, International Week, and Black History Month.

Sports: There are 5 intercollegiate sports for men and 8 for women, and 16 intramural sports for men and 16 for women. Facilities include a football field, a field house, and a recreation building housing basketball and volleyball courts, weight rooms, and a swimming pool.

Disabled Students: All of the campus is accessible. Wheelchair ramps, elevators, special parking, specially equipped rest rooms, special class scheduling, lowered drinking fountains, and lowered telephones are available.

Services: Counseling and information services are available, as is tutoring in some subjects, including math and psychology. There is a reader service for the blind, and remedial math, reading, and writing.

Campus Safety and Security: Measures include 24-hour foot and vehicle patrol, self-defense education, security escort services, and shuttle buses. There are emergency telephones and lighted pathways/sidewalks.

Programs of Study: Master's and doctoral degrees are also awarded. Bachelor's degrees are awarded in BIOLOGICAL SCIENCE (biology/biological science), BUSINESS (accounting, banking and finance, business administration and management, management information systems, management science, and marketing/retailing/merchandising), COMMUNICATIONS AND THE ARTS (broadcasting, communications, dramatic arts, English, fine arts, French, German, journalism, music, Spanish, and speech/debate/rhetoric), COMPUTER AND PHYSICAL SCIENCE (chemistry, computer science, geology, mathematics, and physics), EDUCATION (elementary, physical, and secondary), ENGINEERING AND ENVIRONMENTAL DESIGN (engineering physics), SOCIAL SCIENCE (criminal justice, economics, geography, history, interdisciplinary studies, philosophy, political science/government, psychology, public administration, social work, and sociology). Elementary education, secondary education, and computer science are the largest.

Required: To graduate, students must complete 30 hours of distribution requirements in natural and physical sciences, humanities and fine arts, and social and behavioral sciences; 15 hours in fundamental academic skills in English writing, math, and public speaking; and 6 hours in cultural diversity.

Special: UNOmaha offers internships for business students, cooperative programs, and credit by examination. Students may study abroad in various European countries. There is a freshman honors program.

Faculty/Classroom: In 2002, 58% of faculty were male; 42%, female. 97% teach undergraduates. Graduate students teach 4% of introductory courses. The average class size in an introductory lecture is 37; in a laboratory, 13; and in a regular course, 22.

Admissions: 85% of the 2003-2004 applicants were accepted. The ACT scores for the 2003-2004 freshman class were: 31% below 21, 27% between 21 and 23, 24% between 24 and 26, 10% between 27 and 28, and 8% above 28. 29% of the current freshmen were in the top fifth of their class; 59% were in the top two fifths. 24 freshmen graduated in the top 1% of their class.

Requirements: The SAT I or ACT is required. In addition, students must be graduates of an accredited secondary school. The GED is accepted. Students must have completed 4 units of English and 2 each of math, social sciences, and sciences. UNOmaha requires applicants to be in the upper 50% of their class. A GPA of 2.0 is required. AP and CLEP credits are accepted. Important factors in the admissions decision are recommendations by school officials, evidence of special talent, and personality/intangible qualities.

Procedure: Freshmen are admitted fall, spring, and summer. Entrance exams should be taken by the senior year. There is a rolling admissions plan. Applications should be filed by August 1 for fall entry, December 1 for spring entry, and June 1 for summer entry, along with a $40 fee. Notification is sent on a rolling basis. Applications are accepted on-line.

Transfer: 1155 transfer students enrolled in 2002-2003. Applicants must present evidence of good standing at the last institution they attended. Grades of C or better transfer for credit. A minimum GPA of 2.0 is required. 30 of 125 credits required for the bachelor's degree must be completed at UNOmaha.

Visiting: There are regularly scheduled orientations for prospective students. There are guides for informal visits and visitors may sit in on classes. To schedule a visit, contact the Admissions Office or Office of Orientation at (402) 554-2677.

Financial Aid: In 2003-2004, 44% of all full-time freshmen and 45% of continuing full-time students received some form of financial aid. 42% of full-time freshmen and 43% of continuing full-time students received need-based aid. The average freshman award was $4900. 4% of undergraduates work part time. Average annual earnings from campus work are $2500. The average financial indebtedness of the 2003 graduate was $16,900. The FAFSA is required. The deadline for filing freshman financial aid applications for fall entry is March 1.

International Students: There are 192 international students enrolled. The school actively recruits these students. They must score 500 on the written TOEFL or 173 on the electronic version and also take the SAT I or the ACT.

Computers: The mainframe is a DEC VAX 8650. There are also PCs available in 16 student user rooms. All students may access the system at any time. There are no time limits and no fees.

Graduates: From July 1, 2002 to June 30, 2003, 1525 bachelor's degrees were awarded. The most popular majors were elementry education (10%), criminal justice (9%), and marketing management (7%). In an average class, 8% graduate in 4 years or less, 27% graduate in 5 years or less, and 36% graduate in 6 years or less.

Admissions Contact: Jolene Adams, Associate Director of Admissions. E-mail: *unoadm@unomaha.edu* Web: *www.unomaha.edu*

WAYNE STATE COLLEGE
E-2
Wayne, NE 68787
(402) 375-7000
(800) 228-9972; Fax: (402) 375-7204

Full-time: 1135 men, 1430 women	**Faculty:** 126; IIA, --$
Part-time: 71 men, 133 women	**Ph.D.s:** 80%
Graduate: 161 men, 387 women	**Student/Faculty:** 20 to 1
Year: semesters, summer session	**Tuition:** $3432 ($6042)
Application Deadline: open	**Room & Board:** $3920
Freshman Class: 1321 applied, 1321 accepted, 610 enrolled	
ACT: 21	**NONCOMPETITIVE**

Wayne State College, founded in 1910, is a public liberal arts facility. There are 4 undergraduate and 2 graduate schools. In addition to regional accreditation, Wayne State has baccalaureate program accreditation with NCATE. The library contains 225,308 volumes, 660,271 microform items, and 9622 audio/video tapes/CDs, and subscribes to 466 periodicals. Computerized library services include the card catalog, interlibrary loans, database searching, and Internet access. Special learning facilities include a learning resource center, art gallery, natural history museum, planetarium, radio station, TV station, and an arboretum. The 128-acre campus is in a rural area 45 miles southwest of Sioux City, Iowa. Including any residence halls, there are 25 buildings.

Student Life: 85% of undergraduates are from Nebraska. Students are from 23 states and 19 foreign countries. 90% are from public schools. 92% are white. 49% are Protestant; 31% Catholic; 18% claim no religious affiliation. The average age of freshmen is 18; all undergraduates, 21. 30% do not continue beyond their first year; 44% remain to graduate.

Housing: 1587 students can be accommodated in college housing, which includes single-sex and coed dorms. On-campus housing is guaranteed for the freshman year only and is available on a first-come, first-served basis. 56% of students commute. Alcohol is not permitted. All students may keep cars.

Activities: There are 2 national fraternities and 2 local sororities and 1 national sorority. There are 87 groups on campus, including art, band, cheerleading, choir, chorale, chorus, computers, dance, drama, drill team, ethnic, forensics, gay, honors, international, jazz band, literary magazine, marching band, musical theater, orchestra, pep band, political, professional, radio and TV, religious, social, student government, symphony, and yearbook. Popular campus events include International Dinner, Elizabethan Dinners, and Greek Olympics.

Sports: There are 6 intercollegiate sports for men and 7 for women, and 40 intramural sports for men and 38 for women. Facilities include tennis courts, softball, flag football, and soccer fields, a gym, a 33,000-square-foot recreation center, which has an indoor track, weight room, pool, and handball, volleyball, basketball, and tennis courts, a football stadium, an outdoor track, and a baseball/softball complex.

Disabled Students: 90% of the campus is accessible. Wheelchair ramps, elevators, special parking, specially equipped rest rooms, special class scheduling, lowered drinking fountains, lowered telephones, and special housing are available. The school's pool is equipped with special steps.

Services: Counseling and information services are available, as is tutoring in most subjects. There is a reader service for the blind.

Campus Safety and Security: Measures include 24-hour foot and vehicle patrol, self-defense education, security escort services, and shuttle buses. There are pamphlets/posters/films, emergency telephones, and lighted pathways/sidewalks. In addition, there are articles in the campus newspaper relating to safety and security.

Programs of Study: Wayne State confers B.A. and B.S. degrees. Master's degrees are also awarded. Bachelor's degrees are awarded in BIOLOGICAL SCIENCE (biology/biological science and life science), BUSINESS (business administration and management and sports management), COMMUNICATIONS AND THE ARTS (art, communications, dramatic arts, English, graphic design, modern language, music, Spanish, and speech/debate/rhetoric), COMPUTER AND PHYSICAL SCIENCE (chemistry, computer science, and mathematics), EDUCATION (elementary, foreign languages, health, home economics, industrial arts, music, science, and special), ENGINEERING AND ENVIRONMENTAL DESIGN (technological management), SOCIAL SCIENCE (counseling/psychology, criminal justice, early childhood studies, family/consumer studies, food production/management/services, geography, history, interdisciplinary studies, parks and recreation management, political science/government, psychology, social science, and sociology). Business, education, and social sciences are the largest.

Required: Students must complete a specified 46-credit general education curriculum. A minimum of 125 credit hours is required for graduation, with 30 to 66 in the major and 40 in upper-division courses. Students must maintain at least a 2.0 GPA.

Special: There are co-op programs and cross-registration with Northeast Community College. Also offered are pass/fail options, internships, credit by exam, any combination of dual majors, a B.A.-B.S. degree in certain instances, and some student-designed majors. There is also a Regional Health Opportunities Program. There are 12 national honor societies, a freshman honors program, and 5 departmental honors programs.

Faculty/Classroom: 54% of faculty are male; 46%, female. All teach undergraduates. Graduate students teach 5% of introductory courses. The average class size in an introductory lecture is 26 and in a laboratory, 19.

Admissions: 100% of the 2003-2004 applicants were accepted. The ACT scores for the 2003-2004 freshman class were: 49% below 21, 22% between 21 and 23, 20% between 24 and 26, 6% between 27 and 28, and 3% above 28. 20% of the current freshmen were in the top fifth of their class; 48% were in the top two fifths. 21 freshmen graduated first in their class.

Requirements: Applicants must be graduates of an accredited secondary school. The GED is accepted. Entering freshmen must have completed 16 credits, with a recommended 4 units of English, 3 each of math and social studies, and 2 of science. Additional units in foreign language, fine and performing arts, and computer literacy are recommended. AP and CLEP credits are accepted.

Procedure: Freshmen are admitted to all sessions. Entrance exams should be taken in the spring of the junior year or fall of the senior year. There is a deferred admissions plan and a rolling admissions plan. Application deadlines are open. Application fee is $30. Applications are accepted on-line.

Transfer: 217 transfer students enrolled in 2002-2003. Transfer students must have a minimum GPA of 2.0. Grades of C and above transfer for credit. 40 of 125 credits required for the bachelor's degree must be completed at Wayne State.

Visiting: There are guides for informal visits and visitors may sit in on classes and stay overnight. To schedule a visit, contact the Admissions Office at (402) 375-7234.

Financial Aid: In 2003-2004, 77% of all full-time freshmen and 79% of continuing full-time students received some form of financial aid. 59% of all full-time students received need-based aid. The average freshman award was $3470. Need-based scholarships or need-based grants averaged $1385; and need-based self-help aid (loans and jobs) averaged $1530. Wayne State is a member of CSS. The FAFSA and the college's own financial statement are required. The priority date for freshman financial aid applications for fall entry is May 1. The deadline for filing freshman financial aid applications for fall entry is open.

International Students: There are 22 international students enrolled. They must score 550 on the written TOEFL or 213 on the electronic version.

Computers: There are networked computer labs in the library and the education, business, applied science, and math/science buildings. Dorms are wired for network access. All students may access the system any time. There are no time limits and no fees.

Graduates: From July 1, 2002 to June 30, 2003, 513 bachelor's degrees were awarded. The most popular majors were business (21%), elementary education (12%), and human service counseling (6%). In an average class, 21% graduate in 4 years or less, 40% graduate in 5 years or less, and 44% graduate in 6 years or less. 105 companies recruited on campus in 2002-2003.

Admissions Contact: R. Lincoln Morris, Director of Admissions. E-mail: *admit1@wsc.edu* Web: *www.wsc.edu*

YORK COLLEGE
E-3
York, NE 68467-2699

(402) 363-5608
(800) 950-YORK (9675); Fax: (402) 363-5623

Full-time: 214 men, 218 women	**Faculty:** 33
Part-time: 9 men, 20 women	**Ph.Ds:** 33%
Graduate: none	**Student/Faculty:** 13 to 1
Year: semesters, summer session	**Tuition:** $11,400
Application Deadline: open	**Room & Board:** $3575
Freshman Class: 203 applied, 193 accepted, 112 enrolled	
SAT I Verbal/Math: 509/521	**ACT:** 22	**COMPETITIVE**

York College, founded in 1890, is an independent undergraduate college affiliated with the Churches of Christ. There are 6 undergraduate schools. The library contains 55,062 volumes, 21,074 microform items, and 6169 audio/video tapes/CDs, and subscribes to 344 periodicals. Computerized library services include the card catalog, interlibrary loans, and database searching. The 40-acre campus is in a small town 45 miles west of Lincoln. Including any residence halls, there are 18 buildings.

Student Life: 71% of undergraduates are from out of state, mostly the Midwest. Students are from 30 states, 16 foreign countries, and Canada. 90% are from public schools. 90% are white. 95% are Protestant; 8% claim no religious affiliation. The average age of freshmen is 19; all undergraduates, 20. 15% do not continue beyond their first year; 45% remain to graduate.

Housing: 472 students can be accommodated in college housing, which includes single-sex dorms and on-campus apartments. On-campus housing is guaranteed for all 4 years. 62% of students live on campus; of those, 85% remain on campus on weekends. Alcohol is not permitted. All students may keep cars.

Activities: 54% of men belong to 4 local fraternities; 62% of women belong to 4 local sororities. There are 25 groups on campus, including art, choir, chorus, computers, drama, honors, international, literary magazine, musical theater, newspaper, pep band, photography, political, professional, religious, social, social service, student government, and yearbook. Popular campus events include High School Days, Fall Musical, and All School Banquet.

Sports: There are 6 intercollegiate sports for men and 6 for women, and 6 intramural sports for men and 6 for women. Facilities include basketball and volleyball courts, a gym, soccer, baseball, and intramural fields, a weight room, and an indoor track.

Disabled Students: 50% of the campus is accessible. Wheelchair ramps, elevators, special parking, specially equipped rest rooms, lowered drinking fountains, and lowered telephones are available.

Services: Counseling and information services are available, as is tutoring in most subjects. There is remedial math, reading, and writing. There is a peer tutoring program.

Campus Safety and Security: Measures include self-defense education, pamphlets/posters/films, emergency telephones, lighted pathways/sidewalks, and an evening/night foot patrol.

Programs of Study: York confers B.A., B.S., B.B.A., and B.Mus. degrees. Associate degrees are also awarded. Bachelor's degrees are awarded in BIOLOGICAL SCIENCE (biology/biological science), BUSINESS (accounting, business administration and management, and human resources), COMMUNICATIONS AND THE ARTS (communications, English, music, and music performance), COMPUTER AND PHYSICAL SCIENCE (natural sciences), EDUCATION (education and music), SOCIAL SCIENCE (biblical studies, history, human services, liberal arts/general studies, and psychology). Education, natural science, and psychology are the strongest academically. Education and business are the largest.

Required: To graduate, students must complete a minimum of 128 credits with a 2.0 GPA. Course work includes a general education requirement of 18 hours of humanities, 16 of Bible, 12 of social science, 10 of science, and 3 of math or computer science. The major requirements vary according to concentration; typically, 40 hours or more are required. Some majors and minors require a 2.5 GPA.

Special: Summer internships are required in biblical studies, and work-study is available on campus. Honors and independent study are available as adjuncts to a normal course load. There are 2 national honor societies, a freshman honors program, and 2 departmental honors programs.

Faculty/Classroom: 72% of faculty are male; 28%, female. All teach undergraduates. The average class size in an introductory lecture is 30; in a laboratory, 20; and in a regular course, 25.

Admissions: 95% of the 2003-2004 applicants were accepted. The SAT I scores for the 2003-2004 freshman class were: Verbal--42% below 500, 48% between 500 and 599, 5% between 600 and 700, and 5% above 700; Math--26% below 500, 48% between 500 and 599, and 26% between 600 and 700. The ACT scores were 34% below 21, 34% between 21 and 23, 19% between 24 and 26, 6% between 27 and 28, and 7% above 28. 24% of the current freshmen were in the top fifth of their class; 56% were in the top two fifths. 2 freshmen graduated first in their class.

Requirements: The ACT is recommended. In addition, for regular acceptance, students must meet 2 of the following 3 requirements: a 2.0 cumulative GPA; graduate in the top half of their graduating class; score 18 on the ACT or 860 on the SAT I. York requires applicants to be in the upper 50% of their class. A GPA of 2.0 is required. AP and CLEP credits are accepted. Important factors in the admissions decision are ability to finance college education, personality/intangible qualities, and evidence of special talent.

Procedure: Freshmen are admitted to all sessions. Entrance exams should be taken before April. There is a rolling admissions plan. Application deadlines are open. Application fee is $20.

Transfer: 36 transfer students enrolled in 2002-2003. Transcripts of previous work must be submitted as well as 2 personal references. Cumulative college GPA should not be lower than 2.0 if the student is transferring in more than 60 hours. The last 30 of 128 credits required for the bachelor's degree must be completed at York.

Visiting: There are regularly scheduled orientations for prospective students, including financial aid and admissions consultations and a campus tour. There are guides for informal visits and visitors may sit in on classes and stay overnight. To schedule a visit, contact Keri Mathews at (402) 363-5627 or *kmathews@york.edu.*

Financial Aid: In 2003-2004, 92% of all full-time freshmen and 97% of continuing full-time students received some form of financial aid. The average freshman award was $10,564. 92% of undergraduates work part time. Average annual earnings from campus work are $825. The average financial indebtedness of the 2003 graduate was $15,986. The FAFSA is required. The priority date for freshman financial aid applications for fall entry is April 1.

International Students: There are 26 international students enrolled. They must score 500 on the written TOEFL or 173 on the electronic version. They must also take the SAT I or the ACT, scoring 860 on the SAT I or 18 on the ACT.

Computers: The mainframe is a 586 fileserver in Novell NetWare 3.12. 30 PCs are located in a computer lab. An additional 12 PCs are scattered around the library and other academic buildings. All students may access the system 8 A.M. to 10:30 P.M. weekdays and various times on weekends. There are no time limits and no fees.

Graduates: From July 1, 2002 to June 30, 2003, 78 bachelor's degrees were awarded. The most popular majors were education (33%), business (14%), and psychology (10%). In an average class, 17% graduate in 4 years or less, 14% graduate in 5 years or less, and 6% graduate in 6 years or less. Of the 2002 graduating class, 6% were enrolled in graduate school within 6 months of graduation and 90% were employed.

Admissions Contact: Tod Martin, Director of Admissions.
E-mail: *tjmartin@york.edu* Web: *www.york.edu*

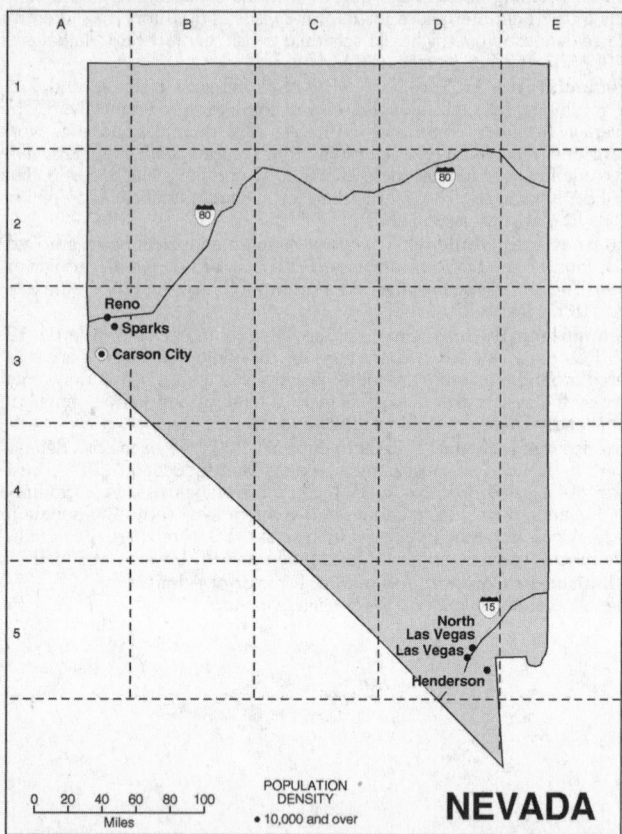

POPULATION DENSITY
● 10,000 and over

0 20 40 60 80 100
Miles

NEVADA

SIERRA NEVADA COLLEGE

Incline Village, NV 89451   A-3

(775) 831-1314
(800) 332-8666; Fax: (775) 831-1347

Full-time: 145 men, 148 women	**Faculty:** 20
Part-time: none	**Ph.D.s:** n/av
Graduate: 59 men, 131 women	**Student/Faculty:** 15 to 1
Year: semesters, summer session	**Tuition:** $18,900
Application Deadline: February 15	**Room & Board:** $7236
Freshman Class: 350 applied, 300 accepted, 67 enrolled	
SAT I Verbal/Math: 524/518	**ACT:** 23	COMPETITIVE

Sierra Nevada College, founded in 1969, is a private institution offering programs in liberal arts, fine arts, business, hotel resort management, ski business management, environmental science, and teacher education. There are 7 undergraduate schools. The library contains 20,000 volumes and 10,000 microform items, and subscribes to 100 periodicals. Computerized library services include interlibrary loans. Special learning facilities include an art gallery, observatory, and recording studio. The 35-acre campus is in a rural area 25 miles west of Reno. Including any residence halls, there are 7 buildings.

Student Life: 70% of undergraduates are from out of state, mostly the West. Students are from 30 states, 8 foreign countries, and Canada. 60% are from public schools. 95% are white. The average age of freshmen is 19; all undergraduates, 22. 20% do not continue beyond their first year; 50% remain to graduate.

Housing: 120 students can be accommodated in college housing, which includes single-sex dorms and on-campus apartments. On-campus housing is guaranteed for all 4 years. 50% of students commute. Alcohol is not permitted. All students may keep cars.

Activities: There are no fraternities or sororities. There are many groups and organizations on campus, including art, choir, chorale, chorus, dance, honors, international, musical theater, newspaper, political, student government, and yearbook. Popular campus events include Bohemia Night, Nevada Day, and a faculty-student softball game.

Sports: There is 1 intercollegiate sport for men and 1 for women, and 2 intramural sports for men and 2 for women. Facilities include nearby ski areas, hiking and mountain biking trails, volleyball and softball areas, community tennis courts and golf courses, and sites for water sports and beach volleyball.

Disabled Students: Wheelchair ramps, specially equipped rest rooms, and special class scheduling are available.

Services: Counseling and information services are available, as is tutoring in most subjects. There is remedial math, reading, and writing.

Campus Safety and Security: Measures include informal discussions.

Programs of Study: SNC confers B.A., B.S., and B.F.A. degrees. Bachelor's degrees are awarded in BUSINESS (business administration and management and recreational facilities management), COMMUNICATIONS AND THE ARTS (fine arts and music), COMPUTER AND PHYSICAL SCIENCE (science), ENGINEERING AND ENVIRONMENTAL DESIGN (environmental science), SOCIAL SCIENCE (humanities). Environmental science/ecology is the strongest academically. Business administration is the largest.

Required: All students must complete at least 120 semester hours, including 40 in upper-division courses with a minimum GPA of 2.0. Students also must pass the writing proficiency exam and meet distribution requirements in 4 interdisciplinary themes: symbols, relationships with nature and humans, memberships in groups and institutions, and ethics, values, and beliefs.

Special: Business administration concentrations are offered in ski business and resort management and in hotel, restaurant, and resort management. Student-designed majors, work-study programs, internships, credit for life experiences and volunteer community work, and nondegree study are available.

Faculty/Classroom: 60% of faculty are male; 40%, female. All teach undergraduates. The average class size in an introductory lecture is 15; in a laboratory, 8; and in a regular course, 15.

Admissions: 86% of the 2003-2004 applicants were accepted.

Requirements: The SAT I or ACT is required. In addition, all applicants are reviewed individually. An essay and 2 letters of recommendation are required, and an interview is recommended. The GED is accepted. A GPA of 2.0 is required. AP and CLEP credits are accepted. Important factors in the admissions decision are ability to finance college education, advanced placement or honor courses, and extracurricular activities record.

Procedure: Freshmen are admitted to all sessions. Entrance exams should be taken in the senior year. There is a deferred admissions plan. Applications should be filed by February 15 for fall entry. Notification is sent on a rolling basis. Applications are accepted on-line.

Transfer: The college accepts applications from students who have completed any course at an accredited postsecondary institution. If fewer than 15 credits have been earned, the high school transcript and standardized test scores are also needed. 96 of 120 credits required for the bachelor's degree must be completed at SNC.

Visiting: There are regularly scheduled orientations for prospective students, consisting of a 2-day campus visit with overnight stay and mandatory class attendance. There are guides for informal visits and visitors may sit in on classes and stay overnight. To schedule a visit, contact the Office of Admissions.

Financial Aid: In 2003-2004, 80% of all full-time students received some form of financial aid, including need-based aid. The average freshman award was $15,000. Need-based scholarships or need-based grants averaged $5000 ($15,000 maximum); need-based self-help aid (loans and jobs) averaged $2000 ($6000 maximum); and other non-need-based awards and non-need-based scholarships averaged $3000 ($10,000 maximum). The FAFSA and the college's own financial statement are required. Check with the school for current deadlines.

International Students: The school actively recruits these students. They must score 500 on the written TOEFL or take any other English proficiency test.

Computers: The mainframe is an IBM. There are computer labs with 25 terminals on campus. The freshman dorm has Internet access. All students may access the system 8 A.M. to 9 P.M. daily. There are no time limits and no fees. It is strongly recommended that all students have a personal computer.

Admissions Contact: Brett Schraeder, Admissions Office.
E-mail: *admissions@sierranevada.edu* Web: *www.sierranevada.edu*

UNIVERSITY AND COMMUNITY COLLEGE SYSTEM OF NEVADA

The University and Community College System of Nevada, established in 1865, is a public system in Nevada. It is governed by a Board of Regents, whose chief administrator is the chancellor. The primary goal of the system is teaching, research, and public service. The main priorities are to provide all public programs of postsecondary instruction in Nevada, to sponsor programs of basic and applied research that contribute to the cultural, economic, and social development of Nevada, and to sponsor programs of public service for citizens of the state. The total enrollment of all 7 campuses usually exceeds 70,000; there were more than 2080 faculty members. Altogether there are 172 baccalaureate, 133 master's, and 65 doctoral programs offered in University and Community College System of Nevada. There is a 4-year campus located in Las Vegas and Reno. Profiles of the 4-year campuses are included in this section.

UNIVERSITY OF NEVADA/LAS VEGAS
Las Vegas, NV 89154-1021   D-5
                                              (702) 774-UNLV
                                           Fax: (702) 774-8008

Full-time: 6295 men, 8080 women	**Faculty:** 676; I, av$
Part-time: 2857 men, 3448 women	**Ph.D.s:** 87%
Graduate: 1833 men, 2617 women	**Student/Faculty:** 21 to 1
Year: semesters; summer session	**Tuition:** $2626 ($11,116)
Application Deadline: April 2	**Room & Board:** $8940
Freshman Class: 6162 applied, 4938 accepted, 2976 enrolled	
SAT I or ACT: required for some programs	**COMPETITIVE**

University of Nevada/Las Vegas, established in 1957, is a state-supported institution offering undergraduate and graduate programs in business, education, health science, engineering, science and math, hotel administration, fine arts, liberal arts, urban affairs, and honors. There are 10 undergraduate schools and 1 graduate school. In addition to regional accreditation, UNLV has baccalaureate program accreditation with AACSB, ABET, CSWE, NASM, NCATE, and NLN. The 4 libraries contain 888,198 volumes, 1,705,020 microform items, and 20,128 audio/video tapes/CDs, and subscribe to 6380 periodicals. Computerized library services include the card catalog and interlibrary loans. Special learning facilities include a learning resource center, art gallery, natural history museum, and radio station. The 335-acre campus is in an urban area. Including any residence halls, there are 60 buildings.

Student Life: 77% of undergraduates are from Nevada. Students are from 49 states, 77 foreign countries, and Canada. 74% are white; 10% Asian American. The average age of freshmen is 18; all undergraduates, 25. 25% do not continue beyond their first year; 74% remain to graduate.

Housing: 1500 students can be accommodated in college housing, which includes single-sex and coed dorms. In addition, there are special-interest houses and substance-free, study-intensive housing. On-campus housing is guaranteed for the freshman year only and is available on a first-come, first-served basis. Priority is given to out-of-town students. 94% of students commute. All students may keep cars.

Activities: 5% of men belong to 15 national fraternities; 5% of women belong to 1 local and 7 national sororities. There are 160 groups on campus, including band, cheerleading, choir, chorus, computers, dance, drama, drill team, ethnic, gay, honors, international, jazz band, marching band, musical theater, newspaper, orchestra, pep band, political, professional, radio and TV, religious, social, student government, and symphony. Popular campus events include Unityfest, Majors Exploration Fair, and Career Day.

Sports: There are 7 intercollegiate sports for men and 8 for women, and 8 intramural sports for men and 8 for women. Facilities include an arena, a football stadium, tennis courts, softball and soccer fields, racquetball courts, a weight room, 2 gyms, and separate athletic/training facilities for intercollegiate athletes.

Disabled Students: All of the campus is accessible. Wheelchair ramps, elevators, special parking, specially equipped rest rooms, special class scheduling, lowered drinking fountains, lowered telephones, and priority class registration are available.

Services: Counseling and information services are available, as is tutoring in every subject. There is a reader service for the blind and remedial math, reading, and writing.

Campus Safety and Security: Measures include 24-hour foot and vehicle patrol, self-defense education, security escort services, and shuttle buses. There are emergency telephones and lighted pathways/sidewalks.

Programs of Study: UNLV confers B.A., B.S., and B.F.A. degrees. Master's and doctoral degrees are also awarded. Bachelor's degrees are awarded in BIOLOGICAL SCIENCE (biology/biological science), BUSINESS (accounting, banking and finance, hotel/motel and restaurant management, human resources, international business management, management information systems, management science, marketing/retailing/merchandising, real estate, and recreational facilities management), COMMUNICATIONS AND THE ARTS (art history and appreciation, communications, dance, dramatic arts, English, film arts, fine arts, French, German, music, romance languages and literature, and Spanish), COMPUTER AND PHYSICAL SCIENCE (applied physics, chemistry, computer science, earth science, geology, mathematics, physics, and radiological technology), EDUCATION (elementary, health, physical, recreation, secondary, special, and trade and industrial), ENGINEERING AND ENVIRONMENTAL DESIGN (architectural engineering, civil engineering, computer engineering, construction management, electrical/electronics engineering, environmental science, interior design, landscape architecture/design, mechanical engineering, and urban planning technology), HEALTH PROFESSIONS (clinical science, exercise sci-

ence, health care administration, nuclear medical technology, nursing, and sports medicine), SOCIAL SCIENCE (anthropology, criminal justice, economics, food production/management/services, history, interdisciplinary studies, philosophy, physical fitness/movement, political science/government, psychology, public administration, social science, social work, sociology, and women's studies). Hotel administration and dance are the strongest academically. Liberal arts and business are the largest.

Required: Students must complete 124 credits, with 45 of these credits in the student's major, and must maintain a minimum GPA of 2.0. All students must meet core requirements that include courses in English, logic and math, the Constitution, social science, fine arts, science, humanities, and international and multicultural diversity.

Special: Opportunities are provided for internships, an accelerated degree program, B.A.-B.S. degrees, dual majors, credit by examination, credit for military service, nondegree study, pass/fail options, and study abroad in 8 countries. There are 16 national honor societies, including Phi Beta Kappa, a freshman honors program, and 11 departmental honors programs.

Faculty/Classroom: 63% of faculty are male; 37%, female. 95% teach undergraduates and 5% do research. The average class size in an introductory lecture is 21 and in a laboratory, 20.

Admissions: 80% of the 2003-2004 applicants were accepted. 47% of the current freshmen were in the top quarter of their class; 83% were in the top half.

Requirements: The SAT I or ACT is required for some programs. In addition, graduation from an accredited secondary school is required. Applicants should submit an academic record distributed as follows: 4 credits in English and 3 each in history, social studies, math, and science. A GPA of 2.5 is required. AP and CLEP credits are accepted. Important factors in the admissions decision are advanced placement or honor courses, recommendations by school officials, and geographic diversity.

Procedure: Freshmen are admitted to all sessions. Entrance exams should be taken by February 1. Applications should be filed by April 2 for fall entry, November 1 for spring entry, and March 1 for summer entry, along with a $40 fee. Notification is sent on a rolling basis. Applications are accepted on-line through the school's web site.

Transfer: Applicants should present a minimum GPA of 2.0. and a minimum of 12 credits for transfer. The SAT I or the ACT is recommended. Applicants must be in good academic standing and eligible to return to the educational institution last attended. 30 of 124 credits required for the bachelor's degree must be completed at UNLV.

Visiting: There are regularly scheduled orientations for prospective students, consisting of a complete introduction to the campus, student services, and parent orientation. There are guides for informal visits and visitors may sit in on classes. To schedule a visit, contact the Admissions Office.

Financial Aid: In 2003-2004, 42% of all full-time freshmen and 60% of continuing full-time students received some form of financial aid. 68% of full-time freshmen and 74% of continuing full-time students received need-based aid. The average freshman award was $5681. Need-based scholarships or need-based grants averaged $2913; and need-based self-help aid (loans and jobs) averaged $4640. 75% of undergraduates work part time. UNLV is a member of CSS. The CSS Profile, FAFSA, FFS, or SFS, the college's own financial statement, and the Singlefile Form are required. Check with the school for current deadlines.

International Students: The school actively recruits these students. They must score 500 on the written TOEFL or take the MELAB, or prove English proficiency by other means.

Computers: The mainframe is a CDC CYBER 830. There are also 100 PCs and Macs available in computer labs. All students may access the system 24 hours a day, 7 days a week. There are no time limits. The fee is $25.

Admissions Contact: Kristi Rodriguez, Assistant Director of Admissions. Web: *http://www.unlv.edu*

UNIVERSITY OF NEVADA/RENO
Reno, NV 89557   A-3
                                              (775) 784-1110
                              (800) 622-4867; Fax: (775) 784-4283

Full-time: 4214 men, 5243 women	**Faculty:** 682; I, av$
Part-time: 1269 men, 1392 women	**Ph.D.s:** 88%
Graduate: 1297 men, 1907 women	**Student/Faculty:** 14 to 1
Year: semesters, summer session	**Tuition:** $2802 ($11,289)
Application Deadline: March 1	**Room & Board:** $6990
Freshman Class: 10,340 applied, 8597 accepted, 5004 enrolled	
SAT I Verbal/Math: 524/531	**ACT:** 22 **COMPETITIVE**

The University of Nevada/Reno, established in 1874, is a land-grant institution and part of the University and Community College System of Nevada. It offers programs in agriculture, arts and science, business administration, education, engineering, human and community sciences, journalism, medicine, and mining, as well as interdisciplinary studies. There are 10 undergraduate schools and 1 graduate school. In addition to regional accreditation, Nevada has baccalaureate program accreditation with AACSB, ABET, ACEJMC, AHEA, CSWE, NASM, NCATE, and

NLN. The 6 libraries contain 1,105,147 volumes, 3,255,565 microform items, and 62,017 audio/video tapes/CDs, and subscribe to 5079 periodicals. Computerized library services include the card catalog, interlibrary loans, database searching, and Internet access. Special learning facilities include a learning resource center, art gallery, planetarium, radio station, TV station, and the Nevada Historical Society Museum. The 200-acre campus is in an urban area 200 miles east of San Francisco. Including any residence halls, there are 86 buildings.

Student Life: 80% of undergraduates are from Nevada. Students are from 49 states, 73 foreign countries, and Canada. 72% are white. The average age of freshmen is 19; all undergraduates, 22. 24% do not continue beyond their first year.

Housing: 1695 students can be accommodated in college housing, which includes single-sex and coed dorms, on-campus apartments, off-campus apartments, and married-student housing. In addition, there are honors houses. On-campus housing is available on a first-come, first-served basis. 89% of students commute. All students may keep cars.

Activities: 7% of men belong to 2 local and 11 national fraternities; 6% of women belong to 4 national sororities. There are 100 groups on campus, including art, band, cheerleading, chess, choir, chorale, chorus, computers, dance, debate, drama, drill team, ethnic, film, gay, honors, international, jazz band, literary magazine, marching band, musical theater, newspaper, orchestra, pep band, photography, political, professional, radio and TV, religious, social, social service, student government, symphony, and yearbook. Popular campus events include Mackay Week and Winter Carnival.

Sports: There are 7 intercollegiate sports for men and 8 for women, and 14 intramural sports for men and 11 for women. Facilities include a recreation center, a 30,000-seat stadium, a 6000-seat gym, a 12,500-seat auditorium, and an 11,600 seat indoor events center.

Disabled Students: 99% of the campus is accessible. Wheelchair ramps, elevators, special parking, specially equipped rest rooms, special class scheduling, lowered drinking fountains, lowered telephones, special housing, and automatic door openers are available.

Services: Counseling and information services are available, as is tutoring in most subjects. There is a reader service for the blind, and remedial math, reading, and writing. Students are mainstreamed with special services for the disabled.

Campus Safety and Security: Measures include 24-hour foot and vehicle patrol, self-defense education, security escort services, and shuttle buses. There are pamphlets/posters/films, emergency telephones, and lighted pathways/sidewalks.

Programs of Study: Nevada confers B.A., B.S., B.A.C.J., B.A.Ed., B.F.A., B.G.S., B.M., B.S.Bus.Ad., B.S.C.E., B.S.Chem.E., B.S.Chem., B.S.C.S., B.S.Ed., B.S.E.E., B.S.E.P., B.S.Geog., B.S.Geol., B.S.Geol.E., B.S.Geophys., B.S.M.E., B.S.Met.E., B.S.Min.E., B.S.Nurs., and B.S.Vet.Sc. degrees. Master's and doctoral degrees are also awarded. Bachelor's degrees are awarded in AGRICULTURE (agricultural economics, animal science, and natural resource management), BIOLOGICAL SCIENCE (biochemistry, biology/biological science, and nutrition), BUSINESS (accounting, banking and finance, business economics, management science, and marketing/retailing/merchandising), COMMUNICATIONS AND THE ARTS (applied music, art, dramatic arts, English, French, German, journalism, music, Spanish, and speech/debate/rhetoric), COMPUTER AND PHYSICAL SCIENCE (chemistry, computer science, geology, geophysics and seismology, hydrology, information sciences and systems, mathematics, and physics), EDUCATION (elementary, music, secondary, and special), ENGINEERING AND ENVIRONMENTAL DESIGN (chemical engineering, civil engineering, electrical/electronics engineering, engineering physics, environmental science, geological engineering, interior design, mechanical engineering, metallurgical engineering, and mining and mineral engineering), HEALTH PROFESSIONS (nursing and speech pathology/audiology), SOCIAL SCIENCE (anthropology, child care/child and family studies, criminal justice, geography, history, human ecology, international relations, liberal arts/general studies, philosophy, political science/government, psychology, social work, and sociology). Psychology, biology, and computer science are the largest.

Required: To graduate, all students must complete 124 to 138 semester credits and earn a GPA of 2.0. The core curriculum includes 9 credits of Western Traditions, 6 each of capstone courses and natural science, 3 to 6 of writing, 3 each of math, social science, and fine arts, and fulfillment of the diversity requirement.

Special: Students may study abroad in 6 countries, pursue internships, and complete dual majors in many subject areas. There is a freshman honors program.

Faculty/Classroom: 59% of faculty are male; 41%, female. All both teach and do research. Graduate students teach 13% of introductory courses. The average class size in an introductory lecture is 36; in a laboratory, 16; and in a regular course, 36.

Admissions: 83% of the 2003-2004 applicants were accepted. The SAT I scores for the 2003-2004 freshman class were: Verbal--37% below 500, 44% between 500 and 599, 18% between 600 and 700, and 2% above 700; Math--34% below 500, 43% between 500 and 599, 20% between 600 and 700, and 2% above 700. The ACT scores were 31% below 21, 30% between 21 and 23, 22% between 24 and 26, 9% between 27 and 28, and 8% above 28.

Requirements: The SAT I or ACT is required, however, test scores are used for placement purposes only. Applicants should have completed 13 1/2 academic credits, including 4 in English, 3 each in math, science, and social studies/history, and a half credit in computer literacy. The GED is not accepted. A GPA of 2.5 is required. AP and CLEP credits are accepted. Important factors in the admissions decision are advanced placement or honor courses, recommendations by school officials, and leadership record.

Procedure: Freshmen are admitted fall and spring. Entrance exams should be taken in October of the senior year. There is a deferred admissions plan and a rolling admissions plan. Applications should be filed by March 1 for fall entry. The college accepts all applicants. The fall 2003 application fee was $60. Notification is sent on a rolling basis.

Transfer: 864 transfer students enrolled in a recent year. Applicants should have a 2.0 GPA and 12 transferable credits. College transcripts are required. 32 of 124 to 138 credits required for the bachelor's degree must be completed at Nevada.

Visiting: There are regularly scheduled orientations for prospective students. There are guides for informal visits and visitors may sit in on classes. To schedule a visit, contact the Office of Outreach Services/the Office for Prospective Students.

Financial Aid: In 2003-2004, 32% of all full-time freshmen and 30% of continuing full-time students received some form of financial aid. At least 14% of full-time freshmen and 21% of continuing full-time students received need-based aid. Need-based scholarships or need-based grants averaged $2908; need-based self-help aid (loans and jobs) averaged $2469; non-need-based athletic scholarships averaged $10,224; and other non-need-based awards and non-need-based scholarships averaged $2735. The average financial indebtedness of the 2003 graduate was $15,548. The FAFSA is required.

International Students: There are 310 international students enrolled. The school actively recruits these students. They must score 500 on the written TOEFL. The SAT I or ACT may also be submitted, with a score of 420 on the verbal portion of the SAT I or 21 on the English section of the ACT.

Computers: The mainframe is a multiple UNIX-based platforms. There are various computer labs within each college designed for local area networks, as well as for networking with the mainframe. All students may access the system. There are no time limits. The fee varies per class laboratory session.

Graduates: From July 1, 2002 to June 30, 2003, 1619 bachelor's degrees were awarded. The most popular majors were biology (6%), elementary education (6%), and general studies (6%). In an average class, 15% graduate in 4 years or less, 39% graduate in 5 years or less, and 39% graduate in 6 years or less.

Admissions Contact: Dr. Melisa N. Choroszy, Assistant Vice President, Records/Enrollment Services. E-mail: *asknevada@unr.edu* Web: *www.unr.edu*

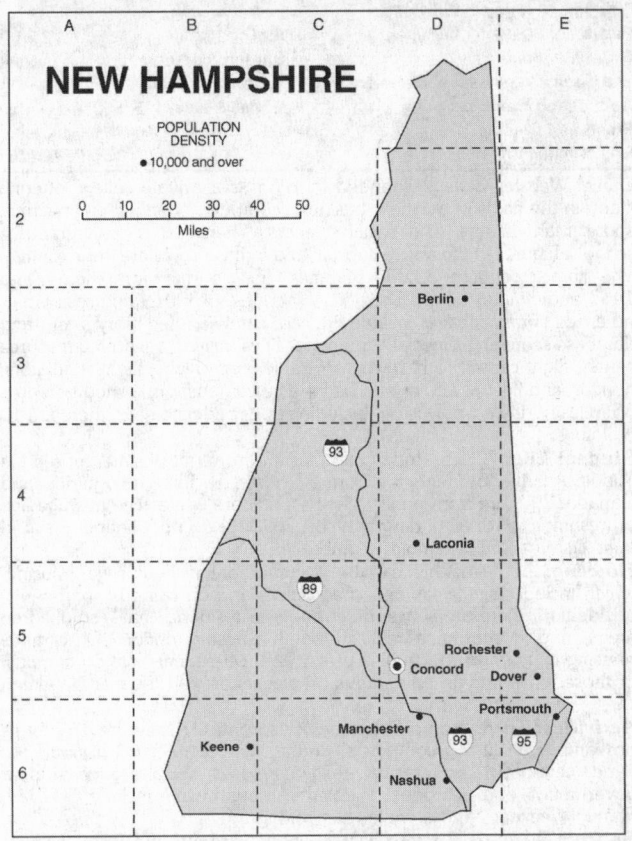

NEW HAMPSHIRE

POPULATION
DENSITY
● 10,000 and over

0 10 20 30 40 50
Miles

COLBY-SAWYER COLLEGE
New London, NH 03257

C-5

(603) 526-3700
(800) 272-1015; Fax: (603) 526-3452

Full-time: 320 men, 555 women	**Faculty:** 49; IIB, -$
Part-time: 10 men, 20 women	**Ph.Ds:** 78%
Graduate: none	**Student/Faculty:** 18 to 1
Year: semesters	**Tuition:** $22,200
Application Deadline: open	**Room & Board:** $8520
Freshman Class: n/av	
SAT I or ACT: required	**LESS COMPETITIVE**

Colby-Sawyer College, established in 1837, is an independent institution offering a variety of undergraduate majors, including fine arts, nursing, business, and communications, as well as education certification. Figures in the above capsule and in this profile are approximate. In addition to regional accreditation, Colby-Sawyer has baccalaureate program accreditation with CAAHEP and NLN. The library contains 92,116 volumes, 197,625 microform items, and 2119 audio/video tapes/CDs, and subscribes to 4148 periodicals. Computerized library services include the card catalog, interlibrary loans, and database searching. Special learning facilities include a learning resource center, art gallery, radio station, academic development center, and laboratory school (K-3). The 200-acre campus is in a small town 100 miles northwest of Boston, MA. Including any residence halls, there are 28 buildings.

Student Life: 69% of undergraduates are from out of state, mostly the Northeast. Students are from 27 states and 9 foreign countries. 79% are from public schools. 95% are white. 39% claim no religious affiliation; 35% are Catholic; 18% Protestant; 7% Buddhist, Hindu, Islamic, Eastern Orthodox, Quaker, and other. The average age of freshmen is 18; all undergraduates, 20. 19% do not continue beyond their first year; 58% remain to graduate.

Housing: 835 students can be accommodated in college housing, which includes single-sex and coed dorms. In addition, there is a substance-free residence hall. On-campus housing is guaranteed for all 4 years. 88% of students live on campus; of those, 70% remain on campus on weekends. All students may keep cars.

Activities: There are no fraternities or sororities. There are 40 groups on campus, including art, chorus, dance, drama, environmental, film, honors, international, Key Association (campus tour guides), literary magazine, musical theater, newspaper, outing, photography, professional, radio and TV, religious, social, social service, student academic counselors, student government, and yearbook. Popular campus events include Fall and Spring Weekends and Mountain Day.

Sports: There are 8 intercollegiate sports for men and 9 for women, and 15 intramural sports for men and 15 for women. Facilities include 6 outdoor and 3 indoor tennis courts, a fitness center, an NCAA-approved swimming pool, a suspended track, squash and racquetball courts, 4 outdoor competitive fields, and nearby golf courses, ski and biking trails, and an indoor riding arena.

Disabled Students: 50% of the campus is accessible. Wheelchair ramps, elevators, special parking, specially equipped rest rooms, special class scheduling, and special housing are available.

Services: Counseling and information services are available, as is tutoring in every subject. There is a reader service for the blind and remedial math, reading, and writing.

Campus Safety and Security: Measures include 24-hour foot and vehicle patrol, self-defense education, security escort services, and shuttle buses. There are informal discussions, pamphlets/posters/films, emergency telephones, lighted pathways/sidewalks, and monthly meetings between students and campus safety personnel.

Programs of Study: Colby-Sawyer confers B.A., B.S., and B.F.A. degrees. Associate degrees are also awarded. Bachelor's degrees are awarded in AGRICULTURE (environmental studies), BIOLOGICAL SCIENCE (biology/biological science), BUSINESS (business administration and management and sports management), COMMUNICATIONS AND THE ARTS (art, communications, design, English, and graphic design), EDUCATION (art, athletic training, early childhood, English, science, and social studies), HEALTH PROFESSIONS (exercise science and nursing), SOCIAL SCIENCE (child psychology/development, history, and psychology). Exercise and sport sciences, business administration, and child development are the largest.

Required: Required courses include writing, math, and computer literacy. Four required interdisciplinary core courses are Creative Expression, Process of Discovery, Social Analysis, and Judgment and Belief. Required electives include 1 each in fine and performing arts and natural sciences, and 2 each in social sciences and humanities. Most majors must also complete an internship or a senior research project. A total of 120 credit hours, with a minimum GPA of 2.0, is needed for graduation.

Special: There is cross-registration through the New Hampshire College and University Council. Students may choose internships (required in some majors) and may study abroad in Australia, Canada, and several European countries. A Washington semester with American University is available. Other options include student-designed majors, education certification, credit by exam, a general studies degree, and interdisciplinary majors such as History, Society, and Culture. There is 1 national honor society, a freshman honors program, and 2 departmental honors programs.

Faculty/Classroom: 45% of faculty are male; 55%, female. All teach undergraduates. The average class size in a regular course is 18.

Requirements: The SAT I or ACT is required. The GED is accepted. A minimum of 15 college preparatory credits is recommended for admission, including 4 years of English, 3 or more of social studies, 3 of math, 2 of the same foreign language, and 2 or more of lab science. An essay is required, as are 2 letters of recommendation. Interviews are strongly recommended. A GPA of 2.0 is required. AP and CLEP credits are accepted. Important factors in the admissions decision are advanced placement or honor courses, recommendations by school officials, and leadership record.

Procedure: Freshmen are admitted fall and spring. Entrance exams should be taken in the fall of the senior year. There is a rolling admissions plan and a deferred admissions plan. Application deadlines are open. Application fee is $40. Applications are accepted on-line through CollegeLink and Common App.

Transfer: 24 transfer students enrolled in a recent year. College-level work will be emphasized. College transcripts, course descriptions, and a dean's form are required in addition to the standard requirements. 60 of 120 credits required for the bachelor's degree must be completed at Colby-Sawyer.

Visiting: There are regularly scheduled orientations for prospective students, including tours and interviews. 2 open house programs offer tours as well as academic, athletic, campus life, career development, and academic development presentations; several visiting-day programs offer tours, interviews, and class visits. There are guides for informal visits and visitors may sit in on classes and stay overnight. To schedule a visit, contact the Admissions Office.

Financial Aid: Colby-Sawyer is a member of CSS. The FAFSA and the college's own financial statement are required. Check with the school for current deadlines.

International Students: The school actively recruits international students. They must score 450 on the written TOEFL.

Computers: There are 3 student computer labs on campus, housing 55 PCs; 2 "smart" classrooms housing 25 PCs; a library with 17 PCs; and a student center with 4 PCs. All students may access the system. There are no time limits and no fees.

Graduates: In a recent year, 167 bachelor's degrees were awarded. The most popular majors were exercise and sports science (16%), child development (16%), and business administration (11%). In an average class, 50% graduate in 4 years or less, 57% graduate in 5 years or less, and 58% graduate in 6 years or less. 5 companies recruited on campus in a recent year. Of a recent graduating class, 12% were enrolled in graduate school within 6 months of graduation and 89% were employed.

Admissions Contact: Office of Admissions and Financial Aid.
E-mail: *csadmiss@colby-sawyer.edu* Web: *http://www.colby-sawyer.edu*

COLLEGE FOR LIFELONG LEARNING
Concord, NH 03301-6430

D-4

(603) 228-3000, ext. 313
(800) 582-7248; Fax: (603) 229-0964

Full-time: 30 men, 60 women	**Faculty:** n/av
Part-time: 460 men, 1650 women	**Ph.D.s:** n/av
Graduate: none	**Student/Faculty:** n/av
Year: trimesters, summer session	**Tuition:** $6300 ($6930)
Application Deadline: open	**Room & Board:** n/app
Freshman Class: n/av	
SAT I or ACT: not required	SPECIAL

The College for Lifelong Learning, established as part of the University System of New Hampshire in 1972, is a state-supported commuter institution offering undergraduate programs in general and professional studies for adults. Figures in the above capsule and in this profile are approximate. Computerized library services include interlibrary loans and database searching. Special learning facilities include a learning resource center. The campus is in a small town.

Student Life: 92% of undergraduates are from New Hampshire. Students are from 4 states and 1 foreign country. 77% are white. The average age of all undergraduates is 35.

Housing: There are no residence halls. All students commute. Alcohol is not permitted.

Activities: There are no fraternities or sororities.

Sports: There is no sports program at CLL.

Disabled Students: All of the campus is accessible. Wheelchair ramps, special parking, and specially equipped rest rooms are available.

Services: There is remedial math, reading, and writing.

Campus Safety and Security: Measures include informal discussions and pamphlets/posters/films.

Programs of Study: CLL confers B.G.S. and B.S. degrees. Associate degrees are also awarded. Bachelor's degrees are awarded in BUSINESS (management science), SOCIAL SCIENCE (behavioral science and liberal arts/general studies). Behavioral science is the largest.

Required: Students must complete 124 credits, 34 to 36 in the major, and must maintain a minimum GPA of 2.0. All students are required to complete courses in computer competency, critical thinking/problem solving, mathematical reasoning, and written and oral communications. General education requirements include courses in humanities/arts, science and technology, and social science.

Special: Opportunities are provided for internships, cross-registration with all USNH schools, student-designed and dual majors, credit by exam, nondegree study, and pass/fail options (for degree students only). CLL offers programs throughout the state through a network of 9 regional centers. There is 1 national honor society.

Faculty/Classroom: 44% of faculty are male; 56%, female. All teach undergraduates. The average class size in a regular course is 10.

Requirements: A GED will be considered if submitted for admission evaluation. An interview is required. AP and CLEP credits are accepted.

Procedure: There is a rolling admissions plan. Application deadlines are open.

Transfer: 30 of 124 credits required for the bachelor's degree must be completed at CLL.

Visiting: There are regularly scheduled orientations for prospective students, consisting of an overview of college programs, financial aid, services, and transfer policies. Visitors may sit in on classes. To schedule a visit, contact a regional center.

Financial Aid: The FAFSA is required.

International Students: International students must score 500 on the written TOEFL.

Computers: The mainframe is a DEC VAX. There are 9 PC labs available for student use. All students may access the system. There are no time limits and no fees.

Admissions Contact: Ruth Nawn, Assistant Registrar.
E-mail: *rnawn@unhf.unh.edu*

DANIEL WEBSTER COLLEGE
Nashua, NH 03063-1300

D-6

(603) 577-6600
(800) 325-6876; Fax: (603) 577-6001

Full-time: 415 men, 100 women	**Faculty:** 33
Part-time: 60 men, 10 women	**Ph.D.s:** 43%
Graduate: none	**Student/Faculty:** 15 to 1
Year: semesters, summer session	**Tuition:** $19,600
Application Deadline: open	**Room & Board:** $7890
Freshman Class: n/av	
SAT I: required	COMPETITIVE

Daniel Webster College, founded in 1965, is a private college offering study in the fields of aviation, business, computer sciences, engineering, sports management, and social sciences. There are 5 undergraduate schools. Figures in the above capsule and in this profile are approximate. The library contains 32,000 volumes, 55,294 microform items, and 1457 audio/video tapes/CDs, and subscribes to 390 periodicals. Computerized library services include the card catalog, interlibrary loans, and database searching. Special learning facilities include a learning resource center, flight center, flight tower, air traffic control labs, flight simulators, hangar, and fleet of airplanes. The 54-acre campus is in a suburban area 35 miles northwest of Boston. Including any residence halls, there are 13 buildings.

Student Life: 72% of undergraduates are from out of state, mostly the Middle Atlantic. Students are from 27 states, 18 foreign countries, and Canada. 79% are from public schools. 91% are white. The average age of freshmen is 18; all undergraduates, 20. 35% do not continue beyond their first year; 51% remain to graduate.

Housing: 500 students can be accommodated in college housing, which includes single-sex and coed dorms and on-campus apartments. In addition, there are suites, quiet floors in residence halls, smoke-free areas, and a substance-free, 10-month housing option. On-campus housing is guaranteed for all 4 years. 72% of students live on campus; of those, 80% remain on campus on weekends. All students may keep cars.

Activities: There are no fraternities or sororities. There are 16 groups on campus, including computers, drama, film, flight team, honors, jazz band, newspaper, professional, religious, social, social service, student government, and yearbook. Popular campus events include Ski Day, Family Weekend, and a whitewater rafting trip.

Sports: There are 7 intercollegiate sports for men and 5 for women, and 6 intramural sports for men and 5 for women. Facilities include an indoor basketball/volleyball court, a weight room, tennis courts, soccer, lacrosse, and softball fields, and cross-country trails.

Disabled Students: 75% of the campus is accessible. Wheelchair ramps, elevators, special parking, specially equipped rest rooms, special class scheduling, and lowered drinking fountains are available.

Services: Counseling and information services are available, as is tutoring in every subject. There is remedial math and writing, study skills and test skills workshops, study groups, a math/science center, a writing center, and accommodations for students with learning disabilities.

Campus Safety and Security: Measures include 24-hour foot and vehicle patrol, self-defense education, security escort services, and informal discussions. There are pamphlets/posters/films, emergency telephones, and lighted pathways/sidewalks.

Programs of Study: DWC confers the B.S. degree. Associate degrees are also awarded. Bachelor's degrees are awarded in BUSINESS (business administration and management, management information systems, and sports management), COMPUTER AND PHYSICAL SCIENCE (computer science and information sciences and systems), ENGINEERING AND ENVIRONMENTAL DESIGN (air traffic control, airline piloting and navigation, aviation administration/management, and computer technology), SOCIAL SCIENCE (social science). Aviation, computer science, and information systems are the strongest academically. Aviation is the largest.

Required: Students must complete general education courses in communication, computer literacy, math, natural science, the humanities, and the social sciences. At least 120 credits, with 45 to 58 in the major, are required for graduation. Students must maintain a minimum overall GPA of 2.0. and grades of C or better in their major.

Special: There is cross-registration with the New Hampshire College and University Council. All programs offer credit by exam. Interdisciplinary majors, including aviation flight operations and aviation management/air traffic management are available. Study abroad, internships in aviation, business management, computer sciences, and sport management, a general studies degree, and a 2-2 engineering program with the Universities of New Hampshire and Massachusetts at Lowell, Kettering University, and Clarkson University are additional options. There is 1 national honor society.

Faculty/Classroom: 76% of faculty are male; 24%, female. All both teach and do research. The average class size in an introductory lecture is 17; in a laboratory, 12; and in a regular course, 20.

Requirements: The SAT I is required. In addition, applicants must be graduates of an accredited secondary school or submit the GED. Students should have taken 4 years of English, 3 of math, 2 each of social studies and science, and 1 of history. An essay and an interview are recommended. AP and CLEP credits are accepted. Important factors in the admissions decision are advanced placement or honor courses, recommendations by school officials, and leadership record.

Procedure: Freshmen are admitted to all sessions. There is a rolling admissions plan. There are early admissions and deferred admissions plans. Application deadlines are open. Application fee is $35. Applications are accepted on-line.

Transfer: Transfer students must have a minimum college GPA of 2.0. The SAT I is required. Grades of C or better transfer for credit. 30 of 120 credits required for the bachelor's degree must be completed at DWC.

Visiting: There are regularly scheduled orientations for prospective students, including a tour and an admissions interview; also available are meetings with faculty and coaches and an aerial tour of the campus. There are guides for informal visits and visitors may sit in on classes and stay overnight. To schedule a visit, contact the Office of Admissions.

Financial Aid: In a recent year, 92% of all full-time freshmen and 90% of continuing full-time students received some form of financial aid. 87% of full-time freshmen and 78% of continuing full-time students received need-based aid. The average freshman award was $13,550. 25% of undergraduates work part time. Average annual earnings from campus work are $1500. The average financial indebtedness of a recent graduate was $18,500. The FAFSA and the college's own financial statement are required. Check with the school for current deadlines.

International Students: International students must score 520 on the written TOEFL.

Computers: There are 14 servers connected to more than 150 PCs for student use. All residence halls are wired for Internet access. All students may access the system when the computer center is open. There are no time limits. There is a one-time technology fee of $120. It is strongly recommended that all students have a personal computer. IBM-compatible is recommended.

Graduates: In a recent year, 76 bachelor's degrees were awarded. The most popular majors were aviation management/flight operations (22%), aviation management (21%), and computer science (13%). In an average class, 46% graduate in 4 years or less, and 49% graduate in 5 years or less. Of a recent graduating class, 10% were enrolled in graduate school within 6 months of graduation and 81% were employed.

Admissions Contact: Jim Thatcher, Enrollment Services.
E-mail: *admissions@dwc.edu* Web: *www.dwc.edu*

DARTMOUTH COLLEGE
Hanover, NH 03755

Full-time: 2060 men, 1968 women	B-4
Part-time: 24 men, 27 women	(603) 646-2875; Fax: (603) 646-1216
Graduate: 920 men, 594 women	**Faculty:** 406; I, ++$
Year: quarters, summer session	**Ph.Ds:** 90%
Application Deadline: January 1	**Student/Faculty:** 10 to 1
Freshman Class: 11,855 applied, 2155 accepted, 1077 enrolled	**Tuition:** $29,145
SAT I Verbal/Math: 710/720	**Room & Board:** $8625
	MOST COMPETITIVE

Dartmouth College, chartered in 1769, is a private liberal arts institution offering a wide range of graduate and undergraduate programs. There is a year-round academic calendar of 4 10-week terms. There are 4 graduate schools. The 10 libraries contain 2,429,072 volumes, 2,554,823 microform items, and 449,291 audio/video tapes/CDs, and subscribe to 20,679 periodicals. Computerized library services include the card catalog, interlibrary loans, database searching, and Internet access. Special learning facilities include a learning resource center, art gallery, radio station, and creative and performing arts center, life sciences lab, physical and social sciences centers, and observatory. The 265-acre campus is in a rural area 140 miles northwest of Boston. Including any residence halls, there are 100 buildings.

Student Life: 97% of undergraduates are from out of state, mostly the Middle Atlantic. Students are from 50 states, 80 foreign countries, and Canada. 63% are from public schools. 58% are white; 14% Asian American. 30% are Protestant; 28% claim no religious affiliation; 23% Catholic; 11% Jewish. The average age of freshmen is 19; all undergraduates, 20. 4% do not continue beyond their first year; 96% remain to graduate.

Housing: 3500 students can be accommodated in college housing, which includes coed dorms, on-campus apartments, married-student housing, fraternity houses, and sorority houses. In addition, there are language houses, special-interest houses, substance and smoke free residence halls, and faculty in-residence and academic affinity programs. On-campus housing is guaranteed for the freshman year only, is available on a first-come, first-served basis, and is available on a lottery system for upperclassmen. 88% of students live on campus. Upperclassmen may keep cars.

Activities: 24% of men belong to 7 local and 7 national fraternities; 22% of women belong to 3 local and 5 national sororities. There are many groups and organizations on campus, including art, band, cheerleading, chess, choir, chorale, chorus, computers, dance, debate, drama, ethnic, film, forensics, gay, honors, international, jazz band, literary mag-

azine, marching band, musical theater, newspaper, opera, orchestra, outing, pep band, photography, political, professional, radio and TV, religious, social, social service, student government, symphony, and yearbook. Popular campus events include Dartmouth Night/Homecoming, Winter and Summer Carnivals, and Green Key Service Weekend.

Sports: There are 17 intercollegiate sports for men and 17 for women, and 25 intramural sports for men and 25 for women. Facilities include a 2100-seat stadium, a fitness center, squash and racquetball courts, a dance studio, a 5000-seat arena, a gym, a 21,000-seat football stadium, a boat house, a tennis center with indoor and outdoor courts, a golf course, a ski slope with 3 chairlifts, and a riding farm.

Disabled Students: All of the campus is accessible. Wheelchair ramps, elevators, special parking, specially equipped rest rooms, special class scheduling, lowered drinking fountains, lowered telephones, and special housing are available.

Services: Counseling and information services are available, as is tutoring in every subject. There is a reader service for the blind. There is an academic skills center for all students. Readers, note takers, tape recorders, and support for learning-disabled students are available.

Campus Safety and Security: Measures include 24-hour foot and vehicle patrol, self-defense education, security escort services, and shuttle buses. There are informal discussions, pamphlets/posters/films, emergency telephones, and lighted pathways/sidewalks.

Programs of Study: Dartmouth confers B.A. and B.Eng. degrees. Master's and doctoral degrees are also awarded. Bachelor's degrees are awarded in BIOLOGICAL SCIENCE (biochemistry, biology/biological science, evolutionary biology, and genetics), COMMUNICATIONS AND THE ARTS (Arabic, art history and appreciation, Chinese, classics, comparative literature, creative writing, dramatic arts, English, English literature, film arts, French, German, Italian, linguistics, music, romance languages and literature, Russian, and Spanish), COMPUTER AND PHYSICAL SCIENCE (chemistry, computer science, earth science, mathematics, and physics), ENGINEERING AND ENVIRONMENTAL DESIGN (engineering and applied science, engineering physics, and environmental science), SOCIAL SCIENCE (African American studies, African studies, anthropology, Asian/Oriental studies, classical/ancient civilization, cognitive science, economics, geography, German area studies, history, Latin American studies, Middle Eastern studies, Native American studies, philosophy, political science/government, psychology, religion, Russian and Slavic studies, social science, sociology, Spanish studies, and women's studies). Economics, psychology, and government are the largest.

Required: All students must pass 35 courses, 10 of which must be distributed in the following fields: arts; social analysis; literature; quantitative or deductive science; philosophical, religious, or historical analysis; natural science; technology or applied science; and international or comparative study. 3 world culture courses are required from the U.S., Europe, and at least 1 non-Western society. A multidisciplinary or interdisciplinary course, a freshman seminar, a senior project, and foreign language proficiency are also required.

Special: Students may design programs using the college's unique Dartmouth Plan, which divides the academic calender into 4 10-week terms, based on the seasons. The plan permits greater flexibility for vacations and for the 39 study-abroad programs in 22 countries, including Italy, France, Scotland, Russia, and Brazil. Cross-registration is offered through the Twelve College Exchange Network, which includes Amherst and Mount Holyoke. Exchange programs also exist with the University of California at San Diego, McGill University in Montreal, selected German universities, Keio University in Tokyo, and Beijing Normal University in China. There are special academic programs in Washington, D.C. and Tucson, Arizona. Students may design their own interdisciplinary majors, involving multiple departments if desired, take dual majors in all fields, or satisfy a modified major involving 2 departments, with emphasis in 1. Hands-on computer science education, internships, combined B.A.-B.S. degrees, and work-study programs also are available. A 3-2 engineering degree is offered with Dartmouth's Thayer School of Engineering. There are 3 national honor societies, including Phi Beta Kappa. All departments have honors programs.

Faculty/Classroom: 66% of faculty are male; 34%, female. 100% both teach and do research. No introductory courses are taught by graduate students. The average class size in an introductory lecture is 34; in a laboratory, 16; and in a regular course, 23.

Admissions: 18% of the 2003-2004 applicants were accepted. The SAT I scores for the 2003-2004 freshman class were: Verbal--1% below 500, 8% between 500 and 599, 32% between 600 and 700, and 59% above 700; Math--1% below 500, 5% between 500 and 599, 28% between 600 and 700, and 66% above 700. 95% of the current freshmen were in the top fifth of their class; 99% were in the top two fifths. There were 63 National Merit finalists and 156 freshmen graduated first in their class in a recent year.

Requirements: The SAT I or ACT is required, as are 3 SAT II: Subject tests. Evidence of intellectual capacity, motivation, and personal integrity are prime considerations in the highly competitive admissions process, which also considers talent, accomplishment, and involvement in nonacademic areas. Course requirements are flexible, but students are urged to take English, foreign language, math, lab science, and history. The GED is accepted. AP credits are accepted.

Procedure: Freshmen are admitted in the fall. Entrance exams should be taken no later than January of the senior year. There are early decision and deferred admissions plans. Early decision applications should be filed by November 1; regular applications, by January 1 for fall entry. The fall 2003 application fee was $70. Notification of early decision is sent December 15; regular decision, April 1. 390 early decision candidates were accepted for the 2003-2004 class. 55 wait-listed applicants were admitted. Applications are accepted on-line through *www.commonapp.org.*

Transfer: 19 transfer students enrolled in 2002-2003. Applicants must demonstrate high achievement and intellectual motivation through college transcripts as well as standardized test scores and high school transcripts. 18 of 35 courses required for the bachelor's degree must be completed at Dartmouth.

Visiting: There are regularly scheduled orientations for prospective students, including tours, group information sessions, and interviews. There are guides for informal visits and visitors may sit in on classes and stay overnight. To schedule a visit, contact the Office of Admissions at (603) 646-2875 or *admissions.office@dartmouth.edu.*

Financial Aid: In 2003-2004, 56% of all full-time freshmen and 50% of continuing full-time students received some form of financial aid. 49% of full-time freshmen and 46% of continuing full-time students received need-based aid. The average freshman award was $27,037. Need-based scholarships or need-based grants averaged $24,176 ($44,510 maximum); and need-based self-help aid (loans and jobs) averaged $4283. The average financial indebtedness of the 2003 graduate was $16,430. Dartmouth is a member of CSS. The CSS/Profile or FAFSA and parents' and student's federal income tax returns. In addition, a Noncustodial Parents' statement, tax returns, and W-2s, and a Business/Farm Supplement may be required. Foreign students must provide a certificate of finances and parents' tax returns are required. The deadline for filing freshman financial aid applications for fall entry is February 1.

International Students: There are 194 international students enrolled. The school actively recruits these students. They must take the TOEFL and the SAT I or the ACT. Students must also take SAT II: Subject tests in any 3 subjects.

Computers: The mainframes are an IBM RS/6000 4P-270, an SG 1 ORIGIN 200, and a Sun E450. More than 12,000 network ports are available for student use. The computer network, which includes wireless network stations, links dorm rooms, administrative and academic buildings, and mainframe computers on and off campus. Students can access scholarly databases, a collegewide e-mail system, and the Internet. All students may access the system 24 hours daily. There are no time limits and no fees. All students are required to have personal computers.

Graduates: From July 1, 2002 to June 30, 2003, 1101 bachelor's degrees were awarded. The most popular majors were economics (12%), psychology and brain sciences (11%), and government and history (10%). In an average class, 88% graduate in 4 years or less, 93% graduate in 5 years or less, and 94% graduate in 6 years or less. 200 companies recruited on campus in 2002-2003. Of the 2002 graduating class, 19% were enrolled in graduate school within 6 months of graduation and 65% were employed.

Admissions Contact: Karl Furstenberg, Dean of Admissions.
E-mail: *undergraduate.admissions@dartmouth.edu*
Web: *www.dartmouth.edu*

FRANKLIN PIERCE COLLEGE

C-8
Rindge, NH 03461-0060
(603) 899-4050
(800) 437-0048; Fax: (603) 899-4394

Full-time: 799 men, 770 women	**Faculty:** 68; IIB, -$
Part-time: 5 men, 4 women	**Ph.D.s:** 79%
Graduate: none	**Student/Faculty:** 23 to 1
Year: semesters, summer session	**Tuition:** $21,680
Application Deadline: open	**Room & Board:** $7300
Freshman Class: 3347 applied, 2895 accepted, 514 enrolled	
SAT I Verbal/Math: 510/490	**LESS COMPETITIVE**

Franklin Pierce College, founded in 1962, is a private liberal arts institution that also has an extensive continuing education program, which offers undergraduate and graduate degrees at locations in Concord, Keene, Lebanon, Salem, Nashua, and Portsmouth in New Hampshire. The library contains 115,252 volumes, 26,165 microform items, and 11,395 audio/video tapes/CDs, and subscribes to 241 periodicals. Computerized library services include the card catalog, interlibrary loans, and database searching. Special learning facilities include a learning resource center, art gallery, radio station, TV station, computer labs, theaters, and studios. The 1000-acre campus is in a rural area 65 miles northwest of Boston. Including any residence halls, there are 30 buildings.

Student Life: 84% of undergraduates are from out of state, mostly the Northeast. Students are from 27 states, 18 foreign countries, and Canada. 87% are from public schools. 80% are white. The average age of freshmen is 18; all undergraduates, 20.

Housing: 1345 students can be accommodated in college housing, which includes single-sex and coed dorms, on-campus apartments, and off-campus apartments. On-campus housing is guaranteed for all 4 years. 87% of students live on campus; of those, 70% remain on campus on weekends. All students may keep cars.

Activities: There are no fraternities or sororities. There are 35 groups on campus, including art, cheerleading, chess, choir, chorale, computers, dance, drama, ethnic, gay, honors, international, jazz band, literary magazine, musical theater, newspaper, outing, photography, political, professional, radio and TV, religious, social, social service, student government, and yearbook. Popular campus events include Winter Carnival, Spring and Fall Weekends, and Up All Night Mardi Gras.

Sports: There are 8 intercollegiate sports for men and 10 for women, and 6 intramural sports for men and 3 for women. Facilities include a 72,000-square-foot airframe activity center, a field house, a fitness center, an 800-seat gym, an athletic trainer, playing fields, a track, a lake with a beach, a fleet of sailboats, cross-country and hiking trails, and courts for tennis, basketball, and volleyball.

Disabled Students: 90% of the campus is accessible. Wheelchair ramps, elevators, special parking, specially equipped rest rooms, special class scheduling, lowered drinking fountains, lowered telephones, and special housing are available.

Services: Counseling and information services are available, as is tutoring in every subject. There is a reader service for the blind, remedial math, reading, and writing, note takers, a professional reading specialist, alternative testing, reduced course loads, study skills workshops, and content-area study skills courses.

Campus Safety and Security: Measures include 24-hour foot and vehicle patrol, security escort services, shuttle buses, and informal discussions. There are pamphlets/posters/films, emergency telephones, and lighted pathways/sidewalks.

Programs of Study: FPC confers B.A. and B.S. degrees. Master's degrees are also awarded. Bachelor's degrees are awarded in BIOLOGICAL SCIENCE (biology/biological science), BUSINESS (accounting, banking and finance, business administration and management, business economics, international economics, management science, marketing/retailing/merchandising, and sports management), COMMUNICATIONS AND THE ARTS (advertising, arts administration/management, communications, dance, dramatic arts, English, fine arts, graphic design, music, performing arts, and theater design), COMPUTER AND PHYSICAL SCIENCE (computer science, information sciences and systems, and mathematics), EDUCATION (education, elementary, and secondary), ENGINEERING AND ENVIRONMENTAL DESIGN (environmental science), SOCIAL SCIENCE (American studies, anthropology, criminal justice, history, political science/government, psychology, social work, and sociology). Anthropology, biology, and environmental science are the strongest academically. Criminal justice, mass communication, and psychology are the largest.

Required: Students must complete 120 semester hours with a cumulative GPA of at least 2.0 and pass exams for writing and math competency. Individual and Community core requirements total 11 courses, including Individual and Community, College Writing, Integrated Science, American Experience, Twentieth Century, Foundations of Mathematics, Experiencing the Arts, Ancient and Medieval Worlds, Reason and Romanticism, Science of Society, and a senior liberal arts seminar.

Special: Cross-registration is offered in nearly every subject through the New Hampshire College and University Council, a 13-member consortium of area institutions. Study at Richmond College in London, Oxford University, and American College in Dublin, internships in most majors on or off campus, a Washington semester, and work-study through the college are possible. In addition, accelerated degree programs in all majors, dual majors in most fields, student-designed majors, credit for life experience, and nondegree study are available. There are 5 national honor societies and a freshman honors program.

Faculty/Classroom: 59% of faculty are male; 41%, female. All teach undergraduates and 50% both teach and do research. The average class size in an introductory lecture is 60; in a laboratory, 16; and in a regular course, 19.

Admissions: 86% of the 2003-2004 applicants were accepted. The SAT I scores for the 2003-2004 freshman class were: Verbal--45% below 500, 43% between 500 and 599, 11% between 600 and 700, and 1% above 700; Math--52% below 500, 37% between 500 and 599, and 11% between 600 and 700. 12% of the current freshmen were in the top fifth of their class; 32% were in the top two fifths.

Requirements: The SAT I or ACT is required, but with no minimum score. Applicants must have earned 10 academic units or 16 Carnegie units in high school, including 4 years of English, 3 each in math and social studies, and 2 in science. An interview is recommended. The GED is accepted. AP and CLEP credits are accepted. Important factors in the admissions decision are recommendations by school officials, advanced placement or honor courses, and leadership record.

Procedure: Freshmen are admitted to all sessions. Entrance exams should be taken in the fall of the senior year. There is a rolling admissions plan. There are early admissions and deferred admissions plans.

Application deadlines are open. Notification is sent on a rolling basis beginning October 15. Applications are accepted on-line although a signed hard copy still needs to be sent.

Transfer: 57 transfer students enrolled in 2002-2003. A minimum 2.0 GPA in college work is required. Students with fewer than 30 credits must submit SAT I results (no minimum score) and official high school transcripts. A personal recommendation is necessary, and an interview recommended. 30 of 120 credits required for the bachelor's degree must be completed at FPC.

Visiting: There are regularly scheduled orientations for prospective students, including open houses held each spring and fall and interviews and tours available weekdays and most Saturdays. There are guides for informal visits and visitors may sit in on classes and stay overnight. To schedule a visit, contact the Admissions Office.

Financial Aid: In 2003-2004, 71% of all full-time freshmen and 73% of continuing full-time students received some form of financial aid. 70% of full-time freshmen and 73% of continuing full-time students received need-based aid. The average freshman award was $15,585. Need-based scholarships or need-based grants averaged $11,535; need-based self-help aid (loans and jobs) averaged $4636; institutional non-need-based athletic scholarships averaged $14,915; and other institutional non-need-based awards and non-need-based scholarships averaged $10,060. The average financial indebtedness of the 2003 graduate was $20,815. The FAFSA is required. The priority date for freshman financial aid applications for fall entry is March 1.

International Students: There were 47 international students enrolled in a recent year. The school actively recruits these students. They must score 500 on the written TOEFL and also take ELS Level 109. The SAT I or ACT may be substituted for the TOEFL.

Computers: There are 3 computer labs (PCs and Macs) available for student use 7 days per week, in addition to Internet access ports in all residence halls for students with PCs. All students may access the system 16 hours daily. There are no time limits and no fees. It is strongly recommended that all students have a personal computer.

Graduates: From July 1, 2002 to June 30, 2003, 263 bachelor's degrees were awarded. The most popular majors were business/marketing (56%), protective services/public administration (36%), and communications/communication technologies (33%). 35 companies recruited on campus in a recent year. Of a recent graduating class, 13% were enrolled in graduate school within 6 months of graduation and 91% were employed.

Admissions Contact: Lucy C. Shonk, Dean of Admissions. A video is available. E-mail: admissions@fpc.edu Web: www.fpc.edu

HESSER COLLEGE
Manchester, NH 03101

(603) 668-6660
(800) 526-9231; Fax: (603) 666-4722

Full-time: 306 men, 438 women	Faculty: 29
Part-time: 22 men, 53 women	Ph.D.s: 1%
Graduate: none	Student/Faculty: 26 to 1
Year: semesters, summer session	Tuition: $11,290
Application Deadline: see profile	Room & Board: $6200
Freshman Class: n/av	
SAT I or ACT: not required	**LESS COMPETITIVE**

Hesser College, founded in 1900, is a small, private institution affiliated with the Kaplan Education Corporation and offering more than 30 associate and 2+2 bachelor degree programs. Students must have an associate degree from Hesser in order to pursue a bachelor's degree. The library contains 26,000 volumes and 2000 audio/video tapes/CDs, and subscribes to 170 periodicals. Computerized library services include the card catalog, interlibrary loans, database searching, and Internet access. Special learning facilities include a learning resource center, radio station, TV station, medical labs, G4 graphic design lab, and massage therapy lab. The 2-acre campus is in a medium-size city. Including any residence halls, there are 2 buildings.

Student Life: 64% of undergraduates are from New Hampshire. Students are from 13 states and 8 foreign countries. The average age of freshmen is 19; all undergraduates, 19.

Housing: 500 students can be accommodated in college housing, which includes single-sex dorms. On-campus housing is guaranteed for the freshman year only and is available on a lottery system for upperclassmen. 50% of students live on campus; of those, 50% remain on campus on weekends. Alcohol is not permitted. All students may keep cars.

Activities: There are no fraternities or sororities. There are some groups and organizations on campus, including cheerleading, honors, international, newspaper, professional, radio and TV, social, and student government.

Sports: There are 4 intercollegiate sports for men and 4 for women, and 5 intramural sports for men and 4 for women. Basketball, volleyball, soccer, and softball programs are available.

Disabled Students: Elevators and special parking are available.

Services: Counseling and information services are available, as is tutoring in every subject. There is remedial math, reading, and writing. There is a center for teaching, learning, and assessment.

Campus Safety and Security: Measures include 24-hour foot and vehicle patrol and security escort services.

Programs of Study: Hesser College confers B.B.A. and B.C.J. degrees. Associate degrees are also awarded. Bachelor's degrees are awarded in BUSINESS (accounting, and business administration and management), SOCIAL SCIENCE (criminal justice). Physical therapist assistant is the strongest academically. Criminal justice is the largest.

Required: A minimum 2.0 GPA is required. Contact the school for specific program information.

Special: Internships and work-study programs are available. The college offers a J.D. degree through an articulation agreement with the Massachusetts School of Law, Andover. There is 1 national honor society, Phi Beta Kappa, and a freshman honors program.

Faculty/Classroom: In a recent year, 54% of faculty were male; 46%, female. The average class size in a regular course is 20.

Admissions: 25% of the current freshmen were in the top fifth of their class; 60% were in the top two fifths.

Requirements: Applicants must be high school graduates. The GED is accepted. An interview is required. A GPA of 2.0 is required. Important factors in the admissions decision are personality/intangible qualities, recommendations by school officials, and leadership record.

Procedure: Freshmen are admitted fall and spring. Entrance exams should be taken at orientation. The application fee is $10. Notification is sent on a rolling basis. Applications are accepted on-line through the school's web site.

Visiting: There are regularly scheduled orientations for prospective students, including campus tours Monday through Friday during the school year and Monday through Thursday during the summer. Open House and Saturday tour days are also available. There are guides for informal visits and visitors may sit in on classes. To schedule a visit, contact Kevin Wilkinson, Director of Admissions at (603) 668-6660, ext. 2110.

Financial Aid: The FAFSA and the college's own financial statement are required. Freshman financial aid applications for fall entry are accepted on a rolling basis.

International Students: In a recent year there were 30 international students enrolled. The school actively recruits these students. They must score 450 on the written TOEFL or take the MELAB, or Kaplan, English Language Proficiency Test.

Computers: There are Dell computer labs and Mac G4 computer labs.

Admissions Contact: Kevin Wilkinson, Director of Admissions. A video is available. E-mail: kwilkinson@hesser.edu Web: www.hesser.edu

KEENE STATE COLLEGE
Keene, NH 03435

B-6
(603) 358-2276
(800) KSC-1909; Fax: (603) 358-2767

Full-time: 1730 men, 2403 women	Faculty: 178; IIA, av$
Part-time: 1297 men, 326 women	Ph.D.s: 81%
Graduate: 20 men, 117 women	Student/Faculty: 23 to 1
Year: semesters, summer session	Tuition: $6530 ($12,580)
Application Deadline: April 1	Room & Board: $5682
Freshman Class: 4207 applied, 2997 accepted, 997 enrolled	
SAT I Verbal/Math: 504/499	ACT: 19 **COMPETITIVE**

Keene State College, founded in 1909, is part of the public University System of New Hampshire and offers a liberal arts program that includes teacher preparation, art, and business emphases. In addition to regional accreditation, KSC has baccalaureate program accreditation with CAAHEP, NASM, and NCATE. The library contains 247,550 volumes, 726,509 microform items, and 5009 audio/video tapes/CDs, and subscribes to 1261 periodicals. Computerized library services include the card catalog, interlibrary loans, and database searching. Special learning facilities include a learning resource center, art gallery, planetarium, radio station, TV station, and the Holocaust Resource Center. The 150-acre campus is in a suburban area 90 miles northwest of Boston. Including any residence halls, there are 60 buildings.

Student Life: 57% of undergraduates are from New Hampshire. Students are from 30 states, 15 foreign countries, and Canada. 80% are from public schools. 90% are white. 48% are Catholic; 21% claim no religious affiliation; 20% Protestant; 10% unspecified. The average age of freshmen is 18; all undergraduates, 21. 23% do not continue beyond their first year; 59% remain to graduate.

Housing: 2196 students can be accommodated in college housing, which includes single-sex and coed dorms, on-campus apartments, married-student housing, fraternity houses, and sorority houses. In addition, there are special-interest houses, wellness areas, drug free areas, environmentally aware housing, and education majors housing. On-campus housing is guaranteed for the freshman year only and is available on a lottery system for upperclassmen. 52% of students live on campus. Upperclassmen may keep cars.

Activities: 3% of men and about 1% of women belong to 3 local fraternities; 4% of women belong to 5 local sororities. There are 80 groups on campus, including art, band, cheerleading, choir, chorale, chorus, computers, dance, drama, ethnic, film, gay, honors, international, jazz band, literary magazine, musical theater, newspaper, orchestra, photography, political, professional, radio and TV, religious, social, social service, student government, and yearbook. Popular campus events include Parent and Family Weekend, Winter Carnival, and Diversity Day.

Sports: There are 7 intercollegiate sports for men and 9 for women, and 11 intramural sports for men and 11 for women. Facilities include a 1500-seat gym, a 1000-seat stadium for soccer and field hockey, an indoor pool, a fitness center, racquetball, tennis, and squash courts, and a training room.

Disabled Students: 90% of the campus is accessible. Wheelchair ramps, elevators, special parking, specially equipped rest rooms, lowered drinking fountains, and lowered telephones are available.

Services: Counseling and information services are available, as is tutoring in most subjects. There is a writing process center, a reading center, and a math center. There is a reader service for the blind and remedial math and reading.

Campus Safety and Security: Measures include 24-hour foot and vehicle patrol, self-defense education, security escort services, and shuttle buses. There are informal discussions, pamphlets/posters/films, emergency telephones, and lighted pathways/sidewalks.

Programs of Study: KSC confers B.A., B.S., B.F.A., and B.M. degrees. Associate and master's degrees are also awarded. Bachelor's degrees are awarded in BIOLOGICAL SCIENCE (biology/biological science), BUSINESS (management science), COMMUNICATIONS AND THE ARTS (art, communications, English, film arts, fine arts, French, journalism, music, music performance, and Spanish), COMPUTER AND PHYSICAL SCIENCE (chemistry, computer mathematics, computer science, geology, mathematics, and physical sciences), EDUCATION (early childhood, education, elementary, foreign languages, mathematics, music, physical, science, secondary, and special), ENGINEERING AND ENVIRONMENTAL DESIGN (environmental science), HEALTH PROFESSIONS (health science), SOCIAL SCIENCE (American studies, dietetics, economics, geography, history, psychology, safety management, social science, and sociology). Education, safety studies, and health science are the strongest academically. Education, management, and psychology are the largest.

Required: All students must take 120 to 142 credits, with 40 to 50 hours in their major, while maintaining a 2.0 GPA. Distribution requirements include 5 courses in the arts and humanities, 4 each in the social sciences, math, and sciences, and 1 in English composition. Students also must demonstrate proficiency in math.

Special: Cross-registration through New Hampshire College and the University Council, internships and co-op programs in all areas of study, study abroad anywhere in the world, and work-study at the college are available. Student teaching is required for education majors. Students also may pursue dual majors, a general studies degree, individualized majors, accelerated degrees in the psychology honors program, and a 3-2 engineering degree with Clarkson University or the University of New Hampshire. In addition, there are pass/fail options and credit for life experience. There are 20 national honor societies and 1 departmental honors program.

Faculty/Classroom: 54% of faculty are male; 46%, female. All teach undergraduates. No introductory courses are taught by graduate students. The average class size in an introductory lecture is 20; in a laboratory, 8; and in a regular course, 13.

Admissions: 71% of the 2003-2004 applicants were accepted. The SAT I scores for the 2003-2004 freshman class were: Verbal--48% below 500, 41% between 500 and 599, 10% between 600 and 700, and 1% above 700; Math--49% below 500, 42% between 500 and 599, 9% between 600 and 700, and 1% above 700. The ACT scores were 66% below 21, 30% between 21 and 23, 2% between 24 and 26, and 3% above 28. 14% of the current freshmen were in the top fifth of their class; 42% were in the top two fifths.

Requirements: The SAT I is required, with scores of 450 verbal and 450 math. Applicants need at least 11 academic credits, including 4 years of English, and 2 each of math, science, social studies, and history. An essay, portfolio, and audition are required for certain programs, and an interview is recommended. A GPA of 2.5 is required. AP and CLEP credits are accepted. Important factors in the admissions decision are advanced placement or honor courses, recommendations by school officials, and evidence of special talent.

Procedure: Freshmen are admitted fall and spring. Entrance exams should be taken during the spring of the junior year or fall of the senior year. There is a deferred admissions plan and a rolling admissions plan. Applications should be filed by April 1 for fall entry and December 1 for spring entry. The fall 2003 application fee was $25. Notification is sent on a rolling basis. Applications are accepted on-line through www.keene.edu\.

Transfer: 137 transfer students enrolled in 2002-2003. Transfer students must have a 2.0 cumulative GPA and at least 12 college credits. An interview is recommended. 24 of 120 credits required for the bachelor's degree must be completed at KSC.

Visiting: There are regularly scheduled orientations for prospective students, consisting of a personal interview with the professional staff and a tour. There are guides for informal visits and visitors may sit in on classes. To schedule a visit, contact the Admissions Office at admissions@keene.edu.

Financial Aid: In 2003-2004, 55% of all full-time freshmen and 52% of continuing full-time students received some form of financial aid. 52% of full-time freshmen and 48% of continuing full-time students received need-based aid. The average freshman award was $6462. Need-based scholarships or need-based grants averaged $4339; and need-based self-help aid (loans and jobs) averaged $3091. 23% of undergraduates work part time. Average annual earnings from campus work are $840. The average financial indebtedness of the 2003 graduate was $18,529. The FAFSA and IRS tax returns are required. The deadline for filing freshman financial aid applications for fall entry is March 1.

International Students: There are 59 international students enrolled. They must score 500 on the written TOEFL.

Computers: The mainframe is an ALPHA 4000. 500 computers are available in discipline-specific and general purpose labs. All students may access the system 24 hours per day. There are no time limits and no fees.

Graduates: From July 1, 2002 to June 30, 2003, 803 bachelor's degrees were awarded. The most popular majors were education (13%), psychology (10%), and management (8%). In an average class, 27% graduate in 4 years or less, 49% graduate in 5 years or less, and 55% graduate in 6 years or less. 20 companies recruited on campus in 2002-2003. Of the 2002 graduating class, 10% were enrolled in graduate school within 6 months of graduation and 46% were employed.

Admissions Contact: Peggy Richmond, Director of Admissions. A video is available. E-mail: admissions@keene.edu Web: www.keene.edu

---

NEW ENGLAND COLLEGE
C-5
Henniker, NH 03242
(603) 428-2223
(800) 521-7642; Fax: (608) 428-7230

Full-time: 397 men, 434 women	Faculty: 53
Part-time: 16 men, 31 women	Ph.Ds: 75%
Graduate: 82 men, 176 women	Student/Faculty: 16 to 1
Year: semesters, summer session	Tuition: $21,120
Application Deadline: open	Room & Board: $7740
Freshman Class: 1023 applied, 994 accepted, 275 enrolled	
SAT I Verbal/Math: 460/450	LESS COMPETITIVE

New England College, founded in 1946, is an independent liberal arts institution emphasizing small classes and a cocurricular leadership program. The library contains 104,000 volumes, 36,000 microform items, and 2000 audio/video tapes/CDs, and subscribes to 650 periodicals. Computerized library services include the card catalog, interlibrary loans, database searching, and Internet access. Special learning facilities include a learning resource center, art gallery, radio station, and the Center for Educational Innovation, with a high-tech classroom building. The 225-acre campus is in a small town 17 miles west of Concord and 80 miles north of Boston, Massachusetts. Including any residence halls, there are 31 buildings.

Student Life: 72% of undergraduates are from out of state, mostly the Northeast. Students are from 9 states, 13 foreign countries, and Canada. 70% are from public schools. 90% are white. The average age of freshmen is 18; all undergraduates, 20. 33% do not continue beyond their first year; 50% remain to graduate.

Housing: 590 students can be accommodated in college housing, which includes coed dorms, on-campus apartments, fraternity houses, and sorority houses. In addition, there are special-interest houses and students may choose to live in cooperative substance-free housing. On-campus housing is guaranteed for all 4 years. 70% of students live on campus; of those, 80% remain on campus on weekends. All students may keep cars.

Activities: 12% of men belong to 3 local fraternities; 17% of women belong to 1 local and 1 national sorority. There are 26 groups on campus, including chorus, dance, drama, ethnic, film, gay, honors, international, literary magazine, newspaper, photography, political, professional, radio and TV, religious, social, social service, sports, student government, and yearbook. Popular campus events include International Week and Spring Weekend.

Sports: There are 7 intercollegiate sports for men and 8 for women, and 7 intramural sports for men and 7 for women. Facilities include a gym, a field house, 26 acres of playing fields, indoor and outdoor basketball and tennis courts, cross-country ski trails, Alpine skiing at a local ski area, and a fitness center.

Disabled Students: 80% of the campus is accessible. Wheelchair ramps, elevators, special parking, specially equipped rest rooms, and special class scheduling are available.

Services: Counseling and information services are available, as is tutoring in every subject. There is a mentor program that provides both academic and social support.

Campus Safety and Security: Measures include 24-hour foot and vehicle patrol, security escort services, shuttle buses, and informal discussions. There are pamphlets/posters/films, emergency telephones, and lighted pathways/sidewalks.

Programs of Study: NEC confers B.A. and B.S. degrees. Associate and master's degrees are also awarded. Bachelor's degrees are awarded in BIOLOGICAL SCIENCE (biology/biological science), BUSINESS (business administration and management and sports management), COMMUNICATIONS AND THE ARTS (art history and appreciation, communications, comparative literature, creative writing, dramatic arts, English literature, and fine arts), COMPUTER AND PHYSICAL SCIENCE (mathematics), EDUCATION (elementary, physical, secondary, and special), ENGINEERING AND ENVIRONMENTAL DESIGN (environmental science), HEALTH PROFESSIONS (health science), SOCIAL SCIENCE (criminal justice, philosophy, physical fitness/movement, political science/government, psychology, sociology, and women's studies). Business, education, and psychology are the strongest academically. Business, education, and kinesiology are the largest.

Required: All students must earn a minimum GPA of 2.0 and take 120 credit hours, including an average of 40 in their major. Distribution requirements cover 5 general education areas, including science, humanities, social science, math, and world culture and human rights. Specific requirements include College Writing I and II, a math course (or a passing grade on a placement test), computer science, and science courses.

Special: Cross-registration is available with the New Hampshire College and University Council. Also available are internships for juniors and seniors with a GPA of 2.5, study abroad in 8 countries, work-study programs, dual majors, student-designed majors, interdisciplinary majors, nondegree study, pass/fail options, and a 3-2 engineering degree with Clarkson University. There is 1 national honor society, a freshman honors program, and all departments have honors programs.

Faculty/Classroom: 50% of faculty are male; 50%, female. All teach undergraduates and 20% both teach and do research. No introductory courses are taught by graduate students. The average class size in an introductory lecture is 20; in a laboratory, 14; and in a regular course, 16.

Admissions: 97% of the 2003-2004 applicants were accepted. The SAT I scores for the 2003-2004 freshman class were: Verbal--62% below 500, 30% between 500 and 599, 6% between 600 and 700, and 2% above 700; Math--70% below 500, 22% between 500 and 599, 7% between 600 and 700, and 1% above 700. 20% of the current freshmen were in the top fifth of their class; 50% were in the top two fifths.

Requirements: 4 years of English, 3 years each of math and social studies, and 2 years each of science and electives are recommended. An essay is required and an interview is recommended. A GPA of 2.0 is required. AP and CLEP credits are accepted. Important factors in the admissions decision are recommendations by school officials, extracurricular activities record, and leadership record.

Procedure: Freshmen are admitted fall, spring, and summer. There is a deferred admissions plan and a rolling admissions plan. Application deadlines are open. Application fee is $30. Applications are accepted on-line through the college's web site or Common App.

Transfer: 45 transfer students enrolled in 2002-2003. Transfer students should have a 2.0 minimum GPA from the previous college. A recommendation from the dean of students is required. An interview is recommended. 30 of 120 credits required for the bachelor's degree must be completed at NEC.

Visiting: There are regularly scheduled orientations for prospective students, including class registration and meeting faculty and other students. There are guides for informal visits and visitors may sit in on classes and stay overnight. To schedule a visit, contact Muriel Schlosser in the Admissions Office at (603) 428-2223 or *mschlosser@nec.edu.*

Financial Aid: In 2003-2004, 91% of all full-time freshmen and 90% of continuing full-time students received some form of financial aid. 78% of full-time freshmen and 79% of continuing full-time students received need-based aid. The average freshman award was $25,247. Need-based scholarships or need-based grants averaged $13,437; need-based self-help aid (loans and jobs) averaged $11,154; and non-need-based awards and non-need-based scholarships averaged $8530. 50% of undergraduates work part time. Average annual earnings from campus work are $1500. The average financial indebtedness of the 2003 graduate was $28,167. The FAFSA is required. The priority date for freshman financial aid applications for fall entry is March 15. The deadline for filing freshman financial aid applications for fall entry is May 3.

International Students: There are 51 international students enrolled. The school actively recruits these students. They must score 450 on the written TOEFL or 213 on the electronic version.

Computers: The mainframe is a Sun server network. 90 PCs are available in the computer labs. All are Internet-connected through a fiber-optic network. There are 16 Macs in the graphic design lab, and 30 PCs in the library. All students may access the system 24 hours a day, 7 days a week. There are no time limits and no fees. It is strongly recommended that all students have a personal computer. A Dell is recommended.

Graduates: From July 1, 2002 to June 30, 2003, 141 bachelor's degrees were awarded. The most popular majors were education (23%),

business (22%), and psychology (8%). In an average class, 48% graduate in 4 years or less, and 52% graduate in 5 years or less. More than 20 companies recruited on campus in 2002-2003. Of the 2002 graduating class, 18% were enrolled in graduate school within 6 months of graduation and 95% were employed.

Admissions Contact: Office of Admissions. A video is available. E-mail: *admis@necl.nec.edu* Web: *www.nec.edu*

PLYMOUTH STATE UNIVERSITY	D-4
Plymouth, NH 03264-1595	(603) 535-2237
	(800) 842-6900; Fax: (603) 535-2714

Full-time: 1826 men, 1881 women	**Faculty:** 156; IIA, +$
Part-time: 130 men, 130 women	**Ph.D.s:** 87%
Graduate: 235 men, 708 women	**Student/Faculty:** 24 to 1
Year: semesters, summer session	**Tuition:** $6240 ($12,290)
Application Deadline: April 1	**Room & Board:** $6058
Freshman Class: 3684 applied, 2601 accepted, 903 enrolled	
SAT I Verbal/Math: 480/480	**ACT:** 18 **LESS COMPETITIVE**

Plymouth State University, formerly Plymouth State College, founded in 1871, is a public institution offering programs in business, education, and liberal arts and sciences. In addition to regional accreditation, PSU has baccalaureate program accreditation with ACBSP, CAAHEP, CSWE, and NCATE. The library contains 306,314 volumes, 796,924 microform items, and 23,095 audio/video tapes/CDs, and subscribes to 1043 periodicals. Computerized library services include the card catalog, interlibrary loans, and database searching. Special learning facilities include a learning resource center, art gallery, planetarium, radio station, a major performing arts center, an NAEYC-accredited lab school for children ages 2 to 6, geographic information systems lab, meteorology lab, graphic design, computer lab, MIDI lab, and weather technology evaluation center. The 170-acre campus is in a small town 2 hours north of Boston. Including any residence halls, there are 66 buildings.

Student Life: 58% of undergraduates are from New Hampshire. Students are from 27 states, 9 foreign countries, and Canada. 96% are from public schools. 90% are white. The average age of freshmen is 18; all undergraduates, 21. 26% do not continue beyond their first year; 53% remain to graduate.

Housing: 2107 students can be accommodated in college housing, which includes coed dorms, on-campus apartments, married-student housing, and sorority houses. In addition, there are special-interest houses, a wellness residence hall, and special-interest areas in the residence halls for skiing, snowboarding, biking, hiking, music/theater, fine arts, community service, and fitness. On-campus housing is guaranteed for the freshman year only. 54% of students live on campus; of those, 70% remain on campus on weekends. All students may keep cars.

Activities: 4% of men belong to 2 national fraternities; 7% of women belong to 2 local and 2 national sororities. There are 100 groups on campus, including Alliance for Women's Awareness, art, band, cheerleading, choir, chorale, computers, dance, debate, drama, ethnic, gay, honors, international, jazz band, Leadership Effectiveness and Development seminar, literary magazine, musical theater, newspaper, OSSIPEE, professional, radio and TV, religious, social, social service, student government, student wellness organization, Students in Adventure Growth Experiences, and yearbook. Popular campus events include Spring Fling, Family Weekend, and Winter Carnival.

Sports: There are 8 intercollegiate sports for men and 9 for women, and 30 intramural sports for men and 30 for women. Facilities include a 2500-seat stadium, a 2000-seat gym, playing fields, and facilities for basketball, racquetball, indoor soccer, swimming, tennis, volleyball, softball, and lacrosse. There is also a 75,000-square-foot recreation student center separate from athletics, as well as a ropes course.

Disabled Students: 75% of the campus is accessible. Wheelchair ramps, elevators, special parking, specially equipped rest rooms, lowered drinking fountains, lowered telephones are available. The shuttle service is wheelchair-accessible, and there are handicap-accessible student apartment units, ADA compliant alarm systems, and TDD/TTY available.

Services: Counseling and information services are available, as is tutoring in some subjects, including 100-and 200-level courses and some upper-level courses. Peer tutoring is available.

Campus Safety and Security: Measures include 24-hour foot and vehicle patrol, self-defense education, security escort services, and shuttle buses. There are informal discussions, pamphlets/posters/films, emergency telephones, lighted pathways/sidewalks. There are also programs in defensive driving, alcohol awareness, drug identification, and personal safety.

Programs of Study: PSU confers B.A., B.S., and B.F.A. degrees. Master's degrees are also awarded. Bachelor's degrees are awarded in BIOLOGICAL SCIENCE (biology/biological science, biotechnology, and environmental biology), BUSINESS (accounting, business administration and management, marketing management, and recreation and leisure services), COMMUNICATIONS AND THE ARTS (art, communications, English, French, graphic design, music, performing arts, and Spanish), COMPUTER AND PHYSICAL SCIENCE (atmospheric sciences and meteorology, chemistry, computer science, information sciences and systems, and mathematics), EDUCATION (art, athletic training, health, music, physical, recreation, and science), ENGINEERING AND ENVIRONMENTAL DESIGN (city/community/regional planning), SOCIAL SCIENCE (anthropology, child care/child and family studies, criminal justice, early childhood studies, economics, geography, history, humanities, interdisciplinary studies, medieval studies, philosophy, political science/government, psychology, public administration, social science, and social work). Meteorology, computer science, and graphic design are the strongest academically. Childhood studies, management, and phys ed are the largest.

Required: All students must maintain a minimum GPA of 2.0 while enrolled in 122 semester hours, including 2 credits in psys ed, 1 credit of introduction to the academic community, and 1 course each in composition and math foundations. Distribution requirements are part of the general education program, which requires 7 credits in scientific and science lab, 6 credits in social and psychological, 3 credits in technological, and 3 credits each in the following perspectives: fine and performing arts, global, historical, literary, philosophical, and quantitative reasoning. Some majors have a higher GPA and total credit requirement.

Special: Cross-registration with the New Hampshire College and University Council is available. Internships, study abroad in 3 countries, and college work-study programs are available. Dual majors, an accelerated degree program, offering an undergraduate business and M.B.A. degree in 5 years, and student-designed majors are possible. There are 9 national honor societies, a freshman honors program, and 2 departmental honors programs.

Faculty/Classroom: 57% of faculty are male; 43%, female. 85% teach undergraduates. The average class size in an introductory lecture is 25; in a laboratory, 17; and in a regular course, 20.

Admissions: 71% of the 2003-2004 applicants were accepted. The SAT I scores for the 2003-2004 freshman class were: Verbal--58% below 500, 36% between 500 and 599, 6% between 600 and 700, and 4% above 700; Math--58% below 500, 35% between 500 and 599, and 7% between 600 and 700. The ACT scores were 68% below 21, 18% between 21 and 23, and 14% between 24 and 26. 12% of the current freshmen were in the top fifth of their class; 39% were in the top two fifths.

Requirements: The SAT I or ACT is required. In addition, PSU requires that applicants have completed 4 units of English, 3 each of math, social studies and science, 2 of history, and recommends 2 in foreign language. An audition for certain programs is required, and an essay is required. The GED is accepted. AP and CLEP credits are accepted. Important factors in the admissions decision are advanced placement or honor courses, recommendations by school officials, and leadership record.

Procedure: Freshmen are admitted fall and spring. Entrance exams should be taken in November of the senior year. There is a deferred admissions plan and a rolling admissions plan. Applications should be filed by April 1 for fall entry and December 1 for spring entry, along with a $35 fee. Notification is sent on a rolling basis. Applications are accepted on-line through the school's web site and CollegeLink.

Transfer: 232 transfer students enrolled in 2002-2003. Transfer students must have a minimum GPA of 2.0 on prior work to be considered. 30 of 122 credits required for the bachelor's degree must be completed at PSU.

Visiting: There are regularly scheduled orientations for prospective students, including an admission presentation, a tour of the campus, and a meal in the dining hall. There are guides for informal visits and visitors may sit in on classes. To schedule a visit, contact the Admission Office at *plymouthadmit@plymouth.edu.*

Financial Aid: In 2003-2004, 61% of all full-time freshmen and 58% of continuing full-time students received some form of financial aid. 58% of full-time freshmen and 56% of continuing full-time students received need-based aid. The average freshman award was $6562. Need-based scholarships or need-based grants averaged $4248; need-based self-help aid (loans and jobs) averaged $4029; and other non-need-based awards and non-need-based scholarships averaged $1930. 14% of undergraduates work part time. Average annual earnings from campus work are $850. The FAFSA is required. The priority date for freshman financial aid applications for fall entry is March 1.

International Students: There are 13 international students enrolled. The school actively recruits these students. They must score 520 on the written TOEFL or 190 on the electronic version.

Computers: The mainframe is a Sun 4800. 445 PCs and 96 Mac workstations are available to students in 39 different computing facilities. In addition, all campus residence halls provide computer ports for students in their rooms. All systems are connected to the campus network and the Internet. All students may access the system. There are no time limits. The fee is $330 annual tech fee. It is strongly recommended that all students have a personal computer.

Graduates: From July 1, 2002 to June 30, 2003, 559 bachelor's degrees were awarded. The most popular majors were childhood studies (14%), management (11%), and communications studies (9%). In an average class, 26% graduate in 4 years or less, 45% graduate in 5 years or less, and 48% graduate in 6 years or less. 68 companies recruited on campus in 2002-2003.

Admissions Contact: Eugene D. Fahey, Senior Associate Director of Admission. E-mail: *plymouthadmit@plymouth.edu*
Web: *www.plymouth.edu*

RIVIER COLLEGE

D-6
Nashua, NH 03060-5086

(603) 897-8507
(800) 44-RIVIER; Fax: (603) 891-1799

Full-time: 267 men, 550 women	**Faculty:** 63; IIA, --$
Part-time: 159 men, 476 women	**Ph.Ds:** 88%
Graduate: 248 men, 617 women	**Student/Faculty:** 13 to 1
Year: semesters, summer session	**Tuition:** $19,125
Application Deadline: open	**Room & Board:** $7092
Freshman Class: 1012 applied, 780 accepted, 314 enrolled	
SAT I Verbal/Math: 492/478	**COMPETITIVE**

Rivier College, founded in 1933 by the Sisters of the Presentation of Mary, is a private Roman Catholic college offering a liberal arts and professional curriculum. In addition to regional accreditation, Rivier has baccalaureate program accreditation with NLN. The library contains 107,200 volumes, 89,572 microform items, and 29,094 audio/video tapes/CDs, and subscribes to 480 periodicals. Computerized library services include the card catalog, interlibrary loans, and database searching. Special learning facilities include a learning resource center, art gallery, radio station, TV station, education curriculum resources center, legal reference center, early childhood center/laboratory school, and language lab. The 68-acre campus is in a suburban area 45 miles north of Boston. Including any residence halls, there are 44 buildings.

Student Life: 68% of undergraduates are from New Hampshire. Students are from 13 states, 13 foreign countries, and Canada. 80% are from public schools. 93% are white. Most are Catholic. The average age of freshmen is 18; all undergraduates, 28. 29% do not continue beyond their first year.

Housing: 425 students can be accommodated in college housing, which includes coed dorms and a substance-free/wellness residence hall. On-campus housing is guaranteed for all 4 years and is available on a first-come, first-served basis. 56% of students commute. All students may keep cars.

Activities: There are no fraternities or sororities. There are 32 groups on campus, including art, behavioral sciences, chorus, computers, debate, drama, ethnic, history, honors, international, literary magazine, newspaper, nursing, paralegal, political, professional, religious, social, social sciences, social service, student government, and yearbook. Popular campus events include Spirit Week, Black History Month, and Women's History Month.

Sports: There are 5 intercollegiate sports for men and 5 for women, and 7 intramural sports for men and 7 for women. Facilities include a 300-seat gym, a weight room, and soccer and softball fields.

Disabled Students: 75% of the campus is accessible. Wheelchair ramps, elevators, special parking, specially equipped rest rooms, and lowered drinking fountains are available.

Services: Counseling and information services are available, as is tutoring in some subjects, including math, English, business, and languages. Tutoring is available in other subjects. There is remedial math and writing. There is a full-service writing center.

Campus Safety and Security: Measures include 24-hour foot and vehicle patrol, security escort services, informal discussions, and pamphlets/posters/films. There are emergency telephones, lighted pathways/sidewalks, and 24-hour access by telephone or walkie-talkie, and electronically operated dorm entrances using security cards.

Programs of Study: Rivier confers B.A., B.S., and B.F.A. degrees. Associate and master's degrees are also awarded. Bachelor's degrees are awarded in BIOLOGICAL SCIENCE (biology/biological science), BUSINESS (business administration and management, management information systems, and management science), COMMUNICATIONS AND THE ARTS (communications, English, graphic design, illustration, and studio art), COMPUTER AND PHYSICAL SCIENCE (computer science and mathematics), EDUCATION (art, early childhood, elementary, English, mathematics, secondary, and social studies), HEALTH PROFESSIONS (nursing, predentistry, premedicine, and preveterinary science), SOCIAL SCIENCE (history, human development, liberal arts/general studies, political science/government, prelaw, psychology, and sociology). Art, education, and nursing are the strongest academically. Education, psychology, and business are the largest.

Required: A writing sample is required at entry, and a demonstration of writing proficiency must be shown prior to graduation. Students must complete at least 120 credit hours, ordinarily consisting of 40 3-credit courses with 35 to 60 credits in the student's major, and they must maintain a minimum GPA of 2.0. Distribution requirements include 17 core courses in basic skills of writing and math, the humanities, and the sciences. These courses include religious studies, philosophy, physical and life sciences, fine arts, modern languages, literature, behavioral and social sciences, and Western civilization.

Special: Rivier offers cross-registration through the New Hampshire College and University Council, internships in most majors, an accelerated master's program in English, dual majors, a liberal studies degree, credit by challenge examination, nondegree study, and pass/fail options. There is 1 national honor society and a freshman honors program.

Faculty/Classroom: 38% of faculty are male; 62%, female. 88% teach undergraduates. No introductory courses are taught by graduate students. The average class size in an introductory lecture is 25; in a laboratory, 20; and in a regular course, 17.

Admissions: 77% of the 2003-2004 applicants were accepted. The SAT I scores for the 2003-2004 freshman class were: Verbal--50% below 500, 35% between 500 and 599, and 15% between 600 and 700; Math--50% below 500, 35% between 500 and 599, and 15% between 600 and 700. 24% of the current freshmen were in the top fifth of their class; 70% were in the top two fifths.

Requirements: The SAT I is required. In addition, applicants must be high school graduates or hold the GED. The recommended college preparatory curriculum includes 4 years of English, 3 of math, 2 or more each of foreign language and social studies, 1 of lab science, and 4 academic electives. An essay and 1 or 2 letters of recommendation are required, and an interview is highly recommended. Prospective art majors must submit a portfolio. Rivier requires applicants to be in the upper 50% of their class. A GPA of 2.5 is required. AP and CLEP credits are accepted. Important factors in the admissions decision are advanced placement or honor courses, recommendations by school officials, and extracurricular activities record.

Procedure: Freshmen are admitted fall and spring. Entrance exams should be taken in the junior or senior year. There is a deferred admissions plan and a rolling admissions plan. The fall 2003 fall application fee was $25. Application deadlines are open. Applications are accepted on-line through the Rivier web site.

Transfer: 160 transfer students enrolled in 2002-2003. Transfer applicants should have a minimum GPA of 2.5 and submit SAT I or ACT scores if they have earned fewer than 12 credits at the previous institution. Official college transcripts are required and an interview is recommended. 60 of 120 credits required for the bachelor's degree must be completed at Rivier.

Visiting: There are regularly scheduled orientations for prospective students, including an opportunity to interview, a tour, class visits, and opportunities to meet with faculty, coaches, and current students. There are guides for informal visits and visitors may sit in on classes and stay overnight. To schedule a visit, contact the Office of Undergraduate Admissions.

Financial Aid: 35% of undergraduates work part time. Average annual earnings from campus work are $546. The average financial indebtedness of the 2003 graduate was $17,500. Rivier is a member of CSS. The FAFSA is required. The deadline for filing freshman financial aid applications for fall entry is March 1.

International Students: The school actively recruits these students. They must score 500 on the written TOEFL and also take the college's own test.

Computers: The mainframes are a Sun SPARC 20 with NEC and DEC Alpha servers. The Academic Computing Center houses high-speed Pentium workstations with a wide range of software and services. All students are provided with private server storage, Internet access, and an e-mail account. Residence halls are wired for access to the college network and the web. All students may access the system 24 hours a day. There are no time limits. The fee varies.

Graduates: The most popular majors were nursing (31%) and education (30%). In a recent year, 21% were enrolled in graduate school within 6 months of graduation and 99% were employed.

Admissions Contact: David A. Boisvert, Director of Undergraduate Admissions. E-mail: *rivadmit@rivier.edu* Web: *www.rivier.edu*

SAINT ANSELM COLLEGE
Manchester, NH 03102

D-6
(603) 641-7500
(888) 4 ANSELM; Fax: (603) 641-7550

Full-time: 833 men, 1106 women	**Faculty:** 122; IIB, av$
Part-time: 30 men, 39 women	**Ph.Ds:** 94%
Graduate: none	**Student/Faculty:** 16 to 1
Year: semesters, summer session	**Tuition:** $22,160
Application Deadline: March 1	**Room & Board:** $8090
Freshman Class: 3033 applied, 2140 accepted, 588 enrolled	
SAT I Verbal/Math: 560/560	**COMPETITIVE**

Saint Anselm College, founded in 1889, is a private Roman Catholic institution offering a liberal arts education. In addition to regional accreditation, Saint Anselm has baccalaureate program accreditation with NLN. The library contains 219,000 volumes, 65,000 microform items, and 8000 audio/video tapes/CDs, and subscribes to 3900 periodicals. Computerized library services include the card catalog, interlibrary loans, database searching, and Internet access. Special learning facilities include a learning resource center, art gallery, planetarium, and TV station. The 404-acre campus is in a suburban area 50 miles north of Boston. Including any residence halls, there are 63 buildings.

Student Life: 74% of undergraduates are from out of state, mostly the Northeast. Students are from 27 states, 16 foreign countries, and Canada. 67% are from public schools. 93% are white. 79% are Catholic; 9% Protestant; 8% claim no religious affiliation. The average age of freshmen is 18; all undergraduates, 20. 20% do not continue beyond their first year; 70% remain to graduate.

Housing: 1644 students can be accommodated in college housing, which includes single-sex and coed dorms and on-campus apartments. In addition, there are special-interest houses and substance-free housing. On-campus housing is guaranteed for all 4 years. 88% of students live on campus; of those, 85% remain on campus on weekends. All students may keep cars.

Activities: There are no fraternities or sororities. There are 64 groups on campus, including art, cheerleading, chess, choir, chorale, chorus, computers, dance, debate, drama, ethnic, honors, international, jazz band, literary magazine, newspaper, orchestra, pep band, photography, political, professional, radio and TV, religious, social, social service, student government, and yearbook. Popular campus events include Winter Weekend, Family Weekend, and Road for Hope.

Sports: There are 10 intercollegiate sports for men and 10 for women, and 13 intramural sports for men and 13 for women. Facilities include a 1500-seat gym, an ice hockey arena, an activity center that houses basketball, volleyball, tennis, and racquetball courts, and weight and training rooms; a 2500-seat football stadium, a 500-seat baseball stadium, and athletic fields.

Disabled Students: 60% of the campus is accessible. Wheelchair ramps, elevators, special parking, specially equipped rest rooms, special class scheduling, and lowered drinking fountains are available.

Services: Counseling and information services are available, as is tutoring in most subjects. There is a reader service for the blind.

Campus Safety and Security: Measures include 24-hour foot and vehicle patrol, informal discussions, pamphlets/posters/films, and emergency telephones. There are lighted pathways/sidewalks and security escort upon request.

Programs of Study: Saint Anselm confers B.A. and B.S.N. degrees. Bachelor's degrees are awarded in BIOLOGICAL SCIENCE (biochemistry and biology/biological science), BUSINESS (accounting, banking and finance, and business administration and management), COMMUNICATIONS AND THE ARTS (classics, English, fine arts, French, and Spanish), COMPUTER AND PHYSICAL SCIENCE (chemistry, computer science, mathematics, and natural sciences), EDUCATION (secondary), ENGINEERING AND ENVIRONMENTAL DESIGN (engineering and environmental science), HEALTH PROFESSIONS (nursing, predentistry, and premedicine), SOCIAL SCIENCE (criminal justice, economics, history, liberal arts/general studies, philosophy, political science/government, prelaw, psychology, sociology, and theological studies). Business, English, and psychology are the largest.

Required: All students must maintain a GPA of 2.0 in the major while completing at least 40 semester courses, including 4 semesters in the humanities, 2 each in English and lab science, 3 each in philosophy and theology, and 2 to 4 in foreign language; 10 to 13 courses are required in the major area of study.

Special: Saint Anselm offers a 5-year liberal arts and a 3-2 engineering program in cooperation with Manhattan College, Notre Dame University, University of Massachusetts Lowell, and Catholic University of America. Cross-registration is possible. In addition, internships, work-study, a Washington semester, study abroad, and nondegree study are available. There are 11 national honor societies, a freshman honors program, and departmental honors programs in all departments.

Faculty/Classroom: 57% of faculty are male; 43%, female. All teach undergraduates. The average class size in an introductory lecture is 20; in a laboratory, 14; and in a regular course, 24.

Admissions: 71% of the 2003-2004 applicants were accepted. The SAT I scores for the 2003-2004 freshman class were: Verbal--18% below 500, 54% between 500 and 599, 26% between 600 and 700, and 2% above 700; Math--17% below 500, 57% between 500 and 599, 24% between 600 and 700, and 2% above 700. 37% of the current freshmen were in the top fifth of their class; 72% were in the top two fifths. 7 freshmen graduated first in their class.

Requirements: The SAT I is required. In addition, applicants must have 16 academic credits and 16 Carnegie units, including 4 years of English, 3 each of math and science, 2 of foreign language, and 1 each of history and social studies. An essay is required and an interview is recommended. The GED is accepted. A GPA of 2.0 is required. AP and CLEP credits are accepted. Important factors in the admissions decision are advanced placement or honor courses, leadership record, and recommendations by school officials.

Procedure: Freshmen are admitted fall and spring. Entrance exams should be taken during the spring of the junior year or fall of the senior year. There are early decision, early admissions, and deferred admissions plans. Early decision applications should be filed by December 1;

regular applications, by March 1 for fall entry and December 1 for spring entry, along with a $50 fee. Notification of early decision is sent December 15; regular decision, on a rolling basis. 46 early decision candidates were accepted for a recent class. A waiting list is an active part of the admissions procedure. Applications are accepted on computer disk and online through Common App.

Transfer: 27 transfer students enrolled in 2002-2003. Transfer students must have a minimum GPA of 2.5 after earning at least 30 college credits. The SAT I is required and an interview is recommended. In addition, 2 letters of recommendation are necessary. 20 of 40 courses required for the bachelor's degree must be completed at Saint Anselm.

Visiting: There are regularly scheduled orientations for prospective students, consisting of daily individual interviews and/or group information sessions followed by a campus tour. There are guides for informal visits and visitors may sit in on classes and stay overnight. To schedule a visit, contact the Office of Admission.

Financial Aid: In a recent year, 82% of all full-time freshmen and 84% of continuing full-time students received some form of financial aid. 85% of full-time freshmen and 84% of continuing full-time students received need-based aid. The average freshman award was $16,189. 45% of undergraduates work part time. Average annual earnings from campus work are $641. The average financial indebtedness of a recent graduate was $17,897. The CSS Profile or FAFSA is required. The deadline for filing freshman financial aid applications for fall entry is March 15.

International Students: There were 16 international students enrolled in a recent year. The school actively recruits these students. They must score 550 on the written TOEFL or 213 on the electronic version and also take the SAT I or the ACT.

Computers: The mainframe is an IBM AS/400. 3 main computer centers on campus contain more than 50 Macs and 125 PCs. All are networked to print- and file-sharing servers and all have high-speed (T3) Internet access. Additional computers are located in psychology, physics, chemistry, biology, and math department labs. All students may access the system 8:30 A.M. to 12 a.m, Monday through Friday; 10 A.M. to 6 P.M. Saturday; 1 P.M. to 12 A.M. Sunday. There are no time limits and no fees.

Graduates: In a recent year, 408 bachelor's degrees were awarded. The most popular majors were economics/business (19%), psychology (12%), and nursing (10%). In an average class, 76% graduate in 4 years or less, and 79% graduate in 5 years or less. 75 companies recruited on campus in a recent year. Of a recent graduating class, 13% were enrolled in graduate school within 6 months of graduation and 80% were employed.

Admissions Contact: Nancy Griffin, Director of Admission.
E-mail: *admission@anselm.edu* Web: *www.anselm.edu*

SOUTHERN NEW HAMPSHIRE UNIVERSITY   D-6
Manchester, NH 03106-1045   **(603) 645-9611**
(800) 642-4968; Fax: (603) 645-9693

Full-time: 1237 men, 1497 women	**Faculty:** IIA, +$
Part-time: 529 men, 964 women	**Ph.D.s:** 70%
Graduate: 850 men, 949 women	**Student/Faculty:** n/av
Year: semesters, summer session	**Tuition:** $18,594
Application Deadline: March 15	**Room & Board:** $7648
Freshman Class: 2413 applied, 1708 accepted, 698 enrolled	
SAT I Verbal/Math: 482/485	**COMPETITIVE**

Southern New Hampshire University, founded in 1932, is a private institution offering business, liberal arts, education, and hospitality-related fields of study. In addition to regional accreditation, SNHU has baccalaureate program accreditation with ACBSP. The library contains 79,621 volumes, 320,236 microform items, and 2105 audio/video tapes/CDs, and subscribes to 529 periodicals. Computerized library services include the card catalog, interlibrary loans, database searching, and Internet access. Special learning facilities include a learning resource center, art gallery, radio station, a center for financial studies, an advertising agency (on campus), an audiovisual studio, and a psychology observation lab. The 280-acre campus is in a suburban area 55 miles north of Boston. Including any residence halls, there are 28 buildings.

Student Life: 69% of undergraduates are from out of state, mostly the Northeast. Students are from 23 states, 35 foreign countries, and Canada. 42% are white. 50% are Catholic; 35% Protestant; 10% Jewish. 25% do not continue beyond their first year; 50% remain to graduate.

Housing: 1224 students can be accommodated in college housing, which includes single-sex and coed dorms and on-campus apartments. In addition, there are special-interest houses and a wellness housing area. On-campus housing is guaranteed for the freshman year only and is available on a first-come, first-served basis. 80% of students live on campus. All students may keep cars.

Activities: 4% of men belong to 3 national fraternities; 5% of women belong to 3 local and 1 national sorority. There are 44 groups on campus, including cheerleading, choir, chorus, crew club, dance, debate club, drama, ethnic, field hockey, honors, international, literary magazine, model UN, musical theater, newspaper, professional, radio and TV, religious, social, social service, student government, and yearbook. Popular campus events include Fall, Winter, and Spring Weekends, Family Weekend, and International Night.

Sports: There are 8 intercollegiate sports for men and 7 for women, and 7 intramural sports for men and 6 for women. Facilities include a gym, an Olympic-size swimming pool, racquetball courts, a fitness center, a field house, a nautilus weight room, a mirrored dance/exercise room, 2 training rooms, an equipment room, 4 tennis courts, baseball and softball fields, a lighted field for soccer and la crosse, and several practice fields.

Disabled Students: 90% of the campus is accessible. Wheelchair ramps, elevators, special parking, specially equipped rest rooms, special class scheduling, lowered drinking fountains, lowered telephones, and automatic door openers are available.

Services: Counseling and information services are available, as is tutoring in every subject. There is a reader service for the blind, and remedial math, reading, and writing.

Campus Safety and Security: Measures include 24-hour foot and vehicle patrol, self-defense education, security escort services, and informal discussions. There are pamphlets/posters/films, emergency telephones, lighted pathways/sidewalks, winter driving seminars for international students, and public safety officers.

Programs of Study: SNHU confers B.A., B.S., and B.A.S.H.A. degrees. Associate, master's, and doctoral degrees are also awarded. Bachelor's degrees are awarded in BUSINESS (accounting, business administration and management, hospitality management services, hotel/motel and restaurant management, international business management, marketing/retailing/merchandising, retailing, sports management, and tourism), COMMUNICATIONS AND THE ARTS (communications, English, and English literature), COMPUTER AND PHYSICAL SCIENCE (information sciences and systems), EDUCATION (business, English, and marketing and distribution), ENGINEERING AND ENVIRONMENTAL DESIGN (technological management), SOCIAL SCIENCE (economics, psychology, and social science). Business administration is the strongest academically. Business administration, sport management, and culinary arts are the largest.

Required: To graduate, students must complete 120 credit hours, including a maximum of 33 in their major, with a GPA of 2.0. Distribution requirements total 69 credits from the college core, including 2 to 3 courses in writing, 2 in economics, and 1 in math, information technology, public speaking, statistics, and social science, plus a freshman seminar and electives in fine arts or humanities, literature, and the social and natural sciences.

Special: Co-op programs with the area business community are strongly promoted, as is cross-registration through the New Hampshire College and University Council. Students may study abroad in England. A general business studies degree with 14 different concentrations, work-study programs, dual majors, an accelerated degree program in business administration, credit for life experience, and nondegree study are available. There are 4 national honor societies, a freshman honors program, and all departments have honors programs.

Faculty/Classroom: 71% of faculty are male; 29%, female. 39% teach undergraduates. No introductory courses are taught by graduate students. The average class size in an introductory lecture is 22; in a laboratory, 15; and in a regular course, 25.

Admissions: 71% of the 2003-2004 applicants were accepted. The SAT I scores for the 2003-2004 freshman class were: Verbal--66% below 500, 30% between 500 and 599, and 4% between 600 and 700; Math--59% below 500, 33% between 500 and 599, and 8% between 600 and 700. 7% of the current freshmen were in the top fifth of their class; 28% were in the top two fifths.

Requirements: The SAT I is required. In addition, students must have completed 4 years of English and 3 of math. An essay, high school transcript, SAT I scores and a letter of recommendation from a guidance counselor or 2 teachers are required. An interview is strongly recommended. The GED is accepted. A GPA of 2.0 is required. AP and CLEP credits are accepted. Important factors in the admissions decision are advanced placement or honor courses, recommendations by school officials, and leadership record.

Procedure: Freshmen are admitted to all sessions. There are early admissions, deferred admissions plans, and rolling admissions. Early decision applications should be filed by November 15; regular applications, by March 15 for fall entry and December 1 for spring entry. The fall 2003 application fee was $35. Notification is sent on a rolling basis. Applications are accepted on-line through ApplyYourself and the school's web site.

Transfer: 151 transfer students enrolled in 2002-2003. Transfer applicants: must submit a completed application, essay, $35 application fee (waved online), official high school transcript, official college transcripts, supplemental transfer form, and a letter of recommendation. An interview is recommended. Most successful applicants for transfer admission have a cumulative GPA of 2.5 or higher. 30 of 120 credits required for the bachelor's degree must be completed at SNHU.

Visiting: There are regularly scheduled orientations for prospective students, including a greeting from college administrators, campus tours with students, and informal discussions with faculty, staff, and students. There are guides for informal visits and visitors may sit in on classes. To schedule a visit, contact the Admission Office at *admission@snhu.edu*.

Financial Aid: In 2003-2004, 80% of all full-time students received some form of financial aid. 80% of all full-time students received need-based aid. The FAFSA is required. The deadline for filing freshman financial aid applications for fall entry is March 15.

International Students: There are 96 international students enrolled. The school actively recruits these students. They must score 500 on the written TOEFL or 173 on the electronic version and also take the SAT I or the ACT.

Computers: The mainframe is an IBM 4381. There are more than 350 terminals, located in computer labs and the library, that provide access to the Internet. All students may access the system 16 hours daily, 8 A.M. to 12 P.M.; extended hours during final exams. There are no time limits and no fees. It is strongly recommended that all students have a personal computer. It is recommended that students in the 3 year honors program in business and information technology have personal computers.

Graduates: From July 1, 2002 to June 30, 2003, 669 bachelor's degrees were awarded. The most popular majors were business administration (37%), hotel and restaurant management (10%), and marketing (6%). In an average class, 25% graduate in 4 years or less, 30% graduate in 5 years or less, and 35% graduate in 6 years or less. 30 companies recruited on campus in 2002-2003.

Admissions Contact: Steven Soba, Director of Admission. A video is available. E-mail: *admission@snhu.edu* Web: *www.snhu.edu*

THOMAS MORE COLLEGE OF LIBERAL ARTS   D-6
Merrimack, NH 03054

(603) 880-8308
(800) 880-8308; Fax: (603) 880-9280

Full-time: 40 men, 30 women	**Faculty:** 5
Part-time: none	**Ph.D.s:** 100%
Graduate: none	**Student/Faculty:** 14 to 1
Year: semesters	**Tuition:** $10,400
Application Deadline: open	**Room & Board:** $7700
Freshman Class: n/av	
SAT I or ACT: required	**COMPETITIVE**

Thomas More College of Liberal Arts, founded in 1978 by Roman Catholic educators, is an undergraduate institution. Figures in the above capsule and in this profile are approximate. In addition to regional accreditation, TMC has baccalaureate program accreditation with AALE. The library contains 50,000 volumes and subscribes to 20 periodicals. The 12-acre campus is in a suburban area between Nashua and Manchester, 40 miles north of Boston. Including any residence halls, there are 5 buildings.

Student Life: 81% of undergraduates are from out of state, mostly the Northeast. Students are from 20 states, 2 foreign countries, and Canada. 84% are white. The average age of freshmen is 18; all undergraduates, 20. 9% do not continue beyond their first year.

Housing: Housing includes single-sex dorms. On-campus housing is guaranteed for all 4 years. Alcohol is not permitted. All students may keep cars.

Activities: There are no fraternities or sororities.

Disabled Students: 70% of the campus is accessible. Wheelchair ramps, special parking, and specially equipped rest rooms are available.

Services: Informal tutoring is available by request.

Campus Safety and Security: Measures include security escort services, informal discussions, and lighted pathways/sidewalks.

Programs of Study: TMC confers the B.A. degree. Bachelor's degrees are awarded in BIOLOGICAL SCIENCE (biology/biological science), COMMUNICATIONS AND THE ARTS (literature), SOCIAL SCIENCE (philosophy and political science/government).

Required: To graduate, students must complete 120 credit hours, (125 for biology majors), including 48 in humanities, 12 in writing workshop, 12 in classical languages, 12 in math and science, 6 in theology, and 3 in fine arts. At least 24 hours (32 for biology majors) in the major are required. In addition, students must complete a junior project of independent study and a senior thesis.

Special: A semester in Rome for sophomores is required unless waived.

Faculty/Classroom: 80% of faculty are male; 20%, female. All teach undergraduates, 80% do research, and 80% do both.

Requirements: The SAT I or ACT is required. In addition, applicants should be high school graduates with 4 college preparatory units of English, 3 of math, and 2 each of foreign language, social science, and lab science. The GED is accepted. An essay and 2 letters of recommendation are required. An interview is strongly recommended. Important factors in the admissions decision are personality/intangible qualities, evidence of special talent, and leadership record.

Procedure: Freshmen are admitted fall and spring. There is a rolling admissions plan. Application deadlines are open. Applications are accepted on-line through the school's web site.

Transfer: 4 transfer students enrolled in a recent year. Applicants must submit a transcript from all higher institutions attended.

Visiting: There are guides for informal visits and visitors may sit in on classes and stay overnight. To schedule a visit, contact Kristen S. Kelly, Director of Admissions.

Financial Aid: TMC is a member of CSS. The FAFSA is required.

International Students: The school actively recruits international students. It is strongly recommended that students take either the SAT I or the ACT.

Computers: There are 6 computers in the library for e-mail, Internet access, and word processing. All students may access the system during library hours. There are no time limits and no fees.

Graduates: In a recent year, 12 bachelor's degrees were awarded. The most popular majors were philosophy (33%), political science (33%), and literature (25%). In an average class, 100% graduate in 4 years or less. Of a recent graduating class, 27% were enrolled in graduate school within 6 months of graduation and 73% were employed.

Admissions Contact: Kristen S. Kelly, Director of Admissions. E-mail: *admissions@thomasmorecollege.edu* Web: *www.thomasmorecollege.edu*

UNIVERSITY OF NEW HAMPSHIRE   E-5
Durham, NH 03824   (603) 862-1360; Fax: (603) 862-0077

Full-time: 4511 men, 6047 women	**Faculty:** 520; I, av$
Part-time: 164 men, 215 women	**Ph.D.s:** 96%
Graduate: 1006 men, 1345 women	**Student/Faculty:** 20 to 1
Year: semesters, summer session	**Tuition:** $8594 ($19,024)
Application Deadline: February 1	**Room & Board:** $6234
Freshman Class: 10,798 applied, 7502 accepted, 2452 enrolled	
SAT I Verbal/Math: 550/560	**VERY COMPETITIVE**

The University of New Hampshire, founded in 1866, is part of the public university system of New Hampshire and offers degree programs in liberal arts, engineering, physical sciences, business, economics, life sciences, agriculture, and health and human services. There are 7 undergraduate schools and 1 graduate school. In addition to regional accreditation, UNH has baccalaureate program accreditation with AACSB, ABET, ADA, AHEA, CAHEA, CSAB, CSWE, NASM, NLN, and SAF. The 5 libraries contain 1,718,808 volumes, 2,964,600 microform items, and 26,640 audio/video tapes/CDs, and subscribe to 27,208 periodicals. Computerized library services include the card catalog, interlibrary loans, and database searching. Special learning facilities include a learning resource center, art gallery, radio station, TV station, optical observatory, marine research laboratory, experiential learning center, electron microscope, child development center, journalism laboratory, various agricultural and equine facilities, and sawmill. The 2600-acre campus is in a rural area 50 miles north of Boston. Including any residence halls, there are 150 buildings.

Student Life: 58% of undergraduates are from New Hampshire. Students are from 42 states, 26 foreign countries, and Canada. 76% are from public schools. 88% are white. 35% are Catholic; 31% claim no religious affiliation; 26% Protestant. The average age of freshmen is 18; all undergraduates, 20. 15% do not continue beyond their first year; 72% remain to graduate.

Housing: 6100 students can be accommodated in college housing, which includes single-sex and coed dorms, on-campus apartments, and married-student housing. In addition, there are honors houses, language houses, special-interest houses, and international and substance-free residence halls. On-campus housing is guaranteed for the freshman year only, is available on a first-come, first-served basis, and is available on a lottery system for upperclassmen. 56% of students live on campus; of those, 65% remain on campus on weekends. Upperclassmen may keep cars.

Activities: 4% of men belong to 1 local and 9 national fraternities; 5% of women belong to 5 national sororities. There are 161 groups on campus, including art, band, cheerleading, chess, choir, chorale, chorus, computers, dance, debate, drama, ethnic, film, gay, honors, international, jazz band, literary magazine, marching band, musical theater, newspaper, opera, orchestra, pep band, photography, political, professional, radio and TV, religious, social, social service, student government, symphony, and yearbook. Popular campus events include International Day, concert and lecture series, and Winter Carnival.

Sports: There are 10 intercollegiate sports for men and 14 for women, and 12 intramural sports for men and 13 for women. Facilities include indoor and outdoor swimming pools, tracks, tennis courts, gyms, wrestling and gymnastics rooms, a dance studio, playing fields, an indoor ice rink, and cross-country ski trails. A 3-story recreation and sports complex, which seats 6000 at hockey and basketball games and special events, includes a fitness center, jogging track, a weight room, racquetball courts, an international squash court, aerobics and martial arts studios, multipurpose courts, and basketball courts.

Disabled Students: 80% of the campus is accessible. Wheelchair ramps, elevators, special parking, specially equipped rest rooms, special class scheduling, lowered drinking fountains, lowered telephones, and special housing are available. Accommodations made on a case-by-case basis include sign language interpreters, reduced course loads, extended exam time, accessible transportation, academic modifications, note takers, text on tape, and readers.

Services: Counseling and information services are available. Instruction in learning strategies, study skills, time management, and organizational skills is available. The university writing center offers free assistance by trained consultants.

Campus Safety and Security: Measures include 24-hour foot and vehicle patrol, self-defense education, security escort services, and shuttle buses. There are informal discussions, pamphlets/posters/films, emergency telephones, lighted pathways/sidewalks, limited access to dorms, and prevention awareness programs.

Programs of Study: UNH confers B.A., B.S., B.F.A., B.M., and B.S.F. degrees. Associate, master's, and doctoral degrees are also awarded. Bachelor's degrees are awarded in AGRICULTURE (animal science, dairy science, equine science, forestry and related sciences, horticulture, natural resource management, plant science, soil science, and wildlife management), BIOLOGICAL SCIENCE (biology/biological science, biotechnology, ecology, marine biology, microbiology, molecular biology, nutrition, and zoology), BUSINESS (business administration and management, hotel/motel and restaurant management, recreation and leisure services, and tourism), COMMUNICATIONS AND THE ARTS (art history and appreciation, classics, communications, dramatic arts, English, English literature, fine arts, French, German, Greek, journalism, Latin, linguistics, music, music history and appreciation, music performance, music theory and composition, performing arts, Russian, Spanish, studio art, and voice), COMPUTER AND PHYSICAL SCIENCE (chemistry, computer science, earth science, geology, hydrology, mathematics, and physics), EDUCATION (athletic training, English, mathematics, music, physical, recreation, and science), ENGINEERING AND ENVIRONMENTAL DESIGN (chemical engineering, city/community/regional planning, civil engineering, computer engineering, electrical/electronics engineering, engineering technology, environmental engineering, environmental science, mechanical engineering, and mechanical engineering technology), HEALTH PROFESSIONS (health care administration, medical laboratory science, nursing, occupational therapy, preveterinary science, and speech pathology/audiology), SOCIAL SCIENCE (anthropology, economics, family/consumer studies, French studies, geography, history, humanities, international studies, philosophy, physical fitness/movement, political science/government, psychology, social work, sociology, water resources, and women's studies). Psychology, English, and biological sciences are the strongest academically. Business administration, English, and psychology are the largest.

Required: To graduate, all students must maintain a GPA of 2.0 and complete at least 128 credits, with a minimum of 36 credits and 10 classes in the major. General education requirements include 4 writing-intensive courses, including freshman composition; 3 courses each in quantitative reasoning and science; and 1 course each in historical perspectives, social science, fine arts, foreign culture, and philosophy/literature. Honors students and most seniors write a thesis or complete a project.

Special: Co-op programs with Cornell University in marine science are available. Extensive cross-registration is possible through the New Hampshire College and University Council Consortium. There also is nationwide study through the National Student Exchange and worldwide study through the Center for International Education. Internships, a Washington semester, work-study, B.A.-B.S. degrees, dual majors, a general studies degree, student-designed majors, extensive 3-2 B.S./M.B.A. programs and other bachelor's/graduate degree plans, nondegree study, and pass/fail options are available. A 3-2 engineering degree is offered with the New Hampshire Technical Institute, Vermont Technical College, Keene State College, and other institutions. There are 22 national honor societies, including Phi Beta Kappa, a freshman honors program, and 41 departmental honors programs.

Faculty/Classroom: 63% of faculty are male; 37%, female. All both teach and do research. Graduate students teach 2% of introductory courses. The average class size in an introductory lecture is 44; in a laboratory, 20; and in a regular course, 18.

Admissions: 69% of the 2003-2004 applicants were accepted. The SAT I scores for the 2003-2004 freshman class were: Verbal--22% below 500, 52% between 500 and 599, 23% between 600 and 700, and 3% above 700; Math--19% below 500, 48% between 500 and 599, 29% between 600 and 700, and 4% above 700. 41% of the current freshmen were in the top fifth of their class; 79% were in the top two fifths. 40 freshmen graduated first in their class.

Requirements: The SAT I or ACT is required. In addition, applicants should have 18 academic credits, including 4 each in English, math, and lab science and 3 each in foreign language and social studies. Students with a specific major in mind are encouraged to take SAT II: Subject tests relating to that major. An essay is required for all students and an informational interview recommended. For art students, a portfolio is required, as is an audition for music students. The GED is accepted. AP and CLEP credits are accepted. Important factors in the admissions decision are advanced placement or honor courses, recommendations by school officials, and evidence of special talent.

Procedure: Freshmen are admitted fall and spring. Entrance exams should be taken before February 1 of the senior year. There are early admissions and deferred admissions plans. Applications should be filed by February 1 for fall entry and November 1 for spring entry, along with a $45 fee. Notification is sent April 15. Applications are accepted on-line through the school's web site, CollegeLink, or Common App.

Transfer: 383 transfer students enrolled in the fall of 2003. Applicants must submit an overall minimum GPA of 2.5 and 3.0 in a general education curriculum. The SAT I or the ACT is required. 32 of 128 credits required for the bachelor's degree must be completed at UNH.

Visiting: There are regularly scheduled orientations for prospective students, including campus tours, a student panel, and general information sessions. There are guides for informal visits and visitors may sit in on classes. To schedule a visit, contact the Admissions Office.

Financial Aid: In 2003-2004, 82% of all full-time freshmen and 71% of continuing full-time students received some form of financial aid. 63% of full-time freshmen and 57% of continuing full-time students received need-based aid. The average freshman award was $12,672. Need-based scholarships or need-based grants averaged $6966 ($17,493 maximum); need-based self-help aid (loans and jobs) averaged $6203 ($6625 maximum); non-need-based athletic scholarships averaged $1788 ($2500 maximum); and other non-need-based awards and non-need-based scholarships averaged $1762. 34% of undergraduates work part time. Average annual earnings from campus work are $1331. The average financial indebtedness of the 2003 graduate was $21,251. UNH is a member of CSS. The FAFSA is required. The deadline for filing freshman financial aid applications for fall entry is March 1.

International Students: There are 75 international students enrolled. The school actively recruits these students. They must score 550 on the written TOEFL or 213 on the electronic version and also take the SAT I or the ACT.

Computers: The mainframe is a Compaq Alpha Server. Each dorm room is fitted with telephone lines for each student to access the university's mainframe and Internet. In addition, there are nearly 220 computers located in 6 clusters on the campus, and more than 100 computers in the library, and 200 active lines available in the library for students with laptop computers. All students may access the system. There are no time limits and no fees.

Graduates: From July 1, 2002 to June 30, 2003, 2242 bachelor's degrees were awarded. The most popular majors were business administration (10%), English (6%), and psychology (6%). In an average class, 49% graduate in 4 years or less, 68% graduate in 5 years or less, and 72% graduate in 6 years or less. More than 200 companies recruited on campus in 2002-2003.

Admissions Contact: Robert McGann, Director, Admissions.
E-mail: *admissions@unh.edu* Web: *www.unh.edu/admissions/*

UNIVERSITY SYSTEM OF NEW HAMPSHIRE

The University System of New Hampshire, established in 1963, is a public system in New Hampshire. It is governed by a board of trustees, whose chief administrator is the chancellor. The primary goal of the system is to serve the higher educational needs of the people of New Hampshire. The main priorities are to provide a well-coordinated system of higher education, student access and diversity, and quality programs through a commitment to excellence. The total enrollment of all 4 campuses is just under 30,000; there were more than 1080 faculty members. Altogether there are 181 baccalaureate, 80 master's, and 21 doctoral programs offered in University System of New Hampshire. 4-year campuses are located in Durham, Keene, and Plymouth. Profiles of the 4-year campuses are included in this section.

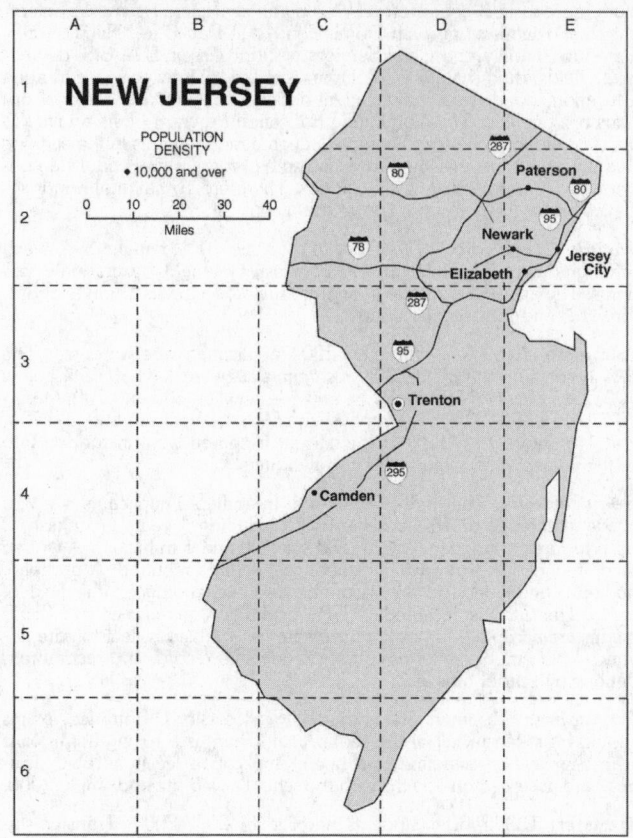

NEW JERSEY

POPULATION
DENSITY
● 10,000 and over

0   10   20   30   40
Miles

Events (including musical events, lectures, speakers, film festivals, and theatrical events).

Sports: There are 4 intercollegiate sports for men and 4 for women, and 4 intramural sports for men and 4 for women. Facilities include a 500-seat gym, weight-lifting facilities, and a basketball and volleyball court.

Disabled Students: 63% of the campus is accessible. Wheelchair ramps, elevators, special parking, specially equipped rest rooms, lowered drinking fountains, lowered telephones, lower fire stations, ADA signage, and lever handles for classroom access are available.

Services: Counseling and information services are available, as is tutoring in most subjects. There is a reader service for the blind, and remedial math, reading, and writing.

Campus Safety and Security: Measures include 24-hour foot and vehicle patrol, security escort services, informal discussions, and pamphlets/posters/films. There are emergency telephones, lighted pathways/sidewalks, and security cameras are installed in all high-traffic areas.

Programs of Study: Bloomfield confers B.A. and B.S. degrees. Bachelor's degrees are awarded in BIOLOGICAL SCIENCE (biology/biological science), BUSINESS (accounting, and business administration and management), COMMUNICATIONS AND THE ARTS (English, fine arts, music technology, and video), COMPUTER AND PHYSICAL SCIENCE (applied mathematics, chemistry, and information sciences and systems), EDUCATION (education), ENGINEERING AND ENVIRONMENTAL DESIGN (graphic arts technology), HEALTH PROFESSIONS (allied health, clinical science, and nursing), SOCIAL SCIENCE (history, philosophy, political science/government, psychology, religion, and sociology). Nursing is the strongest academically. Business, sociology, and psychology are the largest.

Required: All students must complete a Common Core, meet general education requirements, and maintain a 2.0 GPA. At least 132 credits are required for graduation.

Special: Co-op programs, internships, study abroad, and work-study programs are available. Double majors and contract majors are also possible. There are 3 national honor societies, a freshman honors program, and 1 departmental honors program.

Faculty/Classroom: 53% of faculty are male; 47%, female. All teach undergraduates. The average class size in an introductory lecture is 15; in a laboratory, 14; and in a regular course, 13.

Admissions: 13% of the current freshmen were in the top fifth of their class; 39% were in the top two fifths.

Requirements: The SAT I or ACT is required. In addition, the college requires at least 14 academic units, which should include English, math, history, and lab science. An essay and 2 personal recommendations are required. A GPA of 2.77 is required. AP and CLEP credits are accepted. Important factors in the admissions decision are advanced placement or honor courses, recommendations by school officials, and extracurricular activities record.

Procedure: Freshmen are admitted to all sessions. Entrance exams should be taken during the senior year. There are early admissions, deferred admissions, and rolling admission plans. Applications should be filed by March 14 for fall entry and December 1 for spring entry. The fall 2003 fall application fee was $35. Notification is sent on a rolling basis. Applications are accepted on-line through the school's web site and Common App.

Transfer: 313 transfer students enrolled in 2002-2003. Applicants must present a minimum GPA of 2.0 from an accredited institution and submit official transcripts from all previously attended colleges. 32 of 132 credits required for the bachelor's degree must be completed at Bloomfield.

Visiting: There are regularly scheduled orientations for prospective students, consisting of a campus tour, an admissions interview, and other activities by request. There are guides for informal visits and visitors may sit in on classes. To schedule a visit, contact the Office of Admissions at (973) 748-9000, ext. 230.

Financial Aid: In 2003-2004, 96% of all full-time freshmen and 90% of continuing full-time students received some form of financial aid. 75% of full-time freshmen and 68% of continuing full-time students received need-based aid. The average freshman award was $13,188. Need-based scholarships or need-based grants averaged $3567 ($6400 maximum); need-based self-help aid (loans and jobs) averaged $1967 ($2625 maximum); non-need-based athletic scholarships averaged $7097 ($15,700 maximum); and other non-need-based awards and non-need-based scholarships averaged $3690 ($9000 maximum). 5% of undergraduates work part time. Average annual earnings from campus work are $1600. The FAFSA is required. The priority date for freshman financial aid applications for fall entry is March 14. The deadline for filing freshman financial aid applications for fall entry is June 1.

International Students: There are 33 international students enrolled. The school actively recruits these students. They must score 550 on the written TOEFL or 173 on the electronic version.

BLOOMFIELD COLLEGE

Bloomfield, NJ 07003

E-2

(973) 748-9000, ext. 392
(800) 848-4555; Fax: (973) 748-0916

Full-time: 519 men, 1065 women	**Faculty:** 60; IIB, +$
Part-time: 128 men, 363 women	**Ph.D.s:** 77%
Graduate: none	**Student/Faculty:** 26 to 1
Year: semesters, summer session	**Tuition:** $13,100
Application Deadline: March 14	**Room & Board:** $6150
Freshman Class: n/av	
SAT I or ACT: required	**LESS COMPETITIVE**

Bloomfield College, founded in 1868 and affiliated with the Presbyterian Church (U.S.A.), is an independent institution offering programs in liberal arts and sciences, creative arts and technology, professional studies, and the clinical and health sciences. In addition to regional accreditation, Bloomfield has baccalaureate program accreditation with NLN and CCNE. The library contains 64,700 volumes, 59 microform items, and 1148 audio/video tapes/CDs, and subscribes to 456 periodicals. Computerized library services include interlibrary loans and database searching. Special learning facilities include a learning resource center, art gallery, electronic classrooms, and web-based radio station. The 12-acre campus is in a suburban area 15 miles from New York City. Including any residence halls, there are 36 buildings.

Student Life: 96% of undergraduates are from New Jersey. Students are from 13 states and 3 foreign countries. 66% are from public schools. 51% are African American; 18% Hispanic; 15% white. The average age of freshmen is 21; all undergraduates, 27. 30% do not continue beyond their first year; 28% remain to graduate.

Housing: 262 students can be accommodated in college housing, which includes single-sex and coed dorms, fraternity houses, and sorority houses. In addition, there are honors houses, special-interest houses, and theme housing. On-campus housing is available on a first-come, first-served basis. Priority is given to out-of-town students. 87% of students commute. All students may keep cars.

Activities: 5% of men belong to 3 national fraternities; 2% of women belong to 2 national sororities. There are 39 groups on campus, including art, choir, dance, drama, ethnic, film, gay, honors, international, literary magazine, musical theater, newspaper, professional, religious, social, social service, student government, and yearbook. Popular campus events include Formal Dinners, Multicultural Festivals, and Cultural

Computers: The mainframe is a DEC Alpha server DS 20E. Students have access to the Internet and networks through 300 PCs within various computer labs in several buildings. All students may access the system. There are no time limits and no fees.

Graduates: From July 1, 2002 to June 30, 2003, 240 bachelor's degrees were awarded. The most popular majors were business administration (21%), sociology (17%), and nursing (11%). In an average class, 10% graduate in 4 years or less, 23% graduate in 5 years or less, and 28% graduate in 6 years or less. 37 companies recruited on campus in 2002-2003. Of the 2002 graduating class, 6% were enrolled in graduate school within 6 months of graduation and 69% were employed.

Admissions Contact: Lourdes Delgado, Dean of Admissions. E-mail: *admission@bloomfield.edu* Web: *http://www.bloomfield.edu*

CALDWELL COLLEGE
Caldwell, NJ 07006

E-2

(973) 618-3224
(800) 831-9178; Fax: (973) 618-3600

Full-time: 413 men, 678 women	Faculty: 79; IIB, -$
Part-time: 160 men, 585 women	Ph.D.s: 83%
Graduate: 80 men, 303 women	Student/Faculty: 14 to 1
Year: semesters, summer session	Tuition: $17,060
Application Deadline: open	Room & Board: $7000
Freshman Class: 1164 applied, 806 accepted, 283 enrolled	
SAT I Verbal/Math: 440/450	LESS COMPETITIVE

Caldwell College, founded in 1939, is a private school offering programs in liberal arts, science, business, fine arts, and education. It is affiliated with the Roman Catholic Church. In addition to regional accreditation, Caldwell has baccalaureate program accreditation with TEAC. The library contains 142,356 volumes, 5234 microform items, and 2707 audio/video tapes/CDs, and subscribes to 400 periodicals. Computerized library services include the card catalog, interlibrary loans, database searching, and Internet access. Special learning facilities include a learning resource center and art gallery. The 80-acre campus is in a suburban area 20 miles west of New York City. Including any residence halls, there are 9 buildings.

Student Life: 94% of undergraduates are from New Jersey. Students are from 19 states, 27 foreign countries, and Canada. 75% are from public schools. 66% are white; 15% African American; 10% Hispanic. The average age of freshmen is 18; all undergraduates, 34. 30% do not continue beyond their first year; 51% remain to graduate.

Housing: 371 students can be accommodated in college housing, which includes coed dorms. On-campus housing is guaranteed for all 4 years. 71% of students commute. All students may keep cars.

Activities: There are no fraternities or sororities. There are 20 groups on campus, including art, band, cheerleading, choir, ethnic, honors, international, literary magazine, newspaper, orchestra, professional, religious, social, social service, student government, and yearbook. Popular campus events include Founders Day, Freshman Investiture, and Fall Festival.

Sports: There are 5 intercollegiate sports for men and 5 for women, and 4 intramural sports for men and 4 for women. Facilities include a multipurpose gym, a training room, tennis courts, weight rooms, playing fields, and a pool.

Disabled Students: 85% of the campus is accessible. Wheelchair ramps, elevators, special parking, specially equipped rest rooms, special class scheduling, lowered drinking fountains, and lowered telephones are available.

Services: Counseling and information services are available, as is tutoring in most subjects. There is a reader service for the blind, and remedial math, reading, and writing, and a writing lab.

Campus Safety and Security: Measures include 24-hour foot and vehicle patrol, self-defense education, security escort services, and informal discussions. There are pamphlets/posters/films, emergency telephones, and lighted pathways/sidewalks.

Programs of Study: Caldwell confers B.A., B.S., and B.F.A. degrees. Master's degrees are also awarded. Bachelor's degrees are awarded in BIOLOGICAL SCIENCE (biology/biological science), BUSINESS (accounting, business administration and management, international business management, management science, and marketing and distribution), COMMUNICATIONS AND THE ARTS (art, communications, English, fine arts, French, music, Spanish, and studio art), COMPUTER AND PHYSICAL SCIENCE (chemistry, computer management, computer science, information sciences and systems, and mathematics), EDUCATION (elementary), HEALTH PROFESSIONS (medical laboratory technology), SOCIAL SCIENCE (criminal justice, history, political science/government, psychology, social studies, sociology, and theological studies). Liberal arts, education, and sciences are the strongest academically. Business, education, and psychology are the largest.

Required: Students must maintain a minimum GPA of 2.0 while taking 120 credit hours, including a minimum of 30 in the major. The 55-credit core includes 15 credits in religion/philosophy, 6 each in history, English, language, social science, math and computer science, and fine arts, and 2 in communication arts. Students must participate in an outcome as-

sessment that is unique for each department. It is a comprehensive examination for some.

Special: Caldwell offers co-op and internship programs in all majors; study abroad in 3 countries; a Washington semester; 1-semester internships; and work study with Dominican Adult Day Care, Hill Top Day Care, and Family and Child Services of North Essex. B.A.-B.S. degrees in 27 fields, dual majors in all majors, credit for life experience in adult education, nondegree study, student-designed majors, and pass/fail options are possible. The Continuing Education Program offers adults (23 years or older) a chance to complete degree requirements in the evening and on Saturdays, and the External Degree Program gives adults an opportunity to earn a degree off campus. There are 15 national honor societies and a freshman honors program.

Faculty/Classroom: 49% of faculty are male; 51%, female. 89% teach undergraduates. No introductory courses are taught by graduate students. The average class size in an introductory lecture is 15; in a laboratory, 13; and in a regular course, 12.

Admissions: 69% of the 2003-2004 applicants were accepted. The SAT I scores for the 2003-2004 freshman class were: Verbal--69% below 500, 27% between 500 and 599, and 4% between 600 and 700; Math--73% below 500, 23% between 500 and 599, 4% between 600 and 700, and 1% above 700. 12% of the current freshmen were in the top fifth of their class; 27% were in the top two fifths.

Requirements: The SAT I is required. In addition, applicants need 16 academic credits or 16 Carnegie units, including 4 years in English, 2 each in foreign language, math, and science, and 1 in history. A written recommendation from a high school counselor is required. A portfolio, audition, and interview are recommended, depending on the field of study. The GED is accepted. A GPA of 2.0 is required. AP and CLEP credits are accepted. Important factors in the admissions decision are advanced placement or honor courses, leadership record, and recommendations by school officials.

Procedure: Freshmen are admitted to all sessions. Entrance exams should be taken in fall of the senior year. There is a rolling admissions plan. Application deadlines are open. Application fee is $40. Applications are accepted on-line through the school's web site and Apply 2000.

Transfer: 152 transfer students enrolled in 2002-2003. Transfer students must have a minimum GPA of 2.0 (2.5 in teacher education) and 12 transferable credits. 45 of 120 credits required for the bachelor's degree must be completed at Caldwell.

Visiting: There are regularly scheduled orientations for prospective students, including a brief presentation by faculty and students, followed by a tour. There are guides for informal visits and visitors may sit in on classes and stay overnight. To schedule a visit, contact the Admissions Office at (973) 618-3500.

Financial Aid: In 2003-2004, 84% of all full-time freshmen and 79% of continuing full-time students received some form of financial aid. 65% of full-time freshmen and 60% of continuing full-time students received need-based aid. The average freshman award was $8632. Need-based scholarships or need-based grants averaged $3279 ($8820 maximum); need-based self-help aid (loans and jobs) averaged $2123 ($3500 maximum); non-need-based athletic scholarships averaged $5383 ($14,000 maximum); and other non-need-based awards and non-need-based scholarships averaged $6281 ($24,500 maximum). 36% of undergraduates work part time. Average annual earnings from campus work are $850. The average financial indebtedness of the 2003 graduate was $13,225. Caldwell is a member of CSS. The FAFSA and the college's own financial statement are required. The priority date for freshman financial aid applications for fall entry is June 1.

International Students: There are 69 international students enrolled. The school actively recruits these students. They must score 500 on the written TOEFL.

Computers: The mainframe is an IBM AS/400. Some 190 networked PCs located in labs and computer classrooms are available for word processing, spreadsheet, database, desktop publishing, presentation software, and Internet access. 18 Macs are used for similar purposes, except Internet access. All dorm rooms are wired for Internet access. All students may access the system Monday to Thursday 9 A.M. to 9:30 P.M., Friday 10:30 A.M. to 4 P.M., and weekends, 12 P.M. to 5 P.M. There are no time limits and no fees.

Graduates: From July 1, 2002 to June 30, 2003, 272 bachelor's degrees were awarded. The most popular majors were business administration (16%), psychology (15%), and education (12%). In an average class, 1% graduate in 3 years or less, 32% graduate in 4 years or less, 48% graduate in 5 years or less, and 51% graduate in 6 years or less.

Admissions Contact: Richard Ott, Vice President for Enrollment. A video is available. E-mail: *rott@caldwell.edu* Web: *www.caldwell.edu*

CENTENARY COLLEGE
Hackettstown, NJ 07840

C-2

(908) 852-1400
(800) 236-8679; Fax: (908) 852-3454

Full-time: 491 men, 949 women	**Faculty:** 57
Part-time: 96 men, 223 women	**Ph.Ds:** 65%
Graduate: 163 men, 260 women	**Student/Faculty:** 25 to 1
Year: semesters, summer session	**Tuition:** $18,220
Application Deadline: open	**Room & Board:** $7150

Freshman Class: 857 applied, 652 accepted, 236 enrolled
SAT I Verbal/Math: 465/462 **ACT:** 20 **LESS COMPETITIVE**

Centenary College, founded in 1867, is a private institution affiliated with the United Methodist Church. The college offers undergraduate and graduate programs in liberal arts, business, international studies, education, equine studies, fashion, and fine arts. In addition to regional accreditation, Centenary has baccalaureate program accreditation with NASDTEC. The library contains 68,000 volumes, 20,000 microform items, and 5000 audio/video tapes/CDs, and subscribes to 375 periodicals. Computerized library services include the card catalog, interlibrary loans, database searching, and Internet access. Special learning facilities include a learning resource center, art gallery, radio station, TV station, an equestrian center, a CAD lab, and a wireless network. The 42-acre campus is in a suburban area 55 miles west of New York City. Including any residence halls, there are 14 buildings.

Student Life: 83% of undergraduates are from New Jersey. Students are from 16 states, 13 foreign countries, and Canada. 76% are from public schools. 55% are white. The average age of freshmen is 18; all undergraduates, 26. 26% do not continue beyond their first year; 30% remain to graduate.

Housing: 584 students can be accommodated in college housing, which includes single-sex and coed dorms and on-campus apartments. On-campus housing is available on a first-come, first-served basis and is available on a lottery system for upperclassmen. 59% of students live on campus; of those, 50% remain on campus on weekends. All students may keep cars.

Activities: 20% of men belong to 1 local fraternity; 60% of women belong to 3 local sororities. There are 27 groups on campus, including art, cheerleading, chorus, dance, drama, ethnic, honors, international, literary magazine, newspaper, photography, professional, radio and TV, religious, social, social service, student government, and yearbook. Popular campus events include Presidents Ball and Community Plunge.

Sports: There are 7 intercollegiate sports for men and 7 for women. Facilities include a gym, a fitness center and indoor pool, tennis courts, playing fields, and an equine center and stables.

Disabled Students: 50% of the campus is accessible. Wheelchair ramps, special parking, specially equipped rest rooms, special class scheduling, and lowered telephones are available.

Services: Counseling and information services are available, as is tutoring in some subjects, as requested. There is remedial math, reading, and writing. Learning associates provide personalized subject matter support.

Campus Safety and Security: Measures include security escort services, informal discussions, pamphlets/posters/films, and lighted pathways/sidewalks.

Programs of Study: Centenary confers B.A., B.S., and B.F.A. degrees. Associate and master's degrees are also awarded. Bachelor's degrees are awarded in AGRICULTURE (equine science), BIOLOGICAL SCIENCE (biology/biological science), BUSINESS (accounting and business administration and management), COMMUNICATIONS AND THE ARTS (applied art, communications, dramatic arts, and English), COMPUTER AND PHYSICAL SCIENCE (mathematics), EDUCATION (elementary and secondary), SOCIAL SCIENCE (criminal justice, fashion design and technology, history, interdisciplinary studies, international studies, political science/government, psychology, and sociology). Equine studies, business, and education certification are the strongest academically and have the largest enrollments.

Required: Students must complete a distribution of 40 to 46 semester hours in core courses, including college seminars, and 9 credits in liberal arts studies, as well as the required number of credits, usually 48, for their major. At least 128 semester hours and a minimum GPA of 2.0 are needed to earn the bachelor's degree.

Special: Centenary offers internships in every major. The college offers study abroad in England and other countries, dual majors, as long as they are covered under the same degree, an accelerated degree program in liberal arts and bsuiness administration, student-designed majors, work-study on-campus, and a pass/fail option. Students age 25 or older may earn life experience credits. There is 1 national honor society and a freshman honors program.

Faculty/Classroom: 50% of faculty are male; 50%, female. All both teach and do research. No introductory courses are taught by graduate students. The average class size in an introductory lecture is 25; in a laboratory, 20; and in a regular course, 15.

Admissions: 76% of the 2003-2004 applicants were accepted. The SAT I scores for the 2003-2004 freshman class were: Verbal--70% below 500, 22% between 500 and 599, and 8% between 600 and 700; Math--65% below 500, 30% between 500 and 599, 4% between 600 and 700, and 1% above 700. The ACT scores were 100% below 21. 26% of the current freshmen were in the top fifth of their class; 75% were in the top two fifths. 1 freshman graduated first in the class.

Requirements: The SAT I or ACT is required. In addition, minimum scores include an SAT I composite of 800, 400 verbal and 400 math, or an ACT composite of 18. Applicants must be graduates of accredited secondary schools or have earned a GED. Centenary requires 16 academic credits or Carnegie units, based on 4 years of English, math, and science, and 2 years each of foreign language and history. An essay is required for freshmen, and an interview is recommended. Applicants to specific fine arts programs must also submit a portfolio. Centenary requires applicants to be in the upper 50% of their class. A GPA of 2.0 is required. AP and CLEP credits are accepted. Important factors in the admissions decision are advanced placement or honor courses, leadership record, and ability to finance college education.

Procedure: Freshmen are admitted fall and spring. Entrance exams should be taken as early as possible in the senior year. There are early admissions, deferred admissions, and rolling admissions plans. Application deadlines are open. Application fee is $30. Applications are accepted on-line through www.centenarycollege.edu.

Transfer: 114 transfer students enrolled in 2002-2003. Applicants must have a minimum college GPA of 2.0 and submit proof of high school graduation or the equivalent. 32 of 128 credits required for the bachelor's degree must be completed at Centenary.

Visiting: There are regularly scheduled orientations for prospective students, including basic skills testing, advising, registration, and social events. Visitors may sit in on classes and stay overnight. To schedule a visit, contact the Admissions Office at admissions@centenarycollege.edu.

Financial Aid: In 2003-2004, 89% of all full-time freshmen and 86% of continuing full-time students received some form of financial aid. 66% of full-time freshmen and 68% of continuing full-time students received need-based aid. The average freshman award was $12,083. 75% of undergraduates work part time. Average annual earnings from campus work are $1200. The average financial indebtedness of the 2003 graduate was $16,534. Centenary is a member of CSS. The FAFSA and other forms as requested are required. The priority date for freshman financial aid applications for fall entry is March 15. The deadline for filing freshman financial aid applications for fall entry is September 1.

International Students: There are 90 international students enrolled. The school actively recruits these students. They must score 450 on the written TOEFL or 133 on the electronic version and also take the SAT I or the ACT.

Computers: The PC and CAD labs are available for instructional and student use. Access to the Internet is available in the library. All full-time students are issued a laptop. The campus has a wireless network. All students may access the system. Computer and CAD lab use depends on lab hours. The fee is $400 annually.

Graduates: In an average class, 25% graduate in 4 years or less, and 60% graduate in 5 years or less. 35 companies recruited on campus in a recent year. Of the 2002 graduating class, 10% were enrolled in graduate school within 6 months of graduation and 70% were employed.

Admissions Contact: Glenna Warren, Dean of Admissions.
E-mail: admissions@centenarycollege.edu Web: centenarycollege.edu

COLLEGE OF NEW JERSEY, THE
Ewing, NJ 08628-0718

D-3

(609) 771-2131
(800) 624-0967; Fax: (609) 637-5174

Full-time: 2258 men, 3355 women	**Faculty:** 325; IIA, +$
Part-time: 130 men, 195 women	**Ph.Ds:** 90%
Graduate: 201 men, 773 women	**Student/Faculty:** 17 to 1
Year: semesters, summer session	**Tuition:** $8206 ($12,781)
Application Deadline: February 15	**Room & Board:** $7744

Freshman Class: 6373 applied, 3070 accepted, 1178 enrolled
SAT I Verbal/Math: 620/650 **MOST COMPETITIVE**

The College of New Jersey, founded in 1855, is a public institution offering programs in the liberal arts, sciences, business, engineering, nursing, and education. There are 7 undergraduate schools and 1 graduate school. In addition to regional accreditation, TCNJ has baccalaureate program accreditation with AACSB, ABET, CSAB, NASDTEC, NASM, NCATE, and NLN. The library contains 566,460 volumes, 319,021 microform items, and 22,950 audio/video tapes/CDs, and subscribes to 1341 periodicals. Computerized library services include interlibrary loans and database searching. Special learning facilities include a learning resource center, art gallery, planetarium, radio station, TV station, an electron microscopy lab, and greenhouses. The 289-acre campus is in a suburban area between Princeton and Trenton, NJ. Including any residence halls, there are 38 buildings.

Student Life: 95% of undergraduates are from New Jersey. Students are from 22 states and 12 foreign countries. 65% are from public schools. 81% are white. 50% are Catholic; 20% Protestant; 14% claim no religious affiliation; 12% Eastern Orthodox, Buddhist, Muslim, Islamic, Quaker. The average age of freshmen is 18; all undergraduates, 20. 5% do not continue beyond their first year; 83% remain to graduate.

Housing: 3562 students can be accommodated in college housing, which includes single-sex and coed dorms, on-campus apartments, and off-campus apartments. In addition, there are honors houses, special-interest houses, a music house, an engineering house, study floors with extended quiet hours, wellness housing units, and a living-learning center for the First-Year Experience taken by all entering students. On-campus housing is guaranteed for the freshman year only and is available on a lottery system for upperclassmen. 65% of students live on campus; of those, 70% remain on campus on weekends. Upperclassmen may keep cars.

Activities: 2% of men belong to 2 local and 5 national fraternities; 5% of women belong to 7 national sororities. There are 185 groups on campus, including art, band, cheerleading, choir, chorale, chorus, computers, dance, drama, ethnic, film, foreign language, gay, honors, international, jazz band, literary magazine, musical theater, newspaper, opera, orchestra, pep band, photography, political, professional, radio and TV, recreational, religious, social, social service, student government, symphony, and yearbook. Popular campus events include Welcome Week, Ewing Community Day, and Heritage Day.

Sports: There are 12 intercollegiate sports for men and 11 for women, and 7 intramural sports for men and 7 for women. Facilities include a 5000-seat stadium with an Astroturf field, an aquatic center, baseball and softball diamonds, an NCAA-approved all-weather track, lighted tennis courts, a sand volleyball court, a 1200-seat gym, a student recreation center with a wellness center, tennis, racquetball and basketball courts, and a weight room.

Disabled Students: 90% of the campus is accessible. Wheelchair ramps, elevators, special parking, specially equipped rest rooms, special class scheduling, lowered drinking fountains, lowered telephones, TDD machines for the deaf, and a library room equipped for students who are hearing-impaired, visually impaired, or motor impaired are available.

Services: Counseling and information services are available, as is tutoring in every subject. There is a reader service for the blind, and remedial math, reading, and writing. The school also offers science lab tutoring and evaluative testing services.

Campus Safety and Security: Measures include 24-hour foot and vehicle patrol, self-defense education, security escort services, and informal discussions. There are pamphlets/posters/films, emergency telephones, and lighted pathways/sidewalks.

Programs of Study: TCNJ confers B.A., B.S., B.A.B.M.E., B.F.A., B.M., B.S.C., B.S.E.E., B.S.M.E., and B.S.N. degrees. Master's degrees are also awarded. Bachelor's degrees are awarded in BIOLOGICAL SCIENCE (biology/biological science), BUSINESS (accounting, business administration and management, international business management, management science, and marketing/retailing/merchandising), COMMUNICATIONS AND THE ARTS (communications, English, fine arts, graphic design, journalism, music, and Spanish), COMPUTER AND PHYSICAL SCIENCE (chemistry, computer science, mathematics, physics, and statistics), EDUCATION (art, early childhood, education of the deaf and hearing impaired, elementary, English, foreign languages, health, mathematics, music, physical, science, social studies, special, technical, and vocational), ENGINEERING AND ENVIRONMENTAL DESIGN (engineering and applied science), HEALTH PROFESSIONS (nursing), SOCIAL SCIENCE (criminal justice, economics, history, international studies, philosophy, political science/government, psychology, sociology, and women's studies). Biology, English, and computer science are the strongest academically. Elementary education, business, and psychology are the largest.

Required: To graduate, students must earn 120 semester hours, with a minimum GPA of 2.0. Students must complete a liberal learning curriculum of 32 to 34 course units that include diversity and community engagement and major-area proficiencies, as well as student-designed interdisciplinary concentrations in the natural, physical, and social sciences, hummanities, and arts. Students must also complete a first-year seminar, which is discipline-based and thematically relative to important social and cultural issues. The credits required in the major vary by program. A thesis is required for departmental honors.

Special: TCNJ offers cross-registration with the New Jersey Marine Science Consortium, numerous internships in the public and private sectors, and study abroad in more than a dozen countries through the International Student Exchange program (ISEP). Pass/fail options and some dual majors are possible. Specially designed research courses allow students to participate in collaborative scholarly projects with members of the faculty. Combined advanced and accelerated degree programs are offered in law and justice, medicine, and optometry with other area schools. There are 9 national honor societies, a freshman honors program, and 17 departmental honors programs.

Faculty/Classroom: 52% of faculty are male; 48%, female. All teach undergraduates and 50% both teach and do research. No introductory courses are taught by graduate students. The average class size in an introductory lecture is 23; in a laboratory, 20; and in a regular course, 21.

Admissions: 48% of the 2003-2004 applicants were accepted. The SAT I scores for the 2003-2004 freshman class were: Verbal--7% below 500, 31% between 500 and 599, 52% between 600 and 700, and 10% above 700; Math--4% below 500, 18% between 500 and 599, 58% between 600 and 700, and 20% above 700. 87% of the current freshmen were in the top fifth of their class; 98% were in the top two fifths. There were 17 National Merit finalists and 6 semifinalists. 17 freshmen graduated first in their class.

Requirements: The SAT I is required. In addition, applicants must have earned 16 academic credits in high school, consisting of 4 in English, 2 each in math, science, and social studies, and 6 others distributed among math, science, social studies, and a foreign language. An essay is required. Art majors must submit a portfolio, and music majors must audition. The GED is accepted. AP and CLEP credits are accepted. Important factors in the admissions decision are advanced placement or honor courses, leadership record, and evidence of special talent.

Procedure: Freshmen are admitted fall and spring. Entrance exams should be taken by the end of the junior year or early in the senior year. There are early decision, early admissions and rolling admission plans. Early decision applications should be filed by November 15; regular applications, by February 15 for fall entry and November 15 for spring entry, along with a $50 fee. Notification is sent on a rolling basis. 178 early decision candidates were accepted for the 2003-2004 class. 217 were on the 2003 waiting list; 98 were admitted. Applications are accepted online through the college's web site.

Transfer: 186 transfer students enrolled in 2002-2003. Transfer students must have a minimum GPA of 2.5, and those with fewer than 33 credits must submit the SAT I scores. An associate degree is recommended. All transfer students must submit high school transcripts. 42 of 120 credits required for the bachelor's degree must be completed at TCNJ.

Visiting: There are regularly scheduled orientations for prospective students, consisting of an admissions presentation and a tour of campus. Reservations are required. There are guides for informal visits and visitors may sit in on classes and stay overnight. To schedule a visit, contact the Admissions Office at *tcnjinfo@tcnj.edu*.

Financial Aid: In 2003-2004, 49% of all full-time freshmen and 41% of continuing full-time students received some form of financial aid. 21% of full-time freshmen and 18% of continuing full-time students received need-based aid. The average freshman award was $4600. Need-based scholarships or need-based grants averaged $6668 ($15,450 maximum); need-based self-help aid (loans and jobs) averaged $5625 ($20,500 maximum); and other non-need-based awards and non-need-based scholarships averaged $4951 ($15,950 maximum). 95% of undergraduates work part time. Average annual earnings from campus work are $750. The average financial indebtedness of the 2003 graduate was $11,157. The FAFSA and copies of students' and parents' tax returns as applicable are required. The deadline for filing freshman financial aid applications for fall entry is March 5.

International Students: In a recent year, there were 17 international students enrolled. They must score 550 on the written TOEFL and also take the SAT I, or ACT. The SAT I is required for merit scholarship consideration.

Computers: The mainframe is an IBM ES9000 9121-320. There are 500 networked PCs and workstations available in 22 academic computing labs throughout the campus, including 3 in residence halls. Students have access to the campuswide network from their residence hall rooms. In addition, more than 3000 student PCs are connected through the campus residence network. All students may access the system. There are no time limits. The fee is $180 annually. It is strongly recommended that all students have a personal computer.

Graduates: From July 1, 2002 to June 30, 2003, 1298 bachelor's degrees were awarded. The most popular majors were business administration (20%), elementary/early childhood education (10%), and psychology (10%). In an average class, 64% graduate in 4 years or less, 81% graduate in 5 years or less, and 83% graduate in 6 years or less. 608 companies recruited on campus in 2002-2003. Of the 2002 graduating class, 16% were enrolled in graduate school within 6 months of graduation and 82% were employed.

Admissions Contact: Lisa Angeloni, Director of Admissions.
E-mail: *admiss@tcnj.edu* Web: *www.tcnj.edu*

COLLEGE OF SAINT ELIZABETH   E-2
Morristown, NJ 07960-6989   (973) 290-4700
(800) 210-7900; Fax: (973) 290-4710

Full-time: 13 men, 703 women	**Faculty:** 57; IIB, av$
Part-time: 78 men, 482 women	**Ph.D.s:** 80%
Graduate: 34 men, 538 women	**Student/Faculty:** 13 to 1
Year: semesters, summer session	**Tuition:** $17,330
Application Deadline: August 15	**Room & Board:** $8130
Freshman Class: 456 applied, 369 accepted, 151 enrolled	
SAT I Verbal/Math: 470/470	**COMPETITIVE**

The College of St. Elizabeth, founded in 1899, is a private Roman Catholic college primarily for women. Undergraduate programs are offered in the arts and sciences, business administration, education, foods and nutrition, and upper-level nursing. There are graduate programs in education, management, health care management, nutrition, psychology, and theology. Adult undergraduate degree programs and graduate programs are coeducational. There is 1 graduate school. In addition to regional accreditation, CSE has baccalaureate program accreditation with ADA and NLN. The library contains 110,272 volumes, 104,965 microform items, and 1612 audio/video tapes/CDs, and subscribes to 633 periodicals. Computerized library services include the card catalog, interlibrary loans, database searching, and Internet access. Special learning facilities include a learning resource center, art gallery, and a television studio. The 188-acre campus is in a suburban area 40 miles west of New York City. Including any residence halls, there are 11 buildings.

Student Life: 95% of undergraduates are from New Jersey. Students are from 11 states and 16 foreign countries. 68% are from public schools. 62% are white; 11% Hispanic. 50% are Catholic; 25% claim no religious affiliation; 20% Protestant. The average age of freshmen is 18; all undergraduates, 27. 18% do not continue beyond their first year; 62% remain to graduate.

Housing: 402 students can be accommodated in college housing, which includes single-sex dorms and off-campus apartments. On-campus housing is guaranteed for all 4 years. 70% of students live on campus; of those, 22% remain on campus on weekends. All students may keep cars.

Activities: There are no fraternities or sororities. There are 28 groups on campus, including chorale, drama, ethnic, honors, international, literary magazine, newspaper, professional, religious, social, social service, student government, and yearbook. Popular campus events include Oktoberfest, International Night, and Christmas celebrations.

Sports: There are 8 intercollegiate sports for women. Facilities include a student center that houses a swimming pool, a weight room, an archery range, and a gym. Tennis courts are also available, as is a bike and fitness trail.

Disabled Students: 75% of the campus is accessible. Wheelchair ramps, elevators, special parking, specially equipped rest rooms, special class scheduling, and handrails are available.

Services: Counseling and information services are available, as is tutoring in most subjects. There is remedial math, reading, and writing. Other service include books on tape, large monitor computers, and notetakers.

Campus Safety and Security: Measures include 24-hour foot and vehicle patrol, security escort services, informal discussions, and pamphlets/posters/films. There are emergency telephones and lighted pathways/sidewalks.

Programs of Study: CSE confers B.A., B.S., and B.S.N. degrees. Master's degrees are also awarded. Bachelor's degrees are awarded in BIOLOGICAL SCIENCE (biochemistry, biology/biological science, nutrition, and toxicology), BUSINESS (accounting, business administration and management, marketing management, and office supervision and management), COMMUNICATIONS AND THE ARTS (art, communications, English, fine arts, music, and Spanish), COMPUTER AND PHYSICAL SCIENCE (chemistry, computer science, and mathematics), EDUCATION (early childhood, elementary, and special), HEALTH PROFESSIONS (cytotechnology, medical technology, nursing, predentistry, and premedicine), SOCIAL SCIENCE (American studies, economics, history, international studies, peace studies, philosophy, prelaw, psychology, sociology, and theological studies). Math, chemistry, and education are the strongest academically. Business administration, education, and psychology are the largest.

Required: To graduate, students must complete 128 semester hours, with a minimum of 32 in the major, while maintaining a GPA of 2.0, or 2.75 for education majors. Core requirements include 27 credits in specific humanities courses focusing on theology, philosophy, literature, history, foreign language, and fine arts, 6 to 8 in math and science, and 6 in social science. In addition, 2 credits in fitness/wellness and an interdisciplinary course are required. Students must also demonstrate proficiency in writing and complete a comprehensive or capstone experience.

Special: There is cross-registration with Drew and Fairleigh Dickinson Universities. CSE also offers internships in business, law, technology, health, government, sports, and television. On-campus work-study, accelerated degree programs, dual majors, student-designed majors, study abroad, credit for life experience, pass/fail options, and nondegree study are also available. Continuing studies programs are geared to the working student. There are 10 national honor societies and a freshman honors program.

Faculty/Classroom: 34% of faculty are male; 66%, female. 78% teach undergraduates, 5% do research, and 5% do both. No introductory courses are taught by graduate students. The average class size in an introductory lecture is 19; in a laboratory, 13; and in a regular course, 15.

Admissions: 81% of the 2003-2004 applicants were accepted. The SAT I scores for the 2003-2004 freshman class were: Verbal--64% below 500, 30% between 500 and 599, 5% between 600 and 700, and 1% above 700; Math--61% below 500, 32% between 500 and 599, 5% between 600 and 700, and 2% above 700.

Requirements: The SAT I is required, with a minimum composite SAT I score of 1000, 500 on each part, recommended. Applicants must be

graduates of accredited secondary schools or have earned a GED. The college requires 16 academic units, including 3 each in English and math/science, 2 each in foreign language, and 1 in history. An essay and 2 letters of recommendaiton are required and an interview is recommended. CSE requires applicants to be in the upper 50% of their class. A GPA of 2.0 is required. AP and CLEP credits are accepted. Important factors in the admissions decision are advanced placement or honor courses, recommendations by school officials, and leadership record.

Procedure: Freshmen are admitted fall and spring. Entrance exams should be taken early in the senior year. There is a deferred admissions plan and a rolling admissions plan. Applications should be filed by August 15 for fall entry and December 15 for spring entry, along with a $35 fee. Notification is sent on a rolling basis. Applications are accepted online through the school's web site.

Transfer: 100 transfer students enrolled in 2002-2003. Applicants must present a minimum GPA of 2.0 in course work from an accredited college. SAT I or ACT scores, an associate degree, and an interview are also recommended. 56 of 128 credits required for the bachelor's degree must be completed at CSE.

Visiting: There are regularly scheduled orientations for prospective students, including interviews, tours, and class visitation. There are guides for informal visits and visitors may sit in on classes and stay overnight. To schedule a visit, contact Donna Tartarka, Dean of Admission.

Financial Aid: In a recent year, 98% of all full-time freshmen and 71% of continuing full-time students received some form of financial aid. 77% of full-time freshmen and 56% of continuing full-time students received need-based aid. The average freshman award was $15,685. 95% of undergraduates work part time. Average annual earnings from campus work are $1000. The average financial indebtedness of the 2003 graduate was $17,168. CSE is a member of CSS. The FAFSA is required. The deadline for filing freshman financial aid applications for fall entry is March 1.

International Students: There are 45 international students enrolled. The school actively recruits these students. They must take the TOEFL or other approved assessment tests. Applicants from English-speaking countries may submit scores from either the TOEFL or the SAT I.

Computers: The mainframe is a Hewlett-Packard Netfinity LHH Server controlling a Microsoft Windows NT network. There are a total of 152 computers (128 PCs and 24 Macs) in a general and special purpose labs throughout campus. All systems have access to the Internet, and e-mail services from dorm rooms and other locations on campus. All students may access the system. There are no time limits and no fees.

Graduates: From July 1, 2002 to June 30, 2003, 181 bachelor's degrees were awarded. In a recent year the most popular majors were business (30%), education (17%), and psychology (11%). In an average class, 1% graduate in 3 years or less, 56% graduate in 4 years or less, 61% graduate in 5 years or less, and 62% graduate in 6 years or less. 3 companies recruited on campus in a recent year. In a recent year the 2002 graduating class, 21% were enrolled in graduate school within 6 months of graduation and 66% were employed.

Admissions Contact: Donna Tartarka, Dean of Admission. A video is available. E-mail: *apply@www.cse.edu* Web: *www.cse.edu*

DEVRY COLLEGE OF TECHNOLOGY/NORTH BRUNSWICK D-3
North Brunswick, NJ 08902

(732) 435-4850
(800) 33-DEVRY; Fax: (732) 435-4856

Full-time: 1287 men, 308 women	**Faculty:** n/av
Part-time: 714 men, 208 women	**Ph.D.s:** n/av
Graduate: none	**Student/Faculty:** n/av
Year: semesters, summer session	**Tuition:** $10,100
Application Deadline: open	**Room & Board:** n/app
Freshman Class: n/av	
SAT I or ACT: n/av	**LESS COMPETITIVE**

DeVry College of Technology/North Brunswick, founded in 1969, is a private institution offering hands-on programs in electronics, business administration, computer information systems, and information technology. The school is 1 of 67 DeVry University locations throughout the United States and Canada. In addition to regional accreditation, DeVry has baccalaureate program accreditation with ABET. The library contains 32,201 volumes and 1870 audio/video tapes/CDs, and subscribes to 210 periodicals. Computerized library services include the card catalog, interlibrary loans, and database searching. Special learning facilities include a learning resource center. The 15-acre campus is in a small town. There is one building.

Student Life: 43% of students are white; 25% African American; 19% Hispanic. The average age of all undergraduates is 24.

Housing: There are no residence halls. Housing referrals may be obtained through the Student Housing Office. There are private apartments, student-plan housing, and private rooms. All students commute. Alcohol is not permitted. All students may keep cars.

Activities: There are no fraternities or sororities. There are 11 groups on campus, including ethnic, honors, and professional. Popular campus events include Student Appreciation Day.

Sports: There is no sports program at DeVry.

Disabled Students: All of the campus is accessible. Wheelchair ramps, elevators, special parking, specially equipped rest rooms, special class scheduling, lowered drinking fountains, and lowered telephones are available.

Services: Counseling and information services are available, as is tutoring in every subject.

Programs of Study: DeVry confers the B.S. degree. Associate degrees are also awarded. Bachelor's degrees are awarded in COMMUNICATIONS AND THE ARTS (telecommunications), COMPUTER AND PHYSICAL SCIENCE (information sciences and systems), ENGINEERING AND ENVIRONMENTAL DESIGN (electrical/electronics engineering technology). Telecommunications is the largest.

Required: To graduate, students must achieve a GPA of at least 2.0, complete 48 to 154 credit hours, and satisfactorily complete all curriculum requirements. Course requirements vary according to program. All first-semester students take courses in business organization, computer applications, algebra, psychology, and student success strategies.

Special: Evening and weekend classes, distance learning, co-op programs, and an accelerated degree program are offered. There are 2 national honor societies, including Phi Beta Kappa.

Faculty/Classroom: All teach undergraduates.

Requirements: Admissions requirements include graduation from a secondary school; the GED is also accepted. Applicants must pass the DeVry entrance exam or present satisfactory ACT or SAT I scores. An interview is required. CLEP credit is accepted.

Procedure: Freshmen are admitted fall, spring, and summer. There is a rolling admissions plan. There are early admissions and deferred admissions plans. Application deadlines are open. Application fee is $50. Applications are accepted on-line through *https://apply.embark.com/UGrad/DeVry/21.*

Transfer: Applicants must present passing grades in all completed college course work, demonstrate language skills proficiency with at least 24 completed semester hours, and present evidence of math proficiency by appropriate college-level credits. A minimum GPA of 2.0 is required. 25% of 48 to 154 credits required for the bachelor's degree must be completed at DeVry.

Visiting: There are regularly scheduled orientations for prospective students. There are guides for informal visits and visitors may sit in on classes. To schedule a visit, contact Danielle DiNapoli, Dean of Admissions.

Financial Aid: In 2002-2003, 49% of all full-time freshmen and 63% of continuing full-time students received some form of financial aid. At least 48% of full-time freshmen and at least 61% of continuing full-time students received need-based aid. The average freshman award was $6840. Need-based scholarships or need-based grants averaged $5175; need-based self-help aid (loans and jobs) averaged $3542; and institutional non-need-based awards and non-need-based scholarships averaged $9018. The FAFSA is required. The deadline for filing freshman financial aid applications is rolling.

International Students: There were 52 international students enrolled in a recent year. They must score 500 on the written TOEFL or 173 on the electronic version and also take the college's own entrance exam.

Computers: Lab facilities include PCs in stand-alone and network configurations with access to the mainframe. LANs provide access to a wide range of applications software. Hard copy from the mainframe is provided through a local microcomputer and medium- and high-speed printers. Computer information students may access the system during published lab hours. There are no fees. Students in the information technology program must have DeVry-issued laptop computers.

Graduates: From July 1, 2002 to June 30, 2003, 259 bachelor's degrees were awarded. The most popular majors were computer information systems (95%) and electronics engineering technology (5%). 173 companies recruited on campus in a recent year.

Admissions Contact: Danielle DiNapoli, Dean of Admissions.
E-mail: *admissions@devry.edu* Web: *www.nj.devry.edu*

DREW UNIVERSITY/COLLEGE OF LIBERAL ARTS D-2
Madison, NJ 07940 (973) 408-DREW; Fax: (973) 408-3068

Full-time: 607 men, 928 women	**Faculty:** 120; IIA, +$
Part-time: 23 men, 48 women	**Ph.D.s:** 97%
Graduate: 361 men, 356 women	**Student/Faculty:** 13 to 1
Year: semesters, summer session	**Tuition:** $27,906
Application Deadline: February 15	**Room & Board:** $7644
Freshman Class: 2755 applied, 1903 accepted, 420 enrolled	
SAT I Verbal/Math: 610/600	**ACT:** 25 **VERY COMPETITIVE**

The College of Liberal Arts was added to Drew University in 1928 and is part of an educational complex that includes a theological school and a graduate school. Drew is a private, nonprofit, independent institution affiliated with the United Methodist Church. The library contains 499,758 volumes, 373,236 microform items, and 2445 audio/video

tapes/CDs, and subscribes to 2609 periodicals. Computerized library services include the card catalog, interlibrary loans, and database searching. Special learning facilities include a learning resource center, art gallery, radio station, TV station, observatory, photography gallery, and TV satellite dish. The 186-acre campus is in a small town 30 miles west of New York City. Including any residence halls, there are 57 buildings.

Student Life: 57% of undergraduates are from New Jersey. Students are from 37 states and 18 foreign countries. 66% are from public schools. 61% are white. The average age of freshmen is 18; all undergraduates, 20. 87% of freshmen remain to graduate.

Housing: 1306 students can be accommodated in college housing, which includes single-sex and coed dorms, on-campus apartments, and married-student housing. In addition, there are language houses and special-interest houses. On-campus housing is guaranteed for all 4 years. 87% of students live on campus; of those, 70% remain on campus on weekends. Upperclassmen may keep cars.

Activities: There are no fraternities or sororities. There are 80 groups on campus, including art, choir, chorale, computers, dance, drama, ecology, ethnic, film, gay, honors, international, jazz band, literary magazine, newspaper, orchestra, pep band, photography, political, professional, radio and TV, religious, social, social service, student government, women, and yearbook. Popular campus events include Holiday Semiformal, Annual Picnic, and Multicultural Awareness Day.

Sports: There are 11 intercollegiate sports for men and 12 for women, and 12 intramural sports for men and 12 for women. Facilities include an artificial turf athletic field with a 1000-seat gym, a 1000-seat auditorium, a swimming pool, a lighted tennis complex, a weight training room, a game room, an indoor track, a forest preserve, and an arboretum.

Disabled Students: Wheelchair ramps, elevators, special parking, specially equipped rest rooms, special class scheduling, lowered drinking fountains, and lowered telephones are available. The main dining facility, the student center and commons, and the ground floor of every dorm and classroom building are accessible to students with physical disabilities.

Services: Counseling and information services are available, as is tutoring in most subjects. There is a reader service for the blind.

Campus Safety and Security: Measures include 24-hour foot and vehicle patrol, self-defense education, security escort services, and informal discussions. There are pamphlets/posters/films, emergency telephones, and lighted pathways/sidewalks.

Programs of Study: Drew confers the B.A. degree. Master's and doctoral degrees are also awarded. Bachelor's degrees are awarded in BIOLOGICAL SCIENCE (biology/biological science), COMMUNICATIONS AND THE ARTS (art, classics, dramatic arts, English, French, German, music, Russian, and Spanish), COMPUTER AND PHYSICAL SCIENCE (chemistry, computer science, mathematics, and physics), SOCIAL SCIENCE (American studies, anthropology, behavioral science, economics, ethnic studies, history, philosophy, political science/government, psychobiology, psychology, religion, sociology, and women's studies). Psychology, political science, and English are the largest.

Required: To graduate, students must earn at least 128 credits, of which at least 64 must be beyond the lower level and at least 32 must be at the upper level. All students must fulfill the requirements of a major and those of the general education program. For graduation, the cumulative GPA, both overall and in the major, must be at least 2.0. General education requirements include a first-year seminar, demonstration of writing competency, at least 8 credits in foreign language and fulfillment of a language-in-context requirement, and completion of at least 4 credits in each of 2 different departments in the following 4 divisions: natural and mathematical sciences, social sciences, humanities, and arts and literature. Each student must also complete a minor.

Special: Drew offers co-op programs with Duke University, as well as cross-registration with the College of Saint Elizabeth and Fairleigh Dickinson University. There are also dual majors, study abroad, a Wall Street semester, a Washington semester, student-designed majors, internships, 3-2 engineering programs with Washington University in St. Louis, the Stevens Institute of Technology, and Columbia University in New York City, and a 7-year B.A.-M.D. program in medicine with UMDNJ. There are 11 national honor societies, including Phi Beta Kappa, and 12 departmental honors programs.

Faculty/Classroom: 52% of faculty are male; 48%, female. All both teach and do research. Graduate students teach 1% of introductory courses. The average class size in an introductory lecture is 25; in a laboratory, 20; and in a regular course, 18.

Admissions: 69% of the 2003-2004 applicants were accepted. The SAT I scores for the 2003-2004 freshman class were: Verbal--5% below 500, 38% between 500 and 599, 39% between 600 and 700, and 18% above 700; Math--9% below 500, 37% between 500 and 599, 44% between 600 and 700, and 9% above 700. The ACT scores were 7% below 21, 28% between 21 and 23, 28% between 24 and 26, 22% between 27 and 28, and 15% above 28. 65% of the current freshmen were in the top fifth of their class; 35% were in the top two fifths.

Requirements: The SAT I or ACT is required. The SAT I is preferred. The university strongly recommends 18 academic credits or Carnegie units, including 4 in English, 3 in math, and 2 each in foreign language, science, social studies, and history, with the remaining 3 in additional academic courses. 3 SAT II: Subject tests are recommended, including 1 in writing. An essay is also required, and an interview is recommended. AP and CLEP credits are accepted. Important factors in the admissions decision are advanced placement or honor courses, extracurricular activities record, and leadership record.

Procedure: Freshmen are admitted fall and spring. Entrance exams should be taken by January of the senior year. There are early decision, early admissions, and deferred admissions plans. Early decision applications should be filed by December 1; regular applications, by February 15 for fall entry and December 1 for spring entry, along with a $40 fee. Notification of early decision is sent December 24; regular decision, March 15. A waiting list is an active part of the admissions procedure. Applications are accepted on-line through the school's web site and Common App.

Transfer: 39 transfer students enrolled in 2002-2003. Applicants must submit satisfactory high school and college academic records, SAT I or ACT scores, a personal essay, and a statement of good standing from previous schools attended. An interview also may be required. Students with fewer than 12 credits must apply as entering freshmen. 56 of 128 credits required for the bachelor's degree must be completed at Drew.

Visiting: There are regularly scheduled orientations for prospective students. There are guides for informal visits and visitors may sit in on classes and stay overnight. To schedule a visit, contact the Admissions Office.

Financial Aid: In 2003-2004, 50% of all full-time students received some form of financial aid. The average award was $19,955. Need-based scholarships or need-based grants averaged $14,972; and need-based self-help aid (loans and jobs) averaged $5196. 47% of undergraduates work part time. Average annual earnings from campus work are $1080. The average financial indebtedness of the 2003 graduate was $16,381. The CSS Profile or FAFSA is required. The deadline for filing freshman financial aid applications for fall entry is February 15.

International Students: There are 13 international students enrolled. The school actively recruits these students. They must score 550 on the written TOEFL or 213 on the electronic version and also take the SAT I or the ACT.

Computers: The mainframe is a Compaq. All full-time students are provided with a free Pentium notebook computer, a printer, and accompanying software. An extensive software library and additional computers are located on campus. Students also have access to the Internet and e-mail, with connections in many of the residence halls. All students may access the system. There are no time limits and no fees.

Graduates: From July 1, 2002 to June 30, 2003, 349 bachelor's degrees were awarded. The most popular majors were social sciences and history (35%), visual and performing arts (11%), and interdisciplinary studies (11%). In an average class, 75% graduate in 6 years or less. 78 companies recruited on campus in 2002-2003.

Admissions Contact: Mary Beth Carey, Dean of Admissions and Financial Assistance. E-mail: *cadm@drew.edu*
Web: *http://www.drew.edu*

FAIRLEIGH DICKINSON UNIVERSITY SYSTEM

The Fairleigh Dickinson University System, established in 1942, is a private system in New Jersey. It is governed by Board of Trustees, whose chief administrator is president. The primary goal of the system is teaching/research. The main priorities are to provide an academically challenging learning experience to prepare students for employment or enrollment in graduate and professional schools; to promote independent thinking and collaborative learning in students as part of the educational process; and to cultivate a holistic, integrated living-learning experience as part of the educational process, and to foster the ideals of good citizenship and community service. The total enrollment of both campuses usually exceeds 11,000; there were about 670 faculty members. Fairleigh Dickinson University System offers 53 undergraduate and 50 graduate programs. There is a 4-year campus located in Florham Park/Madison Campus. Profiles of the 4-year campuses are included in this section.

FAIRLEIGH DICKINSON UNIVERSITY/COLLEGE AT FLORHAM
Madison, NJ 07940

D-3

(973) 443-8900
(800) 338-8803; Fax: (973) 443-8088

Full-time: 1056 men, 1192 women	**Faculty:** 115; IIA, +$
Part-time: 166 men, 231 women	**Ph.D.s:** 77%
Graduate: 404 men, 694 women	**Student/Faculty:** 20 to 1
Year: semesters, summer session	**Tuition:** $21,880
Application Deadline: March 1	**Room & Board:** $8250
Freshman Class: 2884 applied, 2162 accepted, 616 enrolled	
SAT I Verbal/Math: 510/520	**COMPETITIVE**

Fairleigh Dickinson University/College at Florham, formerly known as the Madison Campus, founded in 1942, is an independent university with 40 acadmeic majors and 35 graduate programs. Studies are rooted in the liberal arts, but they also offer hands-on opportunities in business and professional internships, cooperative education, and global studies abroad. There are 2 undergraduate and 2 graduate schools. In addition to regional accreditation, College at Florham has baccalaureate program accreditation with AACSB, ACS, and APTA. The library contains 150,669 volumes, 108,000 microform items, and 681 audio/video tapes/CDs, and subscribes to 643 periodicals. Computerized library services include the card catalog, interlibrary loans, database searching, and Internet access. Special learning facilities include a learning resource center, art gallery, radio station, a Regional Center for College Students with Learning Disabilities, web lab, ITV multimedia classrooms, and theaters. The 178-acre campus is in a suburban area 27 miles west of New York City, in Morris County. Including any residence halls, there are 33 buildings.

Student Life: 83% of undergraduates are from New Jersey. Students are from 27 states and 21 foreign countries. 75% are white. The average age of freshmen is 18; all undergraduates, 22. 23% do not continue beyond their first year; 51% remain to graduate.

Housing: 1530 students can be accommodated in college housing, which includes coed dorms, on-campus apartments, fraternity houses, and sorority houses. In addition, there are honors houses and special-interest houses. On-campus housing is guaranteed for the freshman year only and is available on a first-come, first-served basis. 53% of students live on campus; of those, 40% remain on campus on weekends. Upperclassmen may keep cars.

Activities: 8% of men belong to 6 national fraternities; 10% of women belong to 4 national sororities. There are 35 groups on campus, including art, cheerleading, computers, debate, drama, ethnic, film, gay, honors, international, jazz band, literary magazine, musical theater, newspaper, pep band, photography, political, professional, radio and TV, religious, social, social service, student government, and yearbook. Popular campus events include Welcome Week, Softball Marathon, and Senior Days.

Sports: There are 9 intercollegiate sports for men and 9 for women, and 11 intramural sports for men and 10 for women. Facilities include a synthetic turf field for football, field hockey, soccer, and lacrosse.

Disabled Students: 40% of the campus is accessible. Wheelchair ramps, elevators, special parking, specially equipped rest rooms, special class scheduling, lowered drinking fountains, lowered telephones, special housing, and oral interpretation for the hearing impaired are available.

Services: Counseling and information services are available, as is tutoring in most subjects. There is a reader service for the blind, and remedial math, reading, and writing. Workshops also offer assistance with study skills and time management, and support services for basic skills students and freshmen are available. There is a Regional Center for College Students with Learning Disabilities that offers comprehensive support to students admitted to the program.

Campus Safety and Security: Measures include 24-hour foot and vehicle patrol, self-defense education, security escort services, and shuttle buses. There are informal discussions, pamphlets/posters/films, emergency telephones, lighted pathways/sidewalks, an active crime prevention program, and a bike patrol.

Programs of Study: College at Florham confers B.A., B.S., B.S.A.H.T., B.S.C.L.S., and B.S.N. degrees. Associate and master's degrees are also awarded. Bachelor's degrees are awarded in BIOLOGICAL SCIENCE (biology/biological science and marine biology), BUSINESS (accounting, business administration and management, entrepreneurial studies, hotel/motel and restaurant management, and marketing/retailing/merchandising), COMMUNICATIONS AND THE ARTS (communications, creative writing, dramatic arts, fine arts, literature, and video), COMPUTER AND PHYSICAL SCIENCE (chemistry, computer science, mathematics, and radiological technology), HEALTH PROFESSIONS (allied health, clinical science, and medical laboratory technology), SOCIAL SCIENCE (economics, French studies, history, humanities, liberal arts/general studies, philosophy, political science/government, psychology, sociology, and Spanish studies). Psychology, business management, and communications are the largest.

Required: To graduate, students must complete a minimum of 128 credits, including 30 to 44 in the major, with an overall minimum 2.0

GPA (2.5 in the major). Distribution requirements include courses in English, communications, math, phys ed, foreign language, humanities, social and behavioral sciences, lab and computer science, an integrated, interdisciplinary university core sequence, and freshman seminar.

Special: The college offers co-op programs in all majors, internships, and study abroad. A Washington semester, work-study, accelerated degrees, and student-designed majors in the humanities and general studies are possible. A prepharmacy program, as well as joint baccalaureate dental programs are available. There are 17 national honor societies, a freshman honors program, and 19 departmental honors programs.

Faculty/Classroom: 63% of faculty are male; 37%, female. All teach undergraduates.

Admissions: 75% of the 2003-2004 applicants were accepted. The SAT I scores for the 2003-2004 freshman class were: Verbal--45% below 500, 43% between 500 and 599, 11% between 600 and 700, and 1% above 700; Math--41% below 500, 45% between 500 and 599, 13% between 600 and 700, and 1% above 700. 1 freshman graduated first in the class.

Requirements: The SAT I or ACT is required. In addition, applicants should be graduates of an accredited high school or have a GED certificate. They should have completed a minimum of 16 academic units, including 4 in English, 3 in math, 2 each in history, foreign language, and lab science (3 are recommended), and 3 in electives. Those students applying to science and health sciences programs must meet additional requirements. An interview may be requested by the college. A GPA of 3.0 is required. AP and CLEP credits are accepted. Important factors in the admissions decision are leadership record, recommendations by school officials, and extracurricular activities record.

Procedure: Freshmen are admitted to all sessions. Entrance exams should be taken in May of the junior year. There are early admissions and deferred admissions plans. There is a rolling admissions plan. Applications should be filed by March 1 for fall entry. The fall 2003 application fee was $40. Notification is sent on a rolling basis. Applications are accepted on-line through CollegeNET, Apply, or the school's web site.

Transfer: 159 transfer students enrolled in 2002-2003. All transfer applicants must submit official transcripts for all college work taken. Those students with fewer than 24 credits must also submit a high school transcript or a copy of their state department of education's equivalency score, and SAT I scores. 60 credits of 128 required for the bachelor's degree must be completed at College at Florham.

Visiting: There are regularly scheduled orientations for prospective students, including standardized placement testing, faculty advisement, class registration, and educational and social activities to prepare students for entrance in the fall. There are guides for informal visits and visitors may sit in on classes and stay overnight. To schedule a visit, contact the Admissions Office at *globaleducation@fdu.edu*.

Financial Aid: College at Florham is a member of CSS. The FAFSA is required. The priority date for freshman financial aid applications for fall entry is February 15. The regular application deadline is rolling.

International Students: There are 35 international students enrolled. The school actively recruits these students. They must score 550 on the written TOEFL or 213 on the electronic version or take the MELAB, the Comprehensive English Language Test, the college's own test, or IELTS. The SAT I or ACT is highly recommended.

Computers: The mainframes are a DEC Alpha 2100 and 4100, Sun 250 and 450, SunFire V880, and Sunblade 2000. There are 7 PC labs, each consisting of 20 or more NetVista Pentium III PCs connected to a central Novell file server and to the network, which is connected to the Internet. Each dorm room has access to the campus LAN and, hence, to the Internet. All students may access the system. There are no time limits. The fee is $480 per year. It is strongly recommended that all students have a personal computer. An IBM ThinkPad or NetVista is recommended.

Graduates: From July 1, 2002 to June 30, 2003, 412 bachelor's degrees were awarded. The most popular majors were psychology (17%), business marketing (10%), and management (9%). In an average class, 30% graduate in 4 years or less, 45% graduate in 5 years or less, and 51% graduate in 6 years or less. 101 companies recruited on campus in 2002-2003.

Admissions Contact: Bernetta Millonde, University Director of Admissions. E-mail: *globaleducation@fdu.edu* Web: *www.fdu.edu*

FAIRLEIGH DICKINSON UNIVERSITY/METROPOLITAN CAMPUS   E-2
(Formerly Fairleigh Dickinson University/Teaneck Campus)
Teaneck, NJ 07666

(973) 443-8900
(800) 338-8803; Fax: (973) 443-8088

Full-time: 871 men, 1230 women	**Faculty:** 172; IIA, +$
Part-time: 1294 men, 1641 women	**Ph.D.s:** 81%
Graduate: 939 men, 1143 women	**Student/Faculty:** 12 to 1
Year: semesters, summer session	**Tuition:** $20,334
Application Deadline: March 1	**Room & Board:** $8250
Freshman Class: 2645 applied, 1787 accepted, 637 enrolled	
SAT I Verbal/Math: 480/490	**COMPETITIVE**

Fairleigh Dickinson University/Metropolitan Campus, formerly known as the Teaneck Campus, founded in 1942, is an independent university offering undergraduate and graduate degrees in business, arts and sciences, professional studies, public administration, and hotel, restaurant, and tourism management. There are 3 undergraduate and 3 graduate schools. In addition to regional accreditation, FDU has baccalaureate program accreditation with AACSB, ABET, APTA, CSAB, NASDTEC, and NLN. The 3 libraries contain 268,865 volumes, 230,266 microform items, and 1884 audio/video tapes/CDs, and subscribe to 1420 periodicals. Computerized library services include the card catalog, interlibrary loans, database searching, and Internet access. Special learning facilities include a learning resource center, radio station, computer labs, ITV multimedia classrooms, photonics lab, a Regional Center for College Students with Learning Disabilities, theater, art galleries, web lab, and Center for Psychological Services. The 88-acre campus is in a suburban area 13 miles from midtown Manhattan. Including any residence halls, there are 53 buildings.

Student Life: 75% of undergraduates are from New Jersey. Students are from 22 states, 51 foreign countries, and Canada. 38% are white; 23% African American; 15% Hispanic; 11% foreign nationals. The average age of freshmen is 20; all undergraduates, 22. 30% do not continue beyond their first year; 48% remain to graduate.

Housing: 1013 students can be accommodated in college housing, which includes single-sex and coed dorms. In addition, there are honors houses and special-interest houses. On-campus housing is available on a first-come, first-served basis and is available on a lottery system for upperclassmen. 74% of students commute. Alcohol is not permitted. All students may keep cars.

Activities: 2% of men belong to 5 national fraternities; 8% of women belong to 7 national sororities. There are 62 groups on campus, including art, cheerleading, choir, computers, dance, drama, ethnic, film, gay, honors, international, literary magazine, musical theater, newspaper, pep band, photography, political, professional, radio and TV, religious, social, social service, student government, student programming board, and yearbook. Popular campus events include Welcome Back Week, Spring Fest, and dances.

Sports: There are 8 intercollegiate sports for men and 10 for women, and 15 intramural sports for men and 15 for women. Facilities include a 5000-seat facility with a 6-lane, 200-meter track, 4 full basketball courts, 2 volleyball courts, 4 racquetball courts, and a fully equipped weight room, 6 outdoor tennis courts, a baseball field and soccer field with bleachers, 2 training room facilities, a softball field, and a fitness center with aerobics room, selectorized weight room, and cardio room.

Disabled Students: 35% of the campus is accessible. Wheelchair ramps, elevators, special parking, specially equipped rest rooms, special class scheduling, lowered drinking fountains, lowered telephones, special housing, and oral interpretation for the hearing impaired are available.

Services: Counseling and information services are available, as is tutoring in every subject. There is a reader service for the blind, and remedial math, reading, and writing. Workshops offer assistance with academic study skills, time management, and advanced reading and writing. Support services for basic skills students and freshmen are available. There is also a Regional Center for College Students with Learning Disabilities that offers comprehensive support to students admitted to the program.

Campus Safety and Security: Measures include 24-hour foot and vehicle patrol, self-defense education, security escort services, and informal discussions. There are pamphlets/posters/films, emergency telephones, lighted pathways/sidewalks, an active crime prevention program, and a bike patrol.

Programs of Study: FDU confers B.A., B.S., B.S.Civ.E.T., B.S.C.L.S., B.S.Con.E.T., B.S.E.E., B.S.E.E.T., B.S.M.E.T., and B.S.N. degrees. Associate, master's, and doctoral degrees are also awarded. Bachelor's degrees are awarded in BIOLOGICAL SCIENCE (biochemistry, biology/biological science, and marine biology), BUSINESS (accounting, business administration and management, entrepreneurial studies, hotel/motel and restaurant management, and marketing/retailing/merchandising), COMMUNICATIONS AND THE ARTS (communications, dramatic arts, English literature, and fine arts), COMPUTER AND PHYSICAL SCIENCE (chemistry, computer science, information sciences and systems, mathematics, radiological technology, and science), ENGINEERING AND ENVIRONMENTAL DESIGN (civil engineering technology, construction engineering, electrical/electronics engineering, electrical/electronics engineering technology, environmental science, and mechanical engineering technology), HEALTH PROFESSIONS (allied health, clinical science, medical laboratory technology, and nursing), SOCIAL SCIENCE (criminal justice, economics, French studies, history, humanities, interdisciplinary studies, international studies, liberal arts/general studies, philosophy, political science/government, psychology, sociology, and Spanish studies). Individualized studies, business management, and psychology are the largest.

Required: To graduate, students must complete 120 to 128 credits, including 30 to 44 in the major, with an overall minimum 2.0 GPA. Students must complete a 4-semester interdisciplinary sequence and 1 course in freshman seminar. Core curriculum includes 12 credits in university core, 6 credits in English, and 3 each in math and computer science.

Special: FDU offers co-op programs in all majors, cross-registration, internships, and study abroad in England. A Washington semester, work-study, accelerated degrees, and student-designed majors in the humanities and general studies are possible. A 7-year medical program is available with Karol Marcinkowski School of Medicine in Poland, as is an accelerated chiropractic progarm with New York Chiropractic College and Logan Chiropractic College. There are 14 national honor societies, a freshman honors program, and 19 departmental honors programs.

Faculty/Classroom: 63% of faculty are male; 37%, female. All teach undergraduates. No introductory courses are taught by graduate students.

Admissions: 68% of the 2003-2004 applicants were accepted. The SAT I scores for the 2003-2004 freshman class were: Verbal--59% below 500, 32% between 500 and 599, and 8% between 600 and 700; Math--53% below 500, 36% between 500 and 599, 10% between 600 and 700, and 1% above 700. 27% of the current freshmen were in the top fifth of their class; 66% were in the top two fifths. 5 freshmen graduated first in their class in a recent year.

Requirements: The SAT I or ACT is required. In addition, applicants should be graduates of an accredited high school or have a GED certificate. They should have completed a minimum of 16 academic units, including 4 in English, 3 in math, 2 each in history, foreign language, and lab science (3 are recommended), and 3 in electives. Those students applying to science, engineering, and health sciences programs must meet additional requirements. An interview may be requested by the university. A GPA of 3.0 is required. AP and CLEP credits are accepted. Important factors in the admissions decision are leadership record, recommendations by school officials, and extracurricular activities record.

Procedure: Freshmen are admitted to all sessions. Entrance exams should be taken in May of the junior year. There are early admissions and deferred admissions plans. Applications should be filed by March 1 for fall entry. The fall 2003 application fee was $40. Applications are accepted on-line through Embark, CollegeNET, Apply, or the school's web site.

Transfer: 407 transfer students enrolled in 2002-2003. All applicants must submit official transcripts for all college work taken. Those students with fewer than 24 credits must also submit a high school transcript or a copy of their state department of education's equivalency score, and SAT I scores. 60 credits of 120 to 128 required for the bachelor's degree must be completed at FDU.

Visiting: There are regularly scheduled orientations for prospective students, including standardized placement testing, faculty advisement, class registration, and educational and social activities to prepare students for entrance in the fall. There are guides for informal visits and visitors may sit in on classes and stay overnight. To schedule a visit, contact the Admissions Office at (201) 692-2553 or *globaleducation@fdu.edu*.

Financial Aid: FDU is a member of CSS. The FAFSA is required. The priority date for freshman financial aid applications for fall entry is February 15. The regular application deadline is rolling.

International Students: There are 199 international students enrolled. The school actively recruits these students. They must score 550 on the written TOEFL or 213 on the electronic version or take the MELAB, the Comprehensive English Language Test, the college's own test, or IELTS. The ACT or SAT I is highly recommended.

Computers: The mainframes are DEC Alpha 4100 and 2100 systems, Sun Enterprise 250 and 450 systems, SunFire V880, and Sunblade 2000. Each PC lab has 20 or more NetVista Pentium III PCs with connectivity to LAN-based file servers and the Internet. Each dorm room has access to the campus LAN and to the Internet. All students may access the system. There are no time limits. The fee is $480 per year. It is strongly recommended that all students have a personal computer. An IBM ThinkPad or NetVista is recommended.

Graduates: From July 1, 2002 to June 30, 2003, 471 bachelor's degrees were awarded. The most popular majors were individualized studies (19%), business management (12%), and psychology (8%). In an average class, 30% graduate in 4 years or less, 44% graduate in 5 years or less, and 58% graduate in 6 years or less. 200 companies recruited on campus in 2002-2003.

Admissions Contact: Bernetta Millonde, University Director of Admissions. E-mail: *globaleducation@fdu.edu* Web: *www.fdu.edu*

FAIRLEIGH DICKINSON UNIVERSITY/TEANECK CAMPUS
(See Fairleigh Dickinson University/Metropolitan Campus)

FELICIAN COLLEGE
E-2
Lodi, NJ 07644   (201) 559-6131; Fax: (201) 559-6188

Full-time: 249 men, 735 women	Faculty: 66
Part-time: 84 men, 348 women	Ph.D.s: 55%
Graduate: 15 men, 95 women	Student/Faculty: 15 to 1
Year: semesters, summer session	Tuition: $17,100
Application Deadline: open	Room & Board: $7200
Freshman Class: 1042 applied, 245 accepted, 240 enrolled	
SAT I Verbal/Math: 440/440	COMPETITIVE

Felician College, founded in 1942, is a private, Roman Catholic, liberal arts school with concentrations in health science, teacher education, and arts and sciences. There are 3 undergraduate and 3 graduate schools. In addition to regional accreditation, Felician has baccalaureate program accreditation with CAHEA and NLN. The library contains 104,000 volumes, 78,039 microform items, and 4202 audio/video tapes/CDs, and subscribes to 401 periodicals. Computerized library services include interlibrary loans and database searching. Special learning facilities include a learning resource center and a nursing clinical lab. The 32-acre campus is in a suburban area 10 miles west of New York City. Including any residence halls, there are 5 buildings.

Student Life: 94% of undergraduates are from New Jersey. Students are from 8 states, 6 foreign countries, and Canada. 65% are from public schools. 52% are white; 15% Hispanic; 11% African American. The average age of freshmen is 19; all undergraduates, 26. 10% do not continue beyond their first year; 35% remain to graduate.

Housing: 700 students can be accommodated in college housing, which includes single-sex and coed dorms. On-campus housing is guaranteed for all 4 years. Alcohol is not permitted. Upperclassmen may keep cars.

Activities: There are no fraternities or sororities. There are 17 groups on campus, including art, cheerleading, chess, choir, computers, drama, education, ethnic, free enterprise, honors, international, karate, literary magazine, professional, religious, science, social service, and student government. Popular campus events include College festival, springfest, and sibling weekend.

Sports: There are 4 intercollegiate sports for men and 4 for women. Facilities include 2 fitness centers and a gym.

Disabled Students: 90% of the campus is accessible. Wheelchair ramps, elevators, special parking, specially equipped rest rooms, lowered drinking fountains, lowered telephones, special housing, and wheelchair lifts are available.

Services: Counseling and information services are available, as is tutoring in most subjects. There is remedial math, reading, and writing.

Campus Safety and Security: Measures include 24-hour foot and vehicle patrol and lighted pathways/sidewalks.

Programs of Study: Felician confers B.A., B.S., and B.S.N. degrees. Associate and master's degrees are also awarded. Bachelor's degrees are awarded in BIOLOGICAL SCIENCE (biology/biological science), BUSINESS (business administration and management and institutional management), COMMUNICATIONS AND THE ARTS (art and English), COMPUTER AND PHYSICAL SCIENCE (computer science and mathematics), EDUCATION (elementary and special), HEALTH PROFESSIONS (clinical science and nursing), SOCIAL SCIENCE (history, humanities, philosophy, psychology, and religion). Education and nursing are the strongest academically.

Required: All students must earn a minimum GPA of 2.0 (2.5 in medical lab technology, 2.75 in nursing, and 3.0 in education), while taking 120 credit hours (128 to 130 in education), with 39 to 57 hours in their majors. Distribution requirements include 45 to 47 hours from a core curriculum, including courses in English, philosophy, religious studies, humanities, historical tradition, science, and social-cultural studies.

Special: Co-op programs are available in clinical lab sciences with the University of Medicine and Dentistry of New Jersey. In addition, internships for credit, work-study at the college, dual majors in education, an interdisciplinary studies degree, an accelerated degree in organizational management, student-designed majors within humanities and social and behavioral sciences, weekend college, and pass/fail options are possible. There is a freshman honors program.

Faculty/Classroom: 51% of faculty are male; 49%, female. The average class size in an introductory lecture is 25; in a laboratory, 20; and in a regular course, 15.

Admissions: 24% of the 2003-2004 applicants were accepted. The SAT I scores for the 2003-2004 freshman class were: Verbal--75% below 500, 21% between 500 and 599, and 4% between 600 and 700; Math--71% below 500, 24% between 500 and 599, and 5% between 600 and 700.

Requirements: The SAT I is required with a minimum composite score of 850 recommended. The college also recommends that applicants have 16 academic credits, including 4 in English, 2 to 3 each in math, science, and social studies, and 3 to 6 in academic electives, including foreign language. An interview is recommended. The GED is accepted. A GPA of 2.0 is required. AP and CLEP credits are accepted. Important factors in the admissions decision are recommendations by school officials, advanced placement or honor courses, and extracurricular activities record.

Procedure: Freshmen are admitted fall, spring, and summer. Application deadlines are open. Application fee is $30. Applications are accepted on-line through the school's web site. Notification is sent on a rolling basis.

Transfer: 155 transfer students enrolled in 2002-2003. Applicants must have maintained a minimum GPA of 2.5 (2.75 in nursing and 3.0 in education). An interview is recommended. Nursing majors require previous college-level lab science. 30 of 120 credits required for the bachelor's degree must be completed at Felician.

Visiting: There are guides for informal visits and visitors may sit in on classes. To schedule a visit, contact the Admissions Office.

Financial Aid: In 2003-2004, all full-time students received some form of financial aid. At least 48% of full-time freshmen and 50% of continuing full-time students received need-based aid. The average freshman award was $11,130. Need-based scholarships or need-based grants averaged $6000; need-based self-help aid (loans and jobs) averaged $3800; non-need-based athletic scholarships averaged $7626; and other non-need-based awards and non-need-based scholarships averaged $7626. 97% of undergraduates work part time. Average annual earnings from campus work are $3000. The average financial indebtedness of the 2003 graduate was $40,000. The FAFSA and the college's own financial statement are required. Check with the school for current deadlines.

International Students: The school actively recruits these students. They must score 500 on the written TOEFL or 200 on the electronic version.

Computers: There are 250 Macs and PCs available for academic use. All students have full access to the Internet. All students may access the system. There are no time limits and no fees.

Graduates: From July 1, 2002 to June 30, 2003, 171 bachelor's degrees were awarded. The most popular majors were business/marketing (43%), education (30%), and psychology (12%). In an average class, 20% graduate in 4 years or less, 10% graduate in 5 years or less, and 2% graduate in 6 years or less.

Admissions Contact: Cynthia Sievewright, Director of Admissions. E-mail: *admissions@inet.felician.edu* Web: *www.felician.edu*

GEORGIAN COURT COLLEGE

E-4

Lakewood, NJ 08701-2697

(732) 364-2200, ext. 760
(800) 458-8422; Fax: (732) 364-4442

Full-time: 50 men, 1000 women	**Faculty:** 82; IIA, --$
Part-time: 100 men, 430 women	**Ph.D.s:** 72%
Graduate: 155 men, 680 women	**Student/Faculty:** 13 to 1
Year: semesters, summer session	**Tuition:** $16,272
Application Deadline: August 1	**Room & Board:** $6600
Freshman Class: n/av	
SAT I or ACT: required	**LESS COMPETITIVE**

Georgian Court College, founded in 1908, is an independent Roman Catholic college. The day division matriculates only women; the evening and graduate divisions are coed. Undergraduate programs are offered in the arts and sciences, business administration, religion, social work, and teacher preparation. Some figures in the above capsule and in this profile are approximate. In addition to regional accreditation, The Court has baccalaureate program accreditation with ACBSP and NASDTEC. The library contains 130,000 volumes, 620,000 microform items, and 2000 audio/video tapes/CDs, and subscribes to 1400 periodicals. Computerized library services include the card catalog, interlibrary loans, and database searching. Special learning facilities include a learning resource center, art gallery, and an arboretum. The 150-acre campus is in a suburban area 60 miles south of New York City and 60 miles east of Philadelphia. Including any residence halls, there are 17 buildings.

Student Life: 99% of undergraduates are from New Jersey. Students are from 5 states and 3 foreign countries. 83% are from public schools. 78% are white. 48% are Catholic; 9% Protestant. The average age of freshmen is 18; all undergraduates, 26. 1% do not continue beyond their first year; 84% remain to graduate.

Housing: 356 students can be accommodated in college housing, which includes single-sex dorms. On-campus housing is guaranteed for all 4 years. 74% of students commute. All students may keep cars.

Activities: There are no fraternities or sororities. There are 38 groups on campus, including art, band, choir, chorale, ethnic, honors, international, literary magazine, newspaper, professional, religious, social, social service, student government, and yearbook. Popular campus events include Irish Afternoon, Family Day, and Christmas Reception.

Sports: There are 4 intercollegiate sports for women. Facilities include a porcelain-faced swimming pool, basketball and volleyball courts, a 300-seat gym, a fitness center, athletic fields, and a tennis court.

Disabled Students: 73% of the campus is accessible. Wheelchair ramps, elevators, special parking, specially equipped rest rooms, special class scheduling, lowered drinking fountains, lowered telephones, and special equipment for the visually and hearing impaired are available.

Services: Counseling and information services are available, as is tutoring in most subjects. There is remedial math, reading, and writing.

Campus Safety and Security: Measures include 24-hour foot and vehicle patrol, security escort services, informal discussions, and pamphlets/posters/films. There are lighted pathways/sidewalks.

Programs of Study: The Court confers B.A., B.S., B.F.A., and B.S.W. degrees. Master's degrees are also awarded. Bachelor's degrees are awarded in BIOLOGICAL SCIENCE (biochemistry and biology/biological science), BUSINESS (accounting and business administration and management), COMMUNICATIONS AND THE ARTS (art, art history and appreciation, English, French, music, and Spanish), COMPUTER AND PHYSICAL SCIENCE (chemistry, mathematics, and physics), EDUCATION (elementary and special), SOCIAL SCIENCE (history, humanities, psychology, religion, social work, and sociology). Education, psychology, and business administration are the largest.

Required: General education requirements include 9 semester courses in humanities, 5 in social science, and 3 in natural science/math. Students under 25 also must complete a semester course in phys ed. The bachelor's degree requires completion of at least 132 credit hours, including a minimum of 30 in a major field. Students must maintain a GPA of at least 2.0 overall and 2.5 in all majors but social work, which requires a 3.0.

Special: Business administration majors may participate in cooperative programs and work-study programs with various employers. Georgian Court also offers study abroad through the College Consortium for International Studies, internships in history, social work, and political science, dual majors in education, a general studies degree in humanities, field experience externships in art, psychology, education, and social work, credit for life experience, and pass/fail options. Nondegree study is possible. There are 15 national honor societies and 13 departmental honors programs.

Faculty/Classroom: 47% of faculty are male; 53%, female. 79% teach undergraduates. No introductory courses are taught by graduate students. The average class size in an introductory lecture is 19; in a laboratory, 7; and in a regular course, 13.

Requirements: The SAT I or ACT is required. In addition, applicants must be graduates of accredited secondary schools or have earned a GED. The college requires 16 academic credits or Carnegie units, based on 6 years of academic electives, 4 of English, 2 each of foreign language and math, and 1 each of history and a lab science. An interview is recommended for all students, and an audition is required for applied music majors. The Court requires applicants to be in the upper 50% of their class. AP and CLEP credits are accepted.

Procedure: Freshmen are admitted fall and spring. Entrance exams should be taken by January of the senior year. There is an early admissions plan. Applications should be filed by August 1 for fall entry and January 1 for spring entry. The application fee is $40. Notification is sent on a rolling basis.

Transfer: Applicants with fewer than 24 credits must fulfill freshman requirements. 50 of 132 credits required for the bachelor's degree must be completed at The Court.

Visiting: There are regularly scheduled orientations for prospective students, including visits with faculty and students and a tour of facilities. There are guides for informal visits and visitors may sit in on classes and stay overnight. To schedule a visit, contact the Director of Admissions.

Financial Aid: The Court is a member of CSS. The FAFSA, the college's own financial statement, and parent and student 1040 tax forms are required.

International Students: The school actively recruits these students. They must score 550 on the written TOEFL.

Computers: 6 modern computer labs with 131 networked computers are available to all students. All students may access the system from 8 A.M. to 10 P.M. daily. There are no time limits and no fees.

Admissions Contact: Director of Admissions.
E-mail: *admissions-ugrad@georgian.edu* Web: *www.georgian.edu*

KEAN UNIVERSITY
Union, NJ 07083-0411

E-2

(908) 737-7100; Fax: (908) 737-7105

Full-time: 2819 men, 4568 women	Faculty: 367; IIA, +$
Part-time: 822 men, 1970 women	Ph.D.s: 90%
Graduate: 623 men, 2172 women	Student/Faculty: 20 to 1
Year: semesters, summer session	Tuition: $6724 ($9086)
Application Deadline: June 15	Room & Board: $7755
Freshman Class: 4300 applied, 2617 accepted, 1376 enrolled	
SAT I Verbal/Math: 499/510	COMPETITIVE

Kean University, founded in 1855, is a public institution offering undergraduate and graduate programs in the arts and sciences, business, education, government, nursing, and technology. Kean is primarily a metropolitan commuter university. There are 4 undergraduate schools and 1 graduate school. In addition to regional accreditation, Kean has baccalaureate program accreditation with APTA, ASLA, CAHEA, CSWE, NASAD, NASDTEC, NASM, NCATE, and NLN. The library contains 271,000 volumes, 792,000 microform items, and 6000 audio/video tapes/CDs, and subscribes to 14,200 periodicals. Computerized library services include the card catalog, interlibrary loans, database searching, and Internet access. Special learning facilities include a learning resource center, art gallery, radio station, TV station, and Holocaust Resource Center. The 151-acre campus is in a suburban area 12 miles west of New York City. Including any residence halls, there are 35 buildings.

Student Life: 96% of undergraduates are from New Jersey. Students are from 17 states and 79 foreign countries. 49% are white; 21% African American; 21% Hispanic. The average age of freshmen is 21; all undergraduates, 26. 21% do not continue beyond their first year; 43% remain to graduate.

Housing: 1300 students can be accommodated in college housing, which includes freshman housing, coed dorms, and on-campus apartments. On-campus housing is guaranteed for all 4 years. 88% of students commute. Alcohol is not permitted. All students may keep cars.

Activities: There are 12 local and 3 national fraternities and 12 local and 4 national sororities. There are 130 groups on campus, including art, cheerleading, choir, chorale, chorus, computers, dance, drama, ethnic, gay, honors, international, jazz band, literary magazine, musical theater, newspaper, orchestra, pep band, photography, political, professional, radio and TV, religious, social, social service, student government, and yearbook. Popular campus events include Campus Awareness Festival and Autumn Food Bank Luncheon.

Sports: There are 8 intercollegiate sports for men and 7 for women, and 13 intramural sports for men and 9 for women. Facilities include a 3000-seat stadium, an 8-lane track, 7 playing fields, 4 gyms, basketball courts, 22 tennis courts, swimming pools, a track, a weight training room, pool tables, and pinball and video machines.

Disabled Students: All of the campus is accessible. Wheelchair ramps, elevators, special parking, specially equipped rest rooms, lowered drinking fountains, and lowered telephones are available.

Services: Counseling and information services are available, as is tutoring in most subjects. There is a reader service for the blind, remedial math, reading, and writing, and a full program for learning-disabled students.

Campus Safety and Security: Measures include 24-hour foot and vehicle patrol, self-defense education, security escort services, and shuttle buses. There are informal discussions, pamphlets/posters/films, emergency telephones, and lighted pathways/sidewalks.

Programs of Study: Kean confers B.A., B.S., B.F.A., B.I.D., B.S.N., and B.S.W. degrees. Master's degrees are also awarded. Bachelor's degrees are awarded in BIOLOGICAL SCIENCE (biology/biological science), BUSINESS (accounting, banking and finance, business administration and management, marketing/retailing/merchandising, and recreation and leisure services), COMMUNICATIONS AND THE ARTS (art history and appreciation, communications, dramatic arts, English, fine arts, graphic design, industrial design, multimedia, music, Spanish, studio art, and telecommunications), COMPUTER AND PHYSICAL SCIENCE (chemistry, computer science, earth science, and mathematics), EDUCATION (drama, early childhood, elementary, industrial arts, music, physical, special, and technical), ENGINEERING AND ENVIRONMENTAL DESIGN (graphic arts technology, industrial engineering technology, and interior design), HEALTH PROFESSIONS (health care administration, medical technology, nursing, occupational therapy, rehabilitation therapy, and speech pathology/audiology), SOCIAL SCIENCE (criminal justice, economics, history, philosophy, political science/government, psychology, public administration, social work, and sociology). Allied health and technology are the strongest academically. Business and education are the largest.

Required: Students must complete a freshman seminar, 18 credits of core requirements, 2 upper-level writing courses, and at least 30 credits in a major field. The bachelor's degree requires completion of 124 to 129 semester hours with a minimum GPA of 2.0.

Special: Students may study abroad in 7 countries, and Kean offers cooperative programs and cross-registration with other members of the Consortium of East New Jersey. There are also dual majors in elementary education, a B.A.- B.S. degree in chemistry, internships in many majors, a Washington semester, accelerated degrees in chemistry and social work, credit for life experience, and pass/fail options. There are 5 national honor societies, a freshman honors program, and 18 departmental honors programs.

Faculty/Classroom: 54% of faculty are male; 46%, female. All teach undergraduates. No introductory courses are taught by graduate students. The average class size in an introductory lecture is 25; in a laboratory, 15; and in a regular course, 22.

Admissions: 61% of the 2003-2004 applicants were accepted. The SAT I scores for the 2003-2004 freshman class were: Verbal--52% below 500, 42% between 500 and 599, and 6% between 600 and 700; Math--50% below 500, 43% between 500 and 599, and 7% between 600 and 700. 18% of the current freshmen were in the top fifth of their class; 49% were in the top two fifths.

Requirements: The SAT I is required, with a minimum composite score of 1000. Applicants must be graduates of accredited secondary schools or have earned a GED. College preparatory study includes 4 courses in English, 3 in math, 2 each in lab science and social studies, and 5 in academic electives. An essay is also required, and an interview is recommended. Kean requires applicants to be in the upper 50% of their class. A GPA of 2.0 is required. AP and CLEP credits are accepted. Important factors in the admissions decision are leadership record, advanced placement or honor courses, and recommendations by school officials.

Procedure: Freshmen are admitted to all sessions. Applications should be filed by June 15 for fall entry and November 1 for spring entry. There is a rolling admissions plan. The fall 2003 fall application fee was $50. Notification is sent on a rolling basis. Applications are accepted on-line.

Transfer: 1073 transfer students enrolled in 2002-2003. Applicants must present a minimum GPA of 2.0. Those students tranferring fewer than 15 credits must also submit SAT I scores. 32 of 124 credits required for the bachelor's degree must be completed at Kean.

Visiting: There are regularly scheduled orientations for prospective students. There are guides for informal visits. To schedule a visit, contact the Admissions Office.

Financial Aid: In 2002-2003, 54% of all full-time freshmen and 48% of continuing full-time students received some form of financial aid. 65% of full-time freshmen and 67% of continuing full-time students received need-based aid. The average freshman award was $5845. Need-based scholarships or need-based grants averaged $4707; need-based self-help aid (loans and jobs) averaged $2302; and other non-need-based awards and non-need-based scholarships averaged $1238. 10% of undergraduates work part time. Average annual earnings from campus work are $1925. The average financial indebtedness of the 2003 graduate was $24,106. The FAFSA is required. The deadline for filing freshman financial aid applications for fall entry is March 15.

International Students: There are 240 international students enrolled. The school actively recruits these students. They must take the SAT I.

Computers: The Computer Services Department operates a Prime 6550 for academic use and a Prime 5340 for CAD/CAM use by the Technology Department. Major buildings are connected by a campuswide fiber-optic backbone to the university's central system. More than 30 discipline-based PC labs with software packages are located throughout the campus. All students may access the system. There are no time limits and no fees.

Graduates: From July 1, 2002 to June 30, 2003, 2313 bachelor's degrees were awarded. The most popular majors were management science (9%), psychology (6%), and accounting (5%). In an average class, 15% graduate in 4 years or less, 35% graduate in 5 years or less, and 43% graduate in 6 years or less.

Admissions Contact: Audley Bridges, Director of Admissions. A video is available. E-mail: *admitme@kean.edu* Web: *www.kean.edu*

MONMOUTH UNIVERSITY
West Long Branch, NJ 07764-1898

E-3

(732) 571-3456
(800) 543-9671; Fax: (732) 263-5166

Full-time: 1697 men, 2208 women	Faculty: 234; IIA, av$
Part-time: 142 men, 334 women	Ph.D.s: 75%
Graduate: 582 men, 1249 women	Student/Faculty: 17 to 1
Year: semesters, summer session	Tuition: $18,766
Application Deadline: March 1	Room & Board: $7568
Freshman Class: 5718 applied, 3785 accepted, 904 enrolled	
SAT I Verbal/Math: 533/549	ACT: 23 COMPETITIVE

Monmouth University, founded in 1933, is a private comprehensive institution offering both undergraduate and graduate programs in the arts and sciences, business, education, upper-level nursing, technology, and professional training. There are 5 undergraduate schools and 1 graduate school. In addition to regional accreditation, Monmouth has baccalaureate program accreditation with AACSB, ABET, ACS, CCNE, CSWE, and NLN. The library contains 253,100 volumes, and subscribes to 11,900 periodicals. Computerized library services include the card catalog, interlibrary loans, database searching, and Internet access. Special learning facilities include a learning resource center, art gallery, radio station, and TV station. The 153-acre campus is in a suburban area 60 miles south of New York City. Including any residence halls, there are 53 buildings.

Student Life: 92% of undergraduates are from New Jersey. Students are from 24 states, 11 foreign countries, and Canada. 79% are white. The average age of freshmen is 18; all undergraduates, 22. 27% do not continue beyond their first year; 52% remain to graduate.

Housing: 1767 students can be accommodated in college housing, which includes coed dorms, on-campus apartments, and off-campus apartments. On-campus housing is available on a first-come, first-served basis. Priority is given to out-of-town students. 55% of students commute. All students may keep cars.

Activities: 3% of men belong to 7 national fraternities; 5% of women belong to 6 national sororities. There are 62 groups on campus, including cheerleading, choir, computers, drama, ethnic, forensics, gay, honors, international, jazz band, literary magazine, musical theater, newspaper, pep band, political, professional, radio and TV, religious, social service, student government, symphony, and yearbook. Popular campus events include Springfest, Ebony Night, and Winter Ball.

Sports: There are 8 intercollegiate sports for men and 8 for women, and 7 intramural sports for men and 7 for women. Facilities include a 2800-seat gym, outdoor tennis courts, 3 basketball courts, an 8-lane all-weather track, an indoor Olympic-size pool, exercise, wrestling, and weight rooms, and baseball, softball, and soccer fields.

Disabled Students: 90% of the campus is accessible. Wheelchair ramps, elevators, special parking, specially equipped rest rooms, special class scheduling, lowered drinking fountains, special housing, and academic assistance provided within the classroom are available.

Services: There is a reader service for the blind, and remedial math, reading, and writing. Tutoring is offered in every subject for learning disabled and physically challenged students. It is available upon request for others.

Campus Safety and Security: Measures include 24-hour foot and vehicle patrol, self-defense education, security escort services, and informal discussions. There are pamphlets/posters/films, emergency telephones, lighted pathways/sidewalks. There is an official Monmouth University police force and a student watch organization.

Programs of Study: Monmouth confers B.A., B.S., B.F.A., B.S.N., and B.S.W. degrees. Associate and master's degrees are also awarded. Bachelor's degrees are awarded in BIOLOGICAL SCIENCE (biology/biological science), BUSINESS (accounting, banking and finance, business administration and management, business economics, and marketing/retailing/merchandising), COMMUNICATIONS AND THE ARTS (art, art history and appreciation, communications, English, modern language, music, and music business management), COMPUTER AND PHYSICAL SCIENCE (chemistry, computer programming, computer science, and mathematics), EDUCATION (art, English, foreign languages, mathematics, music, science, secondary, and special), ENGINEERING AND ENVIRONMENTAL DESIGN (computer graphics), HEALTH PROFESSIONS (clinical science, medical laboratory technology, nursing, and premedicine), SOCIAL SCIENCE (anthropology, criminal justice, history, interdisciplinary studies, political science/government, prelaw, psychology, and social work). Business, education, and communication are the largest.

Required: General education requirements include 6 credits each of English composition, literature, history, natural science, social sciences, and cross-cultural studies; 3 each of math, computer science, critical discourse, and global issues; and 1 of phys ed. Students must also pass a writing proficiency examination. To graduate, students must earn at least 128 credits, including 30 to 81 in a major, with a minimum GPA of 2.0 overall and 2.1 in the major.

Special: Students may study abroad. There are cooperative and internship programs and a Washington semester. Monmouth also offers work-study programs, dual majors, flexible studies programs, and credit for life experience. Nondegree study is possible. There are 7 national honor societies and a freshman honors program.

Faculty/Classroom: 56% of faculty are male; 44%, female. No introductory courses are taught by graduate students. The average class size in a regular course is 22.

Admissions: 66% of the 2003-2004 applicants were accepted. The SAT I scores for the 2003-2004 freshman class were: Verbal--25% below 500, 62% between 500 and 599, 11% between 600 and 700, and 2% above 700; Math--18% below 500, 62% between 500 and 599, 19% between 600 and 700, and 1% above 700. The ACT scores were 18% below 21, 35% between 21 and 23, 41% between 24 and 26, and 6% above 28. 25% of the current freshmen were in the top fifth of their class; 55% were in the top two fifths.

Requirements: The SAT I or ACT is required, with a combined minimum score of 950 on the SAT I. Applicants must be graduates of accredited secondary schools or have earned a GED. The college requires 16 Carnegie units, based on 4 years of English, 3 of math, and 2 each of history and science, with the remaining 5 units in academic electives. An essay and an interview are also recommended. A GPA of 2.25 is required. AP and CLEP credits are accepted. Important factors in the admissions decision are advanced placement or honor courses, extracurricular activities record, and recommendations by school officials.

Procedure: Freshmen are admitted fall, spring, and summer. Entrance exams should be taken by December of the senior year. There are early decision, early admissions, and deferred admissions plans. Early decision applications should be filed by December 1; regular applications, by March 1 for fall entry and January 1 for spring entry, along with a $35 fee. Notification of early decision is sent January 1; regular decision, April 1. 142 early decision candidates were accepted for the 2003-2004 class. 543 applicants were on the 2003 waiting list; 2 were admitted. Applications are accepted on-line through the school's web site.

Transfer: 546 transfer students enrolled in 2002-2003. Transfers with fewer than 24 transferable college credits must provide a high school transcript and SAT I scores. All transfer applicants must submit college transcripts and a statement of good standing. A minimum college GPA of 2.0 is required. 32 of 128 credits required for the bachelor's degree must be completed at Monmouth.

Visiting: There are regularly scheduled orientations for prospective students, including campus tours and interviews. There are guides for informal visits and visitors may sit in on classes. To schedule a visit, contact the Admissions Office at *visitmu@monmouth.edu*.

Financial Aid: In 2003-2004, 95% of all full-time freshmen and 82% of continuing full-time students received some form of financial aid. 60% of all full-time students received need-based aid. 20% of undergraduates work part time. Average annual earnings from campus work are $1500. The average financial indebtedness of the 2003 graduate was $18,500. Monmouth is a member of CSS. The FAFSA is required.

International Students: There are 11 international students enrolled. The school actively recruits these students. They must score 525 on the written TOEFL or 197 on the electronic version. The SAT I may be substituted for the TOEFL, with a minimum 1050 composite score, but no less than 510 verbal. They must take the SAT I or the ACT.

Computers: Classrooms, offices, residence hall rooms, and computer labs are connected via a 10MB Ethernet network encompassing more than 1,000 workstations. More than 500 workstations (Pentium, Mac, SUN, and Silicon Graphics) are dedicated for student use in more than 30 computing labs. There are also areas on campus that are enhanced for laptop connectivity. All students may access the system 24 hours a day, 7 days a week. There are no time limits and no fees.

Graduates: From July 1, 2002 to June 30, 2003, 782 bachelor's degrees were awarded. The most popular majors were business (31%), education (16%), and communication (16%). In an average class, 37% graduate in 4 years or less, 51% graduate in 5 years or less, and 52% graduate in 6 years or less. 207 companies recruited on campus in 2002-2003.

Admissions Contact: Miriam King, Vice President Enrollment Management. E-mail: *admission@monmouth.edu*
Web: *www.monmouth.edu*

MONTCLAIR STATE UNIVERSITY
Upper Montclair, NJ 07043-1624

E-2
(973) 655-4444
(800) 331-9205; Fax: (973) 655-7700

Full-time: 3483 men, 5500 women	**Faculty:** 442; IIA, ++$
Part-time: 869 men, 1523 women	**Ph.D.s:** 90%
Graduate: 1120 men, 2709 women	**Student/Faculty:** 20 to 1
Year: semesters, summer session	**Tuition:** $6410 ($9410)
Application Deadline: March 1	**Room & Board:** $7380
Freshman Class: 8346 applied, 4263 accepted, 1652 enrolled	
SAT I Verbal/Math: 524/543	**COMPETITIVE**

Montclair State University, established in 1908, is a public institution offering programs in liberal arts and sciences, business administration, fine and performing arts, and professional studies. There are 5 undergraduate schools and 1 graduate school. In addition to regional accreditation, Montclair has baccalaureate program accreditation with AACSB, ABET, ADA, AAFCS, ASHA, CSAB, NASAD, NASD, NASDTEC, NASM, NCATE, and NRPA. The library contains 420,000 volumes, 1,300,000 microform items, and 15,000 audio/video tapes/CDs, and subscribes to 3400 periodicals. Computerized library services include the card catalog, interlibrary loans, database searching, and Internet access. Special learning facilities include a learning resource center, art gallery, radio station, TV station, a psychoeducational center, and Academic Success Center. The 275-acre campus is in a suburban area 14 miles west of New York City. Including any residence halls, there are 55 buildings.

Student Life: 95% of undergraduates are from New Jersey. Students are from 31 states, 94 foreign countries, and Canada. 80% are from public schools. 56% are white; 16% Hispanic; 11% African American. 52% are Catholic; 25% Protestant; 8% Islamic, Buddhist, Other 8%. The average age of freshmen is 18; all undergraduates, 24. 19% do not continue beyond their first year; 56% remain to graduate.

Housing: 3140 students can be accommodated in college housing, which includes single-sex and coed dorms and on-campus apartments. In addition, there are honors houses and special-interest houses. On-campus housing is available on a first-come, first-served basis. Priority is given to out-of-town students. 65% of students commute. Alcohol is not permitted. All students may keep cars.

Activities: There are 2 local and 12 national fraternities and 4 local and 9 national sororities. There are 121 groups on campus, including band, cheerleading, choir, chorus, dance, drama, ethnic, gay, honors, international, jazz band, literary magazine, marching band, musical theater, newspaper, orchestra, professional, radio and TV, religious, social, social service, student government, and yearbook. Popular campus events include Carnival, Spring Week, and Greek Week.

Sports: There are 10 intercollegiate sports for men and 11 for women, and 15 intramural sports for men and 10 for women. Facilities include a gym complex with competitive pool, 2 basketball courts, an auxiliary gym, wrestling room, a 6000-seat Astroturf stadium, a baseball stadium, a softball stadium, soccer park, all weather track, tennis courts, and a fitness center.

Disabled Students: 90% of the campus is accessible. Wheelchair ramps, elevators, special parking, specially equipped rest rooms, special class scheduling, lowered drinking fountains, lowered telephones, special housing, curb cuts, speaker phones, special building signs, TDDs, and priority registration are available. An office for students with disabilities has been established.

Services: Counseling and information services are available, as is tutoring in most subjects. There is a reader service for the blind, and remedial math, reading, and writing. Textbooks on tape are available.

Campus Safety and Security: Measures include 24-hour foot and vehicle patrol, self-defense education, security escort services, and shuttle buses. There are informal discussions, pamphlets/posters/films, emergency telephones, lighted pathways/sidewalks, a full-time campus police force, a crime prevention officer, and crime prevention programs.

Programs of Study: Montclair confers B.A., B.S., B.F.A., and B.Mus. degrees. Master's degrees are also awarded. Bachelor's degrees are awarded in BIOLOGICAL SCIENCE (biochemistry, biology/biological science, environmental biology, and molecular biology), BUSINESS (accounting, banking and finance, business administration and management, business economics, hospitality management services, international business management, management information systems, marketing management, recreation and leisure services, retailing, and tourism), COMMUNICATIONS AND THE ARTS (art, art history and appreciation, broadcasting, classics, communications, communications technology, creative writing, dance, dramatic arts, English, fine arts, French, Italian, Latin, linguistics, music, music performance, music theory and composition, public relations, Spanish, speech/debate/rhetoric, studio art, and theater design), COMPUTER AND PHYSICAL SCIENCE (applied mathematics, chemistry, computer science, geoscience, information sciences and systems, mathematics, and physics), EDUCATION (art, athletic training, business, early childhood, health, home economics, music, and physical), HEALTH PROFESSIONS (allied health, community health work, music therapy, predentistry, premedicine, and prepharmacy), SOCIAL SCIENCE (anthropology, criminal justice, economics, food production/management/services, geography, history, home economics, human ecology, humanities, paralegal studies, parks and recreation management, philosophy, political science/government, psychology, religion, sociology, and women's studies). Business administration, psychology, and biology are the largest.

Required: Students must successfully complete a minimum of 120 semester hours, with 33 to 82 in the major, while maintaining a minimum GPA of 2.0. General education requirements include courses in communications, contemporary issues, art appreciation, a foreign language, humanities, math, natural/physical science, social sciences, and multicultural awareness, as well as 1 semester hour in phys ed and 3 semester hours in computer science.

Special: Internships, co-op programs in all majors, credit by exam, pass/fail options, work-study, credit for life experience, independent study, and study abroad in 50 countries are offered. Joint-degree programs are offered in practical anthropology and applied economics, and a 5-year B.A.-B.Mus. program in music is available, as is an articulated medical, dental, physical therapy, and physician assistant program with the University of Medicine and Dentistry of New Jersey and an articulated program leading to a Pharm.D. with Rutgers University. There are 28 national honor societies, a freshman honors program, and 3 departmental honors programs.

Faculty/Classroom: 59% of faculty are male; 41%, female. All teach undergraduates. The average class size in a laboratory is 24 and in a regular course, 24.

Admissions: 51% of the 2003-2004 applicants were accepted. The SAT I scores for the 2003-2004 freshman class were: Verbal--34% below 500, 48% between 500 and 599, 16% between 600 and 700, and 1% above 700; Math--23% below 500, 55% between 500 and 599, 20% between 600 and 700, and 2% above 700. 39% of the current freshmen were in the top fifth of their class; 74% were in the top two fifths. 34 freshmen graduated first in their class.

Requirements: The SAT I is required. In addition, applicants must submit 16 Carnegie units, including 4 in English, 3 to 4 in math (including algebra I and II and geometry), 2 each in lab science, social studies, and

a foreign language, and the remainder in additional courses in these fields. The GED is accepted. A portfolio, audition, or interview is required for students planning to major in fine arts, music, speech, or theater. Admission to computer science requires 4 years of math, including trigonometry. AP and CLEP credits are accepted. Important factors in the admissions decision are advanced placement or honor courses, recommendations by school officials, and leadership record.

Procedure: Freshmen are admitted fall and spring. Entrance exams should be taken in October, November, or December of the senior year. There is a rolling admissions plan. Applications should be filed by March 1 for fall entry and November 1 for spring entry. The fall 2003 application fee was $55. Notification is sent on a rolling basis. 110 applicants were on the 2003 waiting list. Applications are accepted on-line through *www.montclair.edu/applying.shtml.*

Transfer: 1785 transfer students enrolled in 2002-2003. Applicants must have completed a minimum of 15 credits from an accredited college. A cumulative GPA of 2.5 is required for most majors, with higher required in select programs. Applicants must have completed English composition. High school and college transcripts are required. 32 of 120 credits required for the bachelor's degree must be completed at Montclair.

Visiting: There are regularly scheduled orientations for prospective students. There are guides for informal visits. To schedule a visit, contact the Admissions Office at (973) 655-5322 or *www.montclair.edu/admissions/visit.html.*

Financial Aid: In 2003-2004, 71% of all full-time freshmen and 60% of continuing full-time students received some form of financial aid. 47% of full-time freshmen and 46% of continuing full-time students received need-based aid. The average freshman award was $7774. Need-based scholarships or need-based grants averaged $5057 ($10,590 maximum); need-based self-help aid (loans and jobs) averaged $3123 ($6625 maximum); and other non-need-based awards and non-need-based scholarships averaged $4735 ($17,652 maximum). 50% of undergraduates work part time. Average annual earnings from campus work are $976. The average financial indebtedness of the 2003 graduate was $15,872. The FAFSA is required. The priority date for freshman financial aid applications for fall entry is March 1.

International Students: There are 503 international students enrolled. The school actively recruits these students. They must score 500 on the written TOEFL or 173 on the electronic version.

Computers: The mainframes are a DEC VAX cluster and a DEC Alpha cluster. PC and Mac labs are located throughout the campus, with about 218 computers and PC printers. A network of Sun workstations is also available. A wide variety of general and discipline-specific software is offered. Residence hall rooms are wired for network connections, and Internet access is available. All students may access the system. There are no time limits and no fees.

Graduates: From July 1, 2002 to June 30, 2003, 2026 bachelor's degrees were awarded. The most popular majors were business administration (21%), psychology (12%), and human ecology (7%). In an average class, 1% graduate in 3 years or less, 23% graduate in 4 years or less, 50% graduate in 5 years or less, and 56% graduate in 6 years or less. 109 companies recruited on campus in 2002-2003. Of the 2002 graduating class, 18% were enrolled in graduate school within 6 months of graduation and 90% were employed.

Admissions Contact: Dennis Craig, Director of Admissions. A video is available. E-mail: *msuadm@mail.montclair.edu* Web: *www.montclair.edu*

NEW JERSEY CITY UNIVERSITY

Jersey City, NJ 07305

E-2
(201) 200-3234
(888) 441-NJCU; Fax: (201) 200-2044

Full-time: 1630 men, 2575 women	**Faculty:** 233; IIB, ++$
Part-time: 1940 men and women	**Ph.D.s:** 79%
Graduate: 2769 men and women	**Student/Faculty:** 18 to 1
Year: semesters, summer session	**Tuition:** $5264 ($9572)
Application Deadline: April 1	**Room & Board:** $6586
Freshman Class: 2689 applied, 1400 accepted, 763 enrolled	
SAT I Verbal/Math: 450/440	**LESS COMPETITIVE**

New Jersey City University, founded in 1927, is a public institution offering undergraduate and graduate programs in the arts and sciences, business administration, education, health science, upper-level nursing, and other professional fields. There are 3 undergraduate schools and 1 graduate school. In addition to regional accreditation, NJCU has baccalaureate program accreditation with AACSB, NASAD, NASM, NCATE, and NLN. The library contains 250,000 volumes, 600,000 microform items, and 850 audio/video tapes/CDs, and subscribes to 1500 periodicals. Computerized library services include the card catalog, interlibrary loans, database searching, and Internet access. Special learning facilities include a learning resource center, art gallery, radio station, a media arts center, and a lab school for special education instruction. The 17-acre campus is in an urban area 10 miles west of New York City. Including any residence halls, there are 15 buildings.

Student Life: 99% of undergraduates are from New Jersey. Students are from 16 states and 47 foreign countries. 41% are white; 28% Hispanic; 17% African American. The average age of freshmen is 18; all undergraduates, 23. 31% of freshmen remain to graduate.

Housing: 276 students can be accommodated in college housing, which includes coed dorms. On-campus housing is guaranteed for all 4 years. 95% of students commute. Alcohol is not permitted. All students may keep cars.

Activities: 4% of men belong to 5 local fraternities and 1 national fraternity; 3% of women belong to 5 local sororities and 1 national sorority. There are 42 groups on campus, including art, band, choir, chorale, chorus, computers, dance, drama, ethnic, film, gay, honors, international, jazz band, literary magazine, musical theater, newspaper, opera, orchestra, photography, political, professional, radio and TV, religious, social, social service, student government, symphony, and yearbook. Popular campus events include President's Picnic, Town and Gown Concert, and lecture series.

Sports: There are 5 intercollegiate sports for men and 7 for women, and 14 intramural sports for men and 14 for women. Facilities include an athletic and fitness center with a 2000-seat arena, jogging track, fitness facilities, 6-lane pool, sauna, racquetball courts, and soccer, tennis, baseball, and softball facilities.

Disabled Students: All of the campus is accessible. Wheelchair ramps, elevators, special parking, specially equipped rest rooms, special class scheduling, lowered drinking fountains, and lowered telephones are available.

Services: Counseling and information services are available, as is tutoring in most subjects. There is remedial math, reading, and writing.

Campus Safety and Security: Measures include 24-hour foot and vehicle patrol, security escort services, shuttle buses, and informal discussions. There are pamphlets/posters/films, emergency telephones, and lighted pathways/sidewalks.

Programs of Study: NJCU confers B.A., B.S., B.F.A., and B.S.N. degrees. Master's degrees are also awarded. Bachelor's degrees are awarded in BIOLOGICAL SCIENCE (biology/biological science), BUSINESS (business administration and management and retailing), COMMUNICATIONS AND THE ARTS (design, English, fine arts, media arts, music, photography, and Spanish), COMPUTER AND PHYSICAL SCIENCE (chemistry, computer science, geology, mathematics, and physics), EDUCATION (art, early childhood, elementary, health, music, secondary, and special), HEALTH PROFESSIONS (medical laboratory technology, nuclear medical technology, nursing, and public health), SOCIAL SCIENCE (criminal justice, economics, geography, history, philosophy, political science/government, psychology, and sociology). Business, nursing, and criminal justice are the largest.

Required: Students must complete 66 semester hours in general education courses, satisfy college requirements in English, communication, and math, and complete the introductory career exploration and computer usage courses. The bachelor's degree requires completion of at least 128 semester hours, including 36 to 54 in a major field, with a minimum GPA of 2.0. Distribution requirements include 9 credits each in natural science, social science, humanities, and fine and performing arts and 6 credits in communications and contemporary world.

Special: Co-op programs and internships in all majors are available. NJCU also offers study abroad, work-study programs, numerous health science programs, and some programs affiliated with New Jersey College of Medicine and Dentistry in Newark. Nondegree study is possible. There are 4 national honor societies, a freshman honors program, and 1 departmental honors program.

Faculty/Classroom: 53% of faculty are male; 47%, female. All teach undergraduates. No introductory courses are taught by graduate students. The average class size in an introductory lecture is 25; in a laboratory, 15; and in a regular course, 16.

Admissions: 52% of the 2003-2004 applicants were accepted. The SAT I scores for the 2003-2004 freshman class were: Verbal--79% below 500, 19% between 500 and 599, and 3% between 600 and 700; Math--77% below 500, 20% between 500 and 599, and 3% between 600 and 700. 21% of the current freshmen were in the top fifth of their class; 50% were in the top two fifths.

Requirements: The SAT I is required. In addition, applicants must be graduates of accredited secondary schools or have earned a GED. The college requires 16 Carnegie units, including 4 in English, 3 in math, and 2 each in social studies and a lab science, with the remaining 5 units in a foreign language and additional academic courses. An essay is also required, and an interview is recommended. NJCU requires applicants to be in the upper 50% of their class. A GPA of 2.5 is required. AP and CLEP credits are accepted. Important factors in the admissions decision are advanced placement or honor courses, evidence of special talent, and recommendations by school officials.

Procedure: Freshmen are admitted fall and spring. Entrance exams should be taken in the spring of the junior year or fall of the senior year. There are early admissions and deferred admissions plans. Applications should be filed by April 1 for fall entry, along with a $35 fee. Notification is sent on a rolling basis. A waiting list is an active part of the admissions

procedure. Applications are accepted on-line through the school's web site.

Transfer: 622 transfer students enrolled in 2002-2003. Applicants must present a minimum GPA of 2.0 in at least 12 credit hours completed at the college level. Students transferring fewer than 12 credits must also submit SAT I scores of at least 480 verbal and 440 math. An interview is recommended for all transfers. A basic skills test is required for transfers who have fewer than 30 credits or have not taken English or math at their previous school. 36 of 128 credits required for the bachelor's degree must be completed at NJCU.

Visiting: There are regularly scheduled orientations for prospective students, including a financial aid workshop, guided tours, and open house. There is a summer orientation. There are guides for informal visits and visitors may sit in on classes. To schedule a visit, contact the Admissions Office.

Financial Aid: NJCU is a member of CSS. The FAFSA is required. Check with the school for current application deadlines.

International Students: There are about 100 international students enrolled. They must score 500 on the written TOEFL and also take the SAT I, scoring 920.

Computers: The mainframes are a DEC VAX 6510, a VAX 8530, 3 MicroVAX 3100s, and a MicroVAX 3800. Students are able to use the Internet as well as other network systems, and a toll-free dial-up system whereby they may use home computers and the mainframe. There are 3 computer labs. All students may access the system 24 hours a day. There are no time limits and no fees.

Graduates: From July 1, 2002 to June 30, 2003, 868 bachelor's degrees were awarded. The most popular majors were business administration (23%), computer science (10%), and criminal justice (10%). In an average class, 4% graduate in 4 years or less, 17% graduate in 5 years or less, and 31% graduate in 6 years or less. 350 companies recruited on campus in 2002-2003.

Admissions Contact: Jason Hand, Director of Admissions. E-mail: *admissions@njcu.edu* Web: *www.njcu.edu*

NEW JERSEY INSTITUTE OF TECHNOLOGY   E-2
Newark, NJ 07102-1982
(973) 596-3300
(800) 222-NJIT; Fax: (973) 596-6085

Full-time: 3366 men, 873 women	**Faculty:** 301; I, +$
Part-time: 1145 men, 328 women	**Ph.D.s:** 98%
Graduate: 2097 men, 961 women	**Student/Faculty:** 14 to 1
Year: semesters, summer session	**Tuition:** $8500 ($13,868)
Application Deadline: April 1	**Room & Board:** $7896
Freshman Class: 2566 applied, 1747 accepted, 689 enrolled	
SAT I Verbal/Math: 540/600	**VERY COMPETITIVE**

New Jersey Institute of Technology is a public research university providing instruction, research, and public service in engineering, computer science, management, architecture, engineering technology, applied sciences, and related fields. There are 6 undergraduate schools and 1 graduate school. In addition to regional accreditation, NJIT has baccalaureate program accreditation with AACSB, ABET, and NAAB. The 2 libraries contain 220,000 volumes, 7325 microform items, and 73,807 audio/video tapes/CDs, and subscribe to 2500 periodicals. Computerized library services include the card catalog, interlibrary loans, and database searching. Special learning facilities include a learning resource center, art gallery, radio station, and 3 TV studios. NJIT is home to many government- and industry-sponsored labs and research centers, including the EPA Northeast Hazardous Substance Research Center, the National Center for Transportation and Industrial Productivity, the Center for Manufacturing Systems, the Emission Reduction Research Center, the Microelectronics Research Center, the Center for Microwave and Lightwave Engineering, and the Multi-Lifecycle Engineering Center. The 45-acre campus is in an urban area 10 miles west of New York City. Including any residence halls, there are 25 buildings.

Student Life: 94% of undergraduates are from New Jersey. Students are from 36 states, 109 foreign countries, and Canada. 80% are from public schools. 31% are white; 22% Asian American; 14% foreign nationals. The average age of freshmen is 18; all undergraduates, 23. 15% do not continue beyond their first year; 49% remain to graduate.

Housing: 1434 students can be accommodated in college housing, which includes coed dorms. On-campus housing is available on a first-come, first-served basis and is available on a lottery system for upperclassmen. Priority is given to out-of-town students. 75% of students commute. All students may keep cars.

Activities: 7% of men belong to 4 local and 10 national fraternities; 5% of women belong to 4 local and 5 national sororities. There are 92 groups on campus, including art, chess, computers, drama, drum and bugle corps, ethnic, gay, honors, international, musical theater, newspaper, photography, professional, radio and TV, religious, social, social service, student government, and yearbook. Popular campus events include Miniversity, International Students Food Festival, and Leadership Training Weekend.

Sports: There are 9 intercollegiate sports for men and 6 for women, and 13 intramural sports for men and 7 for women. Facilities include a 1000-seat stadium, a fitness center with an indoor track, a 6-lane swimming pool, 4 tennis courts, 4 racquet sport courts, playing fields, bowling lanes, a table tennis and billiards area, and 3 gyms, the largest of which seats 1200.

Disabled Students: 95% of the campus is accessible. Wheelchair ramps, elevators, special parking, specially equipped rest rooms, special class scheduling, lowered drinking fountains, and lowered telephones are available.

Services: Counseling and information services are available, as is tutoring in most subjects. There is a reader service for the blind and remedial math, reading, and writing.

Campus Safety and Security: Measures include 24-hour foot and vehicle patrol, self-defense education, security escort services, and shuttle buses. There are informal discussions, pamphlets/posters/films, emergency telephones, and lighted pathways/sidewalks.

Programs of Study: NJIT confers B.A., B.S., and B.Arch. degrees. Master's and doctoral degrees are also awarded. Bachelor's degrees are awarded in BIOLOGICAL SCIENCE (biology/biological science), BUSINESS (management science), COMMUNICATIONS AND THE ARTS (communications and technical and business writing), COMPUTER AND PHYSICAL SCIENCE (applied mathematics, applied physics, chemistry, computer management, computer science, information sciences and systems, and mathematics), ENGINEERING AND ENVIRONMENTAL DESIGN (architecture, biomedical engineering, chemical engineering, civil engineering, computer engineering, computer technology, electrical/electronics engineering, engineering and applied science, engineering technology, environmental engineering, environmental science, geophysical engineering, industrial engineering, manufacturing engineering, mechanical engineering, technological management, and technology and public affairs), SOCIAL SCIENCE (history). Engineering, computer science, and architecture are the strongest academically. Engineering is the largest.

Required: General university requirements include 9 credits of humanities and social science electives, 7 of natural sciences, 6 each of math, cultural history, basic social sciences, and engineering technology, 3 each of English and management, and 2 each of computer science and phys ed. To graduate, students must earn between 124 and 164 credits, depending on the program, including 50 in the major, with a minimum GPA of 2.0 in upper-level major courses.

Special: Cross-registration is offered in conjunction with Essex County College, Rutgers University's Newark campus, and the University of Medicine and Dentistry of New Jersey. Cooperative programs, available in all majors, include two 6-month internships. There are 3-2 engineering degree programs with Stockton State College and Lincoln and Seton Hall Universities. NJIT also offers work-study programs, study abroad in 18 countries, dual and interdisciplinary majors, accelerated degree programs, distance learning, and nondegree study. There is 1 national honor society and a freshman honors program.

Faculty/Classroom: 84% of faculty are male; 16%, female. 74% teach undergraduates, all do research, and 74% do both. Graduate students teach 10% of introductory courses. The average class size in an introductory lecture is 30; in a laboratory, 27; and in a regular course, 25.

Admissions: 68% of the 2003-2004 applicants were accepted. The SAT I scores for the 2003-2004 freshman class were: Verbal--31% below 500, 46% between 500 and 599, 21% between 600 and 700, and 2% above 700; Math--4% below 500, 43% between 500 and 599, 42% between 600 and 700, and 12% above 700. 1% of the current freshmen were in the top fifth of their class; 7% were in the top two fifths.

Requirements: The SAT I is required. In addition, the SAT II: Subject test in math I or II is also required. Applicants should have completed 16 secondary school units, including 4 each in English and math, 2 in a lab science, and 6 in a distribution of social studies, foreign language, math, and science courses. AP and CLEP credits are accepted. Important factors in the admissions decision are advanced placement or honor courses, recommendations by school officials, and geographic diversity.

Procedure: Freshmen are admitted fall and spring. Entrance exams should be taken in May of the junior year or November of the senior year. There is a rolling admissions plan. Applications should be filed by April 1 for fall entry and November 15 for spring entry, along with a $35 fee. Notification is sent on a rolling basis beginning January 2. 11 applicants were on the 2003 waiting list; 11 were admitted. Applications are accepted on-line through the school's web site.

Transfer: 494 transfer students enrolled in 2002-2003. A minimum college GPA of 2.0 is required, but 2.5 or higher is recommended. Students must submit transcripts of all attempted postsecondary academic work. Applicants with fewer than 30 credits may be asked to provide scores on the SAT I and the SAT II: Subject test in math, as well as high school transcripts. Engineering technology students must present an associate degree. Admission to the School of Architecture is very competitive for transfer students. 33 credits of 124 to 164 required for the bachelor's degree must be completed at NJIT.

Visiting: There are regularly scheduled orientations for prospective students, including tours and meetings with admissions personnel, students,

and faculty. There are guides for informal visits and visitors may sit in on classes and stay overnight. To schedule a visit, contact Kathy Kelly, Director of Admissions.

Financial Aid: In 2003-2004, 70% of all full-time students received some form of financial aid. 65% of all full-time students received need-based aid. Need-based scholarships or need-based grants averaged $4200; need-based self-help aid (loans and jobs) averaged $2800; and non-need-based awards and non-need-based scholarships averaged $2420. 70% of undergraduates work part time. Average annual earnings from campus work are $2150. The average financial indebtedness of the 2003 graduate was $11,000. The FAFSA and the college's own financial statement are required. The priority date for freshman financial aid applications for fall entry is March 15. The deadline for filing freshman financial aid applications for fall entry is May 15.

International Students: There are 289 international students enrolled. The school actively recruits these students. They must score 550 on the written TOEFL or 213 on the electronic version and also take the SAT I. Students must take SAT II: Subject tests in math I or II.

Computers: The mainframes comprise a DEC VAX 6430, which serves as the main VMS computer, and a DEC 5900, which serves as the UNIX engine for academic work. All computing facilities are connected to a campuswide network, which has a fiber-optic spine between buildings; all dorm rooms are wired for access. 150 computer nodes can be accessed from 2500 on-campus locations. All students may access the system. There are no time limits and no fees. All students are required to have personal computers. All full-time freshmen are given a PC and a variety of software.

Graduates: From July 1, 2002 to June 30, 2003, 894 bachelor's degrees were awarded. The most popular majors were computer science (20%), computer engineering (13%), and engineering technology (12%). In an average class, 16% graduate in 4 years or less, 39% graduate in 5 years or less, and 49% graduate in 6 years or less. 200 companies recruited on campus in 2002-2003. Of the 2002 graduating class, 20% were enrolled in graduate school within 6 months of graduation.

Admissions Contact: Kathy Kelly, Director of Admissions.
E-mail: *admissions@admin.njit.edu*

PRINCETON UNIVERSITY D-3
Princeton, NJ 08544-0430 (609) 258-3060; Fax: (609) 258-6743

Full-time: 2428 men, 2247 women	**Faculty:** 797; I, ++$
Part-time: none	**Ph.D.s:** 94%
Graduate: 1242 men, 768 women	**Student/Faculty:** 6 to 1
Year: semesters	**Tuition:** $28,540
Application Deadline: January 2	**Room & Board:** $8109
Freshman Class: 15,726 applied, 1601 accepted, 1175 enrolled	
SAT I: required	**ACT:** n/av **MOST COMPETITIVE**

Princeton University, established in 1746, is a private institution offering degrees in the liberal arts and sciences, engineering, applied science, architecture, public and international affairs, interdisciplinary and regional studies, and the creative arts. In addition to regional accreditation, Princeton has baccalaureate program accreditation with ABET and NAAB. The 16 libraries contain 6 million volumes, 6 million microform items, and 60,000 audio/video tapes/CDs, and subscribe to 15,000 periodicals. Computerized library services include the card catalog, interlibrary loans, and Internet access. Special learning facilities include an art gallery, natural history museum, radio station, a music center, a visual and performing arts center, several theaters, an observatory, a plasma physics lab, and a center for environmental and energy studies. The 500-acre campus is in a small town 50 miles south of New York City. Including any residence halls, there are 160 buildings.

Student Life: 85% of undergraduates are from out of state, mostly the Middle Atlantic. Students are from 50 states, 70 foreign countries, and Canada. 64% are white; 13% Asian American. The average age of freshmen is 18; all undergraduates, 20. 2% do not continue beyond their first year; 97% remain to graduate.

Housing: 4400 students can be accommodated in college housing, which includes coed dorms, on-campus apartments, and married-student housing. Freshmen and sophomores are assigned to 1 of 5 residential colleges; most juniors and seniors live in upper-class dorms and select from among such dining options as co-ops and private clubs. On-campus housing is guaranteed for all 4 years. 98% of students live on campus; of those, 100% remain on campus on weekends. Upperclassmen may keep cars.

Activities: There are no fraternities or sororities. There are 220 groups on campus, including art, band, cheerleading, chess, choir, chorale, chorus, computers, dance, debate, drama, ethnic, film, forensics, gay, honors, international, jazz band, literary magazine, marching band, musical theater, newspaper, opera, orchestra, pep band, photography, political, professional, radio and TV, religious, social, social service, student government, symphony, and yearbook.

Sports: There are 20 intercollegiate sports for men and 18 for women, and 35 intramural sports for men and 35 for women. Facilities include a 30,000-seat football and track stadium, an 18-hole golf course, 2 gyms, an Olympic swimming and diving complex, playing fields, a boathouse and Olympic-level racing course for crew and sailing, a health fitness center, an ice rink, dance studios, and tennis, squash, and volleyball courts.

Disabled Students: Wheelchair ramps, elevators, special parking, specially equipped rest rooms, lowered drinking fountains, lowered telephones, and special housing are available.

Services: Counseling and information services are available, as is tutoring in every subject. There is a reader service for the blind.

Campus Safety and Security: Measures include 24-hour foot and vehicle patrol, self-defense education, security escort services, and shuttle buses. There are informal discussions, pamphlets/posters/films, emergency telephones, and lighted pathways/sidewalks.

Programs of Study: Princeton confers A.B. and B.S.E. degrees. Master's and doctoral degrees are also awarded. Bachelor's degrees are awarded in BIOLOGICAL SCIENCE (biology/biological science), COMMUNICATIONS AND THE ARTS (classics, comparative literature, English, Germanic languages and literature, music, romance languages and literature, and Slavic languages), COMPUTER AND PHYSICAL SCIENCE (astrophysics, chemistry, computer science, geology, mathematics, and physics), ENGINEERING AND ENVIRONMENTAL DESIGN (aeronautical engineering, architectural engineering, architecture, chemical engineering, civil engineering, electrical/electronics engineering, and mechanical engineering), SOCIAL SCIENCE (anthropology, archeology, East Asian studies, economics, history, international relations, Near Eastern studies, philosophy, political science/government, psychology, religion, and sociology).

Required: To graduate, students must complete 8 semesters, or academic units. Candidates for the A.B. degree must demonstrate proficiency in English composition and a foreign language and complete distribution requirements in 7 academic areas. Candidates for the B.S.E. must satisfy the English composition requirement and complete a minimum of 7 courses in the humanities and social sciences spread over 4 distribution areas. A junior project and senior thesis are required of virtually all students.

Special: Princeton offers independent study, preceptorials, accelerated degree programs, a program in teacher preparation, student-proposed courses and majors, field study, study abroad, seminars, and internships in public affairs. The university operates on an honor code whereby exams are not proctored by faculty members. There are 2 national honor societies, including Phi Beta Kappa, and all departments have honors programs.

Faculty/Classroom: 71% of faculty are male; 29%, female. All both teach and do research. No introductory courses are taught by graduate students.

Admissions: 10% of the 2003-2004 applicants were accepted. 98% of the current freshmen were in the top fifth of their class; 99% were in the top two fifths.

Requirements: The SAT I is required. In addition, the ACT is accepted. SAT II: Subject tests are also required. Recommended college preparatory courses include 4 years each of English, math, and a foreign language; 2 years of lab science and history; and some study of art, music, and if possible, a second foreign language. An essay is required and an interview is recommended. Fine arts majors should submit an audition tape or portfolio. AP credits are accepted.

Procedure: Freshmen are admitted in the fall. Entrance exams should be taken by January of the senior year. There are early decision, early admissions, and deferred admissions plans. Early decision applications should be filed by November 1; regular applications, by January 2 for fall entry, along with a $60 fee. Notification of early decision is sent December ; regular decision, April. 27 wait-listed applicants were admitted.

Visiting: There are regularly scheduled orientations for prospective students, including daily tours conducted by student guides, general information sessions, and student sessions with admissions staff. There are guides for informal visits and visitors may sit in on classes.

Financial Aid: In 2003-2004, 75% of all full-time students received some form of financial aid. 52% of all full-time students received need-based aid. The average freshman award was $25,500. 92% of freshmen received need-based scholarships or need-based grants, and 8% received need-based self-help aid (loans and jobs). 67% of undergraduates work part time. Average annual earnings from campus work are $1500. The average financial indebtedness of the 2003 graduate was $10,000. Princeton is a member of CSS. The FAFSA and the college's own financial statement are required. The deadline for filing freshman financial aid applications for fall entry is February 1.

International Students: There are 393 international students enrolled. The school actively recruits these students. They must take the TOEFL or the SAT II: Writing Test may be substituted for the TOEFL. They also have to take the SAT I. These students must take any 3 SAT II: subject tests.

Computers: There are more than 250 workstations and numerous high-quality printers in the two dozen computing clusters around campus that contain a mix of Windows-based Intel computers, Unix workstations, and Macs. All students are given a NetID, which allows access to

central printing server and Unix servers (3 Sun E4500 servers and 3 Dell Poweredge 4400 Systems running Red Hot Linux). All students may access the system. It is strongly recommended that all students have a personal computer.

Graduates: From July 1, 2002 to June 30, 2003, 1108 bachelor's degrees were awarded. In an average class, 91% graduate in 4 years or less, and 97% graduate in 6 years or less. 310 companies recruited on campus in 2002-2003.

Admissions Contact: Janet L. Rapelye, Dean of Admissions. Web: *www.princeton.edu*

RAMAPO COLLEGE OF NEW JERSEY   D-2
Mahwah, NJ 07430
(201) 684-7300
(800) 9-RAMAPO; Fax: (201) 684-7964

Full-time: 1619 men, 2359 women	**Faculty:** 186; IIB, ++$
Part-time: 486 men, 778 women	**Ph.D.s:** 97%
Graduate: 145 men, 244 women	**Student/Faculty:** 21 to 1
Year: semesters, summer session	**Tuition:** $7411 ($11,666)
Application Deadline: March 1	**Room & Board:** $7792
Freshman Class: 4028 applied, 1746 accepted, 725 enrolled	
SAT I Verbal/Math: 573/582	**VERY COMPETITIVE**

Ramapo College, founded in 1971, is a public institution offering undergraduate programs in the arts and sciences, American and international studies, business administration, and human services. Personal interaction is incorporated throughout the curriculum as is an international, multicultural component including telecommunications and computer technology. There are 5 undergraduate and 4 graduate schools. In addition to regional accreditation, Ramapo has baccalaureate program accreditation with NLN. The library contains 110,646 volumes, 802 microform items, and 1726 audio/video tapes/CDs, and subscribes to 910 periodicals. Computerized library services include the card catalog, interlibrary loans, database searching, and Internet access. Special learning facilities include a learning resource center, art gallery, radio station, TV station, and an international telecommunications satellite center. The 314-acre campus is in a suburban area 25 miles northwest of New York City. Including any residence halls, there are 49 buildings.

Student Life: 90% of undergraduates are from New Jersey. Students are from 19 states and 63 foreign countries. 78% are white. The average age of freshmen is 18; all undergraduates, 24. 13% do not continue beyond their first year; 54% remain to graduate.

Housing: 2273 students can be accommodated in college housing, which includes coed dorms and on-campus apartments. In addition, there are special-interest houses and an international house. On-campus housing is available on a first-come, first-served basis. 57% of students live on campus. All students may keep cars.

Activities: 7% of men belong to 6 national fraternities; 6% of women belong to 6 national sororities. There are 60 groups on campus, including cheerleading, choir, chorale, chorus, computers, debate, drama, ethnic, film, gay, honors, international, jazz band, literary magazine, musical theater, newspaper, pep band, photography, political, professional, radio and TV, religious, social, social service, student government, and yearbook. Popular campus events include Welcome Week, Springfest, and Earth Day.

Sports: There are 8 intercollegiate sports for men and 8 for women, and 4 intramural sports for men and 2 for women. Facilities include a 1000-seat stadium, 12 lighted tennis courts, playing fields, a 300-seat arena, a track, a 1000-seat gym with a basketball court, an Olympic-size pool, and a fitness and weight training center.

Disabled Students: All of the campus is accessible. Wheelchair ramps, elevators, special parking, specially equipped rest rooms, special class scheduling, lowered drinking fountains, lowered telephones, and special housing are available.

Services: Counseling and information services are available, as is tutoring in every subject. There is a reader service for the blind, and remedial math, reading, and writing.

Campus Safety and Security: Measures include 24-hour foot and vehicle patrol, security escort services, shuttle buses, and informal discussions. There are pamphlets/posters/films, emergency telephones, lighted pathways/sidewalks, and surveillance cameras.

Programs of Study: Ramapo confers B.A., B.S., B.S.N., and B.S.W. degrees. Master's degrees are also awarded. Bachelor's degrees are awarded in AGRICULTURE (environmental studies), BIOLOGICAL SCIENCE (biochemistry, biology/biological science, and biotechnology), BUSINESS (accounting, business administration and management, and international business management), COMMUNICATIONS AND THE ARTS (art, communications, dramatic arts, literature, music, and visual and performing arts), COMPUTER AND PHYSICAL SCIENCE (chemistry, computer science, information sciences and systems, mathematics, and physics), ENGINEERING AND ENVIRONMENTAL DESIGN (environmental science), HEALTH PROFESSIONS (allied health, clinical science, and nursing), SOCIAL SCIENCE (American studies, economics, history, international studies, law, political science/government, psychology, social science, social work, and sociology). Physics, biochemistry, and nursing are the strongest academically. Business administration, communication arts, and psychology are the largest.

Required: Students must complete general education requirements of approximately 50 credits in science, social science, humanities, and English composition, as well as core requirements in their school of study and their particular major. A senior seminar is also required. To graduate, students must earn at least 128 credits with a minimum GPA of 2.0.

Special: Ramapo's curriculum emphasizes the interdependence of global society and includes an international dimension in all academic programs. Students may study abroad in 8 countries. Cooperative programs are available with various corporations and in 12 foreign countries. Cross-registration is possible with local state colleges. Ramapo also offers a winter session, accelerated degree programs, dual, student-designed, and interdisciplinary majors, including law and society, credit for life experience, pass/fail options, internships, work-study programs, and non-degree study. There are 6 national honor societies, a freshman honors program, and 10 departmental honors programs.

Faculty/Classroom: 58% of faculty are male; 42%, female. All teach undergraduates. The average class size in an introductory lecture is 35; in a laboratory, 11; and in a regular course, 22.

Admissions: 43% of the 2003-2004 applicants were accepted. The SAT I scores for the 2003-2004 freshman class were: Verbal--7% below 500, 60% between 500 and 599, 29% between 600 and 700, and 4% above 700; Math--7% below 500, 53% between 500 and 599, 36% between 600 and 700, and 4% above 700. 42% of the current freshmen were in the top fifth of their class; 81% were in the top two fifths.

Requirements: The SAT I is required. In addition, applicants must be graduates of accredited secondary schools or have earned a GED. The college requires 16 academic credits, including 4 in English, 3 in math, 2 each in science and social studies, and the remaining 5 in academic electives. Students are encouraged to take 2 years of a foreign language. Students must also submit an essay. An interview is recommended. A GPA of 3.0 is required. AP and CLEP credits are accepted. Important factors in the admissions decision are advanced placement or honor courses, recommendations by school officials, and evidence of special talent.

Procedure: Freshmen are admitted fall and spring. Entrance exams should be taken during the senior year. There are early decision, deferred admissions, and rolling admissions plans. Applications should be filed by March 1 for fall entry and December 1 for spring entry. Notification is sent on a rolling basis. The fall 2003 application fee was $55. Applications are accepted on-line.

Transfer: 498 transfer students enrolled in 2002-2003. Applicants must present a minimum GPA of 2.5; however, students applying to the School of Business with at least 45 credits must submit a GPA of 2.5. There are special requirements for social work, nursing, and communications majors. Any applicant transferring fewer than 30 credits must provide a high school transcript. SAT I scores are recommended. Associate degree recipients are encouraged to apply. 45 of 128 credits required for the bachelor's degree must be completed at Ramapo.

Visiting: There are regularly scheduled orientations for prospective students, including orientation, advisement, registration, and immediate decision days. There are guides for informal visits and visitors may sit in on classes. To schedule a visit, contact the Admissions Office at *admissions@ramapo.edu*.

Financial Aid: In 2003-2004, 67% of all full-time freshmen and 54% of continuing full-time students received some form of financial aid. 50% of full-time freshmen and 64% of continuing full-time students received need-based aid. The average freshman award was $10,237. Need-based scholarships or need-based grants averaged $8008; and need-based self-help aid (loans and jobs) averaged $2580. 5% of undergraduates work part time. Average annual earnings from campus work are $1400. The average financial indebtedness of the 2003 graduate was $15,183. The FAFSA is required. The deadline for filing freshman financial aid applications for fall entry is March 15.

International Students: There are 197 international students enrolled. The school actively recruits these students. They must score 550 on the written TOEFL and also take the Comprehensive English Language Test.

Computers: The mainframe is a DEC 5500 running UNIX. In addition, 475 PCs are located in the residence halls, the computing lab, and the library. All students may access the system according to a posted schedules for lab times. There are no time limits and no fees.

Graduates: From July 1, 2002 to June 30, 2003, 770 bachelor's degrees were awarded. The most popular majors were communication arts (15%), psychology (14%), and business administration (13%). In an average class, 29% graduate in 4 years or less, 49% graduate in 5 years or less, and 54% graduate in 6 years or less. 74 companies recruited on campus in 2002-2003.

Admissions Contact: Nancy E. Jaeger, Director of Admissions. A video is available. E-mail: *admissions@ramapo.edu* Web: *www.ramapo.edu*

RICHARD STOCKTON COLLEGE OF NEW JERSEY   D-5
Pomona, NJ 08240-0195   (609) 652-4261; Fax: (609) 748-5541

Full-time: 2293 men, 3146 women	Faculty: 196; IIB, ++$
Part-time: 416 men, 685 women	Ph.Ds: 98%
Graduate: 110 men, 231 women	Student/Faculty: 28 to 1
Year: semesters, summer session	Tuition: $6224 ($9168)
Application Deadline: May 1	Room & Board: $6748
Freshman Class: 3795 applied, 1624 accepted, 825 enrolled	
SAT I Verbal/Math: 550/570	VERY COMPETITIVE

Richard Stockton College of New Jersey, founded in 1969, is a public liberal arts college with 28 undergraduate programs and 6 graduate specialty areas. There is 1 undergraduate and 1 graduate school. In addition to regional accreditation, Stockton has baccalaureate program accreditation with APTA, CSWE, NASDTEC, NCATE, and NLN. The library contains 574,754 volumes, 703,045 microform items, and 14,227 audio/video tapes/CDs, and subscribes to 1333 periodicals. Computerized library services include the card catalog, interlibrary loans, and database searching. Special learning facilities include a learning resource center, art gallery, radio station, TV station, astronomical observatory, marine science field lab, marina with a fleet of small boats, Holocaust resource center, and educational technology training center. The 1600-acre campus is in a suburban area 12 miles northwest of Atlantic City. Including any residence halls, there are 55 buildings.

Student Life: 98% of undergraduates are from New Jersey. Students are from 23 states, 24 foreign countries, and Canada. 74% are from public schools. 82% are white. The average age of freshmen is 18; all undergraduates, 22. 15% do not continue beyond their first year; 65% remain to graduate.

Housing: 2081 students can be accommodated in college housing, which includes coed dorms and on-campus apartments. In addition, there are special-interest houses and wellness, substance-free, academic, and smoke-free housing. On-campus housing is guaranteed for the freshman year only, is available on a first-come, first-served basis, and is available on a lottery system for upperclassmen. 68% of students commute. All students may keep cars.

Activities: 5% of men belong to 9 national fraternities; 9% of women belong to 10 national sororities. There are 75 groups on campus, including art, band, cheerleading, chess, choir, chorale, chorus, computers, dance, drama, ethnic, honors, international, jazz band, literary magazine, newspaper, orchestra, pep band, photography, political, professional, radio and TV, religious, social, social service, student government, and yearbook. Popular campus events include Spring Concert, Spring Fling, and Black History Month.

Sports: There are 7 intercollegiate sports for men and 10 for women, and 10 intramural sports for men and 10 for women. Facilities include an indoor 6-lane swimming pool, an outdoor track, a weight-lifting gym, 2 multipurpose gyms, a sauna, steam baths, and dance studios, as well as playing fields, a 60-acre lake for fishing and canoeing, cross-country courses, bike trails, an all-weather track, and tennis, racquetball, and basketball courts. There are 9 club sports in addition to intramurals.

Disabled Students: 99% of the campus is accessible. Wheelchair ramps, elevators, special parking, specially equipped rest rooms, special class scheduling, lowered drinking fountains, lowered telephones, and electric doors are available.

Services: Counseling and information services are available, as is tutoring in most subjects. There is a reader service for the blind and remedial math, reading, and writing. In addition, there is a skills center and a learning access program for learning-disabled students.

Campus Safety and Security: Measures include 24-hour foot and vehicle patrol, self-defense education, security escort services, and informal discussions. There are pamphlets/posters/films, emergency telephones, lighted pathways/sidewalks, and a fully commissioned police department.

Programs of Study: Stockton confers B.A., B.S., and B.S.N. degrees. Master's degrees are also awarded. Bachelor's degrees are awarded in BIOLOGICAL SCIENCE (biochemistry, biology/biological science, and marine science), BUSINESS (accounting, banking and finance, business administration and management, and management science), COMMUNICATIONS AND THE ARTS (dance, dramatic arts, fine arts, and music), COMPUTER AND PHYSICAL SCIENCE (chemistry, computer science, information sciences and systems, mathematics, and physics), ENGINEERING AND ENVIRONMENTAL DESIGN (environmental science and preengineering), HEALTH PROFESSIONS (nursing, physical therapy, public health, and speech pathology/audiology), SOCIAL SCIENCE (anthropology, criminal justice, economics, history, liberal arts/general studies, philosophy, political science/government, psychology, religion, and social work). Sciences are the strongest academically. Business, psychology, and criminal justice are the largest.

Required: To graduate, students must earn 128 credit hours, with 32 in the general studies curriculum and maintain a minumum GPA of 2.0. 3 quantitative reasoning and 4 writing courses as well as freshman seminar are required.

Special: Stockton offers internships in all fields with a wide variety of companies, work-study with various government agencies and corporations, a Washington semester, independent study, and study abroad in 10 countries. Dual majors in all programs, student-designed majors, an accelerated degree in medicine, 3-2 engineering degrees with the New Jersey Institute of Technology and Rutgers University, and general studies degrees are also offered. Nondegree study, pass/fail options, and credit for life, military, and work experience are possible. There are 5 national honor societies.

Faculty/Classroom: 56% of faculty are male; 44%, female. 91% teach undergraduates and 95% both teach and do research. The average class size in an introductory lecture is 30; in a laboratory, 12; and in a regular course, 17.

Admissions: 43% of the 2003-2004 applicants were accepted. The SAT I scores for the 2003-2004 freshman class were: Verbal--32% below 500, 50% between 500 and 599, 16% between 600 and 700, and 2% above 700; Math--30% below 500, 50% between 500 and 599, 18% between 600 and 700, and 2% above 700. 50% of the current freshmen were in the top fifth of their class; 80% were in the top two fifths. There was 1 National Merit finalist in a recent year.

Requirements: The SAT I or ACT is required. In addition, applicants must be high school graduates; the GED is accepted. 16 academic credits are required, including 4 years in English, 3 each in math and social studies, 2 in science, and 4 additional years of any of the above or a foreign language, or both. An essay and an interview are recommended, and a portfolio or audition is necessary where appropriate. Stockton requires applicants to be in the upper 50% of their class. A GPA of 2.5 is required. AP and CLEP credits are accepted. Important factors in the admissions decision are advanced placement or honor courses, leadership record, and evidence of special talent.

Procedure: Freshmen are admitted fall and spring. Entrance exams should be taken once in the junior year and again before January in the senior year. There is an early admissions plan. Applications should be filed by May 1 for fall entry and December 1 for spring entry. Notification is sent on a rolling basis. A waiting list is an active part of the admissions procedure. Applications are accepted on-line through apply.embark.com/ugrad/stockton/60/.

Transfer: 913 transfer students enrolled in 2002-2003. Transfer students must have earned at least 16 credits at other colleges and must submit college and high school transcripts as well as SAT I scores. 32 of 128 credits required for the bachelor's degree must be completed at Stockton.

Visiting: There are regularly scheduled orientations for prospective students, including academic advising and orientation. There are guides for informal visits and visitors may sit in on classes. To schedule a visit, contact Enrollment Management at (609) 652-4251 or heather.medina@stockton.edu.

Financial Aid: In 2003-2004, 78% of all full-time freshmen and 71% of continuing full-time students received some form of financial aid. 48% of full-time freshmen and 49% of continuing full-time students received need-based aid. The average freshman award was $8462. Need-based scholarships or need-based grants averaged $5814 ($12,372 maximum); need-based self-help aid (loans and jobs) averaged $2288 ($6425 maximum); and non-need-based awards and non-need-based scholarships averaged $1935 ($11,926 maximum). 23% of undergraduates work part time. Average annual earnings from campus work are $1073. The average financial indebtedness of the 2003 graduate was $14,372. The FAFSA is required. The deadline for filing freshman financial aid applications for fall entry is March 1.

International Students: There are 35 international students enrolled. They must score 525 on the written TOEFL.

Computers: The mainframes are a 1 Alpha ES40 and 2 Alpha 2100/275 servers. Students may access the Caucus network for conferencing and linkage to the mainframe and the Internet. There are also more than 950 PCs dispersed in 20 computer labs, 36 electronic classrooms, the library, faculty offices, and academic support facilities. All students may access the system 24 hours a day. There are no time limits and no fees.

Graduates: In a recent year, 1340 bachelor's degrees were awarded. The most popular majors were social science (27%), natural sciences (21%), and business and management (20%). In an average class, 2% graduate in 3 years or less, 30% graduate in 4 years or less, 56% graduate in 5 years or less, and 60% graduate in 6 years or less. Of a recent graduating class, 34% were enrolled in graduate school within 6 months of graduation and 83% were employed.

Admissions Contact: Sal Catalfamo, Dean, Enrollment Management. E-mail: admissions@stockton.edu Web: www.stockton.edu

---

RIDER UNIVERSITY
Lawrenceville, NJ 08648-3099

D-3
(609) 896-5042
(800) 257-9026; Fax: (609) 895-6645

Full-time: 1496 men, 2057 women	**Faculty:** 233; IIA, ++$
Part-time: 265 men, 511 women	**Ph.D.s:** 96%
Graduate: 345 men, 835 women	**Student/Faculty:** 15 to 1
Year: semesters, summer session	**Tuition:** $22,500
Application Deadline: open	**Room & Board:** $8400
Freshman Class: 4329 applied, 3394 accepted, 950 enrolled	
SAT I Verbal/Math: 520/520	**COMPETITIVE**

Rider University, founded in 1865, is a private institution offering undergraduate programs in the areas of business administration, liberal arts, education, sciences, and continuing studies. Westminster Choir College, located in nearby Princeton, is Rider's fourth college. There are 4 undergraduate and 2 graduate schools. In addition to regional accreditation, Rider has baccalaureate program accreditation with AACSB and NCATE. The library contains 452,739 volumes, 639,869 microform items, and 15,326 audio/video tapes/CDs, and subscribes to 1264 periodicals. Computerized library services include the card catalog, interlibrary loans, and database searching. Special learning facilities include a learning resource center, art gallery, radio station, TV station, journalism and sociology labs, and a holocaust/genocide center. The 340-acre campus is in a suburban area 3 miles north of Trenton and 7 miles south of Princeton. Including any residence halls, there are 37 buildings.

Student Life: 72% of undergraduates are from New Jersey. Students are from 30 states, 8 foreign countries, and Canada. 77% are white. 39% are Catholic; 30% claim no religious affiliation; 11% Protestant. The average age of freshmen is 18; all undergraduates, 22. 21% do not continue beyond their first year.

Housing: 2163 students can be accommodated in college housing, which includes single-sex and coed dorms, on-campus apartments, fraternity houses, and sorority houses. In addition, there are special-interest houses, learning community, wellness, quiet, science area, and first-year experience housing. On-campus housing is guaranteed for all 4 years. 56% of students live on campus. All students may keep cars.

Activities: 16% of men belong to 2 local and 5 national fraternities; 14% of women belong to 1 local and 7 national sororities. There are 104 groups on campus, including art, band, cheerleading, choir, chorale, chorus, computers, dance, drama, ethnic, film, gay, honors, international, jazz band, literary magazine, musical theater, newspaper, opera, orchestra, pep band, photography, political, professional, radio and TV, religious, social, social service, student government, symphony, and yearbook. Popular campus events include Cranberry Fest, Family Day, and Unity Day.

Sports: There are 10 intercollegiate sports for men and 10 for women, and 10 intramural sports for men and 6 for women. Facilities include a gym, a swimming pool, a fitness center and spa, lighted outdoor multipurpose courts, outdoor varsity and intramural fields, and an outdoor track.

Disabled Students: 63% of the campus is accessible. Wheelchair ramps, elevators, special parking, specially equipped rest rooms, special class scheduling, lowered drinking fountains, and lowered telephones are available.

Services: Counseling and information services are available, as is tutoring in most subjects. There is remedial math, reading, and writing.

Campus Safety and Security: Measures include 24-hour foot and vehicle patrol, self-defense education, security escort services, and informal discussions. There are pamphlets/posters/films, emergency telephones, lighted pathways/sidewalks, a shuttle car, a staffed kiosk at the entrance, and a security system in residence halls.

Programs of Study: Rider confers B.A., B.S., and B.S.B.A. degrees. Associate and master's degrees are also awarded. Bachelor's degrees are awarded in BIOLOGICAL SCIENCE (biochemistry, biology/biological science, and marine science), BUSINESS (accounting, banking and finance, business administration and management, business economics, human resources, international business management, management science, and marketing/retailing/merchandising), COMMUNICATIONS AND THE ARTS (advertising, art, broadcasting, communications, dance, dramatic arts, English, English literature, fine arts, French, German, journalism, multimedia, music, public relations, Russian, and Spanish), COMPUTER AND PHYSICAL SCIENCE (actuarial science, chemistry, geoscience, information sciences and systems, mathematics, and physics), EDUCATION (early childhood, elementary, English, foreign languages, marketing and distribution, mathematics, science, secondary, and social studies), ENGINEERING AND ENVIRONMENTAL DESIGN (environmental science), HEALTH PROFESSIONS (premedicine), SOCIAL SCIENCE (American studies, biopsychology, economics, history, liberal arts/general studies, philosophy, political science/government, prelaw, psychology, and sociology). Business, actuarial science, and education are the strongest academically. Accounting, elementary education, and finance are the largest.

Required: To graduate, all students must maintain a minimum GPA of 2.0 while taking 120 semester hours. Students also must fulfill core curriculum requirements, including 9 hours in humanities, 7 to 8 in science, 6 each in English writing, foreign language (may be waived if proficiency is demonstrated), social sciences/communications, and history, and 3 in math.

Special: Internships in many programs, a co-op program in marketing, work-study, study abroad in 7 countries, a B.A.-B.S. degree in all liberal arts and sciences, dual majors in education, a liberal studies degree, and nondegree study are possible. There are 28 national honor societies, a freshman honors program, and 19 departmental honors programs.

Faculty/Classroom: 62% of faculty are male; 38%, female. 93% teach undergraduates. No introductory courses are taught by graduate students. The average class size in an introductory lecture is 27; in a laboratory, 11; and in a regular course, 20.

Admissions: 78% of the 2003-2004 applicants were accepted. The SAT I scores for the 2003-2004 freshman class were: Verbal--40% below 500, 45% between 500 and 599, 14% between 600 and 700, and 1% above 700; Math--36% below 500, 46% between 500 and 599, 17% between 600 and 700, and 2% above 700. 24% of the current freshmen were in the top fifth of their class; 54% were in the top two fifths.

Requirements: The SAT I or ACT is required. In addition, applicants need 16 Carnegie units, including 4 years of English and 2 of math. 3 units of math are required for prospective math, science, and business majors. An essay is recommended. An audition is required for theater scholarships. The GED is accepted. Rider requires applicants to be in the upper 50% of their class. A GPA of 2.0 is required. AP and CLEP credits are accepted. Important factors in the admissions decision are advanced placement or honor courses, extracurricular activities record, and leadership record.

Procedure: Freshmen are admitted fall and spring. Entrance exams should be taken by January of the senior year. There is a rolling admissions plan. There are early admissions and deferred admissions plans. Early action applications should be filed November 15; regular application deadlines are open. Application fee is $40. Notification of early action is sent December 15; regular decision, on a rolling basis. Applications are accepted on-line through Common App.

Transfer: 154 transfer students enrolled in 2002-2003. A GPA of 2.5 or better is required for applicants. If students have fewer than 30 credits, they also must submit high school transcripts and SAT I scores. An essay or personal statement is required, and an interview is recommended. 30 credits of 120 required for the bachelor's degree must be completed at Rider.

Visiting: There are regularly scheduled orientations for prospective students, including 4 open houses, with programs that consist of a welcome, a campus tour, and a variety of formal and informal activities to meet faculty, staff, current students, and alumni. There are guides for informal visits and visitors may sit in on classes. To schedule a visit, contact the Office of Admissions.

Financial Aid: In 2003-2004, 91% of all full-time freshmen and 80% of continuing full-time students received some form of financial aid. 70% of full-time freshmen and 61% of continuing full-time students received need-based aid. The average freshman award was $20,471. Need-based scholarships or need-based grants averaged $8697 ($12,603 maximum); need-based self-help aid (loans and jobs) averaged $5524 ($8025 maximum); non-need-based athletic scholarships averaged $10,090 ($27,085 maximum); other non-need-based awards and non-need-based scholarships averaged $7973 ($20,590 maximum); and other awards averaged $10,408 ($29,855 maximum). 15% of undergraduates work part time. The average financial indebtedness of the 2003 graduate was $27,481. The FAFSA is required. The priority date for freshman financial aid applications for fall entry is March 1. The deadline for filing freshman financial aid applications for fall entry is June 30.

International Students: There are 64 international students enrolled. The school actively recruits these students. They must score 563 on the written TOEFL or 202 on the electronic version and also take the SAT I or the ACT.

Computers: The mainframes are 2 DEC VAX 4000s and a MicroVAX 3400. The microcomputer labs have PCs available for general use. There are more than 200 PCs available in departmental labs, many of which are networked. In addition, students have assigned voice mail and e-mail accounts. The campus has a comprehensive light guide voice, data, and video network linking residence halls, classrooms, and faculty/administrative offices. All students may access the system during regular lab hours and at any time in residence halls. There are no time limits.

Graduates: From July 1, 2002 to June 30, 2003, 778 bachelor's degrees were awarded. The most popular majors were business/marketing (37%), education (17%), and English (11%). In an average class, 44% graduate in 4 years or less, 13% graduate in 5 years or less, and 2% graduate in 6 years or less. 128 companies recruited on campus in 2002-2003. Of the 2002 graduating class, 13% were enrolled in graduate school within 6 months of graduation and 81% were employed.

Admissions Contact: Susan C. Christian, Director of Admissions. A video is available. E-mail: *admissions@rider.edu* Web: *www.rider.edu*

ROWAN UNIVERSITY
Glassboro, NJ 08028

C-4

(856) 256-4200
(800) 447-1165; Fax: (856) 256-4430

Full-time: 3077 men, 3727 women	**Faculty:** 380
Part-time: 370 men, 778 women	**Ph.D.s:** 82%
Graduate: 667 men, 335 women	**Student/Faculty:** 18 to 1
Year: semesters, summer session	**Tuition:** $7258 ($12,654)
Application Deadline: March 15	**Room & Board:** $7248
Freshman Class: 6200 applied, 2838 accepted, 1248 enrolled	
SAT I Verbal/Math: 571/592	**VERY COMPETITIVE**

Rowan University was founded in 1923 as a public institution offering undergraduate programs in the arts and sciences, business administration, communication, education, fine and performing arts, and engineering. There are 6 undergraduate schools and 1 graduate school. In addition to regional accreditation, Rowan has baccalaureate program accreditation with AACSB, ABET, CSAB, NASAD, NASDTEC, NASM, NAST, and NCATE. The library contains 345,926 volumes, 497,842 microform items, and 47,525 audio/video tapes/CDs, and subscribes to 5789 periodicals. Computerized library services include the card catalog, interlibrary loans, database searching, and Internet access. Special learning facilities include a learning resource center, art gallery, planetarium, radio station, TV station, and an observatory. The 200-acre campus is in a suburban area 20 miles southeast of Philadelphia. Including any residence halls, there are more than 40 buildings.

Student Life: 95% of undergraduates are from New Jersey. Students are from 11 states, 25 foreign countries, and Canada. 65% are from public schools. 79% are white. The average age of freshmen is 19; all undergraduates, 21. 14% do not continue beyond their first year; 62% remain to graduate.

Housing: 2300 students can be accommodated in college housing, which includes coed dorms, on-campus apartments, off-campus apartments, and married-student housing. In addition, there are honor houses, language houses, and special-interest houses, and healthy living facilities. On-campus housing is guaranteed for all 4 years and is available on a lottery system for upperclassmen. Priority is given to out-of-town students. 60% of students live on campus; of those, 85% remain on campus on weekends. Alcohol is not permitted. Upperclassmen may keep cars.

Activities: 10% of men belong to 1 local and 12 national fraternities; 10% of women belong to 5 local and 8 national sororities. There are 150 groups on campus, including art, band, cheerleading, chess, choir, chorale, chorus, computers, concert band, dance, drama, ethnic, film, gay, honors, international, jazz band, literary magazine, music ensembles, musical theater, newspaper, opera, orchestra, pep band, photography, political, professional, radio and TV, religious, social, social service, student government, symphony, and yearbook. Popular campus events include Spring Fling, Unity Day, and The Big Event.

Sports: There are 8 intercollegiate sports for men and 10 for women, and 7 intramural sports for men and 6 for women. Facilities include a 3000-seat stadium, an 1800-seat gym, a 1000-seat auditorium, a swimming pool, tennis courts, and playing fields.

Disabled Students: 95% of the campus is accessible. Wheelchair ramps, elevators, special parking, specially equipped rest rooms, special class scheduling, lowered drinking fountains, lowered telephones, and special housing are available.

Services: Counseling and information services are available, as is tutoring in every subject. There is remedial math, reading, and writing.

Campus Safety and Security: Measures include 24-hour foot and vehicle patrol, self-defense education, security escort services, and shuttle buses. There are informal discussions, pamphlets/posters/films, emergency telephones, and lighted pathways/sidewalks.

Programs of Study: Rowan confers B.A., B.S., B.F.A., and B.M. degrees. Master's and doctoral degrees are also awarded. Bachelor's degrees are awarded in BIOLOGICAL SCIENCE (biology/biological science), BUSINESS (accounting, business administration and management, marketing/retailing/merchandising, personnel management, and small business management), COMMUNICATIONS AND THE ARTS (art, broadcasting, communications, dramatic arts, English, fine arts, journalism, music, Spanish, and speech/debate/rhetoric), COMPUTER AND PHYSICAL SCIENCE (chemistry, computer science, mathematics, and physics), EDUCATION (early childhood, elementary, foreign languages, music, and science), ENGINEERING AND ENVIRONMENTAL DESIGN (civil engineering and engineering), HEALTH PROFESSIONS (health), SOCIAL SCIENCE (criminal justice, economics, geography, history, liberal arts/general studies, political science/government, psychology, and sociology). Communications, business administration, and elementary education are the strongest academically and are the largest.

Required: General education requirements include 12 to 18 semester hours of social and behavioral sciences, 12 to 16 of science and math, 6 to 9 of communications, 6 of fine and performing arts, and 3 to 6 of history/humanities/languages/arts. Students must also complete 6 semester hours of writing, 3 of phys ed, lab science, computer literacy, and math. Students also must attend the Roman Seminar. The bachelor's degree requires completion of 120 to 132 semester hours, including 30 to 39 in a major field, with a minimum GPA of 2.0.

Special: Students may study abroad in 51 countries. Internships are available in all majors both with and without pay. Rowan also offers accelerated degree programs and 3-2 degrees in optometry, podiatry, and pharmacy. There are dual majors, pass/fail options, and credit for military experience. There are 12 national honor societies, a freshman honors program, and all departments have honors programs.

Faculty/Classroom: 58% of faculty are male; 42%, female. All teach undergraduates. No introductory courses are taught by graduate students. The average class size in an introductory lecture is 22; in a laboratory, 16; and in a regular course, 22.

Admissions: 46% of the 2003-2004 applicants were accepted. The SAT I scores for the 2003-2004 freshman class were: Verbal--9% below 500, 61% between 500 and 599, 26% between 600 and 700, and 3% above 700; Math--5% below 500, 53% between 500 and 599, 37% between 600 and 700, and 5% above 700. 46% of the current freshmen were in the top fifth of their class; 74% were in the top two fifths.

Requirements: The SAT I is required, with a recommended minimum composite score of 1080, or no less than 500 on either part. Students submitting ACT scores should have a minimum composite score of 23. Applicants must be graduates of accredited secondary schools or have earned a GED. Rowan requires 16 academic credits or Carnegie units, including 4 in English, 3 each in math and college preparatory electives, and 2 each in foreign language, history, and lab science. A portfolio or audition is required for specific majors. Rowan requires applicants to be in the upper 75% of their class. A GPA of 3.0 is required. AP and CLEP credits are accepted. Important factors in the admissions decision are advanced placement or honor courses, evidence of special talent, and leadership record.

Procedure: Freshmen are admitted fall and spring. Entrance exams should be taken in May or June of the junior year, or by December of the senior year. There is a deferred admissions plan. Priority decision applications should be filed by January 31; regular applications, by March 15 for fall entry and November 1 for spring entry, along with a $50 fee. Notification of priority decision is sent February 28; regular decision, April 15. 100 applicants were on the 2003 waiting list; 40 were admitted. Applications are accepted on-line through Embark/Princeton Review.

Transfer: 791 transfer students enrolled in 2002-2003. Applicants must have a minimum GPA of 2.0, but should present a GPA of 2.5 to be competitive. An associate degree is recommended. Students who have earned fewer than 24 semester hours must also submit a high school transcript and SAT I results. 30 of 120 to 132 credits required for the bachelor's degree must be completed at Rowan.

Visiting: There are regularly scheduled orientations for prospective students, consisting of a 2-day summer program providing schedule confirmation/adjustment, student activities updates, and workshops for students and parents. There are guides for informal visits and visitors may sit in on classes and stay overnight. To schedule a visit, contact the Admissions Office at *admissions@rowan.edu.*

Financial Aid: In 2003-2004, 70% of all full-time students received some form of financial aid. 70% of all full-time students received need-based aid. The average freshman award was $9093. 10% of undergraduates work part time. Average annual earnings from campus work are $1200. The FAFSA is required. The priority date for freshman financial aid applications for fall entry is January 1. The deadline for filing freshman financial aid applications for fall entry is March 15.

International Students: The school actively recruits these students. They must score 550 on the written TOEFL or 213 on the electronic version and also take the SAT I or ACT. Applicants from English-speaking countries must also submit an SAT I score.

Computers: The mainframes are a The mainframes are 2 DEC VAX 8650, series 6000-410. PCs are available in 43 computer labs with full Internet and network access. On-campus housing is wired with ports for each student, and the library is equipped with portable corrals/ports. All students may access the system 24 hours a day. There are no time limits and no fees. It is recommended that students in engineering have personal computers.

Graduates: In a recent year, 1441 bachelor's degrees were awarded. The most popular majors were business administration (18%), communications (13%), and elementary education (11%). In an average class, 20% graduate in 4 years or less, 48% graduate in 5 years or less, and 55% graduate in 6 years or less. 106 companies recruited on campus in a recent year. Of the 2002 graduating class, 98% were enrolled in graduate school within 6 months of graduation and 98% were employed.

Admissions Contact: Marvin G. Sills, Director of Admissions. E-mail: *admissions@rowan.edu* Web: *rowan.edu/admissions*

RUTGERS, THE STATE UNIVERSITY OF NEW JERSEY

The Rutgers, the State University of New Jersey, established in 1766, is a public system in New Jersey. It is governed by a board of governors, whose chief administrator is the president. The primary goals of the system are instruction, research, and service. The main priorities are to continue development as a distinguished comprehensive public university, to enhance undergraduate education, to strengthen graduate education and research, and to develop and improve programs to serve society New Jersey's needs. The total enrollment of all 3 campuses is usually around 50,000; there are about 1950 faculty members. Altogether there are more than 100 baccalaureate, 100 master's, and 80 doctoral programs offered in Rutgers, the State University of New Jersey. 4-year campuses are located in New Brunswick, Newark, and Camden. Profiles of the 4-year campuses are included in this section.

RUTGERS, THE STATE UNIVERSITY OF NEW JERSEY/CAMDEN CAMPUS		C-4
Camden, NJ 08102-1461	(856) 225-6104; Fax: (856) 225-6498	
Full-time: 1287 men, 1772 women	Faculty: 221; IIA, ++$	
Part-time: 362 men, 517 women	Ph.D.s: 59%	
Graduate: 328 men, 315 women	Student/Faculty: 14 to 1	
Year: semesters, summer session	Tuition: $7590 ($14,104)	
Application Deadline: open	Room & Board: $7400	
Freshman Class: 4697 applied, 2717 accepted, 499 enrolled		
SAT I Verbal/Math: 530/560	VERY COMPETITIVE	

Rutgers, The State University of New Jersey/Camden Campus, founded in 1927, is comprised of 3 undergraduate, degree-granting schools: College of the Arts and Sciences, University College--Camden, and the School of Business--Camden. Each school has individual requirements, policies, and fees. Cost figures in the above capsule are approximate. Applicants should contact the particular school for the most current information. There are 3 undergraduate and 3 graduate schools. In addition to regional accreditation, Camden has baccalaureate program accreditation with AACSB, CCNE, CSWE, and NAACLS. The 2 libraries contain 703,308 volumes, 924,818 microform items, and 260 audio/video tapes/CDs, and subscribe to 4309 periodicals. Computerized library services include the card catalog, interlibrary loans, database searching, and Internet access. Special learning facilities include a learning resource center, art gallery, and radio station. The 40-acre campus is in an urban area 1 mile east of Philadelphia.

Student Life: 96% of undergraduates are from New Jersey. Students are from 5 states. 66% are white; 14% African American. The average age of freshmen is 21; all undergraduates, 25. 18% do not continue beyond their first year.

Housing: College housing includes coed dorms and on-campus apartments. 87% of students commute. Alcohol is not permitted.

Activities: There are no fraternities or sororities. There are 70 groups on campus, including computers, drama, ethnic, gay, honors, international, literary magazine, newspaper, political, professional, radio and TV, religious, social, social service, student government, and yearbook. Popular campus events include Raptor Day, Springfest, and Bill Maher Lecture.

Sports: There is no sports program at Camden.

Disabled Students: 95% of the campus is accessible. Wheelchair ramps, elevators, special parking, specially equipped rest rooms, special class scheduling, lowered drinking fountains, lowered telephones, and special housing are available. Facilities vary from building to building. However, all classes are scheduled in accessible locations for disabled students.

Services: Counseling and information services are available, as is tutoring in some subjects, including introductory classes. There is a reader service for the blind and remedial math, reading, and writing.

Campus Safety and Security: Measures include 24-hour foot and vehicle patrol, self-defense education, security escort services, and shuttle buses. There are informal discussions, pamphlets/posters/films, emergency telephones, lighted pathways/sidewalks, and the police department is supplemented by security guards.

Programs of Study: Camden confers B.A., B.S., and B.H.M. degrees. Master's degrees are also awarded. Bachelor's degrees are awarded in BIOLOGICAL SCIENCE (biochemistry and biology/biological science), BUSINESS (accounting, banking and finance, hospitality management services, management science, and marketing/retailing/merchandising), COMMUNICATIONS AND THE ARTS (art, art history and appreciation, dramatic arts, English, French, German, music, and Spanish), COMPUTER AND PHYSICAL SCIENCE (chemistry, computer science, mathematics, physics, and science), HEALTH PROFESSIONS (medical laboratory technology and nursing), SOCIAL SCIENCE (African American studies, criminal justice, economics, history, liberal arts/general studies, philosophy, political science/government, psychology, religion, social work, sociology, and urban studies). Psychology, computer science, and economics are the largest.

Required: To graduate, students must complete 120 credits, with 30 to 48 in the major, and maintain a minimum GPA of 2.0. A core curriculum of 60 credits is required, including 3 credits each in literary masterpieces, art, music or theater arts, and a foreign language, with an additional 3 credits in English or a foreign language; and 3 credits in math, with an additional 3 credits in math, computer science, or statistics. 1 interdisciplinary course is required, as are 9 credits from social science disciplines, 6 credits in English composition, 6 credits in history, 6 credits in the natural science disciplines, and an additional 9 credits in courses offered outside the major department.

Special: The university offers co-op programs, cross-registration, internships, accelerated degrees, student-designed majors, dual majors, nondegree study, and pass/fail options. Students may study abroad in numerous countries. In addition, there is an 8-year B.A./M.D. program with U.M.D.N.J., and many combined bachelor's and master's programs. There are distance learning, English as a Second Language, honors, and independent study programs. There is a freshman honors program.

Faculty/Classroom: 61% of faculty are male; 39%, female.

Admissions: 58% of the 2003-2004 applicants were accepted. The SAT I scores for the 2003-2004 freshman class were: Verbal--26% below 500, 52% between 500 and 599, 18% between 600 and 700, and 4% above 700; Math--22% below 500, 45% between 500 and 599, 27% between 600 and 700, and 6% above 700. 44% of the current freshmen were in the top fifth of their class; 85% were in the top two fifths.

Requirements: The SAT I or ACT is required, but not for students who have been out of high school for 2 years or more. SAT II: Subject tests are required of students without a high school diploma from an accredited high school and from some GED holders. A high school diploma is required; the GED is accepted. Students must have completed a general college-preparatory program, including 16 academic credits or Carnegie units, with 4 years of English, 3 years of math (4 recommended), and 2 years each of a foreign language and science, plus 5 in electives. AP and CLEP credits are accepted. Important factors in the admissions decision are advanced placement or honor courses, evidence of special talent, and leadership record.

Procedure: Freshmen are admitted in the fall. It is recommended that entrance exams be taken by December of senior year, but it is not a requirement. There is an early admissions plan and a rolling admissions plan. Application deadlines are open. Application fee is $50. 64 applicants were on the 2003 waiting list. Regular decision notification is sent February 28. Freshmen are admitted in the fall and other terms that vary by college. Applications are accepted on-line through *admissions@rutgers.edu.*

Transfer: 409 transfer students enrolled in 2002-2003. Applicants must have a minimum of 12 credit hours. Grades of C or better in courses that correspond in content and credit to those offered by the college transfer for credit. Transfer students are admitted in the fall and spring semesters. All high school and previous college transcripts are required. 30 of the last 42 of 120 credits required for the bachelor's degree must be completed at Camden.

Visiting: There are regularly scheduled orientations for prospective students, including an information session with an admissions officer and a campus tour. Visitors may sit in on classes. To schedule a visit, contact the Admissions Office (Camden).

Financial Aid: In 2003-2004, 64% of all full-time freshmen and 63% of continuing full-time students received some form of financial aid. At least 50% of full-time freshmen and at least 48% of continuing full-time students received need-based aid. The average freshman award was $9253. Need-based scholarships or need-based grants averaged $6732; need-based self-help aid (loans and jobs) averaged $3394; and non-need-based awards and non-need-based scholarships averaged $4234. The average financial indebtedness of the 2003 graduate was $15,432. The FAFSA is required. The deadline for filing freshman financial aid applications for fall entry is open.

International Students: They must score 550 on the written TOEFL and also take the SAT I or the ACT.

Computers: The mainframe consists of a Sun Ultra 2 SPARC Server, Sun 10/51 SPARC Server, and Sun Enterprise 3500. Workstations and networked PCs and Mac (a total of 187 systems) are located in public labs in 2 major academic buildings, the library, the Campus Center, and the dorms. All provide access to the central systems, the Web, and the local Camden campus computers. On-campus computer network services include on-line admission, registration, transcripts, e-mail, library searches, library catalog, and full access to the Internet. A complete intranet web service is available for all aspects of student services. All students may access the system. Public labs are open whenever the building housing the lab is open.

Graduates: From July 1, 2002 to June 30, 2003, 808 bachelor's degrees were awarded. The most popular majors were business/marketing (24%), social sciences/history (18%), and psychology (16%).

Admissions Contact: Dr. Deborah Bowles, Associate Provost for Enrollment Management. Web: *admissions.rutgers.edu*

RUTGERS, THE STATE UNIVERSITY OF NEW JERSEY/NEW BRUNSWICK/PISCATAWAY CAMPUS

D-3

New Brunswick, NJ 08901-1281   (732) 932-4636
Fax: (732) 445-0237

Full-time: 11,767 men, 12,940 women	**Faculty:** 1502; I, +$
Part-time: 1020 men, 1133 women	**Ph.Ds:** 99%
Graduate: 2495 men, 3800 women	**Student/Faculty:** 16 to 1
Year: semesters, summer session	**Tuition:** $7590 ($14,104)
Application Deadline: open	**Room & Board:** $8210
Freshman Class: 26,175 applied, 14,180 accepted, 4717 enrolled	
SAT I Verbal/Math: 590/620	**HIGHLY COMPETITIVE**

Rutgers, The State University of New Jersey, New Brunswick/Piscataway Campus, founded in 1766, is comprised of 12 undergraduate degree-granting colleges. Students in New Brunswick/Piscataway enroll in 1 of 4 liberal arts colleges: Douglass College, Livingston College, Rutgers College, or University College-New Brunswick, or in 1 of 8 professional schools: Cook College, Mason Gross School of the Arts, Ernest Mario School of Pharmacy, Rutgers Business School: Undergraduate-New Brunswick, School of Communication, Information and Library Studies, School of Engineering, Edward J. Bloustein School of Planning and Public Policy, or the School of Management and Labor Relations. Each school within the New Brunswick campus has individual requirements, policies, and fees. Cost figures in the above capsule are approximate. Applicants should contact the particular school for the most current information. There are 12 undergraduate and 10 graduate schools. In addition to regional accreditation, New Brunswick has baccalaureate program accreditation with AACSB, ABET, ASLA, CSWE, NASD, and NASM. The 13 libraries contain 3,362,820 volumes, 4,459,329 microform items, and 133,009 audio/video tapes/CDs, and subscribe to 20,833 periodicals. Computerized library services include the card catalog, interlibrary loans, database searching, and Internet access. Special learning facilities include a learning resource center, art gallery, radio station, TV station, geology museum, and various research centers.

Student Life: 89% of undergraduates are from New Jersey. Students are from 19 states. 55% are white; 20% Asian American. The average age of freshmen is 19; all undergraduates, 21. 11% do not continue beyond their first year.

Housing: College housing includes single-sex and coed dorms, married-student housing, fraternity houses, and sorority houses. In addition, there are language houses, special-interest houses, first year residence, substance-free, transfer, residence for single mothers with children, and a math/science/engineering house for women. 55% of students commute. Alcohol is not permitted.

Activities: There are 27 national fraternities and 15 national sororities. There are 400 groups on campus, including art, band, cheerleading, chess, choir, chorale, chorus, computers, dance, drama, drill team, ethnic, film, gay, honors, international, jazz band, literary magazine, marching band, newspaper, opera, orchestra, pep band, photography, political, professional, radio and TV, religious, social, social service, student government, symphony, and yearbook. Popular campus events include UC Festival, theater trips, and annual picnic.

Sports: There are 15 intercollegiate sports for men and 15 for women.

Disabled Students: Wheelchair ramps, elevators, special parking, specially equipped rest rooms, special class scheduling, lowered drinking fountains, lowered telephones, and special housing are available. Facilities vary from building to building. However, all classes are scheduled in accessible locations for disabled students.

Services: Counseling and information services are available, as is tutoring in most subjects, with specific assistance in difficult first- and second-level courses, as well as learning assistance. There is remedial math, reading, and writing. There is computer software with aids, library technology, and assistance.

Campus Safety and Security: Measures include 24-hour foot and vehicle patrol, self-defense education, security escort services, and shuttle buses. There are informal discussions, pamphlets/posters/films, emergency telephones, lighted pathways/sidewalks, and the police department is supplemented by security guards and student safety officers.

Programs of Study: New Brunswick confers B.A., B.S., B.F.A., and B.Mus. degrees. Master's and doctoral degrees are also awarded. Bachelor's degrees are awarded in AGRICULTURE (agriculture, animal science, natural resource management, and plant science), BIOLOGICAL SCIENCE (biochemistry, biology/biological science, biomathematics, biotechnology, botany, cell biology, ecology, evolutionary biology, genetics, marine science, microbiology, molecular biology, nutrition, and physiology), BUSINESS (accounting, banking and finance, business administration and management, labor studies, management information systems, management science, and marketing/retailing/merchandising), COMMUNICATIONS AND THE ARTS (art, art history and appreciation, Chinese, classics, communications, comparative literature, dance, dramatic arts, East Asian languages and literature, English, French, German, Italian, journalism, Latin, linguistics, music, Portuguese, Russian, Spanish, and visual and performing arts), COMPUTER AND PHYSICAL SCI-

ENCE (astrophysics, chemistry, computer science, geology, information sciences and systems, mathematics, physics, and statistics), ENGINEERING AND ENVIRONMENTAL DESIGN (bioresource engineering, ceramic engineering, chemical engineering, civil engineering, electrical/electronics engineering, engineering and applied science, environmental science, industrial engineering, and mechanical engineering), HEALTH PROFESSIONS (biomedical science, exercise science, medical technology, pharmacy, and public health), SOCIAL SCIENCE (African American studies, American studies, anthropology, Asian/Oriental studies, criminal justice, economics, food science, geography, Hispanic American studies, history, humanities, Judaic studies, Latin American studies, medieval studies, Middle Eastern studies, philosophy, political science/government, psychology, religion, Russian and Slavic studies, social work, sociology, urban studies, and women's studies). Biological sciences, psychology, and English are the largest.

Required: To graduate, students must complete 120 credits, with a minimum GPA of 2.0. A liberal arts core requirement includes 12 credits each of humanities, social sciences, math, and science and 6 credits of English composition. Check with the indivdual college for specific program requirements.

Special: The college offers co-op programs, cross registration, and study abroad in numerous countries. A Washington semester, work-study and accelerated degree programs, B.A.-B.S. degrees, student-designed majors, nondegree study, and pass/fail options are available. There is an 8-year B.A.- or B.S./M.D. program with UMDNJ and several dual degree (5 year and 6 year) programs. There are 2 national honor societies, including Phi Beta Kappa, and a freshman honors program.

Faculty/Classroom: 65% of faculty are male; 35%, female.

Admissions: 54% of the 2003-2004 applicants were accepted. The SAT I scores for the 2003-2004 freshman class were: Verbal--8% below 500, 45% between 500 and 599, 38% between 600 and 700, and 9% above 700; Math--6% below 500, 32% between 500 and 599, 46% between 600 and 700, and 17% above 700. 69% of the current freshmen were in the top fifth of their class; 96% were in the top two fifths.

Requirements: The SAT I or ACT is required. In addition, a high school diploma is required. The GED is accepted. Students must have completed a general college-preparatory program, including 16 academic credits or Carnegie units, with 4 years of English, 3 years of math 4 recommended, including (algebra I and II and geometry), 2 years each of a foreign language and science, and 5 in electives. Engineering students need 4 years of math and must take chemistry and physics for sciences; nursing and pharmacy students must take biology and chemistry. SAT II: Subject tests are required for students without a high school diploma from an accredited high school and from some GED holders. AP and CLEP credits are accepted. Important factors in the admissions decision are evidence of special talent, extracurricular activities record, and ability to finance college education.

Procedure: Freshmen are admitted in the fall. It is recommended that entrance exams be taken by December of senior year, but it is not a requirement. There is an early admissions plan and a rolling admissions plan. Application deadlines are open. Application fee is $50. 1274 applicants were on the 2003 waiting list; 77 were admitted. Regular decision notification is sent February 28. Freshmen are admitted in the fall and other terms that vary by college. Applications are accepted on-line through *admissions.rutgers.edu.*

Transfer: 1183 transfer students enrolled in 2002-2003. Applicants must have a minimum of 12 credit hours earned. High school and college transcripts are required. Transfers are admitted in the fall or spring. 30 of the last 42 of 120 credits required for the bachelor's degree must be completed at New Brunswick.

Visiting: There are regularly scheduled orientations for prospective students, including a preadmission orientation for prospective students. To schedule a visit, contact University Undergraduate Admissions.

Financial Aid: In 2003-2004, 53% of all full-time freshmen and 50% of continuing full-time students received some form of financial aid. At least 45% of full-time freshmen and at least 43% of continuing full-time students received need-based aid. The average freshman award was $10,216. Need-based scholarships or need-based grants averaged $7082; need-based self-help aid (loans and jobs) averaged $3666; non-need-based athletic scholarships averaged $9964; and other non-need-based awards and non-need-based scholarships averaged $4613. The average financial indebtedness of the 2003 graduate was $15,018. The FAFSA is required. The deadline for filing freshman financial aid applications for fall entry is open.

International Students: They must score 550 on the written TOEFL and also take the college's own test.

Computers: Central systems include 11 Sun UNIX servers dedicated to student use. Individual departments have a variety of PCs. The central systems may be accessed from Macs, Windows-based PCs, and X-terminals located in several large public labs. Services include e-mail, newsgroups, software applications, a campuswide information system, and access to the Internet. All students may access the system 24 hours per day. There are no time limits. The fee is $200.

Graduates: From July 1, 2002 to June 30, 2003, 5841 bachelor's degrees were awarded. The most popular majors were social sciences and history (24%), psychology (9%), and biological/life sciences (8%).

Admissions Contact: Office of University Undergraduate Admissions. Web: *admissions.rutgers.edu*

RUTGERS, THE STATE UNIVERSITY OF NEW JERSEY/NEWARK CAMPUS

E-2

Newark, NJ 07102-1897   (973) 353-5205; Fax: (973) 353-1440

Full-time: 2099 men, 2978 women	**Faculty:** 386; I, +$
Part-time: 455 men, 744 women	**Ph.D.s:** 99%
Graduate: 1415 men, 1136 women	**Student/Faculty:** 13 to 1
Year: semesters, summer session	**Tuition:** $7590 ($14,104)
Application Deadline: open	**Room & Board:** $8034
Freshman Class: 7835 applied, 3681 accepted, 987 enrolled	
SAT I Verbal/Math: 540/570	**VERY COMPETITIVE**

Rutgers, The State University of New Jersey/Newark Campus, founded in 1930, is comprised of 4 undergraduate, degree-granting schools: Newark College of Arts and Sciences, University College-Newark, Rutgers Business School: Undergraduate-Newark, and College of Nursing. Each school has individual requirements, policies, and fees. Cost figures in the above capsule are approximate. Applicants should contact the particular school for the most current information. There are 4 undergraduate and 4 graduate schools. In addition to regional accreditation, Newark has baccalaureate program accreditation with AACSB, CCNE, CSWE, and NASM. The 4 libraries contain 1,014,684 volumes, 1,487,235 microform items, and 37,084 audio/video tapes/CDs, and subscribe to 6593 periodicals. Computerized library services include the card catalog, interlibrary loans, database searching, and Internet access. Special learning facilities include a learning resource center, art gallery, radio station, molecular and behavioral neuroscience center, and institutes of jazz and animal behavior. The 34-acre campus is in an urban area 7 miles west of New York City.

Student Life: 92% of undergraduates are from New Jersey. Students are from 9 states and 6 foreign countries. 27% are white; 20% Asian American; 18% African American; 16% Hispanic. The average age of freshmen is 20; all undergraduates, 22. 14% do not continue beyond their first year.

Housing: College housing includes coed on-campus apartments, fraternity houses, and sorority houses. 87% of students commute. Alcohol is not permitted.

Activities: There are no fraternities or sororities. There are 85 groups on campus, including chess, chorale, chorus, drama, newspaper, outreach, radio and TV, student government, and yearbook. Popular campus events include Black History month, Honors convocation, and Alpha Sigma Lambda.

Disabled Students: 80% of the campus is accessible. Wheelchair ramps, elevators, special parking, specially equipped rest rooms, special class scheduling, lowered drinking fountains, lowered telephones, and special housing are available. Facilities vary from building to building. However, all classes are scheduled in accessible locations for disabled students.

Services: Counseling and information services are available, as is tutoring in most subjects. There is a reader service for the blind and remedial math, reading, and writing.

Campus Safety and Security: Measures include 24-hour foot and vehicle patrol, self-defense education, security escort services, and shuttle buses. There are informal discussions, pamphlets/posters/films, emergency telephones, lighted pathways/sidewalks, and security guards assist Rutgers police in providing public safety services. There is also a student marshal program.

Programs of Study: Newark confers B.A., B.S., and B.F.A. degrees. Master's and doctoral degrees are also awarded. Bachelor's degrees are awarded in BIOLOGICAL SCIENCE (biology/biological science, botany, and zoology), BUSINESS (accounting, banking and finance, business administration and management, management science, and marketing/retailing/merchandising), COMMUNICATIONS AND THE ARTS (art, dramatic arts, English, French, German, journalism, music, Portuguese, Spanish, and visual and performing arts), COMPUTER AND PHYSICAL SCIENCE (applied mathematics, applied physics, chemistry, computer science, geology, geoscience, information sciences and systems, mathematics, and physics), ENGINEERING AND ENVIRONMENTAL DESIGN (environmental science), HEALTH PROFESSIONS (allied health, clinical science, and nursing), SOCIAL SCIENCE (African American studies, American studies, anthropology, criminal justice, Eastern European studies, economics, history, medieval studies, philosophy, political science/government, psychology, Puerto Rican studies, science and society, social work, sociology, and women's studies). Accounting, management, and psychology are the largest.

Required: To graduate, students must complete 124 credits with a minimum GPA of 2.0. Distribution requirements include 8 credits in natural science/math or 3 courses in nonlab science, math, or computer science; 6 credits each in history, literature, social sciences, humanities, and fine arts; 1 course in critical thinking; and 15 credits of electives. All students must take English composition and demonstrate math proficiency either by exam or by successfully completing a college algebra course or any other advanced course in math, a college calculus course (with a grade of C or better), or a precalculus course (with a grade of B or better).

Special: Students may cross-register with the New Jersey Institute of Technology and the University of Medicine and Dentistry of New Jersey. Internships are available. The school offers study abroad, accelerated degree programs in business administration and criminal justice, co-op programs, independent study, distance learning, English as a Second Language, dual majors, student-designed majors, nondegree study, and pass/fail options. Contact the school for information on the Honors College. There are 12 national honor societies, including Phi Beta Kappa, and a freshman honors program.

Faculty/Classroom: 61% of faculty are male; 39%, female. All both teach and do research. The average class size in an introductory lecture is 30; in a laboratory, 20; and in a regular course, 30.

Admissions: 47% of the 2003-2004 applicants were accepted. The SAT I scores for the 2003-2004 freshman class were: Verbal--33% below 500, 49% between 500 and 599, 18% between 600 and 700, and 1% above 700; Math--22% below 500, 42% between 500 and 599, 31% between 600 and 700, and 5% above 700. 60% of the current freshmen were in the top fifth of their class; 91% were in the top two fifths.

Requirements: The SAT I or ACT is required. In addition, a high school diploma is required; the GED is accepted. SAT II: Subject tests are required of students without a high school diploma from an accredited high school and from some GED holders. Students should have completed 16 high school academic credits or Carnegie units, with 4 years of English, 3 years of math, (4 recommended) 2 years each of science, a general college-preparatory program, including a foreign language and 5 electives. Biology and chemistry are required for nursing students. AP and CLEP credits are accepted. Important factors in the admissions decision are advanced placement or honor courses, evidence of special talent, and leadership record.

Procedure: Freshmen are admitted in the fall. It is recommended that entrance exams be taken by December of senior year, but it is not a requirement. There is an early admissions plan and a rolling admissions plan. Application deadlines are open. Application fee is $50. 191 applicants were on the 2003 waiting list; 2 were admitted. Regular decision notification is sent February 28. Freshmen are admitted fall and spring and other terms that vary by college. Applications are accepted on-line through admissions@rutgers.edu.

Transfer: 404 transfer students enrolled in 2002-2003. Students who have completed at least 12 credit hours at another college with a cumulative GPA of 2.0 are considered for admission as transfer students. Transfers are admitted in the fall and spring. High school and college transcripts are required. 30 of the last 42 of 124 credits required for the bachelor's degree must be completed at Newark.

Visiting: There are regularly scheduled orientations for prospective students, including an information session with an admissions counselor and a tour of the campus. There are guides for informal visits and visitors may sit in on classes. To schedule a visit, contact the Admissions Office (Newark).

Financial Aid: In 2003-2004, 63% of all full-time freshmen and 62% of continuing full-time students received some form of financial aid. At least 53% of full-time freshmen and at least 50% of continuing full-time students received need-based aid. The average freshman award was $9222. Need-based scholarships or need-based grants averaged $7009; need-based self-help aid (loans and jobs) averaged $3070; and non-need-based awards and non-need-based scholarships averaged $2701. Average annual earnings from campus work are $1365. The average financial indebtedness of the 2003 graduate was $14,757. The FAFSA is required. The deadline for filing freshman financial aid applications for fall entry is open.

International Students: In a recent year, there were 32 international students enrolled. They must score 550 on the written TOEFL and also take the college's own test.

Computers: The mainframe is a Central systems include 11 Sun UNIX servers dedicated to student use. Individual departments also have a variety of PCs. All students can generate their own accounts on this system. Access to the central campus systems, and other university systems is provided through more than 450 networked PCs in 9 campus labs. 1 dorm has a PC lab, and all dorm rooms are wired for direct connection to the network. All students have access to accounts and e-mail. The Internet is available from the campus labs from 8:30 A.M. to midnight, and 24 hours a day from dial-up lines. There are no time limits. The fee is $200. All students are required to have personal computers.

Graduates: From July 1, 2002 to June 30, 2003, 1076 bachelor's degrees were awarded. The most popular majors were business/marketing (28%), computer and information sciences (13%), and social sciences and history (11%).

Admissions Contact: Bruce Neimeyer, Director of Admissions-Newark. Web: admissions.rutgers.edu

SAINT PETER'S COLLEGE
Jersey City, NJ 07306-5997

E-2

(201) 915-9213
(888) SPC-9933; Fax: (201) 432-5860

Full-time: 1100 men, 1150 women	**Faculty:** 112; IIA, -$
Part-time: 160 men, 400 women	**Ph.D.s:** 78%
Graduate: 225 men, 300 women	**Student/Faculty:** 20 to 1
Year: semesters, summer session	**Tuition:** $18,592
Application Deadline: open	**Room & Board:** $8038
Freshman Class: n/av	
SAT I: required	**LESS COMPETITIVE**

Saint Peter's College, founded in 1872, is a private liberal arts and business college affiliated with the Roman Catholic Church and known as New Jersey's Jesuit College. Some figures in the above capsule and in this profile are approximate. There are 2 undergraduate and 3 graduate schools. In addition to regional accreditation, SPC has baccalaureate program accreditation with NLN. The 2 libraries contain 285,000 volumes, 70,000 microform items, and 3800 audio/video tapes/CDs, and subscribe to 1800 periodicals. Computerized library services include the card catalog, interlibrary loans, and database searching. Special learning facilities include a learning resource center, art gallery, radio station, and TV station. The 15-acre campus is in an urban area 2 miles west of New York City. Including any residence halls, there are 29 buildings.

Student Life: 87% of undergraduates are from New Jersey. Students are from 26 states and 10 foreign countries. 56% are from public schools. 48% are white; 27% Hispanic; 16% African American. 68% are Catholic; 8% claim no religious affiliation; 6% Protestant. The average age of freshmen is 18; all undergraduates, 24. 23% do not continue beyond their first year; 51% remain to graduate.

Housing: 863 students can be accommodated in college housing, which includes single-sex and coed dorms and on-campus apartments. In addition, there are community service houses. On-campus housing is guaranteed for all 4 years. 70% of students commute. Upperclassmen may keep cars.

Activities: There are no fraternities or sororities. There are 50 groups on campus, including cheerleading, chess, chorus, computers, debate, drama, ethnic, forensics, honors, international, literary magazine, newspaper, pep band, political, professional, radio and TV, religious, social, social service, student government, and yearbook. Popular campus events include International Day, career fairs, and SpringFest.

Sports: There are 10 intercollegiate sports for men and 8 for women, and 20 intramural sports for men and 18 for women. Facilities include a recreational center, a 2000-seat gym, and an athletic field.

Disabled Students: 80% of the campus is accessible. Wheelchair ramps, elevators, special parking, specially equipped rest rooms, special class scheduling, lowered drinking fountains, lowered telephones, and specially equipped rooms in residence halls are available.

Services: Counseling and information services are available, as is tutoring in every subject. There is a reader service for the blind and remedial math, reading, and writing.

Campus Safety and Security: Measures include 24-hour foot and vehicle patrol, self-defense education, security escort services, and shuttle buses. There are informal discussions, pamphlets/posters/films, emergency telephones, and security desk monitoring of access to residence halls.

Programs of Study: SPC confers B.A., B.S., and B.S.N. degrees. Associate and master's degrees are also awarded. Bachelor's degrees are awarded in BIOLOGICAL SCIENCE (biochemistry and biology/biological science), BUSINESS (accounting, business administration and management, international business management, and marketing/retailing/merchandising), COMMUNICATIONS AND THE ARTS (art history and appreciation, classical languages, classics, English, fine arts, and Spanish), COMPUTER AND PHYSICAL SCIENCE (chemistry, computer science, mathematics, natural sciences, and physics), EDUCATION (elementary and secondary), HEALTH PROFESSIONS (health care administration, medical laboratory technology, nursing, predentistry, and premedicine), SOCIAL SCIENCE (American studies, classical/ancient civilization, criminal justice, economics, history, humanities, philosophy, political science/government, prelaw, psychology, social science, sociology, theological studies, and urban studies). Natural sciences and accounting are the strongest academically. Business management, accounting, and computer sciences are the largest.

Required: To graduate, students must complete 129 credit hours, including 57 in the core curriculum, 12 in core electives, between 30 and 45 in the major, and the rest in subjects related to the major. The core curriculum requires 9 credits of natural sciences, 6 to 8 of math, 3 each of social science, philosophy, history, literature, a modern language, fine arts, and composition. Students must earn a GPA of 2.0.

Special: There are co-op programs with local companies, as well as departmental programs, and many internships available in Jersey City and nearby New York City. A Washington semester and study abroad in any of 60 countries are offered. The college also offers dual majors and student-designed majors, credit for life, military, and work experience, nondegree study, and pass/fail options. There are 9 national honor societies, a freshman honors program, and 1 departmental honors program.

Faculty/Classroom: 65% of faculty are male; 35%, female. All teach undergraduates. No introductory courses are taught by graduate students. The average class size in an introductory lecture is 23; in a laboratory, 14; and in a regular course, 16.

Requirements: The SAT I or ACT is required. In addition, applicants must be high school graduates or submit the GED certificate. Students should have completed 16 Carnegie units of high school study, including 4 years of English, 3 of math, 2 each of science, history, and a foreign language, and another 3 of additional work in any of these subjects. An essay and 2 letters of recommendation are required, and an interview is recommended. AP and CLEP credits are accepted. Important factors in the admissions decision are advanced placement or honor courses, extracurricular activities record, and recommendations by school officials.

Procedure: Freshmen are admitted fall and spring. Entrance exams should be taken by the fall of the senior year. There are early admissions and deferred admissions plans. Application deadlines are open. The fall 2003 application fee was $30. Notification is sent on a rolling basis.

Transfer: The school requires a 2.0 college GPA of transfer students, as well as a high school transcript and an 800 composite SAT I score for students less than 2 years out of high school. An interview is recommended. 30 of 129 credits required for the bachelor's degree must be completed at SPC.

Visiting: There are regularly scheduled orientations for prospective students, including open houses, weekend and weekday visit days with a tour and class and information sessions, as well as tours and interviews by appointment. There are guides for informal visits and visitors may sit in on classes and stay overnight. To schedule a visit, contact the Admissions Office.

Financial Aid: SPC is a member of CSS. The FAFSA is required. The deadline for filing freshman financial aid applications for fall entry is March 1.

International Students: The school actively recruits these students. They must score 500 on the written TOEFL.

Computers: The mainframes are an IBM 9370, a DEC VAX 780, 2 DEC PDP 11/44s, and a DEC PDP 11/24. There are also a number of PCs available in computer labs throughout the campus, and the VAX can be accessed from outside computers by modem. All students may access the system. The system may be used for remote access 24 hours a day; for local access, about 94 hours a week. There are no time limits and no fees.

Admissions Contact: Director of Admissions.
E-mail: *admissions@spcvxa.spc.edu* Web: *www.spc.edu*

SETON HALL UNIVERSITY
South Orange, NJ 07079-2691

E-2

(973) 761-9332
(800) THE-HALL; Fax: (973) 275-2040

Full-time: 2259 men, 2424 women	**Faculty:** 265; I, -$
Part-time: 240 men, 315 women	**Ph.D.s:** 92%
Graduate: 2159 men, 2349 women	**Student/Faculty:** 18 to 1
Year: semesters, summer session	**Tuition:** $21,580
Application Deadline: March 1	**Room & Board:** $8550
Freshman Class: 5750 applied, 4707 accepted, 1249 enrolled	
SAT I Verbal/Math: 550/560	**VERY COMPETITIVE**

Seton Hall University, founded in 1856, is affiliated with the Roman Catholic Church, and offers programs in business, communications, diplomacy, education, engineering, health, and law. It comprises 9 schools and colleges. There are 5 undergraduate and 8 graduate schools. In addition to regional accreditation, Seton Hall has baccalaureate program accreditation with AACSB, CCNE, CSWE, and NLN. The 2 libraries contain 523,000 volumes, 776,500 microform items, and 2225 audio/video tapes/CDs, and subscribe to 1875 periodicals. Computerized library services include the card catalog, interlibrary loans, and database searching. Special learning facilities include a learning resource center, art gallery, natural history museum, radio station, TV station, various institutes, and centers for learning and research. The 58-acre campus is in a suburban area 14 miles west of New York City. Including any residence halls, there are 31 buildings.

Student Life: 75% of undergraduates are from New Jersey. Students are from 45 states, 49 foreign countries, and Canada. 69% are from public schools. 51% are white; 11% African American. 67% are Catholic; 14% Protestant. The average age of freshmen is 18; all undergraduates, 22. 19% do not continue beyond their first year; 60% remain to graduate.

Housing: 2209 students can be accommodated in college housing, which includes single-sex and coed dorms and off-campus apartments. In addition, there are special-interest houses, all-female floors, a freshman interest-group floor, first-year residence halls, and alcohol-free buildings. On-campus housing is available on a first-come, first-served basis and is available on a lottery system for upperclassmen. Priority is given to out-of-town students. 59% of students commute. Upperclassmen may keep cars. Alcohol is permitted for students over 21.

Activities: 15% of men belong to 3 local and 12 national fraternities; 12% of women belong to 4 local and 8 national sororities. There are 100

groups on campus, including art, cheerleading, chess, choir, commuter council, computers, drama, drill team, ethnic, forensics, honors, international, literary magazine, musical theater, newspaper, pep band, photography, political, professional, radio and TV, recreation, religious, social, social service, student ambassador society, student government, and volunteer. Popular campus events include University Day, Theater-in-the-Round, and Welcome Weekend.

Sports: There are 8 intercollegiate sports for men and 9 for women, and 20 intramural sports for men and 20 for women. Facilities include a 2000-seat on-campus area, recreational field house, indoor track, indoor pool, fitness and aerobics rooms, a soccer and baseball field, a softball field, and tennis and racquetball courts. Men's basketball also uses the Continental Arena, which seats 19,759.

Disabled Students: 75% of the campus is accessible. Wheelchair ramps, elevators, special parking, specially equipped rest rooms, special class scheduling, lowered drinking fountains, and lowered telephones are available.

Services: Counseling and information services are available, as is tutoring in most subjects. There is a reader service for the blind and remedial math, reading, and writing. There is also tutorial assistance for disabled students.

Campus Safety and Security: Measures include 24-hour foot and vehicle patrol, security escort services, shuttle buses, and informal discussions. There are pamphlets/posters/films, emergency telephones, and lighted pathways/sidewalks. Paid student security attendants are posted at residence hall entrances.

Programs of Study: Seton Hall confers B.A., B.S., B.A.B.A., B.S.B.A., B.S.Ed., and B.S.N. degrees. Master's and doctoral degrees are also awarded. Bachelor's degrees are awarded in BIOLOGICAL SCIENCE (biochemistry and biology/biological science), BUSINESS (accounting, banking and finance, business administration and management, business economics, management information systems, marketing/retailing/merchandising, and sports management), COMMUNICATIONS AND THE ARTS (art, communications, English, French, Italian, modern language, music, and Spanish), COMPUTER AND PHYSICAL SCIENCE (chemistry, computer science, mathematics, and physics), EDUCATION (elementary, secondary, and special), HEALTH PROFESSIONS (nursing), SOCIAL SCIENCE (African American studies, anthropology, Asian/Oriental studies, Christian studies, classical/ancient civilization, criminal justice, economics, history, international relations, liberal arts/general studies, philosophy, political science/government, psychology, religion, social science, social work, and sociology). Business (accounting, finance), biology, and diplomacy are the strongest academically. Biology, criminal justice, and communication are the largest.

Required: To graduate, students must complete at least 128 to 130 hours, including a minimum of 36 hours in the major, both varying by major. Students must take freshman composition as well as courses in English, math, social science, natural sciences, religious studies, and philosophy, earning a minimum GPA of 2.0 (2.5 in the College of Education and Human Services).

Special: Co-op and work-study are possible through the College of Arts and Sciences and the School of Business; internships are available in many arts and sciences majors. Education majors go into the field during their sophomore year. Cross-registration is available with the University of Medicine and Dentistry of New Jersey and in engineering, including 3-2 engineering degrees, with the New Jersey Institute of Technology. Students may take a Washington semester (political science majors) or study abroad in more than 10 countries. An accelerated B.S.N. degree, a 5-year B.A.-M.A. in diplomacy, a 5-year B.A.-M.B.A., a 5-year B.A.-M.P.A., a 5-year B.A.-B.S. degree in engineering, a 6-year B.S.-M.S. in athletic training, physician assistant, and occupational therapy, and a 7-year B.S.-Doctor of Physical Therapy are offered. Nondegree study is permitted, as are pass/fail options in electives. There are 20 national honor societies, a freshman honors program, and 3 departmental honors programs.

Faculty/Classroom: 57% of faculty are male; 43%, female. 70% teach undergraduates. Graduate students teach 3% of introductory courses. The average class size in an introductory lecture is 30; in a laboratory, 10; and in a regular course, 20.

Admissions: 82% of the 2003-2004 applicants were accepted. The SAT I scores for the 2003-2004 freshman class were: Verbal--24% below 500, 45% between 500 and 599, 26% between 600 and 700, and 5% above 700; Math--21% below 500, 46% between 500 and 599, 29% between 600 and 700, and 4% above 700. 44% of the current freshmen were in the top fifth of their class; 76% were in the top two fifths. 3 freshmen graduated first in their class.

Requirements: The SAT I or ACT is required. In addition, Seton Hall recommends a composite score higher than 1050 on the SAT I, with at least 500 on each part, or a minimum composite score of 24 on the ACT. Applicants must supply high school transcripts or a GED certificate. Students should have completed 16 Carnegie units of high school study, including 4 years of English, 3 of math, 2 each of a foreign language and either history or social studies, 1 of science, and 4 academic electives. An essay is optional and an interview is recommended. A GPA of 2.5 is required. AP and CLEP credits are accepted. Important factors in the admissions decision are advanced placement or honor courses, leadership record, and parents or siblings attending the school.

Procedure: Freshmen are admitted fall and spring. Entrance exams should be taken by January of the senior year. There is a deferred admissions plan and a rolling admissions plan. Applications should be filed by March 1 for fall entry and December 1 for spring entry, along with a $45 fee. Notification is sent on a rolling basis. 1030 applicants were on the 2003 waiting list; 588 were admitted. Applications are accepted online through *admissions.shu.edu* and the application service Applyweb.

Transfer: 325 transfer students enrolled in 2002-2003. Applicants should have earned 30 hours of college credit, with a minimum GPA of 2.5, or 2.8 for the business and science schools. The SAT I is required for students with fewer than 30 credits of college-level work at the time of application, and an interview is recommended. 30 credits of 128 to 130 required for the bachelor's degree must be completed at Seton Hall.

Visiting: There are regularly scheduled orientations for prospective students, including campus tours weekdays and Saturdays during the academic year and on weekdays during the summer. Open houses for prospective applicants are available each fall. Visitors may sit in on classes. To schedule a visit, contact the Enrollment Services Office at *thehall@shu.edu.*

Financial Aid: In 2003-2004, 88% of all full-time freshmen and 77% of continuing full-time students received some form of financial aid. 75% of full-time freshmen and 58% of continuing full-time students received need-based aid. The average freshman award was $15,811. Need-based scholarships or need-based grants averaged $2299 ($8550 maximum); need-based self-help aid (loans and jobs) averaged $1461 ($10,769 maximum); non-need-based athletic scholarships averaged $17,780 ($32,703 maximum); other non-need-based awards and non-need-based scholarships averaged $8523 ($26,056 maximum); and institutional jobs, PLUS loans, NJ Class, and private parent loans averaged $6986 ($15,520 maximum). 21% of undergraduates work part time. Average annual earnings from campus work are $2274. The average financial indebtedness of the 2003 graduate was $18,768. Seton Hall is a member of CSS. The FAFSA is required. The fall financial aid application deadline is open.

International Students: There are 100 international students enrolled. The school actively recruits these students. They must score 550 on the written TOEFL and also take the SAT I or the ACT.

Computers: The mainframe is an IBM Multiprise 3000 (model 7060-HSO). All entering students are required to lease an IBM laptop; in addition, there are more than 300 PCs in public labs. Students have access to the mainframe, networked file servers, the campuswide information system, the library catalog, personal e-mail accounts, and the Internet. Students can connect almost anywhere on campus. All students may access the system. Public labs are available until 11 P.M.; there is 24-hour remote connection available. There are no time limits and no fees. All students are required to have personal computers. Pentium-based IBM laptops are recommended. All entering freshmen are required to participate in the Mobile Computing Program.

Graduates: From July 1, 2002 to June 30, 2003, 969 bachelor's degrees were awarded. The most popular majors were communications (12%), finance (8%), and nursing (7%). In an average class, 38% graduate in 4 years or less, 56% graduate in 5 years or less, and 60% graduate in 6 years or less. 380 companies recruited on campus in 2002-2003. Of the 2002 graduating class, 23% were enrolled in graduate school within 6 months of graduation and 70% were employed.

Admissions Contact: Darryl Jones, Director of Admissions. A video is available. E-mail: *thehall@shu.edu* Web: *www.shu.edu*

STEVENS INSTITUTE OF TECHNOLOGY
Hoboken, NJ 07030

	E-2
	(201) 216-5194
	(800) 458-5323; Fax: (201) 216-8348
Full-time: 1278 men, 423 women	**Faculty:** 206
Part-time: 4 men, 2 women	**Ph.D.s:** 84%
Graduate: 2062 men, 774 women	**Student/Faculty:** 9 to 1
Year: semesters, summer session	**Tuition:** $26,800
Application Deadline: February 15	**Room & Board:** $8500
Freshman Class: 1999 applied, 1018 accepted, 399 enrolled	
SAT I Verbal/Math: 610/670	**ACT:** 28
	HIGHLY COMPETITIVE+

Stevens Institute of Technology, founded in 1870, is a private institution offering programs of study in science, computer science, engineering, business, and humanities. There are 3 undergraduate schools and 1 graduate school. In addition to regional accreditation, Stevens has baccalaureate program accreditation with ABET and CSAB. The library contains 13,176 microform items, and subscribes to 13,000 periodicals. Computerized library services include the card catalog, interlibrary loans, and database searching. Special learning facilities include an art gallery, radio station, TV station, a lab for ocean and coastal engineering, an environmental lab, a design and manufacturing institute, a technology center, telecommunications institute, a computer vision lab, an ultrafast laser spectroscopy and high-speed communications lab, and a wireless net-

work security center. The 55-acre campus is in an urban area 1 mile west of New York City. Including any residence halls, there are 50 buildings.

Student Life: 71% of undergraduates are from New Jersey. Students are from 34 states, 29 foreign countries, and Canada. 51% are white; 20% Asian American. The average age of freshmen is 18; all undergraduates, 20. 10% do not continue beyond their first year; 68% remain to graduate.

Housing: 1000 students can be accommodated in college housing, which includes single-sex and coed dorms, on-campus apartments, off-campus apartments, married-student housing, fraternity houses, and sorority houses. In addition, there are special-interest houses and special-interest floors. On-campus housing is guaranteed for all 4 years. 75% of students live on campus; of those, 60% remain on campus on weekends. Alcohol is not permitted. Upperclassmen may keep cars.

Activities: 30% of men and about 33% of women belong to 9 national fraternities; 35% of women belong to 3 national sororities. There are 70 groups on campus, including art, chess, choir, chorus, computers, drama, ethnic, honors, international, jazz band, literary magazine, musical theater, newspaper, pep band, photography, political, professional, radio and TV, religious, social, social service, student government, and yearbook. Popular campus events include Fall Tech Fest, Spring Boken Festival, and Midnight Breakfast.

Sports: There are 11 intercollegiate sports for men and 11 for women, and 12 intramural sports for men and 12 for women. Facilities include a 6000-square-foot complex with an NCAA regulation swimming pool convertible to international size, squash courts, a 1000-seat basketball arena, fitness rooms, racquetball courts, a playing field, a student union, and several outdoor courts.

Disabled Students: All of the campus is accessible. Wheelchair ramps, elevators, special parking, specially equipped rest rooms, and lowered drinking fountains are available.

Services: Counseling and information services are available, as is tutoring in every subject.

Campus Safety and Security: Measures include 24-hour foot and vehicle patrol, self-defense education, security escort services, and informal discussions. There are pamphlets/posters/films, emergency telephones, and lighted pathways/sidewalks.

Programs of Study: Stevens confers B.A., B.S., and B.E. degrees. Master's and doctoral degrees are also awarded. Bachelor's degrees are awarded in BIOLOGICAL SCIENCE (biochemistry), COMMUNICATIONS AND THE ARTS (literature and music technology), COMPUTER AND PHYSICAL SCIENCE (chemistry, computer science, digital arts/technology, mathematics, physics, and science technology), ENGINEERING AND ENVIRONMENTAL DESIGN (biomedical engineering, chemical engineering, civil engineering, computational sciences, computer engineering, electrical/electronics engineering, engineering, engineering management, engineering physics, environmental engineering, mechanical engineering, and systems engineering), HEALTH PROFESSIONS (predentistry and premedicine), SOCIAL SCIENCE (history, philosophy, and prelaw). Engineering is the strongest academically as well the largest.

Required: To graduate, the student must have earned at least 145 credit hours with a minimum 2.0 GPA; the total hours in the major vary by program. The core curriculum includes courses in engineering, science, computer science, math, liberal arts, and phys ed.

Special: Stevens offers cross-registration and a 3-2 engineering degree with New York University, a work-study program within the school, co-op programs, corporate and research internships through the Undergraduate Projects in Technology and Medicine, study abroad in Scotland and Australia, and pass/fail options for extra courses. Students may undertake dual majors as well as accelerated degree programs in medicine, dentistry, and law, and can receive a B.A.-B.E. degree or a B.A.-B.S. degree in all majors. Undergraduates may take graduate courses. There are 3 national honor societies and a freshman honors program.

Faculty/Classroom: 86% of faculty are male; 14%, female. 83% teach undergraduates and 80% both teach and do research. No introductory courses are taught by graduate students. The average class size in an introductory lecture is 100; in a laboratory, 50; and in a regular course, 20.

Admissions: 51% of the 2003-2004 applicants were accepted. The SAT I scores for the 2003-2004 freshman class were: Verbal--5% below 500, 39% between 500 and 599, 44% between 600 and 700, and 12% above 700; Math--2% below 500, 12% between 500 and 599, 54% between 600 and 700, and 34% above 700. The ACT scores were 4% below 21, 18% between 21 and 23, 21% between 24 and 26, 14% between 27 and 28, and 43% above 28. 72% of the current freshmen were in the top fifth of their class; 92% were in the top two fifths. 7 freshmen graduated first in their class.

Requirements: The SAT I or ACT is required; the SAT I is preferred. Stevens recommends a minimum of 2 SAT II: Subject tests, depending on the intended major. In addition, applicants must provide official high school transcripts. Students should have taken 4 years of English, math, and science. An interview is required. AP credits are accepted. Important factors in the admissions decision are advanced placement or honor courses and extracurricular activities record.

Procedure: Freshmen are admitted in the fall. Entrance exams should be taken by February of the senior year. There are early decision, early admissions, and deferred admissions plans. Early decision applications should be filed by November 15; regular applications, by February 15 for fall entry and December 1 for spring entry, along with a $45 fee. Notification of early decision is sent December 15; regular decision, March 15. 42 early decision candidates were accepted for the 2003-2004 class. 159 applicants were on the 2003 waiting list; 29 were admitted. Applications are accepted on-line through the institute's web site.

Transfer: 47 transfer students enrolled in 2002-2003. Applicants should have a minimum GPA of 3.0. They must submit all college transcripts, including course descriptions; SAT I or ACT scores are required of those students with fewer than 30 hours of college credit. 50 of 145 credits required for the bachelor's degree must be completed at Stevens.

Visiting: There are regularly scheduled orientations for prospective students, including interviews and campus tours. There are guides for informal visits and visitors may sit in on classes and stay overnight. To schedule a visit, contact the Admissions Office.

Financial Aid: In 2003-2004, 94% of all full-time freshmen and 92% of continuing full-time students received some form of financial aid. 82% of full-time freshmen and 81% of continuing full-time students received need-based aid. The average freshman award was $21,842. Need-based scholarships or need-based grants averaged $15,021; need-based self-help aid (loans and jobs) averaged $4613; and non-need-based awards and non-need-based scholarships averaged $7878. 55% of undergraduates work part time. Average annual earnings from campus work are $1000. The average financial indebtedness of the 2003 graduate was $14,113. Stevens is a member of CSS. The FAFSA is required. The priority date for freshman financial aid applications for fall entry is February 15.

International Students: There are 86 international students enrolled. The school actively recruits these students. They must score 550 on the written TOEFL and also take the SAT I or the ACT.

Computers: All students may access campus servers, the Internet, the Web, and specialized facilities via the campuswide wireless network that connects every academic, administrative, and residential building. Connections for notebooks are available throughout the campus, including all residence hall rooms, 1 per person. All students may access the system at all times. There are no time limits and no fees. All students are required to have personal computers. A Compaq Armada EVO N800C with a Pentium IV processor, 1.8 GHz, 256 MB Ram, and a 30-GB hard drive is recommended.

Graduates: The most popular majors were computer engineering (31%), computer science (14%), and mechanical engineering (13%). In an average class, 45% graduate in 4 years or less, 55% graduate in 5 years or less, and 68% graduate in 6 years or less. Of the 2002 graduating class, 17% were enrolled in graduate school within 6 months of graduation and 63% were employed.

Admissions Contact: Daniel Gallagher, Dean of University Admissions. E-mail: *admissions@stevens.edu* Web: *www.stevens.edu*

THOMAS EDISON STATE COLLEGE D-3
Trenton, NJ 08608-1176

(888) 442-8372; Fax: (609) 984-8447

Full-time: none	**Faculty:** n/av
Part-time: 5310 men, 4701 women	**Ph.D.s:** n/av
Graduate: 114 men, 108 women	**Student/Faculty:** n/av
Year: see profile	**Tuition:** $3325 ($4775)
Application Deadline: open	**Room & Board:** n/app
Freshman Class: n/av	
SAT I or ACT: not required	**SPECIAL**

Thomas Edison State College, founded in 1972, is a public institution of higher education. The college provides many ways to complete a degree in more than 100 areas of study, including credit by examination, assessment of experiential learning, guided independent study, and credit for corporate and military training, which enables adults to pursue educational goals while attending to the challenges of career and family. The college offers a comprehensive tuition plan for students who want access to all components of the tuition package. Where only components of the comprehensive tuition plan are required, the college offers an enrolled options plan. There are 5 undergraduate schools and 1 graduate school. In addition to regional accreditation, Thomas Edison State College has baccalaureate program accreditation with NLN. Special learning facilities include the New Jersey State Library, an affiliate of the college. The 2-acre campus is in an urban area 40 miles north of Philadelphia. There are 3 buildings.

Student Life: 50% of undergraduates are from out of state, mostly the Middle Atlantic. Students are from 50 states, 83 foreign countries, and Canada. 65% are white; 10% African American. The average age of all undergraduates is 36.

Housing: There are no residence halls. Alcohol is not permitted.

Activities: There are no fraternities or sororities.

Sports: There is no sports program at Thomas Edison State College.

Disabled Students: 95% of the campus is accessible. Wheelchair ramps, elevators, special parking, specially equipped rest rooms, and lowered drinking fountains are available. Visually impaired students may make use of a "Talking Browser," pwWebSpeak.

Campus Safety and Security: Measures include lighted pathways/sidewalks. There is a guard on the premises 7 A.M. to 11 P.M.; the outside is patrolled by the New Jersey State Police.

Programs of Study: Thomas Edison State College confers B.A., B.S., B.S.A.S.T., B.S.B.A., B.S.H.S., and B.S.N. degrees. Associate and master's degrees are also awarded. Bachelor's degrees are awarded in AGRICULTURE (animal science, environmental studies, forestry and related sciences, and horticulture), BIOLOGICAL SCIENCE (biology/biological science), BUSINESS (accounting, banking and finance, hotel/motel and restaurant management, human resources, institutional management, insurance, international business management, labor studies, logistics, management science, marketing and distribution, office supervision and management, purchasing/inventory management, real estate, recreation and leisure services, retailing, small business management, and transportation management), COMMUNICATIONS AND THE ARTS (advertising, art, communications, dramatic arts, English, journalism, music, and photography), COMPUTER AND PHYSICAL SCIENCE (computer science, information sciences and systems, mathematics, and natural sciences), EDUCATION (foreign languages and health), ENGINEERING AND ENVIRONMENTAL DESIGN (air traffic control, architecture, aviation maintenance management, biomedical equipment technology, civil engineering technology, computer technology, construction engineering, drafting and design, electrical/electronics engineering technology, emergency/disaster science, environmental science, manufacturing technology, marine engineering, mechanical engineering technology, nuclear engineering technology, and survey and mapping technology), HEALTH PROFESSIONS (clinical science, cytotechnology, dental hygiene, health, health care administration, hospital administration, mental health/human services, nuclear medical technology, nursing, radiation therapy, and respiratory therapy), SOCIAL SCIENCE (anthropology, child psychology/development, community services, criminal justice, economics, fire protection, gerontology, history, humanities, liberal arts/general studies, philosophy, political science/government, psychology, public administration, religion, social science, social work, and sociology). Liberal studies, nuclear engineering technology, and general management are the largest.

Required: The baccalaureate student must complete a liberal arts requirement that includes courses in written expression, humanities, social science, math, and natural sciences for a total of at least 50% liberal arts credits. To graduate, 120 semester hours are required, with a minimum GPA of 2.0.

Special: Students may design their own majors and take dual majors in all degree programs except nursing. A B.S. in health sciences is available as a joint degree with the University of Medicine and Dentistry of New Jersey. Credit for college-level knowledge gained through life, military, and work experience is readily granted. Students may receive pass/fail grades. Students work on their own, proceeding at their own pace, depending on the option selected for earning credit. Thomas Edison State College has a 12-semester calendar. There is 1 national honor society.

Requirements: Applicants must have a high school diploma or the equivalent and be at least 21 years old. AP and CLEP credits are accepted.

Procedure: Application deadlines are open. There is a rolling admissions plan. The fall 2003 application fee was $75. Applications are accepted on-line through the school's web site.

Transfer: Transfers, like other students, must be at least 21 and be high school graduates or the equivalent. The granting of credit for course work successfully completed elsewhere is an intrinsic part of the school's system. Transfer credits are awarded with the grades earned.

Visiting: There are regularly scheduled orientations for prospective students, including bimonthly information sessions and individual sessions by appointment. To schedule a visit, contact the Director of Admissions.

Financial Aid: The FAFSA and the college's own financial statement are required.

International Students: There are 276 international students enrolled. They must score 500 on the written TOEFL or 173 on the electronic version.

Computers: The college web site allows students to apply, register for courses, take on-line courses, contact offices via e-mail, and submit course-related forms. Visitors to the college web site may participate in open on-line discussions and chat areas. All students may access the system at the student's convenience. There are no time limits and no fees.

Graduates: From July 1, 2002 to June 30, 2003, 1446 bachelor's degrees were awarded. The most popular majors were liberal studies (34%), nuclear engineering technology (12%), and humanities (6%).

Admissions Contact: Gordon Holly, Director of Admissions. A video is available. E-mail: *info@tesc.edu* Web: *http://www.tesc.edu*

WESTMINSTER CHOIR COLLEGE OF RIDER UNIVERSITY

D-3

Princeton, NJ 08540-3899

(609) 921-7144
(800) 96-CHOIR; Fax: (609) 921-2538

Full-time: 120 men, 200 women	**Faculty:** 37
Part-time: none	**Ph.D.s:** 80%
Graduate: 55 men, 105 women	**Student/Faculty:** 7 to 1
Year: semesters, summer session	**Tuition:** $21,050
Application Deadline: open	**Room & Board:** $8370
Freshman Class: n/av	
SAT I or ACT: required	**SPECIAL**

Westminster Choir College, founded in 1926, is a private school of music within Rider University, that focuses on undergraduate and graduate students seeking positions of music leadership in churches, schools, and communities. Some figures in the above capsule and in this profile are approximate. In addition to regional accreditation, Westminster Choir College has baccalaureate program accreditation with NASM. The library contains 60,000 volumes, 425 microform items, and 9000 audio/video tapes/CDs, and subscribes to 170 periodicals. Computerized library services include the card catalog, interlibrary loans, and database searching. Special learning facilities include a learning resource center, a music computer lab, and a vocal lab. The 23-acre campus is in a suburban area 50 miles south of New York City. Including any residence halls, there are 12 buildings.

Student Life: 66% of undergraduates are from out of state, mostly the Northeast. Students are from 36 states, 24 foreign countries, and Canada. 75% are white; 19% foreign nationals. The average age of freshmen is 18; all undergraduates, 21. 18% do not continue beyond their first year; 50% remain to graduate.

Housing: 206 students can be accommodated in college housing, which includes single-sex and coed dorms. On-campus housing is guaranteed for all 4 years. 70% of students live on campus; of those, 85% remain on campus on weekends. All students may keep cars.

Activities: There are no fraternities or sororities. There are 12 groups on campus, including choir, chorus, drama, ethnic, gay, honors, musical theater, newspaper, opera, orchestra, professional, radio and TV, religious, social, student government, and yearbook. Popular campus events include Spring Fling, Christmas at Westminster, and concerts.

Sports: There are 2 intramural sports for men and 2 for women.

Disabled Students: 42% of the campus is accessible. Wheelchair ramps, elevators, special parking, specially equipped rest rooms, and lowered telephones are available.

Services: Counseling and information services are available, as is tutoring in every subject. There is remedial math, reading, and writing.

Campus Safety and Security: Measures include security escort services, shuttle buses, pamphlets/posters/films, and emergency telephones. There are lighted pathways/sidewalks and increased campus security from 6 P.M. to 6 A.M.

Programs of Study: Westminster Choir College confers B.A. and B.M. degrees. Master's degrees are also awarded. Bachelor's degrees are awarded in COMMUNICATIONS AND THE ARTS (music, music performance, music theory and composition, piano/organ, and voice), EDUCATION (music), SOCIAL SCIENCE (religious music). Music education is the largest.

Required: All students must maintain a minimum GPA of 2.0 (2.5 for music education majors) while completing 124 semester hours, including 92 to 100 in their majors. All students also must meet English reading and writing proficiency requirements. Distribution requirements include 33 semester hours in arts and sciences with at least 1 course from each of the divisions of the department. Satisfactory performance in recital also is needed.

Special: Cross-registration with Drew University, Princeton University, Rider University, and Princeton Theological Seminary, internships in the arts, church, box office management, and arts administration, work-study programs, dual majors in any combination of 7 majors in music, and pass/fail options are all available. In addition, individualized programs of study in Europe may be pursued. There is 1 national honor society.

Faculty/Classroom: All teach undergraduates. No introductory courses are taught by graduate students. The average class size in an introductory lecture is 18; in a laboratory, 8; and in a regular course, 12.

Requirements: The SAT I or ACT is required; SAT I minimum scores should be 800 composite, 400 verbal and 400 math. Applicants must present 4 years of credits in English, 3 in history, 2 in math, and 1 in science. An essay and music audition are required; an interview is recommended. The GED is accepted. A GPA of 2.0 is required. AP credits are accepted. Important factors in the admissions decision are evidence of special talent, recommendations by alumni, and recommendations by school officials.

Procedure: Freshmen are admitted fall and spring. Entrance exams should be taken at the time of the audition. There are early decision, early admissions, and deferred admissions plans. Application deadlines are open. The fall 2003 application fee was $40. Notification is sent on a rolling basis.

Transfer: Applicants must submit high school and college transcripts and 2 letters of recommendation. An audition is required. 65 of 124 credits required for the bachelor's degree must be completed at Westminster Choir College.

Visiting: There are regularly scheduled orientations for prospective students. There are guides for informal visits and visitors may sit in on classes. To schedule a visit, contact the Admissions Office.

Financial Aid: In a recent year, 80% of all full-time freshmen received some form of financial aid. Westminster Choir College is a member of CSS. The FAFSA is required. The priority date for freshman financial aid applications for fall entry is March 1.

International Students: They must score 550 on the written TOEFL.

Computers: PCs are available for academic use in the Music, Arts and Sciences, and Learning Center computer labs. All students may access the system. There are no time limits and no fees.

Admissions Contact: Monica Tritto, Director of Admissions.
E-mail: *wccadmission@rider.edu* Web: *westminster.rider.edu*

WILLIAM PATERSON UNIVERSITY OF NEW JERSEY

E-2

Wayne, NJ 07470

(973) 720-2125; Fax: (973) 720-2910

Full-time: 3116 men, 4245 women	**Faculty:** IIA, ++$
Part-time: 724 men, 1217 women	**Ph.D.s:** 92%
Graduate: 460 men, 1448 women	**Student/Faculty:** n/av
Year: semesters, summer session	**Tuition:** $7120 ($11,510)
Application Deadline: May 1	**Room & Board:** $7330
Freshman Class: 5704 applied, 3469 accepted	
SAT I Verbal/Math: 520/520	**COMPETITIVE**

William Paterson University of New Jersey, founded in 1855 as a college, is a public institution comprised of the colleges of Arts and Communication; Education; Humanities; and Social Sciences; Science and Health; and Business. There are 5 undergraduate and 5 graduate schools. In addition to regional accreditation, WPUNJ has baccalaureate program accreditation with ASLA, NASM, NCATE, and NLN. The library contains 306,673 volumes, 1,080,413 microform items, and 20,124 audio/video tapes/CDs, and subscribes to 4607 periodicals. Computerized library services include the card catalog, interlibrary loans, and database searching. Special learning facilities include an art gallery, radio station, TV station, a speech and hearing clinic, an academic support center, a computerized writing center, and a teleconference center. The 320-acre campus is in a suburban area 25 miles west of New York City. Including any residence halls, there are 35 buildings.

Student Life: 98% of undergraduates are from New Jersey. Students are from 22 states, 58 foreign countries, and Canada. 75% are from public schools. 63% are white; 15% Hispanic; 12% African American. The average age of freshmen is 18; all undergraduates, 24.

Housing: College housing includes coed dorms and on-campus apartments. In addition, there are honors houses. On-campus housing is guaranteed for all 4 years. 76% of students commute. Upperclassmen may keep cars.

Activities: 2% of men belong to 3 local and 8 national fraternities; 3% of women belong to 3 local and 11 national sororities. There are 50 groups on campus, including art, cheerleading, chorus, computers, dance, drama, ethnic, film, gay, honors, international, jazz band, literary magazine, musical theater, newspaper, opera, orchestra, photography, political, professional, radio and TV, religious, student government, and yearbook. Popular campus events include Midday Artist Series, Puerto Rican Heritage Month, and Latin American Week.

Sports: There are 7 intercollegiate sports for men and 7 for women, and 24 intramural sports for men and 24 for women. Facilities include a recreation center with courts for basketball, tennis, racquetball, volleyball, and badminton, weight and exercise rooms, saunas and whirlpools, and a 4000-seat auditorium. The university also offers an Olympic-size pool, 8 additional tennis courts, and an athletic complex with fields for baseball, field hockey, football, soccer, softball, and track.

Disabled Students: Wheelchair ramps, elevators, special parking, specially equipped rest rooms, special class scheduling, lowered drinking fountains, lowered telephones, and special housing are available.

Services: Counseling and information services are available, as is tutoring in most subjects. There is remedial math, reading, and writing. There is a science enrichment center, a writing center, and a business tutorial lab.

Campus Safety and Security: Measures include 24-hour foot and vehicle patrol, security escort services, shuttle buses, and informal discussions. There are pamphlets/posters/films, emergency telephones, and lighted pathways/sidewalks.

Programs of Study: WPUNJ confers B.A., B.S., B.F.A., and B.M. degrees. Master's degrees are also awarded. Bachelor's degrees are awarded in BIOLOGICAL SCIENCE (biology/biological science and biotechnology), BUSINESS (accounting, banking and finance, and business administration and management), COMMUNICATIONS AND THE ARTS (art history and appreciation, communications, dramatic arts, English, fine arts, music, Spanish, and studio art), COMPUTER AND PHYSICAL SCIENCE (chemistry, computer science, and mathematics), EDUCATION (health, music, physical, and special), ENGINEERING AND ENVIRONMENTAL DESIGN (environmental science), HEALTH PROFESSIONS (community health work, health science, and nursing), SOCIAL SCIENCE (African American studies, anthropology, economics, geography, history, philosophy, political science/government, psychology, and sociology). Biology/biotechnology, computer science, and English are the strongest academically. Management, communications, and education are the largest.

Required: All students must maintain a cumulative GPA of at least 2.0 and take 128 credit hours, typically including 30 to 40 in their major. General education requirements include 21 credits in the humanities, 11 or 12 in science, 9 in the social sciences, and 6 in art and communication. Also required are 1 course in health or movement science, 1 course dealing with racism or sexism, and 1 course in non-Western culture. Students also complete 6 credits of general education electives and a minimum of 9 credits of upper-level elective courses.

Special: Study abroad in 33 countries, cross-registration, internships, work-study programs on campus, accelerated degree programs, dual majors, individual curriculum design, and credit for military experience are available. Nondegree study and some pass/fail options are also possible. In the Learning Clusters Project, students experience how 3 general education courses, taken together, reinforce and better integrate each other. There is a professional program in teacher education leading to certification in early childhood, elementary, middle, and secondary education. There are 6 national honor societies and 4 departmental honors programs.

Faculty/Classroom: 52% of faculty are male; 48%, female. All teach undergraduates and 40% do research. No introductory courses are taught by graduate students. The average class size in an introductory lecture is 32; in a laboratory, 24; and in a regular course, 19.

Admissions: 61% of the 2003-2004 applicants were accepted. The SAT I scores for the 2003-2004 freshman class were: Verbal--32% below 500, 54% between 500 and 599, 13% between 600 and 700, and 1% above 700; Math--29% below 500, 56% between 500 and 599, 14% between 600 and 700, and 1% above 700. 28% of the current freshmen were in the top fifth of their class; 59% were in the top two fifths.

Requirements: The SAT I or ACT is required. In addition, applicants must have 16 academic credits or Carnegie units, including 4 in English, 3 in math, 2 each in science lab and social studies, and 5 electives such as foreign language and history. An essay and interview are recommended for some applicants, as are a portfolio and audition. The GED is accepted. AP and CLEP credits are accepted. Important factors in the admissions decision are advanced placement or honor courses, recommendations by school officials, and evidence of special talent.

Procedure: Freshmen are admitted fall and spring. Entrance exams should be taken by January 31. There are early decision, early admissions, and deferred admissions plans. There is a rolling admissions plan. Early decision applications should be filed by April 1; regular applications, by May 1 for fall entry, along with a $50 fee. Notification is sent on a rolling basis. 75 applicants were on the 2003 waiting list; 25 were admitted. Applications are accepted on-line through *www2.wpunj.edu/ admissn/apply_now.cfm.*

Transfer: 896 transfer students enrolled in 2002-2003. Transfer students need a minimum GPA of 2.0 (business, nursing, computer science, and education students need a 2.5 GPA) and at least 12 credit hours earned. 30 of 128 credits required for the bachelor's degree must be completed at WPUNJ.

Visiting: There are regularly scheduled orientations for prospective students, including a campus tour, guest speakers, and dissemination of printed information. There are guides for informal visits and visitors may sit in on classes. To schedule a visit, contact the Admissions Office.

Financial Aid: In 2003-2004, 53% of all full-time freshmen and 47% of continuing full-time students received some form of financial aid. At least 38% of full-time freshmen and 37% of continuing full-time students received need-based aid. The average freshman award was $9113. Need-based scholarships or need-based grants averaged $5789; need-based self-help aid (loans and jobs) averaged $2664; and non-need-based awards and non-need-based scholarships averaged $5561. The average financial indebtedness of the 2003 graduate was $9981. WPUNJ is a member of CSS. The FAFSA and parent and student federal income tax forms are required. The deadline for filing freshman financial aid applications for fall entry is April 1.

International Students: They must score 550 on the written TOEFL.

Computers: The mainframe is an IBM 3099. There are also PCs available for student use. All students may access the system at all times. There are no time limits. The fee is $30.

Graduates: From July 1, 2002 to June 30, 2003, 1449 bachelor's degrees were awarded. The most popular majors were social studies/history (19%), business and marketing (18%), and communications/communicatons technologies (14%).

Admissions Contact: Director of Admissions. Web: *www.wpunj.edu*

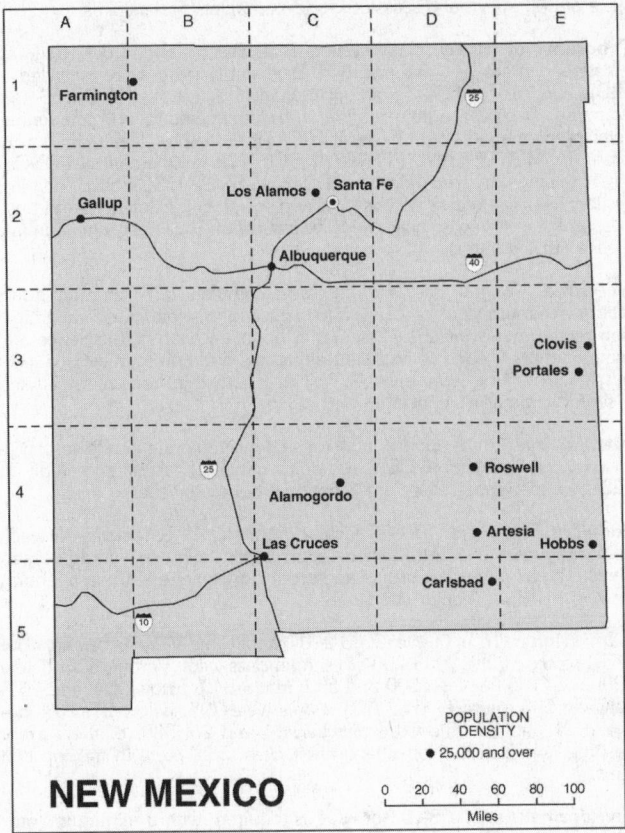

NEW MEXICO

POPULATION DENSITY
● 25,000 and over

0 20 40 60 80 100
Miles

COLLEGE OF SANTA FE
C-2

Santa Fe, NM 87505-7634

(505) 473-6133
(800) 456-2673; Fax: (505) 473-6129

Full-time: 389 men, 565 women	**Faculty:** 63; IIB, -$
Part-time: 214 men, 361 women	**Ph.D.s:** 81%
Graduate: 109 men, 283 women	**Student/Faculty:** 15 to 1
Year: semesters, summer session	**Tuition:** $19,505
Application Deadline: rolling	**Room & Board:** $5788
Freshman Class: 503 applied, 407 accepted, 174 enrolled	
SAT I Verbal/Math: 580/545	**ACT:** 22 **COMPETITIVE+**

The College of Santa Fe, founded in 1874, is a private comprehensive institution grounded in a strong liberal arts curriculum and distinguished by its programs in the creative arts. There are 8 undergraduate and 2 graduate schools. In addition to regional accreditation, CSF has baccalaureate program accreditation with IACBE and NCATE. The 3 libraries contain 145,946 volumes, 88,490 microform items, and 12,114 audio/video tapes/CDs, and subscribe to 411 periodicals. Computerized library services include the card catalog, interlibrary loans, database searching, and Internet access. Special learning facilities include a learning resource center, an art gallery, a professional sound stage for film and video, a visual arts center, a theater center, and a digital center. The 98-acre campus is in a suburban area 60 miles north of Albuquerque. Including any residence halls, there are 100 buildings.

Student Life: 82% of undergraduates are from out of state, mostly the Southwest. Students are from 45 states, 5 foreign countries, and Canada. 68% are from public schools. 75% are white; 12% Hispanic. Most are claim no religious affiliation. The average age of freshmen is 18; all undergraduates, 22. 32% do not continue beyond their first year; 50% remain to graduate.

Housing: 499 students can be accommodated in college housing, which includes single-sex and coed dorms and on-campus apartments. On-campus housing is guaranteed for the freshman year only. 58% of students live on campus; of those, 75% remain on campus on weekends. All students may keep cars.

Activities: There are no fraternities or sororities. There are several groups on campus, including Amnesty International, art, bowling, chorale, craft, crocheting/knitting, dance, drama, ethnic, film, gay, honors, international, Japanese Animation and Cultural Studies Club, literary

magazine, musical theater, newspaper, photography, political, professional, radio and TV, religious, social, social service, student government, Student Writers Association, and yearbook. Popular campus events include Day of Service, Fiesta de Santa Fe, and the semi-formal.

Sports: There is 1 intercollegiate sport for men and 1 for women, and 5 intramural sports for men and 5 for women. Facilities include a fitness center housing a gym, racquetball/squash courts, a weight room, a multipurpose exercise room, and an international-class tennis facility with indoor and outdoor courts.

Disabled Students: 95% of the campus is accessible. Wheelchair ramps, elevators, special parking, specially equipped rest rooms, special class scheduling, lowered drinking fountains, lowered telephones, special housing, and lowered light switches and controls in dorms are available.

Services: Counseling and information services are available, as is tutoring in every subject. There is remedial math, reading, and writing.

Campus Safety and Security: Measures include 24-hour foot and vehicle patrol, self-defense education, informal discussions, and pamphlets/posters/films. There are lighted pathways/sidewalks.

Programs of Study: CSF confers B.A., B.S., B.B.A., and B.F.A. degrees. Associate and master's degrees are also awarded. Bachelor's degrees are awarded in AGRICULTURE (conservation and regulation and environmental studies), BUSINESS (accounting, business administration and management, international business management, management information systems, and organizational behavior), COMMUNICATIONS AND THE ARTS (art history and appreciation, arts administration/management, communications, creative writing, dramatic arts, English, film arts, multimedia, music, musical theater, painting, performing arts, photography, printmaking, sculpture, studio art, technical and business writing, theater design, and theater management), COMPUTER AND PHYSICAL SCIENCE (computer science), EDUCATION (business, early childhood, elementary, English, science, secondary, and social science), ENGINEERING AND ENVIRONMENTAL DESIGN (environmental science), SOCIAL SCIENCE (applied psychology, counseling/psychology, criminal justice, humanities, interdisciplinary studies, pastoral studies, political science/government, psychology, public administration, religion, and Southwest American studies). Social sciences, humanities, and film are the strongest academically. Performing arts, moving image arts, and studio arts are the largest.

Required: Students must successfully complete 128 credit hours with a minimum GPA of 2.0 The 39-credit core curriculum includes courses in sciences, social sciences, humanities, creative expression, cultural diversity, ethical responsibility, and a capstone experience. Freshman are required to complete a 10-credit learning community course.

Special: CSF offers co-op programs in business, studio art, and film, internships in all areas of study, study abroad in 11 countries, work-study programs, dual majors, student-designed majors, a pass/fail option, credit by examination, and credit for life and work experience. There is 1 national honor society.

Faculty/Classroom: 58% of faculty are male; 42%, female. All teach undergraduates. The average class size in an introductory lecture is 19; in a laboratory, 10; and in a regular course, 14.

Admissions: 81% of the 2003-2004 applicants were accepted. The SAT I scores for the 2003-2004 freshman class were: Verbal--16% below 500, 38% between 500 and 599, 38% between 600 and 700, and 8% above 700; Math--32% below 500, 50% between 500 and 599, 15% between 600 and 700, and 3% above 700. The ACT scores were 32% below 21, 33% between 21 and 23, 20% between 24 and 26, 6% between 27 and 28, and 9% above 28. 36% of the current freshmen were in the top fifth of their class; 63% were in the top two fifths.

Requirements: The SAT I or ACT is required. In addition, graduation from an accredited secondary school is required.The GED is accepted. Applicants must have 18 academic credits, including 4 years of English, 2 each of math, science, and social studies, and the remainder in college-prep courses. An essay, an interview, and a letter of recommendation from a teacher and a counselor are required. A portfolio or audition is required for specific majors. AP and CLEP credits are accepted. Important factors in the admissions decision are evidence of special talent, recommendations by school officials, and advanced placement or honor courses.

Procedure: Freshmen are admitted to all sessions. Entrance exams should be taken in the junior year of high school. There are early decision, early admissions, and deferred admissions plans. Early decision applications should be filed by November 15; regular applications are rolling for fall entry. Notification of early decision is sent December 15; regular decision, on a rolling basis. 13 early decision candidates were accepted for the 2003-2004 class The fall 2003 application fee was $35. Applications are accepted on-line through *www.csf.edu*.

Transfer: 186 transfer students enrolled in 2002-2003. Applicants must submit an official high school transcript, official transcripts from all previous colleges, and SAT I or ACT scores. An interview is recommended.

30 of 128 credits required for the bachelor's degree must be completed at CSF.

Visiting: There are regularly scheduled orientations for prospective students, including campus tours, departmental receptions, a meeting with an admissions counselor, a campus event, and an outdoor activity. Students are housed with current students and eat in the campus dining room. There are guides for informal visits and visitors may sit in on classes and stay overnight. To schedule a visit, contact the Office of Admissions at *admissions@csf.edu*.

Financial Aid: In 2003-2004, 80% of all full-time freshmen and 90% of continuing full-time students received some form of financial aid. 54% of full-time freshmen and 67% of continuing full-time students received need-based aid. The average freshman award was $20,814. Need-based scholarships or need-based grants averaged $10,266 ($24,564 maximum); need-based self-help aid (loans and jobs) averaged $5306 ($10,625 maximum); non-need-based athletic scholarships averaged $27,240 (maximum); and other non-need-based awards and non-need-based scholarships averaged $3868 ($5000 maximum). 41% of undergraduates work part time. Average annual earnings from campus work are $2000. The average financial indebtedness of the 2003 graduate was $25,000. CSF is a member of CSS. The FAFSA and tax returns are required. The priority date for freshman financial aid applications for fall entry is March 15. The deadline for filing freshman financial aid applications for fall entry is November 3.

International Students: There are 5 international students enrolled. They must score 550 on the written TOEFL or 213 on the electronic version and also take the SAT I or the ACT.

Computers: The mainframe is an HP D 900. The college has 107 networked computers available for students at 11 different locations. Residence halls and several academic buildings also have wireless access to the Internet. All students may access the system. There are no time limits and no fees.

Graduates: From July 1, 2002 to June 30, 2003, 306 bachelor's degrees were awarded. The most popular majors were studio art (30%), film (16%), and psychology (12%). In an average class, 26% graduate in 4 years or less, 39% graduate in 5 years or less, and 50% graduate in 6 years or less. 60 companies recruited on campus in 2002-2003. Of the 2002 graduating class, 31% were enrolled in graduate school within 6 months of graduation and 88% were employed.

Admissions Contact: Dale H. Reinhart, Vice President for Enrollment. E-mail: *admissions@csf.edu* Web: *www.csf.edu*

COLLEGE OF THE SOUTHWEST
Hobbs, NM 88240-9987

E-4

(505) 392-6563
(800) 530-4400; Fax: (505) 392-6006

Full-time: 155 men, 315 women	**Faculty:** 19
Part-time: 79 men, 147 women	**Ph.D.s:** 38%
Graduate: 35 men, 157 women	**Student/Faculty:** 25 to 1
Year: semesters, summer session	**Tuition:** $7020
Application Deadline: open	**Room & Board:** $2300
Freshman Class: 592 applied, 93 accepted, 64 enrolled	
SAT I Verbal/Math: 436/455	**ACT:** 18 COMPETITIVE+

College of the Southwest, founded in 1962, is a independent college offering undergraduate programs in arts and sciences, business, education, psychology, and criminal justice. Graduate programs are offered in education. Information in this profile refers to the Hobbs and Carlsbad campuses, as well as distance-education students. The library contains 74,049 volumes, 23,209 microform items, and 1538 audio/video tapes/CDs, and subscribes to 302 periodicals. Computerized library services include the card catalog, interlibrary loans, and database searching. Special learning facilities include a learning resource center. The 162-acre campus is in a small town 110 miles southwest of Lubbock, Texas. Including any residence halls, there are 10 buildings.

Student Life: 82% of undergraduates are from New Mexico. Students are from 9 states, 6 foreign countries, and Canada. 66% are white; 26% Hispanic. The average age of freshmen is 19; all undergraduates, 29. 40% do not continue beyond their first year; 30% remain to graduate.

Housing: 119 students can be accommodated in college housing, which includes single-sex dorms and on-campus apartments. On-campus housing is available on a first-come, first-served basis. Priority is given to out-of-town students. 84% of students commute. Alcohol is not permitted. All students may keep cars.

Activities: There are no fraternities or sororities. There are 7 groups on campus, including chorus, drama, honors, newspaper, professional, and student government. Popular campus events include Annual Students in Free Enterprise Dinner and Award Presentation, Family Week, and speakers' presentations.

Sports: There are 3 intercollegiate sports for men and 2 for women, and 5 intramural sports for men and 5 for women. Facilities include soccer and baseball fields, a game room, and a physical fitness center with a multipurpose gym, racquetball courts, and physiology lab.

Disabled Students: All of the campus is accessible. Wheelchair ramps, special parking, and specially equipped rest rooms are available.

Services: Counseling and information services are available, as is tutoring in most subjects. There is remedial math and writing.

Campus Safety and Security: Measures include 24-hour foot and vehicle patrol, informal discussions, and pamphlets/posters/films.

Programs of Study: CSW confers B.S., B.A.S., and B.B.A. degrees. Master's degrees are also awarded. Bachelor's degrees are awarded in BIOLOGICAL SCIENCE (biology/biological science), BUSINESS (accounting, business administration and management, and marketing/retailing/merchandising), COMMUNICATIONS AND THE ARTS (English), COMPUTER AND PHYSICAL SCIENCE (mathematics), EDUCATION (elementary, secondary, and special), SOCIAL SCIENCE (criminal justice, history, prelaw, psychology, and sociology). Education and business are the strongest academically. Education, business, and criminal justice are the largest.

Required: To graduate, students must complete 128 semester hours with a minimum GPA of 2.0 (2.5 for education majors). General education requirements include 12 semester hours each of social science and math/science, 9 each of humanities/fine arts and communications, 6 of religion, and 3 of economics, as well as a course in free enterprise and a senior seminar in leadership and ethics.

Special: Internships are available for students majoring in business, psychology, and education. CSW also offers nondegree study and credit for military experience. There are 2 national honor societies.

Faculty/Classroom: 51% of faculty are male; 49%, female. All teach undergraduates. No introductory courses are taught by graduate students. The average class size in an introductory lecture is 15; in a laboratory, 7; and in a regular course, 12.

Admissions: 16% of the 2003-2004 applicants were accepted. The SAT I scores for the 2003-2004 freshman class were: Verbal--80% below 500, and 20% between 500 and 599; Math--64% below 500, and 36% between 500 and 599. The ACT scores were 70% below 21, 20% between 21 and 23, and 10% between 24 and 26. 28% of the current freshmen were in the top fifth of their class; 53% were in the top two fifths.

Requirements: The SAT I or ACT is required, with a minimum composite score of 19 on the ACT or 910 on the SAT I. Applicants must be graduates of an accredited secondary school or have a GED certificate. CSW requires applicants to be in the upper 50% of their class. A GPA of 2.0 is required. AP and CLEP credits are accepted. Important factors in the admissions decision are advanced placement or honor courses, extracurricular activities record, and ability to finance college education.

Procedure: Freshmen are admitted to all sessions. There is a rolling admissions plan. Application deadlines are open. Notification is sent on a rolling basis. The fall 2003 application fee was $25.

Transfer: 130 transfer students enrolled in a recent year. Applicants must present a minimum GPA of 2.0 and official transcripts from all colleges attended. 30 of 128 credits required for the bachelor's degree must be completed at CSW.

Visiting: There are guides for informal visits and visitors may sit in on classes and stay overnight. To schedule a visit, contact Charlotte Smith, Director of Admissions at *csmith@csw.edu*.

Financial Aid: In a recent year, 93% of all full-time freshmen received some form of financial aid. 43% of full-time freshmen and 84% of continuing full-time students received need-based aid. The average freshman award was $5581. 17% of undergraduates work part time. Average annual earnings from campus work are $2000. The average financial indebtedness of a recent graduate was $10,500. The FAFSA and the college's own financial statement are required. The deadline for filing freshman financial aid applications for fall entry is June 15.

International Students: There were 10 international students enrolled in a recent year. They must score 550 on the written TOEFL and also take the SAT I or the ACT.

Computers: Macs and PCs are located in the computer lab and science building.

Graduates: From July 1, 2002 to June 30, 2003, 131 bachelor's degrees were awarded. The most popular majors were education (40%), psychology (11%), and accounting (8%). In an average class, 19% graduate in 5 years or less. 10 companies recruited on campus in 2002-2003. Of the 2002 graduating class, 13% were enrolled in graduate school within 6 months of graduation and 80% were employed.

Admissions Contact: Karen Workentin, Dean of Admissions. E-mail: *kworkentin@csw.edu* Web: *www.csw.edu*

EASTERN NEW MEXICO UNIVERSITY E-3
Portales, NM 88130
(505) 562-2178
(800) 367-3668; Fax: (505) 562-2118

Full-time: 1094 men, 1363 women	**Faculty:** 134; IIA, --$
Part-time: 185 men, 382 women	**Ph.Ds:** 96%
Graduate: 187 men, 514 women	**Student/Faculty:** 18 to 1
Year: semesters, summer session	**Tuition:** $2472 ($8028)
Application Deadline: open	**Room & Board:** $4290
Freshman Class: 1810 applied, 1342 accepted, 558 enrolled	
SAT I Verbal/Math: 472/461	**ACT:** 19 **LESS COMPETITIVE**

Eastern New Mexico University, founded in 1934, is a public institution offering programs in the liberal arts and sciences, as well as education, business, fine arts, and vocational and technical fields. There are 4 undergraduate schools and 1 graduate school. In addition to regional accreditation, Eastern has baccalaureate program accreditation with ACBSP, ASLA, NASM, NCATE, and NLN. The library contains 305,108 volumes, 738,873 microform items, and 26,408 audio/video tapes/CDs, and subscribes to 1800 periodicals. Computerized library services include the card catalog, interlibrary loans, and database searching. Special learning facilities include a learning resource center, art gallery, natural history museum, radio station, TV station, and nearby important archeological sites. The 400-acre campus is in a small town 120 miles northeast of Lubbock, Texas. Including any residence halls, there are 50 buildings.

Student Life: 83% of undergraduates are from New Mexico. Students are from 41 states, 8 foreign countries, and Canada. 59% are white; 27% Hispanic. 41% are Protestant; 25% Catholic; 8% claim no religious affiliation. The average age of freshmen is 18; all undergraduates, 24. 40% do not continue beyond their first year.

Housing: 1208 students can be accommodated in college housing, which includes single-sex and coed dorms, on-campus apartments, married-student housing, and freshmen-only living areas. On-campus housing is guaranteed for all 4 years. 72% of students commute. Alcohol is not permitted. All students may keep cars.

Activities: There are 2 national sororities. There are 51 groups on campus, including art, band, cheerleading, choir, chorus, computers, dance, debate, drama, drill team, ethnic, forensics, gay, honors, international, jazz band, literary magazine, marching band, musical theater, newspaper, orchestra, pep band, photography, political, professional, radio and TV, religious, social, social service, steel drum band, student government, and yearbook. Popular campus events include Green and Silver Breakthrough, Peanut Valley Festival, and Fiesta International.

Sports: There are 6 intercollegiate sports for men and 8 for women, and 15 intramural sports for men and 15 for women. Facilities include a 5200-seat arena, tennis courts, an indoor pool, a 5300-seat stadium, and handball and racquetball courts.

Disabled Students: All of the campus is accessible. Wheelchair ramps, elevators, special parking, specially equipped rest rooms, special class scheduling, lowered drinking fountains, special housing, automatic door openers, and curb cuts are available.

Services: Counseling and information services are available, as is tutoring in every subject. There is a reader service for the blind, and remedial math, reading, and writing.

Campus Safety and Security: Measures include 24-hour foot and vehicle patrol, self-defense education, security escort services, and pamphlets/posters/films. There are emergency telephones and lighted pathways/sidewalks.

Programs of Study: Eastern confers B.A., B.S., B.A.E., B.B.A., B.F.A., B.M., B.M.E., B.S.E., and B.U.S. degrees. Associate and master's degrees are also awarded. Bachelor's degrees are awarded in AGRICULTURE (agricultural business management, agriculture, and wildlife management), BIOLOGICAL SCIENCE (biology/biological science), BUSINESS (accounting, banking and finance, business administration and management, business economics, marketing/retailing/merchandising, and personnel management), COMMUNICATIONS AND THE ARTS (art, communications, dramatic arts, English, fine arts, journalism, music, music performance, Spanish, and speech/debate/rhetoric), COMPUTER AND PHYSICAL SCIENCE (chemistry, computer science, geology, information sciences and systems, mathematics, physics, and statistics), EDUCATION (agricultural, business, elementary, home economics, music, physical, and special), ENGINEERING AND ENVIRONMENTAL DESIGN (electrical/electronics engineering technology), HEALTH PROFESSIONS (medical laboratory technology, nursing, and speech pathology/audiology), SOCIAL SCIENCE (anthropology, criminal justice, economics, history, human services, political science/government, psychology, religion, social studies, and sociology). Business is the strongest academically. Education, biology, and business administration are the largest.

Required: To graduate, students must earn 128 credit hours, 36 in the major, with a minimum GPA of 2.0. Required courses include those in English, science, math, social studies, humanities, fine arts, and phys ed.

Special: The school offers co-op programs in wildlife and fisheries and communication, internships, study abroad in 3 countries work-study programs, student-designed majors, a general studies degree, credit for life, military, and work experience, nondegree study, and pass/fail options. There are 2 national honor societies and a freshman honors program.

Faculty/Classroom: 54% of faculty are male; 46%, female. 95% teach undergraduates. Graduate students teach 11% of introductory courses.

Admissions: 74% of the 2003-2004 applicants were accepted. The SAT I scores for the 2003-2004 freshman class were: Verbal--60% below 500, 29% between 500 and 599, 8% between 600 and 700, and 3% above 700; Math--63% below 500, 31% between 500 and 599, and 6% between 600 and 700. The ACT scores were 68% below 21, 19% between 21 and 23, 10% between 24 and 26, 2% between 27 and 28, and 2% above 28. 21% of the current freshmen were in the top fifth of their class; 51% were in the top two fifths. 8 freshmen graduated first in their class.

Requirements: The SAT I or ACT is required, with a minimum required composite score of 17 on the ACT or 720 on the SAT I or a GPA of 2.25. Applicants must be high school graduates or have the GED, having earned 20 units, including 4 in English, 3 in math, 2 in science, and 1 each in history, music, and social studies. Provisional and special admissions are available. AP and CLEP credits are accepted.

Procedure: Freshmen are admitted to all sessions. Entrance exams should be taken in the junior or senior year. There is a rolling admissions plan. Application deadlines are open. Applications are accepted on-line through the school's web site.

Transfer: 288 transfer students enrolled in 2002-2003. Transfer students must have a minimum GPA of 2.0. 32 of 128 credits required for the bachelor's degree must be completed at Eastern.

Visiting: There are regularly scheduled orientations for prospective students, including meetings with admissions, financial aid, and faculty, a tour of campus, and a meal in the dining hall. There are guides for informal visits and visitors may sit in on classes and stay overnight. To schedule a visit, contact the Admissions Office.

Financial Aid: In 2003-2004, 69% of all full-time freshmen and 77% of continuing full-time students received some form of financial aid. 60% of full-time freshmen and 47% of continuing full-time students received need-based aid. The average freshman award was $6274. Average annual earnings from campus work are $2800. The average financial indebtedness of the 2003 graduate was $9532. The FAFSA, the college's own financial statement, and an institutional scholarship form are required. The deadline for filing freshman financial aid applications for fall entry is March 1.

International Students: There are 11 international students enrolled. The school actively recruits these students. They must score 500 on the written TOEFL or 175 on the electronic version and also take the SAT I or the ACT, scoring 17 on the ACT.

Computers: The mainframe is an IBM AS/400. Computer accounts are available to all students on campus. Access includes Internet and e-mail. Students have access to the College of Business's 30 PCs, the campuswide computer center that houses 75 PCs, and the 30-station library computer center. Network access is also available from all residence halls. All students may access the system. There are no time limits and no fees.

Graduates: From July 1, 2002 to June 30, 2003, 524 bachelor's degrees were awarded. The most popular majors were elementary education (14%), university studies (11%), and criminal justice (8%). In an average class, 10% graduate in 4 years or less, 23% graduate in 5 years or less, and 31% graduate in 6 years or less. 95 companies recruited on campus in 2002-2003.

Admissions Contact: Phyllis Seefeld, Admissions.
E-mail: *phyllis.seefeld@enmu.edu* Web: *www.enmu.edu*

NEW MEXICO HIGHLANDS UNIVERSITY D-2
Las Vegas, NM 87701
(505) 454-3434
(800) 338-6648; Fax: (505) 454-3552

Full-time: 642 men, 744 women	**Faculty:** 116
Part-time: 214 men, 503 women	**Ph.D.s:** 75%
Graduate: 583 men, 1274 women	**Student/Faculty:** 12 to 1
Year: semesters, summer session	**Tuition:** $2184 ($9096)
Application Deadline: open	**Room & Board:** $3998
Freshman Class: 881 applied, 720 accepted, 227 enrolled	
ACT: 17	**LESS COMPETITIVE**

New Mexico Highlands University, founded in 1893, is a state-supported institution offering undergraduate programs in liberal and fine arts, science and engineering, and professional studies. There are 4 undergraduate schools and 1 graduate school. In addition to regional accreditation, Highlands University has baccalaureate program accreditation with ABET and CSWE. The library contains 522,500 volumes, and subscribes to 1300 periodicals. Computerized library services include the card catalog, interlibrary loans, and database searching. Special learning facilities include a learning resource center, art gallery, radio station, TV station, and a video production studio. The 175-acre campus is in a small town 65 miles northeast of Santa Fe. Including any residence halls, there are 38 buildings.

Student Life: 93% of undergraduates are from New Mexico. Students are from 41 states, 9 foreign countries, and Canada. 97% are from public schools. 58% are Hispanic; 26% white. The average age of freshmen is 19; all undergraduates, 25. 43% do not continue beyond their first year; 24% remain to graduate.

Housing: 480 students can be accommodated in college housing, which includes single-sex and coed dorms, on-campus apartments, and married-student housing. On-campus housing is guaranteed for the freshman year only and is available on a first-come, first-served basis. All students may keep cars.

Activities: There are no fraternities or sororities. There are 31 groups on campus, including art, band, cheerleading, choir, chorale, chorus, departmental, drama, ethnic, film, honors, international, jazz band, marching band, newspaper, photography, political, radio and TV, religious, social service, student government, and yearbook. Popular campus events include Multicultural Week and Career Day.

Sports: There are 4 intercollegiate sports for men and 3 for women, and 8 intramural sports for men and 8 for women. Facilities include a 5000-seat football stadium, a 3600-seat arena, an indoor swimming pool, a weight room, athletic fields, a 9-hole golf course, and tennis, racquetball, and basketball courts. Hiking and skiing are nearby.

Disabled Students: 95% of the campus is accessible. Wheelchair ramps, elevators, special parking, specially equipped rest rooms, lowered drinking fountains, and lowered telephones are available.

Services: Counseling and information services are available, as is tutoring in most subjects. There is a reader service for the blind and remedial math, reading, and writing.

Campus Safety and Security: Measures include 24-hour foot and vehicle patrol, self-defense education, security escort services, and informal discussions. There are pamphlets/posters/films, emergency telephones, and lighted pathways/sidewalks.

Programs of Study: Highlands University confers B.A., B.S., B.B.A., B.F.A., B.S.E., and B.S.W. degrees. Associate and master's degrees are also awarded. Bachelor's degrees are awarded in AGRICULTURE (natural resource management), BIOLOGICAL SCIENCE (biology/biological science), BUSINESS (accounting, banking and finance, business administration and management, management information systems, marketing/retailing/merchandising, and recreation and leisure services), COMMUNICATIONS AND THE ARTS (art, communications, English, graphic design, music, and Spanish), COMPUTER AND PHYSICAL SCIENCE (chemistry, computer science, mathematics, and physics), EDUCATION (early childhood, elementary, science, special, and technical), ENGINEERING AND ENVIRONMENTAL DESIGN (engineering and environmental science), HEALTH PROFESSIONS (health, premedicine, and preveterinary science), SOCIAL SCIENCE (anthropology, history, physical fitness/movement, political science/government, prelaw, psychology, social work, and sociology). Engineering, physical sciences, and psychology are the strongest academically. Education, business administration, and social work are the largest.

Required: Students must complete 40 to 51 credits of core curriculum requirements, including courses in English, history, science, social environment, thought and critical analysis, fine arts, literature, communicating skills, and phys ed. Proficiency in language and math must be demonstrated. A minimum of 128 credits, including at least 30 in the major, with a GPA of at least 2.0 is required to graduate.

Special: Highlands offers practicum, internship, study abroad in 2 countries, and field-study courses; cooperative programs in most majors; internships in education; minors in geology, physics, secondary education, philosophy, and theater; and credit for military training. There are 2 national honor societies, including Phi Beta Kappa, and a freshman honors program.

Faculty/Classroom: 60% of faculty are male; 39%, female. All teach undergraduates and 20% both teach and do research. No introductory courses are taught by graduate students. The average class size in an introductory lecture is 42; in a laboratory, 15; and in a regular course, 18.

Admissions: 82% of the 2003-2004 applicants were accepted. The SAT I scores for the 2003-2004 freshman class were: Verbal--77% below 500, and 23% between 500 and 599; Math--65% below 500, 34% between 500 and 599, and 1% between 600 and 700. The ACT scores were 82% below 21, 16% between 21 and 23, 1% between 24 and 26, and 1% above 28. 18% of the current freshmen were in the top fifth of their class; 55% were in the top two fifths.

Requirements: The ACT is required; SAT I scores may be substituted. Scores are used for placement purposes. Applicants should be graduates of an accredited secondary school; the GED is accepted. A GPA of 2.0 is required. AP and CLEP credits are accepted. Important factors in the admissions decision are advanced placement or honor courses, evidence of special talent, and recommendations by school officials.

Procedure: Freshmen are admitted to all sessions. There are early decision and deferred admissions plans. There is a rolling admissions plan. Application deadlines are open. The fall 2003 application fee was $15. Applications are accepted on computer disk and on-line through the school's web site.

Transfer: Transfer applicants with 16 or more semester credit hours must have at least a 2.0 GPA. 32 of 128 credits required for the bachelor's degree must be completed at Highlands University.

Visiting: There are regularly scheduled orientations for prospective students, available on a call-in basis. There are guides for informal visits and visitors may sit in on classes and stay overnight. To schedule a visit, contact the Admissions Office at (505) 454-3593.

Financial Aid: 25% of undergraduates work part time. Average annual earnings from campus work are $2000. The FAFSA is required.

International Students: They must score 500 on the written TOEFL.

Computers: The mainframe is a Compaq Alpha servers. There are computer labs located in various buildings, including several dorms. All students may access the system 24 hours daily. There are no time limits and no fees. It is strongly recommended that all students have a personal computer.

Graduates: From July 1, 2002 to June 30, 2003, 228 bachelor's degrees were awarded. In an average class, 39% graduate in 6 years or less. 16 companies recruited on campus in 2002-2003. Of the 2002 graduating class, 24% were enrolled in graduate school within 6 months of graduation and 79% were employed.

Admissions Contact: John Coca, Director of Admissions. A video is available. E-mail: *admissions@nmhu.edu* Web: *www.nmhu.edu*

NEW MEXICO INSTITUTE OF MINING AND TECHNOLOGY   C-3
Socorro, NM 87801

(505) 835-5424
(800) 428-TECH; Fax: (505) 835-5989

Full-time: 822 men, 268 women	Faculty: 115
Part-time: 106 men, 168 women	Ph.D.s: 98%
Graduate: 271 men, 162 women	Student/Faculty: 9 to 1
Year: semesters, summer session	Tuition: $3080 ($9601)
Application Deadline: August 1	Room & Board: $4500
Freshman Class: 363 applied, 356 accepted, 285 enrolled	
SAT I Verbal/Math: 620/630	ACT: 26 NONCOMPETITIVE

New Mexico Institute of Mining and Technology, founded in 1889 as the New Mexico School of Mines, is a science and engineering university. It has 4 research-associated divisions: the New Mexico Bureau of Geology and Mineral Resources, the Energetic Materials Research and Testing Center, the Petroleum Recovery Research Center, and the Langmuir Laboratory for Atmospheric Research. There is 1 graduate school. In addition to regional accreditation, New Mexico Tech has baccalaureate program accreditation with ABET. The library contains 321,829 volumes, 217,540 microform items, and 2526 audio/video tapes/CDs, and subscribes to 884 periodicals. Computerized library services include the card catalog, interlibrary loans, database searching, and Internet access. Special learning facilities include a radio station, mineral museum, seismic research mine, and campus astronomical observatory. The 320-acre campus is in a small town 75 miles south of Albuquerque. Including any residence halls, there are 28 buildings.

Student Life: 83% of undergraduates are from New Mexico. Students are from 50 states, 38 foreign countries, and Canada. 70% are white; 19% Hispanic. The average age of freshmen is 18; all undergraduates, 21. 26% do not continue beyond their first year; 40% remain to graduate.

Housing: 644 students can be accommodated in college housing, which includes single-sex and coed dorms, on-campus apartments, off-campus apartments, and married-student housing. On-campus housing is available on a first-come, first-served basis. 56% of students commute. Alcohol is not permitted. All students may keep cars.

Activities: There are no fraternities or sororities. There are 55 groups on campus, including art, band, chess, chorus, computers, drama, ethnic, gay, honors, international, jazz band, musical theater, orchestra, political, professional, radio and TV, religious, social, social service, student government, and yearbook. Popular campus events include 49ers, Spring Fling, and International Student Exhibit.

Sports: There are 9 intramural sports for men and 9 for women. Facilities include 2 gyms, tennis courts, a swimming pool, an 18-hole golf course, an athletic field, sand volleyball courts, a climbing wall, a weight/fitness room, racquetball/squash courts, a Ping-Pong area, and a martial arts/combatives room.

Disabled Students: Wheelchair ramps, elevators, special parking, specially equipped rest rooms, lowered drinking fountains, and lowered telephones are available. Most of the campus is wheelchair accessible.

Services: Counseling and information services are available, as is tutoring in most subjects. There is a reader service for the blind.

Campus Safety and Security: Measures include 24-hour foot and vehicle patrol, self-defense education, security escort services, and informal discussions. There are pamphlets/posters/films, emergency telephones, and lighted pathways/sidewalks.

Programs of Study: New Mexico Tech confers B.S. and B.G.S. degrees. Associate, master's, and doctoral degrees are also awarded. Bachelor's degrees are awarded in BIOLOGICAL SCIENCE (biology/

biological science), BUSINESS (business administration and management), COMMUNICATIONS AND THE ARTS (technical and business writing), COMPUTER AND PHYSICAL SCIENCE (chemistry, computer science, geology, geophysics and seismology, mathematics, and physics), ENGINEERING AND ENVIRONMENTAL DESIGN (chemical engineering, electrical/electronics engineering, engineering, engineering mechanics, environmental engineering, environmental science, materials engineering, metallurgical engineering, mining and mineral engineering, and petroleum/natural gas engineering), SOCIAL SCIENCE (liberal arts/general studies and psychology). Physics and electrical engineering are the strongest academically. Electrical engineering, computer science, and physics are the largest.

Required: The student must earn at least 130 credit hours to graduate, including 42 hours of basic science, consisting in part of 10 hours of physics and 8 each of chemistry, calculus, and biology/geology/engineering. Further distribution requirements include 18 hours of literature, philosophy, the arts, and social science, 9 hours each of written and spoken English, and a senior seminar or senior design project. The credit hours required in the major vary by program. The student must also maintain a cumulative GPA of 2.0.

Special: New Mexico Tech offers co-op programs in computer science and all engineering majors, internships in technical communications, and cross-registration with New Mexico State, University of New Mexico, and Los Alamos National Laboratories in the WERC consortium. There are dual majors offered in engineering, computer science, physics, and math, work programs, and student-designed majors in environmental science, general studies, and basic science. Nondegree study and pass/fail options are also available. There are 3-2 accelerated degree programs in geology and in science or engineering and hydrology. There are 4 national honor societies, and 4 departmental honors programs.

Faculty/Classroom: 81% of faculty are male; 19%, female. 95% teach undergraduates, and 95% both teach and do research. Graduate students teach 12% of introductory courses. The average class size in an introductory lecture is 18; in a laboratory, 12; and in a regular course, 18.

Admissions: 98% of the 2003-2004 applicants were accepted. The SAT I scores for the 2003-2004 freshman class were: Verbal--7% below 500, 27% between 500 and 599, 54% between 600 and 700, and 12% above 700; Math--2% below 500, 28% between 500 and 599, 53% between 600 and 700, and 17% above 700. The ACT scores were 1% between 21 and 23, 30% between 24 and 26, 52% between 27 and 28, and 17% above 28. 54% of the current freshmen were in the top quarter of their class; 88% were in the top half.

Requirements: The ACT is required, with a minimum score of 21. Applicants must be high school graduates or present a GED certificate. Students should have earned 15 academic credits, consisting of 4 units of English, 3 each of social science and math (2 beyond general math), and 2 of science (including 1 of lab science), and electives. A GPA of 2.5 is required. AP credits are accepted. Important factors in the admissions decision are advanced placement or honor courses, evidence of special talent, and extracurricular activities record.

Procedure: Freshmen are admitted to all sessions. Entrance exams should be taken by December of the senior year. There are early decision, early admissions, and deferred admissions plans. Applications should be filed by August 1 for fall entry and December 1 for spring entry. The fall 2003 application fee was $15. Notification is sent on a rolling basis. Applications are accepted on-line through *http://www.nmt.edu/mainpage/uginfo/application.html*, but the printout must be sent to the school.

Transfer: 40 transfer students enrolled in a recent year. Transfer students must have a GPA of 2.0 and have completed 30 semester hours of transferable credit. Those who have fewer than 30 credit hours, or who have not completed freshman English, must present a minimum ACT score of 21, as well as high school transcripts. 30 of 130 credits required for the bachelor's degree must be completed at New Mexico Tech.

Visiting: There are regularly scheduled orientations for prospective students, including 2 days of get-aquainted social activities, information sessions for parents and students, and transition sessions for parents. There are guides for informal visits and visitors may sit in on classes and stay overnight. To schedule a visit, contact the Admission Office.

Financial Aid: The FAFSA is required. The priority date for freshman financial aid applications for fall entry is March 1. The deadline for filing freshman financial aid applications for fall entry is June 1.

International Students: There are 28 international students enrolled. They must score 540 on the written TOEFL or 207 on the electronic version.

Computers: The mainframes are a dual SPARC 20, DEC Alpha 500 and DEC Alpha 400. Students may access the mainframe from PCs located in the computer center and in most departments as well as from their rooms via Ethernet connection or modem. All students may access the system 16 1/2 hours a day on site; and 24 hours a day via network. There are no time limits. The fee is $2 per semester. It is strongly recommended that all students have a personal computer.

Graduates: From July 1, 2002 to June 30, 2003, 179 bachelor's degrees were awarded. The most popular majors were engineering (33%),

physical sciences (23%), and computer and information sciences (16%). In an average class, 33% graduate in 5 years or less, and 40% graduate in 6 years or less.

Admissions Contact: Melissa Jaramillo-Fleming, Director of Admission. E-mail: *admission@admin.nmt.edu* Web: *http://www.nmt.edu*

NEW MEXICO STATE UNIVERSITY
Las Cruces, NM 88003-8001
C-4
(505) 646-3121
(800) 662-6678; Fax: (505) 646-6330

Full-time: 4486 men, 5312 women	Faculty: 660; I, --$
Part-time: 1278 men, 1721 women	Ph.D.s: 83%
Graduate: 1467 men, 1910 women	Student/Faculty: 15 to 1
Year: semesters, summer session	Tuition: $3372 ($11,250)
Application Deadline: open	Room & Board: $4560
Freshman Class: 5630 applied, 4739 accepted, 2067 enrolled	
ACT: 21	COMPETITIVE

New Mexico State University, founded in 1888, is a public institution offering undergraduate and graduate programs that include study in liberal arts, agriculture, business, engineering, health science, education, and visual and performing arts. There are 6 undergraduate schools and 1 graduate school. In addition to regional accreditation, NMSU has baccalaureate program accreditation with AACSB, ABET, ADA, AHEA, APA, CACREP, CAHEA, CCNE, CSWE, NASM, and NCATE. The 2 libraries contain 1,642,678 volumes and 1,410,674 microform items, and subscribe to 5975 periodicals. Computerized library services include the card catalog, interlibrary loans, and database searching. Special learning facilities include a learning resource center, art gallery, natural history museum, radio station, TV station, a 289-acre experimental farm and orchard, a 61,760-acre cattle and experimental ranch, and a 2160-acre recreational area in the Organ Mountains. The 900-acre campus is in an urban area 40 miles north of El Paso. Including any residence halls, there are 289 buildings.

Student Life: 82% of undergraduates are from New Mexico. Students are from 49 states, 71 foreign countries, and Canada. 47% are white; 42% Hispanic. The average age of freshmen is 18; all undergraduates, 23.

Housing: 2255 students can be accommodated in college housing, which includes single-sex and coed dorms, on-campus apartments, married-student housing, fraternity houses, and sorority houses. In addition, there are honors houses. On-campus housing is guaranteed for all 4 years. 82% of students commute. All students may keep cars.

Activities: There are 15 national fraternities and 5 national sororities. There are 253 groups on campus, including art, band, cheerleading, chess, choir, chorale, chorus, computers, dance, drama, drill team, drum and bugle corps, ethnic, gay, honors, international, jazz band, literary magazine, marching band, musical theater, newspaper, opera, orchestra, pep band, photography, political, professional, radio and TV, religious, social, social service, student government, and symphony. Popular campus events include Chicano Week, American Indian Week, and Black Week.

Sports: There are 6 intercollegiate sports for men and 9 for women, and 29 intramural sports for men and 27 for women. Facilities include a game room, a natatorium, tennis courts, playing fields, a gym, and rodeo grounds. One campus stadium seats 30,342 while the other seats more than 13,000.

Disabled Students: 95% of the campus is accessible. Wheelchair ramps, elevators, special parking, specially equipped rest rooms, lowered drinking fountains, lowered telephones, and priority registration are available.

Services: Counseling and information services are available, as is tutoring in most subjects. There is a reader service for the blind. Remedial classes are offered at the Dona Ana Branch Community College. There is also an interpreter for the hearing impaired.

Campus Safety and Security: Measures include 24-hour foot and vehicle patrol, self-defense education, security escort services, and shuttle buses. There are informal discussions, pamphlets/posters/films, emergency telephones, and lighted pathways/sidewalks.

Programs of Study: NMSU confers B.A., B.S., B.Ac., Bachelor of Human and Community Services, B.A.Ec., B.B.A., B.C.J., B.F.A., B.I.S., B.M., B.M.Ed., B.S.Ag., B.S.A.T.Ed., B.S.C.H., B.S.Ed., B.S. in Environmental Science, B.S. in Family and Consumer Sciences, B.S.N., and B.S.W. degrees. Associate, master's, and doctoral degrees are also awarded. Bachelor's degrees are awarded in AGRICULTURE (agricultural business management, agriculture, agronomy, animal science, horticulture, range/farm management, and soil science), BIOLOGICAL SCIENCE (biochemistry, biology/biological science, microbiology, nutrition, and wildlife biology), BUSINESS (accounting, banking and finance, business administration and management, business economics, fashion merchandising, hotel/motel and restaurant management, international business management, management information systems, marketing/retailing/merchandising, recreational facilities management, and tourism), COMMUNICATIONS AND THE ARTS (art, communications, dance, dramatic arts, English, fine arts, journalism, languages, and music), COMPUTER AND PHYSICAL SCIENCE (chemistry, computer science, geology, mathematics, and physics), EDUCATION (agricultural, athletic training, early childhood, elementary, home economics, music, physical, secondary, and special), ENGINEERING AND ENVIRONMENTAL DESIGN (chemical engineering, city/community/regional planning, civil engineering, electrical/electronics engineering, environmental engineering, environmental science, industrial engineering, mechanical engineering, and surveying engineering), HEALTH PROFESSIONS (community health work, nursing, and speech pathology/audiology), SOCIAL SCIENCE (anthropology, child psychology/development, criminal justice, economics, family/consumer studies, geography, history, philosophy, physical fitness/movement, political science/government, psychology, social work, and sociology). Elementary education, business administration, and criminal justice are the largest.

Required: All students must complete a minimum of 128 credits, including at least 50 upper-division credits. A minimum GPA of 2.0 is needed. Distribution requirements include communications, humanities, math, natural sciences, and social sciences.

Special: Internships, cooperative programs in engineering, math, science, teacher education, business, and other majors, dual majors, study abroad in 39 countries, work-study, nondegree study, and B.A.-B.S. degrees in biology, chemistry, and physics are available. There is cross-registration with the Dona Ana Branch Community College. There are 24 national honor societies, a freshman honors program, and 14 departmental honors programs.

Faculty/Classroom: 66% of faculty are male; 34%, female. All both teach and do research. Graduate students teach 10% of introductory courses. The average class size in an introductory lecture is 37; in a laboratory, 16; and in a regular course, 30.

Admissions: 84% of the 2003-2004 applicants were accepted. The ACT scores for the 2003-2004 freshman class were: 51% below 21, 25% between 21 and 23, 16% between 24 and 26, 5% between 27 and 28, and 3% above 28. 38% of the current freshmen were in the top fifth of their class; 69% were in the top two fifths. 28 freshmen graduated first in their class.

Requirements: Applicants must score 20 on the ACT or may take the SAT I (accepted, but not recommended) and submit a composite score of 780. The GED is accepted. Minimum high school preparation of 4 units of English, 3 of math, 2 beyond general science, and 1 foreign language/fine arts is required. A GPA of 2.0 is required. AP and CLEP credits are accepted.

Procedure: Freshmen are admitted to all sessions. Entrance exams should be taken during the high school junior or senior year. There is an early admissions plan. Application deadlines are open. Application fee is $15. Notification is sent on a rolling basis. Applications are accepted online through the school's web site.

Transfer: 756 transfer students enrolled in 2002-2003. Applicants must have a minimum GPA of 2.0. They need 30 credits to avoid freshman admission requirements. If the applicant has earned 30 academic credit hours or more, the ACT score will be waived. If the applicant has earned 48 academic credit hours or more, the high school transcript will be waived. 30 of 128 credits required for the bachelor's degree must be completed at NMSU.

Visiting: There are regularly scheduled orientations for prospective students, including meetings with admissions counselors, faculty members, and financial aid advisers and a tour of campus. There are guides for informal visits and visitors may sit in on classes and stay overnight. To schedule a visit, contact the Office of Admissions.

Financial Aid: In 2003-2004, need-based scholarships or need-based grants averaged $2012 ($4050 maximum); need-based self-help aid (loans and jobs) averaged $2335 ($3000 maximum); non-need-based athletic scholarships averaged $6579 ($10,532 maximum); and other non-need-based awards and non-need-based scholarships averaged $1538 ($18,000 maximum). 6% of undergraduates work part time. NMSU is a member of CSS. The FAFSA is required. The deadline for filing freshman financial aid applications for fall entry is March 1.

International Students: There are 115 international students enrolled. They must score 500 on the written TOEFL or take the MELAB.

Computers: The mainframe is an IBM 9672-R24. A number of PCs are available in academic areas, the library, and the student union. All students may access the system at any time. There are no time limits and no fees.

Graduates: From July 1, 2002 to June 30, 2003, 1927 bachelor's degrees were awarded. The most popular majors were elementary education (9%), criminal justice (4%), and accounting (4%). In an average class, 12% graduate in 4 years or less, 37% graduate in 5 years or less, and 46% graduate in 6 years or less. 636 companies recruited on campus in 2002-2003.

Admissions Contact: Angela Mora-Riley, Director of Admissions. A video is available. E-mail: *admissions@nmsu.edu* Web: *www.nmsu.edu/admissions.html*

SAINT JOHN'S COLLEGE
C-2
Santa Fe, NM 87505
(505) 984-6060
(800) 331-5232; Fax: (505) 984-6162

Full-time: 236 men, 196 women	**Faculty:** 68
Part-time: 1 man, 1 woman	**Ph.D.s:** 79%
Graduate: 62 men, 39 women	**Student/Faculty:** 6 to 1
Year: semesters, summer session	**Tuition:** $29,040
Application Deadline: open	**Room & Board:** $7320
Freshman Class: 338 applied, 275 accepted, 143 enrolled	
SAT I Verbal/Math: 690/600	**ACT:** 29 **VERY COMPETITIVE+**

St. John's College, founded in 1696, offers a curriculum based on the Great Books Program in which students and faculty work together in small discussion classes without lecture courses, written finals, or emphasis on grades. The program is a rigorous interdisciplinary curriculum based on great books—literature, math, philosophy, theology, sciences, political theory, music, history, economics—from Homer to Freud, Euclid to Einstein. The library contains 65,000 volumes and 8205 audio/video tapes/CDs, and subscribes to 135 periodicals. Computerized library services include the card catalog, interlibrary loans, and database searching. Special learning facilities include an art gallery, a music library, a search and rescue headquarters, and music practice rooms. The 250-acre campus is in a suburban area in Santa Fe. Including any residence halls, there are 31 buildings.

Student Life: 90% of undergraduates are from out of state, mostly the Southwest. Students are from 46 states, 8 foreign countries, and Canada. 58% are from public schools. 88% are white. The average age of freshmen is 19; all undergraduates, 20. 10% do not continue beyond their first year; 60% remain to graduate.

Housing: 329 students can be accommodated in college housing, which includes single-sex and coed dorms and on-campus apartments. In addition, there are smoke-free and alcohol-free residences. On-campus housing is guaranteed for the freshman year only and is available on a lottery system for upperclassmen. 75% of students live on campus; of those, all remain on campus on weekends. All students may keep cars.

Activities: There are no fraternities or sororities. There are 32 groups on campus, including art, chess, choir, chorale, chorus, computers, dance, drama, fencing, film, gay, jazz band, literary magazine, newspaper, orchestra, photography, search and rescue, social service, student government, and yearbook. Popular campus events include Oktoberfest, Halloween and Christmas parties, and Reality weekend.

Sports: There are 5 intramural sports for men and 5 for women. Facilities include a soccer field, a track, tennis courts, an outdoor basketball court, a gym with weight room, racquetball, squash, and basketball courts, nearby mountains, and a ski mountain 30 minutes from campus.

Disabled Students: 75% of the campus is accessible. Wheelchair ramps, elevators, special parking, specially equipped rest rooms, and special class scheduling are available.

Services: Counseling and information services are available, as is tutoring in every subject.

Campus Safety and Security: Measures include 24-hour foot and vehicle patrol, self-defense education, security escort services, and shuttle buses. There are informal discussions, pamphlets/posters/films, emergency telephones, and lighted pathways/sidewalks.

Programs of Study: St. John's confers the B.A. degree. Master's degrees are also awarded. Bachelor's degrees are awarded in SOCIAL SCIENCE (liberal arts/general studies).

Required: The college has 1 curriculum, based on the Great Books program for a total of 135 credits. Students attend seminars, preceptorials on specific works or topics, language, music, and math tutorials, and a 3-year science lab. Students take oral exams each semester and write annual essays. Sophomores take a math exam and seniors take a final essay and oral exam.

Special: Internships with alumni in a wide range of fields are available and students may transfer between the Santa Fe and Annapolis campuses. Work study programs are available with the state government, museums, galleries, Santa Fe Institute, businesses, and schools. Premedical studies at universities around the country and 4-1 teaching certification through the University of New Mexico are possible.

Faculty/Classroom: 71% of faculty are male; 29%, female. All teach undergraduates. No introductory courses are taught by graduate students. The average class size in an introductory lecture is 15; in a laboratory, 15; and in a regular course, 15.

Admissions: 81% of the 2003-2004 applicants were accepted. The SAT I scores for the 2003-2004 freshman class were: Verbal--1% below 500, 13% between 500 and 599, 55% between 600 and 700, and 31% above 700; Math--6% below 500, 31% between 500 and 599, 50% between 600 and 700, and 13% above 700. 37% of the current freshmen were in the top fifth of their class; 64% were in the top two fifths. There were 4 National Merit finalists and 12 semifinalists.

Requirements: Applicants must write 3 personal essays and submit 2 teacher references, a secondary school report including a reference from a school official, and transcripts of all academic work in high school and college. A campus visit and interview are recommended. 3 years of math and 2 years of foreign language are required; 4 years each of math, foreign language, English, and science are recommended. The GED is accepted for early admission candidates. The SAT I or ACT is required of early admission candidates. Important factors in the admissions decision are advanced placement or honor courses, evidence of special talent, and recommendations by school officials.

Procedure: Freshmen are admitted fall and spring. There are early admissions, deferred admissions, and rolling admissions plans. Application deadlines are open. It is receommended that regular decision applications for fall entry should be filed by March 1 and December 15 for spring entry.

Transfer: 35 transfer students enrolled in 2002-2003. St. John's accepts transfers only for its freshman class; no previous college credit is recognized. Admission requirements are the same as for freshmen. 135 of 135 credits required for the bachelor's degree must be completed at St. John's.

Visiting: There are regularly scheduled orientations for prospective students, including a tour of the campus and housing, class visits, and an interview. There are guides for informal visits and visitors may sit in on classes and stay overnight. To schedule a visit, contact the Admissions Office at *admissions@sjcsf.edu*.

Financial Aid: In 2003-2004, 69% of all full-time students received some form of financial aid. 66% of full-time freshmen and 68% of continuing full-time students received need-based aid. The average freshman award was $23,160, with $15,960 ($28,937 maximum) from need-based scholarships or need-based grants, and $7200 ($10,500 maximum) from need-based self-help aid (loans and jobs). 63% of undergraduates work part time. Average annual earnings from campus work are $2400. The average financial indebtedness of the 2003 graduate was $22,140. St. John's is a member of CSS. The CSS Profile or FAFSA, the Business/FARM Supplement, and non-custodial parent statement are required. The deadline for filing freshman financial aid applications for fall entry is February 15.

International Students: There are 12 international students enrolled. The school actively recruits these students. They must score 550 on the written TOEFL or 213 on the electronic version and also take the SAT I.

Computers: A computer lab with Macs, PCs, and printers is available to students. All students may access the system. There are no time limits and no fees.

Graduates: From July 1, 2002 to June 30, 2003, 80 bachelor's degrees were awarded. The most popular major was liberal arts (100%). In an average class, 53% graduate in 4 years or less, 63% graduate in 5 years or less, and 64% graduate in 6 years or less. 10 companies recruited on campus in 2002-2003. Of the 2002 graduating class, 9% were enrolled in graduate school within 6 months of graduation and 91% were employed.

Admissions Contact: Larry Clendenin, Director of Admissions. E-mail: *admissions@sjcsf.edu* Web: *http://www.sjcsf.edu*

UNIVERSITY OF NEW MEXICO
Albuquerque, NM 87131
C-2
(505) 277-2446
(800) 225-5866; Fax: (505) 277-6686

Full-time: 6082 men, 8048 women	**Faculty:** 1740; I, -$
Part-time: 1573 men, 2229 women	**Ph.D.s:** 87%
Graduate: 2860 men, 3915 women	**Student/Faculty:** 8 to 1
Year: semesters, summer session	**Tuition:** $3313 ($11,954)
Application Deadline: June 23	**Room & Board:** $5910
Freshman Class: 6752 applied, 5095 accepted, 3004 enrolled	
SAT I Verbal/Math: 540/530	**ACT:** 21	**COMPETITIVE**

The University of New Mexico, founded in 1889, is a public university offering instruction in liberal and fine arts, business, engineering, health science, teacher preparation, law, and technology. In addition to the main campuses, it has 4 campuses for 2-year study and 2 for graduate study. There are 11 undergraduate and 5 graduate schools. In addition to regional accreditation, UNM has baccalaureate program accreditation with AACSB, ABET, ACPE, CAHEA, NAAB, NASM, NCATE, NLN, and NRPA. The 10 libraries contain 2,411,476 volumes, 4,628,643 microform items, and 55,430 audio/video tapes/CDs, and subscribe to 17,607 periodicals. Computerized library services include the card catalog, interlibrary loans, and database searching. Special learning facilities include a learning resource center, art gallery, planetarium, radio station, TV station, robotics lab, photo-history collection, lithography and meteoritic institutes, observatory, and museums of geology, anthropology, biology, and art. The 875-acre campus is in an urban area within the city of Albuquerque. Including any residence halls, there are 229 buildings.

Student Life: 88% of undergraduates are from New Mexico. Students are from 50 states, 90 foreign countries, and Canada. 52% are white; 29% Hispanic. The average age of freshmen is 18; all undergraduates, 24. 24% do not continue beyond their first year; 44% remain to graduate.

Housing: 2547 students can be accommodated in college housing, which includes single-sex and coed dorms, on-campus apartments, married-student housing, fraternity houses, and sorority houses. In addition, there are honors houses and special-interest houses. On-campus housing is guaranteed for all 4 years. 89% of students commute. Alcohol is not permitted. All students may keep cars.

Activities: 4% of men belong to 12 national fraternities; 2% of women belong to 7 national sororities. There are 300 groups on campus, including art, band, cheerleading, chess, choir, chorale, chorus, computers, dance, debate, drama, drill team, ethnic, film, forensics, gay, honors, international, jazz band, literary magazine, marching band, musical theater, newspaper, opera, orchestra, pep band, photography, political, professional, radio and TV, religious, social, social service, student government, symphony, and yearbook. Popular campus events include Spring Fiesta, Welcome Back Days, and Hanging of the Greens.

Sports: There are 10 intercollegiate sports for men and 11 for women, and 22 intramural sports for men and 20 for women. Facilities include 2 gyms, a football field, basketball courts, 2 pools, weights, and racquetball and tennis courts. The stadium seats 30,000, the gym 7000, and the largest arena 20,000.

Disabled Students: 99% of the campus is accessible. Wheelchair ramps, elevators, special parking, specially equipped rest rooms, special class scheduling, and lowered drinking fountains are available.

Services: Counseling and information services are available, as is tutoring in most subjects. There is a reader service for the blind, and remedial math, reading, and writing.

Campus Safety and Security: Measures include 24-hour foot and vehicle patrol, self-defense education, security escort services, and shuttle buses. There are informal discussions, pamphlets/posters/films, emergency telephones, and lighted pathways/sidewalks.

Programs of Study: UNM confers B.A., B.S., B.A.Ed., B.B.A., B.E., B.F.A., B.M., B.S. Ed., and B.U.S. degrees. Associate, master's, and doctoral degrees are also awarded. Bachelor's degrees are awarded in BIOLOGICAL SCIENCE (biochemistry, biology/biological science, life science, and nutrition), BUSINESS (accounting, banking and finance, business administration and management, entrepreneurial studies, international business management, management science, marketing/retailing/merchandising, personnel management, and tourism), COMMUNICATIONS AND THE ARTS (art history and appreciation, classics, communications, comparative literature, creative writing, dance, dramatic arts, English, fine arts, French, German, journalism, languages, linguistics, media arts, music, Portuguese, Spanish, studio art, and technical and business writing), COMPUTER AND PHYSICAL SCIENCE (astrophysics, chemistry, computer science, earth science, mathematics, physics, and planetary and space science), EDUCATION (art, athletic training, bilingual/bicultural, business, early childhood, elementary, health, music, physical, science, special, and teaching English as a second/foreign language (TESOL/TEFOL)), ENGINEERING AND ENVIRONMENTAL DESIGN (architecture, chemical engineering, civil engineering, computer engineering, construction engineering, electrical/electronics engineering, environmental design, manufacturing engineering, mechanical engineering, and nuclear engineering), HEALTH PROFESSIONS (dental hygiene, emergency medical technologies, exercise science, medical laboratory technology, nursing, occupational therapy, pharmacy, physical therapy, physician's assistant, predentistry, premedicine, radiological science, and speech pathology/audiology), SOCIAL SCIENCE (African American studies, American studies, anthropology, Asian/Oriental studies, child care/child and family studies, criminal justice, dietetics, economics, European studies, family/consumer studies, geography, history, interpreter for the deaf, Latin American studies, parks and recreation management, philosophy, physical fitness/movement, political science/government, prelaw, psychology, and sociology). Biology, elementary education, and psychology are the largest.

Required: All students must take 2 English courses, including English composition, and complete the University Core Curriculum. A minimum of 128 credit hours is required, along with a GPA of 2.0.

Special: There is a 3-2 engineering program with the Anderson School of Management. Study abroad is available in 11 countries. The university offers cooperative programs, a Washington semester, work-study, dual and student-designed majors, a general studies degree, credit for military experience, nondegree study, and pass/fall options. There are 20 national honor societies, including Phi Beta Kappa, and a freshman honors program.

Faculty/Classroom: 58% of faculty are male; 42%, female.

Admissions: 75% of the 2003-2004 applicants were accepted. The SAT I scores for the 2003-2004 freshman class were: Verbal--30% below 500, 41% between 500 and 599, 26% between 600 and 700, and 3% above 700; Math--37% below 500, 39% between 500 and 599, 22% between 600 and 700, and 2% above 700. The ACT scores were 43% below 21, 27% between 21 and 23, 18% between 24 and 26, 7% between 27 and 28, and 5% above 28. 36% of the current freshmen were in the top fifth of their class; 66% were in the top two fifths.

Requirements: The SAT I or ACT is required. In addition, a total of 13 academic credits is required, including 4 years of English, 3 years of math, and 2 years each of foreign language, natural science (1 lab), and social science (1 U.S. History). A GED is accepted. A GPA of 2.25 is required. AP and CLEP credits are accepted. Important factors in the admissions decision are leadership record, evidence of special talent, and advanced placement or honor courses.

Procedure: Freshmen are admitted fall, spring, and summer. Entrance exams should be taken late in the junior or early in the senior year. There is an early admissions plan and a rolling admissions plan. Early decision application deadlines are rolling; regular applications should be filed by June 23 for fall entry, November 15 for spring entry, and May 1 for summer entry. Notification is sent on a rolling basis. The fall 2003 application fee was $20. Applications are accepted on-line through http://www.unm.edu.

Transfer: 1802 transfer students enrolled in 2002-2003. Applicants must have at least a 2.0 GPA in all transferable courses. 30 of 128 credits required for the bachelor's degree must be completed at UNM.

Visiting: There are regularly scheduled orientations for prospective students, including academic advisement, admissions and financial aid counseling, and a tour of the campus and housing. There are guides for informal visits and visitors may sit in on classes and stay overnight. To schedule a visit, contact Recruitment Services at (505) 277-2260 or www.unmlobos.edu.

Financial Aid: The FAFSA is required. The deadline for filing freshman financial aid applications for fall entry is March 1.

International Students: The school actively recruits these students. They must score 550 on the written TOEFL or 213 on the electronic version, or take the MELAB or the University of Cambridge English Examination.

Computers: The mainframes are an IBM Z series 800 2066-model, IBM RS 6000/370, 2 IBM RS 6000/390, Operating system: AIX 4.1, and 3 IBM RS6000/370. 451 terminals and PCs are available in 5 computing pods and 9 classrooms in various locations. All students may access the system. There are no time limits and no fees.

Graduates: In a recent year, 2548 bachelor's degrees were awarded. The most popular majors were university studies (9%), elementary education (8%), and biology (7%). In an average class, 46% graduate in 6 years or less. 252 companies recruited on campus in a recent year.

Admissions Contact: Cynthia Stuart, Director of Admissions.
E-mail: apply@unm.edu Web: http://www.unm.edu

WESTERN NEW MEXICO UNIVERSITY   B-4
Silver City, NM 88061

(505) 538-6106
(800) 222-9668; Fax: (505) 538-6127

Full-time: 200 men, 300 women	Faculty: IIA, --$
Part-time: 40 men, 80 women	Ph.D.s: n/av
Graduate: 70 men, 130 women	Student/Faculty: 7 to 1
Year: semesters, summer session	Tuition: $2371 ($8923)
Application Deadline: see profile	Room & Board: $4000
Freshman Class: n/av	
SAT I or ACT: required	LESS COMPETITIVE

Western New Mexico University, founded in 1893, is a public institution offering vocational, liberal arts, science, and professional programs. Some figures in the above capsule and in this profile are approximate. There are 2 undergraduate and 3 graduate schools. The library contains 120,000 volumes, 500,000 microform items, and 500 audio/video tapes/CDs, and subscribes to 950 periodicals. Computerized library services include the card catalog, interlibrary loans, and database searching. Special learning facilities include a learning resource center, art gallery, natu-

ral history museum, and instrumental-vocal music center with individual practice rooms. The 80-acre campus is in a small town 113 miles northwest of Las Cruces and a few minutes from the Gila National Forest. Including any residence halls, there are 40 buildings.

Housing: 285 students can be accommodated in college housing, which includes dorms and married-student housing.

Activities: There are some groups and organizations on campus, including religious, social, and social service.

Programs of Study: WNMU confers B.A., B.S., B.B.A., B.S.V.T., and B.S.W. degrees. Associate and master's degrees are also awarded. Bachelor's degrees are awarded in AGRICULTURE (forestry and related sciences), BIOLOGICAL SCIENCE (biology/biological science, botany, and zoology), BUSINESS (accounting, business administration and management, international business management, management information systems, and marketing/retailing/merchandising), COMMUNICATIONS AND THE ARTS (English, fine arts, music, and Spanish), COMPUTER AND PHYSICAL SCIENCE (chemistry, computer science, mathematics, and science), EDUCATION (art, business, elementary, physical, science, secondary, special, and vocational), HEALTH PROFESSIONS (medical laboratory technology, predentistry, premedicine, prepharmacy, and public health), SOCIAL SCIENCE (Hispanic American studies, history, human services, humanities, law enforcement and corrections, psychology, public administration, social science, social work, and sociology).

Required: To graduate, students must earn at least 128 credit hours, including 30 to 54 in the major, with a minimum GPA of 2.0, and complete 51 hours of general education requirements.

Special: WNMU offers internships, dual and student-designed majors, and work-study programs.

Requirements: The SAT I or ACT is required. In addition, applicants should be graduates of an accredited secondary school or present a GED. Students should have completed at least 3 units of English and 2 of social studies, including U.S. history, as well as 2 each of science and math. Intermediate algebra and plane geometry are advised for students planning to enter certain fields. WNMU recommends a 2.0 GPA, but lower averages will be considered if applicants' test scores and personal recommendations are strong. CLEP credit is accepted.

Procedure: Freshmen are admitted to all sessions. Entrance exams should be taken before registration, preferably in the senior year. There is an early admissions plan. Check with the school for application deadlines and fee. Notification is sent on a rolling basis.

Transfer: Transfer students must have a GPA of 2.0. Those with fewer than 32 hours of college credit must supply ACT or SAT I scores and a high school transcript. 30 of 128 credits required for the bachelor's degree must be completed at WNMU.

Visiting: There are regularly scheduled orientations for prospective students. There are guides for informal visits and visitors may sit in on classes and stay overnight. To schedule a visit, contact the Admissions Office.

Financial Aid: The FAFSA is required. Check with the school for current deadlines.

International Students: The school actively recruits these students. They must score 550 on the written TOEFL and also take the SAT I or the ACT.

Computers: The mainframe is composed of 2 DEX VAX computers. More than 250 Macs and PCs are available to the university community. All are networked for access to e-mail and the Internet. Several campus locations house special-purpose computers. There are no time limits and no fees.

Admissions Contact: Michael Alecksen, Director of Admissions.
E-mail: admstudnt@iron.wnmu.edu Web: www.wnmu.edu

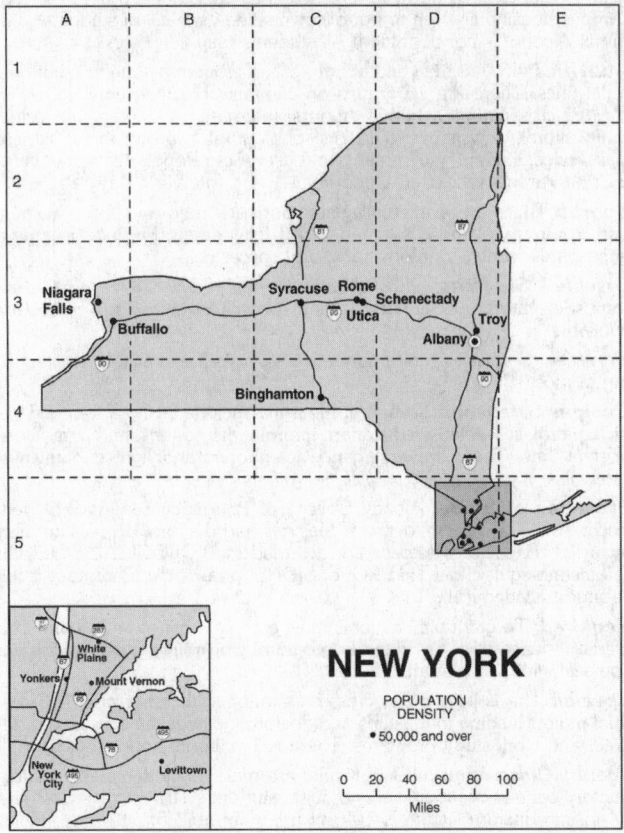

NEW YORK

POPULATION
DENSITY

• 50,000 and over

0 20 40 60 80 100

Miles

professional, radio and TV, religious, social, social service, student government, and yearbook. Popular campus events include Senior Week, Halloween Party, and Fall Fest.

Sports: There are 9 intercollegiate sports for men and 9 for women, and 16 intramural sports for men and 16 for women. Facilities include a 3000-seat stadium, a 600-seat gym, a swimming pool, racquetball, squash, tennis, and handball courts, exercise rooms, a dance studio, a track, and playing fields for baseball, softball, and soccer.

Disabled Students: 95% of the campus is accessible. Wheelchair ramps, elevators, special parking, specially equipped rest rooms, special class scheduling, lowered drinking fountains, lowered telephones, and special housing are available.

Services: Counseling and information services are available, as is tutoring in most subjects. A learning center offers tutoring in writing and quantitative skills, and help with class assignments. There is a reader service for the blind. A writing center is also available.

Campus Safety and Security: Measures include 24-hour foot and vehicle patrol, self-defense education, security escort services, and shuttle buses. There are informal discussions, pamphlets/posters/films, emergency telephones, and lighted pathways/sidewalks. Dorm main entrances are videotaped and dorm doors are locked 24 hours a day.

Programs of Study: Adelphi confers B.A., B.S., B.B.A., B.F.A., B.S.Ed., and B.S.S.W. degrees. Associate, master's, and doctoral degrees are also awarded. Bachelor's degrees are awarded in AGRICULTURE (environmental studies), BIOLOGICAL SCIENCE (biochemistry and biology/biological science), BUSINESS (accounting, banking and finance, business administration and management, and management information systems), COMMUNICATIONS AND THE ARTS (art history and appreciation, communications, dance, design, dramatic arts, English, fine arts, languages, music, performing arts, theater design, and visual and performing arts), COMPUTER AND PHYSICAL SCIENCE (chemistry, computer science, earth science, mathematics, natural sciences, and physics), EDUCATION (art, education of the deaf and hearing impaired, elementary, English, foreign languages, mathematics, music, physical, science, secondary, and social studies), HEALTH PROFESSIONS (nursing and speech pathology/audiology), SOCIAL SCIENCE (anthropology, economics, history, Latin American studies, liberal arts/general studies, philosophy, physical fitness/movement, political science/government, psychology, social science, social work, and sociology). Business management, psychology, and social studies are the largest.

Required: To graduate, students need at least a 2.0 cumulative GPA (higher in some programs) and 120 credit hours with a minimum of 27 in the major. 6 credits each are required in the arts, humanities, and languages, natural sciences and math, and social sciences. Other course requirements include English composition, freshman seminar (3 credits each), and a 1-credit freshman orientation experience. Cross-registration with Tufts, credit for life experience for adult students, nondegree study in special cases, and pass/fail options are possible. A 3-2 engineering degree is offered with Rensselaer Polytechnic, Columbia, Polytechnic, and Stevens Institute of Tech, and joint degree programs are offered in computer science, dentistry, engineering, environmental studies, law, optometry, and physical therapy with other universities and technical institutions.

Special: Internships are available in accounting, banking and money management, and communications, among others. Study abroad is available in more than 20 countries, including Spain, France, Denmark, and England. A 5-year bachelor's/master's degree in a number of fields, including biology, social work, and education is offered. In addition, work-study programs, double majors, the B.A.-B.S. degree, an accelerated degree program, student-designed majors, and a Washington semester are available. There are 19 national honor societies and a freshman honors program.

Faculty/Classroom: 52% of faculty are male; 48%, female. All teach undergraduates. No introductory courses are taught by graduate students. The average class size in a laboratory is 16 and in a regular course, 23.

Admissions: 71% of the 2003-2004 applicants were accepted. The SAT I scores for the 2003-2004 freshman class were: Verbal--31% below 500, 45% between 500 and 599, 21% between 600 and 700, and 3% above 700; Math--23% below 500, 51% between 500 and 599, 23% between 600 and 700, and 4% above 700. 39% of the current freshmen were in the top fifth of their class; 74% were in the top two fifths. 4 freshmen graduated first in their class.

Requirements: The SAT I or ACT is required. In addition, composite scores should be 900 on the SAT I or 19 on the ACT. Applicants should have 16 academic credits, including a recommended 4 units of English, history, and social studies, 3 each of math and science, and 2 or 3 of foreign language. An essay is required and an interview recommended for all applicants. A portfolio for art and technical theater candidates, an audition for music, dance, and theater candidates, and an interview for

ADELPHI UNIVERSITY
Garden City, NY 11530

D-5

(516) 877-3050
(800) ADELPHI; Fax: (516) 877-3039

Full-time: 1026 men, 2402 women	**Faculty:** 228; I, -$
Part-time: 171 men, 558 women	**Ph.D.s:** 87%
Graduate: 660 men, 2538 women	**Student/Faculty:** 15 to 1
Year: semesters, summer session	**Tuition:** $17,800
Application Deadline: open	**Room & Board:** $8500
Freshman Class: 4379 applied, 3089 accepted, 792 enrolled	
SAT I Verbal/Math: 530/550	**VERY COMPETITIVE**

Adelphi University, founded in 1896, is a private (not for profit) liberal arts institution. There are 7 undergraduate and 6 graduate schools. In addition to regional accreditation, Adelphi has baccalaureate program accreditation with CCNE, CSWE, and NLN. The 2 libraries contain 856,909 volumes, 788,698 microform items, and 44,531 audio/video tapes/CDs, and subscribe to 850 periodicals. Computerized library services include the card catalog, interlibrary loans, database searching, and Internet access. Special learning facilities include a learning resource center, art gallery, radio station, observatory, theater, sculpture and ceramics studios, a bronze casting foundry, and language labs. The 75-acre campus is in a suburban area 20 miles east of New York City. Including any residence halls, there are 24 buildings.

Student Life: 89% of undergraduates are from New York. Students are from 37 states, 51 foreign countries, and Canada. 70% are from public schools. 63% are white; 16% African American; 12% Hispanic. 57% are Catholic; 21% Protestant; 9% claim no religious affiliation; 6% Jewish; 6% Greek Orthodox, Hindu, and Muslim. The average age of freshmen is 19; all undergraduates, 25. 21% do not continue beyond their first year; 53% remain to graduate.

Housing: 1086 students can be accommodated in college housing, which includes coed dormitories. On-campus housing is available on a first-come, first-served basis and is available on a lottery system for upperclassmen. Priority is given to out-of-town students. 75% of students commute. Alcohol is not permitted. All students may keep cars.

Activities: 2% of men belong to 1 local and 3 national fraternities; 4% of women belong to 1 local and 6 national sororities. There are 76 groups on campus, including art, band, cheerleading, chorale, chorus, computers, dance, drama, ethnic, film, gay, honors, international, jazz band, literary magazine, musical theater, newspaper, orchestra, political,

nursing, social work, and honors candidates are required. The SAT I is recommended for the general studies and learning disabilities programs. A GPA of 2.5 is required. AP credits are accepted. Important factors in the admissions decision are advanced placement or honor courses, leadership record, and personality/intangible qualities.

Procedure: Freshmen are admitted fall and spring. Entrance exams should be taken in October of the senior year, or May of the junior year. There are early admissions and deferred admissions plans. There is a rolling admissions plan. Application deadlines are open. The fall 2003 application fee was $35. Applications are accepted on-line through the school's web site and via Common App.

Transfer: 646 transfer students enrolled in 2002-2003. A GPA of 2.5 is recommended in addition to an essay, an official high school transcript, and official records of all work completed or in progress from previous colleges and universities. An interview is required for students in social work and nursing, while an audition is needed for music, dance, and theater students, and a portfolio for art and technical theater students. 30 of 120 credits required for the bachelor's degree must be completed at Adelphi.

Visiting: There are regularly scheduled orientations for prospective students, including a campus tour, an interview, and information sessions. There are guides for informal visits and visitors may sit in on classes. To schedule a visit, contact Undergraduate Admissions.

Financial Aid: In 2003-2004, 93% of all full-time freshmen and 88% of continuing full-time students received some form of financial aid. 71% of full-time freshmen and 68% of continuing full-time students received need-based aid. The average freshman award was $13,500. Need-based scholarships or need-based grants averaged $5256 ($7500 maximum); need-based self-help aid (loans and jobs) averaged $4693 ($8000 maximum); and non-need-based athletic scholarships averaged $14,588 ($26,300 maximum). 30% of undergraduates work part time. Average annual earnings from campus work are $1400. The average financial indebtedness of the 2003 graduate was $22,500. Adelphi is a member of CSS. The FAFSA is required. The priority date for freshman financial aid applications for fall entry is March 1. The deadline for filing freshman financial aid applications for fall entry is February 15.

International Students: There are 125 international students enrolled. The school actively recruits these students. They must score 550 on the written TOEFL or 213 on the electronic version and also take the SAT I or the ACT.

Computers: The mainframe is an AV 3700 Data General. There are 540 PC, Mac, and Unix workstations located throughout the campus and in special-purpose labs. There are 6 general-access computer labs. All workstations have the ability to access e-mail and the Internet, and can also utilize the software and services provided on several Unix servers via the campuswide data network. There are 10 laptops students can borrow and use to access the Internet through the wireless network. All students may access the system. There are no time limits. The fee is $100 (full-time), $50 (part-time).

Graduates: From July 1, 2002 to June 30, 2003, 837 bachelor's degrees were awarded. The most popular majors were business (23%), social science (19%), and health professions (10%). In an average class, 3% graduate in 3 years or less, 45% graduate in 4 years or less, 53% graduate in 5 years or less, and 53% graduate in 6 years or less. 247 companies recruited on campus in 2002-2003. Of the 2002 graduating class, 41% were enrolled in graduate school within 6 months of graduation and 87% were employed.

Admissions Contact: Christine Murphy, Director, Office of University Admissions. E-mail: *admissions@adelphi.edu* Web: *www.adelphi.edu*

ALBANY COLLEGE OF PHARMACY
Albany, NY 12208

D-3

(518) 445-7221
(888) 203-8010; Fax: (518) 445-7202

Full-time: 270 men, 431 women	**Faculty:** 63; IIB, +$
Part-time: 2 men	**Ph.D.s:** 75%
Graduate: 61 men, 124 women	**Student/Faculty:** 11 to 1
Year: semesters	**Tuition:** $16,920
Application Deadline: February 1	**Room & Board:** $5400
Freshman Class: n/av	
SAT I Verbal/Math: 590/590	SPECIAL

Albany College of Pharmacy, founded in 1881, is a private, 6-year institution and a division of Union University. In addition to regional accreditation, Albany College of Pharmacy has baccalaureate program accreditation with ACPE. The library contains 12,314 volumes, 28,388 microform items, and 2676 audio/video tapes/CDs, and subscribes to 1399 periodicals. Computerized library services include the card catalog, interlibrary loans, database searching, and Internet access. Special learning facilities include a learning resource center and a pharmacy museum. The 1-acre campus is in an urban area in University Heights area of Albany. Including any residence halls, there are 6 buildings.

Student Life: 90% of undergraduates are from New York. Students are from 11 states, 6 foreign countries, and Canada. 75% are from public schools. 84% are white. The average age of freshmen is 18; all under-

graduates, 21. 18% do not continue beyond their first year; 77% remain to graduate.

Housing: 335 students can be accommodated in college housing, which includes coed dorms and off-campus apartments. Priority for on-campus housing is given to out-of-town students. 52% of students commute. Alcohol is not permitted. All students may keep cars.

Activities: 45% of men and about 43% of women belong to 6 national fraternities. There are 16 groups on campus, including bowling, choir, chorus, cross country, ethnic, honors, international, literary magazine, multicultural, newspaper, outdoors, photography, professional, ski, social service, student government, and yearbook. Popular campus events include Parents Weekend, Open House, and Interview Day.

Sports: There are 4 intercollegiate sports for men and 4 for women, and 3 intramural sports for men and 3 for women. Facilities include a gym, fitness center, outdoor track, and soccer field.

Disabled Students: 98% of the campus is accessible. Wheelchair ramps, elevators, special parking, and specially equipped rest rooms are available.

Services: Counseling and information services are available, as is tutoring in most subjects.

Campus Safety and Security: Measures include 24-hour foot and vehicle patrol, self-defense education, informal discussions, and pamphlets/posters/films. There are emergency telephones and lighted pathways/sidewalks.

Programs of Study: Albany College of Pharmacy confers B.S Med. Tech., and B.S. Pharm. degrees. Master's and doctoral degrees are also awarded. Bachelor's degrees are awarded in BIOLOGICAL SCIENCE (biotechnology), HEALTH PROFESSIONS (pharmacy). Pharmacy is the strongest academically.

Required: To graduate, students must complete between 129 and 162 credits, depending on degree program, including core curriculum courses, with a minimum GPA of 2.0.

Special: The college offers cross-registration with other area colleges, dual majors leading to master's and doctoral degrees, an accelerated degree, and work-study programs. There is 1 national honor society.

Faculty/Classroom: 54% of faculty are male; 46%, female. No introductory courses are taught by graduate students. The average class size in an introductory lecture is 100; in a laboratory, 25; in a regular course, 50.

Admissions: 10 freshmen graduated first in their class.

Requirements: The SAT I or ACT is required. In addition, applicants must be graduates of an accredited high school with at least 17 credits, including 4 each of English and math through precalculus, and 3 of science, including chemistry. The GED is accepted. Albany College of Pharmacy requires applicants to be in the upper 50% of their class. A GPA of 3.0 is required. AP and CLEP credits are accepted. Important factors in the admissions decision are advanced placement or honor courses, extracurricular activities record, and recommendations by alumni.

Procedure: Freshmen are admitted in the fall. Entrance exams should be taken in the junior year. Applications should be filed by February 1 for fall entry. There is a rolling admissions plan. Notification is sent on a rolling basis. The fall 2003 application fee was $50. Applications are accepted on-line through CollegeNET.

Transfer: Applicants must have a GPA of 3.2.

Visiting: There are regularly scheduled orientations for prospective students, including a tour of the school and residence halls and a discussion of admissions requirements, financial aid, and student activities. There are guides for informal visits and visitors may sit in on classes and stay overnight. To schedule a visit, contact the Admissions Office.

Financial Aid: 95% of undergraduates work part time. Average annual earnings from campus work are $800. The FAFSA is required. The priority date for freshman financial aid applications for fall entry is February 1.

International Students: There are 24 international students enrolled. They must score 600 on the written TOEFL or 250 on the electronic version and also take the SAT I or the ACT.

Computers: The mainframe is a DEC VAX 11/750. Entering students receive laptop computers through a lease program. A number of PCs are also available. Dorms and classrooms provide cable and wireless web or Internet access. All students may access the system 24 hours a day. There are no time limits and no fees. All students are required to have personal computers.

Graduates: From July 1, 2002 to June 30, 2003, 40 bachelor's degrees were awarded. The most popular major was pharmacy (100%). In an average class, 76% graduate in 5 years or less, and 76% graduate in 6 years or less. 50 companies recruited on campus in 2002-2003.

Admissions Contact: Michael Green, Admissions Counselor. A video is available. E-mail: *admissions@acp.edu* Web: *www.acp.edu*

ALBERT A. LIST COLLEGE OF JEWISH STUDIES   D-5
New York, NY 10027-4649   **(212) 678-8832; Fax: (212) 678-8947**

Full-time: 80 men, 80 women	**Faculty:** 40
Part-time: 10 men, 10 women	**Ph.D.s:** 98%
Graduate: none	**Student/Faculty:** 4 to 1
Year: semesters, summer session	**Tuition:** $11,260
Application Deadline: January 1	**Room & Board:** $6790
Freshman Class: n/av	
SAT I or ACT: required	**HIGHLY COMPETITIVE+**

Albert A. List College of Jewish Studies, the undergraduate division of the Jewish Theological Seminary, founded in 1886, is a private institution affiliated with the Conservative branch of the Jewish faith. List College offers programs in all aspects of Judaism, including Bible, rabbinics, literature, history, philosophy, education, and communal service. There is a combined liberal arts program with Columbia University and Barnard College. Some figures in the above capsule and in this profile are approximate. The library contains 320,000 volumes and 3500 microform items, and subscribes to 750 periodicals. Computerized library services include the card catalog, interlibrary loans, and database searching. Special learning facilities include a learning resource center, art gallery, a music center, a Jewish education research center, and the Jewish Museum Archives Center. The 1-acre campus is in an urban area on the upper west side of Manhattan. Including any residence halls, there are 6 buildings.

Student Life: 75% of undergraduates are from out of state, mostly the Middle Atlantic. Students are from 12 states, 3 foreign countries, and Canada. 70% are from public schools. Most are white. Most are Jewish. The average age of freshmen is 18; all undergraduates, 20. 96% of freshmen remain to graduate.

Housing: 212 students can be accommodated in college housing, which includes coed dorms, on-campus apartments, off-campus apartments, married-student housing, and kosher housing. On-campus housing is guaranteed for all 4 years. 93% of students live on campus; of those, 95% remain on campus on weekends. Alcohol is not permitted. All students may keep cars.

Activities: Through Columbia University, 12% of men belong to fraternities; 4% of women belong to sororities. There are many groups and organizations on campus, including art, band, choir, chorus, computers, dance, drama, ethnic, film, gay, honors, international, literary magazine, musical theater, newspaper, orchestra, photography, political, professional, radio and TV, religious, social, social service, student government, and yearbook. Popular campus events include Purim, Simchat Torah, and Orientation.

Sports: There are 3 intramural sports for men and 3 for women. List College students may use the facilities at Columbia University.

Disabled Students: All of the campus is accessible. Wheelchair ramps, elevators, special parking, specially equipped rest rooms, lowered drinking fountains, lowered telephones, and elevators with braille panels are available.

Services: Counseling and information services are available, as is tutoring in most subjects.

Campus Safety and Security: Measures include 24-hour foot and vehicle patrol, security escort services, informal discussions, and pamphlets/posters/films. There are emergency telephones and lighted pathways/sidewalks.

Programs of Study: List College confers the B.A. degree. Bachelor's degrees are awarded in SOCIAL SCIENCE (biblical studies and Judaic studies).

Required: Students must take a Hebrew language requirement, 24 credits in Jewish history, 9 in literature, and 6 each in Bible, Jewish philosophy, and Talmud. In addition, there are 60 required credits in liberal arts, including 6 credits each in English, history/philosophy/social science, and math or lab science to be completed at another college or university. A total of 156 credits (96 taken at List College) is required for graduation, with 21 in a major field.

Special: There is a joint program with Columbia University and a double-degree program with Barnard College, which enable students to earn 2 B.A. degrees in 4 to 4 1/2 years. Study abroad is available in Israel, England, France, and Spain. Student-designed majors, credit by exam, and nondegree study are also offered. There is a chapter of Phi Beta Kappa and a freshman honors program.

Faculty/Classroom: 68% of faculty are male; 32%, female. All both teach and do research. The average class size in an introductory lecture is 30 and in a regular course, 10.

Requirements: The school accepts either the SAT I and SAT II: Subject tests in writing or the ACT. Applicants to the double-degree program must take the SAT II: Subject test in writing plus 2 other subject tests and have scores sent to Barnard. Applicants must be graduates of an accredited secondary school or have the GED. An essay and 2 recommendations are required; an interview is strongly recommended. AP credits are accepted. Important factors in the admissions decision are advanced placement or honor courses, extracurricular activities record, and personality/intangible qualities.

Procedure: Freshmen are admitted fall and spring. Entrance exams should be taken in the spring of the junior year. There are early decision, early admissions, and deferred admissions plans. Early decision applications should be filed by November 15; regular applications, by January 1 for fall entry for the double-degree program and February 15 for the joint program. The application fee is $65. Notification of early decision is sent December 15; regular decision, April 1. 14 early decision candidates were accepted for a recent class. Students can print on-line applications and submit them by mail.

Transfer: Applicants must submit SAT I or ACT scores, an essay, high school and college transcripts, and 2 academic recommendations. A minimum college GPA of 2.5 is required. An interview is recommended. 48 of 156 credits required for the bachelor's degree must be completed at List College.

Visiting: There are regularly scheduled orientations for prospective students, including a tour of the campus and of Columbia University, an interview with the dean, and an overnight dorm stay. There are guides for informal visits and visitors may sit in on classes and stay overnight. To schedule a visit, contact the Admissions Director.

Financial Aid: In a recent year, 75% of all full-time freshmen and 65% of continuing full-time students received some form of financial aid. The average freshman award was $17,800. 15% of undergraduates work part time. List College is a member of CSS. The CSS Profile, the college's own financial statement, and 1040 tax forms are required. Check with the school for current deadlines.

International Students: They must score 500 on the written TOEFL and also take the college's own test or the American Language English Placement Test and the SAT I or the ACT.

Computers: All dorms have Internet connections. All students may access the system. There are no time limits and no fees.

Graduates: In a recent year, 39 bachelor's degrees were awarded. In an average class, 60% graduate in 4 years or less, and all graduate in 5 years or less.

Admissions Contact: Director of Admissions.
E-mail: lcadmissions@jtsa.edu Web: www.jtsa.edu

ALFRED UNIVERSITY   B-4
Alfred, NY 14802-1205   **(607) 871-2115**
(800) 541-9229; Fax: (607) 871-2198

Full-time: 929 men, 1015 women	**Faculty:** 173; IIA, -$
Part-time: 49 men, 111 women	**Ph.D.s:** 93%
Graduate: 143 men, 169 women	**Student/Faculty:** 11 to 1
Year: semesters, summer session	**Tuition:** $19,278
Application Deadline: February 1	**Room & Board:** $9012
Freshman Class: 2169 applied, 1493 accepted, 475 enrolled	
SAT I Verbal/Math: 561/557	**COMPETITIVE**

Alfred University, founded in 1836, is a private institution offering programs in business administration, liberal arts and sciences, engineering, and professional studies, and in art and design and ceramic engineering through the New York State College of Ceramics. The above tuition figures are for incoming freshmen. Contact the school for tuition rates at other academic levels. There are 4 undergraduate and 7 graduate schools. In addition to regional accreditation, AU has baccalaureate program accreditation with AACSB, ABET, and NASAD. The 2 libraries contain 323,944 volumes and 94,298 microform items, and subscribe to 6467 periodicals. Computerized library services include the card catalog, interlibrary loans, and database searching. Special learning facilities include a learning resource center, art gallery, radio station, TV station, and observatory. The 232-acre campus is in a rural area 70 miles south of Rochester. Including any residence halls, there are 54 buildings.

Student Life: 69% of undergraduates are from New York. Students are from 38 states, 12 foreign countries, and Canada. 90% are from public schools. 86% are white. The average age of freshmen is 18; all undergraduates, 20. 18% do not continue beyond their first year; 65% remain to graduate.

Housing: 1330 students can be accommodated in college housing, which includes coed dorms, on-campus apartments, fraternity houses, and sorority houses. In addition, there are honors houses, language houses, and special-interest houses. On-campus housing is available on a first-come, first-served basis and is available on a lottery system for upperclassmen. 65% of students live on campus; of those, 90% remain on campus on weekends. All students may keep cars.

Activities: There are no fraternities or sororities. There are more than 100 groups and organizations on campus, including art, band, cheerleading, chess, chorale, chorus, computers, dance, drama, ethnic, film, gay, honors, international, jazz band, literary magazine, musical theater, newspaper, orchestra, pep band, photography, political, professional, radio and TV, religious, social, social service, Student Activities Board, student government, and yearbook. Popular campus events include Alumni Weekend, Hot Dog Day, and Family Weekend.

Sports: There are 10 intercollegiate sports for men and 11 for women, and 14 intramural sports for men and 13 for women. Facilities include an omniturf football surface, a soccer and lacrosse field, an Olympic-size pool, tennis courts, racquetball and squash courts, a weight room, and a dance and exercise studio. The campus stadium seats 4200, the indoor gym, 3000. There is also a fitness center and facilities for horseback riding nearby.

Disabled Students: 50% of the campus is accessible. Wheelchair ramps, elevators, special parking, specially equipped rest rooms, special class scheduling, and lowered drinking fountains are available.

Services: Counseling and information services are available, as is tutoring in most subjects. There is a reader service for the blind, and remedial math, reading, and writing. Time management and study skills workshops and advocacy and support for students with learning and physical disabilities are available.

Campus Safety and Security: Measures include security escort services, informal discussions, pamphlets/posters/films, and emergency telephones. There are lighted pathways/sidewalks and vehicle and foot patrols.

Programs of Study: AU confers B.A.,B.S., and B.F.A. degrees. Master's and doctoral degrees are also awarded. Bachelor's degrees are awarded in BIOLOGICAL SCIENCE (biology/biological science), BUSINESS (accounting, banking and finance, business administration and management, business economics, management science, and marketing/retailing/merchandising), COMMUNICATIONS AND THE ARTS (ceramic art and design, communications, dramatic arts, English, fine arts, French, German, glass, performing arts, and Spanish), COMPUTER AND PHYSICAL SCIENCE (chemistry, computer science, geology, mathematics, physics, and science), EDUCATION (art, athletic training, business, elementary, English, foreign languages, mathematics, science, secondary, and social studies), ENGINEERING AND ENVIRONMENTAL DESIGN (ceramic engineering, electrical/electronics engineering, environmental science, materials engineering, and mechanical engineering), HEALTH PROFESSIONS (health care administration), SOCIAL SCIENCE (criminal justice, crosscultural studies, economics, gerontology, history, interdisciplinary studies, philosophy, political science/government, psychology, public administration, and sociology). Ceramic engineering, electrical engineering, and mechanical engineering are the strongest academically. Art and design, business administration, and ceramic engineering are the largest.

Required: To graduate, students must complete 120 to 137 credits, depending on the major, with 36 to 48 credits in the major. The students must demonstrate basic competencies in writing, oral communication, math, and computers. Freshmen must attend 10 freshman forums and complete a phys ed course. Distribution requirements include 8 credits each of social studies and natural science, and 4 credits each of philosophy or religion, literature, art, and history. A minimum GPA of 2.0 is required.

Special: There are cooperative programs in engineering and business with Duke, Clarkson, and Columbia Universities and SUNY/Brockport. There is cross-registration with the SUNY College of Technology and a 5-year program in environmental management/forestry with Duke. Alfred offers internships in all programs, extensive study abroad, Washington and Albany semesters, work-study, accelerated-degree programs, a general studies degree, student-designed majors, dual majors, credit by examination, and pass/fail options. A special feature is the New York State College of Ceramics, which offers programs and facilities in ceramic engineering and science as well as art and design. There are 12 national honor societies, including Phi Beta Kappa, a freshman honors program, and 42 departmental honors programs.

Faculty/Classroom: 64% of faculty are male; 36%, female. 90% both teach and do research. No introductory courses are taught by graduate students. The average class size in an introductory lecture is 25; in a laboratory, 15; and in a regular course, 18.

Admissions: 69% of the 2003-2004 applicants were accepted. The SAT I scores for the 2003-2004 freshman class were: Verbal--20% below 500, 48% between 500 and 599, 26% between 600 and 700, and 6% above 700; Math--22% below 500, 25% between 600 and 700, and 5% above 700. 72% of the current freshmen were in the top two fifths of their class. There were 7 National Merit finalists. 4 freshmen graduated first in their class.

Requirements: The SAT I or ACT is required. In addition, a GED is accepted. A minimum of 16 Carnegie units is required, including 4 years of English, 2 to 3 years each of math, history/social studies, and science. The remaining units may be either in a foreign language or any of the previously mentioned fields. An essay is required, and applicants to B.F.A. programs must submit a portfolio. Interviews are encouraged. AP credits are accepted. Important factors in the admissions decision are advanced placement or honor courses, personality/intangible qualities, and extracurricular activities record.

Procedure: Freshmen are admitted fall and spring. Entrance exams should be taken in the junior year. There are early decision, early admissions, and deferred admissions plans. Early decision applications should be filed by December 1; regular applications, by February 1 for fall entry and December 1 for spring entry, along with a $40 fee. Notification of early decision is sent December 15; regular decision, March 15. 44 early decision candidates were accepted for the 2003-2004 class. Applications are accepted on-line through the school's web site.

Transfer: 89 transfer students enrolled in 2002-2003. Transfer applicants must have a GPA of at least 2.5. They must submit at least 1 letter of recommendation and official high school and college transcripts. Art students must submit a portfolio. 30 of 120 credits required for the bachelor's degree must be completed at AU.

Visiting: There are regularly scheduled orientations for prospective students, including a campus tour, social activities panel, financial aid presentation, faculty discussions, and on-campus interviews. There are guides for informal visits and visitors may sit in on classes and stay overnight. To schedule a visit, contact the Admissions Office at *admwww@alfred.edu.*

Financial Aid: In 2003-2004, 90% of all full-time students received some form of financial aid. The average freshman award in a recent year was $18,444. 50% of undergraduates work part time. Average annual earnings from campus work are $1000. The average financial indebtedness of the 2003 graduate was $17,500. The FAFSA, the college's own financial statement, the Business/Farm Supplement, and the Non-Custodial Parent statement are required. The deadline for filing freshman financial aid applications for fall entry is May 1.

International Students: There are 45 international students enrolled. The school actively recruits these students. They must score 550 on the written TOEFL or 213 on the electronic version, or take the ACT or SAT I.

Computers: The mainframe is a Compa Alpha ES 40. All buildings are connected to the campus network. There are numerous high-speed, laser, and color printers. More than 400 terminals are located across campus for student use. All students may access the system 24 hours a day, 7 days a week. There are no time limits and no fees.

Graduates: From July 1, 2002 to June 30, 2003, 442 bachelor's degrees were awarded. The most popular majors were art and design (24%), business administration (14%), and ceramic engineering (7%). In an average class, 1% graduate in 3 years or less, 50% graduate in 4 years or less, 65% graduate in 5 years or less, and 66% graduate in 6 years or less. 79 companies recruited on campus in 2002-2003. Of the 2002 graduating class, 32% were enrolled in graduate school within 1 year of graduation and 66% were employed.

Admissions Contact: Scott Hooker, Director of Admissions. A video is available. E-mail: *hooker@alfred.edu* or *admwww@alfred.edu* Web: *http://www.alfred.edu*

AUDREY COHEN COLLEGE
(See Metropolitan College of New York)

BARD COLLEGE
Annandale-on-Hudson, NY 12504-5000

D-4
(845) 758-7472
Fax: (845) 758-5208

Full-time: 558 men, 766 women	**Faculty:** 124
Part-time: 23 men, 30 women	**Ph.D.s:** 98%
Graduate: 64 men, 159 women	**Student/Faculty:** 11 to 1
Year: 4-1-4	**Tuition:** $28,808
Application Deadline: January 15	**Room & Board:** $8544
Freshman Class: 3367 applied, 1310 accepted, 382 enrolled	
SAT I Verbal/Math: 690/630	**HIGHLY COMPETITIVE+**

Bard College, founded in 1860, is an independent liberal arts and sciences institution affiliated historically with the Association of Episcopal Colleges. Discussion-oriented seminars and independent study are encouraged, tutorials are on a one-to-one basis, and most classes are kept small, with fewer than 15 students. The library contains 280,000 volumes, 9050 microform items, and 5800 audio/video tapes/CDs, and subscribes to 13,000 on-line periodicals and 90 on-line databases. Computerized library services include the card catalog, interlibrary loans, database searching, and Internet access. Special learning facilities include a learning resource center, art gallery, radio station, ecology field station, the Levy Economics Institute, the Institute for Writing and Thinking, the Institute for Advanced Theology, the Center for Curatorial Studies and Art in Contemporary Culture, and an archeological field school. The 600-acre campus is in a rural area 100 miles north of New York City. Including any residence halls, there are more than 70 buildings.

Student Life: 71% of undergraduates are from out of state, mostly the Northeast. Students are from 50 states, 43 foreign countries, and Canada. 70% are from public schools. 82% are white. The average age of freshmen is 18; all undergraduates, 20. 13% do not continue beyond their first year; 70% remain to graduate.

Housing: 1200 students can be accommodated in college housing, which includes single-sex and coed dorms. In addition, there are special-interest houses, a single-sex dorm, and quiet dorms. On-campus housing is guaranteed for the freshman year only and is available on a lottery system for upperclassmen. 85% of students live on campus; of those, 75% remain on campus on weekends. All students may keep cars.

Activities: There are no fraternities or sororities. There are 60 groups on campus, including art, band, chamber groups, chess, choir, chorus, computers, dance, drama, ethnic, film, gay, international, jazz band, literary magazine, model UN, newspaper, opera, orchestra, photography, political, radio and TV, religious, social, social service, student government, and yearbook. Popular campus events include Winter Carnival, Spring Festival, and International Students Cultural Show.

Sports: There are 6 intercollegiate sports for men and 5 for women, and 22 intramural sports for men and 22 for women. Facilities include a gym and pool, soccer and softball fields, squash and tennis courts, cross-country trails, bike paths, and the Tivoli bays of the Hudson River.

Disabled Students: 70% of the campus is accessible. Wheelchair ramps, elevators, special parking, specially equipped rest rooms, lowered drinking fountains, and lowered telephones are available.

Services: Counseling and information services are available, as is tutoring in every subject. There is a reader service for the blind.

Campus Safety and Security: Measures include 24-hour foot and vehicle patrol, self-defense education, security escort services, and shuttle buses. There are informal discussions, pamphlets/posters/films, emergency telephones, lighted pathways/sidewalks, volunteer emergency medical technicians on call 24 hours a day, and Bard Response to Rape and Associated Violence Education (BRAVE) volunteers.

Programs of Study: Bard confers B.A. and B.S. degrees. Associate, master's, and doctoral degrees are also awarded. Bachelor's degrees are awarded in BIOLOGICAL SCIENCE (biochemistry, biology/biological science, cell biology, ecology, microbiology, and molecular biology), COMMUNICATIONS AND THE ARTS (American literature, art history and appreciation, Chinese, classical languages, classics, creative writing, dance, dramatic arts, drawing, English, English literature, film arts, French, German, Germanic languages and literature, Italian, music history and appreciation, music performance, music theory and composition, painting, photography, Russian, sculpture, and Spanish), COMPUTER AND PHYSICAL SCIENCE (chemistry, mathematics, natural sciences, and physics), ENGINEERING AND ENVIRONMENTAL DESIGN (environmental science), HEALTH PROFESSIONS (predentistry and premedicine), SOCIAL SCIENCE (African studies, American studies, anthropology, archeology, area studies, Asian/Oriental studies, British studies, Celtic studies, clinical psychology, developmental psychology, Eastern European studies, economics, European studies, French studies, history, history of philosophy, history of science, human development, interdisciplinary studies, Italian studies, Judaic studies, Latin American studies, medieval studies, philosophy, political science/government, prelaw, religion, Russian and Slavic studies, social psychology, social science, sociology, and Spanish studies). Languages and literature, the arts, and social studies are the largest.

Required: All students must complete a 3-week workshop in language and thinking, a first year seminar, and a senior project. A conference in the junior year is required, and through a moderation process in the sophomore year, the student chooses a concentration in an academic department. A distribution of at least 1 course in each of the 7 academic areas, including a quantitative analysis course, is required, with a maximum of 84 hours in the student's major and a total of 124 credit hours needed to graduate.

Special: Bard offers opportunities for study abroad, internships (no academic credit), Washington and New York semesters, dual majors, student-designed majors, accelerated degree programs, and pass/fail options. Cross-registration is available with Vassar College and SUNY/New Paltz. A 3-2 engineering degree is available with the Columbia Univesity School of Engineering. Other 3-2 degrees are available in forestry and environmental studies, social work, architecture, city and regional planning, public health, and business administration. There are also opportunities for independent study, multicultural and ethnic studies, area studies, human rights, and globalization and international affairs.

Faculty/Classroom: 55% of faculty are male; 45%, female. All both teach and do research. No introductory courses are taught by graduate students. The average class size in an introductory lecture is 18; in a laboratory, 14; and in a regular course, 14.

Admissions: 39% of the 2003-2004 applicants were accepted. The SAT I scores for the 2003-2004 freshman class were: Verbal--12% between 500 and 599, 57% between 600 and 700, and 31% above 700; Math--1% below 500, 31% between 500 and 599, 53% between 600 and 700, and 15% above 700. 86% of the current freshmen were in the top fifth of their class; 98% were in the top two fifths.

Requirements: Bard places strong emphasis on the academic background and intellectual curiosity of applicants, as well as indications of the student's commitment to social and environmental concerns, independent research, volunteer work, and other important extracurricular activities. Students applying for admission are expected to have graduated from an accredited secondary school (the GED is accepted) and must submit written essays with the application. The high school record should include a full complement of college-preparatory courses. Honors and advanced placement courses are also considered. An interview is recommended. Bard requires applicants to be in the upper 50% of their class. A GPA of 3.0 is required. AP credits are accepted. Important factors in the admissions decision are advanced placement or honor courses, evidence of special talent, and extracurricular activities record.

Procedure: Freshmen are admitted in the fall. There are early admissions and deferred admissions plans. Early action applications should be filed by November 1; regular applications, by January 15 for fall entry and November 1 for spring entry, along with a $50 fee. Notification of early action is sent January 1; regular decision, April 1. 267 applicants were on the 2003 waiting list; 10 were admitted. Applications are accepted on-line through Common App or Peterson's.

Transfer: 36 transfer students enrolled in 2003-2004. Admission requirements are the same as for regular applicants. A minimum GPA of 3.0 and an interview are recommended. 60 of 124 credits required for the bachelor's degree must be completed at Bard.

Visiting: There are regularly scheduled orientations for prospective students, consisting of regularly scheduled daily tours and information sessions, which are strongly recommended. Visitors may sit in on classes. To schedule a visit, contact the Admissions Office at admission@bard.edu.

Financial Aid: In 2003-2004, 65% of all full-time students received some form of financial aid. 63% of full-time freshmen and 59% of continuing full-time students received need-based aid. The average freshman award was $23,503. Need-based scholarships or need-based grants averaged $20,311 ($37,847 maximum); and need-based self-help aid (loans and jobs) averaged $4641 ($5775 maximum). 50% of undergraduates work part time. Average annual earnings from campus work are $1200. The average financial indebtedness of the 2003 graduate was $16,000. Bard is a member of CSS. The CSS Profile or FAFSA and the state aid form are required. The deadline for filing freshman financial aid applications for fall entry is February 15.

International Students: There are 90 international students enrolled. The school actively recruits these students. They must score 600 on the written TOEFL or 250 on the electronic version.

Computers: The computer center houses more than 160 networked Macs and PCs. There are more than 400 additional terminals and PCs located in the library, academic departments, and throughout the campus. All students may access the system. There are no time limits and no fees.

Graduates: From July 1, 2002 to June 30, 2003, 289 bachelor's degrees were awarded. The most popular majors were social studies (37%), visual and performing arts (30%), and language and literature (25%). In an average class, 3% graduate in 3 years or less, 55% graduate in 4 years or less, 66% graduate in 5 years or less, and 68% graduate in 6 years or less. 100 companies recruited on campus in 2002-2003. Of the 2002 graduating class, 45% were enrolled in graduate school within 6 months of graduation and 50% were employed.

Admissions Contact: Mary Backlund, Director of Admissions. A video is available. E-mail: admission@bard.edu Web: www.bard.edu

BERKELEY COLLEGE
White Plains, NY 10601

D-5
(914) 694-1122
(800) 446-5400; Fax: (914) 328-9469

Full-time: 150 men, 420 women	**Faculty:** n/av
Part-time: 20 men, 100 women	**Ph.D.s:** 54%
Graduate: none	**Student/Faculty:** 38 to 1
Year: quarters, summer session	**Tuition:** $15,900
Application Deadline: open	**Room & Board:** $5850
Freshman Class: n/av	
SAT I or ACT: required	**LESS COMPETITIVE**

Berkeley College, established in 1945, is a private institution with 5 campuses in New York and New Jersey. Its programs are designed to prepare students for careers in business by providing an education that balances academic studies, professional training, and hands-on experience. Some figures in the above capsule and in this profile are approximate. The library contains 9500 volumes and 800 audio/video tapes/CDs, and subscribes to 80 periodicals. Computerized library services include the card catalog, interlibrary loans, and database searching. Special learning facilities include a learning resource center. The 10-acre campus is in a suburban area. Including any residence halls, there are 3 buildings.

Student Life: 80% of undergraduates are from New York. Students are from 8 states and 14 foreign countries. 66% are white; 16% African American; 11% Hispanic. The average age of freshmen is 19; all undergraduates, 20.

Housing: 96 students can be accommodated in college housing, which includes coed dorms. Priority for on-campus housing is given to out-of-town students. 86% of students commute. Alcohol is not permitted. All students may keep cars.

Activities: There are no fraternities or sororities. There are 6 groups on campus, including international, newspaper, professional, social, social service, and student government. Popular campus events include Multicultural Month and Commuter Appreciation Day.

Sports: There is no sports program at Berkeley College. Students have access to the sports and exercise facilities at nearby Manhattanville College.

Disabled Students: Wheelchair ramps, elevators, and special parking are available.

Services: Counseling and information services are available, as is tutoring in every subject. There is remedial math, reading, and writing.

Campus Safety and Security: Measures include lighted pathways/sidewalks and night patrols by trained security personnel.

Programs of Study: Berkeley College confers the B.B.A. degree. Associate degrees are also awarded. Bachelor's degrees are awarded in BUSINESS (accounting, business administration and management, international business management, and marketing/retailing/merchandising).

Required: To graduate, students must complete the prescribed course of study with a minimum GPA of 2.0. A total of 180 credits is required for the bachelor's degree.

Requirements: Graduation from an accredited high school or the equivalent (GED) and an entrance exam or SAT I or ACT scores are basic requirements for admission. A personal interview is strongly recommended. AP and CLEP credits are accepted.

Procedure: Freshmen are admitted to all sessions. Entrance exams should be taken as soon as the application is submitted, if possible. There is a deferred admissions plan. Application deadlines are open. The application fee is $40. Notification is sent on a rolling basis. Applications are accepted on-line at the school's web site.

Transfer: Applicants must submit a transcript from each college attended and a high school transcript or equivalent (GED). 60 of 180 credits required for the bachelor's degree must be completed at Berkeley College.

Visiting: There are guides for informal visits.

Financial Aid: The FAFSA, the college's own financial statement, and the state income tax return are required. Check with the school for current deadlines.

International Students: The school actively recruits these students.

Computers: More than 150 PCs are available to students, all with access to the Internet and the Web. All students may access the system. There are no time limits and no fees.

Admissions Contact: Admissions Officer.
E-mail: *wpcampus@berkeleycollege.edu*
Web: *www.berkeleycollege.edu*

BERKELEY COLLEGE OF NEW YORK CITY — D-5
New York, NY 10017 — (212) 986-4343
(800)446-5400; Fax: (212) 697-3371

Full-time: 400 men, 1120 women	Faculty: n/av
Part-time: 50 men, 150 women	Ph.D.s: 33%
Graduate: none	Student/Faculty: 50 to 1
Year: quarters, summer session	Tuition: $15,900
Application Deadline: open	Room & Board: n/av
Freshman Class: n/av	
SAT I or ACT: required	Less Competitive

Berkeley College of New York City, founded in 1936, is a private institution offering undergraduate programs in business. Some figures in the above capsule and in this profile are approximate. The library contains 11,005 volumes, and subscribes to 130 periodicals. Computerized library services include the card catalog, interlibrary loans, and database searching. Special learning facilities include a learning resource center. The campus is in an urban area in midtown Manhattan, a short walk from Grand Central Station. There are 2 buildings.

Housing: A variety of residence facilities are available in Manhattan and nearby boroughs. Additional information is available at the Admissions Office.

Programs of Study: Berkeley College of New York City confers the B.B.A. degree. Associate degrees are also awarded. Bachelor's degrees are awarded in BUSINESS (accounting, business administration and management, international business management, and marketing/retailing/merchandising).

Required: To graduate, students must complete the prescribed course of study with a minimum GPA of 2.0. A total of 180 credits is required for the bachelor's degree.

Faculty/Classroom: All teach undergraduates.

Requirements: Graduation from an accredited high school or the GED and an entrance exam or SAT I or ACT scores are basic requirements for admission. A personal interview is strongly recommended. AP and CLEP credits are accepted.

Procedure: Freshmen are admitted to all sessions. Entrance exams should be taken any time. There is a deferred admissions plan. Application deadlines are open. The application fee is $40. Notification is sent on a rolling basis. Applications are accepted on-line at the school's web site.

Transfer: A transcript from each college or university attended must be submitted to receive credit. 60 of 180 credits required for the bachelor's degree must be completed at Berkeley College of New York City.

Visiting: There are guides for informal visits.

Financial Aid: The FAFSA, the college's own financial statement, and the state income tax form are required. Check with the school for current deadlines.

International Students: The school actively recruits these students.

Computers: More than 200 PCs are available to students with access to the Internet and Web. All students may access the system. There are no time limits and no fees.

Admissions Contact: Admissions Officer.
E-mail: *nycampus@berkeleycollege.edu*
Web: *www.berkeleycollege.edu*

BORICUA COLLEGE — D-5
New York, NY 10032 — (212) 694-1000 or (718) 782-2200
Fax: (212) 694-1015 or (718) 782-2050

Full-time: 250 men, 900 women	Faculty: n/av
Part-time: none	Ph.D.s: n/av
Graduate: none	Student/Faculty: n/av
Year: semesters, summer session	Tuition: $7100
Application Deadline: open	Room & Board: n/app
Freshman Class: n/av	
SAT I or ACT: not required	COMPETITIVE

Boricua College, founded in 1974, is a private college for bilingual students, designed to meet the needs of a Spanish-speaking population. Some figures in the above capsule and in this profile are approximate. There are 2 graduate schools. The library contains 128,727 volumes and 3000 audio/video tapes/CDs, and subscribes to 227 periodicals. Computerized library services include the card catalog and database searching. Special learning facilities include a learning resource center and art gallery. The campus is in an urban area in Manhattan and Brooklyn. There are 4 buildings.

Student Life: 70% of students are from public schools. 85% are Hispanic; 10% African American. The average age of freshmen is 29; all undergraduates, 32. 12% do not continue beyond their first year; 80% remain to graduate.

Housing: There are no residence halls. Alcohol is not permitted. No one may keep cars.

Activities: There are no fraternities or sororities. There are 5 groups on campus, including art, chorus, drama, newspaper, and student government. Popular campus events include cultural programs, Puerto Rican Discovery Day, and Christmas and spring concerts with chorus and orchestra.

Sports: Facilities include a gym.

Disabled Students: Elevators and specially equipped rest rooms are available.

Services: Counseling and information services are available, as is tutoring in most subjects.

Campus Safety and Security: Measures include shuttle buses, informal discussions, pamphlets/posters/films, and emergency telephones. There are lighted pathways/sidewalks.

Programs of Study: Bachelor's degrees are awarded in BUSINESS (business administration and management), EDUCATION (elementary), SOCIAL SCIENCE (human services and liberal arts/general studies).

Required: A total of 124 credits is required for the bachelor's degree.

Requirements: Boricua administers its own tests to prospective students, although either the SAT I or ACT is accepted. Applicants must be graduates of an accredited secondary school or have a GED. 2 letters of recommendation and an admissions interview are required. Applicants must demonstrate a working knowledge of English and Spanish to a faculty panel. CLEP credit is accepted. Important factors in the admissions decision are leadership record, personality/intangible qualities, and recommendations by school officials.

Procedure: Freshmen are admitted fall, spring, and summer. There is an early decision plan. Application deadlines are open. The fall 2003 application fee was $25. Notification is sent on a rolling basis.

Transfer: Applicants with associate degrees may transfer up to 60 credits. All college credits passed with grade C and above are accepted. 80 of 124 credits required for the bachelor's degree must be completed at Boricua.

Visiting: There are regularly scheduled orientations for prospective students. Letters are sent to prospective students advising them of scheduled orientations. To schedule a visit, contact Abraham Cruz at (212) 694-1000 or Miriam Pfeffer at (718) 782-2200.

Financial Aid: In a recent year, 95% of all full-time freshmen and 70% of continuing full-time students received some form of financial aid. Boricua is a member of CSS. The FAFSA and income tax forms are required. Check with the school for current deadlines.

Computers: The mainframe is an IBM 486 SX. There are computers available for student use in the computer lab. All students may access the system. There are no time limits and no fees.

Admissions Contact: Abraham Cruz, Director of Admissions, Manhattan or Miriam Pfeffer, Director of Admissions, Northside.
E-mail: *acruz@boricuacollege.edu* or *mpfeffer@boricuacolleg*
Web: *www.boricuacollege.edu*

BROOKLYN CAMPUS OF LONG ISLAND UNIVERSITY
(See Long Island University/Brooklyn Campus)

C. W. POST CAMPUS OF LONG ISLAND UNIVERSITY
(See Long Island University/C.W. Post Campus)

CANISIUS COLLEGE
Buffalo, NY 14208

A-3

(716) 888-2200
(800) 843-1517; Fax: (716) 888-3230

Full-time: 1402 men, 1705 women	**Faculty:** 212; IIA, +$
Part-time: 178 men, 250 women	**Ph.D.s:** 97%
Graduate: 846 men, 714 women	**Student/Faculty:** 15 to 1
Year: semesters, summer session	**Tuition:** $20,193
Application Deadline: open	**Room & Board:** $7970
Freshman Class: 3437 applied, 2868 accepted, 839 enrolled	
SAT I Verbal/Math: 552/557	**ACT:** 24	**COMPETITIVE+**

Canisius College, founded in 1870, is a private Roman Catholic college in the Jesuit tradition. It offers undergraduate programs in the liberal arts and sciences, business, education, and human services. There are 3 undergraduate and 3 graduate schools. In addition to regional accreditation, Canisius has baccalaureate program accreditation with AACSB, ACS, and CED. The library contains 331,571 volumes, 595,198 microform items, and 8026 audio/video tapes/CDs, and subscribes to 10,000 periodicals. Computerized library services include the card catalog, interlibrary loans, database searching, and Internet access. Special learning facilities include a learning resource center, art gallery, planetarium, radio station, television studio, foreign language lab, 87 media-assisted classrooms, digital media lab, and musical instrument digital interface classroom. The 36-acre campus is in an urban area in Buffalo. Including any residence halls, there are 51 buildings.

Student Life: 92% of undergraduates are from New York. Others are from 32 states, 14 foreign countries, and Canada. 73% are white. The average age of freshmen is 18; all undergraduates, 24. 16% do not continue beyond their first year; 67% remain to graduate.

Housing: 1472 students can be accommodated in college housing, which includes single-sex and coed dorms, on-campus apartments, and off-campus apartments. In addition, there are honors houses, special-interest houses, an intercultural hall, and townhouses. On-campus housing is guaranteed for all 4 years. 54% of students commute. Alcohol is not permitted. All students may keep cars.

Activities: 2% of men belong to 1 national fraternity; 2% of women belong to 1 national sorority. There are 100 groups on campus, including art, band, cheerleading, chess, choir, chorale, computers, dance, drama, drill team, ethnic, gay, honors, international, jazz band, literary magazine, musical theater, newspaper, orchestra, pep band, political, professional, radio and TV, religious, social, social service, student government, and yearbook. Popular campus events include Fall Semiformal, Senior Week, and Parents Weekend.

Sports: There are 8 intercollegiate sports for men and 8 for women, and 12 intramural sports for men and 12 for women. Facilities include an 1800-seat athletic center with a 25-yard pool, racquetball courts, and training rooms, a 1000-seat sports complex with Astroturf playing fields, a rifle range, and a mirrored dance studio.

Disabled Students: 90% of the campus is accessible. Wheelchair ramps, elevators, special parking, specially equipped rest rooms, special class scheduling, lowered drinking fountains, lowered telephones, automatic doors, TDD, a shuttle service for students with disabilities, distraction-free testing spaces, and adjustable classroom desks are available.

Services: Counseling and information services are available, as is tutoring in every subject. There is a reader service for the blind, and remedial math, reading, and writing.

Campus Safety and Security: Measures include 24-hour foot and vehicle patrol, self-defense education, security escort services, and shuttle buses. There are informal discussions, pamphlets/posters/films, emergency telephones, lighted pathways/sidewalks, a crime prevention officer, and crime prevention programs.

Programs of Study: Canisius confers B.A. and B.S. degrees. Master's degrees are also awarded. Bachelor's degrees are awarded in BIOLOGICAL SCIENCE (biochemistry, bioinformatics, and biology/biological science), BUSINESS (accounting, banking and finance, business administration and management, international business management, management information systems, and marketing/retailing/merchandising), COMMUNICATIONS AND THE ARTS (art history and appreciation, communications, English, French, German, languages, music, and Spanish), COMPUTER AND PHYSICAL SCIENCE (chemistry, computer science, digital arts/technology, mathematics, and physics), EDUCATION (athletic training, business, elementary, English, foreign languages, mathematics, physical, science, secondary, social studies, and special), ENGINEERING AND ENVIRONMENTAL DESIGN (environmental science), HEALTH PROFESSIONS (medical laboratory technology), SOCIAL SCIENCE (anthropology, criminal justice, economics, Eu-

ropean studies, history, humanities, international relations, philosophy, political science/government, psychology, religion, social science, sociology, and urban studies). Accounting, chemistry, and computer science are the strongest academically. Psychology, management, and biology are the largest.

Required: All students must complete a core curriculum consisting of 4 courses in general studies (literature, writing, philosophy, and religion) and 14 courses in area studies (natural sciences, social studies, art and literature, history, philosophy, religious studies, math, and languages). In addition, students must take 10 3-credit courses in the major. A minimum of 120 credit hours and a minimum GPA of 2.0 are required for graduation.

Special: Canisius offers internships, credit by exam, pass/fail options, nondegree studies, dual majors, including anthropology/sociology, a Washington semester, work-study programs, and study abroad in 10 countries. Cooperative programs are available with the Fashion Institute of Technology in New York City and the SUNY College of Environmental Science and Forestry in Syracuse. Cross-registration is permitted with 14 schools in the Western New York Consortium of Higher Education. Canisius also offers early assurance and joint degree programs with SUNY health professions schools in Buffalo and Syracuse, and a 3-2 M.B.A. There are 9 national honor societies, a freshman honors program, and 2 departmental honors programs.

Faculty/Classroom: 62% of faculty are male; 38%, female. 97% teach undergraduates, 75% do research, and 65% do both. No introductory courses are taught by graduate students. The average class size in an introductory lecture is 24; in a laboratory, 21; and in a regular course, 26.

Admissions: 83% of the 2003-2004 applicants were accepted. The SAT I scores for the 2003-2004 freshman class were: Verbal--23% below 500, 50% between 500 and 599, 23% between 600 and 700, and 4% above 700; Math--22% below 500, 46% between 500 and 599, 28% between 600 and 700, and 4% above 700. The ACT scores were 27% below 21, 23% between 21 and 23, 28% between 24 and 26, 11% between 27 and 28, and 11% above 28. 45% of the current freshmen were in the top fifth of their class; 73% were in the top two fifths.

Requirements: The SAT I or ACT is required. In addition, all students must submit an official high school transcript (or GED). College preparatory course work should include 4 units each of English and social science and 3 units each of math, science, and foreign language. Students with a B+ average and 1000 SAT I or higher are most competitive. An essay and an interview are recommended. A GPA of 2.0 is required. AP and CLEP credits are accepted. Important factors in the admissions decision are advanced placement or honor courses, recommendations by school officials, and leadership record.

Procedure: Freshmen are admitted fall and spring. Entrance exams should be taken during the junior or senior year. There are early admissions and deferred admissions plans. Application deadlines are open. The fall 2003 application was $25. Notification is sent on a rolling basis. Applications are accepted on-line.

Transfer: 155 transfer students enrolled in 2002-2003. Applicants must present a minimum GPA of 2.0. 30 of 120 credits required for the bachelor's degree must be completed at Canisius.

Visiting: There are regularly scheduled orientations for prospective students, including campus overnights and single-day visits. Also available are summer visitations for families, an open house in the fall and in the spring, and a financial aid workshop in January. There are guides for informal visits and visitors may sit in on classes and stay overnight. To schedule a visit, contact the Admissions Office at admissions@canisius.edu.

Financial Aid: In 2003-2004, 98% of all full-time freshmen and 89% of continuing full-time students received some form of financial aid. 86% of full-time freshmen and 84% of continuing full-time students received need-based aid. The average freshman award was $16,259. Need-based scholarships or need-based grants averaged $5287 ($25,168 maximum); need-based self-help aid (loans and jobs) averaged $4476 ($8625 maximum); non-need-based athletic scholarships averaged $13,033 ($32,141 maximum); and other non-need-based awards and non-need-based scholarships averaged $9124 ($26,842 maximum). 21% of undergraduates work part time. Average annual earnings from campus work are $1380. The average financial indebtedness of the 2003 graduate was $18,938. Canisius is a member of CSS. The FAFSA and the college's own financial statement are required. The priority date for freshman financial aid applications for fall entry is February 15.

International Students: There are 78 international students enrolled. The school actively recruits these students. They must score 500 on the written TOEFL or 173 on the electronic version and also take the SAT I or the ACT.

Computers: The mainframe is a Sun. All student computers may access the Web, and all students have e-mail. There are a total of 30 labs with 468 computers available for student use. Among them are 5 Internet Plazas with 38 computers where students can check their e-mail or access web sites; 7 general-purpose computer labs with a total of 183 computers; 54 laptops available for use in the library over a wireless network; 4 residence hall computer labs with 33 computers; and a variety of department and special-purpose computer labs. All students may access the system. The Web can be accessed at any time. There are no time limits. The fee is $225. It is strongly recommended that all students have a personal computer.

Graduates: From July 1, 2002 to June 30, 2003, 671 bachelor's degrees were awarded. The most popular majors were education (10%), communication studies (9%), and psychology (7%). In an average class, 51% graduate in 4 years or less, 66% graduate in 5 years or less, and 67% graduate in 6 years or less. 24 companies recruited on campus in 2002-2003. Of the 2002 graduating class, 26% were enrolled in graduate school within 6 months of graduation and 63% were employed.

Admissions Contact: Penelope H. Lips, Director of Admissions. E-mail: *admissions@canisius.edu* Web: *http://www.canisius.edu*

CAZENOVIA COLLEGE	C-3
Cazenovia, NY 13035	(315) 655-7208
	(800) 654-3210; Fax: (315) 655-2190
Full-time: 217 men, 588 women	**Faculty:** 46; IIB, --$
Part-time: 38 men, 141 women	**Ph.D.s:** 63%
Graduate: none	**Student/Faculty:** 18 to 1
Year: semesters, summer session	**Tuition:** $16,980
Application Deadline: open	**Room & Board:** $6960
Freshman Class: 1038 applied, 869 accepted, 274 enrolled	
SAT I Verbal/Math: 480/480	**ACT:** 19 **COMPETITIVE**

Cazenovia College, founded in 1824, is a private institution offering degree programs in applied arts and sciences and preprofessional studies. The library contains 64,000 volumes, 13,000 microform items, and 3000 audio/video tapes/CDs, and subscribes to 456 periodicals. Computerized library services include interlibrary loans and database searching. Special learning facilities include a learning resource center, art gallery, radio station, and a nearby campus farm with equine center. The 40-acre campus is in a small town 18 miles southeast of Syracuse. Including any residence halls, there are 24 buildings.

Student Life: 85% of undergraduates are from New York. Students are from 20 states and 2 foreign countries. 91% are from public schools. 85% are white. The average age of freshmen is 18. 33% do not continue beyond their first year; 32% remain to graduate.

Housing: 600 students can be accommodated in college housing, which includes single-sex and coed dorms and on-campus apartments. In addition, there is a quiet building, wellness center, global awareness cluster, all-female residence hall, and upperclass-only section. On-campus housing is guaranteed for the freshman year only and is available on a lottery system for upperclassmen. 76% of students live on campus; of those, 60% remain on campus on weekends. Alcohol is not permitted. All students may keep cars.

Activities: There are no fraternities or sororities. There are many groups and organizations on campus, including cheerleading, chorale, computers, drama, ethnic, gay, honors, literary magazine, musical theater, newspaper, political, social service, student government, and yearbook. Popular campus events include Spring Day, Parents Weekend, and athletic events.

Sports: There are 5 intercollegiate sports for men and 6 for women, and 8 intramural sports for men and 9 for women. Facilities include an athletic center with a pool, 2 gyms, a weight room, 2 racquetball courts, outdoor tennis courts, and athletic fields.

Disabled Students: 86% of the campus is accessible. Wheelchair ramps, elevators, special parking, specially equipped rest rooms, special class scheduling, lowered telephones, and special housing are available.

Services: Counseling and information services are available, as is tutoring in every subject. There is a reader service for the blind and remedial math, reading, and writing.

Campus Safety and Security: Measures include 24-hour foot and vehicle patrol, security escort services, informal discussions, and pamphlets/posters/films. There are emergency telephones and lighted pathways/sidewalks.

Programs of Study: Cazenovia confers B.A., B.S., B.F.A., and B.P.S. degrees. Associate degrees are also awarded. Bachelor's degrees are awarded in BUSINESS (management science), COMMUNICATIONS AND THE ARTS (English and studio art), EDUCATION (early childhood and elementary), ENGINEERING AND ENVIRONMENTAL DESIGN (commercial art and interior design), SOCIAL SCIENCE (human services, liberal arts/general studies, psychology, and social science). Interior or design, liberal arts, and human services are the strongest academically. Management is the largest.

Required: A total of 120 semester credits and a GPA of 2.0 are required for the bachelor's degree. Students must take courses in speech, academic writing, diversity and social consciousness, science or math, visual literacy, communications, ethics, cultural literacy, and research methods. They must also demonstrate math proficiency and complete a senior capstone course.

Special: Cazenovia offers internships, a Washington semester, work-study, B.A.-B.S. degrees in liberal studies and liberal and professional studies, and study abroad. There is cross-registration with the American International University in London and the Institute for Experimental

Learning. There is 1 national honor society, a freshman honors program, and 2 departmental honors programs.

Faculty/Classroom: 39% of faculty are male; 61%, female. All teach undergraduates and 1% do research. The average class size in an introductory lecture is 22; in a laboratory, 15; and in a regular course, 16.

Admissions: 84% of the 2003-2004 applicants were accepted. The SAT I scores for the 2003-2004 freshman class were: Verbal--57% below 500, 37% between 500 and 599, and 7% between 600 and 700; Math--59% below 500, 35% between 500 and 599, and 6% between 600 and 700. The ACT scores were 60% below 21, 33% between 21 and 23, and 7% between 24 and 26.

Requirements: The SAT I or ACT is recommended. In addition, applicants should be graduates of an accredited secondary school or the equivalent. A recommendation from a guidance counselor or teacher is required. A GPA of 2.0 is required. AP and CLEP credits are accepted. Important factors in the admissions decision are evidence of special talent, personality/intangible qualities, and recommendations by school officials.

Procedure: Freshmen are admitted fall and spring. Entrance exams should be taken by the fall of the senior year. There are early admissions, deferred admissions, and rolling admissions plans. Application deadlines are open. Application fee is $25. A waiting list is an active part of the admissions procedure.

Transfer: 58 transfer students enrolled in a recent year. Applicants must present at least 12 college credits, with a minimum GPA of 2.0, and official transcripts from previous colleges attended. Students with fewer than 24 credits must also submit a high school transcript. 30 of 120 credits required for the bachelor's degree must be completed at Cazenovia.

Visiting: There are regularly scheduled orientations for prospective students, consisting of a welcome by the president and deans, financial aid sessions, placement testing, academic advising, and registration. There are guides for informal visits and visitors may sit in on classes and stay overnight. To schedule a visit, contact the Admissions and Financial Aid Office.

Financial Aid: In a recent year, 85% of all full-time freshmen and 97% of continuing full-time students received some form of financial aid. 82% of full-time freshmen and 93% of continuing full-time students received need-based aid. The average freshman award was $11,664. 22% of undergraduates work part time. Average annual earnings from campus work are $1000. The average financial indebtedness of a recent graduate was $14,808. The FAFSA and Express TAP are required. The deadline for filing freshman financial aid applications for fall entry is March 15.

International Students: In a recent year, there were 2 international students enrolled. They must score 550 on the written TOEFL and also take the SAT I or the ACT.

Computers: The mainframe is a networked IBM-type LAN. Students access a network designed for the computer lab that houses approximately 70 PCs. Network access is also available in residence halls and is linked to the Internet. All students may access the system daily from 8 A.M. to midnight. There are no time limits. The fee is $100.

Graduates: From July 1, 2002 to June 30, 2003, 102 bachelor's degrees were awarded. The most popular majors were management (39%), human services (25%), and visual communications (19%). In an average class, 35% graduate in 5 years or less. 23 companies recruited on campus in 2002-2003.

Admissions Contact: Robert A. Croot, Dean for Admissions and Financial Aid. E-mail: *admission@cazcollege.edu* Web: *www.cazenovia.edu*

CITY UNIVERSITY OF NEW YORK

The City University of New York (CUNY), established in 1847, is a public system in New York City, and the nations's leading urban university. It is governed by a board of trustees whose chief administrator is the chancellor. The mission of the University is to maintain and expand its commitment to academic excellence and to the provision of equal access and opportunity. Its main priorities are providing access for all students who seek to enroll in community or senior colleges, ensuring student success, and enhancing instructional and research excellence. Close to 80 percent of CUNY's nearly 6000 full-time faculty hold the highest degrees in their fields. Many are recipients of such prestigious awards as Pulitzer Prizes, MacArthur "genius awards", Britain's Booker Prize, Academy Awards, and Carnegie Teacher of the Year Awards. The highly competitive university-wide Honors College, established in 2001, has attracted the region's most talented students. CUNY includes 11 senior colleges, 6 community colleges, a graduate school, a law school, and a school of biomedical education, and serves nearly 450,000 degree-credit students and adult, continuing, and professional education students.There are 1400 academic programs offered, with more than 200 majors leading to associate and baccalaureate degrees and more than 100 graduate degree majors. Profiles of the 4-year campuses (located in New York's 5 boroughs of Manhattan, Brooklyn, Queens, Staten Island, and the Bronx) appear in this section.

CITY UNIVERSITY OF NEW YORK/BARUCH COLLEGE D-5

New York, NY 10010-5585   **(646) 312-1400; Fax: (646) 312-1361**

Full-time: 3940 men, 5020 women	**Faculty:** 405
Part-time: 1725 men, 2510 women	**Ph.D.s:** 87%
Graduate: 1400 men, 1400 women	**Student/Faculty:** 22 to 1
Year: semesters, summer session	**Tuition:** $4075 ($10,875)
Application Deadline: February 1	**Room & Board:** n/app
Freshman Class: n/av	
SAT I or ACT: required	**VERY COMPETITIVE+**

Baruch College was founded in 1919 and became a separate unit of the City University of New York in 1968. It offers undergraduate programs in business and public administration and liberal arts and sciences. Some figures in the above capsule and in this profile are approximate. There are 3 undergraduate and 3 graduate schools. In addition to regional accreditation, Baruch has baccalaureate program accreditation with AACSB. The library contains 427,268 volumes, 2,064,811 microform items, and 1017 audio/video tapes/CDs, and subscribes to 4154 periodicals. Computerized library services include the card catalog, interlibrary loans, and database searching. Special learning facilities include a learning resource center, art gallery, and radio station. The campus is in Manhattan. There are 6 buildings.

Student Life: 90% of undergraduates are from New York. Students are from 15 states, 144 foreign countries, and Canada. 70% are from public schools. 26% are Asian American; 26% white; 20% Hispanic; 17% African American; 11% foreign nationals. The average age of freshmen is 18; all undergraduates, 23. 16% do not continue beyond their first year.

Housing: There are no residence halls. All of students commute. Alcohol is not permitted. No one may keep cars.

Activities: 1% of men belong to 1 local fraternity and 2 national fraternities; 1% of women belong to 1 local sorority and 2 national sororities. There are 98 groups on campus, including cheerleading, chess, chorus, computers, drama, ethnic, gay, honors, international, literary magazine, newspaper, photography, political, professional, radio and TV, religious, social, social service, student government, and yearbook. Popular campus events include club fairs, street fairs, and Caribbean Week.

Sports: There are 5 intercollegiate sports for men and 5 for women, and 4 intramural sports for men and 2 for women. Facilities include a gym, a swimming pool, a weight room, an exercise room, and racquetball courts.

Disabled Students: All of the campus is accessible. Wheelchair ramps, elevators, specially equipped rest rooms, and special class scheduling are available.

Services: Counseling and information services are available, as is tutoring in most subjects. There is a reader service for the blind and remedial math, reading, and writing. Note takers, large-print computer screens, and interpreters for the deaf are available.

Campus Safety and Security: Measures include 24-hour foot and vehicle patrol, self-defense education, security escort services, and informal discussions. There are pamphlets/posters/films, lighted pathways/sidewalks, emergency phones, fire safety directors, and an ID system that uses card swipe in turnstiles for entry.

Programs of Study: Baruch confers B.A., B.S., and B.B.A. degrees. Master's and doctoral degrees are also awarded. Bachelor's degrees are awarded in BUSINESS (accounting, investments and securities, management science, marketing management, marketing/retailing/merchandising, operations research, personnel management, and real estate), COMMUNICATIONS AND THE ARTS (advertising, communications, English, journalism, music, and Spanish), COMPUTER AND PHYSICAL SCIENCE (actuarial science, information sciences and systems, mathematics, and statistics), SOCIAL SCIENCE (economics, history, industrial and organizational psychology, philosophy, political science/government, psychology, public affairs, and sociology). Economics, English, and math are the strongest academically. Accounting, finance, and computer information systems are the largest.

Required: Students must complete a minimum of 120 credits for the B.A. or B.S. and 124 for the B.B.A., with at least 24 hours in the major, and maintain a GPA of 2.0 overall in the major. Students' core curriculum should include courses in English, literature, communications, history, philosophy, and fine and performing arts.

Special: Students may take courses at all CUNY schools. The college offers internships and study abroad in Great Britain, France, Germany, Mexico, and Israel. Students may design their own liberal arts major. A federal work-study program is available, and pass/fail options are permitted for liberal arts majors. Students may combine any undergraduate major with a master's in accountancy. There are 7 national honor societies and a freshman honors program.

Faculty/Classroom: 65% of faculty are male; 35%, female. 93% teach undergraduates. Graduate students teach 4% of introductory courses. The average class size in an introductory lecture is 250; in a laboratory, 20; and in a regular course, 35.

Admissions: 45 freshmen graduated first in their class in a recent year.

Requirements: The SAT I or ACT is required. In addition, applicants must present an official high school transcript (a GED will be accepted) indicating a minimum average grade of 81% in academic subjects (minimum of 14 credits). AP and CLEP credits are accepted.

Procedure: Freshmen are admitted fall and spring. Entrance exams should be taken March 1. There is an early decision plan. Applications should be filed by February 1 for fall entry and October 1 for spring entry. The application fee is $50. Admissions processing takes 6 to 8 weeks.

Transfer: 1102 transfer students enrolled in a recent year. All other applicants must have a minimum GPA of 2.5 for 12 to 34.9 credits submitted, a minimum GPA of 2.25 for 35 to 59.9 credits, and a minimum GPA of 2.0 for 60 or more credits. Business applicants must have a 2.75 GPA. Students applying for transfer with fewer than 12 credits earned must have a minimum GPA of 2.5 and a minimum high school average of 80%. 32 of 128 credits required for the bachelor's degree must be completed at Baruch.

Visiting: There are regularly scheduled orientations for prospective students, including a meeting with an admissions counselor. There are guides for informal visits. To schedule a visit, contact the Admissions Office.

Financial Aid: In a recent year, 92% of all full-time freshmen and 68% of continuing full-time students received some form of financial aid. 67% of full-time freshmen and 59% of continuing full-time students received need-based aid. The average freshman award was $2060. 75% of undergraduates work part time. Average annual earnings from campus work are $2500. The average financial indebtedness of a recent year's graduate was $9660. Baruch is a member of CSS. The FAFSA is required. Check with the school for current deadlines.

International Students: There were 1185 international students enrolled in a recent year. They must score 620 on the written TOEFL or 260 on the electronic version and also take the college's own test.

Computers: There are 1200 PCs available in the computer center, media center, resource center, library, computer labs, and classrooms throughout the entire campus for student use. All students may access the system. There are no time limits and no fees.

Graduates: In a recent year, 2356 bachelor's degrees were awarded. The most popular majors were accounting (29%), finance and investments (15%), and human resource management (9%). In an average class, 5% graduate in 4 years or less, 23% graduate in 5 years or less, and 35% graduate in 6 years or less. 350 companies recruited on campus in a recent year.

Admissions Contact: Director of Undergraduate Admissions and Financial Aid. A video is available. E-mail: *admissions@baruch.cuny.edu* Web: *www.baruch.cuny.edu*

CITY UNIVERSITY OF NEW YORK/BROOKLYN COLLEGE D-5

Brooklyn, NY 11210-2889   **(718) 951-5001; Fax: (718) 951-4506**

Full-time: 3198 men, 4501 women	**Faculty:** 509; IIA, ++$
Part-time: 1205 men, 2056 women	**Ph.D.s:** 91%
Graduate: 1444 men, 3109 women	**Student/Faculty:** 15 to 1
Year: semesters, summer session	**Tuition:** $4353 ($8993)
Application Deadline: open	**Room & Board:** n/app
Freshman Class: 7128 applied, 2595 accepted, 1349 enrolled	
SAT I or ACT: required	**COMPETITIVE+**

Brooklyn College, established in 1930, is a publicly supported college of liberal arts, sciences, preprofessional, and professional studies. It is part of the City University of New York and serves the commuter student. There are 2 undergraduate schools and 1 graduate school. In addition to regional accreditation, Brooklyn College has baccalaureate program accreditation with ADA and ASLHA. The library contains 1,299,328 volumes, 1,650,832 microform items, and 22,431 audio/video tapes/CDs, and subscribes to 20,025 periodicals. Computerized library services include the card catalog, interlibrary loans, database searching, and Internet access. Special learning facilities include a learning resource center, art gallery, radio station, TV station, 3 color studios, and a speech and hearing clinic. The 26-acre campus is in an urban area in Brooklyn, New York. There are 8 buildings.

Student Life: 95% of undergraduates are from New York. Students are from 25 states, 75 foreign countries, and Canada. 60% are from public schools. 45% are white; 29% African American; 11% Hispanic; 10% Asian American. The average age of freshmen is 19; all undergraduates, 25. 16% do not continue beyond their first year; 84% remain to graduate.

Housing: There are no residence halls. All students commute. Alcohol is not permitted. No one may keep cars.

Activities: 3% of men belong to 1 local and 6 national fraternities; 3% of women belong to 4 local and 3 national sororities. There are 150 groups on campus, including academic, art, chess, choir, chorus, computers, dance, drama, ethnic, film, forensics, gay, honors, international, literary magazine, musical theater, newspaper, orchestra, photography, political, professional, radio and TV, religious, social, social service, student government, symphony, and yearbook. Popular campus events include Country Fair, Fall Festival, and Black Solidarity Day.

Sports: There are 8 intercollegiate sports for men and 8 for women, and 17 intramural sports for men and 17 for women. Facilities include swimming pools, a soccer field, volleyball, racquetball, squash, tennis, and basketball courts, a weight-training room, and a jogging track.

Disabled Students: All of the campus is accessible. Wheelchair ramps, elevators, special parking, specially equipped rest rooms, special class scheduling, lowered drinking fountains, and lowered telephones are available.

Services: Counseling and information services are available, as is tutoring in every subject. There is a reader service for the blind.

Campus Safety and Security: Measures include 24-hour foot and vehicle patrol, security escort services, shuttle buses, and informal discussions. There are pamphlets/posters/films, emergency telephones, lighted pathways/sidewalks, CCTV cameras, and informational assistants.

Programs of Study: Brooklyn College confers B.A., B.S., B.F.A., and B.Mus. degrees. Master's degrees are also awarded. Bachelor's degrees are awarded in BIOLOGICAL SCIENCE (biology/biological science), BUSINESS (accounting, banking and finance, and business administration and management), COMMUNICATIONS AND THE ARTS (art, art history and appreciation, broadcasting, classics, comparative literature, creative writing, English, film arts, French, German, Greek, Hebrew, Italian, journalism, languages, Latin, linguistics, music, music performance, music theory and composition, radio/television technology, Russian, Spanish, theater management, and visual and performing arts), COMPUTER AND PHYSICAL SCIENCE (chemistry, computer science, geology, information sciences and systems, mathematics, and physics), EDUCATION (art, bilingual/bicultural, early childhood, education of the deaf and hearing impaired, elementary, English, foreign languages, health, mathematics, music, physical, science, secondary, and social studies), HEALTH PROFESSIONS (health science, and speech pathology/audiology), SOCIAL SCIENCE (African studies, American studies, anthropology, archeology, Caribbean studies, economics, Hispanic American studies, history, Judaic studies, Latin American studies, philosophy, political science/government, psychology, religion, sociology, and women's studies). Education, business, and computer science are the largest and the strongest academically.

Required: 14 required, interrelated courses cover the following core curriculum areas: classics, art, music, political science, sociology, history, literature, math, computer science, chemistry, physics, biology, geology, philosophy, and comparative cultures. There are basic skills requirements in reading, composition, speech, and math, as well as a foreign language requirement. A 2.0 GPA and a minimum of 120 credit hours, with 31 to 36 in the major (67 to 70 for chemistry), are required to graduate.

Special: There are numerous cross-registration programs with colleges and universities in the area. Many internships and work-study programs are available. Study abroad is possible in more than 50 countries. A B.A.-M.D., B.S.-M.P.S., and accelerated B.A.-M.A. programs are available. A number of B.A.-B.S. degrees, dual majors, a 3-2 engineering degree, and student-designed majors are possible. Credit by exam, credit for life experience, nondegree study, and pass/fail options are offered. There is a Latin and Greek Institute offered during the summer through the graduate center. There are 13 national honor societies, including Phi Beta Kappa, a freshman honors program, and 26 departmental honors programs.

Faculty/Classroom: 57% of faculty are male; 43%, female. 80% teach undergraduates and 80% do research. The average class size in a laboratory is 15 and in a regular course, 35.

Admissions: 36% of the 2003-2004 applicants were accepted. 37% of the current freshmen were in the top quarter of their class; 69% were in the top half.

Requirements: The SAT I or ACT is required, with an SAT I composite score of 960 (480 verbal and 480 math). Alternatively, the ACT is accepted with 20-20 verbal and math scores. The GED, with a score of 3000 or higher, is accepted. Requirements are higher for B.A.-M.D. entrants and for the scholars program. Applicants not meeting the standard requirements are eligible for admission to the City University's community colleges. AP and CLEP credits are accepted.

Procedure: Freshmen are admitted fall and spring. Entrance exams should be taken prior to admission. There is an early admissions plan. There is a rolling admissions plan. Application deadlines are open. Application fee is $50. Applications are accepted on-line through through the school's web site.

Transfer: 1479 transfer students enrolled in 2002-2003. Transfer students must have a minimum 2.0 GPA with 24 or more credits; 2.25 with 15 to 23 credits; and 2.5 with 7 to 14 credits. Students with less than 7 credits must have an acceptable high school average and a 2.0 college GPA. 30 of 120 credits required for the bachelor's degree must be completed at Brooklyn College.

Visiting: There are regularly scheduled orientations for prospective students, including campus tours, presentations, and meetings with faculty. There are guides for informal visits. To schedule a visit, contact Faride Precil, Admissions at (718) 951-5056 or FPrecil@brooklyn.cuny.edu.

Financial Aid: In 2003-2004, 66% of all full-time freshmen and 62% of continuing full-time students received some form of financial aid. 64%

of full-time freshmen and 65% of continuing full-time students received need-based aid. The average freshman award was $5470. 71% of undergraduates work part time. Average annual earnings from campus work are $1200. The average financial indebtedness of the 2003 graduate was $9700. The FAFSA is required. The priority date for freshman financial aid applications for fall entry is April 1.

International Students: There are 421 international students enrolled. The school actively recruits these students. They must score 500 on the written TOEFL or 173 on the electronic version and also take the college's own test and the SAT I or the ACT, scoring 900 (SAT I).

Computers: The Office of Information Technology Services (ITS) has labs containing 300 networked PCs, all of which provide Internet access, and provide a full complement of adaptive equipment for students with special needs. Wired and wireless connectivity is available for students who wish to use their own laptops. A variety of software applications is available, along with assistance by expert lab technicians, free laser printing, and videoconferencing. Additionally, the Student Union Building Learning Center has 40 Internet-equipped computers and several color printers and 12 workstations. Additional computers are available in the library, with more than 500 PCs and 55 PCs in the library café (24 hours a day, 7 days a week), as well as in individual academic departments.

Graduates: From July 1, 2002 to June 30, 2003, 1600 bachelor's degrees were awarded. The most popular majors were business (16%), elementary education (12%), and computer and information science (11%). In an average class, 15% graduate in 4 years or less, 32% graduate in 5 years or less, and 39% graduate in 6 years or less. 68 companies recruited on campus in 2002-2003. Of the 2002 graduating class, 35% were enrolled in graduate school within 6 months of graduation and 92% were employed.

Admissions Contact: Marianne Booufall Tynan, Director of Admissions. E-mail: adminqry@brooklyn.cuny.edu
Web: www.brooklyn.cuny.edu

CITY UNIVERSITY OF NEW YORK/CITY COLLEGE   D-5

New York, NY 10031-9101   (212) 650-6977; Fax: (212) 650-6417

Full-time: 3114 men, 2801 women	**Faculty:** 479; IIA, ++$
Part-time: 1393 men, 1530 women	**Ph.D.s:** 86%
Graduate: 1496 men, 2066 women	**Student/Faculty:** 12 to 1
Year: semesters, summer session	**Tuition:** $4230 ($11,030)
Application Deadline: December 1	**Room & Board:** n/app
Freshman Class: 6140 applied, 2061 accepted, 1011 enrolled	
SAT I Verbal/Math: 460/490	**COMPETITIVE+**

City College, founded in 1847, is a public liberal arts college that is part of the City University of New York. The college offers programs through 4 undergraduate and 4 graduate schools and 2 professional centers. There are 6 undergraduate and 6 graduate schools. In addition to regional accreditation, CCNY has baccalaureate program accreditation with ABET, ABFSE, NAAB, and NCATE. The 4 libraries contain 1,413,641 volumes, 868,042 microform items, and 21,174 audio/video tapes/CDs, and subscribe to 5156 periodicals. Computerized library services include the card catalog, interlibrary loans, database searching, and Internet access. Special learning facilities include a learning resource center, art gallery, planetarium, radio station, TV station, weather station, laser labs, microwave labs, and Structural Biology Lab. The 34-acre campus is in an urban area in New York City. There are 14 buildings.

Student Life: Students are from 32 states, 140 foreign countries, and Canada. 91% are from public schools. 32% are Hispanic; 27% African American; 16% Asian American; 13% white; 12% foreign nationals. The average age of freshmen is 18; all undergraduates, 26. 12% do not continue beyond their first year; 32% remain to graduate.

Housing: There are no residence halls. All students commute. Alcohol is not permitted. All students may keep cars.

Activities: There are no fraternities or sororities. There are 100 groups on campus, including art, band, cheerleading, chess, chorus, computers, drama, ethnic, gay, honors, international, jazz band, literary magazine, newspaper, orchestra, political, professional, radio and TV, religious, social, social service, student government, and yearbook. Popular campus events include Langston Hughes Poetry Contest, Dance Theater of Harlem performances at Davis Center, and Architecture Lecture Series.

Sports: There are 7 intercollegiate sports for men and 7 for women. Facilities include swimming pools, 2 gyms, a weight room, and an outdoor track and field stadium.

Disabled Students: 90% of the campus is accessible. Wheelchair ramps, elevators, special parking, specially equipped rest rooms, special class scheduling, lowered drinking fountains, and lowered telephones are available.

Services: Counseling and information services are available, as is tutoring in most subjects. There is a reader service for the blind.

Campus Safety and Security: Measures include 24-hour foot and vehicle patrol, security escort services, shuttle buses, and informal discussions. There are pamphlets/posters/films, emergency telephones, lighted pathways/sidewalks, and bicycle patrols, IDs, criminal investigations, and security systems.

Programs of Study: CCNY confers B.A., B.S., B.Arch., B.E., B.F.A., B.M.E., and B.S.Ed. degrees. Master's degrees are also awarded. Bachelor's degrees are awarded in BIOLOGICAL SCIENCE (biology/biological science), BUSINESS (business administration and management), COMMUNICATIONS AND THE ARTS (art, communications, comparative literature, dramatic arts, English, film arts, fine arts, French, multimedia, music, performing arts, romance languages and literature, Spanish, and video), COMPUTER AND PHYSICAL SCIENCE (atmospheric sciences and meteorology, chemistry, computer science, earth science, geology, mathematics, physics, and quantitative methods), EDUCATION (art, bilingual/bicultural, early childhood, education of the emotionally handicapped, education of the mentally handicapped, elementary, English, foreign languages, mathematics, secondary, social studies, and special), ENGINEERING AND ENVIRONMENTAL DESIGN (architecture, biomedical engineering, chemical engineering, civil engineering, computer engineering, electrical/electronics engineering, landscape architecture/design, and mechanical engineering), HEALTH PROFESSIONS (biomedical science, physician's assistant, predentistry, and premedicine), SOCIAL SCIENCE (American studies, anthropology, area studies, Asian/Oriental studies, economics, ethnic studies, history, international studies, Latin American studies, philosophy, political science/government, prelaw, psychology, sociology, and urban studies). Engineering, architecture, and sciences are the strongest academically. Engineering, architecture, and psychology are the largest.

Required: Students must successfully complete 120 credits, with 32 to 48 in the major, and maintain a minimum GPA of 2.0. A core curriculum must be met, and students must complete a college proficiency exam, and courses in basic writing, world humanities, world civilizations, computer literacy, world arts, and U.S. society.

Special: Cross-registration is permitted with other City University colleges. A 6-year urban legal studies degree and a 7-year biomedical education degree are available. Opportunities are provided for a co-op program in engineering, a B.A.-B.S. degree in biomedical engineering, internships, a Washington semester, work-study programs, a wide variety of accelerated degree programs, dual majors, credit by exam, credit for life experience, and study abroad in Vienna and Morocco. There are 2 national honor societies, including Phi Beta Kappa, a freshman honors program, and all departments have honors programs.

Faculty/Classroom: 63% of faculty are male; 37%, female. 68% teach undergraduates, 58% do research, and 40% do both. No introductory courses are taught by graduate students. The average class size in an introductory lecture is 29; in a laboratory, 16; and in a regular course, 19.

Admissions: 34% of the 2002-2003 applicants were accepted. The SAT I scores for the 2003-2004 freshman class were: Verbal--62% below 500, 26% between 500 and 599, 10% between 600 and 700, and 2% above 700; Math--50% below 500, 30% between 500 and 599, 16% between 600 and 700, and 4% above 700. 56% of the current freshmen were in the top fifth of their class; 78% were in the top two fifths.

Requirements: The SAT I is required. A minimum composite SAT I score of 1100 or an ACT score of 22 is recommended. Graduation from an accredited secondary school is generally required, but a GED will be accepted. 14 academic credits should be presented, with a minimum grade average of 80%. AP credits are accepted.

Procedure: Freshmen are admitted fall and spring. Entrance exams should be taken prior to registration. There is an early admissions plan and a rolling admissions plan. Applications should be filed by December 1 for fall entry and October 15 for spring entry. Notification is sent on a rolling basis. The fall 2003 application fee was $40. Applications are accepted on-line through *www.ccny.cuny.edu.*

Transfer: 1070 transfer students enrolled in 2002-2003. Transfer applicants must have earned a minimum of 24 credit hours and maintained a GPA of 2.0. Selected programs have more competitive requirements. 32 of 120 credits required for the bachelor's degree must be completed at CCNY.

Visiting: There are regularly scheduled orientations for prospective students. There are guides for informal visits and visitors may sit in on classes. To schedule a visit, contact the Admissions Office at (212) 650-6476.

Financial Aid: In 2003-2004, 67% of all full-time freshmen and 75% of continuing full-time students received some form of financial aid. 63% of full-time freshmen and 72% of continuing full-time students received need-based aid. The average freshman award was $4860. Need-based scholarships or need-based grants averaged $4600 ($8050 maximum); need-based self-help aid (loans and jobs) averaged $3840 ($4625 maximum); and non-need-based awards and non-need-based scholarships averaged $2900 (maximum). 65% of undergraduates work part time. The average financial indebtedness of the 2003 graduate was $18,408. The FAFSA and the state aid form are required. The priority date for freshman financial aid applications for fall entry is April 1. The deadline for filing freshman financial aid applications for fall entry is rolling.

International Students: There are 997 international students enrolled. They must score 500 on the written TOEFL or 173 on the electronic version and also take the SAT I.

Computers: The mainframe is an IBM 3090 located at the City University central computer facility. A campuswide fiber-optic network is the backbone; more than 5000 PCs are networked throughout campus; 50 computer languages are available. All students may access the system. There are no time limits and no fees.

Graduates: From July 1, 2002 to June 30, 2003, 1363 bachelor's degrees were awarded. The most popular majors were psychology (13%), liberal arts (10%), and computer science (6%). In an average class, 4% graduate in 4 years or less, 22% graduate in 5 years or less, and 32% graduate in 6 years or less. More than 1000 companies recruited on campus in 2002-2003. In a recent graduating class, 14% were enrolled in graduate school within 6 months of graduation.

Admissions Contact: Celia Lloyd, Acting Director of Admissions. A video is available. E-mail: *admissions@admin.ccny.cuny.edu* Web: *www.ccny.cuny.edu*

CITY UNIVERSITY OF NEW YORK/COLLEGE OF STATEN ISLAND   D-5

Staten Island, NY 10314   (718) 982-2010; Fax: (718) 982-2500

Full-time: 3272 men, 3986 women	Faculty: 266; IIA, +$
Part-time: 1294 men, 2549 women	Ph.D.s: 81%
Graduate: 281 men, 1040 women	Student/Faculty: 27 to 1
Year: semesters, summer session	Tuition: $4308 ($11,108)
Application Deadline: open	Room & Board: n/app
Freshman Class: 6487 applied, 6487 accepted, 2344 enrolled	
SAT I Verbal/Math: 430/440	NONCOMPETITIVE

The College of Staten Island, a public institution founded in 1955, offers associate, baccalaureate, and master's degrees and Ph.D.s in conjunction with CUNY Graduate Center. In addition to regional accreditation, CSI has baccalaureate program accreditation with ABET, CAAHEP, CAPTE, CSAB, and NAACLS. The library contains 225,116 volumes, 605,000 microform items, and 13,420 audio/video tapes/CDs, and subscribes to 934 periodicals. Computerized library services include the card catalog, interlibrary loans, database searching, and Internet access. Special learning facilities include an art gallery, radio station, and an astrophysical observatory. The 204-acre campus is in an urban area in New York City's borough of Staten Island. There are 19 buildings.

Student Life: 95% of undergraduates are from New York. Students are from 10 states, 60 foreign countries, and Canada. 44% are white. 54% are Catholic; 22% Islamic, Hindu, Russian/Greek Orthodox, Buddhist; 12% claim no religious affiliation; 7% Protestant. The average age of freshmen is 22; all undergraduates, 25. 20% do not continue beyond their first year; 47% remain to graduate.

Housing: There are no residence halls. All of students commute. Alcohol is not permitted. All students may keep cars.

Activities: There are no fraternities or sororities. There are 50 groups on campus, including art, chorus, computers, dance, drama, ethnic, film, gay, honors, international, jazz band, literary magazine, newspaper, photography, political, professional, radio and TV, religious, social, social service, student government, and yearbook. Popular campus events include Kwanzaa, Spring Festival, and cultural dances.

Sports: There are 5 intercollegiate sports for men and 5 for women, and 7 intramural sports for men and 7 for women. Facilities include a 1200-seat gym, an indoor pool, baseball, softball, and soccer fields, tennis courts, outdoor recreational basketball courts, outdoor track and field facilities, 4 volleyball fields, and an ancillary gym.

Disabled Students: 95% of the campus is accessible. Wheelchair ramps, elevators, special parking, specially equipped rest rooms, special class scheduling, lowered drinking fountains, lowered telephones, wheelchair-accessible campus bus, assistance with registration, and special accommodations in the computer lab are available.

Services: Counseling and information services are available, as is tutoring in most subjects. There is a reader service for the blind, and remedial math, reading, and writing.

Campus Safety and Security: Measures include 24-hour foot and vehicle patrol, security escort services, shuttle buses, and informal discussions. There are pamphlets/posters/films, emergency telephones, lighted pathways/sidewalks, an emergency "blue light" system, radar-controlled traffic monitoring, bicycle patrol, and an emergency broadcast system.

Programs of Study: CSI confers B.A. and B.S. degrees. Associate, master's, and doctoral degrees are also awarded. Bachelor's degrees are awarded in BIOLOGICAL SCIENCE (biochemistry and biology/biological science), BUSINESS (accounting and business administration and management), COMMUNICATIONS AND THE ARTS (art, communications, dramatic arts, English, film arts, music, and Spanish), COMPUTER AND PHYSICAL SCIENCE (chemistry, computer science, information sciences and systems, mathematics, and physics), EDUCATION (education), ENGINEERING AND ENVIRONMENTAL DESIGN (engineering and applied science), HEALTH PROFESSIONS (medical technology, nursing, physical therapy, and physician's assistant), SOCIAL SCIENCE (African American studies, American studies, economics, history, international studies, philosophy, political science/government, psychology, social work, sociology, and women's studies). Business, education, and accounting have the largest enrollments.

Required: The curriculum varies for each degree, but phys ed and English are required for all majors as well as courses from each of 3 areas:

science/technology/math, social sciences/history/philosophy, and humanities. A minimum 2.0 GPA and 120 credit hours are required to graduate.

Special: Cross-registration is available with any other CUNY college. Internships are available in most fields. Study abroad is possible in more than 25 countries, including Italy, Ecuador, England, China, and Greece. There are student-designed majors and interdisciplinary majors, including computer science-math, sociology-anthropology, and science, letters, and society. Credit by exam, credit for life experience, dual majors, and nondegree study are available. There are 7 national honor societies, a freshman honors program, and 19 departmental honors programs.

Faculty/Classroom: 57% of faculty are male; 41%, female. 88% teach undergraduates and 95% both teach and do research. No introductory courses are taught by graduate students. The average class size in an introductory lecture is 33; in a laboratory, 16; and in a regular course, 17.

Admissions: All of the 2003-2004 applicants were accepted. The SAT I scores for the 2003-2004 freshman class were: Verbal--48% below 500, 41% between 500 and 599, 10% between 600 and 700, and 2% above 700; Math--43% below 500, 43% between 500 and 599, 12% between 600 and 700, and 1% above 700.

Requirements: All graduates of an accredited secondary school, or students holding a GED equivalent, are accepted for admission. Applicants must have an 80% grade average or graduate in the upper two thirds of their class to be eligible for admission to the 4-year programs. AP and CLEP credits are accepted.

Procedure: Freshmen are admitted fall and spring. Entrance exams should be taken before registration as a matriculated student. There is a rolling admissions plan. The application deadlines are open. The application fee is $50. Applications are accepted on-line through *www.applyto.uapc.cuny.edu.*

Transfer: 610 transfer students enrolled in 2002-2003. Applicants must have a minimum 2.0 GPA and official transcripts. 30 of 120 credits required for the bachelor's degree must be completed at CSI.

Visiting: There are regularly scheduled orientations for prospective students, including campus tours, presentations, and lunch every Thursday at 3:30 P.M. There are guides for informal visits and visitors may sit in on classes. To schedule a visit, contact the Office of Student Recruitment at (718) 982-2259.

Financial Aid: In 2003-2004, 52% of all full-time freshmen and 50% of continuing full-time students received some form of financial aid. 11% of full-time freshmen and 16% of continuing full-time students received need-based aid. The average freshman award was $4847. Need-based scholarships or need-based grants averaged $4362; need-based self-help aid (loans and jobs) averaged $3869; and other non-need-based awards and non-need-based scholarships averaged $1474. 78% of undergraduates work part time. The FAFSA, the state aid form, and TAP/APTS are required. The deadline for filing freshman financial aid applications for fall entry is May 31.

International Students: There are 260 international students enrolled. The school actively recruits these students. They must score 450 on the written TOEFL or 133 on the electronic version.

Computers: A total of 1086 Macs and PCs are located in 16 computer labs and 15 academic labs. All are connected to the campuswide system and the Internet. All students have e-mail accounts. All students may access the system 8 A.M. to midnight Monday through Thursday, 8.A.M. to 11 P.M. Friday, 9 A.M. to 6 P.M. Saturday, and 9 A.M. to 5 P.M. Sunday. There are no time limits. The fee is $75/semester. It is strongly recommended that all students have a personal computer.

Graduates: From July 1, 2002 to June 30, 2003, 874 bachelor's degrees were awarded. The most popular majors were business (18%), education (10%), and accounting (9%). In an average class, 17% graduate in 4 years or less, 29% graduate in 5 years or less, and 35% graduate in 6 years or less. 110 companies recruited on campus in 2002-2003.

Admissions Contact: Mary Beth Riley, Director of Admissions and Recruitment. E-mail: *reilly@postbox.csi.cuny.edu*
Web: *www.csi.cuny.edu*

CITY UNIVERSITY OF NEW YORK/HERBERT H. LEHMAN COLLEGE   D-5
Bronx, NY 10468

	(718) 960-8700
	(877) LEHMAN-1; Fax: (718) 960-8712
Full-time: 4200 men and women	**Faculty:** 296
Part-time: 3000 men and women	**Ph.D.s:** 89%
Graduate: 1860 men and women	**Student/Faculty:** 14 to 1
Year: semesters, summer session	**Tuition:** $4092 ($10,892)
Application Deadline: rolling	**Room & Board:** n/app
Freshman Class: n/av	
SAT I or ACT: required	**LESS COMPETITIVE**

Lehman College, established in 1968 as an independent unit of the City University of New York, is a commuter institution offering programs in the arts and humanities, natural and social sciences, nursing, and professional studies. Some figures in the above capsule and in this profile are

approximate. There are 5 undergraduate and 4 graduate schools. In addition to regional accreditation, Lehman has baccalaureate program accreditation with ADA, CSWE, NCATE, and NLN. The library contains 556,275 volumes, 620,660 microform items, and 1832 audio/video tapes/CDs, and subscribes to 1513 periodicals. Computerized library services include the card catalog and database searching. Special learning facilities include a learning resource center, art gallery, radio station, TV station, and center for performing arts. The 37-acre campus is in an urban area in the Bronx, New York City. There are 15 buildings.

Student Life: 74% of students are from public schools. 44% are Hispanic; 33% African American; 16% white. 54% are Catholic; 14% claim no religious affiliation. The average age of freshmen is 20; all undergraduates, 29.

Housing: There are no residence halls. All of students commute. Alcohol is not permitted. All students may keep cars.

Activities: There are no fraternities. There are 54 groups on campus, including art, band, chess, choir, chorus, computers, dance, drama, ethnic, film, honors, international, literary magazine, musical theater, newspaper, professional, radio and TV, religious, social, social service, student government, and yearbook.

Sports: There are 9 intercollegiate sports for men and 7 for women, and 9 intramural sports for men and 9 for women. Facilities include 3 gyms, an exercise room, a swimming pool, outdoor tennis courts, soccer and baseball fields, and a dance studio.

Disabled Students: 90% of the campus is accessible. Wheelchair ramps, elevators, special parking, specially equipped rest rooms, and special class scheduling are available.

Services: Counseling and information services are available, as is tutoring in every subject. There is a reader service for the blind and remedial math, reading, and writing. A writing center offers individual and small group tutorials and workshops.

Campus Safety and Security: Measures include 24-hour foot and vehicle patrol, pamphlets/posters/films, emergency telephones, and lighted pathways/sidewalks.

Programs of Study: Lehman confers B.A., B.S., and B.F.A. degrees. Master's degrees are also awarded. Bachelor's degrees are awarded in BIOLOGICAL SCIENCE (biology/biological science), BUSINESS (accounting, business administration and management, and management science), COMMUNICATIONS AND THE ARTS (communications, comparative literature, dance, English, fine arts, French, German, Greek, Hebrew, Italian, languages, Latin, linguistics, music, Russian, Spanish, and speech/debate/rhetoric), COMPUTER AND PHYSICAL SCIENCE (chemistry, computer science, geology, mathematics, and physics), EDUCATION (art, business, early childhood, elementary, foreign languages, health, science, and secondary), HEALTH PROFESSIONS (health care administration, nursing, predentistry, premedicine, and speech pathology/audiology), SOCIAL SCIENCE (African American studies, American studies, anthropology, dietetics, economics, geography, history, international relations, philosophy, political science/government, prelaw, psychology, social work, and sociology). Economics and accounting, education, and nursing are the largest.

Required: To graduate, students must successfully complete 120 credits, including 64 in the major, with a minimum GPA of 2.0. Requirements include 17 credits of core courses, 8 of English composition, 3 to 10 of a foreign language, and 3 of oral communication, as well as 22 credits distributed among courses in comparative culture, historical studies, social science, natural science, literature, art, and knowledge, self, and values. Students must demonstrate proficiency in basic reading, writing, and math skills before entering the upper division.

Special: Lehman offers internships, study abroad, work-study programs, dual and student-designed majors, nondegree study, pass/fail options, and credit for life experience. A 3-2 social work degree is offered in conjunction with the senior college of CUNY, Bard, and Sarah Lawrence. Transfer programs in preengineering, prepharmacy, and preenvironmental science and forestry allow students to complete their degrees at specialized colleges of other New York universities. There are 21 national honor societies, including Phi Beta Kappa, a freshman honors program, and 60 departmental honors programs.

Faculty/Classroom: 53% of faculty are male; 47%, female. No introductory courses are taught by graduate students. The average class size in an introductory lecture is 25 and in a laboratory, 12.

Requirements: The SAT I or ACT is required. Graduation from an accredited secondary school is required; a GED will be accepted. A grade average of 80 is required. AP and CLEP credits are accepted.

Procedure: Freshmen are admitted fall and spring. Entrance exams should be taken before registration. There are early decision, early admissions, and deferred admissions plans. Application deadlines are rolling, but students are encouraged to apply before January for fall entry. The application fee is $50. Notification is sent on a rolling basis.

Transfer: Applicants must submit all educational records and show a minimum GPA of 2.0 in previous college work. Applicants with fewer than 13 college credits must also have a high school average of 80 in academic subjects. 38 of 120 credits required for the bachelor's degree must be completed at Lehman.

Visiting: There are regularly scheduled orientations for prospective students. There are guides for informal visits and visitors may sit in on classes. To schedule a visit, contact the Office of Student Recruitment at (718) 960-8713.

Financial Aid: The college's own financial statement is required. Check with the school for current deadlines.

International Students: They must score 500 on the written TOEFL and also take the college's own test.

Computers: The mainframe is a DEC VAX 11/750. There are Macs and PCs located in the Academic Computer Center and specific classrooms. A UNIX-based network includes an IBM PC/RT file server and 8 IBM 6152 RISC workstations. All students may access the system. There are no time limits and no fees.

Admissions Contact: Clarence A. Wilkes, Director of Admissions. A video is available. E-mail: *enroll@alpha.lehman.cuny.edu*
Web: *www.lehman.cuny.edu*

CITY UNIVERSITY OF NEW YORK/HUNTER COLLEGE   D-5
New York, NY 10021   (212) 772-4490; (800) 772-4000

Full-time: 3176 men, 7313 women	Faculty: 552; IIA, ++$
Part-time: 1612 men, 3804 women	Ph.D.s: 85%
Graduate: 1120 men, 3771 women	Student/Faculty: 19 to 1
Year: semesters, summer session	Tuition: $4329 ($11,129)
Application Deadline: open	Room & Board: $2400
Freshman Class: 10,800 applied, 3913 accepted, 1690 enrolled	
SAT I Verbal/Math: 510/520	COMPETITIVE+

Hunter College, a comprehensive, nonprofit institution established in 1870, is part of the City University of New York and is both city- and state-supported. Primarily a commuter college, it emphasizes liberal arts in its undergraduate and graduate programs. There are 3 undergraduate and 4 graduate schools. In addition to regional accreditation, Hunter has baccalaureate program accreditation with ADA, APTA, ASLA, CSWE, NCATE, and NLN. The library contains 775,000 volumes, 1,186,000 microform items, and 13,300 audio/video tapes/CDs, and subscribes to 2477 periodicals. Computerized library services include the card catalog and database searching. Special learning facilities include a learning resource center, art gallery, radio station, a geography/geology lab, on-campus elementary and secondary schools, and a theater. The 3-acre campus is in an urban area in New York City. Including any residence halls, there are 6 buildings.

Student Life: 98% of undergraduates are from New York: Students are from 35 states, 149 foreign countries, and Canada. 87% are from public schools. 40% are white; 21% Hispanic; 17% African American; 15% Asian American. The average age of freshmen is 18; all undergraduates, 25. 20% do not continue beyond their first year.

Housing: 500 students can be accommodated in college housing, which includes coed dorms. On-campus housing is available on a first-come, first-served basis and is available on a lottery system for upperclassmen. 99% of students commute. No one may keep cars.

Activities: 2% of men belong to 1 local and 1 national fraternity; 1% of women belong to sororities. There are 130 groups on campus, including art, band, cheerleading, choir, chorale, chorus, drama, ethnic, film, gay, honors, international, jazz band, literary magazine, musical theater, newspaper, orchestra, political, professional, radio and TV, religious, social, social service, student government, symphony, and yearbook. Popular campus events include Major Day Fair.

Sports: There are 9 intercollegiate sports for men and 11 for women. Facilities include fencing, dance, and weight rooms, racquetball courts, a pool, outdoor tennis courts, and a gym.

Disabled Students: All of the campus is accessible. Wheelchair ramps, elevators, special parking, specially equipped rest rooms, special class scheduling, lowered drinking fountains, lowered telephones, special advisement office, and a student organization are available.

Services: Counseling and information services are available, as is tutoring in every subject. There is a reader service for the blind, and remedial math, reading, and writing. Review of graduate-level papers through the writing center and a math tutoring center are available.

Campus Safety and Security: Measures include self-defense education, shuttle buses, pamphlets/posters/films, and emergency telephones. There is a 24-hour foot patrol.

Programs of Study: Hunter confers B.A., B.S., B.F.A., B.Mus., and B.S.Ed degrees. Master's degrees are also awarded. Bachelor's degrees are awarded in BIOLOGICAL SCIENCE (biology/biological science and nutrition), BUSINESS (accounting), COMMUNICATIONS AND THE ARTS (Chinese, classics, comparative literature, creative writing, dance, dramatic arts, English, English literature, film arts, fine arts, French, German, Greek, Hebrew, Italian, languages, Latin, media arts, music, Russian, and Spanish), COMPUTER AND PHYSICAL SCIENCE (chemistry, computer science, mathematics, physics, and statistics), EDUCATION (art, early childhood, elementary, foreign languages, health, middle school, music, science, and secondary), ENGINEERING AND ENVIRONMENTAL DESIGN (energy management technology, environmental science, and preengineering), HEALTH PROFESSIONS (medical lab-

oratory technology, nursing, physical therapy, predentistry, premedicine, and public health), SOCIAL SCIENCE (African American studies, anthropology, archeology, economics, geography, Hispanic American studies, history, international relations, Judaic studies, Latin American studies, philosophy, political science/government, prelaw, psychology, religion, social science, sociology, urban studies, and women's studies). Nursing is the strongest academically. Psychology is the largest.

Required: To graduate, students must complete 120 credits. The total number of hours in a major varies from 24 credits for a liberal arts major to 63 credits for a professional concentration; a minimum GPA of 2.0 is needed overall and in the major. Distribution requirements include 12 credits of social sciences, up to 12 credits of a foreign language, 10 or more of math and science, 9 of humanities and the arts, 6 of literature, and 3 of English composition.

Special: Special academic programs include internships, student-designed majors, work-study, study abroad in 20 countries, and dual majors. There is cross-registration with the Brooklyn School of Law, Marymount Manhattan College, and the YIVO Institute. Through the National Student Exchange Program, Hunter students can study for 1 or 2 semesters at any of 150 U.S. campuses. Accelerated degree programs are offered in anthropology, biopharmacology, economics, English, history, math, physics, sociology, and social research. Exchange programs in Paris or Puerto Rico are possible. There are 2 national honor societies, including Phi Beta Kappa, a freshman honors program, and 19 departmental honors programs.

Faculty/Classroom: The average class size in a laboratory is 19 and in a regular course, 30.

Admissions: 36% of the 2003-2004 applicants were accepted. The SAT I scores for the 2003-2004 freshman class were: Verbal--45% below 500, 38% between 500 and 599, 14% between 600 and 700, and 3% above 700; Math--34% below 500, 45% between 500 and 599, 18% between 600 and 700, and 3% above 700.

Requirements: The SAT I is required. Admission is based on a combination of high school grade average, high school academic credits, including English and math, and SAT I scores. AP and CLEP credits are accepted.

Procedure: Freshmen are admitted fall and spring. Entrance exams should be taken by October of the junior year. There are early admissions and deferred admissions plans. There is a rolling admissions plan. Application deadlines are open. Application fee is $50. Notification of early decision is sent December 15; regular decision, on a rolling basis after January 1. 4 early decision candidates were accepted for the 2003-2004 class. Applications are accepted on-line through *www.uapc.cuny.edu*.

Transfer: 2678 transfer students enrolled in 2002-2003. Applicants must have at least a 2.0 GPA. All students must complete 30 credits of the 120 required for a bachelor's degree at the college, including half of those needed for both the major and the minor.

Visiting: There are regularly scheduled orientations for prospective students, presentations and tours every Friday. Please call (212) 772-4490 for details. There are guides for informal visits and visitors may sit in on classes. To schedule a visit, contact the Office of Admissions at *admissions@hunter.cuny.edu*.

Financial Aid: 25% of undergraduates work part time. The college's own financial statement is required. The deadline for filing freshman financial aid applications for fall entry is May 1.

International Students: There are 1238 international students enrolled. They must score 500 on the written TOEFL and also take the college's own test.

Computers: The mainframe is an IBM 3090. There are 600 PCs networked in 26 computer labs. All students may access the system 24 hours a day. There are no time limits and no fees.

Graduates: From July 1, 2002 to June 30, 2003, 2052 bachelor's degrees were awarded. The most popular majors were psychology (15%), English (11%), and sociology (10%). In an average class, 36% graduate in 6 years or less.

Admissions Contact: Office of Admissions.
E-mail: *admissions@hunter.cuny.edu* Web: *www.hunter.cuny.edu*

CITY UNIVERSITY OF NEW YORK/JOHN JAY   D-5
COLLEGE OF CRIMINAL JUSTICE
New York, NY 10019   (212) 237-8878; Fax: (212) 237-8777

Full-time: 3177 men, 5283 women	Faculty: 322; IIA, +$
Part-time: 1306 men, 1743 women	Ph.D.s: 85%
Graduate: 543 men, 974 women	Student/Faculty: 26 to 1
Year: semesters, summer session	Tuition: $4259 ($8899)
Application Deadline: open	Room & Board: n/app
Freshman Class: 5750 applied, 4137 accepted, 2261 enrolled	
SAT I Verbal/Math: 480/470	COMPETITIVE

John Jay College of Criminal Justice, established in 1964, is a liberal arts college and part of the City University of New York, with special emphasis in the fields of criminology, forensic science, correction administration, and other areas of the criminal justice system. The library contains

215,609 volumes, 198,832 microform items, and 3000 audio/video tapes/CDs, and subscribes to 10,335 periodicals. Computerized library services include the card catalog, interlibrary loans, and database searching. Special learning facilities include a learning resource center, art gallery, radio station, TV station, a fire science lab, a security technology lab, and an explosion-proof forensic science/toxicology lab. The 1-acre campus is in an urban area in midtown Manhattan. There are 3 buildings.

Student Life: 95% of undergraduates are from New York. 80% are from public schools. 35% are Hispanic; 25% African American; 23% white. The average age of freshmen is 19; all undergraduates, 23. 26% do not continue beyond their first year; 40% remain to graduate.

Housing: There are no residence halls. All students commute. All students may keep cars.

Activities: There are no fraternities or sororities. There are 26 groups on campus, including art, cheerleading, chess, choir, chorale, chorus, computers, dance, drama, ethnic, film, gay, honors, international, literary magazine, musical theater, newspaper, photography, political, professional, radio and TV, religious, social, social service, student government, and yearbook.

Sports: There are 5 intercollegiate sports for men and 5 for women, and 15 intramural sports for men and 15 for women. Facilities include 2 gyms, 2 racquetball courts, a fitness center, a swimming pool, a strength training center, and a rooftop outdoor tennis court and jogging track.

Disabled Students: 99% of the campus is accessible. Wheelchair ramps, elevators, special parking, specially equipped rest rooms, special class scheduling, lowered drinking fountains, and lowered telephones are available.

Services: Counseling and information services are available, as is tutoring in most subjects, including English, math, and reading. There is a reader service for the blind and remedial math, reading, and writing.

Campus Safety and Security: Measures include 24-hour foot and vehicle patrol, self-defense education, informal discussions, and pamphlets/ posters/films. There are emergency telephones and lighted pathways/ sidewalks.

Programs of Study: John Jay confers B.A. and B.S. degrees. Associate and master's degrees are also awarded. Bachelor's degrees are awarded in BIOLOGICAL SCIENCE (toxicology), COMPUTER AND PHYSICAL SCIENCE (information sciences and systems), SOCIAL SCIENCE (corrections, criminal justice, criminology, fire science, forensic studies, law enforcement and corrections, political science/government, public administration, and safety management). Forensic science is the strongest academically. Criminal justice, forensic psychology, and police science are the largest.

Required: Students are required to complete 128 credit hours, with 36 to 42 of these hours in the student's major, and must maintain a minimum GPA of 2.0. 1 credit in phys ed is required of all students.

Special: The school offers co-op programs, and cross-registration with other schools in the City University of New York. Internships are available with the Manhattan District Attorney, the Queens Supreme Court, the New York City Police Department, the United States Marshal's Service, and the New York City Corrections Department. Opportunities are provided for work-study programs, a Washington semester in public administration, interdisciplinary and student-designed majors, including forensic psychology, pass/fail options, nondegree study, credit for life experience, B.A.-M.A. programs in forensic psychology, criminal justice, and public administration, and study abroad in 5 countries, including England, Barbados, and Israel. There is 1 national honor society and a freshman honors program.

Faculty/Classroom: 54% of faculty are male; 46%, female. 94% teach undergraduates and 80% both teach and do research. Graduate students teach 5% of introductory courses. The average class size in an introductory lecture is 25; in a laboratory, 15; and in a regular course, 20.

Admissions: 72% of the 2003-2004 applicants were accepted. The SAT I scores for the 2003-2004 freshman class were: Verbal--58% below 500, 36% between 500 and 599, 5% between 600 and 700, and 1% above 700; Math--61% below 500, 33% between 500 and 599, 6% between 600 and 700, and 1% above 700.

Requirements: The SAT I is recommended. Admission to associate degree programs requires a minimum SAT I score of 900, a high school average of 72, or a GED score of 300. Admission to baccalaureate degree programs requires a minimum SAT I score of 1020 or a high school average of 80, and 12 academic units, with 4 units in English and math and 1 unit in each discipline. In addition, applicants must have graduated from an accredited secondary school or a GED certificate will be accepted. John Jay requires applicants to be in the upper 50% of their class. AP and CLEP credits are accepted.

Procedure: Freshmen are admitted fall and spring. There is an early admissions plan and a rolling admissions plan. Application deadlines are open. The fall 2003 application fee was $40. Notification is sent on a rolling basis.

Transfer: 2031 transfer students enrolled in 2002-2003. Applicants must have completed 24 credits with a cumulative GPA of 2.0. If fewer

than 24 credits are presented, a high school transcript should be presented. Half of the credits required for the major must be completed at John Jay.

Visiting: There are regularly scheduled orientations for prospective students, consisting of a freshman/transfer workshop. There are guides for informal visits and visitors may sit in on classes. To schedule a visit, call (212) 237-8868.

Financial Aid: In 2003-2004, 70% of all full-time students received some form of financial aid. 85% of full-time freshmen and 75% of continuing full-time students received need-based aid. The average freshman award was $4800. Need-based scholarships or need-based grants averaged $5100; need-based self-help aid (loans and jobs) averaged $2500; and non-need-based awards and non-need-based scholarships averaged $500. 5% of undergraduates work part time. Average annual earnings from campus work are $1000. The average financial indebtedness of the 2003 graduate was $10,000. The FAFSA is required. The fall financial aid application deadline is open.

International Students: There are 185 international students enrolled. They must score 500 on the written TOEFL.

Computers: The mainframe is an IBM 3090/400. Some 540 PCs are available to students. There are open access facilities in the academic computing center and hands-on classes in departmental labs and the library. All students may access the system. There are no time limits and no fees.

Graduates: From July 1, 2002 to June 30, 2003, 1347 bachelor's degrees were awarded. The most popular majors were criminal justice (30%), forensic psychology (26%), and legal studies (7%). In an average class, 2% graduate in 3 years or less, 8% graduate in 4 years or less, 21% graduate in 5 years or less, and 39% graduate in 6 years or less. 75 companies recruited on campus in 2002-2003. Of the 2002 graduating class, 30% were enrolled in graduate school within 6 months of graduation and 88% were employed.

Admissions Contact: Richard Saulnier, Dean of Admissions and Registration. E-mail: *rsaulnier@jjay.cuny.edu*

CITY UNIVERSITY OF NEW YORK/MEDGAR EVERS COLLEGE   D-5

Brooklyn, NY 11225-2201

Full-time: 647 men, 1951 women	**Faculty:** 157
Part-time: 397 men, 1727 women	**Ph.D.s:** 72%
Graduate: none	**Student/Faculty:** 17 to 1
Year: semesters, summer session	**Tuition:** $4232 ($360 per credit)
Application Deadline: open	**Room & Board:** n/app
Freshman Class: 671 enrolled	
SAT I: recommended	**NONCOMPETITIVE**

(718) 270-6021; Fax: (718) 270-6198

Medgar Evers College, established in 1969 as part of the City University of New York, is an undergraduate commuter institution offering programs in business, education, natural sciences and math, nursing, and social sciences. There are 4 undergraduate schools. The library contains 118,000 volumes, 40,000 microform items, and 20,000 audio/video tapes/CDs, and subscribes to 420 periodicals. Computerized library services include the card catalog, interlibrary loans, database searching, and Internet access. Special learning facilities include a learning resource center, radio station, TV station, and a TV lab. The 4-acre campus is in an urban area located in the Crown Heights section of Brooklyn. There are 2 buildings.

Student Life: 88% of undergraduates are from New York. Students are from 3 states and 37 foreign countries. 99% are from public schools. 88% are African American. 50% are Islamic 2%, Buddhist 1%, others 47%; 22% Catholic; 14% Protestant; 12% claim no religious affiliation. The average age of freshmen is 24; all undergraduates, 30. 46% do not continue beyond their first year; 28% remain to graduate.

Housing: There are no residence halls. All students commute. No one may keep cars.

Activities: 2% of men belong to 2 national fraternities. There is 1 national sorority. There are 5 groups on campus, including choir, dance, ethnic, newspaper, political, radio and TV, religious, social service, student government, and yearbook. Popular campus events include Kwaanza and Black Solidarity Day.

Sports: There are 4 intercollegiate sports for men and 3 for women, and 5 intramural sports for men and 3 for women. Facilities include a swimming pool, a gym, and an exercise room.

Disabled Students: All of the campus is accessible. Wheelchair ramps, elevators, special parking, specially equipped rest rooms, lowered drinking fountains, and lowered telephones are available.

Services: Counseling and information services are available, as is tutoring in every subject. There is a reader service for the blind and remedial math, reading, and writing.

Campus Safety and Security: Measures include 24-hour foot and vehicle patrol.

Programs of Study: MEC confers B.A. and B.S. degrees. Associate degrees are also awarded. Bachelor's degrees are awarded in BIOLOGI-

CAL SCIENCE (biology/biological science), BUSINESS (accounting, business administration and management, and management information systems), COMMUNICATIONS AND THE ARTS (English), COMPUTER AND PHYSICAL SCIENCE (mathematics), EDUCATION (elementary and special), ENGINEERING AND ENVIRONMENTAL DESIGN (environmental science), HEALTH PROFESSIONS (nursing), SOCIAL SCIENCE (liberal arts/general studies, psychology, and public administration). Nursing is the strongest academically and is the largest.

Required: To graduate, students must complete 120 credits (depending on program) with a minimum GPA of 2.0. The core curriculum requires a total of 42 credits in English, philosophy, speech, math, liberal arts, career planning, and phys ed. Students must demonstrate proficiency in basic reading, writing, and math skills prior to entering their junior year.

Special: MEC offers exchange programs with other CUNY institutions, evening and weekend classes, credit for military and prior learning experience, pass/fail options, and nondegree study. Study abroad in 3 countries is also possible. There is 1 national honor society, a freshman honors program, and 11 departmental honors programs.

Faculty/Classroom: 53% of faculty are male; 47%, female. All teach undergraduates and 8% both teach and do research. The average class size in an introductory lecture is 25; in a laboratory, 23; and in a regular course, 19.

Requirements: The SAT I is recommended. MEC accepts all applicants who either are graduates of an accredited secondary school or have earned a GED with a score of 225 or higher. Students must meet the university's health standards. CLEP credit is accepted.

Procedure: Freshmen are admitted fall and spring. Entrance exams should be taken during the last year of high school. There is a rolling admissions plan. Application deadlines are open. The fall 2003 application fee was $40.

Transfer: 413 transfer students enrolled in 2002-2003. Applicants must have a minimum GPA of 2.0. Those students with fewer than 24 college credits must also submit a high school transcript. 32 of 120 credits required for the bachelor's degree must be completed at MEC.

Financial Aid: In 2003-2004, 75% of all full-time students received some form of financial aid. 75% of all full-time students received need-based aid. The average freshman award was $3200. Need-based scholarships or need-based grants averaged $3863 ($7200 maximum); and need-based self-help aid (loans and jobs) averaged $1368 ($3700 maximum). 80% of undergraduates work part time. Average annual earnings from campus work are $1500. The FAFSA and CUNY Student Aid Form (CSAF) are required. The deadline for filing freshman financial aid applications for fall entry is August 15.

International Students: There are 192 international students enrolled. The school actively recruits these students. They must score 475 on the written TOEFL and also take the ACT or the college's own entrance exam.

Computers: The mainframe is an IBM 3033. There are PCs and Macs available in the data processing center. All students may access the system. There are no time limits. The fee is $75 per semester.

Graduates: From July 1, 2002 to June 30, 2003, 234 bachelor's degrees were awarded. The most popular majors were business (22%), psychology (14%), and nursing (10%). In an average class, 5% graduate in 4 years or less, 11% graduate in 5 years or less, and 19% graduate in 6 years or less. 15 companies recruited on campus in 2002-2003.

Admissions Contact: Warren Heusner, Director of Admissions. Web: *www.mec.cuny.edu*

CITY UNIVERSITY OF NEW YORK/NEW YORK CITY COLLEGE OF TECHNOLOGY
(Formerly City University of New York/New York City Technical College)
D-5

Brooklyn, NY 11201-2983	**(718) 260-5500; Fax: (718) 260-5504**
Full-time: 3376 men, 3277 women	**Faculty:** IIB, +$
Part-time: 2049 men, 2280 women	**Ph.D.s:** n/av
Graduate: none	**Student/Faculty:** n/av
Year: semesters, summer session	**Tuition:** $4269 ($11,069)
Application Deadline: open	**Room & Board:** n/app
Freshman Class: 3657 accepted, 1838 enrolled	
SAT I Verbal/Math: 388/428	**NONCOMPETITIVE**

New York City College of Technology, formerly New York City Technical College, founded in 1946 and made part of the City University of New York system in 1964, is an undergraduate commuter college offering day and evening programs in technology. In addition to regional accreditation, City Tech has baccalaureate program accreditation with ABET, ADA, NCATE, and NLN. The library contains 185,000 volumes, 11,625 microform items, and 6000 audio/video tapes/CDs, and subscribes to 780 periodicals. Computerized library services include the card catalog, interlibrary loans, and database searching. Special learning facilities include a learning resource center and art gallery. The campus is in an urban area. There are 9 buildings.

Student Life: 95% of undergraduates are from in state. Students are from 6 states. 42% are African American; 29% Hispanic; 14% Asian American; 11% white. The average age of freshmen is 19; all undergraduates, 25.

Housing: There are no residence halls. All students commute. Alcohol is not permitted. All students may keep cars.

Activities: There are no fraternities or sororities. There are more than 25 groups on campus, including computers, drama, ethnic, gay, honors, international, musical theater, newspaper, professional, religious, social, social service, and student government.

Sports: There are 6 intercollegiate sports for men and 7 for women. Facilities include a gym and a weight room.

Services: Counseling and information services are available, as is tutoring in most subjects.

Campus Safety and Security: Measures include 24-hour foot and vehicle patrol, informal discussions, pamphlets/posters/films, and emergency telephones. There are lighted pathways/sidewalks.

Programs of Study: City Tech confers B.S. and B.T. degrees. Associate degrees are also awarded. Bachelor's degrees are awarded in BUSINESS (hotel/motel and restaurant management), COMMUNICATIONS AND THE ARTS (telecommunications), EDUCATION (technical and vocational), ENGINEERING AND ENVIRONMENTAL DESIGN (electromechanical technology and graphic and printing production), SOCIAL SCIENCE (human services). Computer system technology is the strongest academically and is the largest.

Required: Students must receive CUNY certification in reading, writing, and math and complete associate degree requirements. General education requirements include selections from African-American, Puerto Rican, and Latin American studies, sciences, humanities, social sciences, and education. A total of 120 credits is required for the B.S. or B.T. degree.

Special: B.A. and B.S. degrees are offered through CUNY's university-wide bachelor's exchange credits program. An alternative format program for adults offers credit for life/work experience. Nondegree study and work-study are possible.

Admissions: The SAT I scores for the 2003-2004 freshman class were: Verbal--71% below 500, 26% between 500 and 599, and 3% between 600 and 700; Math--66% below 500, 29% between 500 and 599, and 5% between 600 and 700. 15% of the current freshmen were in the top fifth of their class; 46% were in the top two fifths.

Requirements: The SAT I is required for some programs and the ACT is recommended. In addition, applicants should be graduates of an accredited secondary school or have the GED equivalent and meet the university's health standards. Students must first apply to the associate degree program and later to the specific bachelor degree program. A GPA of 2.0 is required. AP and CLEP credits are accepted.

Procedure: Freshmen are admitted fall, spring, and summer.There is a rolling admissions plan. Application deadlines are open. The fall 2003 application fee was $40.

Transfer: 600 transfer students enrolled in 2002-2003. Candidates must have a 2.0 GPA. They must meet CUNY requirements in reading, writing, and math. 34 of 120 credits required for the bachelor's degree must be completed at City Tech.

Visiting: To schedule a visit, contact Joseph Lento at (718) 260-5250 or *Jlento@citytech.cuny.edu*.

Financial Aid: The CUNY Student Aid Form (CSAF) is required.

International Students: There are 274 international students enrolled. They must take the college's own test and also take the college's own entrance exam.

Computers: All students may access the system.

Graduates: From July 1, 2002 to June 30, 2003, 448 bachelor's degrees were awarded. The most popular majors were computer information systems (27%), hospitality management (20%), and human services (13%).

Admissions Contact: Joseph Lento, Director of Admissions. E-mail: *jlento@citytech.cuny.edu* Web: *www.citytech.cuny.edu*

CITY UNIVERSITY OF NEW YORK/NEW YORK CITY TECHNICAL COLLEGE
(See City University of New York/New York City College of Technology)

CITY UNIVERSITY OF NEW YORK/QUEENS COLLEGE
D-5

Flushing, NY 11367-1597	**(718) 997-5608; Fax: (718) 997-5617**
Full-time: 3185 men, 4984 women	**Faculty:** 464; IIA, ++$
Part-time: 1395 men, 2782 women	**Ph.D.s:** 95%
Graduate: 1293 men, 3354 women	**Student/Faculty:** 18 to 1
Year: semesters, summer session	**Tuition:** $4362 ($5682)
Application Deadline: January 1	**Room & Board:** n/app
Freshman Class: 1330 enrolled	
SAT I Verbal/Math: 509/545	**COMPETITIVE**

Queens College, founded in 1937, is a public commuter institution within the City University of New York system. In addition to regional accreditation, Queens has baccalaureate program accreditation with ACS, ADA, APA, and ASLHA. The 2 libraries contain 711,737 volumes, 767,153 microform items, and 27,300 audio/video tapes/CDs, and subscribe to 3156 periodicals. Computerized library services include the card catalog, interlibrary loans, and database searching. Special learning facilities include a learning resource center, art gallery, radio station, a center for the performing arts, and a center for environmental teaching and research located on Long Island. The 76-acre campus is in an urban area 10 miles from Manhattan. There are 20 buildings.

Student Life: 99% of undergraduates are from New York. Students are from 15 states, 118 foreign countries, and Canada. 55% are from public schools. 51% are white; 23% Asian American; 16% Hispanic; 10% African American. 44% are Catholic; 23% Jewish; 11% Protestant; 11% Muslim, Hindu, Buddhist, Taoist. The average age of freshmen is 19; all undergraduates, 26. 15% do not continue beyond their first year; 49% remain to graduate.

Housing: There are no residence halls. All students commute. Alcohol is not permitted. All students may keep cars.

Activities: 1% of men and 1% of women belong to 3 national fraternities. There are 3 national sororities. There are 100 groups on campus, including band, choir, chorus, drama, ethnic, honors, international, jazz band, literary magazine, musical theater, newspaper, orchestra, political, radio and TV, religious, social, social service, student government, symphony, and yearbook. Popular campus events include fall and spring campus fests and a spring job fair.

Sports: There are 10 intercollegiate sports for men and 12 for women, and 10 intramural sports for men and 7 for women. Facilities include a gym complex, a swimming pool, dance studios, weight rooms, an outdoor quarter-mile track, soccer, lacrosse, and baseball fields, and 18 tennis courts.

Disabled Students: 90% of the campus is accessible. Wheelchair ramps, elevators, special parking, specially equipped rest rooms, and special class scheduling are available.

Services: Counseling and information services are available, as is tutoring in most subjects. There is a reader service for the blind.

Campus Safety and Security: Measures include 24-hour foot and vehicle patrol, pamphlets/posters/films, emergency telephones, and lighted pathways/sidewalks.

Programs of Study: Queens confers B.A., B.S., B.B.A., B.F.A., and B.Mus. degrees. Master's degrees are also awarded. Bachelor's degrees are awarded in AGRICULTURE (environmental studies), BIOLOGICAL SCIENCE (biochemistry and biology/biological science), BUSINESS (accounting, business administration and management, and labor studies), COMMUNICATIONS AND THE ARTS (art, art history and appreciation, communications, comparative literature, dance, dramatic arts, English, film arts, French, German, Greek, Hebrew, Italian, Latin, linguistics, media arts, music, Russian, Spanish, and studio art), COMPUTER AND PHYSICAL SCIENCE (chemistry, computer science, geology, mathematics, and physics), EDUCATION (art, early childhood, elementary, home economics, music, and physical), ENGINEERING AND ENVIRONMENTAL DESIGN (environmental science), HEALTH PROFESSIONS (health science, predentistry, and premedicine), SOCIAL SCIENCE (African studies, American studies, anthropology, classical/ancient civilization, East Asian studies, economics, family/consumer studies, history, home economics, interdisciplinary studies, Judaic studies, Latin American studies, philosophy, political science/government, psychology, religion, social work, sociology, urban studies, and women's studies). Music, English, and linguistics are the strongest academically. Accounting, computer science, and psychology are the largest.

Required: To graduate, students must complete 120 credits with a minimum GPA of 2.0. They must fulfill requirements in the major and 35 to 40 credits of a liberal arts core curriculum.

Special: Queens offers co-op programs, cross-registration with other CUNY campuses, internships in business, liberal arts, journalism, and social sciences, study abroad, work-study, accelerated degrees, dual and student-designed majors, pass/fail options, and nondegree study. There are preprofessional programs in engineering, law, medicine, and dentistry. The SEEK program provides financial and educational resources for underprepared freshmen. There are 15 national honor societies, including Phi Beta Kappa, and a freshman honors program.

Faculty/Classroom: 55% of faculty are male; 45%, female. 20% do research and 80% both teach and do research. Graduate students teach 1% of introductory courses. The average class size in an introductory lecture is 35; in a laboratory, 20; and in a regular course, 27.

Admissions: The SAT I scores for the 2003-2004 freshman class were: Verbal--47% below 500, 38% between 500 and 599, 13% between 600 and 700, and 2% above 700; Math--31% below 500, 45% between 500 and 599, 21% between 600 and 700, and 3% above 700.

Requirements: The SAT I is required. In addition, high school preparation should include 4 years each of English and social studies, 3 each of math and foreign language, and 2 of lab science. A GPA of 3.0 is required. AP and CLEP credits are accepted.

Procedure: Freshmen are admitted fall and spring. Entrance exams should be taken in the spring of the junior year or the fall of the senior

year. There is an early admissions plan and a rolling admissions plan. The fall 2003 application fee was $40. For priority consideration, applications should be filed by January 1 for fall entry and October 15 for spring entry. Notification is sent on a rolling basis.

Transfer: 1645 transfer students enrolled in 2002-2003. First-year transfers should have a minimum GPA of 2.5 and must meet freshman criteria; most others need a 2.25 for consideration. 45 of 120 credits required for the bachelor's degree must be completed at Queens.

Visiting: There are regularly scheduled orientations for prospective students, including information sessions and a campus tour. To schedule a visit, contact the Admissions Office at (718) 997-5614.

Financial Aid: In a recent year, 80% of all full-time freshmen and 55% of continuing full-time students received some form of financial aid. 76% of full-time freshmen and 44% of continuing full-time students received need-based aid. The average freshman award was $7500. Average annual earnings from campus work are $2500. The average financial indebtedness of a recent graduate was $12,000. The FAFSA is required. The deadline for filing freshman financial aid applications for fall entry is May 1.

International Students: In a recent year, there were 540 international students enrolled. They must score 500 on the written TOEFL and also take the SAT I or the CUNY Skills Assessment Test. Honors students should take SAT II: Subject tests.

Computers: The mainframe is an IBM. 450 Dell Pentiums and Apple Power Mac computers are available to students in computer labs. All students may access the system during day and evening hours, 7 days a week. There are no time limits. The fee is $75 per year for part-time students and $150 per year for full-time students.

Graduates: From July 1, 2002 to June 30, 2003, 2002 bachelor's degrees were awarded. The most popular majors were sociology (14%), accounting (11%), and political science (10%). In an average class, 3% graduate in 3 years or less, 21% graduate in 4 years or less, 33% graduate in 5 years or less, and 39% graduate in 6 years or less. 100 companies recruited on campus in 2002-2003. Of the 2002 graduating class, 21% were enrolled in graduate school within 6 months of graduation and 70% were employed.

Admissions Contact: Dr. Vincent J. Angrisani, Executive Director of Admissions, Marketing, and Sholarship. A video is available.
Web: *www.qc.edu*

CITY UNIVERSITY OF NEW YORK/YORK COLLEGE   D-5

Jamaica, NY 11451	(718) 262-2165; Fax: (718) 262-2601
Full-time: 890 men, 1970 women	**Faculty:** 168
Part-time: 640 men, 1770 women	**Ph.Ds:** 71%
Graduate: none	**Student/Faculty:** 17 to 1
Year: semesters, summer session	**Tuition:** $4092 ($10,892)
Application Deadline: open	**Room & Board:** n/app
Freshman Class: n/av	
SAT I or ACT: required	**NONCOMPETITIVE**

York College, established in 1966, is a public liberal arts commuter college and part of the City University of New York. Some figures in the above capsule and in this proile are approximate. In addition to regional accreditation, York has baccalaureate program accreditation with ACOTE, CAHEA, CSWE, and NLN. The library contains 180,000 volumes, 154,000 microform items, and 4613 audio/video tapes/CDs, and subscribes to 1100 periodicals. Computerized library services include the card catalog, interlibrary loans, and database searching. Special learning facilities include a learning resource center, art gallery, TV station, a cardio-pneumo simulator, and a theater. The 50-acre campus is in an urban area in New York City. There are 5 buildings.

Student Life: 96% of undergraduates are from New York. Students are from 4 states, 82 foreign countries, and Canada. 44% are African American; 14% Hispanic. The average age of freshmen is 21; all undergraduates, 29. 19% do not continue beyond their first year; 24% remain to graduate.

Housing: There are no residence halls. All students commute. Alcohol is not permitted. All students may keep cars.

Activities: There are no fraternities or sororities. There are 50 groups on campus, including art, cheerleading, choir, chorus, computers, drama, ethnic, honors, international, jazz band, literary magazine, musical theater, newspaper, political, professional, radio and TV, religious, social, social service, student government, and yearbook. Popular campus events include club fairs, talent shows, and ethnic fairs.

Sports: There are 9 intercollegiate sports for men and 10 for women, and 9 intramural sports for men and 10 for women. Facilities include a 1200-seat gym, a 25-meter, 6-lane swimming pool with diving boards, a health risk appraisal center, an exercise therapy room, an outdoor track, tennis courts, a soccer field, an indoor walking/jogging track, a weight room, an aerobics room, handball courts, and a multipurpose room.

Disabled Students: All of the campus is accessible. Wheelchair ramps, elevators, special parking, specially equipped rest rooms, special class scheduling, lowered drinking fountains, and lowered telephones are available.

Services: Counseling and information services are available, as is tutoring in every subject. There is a reader service for the blind and remedial math, reading, and writing.

Campus Safety and Security: Measures include 24-hour foot and vehicle patrol, security escort services, informal discussions, and pamphlets/posters/films. There are emergency telephones and lighted pathways/sidewalks.

Programs of Study: York confers B.A. and B.S. degrees. Bachelor's degrees are awarded in BIOLOGICAL SCIENCE (biology/biological science and biotechnology), BUSINESS (accounting, business administration and management, and marketing/retailing/merchandising), COMMUNICATIONS AND THE ARTS (art history and appreciation, dramatic arts, English, French, music, Spanish, speech/debate/rhetoric, and studio art), COMPUTER AND PHYSICAL SCIENCE (chemistry, geology, information sciences and systems, mathematics, and physics), EDUCATION (physical), HEALTH PROFESSIONS (community health work, environmental health science, exercise science, medical laboratory technology, nursing, and occupational therapy), SOCIAL SCIENCE (African American studies, anthropology, economics, gerontology, history, liberal arts/general studies, philosophy, political science/government, psychology, social work, and sociology). Business, psychology, and social work are the largest.

Required: All students are required to complete 120 credits and maintain a minimum GPA of 2.0. The core curriculum of 61 credits includes courses in humanities, behavioral science, cultural diversity, math, natural science, and junior-level writing. Students must also take a 2-credit phys ed course and complete 2 semesters of English.

Special: Cross-registration with all schools in the City University of New York is permitted. Also provided are work-study programs, credit by exam, dual majors in physics and math, nondegree study, pass/fail options, credit for life experience, internships, cooperative programs with other schools, and student-designed majors. There are 6 national honor societies, and 4 departmental honors programs.

Faculty/Classroom: 56% of faculty are male; 44%, female. 93% teach undergraduates and 7% both teach and do research.

Requirements: The SAT I or ACT is required; students should achieve a minimum composite score of 1100 on the SAT I. Applicants must have graduated from an accredited secondary school or present a GED certificate. An audition is recommended for music majors. AP and CLEP credits are accepted.

Procedure: Freshmen are admitted fall and spring. There are early admissions and deferred admissions plans. Application deadlines are open. The application fee is $50. Notification is sent monthly.

Transfer: Students must present a minimum GPA of 2.0. 40 of 120 credits required for the bachelor's degree must be completed at York.

Visiting: There are regularly scheduled orientations for prospective students, including workshops and group meetings with faculty and staff on matriculation, registration, financial aid, degree requirements, and advisement for classes. Visitors may sit in on classes. To schedule a visit, contact the Director of Admissions or Admissions counselor.

Financial Aid: The FAFSA and the college's own financial statement are required. Check with the school for current deadlines.

International Students: They must score 470 on the written TOEFL and also take the SAT I scoring 1100, ACT, or math placement test if the student comes from a non-English-speaking country.

Computers: The mainframes are an IBM 3090, 3081KX, and 4361-5. There are also 353 Macs and IBM PCs available throughout the school. All students may access the system during hours of operation of college facilities. There are no time limits and no fees.

Admissions Contact: Sally Nelson, Director of Admissions and Enrollment. A video is available. E-mail: *admissions@york.cuny.edu* Web: *www.york.cuny.edu*

CLARKSON UNIVERSITY
Potsdam, NY 13699

D-2
(315) 268-6479
(800) 527-6577; Fax: (315) 268-7647

Full-time: 2057 men, 639 women	Faculty: 141; I, av$
Part-time: 10 men, 17 women	Ph.D.s: 87%
Graduate: 267 men, 115 women	Student/Faculty: 19 to 1
Year: semesters, summer session	Tuition: $23,500
Application Deadline: March 1	Room & Board: $8726
Freshman Class: 2717 applied, 2170 accepted, 721 enrolled	
SAT I Verbal/Math: 570/620	**VERY COMPETITIVE**

Clarkson University, founded in 1896, is a private institution offering undergraduate programs in engineering, business, science, and the liberal arts, and graduate programs in engineering, business, science, and health sciences. There are 4 undergraduate and 4 graduate schools. In addition to regional accreditation, Clarkson has baccalaureate program accreditation with AACSB and ABET. The 2 libraries contain 279,267 volumes, 267,759 microform items, and 2323 audio/video tapes/CDs, and subscribe to 1658 periodicals. Computerized library services include the card catalog, interlibrary loans, and database searching. Special learning facilities include a learning resource center, natural history museum, radio station, and TV station. The 640-acre campus is in a rural area 70 miles north of Watertown and 75 miles south of Ottawa, Canada. Including any residence halls, there are 43 buildings.

Student Life: 75% of undergraduates are from New York. Students are from 38 states, 23 foreign countries, and Canada. 80% are from public schools. 85% are white. 54% are Catholic; 34% Buddhist, Hindu, Muslim, Mormon, Orthodox, and others.; 18% claim no religious affiliation; 6% Protestant. The average age of freshmen is 18; all undergraduates, 20. 12% do not continue beyond their first year; 69% remain to graduate.

Housing: 2182 students can be accommodated in college housing, which includes single-sex and coed dorms, on-campus apartments, married-student housing, fraternity houses, and sorority houses. In addition, there are special-interest houses. On-campus housing is guaranteed for all 4 years. 83% of students live on campus; of those, 90% remain on campus on weekends. Alcohol is not permitted. All students may keep cars.

Activities: 18% of men belong to 4 local and 6 national fraternities; 15% of women belong to 2 national sororities. There are 57 groups on campus, including cheerleading, chess, computers, drama, ethnic, honors, international, jazz band, literary magazine, musical theater, newspaper, orchestra, pep band, photography, professional, radio and TV, religious, social, social service, student government, and yearbook. Popular campus events include Culture Night, Greek Week, and Senior Week.

Sports: There are 10 intercollegiate sports for men and 8 for women, and 10 co-ed intramural sports. 65% of men and 65% of women participate. Facilities include a 3000-seat multipurpose ice arena, a fitness center, a gym, a swimming pool, a weight room, a field house, and racquetball, paddleball, and tennis courts.

Disabled Students: 85% of the campus is accessible. Wheelchair ramps, elevators, special parking, specially equipped rest rooms, special class scheduling, lowered drinking fountains, lowered telephones, and special housing are available.

Services: Counseling and information services are available, as is tutoring in most subjects, including all freshman- and sophomore-level courses and some junior-level courses.

Campus Safety and Security: Measures include 24-hour foot and vehicle patrol, security escort services, shuttle buses, and informal discussions. There are pamphlets/posters/films, emergency telephones, and lighted pathways/sidewalks.

Programs of Study: Clarkson confers B.S. and B.P.S. degrees. Master's and doctoral degrees are also awarded. Bachelor's degrees are awarded in BIOLOGICAL SCIENCE (biology/biological science and molecular biology), BUSINESS (accounting, banking and finance, business administration and management, electronic business, management information systems, and marketing/retailing/merchandising), COMMUNICATIONS AND THE ARTS (technical and business writing), COMPUTER AND PHYSICAL SCIENCE (applied mathematics, chemistry, computer science, information sciences and systems, mathematics, physics, and science), ENGINEERING AND ENVIRONMENTAL DESIGN (aeronautical engineering, chemical engineering, civil engineering, computer engineering, electrical/electronics engineering, engineering management, environmental science, industrial administration/management, and mechanical engineering), HEALTH PROFESSIONS (industrial hygiene), SOCIAL SCIENCE (economics, history, humanities, political science/government, psychology, social science, and sociology). Engineering, business, and sciences are the strongest academically. Mechanical and computer engineering, and engineering and management are the largest.

Required: Students must complete at least 120 credit hours, with 30 in the major and a minimum GPA of 2.0 to graduate. Students must meet a foundation curriculum requirement and take the Personal Wellness unit.

Special: Clarkson offers cross-registration with the Associate Colleges of the St. Lawrence Valley: St. Lawrence University and Potsdam and Canton Colleges. Co-op programs in all academic areas, dual majors in business and liberal arts, interdisciplinary majors, internships, accelerated degree programs, student-designed majors in the B.P.S. degree program, and study abroad in England, Italy, New Zealand, Sweden, Germany, Australia, France, and Canada are possible. There are 3-2 engineering programs with many institutions in the Northeast; students who participate take the first 3 years of the prescribed program at a 4-year liberal arts institution and then transfer with junior standing into one of Clarkson's 4-year engineering curricula. There are interdisciplinary programs in biomolecular science, environmental science and policy, environmental and occupational health, and software engineering. There are 9 national honor societies, including Phi Beta Kappa, a freshman honors program, and all departments have honors programs.

Faculty/Classroom: 79% of faculty are male; 21%, female. 95% teach undergraduates, 40% do research, and 33% do both. No introductory courses are taught by graduate students. The average class size in an introductory lecture is 96; in a laboratory, 32; and in a regular course, 31.

Admissions: 80% of the 2003-2004 applicants were accepted. The SAT I scores for the 2003-2004 freshman class were: Math--2% below

500, 33% between 500 and 599, 51% between 600 and 700, and 14% above 700. 68% of the current freshmen were in the top fifth of their class; 82% were in the top two fifths. 21 freshmen graduated first in their class.

Requirements: The SAT I or ACT is required. In addition, SAT II: Subject tests are also recommended. Applicants must have graduated from an accredited secondary school or have the GED. A campus visit and interview are also recommended. AP and CLEP credits are accepted. Important factors in the admissions decision are advanced placement or honor courses, recommendations by school officials, and extracurricular activities record.

Procedure: Freshmen are admitted fall and spring. Entrance exams should be taken by November. There are early decision, early admissions, and deferred admissions plans. Early decision applications should be filed by December 1 or January 15; regular applications, by March 1 for fall entry and December 1 for spring entry, along with a $30 fee. Notification of early decision is sent January 1; regular decision, February. 168 early decision candidates were accepted for the 2003-2004 class. 2 applicants were on the 2003 waiting list; both were admitted. Applications are accepted on-line.

Transfer: 91 transfer students enrolled in 2002-2003. Transfer students should submit transcripts from all colleges attended and 2 letters of recommendation, including 1 from an academic professsor or instructor. An associate degree will be considered, and an interview is recommended. 30 of 120 credits required for the bachelor's degree must be completed at Clarkson.

Visiting: There are regularly scheduled orientations for prospective students, including meetings with administration and faculty. There are guides for informal visits and visitors may sit in on classes and stay overnight. To schedule a visit, contact the Admissions Office at *admission@clarkson.edu.*

Financial Aid: In 2003-2004, 98% of all full-time freshmen and 94% of continuing full-time students received some form of financial aid. 87% of full-time freshmen and 85% of continuing full-time students received need-based aid. The average freshman award was $19,439. Need-based scholarships or need-based grants averaged $8047 ($20,729 maximum); need-based self-help aid (loans and jobs) averaged $8361 ($11,825 maximum); non-need-based athletic scholarships averaged $19,854 ($33,050 maximum); other non-need-based awards and non-need-based scholarships averaged $8293 ($15,000 maximum); and state awards averaged $2197 ($5000 maximum). 53% of undergraduates work part time. Average annual earnings from campus work are $970. The average financial indebtedness of the 2003 graduate was $18,584. The FAFSA is required. The deadline for filing freshman financial aid applications for fall entry is February 15.

International Students: There are 70 international students enrolled. They must score 550 on the written TOEFL or 213 on the electronic version and also take the SAT I if first-year students.

Computers: The mainframes are an IBM 4381 and an RS 6000. About 100 terminals are available in clusters throughout the campus. All students may access the system. There are no time limits and no fees. It is strongly recommended that all students have a personal computer. Students can bring their own computers; IBM is recommended.

Graduates: From July 1, 2002 to June 30, 2003, 652 bachelor's degrees were awarded. The most popular majors were mechanical engineering (15%), engineering and management (12%), and civil engineering (10%). In an average class, 54% graduate in 4 years or less, 68% graduate in 5 years or less, and 70% graduate in 6 years or less. 91 companies recruited on campus in 2002-2003. Of the 2002 graduating class, 22% were enrolled in graduate school within 6 months of graduation and 46% were employed.

Admissions Contact: Brian T. Grant, Director of Admission. E-mail: *grantbt@clarkson.edu* Web: *http://www.clarkson.edu*

COLGATE UNIVERSITY
Hamilton, NY 13346   C-3

(315) 228-7401; Fax: (315) 228-7544

Full-time: 1379 men, 1390 women	**Faculty:** 241; IIB, ++$
Part-time: 8 men, 19 women	**Ph.D.s:** 91%
Graduate: 4 women	**Student/Faculty:** 11 to 1
Year: semesters	**Tuition:** $29,940
Application Deadline: January 15	**Room & Board:** $7155
Freshman Class: 6789 applied, 2126 accepted, 727 enrolled	
SAT I Verbal/Math: 660/680	**ACT:** 30 **MOST COMPETITIVE**

Colgate University, founded in 1819, is a private liberal arts institution. The 2 libraries contain 1,131,229 volumes, 684,687 microform items, and 34,161 audio/video tapes/CDs, and subscribe to 3170 periodicals. Computerized library services include the card catalog, interlibrary loans, database searching, and Internet access. Special learning facilities include an art gallery, radio station, TV station, an anthropology museum, and observatory. The 515-acre campus is in a rural area 45 miles southeast of Syracuse and 35 miles southwest of Utica. Including any residence halls, there are 86 buildings.

Student Life: 70% of undergraduates are from out of state, mostly the Northeast. Students are from 44 states, 29 foreign countries, and Cana-

da. 71% are from public schools. 81% are white. Most are Jewish. The average age of freshmen is 19; all undergraduates, 20. 4% do not continue beyond their first year; 88% remain to graduate.

Housing: 2400 students can be accommodated in college housing, which includes coed dorms, on-campus apartments, fraternity houses, and sorority houses. In addition, there are language houses and special-interest houses. On-campus housing is guaranteed for all 4 years. 84% of students live on campus; of those, 95% remain on campus on weekends. All students may keep cars.

Activities: 35% of men belong to 8 national fraternities; 32% of women belong to 4 national sororities. There are 150 groups on campus, including art, band, cheerleading, chess, choir, chorale, chorus, computers, dance, debate, drama, ethnic, film, forensics, gay, honors, international, jazz band, literary magazine, musical theater, newspaper, orchestra, pep band, photography, political, professional, radio and TV, religious, social, social service, student government, symphony, and yearbook. Popular campus events include Family Weekend, Peace Jam, and Winter Carnival.

Sports: There are 11 intercollegiate sports for men and 12 for women, and 20 intramural sports for men and 20 for women. Facilities include numerous athletic fields, a softball diamond, an outdoor artificial surface field, a football stadium, an athletic center, a 3000-seat gym, a golf course, a field house, a ski center, a 50-meter pool. a bowling center, a hockey rink, a 9000-square-foot fitness center, running trails, a trap range, and courts for basketball, tennis, squash, handball, and racquetball.

Disabled Students: 20% of the campus is accessible. Wheelchair ramps, elevators, special parking, specially equipped rest rooms, special class scheduling, and lowered drinking fountains are available.

Services: Counseling and information services are available, as is tutoring in every subject. There is a reader service for the blind and remedial writing. There is a note taker service for students with learning and sensory disabilities, and a writing center.

Campus Safety and Security: Measures include 24-hour foot and vehicle patrol, self-defense education, security escort services, and shuttle buses. There are informal discussions, pamphlets/posters/films, emergency telephones, and lighted pathways/sidewalks.

Programs of Study: Colgate confers the B.A. degree. Master's degrees are also awarded. Bachelor's degrees are awarded in BIOLOGICAL SCIENCE (biochemistry, biology/biological science, molecular biology, and neurosciences), COMMUNICATIONS AND THE ARTS (art history and appreciation, Chinese, classics, dramatic arts, English, French, German, Greek, Japanese, Latin, music, Russian, Spanish, and studio art), COMPUTER AND PHYSICAL SCIENCE (astronomy, astrophysics, chemistry, computer science, geology, geophysics and seismology, mathematics, natural sciences, physical sciences, and physics), EDUCATION (education), ENGINEERING AND ENVIRONMENTAL DESIGN (environmental science), SOCIAL SCIENCE (African studies, Asian/Oriental studies, economics, geography, history, humanities, international relations, Latin American studies, Native American studies, peace studies, philosophy, political science/government, psychology, religion, Russian and Slavic studies, social science, sociology, and women's studies). English, economics, and history are the largest.

Required: To graduate, students must complete a First-Year Seminar course and the core curriculum, including 4 general education courses and 2 courses each in the natural sciences, social sciences, and humanities. A total of 32 courses is required, with 8 to 12 courses in the major. Study in a foreign language, phys ed, and a swimming test are also required. Students need a 2.0 GPA in the major.

Special: Colgate offers various internships, semester and summer research opportunities with faculty, work-study, study abroad in 16 countries, accelerated degree programs, dual majors, and student-designed majors. A 3-2 engineering degree with Columbia and Washington Universities and Rensselaer Polytechnic Institute, a 3-4 architecture degree with Washington University, credit by exam, and pass/fail options are available. There are 8 national honor societies, including Phi Beta Kappa, and a freshman honors program.

Faculty/Classroom: 59% of faculty are male; 41%, female. All both teach and do research. No introductory courses are taught by graduate students. The average class size in an introductory lecture is 21; in a laboratory, 17; and in a regular course, 19.

Admissions: 31% of the 2003-2004 applicants were accepted. The SAT I scores for the 2003-2004 freshman class were: Verbal--2% below 500, 16% between 500 and 599, 55% between 600 and 700, and 27% above 700; Math--1% below 500, 9% between 500 and 599, 55% between 600 and 700, and 35% above 700. The ACT scores were 1% below 21, 5% between 21 and 23, 14% between 24 and 26, 7% between 27 and 28, and 74% above 28. 82% of the current freshmen were in the top fifth of their class; 98% were in the top two fifths. 29 freshmen graduated first in their class.

Requirements: The SAT I or ACT is required. In addition, students may submit the SAT I and SAT II: Subject tests in writing and 2 other disciplines, or the ACT. 2 teacher recommendations and a counselor's report are required. An interview, though not evaluated, is recommended. Students should present 16 or more Carnegie credits, based on 4 years each of English and math and at least 3 of lab science, social science, and a foreign language, with electives in the arts. AP and CLEP credits are accepted. Important factors in the admissions decision are advanced placement or honor courses, recommendations by school officials, and leadership record.

Procedure: Freshmen are admitted in the fall. Entrance exams should be taken in time for score reports to reach the University by January 15. There are early decision and deferred admissions plans. Early decision applications should be filed by November 15; regular applications, by January 15 for fall entry, along with a $55 fee. Notification of early decision is sent December 15; regular decision, April 1. 357 early decision candidates were accepted for the 2003-2004 class. 416 applicants were on the 2003 waiting list; 47 were admitted. Applications are accepted on-line through Common App.

Transfer: 19 transfer students enrolled in 2002-2003. Either the SAT I or the ACT is required, as well as college and high school transcripts, a dean's report, and faculty recommendations. 16 of 32 credits required for the bachelor's degree must be completed at Colgate.

Visiting: There are regularly scheduled orientations for prospective students, including nonevaluative interviews, group information sessions, and student-led tours. There are guides for informal visits and visitors may sit in on classes and stay overnight. To schedule a visit, contact the Office of Admission.

Financial Aid: In 2003-2004, 39% of all full-time freshmen and 44% of continuing full-time students received some form of financial aid. 39% of full-time freshmen and 44% of continuing full-time students received need-based aid. The average freshman award was $26,802. Need-based scholarships or need-based grants averaged $23,783; and need-based self-help aid (loans and jobs) averaged $3143. 50% of undergraduates work part time. Average annual earnings from campus work are $890. The average financial indebtedness of the 2003 graduate was $11,104. Colgate is a member of CSS. The CSS Profile or FAFSA is required. The deadline for filing freshman financial aid applications for fall entry is February 1.

International Students: There are 140 international students enrolled. The school actively recruits these students. They must score 600 on the written TOEFL or 250 on the electronic version and also take the SAT I or the ACT.

Computers: The mainframe is a DEC VAX 11/780. There are 400 terminals on campus offering a wide variety of applications software. In addition, all residence halls are wired for networked computers. All students may access the system. There are no time limits and no fees. It is strongly recommended that all students have a personal computer.

Graduates: From July 1, 2002 to June 30, 2003, 631 bachelor's degrees were awarded. In a recent year the most popular majors were economics (12%), English (10%), and history (10%). In an average class, 1% graduate in 3 years or less, 84% graduate in 4 years or less, 88% graduate in 5 years or less, and 89% graduate in 6 years or less. 200 companies recruited on campus in 2002-2003. Of the 2002 graduating class, 16% were enrolled in graduate school within 6 months of graduation and 80% were employed.

Admissions Contact: Gary L. Ross, Dean of Admission.
E-mail: *admission@mail.colgate.edu* Web: *www.colgate.edu*

COLLEGE OF AERONAUTICS   D-5
Flushing, NY 11369

(718) 429-6600
(800) 776-2376; Fax: (718) 779-2231

Full-time: 908 men, 100 women	**Faculty:** n/av
Part-time: 280 men, 20 women	**Ph.Ds:** 10%
Graduate: none	**Student/Faculty:** n/av
Year: semesters, summer session	**Tuition:** $10,790
Application Deadline: open	**Room & Board:** n/app
Freshman Class: 495 applied, 394 accepted, 324 enrolled	
SAT I Verbal/Math: 450/490	SPECIAL

The College of Aeronautics, founded in 1932, is a private aviation school offering undergraduate degrees in aeronautical engineering technology, computerized design/animated graphics, airport management, avionics, aviation maintenance, and aircraft operations In addition to regional accreditation, COA has baccalaureate program accreditation with ABET. The library contains 62,000 volumes and 10,000 microform items. Computerized library services include the card catalog and database searching. Special learning facilities include a learning resource center and a flight simulator, nondestructive testing labs, and a 5000-square-foot hangar facility. The 6-acre campus is in an urban area at LaGuardia Airport, 4 miles east of Manhattan. There are 2 buildings.

Student Life: 95% of undergraduates are from New York. Students are from 9 states, 19 foreign countries, and Canada. 96% are from public schools. 39% are Hispanic; 24% African American; 17% white; 13% Asian American. The average age of freshmen is 21; all undergraduates, 23. 27% do not continue beyond their first year; 68% remain to graduate.

Housing: There are no residence halls. All students commute. Alcohol is not permitted. All students may keep cars.

Activities: There are no fraternities or sororities. There are 4 groups on campus, including ethnic, professional, social, student government, and yearbook. Popular campus events include Open House-Techno Expo, Winter Fest, and Spring Fest.

Sports: There are 3 intramural sports for men and 3 for women. Facilities include nearby areas for softball, flag football, weight lifting, and basketball.

Disabled Students: 95% of the campus is accessible. Wheelchair ramps, elevators, special parking, specially equipped rest rooms, special class scheduling, lowered drinking fountains, and lowered telephones are available.

Services: Counseling and information services are available, as is tutoring in most subjects. There is remedial math, reading, and writing.

Campus Safety and Security: Measures include 24-hour foot and vehicle patrol, informal discussions, and pamphlets/posters/films.

Programs of Study: COA confers the B.S. degree. Associate degrees are also awarded. Bachelor's degrees are awarded in ENGINEERING AND ENVIRONMENTAL DESIGN (aircraft mechanics, airline piloting and navigation, and aviation administration/management). Computerized design, flight operations, and aviation maintenance management are the strongest academically.

Required: All students must satisfy English, math, and science requirements and fulfill appropriate licensing requirements while maintaining a GPA of at least 2.0. Students with advanced credit must complete 30 credits in residency. A total of 134 credits is required to graduate.

Special: Work-study programs are available with the College of Aeronautics, and internships may be arranged through the career development office. B.A.-B.S. degrees are offered.

Faculty/Classroom: 90% of faculty are male; 10%, female. All teach undergraduates. The average class size in an introductory lecture is 25; in a laboratory, 20; and in a regular course, 20.

Admissions: 80% of the 2003-2004 applicants were accepted.

Requirements: The SAT I is recommended. In addition, with scores of 400 verbal and 400 math. Applicants are required to have 3 years of math and 2 years each of English and science. An interview is also recommended. A GPA of 2.5 is required. AP credits are accepted. Important factors in the admissions decision are evidence of special talent, advanced placement or honor courses, and personality/intangible qualities.

Procedure: Freshmen are admitted fall and spring. There are early decision and early admissions plans. There is a rolling admissions plan. Application deadlines are open. 60 early decision candidates were accepted for the 2003-2004 class. The fall application fee was $30.

Transfer: A minimum 2.0 GPA is required. 30 of 134 credits required for the bachelor's degree must be completed at COA.

Visiting: There are regularly scheduled orientations for prospective students, scheduled prior to registration, which include a tour and academic advisement. There are guides for informal visits and visitors may sit in on classes. To schedule a visit, contact the Admissions Office at *admissions@aero.edu*.

Financial Aid: 86% of undergraduates work part time. Average annual earnings from campus work are $2550. The CSS Profile or FAFSA and the college's own financial statement are required. The deadline for filing freshman financial aid applications for fall entry is April 15.

International Students: The school actively recruits these students. They must score 500 on the written TOEFL or have an English Proficiency Certificate.

Computers: The mainframes are an AS400/IBM, networked for both PC and Mac use. All students may access the system. There are no time limits and no fees.

Graduates: In a recent year, 134 bachelor's degrees were awarded. In an average class, 30% graduate in 3 years or less, 60% graduate in 4 years or less, 80% graduate in 5 years or less, and all graduate in 6 years or less. 30 companies recruited on campus in 2002-2003.

Admissions Contact: Ernie Shepelsky, Director of Admissions.
E-mail: *admissions@aero.edu* Web: *www.aero.edu*

COLLEGE OF INSURANCE
(See Saint John's University)

COLLEGE OF MOUNT SAINT VINCENT   D-5
Riverdale, NY 10471

(718) 405-3267
(800) 665-CMSV; Fax: (718) 549-7945

Full-time: 242 men, 866 women	**Faculty:** 71	
Part-time: 24 men, 150 women	**Ph.Ds:** 87%	
Graduate: 83 men, 261 women	**Student/Faculty:** 16 to 1	
Year: semesters, summer session	**Tuition:** $19,000	
Application Deadline: March 1	**Room & Board:** $7800	
Freshman Class: 1608 applied, 1204 accepted, 339 enrolled		
SAT I Verbal/Math: 500/500	**ACT:** 20	COMPETITIVE

The College of Mount Saint Vincent, founded as an academy in 1847 and chartered as a college in 1911, is a private liberal arts institution in the Catholic tradition. In addition to regional accreditation, The Mount has baccalaureate program accreditation with ACBSP and NLN. The library contains 129,000 volumes, 7000 microform items, and 6500 audio/video tapes/CDs, and subscribes to 234 periodicals. Computerized library services include the card catalog, interlibrary loans, database searching, and Internet access. Special learning facilities include a learning resource center, radio station, and TV station. The 70-acre campus is in an urban area 11 miles north of midtown Manhattan. Including any residence halls, there are 11 buildings.

Student Life: 89% of undergraduates are from New York. Students are from 19 states and 4 foreign countries. 46% are from public schools. 38% are white; 32% Hispanic; 14% African American; 10% Asian American. Most are Catholic. The average age of freshmen is 18; all undergraduates, 22. 25% do not continue beyond their first year; 62% remain to graduate.

Housing: 540 students can be accommodated in college housing, which includes coed dorms. On-campus housing is guaranteed for all 4 years. 53% of students commute. All students may keep cars.

Activities: There are no fraternities or sororities. There are 30 groups on campus, including art, cheerleading, chess, choir, chorus, computers, dance, debate, drama, ethnic, film, gay, honors, international, literary magazine, musical theater, newspaper, photography, professional, radio and TV, religious, social, social service, student government, and yearbook. Popular campus events include Annual Block Party, Bachelor Auction, and Battle of the Dorms.

Sports: There are 7 intercollegiate sports for men and 8 for women, and 6 intramural sports for men and 6 for women. Facilities include a gym, a swimming pool, a weight room, a dance studio, a recreation room, a fitness center with aerobic and Nautilus facilities, and basketball, squash, and tennis courts.

Disabled Students: 90% of the campus is accessible. Wheelchair ramps, elevators, special parking, specially equipped rest rooms, lowered drinking fountains, and lowered telephones are available.

Services: Counseling and information services are available, as is tutoring in most subjects, including computer science, math, chemistry, biology, languages, psychology, sociology, writing, and economics. There is a reader service for the blind and remedial math, reading, and writing.

Campus Safety and Security: Measures include 24-hour foot and vehicle patrol, security escort services, shuttle buses, and informal discussions. There are pamphlets/posters/films, emergency telephones, lighted pathways/sidewalks, and a college committee on safety and security on campus.

Programs of Study: The Mount confers B.A. and B.S. degrees. Associate and master's degrees are also awarded. Bachelor's degrees are awarded in BIOLOGICAL SCIENCE (biochemistry and biology/biological science), BUSINESS (business administration and management), COMMUNICATIONS AND THE ARTS (communications, English, French, modern language, and Spanish), COMPUTER AND PHYSICAL SCIENCE (chemistry, computer science, mathematics, and physics), EDUCATION (health, physical, and special), HEALTH PROFESSIONS (allied health and nursing), SOCIAL SCIENCE (economics, history, liberal arts/general studies, philosophy, psychology, religion, sociology, and urban studies). Nursing and biology are the strongest academically. Nursing, psychology, and business are the largest.

Required: All students must complete a 56-credit core curriculum with courses in humanities, social sciences, math and computers, and natural sciences. A total of 120 credits for a B.A. or 126 credits for a B.S., with a minimum of 30 credits in the major, and a minimum GPA of 2.0 are required.

Special: Cross-registration with Manhattan College offers cooperative B.A. programs in international studies, philosophy, phys ed, physics, religious studies, and urban affairs. Internships, work-study, study abroad in 6 countries, a 3-2 engineering degree with Manhattan College, dual majors, and student-designed majors in liberal arts are available. B.A.-B.S. degrees in computer science, health education, math, and psychology, and teacher dual certification programs with special education and elementary, middle school, and secondary education are possible. There are 15 national honor societies, a freshman honors program, and 5 departmental honors programs.

Faculty/Classroom: 39% of faculty are male; 61%, female. All teach undergraduates and 80% both teach and do research. No introductory courses are taught by graduate students. The average class size in an introductory lecture is 25; in a laboratory, 15; and in a regular course, 15.

Admissions: 75% of the 2003-2004 applicants were accepted.

Requirements: The SAT I or ACT is required. In addition, applicants should have completed 4 high school academic units of English, 3 of science, and 2 each of math, foreign language, and social sciences, as well as electives. An essay is required, and an interview is recommended. 1 letter of recommendation is required, and additional letters are encouraged. A grade average of 80 is required. AP and CLEP credits are accepted. Important factors in the admissions decision are advanced placement or honor courses, recommendations by school officials, and extracurricular activities record.

Procedure: Freshmen are admitted fall and spring. Entrance exams should be taken during the junior year and/or fall of the senior year.

There is a rolling admissions plan and an early admissions plan. Early action applications should be filed by November 1; regular applications, by March 1 for fall entry. Notification is sent on a rolling basis beginning in December. Applications are accepted on-line through the school's web site.

Transfer: 113 transfer students enrolled in 2002-2003. Transfer applicants should have a minimum GPA of 2.0. Those majoring in nursing, the sciences, math, or computer science need at least a 2.5 GPA. An interview is recommended. 45 of 120 credits required for the B.A. (126 for the B.S.) must be completed at The Mount.

Visiting: There are regularly scheduled orientations for prospective students. Upon request, students may have an interview with an admissions counselor and tour the campus. All students are invited to an open house. Accepted students may have a one-on-one meeting with a student on campus. There are guides for informal visits and visitors may sit in on classes and stay overnight. To schedule a visit, contact the Admissions Office.

Financial Aid: In 2003-2004, 90% of all full-time freshmen and 75% of continuing full-time students received some form of financial aid. 80% of full-time freshmen and 75% of continuing full-time students received need-based aid. The average freshman award was $9600. 50% of undergraduates work part time. Average annual earnings from campus work are $500. The average financial indebtedness of the 2003 graduate was $17,000. The Mount is a member of CSS. The FAFSA and the TAP application for New York state residents are required. The priority date for freshman financial aid applications for fall entry is February 1. The deadline for filing freshman financial aid applications for fall entry is March 15.

International Students: The school actively recruits these students. They must score 550 on the written TOEFL or 213 on the electronic version or complete ELS Level 109, available on campus, and also take the SAT I, scoring 900, or the ACT.

Computers: The mainframe is a client-server environment running Novell. 176 PCs are available. All students may access the system 9 A.M. to 10 P.M. Monday through Thursday and 9 A.M. to 4 P.M. Friday, Saturday, and Sunday. There are no time limits. The fee is $150.

Graduates: From July 1, 2002 to June 30, 2003, 188 bachelor's degrees were awarded. The most popular majors were nursing (24%), communications (14%), and business (11%). In an average class, 46% graduate in 4 years or less, 60% graduate in 5 years or less, and 62% graduate in 6 years or less. 80 companies recruited on campus in 2002-2003.

Admissions Contact: Timothy P. Nash, Dean of Admission and Financial Aid. A video is available.
E-mail: *admissns@mountsaintvincent.edu* Web: *www.cmsv.edu*

COLLEGE OF NEW ROCHELLE   D-5
New Rochelle, NY 10805-2339   (914) 654-5452
                                      (800) 933-5923; Fax: (914) 654-5464

Full-time: 11 men, 620 women	**Faculty:** 73; IIA, +$
Part-time: 43 men, 294 women	**Ph.D.s:** 84%
Graduate: 213 men, 1147 women	**Student/Faculty:** 9 to 1
Year: semesters, summer session	**Tuition:** $14,650
Application Deadline: August 15	**Room & Board:** $7150
Freshman Class: 1210 applied, 619 accepted, 137 enrolled	
SAT I Verbal/Math: 490/470	**ACT:** 18 **COMPETITIVE**

The College of New Rochelle was founded in 1904 by the Ursuline order as the first Catholic college for women in New York State. Now independent, there are 3 undergraduate schools. The School of Arts and Sciences offers liberal arts baccalaureate education for women only; the School of Nursing is coeducational. The School of New Resources is described in a separate profile. There are 3 undergraduate schools and 1 graduate school. In addition to regional accreditation, CNR has baccalaureate program accreditation with CSWE, NLN, and CCNE. The library contains 224,000 volumes, 277 microform items, and 5700 audio/video tapes/CDs, and subscribes to 1432 periodicals. Computerized library services include the card catalog, interlibrary loans, database searching, and Internet access. Special learning facilities include a learning resource center, art gallery, and , and the Learning Center for Nursing. The 20-acre campus is in a suburban area 12 miles north of New York City. Including any residence halls, there are 20 buildings.

Student Life: 86% of undergraduates are from New York. Others are from 16 states and 10 foreign countries. 73% are from public schools. 48% are African American; 27% white; 18% Hispanic. 77% are Catholic; 18% Protestant. The average age of freshmen is 18; all undergraduates, 21. 23% do not continue beyond their first year; 77% remain to graduate.

Housing: 493 students can be accommodated in college housing, which includes single-sex dormitories. On-campus housing is guaranteed for all 4 years. 61% of students live on campus; of those, 50% remain on campus on weekends. All students may keep cars.

Activities: There are no fraternities or sororities. There are 18 groups on campus, including art, cheerleading, choir, chorus, drama, ethnic, film, honors, international, literary magazine, musical theater, newspaper, photography, political, professional, religious, social, social service, student government, and yearbook. Popular campus events include Junior Celebration, Family Weekend, and Strawberry Festival.

Sports: There are 6 intercollegiate sports for women. Facilities include a fitness center and tennis courts.

Disabled Students: 50% of the campus is accessible. Wheelchair ramps, elevators, special parking, specially equipped rest rooms, and special class scheduling are available.

Services: Counseling and information services are available, as is tutoring in some subjects, including science, languages. There is remedial math, reading, and writing. Individual counseling and educational workshops about self-development and personal concerns are available, as are self-help materials.

Campus Safety and Security: Measures include 24-hour foot and vehicle patrol, self-defense education, security escort services, and shuttle buses. There are informal discussions, pamphlets/posters/films, emergency telephones, lighted pathways/sidewalks, and , card access to dorms, and surveillance cameras.

Programs of Study: CNR confers B.A., B.S., B.F.A., and B.S.N. degrees. Master's degrees are also awarded. Bachelor's degrees are awarded in AGRICULTURE (environmental studies), BIOLOGICAL SCIENCE (biology/biological science), BUSINESS (business administration and management), COMMUNICATIONS AND THE ARTS (art history and appreciation, classics, communications, English, French, and Spanish), COMPUTER AND PHYSICAL SCIENCE (chemistry, and mathematics), EDUCATION (art), HEALTH PROFESSIONS (art therapy, and nursing), SOCIAL SCIENCE (economics, history, international studies, philosophy, political science/government, psychology, religion, social work, sociology, and women's studies). Nursing, art, and psychology are the largest.

Required: Students must complete 120 credit hours, 60 to 90 in liberal arts courses, depending on the major, meet specific course distribution requirements, and maintain a minimum GPA of 2.0 to graduate. 4 phys ed courses are also required.

Special: CNR provides cooperative programs in all disciplines, work-study programs, dual majors in all majors, interdisciplinary studies, an accelerated degree program in nursing, a Washington semester, internships, study abroad in 9 countries, nondegree study, pass/fail options, student-designed majors, and a general studies degree. There is 1 national honor society, a freshman honors program.

Faculty/Classroom: 28% of faculty are male; 72%, female. 100% both teach and do research. No introductory courses are taught by graduate students. The average class size in an introductory lecture is 15; in a laboratory, 10; and in a regular course, 15.

Admissions: 51% of the 2003-2004 applicants were accepted. The SAT I scores for the 2003-2004 freshman class were: Verbal--53% below 500, 35% between 500 and 599, 10% between 600 and 700, and 2% above 700; Math--67% below 500, 25% between 500 and 599, and 8% between 600 and 700. 35% of the current freshmen were in the top fifth of their class; 62% were in the top two fifths.

Requirements: The SAT I is required. In addition, graduation from an accredited secondary school is required; the GED is accepted. Applicants must have completed 15 academic credits, with 4 in English, 3 each in math, science, and social studies, and 2 in a foreign language. A portfolio is required for art majors. An essay and interview are recommended. AP and CLEP credits are accepted. Important factors in the admissions decision are advanced placement or honor courses, recommendations by school officials, and leadership record.

Procedure: Freshmen are admitted to all sessions. Entrance exams should be taken in the junior year or fall of the senior year. There are early decision, early admissions, and deferred admissions plans. Early decision applications should be filed by November 1; regular applications, by August 15 for fall entry and January 10 for spring entry. Notification of early decision is sent December 15; regular decision, on a rolling basis.

Transfer: 70 transfer students enrolled in 2002-2003. Transfer students must submit a transcript from their previous college showing courses completed and a minimum GPA of 2.0. High school records and SAT I scores are required. An interview is recommended. 30 of 120 credits required for the bachelor's degree must be completed at CNR.

Visiting: There are regularly scheduled orientations for prospective students, including several open houses providing information on admission. There are guides for informal visits and visitors may sit in on classes and stay overnight. To schedule a visit, contact the Office of Admissions at *admission@cnr.edu*.

Financial Aid: In 2003-2004, 90% of all full-time freshmen and 80% of continuing full-time students received some form of financial aid. 90% of full-time freshmen and 80% of continuing full-time students received need-based aid. The average freshman award was $14,282. 60% of undergraduates work part time. Average annual earnings from campus work are $1200. The average financial indebtedness of the 2003 graduate was $17,978. The CSS/Profile, FAFSA, FFS or SFS, the college's own financial statement and the income documentation are required.

The deadline for filing freshman financial aid applications for fall entry is open.

International Students: They must score 550 on the written TOEFL or 213 on the electronic version and also take or the ESL Language Test. and also take the SAT I, ACT, or ; the SAT I is preferred.

Computers: The mainframe is an AS400. Students are provided with wired and wireless access points to the college's network throughtout the campus. This provides access to the college intranet, e-mail, Internet, and numerous library databases. More than 500 public access workstations allow network access in the library, residence halls, computer classrooms, and labs. In addition, students may reserve loaner laptops from the library and may access their degree or financial record from a public kiosk. All students may access the system 24 hours per day. There are no time limits and no fees.

Graduates: From July 1, 2002 to June 30, 2003, 208 bachelor's degrees were awarded. In an average class, 37% graduate in 4 years or less, 46% graduate in 5 years or less, and 47% graduate in 6 years or less. 27 companies recruited on campus in 2002-2003. Of the 2002 graduating class, 20% were enrolled in graduate school within 6 months of graduation and 60% were employed.

Admissions Contact: Stephanie Decker, Director of Admission. A video is available. E-mail: *sdecker@cnr.edu* Web: *www.cnr.edu*

COLLEGE OF NEW ROCHELLE - SCHOOL OF NEW RESOURCES   D-5
New Rochelle, NY 10805-2339   (914) 654-5526
(800) 288-4767; Fax: (914) 654-5664

Full-time: 490 men, 3284 women	**Faculty:** 25
Part-time: 60 men, 328 women	**Ph.D.s:** 27%
Graduate: none	**Student/Faculty:** 151 to 1
Year: semesters, summer session	**Tuition:** $5450
Application Deadline: August 15	**Room & Board:** n/app
Freshman Class: 701 enrolled	
SAT I or ACT: not required	**SPECIAL**

The College of New Rochelle's School of New Resources is a liberal arts institution serving adult baccalaureate students. There is 1 undergraduate school. The library contains 224,000 volumes, 277 microform items, and 5700 audio/video tapes/CDs, and subscribes to 1432 periodicals. Computerized library services include the card catalog, interlibrary loans, database searching, and Internet access. Special learning facilities include a learning resource center, art gallery, TV station, and access centers to assist students in improving writing, reading, and math skills. The campus is in an urban area 12 miles north of New York City. Five additional campuses are located within the city. There are 20 buildings.

Student Life: 98% of undergraduates are from New York. Students are from 3 states and 3 foreign countries. 82% are African American; 13% Hispanic. The average age of freshmen is 33; all undergraduates, 37. 35% do not continue beyond their first year; 68% remain to graduate.

Housing: There are no residence halls. All students commute. Alcohol is not permitted. All students may keep cars.

Activities: There are no fraternities or sororities. There are some groups and organizations on campus, including drama, musical theater, religious, and student government. Popular campus events include Founders Day, College Bowl, and numerous women's and ethnic activities.

Sports: There is no sports program at SNR.

Services: Counseling and information services are available, as is tutoring in some subjects, including communication skills, problem solving, and math skills. There is remedial math, reading, and writing.

Campus Safety and Security: Measures include 24-hour foot and vehicle patrol, self-defense education, security escort services, and shuttle buses. There are informal discussions, pamphlets/posters/films, emergency telephones, lighted pathways/sidewalks, and surveillance cameras.

Programs of Study: SNR confers the B.A. degree. Bachelor's degrees are awarded in SOCIAL SCIENCE (liberal arts/general studies).

Required: Students must complete 120 credit hours, meet specific course distribution requirements, and maintain a minimum GPA of 2.0 to graduate. Entrance, core, and exit seminars are required, as are degree-planning courses.

Special: SNR provides a voluntary work-study program. Student-designed internships, courses, and degree plans are available. Credit for prior learning may be obtained.

Faculty/Classroom: 54% of faculty are male; 46%, female. All teach undergraduates. The average class size in an introductory lecture is 15; in a laboratory, 10; and in a regular course, 15.

Requirements: Enrolling students must be age 21 or older, have a high school diploma or its equivalent, and have successfully completed an English assessment. Test scores are not required. New students are expected to attend an orientation workshop. AP and CLEP credits are accepted.

Procedure: Freshmen are admitted to all sessions. Entrance exams should be taken in the junior year or fall of the senior year. Early decision applications should be filed by November 1; regular applications, by

August 15 for fall entry and January 10 for spring entry. Notification of early decision is sent December 15; regular decision, on a rolling basis.

Transfer: 520 transfer students enrolled in a recent year. Transfer students must obtain a transcript from their previous college. With some restrictions, course grades of C- or better will be accepted. 30 of 120 credits required for the bachelor's degree must be completed at SNR.

Financial Aid: In a recent year, 90% of all full-time freshmen received some form of financial aid. The average freshman award was $6899. 5% of undergraduates work part time. Average annual earnings from campus work are $2000. The average financial indebtedness of the 2003 graduate was $9551. The FAFSA, the college's own financial statement, and income documentation are required. The deadline for filing freshman financial aid applications for fall entry is open.

Computers: The mainframe is an AS 400. The main campus has many access points to the Internet and library databases. Branch campuses have access to computers through Access Center labs and computer-assisted classrooms with Internet access. All students may access the system from 8:30 A.M. to 11 P.M. daily. Students may access the system 2 hours during peak usage. There are no fees.

Graduates: From July 1, 2002 to June 30, 2003, 763 bachelor's degrees were awarded. The most popular major was liberal arts/general studies (100%). In an average class, 17% graduate in 4 years or less, 24% graduate in 5 years or less, and 29% graduate in 6 years or less. Of the 2002 graduating class, 18% were enrolled in graduate school within 6 months of graduation.

Admissions Contact: Donna Tyler, Associate Dean. A video is available. Web: www.cnr.edu

---

COLLEGE OF SAINT ROSE
Albany, NY 12203

D-3

(518) 454-5150
(800) 637-8556; Fax: (518) 454-2013

Full-time: 657 men, 1890 women	**Faculty:** 166; IIA, --$
Part-time: 95 men, 256 women	**Ph.D.s:** 77%
Graduate: 465 men, 1303 women	**Student/Faculty:** 15 to 1
Year: semesters, summer session	**Tuition:** $15,638
Application Deadline: February 1	**Room & Board:** $7226
Freshman Class: 1916 applied, 1414 accepted, 535 enrolled	
SAT I Verbal/Math: 530/530	**ACT:** 22 COMPETITIVE

The College of Saint Rose, established in 1920, is an independent liberal arts institution sponsored by the Sisters of St. Joseph of Carondelet. There are 4 undergraduate schools and 1 graduate school. In addition to regional accreditation, CSR has baccalaureate program accreditation with ACBSP, ASLA, and NASAD. The library contains 206,692 volumes, 307,904 microform items, and 1510 audio/video tapes/CDs, and subscribes to 902 periodicals. Computerized library services include the card catalog, interlibrary loans, database searching, and Internet access. Special learning facilities include a learning resource center, art gallery, and TV station. The 28-acre campus is in a suburban area in a residential section, 1 1/2 miles from downtown Albany. Including any residence halls, there are 77 buildings.

Student Life: 93% of undergraduates are from New York. Students are from 20 states, 9 foreign countries, and Canada. 83% are white. The average age of freshmen is 18; all undergraduates, 22. 15% do not continue beyond their first year; 65% remain to graduate.

Housing: 1102 students can be accommodated in college housing, which includes single-sex and coed dorms, on-campus apartments, and married-student housing. On-campus housing is available on a first-come, first-served basis and is available on a lottery system for upperclassmen. 63% of students commute. All students may keep cars.

Activities: There are no fraternities or sororities. There are 37 groups on campus, including cheerleading, chorale, Circle K, commuter, computers, dance, departmental, disabled, drama, ethnic, international, jazz band, literary magazine, newspaper, political, professional, religious, social, social service, student government, women's, and yearbook. Popular campus events include Harvest Fest, Rose Rock, and Land and Water Olympics.

Sports: There are 6 intercollegiate sports for men and 6 for women, and 5 intramural sports for men and 5 for women. Facilities include a gym with basketball and volleyball courts, a weight room, an indoor swimming pool, and access to city soccer fields, baseball fields, and softball fields.

Disabled Students: 98% of the campus is accessible. Wheelchair ramps, elevators, special parking, specially equipped rest rooms, lowered drinking fountains, lowered telephones, and some automatic-open doors are available.

Services: Counseling and information services are available, as is tutoring in most subjects, including writing, math, accounting, computer science, and others as needed. There is a reader service for the blind, and remedial math, reading, and writing. There is also a full-time assistant director of disabled student services.

Campus Safety and Security: Measures include 24-hour foot and vehicle patrol, security escort services, shuttle buses, and informal discus-sions. There are pamphlets/posters/films, emergency telephones, lighted pathways/sidewalks, a student volunteer escort service, and fire drills.

Programs of Study: CSR confers B.A., B.S., and B.F.A. degrees. Master's degrees are also awarded. Bachelor's degrees are awarded in BIOLOGICAL SCIENCE (biochemistry and biology/biological science), BUSINESS (accounting and business administration and management), COMMUNICATIONS AND THE ARTS (communications, English, graphic design, music, Spanish, and studio art), COMPUTER AND PHYSICAL SCIENCE (chemistry, information sciences and systems, and mathematics), EDUCATION (art, early childhood, elementary, English, foreign languages, mathematics, music, science, social studies, special, and technical), ENGINEERING AND ENVIRONMENTAL DESIGN (environmental science), HEALTH PROFESSIONS (cytotechnology, medical technology, and speech pathology/audiology), SOCIAL SCIENCE (American studies, criminal justice, history, interdisciplinary studies, political science/government, psychology, religion, social work, and sociology). Education, art, and music are the strongest academically. Business, special education, and elementary education are the largest.

Required: To graduate, students must complete 122 credits with a minimum GPA of 2.0 overall and in the major; these requirements are higher for certain majors. Liberal education requirements consist of 6 credits in college writing and speech and 30 credits in the humanities, science and math, social science and business, and the arts. Students must also complete 2 credits in phys ed.

Special: CSR offers cross-registration with the Hudson-Mohawk Association and the CSI Consortium, internships, work-study programs, study abroad in several countries, dual and student-designed majors, nondegree study, and pass/fail options. There are 3-2 engineering degree programs with Alfred and Clarkson Universities, Union College, and Rensselaer Polytechnic University, as well as a 6-year law program with Albany Law School. There are 6 national honor societies, and 5 departmental honors programs.

Faculty/Classroom: 42% of faculty are male; 58%, female. No introductory courses are taught by graduate students. The average class size in a laboratory is 14 and in a regular course, 25.

Admissions: 74% of the 2003-2004 applicants were accepted. The SAT I scores for the 2003-2004 freshman class were: Verbal--36% below 500, 48% between 500 and 599, 15% between 600 and 700, and 1% above 700; Math--36% below 500, 48% between 500 and 599, 14% between 600 and 700, and 2% above 700. The ACT scores were 32% below 21, 30% between 21 and 23, 20% between 24 and 26, 14% between 27 and 28, and 4% above 28. 34% of the current freshmen were in the top fifth of their class; 72% were in the top two fifths. 2 freshmen graduated first in their class.

Requirements: The SAT I or ACT is required. In addition, applicants must be graduates of an accredited secondary school or have a GED certificate. They should have completed college preparatory programs. All students must submit a letter of recommendation. Art students must submit portfolios, and music students must audition. AP and CLEP credits are accepted. Important factors in the admissions decision are advanced placement or honor courses, leadership record, and recommendations by school officials.

Procedure: Freshmen are admitted fall and spring. Entrance exams should be taken during spring of junior year or fall of senior year. There are early admissions and deferred admissions plans. There is a rolling admissions plan. Applications should be filed by February 1 for fall entry and November 1 for spring entry. Notification is sent on a rolling basis. The fall 2003 application fee was $35. Applications are accepted on-line through EXPAN.

Transfer: 277 transfer students enrolled in 2002-2003. Applicants must submit official transcripts, a letter of recommendation, and a personal statement of the reasons for seeking transfer. Art majors must submit a portfolio, and music majors must audition. 60 of 122 credits required for the bachelor's degree must be completed at CSR.

Visiting: There are regularly scheduled orientations for prospective students, including visits with admissions and financial aid representatives, an overnight program hosted by students, Saturday information sessions in the fall, open house, and Accepted Student Day in April. There are guides for informal visits and visitors may sit in on classes and stay overnight. To schedule a visit, contact the Admissions Office at admit@mail.strose.edu.

Financial Aid: In a recent year, 95% of all full-time freshmen and 93% of continuing full-time students received some form of financial aid. 73% of full-time freshmen and 76% of continuing full-time students received need-based aid. The average freshman award was $10,140. 16% of undergraduates work part time. Average annual earnings from campus work are $770. The average financial indebtedness of a recent graduate was $16,379. CSR is a member of CSS. The FAFSA is required. The deadline for filing freshman financial aid applications for fall entry is February 1.

International Students: There are 7 international students enrolled. They must score 500 on the written TOEFL or 173 on the electronic version.

Computers: The mainframe is an IBM RS/6000/990. The college network provides connectivity to various application services located throughout the campus. More than 300 PCs are available for student use in computer labs, classrooms, and the library. All dorms are networked with 1 connection per bed. Dial-up access is also available via a modem pool. All PCs have access to the Internet, e-mail, and the World Wide Web. All students may access the system 24 hours a day Monday through Saturday, and additional hours on Sunday. There are no time limits. The fee is $100 per semester.

Graduates: From July 1, 2002 to June 30, 2003, 587 bachelor's degrees were awarded. The most popular majors were elementary education (29%), business (9%), and public communication (7%). In an average class, 47% graduate in 4 years or less, 61% graduate in 5 years or less, and 64% graduate in 6 years or less. 45 companies recruited on campus in 2002-2003. Of the 2002 graduating class, 43% were enrolled in graduate school within 6 months of graduation and 89% were employed.

Admissions Contact: Mary Grondahl, Associate Vice President for Undergraduate Admissions. A video is available.
E-mail: *admit@rosnet.strose.edu* Web: *www.strose.edu*

COLUMBIA UNIVERSITY SYSTEM

The Columbia University System, established in 1754, is a public system in New York. It is governed by a board of trustees, whose chief administrator is president. The primary goals of the system are teaching and research. The main priorities are providing outstanding undergraduate instruction; conducting research to develop new knowledge and methods; and training of professionals in law, business, social work, and medicine. The total enrollment of the 4 campuses is usually about 9000; there were about 2100 faculty members. Altogether there are 110 baccalaureate, 160 master's, and 80 doctoral programs offered in Columbia University System. Profiles of the 4-year campuses are included in this section.

COLUMBIA UNIVERSITY/BARNARD COLLEGE	D-5
New York, NY 10027-6598	(212) 854-2014; Fax: (212) 854-6220
Full-time: 2232 women	**Faculty:** 186; IIB, ++$
Part-time: 49 women	**Ph.D.s:** 93%
Graduate: none	**Student/Faculty:** 12 to 1
Year: semesters	**Tuition:** $26,528
Application Deadline: January 1	**Room & Board:** $10,462
Freshman Class: 4034 applied, 1254 accepted, 554 enrolled	
SAT I Verbal/Math: 690/670	**ACT:** 29 **MOST COMPETITIVE**

Barnard College, founded in 1889, is an independent affiliate of Columbia University. It is an undergraduate women's liberal arts college. The library contains 204,906 volumes, 17,705 microform items, and 17,448 audio/video tapes/CDs, and subscribes to 543 periodicals. Computerized library services include the card catalog, interlibrary loans, database searching, and Internet access. Special learning facilities include a learning resource center, art gallery, radio station, TV station, greenhouse, history of physics lab, child development research and study center, dance studio, modern theater, women's research archives within a women's center, and multimedia labs and classrooms. The 4-acre campus is in an urban area occupying 4 city blocks of Manhattan's Upper West Side. Including any residence halls, there are 15 buildings.

Student Life: 65% of undergraduates are from out of state, mostly the Middle Atlantic. Students are from 48 states, 35 foreign countries, and Canada. 53% are from public schools. 66% are white; 19% Asian American. The average age of freshmen is 18; all undergraduates, 20. 7% do not continue beyond their first year; 84% remain to graduate.

Housing: 2057 students can be accommodated in college housing, which includes dorms, on-campus apartments, and off-campus apartments. In addition, there are special-interest houses. On-campus housing is guaranteed for all 4 years. 89% of students live on campus; of those, 75% remain on campus on weekends. Alcohol is not permitted. All students may keep cars.

Activities: There are no fraternities or sororities. There are 100 groups on campus, including art, band, cheerleading, choir, chorale, chorus, dance, debate, drama, ethnic, film, gay, international, jazz band, literary magazine, marching band, musical theater, newspaper, opera, orchestra, photography, political, professional, radio and TV, religious, social, social service, student government, symphony, and yearbook. Popular campus events include Spring and Winter Festivals, Founders Day, and Take Back the Night.

Sports: Facilities include pools, weight rooms, gyms, tennis courts, an indoor track, and a boat slip.

Disabled Students: 90% of the campus is accessible. Wheelchair ramps, elevators, special parking, specially equipped rest rooms, special class scheduling, lowered drinking fountains, lowered telephones, and special housing are available. The Office of Disability Services provides a variety of support services to students with permanent and temporary disabilities.

Services: Counseling and information services are available, as is tutoring in every subject. There is a reader service for the blind. A student-staffed writing room is available for students of all levels of writing ability, and a math help room is also available to students in all math courses.

Campus Safety and Security: Measures include 24-hour foot and vehicle patrol, security escort services, shuttle buses, and informal discussions. There are pamphlets/posters/films, emergency telephones, lighted pathways/sidewalks, and safety and security education programs.

Programs of Study: Barnard College confers the B.A. degree. Bachelor's degrees are awarded in BIOLOGICAL SCIENCE (biochemistry and biology/biological science), COMMUNICATIONS AND THE ARTS (art history and appreciation, classics, comparative literature, dance, dramatic arts, English, film arts, French, German, Greek, Italian, Latin, linguistics, music, Russian, and Spanish), COMPUTER AND PHYSICAL SCIENCE (astronomy, chemistry, computer science, mathematics, physics, and statistics), ENGINEERING AND ENVIRONMENTAL DESIGN (architecture and environmental science), SOCIAL SCIENCE (American studies, anthropology, biopsychology, classical/ancient civilization, East Asian studies, economics, European studies, history, international studies, medieval studies, Middle Eastern studies, philosophy, political science/government, psychology, religion, sociology, urban studies, and women's studies). English, psychology, and economics are the strongest academically and have the largest enrollments.

Required: A total of 120 credits is required, with a minimum GPA of 2.0. All students must take 4 semesters each of a foreign language, humanities, or social sciences outside the major, and geographic and cultural diversity courses that may satisfy the major or other requirements, 2 semesters each of lab science and phys ed, and 1 semester each in first-year seminar, first-year English, and quantitative reasoning.

Special: Barnard offers cross-registration with Columbia University, more than 2500 internships with New York City firms and institutions, and study abroad worldwide. A 3-2 engineering program with the Columbia School of Engineering and double-degree programs with the Columbia University Schools of International and Public Affairs, Law, and Dentistry, the Juilliard School, and the Jewish Theological Seminary are possible. The college offers dual and student-designed majors and multidisciplinary majors, including economic history. There is 1 national honor society, Phi Beta Kappa.

Faculty/Classroom: 38% of faculty are male; 62%, female. All both teach and do research. The average class size in an introductory lecture is 30; in a laboratory, 11; and in a regular course, 13.

Admissions: 31% of the 2003-2004 applicants were accepted. The SAT I scores for the 2003-2004 freshman class were: Verbal--2% below 500, 7% between 500 and 599, 44% between 600 and 700, and 47% above 700; Math--1% below 500, 10% between 500 and 599, 60% between 600 and 700, and 29% above 700. The ACT scores were 5% between 21 and 23, 10% between 24 and 26, 22% between 27 and 28, and 63% above 28. 96% of the current freshmen were in the top fifth of their class; 99% were in the top two fifths. There were 21 National Merit finalists. 20 freshmen graduated first in their class.

Requirements: The SAT I or ACT is required. In addition, if taking the SAT I, an applicant must also take 3 SAT II: Subject tests, 1 of which must be in writing or literature. A GED is accepted. Applicants should prepare with 4 years of English, 3 of math, 3 or 4 of a foreign language, 2 of a lab science, and 1 of history. An interview is recommended. AP credits are accepted. Important factors in the admissions decision are advanced placement or honor courses, evidence of special talent, and extracurricular activities record.

Procedure: Freshmen are admitted fall and spring. Entrance exams should be taken by January of the senior year. There are early decision and deferred admissions plans. Early decision applications should be filed by November 15; regular applications, by January 1 for fall entry. Notification of early decision is sent December 15; regular decision, April 1. The fall 2003 application fee was $45. 153 early decision candidates were accepted for the 2003-2004 class. 766 applicants were on the 2003 waiting list; 36 were admitted. Applications are accepted on-line through the school's web site.

Transfer: 81 transfer students enrolled in 2002-2003. Applicants must complete at least 1 college course. The SAT I or ACT is required. Deadline for transfer applicants is April 1 (fall term) and November 1 (spring term). 60 of 120 credits required for the bachelor's degree must be completed at Barnard College.

Visiting: There are regularly scheduled orientations for prospective students, consisting of open house programs regularly scheduled throughout the fall. There are guides for informal visits and visitors may sit in on classes and stay overnight. To schedule a visit, contact the Office of Admissions at *admissions@barnard.edu*.

Financial Aid: In 2003-2004, 53% of all full-time students received some form of financial aid. 39% of all full-time students received need-based aid. The average freshman award was $25,424. Need-based scholarships or need-based grants averaged $23,436 ($39,090 maximum); and need-based self-help aid (loans and jobs) averaged $3287

($4400 maximum). 46% of undergraduates work part time. The average financial indebtedness of the 2003 graduate was $16,275. Barnard College is a member of CSS. The CSS Profile or FAFSA, the college's own financial statement, the parents' and student's federal tax returns, and the business and/or noncustodial parent statement, if applicable, are required. The deadline for filing freshman financial aid applications for fall entry is February 1.

International Students: There are 68 international students enrolled. The school actively recruits these students. They must score 600 on the written TOEFL and also take the SAT I or ACT. Applicants who take the SAT I must also take SAT II: Subject tests in writing or literature and 2 others.

Computers: The mainframe is an IBM RS/6000. All students have access to 3 academic computer labs that provide networked access to software, bibliographic searching, and Columbia University mainframe links. Several academic departments maintain computer labs for student use. All dorms are also wired for full Internet access. All students may access the system. There are no time limits and no fees. It is strongly recommended that all students have a personal computer.

Graduates: From July 1, 2002 to June 30, 2003, 597 bachelor's degrees were awarded. The most popular majors were psychology (13%), English (13%), and economics (12%). In an average class, 2% graduate in 3 years or less, 82% graduate in 4 years or less, 88% graduate in 5 years or less, and 84% graduate in 6 years or less. 90 companies recruited on campus in 2002-2003. Of the 2002 graduating class, 24% were enrolled in graduate school within 6 months of graduation and 70% were employed.

Admissions Contact: Jennifer Fondiller, Dean of Admissions.
E-mail: *admissions@barnard.edu* Web: *http://www.barnard.edu*

COLUMBIA UNIVERSITY/COLUMBIA COLLEGE   D-5
New York, NY 10027   (212) 854-2522; Fax: (212) 854-1209

Full-time: 2059 men, 2122 women	**Faculty:** 689; I, ++$
Part-time: none	**Ph.D.s:** 100%
Graduate: none	**Student/Faculty:** 6 to 1
Year: semesters, summer session	**Tuition:** $29,788
Application Deadline: January 2	**Room & Board:** $8802
Freshman Class: 14,665 applied, 1644 accepted, 1011 enrolled	
SAT I Verbal/Math: 710/710	**ACT:** 29 **MOST COMPETITIVE**

Columbia College of Columbia University, founded in 1754, is a private college offering programs in the liberal arts and sciences. The 20 libraries contain 7.2 million volumes. Computerized library services include the card catalog, interlibrary loans, and database searching. Special learning facilities include an art gallery, planetarium, radio station, TV station, and an observatory. The 36-acre campus is in an urban area in New York City. Including any residence halls, there are 50 buildings.

Student Life: 75% of undergraduates are from out of state, mostly the Middle Atlantic. Students are from 50 states, 42 foreign countries, and Canada. 54% are from public schools. 54% are white; 14% Asian American. The average age of freshmen is 18; all undergraduates, 20. 2% do not continue beyond their first year; 91% remain to graduate.

Housing: All students can be accommodated in college housing, which includes single-sex and coed dorms, on-campus apartments, fraternity houses, and sorority houses. In addition, there are language houses and special-interest houses. On-campus housing is guaranteed for all 4 years. 95% of students live on campus. All students may keep cars.

Activities: 15% of men belong to 19 national fraternities; 9% of women belong to 9 national sororities. There are 300 groups on campus, including art, band, cheerleading, chess, choir, chorale, chorus, computers, dance, debate, drama, ethnic, film, gay, honors, international, jazz band, literary magazine, marching band, musical theater, newspaper, opera, orchestra, outdoor, pep band, photography, political, professional, radio and TV, religious, social, social service, student government, symphony, and yearbook. Popular campus events include Columbia Fest, United Minorities Board Ethnic Festival, and Holiday Lighting Ceremony/Yule Log.

Sports: There are 14 intercollegiate sports for men and 15 for women, and 13 intramural sports for men and 13 for women. Facilities include a football stadium, indoor and outdoor track and field facilities, a baseball field, a soccer stadium, a recreational gym with a swimming pool, basketball/volleyball courts, aerobic, fencing, wrestling, martial arts, and weight rooms, a boat house, and tennis, squash, handball, and racquetball courts.

Disabled Students: All of the campus is accessible. Wheelchair ramps, elevators, special parking, specially equipped rest rooms, special class scheduling, lowered drinking fountains, lowered telephones, special housing, and chair lifts are available.

Services: Counseling and information services are available, as is tutoring in every subject. There is a reader service for the blind.

Campus Safety and Security: Measures include 24-hour foot and vehicle patrol, self-defense education, security escort services, and shuttle buses. There are informal discussions, pamphlets/posters/films, emergency telephones, and lighted pathways/sidewalks.

Programs of Study: Columbia confers the A.B. degree. Bachelor's degrees are awarded in BIOLOGICAL SCIENCE (biochemistry, biology/biological science, biophysics, environmental biology, and neurosciences), COMMUNICATIONS AND THE ARTS (art history and appreciation, classics, comparative literature, dance, dramatic arts, English, film arts, French, German, Germanic languages and literature, Greek, Latin, linguistics, music, Russian, Spanish, and visual and performing arts), COMPUTER AND PHYSICAL SCIENCE (astronomy, astrophysics, chemistry, computer science, earth science, geochemistry, geology, geophysics and seismology, mathematics, physics, and statistics), EDUCATION (education), ENGINEERING AND ENVIRONMENTAL DESIGN (architecture and environmental science), SOCIAL SCIENCE (African American studies, American studies, anthropology, archeology, area studies, Asian/American studies, Asian/Oriental studies, classical/ancient civilization, East Asian studies, economics, Hispanic American studies, history, Italian studies, Latin American studies, medieval studies, Middle Eastern studies, philosophy, political science/government, psychology, religion, Russian and Slavic studies, sociology, urban studies, and women's studies). Economics, English, and history are the largest.

Required: All students complete a core curriculum consisting of classes in Western and non-Western cultures, literature and philosophy, history, social science, art, sculpture and architecture, and music of the Western tradition; 2 courses in non-Western areas are also required. Distribution requirements include 2 years of foreign language (unless competency can be demonstrated), 3 semesters of science, 1 year of phys ed, and 1 semester of writing. Courses in logic and rhetoric are also required. A thesis may be required for departmental honors in certain departments. A total of 124 credit hours is required; usually 30 to 40 of these are in the major. The minimum required GPA is 2.0.

Special: There is a study abroad program at more than 100 locations, including France, Oxford and Cambridge Universities in England, and the Kyoto Center for Japanese Studies in Japan. Cross-registration is possible with the Juilliard School and Barnard College. Combined B.A.-B.S. degrees are offered via 3-2 or 4-1 engineering programs. A 3-2 engineering degree is offered with Columbia's Fu Foundation School of Engineering and Applied Science. There is also a 5-year B.A./M.I.A. with Columbia's School of International and Public Affairs. The college offers work-study, internships, credit by exam, pass/fail options, and dual, student-designed, and interdisciplinary majors, including regional studies and ancient studies. There is a chapter of Phi Beta Kappa. 31 departments have honors programs.

Faculty/Classroom: 70% of faculty are male; 30%, female. All both teach and do research. The average class size in an introductory lecture is 70; in a laboratory, 15; and in a regular course, 25.

Admissions: 11% of the 2003-2004 applicants were accepted. The SAT I scores for the 2003-2004 freshman class were: Verbal--8% between 500 and 599, 28% between 600 and 700, and 64% above 700; Math--6% between 500 and 599, 34% between 600 and 700, and 60% above 700. The ACT scores were 4% between 21 and 23, 46% between 27 and 28, and 50% above 28. 95% of the current freshmen were in the top fifth of their class; 99% were in the top two fifths.

Requirements: The SAT I or ACT is required. In addition, 3 SAT II: Subject tests, one of which must be writing, are also required. A GED is accepted. Students should prepare with 4 years of English and 3 or 4 years each of foreign language, social studies/history, math, and lab science. An essay is required; interviews are not required. 2 academic faculty recommendations and a written evaluation or recommendation from a school official are also required. AP credits are accepted. Important factors in the admissions decision are advanced placement or honor courses, recommendations by school officials, and leadership record.

Procedure: Freshmen are admitted in the fall. The college prefers that entrance exams be taken no later than October or November of the senior year. There are early decision, early admissions, and deferred admissions plans. Early decision applications should be filed by November 1; regular applications, by January 2 for fall entry. Notification of early decision is sent December 15; regular decision, April 1. The fall 2003 application fee was $65. 467 early decision candidates were accepted for the 2003-2004 class. 64 applicants were on the 2003 waiting list; all were admitted. Applications are accepted on-line through *www.apply.embark.com/ugrad/columbia.*

Transfer: 61 transfer students enrolled in 2002-2003. Applicants must have completed 1 full year of college (24 credits) with a GPA of at least 3.0. They must submit high school and college transcripts. 60 of 124 credits required for the bachelor's degree must be completed at Columbia.

Visiting: There are regularly scheduled orientations for prospective students, consisting of group information sessions and student-led tours. There are guides for informal visits and visitors may sit in on classes and stay overnight. To schedule a visit, contact Visitors Center at (212) 854-4900 or *www.studentaffairs.columbia.edu/admissions.*

Financial Aid: In 2003-2004, 46% of all full-time freshmen and 55% of continuing full-time students received some form of financial aid. 45% of full-time freshmen and 38% of continuing full-time students received need-based aid. The average freshman award was $24,736. The average financial indebtedness of the 2003 graduate was $15,163. Columbia is a member of CSS. The CSS Profile or FAFSA, the college's own financial statement, federal tax returns, the business/farm supplement, and/or the divorced/separated parents statement, if applicable, are required. The deadline for filing freshman financial aid applications for fall entry is February 10.

International Students: There are 234 international students enrolled. The school actively recruits these students. They must score 600 on the written TOEFL or 250 on the electronic version and also take the SAT I or the ACT. Students must take 3 SAT II: Subject tests, 1 of them in writing.

Computers: The mainframes are comprised of 3 Sun 4/280s, a DEC VAX 8700, and an IBM 4341. There are computer labs and stand-alone terminals throughout the campus and computer clusters in residence halls. Every dorm room has an Ethernet connection. All students may access the system 24 hours a day, 7 days a week. There are no time limits.

Graduates: From July 1, 2002 to June 30, 2003, 994 bachelor's degrees were awarded. The most popular majors were economics (14%), political science (12%), and history (11%). 370 companies recruited on campus in 2002-2003.

Admissions Contact: Admissions Officer, Office of Undergraduate Admissions. A video is available.
Web: *http://www.studentaffairs.columbia.edu/admissions*

COLUMBIA UNIVERSITY/FU FOUNDATION SCHOOL OF ENGINEERING AND APPLIED SCIENCE   D-5

New York, NY 10027   (212) 854-2521; Fax: (212) 854-1209

Full-time: 1007 men, 353 women	**Faculty:** 130; I, ++$
Part-time: none	**Ph.D.s:** 100%
Graduate: none	**Student/Faculty:** 10 to 1
Year: semesters, summer session	**Tuition:** $29,788
Application Deadline: January 2	**Room & Board:** $8802
Freshman Class: 2219 applied, 649 accepted, 314 enrolled	
SAT I Verbal/Math: 700/760	**ACT:** 34 **MOST COMPETITIVE**

The Fu Foundation School of Engineering and Applied Science of Columbia University, founded in 1754, offers undergraduate and graduate degree programs in engineering and applied science. In addition to regional accreditation, Columbia Engineering has baccalaureate program accreditation with ABET. The 20 libraries contain 7.2 million volumes and 48,000 microform items. Computerized library services include the card catalog, interlibrary loans, and database searching. Special learning facilities include an art gallery, radio station, TV station, and an observatory. The 36-acre campus is in an urban area in New York City. Including any residence halls, there are 50 buildings.

Student Life: 70% of undergraduates are from out of state, mostly the Middle Atlantic. Students are from 41 states, 60 foreign countries, and Canada. 66% are from public schools. 41% are Asian American; 35% white; 11% foreign nationals. The average age of freshmen is 18; all undergraduates, 20. 3% do not continue beyond their first year; 89% remain to graduate.

Housing: All students can be accommodated in college housing, which includes single-sex and coed dorms, on-campus apartments, fraternity houses, and sorority houses. In addition, there are language houses and special-interest houses. On-campus housing is guaranteed for all 4 years. 95% of students live on campus. All students may keep cars.

Activities: 15% of men belong to 19 national fraternities; 9% of women belong to 9 national sororities. There are 300 groups on campus, including art, band, cheerleading, chess, choir, chorus, computers, dance, debate, drama, ethnic, film, gay, honors, international, jazz band, literary magazine, marching band, musical theater, newspaper, opera, orchestra, pep band, photography, political, professional, radio and TV, religious, social, social service, student government, symphony, and yearbook. Popular campus events include Columbia Fest, Holiday Lighting Ceremony/Yule Log, and Ethnic Festival.

Sports: There are 14 intercollegiate sports for men and 15 for women, and 13 intramural sports for men and 13 for women. Facilities include a football stadium, indoor and outdoor track-and-field facilities, a baseball field, a soccer stadium, recreational gym with swimming pool, basketball/volleyball courts, aerobic exercise, fencing, wrestling, martial arts, and weight rooms, a boat house, and tennis, squash, handball, and racquetball courts.

Disabled Students: All of the campus is accessible. Wheelchair ramps, elevators, special parking, specially equipped rest rooms, special class scheduling, lowered drinking fountains, lowered telephones, special housing, and chair lifts are available.

Services: Counseling and information services are available, as is tutoring in every subject. There is a reader service for the blind.

Campus Safety and Security: Measures include 24-hour foot and vehicle patrol, self-defense education, security escort services, and shuttle buses. There are pamphlets/posters/films, emergency telephones, and lighted pathways/sidewalks.

Programs of Study: Columbia Engineering confers the B.S. degree. Master's and doctoral degrees are also awarded. Bachelor's degrees are

awarded in BUSINESS (operations research), COMPUTER AND PHYSICAL SCIENCE (applied mathematics, applied physics, and computer science), ENGINEERING AND ENVIRONMENTAL DESIGN (biomedical engineering, chemical engineering, civil engineering, computer engineering, electrical/electronics engineering, engineering management, engineering mechanics, geological engineering, industrial engineering technology, materials science, mechanical engineering, metallurgical engineering, and mining and mineral engineering). Computer science, computer engineering, and biomedical engineering are the largest.

Required: All students must complete 128 semester hours, including 38 hours of technical coursework in math, physics, chemistry, and computer science, and 27 hours in nontechnical courses covering the humanities and economics. Courses in logic and rhetoric, economics, and 1 year of phys ed are required. They must take 66 hours in the major and maintain a 2.5 GPA.

Special: Students may study at Columbia College or any of more than 90 other liberal arts colleges throughout the country in a 5-year program leading to the combined B.A.-B.S. degree or a 3-2 engineering degree. There is cross-registration with Barnard College, Teacher's College, and The Juilliard School. The school offers study abroad in more than 100 locations, including Paris, Kyoto, and Oxford and Cambridge Universities in England, internships, work-study, and pass/fail options. There is a chapter of Phi Beta Kappa.

Faculty/Classroom: 92% of faculty are male; 8%, female. All both teach and do research. The average class size in an introductory lecture is 50; in a laboratory, 15; and in a regular course, 25.

Admissions: 29% of the 2003-2004 applicants were accepted. The SAT I scores for the 2003-2004 freshman class were: Verbal--4% between 500 and 599, 39% between 600 and 700, and 57% above 700; Math--7% between 600 and 700, and 93% above 700. The ACT scores were 4% between 24 and 26, 8% between 27 and 28, and 88% above 28. 94% of the current freshmen were in the top fifth of their class; 99% were in the top two fifths.

Requirements: The SAT I or ACT is required, as are 3 SAT II: Subject tests in math, Level I or II, chemistry or physics, and writing. Applicants must be graduates of an accredited secondary school with a recommended 4 years of English, 3 or 4 of history and social studies, 2 or 3 of a foreign language, 1 each of physics and chemistry, and math courses through calculus. Also required are a written evaluation or recommendation from a college adviser or guidance counselor and 2 recommendations from teachers of academic classroom subjects (1 from a teacher of math). An essay is required and an interview is recommended. AP credits are accepted. Important factors in the admissions decision are advanced placement or honor courses, evidence of special talent, and recommendations by alumni.

Procedure: Freshmen are admitted in the fall. All testing must be completed by November of the senior year of high school (October for early decision applicants). There are early decision, early admissions, and deferred admissions plans. Early decision applications should be filed by November 1; regular applications, by January 2 for fall entry, along with a $65 fee. Notification of early decision is sent December 15; regular decision, April 1. 109 early decision candidates were accepted for the 2003-2004 class. 93 applicants were on the 2003 waiting list; all were admitted. Applications are accepted on-line through *www.apply.embark.com/ugrad/columbia.*

Transfer: 15 transfer students enrolled in 2002-2003. Applicants should have completed 1 year each of calculus, physics, and chemistry with lab, in addition to appropriate liberal arts courses. 60 of 128 credits required for the bachelor's degree must be completed at Columbia Engineering.

Visiting: There are regularly scheduled orientations for prospective students, consisting of group information sessions and student-led tours. There are guides for informal visits and visitors may sit in on classes and stay overnight. To schedule a visit, contact the Visitor Center at (212) 854-4900.

Financial Aid: In 2003-2004, 48% of all full-time freshmen and 45% of continuing full-time students received some form of financial aid. 48% of full-time freshmen and 44% of continuing full-time students received need-based aid. The average freshman award was $22,621. The average financial indebtedness of the 2003 graduate was $15,421. Columbia Engineering is a member of CSS. The CSS Profile or FAFSA and the college's own financial statement are required. The deadline for filing freshman financial aid applications for fall entry is February 10.

International Students: There are 163 international students enrolled. The school actively recruits these students. They must score 600 on the written TOEFL or 250 on the electronic version and also take the college's own test. Students must take SAT II: Subject tests in writing, math Level I or II, and physics or chemistry.

Computers: The mainframes are a comprised of a Prime, 13 DEC VAX 11/750s, 3 AT&T 3B20s, 75 AT&T 3B2 supermicros, an HP 9050, a system of HP 9900s, 2 IRIS computers, and an IBM Interactive Graphics Lab. There are PCs available in labs and classrooms. Academic buildings and residence halls are wired to the campus network. There is a high-speed modem pool for off-campus access. Every residence hall room has an Ethernet connection. All students may access the system 24 hours a day, 7 days a week. There are no time limits. The fee is included in the student fee.

Graduates: From July 1, 2002 to June 30, 2003, 304 bachelor's degrees were awarded. The most popular majors were computer science (17%), operations research (14%), and electrical engineering (13%). 370 companies recruited on campus in 2002-2003.

Admissions Contact: Admissions Officer.
Web: *http://www.studentaffairs.columbia.edu/admissions*

COLUMBIA UNIVERSITY/SCHOOL OF GENERAL STUDIES
New York, NY 10027

D-5

(212) 854-2772
(800) 895-1169; Fax: (212) 854-6316

Full-time: 260 men, 290 women	**Faculty:** n/av
Part-time: 250 men, 340 women	**Ph.D.s:** n/av
Graduate: none	**Student/Faculty:** n/av
Year: semesters, summer session	**Tuition:** $27,780
Application Deadline: June 1	**Room & Board:** $10,000
Freshman Class: n/av	
SAT I or ACT: recommended	**COMPETITIVE**

The School of General Studies of Columbia University, founded in 1947, offers liberal arts degree programs and postgraduate studies for adult men and women whose post-high school education has been interrupted or postponed by at least 1 year. Figures in the above capsule and in this profile are approximate. Computerized library services include the card catalog, interlibrary loans, and database searching. Special learning facilities include a learning resource center, art gallery, and radio station. The campus is in an urban area on the upper west side of Manhattan in New York City.

Student Life: 65% of students are white; 10% foreign nationals. The average age of all undergraduates is 28.

Housing: Available housing includes off-campus apartments, married-student housing, and fraternity houses. On-campus housing is available on a first-come, first-served basis. Alcohol is not permitted. No one may keep cars.

Activities: There are many groups and organizations on campus, including band, cheerleading, chess, choir, computers, drama, ethnic, film, gay, international, jazz band, literary magazine, marching band, musical theater, newspaper, orchestra, photography, political, professional, radio and TV, religious, social, social service, student government, symphony, and yearbook.

Sports: Facilities include 2 gyms, a swimming pool, tennis, squash, and racquetball courts, a training center, 2 dance/martial arts studios, a fencing room, a wrestling room, and an indoor track.

Disabled Students: Wheelchair ramps, elevators, specially equipped rest rooms, lowered drinking fountains, and lowered telephones are available.

Services: Counseling and information services are available, as is tutoring in some subjects, including English composition, math, languages, and sciences.

Campus Safety and Security: Measures include 24-hour foot and vehicle patrol, security escort services, pamphlets/posters/films, and emergency telephones. There are lighted pathways/sidewalks.

Programs of Study: GS confers B.A. and B.S. degrees. Master's and doctoral degrees are also awarded. Bachelor's degrees are awarded in BIOLOGICAL SCIENCE (biology/biological science), COMMUNICATIONS AND THE ARTS (art history and appreciation, classics, comparative literature, dance, dramatic arts, English literature, film arts, French, German, Italian, literature, music, Slavic languages, Spanish, and visual and performing arts), COMPUTER AND PHYSICAL SCIENCE (applied mathematics, astronomy, chemistry, computer science, geoscience, mathematics, physics, and statistics), ENGINEERING AND ENVIRONMENTAL DESIGN (architecture and environmental science), SOCIAL SCIENCE (African American studies, anthropology, archeology, classical/ancient civilization, East Asian studies, economics, French studies, German area studies, Hispanic American studies, history, Italian studies, Latin American studies, Middle Eastern studies, philosophy, political science/government, psychology, religion, sociology, urban studies, and women's studies).

Required: All students must complete 124 credit hours, including 56 distribution requirement credits in literature, humanities, foreign language or literature, social science, science, and cultural diversity. Proficiency in English composition and math is required. A GPA of 2.0 is necessary to graduate.

Special: Preprofessional studies in allied health and medical fields and interdisciplinary majors, minors, and concentrations are offered. Internships in New York City, work-study programs on campus, study abroad, a 3-2 engineering degree at Columbia University School of Engineering and Applied Science, B.A.-B.S. degrees, and dual majors are available. There is a chapter of Phi Beta Kappa.

Requirements: The SAT I or ACT is recommended. SAT I, ACT, or Columbia's General Studies Admissions Exam scores should be submit-

ted along with high school and all college transcripts. An autobiographical statement is required. An interview is encouraged. A GPA of 2.5 is required. AP credits are accepted. Important factors in the admissions decision are advanced placement or honor courses, personality/intangible qualities, and evidence of special talent.

Procedure: Freshmen are admitted to all sessions. Entrance exams should be taken as early as possible. Applications should be filed by June 1 for fall entry, October 15 for spring, and April 1 for summer. The application fee is $65. Notification is sent on a rolling basis. Applications are accepted on-line at the school's web site.

Transfer: 64 of 124 credits required for the bachelor's degree must be completed at GS.

Visiting: There are regularly scheduled orientations for prospective students, consisting of an admissions information session every other Wednesday, preceded by a campus tour. For information, call (212) 854-5109. There are guides for informal visits.

Financial Aid: GS is a member of CSS. The FAFSA and the college's own financial statement are required. Check with the school for current deadlines.

International Students: The school actively recruits these students. They must score 600 on the written TOEFL and also take the college's own test. Submission of recent SAT I scores is encouraged.

Computers: The mainframe is an IBM. Computer accounts allow access to the Internet, e-mail, commercial news wires, labs, and on-line services. All students may access the system. There are no fees. It is strongly recommended that all students have a personal computer.

Admissions Contact: Director of Admissions.
E-mail: *gs-admit@columbia.edu* Web: *www.gs.columbia.edu*

CONCORDIA COLLEGE
Bronxville, NY 10708

D-5

(914) 337-9300
(800) 937-2655; Fax: (914) 395-4636

Full-time: 225 men, 320 women	**Faculty:** 35
Part-time: 40 men, 85 women	**Ph.D.s:** 79%
Graduate: none	**Student/Faculty:** 14 to 1
Year: semesters	**Tuition:** $13,350 ($16,700)
Application Deadline: see profile	**Room & Board:** $5850 ($7500)
Freshman Class: 502 applied, 361 accepted, 132 enrolled	
SAT I Verbal/Math: required	**ACT:** required
	VERY COMPETITIVE

Concordia College, founded in 1881, is a Christian liberal arts college offering undergraduate majors, including business, education, music, social work, and professional training in ministry. Figures in the above capsule and in this profile are approximate. In addition to regional accreditation, Concordia has baccalaureate program accreditation with CSWE. The library contains 85,000 volumes and 25,000 microform items, and subscribes to 450 periodicals. Computerized library services include the card catalog, interlibrary loans, and database searching. Special learning facilities include a learning resource center, art gallery, education center, family center, and Lutheran education service. The 33-acre campus is in a suburban area 15 miles north of New York City. Including any residence halls, there are 21 buildings.

Student Life: 69% of undergraduates are from New York. Students are from 21 states, 31 foreign countries, and Canada. 64% are white; 16% African American; 12% Hispanic. 40% are Protestant; 38% Catholic; 18% Unknown. The average age of freshmen is 18; all undergraduates, 22. 26% do not continue beyond their first year; 60% remain to graduate.

Housing: 420 students can be accommodated in college housing, which includes single-sex dorms. In addition, there are special-interest houses. On-campus housing is guaranteed for all 4 years. 66% of students live on campus; of those, 75% remain on campus on weekends. All students may keep cars.

Activities: There are no fraternities or sororities. There are 25 groups on campus, including art, chamber and jazz ensembles, choir, chorus, drama, ethnic, honors, international, jazz band, literary magazine, musical theater, newspaper, orchestra, organists guild, photography, professional, religious, social, social service, student government, symphony, and yearbook. Popular campus events include guest lectures, dramatic presentations, and spring and fall festivals.

Sports: There are 5 intercollegiate sports for men and 5 for women, and 10 intramural sports for men and 10 for women. Facilities include an athletic center, a field house, indoor and outdoor tennis courts, squash and racquetball courts, a weight room, a fitness center, and 3 athletic fields.

Disabled Students: 50% of the campus is accessible. Elevators, special parking, specially equipped rest rooms, lowered drinking fountains, and lowered telephones are available.

Services: Counseling and information services are available, as is tutoring in most subjects, including reading, writing, and math. There is remedial math, reading, and writing.

Campus Safety and Security: Measures include 24-hour foot and vehicle patrol, security escort services, informal discussions, and emergency telephones. There are lighted pathways/sidewalks.

Programs of Study: Concordia confers B.A., B.S., and B.M. degrees. Associate degrees are also awarded. Bachelor's degrees are awarded in BIOLOGICAL SCIENCE (biology/biological science), BUSINESS (business administration and management), COMMUNICATIONS AND THE ARTS (applied music, arts administration/management, English, and music), COMPUTER AND PHYSICAL SCIENCE (mathematics), EDUCATION (business, early childhood, education, elementary, music, and secondary), ENGINEERING AND ENVIRONMENTAL DESIGN (environmental science), HEALTH PROFESSIONS (physical therapy), SOCIAL SCIENCE (behavioral science, history, interdisciplinary studies, international studies, ministries, religion, religious music, and social work). Education, music, and behavioral science are the strongest academically. Education, business administration, and music are the largest.

Required: To graduate, students must complete 122 semester hours with a minimum GPA of 2.0. General education requirements include 39 semester hours of liberal arts, 18 of foundation courses in basic skills and values, 12 of integrated studies, and 9 of religion. Students are required to take 3 credits each of phys ed and computers. A thesis is required in some majors.

Special: A registered professional nurse program is offered in cooperation with Mount Vernon Hospital School of Nursing. Concordia also offers co-op programs in social work and education, a dual degree program in physical therapy, cross-registration with a consortium of nearby colleges, internships, study abroad in England, B.A.-B.S. degrees, an interdisciplinary studies degree including a major in educational services, and credit for life experience. Accelerated degree programs are available in business administration and behavioral studies. There is 1 national honor society, a freshman honors program, and 10 departmental honors programs.

Faculty/Classroom: 69% of faculty are male; 31%, female. All teach undergraduates. The average class size in an introductory lecture is 19; in a laboratory, 12; and in a regular course, 12.

Requirements: The SAT I or ACT is required. In addition, applicants should be graduates of an accredited secondary school or have a GED certificate. Concordia prefers completion of 16 academic units, including 4 of English, 2 each of math, history or social studies, science (at least 1 with lab), and a foreign language. An interview is recommended, and those students applying to the music program must audition. A GPA of 2.5 is required. AP and CLEP credits are accepted. Important factors in the admissions decision are advanced placement or honor courses, evidence of special talent, and extracurricular activities record.

Procedure: Freshmen are admitted fall and spring. Entrance exams should be taken in the fall of the senior year. There are early decision, early admissions, deferred admissions, and rolling admissions plans. Check with the school for current deadlines. Application fee is $30. Applications are available on disk through College Link and on-line at *concordiany.edu*.

Transfer: 44 transfer students enrolled in a recent year. A 2.0 GPA is recommended. Applicants must submit official transcripts from previous colleges attended. Students must complete the last 30 credits at Concordia College. 30 of 122 credits required for the bachelor's degree must be completed at Concordia.

Visiting: There are regularly scheduled orientations for prospective students. There are guides for informal visits and visitors may sit in on classes and stay overnight. To schedule a visit, contact the Admissions Office.

Financial Aid: In a recent year, 94% of all full-time freshmen and 95% of continuing full-time students received some form of financial aid. 79% of full-time freshmen and 71% of continuing full-time students received need-based aid. The average freshman award was $11,500. 36% of undergraduates work part time. Average annual earnings from campus work are $1275. The average financial indebtedness of a recent graduate was $12,530. The FAFSA is required. Check with the school for current deadlines.

International Students: The school actively recruits these students. They must score 550 on the written TOEFL or 213 on the electronic version or take the SAT I.

Computers: The mainframe is a Condurrent CPU 3212. There are 2 labs with 50 PCs available to students. All students may access the system any time. There are no time limits and no fees.

Admissions Contact: Becky Hendricks, Director of Admission. A video is available. E-mail: *ec@concordia-ny.edu* Web: *concordia-ny.edu*

COOPER UNION FOR THE ADVANCEMENT OF SCIENCE AND ART

D-5

New York, NY 10003-7120   (212) 353-4120; Fax: (212) 353-4342

Full-time: 583 men, 314 women	**Faculty:** 53; II B, ++$
Part-time: 4 men, 2 women	**Ph.D.s:** 82%
Graduate: 32 men, 6 women	**Student/Faculty:** 17 to 1
Year: semesters, summer session	**Tuition:** $1400
Application Deadline: January 1	**Room & Board:** $9000
Freshman Class: 2414 applied, 295 accepted, 208 enrolled	
SAT I Verbal/Math: 680/720	**MOST COMPETITIVE**

The Cooper Union for the Advancement of Science and Art, founded in 1859, is a privately endowed institution. Students who are U.S. residents are admitted under full scholarship, which covers the tuition of $26,000. There is an additional fee of $1400. Cooper Union offers undergraduate degrees in architecture, art, and engineering, and graduate degrees in engineering. There are 3 undergraduate schools and 1 graduate school. In addition to regional accreditation, Cooper Union has baccalaureate program accreditation with ABET, NAAB, and NASAD. The library contains 100,000 volumes, 50,000 microform items, and 300 audio/video tapes/CDs, and subscribes to 350 periodicals. Computerized library services include the card catalog, interlibrary loans, database searching, and Internet access. Special learning facilities include a learning resource center, art gallery, a center for speaking and writing, an electronic resources center, and a visual resources center. The campus is in an urban area located in the heart of lower Manhattan. Including any residence halls, there are 5 buildings.

Student Life: 59% of undergraduates are from New York. Students are from 41 states, 10 foreign countries, and Canada. 75% are from public schools. 54% are white; 25% Asian American. The average age of freshmen is 18; all undergraduates, 20. 6% do not continue beyond their first year; 78% remain to graduate.

Housing: 183 students can be accommodated in college housing, which includes coed on-campus apartments. 78% of students commute. All students may keep cars.

Activities: 20% of men belong to 2 national fraternities; 10% of women belong to 1 local sorority. There are 60 groups on campus, including chorale, computers, drama, environmental, ethnic, film, gay, honors, international, newspaper, political, professional, religious, social, social service, student government, and yearbook. Popular campus events include an end-of-the-year student art and architecture exhibit and ongoing events in the great hall.

Sports: There are 5 intercollegiate sports for men and 2 for women, and 12 intramural sports for men and 12 for women. Facilities include weight, martial arts, and fencing rooms and a nearby swimming pool and basketball courts.

Disabled Students: 60% of the campus is accessible. Wheelchair ramps, elevators, and specially equipped rest rooms are available.

Services: Counseling and information services are available, as is tutoring in some subjects, including math, physics, speech, and writing.

Campus Safety and Security: Measures include pamphlets/posters/films, emergency telephones, lighted pathways/sidewalks, and community security and police.

Programs of Study: Cooper Union confers B.S., B.Arch., B.E., and B.F.A. degrees. Master's degrees are also awarded. Bachelor's degrees are awarded in COMMUNICATIONS AND THE ARTS (fine arts and graphic design), ENGINEERING AND ENVIRONMENTAL DESIGN (architecture, chemical engineering, civil engineering, electrical/electronics engineering, engineering, and mechanical engineering). Engineering is the strongest academically and the largest.

Required: The 5-year architecture program requires 160 credits, including 30 in liberal arts and electives, for graduation. Art students must complete 128 credits, including 38 in liberal arts and electives, with a minimum overall GPA of 2.0 to graduate. A 2.5 GPA is expected in studio work. Engineering students are required to complete a minimum of 135 credits, including a computer literacy course and 24 credits in humanities and social sciences, with a minimum GPA of 2.0.

Special: Cross-registration with New School University, internships, study abroad for art students in 8 countries, and for engineering students in 6 countries, and some pass/fail options are available. Nondegree study is possible. An accelerated degree in engineering is also available. There are 4 national honor societies and 1 departmental honors program.

Faculty/Classroom: 74% of faculty are male; 26%, female. All both teach and do research. No introductory courses are taught by graduate students. The average class size in an introductory lecture is 28; in a laboratory, 20; and in a regular course, 20.

Admissions: 12% of the 2003-2004 applicants were accepted. The SAT I scores for the 2003-2004 freshman class were: Verbal--1% below 500, 14% between 500 and 599, 55% between 600 and 700, and 29% above 700; Math--2% below 500, 12% between 500 and 599, 32% between 600 and 700, and 53% above 700. 75% of the current freshmen were in the top fifth of their class; all were in the top two fifths.

Requirements: The SAT I is required. In addition, engineering applicants must take SAT II: Subject tests in mathematics I or II and physics or chemistry. Graduation from an approved secondary school is required. Applicants should have completed 16 to 18 high school academic credits, depending on their major. An essay is part of the application process. Art students must submit a portfolio. Art and architecture applicants must complete a project called the hometest. AP credits are accepted. Important factors in the admissions decision are evidence of special talent, advanced placement or honor courses, and personality/intangible qualities.

Procedure: Freshmen are admitted in the fall. Entrance exams should be taken before February 1. There are early decision, early admissions, and deferred admissions plans. Early decision applications should be filed by December 1; regular applications, by January 1 for fall entry, along with a $50 fee. Notification of early decision is sent February 1; regular decision, April 1. 60 early decision candidates were accepted for the 2003-2004 class. 33 applicants were on the 2003 waiting list; 12 were admitted. Applications are accepted on-line through the college's web site.

Transfer: 35 transfer students enrolled in 2002-2003. Art and architecture transfer applicants must present a portfolio and a minimum of 24 credits in studio classes. Engineering transfer applicants must submit a transcript with grades of B or better in at least 24 credits of appropriate courses.

Visiting: There are regularly scheduled orientations for prospective students, consisting of open house and portfolio review days for art and open house for engineering; architecture tours are by appointment. Visitors may sit in on classes by appointment. To schedule a visit, contact the Office of Admissions and Records.

Financial Aid: In 2003-2004, all full-time students received some form of financial aid. 33% of full-time freshmen and 31% of continuing full-time students received need-based aid. The average freshman award was $3600. Need-based scholarships or need-based grants averaged $2750 ($5000 maximum); need-based self-help aid (loans and jobs) averaged $2875 ($4425 maximum); and non-need-based awards and non-need-based scholarships averaged $26,000 (maximum). 40% of undergraduates work part time. Average annual earnings from campus work are $1200. The average financial indebtedness of the 2003 graduate was $11,030. Cooper Union is a member of CSS. The FAFSA is required. The deadline for filing freshman financial aid applications for fall entry is April 15.

International Students: There are 70 international students enrolled. They must score 600 on the written TOEFL. All freshman applicants must take the SAT I; art and architecture students must also take the hometest. Engineering students must take SAT II: subject tests in math and physics or chemistry.

Computers: The mainframe is a DEC VAX 11/780. The computer center, located in the Engineering Building, contains more than 100 workstations and PCs, all available for student use. All students have access to e-mail and the Internet. All students may access the system whenever the Engineering Building is open. There are no time limits and no fees.

Graduates: From July 1, 2002 to June 30, 2003, 183 bachelor's degrees were awarded. The most popular majors were fine arts (34%), electrical engineering (18%), and architecture (15%). In an average class, 70% graduate in 4 years or less, and 80% graduate in 5 years or less. 80 companies recruited on campus in 2002-2003. Of the 2002 graduating class, 54% were enrolled in graduate school within 6 months of graduation and 42% were employed.

Admissions Contact: Admissions Representative.
E-mail: *admissions@cooper.edu* Web: *www.cooper.edu*

CORNELL UNIVERSITY
Ithaca, NY 14850

C-3
(607) 255-5241

Full-time: 6895 men, 6760 women	**Faculty:** 1643; I, +$
Part-time: none	**Ph.D.s:** 97%
Graduate: 3467 men, 2498 women	**Student/Faculty:** 8 to 1
Year: semesters, summer session	**Tuition:** $28,724
Application Deadline: January 1	**Room & Board:** $9529
Freshman Class: 20,441 applied, 6334 accepted, 3135 enrolled	
SAT I Verbal/Math: 670/710	**ACT:** 30 **MOST COMPETITIVE**

Cornell University was founded in 1865 as a land-grant institution. Privately supported undergraduate divisions include the College of Architecture, Art, and Planning; the College of Arts and Sciences; the College of Engineering; and the School of Hotel Administration. State-assisted undergraduate divisions include the College of Agriculture and Life Sciences, the College of Human Ecology, and the School of Industrial and Labor Relations. There are 7 undergraduate and 4 graduate schools. In addition to regional accreditation, Cornell has baccalaureate program accreditation with AACSB, ABET, ASLA, CSWE, and FIDER. The 17 libraries contain 7,298,409 volumes, 7,992,461 microform items, and 427,798 audio/video tapes/CDs, and subscribe to 64,760 periodicals. Computerized library services include the card catalog, interlibrary loans, database searching, and Internet access. Special learning facilities include a learning resource center, art gallery, planetarium, radio station, a bird sanctuary, 4 designated national resource centers, and 2 local optical observatories. The 745-acre campus is in a rural area 60 miles south of Syracuse. Including any residence halls, there are 770 buildings.

Student Life: 62% of undergraduates are from out of state, mostly the Middle Atlantic. Students are from 50 states, 107 foreign countries, and Canada. 60% are white; 16% Asian American. The average age of freshmen is 18; all undergraduates, 20. 4% do not continue beyond their first year; 92% remain to graduate.

Housing: 7912 students can be accommodated in college housing, which includes single-sex and coed dorms, on-campus apartments, married-student housing, fraternity houses, and sorority houses. In addition, there are language houses and special-interest houses. On-campus housing is guaranteed for the freshman year only and is available on a lottery system for upperclassmen. 58% of students live on campus; of those, 90% remain on campus on weekends. All students may keep cars.

Activities: 27% of men belong to 3 local and 39 national fraternities; 24% of women belong to 5 local and 18 national sororities. There are 754 groups on campus, including art, band, cheerleading, choir, chorale, chorus, computers, dance, debate, drama, drill team, drum and bugle corps, ethnic, film, forensics, gay, honors, international, literary magazine, marching band, musical theater, newspaper, orchestra, pep band, photography, political, professional, radio and TV, religious, social, social service, student government, symphony, and yearbook. Popular campus events include Third World Festival of the Arts, Student Leadership Conference, and Dragon Day.

Sports: There are 18 intercollegiate sports for men and 18 for women, and 27 intramural sports for men and 27 for women. Facilities include indoor and outdoor tracks, a 5000-seat indoor gym, 3 swimming pools, a 25000-seat stadium, 16 intercollegiate fields, a bowling alley, intramural fields, a boat house, and indoor and outdoor tennis courts.

Disabled Students: 90% of the campus is accessible. Wheelchair ramps, elevators, special parking, specially equipped rest rooms, special class scheduling, lowered drinking fountains, lowered telephones, alternative test arrangements, and bus passes or van transportation are available.

Services: Counseling and information services are available, as is tutoring in most subjects. There is a reader service for the blind. Note takers, biology and math student support centers, and writing workshops are also available.

Campus Safety and Security: Measures include 24-hour foot and vehicle patrol, self-defense education, security escort services, and shuttle buses. There are informal discussions, pamphlets/posters/films, emergency telephones, and lighted pathways/sidewalks.

Programs of Study: Cornell confers B.A., B.S., B.Arch., and B.F.A. degrees. Master's and doctoral degrees are also awarded. Bachelor's degrees are awarded in AGRICULTURE (agricultural business management, agricultural economics, agriculture, agronomy, animal science, horticulture, international agriculture, natural resource management, plant science, and soil science), BIOLOGICAL SCIENCE (biology/biological science, biometrics and biostatistics, botany, entomology, evolutionary biology, genetics, and nutrition), BUSINESS (hotel/motel and restaurant management, labor studies, and operations research), COMMUNICATIONS AND THE ARTS (art history and appreciation, classics, communications, comparative literature, dance, design, dramatic arts, English, film arts, fine arts, French, German, Greek, Italian, languages, Latin, linguistics, music, Russian, and Spanish), COMPUTER AND PHYSICAL SCIENCE (astronomy, atmospheric sciences and meteorology, chemistry, computer science, earth science, geology, mathematics, physics, science technology, and statistics), EDUCATION (education), ENGINEERING AND ENVIRONMENTAL DESIGN (aerospace studies, agricultural engineering, architecture, chemical engineering, city/community/regional planning, civil engineering, computer engineering, electrical/electronics engineering, engineering physics, environmental engineering technology, landscape architecture/design, materials science, and mechanical engineering), SOCIAL SCIENCE (African studies, American studies, anthropology, archeology, Asian/Oriental studies, classical/ancient civilization, economics, family/consumer studies, food production/management/services, food science, German area studies, history, human development, Near Eastern studies, philosophy, political science/government, psychology, public affairs, religion, rural sociology, Russian and Slavic studies, sociology, textiles and clothing, urban studies, and women's studies). Hotel administration, industrial and labor relations, and engineering are the largest.

Required: Entering freshmen must meet basic swimming and water safety competency requirements. All undergraduates must take 2 semesters each of freshman writing seminar and phys ed. Graduation requirements vary by program, including a minimum of 120 credits.

Special: Co-op programs are offered in the College of Engineering and the School of Industrial and Labor Relations. Cross-registration is available with Ithaca College. Public-policy internships are available in Washington, D.C., Albany, and New York City. Cornell also offers study abroad in more than 50 countries, B.A.-B.S. and B.A.-B.F.A. degrees, other dual degrees, interdisciplinary/intercollegiate options, student-designed and dual majors, work-study programs, a Washington semester, accelerated degree programs, pass/fail options, and limited nondegree study. A 6-year B.S./M.B.A/M.Eng. program is offered. There are 5 national honor societies, including Phi Beta Kappa, and many departmental honors programs.

Faculty/Classroom: 77% of faculty are male; 23%, female. All both teach and do research. Graduate students teach 1% of introductory courses. The average class size in an introductory lecture is 53; in a laboratory, 17; and in a regular course, 38.

Admissions: 31% of the 2003-2004 applicants were accepted. The SAT I scores for the 2003-2004 freshman class were: Verbal--1% below 500, 13% between 500 and 599, 48% between 600 and 700, and 37% above 700; Math--1% below 500, 7% between 500 and 599, 33% between 600 and 700, and 58% above 700. The ACT scores were 5% between 21 and 23, 16% between 24 and 26, 17% between 27 and 28, and 62% above 28. 97% of the current freshmen were in the top fifth of their class; 100% were in the top two fifths. There were 178 National Merit finalists. 234 freshmen graduated first in their class.

Requirements: The SAT I or ACT is required. In addition, an essay is required as part of the application process. Other requirements vary by division or program, including specific SAT II: Subject tests, and selection of courses within the minimum 16 secondary-school academic units needed. An interview and/or portfolio is required for specific majors. AP credits are accepted. Important factors in the admissions decision are advanced placement or honor courses, evidence of special talent, and leadership record.

Procedure: Freshmen are admitted fall and spring. Entrance exams should be taken by December of the senior year. There are early decision and deferred admissions plans. Early decision applications should be filed by November 10; regular applications, by January 1 for fall entry, and November 10 for spring entry. Notification of early decision is sent mid-December; regular decision, mid-April. 1709 early decision candidates were accepted for the 2003-2004 class. 1983 applicants were on the 2003 waiting list; 4 were admitted. Applications are accepted online through EXPAN and Apply.

Transfer: 674 transfer students enrolled in 2002-2003. All applicants must submit high school and college transcripts, as well as scores from the SAT I or ACT if taken previously. Other admission requirements vary by program, including the number of credits that must be completed at Cornell. 60 to 75 of a minimum of 120 credits required for the bachelor's degree must be completed at Cornell.

Visiting: There are regularly scheduled orientations for prospective students, including campus tours and information sessions. There are guides for informal visits and visitors may sit in on classes and stay overnight. To schedule a visit, contact the Red Carpet Society at (607) 255-3447 or *redcarpet@cornell.edu.*

Financial Aid: In 2003-2004, 52% of all full-time freshmen and 48% of continuing full-time students received some form of financial aid. 52% of full-time freshmen and 45% of continuing full-time students received need-based aid. The average freshman award was $20,307. Need-based scholarships or need-based grants averaged $14,835 ($42,000 maximum); and need-based self-help aid (loans and jobs) averaged $5471 ($22,500 maximum). 45% of undergraduates work part time. The average financial indebtedness of the 2003 graduate was $21,240. The CSS Profile or FAFSA is required. The IRS form is required after enrollment. The deadline for filing freshman financial aid applications for fall entry is February 11.

International Students: There are 988 international students enrolled. The school actively recruits these students. They must score 600 on the written TOEFL and also take the SAT I or the ACT. Some divisions require SAT II: Subject tests.

Computers: The mainframe is an IBM H55 Multiprise. Students have access to 16 campuswide computer centers and more than 30 departmental facilities with more than 1350 PCs, as well as networks in the residence halls. Wireless connections are available in many locations. All networks are connected to the Internet. All students may access the system. There are no time limits and no fees. It is strongly recommended that all students have a personal computer.

Graduates: From July 1, 2002 to June 30, 2003, 3630 bachelor's degrees were awarded. The most popular majors were engineering (17%), social sciences and history (14%), and biological sciences/life sciences (11%). In an average class, 8% graduate in 3 years or less, 85% graduate in 4 years or less, 91% graduate in 5 years or less, and 92% graduate in 6 years or less. 578 companies recruited on campus in 2002-2003. Of the 2002 graduating class, 32% were enrolled in graduate school within 6 months of graduation and 45% were employed.

Admissions Contact: Jason Locke, Director of Undergraduate Admissions. A video is available. E-mail: *admissions@cornell.edu*
Web: *http://admissions.cornell.edu*

DAEMEN COLLEGE
A-3
Amherst, NY 14226-3592
(716) 839-8225
(800) 462-7652; Fax: (716) 839-8370

Full-time: 353 men, 1055 women	**Faculty:** 70; IIB, -$
Part-time: 39 men, 181 women	**Ph.D.s:** 76%
Graduate: 134 men, 317 women	**Student/Faculty:** 20 to 1
Year: semesters, summer session	**Tuition:** $15,120
Application Deadline: open	**Room & Board:** $7000
Freshman Class: n/av	
SAT I Verbal/Math: 500/510	**ACT:** 21 **COMPETITIVE**

Daemen College, founded in 1947, is a private institution offering undergraduate and graduate programs in the liberal and fine arts, business, education, allied health professions, and natural sciences. There is 1 graduate school. In addition to regional accreditation, Daemen has baccalaureate program accreditation with APTA, ARC-PA, CSWE, and NLN. The library contains 140,176 volumes, 23,778 microform items, and 5045 audio/video tapes/CDs, and subscribes to 945 periodicals. Computerized library services include the card catalog, interlibrary loans, database searching, and Internet access. Special learning facilities include a learning resource center, art gallery, and a video conference center. The 35-acre campus is in a suburban area 5 miles northeast of downtown Buffalo. Including any residence halls, there are 18 buildings.

Student Life: 88% of undergraduates are from New York. Students are from 19 states, 15 foreign countries, and Canada. 75% are white; 13% African American. 44% are Catholic; 21% Protestant; 17% unknown; 15% other. The average age of freshmen is 18; all undergraduates, 24. 27% do not continue beyond their first year; 35% remain to graduate.

Housing: 524 students can be accommodated in college housing, which includes coed dorms and on-campus apartments. There is a quiet dorm. On-campus housing is guaranteed for all 4 years. 62% of students commute. All students may keep cars.

Activities: 3% of men belong to 1 local fraternity; 4% of women belong to 4 local sororities. There are 35 groups on campus, including art, cheerleading, chorale, drama, honors, literary magazine, multicultural, musical theater, newspaper, professional, religious, social, social service, student government, and yearbook. Popular campus events include Welcome Back Week, Springfest, and Fallfest.

Sports: There are 4 intercollegiate sports for men and 4 for women, and 5 intramural sports for men and 4 for women. Facilities include a gym, weight and exercise rooms, saunas, and a volleyball sand court.

Disabled Students: 83% of the campus is accessible. Wheelchair ramps, elevators, special parking, specially equipped rest rooms, lowered drinking fountains, and lowered telephones are available.

Services: Counseling and information services are available, as is tutoring in every subject. There is remedial math, reading, and writing.

Campus Safety and Security: Measures include 24-hour foot and vehicle patrol, security escort services, informal discussions, and pamphlets/posters/films. There are emergency telephones, lighted pathways/sidewalks, and video monitors.

Programs of Study: Daemen confers B.A., B.S., and B.F.A. degrees. Master's and doctoral degrees are also awarded. Bachelor's degrees are awarded in BIOLOGICAL SCIENCE (biochemistry and biology/biological science), BUSINESS (accounting and business administration and management), COMMUNICATIONS AND THE ARTS (applied art, art, English, fine arts, French, graphic design, and Spanish), COMPUTER AND PHYSICAL SCIENCE (mathematics and natural sciences), EDUCATION (art, business, elementary, English, foreign languages, health, mathematics, science, social studies, and special), HEALTH PROFESSIONS (health care administration, nursing, physical therapy, and physician's assistant), SOCIAL SCIENCE (history, humanities, political science/government, psychology, religion, and social work). Physical therapy, physician assistant, and natural science are the strongest academically. Physical therapy, nursing, and special education are the largest.

Required: To graduate, students must complete 120 to 199 hours (depending on the degree program) with a minimum GPA of 2.0. Students are required to complete a minimum of 30 credit hours of course work in residence. The final semester's course work must be taken in residence.

Special: Daemen offers cooperative programs in all majors, internships, cross-registration within the Western New York Consortium of Colleges and Universities, student-designed majors, work-study programs, an accelerated degree program in nursing, dual majors, a Washington semester, and study abroad in Spain, France, Italy, Canada, and Mexico. There are 8 national honor societies and a freshman honors program. All departments have honors programs.

Faculty/Classroom: 54% of faculty are male; 46%, female. 88% teach undergraduates. No introductory courses are taught by graduate students. The average class size in an introductory lecture is 18; in a laboratory, 10; and in a regular course, 16.

Admissions: The SAT I scores for the 2003-2004 freshman class were: Verbal--46% below 500, 45% between 500 and 599, and 9% between

600 and 700; Math--46% below 500, 45% between 500 and 599, and 9% between 600 and 700. The ACT scores were 43% below 21, 38% between 21 and 23, 14% between 24 and 26, 4% between 27 and 28, and 1% above 28. 30% of the current freshmen were in the top fifth of their class; 61% were in the top two fifths.

Requirements: The SAT I or ACT is required. In addition, applicants must be graduates of an accredited secondary school or have the GED equivalent. Some departments have further admissions requirements, including a portfolio review for art majors, 3-year sequences of math and science for all natural science programs, and 2 essays, 3 letters of recommendation, and a supplemental application for the physician assistant program. A GPA of 2.0 is required. AP and CLEP credits are accepted. Important factors in the admissions decision are advanced placement or honor courses, leadership record, and evidence of special talent.

Procedure: Freshmen are admitted fall, spring, and summer. Entrance exams should be taken by the summer following the senior year. There are early admissions and deferred admissions plans. Application deadlines are open. The fall 2003 appliction fee was $25. Notification is sent on a rolling basis. Applications are accepted on-line through the college's web site.

Transfer: 146 transfer students enrolled in 2002-2003. Applicants must present college transcripts and an indication of good standing from the last institution attended and a minimum GPA of 2.0. to 2.8. Physician assistant applicants should submit essays, 3 letters of recommendation, and supplemental applications. 30 of 120 credits required for the bachelor's degree must be completed at Daemen.

Visiting: There are regularly scheduled orientations for prospective students, consisting of a 5-day orientation that includes a campus tour, an interview, and placement testing in math and English during July and August. There are guides for informal visits and visitors may sit in on classes and stay overnight. To schedule a visit, contact the Admissions Office at *admissions@daemen.edu*.

Financial Aid: In a recent year 47% of all full-time freshmen and 72% of continuing full-time students received some form of financial aid. 45% of full-time freshmen and 65% of continuing full-time students received need-based aid. The average freshman award for 2002-2004 was $13,903. Need-based scholarships or need-based grants averaged $7234; need-based self-help aid (loans and jobs) averaged $4227; non-need-based athletic scholarships averaged $5140; and other non-need-based awards and non-need-based scholarships averaged $5823. 21% of undergraduates work part time. Average annual earnings from campus work are $704. The average financial indebtedness of the 2003 graduate was $11,250. The FAFSA, the state aid form, and foreign student certification of finances are required. The priority date for freshman financial aid applications for fall entry is March 15. The deadline for filing freshman financial aid applications for fall entry is rolling.

International Students: There are 271 international students enrolled. The school actively recruits these students. They must score 500 on the written TOEFL or 173 on the electronic version.

Computers: 128 PCs are available on campus in the academic resource center, the library, and departmental computer labs. Internet access is available at all terminals. All students may access the system. There are no time limits and no fees.

Graduates: From July 1, 2002 to June 30, 2003, 316 bachelor's degrees were awarded. The most popular majors were nursing (18%), special education (13%), and natural science (11%). In an average class, 20% graduate in 4 years or less, 33% graduate in 5 years or less, and 36% graduate in 6 years or less. 80 companies recruited on campus in 2002-2003. Of the 2002 graduating class, 19% were enrolled in graduate school within 6 months of graduation and 90% were employed.

Admissions Contact: Patricia Brown, Dean of Enrollment Management. A video is available. E-mail: *admissions@daeman.edu* Web: *http://www.daemen.edu*

DEVRY INSTITUTE OF TECHNOLOGY/NEW YORK   D-5
Long Island City, NY 11101-3051   (718) 472-2728
                                    (888) 713-3879; Fax: (718) 361-0004

Full-time: 998 men, 304 women	**Faculty:** n/av
Part-time: 398 men, 139 women	**Ph.Ds:** n/av
Graduate: n/av	**Student/Faculty:** n/av
Year: semesters, summer session	**Tuition:** $11,860
Application Deadline: open	**Room & Board:** n/app
Freshman Class: n/av	
SAT I or ACT: n/av	**LESS COMPETITIVE**

DeVry Institute of Technology/New York, founded in 1998, is a private institution offering hands-on programs in electronics, business administration, computer information systems, telecommunications, and computer technology. The school is 1 of 67 Devry University locations throughout the United States and Canada. The library contains 9752 volumes and 708 audio/video tapes/CDs, and subscribes to 120 periodicals. Computerized library services include the card catalog, interlibrary loans, and database searching. Special learning facilities include a learning resource center and electronics and other labs. The 2-acre campus is in an urban area. There is one building.

Student Life: 40% of students are African American; 23% Hispanic; 10% white. The average age of all undergraduates is 24.

Housing: There are no residence halls. There are private apartments, student-plan housing, and private rooms. All students commute. Alcohol is not permitted. All students may keep cars.

Activities: There are no fraternities or sororities. There are 7 groups on campus, including chess, international, professional, social, and yearbook. Popular campus events include DSA Time Out, End of Semester Bashment, and Post Ramadan Celebration.

Sports: There is no sports program at DeVry.

Disabled Students: All of the campus is accessible. Elevators, special parking, specially equipped rest rooms, special class scheduling, lowered drinking fountains, and lowered telephones are available.

Services: Counseling and information services are available, as is tutoring in every subject.

Campus Safety and Security: Measures include 24-hour foot and vehicle patrol, security escort services, informal discussions, and pamphlets/posters/films. There are emergency telephones and lighted pathways/sidewalks.

Programs of Study: DeVry confers the B.S. degree. Associate and master's degrees are also awarded. Bachelor's degrees are awarded in BUSINESS (business administration and management), COMMUNICATIONS AND THE ARTS (telecommunications), COMPUTER AND PHYSICAL SCIENCE (information sciences and systems), ENGINEERING AND ENVIRONMENTAL DESIGN (computer technology and electrical/electronics engineering technology). Electronics, computer information systems, and business administration are the largest.

Required: To graduate, students must complete 48 to 154 credit hours with a 2.0 minimum GPA. Course requirements vary according to program. All first-semester students take courses in algebra, psychology, and student success strategies.

Special: Evening and weekend classes, co-op programs, distance learning, and an acclerated degree program are offered.

Faculty/Classroom: All teach undergraduates.

Requirements: Admissions requirements include graduation from a secondary school; the GED is also accepted. Applicants must pass the DeVry entrance exam or present satisfactory ACT or SAT I scores. An interview is required. CLEP credit is accepted.

Procedure: Freshmen are admitted fall, spring, and summer. There is a rolling admissions plan. There are early admissions and deferred admissions plans. Application deadlines are open. Application fee is $50. Applications are accepted on-line through *https://apply.embark.com/UGrad/DeVry/21*.

Transfer: 22 transfer students enrolled in a recent year. Applicants must present passing grades in all completed college course work, demonstrate language skills proficiency with at least 24 completed semester hours, and present evidence of math proficiency by appropriate college-level credits. A minimum GPA of 2.0 is required. 25% of 48 to 154 credits required for the bachelor's degree must be completed at DeVry.

Visiting: There are regularly scheduled orientations for prospective students. There are guides for informal visits and visitors may sit in on classes. To schedule a visit, contact the Director of Admissions.

Financial Aid: In 2002-2003, 66% of all full-time freshmen and 76% of continuing full-time students received some form of financial aid. At least 64% of full-time freshmen and at least 74% of continuing full-time students received need-based aid. The average freshman award was $8821. Need-based scholarships or need-based grants averaged $6115; need-based self-help aid (loans and jobs) averaged $3326; and institutional non-need-based awards and non-need-based scholarships averaged $6490. The FAFSA is required. The deadline for filing freshman financial aid applications is rolling.

International Students: There were 101 international students enrolled in a recent year. They must score 500 on the written TOEFL or 173 on the electronic version and also take the college's own entrance exam.

Computers: Lab facilities include PCs in stand-alone and network configurations, with access to the mainframe. LANs provide access to a wide range of applications software. Hard copy from the mainframe is provided through a local minicomputer and medium- and high-speed printers. Computer information systems students may access the system during lab hours. There are no fees.

Graduates: From July 1, 2002 to June 30, 2003, 204 bachelor's degrees were awarded. The most popular majors were computer information systems (57%), business (25%), and electronics engineering technology (17%). 21 companies recruited on campus in a recent year.

Admissions Contact: Director of Admissions.
E-mail: *nyemailleads@ny.devry.edu* Web: *www.ny.devry.edu*

DOMINICAN COLLEGE
Orangeburg, NY 10962   **D-5**

(845) 359-7800, ext. 208
(866) 432-4636; Fax: (845) 365-3150

Full-time: 337 men, 588 women	**Faculty:** 58; IIB, -$
Part-time: 146 men, 485 women	**Ph.D.s:** 58%
Graduate: 21 men, 81 women	**Student/Faculty:** 16 to 1
Year: semesters, summer session	**Tuition:** $16,650
Application Deadline: open	**Room & Board:** $8160
Freshman Class: 847 applied, 743 accepted, 232 enrolled	
SAT I: required	**LESS COMPETITIVE**

Dominican College, founded in 1952, is a private Catholic institution offering undergraduate programs in business, biology, education, liberal arts, nursing, premedicine, occupational therapy, and social sciences. There is 1 undergraduate and 4 graduate schools. In addition to regional accreditation, Dominican has baccalaureate program accreditation with CCNE, CSWE, and NLN. The library contains 103,000 volumes, 15,000 microform items, and 1000 audio/video tapes/CDs, and subscribes to 650 periodicals. Computerized library services include interlibrary loans, database searching, and Internet access. Special learning facilities include a learning resource center. The 24-acre campus is in a suburban area 17 miles north of New York City. Including any residence halls, there are 10 buildings.

Student Life: 79% of undergraduates are from New York. Students are from 14 states and 2 foreign countries. 70% are from public schools. 61% are white; 15% Hispanic; 14% African American. The average age of freshmen is 18; all undergraduates, 23. 34% do not continue beyond their first year; 39% remain to graduate.

Housing: 351 students can be accommodated in college housing, which includes coed dorms. On-campus housing is guaranteed for all 4 years. 62% of students commute. Alcohol is not permitted. All students may keep cars.

Activities: There are no fraternities or sororities. There are 17 groups on campus, including chorus, computers, drama, honors, international, literary magazine, musical theater, newspaper, professional, religious, social service, student government, and yearbook. Popular campus events include Family Day, Springfest, and Fall Festival.

Sports: There are 6 intercollegiate sports for men and 7 for women, and 3 intramural sports for men and 3 for women. Facilities include soccer and lacrosse field, softball field, gym, track and fitness center.

Disabled Students: All of the campus is accessible. Wheelchair ramps, special parking, specially equipped rest rooms, lowered drinking fountains, and lowered telephones are available.

Services: Counseling and information services are available, as is tutoring in some subjects, including English and math. There is remedial math, reading, and writing. Proofreading and editing services are available for all students in all subjects.

Campus Safety and Security: Measures include 24-hour foot and vehicle patrol, security escort services, shuttle buses, and informal discussions. There are pamphlets/posters/films and lighted pathways/sidewalks.

Programs of Study: Dominican confers B.A., B.S., B.S.Ed., and B.S.N. degrees. Associate and master's degrees are also awarded. Bachelor's degrees are awarded in BIOLOGICAL SCIENCE (biology/biological science), BUSINESS (accounting, banking and finance, business administration and management, business economics, human resources, international business management, and marketing/retailing/merchandising), COMMUNICATIONS AND THE ARTS (English and Spanish), COMPUTER AND PHYSICAL SCIENCE (computer science, information sciences and systems, and mathematics), EDUCATION (athletic training, education of the visually handicapped, elementary, mathematics, science, secondary, and special), HEALTH PROFESSIONS (health care administration, nursing, and occupational therapy), SOCIAL SCIENCE (American studies, history, humanities, psychology, social science, and social work). Occupational therapy and nursing are the strongest academically. Business, nursing, and occupational therapy are the largest.

Required: All students must complete courses in English and speech. Computer courses are required for business majors. In order to graduate, all students must complete 120 semester hours, including a general education curriculum of 36 to 39 credits. A minimum GPA of 2.7 must be maintained by nursing majors; 3.0 for occupational therapy majors. All other majors require a minimum of 2.0.

Special: Accelerated degree programs are available in business majors, as well as co-op programs in business administration, arts and sciences, nursing, social sciences, education, and social work. Individualized internships, work-study programs, B.A.-B.S. degrees, and a 3-2 engineering degree with Manhattan College are also offered. Dual teacher certification in elementary and special education is available. Credit for life experience is granted through submission of a portfolio. Weekend College, offered on a trimester basis, is designed to meet the needs of working adults. There are 5 national honor societies and a freshman honors program.

Faculty/Classroom: 40% of faculty are male; 60%, female. 90% teach undergraduates. No introductory courses are taught by graduate students. The average class size in a regular course is 20.

Admissions: 88% of the 2003-2004 applicants were accepted.

Requirements: The SAT I is required. In addition, applicants should be graduates of an accredited secondary school or possess a GED equivalent. An interview and an essay are required for some professional programs. AP and CLEP credits are accepted. Important factors in the admissions decision are advanced placement or honor courses, leadership record, and extracurricular activities record.

Procedure: Freshmen are admitted to all sessions. Entrance exams should be taken by November of the senior year. There are early decision, early admissions, deferred admissions, and rolling admissions plans. Application deadlines are open. Application fee is $35. Regular decision notification is sent on a rolling basis. Applications are accepted on computer disk and on-line through CollegeLink and Princeton Review.

Transfer: 89 transfer students enrolled in 2002-2003. Applicants must submit a transcript from their previous school. A minimum GPA of 2.0 is required. An interview should be scheduled. Departmental approval is required for acceptance into all major areas of study. 30 of 120 credits required for the bachelor's degree must be completed at Dominican.

Visiting: There are regularly scheduled orientations for prospective students. There are guides for informal visits and visitors may sit in on classes. To schedule a visit, contact Joyce Elbe, Director of Admissions at (866) 432-4636 or joyce.elbe@dc.edu.

Financial Aid: In 2003-2004, 97% of all full-time freshmen and 84% of continuing full-time students received some form of financial aid. 86% of full-time freshmen and 75% of continuing full-time students received need-based aid. The average freshman award was $10,215. Need-based scholarships or need-based grants averaged $10,199 ($15,000 maximum); need-based self-help aid (loans and jobs) averaged $3652 ($4625 maximum); non-need-based athletic scholarships averaged $3178 ($10,000 maximum); and other non-need-based awards and non-need-based scholarships averaged $4695 ($24,000 maximum). 85% of undergraduates work part time. Average annual earnings from campus work are $1500. The average financial indebtedness of the 2003 graduate was $22,318. Dominican is a member of CSS. The FAFSA and the state aid form are required. The priority date for freshman financial aid applications for fall entry is February 15. The deadline for filing freshman financial aid applications for fall entry is June 15.

International Students: The school actively recruits these students. They must score 550 on the written TOEFL or 213 on the electronic version and also take the SAT I or the ACT.

Computers: There are 4 PC labs on campus with more than 75 PCs. One lab is located in the residence hall. All have Internet access. All students may access the system. There are no time limits and no fees.

Graduates: From July 1, 2002 to June 30, 2003, 215 bachelor's degrees were awarded. The most popular majors were business administration (33%), nursing (22%), and occupational therapy (15%). In an average class, 37% graduate in 4 years or less, 42% graduate in 5 years or less, and 47% graduate in 6 years or less. 30 companies recruited on campus in 2002-2003.

Admissions Contact: Joyce Elbe, Director of Admissions. A video is available. E-mail: admissions@dc.edu Web: www.dc.edu

DOWLING COLLEGE
Oakdale, NY 11769-1999   **E-5**

(631) 244-3436
(800) DOWLING; Fax: (631) 563-3827

Full-time: 869 men, 1254 women	**Faculty:** 87
Part-time: 321 men, 622 women	**Ph.D.s:** 92%
Graduate: 1062 men, 1989 women	**Student/Faculty:** 24 to 1
Year: 4-1-4, summer session	**Tuition:** $15,330
Application Deadline: open	**Room & Board:** $8540
Freshman Class: 1970 applied, 1892 accepted, 504 enrolled	
SAT I Verbal/Math: 460/470	**LESS COMPETITIVE**

Dowling College, founded in 1955, is a small, private institution offering programs in the arts and sciences, aviation and transportation, business, and education. There are 4 undergraduate and 3 graduate schools. The library contains 215,000 volumes, 394,000 microform items, and 2626 audio/video tapes/CDs, and subscribes to 961 periodicals. Computerized library services include the card catalog, interlibrary loans, and database searching. Special learning facilities include a learning resource center, art gallery, radio station, government documents, and the Federal Aviation Administration (FAA) Aviation Education Resource Center. The 156-acre campus is in a suburban area 50 miles east of New York City. Including any residence halls, there are 10 buildings.

Student Life: 95% of undergraduates are from New York. Students are from 26 states, 45 foreign countries, and Canada. 89% are from public schools. 65% are white. The average age of freshmen is 19; all undergraduates, 27. 30% do not continue beyond their first year; 37% remain to graduate.

Housing: 481 students can be accommodated in college housing, which includes coed on-campus apartments. On-campus housing is available on a first-come, first-served basis. Priority is given to out-of-town students. 85% of students commute. Alcohol is not permitted. All students may keep cars.

Activities: There are no fraternities or sororities. There are 39 groups on campus, including aeronautics, art, cheerleading, choir, chorus, computers, drama, ethnic, gay, gospel choir, honors, international, literary magazine, martial arts, newspaper, orchestra, photography, professional, psychology, radio and TV, religious, social, student government, and yearbook. Popular campus events include Freshman Mixer, Holiday Party, and Spring Cotillion.

Sports: There are 7 intercollegiate sports for men and 6 for women, and 3 intramural sports for men and 3 for women. Facilities include a basketball court, a weight room, tennis courts, and a fitness center.

Disabled Students: All of the campus is accessible. Wheelchair ramps, elevators, special parking, specially equipped rest rooms, special class scheduling, lowered drinking fountains, and lowered telephones are available.

Services: Counseling and information services are available, as is tutoring in most subjects. There is remedial math, reading, and writing.

Campus Safety and Security: Measures include 24-hour foot and vehicle patrol, security escort services, shuttle buses, and informal discussions. There are pamphlets/posters/films, emergency telephones, and lighted pathways/sidewalks.

Programs of Study: Dowling confers B.A., B.S., and B.B.A. degrees. Master's and doctoral degrees are also awarded. Bachelor's degrees are awarded in BIOLOGICAL SCIENCE (biology/biological science and marine biology), BUSINESS (accounting, banking and finance, business administration and management, international business management, marketing/retailing/merchandising, sports management, tourism, and transportation management), COMMUNICATIONS AND THE ARTS (communications, English, fine arts, languages, music, romance languages and literature, speech/debate/rhetoric, and visual and performing arts), COMPUTER AND PHYSICAL SCIENCE (applied mathematics, computer science, information sciences and systems, mathematics, and natural sciences), EDUCATION (art, elementary, music, secondary, and special), ENGINEERING AND ENVIRONMENTAL DESIGN (aeronautical science, aeronautical technology, and aviation administration/management), SOCIAL SCIENCE (economics, history, humanities, liberal arts/general studies, philosophy, political science/government, psychology, social science, and sociology). Business, education, and computer sciences are the largest.

Required: To graduate, students must complete 122 credits with a minimum GPA of 2.0. The required 36-credit general education core includes a senior seminar.

Special: Dowling offers a B.S. in professional and liberal studies, internships, independent study, work-study, and nondegree study. There are cooperative programs in several majors, including aeronautics and airway science majors, with the FAA. There are 10 national honor societies, a freshman honors program, and 3 departmental honors programs.

Faculty/Classroom: 61% of faculty are male; 39%, female. 64% teach undergraduates. No introductory courses are taught by graduate students. The average class size in an introductory lecture is 20; in a laboratory, 15; and in a regular course, 17.

Admissions: 96% of the 2003-2004 applicants were accepted. The SAT I scores for the 2003-2004 freshman class were: Verbal--66% below 500, 26% between 500 and 599, 7% between 600 and 700, and 1% above 700; Math--59% below 500, 32% between 500 and 599, 8% between 600 and 700, and 1% above 700.

Requirements: The SAT I or ACT is recommended. In addition, applicants should be graduates of an accredited secondary school and have completed at least 16 Carnegie units, including 4 in English. An interview is strongly recommended. AP and CLEP credits are accepted. Important factors in the admissions decision are advanced placement or honor courses, evidence of special talent, and recommendations by school officials.

Procedure: Freshmen are admitted to all sessions. Entrance exams should be taken by January of the senior year. There is a deferred admissions plan and a rolling admissions plan. Application deadlines are open. Application fee is $25. Applications are accepted on-line through the school's web site.

Transfer: 678 transfer students enrolled in 2002-2003. Applicants must submit official transcripts from all colleges attended. Courses completed with a grade of C or better may transfer. 30 of 122 credits required for the bachelor's degree must be completed at Dowling.

Visiting: There are regularly scheduled orientations for prospective students, including a campus tour and meetings with enrollment services members, staff, and faculty. There are guides for informal visits and visitors may sit in on classes and stay overnight. To schedule a visit, contact the Enrollment Services Office at (631) 244-3426.

Financial Aid: In 2003-2004, 85% of all full-time freshmen and 73% of continuing full-time students received some form of financial aid. 77% of full-time freshmen and 70% of continuing full-time students received

need-based aid. The average freshman award was $10,411. Need-based scholarships or need-based grants averaged $7600 ($14,600 maximum); need-based self-help aid (loans and jobs) averaged $4300 ($6625 maximum); non-need-based athletic scholarships averaged $4900 ($20,000 maximum); and other non-need-based awards and non-need-based scholarships averaged $3500 ($13,350 maximum). All undergraduates work part time. Average annual earnings from campus work are $1265. The average financial indebtedness of the 2003 graduate was $16,803. The FAFSA and the college's own financial statement are required. The deadline for filing freshman financial aid applications for fall entry is May 1.

International Students: There are 92 international students enrolled. The school actively recruits these students. They must score 500 on the written TOEFL.

Computers: The mainframe is an IBM RS/6000 Model 7017-570. There are Compaq and IBM PCs in the academic computing center and library. All students may access the system 7 A.M. to 10:45 P.M. Monday through Thursday and 7 A.M. to 5 P.M. Friday through Sunday. There are no time limits and no fees.

Graduates: From July 1, 2002 to June 30, 2003, 569 bachelor's degrees were awarded. The most popular majors were special education (15%), management (11%), and elementary education (9%). In an average class, 3% graduate in 3 years or less, 20% graduate in 4 years or less, 31% graduate in 5 years or less, and 34% graduate in 6 years or less. 100 companies recruited on campus in 2002-2003.

Admissions Contact: Bridget Masturzo, Director of Enrollment Services. A video is available. E-mail: *masturzb@dowling.edu* Web: *www.dowling.edu*

D'YOUVILLE COLLEGE
Buffalo, NY 14201

A-3

(716) 881-7600
(800) 777-3921; Fax: (716) 881-7790

Full-time: 201 men, 582 women	**Faculty:** 100
Part-time: 44 men, 149 women	**Ph.D.s:** 68%
Graduate: 399 men, 1101 women	**Student/Faculty:** 8 to 1
Year: semesters, summer session	**Tuition:** $14,120
Application Deadline: open	**Room & Board:** $6960
Freshman Class: 865 applied, 598 accepted, 139 enrolled	
SAT I Verbal/Math: 460/480	**ACT:** 23 COMPETITIVE

D'Youville College, founded in 1908, is a private, nonsectarian liberal arts institution. In addition to regional accreditation, D'Youville has baccalaureate program accreditation with ADA, APTA, CAHEA, CCNE, and CSWE. The library contains 100,389 volumes, 193,468 microform items, and 3192 audio/video tapes/CDs, and subscribes to 627 periodicals. Computerized library services include the card catalog, database searching, and Internet access. Special learning facilities include a learning resource center and professional theater. The 7-acre campus is in an urban area 1 mile north of Buffalo. Including any residence halls, there are 8 buildings.

Student Life: 94% of undergraduates are from New York. Students are from 23 states, 26 foreign countries, and Canada. 80% are from public schools. 62% are white; 15% foreign nationals; 14% African American. The average age of freshmen is 19; all undergraduates, 25. 30% do not continue beyond their first year; 50% remain to graduate.

Housing: 308 students can be accommodated in college housing, which includes single-sex and coed dormitories. There are quiet floors and 21 and older floors. On-campus housing is guaranteed for all 4 years. 80% of students commute. All students may keep cars.

Activities: There are no fraternities or sororities. There are 35 groups on campus, including cheerleading, chorus, computers, dance, drama, ethnic, gay, honors, international, literary magazine, newspaper, professional, radio and TV, religious, social, social service, student government, and yearbook. Popular campus events include Moving Up Days, Family and Friends, and Honors Convocation.

Sports: There are 5 intercollegiate sports for men and 5 for women, and 9 intramural sports for men and 9 for women. Facilities include a 500-seat gym that houses basketball and volleyball courts and an indoor batting cage, and a fitness facility with aerobic and free weights, swimming pool, and dance studio.

Disabled Students: 95% of the campus is accessible. Wheelchair ramps, elevators, special parking, specially equipped rest rooms, lowered drinking fountains, lowered telephones, and special housing are available.

Services: Counseling and information services are available, as is tutoring in some subjects, based on tutor accessibility. There is a reader service for the blind, and remedial math, reading, and writing.

Campus Safety and Security: Measures include 24-hour foot and vehicle patrol, self-defense education, security escort services, and informal discussions. There are pamphlets/posters/films, emergency telephones, lighted pathways/sidewalks, a special focus program, and a security committee.

Programs of Study: D'Youville confers B.A., B.S., and B.S.N. degrees. Master's and doctoral degrees are also awarded. Bachelor's degrees are awarded in BIOLOGICAL SCIENCE (biology/biological science), BUSINESS (accounting, business administration and management, and international business management), COMMUNICATIONS AND THE ARTS (English), COMPUTER AND PHYSICAL SCIENCE (information sciences and systems), EDUCATION (business, elementary, and special), HEALTH PROFESSIONS (exercise science, nursing, occupational therapy, physical therapy, and physician's assistant), SOCIAL SCIENCE (dietetics, history, philosophy, psychology, and sociology). Education and health professions are the strongest academically. Health professions, business, and nursing are the largest.

Required: All students must complete general program and core curriculum requirements, including 5 courses in humanities, 2 each in English and natural sciences, and 1 each in ethics, philosophy or religion, history, sociology, psychology, economics or political science, math, and computer science. A minimum of 120 to 144 credit hours, varying by major, with a minimum GPA of 2.0, is required to graduate.

Special: D'Youville has cross-registration with member colleges of the Western New York Consortium. Internships, work-study programs, dual majors, study abroad in 3 countries, and pass/fail options are available. Accelerated 5-year B.S.-M.S. programs in physical therapy, occupational therapy, international business, nursing, and dietetics are offered. For freshmen with undecided majors, the Career Discovery Program offers special courses, internships, and faculty advisers. There are 2 national honor societies and 6 departmental honors programs.

Faculty/Classroom: 43% of faculty are male; 57%, female. All both teach and do research. No introductory courses are taught by graduate students. The average class size in an introductory lecture is 30; in a laboratory, 12; and in a regular course, 23.

Admissions: 69% of the 2003-2004 applicants were accepted. The SAT I scores for the 2003-2004 freshman class were: Verbal--58% below 500, 32% between 500 and 599, 8% between 600 and 700, and 2% above 700; Math--60% below 500, 30% between 500 and 599, 7% between 600 and 700, and 3% above 700. The ACT scores were 16% below 21, 50% between 21 and 23, 25% between 24 and 26, and 8% above 28. 36% of the current freshmen were in the top fifth of their class; 71% were in the top two fifths.

Requirements: The SAT I or ACT is required. In addition, applicants should have completed 16 Carnegie units, including 4 years of high school English, 3 of social studies, and 1 each of math and science; some majors require additional years of math and science. The GED is accepted. An interview is recommended. A GPA of 2.0 is required. AP and CLEP credits are accepted.

Procedure: Freshmen are admitted fall and spring. Entrance exams should be taken by the end of the junior year. There is a deferred admissions plan. Application deadlines are open. Application fee is $25. Notification is sent on a rolling basis. Applications are accepted on-line through the school's web site.

Transfer: 113 transfer students enrolled in 2002-2003. Applicants need a minimum GPA of 2.0, or 2.5 for some programs. An interview is recommended. There are very few openings for transfers seeking part-time studies. 30 of 120 credits required for the bachelor's degree must be completed at D'Youville.

Visiting: There are regularly scheduled orientations for prospective students. There are guides for informal visits and visitors may sit in on classes and stay overnight. To schedule a visit, contact the Admissions Office at admiss@dyc.edu.

Financial Aid: In 2003-2004, 98% of all full-time freshmen and 95% of continuing full-time students received some form of financial aid. 88% of all full-time students received need-based aid. The average freshman award was $15,955. Need-based scholarships or need-based grants averaged $10,380 ($3500 maximum); need-based self-help aid (loans and jobs) averaged $6588 ($12,500 maximum); and other non-need-based awards and non-need-based scholarships averaged $5815 ($8700 maximum). 56% of undergraduates work part time. Average annual earnings from campus work are $644. D'Youville is a member of CSS. The FAFSA and the state aid form are required. The priority date for freshman financial aid applications for fall entry is March 1.

International Students: There are 46 international students enrolled. The school actively recruits these students. They must score 500 on the written TOEFL or 200 on the electronic version and also take the SAT I or the ACT.

Computers: The mainframe is a Sun. There are 3 computer labs as well as computers located in the residence hall. Mac and Windows computers are networked. There is a fiber-optic computer network with ports throughout the college, including the dorms. All students may access the system. There are no time limits and no fees. It is strongly recommended that all students have a personal computer.

Graduates: From July 1, 2002 to June 30, 2003, 223 bachelor's degrees were awarded. The most popular majors were physical/occupational therapy (43%), physician assistant (17%), and nursing (13%). In an average class, 50% graduate in 6 years or less. 92 companies recruited on campus in 2002-2003. Of the 2002 graduating class, 10% were enrolled in graduate school within 6 months of graduation and 96% were employed.

Admissions Contact: Ron H. Dannecker, Director of Undergraduate Admissions. E-mail: admiss@dyc.edu Web: www.dyc.edu

EASTMAN SCHOOL OF MUSIC
B-3
Rochester, NY 14604
(585) 274-1060
(800) 388-9695; Fax: (585) 232-8601

Full-time: 239 men, 246 women	**Faculty:** 89
Part-time: 2 men	**Ph.D.s:** 55%
Graduate: 170 men, 223 women	**Student/Faculty:** 5 to 1
Year: semesters	**Tuition:** $24,543
Application Deadline: December 1	**Room & Board:** $9198
Freshman Class: 896 applied, 289 accepted, 148 enrolled	
SAT I or ACT: recommended	**SPECIAL**

Eastman School of Music, founded in 1921, is a private professional school of music within the University of Rochester. In addition to regional accreditation, Eastman has baccalaureate program accreditation with NASM. The library contains 333,014 volumes, 14,116 microform items, and 78,154 audio/video tapes/CDs, and subscribes to 620 periodicals. Computerized library services include the card catalog, interlibrary loans, database searching, and Internet access. Special learning facilities include a learning resource center, art gallery, recording studios, a music library, a theater, and 3 recital halls. The 3-acre campus is in an urban area in downtown Rochester. Including any residence halls, there are 5 buildings.

Student Life: 82% of undergraduates are from out of state, mostly the Middle Atlantic. Students are from 48 states, 32 foreign countries, and Canada. 90% are from public schools. 62% are white; 21% foreign nationals. The average age of freshmen is 18; all undergraduates, 20. 11% do not continue beyond their first year; 78% remain to graduate.

Housing: 360 students can be accommodated in college housing, which includes single-sex and coed dorms, fraternity houses, and sorority houses. The Student Living Center is divided into separate "houses" that can be organized by special interest upon student request. On-campus housing is guaranteed for all 4 years. 72% of students live on campus; of those, all remain on campus on weekends. All students may keep cars.

Activities: 5% of men and about 2% of women belong to 2 national fraternities; 4% of women belong to 1 national sorority. There are more than 20 groups on campus, including Association for Injury Prevention, band, choir, chorale, chorus, computers, dance, gay, international, jazz band, literary magazine, newspaper, opera, orchestra, professional, religious, social, social service, student government, symphony, and yearbook. Popular campus events include Holiday Sing and Boo Blast.

Sports: There is no sports program at Eastman. All athletic facilities of the University of Rochester, as well as a nearby YMCA, are available to students.

Disabled Students: 95% of the campus is accessible. Wheelchair ramps, elevators, special parking, specially equipped rest rooms, lowered drinking fountains, and lowered telephones are available.

Services: Counseling and information services are available, as is tutoring in every subject. There is a reader service for the blind and remedial writing. English tutoring for nonnative English speakers is available.

Campus Safety and Security: Measures include 24-hour foot and vehicle patrol, self-defense education, security escort services, and shuttle buses. There are informal discussions, pamphlets/posters/films, emergency telephones, lighted pathways/sidewalks, and security cameras.

Programs of Study: Eastman confers the B.M. degree. Master's and doctoral degrees are also awarded. Bachelor's degrees are awarded in COMMUNICATIONS AND THE ARTS (jazz, music, music performance, and music theory and composition), EDUCATION (music). Performance is the largest.

Required: All students must complete core requirements in a major instrument or voice, music theory, music history, and Western cultural tradition, as well as English and humanities electives. A total of 120 to 149 credit hours, varying by program, with a minimum GPA of 2.0, is required to graduate.

Special: The school and the University of Rochester cooperatively offer the B.A. degree with a music concentration. All the facilities of the university are open to Eastman students. Cross-registration is also available with colleges in the Rochester Consortium. Dual majors are available in all areas of study. Internships, work-study, and study abroad in 7 countries are also possible. There is 1 national honor society.

Faculty/Classroom: 60% of faculty are male; 40%, female. All both teach and do research. Graduate students teach 10% of introductory courses. The average class size in an introductory lecture is 30 and in a regular course, 15.

Admissions: 32% of the 2003-2004 applicants were accepted.

Requirements: The SAT I or ACT is recommended; the SAT I or ACT is required only of homeschooled applicants. Applicants should be graduates of an accredited secondary school with 16 academic credits, including 4 years of English. The GED is accepted. An audition and an interview are required, as are 3 letters of recommendation. Some majors have other specific requirements. AP credits are accepted. Important factors in the admissions decision are evidence of special talent, recommendations by alumni, and personality/intangible qualities.

Procedure: Freshmen are admitted fall and spring. There is a deferred admissions plan. Applications should be filed by December 1 for fall entry and November 1 for spring entry, along with an $80 fee. Notification is sent before April 15. 72 were on the 2003 waiting list; 3 were admitted. Applications are accepted on-line through the Eastman web site.

Transfer: 8 transfer students enrolled in 2003-2004. Requirements include satisfactory academic standing at the previous institution, a successful audition, and an interview.

Visiting: There are regularly scheduled orientations for prospective students, including group information sessions and a tour of the facilities. To schedule a visit, contact the Admissions Office at *admissions@esm.edu*.

Financial Aid: In 2003-2004, 99% of all full-time freshmen and 98% of continuing full-time students received some form of financial aid. 80% of full-time freshmen and 83% of continuing full-time students received need-based aid. The average freshman award was $22,150, with $7925 ($10,550 maximum) from need-based scholarships or need-based grants, $2725 ($3500 maximum) from need-based self-help aid (loans and jobs) and $11,500 ($17,500 maximum) from non-need-based awards and non-need-based scholarships. 52% of undergraduates work part time. Average annual earnings from campus work are $900. The average financial indebtedness of the 2003 graduate was $14,725. Eastman is a member of CSS. The CSS/Profile or FAFSA, the state aid form, and the college's own financial statement are required. The priority date for freshman financial aid applications for fall entry is December 1. The deadline for filing freshman financial aid applications for fall entry is March 1.

International Students: There are 50 international students enrolled. The school actively recruits these students. They must score 500 on the written TOEFL or 173 on the electronic version.

Computers: PCs and Macs are located in residence halls, the library, and the main building. There is also a computer music center with Musical Instrument Digital Interface. Residence hall rooms are wired for high-speed Internet access. An Internet cafe is located in the main building. All students may access the system. There are no time limits. The fee is $125. It is strongly recommended that all students have a personal computer.

Graduates: From July 1, 2002 to June 30, 2003, 117 bachelor's degrees were awarded. The most popular majors were music performance (73%), music education (12%), and jazz studies and contemporary media (9%). In an average class, 70% graduate in 4 years or less, and 79% graduate in 5 years or less. 35 companies recruited on campus in 2002-2003. Of the 2002 graduating class, 70% were enrolled in graduate school within 6 months of graduation and 16% were employed.

Admissions Contact: Adrian Daly, Director of Admissions.
E-mail: *admissions@esm.rochester.edu*
Web: *http://www.rochester.edu/Eastman*

ELMIRA COLLEGE
Elmira, NY 14901

C-4

(607) 735-1724
(800) 935-6472; Fax: (607) 735-1718

Full-time: 356 men, 906 women	**Faculty:** 86; IIB, -$
Part-time: 70 men, 201 women	**Ph.D.s:** 98%
Graduate: 64 men, 208 women	**Student/Faculty:** 15 to 1
Year: terms, summer session	**Tuition:** $25,740
Application Deadline: March 15	**Room & Board:** $8080
Freshman Class: 1895 applied, 1274 accepted, 353 enrolled	
SAT I Verbal/Math: 580/560	**ACT:** 25 **VERY COMPETITIVE**

Elmira College, founded in 1855, is a private liberal arts institution offering general and preprofessional programs. In addition to regional accreditation, Elmira has baccalaureate program accreditation with NLN. The library contains 389,000 volumes, 1,320,000 microform items, and 6261 audio/video tapes/CDs, and subscribes to 1755 periodicals. Computerized library services include the card catalog, interlibrary loans, database searching, and Internet access. Special learning facilities include a learning resource center, art gallery, radio station, speech and hearing clinic, and Mark Twain's study. The 42-acre campus is in a suburban area 90 miles southwest of Syracuse. Including any residence halls, there are 25 buildings.

Student Life: 55% of undergraduates are from New York. Students are from 35 states, 23 foreign countries, and Canada. 65% are from public schools. 89% are white. The average age of freshmen is 18; all undergraduates, 21. 12% do not continue beyond their first year; 65% remain to graduate.

Housing: 1083 students can be accommodated in college housing, which includes single-sex and coed dorms and on-campus apartments. There are honors floors. On-campus housing is guaranteed for all 4 years. 92% of students live on campus; of those, 90% remain on campus on weekends. All students may keep cars.

Activities: There are no fraternities or sororities. There are 83 groups on campus, including art, band, cheerleading, chorale, chorus, dance,

drama, honors, international, literary magazine, musical theater, newspaper, orchestra, pep band, political, professional, radio station, religious, social, social service, student government, and yearbook. Popular campus events include Mountain Day, Midnight Breakfast, and Spring Weekend.

Sports: There are 6 intercollegiate sports for men and 10 for women, and 21 intramural sports for men and 21 for women. Facilities include 2500-seat and 950-seat gyms, indoor tennis facilities, a 3500-seat hockey arena, racquetball courts, a fitness center, a dance studio, and a swimming pool.

Disabled Students: 25% of the campus is accessible. Wheelchair ramps, elevators, special parking, specially equipped rest rooms, and special class scheduling are available.

Services: Counseling and information services are available, as is tutoring in most subjects. Tutoring in math and freshman English is available in each freshman dorm.

Campus Safety and Security: Measures include 24-hour foot and vehicle patrol, security escort services, informal discussions, and pamphlets/posters/films. There are emergency telephones and lighted pathways/sidewalks.

Programs of Study: Elmira confers B.A. and B.S. degrees. Bachelor's degrees are awarded in BIOLOGICAL SCIENCE (biochemistry and biology/biological science), BUSINESS (accounting, business administration and management, business economics, international business management, and marketing/retailing/merchandising), COMMUNICATIONS AND THE ARTS (art, classics, dramatic arts, English literature, fine arts, French, languages, music, and Spanish), COMPUTER AND PHYSICAL SCIENCE (chemistry and mathematics), EDUCATION (art, elementary, foreign languages, science, and secondary), ENGINEERING AND ENVIRONMENTAL DESIGN (environmental science), HEALTH PROFESSIONS (medical laboratory technology, nursing, predentistry, premedicine, and speech pathology/audiology), SOCIAL SCIENCE (American studies, anthropology, criminal justice, history, human services, international studies, philosophy, political science/government, prelaw, psychology, and sociology). History, theater, and premedicine are the strongest academically. Psychology, management, and education are the largest.

Required: All students must complete general degree requirements, including communication skills, writing courses, math competency, and computer literacy; a core curriculum; distribution requirements in culture and civilization, contemporary social institutions, the scientific method, the creative process, and phys ed; and a field experience program. A total of 120 credit hours with a minimum GPA of 2.0 overall and in the major is required to graduate.

Special: The required field experience program provides a career-related internship as well as community service. A junior year abroad program, a Washington semester, an accelerated degree program, a general studies degree, student-designed majors, and pass/fail options are available. A 3-2 chemical engineering degree is offered with Clarkson University. B.A.-B.S. degrees are offered in biochemistry, biology, chemistry, economics, education, environmental studies, history, math, political science, and psychology. Elmira is a member of the Spring Term Consortium, enabling students to take 6-week courses at participating institutions. There are 10 national honor societies, including Phi Beta Kappa.

Faculty/Classroom: 66% of faculty are male; 34%, female. All both teach and do research. No introductory courses are taught by graduate students. The average class size in an introductory lecture is 24; in a laboratory, 10; and in a regular course, 16.

Admissions: 67% of the 2003-2004 applicants were accepted. The SAT I scores for the 2003-2004 freshman class were: Verbal--26% below 500, 49% between 500 and 599, 21% between 600 and 700, and 4% above 700; Math--28% below 500, 49% between 500 and 599, 19% between 600 and 700, and 4% above 700. The ACT scores were 12% below 21, 22% between 21 and 23, 42% between 24 and 26, 17% between 27 and 28, and 7% above 28. 48% of the current freshmen were in the top fifth of their class; 77% were in the top two fifths. There was 1 National Merit finalist and 8 semifinalists. 26 freshmen graduated first in their class.

Requirements: The SAT I or ACT is required. In addition, applicants should have completed 4 years of high school English, 3 of math, and 2 of science, or GED equivalent. An essay is part of the application process. An interview is strongly recommended. A GPA of 2.0 is required. AP and CLEP credits are accepted. Important factors in the admissions decision are advanced placement or honor courses, extracurricular activities record, and recommendations by school officials.

Procedure: Freshmen are admitted fall and winter. Entrance exams should be taken by January of the entry year. There are early decision, early admissions, deferred admissions, and rolling admissions plans. Early decision applications should be filed by November 1 and January 15; regular applications, by March 15 for fall entry and December 1 for winter entry, along with a $50 fee. Notification of early decision is sent December 15 and January 31; regular decision, on a rolling basis. 68 early decision candidates were accepted for the 2003-2004 class. 56 applicants were on the 2003 waiting list; 4 were admitted. Applications are accepted on-line through CollegeNET and Common App.

Transfer: 74 transfer students enrolled in 2002-2003. Applicants should have a minimum GPA of 2.0. An interview is strongly recommended. 30 of 120 credits required for the bachelor's degree must be completed at Elmira.

Visiting: There are regularly scheduled orientations for prospective students, consisting of an open house format and overview, a tour, lunch, a student panel, a faculty panel, general admissions and scholarship information, and an optional interview. Individual visits for interviews and tours are available year-round, including Saturday mornings. There are guides for informal visits and visitors may sit in on classes and stay overnight. To schedule a visit, contact the Office of Admissions at *admissions@elmira.edu.*

Financial Aid: In 2003-2004, 83% of all full-time freshmen and 82% of continuing full-time students received some form of financial aid. 75% of all full-time students received need-based aid. The average freshman award was $20,700. 50% of undergraduates work part time. Average annual earnings from campus work are $1000. The average financial indebtedness of the 2003 graduate was $19,500. Elmira is a member of CSS. The FAFSA and the state aid form are required. The priority date for freshman financial aid applications for fall entry is February 15. The deadline for filing freshman financial aid applications for fall entry is March 15.

International Students: There are 65 international students enrolled. The school actively recruits these students. They must score 500 on the written TOEFL or 173 on the electronic version.

Computers: More than 90 PCs connected to the Internet and Windows NT file servers are available to students in the computer center and the library. Students have access from their dorm rooms. All students may access the system weekdays 15 hours per day and weekends 8 to 10 hours per day and any time from residence halls. There are no time limits and no fees. It is strongly recommended that all students have a personal computer.

Graduates: From July 1, 2002 to June 30, 2003, 315 bachelor's degrees were awarded. The most popular majors were education (19%), business (15%), and psychology (13%). In an average class, 1% graduate in 3 years or less, 60% graduate in 4 years or less, 65% graduate in 5 years or less, and 65% graduate in 6 years or less. 42 companies recruited on campus in 2002-2003. Of the 2002 graduating class, 43% were enrolled in graduate school within 6 months of graduation and 55% were employed.

Admissions Contact: William S. Neal, Dean of Admissions. E-mail: *admissions@elmira.edu* Web: *elmira.edu*

EUGENE LANG COLLEGE/NEW SCHOOL UNIVERSITY
D-3

New York, NY 10011-8963   **(212) 229-5665; Fax: (212) 229-5166**

Full-time: 227 men, 492 women	**Faculty:** 35
Part-time: 7 men, 7 women	**Ph.D.s:** 100%
Graduate: none	**Student/Faculty:** 21 to 1
Year: semesters	**Tuition:** $24,130
Application Deadline: February 1	**Room & Board:** $10,810
Freshman Class: 862 applied, 560 accepted, 187 enrolled	
SAT I or ACT: required	**COMPETITIVE**

Eugene Lang College, established in 1978, is the liberal arts undergraduate division of New School University. There are 4 undergraduate and 6 graduate schools. The 4 libraries contain 4,137,223 volumes, 4,656,818 microform items, and 52,188 audio/video tapes/CDs, and subscribe to 22,041 periodicals. Computerized library services include the card catalog, interlibrary loans, and database searching. Special learning facilities include an art gallery and writing center. The 5-acre campus is in an urban area in the heart of Greenwich Village. Including any residence halls, there are 14 buildings.

Student Life: 55% of undergraduates are from out of state, mostly the Northeast. Students are from 34 states, 12 foreign countries, and Canada. 60% are from public schools. 52% are white. The average age of freshmen is 18; all undergraduates, 20. 15% do not continue beyond their first year; 85% remain to graduate.

Housing: 500 students can be accommodated in college housing, which includes coed dorms and off-campus apartments. On-campus housing is available on a first-come, first-served basis and is available on a lottery system for upperclassmen. Priority is given to out-of-town students. 57% of students commute. Alcohol is not permitted. All students may keep cars.

Activities: There are no fraternities or sororities. There are 15 groups on campus, including chorus, drama, ethnic, gay, international, jazz band, literary magazine, newspaper, photography, political, social, social service, and student government. Popular campus events include Lang in the City, a program that makes cultural events available to students.

Sports: Students receive discounted rates at area gyms and city recreation facilities.

Disabled Students: Wheelchair ramps, elevators, specially equipped rest rooms, lowered telephones, and special housing are available.

Services: Counseling and information services are available, as is tutoring in some subjects, including writing at the writing center. There is remedial writing.

Campus Safety and Security: Measures include informal discussions, pamphlets/posters/films, and 24-hour dorm security.

Programs of Study: Eugene Lang College confers the B.A. degree. Bachelor's degrees are awarded in COMMUNICATIONS AND THE ARTS (creative writing, dramatic arts, and English), EDUCATION (education), SOCIAL SCIENCE (crosscultural studies, economics, history, political science/government, prelaw, psychology, social science, sociology, urban studies, and women's studies). Creative writing, history, urban studies, and education are the strongest academically. Writing and cultural studies are the largest.

Required: To graduate, students must complete 120 credit hours, with a GPA of 2.0 and a minimum of 36 hours in 1 of 5 areas of concentration: writing, literature, and the arts; urban studies; social and historical inquiry; cultural studies; or mind, nature, and value. Also required are 88 credit hours in Lang College courses and 4 credits of senior work. Required courses include a first-year writing seminar and a freshman workshop program. A senior project must be completed.

Special: Lang College offers a concentration rather than a traditional major; there is no core curriculum and students are instructed in small seminars. Students may cross-register with other New School divisions. A large variety of internships for credit, study abroad, B.A./M.A. and B.A./M.S.T. options, a B.A./B.F.A. degree with Parsons School of Design and the New School's Jazz and Contemporary Music Program, student-designed majors, and nondegree study are available.

Faculty/Classroom: 51% of faculty are male; 49%, female. All teach undergraduates. The average class size in a laboratory is 15 and in a regular course, 15.

Admissions: 65% of the 2003-2004 applicants were accepted.

Requirements: The SAT I or ACT is required. 4 SAT II: Subject tests may be substituted for either test. Applicants must be enrolled in a strong college preparatory program. The GED is accepted. An essay and an interview are required. Art students must present a portfolio and complete a home exam. Jazz students are required to audition. AP credits are accepted. Important factors in the admissions decision are personality/intangible qualities, advanced placement or honor courses, and recommendations by school officials.

Procedure: Freshmen are admitted fall and spring. Entrance exams should be taken in May of the junior year or October of the senior year. There are early decision, early admissions, and deferred admissions plans. Early decision applications should be filed by November 15; regular applications, by February 1 for fall entry and November 15 for spring entry. Notification of early decision is sent December 15; regular decision, by April 1. 38 early decision candidates were accepted for the 2003-2004 class. 70 applicants were on the 2003 waiting list; 21 were admitted.

Transfer: 95 transfer students enrolled in 2003-2004. Applicants must have a minimum college GPA of 2.5 and must submit high school transcripts, ACT or SAT I scores (if taken in the last 5 years), and 2 recommendations. An interview is required. Grades of C or better transfer for credit. 60 of 120 credits required for the bachelor's degree must be completed at Eugene Lang College.

Visiting: There are regularly scheduled orientations for prospective students, including a campus tour, visits to classes, and panel discussions. There are guides for informal visits and visitors may sit in on classes. To schedule a visit, contact the Admissions Office.

Financial Aid: In 2003-2004, 68% of all full-time students received some form of financial aid. At least 66% of all full-time students received need-based aid. The average freshman award was $16,497. Need-based scholarships or need-based grants averaged $13,910; need-based self-help aid (loans and jobs) averaged $3412; and institutional non-need-based awards and non-need-based scholarships averaged $5443. The average financial indebtedness of the 2003 graduate was $20,093. The FAFSA is required. The priority date for freshman financial aid applications for fall entry is March 1.

International Students: The school actively recruits these students. They must score 600 on the written TOEFL and also take the SAT I or the ACT.

Computers: The mainframe is an HP. Macs and IBM PCs are available for student use in an academic computing center. Students can arrange for access for statistical course work and dissertation research. There are no time limits and no fees. It is strongly recommended that all students have a personal computer.

Graduates: From July 1, 2002 to June 30, 2003, 133 bachelor's degrees were awarded. The most popular major was liberal arts/general studies (100%). In an average class, 33% graduate in 4 years or less, 42% graduate in 5 years or less, and 48% graduate in 6 years or less.

Admissions Contact: Terrence Peavy, Director of Admissions. E-mail: *lang@newschool.edu* Web: *www.lang.edu*

EXCELSIOR COLLEGE

Albany, NY 12203-5159

D-3

(518) 464-8500
(888) 674-2388; Fax: (518) 464-8777

Full-time: none	**Faculty:** n/av
Part-time: 8649 men, 13,803 women	**Ph.Ds:** n/av
Graduate: 105 men, 267 women	**Student/Faculty:** n/av
Year: n/app	**Tuition:** $975
Application Deadline: open	**Room & Board:** n/app
Freshman Class: n/av	
SAT I or ACT: not required	**SPECIAL**

Excelsior College, founded in 1971, is an external degree institution that is a member of the University of the State of New York. Students earn credit through proficiency exams, course credit from other accredited colleges, military training, and on-the-job training. There are 4 undergraduate and 2 graduate schools. In addition to regional accreditation, Excelsior has baccalaureate program accreditation with ABET and NLN. Computerized library services include the card catalog, interlibrary loans, database searching, and Internet access. Special learning facilities include an electronic peer network available on the Internet. The campus is in a suburban area in Albany. There are 2 buildings.

Student Life: 90% of undergraduates are from out of state. Students are from 50 states, 52 foreign countries, and Canada. 66% are white; 14% African American. The average age of all undergraduates is 39.

Housing: There are no residence halls.

Activities: There are no fraternities or sororities. Popular campus events include commencement.

Disabled Students: All of the campus is accessible. Wheelchair ramps, elevators, special parking, specially equipped rest rooms, and lowered drinking fountains are available.

Services: Counseling and information services are available, as is tutoring in some subjects, including statistics and writing.

Programs of Study: Excelsior confers B.A., B.S., B.S.Comp.Tech, B.S.Elect.Tech, B.S.N., B.S.Nuc.T, and B.S.T. degrees. Associate and master's degrees are also awarded. Bachelor's degrees are awarded in BUSINESS (accounting, banking and finance, business administration and management, human resources, insurance and risk management, international business management, management information systems, and marketing/retailing/merchandising), COMPUTER AND PHYSICAL SCIENCE (information sciences and systems and nuclear technology), ENGINEERING AND ENVIRONMENTAL DESIGN (computer technology, electrical/electronics engineering technology, and technological management), HEALTH PROFESSIONS (nursing), SOCIAL SCIENCE (liberal arts/general studies). Nursing and liberal studies are the largest.

Required: To graduate, students must complete 120 credits with 30 in the major and a minimum 2.0 GPA. At least 50% of course work must be in the arts and sciences. The required core courses include 6 to 12 credits each in humanities, math/science, and social science/history and 1 credit in information literacy. The nursing program requires a different set of core courses as well as the nursing performance exams. All students must fulfill a written English requirement.

Special: B.A. or B.S. candidates may major in liberal studies or in most traditional academic disciplines. Faculty consultants design curricula, approve sources of credit, create exams, and assess student learning. They do not offer instruction. Students receive academic advising by telephone, letter, computer, or in person. The flexibility of this alternate program enables adults to pursue an undergraduate degree independently. Exams are available. Pass/fail options are possible. There is 1 national honor society.

Faculty/Classroom: 30% of faculty are male; 70%, female.

Requirements: There are no admissions requirements except for nursing students. Applicants need not be residents of New York State. Students without a high school diploma or equivalent are admitted as special students. Nursing enrollment is available only to students with certain health care backgrounds. AP and CLEP credits are accepted.

Procedure: Freshmen are admitted to all sessions. Application deadlines are open.

Transfer: 12880 transfer students enrolled in 2002-2003.

Financial Aid: The college's own financial statement is required. The deadline for filing freshman financial aid applications for fall entry is July 1.

International Students: There are 376 international students enrolled. The school actively recruits these students.

Computers: The mainframe is a DEC Alpha. Students are encouraged to access a database of more than 20,000 exams and courses available through distance learning. They also have access to Excelsior College study groups and administrative offices via the Web. All students may access the system 24 hours a day, 7 days a week, via the Internet. There are no time limits and no fees.

Graduates: From July 1, 2002 to June 30, 2003, 2539 bachelor's degrees were awarded. The most popular majors were liberal arts (72%), technology (16%), and business (10%).

Admissions Contact: Prospective Student Advisor.
E-mail: *info@excelsior.edu* Web: *www.excelsior.edu*

FARMINGDALE STATE UNIVERSITY OF NEW YORK

(Formerly SUNY/College of Technology at Farmingdale)

E-5

Farmingdale, NY 11735   (631) 420-2200; Fax: (631) 420-2633

Full-time: 2291 men, 1353 women	**Faculty:** 151; IIB, ++$
Part-time: 1120 men, 1185 women	**Ph.Ds:** 60%
Graduate: none	**Student/Faculty:** 24 to 1
Year: semesters, summer session	**Tuition:** $5211 ($11,161)
Application Deadline: open	**Room & Board:** $7680
Freshman Class: 3739 applied, 2063 accepted, 876 enrolled	
SAT I Verbal/Math: 471/488	**COMPETITIVE**

Farmingdale State University of New York, formerly State University of New York/College of Technology at Farmingdale, founded in 1912, is a public institution offering associate and bachelor's degrees in the applied sciences and technology. There are 4 undergraduate schools. In addition to regional accreditation, Farmingdale State University of New York has baccalaureate program accreditation with ABET and CAHEA. The library contains 150,000 volumes, 63,000 microform items, and 3100 audio/video tapes/CDs, and subscribes to 900 periodicals. Computerized library services include the card catalog, interlibrary loans, database searching, and Internet access. Special learning facilities include a learning resource center, art gallery, radio station, dental hygiene clinic, CAD/CAM and CIM labs, fleet of multi- and single-engine airplanes, and a greenhouse complex. The 380-acre campus is in a suburban area on Long Island, about 35 miles east of New York City. Including any residence halls, there are 40 buildings.

Student Life: 99% of undergraduates are from New York. Students are from 12 states and 11 foreign countries. 92% are from public schools. 60% are white; 12% African American. The average age of freshmen is 22; all undergraduates, 26. 35% do not continue beyond their first year; 36% remain to graduate.

Housing: 500 students can be accommodated in college housing, which includes coed dorms. In addition, there are honors wings, and residences for students age 23 and older. On-campus housing is available on a first-come, first-served basis and is available on a lottery system for upperclassmen. Priority is given to out-of-town students. 91% of students commute. Alcohol is not permitted. All students may keep cars.

Activities: There are no fraternities or sororities. There are 32 groups on campus, including art, cheerleading, computers, drama, ethnic, honors, literary magazine, musical theater, newspaper, professional, radio and TV, religious, social, student government, and yearbook. Popular campus events include Comedy Nights, Spring Fling, and black, Hispanic, and women's history months.

Sports: There are 7 intercollegiate sports for men and 5 for women, and 11 intramural sports for men and 11 for women. Facilities include basketball, badminton, volleyball, racquetball, handball, squash, and tennis courts, a swimming pool, a wrestling room, bowling alleys, weight training rooms, indoor and outdoor tracks, a golf driving range and 3-hole golf layout, and baseball, softball, soccer/lacrosse, and multipurpose fields.

Disabled Students: 90% of the campus is accessible. Wheelchair ramps, elevators, special parking, specially equipped rest rooms, lowered drinking fountains, and lowered telephones are available.

Services: Counseling and information services are available, as is tutoring in most subjects. There is a reader service for the blind and remedial math, reading, and writing. There is a learning disabilities specialist counselor available.

Campus Safety and Security: Measures include 24-hour foot and vehicle patrol, security escort services, informal discussions, and pamphlets/posters/films. There are emergency telephones and lighted pathways/sidewalks.

Programs of Study: Farmingdale State University of New York confers B.S. and B.Tech. degrees. Associate degrees are also awarded. Bachelor's degrees are awarded in BIOLOGICAL SCIENCE (biology/biological science), ENGINEERING AND ENVIRONMENTAL DESIGN (aeronautical science, automotive technology, aviation administration/management, computer technology, construction management, electrical/electronics engineering technology, graphic arts technology, industrial administration/management, industrial engineering technology, and manufacturing technology), SOCIAL SCIENCE (safety and security technology). Electrical engineering technology and bioscience are the strongest academically. Management of technology and computer programming are the largest.

Required: To graduate, students must complete 124 to 141 credits, including 60 to 70 in the major, with a minimum GPA of 2.0. The core curriculum includes 4 courses each in social science, math/science, and English/humanities, including English composition.

Special: Study abroad in 3 countries is available. There are 3 national honor societies and 1 departmental honors program.

Faculty/Classroom: 59% of faculty are male; 41%, female. All teach undergraduates. The average class size in an introductory lecture is 30; in a laboratory, 15; and in a regular course, 21.

Admissions: 55% of the 2003-2004 applicants were accepted. The SAT I scores for the 2003-2004 freshman class were: Verbal--64% below

500, 32% between 500 and 599, and 4% between 600 and 700; Math--55% below 500, 39% between 500 and 599, and 6% between 600 and 700. 7% of the current freshmen were in the top fifth of their class; 34% were in the top two fifths.

Requirements: The SAT I is required. In addition, applicants must be graduates of an accredited secondary school or have earned a GED. Specific entrance requirements vary by program, but recommended preparation includes 4 units of English and 3 each of math, science, and social science. Art programs require a portfolio and an interview. A GPA of 2.0 is required. AP and CLEP credits are accepted.

Procedure: Freshmen are admitted fall and spring. There are early admissions and deferred admissions plans. There is a rolling admissions plan. Application deadlines are open. Application fee is $40.

Transfer: 745 transfer students enrolled in 2002-2003. Applicants must have a minimum GPA of 2.0 and be eligible to return to their previous college. 30 of 124 to 141 credits required for the bachelor's degree must be completed at Farmingdale State University of New York.

Visiting: There are regularly scheduled orientations for prospective students, including a tour of the campus and general information about the college, admissions, financial aid, and residence life. There are guides for informal visits. To schedule a visit, contact the Admissions Office at admissions@farmingdale.edu.

Financial Aid: The FAFSA, the state aid form, and the college's own financial statement are required. The deadline for filing freshman financial aid applications for fall entry is April 1.

International Students: There are 34 international students enrolled. They must score 500 on the written TOEFL.

Computers: The mainframe is a DEC Alpha cluster. More than 250 PCs, both networked and stand-alone, are located in student labs in several classroom buildings and residence halls. All students may access the system during lab hours of Monday through Friday, 8 A.M. to 10:30 P.M., and Saturday, 9 A.M. to 4 P.M., or through dial-in access. There are no time limits and no fees. It is strongly recommended that all students have a personal computer.

Graduates: From July 1, 2002 to June 30, 2003, 291 bachelor's degrees were awarded. The most popular majors were management of technology (27%), aviation technology (15%), and visual communications (14%). In an average class, 17% graduate in 4 years or less, and 17% graduate in 5 years or less. 72 companies recruited on campus in 2002-2003. Of the 2002 graduating class, 30% were employed within 6 months of graduation.

Admissions Contact: Jim Hall, Admissions Director.
E-mail: jim.hall@farmingdale.edu Web: farmingdale.edu

FASHION INSTITUTE OF TECHNOLOGY/STATE UNIVERSITY OF NEW YORK   D-5
New York, NY 10001-5992
(212) 217-7675
(800) Go-To-FIT; Fax: (212) 217-7481

Full-time: 1025 men, 5568 women	**Faculty:** 208
Part-time: 796 men, 3274 women	**Ph.Ds:** n/av
Graduate: 5 men, 107 women	**Student/Faculty:** 32 to 1
Year: 4-1-4, summer session	**Tuition:** $4620 ($10,570)
Application Deadline: January 1	**Room & Board:** $6549
Freshman Class: 3320 applied, 1531 accepted, 963 enrolled	
SAT I or ACT: not required	**COMPETITIVE+**

The Fashion Institute of Technology, founded in 1944 as part of the State University of New York, is an art and design, business, and technology college that prepares students for careers in fashion and related design professions and industries. In addition to regional accreditation, FIT has baccalaureate program accreditation with FIDER and NASAD. The library contains 168,879 volumes, 4712 microform items, and 244,335 audio/video tapes/CDs, and subscribes to 502 periodicals. Computerized library services include the card catalog, interlibrary loans, and database searching. Special learning facilities include an art gallery, radio station, design lab, lighting lab, quick response center, computer-aided design and communications facility, and the Annette Green Fragrance Foundation Studio Collections of the Museum at FIT. The 5-acre campus is in an urban area in Manhattan. Including any residence halls, there are 8 buildings.

Student Life: 63% of undergraduates are from New York. Students are from 50 states, 80 foreign countries, and Canada. 43% are white; 12% foreign nationals; 10% Asian American; 10% Hispanic. The average age of freshmen is 22; all undergraduates, 29. 81% do not continue beyond their first year; 51% remain to graduate.

Housing: 1250 students can be accommodated in college housing, which includes single-sex and coed dorms and on-campus apartments. On-campus housing is available on a lottery system for upperclassmen. Priority is given to out-of-town students. 83% of students commute. Alcohol is not permitted. No one may keep cars.

Activities: There are no fraternities or sororities. There are 70 groups on campus, including art, cheerleading, choir, dance, drama, ethnic, gay, honors, literary magazine, musical theater, newspaper, photogra-

phy, political, professional, radio and TV, religious, social, social service, student government, and yearbook. Popular campus events include fashion shows, a lecture series, and craft center events.

Sports: There are 4 intercollegiate sports for men and 4 for women, and 4 intramural sports for men and 4 for women. Facilities include 2 gyms, a dance studio, and a weight room.

Disabled Students: 95% of the campus is accessible. Wheelchair ramps, elevators, special parking, specially equipped rest rooms, lowered drinking fountains, lowered telephones, services/facilities for the hearing impaired, and library tapes are available.

Services: Counseling and information services are available, as is tutoring in every subject. There is remedial math, reading, and writing. The school has a special program for the learning disabled.

Campus Safety and Security: Measures include 24-hour foot and vehicle patrol, self-defense education, informal discussions, and pamphlets/posters/films. There are emergency telephones, lighted pathways/sidewalks, and lectures by the New York City Police Department.

Programs of Study: FIT confers B.S. and B.F.A. degrees. Associate and master's degrees are also awarded. Bachelor's degrees are awarded in BUSINESS (apparel and accessories marketing, fashion merchandising, and marketing/retailing/merchandising), COMMUNICATIONS AND THE ARTS (advertising, design, fiber/textiles/weaving, graphic design, illustration, and toy design), ENGINEERING AND ENVIRONMENTAL DESIGN (computer graphics, interior design, and textile technology), SOCIAL SCIENCE (fashion design and technology, home furnishings and equipment management/production/services, and textiles and clothing). Fashion merchandising management, fashion design, and communication design are the largest.

Required: To graduate, students must complete the credit and course requirements for their majors with a 2.0 GPA. Students may qualify for a degree in two ways: by earning 60 credits, with half in the major while in residence at the upper-division level, or by earning 30 credits at the upper-division level in addition to an FIT associate degree. There is a 2-credit phys ed requirement.

Special: Internships are offered, and students may study abroad in 8 countries. Nondegree study is available.

Faculty/Classroom: 48% of faculty are male; 52%, female. All teach undergraduates. No introductory courses are taught by graduate students. The average class size in an introductory lecture is 25; in a laboratory, 18; and in a regular course, 25.

Admissions: 46% of the 2003-2004 applicants were accepted. 36% of the current freshmen were in the top fifth of their class; 72% were in the top two fifths.

Requirements: Applicants must be high school graduates or have a GED certificate. An essay and, when appropriate, a portfolio are required. FIT requires applicants to be in the upper 50% of their class. A GPA of 2.0 is required. AP and CLEP credits are accepted. Important factors in the admissions decision are personality/intangible qualities, leadership record, and evidence of special talent.

Procedure: Freshmen are admitted fall and spring. There is an early decision plan and a rolling admissions plan. Applications should be filed by January 1 for fall entry and October 1 for spring entry, along with a $40 fee. Notification is sent on a rolling basis. 381 early decision candidates were accepted for the 2003-2004 class. A waiting list is an active part of the admissions procedure. Applications are accepted on-line through the school's web site.

Transfer: 1029 transfer students enrolled in 2002-2003. Applicants must have a GPA of 2.0 and at least 30 college credits. An interview is required for art and design applicants, as well as a portfolio when appropriate. 30 credits of 60 required for the bachelor's degree must be completed at FIT.

Visiting: There are regularly scheduled orientations for prospective students, including a presentation and group information session with a counselor. To schedule a visit, contact the Admissions Office at fitinfo@fitnyc.edu.

Financial Aid: In 2002-2003, 70% of all full-time freshmen and 51% of continuing full-time students received some form of financial aid. 51% of full-time freshmen and 40% of continuing full-time students received need-based aid. The average freshman award was $5858. Need-based scholarships or need-based grants averaged $3457 ($9450 maximum); need-based self-help aid (loans and jobs) averaged $3008 ($2625 maximum); and non-need-based awards and non-need-based scholarships averaged $1447 ($1500 maximum). The average financial indebtedness of the 2003 graduate was $9395. FIT is a member of CSS. The FAFSA and the state aid form are required. The priority date for freshman financial aid applications for fall entry is February 15.

International Students: There are 905 international students enrolled. They must score 550 on the written TOEFL.

Computers: There are 240 PCs available in various academic computer labs and college areas. All students may access the system. There are no time limits and no fees.

Graduates: From July 1, 2002 to June 30, 2003, 937 bachelor's degrees were awarded. The most popular majors were fashion merchandising management (32%), advertising, marketing, and communication

(12%), and fashion design (12%). 90 companies recruited on campus in 2002-2003.

Admissions Contact: Dolores Lombardi, Director of Admissions. A video is available. E-mail: *fitinfo@fitnyc.edu* Web: *www.fitnyc.edu*

FIVE TOWNS COLLEGE
Dix Hills, NY 11746

E-5

(631) 424-7000, ext. 2110
Fax: (631) 656-2172

Full-time: 649 men, 387 women	**Faculty:** 49
Part-time: 30 men, 38 women	**Ph.Ds:** 51%
Graduate: 40 men, 38 women	**Student/Faculty:** 21 to 1
Year: semesters, summer session	**Tuition:** $12,850
Application Deadline: open	**Room & Board:** $8200
Freshman Class: 1062 applied, 590 accepted, 381 enrolled	
SAT I Verbal/Math: 484/470	**ACT:** 19 SPECIAL

Five Towns College, founded in 1972, is a private institution offering undergraduate programs in music, music business, business, liberal arts, theater, elementary education, and mass communication (broadcasting, journalism). The library contains 28,000 volumes, 50 microform items, and 9575 audio/video tapes/CDs, and subscribes to 550 periodicals. Computerized library services include interlibrary loans, database searching, and Internet access. Special learning facilities include a learning resource center, radio station, 72-, 48-, and 24-track recording studios, a MIDI studio, and a film/video/TV studio. The 40-acre campus is in a suburban area 48 miles east of New York City. Including any residence halls, there are 3 buildings.

Student Life: 95% of undergraduates are from New York. Students are from 20 states and 7 foreign countries. 91% are from public schools. 62% are white; 15% African American; 14% Hispanic. The average age of freshmen is 19; all undergraduates, 21. 30% do not continue beyond their first year; 58% remain to graduate.

Housing: 180 students can be accommodated in college housing, which includes coed dorms and off-campus apartments. Priority for on-campus housing is given to out-of-town students. 90% of students commute. Alcohol is not permitted. All students may keep cars.

Activities: There are no fraternities or sororities. There are many groups and organizations on campus, including art, band, barbershop quartets, broadcasting, choir, chorale, chorus, drama, film, hip-hop, honors, international, jazz band, live audio, music business, musical theater, newspaper, orchestra, photography, professional, radio and TV, readers theater, social, student government, symphony, theatrical concert, and yearbook. Popular campus events include the Cultural Hour, the Annual Picnic, and spring and fall festivals.

Sports: There are 2 intramural sports for men and 2 for women. Facilities include a gym with basketball and volleyball courts, an outdoor baseball/soccer field, and a fitness center.

Disabled Students: All of the campus is accessible. Wheelchair ramps, special parking, specially equipped rest rooms, special class scheduling, lowered drinking fountains, lowered telephones, and special housing are available.

Services: Counseling and information services are available, as is tutoring in most subjects. There is remedial math, reading, and writing.

Campus Safety and Security: Measures include 24-hour foot and vehicle patrol, shuttle buses, informal discussions, and pamphlets/posters/films. There are lighted pathways/sidewalks.

Programs of Study: FTC confers B.S., B.F.A., B.P.S., and Mus.B. degrees. Associate, master's, and doctoral degrees are also awarded. Bachelor's degrees are awarded in COMMUNICATIONS AND THE ARTS (audio technology, communications, dramatic arts, jazz, music business management, music performance, music theory and composition, and video), EDUCATION (elementary and music). Music and childhood education are the strongest academically. Audio recording technology is the largest.

Required: To graduate, all students must complete a total of 128 credits for a Mus.B. or B.F.A. degree, 120 for a B.P.S. degree, or 130 for a B.S. degree. Students must maintain at least a C average in their major concentration and have a minimum GPA of 2.0 to graduate. Distribution requirements include 45 credits in core courses in liberal arts. The core curriculum consists of English Composition 101 and 102, Speech 101, 3 credits each of either psychology or sociology, and various upper-division liberal arts and social science courses. All music students must pass a jury exam. Music majors and elementary education majors must take a comprehensive exam.

Special: Cross-registration is available with schools in the Long Island Regional Advisory Council on Higher Education. Co-op programs in audio recording technology, music business, film/video arts, and broadcasting are available, and internships are possible. Work-study programs are offered on campus, and B.A./B.S. degrees are possible. Students can have dual majors in music, audio recording technology, business, music business, and video production. There is 1 national honor society and 4 departmental honors programs.

Faculty/Classroom: 66% of faculty are male; 34%, female. All both teach and do research. The average class size in an introductory lecture is 30 and in a laboratory, 24.

Admissions: 56% of the 2003-2004 applicants were accepted. The SAT I scores for the 2003-2004 freshman class were: Verbal--73% below 500, 26% between 500 and 599, and 1% between 600 and 700; Math--71% below 500, 28% between 500 and 599, and 1% between 600 and 700. The ACT scores were 99% below 21, and 1% between 21 and 23. 8% of the current freshmen were in the top fifth of their class; 28% were in the top two fifths.

Requirements: The SAT I or ACT is required. In addition, a minimum high school average of 80 is required. A GED with a minimum score of 280 is accepted. An interview is required for all students, and music and theater students are required to audition. A GPA of 2.0 is required. AP and CLEP credits are accepted. Important factors in the admissions decision are advanced placement or honor courses, evidence of special talent, and personality/intangible qualities.

Procedure: Freshmen are admitted fall, spring, and summer. Entrance exams should be taken prior to admission. There is a deferred admissions plan. Application deadlines are open. The fall 2003 application fee was $25. Notification is sent on a rolling basis. A waiting list is an active part of the admissions procedure.

Transfer: 93 transfer students enrolled in 2002-2003. Students must be in good academic standing at their former school. 45 of 120 credits required for the bachelor's degree must be completed at FTC.

Visiting: There are regularly scheduled orientations for prospective students, including a campus tour, academic counseling, and financial aid counseling. There are guides for informal visits and visitors may sit in on classes. To schedule a visit, contact the Admissions Office at *admissions@ftc.edu*.

Financial Aid: In 2003-2004, 77% of all full-time freshmen and 98% of continuing full-time students received some form of financial aid. 70% of full-time freshmen and 68% of continuing full-time students received need-based aid. The average freshman award was $4500. 74% of undergraduates work part time. Average annual earnings from campus work are $2000. The average financial indebtedness of the 2003 graduate was $18,000. The FAFSA and the college's own financial statement are required.

International Students: There are 14 international students enrolled. They must score 520 on the written TOEFL or 190 on the electronic version and also take the college's own test and the SAT I or the ACT.

Computers: The mainframe is an IBM AS/400. There are 100 terminals available in a computer lab and the library. All students may access the system during school hours.

Graduates: From July 1, 2002 to June 30, 2003, 115 bachelor's degrees were awarded. The most popular majors were business (48%), music education and music performance (25%), and film/video and theater (21%). In an average class, 54% graduate in 4 years or less, 44% graduate in 5 years or less, and 2% graduate in 6 years or less. 64 companies recruited on campus in 2002-2003. Of the 2002 graduating class, 3% were enrolled in graduate school within 6 months of graduation and 88% were employed.

Admissions Contact: Jerry Cohen, Director of Admissions. E-mail: *admissions@ftc.edu* Web: *www.ftc.edu*

FORDHAM UNIVERSITY SYSTEM

The Fordham University System, established in 1841, is a private system in the Jesuit tradition. It is governed by a board of trustees whose chief administrator is the president. The primary goal of the system is to educate talented men and women in the liberal arts, sciences, business, and performing arts. The main priorities are excellence in undergraduate and selected graduate/professional programs, and commitment to teaching, research, and service. The total undergraduate enrollment of all 3 campuses is about 7000, with more than 600 faculty members. There are 69 baccalaureate, 71 master's, and 25 doctoral programs through Fordham University. Profiles of the 4-year campuses are included in this section.

FORDHAM UNIVERSITY
Bronx, NY 10458

D-5

(718) 817-4000
(800) FORDHAM; Fax: (718) 367-3426

Full-time: 2750 men, 3940 women	**Faculty:** 447; I, +$
Part-time: 233 men, 480 women	**Ph.Ds:** 95%
Graduate: 2781 men, 4547 women	**Student/Faculty:** 15 to 1
Year: semesters, summer session	**Tuition:** $25,366
Application Deadline: February 1	**Room & Board:** $9700
Freshman Class: 12,801 applied, 6862 accepted, 1680 enrolled	
SAT I Verbal/Math: 600/601	**ACT:** 26 HIGHLY COMPETITIVE

Fordham University, founded in 1841, is a private institution offering an education based on the Jesuit tradition, with 3 campuses in New York: 1 in the Bronx, 1 in Manhattan near Lincoln Center, and 1 in Tarrytown. There are 5 undergraduate and 6 graduate schools. In addition to regional accreditation, Fordham University has baccalaureate program accreditation with AACSB and NCATE. The 4 libraries contain 2,033,124 volumes, 3,080,449 microform items, and 19,295 audio/video tapes/CDs, and subscribe to 15,940 periodicals. Computerized library services include the card catalog, interlibrary loans, database searching, and Internet access. Special learning facilities include a learning resource center, radio station, a seismic station, an archeological site, and a biological field station. The 85-acre campus is in an urban area adjacent to the Bronx Zoo and New York Botanical Garden. Including any residence halls, there are 32 buildings.

Student Life: 59% of undergraduates are from New York. Students are from 50 states, 50 foreign countries, and Canada. 40% are from public schools. 58% are white; 11% Hispanic. 66% are Catholic; 10% claim no religious affiliation; 9% Protestant. The average age of freshmen is 19; all undergraduates, 20. 10% do not continue beyond their first year; 74% remain to graduate.

Housing: 3947 students can be accommodated in college housing, which includes coed dorms, on-campus apartments, and off-campus apartments. On-campus housing is guaranteed for all 4 years. 59% of students live on campus; of those, 90% remain on campus on weekends. All commuters are guaranteed parking; resident students are usually not permitted to have cars on campus.

Activities: There are no fraternities or sororities. There are 133 groups on campus, including art, band, cheerleading, choir, chorale, chorus, computers, dance, drama, ethnic, film, gay, honors, international, jazz band, literary magazine, marching band, musical theater, newspaper, orchestra, pep band, photography, political, professional, radio and TV, religious, social, social service, student admission ambassadors, student government, symphony, and yearbook. Popular campus events include Spring Weekend, Spring Semiformal, and Senior Week.

Sports: There are 19 intercollegiate sports for men and 17 for women, and 22 intramural sports for men and 22 for women. Facilities include a 6000-seat football stadium, an Olympic-size pool with a separate diving area, an indoor track, a 3200-seat gym, and tennis, squash, and racquetball courts.

Disabled Students: 80% of the campus is accessible. Wheelchair ramps, elevators, special parking, specially equipped rest rooms, special class scheduling, and lowered drinking fountains are available.

Services: Counseling and information services are available, as is tutoring in most subjects.

Campus Safety and Security: Measures include 24-hour foot and vehicle patrol, security escort services, shuttle buses, and informal discussions. There are pamphlets/posters/films, emergency telephones, and lighted pathways/sidewalks.

Programs of Study: Fordham University confers B.A., B.S., and B.F.A. degrees. Master's and doctoral degrees are also awarded. Bachelor's degrees are awarded in BIOLOGICAL SCIENCE (biology/biological science), BUSINESS (accounting, business administration and management, business economics, international business management, and marketing management), COMMUNICATIONS AND THE ARTS (art history and appreciation, broadcasting, classical languages, communications, comparative literature, dance, dramatic arts, English, film arts, fine arts, French, German, Italian, journalism, music, performing arts, Spanish, and visual and performing arts), COMPUTER AND PHYSICAL SCIENCE (chemistry, computer science, information sciences and systems, mathematics, physics, and science), SOCIAL SCIENCE (African American studies, African studies, American studies, anthropology, classical/ancient civilization, economics, French studies, German area studies, history, international studies, Italian studies, Latin American studies, medieval studies, Middle Eastern studies, philosophy, political science/government, psychology, religion, social science, social work, sociology, Spanish studies, theological studies, urban studies, and women's studies). Communications, social sciences, and English are the strongest academically. Business, psychology, and history are the largest.

Required: All students must complete a core curriculum, including 2 courses each in English literature, history, philosophy, theology, natural sciences, and social sciences, 1 each in math, English composition, and fine arts, and foreign language competency. A total of 124 credits with 30 in the major and a 2.0 minimum GPA are required. A thesis is required for the honors program.

Special: Fordham University offers career-oriented internships in communications and other majors during the junior or senior year with New York City companies and institutions. A combined 3-2 engineering program is available with Columbia and Case Western Reserve Universities. Study abroad, a Washington semester, accelerated degrees, dual and student-designed majors, and pass/fail options are available. There are 6 national honor societies, including Phi Beta Kappa, and a freshman honors program.

Faculty/Classroom: 64% of faculty are male; 36%, female. 74% both teach and do research. No introductory courses are taught by graduate students. The average class size in an introductory lecture is 21; in a laboratory, 11; and in a regular course, 17.

Admissions: 54% of the 2003-2004 applicants were accepted. The SAT I scores for the 2003-2004 freshman class were: Verbal--10% below

500, 40% between 500 and 599, 40% between 600 and 700, and 9% above 700; Math--10% below 500, 41% between 500 and 599, 44% between 600 and 700, and 6% above 700. The ACT scores were 2% below 18, 26% between 18 and 23, 58% between 24 and 29, and 14% above 29. 68% of the current freshmen were in the top quarter of their class; 94% were in the top half.

Requirements: The SAT I or ACT is required. In addition, applicants should have completed 4 years of high school English and 3 each of math, science, social studies, history, and foreign language. An essay is part of the application process. An interview is recommended. Auditions are required for theater and dance majors. A GED is accepted (minimum 3000 on new scale; 300 on old scale). AP credits are accepted. Important factors in the admissions decision are leadership record, parents or siblings attending the school, and recommendations by school officials.

Procedure: Freshmen are admitted fall and spring. Entrance exams should be taken by December of the senior year. There are early action and deferred admissions plans. Early action applications should be filed by November 1; regular applications, by February 1 for fall entry and November 1 for spring entry, along with a $50 fee. Notification of early action is sent December 15; regular decision, April 1. 129 early decision candidates were accepted for the 2003-2004 class. 700 applicants were on the 2003 waiting list; 151 were admitted. Applications are accepted on-line through www.fordham.edu.

Transfer: 246 transfer students enrolled in 2002-2003. A 3.0 minimum GPA is recommended. Applicants with less than 1 full year of full-time course work at a postsecondary institution should submit SAT I or ACT scores. An interview is recommended. 64 of 124 credits required for the bachelor's degree must be completed at Fordham University.

Visiting: There are regularly scheduled orientations for prospective students. There are guides for informal visits and visitors may sit in on classes and stay overnight. To schedule a visit, contact the Admissions Office.

Financial Aid: In 2003-2004, 68% of all full-time freshmen and 65% of continuing full-time students received some form of financial aid. 63% of full-time freshmen and 61% of continuing full-time students received need-based aid. The average freshman award was $17,591. Need-based scholarships or need-based grants averaged $14,812; need-based self-help aid (loans and jobs) averaged $3780; non-need-based athletic scholarships averaged $13,259; and other non-need-based awards and non-need-based scholarships averaged $6954. 95% of undergraduates work part time. Average annual earnings from campus work are $1600. The average financial indebtedness of the 2003 graduate was $16,274. Fordham University is a member of CSS. The CSS/Profile or FAFSA is required. The deadline for filing freshman financial aid applications for fall entry is February 1.

International Students: There are 89 international students enrolled. The school actively recruits these students. They must score 575 on the written TOEFL or 231 on the electronic version and also take the college's own test and the SAT I or the ACT.

Computers: The mainframe is a DEC VAX system. More than 900 PCs are available to students in labs throughout the university's campuses. Labs can be found in the libraries, academic buildings, and residence halls. Most are connected to the mainframe and have access to the World Wide Web. All residence halls are also wired for hookup to the university network and the Internet. A wireless network is available. All students may access the system. There are no time limits and no fees.

Graduates: From July 1, 2002 to June 30, 2003, 1487 bachelor's degrees were awarded. The most popular majors were business administration/marketing (24%), social sciences/history (22%), and communications (14%). In an average class, 1% graduate in 3 years or less, 68% graduate in 4 years or less, 72% graduate in 5 years or less, and 73% graduate in 6 years or less. 500 companies recruited on campus in 2002-2003. Of the 2002 graduating class, 25% were enrolled in graduate school within 6 months of graduation and 90% were employed.

Admissions Contact: John W. Buckley, Dean of Admission.
E-mail: *enroll@fordham.edu* Web: *www.fordham.edu*

FRIENDS WORLD PROGRAM
Southampton, NY 11968

E-5
(631) 287-8474
(800)LIU-PLAN; Fax: (631) 287-8463

Full-time: 48 men, 108 women	Faculty: 18
Part-time: 4 men, 3 women	Ph.D.s: 70%
Graduate: none	Student/Faculty: 9 to 1
Year: semesters	Tuition: $20,400
Application Deadline: open	Room & Board: $4400
Freshman Class: 86 applied, 40 accepted, 27 enrolled	
SAT I or ACT: not required	COMPETITIVE

Friends World Program, founded in 1965, offers student-designed majors in the liberal arts and is located on the campus of Southampton College. Some information in the above capsule is approximate. Friends World has campuses in Costa Rica, England, India, China, and Japan, and during the 4-year program, students study at 2 or 3 of them. Much of the learning is through individually designed off-campus field experience and internships in 2 or more cultures. First-year freshman students begin their program in London and complete the senior year in New York. Costs vary by the individual center. Room and board costs range from $1200 to $4400 per semester. Fees (including travel fees) range from $450 to $2200 per semester. Contact the school for current information. The library contains 1 million volumes, 1000 microform items, and 500 audio/video tapes/CDs, and subscribes to 690 periodicals. Computerized library services include the card catalog, interlibrary loans, and database searching. Special learning facilities include a learning resource center, art gallery, radio station, and marine lab. The 110-acre campus is in a rural area 90 miles east of New York City. Including any residence halls, there are 33 buildings.

Student Life: 80% of undergraduates are from out of state, mostly the Northeast. Students are from 29 states, 10 foreign countries, and Canada. 83% are white; 10% foreign nationals. Most claim no religious affiliation. The average age of freshmen is 19; all undergraduates, 22. 20% do not continue beyond their first year; 60% remain to graduate.

Housing: 700 students can be accommodated in college housing, which includes single-sex and coed dorms and off-campus apartments. On-campus housing is guaranteed for the freshman year only. Priority is given to out-of-town students. All students may keep cars.

Activities: There are no fraternities or sororities. There are 50 groups on campus, including art, drama, environmental, ethnic, film, gay, honors, international, literary magazine, newspaper, photography, political, radio and TV, religious, social service, student government, and yearbook. Popular campus events include Ingatherings—weekend events where students on field internships return to campus for sharing and community meetings on college governance. There are also multicultural awareness activities.

Sports: There is no sports program at Friends World.

Disabled Students: 15% of the campus is accessible. Wheelchair ramps and special parking are available.

Services: Counseling and information services are available. The study center offers faculty tutoring in every subject. There is remedial math, reading, and writing.

Campus Safety and Security: Measures include 24-hour foot and vehicle patrol, self-defense education, informal discussions, and pamphlets/posters/films. There are emergency telephones and lighted pathways/sidewalks.

Programs of Study: Friends World confers the B.A. degree. Bachelor's degrees are awarded in SOCIAL SCIENCE (interdisciplinary studies).

Required: All students must complete 1 writing course and the Friends World Education Seminar. Distribution requirements include 12 credits each in area studies, human issues, and foreign language and 24 credits in liberal arts. Students are required to study 2 cultures other than their own. All students demonstrate learning by keeping portfolios. Submission of a completed portfolio is required to advance to the next year of study. There are no grades, but students are required to maintain the equivalent of a 2.0 GPA. A senior thesis and a total of 120 credit hours are required, with at least 24 hours in a major subject area.

Special: There is cross-registration with Long Island University. A work-study program is available for New York-based students. All students carry out fieldwork and internships and live abroad. Friends World offers a liberal arts degree, and the wide range of subjects include women's studies, anthropology, politics, archaeology, comparative religions, music, education, holistic medicine and healing, ecology, the arts, peace studies, and environmental studies. Student-designed majors are available.

Faculty/Classroom: 45% of faculty are male; 55%, female. All teach undergraduates. The average class size in an introductory lecture is 22 and in a regular course, 10.

Admissions: 47% of the 2003-2004 applicants were accepted.

Requirements: The SAT I or ACT is not required for regular admission but is considered if submitted. The GED is accepted, as is evidence of equivalent life experience. An essay and interview are required. A grade average of 80 is required. AP and CLEP credits are accepted. Important factors in the admissions decision are personality/intangible qualities, extracurricular activities record, and evidence of special talent.

Procedure: Freshmen are admitted in the fall. There are early admissions and deferred admissions plans. Application deadlines are open. Application fee is $30. Notification is sent on a rolling basis. Applications are accepted on-line.

Transfer: 23 transfer students enrolled in 2002-2003. Transfer applicants with a 2.0 GPA in 30 academic credits and other candidates showing interest are considered. Applicants with fewer than 30 credits must submit high school as well as college transcripts. All must have an interview. 60 of 120 credits required for the bachelor's degree must be completed at Friends World.

Visiting: There are regularly scheduled orientations for prospective students, including an airport orientation for Foundation Year, London-bound students. There are guides for informal visits and visitors may sit in on classes and stay overnight. To schedule a visit, contact the Admissions Office.

Financial Aid: In 2003-2004, 79% of all full-time freshmen and 87% of continuing full-time students received some form of financial aid. 80% of all full-time students received need-based aid. The average freshman award was $9625. Need-based scholarships or need-based grants averaged $2000 ($7000 maximum); need-based self-help aid (loans and jobs) averaged $3625 (maximum); and non-need-based awards and non-need-based scholarships averaged $1000 ($8000 maximum). The average financial indebtedness of the 2003 graduate was $25,000. Friends World is a member of CSS. The FAFSA and the college's own financial statement are required.

International Students: There are 5 international students enrolled. The school actively recruits these students. They must score 525 on the written TOEFL or 213 on the electronic version.

Computers: The mainframe is an IBM. In Southhampton, students use the LIU network, which is a node on the Internet connecting Friends World students to computers worldwide. There are 125 PCs in 6 campus locations, a 12-to-1 student/computer ratio, and computer hookups in all dorm rooms. Overseas, students have access to Friends World administrative computers, and some centers have PCs for student use. All students may access the system. There are no time limits and no fees. It is strongly recommended that all students have a personal computer.

Graduates: From July 1, 2002 to June 30, 2003, 34 bachelor's degrees were awarded. In an average class, 60% graduate in 4 years or less, 20% graduate in 5 years or less, and 5% graduate in 6 years or less. Of the 2002 graduating class, 2% were enrolled in graduate school within 6 months of graduation and 60% were employed.

Admissions Contact: Stephen Dougherty, Assistant Dean/Enrollment. E-mail: *fw@liu.edu* Web: *www.liu.edu/friendsworld*

GLOBE INSTITUTE OF TECHNOLOGY   D-5
New York, NY 10007
(212) 349-4330
877-39-GLOBE; Fax: (212) 227-5920

Full-time: 500 men, 900 women	**Faculty:** 45
Part-time: 50 men, 50 women	**Ph.D.s:** 50%
Graduate: none	**Student/Faculty:** n/av
Year: semesters, summer session	**Tuition:** $9070
Application Deadline: open	**Room & Board:** $3500
Freshman Class: 1050 applied, 940 accepted, 906 enrolled	
SAT I Verbal/Math: 500/500	**COMPETITIVE**

Globe Institute of Technology, founded in 1984, offers degrees in business administration and technology. Computerized library services include Internet access. Special learning facilities include an art gallery. The campus is in an urban area in New York City. There is 1 building.

Student Life: 90% of undergraduates are from New York. 90% are from public schools. 25% are African American; 25% Asian American; 25% white; 15% Hispanic; 10% foreign nationals.

Housing: College housing includes single-sex dorms, off-campus apartments, and married-student housing. In addition, there are special-interest houses. On-campus housing is guaranteed for all 4 years. 85% of students commute. Alcohol is not permitted. All students may keep cars.

Activities: There are no fraternities or sororities. There are many groups and organizations on campus, including art, cheerleading, chess, computers, dance, international, literary magazine, newspaper, social, student government, and yearbook.

Sports: There are 4 intercollegiate sports for men and 3 for women.

Disabled Students: All of the campus is accessible. Wheelchair ramps, elevators, and special class scheduling are available.

Services: Counseling and information services are available, as is tutoring in every subject. There is remedial math, reading, and writing.

Campus Safety and Security: Measures include informal discussions, pamphlets/posters/films, and lighted pathways/sidewalks.

Programs of Study: Globe confers B.B.A. and B.Tech. degrees. Associate degrees are also awarded. Computer science is the strongest academically. Business management is the largest.

Required: To graduate, students must complete at least 128 credit hours with 64 in the major and a 3.0 GPA.

Special: Credit and noncredit internships, work-study programs, and an accelerated degree program in business management are available. There is a freshman honors program.

Faculty/Classroom: 40% of faculty are male; 60%, female. All teach undergraduates. The average class size in an introductory lecture is 15 and in a regular course, 8.

Admissions: 90% of the 2003-2004 applicants were accepted.

Requirements: The SAT I is recommended. A GPA of 3.0 is required. AP credits are accepted. Important factors in the admissions decision are evidence of special talent, leadership record, and extracurricular activities record.

Procedure: Freshmen are admitted fall, spring, and summer. There is a deferred admissions plan and a rolling admissions plan. Application deadlines are open. The application fee is $50. Applications are accepted on computer disk and on-line through *www.globe.edu*.

Transfer: 32 of 128 credits required for the bachelor's degree must be completed at Globe.

Visiting: There are regularly scheduled orientations for prospective students. There are guides for informal visits and visitors may sit in on classes and stay overnight. To schedule a visit, contact the admissions director at *admission@globe.edu*.

Financial Aid: In 2003–2004, 85% of all students received some form of financial aid, including need-based aid. The FAFSA and the college's own financial statement are required. Check with the school for current deadlines.

International Students: There are 50 international students enrolled. The school actively recruits these students. They must take the college's own test.

Computers: The mainframe is an MVS390. 250 computers are available on campus for student use. All students may access the system 8 A.M. to 10 P.M. There are no time limits and no fees. It is strongly recommended that all students have a personal computer.

Admissions Contact: Tatiana Garelik, Admissions Director. A video is available. E-mail: *admissions@globe.edu* Web: *www.globe.edu*

HAMILTON COLLEGE
Clinton, NY 13323

C-3

(315) 859-4421
(800) 843-2655; Fax: (315) 859-4457

Full-time: 874 men, 901 women	Faculty: 216; IIB, ++$
Part-time: 22 men and women	Ph.D.s: 88%
Graduate: none	Student/Faculty: 8 to 1
Year: semesters	Tuition: $30,200
Application Deadline: see profile	Room & Board: $7360
Freshman Class: 4405 applied, 1459 accepted, 465 enrolled	
SAT I Verbal/Math: 660/670	MOST COMPETITIVE

Hamilton College, founded in 1793, is a private, nonsectarian, liberal arts school offering undergraduate programs in the arts and sciences. The 3 libraries contain 577,031 volumes, 416,230 microform items, and 57,096 audio/video tapes/CDs, and subscribe to 3645 periodicals. Computerized library services include the card catalog and database searching. Special learning facilities include an art gallery, radio station, and an observatory. The 1200-acre campus is in a rural area 9 miles southwest of Utica. Including any residence halls, there are 51 buildings.

Student Life: 63% of undergraduates are from out of state, mostly the Northeast. Students are from 45 states, 29 foreign countries, and Canada. 60% are from public schools. 85% are white. 31% are Catholic; 30% Protestant; 25% claim no religious affiliation; 8% Jewish. The average age of freshmen is 18; all undergraduates, 20. 6% do not continue beyond their first year; 87% remain to graduate.

Housing: 1700 students can be accommodated in college housing, which includes coed dorms, on-campus apartments, and married-student housing. In addition, there are language houses, special-interest houses, quiet floors, substance-free areas, and a cooperative. On-campus housing is guaranteed for all 4 years. 96% of students live on campus; of those, 95% remain on campus on weekends. Upperclassmen may keep cars.

Activities: 34% of men belong to 8 national fraternities; 20% of women belong to 3 local sororities. There are 60 groups on campus, including art, chess, choir, chorale, chorus, computers, dance, drama, ethnic, film, gay, honors, international, jazz band, literary magazine, musical theater, newspaper, pep band, photography, political, professional, radio, religious, social, social service, student government, and yearbook. Popular campus events include Class and Charter Day, Winterfest, and Springfest.

Sports: There are 12 intercollegiate sports for men and 12 for women, and 26 intramural sports for men and 29 for women. Facilities include a gym, a field house, squash and racquetball courts, indoor and outdoor tennis courts, a football stadium, a 9-hole golf course, a swimming pool, indoor and outdoor tracks, numerous grass fields, an artificial turf field, paddle tennis courts, and an ice rink.

Disabled Students: Wheelchair ramps, elevators, special parking, specially equipped rest rooms, and special class scheduling are available.

Services: Counseling and information services are available, as is tutoring in some subjects through the New York State Higher Education Opportunity Program (HEOP).

Campus Safety and Security: Measures include 24-hour foot and vehicle patrol, self-defense education, security escort services, and shuttle buses. There are informal discussions, pamphlets/posters/films, emergency telephones, and lighted pathways/sidewalks.

Programs of Study: Hamilton confers the B.A. degree. Bachelor's degrees are awarded in BIOLOGICAL SCIENCE (biochemistry, biology/biological science, and neurosciences), COMMUNICATIONS AND THE ARTS (art, art history and appreciation, classics, communications, comparative literature, creative writing, dance, dramatic arts, English, French, German, languages, music, Spanish, and studio art), COMPUTER AND PHYSICAL SCIENCE (chemistry, computer science, geology, mathematics, and physics), SOCIAL SCIENCE (African studies, American studies, anthropology, archeology, Asian/Oriental studies, classical/ancient civilization, economics, history, international relations, philosophy, political science/government, psychobiology, psychology, public af-

fairs, religion, Russian and Slavic studies, sociology, and women's studies). Government, economics, and psychology are the largest.

Required: Students must successfully complete 128 credits, with 32 to 40 of these in the student's major, and must maintain at least a 72 average in half the courses taken. Students are required to take 2 courses in each academic division, 3 courses designated as writing intensive, and at least 2 courses covering human diversity and ethical issues, as well as 2 semesters of phys ed. A senior project in the student's major is also required.

Special: Cross-registration is permitted with Colgate University and Utica College of Syracuse University. Opportunities are provided for internships, a cooperative program through the Williams College Mystic Seaport Program in Connecticut, and a Washington semester. Accelerated degree programs, dual majors, nondegree study, pass/fail options, student-designed majors, a program for early assurance of acceptance to medical school, and study abroad in many countries are available. 3-2 engineering degrees are offered with Washington University, Rensselaer Polytechnic Institute, and Columbia University. There are 4 national honor societies, including Phi Beta Kappa.

Faculty/Classroom: 59% of faculty are male; 41%, female. All teach undergraduates.

Admissions: 33% of the 2003-2004 applicants were accepted. The SAT I scores for the 2003-2004 freshman class were: Verbal--3% below 500, 17% between 500 and 599, 50% between 600 and 700, and 30% above 700; Math--2% below 500, 10% between 500 and 599, 59% between 600 and 700, and 29% above 700. 83% of the current freshmen were in the top fifth of their class; 97% were in the top two fifths.

Requirements: The SAT I or ACT is required. In addition, although graduation from an accredited secondary school or a GED is desirable, and a full complement of college-preparatory courses is recommended, Hamilton will consider all highly recommended candidates who demonstrate an ability and desire to perform at intellectually demanding levels. An essay is required, and an interview is recommended. AP credits are accepted. Important factors in the admissions decision are advanced placement or honor courses, recommendations by school officials, and parents or siblings attending the school.

Procedure: Freshmen are admitted in the fall. Entrance exams should be taken prior to February of the senior year. There are early decision, early admissions, and deferred admissions plans. Check with the school for current application deadlines. The fall 2003 application fee was $50. 191 early decision candidates were accepted for the 2003-2004 class. 15 wait-listed applicants were admitted. Applications are accepted on-line through the school's web site at *www.hamilton.edu/admission/application/download.html*.

Transfer: 6 transfer students enrolled in 2002-2003. Transfer applicants must submit high school and college transcripts, an essay or personal statement, and standardized test scores, and must present a minimum GPA of 3.0 in all college-level work. 64 of 128 credits required for the bachelor's degree must be completed at Hamilton.

Visiting: There are regularly scheduled orientations for prospective students, consisting of an interview, tour, class visit, and open house program. There are guides for informal visits and visitors may sit in on classes and stay overnight. To schedule a visit, contact the Admissions Office.

Financial Aid: In a recent year, 55% of all full-time freshmen and 59% of continuing full-time students received some form of financial aid. 52% of full-time freshmen and 56% of continuing full-time students received need-based aid. The average freshman award was $21,520. 48% of undergraduates work part time. Average annual earnings from campus work are $1400. The average financial indebtedness of the 2003 graduate was $16,776. Hamilton is a member of CSS. The CSS Profile or FAFSA is required. The deadline for filing freshman financial aid applications for fall entry is February 1.

International Students: There were 59 international students enrolled in a recent year. The school actively recruits these students. They must take the SAT I, SAT II, or ACT.

Computers: The mainframes are a comprised of a DEC 5100, DEC 5000/25, and DEC 5500. There are 475 college-owned computers accessible to students. Students have full access to the Internet, including in residence halls. All students may access the system. There are no time limits and no fees.

Graduates: From July 1, 2002 to June 30, 2003, 463 bachelor's degrees were awarded. The most popular majors were economics (12%), government (10%), and psychology (7%). In an average class, 1% graduate in 3 years or less, 82% graduate in 4 years or less, 86% graduate in 5 years or less, and 87% graduate in 6 years or less.

Admissions Contact: Lora Schilder, Dean of Admissions.
E-mail: *admission@hamilton.edu* Web: *www.hamilton.edu*

HARTWICK COLLEGE
Oneonta, NY 13820-4020

D-3

(607) 431-4157
(888) HARTWICK; Fax: (607) 431-4102

Full-time: 600 men, 812 women	**Faculty:** 101; IIB, av$
Part-time: 23 men, 31 women	**Ph.D.s:** 94%
Graduate: none	**Student/Faculty:** 14 to 1
Year: 4-1-4	**Tuition:** $27,400
Application Deadline: February 15	**Room & Board:** $7250
Freshman Class: 2056 applied, 1815 accepted, 446 enrolled	
SAT I Verbal/Math: 557/564	**ACT:** 24 COMPETITIVE+

Hartwick College, founded in 1797, is a private undergraduate liberal arts and sciences college. In addition to regional accreditation, Hartwick has baccalaureate program accreditation with NASAD, NASM, and NLN. The library contains 348,699 volumes, 56,817 microform items, and 1400 audio/video tapes/CDs. Computerized library services include the card catalog, interlibrary loans, and database searching. Special learning facilities include an art gallery, radio station, TV station, a museum, 914-acre environmental study center, observatory, and an environmental field station. The 425-acre campus is in a small town 75 miles southwest of Albany. Including any residence halls, there are 28 buildings.

Student Life: 64% of undergraduates are from New York. Students are from 30 states, 35 foreign countries, and Canada. 84% are from public schools. 64% are white. The average age of freshmen is 18; all undergraduates, 20. 22% do not continue beyond their first year; 57% remain to graduate.

Housing: 1259 students can be accommodated in college housing, which includes single-sex and coed dorms, on-campus apartments, fraternity houses, and sorority houses. In addition, there are special-interest houses, substance-free housing, and an environmental campus. On-campus housing is guaranteed for all 4 years. 88% of students live on campus; of those, 90% remain on campus on weekends. All students may keep cars.

Activities: 15% of men belong to 1 local and 4 national fraternities; 17% of women belong to 3 local and 1 national sorority. There are 60 groups on campus, including academic, art, band, cheerleading, choir, chorale, chorus, computers, dance, drama, ethnic, film, gay, honors, international, jazz band, literary magazine, musical theater, newspaper, orchestra, outing, pep band, photography, political, professional, radio and TV, religious, social, social service, student government, and yearbook. Popular campus events include Holiday Ball, Earth Day, and Multicultural Month.

Sports: There are 11 intercollegiate sports for men and 13 for women, and 9 intramural sports for men and 9 for women. Facilities include 2 gyms, an indoor pool, a dance room, athletic and training facilities, a track, a Nautilus exercise gym, a fitness center, a lighted all-weather playing field, a lighted soccer field, a minor league field for baseball, an equestrian complex, and courts for handball, racquetball, squash, and tennis.

Disabled Students: 50% of the campus is accessible. Wheelchair ramps, elevators, special parking, specially equipped rest rooms, special class scheduling, lowered drinking fountains, and lowered telephones are available.

Services: Counseling and information services are available, as is tutoring in every subject. There is a reader service for the blind. There are writing and math centers and an academic center for excellence.

Campus Safety and Security: Measures include 24-hour foot and vehicle patrol, self-defense education, security escort services, and shuttle buses. There are informal discussions, pamphlets/posters/films, emergency telephones, and lighted pathways/sidewalks.

Programs of Study: Hartwick confers B.A. and B.S. degrees. Bachelor's degrees are awarded in BIOLOGICAL SCIENCE (biochemistry and biology/biological science), BUSINESS (accounting and business administration and management), COMMUNICATIONS AND THE ARTS (art, art history and appreciation, dramatic arts, English, French, German, languages, music, and Spanish), COMPUTER AND PHYSICAL SCIENCE (chemistry, computer science, geology, information sciences and systems, mathematics, and physics), EDUCATION (music), HEALTH PROFESSIONS (medical technology and nursing), SOCIAL SCIENCE (anthropology, economics, history, philosophy, political science/government, psychology, religion, and sociology). Anthropology, chemistry, and nursing are the strongest academically. Psychology, management, and nursing are the largest.

Required: Students must complete 36 course units with at least a 2.0 GPA. Core requirements are in the study areas of continuity, interdependence, science and technology, critical thinking, effective communication, and electives. Courses are chosen from offerings in humanities, science and math, social and behavioral sciences, foreign language, and phys ed. A first-year seminar and a contemporary issues seminar for juniors and seniors are required. Students are strongly urged to include an off-campus learning experience.

Special: Students may design their own majors and choose independent study. Cross-registration with SUNY College at Oneonta is possible

and local and international internships are available. There is a January thematic term, a Washington semester, and study abroad in 30 countries. First-year students may participate in specially designated off-campus programs. Experiential programs include Outward Bound and the National Outdoor Leadership School. All departments offer dual majors and accelerated degree options. There is a 3-2 engineering program with Clarkson University or Columbia University, a 3-3 program with Albany Law School, and a 4-1 business program with Clarkson University. There are 10 national honor societies and a freshman honors program.

Faculty/Classroom: 54% of faculty are male; 46%, female. All teach undergraduates. The average class size in an introductory lecture is 20; in a laboratory, 20; and in a regular course, 30.

Admissions: 88% of the 2003-2004 applicants were accepted. The SAT I scores for the 2003-2004 freshman class were: Verbal--18% below 500, 53% between 500 and 599, 26% between 600 and 700, and 3% above 700; Math--17% below 500, 52% between 500 and 599, 28% between 600 and 700, and 4% above 700. 36% of the current freshmen were in the top fifth of their class; 71% were in the top two fifths. 5 freshmen graduated first in their class.

Requirements: Reporting of SAT I and ACT scores is optional. The recommended secondary course of study includes 4 years of English, and 3 years each of math, a foreign language, history, and lab science. Hartwick strongly recommends that applicants plan a campus visit and interview. Prospective art majors should submit a portfolio, and music majors must audition. Computer disks are offered to all prospective students, providing information about the college as well as an application. AP and CLEP credits are accepted. Important factors in the admissions decision are advanced placement or honor courses, recommendations by school officials, and ability to finance college education.

Procedure: Freshmen are admitted to all sessions. Entrance exams should be taken in the spring of the junior year and/or the fall of the senior year. There are early decision and deferred admissions plans. Early decision applications should be filed by January 15; regular applications, by February 15 for fall entry, December 1 for winter entry, and January 1 for spring entry. Notification of early decision is sent on a rolling basis; regular decision, March 15. 75 early decision candidates were accepted for the 2003-2004 class. A waiting list is an active part of the admissions procedure. The fall 2003 application fee was $35. Applications are accepted on-line through the school's web site.

Transfer: 45 transfer students enrolled in a recent year. Applicants should present a minimum GPA of 2.0. 18 of 36 credits required for the bachelor's degree must be completed at Hartwick.

Visiting: There are regularly scheduled orientations for prospective students, consisting of an interview and tour, lunch, departmental open houses, presentations on student life, off-campus programs, and a career planning process. There are guides for informal visits and visitors may sit in on classes and stay overnight. To schedule a visit, contact the Admissions Office.

Financial Aid: In a recent year, 79% of all full-time freshmen and 78% of continuing full-time students received some form of financial aid. The average freshman award was $22,000. 66% of undergraduates work part time. Average annual earnings from campus work are $1400. The average financial indebtedness of a recent graduate was $19,364. Hartwick is a member of CSS. The FAFSA and the college's own financial statement are required. The deadline for filing freshman financial aid applications for fall entry is February 15.

International Students: There are 60 international students enrolled. The school actively recruits these students. They must score 500 on the written TOEFL or take the MELAB.

Computers: The mainframe is comprised of 3 IBM Netfinity 5500 MZ0 servers. All students are provided with a printer and a notebook computer, which they can connect to the network from anywhere on campus. All students may access the system 24 hours per day, 7 days per week. There are no time limits and no fees.

Graduates: From July 1, 2002 to June 30, 2003, 270 bachelor's degrees were awarded. The most popular majors were management (18%), psychology (11%), and history (8%). In an average class, 48% graduate in 4 years or less, 55% graduate in 5 years or less, and 57% graduate in 6 years or less. 20 companies recruited on campus in 2002-2003.

Admissions Contact: Patricia Maben, Director.
E-mail: admissions@hartwick.edu Web: http://www.hartwick.edu

HILBERT COLLEGE
A-3
Hamburg, NY 14075-1597

(716) 649-7900, ext. 211
(800) 649-8003; Fax: (716) 649-0702

Full-time: 308 men, 406 women	**Faculty:** 39; IIB, --$
Part-time: 86 men, 255 women	**Ph.D.s:** 51%
Graduate: none	**Student/Faculty:** 18 to 1
Year: semesters, summer session	**Tuition:** $13,500
Application Deadline: open	**Room & Board:** $5670
Freshman Class: 380 applied, 357 accepted, 162 enrolled	
SAT I Verbal/Math: 467/465	**ACT:** 19 **LESS COMPETITIVE**

Hilbert College, founded in 1957, is a private institution offering degree programs in business, criminal justice, and social sciences. The library contains 41,322 volumes, 22,089 microform items, and 1025 audio/video tapes/CDs, and subscribes to 12,753 periodicals. Computerized library services include the card catalog, interlibrary loans, and database searching. Special learning facilities include a learning resource center. The 44-acre campus is in an urban area about 15 miles south of Buffalo. Including any residence halls, there are 6 buildings.

Student Life: 99% of undergraduates are from New York. Students are from 6 states, 3 foreign countries, and Canada. 86% are from public schools. 88% are white. The average age of freshmen is 24; all undergraduates, 26. 26% do not continue beyond their first year; 74% remain to graduate.

Housing: 134 students can be accommodated in college housing, which includes coed dorms, on-campus apartments, and off-campus apartments. On-campus housing is guaranteed for all 4 years. 88% of students commute. All students may keep cars.

Activities: There are no fraternities or sororities. There are 20 groups on campus, including academic, cheerleading, chorus, ethnic, honors, literary magazine, newspaper, professional, religious, social, social service, and student government. Popular campus events include Quad Party, Welcome Back Picnic, and Fall Family Weekend.

Sports: There are 5 intercollegiate sports for men and 6 for women, and 4 intramural sports for men and 4 for women. Facilities include a soccer/lacrosse field, baseball and softball diamonds, a practice field, a weight room, and a 900-seat NCAA regulation indoor athletic facility.

Disabled Students: 95% of the campus is accessible. Wheelchair ramps, elevators, special parking, specially equipped rest rooms, special class scheduling, lowered drinking fountains, and lowered telephones are available.

Services: Counseling and information services are available, as is tutoring in some subjects, including writing, accounting, and math. There is remedial math and writing.

Campus Safety and Security: Measures include 24-hour foot and vehicle patrol, self-defense education, security escort services, and informal discussions. There are pamphlets/posters/films, emergency telephones, and lighted pathways/sidewalks.

Programs of Study: Hilbert confers B.A. and B.S. degrees. Associate degrees are also awarded. Bachelor's degrees are awarded in BUSINESS (accounting and business administration and management), COMMUNICATIONS AND THE ARTS (English), SOCIAL SCIENCE (criminal justice, criminology, human services, liberal arts/general studies, paralegal studies, and psychology). Economic crime investigation, paralegal studies, and accounting are the strongest academically. Criminal justice, economic crime investigation, and business administration are the largest.

Required: To graduate, students must complete 120 credit hours, including at least 36 in the major and 60 in liberal arts, with a minimum 2.0 GPA. Students must fulfill requirements in English, math, philosophy, social sciences, and senior seminar.

Special: Hilbert offers cross-registration with other members of the Western New York College Consortium, internships in most majors, and work-study programs. The college maintains articulation agreements with New York State community colleges. There are 4 national honor societies, a freshman honors program, and 3 departmental honors programs.

Faculty/Classroom: 60% of faculty are male; 40%, female. All teach undergraduates and 10% do research. The average class size in an introductory lecture is 20; in a laboratory, 4; and in a regular course, 15.

Admissions: 94% of the 2003-2004 applicants were accepted. The SAT I scores for the 2003-2004 freshman class were: Verbal--68% below 500, 26% between 500 and 599, and 6% between 600 and 700; Math--66% below 500, 31% between 500 and 599, and 3% between 600 and 700. The ACT scores were 44% below 21, 36% between 21 and 23, 8% between 24 and 26, and 12% between 27 and 28. 14% of the current freshmen were in the top fifth of their class; 46% were in the top two fifths.

Requirements: The SAT I or ACT is recommended. A grade average of 70 is required. AP and CLEP credits are accepted. Important factors in the admissions decision are leadership record, advanced placement or honor courses, and recommendations by school officials.

Procedure: Freshmen are admitted to all sessions. There is a deferred admissions plan. There is a rolling admissions plan. Application dead-

lines are open. The fall 2003 application fee was $20. Applications are accepted on-line through the school's web site.

Transfer: 145 transfer students enrolled in 2002-2003. Applicants must submit official transcripts from all colleges attended and, in somes cases, the high school transcript. 30 of 120 credits required for the bachelor's degree must be completed at Hilbert.

Visiting: There are regularly scheduled orientations for prospective students, consisting of a campus tour, a student panel, and admissions, financial aid, and academic information sessions. There are guides for informal visits and visitors may sit in on classes and stay overnight. To schedule a visit, contact the Office of Admissions.

Financial Aid: In 2003-2004, 91% of all full-time freshmen and 89% of continuing full-time students received some form of financial aid. 100% of full-time freshmen and 98% of continuing full-time students received need-based aid. The average freshman award was $10,552. Need-based scholarships or need-based grants averaged $2570 ($5000 maximum); need-based self-help aid (loans and jobs) averaged $3642 ($5500 maximum); and non-need-based awards and non-need-based scholarships averaged $2855 ($5000 maximum). 7% of undergraduates work part time. Average annual earnings from campus work are $1735. The average financial indebtedness of the 2003 graduate was $16,295. Hilbert is a member of CSS. The FAFSA is required. The priority date for freshman financial aid applications for fall entry is April 1. The deadline for filing freshman financial aid applications for fall entry is December 1.

International Students: They must score 500 on the written TOEFL or 173 on the electronic version.

Computers: There are 9 computer labs with 156 stations or terminals, all Internet accessible. All students may access the system. There are no time limits. The fee is $25 per semester.

Graduates: From July 1, 2002 to June 30, 2003, 179 bachelor's degrees were awarded. The most popular majors were criminal justice (25%), business administration (18%), and paralegal studies (17%). In an average class, 34% graduate in 3 years or less, 24% graduate in 4 years or less, and 4% graduate in 5 years or less. 40 companies recruited on campus in 2002-2003. Of the 2002 graduating class, 8% were enrolled in graduate school within 6 months of graduation and 69% were employed.

Admissions Contact: Director of Admissions. A video is available. E-mail: *admissions@hilbert.edu* Web: *www.hilbert.edu*

HOBART AND WILLIAM SMITH COLLEGES
C-3
Geneva, NY 14456-3397   H: (315) 781-3622; WS: (315) 781-3472
H: (800) 852-2256; WS: (800) 245-0100; Fax: (315) 781-3471

Full-time: 831 men, 1035 women	**Faculty:** 156; IIB, +$
Part-time: 7 men and women	**Ph.D.s:** 95%
Graduate: none	**Student/Faculty:** 12 to 1
Year: semesters	**Tuition:** $28,948
Application Deadline: February 1	**Room & Board:** $7588
Freshman Class: 3277 applied, 2054 accepted, 517 enrolled	
SAT I or ACT: required	**HIGHLY COMPETITIVE**

Hobart College, a men's college founded in 1822, shares campus, classes, and faculty with William Smith College, a women's college founded in 1908. Together, these coordinate colleges offer degree programs in the liberal arts. The library contains 375,762 volumes, 77,396 microform items, and 9600 audio/video tapes/CDs, and subscribes to 1926 periodicals. Computerized library services include the card catalog, interlibrary loans, database searching, and Internet access. Special learning facilities include a learning resource center, art gallery, radio station, a 100-acre natural preserve, and a 70-foot research vessel. The 170-acre campus is in a small town 50 miles west of Syracuse and 50 miles east of Rochester, on the north shore of Seneca Lake. Including any residence halls, there are 95 buildings.

Student Life: 51% of undergraduates are from out of state, mostly the Northeast. Students are from 40 states, 19 foreign countries, and Canada. 65% are from public schools. 86% are white. 30% are Catholic; 30% Protestant; 20% claim no religious affiliation; 15% Jewish. The average age of freshmen is 18; all undergraduates, 20. 15% do not continue beyond their first year; 75% remain to graduate.

Housing: 1500 students can be accommodated in college housing, which includes single-sex and coed dorms, on-campus apartments, and fraternity houses. In addition, there are honors houses, language houses, special-interest houses, cooperative houses in which students plan and prepare their own meals, and townhouses for upperclassmen. On-campus housing is guaranteed for all 4 years. 90% of students live on campus; of those, 93% remain on campus on weekends. All students may keep cars.

Activities: 15% of men belong to 5 national fraternities. There are no sororities. There are 70 groups on campus, including art, chess, choir, chorale, chorus, computers, dance, debate, drama, ethnic, film, forensics, gay, honors, international, jazz band, literary magazine, musical theater, newspaper, orchestra, photography, political, professional, radio and TV, religious, social, social service, student government, symphony, and yearbook. Popular campus events include Folk Festival, Charter Day, and Moving Up Day.

Sports: There are 11 intercollegiate sports for men and 11 for women, and 23 intramural sports for men and 23 for women. Facilities include a sport and recreation center, 2 gyms, numerous athletic fields, a swimming pool, 5 indoor tennis courts, 3 weight rooms, basketball and racquetball courts, an indoor track, international squash courts, a boat house, and a crew facility.

Disabled Students: Wheelchair ramps, elevators, special parking, specially equipped rest rooms, special class scheduling, and lowered drinking fountains are available.

Services: Counseling and information services are available, as is tutoring in every subject. There is a reader service for the blind, and remedial math, reading, and writing. There is a counseling center staffed by 5 therapists/counselors as well as various support groups and educational workshops.

Campus Safety and Security: Measures include 24-hour foot and vehicle patrol, self-defense education, security escort services, and shuttle buses. There are informal discussions, pamphlets/posters/films, emergency telephones, and lighted pathways/sidewalks.

Programs of Study: HWS confers B.A. and B.S. degrees. Master's degrees are also awarded. Bachelor's degrees are awarded in BIOLOGICAL SCIENCE (biology/biological science), COMMUNICATIONS AND THE ARTS (art history and appreciation, classics, comparative literature, dance, English, fine arts, French, modern language, music, and studio art), COMPUTER AND PHYSICAL SCIENCE (chemistry, computer science, geoscience, mathematics, and physics), ENGINEERING AND ENVIRONMENTAL DESIGN (architecture and environmental science), SOCIAL SCIENCE (African studies, American studies, anthropology, Asian/Oriental studies, economics, European studies, history, international relations, Latin American studies, philosophy, political science/government, psychology, religion, Russian and Slavic studies, sociology, Spanish studies, urban studies, and women's studies). Natural sciences, environmental studies, and creative writing are the strongest academically. English, economics, and political science are the largest.

Required: All first-year students must take a seminar. Students should complete a major of 14 to 18 courses and a minor of 6 to 8 courses, or a second major. Of the major or the minor (or second major), one must be disciplinary and the other interdisciplinary. Minimum grade and GPA standards apply. In addition, all students must meet the 8 goals established by the faculty to ensure breadth across the disciplines as well as depth in the major.

Special: Students are encouraged to spend at least 1 term in a study-abroad program, offered in more than 29 countries and locales within the United States. Options include a United Nations term, a Washington semester, an urban semester, and prearchitecture semesters in New York, Paris, Florence, or Copenhagen. HWS offers dual and student-designed majors, internships, credit for life/military/work experience, nondegree study, and pass/fail options. There are also advanced business degree programs with Clarkson University and Rochester Institute of Technology and 3-2 engineering degrees with Columbia University, Rensselaer Polytechnic Institute, and Dartmouth College. There are 9 national honor societies, including Phi Beta Kappa. All departments have honors program.

Faculty/Classroom: 60% of faculty are male; 40%, female. All both teach and do research. The average class size in an introductory lecture is 40; in a laboratory, 18; and in a regular course, 18.

Admissions: 63% of the 2003-2004 applicants were accepted. The SAT I scores for the 2003-2004 freshman class were: Verbal--11% below 500, 48% between 500 and 599, 36% between 600 and 700, and 5% above 700; Math--7% below 500, 48% between 500 and 599, 41% between 600 and 700, and 5% above 700. 60% of the current freshmen were in the top fifth of their class; 85% were in the top two fifths. 5 freshmen graduated first in their class.

Requirements: The SAT I or ACT is required. SAT II: Subject tests are not required but will be considered if taken. A GED may be accepted. A total of 19 academic credits is required, including 4 years of English, 3 of math, and at least 3 each of lab science, foreign language, and history. An essay is required; an interview is recommended. AP credits are accepted. Important factors in the admissions decision are advanced placement or honor courses, evidence of special talent, and leadership record.

Procedure: Freshmen are admitted in the fall. Entrance exams should be taken no later than December of the senior year. There are early decision, early admissions, and deferred admissions plans. Early decision applications should be filed by November 15 (Early Decision I) and January 1 (Early Decision II); regular applications, by February 1 for fall entry, along with a $45 fee. Notification of early decision is sent December 15 (Early Decision I) and February 1 (Early Decision II); regular decision, late March. 123 early decision candidates were accepted for the 2003-2004 class. 362 were on the 2003 waiting list; 24 were admitted. Applications are accepted on computer disk and on-line through Common Application or the school's web site.

Transfer: 29 transfer students enrolled in 2002-2003. Applicants must have a 2.5 GPA and have completed 1 year of college study. They are

required to take the SAT I or ACT. An interview is recommended. 16 of 32 courses required for the bachelor's degree must be completed at HWS.

Visiting: There are regularly scheduled orientations for prospective students, including 7 open houses in the spring, summer, and fall and daily tours and personal interviews year round. Information sessions are offered February through April and on Saturdays in the summer. There are guides for informal visits and visitors may sit in on classes and stay overnight. To schedule a visit, contact the Office of Admissions at *admissions@hws.edu*.

Financial Aid: In 2003-2004, 70% of all full-time students received some form of financial aid. 60% of full-time freshmen and 65% of continuing full-time students received need-based aid. The average freshman award was $22,963. Need-based scholarships or need-based grants averaged $19,838 ($23,000 maximum); need-based self-help aid (loans and jobs) averaged $5800 ($8425 maximum); and non-need-based awards and non-need-based scholarships averaged $10,847 ($28,400 maximum). 52% of undergraduates work part time. Average annual earnings from campus work are $677. The average financial indebtedness of the 2003 graduate was $20,508. HWS is a member of CSS. The CSS/Profile or FAFSA is required. The priority date for freshman financial aid applications for fall entry is February 1.

International Students: There are 43 international students enrolled. The school actively recruits these students. They must score 550 on the written TOEFL or 220 on the electronic version and also take the SAT I or the ACT.

Computers: The mainframes are a DEC Alpha 2100 and a DEC VAX 6520. There are 122 PCs and 60 terminals directly connected to the mainframe, with 114 PCs networked. The 4 PC labs provide access to the on-line library catalog system, e-mail, and the Internet. All students have e-mail accounts, and computers in student rooms are directly connected to the mainframe. All students may access the system from 8 A.M. to 1 A.M., 7 days a week. There are no time limits and no fees. It is strongly recommended that all students have a personal computer.

Graduates: From July 1, 2002 to June 30, 2003, 365 bachelor's degrees were awarded. The most popular majors were English (10%), economics (9%), and history (8%). In an average class, 65% graduate in 4 years or less, 70% graduate in 5 years or less, and 72% graduate in 6 years or less. Of the 2002 graduating class, 27% were enrolled in graduate school within 6 months of graduation and 82% were employed.

Admissions Contact: Mara O'Laughlin, Director of Admissions. E-mail: *olaughlin@hws.edu* Web: *www.hws.edu*

HOFSTRA UNIVERSITY   D-5
Hempstead, NY 11549   **(516) 463-6700**
                              (800) HOFSTRA; Fax: (516) 560-7660

Full-time: 3882 men, 4487 women	Faculty: 393; I, av$
Part-time: 485 men, 533 women	Ph.D.s: 90%
Graduate: 1358 men, 2476 women	Student/Faculty: 21 to 1
Year: 4-1-4, summer session	Tuition: $18,412
Application Deadline: December 31	Room & Board: $8700
Freshman Class: 11,691 applied, 8000 accepted, 1877 enrolled	
SAT I Verbal/Math: 560/570	ACT: 24 VERY COMPETITIVE

Hofstra University, founded in 1935, is an independent institution offering programs in liberal arts and sciences, business, communications, and education. There are 8 undergraduate and 6 graduate schools. In addition to regional accreditation, Hofstra has baccalaureate program accreditation with AACSB, ABA, ABET, ACEJMC, ACS, APA, ASHA, CAAHEP, CORE, and NCATE. The 3 libraries contain 1.2 million volumes, 3,459,162 microform items, and 10,677 audio/video tapes/CDs, and subscribe to 8556 periodicals. Computerized library services include the card catalog, interlibrary loans, database searching, and Internet access. Special learning facilities include a learning resource center, art gallery, radio station, TV station, museum, arboretum, bird sanctuary, writing center, career center, cultural center, language lab, technology lab, a rooftop observatory, 7 theaters, assessment centers for child observation and mock counseling, and child care institute. The 240-acre campus is in a suburban area 25 miles east of New York City. Including any residence halls, there are 113 buildings.

Student Life: 75% of undergraduates are from New York. Students are from 45 states, 61 foreign countries, and Canada. 61% are white. The average age of freshmen is 18; all undergraduates, 21. 26% do not continue beyond their first year; 56% remain to graduate.

Housing: 4200 students can be accommodated in college housing, which includes single-sex and coed dorms, off-campus apartments, and married-student housing. In addition, there are honors houses, special-interest houses, international student housing, freshman housing, and nonsmoking and quiet floors. There is also some apartment-style housing. On-campus housing is available on a first-come, first-served basis and is available on a lottery system for upperclassmen. 57% of students commute. All students may keep cars.

Activities: 5% of men belong to 2 local and 18 national fraternities; 6% of women belong to 4 local and 8 national sororities. There are 144

groups on campus, including art, band, cheerleading, chess, choir, chorale, chorus, commuter, computers, dance, debate, drama, drum and bugle corps, ethnic, film, forensics, gay, honors, international, jazz band, literary magazine, musical theater, newspaper, opera, orchestra, pep band, photography, political, professional, radio and TV, religious, resident student, social, social service, student government, symphony, and yearbook. Popular campus events include a Shakespeare festival, Italian American, Irish, and Dutch festivals, and Hands Across Hofstra.

Sports: There are 9 intercollegiate sports for men and 9 for women, and 6 intramural sports for men and 6 for women. Facilities include a 15,000-seat stadium, a 5000-seat arena, a 1600-seat soccer stadium, a physical fitness center, a swim center with an Olympic-size swimming pool and high-dive area, a softball stadium, and a recreation center with a multipurpose gym, an indoor track, a weight room, a lounge area, a cardio area, and a mirrored aerobics and martial arts room.

Disabled Students: All of the campus is accessible. Wheelchair ramps, elevators, special parking, specially equipped rest rooms, special class scheduling, lowered drinking fountains, lowered telephones, special housing, automated door openings, and TTY visual telephones are available.

Services: Counseling and information services are available, as is tutoring in most subjects. There is a reader service for the blind, and remedial math, reading, and writing.

Campus Safety and Security: Measures include 24-hour foot and vehicle patrol, self-defense education, security escort services, and shuttle buses. There are informal discussions, pamphlets/posters/films, emergency telephones, lighted pathways/sidewalks, security cameras in residence halls, and a motorist assistance program.

Programs of Study: Hofstra confers B.A., B.S., B.B.A., B.E., B.F.A., and B.S.Ed. degrees. Master's and doctoral degrees are also awarded. Bachelor's degrees are awarded in AGRICULTURE (environmental studies), BIOLOGICAL SCIENCE (biochemistry and biology/biological science), BUSINESS (accounting, banking and finance, business administration and management, business law, entrepreneurial studies, international business management, labor studies, management information systems, management science, and marketing management), COMMUNICATIONS AND THE ARTS (American literature, art history and appreciation, audio technology, ceramic art and design, classics, comparative literature, creative writing, dance, design, dramatic arts, English literature, film arts, fine arts, French, German, Hebrew, Italian, jazz, journalism, media arts, metal/jewelry, music, music business management, music history and appreciation, music performance, music theory and composition, painting, photography, public relations, publishing, radio/television technology, Russian, Spanish, speech/debate/rhetoric, theater design, theater management, video, and visual and performing arts), COMPUTER AND PHYSICAL SCIENCE (actuarial science, applied mathematics, applied physics, chemistry, computer science, geology, mathematics, natural sciences, and physics), EDUCATION (art, athletic training, bilingual/bicultural, business, early childhood, elementary, English, foreign languages, health, mathematics, music, physical, science, secondary, and social studies), ENGINEERING AND ENVIRONMENTAL DESIGN (biomedical engineering, civil engineering, computer engineering, electrical/electronics engineering, environmental engineering, industrial engineering, manufacturing engineering, and mechanical engineering), HEALTH PROFESSIONS (allied health, community health work, exercise science, physician's assistant, predentistry, premedicine, preoptometry, preosteopathy, prepodiatry, preveterinary science, and speech pathology/audiology), SOCIAL SCIENCE (African studies, American studies, anthropology, Asian/Oriental studies, Caribbean studies, economics, geography, Hispanic American studies, history, humanities, interdisciplinary studies, Judaic studies, Latin American studies, liberal arts/general studies, philosophy, political science/government, psychology, social science, and sociology). Accounting, marketing, and English are the strongest academically. Psychology, marketing, and accounting are the largest.

Required: A total of 120 to 147 credit hours is required for graduation, with approximately 30 to 36 in the major depending on degree program and a minimum GPA of 2.0. Students must pass English 1 and 2 and pass a writing proficiency exam. A minimum of 6 semester hours each is required in humanities, in natural sciences, math, and computer science, and in social science, and 3 in cross-cultural courses. Foreign language study is required for the B.A. and the B.B.A. in international business.

Special: Internships in numerous career fields, a Washington semester, and an Albany State Assembly internship, study abroad in 19 countries, and dual and student-designed majors are offered. Credit for military and work experience and credit by exam are given. Hofstra offers nondegree study and pass/fail options. There are 30 national honor societies, including Phi Beta Kappa, a freshman honors program, and 30 departmental honors programs.

Faculty/Classroom: 55% of faculty are male; 45%, female. 73% both teach and do research. No introductory courses are taught by graduate students. The average class size in an introductory lecture is 28; in a laboratory, 22; and in a regular course, 22.

Admissions: 68% of the 2003-2004 applicants were accepted. The SAT I scores for the 2003-2004 freshman class were: Verbal--17% below 500, 54% between 500 and 599, 27% between 600 and 700, and 2% above 700; Math--12% below 500, 53% between 500 and 599, 32% between 600 and 700, and 3% above 700. The ACT scores were 9% below 21, 32% between 21 and 23, 34% between 24 and 26, 16% between 27 and 28, and 9% above 28. 36% of the current freshmen were in the top fifth of their class; 66% were in the top two fifths. 4 freshmen graduated first in their class.

Requirements: The SAT I or ACT is required for some programs. In addition, applicants should graduate from an accredited secondary school or have a GED. Preparatory work should include 4 years of English, 3 each of history and social studies, math, and science, and 2 of foreign language. Engineering students are required to have 4 years of math and 1 each of chemistry and physics. An essay and interview are recommended. One counselor or teacher recommendation is required. AP and CLEP credits are accepted. Important factors in the admissions decision are advanced placement or honor courses, recommendations by school officials, and leadership record.

Procedure: Freshmen are admitted fall and spring. Entrance exams should be taken in the junior or senior year. There are early action, early admissions, deferred, and rolling admissions plans. Early action applications should be filed by November 15; regular applications, by December 31 for fall entry and November 15 for spring entry, for priority consideration, along with a $40 fee. Notification of early action is sent December 15; regular decision, on a rolling basis beginning February 1. 78 early action candidates were accepted for the 2003-2004 class. 438 applicants were on the 2003 waiting list; 49 were admitted. Applications are accepted on-line through the university's web site.

Transfer: 757 transfer students enrolled in 2002-2003. Admission is based primarily on prior college work. A maximum of 64 credits from a 2-year school or 94 credits from a 4-year school is accepted. The minimum GPA is 2.5. 30 of 120 to 147 credits required for the bachelor's degree must be completed at Hofstra.

Visiting: There are regularly scheduled orientations for prospective students, including an open house, a campus tour, and a program in which a prospective student spends the day with a current student in a similar major. There are guides for informal visits and visitors may sit in on classes and stay overnight. To schedule a visit, contact the Ambassador Program at (516) 463-6798.

Financial Aid: In 2003-2004, 85% of all full-time freshmen and 72% of continuing full-time students received some form of financial aid. 51% of full-time freshmen and 56% of continuing full-time students received need-based aid. The average freshman award was $11,220. Need-based scholarships or need-based grants averaged $8636 ($13,572 maximum); need-based self-help aid (loans and jobs) averaged $4289 ($6125 maximum); non-need-based athletic scholarships averaged $21,481 ($31,000 maximum); and other non-need-based awards and non-need-based scholarships averaged $7192 ($17,410 maximum). 37% of undergraduates work part time. Average annual earnings from campus work are $4000. The average financial indebtedness of the 2003 graduate was $17,763. Hofstra is a member of CSS. The FAFSA is required. The priority date for freshman financial aid applications for fall entry is February 15.

International Students: There are 179 international students enrolled. The school actively recruits these students. They must score 550 on the written TOEFL or 213 on the electronic version.

Computers: The mainframes are an IBM 9121, a DEC Alpha, a SUN 880, and 96-CPU Dell Beowulf cluster. The university's computer network provides individual accounts for all students for Internet, e-mail, and more than 250 networked software programs. More than 1100 PC, Mac, and UNIX workstations are available to students in the various labs and classrooms on campus. The labs are staffed, and 1 computer lab is open 24 hours a day, 7 days per week. All campus workstations have high-speed (OC3) Internet access. All resident students are provided with Internet and e-mail access from their dorm rooms, and wireless access is available in several buildings. All students may access the system. There are no time limits. The fee is $100 per semester.

Graduates: From July 1, 2002 to June 30, 2003, 1703 bachelor's degrees were awarded. The most popular majors were psychology (12%), marketing (9%), and management (7%). In an average class, 1% graduate in 3 years or less, 37% graduate in 4 years or less, 53% graduate in 5 years or less, and 56% graduate in 6 years or less. 330 companies recruited on campus in 2002-2003.

Admissions Contact: Gigi Lamens, Vice President for Enrollment Services. A video is available. E-mail: *hofstra@hofstra.edu* Web: *www.hofstra.edu*

HOUGHTON COLLEGE
Houghton, NY 14744

B-3

(585) 567-9353
(800) 777-2556; Fax: (585) 567-9522

Full-time: 417 men, 873 women	**Faculty:** 83; IIB, -$
Part-time: 35 men, 45 women	**Ph.D.s:** 78%
Graduate: 2 men, 7 women	**Student/Faculty:** 15 to 1
Year: 4-1-4	**Tuition:** $17,984
Application Deadline: open	**Room & Board:** $6000
Freshman Class: 987 applied, 911 accepted, 295 enrolled	
SAT I Verbal/Math: 599/579	**ACT:** 25 **VERY COMPETITIVE**

Houghton College, founded in 1883, is a Christian liberal arts college with more than 40 majors and programs. In addition to regional accreditation, Houghton has baccalaureate program accreditation with NASM. The library contains 242,366 volumes, 37,437 microform items, and 9497 audio/video tapes/CDs, and subscribes to 4102 periodicals. Computerized library services include the card catalog, interlibrary loans, database searching, and Internet access. Special learning facilities include an art gallery, radio station, and an equestrian center. The 1300-acre campus is in a rural area 65 miles southeast of Buffalo and 70 miles southwest of Rochester. Including any residence halls, there are 17 buildings.

Student Life: 59% of undergraduates are from New York. Others are from 37 states, 19 foreign countries, and Canada. 70% are from public schools. 90% are white. 66% are Protestant; 23% nondenominational; 7% claim no religious affiliation. The average age of freshmen is 19; all undergraduates, 21. 15% do not continue beyond their first year; 73% remain to graduate.

Housing: 1052 students can be accommodated in college housing, which includes single-sex dormitories, on-campus apartments, and married-student housing. On-campus housing is guaranteed for the freshman year only and is available on a lottery system for upperclassmen. Priority is given to out-of-town students. 80% of students live on campus; of those, 65% remain on campus on weekends. Alcohol is not permitted. All students may keep cars.

Activities: There are no fraternities or sororities. There are 40 groups on campus, including art, bagpipe band, band, cheerleading, choir, chorale, chorus, drama, ethnic, honors, international, jazz band, literary magazine, musical theater, newspaper, opera, orchestra, political, professional, radio and TV, religious, social service, student government, and yearbook. Popular campus events include Christian Life Emphasis Week, Winter Weekend, and Madrigal Dinners.

Sports: There are 4 intercollegiate sports for men and 6 for women, and 8 intramural sports for men and 6 for women. Facilities include 3 basketball and 4 racquetball courts, a swimming pool, an indoor track, a downhill ski slope, cross-country ski trails, 6 tennis courts, a climbing wall, an 8-lane all weather track, and a 386-acre equestrian center with an indoor riding ring. The gym seats 1800; the auditorium, 1300.

Disabled Students: 80% of the campus is accessible. Wheelchair ramps, elevators, special parking, specially equipped rest rooms, special class scheduling, lowered drinking fountains, and lowered telephones are available.

Services: Counseling and information services are available, as is tutoring in some subjects, including general education courses. There is a reader service for the blind. There is support for learning-disabled students.

Campus Safety and Security: Measures include 24-hour foot and vehicle patrol, security escort services, shuttle buses, and informal discussions. There are pamphlets/posters/films, emergency telephones, and lighted pathways/sidewalks.

Programs of Study: Houghton confers B.A., B.S., and B.M. degrees. Associate and master's degrees are also awarded. Bachelor's degrees are awarded in BIOLOGICAL SCIENCE (biology/biological science), BUSINESS (accounting, business administration and management, and recreation and leisure services), COMMUNICATIONS AND THE ARTS (art, communications, creative writing, English, French, music performance, music theory and composition, and Spanish), COMPUTER AND PHYSICAL SCIENCE (chemistry, computer science, mathematics, physics, and science), EDUCATION (elementary, music, physical, science, and secondary), ENGINEERING AND ENVIRONMENTAL DESIGN (environmental science), HEALTH PROFESSIONS (medical technology), SOCIAL SCIENCE (biblical studies, crosscultural studies, history, humanities, international relations, ministries, philosophy, political science/government, psychology, religion, and sociology). Biology, religion, and music are the strongest academically. Education, biology, and psychology are the largest.

Required: Required courses include 10 hours of math and science, 9 of religion, 6 to 9 of English, 6 of social science, 4 each of intermediate language, philosophy, and Western civilization, 3 of fine arts, 2 to 6 of communication, 2 of phys ed, and a research component. A total of between 124 and 129 credits, with at least 24 in the major, and a minimum GPA of 2.0 are required to graduate.

Special: Students may cross-register with members of the Western New York Consortium. Internships are available in psychology (at West Sene-

ca campus), social work, business, accounting, educational ministries, physical fitness, political science, graphic design, communication, athletic training, recreation, English, and Christian education. Study abroad in 25 countries, a Washington semester, dual majors, and a 3-2 engineering degree with Clarkson and Washington Universities are available. Credit for military experience and nondegree study are possible. There are 2 national honor societies, a freshman honors program.

Faculty/Classroom: 73% of faculty are male; 27%, female. All teach undergraduates, 15% do research, and 5% do both. No introductory courses are taught by graduate students. The average class size in an introductory lecture is 29; in a laboratory, 14; and in a regular course, 17.

Admissions: 92% of the 2003-2004 applicants were accepted. The SAT I scores for the 2003-2004 freshman class were: Verbal--15% below 500, 36% between 500 and 599, 35% between 600 and 700, and 13% above 700. The ACT scores were 13% below 21, 26% between 21 and 23, 27% between 24 and 26, 17% between 27 and 28, and 20% above 28. 54% of the current freshmen were in the top fifth of their class; 81% were in the top two fifths. There were 3 National Merit finalists and 2 semifinalists. 21 freshmen graduated first in their class.

Requirements: The SAT I or ACT is required. In addition, a minimum composite score of 900 on the SAT I or 20 on the ACT is recommended. Applicants must graduate from an accredited secondary school or have a GED. A total of 16 academic credits is recommended, including 4 of English, 3 of social studies, and 2 each of foreign language, math, and science. An essay is required. Music students must audition. An interview is recommended. Houghton requires applicants to be in the upper 50% of their class. A GPA of 2.5 is required. AP and CLEP credits are accepted. Important factors in the admissions decision are personality/intangible qualities, recommendations by school officials, and advanced placement or honor courses.

Procedure: Freshmen are admitted fall and spring. Entrance exams should be taken in the spring of the junior year or fall of the senior year. There are early admissions and deferred admissions plans. Application deadlines are open. Applications are accepted on-line.

Transfer: 37 transfer students enrolled in 2002-2003. Applicants should have a 2.5 or better GPA. A pastor's recommendation and high school transcripts must be submitted. The SAT I or ACT and an interview are recommended. 30 of 124 credits required for the bachelor's degree must be completed at Houghton.

Visiting: There are regularly scheduled orientations for prospective students, including a tour, an admissions interview, a financial aid session, a class visit, and academic program sessions. There are guides for informal visits and visitors may sit in on classes and stay overnight.

Financial Aid: In 2003-2004, 97% of all full-time freshmen and 87% of continuing full-time students received some form of financial aid. 84% of full-time freshmen and 78% of continuing full-time students received need-based aid. The average freshman award was $13,350. Need-based scholarships or need-based grants averaged $9510 ($25,795 maximum); need-based self-help aid (loans and jobs) averaged $4125 ($4125 maximum); non-need-based athletic scholarships averaged $3327 ($9000 maximum); and other non-need-based awards and non-need-based scholarships averaged $7178 ($20,500 maximum). 50% of undergraduates work part time. Average annual earnings from campus work are $658. The average financial indebtedness of the 2003 graduate was $10,308. Houghton is a member of CSS. The FAFSA is required. The priority date for freshman financial aid applications for fall entry is March 1.

International Students: There are 62 international students enrolled. The school actively recruits these students. They must score 550 on the written TOEFL and also take .

Computers: The mainframe is a DEC VAX 8200. All students receive a laptop when they enroll full time at Houghton. The laptop is included in tuition. There are data jacks in all residence rooms, 1 per student. The college has several fully wired classrooms as well as access in study areas, the library, and the snack shop. There is a general-use lab that is open 24 hours a day, 7 days a week and various labs for specialized departmental use. All students may access the system. There are no time limits and no fees. All students are required to have personal computers.

Graduates: From July 1, 2002 to June 30, 2003, 340 bachelor's degrees were awarded. The most popular majors were elementary education (11%), biology (8%), and music (7%). In an average class, 3% graduate in 3 years or less, 58% graduate in 4 years or less, 73% graduate in 5 years or less, and 73% graduate in 6 years or less. 33 companies recruited on campus in 2002-2003. Of the 2002 graduating class, 27% were enrolled in graduate school within 6 months of graduation and 82% were employed.

Admissions Contact: Bruce Campbell, Director of Admission.
E-mail: *admission@houghton.edu* Web: *www.houghton.edu*

IONA COLLEGE

New Rochelle, NY 10801-1890

D-5

(914) 633-2503
(800) 231-IONA; Fax: (914) 633-2096

Full-time: 1423 men, 1577 women	**Faculty:** 174; IIA, +$
Part-time: 163 men, 232 women	**Ph.Ds:** 87%
Graduate: 401 men, 592 women	**Student/Faculty:** 17 to 1
Year: semesters, summer session	**Tuition:** $18,290
Application Deadline: March 15	**Room & Board:** $9698
Freshman Class: 4196 applied, 2696 accepted, 860 enrolled	
SAT I Verbal/Math: 550/540	**ACT:** 21 **VERY COMPETITIVE**

Iona College, founded in 1940, is a private, largely commuter college offering programs through schools of general studies, arts and science, and business. It has a campus in Rockland County in addition to the main campus in New Rochelle. There are 2 undergraduate and 2 graduate schools. In addition to regional accreditation, Iona has baccalaureate program accreditation with AACSB, CSWE, and NLN. The 2 libraries contain 268,572 volumes, 499,263 microform items, and 2883 audio/video tapes/CDs, and subscribe to 608 periodicals. Computerized library services include the card catalog, interlibrary loans, database searching, and Internet access. Special learning facilities include a learning resource center, art gallery, radio station, TV station, an electron microscope, and a speech and hearing clinic. The 35-acre campus is in a suburban area 20 miles northeast of New York City. Including any residence halls, there are 44 buildings.

Student Life: 82% of undergraduates are from New York. Students are from 37 states, 30 foreign countries, and Canada. 77% are white; 12% Hispanic. The average age of freshmen is 18; all undergraduates, 19. 21% do not continue beyond their first year; 54% remain to graduate.

Housing: 1000 students can be accommodated in college housing, which includes single-sex and coed dorms and off-campus apartments. On-campus housing is available on a first-come, first-served basis and is available on a lottery system for upperclassmen. Priority is given to out-of-town students. 72% of students commute. Upperclassmen may keep cars.

Activities: 2% of men belong to 1 local fraternity and 2 national fraternities; 4% of women belong to 5 local sororities and 1 national sorority. There are 65 groups on campus, including bagpipe band, cheerleading, choir, chorale, computers, dance, drama, ethnic, honors, international, literary magazine, musical theater, newspaper, pep band, photography, political, professional, radio and TV, religious, social, social service, student government, and yearbook. Popular campus events include Spring Concert, "After-Hours Iona" programming, and Founders Week.

Sports: There are 11 intercollegiate sports for men and 10 for women, and 2 intramural sports for men and 2 for women. Facilities include an all-weather football-soccer field, a gym, a Nautilus fitness center, a baseball field, saunas, a track, and a swimming pool. The campus stadium seats 1200 and the indoor gym, 3000.

Disabled Students: 80% of the campus is accessible. Wheelchair ramps, elevators, special parking, specially equipped rest rooms, special class scheduling, lowered drinking fountains, and lowered telephones are available. All classes are on the first floor.

Services: Counseling and information services are available, as is tutoring in some subjects, including math, statistics, computer science, English composition, history, Spanish, scientific and technological literacy, accounting, business, and management science. There is a reader service for the blind.

Campus Safety and Security: Measures include 24-hour foot and vehicle patrol, security escort services, shuttle buses, and informal discussions. There are pamphlets/posters/films, emergency telephones, and lighted pathways/sidewalks.

Programs of Study: Iona confers B.A., B.S., and B.B.A. degrees. Master's degrees are also awarded. Bachelor's degrees are awarded in BIOLOGICAL SCIENCE (biochemistry, biology/biological science, and ecology), BUSINESS (accounting, banking and finance, business administration and management, international business management, management information systems, management science, and marketing management), COMMUNICATIONS AND THE ARTS (advertising, communications, dramatic arts, English, French, Italian, journalism, public relations, Spanish, speech/debate/rhetoric, and video), COMPUTER AND PHYSICAL SCIENCE (chemistry, computer science, mathematics, and physics), EDUCATION (early childhood, elementary, foreign languages, middle school, science, and secondary), HEALTH PROFESSIONS (health care administration, medical laboratory technology, mental health/human services, predentistry, premedicine, prepharmacy, preveterinary science, and speech pathology/audiology), SOCIAL SCIENCE (behavioral science, criminal justice, economics, history, humanities, international studies, philosophy, political science/government, psychology, religion, social science, social work, and sociology). Accounting, computer science, and management information systems are the strongest academically. Mass communication, accounting, and management are the largest.

Required: The core curriculum includes 24 credits of humanities, 12 credits of natural and symbolic languages, and 6 credits each of commu-

nications, social science, and science and technology. There is an arts and science core and a business core. Computer literacy is required. The total number of credits required in liberal arts is 120, with 39 to 46 in the major; the business program requires 126 credits, with 30 in the major. The minimum GPA is 2.0.

Special: There are internships for upperclassmen. Study abroad is available in Australia, Ireland, Belgium, France, Spain, Italy, and Morocco. There is work-study in Iona offices and academic departments. Students may earn a combined B.A.-B.S. degree in economics, psychology, elementary education, early secondary education, and math education. There is a joint B.S./M.S. program with New York Medical College in physical therapy, and a 6-year joint degree in speech/language pathology and audiology. 5-year programs are offered in computer science, psychology, and history. There are 23 national honor societies and a freshman honors program.

Faculty/Classroom: 62% of faculty are male; 38%, female. All teach undergraduates. No introductory courses are taught by graduate students. The average class size in an introductory lecture is 22; in a laboratory, 16; and in a regular course, 21.

Admissions: 64% of the 2003-2004 applicants were accepted. The SAT I scores for the 2003-2004 freshman class were: Verbal--26% below 500, 49% between 500 and 599, 23% between 600 and 700, and 2% above 700; Math--25% below 500, 50% between 500 and 599, 24% between 600 and 700, and 1% above 700.

Requirements: The SAT I is required and the ACT is recommended. In addition, applicants must complete 16 academic credits, including 4 units of English, 3 of math, 2 of foreign language, and 1 each of history, science, and social studies. A GED is accepted. An essay and an interview are recommended. A GPA of 2.5 is required. AP and CLEP credits are accepted. Important factors in the admissions decision are recommendations by school officials, extracurricular activities record, and leadership record.

Procedure: Freshmen are admitted fall and spring. Entrance exams should be taken in the spring of the senior year. There are early admissions and deferred admissions plans. Applications should be filed by March 15 for fall entry and January 1 for spring entry. The fall 2003 application fee was $40. Notification is sent on a rolling basis.

Transfer: 215 transfer students enrolled in 2002-2003. Transfer applicants must have a GPA of at least 2.5 and must submit high school transcripts if they have earned fewer than 30 college credits. An interview is recommended. 30 of 120 credits required for the bachelor's degree must be completed at Iona.

Visiting: There are regularly scheduled orientations for prospective students, including a meeting with an admissions counselor, a campus tour, and a variety of on-campus programs during the spring and summer. There are guides for informal visits and visitors may sit in on classes. To schedule a visit, contact the Admissions Office at (914) 633-2502 or icad@iona.edu.

Financial Aid: In 2003-2004, 94% of all full-time freshmen and 89% of continuing full-time students received some form of financial aid. 59% of full-time freshmen and 54% of continuing full-time students received need-based aid. The average freshman award was $18,443. Need-based scholarships or need-based grants averaged $2959 ($8050 maximum); need-based self-help aid (loans and jobs) averaged $3977 ($8625 maximum); non-need-based athletic scholarships averaged $8085 ($27,214 maximum); and other non-need-based awards and non-need-based scholarships averaged $13,392 ($31,625 maximum). 16% of undergraduates work part time. Average annual earnings from campus work are $1623. The average financial indebtedness of the 2003 graduate was $18,646. The FAFSA, the college's own financial statement, and the TAP (Tuition Assistance Program) form are required. The priority date for freshman financial aid applications for fall entry is March 15. The deadline for filing freshman financial aid applications for fall entry is April 15.

International Students: There are 55 international students enrolled. The school actively recruits these students. They must score 550 on the written TOEFL and also take the SAT I or the ACT.

Computers: The campus WAN consists of 36 servers (5 Novell, 26 NT, 3 Linux, and 2 UNIX). There are 1300 college- and student-owned Pentium systems available in computing labs, classrooms, residence halls, libraries, and the student center for student use. All students may access the system. Access to PC software, the Internet, and other computing facilities is unlimited. The fee is $85 per semester. It is strongly recommended that all students have a personal computer. The college offers discount pricing for Gateway computers; however, all makes are supported.

Graduates: From July 1, 2002 to June 30, 2003, 654 bachelor's degrees were awarded. The most popular majors were business (31%), mass communication (13%), and psychology (9%). In an average class, 37% graduate in 4 years or less, 50% graduate in 5 years or less, and 52% graduate in 6 years or less. 62 companies recruited on campus in 2002-2003.

Admissions Contact: Thomas Weede, Director of Admissions. E-mail: icad@iona.edu Web: http://www.iona.edu

ITHACA COLLEGE
Ithaca, NY 14850-7020

C-3

(607) 274-3124
(800) 429-4274; Fax: (607) 274-1900

Full-time: 2635 men, 3478 women	**Faculty:** 440; IIA, av$
Part-time: 59 men, 88 women	**Ph.D.s:** 89%
Graduate: 75 men, 161 women	**Student/Faculty:** 14 to 1
Year: semesters, summer session	**Tuition:** $22,264
Application Deadline: March 1	**Room & Board:** $9466
Freshman Class: 10,650 applied, 6756 accepted, 1584 enrolled	
SAT I Verbal/Math: 590/594	**HIGHLY COMPETITIVE**

Ithaca College, founded in 1892, is a private college offering undergraduate and graduate programs in business, communications, health science and human performance, humanities and sciences, and music. There are 5 undergraduate schools and 1 graduate school. In addition to regional accreditation, Ithaca has baccalaureate program accreditation with AOTA, APTA, CAAHEP, CAPTE, NASM, and NRPA. The library contains 304,476 volumes, 249,818 microform items, and 27,982 audio/video tapes/CDs, and subscribes to 2968 periodicals. Computerized library services include the card catalog, interlibrary loans, database searching, and Internet access. Special learning facilities include an art gallery, radio station, TV station, digital audio and video labs, speech, hearing, wellness, and physical therapy clinics, a greenhouse, a financial "trading room," an observatory, and electroacoustic music studios. The 757-acre campus is in a small town 250 miles northwest of New York City. Including any residence halls, there are 60 buildings.

Student Life: 52% of undergraduates are from out of state, mostly the Middle Atlantic. Students are from 45 states, 66 foreign countries, and Canada. 74% are from public schools. 87% are white. The average age of freshmen is 18; all undergraduates, 20. 13% do not continue beyond their first year; 73% remain to graduate.

Housing: 4300 students can be accommodated in college housing, which includes single-sex and coed dorms and on-campus apartments. In addition, there is first-year students only housing, a quiet study residence hall, service and music honor fraternities, smoke-free buildings and floors, coed by door buildings, honors floors, a substance-free building, multicultural housing, and several freshman seminar groups housed together. On-campus housing is guaranteed for all 4 years. 70% of students live on campus; of those, 95% remain on campus on weekends. All students may keep cars.

Activities: 2% of men belong to 4 national fraternities; 2% of women belong to 1 local sorority. There are 165 groups on campus, including art, band, bureau of concerts, chess, choir, chorale, chorus, computers, dance, drama, drum and bugle corps, ethnic, film, gay, honors, international, jazz band, literary magazine, musical theater, newspaper, opera, orchestra, pep band, photography, political, professional, radio and TV, religious, social, social service, student activities board, student government, symphony, and yearbook. Popular campus events include Winter Fest, Fall Madness, and various multicultural awareness events.

Sports: There are 12 intercollegiate sports for men and 13 for women, and 15 intramural sports for men and 15 for women. Facilities include 5 gyms, 2 dance studios, a student union, indoor and outdoor pools, a fitness center and wellness clinic, tennis courts, and baseball, football, lacrosse, field hockey, and soccer fields.

Disabled Students: Wheelchair ramps, elevators, special parking, specially equipped rest rooms, special class scheduling, lowered drinking fountains, and lowered telephones are available.

Services: Nonremedial tutoring is available.

Campus Safety and Security: Measures include 24-hour foot and vehicle patrol, security escort services, pamphlets/posters/films, and emergency telephones. There are lighted pathways/sidewalks and crime prevention programs.

Programs of Study: Ithaca confers B.A., B.S., B.F.A., and Mus.B. degrees. Master's degrees are also awarded. Bachelor's degrees are awarded in BIOLOGICAL SCIENCE (biochemistry and biology/biological science), BUSINESS (accounting, banking and finance, business administration and management, business economics, electronic business, human resources, international business management, management science, marketing management, marketing/retailing/merchandising, organizational behavior, personnel management, recreation and leisure services, and sports management), COMMUNICATIONS AND THE ARTS (art, art history and appreciation, audio technology, broadcasting, communications, creative writing, dramatic arts, English, film arts, fine arts, French, German, jazz, journalism, languages, media arts, modern language, music, music performance, music theory and composition, musical theater, performing arts, photography, public relations, Spanish, speech/debate/rhetoric, studio art, telecommunications, theater design, theater management, video, and visual and performing arts), COMPUTER AND PHYSICAL SCIENCE (chemistry, computer mathematics, computer science, information sciences and systems, mathematics, and physics), EDUCATION (art, athletic training, education, education of the deaf and hearing impaired, educational media, English, foreign languages, health, mathematics, middle school, music, physical, secondary, social studies, and speech correction), ENGI-NEERING AND ENVIRONMENTAL DESIGN (environmental science), HEALTH PROFESSIONS (allied health, clinical science, community health work, exercise science, health, health care administration, health science, hospital administration, occupational therapy, physical therapy, predentistry, premedicine, public health, recreation therapy, rehabilitation therapy, speech pathology/audiology, speech therapy, and sports medicine), SOCIAL SCIENCE (anthropology, economics, gerontology, history, industrial and organizational psychology, interdisciplinary studies, liberal arts/general studies, philosophy, physical fitness/movement, political science/government, prelaw, psychology, social studies, and sociology). Physical therapy, theater, and music are the strongest academically. Music, television-radio, and business administration are the largest.

Required: Students must successfully complete a minimum of 120 credit hours. In addition, each student must meet the requirements of a core curriculum, which varies with each school within the college and includes courses in the liberal arts and professional courses outside the student's major.

Special: Cross-registration is available with Cornell University and Wells College. Opportunities are also provided for internships, work-study programs, dual majors, accelerated degree programs, nondegree study, pass/fail options, student-designed majors, a 3-2 engineering degree with Cornell University, Clarkson University, Rensselaer Polytechnic Institute, and SUNY Binghamton, and study abroad in London, Valencia, and other foreign cities. A 4-1 advanced business degree program, a 3-1 optometry program, and a semester program in marine biology with Duke University are also available. There are 24 national honor societies, a freshman honors program, and 16 departmental honors programs.

Faculty/Classroom: 56% of faculty are male; 44%, female. All teach undergraduates. No introductory courses are taught by graduate students. The average class size in an introductory lecture is 21 and in a regular course, 19.

Admissions: 63% of the 2003-2004 applicants were accepted. The SAT I scores for the 2003-2004 freshman class were: Verbal--10% below 500, 44% between 500 and 599, 40% between 600 and 700, and 6% above 700; Math--7% below 500, 44% between 500 and 599, 44% between 600 and 700, and 5% above 700. 61% of the current freshmen were in the top fifth of their class; 90% were in the top two fifths. There were 7 National Merit finalists. 36 freshmen graduated first in their class.

Requirements: The SAT I or ACT is required. In addition, applicants should be graduates of an accredited secondary school with a minimum of 16 Carnegie units, including 4 years of English, 3 each of math, science, and social studies, 2 of foreign language, and other college-preparatory electives. The GED is accepted. An essay is required, as is an audition for music and theater students. In some majors, a portfolio and an interview are recommended. Ithaca requires applicants to be in the upper 25% of their class. AP and CLEP credits are accepted.

Procedure: Freshmen are admitted fall and spring. Entrance exams should be taken in spring of the junior year or fall of the senior year. There are early decision and deferred admissions plans. Early decision applications should be filed by November 1; regular applications, by March 1 for fall entry and December 1 for spring entry. The fall 2003 application fee was $55. Notification of early decision is sent December 15; regular decision, on a rolling basis. 259 early decision candidates were accepted for the 2003-2004 class. Applications are accepted on-line through the school's web site.

Transfer: 154 transfer students enrolled in 2002-2003. Transfer applicants must submit SAT I or ACT scores, a high school transcript, transcripts from previously attended colleges, and a personal recommendation from their adviser or Dean of Students. A minimum college GPA of 2.75 is recommended. 30 of 120 credits required for the bachelor's degree must be completed at Ithaca.

Visiting: There are regularly scheduled orientations for prospective students, including a campus tour and an interview with an admissions counselor. Fall open house programs offering personal meetings with faculty are available by appointment. There are guides for informal visits and visitors may sit in on classes and stay overnight. To schedule a visit, contact the Director of Admission at admissions@ithaca.edu.

Financial Aid: In 2003-2004, 88% of all full-time freshmen and 82% of continuing full-time students received some form of financial aid. 69% of full-time freshmen and 68% of continuing full-time students received need-based aid. The average freshman award was $17,062. Need-based scholarships or need-based grants averaged $7776 ($30,880 maximum); need-based self-help aid (loans and jobs) averaged $3261 ($7825 maximum); and non-need-based awards and non-need-based scholarships averaged $6230 ($36,056 maximum). 44% of undergraduates work part time. Average annual earnings from campus work are $2200. Ithaca is a member of CSS. The FAFSA is required; the CSS/Profile is required for early decision applicants only and must be filed by November 1. The deadline for filing freshman financial aid applications for fall entry is February 1.

International Students: There are 196 international students enrolled. The school actively recruits these students. They must score 550 on the written TOEFL or 213 on the electronic version and also take the SAT I or the ACT.

Computers: The mainframe is an HP Alpha server ES45. Students may access the mainframe from approximately 624 PCs/terminals in the library, computer labs, and classrooms. All residence halls are fully networked and have access to the Internet and Web. All students may access the system 24 hours a day. There are no time limits and no fees.

Graduates: From July 1, 2002 to June 30, 2003, 1307 bachelor's degrees were awarded. The most popular majors were television-radio (12%), business administration (9%), and music (8%). In an average class, 1% graduate in 3 years or less, 64% graduate in 4 years or less, 72% graduate in 5 years or less, and 73% graduate in 6 years or less. 111 companies recruited on campus in 2002-2003. Of the 2002 graduating class, 33% were enrolled in graduate school within 6 months of graduation and 83% were employed.

Admissions Contact: Paula Mitchell, Director of Admission. A video is available. E-mail: *admission@ithaca.edu* Web: *www.ithaca.edu*

JEWISH THEOLOGICAL SEMINARY/LIST COLLEGE OF JEWISH STUDIES
(See Albert A. List College of Jewish Studies)

JULLIARD SCHOOL
New York, NY 10023-6588   D-5

(212) 799-5000, ext. 223
Fax: (212) 724-6420

Full-time: 246 men, 259 women	**Faculty:** 120
Part-time: 1 man	**Ph.D.s:** n/av
Graduate: 162 men, 145 women	**Student/Faculty:** 4 to 1
Year: semesters	**Tuition:** $21,850
Application Deadline: December 1	**Room & Board:** $10,535
Freshman Class: 1824 applied, 124 accepted, 97 enrolled	
SAT I or ACT: not required	**SPECIAL**

The Juilliard School, founded in 1905, is a private college of dance, music, and drama. The library contains 93,386 volumes, 1399 microform items, and 24,798 audio/video tapes/CDs, and subscribes to 230 periodicals. Computerized library services include the card catalog, interlibrary loans, database searching, and Internet access. Special learning facilities include 200 practice rooms, 5 theaters, scenery and costume shops, and dance studios. The campus is in an urban area at Lincoln Center in New York City. Including any residence halls, there are 2 buildings.

Student Life: 85% of undergraduates are from out of state, mostly the Northeast. Student are from 43 states, 41 foreign countries, and Canada. 57% are white; 29% foreign nationals; 18% Asian American. The average age of freshmen is 18; all undergraduates, 20. 6% do not continue beyond their first year; 75% remain to graduate.

Housing: 350 students can be accommodated in college housing, which includes single-sex and coed dorms. All floors are smoke free. There are quiet, alcohol-free, single sex (all female) floors. In addition, there are special-interest houses. On-campus housing is guaranteed for the freshman year only, is available on a first-come, first-served basis, and is available on a lottery system for upperclassmen. 52% of students commute. All students may keep cars.

Activities: There are no fraternities or sororities. There are 15 groups on campus, including band, book discussion, choir, chorale, chorus, community service, dance, drama, environmental consciousness, ethnic, gay, international, jazz band, marching band, opera, orchestra, professional, recreation, religious, social, social service, student government, and symphony. Popular campus events include performances by the Juilliard orchestras at Lincoln Center, dance concerts, and drama and opera productions.

Sports: There is no sports program at Juilliard. Facilities include a fitness center in the residence hall.

Disabled Students: All of the campus is accessible. Wheelchair ramps, elevators, specially equipped rest rooms, lowered drinking fountains, and lowered telephones are available.

Services: Counseling and information services are available, as is tutoring in some subjects, including ear training, literature and materials of music, and English.

Campus Safety and Security: Measures include 24-hour foot and vehicle patrol, self-defense education, informal discussions, and pamphlets/posters/films. There are emergency telephones, lighted pathways/sidewalks, video cameras, and turnstiles with ID card access.

Programs of Study: Juilliard confers B.Mus. and B.F.A. degrees. Master's and doctoral degrees are also awarded. Bachelor's degrees are awarded in COMMUNICATIONS AND THE ARTS (dance, dramatic arts, music theory and composition, percussion, piano/organ, strings, voice, and winds). Piano, voice, and violin are the largest.

Required: Each division has its own requirements for graduation.

Special: A joint program with Columbia University and Barnard College allows students to obtain a 5-year B.A.-B.Mus. degree. Internships are available with cultural organizations in New York City. There is study abroad in music academies in England, Israel, and Russia. Work-study programs, accelerated degrees and dual majors in music, a combined B.Mus.-M.Mus. degree, nondegree study, and pass/fail options are available.

Faculty/Classroom: 69% of faculty are male; 31%, female. All teach undergraduates. The average class size in a regular course is 12.

Admissions: 7% of the 2003-2004 applicants were accepted.

Requirements: A high school diploma or GED is required. Students are accepted primarily on the basis of personal auditions rather than tests. Important factors in the admissions decision are evidence of special talent and personality/intangible qualities.

Procedure: Freshmen are admitted in the fall. Personal auditions should be completed in December for opera, February for drama and regionals in dance and music, and March for dance and music. Applications should be filed by December 1 for fall entry, along with a $100 fee. Notification is sent April 1. 48 applicants were on the 2003 waiting list; 7 were admitted.

Transfer: 30 transfer students enrolled in 2003-2004. Transfer applicants must audition in person.

Visiting: There are regularly scheduled orientations for prospective students, including guided tours and question-and-answer sessions, Monday to Friday at 2:30 P.M. Visitors may sit in on classes and stay overnight. To schedule a visit, contact Sarah J. Adriance, Admissions Assistant, at *sadriance@juilliard.edu*.

Financial Aid: In 2003-2004, 97% of all full-time freshmen and 94% of continuing full-time students received some form of financial aid. 73% of full-time freshmen and 81% of continuing full-time students received need-based aid. The average freshman award was $20,777. Need-based scholarships or need-based grants averaged $16,074 ($21,250 maximum); need-based self-help aid (loans and jobs) averaged $4653 ($6875 maximum); and non-need-based awards and non-need-based scholarships averaged $3208 ($5000 maximum). 62% of undergraduates work part time. Average annual earnings from campus work are $1210. The average financial indebtedness of the 2003 graduate was $21,447. The FAFSA and the college's own financial statement are required. The deadline for filing freshman financial aid applications for fall entry is March 1.

International Students: There are 118 international students enrolled. They must score 533 on the written TOEFL or 200 on the electronic version and also take the college's own test and the TWE.

Computers: There are 28 Windows and Mac computers in the main PC lab connected to the Internet. Lab PCs are loaded with MS Office applications and a variety of music technology tools such as Sibelius and Finale. Electronic musical equipment, scanners, and printers are also available for student use. 24 other Internet-access terminals are in the library, the lobby, and the residence hall. There is a 16-station state-of-the-art computer training facility. All classrooms and several jacks around the building offer Internet access. More than 70% of students connect to the Internet with their own equipment in their rooms. All students may access the system. Students may access the system during lab hours. There are no fees.

Graduates: From July 1, 2002 to June 30, 2003, 103 bachelor's degrees were awarded. In an average class, 63% graduate in 4 years or less, 76% graduate in 5 years or less, and 80% graduate in 6 years or less.

Admissions Contact: Office of Admissions.
E-mail: *admissions@juilliard.edu* Web: *www.juilliard.edu*

KEUKA COLLEGE
Keuka Park, NY 14478   B-3

(315) 536-5254, ext. 254
(800) 33-KEUKA; Fax: (315) 536-5386

Full-time: 280 men, 750 women	**Faculty:** 50; IIB, --$
Part-time: 10 men, 25 women	**Ph.D.s:** 60%
Graduate: none	**Student/Faculty:** 21 to 1
Year: 4-1-4, summer session	**Tuition:** $15,790
Application Deadline: open	**Room & Board:** $7590
Freshman Class: n/av	
SAT I or ACT: required	**COMPETITIVE**

Keuka College, founded in 1890, is an independent college affiliated with American Baptist Churches, and offers instruction in the liberal arts. Some figures in the above capsule and in this profile are approximate. In addition to regional accreditation, Keuka has baccalaureate program accreditation with AHEA, CSWE, and NLN. The library contains 83,108 volumes, 3991 microform items, and 2764 audio/video tapes/CDs, and subscribes to 17,287 periodicals. Computerized library services include the card catalog, interlibrary loans, and database searching. Special learning facilities include a learning resource center, art gallery, and radio station. The 203-acre campus is in a rural area 60 miles south of Rochester. Including any residence halls, there are 19 buildings.

Student Life: 92% of undergraduates are from New York. Students are from 23 states, 3 foreign countries, and Canada. 80% are from public schools. 92% are white. 30% are Protestant. The average age of freshmen is 18; all undergraduates, 22. 19% do not continue beyond their first year; 52% remain to graduate.

Housing: 719 students can be accommodated in college housing, which includes single-sex and coed dorms. In addition, there are honors houses and special-interest houses. On-campus housing is guaranteed for all 4 years. 68% of students live on campus; of those, 60% remain on campus on weekends. Alcohol is not permitted. Upperclassmen may keep cars.

Activities: There are no fraternities or sororities. There are 42 groups on campus, including art, cheerleading, choir, chorale, dance, drama, ethnic, honors, international, literary magazine, newspaper, political, professional, religious, social, social service, student government, and yearbook. Popular campus events include Spring Weekend, May Day, and Family Weekend.

Sports: There are 5 intercollegiate sports for men and 6 for women, and 8 intramural sports for men and 8 for women. Facilities include an Olympic-size pool, a gym, a fitness center, a weight room, and an outdoor athletic facility.

Disabled Students: 60% of the campus is accessible. Wheelchair ramps, elevators, special parking, specially equipped rest rooms, special class scheduling, lowered drinking fountains, and specially equipped residence rooms are available.

Services: Counseling and information services are available, as is tutoring in every subject. There is a reader service for the blind and remedial math, reading, and writing. Individual and group tutoring is available free through the college's academic support services.

Campus Safety and Security: Measures include 24-hour foot and vehicle patrol, self-defense education, shuttle buses, and informal discussions. There are pamphlets/posters/films, emergency telephones, and lighted pathways/sidewalks.

Programs of Study: Keuka confers B.A. and B.S. degrees. Master's degrees are also awarded. Bachelor's degrees are awarded in BIOLOGICAL SCIENCE (biochemistry and biology/biological science), BUSINESS (accounting, business administration and management, hotel/motel and restaurant management, and marketing/retailing/merchandising), COMMUNICATIONS AND THE ARTS (American Sign Language, communications, and English), EDUCATION (elementary and secondary), ENGINEERING AND ENVIRONMENTAL DESIGN (environmental science), HEALTH PROFESSIONS (medical laboratory technology, nursing, occupational therapy, predentistry, premedicine, and preveterinary science), SOCIAL SCIENCE (criminal justice, political science/government, prelaw, psychology, social work, and sociology). Occupational therapy, biology, and education are the strongest academically. Occupational therapy, education, and management are the largest.

Required: Students must complete 1 field period combining academic study and professional experience for each year of enrollment. The core curriculum consists of 43 to 46 credits, including but not limited to required courses in phys ed, computer science, and integrative studies. A total of 120 credit hours is required for graduation with a minimum of 30 credits in the major and a major and cumulative GPA of 2.0.

Special: There are co-op programs with other members of the Rochester Area Colleges Consortium. The college offers internships, study abroad, a Washington semester, dual majors, and student-designed majors. Credit is also given by exam and for work experience. There are 16 national honor societies.

Faculty/Classroom: 45% of faculty are male; 55%, female. All teach undergraduates. The average class size in an introductory lecture is 22; in a laboratory, 12; and in a regular course, 22.

Requirements: The SAT I or ACT is required. In addition, students should graduate from an accredited secondary school with a minimum GPA of 2.8. The GED is accepted. A minimum of 15 Carnegie units is required, including 4 years of English, 3 of history, 2 to 3 of math and science, 2 of foreign language, and 1 of social studies. An essay is required, and an interview is recommended. Keuka requires applicants to be in the upper 50% of their class. AP and CLEP credits are accepted. Important factors in the admissions decision are recommendations by school officials, extracurricular activities record, and leadership record.

Procedure: Freshmen are admitted fall and spring. Entrance exams should be taken in the spring of the junior year or the fall of the senior year. There are early decision, early admissions, and deferred admissions plans. The deadline for regular applications is open. The application fee is $30. Notification is sent on a rolling basis. Applications are accepted on-line at the school's web site.

Transfer: 69 transfer students enrolled in a recent year. Applicants must take the SAT I or ACT and submit transcripts. An interview is recommended. A minimum GPA of 2.5 is required in college work. 30 of 120 credits required for the bachelor's degree must be completed at Keuka.

Visiting: There are regularly scheduled orientations for prospective students, including open houses held in October and April, when students can speak with faculty, student affairs and financial aid representatives, and current students. There are guides for informal visits and visitors may sit in on classes and stay overnight. To schedule a visit, contact the Admissions Office.

Financial Aid: In a recent year, 96% of all full-time freshmen and 92% of continuing full-time students received some form of financial aid, including need-based aid. The average freshman award was $12,045. 61% of undergraduates work part time. Average annual earnings from campus work are $880. The average financial indebtedness of a recent year's graduate was $18,645. Keuka is a member of CSS. The FAFSA

and the college's own financial statement are required. The deadline for filing freshman financial aid applications for fall entry is April 14.

International Students: There were 8 international students enrolled in a recent year. They must score 588 on the written TOEFL or 238 on the electronic version and also take the SAT I or the ACT.

Computers: The mainframe is a DEC Alpha 4000. 2 fully equipped PC labs provide students with word processing, graphics, spreadsheet, other academic support functions, Internet, and e-mail access. All students may access the system. There are no time limits and no fees. It is strongly recommended that all students have a personal computer.

Graduates: In a recent year, 144 bachelor's degrees were awarded. The most popular majors were occupational therapy (34%), unified elementary/special education (23%), and nursing (7%). In an average class, 35% graduate in 4 years or less, 52% graduate in 5 years or less, and 52% graduate in 6 years or less.

Admissions Contact: Dean of Enrollment Management. A video is available. E-mail: *admissions@mail.keuka.edu* Web: *www.keuka.edu*

LABORATORY INSTITUTE OF MERCHANDISING D-5
New York, NY 10022-5268
(212) 752-1530
(800) 677-1323; Fax: (212) 317-8602

Full-time: 18 men, 467 women	**Faculty:** 9
Part-time: 8 women	**Ph.Ds:** n/av
Graduate: none	**Student/Faculty:** 54 to 1
Year: semesters, summer session	**Tuition:** $15,150
Application Deadline: open	**Room & Board:** $10,000
Freshman Class: 356 applied, 235 accepted, 142 enrolled	
SAT I Verbal/Math: 480/460	**SPECIAL**

The Laboratory Institute of Merchandising, founded in 1939, is a private college offering programs in fashion merchandising, marketing, and visual merchandising. In addition to regional accreditation, LIM has baccalaureate program accreditation with IACBE. The library contains 8600 volumes and 200 audio/video tapes/CDs, and subscribes to 80 periodicals. Computerized library services include database searching. Special learning facilities include a learning resource center and a temporary art gallery. The campus is in an urban area. Including any residence halls, there are 2 buildings.

Student Life: 50% of undergraduates are from out of state, mostly the Middle Atlantic. Students are from 27 states and 7 foreign countries. 58% are from public schools. 64% are white; 18% Hispanic; 11% African American. The average age of freshmen is 18; all undergraduates, 20. 30% do not continue beyond their first year.

Housing: 50 students can be accommodated in college housing, which includes coed dorms. On-campus housing is available on a first-come, first-served basis. Alcohol is not permitted. No one may keep cars.

Activities: There are no fraternities or sororities. There are 10 groups on campus, including art, ethnic, fashion club, film, honors, professional, religious, social service, student government, and yearbook. Popular campus events include an annual fashion show, a ski trip, and a Halloween costume party.

Sports: There is no sports program at LIM.

Disabled Students: Elevators and specially equipped rest rooms are available.

Services: Counseling and information services are available, as is tutoring in most subjects. There is remedial math, reading, and writing.

Campus Safety and Security: Measures include informal discussions and pamphlets/posters/films.

Programs of Study: LIM confers B.B.A. and B.P.S. degrees. Associate degrees are also awarded. Bachelor's degrees are awarded in BUSINESS (fashion merchandising and marketing/retailing/merchandising).

Required: Students must complete 34 credits in the liberal arts and a minimum of 72 in fashion/business courses. Freshmen and sophomores must successfully complete a 3-credit work project each year. Seniors must complete a 13-credit, semester-long co-op program. A total of 126 credits and a GPA of 2.0 are required to graduate.

Special: Internships are required in the first, second, and fourth years. Study abroad is available in China, Italy, Spain, France, and England. There are co-op programs as well as work-study programs with major department stores and specialty shops, manufacturers, showrooms, magazine publishers, and cosmetics companies. There is 1 national honor society.

Faculty/Classroom: 41% of faculty are male; 59%, female. The average class size in an introductory lecture is 19 and in a regular course, 22.

Admissions: 66% of the 2003-2004 applicants were accepted. The SAT I scores for the 2003-2004 freshman class were: Verbal--66% below 500, 30% between 500 and 599, and 4% between 600 and 700; Math--74% below 500, 24% between 500 and 599, and 2% above 700. 14% of the current freshmen were in the top fifth of their class; 34% were in the top two fifths.

Requirements: The SAT I or ACT is required. In addition, an essay and an interview are required. Applicants should be high school graduates or hold the GED. AP and CLEP credits are accepted. Important factors in the admissions decision are recommendations by school officials, leadership record, and personality/intangible qualities.

Procedure: Freshmen are admitted fall and spring. Application deadlines are open. Application fee is $40. Notification is sent on a rolling basis.

Transfer: 75 transfer students enrolled in 2002-2003. Applicants must submit their official high school and college transcripts. Students with fewer than 30 college credits must submit SAT I or ACT scores. Interviews are required of all applicants, and recommendation letters are encouraged but not required. 46 of 126 credits required for the bachelor's degree must be completed at LIM.

Visiting: There are regularly scheduled orientations for prospective students, consisting of the open house program, which includes a tour, 3 presentations, a financial aid overview, breakfast, and interviews. There are guides for informal visits and visitors may sit in on classes. To schedule a visit, contact the Admissions Office.

Financial Aid: In a recent year, 78% of all full-time freshmen and 85% of continuing full-time students received some form of financial aid. The average freshman award was $9000. 5% of undergraduates work part time. Average annual earnings from campus work are $2800. The average financial indebtedness of a recent year's graduate was $15,000. The FAFSA and the college's own financial statement are required. Financial aid is awarded to eligible applicants on a first-come, first-served basis, beginning with applicants who have completed files.

International Students: There are 4 international students enrolled. They must score 550 on the written TOEFL or 213 on the electronic version and also take the SAT I or the ACT.

Computers: All students may access the system. There are no time limits and no fees.

Graduates: From July 1, 2002 to June 30, 2003, 68 bachelor's degrees were awarded. Of the 2002 graduating class, all were employed within 6 months of graduation.

Admissions Contact: Karen Hamill Iglio, Director of Admissions. E-mail: *admissions@limcollege.edu* Web: *www.limcollege.edu*

LE MOYNE COLLEGE
Syracuse, NY 13214-1399

C-3

(315) 445-4300
(800) 333-4733; Fax: (315) 445-4711

Full-time: 892 men, 1374 women	**Faculty:** 153; IIA, +$
Part-time: 116 men, 309 women	**Ph.D.s:** 90%
Graduate: 278 men, 434 women	**Student/Faculty:** 15 to 1
Year: semesters, summer session	**Tuition:** $18,950
Application Deadline: February 1	**Room & Board:** $7450
Freshman Class: 2940 applied, 2118 accepted, 503 enrolled	
SAT I Verbal/Math: 550/560	**ACT:** 23 **VERY COMPETITIVE**

Le Moyne College, founded in 1946, is a private institution in the Catholic and Jesuit tradition offering programs in the liberal arts and sciences. The library contains 247,708 volumes, 584,557 microform items, and 8509 audio/video tapes/CDs, and subscribes to 13,526 periodicals. Computerized library services include the card catalog, interlibrary loans, database searching, and Internet access. Special learning facilities include a learning resource center, art gallery, and radio station. The 151-acre campus is in a suburban area on the eastern edge of Syracuse. Including any residence halls, there are 36 buildings.

Student Life: 93% of undergraduates are from New York. Others are from 23 states and 4 foreign countries. 79% are from public schools. 84% are white. 50% are of unknown religious affiliation, Buddhist, or Muslim; 39% Catholic; 6% Protestant. The average age of freshmen is 18; all undergraduates, 22. 11% do not continue beyond their first year; 76% remain to graduate.

Housing: 1585 students can be accommodated in college housing, which includes single-sex and coed dorms, on-campus apartments, and off-campus apartments. In addition, there are special-interest houses and living learning communities. On-campus housing is guaranteed for all 4 years. 64% of students live on campus; of those, 85% remain on campus on weekends. All students may keep cars.

Activities: There are no fraternities or sororities. There are 70 groups on campus, including art, band, cheerleading, chess, choir, chorale, chorus, computers, dance, drama, ethnic, honors, international, jazz band, literary magazine, musical theater, newspaper, pep band, political, professional, radio and TV, religious, social, social service, student government, and yearbook. Popular campus events include Spring Olympics, Halloween Dance, and Snow Ball Holiday Party.

Sports: There are 8 intercollegiate sports for men and 8 for women, and 8 intramural sports for men and 7 for women. Facilities include a 2500-seat gym, indoor batting cages, team rooms, a 25-yard lap pool with diving capabilities, a whirlpool, a fitness center, an athletic training room, a jogging track, racquetball courts, a recreational gym, and locker rooms. Outdoor facilities include fields for intercollegiate baseball, softball, soccer, and lacrosse, tennis courts, a cross-country trail, and several intramural fields.

Disabled Students: 95% of the campus is accessible. Wheelchair ramps, elevators, special parking, specially equipped rest rooms, lowered drinking fountains, lowered telephones, special housing, and automatic door openers are available.

Services: Counseling and information services are available, as is tutoring in some subjects, including math, biology, chemistry, physics, economics, philosophy, Spanish, French, German, and Latin. There is a reader service for the blind and remedial math and writing. Study groups are available for selected courses.

Campus Safety and Security: Measures include 24-hour foot and vehicle patrol, self-defense education, security escort services, and shuttle buses. There are informal discussions, pamphlets/posters/films, emergency telephones, lighted pathways/sidewalks, 6 Blue Light Security Phones, 23 stationary closed-circuit security cameras, AT&T campuswide card access, and 7 Pan Tilt Zoom closed-circuit security cameras.

Programs of Study: Le Moyne confers B.A. and B.S. degrees. Master's degrees are also awarded. Bachelor's degrees are awarded in BIOLOGICAL SCIENCE (biochemistry and biology/biological science), BUSINESS (accounting, business administration and management, human resources, labor studies, and management information systems), COMMUNICATIONS AND THE ARTS (communications, creative writing, dramatic arts, English, French, and Spanish), COMPUTER AND PHYSICAL SCIENCE (applied mathematics, chemistry, information sciences and systems, mathematics, physical sciences, physics, and science), EDUCATION (elementary, English, foreign languages, mathematics, science, secondary, and social studies), HEALTH PROFESSIONS (physician's assistant, predentistry, premedicine, preoptometry, prepharmacy, prepodiatry, and preveterinary science), SOCIAL SCIENCE (criminology, economics, history, international studies, philosophy, political science/government, prelaw, psychology, religion, and sociology). Business, psychology, and biology are the largest.

Required: A core curriculum of 14 courses in the humanities, natural sciences, and social sciences is required. Students must earn a GPA of 2.0, 30 hours in the major, and 120 total credit hours to graduate.

Special: Internships are available to students in all majors. A campus work-study program, study abroad in 8 countries, dual majors, and a Washington semester are offered. A 3-2 engineering degree is available with Manhattan College, Clarkson University, and University of Detroit Mercy, and there are early assurance medical and dental programs and a physician assistant program. Some pass/fail options are offered. There are 14 national honor societies, a freshman honors program, and 10 departmental honors programs.

Faculty/Classroom: 59% of faculty are male; 41%, female. All both teach and do research. No introductory courses are taught by graduate students. The average class size in an introductory lecture is 25; in a laboratory, 14; and in a regular course, 22.

Admissions: 72% of the 2003-2004 applicants were accepted. The SAT I scores for the 2003-2004 freshman class were: Verbal--22% below 500, 53% between 500 and 599, 23% between 600 and 700, and 2% above 700; Math--17% below 500, 54% between 500 and 599, 27% between 600 and 700, and 2% above 700. The ACT scores were 23% below 21, 31% between 21 and 23, 28% between 24 and 26, 10% between 27 and 28, and 8% above 28. 40% of the current freshmen were in the top fifth of their class; 77% were in the top two fifths. 3 freshmen graduated first in their class.

Requirements: The SAT I or ACT is required. In addition, students should graduate from an accredited high school, having completed 17 academic units that include 4 in English and social studies, 3 to 4 each in math and science, and 3 in foreign language. A personal statement and letters of recommendation from a teacher and a counselor are required. AP and CLEP credits are accepted. Important factors in the admissions decision are recommendations by school officials, advanced placement or honor courses, and extracurricular activities record.

Procedure: Freshmen are admitted fall and spring. Entrance exams should be taken in the spring of the junior year or fall of the senior year. There are early decision, early admissions, and deferred admissions plans. Early decision applications should be filed by December 1; regular applications, by February 1 for fall entry and December 1 for spring entry, along with a $35 fee. Notification of early decision is sent December 15; regular decision, on a rolling basis beginning in January. 47 early decision candidates were accepted for the 2003-2004 class. 103 were on the 2003 waiting list; 39 were admitted. Applications are accepted online through Common App, Princeton Review, NYMentor, and the school's web site.

Transfer: 238 transfer students enrolled in 2002-2003. A 2.6 GPA is usually required. High school and college transcripts, a letter of recommendation from an academic official at the last college attended, and a personal statement must be submitted. SAT I or ACT scores are needed for students out of high school for less than 3 years or with fewer than 30 completed college credits. 30 of 120 credits required for the bachelor's degree must be completed at Le Moyne.

Visiting: There are regularly scheduled orientations for prospective students, including a campus tour and an interview with admissions counselors. Accepted students are invited to attend class and stay overnight in a residence hall. There are guides for informal visits and visitors may sit in on classes and stay overnight. To schedule a visit, contact the Admission Office.

Financial Aid: In 2002-2003, 91% of all full-time freshmen and 89% of continuing full-time students received some form of financial aid. 81% of all full-time students received need-based aid. The average freshman award was $14,780. Need-based scholarships or need-based grants averaged $15,856 ($24,235 maximum); need-based self-help aid (loans and jobs) averaged $3599 ($5625 maximum); non-need-based athletic scholarships averaged $6652 ($24,500 maximum); and other non-need-based awards and non-need-based scholarships averaged $8789 ($15,000 maximum). 90% of undergraduates work part time. Average annual earnings from campus work are $1300. The average financial indebtedness of the 2002 graduate was $18,750. Le Moyne is a member of CSS. The FAFSA and the college's own financial statement are required. The priority date for freshman financial aid applications for fall entry is February 1.

International Students: There are 20 international students enrolled. The school actively recruits these students. They must score 550 on the written TOEFL or 213 on the electronic version and also take the SAT I or the ACT.

Computers: All academic computing for students and faculty is run from Novell and NT servers. Connected to the campus network are about 325 PCs and Macs in public and departmental labs across campus, providing access to the library system, the Internet, and Novell servers with a multitude of applications. There is access to personal space on these servers. Access from residence hall rooms includes the library system, personal space, and the Internet. All students may access the system 24 hours a day. There are no time limits and no fees.

Graduates: From July 1, 2002 to June 30, 2003, 520 bachelor's degrees were awarded. The most popular majors were business (24%), psychology (22%), and English (13%). In an average class, 63% graduate in 4 years or less, 69% graduate in 5 years or less, and 71% graduate in 6 years or less. 73 companies recruited on campus in 2002-2003. Of the 2001 graduating class, 29% were enrolled in graduate school within 12 months of graduation and 72% were employed.

Admissions Contact: Dennis J. Nicholson, Director of Admission. A video is available. E-mail: *admission@lemoyne.edu* Web: *www.lemoyne.edu*

LONG ISLAND UNIVERSITY SYSTEM

Long Island University is a multi-campus, diverse, doctoral institution of higher learning. As the nation's seventh largest private university, it offers 563 undergraduate, graduate, and doctoral degree programs and certificates, and educates more than 31,000 students on six metropolitan area campuses in Brooklyn, Brookville (C.W. Post), Southampton, Brentwood, Rockland, and Westchester. The Arnold & Marie Schwartz College of Pharmacy and Health Sciences prepares students for successful careers in the continually growing fields of pharmacy and health care. The University's Friends World program offers a wide range of study abroad options in North America and at five overseas locations. Nearly 700 full-time faculty members provide outstanding instruction that is supplemented by internships and cooperative education opportunities.

LONG ISLAND UNIVERSITY/BROOKLYN CAMPUS   D-5
Brooklyn, NY 11201   (718) 488-1292
                              (800) LIU-PLAN; Fax: (718) 797-2399

Full-time: 1330 men, 3100 women	**Faculty:** 211; IIA, ++$
Part-time: 260 men, 830 women	**Ph.D.s:** 76%
Graduate: 920 men, 1200 women	**Student/Faculty:** 21 to 1
Year: semesters, summer session	**Tuition:** $17,860
Application Deadline: open	**Room & Board:** $6930
Freshman Class: n/av	
SAT I or ACT: recommended	**COMPETITIVE**

Long Island University/Brooklyn Campus, founded in 1926, is part of the Long Island University system. It is a private institution offering programs in liberal arts and sciences, pharmacy, health professions, education, business, nursing, and special programs. It is largely a commuter school. Some figures in the above capsule and in this profile are approximate. There are 6 undergraduate and 5 graduate schools. In addition to regional accreditation, LIU has baccalaureate program accreditation with ACPE and NLN. The library contains 2,100,000 volumes, 813,544 microform items, and 7902 audio/video tapes/CDs, and subscribes to 8042 periodicals. Computerized library services include the card catalog and interlibrary loans. Special learning facilities include a learning resource center, art gallery, radio station, and TV station. The 10-acre campus is in an urban area. Including any residence halls, there are 11 buildings.

Student Life: 86% of undergraduates are from New York. Students are from 35 states, 21 foreign countries, and Canada. 75% are from public schools. 43% are African American; 27% white; 19% Hispanic; 11% Asian American. The average age of freshmen is 21; all undergraduates, 25. 36% do not continue beyond their first year; 61% remain to graduate.

Housing: 525 students can be accommodated in college housing, which includes single-sex and coed dorms and married-student housing.

On-campus housing is available on a first-come, first-served basis. 89% of students commute. Alcohol is not permitted. No one may keep cars.

Activities: There are 75 groups on campus, including band, cheerleading, chess, chorale, computers, dance, ethnic, honors, international, jazz band, literary magazine, newspaper, pep band, photography, political, radio and TV, religious, student government, and yearbook.

Sports: There are 7 intercollegiate sports for men and 6 for women, and 6 intramural sports for men and 6 for women. Facilities include a baseball/soccer field and a basketball gym.

Disabled Students: All of the campus is accessible. Wheelchair ramps, elevators, specially equipped rest rooms, special class scheduling, lowered drinking fountains, and lowered telephones are available.

Services: Counseling and information services are available, as is tutoring in most subjects. There is remedial math, reading, and writing.

Campus Safety and Security: Measures include 24-hour foot and vehicle patrol, pamphlets/posters/films, emergency telephones, and lighted pathways/sidewalks.

Programs of Study: LIU confers B.A., B.S., and B.F.A. degrees. Associate, master's, and doctoral degrees are also awarded. Bachelor's degrees are awarded in BIOLOGICAL SCIENCE (biology/biological science), BUSINESS (accounting, banking and finance, business administration and management, and marketing/retailing/merchandising), COMMUNICATIONS AND THE ARTS (broadcasting, communications, English, fine arts, journalism, languages, music, and speech/debate/rhetoric), COMPUTER AND PHYSICAL SCIENCE (chemistry, computer science, information sciences and systems, and mathematics), EDUCATION (art, business, early childhood, elementary, music, science, secondary, special, and teaching English as a second/foreign language (TESOL/TEFOL)), HEALTH PROFESSIONS (nursing, occupational therapy, pharmacy, physical therapy, physician's assistant, predentistry, and premedicine), SOCIAL SCIENCE (anthropology, economics, history, philosophy, political science/government, prelaw, psychology, social science, social work, and sociology). Health professions, pharmacy, and liberal arts are the strongest academically. Health professions, liberal arts, and business are the largest.

Required: Proficiency courses include basic English and math, English composition, and speech. Distribution requirements are 6 credits each in foreign language, math, and science. Students must complete a core curriculum of 18 credits in the humanities, 12 in social sciences, 8 in natural sciences, and 6 in math. A total of 128 credits (197 for pharmacy) is required for graduation, with 36 credits in the major, and a GPA of 2.0.

Special: Accelerated degree programs are available in all majors. Students may cross-register with other LIU campuses. Internships in career-related jobs provide cooperative education credits. Study abroad, dual-majors, credit for life, military, and work experience, and pass/fail options are also offered. There is a chapter of Phi Beta Kappa and a freshman honors program.

Faculty/Classroom: All teach undergraduates. The average class size in a regular course is 22.

Requirements: The SAT I or ACT is recommended. LIU requires applicants to be in the upper 75% of their class. A GPA of 2.0 is required. AP and CLEP credits are accepted. Important factors in the admissions decision are recommendations by school officials, advanced placement or honor courses, and evidence of special talent.

Procedure: Freshmen are admitted to all sessions. Entrance exams should be taken by January of the senior year. There is a deferred admissions plan. Application deadlines are open. Application fee is $30. Applications are accepted on-line through *www.liu.edu*.

Transfer: 724 transfer students enrolled in a recent year. A GPA of 2.5 is required. 32 of 128 credits required for the bachelor's degree must be completed at LIU.

Visiting: There are regularly scheduled orientations for prospective students. Visitors may sit in on classes. To schedule a visit, contact the Admissions Office at (718) 488-1011.

Financial Aid: In 2003-2004, 93% of all full-time freshmen received some form of financial aid. The CSS Profile and the college's own financial statement are required. Check with the school for current deadlines.

International Students: There are 95 international students enrolled. The school actively recruits these students. They must score 500 on the written TOEFL and also take the SAT I or the ACT.

Computers: The mainframe is a DEC VAX 8600. PCs are available in the library for academic use. All students may access the system during library hours. There are no time limits and no fees.

Graduates: From July 1, 2002 to June 30, 2003, 552 bachelor's degrees were awarded. The most popular majors were nursing (15%), psychology (9%), and business (8%). In an average class, 30% graduate in 4 years or less, 60% graduate in 5 years or less, and 70% graduate in 6 years or less. 150 companies recruited on campus in a recent year.

Admissions Contact: Richard Sunday, Acting Dean of Admissions. E-mail: *attend@liu.edu* Web: *www.liu.edu*

LONG ISLAND UNIVERSITY/C.W. POST CAMPUS
Brookville, NY 11548-1300

D-5

(516) 299-2900
(800) LIU-PLAN; Fax: (516) 299-2137

Full-time: 1575 men, 2416 women	**Faculty:** IIA, ++$
Part-time: 1155 men, 1473 women	**Ph.D.s:** n/av
Graduate: 1062 men, 2647 women	**Student/Faculty:** n/av
Year: semesters, summer session	**Tuition:** $20,490
Application Deadline: open	**Room & Board:** $7792
Freshman Class: 4520 applied, 3428 accepted, 864 enrolled	
SAT I Verbal/Math: 490/500	**ACT:** 20	**COMPETITIVE**

Long Island University/C.W. Post Campus, founded in 1954 as part of the private Long Island University system, offers 100 undergraduate and 63 graduate majors in education, liberal arts and sciences, accountancy, business, public service, health professions and nursing, and information and computer science. There are 6 undergraduate and 6 graduate schools. In addition to regional accreditation, C.W. Post has baccalaureate program accreditation with AACSB, ADA, ASLA, CAHEA, CSWE, and NLN. The library contains 1,132,318 volumes, 834,413 microform items, and 9606 audio/video tapes/CDs, and subscribes to 10,999 periodicals. Computerized library services include the card catalog, interlibrary loans, and database searching. Special learning facilities include a learning resource center, art gallery, radio station, TV station, art museum, tax institute, speech and hearing center, center for business research, federal depository, and multimedia computer center. The 307-acre campus is in a suburban area 25 miles east of New York City, on the former estate of Marjorie Merriweather Post. Including any residence halls, there are 53 buildings.

Student Life: 91% of undergraduates are from New York. Students are from 32 states, 46 foreign countries, and Canada. 71% are from public schools. 13% are white. The average age of freshmen is 18; all undergraduates, 21. 31% do not continue beyond their first year; 37% remain to graduate.

Housing: 1710 students can be accommodated in college housing, which includes single-sex and coed dorms. On-campus housing is guaranteed for all 4 years. 60% of students commute. All students may keep cars.

Activities: 1% of men belong to 4 national fraternities; 3% of women belong to 9 national sororities. There are 80 groups on campus, including art, band, chamber singing, cheerleading, choir, chorale, chorus, dance, drama, equestrian, ethnic, film, gay, honors, international, jazz band, literary magazine, madigral, musical theater, newspaper, orchestra, pep band, photography, political, professional, radio and TV, religious, Renaissance music, social, social service, student government, vocal jazz, and yearbook. Popular campus events include Theater Festival, Spring Fling, and Cereal Bowl: The Inter-Residential Hall Competition.

Sports: There are 7 intercollegiate sports for men and 10 for women, and 5 intramural sports for men and 5 for women. Facilities include a 5000-seat football stadium, an equestrian center, tennis courts, 70 acres of baseball, soccer, lacrosse, softball, and practice fields, a recreational center with an 8-lane swimming pool, 3 basketball courts with spectator seating for 3000, racquetball courts, an indoor track, and weight and aerobic rooms.

Disabled Students: 75% of the campus is accessible. Wheelchair ramps, elevators, special parking, specially equipped rest rooms, special class scheduling, lowered drinking fountains, lowered telephones, special housing, and electric doors are available.

Services: Counseling and information services are available, as is tutoring in most subjects. There is a reader service for the blind, remedial math, reading, and writing, and an academic resource center for learning-disabled students.

Campus Safety and Security: Measures include 24-hour foot and vehicle patrol, self-defense education, security escort services, and shuttle buses. There are informal discussions, pamphlets/posters/films, emergency telephones, lighted pathways/sidewalks, restricted night access to campus, card-access residence entrances, and an electronic keyless locking system for dorm rooms.

Programs of Study: C.W. Post confers B.A., B.S., B.F.A., and B.S.Ed. degrees. Associate, master's, and doctoral degrees are also awarded. Bachelor's degrees are awarded in AGRICULTURE (conservation and regulation), BIOLOGICAL SCIENCE (biology/biological science, molecular biology, and nutrition), BUSINESS (accounting, banking and finance, business administration and management, and marketing/retailing/merchandising), COMMUNICATIONS AND THE ARTS (arts administration/management, broadcasting, communications, dance, dramatic arts, English, film arts, fine arts, French, German, Italian, journalism, music, photography, public relations, and Spanish), COMPUTER AND PHYSICAL SCIENCE (chemistry, computer science, geology, information sciences and systems, mathematics, physics, and radiological technology), EDUCATION (art, early childhood, elementary, English, foreign languages, health, music, science, and secondary), ENGINEERING AND ENVIRONMENTAL DESIGN (preengineering), HEALTH PROFESSIONS (art therapy, biomedical science, health care administration, medical laboratory technology, medical records administration/

services, nursing, predentistry, premedicine, prepharmacy, and speech pathology/audiology), SOCIAL SCIENCE (criminal justice, economics, geography, history, international studies, philosophy, political science/government, prelaw, psychology, public administration, and social work). Accounting, radiologic technology, and biology are the strongest academically. Business, education, and media arts are the largest.

Required: Core requirements include 9 credits each of history and philosophy, 8 of lab science, 6 each of language and literature, arts, political science and economics, sociology, psychology, and geography or anthropology, and 3 of math. A minimum of 128 credits is required to graduate. GPA requirements range from 2.0 to 2.5 in most departments, 3.0 in interdisciplinary studies. Students must demonstrate competency in writing, quantitative skills, computer skills, oral communications, and library use.

Special: There is cross-registration with several other Long Island colleges. C.W. Post offers co-op programs in all majors, internships, study abroad in 11 countries, work-study in most departments, accelerated degree programs, and a Washington semester for outstanding criminal justice students. Dual and student-designed majors are available. There is a 3-2 engineering degree with Polytechnic University, Pratt Institute, and Arizona State University, and credit is available for life, military, and work experience. Nondegree study is available, as are pass/fail options. There are 14 national honor societies, a freshman honors program, and 16 departmental honors programs.

Faculty/Classroom: No introductory courses are taught by graduate students. The average class size in an introductory lecture is 26; in a laboratory, 20; and in a regular course, 19.

Admissions: 76% of the 2003-2004 applicants were accepted. The ACT scores for the 2003-2004 freshman class were: 52% below 21, 33% between 21 and 23, 5% between 24 and 26, 6% between 27 and 28, and 4% above 28. 30% of the current freshmen were in the top fifth of their class; 61% were in the top two fifths. There were 4 National Merit finalists in a recent year.

Requirements: The SAT I or ACT is required, with a minimum composite SAT I score of 900 or a minimum ACT score of 20. Applicants should be graduates of an accredited secondary school with a B average or have a GED. Preparatory work should include 4 years each of English and social science, and 2 each of foreign language, college preparatory math, and lab science. A grade average of 75 is required. AP and CLEP credits are accepted. Important factors in the admissions decision are advanced placement or honor courses, recommendations by school officials, and evidence of special talent.

Procedure: Freshmen are admitted to all sessions. Entrance exams should be taken from May of the junior year through December of the senior year. There are early admissions, deferred admissions, and rolling admissions plans. Application deadlines are open. The application fee is $30. Applications are accepted on-line through the school's web site.

Transfer: 900 transfer students enrolled in a recent year. Applicants should have appropriate high school credentials and a minimum college GPA of 2.25. 32 of 128 credits required for the bachelor's degree must be completed at C.W. Post.

Visiting: There are regularly scheduled orientations for prospective students, consisting of Post Preview Days, which include meeting the faculty, an admissions and financial aid overview, and a campus tour. There are guides for informal visits and visitors may sit in on classes. To schedule a visit, contact the Office of Admissions.

Financial Aid: In 2003-2004, 85% of all full-time students received some form of financial aid. 85% of all full-time students received need-based aid. The average freshman award was $9600. Need-based scholarships or need-based grants averaged $8574 ($25,000 maximum); need-based self-help aid (loans and jobs) averaged $3538 ($6625 maximum); non-need-based athletic scholarships averaged $6500 ($27,240 maximum); and other non-need-based awards and non-need-based scholarships averaged $6328 ($16,000 maximum). 31% of undergraduates work part time. Average annual earnings from campus work are $1200. The average annual indebtedness of the 2003 graduate was $15,000. C.W. Post is a member of CSS. The CSS Profile or FAFSA is required. The priority date for freshman financial aid applications for fall entry is March 1. The deadline for filing freshman financial aid applications for fall entry is May 15.

International Students: There are 380 international students enrolled. The school actively recruits these students. They must score 525 on the written TOEFL or 197 on the electronic version. SAT I or ACT scores are recommended to help evaluate students' admissions eligibility and enable students to be considered for scholarships.

Computers: The mainframes are a UNIX, NT/2000 servers in the Information Technology Department, and a fiber-based network throughout campus. The Office of Information Technology supports 25 campuswide labs for student use with more than 500 computers (PCs and Macs), free LaserJet printing services, and a wide range of software from graphical to statistical packages; 25 smart classrooms are connected to the Internet; e-mail accounts are provided to every member of the campus community; and all dorm rooms are connected to the campus network. A web-based student information system providing information about grades, bills, degree requirements, and many other services is available.

All students may access the system Monday to Thursday 8 A.M. to 11 P.M. and Friday to Sunday 9 A.M. to 10 P.M. Dial-up capacity is available 24 hours a day. There are no time limits and no fees.

Graduates: In a recent year, 904 bachelor's degrees were awarded. The most popular majors were elementary education (14%), psychology (7%), and criminal justice (6%). 500 companies recruited on campus in a recent year. Of a recent year's graduating class, 29% were enrolled in graduate school within 6 months of graduation and 84% were employed.

Admissions Contact: Beth Carson, Acting Director of Admissions. E-mail: *enroll@cwpost.liu.edu* Web: *www.liu.edu*

LONG ISLAND UNIVERSITY/SOUTHAMPTON COLLEGE

E-5

Southampton, NY 11968   (631) 287-8200
(800) LIU-PLAN, ext. 2; Fax: (631) 287-8130

Full-time: 354 men, 716 women	**Faculty:** 74; IIA, ++$
Part-time: 44 men, 82 women	**Ph.Ds:** 86%
Graduate: 54 men, 203 women	**Student/Faculty:** 14 to 1
Year: semesters, summer session	**Tuition:** $20,560
Application Deadline: open	**Room & Board:** $8810
Freshman Class: 1089 applied, 868 accepted, 197 enrolled	
SAT I Verbal/Math: 531/521	**ACT:** 24 **COMPETITIVE+**

Long Island University/Southampton College, established in 1963, is a private liberal arts institution offering undergraduate and graduate programs in the arts and sciences, business, and education. There are 6 undergraduate and 3 graduate schools. The library contains 150,000 volumes, 1000 microform items, and 500 audio/video tapes/CDs, and subscribes to 700 periodicals. Computerized library services include the card catalog, interlibrary loans, and database searching. Special learning facilities include a learning resource center, art gallery, radio station, on-campus marine station, seawater laboratories, and research vessels. The 110-acre campus is in a rural area 90 miles east of New York City. Including any residence halls, there are 43 buildings.

Student Life: 60% of undergraduates are from New York. Students are from 46 states, 15 foreign countries, and Canada. 85% are from public schools. 82% are white. 65% are Catholic; 20% Protestant. The average age of freshmen is 18; all undergraduates, 21. 10% do not continue beyond their first year; 78% remain to graduate.

Housing: 710 students can be accommodated in college housing, which includes single-sex and coed dorms. In addition, there are honors houses, special-interest houses, a nonsmoking house, and quiet-study, all-women, and smoke-free and substance-free dorms. On-campus housing is guaranteed for all 4 years. 80% of students live on campus; of those, 55% remain on campus on weekends. All students may keep cars.

Activities: There are no fraternities or sororities. There are 50 groups on campus, including art, cheerleading, choir, chorus, computers, dance, drama, environmental, ethnic, film, gay, honors, jazz band, literary magazine, marine science, musical theater, newspaper, photography, political, professional, radio and TV, religious, social, social service, student government, submersibles-scuba diving, and yearbook. Popular campus events include Spring Fest, Fall Fest, and Friday Night Phenomenon.

Sports: There are 5 intercollegiate sports for men and 5 for women, and 6 intramural sports for men and 5 for women. Facilities include a gym, an outdoor swimming pool, basketball and volleyball courts, a weight room, a fitness trail, and soccer, softball, and lacrosse fields.

Disabled Students: 15% of the campus is accessible. Wheelchair ramps, elevators, special parking, specially equipped rest rooms, lowered drinking fountains, and lowered telephones are available.

Services: Counseling and information services are available, as is tutoring in every subject. There is remedial math, reading, and writing.

Campus Safety and Security: Measures include 24-hour foot and vehicle patrol, self-defense education, shuttle buses, and informal discussions. There are pamphlets/posters/films, emergency telephones, and lighted pathways/sidewalks. The college also conducts an alcohol awareness week and date-rape seminars.

Programs of Study: Southampton College confers B.A., B.S., and B.F.A. degrees. Master's degrees are also awarded. Bachelor's degrees are awarded in BIOLOGICAL SCIENCE (biology/biological science and marine science), COMMUNICATIONS AND THE ARTS (communications, English, fine arts, and graphic design), COMPUTER AND PHYSICAL SCIENCE (chemistry), EDUCATION (art and elementary), SOCIAL SCIENCE (history, liberal arts/general studies, political science/government, prelaw, psychology, social science, and sociology). Marine science and fine arts are the strongest academically. Marine science, fine arts, and social science are the largest.

Required: To graduate, students must complete 128 credits with an overall 2.0 GPA and a 2.25 GPA in the major. Core courses consist of 3 required courses in English (including Introduction to Composition), and 2 each in humanities, social science, science/math, and fine arts. 45 to 88 hours must be completed in the major. All students must pass a writing proficiency exam.

Special: Cross-registration is permitted with the C.W. Post and Brooklyn campuses of Long Island University and the Friends World Program. Opportunities are provided for internships in science research, legislative offices, and the Smithsonian Institution. Study abroad, work-study programs, an accelerated degree program in accounting, dual majors in psychology and biology, credit by examination, credit for life experience, nondegree study, and pass/fail options are also available. In liberal studies and the Friends World Program, students design their own majors and receive credit based on experiential education, fieldwork, and overseas travel. There are 2 national honor societies, a freshman honors program, and 2 departmental honors programs.

Faculty/Classroom: 79% of faculty are male; 21%, female. All teach undergraduates and 86% both teach and do research. No introductory courses are taught by graduate students. The average class size in an introductory lecture is 20; in a laboratory, 15; and in a regular course, 15.

Admissions: 80% of the 2003-2004 applicants were accepted. The SAT I scores for the 2003-2004 freshman class were: Verbal--36% below 500, 43% between 500 and 599, 19% between 600 and 700, and 2% above 700; Math--40% below 500, 39% between 500 and 599, 19% between 600 and 700, and 2% above 700. The ACT scores were 13% below 21, 24% between 21 and 23, 21% between 24 and 26, 21% between 27 and 28, and 21% above 28. 32% of the current freshmen were in the top fifth of their class; 61% were in the top two fifths. 5 freshmen graduated first in their class in a recent year.

Requirements: The SAT I or ACT is required. In addition, a minimum composite score of 1000 (500 verbal and 500 math) is required on the SAT I and a score of 21 is required on the ACT. Graduation from an accredited secondary school is required; the GED will be accepted. The academic record should include 4 credits in English, 3 each in history and social studies, 2 each in math and science, and 1 in art. An essay, at least 1 letter of recommendation, portfolio, audition, or interview may be recommended. A grade average of 80 is required. AP and CLEP credits are accepted. Important factors in the admissions decision are advanced placement or honor courses, personality/intangible qualities, and evidence of special talent.

Procedure: Freshmen are admitted fall and spring. Entrance exams should be taken during the junior year. There are early admissions, deferred admissions, and rolling admissions plans. Application deadlines are open for fall and spring entry. The application fee is $30. Notification is sent on a rolling basis. Applications are accepted on computer disk and on-line through *www.southampton.liu.edu*.

Transfer: Applicants must have a 2.0 GPA in previous college work. An interview is recommended. High school grades and SAT I scores are required if the student has fewer than 24 college credits. 30 of 128 credits required for the bachelor's degree must be completed at Southampton College.

Visiting: There are regularly scheduled orientations for prospective students, including an interview, a tour, and lunch or dinner. Students may also attend a class, meet with a coach, and attend a cooperative education meeting. There are guides for informal visits and visitors may sit in on classes and stay overnight. To schedule a visit, contact the Admissions Office at (631) 287-8010 or *admissions@southampton.liu.edu*.

Financial Aid: In 2003-2004, 54% of all full-time freshmen and 70% of continuing full-time students received some form of financial aid. 49% of full-time freshmen received need-based aid. The average freshman award was $29,000. Need-based scholarships or need-based grants averaged $8500 ($10,000 maximum); need-based self-help aid (loans and jobs) averaged $8625 (maximum); non-need-based athletic scholarships averaged $10,000 ($19,510 maximum); and other non-need-based awards and non-need-based scholarships averaged $10,000 ($15,000 maximum). Average annual earnings from campus work are $1200. The average financial indebtedness of the 2003 graduate was $15,235. The FAFSA and the college's own financial statement are required. The deadline for filing freshman financial aid applications for fall entry is June 1.

International Students: They must score 527 on the written TOEFL or 197 on the electronic version and also take the SAT I or the ACT.

Computers: The mainframes are a DEC VAX 750, 8600, and 6210 and an IBM 520. The Long Island University Network is connected to the Internet. There are 120 PCs located at 6 campus locations and there are in-room PC hookups. The student-to-computer ratio is 12 to 1. A Silicon Graphics Lab is also available for student use. All students may access the system 24 hours a day. There are no time limits and no fees.

Graduates: From July 1, 2002 to June 30, 2003, 279 bachelor's degrees were awarded. The most popular majors were marine science (14%), psychology/biology (13%), and liberal studies (12%).

Admissions Contact: Rory Shaffer, Director of Admissions. A video is available. E-mail: *info@southampton.liu.edu* Web: *http://www.southampton.liu.edu*

MANHATTAN COLLEGE
Riverdale, NY 10471

D-5

(718) 862-7200
(800) 622-9235; Fax: (718) 862-8019

Full-time: 1323 men, 1372 women	**Faculty:** 162
Part-time: 119 men, 72 women	**Ph.Ds:** 94%
Graduate: 178 men, 176 women	**Student/Faculty:** 17 to 1
Year: semesters, summer session	**Tuition:** $19,300
Application Deadline: March 1	**Room & Board:** $8100
Freshman Class: n/av	
SAT I: required	**VERY COMPETITIVE**

Manhattan College, founded in 1853, is a private institution affiliated with the Christian Brothers of the Catholic Church. It offers degree programs in the arts and sciences, education and human services, business, and engineering. There are 5 undergraduate and 3 graduate schools. In addition to regional accreditation, Manhattan has baccalaureate program accreditation with ABET, AHEA, and CAHEA. The 4 libraries contain 193,100 volumes, 383,480 microform items, and 3244 audio/video tapes/CDs, and subscribe to 1527 periodicals. Computerized library services include the card catalog, interlibrary loans, and database searching. Special learning facilities include a learning resource center, radio station, nuclear reactor lab, and media center. The 26-acre campus is in an urban area 10 miles north of midtown Manhattan. Including any residence halls, there are 28 buildings.

Student Life: 75% of undergraduates are from New York. Students are from 33 states and 10 foreign countries. 60% are from public schools. 67% are white; 14% Hispanic. The average age of freshmen is 18; all undergraduates, 20. 15% do not continue beyond their first year; 68% remain to graduate.

Housing: 1440 students can be accommodated in college housing, which includes coed dorms and off-campus apartments. On-campus housing is guaranteed for all 4 years. 54% of students live on campus; of those, 80% remain on campus on weekends. All students may keep cars.

Activities: 2% of men belong to 3 local and 1 national fraternities; 1% of women belong to 4 local sororities. There are 70 groups on campus, including bagpipe band, cheerleading, choir, chorus, computers, dance, debate, drama, ethnic, honors, international, jazz band, literary magazine, musical theater, newspaper, orchestra, pep band, political, professional, radio and TV, religious, social, social service, student government, and yearbook. Popular campus events include Annual Springfest, Special Olympics, and Jasper Jingle.

Sports: There are 8 intercollegiate sports for men and 8 for women, and 7 intramural sports for men and 7 for women. Facilities include 5 full basketball courts, which can also be used for volleyball and tennis, an indoor track, a weight room, a swimming pool, and a Nautilus center.

Disabled Students: All of the campus is accessible. Wheelchair ramps, elevators, special parking, and specially equipped rest rooms are available.

Services: Counseling and information services are available, as is tutoring in every subject.

Campus Safety and Security: Measures include 24-hour foot and vehicle patrol, security escort services, informal discussions, and pamphlets/posters/films. There are emergency telephones and lighted pathways/sidewalks.

Programs of Study: Manhattan confers B.A., B.S., and B.S.E. degrees. Master's degrees are also awarded. Bachelor's degrees are awarded in BIOLOGICAL SCIENCE (biochemistry and biology/biological science), BUSINESS (accounting, banking and finance, business economics, international business management, and marketing/retailing/merchandising), COMMUNICATIONS AND THE ARTS (communications, English, French, and Spanish), COMPUTER AND PHYSICAL SCIENCE (chemistry, computer science, information sciences and systems, mathematics, and physics), EDUCATION (early childhood, elementary, foreign languages, health, middle school, physical, science, secondary, and special), ENGINEERING AND ENVIRONMENTAL DESIGN (chemical engineering, civil engineering, electrical/electronics engineering, environmental engineering, and mechanical engineering), HEALTH PROFESSIONS (predentistry, premedicine, and radiological science), SOCIAL SCIENCE (economics, history, peace studies, philosophy, political science/government, prelaw, psychology, religion, sociology, and urban studies). Engineering and business are the strongest academically. Arts, business, and education are the largest.

Required: All students must take courses in English composition and literature, religious studies, philosophy, humanities, social science, science, math, and a modern foreign language. About 130 credit hours are required for graduation, with about 36 in the major. The minimum GPA is 2.0.

Special: Manhattan offers co-op programs in 11 majors, cross-registration with the College of Mount St. Vincent, and off-campus internships in business, industry, government, and social or cultural organizations. Students may study abroad in 10 countries and enter work-study programs with major U.S. corporations, health services, or in the arts. A general studies degree, a 3-2 engineering degree, a dual major in

international business, credit by exam, and nondegree study are also available. There are 22 national honor societies, including Phi Beta Kappa, a freshman honors program, and 28 departmental honors programs.

Faculty/Classroom: 70% of faculty are male; 30%, female. All teach undergraduates and 80% both teach and do research. No introductory courses are taught by graduate students. The average class size in an introductory lecture is 15 and in a regular course, 22.

Admissions: 16 freshmen graduated first in their class in a recent year.

Requirements: The SAT I is required. In addition, applicants must graduate from an accredited secondary school or have earned a GED. 16 academic units are required, including 4 of English, 3 each of math and social studies, and 2 of foreign language, lab sciences, and electives. An essay is required and an interview is recommended. AP and CLEP credits are accepted. Important factors in the admissions decision are advanced placement or honor courses, leadership record, and recommendations by school officials.

Procedure: Freshmen are admitted fall and spring. Entrance exams should be taken in the spring of the junior year or the fall of the senior year. There are early decision and deferred admissions plans. Early decision applications should be filed by November 15; regular applications, by March 1 for fall entry and December 1 for spring entry. Notification of early decision is sent December 1; regular decision, on a rolling basis. 20 early decision candidates were accepted for the 2003-2004 class. A waiting list is an active part of the admissions procedure. Applications are accepted on-line through Common App, EXPAN, CollegeView, CollegeLink, and the college's web site www.manhattan.edu.

Transfer: 125 transfer students enrolled in a recent year. Applicants must have a GPA of 2.5 and meet subject course requirements according to their course of study. They must submit transcripts from colleges and high schools attended. An interview is recommended. 66 of 130 credits required for the bachelor's degree must be completed at Manhattan.

Visiting: There are regularly scheduled orientations for prospective students, during 2 days in the summer, which include scheduling, parent workshops, loan seminars, and English and math testing. There are guides for informal visits and visitors may sit in on classes and stay overnight. To schedule a visit, contact the Admission Center at admit@manhattan.edu.

Financial Aid: In 2003-2004, 82% of all full-time freshmen and 71% of continuing full-time students received some form of financial aid. 73% of full-time freshmen and 63% of continuing full-time students received need-based aid. The average freshman award was $12,688. Need-based scholarships or need-based grants averaged $7179; need-based self-help aid (loans and jobs) averaged $3097; non-need-based athletic scholarships averaged $10,750; and other non-need-based awards and non-need-based scholarships averaged $6988. 15% of undergraduates work part time. Average annual earnings from campus work are $600. The average financial indebtedness of the 2003 graduate was $12,100. The FAFSA and the college's own financial statement are required. The deadline for filing freshman financial aid applications for fall entry is February 1.

International Students: There were 39 international students enrolled in a recent year. The school actively recruits these students. They must score 550 on the written TOEFL and also take the SAT I or the ACT.

Computers: The mainframe is a DEC VAX 8350. Terminals and PCs are located in the computer center and in engineering labs. In addition, all residence halls are capable of providing Internet access to students who have their own computers. All students may access the system 13 hours a day in the labs and 24 hours a day in residence halls or by modem. There are no time limits and no fees.

Graduates: In a recent year, 552 bachelor's degrees were awarded. The most popular majors were arts and science (33%), business (22%), and engineering (18%). In an average class, 53% graduate in 4 years or less, 64% graduate in 5 years or less, and 68% graduate in 6 years or less. 200 companies recruited on campus in 2002-2003. Of the 2002 graduating class, 16% were enrolled in graduate school within 6 months of graduation and 61% were employed.

Admissions Contact: William J. Bisset, Jr., Assistant Vice President for Enrollment Management. A video is available.
E-mail: admit@manhattan.edu Web: www.manhattan.edu

MANHATTAN SCHOOL OF MUSIC
New York, NY 10027-4678

D-5

(212) 749-2802, ext. 4501
Fax: (212) 749-5471

Full-time: 185 men, 190 women	**Faculty:** 35
Part-time: 10 men, 15 women	**Ph.Ds:** 40%
Graduate: 175 men, 265 women	**Student/Faculty:** 11 to 1
Year: semesters	**Tuition:** $23,760
Application Deadline: see profile	**Room & Board:** $11,800
Freshman Class: n/av	
SAT I or ACT: recommended	**SPECIAL**

The Manhattan School of Music, founded in 1917, is a private college offering undergraduate and graduate degrees in music performance and composition. Figures in the above capsule and in this profile are approximate. The library contains 73,405 volumes and 21,074 audio/video tapes/CDs, and subscribes to 128 periodicals. Computerized library services include the card catalog, interlibrary loans, and database searching. Special learning facilities include 2 electronic music studios and a recording studio. The 1-acre campus is in an urban area in New York City. Including any residence halls, there are 2 buildings.

Student Life: 77% of undergraduates are from out of state, mostly the Northeast. Students are from 41 states, 46 foreign countries, and Canada. 81% are from public schools. 36% are foreign nationals; 36% white. The average age of freshmen is 18; all undergraduates, 21. 17% do not continue beyond their first year; 54% remain to graduate.

Housing: 380 students can be accommodated in college housing, which includes single-sex and coed dorms. On-campus housing is guaranteed for the freshman year only and is available on a lottery system for upperclassmen. Priority is given to out-of-town students. 50% of students live on campus; of those, 95% remain on campus on weekends. All students may keep cars.

Activities: 10% of men belong to 2 local fraternities; 20% of women belong to 2 local sororities. There are 13 groups on campus, including choir, chorale, chorus, ethnic, gay, international, jazz band, musical theater, opera, orchestra, student government, and symphony. Popular campus events include a Halloween party, a Christmas/Chanukah party, and post-opera party.

Sports: There is no sports program at MSM.

Disabled Students: 70% of the campus is accessible. Wheelchair ramps, elevators, specially equipped rest rooms, special class scheduling, and lowered telephones are available.

Services: Counseling and information services are available, as is tutoring in most subjects. There is a reader service for the blind.

Campus Safety and Security: Measures include 24-hour foot and vehicle patrol, informal discussions, pamphlets/posters/films, and lighted pathways/sidewalks.

Programs of Study: MSM confers the B.Mus. degree. Master's and doctoral degrees are also awarded. Bachelor's degrees are awarded in COMMUNICATIONS AND THE ARTS (jazz, music, music performance, music theory and composition, piano/organ, strings, and voice). Classical piano, classical voice, and jazz are the largest.

Required: All students must take 4 music theory courses, a 4-course core curriculum in the humanities, and 4 elective humanities courses and perform a final, senior-year recital. Composition majors must complete an original symphonic work. To graduate, students must earn 120 to 130 credit hours, including 90 to 100 in the major, with a minimum GPA of 2.0.

Special: There is cross-registration with Barnard College. Credit by exam in theory and music history is available.

Faculty/Classroom: 69% of faculty are male; 31%, female. All teach undergraduates. Graduate students teach 1% of introductory courses. The average class size in an introductory lecture is 20 and in a regular course, 15.

Requirements: The SAT I or ACT is recommended. In addition, applicants should graduate from an accredited high school with a minimum GPA of 2.5. The GED is accepted. Admission is based on a performance audition, evaluation of scholastic achievements, and available openings in the major field. A GPA of 2.9 is required. AP and CLEP credits are accepted. Important factors in the admissions decision are evidence of special talent, personality/intangible qualities, and extracurricular activities record.

Procedure: Freshmen are admitted in the fall. Check with the school for current application deadlines. The application fee is $100. A waiting list is an active part of the admissions procedure.

Transfer: 67 transfer students enrolled in a recent year. Applicants must audition and submit college transcripts. 60 of 120 credits required for the bachelor's degree must be completed at MSM.

Visiting: There are regularly scheduled orientations for prospective students, consisting of a tour of the facility and a discussion with a counselor. There are guides for informal visits and visitors may sit in on classes. To schedule a visit, contact the Office of Admission and Financial Aid at (212) 749-2802, ext. 2.

Financial Aid: The CSS Profile or FAFSA and the college's own financial statement are required. Check with the school for current deadlines.

International Students: There were 111 international students enrolled in a recent year. The school actively recruits these students. They must score 500 on the written TOEFL or 173 on the electronic version and also take the International English Language Testing System (IELTS).

Computers: Stand-alone PCs are available in the computer lab. All students may access the system. There are no time limits and no fees.

Graduates: In a recent year, 79 bachelor's degrees were awarded. The most popular majors were piano (26%), voice (21%), and strings (14%). In an average class, 4% graduate in 3 years or less, 47% graduate in 4 years or less, 52% graduate in 5 years or less, and 54% graduate in 6 years or less.

Admissions Contact: Lee Cioppa, Director of Admission.
E-mail: *admission@msmnyc.edu* Web: *www.msmnyc.edu*

MANHATTANVILLE COLLEGE   D-5
Purchase, NY 10577   (914) 323-5464
(800) 32 VILLE; Fax: (914) 694-1732

Full-time: 483 men, 1045 women	**Faculty:** 88; IIA, -$
Part-time: 45 men, 98 women	**Ph.D.s:** 93%
Graduate: 187 men, 713 women	**Student/Faculty:** 17 to 1
Year: semesters, summer session	**Tuition:** $23,040
Application Deadline: open	**Room & Board:** $9380
Freshman Class: 2450 applied, 1348 accepted, 418 enrolled	
SAT I Verbal/Math: 540/525	**ACT:** 24 **COMPETITIVE+**

Manhattanville College, founded in 1841, is an independent liberal arts institution offering more than 45 undergraduate areas of study. There is 1 undergraduate and 2 graduate schools. In addition to regional accreditation, M'ville has baccalaureate program accreditation with NASM. The library contains 282,892 volumes, 532,732 microform items, and 3936 audio/video tapes/CDs, and subscribes to 14,227 periodicals. Computerized library services include the card catalog, interlibrary loans, database searching, and Internet access. Special learning facilities include a learning resource center, art gallery, radio station, and TV station. The 100-acre campus is in a suburban area 25 miles north of New York City. Including any residence halls, there are 21 buildings.

Student Life: 66% of undergraduates are from New York. Students are from 35 states, 49 foreign countries, and Canada. 58% are white; 14% Hispanic. The average age of freshmen is 18; all undergraduates, 20. 23% do not continue beyond their first year; 58% remain to graduate.

Housing: 1114 students can be accommodated in college housing, which includes single-sex and coed dorms. On-campus housing is guaranteed for all 4 years. 73% of students live on campus; of those, 75% remain on campus on weekends. All students may keep cars.

Activities: There are no fraternities or sororities. There are 60 groups on campus, including art, band, cheerleading, chess, choir, chorale, chorus, computers, dance, debate, drama, ethnic, film, gay, honors, international, jazz band, literary magazine, musical theater, newspaper, orchestra, pep band, photography, political, professional, radio and TV, religious, social, social service, student government, and yearbook. Popular campus events include Quad Jam, Fall Jam, and The Global Pot.

Sports: There are 7 intercollegiate sports for men and 7 for women, and 3 intramural sports for men and 3 for women. Facilities include a 1000-seat gym, a 25-yard indoor pool, 6 deco-turf tennis courts, a healthworks-wellness center, baseball, lacrosse, field hockey, and softball fields, and batting cages.

Disabled Students: All of the campus is accessible. Wheelchair ramps, elevators, special parking, specially equipped rest rooms, and special class scheduling are available.

Services: Counseling and information services are available, as is tutoring in every subject. There is a program for students with documented learning disabilities.

Campus Safety and Security: Measures include 24-hour foot and vehicle patrol, security escort services, shuttle buses, and informal discussions. There are pamphlets/posters/films, emergency telephones, and lighted pathways/sidewalks.

Programs of Study: M'ville confers B.A., B.F.A., and B.Mus. degrees. Master's degrees are also awarded. Bachelor's degrees are awarded in BIOLOGICAL SCIENCE (biochemistry and biology/biological science), BUSINESS (banking and finance and management science), COMMUNICATIONS AND THE ARTS (art, art history and appreciation, classics, dance, English, French, German, music, romance languages and literature, and Spanish), COMPUTER AND PHYSICAL SCIENCE (chemistry, computer science, mathematics, and physics), EDUCATION (education), SOCIAL SCIENCE (American studies, Asian/Oriental studies, economics, history, international studies, philosophy, political science/government, psychology, religion, and sociology). Management, art, and psychology are the strongest academically. Psychology, management, and history are the largest.

Required: Distribution requirements include 18 credits in social sciences and humanities and either a major or minor in foreign language or 18 credits in Western and non-Western courses, 8 credits in math and natural sciences, and 6 in the arts. A yearlong freshman humanities course, courses in library skills, writing, and global perspective, and a preceptorial are required. A total of 120 credit hours and a minimum GPA of 2.0 are needed to graduate.

Special: Manhattanville offers cross-registration with SUNY Purchase, internships in all majors for credit, a Washington semester, and study abroad in 10 countries. Dual, student-designed, and interdisciplinary majors and pass/fail options are also available. Under the portfolio degree plan, students develop an individualized program combining both academic and nonacademic training. There is a freshman honors program.

Faculty/Classroom: 54% of faculty are male; 46%, female. All teach undergraduates. No introductory courses are taught by graduate students. The average class size in an introductory lecture is 15; in a laboratory, 12; and in a regular course, 10.

Admissions: 55% of the 2003-2004 applicants were accepted. The SAT I scores for the 2003-2004 freshman class were: Verbal--35% below 500, 45% between 500 and 599, 18% between 600 and 700, and 2% above 700; Math--37% below 500, 48% between 500 and 599, 14% between 600 and 700, and 1% above 700.

Requirements: The SAT I or ACT is required. In addition, applicants should graduate in the upper 50% of their class with 4 years of English, 3 each of history, math, and science, including 2 of lab science, and one half year each of art and music. The GED is accepted. Interviews are strongly encouraged. Art applicants must submit a portfolio; music applicants must audition. A GPA of 2.0 is required. AP and CLEP credits are accepted. Important factors in the admissions decision are leadership record, recommendations by alumni, and recommendations by school officials.

Procedure: Freshmen are admitted fall and spring. Entrance exams should be taken in the spring of the junior or fall of the senior year. There is a rolling admissions plan. There are early decision, early admissions, and deferred admissions plans. Application deadlines are open. Application fee is $50. 34 early decision candidates were accepted for the 2003-2004 class. 100 applicants were on the 2003 waiting list. Applications are accepted on-line through the school's web site.

Transfer: 72 transfer students enrolled in 2002-2003. Applicants must submit college transcripts. A minimum GPA of 2.5 and a statement of good standing are required. Applicants with fewer than 40 credits must submit all high school records and SAT I scores. 60 of 120 credits required for the bachelor's degree must be completed at M'ville.

Visiting: There are regularly scheduled orientations for prospective students, including a campus tour, and a meeting in Admissions. There are guides for informal visits and visitors may sit in on classes and stay overnight. To schedule a visit, contact the Office of Admissions.

Financial Aid: In 2003-2004, 68% of all full-time freshmen and 66% of continuing full-time students received some form of financial aid. 63% of full-time freshmen and 58% of continuing full-time students received need-based aid. The average freshman award was $15,500. 31% of undergraduates work part time. Average annual earnings from campus work are $1700. The average financial indebtedness of the 2003 graduate was $21,160. The FAFSA, the state aid form, and the college's own financial statement are required. The deadline for filing freshman financial aid applications for fall entry is March 1.

International Students: There are 131 international students enrolled. The school actively recruits these students. They must score 550 on the written TOEFL or 220 on the electronic version and also take the SAT I or the ACT.

Computers: The mainframe is an HPK 380. Students may access the campus network and the Internet via 170 PCs on campus and in labs in the library. All dorm rooms and public spaces are wired for Internet access. All students may access the system. Internet and intranet are usable 24 hours per day, 7 days a week. Computer labs are open about 64 to 70 hours throughout the week. There are no time limits and no fees.

Graduates: From July 1, 2002 to June 30, 2003, 332 bachelor's degrees were awarded. The most popular majors were management (18%), psychology (13%), and sociology (9%). In an average class, 51% graduate in 4 years or less, 58% graduate in 5 years or less, and 58% graduate in 6 years or less. 34 companies recruited on campus in 2002-2003. Of the 2002 graduating class, 18% were enrolled in graduate school within 6 months of graduation and 64% were employed.

Admissions Contact: Jose Flores, Director of Admissions. A video is available. E-mail: *admissions@mville.edu*
Web: *www.manhattanville.edu*

MANNES COLLEGE OF MUSIC
New York, NY 10024

D-5

(212) 580-0210, ext. 247
(800) 292-3040; Fax: (212) 580-1738

Full-time: 50 men, 80 women	**Faculty:** 23
Part-time: none	**Ph.D.s:** n/av
Graduate: 70 men, 90 women	**Student/Faculty:** 6 to 1
Year: semesters	**Tuition:** $23,530
Application Deadline: December 1	**Room & Board:** $8400
Freshman Class: n/av	
SAT I or ACT: not required	SPECIAL

Mannes College of Music, founded in 1916 and today part of the New School University, is a private institution offering instruction in music. Figures in the above capsule are approximate. There is 1 undergraduate and 1 graduate school. The library contains 36,500 volumes, 3 microform items, and 8800 audio/video tapes/CDs, and subscribes to 77 periodicals. Computerized library services include the card catalog, interlibrary loans, database searching, and Internet access. Special learning facilities include 2 concert/recital halls, recording studio, and electronic music studio. The campus is in an urban area in Manhattan. Including any residence halls, there are 2 buildings.

Student Life: 71% of undergraduates are from out of state, mostly the Northeast. Students are from 18 states, 18 foreign countries, and Canada. The average age of freshmen is 19; all undergraduates, 21. 17% do not continue beyond their first year; 47% remain to graduate.

Housing: 30 students can be accommodated in college housing, which includes coed dorms. On-campus housing is guaranteed for the freshman year only and is available on a first-come, first-served basis. Priority is given to out-of-town students. Alcohol is not permitted.

Activities: There are no fraternities or sororities. There are 6 groups on campus, including choir, chorus, jazz band, opera, orchestra, and symphony. Popular campus events include orchestra/chorus concerts, Christmas parties, and recitals.

Sports: There is no sports program at Mannes.

Disabled Students: All of the campus is accessible. Elevators and specially equipped rest rooms are available.

Services: Counseling and information services are available, as is tutoring in most subjects.

Campus Safety and Security: There is a security guard 24 hours a day at the front entrance of the dorm and from 8 A.M. to 11 P.M. at the front desk of the college lobby.

Programs of Study: Mannes confers B.S. and B.Mus. degrees. Master's degrees are also awarded. Bachelor's degrees are awarded in COMMUNICATIONS AND THE ARTS (music, music performance, music theory and composition, and voice). Voice, piano, and violin are the largest.

Required: The required core curriculum includes courses in English, Western civilization, art history, and literature. Students majoring in instruments and voice must participate in various ensemble classes. Courses are also required in techniques and history of music. To graduate, performance majors must perform before a faculty jury, and composition majors must submit 5 original pieces for juried consideration.

Special: Mannes offers cross-registration with New School University. There are some dual majors by permission.

Faculty/Classroom: No introductory courses are taught by graduate students. The average class size in an introductory lecture is 10 and in a regular course, 6.

Requirements: Applicants must be graduates of an accredited secondary school or have a GED certificate. An audition, an interview, a letter of recommendation, and a written test in music theory and musicianship are required. Important factors in the admissions decision are evidence of special talent, personality/intangible qualities, and recommendations by school officials.

Procedure: Freshmen are admitted in the fall. Entrance exams should be taken at the time of the audition. There is a deferred admissions plan. Applications should be filed by December 1 for fall entry, along with a $100 fee. Notification is sent April 15. 17 applicants were on the 2003 waiting list; 9 were admitted. Applications are accepted on-line through *www.unifiedapps.org*.

Transfer: 27 transfer students enrolled in a recent year. Transfer applicants must complete the same procedures as entering freshmen and submit transcripts from all secondary schools and colleges attended.

Visiting: There are guides for informal visits and visitors may sit in on classes. To schedule a visit, contact the Admissions Office.

Financial Aid: Mannes is a member of CSS. The FAFSA and the college's own financial statement are required. The priority date for freshman financial aid applications for fall entry is December 1. The deadline for filing freshman financial aid applications for fall entry is March 1.

International Students: There are 75 international students enrolled. They must score 550 on the written TOEFL or 213 on the electronic version and also take the college's own test. The college's own entrance exam is also required.

Computers: All students may access the system. There are no time limits and no fees.

Graduates: From July 1, 2002 to June 30, 2003, 21 bachelor's degrees were awarded. The most popular majors were voice (32%), piano (16%), and composition (16%).

Admissions Contact: Allison Scola, Director of Admissions.
E-mail: *mannesadmissions@mannes.edu* Web: *www.mannes.edu*

MARIST COLLEGE
Poughkeepsie, NY 12601

D-4

(845) 575-3226
(800) 436-5483; Fax: (845) 575-3215

Full-time: 1799 men, 2420 women	**Faculty:** 192; IIA, -$
Part-time: 245 men, 309 women	**Ph.D.s:** 78%
Graduate: 404 men, 439 women	**Student/Faculty:** 22 to 1
Year: semesters, summer session	**Tuition:** $18,962
Application Deadline: February 15	**Room & Board:** $8634
Freshman Class: 6606 applied, 3288 accepted, 972 enrolled	
SAT I Verbal/Math: 576/586	**ACT:** 25 VERY COMPETITIVE

Marist College, founded in 1946, is private liberal arts college with a Catholic tradition. In addition to regional accreditation, Marist has baccalaureate program accreditation with CSWE. The library contains 176,347 volumes, 251,683 microform items, and 4940 audio/video tapes/CDs, and subscribes to 12,897 periodicals. Computerized library services include the card catalog, interlibrary loans, and database searching. Special learning facilities include a learning resource center, art gallery, radio station, TV station, a gallery of Lowell Thomas memorabilia, estuarine and environmental studies laboratory, public opinion institute, and economic research center. The 150-acre campus is in a suburban area 75 miles north of New York City on the Hudson River. Including any residence halls, there are 46 buildings.

Student Life: 50% of undergraduates are from out of state, mostly the Northeast. Students are from 35 states, 8 foreign countries, and Canada. 70% are from public schools. 89% are white. 59% are Catholic; 20% Protestant. The average age of freshmen is 18; all undergraduates, 20. 7% do not continue beyond their first year; 73% remain to graduate.

Housing: 2700 students can be accommodated in college housing, which includes coed dorms, on-campus apartments, off-campus apartments, freshmen dorms with mentors, and housing for uppperclassmen. 75% of students live on campus; of those, 90% remain on campus on weekends. Alcohol is not permitted. Upperclassmen may keep cars.

Activities: 2% of men belong to 3 national fraternities; 6% of women belong to 1 local and 4 national sororities. There are 70 groups on campus, including art, band, cheerleading, chess, choir, chorale, chorus, computers, dance, debate, drama, ethnic, film, gay, honors, international, jazz band, literary magazine, marching band, musical theater, newspaper, orchestra, pep band, photography, political, professional, radio and TV, religious, social, social service, student government, symphony, and yearbook. Popular campus events include President's Cup Regatta, Foxfest, and Unity Day.

Sports: There are 11 intercollegiate sports for men and 12 for women, and 9 intramural sports for men and 9 for women. Facilities include a boathouse, a 3600-seat basketball arena, a 3000-seat stadium, 30 acres of playing fields, a field house, a swimming pool, a diving well, racquetball courts, a dance and aerobics studio, a weight room, intramural basketball courts, an all-purpose playing space, and a fitness center.

Disabled Students: All of the campus is accessible. Wheelchair ramps, elevators, special parking, specially equipped rest rooms, special class scheduling, lowered drinking fountains, and lowered telephones are available.

Services: Counseling and information services are available, as is tutoring in every subject. There is a reader service for the blind, and remedial math, reading, and writing.

Campus Safety and Security: Measures include 24-hour foot and vehicle patrol, security escort services, informal discussions, and pamphlets/posters/films. There are emergency telephones, lighted pathways/sidewalks, and security personnel in residence halls.

Programs of Study: Marist confers B.A., B.S., and B.P.S. degrees. Master's degrees are also awarded. Bachelor's degrees are awarded in BIOLOGICAL SCIENCE (biology/biological science), BUSINESS (accounting, business administration and management, and fashion merchandising), COMMUNICATIONS AND THE ARTS (communications, English, fine arts, French, and Spanish), COMPUTER AND PHYSICAL SCIENCE (chemistry, computer mathematics, computer science, digital arts/technology, information sciences and systems, and mathematics), EDUCATION (athletic training and special), ENGINEERING AND ENVIRONMENTAL DESIGN (environmental science), HEALTH PROFESSIONS (medical technology), SOCIAL SCIENCE (American studies, criminal justice, economics, fashion design and technology, history, interdisciplinary studies, philosophy, political science/government, psychology, and social work). Business administration, communications, and psychology are the largest.

Required: To graduate, students must maintain a GPA of 2.0 in the major while taking 120 credits. A 30-credit core curriculum and 30 to 36 credits in a major are required. Distribution requirements include 6 credits each in natural sciences, social sciences, history, literature, and math and 3 credits each in fine arts and philosophy/religious studies. Specific course requirements include English writing skills and foundation courses in those areas defined by major programs.

Special: Marist offers cross-registration with schools in the mid-Hudson area and study abroad in 20 countires. The school also offers a 3-year degree in social work, co-op programs in computer science and computer information systems, marketing, finance, information technology, accounting, and business, work-study programs, and dual abd student-designed majors. There are internships available with more than 250 organizations in the United States abd abroad, including New York State Legislature and White House programs. There are 11 national honor societies and a freshman honors program.

Faculty/Classroom: 62% of faculty are male; 38%, female. All teach undergraduates. No introductory courses are taught by graduate students. The average class size in an introductory lecture is 19; in a laboratory, 7; and in a regular course, 20.

Admissions: 50% of the 2003-2004 applicants were accepted. The SAT I scores for the 2003-2004 freshman class were: Verbal--9% below 500, 54% between 500 and 599, 35% between 600 and 700, and 2% above 700; Math--5% below 500, 51% between 500 and 599, 41% between 600 and 700, and 3% above 700. 50% of the current freshmen were in the top fifth of their class; 88% were in the top two fifths. 3 freshmen graduated first in their class.

Requirements: The SAT I or ACT is required. In addition, applicants should have 16 high school units, including a recommended 4 in En-

glish, 3 in math, 2 each in science, language, and social studies, and 1 in U.S. history, art, and music. The GED is accepted. An essay and campus visit are recommended. Marist requires applicants to be in the upper 50% of their class. A grade average of 83 is required. AP and CLEP credits are accepted. Important factors in the admissions decision are leadership record, advanced placement or honor courses, and recommendations by school officials.

Procedure: Freshmen are admitted fall and spring. Entrance exams should be taken during the fall of the senior year. There are early decision and deferred admissions plans. Early decision applications should be filed by December 1; regular applications, by February 15 for fall entry and November 1 for spring entry, along with a $40 fee. Notification of early decision is sent January 15; regular decision, March 15. 1316 early decision candidates were accepted for the 2003-2004 class. 500 applicants were on the 2003 waiting list. Applications are accepted online through the college's web page.

Transfer: 170 transfer students enrolled in 2002-2003. Applicants must have at least a 2.8 GPA (depending on the college and major program) in at least 30 college credits. Students with fewer than 25 credits will be treated as freshmen. Grades of C or better transfer. 30 of 120 credits required for the bachelor's degree must be completed at Marist.

Visiting: There are regularly scheduled orientations for prospective students, including 1-day June visits for freshmen and a one week welcome program. There are guides for informal visits and visitors may sit in on classes and stay overnight. To schedule a visit, contact the Admissions Office receptionist at *www.marist.edu/admissions*.

Financial Aid: In 2003-2004, 91% of all full-time freshmen and 93% of continuing full-time students received some form of financial aid. 66% of full-time freshmen and 72% of continuing full-time students received need-based aid. The average freshman award was $10,880. Need-based scholarships or need-based grants averaged $5746 ($23,265 maximum); need-based self-help aid (loans and jobs) averaged $4268 ($6625 maximum); non-need based athletic scholarships averaged $8939 ($27,621 maximum); and other non-need based awards and non-need based scholarships averaged $5697 ($14,000 maximum). 22% of undergraduates work part time. Average annual earnings from campus work are $1500. The average financial indebtedness of the 2003 graduate was $7180. The FAFSA is required. The deadline for filing freshman financial aid applications for fall entry is February 15.

International Students: There are 10 international students enrolled. The school actively recruits these students. They must score 550 on the written TOEFL or 213 on the electronic version and also take T.W.E. (Test of Written English).

Computers: The mainframe is an IBM 2900 2064-103. The campus center has a drop-in lab available to all students from 8 A.M. to midnight during the week and longer on weekends. All dorm rooms are equipped with data jacks allowing students to hook up PCs with the mainframe and to access library files. Overall, there are 12 areas on campus providing more than 300 terminals for student use, as well as 185 PCs and numerous printers. All students may access the system. There are no time limits and no fees.

Graduates: From July 1, 2002 to June 30, 2003, 948 bachelor's degrees were awarded. The most popular majors were communications (18%), business (16%), and psychology (13%). In an average class, 56% graduate in 4 years or less, 66% graduate in 5 years or less, and 73% graduate in 6 years or less. 182 companies recruited on campus in 2002-2003. Of the 2002 graduating class, 23% were enrolled in graduate school within 6 months of graduation and 60% were employed.

Admissions Contact: Sean P. Kaylor, Vice President of Admissions and Enrollment. E-mail: *admissions@marist.edu* Web: *www.marist.edu*

MARYMOUNT COLLEGE OF FORDHAM UNIVERSITY   D-5
Tarrytown, NY 10591
(914) 332-8295
(800) 724-4312; Fax: (914) 332-4956

Full-time: 863 women	**Faculty:** 56
Part-time: 1 man, 27 women	**Ph.Ds:** 100%
Graduate: none	**Student/Faculty:** 15 to 1
Year: semesters	**Tuition:** $18,426
Application Deadline: August 1	**Room & Board:** $9260
Freshman Class: 1490 applied, 1224 accepted, 282 enrolled	
SAT I Verbal/Math: 510/470	**ACT:** 21 COMPETITIVE

Marymount College of Fordham University (formerly Marymount College/Tarrytown), founded in 1907, is a private women's undergraduate institution in the Catholic tradition. The college offers programs in liberal arts and career preparation. In addition to regional accreditation, the college has baccalaureate program accreditation with ADA and CSWE. The library contains 135,777 volumes, 14,229 microform items, and 1094 audio/video tapes/CDs, and subscribes to 320 periodicals. Computerized library services include the card catalog, interlibrary loans, database searching, and Internet access. Special learning facilities include a learning resource center and multimedia teaching and learning center. The 25-acre campus is in a suburban area 30 miles north of New York City. Including any residence halls, there are 12 buildings.

Student Life: 67% of undergraduates are from New York. Students are from 32 states and 20 foreign countries. 77% are from public schools. 40% are white; 15% African American; 13% Hispanic. The average age of freshmen is 18; all undergraduates, 21. 35% do not continue beyond their first year; 55% remain to graduate.

Housing: 638 students can be accommodated in college housing, which includes single-sex dorms, honors floors, special-interest floors, an intercultural floor with student-generated programs, and a quiet floor. On-campus housing is guaranteed for all 4 years. 59% of students live on campus. Alcohol is not permitted. All students may keep cars.

Activities: There are no fraternities. There are 25 groups on campus, including art, chorale, commuter, computers, dance, drama, ethnic, gay, honors, international, literary magazine, newspaper, photography, political, professional, radio and TV, religious, social, social service, student government, and yearbook. Popular campus events include Talent Show and Fashion Show and Competition.

Sports: Facilities include a swimming pool, dance studio, fitness center, tennis court, and an athletic field. The campus stadium seats 350, the indoor gym 250.

Disabled Students: 85% of the campus is accessible. Wheelchair ramps, elevators, special parking, specially equipped rest rooms, special class scheduling, automatic door openers, paid note takers, and an ASL interpreter are available.

Services: Counseling and information services are available, as is tutoring in every subject. There is remedial math, reading, and writing. There are writing and math labs.

Campus Safety and Security: Measures include 24-hour foot and vehicle patrol, self-defense education, shuttle buses, and informal discussions. There are pamphlets/posters/films, emergency telephones, and lighted pathways/sidewalks.

Programs of Study: The college confers B.A. and B.S. degrees. Bachelor's degrees are awarded in BIOLOGICAL SCIENCE (biology/biological science), BUSINESS (business administration and management, fashion merchandising, and international business management), COMMUNICATIONS AND THE ARTS (art history and appreciation, dramatic arts, English, fine arts, French, and Spanish), COMPUTER AND PHYSICAL SCIENCE (chemistry, computer science, information sciences and systems, and mathematics), EDUCATION (art, elementary, foreign languages, home economics, mathematics, science, secondary, and special), ENGINEERING AND ENVIRONMENTAL DESIGN (interior design), SOCIAL SCIENCE (American studies, economics, fashion design and technology, food science, history, home economics, interdisciplinary studies, international studies, liberal arts/general studies, political science/government, psychology, public affairs, social work, and sociology). Business, education, and psychology are the largest.

Required: All students must take 19 courses in 10 disciplines. A total of 120 credits is required for graduation, as is a minimum GPA of 2.0. Students must complete 5 courses on college mission themes, and 2 sets of learning community courses.

Special: Juniors and seniors in all disciplines may receive up to 6 credits for on-site internships. The college offers study abroad in 7 countries, a Washington semester, work-study programs, dual and student-designed majors, credit by exam, nondegree study, and pass/fail options. There are 3-2 business and education programs with Fordham University and a 6-year joint program in physical therapy and occupational therapy with Touro College. There are 3 national honor societies, a freshman honors program, and 2 departmental honors programs.

Faculty/Classroom: 35% of faculty are male; 65%, female. All teach undergraduates and 60% do research. The average class size in an introductory lecture is 20; in a laboratory, 16; and in a regular course, 15.

Admissions: 82% of the 2003-2004 applicants were accepted. The SAT I scores for the 2003-2004 freshman class were: Verbal--43% below 500, 43% between 500 and 599, 12% between 600 and 700, and 2% above 700; Math--62% below 500, 31% between 500 and 599, 6% between 600 and 700, and 1% above 700. The ACT scores were 75% below 23, 19% between 24 and 29, and 6% between 30 and 36. 36% of the current freshman were in the top fourth of their class, and 79% were in the top half.

Requirements: The SAT I is required, but ACT scores may be submitted instead. Applicants must complete 16 academic credits, including 4 years of English, and 3 years each of foreign language, math, science, and history or social studies. The GED is accepted. An interview is recommended. A GPA of 2.5 is required. AP and CLEP credits are accepted. Important factors in the admissions decision are recommendations by school officials, extracurricular activities record, and leadership record.

Procedure: Freshmen are admitted fall and spring. Entrance exams should be taken in the fall of the year preceding enrollment. There are early admissions and deferred admissions plans. Early decision applications should be filed by October 31; regular applications, by August 1 for fall entry and January 10 for spring entry. The fall 2003 application fee was $30. Notification of early decision is sent December 1; regular decision, on a rolling basis. Applications are accepted on-line through Common App and NY Mentor.

Transfer: 78 transfer students enrolled in fall 2003. Applicants with fewer than 24 college credits must submit SAT I scores and a high school transcript. A GPA of at least 2.0 is required. 45 of 120 credits required for the bachelor's degree must be completed at the college.

Visiting: There are regularly scheduled orientations for prospective students, including meeting with a counselor and touring the campus. There are guides for informal visits and visitors may sit in on classes. To schedule a visit, contact Daniela Esposito, Director of Admissions.

Financial Aid: In 2003-2004, 77% of all full-time freshmen and 72% of continuing full-time students received some form of financial aid. 73% of full-time freshmen and 69% of continuing full-time students received need-based aid. The average freshman award was $15,085. Need-based scholarships or need-based grants averaged $10,316; need-based self-help aid (loans and jobs) averaged $4158; and non-need-based awards and non-need-based scholarships averaged $7193. The average financial indebtedness of the 2003 graduate was $11,006. The FAFSA is required. The priority date for freshman financial aid applications for fall entry is February 1. The deadline for filing freshman financial aid applications for fall entry is May 1.

International Students: There are 22 international students enrolled. The school actively recruits these students. They must score 500 on the written TOEFL.

Computers: The mainframe is a DEC Alpha. There are about 135 workstations available to students in 5 main labs, a small lab in each dorm, the library, and various other locations. Nearly all are linked with a campuswide LAN. Available software and services include Microsoft Office, graphics, desktop and web publishing, CAD, statistical, e-mail, Internet, and library database access. All dorm rooms provide connectivity, and dial-up service is available off campus. All students may access the system 7 days a week.

Graduates: From July 1, 2002 to June 30, 2003, 134 bachelor's degrees were awarded. The most popular majors were business (19%), education (10%), and psychology (10%). In an average class, 54% graduate in 4 years or less, 58% graduate in 5 years or less, and 58% graduate in 6 years or less. 51 companies recruited on campus in 2002-2003. Of the 2002 graduating class, 30% were enrolled in graduate school within 6 months of graduation and 66% were employed.

Admissions Contact: Daniela Esposito, Director of Admissions. E-mail: *mcenroll@fordham.edu* Web: *www.marymt.edu*

MARYMOUNT MANHATTAN COLLEGE   D-5
New York, NY 10021

(212) 517-0555
(800) MARYMOUNT; Fax: (212) 517-0448

Full-time: 371 men, 1229 women	**Faculty:** 90; IIB, av$
Part-time: 77 men, 506 women	**Ph.D.s:** 77%
Graduate: none	**Student/Faculty:** 18 to 1
Year: semesters, summer session	**Tuition:** $16,292
Application Deadline: open	**Room & Board:** $11,000
Freshman Class: 1597 applied, 1272 accepted, 397 enrolled	
SAT I Verbal/Math: 540/510	**ACT:** 23 **COMPETITIVE**

Marymount Manhattan College is an urban, independent liberal arts college, offering programs in the arts and sciences for all ages, as well as substantial preprofessional preparation. The library contains 75,000 volumes, 70 microform items, and 2000 audio/video tapes/CDs, and subscribes to 740 periodicals. Computerized library services include the card catalog, interlibrary loans, and database searching. Special learning facilities include a learning resource center, art gallery, radio station, TV station, and a communications arts multimedia suite featuring digital editing technology. The 1-acre campus is in an urban area in Manhattan. Including any residence halls, there are 3 buildings.

Student Life: 57% of undergraduates are from New York. Students are from 47 states, 37 foreign countries, and Canada. 50% are from public schools. 61% are white; 17% African American; 14% Hispanic. The average age of freshmen is 18; all undergraduates, 25. 30% do not continue beyond their first year; 45% remain to graduate.

Housing: 642 students can be accommodated in college housing, which includes single-sex and coed dorms and off-campus apartments. On-campus housing is available on a first-come, first-served basis and is available on a lottery system for upperclassmen. Priority is given to out-of-town students. 66% of students commute. Alcohol is not permitted. All students may keep cars.

Activities: 33% of women belong to 1 national sorority. There are no fraternities. There are 20 groups on campus, including art, choir, computers, dance, drama, ethnic, film, gay, honors, international, literary magazine, musical theater, newspaper, photography, political, professional, radio and TV, religious, social, social service, student government, and yearbook. Popular campus events include Strawberry Festival, International Day, and Holiday Soiree.

Sports: There are 3 intramural sports for men and 3 for women. Facilities include a 300-seat auditorium.

Disabled Students: All of the campus is accessible. Wheelchair ramps, elevators, specially equipped rest rooms, special class scheduling, and lowered drinking fountains are available.

Services: Counseling and information services are available, as is tutoring in every subject. There is remedial math, reading, and writing.

Campus Safety and Security: Measures include 24-hour foot and vehicle patrol, self-defense education, shuttle buses, and informal discussions. There are pamphlets/posters/films, lighted pathways/sidewalks, security cameras, and photo ID check-in.

Programs of Study: MMC confers B.A., B.S., and B.F.A. degrees. Bachelor's degrees are awarded in BIOLOGICAL SCIENCE (biology/biological science), BUSINESS (accounting and business administration and management), COMMUNICATIONS AND THE ARTS (communications, dance, dramatic arts, English, and fine arts), COMPUTER AND PHYSICAL SCIENCE (information sciences and systems), EDUCATION (elementary, secondary, and special), HEALTH PROFESSIONS (premedicine and speech pathology/audiology), SOCIAL SCIENCE (history, international studies, liberal arts/general studies, political science/government, psychology, and sociology). Psychology, communication arts, and business are the strongest academically. Psychology, dance, and English are the largest.

Required: To graduate, students must complete 120 credit hours, including 37 to 70 in the major, with a minimum GPA of 2.5. The core curriculum totals 43 credits in the areas of critical thinking, psychology and philosophy, quantitative reasoning and science, the modern world, communications/language, and the arts.

Special: MMC offers study abroad, interdisciplinary courses, pass/fail options, nondegree study, credit for life experience, and some 250 internships in all majors. Cooperative programs in business and finance, dance, music, languages, nursing, and urban education are offered in conjunction with local colleges and institutes. There is a January minisession, cross-registration with Hunter College, and a 5-year master's in publishing with Pace University. There are 7 national honor societies, a freshman honors program, and 6 departmental honors programs.

Faculty/Classroom: 37% of faculty are male; 63%, female. 65% teach undergraduates and 35% both teach and do research. The average class size in an introductory lecture is 30; in a laboratory, 12; and in a regular course, 15.

Admissions: 80% of the 2003-2004 applicants were accepted. The SAT I scores for the 2003-2004 freshman class were: Verbal--30% below 500, 45% between 500 and 599, 23% between 600 and 700, and 3% above 700; Math--44% below 500, 39% between 500 and 599, and 16% between 600 and 700. The ACT scores were 10% below 21, 45% between 21 and 23, and 45% between 24 and 26. 11 freshmen graduated first in their class.

Requirements: The SAT I or ACT is required. In addition, applicants should be graduates of an accredited secondary school or have a GED certificate. MMC recommends completion of 16 academic units, including 4 each in English and electives and 3 each in language, math, social science, and science. Recommendations are required, and an interview is strongly advised. Applicants to the dance and acting programs must audition. A GPA of 2.5 is required. AP and CLEP credits are accepted. Important factors in the admissions decision are personality/intangible qualities, evidence of special talent, and leadership record.

Procedure: Freshmen are admitted to all sessions. Entrance exams should be taken as early as possible. There are early decision and deferred admissions plans. Early decision applications should be filed by November 1; the deadlines are open for regular applications. The fall 2003 application fee was $50. Notification of early decision is sent December 15; regular decision, on a rolling basis. 12 early decision candidates were accepted for the 2003-2004 class. Applications are accepted on-line through Embark or at the college's web site.

Transfer: 121 transfer students enrolled in a recent year. Applicants who have graduated from high school since 1989 must meet standard freshman requirements and must submit official transcripts from all colleges attended. 30 of 120 credits required for the bachelor's degree must be completed at MMC.

Visiting: There are regularly scheduled orientations for prospective students, including an interview with an admissions counselor, a tour of the school and dorms, and a meeting with a financial aid adviser. There are guides for informal visits and visitors may sit in on classes. To schedule a visit, contact the Admissions Office.

Financial Aid: In 2003-2004, 88% of all full-time freshmen and 80% of continuing full-time students received some form of financial aid. 69% of full-time freshmen and 67% of continuing full-time students received need-based aid. The average freshman award was $19,638. Need-based scholarships or need-based grants averaged $7597 ($23,792 maximum); need-based self-help aid (loans and jobs) averaged $10,334 ($24,668 maximum); and non-need-based awards and non-need-based scholarships averaged $12,060 ($30,868 maximum). 65% of undergraduates work part time. Average annual earnings from campus work are $2500. The average financial indebtedness of the 2003 graduate was $21,000. The FAFSA and TAP (New York state residents) are required. The deadline for filing freshman financial aid applications for fall entry is February 15.

International Students: There are 85 international students enrolled. The school actively recruits these students. They must score 500 on the written TOEFL or 173 on the electronic version.

Computers: The mainframe is an IBM RISC 6000. There are 125 laptops for student use in the library and 100 computers in computer labs and banks of computers. All connect to the network. All students may access the system. There are no time limits. There is a $125 technology fee per semester.

Graduates: From July 1, 2002 to June 30, 2003, 395 bachelor's degrees were awarded. The most popular majors were theater/acting (19%), communication arts (19%), and business (13%). In an average class, 32% graduate in 4 years or less, 41% graduate in 5 years or less, and 45% graduate in 6 years or less. 22 companies recruited on campus in 2002-2003. Of the 2002 graduating class, 23% were enrolled in graduate school within 6 months of graduation and 63% were employed.

Admissions Contact: Thomas Friebel, Associate Vice President for Enrollment Services. E-mail: *admissions@mmm.edu* Web: *www.marymount.mmm.edu*

MEDAILLE COLLEGE
Buffalo, NY 14214

C-1
(716) 884-3281
(800) 292-1582; Fax: (716) 884-0291

Full-time: 468 men, 1024 women	**Faculty:** 60; IIB, -$
Part-time: 37 men, 115 women	**Ph.D.s:** 66%
Graduate: 214 men, 403 women	**Student/Faculty:** 25 to 1
Year: semesters, summer session	**Tuition:** $13,660
Application Deadline: August 15	**Room & Board:** $6400
Freshman Class: 772 applied, 508 accepted, 293 enrolled	
SAT I Verbal/Math: 470/450	**COMPETITIVE**

Medaille College, founded in 1875, is a private, nonsectarian institution offering undergraduate programs in liberal arts, education, business, and sciences, and graduate programs in business and education, to a primarily commuter student body. The library contains 55,950 volumes and 2309 audio/video tapes/CDs, and subscribes to 228 periodicals. Computerized library services include the card catalog, interlibrary loans, and database searching. Special learning facilities include a learning resource center, radio station, TV station, and a media institute. The 13-acre campus is in an urban area 3 miles from downtown Buffalo. Including any residence halls, there are 17 buildings.

Student Life: 91% of undergraduates are from New York. Students are from 12 states, 2 foreign countries, and Canada. 67% are white; 15% foreign nationals; 13% African American. The average age of freshmen is 20; all undergraduates, 26. 30% do not continue beyond their first year; 39% remain to graduate.

Housing: 450 students can be accommodated in college housing, which includes single-sex and coed dorms, on-campus apartments, and off-campus apartments. On-campus housing is guaranteed for all 4 years. 82% of students commute. All students may keep cars.

Activities: There are no fraternities or sororities. There are 16 groups on campus, including academic, art, cheerleading, ethnic, honors, literary magazine, newspaper, photography, professional, radio and TV, social, student government, and yearbook. Popular campus events include Founders Day, Silent Auction, and Honors Convocation.

Sports: There are 5 intercollegiate sports for men and 6 for women, and 3 intramural sports for men and 3 for women. Facilities include an NCAA regulation gym located in the student center, and a softball and soccer field.

Disabled Students: All of the campus is accessible. Wheelchair ramps, elevators, special parking, specially equipped rest rooms, lowered drinking fountains, and lowered telephones are available.

Services: Counseling and information services are available, as is tutoring in most subjects. There is a reader service for the blind, and remedial math, reading, and writing.

Campus Safety and Security: Measures include 24-hour foot and vehicle patrol, self-defense education, security escort services, and shuttle buses. There are informal discussions, pamphlets/posters/films, emergency telephones, and lighted pathways/sidewalks.

Programs of Study: Medaille confers B.A., B.S., B.B.A., and B.S.Ed. degrees. Associate and master's degrees are also awarded. Bachelor's degrees are awarded in BIOLOGICAL SCIENCE (biology/biological science), BUSINESS (banking and finance, business administration and management, human resources, and sports management), COMMUNICATIONS AND THE ARTS (communications and visual and performing arts), COMPUTER AND PHYSICAL SCIENCE (information sciences and systems), EDUCATION (elementary), HEALTH PROFESSIONS (veterinary science), SOCIAL SCIENCE (child care/child and family studies, criminal justice, human services, humanities, liberal arts/general studies, political science/government, psychology, and social science). Psychology and humanities are the strongest academically. Education, business administration, and veterinary technology are the largest.

Required: The bachelor's degree requires successful completion of 120 credit hours or 128 for elementary education and biology majors. In addition to specific course requirements for each major, students must maintain a minimum GPA of 2.0. Five theme areas must be satisfied: Theme I - Self and Others; Theme II - Global Perspectives; Theme III - Creative Expression; Theme IV - Science, Technology, and Environment; and Theme V - Communication. Students must also complete 6 credits in capstone courses.

Special: Cross-registration is available with colleges in the Western New York Consortium. Most degree programs require internships. Opportunities are provided for student-designed majors, credit by examination, pass/fail options, accelerated degrees, dual majors, and credit for work experience. The 2-year veterinary technology program combined with additional liberal arts and sciences courses leads to the B.S. in liberal studies degree. A modular program of evening courses, as well as Weekend College classes, enable students to maintain full-time status by attending classes either 2 nights a week or on weekends. There are 2 national honor societies and a freshman honors program.

Faculty/Classroom: 63% of faculty are male; 37%, female. 95% teach undergraduates and 31% both teach and do research. No introductory courses are taught by graduate students. The average class size in an introductory lecture is 20; in a laboratory, 10; and in a regular course, 14.

Admissions: 66% of the 2003-2004 applicants were accepted. The SAT I scores for the 2003-2004 freshman class were: Verbal--70% below 500, 25% between 500 and 599, and 5% between 600 and 700; Math--80% below 500, 18% between 500 and 599, and 2% between 600 and 700. 19% of the current freshmen were in the top fifth of their class; 62% were in the top two fifths.

Requirements: The SAT I is required. In addition, applicants must be graduates of an accredited secondary school or hold the GED. An essay and an interview are required. A GPA of 70.0 is required. AP and CLEP credits are accepted. Important factors in the admissions decision are advanced placement or honor courses, personality/intangible qualities, and leadership record.

Procedure: Freshmen are admitted to all sessions. Entrance exams should be taken in May. There is a deferred admissions plan and a rolling admissions plan. Applications should be filed by August 15 for fall entry, January 15 for spring entry, and June 15 for summer entry, along with a $25 fee. Notification is sent on a rolling basis. Applications are accepted on-line through *www.medaille.edu.*

Transfer: 252 transfer students enrolled in 2002-2003. Transfer applicants must have a minimum GPA of 2.0 in their previous college work. An interview and recommendations are required. 30 of 120 credits required for the bachelor's degree must be completed at Medaille.

Visiting: There are regularly scheduled orientations for prospective students, including campus tours, academic program meetings, icebreakers, and a review of policies and procedures. There are guides for informal visits and visitors may sit in on classes and stay overnight. To schedule a visit, contact Jacqueline S. Matheny at *jmatheny@medaille.edu.*

Financial Aid: In 2003-2004, 95% of all full-time freshmen and 93% of continuing full-time students received some form of financial aid. 85% of all full-time students received need-based aid. The average freshman award was $11,500. 15% of undergraduates work part time. Average annual earnings from campus work are $1500. The average financial indebtedness of the 2003 graduate was $18,500. Medaille is a member of CSS. The FAFSA and the college's own financial statement are required. The deadline for filing freshman financial aid applications for fall entry is April 1.

International Students: There are 230 international students enrolled. They must score 550 on the written TOEFL or 213 on the electronic version and also take the SAT I.

Computers: There are 100 IBM and 25 Mac PCs available for academic use. All students may access the system. There are no time limits and no fees.

Graduates: From July 1, 2002 to June 30, 2003, 394 bachelor's degrees were awarded. The most popular majors were elementary teacher education (54%), business administration (25%), and liberal studies (8%). In an average class, 30% graduate in 4 years or less, 38% graduate in 5 years or less, and 39% graduate in 6 years or less. 65 companies recruited on campus in 2002-2003. Of the 2002 graduating class, 20% were enrolled in graduate school within 6 months of graduation and 95% were employed.

Admissions Contact: Jacqueline S. Matheny, Director Enrollment Management. E-mail: *jmatheny@medaille.edu* Web: *www.medaille.edu*

MERCY COLLEGE
Dobbs Ferry, NY 10522-1189

D-5
(914) 693-7600
(800)MERCY NY; Fax: (914) 674-7382

Full-time: 1262 men, 2859 women	Faculty: 125; IIA, +$
Part-time: 572 men, 1702 women	Ph.D.s: 75%
Graduate: 764 men, 2183 women	Student/Faculty: 33 to 1
Year: semesters, summer session	Tuition: $10,700
Application Deadline: open	Room & Board: $8500
Freshman Class: 884 enrolled	
SAT I Verbal/Math: 500/500	NONCOMPETITIVE

Mercy College, founded in 1950, is a private (not for profit) institution offering programs in liberal arts, business, and health science. In addition to regional accreditation, Mercy has baccalaureate program accreditation

with AACSB, ACOTE, CAPTE, CCNE, CSWE, and NLN. The 8 libraries contain 304,212 volumes and 28,105 microform items, and subscribe to 2099 periodicals. Computerized library services include the card catalog, interlibrary loans, database searching, and Internet access. Special learning facilities include a learning resource center, radio station, TV station, computer lab, reference library, and a digital arts center. The 60-acre campus is in a suburban area 12 miles north of New York City. Including any residence halls, there are 10 buildings.

Student Life: 97% of undergraduates are from New York. Students are from 14 states, 100 foreign countries, and Canada. 95% are from public schools. 29% are white; 25% Hispanic; 24% African American. The average age of freshmen is 19; all undergraduates, 29. 25% do not continue beyond their first year; 60% remain to graduate.

Housing: 165 students can be accommodated in college housing, which includes coed dorms. On-campus housing is guaranteed for all 4 years and is available on a first-come, first-served basis. Priority is given to out-of-town students. 99% of students commute. Alcohol is not permitted. All students may keep cars.

Activities: There are no fraternities or sororities. There are 18 groups on campus, including chess, computers, drama, ethnic, film, gay, honors, international, literary magazine, mentoring program, newspaper, political, professional, radio and TV, religious, social, social service, student government, and veterinary club. Popular campus events include Presidential Lecture Series, Hudson Valley Lecture Series, and Open Houses.

Sports: There are 6 intercollegiate sports for men and 5 for women. Facilities include a gym, a soccer/baseball field, 3 swimming pools, 2 tennis courts, a track, and a basketball court.

Disabled Students: 75% of the campus is accessible. Wheelchair ramps, elevators, special parking, specially equipped rest rooms, special class scheduling, and lowered drinking fountains are available.

Services: Counseling and information services are available, as is tutoring in every subject. There is a reader service for the blind and remedial math, reading, and writing.

Campus Safety and Security: Measures include 24-hour foot and vehicle patrol and lighted pathways/sidewalks.

Programs of Study: Mercy confers B.A. and B.S. degrees. Associate and master's degrees are also awarded. Bachelor's degrees are awarded in BIOLOGICAL SCIENCE (biology/biological science), BUSINESS (accounting and business administration and management), COMMUNICATIONS AND THE ARTS (English, journalism, and music), COMPUTER AND PHYSICAL SCIENCE (computer science, information sciences and systems, and mathematics), EDUCATION (education of the deaf and hearing impaired, elementary, special, and teaching English as a second/foreign language (TESOL/TEFOL)), HEALTH PROFESSIONS (medical laboratory technology, nursing, recreation therapy, and veterinary science), SOCIAL SCIENCE (behavioral science, criminal justice, history, interdisciplinary studies, paralegal studies, political science/government, psychology, social work, and sociology). The health professions programs is the strongest academically. Business and education are the largest.

Required: To graduate, students must complete 120 semester hours with a minimum GPA of 2.0 overall and in the major. Distribution requirements include 12 credits each of math/natural science and philosophy/language/fine arts, 9 of social science, 6 each of English and history, and 3 of speech.

Special: Mercy offers internships in each major, co-op programs in education, work-study programs through the Westchester Employee Association, study abroad, dual majors and degrees, credit for life experience, nondegree study, and pass/fail options. There are 14 national honor societies, including Phi Beta Kappa, a freshman honors program, and 14 departmental honors programs.

Faculty/Classroom: 98% teach undergraduates and 5% do research. No introductory courses are taught by graduate students. The average class size in an introductory lecture is 15; in a laboratory, 12; and in a regular course, 14.

Admissions: All of the 2003-2004 applicants were accepted. There is an open admissions policy.

Requirements: The SAT I or ACT is recommended. In addition, applicants must be graduates of an accredited secondary school or have a GED certificate. They should have completed at least 16 academic units. An interview is required and a letter of recommendation from the high school counselor or principal is required. Art students must submit a portfolio; music students must audition. AP and CLEP credits are accepted.

Procedure: Freshmen are admitted to all sessions. Entrance exams should be taken between January and August of the senior year. There are early decision, early admissions, deferred admissions, and rolling admissions plans. Application deadlines are open. The application fee is $35. Notification is sent on a rolling basis. Applications are accepted online through *www.merlin.mercynet.edu.*

Transfer: Applicants must submit official transcripts from all colleges attended. Students with fewer than 15 college credits must also submit their high school transcript. An interview is required. 30 of 120 credits required for the bachelor's degree must be completed at Mercy.

Visiting: There are regularly scheduled orientations for prospective students, including spring and fall open houses and information sessions. There are guides for informal visits. To schedule a visit, contact the Admissions Office at *admissions@mercy.edu.*

Financial Aid: Mercy is a member of CSS. The FAFSA is required. The deadline for filing freshman financial aid applications for fall entry is May 1.

International Students: There are 208 international students enrolled. The school actively recruits these students. They must score 500 on the written TOEFL or 200 on the electronic version and also take the college's own entrance exam.

Computers: The mainframe is an IBM 4381. There are also 250 IBM PCs and Macs, as well as graphics workstations with IBM XTs and Vectrix graphics boards. All students may access the system. There are no time limits. The fee is $75.

Graduates: 150 companies recruited on campus in 2002-2003.

Admissions Contact: Marie A. Noblitt, Vice President for Enrollment Management. Web: *www.mercy.edu*

METROPOLITAN COLLEGE OF NEW YORK   D-5
(Formerly Audrey Cohen College)

New York, NY 10013   (212) 343-1234, ext. 5001
                                                      (800) 33-THINK; Fax: (212) 343-8470

Full-time: 278 men, 1014 women	**Faculty:** 36
Part-time: none	**Ph.D.s:** 70%
Graduate: 61 men, 278 women	**Student/Faculty:** 36 to 1
Year: trimesters, summer session	**Tuition:** $15,771
Application Deadline: August 1	**Room & Board:** n/app
Freshman Class: 412 applied, 292 accepted, 215 enrolled	
SAT I or ACT: not required	**COMPETITIVE**

Metropolitan College of New York, formerly Audrey Cohen College, founded in 1964, is a private institution offering programs in human services and business management. The college operates on a 3-semester calendar, including a complete summer semester. All bachelor degree programs involve a combination of class work and fieldwork and may be completed in 2 years and 8 months. Master's degree programs can be completed in 1 year. There are 2 undergraduate and 2 graduate schools. The library contains 32,000 volumes and 1800 microform items, and subscribes to 3300 periodicals. Computerized library services include the card catalog, interlibrary loans, database searching, and Internet access. Special learning facilities include a learning resource center. The campus is in an urban area in New York City. There is 1 building.

Student Life: 95% of undergraduates are from New York. Students are from 4 states, 9 foreign countries, and Canada. 68% are from public schools. 61% are African American; 21% Hispanic. The average age of freshmen is 32; all undergraduates, 32. 30% do not continue beyond their first year; 41% remain to graduate.

Housing: There are no residence halls. All students commute. Alcohol is not permitted.

Activities: There are no fraternities or sororities. There are 10 groups on campus, including computers, ethnic, gay, honors, newspaper, professional, social, social service, student government, and yearbook. Popular campus events include career fairs, admissions open house, and dean's list ceremonies.

Sports: There is no sports program at the college.

Disabled Students: All of the campus is accessible. Wheelchair ramps, elevators, specially equipped rest rooms, special class scheduling, lowered drinking fountains, and lowered telephones are available.

Services: Counseling and information services are available, as is tutoring in every subject. There is remedial math, reading, and writing.

Campus Safety and Security: Measures include 24-hour foot and vehicle patrol, pamphlets/posters/films, lighted pathways/sidewalks, fire drills, and a fire escape stairwell.

Programs of Study: The college confers B.B.A. and B.P.S. degrees. Associate and master's degrees are also awarded. Bachelor's degrees are awarded in BUSINESS (business administration and management), EDUCATION (early childhood), HEALTH PROFESSIONS (mental health/human services), SOCIAL SCIENCE (child care/child and family studies, community services, gerontology, human services, prelaw, psychology, and social work). Business management is the strongest academically. Human services is the largest.

Required: To graduate, students must complete 128 credit hours with a minimum GPA of 2.0. The curriculum is prescribed and no electives are featured. A constructive action document based on performance in the field and mastery of course work is required each semester.

Special: Internships, which include required weekly 14-hour field sites, study abroad in 3 countries, work-study programs, B.A.- B.S. degrees and accelerated degree programs in human services and business management, credit by exam, and credit for life experience are offered.

Faculty/Classroom: 72% of faculty are male; 28%, female. 95% teach undergraduates. No introductory courses are taught by graduate students. The average class size in an introductory lecture is 25; in a laboratory, 18; and in a regular course, 20.

Admissions: 71% of the 2003-2004 applicants were accepted.

Requirements: Students must take the Test of Adult Basic Education (TABE) in English, reading, and math; recent high school graduates who have a minimum composite SAT I score of 1050 may present the SAT I instead. Applicants must have graduated from an accredited secondary school. The GED is accepted. An essay and an interview are required. CLEP credit is accepted. Important factors in the admissions decision are evidence of special talent, leadership record, and personality/intangible qualities.

Procedure: Freshmen are admitted to all sessions. Entrance exams should be taken in the senior year. There is a rolling admissions plan. Applications should be filed by August 1 for fall entry, December 1 for spring entry, and April 1 for summer entry, along with a $35 fee. Notification is sent on a rolling basis. Applications are accepted on-line.

Transfer: 90 transfer students enrolled in 2002-2003. Admission is based on current skills and abilities as measured on the entrance exam and essay. 64 credits of 128 required for the bachelor's degree must be completed at the college.

Visiting: There are regularly scheduled orientations for prospective students. There are guides for informal visits and visitors may sit in on classes. To schedule a visit, contact the Admissions Office at *admissions@metropolitan.edu.*

Financial Aid: In 2003-2004, 84% of all full-time freshmen and 85% of continuing full-time students received some form of financial aid. The average freshman award was $19,001. The CSS Profile, FAFSA, and the New York State Higher Education Financial statement are required. The priority date for freshman financial aid applications for fall entry is March. The deadline for filing freshman financial aid applications for fall entry is August 15.

International Students: They must score 550 on the written TOEFL and also take the TABE.

Computers: The mainframe is a Unisys Clearpath. There are 120 Dell PCs available in the computer labs and the library. All students may access the system whenever the college is open. There are no time limits. The fee is $75. It is strongly recommended that all students have a personal computer.

Graduates: From July 1, 2002 to June 30, 2003, 281 bachelor's degrees were awarded. In an average class, 41% graduate in 4 years or less. 55 companies recruited on campus in 2002-2003. Of the 2002 graduating class, 50% were enrolled in graduate school within 6 months of graduation and 85% were employed.

Admissions Contact: Sharon Handelsman, Director of Admissions and Recruitment. E-mail: *shandelsman@metropolitan.edu* Web: *www.metropolitan.edu*

MOLLOY COLLEGE   D-5
Rockville Centre, NY 11570   (516) 678-5000
                                             (888) 466-5569; Fax: (516) 256-2247

Full-time: 410 men, 1212 women	**Faculty:** IIB, +$
Part-time: 113 men, 576 women	**Ph.D.s:** 52%
Graduate: 98 men, 598 women	**Student/Faculty:** n/av
Year: semesters, summer session	**Tuition:** $15,180
Application Deadline: open	**Room & Board:** n/app
Freshman Class: 918 applied, 617 accepted, 299 enrolled	
SAT I Verbal/Math: 522/528	**COMPETITIVE**

Molloy College, founded in 1955 in the Catholic and Dominican tradition, is an independent commuter college. It offers programs in liberal arts and sciences, business, nursing and health professions, social work, teacher certification, and preprofessional studies. In addition to regional accreditation, Molloy has baccalaureate program accreditation with CSWE and NLN. The library contains 110,000 volumes, 13,850 microform items, and 3170 audio/video tapes/CDs, and subscribes to 720 periodicals. Computerized library services include the card catalog, interlibrary loans, database searching, and Internet access. Special learning facilities include a learning resource center, art gallery, and TV station. The 30-acre campus is in a suburban area 20 miles east of New York City. There are 4 buildings.

Student Life: 98% of undergraduates are from New York. Students are from 1 state and 9 foreign countries. 66% are from public schools. 61% are white; 17% African American. 66% are Catholic; 7% Protestant; 6% claim no religious affiliation. The average age of freshmen is 18; all undergraduates, 24. 18% do not continue beyond their first year; 57% remain to graduate.

Housing: There are no residence halls. All students commute. Alcohol is not permitted. All students may keep cars.

Activities: There are no fraternities or sororities. There are 23 groups on campus, including band, cheerleading, choir, chorus, dance, drama, ethnic, honors, international, jazz band, literary magazine, musical theater, newspaper, professional, radio, religious, social, social service, student government, and yearbook. Popular campus events include Senior 55 Nights Party, Junior Ring Night, and Box Town.

Sports: There are 6 intercollegiate sports for men and 7 for women. Facilities include a gym, a dance studio, a weight room, sports fields, and basketball and tennis courts.

Disabled Students: All of the campus is accessible. Wheelchair ramps, elevators, special parking, specially equipped rest rooms, special class scheduling, lowered drinking fountains, and lowered telephones are available.

Services: Counseling and information services are available, as is tutoring in every subject. There is a reader service for the blind, and remedial math, reading, and writing.

Campus Safety and Security: Measures include 24-hour foot and vehicle patrol, security escort services, pamphlets/posters/films, and emergency telephones. There are lighted pathways/sidewalks and a Campus Concerns Committee.

Programs of Study: Molloy confers B.A., B.S., and B.F.A. degrees. Associate and master's degrees are also awarded. Bachelor's degrees are awarded in BIOLOGICAL SCIENCE (biology/biological science), BUSINESS (accounting and business administration and management), COMMUNICATIONS AND THE ARTS (art, communications, English, music, and Spanish), COMPUTER AND PHYSICAL SCIENCE (computer science, information sciences and systems, and mathematics), EDUCATION (elementary, secondary, and special), ENGINEERING AND ENVIRONMENTAL DESIGN (environmental science), HEALTH PROFESSIONS (music therapy, nursing, and speech pathology/audiology), SOCIAL SCIENCE (criminal justice, gerontology, history, interdisciplinary studies, peace studies, philosophy, political science/government, psychology, social work, sociology, and theological studies). Nursing, education, and social work are the strongest academically. Nursing, business, and psychology are the largest.

Required: General education requirements consist of 45 to 54 credits. A total of 128 to 137 credit hours is required for graduation.

Special: Students may cross-register with 16 area colleges. The college offers internships, a Washington semester, study abroad, and dual and student-designed majors. Credit by examination and for life, military, and work experience, nondegree study, and pass/fail options are available. There are 15 national honor societies and a freshman honors program.

Faculty/Classroom: In a recent year 19% of faculty were male; 81%, female. 91% teach undergraduates and 25% do research. No introductory courses are taught by graduate students. The average class size in an introductory lecture is 27; in a laboratory, 15; and in a regular course, 18.

Admissions: 67% of the 2003-2004 applicants were accepted. The SAT I scores for the 2003-2004 freshman class were: Verbal--38% below 500, 47% between 500 and 599, 14% between 600 and 700, and 1% above 700; Math--37% below 500, 46% between 500 and 599, 15% between 600 and 700, and 2% above 700. 39% of the current freshmen were in the top fifth of their class; 59% were in the top two fifths.

Requirements: The SAT I or ACT is required; the SAT I is preferred. In addition, applicants should be graduates of a secondary school or have a GED. Preparation should include 4 years of English, 3 each of math and history, and 2 each of foreign language and science. An essay is required, and an interview is recommended. Music students must audition and take a theory exam. A grade average of 80 is required. AP and CLEP credits are accepted. Important factors in the admissions decision are advanced placement or honor courses, recommendations by school officials, and extracurricular activities record.

Procedure: Freshmen are admitted fall and spring. Entrance exams should be taken in the fall of the senior year. There are early decision, deferred admissions, and rolling admission plans. Application deadlines are open. Application fee is $30. Applications are accepted on-line.

Transfer: 499 transfer students enrolled in 2002-2003. A minimum college GPA of 2.0 is required, with some majors requiring a higher GPA. An interview is recommended. 30 of 128 credits required for the bachelor's degree must be completed at Molloy.

Visiting: There are regularly scheduled orientations for prospective students, including an address by the president of the college, department presentations, campus tours, and admissions, financial aid, and scholarship information. There are guides for informal visits and visitors may sit in on classes. To schedule a visit, contact the Admissions Office.

Financial Aid: In a recent year, 93% of all full-time freshmen and 91% of continuing full-time students received some form of financial aid. 77% of full-time freshmen and 84% of continuing full-time students received need-based aid. The average freshman award was $4125. 23% of undergraduates work part time. Average annual earnings from campus work was $2000. The average financial indebtedness of a recent graduate was $15,000. Molloy is a member of CSS. The FAFSA is required. The deadline for filing freshman financial aid applications for fall entry is May 1.

International Students: There are 19 international students enrolled. They must score 500 on the written TOEFL or take the MELAB.

Computers: Molloy College is a wireless campus. Students can use their own laptop computers or borrow from the lab. There are 244 PCs available to students in 4 campus computer labs. In addition, numerous PCs are available for student use within individual departments. Internet and e-mail access is available to students in the library, computer labs, and many departments. All students may access the system. There are no time limits and no fees.

Graduates: From July 1, 2002 to June 30, 2003, 459 bachelor's degrees were awarded. The most popular majors were nursing (29%), psychology (15%), and business (8%). In a recent year in an average class, 42% graduated in 4 years or less, 55% graduated in 5 years or less, and 57% graduated in 6 years or less. 70 companies recruited on campus in a recent year.

Admissions Contact: Marguerite Lane, Director of Admissions. E-mail: *mlane@molloy.edu* Web: *www.molloy.edu*

MONROE COLLEGE
Bronx, NY 10468

D-5

(718) 933-6700 ext. 250
(800) 55 MONROE; Fax: (718) 364-3552

Full-time: 2300 men, 2700 women	**Faculty:** n/av
Part-time: none	**Ph.D.s:** n/av
Graduate: none	**Student/Faculty:** n/av
Year: semesters, summer session	**Tuition:** $8900
Application Deadline: see profile	**Room & Board:** $6200
Freshman Class: n/av	
SAT I: recommended	**LESS COMPETITIVE**

Monroe College, founded in 1933, offers undergraduate programs in business. Figures in the above capsule and in this profile are approximate.

Housing: College-sponsored living facilities include off-campus apartments. A residence hall is available on the New Rochelle campus.

Programs of Study: Monroe confers B.S. and B.B.A. degrees. Associate degrees are also awarded. Bachelor's degrees are awarded in BUSINESS (accounting and business administration and management), COMPUTER AND PHYSICAL SCIENCE (information sciences and systems), SOCIAL SCIENCE (criminal justice).

Required: To receive a bachelor's degree, students must earn a minimum of 120 total credits, with a minimum of 60 in the major. General education requirements include 9 credits in English and 6 each in math and electives. 2 computer courses are also required.

Special: Internships are available through a cooperative education program, and there are accelerated degree programs.

Requirements: The SAT I is recommended. In addition, the application, an essay, and an interview are required. Monroe College requires applicants to be in the upper 50% of their class. A grade average of 70 is required.

Procedure: Check with the school for current application deadlines. The application fee is $35.

Financial Aid: In a recent year, 80% of all full-time students received some form of financial aid.

Admissions Contact: Luke D. Schultheis, Director of Admissions. A video is available. E-mail: *admissions@monroecollege.edu* Web: *monroecollege.edu*

MOUNT SAINT MARY COLLEGE
Newburgh, NY 12550

D-4

(845) 569-3248
(888) YES-MSMC; Fax: (845) 562-6762

Full-time: 415 men, 1148 women	**Faculty:** 67; IIB, +$
Part-time: 167 men, 400 women	**Ph.D.s:** 84%
Graduate: 94 men, 382 women	**Student/Faculty:** 23 to 1
Year: semesters, summer session	**Tuition:** $14,290
Application Deadline: open	**Room & Board:** $6980
Freshman Class: 1484 applied, 1166 accepted, 347 enrolled	
SAT I or ACT: required	**COMPETITIVE**

MSMC is a private liberal arts college offering undergraduate programs leading to Bachelor of Arts and Bachelor of Science degrees, and graduate programs leading to the masters in education, nursing, and business administration. An accelerated evening program is offered for nontraditional and adult students. There are 3 graduate schools. In addition to regional accreditation, the Mount has baccalaureate program accreditation with CCNE and NLN. The 2 libraries contain 105,683 volumes, 708,609 microform items, and 23,524 audio/video tapes/CDs, and subscribe to 860 periodicals. Computerized library services include the card catalog, interlibrary loans, database searching, and Internet access. Special learning facilities include a learning resource center, radio station, an elementary school, an herbarium field station, and an arboretum. The 70-acre campus is in a rural area 58 miles north of New York City. Including any residence halls, there are 42 buildings.

Student Life: 96% of undergraduates are from New York. Students are from 15 states and 1 foreign country. 60% are from public schools. 81% are white; 10% African American. 54% are Catholic; 39% 7% Christian, 23% unknown, 2% Baptist, 3% Methodist, 4% other. The average age of freshmen is 19; all undergraduates, 26. 28% do not continue beyond their first year; 61% remain to graduate.

Housing: 811 students can be accommodated in college housing, which includes single-sex dorms and on-campus townhouses. On-campus housing is guaranteed for all 4 years. 61% of students commute. All students may keep cars.

Activities: There are no fraternities or sororities. There are 21 groups on campus, including art, choir, computers, dance, drama, ethnic, honors, literary magazine, musical theater, newspaper, photography, political, professional, radio and TV, religious, social, student government, and yearbook. Popular campus events include Octoberfest, Siblings Weekend, and Holiday Formal.

Sports: There are 5 intercollegiate sports for men and 6 for women, and 15 intramural sports for men and 15 for women. Facilities include a gym, a weight room, tennis and handball courts, an indoor running track, a swimming pool, a Nautilus room, a game room, and an aerobics/dance studio.

Disabled Students: All of the campus is accessible. Wheelchair ramps, elevators, special parking, specially equipped rest rooms, lowered telephones, and special equipment in the library and computer centers to accommodate students with low vision is available.

Services: Counseling and information services are available, as is tutoring in every subject. There is remedial math, reading, and writing.

Campus Safety and Security: Measures include 24-hour foot and vehicle patrol, self-defense education, security escort services, and shuttle buses. There are informal discussions, pamphlets/posters/films, emergency telephones, and lighted pathways/sidewalks.

Programs of Study: The Mount confers B.A., B.S., B.S.Ed., and B.S.N. degrees. Master's degrees are also awarded. Bachelor's degrees are awarded in BIOLOGICAL SCIENCE (biology/biological science), BUSINESS (accounting and business administration and management), COMMUNICATIONS AND THE ARTS (communications, English, media arts, and public relations), COMPUTER AND PHYSICAL SCIENCE (chemistry, computer science, information sciences and systems, and mathematics), EDUCATION (elementary, secondary, and special), HEALTH PROFESSIONS (medical laboratory technology, nursing, premedicine, and preveterinary science), SOCIAL SCIENCE (criminal justice, Hispanic American studies, history, human services, interdisciplinary studies, international studies, political science/government, prelaw, psychology, social science, and sociology). Education, nursing, and business are the strongest academically. Education, business, and English are the largest.

Required: The required core curriculum includes 39 credits in natural sciences, math, computer science, philosophy and religion, arts and letters, and social sciences. A total of 120 credit hours is required for the B.A. or B.S., with 24 to 40 in the major and a minimum GPA of 2.0. Overall requirements are higher for nursing, medical technology, and education students. All students must achieve computer literacy before graduation.

Special: Co-op programs and internships are available in all majors. There is cross-registration with other mid-Hudson area colleges, as well as accelerated degree programs in business, accounting, nursing, computer science, and public relations among others. There is a 3-2 degree in physical therapy with New York Medical College, a 3-2 engineering degree with Catholic University, and several other collaborative programs. The college also offers study abroad in more than 22 countries, a Washington semester, work-study, and dual and student-designed majors. Credit by exam and for life, military, and work experience, nondegree study, and pass/fail options are available. There are 9 national honor societies and a freshman honors program.

Faculty/Classroom: 45% of faculty are male; 55%, female. All teach undergraduates, 40% do research, and 40% do both. No introductory courses are taught by graduate students. The average class size in an introductory lecture is 25; in a laboratory, 12; and in a regular course, 20.

Admissions: 79% of the 2003-2004 applicants were accepted. 16% of the current freshmen were in the top fifth of their class; 58% were in the top two fifths.

Requirements: The SAT I or ACT is required. In addition, students should be graduates of an accredited secondary school. The GED is accepted. Applicants should prepare with 4 years each of English and history and at least 3 each of math and science and 2 of foreign language. An essay and an interview are recommended. A grade average of 75 is required. AP and CLEP credits are accepted. Important factors in the admissions decision are advanced placement or honor courses, evidence of special talent, and personality/intangible qualities.

Procedure: Freshmen are admitted to all sessions. Entrance exams should be taken as early as possible. There is a deferred admissions plan and a rolling admissions plan. Notification of regular decision is sent on a rolling basis. Application deadlines are open. The fall 2003 fee was $35. Applications are accepted on-line.

Transfer: 217 transfer students enrolled in 2002-2003. Applicants must have a GPA of at least 2.0 in all college work. The SAT I or ACT and an interview are recommended. 30 of 120 credits required for the bachelor's degree must be completed at the Mount.

Visiting: There are regularly scheduled orientations for prospective students, including 6 open houses per year, a 4-day fall orientation program, and a Spend a Day with a Current Student program in the spring. There are guides for informal visits and visitors may sit in on classes and stay overnight. To schedule a visit, contact Admissions.

Financial Aid: In 2003-2004, 84% of all full-time freshmen and 85% of continuing full-time students received some form of financial aid. 66% of full-time freshmen and 69% of continuing full-time students received need-based aid. The average freshman award was $11,400, with $4200 ($23,000 maximum) from need-based scholarships or need-based grants, $2200 ($4400 maximum) from need-based self-help aid (loans and jobs), $2000 ($16,000 maximum) from non-need-based awards and non-need-based scholarships and $3000 ($23,000 maximum) from other awards. 17% of undergraduates work part time. Average annual earnings from campus work are $1000. The average financial indebtedness of the 2003 graduate was $20,000. The FAFSA and the college's own financial statement are required. The priority date for freshman financial aid applications for fall entry is February 15. The deadline for filing freshman financial aid applications for fall entry is March 15.

International Students: There is 1 international student enrolled. They must score 500 on the written TOEFL and also take the SAT I, ACT, or the college's own entrance exam.

Computers: The mainframe is an IBM AS/400 - Model 270. The student-computer ratio is 14 to 1. PCs are located in the main computer center, labs, classrooms, and the library. There is wireless network access campus wide and access through the web module 24 hours a day, 7 days a week. All students may access the system weekdays from 8 A.M. to 11 P.M., and weekends from 10 A.M. to 5 P.M. or access through the web module 24 hours a day, 7 days a week. There are no time limits and no fees. It is strongly recommended that all students have a personal computer.

Graduates: From July 1, 2002 to June 30, 2003, 454 bachelor's degrees were awarded. The most popular majors were business (25%), education (18%), and English (11%). In an average class, 1% graduate in 3 years or less, 42% graduate in 4 years or less, 57% graduate in 5 years or less, and 61% graduate in 6 years or less. 50 companies recruited on campus in 2002-2003. Of the 2002 graduating class, 25% were enrolled in graduate school within 6 months of graduation and 87% were employed.

Admissions Contact: J. Randall Ognibene, Director of Admissions. A video is available. E-mail: *mtstmary@msmc.edu* Web: *www.msmc.edu*

NAZARETH COLLEGE OF ROCHESTER   B-3
Rochester, NY 14618-3790   (585) 389-2860
(800) 462-3944; Fax: (585) 389-2826

Full-time: 441 men, 1326 women	**Faculty:** 135; IIA, av$
Part-time: 46 men, 184 women	**Ph.D.s:** 94%
Graduate: 204 men, 861 women	**Student/Faculty:** 13 to 1
Year: semesters, summer session	**Tuition:** $17,536
Application Deadline: February 15	**Room & Board:** $7400
Freshman Class: 1627 applied, 1352 accepted, 385 enrolled	
SAT I Verbal/Math: 570/570	**ACT:** 25 **VERY COMPETITIVE**

Nazareth College of Rochester, founded in 1924, is an independent institution offering programs in the liberal arts and sciences and preprofessional areas. There are 4 undergraduate schools. In addition to regional accreditation, Nazareth has baccalaureate program accreditation with CSWE, NASM, ACS, ASHA, CAPTE, and CCNE. The library contains 162,593 volumes, 438,204 microform items, and 12,236 audio/video tapes/CDs, and subscribes to 1888 periodicals. Computerized library services include the card catalog, interlibrary loans, database searching, and Internet access. Special learning facilities include a learning resource center, art gallery, and radio station. The 150-acre campus is in a suburban area 7 miles east of Rochester. Including any residence halls, there are 21 buildings.

Student Life: 93% of undergraduates are from New York. Students are from 23 states, 9 foreign countries, and Canada. 90% are from public schools. 88% are white. The average age of freshmen is 18; all undergraduates, 21. 16% do not continue beyond their first year; 72% remain to graduate.

Housing: 1140 students can be accommodated in college housing, which includes single-sex and coed dorms and on-campus apartments. In addition, there are language houses, special-interest houses, substance-free floors, freshman experience floors, and honors floors. On-campus housing is guaranteed for all 4 years. 62% of students live on campus; of those, 88% remain on campus on weekends. All students may keep cars.

Activities: There are no fraternities or sororities. There are 33 groups on campus, including art, band, cheerleading, choir, chorale, chorus, computers, dance, drama, ethnic, gay, honors, jazz band, literary magazine, musical theater, newspaper, opera, orchestra, political, professional, radio, religious, social, student government, and yearbook. Popular campus events include Springfest, Parents Weekend, and Siblings Weekend.

Sports: There are 8 intercollegiate sports for men and 10 for women, and 20 intramural sports for men and 20 for women. Facilities include

a gym, a 25-meter swimming pool, soccer and lacrosse fields, including an outdoor turf field, tennis and racquetball courts, a fitness center, a sauna, a 2200-seat stadium, and a 400-meter all-weather track.

Disabled Students: 80% of the campus is accessible. Wheelchair ramps, elevators, special parking, specially equipped rest rooms, and special class scheduling are available.

Services: Counseling and information services are available, as is tutoring in every subject.

Campus Safety and Security: Measures include 24-hour foot and vehicle patrol, security escort services, informal discussions, and pamphlets/posters/films. There are emergency telephones, lighted pathways/sidewalks, and an alarm system, and security beepers free to all students.

Programs of Study: Nazareth confers B.A., B.S., and B.Mus. degrees. Master's degrees are also awarded. Bachelor's degrees are awarded in BIOLOGICAL SCIENCE (biochemistry and biology/biological science), BUSINESS (accounting and business administration and management), COMMUNICATIONS AND THE ARTS (art, art history and appreciation, dramatic arts, English, fine arts, French, German, Italian, music, music history and appreciation, music performance, and Spanish), COMPUTER AND PHYSICAL SCIENCE (chemistry, information sciences and systems, and mathematics), EDUCATION (art, business, elementary, English, foreign languages, mathematics, middle school, music, science, social studies, and special), ENGINEERING AND ENVIRONMENTAL DESIGN (environmental science), HEALTH PROFESSIONS (music therapy, nursing, physical therapy, and speech pathology/audiology), SOCIAL SCIENCE (American studies, anthropology, economics, history, international studies, philosophy, political science/government, psychology, religion, social science, social work, and sociology). Physical therapy, math, and English are the strongest academically. Business, psychology, and art are the largest.

Required: All students must take 1 course each in literature, math, lab science, philosophy, social science, history, fine arts, and religious studies. 2 semesters of phys ed, a course in computer literacy, and a writing competency exam in the junior year are required. Other requirements vary according to the major, with a total of 30 to 75 upper-division credits needed. A total of 120 credit hours is required to graduate. The minimum GPA is 2.0.

Special: There is cross-registration with members of the Rochester Area Colleges Consortium. Internships and a Washington semester are offered. There is study abroad in France, Spain, Italy, and Germany, and there are exchange programs in Australia, Japan, Italy, and Wales. There are 20 national honor societies and 13 departmental honors programs.

Faculty/Classroom: 42% of faculty are male; 58%, female. All teach undergraduates. No introductory courses are taught by graduate students. The average class size in an introductory lecture is 22; in a laboratory, 15; and in a regular course, 24.

Admissions: 83% of the 2003-2004 applicants were accepted. The SAT I scores for the 2003-2004 freshman class were: Verbal--19% below 500, 44% between 500 and 599, 33% between 600 and 700, and 5% above 700; Math--16% below 500, 52% between 500 and 599, 29% between 600 and 700, and 4% above 700. The ACT scores were 19% below 21, 30% between 21 and 23, 27% between 24 and 26, 13% between 27 and 28, and 11% above 28. 49% of the current freshmen were in the top fifth of their class; 78% were in the top two fifths. In a recent year, there were 3 National Merit semifinalists and 5 freshmen graduated first in their class.

Requirements: The SAT I or ACT is required with minimum scores of 500 verbal and 500 math on the SAT I and 21 on the ACT. Applicants should graduate from an accredited secondary school or have a GED. A minimum of 16 academic credits is required, including 4 years of English and 3 each of social studies, foreign language, math, and science. An essay is required, as are an audition for music and theater students and a portfolio for art students. An interview is recommended. Nazareth requires applicants to be in the upper 50% of their class. A GPA of 2.75 is required. AP and CLEP credits are accepted. Important factors in the admissions decision are geographic diversity, advanced placement or honor courses, and evidence of special talent.

Procedure: Freshmen are admitted fall and spring. Entrance exams should be taken by December of the senior year. There are early decision, early admissions, and deferred admissions plans. Early decision applications should be filed by November 15; regular applications, by February 15 for fall entry and November 15 for spring entry, along with a $40 fee. Notification of early decision is sent December 15; regular decision, February 1. 54 early decision candidates were accepted for the 2003-2004 class. Applications are accepted on-line through Common App.

Transfer: 158 transfer students enrolled in 2002-2003. Applicants must have a college GPA of 2.5 (2.75 for education and physical therapy students). Those with fewer than 30 credits must submit high school transcripts. 30 of 120 credits required for the bachelor's degree must be completed at Nazareth.

Visiting: There are regularly scheduled orientations for prospective students, including individual appointments, group sessions, campus tours, open houses, and summer academic orientation. There are guides for in-

formal visits and visitors may sit in on classes and stay overnight. To schedule a visit, contact the Admissions Office at *admissions@naz.edu.*

Financial Aid: In 2003-2004, 79% of all full-time freshmen and 81% of continuing full-time students received some form of financial aid. 79% of full-time freshmen and 80% of continuing full-time students received need-based aid. The average freshman award was $14,219. Need-based scholarships or need-based grants averaged $9785; need-based self-help aid (loans and jobs) averaged $4209; and non-need-based awards and non-need-based scholarships averaged $6539. 69% of undergraduates work part time. Average annual earnings from campus work are $1421. The average financial indebtedness of the 2003 graduate was $21,307. Nazareth is a member of CSS. The FAFSA is required. The CSS Profile is required for early decision applicants only. The deadline for filing freshman financial aid applications for fall entry is February 15.

International Students: There were 9 international students enrolled in a recent year. The school actively recruits these students. They must score 550 on the written TOEFL or 213 on the electronic version and also take the SAT I or the ACT.

Computers: The mainframe is a Compact Alpha system. There are 150 PCs available for academic use in 6 labs. Two labs are open 24 hours a day. All students may access the system. There are no time limits and no fees.

Graduates: 439 bachelor's degrees were awarded in a recent year. The most popular majors were business (15%), English (11%), and psychology (10%). In an average class, 71% graduate in 5 years or less, and 72% graduate in 6 years or less. 35 companies recruited on campus in 2002-2003. Of the 2002 graduating class, 47% were enrolled in graduate school within 6 months of graduation and 80% were employed.

Admissions Contact: Thomas DaRin, Vice President of Enrollment Management. E-mail: *admissions@naz.edu* Web: *ww.naz.edu*

NEW YORK INSTITUTE OF TECHNOLOGY   D-5
Old Westbury, NY 11568-8000   (516) 686-7925
(800) 345-NYIT; Fax: (516) 686-7613

Full-time: 2511 men, 1587 women	**Faculty:** 223; IIA, ++$
Part-time: 782 men, 496 women	**Ph.Ds:** 87%
Graduate: 1729 men, 1760 women	**Student/Faculty:** 18 to 1
Year: semesters, summer session	**Tuition:** $17,225
Application Deadline: February 1	**Room & Board:** $6980
Freshman Class: 3564 applied, 2629 accepted, 880 enrolled	
SAT I Verbal/Math: 530/580	**ACT:** 23 **VERY COMPETITIVE**

The New York Institute of Technology, founded in 1955, is a nonsectarian, nonprofit institution of higher learning that provides undergraduate, graduate, and professional programs in allied health, architecture, art, business, culinary arts, communication, arts, education, engineering, hospitality management, and medicine and technology. Traditional, and accelerated formats in day, evening, and weekend sessions are available, in addition to noncredit and personal enrichment programs and off campus independent study. NYIT maintains additional campuses on Long Island, and in Manhattan. NYIT'S on-line campus is an innovative virtual campus. Students can take courses or acquire a 4 year degree entirely through web-based computer conferencing with no campus classes required. There are 7 undergraduate and 8 graduate schools. In addition to regional accreditation, NYIT has baccalaureate program accreditation with ABET, ACOTE, ARC-PA, ADA, FIDER, and NAAB. The 5 libraries contain 206,758 volumes, 857,962 microform items, and 48,950 audio/video tapes/CDs, and subscribe to 2249 periodicals. Computerized library services include the card catalog, interlibrary loans, database searching, and Internet access. Special learning facilities include a learning resource center, art gallery, radio station, TV station, and TV studios. The 525-acre campus is in a suburban area. The Old Westbury campus is 25 miles east of New York City, 10 miles from Queens. Including any residence halls, there are 57 buildings.

Student Life: 90% of undergraduates are from New York. Students are from 30 states, 92 foreign countries, and Canada. 31% are white; 14% foreign nationals; 10% African American. The average age of freshmen is 18; all undergraduates, 23. 29% do not continue beyond their first year; 71% remain to graduate.

Housing: 1000 students can be accommodated in college housing, which includes single-sex and coed dorms, on-campus apartments, and off-campus apartments. In addition, there are special-interest houses, facilities for international, graduate, architecture, first year students, student leaders, student government executive board members, and Greek life organizations. On-campus housing is guaranteed for all 4 years. 89% of students commute. Alcohol is not permitted. All students may keep cars.

Activities: 2% of men belong to 1 local and 4 national fraternities; 1% of women belong to 2 local and 1 national sorority. There are 100 groups on campus, including academic, art, cheerleading, chorale, computers, dance, drama, ethnic, film, honors, international, literary magazine, musical theater, newspaper, political, professional, radio and TV, religious, social, social service, special interest, student government, student media, and yearbook. Popular campus events include May Fest, Club Fair Day, and Earth Day.

Sports: There are 7 intercollegiate sports for men and 7 for women, and 9 intramural sports for men and 9 for women. Facilities include a gym, soccer, softball and baseball fields, a track, courts for tennis, handball, and basketball, a fitness center, aquatic facilities, and a weight room.

Disabled Students: All of the campus is accessible. Wheelchair ramps, elevators, special parking, specially equipped rest rooms, lowered drinking fountains, and special housing are available.

Services: Counseling and information services are available, as is tutoring in every subject. There is remedial math, reading, and writing.

Campus Safety and Security: Measures include 24-hour foot and vehicle patrol, security escort services, shuttle buses, and informal discussions. There are pamphlets/posters/films, emergency telephones, and lighted pathways/sidewalks.

Programs of Study: NYIT confers B.A., B.S., B.Arch., B.F.A., B.P.S., and B.Tech. degrees. Associate, master's, and doctoral degrees are also awarded. Bachelor's degrees are awarded in BIOLOGICAL SCIENCE (biology/biological science, life science, and nutrition), BUSINESS (accounting, banking and finance, business administration and management, hospitality management services, marketing and distribution, and marketing/retailing/merchandising), COMMUNICATIONS AND THE ARTS (advertising, communications, English, fine arts, graphic design, technical and business writing, and telecommunications), COMPUTER AND PHYSICAL SCIENCE (chemistry, computer science, mathematics, and physics), EDUCATION (art, business, education, elementary, health, middle school, science, secondary, technical, and trade and industrial), ENGINEERING AND ENVIRONMENTAL DESIGN (aeronautical engineering, architecture, biomedical engineering, computer engineering, computer graphics, electrical/electronics engineering, electrical/electronics engineering technology, engineering technology, environmental design, environmental engineering technology, industrial engineering, interior design, manufacturing engineering, mechanical engineering, and technological management), HEALTH PROFESSIONS (clinical science, nursing, occupational therapy, physical therapy, physician's assistant, and preosteopathy), SOCIAL SCIENCE (behavioral science, interdisciplinary studies, political science/government, prelaw, social studies, and sociology). Architecture, allied health programs, and engineering are the strongest academically. Computer science, business administration, and architectural technology are the largest.

Required: All students take a core curriculum, sequenced over 8 semesters, that includes 42 credits in English, speech, behavioral and natural science, social science, philosophy, economics, and a capstone course in the major field. A total of 120 to 169 credits and a minimum GPA of 2.0, both overall and in the major, are required for graduation.

Special: NYIT offers cooperative programs, summer study abroad, internships, student-designed majors, a B.A.-B.S. degree in interdisciplinary studies, accelerated degree programs in osteopathic medicine, mechanical engineering, physical therapy, occupational therapy, and criminal justice, and nondegree study. There are 7 national honor societies, a freshman honors program, and 2 departmental honors programs.

Faculty/Classroom: 70% of faculty are male; 30%, female. 88% teach undergraduates, 28% do research, and 28% do both. No introductory courses are taught by graduate students. The average class size in an introductory lecture is 20; in a laboratory, 15; and in a regular course, 17.

Admissions: 74% of the 2003-2004 applicants were accepted. The SAT I scores for the 2003-2004 freshman class were: Verbal--30% below 500, 45% between 500 and 599, 22% between 600 and 700, and 2% above 700; Math--14% below 500, 44% between 500 and 599, 34% between 600 and 700, and 8% above 700. The ACT scores were 28% below 21, 24% between 21 and 23, 16% between 24 and 26, 12% between 27 and 28, and 20% above 28.

Requirements: The SAT I or ACT is required for some programs. In addition, all students must present evidence of completion of high school degree or an equivalence. Architecture, engineering, combined baccalaureate/doctor of osteopathic medicine, nursing, occupational therapy, physical therapy, and physician assistant programs requirements include interviews, essays, letters of recommendation, volunteer hours, and Regents units. Recommendations are required for education program applicants. Portfolios are required for fine arts applicants. AP and CLEP credits are accepted. Important factors in the admissions decision are advanced placement or honor courses, recommendations by school officials, and leadership record.

Procedure: Freshmen are admitted fall, spring, and summer. Entrance exams should be taken in spring for fall enrollment. There is a deferred admissions plan and a rolling admissions plan. Applications should be filed by February 1 for fall entry. The fall 2003 application fee was $50. Notification is sent on a rolling basis. Applications are accepted on-line through the school's web site.

Transfer: 853 transfer students enrolled in 2002-2003. Applicants must submit official transcripts from all colleges attended. Students with less than 30 credits of previous college work must submit a high school transcript and standardized test scores. Some majors have specific require-

ments for their programs. 30 of 120 credits required for the bachelor's degree must be completed at NYIT.

Visiting: There are regularly scheduled orientations for prospective students, including open houses in fall and spring, with campus tours, a president's address, financial aid seminars, honors receptions, sessions with faculty advisers, and major-specific receptions. There are guides for informal visits and visitors may sit in on classes. To schedule a visit, contact the Admissions Office at (516) 686-7520 or *admissions@nyit.edu*.

Financial Aid: In a recent year, 86% of all full-time freshmen and 76% of continuing full-time students received some form of financial aid. 80% of full-time freshmen and 72% of continuing full-time students received need-based aid. 77% of undergraduates work part time. Average annual earnings from campus work were $2000. The average financial indebtedness of a recent graduate was $15,000. The FAFSA and NYS TAP form are required. The priority date for freshman financial aid applications for fall entry is February 1.

International Students: There are 474 international students enrolled. The school actively recruits these students. They must score 550 on the written TOEFL or 213 on the electronic version and also take the college's own test. The SAT I or ACT is required.

Computers: The mainframe is a Sun Ultra Enterprise 4500. There are 3 open access labs with Internet access, 26 classroom labs with 25 computers each, 4 distance learning labs on each campus with full computer capacity, and 718 PC, Mac, and Silicon Graphics workstations available for student use. Open access and reserve computers in 4 libraries are Internet connected. All students may access the system. There are no time limits and no fees. All students are required to have personal computers. It is recommended that students in architecture, engineering, and technology majors have personal computers.

Graduates: From July 1, 2002 to June 30, 2003, 981 bachelor's degrees were awarded. The most popular majors were communication arts (9%), computer science (8%), and architecture (6%). In an average class, 1% graduate in 3 years or less, 15% graduate in 4 years or less, 24% graduate in 5 years or less, and 31% graduate in 6 years or less. 120 companies recruited on campus in 2002-2003. Of the 2002 graduating class, 38% were enrolled in graduate school within 6 months of graduation and 88% were employed.

Admissions Contact: Jacquelyn Nealon, Dean of Admissions and Financial Aid. A video is available. E-mail: *admissions@nyit.edu* Web: *www.nyit.edu*

NEW YORK UNIVERSITY   D-5
New York, NY 10011   (212) 998-4500; Fax: (212) 995-4902

Full-time: 7012 men, 10,706 women	Faculty: 1794; I, ++$
Part-time: 740 men, 1048 women	Ph.Ds: 93%
Graduate: 7968 men, 10,714 women	Student/Faculty: 10 to 1
Year: semesters, summer session	Tuition: $28,496
Application Deadline: January 15	Room & Board: $10,910
Freshman Class: 33,097 applied, 8697 accepted, 3161 enrolled	
SAT I Verbal/Math: 670/680	ACT: 30 MOST COMPETITIVE

New York University, founded in 1831, is a private research university offering undergraduate, graduate, and professional degrees in arts and sciences, business, education, health professions, nursing, social work, performing arts, and individualized study. NYU consists of 14 colleges and schools located in New York City. There are 8 undergraduate and 11 graduate schools. In addition to regional accreditation, NYU has baccalaureate program accreditation with AACSB, ACEJMC, ADA, CSWE, and NLN. The 12 libraries contain 4,618,594 volumes, 6,358,728 microform items, and 1,338,722 audio/video tapes/CDs, and subscribe to 44,066 periodicals. Computerized library services include the card catalog, interlibrary loans, and database searching. Special learning facilities include a learning resource center, art gallery, radio station, TV station, speech/language/hearing clinic, center for students with disabilities, and Speaking Freely (free noncredit foreign language classes). The campus is in an urban area in New York City's Greenwich Village. Including any residence halls, there are 150 buildings.

Student Life: 58% of undergraduates are from out of state, mostly the Northeast. Students are from 50 states, 91 foreign countries, and Canada. 69% are from public schools. 41% are white; 14% Asian American. The average age of freshmen is 18; all undergraduates, 21. 8% do not continue beyond their first year; 78% remain to graduate.

Housing: 10,724 students can be accommodated in college housing, which includes coed dorms, on-campus apartments, and fraternity houses. In addition, there are special-interest houses and SAFE (Substance - Alcohol-Free Environment). On-campus housing is guaranteed for all 4 years. 55% of students live on campus. All students may keep cars.

Activities: 4% of men belong to 13 national fraternities; 2% of women belong to 9 local and 4 national sororities. There are more than 300 groups on campus, including art, bagpipe band, band, cheerleading, chess, choir, chorale, chorus, computers, dance, debate, drama, ethnic, film, forensics, gay, honors, international, jazz band, literary magazine, musical theater, newspaper, orchestra, pep band, photography, political, professional, radio and TV, religious, social, social service, student government, symphony, and yearbook. Popular campus events include Spring Strawberry Festival, Grad Alley, and Career Services Fair.

Sports: There are 12 intercollegiate sports for men and 10 for women, and 11 intramural sports for men and 11 for women. Facilities include 2 state-of-the-art sports and recreation facilities. The sports center houses multipurpose courts for basketball, volleyball, tennnis, and badminton, squash courts, handball and racquetball courts, rooftop tennis courts and running track, 25-meter swimming pool, diving tank, saunas, weight-training facilities, aerobic fitness room, rooms for wrestling, judo, fencing, physical fitness, exercise prescription, and dance, and a rock climbing wall. The athletic center is equipped with a 25-yard swimming pool, basketball/activities courts, foot aerobic fitness room with cardio equipment, and a 30-foot indoor climbing center.

Disabled Students: 95% of the campus is accessible. Wheelchair ramps, elevators, specially equipped rest rooms, special class scheduling, lowered drinking fountains, lowered telephones, special housing, buses with hydraulic lifts, adaptive computer equipment, CART or C-print services, CTV enlargement system, JAWS speech synthesizer, Dragon Dictate Voice Recognition, and Kurzwel Personal Readers are available.

Services: Counseling and information services are available, as is tutoring in every subject. There is a reader service for the blind. Other services include sign language interpreters, scribes, research aides, and notetakers for special needs.

Campus Safety and Security: Measures include 24-hour foot and vehicle patrol, self-defense education, security escort services, and shuttle buses. There are informal discussions, pamphlets/posters/films, emergency telephones, lighted pathways/sidewalks, 24-hour security in residence halls, and a neighborhood-merchant emergency help service.

Programs of Study: NYU confers B.A., B.S., B.F.A., B.S./B.E., and Mus.B. degrees. Associate, master's, and doctoral degrees are also awarded. Bachelor's degrees are awarded in BIOLOGICAL SCIENCE (biochemistry, biology/biological science, neurosciences, and nutrition), BUSINESS (accounting, banking and finance, business administration and management, business economics, hotel/motel and restaurant management, international business management, management science, marketing/retailing/merchandising, operations research, organizational behavior, real estate, recreation and leisure services, and sports management), COMMUNICATIONS AND THE ARTS (American literature, art history and appreciation, classics, communications, communications technology, comparative literature, creative writing, dance, design, dramatic arts, English, English literature, film arts, fine arts, French, German, Germanic languages and literature, Greek, Greek (classical), Hebrew, Italian, journalism, Latin, linguistics, media arts, music, music business management, music performance, music technology, music theory and composition, photography, Portuguese, radio/television technology, romance languages and literature, Russian, Spanish, speech/debate/rhetoric, studio art, and voice), COMPUTER AND PHYSICAL SCIENCE (actuarial science, chemistry, computer science, information sciences and systems, mathematics, physics, and statistics), EDUCATION (early childhood, English, foreign languages, mathematics, music, science, secondary, social studies, and special), ENGINEERING AND ENVIRONMENTAL DESIGN (computer engineering, graphic arts technology, and urban design), HEALTH PROFESSIONS (dental hygiene, health care administration, nursing, predentistry, premedicine, and speech pathology/audiology), SOCIAL SCIENCE (African studies, anthropology, applied psychology, classical/ancient civilization, East Asian studies, economics, European studies, gender studies, history, humanities, international relations, Judaic studies, Latin American studies, Luso-Brazilian studies, medieval studies, Middle Eastern studies, philosophy, political science/government, psychology, religion, social science, social work, sociology, and urban studies). Theater, individualized studies, and finance are the largest.

Required: All students must complete a minimum of 128 credit hours and maintain a minimum GPA of 2.0. A course in expository writing is required. Students must complete a core liberal arts curriculum in addition to major and elective credit.

Special: A 3-2 engineering degree (B.S./B.E.) is available with the Stevens Institute of Technology in New Jersey. A vast array of internships is available, as well as study worldwide at NYU's 5 sites: Florence, Paris, Madrid, Prague, and London. B.A.-B.S. degree options, accelerated degrees in more than 140 majors, dual and student-designed majors, credit by exam, and pass/fail options are also available. A Washington semester is available to political science majors. There are exchange programs with several historically black colleges. There is a chapter of Phi Beta Kappa and a freshman honors program.

Faculty/Classroom: 58% of faculty are male; 42%, female.

Admissions: 26% of the 2003-2004 applicants were accepted. The SAT I scores for the 2003-2004 freshman class were: Verbal--12% between 500 and 599, 52% between 600 and 700, and 36% above 700; Math--1% below 500, 12% between 500 and 599, 49% between 600 and 700, and 39% above 700. The ACT scores were 1% between 21 and 23, 12% between 24 and 26, 15% between 27 and 28, and 71% above 28. 89% of the current freshmen were in the top fifth of their class; 99% were in the top two fifths. There were 133 National Merit finalists. 79 freshmen graduated first in their class.

Requirements: The SAT I or ACT is required. In addition, applicants must graduate from an accredited secondary school. The GED is accepted. Students must present at least 16 Carnegie units, including 4 in English. Some majors require an audition or submission of a creative portfolio. All applicants must submit an essay and 2 letters of recommendation. AP credits are accepted. Important factors in the admissions decision are advanced placement or honor courses, extracurricular activities record, and leadership record.

Procedure: Freshmen are admitted fall, spring, and summer. Entrance exams should be taken by November of the senior year. There is an early decision plan. Early decision applications should be filed by November 1; regular applications, by January 15 for fall entry, December 1 for spring entry, and May 1 for summer entry, along with a $60 fee. Notification of early decision is sent December 15; regular decision, April 1. 1571 early decision candidates were accepted for the 2003-2004 class. 1986 applicants were on the 2003 waiting list; 275 were admitted. Applications are accepted on-line through *http://admissions.nyu.edu/appprocess*, Embark, and Common App.

Transfer: 940 transfer students enrolled in 2003-2004. Students must submit official college transcripts from all postsecondary institutions attended, a final high school transcript, and SAT I scores. 32 of 128 credits required for the bachelor's degree must be completed at NYU.

Visiting: There are regularly scheduled orientations for prospective students, including campus tours and weekday information sessions by appointment. There are also 2 fall open houses. Visitors may sit in on classes. To schedule a visit, contact the Admissions Office at (212) 998-4524 or via the school's web site.

Financial Aid: In 2003-2004, 75% of all full-time freshmen and 73% of continuing full-time students received some form of financial aid. 57% of full-time freshmen and 55% of continuing full-time students received need-based aid. The average freshman award was $18,503. 26% of undergraduates work part time. Average annual earnings from campus work are $2959. The average financial indebtedness of the 2003 graduate was $24,620. The FAFSA is required. The deadline for filing freshman financial aid applications for fall entry is February 15.

International Students: There are 785 international students enrolled. The school actively recruits these students. They must take the college's own test, or have ESL testing and also take the SAT I or the ACT. 3 SAT II: Subject tests are recommended: English and 2 other tests.

Computers: The mainframes are a Sun F15K, 2 Sun F12Ks, 1 IBM RS/6000 SP2 (9076-550), 1 IBM RS/6000 S80 n(7017- S80, 4 IMB pSeries 660 (7026-6H1), 2 IBM RS/6000 H70 (7026-H70) running the IBM AIX Unix OS, 1 IBM zSeries 800 (2066-0A2) running the IMB OS/390 2.8 OS, and multiple Novell, Sun, and AIX servers. Students in degree/diploma programs are eligible for an NYUHome account. This account provides e-mail, a personal web page, software, and easy access to the World Wide Web, Blackboard classes, library resources, network news, and other Internet services. Facilities include Macs and PCs at 4 computer labs, more than 100 public terminals for walk-up access to e-mail and Internet, NYURoam for wireless network access, laptop plug-in ports and circulating laptops at the library, DIAL service for fast PPP phone and modem connectors from home or while traveling, and ResNet for in-room Ethernet access in virtually all residence halls. All students may access the system 24 hours a day, 7 days a week in some cases. There are no time limits and no fees.

Graduates: From July 1, 2002 to June 30, 2003, 4351 bachelor's degrees were awarded. The most popular majors were business (15%), individualized major (9%), and drama/theater arts (8%). In an average class, 71% graduate in 4 years or less, 7% graduate in 5 years or less, and 78% graduate in 6 years or less. 600 companies recruited on campus in 2002-2003. Of the 2002 graduating class, 18% were enrolled in graduate school within 6 months of graduation and 68% were employed.

Admissions Contact: Office of Undergraduate Admissions. A video is available. Web: *http://admissions.nyu.edu*

NIAGARA UNIVERSITY   A-3
Niagara University, NY 14109   **(716) 286-8700**
(800) 462-2111; Fax: (716) 286-8710

Full-time: 1019 men, 1575 women	**Faculty:** 129; IIA, -$
Part-time: 60 men, 80 women	**Ph.Ds:** 93%
Graduate: 273 men, 541 women	**Student/Faculty:** 20 to 1
Year: semesters, summer session	**Tuition:** $17,380
Application Deadline: August 15	**Room & Board:** $7670
Freshman Class: 2658 applied, 2130 accepted, 688 enrolled	
SAT I Verbal/Math: 516/525	**ACT:** 21 **COMPETITIVE**

Niagara University, founded in 1856 by the Vincentian fathers and brothers, is a private institution rooted in a Roman Catholic tradition. Programs offered include those in liberal arts, business, education, nursing, and travel, hotel, and restaurant administration. There are 4 undergraduate and 3 graduate schools. In addition to regional accreditation, Niagara has baccalaureate program accreditation with AACSB, ACCE, CSWE, NCATE, and NLN. The library contains 271,101 volumes,

78,311 microform items, and 772 audio/video tapes/CDs, and subscribes to 4700 periodicals. Computerized library services include the card catalog, interlibrary loans, and database searching. Special learning facilities include a learning resource center, art gallery, radio station, TV station, 2 theaters, and greenhouse. The 160-acre campus is in a suburban area 4 miles north of Niagara Falls, overlooking the Niagara River gorge, 20 miles north of Buffalo. Including any residence halls, there are 25 buildings.

Student Life: 87% of undergraduates are from New York. Students are from 31 states, 10 foreign countries, and Canada. 75% are from public schools. 81% are white. 65% are Catholic; 18%, Protestant; 6% claim no religious affiliation. The average age of freshmen is 18; all undergraduates, 21. 19% do not continue beyond their first year; 60% remain to graduate.

Housing: 1315 students can be accommodated in college housing, which includes single-sex and coed dorms. In addition, there are honors houses, special-interest houses, and international housing. On-campus housing is guaranteed for all 4 years. 51% of students live on campus; of those, 75% remain on campus on weekends. All students may keep cars.

Activities: 2% of men belong to 2 national fraternities. There are no sororities. There are 78 groups on campus, including art, aviation, cheerleading, choir, chorale, computers, drama, drill team, ethnic, film, honors, international, musical theater, newspaper, pep band, political, professional, radio and TV, religious, social, social service, student government, and yearbook. Popular campus events include Orientation, CARE, and University Ball.

Sports: There are 7 intercollegiate sports for men and 6 for women, and 25 intramural sports for men and 25 for women. Facilities include a 3400-seat gym, a 6-lane swimming and diving pool, exercise and weight rooms, saunas and dance areas, outdoor tennis courts, baseball and soccer fields, basketball and racquetball courts, and multipurpose courts with an indoor track. Hiking and biking trails are nearby.

Disabled Students: 75% of the campus is accessible. Wheelchair ramps, elevators, special parking, specially equipped rest rooms, special class scheduling, lowered drinking fountains, and campus accommodation for the vision impaired are available.

Services: Counseling and information services are available, as is tutoring in most subjects. There is a reader service for the blind and remedial math, reading, and writing. Study skills development, note taking, and escort-assistance services are available, as are educational assistance services for the vision impaired, educational/classroom assistance and machines for the hearing impaired, and services for the learning disabled.

Campus Safety and Security: Measures include 24-hour foot and vehicle patrol, self-defense education, security escort services, and informal discussions. There are pamphlets/posters/films, emergency telephones, lighted pathways/sidewalks, and a campus security advisory board.

Programs of Study: Niagara confers B.A., B.S., B.B.A., and B.F.A. degrees. Associate and master's degrees are also awarded. Bachelor's degrees are awarded in BIOLOGICAL SCIENCE (biochemistry, biology/biological science, and life science), BUSINESS (accounting, business administration and management, business economics, hotel/motel and restaurant management, human resources, marketing/retailing/merchandising, tourism, and transportation management), COMMUNICATIONS AND THE ARTS (communications, dramatic arts, English, French, and Spanish), COMPUTER AND PHYSICAL SCIENCE (chemistry, computer science, information sciences and systems, and mathematics), EDUCATION (elementary, English, foreign languages, mathematics, science, secondary, and social studies), ENGINEERING AND ENVIRONMENTAL DESIGN (preengineering), HEALTH PROFESSIONS (nursing, predentistry, and premedicine), SOCIAL SCIENCE (criminal justice, history, international studies, philosophy, political science/government, prelaw, psychology, religion, social science, social work, and sociology). Business, social sciences, and education are the strongest academically. Business administration, travel and tourism, and social services are the largest.

Required: To graduate, students must earn 120 to 126 credit hours and a GPA of at least 2.0; 60 to 66 such hours are required in the major, 20 in specific disciplines, and 20 in liberal arts classes. A comprehensive exam is required in some majors; a thesis is required of honor students and some majors.

Special: Niagara offers a Washington semester, a semester at the state capital in Albany, on-campus work-study, internships in most majors with such companies as the Big 6 accounting firms and Walt Disney World, and co-op programs in all areas except nursing, education, and social work. Students may study abroad in 4 countries and cross-register through the Western New York Consortium. Accelerated degree programs in business and nursing, B.A.-B.S. degrees, dual majors, a 2-3 engineering program with the University of Detroit, nondegree study, credit for life, military, and work experience, pass/fail options, and research are also available. There is also an academic exploration program for undeclared majors. There are 14 national honor societies and a freshman honors program.

Faculty/Classroom: 63% of faculty are male; 37%, female. All teach undergraduates. No introductory courses are taught by graduate students. The average class size in an introductory lecture is 25 and in a regular course, 20.

Admissions: 80% of the 2003-2004 applicants were accepted. The SAT I scores for the 2003-2004 freshman class were: Verbal--43% below 500, 44% between 500 and 599, 13% between 600 and 700, and 1% above 700; Math--38% below 500, 45% between 500 and 599, 16% between 600 and 700, and 2% above 700.

Requirements: The SAT I or ACT is required. In addition, applicants should be graduates of an accredited high school. The GED is accepted. The high school program should include 16 academic credits, with 4 in English and 2 each in foreign language, history, math, science, and social studies, as well as academic electives. Science, math, and computer majors should have 3 credits each in math and science. A grade average of 80 is required. AP and CLEP credits are accepted. Important factors in the admissions decision are advanced placement or honor courses, parents or siblings attending the school, and recommendations by school officials.

Procedure: Freshmen are admitted to all sessions. Entrance exams should be taken in the junior year or fall of the senior year. There are early decision and deferred admissions plans. Applications should be filed by August 15 for fall entry and January 10 for spring entry. The fall 2003 application fee was $30. Notification is sent on a rolling basis. Applications are accepted on-line through EXPAN.

Transfer: 137 transfer students enrolled in a recent year. Applicants must have a minimum GPA of 2.0 in travel, hotel, and restaurant administration, arts and sciences, and academic exploration (except for 2.25 in business and 2.5 for nursing and education majors) and submit all high school and college transcripts. The SAT I or ACT is recommended. 30 of 120 credits required for the bachelor's degree must be completed at Niagara.

Visiting: There are regularly scheduled orientations for prospective students, including informal interviews and campus tours. Other arrangements can be made individually, such as to attend a class, eat in the student cafeteria, and/or speak with a faculty member. There are guides for informal visits and visitors may sit in on classes and stay overnight. To schedule a visit, contact the Admissions Office appointment desk.

Financial Aid: In 2003-2004, 99% of all full-time freshmen and 88% of continuing full-time students received some form of financial aid. 82% of full-time freshmen and 88% of continuing full-time students received need-based aid. The average freshman award was $17,310. 21% of undergraduates work part time. Average annual earnings from campus work are $1592. The average financial indebtedness of a recent year's graduate was $17,606. Niagara is a member of CSS. The FAFSA is required. Check with the school for current deadlines.

International Students: In a recent year, there are 129 international students enrolled. The school actively recruits these students. They must score 500 on the written TOEFL.

Computers: The mainframe is a DEC MicroVAX 3800. There are 150 terminals/PCs available to students in several academic computing labs and in the academic computing center. All dorms are networked, and some rooms are tied in so students can access the system. All students may access the system 9 A.M. to 11 P.M. Monday to Thursday, 9 A.M. to 5 P.M. Friday, noon to 5 P.M. Saturday, and 3 P.M. to 10 P.M. Sunday. There are no time limits and no fees. PCs should be Windows-based for residence hall use.

Graduates: In a recent year, 528 bachelor's degrees were awarded. The most popular majors were commerce and accounting (23%), education (20%), and hospitality/tourism (9%). In an average class, 46% graduate in 4 years or less, 54% graduate in 5 years or less, and 54% graduate in 6 years or less. 139 companies recruited on campus in a recent year. Of a recent graduating class, 22% were enrolled in graduate school within 6 months of graduation and 76% were employed.

Admissions Contact: Mike Koropski, Director of Admissions.
E-mail: *admissions@niagara.edu* Web: *niagara.edu*

NYACK COLLEGE
Nyack, NY 10960

D-5
(845) 358-1710
(800) 336-9225; Fax: (845) 358-3047

Full-time: 685 men, 1035 women	**Faculty:** 71
Part-time: 70 men, 115 women	**Ph.D.s:** 62%
Graduate: 290 men, 270 women	**Student/Faculty:** 16 to 1
Year: semesters, summer session	**Tuition:** $13,500
Application Deadline: open	**Room & Board:** $7000
Freshman Class: n/av	
SAT I or ACT: required	**COMPETITIVE**

Nyack College, founded in 1882, is a private liberal arts institution affiliated with the Christian and Missionary Alliance. The enrollment figures in the above capsule include the Manhattan Center and Adult Degree Completion Program students. There is 1 graduate school. Figures in the above capsule and in this profile are approximate. In addition to regional accreditation, Nyack has baccalaureate program accreditation with NASM. The 3 libraries contain 99,000 volumes and 208,000 microform items, and subscribe to 871 periodicals. Computerized library services include the card catalog, interlibrary loans, and database searching. Special learning facilities include a learning resource center and radio station. The 102-acre campus is in a suburban area 20 miles north of New York City. Including any residence halls, there are 22 buildings.

Student Life: 67% of undergraduates are from New York. Students are from 42 states, 58 foreign countries, and Canada. 36% are white; 27% African American; 23% Hispanic. Most are Protestant. The average age of freshmen is 21; all undergraduates, 27. 35% do not continue beyond their first year; 46% remain to graduate.

Housing: 715 students can be accommodated in college housing, which includes single-sex dorms and on-campus apartments. In addition, there are honors houses. On-campus housing is guaranteed for all 4 years. 81% of students live on campus. Alcohol is not permitted. All students may keep cars.

Activities: There are no fraternities or sororities. There are 17 groups on campus, including band, cheerleading, choir, chorale, drama, ethnic, handbell choir, honors, ladies glee club, literary magazine, musical theater, newspaper, orchestra, professional, radio and TV, religious, social service, student government, and yearbook. Popular campus events include music festivals and the Cultural Events Series.

Sports: There are 5 intercollegiate sports for men and 5 for women. Facilities include a gym, soccer field, fitness center, training room, softball field, tennis courts, outdoor basketball courts, and a baseball field.

Disabled Students: 70% of the campus is accessible. Elevators, special parking, specially equipped rest rooms, and lowered drinking fountains are available.

Services: Counseling and information services are available, as is tutoring in every subject. There is a reader service for the blind.

Campus Safety and Security: Measures include 24-hour foot and vehicle patrol, security escort services, pamphlets/posters/films, and lighted pathways/sidewalks.

Programs of Study: Nyack confers B.A., B.S., B.Mus., and S.M.B. degrees. Associate and master's degrees are also awarded. Bachelor's degrees are awarded in BUSINESS (accounting and business administration and management), COMMUNICATIONS AND THE ARTS (communications, English, music, music performance, music theory and composition, piano/organ, and voice), COMPUTER AND PHYSICAL SCIENCE (computer science and mathematics), EDUCATION (elementary, music, secondary, and teaching English as a second/foreign language (TESOL/TEFOL), SOCIAL SCIENCE (biblical studies, crosscultural studies, history, interdisciplinary studies, missions, pastoral studies, philosophy, psychology, religion, religious education, religious music, social science, social work, and youth ministry). Psychology, education, ministry-related programs, and business are the largest.

Required: To graduate, students must complete 126 to 130 credits with a minimum GPA of 2.0 or 2.5 for education majors. General education and major requirements vary by degree program. Students must adhere to the college's standards of Christian living and behavior and complete Bible courses.

Special: Nyack offers internships, cooperative programs with other schools, study abroad in 6 countries, a semester in Hollywood for communications majors, dual and student-designed majors, independent study, nondegree study, a Washington semester, and pass/fail options. The business program provides advanced standing for the M.B.A. program at St. Thomas Aquinas College in Sparkill, NY. There is a freshman honors program.

Faculty/Classroom: 60% of faculty are male; 40%, female. 70% teach undergraduates. No introductory courses are taught by graduate students. The average class size in a laboratory is 15 and in a regular course, 20.

Admissions: 1 freshman graduated first in the class in a recent year.

Requirements: The SAT I or ACT is required. In addition, high school graduation or its equivalent is essential. Completion of 16 academic credits is required; the college recommends 4 units of English, 3 of history or social science, 3 of any combination of math and science, 2 of a foreign language, and 4 of electives. Students must demonstrate sound Christian character through personal testimony and recommendations. An interview may be required. AP and CLEP credits are accepted.

Procedure: Freshmen are admitted fall and spring. There is a rolling admissions plan. Application deadlines are open. The fall 2003 application fee was $15.

Transfer: 101 transfer students enrolled in a recent year. Applicants must provide all transcripts from previous schools attended. 30 of 126 credits required for the bachelor's degree must be completed at Nyack.

Visiting: There are regularly scheduled orientations for prospective students. There are guides for informal visits and visitors may sit in on classes and stay overnight. To schedule a visit, contact the Office of Admissions.

Financial Aid: The FAFSA and parent and student tax returns, if selected for verification, are required.

International Students: There were 287 international students enrolled in a recent year. The school actively recruits these students. They must score 550 on the written TOEFL and also take the SAT I or the ACT.

Computers: Some 125 PCs are available in computer labs, the libraries, and the resource center. Students may access e-mail to on- and off-campus addresses, as well as the Internet and World Wide Web. All students may access the system. There are no time limits and no fees.

Graduates: In a recent year, 319 bachelor's degrees were awarded. The most popular majors were business (55%), philosophy/religion/theology (10%), and interdisciplinary studies (8%). In an average class, 35% graduate in 4 years or less, 45% graduate in 5 years or less, and 46% graduate in 6 years or less. 50 companies recruited on campus in a recent year.

Admissions Contact: Miguel Sanchez, Director of Admissions. A video is available. E-mail: *enroll@nyack.edu* Web: *www.nyackcollege.edu*

PACE UNIVERSITY D-5
New York, NY 10038-1508   (212) 346-1225 or (914) 773-3321
(800) 874-PACE; Fax: (212) 346-1040 or (914) 773-3851

Full-time: 2653 men, 4240 women	**Faculty:** 438; I, +$
Part-time: 802 men, 1176 women	**Ph.D.s:** 88%
Graduate: 2260 men, 2831 women	**Student/Faculty:** 16 to 1
Year: semesters, summer session	**Tuition:** $21,002
Application Deadline: open	**Room & Board:** $7650
Freshman Class: 7939 applied, 5859 accepted, 1578 enrolled	
SAT I Verbal/Math: 540/540	**ACT:** 22 **VERY COMPETITIVE**

Pace University, founded in 1906, is a private institution offering programs in arts and sciences, business, nursing, education, and computer and information science on 3 campuses, with undergraduate studies in New York City and Pleasantville and graduate studies in White Plains. There are 5 undergraduate and 5 graduate schools. In addition to regional accreditation, Pace has baccalaureate program accreditation with AACSB, ABET, and CCNE. The 3 libraries contain 812,286 volumes, 75,285 microform items, and 976 audio/video tapes/CDs, and subscribe to 1862 periodicals. Computerized library services include the card catalog, interlibrary loans, and database searching. Special learning facilities include a learning resource center, art gallery, radio station, TV station, 2 art galleries, a performing arts center, biological research labs, an environmental center, a language lab, and computer labs. The campus is in an urban area in downtown New York City and there is a 200-acre suburban campus in Pleasantville/Briarcliff Manor. Including any residence halls, there are 41 buildings.

Student Life: 65% of undergraduates are from New York. Students are from 41 states, 30 foreign countries, and Canada. 70% are from public schools. 44% are white; 12% Asian American; 11% African American; 11% Hispanic. The average age of freshmen is 19; all undergraduates, 23. 24% do not continue beyond their first year; 54% remain to graduate.

Housing: 2049 students can be accommodated in college housing, which includes coed dorms, on-campus apartments, and off-campus apartments. In addition, there are honors houses, special-interest houses, and a wellness floor. 75% of students commute. All students may keep cars.

Activities: 5% of men belong to 2 local and 4 national fraternities; 5% of women belong to 4 local and 3 national sororities. There are 159 groups on campus, including art, cheerleading, chorus, computers, dance, debate, drama, ethnic, film, gay, honors, international, literary magazine, musical theater, newspaper, photography, political, professional, radio and TV, religious, social, social service, student government, and yearbook. Popular campus events include Spring Fling, Springcoming, and Diade Comida.

Sports: There are 9 intercollegiate sports for men and 9 for women, and 6 intramural sports for men and 5 for women. Facilities include the Civic Center Gym in New York City and gyms, tennis courts, playing fields, and the Goldstein Health Fitness and Recreation Center at the Pleasantville/Briarcliff Manor campus.

Disabled Students: 70% of the campus is accessible. Wheelchair ramps, elevators, special parking, special class scheduling, lowered drinking fountains, lowered telephones, and other facilities that vary by campus are available.

Services: Counseling and information services are available, as is tutoring in every subject. There is remedial math, reading, and writing. All services are provided in the University's Center for Academic Excellence.

Campus Safety and Security: Measures include 24-hour foot and vehicle patrol, security escort services, shuttle buses, and informal discussions. There are pamphlets/posters/films, emergency telephones, and lighted pathways/sidewalks.

Programs of Study: Pace confers B.A., B.S., B.B.A., B.F.A., and B.S.N. degrees. Associate, master's, and doctoral degrees are also awarded. Bachelor's degrees are awarded in BIOLOGICAL SCIENCE (biology/biological science), BUSINESS (accounting, banking and finance, business economics, international business management, and marketing/retailing/merchandising), COMMUNICATIONS AND THE ARTS (communications, English, Spanish, and theater design), COMPUTER AND PHYSICAL SCIENCE (chemistry, computer science, information sciences and systems, mathematics, and physics), EDUCATION (business, early childhood, and elementary), HEALTH PROFESSIONS (medical laboratory technology, nursing, and physician's assistant), SOCIAL SCIENCE (criminal justice, economics, history, political science/government, psychology, social science, and sociology). Accounting is the strongest academically. Business and finance are the largest.

Required: To graduate, students must complete 128 to 133 credit hours, including 32 to 50 in the major, with a minimum GPA of 2.0. A core curriculum of 60 credits and an introductory computer science course are required.

Special: Internships, study abroad, a Washington semester, and a cooperative education program in all majors are available. Pace also offers accelerated degree programs, B.A.-B.S. degrees, dual majors, general studies degrees, and 3-2 engineering degrees with Manhattan College and Rensselaer Polytechnic Institute. Credit for life, military, and work experience, nondegree study, and pass/fail options are available. There are 13 national honor societies and a freshman honors program.

Faculty/Classroom: 60% of faculty are male; 40%, female. 84% teach undergraduates and 24% do research. No introductory courses are taught by graduate students. The average class size in an introductory lecture is 35; in a laboratory, 11; and in a regular course, 23.

Admissions: 74% of the 2003-2004 applicants were accepted. The SAT I scores for the 2003-2004 freshman class were: Verbal--28% below 500, 51% between 500 and 599, 19% between 600 and 700, and 2% above 700; Math--25% below 500, 50% between 500 and 599, 22% between 600 and 700, and 3% above 700. The ACT scores were 22% below 21, 35% between 21 and 23, 25% between 24 and 26, 11% between 27 and 28, and 7% above 28. 43% of the current freshmen were in the top fifth of their class; 74% were in the top two fifths.

Requirements: The SAT I or ACT is required. In addition, applicants should be graduates of an accredited secondary school, with at least 16 academic credits, including 4 in English, 3 to 4 each in math, science, and history, and 2 to 3 in foreign language. The GED is accepted. An essay and an interview are recommended. A GPA of 3.0 is required. AP and CLEP credits are accepted. Important factors in the admissions decision are advanced placement or honor courses, recommendations by school officials, and leadership record.

Procedure: Freshmen are admitted fall and spring. Entrance exams should be taken by December of the student's senior year. There are early admissions, deferred admissions, and a rolling admission plan. Application deadlines are open. The fall 2003 application fee was $45. Applications are accepted on computer disk and on-line through College Board exam or CollegeView or through the school's web site.

Transfer: 510 transfer students enrolled in 2002-2003. Applicants are admitted in the fall or spring. A college GPA of 2.5 is required. Grades of C or better transfer for credit. A maximum of 68 credits will be accepted from a 2-year school. 32 of 128 to 133 credits required for the bachelor's degree must be completed at Pace.

Visiting: There are regularly scheduled orientations for prospective students, including student-for-a-day programs and overnight visits by appointment. There are guides for informal visits and visitors may sit in on classes and stay overnight. To schedule a visit, contact the Office of Undergraduate Admission at *ugnyc@pace.edu* or *infoctr@pace.edu*.

Financial Aid: In 2003-2004, 78% of all full-time freshmen and 87% of continuing full-time students received some form of financial aid. 76% of full-time freshmen and 81% of continuing full-time students received need-based aid. The average freshman award was $10,507. Average annual earnings from campus work was $3600. The average financial indebtedness of the 2003 graduate was $20,670. The FAFSA is required. The deadline for filing freshman financial aid applications for fall entry is February 15.

International Students: There are 354 international students enrolled. The school actively recruits these students. They must score 550 on the written TOEFL and also take the college's own test.

Computers: The mainframe is an IBM Multiprise 3000 H30-760. There are about 475 terminals on both campuses and at the midtown center. All students may access the system 24 hours a day. There are no time limits and no fees.

Graduates: From July 1, 2002 to June 30, 2003, 1760 bachelor's degrees were awarded. The most popular majors were computer science information systems (18%), finance (15%), and accounting (11%). In an average class, 1% graduate in 3 years or less, 45% graduate in 4 years or less, 52% graduate in 5 years or less, and 56% graduate in 6 years or less. 174 companies recruited on campus in 2002-2003. Of the 2002 graduating class, 81% were employed within 6 months of graduation.

Admissions Contact: Alan Young (NYC) and Joanna Broda, Director(s) of Undergraduate Admissions. E-mail: *infoctr@pace.edu* Web: *www.pace.edu*

PARSONS SCHOOL OF DESIGN
New York, NY 10011

D-5
(877) 528-3321
(877) 528-3324; Fax: (212) 229-5166

Full-time: 550 men, 1575 women	**Faculty:** 56
Part-time: 35 men, 150 women	**Ph.D.s:** n/av
Graduate: 140 men, 280 women	**Student/Faculty:** n/av
Year: semesters, summer session	**Tuition:** $22,630
Application Deadline: open	**Room & Board:** $9615
Freshman Class: n/av	
SAT I or ACT: required	**SPECIAL**

Parsons School of Design, founded in 1896, is a private professional art school and is part of the New School for Social Research. In addition to regional accreditation, Parsons has baccalaureate program accreditation with NASAD. Figures in the above capsule and in this profile are approximate. The 2 libraries contain 177,000 volumes and 5000 audio/video tapes/CDs, and subscribe to 230 periodicals. Computerized library services include the card catalog and database searching. Special learning facilities include an art gallery. The 2-acre campus is in an urban area in Manhattan's Greenwich Village. Including any residence halls, there are 8 buildings.

Student Life: 52% of undergraduates are from New York. Students are from 49 states, 39 foreign countries, and Canada. 80% are from public schools. 32% are white; 29% foreign nationals; 20% Asian American. The average age of freshmen is 19; all undergraduates, 23.

Housing: 700 students can be accommodated in college housing, which includes coed dorms and off-campus apartments. On-campus housing is available on a first-come, first-served basis and is available on a lottery system for upperclassmen. Priority is given to out-of-town students. Alcohol is not permitted. All students may keep cars.

Activities: There are no fraternities or sororities. There are some groups and organizations on campus, including ethnic, gay, international, literary magazine, political, religious, social, student gallery, and student government. Popular campus events include the Fashion Critics Award Show and annual senior shows.

Sports: There is no sports program at Parsons.

Disabled Students: 95% of the campus is accessible. Wheelchair ramps, elevators, and specially equipped rest rooms are available.

Services: Counseling and information services are available, as is tutoring in some subjects, including English and art history. There is remedial reading and writing.

Campus Safety and Security: Measures include informal discussions and pamphlets/posters/films.

Programs of Study: Parsons confers B.A.-B.F.A., B.B.A., and B.F.A. degrees. Associate and master's degrees are also awarded. Bachelor's degrees are awarded in BUSINESS (marketing/retailing/merchandising), COMMUNICATIONS AND THE ARTS (advertising, design, fine arts, graphic design, illustration, photography, and studio art), ENGINEERING AND ENVIRONMENTAL DESIGN (architectural engineering and interior design), SOCIAL SCIENCE (fashion design and technology). Communication design, illustration, and fashion design are the largest.

Required: To graduate, students must complete 134 credit hours, including 97 in the major, with a minimum GPA of 2.0. Parsons requires a minimum of 30 credits in liberal arts and 12 in art history.

Special: Students may cross-register at the New School for Social Research, Cooper Union, and Pratt Institute. Internships are required for some majors. Students may study abroad at the Parsons campus in Paris or in 4 other countries. The 5-year combined B.A.-B.F.A. degree requires 180 credits for graduation. A mobility semester or year at any AICAD school is available, and interdisciplinary majors, including architecture and environmental design and design marketing, are possible.

Faculty/Classroom: 89% teach undergraduates. No introductory courses are taught by graduate students. The average class size in an introductory lecture is 30 and in a regular course, 17.

Requirements: The SAT I or ACT is required. In addition, applicants must be graduates of an accredited secondary school. The GED is accepted. Applicants should have completed 4 years each of art, English, history, and social studies. A portfolio and home exam are required, and an interview is recommended. AP credits are accepted. Important factors in the admissions decision are evidence of special talent, advanced placement or honor courses, and personality/intangible qualities.

Procedure: Freshmen are admitted fall and spring. Entrance exams should be taken by spring of the junior year. There are early admissions and rolling admissions plans. Application deadlines are open. The application fee is $40. A waiting list is an active part of the admissions procedure.

Transfer: 420 transfer students enrolled in a recent year. Applicants will receive credit for grade C work or better in college courses that are similar in content, purpose, and standards to the courses offered at Parsons. A high school transcript is required for undergraduates, and the SAT I or ACT is recommended. All students must present a portfolio and home exam. Transfers are admitted in the fall or spring. 67 of 134 credits required for the bachelor's degree must be completed at Parsons.

Visiting: There are guides for informal visits. To schedule a visit, contact the Office of Admissions.

Financial Aid: In a recent year, 70% of all full-time freshmen and 59% of continuing full-time students received some form of financial aid. 64% of full-time freshmen and 58% of continuing full-time students received need-based aid. The average freshman award was $12,684. The average financial indebtedness of a recent graduate was $23,450. Parsons is a member of CSS. The FAFSA is required, and international students must file an institutional application. Check with the school for current deadlines.

International Students: The school actively recruits these students. They must score 550 on the written TOEFL.

Computers: 800 Macs/PCs are available, as well as graphical software, e-mail and Internet access, and AutoCad and fashion-design labs. All students may access the system. There are no time limits and no fees. It is strongly recommended that all students have a personal computer.

Graduates: In a recent year, 198 bachelor's degrees were awarded. The most popular majors were visual and performing arts (94%) and architecture (6%). In an average class, 46% graduate in 4 years or less, 56% graduate in 5 years or less, and 61% graduate in 6 years or less.

Admissions Contact: Nadine M. Bourgeois, Assistant Dean and Director of Admissions. E-mail: *parsadm@newschool.edu* Web: *www.parsons.edu*

POLYTECHNIC UNIVERSITY/BROOKLYN D-5
Brooklyn, NY 11201-2999

(718) 260-3100
(800) 765-8324; Fax: (718) 260-3136

Full-time: 1217 men, 271 women	**Faculty:** 104; I, av$
Part-time: 63 men, 8 women	**Ph.D.s:** 88%
Graduate: 752 men, 225 women	**Student/Faculty:** 14 to 1
Year: semesters, summer session	**Tuition:** $25,770
Application Deadline: open	**Room & Board:** $8000
Freshman Class: 1300 applied, 955 accepted, 396 enrolled	
SAT I Verbal/Math: 540/640	**VERY COMPETITIVE**

Polytechnic University, founded in 1854, is a private, multicampus university offering undergraduate and graduate programs through the divisions of arts and sciences, engineering, and management. In addition to regional accreditation, Brooklyn Poly has baccalaureate program accreditation with ABET and CSAB. The library contains 212,264 volumes, 60,106 microform items, and 337 audio/video tapes/CDs, and subscribes to 1621 periodicals. Computerized library services include the card catalog, interlibrary loans, and database searching. Special learning facilities include a learning resource center and radio station. The 3-acre campus is in an urban area 5 minutes from downtown Manhattan. Including any residence halls, there are 6 buildings.

Student Life: 88% of undergraduates are from New York. Students are from 18 states, 18 foreign countries, and Canada. 84% are from public schools. 38% are Asian American; 27% white; 10% African American. The average age of freshmen is 19; all undergraduates, 21. 16% do not continue beyond their first year; 54% remain to graduate.

Housing: 400 students can be accommodated in college housing, which includes coed dorms and fraternity houses. On-campus housing is available on a first-come, first-served basis. Priority is given to out-of-town students. 93% of students commute. Alcohol is not permitted. No one may keep cars.

Activities: 12% of men and about 3% of women belong to 2 local and 3 national fraternities; 3% of women belong to 1 national sorority. There are 60 groups on campus, including arts and music, chess, computers, ethnic, film, honors, international, literary magazine, newspaper, photography, professional, radio and TV, religious, social, social service, student government, and yearbook. Popular campus events include Chinese New Year, film festivals, and International Food Fair.

Sports: There are 7 intercollegiate sports for men and 7 for women, and 7 intramural sports for men and 7 for women. Facilities include soccer, lacrosse, and baseball fields, and 2 student centers.

Disabled Students: 70% of the campus is accessible. Wheelchair ramps, elevators, special parking, specially equipped rest rooms, lowered drinking fountains, and lowered telephones are available.

Services: Counseling and information services are available, as is tutoring in every subject. There is remedial math and writing.

Campus Safety and Security: Measures include 24-hour foot and vehicle patrol, informal discussions, pamphlets/posters/films, and emergency telephones. There are lighted pathways/sidewalks.

Programs of Study: Brooklyn Poly confers the B.S. degree. Master's and doctoral degrees are also awarded. Bachelor's degrees are awarded in COMMUNICATIONS AND THE ARTS (technical and business writing), COMPUTER AND PHYSICAL SCIENCE (chemistry, computer science, information sciences and systems, mathematics, and physics), ENGINEERING AND ENVIRONMENTAL DESIGN (chemical engineering, civil engineering, computer engineering, electrical/electronics engineering, and mechanical engineering), SOCIAL SCIENCE (humanities, liberal arts/general studies, and social science). Engineering, management,

and physical sciences are the strongest academically. Electrical engineering, computer engineering, and computer science are the largest.

Required: Students must complete all university and departmental course requirements, including 24 credits in humanities/social science, 16 in math, 12 in chemistry/physics, 4 in computers with Pascal, 4 in engineering design, and 3 in programming methodology. A total of 124 to 128 credits must be earned, with 32 in the major, and a minimum GPA of 2.0, is required to graduate. A senior design project is also required.

Special: Cooperative programs are available in all majors. Opportunities are provided for internships, work-study programs, study abroad, accelerated degree programs in engineering and computer science, dual majors, student-designed majors, and nondegree study. There are 9 national honor societies, a freshman honors program, and 3 departmental honors programs.

Faculty/Classroom: 80% of faculty are male; 20%, female. 67% teach undergraduates. No introductory courses are taught by graduate students. The average class size in an introductory lecture is 22; in a laboratory, 18; and in a regular course, 30.

Admissions: 73% of the 2003-2004 applicants were accepted. The SAT I scores for the 2003-2004 freshman class were: Verbal--25% below 500, 50% between 500 and 599, 22% between 600 and 700, and 3% above 700; Math--4% below 500, 28% between 500 and 599, 52% between 600 and 700, and 17% above 700.

Requirements: The SAT I is required. In addition, graduation from an accredited secondary school is required; a GED will be accepted. Applicants must submit a minimum of 16 credit hours, including 4 each in English, math and science, and 1 each in foreign language, art, music, and social studies. SAT II: Subject tests in writing, math I or II, and chemistry or physics are recommended. An essay and an interview are recommended. AP credits are accepted. Important factors in the admissions decision are advanced placement or honor courses, leadership record, and evidence of special talent.

Procedure: Freshmen are admitted fall, spring, and summer. Entrance exams should be taken by November of the senior year. There is a deferred admissions plan and a rolling admissions plan. Application deadlines are open. The fall 2003 application fee was $50. Applications are accepted on computer disk and on-line through the school's web site.

Transfer: 78 transfer students enrolled in 2002-2003. Transfer applicants must have a 2.75 cumulative GPA. Students with fewer than 30 credits must submit SAT I scores and secondary school transcripts in addition to official college-level transcripts. 36 of 124 credits required for the bachelor's degree must be completed at Brooklyn Poly.

Visiting: There are regularly scheduled orientations for prospective students, including a keynote speaker, major presentations, financial aid and scholarship sessions, and student life and career services sessions. There are guides for informal visits and visitors may stay overnight. To schedule a visit, contact the Dean of Admissions at *admitme@poly.edu*.

Financial Aid: In 2002-2003, 96% of all full-time freshmen and 91% of continuing full-time students received some form of financial aid. 79% of all full-time students received need-based aid. The average freshman award was $20,128. 16% of undergraduates work part time. Average annual earnings from campus work were $1500. The average financial indebtedness of the 2002 graduate was $18,327. The FAFSA and the college's own financial statement are required. The deadline for filing freshman financial aid applications for fall entry is March 1.

International Students: There are 124 international students enrolled. The school actively recruits these students. They must score 500 on the written TOEFL or 213 on the electronic version and also take the SAT I or the ACT.

Computers: Polytechnic University has a wireless network that allows students access to the network and Internet from anywhere on campus. All students may access the system 24-hour dial-up service. Computer labs are open 13 hours a day. There are no time limits and no fees. All students are required to have personal computers. An IBM ThinkPad T40 or its equivalent with XP Professional Operating system is recommended.

Graduates: From July 1, 2002 to June 30, 2003, 263 bachelor's degrees were awarded. The most popular majors were computer science (42%), computer engineering (21%), and electrical engineering (15%). In an average class, 1% graduate in 3 years or less, 36% graduate in 4 years or less, 51% graduate in 5 years or less, and 54% graduate in 6 years or less. 150 companies recruited on campus in 2002-2003. Of the 2002 graduating class, 5% were enrolled in graduate school within 6 months of graduation and 84% were employed.

Admissions Contact: Jonathan Wexler, Dean of Undergraduate Admissions. E-mail: *admitme@poly.edu* Web: *www.poly.edu*

PRATT INSTITUTE
Brooklyn, NY 11205

D-5
(718) 636-3669
(800) 331-0834; Fax: (718) 636-3670

Full-time: 1204 men, 1631 women	**Faculty:** IIA, av$
Part-time: 76 men, 83 women	**Ph.D.s:** 64%
Graduate: 434 men, 1016 women	**Student/Faculty:** n/av
Year: 4-1-4, summer session	**Tuition:** $26,030
Application Deadline: February 1	**Room & Board:** $8320
Freshman Class: 4152 applied, 2180 accepted, 787 enrolled	
SAT I Verbal/Math: 562/561	**SPECIAL**

Pratt Institute, founded in 1887, is a private institution offering undergraduate and graduate programs in architecture, art and design education, art history, industrial, interior, and communication design, fine arts, design management, arts and cultural management, writing for publication, performance and media, and professional studies. There are 2 undergraduate and 3 graduate schools. In addition to regional accreditation, Pratt has baccalaureate program accreditation with FIDER, NAAB, and NASAD. The library contains 208,000 volumes, 50,000 microform items, and 3500 audio/video tapes/CDs, and subscribes to 700 periodicals. Computerized library services include the card catalog, database searching, and Internet access. Special learning facilities include a learning resource center, art gallery, radio station, bronze foundry, and metal forge. The 25-acre campus is in an urban area 3 miles east of downtown Manhattan. Including any residence halls, there are 23 buildings.

Student Life: 53% of undergraduates are from New York. Students are from 46 states, 38 foreign countries, and Canada. 81% are from public schools. 62% are white; 13% Asian American; 10% foreign nationals. The average age of freshmen is 19; all undergraduates, 23. 8% do not continue beyond their first year; 65% remain to graduate.

Housing: 1500 students can be accommodated in college housing, which includes single-sex and coed dorms, on-campus apartments, and married-student housing. In addition, there are honors houses. On-campus housing is guaranteed for the freshman year only, is available on a first-come, first-served basis, and is available on a lottery system for upperclassmen. Priority is given to out-of-town students. 51% of students commute. All students may keep cars.

Activities: 5% of men belong to 1 local and 1 national fraternity; 5% of women belong to 1 local sorority. There are 50 groups on campus, including art, cheerleading, chess, drama, ethnic, film, gay, honors, international, literary magazine, martial arts, musical theater, newspaper, professional, radio and TV, religious, social, student government, and yearbook. Popular campus events include Springfest, International Food Fair, and Holiday Ball.

Sports: There are 6 intercollegiate sports for men and 4 for women, and 3 intramural sports for men and 1 for women. Facilities include an activities resource center containing 5 indoor tennis courts, a 200-meter indoor track, volleyball and basketball courts, a weight room, and 2 dance studios.

Disabled Students: 75% of the campus is accessible. Wheelchair ramps, elevators, special parking, specially equipped rest rooms, lowered drinking fountains, and special housing are available.

Services: Counseling and information services are available, as is tutoring in some subjects, including math, English, science, social science, and art history. There is a reader service for the blind, and individual tutoring and testing services are also available.

Campus Safety and Security: Measures include 24-hour foot and vehicle patrol, security escort services, shuttle buses, and informal discussions. There are pamphlets/posters/films, emergency telephones, lighted pathways/sidewalks, and trained security officers.

Programs of Study: Pratt confers B.Arch., B.F.A., B.I.D., and B.P.S. degrees. Associate and master's degrees are also awarded. Bachelor's degrees are awarded in COMMUNICATIONS AND THE ARTS (art history and appreciation, communications, creative writing, film arts, fine arts, industrial design, and photography), EDUCATION (art), ENGINEERING AND ENVIRONMENTAL DESIGN (architecture, computer graphics, construction management, and interior design), SOCIAL SCIENCE (fashion design and technology). Fine arts, industrial design, and communications design are the strongest academically. Architecture and communications design are the largest.

Required: The number of credits needed for graduation varies with the major, but a minimum of 132 is required, one quarter of which must be in liberal arts. Undergraduates must maintain a GPA of 2.0. All students must take 13 credits (15 for architecture majors) of liberal arts electives, 6 credits each of social sciences or philosophy, English, and cultural history, and 3 credits of science.

Special: Pratt offers co-op programs with the East Coast Consortium (art and design schools) and cross-registration with St. John's College and Queen's College. Internships, study abroad in 4 countries, accelerated degree programs, work-study programs, dual majors, credit for work experience, nondegree study, and pass/fail options are available. There are 4 national honor societies.

Faculty/Classroom: 58% of faculty are male; 42%, female. 92% teach undergraduates and 1% do research. No introductory courses are taught by graduate students. The average class size in an introductory lecture is 22; in a laboratory, 20; and in a regular course, 15.

Admissions: 53% of the 2003-2004 applicants were accepted.

Requirements: The SAT I or ACT is required. In addition, SAT II: Subject tests in writing and mathematics level I or II are recommended for architecture applicants. Applicants must be graduates of an accredited secondary school. The GED is accepted. Students should have completed 4 years of English, 3 of math, and 2 each of science, social studies, and history. A portfolio is required, as is an interview for all applicants who live within 100 miles of Pratt. A GPA of 3.2 is required. AP and CLEP credits are accepted. Important factors in the admissions decision are evidence of special talent, advanced placement or honor courses, and recommendations by school officials.

Procedure: Freshmen are admitted fall and spring. Entrance exams should be taken by November of the senior year. There is an early decision plan. Early decision applications should be filed by November 15; regular applications, by February 1 for fall entry and November 1 for spring entry, along with a $40 fee. A waiting list is an active part of the admissions procedure. Applications are accepted on-line through the school's web site.

Transfer: 216 transfer students enrolled in 2002-2003. Applicants should present college transcripts and recommendations. Students with fewer than 30 college credits must submit SAT I or ACT scores. All transfer applicants without an associate degree must submit high school transcripts as well. A portfolio is required for architecture and art and design students. An interview is recommended. 48 of 132 credits required for the bachelor's degree must be completed at Pratt.

Visiting: There are regularly scheduled orientations for prospective students, including a campus tour, schoolwide presentations, departmental presentations, and financial aid workshops. There are guides for informal visits and visitors may sit in on classes and stay overnight. To schedule a visit, contact the Office of Admissions at (800) 331-0834 or *visit@pratt.edu.*

Financial Aid: In 2003-2004, 78% of continuing full-time students received some form of financial aid. 68% of full-time freshmen and 58% of continuing full-time students received need-based aid. Pratt is a member of CSS. The CSS Profile or FAFSA, the college's own financial statement, and the parents' and student's tax returns are required. The priority date for freshman financial aid applications for fall entry is January 1. The deadline for filing freshman financial aid applications for fall entry is February 1.

International Students: There are 307 international students enrolled. The school actively recruits these students. They must score 530 on the written TOEFL or 197 on the electronic version and also take the college's own test.

Computers: The mainframe is a DEC VAX 6210. The mainframe may be reached via 12 VT340 terminals in the engineering lab or by dial-up modem. All students may access the system 24 hours a day, 7 days a week. There are no time limits and no fees. It is strongly recommended that all students have a personal computer.

Admissions Contact: Judith Aaron, Vice President for Enrollment. A video is available. E-mail: *jaaron@pratt.edu*
Web: *www.pratt.edu/admiss*

PURCHASE COLLEGE, SUNY
(See State University of New York/College at Purchase)

RENSSELAER POLYTECHNIC INSTITUTE
Troy, NY 12180-3590

D-3
(518) 276-6216
(800) 448-6562; Fax: (518) 276-4072

Full-time: 3888 men, 1282 women	**Faculty:** 392; I, +$
Part-time: 27 men, 13 women	**Ph.D.s:** 98%
Graduate: 2190 men, 865 women	**Student/Faculty:** 13 to 1
Year: semesters, summer session	**Tuition:** $28,496
Application Deadline: January 1	**Room & Board:** $9083
Freshman Class: 5252 applied, 4216 accepted, 1341 enrolled	
SAT I Verbal/Math: 630/680	**ACT:** 26
	HIGHLY COMPETITIVE+

Rensselaer Polytechnic Institute, founded in 1824, is a private institution that emphasizes technology in its Schools of Engineering, Architecture, Management, Humanities, Social Sciences, Science, and Information Technology. There are 5 undergraduate and 5 graduate schools. In addition to regional accreditation, Rensselaer has baccalaureate program accreditation with AACSB, ABET, and NAAB. The 2 libraries contain 488,325 volumes, 570,454 microform items, and 91,435 audio/video tapes/CDs, and subscribe to 3112 periodicals. Computerized library services include the card catalog, interlibrary loans, and database searching. Special learning facilities include a learning resource center, art gallery, radio station, and an observatory. The 262-acre campus is in a suburban area 10 miles north of Albany. Including any residence halls, there are 185 buildings.

Student Life: 54% of undergraduates are from out of state, mostly the Northeast. Students are from 50 states, 72 foreign countries, and Canada. 78% are from public schools. 68% are white; 12% Asian American. The average age of freshmen is 18; all undergraduates, 21. 7% do not continue beyond their first year; 81% remain to graduate.

Housing: 2933 students can be accommodated in college housing, which includes single-sex and coed dorms, on-campus apartments, married-student housing, fraternity houses, and sorority houses. In addition, there are special-interest houses and a Black Cultural center. On-campus housing is guaranteed for the freshman year only, is available on a first-come, first-served basis, and is available on a lottery system for upperclassmen. 55% of students live on campus. Upperclassmen may keep cars.

Activities: 39% of men and about 1% of women belong to 1 local and 28 national fraternities; 18% of women belong to 1 local and 4 national sororities. There are 140 groups on campus, including art, band, cheerleading, chess, chorale, chorus, computers, dance, drama, drill team, ethnic, gay, honors, international, jazz band, literary magazine, musical theater, newspaper, orchestra, pep band, photography, political, professional, radio and TV, religious, social, social service, student government, symphony, and yearbook. Popular campus events include Grand Marshal Week, International Festival, and Activities Fair.

Sports: There are 12 intercollegiate sports for men and 11 for women, and 22 intramural sports for men and 21 for women. Facilities include a 5300-seat field house, 2 pools, a stadium, 2 gyms, a sports and recreation center, several playing fields, 2 weight rooms, 6 tennis courts, 7 handball/squash courts, an artificial turf field, an indoor track, an ice hockey rink, and a fitness center.

Disabled Students: 55% of the campus is accessible. Wheelchair ramps, elevators, special parking, specially equipped rest rooms, special class scheduling, lowered drinking fountains, and lowered telephones are available.

Services: Counseling and information services are available, as is tutoring in every subject. There is a reader service for the blind. There is a writing center.

Campus Safety and Security: Measures include 24-hour foot and vehicle patrol, self-defense education, security escort services, and shuttle buses. There are informal discussions, pamphlets/posters/films, emergency telephones, lighted pathways/sidewalks, card-access residence halls, on-campus bicycle patrol, and a student volunteer program.

Programs of Study: Rensselaer confers B.S. and B.Arch. degrees. Master's and doctoral degrees are also awarded. Bachelor's degrees are awarded in BIOLOGICAL SCIENCE (biochemistry, biology/biological science, and biophysics), BUSINESS (management information systems and management science), COMMUNICATIONS AND THE ARTS (communications and media arts), COMPUTER AND PHYSICAL SCIENCE (chemistry, computer science, geology, mathematics, physics, and science technology), ENGINEERING AND ENVIRONMENTAL DESIGN (aeronautical engineering, architecture, biomedical engineering, chemical engineering, civil engineering, computer engineering, construction engineering, electrical/electronics engineering, engineering, engineering physics, environmental engineering, industrial engineering, materials engineering, mechanical engineering, and nuclear engineering), HEALTH PROFESSIONS (predentistry and premedicine), SOCIAL SCIENCE (economics, interdisciplinary studies, philosophy, prelaw, and psychology). Mechanical engineering, electrical engineering, and computer and systems engineering are the strongest academically. General engineering, management, and computer science are the largest.

Required: For graduation, students must earn at least 124 credits in all majors except engineering and B.S. architecture (128 needed) and the B.Arch. program (168 needed). The core curriculum includes 24 credits in physical, life, and engineering sciences and 24 credits in humanities and social sciences. Students must maintain a minimum GPA of 1.8 and must fulfill a writing requirement.

Special: Rensselaer offers an exchange program with Williams and Harvey Mudd Colleges and cross-registration with 14 regional colleges and universities. Co-op programs, internships, study abroad in several countries, and pass/fail options are available. Students may pursue dual and student-designed majors, a 3-2 engineering degree, and accelerated 4-year B.S.-M.S. degrees in engineering, computer science, geophysics, and math. Continuing education programs are broadcast via TV satellite to various industrial locations. There are 14 national honor societies and 3 departmental honors programs.

Faculty/Classroom: 85% of faculty are male; 15%, female. No introductory courses are taught by graduate students. The average class size in an introductory lecture is 75; in a laboratory, 25; and in a regular course, 24.

Admissions: 80% of the 2003-2004 applicants were accepted. The SAT I scores for the 2003-2004 freshman class were: Verbal--6% below 500, 25% between 500 and 599, 51% between 600 and 700, and 19% above 700; Math--1% below 500, 9% between 500 and 599, 46% between 600 and 700, and 44% above 700. The ACT scores were 6% below 21, 15% between 21 and 23, 33% between 24 and 26, 26% between 27 and 28, and 20% above 28. 82% of the current freshmen were in the top fifth of their class; 98% were in the top two fifths. 53 freshmen graduated first in their class.

Requirements: The SAT I or ACT is required. In addition, SAT II: Subject tests in writing, math, and science are recommended (required for accelerated-program applicants). Applicants must be graduates of an accredited secondary school and have completed 4 years each of English, math (through precalculus), and science (including chemistry and physics), and 3 years of social studies. An essay is required. Architecture and electronic arts applicants must submit a portfolio. AP credits are accepted. Important factors in the admissions decision are advanced placement or honor courses, recommendations by school officials, and leadership record.

Procedure: Freshmen are admitted fall and spring. Entrance exams should be taken in the junior or senior year. There are early decision and deferred admissions plans. Early decision applications should be filed by November 15; regular applications, by January 1 for fall entry and November 1 for spring entry, along with a $50 fee. Notification of early decision is sent December 31; regular decision, March 31. 142 early decision candidates were accepted for the 2003-2004 class. Applications are accepted on-line through Embark.com and the school's web site.

Transfer: 165 transfer students enrolled in 2002-2003. The SAT I or ACT is required for applicants with fewer than 30 credits. All students are encouraged to have an interview and must present faculty recommendations; B.Arch. applicants must present a portfolio. Grades of C or better transfer for credit. 48 of 124 credits required for the bachelor's degree must be completed at Rensselaer.

Visiting: There are regularly scheduled orientations for prospective students. There are guides for informal visits and visitors may sit in on classes and stay overnight. To schedule a visit, contact the Admissions Office at *admissions@rpi.edu*.

Financial Aid: In 2003-2004, at least 70% of all full-time freshmen and at least 71% of continuing full-time students received some form of financial aid. At least 70% of full-time freshmen and at least 71% of continuing full-time students received need-based aid. The average freshman award was $24,967. Need-based scholarships or need-based grants averaged $19,532; need-based self-help aid (loans and jobs) averaged $7624; non-need-based institutional athletic scholarships averaged $36,400; and other non-need-based institutional awards and non-need-based scholarships averaged $10,457. 24% of undergraduates work part time. Average annual earnings from campus work are $1000. The average financial indebtedness of the 2003 graduate was $23,725. The FAFSA is required. The deadline for filing freshman financial aid applications for fall entry is February 15.

International Students: There are 238 international students enrolled. The school actively recruits these students. They must score 570 on the written TOEFL or 230 on the electronic version and also take the SAT I or the ACT.

Computers: The mainframe is an IBM ES/9000. There are several PC labs on campus as well as sites in the dorms. Students use more than 500 networked workstations. All students may access the system. All students are required to have personal computers. All undergraduates are required to have a laptop computer. An IBM ThinkPad T40 is recommended.

Graduates: From July 1, 2002 to June 30, 2003, 1267 bachelor's degrees were awarded. The most popular majors were engineering (48%), computer science (21%), and management (12%). In a recent year in an average class, 53% graduated in 4 years or less, 76% graduated in 5 years or less, and 77% graduated in 6 years or less. 370 companies recruited on campus in a recent year. In a recent graduating class, 13% were enrolled in graduate school within 6 months of graduation and 85% were employed.

Admissions Contact: Teresa C. Duffy, Dean, Enrollment Management. E-mail: *admissions@rpi.edu* Web: *http://admissions.rpi.edu*

ROBERTS WESLEYAN COLLEGE
B-3
Rochester, NY 14624-1997
(585) 594-6400
(800) 777-4792; Fax: (585) 594-6371

Full-time: 394 men, 779 women	**Faculty:** 77
Part-time: 49 men, 70 women	**Ph.D.s:** 67%
Graduate: 150 men, 401 women	**Student/Faculty:** 15 to 1
Year: semesters, summer session	**Tuition:** $16,990
Application Deadline: February 1	**Room & Board:** $6200
Freshman Class: 613 applied, 553 accepted, 253 enrolled	
SAT I Verbal/Math: 569/561	**ACT:** 23	**COMPETITIVE+**

Roberts Wesleyan College, founded in 1866, is a private institution affiliated with the Free Methodist Church. The curriculum offers a liberal arts education in the Christian tradition. In addition to regional accreditation, Roberts has baccalaureate program accreditation with ACBSP, CSWE, NASAD, NASM, and NLN. The library contains 121,032 volumes, 171,113 microform items, and 3781 audio/video tapes/CDs, and subscribes to 856 periodicals. Computerized library services include the card catalog, interlibrary loans, database searching, and Internet access. Special learning facilities include a learning resource center, art gallery, and radio station. The 75-acre campus is in a suburban area 8 miles southwest of Rochester. Including any residence halls, there are 32 buildings.

Student Life: 88% of undergraduates are from New York. Students are from 21 states, 18 foreign countries, and Canada. 79% are white. 67% are Protestant; 17% Catholic. The average age of freshmen is 19; all undergraduates, 22. 19% do not continue beyond their first year; 50% remain to graduate.

Housing: 792 students can be accommodated in college housing, which includes single-sex dorms, on-campus apartments, and off-campus apartments. On-campus housing is guaranteed for all 4 years. 65% of students live on campus; of those, 50% remain on campus on weekends. Alcohol is not permitted. All students may keep cars.

Activities: There are no fraternities or sororities. There are many groups and organizations on campus, including band, choir, chorale, drama, ethnic, honors, international, jazz band, musical theater, newspaper, orchestra, pep band, radio and TV, religious, social, social service, student government, and yearbook. Popular campus events include Winter Weekend and Spring Formal.

Sports: There are 6 intercollegiate sports for men and 7 for women, and 6 intramural sports for men and 6 for women. Facilities include an athletic center with facilities for basketball, volleyball, tennis, badminton, track, soccer, weightlifting, walleyball, racquetball, and swimming.

Disabled Students: 60% of the campus is accessible. Wheelchair ramps, elevators, special parking, specially equipped rest rooms, special class scheduling, lowered drinking fountains, and lowered telephones are available.

Services: Counseling and information services are available, as is tutoring in every subject. Note takers for the hearing impaired are available. There is a reader service for the blind, and remedial math, reading, and writing.

Campus Safety and Security: Measures include 24-hour foot and vehicle patrol, self-defense education, security escort services, and informal discussions. There are pamphlets/posters/films, emergency telephones, lighted pathways/sidewalks, and personal-safety education programs.

Programs of Study: Roberts confers B.A. and B.S. degrees. Associate and master's degrees are also awarded. Bachelor's degrees are awarded in BIOLOGICAL SCIENCE (biochemistry and biology/biological science), BUSINESS (accounting and business administration and management), COMMUNICATIONS AND THE ARTS (communications, English, fine arts, and music), COMPUTER AND PHYSICAL SCIENCE (chemistry, computer science, mathematics, and physics), EDUCATION (art, elementary, and music), HEALTH PROFESSIONS (nursing, premedicine, prepharmacy, and preveterinary science), SOCIAL SCIENCE (criminal justice, history, prelaw, psychology, social work, and sociology). Music and teacher education are the strongest academically. Elementary education and organizational management are the largest.

Required: To graduate, students must complete a minimum of 124 credit hours, with a minimum of 30 hours in the major. Required courses include first year experience, phys ed, modern technology, world issues, speech, writing, history, Bible, and philosophy.

Special: Students may cross-register with members of the Rochester Area Colleges consortium. Internships, study abroad in 8 countries, a Washington semester, co-op programs, B.A.-B.S. degrees, dual majors, and 3-2 engineering degrees with Clarkson University, Rensselaer Polytechnic Institute, and Rochester Institute of Technology are available. Nondegree study and credit for life, military, and work experience are also offered. The organizational management program, geared to adults, consists of 4-hour weekly sessions, with reliance on out-of-class work. There is a freshman honors program.

Faculty/Classroom: 59% of faculty are male; 41%, female. 84% teach undergraduates. No introductory courses are taught by graduate students. The average class size in an introductory lecture is 38; in a laboratory, 15; and in a regular course, 23.

Admissions: 90% of the 2003-2004 applicants were accepted. The SAT I scores for the 2003-2004 freshman class were: Verbal--29% below 500, 42% between 500 and 599, 27% between 600 and 700, and 2% above 700; Math--34% below 500, 39% between 500 and 599, 24% between 600 and 700, and 3% above 700. The ACT scores were 30% below 21, 32% between 21 and 23, 21% between 24 and 26, 4% between 27 and 28, and 13% above 28. 42% of the current freshmen were in the top fifth of their class; 69% were in the top two fifths. There was 1 National Merit finalist and 2 semifinalists. 16 freshmen graduated first in their class.

Requirements: The SAT I or ACT is required. In addition, applicants must be graduates of an accredited secondary school. The GED is accepted. At least 12 academic credits are required, including 4 years of English and 2 years each of math and science. A foreign language and 3 years of social studies are recommended. The chosen major may modify requirements. An essay is required and an interview is recommended. Roberts requires applicants to be in the upper 50% of their class. A GPA of 2.3 is required. AP and CLEP credits are accepted. Important factors in the admissions decision are advanced placement or honor courses, personality/intangible qualities, and extracurricular activities record.

Procedure: Freshmen are admitted to all sessions. There are early admissions, deferred admissions plans, and a rolling admissions plan. Applications should be filed by February 1 for fall entry and December 1

for spring entry. The fall 2003 application fee was $35. Notification is sent on a rolling basis. Applications are accepted on-line through *www.roberts.edu* or *www.christiancollegementor.com*.

Transfer: 235 transfer students enrolled in 2002-2003. Applicants must submit transcripts from all previous institutions attended. Credit is usually accepted for courses with grade C or better. 30 of 124 credits required for the bachelor's degree must be completed at Roberts.

Visiting: There are regularly scheduled orientations for prospective students, including a campus tour, class visits, admissions and departmental interviews, and a financial aid presentation. There are guides for informal visits and visitors may sit in on classes and stay overnight. To schedule a visit, contact the Admissions Office.

Financial Aid: In 2003-2004, 91% of all full-time freshmen and 93% of continuing full-time students received some form of financial aid. 88% of full-time freshmen and 89% of continuing full-time students received need-based aid. The average freshman award was $19,363. Need-based scholarships or need-based grants averaged $8787; need-based self-help aid (loans and jobs) averaged $4892; non-need-based athletic scholarships averaged $256; and other non-need-based awards and non-need-based scholarships averaged $5347. 35% of undergraduates work part time. Average annual earnings from campus work are $974. Roberts is a member of CSS. The FAFSA and TAP (New York residents only) are required. The priority date for freshman financial aid applications for fall entry is March 15. The deadline for filing freshman financial aid applications for fall entry is rolling.

International Students: There are 55 international students enrolled. They must score 550 on the written TOEFL or 213 on the electronic version.

Computers: Students have access to nearly 120 public access computers in 10 computer labs on campus. All students may access the system 24 hours a day, 7 days a week. There are no time limits and no fees.

Graduates: From July 1, 2002 to June 30, 2003, 340 bachelor's degrees were awarded. The most popular majors were organizational management (28%), nursing (14%), and elementary education (11%). In an average class, 46% graduate in 4 years or less, 50% graduate in 5 years or less, and 52% graduate in 6 years or less.

Admissions Contact: Linda Kurtz, Vice President for Admissions and Marketing. A video is available. E-mail: *admissions@roberts.edu* Web: *www.roberts.edu*

ROCHESTER INSTITUTE OF TECHNOLOGY
B-3
Rochester, NY 14623   (585) 475-6631; Fax: (585) 475-7424

Full-time: 7705 men, 3504 women	Faculty: 750; IIA, +$
Part-time: 1149 men, 636 women	Ph.D.s: 80%
Graduate: 1436 men, 904 women	Student/Faculty: 15 to 1
Year: quarters, summer session	Tuition: $21,384
Application Deadline: open	Room & Board: $7833
Freshman Class: 8319 applied, 5787 accepted, 2141 enrolled	
SAT I Verbal/Math: 590/630	ACT: 26 VERY COMPETITIVE+

Rochester Institute of Technology, a private institution founded in 1829, offers programs in science, computer science, medical sciences, engineering, fine arts, business, hotel management, graphic arts, and photography, as well as liberal arts, and includes the National Technical Institute for the Deaf. Most programs include a cooperative education component, which provides full-time work experience to complement classroom studies. There are 14 undergraduate and 14 graduate schools. In addition to regional accreditation, RIT has baccalaureate program accreditation with AACSB, ABET, ADA, CAHEA, CSAB, CSWE, FIDER, NASAD, and CAAHEP. The library contains 408,000 volumes, 509,000 microform items, and 47,600 audio/video tapes/CDs, and subscribes to 2800 periodicals. Computerized library services include the card catalog, interlibrary loans, database searching, and Internet access. Special learning facilities include a learning resource center, art gallery, radio station, TV station, a computer chip manufacturing facility, a student-operated restaurant, an electronic prepress lab, an imaging science facility, and an observatory. The 1300-acre campus is in a suburban area 5 miles south of Rochester. Including any residence halls, there are 185 buildings.

Student Life: 55% of undergraduates are from New York. Others are from 50 states, 85 foreign countries, and Canada. 85% are from public schools. 78% are white. The average age of freshmen is 18; all undergraduates, 21. 12% do not continue beyond their first year; 63% remain to graduate.

Housing: 6500 students can be accommodated in college housing, which includes single-sex and coed dorms, on-campus apartments, married-student housing, fraternity houses, and sorority houses. In addition, there are honors houses and special-interest houses. On-campus housing is guaranteed for the freshman year only, is available on a first-come, first-served basis, and is available on a lottery system for upperclassmen. 65% of students live on campus; of those, 90% remain on campus on weekends. All students may keep cars.

Activities: 7% of men belong to 17 national fraternities; 5% of women belong to 7 national sororities. There are 150 groups on campus, including art, band, cheerleading, chess, choir, chorale, chorus, computers, dance, drama, ethnic, film, gay, honors, international, jazz band, literary magazine, newspaper, orchestra, pep band, photography, political, professional, radio and TV, religious, social, social service, student government, and yearbook. Popular campus events include Fall, Spring, and Winter Weekends and Martin Luther King Celebration.

Sports: There are 12 intercollegiate sports for men and 12 for women, and 13 intramural sports for men and 13 for women. Facilities include 3 gyms, an ice rink, 2 swimming pools, 9 tennis courts, a field house, athletic fields, and a student life center with 8 racquetball courts, dance facilities, weight training facilities, and an indoor track.

Disabled Students: 95% of the campus is accessible. Wheelchair ramps, elevators, special parking, specially equipped rest rooms, special class scheduling, lowered drinking fountains, lowered telephones, special housing, and special fire alarm systems for hearing-impaired students are available.

Services: Counseling and information services are available, as is tutoring in most subjects. There is a reader service for the blind. There are comprehensive support services for students with physical or learning disabilities and for first-generation college students.

Campus Safety and Security: Measures include 24-hour foot and vehicle patrol, self-defense education, security escort services, and shuttle buses. There are informal discussions, pamphlets/posters/films, emergency telephones, and lighted pathways/sidewalks.

Programs of Study: RIT confers B.S. and B.F.A. degrees. Associate, master's, and doctoral degrees are also awarded. Bachelor's degrees are awarded in BIOLOGICAL SCIENCE (biochemistry, bioinformatics, biology/biological science, biotechnology, and nutrition), BUSINESS (accounting, banking and finance, business administration and management, business systems analysis, hotel/motel and restaurant management, international business management, management information systems, management science, marketing management, and tourism), COMMUNICATIONS AND THE ARTS (animation, applied art, ceramic art and design, communications, communications technology, crafts, design, film arts, fine arts, glass, graphic design, illustration, industrial design, metal/jewelry, painting, photography, publishing, sculpture, studio art, telecommunications, and video), COMPUTER AND PHYSICAL SCIENCE (applied mathematics, chemistry, computer mathematics, computer science, information sciences and systems, mathematics, physics, polymer science, software engineering, statistics, and systems analysis), EDUCATION (education of the deaf and hearing impaired), ENGINEERING AND ENVIRONMENTAL DESIGN (aerospace studies, biomedical engineering, civil engineering technology, computer engineering, computer graphics, computer technology, electrical/electronics engineering, electrical/electronics engineering technology, engineering, engineering technology, environmental engineering technology, environmental science, furniture design, graphic and printing production, graphic arts technology, industrial engineering, interior design, manufacturing engineering, manufacturing technology, materials science, mechanical engineering, mechanical engineering technology, military science, printing technology, and woodworking), HEALTH PROFESSIONS (allied health, physician's assistant, predentistry, premedicine, preveterinary science, and ultrasound technology), SOCIAL SCIENCE (criminal justice, dietetics, economics, experimental psychology, food production/management/services, interpreter for the deaf, prelaw, psychology, public affairs, and social work). Engineering, computer science, and photography are the strongest academically. Engineering, information technology, and photography are the largest.

Required: Students must have a GPA of 2.0 and have completed 180 quarter credit hours to graduate. Distribution requirements include English, social sciences, and humanities; specific courses include writing and literature, senior seminar, and phys ed. B.S. programs also require a minimum of 20 quarter credit hours in science and math. There are no general science or math requirements for the B.F.A. programs in art, design, photography, or film/video.

Special: RIT offers internships in social science and allied health majors, and cooperative education programs with 1300 co-op employers. Cooperative education is required or recommended in most programs and provides full-time paid work experience. Cross-registration with Rochester-area colleges is available. There are accelerated degree programs in science, engineering, public policy, math, computer science, materials science, imaging science, and business. Students may study abroad in 15 countries, and student-designed majors are permitted in applied arts and sciences. There is an Honors Program in general education and home colleges. There are 6 national honor societies, a freshman honors program, and 7 departmental honors programs.

Faculty/Classroom: 67% of faculty are male; 33%, female. 95% teach undergraduates and 50% both teach and do research. No introductory courses are taught by graduate students. The average class size in an introductory lecture is 30; in a laboratory, 16; and in a regular course, 20.

Admissions: 70% of the 2003-2004 applicants were accepted. The SAT I scores for the 2003-2004 freshman class were: Verbal--10% below 500, 43% between 500 and 599, 39% between 600 and 700, and 8% above 700; Math--4% below 500, 32% between 500 and 599, 48% between 600 and 700, and 16% above 700. The ACT scores were 7% below 21, 16% between 21 and 23, 32% between 24 and 26, 20% be-

tween 27 and 28, and 25% above 28. 57% of the current freshmen were in the top fifth of their class; 86% were in the top two fifths. There were 10 National Merit finalists and 7 semifinalists. 33 freshmen graduated first in their class.

Requirements: The SAT I or ACT is required. In addition, applicants must be high school graduates or have a GED certificate. Applicants are required to submit an essay, and an interview is recommended. The School of Art and the School of Design emphasize a required portfolio of artwork. Required high school math and science credits vary by program, with 3 years in each area generally acceptable. RIT requires applicants to be in the upper 50% of their class. A grade average of 85 is required. AP and CLEP credits are accepted. Important factors in the admissions decision are advanced placement or honor courses, recommendations by school officials, and extracurricular activities record.

Procedure: Freshmen are admitted to all sessions. Entrance exams should be taken during the junior or senior year. There is a rolling admissions plan. There are early decision and deferred admissions plans. Early decision applications should be filed by December 15; regular applications for fall entry are open. There is a $50 fee. Notification of early decision is sent January 15; regular decision, on a rolling basis. 637 early decision candidates were accepted for the 2003-2004 class. 100 applicants were on the 2003 waiting list; 25 were admitted. Applications are accepted on-line through RIT's web site, College Board web site, and Common App.

Transfer: 1234 transfer students enrolled in 2002-2003. Transfer students must have a GPA of 2.5 for admission to most programs; those with fewer than 30 college credits must supply a high school transcript. Other requirements vary by program. 45 of 180 credits required for the bachelor's degree must be completed at RIT.

Visiting: There are regularly scheduled orientations for prospective students, including academic advising and information on housing and student services. There are guides for informal visits and visitors may sit in on classes and stay overnight. To schedule a visit, contact Mary Menard at (585) 475-6736 or *visit.rit.edu*.

Financial Aid: In 2003-2004, 85% of all full-time freshmen and 75% of continuing full-time students received some form of financial aid. 75% of full-time freshmen and 65% of continuing full-time students received need-based aid. The average freshman award was $17,500. 60% of undergraduates work part time. Average annual earnings from campus work are $1800. The FAFSA is required. The priority date for freshman financial aid applications for fall entry is March 1. The deadline for filing freshman financial aid applications for fall entry is June 1.

International Students: There are 525 international students enrolled. The school actively recruits these students. They must score 525 on the written TOEFL or 197 on the electronic version and also take the SAT I or the ACT.

Computers: The mainframes are a VMS cluster of networked Digital VAX and Alpha computers. RIT has 17 computer centers and many computer labs on campus for student use. There are more than 300 terminals available, as well as hundreds of PCs. Students may link their PCs to the campus network system from individual dorm rooms or campus apartments. All students may access the system 7 days per week, 24-hour access. There are no time limits and no fees.

Graduates: From July 1, 2002 to June 30, 2003, 2028 bachelor's degrees were awarded. The most popular majors were engineering (12%), business (12%), and photography (9%). In an average class, 62% graduate in 6 years or less. 500 companies recruited on campus in 2002-2003. Of the 2002 graduating class, 8% were enrolled in graduate school within 6 months of graduation and 90% were employed.

Admissions Contact: Daniel Shelley, Director of Admissions. A video is available. E-mail: *admissions@rit.edu* Web: *http://www.rit.edu*

RUSSELL SAGE COLLEGE
Troy, NY 12180

D-3

(518) 244-2217
(888) Very-Sage; Fax: (518) 244-6880

Full-time: 759 women	**Faculty:** 58; IIA, --$
Part-time: 52 women	**Ph.Ds:** 73%
Graduate: none	**Student/Faculty:** 13 to 1
Year: semesters, summer session	**Tuition:** $19,945
Application Deadline: August 1	**Room & Board:** $6866
Freshman Class: 365 applied, 301 accepted, 129 enrolled	
SAT I Verbal/Math: 539/516	**ACT:** 24	COMPETITIVE

Russell Sage, a private, comprehensive college, was founded in 1916 to prepare women for successful professional careers. Baccalaureate degrees in the traditional arts and sciences are offered, along with professional programs in nutrition, athletic training, nursing, physical and occupational therapy, theater, musical theater, creative arts in therapy, business, forensic science, communications, and education. In addition to regional accreditation, Russell Sage has baccalaureate program accreditation with ADA, AOTA, APTA, NASAD, NCATE, and NLN. The library contains 342,021 volumes, 3341 microform items, and 31,968 audio/video tapes/CDs, and subscribes to 803 periodicals. Computerized library services include the card catalog, interlibrary loans, and database searching. Special learning facilities include a learning resource center and the New York State Theatre Institute, Robinson Athletic Center, and Helen Upton Center for Women's Studies. The 14-acre campus is in an urban area 10 miles from Albany and Schenectady. Including any residence halls, there are 38 buildings.

Student Life: 92% of undergraduates are from New York. Students are from 13 states and 2 foreign countries. 77% are white. The average age of freshmen is 18; all undergraduates, 22. 10% do not continue beyond their first year; 68% remain to graduate.

Housing: 738 students can be accommodated in college housing, which includes single-sex dorms and on-campus apartments. In addition, there are language houses, and special-interest houses, 24-hour quiet housing, and substance-free/wellness housing. On-campus housing is guaranteed for all 4 years and is available on a lottery system for upperclassmen. 55% of students commute. Upperclassmen may keep cars.

Activities: There are no fraternities. There are 26 groups on campus, including academic clubs in each major, choir, chorus, dance, drama, equestrian, ethnic, gay, honors, leadership, literary magazine, musical theater, newspaper, orchestra, political, religious, social, social service, student government, and yearbook. Popular campus events include Rally Day, Sage Fest, and Family Weekend.

Sports: Facilities include a weight and fitness center, a sports medicine facility, swimming pool, 4 tennis courts, a practice field, 2 gyms, and a large multipurpose room for indoor recreation.

Disabled Students: 70% of the campus is accessible. Wheelchair ramps, elevators, special parking, specially equipped rest rooms, special class scheduling, computer center access and electronic access via blackboard for a variety of information and courses. Specially equipped science labs and equipment, and visits to administrative offices by arrangement are available.

Services: Counseling and information services are available, as is tutoring in most subjects. There is remedial math, reading, and writing.

Campus Safety and Security: Measures include 24-hour foot and vehicle patrol, self-defense education, security escort services, and informal discussions. There are pamphlets/posters/films, emergency telephones, lighted pathways/sidewalks, an evening security escort service, and monitored video cameras.

Programs of Study: Russell Sage confers B.A. and B.S. degrees. Master's degrees are also awarded. Bachelor's degrees are awarded in BIOLOGICAL SCIENCE (biochemistry, biology/biological science, and nutrition), BUSINESS (business administration and management), COMMUNICATIONS AND THE ARTS (communications, English, musical theater, and Spanish), COMPUTER AND PHYSICAL SCIENCE (chemistry, computer science, and mathematics), EDUCATION (athletic training and elementary), ENGINEERING AND ENVIRONMENTAL DESIGN (environmental science), HEALTH PROFESSIONS (art therapy, nursing, occupational therapy, physical therapy, and public health), SOCIAL SCIENCE (applied psychology, biopsychology, criminal justice, forensic studies, history, interdisciplinary studies, international studies, political science/government, psychology, and sociology). Psychology, English, and nursing are the strongest academically. Health and rehabilitative sciences, education and psychology are the largest.

Required: To graduate, students must complete 120 credits with a 2.0 GPA overall and at least 30 credits and a 2.2 GPA in the major. B.A. candidates must earn a minimum of 90 credits in the liberal arts and sciences and B.S. candidates must earn a minimum of 60. A general education requirement of 36 credits focuses on the experiences of women in a multicultural society, understanding technology, writing skills, and a broad exposure to the various arts and sciences. There is a course requiring community service and a writing-intensive course in the major. Students must also complete 6 credits in a single language or show proficiency and take technology-intensive and cross-cultured courses.

Special: Students may cross-register with the 14 area schools of the Hudson-Mohawk Association of Colleges. A theater major is offered in conjunction with NYSTI. Study abroad, internships, and work-study programs are available. There are several accelerated 5-year programs in the health sciences, a 5-year B.S./M.B.A., a 3-3 program with Albany Law School, and a 3-2 engineering degree with nearby Rensselaer Polytechnic Institute. 9 centers for interdisciplinary inquiry draw students from across majors. The college confers credit for life, military, or work experience. Nondegree study, student-designed majors, dual majors, and pass/fail options are also available. There are 14 national honor societies and a freshman honors program.

Faculty/Classroom: 38% of faculty are male; 62%, female. 100% both teach and do research. The average class size in an introductory lecture is 19; in a laboratory, 9; and in a regular course, 16.

Admissions: 82% of the 2003-2004 applicants were accepted. The SAT I scores for the 2003-2004 freshman class were: Verbal--31% below 500, 49% between 500 and 599, 18% between 600 and 700, and 2% above 700; Math--37% below 500, 49% between 500 and 599, and 14% between 600 and 700. The ACT scores were 18% below 21, 29% between 21 and 23, 24% between 24 and 26, 18% between 27 and 28, and 12% above 28. 52% of the current freshmen were in the top fifth of their class; 83% were in the top two fifths.

Requirements: The SAT I or ACT is required. In addition, applicants must be graduates of an accredited secondary school or have a GED. A minimum of 16 academic units are required, including courses in English, social sciences, natural sciences, math, and foreign language. An essay, for applicants still in high school, is required, and an interview is recommended. A GPA of 2.0 is required. AP and CLEP credits are accepted. Important factors in the admissions decision are advanced placement or honor courses, leadership record, and evidence of special talent.

Procedure: Freshmen are admitted fall and spring. Entrance exams should be taken during spring of the junior year or fall of the senior year. There are early decision, early admissions, deferred admissions plans, and a rolling admissions plan. Early decision applications should be filed by December 1; regular applications, by August 1 for fall entry and December 15 for spring entry. The fall 2003 application fee was $30. Notification of early decision is sent December 15; regular decision, on a rolling basis. 19 early decision candidates were accepted for the 2003-2004 class. Applications are accepted on-line through www.sage.edu.

Transfer: 121 transfer students enrolled in 2002-2003. Applicants must have a minimum GPA of 2.5. Interviews are strongly encouraged and may be required in some instances. 45 of 120 credits required for the bachelor's degree must be completed at Russell Sage.

Visiting: There are regularly scheduled orientations for prospective students, including meetings with faculty, a campus tour, a financial aid session, and an admissions interview. There are guides for informal visits and visitors may sit in on classes and stay overnight. To schedule a visit, contact the Office of Admission at (518) 244-2218.

Financial Aid: In 2003-2004, 95% of all full-time freshmen and 97% of continuing full-time students received some form of financial aid. 79% of full-time freshmen and 83% of continuing full-time students received need-based aid. The average freshman award was $22,025. 37% of undergraduates work part time. Average annual earnings from campus work are $840. The average financial indebtedness of the 2003 graduate was $18,700. The FAFSA is required. The deadline for filing freshman financial aid applications for fall entry is March 1.

International Students: There are 2 international students enrolled. The school actively recruits these students. They must score 550 on the written TOEFL and for international applicants with English as their native language, also take the SAT I or ACT.

Computers: The mainframes are an HP and a Sun. A campuswide network (SageNet) provides hard-wired and dial-up access to e-mail and the Internet for all students. Labs for student use are equipped with PCs. Word processing, spreadsheet, statistical analysis, graphics, and course-specific software are available. All students may access the system. The public computer labs are open 14 hours per day, 7 days a week; dial-in access is available 24 hours a day. There are no time limits and no fees. It is strongly recommended that all students have a personal computer.

Graduates: From July 1, 2002 to June 30, 2003, 251 bachelor's degrees were awarded. The most popular majors were education (18%), physical therapy (16%), and nursing (11%). In an average class, 33% graduate in 4 years or less, 68% graduate in 5 years or less, and 68% graduate in 6 years or less. 59 companies recruited on campus in 2002-2003. Of the 2002 graduating class, 42% were enrolled in graduate school within 6 months of graduation and 48% were employed.

Admissions Contact: Elizabeth Robertson, Senior Associate Director of Admissions. E-mail: rscadm@sage.edu Web: www.sage.edu

SAINT BONAVENTURE UNIVERSITY
A-3
St. Bonaventure, NY 14778-2284   (716) 375-2400
(800) 462-5050; Fax: (716) 375-4005

Full-time: 1075 men, 1102 women	**Faculty:** 120; IIA, --$
Part-time: 42 men, 72 women	**Ph.D.s:** 85%
Graduate: 180 men, 335 women	**Student/Faculty:** 18 to 1
Year: semesters, summer session	**Tuition:** $17,925
Application Deadline: April 1	**Room & Board:** $6530
Freshman Class: 1829 applied, 1728 accepted, 596 enrolled	
SAT I Verbal/Math: 530/530	**ACT:** 22 **LESS COMPETITIVE**

Saint Bonaventure University, founded in 1858, is a private Roman Catholic institution in the Franciscan tradition, offering programs in the arts and sciences, education, business, and journalism and mass communication. There are 4 undergraduate schools and 1 graduate school. The library contains 241,000 volumes, 97,000 microform items, and 7000 audio/video tapes/CDs, and subscribes to 1500 periodicals. Computerized library services include the card catalog, interlibrary loans, and database searching. Special learning facilities include a learning resource center, art gallery, radio station, TV station, and observatory. The 900-acre campus is in a small town 70 miles southeast of Buffalo. Including any residence halls, there are 29 buildings.

Student Life: 76% of undergraduates are from New York. Students are from 39 states, 10 foreign countries, and Canada. 58% are from public schools. 93% are white. The average age of freshmen is 18; all undergraduates, 21. 15% do not continue beyond their first year; 72% remain to graduate.

Housing: 1450 students can be accommodated in college housing, which includes single-sex and coed dorms and on-campus apartments.

On-campus housing is guaranteed for all 4 years. 76% of students live on campus; of those, 90% remain on campus on weekends. All students may keep cars.

Activities: There are no fraternities or sororities. There are 73 groups on campus, including academic, art, band, cheerleading, chess, choir, chorale, chorus, computers, drama, ethnic, honors, international, jazz band, literary magazine, newspaper, orchestra, pep band, photography, political, professional, radio and TV, religious, social, social service, student government, and yearbook. Popular campus events include Family Weekend, Spring and Winter Weekends, and varsity basketball games.

Sports: There are 7 intercollegiate sports for men and 7 for women, and 10 intramural sports for men and 9 for women. Facilities include a 6000-seat gym with basketball and volleyball courts, an indoor swimming pool, a 9-hole golf course, weight facilities and free weights, and a fitness center with racquetball courts, Nautilus equipment, and an aerobics room. There is also a 77-acre area on campus with soccer, baseball, softball, rugby, and intramural fields.

Disabled Students: 90% of the campus is accessible. Wheelchair ramps, elevators, special parking, specially equipped rest rooms, a counseling center staffed by 2 professionals, and a teaching and learning center with a coordinator for disabled services are available.

Services: Counseling and information services are available, as is tutoring in some subjects. There is remedial math, reading, and writing.

Campus Safety and Security: Measures include 24-hour foot and vehicle patrol, self-defense education, security escort services, and shuttle buses. There are informal discussions, pamphlets/posters/films, emergency telephones, and lighted pathways/sidewalks.

Programs of Study: SBU confers B.A., B.S., B.B.A., and B.S.Ed. degrees. Master's degrees are also awarded. Bachelor's degrees are awarded in BIOLOGICAL SCIENCE (biochemistry, biology/biological science, and biophysics), BUSINESS (accounting, banking and finance, management science, and marketing/retailing/merchandising), COMMUNICATIONS AND THE ARTS (classical languages, English, French, journalism, Spanish, and visual and performing arts), COMPUTER AND PHYSICAL SCIENCE (chemistry, computer science, mathematics, and physics), EDUCATION (elementary and physical), ENGINEERING AND ENVIRONMENTAL DESIGN (engineering physics and environmental science), HEALTH PROFESSIONS (medical laboratory technology and premedicine), SOCIAL SCIENCE (history, philosophy, political science/government, prelaw, psychology, social science, and sociology). Psychology, accounting, and biology are the strongest academically. Mass communication, biology, and elementary education are the largest.

Required: To graduate, students must complete 120 credit hours, 30 of them in the major, with a minimum GPA of 2.0. Students must also demonstrate writing competency through testing or course work.

Special: Cross-registration can be arranged almost anywhere in the United States through the Visiting Student Program. Internships are available in business, mass communication, political science, psychology, and social science. Study abroad in 18 countries, B.A.-B.S. degrees, accelerated degree programs, dual and student-designed majors, a Washington semester with American University, and pass/fail options are offered. Students may complete a 2-2 or 2-3 engineering degree with the University of Detroit or a 2-3 engineering degree with Clarkson University. There are 10 national honor societies and a freshman honors program.

Faculty/Classroom: 80% of faculty are male; 20%, female. 92% teach undergraduates and 1% both teach and do research. Graduate students teach 1% of introductory courses. The average class size in an introductory lecture is 25; in a laboratory, 12; and in a regular course, 18.

Admissions: 94% of the 2003-2004 applicants were accepted. The SAT I scores for the 2003-2004 freshman class were: Verbal--32% below 500, 48% between 500 and 599, 16% between 600 and 700, and 1% above 700. The ACT scores were 36% below 21, 34% between 21 and 23, 19% between 24 and 26, 4% between 27 and 28, and 7% above 28. 27% of the current freshmen were in the top fifth of their class; 58% were in the top two fifths. In a recent year, 1 freshman graduated first in the class.

Requirements: The SAT I or ACT is required, with a minimum composite score of 1000 on the SAT I (500 verbal, 500 math) or 24 on the ACT. In addition, applicants must be graduates of an accredited secondary school or have a GED. 16 academic credits are required, including 4 years each of English and social studies, 3 each of math and science, and 2 of a foreign language. An essay and an interview are recommended. A grade average of 65 is required. AP and CLEP credits are accepted. Important factors in the admissions decision are recommendations by school officials, advanced placement or honor courses, and extracurricular activities record.

Procedure: Freshmen are admitted to all sessions. Entrance exams should be taken during the spring of the junior year or the fall of the senior year. There are early admissions and deferred admissions plans. Applications should be filed by April 1 for fall entry and December 1 for spring entry. The fall 2003 application fee was $30. Notification is sent on a rolling basis. Applications are accepted on-line through NYMentor, CollegeLink, and the Princeton Review (*www.review.com*).

Transfer: 92 transfer students enrolled in a recent year. Applicants must have a minimum 2.5 GPA. Grades of D or better transfer for credit except in the major. 60 of 120 credits required for the bachelor's degree must be completed at SBU.

Visiting: There are regularly scheduled orientations for prospective students, including interviews, tours, class visits, and meetings with professors. There are guides for informal visits and visitors may sit in on classes. To schedule a visit, contact the Admissions Office.

Financial Aid: The average freshman award was $15,270. Need-based scholarships or need-based grants averaged $10,928; need-based self-help aid (loans and jobs) averaged $4219; non-need-based athletic scholarships averaged $11,292; and other non-need-based awards and non-need-based scholarships averaged $7042. 38% of undergraduates work part time. Average annual earnings from campus work are $700. The FAFSA is required. Check with the school for current deadlines.

International Students: They must score 550 on the written TOEFL.

Computers: SBU has 5 PC and 2 Mac labs, housing more than 100 computers connected to a campuswide network. The computer science lab is equipped with 5 Sun workstations and provides a UNIX environment used to support upper-division courses in computer science. Students have full Internet access. All students may access the system 24 hours per day via residence hall rooms or at designated lab hours. There are no time limits and no fees.

Graduates: In an average class, 59% graduate in 4 years or less, 68% graduate in 5 years or less, and 71% graduate in 6 years or less. Of a recent graduating class, 23% were enrolled in graduate school within 6 months of graduation.

Admissions Contact: James Di Risio, Director of Admissions. E-mail: *admissions@sbu.edu* Web: *www.sbu.edu*

SAINT FRANCIS COLLEGE D-5
Brooklyn, NY 11201 (718) 489-5200; Fax: (718) 802-0453

Full-time: 901 men, 1072 women	Faculty: 70; IIB, +$
Part-time: 96 men, 225 women	Ph.D.s: 83%
Graduate: none	Student/Faculty: 28 to 1
Year: semesters, summer session	Tuition: $10,880
Application Deadline: open	Room & Board: n/app
Freshman Class: 1305 applied, 1144 accepted, 428 enrolled	
SAT I Verbal/Math: 470/470	LESS COMPETITIVE

Saint Francis College, chartered in 1884 by the Franciscan Brothers, is an independent Catholic institution conferring degrees in the arts, sciences, business, education, and health sciences. The library contains 120,000 volumes, 16,238 microform items, and 1133 audio/video tapes/CDs, and subscribes to 750 periodicals. Computerized library services include interlibrary loans, database searching, and Internet access. Special learning facilities include a learning resource center, a greenhouse, and a television studio. The 1-acre campus is in an urban area in Brooklyn Heights. There are 6 buildings.

Student Life: 99% of undergraduates are from New York. Students are from 6 states, 42 foreign countries, and Canada. 38% of freshmen are from public schools. 53% are white; 16% African American; 15% foreign nationals; 13% Hispanic. The average age of freshmen is 20; all undergraduates, 24. 24% do not continue beyond their first year; 76% remain to graduate.

Housing: There are no residence halls. Students may apply for housing in the recently-opened dorm at Polytechnic University, a short walk from St. Francis College. All students commute. Alcohol is not permitted. No one may keep cars.

Activities: There is 1 national fraternity; 5% of women belong to 1 local sorority. There are 25 groups on campus, including art, cheerleading, choir, chorus, computers, departmental, drama, ethnic, honors, international, literary magazine, newspaper, political, professional, radio and TV, religious, social, social service, student government, and yearbook. Popular campus events include Hispanic Festival, Thomas J. Volpe Lecture, and Community Day.

Sports: There are 9 intercollegiate sports for men and 9 for women, and 6 intramural sports for men and 6 for women. Facilities include a 1100-seat gym, an Olympic-size swimming pool, a weight-training room, a roof recreation area, and the Genovesi Center.

Disabled Students: All of the campus is accessible. Wheelchair ramps, elevators, specially equipped rest rooms, lowered drinking fountains, and lowered telephones are available.

Services: There is a reader service for the blind, and remedial math, reading, and writing. In addition, there are workshops in academic skills such as note- and test-taking techniques and study skills.

Campus Safety and Security: Measures include informal discussions and pamphlets/posters/films.

Programs of Study: St. Francis confers B.A. and B.S. degrees. Associate degrees are also awarded. Bachelor's degrees are awarded in BIOLOGICAL SCIENCE (biology/biological science), BUSINESS (accounting), COMMUNICATIONS AND THE ARTS (communications and English), COMPUTER AND PHYSICAL SCIENCE (mathematics), EDUCATION (elementary, middle school, physical, and secondary), ENGI-

NEERING AND ENVIRONMENTAL DESIGN (aviation administration/management), HEALTH PROFESSIONS (health care administration, health science, medical laboratory technology, physician's assistant, and radiological science), SOCIAL SCIENCE (criminal justice, economics, history, philosophy, political science/government, psychology, social studies, and sociology). Biology, accounting, and psychology are the strongest academically. Management, communications, and psychology are the largest.

Required: The core curriculum varies according to the major, but all baccalaureate degree programs require courses in communications, English, fine arts, phys ed, history, philosophy, sociology, and science or math. A minimum 2.0 GPA and 128 credit hours are required to graduate.

Special: There are co-op programs in aviation, physical therapy, nursing, and computer science. A variety of internships are available in such areas as industrial and public accounting, and with the NYC Transit Authority, Public Interest Research, the NYS Assembly, and the Urban Fellow Program. Work-study with Methodist Hospital or the borough president's office is possible, and there are pre-professional health programs with the State University of New York Health Science Center at Brooklyn, NY Methodist Hospital, and St. Vincent's Catholic Medical Center. Study abroad in several countries, dual majors, pass/fail options, and credit for life experience are possible. There are 15 national honor societies and a freshman honors program.

Faculty/Classroom: 68% of faculty are male; 32%, female. All teach and do research. The average class size in an introductory lecture is 30; in a laboratory, 17; and in a regular course, 23.

Admissions: 88% of the 2003-2004 applicants were accepted. 7 freshmen graduated first in their class.

Requirements: The SAT I is required. In addition, applicants should graduate from an accredited secondary school or have a GED. An entrance essay is required. A grade average of 80 is required. AP and CLEP credits are accepted. Important factors in the admissions decision are recommendations by school officials, leadership record, and advanced placement or honor courses.

Procedure: Freshmen are admitted to all sessions. Entrance exams should be taken before registration. Application deadlines are open. There is a rolling admissions plan. The fall 2003 application fee was $35. Applications are accepted on-line through the school's web site.

Transfer: 154 transfer students enrolled in 2002-2003. A minimum 2.0 GPA is required for transfer students. Official transcripts from previous colleges and high school transcripts, or a graduation certificate, is also required. 30 of 128 credits required for the bachelor's degree must be completed at St. Francis.

Visiting: There are regularly scheduled orientations for prospective students, including meetings with faculty if desired. There are guides for informal visits and visitors may sit in on classes. To schedule a visit, contact the Office of Admissions at *admissions@stfrancis.edu*.

Financial Aid: In 2003-2004, 89% of all full-time freshmen and 91% of continuing full-time students received some form of financial aid. 58% of full-time freshmen and 59% of continuing full-time students received need-based aid. The average freshman award was $6736. 9% of undergraduates work part time. Average annual earnings from campus work are $1500. The FAFSA, the college's own financial statement, and the NY State TAP application are required. The priority date for freshman financial aid applications for fall entry is February 15.

International Students: There are 283 international students enrolled. The school actively recruits these students. They must score 500 on the written TOEFL.

Computers: There are 6 computer centers including the library, that total 120 PCs. A wireless network in the café, student lounge, and library allows students greatly expanded access to the Internet, research, and communication tools. All students may access the system. There are no time limits. The fee is $50 per year.

Graduates: From July 1, 2002 to June 30, 2003, 487 bachelor's degrees were awarded. The most popular majors were business administration (18%), liberal studies (15%), and psychology (11%). In an average class, 1% graduate in 3 years or less, 31% graduate in 4 years or less, 51% graduate in 5 years or less, and 53% graduate in 6 years or less.

Admissions Contact: Brother George Larkin, O.S.F., Admissions Dean. A video is available. E-mail: *glarkin@stfranciscollege.edu* Web: *www.stfranciscollege.edu*

SAINT JOHN FISHER COLLEGE
Rochester, NY 14618

B-3
(585) 385-8412
(800) 444-4640; Fax: (585) 385-8386

Full-time: 944 men, 1246 women	**Faculty:** 124; IIB, +$
Part-time: 114 men, 192 women	**Ph.D.s:** 82%
Graduate: 199 men, 457 women	**Student/Faculty:** 18 to 1
Year: semesters, summer session	**Tuition:** $17,450
Application Deadline: open	**Room & Board:** $7420
Freshman Class: 2663 applied, 1617 accepted, 540 enrolled	
SAT I Verbal/Math: 520/540	**ACT:** 22 COMPETITIVE

St. John Fisher College is an independent, liberal arts institution in the Catholic tradition of American higher education. Guided since its inception in 1948 by the educational philosophy of the Congregation of St. Basil, the college emphasizes liberal learning for students in traditional academic disciplines, as well as for those in more directly career-oriented fields. The college welcomes qualified students, faculty, and staff regardless of religious or cultural background. There are 2 undergraduate schools and 1 graduate school. In addition to regional accreditation, Fisher has baccalaureate program accreditation with AACSB, ACS, and CCNE. The library contains 176,563 volumes, 203,753 microform items, and 29,000 audio/video tapes/CDs, and subscribes to 11,133 periodicals. Computerized library services include the card catalog, interlibrary loans, database searching, and Internet access. Special learning facilities include a learning resource center, radio station, TV station, multimedia center, "wet" and "dry" multidisciplinary science labs, animal labs, growth chambers, and a dance and fitness facility. The 136-acre campus is in a suburban area 12 miles southeast of Rochester. Including any residence halls, there are 15 buildings.

Student Life: 98% of undergraduates are from New York. Students are from 17 states, 2 foreign countries, and Canada. 65% are from public schools. 89% are white. The average age of freshmen is 18; all undergraduates, 20. 16% do not continue beyond their first year; 64% remain to graduate.

Housing: 1300 students can be accommodated in college housing, which includes single-sex and coed dorms and off-campus apartments. Living facilities include residence halls providing a year-long wellness program. On-campus housing is guaranteed for all 4 years. 59% of students live on campus; of those, 85% remain on campus on weekends. Upperclassmen may keep cars.

Activities: There are no fraternities or sororities. There are 40 groups on campus, including cheerleading, choir, chorale, chorus, College Bowl, computers, drama, ethnic, gay, honors, international, literary magazine, musical theater, newspaper, pep band, photography, political, professional, radio and TV, religious, social, social service, student activities board, student government, and yearbook. Popular campus events include Senior Week, Winter Olympics, and TEDDI, a 24-hour dance marathon for charity.

Sports: There are 8 intercollegiate sports for men and 8 for women, and 5 intramural sports for men and 4 for women. Facilities include racquetball, squash, and tennis courts, baseball and softball fields, an all-weather playing field for football, soccer, lacrosse, and intramural athletics, a 9-hole golf course, weight/exercise facilities, a varsity gym for intercollegiate basketball, and a multipurpose student life center for indoor tennis, volleyball, and basketball.

Disabled Students: 90% of the campus is accessible. Wheelchair ramps, elevators, special parking, specially equipped rest rooms, special class scheduling, lowered drinking fountains, and lowered telephones are available.

Services: Counseling and information services are available, as is tutoring in most subjects. There is a reader service for the blind. Math and writing centers provide help to students at all levels. Peer tutoring is available to all students in most undergraduate subject areas.

Campus Safety and Security: Measures include 24-hour foot and vehicle patrol, security escort services, shuttle buses, and informal discussions. There are pamphlets/posters/films, emergency telephones, and lighted pathways/sidewalks.

Programs of Study: Fisher confers B.A. and B.S. degrees. Master's degrees are also awarded. Bachelor's degrees are awarded in BIOLOGICAL SCIENCE (biology/biological science), BUSINESS (accounting, management science, and sports management), COMMUNICATIONS AND THE ARTS (communications, English, French, and Spanish), COMPUTER AND PHYSICAL SCIENCE (chemistry, computer science, mathematics, physics, and science technology), EDUCATION (early childhood, English, mathematics, science, secondary, social studies, and special), HEALTH PROFESSIONS (nursing), SOCIAL SCIENCE (American studies, anthropology, economics, history, interdisciplinary studies, international studies, philosophy, political science/government, psychology, religion, and sociology). Education and management are the largest.

Required: To graduate, students must complete at least 120 credit hours, including at least 30 in the major, and maintain a 2.0 minimum GPA. Core curriculum requirements include 3 to 4 courses each in literature/foreign languages, social sciences, and religious studies/philosophy,

3 in math/natural science, and up to 3 in arts. Freshmen must participate in one of the integrative learning communities.

Special: The college has cooperative programs with the Pennsylvania College of Optometry, and cross-registration with Rochester area colleges. The college offers internships in most majors, independent research in 16 majors, study abroad, work-study programs, accelerated degree programs in many areas, Washington semesters, dual and student-designed majors, and degrees in interdisciplinary studies or liberal studies. A 3-2 engineering degree is offered with Columbia and Clarkson Universities, University of Detroit-Mercy, SUNY at Buffalo, and Manhattan College. Navy and Marine ROTC is available at the University of Rochester and Air Force and Army ROTC at the Rochester Institute of Technology. There are 10 national honor societies and a freshman honors program.

Faculty/Classroom: 48% of faculty are male; 52%, female. 76% teach undergraduates, 42% do research, and 42% do both. No introductory courses are taught by graduate students. The average class size in an introductory lecture is 24; in a laboratory, 12; and in a regular course, 21.

Admissions: 61% of the 2003-2004 applicants were accepted. The SAT I scores for the 2003-2004 freshman class were: Verbal--30% below 500, 52% between 500 and 599, 15% between 600 and 700, and 2% above 700; Math--25% below 500, 55% between 500 and 599, 19% between 600 and 700, and 1% above 700. The ACT scores were 18% below 21, 38% between 21 and 23, 31% between 24 and 26, 8% between 27 and 28, and 5% above 28. 40% of the current freshmen were in the top fifth of their class; 76% were in the top two fifths. 1 freshman graduated first in the class.

Requirements: The SAT I or ACT is required. In addition, applicants must be graduates of an accredited secondary school. 16 academic credits are required, including 4 years each in English, history, and social studies, 3 years each in math and science, and 2 years in a foreign language. Interviews are recommended. AP and CLEP credits are accepted. Important factors in the admissions decision are advanced placement or honor courses, extracurricular activities record, and evidence of special talent.

Procedure: Freshmen are admitted to all sessions. There are early decision and deferred admissions plans. There is a rolling admissions plan. Early decision applications should be filed by December 1; regular application deadlines are open. Application fee is $25. Notification is sent on a rolling basis beginning November 1. 41 early decision candidates were accepted for the 2003-2004 class. Applications are accepted on-line through *www.sjfc@edu.*

Transfer: 221 transfer students enrolled in 2002-2003. Applicants must have a minimum GPA of 2.0 to be considered (mean GPA is 2.8). A high school transcript is required for students with fewer than 24 college credits. Interviews are recommended. 30 credits of 120 required for the bachelor's degree must be completed at Fisher.

Visiting: There are regularly scheduled orientations for prospective students, including a tour, an interview with a member of the admissions staff, meetings with faculty and coaches, and lunch on campus. There are guides for informal visits and visitors may sit in on classes and stay overnight. To schedule a visit, contact the Admissions Office at (585) 385-8064 or *admissions@sjfc.edu.*

Financial Aid: In 2003-2004, 94% of all full-time freshmen and 82% of continuing full-time students received some form of financial aid. 74% of full-time freshmen and 65% of continuing full-time students received need-based aid. The average freshman award was $12,672. Need-based scholarships or need-based grants averaged $11,602 ($19,000 maximum); and need-based self-help aid (loans and jobs) averaged $5283 ($18,500 maximum). 25% of undergraduates work part time. Average annual earnings from campus work are $1000. The average financial indebtedness of the 2003 graduate was $18,400. Fisher is a member of CSS. The FAFSA is required. The deadline for filing freshman financial aid applications for fall entry is February 15.

International Students: There are 3 international students enrolled. They must score 550 on the written TOEFL or 213 on the electronic version and also take the SAT I or the ACT.

Computers: The mainframes are dual Sun 420Rs and numerous NT and Win 2000 servers. A variety of programming languages is available on the DEC system, including COBOL and FORTRAN. Facilities include Mac and Sun computers, 5 PC labs in the academic computing center, and 3 remote labs on campus. There is also a 50-station PC lab in Kearney Hall. All students may access the system 24 hours daily. There are no time limits and no fees. It is strongly recommended that all students have a personal computer.

Graduates: From July 1, 2002 to June 30, 2003, 523 bachelor's degrees were awarded. The most popular majors were education (24%), business and management (22%), and psychology (9%). In an average class, 52% graduate in 4 years or less, 58% graduate in 5 years or less, and 64% graduate in 6 years or less. 49 companies recruited on campus in 2002-2003. Of the 2002 graduating class, 27% were enrolled in graduate school within 6 months of graduation and 95% were employed.

Admissions Contact: Stacy A. Ledermann, Director of Freshman Admissions. E-mail: *admissions@sjfc.edu* Web: *http://www.sjfc.edu*

SAINT JOHN'S UNIVERSITY
D-5
Jamaica, NY 11439
(718) 990-2000
(888) 9 STJOHNS; Fax: (718) 990-5827

Full-time: 4955 men, 6886 women	**Faculty:** 511; I, +$
Part-time: 1209 men, 1858 women	**Ph.D.s:** 90%
Graduate: 1839 men, 3030 women	**Student/Faculty:** 23 to 1
Year: semesters, summer session	**Tuition:** $20,080
Application Deadline: open	**Room & Board:** $10,000
Freshman Class: 15,383 applied, 10,515 accepted, 2976 enrolled	
SAT I Verbal/Math: 530/540	**COMPETITIVE**

Saint John's University, founded in 1870 by the Vincentian Fathers, is a private Roman Catholic institution offering programs in the arts and sciences, education, business, pharmacy and allied health professions, theology, and professional studies. There are 5 undergraduate and 6 graduate schools. In addition to regional accreditation, St. John's has baccalaureate program accreditation with AACSB and ACPE. The 4 libraries contain 1,168,214 volumes, 2,769,165 microform items, and 22,601 audio/video tapes/CDs, and subscribe to 15,056 periodicals. Computerized library services include the card catalog, interlibrary loans, and database searching. Special learning facilities include a learning resource center, art gallery, radio station, TV station, health education resource center, model pharmacy, speech and hearing clinic, instructional materials center, instructional Media Center, and Institute of Asian Studies. The 98-acre main campus is in a suburban area in the Jamaica section of Queens. There is also a 16-acre branch campus in Staten Island, a campus in Oakdale, Long Island, and a 10-story building located in the Manhattan financial district. Including any residence halls, there are 33 buildings.

Student Life: 90% of undergraduates are from New York. Students are from 44 states, 109 foreign countries, and Canada. 59% are from public schools. 47% are white; 15% Hispanic; 14% African American; 13% Asian American. 50% are Catholic; 21% claim no religious affiliation; 16% Muslim, Hindu, Buddhist, Greek Orthodox, Mormon, Russian Orthodox; 9% Protestant. The average age of freshmen is 18; all undergraduates, 21. 18% do not continue beyond their first year; 64% remain to graduate.

Housing: 2571 students can be accommodated in college housing, which includes coed dorms and off-campus apartments. On-campus housing is available on a first-come, first-served basis and is available on a lottery system for upperclassmen. 87% of students commute. All students may keep cars.

Activities: 7% of men belong to 7 local and 16 national fraternities; 7% of women belong to 12 local and 10 national sororities. There are 175 groups on campus, including art, cheerleading, choir, chorus, computers, dance, debate, drama, environmental, ethnic, film, forensics, honors, human rights, international, jazz band, literary magazine, musical theater, newspaper, pep band, photography, political, professional, radio and TV, religious, social, social service, student government, and yearbook. Popular campus events include International Night, Spring Fling, and Student Activities Fair.

Sports: There are 7 intercollegiate sports for men and 11 for women, and 11 intramural sports for men and 11 for women. Facilities include gyms, a swimming pool, squash and tennis courts, weight and exercise rooms, baseball and softball diamonds, fields for football, lacrosse, and soccer, and basketball and racquetball courts.

Disabled Students: 90% of the campus is accessible. Wheelchair ramps, elevators, special parking, specially equipped rest rooms, special class scheduling, lowered drinking fountains, and lowered telephones are available.

Services: Counseling and information services are available, as is tutoring in most subjects. There is a reader service for the blind, and remedial math, reading, and writing. Note-taking services, tape recorders, assistance in study skills, and a program for at-risk freshmen are available.

Campus Safety and Security: Measures include 24-hour foot and vehicle patrol, security escort services, informal discussions, and pamphlets/posters/films. There are emergency telephones, lighted pathways/sidewalks, and a crime prevention awareness program.

Programs of Study: St. John's confers B.A., B.S., B.F.A., B.S.Ed., and B.S.Med.Tech. degrees. Associate, master's, and doctoral degrees are also awarded. Bachelor's degrees are awarded in BIOLOGICAL SCIENCE (biology/biological science, ecology, and toxicology), BUSINESS (accounting, banking and finance, business administration and management, business economics, funeral home services, hospitality management services, insurance and risk management, management science, marketing and distribution, office supervision and management, real estate, sports management, and transportation management), COMMUNICATIONS AND THE ARTS (art, communications, English, film arts, fine arts, French, German, graphic design, illustration, Italian, journalism, languages, literature, multimedia, photography, Spanish, and speech/debate/rhetoric), COMPUTER AND PHYSICAL SCIENCE (chemistry, computer science, data processing, mathematics, physical sciences, and physics), EDUCATION (art, bilingual/bicultural, early childhood, education of the deaf and hearing impaired, elementary, English, foreign languages, mathematics, middle school, science, secondary, social science, social studies, and special), ENGINEERING AND ENVIRONMENTAL DESIGN (aircraft mechanics, computer technology, environmental science, and preengineering), HEALTH PROFESSIONS (cytotechnology, health care administration, medical technology, nursing, pharmacy, physician's assistant, predentistry, premedicine, and speech pathology/audiology), SOCIAL SCIENCE (American studies, anthropology, Asian/Oriental studies, criminal justice, economics, history, human services, liberal arts/general studies, paralegal studies, philosophy, political science/government, prelaw, psychology, public administration, safety and security technology, social science, sociology, and theological studies). Pharmacy, biology, and psychology are the strongest academically and have the largest enrollments.

Required: To graduate, students must complete at least 126 credit hours, including core courses and distribution requirements, with a minimum GPA of 2.0 overall and in the major. Other requirements vary by program. Core courses include English, theology, philosophy, math/science, Discover NY, history, scientific inquiry, and speech. Distribution requirements include a second language, fine arts, language and culture, math, philosophy, theology, and social science.

Special: St. John's offers internships, cross-registration, study abroad in Europe, Central and South America, Australia, the Caribbean, Africa, and Asia, an accelerated degree program in many majors, via early admissions and early admissions extension programs, B.A.-B.S. degrees, dual majors and combined degree programs, pass/fail options, and some credit for life, military, and work experience. There are cooperative programs in dentistry with Columbia University, in engineering with Manhattan College, in photography with the International Center of Photography, in funeral service administration with the McAllister Institute, and in optometry with SUNY College of Optometry. There is a 6-year doctor of pharmacy program for incoming freshmen. Other combined degree programs are possible. There are 19 national honor societies and a freshman honors program.

Faculty/Classroom: 62% of faculty are male; 38%, female. 87% teach undergraduates, 91% do research, and 78% do both. No introductory courses are taught by graduate students. The average class size in an introductory lecture is 29; in a laboratory, 24; and in a regular course, 27.

Admissions: 68% of the 2003-2004 applicants were accepted. The SAT I scores for the 2003-2004 freshman class were: Verbal--34% below 500, 46% between 500 and 599, 19% between 600 and 700, and 1% above 700; Math--27% below 500, 46% between 500 and 599, 23% between 600 and 700, and 4% above 700. 39% of the current freshmen were in the top fifth of their class; 65% were in the top two fifths. 13 freshmen graduated first in their class.

Requirements: The SAT I or ACT is required. In addition, admissions decisions are made by committee and are based on several criteria, including standardized test scores, academic curriculum, and high school average. A GPA of 3.0 is required. AP and CLEP credits are accepted. Important factors in the admissions decision are advanced placement or honor courses, recommendations by school officials, and extracurricular activities record.

Procedure: Freshmen are admitted fall, spring, and summer. Entrance exams should be taken late in the junior year or early in the senior year. There are early admissions, deferred admissions, and rolling admissions plans. Application deadlines are open. Notification is sent on a rolling basis. The fall 2003 application fee was $30.

Transfer: 619 transfer students enrolled in 2002-2003. Applicants must present official transcripts of high school and college work, as well as a list of courses in progress. If the student has been out of school a semester or more, a letter of explanation is also required. Admissions requirements for transfer students to the 6-year pharmacy program are stricter and placement is limited. 30 of a minimum of 126 credits required for the bachelor's degree must be completed at St. John's.

Visiting: There are regularly scheduled orientations for prospective students, including small group presentations and a tour of the campus. There are guides for informal visits and visitors may sit in on classes. To schedule a visit, contact the Office of Admission at *admissions@stjohns.edu.*

Financial Aid: In 2003-2004, 96% of all full-time freshmen and 88% of continuing full-time students received some form of financial aid. 90% of full-time freshmen and 74% of continuing full-time students received need-based aid. The average freshman award was $18,025. Need-based scholarships or need-based grants averaged $9841 ($25,009 maximum); need-based self-help aid (loans and jobs) averaged $4519 ($8625 maximum); non-need-based athletic scholarships averaged $17,181 ($25,009 maximum); and other non-need-based awards and non-need-based scholarships averaged $6874 ($25,009 maximum). 85% of undergraduates work part time. Average annual earnings from campus work are $5000. The average financial indebtedness of the 2003 graduate was $18,037. The FAFSA is required. The priority date for freshman financial aid applications for fall entry is February 1. The deadline for filing freshman financial aid applications for fall entry is March 1.

International Students: There are 416 international students enrolled. The school actively recruits these students. They must score 500 on the written TOEFL or 173 on the electronic version and also take the col-

lege's own test. Students must also take the SAT I (scoring 1000) or the ACT. This requirement may be waived for international students educated outside of the United States.

Computers: There are more than 1000 workstations available with full access to the Internet and the Web. They are located in the library, computer lab, classrooms, and residence halls. Entering freshmen receive laptops with wireless Internet access. All students may access the system. There are no time limits and no fees.

Graduates: From July 1, 2002 to June 30, 2003, 2320 bachelor's degrees were awarded. The most popular majors were computer science (11%), education (9%), and finance (9%). In an average class, 2% graduate in 3 years or less, 36% graduate in 4 years or less, 60% graduate in 5 years or less, and 64% graduate in 6 years or less. 280 companies recruited on campus in 2002-2003. Of the 2002 graduating class, 27% were enrolled in graduate school within 6 months of graduation and 63% were employed.

Admissions Contact: Matthew Whalen, Director.
E-mail: *admissions@stjohns.edu* Web: *www.stjohns.edu*

SAINT JOSEPH'S COLLEGE, NEW YORK, BROOKLYN CAMPUS   D-5
Brooklyn, NY 11205

(718) 636-6868
(866) AT ST JOE; Fax: (718) 636-8303

Full-time: 105 men, 467 women	**Faculty:** 46
Part-time: 136 men, 418 women	**Ph.D.s:** 80%
Graduate: 30 men, 70 women	**Student/Faculty:** 12 to 1
Year: semesters, summer session	**Tuition:** $10,902
Application Deadline: August 1	**Room & Board:** n/app
Freshman Class: 513 applied, 337 accepted, 112 enrolled	
SAT I Verbal/Math: 498/502	**COMPETITIVE**

Saint Joseph's College, established in 1916, is a private, independent, multicampus, commuter institution offering undergraduate degrees in arts and sciences, child study, business, accounting, health professions, and nursing. There is a branch campus in Patchogue, Long Island. In addition to regional accreditation, Saint Joseph's has baccalaureate program accreditation with NLN. The library contains 75,000 volumes, 4341 microform items, and 4504 audio/video tapes/CDs, and subscribes to 434 periodicals. Computerized library services include interlibrary loans and database searching. Special learning facilities include an on-campus lab preschool. The 3-acre campus is in an urban area 1 mile east of Manhattan. There are 5 buildings.

Student Life: 98% of undergraduates are from New York. Students are from 4 states and 8 foreign countries. 21% are from public schools. 43% are white; 40% African American; 11% Hispanic. The average age of freshmen is 18; all undergraduates, 32. 14% do not continue beyond their first year; 72% remain to graduate.

Housing: There are no residence halls. All students commute. Alcohol is not permitted. All students may keep cars.

Activities: 15% of men belong to 1 local fraternity; 6% of women belong to 1 local sorority. There are 22 groups on campus, including art, cheerleading, chorus, computers, dance, drama, ethnic, honors, literary magazine, newspaper, political, professional, religious, social, social service, student government, and yearbook. Popular campus events include the annual dinner dance, Junior Class Night, and holiday party.

Sports: There are 3 intercollegiate sports for men and 4 for women, and 4 intramural sports for men and 4 for women. Facilities include a gym, a handball court, an outdoor mall, recreation rooms, and an exercise/weight room.

Disabled Students: 10% of the campus is accessible. Wheelchair ramps, elevators, and specially equipped rest rooms are available.

Services: Counseling and information services are available, as is tutoring in most subjects. There is remedial writing.

Campus Safety and Security: Measures include self-defense education, security escort services, informal discussions, and pamphlets/posters/films. There are lighted pathways/sidewalks.

Programs of Study: Saint Joseph's confers B.A. and B.S. degrees. Master's degrees are also awarded. Bachelor's degrees are awarded in BIOLOGICAL SCIENCE (biology/biological science), BUSINESS (accounting, business administration and management, and organizational behavior), COMMUNICATIONS AND THE ARTS (English, Spanish, and speech/debate/rhetoric), COMPUTER AND PHYSICAL SCIENCE (chemistry, information sciences and systems, and mathematics), EDUCATION (early childhood, elementary, secondary, and special), HEALTH PROFESSIONS (community health work, health care administration, and nursing), SOCIAL SCIENCE (history, psychology, and social science). Child study, psychology, and biology are the largest.

Required: To graduate, students must complete a 51-credit core curriculum requirement consisting of 8 courses in humanities, 3 in social science and math/science, and 1 English composition course. The minimum GPA is 2.0. Students must earn 128 credits, with 30 to 36 credits in the major. Most majors require a thesis.

Special: The college offers internship programs in English, history, political science, psychology, sociology, speech and business/accounting, and an interdisciplinary major in human relations. Adult students may pursue a general studies degree in which the college allows credit for life, military, and work experience. Cross-registration with Knowledge Workers Educational Alliance is possible. There are 5 national honor societies and a freshman honors program.

Faculty/Classroom: 44% of faculty are male; 56%, female. All teach undergraduates, 10% do research, and 10% do both. The average class size in an introductory lecture is 16; in a laboratory, 11; and in a regular course, 12.

Admissions: 66% of the 2003-2004 applicants were accepted. The SAT I scores for the 2003-2004 freshman class were: Verbal--45% below 500, 47% between 500 and 599, and 8% between 600 and 700; Math--49% below 500, 33% between 500 and 599, and 18% between 600 and 700. 25% of the current freshmen were in the top fifth of their class; 39% were in the top two fifths.

Requirements: The SAT I is required, with a minimum required composite score of 900. Applicants must graduate from an accredited secondary school or earn a GED. 16 Carnegie units are required, including 4 units of English and social studies, 3 of math, 2 of languages and science, and 3 elective units. Interviews are recommended. A GPA of 3.0 is required. AP and CLEP credits are accepted. Important factors in the admissions decision are advanced placement or honor courses, recommendations by school officials, and leadership record.

Procedure: Freshmen are admitted fall and spring. Entrance exams should be taken. There are early decision, early admissions, deferred admissions, and rolling admissions plans. Applications should be filed by August 1 for fall entry and January 1 for spring entry, along with a $25 fee. Notification is sent on a rolling basis.

Transfer: 34 transfer students enrolled in 2002-2003. Transfer applicants must have a minimum GPA of 2.0. If fewer than 40 credits have been earned, the SAT I is required with a minimum composite score of 900. 48 of 128 credits required for the bachelor's degree must be completed at Saint Joseph's.

Visiting: There are regularly scheduled orientations for prospective students, including meetings with faculty advisers and student-to-student sessions. There are guides for informal visits and visitors may sit in on classes. To schedule a visit, contact the Admissions Office.

Financial Aid: In 2003-2004, 95% of all full-time freshmen and 85% of continuing full-time students received some form of financial aid. 64% of full-time freshmen and 61% of continuing full-time students received need-based aid. The average freshman award was $10,000. Need-based scholarships or need-based grants averaged $10,000 ($13,000 maximum); need-based self-help aid (loans and jobs) averaged $2500 ($5000 maximum); and other non-need-based awards and non-need-based scholarships averaged $10,000 ($13,000 maximum). 4% of undergraduates work part time. Average annual earnings from campus work are $1000. The average financial indebtedness of the 2003 graduate was $156,369. Saint Joseph's is a member of CSS. The FAFSA, the state aid form and the college's own financial statement are required. The priority date for freshman financial aid applications for fall entry is February 25. The deadline for filing freshman financial aid applications for fall entry is rolling.

International Students: They must score 550 on the written TOEFL or 213 on the electronic version and also take SAT I.

Computers: The mainframe is an IBM AS/400/System 36. PCs are available to students in the 3 computer labs, in department offices, and in the library. Students also have access to the Internet and on-line databases at 20 additional workstations. All students may access the system. There are no time limits and no fees.

Graduates: From July 1, 2002 to June 30, 2003, 236 bachelor's degrees were awarded. The most popular majors were child study (21%), organizational management (17%), and community health and human services (17%). In an average class, 64% graduate in 4 years or less, 72% graduate in 5 years or less, and 72% graduate in 6 years or less. 32 companies recruited on campus in 2002-2003. Of the 2002 graduating class, 42% were enrolled in graduate school within 6 months of graduation and 75% were employed.

Admissions Contact: Theresa LaRocca Meyer, Director of Admissions. Web: *www.sjcny.edu*

SAINT JOSEPH'S COLLEGE, NEW YORK, SUFFOLK CAMPUS E-5

Patchogue, NY 11772	(631) 447-3219; Fax: (631) 447-1734
Full-time: 657 men, 1830 women	Faculty: 95; IIB, av$
Part-time: 18 men, 293 women	Ph.Ds: 62%
Graduate: 1 man, 29 women	Student/Faculty: 26 to 1
Year: 4-1-4, summer session	Tuition: $11,297
Application Deadline: March 15	Room & Board: n/app
Freshman Class: 1050 applied, 810 accepted, 410 enrolled	
SAT I Verbal/Math: 530/540	ACT: 22	COMPETITIVE

Saint Joseph's College, established in 1916, is a private, independent, multicampus commuter institution offering a wide variety of undergraduate study options, including traditional liberal arts majors, special course

offerings, and certificate, affiliated, and preprofessional programs. The school offers 12 Career Readiness Tracks. There is a campus in Brooklyn. There are 2 undergraduate and 2 graduate schools. In addition to regional accreditation, SJC has baccalaureate program accreditation with NLN. The library contains 120,000 volumes, and subscribes to 400 periodicals. Computerized library services include the card catalog, database searching, and Internet access. Special learning facilities include a learning resource center. The 25-acre campus is in a suburban area 60 miles east of New York City. There are 5 buildings.

Student Life: 99% of undergraduates are from New York. Students are from 4 states and 4 foreign countries. 85% are from public schools. 86% are white. The average age of freshmen is 18; all undergraduates, 20. 14% do not continue beyond their first year; 67% remain to graduate.

Housing: There are no residence halls. All students commute. Alcohol is not permitted. All students may keep cars.

Activities: 1% of men belong to 1 local fraternity; 4% of women belong to 2 local sororities. There are 31 groups on campus, including cheerleading, chorus, computers, dance, drama, ethnic, jazz band, literary magazine, newspaper, political, religious, social, social service, and student government. Popular campus events include Club Fair, Make a Difference Day, and Spring Fling.

Sports: There are 6 intercollegiate sports for men and 8 for women. Facilities include a swimming pool, a fitness center, an aerobics studio, an indoor running track, and a competition-size basketball court.

Disabled Students: All of the campus is accessible. Wheelchair ramps, elevators, special parking, specially equipped rest rooms, and lowered drinking fountains are available.

Services: Counseling and information services are available, as is tutoring in most subjects.

Campus Safety and Security: Measures include 24-hour foot and vehicle patrol, self-defense education, security escort services, and shuttle buses. There are informal discussions, pamphlets/posters/films, and lighted pathways/sidewalks. The school is monitored through closed-circuit screens.

Programs of Study: SJC confers B.A. and B.S. degrees. Master's degrees are also awarded. Bachelor's degrees are awarded in BIOLOGICAL SCIENCE (biology/biological science), BUSINESS (accounting, business administration and management, and recreation and leisure services), COMMUNICATIONS AND THE ARTS (English and speech/debate/rhetoric), COMPUTER AND PHYSICAL SCIENCE (information sciences and systems and mathematics), EDUCATION (secondary), SOCIAL SCIENCE (child care/child and family studies, history, psychology, and social science). Child study, math/computer science, and business/accounting are the strongest academically. Child study and business/accounting are the largest.

Required: To graduate, students must complete a liberal arts core curriculum. A total of 128 credits is needed to graduate, with a minimum of 33 credits in the major. For education majors, a minimum GPA of 2.8 is required; for all other majors, 2.3.

Special: There is study abroad in approximately 10 countries, an interdisciplinary major in human relations, B.A.-B.S. degrees, and a dual major in child study (elementary and special education). There are 7 national honor societies and 6 departmental honors programs.

Faculty/Classroom: 45% of faculty are male; 55%, female. All teach undergraduates. The average class size in an introductory lecture is 18; in a laboratory, 18; and in a regular course, 18.

Admissions: 77% of the 2003-2004 applicants were accepted. The SAT I scores for the 2003-2004 freshman class were: Verbal--30% below 500, 53% between 500 and 599, 16% between 600 and 700, and 1% above 700; Math--22% below 500, 53% between 500 and 599, 24% between 600 and 700, and 1% above 700. The ACT scores were 37% below 21 and 63% between 21 and 23. 45% of the current freshmen were in the top fifth of their class; 82% were in the top two fifths. 2 freshmen graduated first in their class.

Requirements: The SAT I is required. In addition, high school transcripts, 2 letters of recommendation, a personal essay, and an interview are required. A GPA of 3.0 is required. AP and CLEP credits are accepted.

Procedure: Freshmen are admitted fall and spring. There is a rolling admissions plan. For scholarship consideration, applications should be filed by March 15 for fall entry and January 1 for spring entry, along with a $25 fee. Notification is sent on a rolling basis.

Transfer: 733 transfer students enrolled in 2002-2003. Child study and education majors need a 2.8 GPA; all others, 2.3. 48 of 128 credits required for the bachelor's degree must be completed at SJC.

Visiting: There are regularly scheduled orientations for prospective students, including open houses in fall and spring. There are guides for informal visits and visitors may sit in on classes. To schedule a visit, contact the Admissions office.

Financial Aid: In 2003-2004, 69% of all full-time freshmen and 77% of continuing full-time students received some form of financial aid. 46% of full-time freshmen and 63% of continuing full-time students received need-based aid. The average freshman award was $9798. Need-based scholarships or need-based grants averaged $8136; need-based self-help aid (loans and jobs) averaged $1662; and non-need-based awards and non-need-based scholarships averaged $5085. 5% of undergraduates work part time. Average annual earnings from campus work are $1500. The average financial indebtedness of the 2003 graduate was $15,086. The FAFSA and the college's own financial statement are required. The priority date for freshman financial aid applications for fall entry is February 25.

International Students: There are 5 international students enrolled. They must score 550 on the written TOEFL or 213 on the electronic version and also take the SAT I, scoring 1000, or the ACT.

Computers: The mainframe is an IBM. There are 75 IBM IntelliStations with flat-panel monitors in 5 computer classrooms located in the Business Technology Center. All students may access the system during school hours. There are no time limits and no fees.

Graduates: From July 1, 2002 to June 30, 2003, 691 bachelor's degrees were awarded. The most popular majors were education (63%), business (13%), and psychology (6%).

Admissions Contact: Marion E. Salgado, Director of Admissions. E-mail: *suffolkas@sjcny.edu* Web: *www.sjcny.edu*

SAINT LAWRENCE UNIVERSITY
C-2
Canton, NY 13617

(315) 229-5261
(800) 285-1856; Fax: (315) 229-5818

Full-time: 995 men, 1127 women	**Faculty:** 157; IIB, +$
Part-time: 15 men, 23 women	**Ph.D.s:** 98%
Graduate: 49 men, 80 women	**Student/Faculty:** 14 to 1
Year: semesters, summer session	**Tuition:** $28,190
Application Deadline: February 15	**Room & Board:** $7755
Freshman Class: 3082 applied, 1767 accepted, 566 enrolled	
SAT I Verbal/Math: 570/570	**VERY COMPETITIVE**

St. Lawrence University, established in 1856, is a private liberal arts institution. In addition to regional accreditation, St. Lawrence has baccalaureate program accreditation with ACS. The 2 libraries contain 544,956 volumes, 593,581 microform items, and 4841 audio/video tapes/CDs, and subscribe to 2078 periodicals. Computerized library services include the card catalog, interlibrary loans, database searching, and Internet access. Special learning facilities include a learning resource center, art gallery, radio station, TV station, and a science field station. The 1000-acre campus is in a rural area 80 miles south of Ottawa, Canada. Including any residence halls, there are 30 buildings.

Student Life: 52% of undergraduates are from out of state, mostly the Northeast. Students are from 41 states, 21 foreign countries, and Canada. 73% are from public schools. 69% are white. The average age of freshmen is 18; all undergraduates, 20. 14% do not continue beyond their first year; 74% remain to graduate.

Housing: 1929 students can be accommodated in college housing, which includes coed dorms, on-campus apartments, fraternity houses, and sorority houses. In addition, there are language houses, special-interest houses, and theme cottages, such as Habitat for Humanity. On-campus housing is guaranteed for all 4 years. 95% of students live on campus; of those, 90% remain on campus on weekends. All students may keep cars.

Activities: 15% of men belong to 4 national fraternities; 23% of women belong to 1 local and 3 national sororities. There are 100 groups on campus, including art, chess, choir, chorus, dance, drama, ethnic, forensics, gay, honors, international, literary magazine, newspaper, outdoor, photography, political, professional, radio and TV, religious, social, social service, student government, and yearbook. Popular campus events include St. Lawrence Festival of the Arts, Black History Week, and Holiday Candlelight Service.

Sports: There are 15 intercollegiate sports for men and 16 for women, and 12 intramural sports for men and 9 for women. Facilities include basketball, squash, and tennis courts, a swimming pool, and weight, Nautilus, and exercise rooms. There are also 2 field houses, an arena, an artificial ice rink, an 18-hole golf course, riding stables, jogging and cross-country ski trails, a fitness center, a 9-line track, and soccer, baseball, and softball fields.

Disabled Students: 75% of the campus is accessible. Wheelchair ramps, elevators, special parking, specially equipped rest rooms, special class scheduling, and visual fire alarms are available.

Services: Counseling and information services are available, as is tutoring in every subject. There is a reader service for the blind a writing center, and science and technology counseling.

Campus Safety and Security: Measures include 24-hour foot and vehicle patrol, self-defense education, security escort services, and informal discussions. There are pamphlets/posters/films, emergency telephones, lighted pathways/sidewalks, and student patrols.

Programs of Study: St. Lawrence confers B.A. and B.S. degrees. Master's degrees are also awarded. Bachelor's degrees are awarded in BIOLOGICAL SCIENCE (biochemistry, biology/biological science, and neurosciences), COMMUNICATIONS AND THE ARTS (dramatic arts, English, fine arts, French, German, music, and Spanish), COMPUTER AND PHYSICAL SCIENCE (chemistry, computer science, geology,

mathematics, and physics), ENGINEERING AND ENVIRONMENTAL DESIGN (environmental science), SOCIAL SCIENCE (African studies, anthropology, Asian/Oriental studies, Canadian studies, economics, history, interdisciplinary studies, international studies, philosophy, political science/government, psychology, religion, and sociology). Psychology, English, and economics are the largest.

Required: To graduate, students must maintain a minimum GPA of 2.0 and complete 120 course hours, with 29 to 43 in the major. Freshmen must take a first-year program, a 2-semester team-taught course. Requirements also include 1 course in arts/expression, 1 in humanities, 1 in social science, 1 in math or foreign language, 2 in natural science/science studies, and 2 in diversity.

Special: Students may cross-register with the Associated Colleges of the St. Lawrence Valley. Internships are available through the sociology, psychology, and English departments and through a service learning program. Study-abroad in 14 countries and a Washington semester are offered. Dual majors and student-designed majors can be arranged. Students may earn 3-2 engineering degrees in conjunction with 7 engineering schools. Nondegree study and pass/fail options are available. An Adirondack semester and a leadership academy are also offered. There are 20 national honor societies, including Phi Beta Kappa, and 17 departmental honors programs.

Faculty/Classroom: 55% of faculty are male; 45%, female. 98% teach undergraduates and all do research. No introductory courses are taught by graduate students. The average class size in a regular course is 16.

Admissions: 57% of the 2003-2004 applicants were accepted. The SAT I scores for the 2003-2004 freshman class were: Verbal--17% below 500, 45% between 500 and 599, 33% between 600 and 700, and 5% above 700; Math--13% below 500, 46% between 500 and 599, 36% between 600 and 700, and 4% above 700. 59% of the current freshmen were in the top fifth of their class; 89% were in the top two fifths. 15 freshmen graduated first in their class.

Requirements: The SAT I is required. In addition, applicants must be graduates of an accredited high school. 16 or more academic credits are required, including 4 years of English and 3 years each of foreign languages, math, science, and social studies. Essays are required and interviews are recommended for all applicants. AP and CLEP credits are accepted. Important factors in the admissions decision are advanced placement or honor courses, extracurricular activities record, and recommendations by school officials.

Procedure: Freshmen are admitted fall and spring. Entrance exams should be taken during the spring of the junior year or the fall of the senior year. There are early decision and deferred admissions plans. Early decision applications should be filed by November 15; regular applications, by February 15 for fall entry and December 1 for spring entry, along with a $50 fee. Notification is sent March 15. 134 early decision candidates were accepted for the 2003-2004 class. 476 applicants were on the 2003 waiting list; 23 were admitted. Applications are accepted on-line through the university's web site.

Transfer: 22 transfer students enrolled in 2002-2003. The high school transcript and SAT I scores will be evaluated, but college work is more important. High school and college recommendations are required. 16 of 34 course units required for the bachelor's degree must be completed at St. Lawrence.

Visiting: There are regularly scheduled orientations for prospective students, including interviews and tours. There are guides for informal visits and visitors may sit in on classes and stay overnight. To schedule a visit, contact the Admissions Office at *admissions@stlawu.edu*.

Financial Aid: In 2003-2004, 83% of all full-time freshmen and 85% of continuing full-time students received some form of financial aid. 67% of full-time freshmen and 70% of continuing full-time students received need-based aid. The average freshman award was $15,931. 38% of undergraduates work part time. St. Lawrence is a member of CSS. The CSS Profile or FAFSA and the college's own financial statement are required. The deadline for filing freshman financial aid applications for fall entry is February 15.

International Students: There are 88 international students enrolled. The school actively recruits these students. They must score 600 on the written TOEFL or 250 on the electronic version and also take or the SAT I or ACT.

Computers: 600 PCs are linked to multiple servers and a card catalog. Word processing, spreadsheet, database, and course-specific software, e-mail, calendars, bulletin boards, and Internet and World Wide Web access are available. Computer labs are located throughout campus in academic and resident buildings. All students may access the system 24 hours per day. There are no time limits and no fees.

Graduates: From July 1, 2002 to June 30, 2003, 452 bachelor's degrees were awarded. The most popular majors were economics (11%), English (10%), and government (10%). In an average class, 1% graduate in 3 years or less, 69% graduate in 4 years or less, 74% graduate in 5 years or less, and 74% graduate in 6 years or less. 9 companies recruited on campus in 2002-2003. Of the 2002 graduating class, 20% were enrolled in graduate school within 6 months of graduation and 74% were employed.

Admissions Contact: Teresa Cowdrey, Dean of Admissions and Financial Aid. E-mail: *admissions@stlawu.edu* Web: *www.stlawu.ed*

SAINT THOMAS AQUINAS COLLEGE

D-5

Sparkill, NY 10976

(914) 398-4100

(800) 999-STAC; Fax: (914) 398-4224

Full-time: 1310 men and women	**Faculty:** 76; IIB, +$
Part-time: 700 men and women	**Ph.D:s:** 75%
Graduate: 65 men, 115 women	**Student/Faculty:** 17 to 1
Year: 4-1-4, summer session	**Tuition:** $14,100
Application Deadline: see profile	**Room & Board:** $7980
Freshman Class: n/av	
SAT I or ACT: required	**LESS COMPETITIVE**

Saint Thomas Aquinas College, founded in 1952, is an independent liberal arts institution. Figures in above capsule and in this profile are approximate. The library contains 102,943 volumes and 45,900 microform items, and subscribes to 108 periodicals. Computerized library services include the card catalog, interlibrary loans, and database searching. Special learning facilities include a learning resource center, radio station, and TV station. The 43-acre campus is in a suburban area 15 miles north of New York City. Including any residence halls, there are 12 buildings.

Student Life: 75% of undergraduates are from New York. Students are from 6 states, 8 foreign countries, and Canada. 80% are from public schools. 84% are white. 62% are Catholic; 23% Protestant. The average age of freshmen is 18; all undergraduates, 23. 16% do not continue beyond their first year; 62% remain to graduate.

Housing: 450 students can be accommodated in college housing, which includes single-sex dorms and on-campus apartments. On-campus housing is guaranteed for all 4 years. 65% of students commute. Alcohol is not permitted. All students may keep cars.

Activities: There are no fraternities or sororities. There are 15 groups on campus, including cheerleading, chorus, computers, drama, honors, international, literary magazine, musical theater, newspaper, professional, radio and TV, religious, social service, student government, and yearbook. Popular campus events include trips to Broadway shows and Halloween and Christmas mixers.

Sports: There are 5 intercollegiate sports for men and 4 for women, and 6 intramural sports for men and 5 for women. Facilities include an auditorium, a 750-seat gym, a weight room, and basketball and tennis courts.

Disabled Students: 90% of the campus is accessible. Wheelchair ramps, elevators, special parking, specially equipped rest rooms, special class scheduling, and lowered telephones are available.

Services: Counseling and information services are available, as is tutoring in most subjects. There is remedial math and writing.

Campus Safety and Security: Measures include 24-hour foot and vehicle patrol, security escort services, pamphlets/posters/films, and emergency telephones. There are lighted pathways/sidewalks.

Programs of Study: STAC confers B.A., B.S., and B.S.E. degrees. Associate and master's degrees are also awarded. Bachelor's degrees are awarded in BUSINESS (accounting, banking and finance, business administration and management, marketing/retailing/merchandising, and recreation and leisure services), COMMUNICATIONS AND THE ARTS (communications, English, fine arts, romance languages and literature, and Spanish), EDUCATION (art, bilingual/bicultural, elementary, foreign languages, science, secondary, and special), ENGINEERING AND ENVIRONMENTAL DESIGN (commercial art), HEALTH PROFESSIONS (medical laboratory technology and premedicine), SOCIAL SCIENCE (criminal justice, history, philosophy, prelaw, psychology, religion, and social science). Education, business administration, and natural sciences are the strongest academically. Business administration is the largest.

Required: To graduate, all students must complete a total of 120 credit hours, with 36 to 54 in the major and a minimum GPA of 2.0. A core curriculum of 51 credits in liberal arts courses is required.

Special: The college offers cross-registration with Barry University and Aquinas College and internships in business, criminal justice, commercial design, recreation and leisure, and communications. Study abroad in Europe and Asia, a 3-2 engineering degree with George Washington University and Manhattan College, and in physical therapy with New York Medical College, and work-study programs are available. Nondegree study and pass/fail options are possible. There are 7 national honor societies, including Phi Beta Kappa, and a freshman honors program.

Faculty/Classroom: 55% of faculty are male; 45%, female. 99% teach undergraduates, 50% do research, and 50% do both. No introductory courses are taught by graduate students. The average class size in an introductory lecture is 35; in a laboratory, 15; and in a regular course, 20.

Requirements: The SAT I or ACT is required. In addition, applicants must be graduates of an accredited secondary school or have a GED certificate. 16 Carnegie units are recommended, including 4 years of English, 3 years of social science, 2 years each of math and science, and 1 year each of foreign language and history. An interview is recommended. A GPA of 2.2 is required. AP and CLEP credits are accepted. Impor-

tant factors in the admissions decision are leadership record, extracurricular activities record, and advanced placement or honor courses.

Procedure: Freshmen are admitted fall and spring. Entrance exams should be taken by the spring of the junior year. There are early decision, early admissions, deferred admissions, and rolling admissions plans. Check with the school for current application deadlines. The fall 2003 application fee was $30. Notification is sent on a rolling basis. Applications are accepted on computer disk and on-line via EXPAN or at the college's web site.

Transfer: Applicants must have a 2.0 GPA from the previous school. 30 of 120 credits required for the bachelor's degree must be completed at STAC.

Visiting: There are guides for informal visits and visitors may sit in on classes and stay overnight. To schedule a visit, contact the Admissions Office.

Financial Aid: STAC is a member of CSS. The FAFSA is required. Check with the school for current deadlines.

International Students: The school actively recruits these students. They must score 500 on the written TOEFL.

Computers: The mainframe is an HP 3000. There are also 50 IBM, Zenith, Mac, and HP PCs available throughout campus. The campus is served by an intranet system with access to the Internet and e-mail. All students may access the system. There are no time limits. The fee is $100.

Admissions Contact: Tracey A. Howard-Ubelhoer, Director of Admissions. A video is available. E-mail: *thoward@stac.edu* Web: *www.stac.edu*

SARAH LAWRENCE COLLEGE

D-5

Bronxville, NY 10708

(914) 395-2510

(800) 888-2858; Fax: (914) 395-2515

Full-time: 327 men, 895 women	**Faculty:** 180; IIB, ++$
Part-time: 11 men, 59 women	**Ph.D:s:** n/av
Graduate: 52 men, 262 women	**Student/Faculty:** 7 to 1
Year: semesters	**Tuition:** $30,824
Application Deadline: January 1	**Room & Board:** $10,394
Freshman Class: 2672 applied, 1107 accepted, 322 enrolled	
SAT I Verbal/Math: 650/590	**ACT:** 27 **HIGHLY COMPETITIVE**

Sarah Lawrence College, established in 1926, is an independent institution conferring liberal arts degrees. The academic structure is based on the British don system. Students meet biweekly with professors in tutorials and are enrolled in small seminars. While there are no formal majors, students develop individual concentrations that are usually interdisciplinary. The 3 libraries contain 282,676 volumes, 24,218 microform items, and 9319 audio/video tapes/CDs, and subscribe to 916 periodicals. Computerized library services include the card catalog, interlibrary loans, database searching, and Internet access. Special learning facilities include an art gallery, radio station, a slide library with 75,000 slides of art and architecture, early childhood center, electronic music studio, music library, student-run theater, and student-run art gallery. The 41-acre campus is in a suburban area 15 miles north of midtown Manhattan. Including any residence halls, there are 50 buildings.

Student Life: 81% of undergraduates are from out of state, mostly the Middle Atlantic. Students are from 46 states, 25 foreign countries, and Canada. 65% are from public schools. 70% are white. The average age of freshmen is 18; all undergraduates, 20. 7% do not continue beyond their first year; 72% remain to graduate.

Housing: 965 students can be accommodated in college housing, which includes single-sex and coed dorms and on-campus apartments. A French interest house, the Perkins Art Co-op, and the Good Life House are also available. On-campus housing is guaranteed for all 4 years. 87% of students live on campus; of those, 90% remain on campus on weekends. Upperclassmen may keep cars.

Activities: There are no fraternities or sororities. There are 30 groups on campus, including art, choir, chorale, chorus, computers, dance, drama, ethnic, film, gay, human rights, international, jazz band, literary magazine, musical theater, newspaper, orchestra, philosophy, photography, poetry, political, radio and TV, religious, social, social service, student government, and yearbook. Popular campus events include Mayfair, "Deb Ball," and a student scholarship fundraising auction.

Sports: There are 5 intercollegiate sports for men and 6 for women, and 9 intramural sports for men and 9 for women. Facilities include a sports center with a gym, a jogging track, a 6-lane swimming pool, a rowing tank, a multipurpose studio, and 3 squash courts, a fitness center and weight room, tennis courts, and a number of open fields and lawns. Off-campus, the college has the use of a boat house and stables.

Disabled Students: 50% of the campus is accessible. Wheelchair ramps, elevators, special parking, specially equipped rest rooms, special class scheduling, lowered drinking fountains, and lowered telephones are available.

Services: Counseling and information services are available, as is tutoring in some subjects, including writing. There is a reader service for the blind.

Campus Safety and Security: Measures include 24-hour foot and vehicle patrol, self-defense education, security escort services, and shuttle buses. There are informal discussions, pamphlets/posters/films, emergency telephones, and lighted pathways/sidewalks.

Programs of Study: Sarah Lawrence confers the B.A. degree. Master's degrees are also awarded. Bachelor's degrees are awarded in BIOLOGICAL SCIENCE (biology/biological science), COMMUNICATIONS AND THE ARTS (art history and appreciation, classics, creative writing, dance, dramatic arts, English, film arts, fine arts, French, German, Greek, Italian, Latin, literature, music, Russian, Spanish, and visual and performing arts), COMPUTER AND PHYSICAL SCIENCE (chemistry and mathematics), HEALTH PROFESSIONS (premedicine), SOCIAL SCIENCE (anthropology, Asian/Oriental studies, economics, history, liberal arts/general studies, philosophy, political science/government, psychology, religion, Russian and Slavic studies, sociology, and women's studies).

Required: To graduate, students must complete 120 credit hours and meet distribution requirements in 3 of 4 academic areas, including history and social sciences, creative and performing arts, natural science and math, and humanities. Students must fulfill a first-year studies requirement in one of 18 areas and meet a phys ed requirement. Students must also take 2 lecture courses, where the average class size is 40.

Special: Internships are available in a variety of fields, with the school offering proximity to New York City art galleries and agencies. Study abroad in many countries, work-study programs, dual concentrations, a 3-2 engineering degree with Columbia, and a general degree may be pursued. All concentrations are self-designed and can be combined.

Faculty/Classroom: 49% of faculty are male; 51%, female. All both teach and do research. No introductory courses are taught by graduate students. The average class size in a regular course is 11.

Admissions: 41% of the 2003-2004 applicants were accepted. The SAT I scores for the 2003-2004 freshman class were: Verbal--4% below 500, 19% between 500 and 599, 50% between 600 and 700, and 27% above 700; Math--12% below 500, 41% between 500 and 599, 40% between 600 and 700, and 7% above 700. The ACT scores were 14% between 21 and 23, 31% between 24 and 26, 20% between 27 and 28, and 32% above 28. 66% of the current freshmen were in the top fifth of their class; 95% were in the top two fifths. There were 4 National Merit finalists.

Requirements: Important academic requirements are: secondary school record, teacher recommendation(s) and essay; class rank is considered. Nonacademic requirements include character and personality qualities; extracurricular activities, talent/ability, volunteer work, and work experience. Campus interview, alumnae/i relations, geographical residence, and minority status are considered. AP credits are accepted. Important factors in the admissions decision are recommendations by school officials, personality/intangible qualities, and extracurricular activities record.

Procedure: Freshmen are admitted in the fall. There are early decision, early admissions, and deferred admissions plans. Early decision applications should be filed by November 15; regular applications, by January 1 for fall entry. Notification of early decision is sent December 15; regular decision, April 1. 100 early decision candidates were accepted for the 2003-2004 class. 150 applicants were on the 2003 waiting list; 35 were admitted. The fall 2003 application fee was $50. Applications are acepted on-line through Common App and the college's web site.

Transfer: 50 transfer students enrolled in 2002-2003. Applicants must submit high school and college transcripts, and a statement of good standing from prior institution(s). A GPA of 3.0 is required and transfer applicants must have a minimum of 30 credits completed, or the equivalent of 2 semesters of full-time college work. Also required are a $50 application fee, Admission Information Form (in-house Form 1), essays, a graded academic paper, and 2 teacher/faculty evaluations. An interview is recommended, but not required. November 15 is the application deadline for spring entry.

Visiting: There are regularly scheduled orientations for prospective students, consisting of a full day of faculty and student panels, lectures, tours, and discussion with admissions officers, offered twice per year during the fall. There are guides for informal visits and visitors may sit in on classes and stay overnight. To schedule a visit, contact Linda Bloom, Receptionist, Admissions Office at slcadmit@slc.edu.

Financial Aid: In 2003-2004, 50% of all full-time freshmen and 49% of continuing full-time students received some form of financial aid. 50% of full-time freshmen and 49% of continuing full-time students received need-based aid. The average freshman award was $22,815. 43% of undergraduates work part time. Average annual earnings from campus work are $1000. The average financial indebtedness of the 2003 graduate was $15,023. Sarah Lawrence is a member of CSS. The CSS Profile or FAFSA and non-custodial parent statement are required. The deadline for filing freshman financial aid applications for fall entry is February 1.

International Students: There are 46 international students enrolled. The school actively recruits these students. They must score 600 on the written TOEFL or take the SAT II: English as a second language test.

Computers: There are 60 Macs and PCs with laser printers located in the student computer center, 19 located in the library, and 31 divided between 2 computer classrooms. All PCs are networked with full access to the Internet. All students may access the system 24 hours a day. There are no time limits and no fees.

Graduates: From July 1, 2002 to June 30, 2003, 256 bachelor's degrees were awarded. In an average class, 61% graduate in 4 years or less, 9% graduate in 5 years or less, and 1% graduate in 6 years or less. Of the 2002 graduating class, 30% were enrolled in graduate school within 6 months of graduation and 70% were employed.

Admissions Contact: Thyra L. Briggs, Dean of Admission. E-mail: slcadmit@alc.edu Web: www.sarahlawrence.edu

SCHOOL OF VISUAL ARTS
New York, NY 10010-3994

D-5
(212) 592-2100
(800) 436-4204; Fax: (212) 592-2116

Full-time: 1353 men, 1454 women	**Faculty:** 94
Part-time: 86 men, 79 women	**Ph.D.s:** 42%
Graduate: 148 men, 225 women	**Student/Faculty:** 30 to 1
Year: semesters, summer session	**Tuition:** $18,200
Application Deadline: March 15	**Room & Board:** $12,000
Freshman Class: 1957 applied, 1323 accepted, 488 enrolled	
SAT I Verbal/Math: 520/520	**ACT:** 22 SPECIAL

The School of Visual Arts, established in 1947, is a private institution conferring undergraduate and graduate degrees in fine arts. There are 8 undergraduate and 5 graduate schools. In addition to regional accreditation, SVA has baccalaureate program accreditation with FIDER and NASAD. The library contains 68,800 volumes, 1070 microform items, and 2990 audio/video tapes/CDs, and subscribes to 300 periodicals. Computerized library services include the card catalog, database searching, and Internet access. Special learning facilities include a learning resource center, art gallery, radio station, and 5 student galleries, 3 media arts workshops, 3 film and 2 video studios, numerous editing facilities, animation studio with 3 pencil test facilities, digital audio room, tape transfer room, and multimedia facility with digital printing and editing systems. The campus is in an urban area in the middle of Manhattan. Including any residence halls, there are 8 buildings.

Student Life: 60% of undergraduates are from New York. Students are from 45 states, 19 foreign countries, and Canada. 60% are from public schools. 54% are white; 12% Asian American; 12% foreign nationals. The average age of freshmen is 18; all undergraduates, 21. 10% do not continue beyond their first year; 57% remain to graduate.

Housing: 900 students can be accommodated in college housing, which includes single-sex and coed dorms, on-campus apartments, and off-campus apartments. On-campus housing is available on a first-come, first-served basis. 73% of students commute. Alcohol is not permitted. All students may keep cars.

Activities: There are no fraternities or sororities. There are many groups and organizations on campus, including art, computers, drama, ethnic, film, gay, honors, international, literary magazine, newspaper, photography, political, professional, radio and TV, religious, social, social service, student government, and yearbook. Popular campus events include an annual ski trip, a Halloween party, and 2 annual paintball trips.

Sports: There is no sports program at SVA.

Disabled Students: All of the campus is accessible. Wheelchair ramps, elevators, specially equipped rest rooms, special class scheduling, and lowered telephones are available.

Services: There is remedial reading and writing.

Campus Safety and Security: Measures include 24-hour foot and vehicle patrol, shuttle buses, informal discussions, and pamphlets/posters/films. There are emergency telephones and lighted pathways/sidewalks.

Programs of Study: SVA confers the B.F.A. degree. Master's degrees are also awarded. Bachelor's degrees are awarded in COMMUNICATIONS AND THE ARTS (advertising, animation, film arts, fine arts, graphic design, illustration, photography, and video), ENGINEERING AND ENVIRONMENTAL DESIGN (computer graphics and interior design). Graphic design and advertising, illustration and cartooning, and fine arts are the largest.

Required: To graduate, students must complete 120 credits, including at least 72 in the major, with a minimum GPA of 2.0. These credits must include 30 in humanities and sciences, 12 in art history, and 6 in electives. Students must complete 2 introductory courses in literature and writing and must pass a proficiency exam in the first semester.

Special: SVA offers study abroad in 8 countries, accelerated degree programs, and for-credit internships with more than 200 media-related, design, and advertising firms, including DC Comics, MTV, and Pentagram Design. A summer internship with Walt Disney Studios is possible for illustration/cartooning majors. There is a freshman honors program.

Faculty/Classroom: 60% of faculty are male; 40%, female. 86% teach undergraduates and 12% both teach and do research. No introductory courses are taught by graduate students. The average class size in an introductory lecture is 45 and in a regular course, 20.

Admissions: 68% of the 2003-2004 applicants were accepted. The SAT I scores for the 2003-2004 freshman class were: Math--40% below 500, 36% between 500 and 599, 21% between 600 and 700, and 3% above 700. The ACT scores for the 2003-2004 freshman class were: 32% below 21, 23% between 21 and 23, 10% between 24 and 26, 33% between 27 and 28, and 1% above 28.

Requirements: The SAT I or ACT is required. In addition, applicants must graduate from an accredited secondary school or have a GED. A statement of intent is required of all students. A portfolio is also required, except for film and video applicants, who must submit a 2-part essay. A personal inteview and letters of recommendation are considered helpful. A GPA of 2.5 is required. AP and CLEP credits are accepted. Important factors in the admissions decision are evidence of special talent, personality/intangible qualities, and leadership record.

Procedure: Freshmen are admitted fall and spring. There are early decision and deferred admissions plans. There is a rolling admissions plan. Early decision applications should be filed by December 1; regular applications, by March 15 for fall entry and December 1 for spring entry. Notification of early decision is sent January 14; regular decision, on a rolling basis. A waiting list is an active part of the admissions procedure. Applications are accepted on-line.

Transfer: 60 of 120 credits required for the bachelor's degree must be completed at SVA.

Visiting: There are regularly scheduled orientations for prospective students, including 6 Saturday Open House receptions and weekly tours. There are guides for informal visits. To schedule a visit, contact the Office of Admissions at *admissions@sva.edu.*

Financial Aid: In 2003-2004, 74% of all full-time freshmen and 61% of continuing full-time students received some form of financial aid. 55% of full-time freshmen and 47% of continuing full-time students received need-based aid. The average freshman award was $9400. 5% of undergraduates work part time. Average annual earnings from campus work are $5000. The average financial indebtedness of the 2003 graduate was $14,000. The FAFSA is required. The deadline for filing freshman financial aid applications for fall entry is February 1.

International Students: The school actively recruits these students. They must score 550 on the written TOEFL or 213 on the electronic version and also earn a minimum score of 6 in all categories of the NYU English proficiency exam.

Computers: The mainframe is a Sun Enterprise 3500. There are 555 PCs available in the computer art department, digital imaging center, writing resource center, and library. All students may access the system during normal operating hours of the library and the writing resource center; use in other buildings varies by major. There are no time limits and no fees. It is strongly recommended that all students have a personal computer.

Graduates: The most popular majors were graphic design/advertising (27%), film/video/animation (19%), and photography (16%). In an average class, 35% graduate in 4 years or less, 45% graduate in 5 years or less, and 57% graduate in 6 years or less. 50 companies recruited on campus in 2002-2003. Of the 2002 graduating class, 4% were enrolled in graduate school within 6 months of graduation and 85% were employed.

Admissions Contact: Rick Longo, Executive Director of Admissions. E-mail: *admissions@sva.edu* Web: *www.schoolofvisualarts.edu*

SIENA COLLEGE
Loudonville, NY 12211-1462

D-3

(518) 783-2423
(888) AT SIENA; Fax: (518) 783-2436

Full-time: 1333 men, 1692 women	Faculty: 166; IIB, +$
Part-time: 161 men, 193 women	Ph.D.s: 86%
Graduate: none	Student/Faculty: 18 to 1
Year: semesters, summer session	Tuition: $18,095
Application Deadline: March 1	Room & Board: $7215
Freshman Class: 4112 applied, 2599 accepted, 759 enrolled	
SAT I Verbal/Math: 550/570	ACT: 24 VERY COMPETITIVE

Siena College, founded in 1937, is a coeducational, independent, liberal arts college with a Franciscan and Catholic tradition. Siena offers bachelor's programs in the arts, sciences, and business leading to the baccalaureate. There are 3 undergraduate schools. In addition to regional accreditation, Siena has baccalaureate program accreditation with ACS and CSWE. The library contains 321,801 volumes, 27,527 microform items, and 5516 audio/video tapes/CDs, and subscribes to 1418 periodicals. Computerized library services include the card catalog, interlibrary loans, database searching, and Internet access. Special learning facilities include a radio station. The 164-acre campus is in a suburban area 2 miles north of Albany. Including any residence halls, there are 26 buildings.

Student Life: 86% of undergraduates are from New York. Students are from 31 states, 6 foreign countries, and Canada. 70% are from public schools. 89% are white. The average age of freshmen is 18; all undergraduates, 21. 10% do not continue beyond their first year; 78% remain to graduate.

Housing: 2219 students can be accommodated in college housing, which includes coed dorms and on-campus apartments. In addition, there are special-interest houses. On-campus housing is guaranteed for the freshman year only and is available on a lottery system for upperclassmen. 75% of students live on campus; of those, 90% remain on campus on weekends. Upperclassmen may keep cars.

Activities: There are no fraternities or sororities. There are approximately 75 groups on campus, including cheerleading, choir, chorus, community service, computers, dance, drama, ethnic, film, honors, international, literary magazine, model UN, musical theater, newspaper, opera, orchestra, outing, pep band, political, professional, radio and TV, religious, social, social service, student government, symphony, and yearbook. Popular campus events include Family Weekend, Winter Weekend, and Junior/Senior Formal.

Sports: There are 8 intercollegiate sports for men and 11 for women, and 20 intramural sports for men and 20 for women. Facilities include an athletic complex with free weights, a training facility, an indoor track, an 8-lane 25-meter pool, fitness equipment, life cycles, 4 multipurpose courts, 6 outdoor tennis courts, 5 outdoor fields, 2 squash courts, and racquetball courts.

Disabled Students: 90% of the campus is accessible. Wheelchair ramps, elevators, special parking, specially equipped rest rooms, special class scheduling, and an office for students with disabilities that provides various resources are available.

Services: Counseling and information services are available, as is tutoring in most subjects. There is a reader service for the blind, remedial math and writing, and a writing center that offers free one-to-one assistance.

Campus Safety and Security: Measures include 24-hour foot and vehicle patrol, security escort services, informal discussions, and pamphlets/posters/films. There are emergency telephones, lighted pathways/sidewalks, card access system for residence halls, radio dispatch, and 911 on-campus telephone system.

Programs of Study: Siena confers B.A., B.S., and B.B.A. degrees. Bachelor's degrees are awarded in BIOLOGICAL SCIENCE (biochemistry and biology/biological science), BUSINESS (accounting, banking and finance, business economics, and marketing management), COMMUNICATIONS AND THE ARTS (classical languages, English, French, Spanish, and visual and performing arts), COMPUTER AND PHYSICAL SCIENCE (chemistry, computer science, mathematics, and physics), ENGINEERING AND ENVIRONMENTAL DESIGN (environmental science), SOCIAL SCIENCE (American studies, economics, history, philosophy, political science/government, psychology, religion, social work, and sociology). Biology, political science, and accounting are the strongest academically. Accounting, marketing/management, and biology are the largest.

Required: To graduate, students must earn 120 credits, including 30 to 39 in the major, with at least a 2.0 GPA. The required core curriculum of 42 credits must include 3 math/science courses, 2 foundation courses, 2 social science courses, 1 to 2 courses in English, history, philosophy, and religious studies, and 1 creative arts course.

Special: The college offers a cooperative 4-1 business program with Clarkson University and a cooperative 2-2 program in environmental science and forestry with Syracuse University. Cross-registration with the Hudson-Mohawk Association and a Washington semester with American University are possible. Domestic and international internships, dual majors, B.A.-B.S. degrees, study abroad in 15 countries, and pass/fail options are available. Students may earn 3-2 engineering degrees with Clarkson and Catholic Universities, Manhattan College, Western New England College, SUNY at Binghamton, and Rensselaer Polytechnic Institute. Siena also offers a 4-4 early assurance program with the Columbia University School of Dental and Oral Surgery and SUNY College of Optometry, a 3-4 program with Boston University School of Graduate Dentistry, and a 4-4 medical program with Albany Medical College. There are 7 national honor societies, a freshman honors program, and 4 departmental honors programs.

Faculty/Classroom: 64% of faculty are male; 36%, female. All teach undergraduates. The average class size in an introductory lecture is 25; in a laboratory, 20; in a regular course, 22.

Admissions: 63% of the 2003-2004 applicants were accepted. The SAT I scores for the 2003-2004 freshman class were: Verbal--19% below 500, 55% between 500 and 599, 24% between 600 and 700, and 2% above 700; Math--12% below 500, 52% between 500 and 599, 33% between 600 and 700, and 3% above 700. 50% of the current freshmen were in the top fifth of their class; 80% were in the top two fifths.

Requirements: The SAT I is required. In addition, applicants must be graduates of an accredited secondary school or have a GED. 16 academic credits are required, including 4 years each of English and history, 3 to 4 years each of math and science, and a recommended 3 years of foreign language study. All applicants must submit an essay; an interview is recommended. AP and CLEP credits are accepted. Important factors in the admissions decision are advanced placement or honor courses, personality/intangible qualities, and extracurricular activities record.

Procedure: Freshmen are admitted fall and spring. Entrance exams should be taken during May of the junior year or November of the senior year. There are early decision, early admissions, and deferred admissions plans. Early decision applications should be filed by December 1; regular applications, by March 1 for fall entry, December 1 for spring entry, and January 1 for summer entry, along with a $40 fee. Notification of early decision is sent January 15; regular decision, March 15. 63 early decision candidates were accepted for the 2003-2004 class. 121 applicants were on the 2003 waiting list; 25 were admitted. Applications are accepted on-line through *www.siena.edu/admissions*.

Transfer: 142 transfer students enrolled in 2002-2003. Applicants must have a minimum 2.5 GPA. An interview is recommended. 30 of 120 credits required for the bachelor's degree must be completed at Siena.

Visiting: There are regularly scheduled orientations for prospective students. Students may interview with an admissions counselor, tour campus, or attend a group information session. There are guides for informal visits and visitors may sit in on classes and stay overnight. To schedule a visit, contact the Admissions Office at *admit@siena.edu*.

Financial Aid: In 2003-2004, 95% of all full-time freshmen and 93% of continuing full-time students received some form of financial aid. 62% of full-time freshmen and 63% of continuing full-time students received need-based aid. The average freshman award was $11,892. 13% of undergraduates work part time. Average annual earnings from campus work are $800. The average financial indebtedness of the 2003 graduate was $12,700. The FAFSA and the state aid form are required. The deadline for filing freshman financial aid applications for fall entry is April 1.

International Students: There are 12 international students enrolled. The school actively recruits these students. They must score 550 on the written TOEFL or 213 on the electronic version and also take the SAT I or the ACT.

Computers: The mainframe is a network of more than 25 servers. All students have accounts established for them prior to arrival. Students may access more than 350 PCs, Macs, and terminals in more than a dozen locations, some of which are open 24 hours a day, 7 days a week. Every residence space includes a network connection for student use. All students may access the system 24 hours per day. There are no time limits and no fees.

Graduates: From July 1, 2002 to June 30, 2003, 747 bachelor's degrees were awarded. The most popular majors were marketing/management (26%), psychology (12%), and accounting (11%). In an average class, 70% graduate in 4 years or less, 77% graduate in 5 years or less, and 79% graduate in 6 years or less. 144 companies recruited on campus in 2002-2003. Of the 2002 graduating class, 19% were enrolled in graduate school within 6 months of graduation and 78% were employed.

Admissions Contact: Edward Jones, Assistant Vice President for Admissions. E-mail: *admit@siena.edu* Web: *www.siena.edu*

SKIDMORE COLLEGE
Saratoga Springs, NY 12866-1632

D-3

(518) 580-5570
(800) 867-6007; Fax: (518) 580-5584

Full-time: 952 men, 1329 women	Faculty: 193; IIB, ++$
Part-time: 69 men, 147 women	Ph.D.s: 84%
Graduate: 14 men, 38 women	Student/Faculty: 12 to 1
Year: semesters, summer session	Tuition: $29,630
Application Deadline: January 15	Room & Board: $8300
Freshman Class: 5903 applied, 2724 accepted, 642 enrolled	
SAT I Verbal/Math: 620/630	ACT: 27 HIGHLY COMPETITIVE

Skidmore College, established in 1903, is an independent institution offering undergraduate programs in liberal arts and sciences, as well as business, social work, education, studio art, dance, and theater. In addition to regional accreditation, Skidmore has baccalaureate program accreditation with CSWE and NASAD. The library contains 283,677 volumes, 236,330 microform items, and 138,493 audio/video tapes/CDs, and subscribes to 1178 periodicals. Computerized library services include the card catalog and database searching. Special learning facilities include a learning resource center, art gallery, radio station, TV station, an electronic music studio, music and art studios, theater teaching facility, anthropology lab, and special biological habitats on campus. The 888-acre campus is in a small town 30 miles north of Albany. Including any residence halls, there are 42 buildings.

Student Life: 71% of undergraduates are from out of state, mostly the Northeast. Students are from 44 states, 25 foreign countries, and Canada. 61% are from public schools. 73% are white. The average age of freshmen is 18; all undergraduates, 20. 10% do not continue beyond their first year.

Housing: 1700 students can be accommodated in college housing, which includes single-sex and coed dorms and on-campus apartments. In addition, there are language houses and special-interest houses. On-campus housing is guaranteed for all 4 years. 77% of students live on campus. All students may keep cars.

Activities: There are no fraternities or sororities. There are 80 groups on campus, including art, band, chorale, chorus, computers, dance, drama, ethnic, film, gay, honors, international, jazz band, literary magazine, musical theater, newspaper, opera, orchestra, photography, political,

professional, radio and TV, religious, social, social service, student government, and yearbook. Popular campus events include Martin Luther King Week, Oktoberfest, and Spring Fling.

Sports: There are 10 intercollegiate sports for men and 10 for women, and 15 intramural sports for men and 13 for women. Facilities include a fitness center, an indoor swimming and diving pool, 2 gyms with 4 basketball courts, an indoor jogging track, a weight room, fields for baseball and other sports, dance studios, cross-country ski trails, a riding center, courts for tennis, handball, racquetball, and squash, and an outdoor facility with a synthetic surface soccer/lacrosse field, an all-weather 400-meter track, lights, and permanent stands.

Disabled Students: 75% of the campus is accessible. Wheelchair ramps, elevators, special parking, specially equipped rest rooms, lowered drinking fountains, and special housing are available.

Services: Counseling and information services are available, as is tutoring in most subjects. There is a reader service for the blind. Diagnostic services, note takers, and books on tape are also offered.

Campus Safety and Security: Measures include 24-hour foot and vehicle patrol, security escort services, shuttle buses, and informal discussions. There are pamphlets/posters/films, emergency telephones, lighted pathways/sidewalks, a special security alert system, rigorous fire response procedures, and a lock system on dorm entrances.

Programs of Study: Skidmore confers B.A. and B.S. degrees. Master's degrees are also awarded. Bachelor's degrees are awarded in BIOLOGICAL SCIENCE (biochemistry, biology/biological science, and neurosciences), BUSINESS (business administration and management and business economics), COMMUNICATIONS AND THE ARTS (art, art history and appreciation, classics, dance, dramatic arts, English, fine arts, French, German, music, and Spanish), COMPUTER AND PHYSICAL SCIENCE (chemistry, computer science, geology, mathematics, and physics), EDUCATION (elementary), ENGINEERING AND ENVIRONMENTAL DESIGN (environmental science), HEALTH PROFESSIONS (exercise science), SOCIAL SCIENCE (American studies, anthropology, Asian/Oriental studies, economics, French studies, history, liberal arts/general studies, philosophy, political science/government, psychology, religion, social science, social work, sociology, and women's studies). Business, English, and art are the largest.

Required: To graduate, students must complete 120 credits, including at least 24 at the 300 level, with a minimum GPA of 2.0 overall and in the major. B.A. candidates require 90 credits in the liberal arts to graduate; B.S. candidates require 60 credits. Students must fulfill a 2-course liberal studies sequence and complete distribution requirements of 1 course each in writing, quantitative reasoning, foreign language, lab science, the arts, humanities, and social science, and 1 course in either non-Western cultures or cultural diversity.

Special: Skidmore offers cross-registration with the Hudson-Mohawk Consortium, individually designed internships, various study-abroad programs, a Washington semester in conjunction with American University, dual and student-designed majors, credit for life and experience, and pass/fail options, as well as a nondegree study program for senior citizens. There are cooperative programs in engineering with Dartmouth College and Clarkson University, in business with Clarkson, in education with Union College, and in law with the Benjamin Cardozo Law School. There is a 6-week internship period available at the end of the spring term. There are 9 national honor societies, including Phi Beta Kappa, and a freshman honors program.

Faculty/Classroom: 54% of faculty are male; 46%, female. 90% both teach and do research. No introductory courses are taught by graduate students. The average class size in a regular course is 16.

Admissions: 46% of the 2003-2004 applicants were accepted. The SAT I scores for the 2003-2004 freshman class were: Verbal--5% below 500, 28% between 500 and 599, 51% between 600 and 700, and 16% above 700; Math--3% below 500, 28% between 500 and 599, 57% between 600 and 700, and 12% above 700. The ACT scores were 9% between 21 and 23, 36% between 24 and 26, 23% between 27 and 28, and 32% above 28. 65% of the current freshmen were in the top fifth of their class; 93% were in the top two fifths.

Requirements: The SAT I or ACT is required. AP and CLEP credits are accepted. Important factors in the admissions decision are advanced placement or honor courses, recommendations by school officials, and evidence of special talent.

Procedure: Freshmen are admitted fall and spring. Entrance exams should be taken by December of the senior year. There are early decision, early admissions, and deferred admissions plans. Early decision applications should be filed by December 1; regular applications, by January 15 for fall entry. The fall 2003 application fee was $60. Notification of early decision is sent January 1; regular decision, April 1. A waiting list is an active part of the admissions procedure.

Transfer: Transfer students must have a GPA of 2.7 and must submit a high school transcript, all college transcripts, an essay or personal statement, test scores, and a statement of good standing from prior institutions. At least one professor recommendation from the current institution and a mid-term report are also required. 60 of 120 credits required for the bachelor's degree must be completed at Skidmore.

Visiting: There are regularly scheduled orientations for prospective students, including full day open-house programs. There are guides for informal visits and visitors may sit in on classes and stay overnight. To schedule a visit, contact the Admissions Office at (518) 580-5000.

Financial Aid: In 2003-2004, at least 36% of all full-time freshmen and at least 42% of continuing full-time students received some form of financial aid. At least 36% of full-time freshmen and at least 42% of continuing full-time students received need-based aid. The average freshman award was $22,920. Need-based scholarships or need-based grants averaged $19,072; need-based self-help aid (loans and jobs) averaged $3848; and non-need-based institutional awards and non-need-based scholarships averaged $10,000. The average financial indebtedness of the 2003 graduate was $16,228. The CSS/Profile or FAFSA is required. The deadline for filing freshman financial aid applications for fall entry is January 15.

International Students: The school actively recruits these students. They must score 570 on the written TOEFL and also take the SAT I or the ACT.

Computers: All students may access the system 24 hours per day. There are no time limits and no fees. It is strongly recommended that all students have a personal computer.

Graduates: From July 1, 2002 to June 30, 2003, 539 bachelor's degrees were awarded. The most popular majors were business (13%), English (10%), and art (9%). Of the 2002 graduating class, 13% were enrolled in graduate school within 6 months of graduation and 96% were employed.

Admissions Contact: Mary Lou Bates, Director of Admissions. A video is available. E-mail: *admissions@skidmore.edu* Web: *www.skidmore.edu*

SOUTHAMPTON COLLEGE OF LONG ISLAND UNIVERSITY (See Long Island University/Southampton College)

STATE UNIVERSITY OF NEW YORK

The State University of New York, established in 1948, is a public system in New York. It is governed by a board of trustees, whose chief administrator is the chancellor. The primary goals of the system are teaching, research, and public service. The main priorities are to educate the largest number of people possible at the highest level, including educationally disadvantaged groups; to provide students with enhanced educational skills and techniques; and to enhance the quality of life for all New Yorkers. The total enrollment of all 64 campuses is nearly 400,000; there were 12,000 faculty members. Altogether there are 1720 baccalaureate, 1073 master's, and 312 doctoral programs offered in State University of New York. 4-year campuses are located in Albany, Binghamton, Buffalo, Stony Brook, Brockport, Cortland, Fredonia, Geneseo, New Paltz, Old Westbury, Oneonta, Oswego, Plattsburgh, Potsdam, Purchase, and Saratoga Springs. Profiles of the 4-year campuses are included in this section.

STATE UNIVERSITY OF NEW YORK AT OSWEGO   C-3
Oswego, NY 13126   (315) 312-2250; Fax: (315) 312-3260

Full-time: 3058 men, 3588 women	**Faculty:** 300; IIA, -$
Part-time: 313 men, 378 women	**Ph.D.s:** 76%
Graduate: 495 men, 884 women	**Student/Faculty:** 22 to 1
Year: semesters, summer session	**Tuition:** $5110 ($11,060)
Application Deadline: January 15	**Room & Board:** $7540
Freshman Class: 7438 applied, 4223 accepted, 1332 enrolled	
SAT I or ACT: required	**COMPETITIVE**

State University of New York at Oswego, founded in 1861, is a comprehensive institution offering more than 100 cooperative, preprofessional, and graduate programs in the arts and sciences, business, and education. There are 3 undergraduate and 3 graduate schools. In addition to regional accreditation, Oswego has baccalaureate program accreditation with AACSB, NASM, and NCATE. The library contains 467,346 volumes, 2,106,494 microform items, and 12,540 audio/video tapes/CDs, and subscribes to 1477 periodicals. Computerized library services include the card catalog, interlibrary loans, and database searching. Special learning facilities include a learning resource center, art gallery, planetarium, radio station, TV station, and biological field station. The 696-acre campus is in a small town on the southeast shore of Lake Ontario, 35 miles northwest of Syracuse. Including any residence halls, there are 40 buildings.

Student Life: 98% of undergraduates are from New York. Students are from 28 states, 24 foreign countries, and Canada. 90% are from public schools. 90% are white. 42% are Catholic; 41% Protestant; 14% Jewish. The average age of freshmen is 18; all undergraduates, 21. 28% do not continue beyond their first year; 59% remain to graduate.

Housing: 3600 students can be accommodated in college housing, which includes coed dorms. On-campus housing is guaranteed for all 4 years. 54% of students live on campus; of those, 90% remain on campus on weekends. All students may keep cars.

Activities: 7% of men belong to 7 local and 10 national fraternities; 6% of women belong to 5 local and 7 national sororities. There are 130 groups on campus, including art, band, cheerleading, choir, chorale, chorus, computers, dance, drama, ethnic, gay, honors, international, jazz band, literary magazine, musical theater, newspaper, opera, orchestra, photography, political, professional, radio and TV, religious, social, social service, student government, and yearbook. Popular campus events include Honors Convocations and Quest, Parents Weekend, and College Open House.

Sports: There are 12 intercollegiate sports for men and 11 for women, and 12 intramural sports for men and 12 for women. Facilities include an ice hockey rink, a field house with an artificial-grass practice area, 23 tennis courts, an outdoor track, 3 soccer and 3 lacrosse fields, baseball and softball fields, numerous basketball courts, racquetball and squash courts, 2 indoor pools, and a diving well. The gym seats 3500. There are also 2 fitness centers and weight rooms, a cross-country ski lodge, and a martial arts studio.

Disabled Students: 85% of the campus is accessible. Wheelchair ramps, elevators, special parking, specially equipped rest rooms, special class scheduling, lowered drinking fountains, lowered telephones, special housing, and a student support group are available.

Services: Counseling and information services are available, as is tutoring in every subject. There is a reader service for the blind, and remedial math, reading, and writing. In addition, the Office of Learning Support Services provides general foundation support.

Campus Safety and Security: Measures include 24-hour foot and vehicle patrol, shuttle buses, informal discussions, and pamphlets/posters/films. There are emergency telephones, lighted pathways/sidewalks, a campus police force, programs on safety issues and alcohol education, and a security escort—an electronic device that locates students and alerts the police when triggered.

Programs of Study: Oswego confers B.A., B.S., and B.F.A. degrees. Master's degrees are also awarded. Bachelor's degrees are awarded in BIOLOGICAL SCIENCE (biology/biological science and zoology), BUSINESS (accounting, banking and finance, business administration and management, human resources, international economics, management science, and marketing/retailing/merchandising), COMMUNICATIONS AND THE ARTS (art, broadcasting, communications, dramatic arts, English, French, German, journalism, linguistics, music, public relations, and Spanish), COMPUTER AND PHYSICAL SCIENCE (applied mathematics, atmospheric sciences and meteorology, chemistry, computer science, geochemistry, geology, information sciences and systems, mathematics, and physics), EDUCATION (business, elementary, foreign languages, secondary, and vocational), ENGINEERING AND ENVIRONMENTAL DESIGN (technological management), SOCIAL SCIENCE (American studies, anthropology, cognitive science, criminal justice, economics, history, human development, international studies, philosophy, political science/government, psychology, sociology, and women's studies). Chemistry, computer science, and accounting are the strongest academically. Elementary/secondary education, business administration, and accounting are the largest.

Required: To graduate, all students must complete 42 to 48 general education credits including 6 in human diversity, and 3 to 6 each in expository writing and math. Students must have a minimum 2.0 GPA and complete 122 total credit hours (127 hours for technology and vocational education students). The total number of hours in the major varies from 30 to 78.

Special: Oswego offers cross-registration with ACUSNY-Visiting Student Program. More than 1000 internships are available with business, social, cultural, and government agencies. The university also offers a Washington semester, study abroad in more than 80 programs, a 5-year accounting B.S./M.B.A. program, dual majors, B.A.-B.S. degrees in several sciences and a B.A.-B.F.A. in art, credit for military experience, non-degree study, and pass/fail options. A 3-2 engineering degree is offered with Clarkson University, SUNY at Binghamton, and Case Western Reserve University. A 3-4 degree in optometry with SUNY College of Optometry, a 2-3 degree in zoo technology with Santa Fe Community College, and 2-2 and 2-3 degrees in health sciences with SUNY Health Sciences Center are also possible. There are 21 national honor societies, a freshman honors program, and 9 departmental honors programs.

Faculty/Classroom: 58% of faculty are male; 42%, female. 93% teach undergraduates. No introductory courses are taught by graduate students. The average class size in an introductory lecture is 40; in a laboratory, 18; and in a regular course, 26.

Admissions: 57% of the 2003-2004 applicants were accepted. The SAT I scores for the 2003-2004 freshman class were: Verbal--24% below 500, 59% between 500 and 599, 16% between 600 and 700, and 1% above 700; Math--21% below 500, 59% between 500 and 599, 19% between 600 and 700, and 1% above 700. 27% of the current freshmen were in the top fifth of their class; 64% were in the top two fifths.

Requirements: The SAT I or ACT is required. In addition, applicants must be graduates of an accredited secondary school or have a GED certificate. 18 academic credits are required, including 4 years each of

English and social studies, 3 each of math and science, and 2 of a foreign language. An essay and interview are recommended. A grade average of 80 is required. AP and CLEP credits are accepted. Important factors in the admissions decision are advanced placement or honor courses, extracurricular activities record, and evidence of special talent.

Procedure: Freshmen are admitted fall and spring. Entrance exams should be taken during the spring of the junior year or fall of the senior year. There are early decision, early admissions, deferred admissions, and rolling admissions plans. Early decision applications should be filed by November 15; regular applications, by January 15 for fall entry and November 1 for spring entry, along with a $40 fee. Notification of early decision is sent December 15; regular decision, on a rolling basis. 55 early decision candidates were accepted for a recent class. Applications are accepted on-line through *www.suny.edu/student/apply/apply.cfm*.

Transfer: 700 transfer students enrolled in 2002-2003. Applicants must submit official transcripts from previously attended colleges. Students with a minimum GPA of 2.4 are encouraged to apply. SUNY associate degree holders are given preference. Secondary school records may be required for 1-year transfers. 30 of 122 credits required for the bachelor's degree must be completed at Oswego.

Visiting: There are regularly scheduled orientations for prospective students, usually including a campus tour and a meeting with a counselor. There are guides for informal visits and visitors may sit in on classes and stay overnight. To schedule a visit, contact the Office of Admissions.

Financial Aid: In 2003-2004, 61% of all full-time freshmen and 65% of continuing full-time students received some form of financial aid. 58% of full-time freshmen and 60% of continuing full-time students received need-based aid. The average freshman award was $6729. Need-based scholarships or need-based grants averaged $3867; need-based self-help aid (loans and jobs) averaged $3017; and non-need-based awards and non-need-based scholarships averaged $3426. 33% of undergraduates work part time. Average annual earnings from campus work are $1200. The average financial indebtedness of the 2003 graduate was $16,852. The FAFSA is required. The priority date for freshman financial aid applications for fall entry is April 1.

International Students: There are 78 international students enrolled. The school actively recruits these students. They must score 550 on the written TOEFL or 213 on the electronic version.

Computers: The mainframes are an HP Alpha ES20 and a Sun 450. There are more than 600 PCs available for student access, with labs located throughout the campus for general access and in support of departmental programs. There is an instructional computing center that provides a 24-hour help line. All students may access the system. There are no time limits and no fees. It is recommended that students in business have personal computers.

Graduates: From July 1, 2002 to June 30, 2003, 1345 bachelor's degrees were awarded. The most popular majors were education (28%), business (19%), and communications (7%). In an average class, 1% graduate in 3 years or less, 44% graduate in 4 years or less, 58% graduate in 5 years or less, and 62% graduate in 6 years or less. 90 companies recruited on campus in 2002-2003. Of the 2002 graduating class, 12% were enrolled in graduate school within 6 months of graduation and 79% were employed.

Admissions Contact: Joseph F. Grant, Jr., Dean of Admissions. A video is available. E-mail: *admiss@oswego.edu/admissions* Web: *www.oswego.edu*

STATE UNIVERSITY OF NEW YORK AT POTSDAM
Potsdam, NY 13676

C-2

(315) 267-2180
(877) 768-7326; Fax: (315) 267-2163

Full-time: 1359 men, 1979 women	**Faculty:** 230; IIA, --$
Part-time: 62 men, 84 women	**Ph.D.s:** 80%
Graduate: 222 men, 601 women	**Student/Faculty:** 15 to 1
Year: semesters, summer session	**Tuition:** $5190 ($11,140)
Application Deadline: open	**Room & Board:** $6970
Freshman Class: 3418 applied, 2366 accepted, 677 enrolled	
SAT I Verbal/Math: 540/530	**ACT:** 23 COMPETITIVE

The State University of New York at Potsdam, founded in 1816, joined the state university system in 1948. The school offers more than 40 undergraduate degree programs. There are 3 undergraduate schools and 1 graduate school. In addition to regional accreditation, SUNY Potsdam has baccalaureate program accreditation with NASM and NCATE. The 2 libraries contain 408,484 volumes, 772,029 microform items, and 15,323 audio/video tapes/CDs, and subscribe to 1035 periodicals. Computerized library services include the card catalog, interlibrary loans, database searching, and Internet access. Special learning facilities include a learning resource center, art gallery, natural history museum, planetarium, radio station, electronic music composition lab, recording studios, and seismographic lab. The 240-acre campus is in a rural area 140 miles northeast of Syracuse. Including any residence halls, there are 36 buildings.

Student Life: 94% of undergraduates are from New York. Students are from 23 states, 28 foreign countries, and Canada. 79% are white. The

average age of freshmen is 19; all undergraduates, 23. 27% do not continue beyond their first year; 47% remain to graduate.

Housing: 2400 students can be accommodated in college housing, which includes single-sex and coed dorms and on-campus apartments. In addition, there are honors houses, special-interest houses, substance-free housing, an international house, and first-year experience housing. On-campus housing is guaranteed for all 4 years. 52% of students live on campus; of those, 85% remain on campus on weekends. All students may keep cars.

Activities: 4% of men belong to 3 local and 2 national fraternities; 6% of women belong to 7 local and 1 national sorority. There are 100 groups on campus, including art, band, cheerleading, choir, chorale, chorus, computers, dance, drama, environmental awareness, ethnic, gay, honors, international, jazz band, literary magazine, musical theater, newspaper, opera, orchestra, pep band, photography, political, professional, radio and TV, social, social service, student government, symphony, and yearbook. Popular campus events include Harvest Ball, Spring Fest, and Kwanza Ball.

Sports: There are 7 intercollegiate sports for men and 10 for women, and 9 intramural sports for men and 8 for women. Facilities include a 2400-seat ice arena, an Olympic-size pool, a 3000-seat gym, an indoor field house, indoor and outdoor tracks, tennis, squash, handball, and basketball courts, a weight room, a dance studio, a softball field, and an artificial turf stadium.

Disabled Students: 95% of the campus is accessible. Wheelchair ramps, elevators, special parking, specially equipped rest rooms, special class scheduling, lowered drinking fountains, lowered telephones, special housing, and electric doors are available.

Services: Counseling and information services are available, as is tutoring in most subjects. There is a reader service for the blind, language and math labs, a writing center, and a reading clinic.

Campus Safety and Security: Measures include 24-hour foot and vehicle patrol, self-defense education, security escort services, and informal discussions. There are pamphlets/posters/films, emergency telephones, and lighted pathways/sidewalks.

Programs of Study: SUNY Potsdam confers B.A., B.S., B.A. Mus., and B.M. degrees. Master's degrees are also awarded. Bachelor's degrees are awarded in BIOLOGICAL SCIENCE (biochemistry, biology/biological science, and environmental biology), BUSINESS (business administration and management and business economics), COMMUNICATIONS AND THE ARTS (art history and appreciation, ceramic art and design, dance, dramatic arts, English, French, music, music business management, music performance, music theory and composition, painting, photography, printmaking, sculpture, Spanish, speech/debate/rhetoric, and studio art), COMPUTER AND PHYSICAL SCIENCE (chemistry, computer science, geology, mathematics, and physics), EDUCATION (early childhood, elementary, English, foreign languages, mathematics, middle school, music, science, secondary, and social studies), HEALTH PROFESSIONS (community health work), SOCIAL SCIENCE (anthropology, archeology, criminal justice, economics, history, interdisciplinary studies, philosophy, political science/government, psychology, and sociology). Math, education, and biochemistry are the strongest academically. Music education, elementary education, and psychology are the largest.

Required: To graduate, students must earn 124 to 128 credit hours, with 30 to 33 in the major, and a minimum GPA of 2.0. General education requirements include 21 hours of Modes of Inquiry in liberal arts, 10 to 11 semester hours of freshman course work in verbal and quantitative skills, 4 hours of phys ed, as well as 1 course each in written and oral communication above the freshman level, and demonstrated foreign language proficiency.

Special: Cross-registration is offered with Clarkson, St. Lawrence, and Canton Universities. Political science internships in Albany, and many other internships are possible. SUNY Potsdam also offers work-study opportunities, a 3-2 engineering degree with Clarkson University, study abroad, accelerated degree programs in math, English, and education, 3-2 management and accounting degrees, student-designed majors, dual majors in interdisciplinary natural science, nondegree study, and pass/fail options. There are 23 national honor societies, a freshman honors program, and 18 departmental honors programs.

Faculty/Classroom: 56% of faculty are male; 44%, female. All teach undergraduates. No introductory courses are taught by graduate students.

Admissions: 69% of the 2003-2004 applicants were accepted. The SAT I scores for the 2003-2004 freshman class were: Verbal--35% below 500, 43% between 500 and 599, 20% between 600 and 700, and 2% above 700; Math--35% below 500, 41% between 500 and 599, 22% between 600 and 700, and 2% above 700. The ACT scores were 38% below 21, 18% between 21 and 23, 25% between 24 and 26, 11% between 27 and 28, and 8% above 28. 27% of the current freshmen were in the top fifth of their class; 63% were in the top two fifths. There were 2 National Merit semifinalists. 7 freshmen graduated first in their class.

Requirements: The SAT I or ACT is required. Applicants must be high school graduates in a college preparatory program or hold a GED. 4 years each of English and social studies, 3 each of math and foreign language, 2 of science, and 1 of art or music are recommended. An interview is recommended; an audition, when appropriate, is required. A grade average of 80 is required. AP and CLEP credits are accepted.

Procedure: Freshmen are admitted fall and spring. Entrance exams should be taken in the junior year or early senior year. There are early admissions and deferred admissions plans. There is a rolling admissions plan. Application deadlines are open. Application fee is $40. Notification is sent on a rolling basis beginning October 1. 37 applicants were on the 2003 waiting list; 10 were admitted. Applications are accepted on-line through *www.potsdam.edu/admissions*.

Transfer: 363 transfer students enrolled in 2002-2003. Applicants must have earned 12 hours of college credit. Transfers with fewer than 24 credit hours must submit a high school transcript showing a minimum 2.0 GPA. An interview is recommended, as are supplemental recommendations. 45 credits of 124 to 128 required for the bachelor's degree must be completed at SUNY Potsdam.

Visiting: There are regularly scheduled orientations for prospective students, including a meeting with a counselor and faculty member, and a tour of campus with a student. There are guides for informal visits and visitors may sit in on classes and stay overnight. To schedule a visit, contact the Admissions Office at (877) POTSDAM or *admissions@potsdam.edu*.

Financial Aid: In 2003-2004, 92% of all full-time freshmen and 85% of continuing full-time students received some form of financial aid. 71% of full-time freshmen and 83% of continuing full-time students received need-based aid. The average freshman award was $10,140. Need-based scholarships or need-based grants averaged $4581 ($11,425 maximum); need-based self-help aid (loans and jobs) averaged $7532 ($14,965 maximum); and non-need-based awards and non-need-based scholarships averaged $2328 ($13,660 maximum). Average annual earnings from campus work are $1000. The average financial indebtedness of the 2003 graduate was $17,601. The FAFSA and the state aid form are required. The priority date for freshman financial aid applications for fall entry is January 1. The fall application deadline is rolling.

International Students: There are 113 international students enrolled. The school actively recruits these students. They must score 550 on the written TOEFL or 213 on the electronic version.

Computers: The mainframe is 1 DEC Alpha box (model 4100). About 350 Macs and PCs are networked and connected to all campus buildings and residence hall computer labs. Each has complete access to all networked services, including the Internet. All students may access the system 7 days a week, 24 hours per day. There are no time limits. There is a $125 per semester technology fee for all students.

Graduates: From July 1, 2002 to June 30, 2003, 641 bachelor's degrees were awarded. The most popular majors were psychology (16%), music education (12%), and English (12%). In an average class, 2% graduate in 3 years or less, 25% graduate in 4 years or less, 38% graduate in 5 years or less, and 47% graduate in 6 years or less. 48 companies recruited on campus in 2002-2003. Of the 2002 graduating class, 26% were enrolled in graduate school within 6 months of graduation and 59% were employed.

Admissions Contact: Thomas Nesbitt, Director of Admissions. E-mail: *admissions@potsdam.edu*

STATE UNIVERSITY OF NEW YORK/COLLEGE AT BROCKPORT

B-3

Brockport, NY 14420   (585) 395-2751; Fax: (585) 395-5452

Full-time: 2650 men, 3445 women	**Faculty:** 265; IIA, av$
Part-time: 352 men, 515 women	**Ph.D.s:** 91%
Graduate: 618 men, 1162 women	**Student/Faculty:** 23 to 1
Year: semesters, summer session	**Tuition:** $5221 ($11,171)
Application Deadline: open	**Room & Board:** $6890
Freshman Class: 7282 applied, 3790 accepted, 1046 enrolled	
SAT I Verbal/Math: 540/530	**ACT:** 22 **COMPETITIVE**

The State University of New York/College at Brockport, established in 1867, is a public institution offering undergraduate programs in liberal arts, sciences, business, and teacher preparation. There are 3 undergraduate and 3 graduate schools. In addition to regional accreditation, SUNY Brockport has baccalaureate program accreditation with AACSB, ABET, CSAB, CSWE, NLN, and NRPA. The library contains 610,156 volumes, 2,055,073 microform items, and 8853 audio/video tapes/CDs, and subscribes to 2015 periodicals. Computerized library services include the card catalog, interlibrary loans, database searching, and Internet access. Special learning facilities include a learning resource center, art gallery, planetarium, radio station, aquaculture ponds, weather information system, nuclear lab, high resolution germanium detector, research vessel on Lake Ontario, electron microscope, low-temperature lab, vacuum deposition lab, computational physics lab, 2 supercomputers, Doppler Radar system, ultramodern dance facilities including green room, hydrotherapy room, student learning center, academic computing center, and theater. The 435-acre campus is in a small town 16 miles west of Rochester. Including any residence halls, there are 66 buildings.

Student Life: 98% of undergraduates are from New York. Students are from 29 states, 25 foreign countries, and Canada. 90% are white. The average age of freshmen is 18; all undergraduates, 22. 20% do not continue beyond their first year; 80% remain to graduate.

Housing: 2458 students can be accommodated in college housing, which includes coed dorms. In addition, there are special-interest houses, special residence hall communities for first-year students, and international, 24-hour quiet, scholars/honors, and substance-free floors. On-campus housing is guaranteed for the freshman year only and is available on a first-come, first-served basis. 66% of students commute. All students may keep cars.

Activities: 2% of men belong to 6 national fraternities; 2% of women belong to 4 national sororities. There are 60 groups on campus, including art, business, cheerleading, chess, choir, chorus, computers, criminal justice, dance, drama, ethnic, film, gay, honors, international, jazz band, literary magazine, musical theater, newspaper, outdoors, photography, political, professional, radio and TV, religious, social, social service, and student government. Popular campus events include Health Week, Honors Convocation, and Scholar's Day.

Sports: There are 10 intercollegiate sports for men and 12 for women, and 20 intramural sports for men and 20 for women. Facilities include field hockey, baseball, and softball fields; a soccer pitch; a swimming pool; 6 gyms; a gymnastics area; wrestling and weight rooms; handball, squash, tennis and racquetball courts; an ice arena; and a Special Olympics stadium with a football field and track.

Disabled Students: 95% of the campus is accessible. Wheelchair ramps, elevators, special parking, specially equipped rest rooms, special class scheduling, lowered drinking fountains, lowered telephones, and special classroom accommodations are available.

Services: Counseling and information services are available, as is tutoring in some subjects, which vary from semester to semester. There is remedial math and writing. Study skills support is available to all students.

Campus Safety and Security: Measures include 24-hour foot and vehicle patrol, security escort services, shuttle buses, and informal discussions. There are pamphlets/posters/films, emergency telephones, lighted pathways/sidewalks, a community policing program, bicycle patrols, and 24-hour locked residence halls.

Programs of Study: SUNY Brockport confers B.A., B.S., B.F.A., and B.S.N. degrees. Master's degrees are also awarded. Bachelor's degrees are awarded in AGRICULTURE (environmental studies), BIOLOGICAL SCIENCE (biology/biological science), BUSINESS (accounting, business administration and management, international business management, and recreation and leisure services), COMMUNICATIONS AND THE ARTS (communications, dance, dramatic arts, English, French, journalism, Spanish, and studio art), COMPUTER AND PHYSICAL SCIENCE (actuarial science, atmospheric sciences and meteorology, chemistry, computer science, earth science, geology, information sciences and systems, mathematics, and physics), EDUCATION (physical), ENGINEERING AND ENVIRONMENTAL DESIGN (computational sciences, and environmental science), HEALTH PROFESSIONS (health science, medical technology, and nursing), SOCIAL SCIENCE (African American studies, African studies, anthropology, criminal justice, history, interdisciplinary studies, international studies, philosophy, political science/government, psychology, social work, sociology, water resources, and women's studies). Biological sciences, meteorology, and computer science are the strongest academically. Physical education, business administration, and psychology are the largest.

Required: To graduate, students must complete a minimum of 120 credits, including 30 or more credits in the major, with a 2.0 GPA. The core curriculum includes the SUNY-wide General Education Requirements (one course each in math, natural sciences, social sciences, American History, Western Civilization, World (Non-Western) Civilization, humanities, the arts, foreign language, and basic communication). All students must take courses in contemporary issues, diversity, and perspectives on women, and pass the appropriate competency exams. An academic planning seminar is required of entering freshmen.

Special: Co-op programs, internships in most majors, and work-study programs in education are available. Brockport offers cross-registration with Rochester area colleges, a Washington semester, study abroad in 23 countries, accelerated degree programs, and an interdisciplinary major in arts for children, emphasizing art, dance, music, and theater. Credit for military and work experience, nondegree study, and pass/fail grading options are available. An alternative general education program, Delta College, is an interdisciplinary program that emphasizes global issues and provides opportunities for work or study in other countries, as well as locally, regionally, and nationally. There are 21 national honor societies, a freshman honors program, and 3 departmental honors programs.

Faculty/Classroom: 57% of faculty are male; 43%, female. 90% teach undergraduates. No introductory courses are taught by graduate students. The average class size in an introductory lecture is 25; in a laboratory, 18; and in a regular course, 22.

Admissions: 52% of the 2003-2004 applicants were accepted. The SAT I scores for the 2003-2004 freshman class were: Verbal--26% below 500, 54% between 500 and 599, 18% between 600 and 700, and 2% above 700; Math--32% below 500, 52% between 500 and 599, 15% between 600 and 700, and 1% above 700. The ACT scores were 28% below 21, 37% between 21 and 23, 27% between 24 and 26, 4% between 27 and 28, and 4% above 28. 14% of the current freshmen were in the top fifth of their class; 24% were in the top two fifths. 4 freshmen graduated first in their class.

Requirements: The SAT I or ACT is required. In addition, SUNY Brockport seeks students who have demonstrated academic success and who show persistence. Applicants must have a high school diploma (preferably from the New York State Regents Program) or have completed a minimum of 18 academic units: 4 each in English and social studies, 4 in academic electives, 3 each in math and science (1 with lab). An essay and letters of recommendation are encouraged. An audition is required for dance and theater applicants. SUNY Brockport requires applicants to be in the upper 50% of their class. A grade average of 80 is required. AP and CLEP credits are accepted. Important factors in the admissions decision are advanced placement or honor courses, leadership record, and extracurricular activities record.

Procedure: Freshmen are admitted fall and spring. Entrance exams should be taken during the spring of the junior year and fall of the senior year. There are early admissions and deferred admissions plans. There is a rolling admissions plan. Application deadlines are open. Application fee is $40. Applications are accepted on-line through SUNY Online Direct, EXPAN, and other services.

Transfer: 936 transfer students enrolled in 2002-2003. The applicant must have a minimum GPA of 2.25. Many departments specify prerequisite courses and a higher GPA. SUNY Brockport recommends that transfer applicants have an associate degree or 54 credit hours, with preference given to degree holders. 30 of 120 credits required for the bachelor's degree must be completed at SUNY Brockport.

Visiting: There are regularly scheduled orientations for prospective students, including daily admissions information presentations and campus tours. Visits may be arranged on selected Saturdays and holidays. There are guides for informal visits and visitors may sit in on classes and stay overnight. To schedule a visit, contact the Office of Undergraduate Admissions at *admit@brockport.edu.*

Financial Aid: In 2003-2004, 86% of all full-time freshmen and 84% of continuing full-time students received some form of financial aid. 71% of full-time freshmen and 72% of continuing full-time students received need-based aid. The average freshman award was $7517. Need-based scholarships or need-based grants averaged $2727 ($11,429 maximum); need-based self-help aid (loans and jobs) averaged $2185 ($5500 maximum); and non-need-based awards and non-need-based scholarships averaged $4686 ($17,900 maximum). 71% of undergraduates work part time. Average annual earnings from campus work are $1135. The average financial indebtedness of the 2003 graduate was $17,631. The FAFSA is required. The deadline for filing freshman financial aid applications for fall entry is February 15.

International Students: There are 66 international students enrolled. The school actively recruits these students. They must score 530 on the written TOEFL or take the MELAB. They must also take the SAT I or the ACT.

Computers: The mainframes are a Sun E4500 and Sun 880. More than 500 networked PCs, Macs, and Suns are available for student use in 20 labs distributed throughout the campus. All are connected to the Internet and World Wide Web and include wiring in residence halls. All students may access the system 24 hours per day. There are no time limits. The fee is $222 per year.

Graduates: From July 1, 2002 to June 30, 2003, 1532 bachelor's degrees were awarded. The most popular majors were physical education (12%), business administration (11%), and psychology (9%). In an average class, 1% graduate in 3 years or less, 24% graduate in 4 years or less, 45% graduate in 5 years or less, and 50% graduate in 6 years or less. Of the 2002 graduating class, 7% were enrolled in graduate school within 6 months of graduation and 69% were employed.

Admissions Contact: Bernard S. Valento, Director of Undergraduate Admissions. E-mail: *admit@brockport.edu* Web: *www.brockport.edu*

STATE UNIVERSITY OF NEW YORK/COLLEGE AT BUFFALO
A-3

Buffalo, NY 14222

(716) 878-4017; Fax: (716) 878-6100

Full-time: 3025 men, 4825 women	**Faculty:** 410; IIA, -$
Part-time: 845 men, 900 women	**Ph.D.s:** 89%
Graduate: 635 men, 1520 women	**Student/Faculty:** 19 to 1
Year: semesters, summer session	**Tuition:** $4030 ($8930)
Application Deadline: open	**Room & Board:** $4000
Freshman Class: n/av	
SAT I: required	**COMPETITIVE**

The State University of New York/College at Buffalo, established in 1867, is a public institution conferring undergraduate liberal arts degrees. Figures in the above capsule and in this profile are approximate. In addition to regional accreditation, Buffalo State College has baccalaureate program accreditation with ABET, ADA, ASLA, CSWE, and NCATE. The library contains 470,176 volumes, 910,297 microform items, and 10,863 audio/video tapes/CDs, and subscribes to 2948 periodicals. Computerized library services include the card catalog, interlibrary loans, and database searching. Special learning facilities include a learning resource center, art gallery, planetarium, radio station, speech, language, and hearing clinic, and a center for performing arts. The 115-acre campus is in an urban area in Buffalo. Including any residence halls, there are 36 buildings.

Student Life: 99% of undergraduates are from New York. Students are from 25 states, 28 foreign countries, and Canada. 85% are from public schools. 82% are white; 11% African American. The average age of freshmen is 18; all undergraduates, 24. 23% do not continue beyond their first year; 40% remain to graduate.

Housing: 2086 students can be accommodated in college housing, which includes coed dorms and on-campus apartments. There is also an international student dorm. On-campus housing is available on a first-come, first-served basis. 84% of students commute. Alcohol is not permitted. All students may keep cars.

Activities: There are 1 local and 9 national fraternities and 3 local and 7 national sororities. There are 75 groups on campus, including art, cheerleading, chess, choir, chorus, computers, dance, drama, ethnic, gay, honors, international, jazz band, literary magazine, musical theater, newspaper, orchestra, political, professional, radio and TV, religious, social, social service, student government, and yearbook. Popular campus events include Commuter Daze, The Gathering, and Welcome Back Week.

Sports: There are 8 intercollegiate sports for men and 10 for women, and 5 intramural sports for men and 3 for women. Facilities include a gym, a natatorium, a basketball/volleyball arena, an ice rink, a game field for football, soccer, and lacrosse, a six-lane track, and a softball diamond.

Disabled Students: 93% of the campus is accessible. Wheelchair ramps, elevators, special parking, specially equipped rest rooms, special class scheduling, lowered drinking fountains, lowered telephones, and special dorm accommodations are available.

Services: Counseling and information services are available, as is tutoring in every subject. There is a reader service for the blind and remedial math, reading, and writing. Tutors for visually impaired and hearing-impaired students are also available.

Campus Safety and Security: Measures include 24-hour foot and vehicle patrol, self-defense education, security escort services, and shuttle buses. There are informal discussions, pamphlets/posters/films, emergency telephones, lighted pathways/sidewalks, and community policing.

Programs of Study: Buffalo State College confers B.A., B.S., B.F.A., B.S.Ed., and B.T. degrees. Master's degrees are also awarded. Bachelor's degrees are awarded in BIOLOGICAL SCIENCE (biology/biological science), BUSINESS (business administration and management and hospitality management services), COMMUNICATIONS AND THE ARTS (art, art history and appreciation, broadcasting, communications, design, dramatic arts, English, fine arts, French, Italian, journalism, music, painting, photography, printmaking, sculpture, and Spanish), COMPUTER AND PHYSICAL SCIENCE (chemistry, earth science, geology, information sciences and systems, mathematics, and physics), EDUCATION (art, business, elementary, foreign languages, industrial arts, science, secondary, and special), ENGINEERING AND ENVIRONMENTAL DESIGN (electrical/electronics engineering technology, industrial engineering technology, and mechanical engineering technology), HEALTH PROFESSIONS (health and speech pathology/audiology), SOCIAL SCIENCE (anthropology, criminal justice, dietetics, economics, geography, history, humanities, philosophy, political science/government, psychology, social work, sociology, and urban studies). Elementary education and exceptional education are the strongest academically. Elementary education, psychology, and business studies are the largest.

Required: To graduate, students must complete a 60-hour general education requirement consisting of 42 core credits in applied science and education, arts, humanities, math and science, and social science, and 18 hours of electives. Students must earn 123 credits with a minimum GPA of 2.0. The number of hours in the major varies.

Special: Students may cross-register with the Western New York Consortium and exchange with 160 campus members of the National Student Exchange. Internships, Washington and Albany semesters, study abroad in 5 countries, dual majors, and a general studies degree are offered. Students may earn 3-2 engineeing degrees in association with the State University of New York centers at Buffalo and Binghamton, and Clarkson University. There is a cooperative program with the Fashion Institute of Technology. Credit for life, military, and work experience, non-degree study, and pass/fail grading options are available. There is a chapter of Phi Beta Kappa and a freshman honors program.

Faculty/Classroom: 59% of faculty are male; 41%, female. All teach undergraduates. The average class size in an introductory lecture is 34; in a laboratory, 12; and in a regular course, 18.

Requirements: The SAT I is required. In addition, students must graduate from an accredited secondary school or have a GED. They must complete 4 years of English, 3 years each of math, science, and social studies, and 2 years of a foreign language. A portfolio is required for fine arts applicants. A grade average of 85 is required. AP and CLEP credits are accepted. Important factors in the admissions decision are advanced placement or honor courses, evidence of special talent, and recommendations by school officials.

Procedure: Freshmen are admitted to all sessions. Entrance exams should be taken during the junior or senior years. There are early decision, early admissions, deferred admissions, and rolling admissions plans. Check with the school for current application deadlines. The fall 2003 application fee was $30. A waiting list is an active part of the admissions procedure.

Transfer: 1047 transfer students enrolled in a recent year. Transfer applicants must have a minimum GPA of 2.0. An associate degree is recommended, and a minimum of 15 credit hours must have been earned. 32 of 123 credits required for the bachelor's degree must be completed at Buffalo State College.

Visiting: There are regularly scheduled orientations for prospective students. There are guides for informal visits and visitors may sit in on classes. To schedule a visit, contact the Admissions Office.

Financial Aid: The FAFSA and TAP form are required. Check with the school for current deadlines.

International Students: There were 61 international students enrolled in a recent year. The school actively recruits these students. They must score 500 on the written TOEFL.

Computers: The mainframes are an AXP-7600, OPEN VMS AXP Version 6.1. Students have access to the mainframe and the Internet through the campus local area network. Approximately 750 computers are available at various campus sites including the library, classrooms, Computing Services' general access computing facilities, and departmental computer labs. All students may access the system during site hours. Dial-in access is available 24 hours per day. There are no time limits and no fees.

Graduates: In a recent year, 1640 bachelor's degrees were awarded. The most popular majors were elementary education (11%), business studies (10%), and social work (6%). In an average class, 1% graduate in 3 years or less, 14% graduate in 4 years or less, 34% graduate in 5 years or less, and 40% graduate in 6 years or less. 100 companies recruited on campus in a recent year. Of a recent graduating class, 26% were enrolled in graduate school within 6 months of graduation and 85% were employed.

Admissions Contact: Lesa Loritts, Admissions Director.
E-mail: *admissio@buffalostate.edu* Web: *www.buffalostate.edu*

STATE UNIVERSITY OF NEW YORK/COLLEGE AT CORTLAND
C-3

Cortland, NY 13045

(607) 753-4711; Fax: (607) 753-5998

Full-time: 2293 men, 3211 women	**Faculty:** 266; IIA, -$
Part-time: 122 men, 161 women	**Ph.D.s:** 84%
Graduate: 479 men, 1062 women	**Student/Faculty:** 21 to 1
Year: semesters, summer session	**Tuition:** $5235 ($11,185)
Application Deadline: open	**Room & Board:** $6860
Freshman Class: 9237 applied, 4525 accepted, 1138 enrolled	
SAT I Verbal/Math: 530/550	**ACT:** 24 **COMPETITIVE**

The State University of New York/College at Cortland, founded in 1868, is a public institution offering academic programs leading to baccalaureate and master's degrees in liberal arts and professional studies. There are 3 undergraduate and 3 graduate schools. In addition to regional accreditation, SUNY Cortland has baccalaureate program accreditation with CAHEA and NRPA. The library contains 400,000 volumes, 750,000 microform items, and 5000 audio/video tapes/CDs, and subscribes to 3000 periodicals. Computerized library services include the card catalog, interlibrary loans, and database searching. Special learning facilities include a learning resource center, art gallery, natural history museum, planetarium, radio station, TV station, a natural science museum, a greenhouse, a center for speech and hearing disorders, classrooms equipped with integrated technologies (multimedia enhanced instruction), and many specialized labs to support various program offerings. The 191-acre campus is in a small town 18 miles north of Ithaca and 29 miles south of Syracuse. Including any residence halls, there are 37 buildings.

Student Life: 98% of undergraduates are from New York. Others are from 8 states and 2 foreign countries. 91% are from public schools. 89% are white. The average age of freshmen is 18; all undergraduates, 21. 26% do not continue beyond their first year; 53% remain to graduate.

Housing: 2775 students can be accommodated in college housing, which includes coed dorms, off-campus apartments, fraternity houses, and sorority houses. In addition, there are special-interest houses, a wellness floor in a residence hall, a computer residence hall, quiet residence halls, a residence for Americans majoring in international studies and/or studying abroad, a hall for students 21 years or older, and a leadership house. 55% of students live on campus. All students may keep cars.

Activities: 4% of men belong to 1 national fraternity; 9% of women belong to 1 local and 4 national sororities. There are 100 groups on campus, including art, band, cheerleading, chess, choir, chorale, chorus, computers, dance, drama, ethnic, film, gay, honors, international, jazz band, literary magazine, musical theater, newspaper, orchestra, political, professional, radio and TV, religious, social, social service, student government, symphony, and yearbook. Popular campus events include annual Cortland-Ithaca College football game, Winterfest, and Multicultural Festival.

Sports: There are 11 intercollegiate sports for men and 14 for women, and 55 intramural sports for men and 55 for women. Facilities include an outdoor multipurpose 8000-seat stadium complex, an Olympic-size pool, a 3600-seat gym, an ice arena, a gymnastics arena, wrestling and weight rooms, a dance studio, handball/racquetball courts, squash courts, an athletic training facility, fitness centers, a free-swimming pool, a track, a baseball field, a football/lacrosse/track field seating 4000, a lighted soccer field, a field house, and 50 acres of athletic fields.

Disabled Students: 75% of the campus is accessible. Wheelchair ramps, elevators, special parking, specially equipped rest rooms, special class scheduling, lowered drinking fountains, and lowered telephones are available.

Services: Counseling and information services are available, as is tutoring in some subjects. There is a reader service for the blind. There is a fully staffed Academic Support and Achievement Program for writing, math, study skills, and learning strategies. Specific course tutoring is available with peer tutors.

Campus Safety and Security: Measures include 24-hour foot and vehicle patrol, self-defense education, security escort services, and shuttle buses. There are informal discussions, pamphlets/posters/films, emergency telephones, and lighted pathways/sidewalks. State University police maintain a web site with safety information and links. University police also have a Silent Witness program for reporting crimes anonymously.

Programs of Study: SUNY Cortland confers B.A., B.S., and B.S.E. degrees. Master's degrees are also awarded. Bachelor's degrees are awarded in BIOLOGICAL SCIENCE (biology/biological science), BUSINESS (management science), COMMUNICATIONS AND THE ARTS (art, communications, English, and film arts), COMPUTER AND PHYSICAL SCIENCE (chemistry, geochemistry, geology, geophysics and seismology, mathematics, and physics), EDUCATION (athletic training, foreign languages, health, middle school, physical, recreation, and secondary), ENGINEERING AND ENVIRONMENTAL DESIGN (environmental science), HEALTH PROFESSIONS (health science and speech pathology/audiology), SOCIAL SCIENCE (African American studies, anthropology, economics, geography, history, human services, international studies, philosophy, political science/government, psychology, and sociology). Biology, political science, and speech pathology/audiology are the strongest academically. Elementary education, phys ed, and communication studies are the largest.

Required: To graduate, undergraduates must complete 6 hours in English Composition, and at least 6 hours of writing-intensive courses, with 3 of those in the major. 1 course meeting the Quantitative Skills criteria must also be passed; 28 to 29 hours of courses in the General Education program must also be completed, with no more than 2 courses taken in any 1 of the 8 disciplines in the program. A major of 30 to 36 hours, with no more than 45 credits in discipline-specific courses must be completed. Completion of 90 credits of Liberal Arts and Science courses toward a B.A., 60 credits toward a B.S.E., or 75 credits toward a B.S. is required. A 2.0 GPA, both overall and in all minors and concentrations, must be maintained. Special requirements may be designated by each school of the College.

Special: Cortland offers cross-registration with Tompkins Cortland Community College and has cooperative programs with the State University of New York/College of Environmental Science and Forestry, and Centers at Binghamton and Buffalo, and Cornell and Case Western Reserve Universities. Students may study abroad in 11 countries, and they may enroll in a Washington semester. Work-study programs are available. The college confers an individualized studies degree and allows dual majors. Students may pursue a 3-2 engineering degree in conjunction with Alfred, Case Western Reserve, and Clarkson Universities, and the State University of New York Centers at Binghamton, Buffalo, and Stony Brook. Cortland offers nondegree study opportunities. There are 15 national honor societies, including Phi Beta Kappa, a freshman honors program, and 3 departmental honors programs.

Faculty/Classroom: 53% of faculty are male; 48%, female. All teach undergraduates and 15% also do research. No introductory courses are taught by graduate students. The average class size in an introductory lecture is 38; in a laboratory, 26; and in a regular course, 22.

Admissions: 49% of the 2003-2004 applicants were accepted. The ACT scores for the 2003-2004 freshman class were: 10% below 21, 44% between 21 and 23, 33% between 24 and 26, 8% between 27 and 28, and 5% above 28.

Requirements: The SAT I or ACT is required. In addition, applicants must graduate from an accredited secondary school or have a GED. They must have earned 16 Carnegie units and 16 to 20 academic credits, including 4 units each in English and history or social studies and 2 (3 units preferred) each in math and science; the other 4 units must be taken in areas listed above or in a foreign language. Essays and recommendations are required, and in some cases auditions as well. Interviews are strongly recommended. AP and CLEP credits are accepted. Important factors in the admissions decision are advanced placement or honor courses, extracurricular activities record, and recommendations by school officials.

Procedure: Freshmen are admitted fall and spring. Entrance exams should be taken during the spring of the junior year or fall of the senior year. There are early decision, early admissions, and deferred admissions plans. Early decision applications should be filed by November 15; regular application deadlines are open for fall and spring entry. The fee is $40. Notification of early decision is sent December 15; regular decision, on a rolling basis. There is a rolling admissions plan. 81 early decision candidates were accepted for the 2003-2004 class. Applications are accepted on-line through the State University of New York Common Application Center.

Transfer: 650 transfer students enrolled in a recent year. Applicants must have a minimum GPA of 2.5. Some programs are more competitive. Interviews are encouraged. 45 credits of 124 to 128 required for the bachelor's degree must be completed at SUNY Cortland.

Visiting: There are regularly scheduled orientations for prospective students, consisting of Autumn Preview Days for prospective students as well as a Spring Open House for accepted students. There are guides for informal visits and visitors may sit in on classes. To schedule a visit, contact the Admissions Appointment Secretary.

Financial Aid: In 2003-2004, 61% of all full-time freshmen and 60% of continuing full-time students received some form of financial aid. 56% of full-time freshmen and 54% of continuing full-time students received need-based aid. The average freshman award was $6977. The FAFSA and NYS TAP application are required. The deadline for filing freshman financial aid applications for fall entry is April 1.

International Students: There are 29 international students enrolled. The school actively recruits these students. They must score 550 on the written TOEFL and also take the SAT I. A General Certificate of Education is acceptable in lieu of the TOEFL.

Computers: The mainframes are a Compaq ES 45 and multiple servers. There are also 900 PCs available throughout the campus in 40 student-use labs. There are network connections in all residence hall rooms. All students may access the system 24 hours per day in some labs connected to the campus network. There are no time limits and no fees.

Graduates: From July 1, 2002 to June 30, 2003, 1317 bachelor's degrees were awarded. The most popular majors were health science (31%), education (28%), and social science (16%). In an average class, 30% graduate in 4 years or less, 50% graduate in 5 years or less, and 53% graduate in 6 years or less.

Admissions Contact: Gradin Avery, Director of Admissions. A video is available. E-mail: *admissions@cortland.edu*
Web: *www.cortland.edu/adm.html*

STATE UNIVERSITY OF NEW YORK/COLLEGE AT FREDONIA

A-4

Fredonia, NY 14063

(716) 673-3251
(800) 252-1212; Fax: (716) 673-3249

Full-time: 1932 men, 2718 women	**Faculty:** 253; IIA, av$
Part-time: 75 men, 127 women	**Ph.D.s:** 83%
Graduate: 105 men, 303 women	**Student/Faculty:** 18 to 1
Year: semesters, summer session	**Tuition:** $5362 ($11,312)
Application Deadline: open	**Room & Board:** $6200
Freshman Class: 5961 applied, 3378 accepted, 1089 enrolled	
SAT I Verbal/Math: 550/560	**ACT:** 24 **VERY COMPETITIVE**

The State University of New York at Fredonia, established in 1826, is a public institution offering undergraduate programs in the arts and sciences, business and professional curricula, teacher preparation, and the fine and performing arts. There are 6 undergraduate schools and 1 graduate school. In addition to regional accreditation, Fredonia has baccalaureate program accreditation with NASAD and NASM. The library contains 391,121 volumes, 1,060,631 microform items, and 26,574 audio/video tapes/CDs, and subscribes to 1983 periodicals. Computerized library services include the card catalog, interlibrary loans, and database searching. Special learning facilities include a learning resource center, art gallery, radio station, TV station, a greenhouse, a day-care center, a speech clinic, and an arts center. The 266-acre campus is in a small town 50 miles south of Buffalo and 45 miles north of Erie, Pennsylvania. Including any residence halls, there are 25 buildings.

Student Life: 97% of undergraduates are from New York. Others are from 25 states, 15 foreign countries, and Canada. 65% are from public schools. 94% are white. The average age of freshmen is 19; all undergraduates, 21. 19% do not continue beyond their first year; 61% remain to graduate.

Housing: 2621 students can be accommodated in college housing, which includes single-sex and coed dorms and on-campus apartments. Living space for fraternities and sororities is available in residence halls. In addition, there are special-interest houses for computer and athletics students and quiet-hour centers. On-campus housing is guaranteed for

all 4 years. 50% of students live on campus; of those, 80% remain on campus on weekends. All students may keep cars.

Activities: 7% of men belong to 4 national fraternities; 4% of women belong to 3 national sororities. There are 120 groups on campus, including art, band, cheerleading, choir, chorale, chorus, computers, dance, drama, drill team, ethnic, gay, honors, international, jazz band, literary magazine, musical theater, newspaper, opera, orchestra, pep band, photography, political, professional, radio and TV, religious, ski, social, social service, student government, symphony, and yearbook. Popular campus events include various Art Center presentations, Spring Fest, and Little Siblings Weekend.

Sports: There are 8 intercollegiate sports for men and 9 for women, and 8 intramural sports for men and 8 for women. Facilities include a basketball arena, an ice rink, a swimming pool, a gym, a weight room, dance studios, soccer fields, indoor and outdoor tracks, and racquetball, tennis, and volleyball courts.

Disabled Students: 85% of the campus is accessible. Wheelchair ramps, elevators, special parking, specially equipped rest rooms, special class scheduling, lowered drinking fountains, and lowered telephones are available.

Services: Counseling and information services are available, as is tutoring in most subjects. There is a reader service for the blind.

Campus Safety and Security: Measures include 24-hour foot and vehicle patrol, security escort services, shuttle buses, and informal discussions. There are pamphlets/posters/films, emergency telephones, lighted pathways/sidewalks, and card swipe access to residence halls.

Programs of Study: Fredonia confers B.A., B.S., B.F.A., B.S.Ed., and Mus.B. degrees. Master's degrees are also awarded. Bachelor's degrees are awarded in BIOLOGICAL SCIENCE (biochemistry and biology/biological science), BUSINESS (accounting, business administration and management, and business economics), COMMUNICATIONS AND THE ARTS (audio technology, communications, dramatic arts, English, fine arts, French, graphic design, media arts, music, and Spanish), COMPUTER AND PHYSICAL SCIENCE (chemistry, computer science, earth science, geology, mathematics, and physics), EDUCATION (early childhood, elementary, foreign languages, middle school, music, science, and secondary), HEALTH PROFESSIONS (health care administration, medical laboratory technology, predentistry, premedicine, and speech pathology/audiology), SOCIAL SCIENCE (history, interdisciplinary studies, philosophy, political science/government, psychology, social work, and sociology). Business, communication, and education are the largest.

Required: To graduate, students must complete 120 hours, including 36 to 90 or more in the major, with a 2.0 GPA. Students must take specific courses in English and math and complete 36 hours of general education courses, including writing, statistical/quantitative abilities, oral communication, natural and social sciences, humanities, and arts.

Special: Cooperative programs are available with many other institutions. Students may cross-register with colleges in the Western New York Consortium. Fredonia offers a variety of internships, study-abroad programs in more than 50 countries, and a Washington semester. Accelerated degrees, a general studies degree, dual and student-designed majors, a 3-2 engineering degree program with 14 universities, nondegree study, and pass/fail grading options are available. There are 19 national honor societies, a freshman honors program, and 19 departmental honors programs.

Faculty/Classroom: 57% of faculty are male; 43%, female. All both teach and do research. No introductory courses are taught by graduate students. The average class size in an introductory lecture is 26; in a laboratory, 16; and in a regular course, 20.

Admissions: 57% of the 2003-2004 applicants were accepted. The SAT I scores for the 2003-2004 freshman class were: Verbal--13% below 500, 63% between 500 and 599, 23% between 600 and 700, and 1% above 700; Math--11% below 500, 65% between 500 and 599, 23% between 600 and 700, and 1% above 700. The ACT scores were 4% below 21, 36% between 21 and 23, 42% between 24 and 26, 10% between 27 and 28, and 8% above 28. 34% of the current freshmen were in the top fifth of their class; 76% were in the top two fifths. 10 freshmen graduated first in their class.

Requirements: The SAT I or ACT is required, with a minimum composite score of 950 on the SAT I or 20 on the ACT. Applicants must possess a high school diploma or have a GED. 16 academic credits are recommended, including 4 credits each in English and social studies and 3 each in math, science, and a foreign language. 4 years of math and science are encouraged. Essays are recommended, and, where applicable, an audition or portfolio is required. A GPA of 2.5 is required. AP and CLEP credits are accepted. Important factors in the admissions decision are advanced placement or honor courses, evidence of special talents, and recommendations by school officials.

Procedure: Freshmen are admitted fall and spring. Entrance exams should be taken during the spring of the junior year or fall of the senior year. There are early decision, early admissions, and deferred admissions plans. Early decision applications should be filed by November 1; regular applications deadlines are open for fall entry. There is a $40 fee. There is a rolling admissions plan. Notification of early decision is sent

November 25; regular decision, on a rolling basis after December 15. 52 early decision candidates were accepted for the 2003-2004 class. Applications are accepted on-line through the school's web site.

Transfer: 556 transfer students enrolled in 2002-2003. Applicants should have a minimum GPA of 2.0., and appropriate academic course work to be considered. An interview is recommended. 45 credits of 120 required for the bachelor's degree must be completed at Fredonia.

Visiting: There are regularly scheduled orientations for prospective students, including various open house programs and information sessions and tours Monday through Friday, morning and afternoon, and Saturday tours once a month. Visitors may sit in on classes and stay overnight. To schedule a visit, contact the Office of Admissions at (800) 252-1212 or *admissions.office@fredonia.edu*.

Financial Aid: In 2003-2004, 80% of all full-time freshmen and 77% of continuing full-time students received some form of financial aid. 62% of full-time freshmen and 61% of continuing full-time students received need-based aid. The average freshman award was $5935. 20% of undergraduates work part time. Average annual earnings from campus work are $1369. The average financial indebtedness of the 2003 graduate was $12,430. The FAFSA, the state aid form, and Express TAP Application (ETA) are required. The priority date for freshman financial aid applications for fall entry is February 1.

International Students: There are 42 international students enrolled. The school actively recruits these students. They must score 500 on the written TOEFL or 175 on the electronic version.

Computers: The mainframes are DEC Alpha 4100 servers. PCs for student use are located in the computer center, all academic buildings, and various residence halls. There is Ethernet access in all student residence hall rooms and more than 500 terminals for student use. All students may access the system. There are no time limits and no fees. It is strongly recommended that all students have a personal computer.

Graduates: From July 1, 2002 to June 30, 2003, 1012 bachelor's degrees were awarded. The most popular majors were elementary education (20%), business administration (8%), and psychology (6%). In an average class, 43% graduate in 4 years or less, 55% graduate in 5 years or less, and 57% graduate in 6 years or less. 55 companies recruited on campus in 2002-2003. Of the 2002 graduating class, 29% were enrolled in graduate school within 6 months of graduation and 88% were employed.

Admissions Contact: Daniel Tramuta, Director of Admissions. E-mail: *admissions.office@fredonia.edu* Web: *fredonia.edu*

STATE UNIVERSITY OF NEW YORK/COLLEGE AT GENESEO
B-3

Geneseo, NY 14454

(585) 245-5571
(866) 245-5211; Fax: (585) 245-5550

Full-time: 1939 men, 3262 women	Faculty: 246; IIA, -$
Part-time: 37 men, 69 women	Ph.D.s: 85%
Graduate: 39 men, 204 women	Student/Faculty: 21 to 1
Year: semesters, summer session	Tuition: $5390 ($11,340)
Application Deadline: January 15	Room & Board: $5940
Freshman Class: 8783 applied, 3684 accepted, 988 enrolled	
SAT I Verbal/Math: 621/631	ACT: 27 HIGHLY COMPETITIVE

The State University of New York/College at Geneseo, founded in 1871, is a public institution offering liberal arts, business, and accounting programs, teaching certification, and training in communicative disorders and sciences. In addition to regional accreditation, Geneseo has baccalaureate program accreditation with ASLA. The library contains 529,796 volumes, 819,790 microform items, and 5633 audio/video tapes/CDs, and subscribes to 1769 periodicals. Computerized library services include the card catalog, interlibrary loans, and database searching. Special learning facilities include a learning resource center, art gallery, planetarium, radio station, TV station, and 3 theaters. The 220-acre campus is in a small town 30 miles south of Rochester. Including any residence halls, there are 40 buildings.

Student Life: 96% of undergraduates are from New York. Students are from 20 states, 47 foreign countries, and Canada. 81% are from public schools. 88% are white. 44% are Catholic; 28% Protestant; 21% claim no religious affiliation. The average age of freshmen is 18; all undergraduates, 20. 8% do not continue beyond their first year; 77% remain to graduate.

Housing: 3168 students can be accommodated in college housing, which includes coed dorms. In addition, there are special-interest houses, including science and math houses. On-campus housing is guaranteed for the freshman year only and is available on a first-come, first-served basis. 54% of students live on campus. All students may keep cars.

Activities: 10% of men belong to 7 local and 2 national fraternities; 15% of women belong to 7 local and 6 national sororities. There are 154 groups on campus, including art, band, cheerleading, choir, chorale, chorus, computers, dance, drama, ethnic, gay, honors, international, jazz band, literary magazine, musical theater, newspaper, orchestra, political, professional, radio and TV, religious, social, social service, student gov-

ernment, symphony, and yearbook. Popular campus events include Siblings Weekend, Parents Weekend, and Spring Weekend.

Sports: There are 8 intercollegiate sports for men and 11 for women, and 24 intramural sports for men and 24 for women. Facilities include an ice arena, 2 swimming pools, 3 gyms, 8 squash and 8 tennis courts, an indoor jogging area, Nautilus and weight rooms, a sauna, an outdoor track, and several playing fields. The largest auditorium/arena seats 3000.

Disabled Students: 90% of the campus is accessible. Wheelchair ramps, elevators, special parking, specially equipped rest rooms, special class scheduling, lowered drinking fountains, lowered telephones, and fire alarms for hearing-impaired students are available.

Services: Counseling and information services are available, as is tutoring in every subject. There is a reader service for the blind and remedial math and writing.

Campus Safety and Security: Measures include 24-hour foot and vehicle patrol, self-defense education, security escort services, and informal discussions. There are pamphlets/posters/films, emergency telephones, and lighted pathways/sidewalks.

Programs of Study: Geneseo confers B.A., B.S., and B.S.Ed. degrees. Master's degrees are also awarded. Bachelor's degrees are awarded in BIOLOGICAL SCIENCE (biochemistry, biology/biological science, and biophysics), BUSINESS (accounting and business administration and management), COMMUNICATIONS AND THE ARTS (art history and appreciation, communications, comparative literature, dramatic arts, English, French, music, performing arts, Spanish, and studio art), COMPUTER AND PHYSICAL SCIENCE (applied physics, chemistry, computer science, geochemistry, geology, geophysics and seismology, mathematics, natural sciences, and physics), EDUCATION (elementary and special), HEALTH PROFESSIONS (speech pathology/audiology), SOCIAL SCIENCE (African American studies, American studies, anthropology, economics, geography, history, international relations, philosophy, political science/government, psychology, and sociology). Special education, business administration, and biology are the largest.

Required: To graduate, students must complete 120 credit hours with a minimum 2.0 GPA. The total number of hours in the major varies. The required core curriculum includes 2 courses each in humanities, fine arts, social sciences, and natural sciences, and 1 course each in non-Western tradition, critical writing, and reading.

Special: The college offers a cooperative 3-2 engineering degree with Alfred, Case Western Reserve, Clarkson, Columbia, Penn State, and Syracuse Universities, SUNY at Binghamton and Buffalo, and the University of Rochester, as well as a 3-3 degree with Rochester Institute of Technology. There is also a 3-2 MBA degree offered with Pace, SUNY/Buffalo, or Syracuse; a 4-1 MBA with Alfred, Clarkson, RIT, or Union; and 3-4 degrees with SUNY/Buffalo for Dentistry, SUNY College of Optometry, and NYS College of Osteopathic Medicine. Cross-registration is available with the Rochester Area Colleges Consortium. Geneseo offers internships in all majors, study abroad through more than 95 programs, a Washington semester, dual majors, including theater/English, credit for military experience, and pass/fail options. There are 13 national honor societies, including Phi Beta Kappa, a freshman honors program, and 15 departmental honors programs.

Faculty/Classroom: 56% of faculty are male; 44%, female. All teach undergraduates. No introductory courses are taught by graduate students. The average class size in an introductory lecture is 40; in a laboratory, 18; and in a regular course, 24.

Admissions: 42% of the 2003-2004 applicants were accepted. The SAT I scores for the 2003-2004 freshman class were: Verbal--3% below 500, 27% between 500 and 599, 58% between 600 and 700, and 12% above 700; Math--1% below 500, 22% between 500 and 599, 68% between 600 and 700, and 9% above 700. The ACT scores were 2% below 21, 4% between 21 and 23, 37% between 24 and 26, 33% between 27 and 28, and 24% above 28. 81% of the current freshmen were in the top fifth of their class; 97% were in the top two fifths. 11 freshmen graduated first in their class.

Requirements: The SAT I or ACT is required. In addition, applicants must be graduates of an accredited secondary school or have a GED certificate. The academic program must have included 4 years each of English, math, science, and social studies and 3 years of a foreign language. An essay is required. A portfolio or audition for certain programs and an interview are recommended. Geneseo requires applicants to be in the upper 50% of their class. A GPA of 3.0 is required. AP and CLEP credits are accepted. Important factors in the admissions decision are advanced placement or honor courses, recommendations by school officials, and evidence of special talent.

Procedure: Freshmen are admitted fall and spring. Entrance exams should be taken during the spring of the junior year. There are early decision and deferred admissions plans. There is a rolling admissions plan. Early decision applications should be filed by November 15; regular applications, by January 15 for fall entry and September 15 for spring entry, along with a $40 fee. Notification of early decision is sent December 15; regular decision, on a rolling basis beginning February 15. 133 early decision candidates were accepted for the 2003-2004 class. 1738 applicants were on the 2003 waiting list; 176 were admitted. Applications are accepted on-line.

Transfer: 346 transfer students enrolled in 2002-2003. Applicants must provide transcripts from all previously attended colleges. A minimum 2.0 GPA is required. Students with fewer than 24 credit hours must submit SAT I or ACT scores. An essay is required and an interview is recommended. 30 credits of 120 required for the bachelor's degree must be completed at Geneseo.

Visiting: There are regularly scheduled orientations for prospective students, including a day-and-a-half summer program consisting of academic advisement, registration, and adjustment to college life activities. There are guides for informal visits and visitors may sit in on classes and stay overnight. To schedule a visit, contact the Office of Admissions at *admissions@geneseo.edu*.

Financial Aid: In 2003-2004, 63% of all full-time freshmen and 65% of continuing full-time students received some form of financial aid. 75% of full-time freshmen and 87% of continuing full-time students received need-based aid. The average freshman award was $8040. Need-based scholarships or need-based grants averaged $2790 ($8375 maximum); need-based self-help aid (loans and jobs) averaged $3010 ($5625 maximum); and non-need-based awards and non-need-based scholarships averaged $535 ($4300 maximum). 22% of undergraduates work part time. Average annual earnings from campus work are $2100. The average financial indebtedness of the 2003 graduate was $15,500. Geneseo is a member of CSS. The FAFSA is required. The deadline for filing freshman financial aid applications for fall entry is February 15.

International Students: There are 71 international students enrolled. The school actively recruits these students. They must score 525 on the written TOEFL.

Computers: The mainframe is a DEC Alpha 4100. Mac, DOS/Windows, and Sun workstations are located in more than 30 computer labs, supported by fiber-optic network connectivity and full Internet access. All students may access the system 24 hours a day. There are no time limits. The fee is $125. It is strongly recommended that all students have a personal computer.

Graduates: From July 1, 2002 to June 30, 2003, 1222 bachelor's degrees were awarded. The most popular majors were education (23%), business administration (10%), and psychology (9%). In an average class, 1% graduate in 3 years or less, 62% graduate in 4 years or less, 76% graduate in 5 years or less, and 77% graduate in 6 years or less. 41 companies recruited on campus in 2002-2003. Of the 2002 graduating class, 36% were enrolled in graduate school within 6 months of graduation and 53% were employed.

Admissions Contact: Kris Shay, Director of Admissions. A video is available. E-mail: *admissions@geneseo.edu* Web: *www.geneseo.edu*

STATE UNIVERSITY OF NEW YORK/COLLEGE AT OLD WESTBURY

D-5

Old Westbury, NY 11568-0210

(516) 876-3073
Fax: (516) 876-3307

Full-time: 1048 men, 1444 women	**Faculty:** 118; IIB, +$
Part-time: 274 men, 456 women	**Ph.D.s:** 83%
Graduate: none	**Student/Faculty:** 21 to 1
Year: semesters, summer session	**Tuition:** $5035 ($10,985)
Application Deadline: open	**Room & Board:** $7749
Freshman Class: 2825 applied, 1620 accepted, 330 enrolled	
SAT I Verbal/Math: 470/480	**COMPETITIVE**

The State University of New York/College at Old Westbury, founded in 1965, is a public institution offering degree programs in the arts and sciences, business, education, fine arts, and health science. The library contains 218,718 volumes, 393,382 microform items, and 2175 audio/video tapes/CDs, and subscribes to 784 periodicals. Computerized library services include the card catalog, interlibrary loans, database searching, and Internet access. Special learning facilities include a learning resource center, art gallery, radio station, and TV studio. The 604-acre campus is in a suburban area 20 miles east of New York City. Including any residence halls, there are 22 buildings.

Student Life: 98% of undergraduates are from New York. Others are from 8 states, 20 foreign countries, and Canada. 33% are white; 26% African American; 14% Hispanic. The average age of freshmen is 19; all undergraduates, 26. 28% do not continue beyond their first year; 35% remain to graduate.

Housing: 792 students can be accommodated in college housing, which includes coed dorms. In addition, there are honors houses. On-campus housing is available on a first-come, first-served basis. Priority is given to out-of-town students. 77% of students commute. Alcohol is not permitted. All students may keep cars.

Activities: 6% of men belong to 7 local and 6 national fraternities; 7% of women belong to 6 local and 4 national sororities. There are 55 groups on campus, including art, cheerleading, choir, chorale, computers, ethnic, gay, honors, international, newspaper, political, professional, radio and TV, religious, social, social service, student government, and

yearbook. Popular campus events include Welcome Back Festival, Wellness at Old Westbury, and Mayfest.

Sports: There are 5 intercollegiate sports for men and 5 for women, and 7 intramural sports for men and 7 for women. Facilities include a 3000-seat gym, an auxiliary gym, a cross-country course, playing fields, a swimming pool, a fitness center, a weight room, jogging trails, a student union building, and courts for tennis, paddleball, handball, racquetball, and squash.

Disabled Students: 90% of the campus is accessible. Wheelchair ramps, elevators, special parking, specially equipped rest rooms, special class scheduling, lowered drinking fountains, lowered telephones, and limited volunteer transportation are available.

Services: Counseling and information services are available, as is tutoring in most subjects. There is a reader service for the blind, and remedial math, reading, and writing.

Campus Safety and Security: Measures include 24-hour foot and vehicle patrol, security escort services, shuttle buses, and informal discussions. There are pamphlets/posters/films, emergency telephones, lighted pathways/sidewalks, an officer dormitory patrol from 6 P.M. to 2 A.M., and student safety aides for escort service and night patrol.

Programs of Study: SUNY Old Westbury confers B.A., B.S., and B.P.S. degrees. Master's degrees are also awarded. Bachelor's degrees are awarded in BIOLOGICAL SCIENCE (biochemistry and biology/biological science), BUSINESS (accounting, banking and finance, business administration and management, labor studies, management information systems, and marketing/retailing/merchandising), COMMUNICATIONS AND THE ARTS (communications, media arts, Spanish, and visual and performing arts), COMPUTER AND PHYSICAL SCIENCE (chemistry, computer science, information sciences and systems, and mathematics), EDUCATION (bilingual/bicultural, early childhood, elementary, foreign languages, mathematics, middle school, science, secondary, social studies, and special), HEALTH PROFESSIONS (community health work and health), SOCIAL SCIENCE (American studies, criminology, economics, humanities, international studies, philosophy, political science/government, psychology, religion, and sociology). Teacher education, business, and psychology are the strongest academically and have the largest enrollments.

Required: To graduate, students must maintain a GPA of 2.0 in 120 or 128 semester credits; accounting and special education majors require 128 credits. General education requirements include courses in writing and reasoning skills, creative arts, ideas and ideology, cross-cultural perspectives, U.S. society and history, physical or life science, and foreign language.

Special: SUNY Old Westbury offers cross-registration with SUNY Empire State, Lirache, and colleges in Nassau and Suffolk counties, internships in teacher education, study abroad, a B.A.-B.S. in biological science, dual majors, and a 3-2 engineering degree with SUNY at Stony Brook and SUNY Maritime College. Credit for military and life experience, nondegree study, and pass/fail options are available.

Faculty/Classroom: 48% of faculty are male; 52%, female. All teach undergraduates. The average class size in an introductory lecture is 31; in a laboratory, 10; and in a regular course, 25.

Admissions: 57% of the 2003-2004 applicants were accepted. The SAT I scores for the 2003-2004 freshman class were: Verbal--73% below 500, 23% between 500 and 599, and 4% between 600 and 700; Math--67% below 500, 29% between 500 and 599, and 4% between 600 and 700.

Requirements: The SAT I is required. In addition, applicants must be graduates of an accredited secondary school or have the GED. An essay, portfolio, and interview also are recommended. Students are evaluated according to qualifying categories of academic achievement (80 high school average or 1000 SAT I score), special knowledge and creative ability, paid work experience, and social or personal experience. AP and CLEP credits are accepted. Important factors in the admissions decision are leadership record, recommendations by school officials, and evidence of special talent.

Procedure: Freshmen are admitted fall and spring. There are early decision and deferred admissions plans. Application deadlines are open. The fall 2003 application fee was $30. Notification is sent on a rolling basis. 14 early decision candidates were accepted for the 2003-2004 class. There is a rolling admissions plan. Applications are accepted on-line through the school's web site, *www.http://infostu.suny.edu*.

Transfer: 1078 transfer students enrolled in 2002-2003. Applicants must submit official transcripts from all colleges attended. Those students with fewer than 24 college credits must also submit a high school transcript. The college requires a minimum overall GPA of 2.0. Specific academic majors may require a higher GPA. 48 credits of 120 or 128 required for the bachelor's degree must be completed at SUNY Old Westbury.

Visiting: There are regularly scheduled orientations for prospective students. There are guides for informal visits. To schedule a visit, contact Enrollment Services.

Financial Aid: In 2003-2004, 68% of all full-time freshmen and 59% of continuing full-time students received some form of financial aid. 64%

of full-time freshmen and 54% of continuing full-time students received need-based aid. The average freshman award was $7539. Need-based scholarships or need-based grants averaged $6357; need-based self-help aid (loans and jobs) averaged $1919; and non-need-based awards and non-need-based scholarships averaged $7000. Average annual earnings from campus work are $874. The average financial indebtedness of the 2003 graduate was $22,775. The FAFSA, the college's own financial statement, the IFAA (institutional application), and previous years' household income are required. The deadline for filing freshman financial aid applications for fall entry is April 19.

International Students: There are 37 international students enrolled. The school actively recruits these students. They must score 500 on the written TOEFL or 200 on the electronic version and also take the college's own test.

Computers: The mainframe is a DEC Alpha 4100. There are approximately 300 public access computers around the campus for student use. Each dorm room also has a network connection. Enclosed public spaces have wireless access open to all members of the campus community. Wireless cards can be borrowed from the library for student use. All students may access the system daily. There are no time limits and no fees.

Graduates: From July 1, 2002 to June 30, 2003, 686 bachelor's degrees were awarded. The most popular majors were school of business (31%), teacher education (13%), and psychology (10%).

Admissions Contact: Mary Marquez Bell, Vice President for Enrollment Services. A video is available. E-mail: *enroll@oldwestbury.edu* Web: *www.oldwestbury.edu*

STATE UNIVERSITY OF NEW YORK/COLLEGE AT ONEONTA   D-3

Oneonta, NY 13820-4015

(607) 436-2524
(800) 786-9123; Fax: (607) 436-3074

Full-time: 2196 men, 3147 women	**Faculty:** 244; IIA, -$
Part-time: 80 men, 87 women	**Ph.D.s:** 76%
Graduate: 80 men, 168 women	**Student/Faculty:** 22 to 1
Year: semesters, summer session	**Tuition:** $5256 ($11,206)
Application Deadline: May 1	**Room & Board:** $6614
Freshman Class: 10,200 applied, 4880 accepted, 1211 enrolled	
SAT I Verbal/Math: 538/548	**ACT:** 23 **VERY COMPETITIVE**

The State University of New York/College at Oneonta, founded in 1889, is a public institute that offers undergraduate and graduate programs in the arts and sciences with a campuswide emphasis on educational technology and community service. In addition to regional accreditation, Oneonta has baccalaureate program accreditation with AAFCS, ACS, ADA, and NCATE. The library contains 547,147 volumes, 1,131,652 microform items, and 30,772 audio/video tapes/CDs, and subscribes to 14,452 periodicals. Computerized library services include the card catalog, interlibrary loans, and database searching. Special learning facilities include a learning resource center, art gallery, planetarium, radio station, TV station, an observatory, science discovery center, community service center, college camp, children's center, and off-campus biological field station. The 250-acre campus is in a rural area 75 miles southwest of Albany and 55 miles northeast of Binghamton. Including any residence halls, there are 32 buildings.

Student Life: 97% of undergraduates are from New York. Others are from 12 states and 23 foreign countries. 83% are white. The average age of freshmen is 18; all undergraduates, 20. 25% do not continue beyond their first year; 50% remain to graduate.

Housing: 3019 students can be accommodated in college housing, which includes single-sex and coed dorms. A math and science wing, an international wing, all-freshmen housing, and other special-interest groupings within residence halls are available. On-campus housing is guaranteed for the freshman year only, is available on a first-come, first-served basis, and is available on a lottery system for upperclassmen. 56% of students live on campus; of those, 56% remain on campus on weekends. Alcohol is not permitted. Upperclassmen may keep cars.

Activities: 66% of women belong to 3 local and 4 national sororities. There are no fraternities. There are 70 groups on campus, including academic, art, band, cheerleading, choir, chorale, chorus, computers, culture enrichment, dance, drama, ethnic, film, gay, honors, international, jazz band, musical theater, newspaper, orchestra, pep band, photography, political, professional, radio and TV, religious, social, social service, special interest, student government, volunteer, and yearbook. Popular campus events include Exploration (campus orientation), Into the Streets (community service day), and Reunion Weekend.

Sports: There are 10 intercollegiate sports for men and 11 for women, and 17 intramural sports for men and 17 for women. Facilities include a gym, a field house, dance studios, weight rooms, a pool, indoor racquetball courts, tennis courts, indoor and outdoor tracks, athletic fields, and an all-weather field.

Disabled Students: 75% of the campus is accessible. Wheelchair ramps, elevators, special parking, specially equipped rest rooms, special class scheduling, and lowered drinking fountains are available. All academic buildings and some residence halls are accessible.

Services: Counseling and information services are available, as is tutoring in most subjects. There is a reader service for the blind, and remedial math, reading, and writing.

Campus Safety and Security: Measures include 24-hour foot and vehicle patrol, self-defense education, security escort services, and shuttle buses. There are informal discussions, pamphlets/posters/films, emergency telephones, lighted pathways/sidewalks, and residence hall workshops.

Programs of Study: Oneonta confers B.A. and B.S. degrees. Master's degrees are also awarded. Bachelor's degrees are awarded in BIOLOGICAL SCIENCE (biology/biological science), BUSINESS (accounting, business economics, and fashion merchandising), COMMUNICATIONS AND THE ARTS (art, communications, dramatic arts, English, fine arts, French, music, music business management, Spanish, and speech/debate/rhetoric), COMPUTER AND PHYSICAL SCIENCE (atmospheric sciences and meteorology, chemistry, computer science, earth science, geology, mathematics, physics, and statistics), EDUCATION (business, elementary, English, foreign languages, home economics, mathematics, science, secondary, and social science), ENGINEERING AND ENVIRONMENTAL DESIGN (environmental science), HEALTH PROFESSIONS (predentistry and premedicine), SOCIAL SCIENCE (African studies, anthropology, child care/child and family studies, criminal justice, dietetics, economics, geography, gerontology, Hispanic American studies, history, home economics, interdisciplinary studies, international studies, philosophy, political science/government, prelaw, psychology, sociology, and water resources). Physical and natural sciences, business economics, and education are the strongest academically. Education, business economics, and music industry are the largest.

Required: Students must complete 122 semester hours, with at least 48 hours in upper-division courses and 30 to 36 hours in the major. A minimum GPA of 2.0 (2.5 for education majors) must be maintained. In addition, students must complete a 36-hour general education requirement including courses in math, natural sciences, social sciences, American history, Western civilization, other world civilizations, humanities, the arts, foreign language, basic communications, writing skills and oral communication skills. Students must also pass writing and speech proficiency exams.

Special: Oneonta offers limited cross-registration with Hartwick College, internships in most fields, study abroad through SUNY in 50 countries, a Washington semester, work-study programs, interdisciplinary studies, and dual majors. A 3-2 engineering degree and other cooperative programs are offered. Credit for life experience, nondegree study, and pass/fail options are available. There are 14 national honor societies and a freshman honors program.

Faculty/Classroom: 60% of faculty are male; 40%, female. 99% teach undergraduates. The average class size in an introductory lecture is 25; in a laboratory, 24; and in a regular course, 20.

Admissions: 48% of the 2003-2004 applicants were accepted. The SAT I scores for the 2003-2004 freshman class were: Verbal--24% below 500, 60% between 500 and 599, 15% between 600 and 700, and 1% above 700; Math--16% below 500, 65% between 500 and 599, 18% between 600 and 700, and 1% above 700. The ACT scores were 9% below 21, 52% between 21 and 23, 35% between 24 and 26, and 4% between 27 and 28. 39% of the current freshmen were in the top fifth of their class; 88% were in the top two fifths.

Requirements: The SAT I or ACT is required. In addition, applicants should be graduates of an accredited secondary school and have 16 academic credits, including 4 years each of English and history, and 8 years combined of foreign language, math, and science, with at least 2 years in each of these 3 broad areas. The GED is accepted. A GPA of 2.0 is required. AP and CLEP credits are accepted. Important factors in the admissions decision are advanced placement or honor courses, evidence of special talent, and leadership record.

Procedure: Freshmen are admitted fall and spring. Entrance exams should be taken in the spring of the junior year or the fall of the senior year. There are rolling admissions and deferred admissions plans. Early decision applications should be filed by November 15; regular applications, by May 1 for fall entry and December 15 for spring entry, along with a $40 fee. Notification of early decision is sent November 15; regular decision, on a rolling basis after December 1. 76 early decision candidates were accepted for the 2003-2004 class. 341 were on the 2003 waiting list; 8 were admitted. Applications are accepted on-line through *www.oneonta.edu, www.sony.edu,* and *CollegeNET.*

Transfer: 766 transfer students enrolled in 2002-2003. Official transcripts of all previous college work must be submitted. A minimum of 15 semester hours of transferable credit and a GPA of 2.0 are required. 45 credits of 122 required for the bachelor's degree must be completed at Oneonta.

Visiting: There are regularly scheduled orientations for prospective students, including 2 fall open houses, a summer open house, individual appointments, and group information sessions. There are guides for informal visits and visitors may sit in on classes and stay overnight. To schedule a visit, contact the Admissions Office at *admissions@oneonta.edu.*

Financial Aid: In 2003-2004, 60% of all full-time students received some form of financial aid. 55% of all full-time students received need-based aid. The average freshman award was $5907. 29% of undergraduates work part time. Average annual earnings from campus work are $800. The average financial indebtedness of the 2003 graduate was $16,065. The FAFSA is required. The deadline for filing freshman financial aid applications for fall entry is April 15.

International Students: There are 70 international students enrolled. The school actively recruits these students. They must score 500 on the written TOEFL or 173 on the electronic version. The SAT I or ACT is recommended.

Computers: The mainframes are a Compaq ES40 and two Compaq 2100s. More than 700 PCs and MACs are available in labs on campus. Students have access to e-mail, the Web, the Internet, and on-line registration and other services. All residence halls are wired for high-speed connections. Wireless networking is available in many buildings. All students may access the system any time. There are no time limits and no fees. It is strongly recommended that all students have a personal computer that is network-ready.

Graduates: From July 1, 2002 to June 30, 2003, 1114 bachelor's degrees were awarded. The most popular majors were elementary education (26%), business economics (12%), and human ecology (11%). In an average class, 1% graduate in 3 years or less, 34% graduate in 4 years or less, 45% graduate in 5 years or less, and 47% graduate in 6 years or less. 45 companies recruited on campus in 2002-2003. Of the 2002 graduating class, 47% were enrolled in graduate school within 6 months of graduation and 68% were employed.

Admissions Contact: Karen Brown, Director of Admissions.
E-mail: *admissions@oneonta.edu* Web: *http://www.oneonta.edu*

STATE UNIVERSITY OF NEW YORK/COLLEGE AT PLATTSBURGH

D-2

Plattsburgh, NY 12901-2681

(518) 564-2040
(888) 673-0012; Fax: (518) 564-2045

Full-time: 2121 men, 2873 women	**Faculty:** 250; IIA, -$
Part-time: 151 men, 258 women	**Ph.D.s:** 90%
Graduate: 185 men, 459 women	**Student/Faculty:** 20 to 1
Year: trimesters, summer session	**Tuition:** $5200 ($11,150)
Application Deadline: August 1	**Room & Board:** $6500
Freshman Class: 6798 applied, 4232 accepted, 967 enrolled	
SAT I Verbal/Math: 510/520	**ACT:** 21 **COMPETITIVE**

The State University of New York/College at Plattsburgh, founded in 1889, is a public institution offering degree programs in the liberal arts and professional programs. There are 3 undergraduate and 2 graduate schools. In addition to regional accreditation, Plattsburgh State has baccalaureate program accreditation with AACSB, ADA, ASLA, CSWE, and NLN. The library contains 713,221 volumes, 937,996 microform items, and 23,771 audio/video tapes/CDs, and subscribes to 1283 periodicals. Computerized library services include the card catalog, interlibrary loans, database searching, and Internet access. Special learning facilities include a learning resource center, art gallery, planetarium, radio station, TV station, environmental science institute, child care center, research institute, teacher resource center, speech and hearing clinic, the Alzheimer's Disease Assistance Center, auditory research labs, a virtual reality simulator, and distance learning facilites. The 300-acre campus is in a suburban area 150 miles north of Albany, 25 miles west of Burlington, Vermont, and 65 miles south of Montreal, Canada. Including any residence halls, there are 35 buildings.

Student Life: 90% of undergraduates are from New York. Students are from 18 states, 54 foreign countries, and Canada. 98% are from public schools. 76% are white. The average age of freshmen is 18; all undergraduates, 22. 25% do not continue beyond their first year; 62% remain to graduate.

Housing: 2777 students can be accommodated in college housing, which includes single-sex and coed dorms. In addition, there are special-interest houses, adult student halls/floors, wellness floors, a substance-free building, and vacation housing. On-campus housing is available on a first-come, first-served basis and is available on a lottery system for upperclassmen. 54% of students commute. All students may keep cars.

Activities: 6% of men belong to 3 local and 4 national fraternities; 5% of women belong to 3 local and 4 national sororities. There are 90 groups on campus, including art, band, cheerleading, choir, chorale, chorus, computers, drama, ethnic, film, gay, honors, international, jazz band, literary magazine, musical theater, newspaper, orchestra, photography, political, professional, radio and TV, religious, social, social service, student government, symphony, and yearbook. Popular campus events include Canada Day, Family Weekend, and Arts and Crafts Fair.

Sports: There are 9 intercollegiate sports for men and 10 for women, and 12 intramural sports for men and 9 for women. Facilities include a 3500-seat ice arena, a 1500-seat gym, an indoor track, soccer and volleyball areas, an indoor swimming pool, exercise and weight rooms, an aerobics studio, racquetball courts, lighted tennis courts, softball, lacrosse, and rugby fields, and a fitness center.

Disabled Students: 80% of the campus is accessible. Wheelchair ramps, elevators, special parking, specially equipped rest rooms, special class scheduling, lowered drinking fountains, lowered telephones, curb cuts, and electronic doors are available.

Services: Counseling and information services are available, as is tutoring in every subject. There is a reader service for the blind and remedial math, reading, and writing.

Campus Safety and Security: Measures include 24-hour foot and vehicle patrol, security escort services, shuttle buses, and informal discussions. There are pamphlets/posters/films, emergency telephones, lighted pathways/sidewalks, bicycle patrols, combination locks on student rooms, a computerized keyless entry system for residence hall access, door viewers, and basement and ground-level security windows in residence halls.

Programs of Study: Plattsburgh State confers B.A., B.S., B.F.A., and B.S.Ed. degrees. Master's degrees are also awarded. Bachelor's degrees are awarded in BIOLOGICAL SCIENCE (biochemistry, biology/biological science, and cell biology), BUSINESS (accounting, business administration and management, business economics, and hotel/motel and restaurant management), COMMUNICATIONS AND THE ARTS (communications, dramatic arts, English, French, journalism, music, and Spanish), COMPUTER AND PHYSICAL SCIENCE (chemistry, computer science, geology, mathematics, and physics), EDUCATION (education of the deaf and hearing impaired, elementary, English, mathematics, science, secondary, social studies, and special), ENGINEERING AND ENVIRONMENTAL DESIGN (environmental science), HEALTH PROFESSIONS (medical laboratory technology and nursing), SOCIAL SCIENCE (anthropology, Canadian studies, child care/child and family studies, community services, criminal justice, dietetics, economics, geography, history, home economics, interdisciplinary studies, Latin American studies, philosophy, political science/government, social work, and sociology). Business, accounting, and art are the strongest academically. Psychology, education, and business are the largest.

Required: To graduate, students must have a 2.0 GPA and complete at least 120 semester hours. General education courses total 41 to 46 credits. In addition, all students must demonstrate proficiency in writing by completion of an advanced writing requirement.

Special: The college offers cross-registration with Clinton Community College and Empire State College, internships, study abroad in 6 countries, cooperative programs with a variety of employers, B.A.-B.S. degrees, dual and student-designed majors, and an accelerated degree program in any major except nursing. A 3-2 engineering degree is offered with SUNY Stony Brook and Binghamton, Clarkson, Syracuse, and McGill Universities, and the University of Vermont. Credit for military experience, nondegree study if space permits, and limited pass/fail options are possible. There are 18 national honor societies and a freshman honors program.

Faculty/Classroom: 55% of faculty are male; 45%, female. All both teach and do research. No introductory courses are taught by graduate students. The average class size in an introductory lecture is 27; in a laboratory, 19; and in a regular course, 24.

Admissions: 62% of the 2003-2004 applicants were accepted. The SAT I scores for the 2003-2004 freshman class were: Verbal--39% below 500, 48% between 500 and 599, 12% between 600 and 700, and 1% above 700; Math--35% below 500, 51% between 500 and 599, 14% between 600 and 700, and 1% above 700. The ACT scores were 40% below 21, 34% between 21 and 23, 17% between 24 and 26, 5% between 27 and 28, and 4% above 28. 47% of the current freshmen were in the top fifth of their class; 59% were in the top two fifths. 11% were in the top 10%. 3 freshmen graduated first in their class.

Requirements: The SAT I or ACT is required. In addition, applicants must have at least 12 academic credits, including 4 years of English, 5 combined years of math and science, and 3 years of social studies. An essay, portfolio, audition, and interview may be recommended in some programs. The GED is accepted. Plattsburgh State requires applicants to be in the upper 50% of their class. A grade average of 78 is required. AP and CLEP credits are accepted. Important factors in the admissions decision are advanced placement or honor courses, recommendations by school officials, and leadership record.

Procedure: Freshmen are admitted fall and spring. Entrance exams should be taken during the second half of the junior year or the beginning of the senior year. There are early decision, early admissions, deferred admissions, and rolling admissions plans. Early decision applications should be filed by November 15; regular applications, by August 1 for fall entry and November 1 for spring entry. Notification of early decision is sent December 15; regular decision, on a rolling basis. The fall 2003 application fee was $40. 41 early decision candidates were accepted for the 2003-2004 class. 249 applicants were on the 2003 waiting list; 14 were admitted. Applications are accepted on computer disk and on-line through Apply, Apply Yourself, CollegeLink, CollegeSearch, and EXPAN.

Transfer: 566 transfer students enrolled in 2002-2003. Applicants must have a minimum 2.0 GPA. Most academic programs require a 2.5 GPA or better. 36 of 120 credits required for the bachelor's degree must be completed at Plattsburgh State.

Visiting: There are regularly scheduled orientations for prospective students, including a group, student-led tour, and either a group or individual interview. Special overnight events for accepted freshmen include meals with students and faculty, classroom visits, discussions with faculty, and special workshops. There are guides for informal visits and visitors may sit in on classes and stay overnight. To schedule a visit, contact the Admissions Office at (518) 564-0204 or *admissions@plattsburgh.edu*.

Financial Aid: The average freshman award was $7753. 37% of undergraduates work part time. Average annual earnings from campus work are $1100. The average financial indebtedness of the 2003 graduate was $16,158. The FAFSA is required. In-state students must also file the TAP application. The priority date for freshman financial aid applications for fall entry is March 1. The deadline for filing freshman financial aid applications for fall entry is rolling.

International Students: There are 349 international students enrolled. The school actively recruits these students. They must score 450 on the written TOEFL.

Computers: The mainframes are a DEC VAX 6610 and a DEC VAX 6430. There are 360 student access Macs or PCs located on campus. All students may access the system. There are no time limits. The fee is $50 per semester. It is strongly recommended that all students have a personal computer. Digital, IBM, Zenith, or Mac is recommended.

Graduates: From July 1, 2002 to June 30, 2003, 1088 bachelor's degrees were awarded. The most popular majors were education (23%), business (12%), and mass media (6%). In an average class, 1% graduate in 3 years or less, 33% graduate in 4 years or less, 55% graduate in 5 years or less, and 58% graduate in 6 years or less. 120 companies recruited on campus in 2002-2003. Of the 2002 graduating class, 12% were enrolled in graduate school within 6 months of graduation and 79% were employed.

Admissions Contact: Richard Higgins, Director of Admissions. E-mail: *higginrj@splavb.cc.plattsburgh.edu* Web: *www.plattsburgh.edu*

STATE UNIVERSITY OF NEW YORK/COLLEGE AT PURCHASE   D-5
Purchase, NY 10577-1400   (914) 251-6300; Fax: (914) 251-6314

Full-time: 1350 men, 1690 women	**Faculty:** 136
Part-time: 305 men, 520 women	**Ph.D.s:** 100%
Graduate: 70 men, 85 women	**Student/Faculty:** 22 to 1
Year: semesters, summer session	**Tuition:** $4130 ($9030)
Application Deadline: see profile	**Room & Board:** $6460
Freshman Class: n/av	
SAT I: required	**ACT:** recommended
	VERY COMPETITIVE

State University of New York/College at Purchase, founded in 1967, is a public institution that offers programs in visual arts, music, acting, dance, film, theater/stage design technology, natural science, social science, and humanities. Figures in the above capsule and in this profile are approximate. In addition to regional accreditation, Purchase College SUNY has baccalaureate program accreditation with NASAD and NASM. The library contains 270,090 volumes, 246,975 microform items, and 15,175 audio/video tapes/CDs, and subscribes to 1400 periodicals. Computerized library services include the card catalog, interlibrary loans, and database searching. Special learning facilities include a learning resource center, art gallery, radio station, TV station, listening and viewing center, science and photography labs, music practice rooms and instruments, multitrack synthesizers, experimental stage, typesetting and computer graphics labs, a performing arts complex, an electron microscope, and the Children's Center at Purchase College. The 500-acre campus is in a suburban area 35 miles north of midtown Manhattan. Including any residence halls, there are 40 buildings.

Student Life: 81% of undergraduates are from New York. Students are from 46 states, 30 foreign countries, and Canada. 69% are white. The average age of freshmen is 18; all undergraduates, 22. 23% do not continue beyond their first year; 35% remain to graduate.

Housing: 1850 students can be accommodated in college housing, which includes single-sex and coed dorms, on-campus apartments, and off-campus apartments. In addition, there are special-interest houses, transfer student units, nontraditional age student units, wellness halls, presidential scholars halls, and learning community halls. On-campus housing is available on a first-come, first-served basis and is available on a lottery system for upperclassmen. Priority is given to out-of-town students. 58% of students live on campus. All students may keep cars.

Activities: There are 40 groups on campus, including art, band, choir, chorale, computers, dance, drama, environmental awareness, ethnic, film, gay, jazz band, literary magazine, newspaper, opera, orchestra, photography, political, professional, radio and TV, religious, social, social service, student government, symphony, and visual arts. Popular campus events include Spring Concert, Alcohol Awareness Week, and film programs.

Sports: There are 4 intercollegiate sports for men and 5 for women, and 38 intramural sports for men and 38 for women. Facilities include 3 basketball courts, a fitness center, 6-lane pool, aeorbics studio, 4 raquetball courts, 2 squash courts, 6 lighted tennis courts, and a 4-lane bowling alley.

Disabled Students: All of the campus is accessible. Wheelchair ramps, elevators, special parking, specially equipped rest rooms, note takers, extended test times, quiet rooms for tests, interpreters for the hearing impaired, readers for the visually impaired, a reading machine in the library, and special note-taking paper are available.

Services: Counseling and information services are available, as is tutoring in every subject. There is a reader service for the blind; remedial math, reading, and writing; and math and writing drop-in sessions, "The P.J. Project," offering tutoring in residence halls in evenings, assistive technology, supplemental instructors, and computer lab study groups.

Campus Safety and Security: Measures include 24-hour foot and vehicle patrol, security escort services, informal discussions, and pamphlets/posters/films. There are emergency telephones and lighted pathways/sidewalks.

Programs of Study: Purchase College SUNY confers B.A., B.S., B.A.L.A., B.F.A., and Mus. B. degrees. Master's degrees are also awarded. Bachelor's degrees are awarded in BIOLOGICAL SCIENCE (biology/biological science), COMMUNICATIONS AND THE ARTS (art history and appreciation, creative writing, dance, dramatic arts, film arts, journalism, literature, music, theater design, and visual and performing arts), COMPUTER AND PHYSICAL SCIENCE (chemistry and mathematics), ENGINEERING AND ENVIRONMENTAL DESIGN (environmental science), SOCIAL SCIENCE (anthropology, economics, ethnic studies, history, liberal arts/general studies, philosophy, political science/government, psychology, sociology, and women's studies). Dance, drama, and film are the strongest academically. Visual arts, music, and liberal studies are the largest.

Required: A minimum 2.0 GPA is required with a minimum of 120 credits. Students majoring in the arts complete a minimum of 90 professional credits and the SUNY general education curriculum. Students majoring in the liberal arts and scieces complete the general education curriculum and major requirements, and must complete a senior thesis.

Special: Purchase College offers cross-registration with Empire State colleges, internships with corporations, newspapers, and local agencies, and student-designed majors, dual majors, study abroad, work-study, nondegree study, and pass/fail options. There is also an arts conservatory program.

Faculty/Classroom: 58% of faculty are male; 43%, female. All teach undergraduates. The average class size in an introductory lecture is 29; in a laboratory, 17; and in a regular course, 21.

Requirements: The SAT I is required and the ACT is recommended. Minimum required composite scores are 1100 on the SAT I or 23 on the ACT. Applicants must be graduates of an accredited secondary school and have completed 16 academic credits and 16 Carnegie units. The GED is accepted. Visual arts students must submit an essay and portfolio and have an interview. Film students need an essay and an interview. Design technology students need a portfolio and an interview. Performing arts students must audition. A GPA of 2.0 is required. AP and CLEP credits are accepted. Important factors in the admissions decision are evidence of special talent, recommendations by school officials, and personality/intangible qualities.

Procedure: Freshmen are admitted fall and spring. Entrance exams should be taken by the fall of the senior year. There are early decision, deferred admissions, and rolling admissions plans. Check with the school for current application deadlines. The application fee is $30. A waiting list is an active part of the admissions procedure. Applications are accepted on-line at the school's web site.

Transfer: 426 transfer students enrolled in a recent year. Students transferring to the School of Arts (visual or performing arts) must pass an audition or portfolio review. Transfer credit is limited; students can contact the Office of Admission to get a preliminary credit evaluation. Students transferring to programs in liberal arts and sciences must have a minimum 2.0 GPA if they have completed 30 or more semester hours; if they have fewer than 30 semester hours, the high school transcript is also reviewed. Liberal arts and science transfers can transfer a maximum of 90 semester hours from 4-year colleges and 75 semester hours from 2 year colleges.

Visiting: There are regularly scheduled orientations for prospective students, including group question and answer sessions followed by a tour of the campus. To schedule a visit, contact the Admissions Office.

Financial Aid: In a recent year, 74% of all full-time freshmen and 62% of continuing full-time students received some form of financial aid. 52% of full-time freshmen and 50% of continuing full-time students received need-based aid. The average freshman award was $6160. 12% of undergraduates work part time. Average annual earnings from campus work are $1073. The average financial indebtedness of a recent graduate was $13,510. The FAFSA is required. Check with the school for current deadlines.

International Students: There were 92 international students enrolled in a recent year. The school actively recruits these students. They must score 550 on the written TOEFL or score 430 on the SAT I: Verbal test, and also take the ACT, or SAT I if the TOEFL has not been taken, scoring 1100.

Computers: PCs are available in the computer center in the social sciences building, the humanities building, music building, art and design building, dance hall, natural sciences building, library, and in dorms. There are approximately 350 PCs in total. All students may access the system when the computer center is open. There are no time limits. The fee is $150 per semester. It is strongly recommended that all students have a personal computer.

Graduates: In a recent year, 594 bachelor's degrees were awarded. The most popular majors were visual arts (20%), liberal arts (18%), and music (12%). In an average class, 22% graduate in 4 years or less, 33% graduate in 5 years or less, and 35% graduate in 6 years or less. 50 companies recruited on campus in a recent year.

Admissions Contact: Betsy Immergut, Director of Admissions.
E-mail: *betsy.immergut@purchase.edu* Web: *admissn@purchase.edu*

STATE UNIVERSITY OF NEW YORK/COLLEGE OF AGRICULTURE AND TECHNOLOGY AT COBLESKILL
Cobleskill, NY 12043   D-3

(518) 255-5525
(800) 295-8988; Fax: (518) 234-5333

Full-time: 1300 men, 975 women	**Faculty:** 118; III, av$
Part-time: 75 men, 100 women	**Ph.D.s:** 32%
Graduate: none	**Student/Faculty:** 18 to 1
Year: semesters, summer session	**Tuition:** $4740 ($6540)
Application Deadline: open	**Room & Board:** $6460
Freshman Class: n/av	
SAT I or ACT: recommended	COMPETITIVE+

The State University of New York/College of Agriculture and Technology at Cobleskill, established in 1916, is a public institution conferring the Bachelor of Technology in Agriculture degree. Figures in the above capsule and in this profile are approximate. The library contains 86,000 volumes and 55,000 audio/video tapes/CDs, and subscribes to 1000 periodicals. Computerized library services include the card catalog, interlibrary loans, and database searching. Special learning facilities include a learning resource center, art gallery, and arboretum, greenhouses, and plant nursery. The 750-acre campus is in a rural area 35 miles south of Albany. Including any residence halls, there are 53 buildings.

Student Life: 93% of undergraduates are from New York. Students are from 11 states. 98% are from public schools. 91% are white. The average age of freshmen is 18; all undergraduates, 20. 20% do not continue beyond their first year; 50% remain to graduate.

Housing: College housing includes single-sex and coed dorms. There are special-interest floors in residence halls. On-campus housing is guaranteed for the freshman year only and is available on a lottery system for upperclassmen. 80% of students live on campus; of those, 90% remain on campus on weekends. Alcohol is not permitted. All students may keep cars.

Activities: There are no fraternities or sororities. There are 50 groups on campus, including cheerleading, choir, chorus, computers, departmental, ethnic, honors, jazz band, musical theater, newspaper, professional, religious, social service, student government, and yearbook. Popular campus events include Parents Weekend and Alumni Weekend.

Sports: There are 10 intercollegiate sports for men and 9 for women, and 11 intramural sports for men and 10 for women. Facilities include indoor and outdoor basketball and tennis courts, playing fields, a gym, an exercise room, a swimming pool, bowling lanes, a field house, badminton, volleyball, and handball courts, archery and golf driving areas, a quarter-mile track, a ski center, and a fitness trail.

Disabled Students: 35% of the campus is accessible. Wheelchair ramps, elevators, special parking, specially equipped rest rooms, lowered drinking fountains, and lowered telephones are available.

Services: Counseling and information services are available, as is tutoring in some subjects, including biology, intermediate algebra, and chemistry. There is a reader service for the blind and remedial math, reading, and writing. There is also an academic skills center.

Campus Safety and Security: Measures include 24-hour foot and vehicle patrol, informal discussions, pamphlets/posters/films, and emergency telephones. There are lighted pathways/sidewalks.

Programs of Study: SUNY Cobleskill confers the B.T. in Agriculture degree. Associate degrees are also awarded. Bachelor's degrees are awarded in AGRICULTURE (agricultural business management, agricultural mechanics, animal science, and plant science).

Required: Degree requirements include completion of 126 credit hours, with 30 to 32 upper-division credits in the major, 11 credits of technical electives, 7 to 15 credits in other electives, and a 15-credit internship. Students must maintain a minimum 2.0 GPA.

Special: The college sponsors internship programs and cross-registration is possible with the Hudson-Mohawk Area Consortium. Students may study abroad at Thomas Danby and South Fields Colleges in England. There is 1 national honor society, a freshman honors program, and 1 departmental honors program.

Faculty/Classroom: 70% of faculty are male; 30%, female. 40% do research. The average class size in an introductory lecture is 33; in a laboratory, 15; and in a regular course, 30.

Requirements: The SAT I or ACT is recommended. In addition, applicants must have graduated from an accredited secondary school or earned a GED, and are encouraged to have completed college-preparatory courses. Students planning to enter the agricultural program should also take vocational agricultural courses. Applicants are required to visit the campus. A grade average of 75 is required. AP and CLEP credits are accepted. Important factors in the admissions decision are evidence of special talent, advanced placement or honor courses, and leadership record.

Procedure: Freshmen are admitted fall and spring. There are early admissions, deferred admissions, and rolling admissions plans. Application deadlines are open. The application fee is $30.

Transfer: Applicants must have a minimum GPA of 2.0. 30 of 126 credits required for the bachelor's degree must be completed at SUNY Cobleskill.

Visiting: There are regularly scheduled orientations for prospective students. To schedule a visit, contact the Office of Admissions.

Financial Aid: In a recent year, 64% of all full-time freshmen and 55% of continuing full-time students received some form of financial aid. The average freshman award was $7125. 15% of undergraduates work part time. Average annual earnings from campus work are $675. The average financial indebtedness of a recent graduate was $4213. SUNY Cobleskill is a member of CSS. The FAFSA and the college's own financial statement are required. Check with the school for current deadlines.

International Students: The school actively recruits these students. They must score 500 on the written TOEFL.

Computers: The mainframe is a DEC. There are 3 computer labs, as well as network access in all residence halls. All students may access the system during computer center hours. There are no time limits and no fees.

Graduates: In an average class, 54% graduate in 3 years or less, and 60% graduate in 4 years or less.

Admissions Contact: Dr. Clayton Smith, Director of Admissions.
E-mail: *smithc@cobleskill.edu* Web: *www.cobleskill.edu*

STATE UNIVERSITY OF NEW YORK/COLLEGE OF ENVIRONMENTAL SCIENCE AND FORESTRY
Syracuse, NY 13210-2779   C-3

(315) 470-6600
(800) 777-7373; Fax: (315) 470-6933

Full-time: 735 men, 500 women	**Faculty:** 122; I, -$
Part-time: 153 men, 161 women	**Ph.D.s:** 80%
Graduate: 327 men, 272 women	**Student/Faculty:** 10 to 1
Year: semesters	**Tuition:** $4767 ($10,717)
Application Deadline: March 1	**Room & Board:** $9400
Freshman Class: 796 applied, 499 accepted, 228 enrolled	
SAT I Verbal/Math: 560/570	**ACT:** 24 VERY COMPETITIVE

The College of Environmental Science and Forestry, founded in 1911 and located adjacent to the campus of Syracuse University, is one of the colleges of the State University of New York. The public institution specializes in undergraduate and graduate degrees in agricultural, biological, environmental, health, and physical sciences, landscape architecture, and engineering. Students have access to the academic, cultural, and social life at Syracuse University. In addition to regional accreditation, ESF has baccalaureate program accreditation with ABET, ASLA, and SAF. The library contains 130,305 volumes, 200,090 microform items, and 1118 audio/video tapes/CDs, and subscribes to 2001 periodicals. Computerized library services include the card catalog, interlibrary loans, and database searching. Special learning facilities include a learning resource center, art gallery, natural history museum, radio station, and TV station. The 12-acre campus is in an urban area in Syracuse. Including any residence halls, there are 7 buildings.

Student Life: 91% of undergraduates are from New York. Others are from 25 states, 9 foreign countries, and Canada. 85% are from public schools. 87% are white. The average age of freshmen is 18; all undergraduates, 21. 3% do not continue beyond their first year; 75% remain to graduate.

Housing: 600 students can be accommodated in college housing, which includes single-sex and coed dorms, on-campus apartments, off-campus apartments, and married-student housing. In addition, there are special-interest houses, substance-free floors, quiet floors, and learning communities. On-campus housing is guaranteed for all 4 years. 50% of students live on campus; of those, 90% remain on campus on weekends. Alcohol is not permitted. Upperclassmen may keep cars.

Activities: 3% of men belong to 20 national fraternities; 3% of women belong to 20 national sororities. There are 300 groups on campus, including art, band, cheerleading, choir, chorale, chorus, computers, dance, debate, drama, drum and bugle corps, ethnic, film, gay, honors, international, jazz band, marching band, musical theater, newspaper, orchestra, pep band, photography, political, professional, radio and TV, religious, social, social service, student government, symphony, and yearbook. Popular campus events include Activities Fair, Earth Day, and Awards Banquet.

Sports: There are 21 intercollegiate sports for men and 21 for women, and 30 intramural sports for men and 30 for women. Athletic and recreational facilities are contracted through Syracuse University.

Disabled Students: 90% of the campus is accessible. Wheelchair ramps, elevators, special parking, specially equipped rest rooms, lowered drinking fountains, and lowered telephones are available.

Services: Counseling and information services are available, as is tutoring in some subjects. There is a reader service for the blind.

Campus Safety and Security: Measures include 24-hour foot and vehicle patrol, security escort services, shuttle buses, and informal discussions. There are pamphlets/posters/films, emergency telephones, and lighted pathways/sidewalks.

Programs of Study: ESF confers B.S. and B.L.A. degrees. Associate, master's, and doctoral degrees are also awarded. Bachelor's degrees are awarded in AGRICULTURE (animal science, environmental studies, forest engineering, forestry and related sciences, natural resource management, plant science, soil science, and wood science), BIOLOGICAL SCIENCE (biology/biological science, botany, ecology, entomology, environmental biology, microbiology, molecular biology, plant genetics, and plant physiology), COMPUTER AND PHYSICAL SCIENCE (chemistry and polymer science), EDUCATION (environmental and science), ENGINEERING AND ENVIRONMENTAL DESIGN (chemical engineering, construction management, environmental design, environmental engineering, landscape architecture/design, paper and pulp science, paper engineering, and survey and mapping technology), HEALTH PROFESSIONS (predentistry, premedicine, and prepharmacy), SOCIAL SCIENCE (prelaw). Engineering, chemistry, and biology are the strongest academically. Environmental and forest biology and environmental studies are the largest.

Required: Students must complete 125 to 130 credit hours for the B.S. (160 for the B.L.A.), including 60 in the major, with a minimum 2.0 GPA. Courses in chemistry, English, math, and botany are required.

Special: Cross-registration is offered with Syracuse University. Co-op programs, internships, and dual options in biology and forestry are available. Study abroad is available in landscape architecture and through Syracuse University. There is a 4+1 engineering program with Syracuse University. There is 1 national honor society and a freshman honors program; all departments have honors programs.

Faculty/Classroom: 82% of faculty are male; 18%, female. All both teach and do research. Graduate students teach 1% of introductory courses. The average class size in a regular course is 25.

Admissions: 63% of the 2003-2004 applicants were accepted. The SAT I scores for the 2003-2004 freshman class were: Verbal--9% below 500, 55% between 500 and 599, 34% between 600 and 700, and 2% above 700; Math--10% below 500, 56% between 500 and 599, 32% between 600 and 700, and 2% above 700. The ACT scores were 10% below 21, 40% between 21 and 23, 34% between 24 and 26, 5% between 27 and 28, and 11% above 28.

Requirements: The SAT I or ACT is required. In addition, applicants are required to have a minimum of 3 years of math and science, including chemistry, in a college preparatory curriculum. An essay and an interview are required; letters of recommendation and a personal portfolio or resume are recommended. A high school average of 85 is required. AP and CLEP credits are accepted. Important factors in the admissions decision are advanced placement or honor courses, leadership record, and extracurricular activities record.

Procedure: Freshmen are admitted fall and spring. Entrance exams should be taken by October of the senior year. There are early decision, early admissions, and deferred admissions plans. Early decision applications should be filed by November 15; regular applications, by March 1 for fall entry, along with a $40 fee. There is a rolling admissions plan. Notification of early decision is sent December 15; regular decision, on a rolling basis. 36 early decision candidates were accepted for a recent class. A waiting list is an active part of the admissions procedure. Applications are accepted on-line through SUNY and ESF web sites.

Transfer: 226 transfer students enrolled in a recent year. Transfer requirements vary by major. Students must successfully complete prerequisite course work and must have a 2.0 or higher GPA to be considered. 24 credits of 125 to 130 required for the bachelor's degree must be completed at ESF.

Visiting: There are regularly scheduled orientations for prospective students, including a fall open house, which provides campus tours, faculty sessions, an activities fair, and student affairs presentations. There are guides for informal visits and visitors may sit in on classes. To schedule a visit, contact the Admissions Office.

Financial Aid: In 2003-2004, 80% of all full-time freshmen and 85% of continuing full-time students received some form of financial aid. 80% of all full-time students received need-based aid. The average freshman award was $6425. Need-based scholarships or need-based grants averaged $1400 ($3000 maximum); need-based self-help aid (loans and jobs) averaged $4125 (maximum); and non-need-based awards and

non-need-based scholarships averaged $4350 (maximum). 75% of undergraduates work part time. Average annual earnings from campus work are $1200. The average financial indebtedness of the 2003 graduate was $18,800. ESF is a member of CSS. The FAFSA is required. The deadline for filing freshman financial aid applications for fall entry is March 1.

International Students: There were 7 international students enrolled in a recent year. They must score 550 on the written TOEFL or 213 on the electronic version and also take the SAT I or the ACT.

Computers: The college has a web-based computer system. Public PC clusters offer current technology and software. All are connected to the Web. All students may access the system any time. There are no time limits and no fees.

Graduates: From July 1, 2002 to June 30, 2003, 281 bachelor's degrees were awarded. The most popular majors were environmental and forest biology (38%), environmental studies (19%), and resource management (9%). In an average class, 1% graduate in 3 years or less, 47% graduate in 4 years or less, 68% graduate in 5 years or less, and 69% graduate in 6 years or less. 40 companies recruited on campus in 2002-2003. Of the 2002 graduating class, 25% were enrolled in graduate school within 6 months of graduation and 60% were employed.

Admissions Contact: Susan H. Sanford, Director of Admissions and Inter-Institutional Relations. A video is available.
E-mail: esfinfo@esf.edu Web: www.esf.edu/admissions/htm

STATE UNIVERSITY OF NEW YORK/COLLEGE OF TECHNOLOGY AT ALFRED

B-4

Alfred, NY 14802

(607) 587-4215
(800) 4-ALFRED; Fax: (607) 587-4299

Full-time: 2167 men, 907 women	Faculty: 161; III, -$
Part-time: 99 men, 298 women	Ph.Ds: 14%
Graduate: none	Student/Faculty: 19 to 1
Year: semesters, summer session	Tuition: $5280 ($11,230)
Application Deadline: open	Room & Board: $7136
Freshman Class: 4300 applied, 2537 accepted, 1502 enrolled	
SAT I Verbal/Math: 464/488	ACT: 20 COMPETITIVE

The State University of New York College of Technology at Alfred, founded in 1908, is a public institution conferring associate and bachelor's degrees. There are 3 undergraduate schools. In addition to regional accreditation, Alfred State College has baccalaureate program accreditation with ABET. The 2 libraries contain 71,243 volumes, 594 microform items, and 8148 audio/video tapes/CDs, and subscribe to 448 periodicals. Computerized library services include the card catalog, interlibrary loans, and database searching. Special learning facilities include a learning resource center and radio station. The 150-acre campus is in a rural area 15 miles north of Pennsylvania, 75 miles south of Rochester, and 90 miles southeast of Buffalo. Including any residence halls, there are 48 buildings.

Student Life: 99% of undergraduates are from New York. Students are from 7 states, 5 foreign countries, and Canada. 89% are white. 34% are Catholic; 30% Protestant; 27% claim no religious affiliation; 8% Buddhist, Hindu, and Muslim. The average age of freshmen is 18; all undergraduates, 19. 52% of freshmen remain to graduate.

Housing: 2407 students can be accommodated in college housing, which includes coed dorms. In addition, there are honors houses, special-interest houses, and wellness, computerized, and adult housing. On-campus housing is guaranteed for all 4 years. 70% of students live on campus; of those, 50% remain on campus on weekends. Alcohol is not permitted. All students may keep cars.

Activities: There are 3 local fraternities and 4 local sororities. There are 62 groups on campus, including band, cheerleading, choir, chorale, computers, drama, ethnic, gay, honors, international, jazz band, karate, literary magazine, musical theater, newspaper, peer education network, pep band, professional, radio and TV, rescue and response team, social, social service, student government, and yearbook. Popular campus events include Family Weekend and Hot Dog Day.

Sports: There are 10 intercollegiate sports for men and 8 for women, and 26 intramural sports for men and 23 for women. Facilities include a fitness center/weight room, an indoor swimming pool, a wrestling room, a full gym, tennis courts, an outdoor track, baseball and softball fields, and practice fields.

Disabled Students: All of the campus is accessible. Wheelchair ramps, elevators, special parking, specially equipped rest rooms, special class scheduling, lowered drinking fountains, lowered telephones, and special housing are available.

Services: Counseling and information services are available, as is tutoring in most subjects. There is a reader service for the blind and remedial math, reading, and writing.

Campus Safety and Security: Measures include 24-hour foot and vehicle patrol, self-defense education, security escort services, and shuttle buses. There are informal discussions, pamphlets/posters/films, emergency telephones, and lighted pathways/sidewalks.

Programs of Study: Alfred State College confers B.S., B.B.A., and B.T. degrees. Associate degrees are also awarded. Bachelor's degrees are awarded in COMPUTER AND PHYSICAL SCIENCE (information sciences and systems and web services), ENGINEERING AND ENVIRONMENTAL DESIGN (architectural technology, computer technology, construction management, electrical/electronics engineering technology, electromechanical technology, mechanical engineering technology, and survey and mapping technology). Engineering programs are the strongest academically and have the largest enrollments.

Required: To graduate, candidates for a bachelor's degree must complete a total of 120 credits. A core sequence, including courses in math, physical sciences, and liberal studies, and a year-long senior technical project, are required. A phys ed course is also required.

Special: Cross-registration is offered with Alfred University, Houghton College, Rochester area colleges, and the Western New York Consortium. On-campus work-study programs are available, as are summer internships. There are 2 national honor societies, a freshman honors program, and 52 departmental honors programs.

Faculty/Classroom: 66% of faculty are male; 34%, female. All teach undergraduates. The average class size in an introductory lecture is 40; in a laboratory, 20; and in a regular course, 20.

Admissions: 59% of the 2003-2004 applicants were accepted. 10 freshmen graduated first in their class.

Requirements: The SAT I or ACT is required. In addition, applicants must have graduated from an accredited secondary school or earned a GED. Specific course requirements vary by curriculum. A portfolio is required for applicants interested in computer art and design. A GPA of 3.0 is required. AP and CLEP credits are accepted. Important factors in the admissions decision are recommendations by school officials, advanced placement or honor courses, and leadership record.

Procedure: Freshmen are admitted fall and spring. There is a rolling admissions plan. Application deadlines are open. The application fee is $40. Applications are accepted on-line through the SUNY web site (*www.suny.edu*) or CollegeNET.

Transfer: 226 transfer students enrolled in 2002-2003. Transfer applicants must have a minimum 2.4 GPA. 30 of 120 credits required for the bachelor's degree must be completed at Alfred State College.

Visiting: There are regularly scheduled orientations for prospective students, including open houses during the fall and spring semesters. All aspects of the campus are open for visitation. There are guides for informal visits and visitors may sit in on classes and stay overnight. To schedule a visit, contact the Admissions Office.

Financial Aid: In a recent year, 80% of all full-time freshmen received some form of financial aid. 80% of all full-time students received need-based aid. The average freshman award was $8000. 40% of undergraduates work part time. Average annual earnings from campus work are $1000. The average financial indebtedness of a recent year's graduate was $6000. The FAFSA is required. Check with the school for current application deadlines.

International Students: There were 30 international students enrolled in a recent year. They must score 500 on the written TOEFL.

Computers: The mainframe is a DEC Alpha 1200. There are 1600 PCs available in residence halls, academic buildings, the library, and the Student Development Center. Full Internet access is available via 9 T-1 lines. On-line course registration, student web hosting, on-line library, and a wireless network are also available. All students may access the system 24 hours a day. There are no time limits and no fees.

Graduates: In a recent year, 50 bachelor degrees were awarded. The most popular majors were auto trades (7%), liberal arts and social sciences (6%), and human services (5%). Of a recent year's graduating class, 98% were employed within 6 months of graduation.

Admissions Contact: Deborah Goodrich, Director of Admissions and Enrollment Management. E-mail: *alfredstate.edu*
Web: *www.alfredstate.edu*

STATE UNIVERSITY OF NEW YORK/EMPIRE STATE COLLEGE
D-3

Saratoga Springs, NY 12866-4390   (518) 587-2100, ext. 223
(800) 847-3000, ext. 223; Fax: (518) 580-0105

Full-time: 894 men, 1935 women	**Faculty:** 138; IIB, +$
Part-time: 3337 men, 3189 women	**Ph.D.s:** 91%
Graduate: 132 men, 235 women	**Student/Faculty:** 21 to 1
Year: trimesters	**Tuition:** $4505 ($10,455)
Application Deadline: see profile	**Room & Board:** n/app
Freshman Class: n/av	
SAT I or ACT: not required	**SPECIAL**

Empire State College founded in 1971 as part of the State University of New York, offers degree programs in the arts and sciences through its statewide network of more than 35 regional centers and units. The needs of adult learners are met through guided independent study, distance learning, study groups, cross-registration, and credit for lifelong learning. Administration and coordination is based at the center in Saratoga Springs. Computerized library services include the card catalog, interlibrary loans, and database searching. Special learning facilities include a learning resource center and a technology building.

Student Life: 85% of undergraduates are from New York. Others are from 50 states, 35 foreign countries, and Canada. 65% are white; 12% African American. The average age of all undergraduates is 36. 33% do not continue beyond their first year.

Housing: There are no residence halls. All students commute. Alcohol is not permitted.

Activities: There are 17 groups on campus, including literary magazine and student government. Regional centers sponsor events and outside speakers throughout the year.

Sports: There is no sports program at Empire State College.

Disabled Students: 85% of the campus is accessible.

Programs of Study: Empire State College confers B.A., B.S., and B.P.S. degrees. Associate and master's degrees are also awarded. Bachelor's degrees are awarded in BUSINESS (business administration and management, labor studies, and management science), COMPUTER AND PHYSICAL SCIENCE (mathematics and science), EDUCATION (education), SOCIAL SCIENCE (community services, economics, history, human development, humanities and social science, interdisciplinary studies, liberal arts/general studies, and sociology). Business, management, and economics are the largest.

Required: Students must earn 128 credits, including 24 in their major and 30 credits that meet SUNY general education requirements, to graduate. Degree programs are customized and vary in content.

Special: Empire State College offers cross-registration with 21 other accredited institutions, internships in government, business, nonprofits, and academia, and study abroad in Athens, Thessalonica, Prague, and Cyprus. Accelerated degrees and dual and student-designed majors are possible in all programs, and nondegree study also is possible. Credit is granted for life, military, and work experience.

Faculty/Classroom: 50% of faculty are male; 50%, female. 99% teach undergraduates and 1% both teach and do research. No introductory courses are taught by graduate students.

Requirements: In addition, applicants must be high school graduates, have a GED, or show ability to succeed at the college level. Empire State College also considers the ability of a learning location to meet individual needs. AP and CLEP credits are accepted. Important factors in the admissions decision are recommendations by school officials and personality/intangible qualities.

Procedure: Freshmen are admitted to all sessions. There is a rolling admissions plan. Some programs have open application deadlines; other have specific deadlines, check with the school. Notification is sent on a rolling basis. Applications are accepted on-line through the college's web site at *www.esc.edu/admissions*.

Transfer: 3455 transfer students enrolled in 2002-2003. Empire State College offers maximum flexibility to transfer applicants, who must provide official transcripts from previous colleges attended. 32 of 128 credits required for the bachelor's degree must be completed at Empire State College.

Visiting: There are regularly scheduled orientations for prospective students, by invitation, after students attend an information session. There are guides for informal visits. To schedule a visit, contact Melanie Kaiser at (518) 587-2100, ext. 447 or *melaniekaiser@esc.edu* or contact the individual center of interest.

Financial Aid: In a recent year, 50% of all full-time students received some form of financial aid. 45% of all full-time students received need-based aid. The average financial indebtedness of a recent graduate was $4328. The FAFSA is required.

International Students: There are 35 international students enrolled. They must score 550 on the written TOEFL or 213 on the electronic version.

Computers: The mainframe is an HP Alpha GS-80. There are also 150 PCs distributed among the college's branches and student labs. All students may access the system 24 hours a day. There are no time limits and no fees. It is strongly recommended that all students have a personal computer.

Graduates: In a recent year, 1489 bachelor's degrees were awarded. The most popular majors were business, management, and economics (38%), community and human services (20%), and interdisciplinary studies (7%). In an average class, 42% graduate in 6 years or less.

Admissions Contact: Jennifer Riley, Assistant Director of Admissions. A video is available. E-mail: *admissions@esc.edu* Web: *www.esc.edu*

STATE UNIVERSITY OF NEW YORK/FASHION INSTITUTE OF TECHNOLOGY
(See Fashion Institute of Technology/State University of New York)

STATE UNIVERSITY OF NEW YORK/MARITIME COLLEGE   D-5

Throggs Neck, NY 10465 (718) 409-7220
(800) 642-1874 (Northeast only); Fax: (718) 409-7465

Full-time: 560 men, 80 women	**Faculty:** 56; IIA, -$
Part-time: 10 men, 5 women	**Ph.D.s:** 41%
Graduate: 160 men, 20 women	**Student/Faculty:** 11 to 1
Year: semesters, summer session	**Tuition:** $3525 ($8425)
Application Deadline: open	**Room & Board:** $6500
Freshman Class: n/av	
SAT I: required	**LESS COMPETITIVE**

The Maritime College of the State University of New York, founded in 1874, is a public institution that prepares students for the U.S. Merchant Marine officers' license and for bachelor's degrees in engineering, naval architecture, marine environmental science, and marine transportation/business administration. The college curriculum includes 3 summer semesters at sea aboard the training ship Empire State VI. Tuition and fees total approximately $3525 for students from New York, Connecticut, New Jersey, Pennsylavania, Delaware, Maryland, and Virginia. All others pay approximately $8425. Figures in the above capsule and in this profile are approximate. In addition to regional accreditation, New York Maritime has baccalaureate program accreditation with ABET. The library contains 81,386 volumes, 12,923 microform items, and 3025 audio/video tapes/CDs, and subscribes to 333 periodicals. Computerized library services include interlibrary loans and database searching. Special learning facilities include a learning resource center, planetarium, a 17,000-ton training ship, a tug, a barge, and a center for simulated marine operations, which contains bridge, radar, tanker, and oil spill response simulators. The 55-acre campus is in a suburban area on the Throgs Neck peninsula where Long Island Sound meets the East River. Including any residence halls, there are 27 buildings.

Student Life: 72% of undergraduates are from New York. Students are from 23 states and 15 foreign countries. 57% are from public schools. 78% are white. The average age of freshmen is 18; all undergraduates, 20. 12% do not continue beyond their first year; 62% remain to graduate.

Housing: 800 students can be accommodated in college housing, which includes single-sex and coed dorms. On-campus housing is guaranteed for all 4 years. 97% of students live on campus; of those, 65% remain on campus on weekends. Alcohol is not permitted. Upperclassmen may keep cars.

Activities: There are no fraternities or sororities. There are 38 groups on campus, including art, bagpipe band, band, cheerleading, chess, chorus, computers, drill team, ethnic, honors, international, jazz band, marching band, newspaper, photography, political, professional, religious, social, social service, student government, and yearbook. Popular campus events include spring formal, Friday night mixers, and Admiral's Ball.

Sports: There are 12 intercollegiate sports for men and 8 for women, and 6 intramural sports for men and 4 for women. Facilities include an athletic center containing a 2000-seat gym, a swimming pool, exercise and weight rooms, a rifle and pistol range, and 4 handball/racquetball and squash courts; a sailing center; and baseball, lacrosse, and soccer fields.

Disabled Students: 90% of the campus is accessible. Wheelchair ramps, elevators, special parking, and specially equipped rest rooms are available.

Services: Counseling and information services are available, as is tutoring in every subject.

Campus Safety and Security: Measures include 24-hour foot and vehicle patrol, informal discussions, emergency telephones, and lighted pathways/sidewalks.

Programs of Study: New York Maritime confers B.S. and B.E. degrees. Associate and master's degrees are also awarded. Bachelor's degrees are awarded in BIOLOGICAL SCIENCE (marine science), BUSINESS (business administration and management and transportation management), COMPUTER AND PHYSICAL SCIENCE (atmospheric sciences and meteorology), ENGINEERING AND ENVIRONMENTAL DESIGN (electrical/electronics engineering, engineering, environmental science, marine engineering, maritime science, and naval architecture and marine engineering), SOCIAL SCIENCE (humanities). Engineering, naval architecture, and marine transportation/business administration are the strongest academically. Marine transportation/business administration is the largest.

Required: To graduate, students must complete the U.S. Merchant Marine officers' license program. Bachelor's degree candidates must earn 160 credit hours, with a GPA of 2.0. Distribution requirements and the number of hours required in the major varies. All students must spend 3 summer semesters at sea acquiring hands-on experience aboard the college's training vessel.

Special: The college offers co-op programs in engineering, an accelerated degree program in marine transportation/transportation manage-

ment, and internships as cadet observers aboard commercial ships. There are 2 national honor societies and 2 departmental honors programs.

Faculty/Classroom: 94% teach undergraduates, 12% do research, and 12% do both. No introductory courses are taught by graduate students. The average class size in an introductory lecture is 25; in a laboratory, 15; and in a regular course, 20.

Requirements: The SAT I is required. In addition, applicants must be high school graduates or hold a GED. 16 Carnegie units are required, including 4 years of English, 3 of math (4 are preferred), and 1 of physics or chemistry. An essay is required and an interview is recommended. AP and CLEP credits are accepted. Important factors in the admissions decision are advanced placement or honor courses, extracurricular activities record, and leadership record.

Procedure: Freshmen are admitted in the fall. Entrance exams should be taken during the junior or senior year. There are early decision, early admissions, and deferred admissions plans. Application deadlines are open. Students may apply on-line or on blank preformatted disks available from the Admissions Office.

Transfer: Transfer students must have a 2.5 GPA. All applicants must complete the Indoctrination Program and fulfill degree and license requirements at New York Maritime. All 160 credits required for the bachelor's degree must be completed at New York Maritime.

Visiting: There are regularly scheduled orientations for prospective students, including a tour of the campus and facilities and meetings with faculty and students. There are guides for informal visits and visitors may sit in on classes and stay overnight. To schedule a visit, contact the Admissions Office.

Financial Aid: The FAFSA and student and parent federal income tax returns are required.

International Students: The school actively recruits these students. They must score 500 on the written TOEFL and also take the SAT I or the ACT.

Computers: The mainframe is a Prime 4050. There are 27 terminals, 8 CAD stations, and 58 PCs. All students may access the system from 8:30 A.M. to 11 P.M. The computer center stays open after 11 P.M. when there is sufficient demand. There are no time limits and no fees.

Admissions Contact: Peter Cooney, Director of Admissions and Enrollment Management. A video is available. E-mail: *sunymaritime.edu* Web: *www.sunymaritime.edu*

STATE UNIVERSITY OF NEW YORK/UNIVERSITY AT ALBANY   D-3

Albany, NY 12222 (518) 442-5435
(800) 293-7869; Fax: (518) 442-5383

Full-time: 5356 men, 5362 women	**Faculty:** 382; I, av$
Part-time: 519 men, 559 women	**Ph.D.s:** 97%
Graduate: 1997 men, 3205 women	**Student/Faculty:** 28 to 1
Year: semesters, summer session	**Tuition:** $5770 ($11,720)
Application Deadline: March 1	**Room & Board:** $7181
Freshman Class: 17,328 applied, 9672 accepted, 2161 enrolled	
SAT I: required	**ACT:** n/av
	HIGHLY COMPETITIVE

The State University of New York/University at Albany, established in 1844, is a public institution conferring undergraduate degrees in humanities and fine arts, science and math, social and behavioral sciences, business, public policy, education, and social welfare. There are 7 undergraduate and 9 graduate schools. In addition to regional accreditation, University at Albany has baccalaureate program accreditation with AACSB, ACS, ALA, APA, and CSWE. The 3 libraries contain 2,035,816 volumes, 2,841,494 microform items, and 118,806 audio/video tapes/CDs, and subscribe to 29,598 periodicals. Computerized library services include the card catalog, interlibrary loans, database searching, and Internet access. Special learning facilities include a learning resource center, art gallery, radio station, a linear accelerator, a sophisticated weather data system, a national lightning detection system, an interactive media center, extensive art studios, and a state-of-the-art electronic library. The 560-acre campus is in a suburban area about 5 miles west of downtown Albany. Including any residence halls, there are 90 buildings.

Student Life: 93% of undergraduates are from New York. Students are from 37 states, 51 foreign countries, and Canada. 65% are white. The average age of freshmen is 18; all undergraduates, 21. 16% do not continue beyond their first year; 63% remain to graduate.

Housing: 7200 students can be accommodated in college housing, which includes single-sex and coed dorms, on-campus apartments, and married-student housing. In addition, there are honors houses and special-interest houses. On-campus housing is available on a first-come, first-served basis and is available on a lottery system for upperclassmen. Freshmen are required to live on campus. Priority is given to out-of-town students. 54% of students live on campus. Alcohol is not permitted. Upperclassmen may keep cars.

Activities: 4% of men belong to 2 local and 11 national fraternities; 4% of women belong to 4 local and 13 national sororities. There are 160

groups on campus, including band, chamber singers, cheerleading, chess, chorale, computers, dance, debate, drama, electronic music ensemble, ethnic, gay, honors, international, jazz band, literary magazine, newspaper, orchestra, pep band, percussion ensemble, photography, political, professional, radio and TV, religious, social, social service, student government, symphony, and yearbook. Popular campus events include outdoor concerts, Springtime Fountain Festival, and fall semester "Clash of the Quad."

Sports: There are 8 intercollegiate sports for men and 11 for women, and 13 intramural sports for men and 9 for women. Facilities include a gym with an Olympic-size pool; an ancillary gym with a quarter-mile track; football, softball, soccer, and practice fields; and a 5000-seat recreation and convocation center.

Disabled Students: 99% of the campus is accessible. Wheelchair ramps, elevators, special parking, specially equipped rest rooms, lowered drinking fountains, and lowered telephones are available. Disabled Student Services provides a broad range of personalized services to people with disabilities including preadmission information and accessible housing information.

Services: Counseling and information services are available, as is tutoring in most subjects. There is a reader service for the blind and remedial math, reading, and writing. An Excel program provides low-income of first-generation college students with a variety of mentoring, tutorial, and counseling services.

Campus Safety and Security: Measures include 24-hour foot and vehicle patrol, self-defense education, security escort services, and shuttle buses. There are informal discussions, pamphlets/posters/films, emergency telephones, and lighted pathways/sidewalks.

Programs of Study: University at Albany confers B.A. and B.S. degrees. Master's and doctoral degrees are also awarded. Bachelor's degrees are awarded in BIOLOGICAL SCIENCE (biochemistry, biology/biological science, and molecular biology), BUSINESS (accounting and business administration and management), COMMUNICATIONS AND THE ARTS (art history and appreciation, Chinese, communications, dramatic arts, English, fine arts, French, Hebrew, Italian, Latin, linguistics, music, Russian, and Spanish), COMPUTER AND PHYSICAL SCIENCE (actuarial science, applied mathematics, atmospheric sciences and meteorology, chemistry, computer science, earth science, geology, information sciences and systems, mathematics, and physics), EDUCATION (English, foreign languages, mathematics, science, secondary, and social studies), ENGINEERING AND ENVIRONMENTAL DESIGN (urban design), HEALTH PROFESSIONS (medical laboratory technology, predentistry, and premedicine), SOCIAL SCIENCE (African American studies, anthropology, Asian/Oriental studies, Caribbean studies, classical/ancient civilization, criminal justice, Eastern European studies, economics, geography, Hispanic American studies, history, Latin American studies, medieval studies, philosophy, political science/government, prelaw, psychology, religion, Russian and Slavic studies, social work, sociology, and women's studies). Criminal justice, information technology, and public administration and policy are the strongest academically. Psychology, English, and business are the largest.

Required: To graduate, students must complete a total of 120 credits with a 2.0 GPA in their major and minor, including 30 to 36 credits required in the major for a B.A. degree and 30 to 42 credits for a B.S. degree. B.A. degree candidates must complete 90 credits in liberal arts courses and B.S. candidates must complete 60. All students must complete a writing requirement and a general education core consisting of a minimum of 24 credits in natural sciences, social sciences, humanities, and the arts, 3 credits in an approved course in cultural and historical perspectives, and 3 credits of an approved course in human diversity. Students must also demonstrate a basic proficiency in a language other than English.

Special: Cross-registration is available with Rensselaer Polytechnic Institute, Albany Law School, and Union, Siena, and Russell Sage Colleges. Internships may be arranged with state government agencies and private organizations. Study abroad in many countries, a Washington semester, B.A.-B.S. degrees, and work-study programs are offered. Dual and student-designed majors, nondegree study, and pass/fail grading options are available. A 3-2 engineering degree with 1 of 4 institutions is also possible. There are 15 national honor societies, including Phi Beta Kappa, a freshman honors program, and 29 departmental honors programs.

Faculty/Classroom: 64% of faculty are male; 36%, female. 90% teach undergraduates and 75% do research. Graduate students teach 20% of introductory courses. The average class size in an introductory lecture is 33; in a laboratory, 15; and in a regular course, 29.

Admissions: 56% of the 2003-2004 applicants were accepted. The SAT I scores for the 2003-2004 freshman class were: Verbal--9% below 500, 54% between 500 and 599, 34% between 600 and 700, and 4% above 700; Math--5% below 500, 50% between 500 and 599, 39% between 600 and 700, and 5% above 700. 47% of the current freshmen were in the top fifth of their class; 87% were in the top two fifths. 11 freshmen graduated first in their class.

Requirements: The SAT I is required, with the SAT I preferred, but the ACT accepted. Applicants must be graduates of an accredited secondary school or have a GED. 18 academic credits are required, including 2 to 3 units of math and 2 units of lab sciences. Foreign language study is also recommended. AP and CLEP credits are accepted. Important factors in the admissions decision are advanced placement or honor courses, personality/intangible qualities, and leadership record.

Procedure: Freshmen are admitted fall, spring, and summer. Entrance exams should be taken by November of the senior year. There are early decision, early action, and deferred admissions plans. There is a rolling admissions plan. Early decision applications should be filed by December 1; regular applications, by March 1 for fall entry, December 1 for spring entry, and May 1 for summer entry, along with a $40 fee. Notification of early action is sent before January 1; regular decision, on a rolling basis. A waiting list is an active part of the admissions procedure. Applications are accepted on-line through the school's web site.

Transfer: 1136 transfer students enrolled in 2002-2003. Admission to certain programs is competitive and based not only on a required GPA, but also on completion of a certain set of prerequisite core courses. A grade average of B or better is required for applicants to the accounting, business administration, criminal justice, and social welfare programs. 30 of 120 credits required for the bachelor's degree must be completed at University at Albany.

Visiting: There are regularly scheduled orientations for prospective students, including a 2-day summer orientation session. There are guides for informal visits and visitors may sit in on classes. To schedule a visit, contact the Undergraduate Admissions Office at campusvisit@albany.edu.

Financial Aid: In 2003-2004, 65% of all full-time freshmen and 62% of continuing full-time students received some form of financial aid. 50% of all full-time students received need-based aid. The average freshman award was $7685. 25% of undergraduates work part time. The average financial indebtedness of the 2003 graduate was $16,700. University at Albany is a member of CSS. The FAFSA is required. New York state residents will receive an Express TAP application 1 month after filing FAFSA. The deadline for filing freshman financial aid applications for fall entry is March 15.

International Students: There are 185 international students enrolled. The school actively recruits these students. They must score 550 on the written TOEFL or 213 on the electronic version. International students may submit either their SAT I or TOEFL results.

Computers: The mainframes are an IBM 9672-R21 and VAX and UNIX clusters. The computing services center networks provide e-mail facilities and Internet access. Computer access rooms, terminals in residence halls, and phone hookups provide 24-hour access to mainframe computing facilities. All students may access the system. There are no time limits and no fees.

Graduates: From July 1, 2002 to June 30, 2003, 2640 bachelor's degrees were awarded. The most popular majors were psychology (14%), business (14%), and English (10%). In an average class, 52% graduate in 4 years or less, 60% graduate in 5 years or less, and 63% graduate in 6 years or less. 180 companies recruited on campus in 2002-2003. Of the 2002 graduating class, 33% were enrolled in graduate school within 6 months of graduation and 59% were employed.

Admissions Contact: Robert Andrea, Director, Undergraduate Admissions. E-mail: ugadmissions@albany.edu Web: www.albany.edu

STATE UNIVERSITY OF NEW YORK/UNIVERSITY AT BINGHAMTON   C-4
Binghamton, NY 13902-6000

(607) 777-2171
Fax: (607) 777-4445

Full-time: 5038 men, 5254 women	**Faculty:** 504; I, av$
Part-time: 100 men, 171 women	**Ph.Ds:** 93%
Graduate: 1461 men, 1361 women	**Student/Faculty:** 20 to 1
Year: semesters, summer session	**Tuition:** $5687 ($11,637)
Application Deadline: February 15	**Room & Board:** $7100
Freshman Class: 19,076 applied, 8521 accepted, 2291 enrolled	
SAT I Verbal/Math: 600/630	**ACT:** 27 **HIGHLY COMPETITIVE**

State University of New York/University at Binghamton, founded in 1946, is part of the State University of New York System. The public institution offers programs through the Harpur College of Arts and Sciences and the Schools of Education and Human Development, Nursing, Management, and Engineering and Applied Science. There are 5 undergraduate schools and 1 graduate school. In addition to regional accreditation, Binghamton University has baccalaureate program accreditation with AACSB, ABET, APA, CCNE, CSAB, and NASM. The 2 libraries contain 1,811,142 volumes, 1,833,658 microform items, and 119,047 audio/video tapes/CDs, and subscribe to 6857 periodicals. Computerized library services include the card catalog, interlibrary loans, and database searching. Special learning facilities include a learning resource center, art gallery, radio station, TV station, nature preserve, and a 4-climate greenhouse. The 887-acre campus is in a suburban area 1 mile west of Binghamton. Including any residence halls, there are 90 buildings.

Student Life: 92% of undergraduates are from New York. Students are from 37 states, 58 foreign countries, and Canada. 87% are from public schools. 64% are white; 19% Asian American. 31% are Catholic; 21%

claim no religious affiliation; 21% Jewish; 20% Protestant. The average age of freshmen is 18; all undergraduates, 20. 8% do not continue beyond their first year; 80% remain to graduate.

Housing: 6005 students can be accommodated in college housing, which includes coed dorms, on-campus apartments, and married-student housing. In addition, there are special-interest houses, and chemical-free and smoke-free housing. On-campus housing is available on a lottery system for upperclassmen. 57% of students live on campus; of those, 95% remain on campus on weekends. Upperclassmen may keep cars.

Activities: 8% of men belong to 1 local and 19 national fraternities; 7% of women belong to 15 national sororities. There are 176 groups on campus, including art, band, cheerleading, chess, choir, chorale, chorus, computers, cultural, dance, debate, drama, ethnic, film, gay, honors, international, jazz band, literary magazine, musical theater, newspaper, opera, orchestra, pep band, photography, political, professional, radio and TV, religious, social, social service, student government, symphony, and yearbook. Popular campus events include Caribbean Carnival, Spring Fling, and University Fest.

Sports: There are 10 intercollegiate sports for men and 10 for women, and 20 intramural sports for men and 18 for women. Facilities include 2 gyms with swimming pools, an indoor track, dance and karate studios, basketball, volleyball, squash, racquetball, and tennis courts, a weight room, batting and driving cages, a cross-country course, a fitness center, a 400-meter track and soccer complex, plus many playing fields. The larger gym seats 2600. An Events Center contains basketball/tennis courts and a 200-meter indoor track, with seating for 6000 to 8000.

Disabled Students: 90% of the campus is accessible. Wheelchair ramps, elevators, special parking, specially equipped rest rooms, special class scheduling, lowered drinking fountains, lowered telephones, special housing, a wheelchair van service, adapted computer stations, and a comprehensive array of services for university students with physical or learning disabilities are available.

Services: Counseling and information services are available, as is tutoring in most subjects. There is a reader service for the blind. Some computer-assisted instruction is available, particularly in languages. Peer walk-in tutoring is available 6 days per week.

Campus Safety and Security: Measures include 24-hour foot and vehicle patrol, self-defense education, security escort services, and shuttle buses. There are informal discussions, pamphlets/posters/films, emergency telephones, lighted pathways/sidewalks, police officers, monitored entrance to campus with proper identification between midnight and 5 A.M., keycard entry to residence halls, and formal personal safety programs.

Programs of Study: Binghamton University confers B.A., B.S., B.F.A., and B.Mus. degrees. Master's and doctoral degrees are also awarded. Bachelor's degrees are awarded in BIOLOGICAL SCIENCE (biochemistry and biology/biological science), BUSINESS (accounting and business administration and management), COMMUNICATIONS AND THE ARTS (Arabic, art, art history and appreciation, classics, comparative literature, dramatic arts, English, film arts, fine arts, French, German, Hebrew, Italian, Latin, linguistics, music, music performance, Spanish, speech/debate/rhetoric, and studio art), COMPUTER AND PHYSICAL SCIENCE (actuarial science, chemistry, computer science, geology, mathematics, and physics), ENGINEERING AND ENVIRONMENTAL DESIGN (bioengineering, computer engineering, electrical/electronics engineering, environmental science, industrial engineering, mechanical engineering, and systems engineering), HEALTH PROFESSIONS (nursing), SOCIAL SCIENCE (African American studies, anthropology, Asian/American studies, Caribbean studies, classical/ancient civilization, economics, geography, history, human development, interdisciplinary studies, Judaic studies, Latin American studies, medieval studies, philosophy, political science/government, psychobiology, psychology, and sociology). Accounting and anthropology are the strongest academically. Management, psychology, and economics are the largest.

Required: To graduate, all students must complete 120 to 133 credit hours, with 36 to 72 in the major, and a minimum GPA of 2.0. General education requirements over the first 2 years include courses in language and communication, global vision, science and math, aesthetic perspective, physical activity/wellness, and identity. Other requirements vary by school.

Special: The university offers innovative study through the Innovational Projects Board, internships, study abroad in more than 100 countries, a Washington semester through American University, on- and off-campus work-study programs, and B.A.-B.S. degrees in 28 departments in arts and sciences and in the professional schools. There are also dual and interdisciplinary majors such as philosophy, politics, and law, student-designed majors, pass/fail options, and independent study. The 3-2 engineering degree is possible with SUNY at Buffalo, SUNY at Stony Brook, Columbia University, Rochester Institute of Technology, University of Rochester, Clarkson University, and Binghamton University. Binghamton is also a member of the National Student Exchange and International Student Exchange. Other 3-2 degrees are offered through Harpur College. There are 20 national honor societies, including Phi Beta Kappa, a freshman honors program, and 32 departmental honors programs.

Faculty/Classroom: 64% of faculty are male; 36%, female. All both teach and do research. Graduate students teach 18% of introductory courses. The average class size in an introductory lecture is 59; in a laboratory, 17; and in a regular course, 28.

Admissions: 45% of the 2003-2004 applicants were accepted. The SAT I scores for the 2003-2004 freshman class were: Verbal--5% below 500, 42% between 500 and 599, 46% between 600 and 700, and 7% above 700; Math--2% below 500, 25% between 500 and 599, 56% between 600 and 700, and 17% above 700. The ACT scores were 4% below 21, 10% between 21 and 23, 34% between 24 and 26, 28% between 27 and 28, and 25% above 28. 76% of the current freshmen were in the top fifth of their class; 98% were in the top two fifths. 10 freshmen graduated first in their class.

Requirements: The SAT I or ACT is required. In addition, applicants must be graduates of an accredited secondary school, or have a GED certificate, and complete 16 academic credits. These include 4 units of English, 3 units of 1 foreign language or 2 units each of 2 foreign languages, 2.5 of math, and 2 each of science and social studies. Students may submit slides of artwork, request an audition for music, prepare a videotape for dance or theater, or share athletic achievements. An essay is required. AP and CLEP credits are accepted. Important factors in the admissions decision are advanced placement or honor courses, extracurricular activities record, and evidence of special talent.

Procedure: Freshmen are admitted fall and spring. Entrance exams should be taken in the spring of the junior year or the fall of the senior year. There are early admissions, deferred admissions, early action, and rolling admissions plans. Early action applications should be filed by November 1; regular applications, by February 15 for fall entry and November 15 for spring entry. Notification of early action is sent December 20; regular decision, on a rolling basis.The fall 2003 application fee was $30. 382 applicants were on the 2003 waiting list; 105 were admitted. Applications are accepted on-line through the home page at www.binghamton.edu.

Transfer: 728 transfer students enrolled in 2003–2004. Applicants must submit college transcripts; students who wish to transfer after their first year of college must also submit their high school transcripts. 30 of 120 to 133 credits required for the bachelor's degree must be completed at Binghamton University.

Visiting: There are regularly scheduled orientations for prospective students, including an information session and a tour of campus to be scheduled a week in advance of a visit. Visitors may sit in on classes. To schedule a visit, contact the Office of Undergraduate Admissions at admit@binghamton.edu.

Financial Aid: In 2003-2004, 80% of all full-time freshmen and 71% of continuing full-time students received some form of financial aid. 80% of full-time freshmen and 70% of continuing full-time students received need-based aid. The average freshman award was $13,896. Need-based scholarships or need-based grants averaged $3986 ($20,940 maximum); need-based self-help aid (loans and jobs) averaged $3823 ($20,940 maximum); non-need-based athletic scholarships averaged $7082 ($20,940 maximum); and other non-need-based awards and non-need-based scholarships averaged $8479 ($20,940 maximum). 13% of undergraduates work part time. Average annual earnings from campus work are $1000. The average financial indebtedness of the 2003 graduate was $14,531. Binghamton University is a member of CSS. The FAFSA is required. The deadline for filing freshman financial aid applications for fall entry is March 1.

International Students: There are 327 international students enrolled. The school actively recruits these students. They must score 550 on the written TOEFL. The TOEFL replaces the SAT I or ACT for nonnative speakers of English.

Computers: The mainframes are comprised of 2 IBM 9000 series and a cluster of 5 Sun servers. Each student is given a computer account, e-mail account, and personal web space. Terminals and PCs are available in libraries, some academic areas, and some residence halls. All residence hall rooms have Ethernet and Internet connections. More than 98% of residents bring a computer to campus and connect to the network. Public computer labs are available in the library, in 5 academic buildings, and in 3 residence hall complexes. In labs, students have access to a shared file system and laser printing (75 pages per week). All students may access the system 24 hours per day. There are no time limits and no fees.

Graduates: From July 1, 2002 to June 30, 2003, 2393 bachelor's degrees were awarded. The most popular majors were management (11%), psychology (10%), and economics/English (9%). In an average class, 3% graduate in 3 years or less, 70% graduate in 4 years or less, 78% graduate in 5 years or less, and 80% graduate in 6 years or less. 92 companies recruited on campus in 2002-2003. Of the 2002 graduating class, 38% were enrolled in graduate school within 6 months of graduation and 82% were employed.

Admissions Contact: Cheryl Brown, Director, Undergraduate Admissions. E-mail: admit@binghamton.edu Web: www.binghamton.edu

STATE UNIVERSITY OF NEW YORK/UNIVERSITY AT BUFFALO

A-3

Buffalo, NY 14260

(716) 645-6900
(888) ub-admit; Fax: (716) 645-6498

Full-time: 8921 men, 7298 women	**Faculty:** 1024; I, +$
Part-time: 847 men, 752 women	**Ph.D.s:** 98%
Graduate: 4557 men, 4880 women	**Student/Faculty:** 16 to 1
Year: semesters, summer session	**Tuition:** $5856 ($11,806)
Application Deadline: see profile	**Room & Board:** $6707
Freshman Class: 17,448 applied, 10,890 accepted, 3594 enrolled	
SAT I Verbal/Math: 570/598	**ACT:** 26 **VERY COMPETITIVE**

The State University of New York at Buffalo, established in 1846, is a public institution offering more than 300 bachelor's, master's, and doctoral degree programs. There are 9 undergraduate and 14 graduate schools. In addition to regional accreditation, UB has baccalaureate program accreditation with AACSB, ABA, ABET, ACOTE, ACPE, ADA, ALA, APA, APTA, ASHA, CCNE, CORE, CSWE, JRCNMT, LCM, NAAB, NAACLS, NASAD, and PAB. The 10 libraries contain 3,330,476 volumes, 5,353,719 microform items, and 186,300 audio/video tapes/CDs, and subscribe to 32,796 periodicals. Computerized library services include the card catalog, interlibrary loans, database searching, and Internet access. Special learning facilities include a learning resource center, art gallery, radio station, an anthropology research museum, an observatory, a concert hall, a theater, a nature preserve, a nuclear reactor, and an earthquake research center. The 1350-acre campus is in a suburban area 3 miles north of Buffalo. Including any residence halls, there are 193 buildings.

Student Life: 92% of undergraduates are from New York. Others are from 42 states, 112 foreign countries, and Canada. 71% are white; 10% Asian American. The average age of freshmen is 18; all undergraduates, 22. 15% do not continue beyond their first year; 57% remain to graduate.

Housing: 7547 students can be accommodated in college housing, which includes coed dorms and on-campus apartments. In addition, there are honors houses, special-interest houses, and freshman-only housing. On-campus housing is guaranteed for all 4 years. 63% of students commute. All students may keep cars.

Activities: 2% of men belong to 3 local and 19 national fraternities; 4% of women belong to 4 local and 14 national sororities. There are 200 groups on campus, including art, band, cheerleading, chess, choir, chorale, chorus, computers, dance, drama, ethnic, film, gay, honors, international, jazz band, literary magazine, marching band, musical theater, newspaper, orchestra, pep band, photography, political, professional, radio and TV, religious, social, social service, student government, symphony, and yearbook. Popular campus events include Fall Fest, Spring Fest, and International Fiesta.

Sports: There are 9 intercollegiate sports for men and 9 for women, and 12 intramural sports for men and 12 for women. Facilities include racquetball, squash, tennis, basketball, volleyball, badminton, and handball courts; baseball, soccer, hockey, and multipurpose fields; a football and track and field stadium; an indoor jogging track; an Olympic-size pool and diving well; a triple gym; weight training and wrestling rooms; dance studios; and a spinning room.

Disabled Students: 90% of the campus is accessible. Wheelchair ramps, elevators, special parking, specially equipped rest rooms, special class scheduling, lowered drinking fountains, lowered telephones, special housing, pool accessibility, and wheelchair vans for transport are available.

Services: Counseling and information services are available, as is tutoring in most subjects. There is a reader service for the blind, remedial math, reading, and writing, peer tutoring, and some computer-assisted instruction.

Campus Safety and Security: Measures include 24-hour foot and vehicle patrol, self-defense education, security escort services, and shuttle buses. There are informal discussions, pamphlets/posters/films, emergency telephones, lighted pathways/sidewalks, an alarm system, after-hours card access to academic facilities, community patrols, and a university-wide safety committee.

Programs of Study: UB confers B.A., B.S., B.F.A., B.P.S., and Mus.B. degrees. Master's and doctoral degrees are also awarded. Bachelor's degrees are awarded in BIOLOGICAL SCIENCE (biochemistry, biology/biological science, biophysics, and biotechnology), BUSINESS (business administration and management), COMMUNICATIONS AND THE ARTS (art history and appreciation, classics, communications, dance, dramatic arts, English, fine arts, French, German, Italian, linguistics, media arts, music, music performance, musical theater, Spanish, and studio art), COMPUTER AND PHYSICAL SCIENCE (chemistry, computer science, geology, mathematics, physics, and statistics), ENGINEERING AND ENVIRONMENTAL DESIGN (aeronautical engineering, architectural technology, architecture, chemical engineering, civil engineering, computer engineering, electrical/electronics engineering, engineering physics, environmental design, environmental engineering, industrial en-

gineering, and mechanical engineering), HEALTH PROFESSIONS (exercise science, medical technology, nuclear medical technology, nursing, occupational therapy, pharmacy, physical therapy, and speech pathology/audiology), SOCIAL SCIENCE (African American studies, American studies, anthropology, Asian/Oriental studies, economics, geography, history, philosophy, political science/government, psychology, social science, sociology, and women's studies). Business administration, psychology, and engineering are the strongest academically.

Required: To graduate, students must complete 120 semester hours with a minimum GPA of 2.0. General education requirements include writing, math, and library skills, intermediate language proficiency, and courses in math or computer science, world civilization, American pluralism, scientific literacy, literature and arts, and social and behavioral sciences.

Special: Students may cross-register with the Western New York Consortium. Internships are available, and students may study abroad in 29 countries. UB offers a Washington semester; work-study programs, accelerated degree programs, B.A.-B.S. degrees, dual, student-designed, and interdisciplinary majors, including biochemical pharmacology and medicinal chemistry, nondegree study, and credit for military experience. A 3-2 engineering degree can be pursued. Students may choose a successful/unsuccessful (S/U) grading option for selected courses. There is an early assurance of admission program to medical school for students who have completed 3 semesters with a GPA of 3.5. There are 29 national honor societies, including Phi Beta Kappa, and a freshman honors program. All departments have honors programs.

Faculty/Classroom: 67% of faculty are male; 33%, female. 79% teach undergraduates and all do research. Graduate students teach 20% of introductory courses. The average class size in an introductory lecture is 51; in a laboratory, 26; and in a regular course, 36.

Admissions: 62% of the 2003-2004 applicants were accepted. The SAT I scores for the 2003-2004 freshman class were: Verbal--13% below 500, 53% between 500 and 599, 30% between 600 and 700, and 4% above 700; Math--5% below 500, 45% between 500 and 599, 44% between 600 and 700, and 6% above 700. The ACT scores were 1% below 21, 19% between 21 and 23, 37% between 24 and 26, 22% between 27 and 28, and 21% above 28. 51% of the current freshmen were in the top fifth of their class; 88% were in the top two fifths. 28 freshmen graduated first in their class.

Requirements: The SAT I is required. In addition, applicants must be graduates of an accredited secondary school or have a GED. Art applicants must submit a portfolio; music applicants must audition. AP and CLEP credits are accepted. Important factors in the admissions decision are extracurricular activities record, evidence of special talent, and leadership record.

Procedure: Freshmen are admitted fall and spring. Entrance exams should be taken during the spring of the junior year or the fall of the senior year. There are early decision and early admissions plans. Early decision applications should be filed by November 1. For regular applications, early November is the recommended filing date; applications are considered on a rolling basis until all spaces are filled. The fall 2003 application fee was $40. Notification of early decision is sent December 15; regular decision, on a rolling basis. 296 early decision candidates were accepted for the 2003-2004 class. Applications are accepted on-line through the SUNY web site at http://infostu.suny.edu.

Transfer: 1633 transfer students enrolled in 2003-2004. Applicants must have a minimum GPA of 2.0 with 24 semester hours completed at the time of application. Students with fewer than 24 semester hours will be evaluated according to both college and high school work and SAT I or ACT scores. 30 of 120 credits required for the bachelor's degree must be completed at UB.

Visiting: There are regularly scheduled orientations for prospective students, including the Visit UB program, in which visitors tour the campus and a residence hall as well as attend an information session to learn about application procedures, admissions criteria, housing, financial aid, and scholarship programs. The Visit UB program is offered, with some exceptions, Monday through Friday year-round and on selected Saturdays during the academic year. Reservations are required. Visitors may sit in on classes. To schedule a visit, contact the Office of Admissions or register on-line at www.buffalo.edu/vub.

Financial Aid: In 2003-2004, 69% of all full-time freshmen and 71% of continuing full-time students received some form of financial aid. 66% of full-time freshmen and 77% of continuing full-time students received need-based aid. The average freshman award was $5727. Need-based scholarships or need-based grants averaged $2364; need-based self-help aid (loans and jobs) averaged $2495; and other non-need-based awards and non-need-based scholarships averaged $2700. The average financial indebtedness of the 2003 graduate was $16,418. The FAFSA is required. The priority date for freshman financial aid applications for fall entry is March 1.

International Students: There are 997 international students enrolled. The school actively recruits these students. They must score 550 on the written TOEFL or 213 on the electronic version. The SAT I or ACT is required if the student graduated from an American high school.

Computers: The mainframe is an IBM 2066-OB1. State-of-the-art computing capabilities are available to students in classes, labs, and residence halls, at the library, and off campus. In addition to free Internet access, e-mail accounts, productivity software, and printing for course work, students have 24-hour access to registration, tuition payment, degree audit, parking permit registration, on-line and web-enhanced courses, and UB Wireless. All students may access the system any time. There are no time limits and no fees. It is strongly recommended that all students have a personal computer.

Graduates: From July 1, 2002 to June 30, 2003, 3414 bachelor's degrees were awarded. The most popular majors were business administration (17%), engineering (12%), and communications (11%). In an average class, 1% graduate in 3 years or less, 33% graduate in 4 years or less, 52% graduate in 5 years or less, and 57% graduate in 6 years or less. 454 companies recruited on campus in a recent year. Of a recent year's graduating class, 30% were enrolled in graduate school within 6 months of graduation and 63% were employed.

Admissions Contact: Patricia Armstrong, Director of Admissions. E-mail: *ubadmissions@buffalo.edu* Web: *www.buffalo.edu*

STATE UNIVERSITY OF NEW YORK/UNIVERSITY AT NEW PALTZ
D-4

New Paltz, NY 12561-2443

(845) 257-3200
(888) 639-7589; Fax: (845) 257-3209

Full-time: 1971 men, 3498 women	Faculty: 295; IIA, av$
Part-time: 274 men, 549 women	Ph.D.s: 84%
Graduate: 490 men, 1126 women	Student/Faculty: 19 to 1
Year: semesters, summer session	Tuition: $5145 ($11,095)
Application Deadline: April 1	Room & Board: $6420
Freshman Class: 10,942 applied, 3768 accepted, 914 enrolled	
SAT I Verbal/Math: 545/550	**VERY COMPETITIVE**

State University of New York/University at New Paltz, founded in 1828, is a public institution offering undergraduate and graduate programs in the liberal arts and sciences, business, education, engineering, fine and performing arts, and the health professions. There are 5 undergraduate schools and 1 graduate school. In addition to regional accreditation, SUNY New Paltz has baccalaureate program accreditation with ABET, ASLA, CSAB, NASAD, NASM, and NLN. The library contains 515,224 volumes, 1,092,256 microform items, and 2416 audio/video tapes/CDs, and subscribes to 1392 periodicals. Computerized library services include the card catalog, interlibrary loans, and database searching. Special learning facilities include a learning resource center, planetarium, radio station, TV station, greenhouse, robotics lab, electron microscope facility, speech and hearing clinic, art museum, music therapy training facility, observatory, Fournier transform mass spectrometer, honors center, electronic media center, electronic classroom, and an IBM e-business virtual lab. The 216-acre campus is in a small town 100 miles north of New York City and 65 miles south of Albany. Including any residence halls, there are 57 buildings.

Student Life: 91% of undergraduates are from New York. Students are from 32 states, 51 foreign countries, and Canada. 90% are from public schools. 74% are white; 10% Hispanic. The average age of freshmen is 18; all undergraduates, 20. 16% do not continue beyond their first year; 56% remain to graduate.

Housing: 2541 students can be accommodated in college housing, which includes coed dorms. In addition, there are special-interest houses. On-campus housing is guaranteed for the freshman year only and is available on a first-come, first-served basis. Priority is given to out-of-town students. 51% of students live on campus; of those, 90% remain on campus on weekends. Upperclassmen may keep cars.

Activities: 1% of men belong to 5 local and 5 national fraternities; 3% of women belong to 5 local and 9 national sororities. There are 135 groups on campus, including art, band, cheerleading, chess, choir, chorale, chorus, computers, dance, drama, ethnic, gay, honors, international, jazz band, literary magazine, musical theater, newspaper, orchestra, photography, political, professional, radio and TV, religious, social, social service, student government, and yearbook. Popular campus events include Spirit Weekend, New Paltz Summer Repertory Theater, and Rainbow Month.

Sports: There are 9 intercollegiate sports for men and 11 for women, and 20 intramural sports for men and 15 for women. Facilities include a gym with a swimming pool; numerous playing fields; a 35,000-square-foot air-supported structure for tennis, jogging, volleyball, and basketball; and 24 outdoor tennis courts.

Disabled Students: 90% of the campus is accessible. Wheelchair ramps, elevators, special parking, specially equipped rest rooms, special class scheduling, lowered drinking fountains, lowered telephones, and special housing are available.

Services: Counseling and information services are available, as is tutoring in most subjects. There is a reader service for the blind and remedial math, reading, and writing.

Campus Safety and Security: Measures include 24-hour foot and vehicle patrol, self-defense education, security escort services, and informal

discussions. There are pamphlets/posters/films, emergency telephones, lighted pathways/sidewalks, a bicycle patrol, locked residence halls, and a campus 911 system.

Programs of Study: SUNY New Paltz confers B.A., B.S., B.F.A., B.S.E.E., and B.S.N. degrees. Master's degrees are also awarded. Bachelor's degrees are awarded in BIOLOGICAL SCIENCE (biology/ biological science), BUSINESS (accounting, banking and finance, business administration and management, and marketing/retailing/ merchandising), COMMUNICATIONS AND THE ARTS (art history and appreciation, broadcasting, communications, design, dramatic arts, English, fine arts, French, German, journalism, music, photography, Spanish, speech/debate/rhetoric, and visual and performing arts), COMPUTER AND PHYSICAL SCIENCE (chemistry, computer science, geology, mathematics, and physics), EDUCATION (art, early childhood, elementary, foreign languages, middle school, science, and secondary), ENGINEERING AND ENVIRONMENTAL DESIGN (computer engineering and electrical/electronics engineering), HEALTH PROFESSIONS (premedicine and speech pathology/audiology), SOCIAL SCIENCE (anthropology, Asian/Oriental studies, economics, geography, history, international relations, Latin American studies, philosophy, political science/ government, psychology, social science, sociology, and women's studies). Business, computer science, and math are the strongest academically. Business, visual arts, and elementary education are the largest.

Required: To graduate, students must complete a minimum of 120 credits with a 2.0 GPA. The number of credits required in the major varies. Other requirements include 42 to 52 credits in general education, 1 writing-intensive course in the major, and 60 credits in upper-division courses.

Special: There is cross-registration with the Mid-Hudson Consortium of Colleges. The university offers co-op programs and internships in most majors, work-study programs on campus and at the Children's Center of New Paltz, and opportunities for student-designed or dual majors. Students may study abroad in 18 countries. A 3-2 advanced degree in environmental biology is offered with SUNY Environmental Science and Forestry. There are 7-year medical and optometry accelerated degree programs. There are 4 national honor societies, a freshman honors program, and 6 departmental honors programs.

Faculty/Classroom: 46% of faculty are male; 54%, female. 97% both teach and do research. Graduate students teach 1% of introductory courses. The average class size in an introductory lecture is 19; in a laboratory, 10; and in a regular course, 19.

Admissions: 34% of the 2003-2004 applicants were accepted. The SAT I scores for the 2003-2004 freshman class were: Verbal--22% below 500, 49% between 500 and 599, 26% between 600 and 700, and 3% above 700; Math--21% below 500, 55% between 500 and 599, 22% between 600 and 700, and 3% above 700. 38% of the current freshmen were in the top fifth of their class; 80% were in the top two fifths. There were 5 National Merit semifinalists. 5 freshmen graduated first in their class.

Requirements: The SAT I is required and the ACT is recommended. A minimum composite score of 1100 on the SAT I is recommended. Graduation from an accredited secondary school is required; a GED will be accepted. The applicant's academic record must include a college preparatory program of 4 years of English and 3 to 4 years each of social studies, a foreign language, math, and lab science. Where required, a portfolio and an audition are used for placement purposes only. SUNY New Paltz requires applicants to be in the upper 50% of their class. A GPA of 3.0 is required. AP and CLEP credits are accepted. Important factors in the admissions decision are advanced placement or honor courses, extracurricular activities record, and evidence of special talent.

Procedure: Freshmen are admitted in the fall. Entrance exams should be taken on or before December 31. There is a rolling admissions plan. There are early admissions and deferred admissions plans. Early decision applications should be filed by November 15; regular applications, by April 1 for fall entry. Notification of early decision is sent December 15; regular decision, on a rolling basis. 300 applicants were on the 2003 waiting list; 3 were admitted. Applications are accepted on-line through *http://www.suny.edu/student/apply.apply.cfm*.

Transfer: 767 transfer students enrolled in 2002-2003. To be considered, applicants must have maintained a minimum GPA of 2.5 in all previous college work at accredited institutions. Some programs require a higher GPA for consideration. 30 of 120 credits required for the bachelor's degree must be completed at SUNY New Paltz.

Visiting: Half-hour information sessions are given by admissions staff followed by a campus tour given by a student ambassador. Visitors may sit in on classes. To schedule a visit, contact the Admissions Office.

Financial Aid: In 2003-2004, 75% of all full-time students received some form of financial aid. 60% of full-time freshmen and 75% of continuing full-time students received need-based aid. The average freshman award was $2149. Need-based scholarships or need-based grants averaged $2205; need-based self-help aid (loans and jobs) averaged $1547; and non-need-based awards and non-need-based scholarships averaged $1047. 40% of undergraduates work part time. Average annual earnings from campus work are $800. The average financial indebtedness of the 2003 graduate was $11,000. The FAFSA is required. The deadline for filing freshman financial aid applications for fall entry is March 15.

International Students: There are 174 international students enrolled. The school actively recruits these students. They must score 550 on the written TOEFL or 213 on the electronic version. Conditional acceptance is available, but the applicant must take ESL courses until required proficiency is achieved. The SAT I is required if the TOEFL has not been taken.

Computers: The mainframe is an IBM ES/9000 9121-210. Computer facilities include 6 large public PC labs, PC classrooms, department-based PC labs and clusters, and PC labs in residence halls. Access is provided in all residence hall rooms to local UNIX and mainframe hosts as well as the Internet. All students may access the system during those hours that the buildings are open; residence hall terminals and personal PCs, 24 hours a day. There are no time limits and no fees. It is strongly recommended that all students have a personal computer.

Graduates: From July 1, 2002 to June 30, 2003, 1416 bachelor's degrees were awarded. The most popular majors were education (20%), business and marketing (15%), and visual and performing arts (13%). In an average class, 31% graduate in 4 years or less, 50% graduate in 5 years or less, and 56% graduate in 6 years or less. 457 companies recruited on campus in 2002-2003.

Admissions Contact: Kimberly Lavoie, Director of Freshman/International Admissions. E-mail: *admissions@newpaltz.edu*
Web: *www.newpaltz.edu*

STATE UNIVERSITY OF NEW YORK/UNIVERSITY AT STONY BROOK   E-5

Stony Brook, NY 11794	(631) 632-6868; Fax: 631) 632-9027
Full-time: 6593 men, 6117 women	**Faculty:** I, +$
Part-time: 628 men, 734 women	**Ph.D.s:** n/av
Graduate: 3476 men, 4796 women	**Student/Faculty:** n/av
Year: semesters, summer session	**Tuition:** $5306 ($11,256)
Application Deadline: March 1	**Room & Board:** $7457
Freshman Class: 16,909 applied, 8564 accepted, 2181 enrolled	
SAT I Verbal/Math: 580/620	**HIGHLY COMPETITIVE**

Stony Brook University, founded in 1957 and part of the State University of New York, is a public institution offering degree programs in arts and sciences, engineering and applied sciences, nursing, health technology and management, and social welfare. Professional programs in medicine and dental medicine are offered on the graduate level. There are 5 undergraduate and 8 graduate schools. In addition to regional accreditation, Stony Brook University has baccalaureate program accreditation with ABET, AOTA, APA, APTA, CAAHED, CAHEA, CSWE, NAACLS and NLN. The 7 libraries contain 1,896,697 volumes, 3,770,432 microform items, and 38,926 audio/video tapes/CDs, and subscribe to 11,214 periodicals. Computerized library services include the card catalog, interlibrary loans, and database searching. Special learning facilities include a learning resource center, art gallery, radio station, the Museum of Long Island Natural Sciences, and the Fine Arts Center, which includes a 1100-seat main theater, a 400-seat recital hall, and 3 experimental theaters. The 1100-acre campus is in a suburban area on Long Island, 60 miles from New York City. Including any residence halls, there are 113 buildings.

Student Life: 92% of undergraduates are from New York. Students are from 40 states, 69 foreign countries, and Canada. 85% are from public schools. 35% are white; 23% Asian American. 32% are Catholic; 26% claim no religious affiliation; 22% Protestant; 13% Buddhist, Islamic, Mormon, and Eastern Orthodox; 7% Jewish. The average age of freshmen is 18; all undergraduates, 22. 13% do not continue beyond their first year; 54% remain to graduate.

Housing: 8533 students can be accommodated in college housing, which includes coed dorms, on-campus apartments, and married-student housing. In addition, there are honors houses, special-interest houses, and 7 living/learning centers that integrate academic experience with living environments. On-campus housing is guaranteed for all 4 years. 56% of students live on campus; of those, 65% remain on campus on weekends. Alcohol is not permitted. Upperclassmen may keep cars.

Activities: There are 4 local and 9 national fraternities and 3 local and 8 national sororities. There are 140 groups on campus, including band, cheerleading, choir, chorale, dance, drama, ethnic, film, gay, honors, international, literary magazine, musical theater, newspaper, orchestra, pep band, photography, political, professional, radio and TV, religious, social, student government, and yearbook. Popular campus events include Fall Fest, Opening Week Activities, and Caribbean Weekend.

Sports: There are 10 intercollegiate sports for men and 10 for women, and 25 intramural sports for men and 25 for women. Facilities include a sports complex housing a 5000-seat arena, a 1900-seat gym, an indoor track, a swimming pool, 6 squash and 8 racquetball courts, 3 multipurpose courts, a dance studio, and exercise and Universal gym rooms. Outdoor facilities include 20 tennis courts, a 3000-seat stadium, a 400-meter track, 2 sand volleyball courts, 2 basketball and 4 handball courts,

and separate fields for baseball, soccer, football, lacrosse, and intramural football.

Disabled Students: 75% of the campus is accessible. Wheelchair ramps, elevators, special parking, specially equipped rest rooms, special class scheduling, lowered drinking fountains, lowered telephones, special housing, and automatic door openers are available.

Services: There is a reader service for the blind and remedial math and writing.

Campus Safety and Security: Measures include 24-hour foot and vehicle patrol, self-defense education, security escort services, and shuttle buses. There are informal discussions, pamphlets/posters/films, emergency telephones, lighted pathways/sidewalks, and a campus Crime Stoppers program.

Programs of Study: Stony Brook University confers B.A., B.S., and B.E. degrees. Master's and doctoral degrees are also awarded. Bachelor's degrees are awarded in AGRICULTURE (environmental studies), BIOLOGICAL SCIENCE (biochemistry and biology/biological science), BUSINESS (business administration and management), COMMUNICATIONS AND THE ARTS (art history and appreciation, comparative literature, dramatic arts, English, film arts, Germanic languages and literature, linguistics, music, Russian languages and literature, and studio art), COMPUTER AND PHYSICAL SCIENCE (applied mathematics, astronomy, atmospheric sciences and meteorology, chemistry, computer science, earth science, geology, information sciences and systems, mathematics, and physics), EDUCATION (athletic training), ENGINEERING AND ENVIRONMENTAL DESIGN (biomedical engineering, chemical engineering, computer engineering, electrical/electronics engineering, engineering and applied science, engineering chemistry, and mechanical engineering), HEALTH PROFESSIONS (clinical science, cytotechnology, health science, nursing, pharmacology, physician's assistant, and respiratory therapy), SOCIAL SCIENCE (African studies, American studies, anthropology, economics, ethnic studies, French studies, history, humanities, interdisciplinary studies, Italian studies, philosophy, political science/government, psychology, religion, social science, social work, sociology, Spanish studies, and women's studies). Applied mathematics and statistics, biochemistry, and biology are the strongest academically. Psychology, business, and computer science are the largest.

Required: To graduate, students must have a minimum 2.0 GPA in 120 credit hours (B.A. and B.S.) or 128 (B.E.). The required number of hours in the major varies. At least 39 credits must be earned in upper-division courses. Students must take 14 to 16 courses to satisfy general education requirements in writing and quantitative reasoning skills, literary and philosophic analysis, exposure to the arts, disciplinary diversity, the interrelationship of science and society, and 3 culminating multicultural requirements. Arts and sciences majors must fulfill a foreign language requirement, unless completed through advanced high-school study. Other requirements vary by school.

Special: Cross-registration may be arranged through the Long Island Regional Advisory Council for Higher Education. The university offers a Washington semester and internships with a variety of government, legal, and social agencies, with hospitals and clinics, and in business and industry. The URECA Program allows undergraduates to work with faculty on research and creative projects. An accelerated degree program in nursing, dual majors, student-designed majors, a national student exchange program, study abroad in 10 countries, and pass/fail options are available. There are 4 national honor societies, including Phi Beta Kappa, a freshman honors program, and 30 departmental honors programs.

Faculty/Classroom: Graduate students teach 37% of introductory courses. The average class size in an introductory lecture is 84; in a laboratory, 25; and in a regular course, 38.

Admissions: 51% of the 2003-2004 applicants were accepted. The SAT I scores for the 2003-2004 freshman class were: Verbal--7% below 500, 53% between 500 and 599, 35% between 600 and 700, and 5% above 700; Math--1% below 500, 37% between 500 and 599, 49% between 600 and 700, and 13% above 700. 58% of the current freshmen were in the top fifth of their class. There were 5 National Merit finalists and 6 semifinalists.

Requirements: The SAT I is required. In addition, applicants must be graduates of an accredited secondary school or have a GED certificate. 16 or 17 academic credits are required, including 4 years each of English and social studies, 3 or 4 of math, 3 of science (4 for engineering majors), and 2 or 3 of a foreign language. 3 SAT II: Subject tests, an essay, and an interview are recommended. AP and CLEP credits are accepted. Important factors in the admissions decision are advanced placement or honor courses, extracurricular activities record, and evidence of special talent.

Procedure: Freshmen are admitted fall, spring, and summer. Entrance exams should be taken during the junior year or in the fall of the senior year. There is a rolling admissions plan. There are early action, early admissions, and deferred admissions plans. Early action applications should be filed by November 15; regular applications, by March 1 for fall entry and November 1 for spring entry. Notification of early action is sent January 1; regular decision, on a rolling basis. The fall 2003 application fee was $40. Applications are accepted on-line through the State

University of New York Online Admissions Application System at *www.suny.edu/student/apply/apconline.cfm.*

Transfer: Applicants must have a minimum 2.5 GPA. An associate degree and an interview are recommended. Other requirements vary by program. Applicants who have earned fewer than 24 college credits must submit a high school transcript. 36 of 120 credits required for the bachelor's degree must be completed at Stony Brook University.

Visiting: There are regularly scheduled orientations for prospective students, consisting of 1-, 2-, or 3-day programs during which students may confer with faculty, register for classes, and take placement exams for English and math. There are guides for informal visits and visitors may sit in on classes and stay overnight. To schedule a visit, contact the Admissions Office.

Financial Aid: 10% of undergraduates work part time. Stony Brook University is a member of CSS. The FAFSA and state aid form are required. The deadline for filing freshman financial aid applications for fall entry is March 1.

International Students: In a recent year there were 507 international students enrolled. They must score 550 on the written TOEFL or 213 on the electronic version.

Computers: The mainframes are a consists of a Sun Fire V88 and 2 Sun E420s. There are more than 2000 networked PCs, Macs, and UNIX workstations, all with Internet access, available on campus for student use. All students may access the system 24 hours a day. There are no time limits and no fees.

Graduates: The most popular majors were psychology (14%), business (9%), and computer science (8%). In an average class, 57% graduate in 6 years or less. 500 companies recruited on campus in a recent year. Of a recent graduating class, 47% were enrolled in graduate school within 6 months of graduation and 22% were employed.

Admissions Contact: Judith Burke-Berhanan.
E-mail: *enroll@stonybrook.edu* Web: *www.stonybrook.edu/admissions*

SUNY/COLLEGE OF TECHNOLOGY AT FARMINGDALE
(See Farmingdale State University of New York)

SYRACUSE UNIVERSITY
Syracuse, NY 13244   C-3

Full-time: 4722 men, 6024 women	(315) 443-3611; Fax: (315) 443-4226
Full-time: 4722 men, 6024 women	**Faculty:** 815; I, -$
Part-time: 54 men, 40 women	**Ph.D.s:** 87%
Graduate: 1919 men, 2001 women	**Student/Faculty:** 13 to 1
Year: semesters, summer session	**Tuition:** $25,130
Application Deadline: January 1	**Room & Board:** $9590
Freshman Class: 14,411 applied, 8718 accepted, 2650 enrolled	
SAT I or ACT: required	**HIGHLY COMPETITIVE**

Syracuse University, founded in 1870, is a private institution offering more than 200 undergraduate programs in liberal arts and sciences, architecture, public communications, education, management, human services and health professions, information studies, visual and performing arts, engineering, and computer science. There are 9 undergraduate and 11 graduate schools. In addition to regional accreditation, Syracuse has baccalaureate program accreditation with AACSB, ABET, ACEJMC, ACS, APA, ASHA, CACREP, CSWE, FIDER, NAAB, NASAD, NASM, NASPAA, NCATE, and NLN. The 6 libraries contain 3,115,566 volumes, 4,697,965 microform items, and 858,500 audio/video tapes/CDs, and subscribe to 14,462 periodicals. Computerized library services include the card catalog, interlibrary loans, database searching, and Internet access. Special learning facilities include a learning resource center, art gallery, radio station, TV station, institute for sensory research, center for public and community service, child care and child development laboratory school, English language institute, center for undergraduate research and innovative learning, audio archives, global collaboratory multimedia classroom, center for science and technology, and community darkrooms (photography). The 200-acre campus is in an urban area 250 miles northwest of New York City. Including any residence halls, there are 170 buildings.

Student Life: 58% of undergraduates are from out of state, mostly the Northeast. Students are from 48 states, 61 foreign countries, and Canada. 78% are from public schools. 71% are white. 40% claim no religious affiliation; 27% Catholic; 20% Students represent more than 20 different religions on campus.; 13% Jewish. The average age of freshmen is 18; all undergraduates, 20. 9% do not continue beyond their first year; 77% remain to graduate.

Housing: 7300 students can be accommodated in college housing, which includes coed dorms, on-campus apartments, married-student housing, fraternity houses, and sorority houses. In addition, there are language houses and special-interest houses. There are single-sex floors and wings of residence halls. Learning communities and theme/interest housing are available. On-campus housing is guaranteed for all 4 years and is available on a lottery system for upperclassmen. 73% of students live on campus; of those, 85% remain on campus on weekends. Alcohol is not permitted. Upperclassmen may keep cars.

Activities: 12% of men belong to 1 local and 23 national fraternities; 16% of women belong to 19 national sororities. There are 300 groups on campus, including art, band, cheerleading, chess, choir, chorale, chorus, computers, dance, debate, drama, ethnic, film, gay, honors, international, jazz band, literary magazine, marching band, musical theater, newspaper, orchestra, pep band, photography, political, professional, radio and TV, religious, social, social service, special interest, student government, symphony, and yearbook. Popular campus events include Opening Weekend Activities and Senior Celebration.

Sports: There are 7 intercollegiate sports for men and 10 for women, and 25 intramural sports for men and 25 for women. Facilities include 4 gyms, 2 swimming pools, weight rooms, tennis courts, exercise rooms, a dance studio, courts for racquet sports, an indoor track, grass playing fields, 2 outdoor artificial turf fields, an outdoor track, a soccer stadium, and a softball stadium. The multipurpose domed stadium seats 50,000 for football and 30,000 for basketball.

Disabled Students: 90% of the campus is accessible. Wheelchair ramps, elevators, special parking, specially equipped rest rooms, special class scheduling, lowered drinking fountains, and lowered telephones. There are also special supportive services for the learning disabled: note taking services, oral tests, readers, talking books, a reading machine, tape recorders, a learning center, extended-time tests, a support group, a study circle, and proofreaders are available.

Services: Counseling and information services are available, as is tutoring in most subjects. There is a reader service for the blind. In addition to tutoring and study-group support, the academic support resource center provides workshops on generic study skills such as time management and test anxiety reduction as well as information on departmental academic support resources.

Campus Safety and Security: Measures include 24-hour foot and vehicle patrol, security escort services, shuttle buses, and informal discussions. There are pamphlets/posters/films, emergency telephones, lighted pathways/sidewalks, bicycle registration, a blue light security system placed throughout campus with a direct link to the Department of Public Safety Communications Center in case of an emergency, and a card key access system in all university residence halls.

Programs of Study: Syracuse confers B.A., B.S., B.Arch., B.F.A., B.I.D., and B.Mus. degrees. Master's and doctoral degrees are also awarded. Bachelor's degrees are awarded in BIOLOGICAL SCIENCE (biology/biological science and nutrition), BUSINESS (accounting, banking and finance, business administration and management, entrepreneurial studies, hospitality management services, management information systems, marketing management, marketing/retailing/merchandising, purchasing/inventory management, and retailing), COMMUNICATIONS AND THE ARTS (advertising, art, art history and appreciation, broadcasting, ceramic art and design, classics, communications, comparative literature, design, dramatic arts, English, English literature, fiber/textiles/weaving, film arts, fine arts, French, Germanic languages and literature, graphic design, illustration, industrial design, journalism, languages, linguistics, media arts, metal/jewelry, modern language, music, music business management, music performance, music theory and composition, musical theater, painting, photography, printmaking, public relations, publishing, Russian, sculpture, Spanish, speech/debate/rhetoric, telecommunications, theater design, theater management, and video), COMPUTER AND PHYSICAL SCIENCE (chemistry, computer science, geology, information sciences and systems, mathematics, physics, and statistics), EDUCATION (art, early childhood, elementary, English, mathematics, middle school, music, physical, science, secondary, social studies, and special), ENGINEERING AND ENVIRONMENTAL DESIGN (aeronautical engineering, architecture, bioengineering, chemical engineering, civil engineering, computer engineering, computer graphics, electrical/electronics engineering, engineering physics, environmental design, environmental engineering, environmental science, interior design, and mechanical engineering), HEALTH PROFESSIONS (exercise science, health science, predentistry, premedicine, preveterinary science, and speech pathology/audiology), SOCIAL SCIENCE (African American studies, American studies, anthropology, child care/child and family studies, classical/ancient civilization, consumer services, dietetics, economics, ethics, politics, and social policy, European studies, family/consumer studies, fashion design and technology, food production/management/services, geography, history, international relations, Italian studies, Latin American studies, medieval studies, peace studies, philosophy, political science/government, prelaw, psychology, public affairs, religion, Russian and Slavic studies, social science, social work, sociology, textiles and clothing, and women's studies). Inclusive education, aerospace engineering, and art are the strongest academically. Psychology, political science, and TV-radio-film are the largest.

Required: A minimum of 120 credits with a minimum GPA of 2.0 is required to graduate. All students must take a freshman writing seminar and fulfill core requirements in writing and literature, sciences and math, social sciences, and humanities. Additional requirements vary by college and major. Most programs require an arts and science core and a capstone experience.

Special: The Syracuse University Internship Program (SUIP) places students in off-campus local or national field positions related to their major. Cooperative education programs are available in engineering, retailing, and information studies. Cross-registration is offered with SUNY College of Environmental Science and Forestry. Study abroad is available in 6 university-operated centers and through other special programs, and a Washington semester is offered through the International Relations Program. Syracuse also offers B.A.-B.S. degrees, dual and student-designed majors, accelerated degree programs, work-study programs, a general studies degree, pass/fail options, and nondegree study. There are 36 national honor societies, including Phi Beta Kappa, and a freshman honors program.

Faculty/Classroom: 61% of faculty are male; 39%, female. 98% teach undergraduates, 2% do research, and 98% do both. The average class size in a laboratory is 17 and in a regular course, 28.

Admissions: 60% of the 2003-2004 applicants were accepted. The SAT I scores for the 2003-2004 freshman class were: Verbal--4% below 500, 41% between 500 and 599, 46% between 600 and 700, and 9% above 700; Math--5% below 500, 32% between 500 and 599, 49% between 600 and 700, and 14% above 700. 72% of the current freshmen were in the top fifth of their class; 96% were in the top two fifths. 41 freshmen graduated first in their class in a recent year.

Requirements: The SAT I or ACT is required. In addition, applicants should have a strong college preparatory record from an accredited secondary school or have a GED equivalent. An essay is required. A portfolio is required for art and architecture majors, and an audition is required for music and drama majors. A secondary school counselor evaluation, or 2 academic recommendations, and a high school transcript, are also required. AP and CLEP credits are accepted. Important factors in the admissions decision are advanced placement or honor courses, evidence of special talent, and recommendations by school officials.

Procedure: Freshmen are admitted fall and spring. Entrance exams should be taken before January of the senior year for regular decision, and before November of the senior year for early decision. There are early decision, early admissions, and deferred admissions plans. Early decision applications should be filed by November 15; regular applications, by January 1 for fall entry and November 15 for spring entry, along with a $60 fee. Notification of early decision is sent in late December; regular decision, mid-March. 492 early decision candidates were accepted for the 2003-2004 class. Applications are accepted on-line.

Transfer: 239 transfer students enrolled in 2002-2003. Requirements vary by college. The SAT I or ACT scores and secondary school transcripts are required for applicants with fewer than 30 credit hours. A portfolio is required for art and architecture majors, and an audition for music and drama majors. College transcripts of all post secondary work are required. 30 of 120 credits required for the bachelor's degree must be completed at Syracuse.

Visiting: There are regularly scheduled orientations for prospective students, including information programs, a campus tour, and personal interviews. There are guides for informal visits and visitors may sit in on classes and stay overnight. To schedule a visit, contact the Admissions Office at *orange@syr.edu.*

Financial Aid: In 2003-2004, 75% of all full-time students received some form of financial aid. 55% of full-time freshmen and 56% of continuing full-time students received need-based aid. The average freshman award was $18,000. Need-based scholarships or need-based grants averaged $13,400; and need-based self-help aid (loans and jobs) averaged $4900. 45% of undergraduates work part time. Average annual earnings from campus work are $1700. The average financial indebtedness of the 2003 graduate was $18,925. Syracuse is a member of CSS. The CSS Profile or FAFSA is required. The deadline for filing freshman financial aid applications for fall entry is February 1.

International Students: There are 300 international students enrolled. The school actively recruits these students. They must score 550 on the written TOEFL or 213 on the electronic version and also take the ELPT or APIEL.

Computers: Syracuse has a networked client/server computing environment that gives students access to more than 1000 Macs, and UNIX workstations located throughout the campus. High-speed connections are available in all campus housing. All students may access the system 24 hours per day. It is strongly recommended that all students have a personal computer. Freshmen receive information for purchase of PCs May 1.

Graduates: From July 1, 2002 to June 30, 2003, 2574 bachelor's degrees were awarded. The most popular majors were management (15%), communications (14%), and social sciences (13%). In an average class, 65% graduate in 4 years or less, 75% graduate in 5 years or less, and 77% graduate in 6 years or less. 300 companies recruited on campus in 2002-2003. Of the 2002 graduating class, 20% were enrolled in graduate school within 6 months of graduation and 80% were employed.

Admissions Contact: Susan E. Donovan, Dean of Admissions. A video is available. E-mail: *orange@syr.edu* Web: *http://www.syracuse.edu*

TOURO COLLEGE
New York, NY 10010

D-5

(718) 252-7800 ext. 399
Fax: (718) 253-9455

Full-time: 2758 men, 5140 women	**Faculty:** 240
Part-time: 882 men, 914 women	**Ph.D.s:** 65%
Graduate: 2278 men, 4574 women	**Student/Faculty:** 33 to 1
Year: semesters, summer session	**Tuition:** $10,250
Application Deadline: open	**Room & Board:** $5000
Freshman Class: 4883 applied, 2740 accepted, 1985 enrolled	
SAT I Verbal/Math: 570/550	**ACT:** 23 **VERY COMPETITIVE**

Touro College, founded in 1971, is a private institution offering undergraduate programs primarily through the Lander College of Liberal Arts and Sciences, the School of General Studies, and the School of Health Sciences. Campuses are in midtown Manhattan, Brooklyn, and Queens. There are 6 undergraduate and 7 graduate schools. In addition to regional accreditation, Touro College has baccalaureate program accreditation with AOTA, APTA, and CAHEA. The 11 libraries contain 271,509 volumes, 14,100 microform items, and 4054 audio/video tapes/CDs, and subscribe to 3163 periodicals. Computerized library services include the card catalog, interlibrary loans, and database searching. Special learning facilities include a learning resource center. The campus is in an urban area. Including any residence halls, there are 12 buildings.

Student Life: 95% of undergraduates are from New York. Students are from 25 states, 30 foreign countries, and Canada. 27% do not continue beyond their first year; 47% remain to graduate.

Housing: 200 students can be accommodated in college housing, which includes single-sex dorms, on-campus apartments, and off-campus apartments. On-campus housing is available on a first-come, first-served basis. Priority is given to out-of-town students. Alcohol is not permitted. No one may keep cars.

Activities: There are no fraternities or sororities. There are 8 groups on campus, including computers, debate, literary magazine, newspaper, political, professional, religious, social, student government, and yearbook. Popular campus events include a student-sponsored lecture series and student-faculty social events.

Sports: There is no sports program at Touro College. Facilities include 1 baseball field, 2 tennis courts, and 2 basketball courts.

Disabled Students: All of the campus is accessible. Wheelchair ramps, elevators, specially equipped rest rooms, lowered drinking fountains, and lowered telephones are available.

Services: Counseling and information services are available, as is tutoring in some subjects, including accounting, math, English, and natural sciences. There is remedial math, reading, and writing.

Campus Safety and Security: Measures include 24-hour foot and vehicle patrol and pamphlets/posters/films.

Programs of Study: Touro College confers B.A., B.S., and B.P.S. degrees. Associate, master's, and doctoral degrees are also awarded. Bachelor's degrees are awarded in BIOLOGICAL SCIENCE (biology/biological science), BUSINESS (accounting, banking and finance, business administration and management, management science, and marketing/retailing/merchandising), COMMUNICATIONS AND THE ARTS (English, Hebrew, literature, and speech/debate/rhetoric), COMPUTER AND PHYSICAL SCIENCE (chemistry, computer science, mathematics, and physics), EDUCATION (elementary and special), HEALTH PROFESSIONS (occupational therapy, physical therapy, predentistry, and premedicine), SOCIAL SCIENCE (economics, history, human services, interdisciplinary studies, Judaic studies, liberal arts/general studies, philosophy, political science/government, prelaw, psychology, social science, and sociology). Business/accounting, education, and health sciences are the strongest academically. Psychology, education, and business are the largest.

Required: To graduate, all students must complete at least 120 credit hours (varies by major), with 30 to 70 in the major. A minimum 2.0 GPA is required, with 2.3 in the major. Specific disciplines include Judaic studies or ethnic studies. Required courses include English composition, history, literature, math, and social and natural sciences.

Special: The college offers cross-registration with the Fashion Institute of Technology, internships for juniors and seniors, study abroad in Israel, work-study programs, interdisciplinary majors, an accelerated degree program, credit for life, military, and work experience, pass/fail options, and dual majors. Early and/or preferential admission to professional programs is also possible. There are 2 national honor societies.

Faculty/Classroom: 60% of faculty are male; 40%, female. No introductory courses are taught by graduate students. The average class size in an introductory lecture is 16; in a laboratory, 12; and in a regular course, 15.

Admissions: 56% of the 2003-2004 applicants were accepted. The SAT I scores for the 2003-2004 freshman class were: Verbal--22% below 500, 38% between 500 and 599, 32% between 600 and 700, and 8% above 700; Math--27% below 500, 40% between 500 and 599, 27% between 600 and 700, and 6% above 700. The ACT scores were 8% below 21, 50% between 21 and 23, 8% between 24 and 26, 17% between

27 and 28, and 17% above 28. There were 2 National Merit finalists and 15 semifinalists in a recent year.

Requirements: The SAT I or ACT is recommended. In addition, applicants must be graduates of an accredited secondary school with a satisfactory high school average. SAT I scores of 550 verbal and 550 math are recommended. A GPA of 3.2 is required. AP and CLEP credits are accepted. Important factors in the admissions decision are advanced placement or honor courses, recommendations by school officials, and extracurricular activities record.

Procedure: Freshmen are admitted fall, spring, and summer. Entrance exams should be taken in May of the junior year or fall of the senior year. There are early admissions and deferred admissions plans. Application deadlines are open. Application fee is $50.

Transfer: 726 transfer students enrolled in a recent year. A 2.5 GPA is required. If the student has less than 60 credits, high school documentation is also required. 45 of 120 credits required for the bachelor's degree must be completed at Touro College.

Visiting: There are regularly scheduled orientations for prospective students. There are guides for informal visits and visitors may sit in on classes and stay overnight. To schedule a visit, contact Steven Toplan.

Financial Aid: The CSS Profile is required. Check with the school for current deadlines.

International Students: There were 67 international students enrolled in a recent year. They must score 550 on the written TOEFL or 175 on the electronic version and also take the college's own test.

Computers: The mainframe is an AS/400. Students have access to a LAN (local area network) within Touro's WAN connected to the Internet using a T1 line. More than 500 computers are available for student use. All students may access the system.

Graduates: In a recent year, 900 bachelor's degrees were awarded. The most popular majors were business/accounting (22%), liberal arts (22%), and psychology (12%). In an average class, 47% graduate in 6 years or less. 50 companies recruited on campus in a recent year. Of the 2002 graduating class, 40% were enrolled in graduate school within 6 months of graduation.

Admissions Contact: Steven Toplan, Director of Admissions.
E-mail: *lasadmit@admin.touro.edu* Web: *www.touro.edu*

UNION COLLEGE   D-3
Schenectady, NY 12308-2311   **(518) 388-6112**
(888) 843-6688; Fax: (518) 388-6986

Full-time: 1142 men, 1012 women	**Faculty:** 192; IIA, ++$
Part-time: 13 men, 7 women	**Ph.D.s:** 94%
Graduate: none	**Student/Faculty:** 11 to 1
Year: trimesters, summer session	**Tuition:** $28,928
Application Deadline: January 15	**Room & Board:** $7077
Freshman Class: 4159 applied, 1822 accepted, 559 enrolled	
SAT I Verbal/Math: 610/640	**ACT:** 26 **HIGHLY COMPETITIVE**

Union College, founded in 1795, is an independent liberal arts and engineering college. In addition to regional accreditation, Union has baccalaureate program accreditation with ABET. The library contains 571,508 volumes, 893,493 microform items, and 9044 audio/video tapes/CDs, and subscribes to 3485 periodicals. Computerized library services include the card catalog, interlibrary loans, database searching, and Internet access. Special learning facilities include a radio station, theater, high-tech classroom, lab center, multimedia auditorium, and an art, science, and history gallery. The 100-acre campus is in an urban area 15 miles west of Albany. Including any residence halls, there are 100 buildings.

Student Life: 55% of undergraduates are from out of state, mostly the Northeast. Students are from 36 states, 17 foreign countries, and Canada. 73% are from public schools. 84% are white. The average age of freshmen is 18; all undergraduates, 20. 7% do not continue beyond their first year; 84% remain to graduate.

Housing: 1625 students can be accommodated in college housing, which includes single-sex and coed dorms, on-campus apartments, fraternity houses, and sorority houses. In addition, there are language houses, special-interest houses, 12 theme houses that emphasize various community atmospheres, substance-free lifestyle living, and a 24-hour quiet option. On-campus housing is available on a lottery system for upperclassmen. 80% of students live on campus; of those, 80% remain on campus on weekends. Upperclassmen may keep cars.

Activities: 21% of men belong to 1 local and 13 national fraternities; 19% of women belong to 5 national sororities. There are approximately 100 groups on campus, including art, band, chess, choir, computers, dance, debate, drama, ethnic, gay, honors, international, jazz band, literary magazine, newspaper, orchestra, photography, political, professional, radio and TV, religious, social, social service, student government, and yearbook. Popular campus events include Black History Month, Party in the Garden, and Spring Fest.

Sports: There are 12 intercollegiate sports for men and 13 for women, and 21 intramural sports for men and 14 for women. Facilities include a field house for volleyball, basketball, and track, fields for soccer, foot-

ball, lacrosse, and field hockey, an ice rink, a gym, a swimming pool, weight rooms, and tennis and racquetball/squash courts.

Disabled Students: 60% of the campus is accessible. Wheelchair ramps, elevators, special parking, specially equipped rest rooms, lowered drinking fountains, and lowered telephones are available.

Services: Counseling and information services are available, as is tutoring in most subjects, including science and math. A writing center and a language center are available.

Campus Safety and Security: Measures include 24-hour foot and vehicle patrol, self-defense education, security escort services, and informal discussions. There are pamphlets/posters/films, emergency telephones, lighted pathways/sidewalks, 24-hour locked residence halls, emergency medical assistance, awareness programs, bicycle patrol, trolley escort service, and a shuttle van.

Programs of Study: Union confers B.A., B.S., B.S. Comp. Eng., B.S.E.E., and B.S.M.E. degrees. Bachelor's degrees are awarded in AGRICULTURE (environmental studies), BIOLOGICAL SCIENCE (biochemistry and biology/biological science), BUSINESS (business economics), COMMUNICATIONS AND THE ARTS (classics, English, fine arts, modern language, and studio art), COMPUTER AND PHYSICAL SCIENCE (chemistry, computer science, geology, mathematics, and physics), ENGINEERING AND ENVIRONMENTAL DESIGN (computer engineering, electrical/electronics engineering, and mechanical engineering), SOCIAL SCIENCE (African studies, American studies, anthropology, East Asian studies, economics, history, humanities, interdisciplinary studies, Latin American studies, philosophy, political science/government, psychology, Russian and Slavic studies, sociology, and women's studies). Math, chemistry, and classics are the strongest academically. Political science, psychology, and economics are the largest.

Required: Students must complete a minimum of 36 courses and must maintain a minimum GPA of 1.8 overall and 2.0 in the major. Students must also meet the requirements of the freshman preceptorial and the general education program, which includes courses distributed in 4 areas: history, literature, and civilization; social or behavioral science; math and natural science; and foreign languages and non-Western studies.

Special: Cross-registration is permitted with the Hudson Mohawk Consortium. Opportunities are provided for legislative internships in Albany and Washington, D.C. Union also offers a co-op program for engineering majors, pass/fail options, B.A.-B.S. degrees, dual and student-designed majors, a Washington semester, accelerated degree programs in law and medicine, and study abroad in 25 countries. There are 14 national honor societies, including Phi Beta Kappa, a freshman honors program, and 15 departmental honors programs.

Faculty/Classroom: 60% of faculty are male; 40%, female. All teach undergraduates and 97% both teach and do research. The average class size in an introductory lecture is 22; in a laboratory, 14; and in a regular course, 18.

Admissions: 44% of the 2003-2004 applicants were accepted. The SAT I scores for the 2003-2004 freshman class were: Verbal--3% below 500, 37% between 500 and 599, 48% between 600 and 700, and 12% above 700; Math--1% below 500, 27% between 500 and 599, 50% between 600 and 700, and 22% above 700. 82% of the current freshmen were in the top quarter of their class; 97% were in the top half.

Requirements: The SAT I or ACT is required, or, in place of these, 3 SAT II: Subject tests may be submitted, including 1 in writing. Graduation from an accredited secondary school is required. Applicants must submit a minimum of 16 full-year credits, distributed as follows: 4 years of English, 2 of a foreign language, 2 1/2 to 3 1/2 years of math, 2 years each of science and social studies, and the remainder in college-preparatory courses. Engineering and math majors are expected to have completed additional math and science courses beyond the minimum requirements. An essay is also required, and an interview is recommended. AP credits are accepted. Important factors in the admissions decision are advanced placement or honor courses, recommendations by school officials, and extracurricular activities record.

Procedure: Freshmen are admitted in the fall. Entrance exams should be taken by January of the senior year. There are early decision and deferred admissions plans. Early decision applications should be filed by November 15; regular applications, by January 15 for fall entry. The fall 2003 application fee was $50. Notification of early decision is sent December 15; regular decision, April 1. 194 early decision candidates were accepted for the 2003-2004 class. 912 were on the 2003 waiting list; 41 were admitted. Applications are accepted on-line through the Union web site.

Transfer: 21 transfer students enrolled in 2002-2003. A 3.0 GPA and 1 full year of college academic work are required. Transfer students must study at Union for at least 2 years. 18 credits of 36 required for the bachelor's degree must be completed at Union.

Visiting: There are regularly scheduled orientations for prospective students, including interviews and a tour of the campus. There are guides for informal visits and visitors may sit in on classes and stay overnight. To schedule a visit, contact the Admissions Office, Grant Hall, at *admissions@union.edu*.

Financial Aid: In 2003-2004, 50% of all full-time freshmen and 53% of continuing full-time students received some form of financial aid. 48%

of full-time freshmen and 53% of continuing full-time students received need-based aid. The average freshman award was $23,800. Need-based scholarships or need-based grants averaged $19,675 ($33,000 maximum); need-based self-help aid (loans and jobs) averaged $4125 ($6125 maximum); and non-need-based awards and non-need-based scholarships averaged $12,000 (maximum). 24% of undergraduates work part time. Average annual earnings from campus work are $900. The average financial indebtedness of the 2003 graduate was $17,000. Union is a member of CSS. The CSS/Profile or FAFSA is required. The deadline for filing freshman financial aid applications for fall entry is February 1.

International Students: There are 41 international students enrolled. The school actively recruits these students. They must score 600 on the written TOEFL or 250 on the electronic version and also take SAT I or 3 SAT II: Subject tests, including writing, or the ACT.

Computers: The mainframes are 5 Compaq Alpha servers and 11 Windows NT servers. There are more than 1400 PCs and workstations on campus linking classrooms, labs, offices, and residence hall rooms. There are also 20 electronic classrooms. Departmental computer labs offer Windows and Mac-based systems. 3 computer labs are available 24 hours a day, 7 days a week. Other departmental labs are available, some 24 hours a day, 7 days a week. All students may access the system 24 hours per day, 7 days a week. There are no time limits and no fees.

Graduates: From July 1, 2002 to June 30, 2003, 494 bachelor's degrees were awarded. The most popular majors were political science (10%), psychology (9%), and economics (9%). In an average class, 77% graduate in 4 years or less, 83% graduate in 5 years or less, and 83% graduate in 6 years or less. 43 companies recruited on campus in 2002-2003. Of the 2002 graduating class, 32% were enrolled in graduate school within 6 months of graduation and 67% were employed.

Admissions Contact: Dianne Crozier, Director of Admissions. A video is available. E-mail: *admissions@union.edu*
Web: *http://www.union.edu*

UNITED STATES MERCHANT MARINE ACADEMY   D-5
Kings Point, NY 11024-1699

(516) 773-5391
(800) 732-6267; Fax: (516) 773-5390

Full-time: 842 men, 128 women	**Faculty:** 77
Part-time: none	**Ph.D.s:** 45%
Graduate: none	**Student/Faculty:** 13 to 1
Year: trimesters	**Tuition:** $6250
Application Deadline: March 1	**Room & Board:** n/app
Freshman Class: 1920 applied, 388 accepted, 303 enrolled	
SAT I Verbal/Math: 629/619	**ACT:** 28

HIGHLY COMPETITIVE+

The United States Merchant Marine Academy, founded in 1943, is a publicly supported institution offering maritime, military, and engineering programs for the purpose of training officers for the U.S. merchant marine and the maritime industry. Students make no conventional tuition and board payments. Required fees for freshmen are approximately $6,250; costs in subsequent years are less. In addition to regional accreditation, Kings Point has baccalaureate program accreditation with ABET. The library contains 185,000 volumes, 17,300 microform items, and 2670 audio/video tapes/CDs, and subscribes to 960 periodicals. Computerized library services include the card catalog, interlibrary loans, database searching, and Internet access. Special learning facilities include a learning resource center, planetarium, and a maritime museum. The 80-acre campus is in a suburban area 19 miles east of midtown New York City. Including any residence halls, there are 28 buildings.

Student Life: 89% of undergraduates are from out of state, mostly the Middle Atlantic. Students are from 48 states, 3 foreign countries, and Canada. 75% are from public schools. 91% are white. 49% are Protestant; 38% Catholic; 9% claim no religious affiliation. The average age of freshmen is 18; all undergraduates, 19. 6% do not continue beyond their first year; 94% remain to graduate.

Housing: All students can be accommodated in college housing, which includes coed dormitories. On-campus housing is guaranteed for all 4 years. All students live on campus; of those, 85% remain on campus on weekends. Alcohol is not permitted. Upperclassmen may keep cars.

Activities: There are no fraternities or sororities. There are 26 groups on campus, including band, choir, chorus, computers, debate, drill team, drum and bugle corps, ethnic, marching band, newspaper, pep band, professional, religious, student government, and yearbook.

Sports: There are 14 intercollegiate sports for men and 5 for women, and 5 intramural sports for men. Facilities include a swimming pool and football field.

Disabled Students: 5% of the campus is accessible. Wheelchair ramps, elevators, and special parking are available.

Services: Counseling and information services are available, as is tutoring in most subjects.

Campus Safety and Security: Measures include 24-hour foot and vehicle patrol, self-defense education, informal discussions, and lighted pathways/sidewalks.

Programs of Study: Kings Point confers the B.S. degree. Bachelor's degrees are awarded in BUSINESS (logistics and transportation management), ENGINEERING AND ENVIRONMENTAL DESIGN (engineering, marine engineering, maritime science, naval architecture and marine engineering, and transportation technology). Marine engineering systems is the strongest academically. Logistics and intermodal transportation is the largest.

Required: To graduate, students must complete 164 credit hours with a 2.0 minimum GPA. The required core curriculum includes courses in math, science, English, humanities and history, naval science, phys ed, ship's medicine, and computer science. Students must spend 6 months during their sophomore and junior years at sea on U.S. flagships. All students must pass resident and sea project courses, the U.S. Coast Guard licensing exam and all required certificates, and the academy physical fitness test. Students must apply for and accept, if offered, a commission in the U.S. Naval Reserve.

Special: The college offers internships in the maritime industry and work-study programs with U.S. shipping companies.

Faculty/Classroom: 91% of faculty are male; 9%, female. All teach undergraduates. The average class size in an introductory lecture is 25; in a laboratory, 15; and in a regular course, 20.

Admissions: 20% of the 2003-2004 applicants were accepted. The SAT I scores for the 2003-2004 freshman class were: Verbal--36% between 500 and 599, 42% between 600 and 700, and 22% above 700; Math--39% between 500 and 599, 53% between 600 and 700, and 8% above 700. The ACT scores were 37% between 24 and 26, 47% between 27 and 28, and 16% above 28. 60% of the current freshmen were in the top fifth of their class; 93% were in the top two fifths. 50 freshmen graduated first in their class.

Requirements: The SAT I or ACT is required. In addition, SAT II: Subject tests are recommended. Candidates for admission to the academy must be nominated by a member of the U.S. Congress. They must be between the ages of 17 and 25, U.S. citizens (except by special arrangement), and in excellent physical condition. Applicants should be graduates of an accredited secondary school or have a GED equivalent. 16 academic credits are required, including 4 in English, 3 in math, 1 credit in physics or chemistry with a lab, and 8 in electives. An essay is required. Kings Point requires applicants to be in the upper 40% of their class. AP credits are accepted. Important factors in the admissions decision are advanced placement or honor courses, leadership record, and extracurricular activities record.

Procedure: Freshmen are admitted in the fall. Entrance exams should be taken by the first test date of the year of requested admission. There are early decision and early admissions plans. Early decision applications should be filed by November 1; regular applications, by March 1 for fall entry. Notification of early decision is sent December 15; regular decision, March 31. 130 early decision candidates were accepted for the 2003-2004 class. 293 applicants were on the 2003 waiting list; 3 were admitted. Applications are accepted on-line through *www.usmma.edu*.

Transfer: All students must spend 4 years at the academy. All 164 credits required for the bachelor's degree must be completed at Kings Point.

Visiting: There are guides for informal visits and visitors may sit in on classes and stay overnight. To schedule a visit, contact the Admissions Office at (866) 546-4778.

Financial Aid: In 2003-2004, 34% of all full-time freshmen received some form of financial aid. 15% of full-time freshmen received need-based aid. The average freshman award was $6710. Need-based scholarships or need-based grants averaged $2650 ($5250 maximum); need-based self-help aid (loans and jobs) averaged $5583 ($10,299 maximum); and non-need-based awards and non-need-based scholarships averaged $1835 ($6216 maximum). The average financial indebtedness of the 2003 graduate was $9535. Kings Point is a member of CSS. The FAFSA and the college's own financial statement are required. The priority date for freshman financial aid applications for fall entry is March 1. The deadline for filing freshman financial aid applications for fall entry is May 1.

International Students: There are 19 international students enrolled. They must score 550 on the written TOEFL or 213 on the electronic version and also take the SAT I, scoring 500 on the verbal portion and 550 on the math, or the ACT, scoring 23.

Computers: The mainframe is a Microsoft 2003 network. Dorm rooms are wired for on-line access. All students are issued a laptop. There are an additional 200 terminals in labs, and there is 1 wireless classroom, and wireless access in the library. All students may access the system 24 hours per day. There are no time limits and no fees. All students are required to have personal computers.

Graduates: From July 1, 2002 to June 30, 2003, 200 bachelor's degrees were awarded. The most popular majors were logistics and intermodal transportaion (40%), marine engineering systems (25%), and marine engineering (12%). In an average class, 61% graduate in 4 years or less, and 80% graduate in 5 years or less. 70 companies recruited on campus in 2002-2003. Of the 2002 graduating class, 2% were enrolled in graduate school within 6 months of graduation and 86% were employed.

Admissions Contact: Capt. James Skinner, Director of Admissions. A video is available. E-mail: *admissions@usmma.edu* Web: *www.usmma.edu*

UNITED STATES MILITARY ACADEMY D-4
West Point, NY 10996 (845) 938-4041; Fax: (845) 938-8121

Full-time: 3530 men, 635 women	Faculty: 577; IIA, +$
Part-time: none	Ph.D.s: 39%
Graduate: none	Student/Faculty: 7 to 1
Year: semesters, summer session	Tuition: see profile
Application Deadline: see profile	Room & Board: n/app
Freshman Class: n/av	
SAT I or ACT: required	**MOST COMPETITIVE**

The United States Military Academy, founded in 1802, offers military, engineering, and comprehensive arts and sciences programs leading to a bachelor's degree and a commission as a second lieutenant in the U.S. Army, with a 5-year active duty service obligation. All students receive free tuition and room and board as well as an annual salary of $7200. An initial deposit of $2400 is required. Figures in above capsule and in this profile are approximate. In addition to regional accreditation, West Point has baccalaureate program accreditation with ABET. The library contains 442,169 volumes, 748,443 microform items, and 12,378 audio/video tapes/CDs, and subscribes to 1963 periodicals. Computerized library services include the card catalog, interlibrary loans, and database searching. Special learning facilities include a learning resource center, art gallery, radio station, TV station, and a military museum. Cadets may conduct research in conjunction with the academic departments through the Operations Research Center, the Photonics Research Center, the Mechanical Engineering Research Center, and the Office of Artificial Intelligence, Analysis, and Evaluation. There is also a visiting artist program featuring painting, sculpture, and photography. The 16,080-acre campus is in a small town 56 miles north of New York City. Including any residence halls, there are 902 buildings.

Student Life: 92% of undergraduates are from out of state, mostly the Northeast. Students are from 50 states and 19 foreign countries. 81% are from public schools. 81% are white. 49% are Protestant; 33% Catholic; 15% claim no religious affiliation. The average age of freshmen is 18; all undergraduates, 20. 8% do not continue beyond their first year; 82% remain to graduate.

Housing: 4500 students can be accommodated in college housing. College-sponsored housing is coed. All cadets live in cadet barracks. On-campus housing is guaranteed for all 4 years. All students live on campus. Upperclassmen may keep cars.

Activities: There are no fraternities or sororities. There are 105 groups on campus, including art, astronomy, bagpipe band, band, cheerleading, chess, choir, chorale, chorus, computers, dance, debate, drama, drill team, drum and bugle corps, ethnic, film, flying, forensics, honors, international, language, literary magazine, marching band, musical theater, newspaper, pep band, photography, professional, radio and TV, religious, social, social service, student government, and yearbook. Popular campus events include Ring Weekend and 100th Night for Seniors, 500th Night for Juniors, Yearling Winter Weekend for Sophomores, and Plebe-Parent Weekend for Freshmen.

Sports: There are 15 intercollegiate sports for men and 9 for women, and 18 intramural sports for men and 14 for women. Facilities include a 40,000-seat football stadium, baseball fields, a 2500-seat hockey rink, a 5000-seat basketball arena, 5 gyms for squash, handball, tennis, and racquetball, 3 swimming pools, workout areas, a field house, indoor/outdoor tracks, a golf course and a ski slope, and hunting, fishing, and boating facilities.

Disabled Students: Wheelchair ramps, elevators, special parking, specially equipped rest rooms, lowered drinking fountains, and lowered telephones are available.

Services: Counseling and information services are available, as is tutoring in every subject. The Center for Enhanced Performance offers 2 courses that provide cadets an opportunity to learn and enhance reading, study, and mental skills.

Campus Safety and Security: Measures include 24-hour foot and vehicle patrol, self-defense education, shuttle buses, and lighted pathways/sidewalks.

Programs of Study: West Point confers the B.S. degree. Bachelor's degrees are awarded in BIOLOGICAL SCIENCE (life science), BUSINESS (management science and operations research), COMMUNICATIONS AND THE ARTS (languages and literature), COMPUTER AND PHYSICAL SCIENCE (chemistry, computer science, mathematics, and physics), ENGINEERING AND ENVIRONMENTAL DESIGN (civil engineering, electrical/electronics engineering, engineering management, engineering physics, environmental engineering, mechanical engineering, military science, nuclear engineering, and systems engineering), SOCIAL SCIENCE (behavioral science, economics, geography, history, international studies, law, philosophy, and political science/government). Engineering, behavioral sciences, and history are the largest.

Required: All cadets must complete a core of 31 courses and 9 academic electives pertinent to their field of study. The major requires an additional 1 to 3 electives in the field. In addition, all cadets must complete 4 courses each in phys ed and military science and a senior thesis or design project in the major. A total of 140 credits, including 127 academic, 6 military, and 7 physical, with at least a C average, is required to graduate.

Special: Junior and senior cadets may participate in 3-week summer educational experiences, including Operations Crossroads Africa, research work in technical areas throughout the country, medical internships at Walter Reed Medical Center, workflow positions with federal and Department of Defense agencies, language training in foreign countries, and study at other military and civilian institutions. There are 7 national honor societies, including Phi Beta Kappa, a freshman honors program, and 5 departmental honors programs.

Faculty/Classroom: 88% of faculty are male; 12%, female. 40% do research and 40% both teach and do research. The average class size in an introductory lecture is 15; in a laboratory, 15; and in a regular course, 15.

Requirements: The SAT I or ACT is required. In addition, applicants must be qualified academically, physically, and medically. Candidates must be nominated for admission by members of the U.S. Congress or executive sources. West Point recommends that applicants have 4 years each of English and math, 2 years each of foreign language and lab science, such as chemistry and physics, and 1 year of U.S. history. Courses in geography, government, and economics are also suggested. An essay is required, and an interview is recommended. The GED is accepted. Applicants must be 17 to 22 years old, a U.S. citizen at the time of enrollment (except by agreement with another country), unmarried, and not pregnant or legally obligated to support children. AP credits are accepted. Important factors in the admissions decision are leadership record, extracurricular activities record, and recommendations by school officials.

Procedure: Freshmen are admitted in the summer. Entrance exams should be taken in the spring of the junior year and not later than the fall of the senior year. There are early decision, early admissions, and rolling admissions plans. Check with the school for current application deadlines. Notification is sent on a rolling basis.

Transfer: All applicants must enter as freshmen. 140 of 140 credits required for the bachelor's degree must be completed at West Point.

Visiting: There are regularly scheduled orientations for prospective students, Candidates will be escorted by a cadet, attend class, have lunch with the Corps of Cadets, and talk with cadets about all phases of West Point life. There are guides for informal visits and visitors may sit in on classes and stay overnight. To schedule a visit, contact the Admissions Office.

International Students: They must take the SAT I or the ACT.

Computers: The mainframe is a Unisys 2200/425. Virtually every course requires a computer. There is a PC at each desk, which is connected to academic computing services, word processing, worldwide e-mail, spreadsheets, and database access. All students may access the system 24 hours daily. There are no time limits and no fees. All students are required to have personal computers.

Admissions Contact: Colonel Michael L. Jones, Director of Admissions. A video is available. E-mail: *admissions@usma.edu* Web: *www.usma.edu*

UNIVERSITY OF ROCHESTER B-3
Rochester, NY 14627-0251 (585) 275-3221
(888) 822-2256; Fax: (585) 461-4595

Full-time: 2460 men, 1985 women	Faculty: 499; I, +$
Part-time: 60 men, 165 women	Ph.D.s: 90%
Graduate: 1785 men, 1490 women	Student/Faculty: 9 to 1
Year: semesters, summer session	Tuition: $24,800
Application Deadline: see profile	Room & Board: $8185
Freshman Class: n/av	
SAT I or ACT: required	**HIGHLY COMPETITIVE**

The University of Rochester, founded in 1850, is a private institution offering programs in the arts and sciences, engineering and applied science, nursing, medicine and dentistry, business administration, music, and education. There are 4 undergraduate and 7 graduate schools. Figures in the above capsule and in this profile are approximate. In addition to regional accreditation, UR has baccalaureate program accreditation with AACSB, ABET, ACPE, NASM, and NLN. The 7 libraries contain 2,922,335 volumes, 4,145,264 microform items, and 71,100 audio/video tapes/CDs, and subscribe to 9829 periodicals. Computerized library services include the card catalog, interlibrary loans, and database searching. Special learning facilities include a learning resource center, art gallery, radio station, labs for nuclear structure research and laser energetics, a center for visual science, the Strong Memorial Hospital, an art center, an observatory, an institute of optics, a center for electronic imaging systems, and the National Science Foundation Center for Photoinduced Charge Transfer. The 90-acre campus is in a suburban area 2 miles south of downtown Rochester. Including any residence halls, there are 143 buildings.

Student Life: 50% of undergraduates are from out of state, mostly the Middle Atlantic. Students are from 50 states, 95 foreign countries, and Canada. 76% are white; 12% Asian American.

Housing: 3022 students can be accommodated in college housing, which includes single-sex and coed dorms, on-campus apartments, married-student housing, and fraternity houses. In addition, there are language houses, special-interest houses, drama and medieval houses, and faculty-in-residence housing. On-campus housing is guaranteed for the freshman year only and is available on a lottery system for upperclassmen. 75% of students live on campus; of those, 90% remain on campus on weekends. Upperclassmen may keep cars.

Activities: 25% of men belong to 17 national fraternities; 14% of women belong to 11 national sororities. There are 170 groups on campus, including art, band, campus programming, cheerleading, chess, choir, chorale, chorus, computers, dance, debate, drama, drill team, ethnic, film, gay, honors, international, jazz band, literary magazine, musical theater, newspaper, opera, orchestra, pep band, photography, political, professional, radio and TV, religious, social, social service, student government, symphony, and yearbook. Popular campus events include Dandelion Day, Yellowjacket Day, and Boar's Head Dinner.

Sports: There are 11 intercollegiate sports for men and 11 for women, and 17 intramural sports for men and 17 for women. Facilities include a renovated athletic center, a 5000-seat stadium, a 2500-seat gym, a field house, an ice rink, courts for handball, racquetball, squash, and tennis, an indoor track, a fitness center and weight room, a jogging path, and an aquatic center.

Disabled Students: 75% of the campus is accessible. Wheelchair ramps, elevators, special parking, specially equipped rest rooms, special class scheduling, lowered drinking fountains, lowered telephones, and access to screened reading and adaptive software are available.

Services: Counseling and information services are available, as is tutoring in every subject. There is a reader service for the blind.

Campus Safety and Security: Measures include 24-hour foot and vehicle patrol, self-defense education, security escort services, and shuttle buses. There are informal discussions, pamphlets/posters/films, emergency telephones, and lighted pathways/sidewalks.

Programs of Study: UR confers B.A., B.S., and B.M. degrees. Master's and doctoral degrees are also awarded. Bachelor's degrees are awarded in AGRICULTURE (environmental studies), BIOLOGICAL SCIENCE (biochemistry, biology/biological science, cell biology, ecology, genetics, microbiology, and neurosciences), COMMUNICATIONS AND THE ARTS (American Sign Language, art history and appreciation, classics, comparative literature, English, film arts, fine arts, French, German, Japanese, jazz, linguistics, music, music theory and composition, Russian, Spanish, and studio art), COMPUTER AND PHYSICAL SCIENCE (applied mathematics, chemistry, computer science, geology, mathematics, optics, physics, and statistics), EDUCATION (music), ENGINEERING AND ENVIRONMENTAL DESIGN (biomedical engineering, chemical engineering, electrical/electronics engineering, engineering and applied science, environmental science, geological engineering, and mechanical engineering), HEALTH PROFESSIONS (health, nursing, and public health), SOCIAL SCIENCE (anthropology, cognitive science, economics, history, interpreter for the deaf, philosophy, political science/government, psychology, religion, and women's studies). Psychology, biology, and political science are the largest.

Required: Students focus on the humanities, social sciences, and natural sciences; 1 of the 3 areas will be their major, and they select a 3-course cluster in each of the other 2. A total of 128 credit hours with a minimum GPA of 2.0 is required to graduate. Additionally, all students satisfy a freshman writing requirement and take 2 upper-level courses in their major that are writing intensive.

Special: Cross-registration is offered with other Rochester area colleges. Internships, a Washington semester, B.A.-B.S. degrees, dual and student-designed majors, nondegree study, and pass/fail options are available. Study abroad is possible in 46 university-sponsored programs, including Australia, China, Japan, Egypt, Israel, and the former Soviet Union, and in several European countries. Other options include a fifth year of courses tuition free, courses designed to teach first-year students how to learn and how to make learning a lifetime habit, a management studies certificate, and music lessons for credit at the Eastman School of Music. Qualified freshmen may obtain early assurance of admission to the university's medical school through the Rochester Early Medical Scholars program. Internships are available in the United States and abroad. There are 6 national honor societies, including Phi Beta Kappa, and 13 departmental honors programs.

Faculty/Classroom: 76% of faculty are male; 24%, female. Graduate students teach 5% of introductory courses. The average class size in an introductory lecture is 75; in a laboratory, 20; and in a regular course, 20.

Requirements: The SAT I or ACT is required. In addition, SAT II: Subject tests are recommended. Applicants should be graduates of an accredited secondary school or have a GED equivalent. An audition is re-

quired for music majors. AP credits are accepted. Important factors in the admissions decision are advanced placement or honor courses, recommendations by school officials, and leadership record.

Procedure: Freshmen are admitted fall and spring. Entrance exams should be taken by December of the senior year. There are early decision and deferred admissions plans. Check with the school for current application deadlines. The application fee is $50. A waiting list is an active part of the admissions procedure. The school accepts the institutional application through Embark linked to the UR admissions home page.

Transfer: 90 transfer students enrolled in a recent year. The most important criterion is an applicant's college record. Transfers are accepted on a rolling admissions basis. 32 of 128 credits required for the bachelor's degree must be completed at UR.

Visiting: There are regularly scheduled orientations for prospective students, including campus tours and group information sessions. There are guides for informal visits and visitors may sit in on classes and stay overnight. To schedule a visit, contact the Admissions Office.

Financial Aid: In a recent year, 88% of all full-time students received some form of financial aid. 65% of all full-time students received need-based aid. The average freshman award was $19,400. 50% of undergraduates work part time. Average annual earnings from campus work are $1100. The average financial indebtedness of a recent graduate was $20,998. UR is a member of CSS. The CSS Profile or FAFSA is required. Check with the school for current deadlines.

International Students: There were 191 international students enrolled in a recent year. The school actively recruits these students. They must score 550 on the written TOEFL or 213 on the electronic version and also take the SAT I or the ACT.

Computers: The mainframes are an IBM 4381, DEC VAX systems, Sun systems, and a Solbourne computer. Students have access to hundreds of PCs, workstations, printers, and terminals in the libraries, classrooms, labs, and resource centers on campus. All residence hall rooms have lines accessing the mainframe computers and the Internet. All students may access the system 24 hours daily. There are no time limits and no fees.

Graduates: In a recent year 993, bachelor's degrees were awarded. The most popular majors were psychology (16%), biology (16%), and economics (12%). In an average class, 62% graduate in 4 years or less, and 75% graduate in 6 years or less. 229 companies recruited on campus in a recent year.

Admissions Contact: W. Jamie Hobba, Director of Admissions. A video is available. E-mail: *admit@admissions.rochester.edu* Web: *http://www.rochester.edu*

UTICA COLLEGE C-3
Utica, NY 13502-4892 (315) 792-3006
(800) 782-8884; Fax: (315) 792-3003

Full-time: 774 men, 1095 women	**Faculty:** 108; IIB, av$
Part-time: 109 men, 192 women	**Ph.Ds:** 94%
Graduate: 99 men, 196 women	**Student/Faculty:** 17 to 1
Year: semesters, summer session	**Tuition:** $20,270
Application Deadline: open	**Room & Board:** $8070
Freshman Class: 2475 applied, 1915 accepted, 448 enrolled	
SAT I or ACT: recommended	**COMPETITIVE**

Utica College, formerly Utica College of Syracuse University, is a private liberal arts institution founded by Syracuse University in 1946, which confers the Syracuse University undergraduate degree and Utica College master's degrees. In addition to regional accreditation, UC has baccalaureate program accreditation with AOTA, APTA, and NLN. The library contains 181,050 volumes, 60,431 microform items, and 8823 audio/video tapes/CDs, and subscribes to 1996 periodicals. Computerized library services include the card catalog, interlibrary loans, and database searching. Special learning facilities include a learning resource center, art gallery, radio station, an early childhood education lab, and a math and writing center. The 128-acre campus is in a suburban area 50 miles east of Syracuse. Including any residence halls, there are 18 buildings.

Student Life: 88% of undergraduates are from New York. Students are from 30 states, 47 foreign countries, and Canada. 80% are from public schools. 62% are white. The average age of freshmen is 18; all undergraduates, 22. 31% do not continue beyond their first year; 58% remain to graduate.

Housing: 935 students can be accommodated in college housing, which includes single-sex and coed dorms. On-campus housing is guaranteed for all 4 years. All students may keep cars.

Activities: 2% of men belong to 2 local and 3 national fraternities; 3% of women belong to 2 local and 3 national sororities. There are 86 groups on campus, including art, band, cheerleading, choir, chorus, computers, drama, ethnic, film, gay, honors, international, jazz band, literary magazine, musical theater, newspaper, pep band, photography, political, professional, radio and TV, religious, social, social service, student government, and yearbook. Popular campus events include outdoor concerts, mock elections, and Winter Weekend.

Sports: There are 9 intercollegiate sports for men and 10 for women, and 25 intramural sports for men and 25 for women. Facilities include a 2200-seat gym, a competition-size swimming pool, tennis, racquetball, handball, and squash courts, a sauna, Nautilus and weight rooms, dance and aerobic rooms, playing fields, a stadium, and hockey facilities.

Disabled Students: 89% of the campus is accessible. Wheelchair ramps, elevators, special parking, specially equipped rest rooms, lowered drinking fountains, and automatic doors are available.

Services: Counseling and information services are available, as is tutoring in most subjects. There is a reader service for the blind, and remedial math, reading, and writing as well as a writing center and a math center.

Campus Safety and Security: Measures include 24-hour foot and vehicle patrol, security escort services, shuttle buses, and informal discussions. There are pamphlets/posters/films, emergency telephones, and lighted pathways/sidewalks.

Programs of Study: UC confers B.A. and B.S. degrees. Master's degrees are also awarded. Bachelor's degrees are awarded in BIOLOGICAL SCIENCE (biology/biological science), BUSINESS (accounting, business administration and management, and business economics), COMMUNICATIONS AND THE ARTS (communications, English, fine arts, journalism, and public relations), COMPUTER AND PHYSICAL SCIENCE (actuarial science, chemistry, computer science, mathematics, and physics), ENGINEERING AND ENVIRONMENTAL DESIGN (construction management), HEALTH PROFESSIONS (nursing, occupational therapy, physical therapy, and recreation therapy), SOCIAL SCIENCE (child psychology/development, criminal justice, economics, history, international studies, philosophy, political science/government, psychology, social studies, and sociology). Occupational therapy, psychology, and biology are the strongest academically. Management, psychology, and criminal justice are the largest.

Required: To graduate, students must complete a total of 120 to 128 hours with a minimum 2.0 GPA. They must complete a general education requirement, including basic skills and distribution requirements.

Special: UC offers co-op programs, internships, work-study programs in all majors, accelerated degrees, dual majors, and cross-registration with Hamilton College. Study abroad may be arranged in 9 countries. There is a 2-2 engineering degree with Syracuse University and a cross-registration with the Mohawk Valley Consortium. There are 5 national honor societies and a freshman honors program.

Faculty/Classroom: 55% of faculty are male; 45%, female. All both teach and do research. The average class size in an introductory lecture is 23; in a laboratory, 10; and in a regular course, 17.

Admissions: 77% of the 2003-2004 applicants were accepted.

Requirements: The SAT I or ACT is recommended. In addition, graduation from an accredited secondary school or satisfactory scores on the GED are required. Recommended high school courses include 4 years of English, 3 years each of math and social studies, and 2 years each of foreign language and science. An essay and an interview are also recommended. AP and CLEP credits are accepted. Important factors in the admissions decision are advanced placement or honor courses, extracurricular activities record, and leadership record.

Procedure: Freshmen are admitted fall and spring. Entrance exams should be taken during the junior year. There are early admissions and deferred admissions plans. There is a rolling admissions plan. Application deadlines are open.

Transfer: 240 transfer students enrolled in 2002-2003. Applicants must have a minimum GPA of 2.3. 30 of 120 to 128 credits required for the bachelor's degree must be completed at UC.

Visiting: There are regularly scheduled orientations for prospective students, including an interview, financial aid information, and a tour of the campus. There are guides for informal visits and visitors may sit in on classes and stay overnight. To schedule a visit, contact the Admissions Office at *admiss@utica.edu.*

Financial Aid: In a recent year, 90% of all full-time students received some form of financial aid. 89% of all full-time students received need-based aid. The FAFSA is required. The deadline for filing freshman financial aid applications for fall entry is February 15.

International Students: There were 56 international students enrolled in a recent year. The school actively recruits these students. They must score 529 on the written TOEFL or 195 on the electronic version or take the MELAB, the Comprehensive English Language Test, or the IELTS.

Computers: The mainframe is a Prime 5370. There are also 201 IBMs and Macs available in 8 labs. All students may access the system during posted hours. Time limits are imposed only during peak hours. The fee is $150.

Graduates: From July 1, 2002 to June 30, 2003, 434 bachelor's degrees were awarded. The most popular majors were criminal justice (16%), management (11%), and psychology (10%). In an average class, 1% graduate in 3 years or less, 38% graduate in 4 years or less, 52% graduate in 5 years or less, and 58% graduate in 6 years or less. 168 companies recruited on campus in 2002-2003. Of the 2002 graduating class, 17% were enrolled in graduate school within 6 months of graduation and 78% were employed.

Admissions Contact: Patrick Quinn, Vice President for Enrollment Management. E-mail: *admiss@utica.edu* Web: *www.utica.edu*

VASSAR COLLEGE D-4
Poughkeepsie, NY 12604 (914) 437-7300
(800) 827-7270; Fax: (914) 437-7063

Full-time: 969 men, 1426 women	**Faculty:** 258; IIB, ++$
Part-time: 19 men, 30 women	**Ph.D.s:** 96%
Graduate: none	**Student/Faculty:** 9 to 1
Year: semesters	**Tuition:** $29,540
Application Deadline: January 1	**Room & Board:** $7490
Freshman Class: 6207 applied, 1806 accepted, 636 enrolled	
SAT I Verbal/Math: 696/676	**ACT:** 30 **MOST COMPETITIVE**

Vassar College, founded in 1861, is a private (not for profit), college of the liberal arts and sciences. The 3 libraries contain 844,666 volumes, 608,635 microform items, and 20,487 audio/video tapes/CDs, and subscribe to 2996 periodicals. Computerized library services include the card catalog, interlibrary loans, database searching, and Internet access. Special learning facilities include a learning resource center, art gallery, radio station, studio art building, geological museum, observatory, 3 theaters, concert hall, environmental field station, intercultural center, and research-oriented lab facilities for natural sciences. The 1000-acre campus is in a suburban area 75 miles north of New York City. Including any residence halls, there are 100 buildings.

Student Life: 73% of undergraduates are from out of state, mostly the Middle Atlantic. Students are from 50 states, 49 foreign countries, and Canada. 60% are from public schools. 75% are white. The average age of freshmen is 18; all undergraduates, 20. 4% do not continue beyond their first year; 88% remain to graduate.

Housing: 2305 students can be accommodated in college housing, which includes single-sex and coed dorms, on-campus apartments, off-campus apartments, and married-student housing. There is 1 all-women residence hall and 1 cooperative living unit. On-campus housing is guaranteed for all 4 years. 98% of students live on campus; of those, 90% remain on campus on weekends. All students may keep cars.

Activities: There are no fraternities or sororities. There are 85 groups on campus, including art, band, chess, choir, chorale, chorus, computers, dance, debate, drama, ethnic, film, gay, international, jazz band, literary magazine, newspaper, opera, orchestra, photography, political, radio and TV, religious, social service, student government, and yearbook. Popular campus events include Founders Day, spring and fall formals, and All Parents Weekend.

Sports: There are 12 intercollegiate sports for men and 13 for women, and 18 intramural sports for men and 18 for women. Facilities include a field house with a swimming pool, 5 indoor tennis courts, a weight and conditioning room, a gym with squash and racquetball courts and basketball facilities, a 9-hole golf course, 13 outdoor tennis courts, an all-weather track, 2 soccer fields, a baseball diamond, a rugby field, and various club and intramural fields. An addition to the athletic facilities provides a competition basketball gym, a banked running track, and a 5000-square-foot exercise and fitness center.

Disabled Students: 41% of the campus is accessible. Wheelchair ramps, elevators, special parking, specially equipped rest rooms, special class scheduling, and lowered drinking fountains are available. There is an Office of Disability and Support Services, signage in braille, and assisted listening devices.

Services: Counseling and information services are available, as is tutoring in most subjects. There is a reader service for the blind and remedial math and writing.

Campus Safety and Security: Measures include 24-hour foot and vehicle patrol, self-defense education, security escort services, and shuttle buses. There are informal discussions, pamphlets/posters/films, emergency telephones, and lighted pathways/sidewalks.

Programs of Study: Vassar confers the A.B. degree. Master's degrees are also awarded. Bachelor's degrees are awarded in AGRICULTURE (environmental studies), BIOLOGICAL SCIENCE (biochemistry and biology/biological science), COMMUNICATIONS AND THE ARTS (art, dramatic arts, English, film arts, languages, and music), COMPUTER AND PHYSICAL SCIENCE (astronomy, chemistry, computer science, geology, mathematics, and physics), EDUCATION (foreign languages), ENGINEERING AND ENVIRONMENTAL DESIGN (technology and public affairs), HEALTH PROFESSIONS (premedicine), SOCIAL SCIENCE (African studies, American studies, anthropology, Asian/Oriental studies, biopsychology, classical/ancient civilization, cognitive science, economics, geography, history, international studies, Judaic studies, Latin American studies, medieval studies, philosophy, political science/government, prelaw, psychology, religion, social studies, sociology, Spanish studies, urban studies, and women's studies). English, psychology, and political science are the largest.

Required: To graduate, students must have a total of 34 units equivalent to 120 credit hours, with a minimum GPA of 2.0. Of this total, no more than 17 units may be in a single field of concentration and 8 1/2 units must be outside the major field. Entering freshmen must take the freshman course. All students must meet the foreign language proficiency requirement and must take a quantitative skills course before their third year.

Special: The school offers fieldwork in social agencies and schools, a Washington semester, dual majors, independent majors, a 4-year advanced degree program in chemistry, cross-registration with the 12 College Consortium, and nonrecorded grade options. Study-abroad programs may be arranged in 7 countries. A 3-2 engineering degree with Dartmouth College is offered. There is a chapter of Phi Beta Kappa.

Faculty/Classroom: 52% of faculty are male; 48%, female. All both teach and do research. The average class size in an introductory lecture is 21; in a laboratory, 7; and in a regular course, 17.

Admissions: 29% of the 2003-2004 applicants were accepted. The SAT I scores for the 2003-2004 freshman class were: Verbal--4% between 500 and 599, 47% between 600 and 700, and 50% above 700; Math--8% between 500 and 599, 55% between 600 and 700, and 37% above 700. 90% of the current freshmen were in the top fifth of their class; 98% were in the top two fifths. 30 freshmen graduated first in their class.

Requirements: The SAT I and 3 SAT II: Subject tests, preferably 1 in writing, or the ACT, is required. In addition, graduation from an accredited secondary school or satisfactory scores on the GED are required for admission. The high school program should typically include 4 years each of English, social studies, and math, and 3 or more years each of a foreign language and science. An essay and a writing sample are required. AP credits are accepted. Important factors in the admissions decision are advanced placement or honor courses, recommendations by school officials, and leadership record.

Procedure: Freshmen are admitted in the fall. Entrance exams should be taken as early as possible, but no later than December of the senior year. There are early decision and deferred admissions plans. Early decision applications should be filed by November 15 and January 1; regular applications, by January 1 for fall entry, along with a $60 fee. Notification of early decision is sent December 15 and February 1; regular decision, April 1. 245 early decision candidates were accepted for the 2003-2004 class. 400 were on the 2003 waiting list; 35 were admitted. Applications are accepted on-line through *www.vassar.edu* or via Common App.

Transfer: 26 transfer students enrolled in 2002-2003. Applicants must have at least 1 year of liberal arts course work with a high level of achievement. 17 credits of 34 required for the bachelor's degree must be completed at Vassar.

Visiting: There are regularly scheduled orientations for prospective students, including a campus tour, an information session, and a class visit when possible. There are guides for informal visits and visitors may sit in on classes and stay overnight. To schedule a visit, contact the Admissions Office at *admissions@vassar.edu*.

Financial Aid: In 2003-2004, 56% of all full-time freshmen and 59% of continuing full-time students received some form of financial aid. 47% of full-time freshmen and 52% of continuing full-time students received need-based aid. The average freshman award was $24,008. Need-based scholarships or need-based grants averaged $20,301 ($30,000 maximum); and need-based self-help aid (loans and jobs) averaged $3773 ($5665 maximum). 58% of undergraduates work part time. Average annual earnings from campus work are $956. The average financial indebtedness of the 2003 graduate was $18,728. Vassar is a member of CSS. The CSS/Profile, FAFSA, FFS, and the college's own financial statement are required. The deadline for filing freshman financial aid applications for fall entry is February 10.

International Students: There are 103 international students enrolled. The school actively recruits these students. They must score 600 on the written TOEFL or 250 on the electronic version and also take the SAT I or the ACT. Students must take any 3 SAT II: Subject tests.

Computers: The mainframes are a DEC VAX 6200, an 11/780, an 11/750, and a MicroVAX II. There are also 350 Macs and PCs available throughout the campus. All students may access the system 24 hours per day. There are no time limits and no fees.

Graduates: From July 1, 2002 to June 30, 2003, 616 bachelor's degrees were awarded. The most popular majors were English (11%), political science (10%), and psychology (10%). In an average class, 1% graduate in 3 years or less, 86% graduate in 4 years or less, 91% graduate in 5 years or less, and 91% graduate in 6 years or less. 14 companies recruited on campus in 2002-2003. Of the 2002 graduating class, 17% were enrolled in graduate school within 6 months of graduation and 71% were employed.

Admissions Contact: David Borus, Dean of Admission and Financial Aid. E-mail: *admissions@vassar.edu* Web: *www.vassar.edu*

WAGNER COLLEGE
D-5
Staten Island, NY 10301
(718) 390-3411
(800) 221-1010; Fax: (718) 390-3105

Full-time: 721 men, 1059 women	**Faculty:** 83
Part-time: 13 men, 33 women	**Ph.D.s:** 85%
Graduate: 143 men, 249 women	**Student/Faculty:** n/av
Year: semesters, summer session	**Tuition:** $22,600
Application Deadline: February 15	**Room & Board:** $7300
Freshman Class: 2425 applied, 1609 accepted, 534 enrolled	
SAT I Verbal/Math: 552/549	**ACT:** 25 **VERY COMPETITIVE**

Wagner College, founded in 1883, is a private liberal arts institution. In addition to regional accreditation, Wagner has baccalaureate program accreditation with NLN. The library contains 300,000 volumes and 225,000 microform items, and subscribes to 1000 periodicals. Computerized library services include interlibrary loans and database searching. Special learning facilities include an art gallery and planetarium. The 105-acre campus is in a suburban area 10 miles from Manhattan. Including any residence halls, there are 18 buildings.

Student Life: 69% of undergraduates are from New York. Students are from 36 states and Canada. 63% are from public schools. 85% are white. 44% are Catholic; 36% claim no religious affiliation; 13% Protestant. The average age of freshmen is 18; all undergraduates, 20. 17% do not continue beyond their first year; 68% remain to graduate.

Housing: 1315 students can be accommodated in college housing, which includes coed dorms. There are fraternity/sorority floors and quiet floors in dorms. On-campus housing is guaranteed for all 4 years. 65% of students live on campus; of those, 75% remain on campus on weekends. Alcohol is not permitted. Upperclassmen may keep cars.

Activities: 20% of men belong to 4 local and 4 national fraternities; 20% of women belong to 1 local sorority and 2 national sororities. There are 65 groups on campus, including academic, art, band, cheerleading, chess, choir, chorale, computers, dance, drama, ethnic, gay, honors, international, jazz band, literary magazine, musical theater, newspaper, opera, pep band, political, professional, religious, social service, student government, symphony, women's, and yearbook. Popular campus events include Songfest and Spring Fling Week.

Sports: There are 7 intercollegiate sports for men and 9 for women, and 4 intramural sports for men and 3 for women. Facilities include a football stadium, a gym, a fitness center, a track, and a basketball arena.

Disabled Students: 25% of the campus is accessible. Wheelchair ramps, elevators, special parking, specially equipped rest rooms, and special class scheduling are available.

Services: Counseling and information services are available, as is tutoring in every subject. There is a reader service for the blind and remedial math, reading, and writing.

Campus Safety and Security: Measures include 24-hour foot and vehicle patrol, security escort services, shuttle buses, and informal discussions. There are emergency telephones, lighted pathways/sidewalks, and ID card access into residence halls.

Programs of Study: Wagner confers B.A. and B.S. degrees. Master's degrees are also awarded. Bachelor's degrees are awarded in BIOLOGICAL SCIENCE (biology/biological science and microbiology), BUSINESS (accounting and business administration and management), COMMUNICATIONS AND THE ARTS (arts administration/management, dramatic arts, English, fine arts, and music), COMPUTER AND PHYSICAL SCIENCE (chemistry, computer science, mathematics, and physics), EDUCATION (elementary, middle school, and secondary), HEALTH PROFESSIONS (medical laboratory technology, nursing, and physician's assistant), SOCIAL SCIENCE (anthropology, gerontology, history, political science/government, psychology, public administration, social work, and sociology). Natural sciences is the strongest academically. Business is the largest.

Required: To graduate, students must complete 128 credit hours with 60 hours in the major and a minimum GPA of 2.0. All students must take courses in English, math, and multidisciplinary studies. In addition, students must fulfill distribution requirements in physical science, life science, math and computers, history, literature, philosophy and religion, foreign culture, aesthetics, and human behavior.

Special: Internships are required for business and English majors and are recommended for all majors. Students may earn B.A.-B.S. degrees in math, physics, and psychology. Student-designed and dual majors, credit for life experience, a Washington semester, nondegree study, and pass/fail options are available. Study abroad in 14 countries is possible. There are 9 national honor societies and a freshman honors program.

Faculty/Classroom: 42% of faculty are male; 58%, female. All teach undergraduates. No introductory courses are taught by graduate students. The average class size in an introductory lecture is 23; in a laboratory, 13; and in a regular course, 20.

Admissions: 66% of the 2003-2004 applicants were accepted. The SAT I scores for the 2003-2004 freshman class were: Verbal--18% below 500, 62% between 500 and 599, 19% between 600 and 700, and 1% above 700; Math--19% below 500, 60% between 500 and 599, 20% between 600 and 700, and 1% above 700. The ACT scores were 7% below 21, 13% between 21 and 23, 62% between 24 and 26, 15% between 27 and 28, and 3% above 28. 31% of the current freshmen were in the top fifth of their class; 83% were in the top two fifths.

Requirements: The SAT I or ACT is required. For the SAT I, the recommended minimum scores are 510 verbal and 500 math. A composite score of 21 is recommended on the ACT. Graduation from an accredited secondary school is required, with 18 academic credits or Carnegie units, including 4 years of English, 3 years each of history and math, 2 years each of foreign language, science, and social studies, and 1 year each of art and music. An essay is required, and an interview is recommended. Auditions are required for music and theater applicants. A GPA of 3.0 is required. AP and CLEP credits are accepted. Important factors in the admissions decision are advanced placement or honor courses, recommendations by school officials, and extracurricular activities record.

Procedure: Freshmen are admitted fall and spring. Entrance exams should be taken by December of the senior year. There are early decision, early admissions, and deferred admissions plans. Early decision applications should be filed by December 1; regular applications, by February 15 for fall entry. The fall 2003 application fee was $50. Notification of early decision is sent January 2; regular decision, March 1. 28 early decision candidates were accepted for the 2003-2004 class. Applications are accepted on computer disk.

Transfer: Transfer students should have a minimum of 30 credit hours earned with a GPA of 2.5. Applicants must submit all college and high school transcripts, a letter of recommendation, and a personal statement. An interview is recommended. SAT I or ACT scores taken within the past 5 years may be submitted. 30 of 128 credits required for the bachelor's degree must be completed at Wagner.

Visiting: There are regularly scheduled orientations for prospective students, including a presentation by the Admissions Office, a tour of the campus, and meetings with faculty and staff. There are guides for informal visits and visitors may sit in on classes and stay overnight. To schedule a visit, contact the Admissions Office.

Financial Aid: In 2003-2004, 78% of all full-time freshmen and 80% of continuing full-time students received some form of financial aid. The average freshman award was $6800. Need-based scholarships or need-based grants averaged $1000 ($2500 maximum); need-based self-help aid (loans and jobs) averaged $3500 ($5000 maximum); non-need-based athletic scholarships averaged $3000 ($15,000 maximum); and other non-need-based awards and non-need-based scholarships averaged $6000 ($11,000 maximum). 25% of undergraduates work part time. Average annual earnings from campus work are $800. Wagner is a member of CSS. The FAFSA and the college's own financial statement are required. Check with the school for current deadlines.

International Students: The school actively recruits these students. They must score 550 on the written TOEFL and also take the college's own test.

Computers: The mainframe is a DEC VAX. 75 IBM PCs in the computer center are connected to the mainframe. An additional 52 IBM PCs are available for student use. Printers include 4 HP LaserJet, 2 Epson LQ dot-matrix, and 1 HP PaintJet. All students may access the system Monday through Thursday, 9 A.M. to 10 P.M.; Friday, 9 A.M. to 6 P.M.; and Saturday and Sunday, 11 A.M. to 5 P.M. There are no time limits and no fees. It is strongly recommended that all students have a personal computer.

Admissions Contact: Angelo Araimo, Vice President for Enrollment. E-mail: *admissions@wagner.edu* Web: *www.wagner.edu*

WEBB INSTITUTE   **D-5**
Glen Cove, NY 11542   (516) 671-2213; Fax: (516) 674-9838

Full-time: 60 men, 15 women	**Faculty:** 8
Part-time: none	**Ph.D.s:** 50%
Graduate: none	**Student/Faculty:** 9 to 1
Year: semesters	**Tuition:** see profile
Application Deadline: see profile	**Room & Board:** $6250
Freshman Class: n/av	
SAT I: required	**ACT:** n/av **MOST COMPETITIVE**

Webb Institute, founded in 1889, is a private engineering school devoted to professional knowledge of ship construction, design, and motive power. All students receive 4-year, full-tuition scholarships. Figures in the above capsule and in this profile are approximate. In addition to regional accreditation, Webb has baccalaureate program accreditation with ABET. The library contains 50,598 volumes, 1633 microform items, and 1851 audio/video tapes/CDs, and subscribes to 267 periodicals. Computerized library services include the card catalog, interlibrary loans, and database searching. Special learning facilities include a marine engineering lab and a ship model testing/towing tank. The 26-acre campus is in a suburban area 24 miles east of New York City. Including any residence halls, there are 11 buildings.

Student Life: 70% of undergraduates are from out of state, mostly the Northeast. Students are from 23 states and 2 foreign countries. 70% are from public schools. 98% are white. The average age of freshmen is 18; all undergraduates, 20. 4% do not continue beyond their first year; 73% remain to graduate.

Housing: 110 students can be accommodated in college housing, which includes single-sex dorms. On-campus housing is guaranteed for all 4 years. All students live on campus; 80% remain on campus on weekends. All students may keep cars.

Activities: There are no fraternities or sororities. There are some groups and organizations on campus, including chorale, orchestra, professional, social, student government, yachting, and yearbook. Popular campus events include Parents Day and Webbstock.

Sports: There are 6 intercollegiate sports for men and 6 for women, and 2 intramural sports for men and 2 for women. Facilities include a 60-seat gym, tennis courts, an athletic field, a boat house, and a beachfront dock.

Disabled Students: 90% of the campus is accessible. Elevators and special parking are available.

Services: Counseling and information services are available, as is tutoring in most subjects.

Campus Safety and Security: Measures include 24-hour foot and vehicle patrol, informal discussions, pamphlets/posters/films, and emergency telephones. There are lighted pathways/sidewalks and student and professional security services.

Programs of Study: Webb confers the B.S. degree. Bachelor's degrees are awarded in ENGINEERING AND ENVIRONMENTAL DESIGN (naval architecture and marine engineering).

Required: The curriculum is prescribed, with all students taking the same courses in each of the 4 years. The Webb program has 4 practical 8-week paid work periods: freshman year, a helper mechanic in a shipyard; sophomore year, a cadet in the engine room of a ship; and junior and senior years, a draftsman or junior engineer in a design office. All students must complete a senior seminar, thesis, and technical reports, as well as make engineering inspection visits. A total of 146 credits with a minimum passing grade of 70% is required to graduate.

Special: All students are employed 2 months each year through co-op programs.

Faculty/Classroom: All faculty are male. All teach undergraduates and 40% both teach and do research. The average class size in an introductory lecture is 25; in a laboratory, 9; and in a regular course, 25.

Requirements: The SAT I is required, with minimum scores of 500 verbal and 660 math. Applicants should be graduates of an accredited secondary school with 16 academic credits completed, including 4 each in English and math, 2 each in history and science, 1 in foreign language, and 3 in electives. 3 SAT II: Subject tests in writing, mathematics level I or II, and physics or chemistry are required, as is an interview. Candidates must be U.S. citizens. Webb requires applicants to be in the upper 20% of their class. A GPA of 3.2 is required. Important factors in the admissions decision are advanced placement or honor courses, evidence of special talent, and personality/intangible qualities.

Procedure: Freshmen are admitted in the fall. Entrance exams should be taken by January of the senior year. There is an early decision plan. Check with the school for current application deadlines. The application fee is $25.

Transfer: Transfers must enter as freshmen. A 3.2 GPA is required. SAT I scores and an interview are required. All 146 credits required for the bachelor's degree must be completed at Webb.

Visiting: There are regularly scheduled orientations for prospective students, including an open house one weekend each October. There are guides for informal visits and visitors may sit in on classes and stay overnight. To schedule a visit, contact the Director of Admissions.

Financial Aid: The aid reported here is to assist with room and board. In a recent year, 10% of all full-time freshmen and 19% of continuing full-time students received some form of financial aid. 5% of full-time freshmen and 8% of continuing full-time students received need-based aid. The average freshman award was $5125. The average financial indebtedness of a recent graduate was $900. The CSS Profile and the college's own financial statement are required. Check with the school for current deadlines.

International Students: All applicants must be U.S. citizens.

Computers: There are 9 PCs available on campus. Access to the Internet and Web is available from labs and dorm rooms. All students are issued a laptop, which connects to the network for access to e-mail and the Internet. Students can connect to the network from dorm rooms, classrooms, labs, the library, and other public areas. All students may access the system 24 hours per day.

Graduates: In a recent year, 18 bachelor's degrees were awarded. In an average class, 88% graduate in 4 years or less. 9 companies recruited on campus in a recent year. Of a recent graduating class, 15% were enrolled in graduate school within 6 months of graduation and 85% were employed.

Admissions Contact: William G. Murray, Director of Admissions. E-mail: *admissions@webb-institute.edu* Web: *http://www.webb-institute.edu*

WELLS COLLEGE
Aurora, NY 13026

C-3

(315) 364-3264

(800) 952-9355; Fax: (315) 364-3227

Full-time: 415 men and women	**Faculty:** 50; IIB, av$
Part-time: 21 women	**Ph.Ds:** 100%
Graduate: none	**Student/Faculty:** 8 to 1
Year: semesters	**Tuition:** $14,292
Application Deadline: March 1	**Room & Board:** $6830
Freshman Class: 408 applied, 342 accepted, 100 enrolled	
SAT I Verbal/Math: 580/520	**ACT:** 24 **VERY COMPETITIVE**

Wells College, founded in 1868, is a private liberal arts institution for women. The library contains 252,097 volumes, 13,925 microform items, and 924 audio/video tapes/CDs, and subscribes to 391 periodicals. Computerized library services include the card catalog, interlibrary loans, database searching, and Internet access. Special learning facilities include an art gallery and the Book Arts Center. The 365-acre campus is in a small town on Cayuga Lake, 30 miles north of Ithaca. Including any residence halls, there are 22 buildings.

Student Life: 73% of undergraduates are from New York. Others are from 30 states and 8 foreign countries. 90% are from public schools. 77% are white. The average age of freshmen is 18; all undergraduates, 20. 22% do not continue beyond their first year; 64% remain to graduate.

Housing: 430 students can be accommodated in college housing, which includes single-sex dorms and off-campus apartments. In addition, there are special-interest houses and housing for nontraditional-age students. On-campus housing is guaranteed for all 4 years. 84% of students live on campus; of those, 75% remain on campus on weekends. All students may keep cars.

Activities: There are no sororities. There are 39 groups on campus, including bell ringers, choir, chorale, dance, drama, ethnic, forensics, gay, international, jazz band, literary magazine, musical instrument ensemble, musical theater, newspaper, orchestra, photography, political, professional, religious, social, social service, student government, WILL (Women in Lifelong Learning), women's resource center, and yearbook. Popular campus events include the Odd-Even Basketball Game, Spring Weekend, and 100 Days for Seniors.

Sports: Facilities include a competition-size swimming pool, a gym, a fully equipped fitness center, an athletic training room, 2 indoor tennis courts/practice space, a 9-hole golf course, 4 all-weather tennis courts, and a boat house and dock with canoes and sailboats.

Disabled Students: 51% of the campus is accessible. Wheelchair ramps, elevators, special parking, specially equipped rest rooms, special class scheduling, lowered drinking fountains, lowered telephones, and special housing are available.

Services: Counseling and information services are available, as is tutoring in every subject. Assistance is provided on an individual, as-needed basis. Untimed and extended-time testing options are available.

Campus Safety and Security: Measures include 24-hour foot and vehicle patrol, self-defense education, security escort services, and shuttle buses. There are informal discussions, pamphlets/posters/films, emergency telephones, and lighted pathways/sidewalks. All students must escort their guests on campus at all times.

Programs of Study: Wells confers the B.A. degree. Bachelor's degrees are awarded in AGRICULTURE (environmental studies), BIOLOGICAL SCIENCE (biochemistry, biology/biological science, and molecular biology), BUSINESS (business administration and management), COMMUNICATIONS AND THE ARTS (dance, dramatic arts, English, fine arts, French, German, language arts, music, Spanish, and visual and performing arts), COMPUTER AND PHYSICAL SCIENCE (chemistry, computer science, mathematics, and physics), EDUCATION (elementary), SOCIAL SCIENCE (American studies, anthropology, economics, ethics, politics, and social policy, history, international studies, philosophy, political science/government, psychology, public affairs, religion, sociology, and women's studies). Psychology, English, and mathematical and physical sciences are the largest.

Required: To graduate, students must complete a total of 120 credit hours, including 33 to 63 in the major, with a minimum GPA of 2.0 overall and in the major. All students must complete 2 First-Year Experience courses, a comprehensive exam, and a senior project/thesis. Distribution requirements include 4 courses in phys ed and wellness, 3 in natural and social sciences, 3 in arts and humanities, 2 in a foreign language, and 1 in formal reasoning.

Special: Wells offers cross-registration with Cornell University, Cayuga Community College, and Ithaca College, a Washington semester with American University, internships, and accelerated degree programs in all majors. Study abroad in 13 countries is permitted. A 3-2 engineering degree is available with Columbia, Clarkson, and Cornell Universities. Students may also earn 3-2 degrees in business and community health with the University of Rochester and a 3-4 degree in veterinary medicine with Cornell University. Student-designed majors and pass-fail options are available. Work-study, B.A.-B.S. degrees, and dual majors are also possible. There are 2 national honor societies, including Phi Beta Kappa.

Faculty/Classroom: 39% of faculty are male; 61%, female. All teach undergraduates. The average class size in an introductory lecture is 22; in a laboratory, 15; and in a regular course, 13.

Admissions: 84% of the 2003-2004 applicants were accepted. The SAT I scores for the 2003-2004 freshman class were: Verbal--16% below 500, 41% between 500 and 599, 39% between 600 and 700, and 4% above 700; Math--33% below 500, 41% between 500 and 599, 26% between 600 and 700, and 1% above 700. The ACT scores were 16% below 21, 30% between 21 and 23, 27% between 24 and 26, 16% between 27 and 28, and 11% above 28. 55% of the current freshmen were in the top fifth of their class; 83% were in the top two fifths. 3 freshmen graduated first in their class.

Requirements: The SAT I or ACT is required. In addition, graduation from an accredited secondary school should include 20 academic credits or Carnegie units. High school courses must include 4 years of English, 3 each of a foreign language and math, and 2 each of history and lab science. 2 teacher recommendations and an essay/personal statement are required, and an interview is strongly recommended. AP and CLEP credits are accepted. Important factors in the admissions decision are advanced placement or honor courses, recommendations by school officials, and extracurricular activities record.

Procedure: Freshmen are admitted in the fall. Entrance exams should be taken prior to application. There are early decision, early admissions, and deferred admissions plans. Early decision applications should be filed by December 15; regular applications, by March 1 for fall entry, along with a $40 fee. Notification of early decision is sent January 15; regular decision, April 1. 13 early decision candidates were accepted for the 2003-2004 class. Applications are accepted on-line through Common App, Embark.com, and the school's web site.

Transfer: 33 transfer students enrolled in 2002-2003. Applicants must be in good standing at the institution last attended. A minimum GPA of 2.0 is required. Wells requires official college and high school transcripts, a personal statement, standardized test scores, and a recommendation from a professor. An interview is strongly recommended. 60 of 120 credits required for the bachelor's degree must be completed at Wells.

Visiting: There are regularly scheduled orientations for prospective students, including tours, interviews, class attendance, presentations, open houses, and an overnight hostess program. There are guides for informal visits and visitors may sit in on classes and stay overnight. To schedule a visit, contact the Admissions Office.

Financial Aid: In 2003-2004, 85% of all full-time freshmen and 86% of continuing full-time students received some form of financial aid. 78% of full-time freshmen and 74% of continuing full-time students received need-based aid. The average freshman award was $13,682. 90% of undergraduates work part time. Average annual earnings from campus work are $1200. The average financial indebtedness of the 2003 graduate was $17,125. Wells is a member of CSS. The FAFSA is required; early decision applicants must submit the CSS Profile. The deadline for filing freshman financial aid applications for fall entry is May 1.

International Students: There are 16 international students enrolled. The school actively recruits these students. They must score 550 on the written TOEFL or 213 on the electronic version.

Computers: The mainframe is an IBM AS/400 Model 720. There are 31 Macs (Power Macs and G3s) and 61 Pentium-level PCs available in academic buildings and residence halls. The computer-to-student ratio is 4 to 1. Students have access to the Internet and the World Wide Web. Access to the Internet is available in every dorm room.

Graduates: From July 1, 2002 to June 30, 2003, 120 bachelor's degrees were awarded. The most popular majors were psychology (25%), sociology/anthropology (11%), and visual arts (9%). In an average class, 2% graduate in 3 years or less, 60% graduate in 4 years or less, 62% graduate in 5 years or less, and 64% graduate in 6 years or less. Of the 2002 graduating class, 15% were enrolled in graduate school within 6 months of graduation and 37% were employed.

Admissions Contact: Susan Sloan, Director of Admissions. A video is available. E-mail: *admissions@wells.edu* Web: *www.wells.edu*

YESHIVA UNIVERSITY
New York, NY 10033-3201

D-5

(212) 960-5277; Fax: (212) 960-0086

Full-time: 1280 men, 970 women	**Faculty:** 120
Part-time: 40 men, 20 women	**Ph.Ds:** 79%
Graduate: 1330 men, 1690 women	**Student/Faculty:** 19 to 1
Year: semesters, summer session	**Tuition:** $20,960
Application Deadline: see profile	**Room & Board:** $6570
Freshman Class: n/av	
SAT I or ACT: required	**COMPETITIVE**

Yeshiva University, founded in 1886, is an independent liberal arts institution offering undergraduate programs through Yeshiva College, its undergraduate college for men; Stern College for Women; and Sy Syms School of Business. Figures in the above capsule and in this profile are approximate. There are 7 graduate schools. In addition to regional accreditation, YU has baccalaureate program accreditation with CSWE. The 7 libraries contain 900,000 volumes, 759,000 microform items, and

980 audio/video tapes/CDs, and subscribe to 7790 periodicals. Computerized library services include the card catalog, interlibrary loans, and database searching. Special learning facilities include an art gallery, radio station, and museum. The 26-acre campus is in an urban area.

Student Life: 48% of undergraduates are from New York. Students are from 31 states, 16 foreign countries, and Canada. 14% are from public schools. The average age of freshmen is 17; all undergraduates, 19. 8% do not continue beyond their first year; 90% remain to graduate.

Housing: 1600 students can be accommodated in college housing, which includes single-sex dorms and off-campus apartments. On-campus housing is guaranteed for all 4 years. 85% of students live on campus. Alcohol is not permitted. All students may keep cars.

Activities: There are no fraternities or sororities. There are 70 groups on campus, including art, choir, computers, drama, honors, international, jazz band, literary magazine, musical theater, newspaper, political, professional, radio, religious, social service, special interest, student government, and yearbook. Popular campus events include holiday and dramatic presentations and Parents Day.

Sports: There are 8 intercollegiate sports for men and 2 for women, and 5 intramural sports for men and 4 for women. The athletic center at Yeshiva College houses a variety of facilities, including a 1000-seat gym.

Disabled Students: 95% of the campus is accessible. Wheelchair ramps and elevators are available.

Services: There is remedial reading and writing. There is also a writing center, which helps students with composition and verbal skills.

Campus Safety and Security: Measures include 24-hour foot and vehicle patrol, security escort services, shuttle buses, and informal discussions. There are pamphlets/posters/films, lighted pathways/sidewalks, ID cards, vulnerability surveys, fire drills, alarm systems, emergency telephone numbers, and transportation for routine and special events.

Programs of Study: YU confers B.A. and B.S. degrees. Associate degrees are also awarded. Bachelor's degrees are awarded in BIOLOGICAL SCIENCE (biology/biological science), BUSINESS (accounting, business administration and management, and marketing/retailing/merchandising), COMMUNICATIONS AND THE ARTS (classical languages, communications, English, French, Hebrew, music, and speech/debate/rhetoric), COMPUTER AND PHYSICAL SCIENCE (chemistry, computer science, and mathematics), ENGINEERING AND ENVIRONMENTAL DESIGN (preengineering), HEALTH PROFESSIONS (health science), SOCIAL SCIENCE (economics, history, philosophy, political science/government, psychology, religion, and sociology). The dual program of liberal arts and Jewish studies are the strongest academically. Accounting, psychology, and economics are the largest.

Required: To graduate, students must complete a total of 128 credit hours. Under the dual program, students pursue a liberal arts or business curriculum together with courses in Hebrew language, literature, and culture. Courses in Jewish learning are geared to the student's level of preparation.

Special: YU offers a 3-2 degree in occupational therapy with Columbia and New York Universities; a 3-4 degree in podiatry with the New York College of Podiatric Medicine; and a 3-2 or 4-2 degree in engineering with Columbia University. Stern College students may take courses in advertising, photography, and design at the Fashion Institute of Technology. Study abroad programs may be arranged in Israel. The school offers independent study options and an optional pass/no credit system. There are 9 national honor societies and 20 departmental honors programs.

Faculty/Classroom: 73% of faculty are male; 27%, female. 58% teach undergraduates, 60% do research, and 28% do both. No introductory courses are taught by graduate students. The average class size in an introductory lecture is 38; in a laboratory, 15; and in a regular course, 18.

Requirements: The SAT I or ACT is required. In addition, graduation from an accredited secondary school with 16 academic credits is required for admission. The GED is accepted under limited and specific circumstances. The SAT II: Subject test in Hebrew is recommended for placement purposes. An interview and an essay are required. A GPA of 3.3 is required. AP and CLEP credits are accepted. Important factors in the admissions decision are extracurricular activities record, personality/intangible qualities, and evidence of special talent.

Procedure: Freshmen are admitted to all sessions. There are early admissions, deferred admissions, and rolling admissions plans. Check with the school for current deadlines and fees. A waiting list is an active part of the admissions procedure.

Transfer: 95 of 128 credits required for the bachelor's degree must be completed at YU.

Visiting: There are regularly scheduled orientations for prospective students, YU holds open houses for high school students. There are guides for informal visits and visitors may sit in on classes and stay overnight. To schedule a visit, contact the Office of Admissions.

Financial Aid: YU is a member of CSS. The CSS Profile and the college's own financial statement are required. Check with the school for current deadlines.

International Students: The school actively recruits these students. They must score 500 on the written TOEFL and also take the SAT I or the ACT.

Computers: The mainframe is an IBM RS/6000. There are more than 200 networked and stand-alone PCs and workstations at 4 academic centers, with additional facilities at university libraries. All students may access the system 24 hours per day via modem or when buildings are open. There are no time limits and no fees.

Admissions Contact: Michael Kranzler, Director of Undergraduate Admissions. A video is available. E-mail: *yuadmit@ymail.yu.edu* Web: *www.yu.edu*

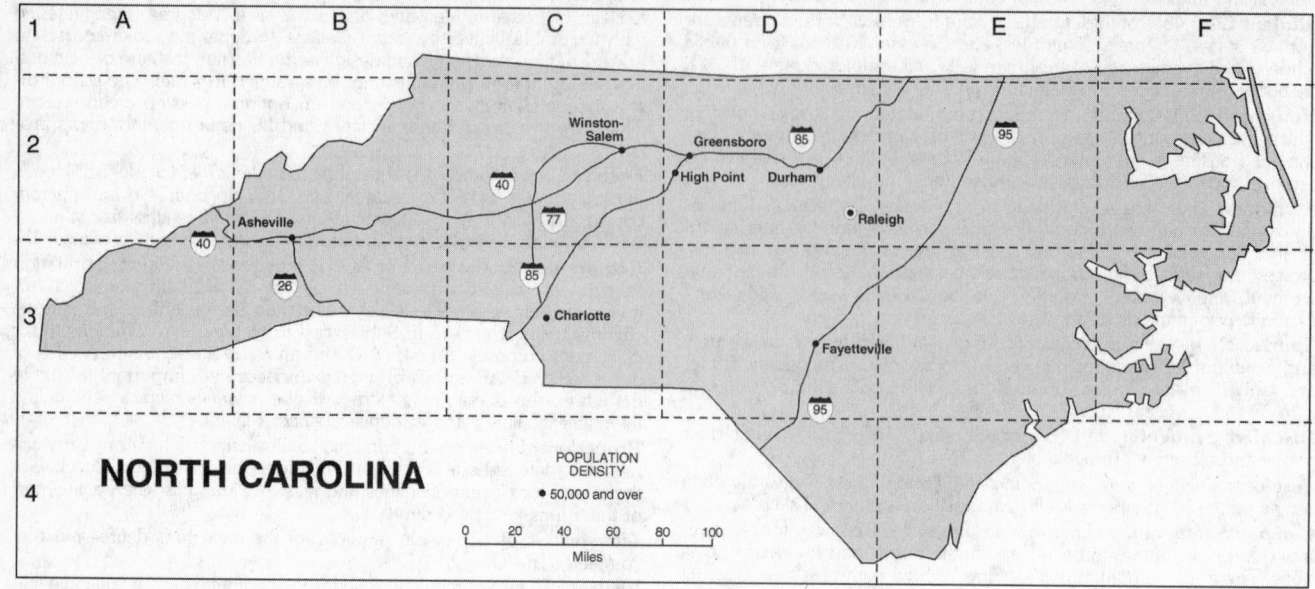

NORTH CAROLINA

POPULATION
DENSITY

• 50,000 and over

0 20 40 60 80 100
Miles

APPALACHIAN STATE UNIVERSITY

B-2

Boone, NC 28608 (828) 262-2120; Fax: (828) 262-3296

Full-time: 5969 men, 5864 women	**Faculty:** IIA, av$
Part-time: 407 men, 694 women	**Ph.Ds:** n/av
Graduate: 403 men, 1006 women	**Student/Faculty:** n/av
Year: semesters, summer session	**Tuition:** $2927 ($12,294)
Application Deadline: open	**Room & Board:** $4710

Freshman Class: 9598 applied, 6293 accepted, 2473 enrolled

SAT I Verbal/Math: 550/560 **VERY COMPETITIVE**

Appalachian State University, founded in 1899 and a member of the University of North Carolina system, is a comprehensive university offering undergraduate and graduate programs in the arts and sciences, business, teacher education, fine and applied arts, and music. There are 5 undergraduate schools and 1 graduate school. In addition to regional accreditation, App State has baccalaureate program accreditation with AACSB, AAFCS, ADA, ASLA, ASLHA, CAAHEP, CSAB, CSWE, NASAD, NASM, NCATE, AND NRPA. The 2 libraries contain 544,299 volumes, 1,481,544 microform items, and 77,899 audio/video tapes/CDs, and subscribe to 40,275 periodicals. Computerized library services include the card catalog, interlibrary loans, and database searching. Special learning facilities include a learning resource center, art gallery, radio station, TV station, an Appalachian cultural center, and the Dark Sky Observatory. The 1337-acre campus is in a rural area in northwest North Carolina. Including any residence halls, there are 86 buildings.

Student Life: 89% of undergraduates are from North Carolina. Students are from 45 states, 54 foreign countries, and Canada. 97% are from public schools. 92% are white. The average age of freshmen is 18; all undergraduates, 21. 18% do not continue beyond their first year; 65% remain to graduate.

Housing: 5081 students can be accommodated in college housing, which includes single-sex and coed dorms, on-campus apartments, and married-student housing. International student housing and a learning community is also available. On-campus housing is guaranteed for the freshman year only and is available on a lottery system for upperclassmen. 62% of students commute. Alcohol is not permitted. All students may keep cars.

Activities: 5% of men belong to 13 national fraternities; 5% of women belong to 9 national sororities. There are more than 200 groups on campus, including art, band, cheerleading, chess, choir, chorale, chorus, computers, dance, debate, drama, drill team, ethnic, film, forensics, gay, honors, international, jazz band, literary magazine, marching band, musical theater, newspaper, opera, orchestra, pep band, photography, political, professional, radio and TV, religious, social, social service, student government, symphony, and yearbook. Popular campus events include Appalachian Summer, fall and spring open houses, and multicultural student weekend.

Sports: There are 11 intercollegiate sports for men and 11 for women, and 43 intramural sports for men and 43 for women. Facilities include a 9,000-seat convocation center, a 7,000-seat varsity gym, an 18,000-seat stadium, an athletic center, facilities for football, soccer, field hockey, basketball, volleyball, wrestling, indoor and outdoor track, golf, baseball, and tennis, a 2000-seat auditorium, and a fitness center.

Disabled Students: All of the campus is accessible. Wheelchair ramps, elevators, special parking, specially equipped rest rooms, special class scheduling, lowered drinking fountains, lowered telephones, and special housing are available.

Services: Counseling and information services are available, as is tutoring in most subjects. There is a reader service for the blind, and remedial math, reading, and writing.

Campus Safety and Security: Measures include 24-hour foot and vehicle patrol, self-defense education, security escort services, and shuttle buses. There are informal discussions, pamphlets/posters/films, emergency telephones, lighted pathways/sidewalks, and bicycle patrol.

Programs of Study: App State confers B.A., B.S., B.F.A., B.M., B.S.B.A., B.S.C.J., and B.S.W. degrees. Master's and doctoral degrees are also awarded. Bachelor's degrees are awarded in BIOLOGICAL SCIENCE (biology/biological science, ecology, and nutrition), BUSINESS (accounting, banking and finance, hospitality management services, insurance and risk management, marketing/retailing/merchandising, and recreational facilities management), COMMUNICATIONS AND THE ARTS (advertising, art, arts administration/management, communications, dramatic arts, English, French, graphic design, journalism, multimedia, music business management, music performance, public relations, Spanish, and studio art), COMPUTER AND PHYSICAL SCIENCE (chemistry, computer science, geology, information sciences and systems, mathematics, physics, and statistics), EDUCATION (art, business, drama, early childhood, elementary, foreign languages, health, industrial arts, middle school, music, physical, science, secondary, social science, and special), ENGINEERING AND ENVIRONMENTAL DESIGN (construction technology, drafting and design, electrical/electronics engineering technology, environmental science, graphic arts technology, industrial engineering technology, and interior design), HEALTH PROFESSIONS (clinical science, exercise science, health care administration, health science, and music therapy), SOCIAL SCIENCE (anthropology, child psychology/development, clothing and textiles management/production/services, criminal justice, economics, family/consumer studies, geography, history, interdisciplinary studies, philosophy, political science/government, psychology, religion, social work, and sociology). Elementary education, management, and information systems are the largest.

Required: To graduate, students must complete 122 credit hours for most programs, including 60 in the major, with a minimum 2.0 GPA. General education requirements include courses in math, science, history, phys ed, English, social sciences, and humanities.

Special: App State offers co-op programs in clinical lab sciences; cross-registration with Auburn University, Wake Forest University, and the University of North Carolina-Greensboro; internships; work-study programs; B.A.-B.S. degrees; dual majors; and study abroad. Student-designed majors are possible in some programs, and a 3-2 engineering degree is possible with Clemson and Auburn Universities. There are 25 national honor societies, a freshman honors program, and 14 departmental honors programs.

Faculty/Classroom: All faculty both teach and do research. Graduate students teach 1% of introductory courses. The average class size in an introductory lecture is 28; in a laboratory, 22; and in a regular course, 23.

Admissions: 66% of the 2003-2004 applicants were accepted. The SAT I scores for the 2003-2004 freshman class were: Verbal--26% below 500, 51% between 500 and 599, 21% between 600 and 700, and 3% above 700; Math--17% below 500, 51% between 500 and 599, 29% between 600 and 700, and 3% above 700. 39% of the current freshmen were in the top fifth of their class; 79% were in the top two fifths.

Requirements: The SAT I or ACT is required. In addition, applicants must be graduates of an accredited secondary school; the GED is also accepted. They must have completed 4 course units in high school English, 3 in math and science, and 2 in social studies. AP and CLEP credits are accepted. Important factors in the admissions decision are advanced placement or honor courses, extracurricular activities record, and evidence of special talent.

Procedure: Freshmen are admitted to all sessions. Entrance exams should be taken by November, if possible. There is a rolling admissions plan. Application deadlines are open. Application fee is $45. 507 applicants were on the 2003 waiting list.

Transfer: 741 transfer students enrolled in 2002-2003. Transfer students must have earned a minimum 2.0 GPA on collegiate work. Those students who have accumulated less than 30 semester credits, or 45 quarter hours, must also meet freshman requirements. 30 of 122 credits required for the bachelor's degree must be completed at App State.

Visiting: There are regularly scheduled orientations for prospective students, beginning in July for all new students. There are guides for informal visits and visitors may sit in on classes. To schedule a visit, contact the Visitors Center at (828) 262-2179.

Financial Aid: In a recent year, 26% of all full-time freshmen received some form of financial aid. 16% of full-time freshmen received need-based aid. The average freshman award was $4378. The FAFSA is required. The priority date for freshman financial aid applications for fall entry is March 31.

International Students: There are 53 international students enrolled. The school actively recruits these students. They must score 500 on the written TOEFL or 173 on the electronic version. The SAT I may be accepted in lieu of the TOEFL.

Computers: The mainframe is clustered Alpha machines. There are more than 750 PCs in classroom buildings and residence halls. All students may access the system. There are no time limits and no fees.

Graduates: From July 1, 2002 to June 30, 2003, 2233 bachelor's degrees were awarded. The most popular majors were elementary education (8%), information technology (6%), and management (5%). In an average class, 1% graduate in 3 years or less, 30% graduate in 4 years or less, 56% graduate in 5 years or less, and 60% graduate in 6 years or less. 275 companies recruited on campus in 2002-2003.

Admissions Contact: Paul Hiatt, Director of Admissions.
E-mail: *admissions@appstate.edu* Web: *appstate.edu*

BARBER-SCOTIA COLLEGE   C-3
Concord, NC 28025   (704) 789-2903
(800) 610-0778; Fax: (704) 789-2958

Full-time: 425 men, 317 women	**Faculty:** 34
Part-time: 2 men, 4 women	**Ph.D.s:** 52%
Graduate: none	**Student/Faculty:** 22 to 1
Year: semesters	**Tuition:** $9448
Application Deadline: open	**Room & Board:** $4452
Freshman Class: 1502 applied, 1058 accepted, 301 enrolled	
SAT I Verbal/Math: 375/370	**LESS COMPETITIVE**

Barber-Scotia College, founded in 1867, is a liberal arts institution affiliated with the Presbyterian Church (U.S.A.) The library contains 44,518 volumes and 90,901 microform items, and subscribes to 180 periodicals. Computerized library services include the card catalog, interlibrary loans, database searching, and Internet access. Special learning facilities include a learning resource center. The 40-acre campus is in a suburban area 20 miles from Charlotte. Including any residence halls, there are 24 buildings.

Student Life: 64% of undergraduates are from North Carolina. Others are from 24 states. 98% are from public schools. 97% are African American. Most are Protestant. The average age of freshmen is 19; all undergraduates, 23. 45% do not continue beyond their first year; 30% remain to graduate.

Housing: 562 students can be accommodated in college housing, which includes single-sex dorms. An honors complex is available. On-campus housing is guaranteed for the freshman year only and is available on a first-come, first-served basis. 66% of students live on campus; of those, 65% remain on campus on weekends. Alcohol is not permitted. Upperclassmen may keep cars.

Activities: There are 4 national fraternities and 4 national sororities. There are 35 groups on campus, including cheerleading, chess, choir, computers, debate, honors, international, newspaper, pep band, politi-

cal, professional, radio and TV, religious, science, social, social service, student government, and yearbook. Popular campus events include Candlelighting Service, Spring Formal, and Fall Convocation.

Sports: There are 4 intercollegiate sports for men and 5 for women. Facilities include a gym, a tennis court, and an athletic field.

Disabled Students: 50% of the campus is accessible. Wheelchair ramps, elevators, special parking, specially equipped rest rooms, and special housing are available.

Services: Counseling and information services are available, as is tutoring in most subjects. There is remedial math, reading, and writing.

Campus Safety and Security: Measures include 24-hour foot and vehicle patrol, informal discussions, pamphlets/posters/films, and lighted pathways/sidewalks.

Programs of Study: Scotia confers B.A. and B.S. degrees. Bachelor's degrees are awarded in BIOLOGICAL SCIENCE (biology/biological science), BUSINESS (business administration and management and recreational facilities management), COMMUNICATIONS AND THE ARTS (communications and English), COMPUTER AND PHYSICAL SCIENCE (mathematics), EDUCATION (early childhood), SOCIAL SCIENCE (political science/government and sociology). Education and biology are the strongest academically. Sociology, political science, and business are the largest.

Required: To graduate, students must complete 125 credit hours, 36 in the major, with a 55-hour general education requirement that includes religion, English, phys ed, computer science, and 6 other areas. A 2.0 minimum GPA, 2 years of foreign language, a senior seminar, and comprehensive exams are required.

Special: The college offers cross-registration with the Charlotte Area Consortium, minority colleges, and the University Consortium. Each major program requires a semester experience. There are 2 national honor societies.

Faculty/Classroom: 66% of faculty are male; 34%, female. All teach undergraduates. The average class size in an introductory lecture is 20; in a laboratory, 20; and in a regular course, 15.

Admissions: 70% of the 2003-2004 applicants were accepted. The SAT I scores for the 2003-2004 freshman class were: Verbal--94% below 500, 4% between 500 and 599, 2% between 600 and 700; Math--91% below 500, 7% between 500 and 599, and 2% between 600 and 700. The ACT scores were 89% below 21, 6% between 21 and 23, 3% between 24 and 26, and 2% above 28. 36% of the current freshmen were in the top fifth of their class; 64% were in the top two fifths. 1 freshman graduated first in the class.

Requirements: The SAT I or ACT is required. AP and CLEP credits are accepted. Important factors in the admissions decision are ability to finance college education, recommendations by school officials, and personality/intangible qualities.

Procedure: Freshmen are admitted fall and spring. There is a deferred admissions plan and a rolling admissions plan. Application deadlines are open. The fall 2003 application fee was $25. The college accepts all applicants. Notification is sent on a rolling basis. Applications are accepted on-line.

Transfer: Applicants for transfer should have a 2.0 GPA. 30 credits of 125 required for the bachelor's degree must be completed at Scotia.

Visiting: There are regularly scheduled orientations for prospective students, consisting of information about the college. There are guides for informal visits and visitors may sit in on classes and stay overnight. To schedule a visit, contact the Admissions Office at (704) 789-2902 or *ealexander@b-sc.edu.*

Financial Aid: In 2003-2004, 92% of all full-time freshmen received some form of financial aid. 92% of all full-time students received need-based aid. The average freshman award was $11,500. Need-based scholarships or need-based grants averaged $2500 ($6050 maximum); need-based self-help aid (loans and jobs) averaged $2600 ($3225 maximum); non-need-based athletic scholarships averaged $4225 ($13,000 maximum); and other non-need-based awards and non-need-based scholarships averaged $4100 ($9000 maximum). 27% of undergraduates work part time. Average annual earnings from campus work are $650. The average financial indebtedness of the 2003 graduate was $14,000. The FAFSA and the state aid form are required. The priority date for freshman financial aid applications for fall entry is April 15. The deadline for filing freshman financial aid applications for fall entry is June 30.

International Students: There are 90 international students enrolled. The school actively recruits these students.

Computers: The mainframes are an IBM and a Dell. Students may use networked labs. All students may access the system 7 A.M. to 9 P.M. Monday through Saturday. There are no time limits and no fees.

Graduates: From July 1, 2002 to June 30, 2003, 108 bachelor's degrees were awarded.

Admissions Contact: Edward Alexander, Interim Director of Admissions. E-mail: *ealexander@b-sc.edu* Web: *www.b-sc.edu*

BARTON COLLEGE
Wilson, NC 27893

E-2

(252) 399-6317
(800) 345-4973; Fax: (252) 399-6572

Full-time: 650 women	**Faculty:** 79; IIB, --$
Part-time: 44 men, 195 women	**Ph.D.s:** 52%
Graduate: none	**Student/Faculty:** 12 to 1
Year: 4-1-4, summer session	**Tuition:** $14,278
Application Deadline: open	**Room & Board:** $5036
Freshman Class: 930 applied, 692 accepted, 250 enrolled	
SAT I Verbal/Math: 480/480	**COMPETITIVE**

Barton College, founded in 1902, is a private baccalaureate college affiliated with the Christian Church (Disciples of Christ). There are 5 undergraduate schools. In addition to regional accreditation, Barton has baccalaureate program accreditation with CAAHEP, CED, CSWE, NCATE, and NLN. The library contains 190,540 volumes, 299,771 microform items, and 3590 audio/video tapes/CDs, and subscribes to 9690 periodicals. Computerized library services include the card catalog, interlibrary loans, and database searching. Special learning facilities include a learning resource center, art gallery, TV station, and writing center. The 62-acre campus is in a suburban area 45 miles east of Raleigh. Including any residence halls, there are 27 buildings.

Student Life: 76% of undergraduates are from North Carolina. Students are from 29 states, 16 foreign countries, and Canada. 80% are from public schools. 73% are white; 20% African American. 50% are Protestant; 31% claim no religious affiliation; 9% Catholic. The average age of freshmen is 18; all undergraduates, 20. 37% do not continue beyond their first year; 46% remain to graduate.

Housing: 561 students can be accommodated in college housing, which includes single-sex and coed dorms. Sorority floors are also available. On-campus housing is guaranteed for the freshman year only and is available on a first-come, first-served basis. 60% of students commute. Alcohol is not permitted. All students may keep cars.

Activities: 13% of men belong to 4 national fraternities; 12% of women belong to 3 national sororities. There are 45 groups on campus, including academic, cheerleading, choir, chorus, drama, ethnic, honors, international, literary magazine, musical theater, newspaper, orchestra, photography, political, professional, radio and TV, religious, social, social service, student government, and symphony. Popular campus events include Pre-exam Jam, Lighting of the Luminaries Christmas Celebration, and Global Focus.

Sports: There are 6 intercollegiate sports for men and 6 for women, and 7 intramural sports for men and 7 for women. Facilities include a gym, a tennis complex, baseball, softball, and soccer fields, community parks for intramural activities, and an indoor pool and track.

Disabled Students: 90% of the campus is accessible. Wheelchair ramps, elevators, special parking, specially equipped rest rooms, special class scheduling, lowered drinking fountains, and special housing are available.

Services: Counseling and information services are available, as is tutoring in some subjects, including math and English. Other services include interpreting in class for hearing impaired students upon request and note takers in class for certain circumstances.

Campus Safety and Security: Measures include 24-hour foot and vehicle patrol, self-defense education, security escort services, and informal discussions. There are pamphlets/posters/films, emergency telephones, lighted pathways/sidewalks, campuswide surveillance cameras, peephole doors to residence rooms, and a city police substation on campus.

Programs of Study: Barton confers B.A., B.S., B.F.A., B.L.S., B.S.N., and B.S.W. degrees. Bachelor's degrees are awarded in BIOLOGICAL SCIENCE (biology/biological science), BUSINESS (accounting, business administration and management, human resources, and sports management), COMMUNICATIONS AND THE ARTS (communications, dramatic arts, English, graphic design, painting, and studio art), COMPUTER AND PHYSICAL SCIENCE (chemistry, information sciences and systems, and mathematics), EDUCATION (art, athletic training, education of the deaf and hearing impaired, elementary, middle school, physical, and specific learning disabilities), ENGINEERING AND ENVIRONMENTAL DESIGN (environmental design), HEALTH PROFESSIONS (exercise science and nursing), SOCIAL SCIENCE (criminal justice, economics, gerontology, history, political science/government, psychology, religion, social studies, social work, and Spanish studies). Nursing, education, and fine arts are the strongest academically. Business, nursing, and education are the largest.

Required: All students must complete a minimum of 126 credit hours, including 36 in the major and 45 to 48 in the core curriculum, with a minimum GPA of 2.0. Core requirements include 12 semester hours in humanities and fine arts, 6 to 9 in global and cross-cultural perspective, 7 in natural sciences, 6 in social sciences, 6 in writing proficiency, 3 each in math, computer proficiency, and first-year seminar (for new freshmen), and 2 in sports science.

Special: Barton offers internships, a Washington semester, a general studies degree, dual majors, work study, and credit by examination in entry-level courses. Preprofessional programs are offered in law, engineering, and a variety of health-related fields, as are 3-2 engineering degrees with North Carolina State and North Carolina Agricultural and Technical State Universities and the University of North Carolina at Charlotte. There are 4 national honor societies and 1 departmental honors program.

Faculty/Classroom: 48% of faculty are male; 52%, female. All teach undergraduates. The average class size in an introductory lecture is 30; in a laboratory, 15; and in a regular course, 25.

Admissions: 74% of the 2003-2004 applicants were accepted. The SAT I scores for the 2003-2004 freshman class were: Verbal--60% below 500, 35% between 500 and 599, and 2% between 600 and 700; Math--56% below 500, 35% between 500 and 599, 7% between 600 and 700, and 2% above 700. 25% of the current freshmen were in the top fifth of their class; 48% were in the top two fifths.

Requirements: The SAT I or ACT is required. In addition, applications must be high school graduates with at least 13 college preparatory credits. Barton recommends 4 units of English, 3 of social science, 3 of math (including algebra), and 2 of natural science (including lab science). A foreign language is encouraged. Admission criteria varies for adult learners. A GPA of 2.0 is required. AP and CLEP credits are accepted.

Procedure: Freshmen are admitted to all sessions. Entrance exams should be taken in the spring of the junior year and fall of the senior year. There is a rolling admissions plan. Application deadlines are open. Application fee is $25. Applications are accepted on-line through Barton's web site.

Transfer: 141 transfer students enrolled in 2002-2003. Applicants must have a college GPA of 2.0 and must be eligible to return to the school they last attended. 45 of 126 credits required for the bachelor's degree must be completed at Barton.

Visiting: There are regularly scheduled orientations for prospective students, including visiting classes, financial aid and freshman advising workshops, tours of the campus, and meeting with administrators, faculty, and students. There are guides for informal visits and visitors may sit in on classes and stay overnight. To schedule a visit, contact the Admissions Office at *enroll@barton.edu*.

Financial Aid: In 2003-2004, 99% of all full-time freshmen and 95% of continuing full-time students received some form of financial aid. 73% of full-time freshmen and 48% of continuing full-time students received need-based aid. The average freshman award was $13,195. 93% of undergraduates work part time. Average annual earnings from campus work are $1108. The average financial indebtedness of the 2003 graduate was $16,900. The FAFSA is required. The priority date for freshman financial aid applications for fall entry is March 15. The deadline for filing freshman financial aid applications for fall entry is June 1.

International Students: There were 26 international students enrolled in a recent year. The school actively recruits these students. They must score 525 on the written TOEFL or 195 on the electronic version.

Computers: The mainframes are an IBM AS/400 and Microsoft network servers. PCs are available in computer labs in major buildings for student use. All residence hall rooms are wired for high-speed connection to the campus network. All students may access the system 24 hours a day, 7 days a week. There are no time limits and no fees.

Graduates: From July 1, 2002 to June 30, 2003, 267 bachelor's degrees were awarded. The most popular majors were business administration (23%), nursing (12%), and elementary education (11%). In an average class, 29% graduate in 4 years or less, 40% graduate in 5 years or less, and 42% graduate in 6 years or less. 102 companies recruited on campus in 2002-2003.

Admissions Contact: Amy Denton, Directors of Admissions.
E-mail: *enroll@barton.edu* Web: *www.barton.edu*

BELMONT ABBEY COLLEGE
Belmont, NC 28012

C-3

(704) 825-6665
(888) BAC-0110; Fax: (704) 825-6220

Full-time: 500 men, 420 women	**Faculty:** 50; IIB, --$
Part-time: 35 men, 100 women	**Ph.D.s:** 85%
Graduate: none	**Student/Faculty:** 18 to 1
Year: semesters, summer session	**Tuition:** $15,778
Application Deadline: open	**Room & Board:** $7964
Freshman Class: 1031 applied, 754 accepted, 211 enrolled	
SAT I Verbal/Math: 510/500	**COMPETITIVE**

Belmont Abbey College, founded in 1876, is a private liberal arts college affiliated with the Roman Catholic Church. In addition to regional accreditation, Belmont Abbey has baccalaureate program accreditation with NCATE. The library contains 110,050 volumes, 59,000 microform items, and 2042 audio/video tapes/CDs, and subscribes to 609 periodicals. Computerized library services include the card catalog, interlibrary loans, database searching, and Internet access. Special learning facilities include a learning resource center and radio station. The 650-acre campus is in a suburban area 12 miles southwest of Charlotte. Including any residence halls, there are 20 buildings.

Student Life: 65% of undergraduates are from North Carolina. Others are from 35 states, 20 foreign countries, and Canada. 81% are white;

10% African American. Most are Catholic. The average age of freshmen is 18; all undergraduates, 23. 30% do not continue beyond their first year; 45% remain to graduate.

Housing: 600 students can be accommodated in college housing, which includes single-sex and coed dormitories and on-campus apartments. In addition, there are special-interest houses and a quiet residence hall. Single-occupancy housing is available for all students. On-campus housing is guaranteed for all 4 years. 51% of students live on campus; of those, 75% remain on campus on weekends. All students may keep cars.

Activities: 40% of men belong to 3 local and 1 national fraternity; 30% of women belong to 3 local and 1 national sorority. There are 34 groups on campus, including cheerleading, chess, choir, chorus, computers, drama, honors, international, literary magazine, newspaper, political, professional, radio and TV, religious, social, social service, student government, and yearbook. Popular campus events include Spring Weekend, Special Olympics, and Greek Week.

Sports: There are 6 intercollegiate sports for men and 6 for women, and 13 intramural sports for men and 13 for women. Facilities include a phys ed center with a 1200-seat gym and a college union with a 225-seat auditorium.

Disabled Students: 60% of the campus is accessible. Wheelchair ramps, elevators, special parking, specially equipped rest rooms, special class scheduling, and lowered drinking fountains are available.

Services: Counseling and information services are available, as is tutoring in some subjects, including math and English. There is a reader service for the blind.

Campus Safety and Security: Measures include 24-hour foot and vehicle patrol, self-defense education, security escort services, and informal discussions. There are pamphlets/posters/films and lighted pathways/sidewalks.

Programs of Study: Belmont Abbey confers B.A. and B.S. degrees. Bachelor's degrees are awarded in BIOLOGICAL SCIENCE (biology/biological science), BUSINESS (accounting, business administration and management, international business management, recreation and leisure services, and sports management), COMMUNICATIONS AND THE ARTS (English), COMPUTER AND PHYSICAL SCIENCE (information sciences and systems), EDUCATION (education, elementary, and secondary), ENGINEERING AND ENVIRONMENTAL DESIGN (preengineering), HEALTH PROFESSIONS (medical laboratory technology, predentistry, premedicine, and prepharmacy), SOCIAL SCIENCE (economics, history, liberal arts/general studies, philosophy, political science/government, prelaw, psychology, sociology, and theological studies). Natural and physical sciences and English are the strongest academically. Business administration, education, and biology are the largest.

Required: To graduate, all students must complete a minimum of 120 credits, including 60 credits of core curriculum and 30 upper-level credits in the major. Among the core requirements are history, math, natural sciences, theology, philosophy, English, fine arts, and Great Books Seminar. A minimum 2.0 GPA must be maintained. Honors students must submit a thesis.

Special: Cross-registration is offered through the Charlotte Area Educational Consortium. There are internships in many majors, including required internships in recreational studies and therapeutic recreation, as well as on-campus work-study, nondegree study, dual majors and study abroad in Guatemala, Germany, and France. There are 5 national honor societies and a freshman honors program.

Faculty/Classroom: 73% of faculty are male; 27%, female. All teach undergraduates and 60% both teach and do research. The average class size in an introductory lecture is 25; in a laboratory, 18; and in a regular course, 17.

Admissions: 73% of the 2003-2004 applicants were accepted. The SAT I scores for the 2003-2004 freshman class were: Verbal--50% below 500, 35% between 500 and 599, 14% between 600 and 700, and 1% above 700; Math--55% below 500, 35% between 500 and 599, and 10% between 600 and 700. 30% of the current freshmen were in the top fifth of their class; 60% were in the top two fifths.

Requirements: The SAT I or ACT is required, with a minimum total score of 850 on the SAT I. Candidates must be graduates of an accredited secondary school. A minimum of 16 academic credits must be completed, including 4 in English, 3 each in math and electives, and 2 each in foreign language, history, and science. An interview is recommended. A GPA of 2.3 is required. AP and CLEP credits are accepted. Important factors in the admissions decision are advanced placement or honor courses, extracurricular activities record, and leadership record.

Procedure: Freshmen are admitted fall and spring. Entrance exams should be taken by October of the senior year. There is a deferred admissions plan and a rolling admission plan. Notification is sent on a rolling basis. There is a $35 fee. Applications are accepted on-line through *www.belmontabbeycollege.edu*. Check with the school for current deadlines.

Transfer: 76 transfer students enrolled in 2002-2003. Students with 24 or more credit hours must submit all college transcripts, and those with fewer than 24 credit hours must also submit a high school transcript and

SAT I scores. All candidates must have a minimum 2.0 GPA and must be eligible to return to the last college attended. An interview is recommended. 30 credits of 120 required for the bachelor's degree must be completed at Belmont Abbey.

Visiting: There are regularly scheduled orientations for prospective students, consisting of a campus tour and meetings with a financial aid adviser, faculty, and students. There are guides for informal visits and visitors may sit in on classes and stay overnight. To schedule a visit, contact the Admissions Office at *admissions@BAC.edu*.

Financial Aid: In 2003-2004, 35% of all full-time freshmen and 90% of continuing full-time students received some form of financial aid. 75% of full-time freshmen and 70% of continuing full-time students received need-based aid. The average freshman award was $12,100. 27% of undergraduates work part time. Average annual earnings from campus work are $1600. The average financial indebtedness of the 2003 graduate was $1050. Belmont Abbey is a member of CSS. The FAFSA is required. The priority date for freshman financial aid applications for fall entry is March 1. The deadline for filing freshman financial aid applications for fall entry is July 1.

International Students: There are 35 international students enrolled. The school actively recruits these students. They must score 550 on the written TOEFL, and also take the SAT I, scoring 900.

Computers: All students may access the system at any time. There are no time limits and no fees.

Graduates: From July 1, 2002 to June 30, 2003, 174 bachelor's degrees were awarded. The most popular majors were business management (40%), education (10%), and accounting (10%). In an average class, 40% graduate in 4 years or less, 45% graduate in 5 years or less, and 46% graduate in 6 years or less. 22 companies recruited on campus in 2002-2003. Of the 2002 graduating class, 25% were enrolled in graduate school within 6 months of graduation and 80% were employed.

Admissions Contact: Michael Poll, Vice President for Enrollment Management. E-mail: *Michaelpoll@BAC.edu*
Web: *www.belmontabbeycollege.edu*

BENNETT COLLEGE

D-2

Greensboro, NC 27401-3239 (336) 370-8624

Full-time: 515 women	**Faculty:** 57; IIB, --$
Part-time: 10 women	**Ph.D.s:** 68%
Graduate: none	**Student/Faculty:** 11 to 1
Year: semesters, summer session	**Tuition:** $7800 ($10,010)
Application Deadline: open	**Room & Board:** $3400 ($4295)
Freshman Class: n/av	
SAT I: required	**COMPETITIVE**

Bennett College, founded in 1873, is a private liberal arts women's institution affiliated with the United Methodist Church. Figures in the above capsule and in this profile are approximate. In addition to regional accreditation, Bennett has baccalaureate program accreditation with ADA, CSWE, and NCATE. The library contains 98,000 volumes, 300 microform items, and 1600 audio/video tapes/CDs, and subscribes to 259 periodicals. Computerized library services include the card catalog, interlibrary loans, and database searching. Special learning facilities include a learning resource center and the Women's Leadership Institute. The 55-acre campus is in an urban area 1 mile from downtown Greensboro. Including any residence halls, there are 31 buildings.

Student Life: 76% of undergraduates are from out of state, mostly the Northeast. Students are from 34 states and 6 foreign countries. 86% are from public schools. 99% are African American. 77% are Protestant; 11% Muslim; 7% claim no religious affiliation. The average age of freshmen is 18; all undergraduates, 21. 21% do not continue beyond their first year; 35% remain to graduate.

Housing: 608 students can be accommodated in college housing, which includes dorms. In addition, there are honors houses. On-campus housing is guaranteed for all 4 years. 80% of students live on campus; of those, 50% remain on campus on weekends. Alcohol is not permitted. All students may keep cars.

Activities: 22% of women belong to 4 national sororities. There are no fraternities. There are 34 groups on campus, including cheerleading, choir, computers, dance, drama, film, honors, international, literary magazine, newspaper, orchestra, professional, religious, student government, and yearbook. Popular campus events include Christmas Concert, President's Ball, and Alumnae Weekend.

Sports: Facilities include a gym, a pool, exercise and gymnastic facilities, an athletic field, and basketball and tennis courts.

Disabled Students: 25% of the campus is accessible. Wheelchair ramps, elevators, special parking, specially equipped rest rooms, and special class scheduling are available.

Services: Counseling and information services are available, as is tutoring in every subject. There is remedial math, reading, and writing.

Campus Safety and Security: Measures include 24-hour foot and vehicle patrol, self-defense education, security escort services, and informal discussions. There are pamphlets/posters/films and lighted pathways/sidewalks.

Programs of Study: Bennett confers B.A., B.S., B.A.S.I.S., and B.S.W. degrees. Associate degrees are also awarded. Bachelor's degrees are awarded in BIOLOGICAL SCIENCE (biology/biological science), BUSINESS (accounting, business administration and management, fashion merchandising, and secretarial studies/office management), COMMUNICATIONS AND THE ARTS (arts administration/management, communications, English, music, and visual and performing arts), COMPUTER AND PHYSICAL SCIENCE (chemistry, computer science, and mathematics), EDUCATION (early childhood, elementary, English, mathematics, middle school, music, science, secondary, and special), SOCIAL SCIENCE (dietetics, interdisciplinary studies, political science/government, psychology, social work, and sociology). Biology, math, and education are the strongest academically. Business administration/accounting and biology are the largest.

Required: All students must take 54 to 64 semester hours of general education courses in communication, humanities, math, natural science, reading, history, foreign language, philosophy, phys ed, religion, and women's studies. A total of 124 semester hours, with 60 to 64 in the major, and at least a 2.0 GPA are required for graduation. Comprehensive exams in math and English are required.

Special: Students may cross-register at member colleges of the Greensboro Regional Consortium, study off campus through exchange programs, take a Washington semester, and study abroad. Bennett offers student-designed majors, dual majors in engineering and nursing, nondegree study, a 3-1 nursing program, a B.A.-B.S. degree in interdisciplinary studies, and a 3-2 engineering degree with North Carolina Agricultural and Technical State University. There are 6 national honor societies and 6 departmental honors programs.

Faculty/Classroom: 38% of faculty are male; 62%, female. All teach undergraduates. The average class size in an introductory lecture is 25; in a laboratory, 30; and in a regular course, 20.

Requirements: The SAT I is required. In addition, applicants must be graduates of accredited high schools or have earned the GED. Secondary preparation should include 4 years of English, 2 of math, 1 of science and social studies, and 4 of other academic courses. A personal essay is required, and an interview is recommended. A GPA of 2.5 is required. CLEP credit is accepted. Important factors in the admissions decision are recommendations by school officials, parents or siblings attending the school, and evidence of special talent.

Procedure: Freshmen are admitted fall and spring. Entrance exams should be taken preferably during the senior year. There is a deferred admissions plan and a rolling admissions plan. Application deadlines are open. The application fee is $20.

Transfer: An official transcript and a catalog from each college previously attended, 2 letters of recommendation, a statement of honorable dismissal from previous colleges, and a personal essay are required. 64 of 124 credits required for the bachelor's degree must be completed at Bennett.

Visiting: There are regularly scheduled orientations for prospective students, including a campus tour and meetings with a financial aid officer and an academic program director. There are guides for informal visits and visitors may sit in on classes and stay overnight. To schedule a visit, contact Linda Torrence, Associate Dean for Enrollment Management.

Financial Aid: In a recent year, 84% of all full-time freshmen and 91% of continuing full-time students received some form of financial aid. 24% of undergraduates work part time. Average annual earnings from campus work are $1000. Bennett is a member of CSS. The FAFSA or FFS is required. Check with the school for current deadlines.

International Students: The school actively recruits these students. They must score 500 on the written TOEFL and also take the SAT I or the ACT.

Computers: The college provides 108 PCs for student use and for computer-assisted instruction. All students may access the system 8 A.M. to 11 P.M. There are no time limits. The fee is $150.

Graduates: In a recent year, 105 bachelor's degrees were awarded. The most popular majors were biology (14%), education (11%), and business administration (10%). In an average class, 24% graduate in 4 years or less, 35% graduate in 5 years or less, and 39% graduate in 6 years or less. 48 companies recruited on campus in a recent year. Of a recent graduating class, 18% were enrolled in graduate school within 6 months of graduation and 40% were employed.

Admissions Contact: Linda Torrence, Associate Dean for Enrollment Management. A video is available.
E-mail: *bcinfo@bennett1.bennett.edu*

CABARRUS COLLEGE OF HEALTH SCIENCES   C-3
Concord, NC 28025-2405   (704) 783-1555; Fax: (704) 783-2077

Full-time: 11 men, 172 women	**Faculty:** n/av
Part-time: 2 men, 57 women	**Ph.D.s:** n/av
Graduate: none	**Student/Faculty:** n/av
Year: semesters	**Tuition:** $7000
Application Deadline: March 1	**Room & Board:** n/app
Freshman Class: 283 applied, 137 accepted, 120 enrolled	
SAT I Verbal/Math: required	**ACT:** required **SPECIAL**

Cabarrus College of Health Sciences, founded in 1942, is a private institution specializing in health science. The library contains 6370 volumes and 776 audio/video tapes/CDs, and subscribes to 263 periodicals. Computerized library services include the card catalog, database searching, and Internet access. Special learning facilities include a learning resource center. The campus is in a suburban area.

Student Life: All undergraduates are from North Carolina.

Housing: There are no residence halls.

Activities: There are some groups and organizations on campus, including honors, professional, and student government.

Disabled Students: All of the campus is accessible. Wheelchair ramps, elevators, special parking, specially equipped rest rooms, lowered drinking fountains, and lowered telephones are available.

Campus Safety and Security: Measures include 24-hour foot and vehicle patrol, emergency telephones, and lighted pathways/sidewalks.

Programs of Study: Cabarrus College of Health Sciences confers the B.S. degree. Associate degrees are also awarded. Bachelor's degrees are awarded in HEALTH PROFESSIONS (health care administration and nursing).

Special: There is 1 national honor society.

Faculty/Classroom: All teach undergraduates. The average class size in an introductory lecture is 20; in a laboratory, 15; and in a regular course, 20.

Admissions: 48% of the 2003-2004 applicants were accepted.

Requirements: The SAT I or ACT is required. Cabarrus College of Health Sciences requires applicants to be in the upper 50% of their class. AP and CLEP credits are accepted.

Procedure: Freshmen are admitted fall and spring. Applications should be filed by March 1 for fall entry and October 1 for spring entry, along with a $35 fee. A waiting list is an active part of the admissions procedure. Applications are accepted on-line.

Visiting: There are regularly scheduled orientations for prospective students.

Financial Aid: In a recent year, 98% of all full-time freshmen received some form of financial aid.

Admissions Contact: Mark Ellison, Director of Admissions.
E-mail: *mellison@cabarruscollege.edu* Web: *www.cabarruscollege.edu*

CAMPBELL UNIVERSITY   D-3
Buies Creek, NC 27506   (800) 334-4111, ext. 1320
Fax: (910) 893-1288

Full-time: 1066 men, 1325 women	**Faculty:** 132
Part-time: 82 men, 62 women	**Ph.D.s:** 90%
Graduate: 175 men, 360 women	**Student/Faculty:** 18 to 1
Year: semesters, summer session	**Tuition:** $13,512
Application Deadline: open	**Room & Board:** $4756
Freshman Class: 2011 applied, 1284 accepted, 679 enrolled	
SAT I Verbal/Math: 544/546	**VERY COMPETITIVE**

Campbell University, founded in 1887, is a private, nonsectarian institution affiliated with the North Carolina Baptist Convention and offering degree programs in liberal arts and sciences, business, and education. There are 5 undergraduate and 5 graduate schools. In addition to regional accreditation, Campbell has baccalaureate program accreditation with ACPE, CAAHEP, CSWE, and NCATE. The 5 libraries contain 210,000 volumes, 750,000 microform items, and 4292 audio/video tapes/CDs, and subscribe to 4440 periodicals. Computerized library services include the card catalog, interlibrary loans, database searching, and Internet access. Special learning facilities include a learning resource center, art gallery, radio station, desktop publishing lab, computerized music lab, family and consumer sciences lab, athletic learning resources center, drug information center for the School of Pharmacy, and pharmacy research facility. The 850-acre campus is in a rural area 28 miles south of Raleigh and 30 miles north of Fayetteville. Including any residence halls, there are 47 buildings.

Student Life: 75% of undergraduates are from North Carolina. Others are from 50 states, 56 foreign countries, and Canada. 90% are from public schools. 82% are white. 76% are Protestant; 8% claim no religious affiliation; 8% Islamic/Muslim, Hindu, Greek Orthodox, Pentecostal; 7% Catholic. The average age of freshmen is 18; all undergraduates, 20. 10% do not continue beyond their first year; 46% remain to graduate.

Housing: 1500 students can be accommodated in college housing, which includes single-sex dorms, on-campus apartments, off-campus apartments, and married-student housing. In addition, there are honors houses. On-campus housing is guaranteed for all 4 years. 60% of students live on campus; of those, 85% remain on campus on weekends. Alcohol is not permitted. All students may keep cars.

Activities: There are no fraternities or sororities. There are 44 groups on campus, including art, band, cheerleading, choir, chorale, chorus, computers, drama, ethnic, honors, international, jazz band, literary magazine, musical theater, newspaper, orchestra, pep band, photography, political, professional, radio and TV, religious, social, social service, student government, and yearbook. Popular campus events include the Staley Lecture Series, Parents Day, and spring and Christmas formals.

Sports: There are 8 intercollegiate sports for men and 9 for women, and 23 intramural sports for men and 23 for women. Facilities include a 2000-seat gym, an athletic complex, a lake, a coffeehouse, a concert hall, a theater, 2 golf courses, and a nature trail.

Disabled Students: 70% of the campus is accessible. Wheelchair ramps, elevators, special parking, specially equipped rest rooms, special class scheduling, lowered drinking fountains, lowered telephones, and special housing are available.

Services: Counseling and information services are available, as is tutoring in most subjects. There is remedial math and writing.

Campus Safety and Security: Measures include 24-hour foot and vehicle patrol, self-defense education, security escort services, and informal discussions. There are pamphlets/posters/films, emergency telephones, and lighted pathways/sidewalks.

Programs of Study: Campbell confers B.A., B.S., B.Applied Sci., B.B.A., B.H.S., and B.S.W. degrees. Associate, master's, and doctoral degrees are also awarded. Bachelor's degrees are awarded in BIOLOGICAL SCIENCE (biochemistry and biology/biological science), BUSINESS (accounting, business administration and management, business economics, international business management, investments and securities, and sports management), COMMUNICATIONS AND THE ARTS (advertising, art, broadcasting, communications, dramatic arts, English, French, journalism, music, and Spanish), COMPUTER AND PHYSICAL SCIENCE (chemistry, computer science, information sciences and systems, and mathematics), EDUCATION (athletic training, elementary, and middle school), ENGINEERING AND ENVIRONMENTAL DESIGN (military science and preengineering), HEALTH PROFESSIONS (clinical science and prepharmacy), SOCIAL SCIENCE (criminal justice, economics, family/consumer studies, history, physical fitness/movement, political science/government, prelaw, psychology, religion, and social work). Trust managemenet, English, and music are the strongest academically. Prepharmacy, mass communication, and business administration are the largest.

Required: To graduate, students must complete 128 credit hours with a minimum GPA of 2.0 overall and in the major. All students must take a core curriculum of 45 to 65 hours including English, math, science, social/science, religion, fine arts, phys ed, and the Cultural Enrichment Program.

Special: Campbell offers co-op programs, internships, study abroad in 7 countries, a Washington semester, numerous apprenticeships, accelerated degrees, dual majors, and a general studies degree. There is credit for military and work experience. Cross-registration with the North Carolina Model Teacher Education Consortium and B.A.-B.S. degrees are also possible. There are 5 national honor societies and a freshman honors program; all departments have honors programs.

Faculty/Classroom: 71% of faculty are male; 29%, female. All teach undergraduates and 40% do research. No introductory courses are taught by graduate students. The average class size in an introductory lecture is 30; in a laboratory, 25; and in a regular course, 25.

Admissions: 64% of the 2003-2004 applicants were accepted. The SAT I scores for the 2003-2004 freshman class were: Verbal--32% below 500, 44% between 500 and 599, 21% between 600 and 700, and 3% above 700; Math--24% below 500, 46% between 500 and 599, 28% between 600 and 700, and 2% above 700. 41% of the current freshmen were in the top fifth of their class; 72% were in the top two fifths. 17 freshmen graduated first in their class.

Requirements: The SAT I or ACT is required, with a minimum recommended composite score of 950 on the SAT I. Applicants should have completed 12 high school academic credits, including 4 credits of English, 3 of math, and 2 each of history or social studies, science, and foreign language. An essay, an interview, and a portfolio are recommended. An audition is required for some majors. Campbell requires applicants to be in the upper 50% of their class. A GPA of 2.7 is required. AP and CLEP credits are accepted. Important factors in the admissions decision are advanced placement or honor courses, leadership record, and personality/intangible qualities.

Procedure: Freshmen are admitted to all sessions. Entrance exams should be taken during the junior year or the fall of senior year. There is a deferred admissions plan and a rolling admissions plan. Applications for fall entry are due August 20; for spring entry, January 7. Application fee is $25. Applications are accepted on computer disk and on-line through *www.applyweb.com/apply/campbell/*.

Transfer: 237 transfer students enrolled in 2002-2003. Applicants should have a minimum GPA of 2.0 and supply transcripts from previously attended colleges. 36 credits of 128 required for the bachelor's degree must be completed at Campbell.

Visiting: There are regularly scheduled orientations for prospective students, including a campus tour, student panel, and department visits. There are guides for informal visits and visitors may sit in on classes. To schedule a visit, contact the Admissions Office at (910) 893-1290 or *adm@mailcenter.campbell.edu*.

Financial Aid: In 2003-2004, 91% of all full-time freshmen and 87% of continuing full-time students received some form of financial aid. 80% of full-time freshmen and 78% of continuing full-time students received need-based aid. The average freshman award was $16,336, with $2049 from need-based scholarships or need-based grants, $3435 from need-based self-help aid (loans and jobs), $492 from non-need-based athletic scholarships, $5207 from other non-need-based awards and non-need based scholarships, and $5153 from non-need-based loans. 30% of undergraduates work part time. Average annual earnings from campus work are $531. The average financial indebtedness of the 2003 graduate was $18,700. The FAFSA is required. The deadline for filing freshman financial aid applications for fall entry is March 15.

International Students: There are 149 international students enrolled. The school actively recruits these students. They must score 500 on the written TOEFL or 173 on the electronic version and also take the SAT I, scoring 850, or the ACT.

Computers: The mainframe is an HP 9000. There are 76 computer terminals in a centralized academic computer center. All students have e-mail accounts, and all dorm rooms have Internet and web access. There are also 21 departmental computer labs ranging from 4 to 25 computers per lab. All students may access the system during posted student hours; generally, Monday through Thursday, 8 A.M. to 11 P.M., with extended hours Friday through Sunday. There are no time limits. There is a $50 Internet fee. It is strongly recommended that all students have a personal computer.

Graduates: From July 1, 2002 to June 30, 2003, 663 bachelor's degrees were awarded. The most popular majors were business administration (33%), education (10%), and history (5%). In an average class, 38% graduate in 4 years or less, 41% graduate in 5 years or less, and 45% graduate in 6 years or less. 14 companies recruited on campus in 2002-2003. Of the 2002 graduating class, 15% were enrolled in graduate school within 6 months of graduation and 85% were employed.

Admissions Contact: Herbert V. Kerner, Jr., Dean of Admissions. A video is available. E-mail: *adm@mailcenter.campbell.edu* Web: *www.campbell.edu*

CATAWBA COLLEGE   C-2
Salisbury, NC 28144   (704) 637-4402
                              (800) 228-2922; Fax: (704) 637-4444

Full-time: 637 men, 752 women	**Faculty:** 75; IIB, -$
Part-time: 22 men, 41 women	**Ph.Ds:** 79%
Graduate: 2 men, 17 women	**Student/Faculty:** 19 to 1
Year: semesters, summer session	**Tuition:** $15,300
Application Deadline: open	**Room & Board:** $5200
Freshman Class: 933 applied, 597 accepted, 252 enrolled	
SAT I Verbal/Math: 510/530	**COMPETITIVE**

Catawba College, founded in 1851, is an independent institution affiliated with the United Church of Christ that offers undergraduate programs in the arts and sciences, business, education, performing arts, forestry and environmental science, social and behavioral sciences, physical education, and preprofessional fields. In addition to regional accreditation, Catawba has baccalaureate program accreditation with NCATE. The 2 libraries contain 158,959 volumes, 593,783 microform items, and 25,985 audio/video tapes/CDs, and subscribe to 1209 periodicals. Computerized library services include the card catalog, interlibrary loans, database searching, and Internet access. Special learning facilities include a curriculum materials center, an observatory, and a nature preserve. The 210-acre campus is in a small town 40 miles northeast of Charlotte. Including any residence halls, there are 30 buildings.

Student Life: 71% of undergraduates are from North Carolina. Students are from 38 states, 8 foreign countries, and Canada. 87% are from public schools. 79% are white; 16% African American. 61% are Protestant; 23% claim no religious affiliation; 12% Catholic. The average age of freshmen is 18; all undergraduates, 22. 35% do not continue beyond their first year; 45% remain to graduate.

Housing: 770 students can be accommodated in college housing, which includes single-sex and coed dorms. In addition, there are nonsmoking and alcohol-free dorms. On-campus housing is guaranteed for the freshman year only. 51% of students commute. All students may keep cars.

Activities: There are no fraternities or sororities. There are 26 groups on campus, including art, band, cheerleading, chess, choir, chorale, chorus, computers, dance, drama, ethnic, honors, jazz band, literary magazine, musical theater, newspaper, orchestra, pep band, political, professional, religious, social, social service, student government, symphony, and yearbook. Popular campus events include Winterfest, Inaugural Ball, and Parents Weekend.

Sports: There are 8 intercollegiate sports for men and 8 for women, and 4 intramural sports for men and 4 for women. Facilities include a 5000-seat stadium and a 3500-seat gym; football, baseball, softball, soccer, and field hockey fields; tennis, volleyball, and racquetball courts; weight lifting; a swimming pool; a challenge course; and table tennis and billiards.

Disabled Students: 90% of the campus is accessible. Wheelchair ramps, elevators, special parking, specially equipped rest rooms, lowered drinking fountains, and lowered telephones are available.

Services: Counseling and information services are available, as is tutoring in most subjects.

Campus Safety and Security: Measures include 24-hour foot and vehicle patrol, self-defense education, security escort services, and informal discussions. There are pamphlets/posters/films, emergency telephones, and lighted pathways/sidewalks.

Programs of Study: Catawba confers B.A., B.S., B.B.A., and B.F.A. degrees. Master's degrees are also awarded. Bachelor's degrees are awarded in AGRICULTURE (environmental studies), BIOLOGICAL SCIENCE (biology/biological science), BUSINESS (accounting, business administration and management, international business management, marketing management, recreation and leisure services, and sports management), COMMUNICATIONS AND THE ARTS (communications, dramatic arts, English, French, language arts, music, musical theater, Spanish, and theater management), COMPUTER AND PHYSICAL SCIENCE (chemistry, information sciences and systems, and mathematics), EDUCATION (athletic training, Christian, education, elementary, mathematics, middle school, music, physical, science, and social studies), ENGINEERING AND ENVIRONMENTAL DESIGN (environmental science), HEALTH PROFESSIONS (medical technology and recreation therapy), SOCIAL SCIENCE (history, philosophy, political science/government, prelaw, psychology, public administration, religion, and sociology). Premedicine, predentistry, and prelaw are the strongest academically. Business, education, and theater arts are the largest.

Required: To graduate, students must complete at least 120 credit hours, including up to 54 in their major, with a minimum GPA of 2.0. General education requirements include 9 semester hours in humanities, 7 in natural sciences, 6 each in social sciences, English composition, and fine arts, 4 to 9 in math, and 1 in physical fitness, information and technology, college orientation, and foreign language through the elementary level. Students must demonstrate proficiency in math, writing, oral communication, and computer technology.

Special: There are cooperative programs in deaf education with Appalachian State University, forestry and environmental science with Duke University, and physician assistant and medical technician training with Wake Forest University. Cross-registration is possible through the Charlotte Area Educational consortium. Catawba also offers internships, study abroad in London, a Washington semester, work-study programs, accelerated degree programs, dual majors, a general studies degree, pass/fail options, and student-designed majors. There are 4 national honor societies and a freshman honors program.

Faculty/Classroom: 59% of faculty are male; 41%, female. All teach undergraduates and 40% both teach and do research. No introductory courses are taught by graduate students. The average class size in an introductory lecture is 20; in a laboratory, 24; and in a regular course, 22.

Admissions: 64% of the 2003-2004 applicants were accepted. The SAT I scores for the 2003-2004 freshman class were: Verbal--45% were 500, 41% between 500 and 599, 12% between 600 and 700, and 2% above 700; Math--33% below 500, 48% between 500 and 599, 18% between 600 and 700, and 1% above 700. 32% of the current freshmen were in the top fifth of their class; 70% were in the top two fifths.

Requirements: The SAT I is required; the ACT may be substituted. A minimum SAT I composite score of 800 or ACT score of 21 is required. Applicants must be graduates of an accredited secondary school or have a GED. They must have completed 16 academic credits, of which 12 must be Carnegie units. An essay is required, and an interview is encouraged for all students. An audition is required for music and drama scholarships. A GPA of 2.0 is required. AP and CLEP credits are accepted. Important factors in the admissions decision are advanced placement or honor courses, evidence of special talent, and extracurricular activities record.

Procedure: Freshmen are admitted to all sessions. Entrance exams should be taken by December of the senior year. There is a deferred admissions plan and a rolling admissions plan. Application deadlines are open. Application fee is $25. Notification is sent on a rolling basis. Applications are accepted on computer disk and on-line through EXPAN, FishNet, ReZun, and the college's web site.

Transfer: 189 transfer students enrolled in 2002-2003. Applicants must present at least 12 semester hours, a GPA of 2.0 or better, and a minimum SAT I score of 800 or ACT score of 21. Students out of high school for 5 or more years are exempt from the SAT I or ACT requirement. 30 credits of 120 required for the bachelor's degree must be completed at Catawba.

Visiting: There are regularly scheduled orientations for prospective students, including campus tours, lunches, meetings with faculty, and financial aid and athletic workshops. There are guides for informal visits and visitors may sit in on classes. To schedule a visit, contact the Office of Admissions at 1-800-CATAWBA or (704) 637-4222 or *admission@catawaba.edu.*

Financial Aid: In 2003-2004, 98% of all full-time freshmen and 94% of continuing full-time students received some form of financial aid. 67% of full-time freshmen and 54% of continuing full-time students received need-based aid. 49% of undergraduates work part time. Average annual earnings from campus work are $1100. The average financial indebtedness of the 2003 graduate was $23,000. Catawba is a member of CSS. The FAFSA and the college's own financial statement are required. The deadline for filing freshman financial aid applications for fall entry is March 15.

International Students: There are 21 international students enrolled. They must score 525 on the written TOEFL.

Computers: The mainframe is an HP3000. All students have access to a PC LAN from their dorm rooms, as well as to 100 PCs in 4 labs on campus. There is full access to the Internet. All students may access the system. There are no time limits and no fees.

Graduates: From July 1, 2002 to June 30, 2003, 236 bachelor's degrees were awarded. The most popular majors were business administration (16%), computer information systems (7%), and communication arts (6%). In an average class, 32% graduate in 4 years or less, 43% graduate in 5 years or less, and 45% graduate in 6 years or less. 15 companies recruited on campus in 2002-2003. Of the 2002 graduating class, 7% were enrolled in graduate school within 6 months of graduation.

Admissions Contact: Dr. Russell Watjen, Vice President and Dean of Admissions. A video is available. E-mail: *lrwatjen@catawba.edu* Web: *http://www.catawba.edu*

DAVIDSON COLLEGE

C-3

Davidson, NC 28035-5000

(704) 894-2230
(800) 768-0380; Fax: (704) 894-2016

Full-time: 857 men, 854 women	**Faculty:** 162; IIB, ++$
Part-time: 1 woman	**Ph.D.s:** 100%
Graduate: none	**Student/Faculty:** 11 to 1
Year: semesters	**Tuition:** $25,903
Application Deadline: January 2	**Room & Board:** $7371
Freshman Class: 3927 applied, 1249 accepted, 492 enrolled	
SAT I Verbal/Math: 680/680	**ACT:** 29 **MOST COMPETITIVE**

Davidson College, founded in 1837, is a private liberal arts institution affiliated with the Presbyterian Church (U.S.A.). In addition to regional accreditation, Davidson has baccalaureate program accreditation with ACS and NCATE. The 3 libraries contain 422,035 volumes, 475,788 microform items, and 9494 audio/video tapes/CDs, and subscribe to 2767 periodicals. Computerized library services include the card catalog, interlibrary loans, and database searching. Special learning facilities include a learning resource center, art gallery, radio station, and arboretum. The 450-acre campus is in a small town 19 miles north of Charlotte. Including any residence halls, there are 98 buildings.

Student Life: 82% of undergraduates are from out of state, mostly the South. Students are from 45 states, 32 foreign countries, and Canada. 53% are from public schools. 81% are white. The average age of freshmen is 18; all undergraduates, 20. 4% do not continue beyond their first year; 90% remain to graduate.

Housing: 1560 students can be accommodated in college housing, which includes single-sex and coed dorms, on-campus apartments, and off-campus apartments. Substance-free housing is available. On-campus housing is guaranteed for the freshman year only and is available on a lottery system for upperclassmen. 92% of students live on campus. All students may keep cars.

Activities: There are 6 national fraternities. There are no sororities. There are 151 groups on campus, including art, cheerleading, choir, chorale, chorus, computers, dance, drama, ethnic, gay, honors, international, jazz band, literary magazine, musical theater, newspaper, opera, orchestra, outing, pep band, political, professional, radio and TV, religious, social, social service, student government, symphony, and yearbook. Popular campus events include Fall Concert, Spring Concert, and convocations.

Sports: There are 11 intercollegiate sports for men and 10 for women, and 16 intramural sports for men and 15 for women. Facilities include indoor and outdoor tennis courts, 3 racquetball courts, a squash court, a natatorium with a diving well, 2 Nautilus rooms, a gym, a wrestling room, a dance studio, a golf course, a cross-country course and trail, a football and soccer stadium, various other playing fields, and facilities for sailing, swimming, water skiing, and canoeing at the Lake campus.

Disabled Students: 90% of the campus is accessible. Wheelchair ramps, elevators, special parking, specially equipped rest rooms, special class scheduling, lowered drinking fountains, and lowered telephones are available.

Services: Counseling and information services are available. Tutoring is available as needed through the Student Affairs Office. There is a reader service for the blind.

Campus Safety and Security: Measures include 24-hour foot and vehicle patrol, self-defense education, security escort services, and informal discussions. There are pamphlets/posters/films, emergency telephones, and lighted pathways/sidewalks.

Programs of Study: Davidson confers A.B. and B.S. degrees. Bachelor's degrees are awarded in BIOLOGICAL SCIENCE (biology/biological science), COMMUNICATIONS AND THE ARTS (art, classics, dramatic arts, English, French, German, music, and Spanish), COMPUTER AND PHYSICAL SCIENCE (chemistry, mathematics, and physics), SOCIAL SCIENCE (anthropology, economics, history, interdisciplinary studies, philosophy, political science/government, psychology, religion, and sociology). Biology, English, and political science are the largest.

Required: Students must complete 32 courses, including 10 to 12 in the major, with a 2.0 GPA in order to graduate. Core curriculum requirements include courses in literature, fine arts, history, religion and philosophy, natural science, math, and social sciences. In addition, students must meet foreign language, composition, cultural diversity, and phys ed requirements. Comprehensive exams and a thesis are required in some majors.

Special: Davidson offers interdisciplinary international and South Asian studies programs and study abroad in 12 countries as well as through other schools' study-abroad programs. A 3-2 engineering program may be arranged with Georgia Institute of Technology and Columbia, Duke, North Carolina State, and Washington Universities. Students may design their own majors, cross-register with any college in the Charlotte Area Educational Consortium, enroll in a Washington or Philadelphia semester or a semester or month-long environmental program at the School for Field Studies, or undertake independent study. There are 15 national honor societies, including Phi Beta Kappa, and 20 departmental honors programs.

Faculty/Classroom: 67% of faculty are male; 33%, female. All both teach and do research. The average class size in an introductory lecture is 16; in a laboratory, 13; and in a regular course, 15.

Admissions: 32% of the 2003-2004 applicants were accepted. The SAT I scores for the 2003-2004 freshman class were: Verbal--1% below 500, 12% between 500 and 599, 49% between 600 and 700, and 38% above 700; Math--1% below 500, 9% between 500 and 599, 52% between 600 and 700, and 39% above 700. 93% of the current freshmen were in the top fifth of their class; 99% were in the top two fifths. 25 freshmen graduated first in their class.

Requirements: The SAT I or ACT is required. In addition, SAT II: Subject tests in writing, mathematics level I or II, and 1 other subject are strongly recommended. At least 16 high school units are required, although 20 units are recommended. These should include 4 units of English, 3 units of math, and 2 units each of the same foreign language, science, and history/social studies. It is strongly recommended that high school students continue for the third and fourth years in science and in the same foreign language, continue math through calculus, and take additional courses in history. AP credits are accepted. Important factors in the admissions decision are advanced placement or honor courses, recommendations by school officials, and leadership record.

Procedure: Freshmen are admitted in the fall. Entrance exams should be taken by the end of the junior year. There are early decision and deferred admissions plans. Early decision applications should be filed by November 15; regular applications, by January 2 for fall entry. The fall 2003 application fee was $50. Notification of early decision is sent December 15; regular decision, April 1. 208 early decision candidates were accepted for the 2003-2004 class; of those on the waiting list, 2 were admitted. Applications are accepted on-line through Apply.

Transfer: 5 transfer students enrolled in 2002-2003. Applicants must have at least 1 full year of college work, generally with a 3.0 GPA. They must submit official college and high school transcripts, as well as required letters of recommendation, and be in good standing at their previous college. 16 credits of 32 required for the bachelor's degree must be completed at Davidson.

Visiting: There are guides for informal visits and visitors may sit in on classes and stay overnight. To schedule a visit, contact the Admissions Office at *admission@davidson.edu.*

Financial Aid: In 2003-2004, 51% of all full-time freshmen and 57% of continuing full-time students received some form of financial aid. 29% of full-time freshmen and 33% of continuing full-time students received need-based aid. The average freshman award was $17,752. Need-based scholarships or need-based grants averaged $15,581; need-based self-help aid (loans and jobs) averaged $3938; non-need-based athletic scholarships averaged $10,040; and other non-need-based awards and non-need-based scholarships averaged $7584. 30% of undergraduates work part time. Average annual earnings from campus work are $2000. The average financial indebtedness of the 2003 graduate was $13,697. The CSS/Profile, FAFSA, and the college's own financial statement are required. The deadline for filing freshman financial aid applications for fall entry is February 15.

International Students: There are 58 international students enrolled. The school actively recruits these students. They must score 600 on the written TOEFL or 250 on the electronic version and also take the SAT I or the ACT.

Computers: The mainframes include 32 servers, including an HP 9000 K360, Digital Alpha Server 1200, and several Dell PowerEdge 2300s and 6350s. Students may use the host computer and PC network for word processing, computation and graphics (Mathematica, Quattro), statistics (SAS, SPSS, Minitab), e-mail, and the Internet. Access is available from 142 networked PCs in academic buildings, with more than 500 PCs and Macs on the campus. All students may access the system 24 hours per day. There are no time limits and no fees.

Graduates: From July 1, 2002 to June 30, 2003, 471 bachelor's degrees were awarded. The most popular majors were English (18%), biology (11%), and economics (10%). In an average class, 87% graduate in 4 years or less, 89% graduate in 5 years or less, and 90% graduate in 6 years or less. 280 companies recruited on campus in 2002-2003. Of the 2002 graduating class, 16% were enrolled in graduate school within 6 months of graduation and 70% were employed.

Admissions Contact: Dr. Nancy J. Cable, Dean of Admission and Financial Aid. E-mail: *admission@davidson.edu*
Web: *www.davidson.edu*

DUKE UNIVERSITY   D-2
Durham, NC 27706   (919) 684-3214; Fax: (919) 681-8941

Full-time: 3119 men, 2944 women	**Faculty:** 762; I, ++$
Part-time: 12 men, 11 women	**Ph.Ds:** 97%
Graduate: 3102 men, 2806 women	**Student/Faculty:** 8 to 1
Year: semesters, summer session	**Tuition:** $29,345
Application Deadline: January 2	**Room & Board:** $8210
Freshman Class: 16,729 applied, 3873 accepted, 1619 enrolled	
SAT I Verbal/Math: 700/720	**ACT:** 31 **MOST COMPETITIVE**

Duke University, founded in 1838, is a private institution affiliated with the United Methodist Church offering undergraduate programs in arts and sciences and engineering. There are 2 undergraduate and 8 graduate schools. In addition to regional accreditation, Duke has baccalaureate program accreditation with AACSB, ABET, ACPE, AHEA, APTA, NCATE, NLN, and SAF. The 9 libraries contain 5,360,303 volumes, 4,256,544 microform units, and 76,371 audio/video tapes/CDs, and subscribe to 38,112 periodicals. Computerized library services include the card catalog, interlibrary loans, database searching, and Internet access. Special learning facilities include a learning resource center, art gallery, radio station, TV station, marine lab at Beaufort, primate center, center for international studies, nuclear lab, free electron laser, science research center, institutes of the arts, statistics and decision sciences, policy sciences and public affairs, and centers for teaching and learning, community service, geometric computing, culture, and women. The 9727-acre campus is in a suburban area 285 miles southwest of Washington, D.C. Including any residence halls, there are 208 buildings.

Student Life: 85% of undergraduates are from out of state, mostly the Middle Atlantic. Students are from 50 states, 55 foreign countries, and Canada. 60% are from public schools. 60% are white; 12% Asian American; 10% African American. 40% are Protestant; 23% claim no religious affiliation; 19% Catholic; 11% Jewish; 8% Muslim and Eastern religions. The average age of freshmen is 18; all undergraduates, 20. 4% do not continue beyond their first year; 93% remain to graduate.

Housing: 5371 students can be accommodated in college housing, which includes single-sex and coed dorms, on-campus apartments, and married-student housing. In addition, there are language houses, special-interest houses, and theme houses in women's studies, the arts, and community service (APO). On-campus housing is guaranteed for all 4 years. 82% of students live on campus. All students may keep cars.

Activities: 29% of men belong to 17 national fraternities; 42% of women belong to 10 national sororities. There are 350 groups on campus, including art, band, cheerleading, chess, choir, chorale, chorus, computers, dance, debate, drama, drill team, ethnic, film, gay, honors, international, jazz band, literary magazine, marching band, musical theater, newspaper, opera, orchestra, pep band, photography, political, professional, radio and TV, religious, social, social service, student government, symphony, and yearbook. Popular campus events include College Bowl, Oktoberfest, and Springfest.

Sports: There are 12 intercollegiate sports for men and 11 for women, and 15 intramural sports for men and 13 for women. Facilities include stadiums for baseball, basketball/volleyball, football, and soccer/lacrosse; squash, racquetball, and tennis courts; an aquatic center; training and weight rooms; a golf course; cross-country and jogging trails; and practice and intramural sport club fields. The largest stadium seats 33941; the largest arena, 8564.

Disabled Students: Wheelchair ramps, elevators, special parking, specially equipped rest rooms, special class scheduling, lowered drinking fountains, lowered telephones, and special housing are available. In addition, activities such as concerts can be moved to accessible facilities upon request.

Services: Counseling and information services are available, as is tutoring in every subject. There is a reader service for the blind.

Campus Safety and Security: Measures include 24-hour foot and vehicle patrol, self-defense education, security escort services, and shuttle buses. There are informal discussions, pamphlets/posters/films, emergency telephones, lighted pathways/sidewalks, and a crime prevention program.

Programs of Study: Duke confers B.S., A.B., and B.S.E. degrees. Master's and doctoral degrees are also awarded. Bachelor's degrees are awarded in BIOLOGICAL SCIENCE (anatomy and biology/biological science), COMMUNICATIONS AND THE ARTS (African languages, art history and appreciation, classical languages, dramatic arts, English, Germanic languages and literature, linguistics, literature, music, Slavic languages, Spanish, and visual and performing arts), COMPUTER AND PHYSICAL SCIENCE (chemistry, computer science, geology, mathematics, and physics), ENGINEERING AND ENVIRONMENTAL DESIGN (biomedical engineering, civil engineering, electrical/electronics engineering, environmental science, materials science, and mechanical engineering), SOCIAL SCIENCE (African American studies, African studies, anthropology, area studies, Asian/Oriental studies, Canadian studies, classical/ancient civilization, economics, French studies, history, Italian studies, medieval studies, philosophy, political science/government, psychology, public affairs, religion, sociology, and women's studies). Public policy studies, political science, and psychology are the strongest academically. Biology, psychology, and history are the largest.

Required: A minimum of 34 course credits is required for graduation including natural sciences, quantitative reasoning, and social sciences. No more than 17 course credits are allowed in a major for the B.A. and no more than 19 for the B.S. At least 12 courses must be at or above the 100 level. At least 3 courses designated as seminars, tutorials, independent study, or thesis completion are required. Computer proficiency must be demonstrated by engineering students.

Special: Duke offers cross-registration with the University of North Carolina/Chapel Hill and North Carolina State and North Carolina Central Universities. Also available are internships through the Career Development Center, study abroad in 27 countries, and a Washington semester. An accelerated degree program is possible, achieving graduation in 3 years or combining the senior year with the first graduate year of the law, business, or environment schools. Several 3-2 and 4-1 medical technology programs (degree completed at Duke) are available. Project Calc, an innovative program in calculus, is also offered. Dual majors of any combination, student-designed majors, nondegree study, and pass/fail options are possible. There are 4 national honor societies, including Phi Beta Kappa.

Faculty/Classroom: 83% of faculty are male; 17%, female. All both teach and do research. Graduate students teach 12% of introductory courses. The average class size in an introductory lecture is 39; in a laboratory, 246; and in a regular course, 21.

Admissions: 23% of the 2003-2004 applicants were accepted. The SAT I scores for the 2003-2004 freshman class were: Verbal--1% below 500, 8% between 500 and 599, 35% between 600 and 700, and 56% above 700; Math--1% below 500, 5% between 500 and 599, 28% between 600 and 700, and 66% above 700. The ACT scores were 2% between 21 and 23, 40% between 27 and 28, and 58% above 28. 96% of the current freshmen were in the top fifth of their class; 99% were in the top two fifths.

Requirements: The SAT I or ACT is required. In addition, 3 SAT II: Subject tests, including writing, are required. Applicants must be graduates of an accredited secondary school and have completed 15 academic credits, with 4 in English and 3 each in math, science, and foreign language; an additional 2 in social studies or history are recommended. Engineering students must have 4 credit units in math and 1 in physics or chemistry. An essay is required and an interview is recommended. A portfolio or audition is advised in appropriate instances. AP credits are accepted. Important factors in the admissions decision are advanced placement or honors courses, recommendations by school officials, and extracurricular activities record.

Procedure: Freshmen are admitted fall and spring. Entrance exams should be taken in October of the junior year for early decision applicants and by January of the senior year for regular decision. There are early decision, early admissions, and deferred admissions plans. Early decision applications should be filed by November 1; regular applications, by January 2 for fall entry and October 15 for spring entry, along with a $70 fee. Notification of early decision is sent December 15; regular decision, April 15. 536 early decision candidates were accepted for the 2003-2004 class. A waiting list is an active part of the admissions procedure.

Transfer: 35 transfer students enrolled in 2002-2003. A minimum 3.6 GPA is recommended. The SAT I, plus 3 SAT II: Subject tests, or the ACT is required. 17 of 34 credits required for the bachelor's degree must be completed at Duke.

Visiting: There are regularly scheduled orientations for prospective students, including student-led tours, counselor-led group information sessions, class visits, and lunch with students. There are guides for informal visits and visitors may sit in on classes and stay overnight.

To schedule a visit, contact Undergraduate Admissions at *studenth@valhalla.oit.duke.edu.*

Financial Aid: In 2003-2004, 42% of all full-time freshmen and 36% of continuing full-time students received some form of financial aid. 35% of full-time freshmen and 34% of continuing full-time students received need-based aid. The average freshman award was $25,832. Need-based scholarships or need-based grants averaged $21,432; need-based self-help aid (loans and jobs) averaged $4711; and non-need-based awards and non-need-based scholarships averaged $7030. 30% of undergraduates work part time. Average annual earnings from campus work are $1839. The average financial indebtedness of the 2003 graduate was $19,737. The CSS Profile or FAFSA is required. The deadline for filing freshman financial aid applications for fall entry is February 1.

International Students: There are 296 international students enrolled. The school actively recruits these students. Students must take the SAT I or ACT. Students taking the SAT I must submit SAT II: Subject tests, one of which must be the SAT II: Writing test. Engineering students must take math.

Computers: The mainframe is an IBM 9672. Students may access a number of computer clusters located throughout the campus, providing access to networked and nonnetworked PCs and to workstations. About 600 terminals/PCs are available for general student use. All students have access to e-mail and the Internet. All students may access the system 24 hours a day. There are no time limits and no fees. It is strongly recommended that all students have a personal computer.

Graduates: From July 1, 2002 to June 30, 2003, 1502 bachelor's degrees were awarded. The most popular majors were economics (18%), psychology (9%), and public policy (8%). In an average class, 1% graduate in 3 years or less, 87% graduate in 4 years or less, and 92% graduate in 5 years or less. 170 companies recruited on campus in 2002-2003. Of the 2002 graduating class, 24% were enrolled in graduate school within 6 months of graduation and 38% were employed.

Admissions Contact: Christoph Guttentag, Director, Undergraduate Admissions. A video is available. E-mail: *askduke@admiss.duke.edu* Web: *http://www.duke.edu/*

EAST CAROLINA UNIVERSITY
E-2
Greenville, NC 27858-4353   (252) 328-6640; Fax: (252) 328-6945

Full-time: 6288 men, 9060 women	Faculty: 814; IIA, -$
Part-time: 624 men, 963 women	Ph.D.s: 68%
Graduate: 1692 men, 3129 women	Student/Faculty: 19 to 1
Year: semesters, summer session	Tuition: $3131 ($13,270)
Application Deadline: March 15	Room & Board: $5540
Freshman Class: 11,005 applied, 8423 accepted, 3534 enrolled	
SAT I Verbal/Math: 518/530	ACT: 20 COMPETITIVE

East Carolina University, founded in 1907, is a state-supported institution offering degree programs in the arts and sciences, business, education, fine arts and communication, health and human performance, human ecology, technology and computer science, medicine, allied health sciences, and nursing. There are 9 undergraduate and 2 graduate schools. In addition to regional accreditation, ECU has baccalaureate program accreditation with AACSB, ACCE, ADA, APTA, CSWE, FIDER, NASAD, NASM, NCATE, NLN, and NRPA. The 2 libraries contain 1,330,787 volumes, 2,461,178 microform items, and 30,128 audio/video tapes/CDs, and subscribe to 4646 periodicals. Computerized library services include the card catalog, interlibrary loans, and database searching. Special learning facilities include a learning resource center, art gallery, and radio station. The 1000-acre campus is in an urban area 90 miles east of Raleigh. Including any residence halls, there are 206 buildings.

Student Life: 85% of undergraduates are from North Carolina. Others are from 47 states, 40 foreign countries, and Canada. 80% are white; 15% African American. The average age of freshmen is 18; all undergraduates, 22.

Housing: 5303 students can be accommodated in college housing, which includes single-sex and coed dorms. In addition, there are honors houses, a first-year students' floor, a leadership hall, an extended-quiet-hours floor, a substance-free hall, a nonsmoking floor, and an academic-year hall. On-campus housing is guaranteed for the freshman year only and is available on a first-come, first-served basis. 71% of students commute. Alcohol is not permitted. All students may keep cars.

Activities: 1% of men belong to 22 national fraternities; 1% of women belong to 13 national sororities. There are 244 groups on campus, including academic, art, band, cheerleading, choir, chorale, chorus, computers, dance, drama, drill team, ethnic, gay, honors, international, jazz band, literary magazine, marching band, military, musical theater, newspaper, opera, orchestra, pep band, photography, political, professional, radio and TV, recreation, religious, social, social service, student government, symphony, and yearbook. Popular campus events include Barefoot on the Mall, Midnight Madness, and Pirate Palooza.

Sports: There are 9 intercollegiate sports for men and 9 for women, and 23 intramural sports for men and 23 for women. Facilities include a 43,000-seat stadium, an 8,000-seat basketball coliseum, a baseball and softball field, a track, and a natatorium. The Student Recreation Center includes a 6-court multipurpose sports area, a cardiovascular and a weight training area, 3 exercise studios, indoor and outdoor pools, an indoor track, a climbing wall, 7 racquetball courts, a squash court, and a fitness assessment center. The Recreational Sports Complex includes 10 football/soccer fields, 5 softball fields, and a ropes challenge course.

Disabled Students: 94% of the campus is accessible. Wheelchair ramps, elevators, special parking, specially equipped rest rooms, special class scheduling, lowered drinking fountains, lowered telephones, automatic doors, and state-of-the-art adaptive equipment are available.

Services: There is a reader service for the blind and remedial math and reading. Tutoring is established on a department-by-department basis.

Campus Safety and Security: Measures include 24-hour foot and vehicle patrol, self-defense education, security escort services, and shuttle buses. There are informal discussions, pamphlets/posters/films, emergency telephones, lighted pathways/sidewalks, bicycle patrols, bicycle registration, motorist assistance, lost and found, operation ID, the Residence Hall Liaison Officer Program, on-and off-campus crime prevention safety tips, Staff and Faculty Eyes (SAFE) Campus Community Watch Program, and alcohol awareness.

Programs of Study: ECU confers B.A., B.S., B.F.A., B.M., B.S.A., B.S.A.P., B.S.B.A., B.S.B.E., B.S.N., B.S.O.T., and B.S.W. degrees. Master's and doctoral degrees are also awarded. Bachelor's degrees are awarded in BIOLOGICAL SCIENCE (biochemistry, biology/biological science, and nutrition), BUSINESS (accounting, banking and finance, business administration and management, hospitality management services, management information systems, marketing management, and recreational facilities management), COMMUNICATIONS AND THE ARTS (art, art history and appreciation, communications, dance, design, dramatic arts, English, French, German, music performance, music theory and composition, and studio art), COMPUTER AND PHYSICAL SCIENCE (applied physics, chemistry, computer science, geology, mathematics, and physics), EDUCATION (art, athletic training, business, dance, drama, early childhood, education of the emotionally handicapped, education of the mentally handicapped, elementary, English, foreign languages, health, home economics, marketing and distribution, mathematics, middle school, music, physical, science, social studies, and special), ENGINEERING AND ENVIRONMENTAL DESIGN (city/community/regional planning, construction management, electrical/electronics engineering technology, environmental engineering technology, industrial engineering technology, interior design, and manufacturing technology), HEALTH PROFESSIONS (environmental health science, exercise science, medical records administration/services, medical technology, music therapy, nursing, occupational therapy, physician's assistant, recreation therapy, rehabilitation therapy, and speech pathology/audiology), SOCIAL SCIENCE (anthropology, child care/child and family studies, clothing and textiles management/production/services, criminal justice, dietetics, economics, family and community services, geography, Hispanic American studies, history, liberal arts/general studies, parks and recreation management, philosophy, physical fitness/movement, political science/government, psychology, social work, sociology, and women's studies). Allied health, art, music, and geology are the strongest academically. Elementary education, nursing, and fine/studio arts are the largest.

Required: To graduate, students must complete 120 to 128 semester hours with a minimum GPA of 2.0 overall and in the major. General education requirements include 12 hours of social science, 10 of humanities and fine arts, 8 of science, 6 of English, 3 of math, and 3 of health and exercise and sport science. The total must include 12 hours of writing-intensive courses and a course in cultural diversity.

Special: ECU offers cooperative programs in most majors, internships, study abroad in 39 countries, dual majors, work-study, and a student-designed major in multidisciplinary studies. There are 19 national honor societies, a freshman honors program, and 39 departmental honors programs.

Faculty/Classroom: 54% of faculty are male; 46%, female. The average class size in an introductory lecture is 52; in a laboratory, 24; and in a regular course, 33.

Admissions: 77% of the 2003-2004 applicants were accepted. The SAT I scores for the 2003-2004 freshman class were: Verbal--40% below 500, 46% between 500 and 599, 13% between 600 and 700, and 1% above 700; Math--32% below 500, 52% between 500 and 599, 15% between 600 and 700, and 1% above 700. The ACT scores were 58% below 21, 28% between 21 and 23, 10% between 24 and 26, 2% between 27 and 28, and 2% above 28. 34% of the current freshmen were in the top fifth of their class; 72% were in the top two fifths. 41 freshmen graduated first in their class.

Requirements: The SAT I or ACT is required. In addition, applicants must be graduates of an accredited secondary school. All degree-seeking students are required to complete 20 academic units, including 4 in English, 3 in math, 3 in science with 1 lab course, 2 in social studies with 1 in U.S. history, and 2 units in a foreign language. 1 unit in fine arts is recommended. 1 unit each in foreign language, natural science, and math should be taken in the senior year. Special circumstances exist for

applicants with a GED. A GPA of 2.0 is required. AP and CLEP credits are accepted.

Procedure: Freshmen are admitted to all sessions. Entrance exams should be taken in the spring of the junior year or the fall of the senior year. There is a deferred admissions plan and a rolling admissions plan. Applications should be filed by March 15 for fall entry, November 1 for spring entry, and March 15 for summer entry. The fall 2003 application fee was $50. Notification is sent on a rolling basis after April 15. Applications are accepted on-line through the school's web site.

Transfer: 1275 transfer students enrolled in 2002-2003. Applicants must submit official transcripts from high school and all colleges attended and have a satisfactory GPA in courses attempted. Applicants who will have completed fewer than 30 semester hours will also be required to meet the freshmen requirements. 30 credits of 120 to 128 required for the bachelor's degree must be completed at ECU.

Visiting: There are regularly scheduled orientations for prospective students, including information sessions and campus tours. There are guides for informal visits. To schedule a visit, contact the Admissions Office at admis@mail.ecu.edu.

Financial Aid: In 2003-2004, 64% of all full-time freshmen and 57% of continuing full-time students received some form of financial aid. 39% of full-time freshmen and 27% of continuing full-time students received need-based aid. The average freshman award was $6736. The average financial indebtedness of the 2003 graduate was $18,318. ECU is a member of CSS. The FAFSA is required. The deadline for filing freshman financial aid applications for fall entry is April 15.

International Students: There are 69 international students enrolled. The school actively recruits these students. They must score 550 on the written TOEFL or 213 on the electronic version. SAT I or ACT scores are required if the student will receive an athletic scholarship or if the student will graduate from a U.S. high school.

Computers: The mainframe is an IBM S390/7060. There are 6100 PCs and Macs currently on the network. E-mail is provided for each enrolled student. Free web access is provided to those students living in the residence halls. Students may register for classes, change their local mailing address, and check housing information, financial aid status, parking fines, hold tags, and so forth, using the ECU web site. Students may also register for classes using the automated voice response system. All students may access the system at all times. There are no time limits and no fees. It is strongly recommended that all students have a personal computer. An 800 MHz Pentium III or the equivalent is recommended.

Graduates: From July 1, 2002 to June 30, 2003, 2849 bachelor's degrees were awarded. The most popular majors were elementary education (6%), nursing (6%), and management (5%). In an average class, 25% graduate in 4 years or less, 48% graduate in 5 years or less, and 54% graduate in 6 years or less. 70 companies recruited on campus in 2002-2003.

Admissions Contact: Thomas E. Powell, Jr., Director of Undergraduate Admissions. E-mail: admis@mail.ecu.edu
Web: www.ecu.ed/admissions

ELIZABETH CITY STATE UNIVERSITY

Elizabeth City, NC 27909

F-2

(252) 335-3305
(800) 347-ECSU; Fax: (252) 335-3537

Full-time: 680 men, 1085 women	**Faculty:** 113; IIB, av$
Part-time: 50 men, 150 women	**Ph.D.s:** 68%
Graduate: none	**Student/Faculty:** 16 to 1
Year: semesters, summer session	**Tuition:** $1650 ($8050)
Application Deadline: open	**Room & Board:** $3900
Freshman Class: n/av	
SAT I or ACT: required	**LESS COMPETITIVE**

Elizabeth City State University, founded in 1891 as part of the University of North Carolina System, is a public institution offering undergraduate programs in liberal arts and sciences, education, and business. Figures in the above capsule and in this profile are approximate. The library contains 174,566 volumes, 486,884 microform items, and 1220 audio/video tapes/CDs, and subscribes to 1698 periodicals. Computerized library services include the card catalog and interlibrary loans. Special learning facilities include a learning resource center, art gallery, planetarium, radio station, TV station, farm, and 639-acre educational research tract. The 829-acre campus is in a small town 55 miles from Norfolk, Virginia.

Student Life: 90% of undergraduates are from North Carolina. Students are from 20 states and 5 foreign countries. 75% are African American; 23% white. 25% do not continue beyond their first year; 50% remain to graduate.

Housing: 1019 students can be accommodated in college housing, which includes single-sex dorms and on-campus apartments. In addition, there are honors houses. On-campus housing is guaranteed for all 4 years. 52% of students commute. Alcohol is not permitted. All students may keep cars.

Activities: There are 4 national fraternities and 4 national sororities. There are many groups and organizations on campus, including band, cheerleading, choir, chorus, dance, drama, honors, international, jazz band, literary magazine, marching band, newspaper, pep band, radio and TV, religious, social, student government, and yearbook.

Sports: Facilities include a 4500-seat gym, a 3500-seat stadium, an all-weather track, a golf range, an Olympic pool, a weight room, 8 tennis courts, dance and exercise studios, handball and racquetball courts, and playing fields.

Disabled Students: Wheelchair ramps, elevators, special parking, specially equipped rest rooms, and lowered drinking fountains are available.

Services: In addition to vocational counseling services, tutoring is available.

Campus Safety and Security: Measures include emergency telephones and ECSU has its own police department on campus.

Programs of Study: ECSU confers B.A., B.S., and B.S.Ed. degrees. Bachelor's degrees are awarded in BIOLOGICAL SCIENCE (biology/biological science), BUSINESS (accounting and business administration and management), COMMUNICATIONS AND THE ARTS (art, English, and music), COMPUTER AND PHYSICAL SCIENCE (chemistry, computer science, geology, mathematics, and physics), EDUCATION (business, elementary, industrial arts, middle school, physical, special, and technical), ENGINEERING AND ENVIRONMENTAL DESIGN (industrial engineering technology), SOCIAL SCIENCE (criminal justice, history, political science/government, psychology, social science, social work, and sociology).

Required: Students must have maintained a minimum GPA of 2.0, fulfilled a major, and completed the requirements of general education courses in the fields of grammar, composition, and literature.

Special: Opportunities are provided for internships, dual majors, weekend/evening degree completion programs, work-study, and credit by exam and for military service. There are 5 national honor societies and a freshman honors program.

Faculty/Classroom: All teach undergraduates.

Requirements: The SAT I or ACT is required. In addition, graduation from an accredited secondary school is required; the GED is accepted. Applicants should submit an academic record with 4 courses in English, 3 each in math and science, and 2 in social studies; it is recommended that applicants have at least 2 course units in foreign languages. Students must also pass the NC Competency Examination or its equivalent. A GPA of 2.0 is required. AP and CLEP credits are accepted.

Procedure: Freshmen are admitted fall, spring, and summer. Entrance exams should be taken as early as possible. There are early admissions and deferred admissions plans. Application deadlines are open. The fall 2003 application fee was $30.

Transfer: Applicants must have a minimum college GPA of 2.0 and submit high school and college transcripts. Those with fewer than 30 credit hours must meet both freshman and transfer admission requirements.

Visiting: There are regularly scheduled orientations for prospective students. There are guides for informal visits. To schedule a visit, contact the Admissions Office.

Financial Aid: The FAFSA, the college's own financial statement, and income tax forms are required. Check with the school for current deadlines.

International Students: They must take the TOEFL or the MELAB, and also take the SAT I or the ACT.

Computers: The mainframe is a DEC VAX 11/780 with an IBM PC network. The Academic Computing Center houses a computer lab that provides access to the state's major computer network and other systems through LINCNET and BITNET. Students in computer-related courses may access the system. There are no time limits and no fees. It is strongly recommended that all students have a personal computer.

Admissions Contact: Bridgett Golham, Director of Admissions and Recruitment. A video is available. E-mail: admissions@alpha.ecsu.edu Web: www.ecsu.edu

---

ELON COLLEGE
(See Elon University)

ELON UNIVERSITY
Elon, NC 27244-2010   D-2

(336) 278-3566
(800) 334-8448; Fax: (336) 278-7699

Full-time: 1663 men, 2646 women	Faculty: 252; II A, av$
Part-time: 41 men, 81 women	Ph.D.s: 85%
Graduate: 74 men, 79 women	Student/Faculty: 17 to 1
Year: 4-1-4, summer session	Tuition: $16,570
Application Deadline: January 10	Room & Board: $5670
Freshman Class: 7053 applied, 3205 accepted, 1227 enrolled	
SAT I Verbal/Math: 570/580	VERY COMPETITIVE

Elon University, founded in 1889 by the United Church of Christ, is a private (not for profit) comprehensive institution that offers programs in the liberal arts and sciences in career-oriented fields of study. There are 4 undergraduate and 3 graduate schools. In addition to regional accreditation, Elon has baccalaureate program accreditation with CAHEA, CAPTE, and NCATE. The library contains 226,576 volumes, 851,327 microform items, and 13,305 audio/video tapes/CDs, and subscribes to 16,152 periodicals. Computerized library services include the card catalog, interlibrary loans, and database searching. Special learning facilities include a learning resource center, art gallery, radio station, TV station, writing center, botanical preserve, and observatory. The 575-acre campus is in a suburban area adjacent to Burlington and 17 miles east of Greensboro. Including any residence halls, there are 108 buildings.

Student Life: 70% of undergraduates are from out of state, mostly the Middle Atlantic. Students are from 47 states, 36 foreign countries, and Canada. 79% are from public schools. 88% are white. 43% are Protestant; 25% Catholic. The average age of freshmen is 18; all undergraduates, 20. 13% do not continue beyond their first year; 71% remain to graduate.

Housing: 2700 students can be accommodated in college housing, which includes single-sex and coed dorms, on-campus apartments, off-campus apartments, fraternity houses, and sorority houses. In addition, there are honors houses, special-interest houses, theme suites, and academic living-learning communities. On-campus housing is guaranteed for the freshman year only and is available on a lottery system for upperclassmen. 62% of students live on campus; of those, 65% remain on campus on weekends. All students may keep cars.

Activities: 26% of men belong to 9 national fraternities; 43% of women belong to 11 national sororities. There are 125 groups on campus, including art, band, cheerleading, choir, chorale, chorus, computers, dance, drama, drill team, ethnic, film, gay, honors, international, jazz band, literary magazine, marching band, musical theater, newspaper, orchestra, pep band, photography, political, professional, radio and TV, religious, social, social service, student government, symphony, and yearbook. Popular campus events include Family Weekend, Greek Week, and College Coffee.

Sports: There are 7 intercollegiate sports for men and 9 for women, and 22 intramural sports for men and 22 for women. Facilities include an 8250-seat stadium, lighted tennis courts, a baseball stadium, a field house, and 15 athletic fields. The athletic center has racquetball courts, aerobic rooms, a human performance lab, a weight room, a fitness center, 2 gyms, and an indoor swimming pool.

Disabled Students: 75% of the campus is accessible. Wheelchair ramps, elevators, special parking, specially equipped rest rooms, special class scheduling, lowered drinking fountains, lowered telephones, special housing, special class locations, and special headphones in auditoriums are available.

Services: Counseling and information services are available, as is tutoring in most subjects, including many lower-level courses. There is remedial math, reading, and writing. Preparatory courses are offered, which count as elective credit toward graduation.

Campus Safety and Security: Measures include 24-hour foot and vehicle patrol, self-defense education, security escort services, and shuttle buses. There are informal discussions, pamphlets/posters/films, emergency telephones, and lighted pathways/sidewalks.

Programs of Study: Elon confers B.A., B.S., and B.F.A. degrees. Master's and doctoral degrees are also awarded. Bachelor's degrees are awarded in BIOLOGICAL SCIENCE (biology/biological science), BUSINESS (accounting, business administration and management, and sports management), COMMUNICATIONS AND THE ARTS (art, broadcasting, communications, dance, dramatic arts, English, film arts, French, journalism, music, music performance, musical theater, and Spanish), COMPUTER AND PHYSICAL SCIENCE (chemistry, computer science, information sciences and systems, mathematics, and physics), EDUCATION (elementary, foreign languages, health, mathematics, middle school, music, physical, science, secondary, social science, and special), ENGINEERING AND ENVIRONMENTAL DESIGN (engineering, environmental science, and military science), HEALTH PROFESSIONS (medical technology and sports medicine), SOCIAL SCIENCE (economics, history, human services, international studies, philosophy, political science/government, psychology, public administration, religion, and sociology). Business, education, and music theater are the strongest academically. Business, education, and journalism and communication are the largest.

Required: To graduate, students must complete 132 semester hours, including 32 to 68 in the major, with a minimum GPA of 2.0. All students must fulfill the requirements of the General Studies program, which includes a first-year core, experiential learning, liberal studies, and advanced studies, for a total of 59 semester hours, and must satisfactorily complete a comprehensive exam in the major.

Special: Elon offers co-op programs in most majors, dual majors, student-designed majors, cross-registration with 6 other colleges and universities in North Carolina, paid and unpaid internships, study abroad in 25 countries, a Washington semester, work-study programs, pass/fail options, and 3-2 dual engineering degree programs. The 3-week January term includes extensive international study opportunities and courses with domestic travel components. There are 24 national honor societies, a freshman honors program, and 16 departmental honors programs.

Faculty/Classroom: 56% of faculty are male; 44%, female. All teach undergraduates and 68% both teach and do research. No introductory courses are taught by graduate students. The average class size in an introductory lecture is 27; in a laboratory, 21; and in a regular course, 22.

Admissions: 45% of the 2003-2004 applicants were accepted. The SAT I scores for the 2003-2004 freshman class were: Verbal--11% below 500, 52% between 500 and 599, 33% between 600 and 700, and 4% above 700; Math--8% below 500, 49% between 500 and 599, 38% between 600 and 700, and 5% above 700. 46% of the current freshmen were in the top fifth of their class; 82% were in the top two fifths. There was 1 National Merit finalist and 3 semifinalists. 9 freshmen graduated first in their class.

Requirements: The SAT I or ACT is required. In addition, students must be graduates of an accredited secondary school or have a GED certificate. They should have completed 4 credits in English, 3 or more in math, 2 or more in a foreign language, 2 or more in science, including at least 1 lab science, and 2 or more in social studies, including U.S. history. A GPA of 2.6 is required. AP and CLEP credits are accepted. Important factors in the admissions decision are advanced placement or honor courses, evidence of special talent, and leadership record.

Procedure: Freshmen are admitted to all sessions. Entrance exams should be taken in the spring of the junior year and the fall of the senior year. There are early decision, deferred admissions, and rolling admissions plans. Early decision applications should be filed by November 15; regular applications, by January 10 (priority deadline) for fall entry. Notification of early decision and regular decision is sent on a rolling basis. 348 early decision candidates were accepted for the 2003-2004 class. 2149 applicants were on the 2003 waiting list; 52 were admitted. Applications are accepted on-line.

Transfer: 70 transfer students enrolled in 2002-2003. Applicants must present a high school transcript and a minimum GPA of 2.5 in college course work from a 4-year college. An interview is recommended. A dean's evaluation form is required from the last college or university attended, and the applicant must be eligible to return to that institution. 33 of 132 credits required for the bachelor's degree must be completed at Elon.

Visiting: There are regularly scheduled orientations for prospective students, consisting of 2 weekends in spring for deposited freshmen and a spring open house for nondeposited students. There are guides for informal visits and visitors may sit in on classes. To schedule a visit, contact the Admissions Office.

Financial Aid: In 2003-2004, 78% of all full-time freshmen and 70% of continuing full-time students received some form of financial aid. 35% of all full-time students received need-based aid. The average freshman award was $11,101. Need-based scholarships or need-based grants averaged $5201 ($19,000 maximum); need-based self-help aid (loans and jobs) averaged $4753 ($8125 maximum); non-need-based athletic scholarships averaged $10,903 ($22,640 maximum); and other non-need-based awards and non-need-based scholarships averaged $4666 ($20,070 maximum). 25% of undergraduates work part time. Average annual earnings from campus work are $1200. The average financial indebtedness of the 2003 graduate was $18,102. Elon is a member of CSS. The CSS Profile, the FAFSA, and the college's own financial statement are required. The priority date for freshman financial aid applications for fall entry is February 15.

International Students: There are 61 international students enrolled. The school actively recruits these students. They must score 550 on the written TOEFL or 213 on the electronic version and also take the SAT I or the ACT, scoring 850 on the SAT I.

Computers: The mainframe is an HP 9000/L3K. The computer labs have 580 workstations connected to the HP mainframe, to 3 Novell servers, to the library, and to the Internet. Macs and PCs are both available. All students may access the system 24 hours a day via modem. It is strongly recommended that all students have a personal computer.

Graduates: From July 1, 2002 to June 30, 2003, 875 bachelor's degrees were awarded. The most popular majors were business (25%), journalism and communications (18%), and education (11%). In an average class, 69% graduate in 4 years or less, 73% graduate in 5 years or less, and 71% graduate in 6 years or less. 205 companies recruited on campus in 2002-2003. Of the 2002 graduating class, 18% were enrolled in graduate school within 6 months of graduation and 79% were employed.

Admissions Contact: Susan Klopman, Dean of Admissions. A video is available. E-mail: *admissions@elon.edu* Web: *www.elon.edu*

FAYETTEVILLE STATE UNIVERSITY   D-3
Fayetteville, NC 28301-4298   (910) 672-1371
(800) 222-2594; Fax: (910) 437-2512

Full-time: 1200 men, 1930 women	**Faculty:** 202; IIA, -$
Part-time: 200 men, 485 women	**Ph.D.s:** n/av
Graduate: 175 men, 555 women	**Student/Faculty:** 15 to 1
Year: semesters, summer session	**Tuition:** $1770 ($9695)
Application Deadline: see profile	**Room & Board:** $3820
Freshman Class: n/av	
SAT I or ACT: required	**LESS COMPETITIVE**

Fayetteville State University, founded in 1867 and today part of the University of North Carolina system, is a public institution offering degree programs in the arts and sciences, business, and teacher preparation. There are 3 undergraduate schools and 1 graduate school. Figures in the above capsule and in this profile are approximate. In addition to regional accreditation, FSU has baccalaureate program accreditation with NCATE. The library contains 241,022 volumes, 936,006 microform items, and 6656 audio/video tapes/CDs. Computerized library services include the card catalog, interlibrary loans, and database searching. Special learning facilities include a planetarium and radio station. The 156-acre campus is in an urban area 60 miles south of Raleigh. Including any residence halls, there are 40 buildings.

Student Life: 90% of undergraduates are from North Carolina. 75% are African American; 19% white. The average age of freshmen is 18; all undergraduates, 24. 29% do not continue beyond their first year; 32% remain to graduate.

Housing: 1200 students can be accommodated in college housing, which includes single-sex and coed dorms, on-campus apartments, and an honors dorm. On-campus housing is available on a first-come, first-served basis. 67% of students commute. Alcohol is not permitted. All students may keep cars.

Activities: 5% of men belong to 5 local and 4 national fraternities; 5% of women belong to 4 national sororities. There are 20 groups on campus, including band, cheerleading, choir, chorus, dance, drama, film, honors, international, jazz band, literary magazine, marching band, newspaper, pep band, political, radio and TV, religious, social service, student government, and yearbook. Popular campus events include The Lyceum, Martin Luther King Day, and Black History Month.

Sports: There are 6 intercollegiate sports for men and 7 for women, and 4 intramural sports for men and 2 for women. Facilities include 2 gyms, a stadium, tennis courts, a bowling alley, a dance studio, a swimming pool, and playing fields.

Disabled Students: 75% of the campus is accessible. Wheelchair ramps, elevators, special parking, specially equipped rest rooms, and lowered drinking fountains are available.

Services: Counseling and information services are available, as is tutoring in some subjects. There is remedial math, reading, and writing.

Campus Safety and Security: Measures include 24-hour foot and vehicle patrol, security escort services, and lighted pathways/sidewalks.

Programs of Study: FSU confers B.A. and B.S. degrees. Master's degrees are also awarded. Bachelor's degrees are awarded in BIOLOGICAL SCIENCE (biology/biological science), BUSINESS (accounting, banking and finance, business administration and management, business economics, and office supervision and management), COMMUNICATIONS AND THE ARTS (dramatic arts, English, Spanish, speech/debate/rhetoric, and visual and performing arts), COMPUTER AND PHYSICAL SCIENCE (chemistry, computer science, and mathematics), EDUCATION (business, early childhood, elementary, health, marketing and distribution, middle school, music, secondary, and social science), HEALTH PROFESSIONS (medical laboratory technology and nursing), SOCIAL SCIENCE (criminal justice, economics, geography, history, political science/government, psychology, public administration, social science, and sociology).

Required: To graduate, students must complete 120 credit hours with a minimum GPA of 2.0 overall and in the major. The core curriculum includes 8 to 11 credits in natural science, 6 to 15 in humanities, 6 to 7 in math, 3 to 9 in social science, 3 each in critical thinking and speech, and 2 each in phys ed/health and university seminar.

Special: FSU offers cooperative programs in business, math, and biological and physical sciences with North Carolina State University, internships, B.A.-B.S. degrees, dual majors, 3-2 engineering degree programs, credit for military experience, and nondegree study. There are 10 national honor societies, a freshman honors program, and 7 departmental honors programs.

Faculty/Classroom: 60% of faculty are male; 40%, female. All both teach and do research. No introductory courses are taught by graduate students. The average class size in an introductory lecture is 30; in a laboratory, 20; and in a regular course, 30.

Requirements: The SAT I or ACT is required. In addition, successful scores are also required on the North Carolina Competency Exam. Applicants must be graduates of an accredited secondary school or have the GED. They should have completed 4 academic units of English, 3 each of math and science with 1 lab course, and 2 of social studies; also recommended are 2 units of a foreign language and completion of 1 unit each of foreign language and math in the senior year. A GPA of 2.0 is required. AP and CLEP credits are accepted. Important factors in the admissions decision are advanced placement or honor courses, recommendations by school officials, and leadership record.

Procedure: Freshmen are admitted to all sessions. Entrance exams should be taken in November. There are early decision, early admissions, deferred admissions, and rolling admissions plans. Check with the school for current deadlines. The fall 2003 application fee was $25. Notification is sent on a rolling basis.

Transfer: 380 transfer students enrolled in a recent year. Applicants must submit official transcripts from all colleges attended, have a minimum GPA of 2.0, and be eligible to return to their previous institution. 30 of 120 credits required for the bachelor's degree must be completed at FSU.

Visiting: There are regularly scheduled orientations for prospective students, including a campus tour, recreational activity, placement tests, preregistration, and orientation to FSU services. There are guides for informal visits and visitors may sit in on classes and stay overnight. To schedule a visit, contact the Director of Enrollment Management at *cdarlington@uncfsu.edu*.

Financial Aid: FSU is a member of CSS. The FAFSA is required. Check with the school for current deadlines.

International Students: They must score 550 on the written TOEFL or take another English proficiency exam administered in their country. They must also take the SAT I (scoring 700) or the ACT.

Computers: The mainframes are a DEC VAX 8530 and 6000-320 and a Sequent Balance. There are PC labs as well as teaching labs available to students. Other PCs are available in academic and administrative units. All students may access the system 24 hours a day. There are no time limits and no fees.

Graduates: In a recent year, 598 bachelor's degrees were awarded. The most popular majors were business administration (19%), criminal justice (15%), and psychology (12%).

Admissions Contact: Charles Darlington, Director of Enrollment Management. A video is available. E-mail: *cdarlington@uncfsu.edu* Web: *www.uncfsu.edu/admissions/index.htm*

GARDNER-WEBB UNIVERSITY
Boiling Springs, NC 28017-9980　　　　　　　　C-3
　　　　　　　　　　　　　　　　(704) 406-4491
　　　　　　　　　　(800) 253-6472; Fax: (704) 406-4488

Full-time: 858 men, 1428 women	**Faculty:** 83; IIA, --$
Part-time: 120 men, 276 women	**Ph.D.s:** 72%
Graduate: 518 men, 668 women	**Student/Faculty:** 28 to 1
Year: semesters, summer session	**Tuition:** $14,160
Application Deadline: open	**Room & Board:** $5140
Freshman Class: 1754 applied, 1303 accepted, 370 enrolled	
SAT I Verbal/Math: 510/520	**COMPETITIVE**

Gardner-Webb University, founded in 1905, is an independent institution affiliated with the Southern Baptist Church and offering undergraduate programs in the arts and sciences, business, education, nursing, and preprofessional studies. There are 3 undergraduate and 4 graduate schools. In addition to regional accreditation, Webb has baccalaureate program accreditation with ATS, CAAHEP, NASM, NCATE, and NLN. The library contains 220,726 volumes, 593,070 microform items, and 9434 audio/video tapes/CDs, and subscribes to 542 periodicals. Computerized library services include interlibrary loans and database searching. Special learning facilities include a learning resource center, radio station, TV station, and an observatory. The 250-acre campus is in a small town 50 miles west of Charlotte. Including any residence halls, there are 37 buildings.

Student Life: 76% of undergraduates are from North Carolina. Students are from 25 states, 30 foreign countries, and Canada. 81% are white; 15% African American. Most are Protestant. The average age of freshmen is 19; all undergraduates, 24. 30% do not continue beyond their first year; 50% remain to graduate.

Housing: 1085 students can be accommodated in college housing, which includes single-sex dorms and on-campus apartments. In addition, there are honors houses. On-campus housing is guaranteed for all 4 years. 65% of students live on campus; of those, 65% remain on campus on weekends. Alcohol is not permitted. All students may keep cars.

Activities: There are no fraternities or sororities. There are 43 groups on campus, including art, band, cheerleading, choir, chorale, chorus, dance, debate, drama, honors, international, jazz band, literary magazine, musical theater, newspaper, opera, orchestra, pep band, photography, political, professional, radio and TV, religious, social, social service, student government, symphony, and yearbook. Popular campus events include Parents Weekend, Spring Jubilee, and Alumni Day.

Sports: There are 10 intercollegiate sports for men and 10 for women, and 16 intramural sports for men and 17 for women. Facilities include a 8500-seat stadium, a gym, tennis and racquetball courts, a weight room, a swimming pool, and playing fields for softball, soccer, football,

and baseball, a 5500-seat arena, aerobics room, and Broyhill Adventure course.

Disabled Students: All of the campus is accessible. Wheelchair ramps, elevators, special parking, specially equipped rest rooms, special class scheduling, lowered drinking fountains, and special housing are available.

Services: Counseling and information services are available, as is tutoring in every subject. There is a reader service for the blind and remedial math, reading, and writing.

Campus Safety and Security: Measures include 24-hour foot and vehicle patrol, security escort services, informal discussions, and pamphlets/posters/films. There are emergency telephones, lighted pathways/sidewalks, and a foot patrol inside the dorm.

Programs of Study: Webb confers B.A., B.S., B.M., and B.S.N. degrees. Associate, master's, and doctoral degrees are also awarded. Bachelor's degrees are awarded in BIOLOGICAL SCIENCE (biology/biological science), BUSINESS (accounting, business administration and management, international business management, and sports management), COMMUNICATIONS AND THE ARTS (American Sign Language, art, communications, English, French, music, and Spanish), COMPUTER AND PHYSICAL SCIENCE (chemistry, computer science, information sciences and systems, and mathematics), EDUCATION (athletic training, elementary, foreign languages, health, middle school, music, physical, and secondary), ENGINEERING AND ENVIRONMENTAL DESIGN (industrial administration/management), HEALTH PROFESSIONS (medical technology, nursing, and physician's assistant), SOCIAL SCIENCE (history, interpreter for the deaf, psychology, religion, religious music, social science, and sociology). Preengineering, computer science, and premedicine are the strongest academically. Business and nursing are the largest.

Required: To graduate, students must complete 128 credit hours, including 24 to 32 in the major, with a minimum GPA of 2.0. The required core curriculum includes courses in English, history, religion, fine arts, foreign language, natural science, and math.

Special: The university offers work-study programs, internships, study abroad in 18 countries, 3-2 engineering degrees with Auburn University and the University of North Carolina at Charlotte, a 3-1 medical technology degree with the Bowman Gray School of Medicine of Wake Forest University, and a 3-2 physician's assistant program with the Wake Forest University School of Medicine. Independent study is encouraged. There are 2 national honor societies, a freshman honors program, and 3 departmental honors programs.

Faculty/Classroom: 49% of faculty are male; 58%, female. All teach undergraduates. No introductory courses are taught by graduate students. The average class size in an introductory lecture is 35; in a laboratory, 9; and in a regular course, 18.

Admissions: 74% of the 2003-2004 applicants were accepted. 29% of the current freshmen were in the top fifth of their class; 49% were in the top two fifths. There was 1 National Merit finalist and 2 semifinalists. 3 freshmen graduated first in their class.

Requirements: The SAT I or ACT is required. In addition, candidates should be graduates of an accredited secondary school or have a GED certificate. The recommended preparatory curriculum includes 4 units of English, 3 of math, and 2 each of social science, natural science, a foreign language, and electives. An interview is encouraged. Webb requires applicants to be in the upper 50% of their class. A GPA of 2.4 is required. AP and CLEP credits are accepted. Important factors in the admissions decision are leadership record, advanced placement or honor courses, and evidence of special talent.

Procedure: Freshmen are admitted to all sessions. Entrance exams should be taken in the senior year. There is a deferred admissions plan and a rolling admissions plan. Application deadlines are open. The fall 2003 application fee was $25. Applications are accepted on-line.

Transfer: 151 transfer students enrolled in 2002-2003. Applicants must submit the standard application and fee, official high school and college transcripts, and SAT I or ACT scores. High school transcripts and test scores are waived for applicants with 30 or more semester credits and a GPA of 2.0. 32 of 128 credits required for the bachelor's degree must be completed at Webb.

Visiting: There are regularly scheduled orientations for prospective students. There are guides for informal visits and visitors may sit in on classes and stay overnight. To schedule a visit, contact the Admissions Office at *admissions@gardner-webb.edu*.

Financial Aid: In 2003-2004, 92% of all full-time freshmen and 78% of continuing full-time students received some form of financial aid. The average freshman award was $9804. Average annual earnings from campus work are $1600. The average financial indebtedness of the 2003 graduate was $11,770. Webb is a member of CSS. The FAFSA and federal tax returns are required.

International Students: There are 48 international students enrolled. The school actively recruits these students. They must score 500 on the written TOEFL or 173 on the electronic version.

Computers: The mainframe is an IBM/34. There are PCs available in 5 computer labs, located in the library and 4 other buildings. All students may access the system 7 A.M. to 11 P.M. except when a class is in progress. There are no time limits and no fees.

Graduates: From July 1, 2002 to June 30, 2003, 573 bachelor's degrees were awarded. The most popular majors were business administration (24%), social science (21%), and accounting (6%). Of the 2002 graduating class, 38% were enrolled in graduate school within 6 months of graduation.

Admissions Contact: Nathan Alexander, Director of Admissions and Enrollment Management. E-mail: *admissions@gardner-webb.edu* Web: *www.gardner-webb.edu*

GREENSBORO COLLEGE
D-2

Greensboro, NC 27401-1875

(336) 272-7102, ext. 211
(800) 346-8226; Fax: (336) 378-0154

Full-time: 428 men, 457 women	**Faculty:** 57; IIB, av$
Part-time: 90 men, 201 women	**Ph.D.s:** 77%
Graduate: 15 men, 57 women	**Student/Faculty:** 16 to 1
Year: semesters, summer session	**Tuition:** $15,720
Application Deadline: open	**Room & Board:** $6030
Freshman Class: 875 applied, 648 accepted, 229 enrolled	
SAT I Verbal/Math: 480/490	**ACT:** 20 **COMPETITIVE**

Greensboro College, founded in 1838, is a private institution affiliated with the United Methodist Church offering undergraduate programs in the arts and sciences, business, education, health sciences, and pre-professional studies, and graduate programs in education. In addition to regional accreditation, Greensboro College has baccalaureate program accreditation with NCATE. The library contains 106,530 volumes, 2981 microform items, and 2695 audio/video tapes/CDs, and subscribes to 282 periodicals. Computerized library services include the card catalog, interlibrary loans, database searching, and Internet access. Special learning facilities include a learning resource center, art gallery, and natural history museum. The 46-acre campus is in an urban area bordering downtown Greensboro. Including any residence halls, there are 23 buildings.

Student Life: 74% of undergraduates are from North Carolina. Students are from 27 states, 24 foreign countries, and Canada. 79% are white; 17% African American. 47% are Protestant; 33% claim no religious affiliation; 11% Catholic. The average age of freshmen is 18; all undergraduates, 23. 31% do not continue beyond their first year; 46% remain to graduate.

Housing: 627 students can be accommodated in college housing, which includes single-sex and coed dorms and on-campus apartments. There is also an on-campus community service house. On-campus housing is guaranteed for all 4 years. 52% of students commute. All students may keep cars.

Activities: 3% of men belong to 2 local and 1 national fraternity; 4% of women belong to 2 local sororities. There are 49 groups on campus, including art, band, cheerleading, choir, chorale, community service, computers, dance, drama, ethnic, honors, international, jazz band, literary magazine, marching band, musical theater, newspaper, opera, pep band, photography, political, professional, programming, religious, social, social service, and student government. Popular campus events include Winter Rose Formal, Festival of Lessons and Carols, and Spring Fling.

Sports: There are 8 intercollegiate sports for men and 8 for women, and 5 intramural sports for men and 5 for women. Facilities include an athletic field for soccer and lacrosse, and tennis and basketball courts.

Disabled Students: 80% of the campus is accessible. Wheelchair ramps, elevators, special parking, specially equipped rest rooms, and special class scheduling are available.

Services: Counseling and information services are available, as is tutoring in most subjects. There is remedial math and writing, a computerized writing center, and a Writing Across the Curriculum program to strengthen communication skills. Professional math tutors are available.

Campus Safety and Security: Measures include 24-hour foot and vehicle patrol, self-defense education, security escort services, and informal discussions. There are pamphlets/posters/films, emergency telephones, lighted pathways/sidewalks, and security entrances to residence halls.

Programs of Study: Greensboro College confers B.A. and B.S. degrees. Master's degrees are also awarded. Bachelor's degrees are awarded in BIOLOGICAL SCIENCE (biology/biological science), BUSINESS (accounting and business administration and management), COMMUNICATIONS AND THE ARTS (art, dramatic arts, English, French, music, and Spanish), COMPUTER AND PHYSICAL SCIENCE (chemistry and mathematics), EDUCATION (art, athletic training, drama, early childhood, elementary, English, foreign languages, mathematics, middle school, music, physical, science, secondary, social studies, and special), HEALTH PROFESSIONS (exercise science), SOCIAL SCIENCE (history, political science/government, psychology, religion, and sociology). Education and business are the strongest academically and have the largest enrollments.

Required: To graduate, students must complete 124 credit hours, including 30 to 48 in the major. They must take courses in social science,

fine arts, lab science, English and literature, religion, history, phys ed, math, and foreign language. They must also take at least 1 course designated as global awareness, and must demonstrate competency in writing, oral communication, and computing.

Special: The college offers cross-registration with members of the Greater Greensboro Consortium and the Piedmont Independent College Association, accelerated degree programs and internships in all majors, B.A.-B.S. degrees, work-study programs, study abroad, dual and student-designed majors, pass/fail options, and credit for life, military, and work experience. Greensboro's Ethics Across the Curriculum program exposes students to ethical issues in a range of disciplines to promote the study and living of ethical principles at the college. There are 12 national honor societies, a freshman honors program, and honors programs in all departments.

Faculty/Classroom: 51% of faculty are male; 49%, female. All teach undergraduates, 50% do research, and 50% do both. The average class size in an introductory lecture is 21; in a laboratory, 16; and in a regular course, 14.

Admissions: 74% of the 2003-2004 applicants were accepted. The SAT I scores for the 2003-2004 freshman class were: Verbal--57% below 500, 33% between 500 and 599, 8% between 600 and 700, and 2% above 700; Math--55% below 500, 36% between 500 and 599, and 9% between 600 and 700. The ACT scores were 64% below 21, 12% between 21 and 23, 16% between 24 and 26, 4% between 27 and 28, and 4% above 28. 10% of the current freshmen were in the top fifth of their class; 38% were in the top two fifths.

Requirements: The SAT I or ACT is required. In addition, applicants must be graduates of an accredited secondary school or have a GED certificate. An essay is required and an interview is recommended. Selected majors must audition or present a portfolio. AP and CLEP credits are accepted. Important factors in the admissions decision are advanced placement or honor courses, leadership record, and evidence of special talent.

Procedure: Freshmen are admitted to all sessions. Entrance exams should be taken in the spring of the junior year. There are early decision, early admissions, and deferred admissions plans. Early decision applications should be filed by December 15; regular applications, by open for fall entry, along with a $35 fee. Notification of early decision is sent January 31; regular decision, on a rolling basis. Applications are accepted on-line through *www.applyweb.com*.

Transfer: 82 transfer students enrolled in a recent year. Official transcripts from any college attended are required. Standardized test scores and high school records are required of applicants with fewer than 30 semester hours. An essay is required, and an interview is recommended. 31 of 124 credits required for the bachelor's degree must be completed at Greensboro College.

Visiting: There are regularly scheduled orientations for prospective students, including an interview, a campus tour, and meetings with faculty and students. There are guides for informal visits and visitors may sit in on classes and stay overnight. To schedule a visit, contact the Admissions Office.

Financial Aid: In 2003-2004, 64% of all full-time freshmen and 80% of continuing full-time students received some form of financial aid. 58% of full-time freshmen and 67% of continuing full-time students received need-based aid. The average freshman award was $15,555. Need-based scholarships or need-based grants averaged $4240; and need-based self-help aid (loans and jobs) averaged $6958. 22% of undergraduates work part time. Average annual earnings from campus work are $700. The average financial indebtedness of the 2003 graduate was $11,802. Greensboro College is a member of CSS. The FAFSA, the state aid form, and the college's own financial statement are required. The priority date for freshman financial aid applications for fall entry is April 15. The deadline for filing freshman financial aid applications for fall entry is rolling.

International Students: There are 53 international students enrolled. They must score 550 on the written TOEFL or 213 on the electronic version.

Computers: There are 95 PCs located in classrooms, computer labs, residence halls, the library, and the student center. Students have access to e-mail, the Internet and World Wide Web, and on-line course support; the campuswide network may be accessed from residence halls and off campus. Students have file sharing space on the server and can have a home page. All students may access the system 24 hours a day. There are no time limits and no fees. It is strongly recommended that all students have a personal computer, preferably one that is networkable.

Graduates: From July 1, 2002 to June 30, 2003, 170 bachelor's degrees were awarded. The most popular majors were business (26%), visual and performing arts (14%), and education (11%). In an average class, 1% graduate in 3 years or less, 30% graduate in 4 years or less, 44% graduate in 5 years or less, and 46% graduate in 6 years or less. 50 companies recruited on campus in 2002-2003. Of the 2002 graduating class, 9% were enrolled in graduate school within 6 months of graduation and 85% were employed.

Admissions Contact: Tim Jackson, Director of Admissions. A video is available. E-mail: *admissions@gborocollege.edu*
Web: *http://www.gborocollege.edu*

GUILFORD COLLEGE
Greensboro, NC 27410

D-2

(336) 316-2100
(800) 992-7759; Fax: (336) 316-2954

Full-time: 711 men, 1023 women	**Faculty:** 92; IIB, --$
Part-time: 103 men, 264 women	**Ph.Ds:** 73%
Graduate: none	**Student/Faculty:** 19 to 1
Year: semesters, summer session	**Tuition:** $19,020
Application Deadline: February 15	**Room & Board:** $5940
Freshman Class: 1647 applied, 1137 accepted, 298 enrolled	
SAT I Verbal/Math: 580/560	**ACT:** 24 **VERY COMPETITIVE**

Guilford College, founded in 1837 by the Religious Society of Friends (Quakers), is a private liberal arts and sciences institution. In addition to regional accreditation, Guilford College has baccalaureate program accreditation with NCATE. The library contains 223,674 volumes, 20,670 microform items, and 9805 audio/video tapes/CDs, and subscribes to 812 periodicals. Computerized library services include the card catalog, interlibrary loans, database searching, and Internet access. Special learning facilities include a learning resource center, art gallery, radio station, an observatory, and a multimedia learning center for cultures and languages. The 340-acre campus is in a suburban area in northwest Greensboro. Including any residence halls, there are 31 buildings.

Student Life: 66% of undergraduates are from North Carolina. Students are from 42 states and 21 foreign countries. 68% are from public schools. 70% are white; 19% African American. 43% are Protestant; 42% claim no religious affiliation. The average age of freshmen is 19; all undergraduates, 22. 29% do not continue beyond their first year; 71% remain to graduate.

Housing: 928 students can be accommodated in college housing, which includes single-sex and coed dorms and on-campus apartments. In addition, there are special-interest houses and alternative houses with themes and community service project requirements. On-campus housing is guaranteed for all 4 years. 73% of students live on campus; of those, 80% remain on campus on weekends. All students may keep cars.

Activities: There are no fraternities or sororities. There are 43 groups on campus, including art, bowling, cheerleading, chess, choir, chorale, chorus, computers, dance, debate, drama, ethnic, film, gay, honors, international, jazz band, literary magazine, musical theater, newspaper, pep band, photography, political, professional, radio and TV, religious, rugby, social, social service, student government, ultimate Frisbee, yachting, and yearbook. Popular campus events include Serendipity Spring Festival, Holiday Choir Concert, and International Dinner and Dance.

Sports: There are 8 intercollegiate sports for men and 8 for women, and 3 intramural sports for men and 3 for women. Facilities include a 3500-seat football/track stadium, a 2500-seat gym, a field house, baseball and softball fields, a swimming pool, playing fields, courts for basketball, tennis, racquetball, badminton, and volleyball, and a weight room.

Disabled Students: 95% of the campus is accessible. Wheelchair ramps, elevators, special parking, specially equipped rest rooms, special class scheduling, lowered drinking fountains, lowered telephones, and an ATM machine are available.

Services: Counseling and information services are available, as is tutoring in every subject. There is a reader service for the blind, and remedial math, reading, and writing. There is faculty tutoring for skills development and student tutoring for course-specific help. Also available are nonremedial writing help, assistance with organizational/time-management skills, and services for students with learning disabilities. Remedial assistance is individually targeted and developmental with a focus on regular assignments.

Campus Safety and Security: Measures include 24-hour foot and vehicle patrol, security escort services, informal discussions, and pamphlets/posters/films. There are emergency telephones, lighted pathways/sidewalks, and a whistle program.

Programs of Study: Guilford College confers A.B., B.S., and B.F.A. degrees. Bachelor's degrees are awarded in AGRICULTURE (environmental studies), BIOLOGICAL SCIENCE (biology/biological science and life science), BUSINESS (accounting, business administration and management, and sports management), COMMUNICATIONS AND THE ARTS (art, dramatic arts, English, French, German, music, and Spanish), COMPUTER AND PHYSICAL SCIENCE (chemistry, earth science, geology, information sciences and systems, mathematics, and physics), EDUCATION (athletic training and education), ENGINEERING AND ENVIRONMENTAL DESIGN (computer technology), HEALTH PROFESSIONS (exercise science and health science), SOCIAL SCIENCE (African American studies, anthropology, community services, criminal justice, economics, forensic studies, German area studies, history, international studies, liberal arts/general studies, peace studies, philosophy, political science/government, psychology, religion, sociology, and women's studies). Psychology, natural sciences, and English are the strongest academically. Business management, psychology, and forensic biology are the largest.

Required: Students must fulfill requirements in fine arts, English, humanities, sciences, social sciences, and foreign language. 128 semester hours and a 2.0 GPA are required. They must take a first-year experience and an interdisciplinary capstone course, and courses in historical perspectives, intercultural studies, social justice and environmental responsibility, diversity, business and policy studies, and quantitative literacy.

Special: There are 3-2 degree programs available in forestry and environmental studies with Duke University, and in physician assistant training with Bowman Gray School of Medicine at Wake Forest University. Guilford also offers many internships, a Washington semester, work-study programs, accelerated degree programs in business management, computer information systems, psychology, and biology, dual majors, student-designed majors, study abroad in 7 countries, B.A.-B.S. degrees, and cross-registration with members of the Greater Greensboro Consortium (8 colleges/universities). There are 2 national honor societies and a freshman honors program.

Faculty/Classroom: 52% of faculty are male; 48%, female. All both teach and do research. The average class size in an introductory lecture is 23; in a laboratory, 19; and in a regular course, 20.

Admissions: 69% of the 2003-2004 applicants were accepted. The SAT I scores for the 2003-2004 freshman class were: Verbal--19% below 500, 37% between 500 and 599, 32% between 600 and 700, and 13% above 700; Math--21% below 500, 44% between 500 and 599, 30% between 600 and 700, and 5% above 700. The ACT scores were 21% below 21, 22% between 21 and 23, 33% between 24 and 26, 9% between 27 and 28, and 15% above 28. 28% of the current freshmen were in the top fifth of their class; 64% were in the top two fifths. There were 2 National Merit semifinalists. 5 freshmen graduated first in their class.

Requirements: The SAT I or ACT is required, with a minimum SAT I composite score of 1000 or ACT score of 22 recommended. Applicants should have completed 20 Carnegie units, including 4 in English, 2 each in foreign language and science, and 1 each in history and social studies. The GED is accepted. An essay is required and an interview is recommended. A GPA of 2.0 is required. AP and CLEP credits are accepted. Important factors in the admissions decision are advanced placement or honor courses, leadership record, and evidence of special talent.

Procedure: Freshmen are admitted fall and spring. Entrance exams should be taken in spring of the junior year or fall of the senior year. There are early admissions and deferred admissions plans. Early action applications should be filed by January 15; regular applications, by February 15 for fall entry and December 1 for spring entry, along with a $25 fee. Notification of early action is sent February 15; regular decision, April 1. 38 early decision candidates were accepted for the 2003-2004 class. 7 applicants were on the 2003 waiting list; 1 was admitted. Applications are accepted on-line through *www.cfnc.org* and the school's web site.

Transfer: 344 transfer students enrolled in 2002-2003. Applicants must have a minimum GPA of 2.5 in at least 12 credit hours, submit either SAT I or ACT scores, and provide a letter from the academic adviser or dean of the previous school. An interview is recommended. 32 credits of 128 required for the bachelor's degree must be completed at Guilford College.

Visiting: There are regularly scheduled orientations for prospective students, including forums, a campus tour, and presentations by faculty, administrators, and students. There are guides for informal visits and visitors may sit in on classes. To schedule a visit, contact the Admission Office at *admission@guilford.edu*.

Financial Aid: In 2003-2004, 98% of all full-time freshmen and 92% of continuing full-time students received some form of financial aid. 62% of full-time freshmen and 56% of continuing full-time students received need-based aid. The average freshman award was $15,950. Need-based scholarships or need-based grants averaged $3172 ($18,700 maximum); need-based self-help aid (loans and jobs) averaged $4000 ($8425 maximum); and non-need-based awards and non-need-based scholarships averaged $3066 ($18,700 maximum). 34% of undergraduates work part time. Average annual earnings from campus work are $765. The average financial indebtedness of the 2003 graduate was $18,500. Guilford College is a member of CSS. The FAFSA is required. The deadline for filing freshman financial aid applications for fall entry is March 1.

International Students: There are 34 international students enrolled. The school actively recruits these students. They must score 550 on the written TOEFL or 213 on the electronic version.

Computers: There are 291 terminals and PCs in the central labs, classroom buildings, and library with access from other buildings through the campus network. All students have e-mail and Internet access, and all residence hall rooms have network connections. All students may access the system 24 hours a day. There are no time limits and no fees.

Graduates: From July 1, 2002 to June 30, 2003, 253 bachelor's degrees were awarded. The most popular majors were business management (13%), English (9%), and psychology (9%). In an average class, 51% graduate in 4 years or less, 55% graduate in 5 years or less, and 57% graduate in 6 years or less. 85 companies recruited on campus in 2002-2003. Of the 2002 graduating class, 17% were enrolled in graduate school within 6 months of graduation and 83% were employed.

Admissions Contact: Randy Doss, Vice President of Enrollment and Marketing. E-mail: *admission@guilford.edu* Web: *www.guilford.edu*

HIGH POINT UNIVERSITY
High Point, NC 27262-3598

D-2

(336) 841-9216
(800) 345-6993; Fax: (336) 888-6382

Full-time: 936 men, 1509 women	**Faculty:** 119; IIB, av$
Part-time: 95 men, 117 women	**Ph.D.s:** 73%
Graduate: 86 men, 148 women	**Student/Faculty:** 21 to 1
Year: semesters, summer session	**Tuition:** $15,700
Application Deadline: August 15	**Room & Board:** $6780
Freshman Class: 1709 applied, 1491 accepted, 550 enrolled	
SAT I Verbal/Math: 510/513	**COMPETITIVE**

High Point University, founded in 1924, is a private institution affiliated with the United Methodist Church. The university offers undergraduate and graduate programs in the arts, science, business, and education, both on its main campus and on its Winston-Salem campus, which accommodates evening students. In addition to regional accreditation, High Point has baccalaureate program accreditation with CAAHEP and NCATE. The library contains 285,000 volumes, 90,000 microform items, 17,000 audio/video tapes/CDs, and 28,967 e-books, and subscribes to 1500 periodicals. Computerized library services include the card catalog, interlibrary loans, and database searching. Special learning facilities include a learning resource center, art gallery, radio station, and TV studio. The 80-acre campus is in a suburban area 15 miles southeast of Winston-Salem and 12 miles southwest of Greensboro. Including any residence halls, there are 26 buildings.

Student Life: 55% of undergraduates are from out of state, mostly the Middle Atlantic. Students are from 36 states and 52 foreign countries. 88% are from public schools. 69% are white; 21% African American. 76% are Protestant; 15% Catholic; 8% claim no religious affiliation. The average age of freshmen is 18; all undergraduates, 20. 24% do not continue beyond their first year.

Housing: 1044 students can be accommodated in college housing, which includes single-sex and coed dorms, on-campus apartments, married-student housing, fraternity houses, and sorority houses. In addition, there are special-interest houses and wellness halls. On-campus housing is guaranteed for all 4 years. 75% of students live on campus; of those, 80% remain on campus on weekends. All students may keep cars.

Activities: 33% of men belong to 4 national fraternities; 33% of women belong to 1 local sorority and 4 national sororities. There are 65 groups on campus, including art, band, cheerleading, choir, chorale, chorus, computers, dance, debate, drama, environmental, ethnic, film, honors, international, literary magazine, musical theater, newspaper, outdoor, pep band, political, professional, radio and TV, religious, social, social service, student government, and yearbook. Popular campus events include Greek Week, Family Weekend, and Winter Festival.

Sports: There are 7 intercollegiate sports for men and 7 for women, and 8 intramural sports for men and 8 for women. Facilities include intramural fields, tennis courts, an intramural gym, a recreation center featuring a swimming pool, racquetball courts, an aerobics center, a weight room, and a 2500-seat arena.

Disabled Students: 90% of the campus is accessible. Wheelchair ramps, elevators, special parking, specially equipped rest rooms, special class scheduling, and lowered drinking fountains are available.

Services: Counseling and information services are available, as is tutoring in every subject. There is remedial math, reading, and writing.

Campus Safety and Security: Measures include 24-hour foot and vehicle patrol, self-defense education, security escort services, and informal discussions. There are pamphlets/posters/films, emergency telephones, lighted pathways/sidewalks, 24-hour secured residence halls, and student bike patrols.

Programs of Study: High Point confers B.A. and B.S. degrees. Master's degrees are also awarded. Bachelor's degrees are awarded in AGRICULTURE (forestry and related sciences), BIOLOGICAL SCIENCE (biology/biological science), BUSINESS (accounting, business administration and management, international business management, marketing/retailing/merchandising, recreation and leisure services, and sports management), COMMUNICATIONS AND THE ARTS (art, dramatic arts, English, fine arts, French, modern language, and Spanish), COMPUTER AND PHYSICAL SCIENCE (chemistry, computer science, information sciences and systems, and mathematics), EDUCATION (art, athletic training, elementary, middle school, physical, secondary, and special), ENGINEERING AND ENVIRONMENTAL DESIGN (interior design), HEALTH PROFESSIONS (exercise science, medical laboratory technology, and sports medicine), SOCIAL SCIENCE (American studies, criminal justice, history, home furnishings and equipment management/production/services, human services, industrial and organizational psychology, international studies, philosophy, physical fitness/movement, political science/government, psychology, religion, and sociology). Business administration, exercise science, and education are the largest.

Required: To graduate, students must complete 124 credit hours, including up to 60 in the major, with a minimum GPA of 2.0. The core curriculum consists of 2 courses each in English, history, social science, phys ed, and a modern foreign language, as well as 1 course each in math, lab science, religion, fine arts, ethics, global studies, and senior seminar.

Special: There is cross-registration with the University of North Carolina at Greensboro, North Carolina Agricultural and Technical State University, and Greensboro, Elon, Guilford, and Bennett Colleges. High Point also offers co-op programs, study abroad in 7 countries, the Student Career Internship Program, a dual major in chemistry and business, accelerated degree programs, unique programs in home furnishings marketing/management studies, work-study programs, student-designed majors, and 3-2 forestry and environmental management programs with Duke University. There are 2 national honor societies, a freshman honors program, and 2 departmental honors programs.

Faculty/Classroom: 60% of faculty are male; 40%, female. All teach undergraduates. No introductory courses are taught by graduate students. The average class size in an introductory lecture is 25; in a laboratory, 20; and in a regular course, 16.

Admissions: 87% of the 2003-2004 applicants were accepted. The SAT I scores for the 2003-2004 freshman class were: Verbal--44% below 500, 40% between 500 and 599, 14% between 600 and 700, and 2% above 700; Math--41% below 500, 44% between 500 and 599, 13% between 600 and 700, and 2% above 700. 28% of the current freshmen were in the top fifth of their class; 54% were in the top two fifths.

Requirements: The SAT I or ACT is required; the SAT I is preferred. Applicants should be graduates of an accredited secondary school or have a GED certificate. They should have completed 14 academic units, including 4 in English, 3 in math, 2 each in science, social studies, and history, and 1 elective. A GPA of 2.0 is required. AP and CLEP credits are accepted. Important factors in the admissions decision are advanced placement or honor courses and evidence of special talent.

Procedure: Freshmen are admitted to all sessions. Entrance exams should be taken prior to high school graduation. There are early admissions and deferred admissions plans. Applications should be filed by August 15 for fall entry, along with a $25 fee. Notification is sent on a rolling basis. Applications are accepted on computer disk and on-line through the university web site.

Transfer: 272 transfer students enrolled in 2002-2003. Applicants must submit official transcripts from colleges and high schools previously attended, as well as SAT I or ACT scores, if available. Generally, a minimum GPA of 2.0 is required. 31 of 124 credits required for the bachelor's degree must be completed at High Point.

Visiting: There are regularly scheduled orientations for prospective students, which are held at the beginning of each term. There are guides for informal visits and visitors may sit in on classes. To schedule a visit, contact the Admissions Office.

Financial Aid: In 2003-2004, 69% of all full-time freshmen and 78% of continuing full-time students received some form of financial aid. At least 59% of full-time freshmen and at least 30% of continuing full-time students received need-based aid. The average freshman award was $11,400. Need-based scholarships or need-based grants averaged $5000; need-based self-help aid (loans and jobs) averaged $4125; institutional non-need-based athletic scholarships averaged $10,000; and other institutional non-need-based awards and non-need-based scholarships averaged $5000. 52% of undergraduates work part time. Average annual earnings from campus work are $1500. The average financial indebtedness of the 2003 graduate was $15,000. High Point is a member of CSS. The FAFSA and the state aid form are required. The priority date for freshman financial aid applications for fall entry is March 1.

International Students: There are 119 international students enrolled. They must score 500 on the written TOEFL or take the MELAB, the Comprehensive English Language Test, or the college's own test.

Computers: The mainframe is an Enterprise 450 mini computer with 13 Intel-based servers. There are 7 computer labs on campus with more than 150 PCs. Student rooms are linked to the Internet. All students may access the system up to 80 hours per week. There are no time limits. The fee is $100. It is strongly recommended that all students have a personal computer.

Graduates: From July 1, 2002 to June 30, 2003, 601 bachelor's degrees were awarded. The most popular majors were business/marketing (42%), computer and information sciences (11%), and education (9%).

Admissions Contact: James L. Schlimmer, Dean of Enrollment Management. E-mail: *admiss@highpoint.edu* Web: *www.highpoint.edu*

JOHNSON C. SMITH UNIVERSITY
Charlotte, NC 28216

C-3
(704) 378-1010
(800) 782-7303; Fax: (704) 378-1242

Full-time: 593 men, 806 women	**Faculty:** 85
Part-time: 30 men, 45 women	**Ph.D.s:** n/av
Graduate: none	**Student/Faculty:** 16 to 1
Year: semesters, summer session	**Tuition:** $13,062
Application Deadline: open	**Room & Board:** $5046
Freshman Class: 3171 applied, 2306 accepted, 472 enrolled	
SAT I Verbal/Math: 493/481	**ACT:** 18 **COMPETITIVE**

Johnson C. Smith University, founded in 1867, is a progressive historically black private institution offering a liberal arts education and affiliated with the Presbyterian Church (U.S.A.). There are 2 undergraduate schools. In addition to regional accreditation, JCSU has baccalaureate program accreditation with ACBSP, CSWE, and NCATE. The library contains 168,621 microform items and 3000 audio/video tapes/CDs, and subscribes to 700 periodicals. Computerized library services include the card catalog, interlibrary loans, database searching, and Internet access. Special learning facilities include a learning resource center and radio station. The 105-acre campus is in an urban area in Charlotte. Including any residence halls, there are 46 buildings.

Student Life: 70% of undergraduates are from out of state, mostly the Northeast. Students are from 35 states, 5 foreign countries, and Canada. 94% are from public schools. 99% are African American. Most are Protestant. The average age of freshmen is 18; all undergraduates, 22. 28% do not continue beyond their first year; 6% remain to graduate.

Housing: 1151 students can be accommodated in college housing, which includes single-sex and coed dorms. In addition, there are honors houses. On-campus housing is available on a first-come, first-served basis. 70% of students live on campus; of those, 76% remain on campus on weekends. Alcohol is not permitted. Upperclassmen may keep cars.

Activities: 7% of men belong to 4 local and 4 national fraternities; 14% of women belong to 4 local and 4 national sororities. There are 46 groups on campus, including art, band, cheerleading, chess, choir, chorale, chorus, computers, dance, debate, drama, ethnic, film, gay, honors, international, jazz band, literary magazine, marching band, newspaper, orchestra, pep band, photography, political, professional, radio and TV, religious, social, social service, student government, symphony, and yearbook. Popular campus events include Founders Day, West Fest, and Family Day.

Sports: There are 6 intercollegiate sports for men and 7 for women, and 5 intramural sports for men and 5 for women. Facilities include a 3200-seat gym, a pool, tennis and basketball courts, a weight room, a training room, an Olympic-size track, a football field, and an on-campus stadium seating 4500.

Disabled Students: 5% of the campus is accessible. Wheelchair ramps, elevators, special parking, specially equipped rest rooms, special class scheduling, and lowered drinking fountains are available.

Services: Counseling and information services are available, as is tutoring in every subject.

Campus Safety and Security: Measures include 24-hour foot and vehicle patrol, self-defense education, security escort services, and informal discussions. There are pamphlets/posters/films, emergency telephones, lighted pathways/sidewalks, and push-button emergency stations.

Programs of Study: JCSU confers B.A., B.S., and B.S.W degrees. Bachelor's degrees are awarded in BIOLOGICAL SCIENCE (biology/biological science), BUSINESS (business administration and management and business economics), COMMUNICATIONS AND THE ARTS (communications, English, music business management, and Spanish), COMPUTER AND PHYSICAL SCIENCE (applied mathematics, chemistry, computer science, mathematics, physics, and science), EDUCATION (elementary, English, health, mathematics, middle school, physical, secondary, and social studies), ENGINEERING AND ENVIRONMENTAL DESIGN (computer engineering, engineering, and preengineering), HEALTH PROFESSIONS (nursing, pharmacy, predentistry, and premedicine), SOCIAL SCIENCE (criminal justice, economics, history, liberal arts/general studies, political science/government, prelaw, psychology, religious music, social science, social work, and sociology). Business administration is the strongest academically. Business and computer science/information systems are the largest.

Required: To graduate, students must complete 122 credit hours, including 30 to 59 in the major, with a minimum GPA of 2.0. Distribution requirements include 47 hours of courses in English, composition, the humanities, social science, health and phys ed, math, computer science, activities, and natural science. Students must take a competency exam in the sophomore year, write a senior paper, and participate in community service and Lyceum, and take Learning Across the Curriculum.

Special: JCSU offers cooperative programs in all majors, student-designed majors, 3-2 engineering degrees with UNCC and Florida A & M University, cross-registration with the Charlotte Area Educational Consortium, dual majors in engineering, nursing, and pharmacy, internships with local businesses, work-study programs, study abroad in 5 countries, and a B.A.-B.S. degree in all majors. Nondegree study in continuing ed-

ucation and pass/fail options are available. There are 9 national honor societies, a freshman honors program, and 1 departmental honors program.

Faculty/Classroom: 58% of faculty are male; 42%, female. All teach undergraduates, 2% do research, and 2% do both. The average class size in an introductory lecture is 30; in a laboratory, 15; and in a regular course, 25.

Admissions: 73% of the 2003-2004 applicants were accepted. The SAT I scores for the 2003-2004 freshman class were: Verbal--89% below 500, 12% between 500 and 599, and 1% between 600 and 700; Math--87% below 500, 13% between 500 and 599, and 1% between 600 and 700. 39% of the current freshmen were in the top fifth of their class; 60% were in the top two fifths. 47 freshmen graduated first in their class.

Requirements: The SAT I or ACT is required. In addition, a minimum SAT I composite score of 830 or ACT score of 17 is recommended. Applicants should have completed 16 Carnegie units, including 4 in English, 3 each in math, 2 in social science, 2 in science, and 5 in electives. The GED is accepted. An essay and an interview are suggested. JCSU requires applicants to be in the upper 50% of their class. A GPA of 2.2 is required. AP credits are accepted. Important factors in the admissions decision are advanced placement or honor courses, recommendations by school officials, and extracurricular activities record.

Procedure: Freshmen are admitted fall and spring. Entrance exams should be taken prior to application. There are early decision, early admissions, deferred admissions, and rolling admissions plans. Application deadlines are open. The application fee is $25. 327 early decision candidates were accepted for the 2003-2004 class.

Transfer: 52 transfer students enrolled in 2002-2003. Applicants need a minimum GPA of 2.0 in 12 semester hours of transferable course work. 32 of 122 credits required for the bachelor's degree must be completed at JCSU.

Visiting: There are regularly scheduled orientations for prospective students, including a campus tour, a classroom visit, and a financial aid meeting. There are guides for informal visits and visitors may sit in on classes and stay overnight. To schedule a visit, contact the Director of Admissions.

Financial Aid: In 2003-2004, 91% of all full-time freshmen and 86% of continuing full-time students received some form of financial aid. 92% of full-time freshmen and 86% of continuing full-time students received need-based aid. The average freshman award was $7500. 60% of undergraduates work part time. Average annual earnings from campus work are $1500. The average financial indebtedness of the 2003 graduate was $21,000. JCSU is a member of CSS. The FAFSA and the state aid form are required. The priority date for freshman financial aid applications for fall entry is April.

International Students: There are 7 international students enrolled. The school actively recruits these students. They must score 540 on the written TOEFL and also take the SAT I or the ACT, scoring 750 on the SAT I.

Computers: The mainframe is an IBM AS/400. More than 400 PCs and printers are located throughout the campus, including some residence halls. Internet access, campus file servers, and e-mail are available. Upon payment of tuition and fees, every student receives an IBM ThinkPad. All students may access the system any time. There are no time limits and no fees.

Graduates: From July 1, 2002 to June 30, 2003, 244 bachelor's degrees were awarded. The most popular majors were business administration (20%), computer science (11%), and communication arts (9%). In an average class, 37% graduate in 4 years or less, 41% graduate in 5 years or less, and 46% graduate in 6 years or less. 117 companies recruited on campus in 2002-2003. Of the 2002 graduating class, 23% were enrolled in graduate school within 6 months of graduation and 57% were employed.

Admissions Contact: Jeffrey A. Smith, Director of Admissions. A video is available. E-mail: *jasmith@jscu.edu* Web: *http://www.jcsu.edu/*

LEES-MCRAE COLLEGE
Banner Elk, NC 28604

B-2
(828) 898-8829
(800) 280-4562; Fax: (828) 898-8707

Full-time: 340 men, 425 women	**Faculty:** 54; III, --$
Part-time: 5 men, 30 women	**Ph.D.s:** 74%
Graduate: none	**Student/Faculty:** 14 to 1
Year: semesters, summer session	**Tuition:** $12,445
Application Deadline: open	**Room & Board:** $4665
Freshman Class: n/av	
SAT I or ACT: required	**LESS COMPETITIVE**

Lees-McRae College, founded in 1900, is an independent nonprofit liberal arts institution affiliated with the Presbyterian Church (U.S.A.). There is 1 undergraduate school. Figures in the above capsule and in this profile are approximate. In addition to regional accreditation, Lees-McRae has baccalaureate program accreditation with NCATE. The library contains 96,628 volumes, 256,447 microform items, and 2326 audio/video tapes/CDs, and subscribes to 343 periodicals. Computerized library services include the card catalog, interlibrary loans, and database searching. Special learning facilities include a learning resource center, art gallery, and an academic advancement center. The 400-acre campus is in a rural area 17 miles south of Boone and 100 miles northwest of Charlotte. Including any residence halls, there are 33 buildings.

Student Life: 61% of undergraduates are from North Carolina. Students are from 30 states, 16 foreign countries, and Canada. 86% are white. 65% are Protestant; 21% claim no religious affiliation; 10% Catholic. The average age of freshmen is 18; all undergraduates, 23. 35% do not continue beyond their first year; 37% remain to graduate.

Housing: 488 students can be accommodated in college housing, which includes single-sex and coed dorms. There is also substance-free housing. On-campus housing is guaranteed for all 4 years. 53% of students live on campus; of those, 30% remain on campus on weekends. Alcohol is not permitted. All students may keep cars.

Activities: There are no fraternities or sororities. There are 20 groups on campus, including cheerleading, choir, chorus, dance, drama, honors, international, musical theater, newspaper, pep band, professional, religious, social, social service, student government, and yearbook. Popular campus events include Staley Distinguished Lectureship, Spring Fling, and Mountain Day.

Sports: There are 8 intercollegiate sports for men and 7 for women, and 11 intramural sports for men and 11 for women. Facilities include a main gym that seats 2000 with basketball/volleyball courts, a match field for soccer/lacrosse, 4 practice fields, a softball field with batting cages, 2 indoor tennis courts, 6 outdoor tennis courts, a secondary gym for intramurals, an indoor Olympic size pool, a fitness center, a weight room facility, outdoor basketball court, and a beach volleyball court.

Disabled Students: 50% of the campus is accessible. Wheelchair ramps, special parking, and specially equipped rest rooms are available.

Services: Counseling and information services are available, as is tutoring in every subject. There is remedial math, reading, and writing.

Campus Safety and Security: Measures include 24-hour foot and vehicle patrol, security escort services, informal discussions, and pamphlets/posters/films. There are emergency telephones and lighted pathways/sidewalks.

Programs of Study: Lees-McRae confers B.A. and B.S. degrees. Bachelor's degrees are awarded in BIOLOGICAL SCIENCE (biology/biological science), BUSINESS (business administration and management), COMMUNICATIONS AND THE ARTS (arts administration/management, communications, dramatic arts, English, and musical theater), COMPUTER AND PHYSICAL SCIENCE (mathematics), EDUCATION (elementary and physical), HEALTH PROFESSIONS (sports medicine), SOCIAL SCIENCE (criminal justice, history, humanities, interdisciplinary studies, international studies, psychology, religion, and sociology). Biology, performing arts, and elementary education are the strongest academically. Business, biology, and performing arts are the largest.

Required: To graduate, students must complete at least 124 credit hours, including 57 in the major, with a GPA of 2.0 overall. Core requirements include courses in English, religion, history, natural sciences, social and behavioral sciences, math, computer science, phys ed, and senior seminar.

Special: The college has work-study programs, student-designed majors in the interdisciplinary studies program, and study-abroad opportunities in Ireland and Great Britain. Cross-registration is available with the Marine Science Education Consortium. There is 1 national honor society, a freshman honors program, and 1 departmental honors program.

Faculty/Classroom: 57% of faculty are male; 43%, female. All teach undergraduates. The average class size in an introductory lecture is 21; in a laboratory, 10; and in a regular course, 11.

Admissions: In a recent year, 1 freshman graduated first in the class.

Requirements: The SAT I or ACT is required. In addition, applicants must have completed 18 units of secondary-school academic courses, including 6 of academic electives, 4 of English, 3 of math, 2 of science (1 with lab work), and 1 each of social studies and history. AP and CLEP credits are accepted. Important factors in the admissions decision are recommendations by school officials, advanced placement or honor courses, and leadership record.

Procedure: Freshmen are admitted to all sessions. Entrance exams should be taken in the fall of the senior year. There is a deferred admissions plan and a rolling admissions plan. The fall 2003 application fee was $15. Application deadlines are open. Applications are accepted online at the school's web site.

Transfer: 124 transfer students enrolled in a recent year. Applicants must submit a college GPA of 2.0 and be in good standing at the previous or current institution. Students who have completed 24 semester hours or more must submit a dean's evaluation form; those with fewer than 24 must also submit high school transcripts and SAT I or ACT scores. 32 of 124 credits required for the bachelor's degree must be completed at Lees-McRae.

Visiting: There are regularly scheduled orientations for prospective students, there are 3 yearly open houses. There are guides for informal visits and visitors may sit in on classes and stay overnight. To schedule a visit, contact the Office of Admissions.

Financial Aid: In a recent, 99% of all full-time freshmen and 98% of continuing full-time students received some form of financial aid. 72% of full-time freshmen and 62% of continuing full-time students received need-based aid. The average freshman award was $12,920. 62% of undergraduates work part time. Average annual earnings from campus work are $1040. The average financial indebtedness of a recent graduate was $6414. Lees-McRae is a member of CSS. The FAFSA is required. Check with the school for the current deadlines.

International Students: In a recent year, there were 35 international students enrolled. The school actively recruits these students. They must score 500 on the written TOEFL and also take the SAT I or the ACT.

Computers: The mainframes are a Microsoft Windows NT server and an IBM/AS400. Students have access to 125 PCs on campus offering Internet, e-mail, word processing, spreadsheet, graphics, and programming languages applications. All students may access the system 24 hours a day. There are no time limits and no fees.

Graduates: In a recent year, 112 bachelor's degrees were awarded. The most popular majors were elementary education (23%), business administration (19%), and criminal justice (13%). In an average class, 24% graduate in 4 years or less, 31% graduate in 5 years or less, and 37% graduate in 6 years or less.

Admissions Contact: Bart Walker, Director of Admissions. A video is available. E-mail: *admissions@lmc.edu* Web: *www.lmc.edu*

LENOIR-RHYNE COLLEGE
C-2
Hickory, NC 28603
(828) 328-7300
(828) 328-7378; Fax: (828) 328-7378

Full-time: 415 men, 745 women	**Faculty:** 107; IIA, --$
Part-time: 55 men, 105 women	**Ph.D.s:** 73%
Graduate: 50 men, 95 women	**Student/Faculty:** 11 to 1
Year: semesters, summer session	**Tuition:** $14,090
Application Deadline: open	**Room & Board:** $5100
Freshman Class: n/av	
SAT I or ACT: required	**COMPETITIVE**

Lenoir-Rhyne College, founded in 1891, is a private institution affiliated with the Lutheran Church, offering liberal arts programs that focus on business, education, and allied health sciences. Figures in the above capsule and in this profile are approximate. In addition to regional accreditation, Lenoir-Rhyne has baccalaureate program accreditation with NCATE and NLN. The library contains 145,960 volumes, 462,878 microform items, and 40,379 audio/video tapes/CDs, and subscribes to 5376 periodicals. Computerized library services include the card catalog, interlibrary loans, and database searching. Special learning facilities include a learning resource center, radio station, TV station, and observatory. The 100-acre campus is in a suburban area 45 miles northwest of Charlotte. Including any residence halls, there are 30 buildings.

Student Life: 70% of undergraduates are from North Carolina. Students are from 29 states, 9 foreign countries, and Canada. 89% are from public schools. 87% are white. 68% are Protestant; 23% claim no religious affiliation; 9% Catholic. The average age of freshmen is 18; all undergraduates, 22. 23% do not continue beyond their first year; 63% remain to graduate.

Housing: 900 students can be accommodated in college housing, which includes single-sex and coed dorms, on-campus apartments, and fraternity houses. In addition, there is honors housing and hearing-impaired housing the first, second, and third years. On-campus housing is guaranteed for all 4 years and is available on a lottery system for upperclassmen. 65% of students live on campus; of those, 70% remain on campus on weekends. All students may keep cars.

Activities: 23% of men belong to 3 national fraternities; 27% of women belong to 4 national sororities. There are 50 groups on campus, including art, band, cheerleading, choir, chorus, computers, dance, debate, drama, ethnic, honors, international, jazz band, literary magazine, marching band, musical theater, newspaper, pep band, photography, political, professional, radio and TV, religious, social, social service, student government, and yearbook. Popular campus events include Spring Fling, Advent Candlelight Service, and Parents Weekend.

Sports: There are 6 intercollegiate sports for men and 6 for women, and 14 intramural sports for men and 14 for women. Facilities include an 8500-seat football stadium, a 3600-seat gym, practice fields, racquetball courts, weight rooms a sauna, a 25-meter swimming pool, 2 intramural fields, and baseball, softball, and soccer fields.

Disabled Students: All of the campus is accessible. Wheelchair ramps, elevators, special parking, specially equipped rest rooms, lowered drinking fountains, and specially equipped residence halls are available.

Services: Counseling and information services are available, as is tutoring in every subject. There is remedial math and writing and interpreters and note takers for hearing-impaired students.

Campus Safety and Security: Measures include 24-hour foot and vehicle patrol, self-defense education, security escort services, and informal discussions. There are pamphlets/posters/films, emergency telephones, and lighted pathways/sidewalks.

Programs of Study: Lenoir-Rhyne confers B.A., B.S., and B.Mus.Ed. degrees. Master's degrees are also awarded. Bachelor's degrees are awarded in BIOLOGICAL SCIENCE (biology/biological science), BUSINESS (accounting, business administration and management, and international business management), COMMUNICATIONS AND THE ARTS (applied music, classics, communications, dramatic arts, English, French, German, music, and Spanish), COMPUTER AND PHYSICAL SCIENCE (chemistry, computer science, mathematics, and physics), EDUCATION (art, business, early childhood, education of the deaf and hearing impaired, elementary, foreign languages, health, middle school, music, science, and secondary), HEALTH PROFESSIONS (medical laboratory technology, nursing, occupational therapy, physician's assistant, and premedicine), SOCIAL SCIENCE (American studies, economics, history, human services, philosophy, political science/government, prelaw, psychology, religious education, religious music, sociology, and theological studies). Business, education, and nursing are the largest.

Required: To graduate, students must complete 128 credit hours, including 56 to 57 in liberal arts courses, with a minimum GPA of 2.0. The total number of hours in a major varies by program.

Special: Lenoir-Rhyne offers cross-registration in design courses at area schools, study abroad in more than 25 countries, a Washington semester at American University and through the Lutheran College Washington Consortium, internships in most majors, dual majors, a general studies degree, work-study programs, 3-2 enginering degrees with North Carolina State, North Carolina Agricultural and Technical, and Clemson Universities and the University of North Carolina at Charlotte, pass/fail options, and auditing for most courses. In addition, the Broyhill institute for Business Leadership offers programs to promote undestanding of the business community, The college uses the Dartmouth method in foreign language and offers an honors program for outstanding students. There are 11 national honor societies, a freshman honors program, and 18 departmental honors programs.

Faculty/Classroom: 55% of faculty are male; 45%, female. All teach undergraduates. No introductory courses are taught by graduate students. The average class size in an introductory lecture is 28; in a laboratory, 20; and in a regular course, 20.

Admissions: In a recent year, 4 freshmen graduated first in their class.

Requirements: The SAT I or ACT is required. In addition, applicants need 16 academic credits and should have 4 units in English, 3 in math, 2 in foreign language, and 1 each in American history and a lab science. An interview is recommended for all students. Music majors must also audition. A GPA of 2.5 is required. AP and CLEP credits are accepted. Important factors in the admissions decision are advanced placement or honor courses, personality/intangible qualities, and leadership record.

Procedure: Freshmen are admitted to all sessions. Entrance exams should be taken in the spring of the junior year and thereafter. There are early admissions, deferred admissions, and rolling admissions plans. Application deadlines are open. The application fee is $25. Applications are accepted on-line at the college's web site.

Transfer: 108 transfer students enrolled in a recent year. Applicants with more than 30 semester hours need a 2.0 minimum GPA in general studies programs or a 2.5 minimum GPA in nursing or education programs. Those with fewer than 30 semester hours must meet freshman entrance criteria. 32 of 128 credits required for the bachelor's degree must be completed at Lenoir-Rhyne.

Visiting: There are regularly scheduled orientations for prospective students, including a meeting with an admissions counselor and a student-guided tour of the campus. There are guides for informal visits and visitors may sit in on classes and stay overnight. To schedule a visit, contact the Admissions Office.

Financial Aid: In a recent year, all full-time freshmen and 92% of continuing full-time students received some form of financial aid. 40% of full-time freshmen and 55% of continuing full-time students received need-based aid. The average freshman award was $18,663. 35% of undergraduates work part time. Average annual earnings from campus work are $1000. The average financial indebtedness of a recent graduate was $30,000. The FAFSA and the college's own financial statement are required. Check with the school for current deadlines.

International Students: In a recent year, there were 12 international students enrolled. The school actively recruits these students. They must score 500 on the written TOEFL.

Computers: There are 4 computer labs with 77 PCs and 17 Macs. All can be used to access e-mail, the Internet, and the World Wide Web. All students may access the system 24 hours per day via modem; computer lab hours are 8 A.M. to 11:30 P.M. There are no time limits and no fees.

Graduates: In a recent year, 275 bachelor's degrees were awarded. The most popular majors were elementary education (12%), psychology (9%), and business (9%). In an average class, 1% graduate in 3 years or less, 53% graduate in 4 years or less, 57% graduate in 5 years or less, and 63% graduate in 6 years or less. 100 companies recruited on campus in a recent year. Of a recent graduating class, 11% were enrolled in graduate school within 6 months of graduation and 96% were employed.

Admissions Contact: Chad A. Spencer, Assistant Director of Admissions. E-mail: admission@lrc.edu Web: http://www.lrc.edu

LIVINGSTONE COLLEGE
C-2
Salisbury, NC 28144   (800) 835-3435

Full-time: 472 men, 515 women	Faculty: 55;
Part-time: 11 men, 7 women	Ph.D.s: 50%
Graduate: none	Student/Faculty: 18 to 1
Year: semesters	Tuition: $12,298
Application Deadline: n/av	Room & Board: $5803

Freshman Class: 1792 applied, 802 accepted, 302 enrolled
SAT I Verbal/Math: 380/365   ACT: 14   **LESS COMPETITIVE**

Livingstone College, founded in 1879 and affiliated with the African Methodist Episcopal Zion Church, is a private institution offering programs in business, engineering, liberal arts, music, and professional and religious training. There are 4 undergraduate schools. In addition to regional accreditation, LC has baccalaureate program accreditation with CSWE. The library contains 80,000 volumes and 1000 microform items, and subscribes to 423 periodicals. Computerized library services include the card catalog, interlibrary loans, database searching, and Internet access. Special learning facilities include a learning resource center and natural history museum. The 272-acre campus is in a small town between Greensboro and Charlotte. Including any residence halls, there are 22 buildings.

Student Life: 54% of undergraduates are from North Carolina. Students are from 22 states and 7 foreign countries. 90% are from public schools. 96% are African American. The average age of freshmen is 18; all undergraduates, 19.

Housing: 700 students can be accommodated in college housing, which includes single-sex dorms and off-campus apartments. In addition, there are honors houses. On-campus housing is guaranteed for all 4 years. 88% of students live on campus; of those, 50% remain on campus on weekends. Alcohol is not permitted. All students may keep cars.

Activities: 40% of men belong to 4 national fraternities; 45% of women belong to 3 national sororities. There are 14 groups on campus, including band, cheerleading, choir, chorus, computers, drama, honors, jazz band, marching band, newspaper, pep band, religious, student government, and yearbook. Popular campus events include Open House.

Sports: There are 4 intercollegiate sports for men and 4 for women, and 5 intramural sports for men and 4 for women. Facilities include a gym and a 4000-seat stadium.

Disabled Students: Wheelchair ramps, special parking, and special class scheduling are available.

Services: Counseling and information services are available, as is tutoring in every subject. There is remedial reading and writing.

Campus Safety and Security: Measures include 24-hour foot and vehicle patrol, security escort services, pamphlets/posters/films, and lighted pathways/sidewalks.

Programs of Study: LC confers B.A., B.S., and B.S.W. degrees. Bachelor's degrees are awarded in BIOLOGICAL SCIENCE (biology/biological science), BUSINESS (accounting and business administration and management), COMMUNICATIONS AND THE ARTS (English and music), COMPUTER AND PHYSICAL SCIENCE (chemistry, computer science, and mathematics), EDUCATION (early childhood, elementary, music, science, and secondary), HEALTH PROFESSIONS (predentistry and premedicine), SOCIAL SCIENCE (history, political science/government, prelaw, psychology, social work, and sociology). Business administration is the largest.

Required: At least 125 semester hours with a minimum GPA of 2.0 are required for graduation. Required courses include freshman English and religion, 2 semesters each of foreign language and phys ed, 8 hours each of natural science, math, and social science, and 9 hours chosen from offerings in art, literature, music, and philosophy.

Special: Upperclassmen are eligible for a cooperative education program. Cross-registration for a dual engineering degree is available with North Carolina Agricultural and Technical State University. There are 2 national honor societies and a freshman honors program.

Faculty/Classroom: 48% of faculty are male; 52%, female. The average class size in an introductory lecture is 28 and in a regular course, 20.

Admissions: 45% of the 2003-2004 applicants were accepted.

Requirements: The SAT I or ACT is required. In addition, applicants should be high school graduates or have earned the GED. Secondary preparation should include 4 academic credits in English, 2 each in history, math, and music, and 1 each in social studies, science, and art. A GPA of 2.0 is required. AP and CLEP credits are accepted. Important factors in the admissions decision are evidence of special talent, leadership record, and extracurricular activities record.

Procedure: Freshmen are admitted fall and spring. Entrance exams should be taken by summer orientation. There is a rolling admissions plan. There is an early decision plan. The fall 2003 application fee was $25. Notification is sent on a rolling basis. A waiting list is an active part of the admissions procedure.

Transfer: 13 transfer students enrolled in 2002-2003. Transfers should have at least a 2.0 GPA in 30 hours of previous college work. Those with fewer hours must meet freshman requirements. 45 of a minimum of 125 credits required for the bachelor's degree must be completed at LC.

Visiting: There are regularly scheduled orientations for prospective students. There are guides for informal visits and visitors may sit in on classes and stay overnight. To schedule a visit, contact Anthony Brooks, Assistant Vice President for Enrollment Management and Admission at (800) 422-5430 or *abrooks@livingstone.edu.*

Financial Aid: In 2003-2004, 90% of all full-time students received some form of financial aid. 50% of undergraduates work part time. Average annual earnings from campus work are $1200. LC is a member of CSS. The FFS is required.

International Students: The school actively recruits these students. They must score 500 on the written TOEFL and also take the SAT I or the ACT.

Computers: The mainframe is an IBM 34. There are also PCs available. All students may access the system. There are no time limits and no fees.

Admissions Contact: Anthony Brooks, Assistant Vice President for Enrollment Management and Admissions.
E-mail: *abrooks@livingstone.edu* Web: *www.livingstone.edu*

MARS HILL COLLEGE
Mars Hill, NC 28754

B-2
(828) 689-1201
(800) 543-1514; Fax: (828) 689-1473

Full-time: 500 men, 605 women	**Faculty:** 80; IIB, --$
Part-time: 40 men, 105 women	**Ph.D.s:** 70%
Graduate: none	**Student/Faculty:** 13 to 1
Year: semesters, summer session	**Tuition:** $13,800
Application Deadline: open	**Room & Board:** $4800
Freshman Class: n/av	
SAT I or ACT: required	**LESS COMPETITIVE**

Mars Hill College, founded in 1856, is a private institution affiliated with the Baptist Church and offers undergraduate programs in the arts and sciences, business, education, and preprofessional studies. Figures in the above capsule and in this profile are approximate. In addition to regional accreditation, Mars Hill has baccalaureate program accreditation with CSWE, NASM, and NCATE. The library contains 98,150 volumes, 1050 microform items, and 6180 audio/video tapes/CDs, and subscribes to 650 periodicals. Computerized library services include the card catalog, interlibrary loans, and database searching. Special learning facilities include an art gallery, radio station, the Southern Appalachian Center of regional history and culture, and the Rural Life Museum. The 180-acre campus is in a rural area 18 miles north of Asheville. Including any residence halls, there are 47 buildings.

Student Life: 60% of undergraduates are from North Carolina. Students are from 19 states, 20 foreign countries, and Canada. 14% are African American. 81% are Protestant; 13% claim no religious affiliation; 7% Catholic. The average age of freshmen is 18; all undergraduates, 21. 20% do not continue beyond their first year; 49% remain to graduate.

Housing: College housing includes single-sex dorms, on-campus apartments, and married-student housing. In addition, there are honors houses. On-campus housing is guaranteed for all 4 years. 80% of students live on campus; of those, 33% remain on campus on weekends. Alcohol is not permitted. All students may keep cars.

Activities: 30% of men belong to 4 local and 2 national fraternities; 12% of women belong to 4 local and 1 national sorority. There are 80 groups on campus, including art, band, cheerleading, choir, chorale, chorus, dance, drama, ethnic, honors, international, jazz band, literary magazine, marching band, musical theater, newspaper, orchestra, photography, political, professional, radio and TV, religious, social, social service, student government, and yearbook. Popular campus events include Culturefest, Spring Fling, and the Bascom Lamar Lunsford Festival.

Sports: There are 7 intercollegiate sports for men and 6 for women, and 5 intramural sports for men and 5 for women. Facilities include a 5000-seat stadium, a 3500-seat gym, an indoor Olympic-size swimming pool, and a 10-acre complex that has a track, baseball diamond, soccer field, all-purpose playing field, and 6 tennis courts.

Disabled Students: 41% of the campus is accessible. Wheelchair ramps, elevators, special parking, and specially equipped rest rooms are available.

Services: Counseling and information services are available, as is tutoring in every subject. There is remedial math, reading, and writing.

Campus Safety and Security: Measures include 24-hour foot and vehicle patrol, self-defense education, security escort services, and informal discussions. There are pamphlets/posters/films, emergency telephones, and lighted pathways/sidewalks.

Programs of Study: Mars Hill confers B.A., B.S., B.F.A., B.M., and B.S.W. degrees. Bachelor's degrees are awarded in BIOLOGICAL SCIENCE (biology/biological science, botany, and zoology), BUSINESS (accounting, business administration and management, fashion merchandising, and recreation and leisure services), COMMUNICATIONS AND THE ARTS (art history and appreciation, communications, dramatic arts, English, music, music performance, musical theater, performing arts, and Spanish), COMPUTER AND PHYSICAL SCIENCE (chemistry,

computer science, and mathematics), EDUCATION (art, athletic training, drama, elementary, mathematics, middle school, music, physical, science, and social studies), HEALTH PROFESSIONS (allied health, physician's assistant, predentistry, premedicine, prepharmacy, and preveterinary science), SOCIAL SCIENCE (history, international studies, political science/government, prelaw, psychology, religion, social work, and sociology). Music, education, and science are the strongest academically. Education is the largest.

Required: To graduate, students must complete at least 128 semester hours with a minimum GPA of 2.0. Distribution requirements include courses in fine arts, literature, American culture, foreign culture, math, natural science, social/behavioral science, ethics, and phys ed.

Special: Mars Hill offers cooperative programs with the Bowman Gray School of Medicine at Wake Forest, internships, study abroad, B.A.-B.S. degrees, dual majors, student-designed majors, and credit for life experience. The Community Life program promotes student involvement in culture and community activities. There are 4 national honor societies and a freshman honors program.

Faculty/Classroom: 58% of faculty are male; 42%, female. All teach undergraduates. The average class size in an introductory lecture is 20; in a laboratory, 15; and in a regular course, 15.

Requirements: The SAT I or ACT is required. In addition, applicants need at least 18 academic credits, including 4 in English, 3 in math, and 2 each in history, science, and foreign language. The GED is accepted. A GPA of 2.0 is required. AP and CLEP credits are accepted. Important factors in the admissions decision are advanced placement or honor courses, leadership record, and extracurricular activities record.

Procedure: Freshmen are admitted to all sessions. There are early decision, early admissions, and rolling admissions plans. Application deadlines are open. The application fee is $25.

Transfer: Transfer applicants must be eligible to return to their previous college or have been out of school for at least 1 semester. They must have a minimum GPA of 2.0 for at least 30 semester credit hours. Remedial and developmental hours do not apply. 32 of 128 credits required for the bachelor's degree must be completed at Mars Hill.

Visiting: There are regularly scheduled orientations for prospective students, consisting of 2 days, during which a variety of special programs are offered. Individual students and their families may visit anytime throughout the year. There are guides for informal visits and visitors may sit in on classes and stay overnight. To schedule a visit, contact the Admissions Office.

Financial Aid: In a recent year, 96% of all full-time freshmen received some form of financial aid. 35% of undergraduates work part time. Average annual earnings from campus work are $1000. Mars Hill is a member of CSS. The FAFSA is required. Check with the school for current deadlines.

International Students: The school actively recruits these students. They must score 500 on the written TOEFL.

Computers: The mainframe is a Wang V565. There are also 90 PCs available, and 10 computer labs fully on-line with the Internet and e-mail. All students may access the system during library hours. Students may access the system for up to 2 hours at a time. There are no fees.

Admissions Contact: Office of Admissions.
E-mail: *admissions@mhc.edu* Web: *www.mhc.edu*

MEREDITH COLLEGE
Raleigh, NC 27607-5298

D-2
(919) 760-8581
(800) MEREDITH; Fax: (919) 760-2348

Full-time: 1564 women	**Faculty:** 137
Part-time: 15 men, 421 women	**Ph.D.s:** 85%
Graduate: 21 men, 131 women	**Student/Faculty:** 11 to 1
Year: semesters, summer session	**Tuition:** $18,065
Application Deadline: February 15	**Room & Board:** $5000
Freshman Class: 1026 applied, 895 accepted, 332 enrolled	
SAT I or ACT: required	**COMPETITIVE**

Meredith College, founded in 1891, is an independent college for women offering a comprehensive undergraduate program with a strong emphasis on the liberal arts. Graduate programs in business, music, education, and nutrition serve both women and men. There are 6 undergraduate schools and 1 graduate school. In addition to regional accreditation, Meredith has baccalaureate program accreditation with ADA, CSWE, FIDER, NASM, and NCATE. The 2 libraries contain 167,000 volumes, 10,395 microform items, and 12,174 audio/video tapes/CDs, and subscribe to 766 periodicals. Computerized library services include the card catalog, interlibrary loans, database searching, and Internet access. Special learning facilities include a learning resource center, art gallery, child-care lab, greenhouse, experimental and clinical psychology labs including one on autism, an electron microscope suite, an astronomy observation deck, and language lab. The 225-acre campus is in an urban area in the city of Raleigh. Including any residence halls, there are 30 buildings.

Student Life: 90% of undergraduates are from North Carolina. Students are from 29 states and 18 foreign countries. 84% are from public schools. 83% are white. 57% are Protestant; 31% claim no religious affiliation; 7% Catholic. The average age of freshmen is 18; all undergraduates, 23. 21% do not continue beyond their first year; 67% remain to graduate.

Housing: 1115 students can be accommodated in college housing, which includes single-sex dorms with nonsmoking halls. On-campus housing is guaranteed for all 4 years. 59% of students commute. Alcohol is not permitted. All students may keep cars.

Activities: There are no fraternities. There are 93 groups on campus, including art, band, Big Sister/Little Sister, chorale, chorus, commuter, computers, dance, drama, environmental, ethnic, foreign language, honors, international, literary magazine, musical theater, newspaper, nutrition and wellness, orchestra, photography, political, professional, religious, social, social service, student government, symphony, and yearbook. Popular campus events include Academics and Leadership Awards Day, White Iris Ball, and Undergraduate Research Conference.

Sports: Facilities include an indoor swimming pool, a dance studio, a fitness center, an archery range, a horseshoe pit, a putting green and driving range, a softball diamond, tennis courts, a soccer field, and a gym with basketball, volleyball, and badminton courts.

Disabled Students: 81% of the campus is accessible. Wheelchair ramps, elevators, special parking, specially equipped rest rooms, special class scheduling, lowered drinking fountains, special housing, a handicap lift in the swimming pool, and lowered fire alarms are available.

Services: Counseling and information services are available, as is tutoring in some subjects, including math, writing, computer lab, French, Spanish, biology, chemistry, study skills, German, GRE prep, Praxis prep, and grammar. There is a reader service for the blind.

Campus Safety and Security: Measures include 24-hour foot and vehicle patrol, self-defense education, security escort services, and informal discussions. There are pamphlets/posters/films, emergency telephones, lighted pathways/sidewalks, controlled campus access at night, and 24-hour locked residence halls.

Programs of Study: Meredith confers B.A., B.S., B.M., and B.S.N. degrees. Master's degrees are also awarded. Bachelor's degrees are awarded in AGRICULTURE (environmental studies), BIOLOGICAL SCIENCE (biology/biological science and nutrition), BUSINESS (accounting, business administration and management, fashion merchandising, and international business management), COMMUNICATIONS AND THE ARTS (applied music, art, communications, dance, dramatic arts, English, fine arts, French, music, music performance, musical theater, and Spanish), COMPUTER AND PHYSICAL SCIENCE (chemistry, computer science, information sciences and systems, and mathematics), EDUCATION (athletic training and music), ENGINEERING AND ENVIRONMENTAL DESIGN (interior design), HEALTH PROFESSIONS (exercise science), SOCIAL SCIENCE (American studies, child psychology/development, economics, family/consumer studies, food science, history, international studies, political science/government, psychology, public affairs, religion, social work, and sociology). Business, psychology, and biology are the largest.

Required: To graduate, students must complete a total of 124 credit hours, including general education requirements, a major field, and electives, with a minimum GPA of 2.0. General Education is comprised of a core curriculum focusing on understanding diverse cultures, fields of knowledge that ensure breadth in the liberal arts, and across-the-curriculum threads and independent learning experiences that build competencies. Some major fields offer or require a concentration, and contract majors are possible. Electives may be used to complete a second major, a minor, teacher licensure, or to explore areas of personal, career or preprofessional interest.

Special: Meredith offers cooperative programs, cross-registration with Cooperating Raleigh Colleges, internships, study abroad in Europe and Asia, a Washington semester at American University, a U.N. semester at Drew University, and work-study programs on campus. Dual majors, interdisciplinary and student-designed majors, preprofessional programs, and pass/fail options are available. Second-degree programs in engineering with North Carolina State University and certification in social work and licensure for teaching are possible. Business administration, management, and social work majors can be completed through evening classes. There are 19 national honor societies and a freshman honors program.

Faculty/Classroom: 32% of faculty are male; 68%, female. All teach undergraduates. No introductory courses are taught by graduate students. The average class size in an introductory lecture is 20; in a laboratory, 14; and in a regular course, 16.

Admissions: 87% of the 2003-2004 applicants were accepted. 37% of the current freshmen were in the top fifth of their class; 72% were in the top two fifths. 4 freshmen graduated first in their class.

Requirements: The SAT I or ACT is required; the SAT I is preferred. Applicants must have a minimum of 16 units of credit, including 4 in English, 3 each in math, history/social studies, and science, 2 in foreign language, and 1 elective. The student is expected to rank in the top half of her class, and grades in academic subjects are very important. An interview may be requested as part of the evaluation process. Meredith re-

quires applicants to be in the upper 50% of their class. A GPA of 2.0 is required. AP and CLEP credits are accepted. Important factors in the admissions decision are recommendations by school officials, advanced placement or honor courses, and evidence of special talent.

Procedure: Freshmen are admitted fall and spring. Entrance exams should be taken by January of the senior year. There are early decision and deferred admissions plans. Early decision applications should be filed by October 15; regular applications, by February 15 for fall entry and December 1 for spring entry, along with a $35 fee. Notification of early decision is sent November 1; regular decision, on a rolling basis. 62 early decision candidates were accepted for the 2003-2004 class. Applications are accepted on computer disk and on-line through *mcmentor.org/xap.com.*

Transfer: 98 transfer students enrolled in 2002-2003. Applicants must have a minimum GPA of 2.0, be eligible to return to the last college attended, and be recommended by college officials. Those students with fewer than 30 hours of credit must also meet freshman admission requirements. 31 of 124 credits required for the bachelor's degree must be completed at Meredith.

Visiting: There are regularly scheduled orientations for prospective students, including Open Days information sessions for senior students and parents, class visitation, informal conversations with students and faculty/staff, and campus tours. Experience Meredith! for accepted students and their parents includes various off-to-college information sessions, an academic fair, a student activities fair, and campus tours. Individual visitors typically have a conference with an admissions counselor and a campus tour. There are also visitation days for juniors and transfers, and a Legacy Day when alumnae bring prospective students for a visit.

Financial Aid: In 2003-2004, 96% of all full-time freshmen and 99% of continuing full-time students received some form of financial aid. 59% of full-time freshmen and 55% of continuing full-time students received need-based aid. The average freshman award was $14,145. Need-based scholarships or need-based grants averaged $11,502 ($23,500 maximum); need-based self-help aid (loans and jobs) averaged $3060 ($5500 maximum); and non-need-based awards and non-need-based scholarships averaged $5798 ($14,100 maximum). 26% of undergraduates work part time. Average annual earnings from campus work are $900. The average financial indebtedness of the 2003 graduate was $14,800. Meredith is a member of CSS. The FAFSA is required. The priority date for freshman financial aid applications for fall entry is March 1.

International Students: There are 14 international students enrolled. The school actively recruits these students. They must score 500 on the written TOEFL or 173 on the electronic version. If English is the student's native language or primary language of instruction, the SAT I should be taken instead of the TOEFL.

Computers: More than 200 PCs are available throughout campus for student use. All are networked for e-mail, the Internet, and the World Wide Web. Residence halls are configured for both wired and wireless connection to the network. All academic buildings and the student center are also configured for wireless network access. All incoming freshmen are provided with a ThinkPad R40 laptop computer. All students may access the system 24 hours per day in residence halls and one lab; 7 A.M. to midnight in other labs. All students are required to have personal computers.

Graduates: From July 1, 2002 to June 30, 2003, 491 bachelor's degrees were awarded. The most popular majors were business administration (17%), psychology (12%), and communications (6%). In an average class, 3% graduate in 3 years or less, 58% graduate in 4 years or less, 66% graduate in 5 years or less, and 67% graduate in 6 years or less. 76 companies recruited on campus in 2002-2003. Of the 2002 graduating class, 17% were enrolled in graduate school within 6 months of graduation and 87% were employed.

Admissions Contact: Carol Kercheval, Director of Admissions. A video is available. E-mail: *admissions@meredith.edu* Web: *www.meredith.edu*

METHODIST COLLEGE   D-3
Fayetteville, NC 28311-1420   (910) 630-7027
                                  (800) 488-7110; Fax: (910) 630-7285

Full-time: 1550 men and women	**Faculty:** 90; IIB, --$
Part-time: 295 men and women	**Ph.D.s:** 54%
Graduate: none	**Student/Faculty:** 19 to 1
Year: semesters, summer session	**Tuition:** $15,776
Application Deadline: open	**Room & Board:** $5940
Freshman Class: n/av	
SAT I or ACT: required	**COMPETITIVE**

Methodist College, founded in 1956, is a private institution affiliated with the United Methodist Church. The college offers programs in the arts and sciences, education, business, and professional training. Figures in the above capsule and in this profile are approximate. There are 2 undergraduate schools and 1 graduate school. In addition to regional accreditation, Methodist has baccalaureate program accreditation with ACBSP,

CAAHEP, CSWE, and NCATE. The library contains 181,833 volumes, 57,759 microform items, and 13,412 audio/video tapes/CDs, and subscribes to 587 periodicals. Computerized library services include the card catalog, interlibrary loans, and database searching. Special learning facilities include a learning resource center, art gallery, and professional golf and tennis management facilities. The 600-acre campus is in a suburban area 5 miles north of Fayetteville. Including any residence halls, there are 30 buildings.

Student Life: 60% of undergraduates are from North Carolina. Students are from 48 states, 37 foreign countries, and Canada. 88% are from public schools. 75% are white; 17% African American. 41% are Protestant; 16% Catholic. The average age of freshmen is 18; all undergraduates, 21. 35% do not continue beyond their first year; 36% remain to graduate.

Housing: 823 students can be accommodated in college housing, which includes single-sex and coed dorms and on-campus apartments. In addition, there are honors houses and a health and wellness hall. On-campus housing is guaranteed for all 4 years. 52% of students live on campus; of those, 70% remain on campus on weekends. Alcohol is not permitted. All students may keep cars.

Activities: 1% of men belong to 2 local fraternities; 1% of women belong to 2 local and 1 national sorority. There are 72 groups on campus, including art, band, cheerleading, chess, choir, chorale, chorus, computers, dance, debate, drama, ethnic, honors, international, jazz band, literary magazine, musical theater, newspaper, orchestra, pep band, photography, political, professional, religious, social, social service, student government, and yearbook. Popular campus events include Show You Care Day, Annual Woodcutting, and Spring Fest.

Sports: There are 9 intercollegiate sports for men and 10 for women, and 7 intramural sports for men and 4 for women. Facilities include a 1200-seat stadium, a 1500-seat gym, a golf course, a track and field area, tennis courts, and fields for baseball, softball, and soccer.

Disabled Students: 90% of the campus is accessible. Wheelchair ramps, special parking, specially equipped rest rooms, and lowered drinking fountains are available.

Services: Counseling and information services are available, as is tutoring in most subjects. There is a reader service for the blind and remedial math, reading, and writing.

Campus Safety and Security: Measures include 24-hour foot and vehicle patrol, self-defense education, security escort services, and shuttle buses. There are informal discussions, pamphlets/posters/films, emergency telephones, and lighted pathways/sidewalks.

Programs of Study: Methodist confers B.A., B.S., B.H.S., B.M., and B.S.W. degrees. Associate and master's degrees are also awarded. Bachelor's degrees are awarded in BIOLOGICAL SCIENCE (biology/biological science), BUSINESS (accounting, business administration and management, marketing/retailing/merchandising, organizational behavior, and sports management), COMMUNICATIONS AND THE ARTS (art, communications, creative writing, dramatic arts, English, French, music, music performance, and Spanish), COMPUTER AND PHYSICAL SCIENCE (chemistry, computer science, and mathematics), EDUCATION (art, athletic training, elementary, middle school, music, physical, secondary, and special), ENGINEERING AND ENVIRONMENTAL DESIGN (computer technology), HEALTH PROFESSIONS (physician's assistant and predentistry), SOCIAL SCIENCE (criminal justice, economics, history, international studies, political science/government, prelaw, psychology, religion, social studies, social work, and sociology). Business administration, biology, and music are the strongest academically. Business administration, education, and biology are the largest.

Required: To graduate, students must complete at least 124 semester hours, including core requirements, with a minimum GPA of 2.0. A liberal arts core, ranging from 36 to 62 hours, is required in all majors.

Special: Methodist offers internships in political science and social work, study abroad in 2 countries, a Washington semester, a general studies degree, a 3-2 engineering degree with North Carolina State University, pass/fail options, dual majors, and nondegree study. The business administration major offers concentrations in professional golf, tennis, and resort management with specialized facilities and co-op programs. There are 7 national honor societies, a freshman honors program, and 3 departmental honors programs.

Faculty/Classroom: 67% of faculty are male; 33%, female. All teach undergraduates. The average class size in an introductory lecture is 25; in a laboratory, 20; and in a regular course, 20.

Requirements: The SAT I or ACT is required. In addition, applicants should be graduates of an accredited secondary school or have a GED certificate. They must have 16 academic credits, including 4 in English and 3 each in history, math, and science. 2 years of foreign language are recommended. An essay and interview are also recommended. AP and CLEP credits are accepted. Important factors in the admissions decision are advanced placement or honor courses, evidence of special talent, and recommendations by school officials.

Procedure: Freshmen are admitted fall, spring, and summer. There is a deferred admissions plan and a rolling admissions plan. Application deadlines are open. The application fee is $25. Applications are accepted on-line at the school's web site.

Transfer: 153 transfer students enrolled in a recent year. Applicants must have a minimum GPA of 2.0. They must also submit a high school transcript, college transcripts, and the SAT I or ACT scores. 30 of 124 credits required for the bachelor's degree must be completed at Methodist.

Visiting: There are regularly scheduled orientations for prospective students, consisting of a 2-day summer orientation in July. There are guides for informal visits and visitors may sit in on classes and stay overnight. To schedule a visit, contact the Admissions Office.

Financial Aid: In a recent year, 84% of all full-time freshmen and 87% of continuing full-time students received some form of financial aid. 78% of full-time freshmen and 83% of continuing full-time students received need-based aid. The average freshman award was $9410. 60% of undergraduates work part time. Average annual earnings from campus work are $1000. The average financial indebtedness of a recent graduate was $15,400. The FAFSA is required. Check with the school for current deadlines.

International Students: In a recent year, there were 60 international students enrolled. The school actively recruits these students. The TOEFL is required with a minimum score of 500 on the written version or 173 on the electronic version. The student may take the SAT I or ACT in place of the TOEFL if English proficiency is demonstrated.

Computers: The mainframe is an IBM. There are also 150 IBM, AT&T, and leading edge PCs available in various labs. All students may access the system during specified hours.

Graduates: In a recent year, 254 bachelor's degrees were awarded. The most popular majors were business (46%), social sciences (11%), and education (7%). In an average class, 1% graduate in 3 years or less, 33% graduate in 4 years or less, 38% graduate in 5 years or less, and 40% graduate in 6 years or less. 180 companies recruited on campus in a recent year.

Admissions Contact: Jamie Legg, Director of Admissions.
E-mail: *jlegg@methodist.edu* Web: *www.methodist.edu*

MONTREAT COLLEGE
B-2
Montreat, NC 28757-1267
(828) 669-8012, ext. 3784
(800) 622-6968; Fax: (828) 669-0120

Full-time: 352 men, 584 women	Faculty: 31; IIB, --$
Part-time: 4 men, 4 women	Ph.D.s: 48%
Graduate: 35 men, 57 women	Student/Faculty: 30 to 1
Year: semesters	Tuition: $14,120
Application Deadline: open	Room & Board: $4642
Freshman Class: 409 applied, 320 accepted, 157 enrolled	
SAT I Verbal/Math: 530/500	ACT: 22 COMPETITIVE

Montreat College, founded in 1916, is a private liberal arts institution affiliated with the Presbyterian Church (U.S.A.) and committed to the integration of faith and learning. In addition to regional accreditation, Montreat has baccalaureate program accreditation with NCATE. The library contains 79,165 volumes, 117,155 microform items, and 3119 audio/video tapes/CDs, and subscribes to 485 periodicals. Computerized library services include the card catalog, interlibrary loans, database searching, and Internet access. Special learning facilities include a learning resource center, art gallery, and the Presbyterian Church (U.S.A.) Historical Foundation. The 100-acre campus is in a rural area 15 miles east of Asheville. Including any residence halls, there are 18 buildings.

Student Life: 79% of undergraduates are from North Carolina. Students are from 21 states and 12 foreign countries. 55% are from public schools. 70% are white; 18% African American. The average age of freshmen is 18. 34% do not continue beyond their first year.

Housing: 392 students can be accommodated in college housing, which includes single-sex dorms. On-campus housing is guaranteed for all 4 years. 76% of students live on campus; of those, 50% remain on campus on weekends. Alcohol is not permitted. All students may keep cars.

Activities: There are no fraternities or sororities. There are 25 groups on campus, including adventure, art, choir, chorus, drama, honors, musical theater, newspaper, photography, political, professional, religious, social, social service, student government, and yearbook.

Sports: There are 6 intercollegiate sports for men and 6 for women, and 4 intramural sports for men and 4 for women. Facilities include standard athletic facilities complemented by opportunities for outdoor recreation activities such as skiing, whitewater sports, mountain climbing, and camping.

Disabled Students: 75% of the campus is accessible. Wheelchair ramps, elevators, special parking, specially equipped rest rooms, special class scheduling, and lowered telephones are available.

Services: Counseling and information services are available, as is tutoring in all academic areas. There is remedial math, reading, and writing.

Campus Safety and Security: Measures include 24-hour foot and vehicle patrol, lighted pathways/sidewalks, and a closed campus.

Programs of Study: Montreat confers B.A., B.S., B.B.A., and B.M. degrees. Associate and master's degrees are also awarded. Bachelor's degrees are awarded in BUSINESS (business administration and management), COMMUNICATIONS AND THE ARTS (English, music business management, and music performance), COMPUTER AND PHYSICAL SCIENCE (mathematics), EDUCATION (elementary), ENGINEERING AND ENVIRONMENTAL DESIGN (environmental science), SOCIAL SCIENCE (American studies, biblical studies, history, human services, liberal arts/general studies, and religion). English is the strongest academically. Business is the largest.

Required: To graduate, students must complete 126 credit hours with a minimum GPA of 2.0. They must pass a comprehensive exam covering math, computation, oral expression, reading, and writing. A thesis is required for some majors.

Special: Montreat offers internships in all majors, study abroad, a Washington semester, work-study programs, alternative majors, and dual majors. There are 2 national honor societies, a freshman honors program, and 3 departmental honors programs.

Faculty/Classroom: 58% of faculty are male; 42%, female. All teach undergraduates. No introductory courses are taught by graduate students. The average class size in an introductory lecture is 30; in a laboratory, 15; and in a regular course, 10.

Admissions: 78% of the 2003-2004 applicants were accepted. The SAT I scores for the 2003-2004 freshman class were: Verbal--41% below 500, 34% between 500 and 599, 21% between 600 and 700, and 4% above 700; Math--45% below 500, 43% between 500 and 599, 10% between 600 and 700, and 3% above 700. The ACT scores were 31% below 21, 35% between 21 and 23, 23% between 24 and 26, 4% between 27 and 28, and 8% above 28. 24% of the current freshmen were in the top fifth of their class; 53% were in the top two fifths.

Requirements: The SAT I or ACT is required, and is rated on a sliding scale with the GPA, with a minimum 860 SAT I score or 18 ACT score needed. Applicants must be graduates of an accredited secondary school and have completed 4 years of English, 3 each of math, science, and social studies, and 1 of foreign language. The GED is accepted. A counselor or teacher recommendation is required, and a short autobiographical essay is required unless the student has been interviewed. Montreat requires applicants to be in the upper 50% of their class. A GPA of 2.25 is required. CLEP credit is accepted. Important factors in the admissions decision are advanced placement or honor courses, extracurricular activities record, and evidence of special talent.

Procedure: Freshmen are admitted to all sessions. Application deadlines are open. Notification is sent on a rolling basis. The fall 2003 application fee was $15.

Transfer: 52 transfer students enrolled in 2002-2003. Applicants must submit official college transcripts, be in good standing at their previous institution, and have completed at least 24 semester hours of college credit with a minimum GPA of 2.0. Students with fewer credits must also submit high school transcripts and SAT I or ACT scores. 18 of 126 credits required for the bachelor's degree must be completed at Montreat.

Visiting: There are regularly scheduled orientations for prospective students, including a campus tour, faculty introduction, and student program. There are guides for informal visits and visitors may sit in on classes and stay overnight. To schedule a visit, contact the Admissions Office.

Financial Aid: In 2003-2004, 98% of all full-time students received some form of financial aid. 71% of full-time freshmen and 75% of continuing full-time students received need-based aid. The average freshman award was $12,337. Need-based scholarships or need-based grants averaged $9758 ($19,125 maximum); need-based self-help aid (loans and jobs) averaged $3880 ($8301 maximum); non-need-based athletic scholarships averaged $9396 ($18,562 maximum); and other non-need-based awards and non-need-based scholarships averaged $4236 ($14,120 maximum). 30% of undergraduates work part time. Average annual earnings from campus work are $1700. The average financial indebtedness of the 2003 graduate was $17,600. Montreat is a member of CSS. The FAFSA and the college's own financial statement are required. The priority date for freshman financial aid applications for fall entry is April 15.

International Students: There are 12 international students enrolled. The school actively recruits these students. They must score 500 on the written TOEFL.

Computers: The student-to-computer ratio is 11:1. PCs in dorm rooms can access the Internet and be linked to the campus network. All students may access the system during computer lab hours or at any time by PC. There are no time limits and no fees. It is strongly recommended that all students have a personal computer. An IBM-compatible unit is recommended.

Graduates: From July 1, 2002 to June 30, 2003, 206 bachelor's degrees were awarded. The most popular majors were business (76%), outdoor education (6%), and human services (3%). In an average class, 26% graduate in 4 years or less, 38% graduate in 5 years or less, and 42% graduate in 6 years or less.

Admissions Contact: Anita F. Darby, Director of Admissions. A video is available. E-mail: admissions@montreat.edu Web: www.montreat.edu

MOUNT OLIVE COLLEGE
Mount Olive, NC 28365

E-3
(919) 658-2502
(800) 653-0854; Fax: (919) 658-7180

Full-time: 650 men, 785 women	**Faculty:** 44
Part-time: 155 men, 195 women	**Ph.D.s:** 79%
Graduate: none	**Student/Faculty:** 33 to 1
Year: semesters, summer session	**Tuition:** $10,010
Application Deadline: open	**Room & Board:** $4400
Freshman Class: n/av	
SAT I or ACT: required	**LESS COMPETITIVE**

Mount Olive College, founded in 1951, is a private liberal arts institution affiliated with the Original Free Will Baptist Church. Figures in the above capsule and in this profile are approximate. The 2 libraries contain 77,545 volumes, 48,735 microform items, and 2005 audio/video tapes/CDs, and subscribe to 5979 periodicals. Computerized library services include the card catalog, interlibrary loans, and database searching. Special learning facilities include a learning resource center, art gallery, and a church archives collection. The 123-acre campus is in a small town 65 miles southeast of Raleigh. Including any residence halls, there are 16 buildings.

Student Life: 92% of undergraduates are from North Carolina. Students are from 21 states, 7 foreign countries, and Canada. 93% are from public schools. 68% are white; 25% African American. The average age of freshmen is 18; all undergraduates, 29. 40% do not continue beyond their first year; 20% remain to graduate.

Housing: 306 students can be accommodated in college housing, which includes single-sex dorms and on-campus apartments. On-campus housing is guaranteed for the freshman year only. 77% of students commute. Alcohol is not permitted. All students may keep cars.

Activities: There are no fraternities or sororities. There are 20 groups on campus, including art, cheerleading, choir, chorale, chorus, drama, honors, international, literary magazine, newspaper, orchestra, pep band, photography, political, professional, religious, student government, and yearbook. Popular campus events include Founders Day, Pickle Classic Weekend, and the North Carolina Pickle Festival.

Sports: There are 6 intercollegiate sports for men and 6 for women, and 10 intramural sports for men and 8 for women. Facilities include a 2000-seat gym, racquetball and tennis courts, a track, wrestling/gymnastics and weight rooms, an athletic field, outdoor basketball areas, a student center, and baseball, softball, and soccer fields.

Disabled Students: 90% of the campus is accessible. Wheelchair ramps, elevators, special parking, specially equipped rest rooms, and special class scheduling are available.

Services: Counseling and information services are available, as is tutoring in most subjects, including math, English, and science. There is remedial math and reading.

Campus Safety and Security: Measures include informal discussions, pamphlets/posters/films, lighted pathways/sidewalks, and evening and weekend patrols.

Programs of Study: Mount Olive confers B.A., B.S., and B.Applied Sc. degrees. Associate degrees are also awarded. Bachelor's degrees are awarded in BIOLOGICAL SCIENCE (biology/biological science), BUSINESS (accounting, business administration and management, human resources, and recreation and leisure services), COMMUNICATIONS AND THE ARTS (art, communications, English, fine arts, and music), COMPUTER AND PHYSICAL SCIENCE (computer management, information sciences and systems, and mathematics), EDUCATION (middle school and secondary), ENGINEERING AND ENVIRONMENTAL DESIGN (environmental science), SOCIAL SCIENCE (criminal justice, history, human services, liberal arts/general studies, ministries, psychology, and religion). Business, accounting, and psychology are the strongest academically. Business, psychology, and recreation are the largest.

Required: To graduate, students must have completed a total of 126 credit hours, with a minimum 2.0 overall GPA in 63 credit hours for the B.S. or in 53 hours for the B. Applied Sc. Distribution requirements include 30 to 36 hours in humanities, 18 in science/math/and 12 in social science. Specific course work includes 6 hours of religion, 4 of phys ed, and 3 hours of computer competency.

Special: Mount Olive offers co-op programs and internships in all majors, work-study, B.A.-B.S. degrees, dual majors, and accelerated degree programs in business, accounting, and criminal justice administration. Cross-registration with James Sprunt Community College and Wayne Community College, study abroad, and credit for life, military, and work experience are also possible. Professional degree completion programs run continuously for 55 to 57 weeks. There is 1 national honor society and a freshman honors program.

Faculty/Classroom: 58% of faculty are male; 42%, female. All teach undergraduates, 14% do research, and 86% do both.

Admissions: In a recent year, 4 freshmen graduated first in their class.

Requirements: The SAT I or ACT is required. A minimum SAT I composite score of 700 or ACT score of 16 is recommended. Applicants must be graduates of an accredited secondary school or have a GED certificate. They must have completed 4 units of English, 3 each of math and science, and 2 of history. An essay and interview are suggested. A GPA of 2.0 is required. AP and CLEP credits are accepted.

Procedure: Freshmen are admitted to all sessions. Entrance exams should be taken in the junior or senior year. There are early admissions, deferred admissions, and rolling admissions plans. Application deadlines are open. The application fee is $20.

Transfer: 131 transfer students enrolled in a recent year. Applicants must have a minimum GPA of 2.0 and submit an official transcript from the previous institution. An interview may be required. 32 of 126 credits required for the bachelor's degree must be completed at Mount Olive.

Visiting: There are regularly scheduled orientations for prospective students, consisting of 2 days of advising, sports, and entertainment. There are guides for informal visits and visitors may sit in on classes. To schedule a visit, contact the Admissions Office at *twoodward@moc.edu*.

Financial Aid: The FAFSA and the college's own financial statement are required. Check with the school for current deadlines.

International Students: In a recent year, there were 8 international students enrolled. The school actively recruits these students. They must score 500 on the written TOEFL and also take the SAT I or the ACT.

Computers: The Internet may be accessed via 45 PCs and Macs located in 2 computer labs, with software and assistance also available. All students may access the system 8 A.M. to 10 P.M. Monday through Friday and during scheduled hours on weekends. Students may access the system for a reasonable length of time. There are no fees. It is strongly recommended that all students have a personal computer.

Graduates: In a recent year, 471 bachelor's degrees were awarded. The most popular majors were business (69%), criminal justice administration (16%), and recreation (4%). In an average class, 1% graduate in 3 years or less, 18% graduate in 4 years or less, and 22% graduate in 5 years or less. 91 companies recruited on campus in a recent year. Of a recent graduating class, 15% were enrolled in graduate school within 6 months of graduation and 8% were employed.

Admissions Contact: Tim Woodard, Director of Admissions. A video is available. E-mail: *admissions@exchanbge.moc.edu* Web: *www.moc.edu*

NORTH CAROLINA AGRICULTURAL AND TECHNICAL STATE UNIVERSITY   D-2
Greensboro, NC 27411

(336) 334-7946
(800) 443-8964; Fax: (336) 334-7136

Full-time: 2800 men, 3100 women	**Faculty:** 442; IIA, av$
Part-time: 350 men, 360 women	**Ph.D.s:** 96%
Graduate: 370 men, 500 women	**Student/Faculty:** 13 to 1
Year: semesters, summer session	**Tuition:** $2190 ($9460)
Application Deadline: see profile	**Room & Board:** $4470
Freshman Class: n/av	
SAT I or ACT: required	**LESS COMPETITIVE**

North Carolina Agricultural and Technical State University, founded in 1891, is a public institution within the University of North Carolina System. A & T offers programs in arts and sciences, education, business and economics, agriculture, nursing, engineering, and technology. Figures in the above capsule and in this profile are approximate. There are 7 undergraduate schools and 1 graduate school. In addition to regional accreditation, A & T has baccalaureate program accreditation with AACSB, ABET, ACCE, CSWE, NCATE, and NLN. The library contains 507,036 volumes, 1,038,474 microform items, and 34,025 audio/video tapes/CDs, and subscribes to 5446 periodicals. Computerized library services include the card catalog, interlibrary loans, and database searching. Special learning facilities include an art gallery, planetarium, radio station, TV station, and African Heritage Center. The 191-acre campus is in an urban area 90 miles northeast of Charlotte. Including any residence halls, there are 107 buildings.

Student Life: 82% of undergraduates are from North Carolina. Students are from 39 states and 25 foreign countries. 89% are African American. The average age of freshmen is 18; all undergraduates, 22. 25% do not continue beyond their first year; 49% remain to graduate.

Housing: 2959 students can be accommodated in college housing, which includes single-sex and coed dorms. In addition, there are honors houses. On-campus housing is available on a first-come, first-served basis and is available on a lottery system for upperclassmen. 53% of students commute. Alcohol is not permitted. All students may keep cars.

Activities: 1% of men belong to 5 national fraternities; 1% of women belong to 4 national sororities. There are 150 groups on campus, including art, band, cheerleading, choir, chorus, computers, dance, drama, drill team, ethnic, film, honors, international, jazz band, marching band, newspaper, orchestra, pep band, photography, political, professional, radio and TV, religious, social, social service, student government, symphony, and yearbook. Popular campus events include Graduation, Martin Luther King's Birthday, and Ron McNair Commemoration.

Sports: There are 7 intercollegiate sports for men and 9 for women, and 12 intramural sports for men and 12 for women. Facilities include

a gym, a sports center, a stadium, tennis courts, a student union, a field house, and softball/baseball facilities.

Disabled Students: 85% of the campus is accessible. Wheelchair ramps, elevators, special parking, specially equipped rest rooms, special class scheduling, lowered drinking fountains, and lowered telephones are available.

Services: Counseling and information services are available, as is tutoring in every subject. There is a reader service for the blind and remedial math, reading, and writing.

Campus Safety and Security: Measures include 24-hour foot and vehicle patrol, self-defense education, security escort services, and shuttle buses. There are informal discussions, pamphlets/posters/films, emergency telephones, and lighted pathways/sidewalks.

Programs of Study: A & T confers B.A., B.S., B.F.A., B.S.I.E., B.S.M.E., B.S.N., and B.S.W. degrees. Master's and doctoral degrees are also awarded. Bachelor's degrees are awarded in AGRICULTURE (agricultural business management, agricultural economics, and animal science), BIOLOGICAL SCIENCE (biology/biological science), BUSINESS (accounting and business administration and management), COMMUNICATIONS AND THE ARTS (communications, dramatic arts, English, French, music, and speech/debate/rhetoric), COMPUTER AND PHYSICAL SCIENCE (chemistry, computer science, mathematics, and physics), EDUCATION (agricultural, art, business, early childhood, English, home economics, industrial arts, mathematics, music, physical, social science, and special), ENGINEERING AND ENVIRONMENTAL DESIGN (architectural engineering, chemical engineering, civil engineering, electrical/electronics engineering, engineering physics, industrial engineering, landscape architecture/design, mechanical engineering, and occupational safety and health), HEALTH PROFESSIONS (nursing), SOCIAL SCIENCE (child psychology/development, clothing and textiles management/production/services, economics, history, political science/government, psychology, social work, and sociology). Business, accounting, and electronics and computer technology are the strongest academically. Accounting and electronics and computer technology are the largest.

Required: To graduate, students must complete a minimum of 124 credit hours, including at least 80 in the major, with an overall GPA of 2.0 or better. Specific course work is required in English, math, natural science, social science, humanities, and health or phys ed.

Special: A & T offers cross-registration with the Greensboro Regional Consortium, internships, B.A.-B.S. degrees, cooperative programs in most majors, study abroad in 5 countries, work-study programs, and dual majors. There are 3 national honor societies, a freshman honors program, and 13 departmental honors programs.

Faculty/Classroom: 65% of faculty are male; 35%, female. All teach undergraduates. The average class size in an introductory lecture is 26; in a laboratory, 17; and in a regular course, 24.

Requirements: The SAT I or ACT is required, with a minimum composite score of 750 on the SAT I or 17 on the ACT. Applicants must be graduates of an accredited secondary school or have a GED certificate. They must have completed at least 16 academic credits, including 4 in English, 3 each in math and science, 2 each in music and social sciences, and a foreign language. An audition is required of fine arts majors, and a portfolio is recommended. An interview is suggested for all applicants. A GPA of 2.0 is required. AP and CLEP credits are accepted. Important factors in the admissions decision are geographic diversity, advanced placement or honor courses, and personality/intangible qualities.

Procedure: Freshmen are admitted to all sessions. Entrance exams should be taken before April 1. There is a deferred admissions plan and a rolling admissions plan. Check with the school for current deadlines. The fall 2003 application fee was $35.

Transfer: Applicants must have a minimum GPA of 2.0 in at least 24 semester hours and must be in good standing at their previous school. Specifically, 6 hours of English, history, college algebra, and science are required. 62 of 124 credits required for the bachelor's degree must be completed at A & T.

Visiting: There are regularly scheduled orientations for prospective students. There are guides for informal visits and visitors may sit in on classes. To schedule a visit, contact the Admissions Office.

Financial Aid: The average financial indebtedness of a recent graduate was $15,008. A & T is a member of CSS. The FAFSA is required. Check with the school for current deadlines.

International Students: They must score 550 on the written TOEFL.

Computers: The mainframes are a DEC VAX 6320 and a DEC VAX 11/785. Mac PCs, IBMs, DEC stations, and X terminals are available. All students may access the system. There are no time limits and no fees.

Admissions Contact: John Smith, Admissions Director. A video is available. E-mail: *uadmit@ncat.edu* Web: *www.ncat.edu*

NORTH CAROLINA CENTRAL UNIVERSITY
Durham, NC 27707

D-2

(919) 560-6298

Fax: (919) 530-7625 or (919) 560-5462

Full-time: 1490 men, 2733 women	**Faculty:** 257; IIA, +$
Part-time: 303 men, 836 women	**Ph.D.s:** 75%
Graduate: 497 men, 1332 women	**Student/Faculty:** 16 to 1
Year: semesters, summer session	**Tuition:** $3223 ($12,587)
Application Deadline: July 1	**Room & Board:** $4311
Freshman Class: 1805 applied, 1566 accepted, 1053 enrolled	
SAT I Verbal/Math: 415/418	**ACT:** 16 **LESS COMPETITIVE**

North Carolina Central University, founded in 1909, is a publicly funded liberal arts institution in the University of North Carolina system. There are 3 undergraduate and 2 graduate schools. In addition to regional accreditation, NCCU has baccalaureate program accreditation with NCATE and NLN. The 6 libraries contain 663,913 volumes, 1,217,019 microform items, and 10,991 audio/video tapes/CDs, and subscribe to 6688 periodicals. Computerized library services include the card catalog and database searching. Special learning facilities include a learning resource center and art gallery. The 103-acre campus is in an urban area 2 miles from the center of Durham. Including any residence halls, there are 57 buildings.

Student Life: 89% of undergraduates are from North Carolina. Students are from 39 states and 17 foreign countries. 80% are African American; 14% white. The average age of freshmen is 19; all undergraduates, 24.

Housing: 2377 students can be accommodated in college housing, which includes single-sex and coed dorms and on-campus apartments. In addition, there are honors houses. On-campus housing is available on a first-come, first-served basis and is available on a lottery system for upperclassmen. 63% of students commute. Alcohol is not permitted. All students may keep cars.

Activities: There are 4 national fraternities and 4 national sororities. There are 45 groups on campus, including art, band, cheerleading, chess, choir, computers, dance, drama, drill team, ethnic, honors, international, jazz band, literary magazine, marching band, newspaper, political, professional, radio and TV, religious, social, social service, student government, symphony, and yearbook.

Sports: There are 6 intercollegiate sports for men and 5 for women. Facilities include a 12,000-seat stadium, a 4500-seat gym, a swimming pool, handball and tennis courts, a track, a bowling alley, dance studios, and a weight room.

Disabled Students: 90% of the campus is accessible. Wheelchair ramps, elevators, special parking, specially equipped rest rooms, special class scheduling, lowered drinking fountains, lowered telephones, lowered dorm intercoms, interpreters, automatic door openers, and adaptive technology are available.

Services: Counseling and information services are available. There is a reader service for the blind, remedial math, reading, and writing, assistance for students in obtaining needed documentation, assistance with registration, and appropriate individual accommodations and assistance as needed.

Campus Safety and Security: Measures include 24-hour foot and vehicle patrol, security escort services, informal discussions, and pamphlets/posters/films. There are emergency telephones and lighted pathways/sidewalks.

Programs of Study: NCCU confers B.A., B.S., B.B.A., B.M., B.S.N., and B.S.W. degrees. Master's degrees are also awarded. Bachelor's degrees are awarded in BIOLOGICAL SCIENCE (biology/biological science and nutrition), BUSINESS (accounting and business administration and management), COMMUNICATIONS AND THE ARTS (art, dramatic arts, English, French, jazz, music, and Spanish), COMPUTER AND PHYSICAL SCIENCE (chemistry, computer science, mathematics, and physics), EDUCATION (elementary, health, middle school, and physical), ENGINEERING AND ENVIRONMENTAL DESIGN (environmental science), HEALTH PROFESSIONS (nursing), SOCIAL SCIENCE (child care/child and family studies, child psychology/development, criminal justice, geography, history, human services, political science/government, psychology, social work, and sociology). Criminal justice and business are the strongest academically. Business, biology, and political science are the largest.

Required: To graduate, students must complete 124 semester hours, including 30 in the major, with a minimum GPA of 2.0. Core requirements include courses in communications, math and natural science, social science, humanities, and health and phys ed.

Special: NCCU offers internships, study abroad, a Washington semester, work-study programs, dual majors, and nondegree study. There are 10 national honor societies, a freshman honors program, and 10 departmental honors programs.

Faculty/Classroom: 53% of faculty are male; 47%, female. All teach undergraduates.

Admissions: 87% of the 2003-2004 applicants were accepted. The SAT I scores for the 2003-2004 freshman class were: Verbal--84% below

500, 13% between 500 and 599, 2% between 600 and 700, and 1% above 700; Math--85% below 500, 13% between 500 and 599, and 2% between 600 and 700. The ACT scores were 89% below 21, 7% between 21 and 23, 2% between 24 and 26, and 2% between 27 and 28. 17% of the current freshmen were in the top fifth of their class; 49% were in the top two fifths.

Requirements: The SAT I or ACT is required. In addition, applicants must be graduates of an accredited secondary school or have a GED certificate. They must have completed 11 academic credits based on 4 years of English, 3 each of math and science, and 2 each of a foreign language and social studies. Music applicants must audition. A GPA of 2.0 is required. AP and CLEP credits are accepted. Important factors in the admissions decision are advanced placement or honor courses, leadership record, and evidence of special talent.

Procedure: Entrance exams should be taken in the spring of the junior year. Applications should be filed by July 1 for fall entry and November 1 for spring entry. The fall 2003 application fee was $30. Notification is sent on a rolling basis. Applications are accepted on-line through the school's web site.

Transfer: 373 transfer students enrolled in 2002-2003. Applicants must have a minimum GPA of 2.0 in all college-level courses. 30 of 124 credits required for the bachelor's degree must be completed at NCCU.

Visiting: There are regularly scheduled orientations for prospective students. There are guides for informal visits and visitors may sit in on classes and stay overnight. To schedule a visit, contact LuAnn Harris at (919) 530-7349.

Financial Aid: In a recent year, 85% of all full-time students received some form of financial aid. 70% of all full-time students received need-based aid. The FAFSA is required. The deadline for filing freshman financial aid applications for fall entry is August 1.

International Students: They must score 500 on the written TOEFL. They must also take the SAT I or the ACT, unless these tests are not administered in their country.

Computers: The mainframe is a Data General MV/15000. All students may access the system 9 A.M. to 5 P.M. Monday through Friday. The computing center also has dial-in service. There are no time limits and no fees. It is strongly recommended that all students have a personal computer.

Graduates: From July 1, 2002 to June 30, 2003, 604 bachelor's degrees were awarded. The most popular majors were business administration (21%), education (11%), and criminal justice (9%). 297 companies recruited on campus in 2002-2003.

Admissions Contact: Jocelyn L. Foy, Director of Admissions. A video is available.

NORTH CAROLINA SCHOOL OF THE ARTS
Winston-Salem, NC 27127-2188

C-2

(336) 770-3290

Fax: (336) 770-3370

Full-time: 952 men and women	**Faculty:** 126
Part-time: 11 men and women	**Ph.D.s:** 70%
Graduate: 79 men and women	**Student/Faculty:** 8 to 1
Year: trimesters	**Tuition:** $3450 ($14,050)
Application Deadline: March 1	**Room & Board:** $5115
Freshman Class: 744 applied, 326 accepted, 215 enrolled	
SAT I Verbal/Math: 567/547	**ACT:** 23 **SPECIAL**

North Carolina School of the Arts, founded in 1963 and part of the University of North Carolina system, is a public institution offering professional training in the performing arts. There are 5 undergraduate and 2 graduate schools. The library contains 114,050 volumes, 25,053 microform items, and 73,025 audio/video tapes/CDs, and subscribes to 490 periodicals. Computerized library services include the card catalog, interlibrary loans, and database searching. Special learning facilities include a learning resource center, art gallery, and numerous performance theaters, screening rooms, and CAD studios. The 67-acre campus is in an urban area in Winston-Salem. Including any residence halls, there are 33 buildings.

Student Life: 55% of undergraduates are from out of state, mostly the Middle Atlantic. Students are from 44 states, 28 foreign countries, and Canada. 80% are from public schools. 84% are white; 10% African American. The average age of freshmen is 19; all undergraduates, 25. 25% do not continue beyond their first year.

Housing: 300 students can be accommodated in college housing, which includes coed dorms and on-campus apartments. On-campus housing is available on a first-come, first-served basis. Priority is given to out-of-town students. 58% of students live on campus; of those, 90% remain on campus on weekends. Alcohol is not permitted. All students may keep cars.

Activities: There are no fraternities or sororities. There are many groups and organizations on campus, including art, band, choir, chorale, chorus, dance, drama, ethnic, film, gay, international, jazz band, musical theater, newspaper, opera, orchestra, radio and TV, student government, and symphony.

Sports: There is no sports program at NCSA. Facilities include a gym, fitness and weight rooms, a swimming pool, a soccer and touch football field, a golf course, and courts for tennis, basketball, and volleyball.

Disabled Students: 85% of the campus is accessible. Wheelchair ramps, elevators, special parking, specially equipped rest rooms, and lowered drinking fountains are available.

Services: Counseling and information services are available, as is tutoring in every subject. There is remedial math, reading, and writing. Private tutoring is also offered on a fee basis.

Campus Safety and Security: Measures include 24-hour foot and vehicle patrol, emergency telephones, and lighted pathways/sidewalks.

Programs of Study: NCSA confers B.F.A. and B.M. degrees. Master's degrees are also awarded. Bachelor's degrees are awarded in COMMUNICATIONS AND THE ARTS (ballet, dance, dramatic arts, film arts, music, performing arts, and theater design).

Required: To earn a bachelor's degree, students must demonstrate satisfactory skills in reading, writing, oral communication, and math, take courses in foundations of Western thought, complete studies in fine arts and humanities, social and behavioral sciences, and math and natural science, and meet all requirements in their arts major.

Special: NCSA offers work-study programs, a general studies major, independent study, and design and production apprenticeships. An accelerated degree program is available to high school students in dance, drama, music, and visual arts.

Faculty/Classroom: 67% of faculty are male; 33%, female. All teach undergraduates. No introductory courses are taught by graduate students. The average class size in a regular course is 10.

Admissions: 44% of the 2003-2004 applicants were accepted. The SAT I scores for the 2003-2004 freshman class were: Verbal--13% below 500, 27% between 500 and 599, 18% between 600 and 700, and 5% above 700; Math--22% below 500, 27% between 500 and 599, 13% between 600 and 700, and 1% above 700. The ACT scores were 1% between 21 and 23, 8% between 24 and 26, 6% between 27 and 28, and 7% above 28. 26% of the current freshmen were in the top fifth of their class; 60% were in the top two fifths.

Requirements: The SAT I or ACT is required. In addition, applicants must be graduates of an accredited secondary school or have a GED certificate. They should have completed 4 units in English, 3 in math, 3 in science with 1 in a lab course, and 2 in social studies with 1 in U.S. history. Also recommended are 2 units in a foreign language and 1 unit each in foreign language and math in the senior year. An audition or interview demonstrating evidence of special talent is the primary admissions criterion. Applicants to the School of Design and Production must submit a portfolio. Filmmaking applicants must submit a creative writing sample. AP and CLEP credits are accepted. Important factors in the admissions decision are recommendations by school officials, evidence of special talent, and recommendations by alumni.

Procedure: Freshmen are admitted fall and winter. Applications should be filed by March 1 for fall entry. There is a rolling admissions plan. Notification is sent on a rolling basis. The fall 2003 application fee was $45.

Transfer: 62 transfer students enrolled in a recent year. Evidence of special talent and good academic standing are required. Placement is based on ability and experience, prior courses, and interviews and auditions.

Visiting: There are regularly scheduled orientations for prospective students, including tours on audition days and question-and-answer sessions with administration and faculty. Visitors may sit in on classes. To schedule a visit, contact the Admissions Office.

Financial Aid: In 2003-2004, 64% of all full-time freshmen received some form of financial aid. 58% of full-time freshmen received need-based aid. The average financial indebtedness of a recent graduate was $15,566. The FAFSA is required. The deadline for filing freshman financial aid applications for fall entry is March 1.

International Students: In a recent year, there were 19 international students enrolled. The school actively recruits these students. They must score 550 on the written TOEFL.

Computers: PCs are available in the student computer lab and the library. All students may access the system. There are no time limits and no fees.

Graduates: In a recent year, 126 bachelor's degrees were awarded. The most popular majors were filmmaking (38%), design and production (23%), and music (21%). In an average class, 3% graduate in 3 years or less, 40% graduate in 4 years or less, 45% graduate in 5 years or less, and 45% graduate in 6 years or less.

Admissions Contact: Sheeler Lawson, Director of Admissions.
E-mail: *admissions@ncarts.edu* Web: *www.ncarts.edu*

NORTH CAROLINA STATE UNIVERSITY   D-2
Raleigh, NC 27695-7103   (919) 515-2434; Fax: (919) 515-5039

Full-time: 10,894 men, 7789 women	**Faculty:** 1607; I, av$
Part-time: 2284 men, 1813 women	**Ph.D.s:** 91%
Graduate: 3774 men, 3083 women	**Student/Faculty:** 12 to 1
Year: semesters, summer session	**Tuition:** $3968 ($15,816)
Application Deadline: February 1	**Room & Board:** $5918
Freshman Class: 12,996 applied, 7998 accepted, 3934 enrolled	
SAT I Verbal/Math: 580/615	**ACT:** 22 **VERY COMPETITIVE**

North Carolina State University, founded in 1887, is a member of the University of North Carolina System. Its degree programs emphasize the arts and sciences, agriculture, business, education, engineering, and pre-professional training. There are 10 undergraduate and 10 graduate schools. In addition to regional accreditation, NC State has baccalaureate program accreditation with ABET, CSAB, CSWE, NAAB, NCATE, NRPA, and SAF. The 5 libraries contain 2.9 million volumes, 4.8 million microform items, and 142,831 audio/video tapes/CDs, and subscribe to 37,000 periodicals. Computerized library services include the card catalog, interlibrary loans, database searching, and Internet access. Special learning facilities include a learning resource center, art gallery, radio station, TV station, nuclear reactor, phytotron, electron microscope facilities, Materials Research Center, Integrated Manufacturing Systems Engineering Institute, Japan Center, and Precision Engineering Center. The 1700-acre campus is in an urban area in Raleigh. Including any residence halls, there are 150 buildings.

Student Life: 87% of undergraduates are from North Carolina. Students are from 50 states, 110 foreign countries, and Canada. 91% are from public schools. 77% are white; 10% African American. 60% are Protestant; 18% claim no religious affiliation; 14% Catholic. The average age of freshmen is 18; all undergraduates, 21. 12% do not continue beyond their first year; 65% remain to graduate.

Housing: 7300 students can be accommodated in college housing, which includes single-sex and coed dorms, married-student housing, fraternity houses, and sorority houses. In addition, there are honors houses, special-interest houses, and international, arts and creative living, computer theme, and first-year-experience halls. On-campus housing is guaranteed for all 4 years. 66% of students commute. Alcohol is not permitted. Upperclassmen may keep cars.

Activities: 10% of men belong to 27 national fraternities; 9% of women belong to 10 national sororities. There are 300 groups on campus, including art, bagpipe band, band, cheerleading, chess, choir, chorale, chorus, computers, dance, drama, drill team, drum and bugle corps, ethnic, film, gay, honors, international, jazz band, literary magazine, marching band, musical theater, newspaper, orchestra, pep band, photography, political, professional, radio and TV, religious, social, social service, student government, symphony, and yearbook. Popular campus events include Pan African Festival, Wolfstock, and Greek Week.

Sports: There are 20 intercollegiate sports for men and 16 for women, and 28 intramural sports for men and 26 for women. Facilities include a 55,000-seat football stadium, a 20,000-seat sports arena, a 5000-seat soccer stadium, a baseball stadium, a 12,500-seat gym, a tennis complex, areas for track, 2 indoor pools, and an indoor rock climbing wall.

Disabled Students: 78% of the campus is accessible. Wheelchair ramps, elevators, special parking, specially equipped rest rooms, special class scheduling, lowered drinking fountains, lowered telephones, and van transportation are available.

Services: Counseling and information services are available, as is tutoring in most subjects. There is a reader service for the blind and remedial math and writing.

Campus Safety and Security: Measures include 24-hour foot and vehicle patrol, self-defense education, security escort services, and shuttle buses. There are informal discussions, pamphlets/posters/films, emergency telephones, lighted pathways/sidewalks, and bicycle patrol.

Programs of Study: NC State confers B.A., B.S., B.Arch., B.E.D.A., B.L.A., and B.S.W. degrees. Associate, master's, and doctoral degrees are also awarded. Bachelor's degrees are awarded in AGRICULTURE (agricultural business management, agricultural economics, agriculture, agronomy, animal science, conservation and regulation, fishing and fisheries, forestry and related sciences, horticulture, natural resource management, poultry science, soil science, and wood science), BIOLOGICAL SCIENCE (biochemistry, biology/biological science, botany, microbiology, and zoology), BUSINESS (accounting, business administration and management, business economics, and recreation and leisure services), COMMUNICATIONS AND THE ARTS (communications, design, English, French, graphic design, industrial design, and Spanish), COMPUTER AND PHYSICAL SCIENCE (atmospheric sciences and meteorology, chemistry, computer science, earth science, geology, mathematics, physics, and statistics), EDUCATION (agricultural, education, foreign languages, industrial arts, marketing and distribution, mathematics, middle school, science, secondary, social studies, technical, and vocational), ENGINEERING AND ENVIRONMENTAL DESIGN (aeronautical engineering, agricultural engineering, architecture, chemical engineering, civil engineering, computer engineering, construction management, electrical/electronics engineering, engineering, environmental design, environmental engineering, environmental science, furniture design, industrial engineering, landscape architecture/design, materials science, mechanical engineering, nuclear engineering, paper and pulp science, and textile engineering), HEALTH PROFESSIONS (medical laboratory technology, predentistry, premedicine, preveterinary science, and speech pathology/audiology), SOCIAL SCIENCE (clothing and textiles management/production/services, criminal justice, economics, food science, history, interdisciplinary studies, parks and recreation management, philosophy, political science/government, prelaw, psychology, religion, social science, social work, sociology, and textiles and clothing). Electrical engineering, chemical engineering, and architecture are the strongest academically. Business management, mechanical engineering, and electrical engineering are the largest.

Required: To graduate, students must complete 120 to 142 semester hours, including 60 to 70 in the major, with a minimum GPA of 2.0. Distribution requirements include 12 to 18 hours in humanities and social sciences, 6 to 8 each in math and science, 6 in English composition, and 4 in phys ed.

Special: NC State offers cross-registration within the Cooperating Raleigh Colleges network, study abroad in more than 90 countries, internships, work-study programs, an accelerated degree plan, dual majors within any program, a general studies degree in education, a 3-2 engineering degree with the University of North Carolina at Asheville, student-designed multidisciplinary studies majors, credit by examination, nondegree study, and pass/fail options. There are 15 national honor societies, including Phi Beta Kappa, a freshman honors program, and 44 departmental honors programs.

Faculty/Classroom: 75% of faculty are male; 25%, female. All both teach and do research. Graduate students teach 8% of introductory courses. The average class size in an introductory lecture is 35; in a laboratory, 20; and in a regular course, 30.

Admissions: 62% of the 2003-2004 applicants were accepted. 87 freshmen graduated first in their class.

Requirements: The SAT I or ACT is required. In addition, the SAT II: Math test is recommended. Applicants must be graduates of an accredited secondary school or have a GED certificate. They must have completed 20 academic credits, including 4 units of English, 3 each of science and math (4 of math is advised), 2 each of social studies and foreign language, and 1 of history. An essay is recommended for all applicants. A portfolio and interview are required for the School of Design. AP and CLEP credits are accepted. Important factors in the admissions decision are advanced placement or honor courses, leadership record, and evidence of special talent.

Procedure: Freshmen are admitted to all sessions. Entrance exams should be taken in the spring of the junior year and the fall of the senior year. There are early admissions and deferred admissions plans. Early decision applications should be filed by November 1; regular applications, by February 1 for fall entry, November 1 for spring entry, and February 1 for summer entry. The fall 2003 application fee was $55. Notification of early decision is sent January 15; regular decision, on a rolling basis. 350 applicants were on the 2003 waiting list; 50 were admitted. Applications are accepted on-line.

Transfer: 1222 transfer students enrolled in a recent year. Applicants must have completed 30 semester hours of college-level work with a minimum GPA of 2.0. Priority is given to students who have completed 60 hours of relevant course work. An associate degree and an interview are recommended. Applicants must have math, English, and foreign language proficiency. 30 of 120 credits required for the bachelor's degree must be completed at NC State.

Visiting: There are regularly scheduled orientations for prospective students, consisting of admissions information sessions. There are guides for informal visits and visitors may sit in on classes. To schedule a visit, contact the Admissions Office at *undergrad-admissions@ncsu.edu.*

Financial Aid: The FAFSA and the university's own financial statement are required. The deadline for filing freshman financial aid applications for fall entry is March 1.

International Students: The school actively recruits these students. They must score 550 on the written TOEFL or 213 on the electronic version and also take the SAT I or ACT, if it is available to students in their country.

Computers: The mainframes are an IBM 3081, an IBM 4381/P12, and a DEC VAX 8700. There are also 2300 computer stations located campuswide. Several departments have additional stations available for their majors only. All students may access the system. Time limits vary by class. The fee is $100.

Admissions Contact: Thomas Griffin, Director of Admissions.
E-mail: *undergrad_admissions@ncsu.edu* Web: *http://www2.ncsu.edu*

NORTH CAROLINA WESLEYAN COLLEGE
Rocky Mount, NC 27804

E-2

(252) 985-5200
(800) 488-NCWC; Fax: (252) 985-5295

Full-time: 449 men, 675 women	**Faculty:** IIB, --$
Part-time: 238 men, 333 women	**Ph.D.s:** 62%
Graduate: none	**Student/Faculty:** n/av
Year: 4-1-4, summer session	**Tuition:** $12,443
Application Deadline: open	**Room & Board:** $5555
Freshman Class: 651 applied, 542 accepted, 200 enrolled	
SAT I or ACT: required	**COMPETITIVE**

North Carolina Wesleyan College, founded in 1956, is a private liberal arts institution affiliated with the United Methodist Church. In addition to regional accreditation, NCWC has baccalaureate program accreditation with NCATE. The library contains 65,721 volumes, 2830 microform items, and 4200 audio/video tapes/CDs, and subscribes to 4645 periodicals. Computerized library services include the card catalog, interlibrary loans, and database searching. Special learning facilities include a learning resource center, art gallery, and a performing arts center. The 200-acre campus is in a suburban area 57 miles east of Raleigh. Including any residence halls, there are 18 buildings.

Student Life: 88% of undergraduates are from North Carolina. Students are from 24 states and 9 foreign countries. 70% are from public schools. 48% are white; 40% African American. 70% are Protestant; 16% Catholic; 14% claim no religious affiliation. The average age of freshmen is 19; all undergraduates, 23.

Housing: 504 students can be accommodated in college housing, which includes single-sex and coed dorms and off-campus apartments. In addition, there are single-occupancy residence halls with kitchens on each floor. On-campus housing is guaranteed for all 4 years. 57% of students live on campus; of those, 60% remain on campus on weekends. All students may keep cars.

Activities: 8% of men belong to 3 national fraternities; 4% of women belong to 3 national sororities. There are 23 groups on campus, including cheerleading, chess, choir, chorus, computers, drama, ethnic, gay, honors, international, jazz band, musical theater, newspaper, political, professional, religious, social, social service, student government, and yearbook. Popular campus events include Spring Fling, Parents Weekend, and Alumni Homecoming.

Sports: There are 5 intercollegiate sports for men and 5 for women, and 13 intramural sports for men and 13 for women. Facilities include a 1200-seat gym with areas for basketball, volleyball, and indoor soccer matches; tennis courts; a skeet range; and fields for intramurals and for varsity baseball, softball, and soccer.

Disabled Students: 90% of the campus is accessible. Wheelchair ramps, elevators, special parking, specially equipped rest rooms, special class scheduling, lowered drinking fountains, lowered telephones, and special housing are available.

Services: Counseling and information services are available, as is tutoring in most subjects. There is remedial math, reading, and writing.

Campus Safety and Security: Measures include 24-hour foot and vehicle patrol, security escort services, informal discussions, and pamphlets/posters/films. There are emergency telephones and lighted pathways/sidewalks.

Programs of Study: NCWC confers B.A. and B.S. degrees. Bachelor's degrees are awarded in BIOLOGICAL SCIENCE (biology/biological science), BUSINESS (accounting, business administration and management, and hotel/motel and restaurant management), COMMUNICATIONS AND THE ARTS (dramatic arts and English), COMPUTER AND PHYSICAL SCIENCE (chemistry, information sciences and systems, and mathematics), EDUCATION (elementary and middle school), ENGINEERING AND ENVIRONMENTAL DESIGN (environmental science), HEALTH PROFESSIONS (exercise science and premedicine), SOCIAL SCIENCE (criminal justice, history, political science/government, psychology, religion, and sociology). Business administration, justice studies, and computer information systems are the largest.

Required: To graduate, students must complete 124 semester hours, including 30 to 54 in the major, with a minimum GPA of 2.0. Distribution requirements consist of 6 semester hours of English composition or demonstrated proficiency; 4 each of biological and physical science; 3 each of ethics, non-Western culture, math, history, social science, psychology or sociology, religion, literature, and fine arts; 2 of phys ed; and 2 of introduction to college life. Some majors require a thesis.

Special: NCWC offers cooperative programs in all majors, internships, work-study programs through the college offices, credit for military experience, nondegree study, and pass/fail options. The B.A.-B.S. degree may be earned in all majors. There are 2 national honor societies and a freshman honors program.

Faculty/Classroom: 55% of faculty are male; 45%, female. All teach undergraduates. The average class size in an introductory lecture is 23; in a laboratory, 15; and in a regular course, 18.

Admissions: 83% of the 2003-2004 applicants were accepted.

Requirements: The SAT I or ACT is required, with a minimum SAT I composite score of 800 or ACT score of 19 recommended. Applicants should be graduates of an accredited secondary school or have a GED. They should have completed at least 13 academic courses, including 4 in English, 3 in math, and 2 each in foreign language, social studies, and lab sciences. An essay and an interview are advised. AP and CLEP credits are accepted. Important factors in the admissions decision are advanced placement or honor courses, extracurricular activities record, and leadership record.

Procedure: Freshmen are admitted fall and spring. Entrance exams should be taken in spring of the junior year or fall or winter of the senior year. Application deadlines are open. Application fee is $25. Applications are accepted on-line through the school's web site.

Transfer: 93 transfer students enrolled in 2003-2004. Applicants must have a minimum GPA of 2.0 in their college courses. They must submit transcripts of all high school and college work, along with proof of high school graduation. 31 of 124 credits required for the bachelor's degree must be completed at NCWC.

Visiting: There are regularly scheduled orientations for prospective students, including an individual campus tour, an interview, a financial aid session, and meetings with faculty and coaches. There are guides for informal visits and visitors may sit in on classes and stay overnight. To schedule a visit, contact the Admissions Office.

Financial Aid: NCWC is a member of CSS. The FAFSA is required. The priority date for freshman financial aid applications for fall entry is March 15.

International Students: They must score 500 on the written TOEFL and also take the SAT I.

Computers: The mainframe is an IBM/36. There are 70 PCs located in the computer lab, residence halls, tutoring center, and library. All students may access the system on a sign-up basis in the computer lab or as available at other locations. There are no time limits and no fees.

Graduates: From July 1, 2002 to June 30, 2003, 401 bachelor's degrees were awarded. The most popular majors were business/marketing (48%), computer and information sciences (24%), and law/legal studies (10%). In an average class, 26% graduate in 4 years or less, 33% graduate in 5 years or less, and 38% graduate in 6 years or less.

Admissions Contact: Cecelia Summers, Director of Admissions. E-mail: adm@ncwc.edu Web: www.ncwc.edu

---

PFEIFFER UNIVERSITY

C-2

Misenheimer, NC 28109

(704) 463-1360, ext. 2079
(800) 338-2060; Fax: (704) 463-1363

Full-time: 433 men, 569 women	**Faculty:** 59; IIA, --$
Part-time: 60 men, 123 women	**Ph.D.s:** 68%
Graduate: 220 men, 370 women	**Student/Faculty:** 17 to 1
Year: semesters, summer session	**Tuition:** $13,550
Application Deadline: August 25	**Room & Board:** $5430
Freshman Class: 562 applied, 416 accepted, 170 enrolled	
SAT I Verbal/Math: 490/510	**ACT:** 21 COMPETITIVE

Pfeiffer University, founded in 1885, is a private institution of liberal arts and sciences affiliated with the United Methodist Church. There are 2 undergraduate schools and 1 graduate school. In addition to regional accreditation, Pfeiffer has baccalaureate program accreditation with NASM and NCATE. The library contains 117,402 volumes, 30,963 microform items, and 2977 audio/video tapes/CDs, and subscribes to 396 periodicals. Computerized library services include the card catalog, interlibrary loans, database searching, and Internet access. Special learning facilities include a learning resource center and art gallery. The 350-acre campus is in a rural area 35 miles east of Charlotte. Including any residence halls, there are 28 buildings.

Student Life: 76% of undergraduates are from North Carolina. Students are from 30 states and 10 foreign countries. 80% are white; 12% African American. 65% are Protestant; 13% claim no religious affiliation; 12% Muslim, Hindu; 10% Catholic. The average age of freshmen is 18; all undergraduates, 22. 33% do not continue beyond their first year; 36% remain to graduate.

Housing: 717 students can be accommodated in college housing, which includes single-sex and coed dorms and married-student housing. In addition, there are honors houses and substance-free and academic emphasis living. On-campus housing is guaranteed for all 4 years. 55% of students live on campus; of those, 60% remain on campus on weekends. All students may keep cars.

Activities: There are no fraternities or sororities. There are 34 groups on campus, including band, cheerleading, chess, choir, chorale, chorus, drama, ethnic, honors, international, jazz band, literary magazine, newspaper, pep band, political, professional, religious, social, social service, student government, and yearbook. Popular campus events include Winterfest, Aprilfest, and coffee houses.

Sports: There are 7 intercollegiate sports for men and 9 for women, and 21 intramural sports for men and 21 for women. Facilities include an 1800-seat main gym, an indoor pool, exercise rooms, training facilities, and weight rooms. The campus also has 6 tennis courts, fields for baseball, softball, lacrosse, and soccer, areas for golf practice and volleyball, and an indoor batting cage.

Disabled Students: 50% of the campus is accessible. Wheelchair ramps, elevators, special parking, specially equipped rest rooms, and special class scheduling are available.

Services: Counseling and information services are available, as is tutoring in most subjects. There is remedial math, reading, and writing.

Campus Safety and Security: Measures include 24-hour foot and vehicle patrol, self-defense education, security escort services, and informal discussions. There are pamphlets/posters/films and lighted pathways/sidewalks.

Programs of Study: Pfeiffer confers A.B. and B.S. degrees. Master's degrees are also awarded. Bachelor's degrees are awarded in BIOLOGICAL SCIENCE (biology/biological science), BUSINESS (accounting, business administration and management, and sports management), COMMUNICATIONS AND THE ARTS (arts administration/management, communications, dramatic arts, English literature, and music), COMPUTER AND PHYSICAL SCIENCE (chemistry, information sciences and systems, and mathematics), EDUCATION (athletic training, Christian, elementary, music, physical, science, secondary, and special), ENGINEERING AND ENVIRONMENTAL DESIGN (environmental science and preengineering), HEALTH PROFESSIONS (premedicine and sports medicine), SOCIAL SCIENCE (American studies, criminal justice, economics, history, human services, political science/government, prelaw, psychology, religion, religious education, religious music, social studies, and sociology). Chemistry, music, and sports medicine and management are the strongest academically. Business administration, criminal justice, and elementary education are the largest.

Required: All students must complete 120 to 124 semester hours, including 60 credits in writing, language and literature, history/political science, music/art/theater, natural science, math, economics/psychology/sociology, religion, and phys ed. Students must maintain an overall minimum GPA of 2.0 and complete 42 to 72 hours in the major.A freshman seminar and senior project in the major are required, as well as participation in the cultural program and basic compentency in computer technology.

Special: A 3-2 program in engineering with Auburn University, work-study programs, many internships in business, education, public service, and phys ed, study abroad in 5 countries, and interdisciplinary majors are offered. There are 5 national honor societies, a freshman honors program, and 10 departmental honors programs.

Faculty/Classroom: 63% of faculty are male; 37%, female. 87% teach undergraduates, 25% do research, and 25% do both. No introductory courses are taught by graduate students. The average class size in an introductory lecture is 24; in a laboratory, 18; and in a regular course, 12.

Admissions: 74% of the 2003-2004 applicants were accepted. The SAT I scores for the 2003-2004 freshman class were: Verbal--51% below 500, 40% between 500 and 599, 8% between 600 and 700, and 1% above 700; Math--43% below 500, 44% between 500 and 599, 12% between 600 and 700, and 1% above 700. The ACT scores were 53% below 21, 33% between 21 and 23, 10% between 24 and 26, and 4% between 27 and 28. 28% of the current freshmen were in the top fifth of their class; 55% were in the top two fifths.

Requirements: The SAT I is required and the ACT is recommended. In addition, all applicants are required to have completed 4 years of English and 3 years of math, including algebra I. The GED is accepted. Pfeiffer requires applicants to be in the upper 50% of their class. A GPA of 2.0 is required. AP and CLEP credits are accepted. Important factors in the admissions decision are advanced placement or honor courses, leadership record, and extracurricular activities record.

Procedure: Freshmen are admitted to all sessions. Entrance exams should be taken by January of the senior year. There are early admissions and deferred admissions plans. Applications should be filed by August 25 for fall entry and January 20 for spring entry, along with a $25 fee. Notification is sent on a rolling basis. Applications are accepted online.

Transfer: 122 transfer students enrolled in 2002-2003. Applicants should be eligible for readmission to the last college attended and have a minimum GPA of 2.0. 45 of 120 credits required for the bachelor's degree must be completed at Pfeiffer.

Visiting: There are regularly scheduled orientations for prospective students, including meetings with faculty/staff, a question-and-answer session, a tour, and a lunch. There are guides for informal visits and visitors may sit in on classes and stay overnight. To schedule a visit, contact the Admissions Office at admissions@pfeiffer.edu.

Financial Aid: In 2003-2004, 79% of all full-time freshmen and 90% of continuing full-time students received some form of financial aid. 94% of full-time freshmen and 90% of continuing full-time students received need-based aid. The average freshman award was $9500. 45% of undergraduates work part time. Average annual earnings from campus work are $1150. The average financial indebtedness of the 2003 graduate was $15,500. Pfeiffer is a member of CSS. The FAFSA is required. The priority date for freshman financial aid applications for fall entry is April 15. The deadline for filing freshman financial aid applications for fall entry is open.

International Students: There are 31 international students enrolled. They must score 500 on the written TOEFL and also take the SAT I or ACT, or show proven success at a U.S. school.

Computers: There are 2 main labs and several smaller ones on campus, each with 24 Pentium II computers, which have Internet access, and are available 24 hours per day. Dorms are wired for Internet access. All students may access the system. There are no time limits and no fees.

Graduates: From July 1, 2002 to June 30, 2003, 229 bachelor's degrees were awarded. The most popular majors were business administration (30%), criminal justice (11%), and education (9%). In an average class, 30% graduate in 4 years or less, 39% graduate in 5 years or less, and 42% graduate in 6 years or less. 112 companies recruited on campus in 2002-2003. Of the 2002 graduating class, 17% were enrolled in graduate school within 6 months of graduation.

Admissions Contact: Steve Cumming, Director of Admissions. E-mail: *admissions@pfeiffer.edu* Web: *www.pfeiffer.edu*

QUEENS UNIVERSITY OF CHARLOTTE   C-3
(Formerly Queens College)
Charlotte, NC 28274

(704) 337-2212
(800) 849-0202; Fax: (704) 337-2403

Full-time: 225 men, 636 women	**Faculty:** 77; IIA, --$
Part-time: 105 men, 445 women	**Ph.D.s:** 81%
Graduate: 172 men, 381 women	**Student/Faculty:** 11 to 1
Year: semesters, summer session	**Tuition:** $15,650
Application Deadline: open	**Room & Board:** $6190
Freshman Class: 839 applied, 619 accepted, 254 enrolled	
SAT I or ACT: required	**COMPETITIVE**

Queens University of Charlotte, formerly Queens College, founded in 1857, is a private liberal arts institution affiliated with the Presbyterian Church (U.S.A.). Undergraduate programs are offered through the College of Arts and Sciences and the Pauline Lewis Hayworth College, a division offering courses in the evening and on Saturday. There are 2 undergraduate schools and 1 graduate school. In addition to regional accreditation, Queens has baccalaureate program accreditation with ACBSP, NASM, NCATE, and NLN. The library contains 142,201 volumes, 87,848 microform items, and 1639 audio/video tapes/CDs, and subscribes to 518 periodicals. Computerized library services include the card catalog, interlibrary loans, and database searching. Special learning facilities include a learning resource center, art gallery, rare books and archival collection, photographic lab, ceramics studio, and recital hall. The 25-acre campus is in a suburban area 2 miles south of uptown Charlotte. Including any residence halls, there are 29 buildings.

Student Life: 64% of undergraduates are from North Carolina. Students are from Canada. 75% are from public schools. 85% are white; 10% African American. The average age of freshmen is 18; all undergraduates, 20. 21% do not continue beyond their first year; 63% remain to graduate.

Housing: 600 students can be accommodated in college housing, which includes single-sex and coed dorms. On-campus housing is guaranteed for the freshman year only and is available on a lottery system for upperclassmen. 72% of students live on campus; of those, 60% remain on campus on weekends. All students may keep pets.

Activities: 20% of men belong to 2 national fraternities; 35% of women belong to 5 national sororities. There are 40 groups on campus, including art, cheerleading, choir, chorale, chorus, dance, drama, ethnic, gay, honors, international, literary magazine, musical theater, newspaper, political, professional, religious, social, social service, student government, and yearbook. Popular campus events include Casino Party, Mardi Gras Festival, and International Symposium.

Sports: There are 6 intercollegiate sports for men and 8 for women. Facilities include an athletic center with a gym, classrooms, dance studios, weight room, training room, and swimming pool. There are also 6 tennis courts (4 lighted) and a soccer/softball complex. In addition, the college center offers various recreational opportunities, and the residence hall has an 8000 square-foot state-of-the-art fitness center.

Disabled Students: 35% of the campus is accessible. Wheelchair ramps, special parking, specially equipped rest rooms, special class scheduling, and elevators in some buildings are available.

Services: There is remedial math, reading, writing, and English.

Campus Safety and Security: Measures include 24-hour foot and vehicle patrol, self-defense education, security escort services, and informal discussions. There are pamphlets/posters/films, emergency telephones, and lighted pathways/sidewalks.

Programs of Study: Queens confers B.A., B.S., B.Mus., and B.S.N. degrees. Master's degrees are also awarded. Bachelor's degrees are awarded in BIOLOGICAL SCIENCE (biochemistry and biology/biological science), BUSINESS (accounting and business administration and management), COMMUNICATIONS AND THE ARTS (communica-

tions, dramatic arts, English, fine arts, French, music, and Spanish), COMPUTER AND PHYSICAL SCIENCE (mathematics), EDUCATION (elementary), HEALTH PROFESSIONS (music therapy and nursing), SOCIAL SCIENCE (American studies, history, international studies, philosophy, political science/government, psychology, and religion). Liberal arts and sciences are the strongest academically. Business and communications are the largest.

Required: To graduate, students must complete a total of 122 credit hours with a minimum GPA of 2.0. For the B.A., between 30 and 40 hours are required in the student's major. For the B.S., 32 are required. All students must take a sequence of 5 courses in the Core Program in the Liberal Arts. In addition, 2 courses in English composition, 2 in phys ed, and 1 in lab science are required. If entering freshmen do not pass the placement exams given in math and a foreign language, additional courses will be required. Some majors require a thesis or research project.

Special: Internships in all majors, cross-registration with colleges of the Charlotte Area Educational Consortium, dual majors, nondegree study, and pass/fail options are available. The school offers a Washington semester. A study tour in Europe and Asia (included in the cost of tuition) may be arranged through the school's International Experience Program. There are 5 national honor societies and a freshman honors program.

Faculty/Classroom: 41% of faculty are male; 59%, female. All teach undergraduates. No introductory courses are taught by graduate students.

Admissions: 74% of the 2003-2004 applicants were accepted. The SAT I scores for the 2003-2004 freshman class were: Verbal--31% below 500, 45% between 500 and 599, 21% between 600 and 700, and 3% above 700; Math--33% below 500, 47% between 500 and 599, 20% between 600 and 700, and 1% above 700. The ACT scores were 25% below 21, 39% between 21 and 23, 28% between 24 and 26, 7% between 27 and 28, and 1% above 28. 40% of the current freshmen were in the top fifth of their class; 70% were in the top two fifths. 2 freshmen graduated first in their class.

Requirements: The SAT I or ACT is required. In addition, applicants should have a college preparatory background in an accredited secondary school. The GED is accepted. High school courses should include 4 years of English, 3 of math, 2 each of history or social studies and a foreign language, and 2 years of science, including 1 of lab science. An interview is recommended. An essay is required. An audition or portfolio is recommended for art and music students. AP and CLEP credits are accepted. Important factors in the admissions decision are recommendations by school officials, advanced placement or honor courses, and leadership record.

Procedure: Freshmen are admitted fall, spring, and summer. Entrance exams should be taken in the junior year or as early as possible in the senior year. There is a rolling admissions plan. Application deadlines are open. Application fee is $40. Applications are accepted on-line through the school's web site.

Transfer: 68 transfer students enrolled in 2002-2003. Transfer students are accepted in all but the senior class. A GPA of 2.0 is required for all previous college-level work. 45 of 122 credits required for the bachelor's degree must be completed at Queens.

Visiting: There are regularly scheduled orientations for prospective students, including a sampling of classes, campus tours, a college overview, a question/answer segment, a meet-the-faculty session, and a scholarship/financial aid session. There are guides for informal visits and visitors may sit in on classes and stay overnight. To schedule a visit, contact the Admissions Office at *admissions@queens.edu.*

Financial Aid: In 2002-2003, 68% of full-time freshmen and 54% of continuing full-time students received need-based aid. The average freshman award was $10,326. Average annual earnings from campus work are $1500. The average financial indebtedness of the 2003 graduate was $15,874. Queens is a member of CSS. The FAFSA is required. The deadline for filing freshman financial aid applications for fall entry is March 1.

International Students: There are 30 international students enrolled. The school actively recruits these students. They must score 550 on the written TOEFL or 213 on the electronic version and also take the SAT I (scoring 450 on Verbal) or the ACT.

Computers: The mainframe is an IBM AS/400. PCs are available for student use in the computer centers, the library, and the residence halls. All students may access the system. There are no time limits and no fees.

Graduates: From July 1, 2002 to June 30, 2003, 216 bachelor's degrees were awarded. The most popular majors were business (29%), communications (17%), and nursing (10%). In an average class, 63% graduate in 6 years or less. 350 companies recruited on campus in 2002-2003.

Admissions Contact: William Lee, Director of Admissions. E-mail: *admissions@queens.edu* Web: *www.queens.edu*

SAINT ANDREWS PRESBYTERIAN COLLEGE   D-3
Laurinburg, NC 28352   (910) 277-5555
                          (800) 763-0198; Fax: (910) 277-5087

Full-time: 267 men, 362 women   **Faculty:** 35; IIB, --$
Part-time: 12 men, 52 women   **Ph.Ds:** 80%
Graduate: none   **Student/Faculty:** 18 to 1
Year: semesters, summer session   **Tuition:** $15,115
Application Deadline: open   **Room & Board:** $5410
Freshman Class: 668 applied, 562 accepted, 196 enrolled
SAT I Verbal/Math: 490/485   COMPETITIVE

St. Andrews Presbyterian College is a private liberal arts institution affiliated with the Presbyterian Church (U.S.A.). The library contains 110,105 volumes, 14,204 microform items, and 1676 audio/video tapes/CDs, and subscribes to 416 periodicals. Computerized library services include the card catalog, interlibrary loans, and database searching. Special learning facilities include a learning resource center, art gallery, a 20,000-square-foot science lab, an artronics lab, and a writing lab. The 600-acre campus is in a small town about 100 miles from Charlotte. Including any residence halls, there are 17 buildings.

Student Life: 52% of undergraduates are from out of state, mostly the South. Students are from 33 states, 13 foreign countries, and Canada. 77% are white; 12% African American. 58% claim no religious affiliation; 30% Protestant; 9% Catholic. The average age of freshmen is 18; all undergraduates, 20. 27% do not continue beyond their first year; 72% remain to graduate.

Housing: 770 students can be accommodated in college housing, which includes single-sex and coed dorms. On-campus housing is guaranteed for all 4 years. 76% of students live on campus; of those, 90% remain on campus on weekends. All students may keep cars.

Activities: There are no fraternities or sororities. There are 32 groups on campus, including art, bagpipe band, cheerleading, chess, chorale, computers, debate, drama, ethnic, film, gay, honors, international, literary magazine, musical theater, newspaper, political, professional, religious, social, social service, and student government. Popular campus events include Writers' Forum, Extravaganza Weekend, and Springfest.

Sports: There are 7 intercollegiate sports for men and 7 for women, and 6 intramural sports for men and 6 for women. Facilities include a basketball and volleyball arena, equestrian facilities, a pool, and soccer, baseball, and softball fields.

Disabled Students: 90% of the campus is accessible. Wheelchair ramps, elevators, special parking, specially equipped rest rooms, lowered drinking fountains, lowered telephones, and personal aides are available.

Services: Counseling and information services are available, as is tutoring in most subjects.

Campus Safety and Security: Measures include 24-hour foot and vehicle patrol, security escort services, informal discussions, and pamphlets/posters/films. There are emergency telephones and lighted pathways/sidewalks.

Programs of Study: St. Andrews confers B.A., B.S., and B.F.A. degrees. Bachelor's degrees are awarded in BIOLOGICAL SCIENCE (biology/biological science, and neurosciences), BUSINESS (business administration and management), COMMUNICATIONS AND THE ARTS (communications, creative writing, English, and visual and performing arts), COMPUTER AND PHYSICAL SCIENCE (chemistry and mathematics), EDUCATION (elementary and physical), SOCIAL SCIENCE (Asian/Oriental studies, forensic studies, history, liberal arts/general studies, philosophy, political science/government, psychology, public history/archives, religion, and therapeutic riding). Business and economics, equine studies, and biology are the strongest academically. Business and economics, elementary education, and phys ed are the largest.

Required: To graduate, students must complete a total of 120 hours with a minimum GPA of 2.0. Between 10 and 15 courses are required in the student's major. All students must complete 15 hours in the interdisciplinary St. Andrews General Education core program. In addition, students must satisfy breadth requirements in the creative arts, humanities, lab sciences, social and behavioral sciences, phys ed, and international studies.

Special: St. Andrew's offers student-designed majors for contract and thematic majors, a Washington semester, nondegree study, on-campus work-study, and pass/fail options. Students may study abroad in 11 countries. A 3-2 engineering degree with North Carolina State University and 3-2 and 4-2 accounting programs with the University of Georgia are available. There are year-long, semester-long, and summer-term internships in all majors. There are 3 national honor societies, a freshman honors program, and 8 departmental honors programs.

Faculty/Classroom: 60% of faculty are male; 40%, female. All teach undergraduates and 50% do research. The average class size in an introductory lecture is 15; in a laboratory, 15; and in a regular course, 15.

Admissions: 84% of the 2003-2004 applicants were accepted. The SAT I scores for the 2003-2004 freshman class were: Verbal--54% below 500, 31% between 500 and 599, 13% between 600 and 700, and 2% above 700; Math--54% below 500, 38% between 500 and 599, and 8% between 600 and 700.

Requirements: The SAT I or ACT is required, with a minimum score of 950 on the SAT I or 20 on the ACT. Graduation from an accredited secondary school or the GED is required for admission. High school courses should include 4 units of English, 3 each of science and math, and 2 each of a foreign language, social studies, and electives. An essay is required. A GPA of 2.5 is required. AP and CLEP credits are accepted. Important factors in the admissions decision are personality/intangible qualities, recommendations by school officials, and evidence of special talent.

Procedure: Freshmen are admitted to all sessions. Entrance exams should be taken as early as possible. There is a deferred admissions plan. Application deadlines are open. The fall 2003 application fee was $30. Applications are accepted on-line through the college's web site.

Transfer: 49 transfer students enrolled in 2002-2003. Transfer students must have a minimum GPA of 2.0. Up to 65 semester or 97 quarter hours may be transferred from a 2-year college and 90 semester or 135 quarter hours from a 4-year college. 30 of 120 credits required for the bachelor's degree must be completed at St. Andrews.

Visiting: There are regularly scheduled orientations for prospective students, including activities, fairs, information sessions, summer orientation sessions with activities, and preregistration. There are guides for informal visits and visitors may sit in on classes and stay overnight. To schedule a visit, contact the Admissions Office.

Financial Aid: In 2003-2004, 97% of all full-time freshmen and 92% of continuing full-time students received some form of financial aid. 43% of full-time freshmen and 47% of continuing full-time students received need-based aid. The average freshman award was $8140. 66% of undergraduates work part time. Average annual earnings from campus work are $1800. The average financial indebtedness of the 2003 graduate was $11,900. The FAFSA is required.

International Students: There are 43 international students enrolled. The school actively recruits these students. They must score 550 on the written TOEFL.

Computers: There is a PC network with computer labs. All students may access the system every day, 24 hours a day. There are no time limits and no fees.

Graduates: The most popular majors were business administration (34%), politics (9%), and therapeutic riding (6%). In an average class, 1% graduate in 3 years or less, 38% graduate in 4 years or less, and 47% graduate in 5 years or less. Of the 2002 graduating class, 24% were enrolled in graduate school within 6 months of graduation and 70% were employed.

Admissions Contact: Glenn Batten, Vice President for Enrollment and Student Services. A video is available. E-mail: *admissions@sapc.edu* Web: *www.sapc.edu*

SAINT AUGUSTINE'S COLLEGE   D-2
Raleigh, NC 27610-2298   (919) 516-4000
                          (800) 948-1126; Fax: (919) 516-5805

Full-time: 515 men, 725 women   **Faculty:** 87
Part-time: 50 men, 80 women   **Ph.Ds:** 59%
Graduate: none   **Student/Faculty:** 16 to 1
Year: semesters, summer session   **Tuition:** $8030
Application Deadline: see profile **Room & Board:** $4960
Freshman Class: n/av
SAT I or ACT: required   LESS COMPETITIVE

Saint Augustine's College, founded in 1867, is a historically black liberal arts institution affiliated with the Episcopal Church. Figures in the above capsule and in this profile are approximate. The library contains 70,200 volumes and 500 microform items, and subscribes to 300 periodicals. Computerized library services include database searching. Special learning facilities include a learning resource center, radio station, and TV station. The 110-acre campus is in an urban area 1 mile northeast of downtown Raleigh. Including any residence halls, there are 37 buildings.

Student Life: 51% of undergraduates are from North Carolina. Students are from 34 states, 16 foreign countries, and Canada. 99% are from public schools. 90% are African American. 58% are Protestant; 39% claim no religious affiliation. The average age of freshmen is 18; all undergraduates, 22. 38% do not continue beyond their first year; 27% remain to graduate.

Housing: 1143 students can be accommodated in college housing, which includes single-sex dorms. In addition, there are honors houses. On-campus housing is guaranteed for all 4 years. 62% of students live on campus; of those, 75% remain on campus on weekends. Alcohol is not permitted. All students may keep cars.

Activities: 6% of men belong to 5 national fraternities; 12% of women belong to 4 national sororities. There are 20 groups on campus, including band, cheerleading, chorale, dance, drama, ethnic, honors, international, newspaper, photography, professional, radio and TV, religious, social service, student government, and yearbook. Popular campus events include opening convocation each semester, CIAA tournament, and career/job fairs.

Sports: There are 5 intercollegiate sports for men and 4 for women, and 4 intramural sports for men and 3 for women. Facilities include a 1700-seat gym, a track, baseball fields, and tennis and basketball courts.

Disabled Students: 64% of the campus is accessible. Wheelchair ramps, elevators, special parking, and specially equipped rest rooms are available.

Services: There is remedial math, reading, and writing. Help with writing and test-taking skills is available.

Campus Safety and Security: Measures include 24-hour foot and vehicle patrol, informal discussions, pamphlets/posters/films, and emergency telephones. There are lighted pathways/sidewalks.

Programs of Study: Saint Augustine's College confers B.A. and B.S. degrees. Bachelor's degrees are awarded in BIOLOGICAL SCIENCE (biology/biological science), BUSINESS (accounting, business administration and management, and international business management), COMMUNICATIONS AND THE ARTS (communications, English, fine arts, French, music, music business management, Spanish, and visual and performing arts), COMPUTER AND PHYSICAL SCIENCE (applied mathematics, chemistry, computer science, information sciences and systems, and mathematics), EDUCATION (business, education of the exceptional child, elementary, English, mathematics, music, physical, science, and social studies), ENGINEERING AND ENVIRONMENTAL DESIGN (industrial administration/management and industrial engineering), HEALTH PROFESSIONS (industrial hygiene, medical laboratory technology, and premedicine), SOCIAL SCIENCE (African American studies, criminal justice, history, physical fitness/movement, political science/government, prelaw, psychology, sociology, and urban studies). Engineering, math, premedicine, and chemistry are the strongest academically. Computer science, business administration, and communications are the largest.

Required: Students must complete at least 120 hours with a minimum 2.0 GPA for graduation. All students must complete a 50 to 55 credit core curriculum that includes courses in reading and communication, foreign language, science, math, philosophy, ethics, humanities, world civilization, psychology, and phys ed. Seniors must pass written and oral examinations in their major fields. Total credit hours required for a degree in offered majors range from 124 to 154.

Special: Students may cross-register at any of 5 area colleges, study abroad, or pursue a 3-2 engineering program with North Carolina State University. There is an accelerated degree program in organizational management for adult learners. Field experience programs, nondegree study, internships, work-study, cooperative programs, and credit for military service are offered. There is 1 national honor society and a freshman honors program.

Faculty/Classroom: 60% of faculty are male; 40%, female. All teach undergraduates. The average class size in an introductory lecture is 22; in a laboratory, 13; and in a regular course, 14.

Requirements: The SAT I or ACT is required. In addition, applicants must be graduates of an accredited secondary school with a C+ average in at least 18 academic units, including 4 in English, 3 in math, and 2 each in social studies and science. A GPA of 2.0 is required. AP credits are accepted. Important factors in the admissions decision are geographic diversity, evidence of special talent, and leadership record.

Procedure: Freshmen are admitted to all sessions. There is a deferred admissions plan and a rolling admissions plan. Check with the school for current application deadlines. The fall 2003 was $25. Notification is sent on a rolling basis.

Transfer: Transfers must submit high school and college transcripts and must be eligible to reenter the last institution attended. 30 of 124 credits required for the bachelor's degree must be completed at Saint Augustine's College.

Visiting: There are guides for informal visits and visitors may sit in on classes. To schedule a visit, contact the Admissions Office at (919) 516-4016.

Financial Aid: In a recent year, 95% of all full-time freshmen and 90% of continuing full-time students received some form of financial aid. 87% of full-time freshmen and 80% of continuing full-time students received need-based aid. The average freshman award was $10,474. 69% of undergraduates work part time. Average annual earnings from campus work are $1572. The average financial indebtedness of a recent graduate was $12,850. Saint Augustine's College is a member of CSS. The FAFSA is required. Check with the school for current deadlines.

International Students: The school actively recruits these students. They must score 500 on the written TOEFL and also take the SAT I or the ACT.

Computers: The mainframe is an IBM RS/6000 Model 590. Students have access to approximately 12 Macs and 150 IBM PCs campuswide that have Microsoft software and are connected to the Internet. All students may access the system. The system may be used during the operating hours of the library, the science building, and the business building. There are no time limits and no fees.

Admissions Contact: Tim Chapman, Interim Director of Admissions. E-mail: *admissions@es.st.aug.edu* Web: *www.st-aug.edu*

SALEM COLLEGE C-2
Winston-Salem, NC 27101 (336) 721-2621
(800) 327-2536; Fax: (336) 917-5572

Full-time: 10 men, 716 women	**Faculty:** 53; IIB, --$
Part-time: 12 men, 172 women	**Ph.D.s:** 85%
Graduate: 19 men, 162 women	**Student/Faculty:** 14 to 1
Year: 4-1-4, summer session	**Tuition:** $15,725
Application Deadline: open	**Room & Board:** $8870
Freshman Class: 438 applied, 305 accepted, 162 enrolled	
SAT I Verbal/Math: 580/540	**ACT:** 25 **VERY COMPETITIVE**

Salem College, founded in 1890, traces its roots back to 1772, when it was begun as a school for girls by the Moravians, an early Protestant denomination. Today the private college, which retains a historical relationship with the church, offers a liberal arts education primarily for women. In addition to regional accreditation, Salem has baccalaureate program accreditation with NASM and NCATE. The 2 libraries contain 132,510 volumes, 302,534 microform items, and 11,699 audio/video tapes/CDs, and subscribe to 284 periodicals. Computerized library services include the card catalog, interlibrary loans, and database searching. Special learning facilities include a learning resource center, art gallery, radio station, and a learning lab (computer lab with multimedia capability). The 57-acre campus is in an urban area in the center of Old Salem, a restored 18th-century village. Including any residence halls, there are 17 buildings.

Student Life: 51% of undergraduates are from out of state, mostly the South. Students are from 25 states and 17 foreign countries. 80% are from public schools. 70% are white; 18% African American. The average age of freshmen is 18; all undergraduates, 27. 20% do not continue beyond their first year; 58% remain to graduate.

Housing: 488 students can be accommodated in college housing, which includes single-sex dorms and off-campus apartments. On-campus housing is guaranteed for all 4 years. 89% of students live on campus; of those, 55% remain on campus on weekends. All students may keep cars.

Activities: There are no fraternities or sororities. There are 41 groups on campus, including chorale, chorus, dance, drama, ethnic, gay, honors, international, literary magazine, marching band, musical theater, newspaper, political, professional, radio and TV, religious, social, social service, student government, and yearbook. Students may also participate in band, marching band, and orchestra at Wake Forest University. Popular campus events include Fall Fest, April Arts, and dance weekends.

Sports: There are 7 intercollegiate sports for women and 7 intramural sports for women. Facilities include 2 athletic fields, a swimming pool, 2 basketball/volleyball and tennis courts, a dance studio, and a universal weight room.

Disabled Students: 75% of the campus is accessible. Special parking, specially equipped rest rooms, special class scheduling, and lowered drinking fountains are available. Many buildings are historic, so disability access is limited to individual areas that have had recent renovations or were already accessible.

Services: Counseling and information services are available, as is tutoring in every subject and a writing center.

Campus Safety and Security: Measures include 24-hour foot and vehicle patrol, security escort services, informal discussions, and pamphlets/posters/films. There are emergency telephones and lighted pathways/sidewalks.

Programs of Study: Salem confers B.A., B.S., B.M., and B.S.B.A. degrees. Master's degrees are also awarded. Bachelor's degrees are awarded in BIOLOGICAL SCIENCE (biology/biological science), BUSINESS (accounting, business administration and management, and international business management), COMMUNICATIONS AND THE ARTS (art history and appreciation, arts administration/management, communications, English, French, German, music, Spanish, and studio art), COMPUTER AND PHYSICAL SCIENCE (chemistry and mathematics), ENGINEERING AND ENVIRONMENTAL DESIGN (interior design), HEALTH PROFESSIONS (medical laboratory technology), SOCIAL SCIENCE (American studies, economics, history, international relations, philosophy, psychology, religion, and sociology). Sociology, business, and communication are the largest.

Required: To graduate, students must complete a total of 36 courses, or 144 semester hours, with a minimum GPA of 2.0. A minimum of 7 courses, or 28 semester hours, is required in the student's major. All students must complete 4 January-term courses, 3 in a modern foreign language, 2 each in English, social science, history, and phys ed, and 1 each in lab science, math, fine arts, and philosophy/religion.

Special: Salem offers an extensive internship program in all majors, cross-registration with Wake Forest University, and study abroad at various locations, including a summer program in Oxford, England. A Washington semester, student-designed and interdisciplinary majors, B.A.-B.S. degrees, nondegree study, and pass/fail options during the January term are available. A 3-2 engineering degree is available with Duke and Vanderbilt Universities. Students may participate in a model U.N. program directed by Drew University in Madison, New Jersey. Interdisciplinary majors are offered in American studies, arts management, international relations, and international business. There are 9 national honor societies, and a freshman honors program.

Faculty/Classroom: 47% of faculty are male; 53%, female. All both teach and do research. No introductory courses are taught by graduate students. The average class size in an introductory lecture is 18; in a laboratory, 15; and in a regular course, 15.

Admissions: 70% of the 2003-2004 applicants were accepted. The SAT I scores for the 2003-2004 freshman class were: Verbal--19% below 500, 41% between 500 and 599, 33% between 600 and 700, and 7% above 700; Math--26% below 500, 44% between 500 and 599, 29% between 600 and 700, and 1% above 700. The ACT scores were 18% below 21, 14% between 21 and 23, 36% between 24 and 26, 23% between 27 and 28, and 9% above 28. 46% of the current freshmen were in the top fifth of their class; 78% were in the top two fifths. In a recent year, 3 freshmen graduated first in their class.

Requirements: The SAT I or ACT is required. In addition, graduation from an accredited secondary school or the GED is needed. Students must have 12 academic credits plus electives, including 4 years of high school English, 3 each of math and science, and 2 each of a foreign language and history. An essay is required for all students. Music students must audition. A GPA of 2.5 is required. AP and CLEP credits are accepted. Important factors in the admissions decision are advanced placement or honor courses, leadership record, and evidence of special talent.

Procedure: Freshmen are admitted fall and spring. Entrance exams should be taken by January of the senior year. There are early admissions and deferred admissions plans. Application deadlines are open. The fall 2003 application fee was $25. Notification is sent on a rolling basis. Applications are accepted on-line through CollegeLink.

Transfer: 17 transfer students enrolled in 2002-2003. Applicants must have a minimum GPA of 2.0 in all previous college work and must submit a statement of good standing from the Dean of Students of the college previously attended, 2 letters of recommendation from teachers, a high school transcript, and a transcript and catalog from each college attended. SAT I or ACT scores may be required on an individual basis. An interview is recommended. 36 of 144 credits required for the bachelor's degree must be completed at Salem.

Visiting: There are regularly scheduled orientations for prospective students. There are guides for informal visits and visitors may sit in on classes and stay overnight. To schedule a visit, contact the Admissions Office.

Financial Aid: In a recent year, 73% of all full-time freshmen and 64% of continuing full-time students received some form of financial aid. 71% of full-time freshmen and 62% of continuing full-time students received need-based aid. The average freshman award was $12,491. 66% of undergraduates work part time. Average annual earnings from campus work are $1600. The average financial indebtedness of the 2003 graduate was $14,881. The FAFSA and the college's own financial statement are required. The deadline for filing freshman financial aid applications for fall entry is March 15.

International Students: There are 43 international students enrolled. The school actively recruits these students. They must score 550 on the written TOEFL.

Computers: The mainframe is a Hewlett-Packard 9000. There are also computers available in the science building, library, and main hall. Salem maintains Mac and Windows labs. All students may access the system when school is in session 24 hours a day. There are no time limits and no fees.

Graduates: From July 1, 2002 to June 30, 2003, 135 bachelor's degrees were awarded. The most popular majors were psychology (13%), sociology (13%), and communication (13%). In an average class, 1% graduate in 3 years or less, 63% graduate in 4 years or less, 64% graduate in 5 years or less, and 64% graduate in 6 years or less. Of the 2002 graduating class, 18% were enrolled in graduate school within 6 months of graduation and 77% were employed.

Admissions Contact: Dama E. Evans, Dean of Admissions and Financial Aid. E-mail: *admissions@salem.edu* Web: *www.salem.edu*

SHAW UNIVERSITY
D-2
Raleigh, NC 27601
(919) 546-8275
(800) 214-6683; Fax: (919) 546-8271

Full-time: 802 men, 1318 women	Faculty: 82; IIB, --$
Part-time: 108 men, 218 women	Ph.D.s: 68%
Graduate: 83 men, 87 women	Student/Faculty: 26 to 1
Year: semesters, summer session	Tuition: $9228
Application Deadline: July 30	Room & Board: $5654
Freshman Class: 3854 applied, 1707 accepted, 509 enrolled	
SAT I or ACT: required	COMPETITIVE+

Shaw University, founded in 1865, is a private liberal arts university affiliated with the Baptist Church. In addition to regional accreditation, Shaw has baccalaureate program accreditation with CAAHEP and NCATE. The library contains 153,304 volumes, 138,950 microform items, and 1306 audio/video tapes/CDs, and subscribes to 15,357 peri-

odicals. Computerized library services include the card catalog, interlibrary loans, database searching, and Internet access. Special learning facilities include a learning resource center, radio station, a praxis lab, Academic Assessment and Achievement Center (AAA), and kinesiotherapy clinic. The 30-acre campus is in an urban area in downtown Raleigh. Including any residence halls, there are 23 buildings.

Student Life: 73% of undergraduates are from North Carolina. Students are from 32 states and 10 foreign countries. 94% are African American. The average age of freshmen is 24; all undergraduates, 28.

Housing: 1293 students can be accommodated in college housing, which includes single-sex dorms. On-campus housing is available on a first-come, first-served basis. 62% of students commute. Alcohol is not permitted. Upperclassmen may keep cars.

Activities: 4% of men belong to 4 national fraternities; 5% of women belong to 4 national sororities. There are 30 groups on campus, including band, business, cheerleading, choir, chorus, criminal justice, dance, drama, ethnic, honors, international, jazz band, marching band, musical theater, newspaper, pep band, professional, radio and TV, religious, social, social service, student government, and yearbook. Popular campus events include Career Day, Awards Day, and Religious Emphasis Week.

Sports: There are 7 intercollegiate sports for men and 7 for women, and 5 intramural sports for men and 4 for women.

Disabled Students: Wheelchair ramps, elevators, special parking, specially equipped rest rooms, lowered drinking fountains, and labels in braille are available.

Services: Counseling and information services are available, as is tutoring in some subjects, including English, math, biology, chemistry, physical science, statistics, and social science. There is remedial math, reading, and writing. There is peer tutoring in accounting.

Campus Safety and Security: Measures include 24-hour foot and vehicle patrol, self-defense education, security escort services, and informal discussions. There are pamphlets/posters/films, lighted pathways/sidewalks, and 24-hour electronic surveillance.

Programs of Study: Shaw confers B.A. and B.S. degrees. Associate and master's degrees are also awarded. Bachelor's degrees are awarded in BIOLOGICAL SCIENCE (biology/biological science), BUSINESS (accounting, business administration and management, and recreation and leisure services), COMMUNICATIONS AND THE ARTS (broadcasting, English, and visual and performing arts), COMPUTER AND PHYSICAL SCIENCE (chemistry, computer science, mathematics, and physics), EDUCATION (athletic training, elementary, English, mathematics, physical, science, secondary, social studies, and special), ENGINEERING AND ENVIRONMENTAL DESIGN (environmental science and preengineering), HEALTH PROFESSIONS (recreation therapy, rehabilitation therapy, and speech pathology/audiology), SOCIAL SCIENCE (African studies, criminal justice, gerontology, international relations, international studies, liberal arts/general studies, political science/government, psychology, public administration, religion, social work, and sociology). Business administration/management, criminal justice, and sociology are the largest.

Required: To graduate (in most majors), students must earn 120 credits, maintain a minimum GPA of 2.0, and successfully complete competency exams in math and English. The general core curriculum includes a total of 54 credits in college orientation, English, math, ethics, humanities, natural sciences, and social sciences.

Special: Shaw offers cross-registration with 4 other North Carolina colleges, internships, a work-study program, a 3-2 engineering degree with North Carolina State University and North Carolina Agricultural and Technical State University, dual and student-designed majors, independent study, and an external degree program for working adults. There are 4 national honor societies and a freshman honors program.

Faculty/Classroom: 68% of faculty are male; 32%, female. 94% teach undergraduates. The average class size in a laboratory is 8 and in a regular course, 13.

Admissions: 44% of the 2003-2004 applicants were accepted.

Requirements: The SAT I or ACT is required. In addition, applicants must be graduates of an accredited secondary school or have a GED certificate. They should have completed 3 units of English, 2 each of math, natural science (with 1 in a lab course), and social science, and 4 of academic electives. Admission to the Teacher Education Program follows separate guidelines. A GPA of 2.0 is required. AP and CLEP credits are accepted. Important factors in the admissions decision are advanced placement or honor courses, personality/intangible qualities, and recommendations by school officials.

Procedure: Freshmen are admitted to all sessions. Entrance exams should be taken prior to enrollment. There is a deferred admissions plan. Applications should be filed by July 30 for fall entry and November 30 for spring entry. The fall 2003 application fee was $25. Notification is sent on a rolling basis. Applications are accepted on computer disk and on-line through the school's web site or Apply software.

Transfer: 148 transfer students enrolled in 2002-2003. Applicants must submit official transcripts from all colleges attended. Transfer credit is given only for course work of grade C or better completed at an accredited degree-granting institution. 30 of 120 credits required for the bachelor's degree must be completed at Shaw.

Visiting: There are regularly scheduled orientations for prospective students, consisting of parent visitation, tours, general administration, and registration. There are guides for informal visits and visitors may sit in on classes. To schedule a visit, contact the Admissions Office at (919) 546-8275 or (919) 546-8276 or *admission@shawu.edu.*

Financial Aid: 2% of undergraduates work part time. Average annual earnings from campus work in a recent year were $12,000. The average financial indebtedness of the recent graduate was $17,125. The FAFSA is required. The priority date for freshman financial aid applications for fall entry is March 1. The deadline for filing freshman financial aid applications for fall entry is open.

International Students: There are 73 international students enrolled. The school actively recruits these students. They must take the SAT I or the ACT.

Computers: The university has Windows 2000 servers. Computer labs are located in libraries, dorms, the science building, and the education building. There are approximately 210 computers with Internet connections. All students may access the system. There are no time limits. The fee is $127 per semester. It is strongly recommended that all students have a personal computer.

Graduates: From July 1, 2002 to June 30, 2003, 367 bachelor's degrees were awarded. The most popular majors were business (24%), criminal justice (14%), and sociology (11%). In an average class, 26% graduate in 4 years or less, 34% graduate in 5 years or less, and 38% graduate in 6 years or less.

Admissions Contact: Paul Vandergrift, Director of Admissions and Recruitment. E-mail: *paulv@shawu.edu* Web: *www.shawuniversity.edu*

UNIVERSITY OF NORTH CAROLINA SYSTEM

The University of North Carolina System, established in 1931, is a public system in North Carolina. It is governed by UNC Board of Governors, whose chief administrator is president. The primary goal of the system is to discover, create, transmit, and apply knowledge to address the needs of North Carolina and its people. The main priorities are teaching/instruction, research/scholarship/creative activities, public service (solving societal problems and enriching quality of life). The total enrollment of all 16 campuses is usually about 170,000; there were about 8500 faculty members. Altogether there are 938 baccalaureate, 676 master's, and 169 doctoral programs offered in University of North Carolina System. Profiles of the 4-year campuses are included in this section.

UNIVERSITY OF NORTH CAROLINA AT ASHEVILLE B-2
Asheville, NC 28804-8510
(828) 251-6481
(800) 531-9842; Fax: (828) 251-6482

Full-time: 1154 men, 1573 women	**Faculty:** 177; IIB, av$
Part-time: 298 men, 385 women	**Ph.D.s:** 88%
Graduate: 16 men, 20 women	**Student/Faculty:** 15 to 1
Year: semesters, summer session	**Tuition:** $3101 ($11,926)
Application Deadline: March 12	**Room & Board:** $4978
Freshman Class: 2293 applied, 1663 accepted, 599 enrolled	
SAT I Verbal/Math: 580/590	**ACT:** 24 **VERY COMPETITIVE**

The University of North Carolina at Asheville is the designated public liberal arts university in the 16-campus UNC system. In addition to regional accreditation, UNCA has baccalaureate program accreditation with NCATE. The library contains 255,805 volumes, 839,718 microform items, and 10,249 audio/video tapes/CDs, and subscribes to 1795 periodicals. Computerized library services include the card catalog, interlibrary loans, and database searching. Special learning facilities include a learning resource center, art gallery, distance learning facility, center for creative retirement, undergraduate research center, botanical gardens, music recording center, and the Environmental Quality Institute. The 265-acre campus is in a suburban area 130 miles west of Charlotte. Including any residence halls, there are 26 buildings.

Student Life: 87% of undergraduates are from North Carolina. Students are from 39 states, 24 foreign countries, and Canada. 85% are from public schools. 90% are white. The average age of freshmen is 18; all undergraduates, 22. 22% do not continue beyond their first year; 51% remain to graduate.

Housing: 1136 students can be accommodated in college housing, which includes single-sex and coed dorms and off-campus apartments. In addition, there are honors houses and substance-free housing. On-campus housing is guaranteed for all 4 years. 64% of students commute. All students may keep cars.

Activities: 4% of men belong to 3 national fraternities; 3% of women belong to 2 national sororities. There are 66 groups on campus, including art, band, cheerleading, choir, chorus, computers, dance, departmental, drama, ethnic, gay, honors, international, jazz band, literary magazine, newspaper, pep band, political, professional, religious, social, social service, and student government. Popular campus events include Spring Lawn Party, Taste of the Holidays, and Chancellor's Campus Community Dinner.

Sports: There are 7 intercollegiate sports for men and 7 for women, and 15 intramural sports for men and 15 for women. Facilities include a sports and health center with a state-of-the-art weight room, 4 basketball courts, volleyball and racquetball courts, a dance studio, an indoor swimming pool, indoor and outdoor tracks, outdoor tennis courts, and soccer and baseball fields.

Disabled Students: 95% of the campus is accessible. Wheelchair ramps, elevators, special parking, specially equipped rest rooms, special class scheduling, lowered drinking fountains, and lowered telephones are available.

Services: Counseling and information services are available, as is tutoring in most subjects. There is a reader service for the blind, and remedial math, reading, and writing.

Campus Safety and Security: Measures include 24-hour foot and vehicle patrol, self-defense education, security escort services, and informal discussions. There are pamphlets/posters/films, emergency telephones, and lighted pathways/sidewalks.

Programs of Study: UNCA confers B.A., B.S., and B.F.A. degrees. Master's degrees are also awarded. Bachelor's degrees are awarded in BIOLOGICAL SCIENCE (biology/biological science), BUSINESS (accounting and business administration and management), COMMUNICATIONS AND THE ARTS (art, classics, communications, dramatic arts, French, German, literature, media arts, multimedia, music, music technology, and Spanish), COMPUTER AND PHYSICAL SCIENCE (atmospheric sciences and meteorology, chemistry, computer science, mathematics, and physics), ENGINEERING AND ENVIRONMENTAL DESIGN (environmental science and industrial administration/management), SOCIAL SCIENCE (economics, history, interdisciplinary studies, philosophy, political science/government, psychology, and sociology). Management, psychology, and environmental science are the largest.

Required: To graduate, students must complete a minimum of 120 credit hours, including 27 to 40 in the major, with a senior capstone experience consisting of undergraduate research, an exam, or a seminar. The core curriculum requires 16 semester hours of humanities, 8 of natural science including lab, 6 of social science, up to 6 of foreign language, 4 each of math and arts, 3 to 7 of English, 2 to 4 of health and fitness, and 1 of library research.

Special: Students may participate in cooperative programs in nursing, forestry, and textile chemistry. UNCA participates in a consortium with Warren Wilson and Mars Hill Colleges, and there is cross-registration with a number of North Carolina universities and colleges. Study-abroad programs are available in more than 7 countries. The school offers internships, dual majors, student-designed interdisciplinary majors, and a 2-2 engineering degree and joint engineering degree with North Carolina State University. Nondegree study is available. There are 13 national honor societies, a freshman honors program, and 11 departmental honors programs.

Faculty/Classroom: 59% of faculty are male; 41%, female. All teach undergraduates. No introductory courses are taught by graduate students. The average class size in an introductory lecture is 22; in a laboratory, 16; and in a regular course, 18.

Admissions: 73% of the 2003-2004 applicants were accepted. The SAT I scores for the 2003-2004 freshman class were: Verbal--13% below 500, 43% between 500 and 599, 38% between 600 and 700, and 5% above 700; Math--12% below 500, 45% between 500 and 599, 41% between 600 and 700, and 3% above 700. The ACT scores were 15% below 21, 27% between 21 and 23, 30% between 24 and 26, 16% between 27 and 28, and 12% above 28. 45% of the current freshmen were in the top fifth of their class; 86% were in the top two fifths. 7 freshmen graduated first in their class.

Requirements: The SAT I or ACT is required, as is graduation from an accredited secondary school. UNCA requires a minimum of 16 high school academic units, including 4 of English, 3 each of math (algebra I, geometry, algebra II) and science (biology, physical science, and a lab course), 2 of social studies/history, and 2 of a foreign language. Applicants are evaluated primarily on their academic achievement record, extracurricular activities that support academic achievement, and SAT I or ACT scores. AP and CLEP credits are accepted. Important factors in the admissions decision are advanced placement or honor courses, leadership record, and evidence of special talent.

Procedure: Freshmen are admitted to all sessions. Entrance exams should be taken at the end of the junior year or the beginning of the senior year. There is a deferred admissions plan and a rolling admissions plan. Applications should be filed by March 12 for fall entry and December 1 for spring entry. The fall 2003 application fee was $60. Notification is sent monthly on a rolling basis. Applications are accepted on-line through the school's web site and Embark.com.

Transfer: 579 transfer students enrolled in 2002-2003. A 2.5 GPA on transfer credit is required; applicants with fewer than 24 semester or 36 quarter credit hours must submit high school transcripts and SAT I or ACT scores. 30 credits of 120 required for the bachelor's degree must be completed at UNCA.

Visiting: There are regularly scheduled orientations for prospective students, including meetings with faculty and with student organizations, an information session for students and families, and a campus tour. Preregistration is prior to fall enrollment during the summer months. There are guides for informal visits and visitors may sit in on classes and stay overnight. To schedule a visit, contact Office of Admissions at *admissions@unca.edu*.

Financial Aid: In 2003-2004, 64% of all full-time freshmen and 63% of continuing full-time students received some form of financial aid. 39% of full-time freshmen and 43% of continuing full-time students received need-based aid. The average freshman award was $5352. Need-based scholarships or need-based grants averaged $3108 ($9406 maximum); need-based self-help aid (loans and jobs) averaged $2816 ($8065 maximum); non-need-based athletic scholarships averaged $5907 ($19,171 maximum); and other non-need-based awards and non-need-based scholarships averaged $2853 ($13,454 maximum). 24% of undergraduates work part time. Average annual earnings from campus work are $1318. The average financial indebtedness of the 2003 graduate was $13,961. The FAFSA is required. The priority date for freshman financial aid applications for fall entry is March 1.

International Students: There are 39 international students enrolled. The school actively recruits these students. They must score 550 on the written TOEFL or 213 on the electronic version and also take the SAT I or the ACT.

Computers: The mainframes are a Compaq Alpha Server 2100 and a Compaq Alpha Server 4100. Students can access the central computing resources and the Internet from one of more than 300 PCs and Macs in campus labs, department labs, residence hall labs, and the library. Additionally, all dorms have a network port for every resident with a PC. Students can register for classes and receive grade reports via the Web. All students may access the system 24 hours a day. There are no time limits and no fees.

Graduates: From July 1, 2002 to June 30, 2003, 571 bachelor's degrees were awarded. The most popular majors were psychology (15%), management (9%), and environmental science (8%). In an average class, 1% graduate in 3 years or less, 28% graduate in 4 years or less, 49% graduate in 5 years or less, and 51% graduate in 6 years or less. 150 companies recruited on campus in 2002-2003. Of the 2002 graduating class, 21% were enrolled in graduate school within 6 months of graduation and 96% were employed.

Admissions Contact: Scot Schaeffer, Director of Admissions and Financial Aid. A video is available. E-mail: *admissions@unca.edu* Web: *www.unca.edu/admissions*

UNIVERSITY OF NORTH CAROLINA AT CHAPEL HILL   D-2
Chapel Hill, NC 27599-2200

(919) 966-3621
Fax: (919) 962-3045

Full-time: 6285 men, 9068 women	**Faculty:** I, +$
Part-time: 175 men, 183 women	**Ph.D.s:** 82%
Graduate: 2889 men, 3907 women	**Student/Faculty:** n/av
Year: semesters, summer session	**Tuition:** $4072 ($15,920)
Application Deadline: January 15	**Room & Board:** $6045
Freshman Class: 17,591 applied, 6441 accepted, 3516 enrolled	
SAT I Verbal/Math: 630/650	**ACT:** 27 **MOST COMPETITIVE**

The University of North Carolina at Chapel Hill, chartered in 1789 and the nation's first public university, offers academic programs leading to 69 bachelor's, 112 master's, and 77 doctoral degrees, as well as 4 professional degrees. There are 9 undergraduate and 12 graduate schools. The 14 libraries contain 5,366,141 volumes, 4,734,753 microform items, and 232,920 audio/video tapes/CDs, and subscribe to 42,238 periodicals. Computerized library services include the card catalog, interlibrary loans, and database searching. Special learning facilities include a learning resource center, art gallery, planetarium, radio station, TV station, botanical garden and theater. The 729-acre campus is in a suburban area 25 miles west of Raleigh. Including any residence halls, there are 292 buildings.

Student Life: 82% of undergraduates are from North Carolina. Students are from 50 states, 105 foreign countries, and Canada. 84% are from public schools. 76% are white; 11% African American. The average age of freshmen is 18; all undergraduates, 20. 5% do not continue beyond their first year; 80% remain to graduate.

Housing: 9715 students can be accommodated in college housing, which includes single-sex and coed dorms, married-student housing, fraternity houses, and sorority houses. In addition, there are language houses, substance-free houses, and special-interest houses. 56% of students commute. Upperclassmen may keep cars.

Activities: 12% of men belong to 29 national fraternities; 12% of women belong to 1 local and 20 national sororities. There are 565 groups on campus, including art, band, cheerleading, chess, choir, chorus, dance, drama, drill team, ethnic, film, gay, honors, international, jazz band, literary magazine, marching band, musical theater, newspaper, orchestra, pep band, photography, political, professional, radio and TV, religious, social, social service, student government, symphony, and yearbook. Popular campus events include Black Greek Council Stepshow, Apple Chill, and Carolina Jazz Festival.

Sports: There are 12 intercollegiate sports for men and 14 for women, and 40 intramural sports for men and 35 for women. Facilities include a 60,000-seat football stadium, 3 swimming pools, a 21,000-seat sports and student activities center, tennis courts, lacrosse and soccer fields, golf course, boathouse, gym facilities, softball fields, and a student recreation center with aerobics, weights, and wellness programs.

Disabled Students: 94% of the campus is accessible. Wheelchair ramps, elevators, special parking, specially equipped rest rooms, special class scheduling, lowered drinking fountains, lowered telephones, and special housing are available.

Services: Counseling and information services are available, as is tutoring in every subject. There is a reader service for the blind and remedial math and writing.

Campus Safety and Security: Measures include 24-hour foot and vehicle patrol, self-defense education, security escort services, and shuttle buses. There are informal discussions, pamphlets/posters/films, emergency telephones, lighted pathways/sidewalks, and building security surveys.

Programs of Study: UNC-Chapel Hill confers B.A., B.S., A.B.J., B.A.Ed., B.F.A., B.M., B.M.Ed., B.S.Applied Sc., and B.S.B.A. degrees. Master's and doctoral degrees are also awarded. Bachelor's degrees are awarded in AGRICULTURE (environmental studies), BIOLOGICAL SCIENCE (biology/biological science, biometrics and biostatistics, and nutrition), BUSINESS (accounting, business administration and management, and recreational facilities management), COMMUNICATIONS AND THE ARTS (art history and appreciation, classics, communications, comparative literature, dramatic arts, English, German, journalism, linguistics, music, music performance, romance languages and literature, Russian, speech/debate/rhetoric, and studio art), COMPUTER AND PHYSICAL SCIENCE (applied science, chemistry, computer science, geology, information sciences and systems, mathematics, and physics), EDUCATION (education, elementary, English, foreign languages, health, mathematics, middle school, music, physical, secondary, and social studies), ENGINEERING AND ENVIRONMENTAL DESIGN (environmental engineering, environmental science, and industrial administration/management), HEALTH PROFESSIONS (clinical science, dental hygiene, exercise science, health care administration, medical laboratory technology, nursing, public health, and radiological science), SOCIAL SCIENCE (African American studies, African studies, American studies, anthropology, Asian/Oriental studies, child care/child and family studies, economics, geography, history, interdisciplinary studies, international studies, Latin American studies, peace studies, philosophy, political science/government, psychology, public affairs, religion, Russian and Slavic studies, sociology, and women's studies). Sociology and journalism are the strongest academically. Biology, psychology, and journalism are the largest.

Required: To graduate, students must complete 120 credits (more for some B.S. degrees) with a 2.0 GPA. The general education requirements fall under 2 headings: Basic Skills (English composition, foreign languages, and mathematical sciences) and Perspectives (aesthetic, natural sciences, philosophical, social sciences, and western historical/nonwestern/comparative). The Basic Skills requirements apply to all students. The Perspectives requirements fall into 2 categories: 9 courses are required of all freshmen and sophomores. 4 more courses, selected from 4 of the 5 perspective areas, are required of juniors and seniors seeking a B.A. degree in the College of Arts and Sciences. 2 phys ed courses are also required.

Special: Students may participate in joint programs with Duke University and North Carolina State University. Internships, study abroad in 64 countries, B.A.-B.S. degrees, and student-designed majors are available. There are pass/fail options and nondegree study. There are 7 national honor societies, including Phi Beta Kappa, and a freshman honors program.

Faculty/Classroom: 62% of faculty are male; 38%, female. All teach undergraduates. Graduate students teach 46% of introductory courses. The average class size in an introductory lecture is 41; in a laboratory, 18; and in a regular course, 28.

Admissions: 37% of the 2003-2004 applicants were accepted. The SAT I scores for the 2003-2004 freshman class were: Verbal--4% below 500, 24% between 500 and 599, 51% between 600 and 700, and 21% above 700; Math--2% below 500, 20% between 500 and 599, 52% between 600 and 700, and 26% above 700. The ACT scores were 6% below 21, 12% between 21 and 23, 27% between 24 and 26, 23% between 27 and 28, and 34% above 28. 91% of the current freshmen were in the top fifth of their class; 98% were in the top two fifths. There were 136 National Merit finalists. 183 freshmen graduated first in their class.

Requirements: The SAT I or ACT is required. In addition, applicants must be graduates of an accredited secondary school. They should complete 16 high school academic credits, including 4 in English, 3 each in math (2 in algebra and 1 in geometry) and science (including at least 1 physical science and 1 lab course), and 2 each in a single foreign language, history, and social studies. A portfolio and an audition are recommended for art and music majors. AP and CLEP credits are accepted.

Procedure: Freshmen are admitted in the fall. Entrance exams should be taken in the junior and senior years. There are early admissions and deferred admissions plans. Applications should be filed by January 15 for fall entry, along with a $60 fee. Applications received by November 1 will receive notification around January 31; regular decision, March 31. 1671 applicants were on the 2003 waiting list; 209 were admitted. Applications are accepted on-line.

Transfer: 829 transfer students enrolled in the fall of 2003. Sophomore transfers need at least 24 credit hours and a minimum GPA of 2.0; junior transfers need at least 51 credit hours and a minimum GPA of 2.0. 45 of 120 (more for some degrees) credits required for the bachelor's degree must be completed at UNC-Chapel Hill.

Visiting: There are regularly scheduled orientations for prospective students, including campus tours and information sessions, offered twice each weekday. There are guides for informal visits and visitors may sit in on classes. To schedule a visit, contact the Office of Undergraduate Admissions at *www.admissions.unc.edu/visit/visit.html*.

Financial Aid: In 2002-2003, 60% of all full-time freshmen and 53% of continuing full-time students received some form of financial aid. 31% of full-time freshmen and 30% of continuing full-time students received need-based aid. The average freshman award was $8693. Need-based scholarships or need-based grants averaged $5524 ($22,700 maximum); need-based self-help aid (loans and jobs) averaged $2774 ($12,132 maximum); non-need-based athletic scholarships averaged $11,215 ($21,726 maximum); and other non-need-based awards and non-need-based scholarships averaged $4740 ($39,500 maximum). The average financial indebtedness of the 2003 graduate was $12,300. UNC-Chapel Hill is a member of CSS. The CSS Profile or FAFSA is required. The deadline for filing freshman financial aid applications for fall entry is March 1.

International Students: There are 184 international students enrolled. The school actively recruits these students. They must score 600 on the written TOEFL or 250 on the electronic version and also take the SAT I or the ACT.

Computers: The mainframes are a CONVEX supercomputer and a variety of UNIX workstations. More than 700 PCs are available for student use throughout the campus and in residence halls. Accounts are available for e-mail and instructional computing. There is a 24-hour help desk and a computer repair center. All students may access the system 24 hours a day. There are no time limits and no fees. All students are required to have personal computers. See the school's web site for university specifications.

Graduates: From July 1, 2002 to June 30, 2003, 3741 bachelor's degrees were awarded. The most popular majors were journalism and mass communication (18%), social sciences and history (18%), and business/marketing (10%). In an average class, 1% graduate in 3 years or less, 67% graduate in 4 years or less, 78% graduate in 5 years or less, and 80% graduate in 6 years or less. 162 companies recruited on campus in 2002-2003. Of the 2002 graduating class, 26% were enrolled in graduate school within 6 months of graduation and 59% were employed.

Admissions Contact: Office of Undergraduate Admissions.
E-mail: *uadm@email.unc.edu* Web: *www.unc.edu*

UNIVERSITY OF NORTH CAROLINA AT CHARLOTTE C-3
Charlotte, NC 28223-0001   (704) 687-2213; Fax: (704) 687-6483

Full-time: 5742 men, 6449 women	**Faculty:** 589; IIA, +$
Part-time: 1543 men, 1960 women	**Ph.D.s:** 85%
Graduate: 1538 men, 2373 women	**Student/Faculty:** 21 to 1
Year: semesters, summer session	**Tuition:** $3109 ($13,146)
Application Deadline: July 1	**Room & Board:** $5076
Freshman Class: 8478 applied, 6085 accepted, 2519 enrolled	
SAT I Verbal/Math: 520/540	**ACT:** 21 **COMPETITIVE**

The University of North Carolina at Charlotte, founded in 1946, is a publicly funded institution in the University of North Carolina System. There are 7 undergraduate schools and 1 graduate school. In addition to regional accreditation, UNC-Charlotte has baccalaureate program accreditation with AACSB, ABET, CSWE, NAAB, NCATE, and NLN. The library contains 1,718,107 volumes, 163,496 microform items, and 48,109 audio/video tapes/CDs, and subscribes to 26,255 periodicals. Computerized library services include the card catalog, interlibrary loans, and database searching. Special learning facilities include a learning resource center, art gallery, on-line teleconferencing facility, high-tech research center in engineering, and botanical garden and greenhouse complex that includes a tropical rain forest. The 1000-acre campus is in a suburban area 8 miles northeast of the center of Charlotte. Including any residence halls, there are 85 buildings.

Student Life: 89% of undergraduates are from North Carolina. Students are from 47 states, 78 foreign countries, and Canada. 74% are white; 16% African American. 64% claim no religious affiliation; 25% Protestant. The average age of freshmen is 18; all undergraduates, 24. 24% do not continue beyond their first year; 45% remain to graduate.

Housing: 4092 students can be accommodated in college housing, which includes single-sex and coed dorms and on-campus apartments. In addition, there are honors houses, special-interest houses, an international floor, and 5 sorority floors. On-campus housing is available on a first-come, first-served basis. 75% of students commute. All students may keep cars.

Activities: 8% of men belong to 13 national fraternities; 6% of women belong to 8 national sororities. There are more than 200 groups on campus, including art, cheerleading, chess, choir, chorale, chorus, computers, dance, debate, drama, ethnic, fashion club, gay, honors, international, jazz band, literary magazine, newspaper, non-traditional students, opera, pep band, photography, political, professional, radio and TV, religious, science fiction and fantasy guild, social, social service, student government, and yearbook. Popular campus events include Greek Week, Miss 49er Pageant, and International Festival.

Sports: There are 7 intercollegiate sports for men and 7 for women, and 39 intramural sports for men and 39 for women. Facilities include a gym, an Olympic-size pool, basketball, tennis, and racquetball courts, a fitness trail, a track, and a training room. There is also a 9100-seat arena, 2 weight rooms, an aerobics studio, an indoor track, indoor basketball/volleyball courts, an indoor climbing wall, and a 7000-square-foot game room.

Disabled Students: 90% of the campus is accessible. Wheelchair ramps, elevators, special parking, specially equipped rest rooms, special class scheduling, lowered drinking fountains, lowered telephones, and limited special housing are available. The Disability Services Office assists students with all academic and physical accommodations.

Services: Counseling and information services are available, as is tutoring in some subjects, including math, science, foreign language, and introductory courses. There is a reader service for the blind.

Campus Safety and Security: Measures include 24-hour foot and vehicle patrol, self-defense education, security escort services, and shuttle buses. There are informal discussions, pamphlets/posters/films, emergency telephones, and lighted pathways/sidewalks.

Programs of Study: UNC-Charlotte confers B.A., B.S., B.Arch., B.F.A., B.M., B.S.B.A, B.S.C.E., B.S.E.E., B.S.E.T., B.S.M.E., B.S.N., and B.S.W. degrees. Master's and doctoral degrees are also awarded. Bachelor's degrees are awarded in BIOLOGICAL SCIENCE (biology/ biological science), BUSINESS (accounting, banking and finance, business administration and management, business economics, international business management, management information systems, and marketing/retailing/merchandising), COMMUNICATIONS AND THE ARTS (art, communications, dance, dramatic arts, English, fine arts, French, German, music, music performance, and Spanish), COMPUTER AND PHYSICAL SCIENCE (chemistry, computer science, earth science, geology, information sciences and systems, mathematics, and physics), EDUCATION (art, athletic training, dance, drama, education of the mentally handicapped, elementary, English, foreign languages, mathematics, middle school, music, science, and social studies), ENGINEERING AND ENVIRONMENTAL DESIGN (architecture, civil engineering, civil engineering technology, computer engineering, electrical/electronics engineering, electrical/electronics engineering technology, industrial administration/ management, manufacturing engineering, manufacturing technology, mechanical engineering, and mechanical engineering technology), HEALTH PROFESSIONS (medical technology and nursing), SOCIAL SCIENCE (African American studies, anthropology, child care/child and family studies, criminal justice, economics, fire control and safety technology, geography, history, international studies, philosophy, physical fitness/movement, political science/government, psychology, religion, social work, and sociology). Architecture, business administration, and geography and earth science are the strongest academically. Business administration, biology, and psychology are the largest.

Required: To graduate, students must complete a minimum of 120 credit hours with an overall minimum GPA of 2.0. Between 30 and 42 hours are required in the major, with a minimum GPA of 2.0 in major and minor courses. All students must complete core requirements in the 6 interrelated areas of communication, problem solving, values, science and technology, arts, literature and ideas, and the individual, society, and culture.

Special: Cross-registration is available through the Charlotte Area Educational Consortium. Also available are cooperative programs in numerous majors and internships of 1 semester arranged with public and private community organizations. Study abroad, B.A.-B.S. degrees, dual majors, and nondegree study are available. Pass/fail options are limited to 1 course per academic year. There are 41 national honor societies, a freshman honors program, and 12 departmental honors programs.

Faculty/Classroom: 61% of faculty are male; 39%, female. 87% teach undergraduates. Graduate students teach 3% of introductory courses. The average class size in a laboratory is 18 and in a regular course, 30.

Admissions: 72% of the 2003-2004 applicants were accepted. The SAT I scores for the 2003-2004 freshman class were: Verbal--36% below 500, 49% between 500 and 599, 14% between 600 and 700, and 1% above 700; Math--27% below 500, 50% between 500 and 599, 21% between 600 and 700, and 2% above 700. The ACT scores were 42% below 21, 33% between 21 and 23, 19% between 24 and 26, 4% between 27 and 28, and 2% above 28. 36% of the current freshmen were in the top fifth of their class; 78% were in the top two fifths. 17 freshmen graduated first in their class.

Requirements: The SAT I or ACT is required. In addition, graduation from an accredited secondary school or the GED is required. The school requires 14 academic credits, including 4 years of English, 3 each of math and science (including 1 physical science and 1 biological science), 2 of a foreign language, and 2 of social studies, including 1 of U.S. history. Priority is given to students whose senior-year courses include a foreign language, math, world history, and health education. A portfolio and interview are required for art and architecture students only. Admission of students is based on overall performance in a select group of academic courses (80%) and SAT I scores (20%). UNC-Charlotte requires applicants to be in the upper 50% of their class. A GPA of 2.0 is required. AP and CLEP credits are accepted. Important factors in the admissions decision are advanced placement or honor courses, leadership record, and recommendations by school officials.

Procedure: Freshmen are admitted to all sessions. Entrance exams should be taken at the end of the junior year or by December of the senior year. There are early admissions and deferred admissions plans. There is a rolling admissions plan. Applications should be filed by July 1 for fall entry, November 15 for spring entry, and May 1 for summer entry. Notification is sent on a rolling basis. The fall 2003 application fee was $35. Applications are accepted on computer disk and on-line through the school's web site.

Transfer: 1774 transfer students enrolled in 2002-2003. Transfer students must have a minimum GPA of 2.0 on all college courses attempted. Certain majors have limited space and require a higher GPA and/or prerequisites. Applicants with fewer than 24 hours of transferable credit must meet both transfer and freshman admissions requirements. An interview is required only for architecture students. 30 of 120 credits required for the bachelor's degree must be completed at UNC-Charlotte.

Visiting: There are regularly scheduled orientations for prospective students, including scheduled tours. There are guides for informal visits and visitors may sit in on classes and stay overnight. To schedule a visit, contact the Admissions Office.

Financial Aid: In 2003-2004, 52% of all full-time freshmen and 49% of continuing full-time students received some form of financial aid. 44% of full-time freshmen and 43% of continuing full-time students received need-based aid. The average freshman award was $6108. Need-based scholarships or need-based grants averaged $3504 ($7250 maximum); need-based self-help aid (loans and jobs) averaged $3865 ($7500 maximum); non-need-based athletic scholarships averaged $7850 ($21,000 maximum); and other non-need-based awards and non-need-based scholarships averaged $1830 ($5500 maximum). 86% of undergraduates work part time. Average annual earnings from campus work are $1800. The average financial indebtedness of the 2003 graduate was $17,144. UNC-Charlotte is a member of CSS. The FAFSA is required. The priority date for freshman financial aid applications for fall entry is April 1.

International Students: There are 320 international students enrolled. They must score 500 on the written TOEFL or 180 on the electronic version or take the MELAB.

Computers: The mainframe is an IBM 9672-R24. About 1,100 PCs are located at various labs on campus. Students can access the Internet and Bitnet. All students may access the system 24 hours per day. There are no time limits. The fee is $25 per semester.

Graduates: From July 1, 2002 to June 30, 2003, 2647 bachelor's degrees were awarded. The most popular majors were business administration (24%), education (7%), and engineering (6%). In an average class, 24% graduate in 4 years or less, 43% graduate in 5 years or less, and 50% graduate in 6 years or less. 97 companies recruited on campus in 2002-2003. Of the 2002 graduating class, 10% were enrolled in graduate school within 6 months of graduation and 81% were employed.

Admissions Contact: Craig Fulton, Director of Admissions. A video is available. E-mail: *unccadm@email.uncc.edu* Web: *http://www.uncc.edu*

UNIVERSITY OF NORTH CAROLINA AT GREENSBORO	**D-2**
Greensboro, NC 27412	(336) 334-5243; Fax: (336) 334-4180
Full-time: 3021 men, 6296 women	**Faculty:** I, --$
Part-time: 583 men, 1206 women	**Ph.D.s:** 78%
Graduate: 1109 men, 2113 women	**Student/Faculty:** 14 to 1
Year: semesters, summer session	**Tuition:** $3038 ($13,412)
Application Deadline: August 1	**Room & Board:** $5210
Freshman Class: 6968 applied, 5353 accepted, 2056 enrolled	
SAT I Verbal/Math: 522/523	**COMPETITIVE**

The University of North Carolina at Greensboro, founded in 1891, is a publicly funded liberal arts institution in the University of North Carolina system. There are 7 undergraduate and 7 graduate schools. In addition to regional accreditation, UNCG has baccalaureate program accreditation with AACSB, ABET, ADA, AHEA, CSWE, FIDER, NASM, NCATE, and NLN. The library contains 844,448 volumes, 1,400,761 microform items, and 59,027 audio/video tapes/CDs, and subscribes to 8714 periodicals. Computerized library services include the card catalog, interlibrary loans, and database searching. Special learning facilities include a learning resource center, art gallery, radio station, and a cooperative observatory-planetarium (off campus). The 200-acre campus is in an urban area in central Greensboro. Including any residence halls, there are 75 buildings.

Student Life: 92% of undergraduates are from North Carolina. Students are from 40 states, 20 foreign countries, and Canada. 95% are from public schools. 69% are white; 20% African American. The average age of freshmen is 18; all undergraduates, 23. 26% do not continue beyond their first year; 48% remain to graduate.

Housing: 3900 students can be accommodated in college housing, which includes single-sex and coed dorms and on-campus apartments. In addition, there are special-interest houses, an international house, and a residential college program. On-campus housing is guaranteed for all 4 years. 66% of students commute. Alcohol is not permitted. All students may keep cars.

Activities: 8% of men belong to 8 national fraternities; 6% of women belong to 8 national sororities. There are 151 groups on campus, including art, band, choir, chorale, chorus, dance, drama, ethnic, film, gay, honors, international, jazz band, literary magazine, musical theater, newspaper, opera, orchestra, pep band, photography, political, professional, radio and TV, religious, social, social service, student government, symphony, and yearbook. Popular campus events include Spring Fling, Fall Kickoff, and Founders Day.

Sports: There are 7 intercollegiate sports for men and 7 for women, and 25 intramural sports for men and 25 for women. Facilities include a physical activities complex and the 44-acre Piney Lake Field Campus, which includes 2 lakes for swimming, boating, and fishing.

Disabled Students: 80% of the campus is accessible. Wheelchair ramps, elevators, special parking, specially equipped rest rooms, special class scheduling, lowered drinking fountains, lowered telephones, and lifts are available.

Services: Counseling and information services are available, as is tutoring in every subject. There is a reader service for the blind and remedial math.

Campus Safety and Security: Measures include 24-hour foot and vehicle patrol, self-defense education, security escort services, and shuttle buses. There are informal discussions, pamphlets/posters/films, emergency telephones, and lighted pathways/sidewalks.

Programs of Study: UNCG confers B.A., B.S., B.F.A., B.M., B.S.M.T., B.S.N., and B.S.W. degrees. Master's and doctoral degrees are also awarded. Bachelor's degrees are awarded in BIOLOGICAL SCIENCE (biochemistry and biology/biological science), BUSINESS (accounting, banking and finance, business administration and management, business economics, hospitality management services, international business management, management information systems, and recreation and leisure services), COMMUNICATIONS AND THE ARTS (art, classics, communications, dance, dramatic arts, English, French, German, jazz, media arts, music, music performance, music theory and composition, Spanish, and studio art), COMPUTER AND PHYSICAL SCIENCE (chemistry, computer science, mathematics, and physics), EDUCATION (art, dance, drama, early childhood, education of the deaf and hearing impaired, elementary, English, foreign languages, health, mathematics, middle school, music, physical, science, secondary, social science, and speech correction), ENGINEERING AND ENVIRONMENTAL DESIGN (interior design), HEALTH PROFESSIONS (community health work, exercise science, medical laboratory technology, nursing, and speech pathology/audiology), SOCIAL SCIENCE (African American studies, anthropology, child care/child and family studies, economics, food production/management/services, geography, history, human development, liberal arts/general studies, philosophy, political science/government, psychology, religion, social work, sociology, textiles and clothing, and women's studies). Nursing, education, and business administration are the largest.

Required: In order to graduate, students must complete a minimum of 122 credit hours with a GPA of at least 2.0. Major requirements vary from a minimum of 30 credit hours. The liberal education curriculum for all students requires 45 credit hours chosen from specified courses in the humanities, math and physical sciences, social and behavioral sciences, and a foreign language. Students must take 36 hours at the upper-division level and earn 31 hours of resident credit.

Special: Cooperative programs, internships, and accelerated degree programs can be arranged in all majors. Cross-registration is offered with the Greater Greensboro Consortium. Students may study abroad in more than 30 countries, including Spain, where UNCG sponsors a semester of study in Madrid. A Washington semester and student-designed majors are also available. The Residential College, a 2-year program for freshmen and sophomores, offers an interdisciplinary curriculum, with faculty and students living in the same residence. Students in this program participate in independent study, community work, and workshops. There are 18 national honor societies, including Phi Beta Kappa, a freshman honors program, and 14 departmental honors programs.

Faculty/Classroom: 49% of faculty are male; 51%, female. 95% teach undergraduates. The average class size in an introductory lecture is 30; in a laboratory, 19; and in a regular course, 21.

Admissions: 77% of the 2003-2004 applicants were accepted. The SAT I scores for the 2003-2004 freshman class were: Verbal--40% below

500, 42% between 500 and 599, 16% between 600 and 700, and 2% above 700; Math--39% below 500, 44% between 500 and 599, 16% between 600 and 700, and 1% above 700. 32% of the current freshmen were in the top fifth of their class; 93% were in the top two fifths.

Requirements: The SAT I is required. In addition, graduation from an accredited secondary school or the GED is required. High school courses must include 4 credits of English, 3 each of math and science, 2 of a foreign language, 1 of U.S. history, and 1 of social studies and an elective. A portfolio or audition is required of art and music students. AP and CLEP credits are accepted. Important factors in the admissions decision are advanced placement or honor courses, leadership record, and evidence of special talent.

Procedure: Freshmen are admitted to all sessions. Entrance exams should be taken in June of the junior year or in the fall of the senior year. There is a rolling admissions plan. Applications should be filed by August 1 for fall entry and December 1 for spring entry. Notification is sent on a rolling basis. The fall 2003 application fee was $35. Applications are accepted on-line.

Transfer: 996 transfer students enrolled in 2002-2003. Transfer students must have a minimum GPA of 2.0. Students having fewer than 24 semester hours must meet the freshman entrance requirements, including satisfactory scores on the SAT I. 31 of 122 credits required for the bachelor's degree must be completed at UNCG.

Visiting: There are regularly scheduled orientations for prospective students. There are guides for informal visits and visitors may sit in on classes and stay overnight. To schedule a visit, contact the Office of Undergraduate Admissions.

Financial Aid: In 2003-2004, 59% of all full-time freshmen and 61% of continuing full-time students received some form of financial aid. 48% of full-time freshmen and 60% of continuing full-time students received need-based aid. The average freshman award was $7706. Need-based scholarships or need-based grants averaged $2480; need-based self-help aid (loans and jobs) averaged $2770; and non-need-based awards and non-need-based scholarships averaged $3025. The average financial indebtedness of the 2003 graduate was $16,942. The FAFSA is required. The deadline for filing freshman financial aid applications for fall entry is March 1.

International Students: There are 103 international students enrolled. They must score 550 on the written TOEFL.

Computers: The mainframe is a DEC VAX 8200. PCs and Macs are in labs in most classroom buildings, the student center, most residence halls, and the library. All students may access the system until late-night hours in labs and 24 hours a day via personal modem. There are no time limits and no fees.

Graduates: From July 1, 2002 to June 30, 2003, 1884 bachelor's degrees were awarded. The most popular majors were business administration (11%), psychology (5%), and elementary education (4%). In an average class, 27% graduate in 4 years or less, 47% in 5 years or less, and 50% graduate in 6 years or less.

Admissions Contact: Lise Keller, Director, Undergraduate Admissions. E-mail: *undergrad_admissions@uncg.edu* Web: *http://www.uncg.edu/adm/*

UNIVERSITY OF NORTH CAROLINA AT PEMBROKE   D-3
Pembroke, NC 28372-1510
                                          (910) 521-6262
                          (800) 949-UNCP; Fax: (910) 521-6497

Full-time: 1332 men, 1960 women	**Faculty:** 162; IIA, -$
Part-time: 214 men, 747 women	**Ph.D.s:** 71%
Graduate: 157 men, 312 women	**Student/Faculty:** 20 to 1
Year: semesters, summer session	**Tuition:** $2565 ($11,929)
Application Deadline: July 15	**Room & Board:** $4364
Freshman Class: 1902 applied, 1633 accepted, 809 enrolled	
SAT I Verbal/Math: 470/470	**LESS COMPETITIVE**

UNC Pembroke, founded in 1887, is part of the University of North Carolina state-supported system. It provides a liberal arts education that includes art, business, health sciences, music, teacher preparation, and preprofessional studies. There are 3 undergraduate schools and 1 graduate school. In addition to regional accreditation, UNCP has baccalaureate program accreditation with CSWE, NASM, and NCATE. The library contains 308,667 volumes, 666,648 microform items, and 1856 audio/video tapes/CDs, and subscribes to 1629 periodicals. Computerized library services include the card catalog, interlibrary loans, database searching, and Internet access. Special learning facilities include an art gallery, TV station, and a Native American resource center. The 152-acre campus is in a small town 30 miles south of Fayetteville, 100 miles south of Raleigh, and 120 miles east of Charlotte. Including any residence halls, there are 38 buildings.

Student Life: 96% of undergraduates are from North Carolina. Students are from 33 states, 20 foreign countries, and Canada. 90% are from public schools. 54% are white; 22% African American; 20% Native American/Eskimo. The average age of freshmen is 19; all undergraduates, 26. 32% do not continue beyond their first year; 68% remain to graduate.

Housing: 1225 students can be accommodated in college housing, which includes coed dorms and on-campus apartments. On-campus housing is guaranteed for all 4 years. 71% of students commute. All students may keep cars.

Activities: 4% of men and about 1% of women belong to 2 local and 8 national fraternities; 3% of women belong to 1 local and 7 national sororities. There are 70 groups on campus, including art, band, cheerleading, choir, chorale, chorus, dance, drama, ethnic, gay, honors, international, jazz band, literary magazine, musical theater, newspaper, pep band, political, professional, radio and TV, religious, social, social service, student government, and yearbook. Popular campus events include the Performing Arts Cultural Series, Miss UNCP Scholarship Pageant, and Pembroke Day.

Sports: There are 7 intercollegiate sports for men and 6 for women, and 13 intramural sports for men and 13 for women. Facilities include a 3200-seat gym, an auxiliary gym, a track, tennis courts, a natatorium, weight rooms, a bowling alley, a 1700-seat auditorium, fields for soccer, baseball, and softball, 2 swimming pools, and a wellness center.

Disabled Students: 98% of the campus is accessible. Wheelchair ramps, elevators, special parking, specially equipped rest rooms, special class scheduling, lowered drinking fountains, and lowered telephones are available.

Services: Counseling and information services are available, as is tutoring in every subject. There is a reader service for the blind, and remedial math, reading, and writing, as well as Americans with Disabilities services.

Campus Safety and Security: Measures include 24-hour foot and vehicle patrol, self-defense education, security escort services, and informal discussions. There are pamphlets/posters/films, emergency telephones, and lighted pathways/sidewalks.

Programs of Study: UNCP confers B.A., B.S., B.M., B.S.A.S., B.S.N., and B.S.W. degrees. Master's degrees are also awarded. Bachelor's degrees are awarded in BIOLOGICAL SCIENCE (biology/biological science), BUSINESS (accounting, business administration and management, and business economics), COMMUNICATIONS AND THE ARTS (art, broadcasting, communications, English, journalism, and music), COMPUTER AND PHYSICAL SCIENCE (chemistry, computer science, and mathematics), EDUCATION (art, elementary, English, mathematics, middle school, music, physical, science, secondary, social studies, and special), HEALTH PROFESSIONS (community health work and premedicine), SOCIAL SCIENCE (American Indian studies, criminal justice, history, parks and recreation management, philosophy, political science/government, prelaw, psychology, public administration, religion, social work, and sociology). Education, business administration, and physical sciences are the strongest academically. Education, business, and social science are the largest.

Required: All students are required to complete 120 to 128 total credits, which include 44 semester hours of general education courses, 39 to 69 hours in a major, and a university orientation class before entrance. A minimum GPA of 2.0 must be maintained.

Special: Co-op programs, cross-registration, internships, study abroad in Sweden, a Washington semester, and work-study programs are available. A 3-1 degree program is offered in medical technology. The B.A.-B.S. degree is available in American Indian studies, broadcasting, or with the B.S.A.S. degree. In addition, dual majors, credit for military experience, and nondegree study are offered. There are 6 national honor societies, including Phi Beta Kappa, a freshman honors program, and 5 departmental honors programs.

Faculty/Classroom: 62% of faculty are male; 38%, female. 98% teach undergraduates, 50% do research, and 80% do both. No introductory courses are taught by graduate students. The average class size in an introductory lecture is 27; in a laboratory, 13; and in a regular course, 20.

Admissions: 86% of the 2003-2004 applicants were accepted. The SAT I scores for the 2003-2004 freshman class were: Verbal--67% below 500, 27% between 500 and 599, 5% between 600 and 700, and 1% above 700; Math--62% below 500, 31% between 500 and 599, 6% between 600 and 700, and 1% above 700. 25% of the current freshmen were in the top fifth of their class; 49% were in the top two fifths.

Requirements: The SAT I or ACT is required. In addition, applicants must be graduates of an accredited secondary school with 20 academic credits, including 4 courses in English, 3 each in math and science, and 2 in history. An essay and an interview are recommended. Students also must submit an official high school transcript that shows their class rank and GPA. The College Opportunity Program is designed to admit a limited number of students who meet most, but not all, of the regular admissions standards. Students who receive the GED should consult an admissions counselor. UNCP requires applicants to be in the upper 50% of their class. A GPA of 2.0 is required. AP and CLEP credits are accepted. Important factors in the admissions decision are advanced placement or honor courses, recommendations by school officials, and evidence of special talent.

Procedure: Freshmen are admitted to all sessions. Entrance exams should be taken during the junior and senior years. There is a deferred admissions plan. Applications should be filed by July 15 for fall entry,

December 1 for spring entry, and May 15 for summer entry. The fall 2003 application fee was $40. Notification is sent on a rolling basis.

Transfer: 429 transfer students enrolled in 2002-2003. Applicants must have a minimum GPA of 2.0, submit transcripts from high school and from all previous colleges, and be eligible to return to the last institution attended. The SAT I and an interview are recommended. 30 of 128 credits required for the bachelor's degree must be completed at UNCP.

Visiting: There are regularly scheduled orientations for prospective students, including open houses in the fall, spring, and winter. There are guides for informal visits and visitors may sit in on classes and stay overnight. To schedule a visit, contact the Office of Admissions at *admissions@papa.uncp.edu*.

Financial Aid: In 2003-2004, 81% of all full-time freshmen and 82% of continuing full-time students received some form of financial aid. 72% of full-time freshmen and 74% of continuing full-time students received need-based aid. The average freshman award was $6792. Need-based scholarships or need-based grants averaged $4178 ($17,559 maximum); need-based self-help aid (loans and jobs) averaged $2574 ($4125 maximum); and non-need-based awards and non-need-based scholarships averaged $4315 ($18,000 maximum). 8% of undergraduates work part time. Average annual earnings from campus work are $1500. The average financial indebtedness of the 2003 graduate was $7457. The FAFSA is required. The deadline for filing freshman financial aid applications for fall entry is March 15.

International Students: There were 24 international students enrolled in a recent year. They must score 520 on the written TOEFL or take the MELAB and also take the SAT I or the ACT.

Computers: The mainframes are an Alpha server 2100 5/250, an Alpha server 2000 4/1233, 2 Compaq DS 20s, a SUN E450, and a SUN E250. There are also PCs available in the computer center classrooms and computer lab. All students may access the system. Students may access the system 1 hour at a time. There are no fees.

Graduates: From July 1, 2002 to June 30, 2003, 536 bachelor's degrees were awarded. The most popular majors were protective services (18%), business (18%), and social services (16%). In an average class, 21% graduate in 4 years or less, and 34% graduate in 5 years or less. 123 companies recruited on campus in 2002-2003. Of the 2002 graduating class, 20% were enrolled in graduate school within 6 months of graduation and 90% were employed.

Admissions Contact: Jacqueline Clark, VC for Enrollment Management. A video is available. E-mail: *admissions@papa.uncp.edu* Web: *www.uncp.edu*

UNIVERSITY OF NORTH CAROLINA AT WILMINGTON   E-4
Wilmington, NC 28403-3297
(910) 962-3243
Fax: (910) 962-3038

Full-time: 3569 men, 5401 women	**Faculty:** 467; IIA, av$
Part-time: 403 men, 601 women	**Ph.D.s:** 84%
Graduate: 355 men, 600 women	**Student/Faculty:** 19 to 1
Year: semesters, summer session	**Tuition:** $3362 ($12,937)
Application Deadline: February 1	**Room & Board:** $5578
Freshman Class: 8325 applied, 4522 accepted, 1722 enrolled	
SAT I Verbal/Math: 543/561	**VERY COMPETITIVE**

The University of North Carolina at Wilmington, founded in 1947, is a publicly funded institution offering programs in the liberal arts and sciences, education, and business. It is a part of the University of North Carolina System. There are 4 undergraduate schools and 1 graduate school. In addition to regional accreditation, UNC at Wilmington has baccalaureate program accreditation with NCATE and NLN. The library contains 517,046 volumes, 785,585 microform items, and 57,323 audio/video tapes/CDs, and subscribes to 3653 periodicals. Computerized library services include the card catalog, interlibrary loans, and database searching. Special learning facilities include a radio station, TV station, wildflower preserve, nature preserve, museum of world cultures, and the research vessel *Seahawk*, used for a marine biology lab and for research. The 661-acre campus is in a suburban area 125 miles southeast of Raleigh. Including any residence halls, there are 71 buildings.

Student Life: 87% of undergraduates are from North Carolina. Students are from 40 states, 37 foreign countries, and Canada. 90% are white. The average age of freshmen is 18; all undergraduates, 22. 21% do not continue beyond their first year; 40% remain to graduate.

Housing: 2364 students can be accommodated in college housing, which includes single-sex and coed dorms and on-campus apartments. In addition, there are honors houses and an international student dorm. On-campus housing is available on a first-come, first-served basis. 77% of students commute. All students may keep cars.

Activities: 7% of men belong to 11 national fraternities; 8% of women belong to 11 national sororities. There are 140 groups on campus, including academic, art, cheerleading, chorale, computers, dance, drama, ethnic, film, gay, honors, international, jazz band, literary magazine, musical theater, pep band, political, radio and TV, readers theater, religious, social, social service, student government, symphony, team, and year-

book. Popular campus events include Business Week, Greek Week, and Spring Week.

Sports: There are 10 intercollegiate sports for men and 11 for women, and 9 intramural sports for men and 9 for women. Facilities include a 6000-seat coliseum, an Olympic-size swimming pool and separate diving tank, a track and field complex, and basketball, tennis, and racquetball courts.

Disabled Students: 98% of the campus is accessible. Wheelchair ramps, elevators, special parking, specially equipped rest rooms, special class scheduling, lowered drinking fountains, and lowered telephones are available.

Services: Counseling and information services are available, as is tutoring in most subjects. There is a reader service for the blind, and remedial math, reading, and writing.

Campus Safety and Security: Measures include 24-hour foot and vehicle patrol, self-defense education, security escort services, and shuttle buses. There are informal discussions, pamphlets/posters/films, emergency telephones, and lighted pathways/sidewalks.

Programs of Study: UNC at Wilmington confers B.A., B.S., B.F.A., and B.S.W. degrees. Master's degrees are also awarded. Bachelor's degrees are awarded in BIOLOGICAL SCIENCE (biology/biological science, marine biology, and marine science), BUSINESS (accounting, banking and finance, business administration and management, business economics, business systems analysis, and marketing/retailing/merchandising), COMMUNICATIONS AND THE ARTS (art history and appreciation, creative writing, dramatic arts, English, film arts, French, music, music performance, Spanish, speech/debate/rhetoric, and studio art), COMPUTER AND PHYSICAL SCIENCE (chemistry, computer science, geology, mathematics, physics, and statistics), EDUCATION (athletic training, early childhood, elementary, middle school, music, physical, secondary, and special), ENGINEERING AND ENVIRONMENTAL DESIGN (environmental science), HEALTH PROFESSIONS (medical laboratory technology, nursing, and recreation therapy), SOCIAL SCIENCE (anthropology, criminal justice, economics, geography, history, parks and recreation management, philosophy, political science/government, psychology, religion, social work, and sociology). Psychology is the largest.

Required: Students may qualify for the bachelor's degree by successfully completing the basic studies requirements, an approved course of study in an academic major, a minimum of 124 semester hours of credit, and a minimum quality point average of 2.0. The final 30 semester hours of course credit, including the final 15 semester hours in the major, must be completed at the University of North Carolina at Wilmington.

Special: UNC at Wilmington offers short-term internships and work-study programs. Dual majors may be pursued if requirements are met, and credit is given for military experience. There are 13 national honor societies, a freshman honors program, and 31 departmental honors programs.

Faculty/Classroom: 60% of faculty are male; 40%, female. 8% do research. The average class size in a regular class is 35.

Admissions: 54% of the 2003-2004 applicants were accepted. The SAT I scores for the 2003-2004 freshman class were: Verbal--29% below 500, 54% between 500 and 599, 16% between 600 and 700, and 1% above 700; Math--20% below 500, 54% between 500 and 599, 24% between 600 and 700, and 2% above 700. The ACT scores were 6% below 21, 31% between 21 and 23, 30% between 24 and 26, 31% between 27 and 28, and 2% above 28. 52% of the current freshmen were in the top fifth of their class; 89% were in the top two fifths.

Requirements: The SAT I or ACT is required; the SAT I is preferred. In addition, graduation from an accredited secondary school or the GED is required for admission. High school courses must include 4 years of English, 3 years of math (algebra I, II, and geometry), 3 units of science (1 year each of biology, physical science, and a lab course), 2 years of social studies including 1 year of U.S. history, and 2 years of a foreign language. Students meeting all requirements except that for foreign language will be accepted with a deficiency and will be required to complete a foreign language sequence before receiving a degree. A GPA of 2.0 is required. AP and CLEP credits are accepted.

Procedure: Freshmen are admitted fall and summer. Entrance exams should be taken during the junior or senior year. Applications should be filed by February 1 for fall entry and May 1 for summer entry, along with a $45 fee. Notification of early decision is sent January 20; regular decision, April 1. A waiting list is an active part of the admissions procedure.

Transfer: 1169 transfer students enrolled in 2002-2003. Transfer students must have a minimum GPA of 2.0 and be eligible to return to the institution last attended. Applicants with fewer than 24 semester hours or 36 quarter hours of transferable credit must also meet the freshman entrance requirements. Prior to admission, transfer applicants must have successfully completed 1 year of freshman-level English and 1 unit of college-level math. One unit of life sciences is also recommended. 30 of 124 credits required for the bachelor's degree must be completed at UNC at Wilmington.

Visiting: There are regularly scheduled orientations for prospective students. There are guides for informal visits. To schedule a visit, contact the Admissions Office.

Financial Aid: In 2003-2004, 60% of all full-time freshmen and 58% of continuing full-time students received some form of financial aid. 34% of full-time freshmen and 38% of continuing full-time students received need-based aid. The average freshman award was $8625. Need-based scholarships or need-based grants averaged $3425 ($16,759 maximum); need-based self-help aid (loans and jobs) averaged $3311 ($9625 maximum); and non-need-based athletic scholarships averaged $4779 ($19,311 maximum). 3% of undergraduates work part time. Average annual earnings from campus work are $1594. The average financial indebtedness of the 2003 graduate was $15,176. The FAFSA and the college's own financial statement are required. The priority date for freshman financial aid applications for fall entry is March 1. The deadline for filing freshman financial aid applications for fall entry is December 17.

International Students: There are 53 international students enrolled. The school actively recruits these students. They must score 550 on the written TOEFL.

Computers: The mainframe is an HP Alpha 6000/420. PCs are available in numerous student computer labs, as well as in academic and administrative departments. All students may access the system from 8 A.M. to 11 P.M. at on-campus clusters and 24-hours daily via the Internet. There are no time limits and no fees. It is strongly recommended that all students have a personal computer. A Dell laptop is recommended.

Graduates: In a recent year, 1891 bachelor's degrees were awarded. The most popular majors were speech communication (9%), biology (8%), and psychology (8%). In an average class, 34% graduate in 4 years or less, 51% graduate in 5 years or less, and 52% graduate in 6 years or less. 153 companies recruited on campus in a recent year. Of a recent graduating class, 16% were enrolled in graduate school within 6 months of graduation.

Admissions Contact: Roxie M. Shabazz, Assistant VC for Admissions. A video is available. Web: *http://www.uncwil.edu*

WAKE FOREST UNIVERSITY

C-2

Winston-Salem, NC 27109-7305   (336) 758-5201

Full-time: 1941 men, 2043 women	**Faculty:** 366; IIA, ++$
Part-time: 28 men, 19 women	**Ph.D.s:** 90%
Graduate: 1358 men, 1062 women	**Student/Faculty:** 11 to 1
Year: semesters, summer session	**Tuition:** $26,490
Application Deadline: January 15	**Room & Board:** $7600
Freshman Class: 5700 applied, 2599 accepted, 1007 enrolled	
SAT I: required	**ACT:** n/av **MOST COMPETITIVE**

Wake Forest University, established in 1834, is a private institution offering undergraduate programs in the liberal arts and sciences, education, and preprofessional fields. There are 2 undergraduate and 5 graduate schools. In addition to regional accreditation, Wake Forest has baccalaureate program accreditation with AACSB and NCATE. The 3 libraries contain 1,742,645 volumes, 2,139,741 microform items, and 9540 audio/video tapes/CDs, and subscribe to 16,082 periodicals. Computerized library services include the card catalog, interlibrary loans, database searching, and Internet access. Special learning facilities include a learning resource center, art gallery, radio station, TV station, and fine arts center, anthropology museum, and laser research facility. The 340-acre campus is in a suburban area 4 miles northwest of Winston-Salem. Including any residence halls, there are 43 buildings.

Student Life: 71% of undergraduates are from out of state, mostly the South. Students are from 50 states, 26 foreign countries, and Canada. 69% are from public schools. 87% are white. 60% are Protestant; 21% Catholic; 14% Muslim, Hindu, Buddhist, Mormon, and Greek Orthodox. The average age of freshmen is 18; all undergraduates, 20. 7% do not continue beyond their first year; 87% remain to graduate.

Housing: 3016 students can be accommodated in college housing, which includes coed dorms and on-campus apartments. In addition, there are honors houses, language houses, and special-interest houses. On-campus housing is guaranteed for all 4 years. 75% of students live on campus; of those, 75% remain on campus on weekends. All students may keep cars.

Activities: 34% of men belong to 14 national fraternities; 52% of women belong to 9 national sororities. There are 125 groups on campus, including art, band, cheerleading, choir, chorale, chorus, computers, dance, debate, drama, drill team, environmental, ethnic, film, gay, honors, international, jazz band, literary magazine, marching band, musical theater, newspaper, orchestra, pep band, photography, political, professional, radio and TV, religious, social, social service, student government, symphony, women's, and yearbook. Popular campus events include Convocation, Moravian Christmas Love Feast, and Family Weekend.

Sports: There are 8 intercollegiate sports for men and 8 for women, and 20 intramural sports for men and 16 for women. Facilities include 7 playing fields, 4 indoor basketball courts, a swimming pool, a track, racquetball and tennis courts, an exercise room and weight room, an indoor tennis center, a fitness center, a soccer complex, a golf practice complex, and a cross-country course.

Disabled Students: 80% of the campus is accessible. Wheelchair ramps, elevators, special parking, specially equipped rest rooms, special class scheduling, lowered drinking fountains, and lowered telephones are available.

Services: Counseling and information services are available, as is tutoring in some subjects, primarily in the sciences, math, and foreign languages. There is a reader service for the blind. The Learning Assistance Center offers instructional support and skill development in writing, reading, and study strategies.

Campus Safety and Security: Measures include 24-hour foot and vehicle patrol, self-defense education, security escort services, and shuttle buses. There are informal discussions, pamphlets/posters/films, emergency telephones, and lighted pathways/sidewalks. There are gatehouses at 2 of the university's 3 entrances that operate from 10 P.M. to 6 A.M. During those hours, the third entrance is closed.

Programs of Study: Wake Forest confers B.A. and B.S. degrees. Master's and doctoral degrees are also awarded. Bachelor's degrees are awarded in BIOLOGICAL SCIENCE (biology/biological science), BUSINESS (accounting, banking and finance, business administration and management, and management information systems), COMMUNICATIONS AND THE ARTS (art, classics, communications, dramatic arts, English, French, German, Greek, Latin, music, and Spanish), COMPUTER AND PHYSICAL SCIENCE (chemistry, computer science, mathematics, and physics), EDUCATION (education), HEALTH PROFESSIONS (exercise science), SOCIAL SCIENCE (anthropology, economics, history, philosophy, political science/government, psychology, religion, and sociology). Business, communication, and political science are the largest.

Required: To graduate, students must complete a total of 112 credits with a minimum GPA of 2.0. The number of hours required in the major varies. All students must take 1 semester of a writing seminar, a first-year seminar, and 1 course in foreign language literature. In addition, students must complete 3 courses each in natural sciences and math, social and behavioral sciences, and history, religion, and philosophy; 2 courses in literature; and 1 course in fine arts.

Special: The school offers cooperative programs in forestry with Duke University. Cross-registration with Salem College is available. The school sponsors study-abroad programs in 9 countries. A Washington semester, internships, work-study programs, dual majors, a 3-2 engineering degree with North Carolina State University, a B.A.-B.S. degree in chemistry/physics, and pass/fail options are available. Accelerated degree programs may be arranged in dentistry and medical technology. Interdisciplinary honors courses and the Open Curriculum program are available for selected students. Wake Forest owns residences in London, Venice, and Vienna where students and professors may attend semester-long courses in a variety of disciplines. There are 11 national honor societies, including Phi Beta Kappa, a freshman honors program, and 23 departmental honors programs.

Faculty/Classroom: 64% of faculty are male; 36%, female. All teach undergraduates. No introductory courses are taught by graduate students. The average class size in a regular course is 19.

Admissions: 46% of the 2003-2004 applicants were accepted. 85% of the current freshmen were in the top fifth of their class; 96% were in the top two fifths. 48 freshmen graduated first in their class.

Requirements: The SAT I is required, and 3 SAT II: Subject tests, including writing and mathematics, are recommended. Graduation from an accredited secondary school or the GED is required. The school requires 16 academic credits, including 4 credits of English, 3 of math, 2 each of a foreign language, history, and social studies, and 1 of science. 1 credit each of art and music is recommended. All students must submit an essay. AP and CLEP credits are accepted. Important factors in the admissions decision are recommendations by school officials, leadership record, and advanced placement or honor courses.

Procedure: Freshmen are admitted fall and spring. Entrance exams should be taken during the junior year, and at least 1 SAT I should be taken during the senior year. There are early decision and deferred admissions plans. Early decision applications should be filed by November 15; regular applications, by January 15 for fall entry and November 15 for spring entry. The fall 2003 application fee was $40. Notification of early decision is sent December 15; regular decision, April 1. 342 early decision candidates were accepted for the 2003-2004 class. A waiting list is an active part of the admissions procedure. Applications are accepted on-line through the school's web site.

Transfer: 49 transfer students enrolled in 2002-2003. Transfer students must have a minimum GPA of 2.0 on all college work attempted. The SAT I is required. 56 credits of 112 required for the bachelor's degree must be completed at Wake Forest.

Visiting: There are regularly scheduled orientations for prospective students, including group information sessions and tours by appointment. There are guides for informal visits and visitors may sit in on classes and stay overnight. To schedule a visit, contact the Admissions Office at *admissions@wfu.edu*.

Financial Aid: In 2003-2004, 69% of all full-time students received some form of financial aid. 34% of full-time freshmen and 28% of continuing full-time students received need-based aid. The average freshman award was $21,109. 25% of undergraduates work part time. Average annual earnings from campus work are $2000. The average financial indebtedness of the 2003 graduate was $19,104. Wake Forest is a member of CSS. The CSS/Profile, FAFSA, and the state aid form are required. The priority date for freshman financial aid applications for fall entry is March 1.

International Students: There are 43 international students enrolled. They must take the TOEFL and also take the SAT I.

Computers: The mainframes are 2 SP2 frames with 47 nodes, 2 HP 3000s, and a 122-node Linux cluster. Each incoming student receives an IBM ThinkPad with mainframe capability. Internet access is available directly from each residence hall room, faculty office, classroom, and the campus library. All have the option of purchasing wireless Ethernet cards. All students may access the system 24 hours per day. There are no time limits and no fees. All students are required to have personal computers.

Graduates: From July 1, 2002 to June 30, 2003, 901 bachelor's degrees were awarded. The most popular majors were business (12%), communication (12%), and political science (10%). In an average class, 86% graduate in 5 years or less, and 87% graduate in 6 years or less. 160 companies recruited on campus in 2002-2003. Of the 2002 graduating class, 30% were enrolled in graduate school within 6 months of graduation and 60% were employed.

Admissions Contact: Martha B. Allman, Director of Admissions. A video is available. E-mail: *admissions@wfu.edu* Web: *www.wfu.edu*

WARREN WILSON COLLEGE   B-2
Asheville, NC 28815-9000

(828) 298-3325
(800) 934-3536; Fax: (828) 298-1440

Full-time: 283 men, 477 women	**Faculty:** 58; IIB, -$
Part-time: 1 man, 8 women	**Ph.D.s:** 95%
Graduate: 14 men, 45 women	**Student/Faculty:** 13 to 1
Year: semesters	**Tuition:** $16,674
Application Deadline: March 15	**Room & Board:** $5120
Freshman Class: 753 applied, 595 accepted, 229 enrolled	
SAT I Verbal/Math: 605/563	**ACT:** 24 **VERY COMPETITIVE**

Warren Wilson College, founded in 1894, is a liberal arts institution affiliated with the Presbyterian Church (U.S.A.). All students work 15 hours per week in jobs related to the operation and maintenance of the college. In exchange, room and board is provided at a low rate. In addition to regional accreditation, Warren Wilson College has baccalaureate program accreditation with CSWE and NCATE. The library contains 101,500 volumes, 33,390 microform items, and 2500 audio/video tapes/CDs, and subscribes to 9251 periodicals. Computerized library services include the card catalog, interlibrary loans, database searching, and Internet access. Special learning facilities include a learning resource center, art gallery, and radio station. The 1175-acre campus is in a small town 5 miles east of Asheville.

Student Life: 79% of undergraduates are from out of state, mostly the South. Students are from 42 states and 21 foreign countries. 74% are from public schools. 90% are white. Most claim no religious affiliation. The average age of freshmen is 18; all undergraduates, 20. 34% do not continue beyond their first year; 46% remain to graduate.

Housing: 684 students can be accommodated in college housing, which includes single-sex and coed dorms, a wellness house, and an eco-dorm. On-campus housing is guaranteed for all 4 years. 87% of students live on campus; of those, 95% remain on campus on weekends. Upperclassmen may keep cars.

Activities: There are no fraternities or sororities. There are many groups and organizations on campus, including art, chess, choir, chorus, computers, dance, drama, environmental, ethnic, film, gay, honors, international, jazz band, literary magazine, musical theater, newspaper, orchestra, outdoor, photography, political, professional, radio and TV, religious, social, social justice, social service, student government, and yearbook. Popular campus events include International Fair, Work Day, and Service Day.

Sports: There are 6 intercollegiate sports for men and 6 for women, and 5 intramural sports for men and 5 for women. Facilities include 2 gyms, an aquatic center, weight and fitness rooms, tennis courts, playing fields, 25 miles of hiking/biking trails, kayak slalom gates, indoor climbing wall, and alpine tower.

Disabled Students: 25% of the campus is accessible. Wheelchair ramps, elevators, special parking, specially equipped rest rooms, special class scheduling, lowered drinking fountains, and lowered telephones are available.

Services: Counseling and information services are available, as is tutoring in most subjects. Tutoring is available through the Peer Assistance Center and the Writing Center. ESL tutoring is also available.

Campus Safety and Security: Measures include 24-hour foot and vehicle patrol, security escort services, informal discussions, and pamphlets/posters/films. There are emergency telephones and lighted pathways/sidewalks.

Programs of Study: Warren Wilson College confers B.A. and B.S. degrees. Master's degrees are also awarded. Bachelor's degrees are award-

ed in AGRICULTURE (environmental studies), BIOLOGICAL SCIENCE (biology/biological science), BUSINESS (business economics), COMMUNICATIONS AND THE ARTS (art, creative writing, English, and Spanish), COMPUTER AND PHYSICAL SCIENCE (chemistry and mathematics), EDUCATION (elementary, English, middle school, and recreation), SOCIAL SCIENCE (anthropology, behavioral science, history, humanities, international studies, philosophy, psychology, social work, sociology, and women's studies). Biology is the strongest academically. Environmental studies, biology, and English are the largest.

Required: To graduate, students must complete a total of 128 semester hours with a minimum GPA of 2.0. Between 32 and 40 hours are required in the student's major. All students must complete 36 hours in the core curriculum. All students must also complete 25 hours of community service each year. A first-year seminar and college composition are required.

Special: Cross-registration is offered with Mars Hill College and the University of North Carolina at Asheville. Internships related to the major may be arranged. Study-abroad programs in South America, Europe, Japan, and India are available. The college offers an accelerated degree program in education, student-designed majors, nondegree study, and pass/fail options. There are dual majors in history/political science and English/theater arts. Cooperative programs are available in engineering with Washington University in St. Louis. On campus work-study is required.

Faculty/Classroom: 51% of faculty are male; 49%, female. 100% both teach and do research. No introductory courses are taught by graduate students. The average class size in an introductory lecture is 16; in a laboratory, 15; and in a regular course, 11.

Admissions: 79% of the 2003-2004 applicants were accepted. The SAT I scores for the 2003-2004 freshman class were: Verbal--9% below 500, 35% between 500 and 599, 42% between 600 and 700, and 15% above 700; Math--19% below 500, 44% between 500 and 599, 31% between 600 and 700, and 5% above 700. 38% of the current freshmen were in the top fifth of their class. There were 5 National Merit finalists. 5 freshmen graduated first in their class.

Requirements: The SAT I or ACT is required, with a score of 500 on each section of the SAT I or a composite score of 21 on the ACT. Graduation from an accredited secondary school or the GED is required. Applicants should have a total of 12 academic credits. An essay and an interview are recommended. A GPA of 2.5 is required. AP credits are accepted. Important factors in the admissions decision are advanced placement or honor courses, evidence of special talent, and recommendations by school officials.

Procedure: Freshmen are admitted fall and winter. Entrance exams should be taken by January 20 of the senior year. There are early decision, early admissions, and deferred admissions plans. Early decision applications should be filed by November 15; regular applications, by March 15 for fall entry and November 1 for winter entry. Notification of early decision is sent December 1; regular decision, April 1. 69 early decision candidates were accepted for the 2003-2004 class. Applications are accepted on computer disk through CollegeLink.

Transfer: 53 transfer students enrolled in 2002-2003. Applicants must have a minimum GPA of 2.75. A year of residence at Warren Wilson is required for graduation. Applicants must be eligible to return to their previous institutions. 32 of 128 credits required for the bachelor's degree must be completed at Warren Wilson College.

Visiting: There are guides for informal visits and visitors may sit in on classes and stay overnight. To schedule a visit, contact the campus visit coordinator at *admit@warren-wilson.edu*.

Financial Aid: In 2003-2004, 90% of all full-time freshmen and 81% of continuing full-time students received some form of financial aid. 61% of full-time freshmen and 55% of continuing full-time students received need-based aid. The average freshman award was $11,344. Need-based scholarships or need-based grants averaged $8826 ($16,800 maximum); need-based self-help aid (loans and jobs) averaged $3224 ($5097 maximum); non-need-based awards and non-need-based scholarships averaged $3178 ($17,322 maximum); and non-need based loans and work averaged $2983 ($13,400 maximum). 89% of undergraduates work part time. Average annual earnings from campus work are $2472. The average financial indebtedness of the 2003 graduate was $14,407. The FAFSA and the college's own financial statement are required. The priority date for freshman financial aid applications for fall entry is April 1.

International Students: There were 38 international students enrolled in a recent year. The school actively recruits these students. They must score 550 on the written TOEFL or 213 on the electronic version.

Computers: The mainframe is a Linux servers. PCs and Macs are available for student use in academic buildings and the library. All students may access the system. There are no time limits and no fees. It is strongly recommended that all students have a personal computer.

Graduates: From July 1, 2002 to June 30, 2003, 96 bachelor's degrees were awarded. The most popular majors were environmental studies (16%), human studies (11%), and psychology (7%). In an average class, 1% graduate in 3 years or less, 33% graduate in 4 years or less, 38% graduate in 5 years or less, and 40% graduate in 6 years or less. 40 companies recruited on campus in 2002-2003.

Admissions Contact: Richard Blomgren, Dean of Admission. A video is available. E-mail: *rickb@warren-wilson.edu*
Web: *www.warren-wilson.edu*

WESTERN CAROLINA UNIVERSITY   B-3
Cullowhee, NC 28723   (828) 227-7317
1-877-WCU4YOU; Fax: (828) 227-7319

Full-time: 2633 men, 2659 women	**Faculty:** 323; IIA, -$
Part-time: 304 men, 491 women	**Ph.Ds:** 80%
Graduate: 569 men, 905 women	**Student/Faculty:** 16 to 1
Year: semesters, summer session	**Tuition:** $2916 ($11,831)
Application Deadline: July 15	**Room & Board:** $3826
Freshman Class: 4606 applied, 3392 accepted, 1495 enrolled	
SAT I Verbal/Math: 500/510	**COMPETITIVE**

Western Carolina University, founded in 1889, is a publicly funded institution in the University of North Carolina system. There are 5 undergraduate schools and 1 graduate school. In addition to regional accreditation, Western has baccalaureate program accreditation with AACSB, ABET, ADA, CSWE, FIDER, NASM, NCATE, and NLN. The library contains 583,694 volumes, 1,352,489 microform items, and 6300 audio/video tapes/CDs, and subscribes to 2928 periodicals. Computerized library services include the card catalog, interlibrary loans, database searching, and Internet access. Special learning facilities include a learning resource center, art gallery, natural history museum, radio station, and a mountain heritage center. The 265-acre campus is in a rural area 160 miles northeast of Atlanta, Georgia, and 50 miles west of Asheville. Including any residence halls, there are 89 buildings.

Student Life: 91% of undergraduates are from North Carolina. Students are from 40 states, 39 foreign countries, and Canada. 95% are from public schools. 88% are white. The average age of freshmen is 17; all undergraduates, 22. 29% do not continue beyond their first year; 46% remain to graduate.

Housing: 3100 students can be accommodated in college housing, which includes single-sex and coed dorms, on-campus apartments, and married-student housing. In addition, there are honors houses. On-campus housing is guaranteed for all 4 years. 55% of students commute. All students may keep cars.

Activities: 13% of men belong to 12 national fraternities; 11% of women belong to 8 national sororities. There are 91 groups on campus, including art, band, cheerleading, choir, chorale, chorus, computers, dance, drama, drill team, ethnic, film, gay, honors, international, literary magazine, marching band, musical theater, newspaper, pep band, photography, political, professional, radio and TV, religious, social, social service, student government, and yearbook. Popular campus events include Mountain Heritage Day, Greek Week, and Madrigal Christmas Dinners.

Sports: There are 6 intercollegiate sports for men and 7 for women, and 38 intramural sports for men and 39 for women. Facilities include a football stadium, a baseball diamond, a track/tennis complex, 6 intramural softball and football fields, a soccer field, 5 gyms, a field house, jogging trails, picnic areas, game rooms, a weight training room, a swimming pool, an archery range, a golf driving range, and a golf putting green.

Disabled Students: 90% of the campus is accessible. Wheelchair ramps, elevators, special parking, specially equipped rest rooms, special class scheduling, lowered drinking fountains, and lowered telephones are available.

Services: Counseling and information services are available, as is tutoring in most subjects. There is a reader service for the blind, and remedial math, reading, and writing.

Campus Safety and Security: Measures include 24-hour foot and vehicle patrol, shuttle buses, informal discussions, and pamphlets/posters/films. There are emergency telephones, lighted pathways/sidewalks, and crime-prevention education programs.

Programs of Study: Western confers B.A., B.S., B.F.A., B.S.B.A., B.S.Ed., and B.S.N. degrees. Master's and doctoral degrees are also awarded. Bachelor's degrees are awarded in AGRICULTURE (natural resource management), BIOLOGICAL SCIENCE (biology/biological science, environmental biology, and nutrition), BUSINESS (accounting, banking and finance, business law, entrepreneurial studies, hospitality management services, international business management, management science, marketing and distribution, marketing management, and sports management), COMMUNICATIONS AND THE ARTS (art, communications, dramatic arts, English, French, German, music, Spanish, speech/debate/rhetoric, and studio art), COMPUTER AND PHYSICAL SCIENCE (chemistry, computer science, geology, information sciences and systems, and mathematics), EDUCATION (art, early childhood, elementary, English, foreign languages, mathematics, middle school, music, physical, science, secondary, social science, special, and speech correction), ENGINEERING AND ENVIRONMENTAL DESIGN (construction management, electrical/electronics engineering technology, emergency/disaster science, engineering technology, industrial engineering technology, interior design, manufacturing technology, and preengineering),

HEALTH PROFESSIONS (clinical science, emergency medical technologies, environmental health science, medical records administration/services, nursing, predentistry, premedicine, preoptometry, prepharmacy, preveterinary science, and recreation therapy), SOCIAL SCIENCE (anthropology, criminal justice, dietetics, geography, history, liberal arts/general studies, parks and recreation management, philosophy, political science/government, prelaw, psychology, social science, social work, and sociology). Elementary education, nursing, and criminal justice are the largest.

Required: In order to graduate, students must complete a total of 120 to 128 credit hours with a minimum GPA of 2.0. Between 30 and 64 hours are required in the major. All students must fulfill liberal studies requirements in writing, oral communication, wellness, social sciences, physical and biological sciences, math, humanities, history, fine and performing arts, world cultures, the freshman seminar, and 1 course in upper level perspectives outside the major.

Special: WCU offers cooperative education programs in most majors, extensive internship opportunities, work-study programs, accelerated degree programs, B.A.-B.S. degrees, dual majors, a special studies degree, nondegree study, pass/fail options in designated courses, and credit for life experience. Study-abroad programs may be arranged in 38 countries. A joint degree program in electrical engineering with the University of North Carolina-Charlotte is possible. There are 15 national honor societies and a freshman honors program.

Faculty/Classroom: 58% of faculty are male; 42%, female. All teach undergraduates. Graduate students teach 5% of introductory courses. The average class size in an introductory lecture is 27; in a laboratory, 15; and in a regular course, 19.

Admissions: 74% of the 2003-2004 applicants were accepted. The SAT I scores for the 2003-2004 freshman class were: Verbal--47% below 500, 40% between 500 and 599, 11% between 600 and 700, and 2% above 700; Math--43% below 500, 42% between 500 and 599, 14% between 600 and 700, and 1% above 700. 21% of the current freshmen were in the top fifth of their class; 51% were in the top two fifths. In a recent year, there were 4 National Merit finalists and 1 semifinalist, and 2 freshmen graduated first in their class.

Requirements: The SAT I is required. In addition, graduation from an accredited secondary school or the GED is required. High school courses must include 4 units of English, 3 each of math and science, 2 of social studies, including 1 of U.S. history, and 2 units of a foreign language. Western requires applicants to be in the upper 25% of their class. A GPA of 2.5 is required. AP and CLEP credits are accepted. Important factors in the admissions decision are advanced placement or honor courses, recommendations by school officials, and evidence of special talent.

Procedure: Freshmen are admitted to all sessions. Entrance exams should be taken during the spring of the junior year or the fall of the senior year. There is an early admissions plan. There is a rolling admissions plan. Applications should be filed by July 15 for fall entry, December 10 for spring entry, and May 1 for summer entry, along with a $40 fee. Notification is sent on a rolling basis. Applications are accepted online through Xap Corporation, but a print application is also required.

Transfer: 598 transfer students enrolled in 2002-2003. Tranfer students must have a minimum GPA of 2.0 and meet freshman admissions requirements. 30 of 120 credits required for the bachelor's degree must be completed at Western.

Visiting: There are regularly scheduled orientations for prospective students, consisting of open houses, 2 in fall, 2 in spring, which include registration, a visit to the department of choice, a campus tour, and an athletic event. There are guides for informal visits and visitors may sit in on classes and stay overnight. To schedule a visit, contact the Admissions Office at *admiss@email.wcu.edu*.

Financial Aid: In 2003-2004, 71% of all full-time students received some form of financial aid. 47% of all full-time students received need-based aid. The average freshman award was $7493. Need-based scholarships or need-based grants averaged $2620 ($6844 maximum); need-based self-help aid (loans and jobs) averaged $3065 ($8025 maximum); non-need-based athletic scholarships averaged $6576 ($16,173 maximum); other non-need-based awards and non-need-based scholarships averaged $2218 ($14,594 maximum); and non-need based loans including PLUS loans averaged $5724 ($20,211 maximum). 15% of undergraduates work part time. Average annual earnings from campus work are $1400. The average financial indebtedness of the 2003 graduate was $16,238. The FAFSA is required. The deadline for filing freshman financial aid applications for fall entry is April 1.

International Students: There are 58 international students enrolled. The school actively recruits these students. They must score 550 on the written TOEFL or 213 on the electronic version and also take the SAT I.

Computers: The mainframes are 2 DEC VAX 4000/700As, 1 DEC Alpha 4100, and 1 DEC Alpha 1000. 10 electronic classrooms are located in 5 classroom buildings. A number of classrooms also contain computer teaching stations. There are also more than 4800 PCs in computer labs, the library, the learning centers, dorm rooms, faculty and staff offices. All buildings and residence hall rooms are wired for network access. All students are required to have a networkable computer. The school provides required specifications. All students may access the system 24 hours a day. There are no time limits and no fees.

Graduates: From July 1, 2002 to June 30, 2003, 1093 bachelor's degrees were awarded. The most popular majors were marketing (7%), criminal justice (7%), and nursing (6%). In an average class, 1% graduate in 3 years or less, 23% graduate in 4 years or less, 46% graduate in 5 years or less, and 46% graduate in 6 years or less. 270 companies recruited on campus in 2002-2003.

Admissions Contact: Phil Cauley, Admissions Officer.
E-mail: *admiss@email.wcu.edu* Web: *http://www.poweryourmind.com/*

WINGATE UNIVERSITY

WINGATE UNIVERSITY	**C-3**
Wingate, NC 28174	**(704) 233-8200**
	(800) 755-5550; Fax: (704) 233-8110
Full-time: 586 men, 691 women	**Faculty:** 85; IIB, --$
Part-time: 18 men, 29 women	**Ph.D.s:** 90%
Graduate: 60 men, 111 women	**Student/Faculty:** 15 to 1
Year: semesters, summer session	**Tuition:** $15,200
Application Deadline: n/av	**Room & Board:** $6000
Freshman Class: 1235 applied, 1011 accepted, 372 enrolled	
SAT I Verbal/Math: 510/520	**ACT:** 20 **COMPETITIVE**

Wingate University, founded in 1896, is a private liberal arts institution affiliated with the Baptist State Convention of North Carolina. There are 3 undergraduate and 2 graduate schools. In addition to regional accreditation, Wingate has baccalaureate program accreditation with ACBSP, NASM, and NCATE. The library contains 110,000 volumes, 14,000 microform items, and 5750 audio/video tapes/CDs, and subscribes to 560 periodicals. Computerized library services include the card catalog, interlibrary loans, and database searching. Special learning facilities include a learning resource center, art gallery, and TV station. The 330-acre campus is in a small town 25 miles east of Charlotte. Including any residence halls, there are 35 buildings.

Student Life: 56% of undergraduates are from North Carolina. Students are from 35 states, 18 foreign countries, and Canada. 90% are from public schools. 81% are white; 11% African American. 67% are Protestant; 15% Catholic; 12% claim no religious affiliation. The average age of freshmen is 18; all undergraduates, 20. 28% do not continue beyond their first year; 43% remain to graduate.

Housing: 1068 students can be accommodated in college housing, which includes single-sex dorms, on-campus apartments, off-campus apartments, married-student housing, and fraternity houses. On-campus housing is guaranteed for all 4 years. 81% of students live on campus; of those, 60% remain on campus on weekends. Alcohol is not permitted. All students may keep cars.

Activities: 9% of men belong to 4 national fraternities; 10% of women belong to 3 national sororities. There are 35 groups on campus, including art, band, cheerleading, choir, chorale, chorus, computers, dance, drama, ethnic, honors, international, jazz band, literary magazine, marching band, musical theater, newspaper, orchestra, pep band, photography, political, professional, radio and TV, religious, running, social, social service, student government, swimming, and yearbook. Popular campus events include Spring Fling and Fall Festival at campus lake, and name-band concerts.

Sports: There are 8 intercollegiate sports for men and 8 for women, and 17 intramural sports for men and 17 for women. Facilities include an athletic complex with a gym, swimming pool, racquetball courts, weight room, and tennis courts, and a student center with bowling, table tennis, pool, and a game room.

Disabled Students: 95% of the campus is accessible. Wheelchair ramps, elevators, special parking, specially equipped rest rooms, special class scheduling, and lowered drinking fountains are available.

Services: Counseling and information services are available, as is tutoring in every subject. Additional academic support is available for students with learning disabilities.

Campus Safety and Security: Measures include 24-hour foot and vehicle patrol, self-defense education, security escort services, and informal discussions. There are pamphlets/posters/films, emergency telephones, and lighted pathways/sidewalks.

Programs of Study: Wingate confers B.A., B.S., B.F.A., B.L.S., and B.M.Ed. degrees. Master's degrees are also awarded. Bachelor's degrees are awarded in BIOLOGICAL SCIENCE (biology/biological science), BUSINESS (accounting, banking and finance, business administration and management, business economics, management information systems, marketing/retailing/merchandising, and sports management), COMMUNICATIONS AND THE ARTS (art, communications, English, fine arts, music, music business management, and Spanish), COMPUTER AND PHYSICAL SCIENCE (applied mathematics, chemistry, computer mathematics, computer science, and mathematics), EDUCATION (art, athletic training, elementary, English, mathematics, middle school, music, physical, reading, and science), ENGINEERING AND ENVIRONMENTAL DESIGN (preengineering), HEALTH PROFESSIONS (predentistry, premedicine, prepharmacy, preveterinary science, and sports medicine), SOCIAL SCIENCE (American studies, history, human services,

law, liberal arts/general studies, parks and recreation management, philosophy, prelaw, psychology, religion, and sociology). Biological sciences, history, and English are the strongest academically. Business, athletic training, and communications are the largest.

Required: To graduate, students must complete a minimum of 125 credit hours with a GPA of 2.0. At least 30 hours must be completed in the student's major. All students must take core courses in English composition, literature, religion, fine arts, history, social sciences, foreign language, math, lab science, fitness and wellness, phys ed, and freshman experience.

Special: Cross-registration through the Charlotte Area Education Consortium, internships, a liberal studies degree, B.A.-B.S. degrees, and nondegree study are available. Wingate conducts foreign study semesters in London, Denmark, and China. The school also sponsors Winternational, a semester seminar with a 10-day trip to a foreign country for which students earn academic credit at little personal cost. Dual majors are offered in biology and education, history and education, art and education, English and education, math and education, and chemistry and business. There are 9 national honor societies and a freshman honors program.

Faculty/Classroom: 57% of faculty are male; 43%, female. All teach undergraduates. No introductory courses are taught by graduate students. The average class size in an introductory lecture is 26; in a laboratory, 15; and in a regular course, 13.

Admissions: 82% of the 2003-2004 applicants were accepted. The SAT I scores for the 2003-2004 freshman class were: Verbal--41% below 500, 43% between 500 and 599, 15% between 600 and 700, and 1% above 700; Math--37% below 500, 43% between 500 and 599, 19% between 600 and 700, and 1% above 700. The ACT scores were 38% below 21, 23% between 21 and 23, 23% between 24 and 26, 10% between 27 and 28, and 7% above 28. 25% of the current freshmen were in the top fifth of their class; 41% were in the top two fifths.

Requirements: The SAT I or ACT is required. In addition, graduation from an accredited secondary school or the GED is required. High school curriculum must include 4 courses in English, 3 in math, 2 each in history and science, and 1 in social studies. 2 courses in a foreign language are recommended. An essay is required of all applicants, and an interview is recommended in some cases. A GPA of 2.7 is required. AP and CLEP credits are accepted. Important factors in the admissions decision are advanced placement or honor courses, leadership record, and recommendations by school officials.

Procedure: Freshmen are admitted fall, spring, and summer. Entrance exams should be taken in spring of the junior year or fall of the senior year. There is an early decision plan. The application fee is $25. Notification is sent on a rolling basis. 35 early decision candidates were accepted for the 2003-2004 class. Applications are accepted on-line through the school's web site.

Transfer: 54 transfer students enrolled in a recent year. Applicants must have a minimum GPA of 2.0 and must be eligible to return to the institution last attended. The SAT I or ACT is required if a student has been out of high school for less than 5 years or has fewer than 24 transferable hours. An interview may be recommended in some cases. 30 of 125 credits required for the bachelor's degree must be completed at Wingate.

Visiting: There are regularly scheduled orientations for prospective students, including Saturday Preview Day 4 times a year, campus tours and presentations of travel programs, academic life, athletics, and student life. New student orientation occurs 4 days prior to opening of school each fall. There are guides for informal visits and visitors may sit in on classes and stay overnight. To schedule a visit, contact the Admissions Office at (704) 233-8201 or *admit@wingate.edu*.

Financial Aid: In a recent year, 95% of all full-time freshmen and 88% of continuing full-time students received some form of financial aid. 22% of full-time freshmen and 33% of continuing full-time students received need-based aid. The average freshman award was $7800. 44% of undergraduates work part time. Average annual earnings from campus work are $1200. The average financial indebtedness of the recent graduate was $24,000. The FAFSA is required. The deadline for filing freshman financial aid applications for fall entry is May 1.

International Students: There are 46 international students enrolled. They must score 550 on the written TOEFL and also take the SAT I or the ACT.

Computers: The mainframe is an HP 3000. PCs are available in labs and offices. All students may access the system 8 A.M. to 11 P.M. Sunday to Thursday.

Graduates: In a recent year, 210 bachelor's degrees were awarded. The most popular majors were business administration (22%), sport management (8%), and athletic training (6%). In an average class, 34% graduate in 4 years or less, 48% graduate in 5 years or less, and 50% graduate in 6 years or less. 45 companies recruited on campus in 2002-2003. Of the 2002 graduating class, 20% were enrolled in graduate school within 6 months of graduation and 80% were employed.

Admissions Contact: Walter Crutchfield, Dean of Admissions. A video is available. E-mail: *admit@wingate.edu* Web: *www.wingate.edu*

WINSTON-SALEM STATE UNIVERSITY   C-2
Winston-Salem, NC 27110

(336) 750-2070
(800) 257-4052; Fax: (336) 750-2079

Full-time: 1075 men, 2237 women	**Faculty:** 194; IIB, +$
Part-time: 177 men, 440 women	**Ph.D.s:** 64%
Graduate: 44 men, 129 women	**Student/Faculty:** 17 to 1
Year: semesters, summer session	**Tuition:** $3620 ($11,885)
Application Deadline: open	**Room & Board:** $5306

Freshman Class: 2597 applied, 1994 accepted, 897 enrolled
SAT I Verbal/Math: 470/470   **LESS COMPETITIVE**

Winston-Salem State University, founded in 1892, is a state-supported liberal arts institution offering undergraduate programs through divisions of arts and sciences, business and economics, education, and nursing and allied health. In addition to regional accreditation, WSSU has baccalaureate program accreditation with NASM, NCATE, and NLN. The library contains 196,168 volumes, 246,029 microform items, and 2198 audio/video tapes/CDs, and subscribes to 1010 periodicals. Computerized library services include the card catalog, interlibrary loans, and database searching. Special learning facilities include a learning resource center, art gallery, radio station, TV station, a PLATO lab, and an enrichment center. The 94-acre campus is in a suburban area in Winston-Salem. Including any residence halls, there are 36 buildings.

Student Life: 92% of undergraduates are from North Carolina. Students are from 34 states and 7 foreign countries. 82% are African American; 16% white. The average age of freshmen is 19; all undergraduates, 24. 23% do not continue beyond their first year; 10% remain to graduate.

Housing: 1228 students can be accommodated in college housing, which includes single-sex and coed dorms. On-campus housing is guaranteed for the freshman year only and is available on a first-come, first-served basis. 59% of students commute. Alcohol is not permitted. All students may keep cars.

Activities: There are 70 groups on campus, including art, band, cheerleading, choir, computers, dance, drama, drill team, ethnic, honors, international, jazz band, marching band, newspaper, photography, political, radio and TV, social, student government, and yearbook.

Sports: There are 4 intercollegiate sports for men and 5 for women. Facilities include 2 gyms, tennis courts, an indoor swimming pool, and a track.

Disabled Students: 90% of the campus is accessible. Wheelchair ramps, elevators, special parking, specially equipped rest rooms, lowered drinking fountains, and lowered telephones are available.

Services: Counseling and information services are available, as is tutoring in most subjects. There is remedial math, reading, and writing.

Campus Safety and Security: Measures include 24-hour foot and vehicle patrol, informal discussions, pamphlets/posters/films, and emergency telephones. There are lighted pathways/sidewalks.

Programs of Study: WSSU confers B.A., B.S., B.S.App.Sci., B.S.Med.Tech., B.S.N., and B.S.P.T. degrees. Master's degrees are also awarded. Bachelor's degrees are awarded in BIOLOGICAL SCIENCE (biology/biological science), BUSINESS (accounting, business administration and management, management information systems, and sports management), COMMUNICATIONS AND THE ARTS (art, communications, English, music business management, and Spanish), COMPUTER AND PHYSICAL SCIENCE (chemistry, computer science, and mathematics), EDUCATION (elementary, music, physical, and special), HEALTH PROFESSIONS (medical technology, nursing, physical therapy, and recreation therapy), SOCIAL SCIENCE (economics, history, political science/government, psychology, public administration, and sociology). Phys ed, computer science, and math are the strongest academically. Nursing, business administration, and education are the largest.

Required: Students must complete a minimum of 121 semester hours, with 40 of these hours in upper-level courses, and must maintain an overall minimum GPA of 2.0. All students must also complete the general education core requirement, which includes courses in English composition, social sciences, math and natural sciences, humanities, and phys ed or military science.

Special: Opportunities are provided for cooperative programs, internships, work-study programs, a B.A.-B.S. degree, a general studies degree, and credit for military experience. The nursing division offers flexible scheduling for employed RNs. There is a freshman honors program.

Faculty/Classroom: 44% of faculty are male; 56%, female. All teach undergraduates. The average class size in an introductory lecture is 60; in a laboratory, 25; and in a regular course, 43.

Admissions: 77% of the 2003-2004 applicants were accepted.

Requirements: The SAT I or ACT is required, with a minimum composite score of 700 on the SAT I recommended. Graduation from an accredited secondary school is required; a GED will be accepted. Applicants should submit an academic record including 4 credits in English, 3 each in math and science, 2 in a foreign language, and 1 each in U.S. history, social studies, and phys ed and health. A GPA of 2.0 is required. AP and CLEP credits are accepted. Important factors in the admissions decision are advanced placement or honor courses, leadership record, and recommendations by school officials.

Procedure: Freshmen are admitted to all sessions. Entrance exams should be taken in the summer or early fall of the senior year in high school. There are early admissions and deferred admissions plans. Application deadlines are open. The fall 2003 application fee was $30. Notification is sent on a rolling basis. Applications are accepted on-line through the university's web site.

Transfer: 335 transfer students enrolled in 2002-2003. Transfer applicants must submit official transcripts from all colleges previously attended, showing no grade lower than C. No more than 64 semester hours (96 quarter hours) will be accepted for transfer. Those applicants transferring fewer than 29 credits will be admitted as freshmen and must meet all freshman admission requirements. 30 of 121 credits required for the bachelor's degree must be completed at WSSU.

Visiting: There are regularly scheduled orientations for prospective students, including summer and fall orientation. There are guides for informal visits and visitors may sit in on classes. To schedule a visit, contact Gilbert Wright in the Admissions Office at wrightg@wssu.edu.

Financial Aid: In 2003-2004, 81% of all full-time freshmen and 80% of continuing full-time students received some form of financial aid. 63% of full-time freshmen and 86% of continuing full-time students received need-based aid. Need-based scholarships or need-based grants averaged $2381; need-based self-help aid (loans and jobs) averaged $1260; non-need-based athletic scholarships averaged $3562; and other non-need-based awards and non-need-based scholarships averaged $2125. The average financial indebtedness of the 2003 graduate was $10,600. WSSU is a member of CSS. The CSS Profile or FFS and the college's own financial statement are required. The deadline for filing freshman financial aid applications for fall entry is April 1.

International Students: They must score 540 on the written TOEFL.

Computers: The academic computer center maintains a DEC VAX 11/750 with 20 terminals and 2 on-line printers. All students may access the system. There are no time limits. The $20 fee is included in tuition.

Graduates: From July 1, 2002 to June 30, 2003, 496 bachelor's degrees were awarded. The most popular majors were nursing (24%), business administration (17%), and psychology (6%). In an average class, 20% graduate in 4 years or less, 38% graduate in 5 years or less, and 80% graduate in 6 years or less.

Admissions Contact: Daniel Lovette, Vice Chancellor of Enrollment Management. A video is available. E-mail: lovetted@wssu.edu Web: www.wssu.edu

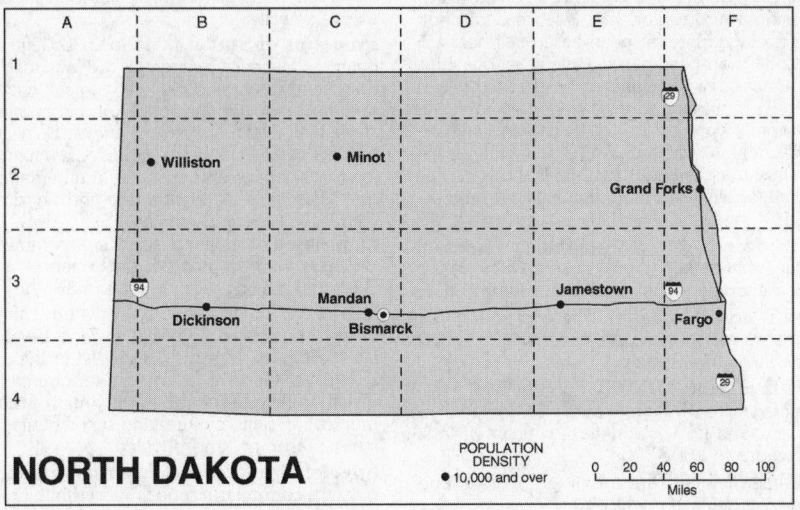

NORTH DAKOTA

POPULATION DENSITY
● 10,000 and over

0 20 40 60 80 100
Miles

DICKINSON STATE UNIVERSITY
B-3
Dickinson, ND 58601-4896
(701) 483-2175
(800) 279-4295; Fax: (701) 483-2409

Full-time: 782 men, 934 women	**Faculty:** 79; IIB, --$
Part-time: 270 men, 465 women	**Ph.D.s:** 55%
Graduate: none	**Student/Faculty:** 20 to 1
Year: semesters, summer session	**Tuition:** $3138 ($7405)
Application Deadline: August 15	**Room & Board:** $3200
Freshman Class: n/av	
SAT I Verbal/Math: 460/490	**ACT:** 22 **NONCOMPETITIVE**

Dickinson State University is a public, regional institution offering undergraduate programs in teacher education, the liberal arts, business, health sciences, agriculture, and computer science. There is opportunity for preprofessional study and vocational training in selected areas. There are 2 undergraduate schools. In addition to regional accreditation, DSU has baccalaureate program accreditation with NCATE and NLN. The library contains 91,870 volumes, 8941 microform items, and 5493 audio/video tapes/CDs, and subscribes to 1748 periodicals. Computerized library services include the card catalog, interlibrary loans, and database searching. Special learning facilities include a learning resource center and art gallery. The 100-acre campus is in a rural area 100 miles west of Bismarck. Including any residence halls, there are 15 buildings.

Student Life: 70% of undergraduates are from North Dakota. Students are from 36 states, 28 foreign countries, and Canada. 95% are from public schools. 76% are white. 50% are Catholic; 50% Protestant. The average age of freshmen is 19; all undergraduates, 22. 2% do not continue beyond their first year; 28% remain to graduate.

Housing: 478 students can be accommodated in college housing, which includes single-sex and coed dorms and married-student housing. In addition, there are honors houses. On-campus housing is guaranteed for the freshman year only and is available on a first-come, first-served basis. 70% of students commute. Alcohol is not permitted. All students may keep cars.

Activities: There are no fraternities or sororities. There are 38 groups on campus, including art, band, cheerleading, choir, chorale, chorus, computers, dance, drama, drill team, ethnic, forensics, honors, international, jazz band, literary magazine, marching band, musical theater, newspaper, pep band, political, professional, religious, social, student government, and yearbook. Popular campus events include Winter, Spring, and Back to School Weeks, and Family Weekend.

Sports: There are 9 intercollegiate sports for men and 8 for women, and 5 intramural sports for men and 3 for women. Facilities include a gym, an outdoor stadium, an indoor/outdoor rodeo arena, and an indoor track.

Disabled Students: 90% of the campus is accessible. Wheelchair ramps, elevators, special parking, specially equipped rest rooms, special class scheduling, lowered drinking fountains, and lowered telephones are available.

Services: Counseling and information services are available, as is tutoring in every subject. There is a reader service for the blind and remedial math, reading, and writing.

Campus Safety and Security: Measures include pamphlets/posters/films, lighted pathways/sidewalks, and 10-hour-a-day security.

Programs of Study: DSU confers B.A., B.S., B.A.S.T., B.S.E., B.S.N., and B.U.S. degrees. Associate degrees are also awarded. Bachelor's degrees are awarded in AGRICULTURE (agricultural business management), BIOLOGICAL SCIENCE (biology/biological science), BUSINESS (accounting, business administration and management, and personnel management), COMMUNICATIONS AND THE ARTS (communications, English, fine arts, journalism, music, Spanish, and speech/debate/rhetoric), COMPUTER AND PHYSICAL SCIENCE (chemistry, computer programming, computer science, earth science, and mathematics), EDUCATION (art, business, early childhood, elementary, middle school, music, science, and secondary), HEALTH PROFESSIONS (nursing), SOCIAL SCIENCE (geography, history, political science/government, social work, and sociology). Elementary education, math, and business are the strongest academically. Education, business, and nursing are the largest.

Required: To graduate, students must complete 128 semester hours, 36 in the major, with a minimum GPA of 2.0. General education requirements include 10 hours in scientific inquiry, including 9 hours each in expressions of human civilizations, understanding human civilization, and communication, 2 hours in phys ed, and 1 computer science course.

Special: DSU offers a co-op program in social work with the University of North Dakota and in agriculture with North Dakota State University. An additional co-op program exists with Bismarck State College and Williston State College. Cross-registration is available within the North Dakota University System. Internships in business and social work, credit for life experience, and pass/fail options are available. Student-designed majors are possible through the Bachelor of University Studies program. There are 5 national honor societies, including Phi Beta Kappa, and a freshman honors program.

Faculty/Classroom: 70% of faculty are male; 30%, female. All teach undergraduates and 5% do research. The average class size in an introductory lecture is 40; in a laboratory, 25; and in a regular course, 20.

Admissions: The SAT I scores for the 2003-2004 freshman class were: Verbal--48% below 500, 45% between 500 and 599, and 6% between 600 and 700; Math--51% below 500, 39% between 500 and 599, and 9% between 600 and 700. The ACT scores were 51% below 21, 25% between 21 and 23, 15% between 24 and 26, 3% between 27 and 28, and 3% above 28. 17% of the current freshmen were in the top fifth of their class; 42% were in the top two fifths.

Requirements: The SAT I or ACT is required; the ACT is preferred. Graduation from an accredited secondary school is recommended. The GED is accepted. Students must have 20 academic credits. An essay is not required. AP and CLEP credits are accepted.

Procedure: Freshmen are admitted to all sessions. Entrance exams should be taken in the spring before fall entrance. Applications should be filed by August 15 for fall entry, January 1 for spring entry, and May 15 for summer entry, along with a $35 fee. The college accepts all applicants. Notification is sent on a rolling basis. Applications are accepted on-line.

Transfer: 299 transfer students enrolled in 2002-2003. Transfer students must have a minimum GPA of 2.0. The ACT is preferred, but applicants may submit the SAT I scores. 32 of 128 credits required for the bachelor's degree must be completed at DSU.

Visiting: There are regularly scheduled orientations for prospective students, consisting of two 2-day orientations and two 1-day sessions in July and August. There are guides for informal visits and visitors may sit in on classes and stay overnight. To schedule a visit, contact the Office of Admissions and Academic Records at *dsu.hawks@dsu.nodak.edu*.

Financial Aid: In 2003-2004, 79% of all full-time students received some form of financial aid. 79% of all full-time students received need-based aid. The average freshman award was $4400. Need-based scholarships or need-based grants averaged $1095; need-based self-help aid (loans and jobs) averaged $2584; non-need-based athletic scholarships averaged $957; and other non-need-based awards and non-need-based scholarships averaged $604. 56% of undergraduates work part time. Average annual earnings from campus work were $1101. The average financial indebtedness of the 2003 graduate was $16,708. The FAFSA is required. The priority date for freshman financial aid applications for fall entry is March 15. The deadline for filing freshman financial aid applications for fall entry is open.

International Students: There are 10 international students enrolled. The school actively recruits these students. They must score 525 on the written TOEFL or 195 on the electronic version and also take the ACT.

Computers: The mainframe is an IBM AS/400. There are 125 PCs available in May Hall and in the residence halls. All students may access the system. There are no time limits and no fees.

Graduates: From July 1, 2002 to June 30, 2003, 265 bachelor's degrees were awarded. In an average class, 8% graduate in 4 years or less, 19% graduate in 5 years or less, and 25% graduate in 6 years or less. 55 companies recruited on campus in 2002-2003.

Admissions Contact: Marshall Melbye, Director of Admissions and Academic Records. E-mail: *dsu.hawk@dsu.nodak.edu*
Web: *www.dickinsonstate.com*

JAMESTOWN COLLEGE
Jamestown, ND 58405   E-3

(701) 252-3467, ext. 2548
(800) 336-2554; Fax: (701) 253-4318

Full-time: 492 men, 595 women	**Faculty:** 56; IIB, --$
Part-time: 24 men, 41 women	**Ph.D.s:** 40%
Graduate: none	**Student/Faculty:** 19 to 1
Year: semesters, summer session	**Tuition:** $8750
Application Deadline: open	**Room & Board:** $3850
Freshman Class: 781 applied, 762 accepted, 261 enrolled	
ACT: 22	**NONCOMPETITIVE**

Jamestown College, founded in 1883, is a private, nonprofit institution affiliated with the Presbyterian Church (U.S.A.). Its emphases are on the liberal arts, business, arts, health science, music, religious studies, and teacher preparation. In addition to regional accreditation, Jamestown College has baccalaureate program accreditation with NLN and IACBE. The library contains 123,750 volumes, 7115 microform items, and 5355 audio/video tapes/CDs, and subscribes to 448 periodicals. Computerized library services include the card catalog, interlibrary loans, database searching, and Internet access. Special learning facilities include a learning resource center and art gallery. The 107-acre campus is in a small town 100 miles west of Fargo, 350 miles west of Minneapolis. Including any residence halls, there are 20 buildings.

Student Life: 57% of undergraduates are from North Dakota. Students are from 30 states, 16 foreign countries, and Canada. 91% are white. 43% are Protestant; 26% claim no religious affiliation; 21% Catholic. The average age of freshmen is 18; all undergraduates, 21. 32% do not continue beyond their first year; 59% remain to graduate.

Housing: 714 students can be accommodated in college housing, which includes coed dorms and on-campus apartments. On-campus housing is guaranteed for the freshman year only, is available on a first-come, first-served basis, and is available on a lottery system for upperclassmen. 61% of students live on campus; of those, 65% remain on campus on weekends. Alcohol is not permitted. All students may keep cars.

Activities: There are no fraternities or sororities. There are 34 groups on campus, including art, band, cheerleading, choir, chorale, chorus, computers, dance, drama, drill team, honors, international, jazz band, literary magazine, musical theater, newspaper, pep band, political, professional, religious, social, social service, student government, and yearbook. Popular campus events include Family Weekend and Jimmie Jive Week.

Sports: There are 8 intercollegiate sports for men and 8 for women, and 6 intramural sports for men and 6 for women. Facilities include an athletics center with a basketball court and wrestling and volleyball practice and composition area; a football stadium with an all-weather track; a soccer field; and a sports center with a swimming pool, weight room, running track, YMCA, and basketball, handball, and racquetball courts. Nearby facilities include a civic arena, softball field, baseball stadium, swimming pool, tennis courts, municipal golf course, and winter sports complex.

Disabled Students: 38% of the campus is accessible. Wheelchair ramps, elevators, special parking, specially equipped rest rooms, special class scheduling, lowered drinking fountains, lowered telephones, and special housing are available.

Services: Counseling and information services are available, as is tutoring in most subjects. There is remedial math, reading, and writing.

Campus Safety and Security: Measures include security escort services, informal discussions, pamphlets/posters/films, and lighted pathways/sidewalks.

Programs of Study: Jamestown College confers B.A., B.S., and B.S.N. degrees. Bachelor's degrees are awarded in BIOLOGICAL SCIENCE (biochemistry and biology/biological science), BUSINESS (accounting and business administration and management), COMMUNICATIONS AND THE ARTS (communications, English, fine arts, and music), COMPUTER AND PHYSICAL SCIENCE (chemistry, computer science, information sciences and systems, mathematics, and radiological technology), EDUCATION (elementary and physical), HEALTH PROFESSIONS (clinical science and nursing), SOCIAL SCIENCE (criminal justice, history, philosophy, political science/government, psychology, and religion). Business, nursing, and physical sciences are the strongest academically. Business, nursing, and education are the largest.

Required: To graduate, students must have a minimum of 128 semester credits, at least 48 of which must be at the upper-division level, with an average of 48 semester credits in the major, and maintain at least a 2.0 GPA. General education requirements include 47 to 56 credits, based on degree sought, in the areas of moral and civic education, communication skills, cultural and social heritage, natural science and quantitative reasoning, and phys ed.

Special: Special academic options include co-op programs in business, nursing, computer science, and criminal justice, on-campus work-study, internships, study abroad, dual majors within any of the concentrations, student-designed majors, nondegree study, pass/fail options, and credit for life, military, and work experience. Directed study is also possible. There are preprofessional programs in law, health-related fields, and engineering, including a 3-2 engineering program with North Dakota State University and the University of North Dakota. Teacher certification may be earned in secondary education. There are 5 national honor societies and 10 departmental honors programs.

Faculty/Classroom: 54% of faculty are male; 46%, female. All teach undergraduates. The average class size in an introductory lecture is 35; in a laboratory, 20; and in a regular course, 24.

Admissions: 98% of the 2003-2004 applicants were accepted. The ACT scores for the 2003-2004 freshman class were: 34% below 21, 35% between 21 and 23, 19% between 24 and 26, 7% between 27 and 28, and 5% above 28. 33% of the current freshmen were in the top fifth of their class; 62% were in the top two fifths.

Requirements: The ACT is recommended. In addition, other admissions requirements include graduation from an accredited secondary school; the GED is also accepted. An interview is highly recommended. Jamestown College requires applicants to be in the upper 50% of their class. A GPA of 2.5 is required. AP and CLEP credits are accepted. Important factors in the admissions decision are evidence of special talent, extracurricular activities record, and leadership record.

Procedure: Freshmen are admitted to all sessions. Entrance exams should be taken before or during the fall of the senior year. There is a deferred admissions plan. Application deadlines are open. Application fee is $20. Notification is on a rolling basis. Applications are accepted on computer disk and on-line through the school's web site or through most on-line application services.

Transfer: 51 transfer students enrolled in a recent year. Applicants must have at least a 2.5 GPA and be in good standing with their previous college; if suspended, the student must allow 1 semester to elapse before applying for probationary admission. 35 of 128 credits required for the bachelor's degree must be completed at Jamestown College.

Visiting: There are regularly scheduled orientations for prospective students, including a campus tour and faculty visits. There are guides for informal visits and visitors may sit in on classes and stay overnight. To schedule a visit, contact the Admissions Office at *admissions@jc.edu*.

Financial Aid: In 2003-2004, all full-time freshmen and 98% of continuing full-time students received some form of financial aid. 82% of full-time freshmen and 89% of continuing full-time students received need-based aid. The average freshman award was $7742. Need-based scholarships or need-based grants averaged $4757 ($12,600 maximum); need-based self-help aid (loans and jobs) averaged $3812 ($10,500 maximum); non-need-based athletic scholarships averaged $1544 ($9360 maximum); and other non-need-based awards and non-need-based scholarships averaged $7119 ($9859 maximum). 36% of undergraduates work part time. Average annual earnings from campus work are $807. The average financial indebtedness of the 2003 graduate was $16,427. Jamestown College is a member of CSS. The FAFSA is required.

International Students: There are 43 international students enrolled. The school actively recruits these students. They must score 525 on the written TOEFL or 197 on the electronic version.

Computers: The mainframes are 7 Compaq Proliant 1600s and 1 Compaq Proliant 6000. There are PCs available in the computer center, labs, college library, faculty offices, and residence halls. All 575 computers are networked and have Internet access. Every residence hall room has a PC. All students may access the system 24 hours a day. There are no time limits and no fees.

Graduates: From July 1, 2002 to June 30, 2003, 163 bachelor's degrees were awarded. The most popular majors were business (23%), nursing (13%), and elementry education (9%). In an average class, 31% graduate in 4 years or less, 43% graduate in 5 years or less, and 49% graduate in 6 years or less. 28 companies recruited on campus in 2002-2003. Of the 2002 graduating class, 11% were enrolled in graduate school within 6 months of graduation and 83% were employed.

Admissions Contact: Judy Erickson, Director of Admissions. E-mail: *admissions@jc.edu* Web: *www.jc.edu*

MAYVILLE STATE UNIVERSITY E-3
Mayville, ND 58257-1299 **(701) 786-4768**
(800) 437-4104; Fax: (701) 786-4748

Full-time: 289 men, 324 women	**Faculty:** 35; IIB, --$
Part-time: 65 men, 139 women	**Ph.Ds:** 48%
Graduate: none	**Student/Faculty:** 18 to 1
Year: semesters, summer session	**Tuition:** $3981 ($8283)
Application Deadline: open	**Room & Board:** $3344
Freshman Class: 263 applied, 254 accepted, 219 enrolled	
ACT: 19	**NONCOMPETITIVE**

Mayville State University, founded in 1889, is a public institution that emphasizes teacher education, business, and information technology. There are 5 undergraduate schools. In addition to regional accreditation, Mayville State has baccalaureate program accreditation with NCATE. The library contains 92,217 volumes, 13,313 microform items, and 1836 audio/video tapes/CDs, and subscribes to 512 periodicals. Computerized library services include the card catalog, interlibrary loans, database searching, and Internet access. Special learning facilities include a learning resource center, art gallery, and a learning services center. The 55-acre campus is in a rural area 58 miles north of Fargo and 42 miles south of Grand Forks. Including any residence halls, there are 19 buildings.

Student Life: 72% of undergraduates are from North Dakota. Students are from 17 states, 6 foreign countries, and Canada. 95% are from public schools. 90% are white. 70% are Protestant; 29% Catholic. The average age of freshmen is 18. 43% do not continue beyond their first year; 38% remain to graduate.

Housing: 410 students can be accommodated in college housing, which includes single-sex and coed dorms, on-campus apartments, and married-student housing. On-campus housing is guaranteed for the freshman year only and is available on a first-come, first-served basis. 69% of students commute. Alcohol is not permitted. All students may keep cars.

Activities: There are no fraternities or sororities. There are 17 groups on campus, including cheerleading, choir, chorus, computers, debate, drama, ethnic, forensics, musical theater, political, professional, religious, student government, and yearbook. Popular campus events include Spring Fling.

Sports: There are 3 intercollegiate sports for men and 3 for women, and 10 intramural sports for men and 9 for women. Facilities include a 4500-seat football stadium, a track and practice field, a baseball diamond, tennis courts, a swimming pool, and handball and racquetball courts.

Disabled Students: 75% of the campus is accessible. Elevators, special parking, special class scheduling, lowered drinking fountains, and lowered telephones are available.

Services: Counseling and information services are available, as is tutoring in some subjects, including writing, math, reading, and study skills. There is remedial math and writing.

Campus Safety and Security: Measures include informal discussions, pamphlets/posters/films, lighted pathways/sidewalks, and a nighttime foot patrol.

Programs of Study: Mayville State confers B.A., B.S., B.A.S., B.G.S., and B.S.Ed. degrees. Associate degrees are also awarded. Bachelor's degrees are awarded in BIOLOGICAL SCIENCE (biology/biological science), BUSINESS (business administration and management and office supervision and management), COMMUNICATIONS AND THE ARTS (English), COMPUTER AND PHYSICAL SCIENCE (chemistry, computer programming, mathematics, physical sciences, and science), EDUCATION (business, elementary, health, physical, science, and secondary), SOCIAL SCIENCE (liberal arts/general studies and social science). Business administration, computer information science, and elementary education are the strongest academically. Business administration and elementary education are the largest.

Required: To graduate, students must complete 128 semester hours with a minimum overall GPA of 2.0 in most programs and 2.5 in education. General requirements include 8 to 10 quarter hours of science, 9 each of humanities and social science, 6 of English, up to 3 of math, and 3 each of computer information systems, psychology, speech, and phys ed.

Special: Through a reciprocity program, residents of all contiguous states and Canadian provinces pay a considerably reduced out-of-state fee. Mayville State also offers preprofessional programs, internships, work-study programs, B.A.-B.S. degrees, dual majors, a general studies degree, credit for life experience, nondegree study, and pass/fail options. Co-op programs are available, including a certified education program for all subject areas. There is also a K-8 math specialist program. There is 1 national honor society.

Faculty/Classroom: 64% of faculty are male; 36%, female. All teach undergraduates. The average class size in an introductory lecture is 20; in a laboratory, 20; and in a regular course, 20.

Admissions: 97% of the 2003-2004 applicants were accepted. The ACT scores for the 2003-2004 freshman class were: 63% below 21, 26% between 21 and 23, 7% between 24 and 26, 1% between 27 and 28, and 2% above 28. 30% of the current freshmen were in the top fifth of their class; 70% were in the top two fifths.

Requirements: The ACT is required. In addition, applicants must be graduates of an accredited secondary school or have a GED certificate. Required core courses include 4 in English, and 3 each in math (algebra I or higher), sciences, and social sciences. A GPA of 2.0 is required. AP and CLEP credits are accepted.

Procedure: Freshmen are admitted to all sessions. Entrance exams should be taken during the senior year. There are early decision and early admissions plans. Application deadlines are open. Application fee is $35. Notification is on a rolling basis. Applications are accepted on-line through the school's web site.

Transfer: 116 transfer students enrolled in 2002-2003. Applicants must submit official transcripts from all colleges attended and should have a minimum GPA of 2.0, with scores on the SAT I or ACT also recommended. 30 of 128 credits required for the bachelor's degree must be completed at Mayville State.

Visiting: There are regularly scheduled orientations for prospective students, including a campus tour, meetings with faculty in fields of interest, and meetings with the financial aid director if needed. There are guides for informal visits and visitors may sit in on classes and stay overnight. To schedule a visit, contact the Office of Enrollment Services at (701) 786-4842.

Financial Aid: In 2002-2003, 60% of all full-time freshmen and 70% of continuing full-time students received some form of financial aid. 56% of full-time freshmen and 65% of continuing full-time students received need-based aid. The average freshman award was $5438. Need-based scholarships or need-based grants averaged $3014; need-based self-help aid (loans and jobs) averaged $2768; non-need-based athletic scholarships averaged $1030; and other non-need-based awards and non-need-based scholarships averaged $722. 30% of undergraduates work part time. The average financial indebtedness of the 2002 graduate was $15,074. Mayville State is a member of CSS. The FAFSA is required. The deadline for filing freshman financial aid applications for fall entry is March 15.

International Students: There are 7 international students enrolled. The school actively recruits these students. They must score 525 on the written TOEFL or 197 on the electronic version.

Computers: All students have laptop computers with access to the LAN and Internet in classrooms, residence halls, and labs. All students may access the system. There are no time limits and no fees.

Graduates: From July 1, 2002 to June 30, 2003, 105 bachelor's degrees were awarded. The most popular majors were elementary education (34%), business administration (30%), and computer information systems (13%). In an average class, 18% graduate in 4 years or less, 37% graduate in 5 years or less, and 42% graduate in 6 years or less. 3 companies recruited on campus in 2002-2003. Of the 2001 graduating class, 8% were enrolled in graduate school within 6 months of graduation and 100% were employed.

Admissions Contact: Brian Larson, Director of Enrollment Services. A video is available. E-mail: *admit@mail.masu.nodak.edu* Web: *www.mayvillestate.edu*

MINOT STATE UNIVERSITY C-2
Minot, ND 58707 **(701) 858-4347**
(800) 777-0750; Fax: (701) 839-6933

Full-time: 944 men, 1569 women	**Faculty:** 159; IIA, --$
Part-time: 427 men, 654 women	**Ph.Ds:** 60%
Graduate: 54 men, 177 women	**Student/Faculty:** 16 to 1
Year: semesters, summer session	**Tuition:** $3228 ($7787)
Application Deadline: open	**Room & Board:** $3374
Freshman Class: 713 applied, 668 accepted, 543 enrolled	
ACT: 22	**LESS COMPETITIVE**

Minot State University, founded in 1913, is a public institution offering undergraduate and graduate programs in arts and sciences, education, business, nursing, and human services. There are 3 undergraduate schools and 1 graduate school. In addition to regional accreditation, MSU has baccalaureate program accreditation with CSWE, NASM, NCATE, and NLN. The library contains 411,678 volumes, 687,708 microform items, and 12,722 audio/video tapes/CDs, and subscribes to 802 periodicals. Computerized library services include the card catalog, interlibrary loans, and database searching. Special learning facilities include a learning resource center, art gallery, natural history museum, radio station, and TV station. The 103-acre campus is in a small town. Including any residence halls, there are 21 buildings.

Student Life: 83% of undergraduates are from North Dakota. Students are from 44 states, 18 foreign countries, and Canada. 95% are from public schools. 84% are white. The average age of freshmen is 19; all undergraduates, 21. 36% do not continue beyond their first year; 32% remain to graduate.

Housing: 643 students can be accommodated in college housing, which includes single-sex and coed dorms, on-campus apartments, and married-student housing. In addition, there are special-interest houses. On-campus housing is guaranteed for the freshman year only, is available on a first-come, first-served basis, and is available on a lottery system for upperclassmen. 88% of students commute. Alcohol is not permitted. All students may keep cars.

Activities: There are no fraternities or sororities. There are 60 groups on campus, including art, band, cheerleading, choir, chorale, chorus, drama, ethnic, honors, international, jazz band, literary magazine, musical theater, newspaper, orchestra, pep band, political, professional, radio and TV, religious, social service, student government, symphony, and yearbook. Popular campus events include Welcome Week, Final Frenzy, and Native American Awareness Week.

Sports: There are 6 intercollegiate sports for men and 6 for women, and 4 intramural sports for men and 4 for women. Facilities include a 10,000-seat field house, a 2800-seat football stadium, and a 3000-seat gym.

Disabled Students: 99% of the campus is accessible. Wheelchair ramps, elevators, special parking, specially equipped rest rooms, special class scheduling, lowered drinking fountains, lowered telephones, and special housing are available.

Services: Counseling and information services are available, as is tutoring in most subjects. Special services are offered for disabled students on request.

Campus Safety and Security: Measures include self-defense education, informal discussions, pamphlets/posters/films, and emergency telephones. There are lighted pathways/sidewalks.

Programs of Study: MSU confers B.A., B.S., B.A.S., B.G.S., B.S. Ed., B.S.N., and B.S.W. degrees. Associate and master's degrees are also awarded. Bachelor's degrees are awarded in BIOLOGICAL SCIENCE (biology/biological science), BUSINESS (accounting, banking and finance, international business management, management information systems, management science, and marketing/retailing/merchandising), COMMUNICATIONS AND THE ARTS (art, broadcasting, communications, English, French, German, multimedia, music, and Spanish), COMPUTER AND PHYSICAL SCIENCE (chemistry, computer science, earth science, geology, mathematics, physical sciences, physics, and radiological technology), EDUCATION (business, drama, education of the deaf and hearing impaired, education of the exceptional child, education of the mentally handicapped, elementary, English, foreign languages, mathematics, music, physical, and science), HEALTH PROFESSIONS (dental laboratory technology, nursing, and speech pathology/audiology), SOCIAL SCIENCE (addiction studies, criminal justice, economics, history, liberal arts/general studies, physical fitness/movement, psychology, social science, social work, and sociology). Communication disorders, special education, and elementary education are the strongest academically. Business, criminal justice, and education are the largest.

Required: Students must take a number of general education courses in humanities, history, communication, math, natural sciences, social and behavorial sciences, and leisure-time education. They must complete at least 128 semester hours, with 30 to 37 in the major and a minimum GPA of 2.0.

Special: A general studies degree, independent research, internships, work-study, and unique programs of study, including student-designed majors, are available. Cross-registration through the North Dakota University System, co-op programs in all majors, and study abroad in 3 countries also are offered. Preliminary programs are available in dental hygiene, dentistry, engineering, law, medicine, and many other areas. There is a freshman honors program.

Faculty/Classroom: 49% of faculty are male; 51%, female. All teach undergraduates and 20% do research. No introductory courses are taught by graduate students. The average class size in an introductory lecture is 60; in a laboratory, 20; and in a regular course, 16.

Admissions: 94% of the 2003-2004 applicants were accepted. The ACT scores for the 2003-2004 freshman class were: 40% below 21, 29% between 21 and 23, 21% between 24 and 26, 6% between 27 and 28, and 4% above 28. 42% of the current freshmen were in the top fifth of their class.

Requirements: The SAT I or ACT is required. In addition, applicants must submit a high school diploma or GED certificate. Core course requirements include 4 years of English and 3 each of math, social studies, and science. AP and CLEP credits are accepted.

Procedure: Freshmen are admitted to all sessions. Entrance exams may be taken any time. There is a deferred admissions plan. Application deadlines are open. Application fee is $35. There is a rolling admissions plan. Applications are accepted on-line, but a print copy must also be submitted.

Transfer: 449 transfer students enrolled in 2002-2003. Transfers must submit transcripts from each college attended. 30 of 128 credits required for the bachelor's degree must be completed at MSU.

Visiting: There are regularly scheduled orientations for prospective students, prior to the beginning of the fall term. There are guides for informal visits and visitors may sit in on classes. To schedule a visit, contact Enrollment Services at (701) 858-3350 or *askmsu@minotstateu.edu*.

Financial Aid: In 2003-2004, 67% of all full-time students received some form of financial aid. 64% of full-time freshmen and 67% of continuing full-time students received need-based aid. The average freshman award was $5802. 1% of undergraduates work part time. Average annual earnings from campus work are $1260. The average financial indebtedness of the 2003 graduate was $12,900. The FAFSA is required. The priority date for freshman financial aid applications for fall entry is March 15. The deadline for filing freshman financial aid applications for fall entry is October 15.

International Students: There are 41 international students enrolled. The school actively recruits these students. They must score 525 on the written TOEFL or 193 on the electronic version.

Computers: The mainframe is 2 Intranet/Novell servers. PCs and Macs are available throughout the campus. Network access to BINET, NWN-WT, and the Internet is available through a campus Ethernet backbone. All students may access the system 24 hours daily. There are no time limits and no fees.

Graduates: From July 1, 2002 to June 30, 2003, 488 bachelor's degrees were awarded. The most popular majors were elementary education (15%), nursing (10%), and criminal justice (9%). In an average class, 37% graduate in 6 years or less. 105 companies recruited on campus in 2002-2003. Of the 2002 graduating class, 11% were enrolled in graduate school within 6 months of graduation and 89% were employed.

Admissions Contact: Alexis Hendricks, Enrollment Services Representative. E-mail: *alexis@minotstateu.edu* Web: *www.minotstateu.edu*

NORTH DAKOTA STATE UNIVERSITY   F-3
Fargo, ND 58105-5454   (701) 231-8643
(800) 488-NDSU; Fax: (701) 231-8802

Full-time: 5140 men, 3841 women	**Faculty:** 468; I, --$
Part-time: 523 men, 644 women	**Ph.D.s:** 91%
Graduate: 816 men, 659 women	**Student/Faculty:** 19 to 1
Year: semesters, summer session	**Tuition:** $3964 ($9599)
Application Deadline: August 15	**Room & Board:** $4471
Freshman Class: 3245 applied, 3153 accepted, 1986 enrolled	
SAT I or ACT: required	**COMPETITIVE**

North Dakota State University, founded in 1890, is a comprehensive, public, land-grant institution. Its undergraduate and graduate programs emphasize the liberal arts and sciences, agricultural and technical studies, architecture, business, engineering, teacher preparation, and pharmaceutical studies. There are 8 undergraduate schools and 1 graduate school. In addition to regional accreditation, NDSU has baccalaureate program accreditation with ABET, ACCE, ACPE, ADA, AHEA, CSAB, FIDER, NAAB, NASM, NCATE, NLN, and ACS. The 4 libraries contain 784,978 volumes, 444,951 microform items, and 2873 audio/video tapes/CDs, and subscribe to 5090 periodicals. Computerized library services include the card catalog, interlibrary loans, database searching, and Internet access. Special learning facilities include a learning resource center, art gallery, and radio station. The 258-acre campus is in an urban area 229 miles northwest of Minneapolis-St. Paul. Including any residence halls, there are 97 buildings.

Student Life: 60% of undergraduates are from North Dakota. Others are from 36 states, 62 foreign countries, and Canada. 95% are white. The average age of freshmen is 18; all undergraduates, 27. 28% do not continue beyond their first year; 41% remain to graduate.

Housing: 3550 students can be accommodated in college housing, which includes single-sex and coed dorms, on-campus apartments, married-student housing, learning communities, an engineering/architecture floor, and first-year student halls. On-campus housing is guaranteed for all 4 years. 72% of students commute. Alcohol is not permitted. All students may keep cars.

Activities: 10% of men belong to 10 national fraternities; 5% of women belong to 5 national sororities. There are 200 groups on campus, including academics, art, band, cheerleading, choir, chorus, computers, dance, debate, drama, drill team, ethnic, forensics, gay, honors, international, jazz band, leisure learning opportunities, marching band, musical theater, newspaper, pep band, political, professional, radio and TV, recreational, religious, social, social service, and student government. Popular campus events include International Students' Week, Spring Blast, and multicultural activities.

Sports: There are 8 intercollegiate sports for men and 8 for women, and 5 intramural sports for men and 6 for women. Facilities include a sports arena, indoor and outdoor tracks, baseball and softball fields, a pool, wrestling and weight rooms, a multipurpose fitness room, and volleyball, tennis, basketball, and racquetball courts, and a wellness center.

Disabled Students: 50% of the campus is accessible. Wheelchair ramps, elevators, special parking, specially equipped rest rooms, special class scheduling, lowered drinking fountains, lowered telephones, and special transportation are available.

Services: Counseling and information services are available, as is tutoring in most subjects. There is a reader service for the blind, remedial math, reading, and writing, and note takers.

Campus Safety and Security: Measures include 24-hour foot and vehicle patrol, self-defense education, security escort services, and shuttle buses. There are informal discussions, pamphlets/posters/films, emergency telephones, and lighted pathways/sidewalks.

Programs of Study: NDSU confers B.A., B.S., B.Arch., B.F.A. in Theater Arts, B.L.A., B.Mus., and B.Univ.Studies degrees. Master's and doctoral degrees are also awarded. Bachelor's degrees are awarded in AGRICULTURE (agricultural business management, agricultural economics, agricultural mechanics, agriculture, animal science, equine science, horticulture, natural resource management, plant protection (pest management), plant science, range/farm management, and soil science), BIOLOGICAL SCIENCE (biology/biological science, biotechnology, botany, microbiology, nutrition, and zoology), BUSINESS (accounting, business administration and management, hotel/motel and restaurant management, institutional management, management information systems, recreation and leisure services, and sports management), COMMUNICATIONS AND THE ARTS (art, communications, dramatic arts, English, French, music, performing arts, and Spanish), COMPUTER AND PHYSICAL SCIENCE (actuarial science, chemistry, computer science, earth science, geology, mathematics, physics, radiological technology, and statistics), EDUCATION (agricultural, athletic training, elementary, health, home economics, music, physical, and secondary), ENGINEERING AND ENVIRONMENTAL DESIGN (agricultural engineering, architecture, civil engineering, computer engineering, construction engineering, construction management, electrical/electronics engineering, engineering management, environmental design, industrial engineering, interior design, landscape architecture/design, manufacturing engineering, and mechanical engineering), HEALTH PROFESSIONS (clinical science, nursing, pharmacy, preveterinary science, respiratory therapy, and veterinary science), SOCIAL SCIENCE (anthropology, child care/child and family studies, criminal justice, economics, food science, history, humanities, international studies, physical fitness/movement, political science/government, psychology, social science, sociology, and textiles and clothing). Biotechnology, polymers and coatings science, and pharmacy are the strongest academically. Sciences, engineering, and human development and education are the largest.

Required: Students must complete at least 122 semester credits, with at least 24 in the major, and maintain at least a 2.0 GPA. General education requirements include: 10 credits in science and technology, including a 1 credit lab course, 9 credits in communication, which includes freshman English and public speaking, 6 credits each in humanities and fine arts, and in social and behavioral science, 3 credits in quantitative reasoning, at least 2 credits in a wellness course, and a first year experience course. Included in these courses must be 1 course designated as a cultural diversity course and 1 designated as a global perspectives course.

Special: Special academic programs include cooperative work programs and internships. There is cross-registration with the Tri-college Consortium and all North Dakota State institutions. Student-designed and dual majors, study abroad, a B.A.-B.S. degree, credit for life, military, and work experience, nondegree study, and pass/fail options are possible. There are 22 national honor societies and a freshman honors program.

Faculty/Classroom: 72% of faculty are male; 28%, female. 97% both teach and do research. Graduate students teach 20% of introductory courses. The average class size in a laboratory is 26 and in a regular course, 42.

Admissions: 97% of the 2003-2004 applicants were accepted. 27% of the current freshmen were in the top fifth of their class; 75% were in the top two fifths. There were 3 National Merit finalists. 100 freshmen graduated first in their class.

Requirements: The SAT I or ACT is required. In addition, applicants must have completed 4 units of English, and 3 each of math (Algebra I or above), laboratory science, and social science. The GED is accepted, with a minimum score of 45 and no subject score lower than 40. A GPA of 2.5 is required. AP and CLEP credits are accepted.

Procedure: Freshmen are admitted to all sessions. Entrance exams should be taken in the spring of the junior year or in the fall of the senior year. There is a rolling admissions plan and a deferred admissions plan. Applications should be filed by August 15 for fall entry, December 16 for spring entry, and May 20 for summer entry. The fall 2003 application fee was $35. Notification is sent on a rolling basis. Applications are accepted on-line through the school's web site.

Transfer: 798 transfer students enrolled in 2002-2003. Transfer students must have a minimum GPA of 2.0; ACT or SAT I scores are required if the applicant has less than 24 semester credits. 36 of 122 credits required for the bachelor's degree must be completed at NDSU.

Visiting: There are regularly scheduled orientations for prospective students, including tours of the campus, academic appointments, and meetings with admissions counselors and financial aid counselors. There are guides for informal visits and visitors may sit in on classes. To schedule a visit, contact the Office of Admission at ndsu.admission@ndsu.nodak.edu.

Financial Aid: In 2003-2004, 80% of all full-time freshmen and 77% of continuing full-time students received some form of financial aid. 55% of full-time freshmen and 54% of continuing full-time students received need-based aid. The average freshman award was $5462. Need-based scholarships or need-based grants averaged $3736; need-based self-help aid (loans and jobs) averaged $3396; non-need based athletic scholarships averaged $3177; and other non-need based awards and non-need based scholarships averaged $2039. 60% of undergraduates work part time. Average annual earnings from campus work are $885. The average financial indebtedness of the 2003 graduate was $20,498. The FAFSA is required. The priority date for freshman financial aid applications for fall entry is March 15. The deadline for filing freshman financial aid applications for fall entry is August 15.

International Students: There are 112 international students enrolled. The school actively recruits these students. They must score 525 on the written TOEFL.

Computers: The mainframes are an RS 6000 and a SUN 3500. Students access the system from various terminal clusters across campus as well as from their living areas via modem. PCs are also available throughout the campus. All students may access the system 24 hours a day or as posted. There are no time limits and no fees. It is recommended that students in architecture and landscape architecture (sophomore level) have personal computers.

Graduates: From July 1, 2002 to June 30, 2003, 1525 bachelor's degrees were awarded. The most popular majors were engineering (20%), business (13%), and health and related sciences (9%). In an average class, 16% graduate in 4 years or less, 25% graduate in 5 years or less, and 40% graduate in 6 years or less. 93 companies recruited on campus in 2002-2003. Of the 2002 graduating class, 18% were enrolled in graduate school within 6 months of graduation and 91% were employed.

Admissions Contact: Dr. Kate Haugen, Associate Dean/Enrollment Management. E-mail: ndsu.admission@ndsu.nodak.edu
Web: www.ndsu.edu

UNIVERSITY OF MARY
Bismarck, ND 58504-9652

C-3

(701) 255-7500
(800) 288-6279; Fax: (701) 255-7687

Full-time: 650 men, 1080 women	**Faculty:** 75
Part-time: 60 men, 150 women	**Ph.D.s:** 38%
Graduate: 80 men, 130 women	**Student/Faculty:** 23 to 1
Year: 4-1-4, summer session	**Tuition:** $9600
Application Deadline: open	**Room & Board:** $3900
Freshman Class: n/av	
SAT I or ACT: recommended	**COMPETITIVE+**

The University of Mary, founded in 1959, is a private institution affiliated with the Roman Catholic Church. Undergraduate and graduate programs emphasize liberal arts, humanities, social sciences, business, health science, music, professional training, philosophy and religious studies, and teacher preparation. Figures in the above capsule and in this profile are approximate. There are 8 undergraduate and 4 graduate schools. In addition to regional accreditation, Mary has baccalaureate program accreditation with CSWE and NLN. The library contains 55,000 volumes and 2500 audio/video tapes/CDs, and subscribes to 550 periodicals. Computerized library services include the card catalog, interlibrary loans, and database searching. Special learning facilities include a learning resource center, art gallery, radio station, and TV station. The 107-acre campus is in a suburban area 7 miles south of Bismarck. Including any residence halls, there are 12 buildings.

Student Life: 70% of undergraduates are from North Dakota. Students are from 26 states, 3 foreign countries, and Canada. 95% are from public schools. 96% are white. 60% are Catholic; 30% Protestant. The average age of freshmen is 18; all undergraduates, 23. 29% do not continue beyond their first year; 40% remain to graduate.

Housing: 755 students can be accommodated in college housing, which includes single-sex and coed dorms and on-campus apartments. On-campus housing is guaranteed for all 4 years. 50% of students commute. Alcohol is not permitted. All students may keep cars.

Activities: There are no fraternities or sororities. There are 22 groups on campus, including band, cheerleading, choir, chorale, chorus, computers, drama, ethnic, forensics, jazz band, musical theater, newspaper, orchestra, pep band, photography, political, professional, radio and TV, religious, social, social service, student government, symphony, and yearbook. Popular campus events include Parents Day, Cultural Day, and Prayer Day.

Sports: There are 8 intercollegiate sports for men and 7 for women, and 10 intramural sports for men and 10 for women. Facilities include an activity center housing a 1200-seat gym, basketball and racquetball courts, wrestling and weight rooms, and a swimming pool. There are also track/football, intramural, and softball fields, tennis courts, a fitness center, and a 1200-seat stadium.

Disabled Students: All of the campus is accessible. Wheelchair ramps, elevators, special parking, specially equipped rest rooms, special class scheduling, and lowered telephones are available.

Services: Counseling and information services are available, as is tutoring in every subject. There is a reader service for the blind and remedial math, reading, and writing.

Campus Safety and Security: Measures include security escort services, shuttle buses, informal discussions, and pamphlets/posters/films. There are emergency telephones and lighted pathways/sidewalks.

Programs of Study: Mary confers B.A., B.S., and B.Univ.Studies degrees. Master's degrees are also awarded. Bachelor's degrees are awarded in BIOLOGICAL SCIENCE (biology/biological science), BUSINESS (accounting, business administration and management, and management information systems), COMMUNICATIONS AND THE ARTS (communications, English, and music), COMPUTER AND PHYSICAL SCIENCE (mathematics and radiological technology), EDUCATION (athletic training, early childhood, elementary, English, mathematics, music, physical, science, social science, and special), HEALTH PROFESSIONS (medical laboratory science, nursing, occupational therapy, physical therapy, premedicine, and respiratory therapy), SOCIAL SCIENCE (addiction studies, behavioral science, ministries, prelaw, psychology, social science, and social work). Business administration, accounting, and nursing are the strongest academically. Business, nursing, and elementary education are the largest.

Required: To graduate, students must complete 128 semester hours, with 32 to 56 in the major and 44 at the 300-400 level, and have a minimum GPA of 2.0. At least 60 semester hours must be in liberal arts courses. In addition, a B.A. degree requires 16 semester hours of a foreign language or 20 semester hours of philosophy/theology, with 12 such hours at the 300-400 level. All students must take 3 courses each in humanities, math/science, philosophy/theology, and social sciences.

Special: A co-op program in engineering is available as is cross-registration with the University of Minnesota. Special academic programs include internships, study abroad in France, Germany, and Spain, on-campus work-study, and a general studies degree. Dual majors include elementary education/early childhood, elementary education/special education, athletic training/biology, athletic training/phys ed, business/accounting, and business/computer. There are accelerated degree programs in several majors, and a 3-2 engineering program with the University of Minnesota. There are 3 national honor societies, a freshman honors program, and 2 departmental honors programs.

Faculty/Classroom: 49% of faculty are male; 51%, female. All teach undergraduates and 15% both teach and do research. No introductory courses are taught by graduate students. The average class size in an introductory lecture is 30; in a laboratory, 20; and in a regular course, 20.

Requirements: The SAT I or ACT is recommended. In addition, applicants should be graduates of an accredited secondary school; the GED is accepted. For automatic acceptance, 3 requirements must be met: a minimum 2.5 GPA; an 18 or higher on the ACT; and rank in the upper half of the graduating class. The school's own testing can also be used to determine acceptance. A recommendation from a school counselor, teacher, or employer is requested. An interview is advised. A GPA of 2.5 is required. AP and CLEP credits are accepted.

Procedure: Freshmen are admitted fall and spring. Entrance exams should be taken in the fall of the senior year. There are early admissions, deferred admissions, and rolling admissions plans. Application deadlines are open. The application fee is $25. Applications are accepted on computer disk and on-line at the school's web site.

Transfer: 223 transfer students enrolled in a recent year. Transfer students should have a 2.0 minimum GPA and should present a recommendation from a school counselor, instructor, or employer. 32 of 128 credits required for the bachelor's degree must be completed at Mary.

Visiting: There are regularly scheduled orientations for prospective students, including a campus tour and meetings with individual professors, coaches, students, and music instructors. There are guides for informal visits and visitors may sit in on classes and stay overnight. To schedule a visit, contact the Admissions Office at marauder@umary.edu.

Financial Aid: In a recent year, 70% of undergraduates worked part time. Average annual earnings from campus work were $1000. The FAFSA is required. Check with the school for current deadlines.

International Students: They must score 500 on the written TOEFL.

Computers: The mainframe is an IBM 5360 System/36. Students have access to the Internet and World Wide Web and general-purpose and course-specific software through PCs in general-use labs and workstations in faculty offices. All students may access the system 24 hours a day. It is recommended that students in computer information systems have personal computers.

Graduates: In a recent year, 470 bachelor's degrees were awarded. The most popular majors were management (16%), nursing (12%), and education (11%). In an average class, 2% graduate in 3 years or less, 35% graduate in 4 years or less, 42% graduate in 5 years or less, and 43% graduate in 6 years or less. 80 companies recruited on campus in a recent year. Of a recent graduating class, 13% were enrolled in graduate school within 6 months of graduation and 97% were employed.

Admissions Contact: Steph Storey, Director of Admissions. A video is available. E-mail: *steph@umary.edu* Web: *www.umary.edu*

UNIVERSITY OF NORTH DAKOTA

E-2

Grand Forks, ND 58202

(701) 777-4463
(800) 225-5863; Fax: (701) 777-2696

Full-time: 5162 men, 4485 women	Faculty: 665; I, --$
Part-time: 535 men, 529 women	Ph.D.s: 86%
Graduate: 1012 men, 1311 women	Student/Faculty: 15 to 1
Year: semesters, summer session	Tuition: $4156 ($9902)
Application Deadline: July 1	Room & Board: $4234
Freshman Class: 4066 applied, 3096 accepted, 2194 enrolled	
SAT I or ACT: required	COMPETITIVE

The University of North Dakota, established in 1883, is a state-supported comprehensive institution. Its undergraduate and graduate programs emphasize the liberal arts, fine arts, engineering, medicine, aerospace sciences, nursing, professional training, business and public administration, health science, teacher preparation, law, and computer science. There are 8 undergraduate and 3 graduate schools. In addition to regional accreditation, UND has baccalaureate program accreditation with AACSB, ABET, ACEJMC, ADA, APTA, CSAB, CSWE, NASAD, NASM, NCATE, and NLN. The 3 libraries contain 1,362,283 volumes, 1,642,898 microform items, and 56,092 audio/video tapes/CDs, and subscribe to 8133 periodicals. Computerized library services include the card catalog, interlibrary loans, and database searching. Special learning facilities include a learning resource center, art gallery, natural history museum, radio station, TV station, an atmospherium, and an art museum and gallery. The 543-acre campus is in an urban area 4 hours from Minneapolis/St. Paul and 2 hours from Winnipeg, Manitoba. Including any residence halls, there are 234 buildings.

Student Life: 51% of undergraduates are from North Dakota. Students are from 50 states, 62 foreign countries, and Canada. 95% are from public schools. 88% are white. The average age of freshmen is 19; all undergraduates, 22. 23% do not continue beyond their first year; 77% remain to graduate.

Housing: 4734 students can be accommodated in college housing, which includes single-sex and coed dorms, on-campus apartments, married-student housing, fraternity houses, and sorority houses. On-campus housing is guaranteed for all 4 years. 67% of students commute. Alcohol is not permitted. All students may keep cars.

Activities: 10% of men belong to 13 national fraternities; 8% of women belong to 7 national sororities. There are 250 groups on campus, including art, band, cheerleading, chess, choir, chorale, chorus, computers, dance, debate, departmental, drama, drill team, ethnic, film, gay, honors, international, jazz band, literary magazine, marching band, musical theater, newspaper, orchestra, pep band, photography, political, professional, radio and TV, religious, social, social service, student government, and symphony. Popular campus events include Honors Day, Time Out/Wacipi, and Potato Bowl.

Sports: There are 8 intercollegiate sports for men and 10 for women, and 21 intramural sports for men and 21 for women. Facilities include an ice arena, a golf course, a 15,000-seat stadium, an 11,499-seat hockey arena, a 6100-seat basketball center, and a sports/field house with racquetball and basketball courts, weight rooms, a dance studio, and a wellness center.

Disabled Students: Wheelchair ramps, elevators, special parking, specially equipped rest rooms, special class scheduling, lowered drinking fountains, lowered telephones, special housing, accessible transportation, and academic and personal support services are available.

Services: Counseling and information services are available, as is tutoring in every subject. There is a reader service for the blind.

Campus Safety and Security: Measures include 24-hour foot and vehicle patrol, self-defense education, security escort services, and shuttle buses. There are informal discussions, pamphlets/posters/films, lighted pathways/sidewalks, and emergency phones throughout the campus.

Programs of Study: UND confers B.A., B.S., B.Acc., B.B.A., B.F.A., B.G.S., B.Mus., B.S.A., B.S.A.T., B.S.At Sc., B.S.C.E., B.S.Ch.E., B.S. Chem., B.S.C.J.S., B.S.C.L.S., B.S.C.N., B.S.C.S.C.I., B.S.Cyto., B.S.D., B.S.Ed., B.S.E.E., B.S.E.G., B.S.E.M., B.S.E.P., B.S.F.W.B., B.S.G., B.S.G.E., B.S.I.T., B.S.M.E., B.S.N., B.S.O.S.E.H., B.S.P.A., B.S.P.E., B.S.R.H.S., B.S.R.L.S., and B.S.S.W. degrees. Master's and doctoral degrees are also awarded. Bachelor's degrees are awarded in AGRICULTURE (fish and game management), BIOLOGICAL SCIENCE (biology/biological science and nutrition), BUSINESS (accounting, banking and finance, business economics, entrepreneurial studies, management information systems, management science, marketing/retailing/

merchandising, recreation and leisure services, and transportation management), COMMUNICATIONS AND THE ARTS (communications, dramatic arts, English, French, German, music, music performance, Scandinavian languages, Spanish, and visual and performing arts), COMPUTER AND PHYSICAL SCIENCE (applied physics, atmospheric sciences and meteorology, chemistry, computer science, geology, information sciences and systems, mathematics, and physics), EDUCATION (athletic training, business, early childhood, elementary, middle school, music, physical, science, social studies, trade and industrial, and vocational), ENGINEERING AND ENVIRONMENTAL DESIGN (aerospace studies, air traffic control, airline piloting and navigation, aviation administration/management, aviation computer technology, chemical engineering, civil engineering, electrical/electronics engineering, environmental engineering technology, geological engineering, industrial engineering technology, mechanical engineering, and occupational safety and health), HEALTH PROFESSIONS (clinical science, community health work, cytotechnology, health science, music therapy, nursing, physical therapy, rehabilitation therapy, and speech pathology/audiology), SOCIAL SCIENCE (anthropology, classical/ancient civilization, criminal justice, dietetics, economics, forensic studies, geography, history, interdisciplinary studies, international studies, liberal arts/general studies, Native American studies, philosophy, political science/government, psychology, public administration, religion, social science, social work, and sociology). Physical therapy is the strongest academically. Health, liberal arts, and business are the largest.

Required: To graduate, students must complete at least 125 credit hours, 30 in the major, with a minimum GPA of 2.0. At least 36 credits must be numbered 300 or above, and at least 60 credits must be from a 4-year institution. Distribution requirements include 12 credits of math, science, and technology, 9 each of social sciences and arts and humanities, and 6 of English composition. One course in social science or arts and humanities must meet the world cultures designation.

Special: Special academic programs include cooperative programs, accelerated degree programs in most majors, internships in many majors, study abroad in at least 20 countries, work-study, and dual majors in all areas. Also offered are a general studies degree, honors programs, student-designed majors, B.A.-B.S. degees, nondegree study, and pass/fail options. Alternative academic programs include the Division of Continuing Education's correspondence study, the Integrated Studies Program, which offers a means of fulfilling general education requirements by a semester of related course work, and study via telecommunications. Cross-registration with all North Dakota 2- and 4-year public institutions is possible. There are 28 national honor societies, including Phi Beta Kappa, a freshman honors program, and 1 departmental honors program.

Faculty/Classroom: 56% of faculty are male; 44%, female. 90% teach undergraduates. The average class size in an introductory lecture is 37; in a laboratory, 23; and in a regular course, 28.

Admissions: 76% of the 2003-2004 applicants were accepted. The ACT scores for the 2003-2004 freshman class were: 28% below 21, 28% between 21 and 23, 25% between 24 and 26, 11% between 27 and 28, and 9% above 28. 32% of the current freshmen were in the top fifth of their class; 62% were in the top two fifths. There were 3 National Merit finalists. 94 freshmen graduated first in their class.

Requirements: The SAT I or ACT is required; the ACT is preferred, but the SAT I will be accepted. Applicants must be graduates of an accredited secondary school or have passed the GED with an average of 50. A GPA of 2.25 is required. AP and CLEP credits are accepted.

Procedure: Freshmen are admitted to all sessions. Entrance exams should be taken in spring of the junior year or fall of the senior year. There are early decision and early admissions plans. Applications should be filed by July 1 for fall entry; deadlines are open for spring and summer entry. The fall 2003 application fee was $35. Notification is sent on a rolling basis.

Transfer: 920 transfer students enrolled in 2002-2003. Transfer students must have a minimum GPA of 2.0 and be in good academic standing. A higher GPA may be required in specific programs. 30 of 125 credits required for the bachelor's degree must be completed at UND.

Visiting: There are regularly scheduled orientations for prospective students, including a visit with an admissions counselor, a campus tour, an academic appointment, and an athletic appointment (if applicable). There are guides for informal visits and visitors may sit in on classes and stay overnight. To schedule a visit, contact Enrollment Services at enrolser@sage.und.nodak.edu.

Financial Aid: In 2003-2004, 81% of all full-time freshmen and 78% of continuing full-time students received some form of financial aid. 47% of full-time freshmen and 50% of continuing full-time students received need-based aid. The average freshman award was $7722. Need-based scholarships or need-based grants averaged $2999 ($4050 maximum); need-based self-help aid (loans and jobs) averaged $4241 ($8820 maximum); non-need-based athletic scholarships averaged $4822 ($14,136 maximum); and other non-need-based awards and non-need-based scholarships averaged $2889 ($3593 maximum). 58% of undergraduates work part time. Average annual earnings from campus work are $2083. The average financial indebtedness of the 2003 graduate was

$22,733. UND is a member of CSS. The FAFSA is required. The priority date for freshman financial aid applications for fall entry is March 15.

International Students: There are 239 international students enrolled. They must score 525 on the written TOEFL.

Computers: The mainframes are a Unisys Clear Path 6600 and an MVS 390. Students may use PCs and Macs at various centrally located campus and departmental labs and residence halls. Network access to mainframe computers and the Internet is available through a dial-in facility (184 lines) and direct access in the PC labs and the residence halls. All students may access the system 24 hours a day. It is recommended that students in aviation and medicine have personal computers. Gateway E6100, E4100, E450 (laptop) are recommended.

Graduates: From July 1, 2002 to June 30, 2003, 1612 bachelor's degrees were awarded. The most popular majors were commercial aviation (9%), elementary education (6%), and psychology (5%). In an average class, 16% graduate in 4 years or less, 41% graduate in 5 years or less, and 49% graduate in 6 years or less. 98 companies recruited on campus in 2002-2003. Of the 2002 graduating class, 20% were enrolled in graduate school within 6 months of graduation and 85% were employed.

Admissions Contact: Kenton Pauls, Director, Enrollment Services. A video is available. E-mail: kenton_pauls@mail.und.nodak.edu; or enrolser@sage.und Web: http://www.und.edu

VALLEY CITY STATE UNIVERSITY
Valley City, ND 58072

E-3
(701) 845-7101
(800) 532-8641; Fax: (701) 845-7245

Full-time: 370 men, 372 women	**Faculty:** 61; IIB, --$
Part-time: 75 men, 181 women	**Ph.D.s:** 43%
Graduate: none	**Student/Faculty:** 12 to 1
Year: semesters, summer session	**Tuition:** $4027 ($8456)
Application Deadline: open	**Room & Board:** $3254
Freshman Class: 266 applied, 233 accepted, 159 enrolled	
SAT I Verbal/Math: 475/460	**ACT:** 21 **LESS COMPETITIVE**

Valley City State University, founded in 1890, is a state-supported institution offering degree programs in the arts and sciences, business, and teacher education. In addition to regional accreditation, VCSU has baccalaureate program accreditation with NASM and NCATE. The library contains 103,174 volumes and 15,069 audio/video tapes/CDs, and subscribes to 2982 periodicals. Computerized library services include the card catalog, interlibrary loans, and database searching. Special learning facilities include a learning resource center, art gallery, and planetarium. The 64-acre campus is in a small town 58 miles west of Fargo. Including any residence halls, there are 29 buildings.

Student Life: 79% of undergraduates are from North Dakota. Students are from 21 states, 8 foreign countries, and Canada. 99% are from public schools. 91% are white. 62% are Protestant; 31% Catholic; 7% claim no religious affiliation. The average age of freshmen is 19; all undergraduates, 23. 39% do not continue beyond their first year.

Housing: 514 students can be accommodated in college housing, which includes single-sex and coed dorms and married-student housing. On-campus housing is guaranteed for all 4 years. 68% of students commute. Alcohol is not permitted. All students may keep cars.

Activities: 1% of men belong to 1 local fraternity; 1% of women belong to 1 local sorority. There are 20 groups on campus, including art, band, cheerleading, choir, chorus, computers, drama, honors, international, jazz band, musical theater, newspaper, pep band, photography, political, professional, religious, social, student government, and yearbook. Popular campus events include Sno-Daze, EBC-Hit Parade, and Medicine Wheel Seasonal Celebrations.

Sports: There are 5 intercollegiate sports for men and 5 for women, and 9 intramural sports for men and 9 for women. Facilities include a 2500-seat football stadium with an all-weather track, a 2500-seat arena, an indoor pool, a field house, tennis and racquetball courts, a cross-country course, softball and baseball fields, a golf course, weight rooms, and a fitness room.

Disabled Students: 85% of the campus is accessible. Wheelchair ramps, elevators, special parking, specially equipped rest rooms, special class scheduling, lowered drinking fountains, and lowered telephones are available.

Services: Counseling and information services are available, as is tutoring in most subjects. There is remedial writing.

Campus Safety and Security: Measures include 24-hour foot and vehicle patrol, self-defense education, informal discussions, and pamphlets/posters/films. There are lighted pathways/sidewalks and a night patrol.

Programs of Study: VCSU confers B.A., B.S., B.S.Ed., and B.University Studies degrees. Bachelor's degrees are awarded in BIOLOGICAL SCIENCE (biology/biological science), BUSINESS (business administration and management, human resources, and office supervision and management), COMMUNICATIONS AND THE ARTS (art, English, music, and Spanish), COMPUTER AND PHYSICAL SCIENCE (chemistry, information sciences and systems, mathematics, and science), EDUCATION (business, elementary, health, physical, technical, and vocational), SOCIAL SCIENCE (history and social science). Education, business, and computer information systems are the strongest academically. Elementary education and business are the largest.

Required: To graduate, students must complete at least 128 semester hours with a minimum GPA of 2.0, or 2.5 for a B.S.Ed. degree. Except for those pursuing the Bachelor of University Studies degree, all students must complete the foundation studies curriculum, which includes 15 to 16 hours in foreign language, 12 in problem solving, 9 in communication, 6 each in wellness and in aesthetic engagement, 5 in global perspective, and 3 in technology. Students must complete 48 hours in their major if they do not have a minor, or 36 hours in their major if they have a minor. All students must complete a digital portfolio specific to their major.

Special: VCSU offers internships, dual majors, on-campus work-study, study abroad in 2 countries, pass/fail options for some courses, and credit for life, military, and work experience. There are 6 national honor societies and 4 departmental honors programs.

Faculty/Classroom: 56% of faculty are male; 44%, female. All teach undergraduates, and 25% both teach and do research. The average class size in an introductory lecture is 40; in a laboratory, 20; and in a regular course, 25.

Admissions: 88% of the 2003-2004 applicants were accepted. The ACT scores for the 2003-2004 freshman class were: 47% below 21, 35% between 21 and 23, 13% between 24 and 26, 3% between 27 and 28, and 2% above 28. 7 freshmen graduated first in their class in a recent year.

Requirements: The ACT is required. In addition, applicants must be graduates of an accredited secondary school or have a GED certificate. Core curriculum requirements include 4 units of English and 3 units each of math, lab science, and social science. AP and CLEP credits are accepted.

Procedure: Freshmen are admitted to all sessions. There is a deferred admissions plan. Application deadlines are open. Application fee is $35. Notification is sent on a rolling basis. Applications are accepted on-line through the school's web site.

Transfer: 165 transfer students enrolled in 2002-2003. Applicants must be in good academic standing, have a minimum GPA of 2.0, and be eligible to return to their previous institution. Official transcripts from all colleges attended are required. Some students may be required to submit high school transcripts and standardized test scores. 24 of 128 credits required for the bachelor's degree must be completed at VCSU.

Visiting: There are regularly scheduled orientations for prospective students. There are guides for informal visits and visitors may sit in on classes and stay overnight. To schedule a visit, contact the Office of Enrollment Services.

Financial Aid: In a recent year, 86% of all full-time freshmen and 74% of continuing full-time students received some form of financial aid. 50% of all full-time students received need-based aid. The average freshman award was $6808. 22% of undergraduates work part time. Average annual earnings from campus work are $1568. The average financial indebtedness of a recent year's graduate was $16,636. VCSU is a member of CSS. The FAFSA is required. The deadline for filing freshman financial aid applications for fall entry is April 15.

International Students: There were 46 international students enrolled in a recent year. They must score 500 on the written TOEFL and also take the SAT I or the ACT.

Computers: Each student is issued an IBM ThinkPad 380ED for use during the school year. Every student has network access 24 hours a day to the Internet, the World Wide Web, and the Groupwise e-mail communication system. There are no time limits and no fees.

Graduates: From July 1, 2002 to June 30, 2003, 188 bachelor's degrees were awarded. The most popular majors were elementary education (50%), business administration (14%), and human resources (6%). In an average class, 23% graduate in 4 years or less, 13% graduate in 5 years or less, and 4% graduate in 6 years or less.

Admissions Contact: Dan Klein, Director of Enrollment Management. E-mail: *enrollment_services@mail.vcsu.nodak.edu* Web: *www.vcsu.edu*

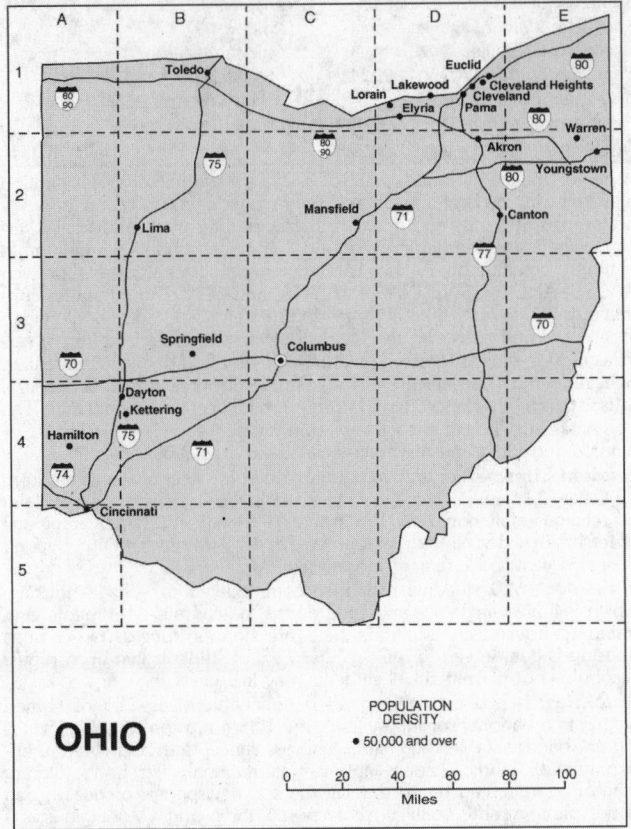

OHIO

POPULATION
DENSITY
● 50,000 and over

0   20   40   60   80   100
Miles

ANTIOCH COLLEGE
Yellow Springs, OH 45387

B-4

(937) 769-1100
(800) 543-9436; Fax: (937) 769-1111

Full-time: 217 men, 347 women	**Faculty:** 47; IIB, --$
Part-time: 2 men, 4 women	**Ph.D.s:** 70%
Graduate: none	**Student/Faculty:** 12 to 1
Year: trimesters, summer session	**Tuition:** $23,275
Application Deadline: February 1	**Room & Board:** $5994
Freshman Class: 599 applied, 402 accepted, 182 enrolled	
SAT I or ACT: recommended	**COMPETITIVE**

Antioch College, established in 1852, is private (not for profit) liberal arts institution where students alternate full-time study on campus with full-time related work experience off campus. The library contains 300,024 volumes, 48,320 microform items, and 6340 audio/video tapes/CDs, and subscribes to 10,920 (print and electronic) periodicals. Computerized library services include the card catalog, interlibrary loans, database searching, and Internet access. Special learning facilities include a learning resource center, art gallery, radio station, and archives. The 100-acre campus is in a small town 18 miles east of Dayton. Including any residence halls, there are 34 buildings.
Student Life: Students are from 43 states and 6 foreign countries. 55% are white. The average age of freshmen is 19; all undergraduates, 21.
Housing: 592 students can be accommodated in college housing, which includes single-sex and coed dorms and on-campus apartments. In addition, there are language houses, special-interest houses, and food cooperatives in the dorms. On-campus housing is guaranteed for all 4 years. 95% of students live on campus; of those, 95% remain on campus on weekends. Alcohol is not permitted. All students may keep cars.
Activities: There are no fraternities or sororities. There are 27 groups on campus, including art, choir, dance, drama, ethnic, film, gay, international, literary magazine, newspaper, photography, political, radio and TV, social, social service, and student government.
Sports: There are 16 intramural sports for men and 16 for women.
Disabled Students: 10% of the campus is accessible. Wheelchair ramps, elevators, special parking, and specially equipped rest rooms are available.
Services: Counseling and information services are available, as is tutoring in most subjects. There is a reader service for the blind and remedial math and writing.

Campus Safety and Security: Measures include 24-hour foot and vehicle patrol, security escort services, informal discussions, and pamphlets/posters/films. There are lighted pathways/sidewalks.
Programs of Study: Antioch confers B.A. and B.S. degrees. Bachelor's degrees are awarded in BUSINESS (entrepreneurial studies), COMMUNICATIONS AND THE ARTS (communications, languages, and visual and performing arts), COMPUTER AND PHYSICAL SCIENCE (physical sciences), ENGINEERING AND ENVIRONMENTAL DESIGN (environmental science), SOCIAL SCIENCE (crosscultural studies, humanities and social science, and interdisciplinary studies). Social sciences and environmental studies are the largest.
Required: To graduate, students must complete at least 107 academic credits, with 40 to 56 in the major, and 5 co-op experiences. The general education program consists of 8 4-credit courses. The core curriculum includes writing, math, and foreign language. Distribution requirements include 32 credits in arts, humanities, social sciences, natural sciences, and physical sciences. In addition, students must demonstrate proficiency in a foreign language and must successfully complete a work-study experience of at least 1 term in an international or cross-cultural setting. Narrative evaluations are used instead of grades.
Special: An alternating work-study program is required of all students; co-op jobs, normally 16 weeks long and resulting in 1 block of co-op credit, are individually arranged according to the needs, interests, and qualifications of each student. There is cross-registration with 17 higher education institutions in southwestern Ohio, and Antioch's membership in the Great Lakes Colleges Association allows for opportunities for special off-campus programs. An extensive study abroad program in 15 countries is based on student-designed majors and accelerated degree programs in all majors. Within the 8 interdisciplinary majors offered at Antioch, there are dual majors and 25 concentrations available. Nondegree study is possible. All courses are graded on a credit/no credit basis with faculty giving narrative evaluations of each student's work.
Faculty/Classroom: 51% of faculty are male; 49%, female. All teach undergraduates. The average class size in a regular course is 12.
Admissions: 67% of the 2003-2004 applicants were accepted.
Requirements: The SAT I or ACT is recommended. A GPA of 2.5 is required. AP and CLEP credits are accepted. Important factors in the admissions decision are personality/intangible qualities, recommendations by school officials, and evidence of special talent.
Procedure: Freshmen are admitted fall, spring, and summer. There are early admissions and deferred admissions plans. Early decision applications should be filed by November 15; regular applications, by February 1 for fall entry, November 1 for spring entry, and April 1 for summer entry, along with a $35 fee. Notification of admission is sent on a rolling basis. Applications are accepted on-line.
Transfer: Official college transcripts from previous institutions and a dean's recommendation form are required. 54 of 107 credits required for the bachelor's degree must be completed at Antioch.
Visiting: There are regularly scheduled orientations for prospective students, including admissions interviews, co-op presentations, tours, and special events. There are guides for informal visits and visitors may sit in on classes and stay overnight. To schedule a visit, contact the Admissions Office at *admissions@antioch-college.edu*.
Financial Aid: The FAFSA and the college's own financial statement are required. Check with the school for current financial aid deadlines.
International Students: There are 10 international students enrolled. They must score 525 on the written TOEFL.
Computers: Students may use PC or Mac labs to access e-mail or the Internet in a variety of labs and/or the library. All students may access the system. There are no time limits. The fee is $140.
Graduates: The most popular majors were cultural and interdisciplinary studies (30%), language, literature, and culture (16%), and self, society, and culture (12%).
Admissions Contact: Michael Thore, Dean of Admission and Financial Aid. A video is available. E-mail: *admissions@antioch-college.edu* Web: *antioch-college.edu*

ART ACADEMY OF CINCINNATI
Cincinnati, OH 45202

A-5

(513) 562-8744
(800) 323-5692; Fax: (513) 562-8778

Full-time: 84 men, 96 women	**Faculty:** 18
Part-time: 7 men, 6 women	**Ph.D.s:** 99%
Graduate: 1 woman	**Student/Faculty:** 10 to 1
Year: semesters, summer session	**Tuition:** $17,300
Application Deadline: June 30	**Room & Board:** n/app
Freshman Class: 144 applied, 143 accepted, 71 enrolled	
SAT I Verbal/Math: 543/516	**ACT:** 21	**SPECIAL**

The Art Academy of Cincinnati, founded in 1887, is a private professional college offering B.F.A. degrees in fine art, communication arts, and art history, an associate degree in graphic design, and a master's degree in art education. In addition to regional accreditation, the art academy has baccalaureate program accreditation with NASAD. The library contains 66,500 volumes, and subscribes to 150 periodicals. Computerized library services include interlibrary loans. Special learning facilities include a learning resource center, art gallery, and an art museum. The 184-acre campus is in an urban area 2 miles northeast of downtown Cincinnati. There are 3 buildings.

Student Life: 75% of undergraduates are from Ohio. Students are from 13 states and 2 foreign countries. 92% are white. The average age of freshmen is 19; all undergraduates, 23. 20% do not continue beyond their first year; 60% remain to graduate.

Housing: There are no residence halls. All students may keep cars.

Activities: There are no fraternities or sororities. Popular campus events include field trips, Career Week, and Performance Day.

Disabled Students: 2% of the campus is accessible. Limited wheelchair ramps and special parking are available.

Services: Counseling and information services are available, as is tutoring in some subjects, including drawing and most academics.

Programs of Study: The art academy confers the B.F.A. degree. Associate and master's degrees are also awarded. Bachelor's degrees are awarded in COMMUNICATIONS AND THE ARTS (art history and appreciation, fine arts, graphic design, and illustration). Art history is the strongest academically. Graphic design is the largest.

Required: To graduate, students must complete 132 semester hours, including 30 to 45 in the major, with a GPA of 2.0. The 21-credit foundation curriculum is required of all students, as are a senior thesis and a senior exhibition. Distribution requirements include 15 credits in art history and 6 each in English, social science, natural science, and humanities, as well as 3 each in a cross-disciplinary, aesthetics, and electives.

Special: Students may cross-register with member institutions of the Greater Cincinnati Consortium. Co-op programs are available in graphic design, illustration, and art history. Art history majors may intern at the Cincinnati Art Museum.

Faculty/Classroom: 60% of faculty are male; 40%, female. All teach undergraduates. The average class size in an introductory lecture is 25 and in a regular course, 12.

Admissions: 99% of the 2003-2004 applicants were accepted. The SAT I scores for the 2003-2004 freshman class were: Verbal--33% below 500, 33% between 500 and 599, 26% between 600 and 700, and 8% above 700; Math--42% below 500, 50% between 500 and 599, and 8% above 700. The ACT scores were 52% below 21, 24% between 21 and 23, 12% between 24 and 26, 4% between 27 and 28, and 8% above 28.

Requirements: The SAT I or ACT is required. In addition, applicants should be graduates of an accredited secondary school. The GED is accepted. A portfolio review and an interview are necessary. A GPA of 2.0 is required. AP and CLEP credits are accepted. Important factors in the admissions decision are evidence of special talent, personality/intangible qualities, and recommendations by school officials.

Procedure: Freshmen are admitted in the fall. There is a deferred admissions plan. Early decision applications should be filed by March 1; regular applications, by June 30 for fall entry, along with a $25 fee. Only transfer students may apply for January admission; that application deadline is December 15. Notification is sent on a rolling basis.

Transfer: 26 transfer students enrolled in 2002-2003. Applicants must present academic transcripts and a portfolio. 66 of 132 credits required for the bachelor's degree must be completed at the art academy.

Visiting: There are guides for informal visits and visitors may sit in on classes. To schedule a visit, contact Mary Jane Zumwalde in Admissions at (513) 721-5205.

Financial Aid: In 2003-2004, 80% of all full-time freshmen and 81% of continuing full-time students received some form of financial aid. 73% of full-time freshmen and 84% of continuing full-time students received need-based aid. The average freshman award was $10,898. All undergraduates work part time. Average annual earnings from campus work are $1750. The average financial indebtedness of the 2003 graduate was $25,233. The FAFSA is required. The priority date for freshman financial aid applications for fall entry is March 1. The deadline for filing freshman financial aid applications for fall entry is rolling.

International Students: There are 3 international students enrolled. They must score 525 on the written TOEFL or 195 on the electronic version and also take the SAT I or the ACT.

Computers: Macs are available to students for art and design functions and word processing. All students may access the system. There are no time limits and no fees.

Graduates: From July 1, 2002 to June 30, 2003, 45 bachelor's degrees were awarded. The most popular majors were fine art (56%), communications design (40%), and art history (4%). In an average class, 73% graduate in 4 years or less. 20 companies recruited on campus in 2002-2003. Of the 2002 graduating class, 5% were enrolled in graduate school within 6 months of graduation and 92% were employed.

Admissions Contact: Mary Jane Zumwalde, Director of Admissions. E-mail: *admissions@artacademy.edu* Web: *artacademy.edu*

ASHLAND UNIVERSITY
Ashland, OH 44805

C-2
(419) 289-5052
(800) 882-1548; Fax: (419) 289-5333

Full-time: 994 men, 1423 women	**Faculty:** 215; IIB, av$
Part-time: 95 men, 270 women	**Ph.D.s:** 79%
Graduate: 1469 men, 2473 women	**Student/Faculty:** 11 to 1
Year: semesters, summer session	**Tuition:** $17,832
Application Deadline: open	**Room & Board:** $6632
Freshman Class: 2137 applied, 1828 accepted, 618 enrolled	
SAT I Verbal/Math: 510/512	**ACT:** 22 **COMPETITIVE**

Ashland University, founded in 1878, is a private liberal arts institution affiliated with the Brethren Church, offering undergraduate and graduate programs in the arts and sciences, business, education, and health services. There are 3 undergraduate and 3 graduate schools. In addition to regional accreditation, AU has baccalaureate program accreditation with AACSB, AHEA, CSWE, NASM, NCATE, and NLN. The 2 libraries contain 270,000 volumes, 250,000 microform items, and 8800 audio/video tapes/CDs, and subscribe to 700 periodicals. Computerized library services include the card catalog, interlibrary loans, and database searching. Special learning facilities include a learning resource center, art gallery, radio station, TV station, writing center, media center, and theater. The 150-acre campus is in a small town midway between Cleveland and Columbus. Including any residence halls, there are 38 buildings.

Student Life: 94% of undergraduates are from Ohio. Students are from 29 states, 13 foreign countries, and Canada. 86% are white. 46% claim no religious affiliation; 34% Protestant; 14% Catholic. The average age of freshmen is 18; all undergraduates, 23. 42% do not continue beyond their first year; 58% remain to graduate.

Housing: 1620 students can be accommodated in college housing, which includes single-sex and coed dorms, on-campus apartments, and fraternity houses. In addition, there are honors houses. On-campus housing is guaranteed for all 4 years. 72% of students live on campus. Alcohol is not permitted. All students may keep cars.

Activities: 14% of men belong to 4 national fraternities; 22% of women belong to 5 national sororities. There are 100 groups on campus, including art, band, cheerleading, choir, chorus, dance, drama, drill team, environmental, ethnic, health, honors, international, jazz band, literary magazine, marching band, musical theater, newspaper, orchestra, pep band, photography, political, professional, radio and TV, religious, social, social service, student government, symphony, and yearbook. Popular campus events include Spectrum Series, plays, and Little Sibs Weekend.

Sports: There are 10 intercollegiate sports for men and 9 for women, and 20 intramural sports for men and 20 for women. Facilities include a 5800-seat stadium, a 3000-seat gym, an all-weather track, a field house, a weight-training center, an 8-lane swimming pool with diving board, saunas, exercise rooms, 3 basketball courts, 2 handball/racquetball courts, playing fields, a fitness center, and a soccer complex with 2 full-size fields.

Disabled Students: 5% of the campus is accessible. Wheelchair ramps, elevators, special parking, specially equipped rest rooms, special class scheduling, lowered drinking fountains, lowered telephones, and special housing are available.

Services: Counseling and information services are available, as is tutoring in every subject. There is a reader service for the blind.

Campus Safety and Security: Measures include 24-hour foot and vehicle patrol, self-defense education, security escort services, and informal discussions. There are pamphlets/posters/films, emergency telephones, lighted pathways/sidewalks, encoded student identification cards, and an electronic-access system in residence halls.

Programs of Study: AU confers B.A., B.S., B.M., B.S.B.A., B.S.Ed., B.S.N., and B.S.W. degrees. Associate, master's, and doctoral degrees are also awarded. Bachelor's degrees are awarded in BIOLOGICAL SCIENCE (biology/biological science and toxicology), BUSINESS (accounting, banking and finance, business administration and management, business economics, fashion merchandising, hotel/motel and restaurant management, management information systems, marketing/retailing/merchandising, and recreational facilities management), COMMUNICATIONS AND THE ARTS (art, broadcasting, communications, creative writing, dramatic arts, English, fine arts, French, journalism, media arts, music, musical theater, Spanish, and speech/debate/rhetoric), COMPUTER AND PHYSICAL SCIENCE (chemistry, computer science, geology, mathematics, and physics), EDUCATION (art, athletic training, early childhood, education administration, education of the exceptional child, elementary, English, foreign languages, health, home economics, music, physical, science, and secondary), ENGINEERING AND ENVIRONMENTAL DESIGN (commercial art and environmental science), HEALTH PROFESSIONS (predentistry, premedicine, preoptometry, preveterinary science, and recreation therapy), SOCIAL SCIENCE (American studies, child care/child and family studies, criminal justice, economics, food science, history, international studies, philosophy, physical fitness/movement, political science/government, prelaw, psychology, religion, social science, social work, and sociology). Preprofessional science is the strongest academically. Business and teacher education are the largest.

Required: To graduate, students must complete at least 128 semester hours with a minimum GPA of 2.0 overall and 2.25 in the major. All students must complete 3 semester hours of freshman studies and 44 semester hours of interdisciplinary studies, including courses in English, phys ed, religion, speech, business or economics, fine arts, humanities, science, and social science.

Special: Opportunities are provided for internships, co-op programs in all business majors, work-study programs, dual majors, credit by exam, study abroad in 27 countries, a Washington semester, and pass/fail options. There are 17 national honor societies, a freshman honors program, and 10 departmental honors programs.

Faculty/Classroom: 61% of faculty are male; 39%, female. 81% teach undergraduates. No introductory courses are taught by graduate students. The average class size in an introductory lecture is 20; in a laboratory, 11; and in a regular course, 18.

Admissions: 86% of the 2003-2004 applicants were accepted. The SAT I scores for the 2003-2004 freshman class were: Verbal--40% below 500, 39% between 500 and 599, 21% between 600 and 700, and 1% above 700; Math--42% below 500, 39% between 500 and 599, 17% between 600 and 700, and 2% above 700. The ACT scores were 34% below 21, 28% between 21 and 23, 24% between 24 and 26, 9% between 27 and 28, and 6% above 28. 40% of the current freshmen were in the top fifth of their class; 70% were in the top two fifths. 13 freshmen graduated first in their class.

Requirements: The SAT I or ACT is required. In addition, applicants must be graduates of an accredited secondary school. The GED is accepted. The recommended preparatory program includes 4 units of English, 3 each of science, social studies, and math, and 2 of foreign language. An interview is recommended. A GPA of 2.5 is required. AP and CLEP credits are accepted. Important factors in the admissions decision are advanced placement or honor courses, evidence of special talent, and leadership record.

Procedure: Freshmen are admitted to all sessions. Entrance exams should be taken in the spring of the junior year. There is a deferred admissions plan. Application deadlines are open. The fall 2003 application fee was $25. Applications are accepted on-line through the university's web site.

Transfer: Official transcripts from all previous colleges, showing course credits and a minimum GPA of 2.25, must be submitted when applying for transfer. Generally, if the student has successfully completed a minimum of 1 year of college, the SAT I or ACT will not be required. 32 of 128 credits required for the bachelor's degree must be completed at AU.

Visiting: There are regularly scheduled orientations for prospective students. There are guides for informal visits and visitors may sit in on classes and stay overnight. To schedule a visit, contact the Office of Admissions at (800) 882-1548, ext. 5052.

Financial Aid: In 2003-2004, 99% of all full-time freshmen and 98% of continuing full-time students received some form of financial aid. 82% of full-time freshmen and 78% of continuing full-time students received need-based aid. The average freshman award was $17,408, with $10,382 ($18,687 maximum) from need-based scholarships or grants, $4785 ($6625 maximum) from need-based self-help aid (loans and jobs), $434 ($24,464 maximum) from non-need-based athletic scholarships, $843 ($17,974 maximum) from other non-need-based awards and non-need-based scholarships, and $964 from outside scholarships. 30% of undergraduates work part time. Average annual earnings from campus work are $954. The average financial indebtedness of the 2003 graduate was $18,250. The FAFSA, the university's own financial statement, and federal tax returns are required. The priority date for freshman financial aid applications for fall entry is March 15. The deadline for filing freshman financial aid applications for fall entry is November 15.

International Students: The school actively recruits these students. They must score 500 on the written TOEFL.

Computers: The mainframes are Sun, NT, and Netware servers. There are 10 Windows-based computerized classrooms with more than 200 Pentium PCs, 1 Mac-based classroom with 28 Macs, and 2 staffed multi-platform open labs with 60 Pentium PCs and several more Macs. More than 200 additional computers exist throughout campus for student use. Laptops are available throughout campus for use in wireless areas. All students may access the system. There are no time limits. The fee is $1.50 per credit hour.

Graduates: Of the 2002 graduating class, 8% were enrolled in graduate school within 6 months of graduation and 34% were employed.

Admissions Contact: Office of Admissions.
E-mail: *auadmsn@ashland.edu* Web: *http://www.ashland.edu*

BALDWIN-WALLACE COLLEGE D-1
Berea, OH 44017-2088 (440) 826-2222; Fax: (440) 826-3830
Full-time: 1273 men, 1781 women | **Faculty:** 163; IIB, +$
Part-time: 245 men, 563 women | **Ph.D.s:** 78%
Graduate: 269 men, 561 women | **Student/Faculty:** 19 to 1
Year: semesters, summer session | **Tuition:** $18,478
Application Deadline: May 1 | **Room & Board:** $6200
Freshman Class: 2026 applied, 1821 accepted, 702 enrolled
SAT I Verbal/Math: 560/550 | **ACT:** 23 | COMPETITIVE

Baldwin-Wallace College, established in 1845, is a private liberal arts institution affiliated with the United Methodist Church. In addition to regional accreditation, B-W has baccalaureate program accreditation with NASM and NCATE. The 3 libraries contain 200,000 volumes and 103,000 microform items, and subscribe to 1000 periodicals. Computerized library services include the card catalog, interlibrary loans, database searching, and Internet access. Special learning facilities include a learning resource center, art gallery, radio station, neuroscience lab, and an observatory. The 100-acre campus is in a suburban area 14 miles southwest of Cleveland. Including any residence halls, there are 60 buildings.

Student Life: 90% of undergraduates are from Ohio. Students are from 30 states, 14 foreign countries, and Canada. 85% are from public schools. 86% are white. 46% are Catholic; 25% Protestant; 17% Buddhist, Hindu, Muslim, Orthodox, Unitarian, and nondenominational. The average age of freshmen is 18; all undergraduates, 23. 16% do not continue beyond their first year; 66% remain to graduate.

Housing: 1955 students can be accommodated in college housing, which includes single-sex and coed dorms and on-campus apartments. In addition, there are honors houses and special-interest houses. On-campus housing is guaranteed for all 4 years. 61% of students live on campus; of those, 40% remain on campus on weekends. Upperclassmen may keep cars.

Activities: 20% of men belong to 5 national fraternities; 22% of women belong to 5 national sororities. There are 135 groups on campus, including art, band, cheerleading, chess, choir, chorale, chorus, computers, dance, drama, drill team, ethnic, gay, honors, international, jazz band, literary magazine, musical theater, newspaper, opera, orchestra, pep band, political, professional, radio and TV, religious, social, social service, student government, symphony, and yearbook. Popular campus events include April Reign Games, Greek Week, and Dance Marathon.

Sports: There are 11 intercollegiate sports for men and 10 for women, and 18 intramural sports for men and 18 for women. Facilities include an 8000-seat stadium with polyturf and an all-weather track, a 3000-seat gym, baseball fields, and a 6-court tennis complex. The recreation center houses a 200-meter track, a swimming pool, a dance studio, wrestling, gymnastics, and weight rooms, and facilities for basketball, racquetball, volleyball, bowling, and billiards.

Disabled Students: 75% of the campus is accessible. Wheelchair ramps, elevators, special parking, specially equipped rest rooms, special class scheduling, and lowered telephones are available.

Services: Counseling and information services are available, as is tutoring in every subject. There is a reader service for the blind and remedial math, reading, and writing.

Campus Safety and Security: Measures include 24-hour foot and vehicle patrol, security escort services, shuttle buses, and informal discussions. There are pamphlets/posters/films, emergency telephones, and lighted pathways/sidewalks.

Programs of Study: B-W confers B.A., B.S., B.M., B.M.E, and B.S.Ed. degrees. Master's degrees are also awarded. Bachelor's degrees are awarded in BIOLOGICAL SCIENCE (biology/biological science and neurosciences), BUSINESS (business administration and management, institutional management, and sports management), COMMUNICATIONS AND THE ARTS (art history and appreciation, broadcasting, communications, dance, dramatic arts, English, French, German, music, music business management, music history and appreciation, music performance, music theory and composition, musical theater, Spanish, and studio art), COMPUTER AND PHYSICAL SCIENCE (chemistry, computer science, geology, information sciences and systems, mathematics, and physics), EDUCATION (art, business, early childhood, education, elementary, health, middle school, music, physical, science, secondary, and specific learning disabilities), ENGINEERING AND ENVIRONMENTAL DESIGN (preengineering), HEALTH PROFESSIONS (exercise science, medical laboratory technology, mental health/human services, music therapy, predentistry, premedicine, speech pathology/audiology, and sports medicine), SOCIAL SCIENCE (criminal justice, economics, family/consumer studies, history, international relations, international studies, philosophy, physical fitness/movement, political science/government, prelaw, psychology, religion, and sociology). Business, education, and sports and fitness administration are the largest.

Required: All students must complete 124 semester hours and have at least a 2.0 GPA. A total of 45 semester hours must be taken in the liberal arts core, including 20 in humanities, 10 each in natural science and social science, 3 in math/computer science/statistics, and 2 in health and phys ed. Comprehensive exams are required in some majors.

Special: Special academic programs include internships that can qualify for credit, work-study programs, student teaching in England, and study abroad in Europe, India, Japan, Central America, and the Middle East. There is cross-registration within the Cleveland Commission on Higher Education, as well as 3-2 programs in social work and biology with Case Western Reserve University, and in engineering with Columbia, Washington, and Case Western Reserve Universities; a 2-2 co-op allied health program is offered with local community colleges and a 3-2 masters program in accounting and human resources. B-W also offers the Consortium for Music Therapy, accelerated degree programs, a general studies degree, a B.A-B.S. degree, dual and student-designed majors, credit for life, military, and work experience, and pass/fail options. The Continuing Education Program offers degrees through evening and weekend colleges. Concentrations in business include accounting, banking and finance, and marketing. There are 5 national honor societies, a freshman honors program, and 8 departmental honors programs.

Faculty/Classroom: 58% of faculty are male; 42%, female. 99% teach undergraduates. No introductory courses are taught by graduate students. The average class size in an introductory lecture is 22; in a laboratory, 25; and in a regular course, 18.

Admissions: 90% of the 2003-2004 applicants were accepted. The SAT I scores for the 2003-2004 freshman class were: Verbal--25% below 500, 42% between 500 and 599, 30% between 600 and 700, and 3% above 700; Math--25% below 500, 44% between 500 and 599, 26% between 600 and 700, and 5% above 700. The ACT scores were 25% below 21, 28% between 21 and 23, 26% between 24 and 26, 9% between 27 and 28, and 11% above 28. 49% of the current freshmen were in the top fifth of their class; 80% were in the top two fifths. There were 4 National Merit finalists. 23 freshmen graduated first in their class.

Requirements: The SAT I or ACT is required. The recommended minimum score for the ACT is 20; for the SAT I, a composite score of 970. The scores are used to support data from the high school record; alternative scores are considered. Applicants must be graduates of an accredited secondary school or have earned a GED. 16 academic credits are required, including 4 in English, 3 each in math, natural science, and social science, and 2 in a foreign language; alternative distributions are considered. A teacher's recommendation is required. B-W requires applicants to be in the upper 50% of their class. A GPA of 2.75 is required. AP and CLEP credits are accepted. Important factors in the admissions decision are leadership record, extracurricular activities record, and recommendations by school officials.

Procedure: Freshmen are admitted to all sessions. Entrance exams should be taken late in the junior year or early in the senior year. There is a deferred admissions plan. Applications should be filed by May 1 for fall entry, March 15 for spring entry, and June 15 for summer entry, along with a $15 fee. Notification is sent on a rolling basis. Applications are accepted on-line.

Transfer: 388 transfer students enrolled in 2002-2003. Students must be in good academic standing at prior institution(s). College achievement is most important. All official high school and college transcripts must be presented at the time of admission. 32 of 124 credits required for the bachelor's degree must be completed at B-W.

Visiting: There are regularly scheduled orientations for prospective students, including an interview, a tour, and classroom visits. There are guides for informal visits and visitors may sit in on classes and stay overnight. To schedule a visit, contact the Admission Office at *admission@bw.edu*.

Financial Aid: The average freshman award was $14,512. Need-based scholarships or need-based grants averaged $4322 ($13,518 maximum); need-based self-help aid (loans and jobs) averaged $3674 ($7425 maximum); and non-need-based awards and non-need-based scholarships averaged $6515 ($16,500 maximum). 80% of undergraduates work part time. Average annual earnings from campus work are $1000. The average financial indebtedness of the 2003 graduate was $13,688. The FAFSA is required. The priority date for freshman financial aid applications for fall entry is May 1. The deadline for filing freshman financial aid applications for fall entry is September 1.

International Students: There are 52 international students enrolled. The school actively recruits these students. They must score 500 on the written TOEFL and also take the SAT I or the ACT.

Computers: The mainframe is an IBM P620. There are 550 computers located in computer labs throughout the campus. In addition, each student has a network drop for Internet access in their residence hall room. Currently, there are 1604 students who have a PC connected in their room for Internet access. All students may access the system 24 hours a day. There are no time limits and no fees.

Graduates: From July 1, 2002 to June 30, 2003, 815 bachelor's degrees were awarded. The most popular majors were business (31%), education (13%), and sport and fitness administration/management (7%). In an average class, 2% graduate in 3 years or less, 48% graduate in 4 years or less, 64% graduate in 5 years or less, and 66% graduate in 6 years or less. 29 companies recruited on campus in 2002-2003. Of the 2002 graduating class, 33% were enrolled in graduate school within 6 months of graduation and 74% were employed.

Admissions Contact: Susan Dileno, Dean of Admission and Financial Aid. E-mail: *sdileno@bw.edu*

BLUFFTON COLLEGE   B-2
Bluffton, OH 45817

(419) 358-3257
(800) 488-3257; Fax: (419) 358-3232

Full-time: 400 men, 571 women	**Faculty:** 63; IIB, -$
Part-time: 24 men, 61 women	**Ph.D.s:** 75%
Graduate: 25 men, 40 women	**Student/Faculty:** 15 to 1
Year: semesters, summer session	**Tuition:** $17,664
Application Deadline: May 31	**Room & Board:** $6030
Freshman Class: 901 applied, 691 accepted, 236 enrolled	
SAT I Verbal/Math: 536/529	**ACT:** 23 **COMPETITIVE**

Bluffton College, founded in 1899, is a private, Christian, liberal arts institution affiliated with the Mennonite Church, U.S.A. In addition to regional accreditation, Bluffton College has baccalaureate program accreditation with ADA, CSWE, and NASM. The library contains 165,679 volumes, 135,354 microform items, and 1295 audio/video tapes/CDs, and subscribes to 5525 periodicals. Computerized library services include the card catalog, interlibrary loans, database searching, and Internet access. Special learning facilities include a learning resource center, art gallery, radio station, and the Lion and the Lamb Peace Arts Center. The 65-acre campus is in a small town 60 miles south of Toledo and 75 miles north of Dayton. Including any residence halls, there are 25 buildings.

Student Life: 88% of undergraduates are from Ohio. Students are from 21 states and 16 foreign countries. 95% are from public schools. 90% are white. 63% are Protestant; 21% Muslim, Hindu, and Buddhist; 16% Catholic. The average age of freshmen is 18; all undergraduates, 22. 27% do not continue beyond their first year; 57% remain to graduate.

Housing: 828 students can be accommodated in college housing, which includes single-sex and coed dorms. On-campus housing is guaranteed for all 4 years. All students must live in residence halls unless commuting from home. 75% of students live on campus; of those, 50% remain on campus on weekends. Alcohol is not permitted. All students may keep cars.

Activities: There are no fraternities or sororities. There are 40 groups on campus, including art, band, cheerleading, choir, chorale, chorus, dance, dance team, drama, ethnic, honors, international, jazz band, literary magazine, musical theater, newspaper, political, professional, radio and TV, religious, social, social service, student government, and yearbook. Popular campus events include International Week, Spiritual Emphasis Weeks, and Artist Series.

Sports: There are 8 intercollegiate sports for men and 8 for women, and 7 intramural sports for men and 7 for women. Facilities include 2 gyms, an athletic complex, baseball/softball and football fields, an all-weather track, and a 2600-seat stadium.

Disabled Students: 33% of the campus is accessible. Wheelchair ramps, elevators, special parking, specially equipped rest rooms, special class scheduling, lowered drinking fountains, lowered telephones, and special computers for visually impaired students are available.

Services: Counseling and information services are available, as is tutoring in every subject. There is a reader service for the blind and remedial math, reading, and writing. Tutoring is available for most students, as are classes at the student's request and/or faculty designation.

Campus Safety and Security: Measures include informal discussions, pamphlets/posters/films, emergency telephones, and lighted pathways/sidewalks. In a town of only 3500, village police cruisers regularly patrol the campus during night hours. There are also two night security officers who communicate directly with village police and routinely patrol the campus at night.

Programs of Study: Bluffton College confers the B.A. degree. Master's degrees are also awarded. Bachelor's degrees are awarded in BIOLOGICAL SCIENCE (biology/biological science), BUSINESS (accounting, apparel and accessories marketing, business administration and management, organizational behavior, recreational facilities management, and sports management), COMMUNICATIONS AND THE ARTS (art, communications, creative writing, English, music, and Spanish), COMPUTER AND PHYSICAL SCIENCE (chemistry, computer science, information sciences and systems, mathematics, and physical sciences), EDUCATION (early childhood, home economics, middle school, music, and physical), HEALTH PROFESSIONS (premedicine), SOCIAL SCIENCE (child psychology/development, criminal justice, economics, family/consumer studies, food science, history, psychology, religion, social science, social work, and sociology). Business, early childhood education, and organizational management are the largest.

Required: To graduate, students must complete 122 semester hours with 40 to 60 in the major, and have a minimum GPA of 2.0. The general education requirements must be met, and satisfactory achievement in departmental senior comprehensives demonstrated. Distribution requirements are approximately one third for general education requirements, including 6 hours of religion, and one third to one half for the major.

Special: Special arrangements include internships in business, recreation, social work, and education, a Washington semester through the Council for Christian Colleges and Universities, and study abroad. Student-designed majors and independent study are possible, as is credit for prior learning and for learning in voluntary service. There is an accelerated degree program in organizational management. Nondegree study and pass/fail options are offered. There are 2 national honor societies and a freshman honors program.

Faculty/Classroom: 63% of faculty are male; 37%, female. All teach undergraduates. No introductory courses are taught by graduate students. The average class size in an introductory lecture is 23; in a laboratory, 12; and in a regular course, 17.

Admissions: 77% of the 2003-2004 applicants were accepted. The SAT I scores for the 2003-2004 freshman class were: Verbal--37% below 500, 46% between 500 and 599, 14% between 600 and 700, and 3% above 700; Math--41% below 500, 32% between 500 and 599, 24% between 600 and 700, and 3% above 700. The ACT scores were 24% below 21, 30% between 21 and 23, 33% between 24 and 26, 10% between 27 and 28, and 3% above 28. 39% of the current freshmen were in the top fifth of their class; 75% were in the top two fifths. 11 freshmen graduated first in their class.

Requirements: The SAT I or ACT is required, with a required minimum of 920 composite on the SAT I or 19 on the ACT. The ACT is preferred. Others admissions requirements include graduation from an accredited secondary school, with a 2.3 GPA or class rank above 50%. Recommended courses include 4 units of English and 3 units each of math, science, social studies, and a foreign language. The GED is accepted. A personal campus visit and an interview are strongly recommended. Music students must audition. AP and CLEP credits are accepted. Important factors in the admissions decision are recommendations by school officials and extracurricular activities record.

Procedure: Freshmen are admitted to all sessions. Entrance exams should be taken in the spring of the junior year or fall of the senior year. There is a deferred admissions plan and a rolling admissions plan. Applications should be filed by May 31 for fall entry, along with a $20 fee. Notification is sent on a rolling basis. Applications are accepted on-line through the school's web site.

Transfer: 87 transfer students enrolled in 2002-2003. Transfer students must have a minimum college GPA of 2.0, meet eligibility criteria from previous institutions, and have met their financial obligations at the former institution. A signed transfer recommendation must be submitted from each college attended. 30 credits of 122 required for the bachelor's degree must be completed at Bluffton College.

Visiting: There are regularly scheduled orientations for prospective students, including high school preview days on Saturdays and overnight visit programs; personal visits are arranged on a daily basis and are strongly encouraged. There are guides for informal visits and visitors may sit in on classes and stay overnight. To schedule a visit, contact the Office of Admission at *admissions@bluffton.edu*.

Financial Aid: In 2003-2004, all full-time students received some form of financial aid. 88% of full-time freshmen and 71% of continuing full-time students received need-based aid. The average freshman award was $16,665. Need-based scholarships or need-based grants averaged $12,061 ($21,565 maximum); need-based self-help aid (loans and jobs) averaged $4927 ($5475 maximum); and non-need-based awards and non-need-based scholarships averaged $8061 ($12,388 maximum). 66% of undergraduates work part time. Average annual earnings from campus work is $1052. The average financial indebtedness of the 2003 graduate was $20,039. The FAFSA is required. The priority date for freshman financial aid applications for fall entry is May 1. The deadline for filing freshman financial aid applications for fall entry is October 1.

International Students: There are 22 international students enrolled. The school actively recruits these students. They must score 500 on the written TOEFL or 180 on the electronic version and also take the college's own entrance exam. The SAT I is preferred for international students, with a score of 750.

Computers: The mainframe is an IBM AS/400. Networked PCs are available to all students in a central lab and other various locations, including many academic departments. All students have e-mail addresses. All students may access the system any time. There are no time limits and no fees.

Graduates: From July 1, 2002 to June 30, 2003, 224 bachelor's degrees were awarded. The most popular majors were organizational management (25%), early childhood education (11%), and business administration (7%). In an average class, 1% graduate in 3 years or less, 49% graduate in 4 years or less, 57% graduate in 5 years or less, and 57% graduate in 6 years or less. 200 companies recruited on campus in 2002-2003. Of the 2002 graduating class, 9% were enrolled in graduate school within 6 months of graduation and 74% were employed.

Admissions Contact: Eric Fulcomer, Director of Admissions. A video is available. E-mail: *admissions@bluffton.edu* Web: *www.bluffton.edu*

BOWLING GREEN STATE UNIVERSITY   B-1
Bowling Green, OH 43403

(419) 372-2086
(866) 246-6732; Fax: (419) 372-6955

Full-time: 6386 men, 8076 women	Faculty: 739; I, --$
Part-time: 485 men, 534 women	Ph.Ds: 80%
Graduate: 1170 men, 1883 women	Student/Faculty: 20 to 1
Year: semesters, summer session	Tuition: $7144 ($14,104)
Application Deadline: July 15	Room & Board: $5892
Freshman Class: 10,281 applied, 9283 accepted, 3541 enrolled	
SAT I Verbal/Math: 511/507	ACT: 22 COMPETITIVE

Bowling Green State University, founded in 1910, is a public research (intensive) institution offering more than 165 undergraduate and 75 graduate programs. There are 6 undergraduate schools and 1 graduate school. In addition to regional accreditation, BGSU has baccalaureate program accreditation with AACSB, ACCE, ACEJMC, ADA, APTA, ASLA, CAHEA, CSWE, NASAD, NASM, NCATE, and NLN. The 2 libraries contain 2,416,042 volumes, 2,330,490 microform items, and 718,734 audio/video tapes/CDs, and subscribe to 4833 periodicals. Computerized library services include the card catalog, interlibrary loans, and database searching. Special learning facilities include a learning resource center, art gallery, planetarium, radio station, and TV station. The 1230-acre campus is in a small town 25 miles south of Toledo. Including any residence halls, there are 118 buildings.

Student Life: 92% of undergraduates are from Ohio. Students are from 50 states, 77 foreign countries, and Canada. 85% are white. The average age of freshmen is 19; all undergraduates, 21. 26% do not continue beyond their first year; 57% remain to graduate.

Housing: 7000 students can be accommodated in college housing, which includes single-sex and coed dorms, on-campus apartments, fraternity houses, and sorority houses. In addition, there are honors houses, language houses, special-interest houses, a living learning center, and accommodations for international students. 56% of students commute. All students may keep cars.

Activities: 11% of men belong to 19 national fraternities; 14% of women belong to 18 national sororities. There are more than 280 groups on campus, including art, band, cheerleading, chess, choir, chorale, chorus, computers, dance, debate, drama, drill team, ethnic, film, gay, honors, international, jazz band, literary magazine, marching band, musical theater, newspaper, opera, orchestra, pep band, photography, political, professional, radio and TV, religious, social, social service, student government, symphony, and yearbook. Popular campus events include Greek Week, International Festival, and all-campus picnic.

Sports: There are 11 intercollegiate sports for men and 11 for women, and 13 intramural sports for men and 13 for women. Facilities include 4 buildings, including a student recreation center and an intramural field house facility, a 30,000-seat football stadium, a 5000-seat gym, tennis courts, a golf course, basketball and ice arenas, and softball and intramural fields.

Disabled Students: 80% of the campus is accessible. Wheelchair ramps, elevators, special parking, specially equipped rest rooms, special class scheduling, lowered drinking fountains, lowered telephones, and a shuttle van with lift capabilities are available.

Services: Counseling and information services are available, as is tutoring in some subjects, including writing, math, and 100-level content area classes such as biology, chemistry, and sociology. There is a reader service for the blind and remedial math, reading, and writing.

Campus Safety and Security: Measures include 24-hour foot and vehicle patrol, security escort services, shuttle buses, and informal discussions. There are pamphlets/posters/films, emergency telephones, lighted pathways/sidewalks, and a campus 911 number.

Programs of Study: BGSU confers B.A., B.S., B.A.C., B.F.A., B.A.H.S., B.L.S., B.Mus., B.S.A.M.P.D., B.S.C.F.R.M., B.S.B.A., B.S. in Econ., B.S.Ed., B.S.F.S.N., B.S.J., B.S.Tech., B.S. Applied Microbiology, B.S.A.Therapy, B.S. Child and Family Community Services, B.S. Criminal Justice, B.S. Dietetics, B.S. Environmental Health, B.S. Gerontology, B.S. Interior Design, B.S. Medical Technology, B.S.N., B.S.N.S., B.S.P.T., B.S.S.W., B.S. Communication Disorders degrees. Master's and doctoral degrees are also awarded. Bachelor's degrees are awarded in BIOLOGICAL SCIENCE (avian sciences, biochemistry, biology/biological science, life science, microbiology, neurosciences, and nutrition), BUSINESS (accounting, apparel and accessories marketing, banking and finance, business administration and management, business economics, business law, fashion merchandising, hospitality management services, hotel/motel and restaurant management, institutional management, international business management, labor studies, management information systems, marketing/retailing/merchandising, personnel management, purchasing/inventory management, recreation and leisure services, sports management, and tourism), COMMUNICATIONS AND THE ARTS (art, art history and appreciation, broadcasting, communications, creative writing, dance, design, dramatic arts, English, film arts, fine arts, French, German, jazz, journalism, Latin, music performance, music theory and composition, Russian, Spanish, technical and business writing, and telecommunications), COMPUTER AND PHYSI-

CAL SCIENCE (chemistry, computer science, geology, information sciences and systems, mathematics, physical sciences, physics, and statistics), EDUCATION (art, business, early childhood, elementary, foreign languages, health, home economics, marketing and distribution, music, physical, secondary, special, and technical), ENGINEERING AND ENVIRONMENTAL DESIGN (computer technology, construction technology, environmental design, environmental science, industrial engineering technology, interior design, manufacturing technology, and mechanical design technology), HEALTH PROFESSIONS (art therapy, environmental health science, exercise science, health care administration, health science, medical laboratory technology, nursing, physical therapy, pre-medicine, and speech pathology/audiology), SOCIAL SCIENCE (African studies, American studies, Asian/Oriental studies, child care/child and family studies, classical/ancient civilization, criminal justice, dietetics, economics, ethnic studies, family/consumer resource management, food science, geography, gerontology, history, international studies, liberal arts/general studies, parks and recreation management, philosophy, physical fitness/movement, political science/government, psychology, public administration, social science, social work, sociology, and women's studies). Education, marketing, and biology are the largest.

Required: To graduate, students must complete a minimum of 122 semester hours, including at least 30 in the major, depending on the major, and maintain a minimum 2.0 GPA. The 8-course mandatory general education core includes 2 courses each from natural sciences, social sciences, and humanities and the arts, 1 course from cultural diversity in the United States, and 1 additional course from among natural sciences, social sciences, humanities and the arts, and foreign languages and cultures. At least one of the courses in the social sciences or humanities and arts must be designated as foreign cultures or foreign language at the 200 level or above.

Special: Special academic programs include co-op programs in all majors with the National Student Exchange, internships, a Washington semester, work-study, and study abroad. Dual majors are available in all programs, and a B.A.-B.S. degree is offered in computer science, geology, math, psychology, statistics, scientific and technical communication, and individualized planned program. Student-designed majors, independent study, credit for experience, nondegree study, and pass/fail options are possible. There are 20 national honor societies, including Phi Beta Kappa, a freshman honors program, and 40 departmental honors programs.

Faculty/Classroom: 56% of faculty are male; 44%, female. 84% teach undergraduates. Graduate students teach 23% of introductory courses. The average class size in an introductory lecture is 28; in a laboratory, 17; and in a regular course, 23.

Admissions: 90% of the 2003-2004 applicants were accepted. The SAT I scores for the 2003-2004 freshman class were: Verbal--46% below 500, 37% between 500 and 599, 13% between 600 and 700, and 3% above 700; Math--48% below 500, 36% between 500 and 599, 14% between 600 and 700, and 3% above 700. The ACT scores were 43% below 21, 32% between 21 and 23, 15% between 24 and 26, 5% between 27 and 28, and 5% above 28. 23% of the current freshmen were in the top fifth of their class; 53% were in the top two fifths. There were 20 National Merit finalists.

Requirements: The ACT is required and the SAT I is recommended. For all freshmen except those out of high school for 3 or more years, the minimum composite SAT I score is 920 and the minimum ACT score is 20. Performance and test scores must be at minimum and above to be considered. There is no automatic admission. Special circumstances are reviewed as applicable. Other admissions requirements include graduation from an accredited secondary school with a recommended 4 years of English, 3 years each of math, science, and social studies/history, 2 years of a foreign language, and 1 year of art or music. The GED is accepted. Music students must audition. A GPA of 2.5 is required. AP and CLEP credits are accepted. Important factors in the admissions decision are advanced placement or honor courses, recommendations by school officials, and evidence of special talent.

Procedure: Freshmen are admitted to all sessions. Entrance exams should be taken in the junior year. There is a deferred admissions plan. Applications should be filed by July 15 for fall entry, December 15 for spring entry, and May 15 for summer entry. The fall 2003 application fee was $35. Notification is sent on a rolling basis. Applications are accepted on-line through the school's web site.

Transfer: 647 transfer students enrolled in 2002-2003. Transfer students who have attempted 12 or more hours at a college are eligible. Applicants with 60 or more semester hours or an associate's degree must have at least a 2.0 GPA; those with fewer hours need a minimum GPA of 2.5 but may petition for admission if it is lower. 30 of 122 credits required for the bachelor's degree must be completed at BGSU.

Visiting: There are regularly scheduled orientations for prospective students. There are guides for informal visits and visitors may sit in on classes and stay overnight. To schedule a visit, contact the Office of Admissions at (419) 372-BGSU or admissions@bgnet.bgsu.edu.

Financial Aid: In 2003-2004, 79% of all full-time freshmen and 75% of continuing full-time students received some form of financial aid. 56% of full-time freshmen and 51% of continuing full-time students received

need-based aid. The average freshman award was $7800. Need-based scholarships or need-based grants averaged $3300; need-based self-help aid (loans and jobs) averaged $2700; and non-need-based athletic scholarships averaged $11,700. The average financial indebtedness of the 2003 graduate was $17,967. BGSU is a member of CSS. The FAFSA is required.

International Students: There are 153 international students enrolled. The school actively recruits these students. They must score 500 on the written TOEFL or 173 on the electronic version or take the MELAB.

Computers: The mainframes are an IBM 9121, an IBM 9221, the Sun SPARCserver cluster, SGI PowerChallenge L, a BGUNIX, a VAX 6620, and Sun workstations. There are about 6240 computers available in computer labs and in residence halls. Students are able to get accounts on university mainframes through specified classes. All students can receive a BGNet account that provides access to the World Wide Web. All students may access the system during operating hours. There are no time limits and no fees.

Graduates: From July 1, 2002 to June 30, 2003, 3104 bachelor's degrees were awarded. The most popular majors were kindergarten/preschool education and teaching (6%), speech and rhetorical studies (5%), and psychology (4%). In an average class, 33% graduate in 4 years or less, 57% graduate in 5 years or less, and 61% graduate in 6 years or less.

Admissions Contact: Gary Swegan, Director of Admissions. A video is available. E-mail: admissions@bgnet.bgsu.edu
Web: www.bgsu.edu/offices/admissions/choose/welcome.html

CAPITAL UNIVERSITY
Columbus, OH 43209-2394

C-3
(614) 236-6101
(800) 289-6289; Fax: (614) 236-6926

Full-time: 818 men, 1335 women	**Faculty:** 178; IIA, -$
Part-time: 188 men, 489 women	**Ph.D.s:** n/av
Graduate: 596 men, 533 women	**Student/Faculty:** 12 to 1
Year: semesters, summer session	**Tuition:** $20,500
Application Deadline: April 15	**Room & Board:** $6050
Freshman Class: n/av	
SAT I or ACT: required	**COMPETITIVE**

Capital University, established in 1830, is a private institution affiliated with the Evangelical Lutheran Church in America. Its undergraduate and graduate programs emphasize the liberal arts and sciences, music, and nursing. There are 4 undergraduate and 3 graduate schools. In addition to regional accreditation, Capital has baccalaureate program accreditation with ABA, ACBSP, ACS, CCNE, CSWE, NASM, NCATE, and NLN. The 2 libraries contain 190,987 volumes, 148,561 microform items, and 15,299 audio/video tapes/CDs, and subscribe to 5765 periodicals. Computerized library services include the card catalog, interlibrary loans, and database searching. Special learning facilities include an art gallery and a TV studio. The 48-acre campus is in a suburban area 3 miles east of downtown Columbus. Including any residence halls, there are 24 buildings.

Student Life: 93% of undergraduates are from Ohio. Students are from 24 states and 11 foreign countries. 78% are white; 14% African American. 51% are Protestant; 20% Catholic; 13% claim no religious affiliation. The average age of freshmen is 18; all undergraduates, 20. 21% do not continue beyond their first year; 57% remain to graduate.

Housing: 1155 students can be accommodated in college housing, which includes coed dorms, on-campus apartments, and off-campus apartments. In addition, there are special-interest floors, substance-free floors, Greek organization floors, and a self-governing unit. On-campus housing is guaranteed for all 4 years. 52% of students commute. Upperclassmen may keep cars.

Activities: There are many groups and organizations on campus, including art, band, cheerleading, choir, chorale, chorus, dance, debate, drama, drill team, ethnic, gay, honors, international, jazz band, literary magazine, musical theater, newspaper, opera, orchestra, pep band, political, professional, radio and TV, religious, social, social service, student government, symphony, and yearbook.

Sports: There are 8 intercollegiate sports for men and 6 for women, and 9 intramural sports for men and 9 for women. Facilities include a 2500-seat football stadium, a 2400-seat gym, tennis courts, and weight and game rooms. The recreation center offers bowling, billiards, and other game facilities.

Disabled Students: Elevators, special parking, specially equipped rest rooms, and special class scheduling are available.

Services: Counseling and information services are available, as is tutoring in most subjects. There is remedial math and writing.

Campus Safety and Security: Measures include 24-hour foot and vehicle patrol, self-defense education, security escort services, and shuttle buses. There are pamphlets/posters/films and lighted pathways/sidewalks.

Programs of Study: Capital confers B.A., B.F.A., B.G.S., B.M., B.S.N., and B.S.W. degrees. Master's degrees are also awarded. Bachelor's degrees are awarded in BIOLOGICAL SCIENCE (biochemistry and biology/biological science), BUSINESS (accounting and business administration and management), COMMUNICATIONS AND THE ARTS (communications, dramatic arts, English, fine arts, French, music, public relations, Spanish, and speech/debate/rhetoric), COMPUTER AND PHYSICAL SCIENCE (chemistry, computer science, and mathematics), EDUCATION (elementary, middle school, physical, and secondary), ENGINEERING AND ENVIRONMENTAL DESIGN (environmental science), HEALTH PROFESSIONS (art therapy, nursing, predentistry, premedicine, and sports medicine), SOCIAL SCIENCE (behavioral science, criminal justice, economics, history, international relations, philosophy, physical fitness/movement, political science/government, prelaw, psychology, religion, social work, and sociology). Business, education, and history are the largest.

Required: To graduate, all students must complete at least 124 semester hours, with a varying number of hours in the major, and maintain a minimum 2.0 GPA. The university core, 36 semester hours, must be followed in an ordered sequence throughout the 4 years; considered an assessment program, it includes specific courses in reading and writing, communication, health, art, science, social science, the humanities, ethics, and religion.

Special: Special academic programs include cross-registration with the Higher Education Council of Columbus, semester internships in most majors, and a Washington semester. Study abroad in 21 countries on 5 continents includes opportunities in Jamaica and at the Kodaly Institute of Music in Hungary. Also possible are a general studies degree and student-designed majors. A dual degree in engineering is offered with Case Western Reserve University and Washington University in St. Louis. Credit for life, military, and work experience may be granted, and non-degree study and pass/fail options are offered. There is a freshman honors program.

Faculty/Classroom: 55% of faculty are male; 45%, female. 80% teach undergraduates. No introductory courses are taught by graduate students. The average class size in an introductory lecture is 30; in a laboratory, 12; and in a regular course, 17.

Admissions: 42% of the current freshmen were in the top fifth of their class; 74% were in the top two fifths.

Requirements: The SAT I or ACT is required. In addition, other admissions requirements include graduation from an accredited secondary school with 16 academic credits, including 4 units of English, 3 each of math, science, and social science, 2 units of a foreign language, and 1 of electives; nursing applicants need chemistry. The GED is accepted. High school students must submit recommendations from their guidance counselor. An interview is recommended. Students must audition for entry to the Conservatory of Music. A GPA of 2.6 is required. AP and CLEP credits are accepted. Important factors in the admissions decision are advanced placement or honor courses, recommendations by school officials, and evidence of special talent.

Procedure: Freshmen are admitted to all sessions. Entrance exams should be taken by December of the senior year. There are early admissions and deferred admissions plans. There is a rolling admissions plan. Applications should be filed by April 15 for fall entry, December 1 for winter entry, and April 1 for summer entry, along with a $25 fee. Notification is sent on a rolling basis beginning October 2. 846 early decision candidates were accepted for the 2003-2004 class. Applications are accepted on-line through the school's web site.

Transfer: 95 transfer students enrolled in 2002-2003. Transfer students must have a minimum college GPA of 2.25. The SAT I or ACT is recommended, as is an interview. 30 credits of 124 required for the bachelor's degree must be completed at Capital.

Visiting: There are regularly scheduled orientations for prospective students, including an interview with a counselor and a campus tour. There are guides for informal visits and visitors may sit in on classes and stay overnight. To schedule a visit, contact the Admissions Office at admissions@capital.edu.

Financial Aid: In 2003-2004, 88% of all full-time freshmen and 82% of continuing full-time students received some form of financial aid. The average freshman award was $15,250. The average financial indebtedness of the 2003 graduate was $25,171. Capital is a member of CSS. The FAFSA is required. The deadline for filing freshman financial aid applications for fall entry is April 1.

International Students: There are 16 international students enrolled. The school actively recruits these students. They must score 500 on the written TOEFL.

Computers: The mainframe is a Sun UltraSPARC II. There are 6 general labs and 90 PCs. The campus is fully networked, including residence hall rooms, a 25-station technology classroom, and an advanced computational lab. All students may access the system 24 hours per day. There are no time limits and no fees.

Graduates: From July 1, 2002 to June 30, 2003, 600 bachelor's degrees were awarded. In an average class, 48% graduate in 4 years or less, 57% graduate in 5 years or less, and 59% graduate in 6 years or less. 27 companies recruited on campus in 2002-2003.

Admissions Contact: Kimberly V. Ebbrecht, Director of Admission. A video is available. E-mail: admissions@capital.edu Web: www.capital.edu

CASE WESTERN RESERVE UNIVERSITY D-1
Cleveland, OH 44106 (216) 368-4450; Fax: (216) 368-5111

Full-time: 2013 men, 1301 women	Faculty: 459; I, +$
Part-time: 159 men, 114 women	Ph.D.s: 95%
Graduate: 2931 men, 2668 women	Student/Faculty: 7 to 1
Year: semesters, summer session	Tuition: $24,342
Application Deadline: January 15	Room & Board: $7660
Freshman Class: 4680 applied, 3525 accepted, 878 enrolled	
SAT I Verbal/Math: 650/680	ACT: 29 MOST COMPETITIVE

Case Western Reserve University, founded in 1826, is a private institution offering undergraduate, graduate, and professional programs in arts and sciences, dentistry, engineering, law, management, medicine, nursing, and social work. There are 4 undergraduate and 7 graduate schools. In addition to regional accreditation, Case has baccalaureate program accreditation with AACSB, ABET, CAHEA, CSAB, NASM, and NLN. The 7 libraries contain 2,236,337 volumes, 2,475,337 microform items, and 49,889 audio/video tapes/CDs, and subscribe to 17,506 periodicals. Computerized library services include the card catalog, interlibrary loans, and database searching. Special learning facilities include a learning resource center, art gallery, natural history museum, planetarium, radio station, and a biology field station. The 155-acre campus is in an urban area 4 miles east of downtown Cleveland. Including any residence halls, there are 87 buildings.

Student Life: 56% of undergraduates are from Ohio. Students are from 49 states, 24 foreign countries, and Canada. 70% are from public schools. 70% are white; 15% Asian American. The average age of freshmen is 18; all undergraduates, 20. 7% do not continue beyond their first year; 77% remain to graduate.

Housing: 2285 students can be accommodated in college housing, which includes single-sex and coed dorms, fraternity houses, sorority houses, and special housing for students in the College Scholars Program. On-campus housing is guaranteed for all 4 years. 76% of students live on campus; of those, 85% remain on campus on weekends. All students may keep cars.

Activities: 34% of men belong to 18 national fraternities; 17% of women belong to 1 local and 4 national sororities. There are 100 groups on campus, including art, cheerleading, chess, choir, chorale, computers, dance, debate, drama, ethnic, film, gay, honors, international, jazz band, literary magazine, marching band, musical theater, newspaper, orchestra, photography, political, professional, radio, religious, social, social service, student government, symphonic winds ensemble, and yearbook. Popular campus events include Hudson Relays, Greek Week, and Springfest.

Sports: There are 10 intercollegiate sports for men and 9 for women, and 30 intramural sports for men and 30 for women. Facilities include a gym with multipurpose rooms, football, baseball, and soccer fields, indoor and all-weather tracks, softball diamonds, a swimming pool, weight, fencing, and wrestling rooms, basketball, badminton, volleyball, squash, tennis, and racquetball courts, and an archery range.

Disabled Students: Wheelchair ramps, elevators, special parking, specially equipped rest rooms, special class scheduling, lowered drinking fountains, lowered telephones, TDD, special testing arrangements, notetaking assistance, and individualized academic counseling and planning are available.

Services: Counseling and information services are available, as is tutoring in every subject. There is a reader service for the blind, seminars to improve computing skills and study strategies, and supplemental instruction in designated courses in biology, chemistry, math, and physics.

Campus Safety and Security: Measures include 24-hour foot and vehicle patrol, self-defense education, security escort services, and shuttle buses. There are informal discussions, pamphlets/posters/films, emergency telephones, lighted pathways/sidewalks, and property crime prevention programs, including bicycle lock rental, vehicle ID etching, and equipment bolting.

Programs of Study: Case confers B.A., B.S., B.S.E., and B.S.N. degrees. Master's and doctoral degrees are also awarded. Bachelor's degrees are awarded in BIOLOGICAL SCIENCE (biochemistry, biology/biological science, evolutionary biology, and nutrition), BUSINESS (accounting and business administration and management), COMMUNICATIONS AND THE ARTS (art history and appreciation, classics, comparative literature, dramatic arts, English, French, German, music, and Spanish), COMPUTER AND PHYSICAL SCIENCE (applied mathematics, astronomy, chemistry, computer science, fluid and thermal science, geology, mathematics, natural sciences, physics, polymer science, and statistics), EDUCATION (art and music), ENGINEERING AND ENVIRONMENTAL DESIGN (aeronautical engineering, biomedical engineering, chemical engineering, civil engineering, computer engineering, electrical/electronics engineering, engineering, engineering physics, environmental science, materials science, mechanical engineering, and systems engineering), HEALTH PROFESSIONS (nursing and speech pathology/audiology), SOCIAL SCIENCE (American studies, anthropology, Asian/Oriental studies, economics, food science, French studies, German area studies, gerontology, history, history of science, international studies, Japanese studies, philosophy, political science/government, psychology, religion, sociology, and women's studies). Engineering, accounting, and biology are the strongest academically. Engineering, biology, and management are the largest.

Required: To graduate, students must complete a minimum of 120 semester hours, with at least 30 hours in the major, and maintain a minimum GPA of 2.0. Students must complete a core curriculum as well as courses in English composition and phys ed.

Special: Case offers co-op programs with more than 160 employers; students may alternate classroom study with full-time employment. Cross-registration with 13 institutions in the Cleveland area is available, as well as internships in government, corporations, and nonprofit agencies. Students may participate in study abroad, a Washington semester, work-study programs, and accelerated-degree programs. B.A.-B.S. degrees, dual and student-designed majors, 3-2 engineering degrees, non-degree study, independent study, and pass/fail options are possible. There are extensive opportunities for undergraduates to work with faculty on research projects. Preprofessional Scholars Programs in medicine, dentistry, and law are available. Interdisciplinary majors, such as environmental geology and a double major in pre-architecture, and intradisciplinary majors, such as nutritional biochemistry and metabolism, are available. There are 3 national honor societies, including Phi Beta Kappa.

Faculty/Classroom: 69% of faculty are male; 31%, female. 77% teach undergraduates, 95% do research, and 77% do both. Graduate students teach 5% of introductory courses. The average class size in an introductory lecture is 35 and in a regular course, 27.

Admissions: 75% of the 2003-2004 applicants were accepted. The SAT I scores for the 2003-2004 freshman class were: Verbal--6% below 500, 21% between 500 and 599, 44% between 600 and 700, and 29% above 700; Math--1% below 500, 15% between 500 and 599, 40% between 600 and 700, and 44% above 700. The ACT scores were 2% below 21, 8% between 21 and 23, 20% between 24 and 26, 16% between 27 and 28, and 54% above 28. 84% of the current freshmen were in the top fifth of their class; 96% were in the top two fifths. There were 59 National Merit finalists. 72 freshmen graduated first in their class.

Requirements: The SAT I or ACT is required. In addition, SAT II: Subject tests in writing plus 2 others of the student's choice are strongly recommended for students who take the SAT I. Applicants must be graduates of an accredited secondary school. The GED is accepted. 16 high school academic credits are required, including 4 years of English, 3 of math, (4 for science, math, and engineering majors), and 1 of lab science (2 for science and math majors and premedical students). 2 to 4 years of foreign language are strongly recommended. Engineering, math, and science students should take the SAT II: Subject tests in math I/IC of IIC and physics and/or chemistry. A writing sample of the student's choice is required, and an interview is recommended. AP credits are accepted. Important factors in the admissions decision are advanced placement or honor courses, leadership record, and recommendations by school officials.

Procedure: Freshmen are admitted fall, spring, and summer. Entrance exams should be taken by the fall of the senior year; CWRU recommends also taking the test during the spring of the junior year. There is a deferred admissions plan. Applications should be filed by January 15 for fall entry. The application fee for fall 2003 was $35 (there is no fee for on-line applications). Notification is sent March 1. 90 early decision candidates were accepted for the 2003-2004 class. 243 applicants were on the 2003 waiting list; 117 were admitted. Applications are accepted on-line through the school's web site and Common Application.

Transfer: 83 transfer students enrolled in 2002-2003. Transfer students should have a minimum GPA of 3.0 and meet all high school requirements. Grades of C or better transfer for credit. 60 of 120 credits required for the bachelor's degree must be completed at Case.

Visiting: There are regularly scheduled orientations for prospective students. There are guides for informal visits and visitors may sit in on classes and stay overnight. To schedule a visit, contact the Office of Undergraduate Admission at *admission@case.edu*.

Financial Aid: In 2002-2003, 90% of all full-time freshmen and 91% of continuing full-time students received some form of financial aid. 63% of full-time freshmen and 51% of continuing full-time students received need-based aid. The average freshman award was $21,877. 70% of undergraduates work part time. Average annual earnings from campus work are $2900. The average financial indebtedness of the 2002 graduate was $21,830. Case is a member of CSS. The CSS Profile or FAFSA and parent and student income tax returns and W-2 forms are required. The deadline for filing freshman financial aid applications for fall entry is February 15.

International Students: There are 158 international students enrolled. The school actively recruits these students. They must score 550 on the written TOEFL or 213 on the electronic version and also complete 30 hours of instruction at Case's English Language Center.

Computers: The mainframe is an IBM 9672-R22. Case's network links more than 12,800 campus locations—classrooms, libraries, residence halls, and labs—with the switched-gigabyte to the desktop standard. There are also more than 1200 wireless access points. All students may

access the system 24 hours a day. There are no time limits and no fees, but students living in residence halls pay a $400 annual technology fee. It is strongly recommended that all students have a personal computer. Windows and Mac models configured to use CWRUnet are recommended.

Graduates: From July 1, 2002 to June 30, 2003, 724 bachelor's degrees were awarded. The most popular majors were management (10%), biology (8%), and mechanical engineering (7%). In an average class, 1% graduate in 3 years or less, 55% graduate in 4 years or less, 75% graduate in 5 years or less, and 77% graduate in 6 years or less. 150 companies recruited on campus in 2002-2003. Of the 2002 graduating class, 41% were enrolled in graduate school within 6 months of graduation and 62% were employed.

Admissions Contact: Director of Undergraduate Admission. A video is available. E-mail: *admission@case.edu* Web: *http://www.case.edu*

CEDARVILLE UNIVERSITY
Cedarville, OH 45314-0601

B-4

(937) 766-3200
(800) CEDARVILLE; Fax: (937) 766-2760

Full-time: 1308 men, 1522 women	**Faculty:** 200; IIB, -$
Part-time: 70 men, 96 women	**Ph.D.s:** 63%
Graduate: 8 men, 12 women	**Student/Faculty:** 14 to 1
Year: semesters, summer session	**Tuition:** $14,944
Application Deadline: open	**Room & Board:** $5010
Freshman Class: 2174 applied, 1762 accepted, 787 enrolled	
SAT I Verbal/Math: 590/590	**ACT:** 25 **VERY COMPETITIVE**

Cedarville University, formerly Cedarville College, founded in 1887, is a private Baptist college of arts and sciences offering programs in engineering, nursing, accounting, computer information systems, and education. The school is known for its religious commitment, conservative values, and community outreach programs. In addition to regional accreditation, Cedarville has baccalaureate program accreditation with ABET and NLN. The library contains 179,306 volumes, 22,001 microform items, and 4939 audio/video tapes/CDs, and subscribes to 929 periodicals. Computerized library services include the card catalog, interlibrary loans, database searching, and Internet access. Special learning facilities include a learning resource center, radio station, media resource center, and observatory. The 400-acre campus is in a small town 12 miles south of Springfield. Including any residence halls, there are 45 buildings.

Student Life: 66% of undergraduates are from out of state, mostly the Midwest. Students are from 47 states, 14 foreign countries, and Canada. 53% are from public schools. 96% are white. All are Protestant. The average age of freshmen is 18; all undergraduates, 20. 14% do not continue beyond their first year; 58% remain to graduate.

Housing: 2523 students can be accommodated in college housing, which includes single-sex dorms and married-student housing. On-campus housing is guaranteed for all 4 years. 82% of students live on campus; of those, 80% remain on campus on weekends. Alcohol is not permitted. All students may keep cars.

Activities: There are no fraternities or sororities. There are 49 groups on campus, including band, cheerleading, choir, chorale, chorus, debate, drama, ethnic, forensics, honors, international, jazz band, newspaper, orchestra, pep band, photography, political, professional, radio and TV, religious, social, social service, student government, and yearbook. Popular campus events include Lil' Sibs Weekend and Homecoming.

Sports: There are 7 intercollegiate sports for men and 7 for women, and 28 intramural sports for men and 28 for women. Facilities include a 3500-seat gym, 5 basketball courts, an indoor track, 3 volleyball courts, 3 racquetball courts, badminton courts, a batting cage, a weight room, a training room, 9 outdoor tennis courts, a 400m 9-lane track, soccer, baseball, softball, and intramural playing fields, and an indoor jogging track.

Disabled Students: 60% of the campus is accessible. Wheelchair ramps, elevators, special parking, specially equipped rest rooms, special class scheduling, lowered drinking fountains, and lowered telephones are available.

Services: Counseling and information services are available, as is tutoring in some subjects, including specific social science, calculus, and science courses. There is a reader service for the blind and remedial math, reading, and writing.

Campus Safety and Security: Measures include 24-hour foot and vehicle patrol, security escort services, informal discussions, and pamphlets/posters/films. There are emergency telephones and lighted pathways/sidewalks.

Programs of Study: Cedarville confers B.A., B.S., B.M.E., B.S.E.E., B.S.M.E., and B.S.N. degrees. Associate and master's degrees are also awarded. Bachelor's degrees are awarded in BIOLOGICAL SCIENCE (biology/biological science), BUSINESS (accounting, banking and finance, business administration and management, management information systems, marketing/retailing/merchandising, and sports management), COMMUNICATIONS AND THE ARTS (communications, dramatic arts, English, graphic design, multimedia, music, Spanish, and technical and business writing), COMPUTER AND PHYSICAL SCI-

ENCE (chemistry, computer science, information sciences and systems, mathematics, and physics), EDUCATION (athletic training, Christian, early childhood, foreign languages, mathematics, middle school, music, physical, science, social studies, and special), ENGINEERING AND ENVIRONMENTAL DESIGN (computer engineering, electrical/electronics engineering, and mechanical engineering), HEALTH PROFESSIONS (exercise science and nursing), SOCIAL SCIENCE (American studies, biblical studies, criminal justice, history, international studies, missions, pastoral studies, philosophy, political science/government, prelaw, psychology, public administration, religious music, social work, and sociology). Business, education, and science are the largest.

Required: To graduate, all students must maintain a minimum GPA of 2.0 while taking 128 semester hours. General education requirements include 16 semester hours of biblical education, 10 of science and math, 9 of humanities, 9 of social sciences and history, 6 of communication, and 2 of phys ed. Students must demonstrate proficiency in English and math and must fulfill the global awareness requirement through foreign language study or intercultural experience.

Special: Internships, study abroad in 15 countries, a Washington semester, dual majors, student-designed majors, B.A.-B.S. degrees in biology, chemistry, and math, work-study programs with the college, and pass/fail options are available. Cross-registration with Southwest Ohio Consortium for Higher Education and the Ohio Learning Network is possible. There are 3 national honor societies, a freshman honors program, and 1 departmental honors program.

Faculty/Classroom: 73% of faculty are male; 27%, female. All teach undergraduates. The average class size in an introductory lecture is 38; in a laboratory, 15; and in a regular course, 20.

Admissions: 81% of the 2003-2004 applicants were accepted. The SAT I scores for the 2003-2004 freshman class were: Verbal--9% below 500, 42% between 500 and 599, 37% between 600 and 700, and 12% above 700; Math--13% below 500, 41% between 500 and 599, 36% between 600 and 700, and 8% above 700. The ACT scores were 5% below 21, 23% between 21 and 23, 30% between 24 and 26, 16% between 27 and 28, and 27% above 28. 54% of the current freshmen were in the top fifth of their class; 84% were in the top two fifths. There were 9 National Merit finalists and 4 semifinalists. 82 freshmen graduated first in their class.

Requirements: The SAT I or ACT (preferred) is required, with scores above the national average preferred. The university recommends that applicants have 4 years of English and 3 each of social studies, math, science, and a foreign language. The GED is accepted. Recommendations from a local pastor and a high school counselor are required. An interview is recommended. Cedarville requires applicants to be in the upper 50% of their class. A GPA of 3.0 is required. AP and CLEP credits are accepted. Important factors in the admissions decision are personality/intangible qualities, recommendations by school officials, and advanced placement or honor courses.

Procedure: Freshmen are admitted to all sessions. Entrance exams should be taken by December of the senior year. There are early admissions and deferred admissions plans. Application deadlines are open. Notification is on a rolling basis. The application fee for fall 2003 was $30. A waiting list is an active part of the admissions procedure. Applications are accepted on-line through the school's web site *www.cedarville.edu\admissions.*

Transfer: 123 transfer students enrolled in 2002-2003. Applicants must have a minimum college GPA of 3.0. The SAT I or ACT (preferred) is required. 32 of 128 credits required for the bachelor's degree must be completed at Cedarville.

Visiting: There are regularly scheduled orientations for prospective students, including campus tours, chapel services, class visits, and meetings with faculty, coaches, and admissions counselors. There are guides for informal visits and visitors may sit in on classes and stay overnight. To schedule a visit, contact the Admissions Office at *admissions@cedarville.edu.*

Financial Aid: In 2003-2004, 94% of all full-time freshmen and 83% of continuing full-time students received some form of financial aid. 72% of full-time freshmen and 66% of continuing full-time students received need-based aid. The average freshman award was $11,931. Need-based scholarships or need-based grants averaged $4162 ($15,941 maximum); need-based self-help aid (loans and jobs) averaged $3069 ($9000 maximum); non-need-based athletic scholarships averaged $4754 ($19,500 maximum); and other non-need-based awards and non-need-based scholarships averaged $9598 ($23,347 maximum). 47% of undergraduates work part time. Average annual earnings from campus work are $709. The average financial indebtedness of the 2003 graduate was $26,739. The FAFSA and the university's own financial statement are required. The deadline for filing freshman financial aid applications for fall entry is March 1.

International Students: There were 12 international students enrolled in a recent year. They must score 550 on the written TOEFL or 213 on the electronic version and also take the SAT I or the ACT.

Computers: The mainframe is an HP 9000/800, model rp5470. A network connects 5 public computer labs with more than 140 PCs and about 1250 residence hall rooms, which are equipped with PCs and printers. The network provides access to more than 150 software packages, library resources, e-mail, and the Internet. Cedarville is a participant in Internet2. All students may access the system 24 hours a day from dorm rooms or up to 93 hours a week in the labs. There are no time limits and no fees.

Graduates: From July 1, 2002 to June 30, 2003, 626 bachelor's degrees were awarded. The most popular majors were communication arts (7%), biology (6%), and nursing (6%). In an average class, 4% graduate in 3 years or less, 57% graduate in 4 years or less, 68% graduate in 5 years or less, and 74% graduate in 6 years or less. 268 companies recruited on campus in 2002-2003. Of the 2002 graduating class, 11% were enrolled in graduate school within 6 months of graduation and 92% were employed.

Admissions Contact: David Ormsbee, Vice President for Enrollment Management. A video is available. E-mail: *admissions@cedarville.edu* Web: *http://www.cedarville.edu*

CENTRAL STATE UNIVERSITY
Wilberforce, OH 45384

B-4
(937) 376-6348
(800) 388-CSU1; Fax: (937) 376-6648

Full-time: 560 men, 645 women	Faculty: 77; IIB, -$
Part-time: 55 men, 70 women	Ph.D.s: 62%
Graduate: 30 men, 55 women	Student/Faculty: 16 to 1
Year: quarters, summer session	Tuition: $3715 ($8120)
Application Deadline: see profile	Room & Board: $5210
Freshman Class: n/av	ACT: required COMPETITIVE+

Central State University, founded in 1887, is a public institution offering programs in liberal arts, business, engineering, teacher preparation, and professional training. There are 3 undergraduate schools and 1 graduate school. Figures in this capsule and in this profile are approximate. In addition to regional accreditation, Central State has baccalaureate program accreditation with ABET and NASM. The library contains 179,241 volumes, 622,727 microform items, and 500 audio/video tapes/CDs, and subscribes to 26,316 periodicals. Computerized library services include the card catalog, interlibrary loans, and database searching. Special learning facilities include a learning resource center, art gallery, radio station, and the National Afro-American Museum and Cultural Center. The 60-acre campus is in a rural area 18 miles east of Dayton. Including any residence halls, there are 34 buildings.

Student Life: 77% of undergraduates are from Ohio. Students are from 24 states and 2 foreign countries. 96% are African American. The average age of freshmen is 18; all undergraduates, 22. 42% do not continue beyond their first year; 23% remain to graduate.

Housing: 745 students can be accommodated in college housing, which includes single-sex dorms. On-campus housing is guaranteed for the freshman year only and is available on a first-come, first-served basis. 57% of students live on campus. Alcohol is not permitted. All students may keep cars.

Activities: 1% of men belong to 2 national fraternities; 1% of women belong to 2 national sororities. There are 30 groups on campus, including art, band, cheerleading, choir, chorale, chorus, drama, drill team, ethnic, honors, jazz band, marching band, pep band, political, professional, radio and TV, religious, social, and student government. Popular campus events include Career Day and May Week.

Sports: There are 3 intercollegiate sports for men and 4 for women, and 8 intramural sports for men and 7 for women. Facilities include 2 gyms, a stadium, a swimming pool, a pool room, a baseball diamond, tennis courts, and a weight room.

Disabled Students: All of the campus is accessible. Wheelchair ramps, elevators, special parking, specially equipped rest rooms, lowered drinking fountains, and lowered telephones are available.

Services: Counseling and information services are available, as is tutoring in most subjects.

Campus Safety and Security: Measures include 24-hour foot and vehicle patrol and lighted pathways/sidewalks.

Programs of Study: Central State confers B.A., B.S., B.M., B.S.Ed., and B.S.M.E. degrees. Master's degrees are also awarded. Bachelor's degrees are awarded in BIOLOGICAL SCIENCE (biology/biological science), BUSINESS (accounting, banking and finance, business administration and management, and marketing/retailing/merchandising), COMMUNICATIONS AND THE ARTS (advertising, broadcasting, English, journalism, and music), COMPUTER AND PHYSICAL SCIENCE (chemistry, computer science, and mathematics), EDUCATION (art, elementary, health, music, physical, secondary, and special), ENGINEERING AND ENVIRONMENTAL DESIGN (graphic arts technology and manufacturing engineering), SOCIAL SCIENCE (economics, history, political science/government, psychology, public administration, social work, sociology, and water resources). Communication, music, and education are the strongest academically. Business administration is the largest.

Required: To graduate, students must complete 186 quarter credits, with a minimum GPA of 2.0 (2.5 in education). Required university core courses include 64 credits in English composition, math, computer skills, humanities, natural sciences, social sciences, health and phys ed, and African American history.

Special: Central State offers co-op programs in all majors, cross-registration with 15 area colleges, study abroad in 3 countries, internships, on-campus work-study programs, and B.A.-B.S. degrees. There is a freshman honors program.

Faculty/Classroom: 77% of faculty are male; 23%, female. All teach undergraduates and 75% both teach and do research. No introductory courses are taught by graduate students. The average class size in an introductory lecture is 25; in a laboratory, 20; and in a regular course, 15.

Requirements: The ACT is required; the SAT I is accepted. Applicants must be graduates of an accredited secondary school. The GED is accepted. Students should have completed 4 years of high school English, 3 years each of math, science, and social studies, and 2 years of the same foreign language. Ohio applicants should have a GPA of 2.0 and a minimum ACT composite score of 15 or SAT I score of 720. Criteria are higher for out-of-state applicants. A GPA of 2.0 is required. AP and CLEP credits are accepted.

Procedure: Freshmen are admitted to all sessions. There are early admissions, deferred admissions, and rolling admissions plans. Check with the school for current deadlines. The application fee is $15. Applications are accepted on-line at *www.centralstate.edu/admissions/apply2.html*.

Transfer: 127 transfer students enrolled in a recent year. Applicants should have a minimum college GPA of 2.0. Grades of C or better transfer for credit. Transfer students with fewer than 47 quarter hours must submit high school transcripts and test scores. Transfers are admitted every term. 45 of 186 credits required for the bachelor's degree must be completed at Central State.

Visiting: There are regularly scheduled orientations for prospective students. There are guides for informal visits and visitors may sit in on classes. To schedule a visit, contact the Admissions Office.

Financial Aid: In a recent year, the average freshman award was $10,765. 48% of undergraduates work part time. Average annual earnings from campus work are $1920. The FAFSA and the college's own financial statement are required. Check with the school for current deadlines.

International Students: In a recent year, there were 8 international students enrolled. They must score 500 on the written TOEFL and also take the SAT I or the ACT, scoring 19.

Computers: The mainframe is a Microsoft NT server. There are 350 individual PCs available to students in 9 computer labs with access to the Internet and Web. All students may access the system.

Graduates: In a recent year, 81 bachelor's degrees were awarded. The most popular majors were education (25%), business (21%), and social sciences and history (17%). In an average class, 1% graduate in 3 years or less, 9% graduate in 4 years or less, 20% graduate in 5 years or less, and 22% graduate in 6 years or less. 135 companies recruited on campus in a recent year. Of a recent graduating class, 37% were enrolled in graduate school within 6 months of graduation and 96% were employed.

Admissions Contact: Thandabantu Maceo, Director of Admissions. A video is available. E-mail: *admissions@csu.ces.edu*
Web: *www.centralstate.edu*

CINCINNATI COLLEGE OF MORTUARY SCIENCE   A-4
Cincinnati, OH 45224-1462
(513) 761-2020
(888) 377-8433; Fax: (513) 761-3333

Full-time: 76 men, 52 women	**Faculty:** 7
Part-time: 1 man, 1 woman	**Ph.D.s:** 33%
Graduate: none	**Student/Faculty:** 18 to 1
Year: quarters, summer session	**Tuition:** $11,865
Application Deadline: October 1	**Room & Board:** n/app
Freshman Class: 19 accepted, 17 enrolled	
SAT I or ACT: required	SPECIAL

The Cincinnati College of Mortuary Science, founded in 1882, is the only private mortuary college in the country that is regionally accredited at the bachelor's level. The curriculum encompasses the embalming sciences, funeral directing, and the liberal arts. In addition to regional accreditation, CCMS has baccalaureate program accreditation with ABFSE. The 2 libraries contain 6000 volumes. Computerized library services include the card catalog. Special learning facilities include a clinical embalming lab. The 16-acre campus is in an urban area 8 miles from downtown Cincinnati. There is one building.

Student Life: 50% of undergraduates are from out of state, mostly the Midwest. Students are from 15 states. 93% are white. The average age of all undergraduates is 24. 15% do not continue beyond their first year; 85% remain to graduate.

Housing: There are no residence halls. Alcohol is not permitted.

Activities: There are no fraternities or sororities. There are some groups and organizations on campus, including student government and yearbook. Popular campus events include field trips, guest lectures, and welcoming and farewell parties.

Sports: There is no sports program at CCMS.

Disabled Students: All of the campus is accessible. Wheelchair ramps, elevators, special parking, and specially equipped rest rooms are available.

Campus Safety and Security: Measures include informal discussions, pamphlets/posters/films, emergency telephones, and lighted pathways/sidewalks.

Programs of Study: CCMS confers the Bachelor of Mortuary Science degree. Associate degrees are also awarded. Bachelor's degrees are awarded in BUSINESS (funeral home services).

Required: To graduate, students must complete 180 quarter credit hours, including 90 in the major, with a minimum GPA of 2.0. General education requirements consist of 18 quarter hours each in natural science/math, social science, and humanities/arts, and 12 each in English composition and literature, business management, and free electives.

Special: Limited credit may be given for life, military, and work experience.

Faculty/Classroom: 87% of faculty are male; 13%, female. All teach undergraduates. The average class size in an introductory lecture is 50 and in a laboratory, 20.

Requirements: The SAT I or ACT is required, with a minimum SAT I composite score of 750 or ACT score of 14. Applicants must be graduates of an accredited secondary school. The GED is accepted. Students must complete 16 high school units, including 8 of electives, 3 of English, 2 each of science and history, and 1 of math. An interview is recommended. A GPA of 2.0 is required. AP and CLEP credits are accepted. Important factors in the admissions decision are leadership record, recommendations by alumni, and parents or siblings attending the school.

Procedure: Freshmen are admitted fall and spring. Applications should be filed by October 1 for fall entry and April 1 for spring entry. The fall 2003 application fee was $25. Notification is sent on a rolling basis. Applications are accepted on-line.

Transfer: Applicants must submit transcripts from all colleges attended. Grades of D+ or better transfer for credit if students have a GPA of 2.0. Transfers are admitted for the fall and spring terms. 90 of 180 quarter credits required for the bachelor's degree must be completed at CCMS.

Visiting: There are regularly scheduled orientations for prospective students, including open house programs in August and February. There are guides for informal visits. To schedule a visit, contact Patsy Leon.

Financial Aid: In 2003-2004, 87% of all full-time freshmen and 89% of continuing full-time students received some form of financial aid. 90% of full-time freshmen and 89% of continuing full-time students received need-based aid. The average freshman award was $6625. Need-based self-help aid (loans and jobs) averaged $6625 (maximum). 80% of undergraduates work part time. The average financial indebtedness of the 2003 graduate was $10,500. CCMS is a member of CSS. The CSS Profile is required. The deadline for filing freshman financial aid applications for fall entry is September 15.

Computers: There are 16 PCs networked in a lab for instruction at a beginning level. All students may access the system during supervised lab hours. There are no fees.

Graduates: From July 1, 2002 to June 30, 2003, 40 bachelor's degrees were awarded. The most popular major was mortuary science (100%). In an average class, 100% graduate in 4 years or less. 4 companies recruited on campus in 2002-2003.

Admissions Contact: Patsy Leon, Admissions/Financial Aid.
E-mail: *ccms@eos.net* Web: *www.ccms.edu*

CLEVELAND INSTITUTE OF ART   D-1
Cleveland, OH 44106
(216) 421-7427
(800) 223-4700; Fax: (216) 421-7438

Full-time: 303 men, 289 women	**Faculty:** 48
Part-time: 8 men, 18 women	**Ph.D.s:** 90%
Graduate: 2 men, 4 women	**Student/Faculty:** 12 to 1
Year: semesters	**Tuition:** $23,335
Application Deadline: July 1	**Room & Board:** $7036
Freshman Class: 390 applied, 369 accepted, 142 enrolled	
SAT I Verbal/Math: 572/509	**ACT:** 21 SPECIAL

Cleveland Institute of Art, founded in 1882, is an independent professional school of art offering a 5-year B.F.A. degree. In addition to regional accreditation, CIA has baccalaureate program accreditation with NASAD. The 3 libraries contain 42,000 volumes and 2800 audio/video tapes/CDs, and subscribe to 260 periodicals. Computerized library services include the card catalog, interlibrary loans, and database searching. Special learning facilities include an art gallery and natural history museum. The 500-acre campus is in an urban area 4 miles east of downtown Cleveland, sharing a campus with Case Western Reserve University. Including any residence halls, there are 4 buildings.

Student Life: 67% of undergraduates are from Ohio. Students are from 31 states, 9 foreign countries, and Canada. 97% are from public schools. 84% are white. The average age of freshmen is 20; all undergraduates, 23. 10% do not continue beyond their first year; 50% remain to graduate.

Housing: 100 students can be accommodated in college housing, which includes single-sex and coed dorms. On-campus housing is guaranteed for the freshman year only, is available on a first-come, first-served basis, and is available on a lottery system for upperclassmen. Priority is given to out-of-town students. 84% of students commute. Alcohol is not permitted. All students may keep cars.

Activities: There are 6 national fraternities and 6 national sororities. There are 7 groups on campus, including art, ethnic, gay, international, photography, professional, and student government. Popular campus events include museum trips, a spring cookout, and student art exhibits. The institute shares many social, cultural, and extracurricular activities with Case Western Reserve University.

Sports: There are 8 intramural sports for men and 8 for women. For a fee, students may use the recreation facilities of Case Western Reserve.

Disabled Students: 90% of the campus is accessible. Wheelchair ramps, elevators, special parking, and specially equipped rest rooms are available.

Services: Counseling and information services are available, as is tutoring in most subjects. There is remedial writing.

Campus Safety and Security: Measures include 24-hour foot and vehicle patrol, security escort services, shuttle buses, and informal discussions. There are pamphlets/posters/films, emergency telephones, and lighted pathways/sidewalks.

Programs of Study: CIA confers the B.F.A. degree. Master's degrees are also awarded. Bachelor's degrees are awarded in COMMUNICATIONS AND THE ARTS (advertising, applied art, design, graphic design, industrial design, painting, photography, and studio art). Industrial design, painting, and metals are the strongest academically. Industrial design, graphic design, and painting are the largest.

Required: To graduate, students must complete 150 to 153 credit hours, with 42 to 51 in the major, and must maintain a minimum GPA of 2.0. Distribution requirements call for 105 studio credits and 48 academic credits. A thesis is required, which is encompassed in the B.F.A. show that each student mounts in the spring of the fifth year.

Special: Cross-registration through the Cleveland Commission on Higher Education, internships for third-, fourth-, and fifth-year students with business and industry, and study abroad in 6 countries are available. There are joint programs with Case Western Reserve University in art education and medical illustration.

Faculty/Classroom: 70% of faculty are male; 30%, female. All teach undergraduates. The average class size in an introductory lecture is 40 and in a regular course, 20.

Admissions: 95% of the 2003-2004 applicants were accepted. The SAT I scores for the 2003-2004 freshman class were: Verbal--18% below 500, 39% between 500 and 599, 37% between 600 and 700, and 6% above 700; Math--38% below 500, 41% between 500 and 599, and 21% between 600 and 700. The ACT scores were 35% below 21, 27% between 21 and 23, 22% between 24 and 26, 11% between 27 and 28, and 5% above 28. 31% of the current freshmen were in the top fifth of their class; 53% were in the top two fifths. 2 freshmen graduated first in their class.

Requirements: The SAT I or ACT is required, with SAT I minimum scores of 350 verbal and 350 math or an ACT minimum composite score of 15. Applicants must be graduates of an accredited secondary school. The GED is accepted. Students should have completed 4 units each of art, English, and math, 2 each of history, science, and social studies, and 1 of a foreign language. An essay and a portfolio are required. An interview is strongly recommended. A GPA of 2.0 is required. AP and CLEP credits are accepted. Important factors in the admissions decision are evidence of special talent, personality/intangible qualities, and leadership record.

Procedure: Freshmen are admitted in the fall. Entrance exams should be taken during the junior year. There are early decision and deferred admissions plans. Applications should be filed by July 1 for fall entry. The fall 2003 application fee was $30. Notification is sent on a rolling basis. A waiting list is an active part of the admissions procedure. Applications are accepted on-line through the school's web site.

Transfer: 73 transfer students enrolled in 2002-2003. Applicants must have a 2.0 GPA and must submit a portfolio. Those who have 30 to 36 credits in comparable studio courses or a strong portfolio will be reviewed by department faculty. Grades of C or better transfer for credit. 3 of 153 credits required for the bachelor's degree must be completed at CIA.

Visiting: There are guides for informal visits and visitors may sit in on classes and stay overnight. To schedule a visit, contact Catherine Redhead, Director of Admissions.

Financial Aid: In 2003-2004, 95% of all full-time students received some form of financial aid. 68% of full-time freshmen and 63% of continuing full-time students received need-based aid. The average freshman award was $20,072. Need-based scholarships or need-based grants averaged $3000 ($7000 maximum); need-based self-help aid (loans and jobs) averaged $4125 ($5625 maximum); and non-need-based awards and non-need-based scholarships averaged $7200 ($21,971 maximum). 33% of undergraduates work part time. Average annual earnings from campus work are $1200. The average financial indebtedness of the 2003 graduate was $21,711. The FAFSA and the college's own financial statement are required. The deadline for filing freshman financial aid applications for fall entry is March 15.

International Students: There are 24 international students enrolled. The school actively recruits these students. They must score 525 on the written TOEFL and also take or complete Level 109 at an ELS center.

Computers: 115 Macs, 65 Windows NT workstations, and 22 Silicon Graphics PCs are available for student use in 8 separate computer labs. Students may access the system for up to 2 hours. There are no fees.

Graduates: From July 1, 2002 to June 30, 2003, 86 bachelor's degrees were awarded. The most popular majors were industrial design (15%), illustration (15%), and interior design and painting (14%). In an average class, 55% graduate in 5 years or less, and 65% graduate in 6 years or less. 82 companies recruited on campus in 2002-2003. Of the 2002 graduating class, 24% were enrolled in graduate school within 6 months of graduation and 74% were employed.

Admissions Contact: Catherine Redhead, Director of Admissions. E-mail: *credhead@gate.cia.edu* Web: *www.cia.edu*

CLEVELAND INSTITUTE OF MUSIC   D-1
Cleveland, OH 44106   (216) 795-3107; Fax: (216) 791-1530

Full-time: 105 men, 120 women	Faculty: 31
Part-time: none	Ph.D.s: 9%
Graduate: 60 men, 90 women	Student/Faculty: 7 to 1
Year: semesters, summer session	Tuition: $20,290
Application Deadline: see profile	Room & Board: $5590
Freshman Class: n/av	
SAT I or ACT: required	SPECIAL

Cleveland Institute of Music, founded in 1920, is a private music conservatory offering education and training in the arts of performance, composition, and related musical disciplines. Figures in the above capsule and in this profile are approximate. In addition to regional accreditation, CIM has baccalaureate program accreditation with NASM. The library contains 47,878 volumes and 20,500 audio/video tapes/CDs, and subscribes to 115 periodicals. Computerized library services include the card catalog, interlibrary loans, and database searching. Special learning facilities include concert and recital halls, teaching studios, practice rooms, a technology learning center, a specially designed eurhythmics studio, an orchestra library, an opera theater workshop and studio, and music store. The 480-acre campus is in an urban area.

Student Life: 68% of undergraduates are from out of state, mostly the Midwest. Students are from 40 states, 21 foreign countries, and Canada. 95% are from public schools. 71% are white; 20% foreign nationals. The average age of freshmen is 18; all undergraduates, 21. 2% do not continue beyond their first year; 85% remain to graduate.

Housing: College-sponsored housing is coed. On-campus housing is guaranteed for the freshman year only. Alcohol is not permitted. All students may keep cars.

Activities: There are no fraternities or sororities. There are 8 groups on campus, including chorale, chorus, jazz band, opera, orchestra, religious, student government, and symphony. Popular campus events include weekly concerts by the Cleveland Orchestra.

Sports: There is no sports program at CIM. Athletic facilities and a fitness center are available.

Disabled Students: Wheelchair ramps, elevators, special parking, specially equipped rest rooms, and lowered drinking fountains are available.

Services: Counseling and information services are available, as is tutoring in some subjects.

Campus Safety and Security: Measures include 24-hour foot and vehicle patrol, security escort services, shuttle buses, and informal discussions. There are pamphlets/posters/films, emergency telephones, and lighted pathways/sidewalks.

Programs of Study: CIM confers B.M.; B.A.Mus.Ed. and B.S.Mus.Ed. degrees. Master's and doctoral degrees are also awarded. Bachelor's degrees are awarded in COMMUNICATIONS AND THE ARTS (music), EDUCATION (music).

Required: CIM requires a minimum of 126 credits with a GPA of 2.0 or higher for graduation. A core curriculum of general education courses, music history, theory, and literature is required. Performance evaluation is based on jury exams and recitals.

Special: Students may take a 5-year double major in performance and audio recording. Cross-registration with schools in the Cleveland Commission on Higher Education Consortium is possible. Music education degrees are offered in conjunction with Case Western Reserve University. There are 2 national honor societies.

Faculty/Classroom: 68% of faculty are male; 32%, female. All teach undergraduates.

Requirements: The SAT I or ACT is required. In addition, an audition and interview are required, at which time freshman applicants must also complete a questionnaire pertaining to general knowledge of music, and diagnostic evaluations of rhythmic comprehension as well as sight singing and ear training. Applicants majoring in composition must submit scores and tapes. Other factors in the admissions decision are GPA, class rank, test scores, and recommendations. Applicants should complete a 16 unit college preparatory program. The GED is accepted. AP credits are accepted.

Procedure: Freshmen are admitted fall and spring. Entrance exams should be taken at the time of the entrance audition. Check with the school for current deadlines. The fall 2003 application fee was $70. A waiting list is an active part of the admissions procedure. Applications are accepted on-line at *www.cim.edu/conserv/admissions.*

Transfer: Applicants must meet the same criteria as entering freshmen and submit transcripts and letters of recommendation. 48 of 126 credits required for the bachelor's degree must be completed at CIM.

Visiting: Visitors may sit in on classes. To schedule a visit, contact the Admission Office.

Financial Aid: CIM is a member of CSS. The CSS Profile or FAFSA is required. Check with the school for current deadlines.

International Students: They must score 550 on the written TOEFL or take the MELAB.

Computers: Each dorm room is connected to CWRUnet, Case Western Reserve University's fiber-optic computer network. Students are encouraged to bring their own PCs for easy access to this extensive system. Computer facilities are available both at CIM and on the CWRU campus. All students may access the system. There are no time limits and no fees. It is strongly recommended that all students have a personal computer.

Admissions Contact: Admission Office.
E-mail: cimadmission@po.cwru.edu Web: www.cim.edu

CLEVELAND STATE UNIVERSITY
Cleveland, OH 44115-2403

D-1

(216) 687-2100
(800) CSU-OHIO; Fax: (216) 687-9210

Full-time: 3113 men, 3592 women	**Faculty:** 486; I, -$
Part-time: 1072 men, 1396 women	**Ph.D.s:** 94%
Graduate: 1516 men, 2144 women	**Student/Faculty:** 14 to 1
Year: semesters, summer session	**Tuition:** $6072 ($11,940)
Application Deadline: July 15	**Room & Board:** $6236
Freshman Class: 2813 applied, 2205 accepted, 987 enrolled	
SAT I Verbal/Math: 470/470	**ACT:** 19 **LESS COMPETITIVE**

Cleveland State University, founded in 1964, is a primarily commuter public institution offering undergraduate and graduate programs through the colleges of arts and sciences, business administration, education, engineering, and urban affairs. There are 7 undergraduate and 7 graduate schools. In addition to regional accreditation, CSU has baccalaureate program accreditation with AACSB, ABET, CSWE, NCATE, and NLN. The 2 libraries contain 484,914 volumes, 690,023 microform items, and 101,376 audio/video tapes/CDs, and subscribe to 6186 periodicals. Computerized library services include the card catalog, interlibrary loans, and database searching. Special learning facilities include a learning resource center, art gallery, and radio station. The 70-acre campus is in an urban area in downtown Cleveland. Including any residence halls, there are 38 buildings.

Student Life: 96% of undergraduates are from Ohio. Students are from 20 states, 79 foreign countries, and Canada. 61% are white; 21% African American. The average age of freshmen is 19; all undergraduates, 27. 37% do not continue beyond their first year; 63% remain to graduate.

Housing: 475 students can be accommodated in college housing, which includes coed dormitories and off-campus apartments. In addition, there are law, quiet study, and first-year experience floors. 95% of students commute. All students may keep cars.

Activities: 1% of men belong to 2 local and 6 national fraternities; 1% of women belong to 8 national sororities. There are 150 groups on campus, including art, cheerleading, chess, choir, chorale, chorus, computers, dance, drama, ethnic, gay, honors, international, jazz band, literary magazine, musical theater, newspaper, opera, orchestra, pep band, photography, political, professional, radio and TV, religious, social, social service, student government, and symphony. Popular campus events include Black Aspiration Week and Springfest.

Sports: There are 8 intercollegiate sports for men and 7 for women, and 5 intramural sports for men and 5 for women. Facilities include a gym, gymnastics and weight rooms, a dance studio, a swimming pool, a fitness trail, an indoor track, handball and squash courts, a 2500-seat soccer stadium, and a convocation center.

Disabled Students: 99% of the campus is accessible. Wheelchair ramps, elevators, special parking, specially equipped rest rooms, and lowered drinking fountains are available.

Services: There is a reader service for the blind, and remedial math, reading, and writing.

Campus Safety and Security: Measures include 24-hour foot and vehicle patrol, security escort services, informal discussions, and pamphlets/posters/films. There are emergency telephones, lighted pathways/sidewalks, and a campus watch organization for faculty and staff.

Programs of Study: CSU confers B.A., B.S., B.B.A., B.C.E., B.Ch.E., B.E.E., B.M., B.M.E., B.S.C.I.S., B.S.Ed., B.S.I.E., B.S.N., and B.S.T. degrees. Master's and doctoral degrees are also awarded. Bachelor's degrees are awarded in BIOLOGICAL SCIENCE (biology/biological science), BUSINESS (accounting, banking and finance, business economics, labor studies, management information systems, management science, and marketing/retailing/merchandising), COMMUNICATIONS AND THE ARTS (art, communications, dramatic arts, English, French, German, linguistics, music, and Spanish), COMPUTER AND PHYSICAL SCIENCE (chemistry, computer science, geology, information sciences and systems, mathematics, and physics), EDUCATION (early childhood, elementary, physical, secondary, and special), ENGINEERING AND ENVIRONMENTAL DESIGN (chemical engineering, civil engineering, electrical/electronics engineering, electromechanical technology, environmental science, industrial engineering, mechanical engineering, and mechanical engineering technology), HEALTH PROFESSIONS (medical technology, nursing, occupational therapy, physical therapy, premedicine, and speech therapy), SOCIAL SCIENCE (anthropology, classical/ancient civilization, economics, history, international relations, liberal arts/general studies, philosophy, political science/government, psychology, religion, social science, social studies, social work, sociology, and urban studies). Communications, psychology, and social work are the largest.

Required: Students must complete at least 120 semester hours with a minimum 2.0 GPA for graduation. Requirements include a core curriculum containing courses in English composition, arts and humanities, social science, natural sciences, math and logic, non-Western culture and civilization, Western culture and civilization, and human diversity and the African American experience.

Special: CSU offers a developmental program for Ohio students not qualified for regular freshman admission. There are also cooperative education programs, nondegree study, work-study programs, internships, pass/fail options, and cross-registration at other Cleveland area colleges. Student-designed and dual majors, study abroad in 10 countries, and volunteer opportunities are available, as well as a combined liberal arts and engineering degree and a 3-2 engineering degree. There are 6 national honor societies, and 5 departmental honors programs.

Faculty/Classroom: 60% of faculty are male; 40%, female.

Admissions: 78% of the 2003-2004 applicants were accepted. The SAT I scores for the 2003-2004 freshman class were: Verbal--61% below 500, 30% between 500 and 599, 8% between 600 and 700, and 1% above 700; Math--61% below 500, 28% between 500 and 599, 9% between 600 and 700, and 2% above 700. The ACT scores were 68% below 21, 19% between 21 and 23, 9% between 24 and 26, 3% between 27 and 28, and 1% above 28. 21% of the current freshmen were in the top fifth of their class; 44% were in the top two fifths.

Requirements: The SAT I or ACT is required. The scores should meet the standards of the specific program for which the student is applying. Advanced placement and honors courses are considered in the admissions decision. AP and CLEP credits are accepted.

Procedure: Freshmen are admitted to all sessions. Entrance exams should be taken prior to application. There is a deferred admissions plan and a rolling admissions plan. Applications should be filed by July 15 for fall entry, December 1 for spring entry, and April 1 for summer entry. The fall 2003 application fee was $30. The college accepts all applicants. Notification is sent on a rolling basis. Applications are accepted on-line through the ApplyYourself Application Network.

Transfer: 1369 transfer students enrolled in 2002-2003. Applicants must have a minimum GPA of 2.0. 30 credits of 120 required for the bachelor's degree must be completed at CSU.

Visiting: There are regularly scheduled orientations for prospective students, including general visitation days for the university (in the fall) and each of the colleges (in the spring). There are guides for informal visits and visitors may sit in on classes and stay overnight. To schedule a visit, contact the Office of Undergraduate Admissions at (216) 687-3755.

Financial Aid: In 2003-2004, 65% of all full-time freshmen and 58% of continuing full-time students received some form of financial aid. At least 50% of full-time freshmen and 41% of continuing full-time students received need-based aid. The average freshman award was $6232. Need-based scholarships or need-based grants averaged $4400; need-based self-help aid (loans and jobs) averaged $3046; institutional non-need-based athletic scholarships averaged $8929; and other institutional non-need-based awards and non-need-based scholarships averaged $6163. The FAFSA is required. The priority date for freshman financial aid applications for fall entry is February 15.

International Students: There were 220 international students enrolled in a recent year. They must score 525 on the written TOEFL.

Computers: The mainframes are a Sun 10,000, 3 DEC VAX 750s, and a VAX 8600. The mainframes are accessible by modem or at the university's 10 stations on campus. PC services are available at several networked PC labs on campus. All students may access the system. Hours vary by input center. Modem access is available 24 hours per day.

Graduates: From July 1, 2002 to June 30, 2003, 1517 bachelor's degrees were awarded. The most popular majors were business/marketing

(22%), education (12%), and communications (10%). In an average class, 7% graduate in 4 years or less, 17% graduate in 5 years or less, and 29% graduate in 6 years or less.

Admissions Contact: Gerald Kiel, Vice Provost of Enrollment Management Services. A video is available. Web: *http://www.csuohio.edu*

COLLEGE OF MOUNT ST. JOSEPH
Cincinnati, OH 45233-1672

A-5

(513) 244-4606
(800) 654-9314; Fax: (513) 244-4851

Full-time: 458 men, 824 women	**Faculty:** 117; IIB, -$
Part-time: 119 men, 475 women	**Ph.D.s:** 60%
Graduate: 45 men, 189 women	**Student/Faculty:** 11 to 1
Year: semesters, summer session	**Tuition:** $17,040
Application Deadline: August 15	**Room & Board:** $5745
Freshman Class: 863 applied, 655 accepted, 267 enrolled	
SAT I Verbal/Math: 500/510	**ACT:** 21 **COMPETITIVE**

The College of Mount St. Joseph, founded in 1920, is a private, liberal arts Catholic institution that fosters a liberal education with career orientation. There is 1 graduate school. In addition to regional accreditation, the Mount has baccalaureate program accreditation with ADA, NASM, NCATE, and NLN. The library contains 97,743 volumes, 393,931 microform items, and 1385 audio/video tapes/CDs, and subscribes to 6230 periodicals. Computerized library services include the card catalog, interlibrary loans, and database searching. Special learning facilities include a learning resource center and art gallery. The 75-acre campus is in a suburban area 7 miles west of downtown Cincinnati. Including any residence halls, there are 7 buildings.

Student Life: 90% of undergraduates are from Ohio. Students are from 16 states and 2 foreign countries. 65% are from public schools. 86% are white; 10% African American. 52% are Catholic; 29% Protestant. The average age of freshmen is 18; all undergraduates, 26. 18% do not continue beyond their first year; 70% remain to graduate.

Housing: 400 students can be accommodated in college housing, which includes coed dorms. On-campus housing is guaranteed for all 4 years. 71% of students commute. All students may keep cars.

Activities: There are no fraternities or sororities. There are 41 groups on campus, including art, band, cheerleading, choir, chorale, chorus, computers, dance, departmental, drama, drill team, ethnic, honors, international, jazz band, literary magazine, marching band, musical theater, newspaper, orchestra, pep band, photography, religious, social, social service, and student government. Popular campus events include the Christmas gala, campus fair, and Mission Exploration Day.

Sports: There are 8 intercollegiate sports for men and 7 for women, and 6 intramural sports for men and 6 for women. Facilities include a gym, a track, a wellness center, a weight room, a hockey field, an aerobics center, racquetball courts, 6 lighted tennis courts, a softball field, and a "home" football and baseball stadium located off campus.

Disabled Students: 95% of the campus is accessible. Wheelchair ramps, elevators, special parking, specially equipped rest rooms, special class scheduling, lowered drinking fountains, lowered telephones, special door openings for wheelchair access, and a chairlift between levels where the science building and classroom building meet are available.

Services: Counseling and information services are available, as is tutoring in most subjects. There is remedial math, reading, and writing, peer tutoring, a skills lab, and a special program for students with learning disabilities.

Campus Safety and Security: Measures include 24-hour foot and vehicle patrol, self-defense education, security escort services, and informal discussions. There are pamphlets/posters/films, emergency telephones, and lighted pathways/sidewalks.

Programs of Study: The Mount confers B.A., B.S., B.F.A., and B.S.N. degrees. Associate and master's degrees are also awarded. Bachelor's degrees are awarded in BIOLOGICAL SCIENCE (biology/biological science), BUSINESS (accounting, business administration and management, and purchasing/inventory management), COMMUNICATIONS AND THE ARTS (art, communications, English, fine arts, graphic design, and music), COMPUTER AND PHYSICAL SCIENCE (chemistry, computer mathematics, computer science, mathematics, and natural sciences), EDUCATION (art, athletic training, early childhood, elementary, middle school, music, physical, science, and special), ENGINEERING AND ENVIRONMENTAL DESIGN (interior design), HEALTH PROFESSIONS (health, health care administration, medical laboratory technology, nursing, premedicine, and recreation therapy), SOCIAL SCIENCE (gerontology, history, human services, humanities, liberal arts/general studies, paralegal studies, pastoral studies, psychology, religion, religious education, social work, sociology, theological studies, and women's studies). Physical therapy, nursing, and biology are the strongest academically. Business, education, and nursing are the largest.

Required: To graduate, students must complete 128 credits with an overall minimum GPA of 2.0 and 2.5 in the major. 48 semester hours of liberal arts and sciences and 36 to 40 hours in the major are required. All students must take 3 credits of computer science, 2 credits of phys ed, and written and oral English courses.

Special: The college offers co-op programs in all majors, cross-registration with the Greater Consortium of Colleges and Universities of Ohio, internships, and study abroad in England, Germany, Spain, and Korea. Work-study programs, accelerated degree programs, dual majors, a general studies degree, nondegree study, and pass/fail options are available. The Weekend College offers students an opportunity to earn a degree by enrolling in specially designed classes that meet only on weekends. There is 1 national honor society, a freshman honors program, and 6 departmental honors programs.

Faculty/Classroom: 39% of faculty are male; 61%, female. All teach undergraduates and 25% both teach and do research. No introductory courses are taught by graduate students. The average class size in an introductory lecture is 25; in a laboratory, 20; and in a regular course, 20.

Admissions: 76% of the 2003-2004 applicants were accepted. The SAT I scores for the 2003-2004 freshman class were: Verbal--48% below 500, 39% between 500 and 599, 12% between 600 and 700, and 1% above 700; Math--45% below 500, 43% between 500 and 599, 11% between 600 and 700, and 1% above 700. The ACT scores were 30% below 21, 26% between 21 and 23, 25% between 24 and 26, 16% between 27 and 28, and 3% above 28. 33% of the current freshmen were in the top fifth of their class; 79% were in the top two fifths. There was 1 National Merit finalist. 2 freshmen graduated first in their class.

Requirements: The SAT I or ACT is required. In addition, applicants must be graduates of an accredited secondary school. The GED (with scores in the 50th percentile) is accepted. Students should have completed the following high school academic credits: 4 years of English, 2 of math (including algebra and geometry), 2 of social studies, 2 of foreign language or 2 additional years of previously listed courses, 2 of science, and 1 of fine arts. Letters of recommendation and a personal essay are required for those students not meeting at least 3 of the 4 following criteria: completion of above-listed high school core subject courses, class rank in upper three fifths, a minimum GPA of 2.25, or minimum testing scores of 19 on the ACT or 480 verbal and 480 math on the SAT I. An audition is required for music students, and a portfolio is recommended for all art students. The Mount requires applicants to be in the upper 60% of their class. A GPA of 2.25 is required. AP and CLEP credits are accepted. Important factors in the admissions decision are recommendations by school officials and extracurricular activities record.

Procedure: Freshmen are admitted to all sessions. There is an early admissions plan and a rolling admissions plan. Applications should be filed by August 15 for fall entry. The fall 2003 application fee was $25. Notification is sent on a rolling basis. Applications are accepted on-line through the school's web site.

Transfer: 122 transfer students enrolled in 2002-2003. Transfer students must meet 3 of 4 freshman criteria or have a college GPA of 2.0 better in a minimum of 12 semester or 18 quarter hours. All college hours must be presented. 27 credits of 128 required for the bachelor's degree must be completed at the Mount.

Visiting: There are regularly scheduled orientations for prospective students, including a meeting with an admissions counselor, a student-guided tour, a visit to financial aid, and a meeting with a faculty member, if requested. There are guides for informal visits and visitors may sit in on classes and stay overnight. To schedule a visit, contact the Admissions Office at (513) 244-4531.

Financial Aid: In 2003-2004, 99% of all full-time freshmen and 90% of continuing full-time students received some form of financial aid. 90% of all full-time students received need-based aid. The average freshman award was $11,560. All undergraduates work part time. Average annual earnings from campus work are $2000. The average financial indebtedness of the 2003 graduate was $9100. The FAFSA is required. The deadline for filing freshman financial aid applications for fall entry is March 1.

International Students: There were 38 international students enrolled in a recent year.

Computers: Students have access to 175 network-based workstations and 5 servers. PCs are in 4 large public labs and some smaller department labs, as well as on each floor of the residence hall. All first time, full-time freshmen are required to lease a computer through the college. The Mount is a wireless college. All students may access the system 24 hours a day. There are no time limits and no fees. It is strongly recommended that all students have a personal computer. An IBM ThinkPad is recommended.

Graduates: From July 1, 2002 to June 30, 2003, 385 bachelor's degrees were awarded. The most popular majors were business administration (11%), rehabilitation science (10%), and nursing (10%). In an average class, 1% graduate in 3 years or less, 68% graduate in 4 years or less, and 70% graduate in 6 years or less. 62 companies recruited on campus in 2002-2003. Of the 2002 graduating class, 15% were enrolled in graduate school within 6 months of graduation and 85% were employed.

Admissions Contact: Peggy Minnich, Director of Admission. A video is available. E-mail: *peggy-minnich@mail.msj.edu* Web: *www.msj.edu*

COLLEGE OF WOOSTER
Wooster, OH 44691

D-2

(330) 263-2322
(800) 877-9905; Fax: (330) 263-2621

Full-time: 853 men, 969 women	**Faculty:** 134; IIB, +$
Part-time: 9 men, 7 women	**Ph.D.s:** 97%
Graduate: none	**Student/Faculty:** 14 to 1
Year: semesters, summer session	**Tuition:** $25,040
Application Deadline: February 15	**Room & Board:** $6260
Freshman Class: 2560 applied, 1780 accepted, 559 enrolled	
SAT I Verbal/Math: 600/600	**ACT:** 25 **HIGHLY COMPETITIVE**

The College of Wooster, founded in 1866, is a private liberal arts college. In addition to regional accreditation, Wooster has baccalaureate program accreditation with NASM. The 3 libraries contain 622,672 volumes, 210,094 microform items, and 24,149 audio/video tapes/CDs, and subscribe to 6696 periodicals. Computerized library services include the card catalog, interlibrary loans, and database searching. Special learning facilities include a learning resource center, art gallery, and radio station. The 240-acre campus is in a suburban area 55 miles southwest of Cleveland. Including any residence halls, there are 37 buildings.

Student Life: 58% of undergraduates are from Ohio. Students are from 44 states, 35 foreign countries, and Canada. 74% are from public schools. 78% are white. The average age of freshmen is 19; all undergraduates, 20. 13% do not continue beyond their first year; 99% remain to graduate.

Housing: 1859 students can be accommodated in college housing, which includes single-sex and coed dorms, fraternity houses, and sorority houses. In addition, there are language houses, special-interest houses, and almost 3 dozen small house residential options, most of which are associated with community service/volunteer programs. On-campus housing is guaranteed for all 4 years. 97% of students live on campus; of those, 80% remain on campus on weekends. All students may keep cars.

Activities: 9% of men belong to 3 local fraternities; 10% of women belong to 6 local sororities. There are 11 groups on campus, including art, bagpipe band, band, cheerleading, chess, choir, chorale, chorus, dance, debate, drama, ethnic, film, forensics, gay, honors, international, jazz band, literary magazine, marching band, musical theater, newspaper, orchestra, pep band, photography, political, radio and TV, religious, social service, student government, symphony, and yearbook. Popular campus events include Party on the Green, Winter Gala, and Scot Spirit Day.

Sports: There are 11 intercollegiate sports for men and 11 for women, and 11 intramural sports for men and 11 for women. Facilities include a phys ed center, a stadium, a golf course, tennis courts, a track, baseball and softball fields, a soccer field, a hockey and lacrosse field, a natatorium, and a fitness center.

Disabled Students: 95% of the campus is accessible. Wheelchair ramps, elevators, special parking, specially equipped rest rooms, special class scheduling, and lowered drinking fountains are available.

Services: Counseling and information services are available, as is tutoring in every subject. There is a reader service for the blind and remedial math, reading, and writing.

Campus Safety and Security: Measures include 24-hour foot and vehicle patrol, security escort services, informal discussions, and pamphlets/posters/films. There are emergency telephones and lighted pathways/sidewalks.

Programs of Study: Wooster confers B.A., B.Mus., and B.Mus.Ed. degrees. Bachelor's degrees are awarded in BIOLOGICAL SCIENCE (biochemistry and biology/biological science), BUSINESS (business economics), COMMUNICATIONS AND THE ARTS (communications, comparative literature, dramatic arts, English, fine arts, French, German, Greek (classical), Latin, music, and Spanish), COMPUTER AND PHYSICAL SCIENCE (chemistry, computer science, geology, mathematics, and physics), SOCIAL SCIENCE (African American studies, anthropology, archeology, area studies, economics, history, interdisciplinary studies, international relations, philosophy, political science/government, psychology, religion, Russian and Slavic studies, sociology, urban studies, and women's studies). Chemistry, history, and English are the strongest academically. History, English, and sociology are the largest.

Required: To graduate, students must complete 32 course credits, with 9 to 13 in the major and a minimum GPA of 2.0. All students must take 1 course each in critical inquiry, studies in cultural differences, religious perspectives, and quantitative reasoning, and demonstrate basic writing and foreign language proficiency. Two courses each in social science/history, natural science/math, and arts/humanities are required.

Special: A 3-2 engineering degree is offered in conjunction with Case Western Reserve and Washington universities. A B.A.-B.S. degree is offered in music/music education. Cross-registration is possible with off-campus programs of the Great Lakes Colleges Association. Internships are available in American politics in Washington, D.C., the Ohio State Legislature, and the U.S. State Department, as well as in professional theater and economics. Student-designed majors, dual majors, study abroad in 50 countries, a Washington semester, accelerated degree programs, nondegree study, and pass/fail options for a limited number of courses are available. All seniors participate in a 2-term independent-study project in the major. The student chooses the topic and works on a one-to-one basis with a faculty mentor. A sophomore research program is available by application. There are 12 national honor societies, including Phi Beta Kappa.

Faculty/Classroom: 59% of faculty are male; 41%, female. All both teach and do research. The average class size in an introductory lecture is 15 and in a regular course, 20.

Admissions: 70% of the 2003-2004 applicants were accepted. The SAT I scores for the 2003-2004 freshman class were: Verbal--10% below 500, 37% between 500 and 599, 39% between 600 and 700, and 15% above 700; Math--9% below 500, 38% between 500 and 599, 44% between 600 and 700, and 9% above 700. 61% of the current freshmen were in the top fifth of their class; 87% were in the top two fifths.

Requirements: The SAT I or ACT is required, with an SAT I composite score of 990 or an ACT minimum composite score of 20. In addition, applicants should be graduates of an accredited secondary school. The GED is accepted. Students should have completed a minimum of 16 high school academic credits. The school also requires an essay and recommends an interview. AP credits are accepted. Important factors in the admissions decision are advanced placement or honor courses, recommendations by school officials, and leadership record.

Procedure: Freshmen are admitted fall and winter. Entrance exams should be taken in the fall of the senior year. There are early decision, early admissions, and deferred admissions plans. Early decision applications should be filed by December 1; regular applications, by February 15 for fall entry. The fall 2003 application fee was $40. Notification of early decision is sent December 15; regular decision, April 1. 70 early decision candidates were accepted for the 2003-2004 class. 249 applicants were on the 2003 waiting list. Applications are accepted on computer disk through Common Application and CollegeLink.

Transfer: 9 transfer students enrolled in 2002-2003. Applicants for transfer must have a minimum GPA of 2.5 and must submit either the SAT I or ACT scores as well as a dean's reference and a high school transcript. An interview is recommended. Grades of C or better transfer for credit. Transfers are admitted every semester. 17 of 32 credits required for the bachelor's degree must be completed at Wooster.

Visiting: There are regularly scheduled orientations for prospective students, including an interview, tour, class visits, and meetings with faculty and coaches. There are guides for informal visits and visitors may sit in on classes and stay overnight. To schedule a visit, contact the Admissions Office at admissions@wooster.edu.

Financial Aid: In 2003-2004, 69% of all full-time freshmen and 63% of continuing full-time students received some form of financial aid. At least 68% of full-time freshmen and 63% of continuing full-time students received need-based aid. The average freshman award was $21,412. Need-based scholarships or need-based grants averaged $15,668; need-based self-help aid (loans and jobs) averaged $4707; and institutional non-need-based awards and non-need-based scholarships averaged $11,355. 50% of undergraduates work part time. The average financial indebtedness of the 2003 graduate was $19,494. Wooster is a member of CSS. The FAFSA and the CSS Profile, or the college's own financial statement are required. The deadline for filing freshman financial aid applications for fall entry is February 15.

International Students: The school actively recruits these students. They must score 550 on the written TOEFL or take the MELAB or American Language Institute test and also take the SAT I or the ACT, scoring 900 on the SAT I.

Computers: The mainframe is a Compaq Alpha server 800 5/500. File servers, laser printers, and other minicomputers are available on campus for student use. More than 500 PCs have been linked to WoosterNet, the campuswide local area network that provides computing capabilities 24 hours a day. All students may access the system any time.

Graduates: From July 1, 2002 to June 30, 2003, 440 bachelor's degrees were awarded. The most popular majors were social sciences and history (36%), English (10%), and visual and performing arts (10%). In an average class, 58% graduate in 4 years or less, and 6% graduate in 5 years or less. Of the 2002 graduating class, 28% were enrolled in graduate school within 6 months of graduation and 70% were employed.

Admissions Contact: Carol Wheatley, Director of Admissions. A video is available. E-mail: admissions@wooster.edu
Web: http://www.wooster.edu

COLUMBUS COLLEGE OF ART AND DESIGN
C-3
Columbus, OH 43215

(614) 222-3261
(877) 997-CCAD; Fax: (614) 232-8344

Full-time: 655 men, 683 women	Faculty: 75
Part-time: 194 men, 205 women	Ph.D.s: 47%
Graduate: none	Student/Faculty: 18 to 1
Year: semesters, summer session	Tuition: $17,880
Application Deadline: open	Room & Board: $6300
Freshman Class: 838 applied, 417 enrolled	
SAT I Verbal/Math: 544/514	ACT: 21	SPECIAL

Columbus College of Art and Design, founded in 1879, is a private institution offering undergraduate programs in art and fine arts. In addition to regional accreditation, CCAD has baccalaureate program accreditation with NASAD. The library contains 41,396 volumes and 13,475 microform items, and subscribes to 254 periodicals. Computerized library services include the card catalog and database searching. Special learning facilities include a learning resource center, art gallery, and art museum. The 17-acre campus is in an urban area in Columbus. Including any residence halls, there are 15 buildings.

Student Life: 63% of undergraduates are from Ohio. Students are from 47 states, 27 foreign countries, and Canada. 89% are white. The average age of freshmen is 19; all undergraduates, 21. 22% do not continue beyond their first year; 36% remain to graduate.

Housing: 300 students can be accommodated in college housing, which includes single-sex and coed dorms and off-campus apartments. On-campus housing is guaranteed for the freshman year only and is available on a first-come, first-served basis. Priority is given to out-of-town students. 82% of students commute. Alcohol is not permitted. Upperclassmen may keep cars.

Activities: There are no fraternities or sororities. There are 7 groups on campus, including ethnic, international, literary magazine, newspaper, professional, religious, and student government. Popular campus events include biannual student art sales, International Reception, and International Students Holiday Brunch.

Sports: There are 4 intramural sports for men and 2 for women. Facilities include a game room in the student center.

Disabled Students: 50% of the campus is accessible. Wheelchair ramps, elevators, special parking, specially equipped rest rooms, special class scheduling, and lowered telephones are available.

Services: There is remedial reading and writing.

Campus Safety and Security: Measures include 24-hour foot and vehicle patrol, security escort services, informal discussions, and pamphlets/posters/films. There are emergency telephones and lighted pathways/sidewalks.

Programs of Study: CCAD confers the B.F.A. degree. Bachelor's degrees are awarded in COMMUNICATIONS AND THE ARTS (advertising, fine arts, graphic design, illustration, industrial design, and media arts), ENGINEERING AND ENVIRONMENTAL DESIGN (interior design), SOCIAL SCIENCE (fashion design and technology). Media arts and fine arts are the largest.

Required: All students must complete foundation studies, including 4 years of drawing and 3 years of design/color, and courses in English, sociology, psychology, science, art history, science, literature, and painting. A total of 129 credit hours, with 75 to 90 in the major depending on the major, and a minimum GPA of 2.0 are required to graduate. A sophomore English exam must be passed. Students must complete a portfolio of professional caliber, and students in fine arts must have an individual showing of recent works.

Special: Cross-registration is offered with Franklin, Ohio State, and Capital Universities, Ohio Dominican, Otterbein, and Pontifical Colleges, Columbus State Community College, Mount Carmel College of Nursing, and DeVry Institute of Technology. Internships are available, as are on-campus work-study, dual majors, and nondegree study.

Faculty/Classroom: 71% of faculty are male; 29%, female. All teach undergraduates. The average class size in an introductory lecture is 23; in a laboratory, 18; and in a regular course, 20.

Requirements: The SAT I or ACT is required. In addition, applicants should be graduates of an accredited secondary school or have the GED. A portfolio of artwork indicative of abilities must be submitted. An interview is advised. A GPA of 2.0 is required. AP credits are accepted. Important factors in the admissions decision are evidence of special talent, recommendations by school officials, and recommendations by alumni.

Procedure: Freshmen are admitted fall and spring. There is a rolling admissions plan. Application deadlines are open. Application fee is $25. Applications are accepted on-line through CollegeNET.

Transfer: 75 transfer students enrolled in 2002-2003. Applicants must submit an acceptable portfolio of artwork as well as all high school and college transcripts. A minimum GPA of 2.0 is required. An interview is recommended. 60 of 129 credits required for the bachelor's degree must be completed at CCAD.

Visiting: There are regularly scheduled orientations for prospective students, including a personal interview, a portfolio review, and a tour.

There are guides for informal visits. To schedule a visit, contact the Admissions Office.

Financial Aid: In 2003-2004, 72% of all full-time freshmen and 85% of continuing full-time students received some form of financial aid. 60% of full-time freshmen and 80% of continuing full-time students received need-based aid. The average freshman award was $6500. Need-based scholarships or need-based grants averaged $8839. 53% of undergraduates work part time. Average annual earnings from campus work are $3126. The average financial indebtedness of the 2003 graduate was $21,730. CCAD is a member of CSS. The FAFSA and the college's own financial statement are required. The deadline for filing freshman financial aid applications for fall entry is March 3.

International Students: There are 73 international students enrolled. The school actively recruits these students. They must score 500 on the written TOEFL or take the MELAB and also take the SAT I or the ACT.

Computers: There are 115 computers available for student use. Primarily Mac systems are available, but several PCs are also used for animation and video editing. All students may access the system during scheduled lab hours and class time. There are no time limits and no fees.

Admissions Contact: Thomas Green, Director of Admissions.
E-mail: *admissions@ccad.edu* Web: *www.ccad.edu*

DAVID N. MYERS COLLEGE
D-1
Cleveland, OH 44115

(216) 523-3800
(877) DNMYERS; Fax: (216) 696-6430

Full-time: 130 men, 445 women	Faculty: 17
Part-time: 195 men, 335 women	Ph.D.s: 23%
Graduate: 50 men, 35 women	Student/Faculty: 12 to 1
Year: semesters, summer session	Tuition: $9475
Application Deadline: open	Room & Board: n/app
Freshman Class: n/av	
SAT I or ACT: required	COMPETITIVE

David H. Myers College, founded in 1848, is a private institution offering undergraduate programs in business to commuting students. Figures in the above capsule and in this profile are approximate. The library contains 13,250 volumes, 616 microform items, and 471 audio/video tapes/CDs, and subscribes to 140 periodicals. Computerized library services include the card catalog, interlibrary loans, and database searching. Special learning facilities include a learning resource center. The 2-acre campus is in an urban area in Cleveland. There is one building.

Student Life: 45% are African American; 42% white. The average age of all undergraduates is 26.

Housing: There are no residence halls. All students commute. Alcohol is not permitted.

Activities: There are no fraternities. There are some groups and organizations on campus, including chorale, student government, and yearbook.

Disabled Students: All of the campus is accessible. Wheelchair ramps, elevators, specially equipped rest rooms, special class scheduling, lowered drinking fountains, and lowered telephones are available.

Services: Counseling and information services are available, as is tutoring in most subjects. There is a reader service for the blind and remedial math, reading, and writing.

Programs of Study: Myers College confers the B.S. degree. Associate and master's degrees are also awarded. Bachelor's degrees are awarded in BUSINESS (accounting, business administration and management, marketing/retailing/merchandising, office supervision and management, real estate, retailing, and secretarial studies/office management), COMPUTER AND PHYSICAL SCIENCE (information sciences and systems), ENGINEERING AND ENVIRONMENTAL DESIGN (industrial administration/management), HEALTH PROFESSIONS (health care administration), SOCIAL SCIENCE (economics, paralegal studies, public administration, and social science).

Required: All students must complete 51 hours of general education requirements, and 27 hours in the business core, plus major requirements and electives. A minimum of 120 semester hours with a minimum GPA of 2.0 is required in order to graduate.

Special: The external degree program enables working adults to earn a bachelor's degree in a nontraditional manner, including credit by exam and credit for life/work experience. Work-study programs, co-op programs in 7 majors, internships, dual majors, pass/fail options, and cross-registration with other area colleges are offered. Evening and Saturday classes are also available.

Faculty/Classroom: 72% of faculty are male; 28%, female. All teach undergraduates. The average class size in an introductory lecture is 11; in a laboratory, 16; and in a regular course, 11.

Requirements: The SAT I or ACT is required for recent high school graduates. Applicants should have completed 19 Carnegie units, including 4 years of high school English, 3 each of math and science, and 2 each of social studies and history. The GED is accepted. An interview is recommended. AP and CLEP credits are accepted. Important factors in the admissions decision are ability to finance college education, advanced placement or honor courses, and recommendations by school officials.

Procedure: Freshmen are admitted to all sessions. Entrance exams should be taken by March of the senior year. There is a deferred admissions plan and a rolling admissions plan. Application deadlines are open. Application fee is $25.

Transfer: 143 transfer students enrolled in a recent year. Applicants should have a minimum GPA of 2.0 in at least 24 semester hours. An associate's degree and an interview are recommended. 30 of 126 credits required for the bachelor's degree must be completed at Myers College.

Visiting: There are guides for informal visits and visitors may sit in on classes. To schedule a visit, contact Admissions Services.

Financial Aid: Myers College is a member of CSS. The FAFSA is required. Check with the school for current deadlines.

International Students: They must score 500 on the written TOEFL.

Computers: The mainframe is a DEC VAX 4000/300. There are 70 IBM and HP PCs available in the computer lab. All students may access the system on or off campus. There are no time limits and no fees.

Graduates: In a recent year, 196 bachelor's degrees were awarded. The most popular majors were business/marketing (50%), information science (8%), and public administration (6%).

Admissions Contact: Tiffiney Payton, Interim Director of Admissions. E-mail: tpayton@dnmyers.edu Web: www.dnmyers.edu

---

DEFIANCE COLLEGE
Defiance, OH 43512   A-2

(419) 783-2361
(800) 520-GODC (4632); Fax: (419) 783-2468

Full-time: 340 men, 382 women	**Faculty:** 45; IIB, --$
Part-time: 69 men, 152 women	**Ph.D.s:** 70%
Graduate: 99 men and women	**Student/Faculty:** 16 to 1
Year: semesters, summer session	**Tuition:** $17,365
Application Deadline: open	**Room & Board:** $5250
Freshman Class: n/av	
SAT I Verbal/Math: 520/470	**ACT:** 20 **COMPETITIVE**

Defiance College, chartered in 1850, is a small liberal arts institution affiliated with the United Church of Christ. In addition to regional accreditation, Defiance has baccalaureate program accreditation with CSWE. The library contains 100,000 volumes and 5000 microform items, and subscribes to 500 periodicals. Computerized library services include the card catalog, interlibrary loans, and database searching. Special learning facilities include a learning resource center, art gallery, a nature sanctuary, and a greenhouse. The 150-acre campus is in a small town 55 miles southwest of Toledo, and 50 miles east of Fort Wayne. Including any residence halls, there are 24 buildings.

Student Life: 89% of undergraduates are from Ohio. Students are from 11 states and 4 foreign countries. 90% are from public schools. 93% are white. 40% are Protestant; 29% Catholic. The average age of freshmen is 18. 31% do not continue beyond their first year; 58% remain to graduate.

Housing: 490 students can be accommodated in college housing, which includes single-sex and coed dorms and on-campus apartments. On-campus housing is guaranteed for all 4 years and is available on a lottery system for upperclassmen. 52% of students commute. Alcohol is not permitted. All students may keep cars.

Activities: 8% of men belong to 1 local and 1 national fraternity; 8% of women belong to 2 national sororities. There are 33 groups on campus, including academic, art, band, cheerleading, chess, choir, drama, ethnic, honors, international, literary magazine, musical theater, newspaper, pep band, photography, professional, religious, social, social service, student government, and yearbook. Popular campus events include Student Senate Service Day, Freshman Service Day, and Arts on the Quad.

Sports: There are 9 intercollegiate sports for men and 9 for women, and 10 intramural sports for men and 10 for women. Facilities include a 4000-seat football stadium, baseball, softball, and soccer fields, a cross-country course, a recreation fitness center with a 5000-seat gym, a racquetball court, an indoor track, a weight-lifting room, basketball and tennis courts, an 8-lane all-weather outdoor track, and a fitness center.

Disabled Students: 80% of the campus is accessible. Wheelchair ramps, elevators, special parking, specially equipped rest rooms, special class scheduling, lowered drinking fountains, and lowered telephones are available.

Services: Counseling and information services are available, as is tutoring in every subject. There is a reader service for the blind, and remedial math, reading, and writing.

Campus Safety and Security: Measures include security escort services, informal discussions, pamphlets/posters/films, and lighted pathways/sidewalks. There are nighttime security guards in residence halls, security cameras in residence hall entrances, and a security guard on the grounds from dusk to dawn.

Programs of Study: Defiance confers B.A. and B.S. degrees. Associate and master's degrees are also awarded. Bachelor's degrees are awarded in BIOLOGICAL SCIENCE (biology/biological science and ecology), BUSINESS (accounting, banking and finance, business administration and management, human resources, management science, marketing/retailing/merchandising, and sports management), COMMUNICATIONS AND THE ARTS (art, communications, and graphic design), COMPUTER AND PHYSICAL SCIENCE (mathematics), EDUCATION (art, Christian, early childhood, elementary, health, mathematics, physical, reading, science, secondary, and social studies), ENGINEERING AND ENVIRONMENTAL DESIGN (environmental science), HEALTH PROFESSIONS (medical laboratory technology), SOCIAL SCIENCE (criminal justice, forensic studies, history, humanities, physical fitness/movement, psychology, religion, and social work). Education and sciences are the strongest academically. Business, forensic sciences, and education are the largest.

Required: All students must fulfill general education requirements, including written and oral communications and foreign language, and distribution studies in sciences, social sciences, humanities, and fine arts. A freshman seminar, a fitness for life course, interdisciplinary studies in Western civilization and the contemporary world, and 2 religion classes, as well as a senior assessment in the major, are also required. A total of 120 semester credits, with at least 30 in the major, and a minimum GPA of 2.0 are required to graduate. Volunteer community service is required in all majors; computer proficiency must be demonstrated.

Special: The college offers a strong interdisciplinary emphasis--as, for example, in the wellness and corporate fitness major--and student-designed majors and courses as well as independent study are available. Work-study programs and dual and student-designed majors are available. Numerous cooperative education programs and internships are also offered. B.A.-B.S. degrees, credit for community service not in the student's major, limited pass/fail options, and some credit for life experience are available. There are 8 national honor societies, a freshman honors program, and 1 departmental honors program.

Faculty/Classroom: 55% of faculty are male; 45%, female. All teach undergraduates and 20% do research. No introductory courses are taught by graduate students. The average class size in an introductory lecture is 22; in a laboratory, 18; and in a regular course, 16.

Admissions: The SAT I scores for the 2003-2004 freshman class were: Verbal--47% below 500, 35% between 500 and 599, and 18% between 600 and 700; Math--55% below 500, 32% between 500 and 599, 10% between 600 and 700, and 3% above 700. The ACT scores were 38% below 21, 27% between 21 and 23, 27% between 24 and 26, 6% between 27 and 28, and 2% above 28. 22% of the current freshmen were in the top fifth of their class; 47% were in the top two fifths.

Requirements: The SAT I or ACT is required. In addition, applicants should be graduates of an accredited secondary school or have a GED, with 15 Carnegie units completed, including 4 in English, 3 each in math, science, and social studies, and 2 in foreign language. An essay and an interview are recommended. A GPA of 2.25 is required. AP and CLEP credits are accepted. Important factors in the admissions decision are advanced placement or honor courses, personality/intangible qualities, and leadership record.

Procedure: Freshmen are admitted to all sessions. Entrance exams should be taken in the spring of the junior year or the fall of the senior year. There are early admissions and deferred admissions plans. There is a rolling admissions plan. Application deadlines are open. Notification is sent on a rolling basis. Application fee is $25. Applications are accepted on-line through the school's web site.

Transfer: 49 transfer students enrolled in 2002-2003. A minimum college GPA of 2.0 is required; an interview is recommended. 35 credits of 120 required for the bachelor's degree must be completed at Defiance.

Visiting: There are regularly scheduled orientations for prospective students, including admissions and financial aid sessions, a campus tour, a complimentary lunch, meetings with faculty, and observing a class in session. Interested applicants can meet with a coach. There are guides for informal visits and visitors may sit in on classes and stay overnight. To schedule a visit, contact the Office of Admission at (419) 783-2359 or admissions@defiance.edu.

Financial Aid: In 2003-2004, all full-time freshmen and 99% of continuing full-time students received some form of financial aid. 70% of all full-time freshmen and 66% of continuing full-time students received need-based aid. The average freshman award was $18,699, with $1707 from need-based scholarships or grants, $1590 from need-based self-help aid (loans and jobs), and $15,402 from non-need-based awards and non-need-based scholarships. 30% of undergraduates work part time. Average annual earnings from campus work are $645. The average financial indebtedness of the 2003 graduate was $14,061. The FAFSA and the college's own financial statement are required. The deadline for filing freshman financial aid applications for fall entry is March 1.

International Students: There are 4 international students enrolled. The school actively recruits these students. They must score 550 on the written TOEFL and also take the SAT I, scoring 850, or the ACT, scoring 18.

Computers: The mainframe is a Compaq DS20. PCs and Macs are available in computer labs and faculty offices. All students may access the system 24 hours a day, every day. There are no time limits. The fee is $120 per semester.

Graduates: From July 1, 2002 to June 30, 2003, 226 bachelor's degrees were awarded. The most popular majors were management (23%), elementary education (13%), and communications (10%). In an average class, 46% graduate in 4 years or less, 56% graduate in 5 years or less, and 58% graduate in 6 years or less. 390 companies recruited on campus in 2002-2003. Of the 2002 graduating class, 10% were enrolled in graduate school within 6 months of graduation and 94% were employed.

Admissions Contact: Mark Thompson, Dean of Admissions and Marketing. E-mail: *admissions@defiance.edu* Web: *www.defiance.edu*

DENISON UNIVERSITY C-3
Granville, OH 43023

(740) 587-6276
(800) DENISON; Fax: (740) 587-6306

Full-time: 954 men, 1167 women	**Faculty:** 180; IIB, +$
Part-time: 8 men, 13 women	**Ph.D.s:** 97%
Graduate: none	**Student/Faculty:** 12 to 1
Year: semesters	**Tuition:** $25,760
Application Deadline: February 1	**Room & Board:** $7290
Freshman Class: 3141 applied, 2125 accepted, 629 enrolled	
SAT I Verbal/Math: 600/610	**ACT:** 26 **HIGHLY COMPETITIVE**

Denison University, founded in 1831, is a private independent institution of liberal arts and sciences. The library contains 333,394 volumes, 105,588 microform items, and 372,970 audio/video tapes/CDs, and subscribes to 6117 periodicals. Computerized library services include the card catalog, interlibrary loans, and database searching. Special learning facilities include a learning resource center, art gallery, planetarium, radio station, TV station, an observatory, a field research station in a 350-acre biological reserve, high resolution spectometer, economics computer labs, and modern languages lab. The 1200-acre campus is in a suburban area 30 miles east of Columbus. Including any residence halls, there are 62 buildings.

Student Life: 59% of undergraduates are from out of state, mostly the Midwest. Students are from 48 states, 32 foreign countries, and Canada. 73% are from public schools. 83% are white. 38% are Protestant; 33% Catholic; 19% other. The average age of freshmen is 18; all undergraduates, 20. 11% do not continue beyond their first year; 78% remain to graduate.

Housing: 2194 students can be accommodated in college housing, which includes single-sex and coed dorms and on-campus apartments. In addition, there are honors houses, special-interest houses, a first-year center, substance-free dorms, quiet dorms, all-women dorms, suite-style dorms, and apartments for juniors and seniors with high GPA/leadership. On-campus housing is guaranteed for all 4 years. 98% of students live on campus; of those, 90% remain on campus on weekends. All students may keep cars.

Activities: 28% of men belong to 8 national fraternities; 41% of women belong to 7 national sororities. There are 157 groups on campus, including art, cheerleading, choir, chorale, chorus, computers, dance, drama, ethnic, film, gay, honors, international, jazz band, literary magazine, musical theater, newspaper, orchestra, pep band, photography, political, professional, radio and TV, religious, social, social service, student government, symphony, and yearbook. Popular campus events include an all-campus community picnic and fair, All-Campus Gala, and Academic Awards Convocation.

Sports: There are 11 intercollegiate sports for men and 11 for women, and 13 intramural sports for men and 13 for women. Facilities include a 6000-seat stadium, a 1500-seat gym, 12 outdoor tennis courts, squash courts, an 8-lane quarter-mile track, a field house with a 200-meter track and 4 tennis courts, baseball/softball fields, a recreation gym with 3 volleyball/basketball courts, weight, aerobic, and fitness rooms, soccer and men's lacrosse stadium, women's field hockey and lacrosse field, and multiple practice fields.

Disabled Students: 62% of the campus is accessible. Wheelchair ramps, elevators, special parking, specially equipped rest rooms, special class scheduling, lowered drinking fountains, and lowered telephones are available.

Services: Counseling and information services are available, as is tutoring in most subjects. There is a reader service for the blind. A reading and writing center is available, as are study sessions for math, chemistry, and some languages, reduced courseloads, special counselor services, note taking services, oral tests, extended time for tests, untimed tests, talking books, tape recorders, and readers.

Campus Safety and Security: Measures include 24-hour foot and vehicle patrol, self-defense education, security escort services, and informal discussions. There are pamphlets/posters/films, emergency telephones, and lighted pathways/sidewalks. Residence halls are locked 24 hours a day with entry through a card access system.

Programs of Study: Denison confers B.A., B.S., and B.F.A. degrees. Bachelor's degrees are awarded in AGRICULTURE (environmental studies), BIOLOGICAL SCIENCE (biochemistry and biology/biological

science), COMMUNICATIONS AND THE ARTS (art history and appreciation, communications, dance, dramatic arts, English, film arts, fine arts, French, German, languages, Latin, media arts, music, Spanish, speech/debate/rhetoric, and studio art), COMPUTER AND PHYSICAL SCIENCE (chemistry, computer science, geology, mathematics, and physics), EDUCATION (education and physical), SOCIAL SCIENCE (African American studies, anthropology, classical/ancient civilization, East Asian studies, economics, history, international studies, Latin American studies, philosophy, political science/government, psychology, religion, sociology, Western European studies, and women's studies). Psychology, philosophy, and physics are the strongest academically. Communication, biology, and economics are the largest.

Required: All students must fulfill aproximately 13 courses of the general education program, including freshman studies in textual, critical, social, scientific, and artistic inquiries, along with oral communication, minority/women's studies, and 2 choices from Western studies, non-Western studies and American social institutions. A total of 127 semester hours, with 36 in the major and a minimum GPA of 2.0, is required to graduate.

Special: Work-study programs, a Washington semester, study-abroad programs in 35 countries, student-designed majors, a math/economics dual major, a dual major in education and various other majors, a philosophy, political science, and economics interdisciplinary major, and pass/fail options are available. A 3-2 engineering program is offered with Rensselaer Polytechnic Institute, Case Western Reserve, and Washington Universities. A May-term internship is available at 200 U.S. locations. A B.A.-B.S. degree, accelerated degree programs, a media technology and arts interdisciplinary major, and nondegree study are possible. There are 15 national honor societies, including Phi Beta Kappa, a freshman honors program, and 100 departmental honors programs.

Faculty/Classroom: 63% of faculty are male; 37%, female. All both teach undergraduates and do research. The average class size in an introductory lecture is 19; in a laboratory, 21; and in a regular course, 20.

Admissions: 68% of the 2003-2004 applicants were accepted. The SAT I scores for the 2003-2004 freshman class were: Verbal--4% below 500, 40% between 500 and 599, 45% between 600 and 700, and 11% above 700; Math--4% below 500, 37% between 500 and 599, 48% between 600 and 700, and 11% above 700. The ACT scores were 6% below 21, 13% between 21 and 23, 32% between 24 and 26, 18% between 27 and 28, and 31% above 28. 71% of the current freshmen were in the top fifth of their class; 99% were in the top two fifths. There were 9 National Merit finalists and 12 semifinalists. 40 freshmen graduated first in their class.

Requirements: The SAT I or ACT is required. In addition, applicants should have completed 19 Carnegie units, including 4 each in English, math and science, 3 in foreign language, 2 in social studies, and 1 each in history and academic electives. An essay is part of the application process. An interview is advised, and a portfolio or an audition is recommended for art or music majors, respectively. AP credits are accepted. Important factors in the admissions decision are personality/intangible qualities, evidence of special talent, and advanced placement or honor courses.

Procedure: Freshmen are admitted in the fall. Entrance exams should be taken by December of the senior year. There are early decision and deferred admissions plans. Early decision applications should be filed by November 15; regular applications, by February 1 for fall entry, along with a $40 fee. Notification of early decision is sent January 1; regular decision, April 1. 93 early decision candidates were accepted for the 2003-2004 class. 164 applicants were on the 2003 waiting list; 13 were admitted. Applications are accepted on-line through the school's web site.

Transfer: 21 transfer students enrolled in 2002-2003. A minimum GPA of 2.75 is required. The SAT I or ACT scores should be submitted. An interview is recommended. 64 credits of 127 required for the bachelor's degree must be completed at Denison.

Visiting: There are regularly scheduled orientations for prospective students, including orientation programs, class visits, tours, and interviews. There are guides for informal visits and visitors may sit in on classes and stay overnight. To schedule a visit, contact the Admissions Office at *www.denison.edu/admissions/visitformfall.html*.

Financial Aid: In 2003-2004, 97% of all full-time freshmen and 95% of continuing full-time students received some form of financial aid. 51% of full-time freshmen and 49% of continuing full-time students received need-based aid. The average freshman award was $22,501. Need-based scholarships or need-based grants averaged $16,913, and need-based self-help aid (loans and jobs) averaged $5422. 51% of undergraduates work part time. Average annual earnings from campus work are $1776. The average financial indebtedness of the 2003 graduate was $15,009. Denison is a member of CSS. The FAFSA and the college's own financial statement are required. The deadline for filing freshman financial aid applications for fall entry is March 1.

International Students: There are 105 international students enrolled. The school actively recruits these students. They must score 550 on the written TOEFL or 213 on the electronic version and also take the SAT I or the ACT.

Computers: The mainframe is a client/server with 20 servers. More than 1000 PCs are connected to the campus network. 450 of those are available to students in public computer clusters and department labs. All residence halls have network services including e-mail, Web, Internet, libraries, directory services, local events calendar, and personal web pages. All students may access the system 24 hours a day. There are no time limits and no fees.

Graduates: From July 1, 2002 to June 30, 2003, 490 bachelor's degrees were awarded. The most popular majors were communications (15%), economics (14%), and English (13%). In an average class, 73% graduate in 4 years or less, 76% graduate in 5 years or less, and 77% graduate in 6 years or less. 90 companies recruited on campus in 2002-2003. Of the 2002 graduating class, 22% were enrolled in graduate school within 6 months of graduation and 65% were employed.

Admissions Contact: Perry Robinson, Director of Admissions.
E-mail: *admissions@denison.edu* Web: *http://denison.edu/admissions/*

DEVRY UNIVERSITY/COLUMBUS
C-3
Columbus, OH 43209-2705

(614) 253-1525
(800) 426-2206; Fax: (614) 253-0843

Full-time: 1696 men, 462 women	**Faculty:** n/av
Part-time: 652 men, 335 women	**Ph.D.s:** n/av
Graduate: n/av	**Student/Faculty:** n/av
Year: semesters, summer session	**Tuition:** $10,670
Application Deadline: open	**Room & Board:** n/app
Freshman Class: n/av	
SAT I or ACT: n/av	**LESS COMPETITIVE**

DeVry University/Columbus, 1 of 67 DeVry University locations in the United States and Canada, opened in 1952. The institute offers undergraduate degrees in business administration, electronics, computer information systems, technical management, information technology, and computer engineering technology. In addition to regional accreditation, DeVry has baccalaureate program accreditation with ABET. The library contains 28,000 volumes, 12,000 e-books, and subscribes to 60 periodicals. Computerized library services include the card catalog, interlibrary loans, and database searching. Special learning facilities include a learning resource center and electronics and other labs. The 13-acre campus is in an urban area. There is one building.

Student Life: 73% of students are white; 20% African American. The average age of all undergraduates is 24.

Housing: There are no residence halls. Housing referrals may be obtained through the Student Housing Office. There are private apartments, student-plan housing, and private rooms. All students commute. Alcohol is not permitted. All students may keep cars.

Activities: There are no fraternities or sororities. There are 9 groups on campus, including ethnic, honors, newspaper, professional, religious, and student government. Popular campus events include Parents Weekend, Student Appreciation Week, and New Student Days.

Sports: There are 3 intramural sports for men and 1 for women.

Disabled Students: 90% of the campus is accessible. Wheelchair ramps, elevators, special parking, specially equipped rest rooms, and special class scheduling are available.

Services: Counseling and information services are available, as is tutoring in every subject.

Campus Safety and Security: Measures include informal discussions, pamphlets/posters/films, emergency telephones, and lighted pathways/sidewalks. Daytime and evening security is provided until the building is closed. Security systems and motion detectors are utilized after business hours.

Programs of Study: DeVry confers the B.S. degree. Associate and master's degrees are also awarded. Bachelor's degrees are awarded in BUSINESS (business administration and management), COMMUNICATIONS AND THE ARTS (telecommunications), COMPUTER AND PHYSICAL SCIENCE (information sciences and systems), ENGINEERING AND ENVIRONMENTAL DESIGN (computer engineering, electrical/electronics engineering technology, and technological management). Computer information systems and computer engineering technology are the largest.

Required: To graduate, students must achieve a GPA of at least 2.0 and satisfactorily complete all curriculum requirements. Course requirements vary according to program. All first-semester students take courses in business organization, computer applications, algebra, psychology, and student success strategies.

Special: Accelerated degrees, co-op programs, nondegree study, distance learning, and evening classes are possible. There is 1 national honor society.

Faculty/Classroom: All teach undergraduates.

Requirements: Admissions requirements include graduation from a secondary school; the GED is also accepted. Applicants must pass the DeVry entrance exam or present satisfactory ACT or SAT I scores. An interview is required. CLEP credit is accepted.

Procedure: Freshmen are admitted fall, spring, and summer. There is a rolling admissions plan. There are early admissions and deferred ad-

missions plans. Application deadlines are open. Application fee is $50. Applications are accepted on-line through *https://apply.embark.com/UGrad/DeVry/21.*

Transfer: 465 transfer students enrolled in a recent year. Applicants must present passing grades in all completed college course work, demonstrate language skills proficiency with at least 24 completed semester hours, and present evidence of math proficiency by appropriate college-level credits. 25% of 48 to 154 credits required for the bachelor's degree must be completed at DeVry.

Visiting: There are regularly scheduled orientations for prospective students. There are guides for informal visits and visitors may sit in on classes. To schedule a visit, contact the New Student Coordinator at (800) 426-3916.

Financial Aid: In 2002-2003, 52% of all full-time freshmen and 73% of continuing full-time students received some form of financial aid. At least 50% of full-time freshmen and at least 72% of continuing full-time students received need-based aid. The average freshman award was $7530. Need-based scholarships or need-based grants averaged $3713; need-based self-help aid (loans and jobs) averaged $4443; and institutional non-need-based awards and non-need-based scholarships averaged $5783. DeVry is a member of CSS. The FAFSA is required. The deadline for filing freshman financial aid applications is rolling.

International Students: There were 31 international students enrolled in a recent year. They must score 500 on the written TOEFL or 173 on the electronic version and also take the college's own entrance exam.

Computers: The mainframes are an IBM 3033 and an IBM System 36. Lab facilities include PCs in stand-alone and network configurations, with access to the mainframe. LANs provide access to a wide range of applications software. Hard copy from the mainframe is provided through a local minicomputer and medium- and high-speed printers. Students in the computer information systems program may access the system during lab hours. There are no fees. Students in the information technology program must have DeVry-issued laptops.

Graduates: From July 1, 2002 to June 30, 2003, 474 bachelor's degrees were awarded. The most popular majors were computer information systems (52%), business (32%), and electronics engineering technology (16%). 175 companies recruited on campus in a recent year.

Admissions Contact: Bill Holtry, Dean of Admissions.
E-mail: *admissions@devry.edu* Web: *www.devry.cols.edu*

FRANCISCAN UNIVERSITY OF STEUBENVILLE
E-3
Steubenville, OH 43952-1763

(740) 283-6226, ext.1220
(800) 783-6220; Fax: (740) 284-5456

Full-time: 673 men, 1017 women	**Faculty:** 96; IIA, --$
Part-time: 58 men, 96 women	**Ph.D.s:** 73%
Graduate: 190 men, 247 women	**Student/Faculty:** 18 to 1
Year: semesters, summer session	**Tuition:** $15,050
Application Deadline: June 30	**Room & Board:** $5250
Freshman Class: 823 applied, 717 accepted, 354 enrolled	
SAT I Verbal/Math: 580/560	**ACT:** 24 **VERY COMPETITIVE**

Franciscan University of Steubenville, founded in 1946 by the Franciscan Friars is a private, liberal arts, professional and preprofessional institution committed to the Catholic Church and its renewal. In addition to regional accreditation, Franciscan University has baccalaureate program accreditation with NLN. The library contains 232,013 volumes, 250,968 microform items, and 892 audio/video tapes/CDs, and subscribes to 5874 periodicals. Computerized library services include the card catalog, interlibrary loans, and database searching. Special learning facilities include a radio station. The 124-acre campus is in a small town 40 miles west of Pittsburgh. Including any residence halls, there are 21 buildings.

Student Life: 76% of undergraduates are from out of state, mostly the Midwest. Students are from 49 states, 23 foreign countries, and Canada. 59% are from public schools. 83% are white. Most are Catholic. The average age of freshmen is 18; all undergraduates, 21. 16% do not continue beyond their first year; 71% remain to graduate.

Housing: 1155 students can be accommodated in college housing, which includes single-sex dorms and Christian faith households in residence halls. On-campus housing is available on a first-come, first-served basis. 61% of students live on campus; of those, 70% remain on campus on weekends. Upperclassmen may keep cars.

Activities: There is 1 local and 1 national fraternity; 1% of women belong to 1 national sorority. There are 25 groups on campus, including choir, chorale, chorus, computers, drama, ethnic, honors, international, literary magazine, newspaper, orchestra, political, professional, prolife, radio and TV, religious, social, social service, student government, and yearbook. Popular campus events include the Feast of St. Francis, Pro-Life Rally, and all school evangelism events.

Sports: There are 4 intramural sports for men and 4 for women. Facilities include a campus athletic center, which houses 2 full-size basketball courts, racquetball courts, saunas, whirlpools, and locker rooms, and provides indoor seating for 2000. Outdoor athletic facilities include a basketball court, 4 tennis courts, and baseball, softball, flag football, and soccer fields.

Disabled Students: 75% of the campus is accessible. Wheelchair ramps, elevators, special parking, specially equipped rest rooms, special class scheduling, lowered drinking fountains, lowered telephones, fire alarm devices, wider doorways, and curb cuts are available.

Services: Counseling and information services are available, as is tutoring in most subjects. There is a reader service for the blind and remedial reading. Tutoring and counseling are available for learning-disabled students. Tutoring is also available for students on academic probation.

Campus Safety and Security: Measures include 24-hour foot and vehicle patrol, self-defense education, security escort services, and shuttle buses. There are informal discussions, pamphlets/posters/films, emergency telephones, and lighted pathways/sidewalks.

Programs of Study: Franciscan University confers B.A., B.S., and B.S.N. degrees. Associate and master's degrees are also awarded. Bachelor's degrees are awarded in BIOLOGICAL SCIENCE (biology/biological science), BUSINESS (accounting and business administration and management), COMMUNICATIONS AND THE ARTS (classics, communications, English, French, German, and Spanish), COMPUTER AND PHYSICAL SCIENCE (chemistry, computer science, information sciences and systems, and mathematics), EDUCATION (elementary), ENGINEERING AND ENVIRONMENTAL DESIGN (engineering and applied science), HEALTH PROFESSIONS (mental health/human services and nursing), SOCIAL SCIENCE (anthropology, economics, history, humanities and social science, paralegal studies, philosophy, political science/government, psychology, religion, religious education, social work, sociology, and theological studies). Theology, psychology, and education are the strongest academically. Theology, education, and business are the largest.

Required: All students must complete core liberal arts courses, including 15 credits each in humanities and communications and 6 credits each in theology, social science, and natural science. A 1-credit thesis seminar is required in all majors. A total of 124 credit hours, with at least 24 in the major, and a minimum GPA of 2.0 are required to graduate.

Special: Dual majors and internships for up to 6 credit hours are available in most majors. A humanities and Catholic culture major in Western tradition and minors in human life issues and music are offered. Study abroad is offered through the university's course location in Gaming, Austria, where students spend a semester studying humanities as well as traveling through Europe. There are 5 national honor societies, a freshman honors program, and 25 departmental honors programs.

Faculty/Classroom: 65% of faculty are male; 35%, female. 93% teach undergraduates. No introductory courses are taught by graduate students. The average class size in an introductory lecture is 28; in a laboratory, 15; and in a regular course, 21.

Admissions: 87% of the 2003-2004 applicants were accepted. The SAT I scores for the 2003-2004 freshman class were: Verbal--12% below 500, 41% between 500 and 599, 37% between 600 and 700, and 10% above 700; Math--18% below 500, 47% between 500 and 599, 31% between 600 and 700, and 4% above 700. 47% of the current freshmen were in the top fifth of their class; 73% were in the top two fifths. 14 freshmen graduated first in their class.

Requirements: The SAT I or ACT is required. In addition, applicants should have completed 15 academic high school units, including 10 in 4 of the 5 following areas: English, foreign language, social science, math, and natural sciences. The GED is accepted. An essay and an interview are recommended. A GPA of 2.4 is required. AP and CLEP credits are accepted. Important factors in the admissions decision are advanced placement or honor courses, evidence of special talent, and leadership record.

Procedure: Freshmen are admitted fall and spring. Entrance exams should be taken in the spring of the junior year or the fall of the senior year. Applications should be filed by June 30 for fall entry and December 15 for spring entry, along with a $20 fee. Notification is sent on a rolling basis. Applications are accepted on-line through the university's web site.

Transfer: 221 transfer students enrolled in 2002-2003. A minimum 2.0 college GPA is required. High school and college transcripts must be submitted. An interview is recommended. 30 of 124 credits required for the bachelor's degree must be completed at Franciscan University.

Visiting: There are regularly scheduled orientations for prospective students, including tours, interviews with professors, admissions, financial aid officers, and class visits. There are guides for informal visits and visitors may sit in on classes and stay overnight. To schedule a visit, contact the Admissions Office at (800) 783-6220 or visit@franciscan.edu.

Financial Aid: In 2003-2004, 92% of all full-time freshmen and 87% of continuing full-time students received some form of financial aid. 61% of full-time freshmen and 67% of continuing full-time students received need-based aid. The average freshman award was $10,126. Need-based scholarships or need-based grants averaged $7190 ($21,000 maximum); and need-based self-help aid (loans and jobs) averaged $3866 ($9625 maximum). 50% of undergraduates work part time. Average annual earnings from campus work are $1000. The average financial indebtedness of the 2003 graduate was $21,616. The FAFSA is required. The deadline for filing freshman financial aid applications for fall entry is March 15.

International Students: There are 61 international students enrolled. The school actively recruits these students. They must score 550 on the written TOEFL or 213 on the electronic version.

Computers: The mainframe is an IBM AS/400. There are also 40 PCs and 30 Macs available in student labs. All students may access the system from 9 A.M. to 11 P.M. Monday through Friday, 10 A.M. to 6 P.M. Saturday, and 1 P.M. to 11 P.M. Sunday. There are no time limits and no fees.

Graduates: From July 1, 2002 to June 30, 2003, 400 bachelor's degrees were awarded. The most popular majors were theology (21%), business (11%), and education (10%). In an average class, 3% graduate in 3 years or less, 63% graduate in 4 years or less, 70% graduate in 5 years or less, and 71% graduate in 6 years or less. 35 companies recruited on campus in a recent year.

Admissions Contact: Margaret Weber, Director of Admissions. A video is available. E-mail: *admissions@franciscan.edu* Web: *www.franciscan.edu*

FRANKLIN UNIVERSITY
Columbus, OH 43215-5399

C-3
(614) 797-4700
(877) 341-6300; Fax: (614) 224-8027

Full-time: 808 men, 1045 women	**Faculty:** 13
Part-time: 1610 men, 1855 women	**Ph.D:s:** 57%
Graduate: 449 men, 519 women	**Student/Faculty:** n/av
Year: trimesters, summer session	**Tuition:** $6720
Application Deadline: open	**Room & Board:** n/app
Freshman Class: n/av	
SAT I or ACT: not required	SPECIAL

Franklin University is a student-centered, independent, regional institution of lifelong higher education (undergraduate and graduate) working in partnership with Central Ohio's business and professional community in a global context. The library contains 15,000 volumes, 7920 microform items, and 132 audio/video tapes/CDs, and subscribes to 200 periodicals. Computerized library services include the card catalog, interlibrary loans, and database searching. Special learning facilities include a learning resource center and art gallery. The 14-acre campus is in an urban area located in downtown Columbus. There are 7 buildings.

Student Life: 82% of undergraduates are from Ohio. Students are from 42 states, 77 foreign countries, and Canada. 66% are white; 18% African American. The average age of freshmen is 28; all undergraduates, 32.

Housing: There are no residence halls. All students commute. Alcohol is not permitted. All students may keep cars.

Activities: There are no fraternities or sororities. There are 6 groups on campus, including computers, international, and professional. Popular campus events include new student orientation, awards/scholarship reception, and opening week activities.

Sports: There is no sports program at Franklin.

Disabled Students: All of the campus is accessible. Wheelchair ramps, elevators, special parking, specially equipped rest rooms, special class scheduling, lowered drinking fountains, and lowered telephones are available.

Services: Counseling and information services are available, as is tutoring in most subjects. There is a reader service for the blind and remedial math, reading, and writing.

Campus Safety and Security: Measures include security escort services and there is a parking guard on duty in each lot and a city police officer on duty during class hours. All such personnel are connected by an emergency radio system.

Programs of Study: Franklin confers the B.S. degree. Associate and master's degrees are also awarded. Bachelor's degrees are awarded in BUSINESS (accounting, banking and finance, business administration and management, human resources, management science, marketing and distribution, and organizational behavior), COMPUTER AND PHYSICAL SCIENCE (computer science), ENGINEERING AND ENVIRONMENTAL DESIGN (technological management), HEALTH PROFESSIONS (health care administration), SOCIAL SCIENCE (safety management). Business administration and computer science are the largest.

Required: Students must complete general education core requirements in communication, math, humanities, socal and behavioral sciences, and science. A total of 122 to 132 semester hours with a minimum GPA of 2.0 (2.25 for some majors) is required to graduate.

Special: Cross-registration is possible with other area colleges and universities through the Higher Education Council of Columbus. Internships are available for accounting, finance, marketing, business administration, computer science, human resources management, and management information sciences. Student-designed majors, ESL, and some pass/fail courses are offered. Bachelor of Science degree completion programs are available through alliances with community colleges in the United States and Canada. Accelerated delivery of specific courses is possible, as are integrated B.S./B.A. degrees in accounting, organizational leadership, financial management, and business administration.

Faculty/Classroom: 60% of faculty are male; 40%, female. 84% teach undergraduates. No introductory courses are taught by graduate students. The average class size in a regular course is 18.

Requirements: Applicants should be graduates of an accredited secondary school or have a GED. AP and CLEP credits are accepted.

Procedure: Freshmen are admitted fall, winter, and summer. There are early admissions and deferred admissions plans. Application deadlines are open. Notification of admission is on a rolling basis.

Transfer: 2528 transfer students enrolled in 2002-2003. The open admission policy applies to transfer students as well as freshmen. 40 of 122 to 132 credits required for the bachelor's degree must be completed at Franklin.

Visiting: There are guides for informal visits and visitors may sit in on classes. To schedule a visit, contact the Admission Office at info@franklin.edu.

Financial Aid: In a recent year, 3% of all full-time freshmen and 2% of continuing full-time students received some form of financial aid. The FAFSA and the university's own financial statement are required. The deadline for filing freshman financial aid applications for fall entry is June 15.

International Students: There are 295 international students enrolled. The school actively recruits these students. They must score 430 on the written TOEFL or 117 on the electronic version or take the MELAB.

Computers: The mainframe is an HP 9000. Students do not use the mainframe but they do access other networked systems like Einstein, Freud, and Newton. Einstein is the UNIX server, Freud is the web server, and Newton is the Oracle server. These support student assignments in computer science courses as well as in general education. There are approximately 350 PCs available for students in labs, the library, and classrooms in 3 locations. These PCs have standard software packages including MS Office XP, Internet Explorer, and other software required by individual courses. All students may access the system. There are no time limits and no fees.

Graduates: From July 1, 2002 to June 30, 2003, 814 bachelor's degrees were awarded. The most popular majors were business administration (39%), accounting (11%), and computer science (9%).

Admissions Contact: Student Services Office.
E-mail: info@franklin.edu Web: www.franklin.edu

HEIDELBERG COLLEGE
Tiffin, OH 44883-2434

C-2

(419) 448-2330
(800) HEIDELBERG; Fax: (419) 448-2334

Full-time: 478 men, 500 women	**Faculty:** 62; IIB, -$
Part-time: 110 men, 173 women	**Ph.D.s:** 77%
Graduate: 73 men, 170 women	**Student/Faculty:** 16 to 1
Year: semesters, summer session	**Tuition:** $13,930 ($13,620)
Application Deadline: May 1	**Room & Board:** $6336
Freshman Class: 1649 applied, 1610 accepted, 296 enrolled	
SAT I Verbal/Math: 515/520	**ACT:** 22 NONCOMPETITIVE

Heidelberg College, founded in 1850, is a private liberal arts institution affiliated with the United Church of Christ/Congregational. In addition to regional accreditation, Heidelberg has baccalaureate program accreditation with NASM. The library contains 260,055 volumes, 108,640 microform items, and 8300 audio/video tapes/CDs, and subscribes to 829 periodicals. Computerized library services include the card catalog, interlibrary loans, and database searching. Special learning facilities include a learning resource center, radio station, TV station, media center, anthropology museum, human cadaver lab, water quality lab, archeology lab, physiology lab, and computer-assisted writing classroom. The 110-acre campus is in a small town 50 miles south of Toledo. Including any residence halls, there are 26 buildings.

Student Life: 94% of undergraduates are from Ohio. Others are from 13 states, 11 foreign countries, and Canada. 61% are from public schools. 90% are white. 61% are Protestant; 33% Catholic. The average age of freshmen is 18; all undergraduates, 24. 27% do not continue beyond their first year; 56% remain to graduate.

Housing: 854 students can be accommodated in college housing, which includes single-sex and coed dorms and special-interest houses. On-campus housing is guaranteed for all 4 years. 86% of students live on campus; of those, 85% remain on campus on weekends. All students may keep cars.

Activities: 30% of men belong to 4 local fraternities; 36% of women belong to 4 local sororities. There are 65 groups on campus, including band, cheerleading, choir, chorale, chorus, computers, dance, drama, drill team, ethnic, forensics, honors, international, jazz band, literary magazine, musical theater, newspaper, opera, orchestra, pep band, political, professional, radio and TV, religious, social, social service, student government, symphony, and yearbook. Popular campus events include Parents Weekend, Greek Sing, and Tuba Christmas.

Sports: There are 9 intercollegiate sports for men and 8 for women, and 9 intramural sports for men and 8 for women. Facilities include a wrestling arena, an all-weather track, indoor courts for volleyball, basketball, racquetball, and tennis, a weight room and fitness area, a sports

medicine clinic, and outdoor tennis, soccer, lacrosse, and football facilities. A YMCA adjacent to the college provides additional recreation options.

Disabled Students: 20% of the campus is accessible. Wheelchair ramps, elevators, special parking, specially equipped rest rooms, special class scheduling, and lowered drinking fountains are available.

Services: Counseling and information services are available, as is tutoring in every subject. There is remedial math.

Campus Safety and Security: Measures include 24-hour foot and vehicle patrol, self-defense education, security escort services, and informal discussions. There are pamphlets/posters/films, emergency telephones, and lighted pathways/sidewalks.

Programs of Study: Heidelberg confers B.A., B.S., and B.Mus. degrees. Master's degrees are also awarded. Bachelor's degrees are awarded in BIOLOGICAL SCIENCE (biology/biological science and environmental biology), BUSINESS (accounting, business administration and management, business economics, management science, and sports management), COMMUNICATIONS AND THE ARTS (communications, dramatic arts, English, German, music, public relations, and Spanish), COMPUTER AND PHYSICAL SCIENCE (chemistry, computer science, information sciences and systems, mathematics, and physics), EDUCATION (athletic training, elementary, foreign languages, middle school, music, physical, science, and secondary), ENGINEERING AND ENVIRONMENTAL DESIGN (preengineering), HEALTH PROFESSIONS (predentistry and premedicine), SOCIAL SCIENCE (anthropology, economics, history, international studies, philosophy, political science/government, prelaw, psychology, public administration, religion, social science, and water resources). Business administration, communications, and sciences are the strongest academically. Business administration, sciences, and psychology are the largest.

Required: Students must fulfill 40 semester hours of general education requirements, including English composition and public speaking, arts, languages and literature, civilization, religion and philosophy, social sciences, natural sciences, and math, and 40 semester hours each in the major and electives. Four units of health and phys ed are needed. A total of 120 semester hours with a minimum GPA of 2.0 overall and 2.5 in the major is required to graduate.

Special: There are co-op programs in preengineering, prenursing, environmental management, and medical technology. A 3-2 engineering degree and a 3-3 nursing degree are offered in cooperation with Case Western Reserve University. Study abroad is possible at the University of Heidelberg, Germany, Seville, Spain, and in Mexico, England, and Cuba. A Washington semester is available at American University. Dual majors in any combination, an honors program, credit for life experience, internships, and pass/fail options are possible. There are 10 national honor societies, a freshman honors program, and 15 departmental honors programs.

Faculty/Classroom: 67% of faculty are male; 33%, female. 93% teach undergraduates. No introductory courses are taught by graduate students. The average class size in an introductory lecture is 30; in a laboratory, 15; and in a regular course, 15.

Admissions: 98% of the 2003-2004 applicants were accepted. The SAT I scores for the 2003-2004 freshman class were: Verbal--55% below 500, 30% between 500 and 599, and 15% between 600 and 700; Math--60% below 500, 33% between 500 and 599, and 7% between 600 and 700. The ACT scores were 48% below 21, 27% between 21 and 23, 13% between 24 and 26, 5% between 27 and 28, and 5% above 28. 30% of the current freshmen were in the top fifth of their class; 60% were in the top two fifths. There were 5 National Merit semifinalists. 6 freshmen graduated first in their class.

Requirements: The SAT I or ACT is required. In addition, applicants should have completed 22 high school academic credits, including 4 years each of English and social studies, 3 each of math and science, and 2 of a foreign language. An audition is required for music majors. Recommendations and an interview are recommended. Heidelberg requires applicants to be in the upper 50% of their class. A GPA of 2.4 is required. AP and CLEP credits are accepted. Important factors in the admissions decision are advanced placement or honor courses, leadership record, and extracurricular activities record.

Procedure: Freshmen are admitted to all sessions. Entrance exams should be taken by the end of the junior year or the beginning of the senior year. There is a rolling admissions plan and a deferred admissions plan. Applications should be filed by May 1 for fall entry, December 1 for spring entry, and June 1 for summer entry, along with a $25 fee. Notification is sent on a rolling basis. Applications are accepted on-line through the college's web site at www.heidelberg.edu.

Transfer: 40 transfer students enrolled in 2002-2003. A minimum GPA of 2.0 and a character reference from the institution most recently attended are required. 30 of 120 credits required for the bachelor's degree must be completed at Heidelberg.

Visiting: There are regularly scheduled orientations for prospective students, including coach and faculty sessions, academic overview, student panel, admissions and financial aid presentations, a tour of the college, and lunch. There are guides for informal visits and visitors may sit in on classes and stay overnight. To schedule a visit, contact the Office of Admission.

Financial Aid: In 2003-2004, 98% of all full-time freshmen and 99% of continuing full-time students received some form of financial aid. 84% of full-time freshmen received need-based aid. The average freshman award was $13,000. Need-based scholarships or need-based grants averaged $8918 ($13,620 maximum); and need-based self-help aid (loans and jobs) averaged $4116 ($5125 maximum). 65% of undergraduates work part time. Average annual earnings from campus work are $800. The average financial indebtedness of the 2003 graduate was $21,682. The FAFSA is required. The priority date for freshman financial aid applications for fall entry is March 1.

International Students: There are 14 international students enrolled. The school actively recruits these students. They must score 500 on the written TOEFL.

Computers: Terminals are located in all residence halls. All Macs and PCs and special use systems are networked through UNIX hosts for use throughout the campus. Almost every department requires some knowledge of computers. Separate computer centers are located in the sciences complex, the library, the business department, the Honors Center, and the administration building. All students may access the system. There are no time limits and no fees.

Graduates: From July 1, 2002 to June 30, 2003, 261 bachelor's degrees were awarded. The most popular majors were education (22%), business (18%), and psychology (15%). In an average class, 50% graduate in 4 years or less, 52% graduate in 5 years or less, and 54% graduate in 6 years or less. 50 companies recruited on campus in 2002-2003. Of the 2002 graduating class, 17% were enrolled in graduate school within 6 months of graduation and 94% were employed.

Admissions Contact: Lindsay Sooy, Interim Director of Admission. E-mail: *adminfo@mail.heidelberg.edu* Web: *http://www.heidelberg.edu*

HIRAM COLLEGE
Hiram, OH 44234

E-1

(330) 569-5169
(800) 362-5280; Fax: (330) 569-5944

Full-time: 390 men, 431 women	**Faculty:** 72; IIB, av$
Part-time: 113 men, 176 women	**Ph.D.s:** 92%
Graduate: none	**Student/Faculty:** 11 to 1
Year: split semesters, summer session	**Tuition:** $21,134
Application Deadline: February 1	**Room & Board:** $7100
Freshman Class: 888 applied, 778 accepted, 226 enrolled	
SAT I Verbal/Math: 560/560	**ACT:** 24 **VERY COMPETITIVE**

Hiram College, founded in 1850, is a private, residential liberal arts and sciences institution. In addition to regional accreditation, Hiram has baccalaureate program accreditation with NASM. The library contains 483,564 volumes, 123,474 microform items, and 8054 audio/video tapes/CDs, and subscribes to 891 periodicals. Computerized library services include the card catalog, interlibrary loans, and database searching. Special learning facilities include a learning resource center, art gallery, planetarium, radio station, 260-acre biological field station, and field station in the Upper Peninsula of Michigan. The 110-acre campus is in a rural area 35 miles southeast of Cleveland. Including any residence halls, there are 28 buildings.

Student Life: 79% of undergraduates are from Ohio. Students are from 23 states and 13 foreign countries. 86% are from public schools. 83% are white; 10% African American. 52% claim no religious affiliation; 21% are Catholic; 21% Protestant. The average age of freshmen is 18; all undergraduates, 20. 14% do not continue beyond their first year; 68% remain to graduate.

Housing: 1000 students can be accommodated in college housing, which includes single-sex and coed dorms. In addition, there is an international theme house. On-campus housing is guaranteed for all 4 years. 93% of students live on campus; of those, 75% remain on campus on weekends. All students may keep cars.

Activities: There are no fraternities or sororities. There are 90 groups on campus, including art, band, cheerleading, choir, chorale, chorus, computers, dance, drama, ethnic, gay, honors, international, jazz band, literary magazine, musical theater, newspaper, opera, orchestra, photography, political, professional, radio and TV, religious, social, social service, student government, and yearbook. Popular campus events include Campus Days, Springfest, and Madrigal Revels.

Sports: There are 9 intercollegiate sports for men and 8 for women, and 10 intramural sports for men and 10 for women. Facilities include a 4000-seat stadium, a gym, sports fields, an all-weather track, a fitness room, a sauna, racquetball and tennis courts, an indoor swimming pool with diving area, an outdoor exercise and fitness trail, a cross-country ski trail, and a fully equipped athletic training facility.

Disabled Students: 40% of the campus is accessible. Wheelchair ramps, elevators, special parking, and specially equipped rest rooms are available.

Services: Counseling and information services are available, as is tutoring in every subject. There is a reader service for the blind. Note takers are available for most classes.

Campus Safety and Security: Measures include 24-hour foot and vehicle patrol, self-defense education, security escort services, and informal discussions. There are pamphlets/posters/films, emergency telephones, and lighted pathways/sidewalks.

Programs of Study: Hiram confers the B.A. degree. Bachelor's degrees are awarded in BIOLOGICAL SCIENCE (biology/biological science), BUSINESS (international economics and management science), COMMUNICATIONS AND THE ARTS (art, art history and appreciation, classics, communications, dramatic arts, English, French, German, language arts, music, and Spanish), COMPUTER AND PHYSICAL SCIENCE (applied physics, chemistry, computer science, and mathematics), EDUCATION (elementary), ENGINEERING AND ENVIRONMENTAL DESIGN (environmental science), SOCIAL SCIENCE (economics, history, philosophy, political science/government, psychobiology, psychology, religion, social studies, and sociology). Biology, computer science, and education are the strongest academically. Biology, education, and management are the largest.

Required: All students must complete distribution requirement courses in the fine arts, humanities, natural sciences, and social sciences; the Freshman Institute and Colloquium; a first-year seminar in writing and speaking skills; and 1 upper-division interdisciplinary requirement. A total of 120 academic semester hours and a minimum GPA of 2.0 are required to graduate.

Special: There is cross-registration through the Cleveland Commission on Higher Education and a 3-2 engineering program with Case Western Reserve and Washington Universities. There is a Washington semester and study abroad in many countries with courses taught by Hiram faculty. Double majors and individually arranged internships in all fields, student-designed majors, and pass/no credit options are possible. There are 8 national honor societies, including Phi Beta Kappa.

Faculty/Classroom: 54% of faculty are male; 46%, female. All teach undergraduates. The average class size in an introductory lecture is 19; in a laboratory, 11; and in a regular course, 13.

Admissions: 88% of the 2003-2004 applicants were accepted. The SAT I scores for the 2003-2004 freshman class were: Verbal--21% below 500, 37% between 500 and 599, 31% between 600 and 700, and 11% above 700; Math--29% below 500, 39% between 500 and 599, 29% between 600 and 700, and 3% above 700. The ACT scores were 28% below 21, 22% between 21 and 23, 23% between 24 and 26, 14% between 27 and 28, and 13% above 28. 53% of the current freshmen were in the top fifth of their class; 78% were in the top two fifths. 16 freshmen graduated first in their class.

Requirements: The SAT I or ACT is required. In addition, applicants should have completed 16 academic units or the GED equivalent. An essay is required. A portfolio, audition, and interview are recommended. AP and CLEP credits are accepted. Important factors in the admissions decision are advanced placement or honor courses, leadership record, and extracurricular activities record.

Procedure: Freshmen are admitted fall and spring. Entrance exams should be taken no later than the fall of the senior year. There is a rolling admissions plan. There are early decision, early admissions, and deferred admissions plans. Early decision applications should be filed by December 1; regular applications, by February 1 for maximum scholarship consideration and December 1 for spring entry, along with a $35 fee. Notification is sent on a rolling basis. 25 early decision candidates were accepted for the 2003-2004 class. Applications are accepted on computer disk and on-line through CollegeLink, CommonApp, and Apply.

Transfer: 27 transfer students enrolled in 2002-2003. Applicants should have at least a 2.5 GPA and be in good academic and social standing with the previous institution. An interview is recommended. 60 of 120 credits required for the bachelor's degree must be completed at Hiram.

Visiting: There are regularly scheduled orientations for prospective students 1 week before the semester begins, and campus visits are encouraged while school is in session. There are guides for informal visits and visitors may sit in on classes and stay overnight. To schedule a visit, contact the Admissions Office.

Financial Aid: In 2003-2004, 94% of all full-time freshmen and 93% of continuing full-time students received some form of financial aid. 82% of all full-time students received need-based aid. The average freshman award was $17,172, with $11,565 from need-based scholarships or need-based grants and $5607 from need-based self-help aid (loans and jobs). 71% of undergraduates work part time. Average annual earnings from campus work are $1251. The average financial indebtedness of the 2003 graduate was $17,125. Hiram is a member of CSS. The FAFSA is required. The deadline for filing freshman financial aid applications for fall entry is March 1.

International Students: There are 39 international students enrolled. The school actively recruits these students. They must score 550 on the written TOEFL and also take the SAT I or the ACT.

Computers: The mainframe is a DEC Alpha Server 2100 5/250. The college network may be accessed from student-owned PCs in residence halls and from PC labs throughout the campus. The network allows access to the Internet and the Web. Each residence hall has a lab with 5 to 8 PCs. More than 60 additional PCs are available in classrooms and other locations. All students may access the system 24 hours a day, 7 days per week. There are no time limits and no fees.

Graduates: From July 1, 2002 to June 30, 2003, 261 bachelor's degrees were awarded. The most popular majors were biology (13%), communication (9%), and history (9%). In an average class, 1% graduate in 3 years or less, 60% graduate in 4 years or less, 66% graduate in 5 years or less, and 68% graduate in 6 years or less. Of the 2002 graduating class, 23% were enrolled in graduate school within 6 months of graduation and 71% were employed.

Admissions Contact: Brenda Swihart-Meyer, Director of Admission. A video is available. E-mail: *admission@hiram.edu* Web: *www.hiram.edu*

JOHN CARROLL UNIVERSITY   D-1
University Heights, OH 44118   **(216) 397-4294**
                                                 Fax: (216) 397-4981

Full-time: 1506 men, 1773 women	**Faculty:** 236; IIA, +$
Part-time: 87 men, 83 women	**Ph.D.s:** 89%
Graduate: 283 men, 510 women	**Student/Faculty:** 14 to 1
Year: semesters, summer session	**Tuition:** $20,766
Application Deadline: February 1	**Room & Board:** $6892
Freshman Class: 2802 applied, 2440 accepted, 859 enrolled	
SAT I Verbal/Math: 570/580	**ACT:** 24 **COMPETITIVE+**

John Carroll University, founded in 1886, is a private Catholic institution operated by the Jesuits. It offers undergraduate degree programs in the arts, sciences, and business. There are 2 undergraduate schools and 1 graduate school. In addition to regional accreditation, John Carroll has baccalaureate program accreditation with AACSB and NCATE. The library contains 710,403 microform items and 4880 audio/video tapes/CDs, and subscribes to 1975 periodicals. Computerized library services include the card catalog, interlibrary loans, and database searching. Special learning facilities include a learning resource center, radio station, and TV station. The 62-acre campus is in a suburban area 10 miles east of Cleveland. Including any residence halls, there are 26 buildings.

Student Life: 75% of undergraduates are from Ohio. Students are from 35 states, 21 foreign countries, and Canada. 53% are from public schools. 87% are white. 71% are Catholic; 15%, Protestant; 7% claim no religious affiliation. The average age of freshmen is 18; all undergraduates, 21. 14% do not continue beyond their first year; 81% remain to graduate.

Housing: 2016 students can be accommodated in college housing, which includes single-sex and coed dorms. 58% of students live on campus. Upperclassmen may keep cars.

Activities: 13% of men belong to 4 national fraternities; 18% of women belong to 5 national sororities. There are 87 groups on campus, including band, cheerleading, chess, choir, chorale, chorus, computers, dance, debate, drama, drill team, ethnic, honors, international, jazz band, literary magazine, musical theater, newspaper, pep band, photography, political, professional, radio and TV, religious, social, social service, student government, symphony, and yearbook. Popular campus events include Welcome Back Week, Little Siblings Weekend, and Dance Marathon.

Sports: There are 11 intercollegiate sports for men and 10 for women, and 8 intramural sports for men and 8 for women. Facilities include a swimming pool and diving well, a 3800-seat football stadium and track, a baseball stadium, soccer and softball fields, an indoor track, tennis, volleyball, racquetball, and basketball courts, a weight room, a fitness center, and a 33-acre off-campus student villa. Club sports include hockey, rugby, lacrosse, skiing, and sailing.

Disabled Students: 96% of the campus is accessible. Wheelchair ramps, elevators, special parking, specially equipped rest rooms, special class scheduling, lowered drinking fountains, and lowered telephones are available.

Services: Counseling and information services are available, as is tutoring in every subject. There is a reader service for the blind.

Campus Safety and Security: Measures include 24-hour foot and vehicle patrol, self-defense education, security escort services, and shuttle buses. There are informal discussions, pamphlets/posters/films, emergency telephones, and lighted pathways/sidewalks.

Programs of Study: John Carroll confers B.A., B.S., B.A.Classics, B.S.B.A., and B.S.Econ. degrees. Master's degrees are also awarded. Bachelor's degrees are awarded in BIOLOGICAL SCIENCE (biology/biological science), BUSINESS (accounting, banking and finance, business administration and management, and marketing/retailing/merchandising), COMMUNICATIONS AND THE ARTS (art history and appreciation, communications, English, French, German, Greek, Latin, literature, and Spanish), COMPUTER AND PHYSICAL SCIENCE (chemistry, computer science, mathematics, and physics), EDUCATION (early childhood, elementary, mathematics, physical, and secondary), ENGINEERING AND ENVIRONMENTAL DESIGN (engineering physics), SOCIAL SCIENCE (economics, history, humanities, philosophy, political science/government, psychology, public administration, religion, and sociology). Accounting, biology, and English are the strongest academically. Communications, biology, and marketing are the largest.

Required: All students must complete a liberal arts core curriculum, which includes 6 credits each in English composition and foreign language, 3 in first-year seminar, and 2 in speech communication. Also, students must take 4 courses each in science/math and the humanities, 3 each in social sciences and philosophy, and 2 in religious studies. Additional requirements include 1 writing-intensive course beyond English composition, 2 international courses, and 1 course in issues of diversity. A total of 128 credit hours with a minimum GPA of 2.0 is required for graduation.

Special: Co-op programs are available, and cross-registration is offered with 16 area colleges through the Northeast Ohio Commission on Higher Education. Study abroad is possible in many countries. Joint engineering degrees are offered with Case Western Reserve University, the University of Detroit Mercy, and Washington University. Work-study programs with local corporations, internships, a Washington semester, student-designed majors, dual majors, and some pass/fail options are available. There are 13 national honor societies and a freshman honors program.

Faculty/Classroom: 59% of faculty are male; 41%, female. All teach undergraduates and 95% do research. Graduate students teach 4% of introductory courses. The average class size in an introductory lecture is 21; in a laboratory, 20; and in a regular course, 21.

Admissions: 87% of the 2003-2004 applicants were accepted. The SAT I scores for the 2003-2004 freshman class were: Verbal--14% below 500, 51% between 500 and 599, 26% between 600 and 700, and 6% above 700; Math--16% below 500, 43% between 500 and 599, 34% between 600 and 700, and 7% above 700. The ACT scores were 22% below 21, 25% between 21 and 23, 34% between 24 and 26, 11% between 27 and 28, and 8% above 28. 45% of the current freshmen were in the top fifth of their class; 77% were in the top two fifths. In a recent year, there were 5 National Merit finalists and 12 freshmen graduated first in their class.

Requirements: The SAT I or ACT is required. In addition, applicants should be graduates of an accredited secondary school with 16 academic credits, including 4 in English, 3 in math, 2 each in foreign language, lab science, and social studies, and 3 in electives. An essay is part of the application process, and an interview is recommended. AP credits are accepted. Important factors in the admissions decision are advanced placement or honor courses, extracurricular activities record, and recommendations by school officials.

Procedure: Freshmen are admitted fall and spring. Entrance exams should be taken in the spring of the junior year or the fall of the senior year. There is a deferred admissions plan. Applications should be filed by February 1 for fall entry, along with a $25 fee. Notification is sent on a rolling basis. Applications are accepted on computer disk and on-line through CollegeLink, Apply, *Embark.com*, or the school's web site.

Transfer: 160 transfer students enrolled in a recent year. Students must be in good standing at the time of application. The most recent term average and the cumulative average at the home school must be 2.0 or better to be considered for admission, and the cumulative average for all schools attended must be 2.0 or better. A GPA of at least 2.5 is recommended. 30 of 128 credits required for the bachelor's degree must be completed at John Carroll.

Visiting: There are regularly scheduled orientations for prospective students, consisting of open houses, admission and financial aid presentations, campus and Cleveland tours, and opportunities to meet faculty and students. There are guides for informal visits and visitors may sit in on classes and stay overnight. To schedule a visit, contact the Office of Admission.

Financial Aid: In 2003-2004, 97% of all full-time freshmen and 94% of continuing full-time students received some form of financial aid. 76% of full-time freshmen and 79% of continuing full-time students received need-based aid. The average freshman award was $15,577. Need-based scholarships or need-based grants averaged $4226 ($8000 maximum); need-based self-help aid (loans and jobs) averaged $4155 ($6425 maximum); and non-need-based awards and non-need-based scholarships averaged $3737 ($13,000 maximum). 34% of undergraduates work part time. The FAFSA is required. Check with the school for current deadlines.

International Students: In a recent year, there were 2 international students enrolled. The school actively recruits these students. They must score 550 on the written TOEFL or 213 on the electronic version and also take the SAT I or the ACT.

Computers: The mainframes are a LAN, Intel-based servers, an Alpha server, RISC-based Sun servers, IBM RS6000 servers, and a clustered network appliance. Any registered student may obtain a user code for the campus network. There are more than 1000 PCs in various locations on campus. PCs are available in the science and math labs. All residence hall rooms are wired, and students may hook directly into the university system as well as the Internet and World Wide Web. All students may access the system 24 hours a day in some locations. There are no time limits. The fee is $300. For those who have their own computers, a PC platform is recommended.

Graduates: In a recent year, 728 bachelor's degrees were awarded. The most popular majors were communications (14%), biology (10%), and marketing (9%). In an average class, 1% graduate in 3 years or less, 70% graduate in 4 years or less, 79% graduate in 5 years or less, and 81% graduate in 6 years or less. 163 companies recruited on campus in a recent year. Of a recent graduating class, 22% were enrolled in graduate school within 6 months of graduation.

Admissions Contact: Thomas P. Fanning, Director of Admission. A video is available. E-mail: *admission@jcu.edu*
Web: *http://explore.jcu.edu*

KENT STATE UNIVERSITY
Kent, OH 44242-0001

D-2

(330) 672-2444
(800) 988-KENT; Fax: (330) 672-2499

Full-time: 6443 men, 9539 women	Faculty: 626; I, --$
Part-time: 1342 men, 1849 women	Ph.D.s: 70%
Graduate: 1704 men, 3365 women	Student/Faculty: 26 to 1
Year: semesters, summer session	Tuition: $6882 ($13,314)
Application Deadline: May 1	Room & Board: $6050
Freshman Class: 11,098 applied, 9922 accepted, 3822 enrolled	
SAT I Verbal/Math: 517/513	ACT: 21	COMPETITIVE

Kent State University, founded in 1910, is a public university offering degree programs in liberal and fine arts, business, health science, teacher and professional training, and aviation. There are 8 undergraduate and 8 graduate schools. In addition to regional accreditation, KSU has baccalaureate program accreditation with AACSB, ABET, ACEJMC, ADA, CAAHEP, FIDER, NAAB, NASAD, NASM, NASPE, NCATE, and NLN. The 6 libraries contain 2,293,371 volumes, 1,286,888 microform items, and 10,266 audio/video tapes/CDs, and subscribe to 11,139 periodicals. Computerized library services include the card catalog, interlibrary loans, database searching, and Internet access. Special learning facilities include an art gallery, planetarium, radio station, TV station, fashion museum, and Liquid Crystal Institute. The 1347-acre campus is in a suburban area 45 miles southeast of Cleveland. Including any residence halls, there are 115 buildings.

Student Life: 90% of undergraduates are from Ohio. Students are from 50 states, 96 foreign countries, and Canada. 84% are white. The average age of freshmen is 18; all undergraduates, 22. 27% do not continue beyond their first year; 44% remain to graduate.

Housing: 6800 students can be accommodated in college housing, which includes single-sex and coed dorms, on-campus apartments, and married-student housing. In addition, there are honors houses and special-interest houses. On-campus housing is guaranteed for all 4 years. 66% of students commute. Alcohol is not permitted. Upperclassmen may keep cars.

Activities: 7% of men belong to 19 national fraternities; 4% of women belong to 1 local and 9 national sororities. There are 175 groups on campus, including academic, art, band, cheerleading, chess, choir, chorale, chorus, computers, dance, drama, ethnic, gay, honors, international, jazz band, marching band, musical theater, newspaper, opera, orchestra, photography, political, professional, radio and TV, religious, social, social service, and student government. Popular campus events include Black Squirrel Festival, Folk Festival, and Experience Kent State-Community/Parents Day.

Sports: There are 8 intercollegiate sports for men and 10 for women, and 22 intramural sports for men and 22 for women. Facilities include a gym, a recreation and wellness center, a football stadium, a field house, 2 fitness circuits, a golf course, a bowling alley, tennis courts, lighted basketball courts, an ice arena, a pool, a weight room, and soccer, lacrosse, rugby, baseball, softball, and field hockey fields, indoor track, outdoor track, and wrestling room.

Disabled Students: 90% of the campus is accessible. Wheelchair ramps, elevators, special parking, specially equipped rest rooms, special class scheduling, lowered drinking fountains, lowered telephones, special housing, and transportation services are available.

Services: Counseling and information services are available, as is tutoring in some subjects. There is a reader service for the blind, remedial math, reading, and writing, and a writing clinic.

Campus Safety and Security: Measures include 24-hour foot and vehicle patrol, security escort services, shuttle buses, and informal discussions. There are pamphlets/posters/films, emergency telephones, lighted pathways/sidewalks, a 24-hour campus police department, overnight security guards, and a 2-key system for residence halls.

Programs of Study: KSU confers B.A., B.S., B.B.A., B.F.A., B.G.S., B.M., B.R.I.T., B.S.E., and B.S.N. degrees. Associate, master's, and doctoral degrees are also awarded. Bachelor's degrees are awarded in AGRICULTURE (conservation and regulation), BIOLOGICAL SCIENCE (biology/biological science, biotechnology, botany, life science, nutrition, and zoology), BUSINESS (accounting, banking and finance, business administration and management, business economics, fashion merchandising, institutional management, international economics, management science, marketing/retailing/merchandising, personnel management, real estate, and recreation and leisure services), COMMUNICATIONS AND THE ARTS (advertising, American Sign Language, art history and appreciation, broadcasting, classics, communications, crafts, dance, design,

dramatic arts, English, film arts, fine arts, French, German, graphic design, illustration, industrial design, journalism, language arts, Latin, music, public relations, radio/television technology, Russian, Spanish, speech/debate/rhetoric, telecommunications, and visual and performing arts), COMPUTER AND PHYSICAL SCIENCE (applied mathematics, chemistry, computer science, earth science, geology, information sciences and systems, mathematics, physical sciences, physics, and science), EDUCATION (art, athletic training, business, early childhood, education, elementary, English, foreign languages, health, marketing and distribution, mathematics, middle school, music, physical, science, secondary, social studies, special, technical, trade and industrial, and vocational), ENGINEERING AND ENVIRONMENTAL DESIGN (aeronautical science, aircraft mechanics, architecture, aviation computer technology, engineering technology, food services technology, industrial administration/management, industrial engineering technology, interior design, and technology and public affairs), HEALTH PROFESSIONS (community health work, cytotechnology, health science, medical technology, nursing, predentistry, premedicine, preveterinary science, radiological science, and speech pathology/audiology), SOCIAL SCIENCE (African studies, American studies, anthropology, criminal justice, Eastern European studies, economics, ethnic studies, family/consumer studies, fashion design and technology, geography, gerontology, history, human development, international relations, Latin American studies, liberal arts/general studies, paralegal studies, peace studies, philosophy, political science/government, prelaw, psychology, Russian and Slavic studies, social studies, and sociology). Architecture, education, and fashion design and merchandising are the strongest academically. Justice studies, psychology, and journalism and mass communication are the largest.

Required: Students are required to complete 121 credit hours, of which 39 must be upper division. Distribution requirements include 9 hours in humanities and fine arts, 9 hours in social sciences and 6 hours each in basic sciences, composition, math, logic, and foreign languages. Students must maintain an overall GPA of 2.0.

Special: A co-op program is available with the School of Technology, and cross-registration is available with the University of Akron, Cleveland State University, and Northeastern Ohio Universities College of Medicine (NEOUCOM). Work-study programs and internships are offered. Study abroad in 18 countries, a Washington semester, an accelerated medical degree program, B.A.-B.S. degrees, dual majors, a general studies degree, student-designed majors, credit for military education, nondegree study, and pass/fail options are also possible. The Honors College provides honors course work in all majors. Dual admission with Cuyahoga Community, Lakeland Community, NEOUCOM, and Lorain County Commmunity Colleges is available. Kent is a member of the national student exchange program. There are 13 national honor societies, including Phi Beta Kappa, and a freshman honors program.

Faculty/Classroom: 52% of faculty are male; 48%, female. Graduate students teach 19% of introductory courses. The average class size in a regular course is 26.

Admissions: 89% of the 2003-2004 applicants were accepted. The SAT I scores for the 2003-2004 freshman class were: Verbal--42% below 500, 40% between 500 and 599, 16% between 600 and 700, and 2% above 700; Math--43% below 500, 40% between 500 and 599, 16% between 600 and 700, and 1% above 700. The ACT scores were 43% below 21, 30% between 21 and 23, 17% between 24 and 26, 6% between 27 and 28, and 4% above 28. 26% of the current freshmen were in the top fifth of their class; 55% were in the top two fifths. 41 freshmen graduated first in their class.

Requirements: The SAT I or ACT is required. Applicants most likely to be admitted will have at least a 2.5 cumulative GPA (on a 4.0 scale) in a solid college-preparatory program and an ACT composite score of at least 21 (or a 980 SAT I combined score). AP and CLEP credits are accepted.

Procedure: Freshmen are admitted fall, spring, and summer. Entrance exams should be taken in the spring of the junior year or the fall of the senior year. There is a rolling admissions plan. Applications should be filed by May 1 for fall entry, along with a $30 fee. Notification is sent on a rolling basis. 1004 applicants were on the 2003 waiting list; 192 were admitted. Applications are accepted on-line through KSU Admissions web site: *www.admissions.kent.edu.*

Transfer: 1345 transfer students enrolled in 2002-2003. Applicants must present a minimum GPA of 2.0 on completed college course work. For students with fewer than 24 semester hours or 36 quarter hours, a high school transcript and ACT or SAT I scores are also required. 30 of 121 credits required for the bachelor's degree must be completed at KSU.

Visiting: There are regularly scheduled orientations for prospective students, including information sessions (financial aid, residence halls, student panel), a campus tour, and meetings with academic representatives. There are guides for informal visits. To schedule a visit, contact the Admissions Office.

Financial Aid: In 2003-2004, 75% of all full-time freshmen and 61% of continuing full-time students received some form of financial aid. 62% of full-time freshmen and 58% of continuing full-time students received need-based aid. The average freshman award was $10,037. The average financial indebtedness of the 2003 graduate was $19,500. KSU is a member of CSS. The FAFSA and the college's own financial statement are required. The priority date for freshman financial aid applications for fall entry is February 1.

International Students: There are 182 international students enrolled. The school actively recruits these students. They must score 525 on the written TOEFL or 197 on the electronic version or take the MELAB.

Computers: The mainframe is an IBM z800. Terminals and PC facilities are available for student use in academic buildings and residence halls. 100 dial-up links provide remote access. Wireless access is available in the library, student center, and Tri-Towers dorms. Students with departmental authorization may access the system 24 hours a day, 7 days a week. There are no time limits and no fees.

Graduates: From July 1, 2002 to June 30, 2003, 3454 bachelor's degrees were awarded. The most popular majors were business (13%), justice studies (6%), and psychology (5%). In an average class, 18% graduate in 4 years or less, 38% graduate in 5 years or less, and 44% graduate in 6 years or less. 179 companies recruited on campus in 2002-2003.

Admissions Contact: Nancy Dellavecchia, Director of Admissions. A video is available. E-mail: *admissions@kent.edu* Web: *www.admissions.kent.edu*

KENYON COLLEGE
Gambier, OH 43022-9623

C-3

(740) 427-5776
(800) 848-2468; Fax: (740) 427-5770

Full-time: 722 men, 870 women	**Faculty:** 144; IIB,
Part-time: 5 men, 15 women	**Ph.D.s:** 96%
Graduate: none	**Student/Faculty:** 11 to 1
Year: semesters	**Tuition:** $30,330
Application Deadline: February 2	**Room & Board:** $5040
Freshman Class: 3364 applied, 1534 accepted, 454 enrolled	
SAT I Verbal/Math: 680/650	**ACT:** 30

HIGHLY COMPETITIVE+

Kenyon College is a private liberal arts and sciences undergraduate college founded in 1824 by Philander Chase, the first Episcopal Bishop of Ohio. The library contains 371,253 volumes, 138,841 microform items, and 171,230 audio/video tapes/CDs, and subscribes to 1178 periodicals. Computerized library services include the card catalog, interlibrary loans, database searching, and Internet access. Special learning facilities include a learning resource center, art gallery, radio station, an obsesrvatory, and an environmental center. The 1000-acre campus is in a rural area 50 miles northeast of Columbus. Including any residence halls, there are 65 buildings.

Student Life: 80% of undergraduates are from out of state, mostly the Midwest. Students are from 49 states, 28 foreign countries, and Canada. 53% are from public schools. 84% are white. 31% claim no religious affiliation; 19% Protestant; 18% Catholic (first-year); 18% a variety of religious practices from Quaker to Zen Buddhist; 14% Jewish. The average age of freshmen is 18; all undergraduates, 20. 8% do not continue beyond their first year; 80% remain to graduate.

Housing: 1579 students can be accommodated in college housing, which includes single-sex and coed dorms and on-campus apartments. In addition, there are special-interest floors, including community service or social group halls, a substance-free hall, a wellness hall, an international wing, Kosher living, and Township Fire Department. On-campus housing is guaranteed for all 4 years. All students live on campus; of those, 99% remain on campus on weekends. All students may keep cars.

Activities: 23% of men belong to 1 local and 7 national fraternities; 8% of women belong to 4 local sororities. There are 120 groups on campus, including art, band, chess, choir, chorale, chorus, dance, debate, drama, environmental/conservation, ethnic, film, gay, international, jazz band, literary magazine, martial arts, musical theater, newspaper, opera, orchestra, pep band, photography, political, professional, radio and TV, religious, social, social service, student government, student lectureship, symphony, and yearbook. Popular campus events include Philander's Phling, Summer Send-Off, and dance, drama, music, and athletic events.

Sports: There are 11 intercollegiate sports for men and 11 for women, and 9 intramural sports for men and 9 for women. Facilities include 70 acres of playing, football, softball, and soccer fields, a 50-yard pool, a field house, a Nautilus center and weight rooms, and basketball, tennis, squash, and racquetball courts.

Disabled Students: 13% of the campus is accessible. Wheelchair ramps, elevators, special parking, specially equipped rest rooms, special class scheduling, lowered drinking fountains, lowered telephones, and audio and visual equipment are available.

Services: Counseling and information services are available, as is tutoring in some subjects upon request. There is a reader service for the blind, remedial writing, note-taking services, oral tests, and extended time on tests.

Campus Safety and Security: Measures include 24-hour foot and vehicle patrol, self-defense education, security escort services, and informal discussions. There are pamphlets/posters/films, emergency telephones, lighted pathways/sidewalks, and formal safety awareness events.

Programs of Study: Kenyon confers the B.A. degree. Bachelor's degrees are awarded in BIOLOGICAL SCIENCE (biochemistry, biology/biological science, molecular biology, and neurosciences), COMMUNICATIONS AND THE ARTS (art history and appreciation, classics, dance, dramatic arts, English, French, German, Greek (classical), Latin, modern language, music, Spanish, and studio art), COMPUTER AND PHYSICAL SCIENCE (chemistry, mathematics, and physics), SOCIAL SCIENCE (anthropology, economics, history, international studies, philosophy, political science/government, psychology, religion, and sociology). English, history, and political science are the largest.

Required: Students are required to complete a total of 16 units, including 4 to 7 units in the major, 1 unit in each of 4 divisions representing the arts, humanities, natural sciences, and social sciences, and 1/2 unit of quantitative reasoning. Students must maintain a minimum GPA of 2.0 and complete the senior exercise in their major.

Special: Students may study abroad in many countries. The college also offers dual and student-designed majors, pass/fail options, internships, winter and/or spring break externship programs, a Washington semester consisting of apprenticeships in any of several U.S. programs, and a 3-2 engineering degree with Case Western Reserve, Washington University in St. Louis, and Rensselaer Polytechnic Institute, as well as a 3-2 nursing degree with Case Western Reserve and a 3-2 environmental studies program with Duke University. 3-2 or 4-1 master's (certification) programs with The Bank Street College of Education are also possible. Kenyon's Interdisciplinary Program in Humane Studies offers a tutorial-based concentration on the human predicament. There are 3 national honor societies, including Phi Beta Kappa, and 30 departmental honors programs.

Faculty/Classroom: 63% of faculty are male; 37%, female. All both teach and do research.

Admissions: 46% of the 2003-2004 applicants were accepted. The SAT I scores for the 2003-2004 freshman class were: Verbal--1% below 500, 15% between 500 and 599, 46% between 600 and 700, and 38% above 700; Math--1% below 500, 23% between 500 and 599, 54% between 600 and 700, and 22% above 700. The ACT scores were 2% between 21 and 23, 22% between 24 and 26, 24% between 27 and 28, and 51% above 28. 79% of the current freshmen were in the top fifth of their class; 95% were in the top two fifths. There were 43 National Merit finalists and 4 semifinalists. 29 freshmen graduated first in their class.

Requirements: The SAT I or ACT is required. In addition, applicants should be graduates of an accredited secondary school. Kenyon recommends 4 units each of English, foreign language, and math, and 3 units each of science and social studies. Candidates are encouraged to exceed the minimum requirements, especially in math and science, and to take advance placement or honors work in at least 2 subjects. An essay and interview are important criteria in the admissions decision. Talent in music, theater, art, writing, and athletics is given extra consideration. AP credits are accepted. Important factors in the admissions decision are advanced placement or honor courses, evidence of special talent, and leadership record.

Procedure: Freshmen are admitted in the fall. Entrance exams should be taken in the fall of the senior year. There are early decision and deferred admissions plans. Early decision applications should be filed by December 1; regular applications, by February 2 for fall entry, along with a $45 fee, which is waived for on-line applications. Notification of early decision is sent December 15; regular decision, April 1. 146 early decision candidates were accepted for the 2003-2004 class. 580 applicants were on the 2003 waiting list; 57 were admitted. Applications are accepted on-line through Common App and *Embark.com*.

Transfer: 27 transfer students enrolled in 2002-2003. Transfer applicants must have a minimum college GPA of 3.0 and a high school record suggesting ability and potential. 8 credits of 16 required for the bachelor's degree must be completed at Kenyon.

Visiting: There are regularly scheduled orientations for prospective students, including interviews with staff, a campus tour, and a class visit. Students may also request to meet with faculty and coaches. Kenyon students are also available to host a prospective student overnight in the dorm weekly Sunday–Thursday. There are guides for informal visits and visitors may sit in on classes and stay overnight. To schedule a visit, contact the Admissions Office at (800) 848-2468 or *admissions@kenyon.edu*.

Financial Aid: In 2003-2004, 49% of all full-time freshmen and 47% of continuing full-time students received some form of financial aid. 49% of full-time freshmen and 45% of continuing full-time students received need-based aid. The average freshman award was $23,891, with $17,513 from need-based scholarships or need-based grants, $2626 need-based self-help aid (loans and jobs), and $3752 from Stafford loans and state and federal loans. 35% of undergraduates work part time. Average annual earnings from campus work are $635. Kenyon is a member of CSS. The CSS/Profile and FAFSA are required. The deadline for filing freshman financial aid applications for fall entry is February 15.

International Students: There are 38 international students enrolled. The school actively recruits these students. They must score 570 on the written TOEFL or 230 on the electronic version.

Computers: The mainframe servers run Windows NT/2000, Linux, and Mac programs. The Student Network Access Plan (SNAP+), Kenyon's residential network program, provides a 10-base-T Ethernet jack in each residence hall room with a direct connection to the campus network and the Internet. There are more than 300 college-owned computers providing student access to network resources, the Internet, library resources, and public access e-mail/Internet stations. The majority of computers are Windows-based, but Mac labs are available. 39 computer labs/classrooms/standalone workstations are available. All students may access the system 24 hours a day. There are no time limits and no fees. It is strongly recommended that all students have a personal computer. A Windows NT, Windows 2000, or any Apple running OSX or higher is recommended.

Graduates: From July 1, 2002 to June 30, 2003, 395 bachelor's degrees were awarded. The most popular majors were English (20%), political science (11%), and history (11%). In an average class, 80% graduate in 4 years or less, 82% graduate in 5 years or less, and 84% graduate in 6 years or less. 40 companies recruited on campus in 2002-2003. Of the 2002 graduating class, 17% were enrolled in graduate school within 6 months of graduation and 95% were employed.

Admissions Contact: Jennifer Britz, Dean of Admissions and Financial Aid. A video is available. E-mail: *admissions@kenyon.edu* Web: *www.kenyon.edu*

LAKE ERIE COLLEGE
E-1
Painesville, OH 44077

(440) 375-7050
(800) 916-0904; Fax: (440) 375-7005

Full-time: 713 men and women	**Faculty:** 27; II B, --$
Part-time: 90 men and women	**Ph.D.s:** 72%
Graduate: none	**Student/Faculty:** 26 to 1
Year: semesters, summer session	**Tuition:** $17,720
Application Deadline: open	**Room & Board:** $5830
Freshman Class: 708 applied, 556 accepted, 215 enrolled	
SAT I Verbal/Math: 580/510	**ACT:** 21 COMPETITIVE

Lake Erie College, founded in 1856, is a private liberal arts institution. The 2 libraries contain 89,232 volumes, 8091 microform items, and 4469 audio/video tapes/CDs, and subscribe to 767 periodicals. Computerized library services include the card catalog, interlibrary loans, and database searching. Special learning facilities include a learning resource center, art gallery, radio station, an American Indian Museum, and an equestrian center. The 150-acre campus is in a small town 30 miles east of Cleveland. Including any residence halls, there are 15 buildings.

Student Life: 85% of undergraduates are from Ohio. Students are from 22 states, 5 foreign countries, and Canada. 90% are from public schools. 96% are white. The average age of freshmen is 18; all undergraduates, 25. 16% do not continue beyond their first year; 65% remain to graduate.

Housing: 256 students can be accommodated in college housing, which includes single-sex and coed dorms. On-campus housing is guaranteed for all 4 years. 52% of students commute. All students may keep cars.

Activities: There are no fraternities or sororities. There are 21 groups on campus, including art, cheerleading, choir, chorus, dance, drama, equestrian, ethnic, honors, international, musical theater, newspaper, pep band, photography, political, professional, religious, social, social service, student government, and yearbook. Popular campus events include Prix de Ville of North America, international dinners, and class dinners.

Sports: There are 5 intercollegiate sports for men and 5 for women, and 5 intramural sports for men and 5 for women. Facilities include a gym, an 85-acre equestrian center, and playing fields.

Disabled Students: 20% of the campus is accessible. Wheelchair ramps, elevators, special parking, specially equipped rest rooms, special class scheduling, lowered drinking fountains, and lowered telephones are available.

Services: Counseling and information services are available, as is tutoring in most subjects. There is remedial math, reading, and writing.

Campus Safety and Security: Measures include 24-hour foot and vehicle patrol, self-defense education, security escort services, and informal discussions. There are pamphlets/posters/films, emergency telephones, and lighted pathways/sidewalks.

Programs of Study: Lake Erie confers B.A., B.S., and B.F.A. degrees. Master's degrees are also awarded. Bachelor's degrees are awarded in AGRICULTURE (equine science), BIOLOGICAL SCIENCE (biology/biological science), BUSINESS (accounting, business administration and management, and international business management), COMMUNICATIONS AND THE ARTS (communications, dance, English, fine arts, French, German, Italian, music, and Spanish), COMPUTER AND PHYSICAL SCIENCE (chemistry and mathematics), EDUCATION (elementary and middle school), ENGINEERING AND ENVIRONMENTAL

DESIGN (environmental science), SOCIAL SCIENCE (paralegal studies, psychology, and social science). Languages, education, and business are the strongest academically. Equestrian science, elementary education, and business are the largest.

Required: General education requirements include 6 hours of computers, 4 hours each of math, English, and either a foreign language or math with application, and 2 hours of public speaking. A computer literacy course is required. There are specific core requirements for 25 additional semester hours. Students must complete 128 credits, including an average of 64 in the major, with a minimum GPA of 2.0.

Special: Students may choose either national or international internships or study abroad in the Netherlands, France, Germany, Spain, England, Italy, or another country, as arranged by the student. B.A.-B.S. degrees, including a B.F.A. in fine arts, music, dance, or an individual major are possible. Student-designed majors and potential credit for life, military, or work experience are offered. Cross-registration is available with the Northeast Ohio Commission on Higher Education. 128 credits are required. There is 1 national honor society.

Faculty/Classroom: 63% of faculty are male; 37%, female. All teach undergraduates. The average class size in an introductory lecture is 15; in a laboratory, 16; and in a regular course, 11.

Admissions: 79% of the 2003-2004 applicants were accepted. The SAT I scores for the 2003-2004 freshman class were: Verbal--52% below 500, 28% between 500 and 599, 15% between 600 and 700, and 5% above 700; Math--55% below 500, 35% between 500 and 599, and 10% between 600 and 700. The ACT scores were 46% below 21, 27% between 21 and 23, 18% between 24 and 26, 8% between 27 and 28, and 1% above 28. 3 freshmen graduated first in their class.

Requirements: The SAT I or ACT is required. In addition, applicants should be graduates of an accredited secondary school with a minimum GPA of 2.75. The high school program should include 4 years each of English, math, and science (including 2 years of lab science), and 2 years each of history and social studies, with 2 years of a foreign language recommended. A GPA of 2.0 is required. AP and CLEP credits are accepted. Important factors in the admissions decision are advanced placement or honor courses, recommendations by school officials, and extracurricular activities record.

Procedure: Freshmen are admitted fall, spring, and summer. Entrance exams should be taken by November of the senior year. There is a deferred admissions plan and a rolling admissions plan. Application deadlines are open. Notification is sent on a rolling basis. Application fee is $25. Applications are accepted on-line through Next Stop College.

Transfer: 94 transfer students enrolled in 2002-2003. Applicants should submit transcripts from all schools attended and show a GPA of 2.0 in all college work. 32 credits of 128 required for the bachelor's degree must be completed at Lake Erie.

Visiting: There are regularly scheduled orientations for prospective students, including a campus tour, a financial aid information session, classroom observation, and faculty or department head interviews. There are guides for informal visits and visitors may sit in on classes and stay overnight. To schedule a visit, contact the Admissions Office at *admissions@lec.edu*.

Financial Aid: 25% of undergraduates work part time. Average annual earnings from campus work are $2000. The FAFSA and the college's own financial statement are required. The fall application deadline is rolling.

International Students: There are 7 international students enrolled. They must score 550 on the written TOEFL or take the MELAB, and also take the SAT I, scoring 850, or the ACT, scoring 18.

Computers: The mainframe is an HP G-30. PCs are available in residence halls, the computer center, and the library. There are no time limits and no fees.

Admissions Contact: Jennifer Calhoun, Director of Admissions. E-mail: *lecadmit@lec.edu* Web: *www.lec.edu*

LOURDES COLLEGE
B-1
Sylvania, OH 43560

(419) 885-5291, ext. 299
(800) 878-3210, ext. 1299; Fax: (419) 882-3987

Full-time: 90 men, 405 women	**Faculty:** 60; IIB, --$
Part-time: 106 men, 601 women	**Ph.D.s:** 32%
Graduate: 11 men, 36 women	**Student/Faculty:** 8 to 1
Year: semesters, summer session	**Tuition:** $15,300
Application Deadline: open	**Room & Board:** n/app
Freshman Class: 283 applied, 224 accepted, 70 enrolled	
SAT I Verbal/Math: 430/460	**ACT:** 20 LESS COMPETITIVE

Lourdes College, founded in 1958, is a private liberal arts college affiliated with the Roman Catholic Church and sponsored by the Sisters of St. Francis. In addition to regional accreditation, Lourdes has baccalaureate program accreditation with CSWE and NLN. The library contains 59,236 volumes, 10,807 microform items, and 1451 audio/video tapes/CDs, and subscribes to 388 periodicals. Computerized library services include the card catalog, interlibrary loans, and database searching. Special learning facilities include a learning resource center, art gallery, planetarium, and an environmental science lab. The 89-acre campus is in a suburban area 10 miles west of Toledo. There are 8 buildings.

Student Life: 93% of undergraduates are from Ohio. Students are from 2 states and 2 foreign countries. 12% are African American. The average age of freshmen is 21; all undergraduates, 30.

Housing: There are no residence halls. All of students commute. Alcohol is not permitted. All students may keep cars.

Activities: There are no fraternities or sororities. There are 15 groups on campus, including art, choir, chorus, honors, international, literary magazine, newspaper, political, professional, religious, social service, and student government. Popular campus events include End-of-the-Year Picnic, Convocation, and Christmas dinner.

Sports: There are 4 intramural sports for men and 4 for women. Facilities include a gym and exercise room.

Disabled Students: 95% of the campus is accessible. Wheelchair ramps, elevators, special parking, specially equipped rest rooms, special class scheduling, lowered drinking fountains, lowered telephones, and accessible computer stations are available.

Services: Counseling and information services are available, as is tutoring in most subjects. There is remedial math, reading, and writing. Windows for Intellectual Networking Center offers computer-assisted instruction for self-paced learning/tutoring in remedial math, reading, writing, study skills, APA style documentation, Spanish tutorials, advanced math programs, as well as offering professional tutoring services in writing. The center also works with instructors to offer in-class tutorial workshops on specific topics as requested.

Campus Safety and Security: Measures include security escort services, pamphlets/posters/films, and lighted pathways/sidewalks.

Programs of Study: Lourdes confers B.A., B.S., B.I.S., and B.S.N. degrees. Associate and master's degrees are also awarded. Bachelor's degrees are awarded in BIOLOGICAL SCIENCE (biology/biological science), BUSINESS (accounting, business administration and management, human resources, and marketing management), COMMUNICATIONS AND THE ARTS (art, art history and appreciation, English, and fine arts), EDUCATION (education), ENGINEERING AND ENVIRONMENTAL DESIGN (environmental science), HEALTH PROFESSIONS (health care administration and nursing), SOCIAL SCIENCE (criminal justice, history, psychology, religion, social work, and sociology). Nursing, chemistry, and education are the strongest academically. Business, nursing, and criminal justice are the largest.

Required: Students are required to maintain at least a 2.0 overall GPA, although most disciplines require 2.5. The total number of hours in the major varies from 36 to 59 semester hours depending on the major. Students must complete 120 credit hours, the requirements varying according to the degree sought. Most students will need courses in art/music, religious studies, composition, literature, phys ed, social science, and philosophy.

Special: The college offers internships in social work, criminal justice, occupational therapy, and business, co-op programs in business, work-study programs, B.A.-B.S. degrees in biology, chemistry, and education, and an accelerated degree program in business and criminal justice. Students may pursue dual majors, nondegree study, student-designed majors, or select pass/fail options. The college gives credit for life, military, or work experience.

Faculty/Classroom: 30% of faculty are male; 70%, female. 99% teach undergraduates. No introductory courses are taught by graduate students. The average class size in an introductory lecture is 16; in a laboratory, 8; and in a regular course, 12.

Admissions: 79% of the 2003-2004 applicants were accepted. The SAT I scores for the 2003-2004 freshman class were: Verbal--100% below 500; Math--100% below 500. The ACT scores were 63% below 21, 27% between 21 and 23, 8% between 24 and 26, and 2% above 28.

Requirements: The SAT I or ACT is required, with an ACT composite of 19 or higher. Candidates for admission should have completed 4 units of English and 3 each of math, science, and social studies. If a GED recipient, a passing score on the GED and satisfactory placement test scores are required. A GPA of 2.0 is required. AP and CLEP credits are accepted.

Procedure: Freshmen are admitted to all sessions. Entrance exams should be taken at least 30 days prior to the beginning of the freshman year of college. There are early admissions and deferred admissions plans. There is a rolling admissions plan. Application deadlines are open. The fall 2003 fee was $25. Notification is sent out on a rolling basis. Applications are accepted on-line through the school's web site.

Transfer: 200 transfer students enrolled in 2002-2003. Transfer students need to submit official transcripts from previously attended colleges/universities, a completed application and fee, and placement tests when necessary. Regular admission is granted to transfer students with a GPA of 2.0 or better and satisfactory placement test scores, if required. 30 credits of 120 required for the bachelor's degree must be completed at Lourdes.

Visiting: There are guides for informal visits and visitors may sit in on classes. To schedule a visit, contact the Office of Admissions at (419) 885-3211.

Financial Aid: In 2003-2004, 91% of all full-time freshmen and 96% of continuing full-time students received some form of financial aid. 93% of full-time freshmen and 94% of continuing full-time students received need-based aid. The average freshman award was $13,732. Need-based scholarships or need-based grants averaged $4475 ($5466 maximum); need-based self-help aid (loans and jobs) averaged $6620 ($7876 maximum); and non-need-based awards and non-need-based scholarships averaged $4439 ($5000 maximum). 6% of undergraduates work part time. Lourdes is a member of CSS. The FAFSA is required. The priority date for freshman financial aid applications for fall entry is March 31.

International Students: There are 2 international students enrolled. They must score 500 on the written TOEFL or 173 on the electronic version.

Computers: The mainframes are Dell Poweredge servers. There are 86 computers available for student use. Students have web and e-mail access. All students may access the system. PCs may be used any time during open lab hours. There are no time limits and no fees.

Graduates: From July 1, 2002 to June 30, 2003, 195 bachelor's degrees were awarded. The most popular majors were business (25%), nursing (20%), and education (15%). In an average class, 28% graduate in 6 years or less. 7 companies recruited on campus in 2002-2003.

Admissions Contact: Amy L. Megen, Director of Admissions.
E-mail: *lcadmits@lourdes.edu* Web: *www.lourdes.edu*

MALONE COLLEGE
Canton, OH 44709
D-2
(330) 471-8139
(800) 521-1146; Fax: (330) 471-8149

Full-time: 658 men, 1002 women	Faculty: 99; IIA, --$
Part-time: 94 men, 183 women	Ph.D.s: 60%
Graduate: 91 men, 178 women	Student/Faculty: 17 to 1
Year: semesters, summer session	Tuition: $14,995
Application Deadline: July 1	Room & Board: $6000
Freshman Class: 992 applied, 842 accepted, 401 enrolled	
SAT I Verbal/Math: 550/535	ACT: 23	COMPETITIVE

Malone College, founded in 1892, is a private Christian college for the arts, sciences, and professions in the liberal arts tradition. There are 6 undergraduate schools and 1 graduate school. In addition to regional accreditation, Malone has baccalaureate program accreditation with CSWE, IACBE, and NLN. The library contains 161,889 volumes, 620,013 microform items, and 10,943 audio/video tapes/CDs, and subscribes to 1193 periodicals. Computerized library services include the card catalog, interlibrary loans, database searching, and Internet access. Special learning facilities include a learning resource center, radio station, a writing lab, and a math tutoring lab. The 78-acre campus is in a suburban area 56 miles southeast of Cleveland. Including any residence halls, there are 21 buildings.

Student Life: 89% of undergraduates are from Ohio. Students are from 24 states and 12 foreign countries. 82% are from public schools. 92% are white. 86% are Protestant; 8% Catholic; 6% claim no religious affiliation. The average age of freshmen is 18; all undergraduates, 24. 25% do not continue beyond their first year; 50% remain to graduate.

Housing: 961 students can be accommodated in college housing, which includes single-sex dorms and special topic/discipleship floors for upperclassmen. On-campus housing is guaranteed for the freshman year only, is available on a first-come, first-served basis, and is available on a lottery system for upperclassmen. 55% of students live on campus; of those, 40% remain on campus on weekends. Alcohol is not permitted. All students may keep cars.

Activities: There are no fraternities or sororities. There are 52 groups on campus, including art, band, cheerleading, choir, chorale, chorus, computers, debate, drama, drill team, ethnic, forensics, honors, international, jazz band, literary magazine, marching band, musical theater, newspaper, pep band, photography, political, professional, radio and TV, religious, social, social service, student government, and yearbook. Popular campus events include Little Sibs Weekend, Staley Lecture, and Spring Fest.

Sports: There are 9 intercollegiate sports for men and 9 for women, and 14 intramural sports for men and 13 for women. Facilities include a gym, weight room, outdoor track, baseball, softball, and soccer fields, practice soccer and football fields, intramural fields, cross-country course, fitness room, and outdoor volleyball and basketball courts.

Disabled Students: 90% of the campus is accessible. Wheelchair ramps, elevators, special parking, specially equipped rest rooms, special class scheduling, lowered drinking fountains, and lowered telephones are available.

Services: Counseling and information services are available, as is tutoring in most subjects. There is a reader service for the blind and remedial math and writing. There are also disability support services such as a distraction-free testing area.

Campus Safety and Security: Measures include 24-hour foot and vehicle patrol, self-defense education, security escort services, and shuttle buses. There are informal discussions, emergency telephones, and lighted pathways/sidewalks.

Programs of Study: Malone confers B.A., B.S.Ed., and B.S.N. degrees. Master's degrees are also awarded. Bachelor's degrees are awarded in BIOLOGICAL SCIENCE (biology/biological science and life science), BUSINESS (accounting, business administration and management, recreational facilities management, and sports management), COMMUNICATIONS AND THE ARTS (art, communications, English, language arts, music, music technology, and Spanish), COMPUTER AND PHYSICAL SCIENCE (chemistry, computer science, mathematics, physical sciences, and science), EDUCATION (art, Christian, early childhood, elementary, foreign languages, health, middle school, music, physical, science, secondary, social studies, and special), HEALTH PROFESSIONS (community health work, exercise science, medical laboratory technology, and nursing), SOCIAL SCIENCE (biblical studies, history, liberal arts/general studies, ministries, physical fitness/movement, political science/government, psychology, religious music, social work, theological studies, and youth ministry). Biology, chemistry, and math are the strongest academically. Business administration, early childhood education, and communication arts are the largest.

Required: Students must maintain a GPA of 2.0 overall and 2.25 to 2.75 in the major, depending upon the major. At least 30 hours in the major and 39 hours at the 300 or 400 level are required. To graduate, all students must complete at least 124 credit hours, including a general education curriculum requiring 63 to 64 semester hours focusing on stewardship: Stewardship Under God (14 hours), Stewardship and Skills (15 to 16 hours), Stewardship and the Sciences (12 to 13 hours), and Stewardship and Society (15 to 18 hours). Courses in phys ed and data analysis are also required.

Special: Students may participate in co-op programs and internships in all majors and may cross-register within the Christian College Consortium. Malone offers study abroad in Guatemala, Costa Rica, England, Russia, China, Egypt, Australia, and Kenya; Hollywood or Washington semesters through the Council for Christian Colleges and Universities; work-study programs; and accelerated degree completion programs in management and nursing. A liberal arts degree, dual and student-designed majors, and credit for life, military, or work experience are also available. The Malone College Management Program offers degree completion for students age 25 or older who have the equivalent of 2 years of college. The BSNDC program offers degree completion for RNs. There are 8 national honor societies and a freshman honors program.

Faculty/Classroom: 53% of faculty are male; 48%, female. 99% teach undergraduates and 40% both teach and do research. No introductory courses are taught by graduate students. The average class size in an introductory lecture is 27; in a laboratory, 13; and in a regular course, 20.

Admissions: 85% of the 2003-2004 applicants were accepted. The SAT I scores for the 2003-2004 freshman class were: Verbal--27% below 500, 40% between 500 and 599, 30% between 600 and 700, and 3% above 700; Math--35% below 500, 41% between 500 and 599, 19% between 600 and 700, and 4% above 700. The ACT scores were 27% below 21, 33% between 21 and 23, 24% between 24 and 26, 8% between 27 and 28, and 8% above 28. 43% of the current freshmen were in the top fifth of their class; 68% were in the top two fifths. 12 freshmen graduated first in their class.

Requirements: The ACT is required for traditional students. The SAT I is accepted. Applicants should be graduates of an accredited secondary school with a minimum GPA of 2.5. The GED is accepted. A GPA of 2.5 is required. AP and CLEP credits are accepted.

Procedure: Freshmen are admitted to all sessions. Entrance exams should be taken in the junior year. There is a deferred admissions plan and a rolling admissions plan. Applications should be filed by July 1 for fall entry. The fall 2003 application fee was $20. Notification is sent on a rolling basis. Applications are accepted on-line through the school's web site.

Transfer: 85 transfer students enrolled in 2002-2003. Applicants must submit an official transcript and a financial aid transcript from each college attended and a transfer reference form from the most recent school. 30 credits of 124 required for the bachelor's degree must be completed at Malone.

Visiting: There are regularly scheduled orientations for prospective students. There are guides for informal visits and visitors may sit in on classes and stay overnight. To schedule a visit, contact Jody Dimit, Campus Visit Coordinator at (330) 471-8147 or jdimit@malone.edu.

Financial Aid: In 2003-2004, 99% of all full-time freshmen and 91% of continuing full-time students received some form of financial aid. 72% of full-time freshmen and 63% of continuing full-time students received need-based aid. The average freshman award was $14,453. Need-based scholarships or need-based grants averaged $5042 ($14,412 maximum); need-based self-help aid (loans and jobs) averaged $4144 ($6625 maximum); non-need-based athletic scholarships averaged $5169 ($12,500 maximum); other non-need-based awards and non-need-based scholarships averaged $5731 ($20,502 maximum); and parent loans averaged $10,285 ($18,800 maximum). 20% of undergraduates work part time. Average annual earnings from campus work are $1794. The average financial indebtedness of the 2003 graduate was $16,465. Malone is a member of CSS. The FAFSA and the college's own form, only required for returning students, are required. The deadline for filing freshman financial aid applications for fall entry is March 1.

International Students: There are 11 international students enrolled. They must score 550 on the written TOEFL or 213 on the electronic version.

Computers: The mainframe is a Compaq server Model ML 570. Malone has 181 PCs available to students, 89 of which are in 5 different labs, 64 in residence halls, and 28 in the library. Students use them for information retrieval from the Web, for looking up library research materials, for e-mail, for class assignments involving word processing, spreadsheets, databases, and presentations, for on-line courses, for accessing faculty web sites, and for specialized software in accounting, music, and graphic arts. All students may access the system Monday to Thursday, 8 A.M. to 11:30 P.M.; Friday, 8 A.M. to 5 P.M.; Saturday, 10 A.M. to 5 P.M.; and Sunday, 2 P.M. to 10 P.M. There are no time limits and no fees.

Graduates: From July 1, 2002 to June 30, 2003, 511 bachelor's degrees were awarded. The most popular majors were business administration (6%), communication arts (6%), and nursing (5%). In an average class, 35% graduate in 4 years or less, 48% graduate in 5 years or less, and 50% graduate in 6 years or less. 59 companies recruited on campus in 2002-2003. Of the 2002 graduating class, 32% were enrolled in graduate school within 1 year of graduation and 82% were employed.

Admissions Contact: John Russell, Director of Admissions. A video is available. E-mail: admissions@malone.edu
Web: http://www.malone.edu

MARIETTA COLLEGE
E-5
Marietta, OH 45750-4005
(740) 376-4600
(800)331-7896; Fax: (740) 376-8888

Full-time: 598 men, 546 women	**Faculty:** 78; IIB, -$
Part-time: 25 men, 58 women	**Ph.D.s:** 92%
Graduate: 27 men, 52 women	**Student/Faculty:** 15 to 1
Year: semesters, summer session	**Tuition:** $21,100
Application Deadline: April 15	**Room & Board:** $5947
Freshman Class: 1565 applied, 1480 accepted, 466 enrolled	
SAT I Verbal/Math: 540/540	**ACT:** 23 COMPETITIVE

Marietta College, founded in 1835, is a private liberal arts college. In addition to regional accreditation, Marietta has baccalaureate program accreditation with ABET and CAAHEP. The library contains 249,122 volumes and 133,116 microform items, and subscribes to 550 print and 3400 electronic periodicals. Computerized library services include the card catalog, interlibrary loans, database searching, and Internet access. Special learning facilities include a learning resource center, art gallery, radio station, TV station, an observatory, and a greenhouse. The 120-acre campus is in a small town 115 miles southeast of Columbus. Including any residence halls, there are 40 buildings.

Student Life: 50% of undergraduates are from out of state, mostly the Middle Atlantic. Students are from 42 states, 13 foreign countries, and Canada. 89% are from public schools. 88% are white. 60% are Protestant; 30% Catholic; 10% Jewish. The average age of freshmen is 18; all undergraduates, 20. 12% do not continue beyond their first year; 65% remain to graduate.

Housing: 1045 students can be accommodated in college housing, which includes single-sex and coed dorms, on-campus apartments, fraternity houses, and sorority houses. In addition, there are honors houses and special-interest houses. On-campus housing is guaranteed for all 4 years. 85% of students live on campus; of those, 80% remain on campus on weekends. All students may keep cars.

Activities: 20% of men belong to 3 national fraternities; 25% of women belong to 3 national sororities. There are 100 groups on campus, including Amnesty International, art, Arts and Humanities Council, band, cheerleading, choir, chorale, chorus, circle K, computers, dance, debate, drama, drill team, ethnic, film, forensics, Friends of Marietta, gay, Great Outdoors, honors, international, jazz band, literary magazine, musical theater, newspaper, orchestra, pep band, Philanthropy Connection, photography, political, professional, radio and TV, religious, rowing, ski, social, social service, student government, swing dance, and yearbook. Popular campus events include DooDah Day, Winter Weekend, and Little Sibs Weekend.

Sports: There are 8 intercollegiate sports for men and 8 for women, and 12 intramural sports for men and 12 for women. Facilities include a 7000-seat stadium, a 3000-seat field house, baseball and soccer fields, a boat house, a cross-country course, tennis courts, and a recreational center housing a 200-meter track, multipurpose and racquetball courts, an ergometer training room, cardio equipment, and a climbing wall.

Disabled Students: 70% of the campus is accessible. Wheelchair ramps, elevators, special parking, specially equipped rest rooms, and special class scheduling are available.

Services: Counseling and information services are available, as is tutoring in most subjects. There is a reader service for the blind, remedial math and writing, and a peer tutoring program.

Campus Safety and Security: Measures include 24-hour foot and vehicle patrol, self-defense education, security escort services, and informal

discussions. There are pamphlets/posters/films, emergency telephones, and lighted pathways/sidewalks.

Programs of Study: Marietta confers B.A., B.S., Bach. of Petrol. Engin., and B.F.A. degrees. Associate and master's degrees are also awarded. Bachelor's degrees are awarded in AGRICULTURE (environmental studies), BIOLOGICAL SCIENCE (biochemistry and biology/biological science), BUSINESS (accounting, human resources, international business management, management information systems, management science, and marketing/retailing/merchandising), COMMUNICATIONS AND THE ARTS (advertising, broadcasting, communications, dramatic arts, English, fine arts, graphic design, journalism, music, musical theater, public relations, Spanish, speech/debate/rhetoric, and studio art), COMPUTER AND PHYSICAL SCIENCE (chemistry, computer science, geology, information sciences and systems, mathematics, and physics), EDUCATION (elementary), ENGINEERING AND ENVIRONMENTAL DESIGN (environmental engineering, environmental science, and petroleum/natural gas engineering), HEALTH PROFESSIONS (sports medicine), SOCIAL SCIENCE (economics, history, international studies, political science/government, and psychology). Petroleum engineering is the strongest academically. Economics, management and accounting, and elementary education are the largest.

Required: To graduate, students must complete at least 120 total credit hours, with general education requirements of 4 hours in the humanities and 2 each in fine arts, lab, and social sciences. All students must also take a freshman seminar, English, and speech, and successfully complete at least 1 math course. The minimum number of hours required for a major is 36. A minimum GPA of 2.0 must be maintained. Seniors must complete a capstone project.

Special: There are binary programs with Case Western Reserve, Columbia, and Duke Universities and the Universities of Pennsylvania and Michigan. Internships are available in many majors, and students may study abroad in numerous countries and participate in a Washington semester through American University. Preprofessional programs, work-study programs, B.A.-B.S. degrees in all majors, student-designed majors, a 3-2 engineering degree with several universities, pass/fail options, and credit for life, military, and work experience are also available. The freshman year program is designed to assist with the student's academic and social transition to college life. There are 20 national honor societies, including Phi Beta Kappa, a freshman honors program, and 20 departmental honors programs.

Faculty/Classroom: 57% of faculty are male; 43%, female. All teach undergraduates and 30% both teach and do research. No introductory courses are taught by graduate students. The average class size in an introductory lecture is 25; in a laboratory, 12; and in a regular course, 22.

Admissions: 95% of the 2003-2004 applicants were accepted. The SAT I scores for the 2003-2004 freshman class were: Math--33% below 500, 41% between 500 and 599, 23% between 600 and 700, and 3% above 700. The ACT scores for the 2003-2004 freshman class were: 24% below 21, 30% between 21 and 23, 27% between 24 and 26, 14% between 27 and 28, and 5% above 28. 39% of the current freshmen were in the top fifth of their class; 69% were in the top two fifths. There were 10 National Merit semifinalists. 26 freshmen graduated first in their class.

Requirements: The SAT I or ACT is required. In addition, students seeking admission should have completed 4 years of English and 3 of history, math, and science; 2 years of a foreign language is also recommended. An interview is strongly recommended. A GPA of 2.0 is required. AP and CLEP credits are accepted. Important factors in the admissions decision are advanced placement or honor courses, evidence of special talent, and leadership record.

Procedure: Freshmen are admitted fall and spring. Entrance exams should be taken no later than February of the senior year. There is a rolling admissions plan. Applications should be filed by April 15 for fall entry. The fall 2003 application fee was $25. Notification is sent on a rolling basis. Applications are accepted on-line through the Marietta web site, Common Application, Peterson's, CollegeView, EXPAN, and Apply.

Transfer: 63 transfer students enrolled in 2002-2003. A minimum GPA of 2.5, a recommendation, and an essay are required. 36 credits of 120 required for the bachelor's degree must be completed at Marietta.

Visiting: There are regularly scheduled orientations for prospective students, including fall and spring open houses, tours, and meetings with faculty, coaches, and financial aid representatives. There are guides for informal visits and visitors may sit in on classes and stay overnight. To schedule a visit, contact the Office of Admissions.

Financial Aid: In 2003-2004, 96% of all full-time freshmen and 93% of continuing full-time students received some form of financial aid. 77% of full-time freshmen and 70% of continuing full-time students received need-based aid. The average freshman award was $19,000. 77% of undergraduates work part time. Average annual earnings from campus work are $2000. The average financial indebtedness of the 2003 graduate was approximately $17,000. Marietta is a member of CSS. The FAFSA is required. The deadline for filing freshman financial aid applications for fall entry is March 1.

International Students: There are 60 international students enrolled. The school actively recruits these students. They must score 550 on the written TOEFL.

Computers: The mainframes are a DEC Alpha 2100 RISC system, a DEC Alpha RISC, an IBM RS/6000, and a Multimax 510. The campus-wide network includes 120 PCs and some 80 terminals in 10 academic labs, and offers e-mail, Internet, and web access. There are also 150 Macs available for student use. All students may access the system. It is strongly recommended that all students have a personal computer.

Graduates: From July 1, 2002 to June 30, 2003, 222 bachelor's degrees were awarded. The most popular majors were management (11%), elementary education (9%), and psychology (8%). 45 companies recruited on campus in 2002-2003. Of the 2002 graduating class, 25% were enrolled in graduate school within 6 months of graduation and 70% were employed.

Admissions Contact: Marke M. Vickers, Director of Admission. A video is available. E-mail: *admit@mcnet.marietta.edu*
Web: *http://www.marietta.edu*

MIAMI UNIVERSITY

A-4

Oxford, OH 45056   (513) 529-2531; Fax: (513) 529-1550

Full-time: 6734 men, 8052 women	**Faculty:** 825; I, -$
Part-time: 207 men, 181 women	**Ph.D.s:** 86%
Graduate: 604 men, 1017 women	**Student/Faculty:** 18 to 1
Year: semesters, summer session	**Tuition:** $8353 ($18,123)
Application Deadline: January 31	**Room & Board:** $6680
Freshman Class: 13,859 applied, 9842 accepted, 3309 enrolled	
SAT I Verbal/Math: 610/630	**ACT:** 27 HIGHLY COMPETITIVE

Miami University, founded in 1809, is a public institution offering a variety of programs in the liberal arts and preprofessional-vocational training. There are 6 undergraduate schools and 1 graduate school. In addition to regional accreditation, Miami University has baccalaureate program accreditation with AACSB, ABET, ADA, AHEA, ASLA, NAAB, NASAD, NASM, NCATE, and NLN. The 4 libraries contain 2,373,050 volumes, 3,031,242 microform items, and 26,468 audio/video tapes/CDs, and subscribe to 13,710 periodicals. Computerized library services include the card catalog, interlibrary loans, and database searching. Special learning facilities include a learning resource center, art gallery, natural history museum, radio station, and TV station. The 1921-acre campus is in a small town 35 miles northwest of Cincinnati. Including any residence halls, there are 162 buildings.

Student Life: 72% of undergraduates are from Ohio. Students are from 48 states, 59 foreign countries, and Canada. 75% are from public schools. 90% are white. The average age of freshmen is 18; all undergraduates, 20. 10% do not continue beyond their first year; 80% remain to graduate.

Housing: 7080 students can be accommodated in college housing, which includes single-sex and coed dorms, married-student housing, and sorority houses. In addition, there are honors houses, language houses, special-interest houses, international houses, and freshmen-only houses. On-campus housing is guaranteed for the freshman year only and is available on a lottery system for upperclassmen. 55% of students commute. Alcohol is not permitted. All students may keep cars.

Activities: 24% of men belong to 28 national fraternities; 27% of women belong to 22 national sororities. There are 350 groups on campus, including art, band, cheerleading, choir, chorale, chorus, dance, debate, drama, drill team, ethnic, forensics, gay, honors, international, jazz band, literary magazine, marching band, musical theater, newspaper, opera, orchestra, pep band, political, professional, radio and TV, religious, social, social service, student government, symphony, and yearbook. Popular campus events include Parents Weekend, Kidsfest Weekend, and Unity Fest.

Sports: There are 8 intercollegiate sports for men and 11 for women, and 25 intramural sports for men and 25 for women. Facilities include a 25,000-seat football stadium, 70 acres of playing fields, 30 outdoor tennis courts, a recreational sports center, 10 indoor basketball/volleyball courts, racquetball, handball, and squash courts, a floor hockey/indoor soccer court, a climbing wall, equestrian stables and dressage course, an aquatic center containing 3 indoor swimming pools, jogging paths, a par course, sand volleyball courts, aerobics and weight rooms, a Frisbee golf course, and an outdoor in-line skating court.

Disabled Students: All of the campus is accessible. Wheelchair ramps, elevators, special parking, specially equipped rest rooms, special class scheduling, lowered drinking fountains, and lowered telephones are available.

Services: Counseling and information services are available, as is tutoring in most subjects. There is a reader service for the blind. Assistance in study skills is available.

Campus Safety and Security: Measures include 24-hour foot and vehicle patrol, self-defense education, security escort services, and shuttle buses. There are informal discussions, pamphlets/posters/films, emergency telephones, lighted pathways/sidewalks, formal crime prevention programs, a community relations officer, a bicycle patrol, and card access into dorms.

Programs of Study: Miami University confers B.A., B.S., B.E.D., B.F.A., B.Mus., and B.Phil. degrees. Master's and doctoral degrees are also awarded. Bachelor's degrees are awarded in BIOLOGICAL SCIENCE (biochemistry, biology/biological science, botany, microbiology, and zoology), BUSINESS (accounting, banking and finance, business administration and management, business economics, human resources, management information systems, management science, marketing/retailing/merchandising, operations research, organizational behavior, personnel management, purchasing/inventory management, and sports management), COMMUNICATIONS AND THE ARTS (art, art history and appreciation, broadcasting, communications, dramatic arts, English, fine arts, French, German, graphic design, Greek, Latin, linguistics, music, music performance, Russian, Spanish, speech/debate/rhetoric, and telecommunications), COMPUTER AND PHYSICAL SCIENCE (chemistry, computer science, geology, mathematics, physics, and statistics), EDUCATION (art, athletic training, early childhood, elementary, foreign languages, health, middle school, music, physical, science, secondary, and special), ENGINEERING AND ENVIRONMENTAL DESIGN (architecture, electrical/electronics engineering, engineering, engineering management, engineering physics, engineering technology, environmental design, environmental science, interior design, manufacturing engineering, mechanical engineering, and paper and pulp science), HEALTH PROFESSIONS (exercise science, health, medical technology, nursing, premedicine, and speech pathology/audiology), SOCIAL SCIENCE (African American studies, American studies, anthropology, classical/ancient civilization, dietetics, economics, family/consumer studies, geography, history, interdisciplinary studies, international relations, international studies, philosophy, physical fitness/movement, political science/government, prelaw, psychology, public administration, religion, social science, social work, sociology, urban studies, and women's studies). Zoology, chemistry, and accountancy are the strongest academically. Accountancy, elementary education, and marketing are the largest.

Required: To graduate, students must complete 128 semester hours, with a minimum 2.0 GPA. Distribution requirements include a total of 36 hours in English composition, fine arts, humanities, social science, world cultures, natural science, math, formal reasoning, and technology. A minimum of 9 hours in a Thematic Sequence outside the major department, and a 3-hour Senior Capstone Experience, which integrates liberal learning and specialized knowledge, are also required.

Special: The university offers cross-registration with Cincinnati area colleges, study abroad in 15 countries, co-op programs in the School of Applied Science, internships in health and sport studies and applied science, a 3-2 engineering degree with Case Western Reserve and Columbia Universities, and a 3-2 forestry degree with Duke University. Students may pursue student-designed majors through the School of Interdisciplinary Studies or interdisciplinary majors, including decision sciences and history of art and architecture. There are 30 national honor societies, including Phi Beta Kappa, and a freshman honors program.

Faculty/Classroom: 64% of faculty are male; 36%, female. Graduate students teach 25% of introductory courses. The average class size in a laboratory is 15 and in a regular course, 28.

Admissions: 71% of the 2003-2004 applicants were accepted. The SAT I scores for the 2003-2004 freshman class were: Verbal--4% below 500, 42% between 500 and 599, 47% between 600 and 700, and 8% above 700; Math--3% below 500, 28% between 500 and 599, 59% between 600 and 700, and 11% above 700. The ACT scores were 2% below 21, 11% between 21 and 23, 35% between 24 and 26, 24% between 27 and 28, and 28% above 28. 67% of the current freshmen were in the top fifth of their class; 94% were in the top two fifths. There were 29 National Merit finalists and 9 semifinalists.

Requirements: The SAT I or ACT is required. In addition, candidates for admission must ordinarily be graduates of accredited secondary schools or hold the GED and should have completed 4 units of English, 3 each of math, science, and social studies/history, 2 of a foreign language, and 1 of fine arts. An audition, a portfolio, or an interview is required for direct admission to majors in the School of Fine Arts. AP and CLEP credits are accepted. Important factors in the admissions decision are advanced placement or honor courses, evidence of special talent, and extracurricular activities record.

Procedure: Freshmen are admitted to all sessions. Entrance exams should be taken no later than December of the senior year. There is an early decision plan. Early decision applications should be filed by November 1; regular applications, by January 31 for fall entry and November 15 for spring entry, along with a $45 fee. Notification of early decision is sent December 15; regular decision, March 15. A waiting list is an active part of the admissions procedure. Applications are accepted online through *www.muohio.edu/admission*.

Transfer: 406 transfer students enrolled in 2002-2003. A limited number of transfer students can be accepted. A GPA of 2.0 or higher is necessary. 32 credits of 128 required for the bachelor's degree must be completed at Miami University.

Visiting: There are regularly scheduled orientations for prospective students, consisting of open houses in February and April. There are guides for informal visits and visitors may sit in on classes and stay overnight.

To schedule a visit, contact the Office of Admissions, Visit Coordinator at (513) 529-4632 or *visitcoor@muohio.edu*.

Financial Aid: In a recent year, 67% of all full-time freshmen and 46% of continuing full-time students received some form of financial aid. 34% of full-time freshmen and 31% of continuing full-time students received need-based aid. The average freshman award was $6636. 30% of undergraduates work part time. Average annual earnings from campus work are $1084. The average financial indebtedness of a recent graduate was $16,379. The FAFSA is required. The deadline for filing freshman financial aid applications for fall entry is February 15.

International Students: There are 122 international students enrolled. They must score 530 on the written TOEFL or take the MELAB. The SAT I or ACT is required only for Canadian applicants, athletes, and those students who have followed a U.S. high school curriculum at a secondary school in the United States or abroad.

Computers: Computer facilities include statistical analysis, database programming, and e-mail, via student computing facilities in academic departments, residence halls, or dial-up. More than 1000 PCs and terminals are available. All residence halls have direct connections to the university network. All students may access the system. There are no time limits. The fee is $90 per semester for full-time on campus and $15 per semester for part-time and off campus. It is strongly recommended that all students have a personal computer.

Graduates: From July 1, 2002 to June 30, 2003, 3744 bachelor's degrees were awarded. The most popular majors were marketing (11%), finance (8%), and psychology (6%). In an average class, 3% graduate in 3 years or less, 64% graduate in 4 years or less, 78% graduate in 5 years or less, and 80% graduate in 6 years or less. 336 companies recruited on campus in 2002-2003.

Admissions Contact: Michael Mills, Asst Vice President/Director of Admissions. A video is available. E-mail: *millsme@muohio.edu* Web: *www.muohio.edu*

MOUNT UNION COLLEGE
Alliance, OH 44601

E-2
(330) 821-5320
(800) 992-6682; Fax: (330) 823-3457

Full-time: 905 men, 1160 women	**Faculty:** 118; IIB, -$
Part-time: 95 men, 215 women	**Ph.D.s:** 97%
Graduate: none	**Student/Faculty:** 17 to 1
Year: semesters, summer session	**Tuition:** $16,310
Application Deadline: open	**Room & Board:** $4810
Freshman Class: n/av	
SAT I or ACT: required	**COMPETITIVE**

Mount Union College, founded in 1846, is a private, liberal arts college affiliated with the United Methodist Church. Figures in the above capsule and in this profile are approximate. In addition to regional accreditation, Mount Union has baccalaureate program accreditation with NASM. The 3 libraries contain 230,000 volumes and 43,000 microform items, and subscribe to 950 periodicals. Special learning facilities include a learning resource center, art gallery, radio station, two astronomical observatories, a university theater, a playhouse, and a nature center. The 115-acre campus is in a suburban area 20 miles east of Canton. Including any residence halls, there are 26 buildings.

Student Life: 88% of undergraduates are from Ohio. Students are from 20 states, 15 foreign countries, and Canada. 89% are from public schools. 94% are white. 39% are Protestant; 31% Catholic; 30% claim no religious affiliation. The average age of freshmen is 19; all undergraduates, 22. 12% do not continue beyond their first year; 61% remain to graduate.

Housing: 1385 students can be accommodated in college housing, which includes single-sex and coed dorms. In addition, there are honors houses, special-interest houses, and substance-free (tobacco/alcohol) houses. On-campus housing is guaranteed for the freshman year only, is available on a first-come, first-served basis, and is available on a lottery system for upperclassmen. 68% of students live on campus; of those, 70% remain on campus on weekends. All students may keep cars.

Activities: 28% of men belong to 4 national fraternities; 30% of women belong to 1 local and 4 national sororities. There are 74 groups on campus, including art, band, cheerleading, chess, choir, chorale, chorus, computers, dance, debate, drama, drill team, ethnic, forensics, gay, honors, international, jazz band, literary magazine, marching band, musical theater, newspaper, orchestra, pep band, political, professional, radio and TV, religious, social, social service, student government, and yearbook. Popular campus events include Spring Fest, Greek Week, and Schooler Lecture series.

Sports: There are 12 intercollegiate sports for men and 11 for women, and 16 intramural sports for men and 16 for women. Facilities include a gym, field house, stadium, tennis courts, wellness center, exercise and aerobics rooms, and the Hoover-Price Campus Center.

Disabled Students: 90% of the campus is accessible. Wheelchair ramps, elevators, special parking, specially equipped rest rooms, special class scheduling, lowered drinking fountains, and specially equipped residence hall rooms are available.

Services: Counseling and information services are available, as is tutoring in most subjects, including general education courses and most introductory courses. There is a reader service for the blind and remedial writing and facilitated study groups for most general education courses that meet once a week.

Campus Safety and Security: Measures include 24-hour foot and vehicle patrol, self-defense education, informal discussions, and pamphlets/posters/films. There are emergency telephones and lighted pathways/sidewalks.

Programs of Study: Mount Union confers B.A., B.S., B.Mus., and B.Mus.Ed. degrees. Bachelor's degrees are awarded in BIOLOGICAL SCIENCE (biology/biological science and environmental biology), BUSINESS (accounting, business administration and management, international business management, and sports management), COMMUNICATIONS AND THE ARTS (art, communications, creative writing, dramatic arts, English, French, German, Japanese, media arts, music, music performance, and Spanish), COMPUTER AND PHYSICAL SCIENCE (astronomy, chemistry, computer science, geology, information sciences and systems, mathematics, and physics), EDUCATION (athletic training, early childhood, elementary, middle school, music, and physical), SOCIAL SCIENCE (American studies, economics, history, international studies, Near Eastern studies, philosophy, physical fitness/movement, political science/government, psychology, religion, social science, and sociology). Biology, athletic training, and exercise science are the strongest academically. Business, education, and psychology are the largest.

Required: To graduate, students must complete a minimum of 120 semester hours, including 30 in upper division courses and up to 48 in the major, with a minimum GPA of 2.0. General requirements include 49 hours in a core curriculum encompassing communication skills, analytical skills, religion/philosophy, international studies, Western history, literature, fine arts, phys ed, and the freshman liberal arts experience. Students must also complete a minor requirement and the senior year culminating experience.

Special: Mount Union offers internships for credit in many majors, study abroad in 12 countries, co-op programs in business, work-study programs with various employers, student-designed majors, and pass/fail options. Adults in the nontraditional study program may receive credit for life, military, or work experience. There are 18 national honor societies, a freshman honors program, and 18 departmental honors programs.

Faculty/Classroom: 63% of faculty are male; 37%, female. All teach undergraduates. The average class size in an introductory lecture is 21; in a laboratory, 14; and in a regular course, 16.

Admissions: In a recent year, 14 freshmen graduated first in their class.

Requirements: The SAT I or ACT is required. Preference is given to high school graduates who have completed a minimum of 15 academic units, including 4 in English, 3 each in math, social science, and lab science, and 2 in foreign language. A GPA of 2.0 is required. AP and CLEP credits are accepted. Important factors in the admissions decision are advanced placement or honor courses, recommendations by school officials, and personality/intangible qualities.

Procedure: Freshmen are admitted fall and spring. Entrance exams should be taken for the first time in the spring of the junior year. There is a deferred admissions plan and a rolling admissions plan. Application deadlines are open. Applications are accepted on-line with the form available at the school's web site. Check with the school for current fees.

Transfer: Applicants must have a college GPA of 2.0 for consideration and must submit a statement of honorable dismissal and an official transcript from the last college attended. A personal statement must accompany the transfer application. 45 of 120 credits required for the bachelor's degree must be completed at Mount Union.

Visiting: There are regularly scheduled orientations for prospective students, including interviews, a campus tour, meetings with faculty, and classroom visits. There are guides for informal visits and visitors may sit in on classes and stay overnight. To schedule a visit, contact the Admissions Office at (330) 823-2590 or admission@muc.edu.

Financial Aid: Mount Union is a member of CSS. The FAFSA is required. Check with the school for current deadlines.

International Students: The school actively recruits these students. They must score 500 on the written TOEFL.

Computers: Students have network hook-ups in each residence hall-room that provide access to the campus network, including e-mail and the Internet. Students can also use various computer labs located on campus. Students, faculty, and staff share a common e-mail system. All students may access the system. There are no time limits and no fees. It is strongly recommended that all students have a personal computer.

Graduates: In a recent year, 420 bachelor's degrees were awarded. The most popular majors were business administration (17%), education (16%), and biology (8%). In an average class, 57% graduate in 4 years or less, 63% graduate in 5 years or less, and 65% graduate in 6 years or less. Of a recent graduating class, 25% were enrolled in graduate school within 6 months of graduation and 85% were employed.

Admissions Contact: Amy Tomko, Vice President, Enrollment Services. A video is available. E-mail: kinggl@muc.edu
Web: www.muc.edu

MOUNT VERNON NAZARENE UNIVERSITY

C-3

Mt. Vernon, OH 43050

(740) 392-6868, ext. 4510
(800) 782-2435; Fax: (740) 393-0511

Full-time: 819 men, 1125 women	Faculty: 98
Part-time: 133 men, 129 women	Ph.Ds: 63%
Graduate: 65 men, 121 women	Student/Faculty: 20 to 1
Year: 4-1-4, summer session	Tuition: $14,272
Application Deadline: May 31	Room & Board: $4653
Freshman Class: 699 applied, 602 accepted, 375 enrolled	
SAT I Verbal/Math: 560/540	ACT: 22	COMPETITIVE

Mount Vernon Nazarene University, formerly Mount Vernon Nazarene College, founded in 1964, is a private liberal arts college affiliated with the Church of the Nazarene. The library contains 101,754 volumes, 3382 microform items, and 7143 audio/video tapes/CDs, and subscribes to 511 periodicals. Computerized library services include the card catalog, interlibrary loans, database searching, and Internet access. Special learning facilities include a learning resource center, art gallery, radio station, and a nature center. The 401-acre campus is in a small town 45 miles northeast of Columbus. Including any residence halls, there are 37 buildings.

Student Life: 85% of undergraduates are from Ohio. Students are from 24 states, 8 foreign countries, and Canada. 82% are from public schools. 96% are white. Most are Protestant. The average age of freshmen is 18; all undergraduates, 20. 30% do not continue beyond their first year; 50% remain to graduate.

Housing: 1134 students can be accommodated in college housing, which includes single-sex dorms and on-campus apartments. On-campus housing is available on a first-come, first-served basis. 77% of students live on campus; of those, 55% remain on campus on weekends. Alcohol is not permitted. All students may keep cars.

Activities: There are no fraternities or sororities. There are 37 groups on campus, including art, band, cheerleading, choir, chorale, chorus, computers, drama, ethnic, honors, international, jazz band, musical theater, newspaper, orchestra, pep band, photography, political, professional, radio and TV, religious, social, social service, student government, symphony, and yearbook. Popular campus events include Sonfest, community service week, and concerts.

Sports: There are 4 intercollegiate sports for men and 4 for women, and 9 intramural sports for men and 9 for women. Facilities include a main gym, an intramural/practice gym, a weight room, tennis courts, intramural, baseball, softball, and soccer fields, and a baseball/softball batting facility.

Disabled Students: 91% of the campus is accessible. Wheelchair ramps, elevators, special parking, specially equipped rest rooms, special class scheduling, lowered drinking fountains, and lowered telephones are available.

Services: Counseling and information services are available, as is tutoring in most subjects. There is a reader service for the blind, and remedial math, reading, and writing. Students in the at-risk program are required to take College Survival Skills, Critical Thinking, to meet weekly with academic peer mentors, and take supplemental and peer instruction.

Campus Safety and Security: Measures include 24-hour foot and vehicle patrol, self-defense education, informal discussions, and pamphlets/posters/films. There are emergency telephones, lighted pathways/sidewalks, fire safety training with Student Leadership, blood-borne pathogen seminars, and Campus Safety and Security Review Committee.

Programs of Study: MVNU confers B.A., B.S., and B.B.A. degrees. Associate and master's degrees are also awarded. Bachelor's degrees are awarded in BIOLOGICAL SCIENCE (biology/biological science), BUSINESS (accounting, business administration and management, office supervision and management, and sports management), COMMUNICATIONS AND THE ARTS (art, communications, English, graphic design, journalism, music, music performance, and Spanish), COMPUTER AND PHYSICAL SCIENCE (chemistry, computer science, and mathematics), EDUCATION (art, business, Christian, early childhood, elementary, English, foreign languages, home economics, mathematics, middle school, music, physical, science, secondary, social studies, and special), HEALTH PROFESSIONS (exercise science and medical technology), SOCIAL SCIENCE (family/consumer studies, history, philosophy, psychology, religion, religious education, social work, sociology, and youth ministry). Premedicine, biology, and accounting are the strongest academically. Business, teacher education, and religion are the largest.

Required: Students must complete 124 semester hours, at least 40 to 60 hours in the major and 40 in upper-division courses, and maintain a minimum GPA of 2.0. The 43- to 48-hour B.A. general education core includes 12 to 15 hours of general requirements, 18 to 19 in the humanities, 7 to 8 in natural sciences, and 6 in social sciences. Students must also complete 1 semester of a foreign language (or 2 years of 1 language in high school), intermediate algebra (or complete 2 years of algebra and/or geometry in high school), and the junior-senior testing program.

Special: MVNU offers internships with local businesses/organizations, on-campus work-study programs, travel abroad during the January interim, dual majors, a general studies degree, and nondegree study. A 2-2 nursing degree in cooperation with Capital University is also available, as is a 2-2 engineering degree with Olivet Nazarene University. Cross-registration is available with Nazarene Colleges and Universities, and a Washington semester is offered through the American Studies Program. There are 3 national honor societies, a freshman honors program, and 19 departmental honors programs.

Faculty/Classroom: 66% of faculty are male; 34%, female. 97% teach undergraduates and 20% both teach and do research. No introductory courses are taught by graduate students. The average class size in an introductory lecture is 22; in a laboratory, 17; and in a regular course, 19.

Admissions: 86% of the 2003-2004 applicants were accepted. The SAT I scores for the 2003-2004 freshman class were: Verbal--30% below 500, 37% between 500 and 599, 29% between 600 and 700, and 4% above 700; Math--30% below 500, 43% between 500 and 599, 24% between 600 and 700, and 3% above 700. The ACT scores were 32% below 21, 30% between 21 and 23, 21% between 24 and 26, 9% between 27 and 28, and 8% above 28. 34% of the current freshmen were in the top fifth of their class; 62% were in the top two fifths. 14 freshmen graduated first in their class.

Requirements: The ACT is required, and a minimum score of 18 is recommended. Applicants should be graduates of an accredited high school and be in the upper two-thirds of their class. Required preparatory courses include 3 units in English, 2 units each in math (algebra I and II, and geometry) and social studies, and 1 unit in science. 2 units of 1 foreign language and a second science course are recommended. A GPA of 2.5 is required. AP and CLEP credits are accepted. Important factors in the admissions decision are recommendations by school officials, personality/intangible qualities, and leadership record.

Procedure: Freshmen are admitted fall, winter, and spring. Entrance exams should be taken in early fall. Applications should be filed by May 31 for fall entry, December 3 for winter entry, December 17 for spring entry, and May 15 for summer entry, along with a $25 fee. There is a rolling admissions plan. Notification is sent on a rolling basis. Applications are accepted on-line.

Transfer: 60 transfer students enrolled in 2003-2004. Transfer students must be in good standing academically and financially. Official transcripts from all colleges attended must be submitted. 30 credits of 124 required for the bachelor's degree must be completed at MVNU.

Visiting: There are regularly scheduled orientations for prospective students. There are guides for informal visits and visitors may sit in on classes and stay overnight. To schedule a visit, contact the Admissions Office at (866) 462-6868 or admissions@mvnu.edu.

Financial Aid: In 2003-2004, all full-time freshmen and 99% of continuing full-time students received some form of financial aid. 86% of all full-time students received need-based aid. The average freshman award was $14,436. Need-based scholarships or need-based grants averaged $3820 ($14,250 maximum); need-based self-help aid (loans and jobs) averaged $5403 ($19,125 maximum); non-need-based athletic scholarships averaged $2643 ($12,500 maximum); and other non-need-based awards and non-need-based scholarships averaged $4930 ($21,866 maximum). 37% of undergraduates work part time. Average annual earnings from campus work are $1400. The average financial indebtedness of the 2003 graduate was $17,677. The FAFSA and the college's own financial statement are required. The priority date for freshman financial aid applications for fall entry is April 15.

International Students: There are 9 international students enrolled. They must score 500 on the written TOEFL and also take the SAT I or the ACT, scoring 19.

Computers: The mainframe is an HP 9000/L2000. A campuswide network includes Macs and PCs in 5 major computing labs and many other specialized labs. Internet and Web access are available in the library, classrooms, and residential facilities. All students may access the system 24 hours, 7 days a week. There are no time limits and no fees.

Graduates: From July 1, 2002 to June 30, 2003, 466 bachelor's degrees were awarded. The most popular majors were business (16%), education (14%), and religion (12%). In an average class, 1% graduate in 3 years or less, 37% graduate in 4 years or less, 61% graduate in 5 years or less, and 55% graduate in 6 years or less. 63 companies recruited on campus in 2002-2003. Of the 2002 graduating class, 26% were enrolled in graduate school within 6 months of graduation and 96% were employed.

Admissions Contact: Tim Eades, Director of Admissions and Recruitment. E-mail: admissions@mvnu.edu Web: www.mvnu.edu

MUSKINGUM COLLEGE
New Concord, OH 43762

D-3
(740) 826-8137
(800) 752-6082; Fax: (740) 826-8100

Full-time: 787 men, 751 women	**Faculty:** 99; IIB, -$
Part-time: 26 men, 48 women	**Ph.D.s:** 92%
Graduate: 181 men, 316 women	**Student/Faculty:** 16 to 1
Year: semesters, summer session	**Tuition:** $14,800
Application Deadline: June 1	**Room & Board:** $5880
Freshman Class: 1703 applied, 1360 accepted, 386 enrolled	
SAT I Verbal/Math: 510/530	**ACT:** 21 — COMPETITIVE

Muskingum College, founded in 1837, is a private liberal arts and sciences institution affiliated with the Presbyterian Church (U.S.A.). In addition to regional accreditation, Muskingum has baccalaureate program accreditation with NASM and NCATE. The library contains 218,000 volumes, 5772 microform items, and 3111 audio/video tapes/CDs, and subscribes to 10,000 periodicals. Computerized library services include the card catalog, interlibrary loans, database searching, and Internet access. Special learning facilities include a learning resource center, art gallery, radio station, TV station, and greenhouse. The 215-acre campus is in a small town 9 miles west of Cambridge and 50 miles east of Columbus. Including any residence halls, there are 34 buildings.

Student Life: 88% of undergraduates are from Ohio. Students are from 23 states and 15 foreign countries. 85% are from public schools. 92% are white. 45% are Protestant; 35% claim no religious affiliation; 19% Catholic. The average age of freshmen is 18; all undergraduates, 21. 23% do not continue beyond their first year; 62% remain to graduate.

Housing: 1100 students can be accommodated in college housing, which includes single-sex and coed dorms, on-campus apartments, fraternity houses, and sorority houses. In addition, there are language houses, special-interest houses, upperclassmen apartments, and townhouses. On-campus housing is guaranteed for all 4 years. 80% of students live on campus; of those, 70% remain on campus on weekends. All students may keep cars.

Activities: 30% of men belong to 3 local and 2 national fraternities; 35% of women belong to 3 local and 2 national sororities. There are 90 groups on campus, including art, band, cheerleading, choir, chorus, computers, dance, dance team, debate, drama, forensics, gay, honors, international, jazz band, literary magazine, musical theater, newspaper, orchestra, pep band, political, professional, radio and TV, religious, social, social service, student government, symphony, and yearbook. Popular campus events include Parents Weekend, Li'l Sibs Weekend, and Muskiepalooza.

Sports: There are 9 intercollegiate sports for men and 8 for women, and 8 intramural sports for men and 8 for women. Facilities include gyms, weightlifting/training rooms, an aerobics room, a baseball batting cage, a swimming pool, a walking/jogging trail, an all-weather track, football, baseball, and soccer fields, and tennis, basketball, and racquetball courts.

Disabled Students: 40% of the campus is accessible. Wheelchair ramps, elevators, special parking, and lowered drinking fountains are available.

Services: Counseling and information services are available, as is tutoring in every subject. There is a reader service for the blind. The PLUS program is available for learning-disabled and disabled students. The Center for the Advancement of Learning assists all students with study strategies.

Campus Safety and Security: Measures include 24-hour foot and vehicle patrol, security escort services, informal discussions, and pamphlets/posters/films. There are emergency telephones and lighted pathways/sidewalks.

Programs of Study: Muskingum confers B.A. and B.S. degrees. Master's degrees are also awarded. Bachelor's degrees are awarded in AGRICULTURE (conservation and regulation), BIOLOGICAL SCIENCE (biology/biological science, molecular biology, and neurosciences), BUSINESS (accounting, business administration and management, and international business management), COMMUNICATIONS AND THE ARTS (art, communications, dramatic arts, English, French, German, journalism, music, Spanish, and speech/debate/rhetoric), COMPUTER AND PHYSICAL SCIENCE (chemistry, computer science, earth science, geology, mathematics, and physics), EDUCATION (Christian, early childhood, elementary, foreign languages, music, physical, reading, science, secondary, and special), ENGINEERING AND ENVIRONMENTAL DESIGN (environmental science), SOCIAL SCIENCE (American studies, criminal justice, economics, history, international relations, philosophy, political science/government, psychology, public affairs, religion, religious education, social science, and sociology). Sciences, education, and history are the strongest academically. Education, business, and psychology are the largest.

Required: To graduate, students must complete a minimum of 124 credit hours, including at least 30 in a major and 40 in upper-level courses. Students must maintain a GPA of at least 2.0, and must also complete the 50 to 55 credit hours of Liberal Arts Essentials, with courses in writing, speech, math, arts and humanities, religion and ethics, science, social science, American studies, and phys ed. Senior capstone experience is required in all areas.

Special: Internships, both national and regional, work-study programs, study abroad in 12 countries, and a Washington semester are possible. Students may earn a 3-2 engineering degree with Case Western Reserve University, a B.A.-B.S. degree, or a general studies degree; nearly a third of students pursue dual and student-designed majors. Nondegree study, pass/fail options, and credit for life, military, or work experience are also available. There are 13 national honor societies.

Faculty/Classroom: 60% of faculty are male; 40%, female. All teach undergraduates; 90% both teach and do research. No introductory courses are taught by graduate students. The average class size in an introductory lecture is 30; in a laboratory, 16; and in a regular course, 25.

Admissions: 80% of the 2003-2004 applicants were accepted. The SAT I scores for the 2003-2004 freshman class were: Verbal--45% below 500, 30% between 500 and 599, 20% between 600 and 700, and 5% above 700; Math--44% below 500, 30% between 500 and 599, 22% between 600 and 700, and 4% above 700. The ACT scores were 47% below 21, 26% between 21 and 23, 16% between 24 and 26, 6% between 27 and 28, and 5% above 28. 36% of the current freshmen were in the top fifth of their class; 64% were in the top two fifths. 9 freshmen graduated first in their class.

Requirements: The SAT I or ACT is required. In addition, candidates for admission must have a high school diploma or its equivalent, and should have 4 years of English, 3 years of college preparatory math, and 2 years each of science, social science, and foreign language. A GPA of 2.2 is required. AP and CLEP credits are accepted. Important factors in the admissions decision are advanced placement or honor courses, extracurricular activities record, and leadership record.

Procedure: Freshmen are admitted to all sessions. Entrance exams should be taken in the junior year or the fall of the senior year. There are early admissions and deferred admissions plans. There is a rolling admissions plan. Applications should be filed by June 1 for fall entry. Notification is sent on a rolling basis, beginning October 1. Applications are accepted on computer disk and on-line through Muskingum's web site, Princeton Review (Embark.com), CollegeLink, or Apply.

Transfer: 46 transfer students enrolled in 2002-2003. Applicants must submit an official college transcript and be in good academic standing from their previous institution. 48 credits of 124 required for the bachelor's degree must be completed at Muskingum.

Visiting: There are regularly scheduled orientations for prospective students, consisting of an admission presentation, faculty and student panels, and class attendance. There are guides for informal visits and visitors may sit in on classes and stay overnight. To schedule a visit, contact the Admission Office at *adminfo@muskingum.edu.*

Financial Aid: In 2003-2004, 94% of all full-time freshmen and 95% of continuing full-time students received some form of financial aid. 84% of full-time freshmen and 76% of continuing full-time students received need-based aid. The average freshman award was $14,200. 45% of undergraduates work part time. Average annual earnings from campus work are $1000. The average financial indebtedness of the 2003 graduate was $17,500. Muskingum is a member of CSS. The FAFSA and student and parents' tax returns are required. The priority date for freshman financial aid applications for fall entry is March 15. The regular fall application deadline is open.

International Students: There are 33 international students enrolled. The school actively recruits these students. They must score 550 on the written TOEFL or 213 on the electronic version. Either the SAT I or ACT is recommended.

Computers: There are 7 computing labs on the quad, and 4 additional labs in the residence halls. All residence halls have network access. All students may access the system 24 hours a day. There are no time limits and no fees.

Graduates: From July 1, 2002 to June 30, 2003, 312 bachelor's degrees were awarded. The most popular majors were business (22%), early childhood education (12%), and history (9%). In an average class, 50% graduate in 4 years or less, and 61% graduate in 5 years or less. 36 companies recruited on campus in 2002-2003. Of the 2002 graduating class, 8% were enrolled in graduate school within 6 months of graduation and 96% were employed.

Admissions Contact: Beth DaLonzo, Director of Admission. E-mail: *adminfo@muskingum.edu* Web: *www.muskingum.edu*

NOTRE DAME COLLEGE   D-1
South Euclid, OH 44121   (216) 373-5383
(800) NDC-1680, ext. 355; Fax: (216) 381-3802

Full-time: 60 men, 245 women	**Faculty:** 26; IIB, --$
Part-time: 495 men and women	**Ph.D.s:** 65%
Graduate: 125 men and women	**Student/Faculty:** 12 to 1
Year: semesters, summer session	**Tuition:** $14,800
Application Deadline: open	**Room & Board:** $5625
Freshman Class: n/av	
SAT I or ACT: required	**COMPETITIVE**

Notre Dame College, founded in 1922, is a private liberal arts and sciences college affiliated with the Roman Catholic Church. In addition to regional accreditation, NDC has baccalaureate program accreditation with ADA. Figures in the above capsule and in this profile are approximate. The library contains 89,292 volumes, 14,200 microform items, and 1768 audio/video tapes/CDs, and subscribes to 300 periodicals. Computerized library services include the card catalog, interlibrary loans, and database searching. Special learning facilities include a learning resource center and tolerance resource center. The 53-acre campus is in a suburban area 13 miles east of Cleveland. Including any residence halls, there are 6 buildings.

Student Life: 95% of undergraduates are from Ohio. Students are from 8 states, 7 foreign countries, and Canada. 65% are from public schools. 65% are white; 23% African American. 55% are Catholic; 20% Baptist, Muslim, and other Christian; 15% Protestant; 8% claim no religious affiliation. The average age of freshmen is 18; all undergraduates, 26. 34% do not continue beyond their first year; 52% remain to graduate.

Housing: 222 students can be accommodated in college housing, which includes dorms. There are also nonsmoking floors and quiet floors. Housing is available for weekend college students on WECO weekends. On-campus housing is guaranteed for all 4 years. 78% of students commute. Alcohol is not permitted. All students may keep cars.

Activities: There are no fraternities or sororities. There are 32 groups on campus, including art, choir, computers, dance, drama, ethnic, honors, international, literary magazine, newspaper, political, professional, religious, social, social service, and student government. Popular campus events include Parents Day, Founders Weekend, and Christmas Happening.

Sports: There are 5 intercollegiate sports for men and 7 for women, and 4 intramural sports for men and 4 for women. Facilities include a 500-seat gym, a pool, and a fitness center.

Disabled Students: 75% of the campus is accessible. Wheelchair ramps, elevators, special parking, specially equipped rest rooms, lowered drinking fountains, and lowered telephones are available.

Services: Counseling and information services are available, as is tutoring in most subjects. There is remedial math, reading, and writing.

Campus Safety and Security: Measures include 24-hour foot and vehicle patrol, security escort services, informal discussions, and pamphlets/posters/films. There are emergency telephones and lighted pathways/sidewalks.

Programs of Study: NDC confers B.A. and B.S. degrees. Associate and master's degrees are also awarded. Bachelor's degrees are awarded in BIOLOGICAL SCIENCE (biology/biological science), BUSINESS (accounting, business economics, human resources, management science, and marketing/retailing/merchandising), COMMUNICATIONS AND THE ARTS (art, communications, English, graphic design, studio art, and visual and performing arts), COMPUTER AND PHYSICAL SCIENCE (chemistry, information sciences and systems, and mathematics), EDUCATION (early childhood, elementary, middle school, and secondary), ENGINEERING AND ENVIRONMENTAL DESIGN (environmental science), SOCIAL SCIENCE (economics, history, ministries, political science/government, psychology, and theological studies). Business, education, and science are the strongest academically. Business administration, education, and sciences are the largest.

Required: To graduate, students must complete 128 semester hours with a minimum GPA of 2.0. Core requirements include English, speech, literature, fine arts, foreign language, health and phys ed, math, science, social or behavioral science, philosophy/theology, world civilization, and senior seminar.

Special: Students may cross-register with the Cleveland Institutes of Music and Art and through the Northeast Ohio Council on Higher Education. The college offers co-op programs in most majors, internships with local businesses, special degrees, including a B.A. with a diploma in theology, and interdisciplinary majors, including visual arts management, credit by exam, nondegree study, and pass/fail options. NDC also offers Weekend College. There are 5 national honor societies.

Faculty/Classroom: 30% of faculty are male; 70%, female. All teach undergraduates. No introductory courses are taught by graduate students. The average class size in an introductory lecture is 20; in a laboratory, 11; and in a regular course, 11.

Requirements: The SAT I or ACT is required, with a minimum composite score of 900 on the SAT I or 19 on the ACT. Applicants should be graduates of an accredited secondary school with 15 academic credits, including 4 of English, 2 of foreign language, 1 each of math, social studies, and science, plus 5 electives. The GED is accepted. An interview is recommended. A GPA of 2.5 is required. AP and CLEP credits are accepted. Important factors in the admissions decision are advanced placement or honor courses, evidence of special talent, and extracurricular activities record.

Procedure: Freshmen are admitted fall and spring. Entrance exams should be taken in the spring of the junior year or the fall of the senior year. There are deferred admissions and rolling admissions plans. Application deadlines are open. The fall 2003 application fee was $30. Notification is sent on a rolling basis.

Transfer: 37 transfer students enrolled in a recent year. Applicants must have a college GPA of at least 2.5. An interview is required. 32 of 128 credits required for the bachelor's degree must be completed at NDC.

Visiting: There are regularly scheduled orientations for prospective students, including placement testing, academic advising, scheduling, an overview of student services, and a tour of Cleveland. There are guides for informal visits and visitors may sit in on classes and stay overnight. To schedule a visit, contact the Admissions Office.

Financial Aid: In a recent year, all full-time freshmen and 90% of continuing full-time students received some form of financial aid. 92% of full-time freshmen and 90% of continuing full-time students received need-based aid. The average freshman award was $13,200. 20% of undergraduates work part time. Average annual earnings from campus work are $1500. The average financial indebtedness of a recent graduate was $14,825. The FAFSA is required.

International Students: There were 7 international students enrolled in a recent year. The school actively recruits these students. They must score 550 on the written TOEFL or take the ELS Proficiency Test 109.

Computers: NDC has a Unisys system, and students use individual PCs in the computer lab networked for classroom and homework. There are also PCs located in education and writing labs in dorms. The learning center computer classroom has 31 Pentium MMX computers, and its lab has 16 Pentium computers, all with full Internet access. There is also a 5-seat lab in the residence halls and a Mac lab with 14 power Mac 5400s. All students may access the system. There are no time limits. The fee is $200.

Graduates: In a recent year, 92 bachelor's degrees were awarded. The most popular majors were accounting (19%), human resources (16%), and management (14%). In an average class, 35% graduate in 4 years or less, and 48% graduate in 5 years or less. 85 companies recruited on campus in a recent year. Of a recent graduating class, 10% were enrolled in graduate school within 6 months of graduation and 85% were employed.

Admissions Contact: Meredith Young, Director of Admissions. E-mail: *myoung@ndc.edu* Web: *http://www.ndc.edu*

OBERLIN COLLEGE
Oberlin, OH 44074

D-2

(440) 775-8411
(800) 622-6243; Fax: (440) 775-6905

Full-time: 1261 men, 1548 women	Faculty: 272; IIB, ++$
Part-time: 33 men, 41 women	Ph.D.s: 94%
Graduate: 6 men, 9 women	Student/Faculty: 10 to 1
Year: 4-1-4	Tuition: $29,688
Application Deadline: January 15	Room & Board: $7250
Freshman Class: 4934 applied, 1904 accepted, 659 enrolled	
SAT I Verbal/Math: 690/660	ACT: 29 **MOST COMPETITIVE**

Oberlin College, founded in 1833, is an independent institution offering degree programs in the liberal arts and sciences and music. There are 2 undergraduate schools. In addition to regional accreditation, Oberlin has baccalaureate program accreditation with NASM. The 4 libraries contain 1,275,338 volumes, 339,260 microform items, and 75,045 audio/video tapes/CDs, and subscribe to 13,403 periodicals. Computerized library services include the card catalog, interlibrary loans, database searching, and Internet access. Special learning facilities include a learning resource center, art gallery, radio station, an observatory, an art museum, an art library, an arboretum, a conservatory of music, and a music library. The 440-acre campus is in a small town 35 miles southwest of Cleveland. Including any residence halls, there are 65 buildings.

Student Life: 90% of undergraduates are from out of state, mostly the Middle Atlantic. Students are from 47 states, 44 foreign countries, and Canada. 61% are from public schools. 74% are white. 43% claim no religious affiliation; 23% Protestant; 16% Jewish; 11% Islamic, Buddhist; 7% Catholic. The average age of freshmen is 18; all undergraduates, 20. 10% do not continue beyond their first year; 81% remain to graduate.

Housing: 2072 students can be accommodated in college housing, which includes single-sex and coed dorms and on-campus apartments. In addition, there are language houses, special-interest houses, and co-ops. On-campus housing is guaranteed for all 4 years. 75% of students live on campus; of those, 99% remain on campus on weekends. All students may keep cars.

Activities: There are no fraternities or sororities. There are 120 groups on campus, including art, band, cheerleading, chess, choir, chorale, chorus, computers, dance, drama, ethnic, film, gay, honors, international, jazz band, literary magazine, marching band, musical theater, newspaper, opera, orchestra, photography, political, professional, radio and TV, religious, social, social service, student government, symphony, and yearbook. Popular campus events include Mayfair, Octoberfest, and Mardi Gras.

Sports: There are 11 intercollegiate sports for men and 11 for women, and 10 intramural sports for men and 10 for women (intercollegiate only). Facilities include a gym, an enclosed and a semienclosed field house, a stadium, an indoor 6-lane, 200-meter track, an 8-lane outdoor track, 12 outdoor and 4 indoor tennis courts, a cross-country course, a fitness trail, a swimming pool, a Nautilus center, a free-weight room, 22 practice/play fields, and indoor space for football, soccer, and lacrosse practice.

Disabled Students: 90% of the campus is accessible. Wheelchair ramps, elevators, special parking, specially equipped rest rooms, special class scheduling, lowered drinking fountains, lowered telephones, special housing, and an indoor/outdoor lift are available.

Services: Counseling and information services are available, as is tutoring in every subject. There is a reader service for the blind, and remedial math, reading, and writing. Computer-assisted services for hearing and visually impaired students and special tutoring and peer-counseling services for learning-disabled students are available.

Campus Safety and Security: Measures include 24-hour foot and vehicle patrol, self-defense education, security escort services, and informal discussions. There are pamphlets/posters/films, emergency telephones, lighted pathways/sidewalks, a full-time crime prevention officer, a 24-hour headquarters facility staffed by professional dispatchers, and an electronic card-access system in all dorms. All security officers are state-certified academy graduates.

Programs of Study: Oberlin confers B.A. and B.Mus. degrees. Master's degrees are also awarded. Bachelor's degrees are awarded in BIOLOGICAL SCIENCE (biochemistry, biology/biological science, and neurosciences), COMMUNICATIONS AND THE ARTS (art, classics, comparative literature, creative writing, dance, dramatic arts, English, film arts, fine arts, French, German, music, music history and appreciation, music performance, music theory and composition, romance languages and literature, Russian, and Spanish), COMPUTER AND PHYSICAL SCIENCE (astronomy, chemistry, computer science, geology, mathematics, and physics), EDUCATION (music), ENGINEERING AND ENVIRONMENTAL DESIGN (environmental science), SOCIAL SCIENCE (African American studies, American studies, anthropology, archeology, East Asian studies, economics, history, humanities, Judaic studies, Latin American studies, law, Near Eastern studies, philosophy, political science/government, psychology, religion, sociology, and women's studies). Sciences, art and humanities, and music are the strongest academically. English, biology, and history are the largest.

Required: Students are required to complete 112 to 124 total credit hours, including 9 hours each in arts/humanities, social/behavioral sciences, natural science/math, and courses dealing with cultural diversity, and 3 winter term projects. In addition, they must earn writing and quantitative proficiency certification. A minimum of 24 credits is required for the major.

Special: Internships are available through the Business Initiatives Program. Students may study abroad in more than 25 countries. The college offers independent and dual majors, 3-2 engineering programs with other institutions, nondegree study for special and visiting students, and a 5-year B.A.-B.Mus. double degree. Pass/no credit options are available to all students. There are 4 national honor societies, including Phi Beta Kappa, and 25 departmental honors programs.

Faculty/Classroom: 64% of faculty are male; 36%, female. All both teach and do research. No introductory courses are taught by graduate students. The average class size in a laboratory is 14 and in a regular course, 18.

Admissions: 39% of the 2003-2004 applicants were accepted. The SAT I scores for the 2003-2004 freshman class were: Verbal--2% below 500, 12% between 500 and 599, 43% between 600 and 700, and 43% above 700; Math--3% below 500, 18% between 500 and 599, 49% between 600 and 700, and 30% above 700. The ACT scores were 3% below 21, 5% between 21 and 23, 15% between 24 and 26, 27% between 27 and 28, and 51% above 28. 82% of the current freshmen were in the top fifth of their class; 96% were in the top two fifths. There were 33 National Merit finalists in a recent year. 36 freshmen graduated first in their class.

Requirements: The SAT I or ACT is required. In addition, candidates for admission should have completed 4 years each of English and math and 3 each of science, social studies, and a foreign language. AP credits are accepted. Important factors in the admissions decision are advanced placement or honor courses, personality/intangible qualities, and leadership record.

Procedure: Freshmen are admitted in the fall. Entrance exams should be taken in the junior year or early in the senior year. There are early decision and deferred admissions plans. There is a rolling admissions plan. Early decision applications should be filed by November 15; regular applications, by January 15 for fall entry and November 15 for spring entry, along with a $35 fee. Notification of early decision is sent December 15; regular decision, April 1. 236 early decision candidates were accepted for the 2003-2004 class. 545 applicants were on the 2003 waiting list; 125 were admitted. Applications are accepted on-line.

Transfer: 44 transfer students enrolled in 2002-2003. Applicants should submit official transcripts of all college work completed, plus a list of current courses and midterm grades. An average of B or better should be presented. A high school transcript, recommendations, and standardized test scores are also required. 56 credits of 112 to 124 required for the bachelor's degree must be completed at Oberlin.

Visiting: There are regularly scheduled orientations for prospective students, including campus tours, class visits, an interview with an admissions staff member, and an overnight stay in the dorm. There are guides for informal visits and visitors may sit in on classes and stay overnight. To schedule a visit, contact the Admissions Office.

Financial Aid: In 2003-2004, 65% of all full-time freshmen and 60% of continuing full-time students received some form of financial aid. 56% of full-time freshmen and 58% of continuing full-time students received need-based aid. The average freshman award was $21,413. Need-based scholarships or need-based grants averaged $14,590 ($32,971 maximum); need-based self-help aid (loans and jobs) averaged $3058 ($8275 maximum); and non-need-based awards and non-need-based scholarships averaged $2459 ($36,938 maximum). 57% of undergraduates work part time. Average annual earnings from campus work are $1450. The average financial indebtedness of the 2003 graduate was $13,926. Oberlin is a member of CSS. The CSS/Profile, FAFSA, and the college's own financial statement are required. The deadline for filing freshman financial aid applications for fall entry is February 15.

International Students: There are 177 international students enrolled. The school actively recruits these students. They must score 600 on the written TOEFL.

Computers: There are 10 computer labs throughout campus for general use and 6 departmental computer labs. There are approximately 350 Windows and Mac computers available for student use. Every residence hall room has Internet access and many parts of campus have wireless Internet access. All students may access the system. There are no time limits and no fees.

Graduates: From July 1, 2002 to June 30, 2003, 676 bachelor's degrees were awarded. The most popular majors were English (12%), politics (9%), and biology (8%). In an average class, 1% graduate in 3 years or less, 67% graduate in 4 years or less, 80% graduate in 5 years or less, and 81% graduate in 6 years or less. 18 companies recruited on campus in 2002-2003. Of the 2002 graduating class, 20% were enrolled in graduate school within 6 months of graduation and 77% were employed.

Admissions Contact: Debra Chermonte, Dean of Admissions and Financial Aid. E-mail: *college.admissions@oberlin.edu*
Web: *www.oberlin.edu*

OHIO DOMINICAN UNIVERSITY
Columbus, OH 43219

C-3
(614) 251-4500
(800) 955-OHIO; Fax: (614) 252-0776

Full-time: 519 men, 1159 women	**Faculty:** 60; IIB, -$
Part-time: 177 men, 453 women	**Ph.D.s:** 90%
Graduate: none	**Student/Faculty:** 28 to 1
Year: semesters, summer session	**Tuition:** $17,200
Application Deadline: open	**Room & Board:** $5500
Freshman Class: 1193 applied, 902 accepted, 312 enrolled	
SAT I or ACT: required	**COMPETITIVE**

Ohio Dominican University, formerly Ohio Dominican College, founded in 1911 by the Dominican Sisters of St. Mary of the Springs, is a private liberal arts university affiliated with the Roman Catholic Church. There are 2 undergraduate schools and 1 graduate school. The library contains 109,606 volumes, 7211 microform items, and 3932 audio/video tapes/ CDs, and subscribes to 575 periodicals. Computerized library services include the card catalog, interlibrary loans, database searching, and Internet access. Special learning facilities include a learning resource center, art gallery, and radio station. The 62-acre campus is in an urban area 5 miles from downtown Columbus. Including any residence halls, there are 9 buildings.

Student Life: 97% of undergraduates are from Ohio. Students are from 14 states, 16 foreign countries, and Canada. 71% are from public schools. 69% are white; 23% African American. 41% are Protestant; 28% Catholic. The average age of freshmen is 19; all undergraduates, 28. 42% do not continue beyond their first year; 49% remain to graduate.

Housing: 411 students can be accommodated in college housing, which includes single-sex and coed dorms. On-campus housing is available on a first-come, first-served basis. 83% of students commute. Alcohol is not permitted. All students may keep cars.

Activities: There are no fraternities or sororities. There are 25 groups on campus, including academic, art, association of commuters, associa-

tion of resident students, band, board games, cheerleading, choir, dance, drama, drill team, English circle, ethnic, honors, international, literary magazine, newspaper, Palette Club, political, professional, radio and TV, religious, social, social service, and student government. Popular campus events include Black History Week, International Student Week, and ODU Day in the Spring.

Sports: There are 7 intercollegiate sports for men and 7 for women, and 6 intramural sports for men and 6 for women. Facilities include an athletic center, a gym, a baseball and softball field, a soccer field, and tennis courts.

Disabled Students: 90% of the campus is accessible. Wheelchair ramps, elevators, special parking, specially equipped rest rooms, and special class scheduling are available.

Services: Counseling and information services are available, as is tutoring in most subjects. There is remedial math, reading, and writing. The Academic Center is a support unit designed to help all students meet their academic commitment and improve their learning skills. The staff offers workshops in study-related topics, provides professional and peer tutoring in a variety of subjects, and counsels students and faculty on learning and study problems.

Campus Safety and Security: Measures include 24-hour foot and vehicle patrol, self-defense education, security escort services, and shuttle buses. There are informal discussions, pamphlets/posters/films, emergency telephones, and lighted pathways/sidewalks.

Programs of Study: ODU confers B.A., B.S., and B.S.Ed. degrees. Associate and master's degrees are also awarded. Bachelor's degrees are awarded in BIOLOGICAL SCIENCE (biology/biological science), BUSINESS (accounting, banking and finance, business administration and management, international business management, and management information systems), COMMUNICATIONS AND THE ARTS (art, communications, English, graphic design, public relations, and technical and business writing), COMPUTER AND PHYSICAL SCIENCE (chemistry, computer science, information sciences and systems, and mathematics), EDUCATION (early childhood, middle school, special, and teaching English as a second/foreign language (TESOL/TEFOL)), SOCIAL SCIENCE (criminal justice, economics, history, interdisciplinary studies, liberal arts/general studies, philosophy, political science/government, psychology, social work, and sociology). Business, education, and computer science and information systems are the largest.

Required: Core curriculum requirements include 4 semester credits each in philosophy and theology, plus 4 additional credits in either, 8 each in humanities, English, and behavioral science, 4 each in literature, math, and science, 4 or 8 in language, and 1 in phys ed. All students beyond the freshman year must maintain a GPA of 2.0. Students must complete 124 semester credits. The total hours in the major is set by individual departments.

Special: Students may cross-register with members of the Higher Education Council of Columbus Consortium, study abroad in various countries, and participate in a Washington semester. Internships are required in some majors. ODU offers dual majors and pass/fail options in some courses. Nondegree study and credit for life, military, and work experience are available. The Weekend College Program allows students to attend classes scheduled every other weekend. There are 4 national honor societies and a freshman honors program.

Faculty/Classroom: 43% of faculty are male; 57%, female. All teach undergraduates. The average class size in an introductory lecture is 20 and in a regular course, 20.

Admissions: 76% of the 2003-2004 applicants were accepted. The ACT scores for the 2003-2004 freshman class were: 52% below 21, 29% between 21 and 23, 14% between 24 and 26, 4% between 27 and 28, and 1% above 28.

Requirements: The SAT I or ACT is required. In addition, candidates for admission should have completed 4 units of English and 3 units each of a foreign language, math, science, and social studies. The freshman applicant is required to submit a completed application, transcripts of secondary courses and grades, and official scores from standardized testing (ACT or SAT I). An essay and an interview (in-state applicants) are required. A GPA of 2.0 is required. AP and CLEP credits are accepted.

Procedure: Freshmen are admitted to all sessions. There is a deferred admissions plan and a rolling admissions plan. Application deadlines are open. Notification is sent on a rolling basis. Application fee is $25.

Transfer: 238 transfer students enrolled in 2002-2003. A completed application, an interview, and transcripts of all college work are required of transfer applicants. 32 credits of 124 required for the bachelor's degree must be completed at ODU.

Visiting: There are regularly scheduled orientations for prospective students, including an August orientation for fall entry and a January orientation for the second semester. Individual appointments can be arranged. There are guides for informal visits and visitors may sit in on classes and stay overnight. To schedule a visit, contact Victoria Thompson-Campbell, Director of Admissions at *thompson@ohiodominican.edu*.

Financial Aid: In 2003-2004, 97% of all full-time freshmen and 67% of continuing full-time students received some form of financial aid. 80%

of full-time freshmen and 78% of continuing full-time students received need-based aid. The average freshman award was $18,242. 93% of undergraduates work part time. Average annual earnings from campus work are $2000. ODU is a member of CSS. The FAFSA is required. The deadline for filing freshman financial aid applications for fall entry is April 1.

International Students: There are 27 international students enrolled. The school actively recruits these students. They must score 500 on the written TOEFL or 173 on the electronic version or take the MELAB and the college's own test.

Computers: ODU has a Windows NT network, with 336 PCs available to students in the library, the science and art buildings, and residence halls. Software for the World Wide Web, word processing, spreadsheet, and database functions is provided, as well as languages for computer science courses. All students may access the system. There are no time limits and no fees. It is strongly recommended that all students have a personal computer.

Graduates: From July 1, 2002 to June 30, 2003, 357 bachelor's degrees were awarded. The most popular majors were business administration/international business (38%), early childhood education (13%), and information systems (5%). In an average class, 1% graduate in 3 years or less, 33% graduate in 4 years or less, 47% graduate in 5 years or less, and 49% graduate in 6 years or less. 15 companies recruited on campus in 2002-2003.

Admissions Contact: Victoria Thompson-Campbell, Director of Admissions. E-mail: *admissions@ohiodominion.edu* Web: *www.ohiodominion.edu*

OHIO NORTHERN UNIVERSITY
Ada, OH 45810

B-2

(419) 772-2260
(800) 408-4668; Fax: (419) 772-2313

Full-time: 1185 men, 1050 women	Faculty: 169; IIB, +$
Part-time: 30 men, 30 women	Ph.D.s: 82%
Graduate: 410 men, 570 women	Student/Faculty: 13 to 1
Year: quarters, summer session	Tuition: $22,275
Application Deadline: see profile	Room & Board: $5490
Freshman Class: n/av	
SAT I or ACT: required	VERY COMPETITIVE

Ohio Northern University, founded in 1871, is a private institution affiliated with the United Methodist Church. Undergraduate programs are offered in arts and sciences, business administration, engineering, and pharmacy. There are 4 undergraduate schools and 1 graduate school. Figures in the above capsule and in this profile are approximate. In addition to regional accreditation, ONU has baccalaureate program accreditation with ABET, ACPE, ACS, CAAHEP, NASM, and NCATE. The 2 libraries contain 250,518 volumes, 72,067 microform items, and 10,815 audio/video tapes/CDs, and subscribe to 1038 periodicals. Computerized library services include the card catalog, interlibrary loans, and database searching. Special learning facilities include a learning resource center, art gallery, radio station, TV station, and pharmacy museum. The 285-acre campus is in a small town about 75 miles south of Toledo. Including any residence halls, there are 39 buildings.

Student Life: 86% of undergraduates are from Ohio. Students are from 42 states, 17 foreign countries, and Canada. 82% are from public schools. 95% are white. 43% are Baptist, Muslim, Lutheran, Presbyterian, United Church of Christ; 26% Catholic; 12% claim no religious affiliation. The average age of freshmen is 18; all undergraduates, 20. 18% do not continue beyond their first year; 66% remain to graduate.

Housing: 1915 students can be accommodated in college housing, which includes single-sex and coed dorms, on-campus apartments, off-campus apartments, fraternity houses, and sorority houses. In addition, there are honors houses and special-interest houses. On-campus housing is guaranteed for all 4 years. 64% of students live on campus; of those, 70% remain on campus on weekends. All students may keep cars.

Activities: 25% of men belong to 8 national fraternities; 22% of women belong to 4 national sororities. There are 170 groups on campus, including art, band, cheerleading, chess, choir, chorale, chorus, computers, dance, debate, drama, drill team, ethnic, honors, international, jazz band, literary magazine, marching band, musical theater, newspaper, orchestra, pep band, political, professional, radio and TV, religious, social, social service, student government, symphony, and yearbook. Popular campus events include Tunes on the Tundra, International Week, and Little Sibs Weekend.

Sports: There are 11 intercollegiate sports for men and 10 for women, and 12 intramural sports for men and 11 for women. Facilities include a 6-lane pool, a wrestling room, weight rooms, indoor/outdoor tennis courts, 3 basketball courts, a football stadium, a training room, bowling lanes, a billiards room, a dance room, a fitness lab, a 200-meter indoor track, an 8-lane, 400-meter outdoor track, 3 racquetball courts, a Nautilus room, and a 2.5-mile jogging/walking path.

Disabled Students: 95% of the campus is accessible. Wheelchair ramps, elevators, special parking, specially equipped rest rooms, special

class scheduling, lowered drinking fountains, and lowered telephones are available.

Services: Counseling and information services are available, as is tutoring in most subjects. There is a reader service for the blind and remedial math and writing.

Campus Safety and Security: Measures include 24-hour foot and vehicle patrol, self-defense education, security escort services, and informal discussions. There are pamphlets/posters/films, emergency telephones, and lighted pathways/sidewalks.

Programs of Study: ONU confers B.A., B.S., B.F.A., B.M., B.S.B.A., B.S.C.E., B.S.C.P.E., B.S.E.E., B.S.M.E., B.S.M.T., and B.S.Ph. degrees. Doctoral degrees are also awarded. Bachelor's degrees are awarded in AGRICULTURE (environmental studies), BIOLOGICAL SCIENCE (biochemistry, biology/biological science, and molecular biology), BUSINESS (accounting, business administration and management, business economics, international business management, management science, and sports management), COMMUNICATIONS AND THE ARTS (broadcasting, ceramic art and design, communications, creative writing, dramatic arts, English, fine arts, French, graphic design, journalism, language arts, literature, music, music business management, music performance, music theory and composition, public relations, and Spanish), COMPUTER AND PHYSICAL SCIENCE (chemistry, computer science, mathematics, physics, and statistics), EDUCATION (athletic training, early childhood, health, middle school, music, and physical), ENGINEERING AND ENVIRONMENTAL DESIGN (civil engineering, computer engineering, electrical/electronics engineering, mechanical engineering, and technological management), HEALTH PROFESSIONS (health, medical technology, and pharmacy), SOCIAL SCIENCE (criminal justice, history, international studies, philosophy, political science/government, psychology, religion, social studies, sociology, and youth ministry). Chemistry, engineering, and pharmacy are the strongest academically. Pharmacy, engineering, and biology are the largest.

Required: To graduate, students must complete a minimum of 182 quarter hours, maintain a cumulative GPA of 2.0, and fulfill all departmental/college core requirements. Also, students must submit a formal application for graduation.

Special: Co-op programs are available in civil, electrical, computer, and mechanical engineering and technology, computer science, and math. Students may take internships in pharmacy, engineering, and business and may study abroad in 15 countries. B.A.-B.S. degrees and dual majors are available in arts/engineering, arts/pharmacy, and arts/business. The university also offers pass/fail options and work-study programs. There are 38 national honor societies, a freshman honors program, and 21 departmental honors programs.

Faculty/Classroom: 67% of faculty are male; 33%, female. 90% teach undergraduates. No introductory courses are taught by graduate students. The average class size in an introductory lecture is 29; in a laboratory, 14; and in a regular course, 25.

Admissions: There were 11 National Merit finalists in a recent year. 85 freshmen graduated first in their class.

Requirements: The SAT I or ACT is required. In addition, the preparatory program should include 4 years of English, 3 of math, and 2 each of science, social studies, art, history, and music; 2 years of foreign language are recommended. Applications are accepted on-line via EXPAN and at *embark.com*. ONU requires applicants to be in the upper 50% of their class. A GPA of 2.5 is required. AP and CLEP credits are accepted. Important factors in the admissions decision are advanced placement or honor courses, leadership record, and extracurricular activities record.

Procedure: Freshmen are admitted to all sessions. Entrance exams should be taken in the spring of the junior year or the fall of the senior year. There are deferred admissions and rolling admissions plans. Check with the school for current application deadlines. The application fee is $30. Notification is sent on a rolling basis. Applications are accepted online.

Transfer: 88 transfer students enrolled in a recent year. Applicants should have a minimum college GPA of 2.0 and submit official transcripts from all the schools they have attended. 45 of 182 credits required for the bachelor's degree must be completed at ONU.

Visiting: There are regularly scheduled orientations for prospective students, including a tour, lunch, and appointments in academics, admissions, and financial aid. A meeting with a coach can also be arranged. There are guides for informal visits and visitors may sit in on classes and stay overnight. To schedule a visit, contact the Admissions Office.

Financial Aid: 65% of undergraduates work part time. Average annual earnings from campus work are $1320. ONU is a member of CSS. The FAFSA and the college's own financial statement are required. Check with the school for current deadlines.

International Students: There were 23 international students enrolled in a recent year. The school actively recruits these students. They must score 550 on the written TOEFL or 213 on the electronic version or take the MELAB.

Computers: The mainframe is an IBM RISC System/6000. PCs for general use are located in all academic buildings and in 9 residence halls. PCs access the other computer hosts around campus via a network.

Modem ports may be accessed through telephones on and off campus. The network is connected to OARnet, which provides contact to other research, academic, and commercial institutions connected to the global Internet. All students may access the system during building hours and 24 hours a day via modem. There are no time limits and no fees.

Graduates: In a recent year, 475 bachelor's degrees were awarded. The most popular majors were pharmacy (24%), mechanical engineering (7%), and education (6%). In an average class, 66% graduate in 6 years or less. 342 companies recruited on campus in a recent year. Of a recent graduating class, 16% were enrolled in graduate school within 6 months of graduation and 84% were employed.

Admissions Contact: Karen P. Condeni, VP, Admissions. A video is available. E-mail: *admissions-ug@onu.edu* Web: *www.onu.edu*

OHIO STATE UNIVERSITY SYSTEM

The Ohio State University System, established in 1870, is a land-grant university. It is governed by a board of trustees, publicly funded through the Ohio Board of Regents. The chief administrator is the president. As a comprehensive flagship institution, its mission includes teaching, research, and public service. The main campus is in Columbus, and regional campuses are located in Lima, Mansfield, Marion, and Newark, while the 2-year Agricultural Technical Institute is in Wooster. The undergraduate enrollment of the 5 4-year campuses is about 57,000, with some 4500 faculty members. There are more than 170 baccalaureate, 116 master's, and 88 doctoral programs offered through The Ohio State University. Profiles of the 4-year campuses are included in this section.

OHIO STATE UNIVERSITY
C-3
Columbus, OH 43210-1200   (614) 292-3980; Fax: (614) 292-4818

Full-time: 17,487 men, 15,934 women	**Faculty:** 1903; I, +$
Part-time: 2196 men, 1988 women	**Ph.D.s:** 99%
Graduate: 4591 men, 5340 women	**Student/Faculty:** 18 to 1
Year: quarters, summer session	**Tuition:** $6651 ($16,638)
Application Deadline: February 1	**Room & Board:** $6429
Freshman Class: 19,211 applied, 14,355 accepted, 6258 enrolled	
SAT I Verbal/Math: 580/610	**ACT:** 26 **VERY COMPETITIVE+**

The Ohio State University, founded in 1870, is a public land-grant institution offering programs in agriculture and natural resources, arts and sciences, business, education, architecture and engineering, nursing, pharmacy, social work, dental hygiene, and human ecology. There are 5 other campuses. There are 14 undergraduate schools and 1 graduate school. In addition to regional accreditation, Ohio State has baccalaureate program accreditation with AACSB, ABET, ACPE, ADA, APTA, ASLA, CAAHEP, CSAB, FIDER, NASAD, NASM, NCATE, NLN, and SAF. The 18 libraries contain 5,674,784 volumes, 5,671,780 microform items, and 51,500 audio/video tapes/CDs, and subscribe to 42,847 periodicals. Computerized library services include the card catalog, interlibrary loans, and database searching. Special learning facilities include a learning resource center, art gallery, planetarium, radio station, TV station, the Museum of Biological Diversity, the John Glenn Institute for Public Service and Public Policy, and the Cartoon Research Library. The 1741-acre campus is in an urban area 2 miles north of downtown Columbus. Including any residence halls, there are 424 buildings.

Student Life: 91% of undergraduates are from Ohio. Students are from 49 states, 85 foreign countries, and Canada. 87% are from public schools. 79% are white. 44% are Protestant; 31% Catholic; 22% Buddhist, Islamic; 17% claim no religious affiliation. The average age of freshmen is 18; all undergraduates, 21. 12% do not continue beyond their first year; 62% remain to graduate.

Housing: 10,104 students can be accommodated in college housing, which includes single-sex and coed dorms, on-campus apartments, off-campus apartments, and married-student housing. In addition, there are honors houses and special-interest houses. On-campus housing is guaranteed for the freshman year only and is available on a first-come, first-served basis. 76% of students commute. All students may keep cars.

Activities: 5% of men belong to 1 local and 35 national fraternities; 6% of women belong to 1 local and 20 national sororities. There are 750 groups on campus, including art, band, cheerleading, chess, choir, chorale, chorus, computers, dance, debate, drama, drill team, ethnic, film, forensics, gay, honors, international, jazz band, literary magazine, marching band, musical theater, newspaper, orchestra, pep band, photography, political, professional, radio and TV, religious, social, social service, student government, symphony, and yearbook. Popular campus events include United Black World Month, Medieval and Renaissance Festival, and Greek Week.

Sports: There are 18 intercollegiate sports for men and 19 for women, and 48 intramural sports for men and 47 for women. Facilities include a 100,000-seat football stadium, a 17,500-to-21,000-seat multipurpose event center, a 13,000-seat arena, an archery range, a running track, sand volleyball courts, a cricket field, an in-line hockey rink, weight rooms, swimming pools, basketball, volleyball, and racquetball courts,

field houses for tennis, volleyball, basketball, soccer, and baseball and softball fields.

Disabled Students: 85% of the campus is accessible. Wheelchair ramps, elevators, special parking, specially equipped rest rooms, special class scheduling, lowered drinking fountains, lowered telephones, special housing, and adaptive transportation are available.

Services: Counseling and information services are available, as is tutoring in most subjects. There is a reader service for the blind, and remedial math, reading, and writing.

Campus Safety and Security: Measures include 24-hour foot and vehicle patrol, self-defense education, security escort services, and shuttle buses. There are informal discussions, pamphlets/posters/films, emergency telephones, lighted pathways/sidewalks, crisis action teams, and off-campus patrols in cooperation with the city police.

Programs of Study: Ohio State confers B.A., B.S., B. A. E., B.F.A., B.Mus., and B.Mus.Ed. degrees. Master's and doctoral degrees are also awarded. Bachelor's degrees are awarded in AGRICULTURE (agricultural economics, animal science, fishing and fisheries, forestry and related sciences, natural resource management, and plant science), BIOLOGICAL SCIENCE (biochemistry, biology/biological science, entomology, evolutionary biology, microbiology, nutrition, plant physiology, and zoology), BUSINESS (accounting, banking and finance, business economics, hospitality management services, human resources, insurance and risk management, international business management, management information systems, marketing and distribution, real estate, and transportation management), COMMUNICATIONS AND THE ARTS (Arabic, art, Chinese, classics, communications, dance, English, French, German, Greek, Hebrew, industrial design, Italian, Japanese, jazz, journalism, linguistics, music, music history and appreciation, music performance, music theory and composition, Portuguese, Russian, and Spanish), COMPUTER AND PHYSICAL SCIENCE (actuarial science, astronomy, chemistry, computer science, geology, information sciences and systems, mathematics, and physics), EDUCATION (agricultural, art, dance, environmental, music, and technical), ENGINEERING AND ENVIRONMENTAL DESIGN (aeronautical engineering, architecture, ceramic engineering, chemical engineering, civil engineering, computer engineering, electrical/electronics engineering, engineering physics, environmental science, industrial engineering, interior design, landscape architecture/design, materials engineering, materials science, mechanical engineering, metallurgical engineering, and welding engineering), HEALTH PROFESSIONS (dental hygiene, medical technology, nursing, occupational therapy, physical therapy, radiograph medical technology, respiratory therapy, and speech pathology/audiology), SOCIAL SCIENCE (African American studies, anthropology, clothing and textiles management/production/services, criminology, economics, geography, history, human development, human ecology, industrial and organizational psychology, international studies, Islamic studies, Judaic studies, medieval studies, philosophy, political science/government, psychology, social work, sociology, and women's studies). Engineering, business, and social and behavioral sciences are the largest.

Required: To graduate, students must complete 181 to 220 quarter hours, including 40 to 60 in the major, with a minimum GPA of 2.0. The core curriculum consists of courses in writing skills, quantitative and logical skills, foreign language, the sciences, math, and the arts. Distribution requirements include 4 to 5 courses in natural science, 3 in social science, and 5 in arts and humanities.

Special: Students may cross-register with all central Ohio colleges. OSU offers internships, co-op programs, extensive study abroad, work-study programs, dual and student-designed majors, a general degree, credit by examination, nondegree study, and pass/fail options. There are 39 national honor societies, including Phi Beta Kappa, a freshman honors program, and all undergraduate colleges have honors programs.

Faculty/Classroom: 68% of faculty are male; 32%, female. 75% teach undergraduates, 98% do research, and 74% do both. Graduate students teach 38% of introductory courses.

Admissions: 75% of the 2003-2004 applicants were accepted. The SAT I scores for the 2003-2004 freshman class were: Verbal--12% below 500, 44% between 500 and 599, 38% between 600 and 700, and 6% above 700; Math--7% below 500, 37% between 500 and 599, 46% between 600 and 700, and 10% above 700. The ACT scores were 5% below 21, 19% between 21 and 23, 36% between 24 and 26, 19% between 27 and 28, and 21% above 28. 60% of the current freshmen were in the top fifth of their class; 88% were in the top two fifths. 240 freshmen graduated first in their class.

Requirements: The SAT I or ACT is required. In addition, applicants must complete high school with at least 18 academic credits, including 4 in English, 3 in math, 2 each in foreign language, science, and history or social studies, and 1 in art or music. The GED is accepted. AP and CLEP credits are accepted. Important factors in the admissions decision are advanced placement or honor courses and evidence of special talent.

Procedure: Freshmen are admitted to all sessions. Entrance exams should be taken by October of the senior year. Applications should be filed by February 1 for fall entry, November 1 for winter entry, February 1 for spring entry, and February 1 for summer entry, along with a $40 fee. There is a rolling admissions plan. Notification is sent on a rolling basis. 669 applicants were on the 2003 waiting list; 7 were admitted. Applications are accepted on-line through the university's web site.

Transfer: 2047 transfer students enrolled in 2002-2003. High school graduates with 45 hours of college credit and a minimum GPA of 2.0 are admitted for transfer. Those with fewer than 45 hours apply on a competitive basis. 45 of 181 to 220 credits required for the bachelor's degree must be completed at Ohio State.

Visiting: There are regularly scheduled orientations for prospective students, including campus tours, placement tests, course scheduling, and special sessions designed for parents. There are guides for informal visits and visitors may sit in on classes and stay overnight. To schedule a visit, contact the Student Visitor Center.

Financial Aid: In 2003-2004, 86% of all full-time freshmen and 74% of continuing full-time students received some form of financial aid. 50% of full-time freshmen and 48% of continuing full-time students received need-based aid. The average freshman award was $6795. Need-based scholarships or need-based grants averaged $3312 ($16,753 maximum); need-based self-help aid (loans and jobs) averaged $4060 ($13,765 maximum); non-need-based athletic scholarships averaged $13,833 ($34,154 maximum); and other non-need-based awards and non-need-based scholarships averaged $4866 ($30,047 maximum). 27% of undergraduates work part time. Average annual earnings from campus work are $2609. The average financial indebtedness of the 2003 graduate was $14,869. Ohio State is a member of CSS. The FAFSA is required. The deadline for filing freshman financial aid applications for fall entry is March 1.

International Students: There are 1289 international students enrolled. They must score 527 on the written TOEFL or 197 on the electronic version or take the MELAB or take the SAT I or the ACT.

Computers: The mainframe is an IBM zSeries enterprise server. Students have access to the Internet and university services through more than 3500 PCs in public student computer centers, college and department labs, libraries, and residence halls. Many of these facilities also provide access for personal laptops. In addition, all residence halls have high-speed network access for all residents. Off-campus students may connect through university dial-up access or commercial dial-up and high-speed access. All students may access the system 24 hours a day. There are no time limits and no fees. It is strongly recommended that all students have a personal computer.

Graduates: From July 1, 2002 to June 30, 2003, 7903 bachelor's degrees were awarded. In an average class, 56% graduate in 5 years or less, and 62% graduate in 6 years or less.

Admissions Contact: Admissions Information Center Representative. A video is available. E-mail: *askabuckeye@osu.edu*
Web: *www.osu.edu*

OHIO STATE UNIVERSITY AT LIMA
B-2
Lima, OH 45804   **(419) 995-8396**

Full-time: 549 men, 789 women	**Faculty:** 56; IIB, av$
Part-time: 431 men, 570 women	**Ph.D.s:** 84%
Graduate: 15 men, 75 women	**Student/Faculty:** 15 to 1
Year: quarters, summer session	**Tuition:** $4416 ($14,403)
Application Deadline: July 1	**Room & Board:** n/app
Freshman Class: n/av	
SAT I: n/av	**ACT:** required

NONCOMPETITIVE

Ohio State University at Lima, founded in 1960, is a regional commuter campus in the Ohio State University system. At Lima, students may earn a bachelor's degree in education, English, and psychology as well as 1 to 3 years of credit toward any degree conferred by OSU. The student may finish the degree at the Columbus campus or transfer to another institution. There are 19 undergraduate and 2 graduate schools. In addition to regional accreditation, Ohio State Lima has baccalaureate program accreditation with NCATE. The library contains 77,984 volumes, 9040 microform items, and 7715 audio/video tapes/CDs, and subscribes to 517 periodicals. Computerized library services include the card catalog, interlibrary loans, and database searching. Special learning facilities include a learning resource center, greenhouse, and geology museum. The 565-acre campus is in a suburban area 3 miles east of Lima. There are 7 buildings.

Student Life: 95% of students are from public schools. 94% are white. 27% are Protestant; 25% Catholic; 10% claim no religious affiliation. The average age of freshmen is 19; all undergraduates, 24. 35% do not continue beyond their first year; 50% remain to graduate.

Housing: There are no residence halls. Alcohol is not permitted. All students may keep cars.

Activities: There are no fraternities or sororities. There are 24 groups on campus, including cheerleading, chess, chorus, computers, drama, ethnic, honors, musical theater, political, religious, social, and student government. Popular campus events include May Week, Back to School Weiner Roast, and movies.

Sports: There are 3 intramural sports for men and 3 for women. Facilities include a gym and a weight room.

Disabled Students: All of the campus is accessible. Wheelchair ramps, elevators, special parking, specially equipped rest rooms, special class scheduling, and lowered drinking fountains are available.

Services: Counseling and information services are available, as is tutoring in most subjects. There is a reader service for the blind and remedial math, reading, and writing. Developmental education, taped textbooks, oral testing, test readers and scribes, tape recorders, note takers, and a learning disabilities coordinator/counselor are also available.

Campus Safety and Security: Measures include 24-hour foot and vehicle patrol, self-defense education, security escort services, and informal discussions. There are pamphlets/posters/films, emergency telephones, and lighted pathways/sidewalks.

Programs of Study: Ohio State Lima confers B.A., B.S., and B.S.Ed. degrees. Associate and master's degrees are also awarded. Bachelor's degrees are awarded in BUSINESS (business administration and management and hospitality management services), COMMUNICATIONS AND THE ARTS (English), EDUCATION (education), SOCIAL SCIENCE (family/consumer resource management, history, and psychology). Education is the strongest academically.

Required: To graduate, all students must complete 181 to 220 quarter hours, with a minimum GPA of 2.0, and fulfill the general education curriculum requirements.

Special: Students may cross-register with Rhodes State College. Work-study programs, nondegree study, pass/fail options, and credit for life, military, or work experience are available. There is 1 national honor society, a freshman honors program, and 4 departmental honors programs.

Faculty/Classroom: 60% of faculty are male; 40%, female. All teach undergraduates and 50% do research. No introductory courses are taught by graduate students. The average class size in an introductory lecture is 35; in a laboratory, 25; and in a regular course, 20.

Requirements: The ACT is required. In addition, candidates should be high school graduates with 4 years of English, 3 of math, 2 each of foreign language, science, and social studies, 1 of visual or performing arts, and 2 additional years of any of the above subjects. AP and CLEP credits are accepted.

Procedure: Freshmen are admitted to all sessions. Entrance exams should be taken in the spring of the junior year or early fall of the senior year. Applications should be filed by July 1 for fall entry, December 1 for winter entry, March 1 for spring entry, and June 1 for summer entry, along with a $40 fee. The college accepts all in-state residents. Notification is sent on a rolling basis.

Transfer: An overall GPA of 2.0 on all previous college work is required of transfer applicants. 45 of 181 credits required for the bachelor's degree must be completed at Ohio State Lima.

Visiting: There are regularly scheduled orientations for prospective students. There are guides for informal visits and visitors may sit in on classes. To schedule a visit, contact the Admissions Office.

Financial Aid: In 2003-2004, 56% of all full-time freshmen and 58% of continuing full-time students received some form of financial aid. 45% of full-time freshmen and 50% of continuing full-time students received need-based aid. The average freshman award was $3160. Need-based scholarships or need-based grants averaged $450 ($4050 maximum); need-based self-help aid (loans and jobs) averaged $2625 ($10,000 maximum); and non-need-based awards and non-need-based scholarships averaged $450 ($1500 maximum). 95% of undergraduates work part time. Average annual earnings from campus work are $2000. The average financial indebtedness of the 2003 graduate was $12,000. The FAFSA is required. The deadline for filing freshman financial aid applications for fall entry is March 1.

International Students: They must score 500 on the written TOEFL and also take the ACT.

Computers: There are 77 PCs available for student use in labs, the library, and the career center. All students may access the system. There are no time limits and no fees.

Graduates: In an average class, 15% graduate in 4 years or less, 49% graduate in 5 years or less, and 65% graduate in 6 years or less.

Admissions Contact: Admissions Office.
Web: *www.lima.ohio-state.edu*

OHIO STATE UNIVERSITY AT MANSFIELD
C-2
Mansfield, OH 44906   **(419) 755-4226**

Full-time: 330 men, 450 women	**Faculty:** 42; IIB, av$
Part-time: 150 men, 300 women	**Ph.D.s:** 95%
Graduate: 20 men, 95 women	**Student/Faculty:** 19 to 1
Year: quarters, summer session	**Tuition:** $3610 ($12,375)
Application Deadline: open	**Room & Board:** n/app
Freshman Class: n/av	
SAT I or ACT: required	

NONCOMPETITIVE

Ohio State University at Mansfield, founded in 1958, is a regional commuter campus of the Ohio State University system. At Mansfield, students may earn an undergraduate degree in elementary education. Figures in the above capsule and in this profile are approximate. There are

19 undergraduate schools and 1 graduate school. In addition to regional accreditation, OSU Mansfield has baccalaureate program accreditation with NCATE. The library contains 38,874 volumes, 17,559 microform items, and 2155 audio/video tapes/CDs, and subscribes to 410 periodicals. Special learning facilities include a learning resource center, art gallery, radio station, and TV station. The 600-acre campus is in a suburban area 2 miles from Mansfield. There are 7 buildings.

Student Life: 91% are white. The average age of freshmen is 19; all undergraduates, 24.

Housing: There are no residence halls. All students commute. Alcohol is not permitted.

Activities: There are no fraternities or sororities. There are 50 groups on campus, including chorale, drama, ethnic, film, musical theater, newspaper, radio and TV, religious, social, social service, student ambassadors, and student government. Popular campus events include May Day and Buckeye Week.

Sports: There are 12 intramural sports for men and 12 for women. Facilities include a gym and a weight room.

Disabled Students: All of the campus is accessible. Wheelchair ramps, elevators, special parking, specially equipped rest rooms, special class scheduling, lowered drinking fountains, and lowered telephones are available.

Services: Counseling and information services are available, as is tutoring in most subjects. There is a reader service for the blind and remedial math, reading, and writing. Writing and math labs are provided. Books on tape, test readers and scribes, and priority scheduling are available.

Campus Safety and Security: Measures include 24-hour foot and vehicle patrol, self-defense education, security escort services, and informal discussions. There are pamphlets/posters/films, emergency telephones, and lighted pathways/sidewalks.

Programs of Study: OSU Mansfield confers the B.S. in Elem.Ed. degree. Associate degrees are also awarded. Bachelor's degrees are awarded in EDUCATION (elementary).

Required: To graduate, all students must complete 181 to 220 quarter hours, with a minimum GPA of 2.0. General education curriculum requirements must be met.

Special: OSU Mansfield offers co-op programs, study abroad, internships, a general studies degree (no major), nondegree study, pass/fail options, and work-study programs. There are 3 national honor societies and a freshman honors program.

Faculty/Classroom: 92% teach undergraduates.

Requirements: The SAT I or ACT is required. The GED is accepted. OSU Mansfield follows an open admissions policy. AP and CLEP credits are accepted.

Procedure: Freshmen are admitted to all sessions. There are early admissions and deferred admissions plans. Application deadlines are open. Check with the school for current deadlines and fees.

Transfer: Applicants must present a minimum 2.0 GPA on previous university course work. 45 of 181 credits required for the bachelor's degree must be completed at OSU Mansfield.

Visiting: There are regularly scheduled orientations for prospective students. There are guides for informal visits and visitors may sit in on classes. To schedule a visit, contact Henry Thomas, Coordinator of Admissions.

Financial Aid: OSU Mansfield is a member of CSS. The FAFSA is required. Check with the school for current deadlines.

International Students: They must score 500 on the written TOEFL.

Computers: The mainframe is an Amdahl V8. There are 47 PCs in labs and the library. All students may access the system. There are no time limits and no fees.

Admissions Contact: Henry Thomas, Coordinator of Admissions. Web: *www.mansfield.ohio-state.edu*

OHIO STATE UNIVERSITY AT MARION   C-3
Marion, OH 43302   (614) 389-6786, ext. 6337; Fax: (614) 292-5817

Total enrollment: 1360 men and women	**Faculty:** 26; IIB, +$
	Ph.D.s: 94%
Year: quarters, summer session	**Student/Faculty:** 18 to 1
Application Deadline: open	**Tuition:** $4801 ($12,273)
	Room & Board: n/app
Freshman Class: n/av	
SAT I or ACT: recommended	**NONCOMPETITIVE**

Ohio State University at Marion, founded in 1957, is a commuter campus of the Ohio State University system. At Marion, students may earn a bachelor's degree in elementary education, English, accounting, business management, and psychology as well as 1 to 3 years of credit applicable to any other degree, including more than 170 academic programs, conferred by OSU, provided the program is completed at the main campus in Columbus. Some figures in the above capsule are approximate. In addition to regional accreditation, OSU Marion has baccalaureate program accreditation with NCATE. The library contains 44,000 volumes, 2906 microform items, and 8000 audio/video tapes/CDs, and

subscribes to 322 periodicals. Computerized library services include the card catalog, interlibrary loans, and database searching. Special learning facilities include a learning resource center, art gallery, natural reconstructed prairie site, greenhouse, psychology lab, and early childhood education center. The 180-acre campus is in a rural area 45 miles north of Columbus. There are 6 buildings.

Student Life: Others are from 3 states. 98% are from public schools. 86% are white. The average age of freshmen is 20; all undergraduates, 24.

Housing: There are no residence halls. All students commute. Alcohol is not permitted. All students may keep cars.

Activities: There are no fraternities or sororities. There are 8 groups on campus, including art, choir, chorale, chorus, dance, drama, ethnic, honors, international, jazz band, literary magazine, musical theater, newspaper, political, professional, religious, social, social service, and student government. Popular campus events include Buckeye Week, May Day, and cultural arts events.

Sports: There are 4 intercollegiate sports for men and 3 for women, and 5 intramural sports for men and 5 for women. Facilities include a 740-seat gym, an outdoor fitness court, a weight room, a game room, a rock climbing wall, volleyball courts, and an exercise room.

Disabled Students: All of the campus is accessible. Wheelchair ramps, elevators, special parking, specially equipped rest rooms, lowered drinking fountains, and lowered telephones are available.

Services: Counseling and information services are available, as is tutoring in most subjects. There is remedial math, reading, and writing.

Campus Safety and Security: Measures include self-defense education, informal discussions, pamphlets/posters/films, and emergency telephones. There are lighted pathways/sidewalks.

Programs of Study: OSU Marion confers B.A., B.S., and B.S.Ed. degrees. Associate and master's degrees are also awarded. Bachelor's degrees are awarded in BUSINESS (accounting), COMMUNICATIONS AND THE ARTS (English), EDUCATION (elementary), SOCIAL SCIENCE (psychology). Elementary education and psychology are the strongest academically. Elementary education, psychology, and English are the largest.

Required: Between 181 and 220 credit hours are needed for graduation. Students must complete general education curriculum requirements and maintain a 2.0 GPA.

Special: OSU Marion offers cross-registration with Ohio State University Columbus, various co-op and work-study programs, nondegree study in continuing education, and pass/fail options. There is a freshman honors program.

Faculty/Classroom: 70% of faculty are male; 30%, female. All both teach and do research. The average class size in an introductory lecture is 18; in a laboratory, 24; and in a regular course, 25.

Requirements: The SAT I or ACT is recommended. In addition, OSU Marion follows an open admissions policy for in-state students. Applicants should be high school graduates with 4 units of English, 3 of math, 2 each of foreign language, history or social studies, and science, and 1 of art or music. AP and CLEP credits are accepted.

Procedure: Freshmen are admitted to all sessions. Entrance exams should be taken before fall of the senior year in high school. Application deadlines are open. Applications are accepted on-line through the school's web site.

Transfer: A GPA of 2.0 is required. 45 of 181 to 220 credits required for the bachelor's degree must be completed at OSU Marion.

Visiting: There are regularly scheduled orientations for prospective students. There are guides for informal visits and visitors may sit in on classes. To schedule a visit, contact the Admissions Office.

Financial Aid: Average annual earnings from campus work are $2500. The FAFSA is required. The deadline for filing freshman financial aid applications for fall entry is March 1.

International Students: They must score 500 on the written TOEFL.

Computers: 174 PCs are available for student use in a computer center and in labs. All students may access the system. There are no time limits and no fees. It is strongly recommended that all students have a personal computer.

Admissions Contact: Mathieu Moreau, Director of Admissions. E-mail: *moreau.1@osu.edu* Web: *www.marion.ohio-state.edu*

OHIO STATE UNIVERSITY AT NEWARK

Newark, OH 43055

C-3

(740) 292-4095
(800) 9NEWARK; Fax: (740) 366-9460

Full-time: 615 men, 899 women	**Faculty:** 59; IIB, av$
Part-time: 201 men, 354 women	**Ph.D.s:** 88%
Graduate: 5 men, 74 women	**Student/Faculty:** 26 to 1
Year: quarters, summer session	**Tuition:** $4281 ($14,403)
Application Deadline: July 1	**Room & Board:** $5600
Freshman Class: 1159 applied, 1142 accepted, 1000 enrolled	
SAT I Verbal/Math: 490/485	**ACT:** 19 **NONCOMPETITIVE**

The Ohio State University at Newark, founded in 1957, is a regional commuter campus of the Ohio State University system. At Newark, students may earn a bachelor's degree in elementary education, psychology, history, or English as well as 1 to 3 years of credit applicable to any other degree, including 219 academic programs, conferred by OSU, provided the program is completed at the main campus in Columbus. The library contains 50,008 volumes, 17,465 microform items, and 3649 audio/video tapes/CDs, and subscribes to 427 periodicals. Computerized library services include the card catalog, interlibrary loans, database searching, and Internet access. Special learning facilities include a learning resource center and art gallery. The 150-acre campus is in a suburban area 40 miles east of Columbus. Including any residence halls, there are 5 buildings.

Student Life: 99% of undergraduates are from Ohio. Students are from 3 states and 1 foreign country. 98% are from public schools. 92% are white. The average age of freshmen is 19; all undergraduates, 24. 65% do not continue beyond their first year.

Housing: 140 students can be accommodated in college housing, which includes coed on-campus apartments. On-campus housing is available on a first-come, first-served basis. 95% of students commute. Alcohol is not permitted. All students may keep cars.

Activities: There are no fraternities or sororities. There are 25 groups on campus, including cheerleading, choir, chorale, chorus, Circle K, drama, Ebony Horizons, ethnic, gay, honors, professional, religious, social, social service, student government, and Young Democrats. Popular campus events include Welcome Week, Spring Fling, and Community Service Programs.

Sports: There are 3 intercollegiate sports for men and 3 for women, and 7 intramural sports for men and 7 for women. Facilities include 2 weight rooms, a double gym, and a vita course.

Disabled Students: All of the campus is accessible. Wheelchair ramps, elevators, special parking, specially equipped rest rooms, special class scheduling, lowered drinking fountains, and lowered telephones are available.

Services: Counseling and information services are available, as is tutoring in every subject. There is a reader service for the blind and remedial math and writing. Books on tape, extended test time, readers, scribes, word processing assistance, and loans of specialized equipment are available.

Campus Safety and Security: Measures include 24-hour foot and vehicle patrol, self-defense education, security escort services, and informal discussions. There are pamphlets/posters/films and emergency telephones.

Programs of Study: OSU Newark confers B.A. and B.S.Ed. degrees. Associate and master's degrees are also awarded. Bachelor's degrees are awarded in BUSINESS (business administration and management), COMMUNICATIONS AND THE ARTS (English), EDUCATION (elementary), SOCIAL SCIENCE (history and psychology). Elementary education, English, and psychology are the strongest academically. Elementary education is the largest.

Required: Between 181 and 220 credit hours are necessary for graduation, as is a GPA of 2.0. General education requirements include courses in English, math, natural sciences, social sciences, humanities, and foreign language.

Special: Co-op programs and internships are available in some majors, and study abroad in some departments. Cross-registration is possible with Central Ohio Technical College and HECC member schools, and there is work-study with Ohio State. B.A.-B.S. degrees are offered in elementary education, general business, English, history, and psychology. Dual and student-designed majors and nondegree study are possible, and pass/fail options are available. There is a freshman honors program and 4 departmental honors programs.

Faculty/Classroom: 60% of faculty are male; 40%, female. All teach undergraduates. Graduate students teach 10% of introductory courses. The average class size in an introductory lecture is 35; in a laboratory, 24; and in a regular course, 24.

Admissions: 99% of the 2003-2004 applicants were accepted. The ACT scores for the 2003-2004 freshman class were: 77% below 21, 15% between 21 and 23, 4% between 24 and 26, 3% between 27 and 28, and 1% above 28. 3 freshmen graduated first in their class.

Requirements: The SAT I or ACT is recommended for applicants who graduated from high school within the previous 3 years. Candidates should be high school graduates with 4 units of English, 3 of math, 2 each of science, foreign language, and history or social studies, and 1 of visual or performing arts. OSU Newark follows an open admissions policy for Ohio resident applicants. AP and CLEP credits are accepted.

Procedure: Freshmen are admitted to all sessions. Entrance exams should be taken in the junior year of high school. Applications should be filed by July 1 for fall entry, December 1 for winter entry, March 1 for spring entry, and June 1 for summer entry, along with a $40 fee. There is a rolling admissions plan. The college accepts all in-state residents. Notification is sent on a rolling basis. Applications are accepted on-line through *www.osu.edu.*.

Transfer: 132 transfer students enrolled in 2002-2003. A GPA of 2.0 is required. 45 credits of 181 to 220 required for the bachelor's degree must be completed at OSU Newark.

Visiting: There are regularly scheduled orientations for prospective students, including a campus tour, meeting with faculty, financial aid, and student services, a placement test, and class scheduling. There are guides for informal visits and visitors may sit in on classes and stay overnight. To schedule a visit, contact Admissions at (740) 366-9333 or *bruner.4@osu.edu.*

Financial Aid: In 2003-2004, 75% of all full-time freshmen and 62% of continuing full-time students received some form of financial aid. 67% of full-time freshmen and 60% of continuing full-time students received need-based aid. The average freshman award was $11,000, with $3000 ($9000 maximum) from need-based scholarships or need-based grants, $7000 ($23,000 maximum) from need-based self-help aid (loans and jobs), and $1000 ($4000 maximum) from non-need-based awards and non-need-based scholarships. 7% of undergraduates work part time. Average annual earnings from campus work are $1250. The average financial indebtedness of the 2003 graduate was $12,250. The FAFSA is required. The priority date for freshman financial aid applications for fall entry is April 1; regular deadline is open.

International Students: They must score 527 on the written TOEFL or 197 on the electronic version or take the MELAB.

Computers: The mainframe is an IBM. Some 450 PCs are available for academic use in computer labs. All students may access the system. There are no time limits and no fees.

Graduates: From July 1, 2002 to June 30, 2003, 125 bachelor's degrees were awarded. The most popular majors were elementary education (50%), arts and sciences (40%), and business (10%). Of the 2002 graduating class, 24% were enrolled in graduate school within 6 months of graduation and 97% were employed.

Admissions Contact: Ann Donahue, Director of Enrollment. A video is available. E-mail: *donahue.5@osu.edu* Web: *http://newark.osu.edu*

OHIO UNIVERSITY

Athens, OH 45701-2979

D-4

(740) 593-4100; Fax: (740) 593-0560

Full-time: 7476 men, 8569 women	**Faculty:** 918; I, -$
Part-time: 461 men, 686 women	**Ph.D.s:** 88%
Graduate: 1341 men, 1435 women	**Student/Faculty:** 17 to 1
Year: quarters, summer session	**Tuition:** $7128 ($15,351)
Application Deadline: February 1	**Room & Board:** $7320
Freshman Class: 12,937 applied, 10,235 accepted, 3672 enrolled	
SAT I Verbal/Math: 550/550	**ACT:** 23 **COMPETITIVE**

Ohio University, founded in 1804, is a public university offering programs in liberal and fine arts, aviation, business, communication, engineering, health science, osteopathic medicine, professional training, sciences, and teacher preparation. There are 9 undergraduate and 8 graduate schools. In addition to regional accreditation, Ohio has baccalaureate program accreditation with AACSB, ABET, ACEJMC, ADA, AHEA, CSWE, FIDER, NASAD, NASM, NCATE, and NLN. The 9 libraries contain 2,405,884 volumes, 3,152,947 microform items, and 111,579 audio/video tapes/CDs, and subscribe to 15,906 periodicals. Computerized library services include the card catalog, interlibrary loans, and database searching. Special learning facilities include a learning resource center, art gallery, radio station, TV station, quarterly magazine, accelerator lab, and hearing and speech clinic. The 1700-acre campus is in a small town 75 miles southeast of Columbus. Including any residence halls, there are 201 buildings.

Student Life: 91% of undergraduates are from Ohio. Students are from 50 states, 100 foreign countries, and Canada. 80% are from public schools. 93% are white. 40% are Protestant; 31% Catholic. The average age of freshmen is 18; all undergraduates, 20. 17% do not continue beyond their first year; 70% remain to graduate.

Housing: 7649 students can be accommodated in college housing, which includes single-sex and coed dorms, on-campus apartments, married-student housing, fraternity houses, and sorority houses. In addition, there are honors houses, language houses, special-interest houses, international houses, quiet halls, and engineering, business, and communication halls. On-campus housing is guaranteed for all 4 years. 56% of students commute. Alcohol is not permitted. Upperclassmen may keep cars.

Activities: 13% of men belong to 20 national fraternities; 14% of women belong to 12 national sororities. There are 372 groups on campus, including art, band, cheerleading, chess, choir, chorale, chorus, computers, dance, drama, ethnic, film, forensics, gay, honors, international, jazz band, literary magazine, marching band, musical theater, newspaper, opera, orchestra, pep band, photography, political, professional, radio and TV, religious, social, social service, student government, symphony, and yearbook. Popular campus events include Parents Weekend, International Street Fair, and Communication Week.

Sports: There are 9 intercollegiate sports for men and 12 for women, and 46 intramural sports for men and 46 for women. Facilities include a recreation center, a football stadium, a basketball and convocation center, an aquatic center, an ice rink, tennis courts, a golf course, an intramural gym, a running track, a fitness and aerobics center, baseball, softball, and soccer fields, and an artificial turf field with track.

Disabled Students: 77% of the campus is accessible. Wheelchair ramps, elevators, special parking, specially equipped rest rooms, special class scheduling, lowered drinking fountains, and lowered telephones are available.

Services: Counseling and information services are available, as is tutoring in most subjects. There is a reader service for the blind and remedial math, reading, and writing.

Campus Safety and Security: Measures include 24-hour foot and vehicle patrol, self-defense education, security escort services, and pamphlets/posters/films. There are emergency telephones and lighted pathways/sidewalks.

Programs of Study: Ohio confers B.A., B.S., B.B.A., B.C.J., B.F.A., B.Mus., B.S.A., B.S.A.S., B.S.A.T., B.S.C., B.S.C.E., B.S.Ch.E., B.S.C.S., B.S.Ed., B.S.E.E., B.S.E.H., B.S.H., B.S.H.C.S., B.S.H.L.S., B.S.I.H., B.S.I.S.E., B.S.I.T., B.S.J., B.S.M.E., B.S.N., B.S.P.E., B.S.R.S., B.S.S., B.S.S.P.S., and B.S.V.C. degrees. Associate, master's, and doctoral degrees are also awarded. Bachelor's degrees are awarded in AGRICULTURE (plant science), BIOLOGICAL SCIENCE (biochemistry, biology/biological science, cell biology, environmental biology, microbiology, nutrition, and wildlife biology), BUSINESS (accounting, banking and finance, business administration and management, business economics, business law, international business management, marketing management, personnel management, recreation and leisure services, and sports management), COMMUNICATIONS AND THE ARTS (art, art history and appreciation, broadcasting, ceramic art and design, classical languages, communications, creative writing, dance, dramatic arts, English, fiber/textiles/weaving, fine arts, French, German, Greek (classical), journalism, linguistics, music, music history and appreciation, music theory and composition, painting, printmaking, Russian, Spanish, speech/debate/rhetoric, telecommunications, visual and performing arts, and voice), COMPUTER AND PHYSICAL SCIENCE (actuarial science, applied mathematics, chemistry, computer science, earth science, geology, mathematics, and physics), EDUCATION (art, athletic training, business, early childhood, education of the multiply handicapped, education of the physically handicapped, elementary, music, science, and secondary), ENGINEERING AND ENVIRONMENTAL DESIGN (airline piloting and navigation, aviation administration/management, cartography, chemical engineering, civil engineering, computer engineering, electrical/electronics engineering, and industrial engineering), HEALTH PROFESSIONS (community health work, health care administration, nursing, predentistry, premedicine, prepharmacy, and sports medicine), SOCIAL SCIENCE (African American studies, African studies, anthropology, child care/child and family studies, community services, criminal justice, dietetics, economics, family/consumer resource management, food production/management/services, geography, history, international studies, Latin American studies, parks and recreation management, philosophy, political science/government, prelaw, psychology, social studies, social work, sociology, urban studies, and water resources). Education, business, and communication are the strongest academically. Recreation, journalism, and biological sciences are the largest.

Required: To graduate, students must complete 192 quarter hours, including 45 to 55 in the major, with a minimum GPA of 2.0 in most departments. General education requirements include 2 courses in English composition plus 30 quarter hours in social sciences, natural sciences, humanities, and third world cultures, a minimum of 1 course in math or quantitative skills, and a senior year interdisciplinary course.

Special: The university offers co-op programs in engineering and computer science, internships, study abroad, work-study programs, and an accelerated degree program for students in the Honors Tutorial College. Students may earn a B.A.-B.S. degree in most arts and sciences majors, or a general studies degree. Dual and student-designed majors, nondegree study, limited pass/fail options, and credit for life, military, or work experience are also available. There are 36 national honor societies, including Phi Beta Kappa, and a freshman honors program.

Faculty/Classroom: 66% of faculty are male; 34%, female. All both teach and do research. Graduate students teach 16% of introductory courses. The average class size in an introductory lecture is 38; in a laboratory, 16; and in a regular course, 24.

Admissions: 79% of the 2003-2004 applicants were accepted. The SAT I scores for the 2003-2004 freshman class were: Verbal--23% below 500, 49% between 500 and 599, 25% between 600 and 700, and 3% above 700; Math--23% below 500, 49% between 500 and 599, 25% be-

tween 600 and 700, and 3% above 700. The ACT scores were 15% below 21, 36% between 21 and 23, 28% between 24 and 26, 11% between 27 and 28, and 10% above 28. 40% of the current freshmen were in the top fifth of their class; 77% were in the top two fifths. There were 5 National Merit finalists. 116 freshmen graduated first in their class.

Requirements: The SAT I or ACT is required. In addition, applicants should graduate with 4 units of English, 3 each of math, science, and social studies, 2 of foreign language, and 1 each of history and visual or performing arts. Ohio requires applicants to be in the upper 50% of their class. A GPA of 2.0 is required. AP and CLEP credits are accepted. Important factors in the admissions decision are advanced placement or honor courses, recommendations by school officials, and evidence of special talent.

Procedure: Freshmen are admitted to all sessions. Entrance exams should be taken in spring of the junior year or fall of the senior year. There is a rolling admissions plan. Applications should be filed by February 1 for fall entry, December 1 for winter entry, March 1 for spring entry, and May 1 for summer entry. The fall 2003 application fee was $45. Notification is sent on a rolling basis.

Transfer: 470 transfer students enrolled in 2002-2003. Transfer students are evaluated individually but must have a GPA of at least 2.5 and 30 quarter hours of transferable college credit. Business and journalism majors usually require a GPA of 3.0 or higher. 48 credits of 192 required for the bachelor's degree must be completed at Ohio.

Visiting: There are regularly scheduled orientations for prospective students, including information sessions and campus tours conducted daily Monday to Saturday. There are guides for informal visits and visitors may sit in on classes. To schedule a visit, contact the Admissions Office.

Financial Aid: In 2003-2004, 73% of all full-time freshmen and 69% of continuing full-time students received some form of financial aid. 44% of all full-time students received need-based aid. The average freshman award was $10,405. Need-based scholarships or need-based grants averaged $3376 ($12,500 maximum); need-based self-help aid (loans and jobs) averaged $2801 ($5500 maximum); non-need-based athletic scholarships averaged $11,198 ($23,071 maximum); and other non-need-based awards and non-need-based scholarships averaged $8873 ($33,497 maximum). 34% of undergraduates work part time. Average annual earnings from campus work are $1385. The average financial indebtedness of the 2003 graduate was $16,307. The FAFSA is required.

International Students: There are 285 international students enrolled. They must take the TOEFL or the MELAB.

Computers: The mainframes are an IBM Multiprise 3000, 3006 integrated server, and IBM Z800. More than 6000 PCs are available to students in various campus locations. All students may access the system. There are no time limits and no fees.

Graduates: From July 1, 2002 to June 30, 2003, 3991 bachelor's degrees were awarded. The most popular majors were early childhood/middle childhood education (8%), human and consumer sciences (7%), and journalism (6%). In an average class, 45% graduate in 4 years or less, 66% graduate in 5 years or less, and 70% graduate in 6 years or less. 574 companies recruited on campus in 2002-2003. Of the 2002 graduating class, 28% were enrolled in graduate school within 6 months of graduation and 85% were employed.

Admissions Contact: N. Kip Howard, Director of Admissions.
E-mail: *admissions.freshmen@ohiou.edu*

OHIO WESLEYAN UNIVERSITY   C-3
Delaware, OH 43015

(740) 368-3020
(800) 922-8953; Fax: (740) 368-3314

Full-time: 877 men, 1027 women	**Faculty:** 126; IIB, +$
Part-time: 11 men, 14 women	**Ph.Ds:** 99%
Graduate: none	**Student/Faculty:** 15 to 1
Year: semesters, summer session	**Tuition:** $25,440
Application Deadline: open	**Room & Board:** $7110
Freshman Class: 2580 applied, 1914 accepted, 567 enrolled	
SAT I Verbal/Math: 605/610	**ACT:** 27 **VERY COMPETITIVE+**

Ohio Wesleyan University, founded in 1842, is an independent liberal arts institution affiliated with the United Methodist Church. In addition to regional accreditation, Ohio Wesleyan has baccalaureate program accreditation with NASM. The 5 libraries contain 441,912 volumes, 110,048 microform items, and 3197 audio/video tapes/CDs, and subscribe to 1073 periodicals. Computerized library services include the card catalog, interlibrary loans, and database searching. Special learning facilities include a learning resource center, art gallery, radio station, TV station, and an astronomical observatory. The 200-acre campus is in a small town 20 miles north of Columbus. Including any residence halls, there are 55 buildings.

Student Life: 59% of undergraduates are from out of state, mostly the Northeast. Students are from 44 states and 52 foreign countries. 75% are from public schools. 81% are white; 10% nonresident aliens. The average age of freshmen is 18; all undergraduates, 20. 22% do not continue beyond their first year; 98% remain to graduate.

Housing: 1720 students can be accommodated in college housing, which includes single-sex and coed dorms, on-campus apartments, and fraternity houses. In addition, there are honors houses, language houses, and special-interest houses. Students are invited to submit theme proposals to run a residential house for 8 to 20 students. On-campus housing is guaranteed for all 4 years. 85% of students live on campus; of those, 93% remain on campus on weekends. Upperclassmen may keep cars.

Activities: 44% of men belong to 11 national fraternities; 34% of women belong to 7 national sororities. There are 100 groups on campus, including art, cheerleading, choir, chorale, chorus, computers, dance, drama, ethnic, honors, international, jazz band, literary magazine, newspaper, opera, orchestra, pep band, political, professional, radio and TV, religious, social, social service, student government, symphony, and yearbook. Popular campus events include National Colloquium, Fallfest, and Monett Weekend.

Sports: There are 11 intercollegiate sports for men and 11 for women, and 17 intramural sports for men and 17 for women. Facilities include a gym, a football and lacrosse stadium, field hockey and soccer fields, practice fields, a weight room, indoor and outdoor tracks, handball and squash courts, and an indoor pool.

Disabled Students: 60% of the campus is accessible. Wheelchair ramps, special parking, specially equipped rest rooms, special class scheduling, and special housing are available.

Services: Counseling and information services are available, as is tutoring in most subjects. Students with learning disabilities may receive special help in writing and organization.

Campus Safety and Security: Measures include 24-hour foot and vehicle patrol, self-defense education, security escort services, and informal discussions. There are pamphlets/posters/films, emergency telephones, and lighted pathways/sidewalks.

Programs of Study: Ohio Wesleyan confers B.A., B.F.A., and B.M. degrees. Bachelor's degrees are awarded in BIOLOGICAL SCIENCE (biochemistry, biology/biological science, botany, genetics, microbiology, and zoology), BUSINESS (accounting, business administration and management, business economics, and international business management), COMMUNICATIONS AND THE ARTS (broadcasting, dramatic arts, English, fine arts, French, German, journalism, music, and Spanish), COMPUTER AND PHYSICAL SCIENCE (chemistry, computer science, earth science, geology, mathematics, and physics), EDUCATION (art, early childhood, elementary, foreign languages, middle school, music, physical, science, and secondary), ENGINEERING AND ENVIRONMENTAL DESIGN (environmental science), HEALTH PROFESSIONS (predentistry, premedicine, and preveterinary science), SOCIAL SCIENCE (African American studies, anthropology, economics, geography, history, international relations, philosophy, political science/government, prelaw, psychology, religion, social science, sociology, and women's studies). Psychology, political science and prelaw, and biological sciences are the strongest academically. Economics and business, biological sciences, and political science are the largest.

Required: Most students are required to complete at least 34 units, including 3 units each of humanities/English, social sciences, science/math, and foreign languages, and 1 unit of fine or performing arts. Each unit equals a full course and 3.75 semester hours. All students must also take 8 to 12 units in the major, maintain a minimum GPA of 2.0, and satisfy the university writing skills requirements.

Special: Cross-registration is available with members of the Great Lakes College Association. Students may study abroad in 20 countries or participate in a Washington semester, a departmental internship, or a work-study program. Students may also take dual majors in any combination, design their own majors, or pursue a 3-2 engineering degree in conjunction with 4 major universities. Nondegree study and pass/fail options are available. There are 23 national honor societies, including Phi Beta Kappa, and a freshman honors program.

Faculty/Classroom: 58% of faculty are male; 42%, female. All teach undergraduates and 90% both teach and do research. The average class size in an introductory lecture is 22; in a laboratory, 15; and in a regular course, 12.

Admissions: 74% of the 2003-2004 applicants were accepted. The SAT I scores for the 2003-2004 freshman class were: Verbal--12% below 500, 34% between 500 and 599, 41% between 600 and 700, and 14% above 700; Math--10% below 500, 37% between 500 and 599, 42% between 600 and 700, and 11% above 700. The ACT scores were 16% between 21 and 23, 33% between 24 and 26, 24% between 27 and 28, and 28% above 28. 49% of the current freshmen were in the top fifth of their class; 71% were in the top two fifths.

Requirements: The SAT I or ACT is required. In addition, candidates for admission should complete a recommended 4 units of English and 3 each of math, foreign language, social studies, and science. AP credits are accepted. Important factors in the admissions decision are recommendations by school officials, extracurricular activities record, and advanced placement or honor courses.

Procedure: Freshmen are admitted fall and spring. Entrance exams should be taken in the spring of the junior year or fall of the senior year.

There are early decision, early admissions, and deferred admissions plans. There is a rolling admissions plan. Early decision applications should be filed by December 1; regular application deadlines are open. Application fee is $35. Notification of early decision is sent December 30; regular decision, on a rolling basis. 21 early decision candidates were accepted for the 2003-2004 class. 26 applicants were on the 2003 waiting list; 13 were admitted. Applications are accepted on-line through the school's web site.

Transfer: 28 transfer students enrolled in 2002-2003. Applicants should have better than a 2.5 college GPA and at least 8 course units of credit. High school and college transcripts and an essay are required, along with a statement of good standing from the previous institution. An interview is recommended. 16 credits of 34 required for the bachelor's degree must be completed at Ohio Wesleyan.

Visiting: There are regularly scheduled orientations for prospective students. There are guides for informal visits and visitors may sit in on classes and stay overnight. To schedule a visit, contact the Office of Admission.

Financial Aid: In 2003-2004, 63% of all full-time freshmen and 56% of continuing full-time students received some form of financial aid. At least 63% of full-time freshmen and at least 56% of continuing full-time students received need-based aid. The average freshman award was $23,268. Need-based scholarships or need-based grants averaged $21,561; need-based self-help aid (loans and jobs) averaged $5716; and non-need-based awards and non-need-based scholarships averaged $11,513. The average financial indebtedness of the 2003 graduate was $22,166. Ohio Wesleyan is a member of CSS. The FAFSA and the college's own financial statement are required. The priority date for freshman financial aid applications for fall entry is March 15. The deadline for filing freshman financial aid applications for fall entry is May 15.

International Students: There are 191 international students enrolled. The school actively recruits these students. They must score 550 on the written TOEFL and also take the SAT I or the ACT.

Computers: The mainframes are a DEC Alpha 2100 and DEC Alpha 3000. More than 120 PCs are available for student use in 5 computer labs and in academic departments. Students with their own PCs may network the campus computer. All students may access the system 24 hours a day. There are no time limits and no fees.

Graduates: From July 1, 2002 to June 30, 2003, 316 bachelor's degrees were awarded. The most popular majors were social science and history (24%), business/marketing (14%), and psychology (8%). In an average class, 59% graduate in 4 years or less. 20 companies recruited on campus in 2002-2003. Of the 2002 graduating class, 30% were enrolled in graduate school within 6 months of graduation.

Admissions Contact: Margaret Drugovich, Vice President of Admission and Financial Aid. E-mail: owuadmit@cc.owu.edu
Web: www.owu.edu

OTTERBEIN COLLEGE
Westerville, OH 43081

C-3
(614) 823-1500
(800) 488-8144; Fax: (614) 823-1200

Full-time: 765 men, 1323 women	**Faculty:** 143
Part-time: 141 men, 444 women	**Ph.D.s:** 91%
Graduate: 122 men, 236 women	**Student/Faculty:** 15 to 1
Year: quarters, summer session	**Tuition:** $20,133
Application Deadline: March 1	**Room & Board:** $5952
Freshman Class: 2305 applied, 1929 accepted, 633 enrolled	
SAT I or ACT: required	**COMPETITIVE**

Otterbein College, founded in 1847, is an independent institution affiliated with the United Methodist Church. The college provides a solid liberal arts education combined with professional/career preparation. In addition to regional accreditation, Otterbein College has baccalaureate program accreditation with CAAHEP, NASM, NCATE, and NLN. The library contains 300,000 volumes. Computerized library services include the card catalog, interlibrary loans, and database searching. Special learning facilities include a learning resource center, art gallery, planetarium, radio station, TV station, an equine facility, 2 theaters, and a recital hall. The 142-acre campus is in a suburban area 12 miles northeast of Columbus. Including any residence halls, there are 28 buildings.

Student Life: 89% of undergraduates are from Ohio. Students are from 29 states, 28 foreign countries, and Canada. 88% are white. 76% are Protestant; 22% Catholic; 12% claim no religious affiliation. The average age of freshmen is 18; all undergraduates, 22. 7% do not continue beyond their first year; 74% remain to graduate.

Housing: 1029 students can be accommodated in college housing, which includes single-sex and coed dorms, on-campus apartments, fraternity houses, and sorority houses. In addition, there are honors houses and special-interest houses. On-campus housing is guaranteed for the freshman year only, is available on a first-come, first-served basis, and is available on a lottery system for upperclassmen. Priority is given to out-of-town students. 60% of students live on campus; of those, 55% remain on campus on weekends. Alcohol is not permitted. All students may keep cars.

Activities: 28% of men belong to 5 local and 1 national fraternity; 28% of women belong to 6 local sororities. There are 90 groups on campus, including art, band, cheerleading, choir, chorale, chorus, dance, debate, drama, drill team, equestrian, ethnic, forensics, gay, honors, international, intramurals, jazz band, literary magazine, marching band, musical theater, newspaper, opera, orchestra, pep band, photography, political, professional, radio and TV, religious, social, social service, student government, symphony, and yearbook. Popular campus events include athletics, and music and theater events.

Sports: There are 8 intercollegiate sports for men and 8 for women, and 11 intramural sports for men and 11 for women. Facilities include a basketball and volleyball center, a football stadium, a soccer field, a weight room, tennis courts, a cross-country course, and a student recreation center.

Disabled Students: 81% of the campus is accessible. Wheelchair ramps, elevators, special parking, specially equipped rest rooms, special class scheduling, lowered drinking fountains, and lowered telephones are available.

Services: Counseling and information services are available, as is tutoring in every subject. There is a reader service for the blind, and remedial math, reading, and writing.

Campus Safety and Security: Measures include 24-hour foot and vehicle patrol, self-defense education, security escort services, and informal discussions. There are pamphlets/posters/films, emergency telephones, lighted pathways/sidewalks, and 24-hour locked dorm facilities.

Programs of Study: Otterbein College confers B.A., B.S., B.F.A., B.M., B.Mus.Ed., B.S.E., and B.S.N. degrees. Master's degrees are also awarded. Bachelor's degrees are awarded in AGRICULTURE (equine science), BIOLOGICAL SCIENCE (biochemistry, life science, and molecular biology), BUSINESS (accounting and business administration and management), COMMUNICATIONS AND THE ARTS (art, broadcasting, communications, dramatic arts, English, French, journalism, music, music performance, musical theater, public relations, Spanish, speech/debate/rhetoric, and visual and performing arts), COMPUTER AND PHYSICAL SCIENCE (chemistry, computer science, mathematics, and physics), EDUCATION (athletic training, elementary, health, music, and physical), HEALTH PROFESSIONS (nursing), SOCIAL SCIENCE (economics, history, international studies, liberal arts/general studies, philosophy, political science/government, psychology, religion, and sociology). Life science, chemistry, and athletic training are the strongest academically. Business, education, and communications are the largest.

Required: All students must complete 180 quarter hours, including 50 to 100 in the major, with a minimum GPA of 2.0. The liberal arts core includes 15 hours in English composition and literature, 10 hours each in natural and social sciences, 5 hours each in religion/philosophy, fine arts, and non-Western cultures, and 3 in phys ed.

Special: Students may cross-register with members of the Higher Education Council of Columbus, study abroad in 9 countries, have an internship in most majors, or participate in a Washington semester. B.A.-B.S. degrees, 3-2 engineering degrees with Case Western Reserve and Washington Universities, credit for military experience, student-designed majors, nondegree study, and limited pass/fail options are also available. There are 9 national honor societies and a freshman honors program.

Faculty/Classroom: 52% of faculty are male; 48%, female. All teach undergraduates. No introductory courses are taught by graduate students. The average class size in an introductory lecture is 20; in a laboratory, 10; and in a regular course, 20.

Admissions: 84% of the 2003-2004 applicants were accepted.

Requirements: The SAT I or ACT is required. In addition, applicants should be graduates of an accredited secondary school. The recommended preparatory program includes 4 units of English, 3 to 4 units each of math, science, and social studies, 2 to 3 units of foreign language, and 1 to 2 units of performing arts. A high school GPA of 2.5 or better is recommended. Otterbein College requires applicants to be in the upper 50% of their class. A GPA of 2.5 is required. AP and CLEP credits are accepted. Important factors in the admissions decision are advanced placement or honor courses, evidence of special talent, and geographic diversity.

Procedure: Freshmen are admitted to all sessions. Entrance exams should be taken in the spring of the junior year. There is a deferred admissions plan and a rolling admissions plan. Applications should be filed by March 1 for fall entry, along with a $25 fee. Notification is sent on a rolling basis. Applications are accepted on-line through the school's web site.

Transfer: 74 transfer students enrolled in 2002-2003. Applicants should present a college GPA of 2.5. 60 credits of 180 required for the bachelor's degree must be completed at Otterbein College.

Visiting: There are regularly scheduled orientations for prospective students, including a conference with an admissions counselor, and a campus tour. There are guides for informal visits and visitors may sit in on classes and stay overnight. To schedule a visit, contact Debbie Jamieson at *uotterb@otterbein.edu.*

Financial Aid: In a recent year, 76% of all full-time freshmen and 78% of continuing full-time students received some form of financial aid, including need-based aid. The average freshman award was $13,739. 28% of undergraduates work part time. Average annual earnings from campus work are $1500. The FAFSA is required. The deadline for filing freshman financial aid applications for fall entry is April 1.

International Students: There were 56 international students enrolled in a recent year. The school actively recruits these students. They must score 500 on the written TOEFL and also take the SAT I or the ACT.

Computers: The mainframe is a DEC VAX/VMS. Terminals and PCs are available in several campus locations. All students may access the system. There are no time limits and no fees.

Graduates: In an average class, 4% graduate in 3 years or less, 80% graduate in 4 years or less, and 88% graduate in 5 years or less. Of the 2002 graduating class, 95% were employed within 6 months of graduation.

Admissions Contact: Dr. Cass Johnson, Director of Admissions. E-mail: *uotterb@otterbein.edu* Web: *www.otterbein.edu*

SHAWNEE STATE UNIVERSITY
Portsmouth, OH 45662

C-5
(740) 351-4778
(800) 959-2778; Fax: (740) 351-3111

Full-time: 1279 men, 1768 women	Faculty: 127; IIB, av$
Part-time: 214 men, 432 women	Ph.D.s: 52%
Graduate: none	Student/Faculty: 24 to 1
Year: quarters, summer session	Tuition: $4734 ($8019)
Application Deadline: open	Room & Board: $6297
Freshman Class: 2624 applied, 2624 accepted, 835 enrolled	
ACT: 19	NONCOMPETITIVE

Shawnee State University, founded in 1975, is a public institution offering programs in arts and sciences, business, engineering, health sciences, and education. There are 2 undergraduate schools. In addition to regional accreditation, Shawnee State has baccalaureate program accreditation with ACBSP and ADA. The library contains 140,232 volumes, 39,167 microform items, and 38,552 audio/video tapes/CDs, and subscribes to 5344 periodicals. Computerized library services include interlibrary loans and database searching. Special learning facilities include a learning resource center and planetarium. The 50-acre campus is in a small town 90 miles south of Columbus. Including any residence halls, there are 27 buildings.

Student Life: 91% of undergraduates are from Ohio. Students are from 13 states, 9 foreign countries, and Canada. 88% are white. The average age of freshmen is 20; all undergraduates, 24. 41% do not continue beyond their first year; 59% remain to graduate.

Housing: 296 students can be accommodated in college housing, which includes single-sex on-campus apartments. On-campus housing is available on a first-come, first-served basis. 90% of students commute. Alcohol is not permitted. All students may keep cars.

Activities: 5% of men belong to 3 national fraternities; 3% of women belong to 2 local sororities. There are 15 groups on campus, including art, cheerleading, choir, chorus, computers, ethnic, honors, international, literary magazine, newspaper, pep band, photography, professional, social, and student government. Popular campus events include Founders Day.

Sports: There are 5 intercollegiate sports for men and 5 for women, and 19 intramural sports for men and 19 for women. Facilities include an activities center with basketball and volleyball courts; a sports center with racquetball courts, Nautilus and weight rooms, a pool, a sauna, and a whirlpool; and a soccer field.

Disabled Students: All of the campus is accessible. Wheelchair ramps, elevators, special parking, specially equipped rest rooms, lowered drinking fountains, and lowered telephones are available.

Services: Counseling and information services are available, as is tutoring in most subjects. There is a reader service for the blind and remedial math, reading, and writing.

Campus Safety and Security: Measures include 24-hour foot and vehicle patrol, pamphlets/posters/films, emergency telephones, and lighted pathways/sidewalks.

Programs of Study: Shawnee State confers B.A., B.S., B.F.A., B.I.S., and B.S.N. degrees. Associate degrees are also awarded. Bachelor's degrees are awarded in BIOLOGICAL SCIENCE (biology/biological science), BUSINESS (business administration and management and sports management), COMMUNICATIONS AND THE ARTS (English and fine arts), COMPUTER AND PHYSICAL SCIENCE (chemistry, mathematics, natural sciences, and physical sciences), EDUCATION (education and elementary), ENGINEERING AND ENVIRONMENTAL DESIGN (computer technology, environmental engineering technology, and plastics technology), HEALTH PROFESSIONS (medical laboratory science, nursing, occupational therapy, and premedicine), SOCIAL SCIENCE (history, humanities, interdisciplinary studies, international relations, prelaw, psychology, social science, and sociology). Engineering technologies is the strongest academically. Early childhood education is the largest.

Required: To graduate, students must complete a general education program and a senior seminar. A total of 180 to 190 quarter credit hours, with a 2.0 GPA in all course work and in the major, is required.

Special: Study abroad in China, Germany, and Spain, internships, and student-designed programs are available. There is 1 national honor society and a freshman honors program.

Faculty/Classroom: 61% of faculty are male; 39%, female. All teach undergraduates. The average class size in an introductory lecture is 22; in a laboratory, 15; and in a regular course, 18.

Admissions: All of the 2003-2004 applicants were accepted. The ACT scores for the 2003-2004 freshman class were: 61% below 21, 24% between 21 and 23, 11% between 24 and 26, 3% between 27 and 28, and 1% above 28.

Requirements: Applicants must graduate from an accredited high school or have a GED. AP and CLEP credits are accepted.

Procedure: Freshmen are admitted to all sessions. Entrance exams should be taken in late spring or early summer. There is a rolling admissions plan. Application deadlines are open. Notification is sent on a rolling basis. Applications are accepted on-line through the university's web site.

Transfer: 187 transfer students enrolled in 2002-2003. A completed application and college and high school transcripts sent directly to SSU from previous institutions are required. 45 credits of 180 to 190 required for the bachelor's degree must be completed at Shawnee State.

Visiting: There are regularly scheduled orientations for prospective students, including fall and spring visitation days, which consist of small sessions with deans and faculty, orientation by student affairs officers, and tours with current college students. There are guides for informal visits and visitors may sit in on classes. To schedule a visit, contact the Office of Admissions at to_ssu@shawner.edu.

Financial Aid: The FAFSA is required. The deadline for filing freshman financial aid applications for fall entry is March 1.

International Students: There are 24 international students enrolled. The school actively recruits these students. They must score 500 on the written TOEFL and also take the college's own test.

Computers: The mainframe is a Compaq Alpha 4/275. PCs are available in the College of Business and College of Engineering Technologies, Internet Café, and library. All students may access the system. There are no time limits and no fees.

Graduates: From July 1, 2002 to June 30, 2003, 278 bachelor's degrees were awarded. The most popular majors were business administration (15%), social sciences (14%), and early childhood education (11%). In an average class, 19% graduate in 4 years or less, 28% graduate in 5 years or less, and 30% graduate in 6 years or less. 200 companies recruited on campus in 2002-2003.

Admissions Contact: Bob Trusz, Director of Admissions and Retention. A video is available. E-mail: To_SSU@shawnee.edu
Web: www.shawnee.edu

TIFFIN UNIVERSITY
Tiffin, OH 44883

C-2

(419) 447-6443
(800) 968-6446; Fax: (419) 443-5006

Full-time: 420 men, 450 women	**Faculty:** 49; IIB, av$
Part-time: 51 men, 105 women	**Ph.D.s:** 69%
Graduate: 174 men, 209 women	**Student/Faculty:** 18 to 1
Year: semesters, summer session	**Tuition:** $13,590
Application Deadline: open	**Room & Board:** $5900
Freshman Class: 1000 applied, 911 accepted, 262 enrolled	
SAT I Verbal/Math: 465/465	**ACT:** 19 **LESS COMPETITIVE**

Tiffin University, established in 1888, is a private institution emphasizing degree programs in business, liberal studies, and criminal justice. There are 3 undergraduate and 2 graduate schools. In addition to regional accreditation, TU has baccalaureate program accreditation with ACBSP. The library contains 30,000 volumes, 32,500 microform items, and 830 audio/video tapes/CDs, and subscribes to 255 periodicals. Computerized library services include the card catalog, interlibrary loans, database searching, and Internet access. Special learning facilities include a learning resource center, art gallery, and the Ohio Council on Holocaust Education Information Center. The 110-acre campus is in a small town 90 miles north of Columbus and 60 miles southeast of Toledo. Including any residence halls, there are 25 buildings.

Student Life: 85% of undergraduates are from Ohio. Students are from 19 states, 13 foreign countries, and Canada. 78% are from public schools. 85% are white; 10% African American. The average age of freshmen is 18; all undergraduates, 24. 39% do not continue beyond their first year; 25% remain to graduate.

Housing: 450 students can be accommodated in college housing, which includes single-sex and coed dorms, on-campus apartments, off-campus apartments, fraternity houses, and sorority houses. In addition, there are honors houses and student development housing, bringing together students who are involved in a number of activities and maintain a 3.2 GPA. On-campus housing is guaranteed for all 4 years. 50% of

students live on campus; of those, 60% remain on campus on weekends. All students may keep cars.

Activities: 1% of men belong to 1 local and 1 national fraternity; 1% of women belong to 2 local and 1 national sorority. There are 22 groups on campus, including band, cheerleading, choir, chorale, chorus, computers, drama, drill team, ethnic, gay, honors, international, jazz band, marching band, pep band, political, professional, religious, social, social service, student government, and vocal jazz. Popular campus events include Spring Fest and the faculty/student basketball game.

Sports: There are 9 intercollegiate sports for men and 9 for women, and 10 intramural sports for men and 8 for women. Facilities include a student center gym, indoor batting cages, a weight room, tennis courts, and soccer, baseball, and softball fields.

Disabled Students: 90% of the campus is accessible. Wheelchair ramps, elevators, special parking, specially equipped rest rooms, special class scheduling, lowered drinking fountains, and lowered telephones are available.

Services: Counseling and information services are available, as is tutoring in most subjects. There is a reader service for the blind and remedial math, reading, and writing.

Campus Safety and Security: Measures include self-defense education, security escort services, informal discussions, and pamphlets/posters/films. There are lighted pathways/sidewalks.

Programs of Study: TU confers B.A., B.B.A., and B.C.J. degrees. Associate and master's degrees are also awarded. Bachelor's degrees are awarded in BUSINESS (accounting, banking and finance, business administration and management, hotel/motel and restaurant management, marketing/retailing/merchandising, and personnel management), COMPUTER AND PHYSICAL SCIENCE (information sciences and systems), SOCIAL SCIENCE (corrections, criminology, international studies, law enforcement and corrections, and liberal arts/general studies). Accounting and forensic psychology are the strongest academically. Accounting and management are the largest.

Required: To graduate, all students must complete 130 to 133 semester hours, including 51 to 54 in the major, with a GPA of 2.0 cumulatively and 2.5 in the major. The 61-semester-hour integrated core curriculum includes courses in computer systems, speech and writing, math and statistics, economics, psychology, sociology, history, literature, philosophy, and cultural heritage.

Special: Internships are recommended for all students. An accelerated degree program in finance, work-study programs, a junior semester in England, nondegree study, and pass/fail options are also available. There is 1 national honor society.

Faculty/Classroom: 70% of faculty are male; 30%, female. All teach undergraduates. No introductory courses are taught by graduate students. The average class size in an introductory lecture is 24 and in a regular course, 23.

Admissions: 91% of the 2003-2004 applicants were accepted. The SAT I scores for the 2003-2004 freshman class were: Verbal--68% below 500, and 32% between 500 and 599; Math--67% below 500, 28% between 500 and 599, 3% between 600 and 700, and 2% above 700. The ACT scores were 65% below 21, 22% between 21 and 23, 11% between 24 and 26, and 2% between 27 and 28. 17% of the current freshmen were in the top fifth of their class; 48% were in the top two fifths.

Requirements: The SAT I or ACT is required. In addition, candidates should be graduates of an accredited secondary school, with 4 units of English, 3 of math, 2 each of science and social studies, and 5 of electives. The GED is accepted. An interview is recommended. A GPA of 3.0 is required. AP and CLEP credits are accepted. Important factors in the admissions decision are leadership record, recommendations by school officials, and extracurricular activities record.

Procedure: Freshmen are admitted to all sessions. Entrance exams should be taken as early as possible. There is a rolling admissions plan. Application deadlines are open. The fall 2003 application fee was $20. Notification is sent on a rolling basis. Applications are accepted on-line.

Transfer: 21 transfer students enrolled in 2002-2003. Applicants with 12 or more hours of credit must have a minimum college GPA of 2.0; applicants with fewer hours of credit need a minimum GPA of 1.8 to enter in good standing. The SAT I or ACT and an interview are recommended. 30 credits of 130 to 133 required for the bachelor's degree must be completed at TU.

Visiting: There are regularly scheduled orientations for prospective students, consisting of placement testing, tours of the campus, lunch with advisers, and an appointment with an individual adviser to schedule fall classes. There are guides for informal visits and visitors may sit in on classes and stay overnight. To schedule a visit, contact the Admissions Office at (419) 448-3423.

Financial Aid: In 2003-2004, 90% of all full-time freshmen and 87% of continuing full-time students received some form of financial aid. 88% of full-time freshmen and 86% of continuing full-time students received need-based aid. The average freshman award was $12,458. Need-based scholarships or need-based grants averaged $5180 ($11,016 maximum); need-based self-help aid (loans and jobs) averaged $3294 ($6500 maximum); non-need-based athletic scholarships averaged $4243 ($13,590 maximum); and other non-need-based awards and non-need-based scholarships averaged $6192 ($19,492 maximum). 13% of undergraduates work part time. Average annual earnings from campus work are $874. The average financial indebtedness of the 2003 graduate was $17,125. The FAFSA is required. The deadline for filing freshman financial aid applications for fall entry is August 1.

International Students: There are 26 international students enrolled. The school actively recruits these students. They must score 500 on the written TOEFL.

Computers: The computer system operates on a Novell Network, with 60 PCs distributed among 3 computer labs in classroom buildings. All students may access the system. There are no time limits. The fee is $35.

Graduates: From July 1, 2002 to June 30, 2003, 268 bachelor's degrees were awarded. The most popular majors were management (59%), forensic psychology (8%), and accounting (5%). 8 companies recruited on campus in 2002-2003. Of the 2002 graduating class, 18% were enrolled in graduate school within 6 months of graduation and 97% were employed.

Admissions Contact: Cam Cruickshank, Director of Admissions. A video is available. E-mail: *cacruick@tiffin.edu* Web: *www.tiffin.edu*

UNION INSTITUTE AND UNIVERSITY
A-5
Cincinnati, OH 45206-1925
(513) 861-6400
(800) 486-3116; Fax: (513) 861-0779

Full-time: 197 men, 629 women	**Faculty:** 42
Part-time: 174 men, 288 women	**Ph.D.s:** 86%
Graduate: 530 men, 1092 women	**Student/Faculty:** 20 to 1
Year: semesters, summer session	**Tuition:** $7848
Application Deadline: October 1	**Room & Board:** n/app
Freshman Class: n/av	
SAT I or ACT: not required	**SPECIAL**

Union Institute & University, established in 1964, serves the academic needs of mature working adults seeking to earn the B.A. or B.S. degree. In addition to the main Cincinnati campus, there are learning centers in Miami, Los Angeles, San Diego, and Sacramento. The Institute's Center for Distance Learning enables individuals to earn their degrees through a computer-based educational delivery system. There are 2 undergraduate and 2 graduate schools. The library contains 45,000 volumes and 450 audio/video tapes/CDs, and subscribes to 150 periodicals. Computerized library services include database searching. Special learning facilities include a learning resource center and art gallery. The campus is in an urban area 2 miles from downtown Cincinnati. There are 3 buildings.

Student Life: 77% of undergraduates are from Ohio. Students are from 45 states, 6 foreign countries, and Canada. 52% are white; 26% African American. The average age of freshmen is 38; all undergraduates, 38.

Housing: There are no residence halls. 90% of students commute. The other 10% are distance learners. Alcohol is not permitted. All students may keep cars.

Activities: There are no fraternities or sororities. Popular campus events include Commencement.

Sports: There is no sports program at Union.

Disabled Students: All of the campus is accessible. Wheelchair ramps, elevators, special parking, specially equipped rest rooms, lowered drinking fountains, lowered telephones, and audio/visual fire alarms are available.

Services: Scholar skills development is available.

Campus Safety and Security: Measures include lighted pathways/sidewalks and a security guard during operating hours.

Programs of Study: Union confers B.A. and B.S. degrees. Master's and doctoral degrees are also awarded. Bachelor's degrees are awarded in BUSINESS (business administration and management), COMMUNICATIONS AND THE ARTS (communications), COMPUTER AND PHYSICAL SCIENCE (computer science), EDUCATION (education), HEALTH PROFESSIONS (health), SOCIAL SCIENCE (criminal justice, liberal arts/general studies, psychology, public administration, social science, and social work). Criminal justice studies, business, and education are the largest.

Required: To graduate, students must complete a total of 128 semester credit hours. Distribution requirements include a minimum of 16 semester credits each in humanities and arts, social sciences, language and communications, and natural sciences and math, plus 64 credits in electives and the area of concentration. A senior project, including an oral presentation and thesis, is required.

Special: Programs are designed to meet individual learning needs, with tutorial-based courses, often one-on-one. Scheduling is flexible, and there are part-time enrollment options. Dual majors and student-designed majors are offered.

Faculty/Classroom: 46% of faculty are male; 54%, female. 35% teach undergraduates. No introductory courses are taught by graduate students. The average class size in an introductory lecture is 8 and in a regular course, 1.

Requirements: Applicants must show evidence of ability to do college-level work, to be highly motivated, and to have the capacity for self-directed learning. All applicants should present 2 letters of recommendation, a structured personal essay, and transcripts of any previous college work. An interview is required. AP and CLEP credits are accepted. Important factors in the admissions decision are evidence of special talent, personality/intangible qualities, and leadership record.

Procedure: Freshmen are admitted to all sessions. There is a deferred admissions plan and a rolling admissions plan. Applications should be filed by October 1 for fall entry, February 1 for spring entry, and June 1 for summer entry. These dates vary by program. The fall 2003 application fee was $50. Notification is sent on a rolling basis. Applications are accepted on computer disk and on-line through the school's web site.

Transfer: Grades of C or better from a regionally accredited institution may be transferable. 32 credits of 128 required for the bachelor's degree must be completed at Union.

Visiting: There are guides for informal visits and visitors may sit in on classes. To schedule a visit, contact local campuses.

Financial Aid: 94% of undergraduates work part time. The FAFSA and the college's own financial statement are required.

International Students: There are 8 international students enrolled.

Computers: The mainframes are an AS400 and an S30. Learners may access the Internet from privately owned PCs. All students may access the system. There are no time limits and no fees. It is strongly recommended that all students have a personal computer.

Graduates: From July 1, 2002 to June 30, 2003, 260 bachelor's degrees were awarded. The most popular majors were criminal justice studies (22%), education (19%), and liberal studies (17%).

Admissions Contact: Admissions Office. E-mail: *admissions@tui.edu* Web: *www.tui.edu*

UNIVERSITY OF AKRON
D-2
Akron, OH 44325
(330) 972-7077
(800) 655-4884; Fax: (330) 972-7676

Full-time: 6574 men, 7352 women	**Faculty:** 715; I, -$
Part-time: 2591 men, 3594 women	**Ph.D.s:** 87%
Graduate: 1850 men, 2374 women	**Student/Faculty:** 19 to 1
Year: semesters, summer session	**Tuition:** $6808 ($14,298)
Application Deadline: August 15	**Room & Board:** $6326
Freshman Class: 8254 applied, 5690 accepted, 3193 enrolled	
SAT I Verbal/Math: 500/510	**ACT:** 20 **NONCOMPETITIVE**

University of Akron, founded in 1870, is the public research university for northern Ohio. Primarily a commuter institution, the university offers more than 350 associate, bachelor's, master's, doctoral, and law degree programs and approximately 100 certificate programs at its main campus in Akron, its Wayne College branch campus in Orrville, and in sites throughout Medina and Summit counties. There are 9 undergraduate and 8 graduate schools. In addition to regional accreditation, UA has baccalaureate program accreditation with AACSB, ABET, ADA, CAHEA, CSWE, NASAD, NASD, NASM, NATA, NCATE, and NLN. The 4 libraries contain 1,180,014 volumes, 1,614,271 microform items, and 43,938 audio/video tapes/CDs, and subscribe to 8209 periodicals. Computerized library services include the card catalog, interlibrary loans, database searching, and Internet access. Special learning facilities include a learning resource center, art gallery, radio station, TV station, a nursing center, speech and hearing center, dance institute, educational media lab, and synchronous learning classrooms. The 170-acre campus is in an urban area in downtown Akron, 35 miles south of Cleveland. Including any residence halls, there are 78 buildings.

Student Life: 98% of undergraduates are from Ohio. Students are from 42 states, 86 foreign countries, and Canada. 77% are white; 13% African American. The average age of freshmen is 22; all undergraduates, 25. 34% do not continue beyond their first year; 41% remain to graduate.

Housing: 2064 students can be accommodated in college housing, which includes single-sex and coed dorms and on-campus apartments. In addition, there are honors houses, special-interest houses, fraternity and sorority houses, private apartment-type halls, and private residence halls. On-campus housing is available on a first-come, first-served basis. Priority is given to out-of-town students. 90% of students commute. Alcohol is not permitted. All students may keep cars.

Activities: 5% of men belong to 1 local and 17 national fraternities; 3% of women belong to 8 national sororities. There are 200 groups on campus, including art, band, cheerleading, chess, choir, chorale, chorus, computers, dance, drama, ethnic, gay, honors, international, jazz band, marching band, musical theater, newspaper, opera, orchestra, pep band, photography, political, professional, radio and TV, religious, social, social service, student government, symphony, and yearbook. Popular campus events include May Day, Parents/Family Day, and All Campus Leadership Conference.

Sports: There are 9 intercollegiate sports for men and 9 for women, and 12 intramural sports for men and 12 for women. Facilities include a 5500-seat gym, a 35,000-seat stadium, an indoor pool, a student center, indoor and outdoor tracks, 9 racquetball courts, gymnastics and combatives areas, and weight-training and fitness rooms.

Disabled Students: 90% of the campus is accessible. Wheelchair ramps, elevators, special parking, specially equipped rest rooms, special class scheduling, lowered drinking fountains, lowered telephones, and city/campus bus service are available.

Services: Counseling and information services are available, as is tutoring in most subjects. There is a reader service for the blind, remedial math, reading, and writing, and TDDs.

Campus Safety and Security: Measures include 24-hour foot and vehicle patrol, self-defense education, security escort services, and shuttle buses. There are informal discussions, pamphlets/posters/films, emergency telephones, and lighted pathways/sidewalks.

Programs of Study: UA confers B.A., B.S., and B.F.A. degrees. Associate, master's, and doctoral degrees are also awarded. Bachelor's degrees are awarded in BIOLOGICAL SCIENCE (biology/biological science, botany, microbiology, and zoology), BUSINESS (accounting, banking and finance, business administration and management, business economics, hospitality management services, international business management, marketing/retailing/merchandising, and personnel management), COMMUNICATIONS AND THE ARTS (advertising, art, broadcasting, classics, communications, dance, design, dramatic arts, English, fine arts, French, German, Latin, music, photography, Russian, Spanish, and speech/debate/rhetoric), COMPUTER AND PHYSICAL SCIENCE (chemistry, computer science, earth science, geology, mathematics, natural sciences, physics, and statistics), EDUCATION (art, athletic training, business, early childhood, elementary, foreign languages, guidance, health, home economics, music, physical, science, secondary, special, and technical), ENGINEERING AND ENVIRONMENTAL DESIGN (biomedical engineering, chemical engineering, civil engineering, computer engineering, construction technology, electrical/electronics engineering, emergency/disaster science, manufacturing technology, mechanical engineering, mechanical engineering technology, and survey and mapping technology), HEALTH PROFESSIONS (emergency medical technologies, medical laboratory technology, nursing, predentistry, premedicine, prepharmacy, preveterinary science, and speech pathology/audiology), SOCIAL SCIENCE (anthropology, criminal justice, dietetics, economics, family/consumer studies, geography, history, home economics, humanities, philosophy, political science/government, prelaw, psychology, public administration, social science, social work, and sociology). Engineering, nursing, and business are the strongest academically. Arts and sciences, business, and engineering are the largest.

Required: To graduate, all students must complete at least 128 credits, with a varying number of hours in the major, and maintain a GPA of 2.0. Specific course requirements include English, Western cultural traditions, math, natural science, social science, humanities, speech, cultural diversity, and phys ed.

Special: UA offers co-op programs with local and out-of-state employers, study abroad in 22 countries, internships and work-study opportunities with community employers, a 6-year accelerated B.S.-M.D. program, a 3-2 engineering degree with Ashland University, B.A.-B.S. degrees in 10 majors, credit for military experience, nondegree study, and pass/fail options. There are 25 national honor societies and a freshman honors program; all departments have honors programs.

Faculty/Classroom: 53% of faculty are male; 47%, female. The average class size in a laboratory is 21 and in a regular course, 26.

Admissions: All of the 2003-2004 applicants were accepted. The SAT I scores for the 2003-2004 freshman class were: Verbal--48% below 500, 34% between 500 and 599, 16% between 600 and 700, and 2% above 700; Math--46% below 500, 30% between 500 and 599, 20% between 600 and 700, and 4% above 700. The ACT scores were 56% below 21, 22% between 21 and 23, 13% between 24 and 26, 5% between 27 and 28, and 4% above 28. 21% of the current freshmen were in the top fifth of their class; 44% were in the top two fifths. 55 freshmen graduated first in their class.

Requirements: The SAT I or ACT is required. UA follows an open admissions policy for in-state applicants. Applicants must have a diploma from an accredited secondary school or hold the GED. Applicants for unconditional admission must have the following secondary school credits: 4 of English, 3 each of math, science, and social studies, and 2 of foreign language. A portfolio is recommended for art and graphic design students, an audition is required for music and dance students, and an interview is advised for nursing and engineering students. AP and CLEP credits are accepted.

Procedure: Freshmen are admitted to all sessions. Entrance exams should be taken by December 1 for scholarship consideration. There are early admissions and deferred admissions plans. There is a rolling admissions plan. Early decision applications should be filed by February 1; regular applications, by August 15 for fall entry, December 31 for spring entry, and May 27 for summer entry, along with a $30 fee. The college accepts all in-state residents. Notification of early decision is sent March 15; regular decision, on a rolling basis. Applications are accepted on-line through *www.uakron.edu.*

Transfer: 867 transfer students enrolled in 2002-2003. In-state applicants should present a minimum college GPA of 2.0; out-of-state applicants, a GPA of 2.5. There are other requirements for specific academic

programs. 32 credits of 128 required for the bachelor's degree must be completed at UA.

Visiting: There are regularly scheduled orientations for prospective students, including small groups for information on financial aid, student organizations, campus tours, and meetings with college faculty. There are guides for informal visits and visitors may sit in on classes. To schedule a visit, contact the Office of Undergraduate Admissions at *admissions@uakron.edu.*

Financial Aid: In 2002-2003, 74% of all full-time freshmen and 79% of continuing full-time students received some form of financial aid. 61% of full-time freshmen and 53% of continuing full-time students received need-based aid. The average freshman award was $3453. Need-based scholarships or need-based grants averaged $2000 ($4050 maximum); need-based self-help aid (loans and jobs) averaged $2700 ($5425 maximum); non-need-based athletic scholarships averaged $7112 ($14,225 maximum); and other non-need-based awards and non-need-based scholarships averaged $2000 ($14,500 maximum). 57% of undergraduates work part time. Average annual earnings from campus work are $1350. UA is a member of CSS. The FAFSA is required. The priority date for freshman financial aid applications for fall entry is March 1. The deadline for filing freshman financial aid applications for fall entry is June 30.

International Students: There are 244 international students enrolled. The school actively recruits these students. They must score 500 on the written TOEFL or 173 on the electronic version and also take the SAT I or ACT, if under age 21 or transferring with fewer than 12 credits.

Computers: The mainframe is an IBM system/390 Enterprise server. There are 8 public computer labs with 177 workstations, 91 departmental labs with 1749 workstations, and 2 mobile labs with 60 workstations. All students may access the system from 7 A.M. to 1 A.M. at the computer center. There are no time limits and no fees. Honors students are given an IBM laptop for use while enrolled in courses.

Graduates: From July 1, 2002 to June 30, 2003, 2143 bachelor's degrees were awarded. The most popular majors were early childhood education (4%), nursing (4%), and accounting (4%). In an average class, 10% graduate in 4 years or less, 27% graduate in 5 years or less, and 36% graduate in 6 years or less. 200 companies recruited on campus in 2002-2003.

Admissions Contact: Diane Raybuck, Director of Admissions. A video is available. E-mail: *admissions@uakron.edu*
Web: *www.uakron.edu/admissions*

UNIVERSITY OF CINCINNATI
A-5
Cincinnati, OH 45221-0127 (513) 556-1100; Fax: (513) 556-1105

Full-time: 8368 men, 7357 women	**Faculty:** 1111; I, -$
Part-time: 1553 men, 1881 women	**Ph.D.s:** 82%
Graduate: 3163 men, 3522 women	**Student/Faculty:** 14 to 1
Year: quarters, summer session	**Tuition:** $7623 ($19,230)
Application Deadline: July 31	**Room & Board:** $7113
Freshman Class: 10,836 applied, 9673 accepted, 3724 enrolled	
SAT I Verbal/Math: 518/533	**ACT:** 22 COMPETITIVE

The University of Cincinnati, founded in 1819, is a state-supported institution offering undergraduate programs in art and architecture, business, engineering, health science, liberal arts and sciences, music, and technical training. There are 17 undergraduate and 10 graduate schools. In addition to regional accreditation, UC has baccalaureate program accreditation with AACSB and NCATE. The 18 libraries contain 2,977,475 volumes, 3,287,318 microform items, and 544,245 audio/video tapes/CDs, and subscribe to 33,568 periodicals. Computerized library services include the card catalog, interlibrary loans, database searching, and Internet access. Special learning facilities include a learning resource center, art gallery, and radio station. The 270-acre campus is in an urban area in downtown Cincinnati. Including any residence halls, there are 90 buildings.

Student Life: 93% of undergraduates are from Ohio. Students are from 48 states, 93 foreign countries, and Canada. 76% are white; 14% African American. The average age of freshmen is 19; all undergraduates, 24. 24% do not continue beyond their first year.

Housing: 3400 students can be accommodated in college housing, which includes coed dorms and on-campus apartments. On-campus housing is guaranteed for the freshman year only. Priority is given to out-of-town students. 86% of students commute. Alcohol is not permitted. All students may keep cars.

Activities: 11% of men belong to 24 local fraternities; 10% of women belong to 11 local sororities. There are many groups and organizations on campus, including art, band, cheerleading, chess, choir, chorale, chorus, computers, dance, drama, ethnic, gay, honors, international, jazz band, literary magazine, marching band, musical theater, newspaper, opera, orchestra, pep band, photography, political, professional, radio and TV, religious, social, social service, student government, symphony, and yearbook. Popular campus events include College Conservatory of Music productions.

Sports: There are 8 intercollegiate sports for men and 10 for women, and 32 intramural sports for men and 32 for women. Athletic and recreation facilities include a 30,000-seat stadium, a field house, a 13,000-seat gym, indoor and outdoor tracks, a swimming pool, tennis courts, and athletic fields.

Disabled Students: 95% of the campus is accessible. Wheelchair ramps, elevators, special parking, specially equipped rest rooms, special class scheduling, lowered drinking fountains, and lowered telephones are available.

Services: Counseling and information services are available, as is tutoring in most subjects. There is remedial math, reading, and writing, note taking and reading services for the blind, and interpreting services for the hearing-impaired.

Campus Safety and Security: Measures include security escort services, shuttle buses, emergency telephones, and lighted pathways/sidewalks.

Programs of Study: UC confers B.A., B.S., B.Arch., B.B.A., B.F.A., B.G.S., B.M., B.S.Des., B.S.E., B.S.I.M., B.S.N., B.S.Pharm., B.S.W., and B.U.P. degrees. Associate, master's, and doctoral degrees are also awarded. Bachelor's degrees are awarded in BIOLOGICAL SCIENCE (biochemistry and biology/biological science), BUSINESS (accounting, banking and finance, business administration and management, management science, marketing/retailing/merchandising, and real estate), COMMUNICATIONS AND THE ARTS (broadcasting, communications, comparative literature, dance, design, dramatic arts, English, fine arts, French, German, jazz, linguistics, music, music history and appreciation, music theory and composition, piano/organ, Spanish, theater design, and voice), COMPUTER AND PHYSICAL SCIENCE (chemical technology, chemistry, computer science, geology, information sciences and systems, mathematics, physics, and quantitative methods), EDUCATION (art, business, early childhood, elementary, foreign languages, guidance, health, industrial arts, middle school, music, nutrition, science, secondary, and special), ENGINEERING AND ENVIRONMENTAL DESIGN (aeronautical engineering, architectural engineering, architectural technology, chemical engineering, city/community/regional planning, civil engineering, computer engineering, construction management, electrical/electronics engineering, electrical/electronics engineering technology, engineering, engineering mechanics, engineering technology, industrial administration/management, industrial engineering technology, materials engineering, mechanical engineering, mechanical engineering technology, metallurgical engineering, and nuclear engineering), HEALTH PROFESSIONS (medical laboratory technology, nuclear medical technology, nursing, pharmacy, predentistry, premedicine, and speech pathology/audiology), SOCIAL SCIENCE (African American studies, anthropology, Asian/Oriental studies, classical/ancient civilization, criminal justice, economics, geography, history, international studies, Judaic studies, Latin American studies, philosophy, political science/government, prelaw, psychology, social science, social work, sociology, and urban studies). Engineering is the strongest academically. Arts and sciences are the largest.

Required: All students must complete English and humanities requirements. A minimum of 185 quarter credits is required for the baccalaureate degree.

Special: The Professional Practice Program, a 5-year cooperative plan offering alternate work in academic subjects and industry, is available for students in engineering, business, arts and sciences, design, architecture, and art. Study-abroad opportunities include a winter quarter in Spain, an academic program in Paris, and a language/area studies work program in Germany. A general studies degree and nondegree study are available. There is a chapter of Phi Beta Kappa and a freshman honors program.

Faculty/Classroom: 66% of faculty are male; 34%, female.

Admissions: 89% of the 2003-2004 applicants were accepted. The SAT I scores for the 2003-2004 freshman class were: Verbal--36% below 500, 40% between 500 and 599, 21% between 600 and 700, and 3% above 700; Math--35% below 500, 36% between 500 and 599, 24% between 600 and 700, and 5% above 700. The ACT scores were 37% below 21, 23% between 21 and 23, 19% between 24 and 26, 10% between 27 and 28, and 9% above 28. 29% of the current freshmen were in the top fifth of their class; 54% were in the top two fifths.

Requirements: The SAT I or ACT is required. In addition, applicants should be graduates of an accredited secondary school with 4 units of high school English, 3 of math, 2 each of science, social science, foreign language, and electives, and 1 of fine arts. A GPA of 2.0 is required.

Procedure: Freshmen are admitted to all sessions. Entrance exams should be taken in May of the junior year or January or March of the senior year. There is a rolling admissions plan. Applications should be filed by July 31 for fall entry, along with a $35 fee. Notification is sent on a rolling basis.

Transfer: 1166 transfer students enrolled in 2002-2003. A GPA of 2.0 is required to apply from a 4-year college; a GPA of 2.5 or an associate degree if applying from a 2-year college.

Visiting: There are regularly scheduled orientations for prospective students. There are guides for informal visits and visitors may sit in on classes and stay overnight. To schedule a visit, contact the Admissions Office.

Financial Aid: In 2003-2004, 57% of all full-time freshmen and 52% of continuing full-time students received some form of financial aid. 41%

of full-time freshmen and 35% of continuing full-time students received need-based aid. The average freshman award was $6840. Need-based scholarships or need-based grants averaged $3888; need-based self-help aid (loans and jobs) averaged $1835; and non-need-based athletic scholarships averaged $5171. The CSS Profile and FAFSA are required.

International Students: International students must score 515 on the written TOEFL.

Computers: The mainframes are an Amdahl 5880 and 470, and a DEC VAX. There are also 350 Macs and PCs available in all colleges and in the library. All students may access the system. There are no time limits and no fees.

Graduates: From July 1, 2002 to June 30, 2003, 2905 bachelor's degrees were awarded. In an average class, 14% graduate in 4 years or less, 40% graduate in 5 years or less, and 49% graduate in 6 years or less.

Admissions Contact: Director of Admissions.
E-mail: *admissions@uc.edu* Web: *www.uc.edu*

UNIVERSITY OF DAYTON B-4
Dayton, OH 45469

(937) 229-4411
(800) 837-7433; Fax: (937) 229-4729

Full-time: 3289 men, 3293 women	Faculty: 353; IIA, +$
Part-time: 276 men, 245 women	Ph.Ds: 94%
Graduate: 1073 men, 1630 women	Student/Faculty: 19 to 1
Year: semesters, summer session	Tuition: $18,960
Application Deadline: open	Room & Board: $5890
Freshman Class: 7626 applied, 6247 accepted, 1874 enrolled	
SAT I Verbal/Math: 560/580	ACT: 25 VERY COMPETITIVE

The University of Dayton, founded in 1850, is a nonprofit, private, comprehensive institution affiliated with the Roman Catholic Church. Part of the Southwestern Ohio Council for Higher Education, it has undergraduate and graduate programs emphasizing the arts and sciences, business administration, engineering, education, allied professions and law. There are 4 undergraduate schools and 1 graduate school. In addition to regional accreditation, UD has baccalaureate program accreditation with AACSB, ABET, ADA, NASM, and NCATE. The 3 libraries contain 905,924 volumes, 795,807 microform items, and 3030 audio/video tapes/CDs, and subscribe to 7554 periodicals. Computerized library services include the card catalog, interlibrary loans, and database searching. Special learning facilities include a learning resource center, art gallery, radio station, TV station, UD Research Institute, Bombeck Family Learning Center, a learning teaching center, and Davis Center for Portfolio Management. The 123-acre campus is in a suburban area 2 miles south of downtown Dayton. Including any residence halls, there are 46 buildings.

Student Life: 66% of undergraduates are from Ohio. Students are from 46 states, 32 foreign countries, and Canada. 52% are from public schools. 87% are white. 67% are Catholic; 12% Protestant. The average age of freshmen is 18; all undergraduates, 19. 14% do not continue beyond their first year; 73% remain to graduate.

Housing: 5760 students can be accommodated in college housing, which includes single-sex and coed dorms, on-campus apartments, fraternity houses, and sorority houses. In addition, there are honors houses and special-interest houses. On-campus housing is available on a first-come, first-served basis and is available on a lottery system for upperclassmen. First- and second-year students are required to live on campus. 95% of students live on campus; of those, 85% remain on campus on weekends. Upperclassmen may keep cars.

Activities: 15% of men belong to 2 local and 11 national fraternities; 18% of women belong to 1 local and 9 national sororities. There are 190 groups on campus, including art, band, cheerleading, chess, choir, chorale, chorus, computers, dance, debate, drama, drill team, ethnic, gay, honors, international, jazz band, literary magazine, marching band, musical theater, newspaper, orchestra, pep band, photography, political, professional, radio and TV, religious, social, social service, student government, symphony, and yearbook. Popular campus events include Christmas on Campus, Distinguished Speakers Series, and The Weekend Scene.

Sports: There are 7 intercollegiate sports for men and 10 for women, and 13 intramural sports for men and 13 for women. Facilities include a physical activities center, a field house, a 13,455-seat arena, a 11,000-seat football stadium, soccer and baseball fields, an outdoor track, indoor and outdoor tennis courts, racquetball and squash courts, a swimming pool, a basketball court, weight rooms, a fully equipped aerobic conditioning center, a strength and conditioning facility, a weight room, and a sports medicine complex.

Disabled Students: Wheelchair ramps, elevators, special parking, specially equipped rest rooms, special class scheduling, lowered drinking fountains, lowered telephones, a note-taking service, Braille services, interpreters for hearing impaired, talking books, electronic text, adaptive computer lab, oral tests, and untimed tests are available.

Services: Counseling and information services are available, as is tutoring in every subject. There is a reader service for the blind and remedial math. Developmental math, reading and writing, and nonremedial tutoring are available.

Campus Safety and Security: Measures include 24-hour foot and vehicle patrol, security escort services, informal discussions, and pamphlets/posters/films. There are emergency telephones, lighted pathways/ sidewalks, bike patrol, controlled dorm access, video cameras, and on-campus EMTs.

Programs of Study: UD confers B.A., B.S., B.C.E., B.Ch.E., B.E.E., B.F.A., B.G.S., B.M.E., and B.Mus. degrees. Master's and doctoral degrees are also awarded. Bachelor's degrees are awarded in BIOLOGICAL SCIENCE (biochemistry, biology/biological science, environmental biology, and nutrition), BUSINESS (accounting, banking and finance, business economics, international business management, management information systems, management science, marketing/retailing/merchandising, operations research, and sports management), COMMUNICATIONS AND THE ARTS (art history and appreciation, broadcasting, communications, design, dramatic arts, English, fine arts, French, German, journalism, music, music performance, music theory and composition, photography, public relations, and Spanish), COMPUTER AND PHYSICAL SCIENCE (chemistry, computer science, geology, information sciences and systems, mathematics, physical sciences, and physics), EDUCATION (art, early childhood, elementary, music, physical, secondary, and special), ENGINEERING AND ENVIRONMENTAL DESIGN (chemical engineering, civil engineering, computer engineering, computer technology, electrical/electronics engineering, electrical/ electronics engineering technology, engineering technology, industrial engineering technology, manufacturing technology, mechanical engineering, and mechanical engineering technology), HEALTH PROFESSIONS (exercise science, music therapy, predentistry, and premedicine), SOCIAL SCIENCE (American studies, criminal justice, dietetics, economics, history, international studies, philosophy, political science/ government, prelaw, psychology, religion, and sociology). Engineering, business, and exercise science/prephysical therapy are the strongest academically. Business/marketing and engineering/engineering technologies are the largest.

Required: To graduate, all students must complete a minimum of 120 semester hours with at least 30 hours of residence, and maintain a minimum GPA of 2.0. The curricula must include general education requirements, including 4 classes in religious studies and philosophy as well as basic skills requirements. Departmental requirements vary.

Special: Co-op programs are available in 24 majors; students in other majors may participate in the co-op program with the approval of their department. Internships are available in all majors. More than 100 companies participate in the work-study program. Cross-registration is available with the Southwestern Ohio Council for Higher Education. Study abroad, a Washigton semester, accelerated degree programs in business and engineering, and B.A.-B.S. degrees in chemistry, math, economics, and psychology are available. For students who wish to have a dual major, almost all programs may be combined. Student designed majors include general studies and interdisciplinary studies. An engineering curriculum agreement exist with Sinclair Community College. There are 14 national honor societies, a freshman honors program, and all departments have honors programs.

Faculty/Classroom: 73% of faculty are male; 27%, female. 88% teach undergraduates. Less than 5% of introductory courses are taught by graduate students. The average class size in an introductory lecture is 32; in a laboratory, 15; and in a regular course, 27.

Admissions: 82% of the 2003-2004 applicants were accepted. The SAT I scores for the 2003-2004 freshman class were: Verbal--20% below 500, 45% between 500 and 599, 30% between 600 and 700, and 5% above 700; Math--18% below 500, 38% between 500 and 599, 37% between 600 and 700, and 8% above 700. The ACT scores were 14% below 21, 24% between 21 and 23, 28% between 24 and 26, 15% between 27 and 28, and 19% above 28. 39% of the current freshmen were in the top fifth of their class; 66% were in the top two fifths. There were 12 National Merit finalists and 4 semifinalists. 46 freshmen graduated first in their class.

Requirements: The SAT I or ACT is required. In addition, applicants should be graduates of an accredited secondary school with 16 units in English, math, science, social studies, and academic electives. In addition, 2 units of foreign language are required for admission to the College of Arts and Sciences. The GED is accepted. High school transcripts and official scores from the ACT or SAT I must be submitted. An essay or personal statement, recommendation from the high school guidance counselor, and an interview are recommended. Music students must audition. AP and CLEP credits are accepted.

Procedure: Freshmen are admitted fall, winter, and summer. Entrance exams should be taken by December of the senior year. There is a deferred admissions plan. There is a rolling admissions plan. Application deadlines are open. 15 applicants were on the 2003 waiting list; 6 were admitted. Applications are accepted on-line through at the school's web site. The on-line application is required and free.

Transfer: 112 transfer students enrolled in 2002-2003. Attention is directed to college and high school GPA and course selection. The minimum grade point average is 2.0. The School of Education and Allied

Professions requires a minimum 2.5 GPA in previous college work. Achievement of the minimum GPA does not guarantee admission. For students under 21 years of age, results of the SAT I or ACT are required. All students applying to the School of Education and Allied Professions, must submit SAT I or ACT and Praxis I scores. 30 of 120 credits required for the bachelor's degree must be completed at UD.

Visiting: There are regularly scheduled orientations for prospective students, including an admission interview, financial aid consultation, campus tour, residence hall tour, faculty or class visit. High school seniors who have been accepted to the University of Dayton may participate in an overnight visit during the winter semester. There are guides for informal visits. To schedule a visit, contact campus visit coordinator, Office of Admission at *admission@udayton.edu.*

Financial Aid: In 2002-2003, 93% of all full-time freshmen and 90% of continuing full-time students received some form of financial aid. 57% of full-time freshmen and 58% of continuing full-time students received need-based aid. The average freshman award was $13,418. Need-based scholarships or need-based grants averaged $8691; need-based self-help aid (loans and jobs) averaged $4079; non-need-based athletic scholarships averaged $14,716; and other non-need-based awards and non-need-based scholarships averaged $3812. The average financial indebtedness of the 2003 graduate was $21,467. The FAFSA is required. The priority date for freshman financial aid applications for fall entry is March 31.

International Students: There are 39 international students enrolled. The school actively recruits these students. They must score 523 on the written TOEFL or 193 on the electronic version or take the English Language Proficiency Test or the Advanced Placement International English Language Examination.

Computers: The mainframe is an Alpha server 2100 4/275. Approximately 1000 workstations are available for student use in 21 central labs, 12 departmental or other labs, and 40 classrooms. All student housing is networked, and a wireless network is available in several locations. All students may access the system 24 hours a day, 7 day a week. There are no time limits and no fees. All students are required to have personal computers. The Tangent Shuttle 2.5 GHz, Tangent Shuttle 1.4 GHz, or Tangent Shuttle 1.7 Ghz is recommended.

Graduates: From July 1, 2002 to June 30, 2003, 1654 bachelor's degrees were awarded. The most popular majors were business/marketing (26%), engineering/engineering technologies (15%), and education (12%). In an average class, 57% graduate in 4 years or less, 75% graduate in 5 years or less, and 76% graduate in 6 years or less. 210 companies recruited on campus in 2002-2003.

Admissions Contact: Robert F. Durkle, Director of Admission.
E-mail: *admission@udayton.edu* Web: *http://admission@udayton.edu*

UNIVERSITY OF FINDLAY   B-2
Findlay, OH 45840   (419) 424-4732
(800) 548-0932; Fax: (419) 424-4822

Full-time: 1130 men, 1485 women	**Faculty:** 160; IIA, --$
Part-time: 335 men, 435 women	**Ph.D.s:** 51%
Graduate: 490 men, 715 women	**Student/Faculty:** 16 to 1
Year: semesters, summer session	**Tuition:** $17,530
Application Deadline: see profile	**Room & Board:** $6435
Freshman Class: n/av	
SAT I or ACT: required	**NONCOMPETITIVE**

The University of Findlay, founded in 1882, is a private, independent institution affiliated with the Churches of God, General Conference, offering liberal arts and sciences and career preparation programs. There are 4 undergraduate and 7 graduate schools. Figures in the above capsule and in this profile are approximate. In addition to regional accreditation, Findlay has baccalaureate program accreditation with NCATE. The library contains 135,000 volumes, 90,400 microform items, and 1200 audio/video tapes/CDs, and subscribes to 2511 periodicals. Computerized library services include interlibrary loans and database searching. Special learning facilities include a learning resource center, art gallery, planetarium, radio station, university-owned farm, equine facility, and emergency response training center. The 135-acre campus is in a small town 45 miles south of Toledo and 100 miles north of Columbus. Including any residence halls, there are 55 buildings.

Student Life: 80% of undergraduates are from Ohio. Students are from 45 states, 41 foreign countries, and Canada. 80% are from public schools. 85% are white. 60% are Protestant; 35% Catholic. The average age of freshmen is 18; all undergraduates, 22. 25% do not continue beyond their first year; 55% remain to graduate.

Housing: 1000 students can be accommodated in college housing, which includes single-sex dorms, on-campus apartments, fraternity houses, and sorority houses. In addition, there are honors houses, language houses, and special-interest houses. On-campus housing is guaranteed for all 4 years. 65% of students commute. Alcohol is not permitted. All students may keep cars.

Activities: 4% of men belong to 3 national fraternities; 1% of women belong to 2 national sororities. There are 40 groups on campus, including art, band, cheerleading, choir, chorale, chorus, computers, drama, drum and bugle corps, equestrian, ethnic, honors, international, jazz band, literary magazine, marching band, musical theater, newspaper, pep band, political, preveterinary, professional, radio and TV, religious, social, social service, student government, and yearbook. Popular campus events include Family Weekend, International Night, and Spring Bash.

Sports: There are 14 intercollegiate sports for men and 12 for women, and 15 intramural sports for men and 15 for women. Facilities include a fitness center, a 7200-seat stadium, a 25-meter pool, racquetball courts, a phys ed center with a 3200-seat gym, an ice arena, indoor track, and four-court athletic building.

Disabled Students: 90% of the campus is accessible. Wheelchair ramps, elevators, special parking, specially equipped rest rooms, special class scheduling, lowered drinking fountains, and specially equipped residence hall rooms are available.

Services: Counseling and information services are available, as is tutoring in most subjects. There is a reader service for the blind and remedial math, reading, and writing. Other services include assistance with note taking, test taking, research papers, study skills, and support for the hearing impaired, including interpreters.

Campus Safety and Security: Measures include 24-hour foot and vehicle patrol, self-defense education, security escort services, and informal discussions. There are pamphlets/posters/films, emergency telephones, and lighted pathways/sidewalks.

Programs of Study: Findlay confers B.A. and B.S. degrees. Associate and master's degrees are also awarded. Bachelor's degrees are awarded in AGRICULTURE (equine science), BIOLOGICAL SCIENCE (biology/biological science), BUSINESS (accounting, banking and finance, business administration and management, business economics, business systems analysis, hospitality management services, human resources, international business management, and marketing/retailing/merchandising), COMMUNICATIONS AND THE ARTS (arts administration/management, broadcasting, communications, dramatic arts, English, English as a second/foreign language, illustration, Japanese, Spanish, studio art, and technical and business writing), COMPUTER AND PHYSICAL SCIENCE (computer science, mathematics, and science), EDUCATION (art, athletic training, bilingual/bicultural, business, elementary, foreign languages, middle school, physical, and secondary), ENGINEERING AND ENVIRONMENTAL DESIGN (environmental science, occupational safety and health, preengineering, and technological management), HEALTH PROFESSIONS (health science, nuclear medical technology, nursing, occupational therapy, physician's assistant, premedicine, and preveterinary science), SOCIAL SCIENCE (criminal justice, economics, history, international studies, philosophy, political science/government, prelaw, psychology, religion, social work, and sociology). Business administration, preveterinary medicine, and education are the strongest academically. Business administration, equestrian studies, and education are the largest.

Required: All students must complete 33 semester hours of general education requirements, including fine arts, humanities, natural science, math, social science, and religion or philosophy, and most take courses in wellness, computer science, and statistics. There are competency requirements in library use, English and reading, and a wellness course. A total of 124 semester hours with a minimum GPA of 2.0 is required in order to graduate.

Special: Co-op programs are available in accounting and occupational health and safety. There is cross-registration with Mount Carmel College of Nursing and a 3-2 engineering program with the University of Toledo, Ohio Northern University, and Washington University. The field experience program provides up to 20 semester hours in field placement. Internships are available for business, business education, communication, hazardous materials management, and theater majors. Through the College Consortium for International Studies, study abroad is possible in 16 countries. Work-study, a Washington semester, dual and student-designed majors, a general studies degree, pass/fail options, and credit for life experience are offered. Nondegree study is possible. There is a freshman honors program.

Faculty/Classroom: 60% of faculty are male; 40%, female. All teach undergraduates. No introductory courses are taught by graduate students. The average class size in an introductory lecture is 23; in a laboratory, 15; and in a regular course, 22.

Admissions: 21 freshmen graduated first in their class in a recent year.

Requirements: The SAT I or ACT is required. In addition, applicants should have completed 16 high school credits or GED equivalents, including 4 years of English, 2 years of social studies/history, 3 to 4 math courses, and 2 to 3 science courses. A GPA of 2.3 is required. AP and CLEP credits are accepted. Important factors in the admissions decision are advanced placement or honor courses, evidence of special talent, and extracurricular activities record.

Procedure: Freshmen are admitted to all sessions. Entrance exams should be taken during fall of the senior year or the spring of the junior year. There is a deferred admissions plan and a rolling admissions plan. Check with the school for current deadlines. Notification is sent on a roll-ing basis. Applications are accepted on-line via the university's web site, CollegeView, *Review.com*, CollegeNET, and CollegeLink.

Transfer: 100 transfer students enrolled in a recent year. A minimum 2.0 GPA and eligibility to return to the current institution are required. An interview is recommended. 30 of 124 credits required for the bachelor's degree must be completed at Findlay.

Visiting: There are regularly scheduled orientations for prospective students, including a tour, interview, coach/faculty visits, and lunch. There are guides for informal visits and visitors may sit in on classes and stay overnight. To schedule a visit, contact the Admissions Office at (800) 548-0932, ext. 4732.

Financial Aid: In a recent year, 90% of all full-time students received some form of financial aid. 75% of full-time freshmen and 80% of continuing full-time students received need-based aid. The average freshman award was $11,700. 80% of undergraduates work part time. Average annual earnings from campus work are $800. The average financial indebtedness of a recent graduate was $14,000. The FAFSA is required. Check with the school for current deadlines.

International Students: In a recent year, there were 426 international students enrolled. The school actively recruits these students. They must score 500 on the written TOEFL.

Computers: The mainframe is an HP G-30. There are 7 student computer labs with networked Pentium-based PCs and Mac G-3s. More than 200 student workstations are available. All residence hall rooms are networked, and off-campus students have free modem access. All students may access the system. There are no time limits and no fees.

Graduates: In a recent year, 690 bachelor's degrees were awarded. The most popular majors were business management (15%), business administration (9%), and education (5%). In an average class, 2% graduate in 3 years or less, 55% graduate in 4 years or less, 57% graduate in 5 years or less, and 58% graduate in 6 years or less. 200 companies recruited on campus in a recent year. Of a recent graduating class, 10% were enrolled in graduate school within 6 months of graduation and 85% were employed.

Admissions Contact: Michael Momany, Executive Director of Enrollment Services. E-mail: *admissions@findlay.edu* Web: *www.findlay.edu*

UNIVERSITY OF RIO GRANDE   D-5
Rio Grande, OH 45674

(740) 245-5353
(800) 282-7201; Fax: (740) 245-7260

Full-time: 620 men, 900 women	**Faculty:** 84; IIB, -$
Part-time: 115 men, 220 women	**Ph.D.s:** 52%
Graduate: 25 men, 75 women	**Student/Faculty:** 20 to 1
Year: quarters, summer session	**Tuition:** $4495 ($4950)
Application Deadline: see profile	**Room & Board:** $4240
Freshman Class: n/av	**ACT:** required
	NONCOMPETITIVE

The University of Rio Grande, founded in 1876, is a private institution offering degree programs in the liberal arts and sciences, business, and education. Check with the school for specific tuition rates that vary by program. Figures in the above capsule and in this profile are approximate. There are 9 undergraduate schools and 1 graduate school. In addition to regional accreditation, Rio has baccalaureate program accreditation with CSWE, NASDTEC, and NLN. The library contains 96,731 volumes, 274,400 microform items, and 1835 audio/video tapes/CDs, and subscribes to 850 periodicals. Computerized library services include the card catalog, interlibrary loans, and database searching. Special learning facilities include a learning resource center, art gallery, radio station, and TV station. The 194-acre campus is in a rural area 100 miles southeast of Columbus. Including any residence halls, there are 27 buildings.

Student Life: 94% of undergraduates are from Ohio. Students are from 12 states, 15 foreign countries, and Canada. 98% are from public schools. 97% are white. The average age of freshmen is 23; all undergraduates, 24.

Housing: 640 students can be accommodated in college housing, which includes single-sex and coed dorms. In addition, there are special-interest houses. On-campus housing is guaranteed for all 4 years. 76% of students commute. All students may keep cars.

Activities: 6% of men belong to 2 local and 2 national fraternities; 4% of women belong to 5 local sororities. There are 39 groups on campus, including band, cheerleading, choir, chorale, chorus, drama, ecology, ethnic, gay, honors, international, jazz band, musical theater, newspaper, orchestra, pep band, photography, political, professional, radio and TV, religious, social, social service, and student government. Popular campus events include Ethnofest, Bob Evans Farm Festival, and Community Service Day.

Sports: There are 5 intercollegiate sports for men and 5 for women, and 10 intramural sports for men and 10 for women. Facilities include 2 gyms, tennis courts, an indoor Olympic-size pool, an outdoor track, handball, racquetball, and sand volleyball courts, a fitness center, a cross-country track, and soccer, baseball, and softball fields.

Disabled Students: 70% of the campus is accessible. Wheelchair ramps, elevators, special parking, specially equipped rest rooms, special class scheduling, lowered drinking fountains, lowered telephones, note takers, tape recorders, and closed-caption TV are available.

Services: Counseling and information services are available, as is tutoring in every subject. There is a reader service for the blind and remedial math, reading, and writing. There is also an Accessibility Office.

Campus Safety and Security: Measures include 24-hour foot and vehicle patrol, security escort services, informal discussions, and pamphlets/posters/films. There are emergency telephones and lighted pathways/sidewalks.

Programs of Study: Rio confers B.A., B.S., B.S.I.T., B.S.N., and B.S.W. degrees. Associate and master's degrees are also awarded. Bachelor's degrees are awarded in BIOLOGICAL SCIENCE (biology/biological science), BUSINESS (accounting, business administration and management, business economics, international business management, and marketing management), COMMUNICATIONS AND THE ARTS (art, communications, English, fine arts, music, and public relations), COMPUTER AND PHYSICAL SCIENCE (chemistry, computer science, mathematics, and physical sciences), EDUCATION (art, business, early childhood, education of the mentally handicapped, elementary, English, health, mathematics, music, physical, psychology, reading, science, secondary, social science, and social studies), ENGINEERING AND ENVIRONMENTAL DESIGN (computer technology, drafting and design technology, electrical/electronics engineering technology, environmental science, industrial engineering technology, manufacturing technology, preengineering, and woodworking), HEALTH PROFESSIONS (medical technology, nursing, predentistry, premedicine, and preveterinary science), SOCIAL SCIENCE (American studies, behavioral science, economics, history, humanities, physical fitness/movement, political science/government, prelaw, psychology, social work, and sociology). Education, business, and nursing are the strongest academically. Education, general studies, and business are the largest.

Required: Students must complete 190 to 198 quarter hours, including 47 to 53 in the major, with a minimum GPA of 2.0. The required general studies program, for all but teacher certification and industrial technology majors, includes 13 credit hours in communication skills, 12 hours each in the humanities, math, natural sciences, and social sciences, 3 hours in health and phys ed, and 1 hour in liberal arts.

Special: Rio offers internships in social work, communications, and business, a Washington semester, student-designed majors, limited pass/fail options, and credit for life, military, or work experience. Nondegree study for 1-year certificates in secretarial science and personal computer applications is also available. A community college on the same campus offers technical degree programs that are built into 4-year degrees. There are 3 national honor societies, a freshman honors program, and 1 departmental honors program.

Faculty/Classroom: 67% of faculty are male; 33%, female. All teach undergraduates. The average class size in an introductory lecture is 30; in a laboratory, 20; and in a regular course, 20.

Requirements: The ACT is required for applicants who are less than 5 years out of high school. Rio follows an open admissions policy for all applicants. A high school diploma or GED is required. A GPA of 2.0 is required. AP and CLEP credits are accepted.

Procedure: Freshmen are admitted to all sessions. Entrance exams should be taken no later than December of the senior year for those entering college the following fall. There is an early admissions plan and a rolling admissions plan. The college accepts all applicants. Check with the school for current deadlines. The application fee is $15. For an online application, consult the Rio web site.

Transfer: Candidates must submit a final transcript and a dean's evaluation form from the last school attended. 45 of 190 credits required for the bachelor's degree must be completed at Rio.

Visiting: There are regularly scheduled orientations for prospective students, with parents and students participating in 1- or 2-day sessions. The program includes half-day placement testing and presentations from various offices, campus e-mail, advising, and registration. Residential students stay in the dorms and have dinner with the president. There are guides for informal visits and visitors may sit in on classes and stay overnight. To schedule a visit, contact the Admissions Office.

Financial Aid: In a recent year, 87% of all full-time freshmen and 85% of continuing full-time students received some form of financial aid. 75% of full-time freshmen and 69% of continuing full-time students received need-based aid. The average freshman award was $4650. Rio is a member of CSS. The FAFSA and the college's own financial statement are required. Check with the school for current deadlines.

International Students: The school actively recruits these students. They must score 400 on the written TOEFL.

Computers: The mainframe is an IBM AS/400 Series 3 for administrative use only. Rio maintains more than 200 PCs on a switched Ethernet local area network. Students have full access to the Web, e-mail, and other Internet services. All students may access the system. The fee is $7 per quarter. It is strongly recommended that all students have a personal computer.

Admissions Contact: Mark F. Abell, Executive Director, Admissions. E-mail: mabell@rio.edu Web: www.rio.edu

UNIVERSITY OF TOLEDO	B-1
Toledo, OH 43606-3398	(419) 530-2696
	(800) 5TOLEDO; Fax: (419) 530-5835

Full-time: 6901 men, 6872 women	**Faculty:** 710; I, --$
Part-time: 1968 men, 1647 women	**Ph.Ds:** 78%
Graduate: 1475 men, 1731 women	**Student/Faculty:** 19 to 1
Year: semesters, summer session	**Tuition:** $5849 ($14,302)
Application Deadline: open	**Room & Board:** $6630
Freshman Class: 8866 applied, 8656 accepted, 3642 enrolled	
SAT I Verbal/Math: 511/521	**ACT:** 22 **NONCOMPETITIVE**

The University of Toledo, founded in 1872, is a public comprehensive institution emphasizing undergraduate degree programs in the liberal arts and sciences, business, engineering, teacher preparation, and health professions. There are 8 undergraduate and 7 graduate schools. In addition to regional accreditation, UT has baccalaureate program accreditation with AACSB, ABET, ACPE, APTA, NASM, and NCATE. The 3 libraries contain 1,610,000 volumes, 1,614,490 microform items, and 7800 audio/video tapes/CDs, and subscribe to 8000 periodicals. Computerized library services include the card catalog, interlibrary loans, and database searching. Special learning facilities include a learning resource center, art gallery, planetarium, and radio station. The 450-acre campus is in a suburban area 6 miles northwest of downtown Toledo. Including any residence halls, there are 85 buildings.

Student Life: 90% of undergraduates are from Ohio. Students are from 45 states, 105 foreign countries, and Canada. 76% are white; 12% African American. The average age of freshmen is 19; all undergraduates, 22. 28% do not continue beyond their first year; 40% remain to graduate.

Housing: 3500 students can be accommodated in college housing, which includes single-sex and coed dorms, fraternity houses, and sorority houses. In addition, there are honors houses, special-interest houses, and an international house. On-campus housing is available on a first-come, first-served basis. 86% of students commute. All students may keep cars.

Activities: 10% of men belong to 1 local and 13 national fraternities; 9% of women belong to 13 national sororities. There are 200 groups on campus, including art, band, cheerleading, chess, choir, chorale, chorus, computers, dance, drama, drill team, ethnic, film, gay, honors, international, jazz band, literary magazine, marching band, musical theater, newspaper, orchestra, pep band, photography, political, professional, radio and TV, religious, social, social service, student government, and symphony. Popular campus events include Songfest, Spring Release, and International Student Dinner.

Sports: There are 9 intercollegiate sports for men and 10 for women, and 48 intramural sports for men and 48 for women. Facilities include a recreation center, a 27,000-seat stadium, a 9000-seat arena, a field house, 3 pools, 12 tennis courts, an indoor/outdoor track, a 4-field recreational softball complex, and recreational/sport club fields.

Disabled Students: 96% of the campus is accessible. Wheelchair ramps, elevators, special parking, specially equipped rest rooms, special class scheduling, lowered drinking fountains, and lowered telephones are available.

Services: Counseling and information services are available, as is tutoring in every subject. There is a reader service for the blind and remedial math, reading, and writing.

Campus Safety and Security: Measures include 24-hour foot and vehicle patrol, self-defense education, security escort services, and shuttle buses. There are informal discussions, pamphlets/posters/films, emergency telephones, lighted pathways/sidewalks, and student patrols. All security officers are state-certified with full arrest authority.

Programs of Study: UT confers B.A., B.S., B.B.A., B.Ed. B. in Eng., B.Eng.Tech., B.F.A., B.Mus., B.S.Admin.Serv., B.S.Criminal Justice, B.S.Exercise Science, B.S.Institutional Health Care, B.S.Med.Tech., B.S.N., B.S.Pharm., B.S. in Physical Therapy, and B.Voc.Ed. degrees. Associate, master's, and doctoral degrees are also awarded. Bachelor's degrees are awarded in BIOLOGICAL SCIENCE (biology/biological science), BUSINESS (accounting, banking and finance, business administration and management, marketing/retailing/merchandising, and recreation and leisure services), COMMUNICATIONS AND THE ARTS (art history and appreciation, communications, dramatic arts, English, film arts, fine arts, French, German, linguistics, music, and Spanish), COMPUTER AND PHYSICAL SCIENCE (chemistry, computer science, geology, information sciences and systems, mathematics, and physics), EDUCATION (art, business, early childhood, elementary, foreign languages, health, music, physical, science, secondary, special, and vocational), ENGINEERING AND ENVIRONMENTAL DESIGN (bioengineering, chemical engineering, civil engineering, computer engineering, electrical/electronics engineering, electromechanical technology, engineering, engineering technology, environmental science, industrial engineering, and mechanical engineering), HEALTH PROFESSIONS (nursing, pharmacy, physical therapy, and speech pathology/audiology), SOCIAL SCIENCE (anthropology, community services, criminal justice, economics, geography, history, humanities, international relations, philosophy, physical fitness/movement, political science/government, psychology, social work, sociology, and women's studies). Engineering, pharmacy, and business are the strongest academically.

Required: To graduate, all students must complete 124 to 169 hours of credit, with a minimum of 60 in the major, and maintain a minimum GPA of 2.0. A core curriculum is required of all students. A thesis is required in the honors program.

Special: Special academic programs include internships in most majors, study abroad in 14 countries, and on-campus employment through the Financial Aid Office. There is a co-op program with the College of Engineering and cross-registration with Bowling Green State University. The B.A.-B.S. degree and dual majors are available in many areas of study. A general studies degree, student-designed majors, credit for life, military, and work experience, nondegree study, and pass/fail options are also offered. There are 56 national honor societies and a freshman honors program.

Faculty/Classroom: 60% of faculty are male; 40%, female. The average class size in an introductory lecture is 33; in a laboratory, 19; and in a regular course, 28.

Admissions: 98% of the 2003-2004 applicants were accepted. The SAT I scores for the 2003-2004 freshman class were: Verbal--44% below 500, 38% between 500 and 599, 16% between 600 and 700, and 2% above 700; Math--40% below 500, 35% between 500 and 599, 21% between 600 and 700, and 4% above 700. The ACT scores were 42% below 21, 27% between 21 and 23, 19% between 24 and 26, 6% between 27 and 28, and 6% above 28. 30% of the current freshmen were in the top fifth of their class; 53% were in the top two fifths. 46 freshmen graduated first in their class.

Requirements: The SAT I or ACT is required for some programs. The university follows an open admissions policy for Ohio applicants. Students should be graduates of an accredited secondary school or hold the GED. The preparatory program should include 4 years of English, 3 each of math, natural science, and social studies, and 2 of a foreign language. An interview is advised. AP and CLEP credits are accepted.

Procedure: Freshmen are admitted to all sessions. Entrance exams should be taken late in the junior year or early in the senior year. There is a deferred admissions plan and a rolling admissions plan. Application deadlines are open. Application fee is $40. Notification is sent on a rolling basis. Applications are accepted on-line through Ohio Mentor.

Transfer: 1336 transfer students enrolled in 2002-2003. Applicants must have a minimum of 12 quarter or 8 semester college credits and a GPA of 2.0. An interview is recommended.

Visiting: There are regularly scheduled orientations for prospective students, including an interview with an admissions counselor and a student-guided campus tour. There are guides for informal visits and visitors may sit in on classes and stay overnight. To schedule a visit, contact the Office of Admissions at (419) 530-8700 or enroll@utoledo.edu.

Financial Aid: In 2003-2004, 80% of all full-time freshmen and 75% of continuing full-time students received some form of financial aid. 58% of full-time freshmen and 52% of continuing full-time students received need-based aid. The average freshman award was $10,211. Need-based scholarships or need-based grants averaged $3865 ($7840 maximum); need-based self-help aid (loans and jobs) averaged $3512 ($8945 maximum); non-need-based athletic scholarships averaged $13,532 ($23,236 maximum); and other non-need-based awards and non-need-based scholarships averaged $11,801 ($24,157 maximum). Average annual earnings from campus work are $2044. The average financial indebtedness of the 2003 graduate was $19,390. UT is a member of CSS. The FAFSA is required. The priority date for freshman financial aid applications for fall entry is April 1. The deadline for filing freshman financial aid applications for fall entry is the same as the FAFSA last date to file.

International Students: The school actively recruits these students. They must score 500 on the written TOEFL.

Computers: The mainframe is an IBM 7060-H50. Networked PCs are available at many campus locations. Dorm rooms have Internet access. All students may access the system 24 hours per day, except from Saturday at 5 P.M. to Sunday at noon. There are no time limits and no fees.

Graduates: From July 1, 2002 to June 30, 2003, 2086 bachelor's degrees were awarded. The most popular majors included business (18%), education (15%), and engineering (14%).

Admissions Contact: Carolyn Baumgartner, Director of Undergraduate Admissions. A video is available. E-mail: enroll@utnet.utoledo.edu Web: www.utoledo.edu

URBANA UNIVERSITY
Urbana, OH 43078-2091

B-3
(937) 484-1356
(800) 7-URBANA; Fax: (937) 484-1322

Full-time: 469 men, 415 women	**Faculty:** 49
Part-time: 186 men, 371 women	**Ph.Ds:** 74%
Graduate: 28 men, 58 women	**Student/Faculty:** 18 to 1
Year: semesters, summer session	**Tuition:** $13,705
Application Deadline: open	**Room & Board:** $5410
Freshman Class: 538 applied, 312 accepted, 199 enrolled	
SAT I or ACT: required	**COMPETITIVE**

Urbana University, founded in 1850 and affiliated with the Swedenborgian Church, is a nonprofit, independent institution emphasizing programs in liberal arts, business, professional training, and teacher preparation. Some of the figures in the above capsule and in this profile are approximate. The library contains 70,000 volumes, 8176 microform items, and 2099 audio/video tapes/CDs, and subscribes to 328 periodicals. Computerized library services include interlibrary loans and database searching. Special learning facilities include a learning resource center, radio station, TV station, rare book room, and history museum. The 128-acre campus is in a small town 40 miles west of Columbus and 50 miles north of Dayton. Including any residence halls, there are 29 buildings.

Student Life: 90% of undergraduates are from Ohio. Students are from 5 states and 5 foreign countries. 95% are from public schools. 79% are white; 17% African American. The average age of freshmen is 20; all undergraduates, 24. 23% do not continue beyond their first year; 35% remain to graduate.

Housing: 350 students can be accommodated in college housing, which includes single-sex and coed dorms. In addition, there are honors houses. On-campus housing is available on a lottery system for upperclassmen. 58% of students commute. All students may keep cars.

Activities: There are no fraternities or sororities. There are 20 groups on campus, including band, cheerleading, choir, chorus, drama, ethnic, honors, international, literary magazine, musical theater, newspaper, pep band, political, professional, radio and TV, religious, social service, student government, and yearbook. Popular campus events include Spring Week, Founders Day, and Activities Fair.

Sports: There are 5 intercollegiate sports for men and 4 for women, and 6 intramural sports for men and 6 for women. Facilities include a community center with a 3500-seat gym, a pool, handball and racquetball courts, a weight room, and outdoor tennis courts.

Disabled Students: 30% of the campus is accessible. Wheelchair ramps, elevators, special parking, and special class scheduling are available.

Services: Counseling and information services are available, as is tutoring in most subjects. There is remedial math, reading, and writing, taped textbooks, reading and writing labs, and study skills seminars.

Campus Safety and Security: Measures include 24-hour foot and vehicle patrol, self-defense education, security escort services, and informal discussions. There are pamphlets/posters/films, emergency telephones, and lighted pathways/sidewalks.

Programs of Study: Urbana confers B.A., B.S., and B.S.Ed. degrees. Associate and master's degrees are also awarded. Bachelor's degrees are awarded in BUSINESS (business administration and management and sports management), COMMUNICATIONS AND THE ARTS (communications and English), COMPUTER AND PHYSICAL SCIENCE (science), EDUCATION (elementary, middle school, and secondary), HEALTH PROFESSIONS (premedicine and sports medicine), SOCIAL SCIENCE (criminal justice, liberal arts/general studies, philosophy, physical fitness/movement, prelaw, psychology, and sociology). Business and education are the strongest academically. Business and education are the largest.

Required: To graduate, all students must complete 126 semester hours, with a minimum overall GPA of 2.0 and 2.5 in the major. Distribution requirements include 12 to 13 credit hours in math and science, 12 each in humanities and social sciences, 9 in communications, and 2 to 3 in health, phys ed, and recreation.

Special: Special academic programs include internships, cross-registration with the Southwestern Ohio Council for Higher Education, study abroad, and accelerated degree programs in teacher certification. B.A.-B.S. degrees, dual and student-designed majors, credit for life, military, and work experience, and nondegree study are also available. There is 1 national honor society and 4 departmental honors programs.

Faculty/Classroom: 60% of faculty are male; 40%, female. All teach undergraduates. No introductory courses are taught by graduate students. The average class size in an introductory lecture is 18; in a laboratory, 7; and in a regular course, 19.

Admissions: 58% of the 2003-2004 applicants were accepted.

Requirements: The SAT I or ACT is required for applicants under 23 years of age, with the ACT preferred. The minimum SAT I score should be 700, and the minimum ACT score, 18. Applicants must be graduates of an accredited secondary school with a GPA of 2.0. The GED is accepted. An essay is required of all applicants, and an interview is recommended. A GPA of 2.0 is required. CLEP credit is accepted. Important factors in the admissions decision are advanced placement or honor courses, evidence of special talent, and extracurricular activities record.

Procedure: Freshmen are admitted to all sessions. Entrance exams should be taken during the junior or senior year. There is a deferred admissions plan. Application deadlines are open. Applications are accepted on computer disk and on-line through the school's web site. Notification is sent on a rolling basis.

Transfer: Applicants must have at least 30 college credits with a GPA of 2.25 and must be in good standing at their previous institution. 30 of 126 credits required for the bachelor's degree must be completed at Urbana.

Visiting: There are regularly scheduled orientations for prospective students, consisting of a campus tour and sessions on academics, athletics, performing arts, financial aid, and student life. There are guides for informal visits and visitors may sit in on classes and stay overnight. To schedule a visit, contact the Admissions Office.

Financial Aid: Need-based scholarships or need-based grants averaged $10,343; need-based self-help aid (loans and jobs) averaged $7532; non-need-based awards and non-need-based scholarships averaged $3445; and need-based loans averaged $3157. Urbana is a member of CSS. The FAFSA, the college's own financial statement and the state aid form for residents are required. Check with the school for current deadlines.

International Students: There are 4 international students enrolled. The school actively recruits these students. They must score 500 on the written TOEFL.

Computers: The mainframe is a DEC PDP 11/84. Macs and PCs are available for student use in 4 computer labs, the education department, and the library. All students have e-mail accounts. All students may access the system. There are no time limits and no fees.

Admissions Contact: Melissa Tolle, Director of Admissions.
E-mail: *mtolle@urbana.edu* Web: *www.urbana.edu*

URSULINE COLLEGE

Pepper Pike, OH 44124

D-1

(440) 442-4203
(888) URSULINE; Fax: (440) 684-6138

Full-time: 36 men, 625 women	**Faculty:** 53; IIB, --$
Part-time: 62 men, 372 women	**Ph.D.s:** 67%
Graduate: 38 men, 276 women	**Student/Faculty:** 13 to 1
Year: semesters, summer session	**Tuition:** $17,270
Application Deadline: open	**Room & Board:** $5458
Freshman Class: 351 applied, 244 accepted, 118 enrolled	
SAT I Verbal/Math: 490/490	**ACT:** 20 **LESS COMPETITIVE**

Ursuline College, established in 1871, is a private, liberal arts, primarily women's college affiliated with the Roman Catholic Church. There are 3 undergraduate schools and 1 graduate school. In addition to regional accreditation, Ursuline has baccalaureate program accreditation with CSWE and NLN. The library contains 129,096 volumes, 4963 microform items, and 7871 audio/video tapes/CDs, and subscribes to 332 periodicals. Computerized library services include the card catalog, interlibrary loans, database searching, and Internet access. Special learning facilities include a learning resource center, art gallery, media center, and curriculum library. The 112-acre campus is in a suburban area 13 miles east of Cleveland. Including any residence halls, there are 13 buildings.

Student Life: 99% of undergraduates are from Ohio. Students are from 6 states, 9 foreign countries, and Canada. 72% are from public schools. 71% are white; 23% African American. 42% claim no religious affiliation; 34% Catholic; 10% Protestant. The average age of freshmen is 19; all undergraduates, 29. 32% do not continue beyond their first year; 40% remain to graduate.

Housing: 164 students can be accommodated in college housing, which includes single-sex and coed dorms. On-campus housing is guaranteed for all 4 years. 86% of students commute. Alcohol is not permitted. All students may keep cars.

Activities: There are no fraternities or sororities. There are 19 groups on campus, including drama, ethnic, international, literary magazine, professional, religious, social, social service, and student government. Popular campus events include All College Day, a formal dance, and charity benefits.

Sports: There are 6 intercollegiate sports for women and 6 intramural sports for women. Facilities include a fitness center, a swimming pool, a gym, and a campus center.

Disabled Students: 90% of the campus is accessible. Wheelchair ramps, elevators, special parking, and specially equipped rest rooms are available.

Services: Counseling and information services are available, as is tutoring in most subjects. There is a reader service for the blind and remedial math, reading, and writing.

Campus Safety and Security: Measures include 24-hour foot and vehicle patrol, security escort services, informal discussions, and pamphlets/posters/films. There are emergency telephones and lighted pathways/sidewalks.

Programs of Study: Ursuline confers B.A. and B.S.N. degrees. Master's degrees are also awarded. Bachelor's degrees are awarded in BIOLOGICAL SCIENCE (biology/biological science and biotechnology), BUSINESS (accounting, business administration and management, fashion merchandising, human resources, management information systems, and marketing management), COMMUNICATIONS AND THE ARTS (art, English, graphic design, historic preservation, and public relations), COMPUTER AND PHYSICAL SCIENCE (mathematics), EDUCATION (early childhood, elementary, middle school, secondary, and special), HEALTH PROFESSIONS (allied health, health care administration, nursing, and premedicine), SOCIAL SCIENCE (American studies, child care/child and family studies, fashion design and technology, history, humanities, law, philosophy, prelaw, psychology, religion, social work, and sociology). Nursing is the strongest academically. Nursing and business are the largest.

Required: To graduate, students must complete 128 semester hours for the B.A. and 129 for the B.S.N., with a minimum GPA of 2.0 (2.5 in education courses). All students must take 49 credits of general education courses, structured to develop progressive stages of learning.

Special: Ursuline offers co-op programs in business, public relations, and fashion merchandising, and cross-registration with colleges in the Northeast Ohio Commission of Higher Education. Internships, a general studies degree, dual and student-designed majors, nondegree study, and accelerated degree programs in business management, health care administration, legal studies, and management information systems are available. Students may receive credit for life, military, or work experience. There are pass/fail options and a continuing studies program for nontraditional students. There are 2 national honor societies.

Faculty/Classroom: 25% of faculty are male; 75%, female. 89% teach undergraduates. No introductory courses are taught by graduate students. The average class size in an introductory lecture is 15; in a laboratory, 10; and in a regular course, 11.

Admissions: 70% of the 2003-2004 applicants were accepted. The SAT I scores for the 2003-2004 freshman class were: Verbal--49% below 500, 39% between 500 and 599, and 12% between 600 and 700; Math--51% below 500, 42% between 500 and 599, and 7% between 600 and 700. The ACT scores were 67% below 21, 19% between 21 and 23, 11% between 24 and 26, 2% between 27 and 28, and 1% above 28. 26% of the current freshmen were in the top fifth of their class; 62% were in the top two fifths.

Requirements: The SAT I or ACT is required. In addition, students should be graduates of an accredited secondary school and have a GPA of 2.5. Recommended college preparatory courses include 4 units of English, 3 each of social studies, math, and science, 2 of a foreign language, and 1 each of fine/performing arts and phys ed/health. A recommendation from a teacher or counselor is required and an interview is encouraged. A GPA of 2.5 is required. AP and CLEP credits are accepted. Important factors in the admissions decision are advanced placement or honor courses, recommendations by school officials, and leadership record.

Procedure: Freshmen are admitted to all sessions. Entrance exams should be taken in the junior year. There is a deferred admissions plan and a rolling admissions plan. Application deadlines are open. Application fee is $25. Notification is sent on a rolling basis.

Transfer: 189 transfer students enrolled in 2002-2003. Offical copies of all transcripts and a 2.5 GPA are required. Students with fewer than 24 semester hours must provide high school transcripts. 43 credits of 128 required for the bachelor's degree must be completed at Ursuline.

Visiting: There are regularly scheduled orientations for prospective students, including an open house and overnight visit. There are guides for informal visits and visitors may sit in on classes and stay overnight. To schedule a visit, contact the Admissions Office at *admission@ursuline.edu.*

Financial Aid: In 2003-2004, 88% of all full-time freshmen and 77% of continuing full-time students received some form of financial aid. 84% of full-time freshmen received need-based aid. The average freshman award was $15,901. Need-based scholarships or need-based grants averaged $8055; need-based self-help aid (loans and jobs) averaged $4491; non-need-based athletic scholarships averaged $8750; and other non-need-based awards and non-need-based scholarships averaged $6875. All undergraduates work part time. Average annual earnings from campus work are $825. The average financial indebtedness of the 2003 graduate was $22,111. Ursuline is a member of CSS. The FAFSA and the college's own financial statement are required. The deadline for filing freshman financial aid applications for fall entry is March 1.

International Students: There are 10 international students enrolled. The school actively recruits these students. They must score 500 on the written TOEFL or 173 on the electronic version and also take the SAT I or the ACT, scoring 850 on the SAT I.

Computers: The mainframe is a Unisys. There are 8 computer labs on campus for student use. 2 are located in the residence halls. 7 of the labs have PCs and one is a Mac lab. Residence hall rooms are wired so students with their own computers can access the college's network. All students may access the system daily at designated hours. There are no time limits. The fee is $85 per semester.

Graduates: From July 1, 2002 to June 30, 2003, 217 bachelor's degrees were awarded. The most popular majors were business (31%), nursing (29%), and education (6%). In an average class, 26% graduate in 4 years or less, 39% graduate in 5 years or less, and 40% graduate in 6 years or less.

Admissions Contact: Sarah Carr, Director of Admission.
E-mail: *admission@ursuline.edu* Web: *ursuline.edu*

WALSH UNIVERSITY   D-2
North Canton, OH 44720-3396   (330) 490-7172
(800) 362-9846; Fax: (330) 490-7165

Full-time: 492 men, 657 women	**Faculty:** 76; IIB, -$
Part-time: 143 men, 281 women	**Ph.D.s:** 72%
Graduate: 77 men, 151 women	**Student/Faculty:** 15 to 1
Year: semesters, summer session	**Tuition:** $14,490
Application Deadline: August 25	**Room & Board:** $6400
Freshman Class: 850 applied, 792 accepted, 293 enrolled	
ACT: 22	**COMPETITIVE**

Walsh University was established in 1958 by the Brothers of Christian Instruction, a religious order of the Roman Catholic Church. The private institution offers undergraduate programs in liberal arts, business, communication, education, professional training, and nursing. In addition to regional accreditation, Walsh has baccalaureate program accreditation with NLN. The library contains 135,946 volumes, 8626 microform items, and 1625 audio/video tapes/CDs, and subscribes to 550 periodicals. Computerized library services include the card catalog, interlibrary loans, database searching, and Internet access. Special learning facilities include a learning resource center, radio station, and a child development center. The 107-acre campus is in a small town 20 miles south of Akron. Including any residence halls, there are 13 buildings.

Student Life: 97% of undergraduates are from Ohio. Students are from 15 states, 6 foreign countries, and Canada. 73% are from public schools. 82% are white. Most are Catholic. The average age of freshmen is 22.8; all undergraduates, 25. 30% do not continue beyond their first year; 55% remain to graduate.

Housing: 591 students can be accommodated in college housing, which includes single-sex and coed dorms and on-campus apartments. In addition, there are special-interest houses, study floors, and substance-free floors. On-campus housing is guaranteed for all 4 years. 65% of students commute. All students may keep cars.

Activities: There are no fraternities or sororities. There are 25 groups on campus, including cheerleading, choir, chorale, computers, dance, drama, ethnic, forensics, honors, international, leadership honor societies, literary magazine, newspaper, pep band, political, professional, radio and TV, religious, social, social service, student government, and yearbook. Popular campus events include Apollo Night, Late Night Finals Breakfast, and World Week.

Sports: There are 8 intercollegiate sports for men and 8 for women, and 9 intramural sports for men and 9 for women. Facilities include a 1200-seat gym, outdoor basketball and tennis courts, a track, softball and baseball fields, practice and intramural fields, a soccer field, a game room, and a student exercise and weight room.

Disabled Students: All of the campus is accessible. Wheelchair ramps, elevators, special parking, specially equipped rest rooms, special class scheduling, lowered drinking fountains, lowered telephones, and special housing are available.

Services: Counseling and information services are available, as is tutoring in every subject. There is remedial math, reading, and writing.

Campus Safety and Security: Measures include 24-hour foot and vehicle patrol, self-defense education, security escort services, and informal discussions. There are pamphlets/posters/films, emergency telephones, and lighted pathways/sidewalks.

Programs of Study: Walsh confers B.A., B.S., B.S.Ed., and B.S.N. degrees. Associate and master's degrees are also awarded. Bachelor's degrees are awarded in BIOLOGICAL SCIENCE (biology/biological science), BUSINESS (accounting, banking and finance, business administration and management, and marketing/retailing/merchandising), COMMUNICATIONS AND THE ARTS (communications, English, French, and Spanish), COMPUTER AND PHYSICAL SCIENCE (chemistry, computer science, mathematics, and science), EDUCATION (early childhood, elementary, middle school, physical, secondary, and special), HEALTH PROFESSIONS (clinical science, nursing, physical therapy, predentistry, premedicine, and preveterinary science), SOCIAL SCIENCE (history, international studies, pastoral studies, philosophy, political science/government, prelaw, psychology, religion, sociology, and theological studies). Business, psychology, and nursing are the strongest academically. Education, business, and biology are the largest.

Required: To graduate, students must complete 130 semester hours with a minimum 2.0 GPA. The number of hours required in the major varies. A core curriculum of 68 to 71 hours is required, including courses in English, art and music appreciation, economics, social science, math,

science, humanities, phys ed, theology, philosophy, and possibly a foreign language.

Special: Work-study programs are available to students having substantial financial need. A 3-2 program in natural resources, including forestry, conservation teaching, fisheries, and wildlife management, is offered with the University of Michigan. Walsh offers co-op programs in business, internships in several majors, study abroad in 6 countries, accelerated degree programs in business, management, and nursing, evening and continuing education programs, and credit for life experience. There is a freshman honors program and 10 departmental honors programs.

Faculty/Classroom: 55% of faculty are male; 43%, female. All both teach undergraduates and do research. No introductory courses are taught by graduate students. The average class size in an introductory lecture is 25; in a laboratory, 22; and in a regular course, 18.

Admissions: 93% of the 2003-2004 applicants were accepted. The ACT scores for the 2003-2004 freshman class were: 42% below 21, 28% between 21 and 23, 18% between 24 and 26, 7% between 27 and 28, and 4% above 28. 37% of the current freshmen were in the top fifth of their class; 61% were in the top two fifths. 8 freshmen graduated first in their class.

Requirements: The SAT I or ACT is required. In addition, the applicant must be a graduate of an accredited secondary school; the GED is accepted. Walsh recommends completion of 4 units of English, 3 each of math, science, and social studies, 2 of foreign language, and 1 of fine or performing arts. An essay and an interview are recommended. A GPA of 2.1 is required. AP and CLEP credits are accepted. Important factors in the admissions decision are recommendations by school officials, leadership record, and personality/intangible qualities.

Procedure: Freshmen are admitted to all sessions. Entrance exams should be taken during the junior year. There is a deferred admissions plan and a rolling admissions plan. Applications should be filed by August 25 for fall entry and January 5 for spring entry, along with a $25 fee. Notification is sent on a rolling basis. Applications are accepted online through the school's web site.

Transfer: 150 transfer students enrolled in 2002-2003. Applicants must have a minimum GPA of 2.0 from previous colleges attended. 32 credits of 130 required for the bachelor's degree must be completed at Walsh.

Visiting: There are regularly scheduled orientations for prospective students, consisting of a campus tour, a session with financial aid and admissions staff, and an opportunity to meet with faculty, coaches, and other personnel. There are guides for informal visits and visitors may sit in on classes and stay overnight. To schedule a visit, contact the Admissions Office at *bfreshour@walsh.edu*.

Financial Aid: In 2003-2004, 95% of all full-time freshmen and 90% of continuing full-time students received some form of financial aid. 78% of full-time freshmen and 75% of continuing full-time students received need-based aid. The average freshman award was $10,605. Need-based scholarships or need-based grants averaged $2000 ($6000 maximum); need-based self-help aid (loans and jobs) averaged $4452 ($5125 maximum); non-need-based athletic scholarships averaged $2370 ($10,000 maximum); and other non-need-based awards and non-need-based scholarships averaged $5002 ($22,643 maximum). 22% of undergraduates work part time. Average annual earnings from campus work are $1360. The average financial indebtedness of the 2003 graduate was $17,000. Walsh is a member of CSS. The FAFSA and the college's own financial statement are required. The priority date for freshman financial aid applications for fall entry is March 1. The regular freshman application deadline for fall entry is rolling.

International Students: There are 28 international students enrolled. The school actively recruits these students. They must score 550 on the written TOEFL or 173 on the electronic version.

Computers: There are 160 networked PCs located in 10 computer labs, 3 of which are located in a residence hall. Student access to the Internet is available in the labs. All students may access the system. There are no time limits and no fees.

Graduates: From July 1, 2002 to June 30, 2003, 282 bachelor's degrees were awarded. The most popular majors were management (22%), biology (8%), and marketing (6%). In an average class, 24% graduate in 4 years or less, 39% graduate in 5 years or less, and 49% graduate in 6 years or less. 21 companies recruited on campus in 2002-2003. Of the 2002 graduating class, 12% were enrolled in graduate school within 6 months of graduation and 86% were employed.

Admissions Contact: Brett Freshhour, Dean of Enrollment Management. E-mail: *admissions@walsh.edu* Web: *www.walsh.edu*

WILBERFORCE UNIVERSITY
B-4
Wilberforce, OH 45384-1091

(937) 376-2911, ext. 721
(800) 367-8568; Fax: (937) 376-4751

Full-time: 300 men, 480 women	**Faculty:** 46
Part-time: 10 men, 10 women	**Ph.Ds:** 53%
Graduate: none	**Student/Faculty:** 17 to 1
Year: semesters	**Tuition:** $10,640
Application Deadline: open	**Room & Board:** $4300
Freshman Class: n/av	
SAT I or ACT: recommended	**LESS COMPETITIVE**

Wilberforce University, founded in 1856, is a nonprofit, private institution operated under the auspices of the African Methodist Episcopal Church; it was the first black college in America. Its programs emphasize the liberal arts, business, art and fine arts, engineering, and music. Figures in the above capsule and in this profile are approximate. The library contains 60,000 volumes, 12,000 microform items, and 200 audio/video tapes/CDs, and subscribes to 350 periodicals. Special learning facilities include a learning resource center, radio station, and the nearby National Afro-American Museum. The 125-acre campus is in a rural area 20 miles east of Dayton. Including any residence halls, there are 21 buildings.

Student Life: 64% of undergraduates are from out of state, mostly the Midwest. Students are from 32 states and 2 foreign countries. All are African American. The average age of freshmen is 18; all undergraduates, 20.

Housing: 775 students can be accommodated in college housing, which includes dorms and married-student housing. In addition, there are honors houses. On-campus housing is guaranteed for all 4 years. 85% of students live on campus; of those, 70% remain on campus on weekends. Alcohol is not permitted. All students may keep cars.

Activities: 10% of men belong to 3 national fraternities; 10% of women belong to 3 national sororities. There are 30 groups on campus, including choir, computers, dance, ethnic, honors, international, literary magazine, newspaper, political, religious, social, student government, and yearbook. Popular campus events include Fall Festival and Dawn Dance.

Sports: There are 5 intercollegiate sports for men and 4 for women, and 4 intramural sports for men and 4 for women. Facilities include a 1500-seat gym, outdoor and cross-country track, a softball field, and basketball, volleyball, and tennis courts.

Disabled Students: 50% of the campus is accessible. Wheelchair ramps, special parking, specially equipped rest rooms, and limited elevator service in classroom buildings only are available.

Services: Counseling and information services are available, as is tutoring in most subjects. There is a reader service for the blind and remedial math, reading, and writing.

Programs of Study: Wilberforce confers B.A. and B.S. degrees. Bachelor's degrees are awarded in BIOLOGICAL SCIENCE (biology/biological science), BUSINESS (accounting, banking and finance, business administration and management, business economics, management science, and marketing/retailing/merchandising), COMMUNICATIONS AND THE ARTS (communications, fine arts, literature, and music), COMPUTER AND PHYSICAL SCIENCE (chemistry, computer science, information sciences and systems, mathematics, and science), ENGINEERING AND ENVIRONMENTAL DESIGN (preengineering), HEALTH PROFESSIONS (health care administration and rehabilitation therapy), SOCIAL SCIENCE (economics, liberal arts/general studies, political science/government, prelaw, psychology, social science, social work, and sociology). Business administration, accounting, and banking and finance are the strongest academically.

Required: To graduate, students must complete 126 credit hours with a minimum GPA of 2.0 and no grade in the major below a C. To fulfill the general studies requirements, all students must complete a first-year program, which includes composition and computer literacy courses, and they must also take at least 1 course from each of the following areas: humanistic traditions, music, art, religion, communication arts, literature and language, non-Western studies, behavioral sciences, economics and political science, physical sciences, and life science. 2 credits in health and phys ed and completion of 2 cooperative education experiences are also required.

Special: Wilberforce offers a co-op arrangement with St. John's University School of Law and cross-registration through the Southwestern Ohio Council for Higher Education. B.A.-B.S. degrees are available in all majors, and there are dual majors in engineering along with a 3-2 engineering degree with the University of Dayton. Credit is given for the mandatory co-op education program, in which students participate in paid work experience in their chosen field. Nondegree study is possible in military science. There is 1 national honor society, including Phi Beta Kappa, a freshman honors program, and 4 departmental honors programs.

Faculty/Classroom: 50% of faculty are male; 50%, female. The average class size in an introductory lecture is 12 and in a regular course, 18.

Requirements: The SAT I or ACT is recommended. In addition, students should be graduates of an accredited secondary school and have 15 Carnegie units, including 4 units of English, 2 to 3 of math, including algebra, 2 to 3 of science, including a lab course, and 2 of social studies, including U.S. history. The GED is accepted with a score of 45 or better. SAT II: Subject tests are recommended. A GPA of 2.0 is required. AP and CLEP credits are accepted. Important factors in the admissions decision are recommendations by school officials, advanced placement or honor courses, and evidence of special talent.

Procedure: Freshmen are admitted fall and spring. Entrance exams should be taken by the fall of the senior year. There are early decision, early admissions, and rolling admissions plans. Application deadlines are open. A waiting list is an active part of the admissions procedure. Check with the school for current application fee.

Transfer: A minimum college GPA of 2.0 is required. 30 of 126 credits required for the bachelor's degree must be completed at Wilberforce.

Visiting: There are regularly scheduled orientations for prospective students. There are guides for informal visits. To schedule a visit, contact the Office of Admissions.

Financial Aid: Wilberforce is a member of CSS. The FAFSA, the college's own financial statement, and the parent and student federal income tax returns are required. Check with the school for current deadlines.

International Students: They must score 500 on the written TOEFL and also take the SAT I or the ACT.

Computers: The mainframe is an NCR Tower Series 32/650. There are also 85 NCR 710 PCs available in the computer center. Students enrolled in computer and engineering programs may access the system. There are no time limits and no fees.

Admissions Contact: Kenneth C. Christmon, Director of Admissions. E-mail: *admissions@payne.wilberforce.edu* Web: *www.wilberforce.edu*

WILMINGTON COLLEGE
B-4
Wilmington, OH 45177

(937) 382-6661
(800) 341-9318; Fax: (937) 383-8542

Full-time: 537 men, 634 women	**Faculty:** 70; IIB, --$
Part-time: 30 men, 47 women	**Ph.Ds:** 69%
Graduate: none	**Student/Faculty:** 17 to 1
Year: semesters, summer session	**Tuition:** $17,682
Application Deadline: open	**Room & Board:** $6490
Freshman Class: 835 applied, 781 accepted, 305 enrolled	
ACT: 21	**LESS COMPETITIVE**

Wilmington College, established in 1870, is a private institution sponsored by the Society of Friends. The college offers programs in the liberal arts, business, health science, teacher preparation, agricultural studies, religious studies, and athletic training. In addition to regional accreditation, Wilmington has baccalaureate program accreditation with CAAHEP and NCATE. The library contains 110,000 volumes, 42,000 microform items, and 1400 audio/video tapes/CDs, and subscribes to 400 periodicals. Computerized library services include the card catalog, interlibrary loans, and database searching. Special learning facilities include a learning resource center, art gallery, Peace Resource Center, Quaker museum, observatory, greenhouse, and academic farm. The 65-acre campus is in a small town 50 miles from Cincinnati and from Columbus. Including any residence halls, there are 20 buildings.

Student Life: 96% of undergraduates are from Ohio. Students are from 13 states and 4 foreign countries. 74% are white. 40% claim no religious affiliation; 17% Catholic. The average age of freshmen is 18; all undergraduates, 21. 22% do not continue beyond their first year; 53% remain to graduate.

Housing: 833 students can be accommodated in college housing, which includes single-sex and coed dorms, on-campus apartments, fraternity houses, and sorority houses. On-campus housing is guaranteed for all 4 years. 70% of students live on campus. All students may keep cars.

Activities: 17% of men belong to 1 national and 4 local fraternities; 16% of women belong to 4 local sororities. There are 63 groups on campus, including cheerleading, choir, chorale, drama, ethnic, gay, honors, international, jazz band, literary magazine, musical theater, newspaper, orchestra, photography, political, professional, religious, social, social service, student government, and yearbook. Popular campus events include Community Day, Westheimer Peace Symposium, and Fall Fest.

Sports: There are 11 intercollegiate sports for men and 10 for women, and 8 intramural sports for men and 8 for women. Facilities include an Olympic-size pool, a Nautilus weight-training room, an exercise room, racquetball courts, a 4500-seat gym, and a 3000-seat stadium.

Disabled Students: 20% of the campus is accessible. Wheelchair ramps, elevators, special parking, specially equipped rest rooms, and special class scheduling are available.

Services: Counseling and information services are available, as is tutoring in every subject. There is remedial math, reading, and writing.

Campus Safety and Security: Measures include 24-hour foot and vehicle patrol, security escort services, informal discussions, and pamphlets/posters/films. There are emergency telephones and lighted pathways/sidewalks.

Programs of Study: Wilmington confers B.A. and B.S. degrees. Master's degrees are also awarded. Bachelor's degrees are awarded in AGRICULTURE (agriculture), BIOLOGICAL SCIENCE (biology/biological science), BUSINESS (accounting, business administration and management, organizational behavior, and sports management), COMMUNICATIONS AND THE ARTS (art, communications, dramatic arts, English, and Spanish), COMPUTER AND PHYSICAL SCIENCE (chemistry, computer science, and mathematics), EDUCATION (athletic training, early childhood, elementary, physical, and secondary), HEALTH PROFESSIONS (predentistry, premedicine, and preveterinary science), SOCIAL SCIENCE (criminal justice, history, liberal arts/general studies, prelaw, psychology, religion, social science, social work, and sociology). Chemistry, biology, and athletic training are the strongest academically. Business, agriculture, and athletic training are the largest.

Required: To graduate, students must complete 124 semester hours, with no more than 60 hours in the major, with a minimum GPA of 2.0. At least 40 hours must be in upper-division work. General education requirements include courses in English and math competence, international knowledge, basic areas of thought and expression, and personal fitness.

Special: Special academic programs include work-study, internships, a Washington semester, and cross-registration with the Southwest Ohio Consortium. Study abroad may be arranged in Mexico, Austria, France, and other countries. Dual majors in any subject and student-designed majors are offered. Credit for experience, nondegree study, and pass/fail options are possible. There are 5 national honor societies, a freshman honors program, and 3 departmental honors programs.

Faculty/Classroom: 57% of faculty are male; 43%, female. All teach undergraduates. The average class size in an introductory lecture is 25 and in a regular course, 19.

Admissions: 94% of the 2003-2004 applicants were accepted. The ACT scores for the 2003-2004 freshman class were: 50% below 21, 24% between 21 and 23, 20% between 24 and 26, 4% between 27 and 28, and 2% above 28. 35% of the current freshmen were in the top fifth of their class; 65% were in the top two fifths. 8 freshmen graduated first in their class.

Requirements: The SAT I or ACT is required. In addition, applicants must be graduates of an accredited secondary school, with 4 units of English, 2 units each of math, science, and social studies, and a recommended 2 units of a foreign language. An additional 6 units is required in other areas. The GED is accepted. An interview is recommended. An essay may be required. AP and CLEP credits are accepted. Important factors in the admissions decision are recommendations by school officials, parents or siblings attending the school, and recommendations by alumni.

Procedure: Freshmen are admitted fall and spring. Entrance exams should be taken as early as possible. There is a deferred admissions plan. Application deadlines are open. Application fee is $25.

Transfer: 70 transfer students enrolled in a recent year. Applicants' college and high school transcripts are evaluated on an individual basis. They must have a 2.0 GPA and a completed transfer recommendation form. 30 of 124 credits required for the bachelor's degree must be completed at Wilmington.

Visiting: There are regularly scheduled orientations for prospective students, including meetings with faculty and a tour of the campus. There are guides for informal visits and visitors may sit in on classes and stay overnight. To schedule a visit, contact the Admissions Office.

Financial Aid: In 2003-2004, 99% of all full-time students received some form of financial aid. 84% of full-time freshmen and 83% of continuing full-time students received need-based aid. The average freshman award was $17,520 with $5816 ($15,300 maximum) from need-based scholarships or need-based grants; $4096 ($8175 maximum) from need-based self-help aid (loans and jobs); $6678 ($15,002 maximum) from non-need-based awards and non-need-based scholarships; and $930 ($6625 maximum) from unsubsidized Stafford Loans. Total award does not include Parent Plus loans or alternative educational loans. 35% of undergraduates work part time. Average annual earnings from campus work are $1400. The average financial indebtedness of the 2003 graduate was $19,306. The FAFSA is required. The priority date for freshman financial aid applications for fall entry is March 15.

International Students: There are 5 international students enrolled. The school actively recruits these students. They must score 500 on the written TOEFL or 173 on the electronic version. The TOEFL is not required if the SAT I is taken. Students who have been previously enrolled in a U.S. high school must also take the SAT I or ACT, scoring 900.

Computers: The mainframe consists of 2 HP 9000s. There are 150 networked PCs available in public areas. There is full access to the Internet and the Web, Windows 95, Office 97, and 100 other titles on-line. All students may access the system at any time. There are no time limits and no fees.

Graduates: In a recent year, 145 bachelor's degrees were awarded. The most popular majors were business (38%), education (14%), and agriculture (11%). 52 companies recruited on campus in 2002-2003. Of the 2002 graduating class, 5% were enrolled in graduate school within 6 months of graduation and 21% were employed.

Admissions Contact: Tina Garland, Director of Admissions.
E-mail: *admission@wilmington.edu* Web: *www.wilmington.edu*

WITTENBERG UNIVERSITY   B-3
Springfield, OH 45501   (937) 327-6314
(800) 677-7558; Fax: (937) 327-6379

Full-time: 872 men, 1183 women	**Faculty:** 147; IIB, av$
Part-time: 35 men, 62 women	**Ph.D.s:** 89%
Graduate: 6 men, 30 women	**Student/Faculty:** 14 to 1
Year: semesters, summer session	**Tuition:** $24,948
Application Deadline: March 15	**Room & Board:** $6368
Freshman Class: 2516 applied, 2269 accepted, 606 enrolled	
SAT I Verbal/Math: 578/578	**ACT:** 24 **VERY COMPETITIVE**

Wittenberg University, founded in 1845, is a private liberal arts and sciences institution affiliated with the Evangelical Lutheran Church in America. In addition to regional accreditation, Wittenberg has baccalaureate program accreditation with ACS, NASM, and NCATE. The 2 libraries contain 402,297 volumes, 81,966 microform items, and 21,732 audio/video tapes/CDs, and subscribe to 5574 periodicals. Computerized library services include the card catalog, interlibrary loans, database searching, and Internet access. Special learning facilities include a learning resource center, art gallery, radio station, geology museum, and observatory. The 100-acre campus is in a suburban area 25 miles east of Dayton, 40 miles west of Columbus, and 75 miles from Cincinatti. Including any residence halls, there are 35 buildings.

Student Life: 72% of undergraduates are from Ohio. Students are from 44 states and 37 foreign countries. 80% are from public schools. 88% are white. 37% claim no religious affiliation; 21% Protestant; 20% Catholic. The average age of freshmen is 18; all undergraduates, 20. 35% do not continue beyond their first year; 59% remain to graduate.

Housing: 1200 students can be accommodated in college housing, which includes single-sex and coed dorms, on-campus apartments, off-campus apartments, married-student housing, fraternity houses, and sorority houses. In addition, there are honors houses, language houses, special-interest houses, and a substance-free residence hall. On-campus housing is guaranteed for all 4 years. 96% of students live on campus; of those, 85% remain on campus on weekends. All students may keep cars.

Activities: 20% of men belong to 5 national fraternities; 35% of women belong to 7 national sororities. There are 110 groups on campus, including art, band, caving, cheerleading, chess, choir, chorale, chorus, computers, dance, drama, ethnic, forensics, gay, honors, international, jazz band, literary magazine, musical theater, newspaper, orchestra, pep band, photography, political, professional, radio and TV, religious, social, social service, student government, symphony, and yearbook. Popular campus events include Wittenberg Series, International Festival, and Professional Alumni Days.

Sports: There are 11 intercollegiate sports for men and 11 for women, and 15 intramural sports for men and 12 for women. Facilities include a multipurpose field house, a swimming pool, 6 racquetball/handball courts, a fitness center, and sports medicine rooms. There is also a 3200-seat gym, a 3200-seat arena, 12 acres of playing fields, and a 500-seat stadium with an artificially lit playing field, a track, and 12 tennis courts.

Disabled Students: 75% of the campus is accessible. Wheelchair ramps, elevators, special parking, specially equipped rest rooms, special class scheduling, lowered drinking fountains, and lowered telephones are available.

Services: Counseling and information services are available, as is tutoring in most subjects. There are also math and writers' workshops.

Campus Safety and Security: Measures include 24-hour foot and vehicle patrol, self-defense education, security escort services, and informal discussions. There are pamphlets/posters/films, emergency telephones, and lighted pathways/sidewalks. City police support campus police during the evening. There is also a student Eyes and Ears Program and a campus security committee made up of students and faculty.

Programs of Study: Wittenberg confers B.A., B.S., B.F.A., B.M., and B.M.E. degrees. Master's degrees are also awarded. Bachelor's degrees are awarded in BIOLOGICAL SCIENCE (biology/biological science), BUSINESS (business administration and management), COMMUNICATIONS AND THE ARTS (communications, dramatic arts, English, fine arts, French, German, music, Russian, and Spanish), COMPUTER AND PHYSICAL SCIENCE (chemistry, computer science, geology, mathematics, and physics), EDUCATION (elementary, foreign languages, middle school, music, science, secondary, and special), HEALTH PROFESSIONS (predentistry and premedicine), SOCIAL SCIENCE (American studies, East Asian studies, economics, geography, history, international relations, philosophy, political science/government, prelaw, psychology, religion, and sociology). Biology, education, and English are the strongest academically. Business, education, and biology are the largest.

Required: To graduate, students must complete at least 130 credits. The required minimum GPA and number of hours in the major varies by department. The liberal arts core includes courses distributed in various areas. All students must take a Common Learning course, and courses in writing proficiency, services, phys ed, and math/computer science. Comprehensive exams are required in some departments. Sophomores must spend 30 hours in volunteer service.

Special: Special academic programs include internships, cross-registration through the Southwest Ohio Consortium, a Washington semester, work-study programs, study-abroad opportunities in many countries, accelerated degree programs, dual and student-designed majors, nondegree study, and pass/fail options. A 3-2 engineering degree is offered through Washington, Columbia, and Case Western Reserve Universities and Georgia Institute of Technology. There is also a 3-2 nursing program with Johns Hopkins University and an occupational therapy program with Washington University. There are 6 national honor societies, including Phi Beta Kappa, a freshman honors program, and 10 departmental honors programs.

Faculty/Classroom: 56% of faculty are male; 44%, female. All teach undergraduates. No introductory courses are taught by graduate students. The average class size in an introductory lecture is 25; in a laboratory, 20; and in a regular course, 18.

Admissions: 90% of the 2003-2004 applicants were accepted. The SAT I scores for the 2003-2004 freshman class were: Verbal--13% below 500, 46% between 500 and 599, 34% between 600 and 700, and 7% above 700; Math--15% below 500, 45% between 500 and 599, 35% between 600 and 700, and 5% above 700. The ACT scores were 24% below 21, 27% between 21 and 23, 25% between 24 and 26, 12% between 27 and 28, and 12% above 28. 52% of the current freshmen were in the top fifth of their class; 74% were in the top two fifths. There were 2 National Merit finalists. 20 freshmen graduated first in their class.

Requirements: The SAT I or ACT is required. In addition, students should have graduated from an accredited secondary school with 16 academic credits, including 4 units of English and 3 each of a foreign language, math, science, and social studies, which includes history. The SAT II: Writing test is recommended. An essay is required and an interview advised. Art students must present a portfolio, and music students must audition. AP credits are accepted. Important factors in the admissions decision are advanced placement or honor courses, evidence of special talent, and extracurricular activities record.

Procedure: Freshmen are admitted to all sessions. Entrance exams should be taken by the fall of the senior year, but as early as possible. There are early decision, early admissions, and deferred admissions plans. There is a rolling admissions plan. Early decision applications should be filed by November 15; regular applications, by March 15 for fall entry, December 1 for winter entry, and May 1 for summer entry, along with a $40 fee. Notification of early decision is sent January 1; regular decision, on a rolling basis. 31 early decision candidates were accepted for the 2003-2004 class. Applications are accepted on-line through Common App, CollegeLink, Apply, and the school's web site.

Transfer: 34 transfer students enrolled in 2002-2003. Applicants should have a minimum GPA of 2.25 at an accredited college and be in good academic and social standing. High school transcripts are required in some cases. An interview is recommended. 75 credits of 130 required for the bachelor's degree must be completed at Wittenberg.

Visiting: There are regularly scheduled orientations for prospective students, including interviews, tours, and a faculty panel. There are guides for informal visits and visitors may sit in on classes and stay overnight. To schedule a visit, contact the Admissions Office at admission@wittenberg.edu.

Financial Aid: In 2003-2004, 98% of all full-time freshmen and 72% of continuing full-time students received some form of financial aid. 73% of full-time freshmen and 72% of continuing full-time students received need-based aid. The average freshman award was $19,921. Need-based scholarships or need-based grants averaged $16,342; need-based self-help aid (loans and jobs) averaged $370; and non-need-based awards and non-need-based scholarships averaged $10,244. 55% of undergraduates work part time. Average annual earnings from campus work are $1500. The average financial indebtedness of the 2003 graduate was $19,191. The FAFSA is required. The deadline for filing freshman financial aid applications for fall entry is March 15.

International Students: There are 52 international students enrolled. The school actively recruits these students. They must score 550 on the written TOEFL or 213 on the electronic version and also take the ACT or SAT I, if available, and IELTS.

Computers: The mainframe is a DEC VAX 11/750. There are 500 terminals and PCs located in residence halls and all academic buildings and libraries. All students may access the system 24 hours a day. There are no time limits and no fees. It is strongly recommended that all students have a personal computer.

Graduates: From July 1, 2002 to June 30, 2003, 422 bachelor's degrees were awarded. The most popular majors were business (15%), English (10%), and education (10%). In an average class, 1% graduate in 3 years or less, 68% graduate in 4 years or less, 71% graduate in 5 years or less, and 72% graduate in 6 years or less. 75 companies recruited on campus in 2002-2003. Of the 2002 graduating class, 16% were enrolled in graduate school within 6 months of graduation and 96% were employed.

Admissions Contact: Kenneth G. Benne, Dean of Admissions. A video is available. E-mail: *admission@wittenberg.edu*
Web: *www.wittenberg.edu*

WRIGHT STATE UNIVERSITY
B-4
Dayton, OH 45435 (937) 775-5700
(800) 247-1770; Fax: (937) 775-5795

Full-time: 4280 men, 5500 women	**Faculty:** 487; I, --$
Part-time: 1040 men, 1400 women	**Ph.D.s:** 87%
Graduate: 1480 men, 2120 women	**Student/Faculty:** 20 to 1
Year: quarters, summer session	**Tuition:** $5470 ($10,945)
Application Deadline: open	**Room & Board:** $6020
Freshman Class: 5104 applied, 4650 accepted, 2254 enrolled	
SAT I Verbal/Math: 510/510	**ACT:** 21 **LESS COMPETITIVE**

Wright State University, founded in 1964, is a state-supported institution offering undergraduate programs in business and administration, education and human services, engineering and computer science, liberal arts, math and science, and nursing and health. Figures in the above capsule are approximate. There are 6 undergraduate and 5 graduate schools. In addition to regional accreditation, Wright State has baccalaureate program accreditation with AACSB, ABET, CSWE, NASM, NCATE, and NLN. The 2 libraries contain 695,805 volumes and 1,278,767 microform items, and subscribe to 5523 periodicals. Computerized library services include the card catalog, interlibrary loans, and database searching. Special learning facilities include a learning resource center, art gallery, radio station, TV station, and TV production studio. The Department of Archives and Special Collections houses one of the most complete depositories of information on the Wright brothers in the world. The 645-acre campus is in a suburban area 8 miles northeast of Dayton. Including any residence halls, there are 53 buildings.

Student Life: 98% of undergraduates are from Ohio. Students are from 49 states, 71 foreign countries, and Canada. 82% are white. The average age of freshmen is 19; all undergraduates, 24. 28% do not continue beyond their first year; 42% remain to graduate.

Housing: 2300 students can be accommodated in college housing, which includes coed dorms, on-campus apartments, and married-student housing. In addition, there are honors houses and special-interest houses. On-campus housing is available on a first-come, first-served basis and is available on a lottery system for upperclassmen. 80% of students commute. All students may keep cars.

Activities: 5% of men belong to 2 local and 8 national fraternities; 3% of women belong to 5 national sororities. There are 140 groups on campus, including band, cheerleading, chess, choir, chorale, chorus, computers, drill team, ethnic, film, gay, honors, international, jazz band, literary magazine, newspaper, orchestra, pep band, political, professional, radio and TV, religious, social, social service, and student government. Popular campus events include October Daze, May Daze, and Madrigal Dinner.

Sports: There are 7 intercollegiate sports for men and 7 for women, and 12 intramural sports for men and 12 for women. Facilities include an athletic and entertainment center with an arena seating 13,000 spectators, break-off rooms, auxiliary gym, and baseball and practice fields. The student union houses a natatorium, weight rooms, game rooms, and playing courts.

Disabled Students: All of the campus is accessible. Wheelchair ramps, elevators, special parking, specially equipped rest rooms, lowered drinking fountains, lowered telephones, special housing, and adaptive technology are available. An underground tunnel system connects all academic buildings.

Services: Counseling and information services are available, as is tutoring in most subjects. There is a reader service for the blind and remedial math, reading, and writing.

Campus Safety and Security: Measures include 24-hour foot and vehicle patrol, self-defense education, security escort services, and shuttle buses. There are informal discussions, pamphlets/posters/films, emergency telephones, and lighted pathways/sidewalks.

Programs of Study: Wright State confers B.A., B.S., B.F.A., B.Mus., B.S.B., B.S.Comp.Eng., B.S.E., B.S.Ed., B.S.M.T., and B.S.N. degrees. Master's and doctoral degrees are also awarded. Bachelor's degrees are awarded in BIOLOGICAL SCIENCE (biology/biological science), BUSINESS (accounting, banking and finance, business economics, management information systems, management science, and marketing/retailing/merchandising), COMMUNICATIONS AND THE ARTS (art history and appreciation, arts administration/management, classical languages, communications, dance, dramatic arts, English, film arts, fine arts, French, German, modern language, music, music history and appreciation, music theory and composition, Spanish, and theater design), COMPUTER AND PHYSICAL SCIENCE (chemistry, computer science, geology, geophysics and seismology, mathematics, and physics), EDUCATION (art, business, elementary, foreign languages, music, physical, science, secondary, and special), ENGINEERING AND ENVIRONMENTAL DESIGN (biomedical engineering, computer engineering, electrical/electronics engineering, engineering physics, materials engineering, mechanical engineering, systems engineering, and water and wastewater technology), HEALTH PROFESSIONS (environmental health science, medical laboratory technology, nursing, predentistry, premedicine, and rehabilitation therapy), SOCIAL SCIENCE (anthropology, economics, geography, history, humanities, international relations, philosophy, political science/government, prelaw, psychology, religion, social work, sociology, and urban studies). Business education, theater arts, and engineering are the strongest academically. Elementary education, accounting, and nursing are the largest.

Required: To graduate, students must complete 183 quarter hours, with a minimum GPA of 2.0. All students are required to take 57 credit hours of general education courses in 4 areas: communication and math skills, the Western experience, the non-Western world, and understanding the contemporary world.

Special: B.A.-B.S. degrees are offered in computer science, geography, urban affairs, biological sciences, chemistry, geological sciences, math, and psychology. Cross-registration with other area colleges is available through the Southwestern Ohio Council for Higher Education. Dual majors, co-op programs, internships, study abroad, work-study programs, student-designed majors, nondegree study, and credit for military experience are available. There are 13 national honor societies, a freshman honors program, and 62 departmental honors programs.

Faculty/Classroom: 64% of faculty are male; 36%, female. The average class size in an introductory lecture is 41; in a laboratory, 27; and in a regular course, 32.

Admissions: 91% of the 2003-2004 applicants were accepted. The SAT I scores for the 2003-2004 freshman class were: Verbal--48% below 500, 37% between 500 and 599, 14% between 600 and 700, and 1% above 700; Math--49% below 500, 35% between 500 and 599, 14% between 600 and 700, and 2% above 700. The ACT scores were 50% below 21, 25% between 21 and 23, 15% between 24 and 26, 6% between 27 and 28, and 4% above 28. 33% of the current freshmen were in the top fifth of their class; 56% were in the top two fifths.

Requirements: The SAT I or ACT is required. In addition, applicants should be graduates of an accredited secondary school and have 4 units in English, 3 units each in math, science, and social studies, 2 units in a foreign language, and 1 unit in the arts. A portfolio is required for art majors, an audition for theater and music majors. The GED is accepted. AP and CLEP credits are accepted.

Procedure: Freshmen are admitted to all sessions. Entrance exams should be taken in the spring of the junior year. There is a deferred admissions plan. Application deadlines are open. The fall 2003 application fee was $30. There is a rolling admissions plan. Applications are accepted on computer disk and on-line.

Transfer: Applicants must have a 2.0 GPA. 45 of 183 credits required for the bachelor's degree must be completed at Wright State.

Visiting: There are regularly scheduled orientations for prospective students, including a campus tour and information on academic and student services. There are guides for informal visits and visitors may sit in on classes. To schedule a visit, contact the Office of Admissions.

Financial Aid: In 2003-2004, 78% of all full-time students received some form of financial aid. 55% of full-time freshmen and 74% of continuing full-time students received need-based aid. The average freshman award was $8894. Need-based scholarships or need-based grants averaged $2983 ($4050 maximum); need-based self-help aid (loans and jobs) averaged $3729 ($10,500 maximum); non-need-based athletic scholarships averaged $9226 ($17,700 maximum); and other non-need-based awards and non-need-based scholarships averaged $2648 ($6000 maximum). Wright State is a member of CSS. The CSS Profile, FAFSA, FFS, or SFS, and the college's own financial statement are required. Check with the school for current deadlines.

International Students: They must score 500 on the written TOEFL.

Computers: The mainframe is a Hitachi AS/EX 44. Students may access the system through many labs on campus and through the network from remote locations, including residence halls. All students may access the system. There are no time limits and no fees.

Graduates: In an average class, 25% graduate in 5 years or less, and 35% graduate in 6 years or less.

Admissions Contact: Cathy Davis, Director of Undergraduate Admissions. E-mail: *admissions@wright.edu* Web: *www.wright.edu*

XAVIER UNIVERSITY
Cincinnati, OH 45207

A-5

(513) 745-3301
(877) 982-3648; Fax: (513) 745-4319

Full-time: 1447 men, 1857 women	**Faculty:** 269; IIA, -$
Part-time: 259 men, 352 women	**Ph.Ds:** 85%
Graduate: 1076 men, 1635 women	**Student/Faculty:** 12 to 1
Year: semesters, summer session	**Tuition:** $19,150
Application Deadline: February 1	**Room & Board:** $7700
Freshman Class: 4366 applied, 3421 accepted, 786 enrolled	
SAT I Verbal/Math: 580/590	**ACT:** 26 **VERY COMPETITIVE+**

Xavier University, founded in 1831, is a comprehensive Jesuit institution affiliated with the Roman Catholic Church. There are 3 undergraduate and 10 graduate schools. In addition to regional accreditation, Xavier has baccalaureate program accreditation with AACSB, ACOTE, AOTA, CAAHEP, CCNE, and CSWE. The library contains 364,962 volumes, 713,188 microform items, and 8627 audio/video tapes/CDs, and subscribes to 1615 periodicals. Computerized library services include the card catalog, interlibrary loans, database searching, and Internet access. Special learning facilities include a learning resource center, art gallery, radio station, TV station, and an observatory. The 131-acre campus is in a suburban area 5 miles northeast of the center of Cincinnati in a residential area. Including any residence halls, there are 31 buildings.

Student Life: 65% of undergraduates are from Ohio. Students are from 46 states, 53 foreign countries, and Canada. 46% are from public schools. 86% are white. 63% are Catholic; 15% claim no religious affiliation. The average age of freshmen is 18.5; all undergraduates, 21. 11% do not continue beyond their first year; 80% remain to graduate.

Housing: 1845 students can be accommodated in college housing, which includes coed dorms, on-campus apartments, and off-campus apartments. In addition, there are honors houses and special-interest houses. On-campus housing is available on a first-come, first-served basis and is available on a lottery system for upperclassmen. 52% of students commute. All students may keep cars.

Activities: There are no fraternities or sororities. There are 100 groups on campus, including art, band, cheerleading, choir, chorale, chorus, computers, dance, drama, ethnic, film, gay, honors, international, jazz band, literary magazine, musical theater, newspaper, pep band, photography, political, professional, radio and TV, religious, social, social service, student government, and yearbook. Popular campus events include Family Weekend and Spring Break Away.

Sports: There are 8 intercollegiate sports for men and 8 for women, and 10 intramural sports for men and 10 for women. Facilities include a field house, a sports center, basketball and volleyball courts, baseball, soccer, and softball fields, a rifle range, and tennis courts.

Disabled Students: 98% of the campus is accessible. Wheelchair ramps, elevators, special parking, specially equipped rest rooms, lowered drinking fountains, and lowered telephones are available.

Services: Counseling and information services are available, as is tutoring in most subjects. There are math and writing labs and an efficient reading and study skills class. There is a reader service for the blind and remedial math.

Campus Safety and Security: Measures include 24-hour foot and vehicle patrol, self-defense education, security escort services, and shuttle buses. There are informal discussions, pamphlets/posters/films, emergency telephones, lighted pathways/sidewalks, and alcohol awareness, drug awareness, and sexual assault programs.

Programs of Study: Xavier confers B.A., B.S., Honors A.B., B.F.A., B.L.A., B.S.B.A., B.S.N., B.S.O.T., and B.S.W. degrees. Associate, master's, and doctoral degrees are also awarded. Bachelor's degrees are awarded in BIOLOGICAL SCIENCE (biology/biological science), BUSINESS (accounting, banking and finance, business administration and management, business economics, entrepreneurial studies, human resources, international business management, management science, marketing/retailing/merchandising, and sports management), COMMUNICATIONS AND THE ARTS (advertising, art, classics, communications, English, fine arts, French, German, music, public relations, and Spanish), COMPUTER AND PHYSICAL SCIENCE (applied physics, chemistry, computer science, information sciences and systems, mathematics, natural sciences, and physics), EDUCATION (athletic training, early childhood, education, middle school, music, science, and special), ENGINEERING AND ENVIRONMENTAL DESIGN (chemical engineering), HEALTH PROFESSIONS (medical laboratory technology, nursing, occupational therapy, and prepharmacy), SOCIAL SCIENCE (criminal justice, economics, history, humanities, international relations, liberal arts/general studies, philosophy, political science/government, psychology, social work, sociology, and theological studies). Physics, Honors A.B., and natural science are the strongest academically. Business, communications, and education are the largest.

Required: To graduate, students must complete a minimum of 120 credit hours with a minimum GPA of 2.0. The total number of hours required in the major varies. All students must take core curriculum courses in English composition, cultural diversity, math, science, social science, history, theology, philosophy, a foreign language, literature, fine arts, and an ethics/religion and society focus.

Special: Xavier offers internships related to some majors, cross-registration through the Greater Cincinnati Consortium, and co-op programs in business and computer science. Students may study abroad in 13 countries. A Washington semester and nondegree study are available. A 3-2 engineering degree is offered with the University of Cincinnati, and a 3-2 applied biology degree is offered with Duke University. There are 8 national honor societies and a freshman honors program.

Faculty/Classroom: 52% of faculty are male; 48%, female. 97% teach undergraduates. No introductory courses are taught by graduate students. The average class size in an introductory lecture is 24; in a laboratory, 17; and in a regular course, 19.

Admissions: 78% of the 2003-2004 applicants were accepted. The SAT I scores for the 2003-2004 freshman class were: Verbal--12% below

500, 43% between 500 and 599, 37% between 600 and 700, and 8% above 700; Math--10% below 500, 46% between 500 and 599, 36% between 600 and 700, and 8% above 700. The ACT scores were 10% below 21, 20% between 21 and 23, 25% between 24 and 26, 19% between 27 and 28, and 26% above 28. 48% of the current freshmen were in the top fifth of their class; 77% were in the top two fifths. There were 12 National Merit finalists.

Requirements: The SAT I or ACT is required. In addition, graduation from an accredited secondary school or satisfactory scores on the GED is required for admission. The school requires 21 academic credits, including 4 years of English, 3 each of math, social studies, and science, 2 of foreign language, 1 of health/phys ed, plus 5 electives. Xavier recommends an interview. AP and CLEP credits are accepted. Important factors in the admissions decision are advanced placement or honor courses, leadership record, and extracurricular activities record.

Procedure: Freshmen are admitted fall and spring. There is a deferred admissions plan and a rolling admissions plan. Applications should be filed by February 1 for fall entry, along with a $35 fee. Notification is sent on a rolling basis beginning October 15. 225 applicants were on the 2003 waiting list; 31 were admitted. Applications are accepted on-line through Common App or the school's web site.

Transfer: 78 transfer students enrolled in 2002-2003. Transfer students must have a minimum GPA of 2.0 in all college-level work. An interview is also recommended. Students who transfer to Xavier with 30 or more semester hours are not required to submit an essay or the results of the ACT or SAT I tests. 30 credits of 120 required for the bachelor's degree must be completed at Xavier.

Visiting: There are regularly scheduled orientations for prospective students, including an interview and a tour of the campus. There are guides for informal visits and visitors may sit in on classes and stay overnight. To schedule a visit, contact the Admissions Office at *xuadmit@xavier.edu.*

Financial Aid: In 2003-2004, 98% of all full-time freshmen and 83% of continuing full-time students received some form of financial aid. 62% of full-time freshmen and 48% of continuing full-time students received need-based aid. The average freshman award was $12,715. Need-based scholarships or need-based grants averaged $10,512; need-based self-help aid (loans and jobs) averaged $4350; and non-need-based athletic scholarships averaged $19,327. 19% of undergraduates work part time. Average annual earnings from campus work are $2080. The average financial indebtedness of the 2003 graduate was $17,981. Xavier is a member of CSS. The FAFSA is required. The deadline for filing freshman financial aid applications for fall entry is February 15.

International Students: There are 48 international students enrolled. The school actively recruits these students. They must score 500 on the written TOEFL or 173 on the electronic version and also take the SAT I or ACT.

Computers: The mainframe is a DEC VAX 6620. Students have network accounts on the university network from any of the 200 or more PCs or Macs in the 6 academic computing labs or from their own PC. All residence hall rooms are connected to the network and have full Internet access. All students may access the system 24 hours a day, 7 days a week. There are no time limits. The fee is $150 per semester.

Graduates: From July 1, 2002 to June 30, 2003, 827 bachelor's degrees were awarded. The most popular majors were business/marketing (25%), liberal arts (15%), and communications (12%). In an average class, 68% graduate in 4 years or less, 78% graduate in 5 years or less, and 80% graduate in 6 years or less. 115 companies recruited on campus in 2002-2003. Of the 2002 graduating class, 23% were enrolled in graduate school within 6 months of graduation and 68% were employed.

Admissions Contact: Marc Camille, Dean of Admission. A video is available. E-mail: *xuadmit@xu.edu* Web: *www.xavier.edu*

YOUNGSTOWN STATE UNIVERSITY

Youngstown, OH 44555-0001	**C-2**
	(330) 941-2000
	(877) 468-6978; Fax: (330) 941-3674
Full-time: 4211 men, 4947 women	**Faculty:** 407; IIA, +$
Part-time: 1027 men, 1413 women	**Ph.D.s:** 83%
Graduate: 451 men, 809 women	**Student/Faculty:** 23 to 1
Year: semesters, summer session	**Tuition:** $5448 ($10,656)
Application Deadline: August 15	**Room & Board:** $5700
Freshman Class: 3761 applied, 3647 accepted, 2191 enrolled	
ACT: 20	**NONCOMPETITIVE**

Youngstown State University, founded in 1908, is a publicly funded, primarily commuter institution offering undergraduate and graduate programs in the arts and sciences, education, business, engineering, fine and performing arts, and health and human services. There are 6 undergraduate schools and 1 graduate school. In addition to regional accreditation, YSU has baccalaureate program accreditation with AACSB, ABET, ADA, CAAHEP, CAHEA, CSWE, NAACLS, NASAD, NASM, NCATE, and NLN. The library contains 897,608 volumes, 911,738 microform items, and 19,116 audio/video tapes/CDs, and subscribes to

2500 periodicals. Computerized library services include the card catalog, interlibrary loans, database searching, and Internet access. Special learning facilities include a learning resource center, art gallery, planetarium, radio station, and center for historic preservation. The 200-acre campus is in an urban area 65 miles southeast of Cleveland. Including any residence halls, there are 47 buildings.

Student Life: 90% of undergraduates are from Ohio. Students are from 40 states, 58 foreign countries, and Canada. 80% are white; 10% African American. The average age of freshmen is 20; all undergraduates, 24. 31% do not continue beyond their first year; 38% remain to graduate.

Housing: 1300 students can be accommodated in college housing, which includes single-sex and coed dorms and on-campus apartments. In addition, there are honors houses, an international living-learning center, off-campus fraternity and sorority houses, and junior, senior, and graduate housing. On-campus housing is available on a first-come, first-served basis and is available on a lottery system for upperclassmen. 90% of students commute. Alcohol is not permitted. All students may keep cars.

Activities: 4% of men belong to 8 national fraternities; 3% of women belong to 1 local and 4 national sororities. There are 130 groups on campus, including art, band, cheerleading, chess, choir, chorale, chorus, computers, dance, drama, ethnic, film, gay, honors, international, jazz band, literary magazine, marching band, musical theater, newspaper, opera, orchestra, pep band, photography, political, professional, radio and TV, religious, social, social service, student government, and symphony. Popular campus events include Organizational Fair, Greek Sing, and Career Night.

Sports: There are 8 intercollegiate sports for men and 10 for women, and 26 intramural sports for men and 26 for women. Facilities include a sports complex with a 20,360-seat stadium, an artificial turf field for football and soccer, racquetball courts, gyms, weight rooms, an all-weather 400-meter track, outdoor basketball, handball, and volleyball courts, and 10 lighted tennis courts. There is also a phys ed center with a 7000-spectator gym, an Olympic-size swimming pool, a dance studio, a rifle range, a fitness center, racquetball and squash courts, and separate gyms for wrestling, weight lifting, gymnastics, and the disabled.

Disabled Students: 98% of the campus is accessible. Wheelchair ramps, elevators, special parking, specially equipped rest rooms, special class scheduling, lowered drinking fountains, lowered telephones, an escort service, a mobility cart, adaptive computers, a lounge, books on tape, institutional memberships, interpreters, a test proctoring program, TDD, and other adaptive equipment are available.

Services: Counseling and information services are available, as is tutoring in most subjects. There is a reader service for the blind and remedial math, reading, and writing. A foreign language lab is also available.

Campus Safety and Security: Measures include 24-hour foot and vehicle patrol, self-defense education, security escort services, and shuttle buses. There are informal discussions, pamphlets/posters/films, emergency telephones, lighted pathways/sidewalks, night security posts in dorms, and concentrated security in parking and other critical areas.

Programs of Study: YSU confers A.B., B.S., B.Eng., B.F.A., B.M., B.S.Appl.Sci., B.S.B.A., B.S.Ed., B.S.N., B.S.R.C., and B.S.W. degrees. Associate, master's, and doctoral degrees are also awarded. Bachelor's degrees are awarded in BIOLOGICAL SCIENCE (biology/biological science and nutrition), BUSINESS (accounting, apparel and accessories marketing, banking and finance, business administration and management, business economics, fashion merchandising, hospitality management services, hotel/motel and restaurant management, international economics, labor studies, management information systems, marketing and distribution, marketing management, marketing/retailing/merchandising, office supervision and management, personnel management, retailing, and secretarial studies/office management), COMMUNICATIONS AND THE ARTS (advertising, art, art history and appreciation, broadcasting, communications, dramatic arts, drawing, English, French, graphic design, Italian, journalism, languages, music, music history and appreciation, music performance, music theory and composition, musical theater, painting, percussion, performing arts, photography, piano/organ, printmaking, public relations, Spanish, speech/debate/rhetoric, studio art, technical and business writing, telecommunications, voice, and winds), COMPUTER AND PHYSICAL SCIENCE (astronomy, chemistry, computer programming, computer science, data processing, earth science, geology, information sciences and systems, mathematics, physics, and science), EDUCATION (art, business, computer, drama, early childhood, education, education of the emotionally handicapped, education of the mentally handicapped, education of the multiply handicapped, elementary, English, foreign languages, health, home economics, mathematics, middle school, music, physical, science, secondary, social science, social studies, special, specific learning disabilities, and vocational), ENGINEERING AND ENVIRONMENTAL DESIGN (chemical engineering, civil engineering, civil engineering technology, computer technology, drafting and design, drafting and design technology, electrical/electronics engineering, electrical/electronics engineering technology, engineering, engineering technology, environmental science, industrial administration/management, industrial engineering, materials engineering, mechanical engineering, mechanical engineering technology, preengineering, and systems engineering), HEALTH PROFESSIONS (allied health, community health work, dental hygiene, health, health science, medical laboratory technology, medical technology, nursing, physical therapy, predentistry, premedicine, preoptometry, preosteopathy, prepharmacy, preveterinary science, and respiratory therapy), SOCIAL SCIENCE (African studies, American studies, anthropology, child care/child and family studies, corrections, criminal justice, dietetics, early childhood studies, economics, family and community services, family/consumer studies, fashion design and technology, forensic studies, geography, history, home economics, human ecology, law enforcement and corrections, philosophy, physical fitness/movement, political science/government, prelaw, psychology, public administration, religion, safety and security technology, social science, social studies, social work, and sociology). Early childhood education, management, and nursing are the largest.

Required: To graduate, students must complete 124 to 132 semester hours, depending on the major, with a minimum GPA of 2.0. At least 60 semester hours in the major are required. All students must fulfill core requirements, including 2 to 3 courses each in natural science, artistic and literary perspective, and societies and institutions, and 2 courses in personal and social responsibility. Requirements must also be met in English, speech, and math.

Special: YSU offers co-op programs in business and engineering, internships, dual majors, credit for military experience, nondegree study, honors degree programs, distance learning, a joint engineering program, accelerated degrees in medicine and chemistry, and pass/fail options. Student-designed majors are available through the Individualized Curriculum Program. There are 25 national honor societies, a freshman honors program, and 6 departmental honors programs.

Faculty/Classroom: 64% of faculty are male; 36%, female. All teach undergraduates. Graduate students teach 10% of introductory courses. The average class size in an introductory lecture is 32; in a laboratory, 10; and in a regular course, 22.

Admissions: 97% of the 2003-2004 applicants were accepted. The ACT scores for the 2003-2004 freshman class were: 54% below 21, 24% between 21 and 23, 14% between 24 and 26, 5% between 27 and 28, and 3% above 28. 21% of the current freshmen were in the top fifth of their class; 41% were in the top two fifths.

Requirements: The SAT I or ACT is required. Those who have been out of school for 2 or more years, and who are not pursuing a restricted program of study, are exempt from test requirements. Out-of-state applicants must rank in the upper two thirds of their class or have a combined SAT I score of 820 or higher or 17 or higher composite on the ACT. Graduation from an accredited secondary school or satisfactory scores on the GED are required for all applicants. High school courses must include 4 units of English, 3 each of math, science, and social studies, 2 of foreign language, and 1 of fine or performing arts. AP and CLEP credits are accepted.

Procedure: Freshmen are admitted fall, spring, and summer. Entrance exams should be taken in spring of the junior year or fall of the senior year. There are early admissions and deferred admissions plans. There is a rolling admissions plan. Early decision applications should be filed by February 15; regular applications, by August 15 for fall entry, December 15 for spring entry, and April 15 for summer entry. The fall 2003 application fee was $30. The college accepts all in-state residents. Notification is sent on a rolling basis.

Transfer: 549 transfer students enrolled in 2002-2003. Transfer students must provide transcripts from all secondary schools and colleges attended. Non-Ohio residents must have a minimum GPA of 2.0; those with a lower GPA may be admitted if high school grades and test scores show potential. Ohio residents with a GPA of 2.0 or higher are accepted in good standing; those with a GPA of less than 2.0 or on probation are admitted on probation. If the GPA is below 2.0, the student will be automatically subjected to an appeal process for possible entrance into the university. 30 credits of 124 to 132 required for the bachelor's degree must be completed at YSU.

Visiting: There are regularly scheduled orientations for prospective students. There are guides for informal visits and visitors may sit in on classes. To schedule a visit, contact the Office of Undergraduate Admissions at *enroll@ysu.edu.*

Financial Aid: In 2002-2003, 87% of all full-time freshmen and 82% of continuing full-time students received some form of financial aid. 42% of full-time freshmen and 40% of continuing full-time students received need-based aid. The FAFSA and the college's own financial statement are required. The deadline for filing freshman financial aid applications for fall entry is February 15.

International Students: There are 135 international students enrolled. The school actively recruits these students. They must score 500 on the written TOEFL or 173 on the electronic version or take the MELAB, and also take SAT II: Subject tests.

Computers: The mainframe is an IBM 7060-H30 multiprise 3000 server. There are approximately 100 terminals in various locations to access student on-line registration and on-line transcripts. There are approximately 1620 PCs that access the mainframe and Internet. There are 55 computer labs. All students may access the system. There are no time limits and no fees.

Graduates: From July 1, 2002 to June 30, 2003, 1387 bachelor's degrees were awarded. The most popular majors were teacher education (15%), criminal justice (5%), and management (4%). In an average class, 1% graduate in 3 years or less, 14% graduate in 4 years or less, 30% graduate in 5 years or less, and 38% graduate in 6 years or less.

Admissions Contact: Sue Davis, Director, Undergraduate Admissions. E-mail: *enroll@.ysu.edu* Web: *www.ysu.edu*

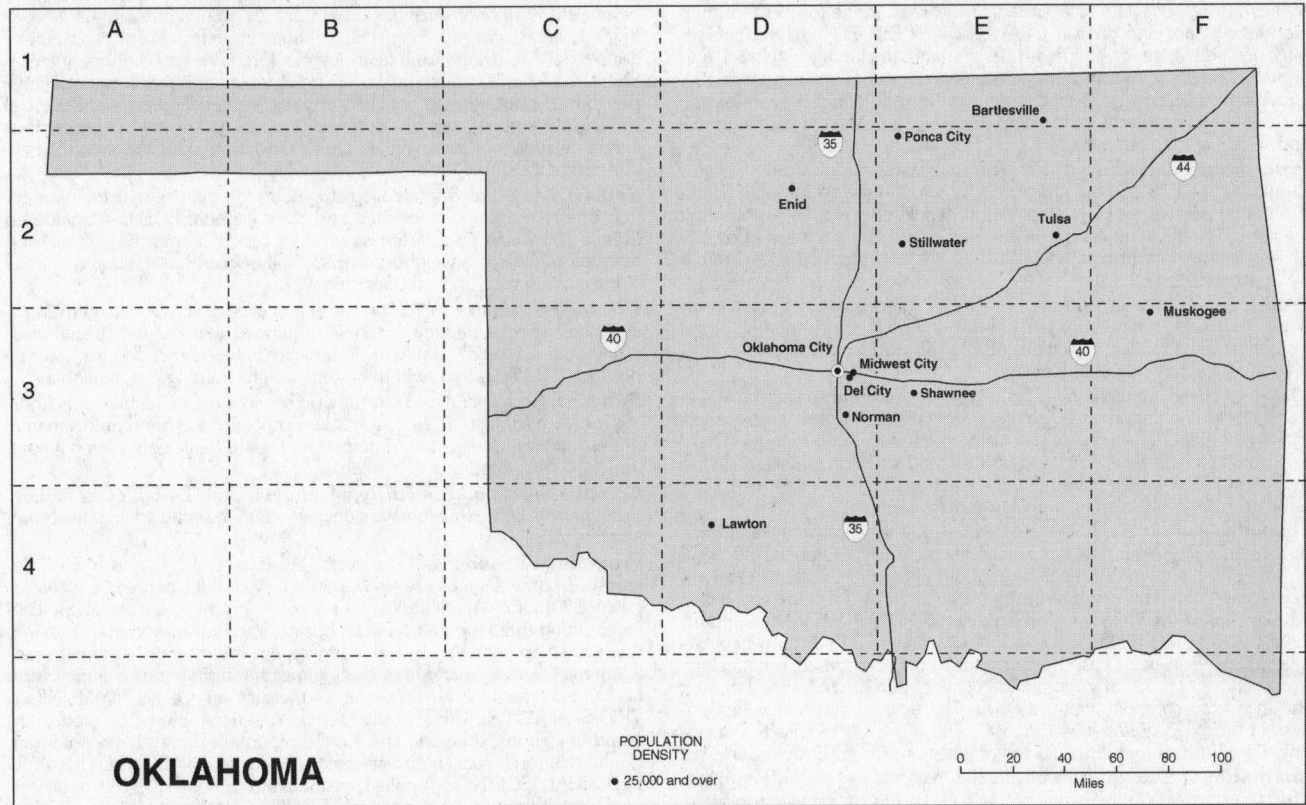

OKLAHOMA

POPULATION
DENSITY

● 25,000 and over

0 20 40 60 80 100
Miles

BARTLESVILLE WESLEYAN COLLEGE
(See Oklahoma Wesleyan University)

CAMERON UNIVERSITY
Lawton, OK 73505-6377

D-4

(580) 581-2230 or 2289
(888)-454-7600; Fax: (580) 581-5514

Full-time: 1311 men, 1786 women	**Faculty:** 192; IIB, --$
Part-time: 912 men, 1196 women	**Ph.D.s:** 63%
Graduate: 124 men, 297 women	**Student/Faculty:** 16 to 1
Year: semesters, summer session	**Tuition:** $2838 ($6738)
Application Deadline: open	**Room & Board:** $2854
Freshman Class: n/av	
ACT: 19	**NONCOMPETITIVE**

Cameron University, founded in 1908, is a publicly funded institution offering undergraduate programs in business, education and psychology, fine arts, liberal arts, science, mathematics, and technology. There are 3 undergraduate schools and 1 graduate school. In addition to regional accreditation, Cameron has baccalaureate program accreditation with ACBSP, ADDA, NASM, NCATE, and NLN. The library contains 263,251 volumes, 540,706 microform items, and 7918 audio/video tapes/CDs, and subscribes to 1140 periodicals. Computerized library services include the card catalog, interlibrary loans, database searching, and Internet access. Special learning facilities include a learning resource center, art gallery, radio station, and TV station. The 160-acre campus is in a suburban area 90 miles southwest of Oklahoma City. Including any residence halls, there are 30 buildings.

Student Life: 88% of undergraduates are from Oklahoma. Students are from 21 states, 36 foreign countries, and Canada. 97% are from public schools. 60% are white; 19% African American. The average age of freshmen is 23; all undergraduates, 25.

Housing: 512 students can be accommodated in college housing, which includes single-sex dorms. On-campus housing is guaranteed for all 4 years. 99% of students commute. Alcohol is not permitted. All students may keep cars.

Activities: 4% of men belong to 2 national fraternities; 6% of women belong to 2 national sororities. There are 65 groups on campus, including art, band, cheerleading, computers, debate, drama, drill team, ethnic, forensics, gay, honors, international, jazz band, literary magazine, newspaper, orchestra, pep band, political, professional, radio and TV,

religious, social, social service, student government, and yearbook. Popular campus events include Spring Fling, Diversity Week, and Organizational Day.

Sports: There are 4 intercollegiate sports for men and 4 for women, and 6 intramural sports for men and 6 for women. Facilities include a 10,000-seat football stadium, an 1800-seat gym, an 800-seat baseball park, a running track, Nautilus and free-weight rooms, an indoor swimming pool, and basketball, volleyball, and racquetball courts.

Disabled Students: 80% of the campus is accessible. Wheelchair ramps, elevators, special parking, specially equipped rest rooms, special class scheduling, lowered drinking fountains, and lowered telephones are available.

Services: Counseling and information services are available, as is tutoring in some subjects, including writing, reading, accounting, math, fine arts, technology, and computer science. There is remedial math, reading, and writing.

Campus Safety and Security: Measures include 24-hour foot and vehicle patrol, security escort services, pamphlets/posters/films, and emergency telephones. There are lighted pathways/sidewalks.

Programs of Study: Cameron confers B.A., B.S., B.Acctg., B.B.A., B.F.A., and B.Mus. degrees. Associate and master's degrees are also awarded. Bachelor's degrees are awarded in AGRICULTURE (agriculture), BIOLOGICAL SCIENCE (biology/biological science), BUSINESS (accounting and business administration and management), COMMUNICATIONS AND THE ARTS (art, communications, English, multimedia, music, and romance languages and literature), COMPUTER AND PHYSICAL SCIENCE (chemistry, computer science, mathematics, natural sciences, and physics), EDUCATION (elementary and physical), ENGINEERING AND ENVIRONMENTAL DESIGN (technology and public affairs), HEALTH PROFESSIONS (health), SOCIAL SCIENCE (criminal justice, history, human ecology, interdisciplinary studies, liberal arts/general studies, political science/government, psychology, and sociology). Elementary education and criminal justice are the largest.

Required: To graduate, students must complete a total of 128 credit hours with a minimum GPA of 2.0. All students must take courses in English, math, science, U.S. history and government, humanities, behavioral science, economics, and phys ed.

Special: Cameron offers dual majors in several fields, an interdisciplinary studies degree, nondegree study, and credit for military experience. There are 18 national honor societies, a freshman honors program, and 11 departmental honors programs.

Faculty/Classroom: 63% of faculty are male; 36%, female. All both teach and do research. The average class size in an introductory lecture is 50; in a laboratory, 30; and in a regular course, 30.

Requirements: The SAT I or ACT is required, with minimum scores of 890 or 20, respectively, or applicants must rank in the top 50% of their graduating class and have a GPA of at least 2.7. High school courses must include 4 years of English, 3 of math (including algebra I and above), 2 each of history and lab science, 1 of economics, geography, government, or non-Western culture, and an additional 3 years of any of the previous subjects, or of computer science or foreign language. AP and CLEP credits are accepted.

Procedure: Freshmen are admitted to all sessions. Entrance exams should be taken late in the junior year or early in the senior year. There is a rolling admissions plan. Application deadlines are open. Application fee is $15. Notification is sent on a rolling basis, within a week of receipt of application documents. Applications are accepted on-line through *www.cameron.edu.*

Transfer: 365 transfer students enrolled in a recent year. Transfer students must have a minimum GPA of 2.0 and be in good standing at the institution last attended. 30 credits of 128 required for the bachelor's degree must be completed at Cameron.

Visiting: There are regularly scheduled orientations for prospective students, including introductory sessions on college life and student services, with department chairs and enrollment, and campus tours. There are guides for informal visits and visitors may sit in on classes and stay overnight. To schedule a visit, contact Brenda Dally, Admissions Counselor at (580) 581-2837 or *brenda@cameron.edu.*

Financial Aid: In 2003-2004, 90% of all full-time freshmen and 85% of continuing full-time students received some form of financial aid. 85% of full-time freshmen and 83% of continuing full-time students received need-based aid. The average freshman award was $3000. Need-based scholarships or need-based grants averaged $2000 ($9376 maximum); need-based self-help aid (loans and jobs) averaged $1500 ($4625 maximum); and non-need-based awards and non-need-based scholarships averaged $800. 70% of undergraduates work part time. Average annual earnings from campus work are $800. The average financial indebtedness of the 2003 graduate was $6300. The FAFSA is required. The priority date for freshman financial aid applications for fall entry is June 15.

International Students: There are 202 international students enrolled. They must score 500 on the written TOEFL or 173 on the electronic version if from non-English speaking countries, and also take the SAT I or the ACT, scoring 19 on the ACT, if under 21 years of age.

Computers: The mainframe is an HP/3000 Series 960. Students may access the Internet and various academic programs using more than 800 PCs in 15 labs. Dorm rooms have network connections. All students may access the system 7:30 A.M. to 11 P.M. daily. There are no time limits and no fees.

Graduates: From July 1, 2002 to June 30, 2003, 540 bachelor's degrees were awarded. The most popular majors were criminal justice (9%), elementary education (9%), and accounting (8%). In an average class, 31% graduate in 6 years or less. Approximately 50 companies recruited on campus in 2002-2003.

Admissions Contact: Zoe Du Rant, Director of Admissions.
E-mail: *zoed@cameron.edu* Web: *www.cameron.edu*

EAST CENTRAL UNIVERSITY
Ada, OK 74820

E-4

(580) 332-8000; Fax: (580) 310-5432

Full-time: 1342 men, 1817 women	Faculty: 157; IIA, --$
Part-time: 168 men, 361 women	Ph.D.s: 70%
Graduate: 227 men, 559 women	Student/Faculty: 20 to 1
Year: semesters, summer session	Tuition: $2194 ($5314)
Application Deadline: open	Room & Board: $2774
Freshman Class: 642 enrolled	
ACT: 21	COMPETITIVE

East Central University, founded in 1909, is a publicly funded institution offering undergraduate programs in liberal arts and sciences, education, business, and health-related fields. There are 4 undergraduate schools and 1 graduate school. In addition to regional accreditation, ECU has baccalaureate program accreditation with ACBSP, CSWE, NASM, NCATE, and NLN. The library contains 215,000 volumes, 1 million microform items, and 7000 audio/video tapes/CDs, and subscribes to 1200 periodicals. Computerized library services include the card catalog, interlibrary loans, database searching, and Internet access. Special learning facilities include a learning resource center, art gallery, and an observatory. The 140-acre campus is in a small town 90 miles south of Oklahoma City. Including any residence halls, there are 28 buildings.

Student Life: 97% of undergraduates are from Oklahoma. Students are from 25 foreign countries and Canada. 99% are from public schools. 72% are white; 18% Native American/Eskimo. The average age of freshmen is 19; all undergraduates, 24. 38% do not continue beyond their first year.

Housing: 1121 students can be accommodated in college housing, which includes single-sex and coed dorms, on-campus apartments, married-student housing, fraternity houses, and sorority houses. On-campus housing is available on a first-come, first-served basis. Alcohol is not permitted. All students may keep cars.

Activities: 8% of men belong to 4 national fraternities; 8% of women belong to 3 national sororities. There are 76 groups on campus, including art, band, cheerleading, chess, choir, chorale, chorus, computers, dance, debate, drama, drill team, ethnic, forensics, gay, honors, international, jazz band, marching band, newspaper, nontraditional students, pep band, photography, political, professional, religious, social, social service, student government, symphony, and yearbook. Popular campus events include Welcome Week, Don't Go Home This Weekend Weekend, and Christmas in the Eyes of a Child.

Sports: There are 6 intercollegiate sports for men and 5 for women, and 8 intramural sports for men and 8 for women. Facilities include an indoor swimming pool, a fitness/aerobics center, tennis, basketball, and racquetball courts, a weight room, football, soccer, baseball, and softball fields, and indoor and outdoor tracks.

Disabled Students: All of the campus is accessible. Wheelchair ramps, elevators, special parking, specially equipped rest rooms, special class scheduling, lowered drinking fountains, lowered telephones, special housing, and adaptive swimming and weight training are available.

Services: Counseling and information services are available, as is tutoring in every subject. There is a reader service for the blind and remedial math, reading, and writing. Interpreters for the deaf, note taking/typing, and tape transcription are available.

Campus Safety and Security: Measures include 24-hour foot and vehicle patrol, lighted pathways/sidewalks, and training in the freshman seminar class.

Programs of Study: ECU confers B.A., B.S., B.S.Ed., and B.S.W. degrees. Master's degrees are also awarded. Bachelor's degrees are awarded in BIOLOGICAL SCIENCE (biology/biological science), BUSINESS (accounting, banking and finance, business administration and management, fashion merchandising, management information systems, management science, marketing/retailing/merchandising, office supervision and management, and recreation and leisure services), COMMUNICATIONS AND THE ARTS (advertising, American Sign Language, art, communications, dramatic arts, English, journalism, music, piano/organ, public relations, speech/debate/rhetoric, and voice), COMPUTER AND PHYSICAL SCIENCE (applied mathematics, chemistry, computer science, mathematics, and physics), EDUCATION (art, athletic training, business, drama, early childhood, elementary, English, health, home economics, mathematics, music, physical, science, secondary, and special), ENGINEERING AND ENVIRONMENTAL DESIGN (cartography), HEALTH PROFESSIONS (environmental health science, exercise science, medical laboratory technology, medical records administration/services, nursing, and rehabilitation therapy), SOCIAL SCIENCE (criminal justice, family/consumer resource management, gerontology, history, human services, liberal arts/general studies, paralegal studies, political science/government, prelaw, psychology, social work, and sociology). Nursing, human resources, and elementary education are the largest.

Required: To graduate, students must complete a minimum of 124 credit hours with a minimum GPA of 2.0. Between 45 and 55 hours must be completed in the major and 18 to 21 hours in the minor. All students must take 40 hours of upper-level courses, as well as 45 hours in general studies, and must meet computer proficiency requirements.

Special: The school offers co-op programs with the Ardmore Higher Education Center and is a member of the National Student Exchange Program. Internships are available in human resources, environmental health, political science, office technology, mass communications, and cartography. Students may participate in a work-study program with the Veterans Administration. Nondegree study and credit for military experience are available. The school offers special rates for nonresidents from approved states who wish to major in specialized fields. There is 1 national honor society, Phi Beta Kappa, and a freshman honors program.

Faculty/Classroom: 61% of faculty are male; 39%, female. No introductory courses are taught by graduate students. The average class size in an introductory lecture is 30 and in a laboratory, 30.

Admissions: The ACT scores for the 2003-2004 freshman class were: 53% below 21, 25% between 21 and 23, 14% between 24 and 26, 5% between 27 and 28, and 3% above 28. 43% of the current freshmen were in the top quarter of their class; 77% were in the top half.

Requirements: The ACT is required, with a minimum composite score of 20. The SAT I will be accepted in place of the ACT. Applicants must be graduates of an accredited secondary school or have the GED. High school courses must include 4 years of English, 3 years of math, and 2 years each of history and science. ECU requires applicants to be in the upper 50% of their class. A GPA of 2.7 is required. AP and CLEP credits are accepted.

Procedure: Freshmen are admitted to all sessions. Entrance exams should be taken during the junior or senior year of high school. Application deadlines are open. Applications are accepted on-line.

Transfer: 384 transfer students enrolled in a recent year. Applicants having fewer than 24 credit hours must meet the criteria for entering freshmen. The required minimum GPA for transfer students is 2.0. 30

credits of 124 required for the bachelor's degree must be completed at ECU.

Visiting: There are regularly scheduled orientations for prospective students. There are guides for informal visits. To schedule a visit, contact the Student Services Office at (877) 310-5628.

Financial Aid: 22% of undergraduates work part time. Average annual earnings from campus work are $1732. The average financial indebtedness of a recent graduate was $13,243. The FAFSA, the college's own financial statement, and federal tax returns are required. Check with the school for current application deadlines.

International Students: There were 83 international students enrolled in a recent year. The school actively recruits these students. They must score 500 on the written TOEFL. Students may be required to take the ACT upon arrival.

Computers: The mainframe is an HP 3000. There are PCs available in the library and in various departments. All students have access to the Internet. All students may access the system when labs are open. There are no time limits and no fees.

Graduates: In a recent year, 513 bachelor's degrees were awarded.

Admissions Contact: Pamla Armstrong, Registrar and Director of Admissions. E-mail: *parmstro@mailclerk.ecok.edu* Web: *www.ecok.edu*

LANGSTON UNIVERSITY
Langston, OK 73050

D-3

(405) 466-3224; Fax: (405) 466-3381

Full-time: 1290 men, 1920 women	Faculty: 105
Part-time: 290 men, 520 women	Ph.D.s: 50%
Graduate: 20 men, 40 women	Student/Faculty: 31 to 1
Year: semesters, summer session	Tuition: $2310 ($5055)
Application Deadline: open	Room & Board: n/app
Freshman Class: n/av	
SAT I or ACT: required	LESS COMPETITIVE

Langston University, founded in 1897 as the Colored Agricultural and Normal University, is today a multiracial, public institution offering programs in liberal arts, business, allied health, and teacher preparation. Figures in the above capsule and in this profile are approximate. In addition to regional accreditation, Langston has baccalaureate program accreditation with ADA, APTA, NCATE, and NLN. The 6 libraries contain 110,248 volumes and 465,319 microform items, and subscribe to 80 periodicals. Computerized library services include the card catalog and interlibrary loans. Special learning facilities include a learning resource center, satellite teaching, a black heritage center, an institute for goat research, and a state research group in catfish production. The 40-acre campus is in a rural area 45 miles from Oklahoma City. Including any residence halls, there are 20 buildings.

Student Life: 98% are from public schools. 50% are African American; 50% white. 65% of freshmen remain to graduate.

Housing: 676 students can be accommodated in college housing, which includes dorms and married-student housing. Alcohol is not permitted. All students may keep cars.

Activities: 25% of men belong to 4 national fraternities; 30% of women belong to 4 national sororities. There are 30 groups on campus, including band, cheerleading, choir, drama, ethnic, international, jazz band, marching band, newspaper, professional, religious, social service, student government, and yearbook. Popular campus events include student theater productions and a performing arts series.

Sports: There are 4 intercollegiate sports for men and 2 for women, and 6 intramural sports for men and 5 for women. Facilities include a gym, tennis courts, a baseball field, and a track.

Disabled Students: 70% of the campus is accessible. Wheelchair ramps, elevators, special parking, specially equipped rest rooms, and special class scheduling are available.

Services: Counseling and information services are available, as is tutoring in some subjects. There is remedial math, reading, and writing.

Programs of Study: Langston confers B.A., B.B.A., B.S., B.S.Ed., and B.S.N. degrees. Associate and master's degrees are also awarded. Bachelor's degrees are awarded in AGRICULTURE (agricultural economics and animal science), BIOLOGICAL SCIENCE (biology/biological science and nutrition), BUSINESS (accounting, business administration and management, and management science), COMMUNICATIONS AND THE ARTS (dramatic arts, English, music, and speech/debate/rhetoric), COMPUTER AND PHYSICAL SCIENCE (chemistry, computer science, and mathematics), EDUCATION (business, elementary, home economics, industrial arts, mathematics, physical, and science), ENGINEERING AND ENVIRONMENTAL DESIGN (industrial engineering technology), HEALTH PROFESSIONS (health care administration, medical laboratory technology, nursing, and physical therapy), SOCIAL SCIENCE (criminal justice, early childhood studies, economics, gerontology, history, home economics, psychology, social science, sociology, and urban studies).

Required: To graduate, students must complete a total of 124 semester hours, with a GPA of 2.0. The required general education core consists of 50 credits in English, math, computer science, biological and physical sciences, social science, and health and phys ed. 6 credits are required

in American history and government, and all students must complete an internship or field experience.

Special: Work-study programs, internships, and nondegree and noncredit study are available. There are 6 national honor societies and a freshman honors program.

Faculty/Classroom: All teach undergraduates.

Requirements: The SAT I or ACT is required. In general, test scores should place students in the upper 60 percent of Oklahoma high school seniors. Applicants should be graduates of accredited high schools with at least a C average (2.7 on a 4.0 scale) and rank in the upper 60 percent of their graduating classes. Required secondary preparation includes 4 years of English, 3 years of math, and 2 years each of lab science and history, including 1 year of American history. 4 additional academic units, including a foreign language, are strongly recommended. There are alternative admission programs for students with varying backgrounds. Langston requires applicants to be in the upper 50% of their class. A GPA of 2.7 is required. AP and CLEP credits are accepted.

Procedure: Freshmen are admitted to all sessions. There is a rolling admissions plan. Application deadlines are open. The fall 2003 application fee was $15.

Transfer: Applicants should be in good standing and have earned at least a C average in previous college work. 30 of 124 credits required for the bachelor's degree must be completed at Langston.

Visiting: There are regularly scheduled orientations for prospective students. There are guides for informal visits and visitors may sit in on classes and stay overnight. To schedule a visit, contact the High School/College Relations Office.

Financial Aid: The CSS Profile, FAFSA, FFS, or SFS is required. Check with the school for current deadlines.

International Students: They must score 500 on the written TOEFL.

Computers: The mainframes are a DEC VAX 11/750 and an IBM 34. There are also 40 PCs available in academic labs. There are no time limits and no fees.

Admissions Contact: Ms. Gayle T. Robertson, Driector of Admissions and Enrollment Management. E-mail: *gtrobertson@lunet.edu*

NORTHEASTERN STATE UNIVERSITY
Tahlequah, OK 74464

F-3

(918) 456-5511, ext. 2200
(800) 722-9614; Fax: (918) 458-2342

Full-time: 3300 men, 4210 women	Faculty: II A, --$
Part-time: 600 men, 1187 women	Ph.D.s: n/av
Graduate: 393 men, 271 women	Student/Faculty: n/av
Year: semesters, summer session	Tuition: $2100 ($4650)
Application Deadline: open	Room & Board: $2850
Freshman Class: 1832 applied, 1751 accepted, 1270 enrolled	
ACT: 24	LESS COMPETITIVE

Northeastern State University, founded in 1846, is a public institution offering programs in arts and sciences, professional training, teacher preparation, and business. There are 5 undergraduate schools and 1 graduate school. In addition to regional accreditation, NSU has baccalaureate program accreditation with ACBSP, ADA, ASLA, CSWE, NASM, NCATE, and NLN. The library contains 380,000 volumes, 604,000 microform items, and 7880 audio/video tapes/CDs, and subscribes to 3442 periodicals. Computerized library services include the card catalog and interlibrary loans. Special learning facilities include a learning resource center. The 200-acre campus is in a small town 70 miles from Tulsa. Including any residence halls, there are 43 buildings.

Student Life: 95% of undergraduates are from Oklahoma. Students are from 30 states, 41 foreign countries, and Canada. 64% are white; 28% Native American/Eskimo. The average age of freshmen is 19; all undergraduates, 26. 30% do not continue beyond their first year.

Housing: 1653 students can be accommodated in college housing, which includes single-sex and coed dorms and married-student housing. There are also rooming arrangements for special-interest groups. On-campus housing is available on a first-come, first-served basis. 80% of students commute. Alcohol is not permitted. All students may keep cars.

Activities: 10% of men belong to 6 national fraternities; 10% of women belong to 3 national sororities. There are 75 groups on campus, including art, band, cheerleading, choir, dance, drama, drill team, ethnic, honors, international, jazz band, literary magazine, marching band, newspaper, orchestra, pep band, political, professional, religious, social service, student government, and yearbook. Popular campus events include the Lyceum Series, Cherokee Seminaries, and NSU Playhouse events.

Sports: There are 7 intercollegiate sports for men and 5 for women, and 4 intramural sports for men and 3 for women. Facilities include a swimming pool, a softball/soccer complex, a weight room, playing fields, a 10,000-seat track and football stadium, and basketball, handball, and racquetball courts.

Disabled Students: 98% of the campus is accessible. Wheelchair ramps, elevators, special parking, specially equipped rest rooms, lowered drinking fountains, and lowered telephones are available.

Services: Counseling and information services are available, as is tutoring in most subjects. There is remedial math, reading, and writing.

Campus Safety and Security: Measures include 24-hour foot and vehicle patrol, security escort services, shuttle buses, and informal discussions. There are pamphlets/posters/films, emergency telephones, and lighted pathways/sidewalks. There is a campus security police department.

Programs of Study: NSU confers B.A., B.S., B.A.Ed., B.B.A., B.S.Ed., B.S.Sci.Ed., B.S.N., and B.S.W. degrees. Master's and doctoral degrees are also awarded. Bachelor's degrees are awarded in BIOLOGICAL SCIENCE (biology/biological science and zoology), BUSINESS (accounting, banking and finance, business administration and management, and marketing/retailing/merchandising), COMMUNICATIONS AND THE ARTS (advertising, communications, English, fine arts, journalism, music, Spanish, and speech/debate/rhetoric), COMPUTER AND PHYSICAL SCIENCE (chemistry, computer science, information sciences and systems, mathematics, and physics), EDUCATION (art, early childhood, elementary, health, home economics, industrial arts, music, science, secondary, and special), HEALTH PROFESSIONS (medical laboratory technology, nursing, predentistry, and premedicine), SOCIAL SCIENCE (criminal justice, geography, history, political science/government, prelaw, psychology, social science, social work, and sociology).

Required: To graduate, students must complete at least 124 credit hours, with 24 to 50 in the major. General education requirements include 40 hours in language arts, social science, natural science, humanities, and phys ed. Freshman orientation and English proficiency are required.

Special: NSU offers educational tours for academic credit, B.A.-B.S. degrees, a weekend program, nondegree study, credit by exam or for military experience, and a pass/fail option. There are 10 national honor societies, a freshman honors program, and 5 departmental honors programs.

Admissions: 96% of the 2003-2004 applicants were accepted.

Requirements: The ACT is required, with a minimum composite score of 20. Applicants should be high school graduates or have a GED. Students should have completed 4 years of English, 3 of math, and 2 each of history and science. NSU requires applicants to be in the upper 50% of their class. A GPA of 2.7 is required. AP and CLEP credits are accepted.

Procedure: Freshmen are admitted to all sessions. There is an early admissions plan. Application deadlines are open. Notification is sent on a rolling basis.

Transfer: Transfer applicants must have a minimum GPA of 2.0, with 24 transfer hours completed, and be in good standing at the last institution attended. 30 credits of 124 required for the bachelor's degree must be completed at NSU.

Visiting: There are regularly scheduled orientations for prospective students, including a general campus visit with highlights presented by trained tour guides. Visitors may sit in on classes and stay overnight. To schedule a visit, contact High School and College Relations at (918) 458-2130.

Financial Aid: In a recent year, 62% of all full-time freshmen and 69% of continuing full-time students received some form of financial aid. 57% of full-time freshmen and 69% of continuing full-time students received need-based aid. The average freshman award was $7075. 41% of undergraduates work part time. Average annual earnings from campus work are $2480. The average financial indebtedness of a recent graduate was $7436. The FAFSA and the college's own financial statement are required. The deadline for filing freshman financial aid applications for fall entry is April 30.

International Students: There were 41 international students enrolled in a recent year. They must score 500 on the written TOEFL or 173 on the electronic version.

Computers: Macs and TRS 80 PCs are available in classrooms and labs. Computer labs are located all over campus; there are terminal ports in each dorm room. All students may access the system.

Graduates: In a recent year, 1258 bachelor's degrees were awarded.

Admissions Contact: Dawn Cain, Director of Admissions.
E-mail: *nsuinfo@nsuok.edu* Web: *www.nsuok.edu*

NORTHWESTERN OKLAHOMA STATE UNIVERSITY   C-1
Alva, OK 73717   (580) 327-8546; Fax: (580) 327-8413

Full-time: 560 men, 707 women	**Faculty:** 85
Part-time: 208 men, 330 women	**Ph.D.s:** 51%
Graduate: 74 men, 169 women	**Student/Faculty:** 15 to 1
Year: semesters, summer session	**Tuition:** $2713 ($6613)
Application Deadline: open	**Room & Board:** $2720
Freshman Class: 376 applied, 308 enrolled	
ACT: 20	**NONCOMPETITIVE**

Northwestern Oklahoma State University, founded in 1897, is a public institution offering programs in liberal and fine arts, agriculture, business, professional training, and teacher preparation. Enrollment figures in the above capsule are from 2002. There are 2 undergraduate schools and 1 graduate school. In addition to regional accreditation, Northwestern has baccalaureate program accreditation with NCATE and NLN. The library contains 135,000 volumes, 366,000 microform items, and 1100 audio/video tapes/CDs, and subscribes to 1480 periodicals. Computerized library services include interlibrary loans, database searching, and Internet access. Special learning facilities include a learning resource center, natural history museum, radio station, TV station, and a cable channel. The 70-acre campus is in a small town 150 miles northwest of Oklahoma City. Including any residence halls, there are 35 buildings.

Student Life: 83% of undergraduates are from Oklahoma. Students are from 29 states, 27 foreign countries, and Canada. 89% are white. The average age of freshmen is 21; all undergraduates, 24. 34% do not continue beyond their first year; 35% remain to graduate.

Housing: 872 students can be accommodated in college housing, which includes single-sex dorms and a dorm with all private rooms for junior and senior women. On-campus housing is guaranteed for all 4 years. Alcohol is not permitted. All students may keep cars.

Activities: 1% of men belong to 1 national fraternity; there is 1 local and 1 national sorority. There are 39 groups on campus, including art, band, cheerleading, choir, chorale, computers, dance, drama, ethnic, forensics, honors, international, jazz band, marching band, musical theater, newspaper, pep band, photography, political, professional, radio and TV, religious, social, student government, and yearbook. Popular campus events include Foundation Scholarship Banquet, Alumni Banquet, and Science Fair.

Sports: There are 4 intercollegiate sports for men and 2 for women, and 4 intramural sports for men and 4 for women. Facilities include a field house, playing fields, a basketball court, a pool, and racquetball and tennis courts.

Disabled Students: Wheelchair ramps, elevators, special parking, specially equipped rest rooms, special class scheduling, and lowered drinking fountains, are available. Northwestern works with disabled students to accommodate their special needs.

Services: Counseling and information services are available, as is tutoring in most subjects. There is remedial math, reading, and writing.

Campus Safety and Security: Measures include 24-hour foot and vehicle patrol and lighted pathways/sidewalks.

Programs of Study: Northwestern confers B.A., B.S., B.A.Ed., B.S.Ed., and B.S.N. degrees. Master's degrees are also awarded. Bachelor's degrees are awarded in AGRICULTURE (agricultural business management, agriculture, and conservation and regulation), BIOLOGICAL SCIENCE (biology/biological science), BUSINESS (accounting, business administration and management, and office supervision and management), COMMUNICATIONS AND THE ARTS (broadcasting, communications, dramatic arts, English, music, public relations, and speech/debate/rhetoric), COMPUTER AND PHYSICAL SCIENCE (chemistry, computer science, mathematics, and physics), EDUCATION (business, early childhood, elementary, English, library science, mathematics, music, physical, science, secondary, and special), HEALTH PROFESSIONS (medical laboratory technology and nursing), SOCIAL SCIENCE (criminal justice, economics, history, political science/government, psychology, social science, social work, and sociology). Education and business are the strongest academically and the largest.

Required: A total of 124 credit hours is required, including at least 40 in the major, with a minimum GPA of 2.0. General education courses total 54 semester hours, including 19 hours in communication and humanities, 15 in social and behavioral science, 11 in math and natural science, and 9 in phys ed and other practical arts. This general sequence totals 50 hours for education majors.

Special: Northwestern offers credit by exam and for military experience. There are 4 national honor societies and a freshman honors program.

Faculty/Classroom: 49% of faculty are male; 51%, female. All teach undergraduates. No introductory courses are taught by graduate students. The average class size in an introductory lecture is 38; in a laboratory, 24; and in a regular course, 19.

Admissions: The ACT scores for the 2003-2004 freshman class were: 56% below 21, 25% between 21 and 23, 12% between 24 and 26, 5% between 27 and 28, and 2% above 28.

Requirements: The ACT is required, with a minimum required score of 19. Applicants must be graduates of an accredited secondary school or have earned a GED. Northwestern requires 20 academic credits, including 4 in English, 3 in math, and 2 each in history and lab science. Northwestern requires applicants to be in the upper 50% of their class. A GPA of 2.7 is required. CLEP credit is accepted.

Procedure: Freshmen are admitted to all sessions. Entrance exams should be taken in the junior or senior year. Application deadlines are open. The fall 2003 application fee was $15. Notification is sent on a rolling basis.

Transfer: 242 transfer students enrolled in 2002-2003. Applicants must have a GPA of at least 2.0. 40 credits of 124 required for the bachelor's degree must be completed at Northwestern.

Visiting: There are regularly scheduled orientations for prospective students. In April, usually during 2 sessions, entering freshmen receive information, tour the campus, and enroll. There are guides for informal visits and visitors may sit in on classes and stay overnight. To schedule a visit, contact the Recruitment Office.

Financial Aid: 57% of undergraduates work part time. Average annual earnings from campus work are $2040. The FAFSA is required. The deadline for filing freshman financial aid applications for fall entry is June 1.

International Students: There are 27 international students enrolled. The school actively recruits these students. They must score 500 on the written TOEFL.

Computers: The mainframe is a DEC Alpha 2000 Model 4/233. More than 100 PCs provide students with mainframe access as well as applications software, web access, and e-mail. Computer labs are distributed across the campus. All students may access the system 8 A.M. to 8 P.M. There are no time limits and no fees.

Graduates: From July 1, 2002 to June 30, 2003, 306 bachelor's degrees were awarded. The most popular majors were business administration (15%), elementary education (9%), and psychology (9%). In an average class, 25% graduate in 4 years or less, 32% graduate in 5 years or less, and 35% graduate in 6 years or less. 25 companies recruited on campus in 2002-2003.

Admissions Contact: Dustin Smith, Director of Recruitment. A video is available. E-mail: *dpsmith@nwosu.edu* Web: *www.nwosu.edu*

OKLAHOMA BAPTIST UNIVERSITY
E-3
Shawnee, OK 74804

(405) 878-2033
(800) 654-3285; Fax: (405) 878-2046

Full-time: 593 men, 906 women	**Faculty:** 118; IIB, --$
Part-time: 232 men, 126 women	**Ph.D.s:** 77%
Graduate: 4 men, 13 women	**Student/Faculty:** 13 to 1
Year: 4-1-4, summer session	**Tuition:** $11,580
Application Deadline: August 1	**Room & Board:** $3640
Freshman Class: 1026 applied, 972 accepted, 404 enrolled	
SAT I Verbal/Math: 590/560	**ACT:** 25 **VERY COMPETITIVE**

Oklahoma Baptist University, founded in 1910, is a liberal arts institution affiliated with the Southern Baptist Convention. OBU offers degrees in Christian service, business, nursing, fine arts, telecommunications, teacher education, and the traditional liberal arts areas. There are 5 undergraduate schools and 1 graduate school. In addition to regional accreditation, OBU has baccalaureate program accreditation with ACBSP, NASM, NCATE, and NLN. The library contains 290,000 volumes, 230,000 microform items, and 1500 audio/video tapes/CDs, and subscribes to 600 periodicals. Computerized library services include the card catalog, interlibrary loans, and database searching. Special learning facilities include a learning resource center, planetarium, TV station, a language lab, and a Biblical research library. The 189-acre campus is in a small town 30 miles east of Oklahoma City and 90 miles southwest of Tulsa. Including any residence halls, there are 50 buildings.

Student Life: 61% of undergraduates are from Oklahoma. Students are from 42 states, 20 foreign countries, and Canada. 84% are from public schools. 85% are white; 11% Asian American. 88% are Protestant; 11% claim no religious affiliation. The average age of freshmen is 18; all undergraduates, 22. 24% do not continue beyond their first year; 58% remain to graduate.

Housing: 1390 students can be accommodated in college housing, which includes single-sex dorms, on-campus apartments, and married-student housing. On-campus housing is guaranteed for all 4 years. 70% of students live on campus; of those, 75% remain on campus on weekends. Alcohol is not permitted. All students may keep cars.

Activities: 16% of men belong to 5 local fraternities; 15% of women belong to 5 local sororities. There are 95 groups on campus, including art, band, cheerleading, choir, chorale, chorus, computers, drama, ethnic, film, honors, international, jazz band, literary magazine, musical theater, newspaper, opera, orchestra, pep band, photography, political, professional, radio and TV, religious, social, social service, student government, and yearbook. Popular campus events include Stampede of Stars, International Awareness Day, and Hanging of the Green.

Sports: There are 7 intercollegiate sports for men and 7 for women, and 10 intramural sports for men and 8 for women. Facilities include a sports complex, which houses a 2500-seat arena, a swimming pool, tennis and racquetball courts, weight rooms, an all-weather track, and baseball, softball, and sand volleyball facilities.

Disabled Students: 95% of the campus is accessible. Wheelchair ramps, elevators, special parking, specially equipped rest rooms, lowered drinking fountains, lowered telephones, and special housing are available.

Services: Counseling and information services are available, as is tutoring in most subjects. There is a reader service for the blind and remedial math, reading, and writing.

Campus Safety and Security: Measures include 24-hour foot and vehicle patrol, self-defense education, security escort services, and pamphlets/posters/films. There are emergency telephones and lighted pathways/sidewalks.

Programs of Study: OBU confers B.A., B.S., B.B.A., B.F.A., B.Hum., B.M., B.M.A., B.Mus.Ed., and B.S.E. degrees. Associate and master's degrees are also awarded. Bachelor's degrees are awarded in BIOLOGI-CAL SCIENCE (biology/biological science), BUSINESS (accounting, banking and finance, business administration and management, and marketing/retailing/merchandising), COMMUNICATIONS AND THE ARTS (broadcasting, communications, dramatic arts, English, fine arts, French, German, journalism, music, Spanish, speech/debate/rhetoric, and telecommunications), COMPUTER AND PHYSICAL SCIENCE (chemistry, computer science, information sciences and systems, mathematics, and physics), EDUCATION (art, early childhood, elementary, foreign languages, music, physical, science, and secondary), HEALTH PROFESSIONS (nursing, physical therapy, predentistry, and premedicine), SOCIAL SCIENCE (history, political science/government, prelaw, psychology, religion, social science, social work, and sociology). Teacher education, biology, and religion are the strongest academically. Biology, elementary education, and nursing are the largest.

Required: To graduate, students must complete a total of 128 credit hours, including 30 to 48 hours in the major, with a 2.0 GPA. Students are also required to complete 6 credits each of English, literature, history, science, Bible, social sciences, and language; 3 each in math, fine arts, and comparative civilization; 2 each in speech, philosophy, and phys ed; and 1 in computer literacy.

Special: OBU offers co-op programs in business, cross-registration with Saint Gregory's University, and a 3-2 engineering degree with Oklahoma State University. Students may study abroad in Europe, South America, Hungary, China, Japan, Spain, and Russia. Internships in several fields, student-designed majors, including an interdisciplinary program in humanities, and pass/fail options are available. There are 4 national honor societies and a freshman honors program.

Faculty/Classroom: 58% of faculty are male; 42%, female. All teach undergraduates. No introductory courses are taught by graduate students. The average class size in an introductory lecture is 25; in a laboratory, 19; and in a regular course, 18.

Admissions: 95% of the 2003-2004 applicants were accepted. The SAT I scores for the 2003-2004 freshman class were: Verbal--16% below 500, 36% between 500 and 599, 36% between 600 and 700, and 12% above 700; Math--21% below 500, 41% between 500 and 599, 29% between 600 and 700, and 9% above 700. The ACT scores were 10% below 21, 30% between 21 and 23, 25% between 24 and 26, 16% between 27 and 28, and 19% above 28. 60% of the current freshmen were in the top fifth of their class; 83% were in the top two fifths. There were 5 National Merit finalists and 5 semifinalists in a recent year. 36 freshmen graduated first in their class.

Requirements: The SAT I or ACT is required. Admission is granted to students with composite scores of 950 on the SAT I or 20 on the ACT, with a 2.5 GPA. Graduation from an accredited secondary school or satisfactory scores on the GED are required for admission. The recommended high school courses should include 4 units of English, 3 units of math, and 2 units each of social studies, lab science, and a foreign language. OBU requires applicants to be in the upper 50% of their class. A GPA of 2.5 is required. AP and CLEP credits are accepted. Important factors in the admissions decision are advanced placement or honor courses, recommendations by school officials, and leadership record.

Procedure: Freshmen are admitted to all sessions. Entrance exams should be taken during the spring of the junior year. There are early admissions and deferred admissions plans. There is a rolling admissions plan. Applications should be filed by August 1 for fall entry, December 15 for winter entry, January 15 for spring entry, and May 15 for summer entry. The fall 2003 application fee was $25. Notification is sent on a rolling basis. Applications are accepted on-line through the university's web site.

Transfer: Transfer students must have a GPA of 2.5 for all college work attempted. 33 credits of 128 required for the bachelor's degree must be completed at OBU.

Visiting: There are regularly scheduled orientations for prospective students, including tours, faculty visits, and general information sessions. There are guides for informal visits and visitors may sit in on classes and stay overnight. To schedule a visit, contact the Admissions Office.

Financial Aid: In 2003-2004, 94% of all full-time freshmen and 92% of continuing full-time students received some form of financial aid. 62% of full-time freshmen and 65% of continuing full-time students received need-based aid. The average freshman award was $8949. 95% of undergraduates work part time. Average annual earnings from campus work are $843. The average financial indebtedness of the 2003 graduate was $14,000. The FAFSA is required. The deadline for filing freshman financial aid applications for fall entry is April 15.

International Students: The school actively recruits these students. They must score 500 on the written TOEFL or 173 on the electronic version and also take the SAT I or the ACT, scoring 20 on the ACT.

Computers: The mainframe is an HP 3000/979. Students have access to about 175 networked Windows 95 and Macs in residence halls, labs, and elsewhere on campus. All students have access to e-mail and the World Wide Web. All students may access the system 75 hours per week. There are no time limits and no fees.

Admissions Contact: Trent Argo, Enrollment Management. A video is available. E-mail: *admissions@okbu.edu* Web: *www.okbu.edu*

OKLAHOMA CHRISTIAN UNIVERSITY
Oklahoma City, OK 73136-1100

D-3

(405) 425-5050
(800) 877-5010; Fax: (405) 425-5069

Full-time: 712 men, 739 women	**Faculty:** 88; IIB, -$
Part-time: 38 men, 37 women	**Ph.D.s:** 67%
Graduate: 90 men, 41 women	**Student/Faculty:** 16 to 1
Year: semesters, summer session	**Tuition:** $13,090
Application Deadline: open	**Room & Board:** $4600
Freshman Class: 1271 applied, 1250 accepted, 387 enrolled	
SAT I Verbal/Math: 560/560	**ACT:** 23 **NONCOMPETITIVE**

Oklahoma Christian University, founded in 1950, is a private liberal arts institution affiliated with the Church of Christ. There are 3 undergraduate and 2 graduate schools. In addition to regional accreditation, OC has baccalaureate program accreditation with ABET, ACBSP, NASM, and NCATE. The library contains 96,581 volumes, 732,357 microform items, and 5396 audio/video tapes/CDs, and subscribes to 891 periodicals. Computerized library services include the card catalog, interlibrary loans, and database searching. Special learning facilities include a learning resource center, art gallery, radio station, free enterprise museum, and journalism lab. The 200-acre campus is in a suburban area on the north side of Oklahoma City. Including any residence halls, there are 33 buildings.

Student Life: 53% of undergraduates are from out of state, mostly the Midwest. Students are from 47 states, 33 foreign countries, and Canada. 85% are white. Most are Protestant. The average age of freshmen is 18. 34% do not continue beyond their first year; 41% remain to graduate.

Housing: 1254 students can be accommodated in college housing, which includes single-sex dorms, on-campus apartments, and married-student housing. In addition, there are honors houses. On-campus housing is guaranteed for all 4 years. 68% of students live on campus. Alcohol is not permitted. All students may keep cars.

Activities: There are no fraternities or sororities. There are 24 groups on campus, including band, cheerleading, choir, chorale, computers, drama, ethnic, honors, international, jazz band, literary magazine, musical theater, newspaper, opera, pep band, photography, political, professional, radio and TV, religious, social service, student government, symphony, and yearbook. Popular campus events include High School Day, Spring Sing, and Special Olympics Banquet.

Sports: There are 6 intercollegiate sports for men and 6 for women, and 13 intramural sports for men and 13 for women. Facilities include 3 gyms, a swimming pool, softball, football, and soccer fields, a fitness center with weight training, stair, and bicycle machines, 3 volleyball courts, and water and land aerobics.

Disabled Students: 98% of the campus is accessible. Wheelchair ramps, elevators, special parking, specially equipped rest rooms, special class scheduling, lowered drinking fountains, and lowered telephones are available.

Services: Counseling and information services are available, as is tutoring in some subjects, including English, math, speech, chemistry, physics, business, education, and computer science. There is remedial math, reading, and writing.

Campus Safety and Security: Measures include 24-hour foot and vehicle patrol, security escort services, informal discussions, and pamphlets/posters/films. There are lighted pathways/sidewalks and security officers.

Programs of Study: OC confers B.A., B.S., B.B.A., B.F.A., B.M.E., B.Mus.Ed., B.S.C.E., B.S.E., B.S.Ed., B.S.E.E., and B.S.M.E. degrees. Master's degrees are also awarded. Bachelor's degrees are awarded in BIOLOGICAL SCIENCE (biochemistry and biology/biological science), BUSINESS (accounting, business administration and management, and marketing/retailing/merchandising), COMMUNICATIONS AND THE ARTS (advertising, art, broadcasting, communications, creative writing, design, English, journalism, music, and Spanish), COMPUTER AND PHYSICAL SCIENCE (chemistry, computer science, information sciences and systems, and mathematics), EDUCATION (art, early childhood, elementary, English, mathematics, middle school, music, physical, science, social studies, special, and teaching English as a second/foreign language (TESOL/TEFOL)), ENGINEERING AND ENVIRONMENTAL DESIGN (computer engineering, electrical/electronics engineering, engineering physics, interior design, and mechanical engineering), HEALTH PROFESSIONS (medical laboratory technology and premedicine), SOCIAL SCIENCE (biblical studies, child care/child and family studies, history, liberal arts/general studies, ministries, missions, prelaw, psychology, religious education, and youth ministry). Business, science and engineering, and communication and fine arts are the largest.

Required: To graduate, students must have a minimum of 126 credit hours, including 30 to 104 in the major, with a GPA of 2.0. All students must complete 60 to 61 hours in the general education program, which includes courses in Bible, English, speech, American studies, math, literature, fine arts, economics, biology, physical science, philosophy, Western civilization, phys ed, personal development, and social science.

Special: OC offers cross-registration with the University of Central Oklahoma, a liberal studies degree, internships in various majors, on-campus work-study, and credit for military experience. Students may study abroad in Austria, Japan, and the Pacific Rim. Major-minor combinations are offered in mass communication, family life, engineering, prelaw, advertising design, speech communication, English, music, education, and math. There are 3 national honor societies, a freshman honors program, and 1 departmental honors program.

Faculty/Classroom: 74% of faculty are male; 26%, female. All teach undergraduates and 20% both teach and do research. No introductory courses are taught by graduate students. The average class size in an introductory lecture is 50; in a laboratory, 19; and in a regular course, 30.

Admissions: 98% of the 2003-2004 applicants were accepted. The SAT I scores for the 2003-2004 freshman class were: Verbal--26% below 500, 40% between 500 and 599, 29% between 600 and 700, and 5% above 700; Math--29% below 500, 34% between 500 and 599, 31% between 600 and 700, and 6% above 700. The ACT scores were 38% below 21, 14% between 21 and 23, 23% between 24 and 26, 11% between 27 and 28, and 14% above 28.

Requirements: The SAT I or ACT is required. In addition, graduation from an accredited secondary school or satisfactory scores on the GED are required for admission. AP and CLEP credits are accepted.

Procedure: Freshmen are admitted to all sessions. There is a deferred admissions plan and a rolling admissions plan. The fall 2003 application fee was $25. Notification is sent on a rolling basis. Application deadlines are open.

Transfer: 61 transfer students enrolled in 2002-2003. Applicants must be eligible to return to the school from which they are transferring. 30 credits of 126 required for the bachelor's degree must be completed at OC.

Visiting: There are regularly scheduled orientations for prospective students, including fall and spring visits in September and February. There are guides for informal visits and visitors may sit in on classes and stay overnight. To schedule a visit, contact the Admissions Office at *info@oc.edu*.

Financial Aid: In 2003-2004, 76% of all full-time freshmen and 64% of continuing full-time students received some form of financial aid. 50% of full-time freshmen and 40% of continuing full-time students received need-based aid. The average freshman award was $8025. Need-based scholarships or need-based grants averaged $4000 ($7200 maximum); need-based self-help aid (loans and jobs) averaged $8000 ($12,000 maximum); and non-need-based athletic scholarships averaged $3714 ($11,490 maximum). 36% of undergraduates work part time. Average annual earnings from campus work are $1219. The average financial indebtedness of the 2003 graduate was $18,065. The FAFSA is required. The priority date for freshman financial aid applications for fall entry is March 15. The deadline for filing freshman financial aid applications for fall entry is April 15.

International Students: There are 48 international students enrolled. The school actively recruits these students. They must score 500 on the written TOEFL or 173 on the electronic version.

Computers: All students have a university-owned laptop issued to them. All students may access the system 24 hours, 7 days a week. There are no time limits and no fees. It is strongly recommended that all students have a personal computer.

Graduates: From July 1, 2002 to June 30, 2003, 320 bachelor's degrees were awarded. The most popular majors were liberal studies (34%), engineering (18%), and biology (16%). In an average class, 23% graduate in 4 years or less, 39% graduate in 5 years or less, and 41% graduate in 6 years or less. 50 companies recruited on campus in 2002-2003.

Admissions Contact: Risa Forrester, Director of Enrollment Development. A video is available. E-mail: *info@oc.edu* Web: *oc.edu*

OKLAHOMA CITY UNIVERSITY
Oklahoma City, OK 73106-1493

D-3

(405) 521-5050
(800) 633-7242; Fax: (405) 521-5916

Full-time: 524 men, 820 women	**Faculty:** 139; IIA, -$
Part-time: 159 men, 290 women	**Ph.D.s:** 78%
Graduate: 1082 men, 793 women	**Student/Faculty:** 1 to 1
Year: semesters, summer session	**Tuition:** $14,030
Application Deadline: August 20	**Room & Board:** $5550
Freshman Class: 822 applied, 639 accepted, 319 enrolled	
SAT I Verbal/Math: 570/560	**ACT:** 24 **VERY COMPETITIVE**

Oklahoma City University, founded in 1904, is a private, comprehensive university affiliated with the United Methodist Church, offering undergraduate and graduate programs in arts and sciences, business, music and performing arts, religion and church vocations, nursing, and law. There are 6 undergraduate and 6 graduate schools. In addition to regional accreditation, OCU has baccalaureate program accreditation with ACBSP, NASM, and NLN. The 2 libraries contain 440,374 volumes, 975,580 microform items, and 10,948 audio/video tapes/CDs, and subscribe to 6017 periodicals. Computerized library services include the card catalog, interlibrary loans, and database searching. Special learning facilities include a learning resource center, art gallery, and TV station.

The 68-acre campus is in an urban area within Oklahoma City. Including any residence halls, there are 35 buildings.

Student Life: 69% of undergraduates are from Oklahoma. Students are from 48 states, 67 foreign countries, and Canada. 60% are white; 23% foreign nationals. 39% are Protestant; 30% claim no religious affiliation; 9% Catholic. The average age of freshmen is 19; all undergraduates, 21. 27% do not continue beyond their first year; 53% remain to graduate.

Housing: 1021 students can be accommodated in college housing, which includes single-sex dorms, on-campus apartments, and fraternity houses. In addition, there are special-interest houses. On-campus housing is guaranteed for all 4 years. 64% of students commute. Alcohol is not permitted. All students may keep cars.

Activities: 11% of men belong to 3 national fraternities; 15% of women belong to 3 national sororities. There are 42 groups on campus, including art, band, cheerleading, choir, chorus, computers, dance, drama, drill team, ethnic, film, gay, honors, international, jazz band, literary magazine, musical theater, newspaper, opera, orchestra, pep band, photography, political, professional, radio and TV, religious, social, social service, student government, symphony, and yearbook. Popular campus events include sports, theater, dance, and music programs; international fair; and oozeball.

Sports: There are 4 intercollegiate sports for men and 4 for women, and 9 intramural sports for men and 8 for women. Facilities include a field house, tennis courts, baseball and soccer fields, and a wellness and activity center.

Disabled Students: 96% of the campus is accessible. Wheelchair ramps, elevators, special parking, specially equipped rest rooms, lowered drinking fountains, and lowered telephones are available.

Services: Counseling and information services are available, as is tutoring in most subjects. There is remedial math, reading, and writing. There are writing and learning enhancement centers and a math lab.

Campus Safety and Security: Measures include 24-hour foot and vehicle patrol, security escort services, informal discussions, and pamphlets/posters/films. There are emergency telephones, lighted pathways/sidewalks, and an inner-campus bicycle patrol.

Programs of Study: OCU confers B.A., B.S., B.F.A., B.M., B.Perf.Arts, B.S.B., and B.S.N. degrees. Master's degrees are also awarded. Bachelor's degrees are awarded in BIOLOGICAL SCIENCE (biochemistry, biology/biological science, and biophysics), BUSINESS (accounting, banking and finance, and business administration and management), COMMUNICATIONS AND THE ARTS (advertising, art, broadcasting, communications, dance, dramatic arts, English, French, German, graphic design, journalism, music, piano/organ, Spanish, and speech/debate/rhetoric), COMPUTER AND PHYSICAL SCIENCE (chemistry, computer management, computer science, mathematics, physics, and science), EDUCATION (early childhood, elementary, foreign languages, music, physical, and science), HEALTH PROFESSIONS (nursing and premedicine), SOCIAL SCIENCE (criminal justice, economics, history, humanities, philosophy, political science/government, prelaw, psychology, religion, and sociology). Business, performing arts, and dance are the strongest academically. Business, performing arts, and mass communications are the largest.

Required: To graduate, students must complete a total of 124 credit hours, including 30 to 80 in the major, with a minimum GPA of 2.0. Students must complete their last 15 hours, including the last 6 in the major, at OCU, with a minimum GPA of 2.0. All students must take 43 hours in the core curriculum as specified by their college or department.

Special: OCU offers internships, a Washington semester, work-study programs, a general studies degree, dual and student-designed majors, credit for life experience, and study-abroad programs in 5 countries. B.A.-B.S. degrees and an accelerated degree program in nursing are also available. There are 9 national honor societies, a freshman honors program, and 10 departmental honors programs.

Faculty/Classroom: 53% of faculty are male; 47%, female. 80% teach undergraduates. No introductory courses are taught by graduate students. The average class size in an introductory lecture is 22; in a laboratory, 9; and in a regular course, 13.

Admissions: 78% of the 2003-2004 applicants were accepted. The SAT I scores for the 2003-2004 freshman class were: Verbal--18% below 500, 49% between 500 and 599, 32% between 600 and 700, and 1% above 700; Math--28% below 500, 35% between 500 and 599, 33% between 600 and 700, and 4% above 700. The ACT scores were 19% below 21, 26% between 21 and 23, 26% between 24 and 26, 12% between 27 and 28, and 17% above 28. 52% of the current freshmen were in the top fifth of their class; 80% were in the top two fifths.

Requirements: The SAT I or ACT is required, with a minimum composite score of 1020 on the SAT I or a minimum of 20 on the ACT. Graduation from an accredited secondary school or satisfactory scores on the GED are also required for admission. High school courses must include 4 units of English, 3 units each of science, social studies, and math, and 2 units of a foreign language. Music and dance students are required to audition. OCU requires applicants to be in the upper 50% of their class. A GPA of 3.0 is required. AP and CLEP credits are accepted.

Important factors in the admissions decision are evidence of special talent, advanced placement or honor courses, and leadership record.

Procedure: Freshmen are admitted to all sessions. Entrance exams should be taken by February of the senior year. There are early admissions and deferred admissions plans. There is a rolling admissions plan. Applications should be filed by August 20 for fall entry. The fall 2003 application fee was $35. Notification is sent on a rolling basis. Applications are accepted on computer disk and on-line through CollegeNET.

Transfer: 155 transfer students enrolled in 2002-2003. Applicants must submit a transcript from each college attended and must have a minimum GPA of 2.0 from an accredited institution. Applicants having fewer than 29 credit hours must submit a high school transcript and ACT or SAT I scores. 30 credits of 124 required for the bachelor's degree must be completed at OCU.

Visiting: There are regularly scheduled orientations for prospective students. There are guides for informal visits and visitors may sit in on classes and stay overnight. To schedule a visit, contact Visitor Services or Undergraduate Admissions at *visitocu@okcu.edu*.

Financial Aid: In 2003-2004, 99% of all full-time freshmen and 79% of continuing full-time students received some form of financial aid. 80% of full-time freshmen and 66% of continuing full-time students received need-based aid. The average freshman award was $14,230. Need-based scholarships or need-based grants averaged $9847 ($21,204 maximum); need-based self-help aid (loans and jobs) averaged $7776 ($23,125 maximum); non-need-based athletic scholarships averaged $2442 ($9916 maximum); and other non-need-based awards and non-need-based scholarships averaged $6526 ($20,997 maximum). 18% of undergraduates work part time. Average annual earnings from campus work are $2194. The average financial indebtedness of the 2003 graduate was $18,669. The FAFSA and tax returns, if selected for verification, are required. The deadline for filing freshman financial aid applications for fall entry is March 1.

International Students: There were 370 international students enrolled in a recent year. The school actively recruits these students. They must score 500 on the written TOEFL or take the MELAB.

Computers: The mainframes are an NCR 3455, NCR 3550, 2 DEC Alphas, a DEC 8250, and a VAX 4500. Students have access to academic computer systems and the Internet from the labs, dorm rooms, and through a dial-up remote system. Students can access e-mail from any browser on-and off campus. Home directories are only accessible on campus. Approximately 130 open access PCs are available to students in labs on campus. All students may access the system 24 hours a day. There are no time limits. The fee is $150.

Graduates: From July 1, 2002 to June 30, 2003, 446 bachelor's degrees were awarded. The most popular majors were business (15%), nursing (6%), and dance (5%). In an average class, 36% graduate in 4 years or less, 46% graduate in 5 years or less, and 49% graduate in 6 years or less. 65 companies recruited on campus in 2002-2003.

Admissions Contact: Shery Boyles, Director, Undergraduate Admissions. A video is available. E-mail: uadmissions@okcu.edu
Web: *www.okcu.edu* or *www.youatokcu.com*

OKLAHOMA PANHANDLE STATE UNIVERSITY   B-2
Goodwell, OK 73939
(580) 349-1312
(800) 664-6778; Fax: (580) 349-2302

Full-time: 500 men, 453 women	**Faculty:** 50
Part-time: 53 men, 139 women	**Ph.D.s:** 52%
Graduate: none	**Student/Faculty:** 19 to 1
Year: semesters, summer session	**Tuition:** $2500 ($3159)
Application Deadline: open	**Room & Board:** $2870
Freshman Class: 947 applied, 787 accepted, 594 enrolled	
ACT: 21	**COMPETITIVE**

Oklahoma Panhandle State University, founded in 1909, is a publicly funded institution offering undergraduate programs in the liberal arts, business, education, agriculture, technology, and preprofessional training. There are 5 undergraduate schools. In addition to regional accreditation, OPSU has baccalaureate program accreditation with NCATE and NLN. The library contains 113,733 volumes, 13,038 microform items, and 8487 audio/video tapes/CDs, and subscribes to 498 periodicals. Computerized library services include the card catalog, interlibrary loans, and database searching. Special learning facilities include a learning resource center, natural history museum, radio station, writing lab, academic support lab, farm lab, children's collection library, and 2 instructional TV facilities. The 120-acre campus is in a rural area 100 miles north of Amarillo, Texas. Including any residence halls, there are 27 buildings.

Student Life: 53% of undergraduates are from out of state, mostly the Midwest. Students are from 36 states, 25 foreign countries, and Canada. 98% are from public schools. 80% are white; 10%, Hispanic. The average age of freshmen is 21; all undergraduates, 25. 50% do not continue beyond their first year; 10% remain to graduate.

Housing: 412 students can be accommodated in college housing, which includes single-sex and coed dorms, on-campus apartments, and married-student housing. In addition, there are honors houses. On-campus housing is guaranteed for all 4 years. 66% of students commute. Alcohol is not permitted. All students may keep cars.

Activities: There are no fraternities or sororities. There are 45 groups on campus, including art, band, cheerleading, choir, chorale, chorus, computers, dance, debate, drama, drill team, ethnic, forensics, honors, jazz band, marching band, musical theater, newspaper, pep band, photography, professional, radio and TV, religious, rodeo, social, student government, and yearbook. Popular campus events include Annual Rodeo and a Broadway play.

Sports: There are 4 intercollegiate sports for men and 4 for women, and 12 intramural sports for men and 12 for women. Facilities include a field house, an athletic field, a golf course, tennis courts, and an activity center. Water skiing and fishing spots are nearby.

Disabled Students: 90% of the campus is accessible. Wheelchair ramps, elevators, special parking, and special class scheduling are available.

Services: Counseling and information services are available, as is tutoring in every subject. There is remedial math, reading, and writing. Free tutoring is provided through the peer counseling center.

Campus Safety and Security: Measures include 24-hour foot and vehicle patrol, self-defense education, pamphlets/posters/films, and emergency telephones. There are lighted pathways/sidewalks.

Programs of Study: OPSU confers B.A., B.S., B.B.A., B.H.P.E., B.I.B.M., B.M.E., B.S.N., and B.T. degrees. Associate degrees are also awarded. Bachelor's degrees are awarded in AGRICULTURE (agricultural business management, agronomy, and animal science), BIOLOGICAL SCIENCE (biology/biological science), BUSINESS (accounting and business administration and management), COMMUNICATIONS AND THE ARTS (English and music), COMPUTER AND PHYSICAL SCIENCE (chemistry, information sciences and systems, mathematics, and physical sciences), EDUCATION (agricultural, business, elementary, English, health, mathematics, music, physical, science, and social studies), ENGINEERING AND ENVIRONMENTAL DESIGN (industrial engineering technology), HEALTH PROFESSIONS (medical technology and nursing), SOCIAL SCIENCE (fire protection, history, humanities, psychology, and social studies). Business, agriculture, and education are the strongest academically. Education, agriculture, and business are the largest.

Required: To graduate, students must complete a total of 124 semester hours with a minimum GPA of 2.0. The number of hours required in the major varies. All students must complete 45 hours of general education courses, with at least 1 course at the upper-division level.

Special: Oklahoma Panhandle State University offers dual majors and the B.A.-B.S. degree in most areas. There is 1 national honor society and 1 departmental honors program.

Faculty/Classroom: 50% of faculty are male; 50%, female. All teach undergraduates. The average class size in an introductory lecture is 35; in a laboratory, 24; and in a regular course, 20.

Admissions: 83% of the 2003-2004 applicants were accepted. 5% of the current freshmen were in the top fifth of their class; 37% were in the top two fifths.

Requirements: The SAT I or ACT is required, with a minimum composite score of 19 on the ACT. In addition, graduation from an accredited secondary school or satisfactory scores on the GED are required. High school courses must include 4 units of English, 3 units of math (beginning with algebra I), 3 units of other courses such as foreign language or computer application courses, 2 units each of history (including 1 unit of American history) and lab science, and 1 unit of citizenship (for example, government or civics). AP and CLEP credits are accepted.

Procedure: Freshmen are admitted to all sessions. Application deadlines are open. There is a rolling admissions plan.

Transfer: 164 transfer students enrolled in a recent year. An application for admission, a medical history form, college transcripts, high school transcripts, and ACT scores are required. If students are transferring in with a GPA below 2.0, they come in on academic probation. 30 of 124 credits required for the bachelor's degree must be completed at OPSU.

Visiting: There are regularly scheduled orientations for prospective students. There are guides for informal visits and visitors may sit in on classes and stay overnight. To schedule a visit, contact High School and Community Relations.

Financial Aid: 16% of undergraduates work part time. Average annual earnings from campus work are $3000. The FAFSA and the college's own financial statement are required. Check with the school for current application deadlines.

International Students: In a recent year, there were 55 international students enrolled. The school actively recruits these students. They must score 500 on the written TOEFL and also take the SAT I or ACT, or any other country's equivalent, scoring 19 on the ACT.

Computers: The mainframe is an HP 9000/8275. There are 40 Macs and PCs available in labs. Students enrolled in computer information system classes may access the system 5 A.M. to 11 P.M. There are no time limits and no fees.

Graduates: In a recent year, 211 bachelor's degrees were awarded.

Admissions Contact: Alesha Cruz, Admissions Counselor.
E-mail: *opsu@opsu.edu* Web: *www.opsu.edu*

OKLAHOMA STATE SYSTEM OF HIGHER EDUCATION

The Oklahoma State System of Higher Education, established in 1941, is a public system in Oklahoma. It is governed by the Oklahoma State Regents for Higher Education, whose chief administrator is the chancellor. The primary goals of the system are teaching, research, and public service. The main priorities are student success, excellence, and system efficiency. The total enrollment of all 25 campuses is usually about 213,000; there were about 6780 faculty members. Altogether there are 596 baccalaureate, 266 master's, and 106 doctoral programs offered in Oklahoma State System of Higher Education. 4-year campuses are located in Stillwater, Norman, Edmond, Ada, Tahlequah, Alva, Durant, Weatherford, Lawton, Langston, Goodwell, and Chickasha. Profiles of the 4-year campuses are included in this section.

OKLAHOMA STATE UNIVERSITY
Stillwater, OK 74078

E-2

(405) 744-6858
(800) 852-1255; Fax: (405) 744-5285

Full-time: 8360 men, 8042 women	**Faculty:** I, --$
Part-time: 1145 men, 1082 women	**Ph.D.s:** 82%
Graduate: 2366 men, 1772 women	**Student/Faculty:** n/av
Year: semesters, summer session	**Tuition:** $3748 ($10,066)
Application Deadline: open	**Room & Board:** $5468
Freshman Class: 6629 applied, 5930 accepted, 3488 enrolled	
SAT I Verbal/Math: 550/560	**ACT:** 24 **VERY COMPETITIVE**

Oklahoma State University, founded in 1890, is a publicly funded land-grant institution, offering undergraduate programs in agricultural sciences and natural resources, arts and sciences, business, education, engineering, architecture, technology, and human environmental resources. There are 6 undergraduate schools and 1 graduate school. In addition to regional accreditation, OSU has baccalaureate program accreditation with AACSB, ABET, ACEJMC, ACS, ADA, AHEA, APA, ASLA, ASLHA, FIDER, NAAB, NAACLS, NASM, NRPA, and SAF. The 5 libraries contain 2,297,246 volumes, 3,842,656 microform items, and 18,326 audio/video tapes/CDs, and subscribe to 16,737 periodicals. Computerized library services include interlibrary loans and database searching. Special learning facilities include an art gallery, natural history museum, and radio station. The 840-acre campus is in a small town 65 miles north of Oklahoma City. Including any residence halls, there are 200 buildings.

Student Life: 87% of undergraduates are from Oklahoma. Students are from 50 states, 119 foreign countries, and Canada. 65% are white. The average age of freshmen is 19; all undergraduates, 22. 20% do not continue beyond their first year.

Housing: 5813 students can be accommodated in college housing, which includes single-sex and coed dorms, on-campus apartments, off-campus apartments, married-student housing, fraternity houses, and sorority houses. In addition, there are honors houses, language houses, special-interest houses, and floors for fine arts, engineering, and fire protection majors. On-campus housing is guaranteed for all 4 years. 61% of students commute. Alcohol is not permitted. All students may keep cars.

Activities: 14% of men belong to 20 national fraternities; 18% of women belong to 14 national sororities. There are 374 groups on campus, including art, band, cheerleading, choir, chorale, chorus, computers, dance, drama, ethnic, gay, honors, international, jazz band, literary magazine, marching band, musical theater, newspaper, opera, orchestra, pep band, political, professional, radio and TV, religious, social, social service, student government, and symphony. Popular campus events include Spring Sing, Freshmen Follies, and Special Olympics.

Sports: There are 9 intercollegiate sports for men and 7 for women, and 40 intramural sports for men and 40 for women. Facilities include a phys ed center with an indoor climbing wall and activity areas for basketball, volleyball, racquetball, squash, badminton, fencing, golf, table tennis, billiards, wrestling, dance, weight lifting, and indoor and outdoor swimming. There are also outdoor basketball and tennis courts, archery and golf ranges, a jogging track, and playing fields.

Disabled Students: 95% of the campus is accessible. Wheelchair ramps, elevators, special parking, specially equipped rest rooms, special class scheduling, lowered drinking fountains, lowered telephones, special housing, and adaptive technology are available.

Services: Counseling and information services are available, as is tutoring in most subjects, including math. Tutoring is not disability-specific. There is a reader service for the blind and remedial math, reading, and writing. Academic assessment and minority programs are also available.

Campus Safety and Security: Measures include 24-hour foot and vehicle patrol, self-defense education, security escort services, and shuttle buses. There are informal discussions, pamphlets/posters/films, emergency telephones, and lighted pathways/sidewalks.

Programs of Study: OSU confers B.A., B.S., B.Arch., B.Arch.Eng., B.F.A., B.Land.Arch., B.M., and B.U.S. degrees. Master's and doctoral degrees are also awarded. Bachelor's degrees are awarded in AGRICULTURE (agricultural business management, agricultural economics, animal science, fish and game management, forestry and related sciences, horticulture, and plant science), BIOLOGICAL SCIENCE (biochemistry, biology/biological science, botany, cell biology, entomology, microbiology, molecular biology, nutrition, physiology, and zoology), BUSINESS (accounting, banking and finance, business administration and management, business economics, hotel/motel and restaurant management, international business management, management information systems, management science, marketing/retailing/merchandising, and recreation and leisure services), COMMUNICATIONS AND THE ARTS (art, communications, design, dramatic arts, English, French, German, journalism, music, Russian, and Spanish), COMPUTER AND PHYSICAL SCIENCE (chemistry, computer science, geology, mathematics, physics, and statistics), EDUCATION (agricultural, elementary, health, music, physical, secondary, and technical), ENGINEERING AND ENVIRONMENTAL DESIGN (aeronautical engineering, architectural engineering, architecture, aviation computer technology, bioengineering, chemical engineering, civil engineering, construction management, electrical/electronics engineering, electrical/electronics engineering technology, engineering, environmental science, industrial engineering, landscape architecture/design, mechanical engineering, and mechanical engineering technology), HEALTH PROFESSIONS (biomedical science, medical technology, premedicine, preveterinary science, and speech pathology/audiology), SOCIAL SCIENCE (American studies, child care/child and family studies, economics, fire control and safety technology, geography, history, liberal arts/general studies, philosophy, political science/government, prelaw, psychology, and sociology). Engineering and business are the strongest academically. Animal sciences is the largest.

Required: To graduate, students must have a minimum GPA of 2.0 and at least 120 hours, including 40 to 60 in the major, for most programs. A higher GPA may be required in some majors. All students must take a minimum of 40 credit hours of core courses, including 6 each of English, humanities, analytical and quantitative thought, natural sciences, and social and behavioral sciences, 3 each of American history and government, and 1 each of scientific investigation and international studies.

Special: OSU offers internships in medical technology, engineering, home economics, and arts and sciences. A B.A.-B.S. degree, dual majors, an individualized university studies degree, a 3-2 engineering degree, an engineering co-op program, multidisciplinary majors in biosystems engineering and in cell and molecular biology, credit for life experience, nondegree study, and pass/fail options are available. Students may study abroad in several countries. The school also sponsors Semester at Sea, a 1-semester program of study on a ship traveling to ports throughout the world. There are 25 national honor societies and a freshman honors program.

Faculty/Classroom: 69% of faculty are male; 31%, female. 58% teach undergraduates, 73% do research, and 44% do both. Graduate students teach 20% of introductory courses. The average class size in an introductory lecture is 30.

Admissions: 89% of the 2003-2004 applicants were accepted. The SAT I scores for the 2003-2004 freshman class were: Verbal--19% below 500, 55% between 500 and 599, 22% between 600 and 700, and 4% above 700; Math--17% below 500, 50% between 500 and 599, 27% between 600 and 700, and 6% above 700. The ACT scores were 19% below 21, 29% between 21 and 23, 25% between 24 and 26, 13% between 27 and 28, and 14% above 28. 43% of the current freshmen were in the top fifth of their class; 72% were in the top two fifths. In a recent year, there were 23 National Merit finalists, and 312 freshmen graduated first in their class.

Requirements: The SAT I or ACT is required. The ACT is preferred. For admission in good standing, freshman applicants must have a cumulative high school GPA of 3.0 and rank in the upper third of their graduating class, or achieve at least a 22 composite score on the ACT or 1020 on the SAT I, or have a 3.0 GPA in the required 15 curricular units, which include 4 years of English, 3 of math (algebra I and above), 2 each of history and lab science, 1 of citizenship skills, and 3 more from any of the above or computer science or foreign language. A GPA of 3.0 is required. AP and CLEP credits are accepted. Important factors in the admissions decision are advanced placement or honor courses, evidence of special talent, and recommendations by school officials.

Procedure: Freshmen are admitted to all sessions. Entrance exams should be taken during the junior or senior year. There is a rolling admissions plan. Application deadlines are open. Application fee is $25. Applications are accepted on-line through *www.okstate.edu.*

Transfer: 1859 transfer students enrolled in 2002-2003. Applicants must submit official transcripts from all colleges attended. Students having fewer than 24 credit hours must also meet the requirements for entering freshmen. Nonresidents must have a minimum GPA of 2.0 and a total of 24 credit hours. In-state applicants must meet the requirements on a scaled GPA. 30 of 120 credits required for the bachelor's degree must be completed at OSU.

Visiting: There are regularly scheduled orientations for prospective students, including personal meetings and tours. Appointments are scheduled with other campus departments, as needed, to assist prospective students. There are guides for informal visits and visitors may sit in on classes and stay overnight. To schedule a visit, contact High School and College Relations at (405) 744-5358 or (800) 852-1255.

Financial Aid: In 2003-2004, 41% of all full-time freshmen and 48% of continuing full-time students received some form of financial aid. At least 28% of full-time freshmen and 35% of continuing full-time students received need-based aid. The average freshman award was $7250. 19% of undergraduates work part time. Average annual earnings from campus work are $2000. The average financial indebtedness of the 2003 graduate was $16,268. The FAFSA is required. The deadline for filing freshman financial aid applications for fall entry is March 1.

International Students: There are 806 international students enrolled. The school actively recruits these students. They must score 500 on the written TOEFL or 173 on the electronic version and also take the SAT I or the ACT.

Computers: The mainframe is an IBM 9672/R25. There are some 2000 Macs and PCs available throughout the campus, with more than 15,000 active data ports. Access is also available in most residence halls. All students may access the system. There are no time limits. The fee is $5 per credit.

Graduates: From July 1, 2002 to June 30, 2003, 3221 bachelor's degrees were awarded. The most popular majors were business/marketing (30%), engineering/engineering technologies (11%), and education (9%). In an average class, 25% graduate in 4 years or less, 27% graduate in 5 years or less, and 7% graduate in 6 years or less. 460 companies recruited on campus in a recent year.

Admissions Contact: Gordon L. Reese, Director of Admissions. E-mail: *admit@okstate.edu* Web: *www.okstate.edu*

OKLAHOMA WESLEYAN UNIVERSITY   E-1
(Formerly Bartlesville Wesleyan College)
Bartlesville, OK 74006   (918) 335-6219
(800) 468-6292; Fax: (918) 335-6229

Full-time: 150 men, 230 women	**Faculty:** 34; IIB
Part-time: 50 men, 110 women	**Ph.D.s:** 51%
Graduate: none	**Student/Faculty:** 11 to 1
Year: semesters, summer session	**Tuition:** $10,400
Application Deadline: open	**Room & Board:** $3700
Freshman Class: n/av	
SAT I or ACT: recommended	**LESS COMPETITIVE**

Oklahoma Wesleyan College, founded in 1909, is a private liberal arts institution affiliated with the Wesleyan Church. Figures in the above capsule and in this profile are approximate. The library contains 120,000 volumes, 20,000 microform items, and 500 audio/video tapes/CDs, and subscribes to 18,000 periodicals. Computerized library services include the card catalog, interlibrary loans, and database searching. Special learning facilities include a learning resource center. The 101-acre campus is in a suburban area 40 miles north of Tulsa. Including any residence halls, there are 15 buildings.

Student Life: 53% of undergraduates are from Oklahoma. Students are from 28 states and 12 foreign countries. 85% are from public schools. 80% are white. 49% are Protestant; 10% claim no religious affiliation. The average age of freshmen is 18; all undergraduates, 26. 10% do not continue beyond their first year; 60% remain to graduate.

Housing: 300 students can be accommodated in college housing, which includes single-sex dorms. On-campus housing is guaranteed for all 4 years and is available on a first-come, first-served basis. 53% of students commute. Alcohol is not permitted. All students may keep cars.

Activities: There are no sororities. There are 10 groups on campus, including band, cheerleading, choir, chorale, chorus, computers, debate, drama, ethnic, forensics, honors, international, newspaper, photography, political, professional, religious, social service, student government, and yearbook. Popular campus events include Spiritual Emphasis Week and Youth Conference.

Sports: There are 2 intercollegiate sports for men and 3 for women, and 10 intramural sports for men and 10 for women. Facilities include a 2000-seat indoor gym and an 8-acre athletic field.

Disabled Students: 73% of the campus is accessible. Wheelchair ramps, elevators, special parking, and specially equipped rest rooms are available.

Services: Counseling and information services are available, as is tutoring in most subjects. There is remedial math, reading, and writing.

Campus Safety and Security: Measures include informal discussions, lighted pathways/sidewalks, and an evening patrol by a security guard.

Programs of Study: BWC confers B.A. and B.S. degrees. Associate degrees are also awarded. Bachelor's degrees are awarded in BIOLOGICAL SCIENCE (biology/biological science), BUSINESS (accounting, business administration and management, and human resources), COMMUNICATIONS AND THE ARTS (communications, English, and music), COMPUTER AND PHYSICAL SCIENCE (chemistry, computer science, information sciences and systems, mathematics, and science),

EDUCATION (art, athletic training, business, elementary, English, mathematics, middle school, music, physical, science, secondary, and social studies), HEALTH PROFESSIONS (predentistry and premedicine), SOCIAL SCIENCE (behavioral science, history, liberal arts/general studies, pastoral studies, political science/government, prelaw, religion, religious music, social studies, sociology, and youth ministry). Business and education are the strongest academically and are the largest.

Required: To graduate, students must complete a total of 126 credit hours with a minimum GPA of 2.0. About 30 hours are required in the major. All students must take 9 hours of religion and a writing proficiency exam.

Special: BWC offers cross-registration with Tri-County Tech, a Washington semester, a co-op program, internships, a general studies degree, credit for life experience, an accelerated degree program in management of human resources, and nondegree study. There is an accelerated program for adult learners, a pretherapy program, and a leadership in business program.

Faculty/Classroom: 60% of faculty are male; 40%, female. The average class size in an introductory lecture is 20; in a laboratory, 20; and in a regular course, 20.

Requirements: The SAT I or ACT is recommended. In addition, graduation from an accredited secondary school or satisfactory scores on the GED are required for admission. 18 academic credits must be completed, including 4 credits of English and 2 credits each of history, math, science, and social studies. BWC requires applicants to be in the upper 50% of their class. A GPA of 2.0 is required. AP and CLEP credits are accepted. Important factors in the admissions decision are leadership record, personality/intangible qualities, and geographic diversity.

Procedure: Freshmen are admitted to all sessions. Entrance exams should be taken during the senior year. There is a rolling admissions plan. Application deadlines are open. Applications are accepted on-line at BWC's web site.

Transfer: Applicants must have a minimum GPA of 2.0. 24 of 126 credits required for the bachelor's degree must be completed at BWC.

Visiting: There are regularly scheduled orientations for prospective students. There are guides for informal visits and visitors may sit in on classes and stay overnight. To schedule a visit, contact the Enrollment Services Office.

Financial Aid: The FAFSA and the college's own financial statement are required. The deadline for filing freshman financial aid applications for fall entry is open.

International Students: The school actively recruits these students. They must score 500 on the written TOEFL and also take the college's own entrance exam and placement tests.

Computers: There is a computer lab housing both IBM and Mac PCs. All students may access the system 8 A.M. to 10 P.M. There are no time limits and no fees.

Admissions Contact: Jere Johnson, Enrollment Services Administrator. E-mail: *admissions@bwc.edu* Web: *www.bwc.edu*

ORAL ROBERTS UNIVERSITY
Tulsa, OK 74171

E-2

(918) 495-6529
(800) 678-8876; Fax: (918) 495-6222

Full-time: 1190 men, 1635 women	**Faculty:** 152
Part-time: 100 men, 170 women	**Ph.D.s:** 50%
Graduate: 305 men, 290 women	**Student/Faculty:** 16 to 1
Year: semesters, summer session	**Tuition:** $12,920
Application Deadline: open	**Room & Board:** $5570
Freshman Class: n/av	
SAT I or ACT: required	**COMPETITIVE**

Oral Roberts University, founded in 1963, is a private liberal arts university committed to the Christian faith. Figures in the above capsule and in this profile are approximate. There are 6 undergraduate and 3 graduate schools. In addition to regional accreditation, ORU has baccalaureate program accreditation with ABET, CSWE, NASM, and NLN. The library contains 750,000 volumes, 200,000 microform items, and 500,000 audio/video tapes/CDs, and subscribes to 2100 periodicals. Computerized library services include the card catalog and database searching. Special learning facilities include a learning resource center, natural history museum, radio station, TV station, and a TV production studio. The 400-acre campus is in a suburban area. Including any residence halls, there are 22 buildings.

Student Life: 86% of undergraduates are from out of state, mostly the Midwest. Students are from 50 states, 51 foreign countries, and Canada. 50% are from public schools. 63% are white; 23% African American. Most are Protestant. The average age of freshmen is 20. 15% do not continue beyond their first year; 42% remain to graduate.

Housing: 3000 students can be accommodated in college housing, which includes single-sex dorms. On-campus housing is available on a first-come, first-served basis. 57% of students live on campus; of those, 99% remain on campus on weekends. Alcohol is not permitted. All students may keep cars.

Activities: There are no fraternities or sororities. There are 60 groups on campus, including art, band, cheerleading, choir, chorale, chorus, community outreach, computers, drama, ethnic, film, honors, international, jazz band, newspaper, opera, pep band, photography, political, professional, radio and TV, religious, social, social service, student government, summer mission, symphony, and yearbook. Popular campus events include Fall Break and College Weekend.

Sports: There are 8 intercollegiate sports for men and 8 for women, and 20 intramural sports for men and 20 for women. Facilities include a physical fitness center, a track, tennis, racquetball, squash, volleyball, and basketball courts, and baseball and soccer fields.

Disabled Students: 90% of the campus is accessible. Wheelchair ramps, elevators, special parking, specially equipped rest rooms, special class scheduling, lowered drinking fountains, and lowered telephones are available.

Services: Counseling and information services are available, as is tutoring in most subjects. There is a reader service for the blind and remedial math, reading, and writing.

Campus Safety and Security: Measures include 24-hour foot and vehicle patrol, self-defense education, security escort services, and shuttle buses. There are lighted pathways/sidewalks.

Programs of Study: ORU confers B.A., B.S., B.M., B.Mus.Ed., B.S.E., B.S.N., and B.S.W. degrees. Master's and doctoral degrees are also awarded. Bachelor's degrees are awarded in BIOLOGICAL SCIENCE (biology/biological science), BUSINESS (accounting, banking and finance, business administration and management, international business management, management information systems, management science, marketing/retailing/merchandising, organizational behavior, and recreation and leisure services), COMMUNICATIONS AND THE ARTS (applied art, broadcasting, communications, dramatic arts, English, English literature, film arts, French, German, literature, music, music performance, music theory and composition, Spanish, speech/debate/rhetoric, and studio art), COMPUTER AND PHYSICAL SCIENCE (chemistry, computer science, mathematics, and physics), EDUCATION (art, business, drama, early childhood, elementary, English, foreign languages, health, mathematics, music, physical, recreation, science, social studies, and special), ENGINEERING AND ENVIRONMENTAL DESIGN (bioengineering, commercial art, computer engineering, electrical/electronics engineering, engineering, engineering management, mechanical engineering, and preengineering), HEALTH PROFESSIONS (biomedical science, health science, medical laboratory technology, nursing, optometry, predentistry, and premedicine), SOCIAL SCIENCE (biblical studies, history, international relations, international studies, liberal arts/general studies, ministries, philosophy, political science/government, prelaw, psychology, religion, religious education, religious music, and social work). All science programs, music, and theology are the strongest academically. Business is the largest.

Required: A minimum of 128 credit hours, with a minimum of 30 hours in the major, and a 2.0 GPA are required to graduate. All students must complete specific courses in the Bible, theology, and English, plus 12 hours in social sciences, 11 in biological, physical, and mathematical sciences, 6 to 7 in a modern foreign language, 3 in communication arts, and 2 in fine arts. 1 physical activity course is required per semester, along with regular, semiweekly chapel attendance. A senior paper must be completed in most majors.

Special: ORU offers combined B.A.-B.S. degrees, internships, 3-2 programs, work-study programs, dual and student-designed majors, study abroad in 5 countries, independent study, nondegree study, an accelerated degree in business and education, and a liberal arts degree. There are 3 national honor societies, a freshman honors program, and 7 departmental honors programs.

Faculty/Classroom: 68% of faculty are male; 32%, female. 78% both teach and do research. No introductory courses are taught by graduate students. The average class size in an introductory lecture is 30; in a laboratory, 20; and in a regular course, 20.

Requirements: The SAT I or ACT is required. In addition, students should be graduates of an accredited secondary school or hold a GED. High school preparation should include 4 years of English, 2 of math, including algebra and geometry or 2 years of algebra, and 2 each of foreign language, social studies, and science, including lab science. A recommendation from the student's minister is required. An academic recommendation and an interview are recommended. AP and CLEP credits are accepted.

Procedure: Freshmen are admitted to all sessions. Entrance exams should be taken during the last semester of the junior year or during the senior year. There are early decision, early admissions, deferred and rolling admissions plans. Application deadlines are open. The fall 2003 application fee was $35. 80 early decision candidates were accepted for the 2003-2004 class.

Transfer: An official transcript showing honorable dismissal from each previous institution is required. 30 of 128 credits required for the bachelor's degree must be completed at ORU.

Visiting: There are regularly scheduled orientations for prospective students, including College Weekend, which consists of visiting classes, meeting with faculty and staff, attending chapel services, and attending student life events. Visitors may sit in on classes and stay overnight. To schedule a visit, contact LeAnne Langley, the Admissions Office.

Financial Aid: In a recent year, 72% of all full-time freshmen and 67% of continuing full-time students received some form of financial aid. The FAFSA and the federal income tax return are required. Check with the school for current deadlines.

International Students: They must score 500 on the written TOEFL or take the SAT I or ACT.

Computers: The mainframe is an IBM. Academic Computing provides access to 4 teaching areas that may be used as both classrooms and walk-in labs. There are 14 computer labs available for students in the residence halls and all student rooms are wired for computer access. Business students may access the system. There are no time limits. The fee is $10 per credit hour.

Admissions Contact: Chris Belcher, Admissions.
E-mail: *admission@oru.edu* Web: *www.oru.edu*

SAINT GREGORY'S UNIVERSITY
Shawnee, OK 74804

E-3

(405) 878-5444
(888) 784-7847; Fax: (405) 878-5198

Full-time: 280 men, 335 women	**Faculty:** 38
Part-time: 65 men, 90 women	**Ph.Ds:** 42%
Graduate: none	**Student/Faculty:** 16 to 1
Year: semesters, summer session	**Tuition:** $9505
Application Deadline: open	**Room & Board:** $4480
Freshman Class: n/av	
ACT: required	**NONCOMPETITIVE**

Saint Gregory's University, founded in 1875, is a private instituition affiliated with the Roman Catholic Church. Students design personalized degree programs within the integrative areas of humanities, natural science, social science, business, and theology. There are 5 undergraduate schools. The figures in the above capsule and in this profile are approximate. The library contains 70,000 volumes, 3526 microform items, and 450 audio/video tapes/CDs, and subscribes to 150 periodicals. Computerized library services include the card catalog, interlibrary loans, and database searching. Special learning facilities include an art gallery. The 300-acre campus is in a suburban area about 30 miles east of Oklahoma City. Including any residence halls, there are 12 buildings.

Student Life: 70% of undergraduates are from Oklahoma. Students are from 13 states, 15 foreign countries, and Canada. 80% are from public schools. 65% are white; 15% foreign nationals. 40% are Catholic; 24% claim no religious affiliation. The average age of freshmen is 18. 35% do not continue beyond their first year.

Housing: 415 students can be accommodated in college housing, which includes single-sex and coed dorms. In addition, there are language houses and a dorm floor dedicated to honors students. On-campus housing is guaranteed for the freshman year only and is available on a first-come, first-served basis. Priority is given to out-of-town students. 70% of students live on campus; of those, 60% remain on campus on weekends. Alcohol is not permitted. All students may keep cars.

Activities: 10% of men belong to 3 local fraternities; 10% of women belong to 3 local sororities. There are 24 groups on campus, including art, cheerleading, choir, chorale, computers, dance, drama, ethnic, history, honors, international, musical theater, newspaper, photography, professional, radio and TV, religious, social, social service, student government, and yearbook. Popular campus events include sporting events, movie nights, and Hanging of the Green.

Sports: There are 5 intercollegiate sports for men and 7 for women, and 4 intramural sports for men and 4 for women. Facilities include soccer, baseball, and softball facilities, a wellness center with 2 gyms, Cybex equipment, and a free weight facility.

Disabled Students: 90% of the campus is accessible. Wheelchair ramps, elevators, special parking, specially equipped rest rooms, special class scheduling, and lowered drinking fountains are available.

Services: Counseling and information services are available, as is tutoring in every subject. Partners In Learning is a program designed to aid those students with learning disabilities. There is a reader service for the blind.

Campus Safety and Security: Measures include 24-hour foot and vehicle patrol, security escort services, informal discussions, lighted pathways/sidewalks, and card access to residence halls.

Programs of Study: St. Greg's confers B.A. in Humanities, B.A. in Theology, B.S. in Business, B.S. in Natural Science, and B.S. in Social Science. Students follow personalized degree programs under these five integrative degrees. Associate degrees are also awarded. Life sciences, premedicine, and conservation biology are the strongest academically. Natural sciences, business, and social sciences are the largest.

Required: To graduate, students must complete 128 credits, including approximately 40 in the major, with a minimum 2.0 GPA. The core curriculum focuses on professional communication, creative thinking, self leadership, and informational technology, including specific courses in English, speech, math, life science, physical science, philosophy, and theology. Students must pass a comprehensive exam at the end of sophomore year and complete a senior research project.

Special: Cross-registration is available through Oklahoma Baptist University. Each student designs a personalized program of study within the 5 integrative fields offered. The program should include one or more internships. Accelerated degree programs and study abroad in England and Mexico are offered. Directed study is available for further exploration of topics. There are 4 national honor societies, a freshman honors program, and all departments have honors programs.

Faculty/Classroom: 55% of faculty are male; 45%, female. All teach undergraduates. The average class size in an introductory lecture is 16; in a laboratory, 14; and in a regular course, 9.

Admissions: In a recent year, there were 2 National Merit semifinalists. 10 freshmen graduated first in their class.

Requirements: The ACT is required, with a minumum score of 18. St. Greg's requires applicants to be in the upper 50% of their class. A GPA of 2.0 is required. AP and CLEP credits are accepted. Important factors in the admissions decision are leadership record, parents or siblings attending the school, and recommendations by alumni.

Procedure: Freshmen are admitted to all sessions. Entrance exams should be taken in October. There is a deferred admissions plan and a rolling admissions plan. Application deadlines are open. Application fee is $25. Applications are accepted on-line via CollegeNET or the school's web site.

Transfer: 40 transfer students enrolled in a recent year. Applicants must have either an associate degree or a cumulative 2.0 GPA in all completed college courses. 30 of 128 credits required for the bachelor's degree must be completed at St. Greg's.

Visiting: There are regularly scheduled orientations for prospective students, consisting of a private tour by an admissions counselor. There are guides for informal visits and visitors may sit in on classes and stay overnight. To schedule a visit, contact the Office of Admissions at (405) 878-5100 or *drutledge@sgc.edu*.

Financial Aid: In a recent year, 62% of all full-time freshmen and 57% of continuing full-time students received some form of financial aid. 60% of full-time freshmen and 56% of continuing full-time students received need-based aid. The average freshman award was $7438. 38% of undergraduates work part time. Average annual earnings from campus work are $1000. The average financial indebtedness of a recent graduate was $12,516. The FAFSA is required. Check with the school for current deadlines.

International Students: In a recent year, there were 60 international students enrolled. The school actively recruits these students. They must score 500 on the written TOEFL or 173 on the electronic version or complete an on-campus intensive English program.

Computers: The mainframes are an IBM PC servers and a clone server. 30 PCs are available for student use, and each dorm room has Internet access. The computer lab is open 10 hours a day. There are no time limits and no fees. All students are required to have personal computers. Any model that meets minimum 650 MHz, 10 GB hard disk, and 128 M is recommended.

Graduates: In a recent year, 78 bachelor's degrees were awarded. The most popular majors were social science (38%), natural science (24%), and humanities (23%). 10 companies recruited on campus in a recent year. Of a recent graduating class, 6% were enrolled in graduate school within 6 months of graduation and 40% were employed.

Admissions Contact: Dan Rutledge, Director of Admissions.
E-mail: *drutledge@sgc.edu* Web: *www.sgc.edu*

SOUTHEASTERN OKLAHOMA STATE UNIVERSITY
Durant, OK 74701

D-3

(580) 745-2060; Fax: (580) 745-7502

Full-time: 1427 men, 1539 women	**Faculty:** 153; IIA, --$
Part-time: 283 men, 489 women	**Ph.D.s:** 65%
Graduate: 177 men, 288 women	**Student/Faculty:** 19 to 1
Year: semesters, summer session	**Tuition:** $2947 ($6847)
Application Deadline: open	**Room & Board:** $3200
Freshman Class: 1067 applied, 856 accepted, 649 enrolled	
ACT: 20	**COMPETITIVE**

Southeastern Oklahoma State University, founded in 1909, is a public institution offering programs in the arts and sciences, business, education, music, and technology to a primarily commuter student body. There are 3 undergraduate schools and 1 graduate school. In addition to regional accreditation, Southeastern has baccalaureate program accreditation with AACSB, ACBSP, NASM, and NCATE. The library contains 288,030 volumes, 563,955 microform items, and 7084 audio/video tapes/CDs, and subscribes to 1017 periodicals. Computerized library services include the card catalog, interlibrary loans, database searching, and Internet access. Special learning facilities include a learning resource center, radio station, and an herbarium. The 177-acre campus is in a rural area 90 miles north of Dallas. Including any residence halls, there are 46 buildings.

Student Life: 77% of undergraduates are from Oklahoma. Students are from 34 states, 34 foreign countries, and Canada. 99% are from public schools. 64% are white; 28% Native American/Eskimo. The average age of freshmen is 22; all undergraduates, 25. 42% do not continue beyond their first year; 40% remain to graduate.

Housing: 648 students can be accommodated in college housing, which includes single-sex and coed dorms, on-campus apartments, and married-student housing. In addition, there are special-interest houses. On-campus housing is guaranteed for all 4 years. 80% of students commute. Alcohol is not permitted. All students may keep cars.

Activities: 1% of men belong to 3 national fraternities; 5% of women belong to 2 national sororities. There are 70 groups on campus, including art, band, cheerleading, chess, choir, chorale, chorus, computers, dance, debate, drama, ethnic, forensics, honors, international, jazz band, literary magazine, marching band, musical theater, newspaper, opera, pep band, photography, political, professional, radio and TV, religious, social, social service, student government, and yearbook. Popular campus events include Parents Day, Candlelighting, and Springfest.

Sports: There are 4 intercollegiate sports for men and 5 for women, and 2 intramural sports for men and 1 for women. Facilities include a 4000-seat football stadium, a 2000-seat gym, baseball and softball fields, a track, tennis courts, playing fields, and a swimming pool.

Disabled Students: 70% of the campus is accessible. Wheelchair ramps, elevators, special parking, specially equipped rest rooms, special class scheduling, lowered drinking fountains, lowered telephones, and special housing are available.

Services: Counseling and information services are available, as is tutoring in every subject. There is a reader service for the blind, remedial math, reading, and writing, and tutoring in study skills.

Campus Safety and Security: Measures include 24-hour foot and vehicle patrol, self-defense education, security escort services, and informal discussions. There are pamphlets/posters/films, lighted pathways/sidewalks, and safety training.

Programs of Study: Southeastern confers B.A., B.S., B.A.A.S., B.B.A., B.G.S., B.M., and B.M.Ed. degrees. Master's degrees are also awarded. Bachelor's degrees are awarded in AGRICULTURE (conservation and regulation and environmental studies), BIOLOGICAL SCIENCE (biology/biological science and biotechnology), BUSINESS (accounting, business administration and management, recreation and leisure services, and secretarial studies/office management), COMMUNICATIONS AND THE ARTS (art, communications, dramatic arts, English, fine arts, music, and speech/debate/rhetoric), COMPUTER AND PHYSICAL SCIENCE (chemistry, computer science, information sciences and systems, mathematics, and physics), EDUCATION (art, business, early childhood, education of the mentally handicapped, elementary, mathematics, music, physical, science, secondary, and social studies), ENGINEERING AND ENVIRONMENTAL DESIGN (aviation administration/management and occupational safety and health), HEALTH PROFESSIONS (medical laboratory technology), SOCIAL SCIENCE (criminal justice, economics, gerontology, history, political science/government, psychology, social science, and sociology). Chemistry, history, and music are the strongest academically. Occupational safety and health, elementary education, and criminal justice are the largest.

Required: A total of 124 credit hours with a minimum GPA of 2.0 (2.5 for teacher education majors) is required for graduation. All students must complete 41 semester hours of general education requirements, including English, American history, government, humanities, arts, social and lab sciences, math, communications, and health education, and 3 hours of computer science.

Special: Internships, study abroad, credit for military experience, pass/fail options in some courses, and nondegree study are available. There are 15 national honor societies and 9 departmental honors programs.

Faculty/Classroom: 64% of faculty are male; 36%, female. All teach undergraduates and 10% do research. No introductory courses are taught by graduate students. The average class size in an introductory lecture is 28; in a laboratory, 18; and in a regular course, 23.

Admissions: 80% of the 2003-2004 applicants were accepted. The ACT scores for the 2003-2004 freshman class were: 60% below 21, 23% between 21 and 23, 12% between 24 and 26, 4% between 27 and 28, and 1% above 28. 30% of the current freshmen were in the top fifth of their class; 60% were in the top two fifths. 16 freshmen graduated first in their class.

Requirements: The ACT is required. In addition, applicants should be graduates of an accredited secondary school or have earned a GED. High school courses must include 4 years of English, 3 of math, 2 each of lab science and history, 1 of citizenship skills (from the subjects of economics, geography, government, or non-Western culture), and 3 additional units of subjects previously listed or of computer science or foreign language. Southeastern requires applicants to be in the upper 50% of their class. A GPA of 2.7 is required. AP and CLEP credits are accepted.

Procedure: Freshmen are admitted to all sessions. Entrance exams should be taken by the fall of the senior year. There is a rolling admissions plan. Application deadlines are open. Application fee is $20. Notification is sent on a rolling basis. Applications are accepted on-line.

Transfer: 445 transfer students enrolled in 2002-2003. Out-of-state applicants must have a 2.0 GPA. In-state applicants must have a 1.7 GPA with 24 to 36 credit hours earned, 1.8 with 37 to 72 hours, and 2.0 with 73 or more hours. 30 credits of 124 required for the bachelor's degree must be completed at Southeastern.

Visiting: There are guides for informal visits and visitors may sit in on classes. To schedule a visit, contact Admissions and Recruitment Services at (800) 435-1327, ext. 2060 or admissions@sosu.edu.

Financial Aid: In 2003-2004, 76% of all full-time freshmen and 70% of continuing full-time students received some form of financial aid. 51% of full-time freshmen and 55% of continuing full-time students received need-based aid. The average freshman award was $2585. Need-based scholarships or need-based grants averaged $1171 ($6050 maximum); need-based self-help aid (loans and jobs) averaged $1226 ($7560 maximum); non-need-based athletic scholarships averaged $1678 ($6764 maximum); and other non-need-based awards and non-need-based scholarships averaged $1350 ($3000 maximum). 45% of undergraduates work part time. Average annual earnings from campus work are $1200. The average financial indebtedness of the 2003 graduate was $8000. Southeastern is a member of CSS. The FAFSA is required. The priority date for freshman financial aid applications for fall entry is April 1.

International Students: There are 46 international students enrolled. They must score 550 on the written TOEFL or 213 on the electronic version and also take the SAT I or the ACT.

Computers: The mainframe is a Digital Alpha DS25 EV68. Students have access to the Internet and Web via 390 PCs in general-use student labs and teaching labs. Students are mainly served by Windows NT and Windows 2000 servers. All students may access the system. There are no time limits. The fee is $11 per credit hour.

Graduates: From July 1, 2002 to June 30, 2003, 618 bachelor's degrees were awarded. The most popular majors were elementary education (27%), business and marketing (17%), and engineering (9%). In an average class, 2% graduate in 3 years or less, 18% graduate in 4 years or less, 35% graduate in 5 years or less, and 40% graduate in 6 years or less. 130 companies recruited on campus in 2002-2003.

Admissions Contact: Kyle Stafford, Director, Admissions and Recruitment Services. E-mail: admissions@sosu.edu Web: www.sosu.edu

SOUTHERN NAZARENE UNIVERSITY
Bethany, OK 73008   D-3
(405) 491-6324
(800) 648-9899; Fax: (405) 491-6320

Full-time: 765 men, 860 women	**Faculty:** 53
Part-time: 30 men, 50 women	**Ph.D.s:** 58%
Graduate: 135 men, 170 women	**Student/Faculty:** 31 to 1
Year: semesters, summer session	**Tuition:** $10,315
Application Deadline: see profile	**Room & Board:** $4320
Freshman Class: n/av	
SAT I or ACT: required	**NONCOMPETITIVE**

Southern Nazarene University, founded in 1899, is a private, coeducational institution affiliated with the Church of the Nazarene. It offers programs in liberal arts and sciences, health fields, business, and education. Figures in above capsule and in this profile are approximate. There are 3 undergraduate schools and 1 graduate school. In addition to regional accreditation, SNU has baccalaureate program accreditation with NASM, NCATE, and NLN. The library contains 112,673 volumes, 219,576 microform items, and 3543 audio/video tapes/CDs, and subscribes to 667 periodicals. Computerized library services include the card catalog, interlibrary loans, and database searching. Special learning facilities include a learning resource center and TV station. The 40-acre campus is in a suburban area 10 miles northwest of Oklahoma City. Including any residence halls, there are 20 buildings.

Student Life: 55% of undergraduates are from out of state, mostly the South. Students are from 31 states, 22 foreign countries, and Canada. 90% are white. 90% are Protestant; 7% claim no religious affiliation. The average age of freshmen is 18; all undergraduates, 23. 10% do not continue beyond their first year; 45% remain to graduate.

Housing: 938 students can be accommodated in college housing, which includes single-sex dorms, on-campus apartments, and married-student housing. On-campus housing is guaranteed for all 4 years. 55% of students live on campus; of those, 80% remain on campus on weekends. Alcohol is not permitted. All students may keep cars.

Activities: There are no fraternities or sororities. There are 40 groups on campus, including band, cheerleading, choir, chorale, chorus, computers, drama, drum and bugle corps, honors, international, jazz band, literary magazine, musical theater, newspaper, orchestra, pep band, photography, political, professional, radio and TV, religious, social, social service, student government, symphony, and yearbook. Popular campus events include Valentine Banquet, Fall Fest, and Yule Feast.

Sports: There are 7 intercollegiate sports for men and 7 for women, and 3 intramural sports for men and 3 for women. Facilities include a 1824-seat phys ed center, gyms, a soccer complex, tennis courts, and an athletic convocation center that seats 4000.

Disabled Students: 95% of the campus is accessible. Wheelchair ramps, elevators, special parking, specially equipped rest rooms, special class scheduling, lowered drinking fountains, lowered telephones are available. Dorm rooms may be adapted for handicapped students.

Services: Counseling and information services are available, as is tutoring in most subjects. There is remedial math, reading, and writing. Services may be arranged for deaf or learning-disabled students.

Campus Safety and Security: Measures include 24-hour foot and vehicle patrol, self-defense education, security escort services, and informal discussions. There are lighted pathways/sidewalks and 24-hour controlled access into dorms.

Programs of Study: SNU confers A.B., B.S., and B.Mus.Ed. degrees. Associate and master's degrees are also awarded. Bachelor's degrees are awarded in AGRICULTURE (agriculture), BIOLOGICAL SCIENCE (biology/biological science), BUSINESS (accounting, banking and finance, business administration and management, business economics, management information systems, marketing/retailing/merchandising, office supervision and management, personnel management, and sports management), COMMUNICATIONS AND THE ARTS (communications, creative writing, English, fine arts, journalism, music, music business management, music performance, piano/organ, Spanish, speech/debate/rhetoric, and voice), COMPUTER AND PHYSICAL SCIENCE (chemistry, computer science, mathematics, and physics), EDUCATION (athletic training, business, early childhood, elementary, foreign languages, music, physical, and secondary), ENGINEERING AND ENVIRONMENTAL DESIGN (aviation administration/management and preengineering), HEALTH PROFESSIONS (exercise science, nursing, physical therapy, predentistry, premedicine, and prepharmacy), SOCIAL SCIENCE (biblical languages, criminal justice, history, international studies, missions, philosophy, political science/government, prelaw, psychology, religion, religious education, social science, and sociology). Premedicine, physics, and theology are the strongest academically. Business and education are the largest.

Required: A total of 124 semester hours, including at least 32 hours in the major, with a minimum GPA of 2.0 is required to graduate. All students must complete 53 hours of general education requirements covering core areas of self and identity, faith and tradition, and service and society. Skills courses must be taken in computer science, composition, speech communication, math, natural science, citizenship, foreign language, and phys ed.

Special: Cross-registration and co-op programs are available through the Southwestern Colleges of Christian Ministry. Internships may be arranged in the major. A Washington semester, study abroad in Latin America, England, Russia, and the Middle East, work-study programs in sociology, and dual and student-designed majors are available. There is an accelerated degree program in management of human resources and family studies and gerontology. SNU offers nondegree study for life/military/work experience. A Hollywood semester may be arranged through the Christian College Coalition. There are 6 national honor societies, including Phi Beta Kappa, and a freshman honors program.

Faculty/Classroom: 57% of faculty are male; 43%, female. All teach undergraduates and 15% do research. Graduate students teach 1% of introductory courses. The average class size in an introductory lecture is 20 and in a laboratory, 15.

Requirements: The SAT I or ACT is required. In addition, applicants must be graduates of an accredited secondary school or have a GED. SNU requires applicants to be in the upper 40% of their class. A GPA of 2.5 is required. AP and CLEP credits are accepted. Important factors in the admissions decision are advanced placement or honor courses, extracurricular activities record, and leadership record.

Procedure: Freshmen are admitted fall and spring. Entrance exams should be taken by April of the senior year or at orientation prior to the beginning of classes. There are early admissions, deferred admissions, and rolling admissions plans. Check with the school for current deadlines. The fall 2003 application fee was $25. The college accepts all applicants.

Transfer: Transfer applicants must have a 2.0 GPA and be in good standing at their previous college. 30 of 124 credits required for the bachelor's degree must be completed at SNU.

Visiting: There are regularly scheduled orientations for prospective students, including visits with faculty and students and seminars on financial aid and admissions. There are campus tours, group social activities, and small group mentoring throughout the fall semester. There are guides for informal visits and visitors may sit in on classes and stay overnight. To schedule a visit, contact the Office of Admissions.

Financial Aid: The FAFSA is required. Check with the school for current deadlines.

International Students: They must take the TOEFL.

Computers: The mainframe is an IBM AS 400. Students have access to 75 networked and 15 nonnetworked computers. DOS-based students may access an IBM S/36 and a MicroVAX II. All students may access the system Monday through Saturday. There are no time limits. The fee is $140 per year.

Admissions Contact: Brad Townley, Director of Admissions. A video is available. E-mail: *admiss@snu.edu* Web: *www.snu.edu*

SOUTHWESTERN OKLAHOMA STATE UNIVERSITY   D-3
Weatherford, OK 73096   (580) 774-3009; Fax: (580) 774-3795

Full-time: 1525 men, 1895 women	**Faculty:** 190; IIA, --$
Part-time: 170 men, 275 women	**Ph.D.s:** 65%
Graduate: 245 men, 365 women	**Student/Faculty:** 18 to 1
Year: semesters, summer session	**Tuition:** $2125 ($4870)
Application Deadline: see profile	**Room & Board:** $2680
Freshman Class: n/av	
ACT: required	**COMPETITIVE**

Southwestern Oklahoma State University, founded in 1901, is a public institution offering programs in education, arts and sciences, business, health sciences, and pharmacy. There are 4 undergraduate and 3 graduate schools. Figures in the above capsule and in this profile are approximate. In addition to regional accreditation, SWOSU has baccalaureate program accreditation with ABET, ABHES, ACBSP, ACOTE, ACPE, ACS, APTA, CAAHEP, CAHEA, CSWE, JRCERT, NAMT, NASM, NCATE, and NLN. The library contains 287,572 volumes, 1,168,558 microform items, and 872 audio/video tapes/CDs, and subscribes to 1551 periodicals. Computerized library services include the card catalog, interlibrary loans, and database searching. The 73-acre campus is in a small town 70 miles west of Oklahoma City. Including any residence halls, there are 30 buildings.

Student Life: 90% of undergraduates are from Oklahoma. Students are from 37 states, 36 foreign countries, and Canada. 98% are from public schools. 86% are white. The average age of freshmen is 19; all undergraduates, 23. 35% do not continue beyond their first year; 32% remain to graduate.

Housing: 1255 students can be accommodated in college housing, which includes single-sex dorms and married-student housing. On-campus housing is guaranteed for all 4 years. 73% of students commute. Alcohol is not permitted. All students may keep cars.

Activities: 2% of men belong to 2 local and 1 national fraternity; 2% of women belong to 3 local sororities. There are 66 groups on campus, including art, band, cheerleading, choir, chorale, chorus, computers, debate, drama, drill team, ethnic, forensics, honors, international, jazz band, marching band, musical theater, newspaper, opera, orchestra, pep band, political, professional, religious, social, social service, student government, symphony, and yearbook. Popular campus events include Howdy Week, Miss Southwestern Pageant, and Panorama Series.

Sports: There are 6 intercollegiate sports for men and 6 for women, and 8 intramural sports for men and 8 for women. Facilities include 2 gyms, a weight room, an indoor pool, an outdoor track, tennis courts, an outdoor football field and baseball diamond, 2 football practice fields, a rodeo arena, an exercise equipment room, a ropes course, and a lake. A soccer practice field, sand volleyball courts, and outdoor basketball courts are also available.

Disabled Students: 98% of the campus is accessible. Wheelchair ramps, elevators, special parking, specially equipped rest rooms, special class scheduling, lowered drinking fountains, and lowered telephones are available.

Services: Counseling and information services are available, as is tutoring in some subjects, including math, science, business, English, and social sciences. There is remedial math, reading, and writing. A student development center offers counseling and tutoring on an individual basis.

Campus Safety and Security: Measures include 24-hour foot and vehicle patrol, self-defense education, informal discussions, and pamphlets/posters/films. There are emergency telephones and lighted pathways/sidewalks.

Programs of Study: SWOSU confers B.A., B.S., B.A.Ed., B.Art, B.B.A., B.Comm.Art, B.Gen.Tech., B.M., B.M.Ed., B.Rec., B.S.Ed., B.S.Eng.Tech., B.S.H.I.M., B.S.M.T., B.S.N., and B.S.P. degrees. Associate, master's, and doctoral degrees are also awarded. Bachelor's degrees are awarded in BIOLOGICAL SCIENCE (biology/biological science, and biophysics), BUSINESS (accounting, banking and finance, business administration and management, management information systems, management science, marketing/retailing/merchandising, and recreational facilities management), COMMUNICATIONS AND THE ARTS (communications, English, and graphic design), COMPUTER AND PHYSICAL SCIENCE (chemistry, computer programming, computer science, information sciences and systems, mathematics, natural sciences, and physics), EDUCATION (art, athletic training, education administration, elementary, English, health, industrial arts, mathematics, music, physical, school psychology, science, secondary, social science, special, and technical), ENGINEERING AND ENVIRONMENTAL DESIGN (computer engineering, electrical/electronics engineering technology, engineering physics, engineering technology, environmental engineering technology, industrial administration/management, industrial engineering technology, manufacturing engineering, and manufacturing technology), HEALTH PROFESSIONS (health care administration, health science, medical records administration/services, medical technology, music therapy, and nursing), SOCIAL SCIENCE (community psychology, criminal justice, history, political science/government, psychology, and social work). Chemistry is the strongest academically. Business and education are the largest.

Required: To graduate, students must complete 124 semester hours with a minimum GPA of 2.0. Distribution requirements include 8 hours in communication and natural sciences, 6 each in history and government, fine arts and humanities, and international and cultural studies, 3 each in economics, health and phys ed, behavioral/social science, and math, and 2 in computer applications.

Special: SWOSU offers work-study programs and a program allowing high school seniors to earn college credits. Preprofessional curricula are offered in numerous areas including medicine, law, engineering, and allied health professions. There are 4 national honor societies.

Faculty/Classroom: 63% of faculty are male; 37%, female. All teach undergraduates, 10% do research, and 10% do both. Graduate students teach 1% of introductory courses. The average class size in a laboratory is 15 and in a regular course, 27.

Admissions: In a recent year, 55 freshmen graduated first in their class.

Requirements: The ACT is required, with a minimum composite score of 19. Applicants should be graduates of an accredited secondary school. The GED is accepted. Students should present at least 15 academic credits, including 4 in English, 3 in math, 2 each in history and lab science, 1 in citizenship, and 3 additional units in computer science or foreign language. SWOSU requires applicants to be in the upper 50% of their class. A GPA of 2.7 is required. AP and CLEP credits are accepted.

Procedure: Freshmen are admitted to all sessions. Entrance exams should be taken during the senior year. There is a rolling admissions plan. The fall 2003 application fee was $15. Check with the school for current deadlines.

Transfer: 299 transfer students enrolled in a recent year. Applicants must have a minimum college GPA of 2.0 and submit official transcripts from all institutions attended. 30 of 124 credits required for the bachelor's degree must be completed at SWOSU.

Visiting: There are regularly scheduled orientations for prospective students, including counseling sessions on careers, financial aid, social activities, and enrollment procedures. There are guides for informal visits and visitors may sit in on classes and stay overnight. To schedule a visit, contact the Director of High School and College Relations at (580) 774-3782 or *boydt@swosu.edu.*

Financial Aid: The FAFSA and the college's own financial statement are required. Check with the school for current deadlines.

International Students: In a recent year, there were 85 international students enrolled. They must score 500 on the written TOEFL and also take the ACT, scoring 19.

Computers: The mainframes are a DEC VAX 4700, a DEC VAX 4100, and a DEC Alpha. Macs, IBM PCs, and terminals are available in labs across campus. All students may access the system from 8 A.M. to midnight Monday through Thursday, 8 A.M. to 5 P.M. Friday, 10 A.M. to 2 P.M. Saturday, and 2 P.M. to midnight Sunday. There are no time limits and no fees.

Graduates: In a recent year, 553 bachelor's degrees were awarded. The most popular majors were accounting (7%), nursing (7%), and elementary education (6%). In an average class, 12% graduate in 4 years or less, 26% graduate in 5 years or less, and 32% graduate in 6 years or less. 140 companies recruited on campus in a recent year.

Admissions Contact: Connie Phillips, Admissions Coordinator. A video is available. E-mail: *phillic@swosu.edu* Web: *www.swosu.edu*

UNIVERSITY OF CENTRAL OKLAHOMA

E-5

Edmond, OK 73034

(405) 974-2338
(800) 254-4215; Fax: (405) 341-4964

Full-time: 4028 men, 5543 women	**Faculty:** 381; IIA, -$
Part-time: 1671 men, 2324 women	**Ph.D.s:** 73%
Graduate: 561 men, 1119 women	**Student/Faculty:** 25 to 1
Year: semesters, summer session	**Tuition:** $2714 ($6614)
Application Deadline: August 15	**Room & Board:** $4006
Freshman Class: 3791 applied, 3346 accepted, 2009 enrolled	
ACT: 22	**COMPETITIVE**

The University of Central Oklahoma, founded in 1890, is a state-supported institution offering undergraduate and graduate programs in the liberal arts and sciences, education, business, and music. There are 5 undergraduate schools and 1 graduate school. In addition to regional accreditation, UCO has baccalaureate program accreditation with ABFSE, ACBSP, ADA, NASM, NCATE, and NLN. The library contains 438,975 volumes, 989,936 microform items, and 30,202 audio/video tapes/CDs, and subscribes to 5244 periodicals. Computerized library services include the card catalog, interlibrary loans, database searching, and Internet access. Special learning facilities include a learning resource center, art gallery, radio station, and TV station. The 200-acre campus is in a suburban area north of Oklahoma City. Including any residence halls, there are 43 buildings.

Student Life: 87% of undergraduates are from Oklahoma. Students are from 38 states, 100 foreign countries, and Canada. 83% are from public schools. 68% are white; 10% foreign nationals. The average age

of freshmen is 21; all undergraduates, 24. 33% do not continue beyond their first year; 27% remain to graduate.

Housing: 1550 students can be accommodated in college housing, which includes single-sex and coed dorms, on-campus apartments, off-campus apartments, and married-student housing. On-campus housing is available on a first-come, first-served basis and is available on a lottery system for upperclassmen. 90% of students commute. Alcohol is not permitted. All students may keep cars.

Activities: 5% of men belong to 11 national fraternities; 7% of women belong to 7 national sororities. There are 170 groups on campus, including art, band, cheerleading, choir, computers, dance, debate, ethnic, gay, honors, international, jazz band, literary magazine, marching band, musical theater, newspaper, opera, orchestra, political, professional, radio and TV, religious, social, student government, and yearbook. Popular campus events include International Week, Black Heritage Week, and Indian Heritage Week.

Sports: There are 8 intercollegiate sports for men and 7 for women, and 21 intramural sports for men and 21 for women. Facilities include a field house with a gym, a swimming pool, a track, a weight room, a stadium with a track and a softball field, and a wellness center with basketball courts, aerobic classes, cardiovascular equipment, weights, and various classes.

Disabled Students: All of the campus is accessible. Wheelchair ramps, elevators, special parking, specially equipped rest rooms, special class scheduling, and lowered drinking fountains are available.

Services: Counseling and information services are available, as is tutoring in some subjects, including English, math, reading, and writing. There is remedial math.

Campus Safety and Security: Measures include 24-hour foot and vehicle patrol, security escort services, emergency telephones, lighted pathways/sidewalks, and a crime and terrorism tip line.

Programs of Study: UCO confers B.A., B.S., B.A.Ed., B.B.A., B.F.A., B.F.A.Ed., B.M.Ed., B.Mus., and B.S.Ed. degrees. Master's degrees are also awarded. Bachelor's degrees are awarded in BIOLOGICAL SCIENCE (biology/biological science and nutrition), BUSINESS (accounting, banking and finance, business administration and management, business economics, fashion merchandising, funeral home services, hotel/motel and restaurant management, human resources, insurance, management information systems, marketing/retailing/merchandising, and recreational facilities management), COMMUNICATIONS AND THE ARTS (advertising, broadcasting, communications, creative writing, dramatic arts, English, fine arts, French, German, graphic design, journalism, music, photography, public relations, Spanish, and speech/debate/rhetoric), COMPUTER AND PHYSICAL SCIENCE (actuarial science, chemistry, computer science, and mathematics), EDUCATION (art, business, dance, early childhood, elementary, English, foreign languages, industrial arts, marketing and distribution, mathematics, museum studies, music, physical, science, social studies, and special), ENGINEERING AND ENVIRONMENTAL DESIGN (engineering physics and interior design), HEALTH PROFESSIONS (community health work, industrial hygiene, medical laboratory technology, nursing, and speech pathology/audiology), SOCIAL SCIENCE (addiction studies, criminal justice, economics, family/consumer studies, forensic studies, geography, history, liberal arts/general studies, philosophy, physical fitness/movement, political science/government, psychology, public administration, and sociology). Nursing, business administration, and elementary education are the largest.

Required: Students must complete 124 semester hours with a 2.25 GPA. At least 15 hours in upper-division courses in the major are required. Students must also complete a maximum of 12 semester hours in general education requirements, including phys ed.

Special: There is cross-registration with the Downtown Consortium. Opportunities are provided for internships, B.A.-B.S. degrees, dual majors, a general studies degree, credit by exam, nondegree study, and credit for military experience. Work-study programs may be arranged through the Federal College Work-Study Program. There are 6 national honor societies.

Faculty/Classroom: 54% of faculty are male; 46%, female. No introductory courses are taught by graduate students.

Admissions: 88% of the 2003-2004 applicants were accepted. The ACT scores for the 2003-2004 freshman class were: 41% below 21, 31% between 21 and 23, 17% between 24 and 26, 7% between 27 and 28, and 4% above 28.

Requirements: The ACT is required, with a minimum composite score of 19. Graduation from an accredited secondary school is required. A GED will be accepted for adult students. The applicant's academic record should include 4 years of English, 3 years of math, first-year algebra and beyond, and 2 years each of lab science and history, of which 1 year must be in American history. UCO requires applicants to be in the upper 50% of their class. A GPA of 2.7 is required. AP and CLEP credits are accepted. Important factors in the admissions decision are evidence of special talent, extracurricular activities record, and leadership record.

Procedure: Freshmen are admitted to all sessions. Entrance exams should be taken within 30 days of submitting the application. There is an early admissions plan and a rolling admissions plan. Applications should be filed by August 15 for fall entry, January 2 for spring entry, and May 25 for summer entry, along with a $25 fee. Notification is sent on a rolling basis.

Transfer: 1545 transfer students enrolled in 2002-2003. Applicants must submit official transcripts from previous colleges attended and have a minimum GPA of 2.0. Students who have completed fewer than 24 hours of transferable credit must meet the requirements for entering freshmen. 30 credits of 124 required for the bachelor's degree must be completed at UCO.

Visiting: There are regularly scheduled orientations for prospective students, including a brief tour, a question-and-answer period, and access to an information booth. There are guides for informal visits and visitors may sit in on classes. To schedule a visit, contact Prospective Student Services at (405) 974-2727 or *4ucoinfo@ucok.edu*.

Financial Aid: 50% of undergraduates work part time. Average annual earnings from campus work are $2500. The CSS Profile, FFS, and the college's own financial statement are required. The deadline for filing freshman financial aid applications for fall entry is April 1.

International Students: There are 1226 international students enrolled. The school actively recruits these students. They must score 500 on the written TOEFL and also take the ACT, scoring 20.

Computers: Students may access some 140 terminals located in computer labs and in the library during scheduled hours. All students may access the system. There are no time limits and no fees.

Graduates: From July 1, 2002 to June 30, 2003, 1913 bachelor's degrees were awarded. The most popular majors were general studies (11%), information and operations management (7%), and accounting (5%). In an average class, 9% graduate in 4 years or less, 24% graduate in 5 years or less, and 27% graduate in 6 years or less. 68 companies recruited on campus in 2002-2003.

Admissions Contact: Linda Lofton, Director, Admissions.
E-mail: *admissions@ucok.edu* Web: *www.ucok.edu*

UNIVERSITY OF OKLAHOMA
Norman, OK 73019

D-3

(405) 325-2252
(800) 234-6868; Fax: (405) 325-7124

Full-time: 8897 men, 8750 women	**Faculty:** 1011; I, --$
Part-time: 1380 men, 1244 women	**Ph.D.s:** 86%
Graduate: 2221 men, 2008 women	**Student/Faculty:** 17 to 1
Year: semesters, summer session	**Tuition:** $3741 ($10,254)
Application Deadline: June 1	**Room & Board:** $5485
Freshman Class: 8140 applied, 6638 accepted, 3808 enrolled	
SAT I Verbal/Math: 592/598	**ACT:** 25 **VERY COMPETITIVE**

The University of Oklahoma, founded in 1890, is a comprehensive research university offering 160 areas for undergraduate study. There are 9 undergraduate and 9 graduate schools. In addition to regional accreditation, OU has baccalaureate program accreditation with AACSB, ABA, ABET, ACCE, ACEJMC, ADA, APA, APTA, CSAB, CSWE, FIDER, NAAB, NASM, and NCATE. The 9 libraries contain 4,088,505 volumes, 4,102,931 microform items, and 9064 audio/video tapes/CDs, and subscribe to 24,204 periodicals. Computerized library services include the card catalog, interlibrary loans, database searching, and Internet access. Special learning facilities include an art gallery, natural history museum, radio station, TV station, and observatory. The 3182-acre campus is in a suburban area 18 miles south of Oklahoma City. Including any residence halls, there are 232 buildings.

Student Life: 76% of undergraduates are from Oklahoma. Students are from 50 states, 105 foreign countries, and Canada. 72% are white. The average age of freshmen is 19; all undergraduates, 21. 17% do not continue beyond their first year; 54% remain to graduate.

Housing: 5500 students can be accommodated in college housing, which includes single-sex and coed dorms, on-campus apartments, and married-student housing. In addition, there are honors houses, special-interest houses, international floors, and intensive-study housing. On-campus housing is guaranteed for the freshman year only and is available on a first-come, first-served basis. 80% of students commute. All students may keep cars.

Activities: 17% of men belong to 1 local and 24 national fraternities; 25% of women belong to 1 local and 18 national sororities. There are more than 300 groups on campus, including art, band, cheerleading, chess, choir, chorale, chorus, computers, dance, debate, drama, drill team, ethnic, film, forensics, gay, honors, international, jazz band, literary magazine, marching band, musical theater, newspaper, opera, orchestra, pep band, photography, political, professional, radio and TV, religious, social, social service, student government, symphony, and yearbook. Popular campus events include Moms and Dads Days, Theater and Dance season, and Big Event Community Service.

Sports: There are 10 intercollegiate sports for men and 10 for women, and 35 intramural sports for men and 35 for women. Facilities include a golf course, a field house, an arena, a gymnastics center, tennis courts, a swimming pool complex, a fitness center, a football stadium, track and field facilities, and baseball, soccer, and softball fields.

Disabled Students: 90% of the campus is accessible. Wheelchair ramps, elevators, special parking, specially equipped rest rooms, special class scheduling, lowered drinking fountains, lowered telephones, special housing, 25 TDDs, automatic door openers, adaptive computers labs, and an office of disability services are available.

Services: Counseling and information services are available, as is tutoring in most subjects. There is a reader service for the blind and remedial math, reading, and writing. There are also volunteer note takers, interpreter and real-time reporting services for the deaf or hearing impaired, and alternative testing services. Tutoring is a personal service and therefore available to students with disabilities only as offered to the general student population.

Campus Safety and Security: Measures include 24-hour foot and vehicle patrol, self-defense education, security escort services, and shuttle buses. There are informal discussions, pamphlets/posters/films, emergency telephones, lighted pathways/sidewalks, a modified 911 system, and a bicycle patrol.

Programs of Study: OU confers B.A., B.S., B.B.A., B.F.A., and B.Mus. degrees. Master's and doctoral degrees are also awarded. Bachelor's degrees are awarded in BIOLOGICAL SCIENCE (botany, microbiology, and zoology), BUSINESS (accounting, banking and finance, business administration and management, business economics, international business management, management information systems, marketing/retailing/merchandising, and real estate), COMMUNICATIONS AND THE ARTS (advertising, art, art history and appreciation, broadcasting, classics, communications, dance, dramatic arts, English, film arts, fine arts, French, German, journalism, languages, linguistics, music, photography, public relations, Russian, Spanish, and video), COMPUTER AND PHYSICAL SCIENCE (astronomy, astrophysics, atmospheric sciences and meteorology, chemistry, computer science, geology, geophysics and seismology, geoscience, information sciences and systems, mathematics, and physics), EDUCATION (early childhood, elementary, foreign languages, mathematics, music, science, social studies, and special), ENGINEERING AND ENVIRONMENTAL DESIGN (aeronautical engineering, architecture, aviation administration/management, chemical engineering, civil engineering, computer engineering, construction management, electrical/electronics engineering, engineering, engineering physics, environmental design, environmental engineering, environmental science, geological engineering, industrial engineering, interior design, land use management and reclamation, mechanical engineering, and petroleum/natural gas engineering), HEALTH PROFESSIONS (health science and medical laboratory technology), SOCIAL SCIENCE (African American studies, anthropology, area studies, Asian/Oriental studies, economics, geography, history, international studies, liberal arts/general studies, Native American studies, philosophy, political science/government, psychology, public affairs, religion, social work, sociology, and women's studies). Meteorology, finance and accounting, and chemistry and biochemistry are the strongest academically. Psychology, sociology, and zoology are the largest.

Required: To graduate, students must have a minimum 2.0 GPA, depending on the major, and complete a minimum of 124 semester hours, the last 30 hours of which must be in residence. The number of hours required in the major varies. A 40-hour general education core includes courses in arts and humanities, oral and symbolic communication, natural science, and social science. All students must take 6 hours each of English composition, American history and government, and general education requirements. Seniors must take a 3-credit-hour capstone experience course integrating their undergraduate studies, and it must include writing.

Special: Co-op programs are available in engineering and business. A variety of voluntary and required internships is available in more than 50 fields of study. OU offers study abroad in 50 countries, work-study programs, a Washington semester, a general studies degree, dual and student-designed majors, nondegree study, pass/fail options, and credit for life experience. B.A.-B.S. degrees are offered in many subjects and an accelerated degree is offered in 11 majors. The interdisciplinary major in letters combines the classics, history, philosophy, and languages. A professional studies major is offered through the continuing education program. There are 37 national honor societies, including Phi Beta Kappa, a freshman honors program, and all departments have honors programs.

Faculty/Classroom: 66% of faculty are male; 34%, female. Graduate students teach 32% of introductory courses. The average class size in an introductory lecture is 46.

Admissions: 82% of the 2003-2004 applicants were accepted. The ACT scores for the 2003-2004 freshman class were: 9% below 21, 15% between 21 and 23, 36% between 24 and 26, 17% between 27 and 28, and 23% above 28. 62% of the current freshmen were in the top fifth of their class; 77% were in the top two fifths. There were 170 National Merit finalists. 302 freshmen graduated first in their class.

Requirements: The SAT I or ACT is required. In addition, performance requirements can be met by residents of Oklahoma with a high school GPA of 3.0 and a class ranking in the upper 25% or a minimum composite score of 1090 on the SAT I or 24 on the ACT. Nonresidents must have a high school GPA of 3.5 and rank in the top 25% or have a composite score of 26 on the ACT or an 1170 combined verbal and math score on the SAT I. Graduation from an accredited secondary school or a satisfactory score on the GED is required. Students must have a total of 15 curricular units, including 4 years of English, 3 of math, 2 each of history and lab science, 1 unit of citizenship skills, and 3 elective units from areas previously mentioned or computer science or foreign language. Some alternative admission opportunities are available but are limited. OU requires applicants to be in the upper 25% of their class. A GPA of 3.0 is required. AP and CLEP credits are accepted.

Procedure: Freshmen are admitted to all sessions. Entrance exams should be taken during the junior year or the first part of the senior year. Applications should be filed by June 1 for fall entry, November 1 for spring entry, and April 1 for summer entry, along with a $25 fee or $75 for international applicants. There is a rolling admissions plan. Notification is sent on a rolling basis. 706 applicants were on the 2003 waiting list; 190 were admitted.

Transfer: 1561 transfer students enrolled in 2002-2003. Applicants who have attempted 7 to 59 semester hours of college work must have a minimum GPA of 2.5. Applicants with 60 or more semester hours attempted must have a minimum GPA of 2.0; nonresident applicants with engineering majors must have a minimum 3.0 GPA. Applicants with fewer than 24 semester hours of college level work must also meet freshman admission requirements. Nonresidents must be in good standing at the last institution attended. 30 of 124 credits required for the bachelor's degree must be completed at OU.

Visiting: There are regularly scheduled orientations for prospective students, consisting of sessions tailored to individual needs and interests. There are guides for informal visits and visitors may sit in on classes and stay overnight. To schedule a visit, contact Prospective Student Services at (405) 325-2151 or *ou-pss@ou.edu.*

Financial Aid: In 2003-2004, 74% of all full-time freshmen and 76% of continuing full-time students received some form of financial aid. 58% of full-time freshmen and 57% of continuing full-time students received need-based aid. The average freshman award was $6524. Need-based scholarships or need-based grants averaged $3700 ($10,132 maximum); need-based self-help aid (loans and jobs) averaged $6200 ($9825 maximum); non-need-based athletic scholarships averaged $5083 ($20,748 maximum); and other non-need-based awards and non-need-based scholarships averaged $3566. 55% of undergraduates work part time. Average annual earnings from campus work are $2092. The average financial indebtedness of the 2003 graduate was $17,445. OU is a member of CSS. The FAFSA is required. The priority date for freshman financial aid applications for fall entry is March 1. The deadline for filing freshman financial aid applications for fall entry is June 1.

International Students: There are 606 international students enrolled. They must score 550 on the written TOEFL or 213 on the electronic version.

Computers: The mainframe is an IBM 9672-R14. Students may access several hundred computers distributed throughout the campus with a wide range of software, including word processing, presentation graphics, Internet access, and other tools and applications. Off-campus access is available via dial-up or commercial broadband access. All students may access the system 24 hours per day. There are no time limits. The fee is $10. It is strongly recommended that all students have a personal computer. It is required that students in engineering programs have personal computers. A special OU student PC package is available through Dell.

Graduates: From July 1, 2002 to June 30, 2003, 2981 bachelor's degrees were awarded. The most popular majors were management information (8%), marketing (6%), and sociology (5%). In an average class, 1% graduate in 3 years or less, 19% graduate in 4 years or less, 44% graduate in 5 years or less, and 54% graduate in 6 years or less. 1120 companies recruited on campus in 2002-2003.

Admissions Contact: Pat Lynch, Director of Admissions. A video is available. E-mail: *admrec@ou.edu* Web: *www.ou.edu*

UNIVERSITY OF SCIENCE AND ARTS OF OKLAHOMA D-4
Chickasha, OK 73018-5322 (405) 574-1204
(800) 933-8726; Fax: (405) 574-1220

Full-time: 419 men, 640 women	**Faculty:** 48; IIB, --$
Part-time: 108 men, 282 women	**Ph.D.s:** 88%
Graduate: none	**Student/Faculty:** 22 to 1
Year: trimesters, summer session	**Tuition:** $2312 ($5432)
Application Deadline: September 8	**Room & Board:** $3670
Freshman Class: 523 applied, 448 accepted, 296 enrolled	
ACT: 20	COMPETITIVE

The University of Science and Arts of Oklahoma, founded in 1908, is a publicly funded liberal arts institution, providing interdisciplinary learning opportunities. In addition to regional accreditation, USAO has baccalaureate program accreditation with CED, NASM, and NCATE, The library contains 72,716 volumes, 153,126 microform items, and 4608 audio/video tapes/CDs, and subscribes to 137 periodicals. Computerized library services include the card catalog, interlibrary loans, database searching, and Internet access. Special learning facilities include a learn-

ing resource center, art gallery, a commercial art computer lab, and a speech pathology clinic. The 75-acre campus is in a small town 40 miles southwest of Oklahoma City. Including any residence halls, there are 14 buildings.

Student Life: 94% of undergraduates are from Oklahoma. Students are from 15 states, 14 foreign countries, and Canada. 94% are from public schools. 76% are white; 15% Native American/Eskimo. The average age of freshmen is 19; all undergraduates, 23. 43% do not continue beyond their first year; 27% remain to graduate.

Housing: 504 students can be accommodated in college housing, which includes single-sex and coed dorms and on-campus apartments. On-campus housing is guaranteed for the freshman year only and is available on a first-come, first-served basis. 73% of students commute. All students may keep cars.

Activities: 5% of men belong to 1 national fraternity. There are no sororities. There are 26 groups on campus, including art, band, cheerleading, choir, chorale, chorus, computers, drama, drill team, ethnic, honors, international, jazz band, literary magazine, musical theater, newspaper, opera, orchestra, pep band, photography, political, professional, radio and TV, religious, social, and student government. Popular campus events include Montmartre Festival, Curriculum Contest, and Christmas fine arts productions.

Sports: There are 3 intercollegiate sports for men and 3 for women, and 4 intramural sports for men and 4 for women. Facilities include a field house, a 2000-seat gym, a 1000-seat auditorium, a ballpark with baseball and softball fields, each seating 200, a soccer field with seating for 250, tennis courts, a pool, and a weight room.

Disabled Students: All of the campus is accessible. Wheelchair ramps, elevators, special parking, specially equipped rest rooms, special class scheduling, lowered drinking fountains, and lowered telephones are available.

Services: Counseling and information services are available, as is tutoring in some subjects, including math, writing, and reading. There is remedial math, reading, and writing. Tutors and interpreters are available for hearing-impaired students.

Campus Safety and Security: Measures include 24-hour foot and vehicle patrol, informal discussions, pamphlets/posters/films, and lighted pathways/sidewalks.

Programs of Study: USAO confers B.A., B.S., and B.F.A. degrees. Bachelor's degrees are awarded in BIOLOGICAL SCIENCE (biology/biological science), BUSINESS (business administration and management), COMMUNICATIONS AND THE ARTS (art, communications, dramatic arts, English, fine arts, and music), COMPUTER AND PHYSICAL SCIENCE (chemistry, computer science, mathematics, natural sciences, and physics), EDUCATION (early childhood, education of the deaf and hearing impaired, elementary, and physical), HEALTH PROFESSIONS (speech pathology/audiology), SOCIAL SCIENCE (American Indian studies, economics, history, political science/government, psychology, and sociology). Business, social science, and arts and humanities are the strongest academically. Business, art, and physical education are the largest.

Required: To graduate, students must complete a total of 124 credit hours with a minimum GPA of 2.0. Required core courses include 29 hours of team-taught interdisciplinary ideas in math, science, and social science, 15 of interdisciplinary skills in logic and critical thinking, writing, and computer science, 3 of freshman seminar, and 2 each of artistic and physical expression. Other requirements include a 2-hour senior seminar, an English proficiency exam, and entry-, junior-, and senior-level academic assessments.

Special: USAO offers dual majors, accelerated degree programs in all majors through year-round study, work-study programs, internship placement in community institutions, a Tutorial Scholars Program for student-designed majors, an interdisciplinary studies program, and a limited number of pass/fail options. There are 5 national honor societies, a freshman honors program, and 1 departmental honors program.

Faculty/Classroom: 62% of faculty are male; 38%, female. All teach undergraduates; 56% both teach and do research. The average class size in an introductory lecture is 22; in a laboratory, 18; and in a regular course, 21.

Admissions: 86% of the 2003-2004 applicants were accepted. The ACT scores for the 2003-2004 freshman class were: 55% below 21, 24% between 21 and 23, 14% between 24 and 26, 4% between 27 and 28, and 3% above 28. 23% of the current freshmen were in the top fifth of their class; 56% were in the top two fifths. 11 freshmen graduated first in their class.

Requirements: The ACT is required, with a minimum composite score of 20. Applicants must be graduates of an accredited secondary school or have a GED. They must complete 20 high school academic credits, including 4 years of English, 3 of math, and 2 each of lab science and history, 1 of which is American history. USAO requires applicants to be in the upper 50% of their class. A GPA of 2.7 is required. AP and CLEP credits are accepted.

Procedure: Freshmen are admitted to all sessions. Entrance exams should be taken by May of the preceding spring. There is a rolling admissions plan. Applications should be filed by September 8 for fall entry. The fall 2003 application fee was $15. Notification is sent on a rolling basis. Applications are accepted on computer disk and on-line through Apply or the school's web site.

Transfer: 101 transfer students enrolled in 2002-2003. Applicants must have a minimum GPA of 2.0. Those students with fewer than 30 college-level credit hours must submit a high school transcript or GED and ACT scores. 30 credits of 124 required for the bachelor's degree must be completed at USAO.

Visiting: There are guides for informal visits and visitors may sit in on classes. To schedule a visit, contact the Admissions Office at (405) 574-1357 or usao-admissions@usao.edu.

Financial Aid: In 2003-2004, 87% of all full-time freshmen and 86% of continuing full-time students received some form of financial aid. 71% of full-time freshmen and 72% of continuing full-time students received need-based aid. The average freshman award was $5303. Need-based scholarships or need-based grants averaged $4319 ($11,640 maximum); need-based self-help aid (loans and jobs) averaged $2525 ($4625 maximum); non-need-based athletic scholarships averaged $4270 ($9956 maximum); and other non-need-based awards and non-need-based scholarships averaged $1809 ($7370 maximum). 23% of undergraduates work part time. Average annual earnings from campus work are $1012. The average financial indebtedness of the 2003 graduate was $12,268. The FAFSA and Institution Information Sheet are required. The priority date for freshman financial aid applications for fall entry is March 15. The regular fall application deadline is rolling.

International Students: There are 20 international students enrolled. The school actively recruits these students. They must score 500 on the written TOEFL or 170 on the electronic version and also take the ACT, scoring 20.

Computers: The mainframe is a DEC VAX 4700A. There are computer labs campuswide with networked PCs and Macs, all with Internet access. The library also has PCs available. Dorms are wired to the bedside. All students may access the system at any time. There are no time limits and no fees.

Graduates: From July 1, 2002 to June 30, 2003, 195 bachelor's degrees were awarded. The most popular majors were business administration (14%), elementary education (9%), and physical education (9%). In an average class, 17% graduate in 4 years or less, 28% graduate in 5 years or less, and 30% graduate in 6 years or less. 30 companies recruited on campus in 2002-2003. Of the 2002 graduating class, 10% were enrolled in graduate school within 6 months of graduation and 91% were employed.

Admissions Contact: Joe Evans, Director of Admissions/Registrar. E-mail: jwevans@usao.edu Web: http://www.usao.edu

UNIVERSITY OF TULSA
Tulsa, OK 74104-3189

E-2

(918) 631-2307
(800) 331-3050; Fax: (918) 631-5003

Full-time: 1232 men, 1229 women	**Faculty:** 260; IIA, +$
Part-time: 103 men, 108 women	**Ph.D.s:** 96%
Graduate: 793 men, 607 women	**Student/Faculty:** 9 to 1
Year: semesters, summer session	**Tuition:** $16,480
Application Deadline: open	**Room & Board:** $5610
Freshman Class: 2292 applied, 1747 accepted, 590 enrolled	
SAT I Verbal/Math: 600/600	**ACT:** 26 **VERY COMPETITIVE+**

The University of Tulsa, founded in 1894, is a private comprehensive institution offering 60 undergraduate major areas of study through its programs in liberal arts and sciences, engineering and natural sciences, and business administration. There are 3 undergraduate and 2 graduate schools. In addition to regional accreditation, TU has baccalaureate program accreditation with AACSB, ABET, CSAB, NASM, NCATE, and NLN. The 2 libraries contain 1,003,918 volumes, 3,206,420 microform items, and 14,726 audio/video tapes/CDs, and subscribe to 16,324 periodicals. Computerized library services include the card catalog, interlibrary loans, database searching, and Internet access. Special learning facilities include an art gallery, radio station, and TV station. The 209-acre campus is in an urban area in the city of Tulsa. Including any residence halls, there are 77 buildings.

Student Life: 64% of undergraduates are from Oklahoma. Others are from 37 states, 56 foreign countries, and Canada. 81% are from public schools. 64% are white; 11% foreign nationals. 45% are Protestant; 38% claim no religious affiliation; 12% Catholic. The average age of freshmen is 18; all undergraduates, 21. 22% do not continue beyond their first year; 54% remain to graduate.

Housing: 2192 students can be accommodated in college housing, which includes single-sex and coed dorms, on-campus apartments, off-campus apartments, married-student housing, and sorority houses. In addition, there are honors houses and language houses. On-campus housing is guaranteed for all 4 years. 65% of students live on campus; of those, 92% remain on campus on weekends. All students may keep cars.

Activities: 21% of men belong to 7 national fraternities; 23% of women belong to 9 national sororities. There are 272 groups on campus, including art, band, cheerleading, chess, choir, chorale, chorus, computers, dance, drama, drill team, ethnic, film, gay, honors, international, jazz band, literary magazine, marching band, musical theater, newspaper, opera, orchestra, pep band, photography, political, professional, radio and TV, religious, social, social service, student government, symphony, and yearbook. Popular campus events include Parents Weekend, Springfest, and Black Heritage Month.

Sports: There are 8 intercollegiate sports for men and 10 for women, and 25 intramural sports for men and 25 for women. Facilities include a 40,000-seat stadium, an 8300-seat baketball arena, a gym, an athletic field, indoor racquetball courts, basketball and tennis courts, an indoor swimming pool, a handball court, a weight room, a dance studio, student fitness center, soccer fields, softball field, track, multi-purpose recreational field, and outdoor tennis courts.

Disabled Students: 80% of the campus is accessible. Wheelchair ramps, elevators, special parking, specially equipped rest rooms, special class scheduling, lowered drinking fountains, lowered telephones, and sidewalks and curb cuts are available.

Services: Counseling and information services are available, as is tutoring in most subjects. There is a reader service for the blind. Special labs are available to students in need of assistance in math and writing courses, and study skills classes are available free of charge. Special-needs students are assisted on an individual basis.

Campus Safety and Security: Measures include 24-hour foot and vehicle patrol, self-defense education, security escort services, and informal discussions. There are pamphlets/posters/films, emergency telephones, and lighted pathways/sidewalks. Electronic door locks on residence halls open only with student identification.

Programs of Study: TU confers B.A., B.S., B.F.A., B.Mus.Ed., B.S.A.M., B.S.A.T., B.S.B., B.S.B.A., B.S.C., B.S.C.E., B.S.C.S., B.S.D.E., B.S.E., B.S.E.E., B.S.E.P., B.S.E.S.S., B.S.G.S., B.S.I.B.L., B.S.M.E., B.S.N., B.S.P.E., and B.S.S.P. degrees. Master's and doctoral degrees are also awarded. Bachelor's degrees are awarded in AGRICULTURE (environmental studies), BIOLOGICAL SCIENCE (biochemistry and biology/biological science), BUSINESS (accounting, banking and finance, international business management, management information systems, management science, marketing/retailing/merchandising, and sports management), COMMUNICATIONS AND THE ARTS (art, arts administration/management, communications, English, film arts, French, German, music, music performance, musical theater, piano/organ, Spanish, and voice), COMPUTER AND PHYSICAL SCIENCE (chemistry, computer science, geology, geoscience, information sciences and systems, mathematics, and physics), EDUCATION (athletic training, education, education of the deaf and hearing impaired, elementary, and music), ENGINEERING AND ENVIRONMENTAL DESIGN (chemical engineering, electrical/electronics engineering, engineering physics, mechanical engineering, and petroleum/natural gas engineering), HEALTH PROFESSIONS (exercise science, nursing, premedicine, and speech pathology/audiology), SOCIAL SCIENCE (anthropology, economics, history, philosophy, political science/government, prelaw, psychology, religion, Russian and Slavic studies, and sociology). Petroleum engineering, psychology, and English are the strongest academically. Management, mechanical engineering, and computer science are the largest.

Required: To graduate, students must complete 124 to 136 credit hours, including 24 to 51 in the major, with a minimum GPA determined by the major. Freshmen in liberal arts and business administration must complete the First Seminar. All students must complete the core curriculum, which includes 3 writing courses and at least 1 course in math. All students must also complete the general curriculum, which requires 8 courses in 4 categories (artistic imagination, social inquiry, cultural interpretation, and scientific investigation). A foreign language requirement of 2 years for liberal arts and sciences students and 1 year for business majors must be completed.

Special: Internships are available in the Tulsa area during the school year and in cities throughout the United States during the summer. Students may participate in more than 40 study-abroad programs, most of them arranged through the Institute of European Studies. TU offers a Washington semester, B.A.-B.S. degrees, cross-registration with the 3 undergraduate schools, dual and student-designed majors, accelerated degree programs, nondegree study, work-study programs, and pass/fail options. There are 37 national honor societies, including Phi Beta Kappa, and a freshman honors program.

Faculty/Classroom: 66% of faculty are male; 34%, female. All both teach and do research. No introductory courses are taught by graduate students. The average class size in an introductory lecture is 23; in a laboratory, 16; and in a regular course, 19.

Admissions: 76% of the 2003-2004 applicants were accepted. The SAT I scores for the 2003-2004 freshman class were: Verbal--17% below 500, 29% between 500 and 599, 32% between 600 and 700, and 22% above 700; Math--16% below 500, 33% between 500 and 599, 33% between 600 and 700, and 18% above 700. The ACT scores were 14% below 21, 18% between 21 and 23, 25% between 24 and 26, 15% between 27 and 28, and 28% above 28. 74% of the current freshmen were in the top fifth of their class; 90% were in the top two fifths. There were 48 National Merit finalists. 39 freshmen graduated first in their class.

Requirements: The SAT I or ACT is required for some programs. In addition, graduation from an accredited secondary school or satisfactory scores on the GED are also required for admission. The school recommends a minimum of 15 academic credits, including 4 years of English, 3 to 4 years each of math, science, and social studies (including history), and 2 years of a single foreign language. An essay and an interview are highly recommended. An audition or a portfolio is required for students applying for music, theater, or art scholarships. TU requires applicants to be in the upper 33% of their class. A GPA of 3.0 is required. AP and CLEP credits are accepted. Important factors in the admissions decision are advanced placement or honor courses, leadership record, and extra-curricular activities record.

Procedure: Freshmen are admitted fall, spring, and summer. Entrance exams should be taken during spring of the junior year or fall of the senior year. There is a rolling admissions plan and a deferred admissions plan. Application deadlines are open. Application fee is $35. Applications are accepted on computer disk and on-line through College Link.

Transfer: 200 transfer students enrolled in 2002-2003. Transfer students must submit official transcripts from all colleges attended and should have a minimum GPA of 2.5 for all college and high school work. Applicants with fewer than 30 credit hours must submit ACT or SAT I scores. Those with fewer than 60 credit hours must submit an official high school transcript. Applicants 25 years of age or older are exempt from submitting ACT or SAT I scores unless requested to do so by the Admission Office. 45 of 126 credits required for the bachelor's degree must be completed at TU.

Visiting: There are regularly scheduled orientations for prospective students, including overnight programs in the fall and spring. Students stay on campus and attend special information sessions. There are guides for informal visits and visitors may sit in on classes and stay overnight. To schedule a visit, contact the Office of Admission at *admission@utulsa.edu.*

Financial Aid: In 2003-2004, 98% of all full-time freshmen and 77% of continuing full-time students received some form of financial aid. 47% of full-time freshmen and 36% of continuing full-time students received need-based aid. The average freshman award was $20,760. Need-based scholarships or need-based grants averaged $3583 ($5300 maximum); need-based self-help aid (loans and jobs) averaged $6266 ($8925 maximum); non-need based athletic scholarships averaged $8844 ($22,615 maximum); and other non-need based awards and non-need based scholarships averaged $7859 ($16,400 maximum). 21% of undergraduates work part time. Average annual earnings from campus work are $2300. The average financial indebtedness of the 2003 graduate was $14,546. The FAFSA and the college's own financial statement are required. The deadline for filing freshman financial aid applications for fall entry is April 1.

International Students: There are 274 international students enrolled. The school actively recruits these students. They must score 500 on the written TOEFL or 173 on the electronic version.

Computers: The mainframes are a Sun E-3500 and Sun 450. There are more than 900 PCs and Macs available throughout the campus. Connections are available in university housing, as are e-mail and Internet access. All students may access the system 24 hours per day. There are no time limits and no fees.

Graduates: From July 1, 2002 to June 30, 2003, 530 bachelor's degrees were awarded. The most popular majors were marketing (8%), management (7%), and psychology (6%). In an average class, 37% graduate in 4 years or less, 53% graduate in 5 years or less, and 54% graduate in 6 years or less. 197 companies recruited on campus in 2002-2003. Of the 2002 graduating class, 22% were enrolled in graduate school within 6 months of graduation and 78% were employed.

Admissions Contact: John C. Corso, Associate Vice President for Administration/Dean of Admission. A video is available.
E-mail: *admission@utulsa.edu* Web: *www.utulsa.edu*

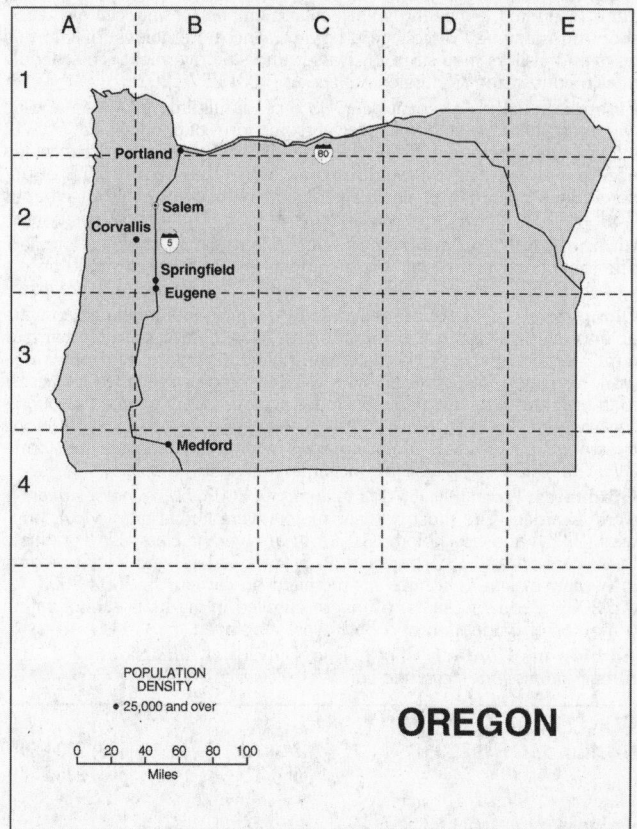

A B C D E

1

Portland

2
Salem
Corvallis

Springfield
Eugene

3

Medford

4

POPULATION
DENSITY
● 25,000 and over

0 20 40 60 80 100
Miles

OREGON

ART INSTITUTE OF PORTLAND
Portland, OR 97209-2911

B-1

(503) 228-6528
(888) 228-6528; Fax: (503) 227-1945

Full-time: 466 men, 534 women	**Faculty:** 27
Part-time: 150 men, 177 women	**Ph.D.s:** 52%
Graduate: none	**Student/Faculty:** 37 to 1
Year: quarters, summer session	**Tuition:** $15,345
Application Deadline: open	**Room & Board:** $7695
Freshman Class: n/av	
SAT I or ACT: recommended	**SPECIAL**

The Art Institute of Portland is a private institution offering undergraduate programs in interior, graphic, and apparel design; media arts and animation; multimedia and web design; game art and design; digital media production; and advertising. The library contains 22,289 volumes and 1000 audio/video tapes/CDs, and subscribes to 200 periodicals. Computerized library services include the card catalog, interlibrary loans, database searching, and Internet access. Special learning facilities include a learning resource center. The 1-acre campus is in an urban area in downtown Portland. Including any residence halls, there are 2 buildings.

Student Life: 69% of undergraduates are from Oregon. 81% are white. The average age of freshmen is 23; all undergraduates, 25.

Housing: 110 students can be accommodated in college housing, which includes coed off-campus apartments. On-campus housing is available on a first-come, first-served basis. 92% of students commute. Alcohol is not permitted. No one may keep cars.

Activities: There are no fraternities or sororities. There are 6 groups on campus, including art, computers, film, international, professional, and student government. Popular campus events include portfolio review, animation shows, and Halloween and Valentine's Day activities.

Sports: There is no sports program at AIPD.

Disabled Students: All of the campus is accessible. Wheelchair ramps, elevators, special parking, specially equipped rest rooms, special class scheduling, lowered drinking fountains, and lowered telephones are available.

Services: Counseling and information services are available, as is tutoring in most subjects. There is remedial math, reading, and writing.

Campus Safety and Security: Measures include informal discussions, pamphlets/posters/films, emergency telephones, lighted pathways/sidewalks, and a night security guard.

Programs of Study: AIPD confers the B.S. degree. Associate degrees are also awarded. Bachelor's degrees are awarded in COMMUNICATIONS AND THE ARTS (advertising, animation, apparel design, graphic design, media arts, and multimedia), ENGINEERING AND ENVIRONMENTAL DESIGN (interior design). Interior design is the strongest academically. Graphic design is the largest.

Required: To graduate, students must complete 180 quarter hours, including 111 in the major, with a minimum GPA of 2.0. Distribution requirements include 9 credits each in English composition and history of material culture, 6 credits in basic design, and 3 credits each in drawing, computer fundamentals, physics, math, art history, and critical thinking.

Special: Accelerated degree programs and field trips to San Francisco and annually to Europe are available. Internships are required for most programs.

Faculty/Classroom: 44% of faculty are male; 56%, female. All teach undergraduates. The average class size in an introductory lecture is 25; in a laboratory, 25; and in a regular course, 20.

Requirements: The SAT I or ACT is recommended. In addition, a high school diploma or GED is required. An essay, and an interview with an admissions officer are required. A GPA of 2.5 is required. AP and CLEP credits are accepted. Important factors in the admissions decision are evidence of special talent, personality/intangible qualities, and recommendations by school officials.

Procedure: Freshmen are admitted to all sessions. There is a deferred admissions plan and a rolling admissions plan. Application deadlines are open. Application fee is $50. Notification is sent on a rolling basis. 169 early decision candidates were accepted for the 2003-2004 class. Applications are accepted on-line through the institute's web site.

Transfer: 185 transfer students enrolled in 2002-2003. Requirements are the same as for new students. 45 credits of 180 required for the bachelor's degree must be completed at AIPD.

Visiting: There are regularly scheduled orientations for prospective students, including college tours, mini class sessions, financial aid and financial planning meetings, and career assessment. There are guides for informal visits and visitors may sit in on classes. To schedule a visit, contact the Admissions Office at aipdadm@aii.edu.

Financial Aid: In 2003-2004, 84% of all full-time freshmen and 80% of continuing full-time students received some form of financial aid. 82% of full-time freshmen and 75% of continuing full-time students received need-based aid. The average freshman award was $11,093. Need-based scholarships or need-based grants averaged $3784 ($4050 maximum); need-based self-help aid (loans and jobs) averaged $3051 ($5500 maximum); and non-need-based awards and non-need-based scholarships averaged $3495 ($6252 maximum). 4% of undergraduates work part time. Average annual earnings from campus work are $2431. The average financial indebtedness of the 2003 graduate was $19,400. AIPD is a member of CSS. The FAFSA is required. The priority date for freshman financial aid applications for fall entry is March 1. The regular fall application deadline is rolling.

International Students: There are 37 international students enrolled. The school actively recruits these students. They must score 480 on the written TOEFL or 157 on the electronic version.

Computers: Students have access to more than 280 computers on campus, which are all Internet ready. All students may access the system weekdays and weekends, daytime and evening. There are no time limits and no fees. It is strongly recommended that all students have a personal computer.

Graduates: The most popular majors were graphic design (27%), multimedia (18%), and apparel design (17%). 375 companies recruited on campus in 2002-2003. Of the 2002 graduating class, 1% were enrolled in graduate school within 6 months of graduation and 90% were employed.

Admissions Contact: Kelly Alston, Director of Admissions.
E-mail: aipdadm@aii.edu Web: www.aipd.artinstitutes.edu

CASCADE COLLEGE
B-2
Portland, OR 97216-1515
(503) 255-7060
(800) 550-7678; Fax: (503) 257-1222

Full-time: 132 men, 132 women	Faculty: 15
Part-time: 6 men, 10 women	Ph.Ds: 53%
Graduate: none	Student/Faculty: 18 to 1
Year: semesters, summer session	Tuition: $11,000
Application Deadline: open	Room & Board: $5700
Freshman Class: 243 applied, 243 accepted, 73 enrolled	
SAT I Verbal/Math: 485/440	ACT: 21 NONCOMPETITIVE

Cascade College is a Christian liberal arts college offering bachelor's degrees in interdisciplinary studies, business, biblical studies, English, psychology, and early childhood education. The library contains 25,000 volumes, 62,045 microform items, and 1200 audio/video tapes/CDs, and subscribes to 110 periodicals. Computerized library services include the card catalog, interlibrary loans, database searching, and Internet access. Special learning facilities include a learning resource center. The 12-acre campus is in a suburban area 8 miles east of downtown Portland. Including any residence halls, there are 16 buildings.

Student Life: 64% of undergraduates are from out of state, mostly the Northwest. Students are from 20 states, 6 foreign countries, and Canada. 85% are from public schools. 82% are white. 85% are Protestant. The average age of freshmen is 19; all undergraduates, 20. 40% do not continue beyond their first year; 25% remain to graduate.

Housing: 233 students can be accommodated in college housing, which includes single-sex dorms. On-campus housing is guaranteed for all 4 years. 75% of students live on campus; of those, 65% remain on campus on weekends. Alcohol is not permitted. All students may keep cars.

Activities: There are no fraternities or sororities. There are 18 groups on campus, including band, cheerleading, choir, chorale, chorus, drama, honors, jazz band, literary magazine, professional, religious, social service, student government, and yearbook. Popular campus events include a campus variety show, formal banquets, and Youth Venture.

Sports: There are 4 intercollegiate sports for men and 5 for women, and 5 intramural sports for men and 5 for women. Facilities include a gym, a weight room, a team room, a soccer field, and basketball, volleyball, badminton, and tennis courts.

Disabled Students: 70% of the campus is accessible. Wheelchair ramps, elevators, special parking, and specially equipped rest rooms are available.

Services: Counseling and information services are available, as is tutoring in most subjects. There is remedial math, reading, and writing. Other services may be available as needed.

Campus Safety and Security: Measures include informal discussions, pamphlets/posters/films, lighted pathways/sidewalks, and a nighttime security patrol.

Programs of Study: Cascade confers B.A., B.S., and B.S.E. degrees. Bachelor's degrees are awarded in BUSINESS (business administration and management), COMMUNICATIONS AND THE ARTS (English), SOCIAL SCIENCE (biblical studies, interdisciplinary studies, missions, psychology, and youth ministry). Business, psychology, and elementary education are the largest.

Required: To graduate, students must complete 126 to 131 semester hours, including 45 in upper-division courses, with a GPA of 2.0. At least 30 hours must be taken in the major, 20 of them being upper division. In addition to biblical and religious curriculum requirements, 1 hour of phys ed is required.

Special: Cascade College offers internships and practica in some areas of study, including psychology, business, and ministry. Study abroad in Austria and the Pacific Rim is possible, as are student-designed majors. Christian service is available as a second major. There is 1 national honor society.

Faculty/Classroom: 67% of faculty are male; 33%, female. All teach undergraduates. The average class size in an introductory lecture is 28; in a laboratory, 20; and in a regular course, 20.

Admissions: All of the 2003-2004 applicants were accepted. The SAT I scores for the 2003-2004 freshman class were: Verbal--34% below 500, 46% between 500 and 599, and 20% between 600 and 700; Math--54% below 500, 37% between 500 and 599, and 9% between 600 and 700. The ACT scores were 44% below 21, 21% between 21 and 23, 26% between 24 and 26, and 9% between 27 and 28.

Requirements: The SAT I or ACT is required; the ACT is preferred. Applicants should be graduates of an accredited secondary school with a minimum GPA of 2.0. The GED is accepted. AP and CLEP credits are accepted.

Procedure: Freshmen are admitted to all sessions. The school accepts all applicants. Entrance exams should be taken at any test date prior to fall enrollment. There is an early admissions plan and a rolling admissions plan. Application deadlines are open. The fall 2003 application fee was $25. Notification is sent on a rolling basis.

Transfer: 66 transfer students enrolled in 2002-2003. Official transcripts from all institutions attended are required. 30 credits of 126 to 131 required for the bachelor's degree must be completed at Cascade.

Visiting: There are regularly scheduled orientations for prospective students, including a meeting with faculty members, a financial aid workshop, and a survey of college programs. There are guides for informal visits and visitors may sit in on classes and stay overnight. To schedule a visit, contact the Admissions Office at (503) 257-1202.

Financial Aid: In a recent year, 95% of all full-time freshmen and all continuing full-time students received some form of financial aid. 60% of full-time freshmen and 80% of continuing full-time students received need-based aid. The average freshman award was $8100. 26% of undergraduates work part time. Average annual earnings from campus work are $1400. Cascade is a member of CSS. The FAFSA is required.

International Students: There are 6 international students enrolled. The school actively recruits these students. They must score 500 on the written TOEFL and also take the SAT I or ACT, with the ACT preferred.

Computers: There are 35 networked PCs, including multimedia, available for student use in 4 computer labs, allowing access to the campus e-mail system, network data storage, network printing, and other network resources, including the Web. All dorm rooms are wired for access to the campus network, which includes access to all networked resources such as e-mail and the Web. Wireless network access is available in the classrooms and student center area. All students may access the system 8 A.M. to 10:30 P.M. There are no time limits and no fees.

Graduates: From July 1, 2002 to June 30, 2003, 50 bachelor's degrees were awarded. The most popular majors were liberal arts (54%), business (22%), and psychology (10%). In an average class, 11% graduate in 4 years or less, 18% graduate in 5 years or less, and 21% graduate in 6 years or less. 3 companies recruited on campus in 2002-2003. Of the 2002 graduating class, 6% were enrolled in graduate school within 6 months of graduation and 85% were employed.

Admissions Contact: Clint LaRue, Director of Admissions.
E-mail: *admissions@cascade.edu* Web: *www.cascade.edu*

CONCORDIA UNIVERSITY
B-1
Portland, OR 97211
(503) 280-8501
(800) 321-9371; Fax: (503) 280-8531

Full-time: 275 men, 470 women	Faculty: 40; IIB, --$
Part-time: 71 men, 89 women	Ph.D.s: 57%
Graduate: 130 men, 239 women	Student/Faculty: 19 to 1
Year: semesters, summer session	Tuition: $17,400
Application Deadline: open	Room & Board: $5050
Freshman Class: 632 applied, 453 accepted, 128 enrolled	
SAT I Verbal/Math: 520/510	ACT: 21 COMPETITIVE

Concordia University, founded in 1905, is a private liberal arts institution affiliated with the Lutheran Church – Missouri Synod and is 1 of 10 institutions of the Concordia University System. There are 3 undergraduate and 2 graduate schools. The library contains 55,000 volumes, 56,706 microform items, and 2888 audio/video tapes/CDs, and subscribes to 424 periodicals. Computerized library services include the card catalog, interlibrary loans, database searching, and Internet access. Special learning facilities include a video conference classroom. The 13-acre campus is in an urban area in Portland. Including any residence halls, there are 20 buildings.

Student Life: 75% of undergraduates are from Oregon. Students are from 14 states, 18 foreign countries, and Canada. 77% are white. 59% are Protestant; 30% claim no religious affiliation. The average age of freshmen is 19; all undergraduates, 25. 25% do not continue beyond their first year; 45% remain to graduate.

Housing: 400 students can be accommodated in college housing, which includes single-sex and coed dorms, on-campus apartments, and married-student housing. On-campus housing is guaranteed for the freshman year only and is available on a first-come, first-served basis. Alcohol is not permitted. All students may keep cars.

Activities: There are no fraternities or sororities. There are many groups and organizations on campus, including choir, chorus, drama, honors, international, literary magazine, musical theater, newspaper, professional, religious, social, social service, and student government.

Sports: There are 4 intercollegiate sports for men and 5 for women, and 10 intramural sports for men and 10 for women. Facilities include a weight room, a 1200-seat gym, and a baseball/soccer field.

Disabled Students: 80% of the campus is accessible. Wheelchair ramps, elevators, special parking, specially equipped rest rooms, special class scheduling, and lowered telephones are available.

Services: Counseling and information services are available, as is tutoring in most subjects. There is remedial math, reading, and writing, student-supported individual help, and media resources.

Campus Safety and Security: Measures include 24-hour foot and vehicle patrol, self-defense education, security escort services, and informal discussions. There are pamphlets/posters/films and lighted pathways/sidewalks.

Programs of Study: Concordia confers B.A. and B.S. degrees. Associate and master's degrees are also awarded. Bachelor's degrees are awarded in BIOLOGICAL SCIENCE (biology/biological science), BUSINESS (business administration and management), COMMUNICATIONS AND THE ARTS (English), COMPUTER AND PHYSICAL SCIENCE (chemistry), EDUCATION (early childhood, elementary, and secondary), ENGINEERING AND ENVIRONMENTAL DESIGN (environmental science), HEALTH PROFESSIONS (health care administration and premedicine), SOCIAL SCIENCE (humanities, psychology, social work, theological studies, and youth ministry). Business administration, education, and psychology are the strongest academically. Education and business are the largest.

Required: To graduate, students must complete a total of 124 semester hours, with a minimum GPA of 2.0. General education requirements total 48 semester hours. All students must take freshman composition and courses in math, phys ed, humanities, religion, science, writing, fine arts, and social sciences.

Special: Cross-registration may be arranged through the Concordia University System and with Oregon Independent College. There are also internships, study abroad in 3 countries, and an accelerated degree program in management, communication, and leadership. There is 1 national honor society and a freshman honors program.

Faculty/Classroom: 67% of faculty are male; 33%, female. All teach undergraduates and 5% do research. No introductory courses are taught by graduate students. The average class size in an introductory lecture is 19; in a laboratory, 19; and in a regular course, 17.

Admissions: 72% of the 2003-2004 applicants were accepted. The SAT I scores for the 2003-2004 freshman class were: Verbal--41% below 500, 45% between 500 and 599, 12% between 600 and 700, and 2% above 700; Math--42% below 500, 40% between 500 and 599, 17% between 600 and 700, and 1% above 700. The ACT scores were 43% below 21, 24% between 21 and 23, 24% between 24 and 26, 3% between 27 and 28, and 5% above 28. 32% of the current freshmen were in the top fifth of their class; 62% were in the top two fifths.

Requirements: The SAT I or ACT is required, with a minimum SAT I verbal score of 480 recommended. Graduation from an accredited secondary school or satisfactory scores on the GED are required. The school recommends that high school courses include 4 units of English, 3 units each of social studies, math, and science, 2 units of a foreign language, and 1 unit of art and music. An interview is recommended. A GPA of 2.5 is required. AP and CLEP credits are accepted. Important factors in the admissions decision are recommendations by school officials, leadership record, and personality/intangible qualities.

Procedure: Freshmen are admitted fall, spring, and summer. Entrance exams should be taken during the junior year or early in the senior year. Early decision applications should be filed by March 1; regular application deadlines are open for fall entry. There is a $20 fee. Notification is sent on a rolling basis. Applications are accepted on-line through the school's web site.

Transfer: 141 transfer students enrolled in 2002-2003. Transfer students must have a minimum GPA of 2.0. 45 credits of 124 required for the bachelor's degree must be completed at Concordia.

Visiting: There are regularly scheduled orientations for prospective students, including class visitations and meetings with program deans and faculty. There are guides for informal visits and visitors may sit in on classes and stay overnight. To schedule a visit, contact the Admissions Office at *admissions@cu-portland.edu*.

Financial Aid: The average freshman award was $9500. The average financial indebtedness of the 2003 graduate was $18,000. Concordia is a member of CSS. The FAFSA is required.

International Students: There are 18 international students enrolled. The school actively recruits these students. They must score 525 on the written TOEFL or 195 on the electronic version.

Computers: The mainframe is a Compaq Alpha. There are 2 IBM labs with 48 PCs located in the library. There are 2 mobile labs each with 24 networked notebook PCs. Students can also access the campus network from all residence hall rooms and by broadband from off campus. All students may access the system. There are no time limits and no fees. All students are required to have personal computers. Windows 2000 or greater compatible models are recommended.

Graduates: From July 1, 2002 to June 30, 2003, 219 bachelor's degrees were awarded. The most popular majors were business administration (36%), education (34%), and health care administration (7%). In an average class, 30% graduate in 4 years or less, 39% graduate in 5 years or less, and 43% graduate in 6 years or less. 35 companies recruited on campus in 2002-2003.

Admissions Contact: Admissions Office.
E-mail: *admissions@cu-portland.edu* Web: *www.cu-portland.edu*

EASTERN OREGON UNIVERSITY D-2
La Grande, OR 97850-2807 (541) 962-3393
(800) 452-8639; Fax: (541) 962-3418

Full-time: 857 men, 1088 women	**Faculty:** 93; IIB, --$
Part-time: 416 men, 680 women	**Ph.D.s:** 88%
Graduate: 58 men, 188 women	**Student/Faculty:** 21 to 1
Year: terms, summer session	**Tuition:** $4305
Application Deadline: open	**Room & Board:** $5775
Freshman Class: 714 applied, 709 accepted, 305 enrolled	
SAT I Verbal/Math: 485/484	**ACT:** 22 NONCOMPETITIVE

Eastern Oregon University, founded in 1929, is a public institution that is part of the Oregon University System. It offers programs in liberal and fine arts, agriculture, business, health science, and teacher preparation. There are 3 undergraduate schools and 1 graduate school. In addition to regional accreditation, Eastern has baccalaureate program accreditation with NCATE. The library contains 335,455 volumes, 250,834 microform items, and 34,176 audio/video tapes/CDs, and subscribes to 893 periodicals. Computerized library services include the card catalog, interlibrary loans, database searching, and Internet access. Special learning facilities include a learning resource center, art gallery, natural history museum, and radio station. The 121-acre campus is in a rural area 260 miles east of Portland. Including any residence halls, there are 13 buildings.

Student Life: 70% of undergraduates are from Oregon. Students are from 42 states, 25 foreign countries, and Canada. 96% are from public schools. 82% are white. The average age of freshmen is 19; all undergraduates, 27. 32% do not continue beyond their first year; 37% remain to graduate.

Housing: 436 students can be accommodated in college housing, which includes single-sex and coed dorms and married-student housing. In addition, there is a wellness floor and an academic focus floor. On-campus housing is available on a first-come, first-served basis. 85% of students commute. All students may keep cars.

Activities: There are no fraternities or sororities. There are 44 groups on campus, including art, band, cheerleading, choir, chorale, chorus, computers, dance, drama, ethnic, international, jazz band, literary magazine, musical theater, newspaper, orchestra, pep band, photography, professional, radio and TV, religious, social, student government, symphony, and yearbook. Popular campus events include Casino Night, Spring Fling, and Spring Symposium.

Sports: There are 6 intercollegiate sports for men and 6 for women, and 6 intramural sports for men and 6 for women. Facilities include racquetball courts, a weight room, 3 gyms, a swimming pool, aerobics facilities, a track, and indoor and outdoor tennis courts.

Disabled Students: 80% of the campus is accessible. Wheelchair ramps, elevators, special parking, and specially equipped rest rooms are available.

Services: Counseling and information services are available, as is tutoring in most subjects. There is a reader service for the blind and remedial math, reading, and writing.

Campus Safety and Security: Measures include 24-hour foot and vehicle patrol, security escort services, informal discussions, and pamphlets/posters/films. There are emergency telephones and lighted pathways/sidewalks.

Programs of Study: Eastern confers B.A. and B.S degrees. Master's degrees are also awarded. Bachelor's degrees are awarded in AGRICULTURE (agricultural business management, agricultural economics, forestry and related sciences, range/farm management, and soil science), BIOLOGICAL SCIENCE (biology/biological science), BUSINESS (accounting and business administration and management), COMMUNICATIONS AND THE ARTS (art, dramatic arts, English, and music), COMPUTER AND PHYSICAL SCIENCE (chemistry, computer science, mathematics, and physics), EDUCATION (education and physical), HEALTH PROFESSIONS (health and nursing), SOCIAL SCIENCE (anthropology, history, liberal arts/general studies, psychology, and sociology). Sciences is the strongest academically. Business and education are the largest.

Required: Students must complete 180 credit hours, including 60 hours of general education courses that include 15 hours each of social science, natural science, humanities, art, language, and logic, with a GPA of at least 2.0. They must demonstrate computer competency and pass a writing proficiency exam. A senior capstone experience is required.

Special: There are cooperative and 3-2 engineering degree programs with Oregon State University. The university offers internships, work-study with federal agencies, accelerated degree program, student-designed and dual majors, study abroad in 8 countries, a general studies degree, B.A.-B.S. degrees, a multidisciplinary degree, numerous preprofessional programs, credit by exam, and for life/military/work experience, external degrees, and pass/fail options. The university also serves students with course work via telecommunications and video and with a weekend University. There are 6 national honor societies, including Phi Beta Kappa, and 6 departmental honors programs.

Faculty/Classroom: 57% of faculty are male; 43%, female. All both teach and do research. No introductory courses are taught by graduate students. The average class size in an introductory lecture is 60; in a laboratory, 20; and in a regular course, 35.

Admissions: 99% of the 2003-2004 applicants were accepted. The SAT I scores for the 2003-2004 freshman class were: Verbal--49% below 500, 36% between 500 and 599, 13% between 600 and 700, and 2% above 700; Math--51% below 500, 35% between 500 and 599, 12% between 600 and 700, and 2% above 700. The ACT scores were 18% between 12 and 17, 62% between 18 and 23, and 20% between 24 and 29. 39% of the current freshmen were in the top fifth of their class; 71% were in the top two fifths.

Requirements: The SAT I or ACT is required. A GED is accepted. Applicants must complete 14 academic credits, including 4 years of English, 3 each of math and social studies, and 2 of science. A GPA of 3.0 is required. AP and CLEP credits are accepted. Important factors in the admissions decision are extracurricular activities record and geographic diversity.

Procedure: Freshmen are admitted to all sessions. Entrance exams should be taken in the senior year. There is a deferred admissions plan. There is a rolling admissions plan. Application deadlines are open. Application fee is $50.

Transfer: 463 transfer students enrolled in 2002-2003. Applicants must have 30 credits of transferable academic work with a GPA of 2.25. 45 of 180 credits required for the bachelor's degree must be completed at Eastern.

Visiting: There are regularly scheduled orientations for prospective students, including a campus tour, academic advising, and information sessions on financial aid and residence life. There are guides for informal visits and visitors may sit in on classes and stay overnight. To schedule a visit, contact Admissions/New Student Programs at admissions@eou.edu.

Financial Aid: In 2003-2004, 60% of all full-time freshmen and 66% of continuing full-time students received some form of financial aid. 37% of full-time freshmen and 44% of continuing full-time students received need-based aid. The average freshman award was $7558. 35% of undergraduates work part time. Average annual earnings from campus work are $1003. The average financial indebtedness of the 2003 graduate was $14,185. Eastern is a member of CSS. The FAFSA is required. The deadline for filing freshman financial aid applications for fall entry is March 1.

International Students: There are 92 international students enrolled. They must score 520 on the written TOEFL or 190 on the electronic version or take the IELTS, with a minimum score of 6.

Computers: There are 36 PCs in the classroom computer center, 20 in the learning center, 30 in the library, and a number in the residence halls. All students may access the system at various posted hours. There are no time limits and no fees.

Graduates: From July 1, 2002 to June 30, 2003, 494 bachelor's degrees were awarded. The most popular majors were liberal studies (25%), interdisciplinary studies (20%), and business marketing (19%). In an average class, 20% graduate in 4 years or less, 45% graduate in 5 years or less, and 37% graduate in 6 years or less. 30 companies recruited on campus in 2002-2003.

Admissions Contact: Sherri Edvalson, Director of Admissions. E-mail: admissions@eou.edu Web: http://www.eou.edu

---

GEORGE FOX UNIVERSITY
B-2
Newberg, OR 97132

(503) 554-2240
(800) 765-4369; Fax: (503) 538-7234

Full-time: 543 men, 791 women	**Faculty:** n/av
Part-time: 151 men, 178 women	**Ph.D.s:** 66%
Graduate: 510 men, 727 women	**Student/Faculty:** n/av
Year: semesters	**Tuition:** $19,810
Application Deadline: June 1	**Room & Board:** $6300
Freshman Class: 935 applied, 827 accepted, 343 enrolled	
SAT I Verbal/Math: 560/550	**ACT:** 24 **VERY COMPETITIVE**

George Fox University, founded in 1891, is a private school of liberal arts and sciences operated by the Northwest Yearly Meeting of Friends (Quaker). In addition to regional accreditation, George Fox has baccalaureate program accreditation with NASM. The 2 libraries contain 139,571 volumes, 209,902 microform items, and 5171 audio/video tapes/CDs, and subscribe to 1203 periodicals. Computerized library services include the card catalog, interlibrary loans, and database searching. Special learning facilities include a learning resource center, art gallery, radio station, a television production studio, and a Quaker museum. The 75-acre campus is in a small town 23 miles southwest of Portland. Including any residence halls, there are 60 buildings.

Student Life: 64% of undergraduates are from Oregon. 92% are from public schools. 85% are white. The average age of freshmen is 18; all undergraduates, 24.

Housing: 1000 students can be accommodated in college housing, which includes single-sex dorms, on-campus apartments, off-campus

apartments, and married-student housing. In addition, there are special-interest houses. On-campus housing is available on a first-come, first-served basis. 75% of students live on campus; of those, 50% remain on campus on weekends. Alcohol is not permitted. All students may keep cars.

Activities: There are no fraternities or sororities. There are 27 groups on campus, including band, cheerleading, chess, choir, chorale, chorus, computers, drama, drill team, ethnic, film, forensics, honors, international, newspaper, orchestra, pep band, political, professional, radio, religious, social, social service, student government, symphony, and yearbook. Popular campus events include Quaker Heritage Week, Christian Emphasis Week, and a raft race.

Sports: There are 6 intercollegiate sports for men and 7 for women, and 4 intramural sports for men and 4 for women. Facilities include an all-weather track, a weight room, tennis and handball/racquetball courts, a 2500-seat gym, and baseball, softball, and soccer fields.

Disabled Students: 80% of the campus is accessible. Wheelchair ramps, elevators, special parking, specially equipped rest rooms, special class scheduling, lowered drinking fountains, lowered telephones, and special housing are available.

Services: Counseling and information services are available, as is tutoring in some subjects. There is a reader service for the blind and remedial math, reading, and writing.

Campus Safety and Security: Measures include 24-hour foot and vehicle patrol, self-defense education, security escort services, and informal discussions. There are emergency telephones and lighted pathways/sidewalks.

Programs of Study: George Fox confers B.A. and B.S. degrees. Master's and doctoral degrees are also awarded. Bachelor's degrees are awarded in BIOLOGICAL SCIENCE (biology/biological science), BUSINESS (business economics, human resources, and management science), COMMUNICATIONS AND THE ARTS (art, communications, literature, music, Spanish and telecommunications), COMPUTER AND PHYSICAL SCIENCE (chemistry, computer science, information sciences and systems, and mathematics), EDUCATION (elementary, health, home economics, mathematics, middle school, music, physical, science, secondary, and social studies), ENGINEERING AND ENVIRONMENTAL DESIGN (engineering), HEALTH PROFESSIONS (predentistry, premedicine, and preveterinary science), SOCIAL SCIENCE (biblical studies, cognitive science, economics, history, home economics, international studies, ministries, political science/government, prelaw, psychology, religion, social work, and sociology). Natural sciences is the strongest academically. Business is the largest.

Required: To graduate, students must have a minimum 2.0 GPA and complete 126 semester hours, including 48 in the major. The required core curriculum of 57 semester hours includes 18 hours total in math/language, natural science, and social science, 14 to 15 hours of humanities, 10 hours of Bible/religious studies, 6 hours in communication, 6 hours in language and global studies, and 3 hours of health/phys ed.

Special: There is a 3-2 engineering degree with the University of Portland, Oregon State University, and Washington University in St. Louis, and cross-registration through the Oregon Independent College Association. George Fox also offers internships with area companies, study abroad, and a Washington semester through the Christian College Coalition. Work-study programs with the college, B.A.-B.S. degrees in all majors, dual and student-designed interdisciplinary majors, and pass/fail options in upper-division courses outside of the major also are offered. There are 3 national honor societies and a freshman honors program.

Faculty/Classroom: 56% of faculty are male; 44%, female. The average class size in an introductory lecture is 50; in a laboratory, 20; and in a regular course, 25.

Admissions: 88% of the 2003-2004 applicants were accepted. The SAT I scores for the 2003-2004 freshman class were: Verbal--22% below 500, 45% between 500 and 599, 28% between 600 and 700, and 5% above 700; Math--25% below 500, 44% between 500 and 599, 26% between 600 and 700, and 5% above 700. The ACT scores were 27% below 21, 21% between 21 and 23, 30% between 24 and 26, 12% between 27 and 28, and 10% above 28. 42% of the current freshmen were in the top fifth of their class; 87% were in the top two fifths.

Requirements: The SAT I or ACT is required. In addition, applicants need 16 academic credits or 14 Carnegie units, including a suggested 4 units of English and 2 units each of a foreign language, math, science, and social studies. An essay and 2 personal recommendations are required; a portfolio, audition, and interview are recommended in certain majors. A GPA of 2.6 is required. AP and CLEP credits are accepted. Important factors in the admissions decision are advanced placement or honor courses, recommendations by school officials, and recommendations by alumni.

Procedure: Freshmen are admitted fall and spring. Entrance exams should be taken in fall or winter. There is a deferred admissions plan. Applications should be filed by June 1 for fall entry and December 1 for spring entry. The fall 2003 application fee was $40. Notification is sent on a rolling basis. Applications are accepted on-line through www.apply.com.

Transfer: 117 transfer students enrolled in 2002-2003. Transfers must have a minimum 2.3 GPA and 14 earned credits from their previous college. A personal recommendation is required. 30 of 126 credits required for the bachelor's degree must be completed at George Fox.

Visiting: There are regularly scheduled orientations for prospective students, including observation of classes and talking with professors. There are guides for informal visits and visitors may sit in on classes and stay overnight. To schedule a visit, contact the Office of Admissions.

Financial Aid: In 2003-2004, 78% of all full-time freshmen and 81% of continuing full-time students received some form of financial aid. 78% of all full-time students received need-based aid. The average freshman award was $15,611. Need-based scholarships or need-based grants averaged $11,721; need-based self-help aid (loans and jobs) averaged $4256; and institutional non-need-based awards and non-need-based scholarships averaged $7551. The FAFSA is required. The priority date for freshman financial aid applications for fall entry is February 1.

International Students: There are 48 international students enrolled. The school actively recruits these students. They must score 500 on the written TOEFL or 213 on the electronic version.

Computers: The mainframe is a DEC Alpha 2000. Computers Across the Curriculum provides each entering freshman with a computer to use while a student and to keep after graduation. Students also have access to a full computer resource area, including a training center. There is a Mac lab with 21 computers and an IBM lab with 25 Pentium computers. Network and Internet access is provided in all residences and at other plug-in locations on campus. All students may access the system. There are no time limits and no fees.

Graduates: From July 1, 2002 to June 30, 2003, 505 bachelor's degrees were awarded.

Admissions Contact: Dale Seipp, Director of Undergraduate Admission. E-mail: *admissions@georgefox.edu* Web: *www.georgefox.edu*

LEWIS AND CLARK COLLEGE
Portland, OR 97219-7899

B-1

(503) 768-7040
(800) 444-4111; Fax: (503) 768-7055

Full-time: 685 men, 1072 women	Faculty: 118; IIB, +$
Part-time: 19 men, 16 women	Ph.D.s: 97%
Graduate: 503 men, 776 women	Student/Faculty: 15 to 1
Year: semesters, summer session	Tuition: $23,730
Application Deadline: February 1	Room & Board: $6890
Freshman Class: 3410 applied, 2311 accepted, 493 enrolled	
SAT I Verbal/Math: 600-690/570-670	ACT: 26-30

VERY COMPETITIVE

Lewis & Clark College, founded in 1867, is a private, independent liberal arts and sciences institution, with a global reach. In addition to regional accreditation, LC has baccalaureate program accreditation with NASM. The 2 libraries contain 480,501 volumes, 2,043,167 microform items, and 13,146 audio/video tapes/CDs, and subscribe to 6481 periodicals. Computerized library services include the card catalog, interlibrary loans, database searching, and Internet access. Special learning facilities include a learning resource center, art gallery, radio station, TV station, a telescope, a research astronomical observatory, a language lab, and a greenhouse. The 137-acre campus is in a suburban area 6 miles south of downtown Portland. Including any residence halls, there are 54 buildings.

Student Life: 80% of undergraduates are from out of state, mostly the West. Students are from 49 states, 40 foreign countries, and Canada. 74% are from public schools. 65% are white. 72% claim no religious affiliation; 14% Protestant; 7% Catholic. The average age of freshmen is 18; all undergraduates, 20. 16% do not continue beyond their first year; 71% remain to graduate.

Housing: 1165 students can be accommodated in college housing, which includes single-sex and coed dorms and on-campus apartments. In addition, there are langauge, international awareness, outdoor pursuits, visual and performance arts, and substance-free floors. On-campus housing is guaranteed for the freshman and sophomore years only and is available on a lottery system for upperclassmen. 64% of students live on campus; of those, 98% remain on campus on weekends. Upperclassmen may keep cars.

Activities: There are no fraternities or sororities. There are 75 groups on campus, including art, band, choir, chorale, chorus, computers, cross-cultural journal, dance, debate, drama, ethnic, film, forensics, gay, honors, international, jazz band, literary magazine, newspaper, orchestra, outdoors, pep band, photography, political, professional, radio and TV, religious, social, social service, student government, symphony, and yearbook. Popular campus events include Gender Studies Symposium, International Affairs Symposium, and Environmental Studies Symposium.

Sports: There are 9 intercollegiate sports for men and 10 for women, and 10 intramural sports for men and 10 for women. Facilities include indoor and outdoor swimming pools, 6 tennis courts (3 covered), Astroturf football field, basketball and volleyball courts, softball and baseball fields, a track, and weight and aerobics rooms. There is also a 3700-seat stadium and a 2200-seat auditorium/arena.

Disabled Students: 80% of the campus is accessible. Wheelchair ramps, elevators, special parking, specially equipped rest rooms, special class scheduling, lowered drinking fountains, lowered telephones, and special housing are available.

Services: Counseling and information services are available, as is tutoring in every subject. There are also mentors, note takers, books on tape, and math and writing skills centers. There is a reader service for the blind.

Campus Safety and Security: Measures include 24-hour foot and vehicle patrol, self-defense education, security escort services, and shuttle buses. There are informal discussions, pamphlets/posters/films, emergency telephones, lighted pathways/sidewalks, and card key locks in all residence halls.

Programs of Study: LC confers the B.A. degree. Master's degrees are also awarded. Bachelor's degrees are awarded in AGRICULTURE (environmental studies), BIOLOGICAL SCIENCE (biochemistry and biology/biological science), COMMUNICATIONS AND THE ARTS (art history and appreciation, communications, dramatic arts, English, fine arts, languages, music, and studio art), COMPUTER AND PHYSICAL SCIENCE (chemistry, computer science, mathematics, and physics), SOCIAL SCIENCE (anthropology, East Asian studies, economics, French studies, German area studies, Hispanic American studies, history, interdisciplinary studies, international relations, philosophy, political science/government, psychology, religion, and sociology). Psychology, English, and biology are the strongest academically. Psychology, international affairs, and English are the largest.

Required: To graduate, students must complete a total of 128 semester hours with a 2.0 GPA. A third of this total generally falls in the major program, a third in electives, and a third in general requirements, which includes a required first-year course, 12 hours in scientific and quantitative reasoning, 8 hours in international studies, 3 semesters of a foreign language, 2 semesters of phys ed, and 1 course in creative arts. Certain majors require a thesis or a senior project/recital.

Special: LC offers cross-registration with the Oregon Independent College Association, which includes Reed College and the University of Portland; internships; study-abroad programs encompassing 60 countries; semesters in Washington and New York City; and dual and student-designed majors. A 3-2 engineering program is available with Columbia and Washington Universities, the University of Southern California, and the Oregon Graduate Institute. There are 5 national honor societies, including Phi Beta Kappa; all 100 departments have honors programs.

Faculty/Classroom: 44% of faculty are male; 36%, female. All both teach and do research. No introductory courses are taught by graduate students. The average class size in an introductory lecture is 24; in a laboratory, 16; and in a regular course, 19.

Admissions: 68% of the 2003-2004 applicants were accepted. The SAT I scores for the 2003-2004 freshman class were: Verbal--1% below 500, 21% between 500 and 599, 48% between 600 and 700, and 30% above 700; Math--1% below 500, 31% between 500 and 599, 51% between 600 and 700, and 17% above 700. The ACT scores were 3% below 21, 12% between 21 and 23, 18% between 24 and 26, 23% between 27 and 28, and 44% above 28. 70% of the current freshmen were in the top fifth of their class; 93% were in the top two fifths. There were 8 National Merit finalists. 30 freshmen graduated first in their class.

Requirements: The SAT I or ACT is required; a GED may be accepted. It is recommended that applicants have 4 years each of English and math, 3 to 4 years of science, 3 years each of history/social studies and foreign language, and 1 year of fine arts. An essay is required and an interview recommended. The college also admits exceptional students through the Portfolio Path option. Portfolios should include 4 samples of graded work from junior or senior year: 2 writing, 1 quantitative, and 1 of the student's choice. A GPA of 2.0 is required. AP credits are accepted. Important factors in the admissions decision are advanced placement or honor courses and recommendations by school officials.

Procedure: Freshmen are admitted fall and spring. Entrance exams should be taken during the spring of the junior year and the fall of the senior year. There are early admissions and deferred admissions plans. Early decision applications should be filed by December 1; regular applications, by February 1 for fall entry, December 1 for spring entry, and May 1 for summer entry, along with a $50 fee. The on-line application is free. Notification of early decision is sent January 15; regular decision, April 1. 122 applicants were on the 2003 waiting list; 14 were admitted. Applications are accepted on computer disk and on-line through CollegeNET, CollegeLink, Apply, Common App, or LC's web site.

Transfer: 56 transfer students enrolled in 2002-2003. Applicants must submit high school and college transcripts, 2 essays, and SAT I or ACT scores, if they have fewer than 2 years of transferable credit. 60 credits of 128 required for the bachelor's degree must be completed at LC.

Visiting: There are regularly scheduled orientations for prospective students, including campus tours, class visits, interviews, special-interest appointments, overnight stays in residence halls, and 4 open house events.

There are guides for informal visits and visitors may sit in on classes and stay overnight. To schedule a visit, contact the Visit Coordinator, Office of Admissions.

Financial Aid: In 2003-2004, 84% of all full-time freshmen and 74% of continuing full-time students received some form of financial aid. 74% of full-time freshmen and 68% of continuing full-time students received need-based aid. The average freshman award was $18,049, with $15,740 ($34,440 maximum) from need-based scholarships or need-based grants, and $2310 ($7125 maximum) from need-based self-help aid (loans and jobs). 42% of undergraduates work part time. Average annual earnings from campus work are $1832. The average financial indebtedness of the 2003 graduate was $17,055. The FAFSA is required. The deadline for filing freshman financial aid applications for fall entry is March 1.

International Students: There are 96 international students enrolled. The school actively recruits these students. They must score 550 on the written TOEFL or 213 on the electronic version or take the MELAB. They also must take ECPE, FCE, CAE, CPE, or IELTS.

Computers: The mainframes are a Sun DEC Alpha Server 2100/A500 and an Alpha Server 2000/400. The campus servers are networked with 6 UNIX workstations and 5 X-Windows terminals. They run the UNIX operating system and are interconnected through Ethernet on campus with the library, residence halls, and academic buildings. Mac and PC clusters are available in the library and residence halls. All students may access the system 24 hours a day. There are no time limits and no fees.

Graduates: From July 1, 2002 to June 30, 2003, 407 bachelor's degrees were awarded. The most popular majors were psychology (11%), international affairs (9%), and English (8%). In an average class, 1% graduate in 3 years or less, 62% graduate in 4 years or less, 70% graduate in 5 years or less, and 71% graduate in 6 years or less. 37 companies recruited on campus in 2002-2003. Of the 2002 graduating class, 13% were enrolled in graduate school within 6 months of graduation and 70% were employed.

Admissions Contact: Michael B. Sexton, Dean of Admissions. E-mail: *admissions@lclark.edu* Web: *www.lclark.edu*

LINFIELD COLLEGE
McMinnville, OR 97128

B-2

(503) 883-2213
(800) 883-2287; Fax: (503) 883-2472

Full-time: 716 men, 893 women	Faculty: 111; IIB, av$
Part-time: 29 men, 21 women	Ph.Ds: 98%
Graduate: none	Student/Faculty: 14 to 1
Year: 4-1-4, summer session	Tuition: $20,970
Application Deadline: February 15	Room & Board: $6120
Freshman Class: 2145 applied, 1644 accepted, 453 enrolled	
SAT I Verbal/Math: 550/570	ACT: 24 VERY COMPETITIVE

Linfield College, founded in 1849, is a private liberal arts school affiliated with the American Baptist Church. In addition to regional accreditation, Linfield has baccalaureate program accreditation with CAHEA and NASM. The library contains 164,985 volumes, 16,725 microform items, and 22,679 audio/video tapes/CDs, and subscribes to 1309 periodicals. Computerized library services include the card catalog, interlibrary loans, database searching, and Internet access. Special learning facilities include a learning resource center, art gallery, radio station, writing center, psychology lab, computer lab, anthropology museum, multimedia studio, speaking center, and research institute. The 193-acre campus is in a small town 40 miles southwest of Portland. Including any residence halls, there are 66 buildings.

Student Life: 55% of undergraduates are from Oregon. Students are from 26 states, 19 foreign countries, and Canada. 83% are from public schools. 79% are white. 39% are Protestant; 11% Catholic; 11% claim no religious affiliation. The average age of freshmen is 18; all undergraduates, 20. 19% do not continue beyond their first year; 67% remain to graduate.

Housing: 1287 students can be accommodated in college housing, which includes single-sex and coed dorms, on-campus apartments, off-campus apartments, and fraternity houses. On-campus housing is guaranteed for the freshman year only. 77% of students live on campus; of those, 80% remain on campus on weekends. All students may keep cars.

Activities: 22% of men belong to 1 local and 3 national fraternities; 28% of women belong to 1 local and 3 national sororities. There are 60 groups on campus, including art, band, bowling, cheerleading, choir, chorale, chorus, computers, dance, debate, drama, ethnic, forensics, gay, honors, international, jazz band, literary magazine, musical theater, newspaper, opera, orchestra, outdoor, pep band, photography, political, professional, radio and TV, religious, social, social service, student government, symphony, women, and yearbook. Popular campus events include Cultural Awareness Week, Oregon Nobel Laureate Symposium, and Christmas Choral Concert.

Sports: There are 9 intercollegiate sports for men and 10 for women, and 8 intramural sports for men and 8 for women. Facilities include a complex with a 2200-seat gym, 3 basketball courts, a 25-yard swimming pool, 4 racquetball courts, a 3200-square-foot weight room, a field

house with 3 tennis courts, 4 hitting cages, and an indoor track, and a baseball facility. There also are soccer and football fields, an all-weather track, and additional basketball, tennis, and racquetball courts.

Disabled Students: 70% of the campus is accessible. Wheelchair ramps, elevators, special parking, specially equipped rest rooms, special class scheduling, lowered drinking fountains, and lowered telephones are available.

Services: Counseling and information services are available, as is tutoring in every subject. There is a reader service for the blind and remedial math. There is a writing lab and a speaking center.

Campus Safety and Security: Measures include 24-hour foot and vehicle patrol, self-defense education, security escort services, and informal discussions. There are pamphlets/posters/films, emergency telephones, and lighted pathways/sidewalks.

Programs of Study: Linfield confers B.A. and B.S. degrees. Bachelor's degrees are awarded in BIOLOGICAL SCIENCE (biology/biological science), BUSINESS (accounting, banking and finance, business administration and management, and international business management), COMMUNICATIONS AND THE ARTS (art, communications, creative writing, dramatic arts, English, French, German, music, and Spanish), COMPUTER AND PHYSICAL SCIENCE (applied physics, chemistry, computer science, mathematics, physics, and science), EDUCATION (athletic training, elementary, health, and physical), ENGINEERING AND ENVIRONMENTAL DESIGN (environmental science), HEALTH PROFESSIONS (exercise science), SOCIAL SCIENCE (anthropology, economics, history, philosophy, political science/government, psychology, religion, and sociology). Business, elementary education, and communication are the strongest academically.

Required: To graduate, students must have a 2.0 GPA and complete 125 credit hours, including 35 to 48 in the major. Core requirements include courses from the sciences, literature, fine arts, religion or philosophy, the social sciences, and history. Students must also take courses in American pluralism and global diversity.

Special: Students may study abroad in 10 countries and during the January term, academic classes are conducted in such areas as New York City, Hawaii, China, Japan, Ireland, Mexico, and Ghana. Internships and work-study programs, B.A.-B.S. degrees, and pass/fail options are also offered. A 3-2 engineering degree may be arranged with Oregon State and Washington State Universities, and the University of Southern California. There is also an adult degree program with courses throughout Oregon and on-line. There are 14 national honor societies.

Faculty/Classroom: 54% of faculty are male; 44%, female. All both teach and do research. The average class size in an introductory lecture is 34; in a laboratory, 14; and in a regular course, 16.

Admissions: 77% of the 2003-2004 applicants were accepted. The SAT I scores for the 2003-2004 freshman class were: Verbal--25% below 500, 45% between 500 and 599, 24% between 600 and 700, and 5% above 700; Math--19% below 500, 47% between 500 and 599, 30% between 600 and 700, and 5% above 700. The ACT scores were 27% below 21, 22% between 21 and 23, 28% between 24 and 26, 13% between 27 and 28, and 10% above 28. 58% of the current freshmen were in the top fifth of their class; 84% were in the top two fifths. There were 2 National Merit semifinalists. 45 freshmen graduated first in their class.

Requirements: The SAT I or ACT is required. In addition, applicants must have 17 to 20 academic credits, including a recommended 4 years each in English and math, 3 years in science, and 2 years each in foreign language, history, and social studies. An essay is required, and an interview is recommended. The GED is accepted. AP and CLEP credits are accepted. Important factors in the admissions decision are extracurricular activities record, evidence of special talent, and advanced placement or honor courses.

Procedure: Freshmen are admitted fall and spring. Entrance exams should be taken during the fall of the senior year. There are early admissions and deferred admissions plans. Early action applications should be filed by November 15; regular applications, by February 15 for fall entry and December 1 for spring entry, along with a $40 fee. Notification of early decision is sent January 15; regular decision, April 1. 31 applicants were on the 2003 waiting list; 15 were admitted. Applications are accepted on computer disk and on-line.

Transfer: 90 transfer students enrolled in 2002-2003. Applicants must have a minimum 2.0 GPA from an accredited institution to be considered. An interview is also recommended. 30 credits of 125 required for the bachelor's degree must be completed at Linfield.

Visiting: There are regularly scheduled orientations for prospective students, including tours and interviews. There are guides for informal visits and visitors may sit in on classes and stay overnight. To schedule a visit, contact the Admissions Office at *admission@linfield.edu*.

Financial Aid: In 2003-2004, 95% of all full-time freshmen and 93% of continuing full-time students received some form of financial aid. 69% of full-time freshmen and 71% of continuing full-time students received need-based aid. The average freshman award was $15,494. Need-based scholarships or need-based grants averaged $6801 ($18,730 maximum); and need-based self-help aid (loans and jobs) averaged $7001 ($22,020 maximum). 78% of undergraduates work part time. Average annual earnings from campus work are $1603. The average financial indebtedness of the 2003 graduate was $20,537. Linfield is a member of CSS. The FAFSA and CSS profile (for early action applicants only) are required. The priority date for freshman financial aid applications for fall entry is February 1.

International Students: There are 55 international students enrolled. The school actively recruits these students. They must score 550 on the written TOEFL or 213 on the electronic version or take the MELAB.

Computers: The mainframes are a variety of Intel and Sun servers running Linux and UNIX operating systems. 5 main PC labs provide 123 stations for both instruction and access to a wide range of programming, word processing, graphics, analysis, and Internet access tools. Several departmental PC labs provide access to 149 additional stations. Residence halls have small computer labs with access to the Internet and Web. All students may access the system. There are no time limits and no fees.

Graduates: From July 1, 2002 to June 30, 2003, 331 bachelor's degrees were awarded. The most popular majors were elementary education (14%), business (9%), and international business (9%). In an average class, 1% graduate in 3 years or less, 58% graduate in 4 years or less, 66% graduate in 5 years or less, and 69% graduate in 6 years or less. 8 companies recruited on campus in 2002-2003. Of the 2002 graduating class, 22% were enrolled in graduate school within 6 months of graduation and 84% were employed.

Admissions Contact: Lisa Knodle-Bragiel, Director of Admissions. E-mail: *admission@linfield.edu* Web: *www.linfield.edu*

MARYLHURST UNIVERSITY   B-1
Marylhurst, OR 97036   (503) 699-6268
                                    (800) 634-9982; Fax: (503) 635-6585

Full-time: 66 men, 157 women	**Faculty:** 31
Part-time: 105 men, 373 women	**Ph.D s:** 28%
Graduate: 129 men, 220 women	**Student/Faculty:** 7 to 1
Year: quarters, summer session	**Tuition:** $12,465
Application Deadline: open	**Room & Board:** $6000
Freshman Class: n/av	
SAT I or ACT: not required	**NONCOMPETITIVE**

Marylhurst University, founded in 1893, is a private, commuter, liberal arts institution affiliated with the Roman Catholic Church. The primary emphasis is on innovative programs such as the Weekend College for adult students. There are 10 undergraduate and 4 graduate schools. In addition to regional accreditation, Marylhurst has baccalaureate program accreditation with NASM. The library contains 89,428 volumes, 18 microform items, and 2873 audio/video tapes/CDs, and subscribes to 522 periodicals. Computerized library services include the card catalog, interlibrary loans, and database searching. Special learning facilities include an art gallery. The 68-acre campus is in a suburban area 10 miles south of Portland. Including any residence halls, there are 14 buildings.

Student Life: 88% of undergraduates are from Oregon. Students are from 9 states, 22 foreign countries, and Canada. 85% are white. The average age of freshmen is 34; all undergraduates, 37.

Housing: 50 students can be accommodated in college housing, which includes coed dorms. Priority for on-campus housing is given to out-of-town students. 97% of students commute. Alcohol is not permitted. All students may keep cars.

Activities: There are no fraternities or sororities. There are 6 groups on campus, including art, chorale, international, jazz band, orchestra, professional, and symphony. Popular campus events include Alumni Days and Commencement Weekend.

Sports: There is no sports program at Marylhurst.

Disabled Students: 75% of the campus is accessible. Wheelchair ramps, elevators, special parking, specially equipped rest rooms, lowered drinking fountains, and lowered telephones are available.

Services: Counseling and information services are available, as is tutoring in some subjects, including math and writing. There is a reader service for the blind.

Campus Safety and Security: Measures include 24-hour foot and vehicle patrol, self-defense education, security escort services, and emergency telephones. There are lighted pathways/sidewalks.

Programs of Study: Marylhurst confers B.A., B.S., B.F.A., and B.M. degrees. Master's degrees are also awarded. Bachelor's degrees are awarded in BUSINESS (management science), COMMUNICATIONS AND THE ARTS (art, communications, fine arts, music, and technical and business writing), COMPUTER AND PHYSICAL SCIENCE (science), SOCIAL SCIENCE (human development, interdisciplinary studies, ministries, and social science). Management, social science, and communication are the largest.

Required: To graduate, students must have a minimum 2.0 GPA and complete 180 quarter credits, including 60 to 129 in the major. Distribution requirements vary according to major but include 15 credits each (10 for the B.M. degree) in communications, arts and letters, science/math, and social science. An interdisciplinary seminar is also required, as are internships in some majors.

Special: Cross-registration may be arranged through the Oregon Independent College Association. Marylhurst offers work-study programs, B.A.-B.S. degrees, internships, an interdisciplinary studies degree, dual and student-designed majors, accelerated degree programs in all majors, credit for life experience, nondegree study, and pass/fail options.

Faculty/Classroom: 48% of faculty are male; 52%, female. 94% teach undergraduates. No introductory courses are taught by graduate students. The average class size in an introductory lecture is 15 and in a regular course, 15.

Requirements: Only the Early Scholars Program has specific requirements including the SAT I, essays, a college interview, and recommendations by school officials. CLEP credit is accepted.

Procedure: Freshmen are admitted to all sessions. Application deadlines are open. The fall 2003 application fee was $20. Notification is sent on a rolling basis.

Transfer: 116 transfer students enrolled in a recent year. Almost all students are returning adults who have transferred prior to college credit. Grades of C or better transfer for credit. 45 of 180 credits required for the bachelor's degree must be completed at Marylhurst.

Visiting: There are regularly scheduled orientations for prospective students, including addressing registration and financial aid issues, academic advising, and use of the library, cafeteria, and bookstore. There are guides for informal visits and visitors may sit in on classes and stay overnight. To schedule a visit, contact the Dean of Admissions.

Financial Aid: The average freshman award was $10,000. The FAFSA and an institutional application are required. Check with the school for current deadlines.

International Students: They must score 550 on the written TOEFL and also take the college's own test.

Computers: The mainframe is an NT Server. Students may use independent PCs available in the computer center. All students may access the system. There are no time limits and no fees.

Admissions Contact: John French, Academic Advising Specialist. E-mail: *admissions@marylhurst.edu* Web: *www.marylhurst.edu*

NORTHWEST CHRISTIAN COLLEGE   B-2
Eugene, OR 97401-3727   (541) 684-7201
                                    (877) 463-6622; Fax: (541) 684-7317

Full-time: 147 men, 209 women	**Faculty:** 23
Part-time: 15 men, 21 women	**Ph.D s:** 67%
Graduate: 42 men, 57 women	**Student/Faculty:** 15 to 1
Year: quarters, summer session	**Tuition:** $16,350
Application Deadline: n/av	**Room & Board:** $5510
Freshman Class: 168 applied, 109 accepted, 53 enrolled	
SAT I Verbal/Math: 480/520	**ACT:** 20 **COMPETITIVE**

Northwest Christian College, founded in 1895, is a private institution affiliated with the Christian Church, offering programs in the arts and sciences, business, education, and ministries. In addition to regional accreditation, NCC has baccalaureate program accreditation with IACBE. The library contains 62,200 volumes, 128 microform items, and 8677 audio/video tapes/CDs, and subscribes to 261 periodicals. Computerized library services include the card catalog, interlibrary loans, database searching, and Internet access. Special learning facilities include a learning resource center. The 8-acre campus is in an urban area 125 miles south of Portland. Including any residence halls, there are 14 buildings.

Student Life: 88% of undergraduates are from Oregon. Students are from 6 states and 3 foreign countries. 94% are from public schools. 86% are white. 64% claim no religious affiliation; 35% Protestant. The average age of freshmen is 18; all undergraduates, 25. 37% do not continue beyond their first year; 31% remain to graduate.

Housing: 213 students can be accommodated in college housing, which includes single-sex and coed dorms, off-campus apartments, and married-student housing. On-campus housing is guaranteed for the freshman year only. 67% of students commute. Alcohol is not permitted. All students may keep cars.

Activities: There are no fraternities or sororities. There are 15 groups on campus, including cheerleading, choir, chorale, debate, drama, forensics, literary magazine, musical theater, newspaper, religious, social service, student government, and yearbook. Popular campus events include Annual Musical, Spirit Week, and Wellness Week.

Sports: There is 1 intercollegiate sport for men and 2 for women, and 4 intramural sports for men and 4 for women. Facilities include an event center with a basketball court, fitness rooms, locker rooms, and softball practice area.

Disabled Students: 60% of the campus is accessible. Wheelchair ramps, elevators, special parking, specially equipped rest rooms, special class scheduling, lowered drinking fountains, and lowered telephones are available.

Services: Counseling and information services are available, as is tutoring in most subjects. There is remedial math, reading, and writing.

Campus Safety and Security: Measures include security escort services, emergency telephones, and lighted pathways/sidewalks.

Programs of Study: NCC confers B.A. and B.S. degrees. Associate and master's degrees are also awarded. Bachelor's degrees are awarded in BUSINESS (business administration and management), COMMUNICATIONS AND THE ARTS (communications and music), COMPUTER AND PHYSICAL SCIENCE (information sciences and systems), EDUCATION (elementary), SOCIAL SCIENCE (human services, humanities, interdisciplinary studies, international studies, ministries, psychology, and social science). Business administration, ministry, and elementary education are the strongest academically. Elementary education and psychology are the largest.

Required: To graduate, students must complete 186 quarter credits with at least 40 in the major and a minimum GPA of 2.0. The core curriculum consists of 86 credit hours in humanities, social sciences, math and science, and Bible; a 1-credit-hour chapel for every term enrolled is also required as are 3 service credits.

Special: NCC offers internships, study abroad in 4 countries, a Washington semester, work study, accelerated degree programs, and student-designed majors.

Faculty/Classroom: 67% of faculty are male; 33%, female. All teach undergraduates. No introductory courses are taught by graduate students. The average class size in an introductory lecture is 40 and in a regular course, 25.

Admissions: 65% of the 2003-2004 applicants were accepted. The SAT I scores for the 2003-2004 freshman class were: Verbal--55% below 500, 32% between 500 and 599, 10% between 600 and 700, and 3% above 700; Math--42% below 500, 45% between 500 and 599, 13% between 600 and 700. The ACT scores were 55% below 21, 13% between 21 and 23, 18% between 24 and 26, 11% between 27 and 28, and 3% above 28. 40% of the current freshmen were in the top fifth of their class; 58% were in the top two fifths. 2 freshmen graduated first in their class.

Requirements: The SAT I or ACT is required. In addition, students are required to submit a completed admission application, high school transcripts, and 2 references. An interview is recommended. A GPA of 2.5 is required. AP and CLEP credits are accepted. Important factors in the admissions decision are advanced placement or honor courses, recommendations by school officials, and extracurricular activities record.

Procedure: Freshmen are admitted fall, winter, and spring. There are early admissions and deferred admissions plans. There is a rolling admissions plan. The fee is $25. Notification is sent on a rolling basis. Check with the school for current application deadlines. Applications are accepted on-line through the school's web site.

Transfer: 55 transfer students enrolled in 2002-2003. Students are required to submit a completed application, official transcripts from each college or university attended, an academic reference, and official high school transcripts if they have fewer than 36 transferable credits. 45 credits of 186 required for the bachelor's degree must be completed at NCC.

Visiting: There are regularly scheduled orientations for prospective students. There are guides for informal visits and visitors may sit in on classes and stay overnight. To schedule a visit, contact Admissions at (541) 684-7209.

Financial Aid: In 2003-2004, all full-time students received some form of financial aid. NCC is a member of CSS. The FAFSA and the college's own financial statement are required.

International Students: There are 3 international students enrolled. They must score 500 on the written TOEFL.

Computers: The mainframes are 4 Dell servers in a Windows 2000 network. A computer lab with more than 20 terminals, Internet access, and e-mail is available. There are also 20 networked terminals in a computer classroom and 12 networked terminals in the library. Students also have Internet access from dorm rooms. All students may access the system during open library hours. There are no time limits and no fees. It is strongly recommended that all students have a personal computer.

Graduates: From July 1, 2002 to June 30, 2003, 116 bachelor's degrees were awarded. The most popular majors were management (37%), teacher education (31%), and psychology (8%). In an average class, 31% graduate in 4 years or less, 37% graduate in 5 years or less, and 39% graduate in 6 years or less.

Admissions Contact: Randy Jones, Dean of Admissions.
E-mail: *admissions@nwcc.edu* Web: *www.nwcc.edu*

OREGON INSTITUTE OF TECHNOLOGY	B-4
Klamath Falls, OR 97601-8801	**(541) 885-1150**
	Fax: (541) 885-1115
Full-time: 1110 men, 835 women	Faculty: 107; IIB, -$
Part-time: 590 men, 555 women	Ph.D.s: 31%
Graduate: 15 men	Student/Faculty: 18 to 1
Year: quarters, summer session	Tuition: $3565 ($12,525)
Application Deadline: see profile	Room & Board: $5155
Freshman Class: n/av	
SAT I or ACT: required	COMPETITIVE

Oregon Institute of Technology, the only public institute of technology in the Pacific Northwest, provides degree programs in engineering and health technologies, management, communications and applied sciences that prepare students to be effective participants in their professional, public and international communities. Figures in the above capsule and in this profile are approximate. There are 3 undergraduate schools and 1 graduate school. In addition to regional accreditation, OIT has baccalaureate program accreditation with ABET and NLN. The library contains 145,988 volumes, 158,278 microform items, and 2069 audio/video tapes/CDs, and subscribes to 1815 periodicals. Computerized library services include the card catalog, interlibrary loans, and database searching. Special learning facilities include a learning resource center, art gallery, and radio station. The 173-acre campus is in a small town 60 miles east of Medford in south central Oregon. Including any residence halls, there are 12 buildings.

Student Life: 85% of undergraduates are from Oregon. Students are from 35 states and 17 foreign countries. 95% are from public schools. 80% are white. The average age of freshmen is 23; all undergraduates, 26. 26% do not continue beyond their first year; 29% remain to graduate.

Housing: 500 students can be accommodated in college housing, which includes single-sex and coed dorms. On-campus housing is guaranteed for all 4 years. 82% of students commute. All students may keep cars.

Activities: 3% of men belong to 1 local and 1 national fraternity; 3% of women belong to 1 local and 1 national sorority. There are 37 groups on campus, including cheerleading, computers, ethnic, honors, international, newspaper, outdoor, pep band, professional, radio and TV, religious, social, and student government. Popular campus events include Tech Challenge, Family Weekend Tech Fest, and a skills contest for business and math students.

Sports: There are 4 intercollegiate sports for men and 6 for women. Facilities include a 3000-seat stadium, a 2066-seat gym, football, baseball, and softball fields, free weights and aerobics areas, an indoor swimming pool, a track, and tennis, volleyball, basketball, and badminton courts.

Disabled Students: 90% of the campus is accessible. Wheelchair ramps, elevators, special parking, specially equipped rest rooms, and special class scheduling are available.

Services: Counseling and information services are available, as is tutoring in some subjects, including math, sciences, and computers. There is a reader service for the blind and remedial math, reading, and writing.

Campus Safety and Security: Measures include 24-hour foot and vehicle patrol, security escort services, and lighted pathways/sidewalks.

Programs of Study: OIT confers the B.S. degree. Associate and master's degrees are also awarded. Bachelor's degrees are awarded in BUSINESS (management information systems), ENGINEERING AND ENVIRONMENTAL DESIGN (civil engineering, computer technology, electrical/electronics engineering technology, engineering technology, environmental science, industrial administration/management, laser electro-optics technology, manufacturing technology, mechanical engineering technology, and surveying engineering), HEALTH PROFESSIONS (dental hygiene, health science, radiograph medical technology, and ultrasound technology), SOCIAL SCIENCE (industrial and organizational psychology). Engineering technology programs are the largest.

Required: General education requirements include 12 hours in social science and 9 hours each in communication, business, and humanities. Students also must take 9 hours in English composition and technical report writing. Completion of about 200 quarter hours, with a minimum GPA of 2.0, is required to graduate.

Special: Cross-registration with Klamath Community College, internships in all majors, and co-op programs in all engineering technologies are available. OIT also offers advanced degree programs in software engineering technology and vascular imaging. There are 2 national honor societies.

Faculty/Classroom: 77% of faculty are male; 23%, female. All teach undergraduates. The average class size in an introductory lecture is 30; in a laboratory, 18; and in a regular course, 30.

Requirements: The SAT I or ACT is required for placement purposes; however, a composite score of 1000 on the SAT I or 21 on the ACT is required for applicants who do not meet the minimum GPA requirement. Applicants must have 14 academic units, including 4 years of English, 3 each of math and social sciences, and 2 each of science and a foreign language. The GED is accepted. A GPA of 2.5 is required. AP and CLEP credits are accepted.

Procedure: Freshmen are admitted to all sessions. The SAT I or ACT should be taken during the senior year, and placement tests just prior to registration. There is an early admissions plan and a rolling admissions plan. Check with the school for current deadlines. Notification is sent on a rolling basis. Applications are accepted on computer disk.

Transfer: 168 transfer students enrolled in a recent year. Applicants must have a minimum GPA of 2.0 and at least 24 quarter credit hours; students with fewer credit hours must submit high school transcripts or GED scores. An associate degree is recommended. 45 of 190 credits required for the bachelor's degree must be completed at OIT.

Visiting: There are regularly scheduled orientations for prospective students, including tours and meetings with admissions counselors, faculty, and students. There are guides for informal visits and visitors may sit in on classes and stay overnight. To schedule a visit, contact the Admissions Office at oit@oit.edu.

Financial Aid: In a recent year, 85% of all full-time freshmen and 60% of continuing full-time students received some form of financial aid. 80% of full-time freshmen and 75% of continuing full-time students received need-based aid. The average freshman award was $9700. 40% of undergraduates work part time. Average annual earnings from campus work are $1200. The average financial indebtedness of a recent graduate was $22,629. The FAFSA is required. Check with the school for current deadlines.

International Students: In a recent year, there were 29 international students enrolled. The school actively recruits these students. They must score 520 on the written TOEFL.

Computers: The mainframes are a Prime EXL-316, a DEC PDP 11/44, and a DEC Alpha 2100. More than 700 terminals and PCs are available on campus. Modem access is available to students off campus. All students may access the system 24 hours daily during the last 2 weeks of the quarter and 18 hours daily otherwise. There are no time limits and no fees.

Graduates: 76 companies recruited on campus in a recent year. Of a recent graduating class, 11% were enrolled in graduate school within 6 months of graduation and 86% were employed.

Admissions Contact: Palmer Muntz, Director of Admissions. A video is available. E-mail: muntzp@oit.edu Web: www.oit.edu

OREGON STATE UNIVERSITY
Corvallis, OR 97331-2106

B-2

(541) 737-4411
(800) 291-4192; Fax: (541) 737-2482

Full-time: 7509 men, 6478 women	**Faculty:** 1352; I, --$
Part-time: 808 men, 804 women	**Ph.D.s:** 85%
Graduate: 1710 men, 1650 women	**Student/Faculty:** 10 to 1
Year: quarters, summer session	**Tuition:** $4719 ($17,475)
Application Deadline: see profile	**Room & Board:** $6336
Freshman Class: 7410 applied, 6529 accepted, 2949 enrolled	
SAT I or ACT: required	**COMPETITIVE**

Oregon State University, founded in 1868, is the oldest institution in the Oregon state system, offering liberal arts and preprofessional programs. There are 10 undergraduate and 12 graduate schools. In addition to regional accreditation, OSU has baccalaureate program accreditation with AACSB, ABET, ACCE, ACEJMC, ACPE, AHEA, NASM, NCATE, and SAF. The 4 libraries contain 1,403,451 volumes, 1,912,023 microform items, and 6225 audio/video tapes/CDs, and subscribe to 14,777 periodicals. Computerized library services include the card catalog and database searching. Special learning facilities include a learning resource center, art gallery, natural history museum, radio station, TV station, arboretum, wave research lab, research farm, research vessel, and the Linus Pauling Collection. The 400-acre campus is in a small town 80 miles south of Portland. Including any residence halls, there are 203 buildings.

Student Life: 85% of undergraduates are from Oregon. Students are from 50 states, 90 foreign countries, and Canada. 75% are white. The average age of freshmen is 19; all undergraduates, 23. 20% do not continue beyond their first year; 60% remain to graduate.

Housing: 5593 students can be accommodated in college housing, which includes coed dorms, married-student housing, fraternity houses, and sorority houses. In addition, there are honors houses, special-interest houses, and cooperative houses. All residences are smoke-free. On-campus housing is available on a first-come, first-served basis. 71% of students commute. Alcohol is not permitted. All students may keep cars.

Activities: 15% of men belong to 25 national fraternities; 11% of women belong to 13 national sororities. There are 350 groups on campus, including art, band, cheerleading, chess, choir, chorale, chorus, computers, dance, drama, drill team, drum and bugle corps, ethnic, film, gay, honors, international, jazz band, literary magazine, marching band, musical theater, newspaper, orchestra, pep band, photography, political, professional, radio and TV, religious, social, social service, student government, symphony, and yearbook. Popular campus events include Renaissance Fair and Native American Pow Wow.

Sports: There are 7 intercollegiate sports for men and 8 for women, and 19 intramural sports for men and 17 for women. Facilities include 2 fitness centers, a 10,400-seat gym, a 40,000-seat stadium, indoor and outdoor recreation centers, weight and exercise rooms, bowling alleys, and numerous courts and playing fields.

Disabled Students: 92% of the campus is accessible. Wheelchair ramps, elevators, special parking, specially equipped rest rooms, special class scheduling, lowered drinking fountains, lowered telephones, note takers, interpreters for the deaf, and visual-aid equipment for the blind are available.

Services: Counseling and information services are available, as is tutoring in most subjects, including chemistry, computer science, math, psychology and counseling, and physics. There is a reader service for the blind and remedial math, reading, and writing. Facilities include a communication skills center and a math sciences learning center.

Campus Safety and Security: Measures include emergency telephones and lighted pathways/sidewalks.

Programs of Study: OSU confers B.A., B.S., and B.F.A. degrees. Master's and doctoral degrees are also awarded. Bachelor's degrees are awarded in AGRICULTURE (agricultural business management, agricultural economics, agriculture, animal science, fishing and fisheries, forest engineering, forestry and related sciences, forestry production and processing, horticulture, poultry science, range/farm management, and soil science), BIOLOGICAL SCIENCE (biochemistry, biology/biological science, biophysics, botany, entomology, microbiology, nutrition, plant pathology, wildlife biology, and zoology), BUSINESS (accounting, business administration and management, hotel/motel and restaurant management, marketing management, and marketing/retailing/merchandising), COMMUNICATIONS AND THE ARTS (apparel design, art, dramatic arts, English, French, German, music, Spanish, speech/debate/rhetoric, and visual and performing arts), COMPUTER AND PHYSICAL SCIENCE (chemistry, computer science, geology, mathematics, physics, and science), EDUCATION (health), ENGINEERING AND ENVIRONMENTAL DESIGN (chemical engineering, civil engineering, computer engineering, construction management, environmental science, industrial engineering technology, landscape architecture/design, mechanical engineering, nuclear engineering, and urban design), HEALTH PROFESSIONS (environmental health science, health, health care administration, medical technology, and nursing), SOCIAL SCIENCE (American studies, anthropology, economics, family/consumer studies, fashion design and technology, food science, geography, history, home economics, human development, liberal arts/general studies, philosophy, political science/government, psychology, sociology, and textiles and clothing). Engineering, biochemistry, and forestry are the strongest academically. Business, liberal arts, and mechanical engineering are the largest.

Required: To graduate, students must complete at least 192 quarter credits with a GPA of 2.0. The required core curriculum includes a total of 37 credits in writing and communications, math, humanities and social studies, natural sciences, and fitness. Students must take a writing-intensive course in their major field and meet additional distribution requirements.

Special: OSU offers cooperative veterinary medicine programs with Washington State University and the University of Idaho; geological, metallurgical, and mining engineering programs with the University of Idaho; and an education program with the University of Oregon. Students may cross-register at any college in the Oregon state system, at member colleges of the Western Interstate Commission, and with any member of the National Student Exchange. Study abroad is possible in any of 13 countries, including New Zealand and the former Soviet Union. There is a 5-year B.A.-B.S. program in civil engineering and forest engineering, and a 3-2 engineering program with the University of Oregon. Internships, a liberal studies degree, nondegree study, and pass/fail options are also available. There are 7 national honor societies, a freshman honors program, and 20 departmental honors programs.

Faculty/Classroom: 58% of faculty are male; 42%, female. 67% teach undergraduates and do research.

Admissions: 88% of the 2003-2004 applicants were accepted. The SAT I scores for the 2003-2004 freshman class were: Verbal--35% below 500, 42% between 500 and 599, 21% between 600 and 700, and 2% above 700; Math--29% below 500, 42% between 500 and 599, 26% between 600 and 700, and 3% above 700. The ACT scores were 31% below 21, 28% between 21 and 23, 22% between 24 and 26, 9% between 27 and 28, and 10% above 28. 37% of the current freshmen were in the top fifth of their class; 69% were in the top two fifths.

Requirements: The SAT I or ACT is required. In addition, applicants should be high school graduates or hold the GED. Required high school preparation includes 4 years of English; 3 years of math, including algebra I; 2 years of natural science; and 1 year each of U.S history, world history, and social science. Among electives, government and foreign language are strongly recommended. Some subject requirements may be fulfilled by test scores. A GPA of 3.0 is required. AP and CLEP credits are accepted. Advanced placement or honor courses are an important factor in the admissions decision.

Procedure: Freshmen are admitted to all sessions. Entrance exams should be taken during the junior or senior year. There is an early admissions plan. Check with the school for current deadlines. The fall 2003 application fee was $50. Notification is sent on a rolling basis.

Transfer: 1141 transfer students enrolled in a recent year. Applicants who are Oregon residents must present a GPA of at least 2.25 in previous college work; for nonresidents, a GPA of 2.5. Students should have completed at least 36 hours of college credit. Either SAT I or ACT scores must be submitted. 36 of 192 credits required for the bachelor's degree must be completed at OSU.

Visiting: There are regularly scheduled orientations for prospective students. There are guides for informal visits and visitors may sit in on classes and stay overnight. To schedule a visit, contact the Office of New Student Programs.

Financial Aid: OSU is a member of CSS. The FAFSA is required. Check with the school for current deadlines.

International Students: The school actively recruits these students. They must score 550 on the written TOEFL.

Computers: The mainframes are 2 Digital 7000/620 AXP open/VMS machines and 1 Digital 2100 AXP OSF/1. There are more than 2200 PC and Mac systems available to students in the computer lab, the library, and various academic buildings. All students may access the system at any time. There are no time limits and no fees.

Graduates: In a recent year, 2600 bachelor's degrees were awarded. The most popular majors were business administration (13%), liberal studies (6%), and human development and family studies (4%). In an average class, 1% graduate in 3 years or less, 28% graduate in 4 years or less, 54% graduate in 5 years or less, and 59% graduate in 6 years or less.

Admissions Contact: Michelle Sandlin, Director of Admissions.
E-mail: *osuadmit@orst.edu*
Web: *http://www.oregonstate.edu/admissions*

OREGON UNIVERSITY SYSTEM

The Oregon University System (OUS), is comprised of 7 distinguished public universities, reaching more than 1 million persons each year through on-campus classes, statewide public services, and lifelong learning. OUS provides the central administration for the Oregon State Board of Higher Education, an 11-member volunteer board appointed by the governor and confirmed by the Oregon legislature. The chancellor serves as the system's chief administrative officer. OUS has a three-part mission: to provide affordable access to high-quality post-secondary education for all qualified Oregonians; to improve and enrich learning in the sciences, the social sciences, the humanities, the arts, and the professions; and to help Oregon respond effectively to social, economic, and environmental challenges and opportunities. Total campus enrollment exceeds 75,000 with nearly 3400 faculty. Academic offerings include 327 baccalaureate, 272 master's, and 134 doctoral programs. Campuses of the system include Eastern Oregon University, Oregon Institute of Technology, Oregon State University, Portland State University, Southern Oregon University, the University of Oregon, and Western Oregon University.

PACIFIC NORTHWEST COLLEGE OF ART
B-1
Portland, OR 97209 — (503) 821-8972; Fax: (503) 821-8978

Full-time: 128 men, 140 women	**Faculty:** 14
Part-time: 18 men, 20 women	**Ph.D.s:** 79%
Graduate: none	**Student/Faculty:** 19 to 1
Year: semesters	**Tuition:** $14,890
Application Deadline: March 1	**Room & Board:** n/app
Freshman Class: 91 applied, 83 accepted, 30 enrolled	
SAT I or ACT: not required	**SPECIAL**

Pacific Northwest College of Art, founded in 1909, offers professional training in the fine and visual arts. In addition to regional accreditation, PNCA has baccalaureate program accreditation with NASAD. The library contains 12,742 volumes and 459 audio/video tapes/CDs, and subscribes to 65 periodicals. Computerized library services include interlibrary loans. Special learning facilities include an art gallery. The 1-acre campus is in an urban area in downtown Portland. There are 3 buildings.

Student Life: 74% of undergraduates are from Oregon. Students are from 20 states, 5 foreign countries, and Canada. 87% are white. The average age of freshmen is 20; all undergraduates, 25. 37% do not continue beyond their first year; 35% remain to graduate.

Housing: There are no residence halls. All students commute.

Activities: There are no fraternities or sororities. There are some groups and organizations on campus, including art, photography, professional, and student government.

Sports: There is no sports program at PNCA.

Disabled Students: 90% of the campus is accessible. Wheelchair ramps, elevators, specially equipped rest rooms, and lowered drinking fountains are available.

Services: There is remedial writing.

Campus Safety and Security: Measures include pamphlets/posters/films, emergency telephones, and guards at building entrances.

Programs of Study: PNCA confers the B.F.A. degree. Bachelor's degrees are awarded in COMMUNICATIONS AND THE ARTS (fine arts, graphic design, illustration, painting, photography, printmaking, and sculpture). Painting is the largest.

Required: To graduate, all students must complete 120 credits, including 45 in liberal arts and science courses and 57 in a studio major. All seniors must earn a 2.0 GPA for both semesters and must complete a thesis, which is critiqued by the faculty and later exhibited.

Special: A joint B.A./B.F.A. degree is offered with Reed College. Students may cross-register with members of the Oregon Independent Col-

leges Association. There is a Mobility Program for 1 semester or 1 year with member schools of the Association of Schools of Art and Design. Fourth-year graphic design majors may undertake a 1-semester professional internship; internships also are strongly encouraged for juniors in all majors. Students may study abroad in 3 countries through PNCA's program or in any other country through the programs of other accredited institutions. Nondegree study and student-designed majors are possible.

Faculty/Classroom: 62% of faculty are male; 38%, female. All teach undergraduates. The average class size in a regular course is 17.

Admissions: 91% of the 2003-2004 applicants were accepted. The SAT I scores for the 2003-2004 freshman class were: Verbal--41% below 500, 42% between 500 and 599, and 17% between 600 and 700; Math--50% below 500, 17% between 500 and 599, and 33% between 600 and 700. The ACT scores were 33% below 21 and 67% between 21 and 23. 19% of the current freshmen were in the top fifth of their class; 24% were in the top two fifths.

Requirements: Applicants should be high school graduates or have earned the GED. The application consists of high school transcripts, a personal statement about the applicant's decision to become an artist, 1 letter of recommendation, and a portfolio of at least 12 pieces of artwork. The portfolio must consist of 6 drawings from life and at least 6 additional pieces. A GPA of 2.0 is required. AP credits are accepted. Evidence of special talent is an important factor in the admission decision.

Procedure: Freshmen are admitted fall and spring. There is a rolling admissions plan and a deferred admissions plan. Applications should be filed by March 1 for fall entry and December 15 for spring entry. Notification is sent on a rolling basis.

Transfer: 70 transfer students enrolled in 2002-2003. Applicants must submit college and in some cases, high school transcripts. Students may submit up to 40 slides or up to 20 original pieces of artwork, at least 6 of which must be drawings. Potential graphic design majors must submit samples of their work. A minimum 2.0 GPA is required. 48 of 120 credits required for the bachelor's degree must be completed at PNCA.

Visiting: There are guides for informal visits and visitors may sit in on classes. To schedule a visit, contact the Admissions Office.

Financial Aid: The average financial indebtedness of a recent graduate was $18,917. The FAFSA is required. The priority date for freshman financial aid applications for fall entry is March 1. The deadline for filing freshman financial aid applications for fall entry is August 1.

International Students: International students must score 550 on the written TOEFL.

Computers: All students may access the system. There are no time limits and no fees.

Graduates: From July 1, 2002 to June 30, 2003, 57 bachelor's degrees were awarded. The most popular majors were painting (32%), graphic design (18%), and photography (15%). In an average class, 26% graduate in 4 years or less, and 26% graduate in 6 years or less.

Admissions Contact: Rebecca Haas, Director of Admissions.
E-mail: *admissions@pnca.edu* Web: *www.pnca.edu*

PACIFIC UNIVERSITY
B-1
Forest Grove, OR 97116 — (503) 359-2218
(800) PAC-UNIV; Fax: (503) 359-2975

Full-time: 380 men, 620 women	**Faculty:** 87; IIA, --$
Part-time: 35 men, 40 women	**Ph.D.s:** 78%
Graduate: 365 men, 625 women	**Student/Faculty:** 12 to 1
Year: 4-1-4, summer session	**Tuition:** $19,840
Application Deadline: see profile	**Room & Board:** $5740
Freshman Class: n/av	
SAT I or ACT: required	**COMPETITIVE**

Pacific University, founded in 1849, is an independent institution affiliated with the Congregational Church (United Church of Christ), offering degree programs in liberal arts, science, business, education, and health professions. Figures in the above capsule and in this profile are approximate. In addition to regional accreditation, Pacific has baccalaureate program accreditation with NASM. The library contains 152,060 volumes, 76,609 microform items, and 3708 audio/video tapes/CDs, and subscribes to 945 periodicals. Computerized library services include the card catalog, interlibrary loans, and database searching. Special learning facilities include a learning resource center, art gallery, radio station, TV station, and museum of the history of the university. The 55-acre campus is in a small town 25 miles west of Portland. Including any residence halls, there are 18 buildings.

Student Life: 50% of undergraduates are from out of state, mostly the West. Students are from 31 states, 7 foreign countries, and Canada. 91% are from public schools. 64% are white; 17% Asian American. The average age of freshmen is 18; all undergraduates, 20. 22% do not continue beyond their first year; 54% remain to graduate.

Housing: 680 students can be accommodated in college housing, which includes single-sex and coed dorms, off-campus apartments, and married-student housing. In addition, there are special-interest houses. On-campus housing is guaranteed for the freshman year only, is available on a first-come, first-served basis, and is available on a lottery system for upperclassmen. 50% of students live on campus; of those, 90% remain on campus on weekends. All students may keep cars.

Activities: 2% of men belong to 3 local fraternities; 6% of women belong to 3 local sororities. There are 35 groups on campus, including art, band, cheerleading, choir, chorale, chorus, computers, dance, debate, drama, ethnic, forensics, gay, honors, international, jazz band, literary magazine, musical theater, newspaper, opera, orchestra, outdoor and urban recreation, pep band, photography, political, professional, radio and TV, religious, social, social service, student government, and yearbook. Popular campus events include Hawaiian Club Luau, International Club Banquet, and Japan Day.

Sports: There are 8 intercollegiate sports for men and 8 for women, and 10 intramural sports for men and 10 for women. Facilities include a gym, various courts, a sauna, weight and wrestling rooms, a dance studio, outdoor playing fields, a field house, and racquetball courts.

Disabled Students: 80% of the campus is accessible. Wheelchair ramps, elevators, special parking, specially equipped rest rooms, and lowered drinking fountains are available.

Services: Counseling and information services are available, as is tutoring in most subjects. There is a reader service for the blind.

Campus Safety and Security: Measures include 24-hour foot and vehicle patrol, security escort services, informal discussions, and pamphlets/posters/films. There are emergency telephones and lighted pathways/sidewalks.

Programs of Study: Pacific confers B.A., B.S., and B.M. degrees. Master's and doctoral degrees are also awarded. Bachelor's degrees are awarded in BIOLOGICAL SCIENCE (biology/biological science), BUSINESS (business administration and management), COMMUNICATIONS AND THE ARTS (creative writing, dramatic arts, Japanese, literature, music, and Spanish), COMPUTER AND PHYSICAL SCIENCE (chemistry, computer science, mathematics, and physics), SOCIAL SCIENCE (economics, history, humanities, philosophy, political science/government, psychology, social work, and sociology). Natural sciences, literature, and creative writing are the strongest academically. Business administration, English, and psychology are the largest.

Required: All students take a core curriculum that includes a first-year seminar and courses in writing, foreign language, social and natural sciences, art, and cross-cultural studies. A cumulative GPA of 2.0 in 124 semester hours is required for graduation. 34 to 64 hours are required in the major, depending on the discipline.

Special: Cross-registration is available with Oregon Independent Colleges and Oregon Graduate Institute of Science and Technology (OGIST). The university also offers cooperative programs with Washington University in St. Louis, OGIST, and Oregon School of Arts and Crafts, as well as study abroad in 13 countries. Full-time, semester-long internships, including one in Washington D.C., are possible. Dual majors, a general studies degree in humanities, nondegree study, 3-2 engineering programs with Washington University in St. Louis and OGIST, and an interdisciplinary program in peace and conflict studies are available. There are 2 national honor societies, a freshman honors program, and 1 departmental honors program.

Faculty/Classroom: 52% of faculty are male; 48%, female. All both teach and do research. No introductory courses are taught by graduate students. The average class size in an introductory lecture is 35; in a laboratory, 20; and in a regular course, 19.

Requirements: The SAT I or ACT is required. In addition, applicants are expected to be high school graduates or to hold the GED. A personal essay is required, and an interview is recommended. A GPA of 3.0 is required. AP and CLEP credits are accepted. Important factors in the admissions decision are advanced placement or honor courses, recommendations by school officials, and extracurricular activities record.

Procedure: Freshmen are admitted fall and spring. There is a deferred admissions plan and a rolling admissions plan. Check with the school for current deadlines. Application fee is $30. Applications are accepted online at the school's web site or through AppliedTechnology (Princeton Review).

Transfer: Transfer applicants must present at least a 2.75 GPA in previous college work; those with fewer than 30 semester hours or 45 quarter hours must also submit SAT I or ACT test scores and high school transcripts. A personal interview is strongly recommended. 30 of 124 credits required for the bachelor's degree must be completed at Pacific.

Visiting: There are regularly scheduled orientations for prospective students, including overnight housing with current students, a campus tour, classroom visitations, and meetings with faculty and coaches. There are guides for informal visits and visitors may sit in on classes and stay overnight. To schedule a visit, contact the Admissions Office.

Financial Aid: Pacific is a member of CSS. The FAFSA is required. Check with the school for current deadlines.

International Students: The school actively recruits these students. They must score 550 on the written TOEFL.

Computers: There is a Mac-based LAN with 45 student terminals, plus 6 student-use PCs, 18 Mac standalones in residence halls, a Sequent S-81, an Intel System 303 running UNIX System 5, and a Sun 3/80 work-

station. All students may access the system. There are no time limits and no fees.

Admissions Contact: Beth Woodward, Director of Admissions. E-mail: *admissions@pacificu.edu* Web: *www.pacificu.edu*

PORTLAND STATE UNIVERSITY
Portland, OR 97207-0751

B-1

(503) 725-3511
(800) 547-8887; Fax: (503) 725-5525

Full-time: 4673 men, 5415 women	**Faculty:** 635; I, --$
Part-time: 2655 men, 3174 women	**Ph.D.s:** 78%
Graduate: 2118 men, 2995 women	**Student/Faculty:** 16 to 1
Year: quarters, summer session	**Tuition:** $4278 ($13,674)
Application Deadline: open	**Room & Board:** $8175
Freshman Class: 3019 applied, 2465 accepted, 1536 enrolled	
SAT I Verbal/Math: 520/520	**ACT:** 21 COMPETITIVE

Portland State University, founded in 1946, is a comprehensive public institution serving a primarily commuter student body. Graduate and undergraduate degree programs are offered in liberal arts and sciences, business, education, engineering and applied science, fine and performing arts, social work, and urban and public affairs. There are 5 undergraduate and 7 graduate schools. In addition to regional accreditation, PSU has baccalaureate program accreditation with AACSB, ABET, ASLA, NASAD, and NASM. The library contains 1,300,919 volumes, 2,362,836 microform items, and 87,092 audio/video tapes/CDs, and subscribes to 9730 periodicals. Computerized library services include the card catalog, interlibrary loans, database searching, and Internet access. Special learning facilities include a learning resource center, art gallery, radio station, a multicultural center, and a Native American center. The 49-acre campus is in an urban area in the center of Portland. Including any residence halls, there are 43 buildings.

Student Life: 87% of undergraduates are from Oregon. Students are from 47 states, 67 foreign countries, and Canada. 66% are white; 10% Asian American. The average age of freshmen is 19; all undergraduates, 26. 34% do not continue beyond their first year; 32% remain to graduate.

Housing: 1600 students can be accommodated in college housing, which includes coed dorms, on-campus apartments, off-campus apartments, fraternity houses, sorority houses, and freshmen experience. On-campus housing is available on a first-come, first-served basis. Priority is given to out-of-town students. 89% of students commute. All students may keep cars.

Activities: 1% of men belong to 3 national fraternities; 1% of women belong to 1 local and 2 national sororities. There are 148 groups on campus, including art, band, cheerleading, chess, choir, chorale, chorus, computers, dance, debate, drama, drill team, ethnic, film, forensics, gay, honors, international, jazz band, literary magazine, musical theater, newspaper, opera, orchestra, outdoor, pep band, photography, political, professional, radio and TV, religious, social, social service, student government, students with disabilities, symphony, and yearbook. Popular campus events include International Student Cultural Night, Friends of Chamber Music, and LunchBox Theater.

Sports: There are 8 intercollegiate sports for men and 9 for women, and 7 intramural sports for men and 6 for women. Facilities include a practice field, a swimming pool, an all-weather tennis facility, gyms, circuit training and weight rooms, a golf putting green, a running track, and racquetball, handball, and squash courts. Nearby Civic Stadium and Duniway Park provide football, baseball, and track and field facilities.

Disabled Students: 95% of the campus is accessible. Wheelchair ramps, elevators, special parking, specially equipped rest rooms, special class scheduling, lowered drinking fountains, lowered telephones, and special housing are available.

Services: Counseling and information services are available, as is tutoring in most subjects. There is a reader service for the blind, remedial math and writing, and Student Support Services, a program that provides assistance to students who are low-income, who have a physical disability, or whose parents did not graduate from college.

Campus Safety and Security: Measures include 24-hour foot and vehicle patrol, self-defense education, security escort services, and informal discussions. There are pamphlets/posters/films, emergency telephones, lighted pathways/sidewalks, a campus watch newsletter, information lectures, and community liaison.

Programs of Study: PSU confers B.A., B.S., and B.M. degrees. Master's and doctoral degrees are also awarded. Bachelor's degrees are awarded in BIOLOGICAL SCIENCE (biochemistry and biology/biological science), BUSINESS (accounting, business administration and management, management science, marketing/retailing/merchandising, and personnel management), COMMUNICATIONS AND THE ARTS (advertising, art history and appreciation, Chinese, dramatic arts, English, fine arts, French, German, Japanese, languages, music, Russian, Spanish, and speech/debate/rhetoric), COMPUTER AND PHYSICAL SCIENCE (chemistry, computer science, geology, information sciences and systems, mathematics, and physics), EDUCATION (health), ENGINEERING AND ENVIRONMENTAL DESIGN (architecture, civil engineering, computer engineering, electrical/electronics engineering, and environmental science), SOCIAL SCIENCE (anthropology, child care/child and family studies, community services, economics, geography, history, international studies, law enforcement and corrections, liberal arts/general studies, philosophy, political science/government, psychology, sociology, and women's studies). Electrical engineering, environmental science, and physics are the strongest academically. Psychology, business administration, and art are the largest.

Required: All students must complete at least 180 quarter credits with a 2.0 GPA. Other requirements and the number of hours that must be completed in the major vary by degree program. Freshmen must complete 3 5-credit freshman inquiry courses; sophomores, 3 4-credit courses from different interdisciplinary programs or general education clusters; juniors and seniors, 1 interdisciplinary program or general education cluster (4 3-credit courses); and seniors must complete a Senior Capstone.

Special: Students may study abroad in 34 countries. Numerous internships, a Washington semester, and work-study programs are available. Most undergraduate programs may be taken on an accelerated basis, and students in all programs may undertake dual majors or design their own majors. A general studies program is available in arts and letters, science, or social science. Nondegree study and pass/fail grading options are possible. Students may enroll for 7 or fewer credits per term without formal admission. There are 18 national honor societies, a freshman honors program, and 10 departmental honors programs.

Faculty/Classroom: 55% of faculty are male; 45%, female. All both teach and do research. The average class size in an introductory lecture is 23; in a laboratory, 19; and in a regular course, 28.

Admissions: 82% of the 2003-2004 applicants were accepted. The SAT I scores for the 2003-2004 freshman class were: Verbal--41% below 500, 39% between 500 and 599, 18% between 600 and 700, and 2% above 700; Math--40% below 500, 41% between 500 and 599, 18% between 600 and 700, and 1% above 700. The ACT scores were 39% below 21, 30% between 21 and 23, 20% between 24 and 26, 8% between 27 and 28, and 3% above 28. 18 freshmen graduated first in their class in a recent year.

Requirements: The SAT I or ACT is required, with a suggested minimum composite SAT I score of 1000 and a minimum composite ACT score of 21. Applicants should be high school graduates or have earned the GED. Secondary preparation should include 4 years of English, 3 years each of social studies and math, and 2 years each of science and foreign language. A GPA of 3.0 is required. AP and CLEP credits are accepted.

Procedure: Freshmen are admitted to all sessions. Entrance exams should be taken as early as possible. There is a deferred admissions plan and a rolling admissions plan. Application deadlines are open. Application fee is $50. Notification is sent on a rolling basis. Applications are accepted on-line through the school's web site.

Transfer: 2516 transfer students enrolled in 2002-2003. Applicants who are Oregon residents must have earned at least a 2.0 GPA in 30 college credits; those with 12 to 30 credits must meet freshman admission requirements and have a 2.0 GPA in all college work attempted. Nonresident applicants must have at least a 2.25 GPA in 30 hours of college work; those with 12 to 30 hours must meet freshman requirements and have a 2.5 GPA in all college work attempted. 45 credits of 180 required for the bachelor's degree must be completed at PSU.

Visiting: There are regularly scheduled orientations for prospective students, including twice-daily campus tours led by student guides and opportunities for prospective students to meet with faculty, staff, and advisers. There are guides for informal visits and visitors may sit in on classes and stay overnight. To schedule a visit, contact Campus Tour Coordinator, Office of Admissions and Records at (503) 725-5555 or psutours@pdx.edu.

Financial Aid: In 2003-2004, 63% of all full-time freshmen and 58% of continuing full-time students received some form of financial aid. 46% of full-time freshmen and 51% of continuing full-time students received need-based aid. The average freshman award was $6203. Need-based scholarships or need-based grants averaged $7343 ($21,681 maximum). 80% of undergraduates work part time. Average annual earnings from campus work are $1716. The FAFSA and the college's own financial statement are required. The deadline for filing freshman financial aid applications for fall entry is June 15.

International Students: There are 363 international students enrolled. The school actively recruits these students. They must score 525 on the written TOEFL and also take the college's own test. Only the international TOEFL exam or the PSU institutional TOEFL exam will be accepted.

Computers: The mainframes are a Sequent NUMAQ and Sun Enterprise servers. There are 12 computer labs and several smaller departmental sites. The open-access PC and Mac labs are open to all students. Labs are available in Smith Center, Shattuck Hall, Millar Library, and various departmental locations throughout campus. All students may get student accounts for access to the Internet and the Web and for use of e-mail. There are also several servers across campus for student access and data storage. All students may access the system 24 hours a day, except during the scheduled weekly maintenance period. Lab time is not limited, but dial-in is 90 minutes per session. There are no fees.

Graduates: From July 1, 2002 to June 30, 2003, 2596 bachelor's degrees were awarded. The most popular majors were general studies/social science (11%), management (8%), and psychology (7%). In an average class, 8% graduate in 4 years or less, 24% graduate in 5 years or less, and 32% graduate in 6 years or less. 130 companies recruited on campus in 2002-2003.

Admissions Contact: Samuel Collie, Executive Director of Admissions, Records and Financial Aid. E-mail: askadm@ess.pdx.edu Web: http://www.ess.pdx.edu/adm/

REED COLLEGE
Portland, OR 97202-8199

B-1

(503) 777-7511
(800) 547-4750; Fax: (503) 777-7553

Full-time: 578 men, 688 women	**Faculty:** 120; IIB, ++$
Part-time: 20 men, 26 women	**Ph.Ds:** 87%
Graduate: 12 men, 16 women	**Student/Faculty:** 11 to 1
Year: semesters	**Tuition:** $29,200
Application Deadline: January 15	**Room & Board:** $7750
Freshman Class: 2282 applied, 1044 accepted, 301 enrolled	
SAT I Verbal/Math: 700/660	**ACT:** 30 MOST COMPETITIVE

Reed College, founded in 1908, is a private, nonsectarian institution offering programs in liberal arts and sciences, and emphasizing instruction through small conference-style classes. In addition to regional accreditation, Reed has baccalaureate program accreditation with ACS. The library contains 512,115 volumes, 239,479 microform items, and 16,339 audio/video tapes/CDs, and subscribes to 2466 periodicals. Computerized library services include the card catalog, interlibrary loans, and database searching. Special learning facilities include a learning resource center, art gallery, and radio station. The 100-acre campus is in an urban area in Portland. Including any residence halls, there are 37 buildings.

Student Life: 84% of undergraduates are from out of state, mostly the Northwest. Students are from 38 foreign countries and Canada. 66% are from public schools. 65% are white. The average age of freshmen is 18; all undergraduates, 20. 10% do not continue beyond their first year; 72% remain to graduate.

Housing: 784 students can be accommodated in college housing, which includes coed dorms, on-campus apartments, and off-campus apartments. In addition, there are language houses, special-interest houses, and quiet, substance-free, and no-smoking dorms. On-campus housing is guaranteed for the freshman year only, is available on a first-come, first-served basis, and is available on a lottery system for upperclassmen. 65% of students live on campus; of those, 95% remain on campus on weekends. Alcohol is not permitted. All students may keep cars.

Activities: There are no fraternities or sororities. There are 65 groups on campus, including art, chess, choir, chorale, chorus, computers, dance, debate, drama, ethnic, gay, international, literary magazine, newspaper, orchestra, photography, radio and TV, religious, social service, student government, and yearbook. Popular campus events include Performing Arts Festival, Campus Clean Up Day (Canyon Day), and Renaissance Fair.

Sports: There are 6 intercollegiate sports for men and 4 for women, and 4 intramural sports for men and 4 for women. Facilities include a sports center that houses 2 gyms (1 seating 1200), an indoor pool, squash and racquetball courts, saunas, a weight room, an exercise room, and a dance studio. Outdoor facilities include tennis courts, a track, and areas for soccer, rugby, volleyball, and baseball.

Disabled Students: 68% of the campus is accessible. Wheelchair ramps, elevators, special parking, specially equipped rest rooms, special class scheduling, lowered drinking fountains, and lowered telephones are available.

Services: Counseling and information services are available, as is tutoring in every subject. There is a reader service for the blind and remedial math, reading, and writing.

Campus Safety and Security: Measures include 24-hour foot and vehicle patrol, self-defense education, security escort services, and shuttle buses. There are informal discussions, pamphlets/posters/films, emergency telephones, and lighted pathways/sidewalks.

Programs of Study: Reed confers the B.A. degree. Master's degrees are also awarded. Bachelor's degrees are awarded in BIOLOGICAL SCIENCE (biology/biological science), COMMUNICATIONS AND THE ARTS (art, Chinese, classics, dramatic arts, English literature, Germanic languages and literature, linguistics, music, and Russian languages and literature), COMPUTER AND PHYSICAL SCIENCE (chemistry, mathematics, and physics), SOCIAL SCIENCE (anthropology, economics, French studies, history, philosophy, political science/government, psychology, religion, sociology, and Spanish studies). Biology, history, and psychology are the largest.

Required: All students are required to maintain a C average while taking 120 semester hours. The liberal arts program also requires 1 year of humanities and 1 year for a senior research project, in addition to 1 year each from literature and the arts, history, social science, psychology, natural science, math, logic, foreign languages, and linguistics. Students also must take 3 semesters of phys ed.

Special: Cross-registration is available through the Oregon Independent Colleges organization and Pacific Northwest College of Art. Also available are 3-2 engineering degrees with California Institute of Technology, Columbia University, and Rensselaer Polytechnic Institute, combined 3-2 programs in science, and programs with the Pacific Northwest College of Art. Study abroad in 12 countries, a domestic exchange program with Howard University in Washington, D.C., accelerated degree programs, dual majors, student-designed majors, numerous interdisciplinary majors, nondegree study, and pass/fail options are also offered. There is a chapter of Phi Beta Kappa.

Faculty/Classroom: 64% of faculty are male; 36%, female. All both teach and do research. No introductory courses are taught by graduate students. The average class size in a laboratory is 17 and in a regular course, 13.

Admissions: 46% of the 2003-2004 applicants were accepted. The SAT I scores for the 2003-2004 freshman class were: Verbal--1% below 500, 6% between 500 and 599, 38% between 600 and 700, and 55% above 700; Math--1% below 500, 15% between 500 and 599, 53% between 600 and 700, and 31% above 700. The ACT scores were 1% between 21 and 23, 8% between 24 and 26, 24% between 27 and 28, and 67% above 28. 84% of the current freshmen were in the top fifth of their class; 97% were in the top two fifths. There were 19 National Merit finalists. 11 freshmen graduated first in their class.

Requirements: The SAT I is required. In addition, the SAT II: Subject test in writing is recommended. Reed strongly recommends that applicants have 4 years of English, 3 each of math and science, and 2 each of foreign language, history, and social studies. An essay is required, and an interview is recommended. The GED is accepted. AP credits are accepted. Important factors in the admissions decision are advanced placement or honor courses, personality/intangible qualities, and evidence of special talent.

Procedure: Freshmen are admitted fall and spring. There are early decision, early admissions, and deferred admissions plans. Early decision applications should be filed by November 15; regular applications, by January 15 for fall entry and November 15 for winter entry. The fall 2003 application fee was $40. Notification of early decision is sent December 15; regular decision, April 1. 110 early decision candidates were accepted for the 2003-2004 class. 551 applicants were on the 2003 waiting list; 47 were admitted. Applications are accepted on-line through Common App.

Transfer: 31 transfer students enrolled in 2002-2003. Transfer students must have a GPA of 3.0. 60 of 120 credits required for the bachelor's degree must be completed at Reed.

Visiting: There are regularly scheduled orientations for prospective students, including an information session, campus tour, and an admission interview. Visitors may sit in on classes and stay overnight. To schedule a visit, contact the Office of Admission at admission@reed.edu.

Financial Aid: In 2003-2004, 48% of all full-time freshmen and 55% of continuing full-time students received some form of financial aid. 48% of full-time freshmen and 55% of continuing full-time students received need-based aid. The average freshman award was $23,800. Need-based scholarships or need-based grants averaged $22,032; and need-based self-help aid (loans and jobs) averaged $4992. 56% of undergraduates work part time. Average annual earnings from campus work are $1640. The average financial indebtedness of the 2003 graduate was $13,692. The CSS Profile or FAFSA, the college's own financial statement and the parent and student federal tax forms are required. The deadline for filing freshman financial aid applications for fall entry is March 1.

International Students: There are 77 international students enrolled. The school actively recruits these students. They must score 600 on the written TOEFL and also take the SAT I or the ACT. Students must take SAT II: Subject tests in writing and 2 others.

Computers: The mainframes are a Sun Alphaserver, Sun Ultra, and SunFire servers. There are more than 800 Macs, 130 Windows, and 25 Unix boxes available. Various labs and workstations offer UNIX workstations and servers. The entire campus is networked with fiber-optic cable and there is network access in each residence hall room. The library is also accessible on-line. There are central computer labs in addition to computerized departmental classrooms and teaching labs. All students may access the system 24 hours daily. There are no time limits and no fees.

Graduates: From July 1, 2002 to June 30, 2003, 291 bachelor's degrees were awarded. The most popular majors were biology (17%), English (15%), and psychology (9%). In an average class, 52% graduate in 4 years or less, 66% graduate in 5 years or less, and 72% graduate in 6 years or less. 12 companies recruited on campus in 2002-2003.

Admissions Contact: Paul Marthers, Dean.
E-mail: admission@reed.edu Web: http://www.reed.edu

SOUTHERN OREGON UNIVERSITY
B-4
Ashland, OR 97520-5005
(541) 552-6411
(800) 482-7672; Fax: (541) 552-6614

Full-time: 3863 men and women	**Faculty:** 203; IIA, --$
Part-time: 1101 men and women	**Ph.D.s:** 93%
Graduate: 542 men and women	**Student/Faculty:** 19 to 1
Year: quarters, summer session	**Tuition:** $4152 ($12,825)
Application Deadline: open	**Room & Board:** $6210
Freshman Class: 2341 applied, 1997 accepted, 998 enrolled	
SAT I Verbal/Math: 520/510	**ACT:** 21 **COMPETITIVE**

Southern Oregon University, founded in 1882, is a public comprehensive university providing undergraduate and graduate programs in humanities, science, business, fine and performing arts, social sciences, and teacher education. There are 4 undergraduate schools and 1 graduate school. In addition to regional accreditation, Southern has baccalaureate program accreditation with NASM and NLN. The library contains 300,000 volumes, 750,000 microform items, and 6000 audio/video tapes/CDs, and subscribes to 2000 periodicals. Computerized library services include interlibrary loans, database searching, and Internet access. Special learning facilities include a learning resource center, art gallery, radio station, TV station, an art museum, 8 art galleries, a wildlife forensics lab, a music recital hall, 2 theaters, a greenhouse, and an ecology center. The 175-acre campus is in a small town 10 miles southeast of Medford. Including any residence halls, there are 36 buildings.

Student Life: 79% of undergraduates are from Oregon. Students are from 43 states, 35 foreign countries, and Canada. 85% are from public schools. 86% are white. The average age of all undergraduates is 24. 30% do not continue beyond their first year; 37% remain to graduate.

Housing: 1100 students can be accommodated in college housing, which includes coed dorms, off-campus apartments, and married-student housing. In addition, there are special-interest houses, 24-hour and 12-hour quiet halls, a wellness hall, a freshman hall, a smoke-and incense-free hall, and an age 21+ hall. On-campus housing is guaranteed for the freshman year only and is available on a first-come, first-served basis. 75% of students commute. Alcohol is not permitted. All students may keep cars.

Activities: There are no fraternities or sororities. There are 84 groups on campus, including art, band, cheerleading, choir, chorale, chorus, computers, dance, drama, ethnic, gay, honors, international, jazz band, literary magazine, musical theater, newspaper, pep band, photography, political, professional, radio and TV, religious, social, student government, and symphony. Popular campus events include Commencement and Parents weekends, International Week, and One World Series.

Sports: There are 6 intercollegiate sports for men and 7 for women, and 11 intramural sports for men and 7 for women. Facilities include an indoor swimming pool, 6 racquetball courts, 12 tennis courts, 4 gyms, a climbing-wall gym, a dance studio, wrestling and weight rooms, a sauna, a football stadium, and an all-weather track.

Disabled Students: 95% of the campus is accessible. Wheelchair ramps, elevators, special parking, specially equipped rest rooms, lowered drinking fountains, and individualized programming are available.

Services: Counseling and information services are available, as is tutoring in some subjects, including math and writing. There is a reader service for the blind and remedial math and writing. Program design is offered for students with learning disabilities.

Campus Safety and Security: Measures include 24-hour foot and vehicle patrol, self-defense education, informal discussions, and pamphlets/posters/films. There are emergency telephones and lighted pathways/sidewalks.

Programs of Study: Southern confers B.A., B.S., and B.F.A. degrees. Master's degrees are also awarded. Bachelor's degrees are awarded in BIOLOGICAL SCIENCE (biology/biological science), BUSINESS (accounting, business administration and management, and marketing/retailing/merchandising), COMMUNICATIONS AND THE ARTS (art, communications, dramatic arts, English, languages, music, music business management, Spanish, and visual and performing arts), COMPUTER AND PHYSICAL SCIENCE (chemistry, computer science, geology, mathematics, physics, and science), EDUCATION (physical), HEALTH PROFESSIONS (health, nursing, and premedicine), SOCIAL SCIENCE (anthropology, criminology, economics, geography, history, international studies, liberal arts/general studies, political science/government, prelaw, psychology, social science, and sociology). Fine and performing arts, sciences, and social sciences are the strongest academically. Business and social sciences are the largest.

Required: Students need a minimum GPA of 2.0 earned over 180 quarter hours, with 50 to 100 in the major and at least 60 in upper-division course work. Competency must be demonstrated through course work in writing and research. General education requirements include a year-long course in speaking, writing, and critical thinking, and both lower- and upper-division courses in arts and letters, natural sciences, social sciences, and quantitative reasoning. There is a required senior capstone experience.

Special: Cross-registration through the National Student and Western Student Exchanges, study abroad in 16 countries, internships, and federal work-study are all available. Accelerated degrees in business, communication, computer science, economics, geography, math, political science, and foreign languages and literature; dual majors in business and chemistry, physics, math, or music, and in math and computer science; and interdisciplinary majors in environmental or international studies are all offered. There are 13 national honor societies, a freshman honors program, and 3 departmental honors programs.

Faculty/Classroom: 56% of faculty are male; 44%, female. All teach undergraduates and 50% do research. No introductory courses are taught by graduate students.

Admissions: 85% of the 2003-2004 applicants were accepted. The SAT I scores for the 2003-2004 freshman class were: Verbal--39% below 500, 39% between 500 and 599, 19% between 600 and 700, and 3% above 700; Math--41% below 500, 43% between 500 and 599, 15% between 600 and 700, and 2% above 700. The ACT scores were 36% below 21, 34% between 21 and 23, 20% between 24 and 26, 5% between 27 and 28, and 5% above 28.

Requirements: The SAT I or ACT is required. In addition, a minimum composite score of 1010 on the SAT I is needed if the high school GPA is less than 2.75. Applicants need 14 academic credits, including 4 years of English, 3 each of math and social studies, 2 of science, and 2 years of one foreign language. SAT II: Subject tests in writing, math, and another area are needed if there is insufficient college-preparatory course work. The GED is accepted. A GPA of 2.75 is required. AP and CLEP credits are accepted.

Procedure: Freshmen are admitted to all sessions. Entrance exams should be taken in the senior year. There is a deferred admissions plan and a rolling admissions plan. Application deadlines are open. The fall 2003 application fee was $50. Applications are accepted on-line through the university's web site.

Transfer: 468 transfer students enrolled in 2002-2003. Transfer students need a minimum GPA of 2.25 and at least 36 quarter credits. 45 of 180 credits required for the bachelor's degree must be completed at Southern.

Visiting: There are regularly scheduled orientations for prospective students, including tours of the campus and residence halls, and a meeting with an admissions representative. Appointments with faculty and class visits can be arranged. There are guides for informal visits and visitors may sit in on classes. To schedule a visit, contact the Admissions Office at (541) 552-6411 or (800) 482-7672 or *admissions@sou.edu*.

Financial Aid: 46% of undergraduates work part time. Average annual earnings from campus work are $809. Southern is a member of CSS. The FAFSA is required. The deadline for filing freshman financial aid applications for fall entry is March 1.

International Students: There are 153 international students enrolled. The school actively recruits these students. They must score 520 on the written TOEFL.

Computers: The mainframe is a Novell NetWare server. The main computing services lab and 22 other labs contain a total of 620 PCs available for student use. All students may access the system 7:30 A.M. to 10 P.M. Monday through Thursday, 7:30 A.M. to 5 P.M. Friday, 10 A.M. to 5 P.M. Saturday, and 10 A.M. to 10 P.M. Sunday.

Graduates: In a recent year, 771 bachelor's degrees were awarded. The most popular majors were business (20%), communication (10%), and psychology (9%). In an average class, 1% graduate in 3 years or less, 15% graduate in 4 years or less, 30% graduate in 5 years or less, and 42% graduate in 6 years or less. 93 companies recruited on campus in a recent year. Of a recent graduating class, 83% were employed within 6 months of graduation.

Admissions Contact: Mara Affre, Director of Admissions.
E-mail: *admissions@sou.edu* Web: *www.sou.edu*

UNIVERSITY OF OREGON
B-2
Eugene, OR 97403-1226

(541) 346-3201
(800) 232-3825; Fax: (541) 346-5815

Full-time: 6742 men, 7710 women	**Faculty:** 798; I, --$
Part-time: 761 men, 770 women	**Ph.D.s:** 95%
Graduate: 1872 men, 2137 women	**Student/Faculty:** 18 to 1
Year: quarters, summer session	**Tuition:** $4913 ($16,350)
Application Deadline: January 15	**Room & Board:** $6565
Freshman Class: 10,193 applied, 8602 accepted, 2819 enrolled	
SAT I Verbal/Math: 550/556	**VERY COMPETITIVE**

The University of Oregon, founded in 1876, is a public liberal arts institution within the Oregon University System. There are 8 undergraduate and 7 graduate schools. In addition to regional accreditation, UO has baccalaureate program accreditation with AACSB, ACEJMC, ASLA, FIDER, NAAB, NASM, and NRPA. The 6 libraries contain 2,490,159 volumes, 2,887,172 microform items, and 74,429 audio/video tapes/CDs, and subscribe to 17,840 periodicals. Computerized library services include the card catalog, interlibrary loans, and database searching. Special learning facilities include a learning resource center, art gallery, natu-

ral history museum, radio station, TV station, 13 specialized science institutes, including a center for volcanology, a neuroscience institute, a marine biology institute, and an observatory, 7 humanities and social science centers, and 12 other research facilities. The 295-acre campus is in a suburban area near downtown Eugene. Including any residence halls, there are 100 buildings.

Student Life: 77% of undergraduates are from Oregon. Students are from 50 states, 86 foreign countries, and Canada. 91% are from public schools. 82% are white. The average age of freshmen is 19; all undergraduates, 22. 18% do not continue beyond their first year; 61% remain to graduate.

Housing: 3250 students can be accommodated in college housing, which includes single-sex and coed dorms and married-student housing. In addition, there are honors houses, language houses, special-interest houses, an international house, and a graduate student residence hall. On-campus housing is available on a first-come, first-served basis. 82% of students commute. Alcohol is not permitted. All students may keep cars.

Activities: 8% of men belong to 13 national fraternities; 10% of women belong to 9 national sororities. There are 300 groups on campus, including art, band, cheerleading, choir, chorale, chorus, computers, dance, drama, drill team, ethnic, film, forensics, gay, honors, international, jazz band, literary magazine, marching band, musical theater, newspaper, opera, orchestra, pep band, photography, political, professional, radio and TV, religious, social, social service, student government, symphony, and yearbook. Popular campus events include University Day, Family and Friends Weekend, and Martin Luther King Day.

Sports: There are 8 intercollegiate sports for men and 9 for women, and 19 intramural sports for men and 17 for women. Facilities include a 41,000-seat stadium, a 10,000-seat arena, a swimming pool, several gyms, 15 tennis courts, running tracks, fields for outdoor sports, and a student recreation center with an indoor track, exercise and weight training equipment, a juice bar, and an indoor practice facility for athletic teams.

Disabled Students: 90% of the campus is accessible. Wheelchair ramps, elevators, special parking, specially equipped rest rooms, special class scheduling, lowered drinking fountains, lowered telephones, special housing, and a counselor for students with disabilities are available. Other accommodations are made upon request.

Services: Counseling and information services are available, as is tutoring in every subject. There is a reader service for the blind and remedial math and writing. Peer tutors in entry-level undergraduate courses are available through the Academic Learning Services Center. Students may drop in to receive free assistance with math and writing at the center's lab.

Campus Safety and Security: Measures include 24-hour foot and vehicle patrol, self-defense education, security escort services, and shuttle buses. There are informal discussions, pamphlets/posters/films, emergency telephones, and lighted pathways/sidewalks.

Programs of Study: UO confers B.A., B.S., B.Arch., B.Ed., B.F.A., B.I.Arch., B.L.A., and B.Mus. degrees. Master's and doctoral degrees are also awarded. Bachelor's degrees are awarded in BIOLOGICAL SCIENCE (biochemistry and biology/biological science), BUSINESS (accounting and business administration and management), COMMUNICATIONS AND THE ARTS (art history and appreciation, ceramic art and design, Chinese, classics, comparative literature, dance, dramatic arts, English, fiber/textiles/weaving, fine arts, French, German, graphic design, Greek, Italian, Japanese, jazz, journalism, Latin, linguistics, metal/jewelry, multimedia, music, music performance, music theory and composition, painting, photography, printmaking, romance languages and literature, Russian, sculpture, and Spanish), COMPUTER AND PHYSICAL SCIENCE (chemistry, computer science, geology, mathematics, physics, and science), EDUCATION (education and music), ENGINEERING AND ENVIRONMENTAL DESIGN (architecture, environmental science, interior design, and landscape architecture/design), HEALTH PROFESSIONS (exercise science and speech pathology/audiology), SOCIAL SCIENCE (anthropology, Asian/Oriental studies, classical/ancient civilization, economics, ethnic studies, family and community services, geography, history, humanities, international studies, Judaic studies, philosophy, political science/government, psychology, public administration, religion, sociology, and women's studies). Architecture, journalism, and biology are the strongest academically. Business, psychology, and journalism are the largest.

Required: For graduation, at least 180 quarter credits are required of all students, with a minimum GPA of 2.0. A minimum of 36 credits must be in the major, including 24 in upper-division work. Basic courses vary by major, but all students must complete 12 to 16 credits each in the areas of arts and letters, social science, and science, and 2 courses each in written English and multicultural studies.

Special: UO offers cross-registration with other schools in the Oregon University System, study abroad in at least 30 countries, preengineering in conjunction with Lane Community College, an engineering/physics program with Oregon State University, and internships. A B.A.-B.S. degree, dual majors, a 3-2 engineering degree, and pass/fail options are available. There are 24 national honor societies, including Phi Beta Kappa, a freshman honors program, and 54 departmental honors programs.

Faculty/Classroom: 59% of faculty are male; 41%, female. All teach undergraduates. Graduate students teach 14% of introductory courses. The average class size in a regular course is 26.

Admissions: 84% of the 2003-2004 applicants were accepted. The SAT I scores for the 2003-2004 freshman class were: Verbal--31% below 500, 41% between 500 and 599, 23% between 600 and 700, and 5% above 700; Math--28% below 500, 41% between 500 and 599, 26% between 600 and 700, and 5% above 700. There were 10 National Merit finalists. 122 freshmen graduated first in their class.

Requirements: The SAT I or ACT is required. In addition, students should be graduates from standard or accredited high schools and have obtained a score of 30 on the TSWE or 12 on the English portion of the ACT. The GED is accepted. Specific subject requirements include 4 years of English, 3 each of math and social studies, and 2 each of science and a foreign language. A GPA of 3.25 is required. AP and CLEP credits are accepted.

Procedure: Freshmen are admitted to all sessions. Entrance exams should be taken after October 15 of the junior year and before March of the senior year. There is a rolling admissions plan. Applications should be filed by January 15 for fall entry, October 15 for winter entry, January 18 for spring entry, and March 1 for summer entry, along with a $50 fee. Notification is sent on a rolling basis. Applications are accepted on-line through the school's web site.

Transfer: 1373 transfer students enrolled in 2002-2003. Students who have completed 36 or more credits with a minimum 2.25 GPA for residents and 2.5 for nonresidents, and whose college record includes passing 1 college-level course each in writing and math with a C- or better, may be admitted as transfer students. An official transcript from each college and university attended must be submitted. Students who have completed 12 to 35 credits must also meet freshman requirements. 45 credits of 180 required for the bachelor's degree must be completed at UO.

Visiting: There are regularly scheduled orientations for prospective students, including 2-day programs scheduled for late July that include both advising and telephone registration. There are guides for informal visits and visitors may sit in on classes. To schedule a visit, contact the Ambassador Program at (541) 346-1274.

Financial Aid: In 2003-2004, 40% of all full-time students received some form of financial aid. 35% of full-time freshmen and 36% of continuing full-time students received need-based aid. The average freshman award was $7118. The average financial indebtedness of the 2003 graduate was $17,111. The FAFSA is required. The deadline for filing freshman financial aid applications for fall entry is March 1.

International Students: There are 783 international students enrolled. The school actively recruits these students. They must score 500 on the written TOEFL or score 6.5 on the International English Language Testing Systems (IELTS) and also take the SAT I or the ACT.

Computers: The mainframes are a DEC 7000 VMS cluster and several Sun SPARC centers. There are approximately 500 networked PCs and terminals available on campus in 6 instructional and open labs, the student union, and various academic departments. All students may access the system 24 hours a day. There are no time limits. The fee is $75 per term. It is strongly recommended that all students have a personal computer. Students in architecture and law must have personal computers.

Graduates: From July 1, 2002 to June 30, 2003, 2895 bachelor's degrees were awarded. The most popular majors were business administration (10%), architecture and arts (10%), and journalism/communications (10%). In an average class, 1% graduate in 3 years or less, 37% graduate in 4 years or less, 56% graduate in 5 years or less, and 61% graduate in 6 years or less. 180 companies recruited on campus in 2002-2003. Of the 2002 graduating class, 20% were enrolled in graduate school within 6 months of graduation and 81% were employed.

Admissions Contact: Martha Pitts, Assistant Vice President for Enrollment Services. A video is available.
E-mail: *uoadmit@oregon.uoregon.edu* Web: *www.uoregon.edu*

UNIVERSITY OF PORTLAND
Portland, OR 97203

B-1

(503) 943-7147
(888) 627-5601; Fax: (503) 943-7315

Full-time: 1050 men, 1575 women	**Faculty:** 196; IIA, av$
Part-time: 18 men, 28 women	**Ph.D.s:** 98%
Graduate: 187 men, 255 women	**Student/Faculty:** 13 to 1
Year: semesters, summer session	**Tuition:** $22,100
Application Deadline: February 1	**Room & Board:** $6400
Freshman Class: 2964 applied, 2136 accepted, 673 enrolled	
SAT I Verbal/Math: 588/585	**ACT:** 29 **VERY COMPETITIVE**

The University of Portland, founded in 1901, is an independent institution affiliated with the Roman Catholic Church. It offers degree programs in the arts and sciences, business administration, education, engineering, and nursing. There are 5 undergraduate schools and 1 graduate school. In addition to regional accreditation, UP has baccalaureate program accreditation with AACSB, ABET, NASM, NCATE, and NLN. The library contains 380,000 volumes, 524,861 microform items, and 7827 audio/video tapes/CDs, and subscribes to 1446 periodicals. Computerized library services include interlibrary loans, database searching, and Internet access. Special learning facilities include a learning resource center, art gallery, radio station, and an observatory. The 155-acre campus is in a suburban area 4 miles north of downtown Portland. Including any residence halls, there are 30 buildings.

Student Life: 61% of undergraduates are from out of state, mostly the West. Students are from 44 states, 37 foreign countries, and Canada. 62% are from public schools. 81% are white. Most are Catholic. The average age of freshmen is 19; all undergraduates, 21. 14% do not continue beyond their first year; 71% remain to graduate.

Housing: 1425 students can be accommodated in college housing, which includes single-sex and coed dorms, off-campus apartments, and special-interest houses. On-campus housing is guaranteed for all 4 years. 58% of students live on campus; of those, 85% remain on campus on weekends. Upperclassmen may keep cars.

Activities: There are no fraternities or sororities. There are 62 groups on campus, including art, band, cheerleading, choir, chorale, chorus, computers, dance, debate, drama, ethnic, honors, international, jazz band, literary magazine, musical theater, newspaper, orchestra, pep band, photography, political, professional, radio and TV, religious, social, social service, student government, symphony, and yearbook. Popular campus events include Christmas in April, Casino Night, and Luau.

Sports: There are 7 intercollegiate sports for men and 7 for women, and 20 intramural sports for men and 20 for women. Facilities include weight rooms, an indoor track, a gym, a swimming pool, and a 5000-seat athletic and convocation center. Rental equipment is available for biking and camping activities.

Disabled Students: 95% of the campus is accessible. Wheelchair ramps, elevators, special parking, specially equipped rest rooms, special class scheduling, lowered drinking fountains, and lowered telephones are available.

Services: Counseling and information services are available, as is tutoring in most subjects, including English and math. The faculty is available for individual assistance.

Campus Safety and Security: Measures include 24-hour foot and vehicle patrol, self-defense education, security escort services, and informal discussions. There are pamphlets/posters/films, emergency telephones, and lighted pathways/sidewalks.

Programs of Study: UP confers B.A., B.S., B.A.Ed., B.B.A., B.M.Ed., B.S.C.E., B.S.E.E., B.S.E.M., B.S.E.S., B.S.M.E., B.S.N., and B.S.S.E. degrees. Master's degrees are also awarded. Bachelor's degrees are awarded in BIOLOGICAL SCIENCE (biology/biological science), BUSINESS (accounting, banking and finance, international business management, and marketing/retailing/merchandising), COMMUNICATIONS AND THE ARTS (communications, dramatic arts, English, music, Spanish, and theater management), COMPUTER AND PHYSICAL SCIENCE (chemistry, computer science, mathematics, and physics), EDUCATION (elementary, music, and secondary), ENGINEERING AND ENVIRONMENTAL DESIGN (civil engineering, electrical/electronics engineering, engineering, engineering management, environmental science, and mechanical engineering), HEALTH PROFESSIONS (nursing), SOCIAL SCIENCE (criminal justice, history, interdisciplinary studies, philosophy, political science/government, psychology, social work, sociology, and theological studies). Engineering, business, and nursing are the strongest academically. Business administration, education, and nursing are the largest.

Required: To graduate, students must complete 120 credit hours, including at least 24 upper-division classes in the major, with a minimum GPA of 2.0. Required courses include 9 hours each of philosophy and theology, 6 each of science, social sciences, and electives, and 3 each of fine arts, history, math, and literature.

Special: UP offers internships through individual departments, cross-registration with members of the Oregon Independent College Association, dual and interdisciplinary majors, including engineering chemistry and organizational communications, work-study programs, and pass/fail options. Study abroad may be arranged in Japan, Mexico, Australia, Chile, and several European countries. There are 9 national honor societies and a freshman honors program.

Faculty/Classroom: 60% of faculty are male; 40%, female. All teach undergraduates. No introductory courses are taught by graduate students. The average class size in an introductory lecture is 25; in a laboratory, 20; and in a regular course, 20.

Admissions: 72% of the 2003-2004 applicants were accepted. The SAT I scores for the 2003-2004 freshman class were: Verbal--5% below 500, 41% between 500 and 599, 42% between 600 and 700, and 12% above 700; Math--5% below 500, 40% between 500 and 599, 43% between 600 and 700, and 12% above 700. 74% of the current freshmen were in the top fifth of their class; 96% were in the top two fifths. There were 5 National Merit finalists and 13 semifinalists. 34 freshmen graduated first in their class.

Requirements: The SAT I or ACT is required with a minimum score of 550 on each section of the SAT I or a composite of 19 on the ACT.

Graduation from an accredited secondary school or satisfactory scores on the GED are required. The high school curriculum should include courses in English composition, math, social studies, science, and a foreign language. 2 essays are required, as is a letter of recommendation from the high school counselor or principal. UP requires applicants to be in the upper 50% of their class. A GPA of 3.0 is required. AP and CLEP credits are accepted.

Procedure: Freshmen are admitted to all sessions. Entrance exams should be taken preferably before February 1 but no later than June 1 of the senior year. There is a rolling admissions plan and a deferred admissions plan. Applications should be filed by February 1 for fall entry, along with a $50 fee. Notification is sent on a rolling basis. 134 were on the 2003 waiting list; 13 were admitted. Applications are accepted online through the university's web site or Common App.

Transfer: 167 transfer students enrolled in 2002-2003. Applicants with 26 or more credits must have a minimum GPA of 2.5 and be in good standing at their previous school. Students with fewer credits may need to meet freshman requirements. 30 of 120 credits required for the bachelor's degree must be completed at UP.

Visiting: There are regularly scheduled orientations for prospective students, including a campus tour, class attendance, and a meeting with an admissions counselor. There are guides for informal visits and visitors may sit in on classes and stay overnight. To schedule a visit, contact the Office of Admissions at *admissio@up.edu*.

Financial Aid: In 2003-2004, 93% of all full-time freshmen and 89% of continuing full-time students received some form of financial aid. 58% of full-time freshmen and 57% of continuing full-time students received need-based aid. The average freshman award was $15,450. 55% of undergraduates work part time. Average annual earnings from campus work are $2100. The average financial indebtedness of the 2003 graduate was $17,500. The FAFSA and the college's own financial statement are required. The deadline for filing freshman financial aid applications for fall entry is March 1.

International Students: There are 61 international students enrolled. The school actively recruits these students. They must score 540 on the written TOEFL.

Computers: The mainframe is a Sun UNIX. All students may utilize more than 375 PCs for various projects, with additional terminals designated specifically for computer-intensive majors such as computer science, engineering, and education. Students have access to the Internet and to e-mail. All students may access the system. There are no time limits and no fees. It is strongly recommended that all students have a personal computer.

Graduates: From July 1, 2002 to June 30, 2003, 545 bachelor's degrees were awarded. The most popular majors were business (19%), nursing (14%), and engineering (13%). In an average class, 63% graduate in 4 years or less, and 72% graduate in 5 years or less. 85 companies recruited on campus in 2002-2003.

Admissions Contact: James Lyons, Dean of Admissions. A video is available. E-mail: *admissio@up.edu* Web: *www.up.edu*

WARNER PACIFIC COLLEGE
B-1
Portland, OR 97215

(503) 517-1024
(800) 582-7885; Fax: (503) 517-1352

Full-time: 190 men, 360 women	**Faculty:** 39
Part-time: 30 men, 65 women	**Ph.D.s:** 50%
Graduate: 5 men and women	**Student/Faculty:** 14 to 1
Year: semesters, summer session	**Tuition:** $16,910
Application Deadline: open	**Room & Board:** $4990
Freshman Class: n/av	
SAT I or ACT: required	**COMPETITIVE**

Warner Pacific College, founded in 1937, is a private Christian liberal arts college affiliated with the Church of God. Enrollment figures in above capsule are approximate. The library contains 53,000 volumes, 1155 microform items, and 1110 audio/video tapes/CDs, and subscribes to 400 periodicals. Computerized library services include the card catalog, interlibrary loans, and database searching. Special learning facilities include a learning resource center, 2 electron microscopes, and an early childhood learning center. The 14-acre campus is in an urban area 5 miles east of downtown Portland. Including any residence halls, there are 30 buildings.

Student Life: 80% of undergraduates are from Oregon. Students are from 18 states, 7 foreign countries, and Canada. 78% are from public schools. 83% are white. 51% claim no religious affiliation; 42% Protestant. The average age of freshmen is 21; all undergraduates, 28. 25% do not continue beyond their first year; 45% remain to graduate.

Housing: 250 students can be accommodated in college housing, which includes single-sex dorms, on-campus apartments, and married-student housing. On-campus housing is guaranteed for the freshman year only, is available on a first-come, first-served basis, and is available on a lottery system for upperclassmen. Priority is given to out-of-town students. 70% of students commute. Alcohol is not permitted. All students may keep cars.

Activities: There are no fraternities or sororities. There are 6 groups on campus, including art, band, Bible study, choir, chorale, chorus, dance, drama, ethnic, international, jazz band, musical theater, orchestra, photography, professional, religious, social, social service, spiritual growth groups, student government, and yearbook. Popular campus events include Winter Banquet, Spring Banquet, and Western Fling.

Sports: There are 4 intercollegiate sports for men and 5 for women, and 10 intramural sports for men and 10 for women. Facilities include a gym, a weight-training room, and hiking trails.

Disabled Students: 75% of the campus is accessible. Wheelchair ramps, special parking, specially equipped rest rooms, special class scheduling, lowered drinking fountains, and personalized care and services are available.

Services: Counseling and information services are available, as is tutoring in most subjects. There is remedial math, reading, and writing and testing and study skills workshops.

Campus Safety and Security: Measures include 24-hour foot and vehicle patrol, self-defense education, security escort services, and informal discussions. There are pamphlets/posters/films and lighted pathways/sidewalks.

Programs of Study: Warner Pacific confers B.A. and B.S degrees. Associate and master's degrees are also awarded. Bachelor's degrees are awarded in BIOLOGICAL SCIENCE (biology/biological science), BUSINESS (business administration and management), COMMUNICATIONS AND THE ARTS (English and music), EDUCATION (music and physical), SOCIAL SCIENCE (American studies, history, human development, liberal arts/general studies, ministries, religious music, social science, and sociology). Biological science and business administration are the strongest academically. Business administration, human development, and music education are the largest.

Required: To graduate, students must complete 124 credits with a minimum GPA of 2.0. All students must take a core curriculum of 42 credits, consisting of 15 hours in humanities, 9 in communication, 7 to 9 in religion, 6 in social science, 4 in fine arts, and 3 each in science and health and phys ed.

Special: Warner Pacific offers cross-registration through OICA, a Washington semester, a co-op nursing program, accelerated degree programs in human development and business administration, and study abroad in Latin America, the Middle East, and Russia. Internships, work-study programs, double majors, individualized majors, independent study credit for life and military experience, and pass/fail options are available.

Faculty/Classroom: 62% of faculty are male; 38%, female. All teach undergraduates and 40% do research. No introductory courses are taught by graduate students. The average class size in an introductory lecture is 15; in a laboratory, 10; and in a regular course, 15.

Requirements: The SAT I or ACT is required. In addition, applicants must be graduates of an accredited secondary school. The GED is accepted. High school preparation should include 4 years of English, 3 of social studies, and 2 each of math and lab science. A GPA of 2.25 is required. AP and CLEP credits are accepted. Important factors in the admissions decision are evidence of special talent, leadership record, and advanced placement or honor courses.

Procedure: Freshmen are admitted to all sessions. Entrance exams should be taken no later than the early fall of the senior year. Application deadlines are open. Application fee is $25. Applications are accepted on-line.

Transfer: 54 transfer students enrolled in 2002-2003. Applicants must provide transcripts from their previous college. A minimum GPA of 2.0 is required. 30 of 124 credits required for the bachelor's degree must be completed at Warner Pacific.

Visiting: There are regularly scheduled orientations for prospective students, including 6 visitation weekends, academic fairs, scholarship days, and a retreat. There are guides for informal visits and visitors may sit in on classes and stay overnight. To schedule a visit, contact Office of Admissions and Financial Aid.

Financial Aid: In 2003-2004, 98% of all full-time students received some form of financial aid. 98% of all full-time students received need-based aid. The average freshman award was $18,282. Average annual earnings from campus work are $2000. Warner Pacific is a member of CSS. The FAFSA is required. The deadline for filing freshman financial aid applications for fall entry is April 15.

International Students: There are 12 international students enrolled. The school actively recruits these students. They must score 525 on the written TOEFL or 195 on the electronic version and also take the college's own test.

Computers: The mainframes are an AS400 and a 9404-200. The library houses a 24-hour computer lab and all campus housing has networking for PCs. All students may access the system 24 hours a day. There are no time limits and no fees. It is strongly recommended that all students have a personal computer.

Graduates: From July 1, 2002 to June 30, 2003, 149 bachelor's degrees were awarded. The most popular majors were psychology (48%), business (34%), and religion (5%). In an average class, 2% graduate in 3 years or less, 29% graduate in 4 years or less, 8% graduate in 5 years or less, and 2% graduate in 6 years or less.

Admissions Contact: Dr. Jack P. Powell, Dean of Enrollment Management. E-mail: *admiss@warnerpacific.edu*
Web: *www.warnerpacific.edu*

WESTERN BAPTIST COLLEGE

B-2

Salem, OR 97301-9392

(503) 375-7005
(800) 845-3005; Fax: (503) 585-4316

Full-time: 242 men, 376 women	**Faculty:** 33
Part-time: 60 men, 59 women	**Ph.Ds:** 39%
Graduate: none	**Student/Faculty:** 19 to 1
Year: semesters, summer session	**Tuition:** $16,084
Application Deadline: August 1	**Room & Board:** $5724
Freshman Class: 550 applied, 460 accepted, 167 enrolled	
SAT I Verbal/Math: 550/540	**ACT:** 21 COMPETITIVE

Western Baptist College is a Christian, liberal arts institution offering degrees in biblical-theological studies, business administration, education, humanities, math, phys ed, social sciences, psychology, intercultural studies, and youth work. The library contains 82,000 volumes, 4100 microform items, and 4532 audio/video tapes/CDs, and subscribes to 552 periodicals. Computerized library services include the card catalog, interlibrary loans, database searching, and Internet access. Special learning facilities include a learning resource center and an archaeological museum. The 107-acre campus is in a suburban area in Salem. Including any residence halls, there are 20 buildings.

Student Life: 70% of undergraduates are from Oregon. Students are from 30 states and 5 foreign countries. 72% are from public schools. 93% are white. Most are Protestant. The average age of freshmen is 19; all undergraduates, 23. 30% do not continue beyond their first year; 50% remain to graduate.

Housing: 390 students can be accommodated in college housing, which includes single-sex dorms, on-campus apartments, and married-student housing. On-campus housing is guaranteed for the freshman year only and is available on a first-come, first-served basis. Priority is given to out-of-town students. 53% of students live on campus; of those, 90% remain on campus on weekends. Alcohol is not permitted. All students may keep cars.

Activities: There are no fraternities or sororities. There are 16 groups on campus, including band, cheerleading, choir, chorale, chorus, drama, honors, jazz band, literary magazine, newspaper, orchestra, pep band, religious, social, social service, student government, and yearbook. Popular campus events include Western Weekends, Sports Weekends, and chapel services.

Sports: There are 4 intercollegiate sports for men and 5 for women, and 3 intramural sports for men and 3 for women. Facilities include a sports center with a gym and soccer and baseball fields.

Disabled Students: 95% of the campus is accessible. Elevators, special parking, specially equipped rest rooms, and lowered telephones are available.

Services: Counseling and information services are available, as is tutoring in most subjects.

Campus Safety and Security: Measures include security escort services, informal discussions, emergency telephones, and lighted pathways/sidewalks. There is a campus security patrol and a vehicle patrol.

Programs of Study: Western confers B.A., B.S., and Th.B. degrees. Associate degrees are also awarded. Bachelor's degrees are awarded in BUSINESS (accounting and business administration and management), COMMUNICATIONS AND THE ARTS (communications, English, and music), COMPUTER AND PHYSICAL SCIENCE (computer science and mathematics), EDUCATION (education and physical), HEALTH PROFESSIONS (health science), SOCIAL SCIENCE (biblical studies, crosscultural studies, history, humanities, ministries, psychology, and social science). Education, psychology, and business are the largest.

Required: To graduate, students must complete 128 credits, with 40 to 64 in the major. The minimum required GPA is 2.0 for most programs; the education major requires a 3.0 GPA. The general education core consists of 68 credits. Courses must be taken in the Bible, humanities, social sciences, math, science, and phys ed.

Special: Western offers a preseminary co-op program, cross-registration with Oregon Independent Colleges, study abroad in 4 countries, a Washington semester, internships with the approval of a program adviser, accelerated programs in management and communication and in family studies, and student-designed majors with adviser approval. There is a freshman honors program.

Faculty/Classroom: 79% of faculty are male; 21%, female. All teach undergraduates. The average class size in an introductory lecture is 38; in a laboratory, 15; and in a regular course, 25.

Admissions: 84% of the 2003-2004 applicants were accepted. The SAT I scores for the 2003-2004 freshman class were: Verbal--24% below 500, 45% between 500 and 599, 28% between 600 and 700, and 3% above 700; Math--31% below 500, 44% between 500 and 599, 22% between 600 and 700, and 3% above 700. The ACT scores were 7% below 21, 60% between 21 and 23, 6% between 24 and 26, 7% between 27 and 28, and 20% above 28. 47% of the current freshmen were in the top fifth of their class; 72% were in the top two fifths. 6 freshmen graduated first in their class.

Requirements: The SAT I or ACT is required, as is an essay. A GPA of 2.5 is required. AP and CLEP credits are accepted. Important factors in the admissions decision are extracurricular activities record, leadership record, and evidence of special talent.

Procedure: Freshmen are admitted fall and spring. Applications should be filed by August 1 for fall entry and December 1 for spring entry, along with a $35 fee. There is a rolling admissions plan. Notification is sent on a rolling basis. Applications are accepted on computer disk and on-line through Western's home page at *www.wbc.edu*.

Transfer: 117 transfer students enrolled in 2002-2003. Transfer applicants are required to have a minimum 2.0 cumulative college GPA and submit the college transcript and 3 references. 30 of 128 credits required for the bachelor's degree must be completed at Western.

Visiting: There are regularly scheduled orientations for prospective students, including scheduled weekend visits and Western Daze. There are guides for informal visits and visitors may sit in on classes and stay overnight. To schedule a visit, contact the Admissions Office at (503) 581-8600.

Financial Aid: In a recent year, 98% of all full-time students received some form of financial aid. 87% of continuing full-time students received need-based aid. The average freshman award was $12,505. 30% of undergraduates work part time. Average annual earnings from campus work are $1000. The average financial indebtedness of a recent graduate was $14,000. The FAFSA is required. The deadline for filing freshman financial aid applications for fall entry is March 1.

International Students: There are 5 international students enrolled. They must score 500 on the written TOEFL and also take the SAT I or the ACT.

Computers: The 6 labs contain 35 PCs, and students have campuswide e-mail and Internet access on their personal computers. All students may access the system 7 days per week/24 hours per day. There are no time limits and no fees. It is strongly recommended that all students have a personal computer. Students in business information systems and computer science must have personal computers.

Graduates: From July 1, 2002 to June 30, 2003, 173 bachelor's degrees were awarded. The most popular majors were business (26%), pyschology (24%), and education (14%). In an average class, 2% graduate in 3 years or less, 49% graduate in 4 years or less, 54% graduate in 5 years or less, and 54% graduate in 6 years or less.

Admissions Contact: Marty Ziesemer, Dean of Enrollment Management. E-mail: *admissions@wbc.edu* Web: *www.wbc.edu*

WESTERN OREGON UNIVERSITY

B-2

Monmouth, OR 97361

(503) 838-8211
(877) 877-1593; Fax: (503) 838-8067

Full-time: 1595 men, 2421 women	**Faculty:** 182; IIA, --$
Part-time: 245 men, 209 women	**Ph.Ds:** 81%
Graduate: 172 men, 390 women	**Student/Faculty:** 22 to 1
Year: quarters, summer session	**Tuition:** $4305 ($12,570)
Application Deadline: open	**Room & Board:** $5976
Freshman Class: 1809 applied, 1694 accepted, 926 enrolled	
SAT I Verbal/Math: 495/485	**ACT:** 21 COMPETITIVE

Western Oregon University, founded in 1856, is a publicly funded institution and a member of the Oregon University System. WOU offers undergraduate programs through the Colleges of Education and Liberal Arts and Sciences. There are 2 undergraduate schools and 1 graduate school. In addition to regional accreditation, WOU has baccalaureate program accreditation with NASM and NCATE. Computerized library services include the card catalog, interlibrary loans, and database searching. Special learning facilities include a learning resource center, art gallery, TV station, and the Paul Jensen Arctic Museum. The 157-acre campus is in a rural area 15 miles west of Salem. Including any residence halls, there are 36 buildings.

Student Life: 91% of undergraduates are from Oregon. Students are from 23 states, 19 foreign countries, and Canada. 99% are from public schools. 81% are white. The average age of freshmen is 19; all undergraduates, 22. 29% do not continue beyond their first year; 50% remain to graduate.

Housing: 1275 students can be accommodated in college housing, which includes coed dorms and married-student housing. In addition, there are wellness, honors, multicultural, and quiet communities. On-campus housing is guaranteed for the freshman year only and is available on a first-come, first-served basis. 76% of students commute. Alcohol is not permitted. All students may keep cars.

Activities: There are no fraternities or sororities. There are 50 groups on campus, including art, band, cheerleading, chess, choir, chorale, chorus, computers, dance, debate, drama, drill team, ethnic, gay, honors, international, jazz band, literary magazine, marching band, model U.N., musical theater, newspaper, orchestra, pep band, political, radio and TV, religious, social, social service, and student government. Popular campus events include Annual Christmas Tree Lighting, Alcohol Awareness Week, and Family Day.

Sports: There are 5 intercollegiate sports for men and 6 for women, and 25 intramural sports for men and 25 for women. Facilities include a sports field, a phys ed building, a swimming pool, a weight room, indoor/outdoor tennis courts, handball and racquetball courts, a dance studio, archery facilities, and baseball, softball, and soccer fields.

Disabled Students: 90% of the campus is accessible. Wheelchair ramps, elevators, special parking, specially equipped rest rooms, special class scheduling, lowered drinking fountains, lowered telephones, and the Regional Resource Center of Deafness are available.

Services: Counseling and information services are available, as is tutoring in most subjects. There is a reader service for the blind, and remedial math, reading, and writing. There is also a student support and services program for first-generation, low-income, and physically disabled students.

Campus Safety and Security: Measures include 24-hour foot and vehicle patrol, self-defense education, security escort services, and informal discussions. There are pamphlets/posters/films, emergency telephones, and lighted pathways/sidewalks.

Programs of Study: WOU confers B.A., B.S., and B.Mus. degrees. Associate and master's degrees are also awarded. Bachelor's degrees are awarded in BIOLOGICAL SCIENCE (biology/biological science), BUSINESS (business administration and management), COMMUNICATIONS AND THE ARTS (American Sign Language, art, dance, dramatic arts, English, music, Spanish, and speech/debate/rhetoric), COMPUTER AND PHYSICAL SCIENCE (chemistry, computer science, earth science, information sciences and systems, mathematics, and natural sciences), EDUCATION (education and health), SOCIAL SCIENCE (anthropology, corrections, economics, fire protection, geography, history, humanities, interdisciplinary studies, international studies, interpreter for the deaf, law enforcement and corrections, philosophy, political science/government, psychology, public administration, social science, and sociology). Education, business, and psychology are the strongest academically. Education, criminal justice, and psychology are the largest.

Required: To graduate, students must complete a total of 180 quarter hours with a minimum GPA of 2.0. Between 45 and 120 quarter hours are required in the major. All students must fulfill the requirements of the 55-quarter-hour liberal arts core curriculum, which includes 12 credits each of lab science and social sciences, 9 each of literature and fine arts, 4 of phys ed, and 3 each of philosophy, speech, and writing. Students must also satisfy graduation requirements in math, computer science or technology, writing-intensive course work, and cultural diversity.

Special: Most academic majors in liberal arts and sciences offer a B.A.-B.S degree option. Dual majors, internships, study abroad through international exchange programs and the Oregon University System, and student-designed majors in interdisciplinary studies are available. Nondegree study and pass/fail options are possible. There are 7 national honor societies and a freshman honors program.

Faculty/Classroom: 51% of faculty are male; 49%, female. All teach undergraduates. Graduate students teach 1% of introductory courses. The average class size in an introductory lecture is 40; in a laboratory, 25; and in a regular course, 30.

Admissions: 94% of the 2003-2004 applicants were accepted. The SAT I scores for the 2003-2004 freshman class were: Verbal--52% below 500, 37% between 500 and 599, and 11% between 600 and 700; Math--55% below 500, 35% between 500 and 599, 9% between 600 and 700, and 1% above 700. The ACT scores were 23% below 21, 50% between 21 and 23, 23% between 24 and 26, 2% between 27 and 28, and 2% above 28. 36% of the current freshmen were in the top fifth of their class; 74% were in the top two fifths.

Requirements: The SAT I or ACT is required. In addition, graduation from an accredited secondary school or satisfactory scores on the GED are required. Students must have 14 academic credits or Carnegie units. High school courses must include 4 years of English, 3 each of math and social studies, and 2 each of science and a foreign language. A GPA of 2.75 is required. AP and CLEP credits are accepted. Important factors in the admissions decision are evidence of special talent, recommendations by alumni, and parents or siblings attending the school.

Procedure: Freshmen are admitted to all sessions. Entrance exams should be taken during the junior or senior year. Application deadlines are open. There is a rolling admissions plan. Application fee is $50. Notification is sent on a rolling basis. Applications are accepted on-line.

Transfer: 509 transfer students enrolled in a recent year. Applicants must have a minimum GPA of 2.0. Applicants with fewer than 24 quarter hours must also meet freshman admission requirements. 45 credits of 180 required for the bachelor's degree must be completed at WOU.

Visiting: There are regularly scheduled orientations for prospective students, consisting of a 1-day program for students and a parent program; all newly admitted students must make arrangements to register during orientation in July to reserve their enrollment slot. There are guides for informal visits and visitors may sit in on classes. To schedule a visit, contact the Admissions Office at *wolfgram@wou.edu*.

Financial Aid: In a recent year, 80% of all full-time freshmen and 79% of continuing full-time students received some form of financial aid. 36%

of full-time freshmen and 79% of continuing full-time students received need-based aid. The average freshman award was $5739. The average financial indebtedness of a recent graduate was $16,383. The FAFSA is required. The priority date for freshman financial aid applications for fall entry is March 1.

International Students: There are 75 international students enrolled. The school actively recruits these students. They must score 520 on the written TOEFL or 190 on the electronic version or take the MELAB.

Computers: The mainframe is a Sun 420R. There are PC and Mac labs located in the instructional technology center, natural science building, Werner University Center, education building, and the Hamersly Library. All students may access the system. There are no time limits. The fee is $70.

Graduates: The most popular majors were business (15%), corrections/law enforcement (14%), and social sciences and history (11%). In an average class, 37% graduate in 4 years or less, 51% graduate in 5 years or less, and 12% graduate in 6 years or less.

Admissions Contact: Rob Kvidt, Director of Admissions.
E-mail: *wolfgram@wou.edu* Web: *www.wou.edu*

WILLAMETTE UNIVERSITY

Salem, OR 97301

B-2

(503) 370-6303

(877) 542-2787; Fax: (503) 375-5363

Full-time: 796 men, 1012 women	**Faculty:** 145
Part-time: 77 men, 60 women	**Ph.Ds:** 91%
Graduate: 348 men, 297 women	**Student/Faculty:** 12 to 1
Year: semesters	**Tuition:** $25,432
Application Deadline: February 1	**Room & Board:** $6600
Freshman Class: 2164 applied, 1603 accepted, 541 enrolled	
SAT I Verbal/Math: 620/620	**ACT:** 27 **VERY COMPETITIVE+**

Willamette University, founded in 1842, is an independent liberal arts institution affiliated with the Methodist Church. There are 3 graduate schools. In addition to regional accreditation, Willamette has baccalaureate program accreditation with NASM. The 2 libraries contain 372,571 volumes, 333,664 microform items, and 10,440 audio/video tapes/CDs, and subscribe to 1623 periodicals. Computerized library services include the card catalog, interlibrary loans, database searching, and Internet access. Special learning facilities include a learning resource center, art gallery, natural history museum, radio station, botanical and Japanese gardens, multimedia center, and "smart" classrooms. The 72-acre campus is in an urban area 50 minutes south of Portland. Including any residence halls, there are 44 buildings.

Student Life: 59% of undergraduates are from out of state, mostly the West. Students are from 39 states, 23 foreign countries, and Canada. 81% are from public schools. 57% are white. 66% claim no religious affiliation; 24% are Protestant; 8%, Catholic. The average age of freshmen is 18; all undergraduates, 20. 13% do not continue beyond their first year; 85% remain to graduate.

Housing: 1366 students can be accommodated in college housing, which includes single-sex and coed dorms, on-campus apartments, fraternity houses, and sorority houses. In addition, there are language houses, special-interest houses, a 24-hour quiet-hour dorm, and substance-free options. On-campus housing is guaranteed for the freshman year only and is available on a lottery system for upperclassmen. 69% of students live on campus; of those, 65% remain on campus on weekends. All students may keep cars.

Activities: 25% of men belong to 5 national fraternities; 25% of women belong to 3 national sororities. There are 100 groups on campus, including art, band, cheerleading, chess, choir, chorale, chorus, computers, dance, debate, drama, ethnic, film, forensics, gay, honors, international, jazz band, literary magazine, musical theater, newspaper, orchestra, pep band, photography, political, professional, radio and TV, religious, social, social service, student government, symphony, and yearbook. Popular campus events include International Extravaganza, Black Tie Affair, and Hawaiian Luau.

Sports: There are 10 intercollegiate sports for men and 10 for women, and 17 intramural sports for men and 17 for women. Facilities include a phys ed and recreation center, a 4000-seat football stadium, a 3000-seat indoor gym, a 1200-seat auditorium, a baseball stadium, a soccer field, an all-weather track, a track building, 2 other gyms, a mini-Olympic-size indoor swimming pool, an outdoor swimming pool, 3 indoor and 10 outdoor tennis courts, handball/racquetball courts, weight training facilities, and other practice fields.

Disabled Students: 90% of the campus is accessible. Wheelchair ramps, elevators, special parking, specially equipped rest rooms, special class scheduling, lowered drinking fountains, lowered telephones, special equipment, readers, and braille services are available.

Services: Counseling and information services are available, as is tutoring in most subjects. There is a reader service for the blind. Therapists are available for students on an individual need basis.

Campus Safety and Security: Measures include 24-hour foot and vehicle patrol, self-defense education, security escort services, and informal discussions. There are pamphlets/posters/films, emergency telephones, lighted pathways/sidewalks, formal programs and education, and a weekly published campus safety report.

Programs of Study: Willamette confers B.A. and B.M. degrees. Master's and doctoral degrees are also awarded. Bachelor's degrees are awarded in BIOLOGICAL SCIENCE (biology/biological science), COMMUNICATIONS AND THE ARTS (art history and appreciation, comparative literature, dramatic arts, English, French, German, music, music performance, music theory and composition, Spanish, speech/debate/rhetoric, and studio art), COMPUTER AND PHYSICAL SCIENCE (chemistry, computer science, mathematics, and physics), EDUCATION (music), ENGINEERING AND ENVIRONMENTAL DESIGN (environmental science), HEALTH PROFESSIONS (exercise science), SOCIAL SCIENCE (American studies, anthropology, classical/ancient civilization, economics, history, humanities, international studies, Japanese studies, Latin American studies, philosophy, political science/government, psychology, religion, and sociology). Social sciences, natural science, and humanities are the strongest academically. Economics, politics, and psychology are the largest.

Required: To graduate, students must complete a total of 124 semester hours, including a minimum of 32 in the major, with a minimum GPA of 2.0. All students must complete general education requirements in fine arts, humanities, literature, foreign language, interdisciplinary courses, natural sciences, and social sciences, and meet math and English proficiency levels. Freshmen are required to take a World Views seminar. Seniors are required to complete a senior thesis or other project in their major.

Special: Willamette offers internships with the state and city governments, a Chicago semester, a Washington semester, and a 3-2 engineering degree with Washington University, University of Southern California, and Columbia University. Nondegree study, B.A.-B.S. degrees, dual majors, work-study programs with numerous employers in the Salem area and at the university, and credit/no-credit options are also available. Study abroad programs are available in 14 countries. There are 3-2 degrees in management, forestry, and computer science. There are 11 national honor societies, including Phi Beta Kappa.

Faculty/Classroom: 63% of faculty are male; 37%, female. All both teach and do research. No introductory courses are taught by graduate students. The average class size in an introductory lecture is 19; in a laboratory, 13; and in a regular course, 17.

Admissions: 74% of the 2003-2004 applicants were accepted. The SAT I scores for the 2003-2004 freshman class were: Verbal--6% below 500, 30% between 500 and 599, 47% between 600 and 700, and 17% above 700; Math--5% below 500, 31% between 500 and 599, 51% between 600 and 700, and 14% above 700. The ACT scores were 4% below 21, 11% between 21 and 23, 31% between 24 and 26, 23% between 27 and 28, and 31% above 28. 74% of the current freshmen were in the top fifth of their class; 94% were in the top two fifths. In a recent year, there were 10 National Merit finalists and 23 semifinalists. 60 freshmen graduated first in their class.

Requirements: The SAT I or ACT is required. In addition, graduation from an accredited secondary school or satisfactory scores on the GED are required. Institutional preferences include 4 years each of English and math, and 3 years each of foreign language, lab science, and social studies or history. 2 essays are required, and an interview is recommended. Portfolios or auditions are recommended for art and music students.

A GPA of 2.0 is required. AP credits are accepted. Important factors in the admissions decision are advanced placement or honor courses and recommendations by school officials.

Procedure: Freshmen are admitted fall and spring. Entrance exams should be taken by the end of December. There are early admissions and deferred admissions plans. Applications should be filed by February 1 for fall entry and November 1 for spring entry, along with a $50 fee. Notification is sent April 1. 409 early action candidates were accepted for the 2003-2004 class. 182 applicants were on the 2003 waiting list. Applications are accepted on computer disk and on-line through Common App, CollegeNET, and Embark.

Transfer: 68 transfer students enrolled in 2002-2003. Transfer students must submit transcripts for all college and high school courses. A minimum GPA of 2.0 is required, as is a Transfer Reference Form (recommendation form). 60 of 124 credits required for the bachelor's degree must be completed at Willamette.

Visiting: There are regularly scheduled orientations for prospective students, consisting of fall and spring campus preview days, tours, and faculty and student presentations. There are guides for informal visits and visitors may sit in on classes and stay overnight. To schedule a visit, contact Martha Cripe at *libarts@willamette.edu*.

Financial Aid: In 2003-2004, all full-time freshmen and 95% of continuing full-time students received some form of financial aid. All full-time freshmen and 94% of continuing full-time students received need-based aid. The average freshman award was $21,119. Need-based scholarships or need-based grants averaged $17,920 ($31,954 maximum); need-based self-help aid (loans and jobs) averaged $3888 ($7313 maximum); and non-need-based awards and non-need-based scholarships averaged $11,645 ($33,686 maximum). 55% of undergraduates work part time. Average annual earnings from campus work are $1855. The average financial indebtedness of the 2003 graduate was $18,689. Willamette is a member of CSS. The FAFSA is required, and students applying for admission under the early action program must also file the CSS Profile. The deadline for filing freshman financial aid applications for fall entry is February 1.

International Students: There are 20 international students enrolled. The school actively recruits these students. They must score 550 on the written TOEFL or 213 on the electronic version and also take the ELPT (English Language Placement Test), as well as the SAT I or the ACT.

Computers: About 400 PCs and Macs are available for student use in the computer lab, library, and science building. Students may access the mainframe from their residence hall rooms through a network hookup. All students may access the system 24 hours per day. There are no time limits and no fees.

Graduates: From July 1, 2002 to June 30, 2003, 386 bachelor's degrees were awarded. The most popular majors were economics (10%), biology (10%), and politics (9%). In an average class, 1% graduate in 3 years or less, 76% graduate in 4 years or less, and 85% graduate in 5 years or less. 100 companies recruited on campus in 2002-2003. Of the 2002 graduating class, 22% were enrolled in graduate school within 6 months of graduation and 69% were employed.

Admissions Contact: Robin Brown, Vice President, Enrollment.
E-mail: *undergrad-admission@willamette.edu*
Web: *http://www.willamette.edu*

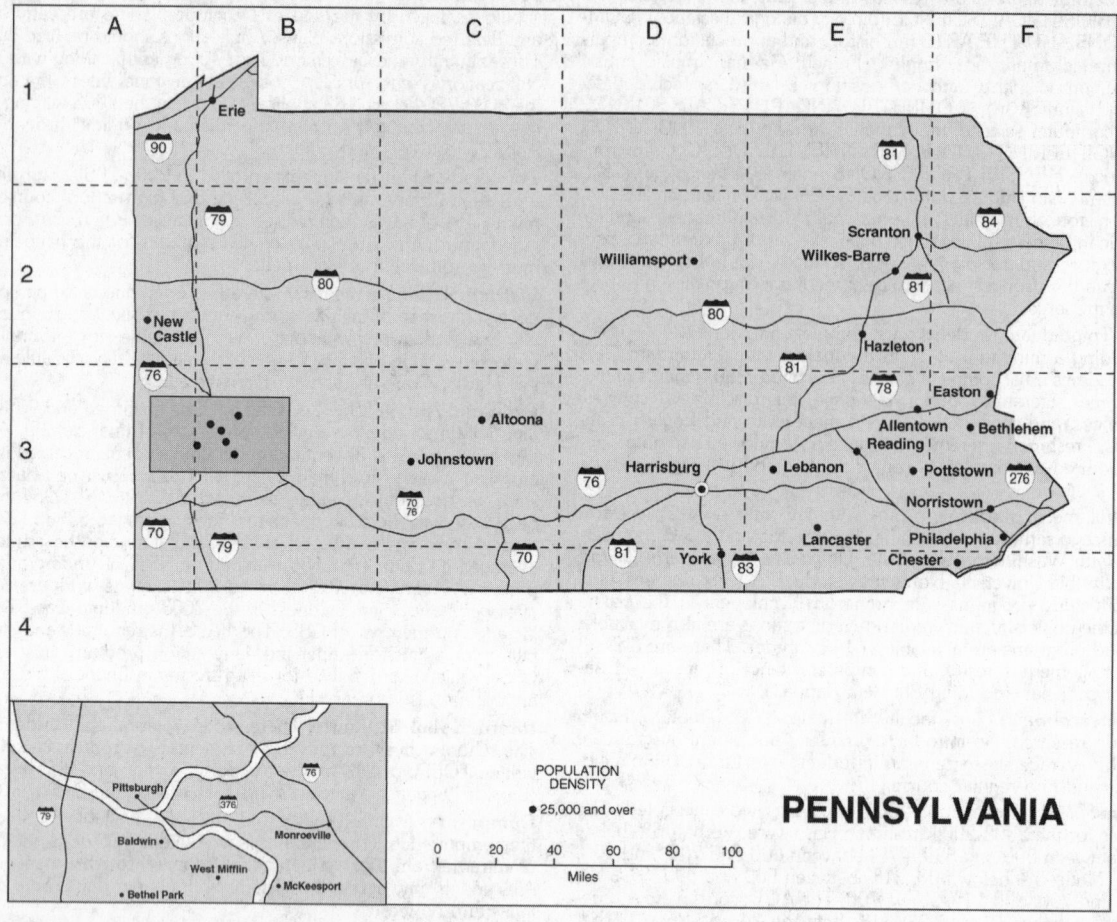

POPULATION DENSITY
● 25,000 and over

PENNSYLVANIA

0 20 40 60 80 100
Miles

ALBRIGHT COLLEGE
Reading, PA 19612-5234

E-3

(610) 921-7512
(800) 252-1856; Fax: (610) 921-7294

Full-time: 888 men, 1106 women	**Faculty:** 104; IIB, av$
Part-time: 20 men, 36 women	**Ph.D.s:** 77%
Graduate: 37 men, 43 women	**Student/Faculty:** 19 to 1
Year: 4-1-4, summer session	**Tuition:** $23,430
Application Deadline: open	**Room & Board:** $7149
Freshman Class: 2967 applied, 2137 accepted, 456 enrolled	
SAT I Verbal/Math: 520/510	**COMPETITIVE**

Albright College, founded in 1856, is a private liberal arts institution affiliated with the United Methodist Church. The 2 libraries contain 218,465 volumes, 83,934 microform items, and 23,435 audio/video tapes/CDs, and subscribe to 725 periodicals. Computerized library services include the card catalog, interlibrary loans, database searching, and Internet access. Special learning facilities include a learning resource center, art gallery, radio station, multicultural center, and centers for women and child development. The 110-acre campus is in a suburban area 55 miles west of Philadelphia. Including any residence halls, there are 36 buildings.

Student Life: 66% of undergraduates are from Pennsylvania. Others are from 21 states and 22 foreign countries. 73% are from public schools. 79% are white. 48% claim no religious affiliation; 25% are Catholic; 24% Protestant. The average age of freshmen is 18; all undergraduates, 20. 18% do not continue beyond their first year; 67% remain to graduate.

Housing: 1068 students can be accommodated in college housing, which includes single-sex and coed dorms and on-campus apartments. In addition, there are honors houses and special-interest houses. On-campus housing is guaranteed for all 4 years. 69% of students live on campus; of those, 95% remain on campus on weekends. Upperclassmen may keep cars.

Activities: 28% of men belong to 3 national fraternities; 32% of women belong to 3 national sororities. There are 70 groups on campus, including band, cheerleading, chess, choir, chorus, computers, dance, drama, ethnic, film, honors, international, jazz band, literary magazine, musical theater, newspaper, photography, political, professional, radio and TV, religious, social, social service, student government, and yearbook. Popular campus events include Dance Marathon, Greek Weekend, and Spring Fever Weekend.

Sports: There are 11 intercollegiate sports for men and 11 for women, and 3 intramural sports for men and 4 for women. Facilities include a 7500-seat stadium, baseball, softball, and soccer fields, fitness center, weight room, indoor and outdoor tracks, bowling alley, a swimming pool, and racquetball courts.

Disabled Students: 75% of the campus is accessible. Wheelchair ramps, elevators, special parking, specially equipped rest rooms, and special class scheduling are available.

Services: Counseling and information services are available, as is tutoring in most subjects. There is a reader service for the blind. An academic learning center, a writing center, and an ESL program are available.

Campus Safety and Security: Measures include 24-hour foot and vehicle patrol, self-defense education, security escort services, and shuttle buses. There are informal discussions, pamphlets/posters/films, emergency telephones, lighted pathways/sidewalks, a Comprehensive Crisis Action Plan, and a bicycle patrol. All officers are CPR, AED, and first aid certified.

Programs of Study: Albright confers B.A. and B.S. degrees. Master's degrees are also awarded. Bachelor's degrees are awarded in BIOLOGICAL SCIENCE (biochemistry and biology/biological science), BUSINESS (accounting, business administration and management, and fashion merchandising), COMMUNICATIONS AND THE ARTS (art, communications, dramatic arts, English, French, and Spanish), COMPUTER AND PHYSICAL SCIENCE (chemistry, computer science, information sciences and systems, mathematics, and physics), EDUCATION (elementary, secondary, and special), ENGINEERING AND ENVIRONMENTAL DESIGN (environmental science), SOCIAL SCIENCE (American studies, child care/child and family studies, criminal justice, economics, history, Latin American studies, philosophy, political science/government, psychobiology, psychology, religion, and textiles and clothing). Biology, psychology, and business are the largest.

Required: To graduate, students must complete 32 courses, including 13 to 14 in the major, with a minimum GPA of 2.0. All students take 1 interdisciplinary course, and they must fulfill the cultural experience requirement. General studies requirements include 11 to 15 courses in English composition, a foreign language, natural science, quantitative reasoning, social science, the arts, and humanities (literature, history, philosophy, and religion).

Special: Co-op programs are available in forestry, environmental studies, and natural resources with Duke University and the University of Michigan. The school offers credit and noncredit internships, a Washington semester, an accelerated degree program, cross-registration, dual majors, student-designed majors, nondegree study, and pass/fail options. Study abroad may be arranged in any country. There are 11 national honor societies and a freshman honors program.

Faculty/Classroom: 52% of faculty are male; 48%, female. All teach undergraduates. The average class size in an introductory lecture is 25; in a laboratory, 15; and in a regular course, 18.

Admissions: 72% of the 2003-2004 applicants were accepted. The SAT I scores for the 2003-2004 freshman class were: Verbal--42% between 500 and 599 and 18% between 600 and 700; Math--41% below 500, 40% between 500 and 599, 18% between 600 and 700, and 1% above 700. 39% of the current freshmen were in the top fifth of their class; 67% were in the top two fifths. 2 freshmen graduated first in their class.

Requirements: The SAT I is required. In addition, graduation from an accredited secondary school or satisfactory scores on the GED are required for admission. Students must have a total of 16 Carnegie units, including 4 years of English, 3 in science, including 1 lab, 2 years each of a foreign language, math, and social studies, and 3 electives in college preparatory subjects. An essay is required and an interview recommended. AP and CLEP credits are accepted. Important factors in the admissions decision are advanced placement or honor courses, leadership record, and recommendations by school officials.

Procedure: Freshmen are admitted fall, spring, and summer. Entrance exams should be taken during the spring of the junior year or the fall of the senior year. There is a rolling admissions plan and a deferred admissions plan. Application deadlines are open. The fall 2003 application fee was $25. Applications are accepted on-line through Common App and the school's web site.

Transfer: 40 transfer students enrolled in 2002-2003. Transfer students must have a minimum GPA of 2.5 and be in good standing. 64 of 128 credits required for the bachelor's degree must be completed at Albright.

Visiting: There are regularly scheduled orientations for prospective students, including an interview with a counselor and a tour of the campus with a currently enrolled student. There are guides for informal visits and visitors may sit in on classes and stay overnight. To schedule a visit, contact the Admissions Office.

Financial Aid: In a recent year, 95% of all full-time freshmen and 90% of continuing full-time students received some form of financial aid. 88% of all full-time students received need-based aid. The average freshman award was $21,963. 35% of undergraduates work part time. Average annual earnings from campus work are $903. The average financial indebtedness of a recent graduate was $23,000. Albright is a member of CSS. The FAFSA is required. The deadline for filing freshman financial aid applications for fall entry is March 1.

International Students: There were 71 international students enrolled in a recent year . The school actively recruits these students. They must take the SAT I or the ACT, or they can take the TOEFL in lieu of the SAT I.

Computers: Students do not access our mainframe system. Instead, there are approximately 200 workstations dedicated for student use, located across campus, networked to provide access to client/server systems. All students may access the system 8 A.M. to 1 A.M. There are no time limits. The fee is $200 per year. It is strongly recommended that all students have a personal computer. Dell, Gateway, Apple, or IBM is recommended.

Graduates: From July 1, 2002 to June 30, 2003, 273 bachelor's degrees were awarded. The most popular majors were business administration (22%), psychology/psychobiology (18%), and biology/biochemistry (17%). In an average class, 1% graduate in 3 years or less, 60% graduate in 4 years or less, 67% graduate in 5 years or less, and 67% graduate in 6 years or less. 68 companies recruited on campus in 2002-2003. Of the 2002 graduating class, 23% were enrolled in graduate school within 6 months of graduation and 98% were employed.

Admissions Contact: Gregory E. Eichhorn, Vice President for Enrollment Management and Dean of Admissions. E-mail: *albright@alb.edu* Web: *www.albright.edu*

ALLEGHENY COLLEGE
B-1
Meadville, PA 16335
(814) 332-4351
(800) 521-5293; Fax: (814) 337-0431

Full-time: 882 men, 927 women	**Faculty:** 134; IIB, +$
Part-time: 14 men, 26 women	**Ph.D.s:** 90%
Graduate: none	**Student/Faculty:** 14 to 1
Year: semesters	**Tuition:** $24,400
Application Deadline: February 15	**Room & Board:** $5880
Freshman Class: 2438 applied, 2001 accepted, 478 enrolled	
SAT I Verbal/Math: 600/600	**ACT:** 25 **VERY COMPETITIVE**

Allegheny College, founded in 1815, is a private liberal arts institution affiliated with the United Methodist Church. The library contains 796,762 volumes, 504,636 microform items, and 7502 audio/video tapes/CDs, and subscribes to 3500 periodicals. Computerized library services include the card catalog, interlibrary loans, database searching, and Internet access. Special learning facilities include a learning resource center, art gallery, planetarium, radio station, TV studio, observatory, 283-acre experimental research reserve, art studio, 80-acre protected forest, dance studio, Geographic Information Systems Learning Laboratory, and a language learning center. The 254-acre campus is in a small town 90 miles north of Pittsburgh and east of Cleveland. Including any residence halls, there are 34 buildings.

Student Life: 67% of undergraduates are from Pennsylvania. Students are from 33 states, 25 foreign countries, and Canada. 82% are from public schools. 94% are white. 39% are Catholic; 31% Protestant; 22% claim no religious affiliation. The average age of freshmen is 19; all undergraduates, 20. 15% do not continue beyond their first year; 70% remain to graduate.

Housing: 1450 students can be accommodated in college housing, which includes single-sex and coed dorms, on-campus apartments, off-campus apartments, and fraternity houses. In addition, there are language houses and special-interest houses. On-campus housing is guaranteed for all 4 years. 73% of students live on campus; of those, 75% remain on campus on weekends. All students may keep cars.

Activities: 26% of men belong to 5 national fraternities; 29% of women belong to 4 national sororities. There are 107 groups on campus, including academic, art, band, cheerleading, choir, chorale, chorus, computers, dance, debate, drama, environmental, ethnic, film, gay, honors, international, jazz band, literary magazine, music ensembles, musical theater, newspaper, orchestra, outdoor, photography, political, professional, radio and TV, religious, social, social service, student government, symphony, and yearbook. Popular campus events include Centerstage (arts and lecture) Series, Black History Month, and Latino Heritage Month.

Sports: There are 10 intercollegiate sports for men and 10 for women, and 8 intramural sports for men and 8 for women. Facilities include a sports and fitness center that includes a training track, weight rooms, a variety of cardio machines, 4 multipurpose courts (volleyball, basketball, tennis, badminton, putting green, batting cage), a natatorium, a dance studio, 3 racquetball courts, and a performance floor; and an outdoor complex with a stadium, cross-country course, 8 fields, 12 lighted tennis courts, a challenge course, and picnic shelter. In addition, there are 100 wooded acres for mountain biking, hiking, and cross-country skiing.

Disabled Students: 30% of the campus is accessible. Wheelchair ramps, elevators, special parking, specially equipped rest rooms, special class scheduling, and special housing, are available. Reasonable accommodations are made for all special needs.

Services: Counseling and information services are available, as is tutoring in some subjects, including biology, chemistry, economics, computer science, environmental science, geology, math, physics, psychology, and writing. There is a reader service for the blind, and remedial math, reading, and writing. There is also help with study skills, a speech center, and a learning center.

Campus Safety and Security: Measures include 24-hour foot and vehicle patrol, self-defense education, security escort services, and informal discussions. There are pamphlets/posters/films, emergency telephones, lighted pathways/sidewalks, and TTY phones.

Programs of Study: Allegheny confers B.A. and B.S. degrees. Bachelor's degrees are awarded in AGRICULTURE (environmental studies), BIOLOGICAL SCIENCE (biochemistry, biology/biological science, and neurosciences), COMMUNICATIONS AND THE ARTS (art, art history and appreciation, communications, dramatic arts, English, French, German, music, Spanish, and studio art), COMPUTER AND PHYSICAL SCIENCE (chemistry, computer science, geology, mathematics, and physics), ENGINEERING AND ENVIRONMENTAL DESIGN (environmental science), SOCIAL SCIENCE (economics, history, international studies, philosophy, political science/government, psychology, religion, and women's studies). Physical and biological sciences, political science, and English are the strongest academically. Psychology, environmental science/studies, and economics are the largest.

Required: To graduate, students must complete 131 credit hours with a minimum GPA of 2.0. Between 32 and 64 hours are required in the major, including the junior seminar and senior research project. All students must fulfill liberal studies requirements of 8 credits each in arts and humanities, natural sciences, and social sciences. The liberal studies program extends through all 4 years and promotes breadth at both introductory and advanced levels of study. Additional required courses include freshman first seminar, freshman second seminar, a sophomore writing and speaking seminar, and academic planning seminars. All graduating seniors complete an independent research project. Most departments require an oral defense of the project.

Special: Allegheny offers a Washington semester, internships, dual majors, student-designed majors, study abroad in 13 countries, nondegree study, and pass/fail options. A 3-2 engineering degree is available with Case Western Reserve, Columbia, Duke, Pittsburgh, and Washington Universities. There also are cooperative arrangements in medical technology and nursing with Rochester and Case Western Reserve Universities. Allegheny students can graduate with a bachelor's degree from Allegheny, a Master's degree from the University of Pittsburgh, and Pennsylvania teaching certification in 5 years. Preprofessional programs, independent study, a marine biology study program, and an experiential learning term are also available. There are 13 national honor societies, including Phi Beta Kappa, and 17 departmental honors programs.

Faculty/Classroom: 66% of faculty are male; 34%, female. All both teach and do research. The average class size in an introductory lecture is 22; in a laboratory, 17; and in a regular course, 22.

Admissions: 82% of the 2003-2004 applicants were accepted. The SAT I scores for the 2003-2004 freshman class were: Verbal--11% below 500, 35% between 500 and 599, 45% between 600 and 700, and 9% above 700; Math--7% below 500, 41% between 500 and 599, 43% between 600 and 700, and 9% above 700. The ACT scores were 11% below 21, 15% between 21 and 23, 36% between 24 and 26, 22% between 27 and 28, and 16% above 28. 65% of the current freshmen were in the top fifth of their class; 90% were in the top two fifths. There were 2 National Merit semifinalists in a recent year.

Requirements: The SAT I or ACT is required. In addition, SAT II: Subject tests are recommended in writing and in the student's expected major. Graduation from an accredited secondary school is required for admission. Students must have 16 Carnegie units, including 4 years of English, 3 years each of math, science, and social studies, and 2 years of a foreign language. An essay is required, and an interview is recommended. The GED is accepted. AP and CLEP credits are accepted. Important factors in the admissions decision are advanced placement or honor courses, recommendations by school officials, and extracurricular activities record.

Procedure: Freshmen are admitted fall and spring. Entrance exams should be taken by December of the senior year. There are early decision, early admissions, and deferred admissions plans. Early decision applications should be filed by January 15; regular applications, by February 15 for fall entry and November 1 for spring entry, along with a $35 fee. Notification of early decision is sent October 15; regular decision, April 1. 75 early decision candidates were accepted for the 2003-2004 class. 62 applicants were on the 2003 waiting list; 14 were admitted. Applications are accepted on computer disk and on-line through the school's web site, Embark.com, Apply Yourself, and Common App.

Transfer: 13 transfer students enrolled in 2002-2003. Transfer applicants must submit a transcript of all college courses, a high school transcript, standardized test scores, a statement of good standing, and a letter describing reasons for transfer, and have a minimum GPA of 2.5, with 3.0 recommended. 64 credits of 131 required for the bachelor's degree must be completed at Allegheny.

Visiting: There are regularly scheduled orientations for prospective students, consisting of tours, panels, and presentations on academic programs, student life, admissions, and financial aid. There are guides for informal visits and visitors may sit in on classes and stay overnight. To schedule a visit, contact the Office of Admissions at *admissions@allegheny.edu.*

Financial Aid: In 2003-2004, 96% of all full-time students received some form of financial aid. 73% of all full-time students received need-based aid. The average freshman award was $19,257. Need-based scholarships or need-based grants averaged $15,172 ($25,400 maximum); need-based self-help aid (loans and jobs) averaged $5383 ($6625 maximum); non-need-based awards and non-need-based scholarships averaged $9601 ($16,500 maximum); and tuition remission to students with no financial need averaged $21,425 ($24,100 maximum). 66% of undergraduates work part time. Average annual earnings from campus work are $800..The average financial indebtedness of the 2003 graduate was $23,735. The FAFSA is required. The priority date for freshman financial aid applications for fall entry is February 15.

International Students: There are 34 international students enrolled. The school actively recruits these students. They must score 550 on the written TOEFL or 213 on the electronic version and also take the SAT I or the ACT.

Computers: The mainframes are a TCP/IP network of 30 UNIX servers and 15 Windows servers. 336 PCs are networked and available to students in the library, all academic buildings, the computer center, and the campus center. Residence hall rooms and lounges are wired to the campus network. All students may access the system 24 hours per day. There

are no time limits and no fees. It is strongly recommended that all students have a personal computer. An Intel/Windows PC is recommended.

Graduates: From July 1, 2002 to June 30, 2003, 444 bachelor's degrees were awarded. The most popular majors were economics (12%), psychology (10%), and political science (10%). In an average class, 62% graduate in 4 years or less, 68% graduate in 5 years or less, and 70% graduate in 6 years or less. 40 companies recruited on campus in 2002-2003. Of the 2002 graduating class, 31% were enrolled in graduate school within 6 months of graduation and 83% were employed.

Admissions Contact: Dr. W. Scott Friedhoff, Vice President for Enrollment. E-mail: *admissions@allegheny.edu* Web: *www.allegheny.edu*

ALVERNIA COLLEGE
Reading, PA 19607

E-3

(610) 796-8362
(888) Alvernia; Fax: (610) 796-8336

Full-time: 397 men, 737 women	**Faculty:** 65; IIB, -$
Part-time: 134 men, 329 women	**Ph.D.s:** 62%
Graduate: 149 men, 240 women	**Student/Faculty:** 17 to 1
Year: semesters, summer session	**Tuition:** $16,362
Application Deadline: open	**Room & Board:** $6850
Freshman Class: 910 applied, 750 accepted, 290 enrolled	
SAT I Verbal/Math: 470/465	**LESS COMPETITIVE**

Alvernia College, established in 1958, is a Roman Catholic liberal arts institution. In addition to regional accreditation, Alvernia has baccalaureate program accreditation with ACOTE, APTA, CCNE, CSWE, NCATE, and NLN. The library contains 86,647 volumes and 1967 audio/video tapes/CDs, and subscribes to 390 periodicals. Computerized library services include the card catalog, interlibrary loans, and database searching. The 85-acre campus is in a suburban area 3 miles southwest of Reading. Including any residence halls, there are 14 buildings.

Student Life: 88% of undergraduates are from Pennsylvania. Students are from 12 states and 9 foreign countries. 76% are from public schools. 84% are white. 29% are Catholic; 19% claim no religious affiliation. The average age of freshmen is 19; all undergraduates, 24.

Housing: 500 students can be accommodated in college housing, which includes single-sex and coed dorms and on-campus apartments. In addition, there are honors houses. On-campus housing is guaranteed for the freshman year only and is available on a first-come, first-served basis. Priority is given to out-of-town students. 60% of students commute. Alcohol is not permitted. All students may keep cars.

Activities: There are no fraternities or sororities. There are 31 groups on campus, including cheerleading, chorus, computers, drama, ethnic, honors, international, literary magazine, newspaper, political, professional, religious, student government, and yearbook. Popular campus events include Christmas on Campus, Spring Fling, and Club Fair.

Sports: There are 6 intercollegiate sports for men and 8 for women, and 4 intramural sports for men and 2 for women. Facilities include a gym, a physical fitness and recreation center, playing fields, and outdoor tennis, basketball, and volleyball courts.

Disabled Students: 75% of the campus is accessible. Wheelchair ramps, elevators, special parking, specially equipped rest rooms, special class scheduling, lowered drinking fountains, lowered telephones, and special housing are available.

Services: Counseling and information services are available, as is tutoring in every subject. There is remedial math, reading, and writing. Facilities include a writing center and a math/science tutorial lab.

Campus Safety and Security: Measures include 24-hour foot and vehicle patrol, security escort services, informal discussions, and pamphlets/posters/films. There are emergency telephones, lighted pathways/sidewalks, and Photo ID cards must be carried by students.

Programs of Study: Alvernia confers B.A., B.S., B.S.N., and B.S.W. degrees. Associate and master's degrees are also awarded. Bachelor's degrees are awarded in BIOLOGICAL SCIENCE (biochemistry and biology/biological science), BUSINESS (accounting, business administration and management, marketing and distribution, and sports management), COMMUNICATIONS AND THE ARTS (communications and English), COMPUTER AND PHYSICAL SCIENCE (chemistry, information sciences and systems, mathematics, and science), EDUCATION (athletic training, elementary, and secondary), HEALTH PROFESSIONS (nursing), SOCIAL SCIENCE (addiction studies, criminal justice, forensic studies, history, liberal arts/general studies, philosophy, political science/government, psychology, social studies, social work, and theological studies). Biology, chemistry, and occupational therapy are the strongest academically. Criminal justice, education, and forensic science are the largest.

Required: To graduate, all students must complete at least 123 credit hours with a minimum GPA of 2.0 overall and in the major (2.5 for elementary education and nursing majors). Requirements include 54 to 55 credits in a liberal arts core, consisting of theology and philosophy, social science, communications, literature, fine arts, math, and science. All students also must perform 40 clock hours of service to others before graduation, complete course work in college success skills and in human diversity, and demonstrate computer proficiency.

Special: The college offers co-op programs in business and sports management, internships, cross-registration with Kutztown University, Pennsylvania State University, Albright College, and Reading area community colleges, a Washington semester, dual and student-designed majors, and practicums in psychology, criminal justice, education, addiction studies, social work, athletic training, and occupational therapy. There is a freshman honors program.

Faculty/Classroom: 43% of full-time faculty are male; 57%, female. All teach undergraduates. No introductory courses are taught by graduate students. The average class size in an introductory lecture is 21; in a laboratory, 15; and in a regular course, 18.

Admissions: 82% of the 2003-2004 applicants were accepted. The SAT I scores for the 2003-2004 freshman class were: Verbal--68% below 500, 25% between 500 and 599, 7% between 600 and 700, and 1% above 700; Math--67% below 500, 27% between 500 and 599, and 6% between 600 and 700. 26% of the current freshmen were in the top fifth of their class; 48% were in the top two fifths.

Requirements: The SAT I is required and the ACT is recommended. In addition, all applicants must be graduates of an accredited secondary school or have a GED certificate. They should have completed at least 16 academic units, including 4 in English and electives and 2 each in math, foreign language, science, and social studies. An interview is required for nursing applicants and strongly recommended for all others. Nursing candidates also must submit results of the NLN prenursing test. A GPA of 2.0 is required. AP and CLEP credits are accepted. Important factors in the admissions decision are advanced placement or honor courses, recommendations by school officials, and extracurricular activities record.

Procedure: Freshmen are admitted fall and spring. Entrance exams should be taken in the spring of the junior year or fall of the senior year. There is a deferred admissions plan and a rolling admissions plan. Application deadlines are open. The fall 2003 application fee was $25. Applications are accepted on-line.

Transfer: 75 transfer students enrolled in 2002-2003. Applicants must have a college GPA of 2.0 or better. 45 of 123 credits required for the bachelor's degree must be completed at Alvernia.

Visiting: There are regularly scheduled orientations for prospective students, including faculty displays, lunch, tours of the campus, and the opportunity to interact with current students. There are guides for informal visits and visitors may sit in on classes and stay overnight. To schedule a visit, contact the Admissions Office.

Financial Aid: In 2003-2004, 81% of all full-time freshmen and 86% of continuing full-time students received some form of financial aid. At least 80% of full-time freshmen and at least 82% of continuing full-time students received need-based aid. The average freshman award was $13,704. Need-based scholarships or need-based grants averaged $9768; need-based self-help aid (loans and jobs) averaged $4605; and non-need-based awards and non-need-based scholarships averaged $10,371. 80% of undergraduates work part time. Average annual earnings from campus work are $1000. The average financial indebtedness of the 2003 graduate was $6749. Alvernia is a member of CSS. The FAFSA, the state aid form, and the noncustodial parent's statement, if applicable are required.

International Students: In a recent year, there were 12 international students enrolled. They must score 550 on the written TOEFL.

Computers: The mainframe is an NT Network environment. PCs are available to students in the science and math building. Network jacks are available in the student center, residence halls, and library. All students may access the system. Labs are open 17 hours per day, and the network is available 24 hours per day. There are no time limits and no fees. It is strongly recommended that all students have a personal computer. A Pentium processor or equivalent is recommended.

Graduates: In a recent year, 263 bachelor's degrees were awarded. The most popular majors were business management (15%), criminal justice (14%), and health science (11%). In an average class, 65% graduate in 4 years or less, 76% graduate in 5 years or less, and 78% graduate in 6 years or less. 49 companies recruited on campus in a recent year.

Admissions Contact: Jack Moser, Director of Admissions. E-mail: *admissions@alvernia.edu* Web: *www.alvernia.edu*

ARCADIA UNIVERSITY	F-3
Glenside, PA 19038	**(215) 572-2910**
	(877) ARCADIA; Fax: (215) 572-4049
Full-time: 403 men, 1167 women	**Faculty:** 97; IIA, +$
Part-time: 77 men, 193 women	**Ph.D.s:** n/av
Graduate: 363 men, 1214 women	**Student/Faculty:** 16 to 1
Year: semesters, summer session	**Tuition:** $21,270
Application Deadline: open	**Room & Board:** $8620
Freshman Class: 2691 applied, 2014 accepted, 501 enrolled	
SAT I Verbal/Math: 540/510	**COMPETITIVE**

Arcadia University, founded in 1853, is a private institution affiliated with the Presbyterian Church (U.S.A.). It offers undergraduate and graduate programs in the fine arts, the sciences, business, education, and preprofessional fields. In addition to regional accreditation, Arcadia University has baccalaureate program accreditation with APTA and NASAD. The library contains 139,903 volumes, 50,301 microform items, and 2861 audio/video tapes/CDs, and subscribes to 798 periodicals. Computerized library services include the card catalog, interlibrary loans, database searching, and Internet access. Special learning facilities include a learning resource center, art gallery, radio station, observatory, theater, computer graphics and communication labs, and multimedia classrooms. The 60-acre campus is in a suburban area 10 miles north of Philadelphia. Including any residence halls, there are 21 buildings.

Student Life: 72% of undergraduates are from Pennsylvania. Students are from 23 states and 23 foreign countries. 70% are from public schools. 74% are white; 10% African American. The average age of freshmen is 19; all undergraduates, 23.

Housing: College housing includes single-sex and coed dorms and off-campus apartments. On-campus housing is guaranteed for all 4 years. 68% of students live on campus. Upperclassmen may keep cars.

Activities: There are no fraternities or sororities. There are 40 groups on campus, including art, cheerleading, choir, chorale, chorus, computers, dance, drama, ethnic, gay, honors, international, literary magazine, musical theater, newspaper, photography, political, professional, radio and TV, religious, social, social service, student government, and yearbook. Popular campus events include Mr. Beaver contest, Woodstock Weekend, and Spring Fling.

Sports: There are 7 intercollegiate sports for men and 9 for women, and 5 intramural sports for men and 5 for women. Facilities include a softball field, outdoor tennis and basketball courts, field hockey and soccer/lacrosse fields, and an athletic and recreation center with a 1500-seat gym for basketball and volleyball, an indoor track, an indoor NCAA regulation swimming pool, an aerobics and dance studio, and fitness and training rooms.

Disabled Students: 70% of the campus is accessible. Wheelchair ramps, elevators, special parking, specially equipped rest rooms, special class scheduling, lowered drinking fountains, and lowered telephones are available.

Services: Counseling and information services are available, as is tutoring in every subject. There is a reader service for the blind and remedial math, reading, and writing.

Campus Safety and Security: Measures include 24-hour foot and vehicle patrol, self-defense education, security escort services, and shuttle buses. There are informal discussions, pamphlets/posters/films, emergency telephones, lighted pathways/sidewalks, alarmed doors, night receptionists, and card access to residence halls.

Programs of Study: Arcadia University confers B.A., B.S., and B.F.A. degrees. Master's and doctoral degrees are also awarded. Bachelor's degrees are awarded in BIOLOGICAL SCIENCE (biology/biological science), BUSINESS (accounting, banking and finance, business administration and management, marketing/retailing/merchandising, and personnel management), COMMUNICATIONS AND THE ARTS (communications, dramatic arts, English, fine arts, graphic design, illustration, photography, and theater design), COMPUTER AND PHYSICAL SCIENCE (chemistry, computer science, mathematics, and science), EDUCATION (art, early childhood, elementary, secondary, and special), ENGINEERING AND ENVIRONMENTAL DESIGN (engineering, environmental science, and interior design), HEALTH PROFESSIONS (art therapy, health care administration, predentistry, premedicine, preoptometry, and preveterinary science), SOCIAL SCIENCE (history, liberal arts/general studies, philosophy, political science/government, prelaw, psychobiology, psychology, and sociology). Education, psychology, and chemistry are the strongest academically. Fine arts, business, and biology are the largest.

Required: Students must take English composition, math, 2 semesters each of a lab science and a foreign language, and 1 semester of computer science. They must also fulfill 24 credits of distribution requirements in the arts, humanities, and social sciences; core courses in American pluralism and non-Western cultures; and a final project or thesis. 128 credit hours are required to graduate, including 40 to 52 in the major, with a minimum GPA of 2.0.

Special: Internships are encouraged in all majors. There are study-abroad programs in 9 countries and co-op programs in business, computer science, chemistry, actuarial science, and accounting. There is a 3-2 engineering program with Columbia University and a 3-4 optometry program with the Pennsylvania College of Optometry. Arcadia also offers a Washington semester, work-study, student-designed majors, a dual major in chemistry and business, interdisciplinary majors in artificial intelligence and scientific illustration, credit by exam and for life/military/work experience, and nondegree study. There are 3 national honor societies, including Phi Beta Kappa, and a freshman honors program.

Faculty/Classroom: All faculty do research. No introductory courses are taught by graduate students. The average class size in an introductory lecture is 28; in a laboratory, 20; and in a regular course, 16.

Admissions: 75% of the 2003-2004 applicants were accepted. The SAT I scores for the 2003-2004 freshman class were: Verbal--31% below

500, 43% between 500 and 599, 25% between 600 and 700, and 1% above 700; Math--35% below 500, 43% between 500 and 599, 20% between 600 and 700, and 2% above 700. 52% of the current freshmen were in the top fifth of their class; 86% were in the top two fifths.

Requirements: The SAT I is required and the ACT is recommended. In addition, applicants must be graduates of an accredited secondary school or have a GED. A total of 16 academic credits is required, including 4 years of English, 3 each of math and social studies, and 2 each of a foreign language and science. An essay is required. All art and illustration majors (except art education) must submit a portfolio. AP and CLEP credits are accepted. Important factors in the admissions decision are advanced placement or honor courses, recommendations by school officials, and extracurricular activities record.

Procedure: Freshmen are admitted fall and spring. Entrance exams should be taken during orientation. There are early decision and deferred admissions plans. There is a rolling admissions plan. Application deadlines are open. The fall 2003 application fee was $30. 12 early decision candidates were accepted for the 2003-2004 class. Applications are accepted on-line through the Common App and the university's web site, *www.arcadia.edu.*

Transfer: 132 transfer students enrolled in 2002-2003. Applicants must have a GPA of 2.5. Art majors must submit a portfolio. The SAT I or the ACT is required if the student has earned less than 1 year of college credit. An interview is encouraged. 32 of 128 credits required for the bachelor's degree must be completed at Arcadia University.

Visiting: There are regularly scheduled orientations for prospective students, including personal interviews Monday through Saturday, open houses, and opportunities to dine on campus and to meet with faculty, financial aid officers, and current students. There are guides for informal visits and visitors may sit in on classes and stay overnight. To schedule a visit, contact the Office of Enrollment Management at *admiss@arcadia.edu.*

Financial Aid: In 2003-2004, 84% of all full-time freshmen received some form of financial aid. 81% of full-time freshmen received need-based aid. Need-based scholarships or need-based grants averaged $7857; need-based self-help aid (loans and jobs) averaged $5400; and non-need-based awards and non-need-based scholarships averaged $4523. The average financial indebtedness of the 2003 graduate was $29,145. The FAFSA, the college's own financial statement, the PHEAA, and parent and student tax returns are required. The deadline for filing freshman financial aid applications for fall entry is March 1.

International Students: The school actively recruits these students. They must score 520 on the written TOEFL and also take the SAT I or the ACT.

Computers: PCs and Macs are available in 8 computer labs across campus. Residence halls, offices, and classrooms are networked, and all have access to the Internet and the World Wide Web. The campus is wireless. All students may access the system. There are no time limits and no fees.

Graduates: From July 1, 2002 to June 30, 2003, 328 bachelor's degrees were awarded. The most popular majors were business (17%), education (15%), and psychology (13%).

Admissions Contact: Office of Enrollment Management. A video is available. E-mail: *admiss@arcadia.edu* Web: *www.arcadia.edu*

BLOOMSBURG UNIVERSITY OF PENNSYLVANIA   E-2
Bloomsburg, PA 17815   **(570) 389-4316; Fax: (570) 389-4741**

Full-time: 2747 men, 4227 women	**Faculty:** 335; IIA, +$
Part-time: 194 men, 353 women	**Ph.D.s:** 75%
Graduate: 221 men, 542 women	**Student/Faculty:** 21 to 1
Year: semesters, summer session	**Tuition:** $5844 ($12,792)
Application Deadline: open	**Room & Board:** $5000
Freshman Class: 7274 applied, 5123 accepted, 1671 enrolled	
SAT I Verbal/Math: 510/510	**COMPETITIVE**

Bloomsburg University of Pennsylvania, founded in 1839, is a public institution offering undergraduate programs in the liberal arts, sciences, business, teacher education, technology, and health professions. There are 4 undergraduate schools and 1 graduate school. In addition to regional accreditation, BU has baccalaureate program accreditation with CSWE, NCATE, and NLN. The library contains 441,314 volumes, 2,108,716 microform items, and 8223 audio/video tapes/CDs, and subscribes to 2399 periodicals. Computerized library services include the card catalog, interlibrary loans, database searching, and Internet access. Special learning facilities include a learning resource center, art gallery, radio station, and TV station. The 282-acre campus is in a small town 80 miles northeast of Harrisburg. Including any residence halls, there are 54 buildings.

Student Life: 89% of undergraduates are from Pennsylvania. Students are from 25 states, 34 foreign countries, and Canada. 91% are from public schools. 91% are white. The average age of freshmen is 18; all undergraduates, 21. 19% do not continue beyond their first year; 61% remain to graduate.

Housing: 2966 students can be accommodated in college housing, which includes single-sex and coed dorms and on-campus apartments.

In addition, there are honors houses and special-interest houses. On-campus housing is guaranteed for the freshman year only and is available on a first-come, first-served basis. Alcohol is not permitted. All students may keep cars.

Activities: 4% of men belong to 2 local and 9 national fraternities; 6% of women belong to 5 local and 8 national sororities. There are more than 160 groups on campus, including art, band, cheerleading, chess, choir, chorale, chorus, computers, dance, drama, drill team, ethnic, film, forensics, gay, honors, international, jazz band, literary magazine, marching band, musical theater, newspaper, orchestra, pep band, political, professional, radio and TV, religious, social, social service, student government, and yearbook. Popular campus events include Parents Weekend, Renaissance Jamboree, and Siblings and Children Weekend.

Sports: There are 9 intercollegiate sports for men and 9 for women. Facilities include a 5000-seat stadium, a gym, an athletic field, an indoor track, a 6-lane swimming pool, 9 practice fields, 18 Grasstex tennis courts, racquetball/handball courts, and a 57,000-square-foot recreation facility.

Disabled Students: Wheelchair ramps, elevators, special parking, specially equipped rest rooms, special class scheduling, lowered drinking fountains, and lowered telephones are available.

Services: Counseling and information services are available, as is tutoring in some subjects. There is a reader service for the blind, and remedial math, reading, and writing.

Campus Safety and Security: Measures include 24-hour foot and vehicle patrol, self-defense education, security escort services, and shuttle buses. There are emergency telephones, lighted pathways/sidewalks, monitored surveillance cameras, and strict residence hall security.

Programs of Study: BU confers B.A., B.S., B.S.Ed., and B.S.N. degrees. Associate and master's degrees are also awarded. Bachelor's degrees are awarded in BIOLOGICAL SCIENCE (biology/biological science), BUSINESS (accounting, business administration and management, and business economics), COMMUNICATIONS AND THE ARTS (art history and appreciation, communications, dramatic arts, English, French, German, music, Spanish, speech/debate/rhetoric, and studio art), COMPUTER AND PHYSICAL SCIENCE (chemistry, computer science, earth science, geology, mathematics, natural sciences, physics, and radiological technology), EDUCATION (business, early childhood, elementary, science, secondary, social studies, and special), ENGINEERING AND ENVIRONMENTAL DESIGN (electrical/electronics engineering), HEALTH PROFESSIONS (health, medical laboratory technology, nursing, and speech pathology/audiology), SOCIAL SCIENCE (anthropology, criminal justice, economics, ethics, politics, and social policy, geography, history, humanities, interpreter for the deaf, philosophy, physical fitness/movement, political science/government, psychology, social science, social work, and sociology). Elementary education, business management, and special education are the largest.

Required: To graduate, students must complete 120 credit hours with a minimum GPA of 2.0. BU requires 12 semester hours each in humanities, social sciences, natural sciences, and math. There are specific course requirements in communication, quantitative/analytical reasoning, values, ethics, responsible decision making, and survival, fitness, and recreational skills.

Special: Internships for upperclassmen, study abroad in more than 11 countries, work-study programs, and dual majors are available. BU offers a 3-2 engineering degree with Pennsylvania State and Wilkes Universities. There is nondegree study, pass/fail options, and credit for life, military, and work experience. The school uses telecourses and interactive video. There are 9 national honor societies, a freshman honors program, and 15 departmental honors programs.

Faculty/Classroom: 61% of faculty are male; 39%, female. No introductory courses are taught by graduate students. The average class size in a laboratory is 14 and in a regular course, 29.

Admissions: 70% of the 2003-2004 applicants were accepted. The SAT I scores for the 2003-2004 freshman class were: Verbal--44% below 500, 46% between 500 and 599, and 9% between 600 and 700; Math--40% below 500, 48% between 500 and 599, 11% between 600 and 700, and 1% above 700. 22% of the current freshmen were in the top fifth of their class; 59% were in the top two fifths. 6 freshmen graduated first in their class.

Requirements: The SAT I or ACT is required, with a minimum composite score of 1050 on the SAT I. In additon, applicants must be graduates of an accredited secondary school. To be competitive, a student should also rank in the top 30% of the high school class with a B average. The GED is accepted. Applicants should complete 4 years each of English and social studies, 3 years each of math and science, and 2 years of a foreign language. An interview is recommended. AP and CLEP credits are accepted.

Procedure: Freshmen are admitted to all sessions. Entrance exams should be taken during the junior year. There are early decision, early admissions, and deferred admissions plans. Early decision applications should be filed by November 15; deadlines are open for regular applications. The fall 2003 application fee was $30. Notification of early decision is sent December 1; regular decision, on a rolling basis. 213 early decision candidates were accepted for the 2003-2004 class. 88 applicants were on the 2003 waiting list. Applications are accepted on-line through *www.bloomu.edu*.

Transfer: 379 transfer students enrolled in 2002-2003. Either the SAT I or ACT is required from applicants who have completed fewer than 24 semester hours of college credits. An official secondary school transcript or a GED and official transcripts from any postsecondary schools attended are also required. Applicants must have a minimum GPA of 2.0 (2.5 or 2.8 for some majors) and be in good standing at the college last attended. Those who have completed 30 semester hours must select a major upon entering BU. 32 of 120 credits required for the bachelor's degree must be completed at BU.

Visiting: There are regularly scheduled orientations for prospective students, consisting of a general meeting with admissions staff, a question-and-answer session, a campus tour, lunch, and meetings with academic faculty. There are guides for informal visits and visitors may sit in on classes. To schedule a visit, contact the Admissions Office at *buadmiss@bloomu.edu*.

Financial Aid: In 2003-2004, 65% of all full-time freshmen and 61% of continuing full-time students received some form of financial aid. The average freshman award was $11,408. Need-based scholarships or need-based grants averaged $3824; need-based self-help aid (loans and jobs) averaged $3501; and non-need-based athletic scholarships averaged $2271. The average financial indebtedness of the 2003 graduate was $15,743. The FAFSA and PHEAA Aid Information Request (PAIR) are required. The priority date for freshman financial aid applications for fall entry is March 15.

International Students: They must score 500 on the written TOEFL.

Computers: The mainframes are a Unisys 2200/402 and a Unisys U6000 UNIX System. Terminal direct attachment to the mainframe system is provided in several campus labs for use in instruction and research. Students can access the system through a modem over Ethernet lines. Students may access the system on a selected-service basis. There are no time limits and no fees.

Graduates: From July 1, 2002 to June 30, 2003, 1386 bachelor's degrees were awarded. The most popular majors were elementary education (10%), management (9%), and psychology (5%). In an average class, 36% graduate in 4 years or less, 59% graduate in 5 years or less, and 61% graduate in 6 years or less. Of the 2002 graduating class, 15% were enrolled in graduate school within 6 months of graduation and 89% were employed.

Admissions Contact: Christopher Keller, Director of Admissions. E-mail: *buadmiss@bloomu.edu* Web: *www.bloomu.edu/admissions/*

BRYN ATHYN COLLEGE OF THE NEW CHURCH   F-3

Bryn Athyn, PA 19009   **(215) 938-2511; Fax: (215) 938-2658**

Full-time: 54 men, 66 women	Faculty: 15
Part-time: 7 men, 6 women	Ph.D.s: 80%
Graduate: 3 men, 9 women	Student/Faculty: 8 to 1
Year: trimesters	Tuition: $7656
Application Deadline: February 1	Room & Board: $4956
Freshman Class: 53 applied, 52 accepted, 49 enrolled	
SAT I Verbal/Math: 580/560	NONCOMPETITIVE

Bryn Athyn College of the New Church, founded in 1877, is a private independent liberal arts institution affiliated with the General Church of the New Jerusalem. There is 1 graduate school. The 2 libraries contain 102,713 volumes, 3084 microform items, and 590 audio/video tapes/CDs, and subscribe to 159 periodicals. Computerized library services include the card catalog, interlibrary loans, database searching, and Internet access. Special learning facilities include a museum, performing arts center, and archives. The 130-acre campus is in a suburban area 15 miles northeast of Philadelphia. Including any residence halls, there are 13 buildings.

Student Life: 53% of undergraduates are from Pennsylvania. Students are from 17 states, 10 foreign countries, and Canada. 23% are from public schools. 72% are white; 23% foreign nationals. 93% are of the General Church of the New Jerusalem. The average age of freshmen is 19; all undergraduates, 21. 35% do not continue beyond their first year; 29% remain to graduate.

Housing: 91 students can be accommodated in college housing, which includes single-sex dorms and off-campus apartments. On-campus housing is guaranteed for all 4 years. 69% of students live on campus; of those, all remain on campus on weekends. Alcohol is not permitted. All students may keep cars.

Activities: There are no fraternities or sororities. There are 10 groups on campus, including art, business, chorale, drama, international, newspaper, outing, social, social service, and student government. Popular campus events include Charter Day, service day, and alumni weekend.

Sports: There are 5 intercollegiate sports for men and 4 for women. Facilities include a 500-seat gym, an outdoor skating rink, tennis courts, 2 athletic fields, a fitness center, and a dance studio.

Disabled Students: 65% of the campus is accessible. Wheelchair ramps, elevators, special parking, and specially equipped rest rooms are available.

Services: Counseling and information services are available, as is tutoring in most subjects.

Campus Safety and Security: Measures include informal discussions, emergency telephones, lighted pathways/sidewalks, and an 18-hour foot and vehicle patrol.

Programs of Study: Bryn Athyn College confers B.A. and B.S. degrees. Associate and master's degrees are also awarded. Bachelor's degrees are awarded in BIOLOGICAL SCIENCE (biology/biological science), COMMUNICATIONS AND THE ARTS (English), EDUCATION (education), SOCIAL SCIENCE (history, interdisciplinary studies, and religion). Interdisciplinary studies, history, and biology/biological science are the largest.

Required: To graduate, students must complete a total of 136 credit hours with a minimum GPA of 1.9. All students must take required courses in religion, English composition, introduction to literature, and philosophy. Some majors require a comprehensive exam or thesis.

Special: Cross-registration is available with Holy Family College. Also available are co-op interdisciplinary programs, internships, a general studies degree, student-designed majors, nondegree study, and study abroad in Scotland and England in association with Beaver College.

Faculty/Classroom: 52% of faculty are male; 48%, female. 92% teach undergraduates and 8% both teach and do research. No introductory courses are taught by graduate students. The average class size in an introductory lecture is 10; in a laboratory, 10; and in a regular course, 8.

Admissions: 98% of the 2003-2004 applicants were accepted. The SAT I scores for the 2003-2004 freshman class were: Verbal--24% below 500, 31% between 500 and 599, 31% between 600 and 700, and 13% above 700; Math--17% below 500, 52% between 500 and 599, 24% between 600 and 700, and 7% above 700. There were 3 National Merit semifinalists.

Requirements: The SAT I or ACT is required with a minimum SAT I score of 920 or ACT score of 19. Applicants must be graduates of an accredited secondary school or achieve satisfactory scores on the GED. An interview is recommended. A GPA of 2.2 is required. AP and CLEP credits are accepted. Important factors in the admissions decision are recommendations by school officials, personality/intangible qualities, and advanced placement or honor courses.

Procedure: Freshmen are admitted to all sessions. Entrance exams should be taken by fall of senior year. There is a rolling admissions plan. Applications should be filed by February 1 for fall entry, October 15 for winter entry, and January 1 for spring entry, along with a $30 fee. Notification is sent on a rolling basis. Applications are accepted on-line through the college's web site.

Transfer: 3 transfer students enrolled in a recent year. Transfer students must supply SAT I or ACT scores, transcripts, course descriptions, and teacher, adviser, and employer recommendations. An interview is recommended. 68 of 136 credits required for the bachelor's degree must be completed at Bryn Athyn College.

Visiting: There are regularly scheduled orientations for prospective students, consisting of campus tours, chapel attendance, and visiting classes. There are guides for informal visits and visitors may sit in on classes and stay overnight. To schedule a visit, contact Dee Smith-Johns at *dsjohns@newchurch.edu*.

Financial Aid: In a recent year, 39% of all full-time freshmen and 40% of continuing full-time students received some form of financial aid. 39% of full-time freshmen received need-based aid. The average freshman award was $4382. 27% of undergraduates work part time. Average annual earnings from campus work are $1100. The college's own financial statement is required. The deadline for filing freshman financial aid applications for fall entry is June 1.

International Students: There are 27 international students enrolled. They must score 520 on the written TOEFL or 190 on the electronic version and also take the SAT I or the ACT, scoring 920 (SAT I) or 19 (ACT).

Computers: The mainframe is a Novell network with Compaq servers. The school provides 32 PCs for academic use in 2 computer labs. All academic buildings and residence halls have access to the network. All students may access the system 8 A.M. to 1 A.M. There are no time limits and no fees.

Graduates: From July 1, 2002 to June 30, 2003, 23 bachelor's degrees were awarded. The most popular majors were interdisciplinary studies (43%), English (22%), and education (17%).

Admissions Contact: Dee Smith-Johns, Director of Admissions. A video is available. E-mail: *dsjohns@newchurch.edu* Web: *www.newchurch.edu/college* or *www.brynathyncollege.org*

BRYN MAWR COLLEGE
Bryn Mawr, PA 19010-2899

F-3

(610) 526-5152
(800) 262-1885; Fax: (610) 526-7471

Full-time: 25 men, 1259 women
Part-time: 50 women
Graduate: 81 men, 366 women
Year: semesters, summer session
Application Deadline: January 15
Freshman Class: 1748 applied, 899 accepted, 352 enrolled
SAT I Verbal/Math: 670/630

Faculty: 146; IIA, ++$
Ph.D.s: 97%
Student/Faculty: 9 to 1
Tuition: $27,520
Room & Board: $9370

HIGHLY COMPETITIVE+

Bryn Mawr College, founded in 1885, is an independent liberal arts institution, primarily for women. The undergraduate college is for women only. The two graduate schools and postbaccalaureate program are co-educational. The 4 libraries contain 1,125,116 volumes, 157,521 microform items, and 4008 audio/video tapes/CDs, and subscribe to 1859 periodicals. Computerized library services include the card catalog, interlibrary loans, database searching, and Internet access. Special learning facilities include a learning resource center, art gallery, radio station, an archeological museum, and a language learning center with audio, video, and computer technology. The 135-acre campus is in a suburban area 11 miles west of Philadelphia. Including any residence halls, there are 57 buildings.

Student Life: 80% of undergraduates are from out of state, mostly the Middle Atlantic. Students are from 47 states, 44 foreign countries, and Canada. 62% are from public schools. 50% are white; 12% Asian American. The average age of freshmen is 18; all undergraduates, 20. 3% do not continue beyond their first year; 85% remain to graduate.

Housing: 1218 students can be accommodated in college housing, which includes single-sex and coed dorms and off-campus apartments. In addition, there are language houses, special-interest houses, an African American culture center that houses several students, and a co-op house. On-campus housing is guaranteed for all 4 years. 95% of students live on campus; of those, 85% remain on campus on weekends. Alcohol is not permitted. Upperclassmen may keep cars.

Activities: There are no fraternities. There are 100 groups on campus, including art, chess, choir, chorale, chorus, computers, dance, drama, environmental, ethnic, film, gay, honors, international, literary magazine, musical theater, newspaper, orchestra, photography, political, professional, radio and TV, religious, science fiction, social, social service, student government, and yearbook. Popular campus events include May Day, Lantern Night, and Fall Frolic.

Sports: Facilities include 3 playing fields with access to an indoor track, a gym with an 8-lane pool and diving well, basketball, badminton, and volleyball courts, a gymnastics room and dance studio, a weight-training and fitness room, a 1000-seat auditorium, and a student center.

Disabled Students: Wheelchair ramps, elevators, special parking, specially equipped rest rooms, special class scheduling, lowered drinking fountains, lowered telephones, and special housing are available.

Services: Counseling and information services are available, as is tutoring in every subject. There is a reader service for the blind.

Campus Safety and Security: Measures include 24-hour foot and vehicle patrol, self-defense education, security escort services, and shuttle buses. There are informal discussions, pamphlets/posters/films, emergency telephones, lighted pathways/sidewalks, a web page, and bicycle registration.

Programs of Study: Bryn Mawr confers the A.B. degree. Master's and doctoral degrees are also awarded. Bachelor's degrees are awarded in BIOLOGICAL SCIENCE (biology/biological science), COMMUNICATIONS AND THE ARTS (art history and appreciation, classical languages, classics, comparative literature, English, fine arts, French, German, Greek, Italian, Latin, music, romance languages and literature, Russian, and Spanish), COMPUTER AND PHYSICAL SCIENCE (astronomy, chemistry, geology, mathematics, and physics), SOCIAL SCIENCE (anthropology, archeology, East Asian studies, economics, history, philosophy, political science/government, psychology, religion, sociology, and urban studies). Growth and structure of cities, classical and Near Eastern archeology, and physics are the strongest academically. English, math, and biology are the largest.

Required: To graduate, students must complete 128 semester hours, with 40 to 60 in the major and a minimum GPA of 2.0. All students must complete 2 courses each in the social sciences, the humanities, and natural sciences or math, including 1 lab science. Additional required courses include 2 college seminars and 1 quantitative skills course. Students must be able to demonstrate proficiency in 1 foreign language.

Special: Students may cross-register with Haverford and Swarthmore colleges and the University of Pennsylvania. Internships are available in the cities, sociology, education, and science programs through the Career Development Office. Bryn Mawr sponsors and cosponsors study abroad in 27 countries. Student-designed and dual majors are possible. Pass/fail options, work-study programs, and 3-2 degrees in engineering and city and regional planning with the University of Pennsylvania are offered.

Faculty/Classroom: 50% of faculty are male; 50%, female. All both teach and do research. No introductory courses are taught by graduate students. The average class size in an introductory lecture is 25; in a laboratory, 15; and in a regular course, 16.

Admissions: 51% of the 2003-2004 applicants were accepted. The SAT I scores for the 2003-2004 freshman class were: Verbal--2% below 500, 16% between 500 and 599, 44% between 600 and 700, and 38% above 700; Math--1% below 500, 31% between 500 and 599, 53% between 600 and 700, and 15% above 700. 84% of the current freshmen were in the top fifth of their class; 99% were in the top two fifths.

Requirements: The SAT I is required, but the ACT may be substituted. SAT II: Subject tests in writing and 2 other areas are required. Applicants must be graduates of an accredited secondary school. The GED is accepted. Applicants should complete 4 years of English, at least 3 years of foreign language, 3 years of math, and 1 year each of science and history. An essay is required. An interview is strongly recommended. AP credits are accepted. Important factors in the admissions decision are advanced placement or honors courses, evidence of special talent, and extracurricular activities record.

Procedure: Freshmen are admitted in the fall. Entrance exams should be taken in the spring of the junior year or the fall of the senior year. There are early decision and deferred admissions plans. Early decision applications should be filed by November 15; regular applications, by January 15 for fall entry, along with a $50 fee. Notification of early decision is sent December 15; regular decision, March 20. 78 early decision candidates were accepted for the 2003-2004 class. 176 applicants were on the 2003 waiting list; 1 was admitted. Applications are accepted on computer disk and on-line through Common App and Embark.com.

Transfer: 14 transfer students enrolled in a recent year. Applicants for transfer must have a minimum college GPA of 3.0. The SAT I and recommendations from both college and high school are required. 96 of 128 credits required for the bachelor's degree must be completed at Bryn Mawr.

Visiting: There are regularly scheduled orientations for prospective students, including student-guided campus tours. Interviews can be arranged. There are guides for informal visits and visitors may sit in on classes and stay overnight. To schedule a visit, contact the Office of Admissions at admissions@brynmawr.edu.

Financial Aid: In 2003-2004, 59% of all full-time freshmen and 62% of continuing full-time students received some form of financial aid. 58% of full-time freshmen and 56% of continuing full-time students received need-based aid. The average freshman award was $24,500. Need-based scholarships or need-based grants averaged $21,413; and need-based self-help aid (loans and jobs) averaged $5721. 75% of undergraduates work part time. Average annual earnings from campus work are $1500. The average financial indebtedness of the 2003 graduate was $17,827. Bryn Mawr is a member of CSS. The CSS Profile or FAFSA and the prior year's tax returns, the noncustodial parent statement, and the business/farm supplement are required. The deadline for filing freshman financial aid applications for fall entry is February 2.

International Students: There are 100 international students enrolled. The school actively recruits these students. They must score 600 on the written TOEFL or 250 on the electronic version and also take the SAT I or the ACT.

Computers: The mainframes consist of HP, Sun, and UNIX systems. More than 270 computers are available for student use, including more than 100 in science and math labs and 10 loaner laptops. All dorm rooms are networked, and all students have e-mail accounts and Internet access. All students may access the system every day. There are no time limits and no fees.

Graduates: From July 1, 2002 to June 30, 2003, 304 bachelor's degrees were awarded. The most popular majors were political science (12%), English (11%), and biology (9%). In an average class, 2% graduate in 3 years or less, 78% graduate in 4 years or less, 84% graduate in 5 years or less, and 85% graduate in 6 years or less. 175 companies recruited on campus in 2002-2003. Of the 2002 graduating class, 20% were enrolled in graduate school within 6 months of graduation and 64% were employed.

Admissions Contact: Jennifer Rickard, Dean of Admissions and Financial Aid. A video is available. E-mail: admissions@brynmawr.edu Web: http://www.brynmawr.edu

BUCKNELL UNIVERSITY
Lewisburg, PA 17837

D-2

(570) 577-1101; Fax: (570) 577-3760

Full-time: 1712 men, 1736 women
Part-time: 18 men, 19 women
Graduate: 79 men, 113 women
Year: semesters, summer session
Application Deadline: January 1
Freshman Class: 7706 applied, 2961 accepted, 906 enrolled
SAT I Verbal/Math: 640/670

Faculty: 291; IIA, ++$
Ph.D.s: 95%
Student/Faculty: 12 to 1
Tuition: $28,960
Room & Board: $6302

HIGHLY COMPETITIVE+

Bucknell University, established in 1846, is a private independent institution offering undergraduate and graduate programs in arts, music, education, humanities, management, engineering, sciences, and social sciences. There are 2 undergraduate schools and 1 graduate school. In addition to regional accreditation, Bucknell has baccalaureate program accreditation with ABET, ACS, CSAB, and NASM. The library contains 782,936 volumes, 63 microform items, and 16,496 audio/video tapes/CDs, and subscribes to 6059 periodicals. Computerized library services include the card catalog, interlibrary loans, and database searching. Special learning facilities include an art gallery, radio station, outdoor natural area, greenhouse, primate facility, observatory, photography lab, race and gender resource center, library resources training lab, electronic classroom, multimedia lab, conference center, performing arts center, and multicultural, writing, craft, and poetry centers, herbarium, and engineering structural test lab. The 396-acre campus is in a small town 75 miles north of Harrisburg. Including any residence halls, there are 113 buildings.

Student Life: 70% of undergraduates are from out of state, mostly the Middle Atlantic. Students are from 48 states, 46 foreign countries, and Canada. 85% are white. 30% are Catholic; 29% claim no religious affiliation; 26% Protestant; 6% Jewish. The average age of freshmen is 18; all undergraduates, 20. 6% do not continue beyond their first year; 86% remain to graduate.

Housing: 2639 students can be accommodated in college housing, which includes single-sex and coed dorms, on-campus apartments, and fraternity houses. In addition, there are special-interest houses and 6 residential colleges for the first year (arts, environmental, humanities, global, science and technology, and social justice). On-campus housing is guaranteed for all 4 years. 89% of students live on campus; of those, 85% remain on campus on weekends. Upperclassmen may keep cars.

Activities: 38% of men belong to 11 national fraternities; 38% of women belong to 8 national sororities. There are 135 groups on campus, including art, band, cheerleading, chess, choir, chorale, chorus, dance, drama, ethnic, film, gay, honors, international, jazz band, literary magazine, newspaper, opera, orchestra, pep band, photography, political, professional, radio, religious, social, social service, student government, symphony, and yearbook. Popular campus events include Celebration for the Arts, Parents Weekend, and Spring Greek Weekend.

Sports: There are 12 intercollegiate sports for men and 14 for women, and 18 intramural sports for men and 18 for women. Facilities include an athletic and recreation center with an Olympic-size pool, 16,000-sq. foot fitness center; a 4000-seat basketball arena, a 13,000-seat stadium with 8-lane track; hockey and lacrosse fields, baseball fields, and recreational fields for soccer, softball, and other activities; a field house with a 4-lane track, tennis, squash, and racquetball courts, climbing wall, and dance studio; an 18-hole golf course, and tennnis courts.

Disabled Students: 70% of the campus is accessible. Wheelchair ramps, elevators, special parking, specially equipped rest rooms, lowered drinking fountains, and lowered telephones are available. Individual arrangements may be made with faculty for students with disabilities.

Services: Counseling and information services are available, as is tutoring in some subjects, including biology, chemistry, physics, math, and writing across the curriculum.

Campus Safety and Security: Measures include 24-hour foot and vehicle patrol, self-defense education, security escort services, and informal discussions. There are pamphlets/posters/films, emergency telephones, lighted pathways/sidewalks, campus safety alerts, and intrusion alarms in residence halls.

Programs of Study: Bucknell confers B.A., B.S., B.Mus., B.S.B.A., B.S.B.E., B.S.C.E., B.S.Ch.E., B.S.C.S.E., B.S.Ed., B.S.E.E., and B.S.M.E. degrees. Master's degrees are also awarded. Bachelor's degrees are awarded in BIOLOGICAL SCIENCE (biochemistry, biology/biological science, and cell biology), BUSINESS (accounting and business administration and management), COMMUNICATIONS AND THE ARTS (art, art history and appreciation, classics, dramatic arts, English, fine arts, French, German, music, music history and appreciation, music performance, music theory and composition, Russian, and Spanish), COMPUTER AND PHYSICAL SCIENCE (chemistry, computer science, geology, mathematics, and physics), EDUCATION (early childhood, education, educational statistics and research, elementary, music, and secondary), ENGINEERING AND ENVIRONMENTAL DESIGN (biomedical engineering, chemical engineering, civil engineering, computer engineering, electrical/electronics engineering, engineering, environmental science, and mechanical engineering), SOCIAL SCIENCE (anthropology, East Asian studies, economics, geography, history, humanities, interdisciplinary studies, international relations, Latin American studies, philosophy, political science/government, psychology, religion, sociology, and women's studies). Humanities, biology, and English are the strongest academically. Biology, management, and economics are the largest.

Required: All students enrolled in the College of Arts and Sciences must complete a foundation seminar during the first semester; distribution selections include 4 courses in humanities, 3 in natural science and math, 2 in social science, 2 in broadened perspectives for the 21st century addressing issues of the natural and fabricated worlds and issues in human diversity, and a capstone seminar or experience during the senior year.

In addition, Bucknell requires a minimum writing competency for graduation. All students enrolled in the College of Engineering have a common first semester and must complete Exploring Engineering (EG 100). A total of 32 courses (34 courses for engineering) and a minimum GPA of 2.0 are required to graduate.

Special: Bucknell offers internships, study abroad in more than 60 countries, a Washington semester, a 5-year B.A.-B.S. degree in arts and engineering, a 3-2 engineering degree, and dual and student-designed majors. An interdisciplinary major in animal behavior is offered through the biology and psychology departments. Nondegree study is possible, and a pass/fail grading option is offered in some courses. The Residential College program offers opportunities for an academic-residential mix and faculty-student collaborative learning. Undergraduate research opportunities are available in the humanities/social sciences and the sciences and engineering. There are 23 national honor societies, including Phi Beta Kappa.

Faculty/Classroom: 65% of faculty are male; 35%, female. All teach undergraduates and do research. No introductory courses are taught by graduate students. The average class size in an introductory lecture is 24; in a laboratory, 17; and in a regular course, 21.

Admissions: 38% of the 2003-2004 applicants were accepted. The SAT I scores for the 2003-2004 freshman class were: Verbal--1% below 500, 22% between 500 and 599, 62% between 600 and 700, and 15% above 700; Math--12% between 500 and 599, 59% between 600 and 700, and 29% above 700. 89% of the current freshmen were in the top fifth of their class; 98% were in the top two fifths.

Requirements: The SAT I is required. In addition, applicants must graduate from an accredited secondary school or have a GED. 16 units must be earned, including 4 in English, 3 in math, and 2 each in history, science, social studies, and a foreign language. An essay is required, and an interview is recommended. Music applicants are required to audition. A portfolio is recommended for art applicants. A GPA of 2.5 is required. AP credits are accepted. Important factors in the admissions decision are advanced placement or honor courses, recommendations by school officials, and evidence of special talent.

Procedure: Freshmen are admitted in the fall. Entrance exams should be taken before January 1. There are early decision and deferred admissions plans. Early decision applications should be filed by November 15; regular applications, by January 1 for fall entry. The fall 2003 application fee was $60. Notification of early decision is sent December 15; regular decision, April 1. 323 early decision candidates were accepted for the 2003-2004 class. 688 applicants were on the 2003 waiting list; 46 were admitted. Applications are accepted on-line through CollegeNET.

Transfer: 30 transfer students enrolled in 2002-2003. Transfer students must have a minimum GPA of 2.5 in courses comparable to those offered at Bucknell. The SAT I or ACT is required. A minimum of 16 credit hours must have been earned; 32 are recommended. Students are accepted on a space-available basis. An interview is recommended. 48 of 128 credits required for the bachelor's degree must be completed at Bucknell.

Visiting: There are regularly scheduled orientations for prospective students, including an open house for admitted students on the middle Saturday in April and fall visitation program for minority students, and open houses for prospective students in September and November. There are guides for informal visits and visitors may sit in on classes and stay overnight. To schedule a visit, contact the Admissions Office at admissions@bucknell.edu.

Financial Aid: In 2003-2004, 49% of all full-time freshmen and 52% of continuing full-time students received some form of financial aid. 49% of full-time freshmen and 56% of continuing full-time students received need-based aid. The average freshman award was $20,200. 47% of undergraduates work part time. Average annual earnings from campus work are $1500. The average financial indebtedness of the 2003 graduate was $16,500. Bucknell is a member of CSS. The CSS Profile or FAFSA, noncustodial parent's statement, and business/farm supplement are required. The deadline for filing freshman financial aid applications for fall entry is January 1.

International Students: There are 74 international students enrolled. The school actively recruits these students. They must score 550 on the written TOEFL or 213 on the electronic version.

Computers: More than 620 PCs with network access are available in labs, classrooms, the library, lounges, collaborative work spaces, and student housing. All students have free unlimited access to network resources and the Internet. All students may access the system 24 hours per day, 7 days per week. There are no time limits and no fees. It is strongly recommended that all students have a personal computer.

Graduates: From July 1, 2002 to June 30, 2003, 850 bachelor's degrees were awarded. The most popular majors were management (16%), economics (13%), and English (8%). In an average class, 84% graduate in 4 years or less, 89% graduate in 5 years or less, and 89% graduate in 6 years or less. 256 companies recruited on campus in 2002-2003. Of the 2002 graduating class, 21% were enrolled in graduate school within 6 months of graduation and 65% were employed.

Admissions Contact: Mark D. Davies, Director of Admissions. A video is available. E-mail: *admissions@bucknell.edu* Web: *http://www.bucknell.edu*

CABRINI COLLEGE
Radnor, PA 19087-3698
F-4

(610) 902-8552
(800) 848-1003; Fax: (610) 902-8508

Full-time: 510 men, 921 women	**Faculty:** 60; IIB, -$
Part-time: 111 men, 173 women	**Ph.D.s:** 75%
Graduate: 137 men, 351 women	**Student/Faculty:** 24 to 1
Year: semesters, summer session	**Tuition:** $20,470
Application Deadline: open	**Room & Board:** $8550
Freshman Class: 2302 applied, 1910 accepted, 407 enrolled	
SAT I Verbal/Math: 490/480	**COMPETITIVE**

Cabrini College, founded in 1957, is a private liberal arts institution affiliated with the Roman Catholic Church and founded by the Missionary Sisters of the Sacred Heart. The college is known for its service learning emphasis. In addition to regional accreditation, Cabrini has baccalaureate program accreditation with CSWE. The library contains 213,883 volumes, 118,585 microform items, and 1255 audio/video tapes/CDs, and subscribes to 465 periodicals. Computerized library services include the card catalog, interlibrary loans, database searching, and Internet access. Special learning facilities include a learning resource center, art gallery, radio station, and a communications lab with a TV studio. The 112-acre campus is in a suburban area 20 miles west of Philadelphia. Including any residence halls, there are 22 buildings.

Student Life: 67% of undergraduates are from Pennsylvania. Students are from 20 states, 30 foreign countries, and Canada. 48% are from public schools. 82% are white. 70% are Catholic; 19% Jewish; 13% Protestant; 7% claim no religious affiliation. The average age of freshmen is 18; all undergraduates, 23. 25% do not continue beyond their first year; 60% remain to graduate.

Housing: 938 students can be accommodated in college housing, which includes single-sex and coed dorms, on-campus apartments, and off-campus apartments. In addition, there are honors houses, language houses, and special-interest houses. On-campus housing is available on a first-come, first-served basis and is available on a lottery system for upperclassmen. Priority is given to out-of-town students. 66% of students live on campus; of those, 60% remain on campus on weekends. Upperclassmen may keep cars.

Activities: There are no fraternities or sororities. There are 27 groups on campus, including cheerleading, chess, choir, chorus, computers, dance, drama, ethnic, honors, international, literary magazine, musical theater, newspaper, photography, political, professional, radio and TV, religious, social, social service, student government, and yearbook. Popular campus events include Cabrini Day, Yule Log, and Superthon.

Sports: There are 7 intercollegiate sports for men and 9 for women, and 12 intramural sports for men and 12 for women. Facilities include a weight room, athletic fields, a 1500-seat gym, tennis courts, an Olympic-size pool, an indoor jogging track, squash courts, and an aerobic dance studio.

Disabled Students: 90% of the campus is accessible. Wheelchair ramps, elevators, special parking, specially equipped rest rooms, special class scheduling, lowered drinking fountains, and lowered telephones. Accommodations are made on an individual basis, with appropriate documentation.

Services: Counseling and information services are available, as is tutoring in most subjects. There is a reader service for the blind. Students may enroll in a study skills course or utilize individual tutoring to acquire learning skills.

Campus Safety and Security: Measures include 24-hour foot and vehicle patrol, self-defense education, security escort services, and shuttle buses. There are informal discussions, pamphlets/posters/films, emergency telephones, and lighted pathways/sidewalks.

Programs of Study: Cabrini confers B.A., B.S., B.S.Ed., and B.S.W. degrees. Master's degrees are also awarded. Bachelor's degrees are awarded in BIOLOGICAL SCIENCE (biology/biological science and biotechnology), BUSINESS (accounting, banking and finance, business administration and management, human resources, and marketing/retailing/merchandising), COMMUNICATIONS AND THE ARTS (communications, English, French, graphic design, Spanish, and visual and performing arts), COMPUTER AND PHYSICAL SCIENCE (chemistry, information sciences and systems, mathematics, and web technology), EDUCATION (early childhood, education, elementary, and special), HEALTH PROFESSIONS (medical laboratory technology and sports medicine), SOCIAL SCIENCE (American studies, criminal justice, history, liberal arts/general studies, philosophy, political science/government, psychology, religion, social work, and sociology). Education and English and communication are the strongest academically. Business, education, and English and communication are the largest.

Required: To graduate, students must complete a minimum of 123 credits with a minimum GPA of 2.0. All students must complete a core curriculum, which includes English, math, foreign language, computers,

an interdisciplinary seminar in self-understanding, and a junior seminar exploring the common good. Distribution requirements cover science, heritage, cultural diversity, values, the individual and society, contemporary issues, creativity, and religious studies. A thesis is required in some majors, a community service project is part of the junior seminar, and senior capstone seminar courses are required in many majors.

Special: Cabrini offers cooperative programs, internships, study abroad, work-study programs, and cross-registration with Eastern, Rosemont, and Valley Forge Colleges and other SEPCHE colleges and universities. B.A.-B.S. degrees, dual majors and minors, a liberal arts degree, and student-designed majors are available, as well as an accelerated interdisciplinary degree program in organizational management. Credit by examination, credit for life/military/work experience, nondegree study, and pass/fail options are also offered. There are 15 national honor societies, a freshman honors program, and 11 departmental honors programs.

Faculty/Classroom: 45% of faculty are male; 55%, female. 86% teach undergraduates and 45% both teach and do research. No introductory courses are taught by graduate students. The average class size in an introductory lecture is 19; in a laboratory, 10; and in a regular course, 18.

Admissions: 83% of the 2003-2004 applicants were accepted. The SAT I scores for the 2003-2004 freshman class were: Verbal--53% below 500, 39% between 500 and 599, 7% between 600 and 700, and 1% above 700; Math--59% below 500, 34% between 500 and 599, 6% between 600 and 700, and 1% above 700. 20% of the current freshmen were in the top fifth of their class; 42% were in the top two fifths.

Requirements: The SAT I is required, with a minimum composite score of 1000 (500 each on the verbal and math) recommended. All students must be graduates of an accredited secondary school or have a GED. A minimum of 17 Carnegie units are required, consisting of 4 in English, 3 each in math, science, and social studies, 2 in a foreign language, and the rest in electives. An interview is recommended. A GPA of 2.0 is required. AP and CLEP credits are accepted. Important factors in the admissions decision are advanced placement or honor courses, extracurricular activities record, and leadership record.

Procedure: Freshmen are admitted to all sessions. Entrance exams should be taken before December of the senior year. There are early admissions, deferred admissions, and rolling admissions plans. Application deadlines are open. The fall 2003 application fee was $25. Applications are accepted on-line through CollegeNET, linked from Cabrini's web site.

Transfer: 77 transfer students enrolled in 2002-2003. A minimum of 15 credit hours with at least a GPA of 2.2 overall is required; a 2.5 GPA is preferred. Some programs may have higher requirements. 45 of 123 credits required for the bachelor's degree must be completed at Cabrini.

Visiting: There are regularly scheduled orientations for prospective students, consisting of summer preview programs during which students register for classes. Fall and spring orientations are held 2 to 3 days before classes begin. There are guides for informal visits and visitors may sit in on classes and stay overnight. To schedule a visit, contact the Admissions Office.

Financial Aid: In 2003-2004, 96% of all full-time freshmen and 95% of continuing full-time students received some form of financial aid. 93% of full-time freshmen and 92% of continuing full-time students received need-based aid. The average freshman award was $14,785. Need-based scholarships or need-based grants averaged $8821 ($12,300 maximum); need-based self-help aid (loans and jobs) averaged $3290 ($4625 maximum); and non-need-based awards and non-need-based scholarships averaged $6586 ($20,470 maximum). 15% of undergraduates work part time. Average annual earnings from campus work are $765. The average financial indebtedness of the 2003 graduate was $17,500. The FAFSA is required.

International Students: There are 11 international students enrolled. The school actively recruits these students. They must score 500 on the written TOEFL and also take or successfully complete ESL if not from an English-speaking country. They must also take the SAT I or ACT, but it is optional for students whose native language is not English.

Computers: The mainframes are a SUN server and an Oracle database. There are approximately 150 networked PCs in the main classsroom building with other PCs located in the library and residence halls. All students may access the system 24 hours a day, 7 days a week. There are no time limits and no fees. It is strongly recommended that all students have a personal computer. A Celeron at 600MHz or a 1-GHz or faster PowerMac G4, Dell, Gateway, or Apple is recommended.

Graduates: From July 1, 2002 to June 30, 2003, 273 bachelor's degrees were awarded. The most popular majors were elementary education (13%), English and communication (12%), and psychology (6%). In an average class, 1% graduate in 3 years or less, 53% graduate in 4 years or less, 58% graduate in 5 years or less, and 61% graduate in 6 years or less. 85 companies recruited on campus in 2002-2003. Of the 2002 graduating class, 20% were enrolled in graduate school within 6 months of graduation and 90% were employed.

Admissions Contact: Gary Johnson, Dean of Enrollment.
E-mail: *admit@cabrini.edu* Web: *http://www.cabrini.edu*

CALIFORNIA UNIVERSITY OF PENNSYLVANIA
California, PA 15419-1394

B-3
(724) 938-4404; Fax: (724) 938-4564

Full-time: 2140 men, 2280 women
Part-time: 420 men, 245 women
Graduate: 310 men, 565 women
Year: semesters, summer session
Application Deadline: open
Freshman Class: n/av
SAT I: required

Faculty: 266; IIA, +$
Ph.D.s: 55%
Student/Faculty: 17 to 1
Tuition: $5205 ($11,590)
Room & Board: $5135

COMPETITIVE

California University of Pennsylvania, founded in 1852, is a state-supported institution offering degree programs in the arts and sciences, engineering, and education. There are 3 undergraduate schools and 1 graduate school. Figures in the above capsule and in this profile are approximate. In addition to regional accreditation, the university has baccalaureate program accreditation with CSWE, NCATE, and NLN. The library contains 431,300 volumes, 830,727 microform items, and 60,416 audio/video tapes/CDs, and subscribes to 9314 periodicals. Computerized library services include the card catalog, interlibrary loans, and database searching. Special learning facilities include a learning resource center, art gallery, natural history museum, radio station, and TV station. The 148-acre campus is in a small town 35 miles south of Pittsburgh. Including any residence halls, there are 38 buildings.

Student Life: 95% of undergraduates are from Pennsylvania. Students are from 21 states, 10 foreign countries, and Canada. 95% are from public schools. 94% are white. The average age of freshmen is 19; all undergraduates, 23. 26% do not continue beyond their first year; 47% remain to graduate.

Housing: 1450 students can be accommodated in college housing, which includes single-sex and coed dorms and off-campus apartments. On-campus housing is available on a first-come, first-served basis. 74% of students commute. Alcohol is not permitted. All students may keep cars.

Activities: 10% of men belong to 13 national fraternities; 6% of women belong to 9 national sororities. There are 19 groups on campus, including art, band, cheerleading, chess, choir, chorale, chorus, computers, dance, debate, drama, drill team, ethnic, forensics, honors, international, jazz band, literary magazine, marching band, musical theater, newspaper, pep band, professional, radio and TV, religious, student government, and yearbook.

Sports: There are 6 intercollegiate sports for men and 7 for women, and 20 intramural sports for men and 2 for women. Facilities include tennis and basketball courts, an all-weather track, a swimming pool, and a 4500-seat stadium.

Disabled Students: 95% of the campus is accessible. Wheelchair ramps, elevators, special parking, specially equipped rest rooms, special class scheduling, lowered drinking fountains, and lowered telephones are available.

Services: Counseling and information services are available, as is tutoring in most subjects. There is a reader service for the blind and remedial math, reading, and writing.

Campus Safety and Security: Measures include 24-hour foot and vehicle patrol, self-defense education, security escort services, and shuttle buses. There are informal discussions, pamphlets/posters/films, and lighted pathways/sidewalks.

Programs of Study: the university confers B.A., B.S., B.S.Ed., and B.S.N. degrees. Associate and master's degrees are also awarded. Bachelor's degrees are awarded in BIOLOGICAL SCIENCE (biology/biological science), BUSINESS (business administration and management), COMMUNICATIONS AND THE ARTS (art, communications, dramatic arts, English, French, German, and Spanish), COMPUTER AND PHYSICAL SCIENCE (chemistry, computer programming, computer science, earth science, geology, mathematics, and physics), EDUCATION (athletic training, early childhood, education of the mentally handicapped, education of the physically handicapped, elementary, English, foreign languages, industrial arts, mathematics, science, secondary, social studies, and special), ENGINEERING AND ENVIRONMENTAL DESIGN (electrical/electronics engineering technology, environmental science, graphic arts technology, industrial administration/management, and manufacturing technology), HEALTH PROFESSIONS (medical laboratory technology, nursing, predentistry, premedicine, and speech pathology/audiology), SOCIAL SCIENCE (anthropology, economics, geography, gerontology, history, humanities, industrial and organizational psychology, international studies, parks and recreation management, philosophy, political science/government, psychology, social science, social work, and sociology).

Required: Students must complete a minimum of 128 semester credits and must maintain a minimum GPA of 2.5 in teacher education curricula, 2.3 in the student's area of concentration, and 2.0 overall.

Special: Cooperative programs are available with Pennsylvania State University and the University of Pittsburgh. Opportunities are provided for internships, study abroad, work-study programs, a B.A.-B.S. degree, a general studies degree, a 3-2 engineering degree, credit by exam, non-degree study, and pass/fail options. There is also an accelerated degree

program in justice studies. There are 3 national honor societies and a freshman honors program.

Faculty/Classroom: 76% of faculty are male; 24%, female. All teach undergraduates. No introductory courses are taught by graduate students. The average class size in an introductory lecture is 35; in a laboratory, 24; and in a regular course, 26.

Requirements: The SAT I is required, with a minimum composite score of 800 (400 verbal, 400 math); the ACT may be substituted, with a minimum score of 20. Graduation from an accredited secondary school is required; a GED will be accepted. Applicants should submit an academic record that includes 4 credits each in English and history, 3 each in math and academic electives, 2 in science, and 1 each in social studies and a foreign language. An essay and an interview are recommended. The university requires applicants to be in the upper 60% of their class. A GPA of 2.5 is required. AP and CLEP credits are accepted. Important factors in the admissions decision are advanced placement or honor courses, evidence of special talent, and leadership record.

Procedure: Freshmen are admitted to all sessions. Entrance exams should be taken during the senior year. There is a rolling admissions plan. Application deadlines are open. Application fee is $25.

Transfer: 499 transfer students enrolled in a recent year. Applicants must submit official transcripts from all previous colleges attended. If fewer than 30 transferable credits are submitted, applicants must also include a high school transcript and standardized test score. Grades of D are not transferable. 38 of 128 credits required for the bachelor's degree must be completed at the university.

Visiting: There are regularly scheduled orientations for prospective students. There are guides for informal visits and visitors may sit in on classes and stay overnight. To schedule a visit, contact the Admissions Office.

Financial Aid: The FAFSA, Pennsylvania State Grant, and Federal Financial Aid Application are required. Check with the school for current deadlines.

International Students: In a recent year, there were 41 international students enrolled. The school actively recruits these students. They must score 450 on the written TOEFL. The SAT I is recommended, with a minimum composite score of 800.

Computers: The mainframe is a DEC VAX 11/780. 350 terminals and PCs provide access to the mainframe. In addition, there are 700 IBM and Mac PCs on campus in various labs and offices. All students may access the system. There are no time limits and no fees.

Graduates: In a recent year, 821 bachelor's degrees were awarded. The most popular majors were education (30%), business (12%), and social sciences (7%). In an average class, 16% graduate in 4 years or less, 31% graduate in 5 years or less, and 37% graduate in 6 years or less. 62 companies recruited on campus in a recent year. Of a recent graduating class, 18% were enrolled in graduate school within 6 months of graduation and 95% were employed.

Admissions Contact: William Edmonds, Director of Admissions. A video is available. E-mail: *inquiry@cup.edu* Web: *www.cup.edu*

CARLOW COLLEGE
Pittsburgh, PA 15213

B-3
(412) 578-6059
(800) 333-CARLOW; Fax: (412) 578-6668

Full-time: 54 men, 1042 women
Part-time: 57 men, 603 women
Graduate: 38 men, 333 women
Year: semesters, summer session
Application Deadline: open
Freshman Class: 1123 applied, 644 accepted, 236 enrolled
SAT I Verbal/Math: 490/460

Faculty: 72; IIA, --$
Ph.D.s: 77%
Student/Faculty: 15 to 1
Tuition: $15,224
Room & Board: $6110

ACT: 20   COMPETITIVE

Carlow College, founded in 1929, is a private, primarily women's college affiliated with the Roman Catholic Church, offering programs in liberal and fine arts, business, health science, professional training, and teacher preparation. In addition to regional accreditation, Carlow has baccalaureate program accreditation with AACN, CCNE, and CSWE. The library contains 124,374 volumes, 11,603 microform items, and 4684 audio/video tapes/CDs, and subscribes to 381 periodicals. Computerized library services include the card catalog, interlibrary loans, database searching, and Internet access. Special learning facilities include a learning resource center, art gallery, and TV studio. The 14-acre campus is in an urban area, the Oakland section of Pittsburgh. Including any residence halls, there are 14 buildings.

Student Life: 95% of undergraduates are from Pennsylvania. Students are from 11 states, 20 foreign countries, and Canada. 83% are from public schools. 69% are white; 22% African American. 41% are Catholic; 16% Protestant; 13% claim no religious affiliation. The average age of freshmen is 18; all undergraduates, 31. 22% do not continue beyond their first year; 59% remain to graduate.

Housing: 393 students can be accommodated in college housing, which includes single-sex dorms. In addition, there are quiet floors. On-campus housing is available on a first-come, first-served basis and is available on a lottery system for upperclassmen. 85% of students commute. Alcohol is not permitted. All dorm students with documented need may keep cars.

Activities: There are no fraternities or sororities. There are 25 groups on campus, including art, choir, drama, ethnic, honors, instrumental ensembles, international, literary magazine, newspaper, philosophy, political, professional, religious, social, social service, student government, and yearbook. Popular campus events include International Fair, Spring Carnival, and Wellness Fair.

Sports: There are 5 intercollegiate sports for women. Facilities include a gym, a pool, a fitness center, and an aerobics room.

Disabled Students: 10% of the campus is accessible. Wheelchair ramps, elevators, special parking, specially equipped rest rooms, special class scheduling, lowered drinking fountains, and lowered telephones are available.

Services: Counseling and information services are available, as is tutoring in most subjects. There is remedial math, reading, and writing. Professional tutoring is available for reading, writing, study skills, math, and sciences. Peer tutoring is available in other subject areas.

Campus Safety and Security: Measures include 24-hour foot and vehicle patrol, self-defense education, security escort services, and shuttle buses. There are informal discussions, pamphlets/posters/films, emergency telephones, lighted pathways/sidewalks, and an electronically operated dorm entrance.

Programs of Study: Carlow confers B.A., B.S., B.S.N., and B.S.W. degrees. Master's degrees are also awarded. Bachelor's degrees are awarded in BIOLOGICAL SCIENCE (biology/biological science), BUSINESS (accounting, business administration and management, human resources, and international business management), COMMUNICATIONS AND THE ARTS (art, art history and appreciation, communications, creative writing, English, Spanish, and technical and business writing), COMPUTER AND PHYSICAL SCIENCE (chemistry, computer science, information sciences and systems, and mathematics), EDUCATION (art, early childhood, elementary, secondary, and special), ENGINEERING AND ENVIRONMENTAL DESIGN (computer graphics), HEALTH PROFESSIONS (art therapy, health science, and nursing), SOCIAL SCIENCE (criminal justice, history, liberal arts/general studies, philosophy, psychology, social studies, social work, sociology, and theological studies). Nursing, creative writing, and education are the strongest academically. Nursing, business management, and elementary education are the largest.

Required: A total of 120 credit hours (125 for nursing students), including 27 to 44 in the major, is required to graduate. Credits must be earned in history, literature, art or music, math or logic, theology, philosophy, psychology or sociology, biology or chemistry, and women's studies. An interdisciplinary course, a course with a peace and justice overlay, English, and communication studies are also required. A minimum GPA of 2.0 is required. All students must demonstrate competence in writing, reading comprehension, and math, and must take basic skills courses in public speaking and research paper writing. All students undergo a comprehensive evaluation in their senior year.

Special: Carlow offers cross-registration through the Pittsburgh Council for Higher Education, internships in all areas, and work-study. There are accelerated degree programs in health science and professional writing. Dual majors are possible in most majors, as are student-designed majors. There are 3-2 engineering programs with Carnegie Mellon University, as well as 2-2 and 3-3 programs in athletic training, physician assistant, physical therapy, and occupational therapy with Duquesne University. There are 4 national honor societies and a freshman honors program.

Faculty/Classroom: 34% of faculty are male; 66%, female. 93% teach undergraduates. No introductory courses are taught by graduate students. The average class size in an introductory lecture is 14; in a laboratory, 12; and in a regular course, 13.

Admissions: 57% of the 2003-2004 applicants were accepted. The SAT I scores for the 2003-2004 freshman class were: Verbal--50% below 500, 41% between 500 and 599, 8% between 600 and 700, and 1% above 700; Math--62% below 500, 31% between 500 and 599, 6% between 600 and 700, and 1% above 700. The ACT scores were 56% below 21, 17% between 21 and 23, 17% between 24 and 26, 8% between 27 and 28, and 2% above 28. 27% of the current freshmen were in the top fifth of their class; 59% were in the top two fifths. 2 freshmen graduated first in their class.

Requirements: The SAT I or ACT is required; the minimum scores depend on the major selected. Candidates must be graduates of an accredited secondary school. 18 Carnegie units are required, including 4 each in English and arts/humanities, 3 each in math and science, and 4 in electives. Applicants for nursing must have completed a minimum 4 units in English, 3 in social studies, and 2 each in math (including algebra) and lab science, as required by the State Board of Nursing. The GED is accepted. An essay and/or interview may be required. Art majors may submit a portfolio. In some cases where preferred admission requirements are not met, conditional admission may be granted. Carlow prefers applicants to be in the upper 40% of their class. A GPA of 2.0 is required; a 3.0 is preferred. AP and CLEP credits are accepted. Important factors in the admissions decision are advanced placement or honor courses, leadership record, and recommendations by school officials.

Procedure: Freshmen are admitted fall and spring. Entrance exams should be taken early in the senior year. There are early decision, early admissions, and deferred admissions plans. There is a rolling admissions plan. Application deadlines are open. Application fee is $20. Notification is sent on a rolling basis. Applications are accepted on-line through the college's web site.

Transfer: 103 transfer students enrolled in 2002-2003. Transfer students must have a minimum GPA of 2.0 and submit high school and college transcripts. A 2.5 cumulative GPA for nursing and social work and 2.8 for perfusion technology is required. A 3.0 GPA is required for education. An interview is also recommended. 32 credits of 120 required for the bachelor's degree must be completed at Carlow.

Visiting: There are regularly scheduled orientations for prospective students, including a campus tour, information sessions on admission and financial aid, and interaction with faculty and students regarding academic and student life. There are guides for informal visits and visitors may sit in on classes and stay overnight. To schedule a visit, contact the Admissions Office.

Financial Aid: In 2003-2004, 98% of all full-time students received some form of financial aid. 86% of full-time freshmen and 76% of continuing full-time students received need-based aid. The average freshman award was $15,942. Need-based scholarships or need-based grants averaged $3321 ($9060 maximum); need-based self-help aid (loans and jobs) averaged $1572 ($2625 maximum); non-need-based athletic scholarships averaged $3091 ($5000 maximum); and other non-need-based awards and non-need-based scholarships averaged $4052 ($14,776 maximum). 12% of undergraduates work part time. Average annual earnings from campus work are $796. The average financial indebtedness of the 2003 graduate was $17,833. Carlow is a member of CSS. The FAFSA, verification worksheets, and tax returns when applicable are required. The deadline for filing freshman financial aid applications for fall entry is April 1.

International Students: There are 14 international students enrolled. They must score 550 on the written TOEFL or 173 on the electronic version (213 for nursing students). In some cases SAT I can replace TOEFL; otherwise, it is recommended only.

Computers: The mainframe is an HP 9000-L2000. There are 258 computer terminals/PCs available on campus for student use in computer labs located in the library, residence halls, the computer center, the student center, remote sites, and classroom buildings. Students can access e-mail, the Internet, and application software. All students may access the system 24 hours a day, 7 days a week. There are no time limits and no fees. It is strongly recommended that all students have a personal computer. An IBM ThinkPad is recommended.

Graduates: From July 1, 2002 to June 30, 2003, 323 bachelor's degrees were awarded. The most popular majors were nursing (21%), education (12%), and business management (11%). In an average class, 46% graduate in 4 years or less, 57% graduate in 5 years or less, and 59% graduate in 6 years or less. 3 companies recruited on campus in 2002-2003. Of the 2002 graduating class, 26% were enrolled in graduate school within 6 months of graduation and 67% were employed.

Admissions Contact: Christine Devine, Director of Admissions. A video is available. E-mail: admissions@carlow.edu Web: www.carlow.edu

CARNEGIE MELLON UNIVERSITY
B-3
Pittsburgh, PA 15213 (412) 268-2082; Fax: (412) 268-7838

Full-time: 3240 men, 1805 women	**Faculty:** 1042; I, +$
Part-time: 60 men, 30 women	**Ph.D.s:** 96%
Graduate: 2230 men, 945 women	**Student/Faculty:** 5 to 1
Year: semesters, summer session	**Tuition:** $25,875
Application Deadline: open	**Room & Board:** $6810
Freshman Class: n/av	
SAT I or ACT: required	**MOST COMPETITIVE**

Carnegie Mellon University, established in 1900, is a private nonsectarian institution offering undergraduate programs in liberal arts and science and professional technology. Figures in above capsule and in this profile are approximate. There are 6 undergraduate and 7 graduate schools. In addition to regional accreditation, Carnegie Mellon has baccalaureate program accreditation with AACSB, ABET, NAAB, NASAD, and NASM. The 3 libraries contain 935,888 volumes, 885,422 microform items, and 50,465 audio/video tapes/CDs, and subscribe to 3209 periodicals. Computerized library services include the card catalog, interlibrary loans, and database searching. Special learning facilities include a learning resource center, art gallery, and radio station. The 103-acre campus is in a suburban area 4 miles from downtown Pittsburgh. Including any residence halls, there are 80 buildings.

Student Life: 78% of undergraduates are from out of state, mostly the Middle Atlantic. Students are from 50 states, 102 foreign countries, and Canada. 70% are from public schools. 53% are white; 21% foreign nationals; 17% Asian American. The average age of freshmen is 18; all undergraduates, 20. 8% do not continue beyond their first year; 76% remain to graduate.

Housing: 3538 students can be accommodated in college housing, which includes single-sex and coed dorms, on-campus apartments, off-campus apartments, fraternity houses, and sorority houses. In addition, there are honors houses, language houses, and special-interest houses. On-campus housing is guaranteed for all 4 years. 59% of students live on campus; of those, 90% remain on campus on weekends. Alcohol is not permitted. Upperclassmen may keep cars.

Activities: 13% of men belong to 13 national fraternities; 9% of women belong to 1 local and 4 national sororities. There are 120 groups on campus, including art, bagpipe band, band, cheerleading, chess, choir, chorale, chorus, computers, debate, drama, ethnic, film, gay, honors, international, jazz band, literary magazine, marching band, musical theater, newspaper, opera, orchestra, pep band, photography, political, professional, radio and TV, religious, social, social service, student government, symphony, and yearbook. Popular campus events include Spring Carnival, International Festival, and Watson Arts Festival.

Sports: There are 9 intercollegiate sports for men and 8 for women, and 22 intramural sports for men and 16 for women. Facilities include a gym, a stadium, athletic fields, tennis and racquetball courts, and a pool.

Disabled Students: 98% of the campus is accessible. Wheelchair ramps, elevators, special parking, specially equipped rest rooms, special class scheduling, lowered drinking fountains, and lowered telephones are available.

Services: Counseling and information services are available, as is tutoring in most subjects. There is a reader service for the blind.

Campus Safety and Security: Measures include 24-hour foot and vehicle patrol, self-defense education, security escort services, and shuttle buses. There are informal discussions, pamphlets/posters/films, emergency telephones, lighted pathways/sidewalks, and a SafeWalk Program.

Programs of Study: Carnegie Mellon confers B.A., B.S., B.A.H., B.Arch., B.F.A., and B.S.A. degrees. Master's and doctoral degrees are also awarded. Bachelor's degrees are awarded in BIOLOGICAL SCIENCE (biology/biological science), BUSINESS (business administration and management, business economics, and marketing/retailing/merchandising), COMMUNICATIONS AND THE ARTS (communications, design, dramatic arts, English, fine arts, French, German, journalism, languages, music, and Spanish), COMPUTER AND PHYSICAL SCIENCE (chemistry, computer programming, computer science, information sciences and systems, mathematics, physics, and statistics), EDUCATION (music), ENGINEERING AND ENVIRONMENTAL DESIGN (chemical engineering, civil engineering, computer engineering, electrical/electronics engineering, engineering, and mechanical engineering), SOCIAL SCIENCE (economics, history, philosophy, political science/government, psychology, public administration, social science, and urban studies). Computer Science, engineering, and business administration are the strongest academically. Engineering is the largest.

Required: To graduate, students must complete requirements in English, history, and computing skills, and they must have a GPA of 2.0. Distribution requirements, the number of credits needed to graduate, and the number of credits required in the major vary by college.

Special: Students may cross-register with other Pittsburgh Council of Higher Education institutions. Also available are internships, work-study programs, study abroad in Germany, Switzerland, and Japan, a Washington semester, accelerated degrees, B.A.-B.S. degrees, co-op programs, dual majors, and limited student-designed majors. There are 10 national honor societies, including Phi Beta Kappa, and a freshman honors program.

Faculty/Classroom: 72% of faculty are male; 28%, female. All both teach and do research.

Requirements: The SAT I or ACT is required. In addition, SAT II: Subject tests in writing and math are required for all applicants. Engineering applicants must take the chemistry or physics test. Science applicants may take either of these or the biology test. Business and liberal arts applicants must take a third test of their choice. Applicants must graduate from an accredited secondary school or have a GED. They must earn 16 Carnegie units. All applicants must have completed 4 years of English. Applicants to the Carnegie Institute of Technology and the Mellon College of Science must take 4 years of math and 1 year each of biology, chemistry, and physics. Essays are required, and interviews are recommended. Art and design applicants must submit a portfolio. Drama and music applicants must audition. AP credits are accepted. Important factors in the admissions decision are advanced placement or honor courses, leadership record, and evidence of special talent.

Procedure: Freshmen are admitted in the fall. Entrance exams should be taken be received by February 15. There are early decision, early admissions, and deferred admissions plans. Check with the school for current deadlines. The fall 2003 application fee was $50. 95 early decision candidates were accepted for the 2003-2004 class. A waiting list is an active part of the admissions procedure. Applications are accepted on-line at the school's web site.

Transfer: Applicants must have a minimum GPA of 3.3 in all previous college-level work. 1 academic year must be completed at Carnegie Mellon.

Visiting: There are regularly scheduled orientations for prospective students, including Saturday group sessions in September, October, No-

vember, and April. There are guides for informal visits and visitors may sit in on classes and stay overnight. To schedule a visit, contact the Admissions Office.

Financial Aid: Carnegie Mellon is a member of CSS. The FAFSA, the college's own financial statement, and the parent and student federal tax returns and W-2 forms are required.

International Students: The school actively recruits these students. They must score 600 on the written TOEFL or take the MELAB and also take the SAT I or the ACT. Students must take SAT II: Subject tests in writing and math level I or II.

Computers: The mainframes are a DEC VAX 6320, 6330, and 11/780 models and a Sun 3280. The campuswide computer network extends to every office and dorm room, connecting hundreds of PCs and advanced workstations. All students may access the system 24 hours per day. There are no time limits and no fees.

Admissions Contact: Michael Steidel, Director of Admissions.
E-mail: *undergraduate-admissions+@andrew.cmu.edu*
Web: *www.cmu.edu/enrollment/admission*

CEDAR CREST COLLEGE
Allentown, PA 18104-6196

E-3
(610) 740-3780
(800) 360-1222; Fax: (610) 606-4647

Full-time: 10 men, 775 women	**Faculty:** 69
Part-time: 70 men, 740 women	**Ph.Ds:** 78%
Graduate: none	**Student/Faculty:** 11 to 1
Year: semesters, summer session	**Tuition:** $18,680
Application Deadline: open	**Room & Board:** $6465
Freshman Class: n/av	
SAT I or ACT: required	**COMPETITIVE+**

Cedar Crest College, founded in 1867, by the United Church of Christ is a private, women's, liberal arts college. In addition to regional accreditation, Cedar Crest has baccalaureate program accreditation with CAHEA, CSWE, and NLN. Figures in the above capsule and in this profile are approximate. The library contains 135,088 volumes, 12,941 microform items, and 16,126 audio/video tapes/CDs, and subscribes to 6650 periodicals. Computerized library services include the card catalog, interlibrary loans, and database searching. Special learning facilities include a learning resource center, art gallery, radio station, arboretum, theaters, and sculpture garden. The 84-acre campus is in a suburban area 55 miles north of Philadelphia and 90 miles west of New York City. Including any residence halls, there are 18 buildings.

Student Life: 82% of undergraduates are from Pennsylvania. Students are from 31 states, 35 foreign countries, and Canada. 95% are from public schools. 83% are white. 45% claim no religious affiliation; 26% are Protestant; 25% Catholic. The average age of freshmen is 18; all undergraduates, 29. 20% do not continue beyond their first year; 83% remain to graduate.

Housing: 550 students can be accommodated in college housing, which includes single-sex dorms and smoke-free floors. On-campus housing is guaranteed for all 4 years. 80% of students live on campus; of those, 70% remain on campus on weekends. All students may keep cars.

Activities: There are no fraternities. There are 46 groups on campus, including art, choir, chorus, computers, dance, drama, ethnic, gay, honors, international, literary magazine, musical theater, newspaper, political, professional, radio and TV, religious, social, social service, student government, and yearbook. Popular campus events include Student Faculty Frolic, Midnight Breakfast, and Ring Ceremony.

Sports: Facilities include 5 tennis courts, softball, field hockey, soccer, and lacrosse fields, a cross-country course, a gym with basketball, volleyball, and badminton courts, dance and aerobics studios, weight training, and a fitness center.

Disabled Students: 35% of the campus is accessible. Wheelchair ramps, elevators, special parking, specially equipped rest rooms, special class scheduling, lowered drinking fountains, and lowered telephones are available.

Services: Counseling and information services are available, as is tutoring in most subjects. There is remedial math and writing and a computer software skills program for underprepared students.

Campus Safety and Security: Measures include 24-hour foot and vehicle patrol, self-defense education, security escort services, and informal discussions. There are pamphlets/posters/films, emergency telephones, and lighted pathways/sidewalks. Residence halls are equipped with fire/intrusion alarms, which are monitored 24 hours a day. A keyless access system is in place; exterior doors are locked 24 hours a day.

Programs of Study: Cedar Crest confers B.A. and B.S degrees. Associate degrees are also awarded. Bachelor's degrees are awarded in BIOLOGICAL SCIENCE (biochemistry, biology/biological science, genetics, and neurosciences), BUSINESS (accounting and business administration and management), COMMUNICATIONS AND THE ARTS (art, communications, comparative literature, dance, dramatic arts, English, fine arts, French, music, and Spanish), COMPUTER AND PHYSICAL SCIENCE (chemistry, computer science, information sciences and systems, and mathematics), EDUCATION (elementary, science, and secondary), ENGINEERING AND ENVIRONMENTAL DESIGN (environmental science), HEALTH PROFESSIONS (medical laboratory technology, nuclear medical technology, and nursing), SOCIAL SCIENCE (history, liberal arts/general studies, philosophy, political science/government, prelaw, psychology, social work, and sociology). Genetic engineering, nursing, and sciences are the strongest academically. Sciences, nursing, and psychology are the largest.

Required: To graduate, students must complete 120 credit hours (122 for nursing) with a minimum GPA of 2.0 (some majors have higher requirements). Distribution requirements include 8 credits in science; 6 each in humanistic studies, primary texts, creativity and the arts, and global issues and world cultures; and 3 each in writing, research, math, and ethics. A major capstone experience is required.

Special: Cross-registration is available through the Lehigh Valley Association of Independent Colleges. Also available are internships, a Washington semester with American University, work-study programs, an accelerated degree program in business, B.A.-B.S. degrees in math, biology, and psychology. Dual majors, student-designed majors, 3-2 engineering degrees with Georgia Institute of Technology and Washington University, pass/fail options, and credit for life, military, and work experience are offered. There are 13 national honor societies, a freshman honors program, and 1 departmental honors program.

Faculty/Classroom: 41% of faculty are male; 59%, female. All teach undergraduates. The average class size in an introductory lecture is 20; in a laboratory, 13; and in a regular course, 14.

Requirements: The SAT I or ACT is required. In addition, applicants must be graduates of an accredited secondary school. The GED is accepted. Students should have completed 16 high school academic credits, including 4 years of English, 3 of math, 2 each of science, history, and foreign language, and 1 each of art, music, and social studies. An essay and an interview are required. A portfolio is recommended for art students and an audition for music students. Cedar Crest requires applicants to be in the upper 50% of their class. A GPA of 2.0 is required. AP and CLEP credits are accepted. Important factors in the admissions decision are advanced placement or honor courses, leadership record, and evidence of special talent.

Procedure: Freshmen are admitted fall and spring. Entrance exams should be taken in the junior year or early in the senior year. There are early admissions, deferred admissions, and rolling admissions plans. Application deadlines are open. The fall 2003 application fee was $30. Applications are accepted on computer disk and on-line.

Transfer: 27 transfer students enrolled in a recent year. Applicants should have a minimum college GPA of 2.0. An interview is recommended. 30 of 120 credits required for the bachelor's degree must be completed at Cedar Crest.

Visiting: There are regularly scheduled orientations for prospective students. There are guides for informal visits and visitors may sit in on classes and stay overnight. To schedule a visit, contact the Admissions Office at cccadmis@cedarcrest.edu.

Financial Aid: In a recent year, 98% of all full-time freshmen and 96% of continuing full-time students received some form of financial aid. 90% of full-time freshmen and 91% of continuing full-time students received need-based aid. The average freshman award was $18,487. 50% of undergraduates work part time. Average annual earnings from campus work are $1100. The average financial indebtedness of a recent graduate was $20,514. Cedar Crest is a member of CSS. The FAFSA and the college's own financial statement are required. Check with the school for current deadlines.

International Students: The school actively recruits these students. They must score 500 on the written TOEFL and also take the SAT I or the ACT.

Computers: There are 7 Compaq servers. A total of 240 PCs are available in 13 computer labs, classrooms, and 4 residence hall labs. The network provides a range of word processing, spreadsheet, and database applications, and high-speed, full Internet access and e-mail. Niche software such as multimedia tools, graphics software, and statistical analysis packages are available in specific labs and work areas across campus. Web access to e-mail is available to all, from any Internet connection worldwide. All students may access the system. There are no time limits and no fees. It is strongly recommended that all students have a personal computer.

Graduates: In a recent year, 235 bachelor's degrees were awarded. The most popular majors were psychology (20%), health and related sciences (19%), and business administration (15%). In an average class, 1% graduate in 3 years or less, 63% graduate in 4 years or less, and 68% graduate in 5 years or less. 32 companies recruited on campus in a recent year. Of a recent graduating class, 30% were enrolled in graduate school within 6 months of graduation and 81% were employed.

Admissions Contact: Judith Neyhart, Vice President for Enrollment and Advancement. A video is available.
E-mail: *judyn.@cedarcrest.edu* Web: *www.cedarcrest.edu*

CHATHAM COLLEGE
B-3
Pittsburgh, PA 15232
(412) 365-1290
(800) 837-1290; Fax: (412) 365-1609

Full-time: 407 women	**Faculty:** 71; IIA, --$
Part-time: 261 women	**Ph.D.s:** 89%
Graduate: 92 men, 460 women	**Student/Faculty:** 6 to 1
Year: 4-1-4, summer session	**Tuition:** $20,552
Application Deadline: open	**Room & Board:** $6714
Freshman Class: 243 applied, 149 accepted, 75 enrolled	
SAT I Verbal/Math: 550/480	**ACT:** 24 COMPETITIVE+

Chatham College, founded in 1869, is a private college offering undergraduate degree programs only to women in more than 30 liberal arts and preprofessional majors. Graduate degree programs in health sciences, education, management, writing, biology, counseling psychology, and landscape architecture are coeducational. In addition to regional accreditation, Chatham has baccalaureate program accreditation with ACS. The library contains 93,100 volumes, 8500 microform items, and 385 audio/video tapes/CDs, and subscribes to 8500 periodicals. Computerized library services include the card catalog, interlibrary loans, database searching, and Internet access. Special learning facilities include a learning resource center, art gallery, theaters, a media center, and an arboretum. The 32-acre campus is in an urban area 8 miles east of downtown Pittsburgh. Including any residence halls, there are 33 buildings.

Student Life: 75% of undergraduates are from Pennsylvania. Students are from 25 states, 18 foreign countries, and Canada. 96% are from public schools. 77% are white; 10% African American. The average age of freshmen is 18; all undergraduates, 21. 35% do not continue beyond their first year; 54% remain to graduate.

Housing: 380 students can be accommodated in college housing, which includes single-sex dorms, on-campus apartments, and off-campus apartments. In addition, there are special-interest houses and an intercultural residence hall. On-campus housing is available on a lottery system for upperclassmen. 66% of students live on campus; of those, 75% remain on campus on weekends. Upperclassmen may keep cars.

Activities: There are 28 groups on campus, including choir, dance, drama, environmental, ethnic, feminist, film, gay, honors, international, literary magazine, newspaper, photography, political, professional, religious, social service, student government, and yearbook. Popular campus events include Fall Festival, Spring Fling, and Air Band Contest.

Sports: Facilities include a swimming pool, a gym, an athletic and fitness center, a dance studio, an athletic field, free weights, a cardiovascular room, and a Cybex system.

Disabled Students: 75% of the campus is accessible. Wheelchair ramps, elevators, special parking, specially equipped rest rooms, and special class scheduling are available.

Services: Counseling and information services are available, as is tutoring in every subject. There is a reader service for the blind and remedial math, reading, and writing. One-on-one and group tutoring are available by both students and professional specialists, and there is also computer-aided tutoring and an organized study group.

Campus Safety and Security: Measures include 24-hour foot and vehicle patrol, self-defense education, security escort services, and shuttle buses. There are informal discussions, pamphlets/posters/films, emergency telephones, and lighted pathways/sidewalks.

Programs of Study: Chatham confers B.A., B.S., and B.S.W. degrees. Master's and doctoral degrees are also awarded. Bachelor's degrees are awarded in AGRICULTURE (environmental studies), BIOLOGICAL SCIENCE (biochemistry, bioinformatics, and biology/biological science), BUSINESS (accounting, business administration and management, international business management, management information systems, and marketing management), COMMUNICATIONS AND THE ARTS (art history and appreciation, arts administration/management, communications, dramatic arts, English, English literature, French, media arts, music, Spanish, and visual and performing arts), COMPUTER AND PHYSICAL SCIENCE (chemistry, computer science, mathematics, and physics), EDUCATION (education), ENGINEERING AND ENVIRONMENTAL DESIGN (environmental science), HEALTH PROFESSIONS (exercise science), SOCIAL SCIENCE (crosscultural studies, economics, forensic studies, history, interdisciplinary studies, international relations, political science/government, psychology, public affairs, social work, and women's studies). Biology, psychology, and English have the largest enrollments and are the strongest academically.

Required: To graduate, students must complete 120 credit hours, including a general education curriculum of 7 courses and a senior tutorial, with a minimum GPA of 2.0. Students must also demonstrate proficiencies in writing, math, and computer literacy.

Special: Chatham offers a study-abroad program in 7 countries, cross-registration with other Pittsburgh Council on Higher Education institutions, co-op programs in all majors, several multidisciplinary majors, internships in the public and private sectors, and a Washington semester in conjunction with American University and the Public Leadership Education Network. Accelerated degree programs, work-study, combined

B.A.-B.S. degrees, multidisciplinary majors, and dual and student-designed majors are available. There are 3-2 engineering degrees with Carnegie Mellon and Penn State Universities and the University of Pittsburgh, dual degree programs, and an accelerated Master's program with Carnegie Mellon's Heinz School is also available. There are 7 national honor societies, including Phi Beta Kappa, and all departments have honors programs.

Faculty/Classroom: 37% of faculty are male; 63%, female. 100% both teach and do research. No introductory courses are taught by graduate students. The average class size in an introductory lecture is 16; in a laboratory, 12; and in a regular course, 12.

Admissions: 61% of the 2003-2004 applicants were accepted. The SAT I scores for the 2003-2004 freshman class were: Verbal--26% below 500, 40% between 500 and 599, 31% between 600 and 700, and 3% above 700; Math--59% below 500, 28% between 500 and 599, 12% between 600 and 700, and 1% above 700. The ACT scores were 31% below 21, 18% between 21 and 23, 38% between 24 and 26, and 13% between 27 and 28. 34% of the current freshmen were in the top fifth of their class; 58% were in the top two fifths.

Requirements: The SAT I or ACT is required. In addition, applicants must be graduates of an accredited secondary school or have earned the GED. Students are encouraged to have completed 4 years of high school English and 2 years each of math, science, and social studies. A foreign language and an interview are recommended. An essay is required. Chatham requires applicants to be in the upper 50% of their class. A GPA of 2.8 is required. AP and CLEP credits are accepted. Important factors in the admissions decision are recommendations by school officials, leadership record, and extracurricular activities record.

Procedure: Freshmen are admitted fall, winter, and spring. Entrance exams should be taken by fall of the senior year. There is a deferred admissions plan and a rolling admissions plan. Application deadlines are open. Application fee is $35. Applications are accepted on-line through www.chatham.edu or through the Common Application.

Transfer: 28 transfer students enrolled in 2002-2003. Applicants must present high school and college transcripts. The SAT I or ACT and an interview are required. 45 of 120 credits required for the bachelor's degree must be completed at Chatham.

Visiting: There are regularly scheduled orientations for prospective students, including campus tours, student and faculty panels, financial aid presentations, and athletic coach meetings. There are guides for informal visits and visitors may sit in on classes and stay overnight. To schedule a visit, contact the Admissions Office at admissions@chatham.edu.

Financial Aid: In 2003-2004, 99% of all full-time freshmen and 95% of continuing full-time students received some form of financial aid. 86% of full-time freshmen and 80% of continuing full-time students received need-based aid. The average freshman award was $18,231. Need-based scholarships or need-based grants averaged $9427 ($16,330 maximum); need-based self-help aid (loans and jobs) averaged $4746 ($7779 maximum); non-need-based awards and non-need-based scholarships averaged $2397 ($7000 maximum); and parent Plus averaged $9794 ($18,642 maximum). 90% of undergraduates work part time. Average annual earnings from campus work are $2200. The average financial indebtedness of the 2003 graduate was $20,125. The FAFSA is required. The deadline for filing freshman financial aid applications for fall entry is May 1.

International Students: There are 29 international students enrolled. The school actively recruits these students. They must score 550 on the written TOEFL or 210 on the electronic version or take the MELAB. The SAT I is required unless TOEFL score is available.

Computers: The mainframe consists of Microsoft 2000 servers. There are 300 computers connected to the campuswide Microsoft 2000 network, through which Internet access is provided. Clusters are located in each residence hall, in off-campus apartments, and in the library. Network access ports are provided in all residence hall and apartment rooms. All students may access the system 24 hours per day from their own or residence hall cluster computers. There are no time limits and no fees. The college specifies minimum capabilities and software for students to be able to connect into the college network.

Graduates: From July 1, 2002 to June 30, 2003, 118 bachelor's degrees were awarded. The most popular majors were biology (15%), psychology (15%), and English (10%). In an average class, 54% graduate in 4 years or less, 59% graduate in 5 years or less, and 60% graduate in 6 years or less. 62 companies recruited on campus in 2002-2003. Of the 2002 graduating class, 36% were enrolled in graduate school within 6 months of graduation and 53% were employed.

Admissions Contact: Alan G. McIvor, Vice President of Enrollment Management. E-mail: admissions@chatham.edu
Web: www.chatham.edu

CHESTNUT HILL COLLEGE
Philadelphia, PA 19118-2693

F-3
(215) 248-7001
(800) 248-0052; Fax: (215) 248-7082

Full-time: 119 men, 525 women	**Faculty:** 56
Part-time: 54 men, 208 women	**Ph.Ds:** 82%
Graduate: 118 men, 531 women	**Student/Faculty:** 12 to 1
Year: semesters, summer session	**Tuition:** $19,050
Application Deadline: open	**Room & Board:** $7400
Freshman Class: 973 applied, 751 accepted, 193 enrolled	
SAT I Verbal/Math: 480/460	**ACT:** 18 **LESS COMPETITIVE**

Chestnut Hill College, founded in 1924, is a private, liberal arts, institution, affiliated with the Roman Catholic Church. In addition to the traditional program, CHC also offers an accelerated evening and weekend program for working adults. Courses in the accelerated program are offered in 6 8-week sessions per year, with 11 career-oriented majors. There are 2 undergraduate schools and 1 graduate school. The library contains 128,489 volumes, 203,958 microform items, and 2089 audio/video tapes/CDs, and subscribes to 484 periodicals. Computerized library services include the card catalog, interlibrary loans, database searching, and Internet access. Special learning facilities include a learning resource center, art gallery, planetarium, rotating observatory, and technology center. The 45-acre campus is in a suburban area 25 miles northwest of downtown Philadelphia. Including any residence halls, there are 11 buildings.

Student Life: 85% of undergraduates are from Pennsylvania. Students are from 13 states, 12 foreign countries, and Canada. 47% are from public schools. 64% are white; 28% African American. 59% are Catholic; 26% claim no religious affiliation; 11% Protestant. The average age of freshmen is 18; all undergraduates, 21. 25% do not continue beyond their first year; 66% remain to graduate.

Housing: 350 students can be accommodated in college housing, which includes coed dorms. On-campus housing is guaranteed for all 4 years. 66% of students live on campus; of those, 60% remain on campus on weekends. Alcohol is not permitted. All students may keep cars.

Activities: There are no fraternities or sororities. There are 25 groups on campus, including chorale, chorus, drama, environmental, ethnic, honors, instrumental ensemble, international, literary magazine, musical theater, newspaper, opera, orchestra, political, professional, religious, social, social service, student government, and yearbook. Popular campus events include International Gourmet Day, Intramural One-Act Play Night, and concerts.

Sports: There are 5 intercollegiate sports for men and 7 for women. Facilities include a gym and an auxiliary gym, an athletic training room, locker facilities, fitness room, indoor swimming pool, 8 tennis courts, playing fields for hockey, lacrosse, softball, and soccer, as well as neighboring stables and a golf course.

Disabled Students: 90% of the campus is accessible. Wheelchair ramps, elevators, special parking, specially equipped rest rooms, and a shower area in residence halls are available.

Services: Counseling and information services are available, as is tutoring in most subjects. There is a reader service for the blind and remedial math and writing.

Campus Safety and Security: Measures include 24-hour foot and vehicle patrol, security escort services, informal discussions, and pamphlets/posters/films. There are lighted pathways/sidewalks. Doors are locked after 6 P.M. and on weekends and are monitored by cameras. Escorted shuttle cars to parking lots are available in the evenings.

Programs of Study: CHC confers B.A. and B.S. degrees. Associate, master's, and doctoral degrees are also awarded. Bachelor's degrees are awarded in BIOLOGICAL SCIENCE (biochemistry, biology/biological science, and molecular biology), BUSINESS (accounting, banking and finance, business administration and management, business communications, human resources, management science, and marketing/retailing/merchandising), COMMUNICATIONS AND THE ARTS (art history and appreciation, communications technology, English, French, and Spanish), COMPUTER AND PHYSICAL SCIENCE (chemistry, computer science, and mathematics), EDUCATION (early childhood and elementary), ENGINEERING AND ENVIRONMENTAL DESIGN (environmental science), HEALTH PROFESSIONS (health care administration), SOCIAL SCIENCE (child care/child and family studies, criminal justice, gerontology, history, human services, political science/government, psychology, and sociology). Biological/computer/physical sciences, humanities, and social sciences are the strongest academically. Education, biological sciences, and psychology are the largest.

Required: To graduate, students must complete at least 120 credit hours with a general average of 2.0 overall and in the major. Course work must include 12 to 15 courses in the major; Introduction to the Liberal Arts; Interdisciplinary Global Studies Seminar; a writing course; 2 courses in religious studies; the College Experience; Career Connections: 2 1-credit courses in phys ed; courses in various ways of knowing, including historical (2 courses), literary (1), aesthetic (1), scientific (2 or 3), analytic (1) and interpreting human behavior (2); and a senior seminar and senior thesis. Proficiency must be demonstrated in math, computers, oral communication, and swimming. Students may choose from a wide variety of minors.

Special: Cross-registration is available with LaSalle University and at the 10 colleges in the Sisters of St. Joseph College Consortium Student Exchange Program. The college offers internships, study abroad in England, Spain, Italy, Austria, and France, work-study programs, interdisciplinary majors, and dual and student-designed majors. Up to 6 credits may be given for life experience. Nondegree study and pass/fail options are available. The school offers unique career preparation programs in communications, international studies, environmental science, and international business. There are 4 national honor societies, a freshman honors program, and 11 departmental honors programs.

Faculty/Classroom: 39% of faculty are male; 61%, female. 92% teach undergraduates and 40% both teach and do research. No introductory courses are taught by graduate students. The average class size in an introductory lecture is 25; in a laboratory, 15; and in a regular course, 15.

Admissions: 77% of the 2003-2004 applicants were accepted. The SAT I scores for the 2003-2004 freshman class were: Verbal--58% below 500, 33% between 500 and 599, 8% between 600 and 700, and 1% above 700; Math--66% below 500, 29% between 500 and 599, and 5% between 600 and 700. The ACT scores were 75% below 21, and 25% between 21 and 23. 29% of the current freshmen were in the top fifth of their class; 51% were in the top two fifths.

Requirements: The SAT I or ACT is required, with a recommended minimum composite score on the SAT I of 900 to 1000. Applicants must be graduates of an accredited secondary school. 16 Carnegie units are required, with a recommended 4 units each of English, math, science, and social studies and 3 of foreign language. An interview is recommended for all students. An essay is required. A GPA of 2.0 is required. AP and CLEP credits are accepted. Important factors in the admissions decision are leadership record, recommendations by alumni, and evidence of special talent.

Procedure: Freshmen are admitted fall and spring. Entrance exams should be taken early in the senior year. There are early admissions and deferred admissions plans. There is a rolling admissions plan. Application deadlines are open. Application fee is $35. Applications are accepted on-line through *www.chc.edu.*

Transfer: 39 transfer students enrolled in 2002-2003. Applicants must have a minimum GPA of 2.0; a 2.5 is recommended. 45 of 120 credits required for the bachelor's degree must be completed at CHC.

Visiting: There are regularly scheduled orientations for prospective students, including faculty presentations and workshops on specific issues. There are guides for informal visits and visitors may sit in on classes and stay overnight. To schedule a visit, contact the Admissions Office at *chcapply@chc.edu.*

Financial Aid: In 2003-2004, 83% of all full-time freshmen and 93% of continuing full-time students received some form of financial aid. 77% of full-time freshmen and 90% of continuing full-time students received need-based aid. The average freshman award was $14,050. Need-based scholarships or need-based grants averaged $8125; need-based self-help aid (loans and jobs) averaged $4625; and non-need-based awards and non-need-based scholarships averaged $6050. 50% of undergraduates work part time. Average annual earnings from campus work are $1500. The average financial indebtedness of the 2003 graduate was $17,125. CHC is a member of CSS. The FAFSA is required. The deadline for filing freshman financial aid applications for fall entry is April 15.

International Students: There are 12 international students enrolled. The school actively recruits these students. They must score 550 on the written TOEFL.

Computers: The mainframe is an IBM/AS400. Students use Mac and IBM PCs in the multimedia technology center, other computer labs, science labs, computer classrooms, smart classrooms, and dorms. All students may access the system. There are no time limits and no fees. All students are required to have personal computers. The IBM Mobile/Wireless (Centrino) laptop is recommended.

Graduates: From July 1, 2002 to June 30, 2003, 205 bachelor's degrees were awarded. The most popular majors were business (26%), sociology (25%), and education (11%). In an average class, 58% graduate in 4 years or less, 60% graduate in 5 years or less, and 62% graduate in 6 years or less. 25 companies recruited on campus in 2002-2003.

Admissions Contact: Jodie King, Director of Admissions. A video is available. E-mail: *chcapply@chc.edu* Web: *www.chc.edu*

CHEYNEY UNIVERSITY OF PENNSYLVANIA

F-4
Cheyney, PA 19319 (610) 399-2275
(800) 223-3608; Fax: (610) 399-2099

Full-time: 515 men, 550 women	**Faculty:** 83; IIB, +$
Part-time: 35 men, 110 women	**Ph.D.s:** 33%
Graduate: 85 men, 235 women	**Student/Faculty:** 13 to 1
Year: semesters, summer session	**Tuition:** $4675 ($10,695)
Application Deadline: see profile	**Room & Board:** $5325
Freshman Class: n/av	
SAT I or ACT: required	**COMPETITIVE**

Cheyney University of Pennsylvania, founded in 1837, is a public, liberal arts institution offering programs in art, business, music, and teacher preparation. There are 2 undergraduate schools and 1 graduate school. Figures in the above capsule and in this profile are approximate. In addition to regional accreditation, Cheyney has baccalaureate program accreditation with IACBE and NCATE. The library contains 162,878 volumes, 781,388 microform items, and 1434 audio/video tapes/CDs, and subscribes to 414 periodicals. Computerized library services include the card catalog. Special learning facilities include a planetarium, radio station, TV station, weather station, world cultures center, and theater arts center. The 275-acre campus is in a suburban area 24 miles west of Philadelphia. Including any residence halls, there are 33 buildings.

Student Life: 83% of undergraduates are from Pennsylvania. Students are from 14 states and 5 foreign countries. 98% are African American. The average age of freshmen is 25; all undergraduates, 22.

Housing: 1300 students can be accommodated in college housing, which includes single-sex and coed dorms. In addition, there are honors houses. On-campus housing is available on a first-come, first-served basis. 69% of students live on campus. Alcohol is not permitted. All students may keep cars.

Activities: There are 5 national fraternities and 4 national sororities. There are 30 groups on campus, including art, cheerleading, chess, choir, computers, drama, ethnic, honors, international, newspaper, political, professional, radio and TV, religious, social, social service, student government, and yearbook. Popular campus events include Founders Day Ball and Wade Wilson Football Classic.

Sports: There are 5 intercollegiate sports for men and 5 for women, and 3 intramural sports for men and 2 for women. Facilities include a track, tennis courts, outdoor and indoor basketball courts, a pool, a gym, and a weight room.

Disabled Students: 86% of the campus is accessible. Wheelchair ramps, elevators, special parking, specially equipped rest rooms, lowered drinking fountains, and lowered telephones are available.

Services: Counseling and information services are available, as is tutoring in most subjects. There is remedial math, reading, and writing. Both peers and professionals serve as tutors.

Campus Safety and Security: Measures include 24-hour foot and vehicle patrol, shuttle buses, informal discussions, and pamphlets/posters/films. There are emergency telephones and lighted pathways/sidewalks.

Programs of Study: Cheyney confers B.A., B.S., and B.S.Ed. degrees. Master's degrees are also awarded. Bachelor's degrees are awarded in BIOLOGICAL SCIENCE (biology/biological science), BUSINESS (business administration and management and hotel/motel and restaurant management), COMMUNICATIONS AND THE ARTS (communications, dramatic arts, English, and music), COMPUTER AND PHYSICAL SCIENCE (chemistry, computer science, mathematics, and science), EDUCATION (early childhood, elementary, home economics, secondary, and special), HEALTH PROFESSIONS (medical laboratory technology), SOCIAL SCIENCE (clothing and textiles management/production/services, economics, geography, parks and recreation management, political science/government, psychology, and social science). Psychology, political science, and social relations are the strongest academically. Business administration and social relations are the largest.

Required: To graduate, students must complete at least 124 credit hours, with 30 in the major and a minimum GPA of 2.0. Distribution requirements include 6 credits each in communications, humanities, science, and social science, 4 in health and phys ed, and 3 in math.

Special: Students may participate in a co-op program and cross-register with West Chester University of Pennsylvania. Internships, study abroad, work-study programs, a chemistry-biology dual degree, nondegree study, pass/fail options, and credit for life, military, and work experience are available. There are 10 national honor societies, a freshman honors program, and 6 departmental honors programs.

Faculty/Classroom: 50% of faculty are male; 50%, female. 76% teach undergraduates. No introductory courses are taught by graduate students.

Requirements: The SAT I or ACT is required. In addition, applicants must be graduates of an accredited secondary school or hold a GED. An interview is recommended. CLEP credit is accepted. Important factors in the admissions decision are ability to finance college education, extracurricular activities record, and geographic diversity.

Procedure: Freshmen are admitted fall and spring. Entrance exams should be taken during the junior or senior year. There are early decision and early admissions plans and a rolling admissions plan. Check with the school for current deadlines. The fall 2003 application fee was $20.

Transfer: 66 transfer students enrolled in a recent year. Applicants must have a C average from an accredited postsecondary institution; others may be admitted on probation. Students with fewer than 30 credits must submit a high school transcript. 30 of 124 credits required for the bachelor's degree must be completed at Cheyney.

Visiting: There are regularly scheduled orientations for prospective students. There are guides for informal visits and visitors may sit in on classes. To schedule a visit, contact the Office of Admissions at (800) Cheyney.

Financial Aid: In a recent year, 87% of all full-time freshmen and 90% of continuing full-time students received some form of financial aid. 82% of full-time freshmen and 85% of continuing full-time students received need-based aid. The average freshman award was $7200. 43% of undergraduates work part time. Average annual earnings from campus work are $1650. The average financial indebtedness of a recent graduate was $16,650. Cheyney is a member of CSS. The FAFSA is required. Check with the school for current deadlines.

International Students: In a recent year, there were 14 international students enrolled. The school actively recruits these students. They must score 500 on the written TOEFL.

Computers: 150 Macs and PCs are available in the library and departmental offices. Only authorized terminal operators may access the system 24 hours a day. There are no time limits and no fees.

Graduates: In a recent year, 123 bachelor's degrees were awarded. The most popular majors were elementary education (28%), social relations (26%), and business administration (21%).

Admissions Contact: James Brown, Director of Admission. A video is available. E-mail: jbrown@cheyney.edu Web: www.cheyney.edu

---

CLARION UNIVERSITY OF PENNSYLVANIA   B-2
Clarion, PA 16214

(814) 393-2306
(800) 672-7171; Fax: (814) 393-2030

Full-time: 2070 men, 3180 women	**Faculty:** 323; IIA
Part-time: 155 men, 415 women	**Ph.D.s:** 59%
Graduate: 115 men, 345 women	**Student/Faculty:** 16 to 1
Year: semesters, summer session	**Tuition:** $7225 ($11,240)
Application Deadline: open	**Room & Board:** $4050
Freshman Class: n/av	
SAT I: recommended	**LESS COMPETITIVE**

Clarion University of Pennsylvania, founded in 1867, is a public institution, and part of the Pennsylvania State System of Higher Education. There are 4 undergraduate and 4 graduate schools. Figures in the above capsule and in this profile are approximate. In addition to regional accreditation, Clarion University has baccalaureate program accreditation with AACSB, NASM, NCATE, and NLN. The library contains 16,111 volumes, 12,191 microform items, and 461 audio/video tapes/CDs, and subscribes to 4412 periodicals. Computerized library services include the card catalog, interlibrary loans, and database searching. Special learning facilities include a learning resource center, art gallery, planetarium, radio station, and TV station. The 99-acre campus is in a small town 85 miles northeast of Pittsburgh. Including any residence halls, there are 45 buildings.

Student Life: 96% of undergraduates are from Pennsylvania. Students are from 28 states, 30 foreign countries, and Canada. 90% are from public schools. 94% are white. The average age of freshmen is 18; all undergraduates, 23. 27% do not continue beyond their first year; 59% remain to graduate.

Housing: 2029 students can be accommodated in college housing, which includes single-sex and coed dorms. In addition, there are special-interest floors, nonsmoking floors, older student floors, and quiet floors. Alcohol is not permitted. All students may keep cars.

Activities: 11% of men belong to 11 national fraternities; 10% of women belong to 9 national sororities. There are 125 groups on campus, including art, band, cheerleading, chess, choir, chorus, computers, concert band, dance, debate, drama, ethnic, forensics, gay, honors, international, jazz band, marching band, musical theater, music ensembles, newspaper, orchestra, photography, political, professional, radio and TV, religious, social, social service, student government, symphony, and yearbook. Popular campus events include Autumn Leaf Festival, Activities Day, and Martin Luther King Cultural Series.

Sports: There are 8 intercollegiate sports for men and 7 for women, and 35 intramural sports for men and 35 for women. Facilities include a 5000-seat stadium, a gym with physical fitness center and recreational swimming, and a natatorium.

Disabled Students: 85% of the campus is accessible. Wheelchair ramps, elevators, special parking, specially equipped rest rooms, special class scheduling, lowered drinking fountains, lowered telephones, and priority registration are available.

Services: Counseling and information services are available, as is tutoring in most subjects. There is a reader service for the blind and remedial math, reading, and writing. Computer-assisted instruction and a learning skills lab are also available.

Campus Safety and Security: Measures include 24-hour foot and vehicle patrol, self-defense education, security escort services, and informal discussions. There are pamphlets/posters/films, emergency telephones, lighted pathways/sidewalks, video surveillance cameras on campus, a bicycle patrol program, and a rape/aggressive defense program.

Programs of Study: Clarion University confers B.A., B.S., B.F.A., B.Mus., B.S.B.A., B.S.E., and B.S.N. degrees. Associate and master's degrees are also awarded. Bachelor's degrees are awarded in BIOLOGICAL SCIENCE (biology/biological science and molecular biology), BUSINESS (accounting, banking and finance, business administration and management, business economics, international business management, marketing/retailing/merchandising, and real estate), COMMUNICATIONS AND THE ARTS (art, communications, dramatic arts, English, French, music, Spanish, and speech/debate/rhetoric), COMPUTER AND PHYSICAL SCIENCE (chemistry, computer management, computer science, earth science, geology, information sciences and systems, mathematics, natural sciences, physics, and radiological technology), EDUCATION (early childhood, elementary, foreign languages, library science, music, secondary, and special), ENGINEERING AND ENVIRONMENTAL DESIGN (environmental science and industrial administration/management), HEALTH PROFESSIONS (medical technology, nursing, rehabilitation therapy, and speech pathology/audiology), SOCIAL SCIENCE (anthropology, economics, geography, history, humanities, liberal arts/general studies, philosophy, political science/government, psychology, social science, and sociology). Elementary education, communication, and marketing are the largest.

Required: To graduate, students must complete at least 128 credits, with a minimum GPA of 2.0 (2.5 for the College of Education and Human Services). Degree requirements include 15 credits of liberal education skills, 9 credits each in physical and biological sciences, social and behavioral sciences, and arts and humanities; and 4 credits in health and personal performance.

Special: Clarion University has co-op programs in engineering with the University of Pittsburgh and Case Western Reserve University and in speech pathology and audiology with Gallaudet University. Internships, study abroad, work-study programs, and dual and student-designed majors are also available. There are 12 national honor societies and a freshman honors program.

Faculty/Classroom: 54% of faculty are male; 46%, female. All teach undergraduates. No introductory courses are taught by graduate students. The average class size in a regular course is 25.

Requirements: The SAT I is recommended. In addition, applicants must be graduates of an accredited secondary school. The GED is accepted. Students should have completed 4 years each of English and social studies, and 2 years each of math, science, and foreign language. An essay and interview are recommended. A GPA of 2.0 is required. AP and CLEP credits are accepted. Important factors in the admissions decision are advanced placement or honor courses, evidence of special talent, and leadership record.

Procedure: Freshmen are admitted fall and spring. Entrance exams should be taken in the spring of the junior year or early fall of the senior year. There are early admissions, deferred admissions, and rolling admissions plans. Application deadlines are open. Application fee is $30. Applications are accepted on computer disk and on-line.

Transfer: 359 transfer students enrolled in a recent year. Applicants for transfer should have completed at least 12 college credit hours with a GPA of 2.75 for speech pathology and audiology majors, 2.5 for business and education majors, and 2.0 for other programs. An audition is required for music majors, and an interview and national test are required for nursing students. 45 of 128 credits required for the bachelor's degree must be completed at Clarion University.

Visiting: There are regularly scheduled orientations for prospective students, including a 1 1/2-day summer program for committed students. There are guides for informal visits and visitors may sit in on classes. To schedule a visit, contact the Admissions Office.

Financial Aid: The average financial indebtedness of a recent graduate was $12,858. The FAFSA is required. Check with the school for current deadlines.

International Students: The school actively recruits these students. They must score 550 on the written TOEFL.

Computers: The mainframe is a DEC VAX 8810. There are also more than 350 PCs and Apple IIe's available in student labs, all with access to the Web. All students may access the system 24 hours a day. There are no time limits and no fees.

Graduates: In a recent year, 923 bachelor's degrees were awarded. The most popular majors were education (32%), business (17%), and health professions and related sciences (11%). In an average class, 38% graduate in 4 years or less, and 55% graduate in 5 years or less.

Admissions Contact: Admissions Officer. A video is available. E-mail: admissions@clarion.edu Web: www.clarion.edu

COLLEGE MISERICORDIA
Dallas, PA 18612

B-2

(570) 674-6400
(866) 262-6363; Fax: (570) 675-2441

Full-time: 379 men, 1005 women	**Faculty:** 90; IIB, av$
Part-time: 143 men, 440 women	**Ph.Ds:** 52%
Graduate: 54 men, 101 women	**Student/Faculty:** 15 to 1
Year: semesters	**Tuition:** $18,850
Application Deadline: open	**Room & Board:** $7500
Freshman Class: 1267 applied, 975 accepted, 433 enrolled	
SAT I Verbal/Math: 508/510	**ACT:** 23 **COMPETITIVE**

College Misericordia, established in 1924 and sponsored by the Religious Sisters of Mercy, is a private liberal arts institution affiliated with the Roman Catholic Church and offering professional programs in health-related fields. In addition to regional accreditation, College Misericordia has baccalaureate program accreditation with CAHEA, CSWE, and NLN. The library contains 72,836 volumes, 6666 microform items, and 2240 audio/video tapes/CDs, and subscribes to 590 periodicals. Computerized library services include the card catalog, interlibrary loans, database searching, and Internet access. Special learning facilities include a learning resource center, art gallery, radio station, and TV station. The 120-acre campus is in a suburban area 9 miles north of Wilkes-Barre. Including any residence halls, there are 16 buildings.

Student Life: 73% of undergraduates are from Pennsylvania. Students are from 12 states and 2 foreign countries. 45% are from public schools. 96% are white. 65% are Catholic; 32% Protestant. The average age of freshmen is 18; all undergraduates, 21. 9% do not continue beyond their first year; 63% remain to graduate.

Housing: 720 students can be accommodated in college housing, which includes single-sex and coed dorms, on-campus apartments, and off-campus apartments. In addition, there are special-interest houses. On-campus housing is guaranteed for all 4 years. 55% of students live on campus; of those, 70% remain on campus on weekends. Upperclassmen may keep cars.

Activities: There are no fraternities or sororities. There are 26 groups on campus, including cheerleading, choir, chorus, computers, drama, ethnic, honors, international, literary magazine, musical theater, newspaper, political, professional, religious, social service, student government, and yearbook. Popular campus events include Spring Fling, Winter Weekend, and Junior Ring Day.

Sports: There are 9 intercollegiate sports for men and 10 for women, and 11 intramural sports for men and 11 for women. Facilities include a sports-health center and athletic fields, a 24,000-square foot athletic center, an Olympic-size pool, a dance studio, a fitness center, natural and synthetic basketball courts, an indoor walking track, and 3 racquetball courts.

Disabled Students: 95% of the campus is accessible. Wheelchair ramps, elevators, special parking, specially equipped rest rooms, and special class scheduling are available.

Services: Counseling and information services are available, as is tutoring in every subject. There is remedial math and reading. Services for students with disabilities are provided through the Alternative Learners Program.

Campus Safety and Security: Measures include 24-hour foot and vehicle patrol, security escort services, informal discussions, and pamphlets/posters/films. There are emergency telephones and lighted pathways/sidewalks.

Programs of Study: College Misericordia confers B.A., B.S., B.S.N., and B.S.W. degrees. Master's degrees are also awarded. Bachelor's degrees are awarded in BIOLOGICAL SCIENCE (biochemistry and biology/biological science), BUSINESS (accounting, business administration and management, marketing/retailing/merchandising, and sports management), COMMUNICATIONS AND THE ARTS (communications and English), COMPUTER AND PHYSICAL SCIENCE (chemistry, computer science, information sciences and systems, and mathematics), EDUCATION (early childhood, elementary, secondary, and special), HEALTH PROFESSIONS (medical laboratory technology, nursing, occupational therapy, physical therapy, predentistry, premedicine, radiograph medical technology, and speech therapy), SOCIAL SCIENCE (history, interdisciplinary studies, liberal arts/general studies, philosophy, prelaw, psychology, and social work). Occupational therapy, physical therapy, and nursing are the strongest programs academically and have the largest enrollments.

Required: To graduate, students must earn a minimum of 120 credits, with at least 60 credits in the major. The required 54-credit core curriculum includes courses in anthropology, English composition and literature, fine arts, history, math, philosophy, political science, psychology, religious studies, and science. A minimum GPA of 2.0 is required.

Special: Students may cross-register with King's College and Wilkes University. The college offers co-op programs, internships for all majors, work-study programs, study abroad in Guyana, Haiti, and Ireland, an accelerated degree program in business and nursing for adult students, student-designed majors, and dual majors in elementary and early childhood education, elementary and special education, and math and com-

puter science. Credit may be granted for life, military, and work experience. Nondegree study is also available. The college offers an alternative learner's project, which accepts a limited number of learning disabled students each year. There is 1 national honor society, a freshman honors program, and 1 departmental honors program.

Faculty/Classroom: 49% of faculty are male; 51%, female. 90% teach undergraduates, 40% do research, and 45% do both. No introductory courses are taught by graduate students. The average class size in an introductory lecture is 25; in a laboratory, 20; and in a regular course, 18.

Admissions: 77% of the 2003-2004 applicants were accepted. The SAT I scores for the 2003-2004 freshman class were: Verbal--47% below 500, 42% between 500 and 599, and 11% between 600 and 700; Math--45% below 500, 44% between 500 and 599, and 11% between 600 and 700. The ACT scores were 29% below 21, 24% between 21 and 23, 35% between 24 and 26, 6% between 27 and 28, and 6% above 28. 35% of the current freshmen were in the top fifth of their class; 65% were in the top two fifths. 2 freshmen graduated first in their class.

Requirements: The SAT I is required. In addition, applicants must graduate from an accredited secondary school or have a GED. 16 Carnegie units must be earned, and students must complete 3 years each in English, math, history, and science, and 2 to 3 years in social studies. Radiography applicants must take physics. Physical therapy students must take calculus. College Misericordia requires applicants to be in the upper 50% of their class. A GPA of 2.0 is required. AP and CLEP credits are accepted. Important factors in the admissions decision are advanced placement or honor courses, personality/intangible qualities, and extracurricular activities record.

Procedure: Freshmen are admitted fall and spring. Entrance exams should be taken during the junior year. There are early admissions, deferred admissions, and rolling admissions plans. Application deadlines are open. Application fee is $25. 31 applicants were on the 2003 waiting list; none were admitted. Applications are accepted on computer disk and on-line through AES Mentor and the College Board Common App.

Transfer: 119 transfer students enrolled in 2002-2003. Applicants must have a minimum GPA of 2.0. Requirements may be higher for selected majors. 30 of 120 credits required for the bachelor's degree must be completed at College Misericordia.

Visiting: There are regularly scheduled orientations for prospective students, including meetings with admissions and financial aid counselors, a tour of the campus, and optional meetings with faculty and coaches. There are guides for informal visits and visitors may sit in on classes and stay overnight. To schedule a visit, contact the Admissions Office.

Financial Aid: In 2003-2004, 98% of all full-time freshmen and 93% of continuing full-time students received some form of financial aid. 94% of full-time freshmen and 91% of continuing full-time students received need-based aid. The average freshman award was $14,019. Need-based scholarships or need-based grants averaged $4227 ($12,850 maximum); need-based self-help aid (loans and jobs) averaged $3716 ($5525 maximum); and non-need-based awards and non-need-based scholarships averaged $9418 ($18,000 maximum). 18% of undergraduates work part time. Average annual earnings from campus work are $784. The average financial indebtedness of the 2003 graduate was $13,000. College Misericordia is a member of CSS. The FAFSA and the college's own financial statement are required. The priority date for freshman financial aid applications for fall entry is March 1.

International Students: They must score 500 on the written TOEFL.

Computers: The mainframe is an IBM AS/400. There are 7 computer labs on campus. PC- and Mac-available in residence halls are Internet and e-mail accessible. All students may access the system. There are no time limits and no fees.

Graduates: In an average class, 26% graduate in 4 years or less, 65% graduate in 5 years or less, and 3% graduate in 6 years or less.

Admissions Contact: Jane F. Dessoye, Executive Director of Admissions and Financial Aid. E-mail: *admiss@misericordia.edu* Web: *www.misericordia.edu*

CURTIS INSTITUTE OF MUSIC
Philadelphia, PA 19103-6187

F-3

(215) 893-5262
Fax: (215) 893-9065

Full-time: 40 men, 80 women	**Faculty:** n/av
Part-time: none	**Ph.Ds:** n/av
Graduate: 10 men, 10 women	**Student/Faculty:** n/av
Year: n/app	**Tuition:** 0
Application Deadline: open	**Room & Board:** n/app
Freshman Class: n/av	
SAT I: required	**SPECIAL**

Curtis Institute of Music, founded in 1924, is a private conservatory offering undergraduate, graduate, and professional programs in music. The institution serves an entirely commuter student body. All applicants are accepted on full-tuition scholarships. However, they must pay about $700 in fees and provide all their living expenses. Figures given in the above capsule and in this profile are approximate. In addition to regional accreditation, Curtis has baccalaureate program accreditation with

NASM. The library contains 60,000 volumes, 100 microform items, and 10,000 audio/video tapes/CDs, and subscribes to 40 periodicals. Special learning facilities include the Leonard Stolowski Collection. The campus is in an urban area. There are 3 buildings.

Student Life: 92% of undergraduates are from out of state, mostly the Northeast. Students are from 30 states, 21 foreign countries, and Canada. 90% are from public schools. 62% are white. The average age of freshmen is 18. 2% do not continue beyond their first year; 98% remain to graduate.

Housing: There are no residence halls. Alcohol is not permitted.

Activities: There are no fraternities or sororities. There are some groups and organizations on campus, including student government.

Sports: There is no sports program at Curtis.

Disabled Students: 1% of the campus is accessible. Elevators and specially equipped rest rooms are available.

Services: Counseling and information services are available. Tutoring is provided on an individual basis in every subject.

Campus Safety and Security: Measures include informal discussions, 24-hour security guards in the main building, and buzzer entry to other buildings.

Programs of Study: Bachelor's degrees are awarded in COMMUNICATIONS AND THE ARTS (music).

Requirements: The SAT I is required. In addition, applicants must be graduates of an accredited secondary school or have earned a GED. Confidential letters of recommendation from 2 qualified musicians are required. Admission is based primarily on evidence of the applicant's special talent. An audition is required. AP and CLEP credits are accepted.

Procedure: Freshmen are admitted in the fall. Entrance exams should be taken by March of the senior year. Application deadlines are open. Check with the school for the current fee.

Transfer: 97 of 131 credits required for the bachelor's degree must be completed at Curtis.

Financial Aid: Curtis is a member of CSS. The CSS Profile and the college's own financial statement are required. Check with the school for current deadlines.

International Students: They must score 500 on the written TOEFL and also take the SAT I.

Computers: All students may access the system. There are no time limits and no fees.

Admissions Contact: Judi L. Gattone, Director of Admissions.

DE SALES UNIVERSITY
Center Valley, PA 18034-9568

E-3

(610) 282-1100, ext. 1475
(877) 433-7253; Fax: (610) 282-0131

Full-time: 753 men, 921 women	**Faculty:** 90; IIA, --$
Part-time: 217 men, 276 women	**Ph.Ds:** 73%
Graduate: 747 men and women	**Student/Faculty:** 19 to 1
Year: semesters, summer session	**Tuition:** $18,390
Application Deadline: open	**Room & Board:** $7080
Freshman Class: 1678 applied, 1284 accepted, 398 enrolled	
SAT I Verbal/Math: 530/540	COMPETITIVE

De Sales University, founded in 1964, is a private liberal arts institution affiliated with the Roman Catholic Church. In addition to regional accreditation, DSU has baccalaureate program accreditation with ARC-PA and NLN. The library contains 140,629 volumes, 454,163 microform items, and 6264 audio/video tapes/CDs, and subscribes to 541 periodicals. Computerized library services include the card catalog, interlibrary loans, and database searching. Special learning facilities include a learning resource center, radio station, TV station, 2 theaters, 2 dance studios, a distant learning center, and a science center. The 400-acre campus is in a suburban area 50 miles north of Philadelphia. Including any residence halls, there are 24 buildings.

Student Life: 85% of undergraduates are from Pennsylvania. Students are from 10 states and 5 foreign countries. 46% are from public schools. 94% are white. 73% are Catholic; 12% Protestant; 6% claim no religious affiliation. The average age of freshmen is 18. 17% do not continue beyond their first year; 65% remain to graduate.

Housing: 823 students can be accommodated in college housing, which includes single-sex and coed dorms. In addition, there are special-interest houses. On-campus housing is guaranteed for all 4 years. 70% of students live on campus; of those, 60% remain on campus on weekends. All students may keep cars.

Activities: There is 1 local sororitiy. There are no fraternities. There are 32 groups on campus, including cheerleading, chorale, chorus, computers, dance, debate, drama, ethnic, honors, international, literary magazine, musical theater, newspaper, political, professional, radio and TV, religious, social, social service, student government, and yearbook. Popular campus events include Act One Plays, Annual Lecture Series, and Fall Fest.

Sports: There are 8 intercollegiate sports for men and 7 for women, and 8 intramural sports for men and 8 for women. Facilities include facilities for soccer, baseball, softball, tennis, basketball, lacrosse, track and cross country, and volleyball, and a state-of-the-art sports and recreation facility featuring a state-of-the-art fitness center, a student lounge, and multi-purpose athletic courts.

Disabled Students: 95% of the campus is accessible. Wheelchair ramps, elevators, special parking, specially equipped rest rooms, special class scheduling, lowered drinking fountains, and lowered telephones are available.

Services: Counseling and information services are available, as is tutoring in most subjects. There is a reader service for the blind and remedial reading and writing. Learning Center resources (including tutoring) are available to all students.

Campus Safety and Security: Measures include 24-hour foot and vehicle patrol, security escort services, informal discussions, and pamphlets/posters/films. There are emergency telephones, lighted pathways/sidewalks, and 24-hour desk security in residence halls.

Programs of Study: DSU confers B.A., B.S., and B.S.N. degrees. Master's degrees are also awarded. Bachelor's degrees are awarded in BIOLOGICAL SCIENCE (biology/biological science), BUSINESS (accounting, banking and finance, business administration and management, electronic business, human resources, management information systems, marketing/retailing/merchandising, and sports management), COMMUNICATIONS AND THE ARTS (communications, dance, dramatic arts, English, film arts, performing arts, radio/television technology, and Spanish), COMPUTER AND PHYSICAL SCIENCE (chemistry, computer science, and mathematics), EDUCATION (elementary), ENGINEERING AND ENVIRONMENTAL DESIGN (environmental science), HEALTH PROFESSIONS (nursing, physician's assistant, and sports medicine), SOCIAL SCIENCE (criminal justice, family/consumer studies, history, liberal arts/general studies, philosophy, political science/government, psychology, social work, and theological studies). Performing arts, nursing, and natural sciences are the strongest academically. Elementary education, theater/tv/film, and criminal justice are the largest.

Required: For graduation, students must complete a minimum of 120 credit hours, including a maximum of 48 in the major, with a minimum GPA of 2.0. Liberal arts distribution requirements consist of 12 to 16 courses including cultural literacy, modes of thinking, and Christian values and theology, as well as 3 units in phys ed. Internships are strongly encouraged for all majors.

Special: Students may cross-register with schools in the Lehigh Valley Association of Independent Colleges. Internships are strongly encouraged in all majors and study abroad in 2 countries is possible. Dual majors, a Washington semester, pass/fail options, accelerated degree programs, and credit for life, military, and work experience are offered. There are 10 national honor societies and a freshman honors program.

Faculty/Classroom: 63% of faculty are male; 37%, female. All teach undergraduates and do research. No introductory courses are taught by graduate students. The average class size in an introductory lecture is 20; in a laboratory, 20; and in a regular course, 20.

Admissions: 77% of the 2003-2004 applicants were accepted. The SAT I scores for the 2003-2004 freshman class were: Verbal--31% below 500, 45% between 500 and 599, 21% between 600 and 700, and 3% above 700; Math--29% below 500, 46% between 500 and 599, 23% between 600 and 700, and 2% above 700. 38% of the current freshmen were in the top fifth of their class; 65% were in the top two fifths.

Requirements: The SAT I is required. In addition, applicants must be graduates of an accredited secondary school. The GED is accepted. Applicants should have completed 17 college preparatory courses, including 4 years each of English, history, and math, 3 years of science, and 2 years of foreign language. The school will accept an essay, but strongly recommends an interview. For theater students, a performance appraisal is required. For dance students an audition is required. A GPA of 3.0 is required. AP and CLEP credits are accepted. Important factors in the admissions decision are advanced placement or honor courses, leadership record, and evidence of special talent.

Procedure: Freshmen are admitted fall and spring. Entrance exams should be taken during the junior or senior year. There is a deferred admissions plan and a rolling admissions plan. Application deadlines are open. Application fee is $30. Applications are accepted on-line through Apply, EXPAN, and the school's web site.

Transfer: 68 transfer students enrolled in 2002-2003. Applicants for transfer should have completed a minimum of 24 college credit hours with a GPA of 2.5. An interview is recommended. 45 of 120 credits required for the bachelor's degree must be completed at DSU.

Visiting: There are regularly scheduled orientations for prospective students, including meetings with faculty advisers and social activities. There are guides for informal visits and visitors may sit in on classes and stay overnight. To schedule a visit, contact the Enrollment Management Office at (610) 282-4443 or admiss@desales.edu.

Financial Aid: In a recent year, 80% of all full-time freshmen and 84% of continuing full-time students received some form of financial aid. 76% of full-time freshmen and 83% of continuing full-time students received need-based aid. The average freshman award was $12,587. 51% of undergraduates work part time. Average annual earnings from campus work are $833. The average financial indebtedness of a recent graduate was $13,997. The FAFSA and the college's own financial statement are required. The deadline for filing freshman financial aid applications for fall entry is February 1.

International Students: There are 10 international students enrolled. They must score 550 on the written TOEFL. The SAT I is recommended, but not required.

Computers: There are 200 public computing/classroom PCs, fully network compliant, and network connections are supplied to all residence hall rooms. Students use their own PCs in their residence hall room. Wireless networks are available in student lounges and in the library. Internet access is available on all networks. All students may access the system 24/hours a day from residence hall rooms, and 7 A.M. to 11 P.M. in public computing rooms. There are no time limits and no fees. It is strongly recommended that all students have a personal computer. A 100 MHz processor is recommended.

Graduates: From July 1, 2002 to June 30, 2003, 410 bachelor's degrees were awarded. The most popular majors were business (28%), visual and performing arts (12%), and computer science/mathematics (9%). In an average class, 59% graduate in 4 years or less, 59% graduate in 5 years or less, and 64% graduate in 6 years or less. 41 companies recruited on campus in 2002-2003. Of the 2002 graduating class, 17% were enrolled in graduate school within 6 months of graduation and 82% were employed.

Admissions Contact: Jerry Joyce, Dean of Enrollment Management. E-mail: admiss@desales.edu Web: www.desales.edu

DELAWARE VALLEY COLLEGE
Doylestown, PA 18901-2697

F-3

(215) 489-2372
(800) 2-DEL-VAL; Fax: (215) 230-2968

Full-time: 728 men, 730 women	**Faculty:** 76; IIB, -$
Part-time: 237 men, 263 women	**Ph.D.s:** 63%
Graduate: 36 men, 43 women	**Student/Faculty:** 19 to 1
Year: semesters, summer session	**Tuition:** $19,304
Application Deadline: open	**Room & Board:** $7372
Freshman Class: 1556 applied, 1283 accepted, 440 enrolled	
SAT I Verbal/Math: 497/494	**ACT:** 21 COMPETITIVE

Delaware Valley College, founded in 1896, is a private institution offering undergraduate programs in specialized fields of agriculture, business administration, English, the sciences, math, criminal justice administration, and secondary education. The library contains 57,342 volumes and 162,914 microform items, and subscribes to 728 periodicals. Computerized library services include interlibrary loans and database searching. Special learning facilities include a learning resource center, radio station, a dairy science center, a livestock farm, horse facilities, an apiary, a small animal lab, a tissue culture lab, an arboretum, and greenhouses. The 600-acre campus is in a suburban area 20 miles north of Philadelphia. Including any residence halls, there are 36 buildings.

Student Life: 64% of undergraduates are from Pennsylvania. Students are from 20 states, 4 foreign countries, and Canada. 84% are from public schools. 76% are white. 35% are Catholic; 32% Protestant; 16% claim no religious affiliation; 14% Buddhist, Seventh-day Adventist, and others. The average age of freshmen is 18; all undergraduates, 20. 28% do not continue beyond their first year; 72% remain to graduate.

Housing: 895 students can be accommodated in college housing, which includes single-sex and coed dorms. In addition, there are honors houses. On-campus housing is available on a first-come, first-served basis and is available on a lottery system for upperclassmen. 63% of students live on campus; of those, 50% remain on campus on weekends. All students may keep cars.

Activities: 4% of men belong to 5 national fraternities; 5% of women belong to 3 national sororities. There are 40 groups on campus, including art, band, cheerleading, chess, choir, chorale, chorus, computers, dance, drama, ethnic, honors, international, literary magazine, newspaper, pep band, photography, professional, radio and TV, religious, social, social service, student government, and yearbook. Popular campus events include A-Day, Parents Day, and Family Weekend.

Sports: There are 8 intercollegiate sports for men and 7 for women, and 9 intramural sports for men and 9 for women. Facilities include 2 gyms, tennis courts, outdoor playing courts and fields, a football stadium, a running track, a small lake, a video game room, picnic areas, nature walks, riding trails, and indoor and outdoor equine facilities.

Disabled Students: 85% of the campus is accessible. Wheelchair ramps, elevators, special parking, specially equipped rest rooms, special class scheduling, and lowered drinking fountains are available.

Services: Counseling and information services are available, as is tutoring in most subjects. There is a reader service for the blind, and remedial math, reading, and writing.

Campus Safety and Security: Measures include 24-hour foot and vehicle patrol, self-defense education, security escort services, and shuttle buses. There are informal discussions, pamphlets/posters/films, emergency telephones, and lighted pathways/sidewalks.

Programs of Study: DVC confers B.A. and B.S. degrees. Associate and master's degrees are also awarded. Bachelor's degrees are awarded in AGRICULTURE (agriculture, animal science, dairy science, horticulture, and wildlife management), BIOLOGICAL SCIENCE (biology/biological science), BUSINESS (accounting, business administration and management, and marketing/retailing/merchandising), COMMUNICATIONS AND THE ARTS (English), COMPUTER AND PHYSICAL SCIENCE (chemistry, computer science, and mathematics), EDUCATION (secondary), ENGINEERING AND ENVIRONMENTAL DESIGN (food services technology), SOCIAL SCIENCE (criminal justice, food production/management/services, and food science). Physical and biological science and animal science are the strongest academically. Business administration and animal science are the largest.

Required: The bachelor's degree requires completion of at least 128 credits, including 48 in the major, with a minimum GPA of 2.0. The core curriculum consists of 48 credits of liberal arts courses, including cultural enrichment, phys ed, and an introduction to computers. Students must also fulfill employment program requirements.

Special: DVC offers a specialized methods and techniques program that enables students to learn lab techniques and gain experience in the practical aspects of their majors. There is a zoo science major that prepares students for careers in zoo management and animal conservation. There are co-op programs in all majors, dual majors, study abroad in England, internships, and work-study programs in a wide variety of employment and research settings. Cross-registration is available with Rutgers University and Middle Bucks Technical Institute. Nondegree study and pass/fail options are also available. There are 3 national honor societies, a freshman honors program, and 2 departmental honors programs.

Faculty/Classroom: 71% of faculty are male; 29%, female. All teach undergraduates. The average class size in an introductory lecture is 50; in a laboratory, 22; and in a regular course, 35.

Admissions: 82% of the 2003-2004 applicants were accepted. The SAT I scores for the 2003-2004 freshman class were: Verbal--54% below 500, 35% between 500 and 599, 10% between 600 and 700, and 1% above 700; Math--52% below 500, 39% between 500 and 599, and 9% between 600 and 700. The ACT scores were 42% below 21, 42% between 21 and 23, and 16% between 24 and 26. 23% of the current freshmen were in the top fifth of their class; 52% were in the top two fifths. 1 freshman graduated first in the class.

Requirements: The ACT is required. In addition, applicants must be graduates of accredited secondary schools or have earned a GED. The college requires 15 academic units, including 6 in electives, 3 in English, and 2 each in math, science, and social studies. An interview is recommended. DVC requires applicants to be in the upper 50% of their class. A GPA of 2.75 is required. AP and CLEP credits are accepted. Important factors in the admissions decision are leadership record, personality/intangible qualities, and extracurricular activities record.

Procedure: Freshmen are admitted fall and spring. Entrance exams should be taken in the junior or senior year. Application deadlines are open. There is a rolling admissions plan. Notification is sent on a rolling basis. Application fee is $35. Applications are accepted on-line through CollegeNET and the college's web site.

Transfer: 79 transfer students enrolled in 2002-2003. Applicants must have a minimum GPA of 2.0 and must submit SAT I scores. An interview is recommended. 60 credits of 128 required for the bachelor's degree must be completed at DVC.

Visiting: There are regularly scheduled orientations for prospective students, consisting of a student panel, meetings with department chairs, and general information sessions. There are guides for informal visits and visitors may sit in on classes and stay overnight. To schedule a visit, contact the Admissions Department.

Financial Aid: In 2003-2004, 96% of all full-time freshmen and 92% of continuing full-time students received some form of financial aid. 77% of full-time freshmen and 74% of continuing full-time students received need-based aid. The average freshman award was $15,196. 27% of undergraduates work part time. Average annual earnings from campus work was $1600. The average financial indebtedness of the 2003 graduate was $17,790. The FAFSA is required. The deadline for filing freshman financial aid applications for fall entry is April 1.

International Students: There are 3 international students enrolled. They must score 500 on the written TOEFL and also take the SAT I or the ACT.

Computers: There are 150 PCs in the computer center, labs, the library, the tutoring center, and residence hall lounges. All students may access the system at designated times in the labs and 24 hours per day in most other areas. There are no time limits and no fees.

Graduates: From July 1, 2002 to June 30, 2003, 278 bachelor's degrees were awarded. The most popular majors were business administration (25%), animal science (20%), and ornamental horticulture (10%). In an average class, 40% graduate in 4 years or less, 50% graduate in 5 years or less, and 52% graduate in 6 years or less. 310 companies recruited on campus in 2002-2003. Of the 2002 graduating class, 9% were enrolled in graduate school within 6 months of graduation and 95% were employed.

Admissions Contact: Stephen W. Zenko, Director of Admissions. A video is available. E-mail: *admitme@devalcol.edu* Web: *www.devalcol.edu*

DEVRY UNIVERSITY/FORT WASHINGTON
Fort Washington, PA 19034-3204

(215) 591-5700
(866) 303-3879; Fax: (251) 591-5745

Full-time: 350 men, 93 women	**Faculty:** n/av
Part-time: 147 men, 73 women	**Ph.D.s:** n/av
Graduate: n/av	**Student/Faculty:** n/av
Year: semesters, summer session	**Tuition:** $11,860
Application Deadline: open	**Room & Board:** n/app
Freshman Class: n/av	
SAT I or ACT: n/av	**LESS COMPETITIVE**

DeVry University/Fort Washington. 1 of 67 DeVry University locations in the United States and Canada, opened in 2002. It offers programs in business administration, computer engineering technology, computer information systems, electronics engineering technology, network and communications management, and technical management. The library contains 4211 volumes and 618 audio/video tapes/CDs, and subscribes to 68 periodicals. The campus is located 25 miles from downtown Philadelphia.

Student Life: 46% are white; 39% African American.

Housing: There are no residence halls. All students commute.

Activities: There are no fraternities or sororities.

Programs of Study: DeVry confers B.A. degrees. Associate and master's degrees are also awarded. Bachelor's degrees are awarded in BUSINESS (business administration and management), COMMUNICATIONS AND THE ARTS (telecommunications), COMPUTER AND PHYSICAL SCIENCE (information sciences and systems), ENGINEERING AND ENVIRONMENTAL DESIGN (computer engineering, electrical/electronics engineering technology, and technological management).

Required: To graduate, students must achieve a GPA of at least 2.0, complete 48 to 154 credit hours, and satisfactorily complete all curriculum requirements. Course requirements vary according to program. All first-semester students take course in business organization, computer applications, algebra, psychology, and student success strategies.

Special: Accelerated degree programs in computer information systems and technical management, co-op programs, and distance learning are available.

Requirements: Admissions requirements include graduation from a secondary school; the GED is accepted. Applicants must pass the DeVry entrance exam or present satisfactory SAT I or ACT scores. An interview is required.

Procedure: Freshmen are admitted fall, spring, and summer. There are early admissions, deferred admissions, and rolling admissions plans. Application deadlines are open. Application fee is $50. Applications are accepted on-line through *https://apply.embark.edu/UGrad/DeVry/21/*.

Transfer: 25 of 48 credits required for the bachelor's degree must be completed at DeVry University/Fort Washington.

Financial Aid: In 2002-2003, 74% of all full-time freshmen and 75% of continuing full-time students received some form of financial aid. At least 73% of all full-time students received need-based aid. The average freshman award was $6884. Need-based scholarships or need-based grants averaged $4120; need-based self-help aid (loans and jobs) averaged $4201; and other institutional non-need-based awards and non-need-based scholarships averaged $8122. The FAFSA is required. The deadline for filing freshman financial aid applications for fall entry is rolling.

International Students: They must score 500 on the written version or 173 on the electronic version of the TOEFL and also take the college's own entrance exam.

Admissions Contact: Director of Admissions.
E-mail: *admissions@phi.devry.edu*
Web: *www.devry.edu/fortwashington*

DICKINSON COLLEGE
Carlisle, PA 17013

D-3
(717) 245-1231
(800) 644-1773; Fax: (717) 245-1442

Full-time: 979 men, 1262 women	**Faculty:** 166; IIB, +$
Part-time: 14 men, 21 women	**Ph.D.s:** 90%
Graduate: none	**Student/Faculty:** 14 to 1
Year: semesters, summer session	**Tuition:** $28,615
Application Deadline: February 1	**Room & Board:** $7210
Freshman Class: 4633 applied, 2394 accepted, 624 enrolled	
SAT I Verbal/Math: 640/640	**ACT: 27 HIGHLY COMPETITIVE**

Dickinson College, founded in 1783, is a private institution offering a liberal arts curriculum including international education and science. The library contains 512,232 volumes, 166,352 microform items, and 16,736 audio/video tapes/CDs, and subscribes to 1600 periodicals. Computerized library services include the card catalog, interlibrary loans,

database searching, and Internet access. Special learning facilities include an art gallery, planetarium, radio station, fiber optic and satellite telecommunications networks, telescope observatory, and an archival collection. The 115-acre campus is in a suburban area about 20 miles west of Harrisburg and 2 hours from Washington, DC. Including any residence halls, there are 113 buildings.

Student Life: 65% of undergraduates are from out of state, mostly the Middle Atlantic. Students are from 43 states, 20 foreign countries, and Canada. 62% are from public schools. 90% are white. 35% are Protestant; 31% Catholic; 20% claim no religious affiliation. The average age of freshmen is 18; all undergraduates, 20. 10% do not continue beyond their first year; 76% remain to graduate.

Housing: 1931 students can be accommodated in college housing, which includes coed dorms, on-campus apartments, fraternity houses, and sorority houses. In addition, there are language houses and special-interest houses, including arts, Asian, environmental, equality, Hillel, and multicultural. On-campus housing is guaranteed for all 4 years. 91% of students live on campus; of those, 85% remain on campus on weekends. Upperclassmen may keep cars.

Activities: 23% of men belong to 8 national fraternities; 24% of women belong to 1 local and 3 national sororities. There are 120 groups on campus, including art, band, cheerleading, chess, choir, chorale, chorus, computers, dance, debate, drama, ethnic, film, gay, honors, international, jazz band, literary magazine, musical theater, newspaper, orchestra, photography, political, professional, radio and TV, religious, social, social service, student government, symphony, and yearbook. Popular campus events include Black Arts Festival, Multicultural Fair, and Public Affairs Symposium.

Sports: There are 11 intercollegiate sports for men and 12 for women, and 16 intramural sports for men and 15 for women. Facilities include an 8,000-square-foot fitness center with weight training and 40 cardiorespiratory conditioning machines. The 38,600-square-foot Kline Center includes basketball, squash, racquetball, and handball courts. The gym area features a multipurpose synthetic floor covering that includes an indoor 200-meter 4-lane track with a jump pit. There is a 20-yard competition swimming pool with separate diving well and seating for 350 spectators, tennis courts, a varsity football field, and lacrosse, baseball, and soccer fields, all comprising nearly 30 acres. There is also an outdoor track, jogging trails, and an indoor rock-climbing wall.

Disabled Students: 56% of the campus is accessible. Wheelchair ramps, elevators, special parking, specially equipped rest rooms, special class scheduling, lowered drinking fountains, lowered telephones, and special housing are available.

Services: Counseling and information services are available, as is tutoring in every subject. Services are provided as necessary on a case-by-case basis. There is a reader service for the blind. There also is a writing center.

Campus Safety and Security: Measures include 24-hour foot and vehicle patrol, self-defense education, security escort services, and informal discussions. There are pamphlets/posters/films, emergency telephones, lighted pathways/sidewalks, and electronic access to residence halls.

Programs of Study: Dickinson confers B.A. and B.S. degrees. Bachelor's degrees are awarded in BIOLOGICAL SCIENCE (biochemistry and biology/biological science), BUSINESS (international business management), COMMUNICATIONS AND THE ARTS (classical languages, dance, dramatic arts, English, fine arts, French, German, Greek, Latin, music, Russian, Spanish, and theater design), COMPUTER AND PHYSICAL SCIENCE (chemistry, computer science, geology, mathematics, and physics), ENGINEERING AND ENVIRONMENTAL DESIGN (environmental science), HEALTH PROFESSIONS (environmental health science), SOCIAL SCIENCE (American studies, anthropology, archeology, classical/ancient civilization, East Asian studies, economics, history, international studies, Italian studies, Judaic studies, medieval studies, philosophy, political science/government, psychology, public affairs, religion, Russian and Slavic studies, sociology, and women's studies). International education/foreign languages, natural sciences, and preprofessional programs are the strongest academically. English, political science, international business and management are the largest.

Required: To graduate, students must complete 32 courses with a minimum GPA of 2.0. The school requires 2 courses each in humanities, social sciences, and lab sciences. Also required are 3 courses of crosscultural studies (including foreign language and U.S. diversity), a freshman seminar, phys ed, and the completion of a major averaging 9 to 10 courses. Writing-intensive and quantitative reasoning courses are also required.

Special: Students may cross-register with Central Pennsylvania Consortium Colleges. 32 academic year or summer study-abroad programs are offered in 22 countries. A Washington semester, work-study, and accelerated degree programs are available, as are dual majors, student-designed majors, nondegree study, pass/fail options, and a 3-3 law degree with the Dickinson School of Law of Pennsylvania State University. There are 3-2 engineering degrees offered with Case Western Reserve University, Rensselaer Polytechnic Institute, and the University of Pennsylvania. Instruction in 11 languages is available. There are certification programs in Latin American studies and secondary education. Linkage programs are available with 7 graduate programs in business, accounting, and public administration at various institutions. There are 15 national honor societies, including Phi Beta Kappa, and 39 departmental honors programs.

Faculty/Classroom: 59% of faculty are male; 41%, female. All both teach and do research. The average class size in an introductory lecture is 35; in a laboratory, 18; and in a regular course, 18.

Admissions: 52% of the 2003-2004 applicants were accepted. The SAT I scores for the 2003-2004 freshman class were: Verbal--26% between 500 and 599, 59% between 600 and 700, and 14% above 700; Math--2% below 500, 24% between 500 and 599, 56% between 600 and 700, and 18% above 700. The ACT scores were 1% below 21, 3% between 21 and 23, 34% between 24 and 26, 29% between 27 and 28, and 32% above 28. 73% of the current freshmen were in the top fifth of their class; 94% were in the top two fifths. 17 freshmen graduated first in their class.

Requirements: The SAT I or ACT is recommended. SAT II: Subject tests are optional submissions. The GED is accepted. Applicants should have completed 16 academic credits, including 4 years of English, 3 each of math and science, 2 (preferably 3) of foreign language, 2 of social studies, and 2 additional courses drawn from the above areas. An essay is required and an interview is recommended. AP credits are accepted. Important factors in the admissions decision are advanced placement or honor courses, extracurricular activities record, and recommendations by school officials.

Procedure: Freshmen are admitted in the fall. Entrance exams should be taken in the spring of the junior year or the fall of the senior year. There are early decision, early admissions, and deferred admissions plans. Early decision applications should be filed by January 15; regular applications, by February 1 for fall entry. The fall 2003 application fee was $50. Notification of early decision is sent February 15; regular decision, March 31. 286 early decision candidates were accepted for the 2003-2004 class. 292 were on the 2003 waiting list; 17 were admitted. Applications are accepted on computer disk and on-line through Common App, CollegeView, CollegeLink, and others.

Transfer: 30 transfer students enrolled in 2002-2003. Applicants for transfer will normally have at least a 2.0 cumulative GPA and must submit secondary school and college transcripts and a dean's report form in addition to the standard application for admission. 16 credits of 32 required for the bachelor's degree must be completed at Dickinson.

Visiting: There are regularly scheduled orientations for prospective students, including campus tours, individual interviews, group information sessions, class visits, overnight stays in residence halls, and open houses. There are guides for informal visits and visitors may sit in on classes and stay overnight. To schedule a visit, contact the Admissions Office.

Financial Aid: In 2003-2004, 68% of all full-time freshmen and 70% of continuing full-time students received some form of financial aid. 47% of full-time freshmen and 52% of continuing full-time students received need-based aid. The average freshman award was $20,881, with $15,118 ($35,540 maximum) from need-based scholarships or need-based grants, $4218 ($13,200 maximum) from need-based self-help aid (loans and jobs), and $1545 ($38,000 maximum) from federal, state, and outside grants/scholarships. 55% of undergraduates work part time. Average annual earnings from campus work are $1289. The average financial indebtedness of the 2003 graduate was $19,207. Dickinson is a member of CSS. The CSS/Profile, FAFSA, the state aid form, noncustodial parent statement, and business farm supplement are required. The deadline for filing freshman financial aid applications for fall entry is February 1.

International Students: There are 43 international students enrolled. The school actively recruits these students. They must score 550 on the written TOEFL.

Computers: The mainframe is an HP Alpha Server E547. A fiber-optic network enables students to have private PC hookup to the mainframe from their residence hall rooms. All students are assigned Alpha accounts for e-mail and Internet communications. There are more than 596 PCs and Macs in public areas and instructional spaces. All students may access the system. There are no time limits and no fees.

Graduates: From July 1, 2002 to June 30, 2003, 542 bachelor's degrees were awarded. The most popular majors were English (12%), political science (12%), and international studies (12%). In an average class, 76% graduate in 4 years or less, 78% graduate in 5 years or less, and 79% graduate in 6 years or less. 34 companies recruited on campus in 2002-2003. Of the 2002 graduating class, 20% were enrolled in graduate school within 6 months of graduation and 79% were employed.

Admissions Contact: Christopher Seth Allen, Director of Admissions. E-mail: *admit@dickinson.edu* Web: *http://www.dickinson.edu*

DREXEL UNIVERSITY
Philadelphia, PA 19104

F-3

(215) 895-2400
(800) 2-DREXEL; Fax: (215) 895-5939

Full-time: 5693 men, 3645 women
Part-time: 941 men, 732 women
Graduate: 1980 men, 2260 women
Year: quarters, summer session
Application Deadline: March 1
Freshman Class: n/av
SAT I Verbal/Math: 580/620

Faculty: 653; I, -$
Ph.D.s: 90%
Student/Faculty: 14 to 1
Tuition: $18,960
Room & Board: $8695

VERY COMPETITIVE

Drexel University, established in 1891, is a private institution with undergraduate programs in business and administration, engineering, information studies, design arts, and arts and sciences. Cost figures in the above capsule are approximate. There are 9 undergraduate and 8 graduate schools. In addition to regional accreditation, Drexel has baccalaureate program accreditation with AACSB, ABET, ADA, APA, CSAB, FIDER, and NAAB. The library contains 290,000 volumes, 651,500 microform items, and 32,935 audio/video tapes/CDs, and subscribes to 9662 periodicals. Computerized library services include the card catalog, interlibrary loans, and database searching. Special learning facilities include a learning resource center, art gallery, radio station, and TV station. The 49-acre campus is in an urban area near the center of Philadelphia. Including any residence halls, there are 34 buildings.

Student Life: 40% of undergraduates are from out of state, mostly the Middle Atlantic. Students are from 40 states, 121 foreign countries, and Canada. 61% are white; 13% Asian American; 10% African American. The average age of freshmen is 18; all undergraduates, 21. 14% do not continue beyond their first year; 54% remain to graduate.

Housing: 2600 students can be accommodated in college housing, which includes coed dorms, on-campus apartments, and fraternity houses. In addition, there are honorss floors in residence halls and international student housing. On-campus housing is available on a first-come, first-served basis and is available on a lottery system for upperclassmen. Freshmen are required to live on campus unless they live with their parents. 63% of students commute. All students may keep cars.

Activities: 12% of men belong to 14 national fraternities; 8% of women belong to 4 national sororities. There are 103 groups on campus, including art, band, cheerleading, chess, choir, chorus, computers, dance, drama, ethnic, film, gay, honors, international, jazz band, literary magazine, musical theater, newspaper, orchestra, pep band, photography, political, professional, radio and TV, religious, social, social service, student government, and yearbook. Popular campus events include Spring Jam, Winter Weekend, and an ongoing program of musical, cultural, and art events.

Sports: There are 10 intercollegiate sports for men and 10 for women, and 15 intramural sports for men and 12 for women. Facilities include a phys ed and activity center with 3 gyms, 6 squash courts, a swimming pool, a diving well, a wrestling room, a dance studio, a fencing room, Nautilus weight training rooms, and special exercise rooms; a field house; a bowling alley and game room with billiard, table tennis, and arcade games; and an outdoor volleyball court.

Disabled Students: 75% of the campus is accessible. Wheelchair ramps, elevators, special parking, specially equipped rest rooms, special class scheduling, lowered drinking fountains, lowered telephones, and special housing are available.

Services: Counseling and information services are available, as is tutoring in most subjects. There is remedial math, reading, and writing, and a resident tutor program.

Campus Safety and Security: Measures include 24-hour foot and vehicle patrol, self-defense education, security escort services, and shuttle buses. There are pamphlets/posters/films, emergency telephones, lighted pathways/sidewalks, and residential and commuter safety and security programs.

Programs of Study: Drexel confers B.A., B.S., and B.Arch. degrees. Master's and doctoral degrees are also awarded. Bachelor's degrees are awarded in BIOLOGICAL SCIENCE (biology/biological science and nutrition), BUSINESS (business administration and management, fashion merchandising, hotel/motel and restaurant management, and marketing/retailing/merchandising), COMMUNICATIONS AND THE ARTS (communications, creative writing, design, film arts, graphic design, literature, music, photography, and video), COMPUTER AND PHYSICAL SCIENCE (chemistry, computer science, digital arts/technology, information sciences and systems, mathematics, physics, and science), EDUCATION (education), ENGINEERING AND ENVIRONMENTAL DESIGN (architectural engineering, architecture, biomedical engineering, chemical engineering, civil engineering, computer engineering, construction management, electrical/electronics engineering, environmental engineering, environmental science, interior design, materials engineering, and mechanical engineering), HEALTH PROFESSIONS (predentistry and premedicine), SOCIAL SCIENCE (fashion design and technology, food production/management/services, history, international studies, political science/government, prelaw, psychology, and sociology). Engineering, business, and design arts are the strongest academically. Electrical and computer engineering, business, and architecture are the largest.

Required: To graduate, students must complete 180 to 192 term credits with a minimum GPA of 2.0 and must earn the number of Drexel Co-op Units determined by the major. There are requirements in math, computer literacy, English, lab science, humanities, and history.

Special: The Drexel Plan of Cooperative Education enables students to alternate periods of full-time classroom studies and full-time employment with university-approved employers. Participation in cooperative education is mandatory, for most students. Cross-registration is available with Eastern Mennonite College, Indiana University of Pennsylvania, and Lincoln University. Drexel also offers study abroad, internships, accelerated degrees, 3-3 engineering degrees, dual majors, nondegree study, credit/no credit options, and a Sea Education Association semester. There is a freshman honors program.

Faculty/Classroom: 63% of faculty are male; 37%, female. The average class size in an introductory lecture is 35; in a laboratory, 24; and in a regular course, 24.

Admissions: The SAT I scores for the 2003-2004 freshman class were: Verbal--10% below 500, 47% between 500 and 599, 38% between 600 and 700, and 5% above 700; Math--5% below 500, 34% between 500 and 599, 50% between 600 and 700, and 11% above 700. 56% of the current freshmen were in the top fifth of their class; 85% were in the top two fifths. 21 freshmen graduated first in their class in a recent year.

Requirements: The SAT I or ACT is required; the SAT I is preferred. Applicants must be graduates of an accredited secondary school. The GED is accepted. An interview is recommended. A GPA of 2.0 is required. AP and CLEP credits are accepted. Important factors in the admissions decision are advanced placement or honor courses, evidence of special talent, and recommendations by school officials.

Procedure: Freshmen are admitted to all sessions. Entrance exams should be taken by January 1 of the senior year. There are early admissions and deferred admissions plans. There is a rolling admissions plan. Applications should be filed by March 1 for fall entry, along with a $50 fee. Notification is sent on a rolling basis. A waiting list is an active part of the admissions procedure. Applications are accepted on-line through the school's web site.

Transfer: 850 transfer students enrolled in 2003-2004. Applicants must have a minimum GPA of 2.5. Other requirements vary among the individual colleges within the university. 45 of 192 credits required for the bachelor's degree must be completed at Drexel.

Visiting: There are regularly scheduled orientations for prospective students, consisting of a 2-day program for new freshmen and their parents in late July. There are guides for informal visits and visitors may sit in on classes and stay overnight. To schedule a visit, contact the Admissions Office at *enroll@drexel.edu.*

Financial Aid: In 2003-2004, 70% of all full-time freshmen and 89% of continuing full-time students received some form of financial aid. The average freshman award was $10,728. Need-based scholarships or need-based grants averaged $4603; need-based self-help aid (loans and jobs) averaged $4989; non-need-based athletic scholarships averaged $24,014; and other non-need-based awards and non-need-based scholarships averaged $7045. 16% of undergraduates work part time. Average annual earnings from campus work are $800. The average financial indebtedness of the 2003 graduate was $22,234. The FAFSA is required. The deadline for filing freshman financial aid applications for fall entry is February 15.

International Students: There are 594 international students enrolled. The school actively recruits these students. They must score 510 on the written TOEFL.

Computers: The mainframes are an IBM 9121/320 and a Sun Server 670. Students may access the mainframe, the library, and the Internet through PCs in dorms or residences. There are also 610 networked public computers available. Drexel also offers completely wireless Internet access throughout the campus. All students may access the system 24 hours a day. There are no time limits and no fees. All students are required to have personal computers.

Graduates: From July 1, 2002 to June 30, 2003, 1942 bachelor's degrees were awarded. The most popular majors were business/marketing (27%), engineering/engineering technologies (23%), and computer and information sciences (15%). In an average class, 57% graduate in 6 years or less. 300 companies recruited on campus in 2002-2003. Of the 2002 graduating class, 14% were enrolled in graduate school within 6 months of graduation and 81% were employed.

Admissions Contact: David Eddy, Director of Admissions. A video is available. E-mail: *enroll@drexel.edu* Web: *www.drexel.edu*

DUQUESNE UNIVERSITY
Pittsburgh, PA 15282-0201

B-3
(412) 396-5002
(800) 456-0590; Fax: (412) 396-6223

Full-time: 2182 men, 3180 women	**Faculty:** 425; IIA, +$
Part-time: 175 men, 187 women	**Ph.D.s:** n/av
Graduate: 1622 men, 2355 women	**Student/Faculty:** 13 to 1
Year: semesters, summer session	**Tuition:** $19,425
Application Deadline: July 1	**Room & Board:** $7482
Freshman Class: 3856 applied, 3280 accepted, 1492 enrolled	
SAT I Verbal/Math: 560/560	**ACT:** 24 **VERY COMPETITIVE**

Duquesne University, founded in 1878 by the Spiritan Congregation, is a private Roman Catholic institution offering programs in liberal arts, natural and environmental sciences, nursing, health sciences, pharmacy, business, music, teacher preparation, preprofessional training, law, and leadership and professional development. There are 9 undergraduate and 10 graduate schools. In addition to regional accreditation, Duquesne has baccalaureate program accreditation with AACSB, ACOTE, ACPE, ACS, APTA, CAAHEP, CAPTE, and NASM. The 2 libraries contain 707,071 volumes and 312,682 microform items, and subscribe to 7880 periodicals. Computerized library services include the card catalog, interlibrary loans, database searching, and Internet access. Special learning facilities include a learning resource center, art gallery, radio station, TV station, and 123 multimedia enhanced teaching facilities. The 43-acre campus is in an urban area on a private, self-contained campus in the center of Pittsburgh. Including any residence halls, there are 26 buildings.

Student Life: 79% of undergraduates are from Pennsylvania. Students are from 46 states, 58 foreign countries, and Canada. 78% are from public schools. 84% are white. 55% are Catholic; 25% claim no religious affiliation. The average age of freshmen is 18; all undergraduates, 22. 14% do not continue beyond their first year; 72% remain to graduate.

Housing: 2849 students can be accommodated in college housing, which includes single-sex and coed dorms. In addition, there are honors houses, special-interest houses, fraternity and sorority wings, no smoking wings, international wings, and club wings. On-campus housing is guaranteed for the freshman year only on a first-come, first-served basis, and is available on a lottery system for upperclassmen. 51% of students commute. All students may keep cars, except resident freshmen and residents in Citiline Towers, Chatham Center, and Washington Plaza.

Activities: 14% of men belong to 2 local and 7 national fraternities; 14% of women belong to 1 local and 8 national sororities. There are 134 groups on campus, including art, band, cheerleading, chess, choir, chorale, chorus, computers, dance, debate, drama, ethnic, film, honors, international, jazz band, literary magazine, marching band, musical theater, newspaper, opera, orchestra, pep band, photography, political, professional, radio and TV, religious, social, social programming, social service, student government, symphony, and yearbook. Popular campus events include Carnival, Dance Marathon, and Valentine, Halloween, and Christmas balls.

Sports: There are 10 intercollegiate sports for men and 10 for women, and 9 intramural sports for men and 9 for women. Facilities include an athletic center, a swimming pool, a football and soccer field, a baseball field, an intramural field with an all weather track, a weight room and exercise facilities, volleyball courts, 4 tennis courts, a squash court, racquetball courts, and a street hockey court.

Disabled Students: All of the campus is accessible. Wheelchair ramps, elevators, special parking, specially equipped rest rooms, special class scheduling, lowered drinking fountains, lowered telephones, and special housing are available.

Services: Counseling and information services are available, as is tutoring in every subject, including special tutorials for chemistry, biology, physics, and math. There is a reader service for the blind and remedial math, reading, and writing.

Campus Safety and Security: Measures include 24-hour foot and vehicle patrol, self-defense education, security escort services, and informal discussions. There are pamphlets/posters/films, emergency telephones, lighted pathways/sidewalks, and security cameras throughout campus that monitor exterior areas. All academic buildings have card access. Security measures for residence halls include card access, security cameras, and entrances that are monitored by residence life staff 24 hours a day.

Programs of Study: Duquesne confers B.A., B.S., B.M., B.S.A.T., B.S.B.A., B.S.Ed., B.S.H.M.S., B.S.H.S., B.S.M.E., B.S.M.T., B.S.N., and B.S.P.S. degrees. Master's and doctoral degrees are also awarded. Bachelor's degrees are awarded in BIOLOGICAL SCIENCE (biochemistry, biology/biological science, and microbiology), BUSINESS (accounting, banking and finance, business administration and management, entrepreneurial studies, international business management, investments and securities, logistics, management information systems, management science, marketing and distribution, marketing/retailing/merchandising, and purchasing/inventory management), COMMUNICATIONS AND THE ARTS (art history and appreciation, classical languages, classics, communications, dramatic arts, English, Greek (classical), journalism, Latin, literature, music, music performance, Spanish, speech/debate/

rhetoric, and studio art), COMPUTER AND PHYSICAL SCIENCE (chemistry, computer science, mathematics, physics, and web technology), EDUCATION (athletic training, early childhood, education, educational media, elementary, English, foreign languages, mathematics, music, science, secondary, social studies, and special), ENGINEERING AND ENVIRONMENTAL DESIGN (environmental science), HEALTH PROFESSIONS (health care administration, health science, music therapy, nursing, occupational therapy, pharmacy, physical therapy, physician's assistant, and speech pathology/audiology), SOCIAL SCIENCE (classical/ancient civilization, economics, history, international relations, liberal arts/general studies, philosophy, political science/government, psychology, sociology, and theological studies). Liberal arts, business, and health sciences are the largest.

Required: To graduate, students are required to complete at least 120 credit hours, including a specified number in the major (varies by program), with a minimum 2.0 GPA. General requirements vary by department, but there is a 27-credit liberal arts core curriculum.

Special: The university offers cross-registration through the Pittsburgh Council on Higher Education, internships, study abroad in 25 countries, and a Washington semester. Also available are B.A.-B.S. degrees, Saturday College, a general studies degree, an accelerated degree program, dual and student-designed majors, a 3-2 engineering program with Case Western Reserve University and University of Pittsburgh, pass/fail options, and credit for life, military, and work experience. There are 5 national honor societies, a freshman honors program, and 7 departmental honors programs.

Faculty/Classroom: 61% of faculty are male; 39%, female. The average class size in an introductory lecture is 31; in a laboratory, 19; and in a regular course, 25.

Admissions: 85% of the 2003-2004 applicants were accepted. The SAT I scores for the 2003-2004 freshman class were: Verbal--21% below 500, 49% between 500 and 599, 27% between 600 and 700, and 3% above 700; Math--21% below 500, 46% between 500 and 599, 30% between 600 and 700, and 3% above 700. The ACT scores were 19% below 21, 25% between 21 and 23, 30% between 24 and 26, 15% between 27 and 28, and 11% above 28. 47% of the current freshmen were in the top fifth of their class; 78% were in the top two fifths. 46 freshmen graduated first in their class.

Requirements: The SAT I or ACT is required. In addition, students should have either a high school diploma or the GED. Applicants are required to have 16 academic credits, including 4 each in English and academic electives, and 8 combined in social studies, language, math,and science. An audition is required for music majors. An essay is required and an interview is recommended. A GPA of 3.0 is required. AP and CLEP credits are accepted.

Procedure: Freshmen are admitted to all sessions. Entrance exams should be taken during the spring of the junior year or the fall of the senior year. There are early decision, early admissions, and rolling and deferred admissions plans. Early decision applications should be filed by November 1; regular applications, by July 1 for fall entry, December 1 for spring entry, and April 1 for summer entry, along with a $50 fee. Notification of early decision is sent December 15; regular decision, on a rolling basis. 96 early decision candidates were accepted for the 2003-2004 class. Applications are accepted on-line through the school's web site.

Transfer: 172 transfer students enrolled in 2002-2003. Applicants must submit complete high school and college transcripts. Students should have a minimum GPA of 2.5 for the university, but some schools require a higher average. A minimum of 12 credits earned is required and an interview is recommended. 30 of 120 credits required for the bachelor's degree must be completed at Duquesne.

Visiting: There are regularly scheduled orientations for prospective students, consisting of a campus tour and individual interviews with counselors and professors. There are guides for informal visits and visitors may sit in on classes. To schedule a visit, contact the Office of Admissions at (412) 396-6222 or *admissions@duq.edu*.

Financial Aid: In 2003-2004, 97% of all full-time freshmen and 88% of continuing full-time students received some form of financial aid. 68% of full-time freshmen and 63% of continuing full-time students received need-based aid. The average freshman award was $15,555. Need-based scholarships or need-based grants averaged $2776 ($10,850 maximum); need-based self-help aid (loans and jobs) averaged $4339 ($6825 maximum); non-need-based athletic scholarships averaged $545 ($29,755 maximum); and other non-need-based awards and non-need-based scholarships averaged $6285 ($22,093 maximum). The average financial indebtedness of the 2003 graduate was $15,437. Duquesne is a member of CSS. The FAFSA and the college's own financial statement are required. The deadline for filing freshman financial aid applications for fall entry is May 1.

International Students: There are 130 international students enrolled. The school actively recruits these students. They must score 525 on the written TOEFL or 195 on the electronic version or take the MELAB.

Computers: The campus is covered by a 7000 Node Ethernet network, wireless network, and more than 700 computers in public and semi-public computer labs. All students may access the system. There are no time limits and no fees. It is strongly recommended that all students have a Dell, IBM, or Apple personal computer.

Graduates: From July 1, 2002 to June 30, 2003, 1060 bachelor's degrees were awarded. The most popular majors were liberal arts (29%), business (28%), and education (14%). In an average class, 56% graduate in 4 years or less, 68% graduate in 5 years or less, and 70% graduate in 6 years or less. 80 companies recruited on campus in 2002-2003. Of the 2002 graduating class, 23% were enrolled in graduate school within 6 months of graduation and 75% were employed.

Admissions Contact: Paul-James Cukanna, Director of Admissions. A video is available. E-mail: *admissions@duq.edu* Web: *www.admissions.duq.edu*

EAST STROUDSBURG UNIVERSITY OF PENNSYLVANIA

East Stroudsburg, PA 18301

F-2

(570) 422-3542
(877) 230-5547; Fax: (570) 422-3933

Full-time: 1935 men, 2715 women	**Faculty:** n/av
Part-time: 207 men, 264 women	**Ph.D.s:** n/av
Graduate: 314 men, 727 women	**Student/Faculty:** n/av
Year: semesters, summer session	**Tuition:** $5946 ($12,892)
Application Deadline: March 1	**Room & Board:** $4390

Freshman Class: 4280 applied, 3067 accepted, 1085 enrolled
SAT I Verbal/Math: 490/490

COMPETITIVE

East Stroudsburg University of Pennsylvania, founded in 1893, is a part of the Pennsylvania State System of Higher Education and offers programs in arts and science, health sciences and human performance, and professional studies. There are 3 undergraduate schools and 1 graduate school. In addition to regional accreditation, East Stroudsburg has baccalaureate program accreditation with NLN. The library contains 428,000 volumes, 1,238,040 microform items, and 7650 audio/video tapes/CDs, and subscribes to 2200 periodicals. Computerized library services include the card catalog, interlibrary loans, and database searching. Special learning facilities include a learning resource center, art gallery, radio station, and wildlife museum. The 183-acre campus is in a small town 75 miles west of New York City. Including any residence halls, there are 39 buildings.

Student Life: 81% of undergraduates are from Pennsylvania. Students are from 22 states, 21 foreign countries, and Canada. 92% are white. The average age of freshmen is 18; all undergraduates, 23. 17% do not continue beyond their first year; 60% remain to graduate.

Housing: 2140 students can be accommodated in college housing, which includes single-sex and coed dorms and on-campus apartments. There are honors floors. 53% of students commute. Alcohol is not permitted. Upperclassmen may keep cars.

Activities: 12% of men belong to 8 national fraternities; 15% of women belong to 2 local and 6 national sororities. There are 76 groups on campus, including art, band, cheerleading, chess, choir, chorus, computers, dance, drama, ethnic, gay, honors, international, jazz band, literary magazine, musical theater, newspaper, pep band, political, professional, radio and TV, religious, social, social service, student government, and yearbook. Popular campus events include concerts, Spring Music Festival, and International Celebrations.

Sports: There are 9 intercollegiate sports for men and 9 for women, and 11 intramural sports for men and 11 for women. Facilities include a 5000-seat stadium, a 2600-seat gym, another gym, 8 athletic fields, 12 outdoor tennis courts, 1 indoor tennis court, a swimming pool, indoor and outdoor tracks, and weight rooms.

Disabled Students: 98% of the campus is accessible. Wheelchair ramps, elevators, special parking, specially equipped rest rooms, special class scheduling, lowered drinking fountains, lowered telephones, and visual fire alarms for hearing impaired persons are available.

Services: Counseling and information services are available, as is tutoring in every subject. There is remedial math, reading, and writing.

Campus Safety and Security: Measures include 24-hour foot and vehicle patrol, self-defense education, security escort services, and informal discussions. There are pamphlets/posters/films, emergency telephones, lighted pathways/sidewalks, and a police bicycle patrol.

Programs of Study: East Stroudsburg confers B.A. and B.S. degrees. Master's degrees are also awarded. Bachelor's degrees are awarded in BIOLOGICAL SCIENCE (biochemistry, biology/biological science, and marine science), BUSINESS (business administration and management and hotel/motel and restaurant management), COMMUNICATIONS AND THE ARTS (art, communications, dramatic arts, English, fine arts, French, media arts, music, and Spanish), COMPUTER AND PHYSICAL SCIENCE (chemistry, computer science, earth science, mathematics, physical sciences, and science), EDUCATION (early childhood, elementary, foreign languages, health, secondary, and special), ENGINEERING AND ENVIRONMENTAL DESIGN (environmental science), HEALTH PROFESSIONS (allied health, medical laboratory technology, nursing, premedicine, and speech pathology/audiology), SOCIAL SCIENCE (economics, geography, history, parks and recreation management, philosophy, physical fitness/movement, political science/government, psychology, social studies, and sociology). Computer science, nursing, and math are the strongest academically. Education, hospitality management, and phys ed are the largest.

Required: All students must maintain a GPA of at least 2.0 while taking 128 semester hours, including 27 to 83 hours in the major. General education courses total 50 credits, with English composition and phys ed required courses. Distribution requirements include 15 hours in arts and letters, science, and social science.

Special: Internships are offered in most programs, as are dual majors. Also offered are B.A.-B.S. degrees, 3-2 engineering degrees with Pennsylvania State University or the University of Pittsburgh, and a transfer program in podiatry. Nondegree study, study abroad, and cross-registration through the National Student Exchange are possible. There are 16 national honor societies and a freshman honors program.

Faculty/Classroom: All teach undergraduates. No introductory courses are taught by graduate students. The average class size in an introductory lecture is 40; in a laboratory, 25; and in a regular course, 25.

Admissions: 72% of the 2003-2004 applicants were accepted. The SAT I scores for the 2003-2004 freshman class were: Verbal--57% below 500, 36% between 500 and 599, 6% between 600 and 700, and 1% above 700; Math--53% below 500, 38% between 500 and 599, 8% between 600 and 700, and 1% above 700. 16% of the current freshmen were in the top fifth of their class; 48% were in the top two fifths.

Requirements: The SAT I is required. In addition, applicants must be graduates of an accredited secondary school. The GED is accepted. AP and CLEP credits are accepted. Important factors in the admissions decision are advanced placement or honor courses, evidence of special talent, and leadership record.

Procedure: Freshmen are admitted in the fall. Entrance exams should be taken during the fall of the senior year. Applications should be filed by March 1 for fall entry for priority consideration. The fall 2003 application fee was $35. Notification is sent March 1.

Transfer: Transfer students must have a 2.0 GPA earned over at least 24 credit hours. 32 of 128 credits required for the bachelor's degree must be completed at East Stroudsburg.

Visiting: There are regularly scheduled orientations for prospective students. There are guides for informal visits and visitors may sit in on classes. To schedule a visit, contact the Admissions Office.

Financial Aid: In 2003-2004, 67% of all full-time freshmen and 72% of continuing full-time students received some form of financial aid. East Stroudsburg is a member of CSS. The FAFSA is required. Check with the school for current deadlines.

International Students: They must score 500 on the written TOEFL.

Computers: The mainframe is a Unisys A-11. There are 14 file servers connected to 400 PCs located in 15 computer labs. All students may access the system. Most computers are available 7 A.M. to 10 P.M., with some available on a 24-hour basis. There are no time limits and no fees.

Graduates: In an average class, 1% graduate in 3 years or less, 25% graduate in 4 years or less, 45% graduate in 5 years or less, and 50% graduate in 6 years or less.

Admissions Contact: Alan T. Chesterton, Director of Admission. E-mail: *undergrads@esu.edu* Web: *www.esu.edu*

EASTERN UNIVERSITY
St. Davids, PA 19087-3696

F-3
(610) 341-5967
(800) 452-0996; Fax: (610) 341-1723

Full-time: 520 men, 1030 women	**Faculty:** 64; IIA, --$
Part-time: 120 men, 230 women	**Ph.D.s:** 75%
Graduate: 330 men, 530 women	**Student/Faculty:** 24 to 1
Year: semesters, summer session	**Tuition:** $16,820
Application Deadline: May 1	**Room & Board:** $7200
Freshman Class: n/av	
SAT I or ACT: required	**COMPETITIVE**

Eastern University, founded in 1932, is a private liberal arts institution affiliated with the American Baptist Church. Enrollment and faculty information in the above capsule is approximate. In addition to regional accreditation, Eastern has baccalaureate program accreditation with CSWE and NLN. The 2 libraries contain 131,000 volumes, 716,396 microform items, and 13,242 audio/video tapes/CDs, and subscribe to 1079 periodicals. Computerized library services include the card catalog, interlibrary loans, and database searching. Special learning facilities include a planetarium and radio station. The 106-acre campus is in a small town 20 miles northwest of Philadelphia. Including any residence halls, there are 23 buildings.

Student Life: 60% of undergraduates are from Pennsylvania. Students are from 38 states, 26 foreign countries, and Canada. 72% are from public schools. 81% are white; 14% African American. 68% are Assembly of God, Christian, Evangelical, Mennonite, Pentecostal; 13% claim no religious affiliation; 11% Catholic. The average age of freshmen is 19; all undergraduates, 27. 28% do not continue beyond their first year; 55% remain to graduate.

Housing: 840 students can be accommodated in college housing, which includes single-sex and coed dorms and on-campus apartments. On-campus housing is guaranteed for all 4 years. 53% of students commute. Alcohol is not permitted. All students may keep cars.

Activities: There are no fraternities or sororities. There are 70 groups on campus, including band, cheerleading, choir, chorale, chorus, computers, dance, drama, drill team, ethnic, honors, international, jazz band, literary magazine, musical theater, newspaper, orchestra, pep band, political, professional, radio and TV, religious, social, social service, student government, and yearbook. Popular campus events include President's Christmas Party, Spring Banquet, and World Culture Day.

Sports: There are 5 intercollegiate sports for men and 7 for women, and 3 intramural sports for men and 3 for women. Facilities include a gym, a soccer pitch, a baseball/field hockey/softball field, a weight room, an outdoor track, 4 tennis courts, a health fitness trail, an outdoor pool, and basketball/volleyball courts.

Disabled Students: 75% of the campus is accessible. Wheelchair ramps, elevators, special parking, specially equipped rest rooms, special class scheduling, lowered drinking fountains, lowered telephones, and special housing are available.

Services: Counseling and information services are available, as is tutoring in every subject. There is a reader service for the blind, remedial math, reading, and writing, and a summer skills workshop.

Campus Safety and Security: Measures include 24-hour foot and vehicle patrol, self-defense education, security escort services, and shuttle buses. There are informal discussions, pamphlets/posters/films, emergency telephones, and lighted pathways/sidewalks.

Programs of Study: Eastern confers B.A., B.S., B.S.N., and B.S.W. degrees. Associate and master's degrees are also awarded. Bachelor's degrees are awarded in AGRICULTURE (environmental studies), BIOLOGICAL SCIENCE (biochemistry and biology/biological science), BUSINESS (accounting, business administration and management, management information systems, and marketing/retailing/merchandising), COMMUNICATIONS AND THE ARTS (art history and appreciation, communications, dance, English literature, French, music, Spanish, and studio art), COMPUTER AND PHYSICAL SCIENCE (astronomy, chemistry, and mathematics), EDUCATION (elementary, English, secondary, and special), ENGINEERING AND ENVIRONMENTAL DESIGN (city/community/regional planning), HEALTH PROFESSIONS (health care administration and health science), SOCIAL SCIENCE (biblical studies, history, missions, political science/government, psychology, social work, sociology, theological studies, urban studies, and youth ministry). Biblical/theological studies and English literature are the strongest academically. Youth ministries and elementary education are the largest.

Required: To graduate, all students must complete at least 127 credit hours with a minimum 2.0 GPA. The required hours in the major vary. Students must take courses in the Old and New Testament, humanities, social sciences, non-Western heritage, natural sciences, college writing, Living and Learning in Community, Heritage of Western Thought and Civilization, Science Technology and Values, and Justice in a Pluralistic Society and complete a capstone.

Special: The college offers cross-registration with Cabrini and Rosemont Colleges, Valley Forge Military Academy, and Villanova University, internships, a Washington semester in the American studies program, and student-designed majors. Also available are accelerated degree programs in organizational management and management of information systems, credit for experience, nondegree study, and pass/fail options. There is a different calendar for the organizational management program. There are 10 national honor societies, a freshman honors program, and 1 departmental honors program.

Faculty/Classroom: 54% of faculty are male; 46%, female. 83% teach undergraduates. No introductory courses are taught by graduate students. The average class size in an introductory lecture is 45; in a laboratory, 14; and in a regular course, 14.

Requirements: The SAT I or ACT is required. A GPA of 2.0 is required. AP and CLEP credits are accepted.

Procedure: Freshmen are admitted to all sessions. Entrance exams should be taken as early as possible. There are early admissions and deferred admissions plans. Applications should be filed by May 1 for fall entry. The fall 2003 application fee was $25. Notification is sent 4 to 6 weeks after receipt of the completed application. Applications are accepted on-line through the school's web site.

Transfer: Applicants should have a 2.0 GPA with more than 24 credits, and a 2.5 GPA with fewer than 24 credits. Candidates must be in good standing at their previous institution. 32 of 127 credits required for the bachelor's degree must be completed at Eastern.

Visiting: There are regularly scheduled orientations for prospective students, including a preview of academics, student life, and athletics. There are guides for informal visits and visitors may sit in on classes and stay overnight. To schedule a visit, contact the Admissions Office.

Financial Aid: In 2003-2004, 95% of all full-time freshmen received some form of financial aid, including need-based aid. Eastern is a member of CSS. The FAFSA, the college's own financial statement, and income tax forms are required. Check with the school for current deadlines.

International Students: The school actively recruits these students. They must score 550 on the written TOEFL.

Computers: Students may access the Novell on-campus network from 3 labs, residence hall lounge areas, the library, and individual residence hall rooms. All students may access the system. There are no time limits and no fees. It is strongly recommended that all students have a personal computer.

Admissions Contact: David Urban, Executive Director of Enrollment Management. E-mail: *ugadm@eastern.edu* Web: *www.eastern.edu*

EDINBORO UNIVERSITY OF PENNSYLVANIA   B-1
Edinboro, PA 16444

(814) 732-2761
(800) 626-2203; Fax: (814) 732-2420

Full-time: 2669 men, 3572 women	**Faculty:** 356; IIA, +$
Part-time: 295 men, 493 women	**Ph.D.s:** 64%
Graduate: 315 men, 701 women	**Student/Faculty:** 18 to 1
Year: semesters, summer session	**Tuition:** $5764 ($8114)
Application Deadline: open	**Room & Board:** $5086
Freshman Class: 3950 applied, 2710 accepted, 1455 enrolled	
SAT I Verbal/Math: 470/470	**ACT:** 18 **LESS COMPETITIVE**

Edinboro University of Pennsylvania, founded in 1857, is a public institution and a member of the Pennsylvania State System of Higher Education. The university offers programs in fine and liberal arts, business, engineering, health science, and teacher preparation. There are 3 undergraduate schools and 1 graduate school. In addition to regional accreditation, EUP has baccalaureate program accreditation with ACBSP, ADA, CSWE, NASM, NCATE, and NLN. The 2 libraries contain 468,887 volumes, 1,354,837 microform items, and 32,413 audio/video tapes/CDs, and subscribe to 1669 periodicals. Computerized library services include the card catalog, interlibrary loans, and database searching. Special learning facilities include an art gallery, planetarium, radio station, TV station, and a newspaper. The 585-acre campus is in a small town 18 miles south of Erie. Including any residence halls, there are 43 buildings.

Student Life: 89% of undergraduates are from Pennsylvania. Students are from 34 states, 49 foreign countries, and Canada. 89% are white. The average age of freshmen is 19; all undergraduates, 22. 31% do not continue beyond their first year; 50% remain to graduate.

Housing: 2500 students can be accommodated in college housing, which includes single-sex and coed dorms. In addition, there are honors houses and special-interest houses, floors by academic major, quiet floors, and non-smoking residence halls. On-campus housing is guaranteed for the freshman year only and is available on a first-come, first-served basis. 58% of students commute. Alcohol is not permitted. All students may keep cars.

Activities: 7% of men belong to 8 national fraternities; 7% of women belong to 8 national sororities. There are 129 groups on campus, including art, bagpipe band, band, cheerleading, chess, choir, chorale, chorus, computers, dance, debate, drama, drill team, ethnic, film, forensics, gay, honors, international, literary magazine, marching band, musical theater, opera, orchestra, pep band, photography, political, professional, radio and TV, religious, social, social service, student government, symphony, and yearbook. Popular campus events include Academic Festival, Snowfest, and Greek Week.

Sports: There are 6 intercollegiate sports for men and 7 for women, and 12 intramural sports for men and 12 for women. Facilities include a field house, a stadium, a gym, a swimming pool, racquetball courts, an aerobics room, an indoor track, a fitness center, saunas, steamrooms, 2 weight rooms, and a climbing wall.

Disabled Students: 97% of the campus is accessible. Wheelchair ramps, elevators, special parking, specially equipped rest rooms, special class scheduling, lowered drinking fountains, lowered telephones, special housing, computer facilities, and transportation services are available.

Services: Counseling and information services are available, as is tutoring in most subjects. There is a reader service for the blind and remedial math, reading, and writing. Academic aides are available as are services in the academic support library. Also available are alternative test arrangements, peer-mentoring, priority scheduling, and recordings for the blind or dyslexic.

Campus Safety and Security: Measures include 24-hour foot and vehicle patrol, self-defense education, informal discussions, and pamphlets/posters/films. There are emergency telephones, lighted pathways/sidewalks, and there are 14 commissioned police officers and optional engraving of personal property.

Programs of Study: EUP confers B.A., B.S., B.S.Ed., B.F.A., B.S.A.E., B.S.H.P.E., and B.S.N. degrees. Associate and master's degrees are also awarded. Bachelor's degrees are awarded in BIOLOGICAL SCIENCE (biochemistry, biology/biological science, and nutrition), BUSINESS (accounting, banking and finance, business administration and management, marketing management, and sports management), COMMUNICATIONS AND THE ARTS (advertising, applied art, art, art history and appreciation, broadcasting, ceramic art and design, creative writing, dramatic arts, drawing, English, English literature, fiber/textiles/weaving, film arts, fine arts, German, graphic design, media arts, metal/jewelry, music, painting, photography, printmaking, sculpture, Spanish, and speech/

debate/rhetoric), COMPUTER AND PHYSICAL SCIENCE (chemistry, computer science, earth science, geology, mathematics, natural sciences, and physics), EDUCATION (art, early childhood, elementary, English, foreign languages, health, mathematics, music, physical, science, secondary, social studies, and special), ENGINEERING AND ENVIRONMENTAL DESIGN (engineering physics, environmental science, and woodworking), HEALTH PROFESSIONS (medical laboratory technology, nuclear medical technology, nursing, predentistry, premedicine, preveterinary science, public health, and speech pathology/audiology), SOCIAL SCIENCE (anthropology, criminal justice, economics, forensic studies, geography, history, humanities, liberal arts/general studies, philosophy, political science/government, prelaw, psychology, social work, and sociology). Applied media arts, business administration, and criminal justice are the largest.

Required: To graduate, students must complete a minimum of 120 semester hours with a minimum GPA of 2.0. General education requirements include 48 hours of courses, consisting of a 21-semester-hour core with 3 hours each in artistic expression, world civilizations, American civilizations, human behavior, cultural diversity and social pluralism, ethics, and science and technology; a 12-hour distribution with 9 hours in English and math skills, and 3 hours of health and phys ed.

Special: The university offers cooperative programs in engineering, prelaw, and osteopathic medicine, and cross-registration through the Pennsylvania State System of Higher Education and the Marine Science Consortium at Wallops Island, Virginia, and with Mercyhurst College and Gannon University. A Harrisburg semester, internships in most majors, a general studies program, student-designed majors, dual majors in education, a 3-2 engineering degree, study abroad in more than 10 countries, and nondegree study are also offered. Students may select pass/fail options and receive credit for life, military, and work experience. There are 10 national honor societies, a freshman honors program, and 9 departmental honors programs.

Faculty/Classroom: 56% of faculty are male; 44%, female. 92% teach undergraduates. No introductory courses are taught by graduate students. The average class size in an introductory lecture is 30.

Admissions: 69% of the 2003-2004 applicants were accepted. The SAT I scores for the 2003-2004 freshman class were: Verbal--61% below 500, 31% between 500 and 599, 7% between 600 and 700, and 1% above 700; Math--62% below 500, 31% between 500 and 599, and 7% between 600 and 700. The ACT scores were 69% below 21, 21% between 21 and 23, 9% between 24 and 26, 1% between 27 and 28, and 1% above 28. 15% of the current freshmen were in the top fifth of their class; 39% were in the top two fifths. 5 freshmen graduated first in their class.

Requirements: The SAT I or ACT is required. In addition, candidates for admission should be graduates of an accredited secondary school or the equivalent. The GED is accepted. A GPA of 2.0 is recommended. A portfolio is recommended for art students and an audition is required for music students. An interview is recommended for all. Admissions decisions are based upon the academic major requested, high school curriculum, grades, GPA, class rank, SAT I or ACT scores, and leadership and extracurricular activities record. AP and CLEP credits are accepted. Important factors in the admissions decision are advanced placement or honor courses, extracurricular activities record, and personality/intangible qualities.

Procedure: Freshmen are admitted to all sessions. Entrance exams should be taken in the junior year or early in the senior year. There are early admissions, deferred admissions, and rolling admissions plans. Application deadlines are open. Application fee is $25. Applications are accepted on-line through the school's web site *http://iis1.edinboro.edu/pubrel/admissions/application.asp*.

Transfer: 466 transfer students enrolled in 2002-2003. Applicants should have a 2.0 GPA and must submit transcripts from previous institutions. An interview is recommended. 32 of 120 credits required for the bachelor's degree must be completed at EUP.

Visiting: There are regularly scheduled orientations for prospective students, including admissions, financial aid, and academic affairs presentations followed by campus tours. There are guides for informal visits and visitors may sit in on classes and stay overnight. To schedule a visit, contact the Admissions Office at *eup_admissions@edinboro.edu*.

Financial Aid: In 2003-2004, 67% of all full-time freshmen and 57% of continuing full-time students received some form of financial aid. 64% of full-time freshmen and 56% of continuing full-time students received need-based aid. The average freshman award was $5658. 10% of undergraduates work part time. Average annual earnings from campus work are $1800. The average financial indebtedness of the 2003 graduate was $15,935. The FAFSA is required. The deadline for filing freshman financial aid applications for fall entry is March 15.

International Students: There are 215 international students enrolled. The school actively recruits these students. They must score 450 on the written TOEFL or 133 on the electronic version.

Computers: The mainframe is a Digital Alpha Series server. More than 2070 Windows, Mac systems, and Notebooks are available to students in locations across campus. Workstations are located in the library, specific residence halls, the student union, the main computer lab, and academic-specific labs. All students may access the system. Lab hours vary. There are no time limits and no fees.

Graduates: From July 1, 2002 to June 30, 2003, 1047 bachelor's degrees were awarded. The most popular majors were elementary education (8%), applied media arts (7%), and business administration (6%). In an average class, 20% graduate in 4 years or less, 25% graduate in 5 years or less, and 50% graduate in 6 years or less.

Admissions Contact: Admissions Office.
E-mail: *eup_admissions@edinboro.edu* Web: *http://www.edinboro.edu*

ELIZABETHTOWN COLLEGE
Elizabethtown, PA 17022

D-3

(717) 361-1400; Fax: (717) 361-1365

Full-time: 617 men, 1161 women	**Faculty:** 126; IIB, +$
Part-time: 68 men, 129 women	**Ph.D.s:** 90%
Graduate: none	**Student/Faculty:** 14 to 1
Year: semesters, summer session	**Tuition:** $22,500
Application Deadline: open	**Room & Board:** $6300
Freshman Class: 2541 applied, 1780 accepted, 496 enrolled	
SAT I Verbal/Math: 500–600/510–610	**COMPETITIVE**

Elizabethtown College, founded in 1899, is a private college founded by members of the Church of the Brethren and offering 43 undergraduate degrees in the arts, sciences, humanities and professional programs. In addition to regional accreditation, E-town has baccalaureate program accreditation with ACBSP, CSWE, and NASM. The library contains 190,261 volumes, 17,763 microform items, and 31,523 audio/video tapes/CDs, and subscribes to 1055 periodicals. Computerized library services include the card catalog, interlibrary loans, database searching, and Internet access. Special learning facilities include a learning resource center, art gallery, radio station, TV station, and a center for the study of Anabaptist and Pietist groups. The 185-acre campus is in a small town 20 miles southeast of Harrisburg, 10 miles south of Hershey. Including any residence halls, there are 28 buildings.

Student Life: 68% of undergraduates are from Pennsylvania. Students are from 35 states and 40 foreign countries. 82% are from public schools. 90% are white. 45% are Catholic; 30% Protestant; 25% claim no religious affiliation. The average age of freshmen is 18; all undergraduates, 20. 16% do not continue beyond their first year; 72% remain to graduate.

Housing: 1470 students can be accommodated in college housing, which includes single-sex and coed dorms and on-campus apartments. In addition, there are honors houses, special-interest houses, and chemical-free, healthy-living, and quiet areas. On-campus housing is guaranteed for all 4 years. 85% of students live on campus; of those, 70% remain on campus on weekends. All students may keep cars.

Activities: There are no fraternities or sororities. There are 80 groups on campus, including art, band, cheerleading, choir, chorale, chorus, computers, dance, departmental, drama, ethnic, forensics, gay, honors, international, jazz band, literary magazine, musical theater, newspaper, orchestra, photography, political, professional, radio and TV, religious, residence hall, social, social service, student government, and yearbook. Popular campus events include Family Weekend, theme weekends, and Spring Arts Festival.

Sports: There are 10 intercollegiate sports for men and 10 for women, and 7 intramural sports for men and 7 for women. Facilities include a swimming pool, weight training rooms, a 2200-seat soccer complex, a 2400-seat gym, a track and field complex, racquetball and tennis courts, basketball courts, sand volleyball courts, aerobic classes, a fitness center, baseball, softball, lacrosse, and hockey fields, and an artificial turf field for field hockey and lacrosse.

Disabled Students: 85% of the campus is accessible. Wheelchair ramps, elevators, special parking, specially equipped rest rooms, special class scheduling, lowered drinking fountains, and lowered telephones are available.

Services: Counseling and information services are available, as is tutoring in most subjects. There is remedial writing. Workshops and individual help with study skills are also available.

Campus Safety and Security: Measures include 24-hour foot and vehicle patrol, self-defense education, security escort services, and shuttle buses. There are informal discussions, pamphlets/posters/films, emergency telephones, lighted pathways/sidewalks, a student patrol, and a crime prevention program.

Programs of Study: E-town confers B.A., B.S., and B.M. degrees. Associate and master's degrees are also awarded. Bachelor's degrees are awarded in AGRICULTURE (forestry and related sciences), BIOLOGICAL SCIENCE (biochemistry, biology/biological science, and biotechnology), BUSINESS (accounting, business administration and management, and international business management), COMMUNICATIONS AND THE ARTS (art, communications, English, French, German, music, and Spanish), COMPUTER AND PHYSICAL SCIENCE (chemistry, computer science, mathematics, physics, and science), EDUCATION (early childhood, elementary, music, and secondary), ENGINEERING AND ENVIRONMENTAL DESIGN (computer engineering, engineering, engineering physics, environmental science, and industrial engineering),

HEALTH PROFESSIONS (clinical science, music therapy, and occupational therapy), SOCIAL SCIENCE (economics, history, philosophy, political science/government, psychology, religion, social studies, social work, and sociology). Sciences, occupational therapy, and international business are the strongest academically. Business administration, communications, and elementary and early childhood education are the largest.

Required: The core curriculum includes a first year seminar, a colloquium, courses in foreign cultures and international studies, math analysis, the power of language, creative expression, cultural heritage, foreign language, the natural and social worlds, and values and choice. Distribution requirements include 37 to 39 hours in 9 areas of understanding. Students must complete 125 credit hours, with at least 30 in the major, and maintain a GPA of 2.0 overall and in the major.

Special: Cross-registration with Brethren Colleges Abroad, work-study programs, internships, study abroad in 12 countries, a Washington semester, accelerated degrees, and dual majors, including sociology/anthropology, are available. A 3-2 engineering degree is offered with Pennsylvania State University; a 2-2 allied health degree and a 4-2 physical therapy (D.P.T.) degree with Thomas Jefferson University, Widener University, and the University of Maryland/Baltimore County; and a 3-2 forestry or environmental management degree with Duke University. There are 13 national honor societies, a freshman honors program, and 19 departmental honors programs.

Faculty/Classroom: 56% of faculty are male; 44%, female. 33% both teach and do research. The average class size in an introductory lecture is 23; in a laboratory, 18; and in a regular course, 20.

Admissions: 70% of the 2003-2004 applicants were accepted. The SAT I scores for the 2003-2004 freshman class were: Verbal--22% below 500, 49% between 500 and 599, 25% between 600 and 700, and 4% above 700; Math--20% below 500, 48% between 500 and 599, 28% between 600 and 700, and 4% above 700. The ACT scores were 6% above 28. 55% of the current freshmen were in the top fifth of their class; 83% were in the top two fifths. There were 6 National Merit semifinalists. 11 freshmen graduated first in their class.

Requirements: The SAT I or ACT is required. Recommended composite scores for the SAT I range from 1040 to 1190; for the ACT, 19 to 24. Applicants must be graduates of an accredited secondary school or have earned a GED. The college encourages completion of 18 academic credits, based on 4 years of English, 3 of math, 2 each of lab science, social studies, and consecutive foreign language, and 5 additional college preparatory units. An audition is required for music majors and an interview is required for occupational therapy majors. AP and CLEP credits are accepted. Important factors in the admissions decision are advanced placement or honor courses, recommendations by school officials, and extracurricular activities record.

Procedure: Freshmen are admitted to all sessions. Entrance exams should be taken in spring of the junior year or fall of the senior year. There are early admissions and deferred admissions plans. There is a rolling admissions plan, but applications are preferred by March 1. Application deadlines are open. Application fee is $30. Applications are accepted on computer disk and on-line through the Common Application, CollegeLink, Apply, or the school's own on-line application.

Transfer: 60 transfer students enrolled in 2002-2003. Applicants should present a minimum GPA of 3.0 in at least 15 credit hours earned from a community college, or 2.5 from a 4-year institution. 30 of 125 credits required for the bachelor's degree must be completed at E-town.

Visiting: There are regularly scheduled orientations for prospective students, including 5 open houses and weekday appointments throughout the year. Special academic department days are also hosted. There are guides for informal visits and visitors may sit in on classes and stay overnight. To schedule a visit, contact the Admissions Office.

Financial Aid: In 2003-2004, 96% of all full-time freshmen and 93% of continuing full-time students received some form of financial aid. 74% of full-time freshmen and 72% of continuing full-time students received need-based aid. The average freshman award was $15,322. 68% of undergraduates work part time. The average financial indebtedness of the 2003 graduate was $19,025. E-town is a member of CSS. The FAFSA, the college's own financial statement, and the family federal tax returns are required. The deadline for filing freshman financial aid applications for fall entry is March 15.

International Students: There are 83 international students enrolled. The school actively recruits these students. They must score 525 on the written TOEFL.

Computers: A 24-hour terminal room allows student access to e-mail and word processing. Several labs house a total of 40 Macs and 43 PCs, all connected to the Internet. All residence hall rooms also have Internet access. Approximately 90% of freshmen have their own computers. All students may access the system any time from residence hall rooms. There are no time limits and no fees. It is strongly recommended that all students have a personal computer.

Graduates: From July 1, 2002 to June 30, 2003, 371 bachelor's degrees were awarded. The most popular majors were business (22%), education (21%), and health professional and related science (10%). In an average class, 65% graduate in 4 years or less, 66% graduate in 5 years or less, and 67% graduate in 6 years or less. 70 companies recruited on campus in 2002-2003. Of the 2002 graduating class, 20% were enrolled in graduate school within 6 months of graduation and 83% were employed.

Admissions Contact: W. Kent Barnds, Dean of Admissions and Enrollment Management. E-mail: *admissions@etown.edu* Web: *www.etown.edu*

FRANKLIN AND MARSHALL COLLEGE   E-3
Lancaster, PA 17604-3003   (717) 291-3953; Fax: (717) 291-4389

Full-time: 987 men, 896 women	**Faculty:** 167; IIB, ++$
Part-time: 21 men, 19 women	**Ph.D.s:** 97%
Graduate: none	**Student/Faculty:** 11 to 1
Year: semesters, summer session	**Tuition:** $28,860
Application Deadline: February 1	**Room & Board:** $7070
Freshman Class: 3616 applied, 2085 accepted, 503 enrolled	
SAT I Verbal/Math: 620/640	**ACT:** 29
	HIGHLY COMPETITIVE+

Franklin and Marshall College, founded in 1787, is a private liberal arts institution. The 2 libraries contain 473,036 volumes, 136,915 microform items, and 12,651 audio/video tapes/CDs, and subscribe to 1790 periodicals. Computerized library services include the card catalog, interlibrary loans, database searching, and Internet access. Special learning facilities include an art gallery, natural history museum, planetarium, radio station, TV station, academic technology services, an advanced language lab, a writing center, and a student newspaper. The 125-acre campus is in a suburban area 60 miles west of Philadelphia. Including any residence halls, there are 44 buildings.

Student Life: 64% of undergraduates are from out of state, mostly the Middle Atlantic. Students are from 42 states, 40 foreign countries, and Canada. 58% are from public schools. 78% are white. 37% claim no religious affiliation; 22% Catholic; 19% Protestant; 11% Jewish; 11% Orthodox Christian, Moslem, Hindu, Buddhist, Unitarian. The average age of freshmen is 18; all undergraduates, 20. 10% do not continue beyond their first year; 84% remain to graduate.

Housing: 1275 students can be accommodated in college housing, which includes single-sex and coed dorms and off-campus apartments. In addition, there are language houses and special-interest houses, including a French house, an arts house, an international living center, and a community outreach house. On-campus housing is guaranteed for the freshman and sophomore years only and is available on a lottery system for upperclassmen. 67% of students live on campus; of those, 85% remain on campus on weekends. All students may keep cars.

Activities: There are 110 groups on campus, including art, band, Ben's Underground (a student-run club/restaurant), chess, choir, chorale, chorus, computers, dance, debate, drama, ethnic, film, forensics, gay, honors, international, jazz band, literary magazine, musical theater, newspaper, orchestra, photography, political, professional, radio and TV, religious, social, social service, student government, symphony, and yearbook. Popular campus events include Spring Arts Weekend, Freshman Feast, and Senior Surprise.

Sports: There are 13 intercollegiate sports for men and 13 for women, and 12 intramural sports for men and 12 for women. Facilities include a 3000-seat gym, 4 squash courts, a wrestling room, 54 acres of playing fields, a 400-meter all-weather track, a wellness/aerobic center, a strength training center, and tennis courts. A sport center features a fitness center, 5 multipurpose courts, 2 jogging tracks, and an Olympic-size pool.

Disabled Students: 70% of the campus is accessible. Wheelchair ramps, elevators, special parking, specially equipped rest rooms, special class scheduling, lowered drinking fountains, lowered telephones, and special housing are available.

Services: Counseling and information services are available, as is tutoring in *every* subject.

Campus Safety and Security: Measures include 24-hour foot and vehicle patrol, self-defense education, security escort services, and informal discussions. There are pamphlets/posters/films, emergency telephones and lighted pathways/sidewalks. Regular fire safety drills are held in residence halls and academic buildings and residence hall access requires a security code.

Programs of Study: F & M confers the B.A. degree. Bachelor's degrees are awarded in AGRICULTURE (environmental studies), BIOLOGICAL SCIENCE (biochemistry, biology/biological science, and neurosciences), BUSINESS (accounting, banking and finance, and business administration and management), COMMUNICATIONS AND THE ARTS (art history and appreciation, classics, dramatic arts, English, fine arts, French, German, Greek, Latin, music, Spanish, and studio art), COMPUTER AND PHYSICAL SCIENCE (astronomy, astrophysics, chemistry, geology, mathematics, and physics), ENGINEERING AND ENVIRONMENTAL DESIGN (environmental science), SOCIAL SCIENCE (African studies, American studies, anthropology, economics, history, interdisciplinary studies, philosophy, political science/government, psychology, re-

ligion, and sociology). Chemistry, geosciences, and psychology are the strongest academically. Government, business administration, and biology are the largest.

Required: General eduation requirements proceed from 3 foundations courses and a distribution requirement to an upper-level coherent exploration and a major. Students must take at least one course in arts, humanities, social science, and natural sciences. There are also language studies and non-Western culture studies requirements. Students must also satisfy the writng proficiency requirement. The bachelor's degree requires completion of 32 courses, including a minimum of 8 in the major, with a minimum GPA of 2.0.

Special: There is a 3-2 degree program in forestry and environmental studies with Duke University as well as 3-2 degree programs in engineering with the University of Pennsylvania, Columbia University, Rensselaer Polytechnic Institute, Case Western Reserve, Georgia Institute of Technology, and Washington University at St. Louis. Cross-registration with the Central Pennsylvania Consortium and Millersville University allows students to study at nearby Dickinson College or Gettysburg College. Students may also study architecture and urban planning at Columbia University, studio art at the School of Visual Arts in New York City, theater in Connecticut, oceanography in Massachusetts, and American studies at American University. There are study-abroad programs in England, France, Germany, Greece, Italy, Denmark, India, Japan, and other countries. There are internships for credit, joint majors, student-designed majors, independent study, interdisciplinary studies, optional first-year seminars, collaborative projects, pass/fail options, and nondegree study. There are 12 national honor societies, including Phi Beta Kappa.

Faculty/Classroom: 62% of faculty are male; 38%, female. All teach undergraduates and do research. The average class size in an introductory lecture is 23; in a laboratory, 19; and in a regular course, 19.

Admissions: 58% of the 2003-2004 applicants were accepted. The SAT I scores for the 2003-2004 freshman class were: Verbal--5% below 500, 31% between 500 and 599, 48% between 600 and 700, and 15% above 700; Math--3% below 500, 28% between 500 and 599, 48% between 600 and 700, and 21% above 700. 69% of the current freshmen were in the top fifth of their class; 94% were in the top two fifths. There were 2 National Merit finalists.

Requirements: The SAT I is required. In addition, SAT II: Writing test is also required. Standardized tests are optional for students in the top 10% of their class; if this option is selected, 2 graded writing samples are required. Applicants must be graduates of accredited secondary schools. Recommended college preparatory study includes 4 years each of English and math, 3 or 4 of foreign language, 3 each of lab science and history/social studies, and 1 or 2 courses in art or music. All students must also submit their high school transcripts, recommendations from a teacher and a counselor, and a personal essay. An interview is recommended. AP and CLEP credits are accepted. Important factors in the admissions decision are advanced placement or honor courses, recommendations by school officials, and extracurricular activities record.

Procedure: Freshmen are admitted fall and spring. Entrance exams should be taken by December of the senior year. There are early decision and deferred admissions plans. Early decision applications should be filed by November 15 (round 1); January 15 (round 2); regular applications, by February 1 for fall entry, along with a $50 fee. Notification of early decision is sent December 15 (round 1); February 15 (round 2); regular decision, April 1. 179 early decision candidates were accepted for the 2003-2004 class. 686 applicants were on the 2003 waiting list; 59 were admitted. Applications are accepted on-line.

Transfer: 13 transfer students enrolled in 2002-2003. Applicants must present a minimum of 4 course credits (16 semester hours) completed at an accredited college. An interview, SAT I or ACT scores, college and secondary school transcripts, a dean's form, recommendations from 2 professors, and a letter explaining the reason for transfer are also required. 16 of 32 credits required for the bachelor's degree must be completed at F & M.

Visiting: There are regularly scheduled orientations for prospective students, including a campus tour, an interview, a class visit, and an overnight stay. There are guides for informal visits and visitors may sit in on classes and stay overnight. To schedule a visit, contact the Admission Office.

Financial Aid: In 2003-2004, 70% of all full-time freshmen and 65% of continuing full-time students received some form of financial aid. 50% of full-time freshmen and 46% of continuing full-time students received need-based aid. The average freshman award was $19,719. Need-based scholarships or need-based grants averaged $18,551; need-based self-help aid (loans and jobs) averaged $5037; and non-need-based awards and non-need-based scholarships averaged $14,949. 44% of undergraduates work part time. Average annual earnings from campus work are $1390. The average financial indebtedness of the 2003 graduate was $18,370. F & M is a member of CSS. The CSS Profile or FAFSA, the state aid form, the college's own financial statement, and if applicable, the Business/Farm Supplement and noncustodial parents statement are required. The deadline for filing freshman financial aid applications for fall entry is February 1.

International Students: There are 167 international students enrolled. The school actively recruits these students. They must score 600 on the written TOEFL or 250 on the electronic version and also take the SAT I or the ACT. Students must take SAT II: Subject tests in writing, unless using ACT or no SAT I option (top decile of high school class).

Computers: The mainframes are a series of VAX and other servers. A computer workroom houses 32 Macs, 6 Apple LaserWriter printers, 1 color Apple printer, and 1 HP laser printer that is directly connected to the mainframe. All of the Macs are on the campuswide network for access to file servers and the academic VAX. The campus is 100% networked, both Ethernet and wireless. All students may access the system 24 hours a day, 7 days a week. There are no time limits. The fee is $100 for students residing on campus. It is strongly recommended that all students have a personal computer. An iMac or iBook is recommended.

Graduates: From July 1, 2002 to June 30, 2003, 443 bachelor's degrees were awarded. The most popular majors were government (17%), business management (11%), and biology (8%). In an average class, 80% graduate in 4 years or less, 82% graduate in 5 years or less, and 84% graduate in 6 years or less. 26 companies recruited on campus in 2002-2003. Of the 2002 graduating class, 25% were enrolled in graduate school within 6 months of graduation and 75% were employed.

Admissions Contact: Dennis Trotter, Vice President for Enrollment Management and Dean of Admissions. A video is available.
E-mail: *admission@fandm.edu* Web: *www.fandm.edu/admission.html*

GANNON UNIVERSITY
Erie, PA 16541

B-1

(814) 871-5696
(800) GANNON U; Fax: (814) 871-5803

Full-time: 909 men, 1236 women	**Faculty:** 165
Part-time: 108 men, 182 women	**Ph.D.s:** n/av
Graduate: 377 men, 647 women	**Student/Faculty:** 13 to 1
Year: semesters, summer session	**Tuition:** $16,670
Application Deadline: open	**Room & Board:** $6590
Freshman Class: 2277 applied, 1872 accepted, 588 enrolled	
SAT I Verbal/Math: 520/529	**ACT:** 23 COMPETITIVE

Gannon University, founded in 1925, is a private liberal arts and teacher preparation university affiliated with the Roman Catholic Church. There are 2 undergraduate schools and 1 graduate school. In addition to regional accreditation, Gannon has baccalaureate program accreditation with ABET, ADA, CAHEA, CSWE, and NLN. The library contains 253,617 volumes, 48,302 microform items, and 3011 audio/video tapes/CDs, and subscribes to 2073 periodicals. Computerized library services include the card catalog, interlibrary loans, and database searching. Special learning facilities include a learning resource center, art gallery, and radio station. The 13-acre campus is in an urban area 128 miles north of Pittsburgh, 99 miles east of Cleveland, and 106 miles southwest o. Including any residence halls, there are 27 buildings.

Student Life: 78% of undergraduates are from Pennsylvania. Students are from 25 states, 20 foreign countries, and Canada. 80% are from public schools. 92% are white. 58% are Catholic; 27% Protestant; 15% Buddhist, Hindu, Muslim, and Orthodox. The average age of freshmen is 18; all undergraduates, 21. 12% do not continue beyond their first year; 64% remain to graduate.

Housing: 1110 students can be accommodated in college housing, which includes coed dorms, on-campus apartments, fraternity houses, and sorority houses. On-campus housing is guaranteed for the freshman year only. 67% of students live on campus; of those, 85% remain on campus on weekends. Alcohol is not permitted. Upperclassmen may keep cars.

Activities: 18% of men belong to 6 national fraternities; 16% of women belong to 6 national sororities. There are 70 groups on campus, including Activiities Programming Board, art, cheerleading, chess, chorus, computers, debate, drama, ethnic, honors, international, literary magazine, musical theater, newspaper, orchestra, pep band, political, professional, radio, religious, Residence Union, social, social service, student government, and yearbook. Popular campus events include Family Weekend, Distinguished Speaker Series, and Springtopia.

Sports: There are 10 intercollegiate sports for men and 9 for women, and 22 intramural sports for men and 11 for women. Facilities include a pool, 3 indoor gyms, a track, 6 racquetball courts, an outdoor recreation field, outdoor sand volleyball and tennis courts, a 3000-seat basketball and volleyball venue, exercise equipment, and a dance room.

Disabled Students: 80% of the campus is accessible. Wheelchair ramps, elevators, special parking, specially equipped rest rooms, special class scheduling, lowered drinking fountains, lowered telephones, and special drop-off points are available.

Services: Counseling and information services are available, as is tutoring in some subjects. There is remedial math and writing. There are math, writing, and advising centers.

Campus Safety and Security: Measures include 24-hour foot and vehicle patrol, security escort services, informal discussions, and pamphlets/posters/films. There are emergency telephones, lighted pathways/sidewalks, and security cameras in buildings.

Programs of Study: Gannon confers B.A., B.S., B.S.E.E., B.S.M.E., and B.S.N. degrees. Associate, master's, and doctoral degrees are also awarded. Bachelor's degrees are awarded in BIOLOGICAL SCIENCE (biology/biological science), BUSINESS (accounting, banking and finance, business administration and management, entrepreneurial studies, international business management, management information systems, and marketing/retailing/merchandising), COMMUNICATIONS AND THE ARTS (advertising, communications, dramatic arts, English, and languages), COMPUTER AND PHYSICAL SCIENCE (chemistry, computer programming, computer science, mathematics, and science), EDUCATION (early childhood, elementary, foreign languages, secondary, and special), ENGINEERING AND ENVIRONMENTAL DESIGN (electrical/electronics engineering, environmental science, and mechanical engineering), HEALTH PROFESSIONS (medical laboratory technology, nursing, physician's assistant, predentistry, premedicine, preoptometry, preosteopathy, prepharmacy, prepodiatry, preveterinary science, radiological science, and respiratory therapy), SOCIAL SCIENCE (criminal justice, dietetics, history, international studies, liberal arts/general studies, paralegal studies, philosophy, political science/government, prelaw, psychology, social science, social work, and theological studies). Engineering, preprofessional, and nursing are the strongest academically. Occupational therapy, elementary education, and biology are the largest.

Required: Students must complete at least 128 hours of academic work. Each academic program has specific course requirements. Students must have a cumulative GPA of at least 2.0 overall and in the area of concentration. 3 writing-intensive courses must be completed after the freshman year; 1 must be taken in the senior year. There is a liberal studies core curriculum.

Special: The university offers study abroad in more than 5 countries, co-op programs, dual majors, B.A.-B.S. degrees, summer internships, cross-registration with Mercyhurst College, Washington semesters, pass/fail options, work-study programs, a general studies program, accelerated degree programs in law, optometry, podiatry, and pharmacy, a 3-2 chemical engineering degree with the Universities of Akron, Pittsburgh, and Detroit Mercy, and nondegree study. The B.S. in mortuary science program consists of 2 or 3 years of study at Gannon with degree completion at a school of mortuary science. Gannon also offers a medical degree program in conjunction with Hahnemann University, and pharmacy and law programs with Duquesne University. There is an honors program. There are 11 national honor societies and a freshman honors program.

Faculty/Classroom: 57% of faculty are male; 43%, female. 91% teach undergraduates and 6% do research. No introductory courses are taught by graduate students. The average class size in an introductory lecture is 25; in a laboratory, 15; and in a regular course, 17.

Admissions: 82% of the 2003-2004 applicants were accepted. The SAT I scores for the 2003-2004 freshman class were: Verbal--39% below 500, 44% between 500 and 599, 15% between 600 and 700, and 2% above 700; Math--34% below 500, 45% between 500 and 599, 20% between 600 and 700, and 1% above 700. 44% of the current freshman class ranked in the upper quarter of their high school class; 72% were in the top half.

Requirements: The SAT I or ACT is required. In addition, candidates should have completed 16 academic units including 4 in English and 12 in social sciences, foreign languages, math, and science, depending on the degree sought. Specific courses in math and science are required for some majors in health sciences and engineering. Gannon requires applicants to be in the upper 60% of their class. A GPA of 2.0 is required. AP and CLEP credits are accepted. Important factors in the admissions decision are advanced placement or honor courses, leadership record, and recommendations by school officials.

Procedure: Freshmen are admitted to all sessions. Entrance exams should be taken at the end of the junior year or the beginning of the senior year. There is a deferred admissions plan. Application deadlines are open. Application fee is $25. A waiting list is an active part of the admissions procedure. Applications are accepted on-line through EXPAN. Notification is sent on a rolling basis.

Transfer: Transfer students should be in good standing at their previous institution with at least a 2.0 GPA. They must submit a college clearance from the college most recently attended and all transcripts. A high school transcript is required from transfer students with fewer than 60 credits. Several health science programs are not designed to accommodate transfers. 30 of 128 credits required for the bachelor's degree must be completed at Gannon.

Visiting: There are regularly scheduled orientations for prospective students, consisting of open houses for prospective students in the fall and spring. Students may meet with faculty, tour the campus, and sit in on a variety of presentations. There are guides for informal visits and visitors may sit in on classes and stay overnight. To schedule a visit, contact the Admissions Office.

Financial Aid: In 2003-2004, 88% of all full-time freshmen and 90% of continuing full-time students received some form of financial aid. 88% of full-time freshmen and 91% of continuing full-time students received need-based aid. The average freshman award was $10,900. Need-based

scholarships or need-based grants averaged $10,488; need-based self-help aid (loans and jobs) averaged $5900; non-need-based athletic scholarships for freshmen averaged $1000 ($23,260 maximum); and other non-need-based awards and non-need-based scholarships averaged $4600. 82% of undergraduates work part time. Average annual earnings from campus work are $1700. Gannon is a member of CSS. The FAFSA and the college's own financial statement are required. Check with the school for current deadlines.

International Students: The school actively recruits these students. They must score 500 on the written TOEFL.

Computers: The mainframes are a DEC VAX 6000-410 cluster, 2 DEC VAX 6410 clusters, and a Sun 2000. There is 1 mainframe lab and 2 PC labs with about 30 PCs in each. The departments of business, engineering, and education maintain special computer labs. All students may access the system Monday through Friday 9 A.M. to midnight, Saturday noon to 6 P.M., and Sunday noon to midnight. There are no time limits and no fees. It is strongly recommended that all students have a personal computer.

Graduates: Of the 2002 graduating class, 22% were enrolled in graduate school within 6 months of graduation and 73% were employed.

Admissions Contact: Bill Eilola, Dean of Enrollment.
E-mail: *admissions@gannon.edu* Web: *www.gannon.edu*

GENEVA COLLEGE
Beaver Falls, PA 15010

A-3
(724) 847-6500
(800) 847-8255; Fax: (724) 847-6776

Full-time: 598 men, 723 women	**Faculty:** 75; IIB, -$
Part-time: 27 men, 29 women	**Ph.D.s:** 76%
Graduate: 122 men, 182 women	**Student/Faculty:** 18 to 1
Year: semesters, summer session	**Tuition:** $15,480
Application Deadline: open	**Room & Board:** $6370
Freshman Class: 984 applied, 787 accepted, 298 enrolled	
SAT I Verbal/Math: 540/550	**ACT:** 23

COMPETITIVE

Geneva College, founded in 1848, is a private institution affiliated with the Reformed Presbyterian Church of North America. The college offers undergraduate programs in the arts and sciences, business, education, health science, biblical and religious studies, engineering, and preprofessional training. In addition to the above figures, there are 440 nontraditional undergraduates. In addition to regional accreditation, Geneva has baccalaureate program accreditation with ABET and ACBSP. The library contains 167,206 volumes, 198,624 microform items, and 12,901 audio/video tapes/CDs, and subscribes to 879 periodicals. Computerized library services include the card catalog, interlibrary loans, database searching, and Internet access. Special learning facilities include a radio station, TV station, and an observatory. The 50-acre campus is in a small town 35 miles northwest of Pittsburgh. Including any residence halls, there are 30 buildings.

Student Life: 73% of undergraduates are from Pennsylvania. Students are from 37 states, 19 foreign countries, and Canada. 87% are from public schools. 91% are white. 89% are Protestant; 7% Catholic. The average age of freshmen is 19; all undergraduates, 26. 23% do not continue beyond their first year; 55% remain to graduate.

Housing: 994 students can be accommodated in college housing, which includes single-sex dorms, on-campus apartments, and off-campus apartments. Discipleship House is also available for those interested in structural growth opportunities. On-campus housing is guaranteed for all 4 years. 73% of students live on campus; of those, 70% remain on campus on weekends. Alcohol is not permitted. Upperclassmen may keep cars.

Activities: There are no fraternities or sororities. There are 50 groups on campus, including band, cheerleading, chess, choir, chorale, chorus, computers, drama, ethnic, forensics, honors, international, literary magazine, marching band, newspaper, photography, political, professional, radio, religious, social, social service, student government, and yearbook. Popular campus events include International Day, Fall Fest, and The Big Event.

Sports: There are 6 intercollegiate sports for men and 5 for women, and 6 intramural sports for men and 5 for women. Facilities include a 5600-seat stadium, a field house, a 3200-seat gym, a practice gym, a track, athletic fields, racquetball and tennis courts, weight training rooms, and the Merriman Athletic Soccer/Track Complex.

Disabled Students: 90% of the campus is accessible. Wheelchair ramps, elevators, special parking, specially equipped rest rooms, special class scheduling, lowered drinking fountains, and lowered telephones are available.

Services: Counseling and information services are available, as is tutoring in most subjects. There is remedial math, reading, and writing.

Campus Safety and Security: Measures include security escort services, informal discussions, pamphlets/posters/films, and emergency telephones. There are lighted pathways/sidewalks, off-duty city policemen on campus from 4:30 P.M. to 7 A.M. daily, and a full-time Director of Campus Security.

Programs of Study: Geneva confers B.A., B.S., B.S.B.A., B.S.E., and B.S.Ed. degrees. Associate and master's degrees are also awarded. Bachelor's degrees are awarded in BIOLOGICAL SCIENCE (biology/biological science), BUSINESS (accounting and business administration and management), COMMUNICATIONS AND THE ARTS (applied music, broadcasting, communications, creative writing, English, music, music business management, Spanish, and speech/debate/rhetoric), COMPUTER AND PHYSICAL SCIENCE (applied mathematics, chemistry, computer science, and physics), EDUCATION (elementary, mathematics, and music), ENGINEERING AND ENVIRONMENTAL DESIGN (aviation administration/management, chemical engineering, and engineering), HEALTH PROFESSIONS (speech pathology/audiology), SOCIAL SCIENCE (biblical studies, counseling/psychology, history, human services, interdisciplinary studies, ministries, philosophy, political science/government, psychology, and sociology). Engineering, business administration, and education are the strongest academically. Elementary education, business administration, and psychology are the largest.

Required: The core curriculum includes 12 hours of humanities, 9 each of biblical studies and social science, 8 to 10 of natural science, 6 of communications, 2 of phys ed, and the 1-hour Freshman Experience course. Students must also fulfill a chapel requirement per semester. To graduate, students must complete 126 to 138 semester hours, including those required for a major, with a minimum GPA of 2.0 in the major.

Special: Cross-registration is offered in conjunction with Pennsylvania State University/Beaver Campus and Community College of Beaver County. There is a 3-1 degree program in cardiovascular technology, and an accelerated degree programs in human resources and community ministry. Off-campus study includes programs at the Philadelphia Center for Urban Theological Studies, a Washington semester, a summer program at AuSable, Institute of Environmental Studies in Michigan, art studies in Pittsburgh, CCCU music program in Martha's Vineyard, film studies in Los Angeles, and study abroad in Costa Rica, Egypt, China, England, Russia, and Israel. Geneva also offers internships, independent study, and credit by proficiency exam. Nondegree study is available through adult education programs. There are 2 national honor societies, a freshman honors program, and 1 departmental honors program.

Faculty/Classroom: 76% of faculty are male; 24%, female. 95% teach undergraduates. No introductory courses are taught by graduate students. The average class size in an introductory lecture is 135; in a laboratory, 22; and in a regular course, 20.

Admissions: 80% of the 2003-2004 applicants were accepted. The SAT I scores for the 2003-2004 freshman class were: Verbal--28% below 500, 45% between 500 and 599, 23% between 600 and 700, and 4% above 700; Math--40% below 500, 38% between 500 and 599, 20% between 600 and 700, and 2% above 700. 25% of the current freshmen were in the top fifth of their class; 34% were in the top two fifths. There were 3 National Merit finalists and 2 semifinalists. 10 freshmen graduated first in their class.

Requirements: The SAT I or ACT is required. In addition, applicants must be graduates of an accredited secondary school or have earned a GED. Geneva requires 16 academic units, based on 4 each of English and electives, 3 of social studies, 2 each of math and foreign language, and 1 of science. An essay is required and an interview is recommended. Geneva requires applicants to be in the upper 50% of their class. A GPA of 2.5 is required. AP and CLEP credits are accepted. Important factors in the admissions decision are recommendations by school officials, advanced placement or honor courses, and leadership record.

Procedure: Freshmen are admitted to all sessions. Entrance exams should be taken during the junior or senior year. There is a deferred admissions plan. There is a rolling admissions plan. Application deadlines are open. Application fee is $25. Applications are accepted on-line through the college's web site, CollegeLink, and Mac Apply.

Transfer: 96 transfer students enrolled in 2002-2003. Applicants must have a GPA of 2.0 from College, must complete 48 semester hours at Geneva, including 15 in a chosen major, have a high school diploma or GED, and take the SAT I or the ACT if less than 3 years out of high school. Letters of recommendation are required. 48 of 126 credits required for the bachelor's degree must be completed at Geneva.

Visiting: There are regularly scheduled orientations for prospective students, including class visits, a campus tour, meetings with faculty, admissions, and financial aid counselors, and meetings with coaches. There are guides for informal visits and visitors may sit in on classes and stay overnight. To schedule a visit, contact Victoria Chapoloko, Campus Visit Coordinator at (724) 847-6501 or *vmchapol@geneva.edu*.

Financial Aid: In 2003-2004, 90% of all full-time students received some form of financial aid. 70% of all full-time students received need-based aid. The average freshman award was $13,785. Need-based scholarships or need-based grants averaged $10,241 ($22,000 maximum); need-based self-help aid (loans and jobs) averaged $4212 ($5625 maximum); and non-need-based athletic scholarships averaged $2542 ($14,980 maximum). 75% of undergraduates work part time. Average annual earnings from campus work are $1000. The average financial indebtedness of the 2003 graduate was $20,000. Geneva is a member of CSS. The FAFSA is required. The priority date for freshman financial aid applications for fall entry is March 15. The deadline for filing freshman financial aid applications for fall entry is April 15.

International Students: There are 18 international students enrolled. The school actively recruits these students. They must score 480 on the written TOEFL or take the college's own test.

Computers: The mainframe is an IBM AS/400. Access to the campus network and to the Internet is provided to all students. There are more than 150 PCs throughout the campus that students can use. Some of these are general purpose labs and others in discipline-specify labs. Many residence hall rooms are also wired for connection to the campus network. All students may access the system. There are no time limits. The fee is $100 per semester.

Graduates: From July 1, 2002 to June 30, 2003, 454 bachelor's degrees were awarded. The most popular majors were business and marketing (40%), philosophy/religion/theology (14%), and education (12%). In an average class, 1% graduate in 3 years or less, 42% graduate in 4 years or less, 55% graduate in 5 years or less, and 56% graduate in 6 years or less.

Admissions Contact: Director of Admissions. A video is available. E-mail: *admissions@geneva.edu* Web: *www.geneva.edu*

GETTYSBURG COLLEGE

Gettysburg, PA 17325-1484   **D-4**

(717) 337-6100
(800) 431-0803; Fax: (717) 337-6145

Full-time: 1231 men, 1353 women	**Faculty:** IIB, +$
Part-time: 9 men, 4 women	**Ph.D.s:** 95%
Graduate: none	**Student/Faculty:** n/av
Year: semesters	**Tuition:** $28,674
Application Deadline: February 15	**Room & Board:** $3972
Freshman Class: 5017 applied, 2317 accepted, 695 enrolled	
SAT I Verbal/Math: 630/630	**HIGHLY COMPETITIVE**

Gettysburg College, founded in 1832, is a nationally ranked, residential college affiliated with the Lutheran Church. It offers programs in the liberal arts and sciences. The library contains 464,357 volumes, 75,066 microform items, and 21,269 audio/video tapes/CDs, and subscribes to 17,583 periodicals. Computerized library services include the card catalog, interlibrary loans, database searching, and Internet access. Special learning facilities include an art gallery, planetarium, radio station, TV station, electron microscopes, spectrometers, an optics lab, plasma physics lab, greenhouse, observatory, child study lab, fine and performing arts facilities, and a challenge course. The 200-acre campus is in a suburban area 30 miles south of Harrisburg, 55 miles from Baltimore, MD, and 80 miles from Washington, D.C. Including any residence halls, there are 60 buildings.

Student Life: 72% of undergraduates are from out of state, mostly the Middle Atlantic. Students are from 40 states, 32 foreign countries, and Canada. 70% are from public schools. 91% are white. 34% are Protestant; 31% Catholic; 6% claim no religious affiliation. The average age of freshmen is 18; all undergraduates, 20. 10% do not continue beyond their first year; 75% remain to graduate.

Housing: 2220 students can be accommodated in college housing, which includes single-sex and coed dorms, on-campus apartments, off-campus apartments, and fraternity houses. In addition, there are honors houses, language houses, and special-interest houses. On-campus housing is guaranteed for all 4 years. 93% of students live on campus; of those, 95% remain on campus on weekends. All students may keep cars.

Activities: 44% of men belong to 10 national fraternities; 26% of women belong to 5 national sororities. There are 100 groups on campus, including art, band, cheerleading, choir, chorale, chorus, computers, dance, dance ensemble, drama, drill team, ethnic, film, gay, honors, international, jazz band, literary magazine, marching band, musical theater, newspaper, opera, orchestra, outdoor recreation program, pep band, photography, political, professional, radio and TV, religious, social, social service, student activities council, student government, symphony, and yearbook. Popular campus events include Holiday Concert, all-campus picnics, and Family Weekend.

Sports: There are 12 intercollegiate sports for men and 12 for women. Facilities include basketball courts, indoor and outdoor tennis courts, a pool, several tracks and fields, a field house, fitness and weight rooms, and an athletic complex.

Disabled Students: 90% of the campus is accessible. Wheelchair ramps, elevators, special parking, specially equipped rest rooms, and special class scheduling are available.

Services: Counseling and information services are available, as is tutoring in most subjects.

Campus Safety and Security: Measures include 24-hour foot and vehicle patrol, self-defense education, security escort services, and informal discussions. There are pamphlets/posters/films, emergency telephones, and lighted pathways/sidewalks.

Programs of Study: Gettysburg confers B.A., B.S., and B.S.M.E. degrees. Bachelor's degrees are awarded in BIOLOGICAL SCIENCE (biochemistry and biology/biological science), BUSINESS (business administration and management), COMMUNICATIONS AND THE ARTS (art

history and appreciation, classics, dramatic arts, English, French, German, Greek, Latin, music, Spanish, and studio art), COMPUTER AND PHYSICAL SCIENCE (chemistry, computer science, mathematics, and physics), EDUCATION (elementary, foreign languages, music, science, and secondary), ENGINEERING AND ENVIRONMENTAL DESIGN (environmental science), HEALTH PROFESSIONS (health science, predentistry, and premedicine), SOCIAL SCIENCE (anthropology, economics, history, international relations, Japanese studies, philosophy, political science/government, prelaw, psychology, religion, sociology, and women's studies). The sciences, psychology, and history are the strongest academically. Management, political science, and psychology are the largest.

Required: All students must complete 32 courses including a concentration in a major field of study culminating with a capstone experience; 1 course each in humanities, social studies, reasoning, composition, diversity: non-western culture; diversity: domestic and conceptual; science, technology, and society; 2 courses in natural sciences and 4 courses in a foreign language. The minimum GPA is 2.0.

Special: The college offers cross-registration with the Central Pennsylvania Consortium, an extensive study-abroad program and has special centers worldwide. There are summer internships and a Washington semester with American University. There is a United Nations semester at Drew University, and a 3-2 engineering program with Columbia University, Rensselaer Polytechnic, and Washington University in St. Louis. There are also joint programs in optometry with the Pennsylvania College of Optometry, and forestry and environmental studies with Duke University. The college also offers double majors, student-designed majors, and B.A.-B.S. degrees in biology, math, chemistry, physics, biochemistry, molecular biology, and music education. Education certification is also available. There are 16 national honor societies, including Phi Beta Kappa.

Faculty/Classroom: 55% of faculty are male; 45%, female. All both teach and do research. The average class size in an introductory lecture is 19; in a laboratory, 15; and in a regular course, 19.

Admissions: 46% of the 2003-2004 applicants were accepted. The SAT I scores for the 2003-2004 freshman class were: Verbal--34% between 500 and 599, 56% between 600 and 700, and 9% above 700; Math--28% between 500 and 599, 63% between 600 and 700, and 8% above 700. 75% of the current freshmen were in the top fifth of their class; 99% were in the top two fifths.

Requirements: The SAT I or ACT is required. In addition, an essay is required. Art students can submit a portfolio, and music students must audition. An interview and SAT II: Subject tests are recommended. A GPA of 3.0 is required. AP credits are accepted. Important factors in the admissions decision are evidence of special talent, recommendations by school officials, and advanced placement or honor courses.

Procedure: Freshmen are admitted fall and spring. Entrance exams should be taken by the January testing date of the senior year. There are early decision, early admissions, and deferred admissions plans. Early decision applications should be filed by February 1; regular applications, by February 15 for fall entry and December 1 for spring entry, along with a $45 fee. Notification is sent April 1. 196 early decision candidates were accepted for the 2003-2004 class. A waiting list is an active part of the admissions procedure. Applications are accepted on-line through CommonApp or the school's web site.

Transfer: 25 transfer students enrolled in 2002-2003. Transfer applicants must have a GPA of at least 2.0. An interview is recommended. The high school record, test scores, and a Dean's transfer recommendation form are also considered. 16 of 32 credits required for the bachelor's degree must be completed at Gettysburg.

Visiting: There are regularly scheduled orientations for prospective students, including interviews, tours, day and overnight visits, open houses, and group sesions. There are guides for informal visits and visitors may sit in on classes and stay overnight. To schedule a visit, contact the Admissions Office at *admiss@gettysburg.edu*.

Financial Aid: In 2003-2004, 67% of all full-time freshmen and 65% of continuing full-time students received some form of financial aid. 61% of full-time freshmen and 60% of continuing full-time students received need-based aid. The average freshman award was $23,640. 37% of undergraduates work part time. Average annual earnings from campus work are $1500. The average financial indebtedness of the 2003 graduate was $15,500. Gettysburg is a member of CSS. The CSS Profile or FAFSA and are required. The deadline for filing freshman financial aid applications for fall entry is February 15.

International Students: There are 54 international students enrolled. The school actively recruits these students. They must score 550 on the written TOEFL and also take the SAT I or the ACT.

Computers: A campuswide network has connections to the Internet. PCs are available in labs and other locations throughout the campus. Wireless connections are available. College navigation (CNAV) is a web portal that gives students access to personal information, and provides connections to courses, faculty, and students with similar interests. All students may access the system 24 hours a day. There are no time limits and no fees. It is strongly recommended that all students have a personal computer.

Graduates: From July 1, 2002 to June 30, 2003, 620 bachelor's degrees were awarded. The most popular majors were management (22%), political science (10%), and history (8%). In an average class, 75% graduate in 4 years or less, 76% graduate in 5 years or less, and 77% graduate in 6 years or less. 145 companies recruited on campus in 2002-2003. Of the 2002 graduating class, 35% were enrolled in graduate school within 6 months of graduation and 63% were employed.

Admissions Contact: Gail Sweezey, Director of Admissions.
E-mail: *admiss@gettysburg.edu* Web: *www.gettysburg.edu*

GROVE CITY COLLEGE
B-2

Grove City, PA 16127-2104   (724) 458-2100; Fax: (724) 458-3395

Full-time: 1130 men, 1137 women	**Faculty:** 125
Part-time: 5 men, 4 women	**Ph.D.s:** 75%
Graduate: none	**Student/Faculty:** 18 to 1
Year: semesters	**Tuition:** $9376
Application Deadline: February 1	**Room & Board:** $4852
Freshman Class: 2199 applied, 893 accepted, 567 enrolled	
SAT I Verbal/Math: 631/637	**ACT:** 27 **HIGHLY COMPETITIVE**

Grove City College, founded in 1876, is a private, liberal arts and science college affiliated with the Presbyterian Church (U.S.A.). There are 2 undergraduate schools. In addition to regional accreditation, Grove City has baccalaureate program accreditation with ABET. The library contains 158,000 volumes, 230,000 microform items, and 520 audio/video tapes/CDs, and subscribes to 1200 periodicals. Computerized library services include the card catalog, interlibrary loans, database searching, and Internet access. Special learning facilities include an art gallery and radio station. The 150-acre campus is in a small town 60 miles north of Pittsburgh. Including any residence halls, there are 27 buildings.

Student Life: 52% of undergraduates are from Pennsylvania. Others are from 43 states, 13 foreign countries, and Canada. 81% are from public schools. 98% are white. 67% are Protestant; 24% claim no religious affiliation; 9% Catholic. The average age of freshmen is 18; all undergraduates, 20. 10% do not continue beyond their first year; 75% remain to graduate.

Housing: 2048 students can be accommodated in college housing, which includes single-sex dorms. On-campus housing is guaranteed for all 4 years. 91% of students live on campus; of those, 90% remain on campus on weekends. Alcohol is not permitted. Upperclassmen may keep cars.

Activities: 9% of men belong to 7 local fraternities; 20% of women belong to 8 local sororities. There are 120 groups on campus, including art, band, cheerleading, choir, chorale, chorus, computers, dance, debate, drama, drill team, ethnic, film, forensics, honors, international, jazz band, literary magazine, marching band, musical theater, newspaper, opera, orchestra, pep band, photography, political, professional, radio and TV, religious, social, social service, student government, symphony, and yearbook. Popular campus events include Parents Weekend, Christmas Candlelight Service, and President's Gala.

Sports: There are 10 intercollegiate sports for men and 10 for women, and 4 intramural sports for men and 11 for women. Facilities include a field house, a recreation building that includes 2 indoor pools, an indoor running track, 4 basketball, volleyball, or tennis courts, 3 racquetball courts, bowling lanes, and a weight room, 10 outdoor tennis courts, a football stadium with an all-weather track, baseball, soccer, and softball fields, and a basketball arena.

Disabled Students: All of the campus is accessible. Wheelchair ramps, elevators, special parking, specially equipped rest rooms, special class scheduling, lowered drinking fountains, and lowered telephones are available. The college's hillside location presents some difficulty for the seriously disabled.

Services: Counseling and information services are available, as is tutoring in most subjects. A student tutoring program is available for a small fee.

Campus Safety and Security: Measures include 24-hour foot and vehicle patrol, self-defense education, security escort services, and pamphlets/posters/films. There are emergency telephones and lighted pathways/sidewalks.

Programs of Study: Grove City confers B.A., B.S., B.Mus., B.S.E.E., and B.S.M.E. degrees. Bachelor's degrees are awarded in BIOLOGICAL SCIENCE (biochemistry and biology/biological science), BUSINESS (accounting, banking and finance, business administration and management, international business management, management information systems, and marketing/retailing/merchandising), COMMUNICATIONS AND THE ARTS (communications, English, French, music, music business management, music performance, and Spanish), COMPUTER AND PHYSICAL SCIENCE (chemistry, computer science, mathematics, and physics), EDUCATION (elementary, music, science, and secondary), ENGINEERING AND ENVIRONMENTAL DESIGN (electrical/electronics engineering, industrial administration/management, and mechanical engineering), HEALTH PROFESSIONS (predentistry and premedicine), SOCIAL SCIENCE (economics, history, philosophy, political

science/government, prelaw, psychology, religion, and religious music). Engineering, education, and premedicine are the strongest academically. Business, education, and engineering are the largest.

Required: Students are required to complete a minimum of 128 credit hours (136 for engineering students). All students must complete the 38-semester-hour general education curriculum, which includes 18 hours of humanities, 8 of natural science, and 6 each of social science and quantitative and logical reasoning, 2 hours in phys ed, 4 chapel credits, and 2 years of foreign language. A minimum GPA of 2.0 is required.

Special: The college offers study abroad, summer internships, 3 accelerated degree programs, student-designed interdisciplinary majors, non-degree study for special students, and a Washington semester. There are 9 national honor societies and 14 departmental honors programs.

Faculty/Classroom: 72% of faculty are male; 28%, female. 99% teach undergraduates and 20% both teach and do research. The average class size in an introductory lecture is 42; in a laboratory, 22; and in a regular course, 25.

Admissions: 41% of the 2003-2004 applicants were accepted. The SAT I scores for the 2003-2004 freshman class were: Verbal--4% below 500, 25% between 500 and 599, 52% between 600 and 700, and 19% above 700; Math--2% below 500, 24% between 500 and 599, 51% between 600 and 700, and 23% above 700. The ACT scores were 2% below 21, 10% between 21 and 23, 26% between 24 and 26, 24% between 27 and 28, and 38% above 28. 79% of the current freshmen were in the top fifth of their class; 96% were in the top two fifths. There were 18 National Merit finalists and 3 semifinalists. 67 freshmen graduated first in their class.

Requirements: The SAT I or ACT is required. In addition, the academic or college preparatory course is highly recommended, including 4 units each of English, history, math, science, and a foreign language. An essay is required of all applicants, and an audition is required of music students. An interview is highly recommended. AP and CLEP credits are accepted. Important factors in the admissions decision are extracurricular activities record, personality/intangible qualities, and ability to finance college education.

Procedure: Freshmen are admitted fall and spring. Entrance exams should be taken in the spring of the junior year or the fall of the senior year. There are early decision and deferred admissions plans. Early decision applications should be filed by November 15; regular applications, by February 1 for fall entry and January 1 for spring entry, along with a $50 fee. Notification of early decision is sent December 15; regular decision, March 15. 337 early decision candidates were accepted for the 2003-2004 class. 220 applicants were on the 2003 waiting list; 76 were admitted. Applications are accepted on-line through the college's web site.

Transfer: 33 transfer students enrolled in 2002-2003. Applicants should have a minimum of 17 credit hours earned with a 2.0 minimum GPA. Either the SAT I or the ACT is recommended, as is an interview. 64 of 128 credits required for the bachelor's degree must be completed at Grove City.

Visiting: There are regularly scheduled orientations for prospective students, consisting of daily interviews and tours, 2 high school visitation days in the fall, and a career day in the spring. There is a science and engineering open house in the fall. There are guides for informal visits and visitors may sit in on classes and stay overnight. To schedule a visit, contact the Admissions Office.

Financial Aid: In 2003-2004, 71% of all full-time freshmen and 51% of continuing full-time students received some form of financial aid. 43% of full-time freshmen and 32% of continuing full-time students received need-based aid. The average freshman award was $7370. Need-based scholarships or need-based grants averaged $3722 ($15,978 maximum) and non-need-based awards and non-need-based scholarships averaged $2777 ($15,978 maximum). 50% of undergraduates work part time. Average annual earnings from campus work are $500. The average financial indebtedness of the 2003 graduate was $12,500. The college's own financial statement is required. The deadline for filing freshman financial aid applications for fall entry is April 15.

International Students: There are 19 international students enrolled. They must score 550 on the written TOEFL or 213 on the electronic version. If the TOEFL is not available, either the SAT I or the ACT is required.

Computers: The mainframe is an HP ProLiant. The technological learning center houses 40 PCs and terminal stations. Every full-time student has a laptop computer with the ability to connect to the Internet, Intranet, and e-mail accounts. All students may access the system 8 A.M. to 11 P.M., Monday through Friday; 8 A.M. to 5 P.M., Saturday; and 2 P.M. to 11 P.M., Sunday. There are no time limits and no fees. All students are required to have personal computers. All freshman receive a Compaq color notebook computer.

Graduates: From July 1, 2002 to June 30, 2003, 487 bachelor's degrees were awarded. The most popular majors were elementary education (11%), business management (9%), and molecular biology (6%). In an average class, 2% graduate in 3 years or less, 78% graduate in 4 years or less, 85% graduate in 5 years or less, and 85% graduate in 6 years or less. 116 companies recruited on campus in 2002-2003. Of the 2002 graduating class, 15% were enrolled in graduate school within 6 months of graduation and 60% were employed.

Admissions Contact: Jeffrey C. Mincey, Director of Admissions. E-mail: *admissions@gcc.edu* Web: *www.gcc.edu*

GWYNEDD-MERCY COLLEGE F-4
Gwynedd Valley, PA 19437

(215) 641-5510
(800) DIAL-GMC; Fax: (215) 641-5556

Full-time: 286 men, 944 women	**Faculty:** 75; IIB, av$
Part-time: 225 men, 722 women	**Ph.Ds:** 61%
Graduate: 97 men, 341 women	**Student/Faculty:** 16 to 1
Year: semesters, summer session	**Tuition:** $16,700
Application Deadline: August 1	**Room & Board:** $7525
Freshman Class: 2658 applied, 1442 accepted, 446 enrolled	
SAT I Verbal/Math: 485/480	**COMPETITIVE**

Gwynedd-Mercy College, founded in 1948, is a private institution affiliated with the Roman Catholic Church and offering degree programs in the arts and sciences, business, education, and health fields. There are 5 undergraduate and 2 graduate schools. In addition to regional accreditation, Gwynedd-Mercy has baccalaureate program accreditation with NLN. The library contains 101,018 volumes, 14,802 microform items, and 51,604 audio/video tapes/CDs, and subscribes to 872 periodicals. Computerized library services include the card catalog and database searching. Special learning facilities include a learning resource center and a lab school for education majors. The 170-acre campus is in a suburban area 20 miles northwest of Philadelphia. Including any residence halls, there are 20 buildings.

Student Life: 95% of undergraduates are from Pennsylvania. Students are from 9 states and 54 foreign countries. 51% are from public schools. 81% are white; 13% African American. 55% are Catholic; 20% Protestant; 8% claim no religious affiliation. The average age of freshmen is 23; all undergraduates, 28. 12% do not continue beyond their first year; 70% remain to graduate.

Housing: 467 students can be accommodated in college housing, which includes coed dorms. On-campus housing is available on a first-come, first-served basis. 77% of students commute. Alcohol is not permitted. All students may keep cars.

Activities: There are no fraternities or sororities. There are 21 groups on campus, including choir, chorus, drama, ethnic, honors, international, literary magazine, newspaper, professional, religious, social, social service, student government, and yearbook. Popular campus events include Fall Fest, Carol Night, and International Night.

Sports: There are 8 intercollegiate sports for men and 10 for women. Facilities include a recreation center housing men's and women's basketball, women's volleyball, a walking track, indoor racquetball courts, a weight room, team locker rooms, and a sauna. Outdoor facilities include soccer, baseball, softball, and field hockey fields.

Disabled Students: 75% of the campus is accessible. Wheelchair ramps, elevators, special parking, specially equipped rest rooms, and special class scheduling are available.

Services: Counseling and information services are available, as is tutoring in most subjects. There is remedial math, reading, and writing. Tutoring is made available in conjunction with student needs.

Campus Safety and Security: Measures include 24-hour foot and vehicle patrol, security escort services, shuttle buses, and informal discussions. There are emergency telephones and lighted pathways/sidewalks.

Programs of Study: Gwynedd-Mercy confers B.A., B.S., and B.H.S. degrees. Associate and master's degrees are also awarded. Bachelor's degrees are awarded in BIOLOGICAL SCIENCE (biology/biological science), BUSINESS (accounting, banking and finance, business administration and management, human resources, international business management, management science, marketing and distribution, office supervision and management, and sports management), COMMUNICATIONS AND THE ARTS (communications, English, and public relations), COMPUTER AND PHYSICAL SCIENCE (computer science, information sciences and systems, mathematics, and natural sciences), EDUCATION (business, elementary, mathematics, science, secondary, social studies, and special), HEALTH PROFESSIONS (clinical science, health care administration, medical laboratory technology, nursing, radiation therapy, and respiratory therapy), SOCIAL SCIENCE (criminal justice, history, psychology, social work, and sociology). Nursing, biology, and medical technology are the strongest academically. Nursing, business, and education are the largest.

Required: All students must complete at least 125 credit hours, including 60 in the major, with a minimum GPA of 2.0. (Some programs require a higher GPA.) General education courses cover language, literature and fine arts, behavioral and social sciences, humanities, and natural science. Specific courses in English composition, literature, philosophy, and religious studies are required.

Special: The college offers co-op programs in computer science, business administration, and accounting, as well as internships, dual majors, accelerated degree programs, B.A.-B.S. degrees, and pass/fail options.

Cross-registration is offered with South Eastern Pennsylvania Consortium for Higher Education. All programs require or have the option for hands-on experience. There is a 3-1 program in medical technology available wherein the last year is a hospital rotation. There are 4 national honor societies, a freshman honors program, and 1 departmental honors program.

Faculty/Classroom: 30% of faculty are male; 70%, female. 97% teach undergraduates. No introductory courses are taught by graduate students. The average class size in an introductory lecture is 17; in a laboratory, 10; and in a regular course, 17.

Admissions: 54% of the 2003-2004 applicants were accepted. The SAT I scores for the 2003-2004 freshman class were: Verbal--55% below 500, 38% between 500 and 599, 6% between 600 and 700, and 1% above 700; Math--58% below 500, 35% between 500 and 599, and 7% between 600 and 700. 21% of the current freshmen were in the top fifth of their class; 46% were in the top two fifths. 1 freshman graduated first in the class.

Requirements: The SAT I is required. In addition, candidates for admission must be graduates of accredited secondary schools and have completed 16 academic credits/Carnegie units, including 4 credits in English, 3 each in math, science, and college preparatory electives, 2 in a foreign language, and 1 in history. The GED is accepted. An interview is recommended for all candidates and is required for some programs. Gwynedd-Mercy requires applicants to be in the upper 71% of their class. A GPA of 2.0 is required. AP and CLEP credits are accepted. Important factors in the admissions decision are advanced placement or honor courses, parents or siblings attending the school, and recommendations by alumni.

Procedure: Freshmen are admitted fall and spring. Entrance exams should be taken in the spring of the junior year or the fall of the senior year. There is a deferred admissions plan and a rolling admissions plan. Applications should be filed by August 1 for fall entry and December 15 for spring entry, along with a $25 fee. Notification is sent on a rolling basis. Applications are accepted on-line through *http://www.gmc.edu/admissions/how.html*.

Transfer: 134 transfer students enrolled in 2002-2003. Neither the SAT I nor the ACT is required for transfer students out of high school for 2 or more years. A minimum GPA of 2.0 is necessary; some programs require a higher GPA. An interview is recommended. 45 of 125 credits required for the bachelor's degree must be completed at Gwynedd-Mercy.

Visiting: There are regularly scheduled orientations for prospective students, consisting of open houses with formal presentations and campus tours, and class days with class visitations and campus tours. There are guides for informal visits and visitors may sit in on classes and stay overnight. To schedule a visit, contact the Admissions Office at *admissions@gmc.edu*.

Financial Aid: In 2003-2004, 94% of all full-time freshmen and 75% of continuing full-time students received some form of financial aid. 69% of full-time freshmen and 46% of continuing full-time students received need-based aid. The average freshman award was $13,343. 122% of undergraduates work part time. Average annual earnings from campus work are $503. The average financial indebtedness of the 2003 graduate was $15,510. The FAFSA, the college's own financial statement, and the federal income tax returns are required. The deadline for filing freshman financial aid applications for fall entry is March 15.

International Students: There are 38 international students enrolled. They must score 500 on the written TOEFL or take the MELAB.

Computers: There are 34 Compaq multimedia PCs in a Novell Network connected to the campus network and the Internet, with additional desktop packages available. All students may access the system 65 hours a week.

Graduates: From July 1, 2002 to June 30, 2003, 332 bachelor's degrees were awarded. The most popular majors were nursing (33%), business administration (28%), and education (15%). In an average class, 57% graduate in 4 years or less, and 7% graduate in 5 years or less.

Admissions Contact: Dennis Murphy, Vice President of Enrollment Management. E-mail: *admissions@gmc.edu* Web: *www.gmc.edu*

HAVERFORD COLLEGE E-4
Haverford, PA 19041-1392

(610) 896-1350; Fax: (610) 896-1338

Full-time: 554 men, 609 women	**Faculty:** 108; IIB, +$
Part-time: none	**Ph.Ds:** 98%
Graduate: none	**Student/Faculty:** 11 to 1
Year: semesters	**Tuition:** $28,880
Application Deadline: January 15	**Room & Board:** $9020
Freshman Class: 2973 applied, 878 accepted, 313 enrolled	
SAT I Verbal/Math: 690/690	**MOST COMPETITIVE**

Haverford College, founded in 1833, is a private liberal arts college. The 5 libraries contain 757,759 volumes, 4809 microform items, and 11,921 audio/video tapes/CDs, and subscribe to 4506 periodicals. Computerized library services include the card catalog, interlibrary loans, and database searching. Special learning facilities include an art gallery, radio station, an observatory, and an arboretum. The 200-acre campus is in a suburban area 10 miles west of Philadelphia. Including any residence halls, there are 71 buildings.

Student Life: 83% of undergraduates are from out of state, mostly the Middle Atlantic. Students are from 48 states, 35 foreign countries, and Canada. 61% are from public schools. 72% are white; 14% Asian American. The average age of freshmen is 18; all undergraduates, 20. 4% do not continue beyond their first year; 92% remain to graduate.

Housing: 1141 students can be accommodated in college housing, which includes single-sex and coed dorms and on-campus apartments. In addition, there are language houses, special-interest houses, and Haverford students may live at Bryn Mawr College through a dorm exchange program. On-campus housing is guaranteed for all 4 years. 98% of students live on campus; of those, 90% remain on campus on weekends. Upperclassmen may keep cars.

Activities: There are no fraternities or sororities. There are 75 groups on campus, including chorale, dance, drama, ethnic, gay, international, jazz band, literary magazine, musical theater, newspaper, orchestra, political, radio and TV, religious, social service, student government, and yearbook. Popular campus events include Haverfest, Snowball, and Swarthmore athletic competitions.

Sports: There are 10 intercollegiate sports for men and 11 for women, and 4 intramural sports for men and 4 for women. Facilities include a field house with an indoor track, extensive outdoor fields, a 400-meter, 8-lane, all-weather track, and tennis, squash, and basketball courts.

Disabled Students: 60% of the campus is accessible. Wheelchair ramps, elevators, special parking, specially equipped rest rooms, special class scheduling, lowered drinking fountains, lowered telephones, and reasonable accommodation are available.

Services: Counseling and information services are available, as is tutoring in every subject. There is a reader service for the blind.

Campus Safety and Security: Measures include 24-hour foot and vehicle patrol, self-defense education, security escort services, and shuttle buses. There are informal discussions, pamphlets/posters/films, emergency telephones, lighted pathways/sidewalks, and a fire safety program.

Programs of Study: Haverford confers B.A. and B.S. degrees. Bachelor's degrees are awarded in BIOLOGICAL SCIENCE (biology/biological science), COMMUNICATIONS AND THE ARTS (art history and appreciation, classics, comparative literature, English, fine arts, French, German, Italian, linguistics, music, romance languages and literature, Russian, Spanish, and visual and performing arts), COMPUTER AND PHYSICAL SCIENCE (astronomy, chemistry, geology, information sciences and systems, mathematics, and physics), SOCIAL SCIENCE (anthropology, archeology, East Asian studies, economics, history, interdisciplinary studies, liberal arts/general studies, philosophy, political science/government, psychology, religion, sociology, and urban studies). Natural and physical sciences, English, and history are the strongest academically. English, biology, and history are the largest.

Required: All students must take a minimum of 32 course credits, including freshman writing and 3 courses each in social science, natural science, and the humanities. One of the distribution courses must be quantitative and 1 must meet the social justice requirement. Students must also take 3 semesters of phys ed and demonstrate proficiency in a foreign language. Students must take a minimum of 6 courses in the major and 6 in related fields. Each major includes a capstone experience (a comprehensive exam, thesis, or advanced project, a specially-designed course, or some combination), which varies by department.

Special: Haverford offers internship programs, cross-registration with Bryn Mawr College, Swarthmore College, and study abroad in 33 countries, dual majors, student-designed majors. Pass/fail options are limited to 4 in 4 years. There is 1 national honor society, including Phi Beta Kappa, and 28 departmental honors programs.

Faculty/Classroom: 57% of faculty are male; 43%, female. All teach undergraduates. The average class size in an introductory lecture is 30; in a laboratory, 13; and in a regular course, 17.

Admissions: 30% of the 2003-2004 applicants were accepted. The SAT I scores for the 2003-2004 freshman class were: Verbal--1% below 500, 7% between 500 and 599, 46% between 600 and 700, and 46% above 700; Math--1% below 500, 7% between 500 and 599, 48% between 600 and 700, and 44% above 700. 98% of the current freshmen were in the top fifth of their class.

Requirements: The SAT I or ACT is required. In addition, the SAT II: writing test is required, plus 2 others. Candidates for admission must be graduates of an accredited secondary school and have taken 4 courses in English, 3 each in a foreign language and math, and 1 each in science and history. The GED is accepted. An essay is required and an interview is recommended. AP credits are accepted. Important factors in the admissions decision are advanced placement or honor courses, leadership record, and recommendations by school officials.

Procedure: Freshmen are admitted in the fall. Entrance exams should be taken before January 15. There are early decision, early admissions, and deferred admissions plans. Early decision applications should be filed by November 15; regular applications, by January 15 for fall entry, along with a $60 fee. Notification of early decision is sent December 15; regular decision, by April 15. 103 early decision candidates were accept-

ed for the 2003-2004 class. A waiting list is an active part of the admissions procedure. Applications are accepted on computer disk and on-line through *Embark.com* and CollegeLink.

Transfer: 2 transfer students enrolled in 2002-2003. Transfer students must be able to enter the sophomore or junior class. Admission depends mainly on the strength of college grades. A minimum GPA of 3.0 is necessary and the SAT I is recommended. The equivalent of 1 year of courses must have been earned. A liberal arts curriculum is also recommended. 64 of 128 credits required for the bachelor's degree must be completed at Haverford.

Visiting: There are guides for informal visits and visitors may sit in on classes and stay overnight. To schedule a visit, contact the Admissions Office at *admission@haverford.edu*.

Financial Aid: In 2003-2004, 39% of all full-time freshmen and 43% of continuing full-time students received some form of financial aid. 37% of full-time freshmen and 41% of continuing full-time students received need-based aid. The average freshman award was $23,617. The average financial indebtedness of the 2003 graduate was $15,362. The CSS Profile or FAFSA is required. The deadline for filing freshman financial aid applications for fall entry is January 31.

International Students: There are 35 international students enrolled. The school actively recruits these students. They must score 600 on the written TOEFL or 250 on the electronic version and also take the SAT I or the ACT.

Computers: 201 computers are available for student use, 96 in public computing labs, 75 in department specific labs, and 30 in the library and other buildings. All students may access the system. There are no time limits and no fees.

Graduates: From July 1, 2002 to June 30, 2003, 291 bachelor's degrees were awarded. The most popular majors were English (17%), biology (14%), and history (9%). In an average class, 88% graduate in 4 years or less, 90% graduate in 5 years or less, and 92% graduate in 6 years or less. 172 companies recruited on campus in 2002-2003. Of the 2002 graduating class, 17% were enrolled in graduate school within 6 months of graduation and 55% were employed.

Admissions Contact: Rob Killion, Director of Admission. A video is available. E-mail: *admitme@haverford.edu*
Web: *http://www.haverford.edu*

HOLY FAMILY COLLEGE
Philadelphia, PA 19114

F-3
(215) 637-3050
(800) 637-1191; Fax: (215) 281-1022

Full-time: 235 men, 840 women	**Faculty:** 75; IIB, -$
Part-time: 195 men, 585 women	**Ph.Ds:** 69%
Graduate: 180 men, 640 women	**Student/Faculty:** 14 to 1
Year: semesters, summer session	**Tuition:** $13,710
Application Deadline: open	**Room & Board:** n/app
Freshman Class: n/av	
SAT I or ACT: required	**LESS COMPETITIVE**

Holy Family College, established in 1954 and affiliated with the Roman Catholic Church, is a private, nonresidential institution with a liberal arts core. Figures in the above capsule and in this profile are approximate. In addition to regional accreditation, Holy Family has baccalaureate program accreditation with AACSB and NLN. The library contains 101,392 volumes, 8588 microform items, and 2975 audio/video tapes/CDs, and subscribes to 709 periodicals. Computerized library services include the card catalog, interlibrary loans, and database searching. Special learning facilities include a learning resource center and writing resource center. The 46-acre campus is in a suburban area within city limits. There are 8 buildings.

Student Life: 90% of undergraduates are from Pennsylvania. Students are from 7 states and 17 foreign countries. 24% are from public schools. 92% are white. 78% are Catholic; 9% Protestant. The average age of freshmen is 18; all undergraduates, 21. 18% do not continue beyond their first year; 65% remain to graduate.

Housing: There are no residence halls. All students commute. Alcohol is not permitted. All students may keep cars.

Activities: There are no fraternities or sororities. There are 62 groups on campus, including cheerleading, drama, honors, international, literary magazine, newspaper, professional, religious, social service, student government, and yearbook. Popular campus events include Buddy Day, Christmas Rose, and Spring Fling.

Sports: There are 3 intercollegiate sports for men and 4 for women, and 5 intramural sports for men and 5 for women. Facilities include a gym, a weight room, racquetball courts, and soccer and softball fields.

Disabled Students: All of the campus is accessible. Wheelchair ramps, elevators, special parking, specially equipped rest rooms, lowered drinking fountains, and lowered telephones are available.

Services: Counseling and information services are available, as is tutoring in some subjects, including writing, reading, and math.

Campus Safety and Security: Measures include 24-hour foot and vehicle patrol, security escort services, pamphlets/posters/films, and emergency telephones. There are lighted pathways/sidewalks.

Programs of Study: Holy Family confers B.A., B.S., and B.S.N. degrees. Associate and master's degrees are also awarded. Bachelor's degrees are awarded in BIOLOGICAL SCIENCE (biochemistry and biology/biological science), BUSINESS (accounting, business administration and management, and marketing/retailing/merchandising), COMMUNICATIONS AND THE ARTS (art, English, French, and Spanish), COMPUTER AND PHYSICAL SCIENCE (chemistry, information sciences and systems, and mathematics), EDUCATION (early childhood, elementary, foreign languages, science, secondary, and special), HEALTH PROFESSIONS (medical laboratory technology, nursing, and premedicine), SOCIAL SCIENCE (criminal justice, economics, history, humanities, prelaw, psychology, religion, social work, and sociology). Nursing, elementary education, and accounting are the strongest academically. Nursing, education, and business are the largest.

Required: Students must complete 120 to 130 semester hours, including at least 30 in the major, with a minimum GPA of 2.0. Nursing, medical technology, and education majors must maintain a GPA of 2.5. Specific discipline requirements include English, science, math, philosophy, religious studies, social studies, humanities, and foreign language. A core curriculum of communication, quantification, philosophy, humanities, social science, natural sciences, senior ethics, and religious studies must be fulfilled. All majors require satisfactory performance on a comprehensive exam.

Special: Opportunities are provided for study abroad, co-op programs in 23 majors with more than 200 companies, a B.A.-B.S. degree, an accelerated degree program, independent study, credit by exam, nondegree study, and pass/fail options. Students may pursue dual majors in business and French or Spanish, international business and French or Spanish, and elementary and special education. There are 10 national honor societies, a freshman honors program, and 2 departmental honors programs.

Faculty/Classroom: 44% of faculty are male; 56%, female. No introductory courses are taught by graduate students. The average class size in an introductory lecture is 20; in a laboratory, 17; and in a regular course, 21.

Requirements: The SAT I or ACT is required. In addition, graduation from an accredited secondary school is required; a GED is accepted. Applicants must submit 16 academic credits, including 4 courses in English, 3 each in history and math, 2 each in foreign language and science, 1 in social studies, and the remainder in academic electives. Holy Family requires applicants to be in the upper 40% of their class. A GPA of 2.0 is required. AP and CLEP credits are accepted. Important factors in the admissions decision are recommendations by school officials, recommendations by alumni, and personality/intangible qualities.

Procedure: Freshmen are admitted to all sessions. Entrance exams should be taken by October or November of the senior year. There are early decision and deferred admissions plans and rolling admissions plans. Application deadlines are open. The fall 2003 application fee was $25.

Transfer: 120 transfer students enrolled in a recent year. Applicants must submit official transcripts from all previous colleges. Grades of D are not transferable. A maximum of 75 credits will be accepted for transfer. 45 of 120 credits required for the bachelor's degree must be completed at Holy Family.

Visiting: There are regularly scheduled orientations for prospective students, consisting of an interview and a tour. There are guides for informal visits and visitors may sit in on classes. To schedule a visit, contact the Office of Admissions.

Financial Aid: Holy Family is a member of CSS. The FAFSA is required. Check with the school for current deadline.

International Students: In a recent year, there were 13 international students enrolled. They must score 530 on the written TOEFL.

Computers: There are more than 100 PCs networked in 4 to 6 labs available for student use. All students may access the system 6 days a week (7-day remote Internet access for subscribers). There are no time limits and no fees.

Graduates: In a recent year, 306 bachelor's degrees were awarded. The most popular majors were education (35%), business/marketing (19%), and health professions (11%). In an average class, 4% graduate in 3 years or less, 46% graduate in 4 years or less, 58% graduate in 5 years or less, and 60% graduate in 6 years or less. 85 companies recruited on campus in a recent year. Of a recent graduating class, 5% were enrolled in graduate school within 6 months of graduation and 90% were employed.

Admissions Contact: Roberta Nolan, Director of Undergraduate Admissions. E-mail: *rnolan@hfc.edu* Web: *www.hfc.edu*

IMMACULATA UNIVERSITY
Immaculata, PA 19345

E-4
(610) 647-4400, ext. 3015
(877) IC-TODAY; Fax: (610) 640-0836

Full-time: 389 women	**Faculty:** 76; IIA, --$
Part-time: none	**Ph.D.s:** 64%
Graduate: none	**Student/Faculty:** 5 to 1
Year: semesters, summer session	**Tuition:** $17,200
Application Deadline: May 1	**Room & Board:** $8000
Freshman Class: n/av	
SAT I: required	**ACT:** n/av **COMPETITIVE**

Immaculata University, founded in 1920, is a private Catholic, women's liberal arts and career preparation college. In addition to regional accreditation, Immaculata has baccalaureate program accreditation with ADA, AHEA, NASM, and NLN. The library contains 130,000 volumes, 1373 microform items, and 1500 audio/video tapes/CDs, and subscribes to 760 periodicals. Computerized library services include the card catalog, interlibrary loans, database searching, and Internet access. Special learning facilities include a learning resource center and computer and language labs. The 400-acre campus is in a suburban area 20 miles west of Philadelphia. Including any residence halls, there are 13 buildings.

Student Life: 71% of undergraduates are from Pennsylvania. Students are from 10 states and 1 foreign countries. 38% are from public schools. 85% are white. 76% are Catholic; 16% Protestant; 7% Muslim, Hindu, and Shinto. The average age of freshmen is 18; all undergraduates, 20. 31% do not continue beyond their first year; 55% remain to graduate.

Housing: 380 students can be accommodated in college housing, which includes single-sex dorms. On-campus housing is guaranteed for all 4 years. 74% of students live on campus; of those, 55% remain on campus on weekends. Alcohol is not permitted. All students may keep cars.

Activities: There are no fraternities. There are 32 groups on campus, including art, choir, chorale, chorus, computers, dance, debate, drama, ethnic, honors, international, literary magazine, musical theater, newspaper, orchestra, photography, political, professional, religious, social, social service, student government, and yearbook. Popular campus events include Rose Arbor Dinner, class proms, and Friday's Pub.

Sports: Facilities include tennis courts, a full gym, a handball gym, an Olympic-size swimming pool, hockey and softball fields, and a weight room.

Disabled Students: All of the campus is accessible. Wheelchair ramps, elevators, special parking, specially equipped rest rooms, special class scheduling, lowered drinking fountains, lowered telephones, and special housing are available.

Services: Counseling and information services are available, as is tutoring in most subjects. There is a reader service for the blind and remedial math, reading, and writing.

Campus Safety and Security: Measures include 24-hour foot and vehicle patrol, self-defense education, security escort services, and informal discussions. There are pamphlets/posters/films, emergency telephones, and lighted pathways/sidewalks.

Programs of Study: Immaculata confers B.A., B.S., B.Mus., and B.S.N. degrees. Associate, master's, and doctoral degrees are also awarded. Bachelor's degrees are awarded in BIOLOGICAL SCIENCE (biochemistry and biology/biological science), BUSINESS (accounting, banking and finance, business administration and management, and fashion merchandising), COMMUNICATIONS AND THE ARTS (English, French, music, and Spanish), COMPUTER AND PHYSICAL SCIENCE (information sciences and systems and mathematics), EDUCATION (early childhood, elementary, foreign languages, home economics, middle school, music, science, and secondary), HEALTH PROFESSIONS (music therapy, nursing, and premedicine), SOCIAL SCIENCE (dietetics, economics, experimental psychology, food science, history, international relations, prelaw, psychology, social science, sociology, and theological studies). Premedicine, education, and dietetics are the strongest academically. Education, business, and music therapy are the largest.

Required: To graduate, all students must complete 54 credits in liberal arts, including distribution requirements in humanities, social sciences, and sciences. Students must take a minimum of 126 credits, including 36 to 52 in the major. 2 credits of phys ed are also required. The college requires a minimum GPA of 2.0. A thesis, which is the outcome of a required senior seminar, is also required. Internships are required for dietetics, music therapy, and education.

Special: All majors offer opportunities for internships, and most require them. Students may study abroad in 6 countries. The college offers dual-majors, 3 accelerated degree programs in organization dynamics, human resource management, and nursing, and nondegree study and pass/fail options. There are 16 national honor societies, including Phi Beta Kappa, a freshman honors program, and 13 departmental honors programs.

Faculty/Classroom: 28% of faculty are male; 72%, female. 92% teach undergraduates and 4% both teach and do research. The average class size in an introductory lecture is 15; in a laboratory, 12; and in a regular course, 15.

Admissions: 24% of the current freshmen were in the top fifth of their class; 52% were in the top two fifths. In a recent year, 2 freshmen graduated first in their class.

Requirements: The SAT I is required, with a minimum composite score of 800, 400 verbal and 400 math. Candidates for admission should be graduates of an accredited secondary school with a minimum of 16 academic credits including 4 in English, 2 each in a foreign language, math, science, and social studies, 1 in history, and 3 more in college preparatory courses. The GED is accepted. An audition is required for music students and an essay and an interview are recommended for all. Immaculata requires applicants to be in the upper 60% of their class. A GPA of 2.0 is required. AP and CLEP credits are accepted. Important factors in the admissions decision are advanced placement or honor courses, recommendations by school officials, and extracurricular activities record.

Procedure: Freshmen are admitted fall and spring. Entrance exams should be taken in the spring of the junior year. There are early decision, deferred admissions, and rolling admissions plans. Early decision applications should be filed by November 1; regular applications, by May 1 for fall entry and November 1 for spring entry, along with a $25 fee. Notification of early decision is sent December 1; regular decision, on a rolling basis.

Transfer: 23 transfer students enrolled in 2002-2003. In addition to high school credentials, transfer applicants must present college transcripts. Courses in which the student has achieved a C or better are accepted if they are comparable to Immaculata's courses. A minimum composite score of 800 on the SAT I is required, as is an interview. Students must have a minimum GPA of 2.0. 36 of 126 credits required for the bachelor's degree must be completed at Immaculata.

Visiting: There are regularly scheduled orientations for prospective students, including an open house and class visit. There are guides for informal visits and visitors may sit in on classes and stay overnight. To schedule a visit, contact the Office of Admissions at *pbarry@immaculata.edu*.

Financial Aid: In 2003-2004, 91% of all full-time freshmen and 86% of continuing full-time students received some form of financial aid. 91% of full-time freshmen and 75% of continuing full-time students received need-based aid. The average freshman award was $13,500. Need-based scholarships or need-based grants averaged $2318 ($4050 maximum); need-based self-help aid (loans and jobs) averaged $1578 ($2625 maximum); and non-need-based awards and non-need-based scholarships averaged $15,488 ($17,200 maximum). All of undergraduates work part time. Average annual earnings from campus work are $700. The average financial indebtedness of the 2003 graduate was $17,125. Immaculata is a member of CSS. The FAFSA is required. The priority date for freshman financial aid applications for fall entry is February 15. The deadline for filing freshman financial aid applications for fall entry is April 15.

International Students: In a recent year, there were 35 international students enrolled. The school actively recruits these students. They must score 550 on the written TOEFL.

Computers: Students may use the networked computer terminals in the administrative offices, computer centers labs, and library. There is Internet and e-mail access for all students in residence halls. All students may access the system. There are no time limits and no fees.

Graduates: From July 1, 2002 to June 30, 2003, 94 bachelor's degrees were awarded. In an average class, 1% graduate in 3 years or less, 71% graduate in 4 years or less, 3% graduate in 5 years or less, and 4% graduate in 6 years or less. 18 companies recruited on campus in 2002-2003. Of the 2002 graduating class, 7% were enrolled in graduate school within 6 months of graduation and 85% were employed.

Admissions Contact: Sarah Fox, Assistant Director of Admissions. A video is available. E-mail: *admiss@immaculata.edu* Web: *http://www.immaculata.edu*

INDIANA UNIVERSITY OF PENNSYLVANIA — B-3
Indiana, PA 15705   (724) 357-2230; (800) 442-6830

Full-time: 4875 men, 6316 women	Faculty: 632; I, -$
Part-time: 413 men, 515 women	Ph.D.s: 96%
Graduate: 639 men, 1110 women	Student/Faculty: 18 to 1
Year: semesters, summer session	Tuition: $5785 ($12,685)
Application Deadline: open	Room & Board: $4704
Freshman Class: 8618 applied, 5136 accepted, 2761 enrolled	
SAT I Verbal/Math: 522/517	COMPETITIVE

Indiana University of Pennsylvania, founded in 1875, is a public member of the Pennsylvania State System of Higher Education offering programs in liberal and fine arts, business, preengineering, health science, military science, teacher preparation, basic and applied science, social science and humanities, criminology, and safety science. There are 7 undergraduate schools and 1 graduate school. In addition to regional accreditation, IUP has baccalaureate program accreditation with AACSB, ABET, ACPHA, ACS, ADA, APA, ASHA, CAHEA, CCNE, JRCERT, NASM, NASP, NAST, and NCATE. The library contains 836,151 volumes, 2,376,446 microform items, and 110,395 audio/video tapes/CDs, and subscribes to 2622 periodicals. Computerized library services include the card catalog, interlibrary loans, database searching, and Internet access. Special learning facilities include a learning resource center, art gallery, planetarium, radio station, and TV station. The 342-acre campus is in a small town 50 miles northeast of Pittsburgh. Including any residence halls, there are 79 buildings.

Student Life: 97% of undergraduates are from Pennsylvania. Students are from 41 states and 83 foreign countries. 95% are from public schools. 89% are white. The average age of freshmen is 18; all undergraduates, 21. 27% do not continue beyond their first year; 49% remain to graduate.

Housing: 3993 students can be accommodated in college housing, which includes single-sex and coed dorms and on-campus apartments. In addition, there are honors houses, 24-hour intensified study floors, substance-free housing, academic specialty housing, and an international house. On-campus housing is guaranteed for the freshman year only and is available on a lottery system for upperclassmen. Alcohol is not permitted. No one may keep cars.

Activities: 10% of men belong to 19 national fraternities; 11% of women belong to 14 national sororities. There are 200 groups on campus, including art, band, cheerleading, choir, chorale, chorus, computers, dance, drama, ethnic, film, gay, honors, international, jazz band, marching band, musical theater, newspaper, opera, orchestra, pep band, political, professional, radio and TV, religious, social, social service, student government, symphony, and yearbook. Popular campus events include Family Weekend and International Day.

Sports: There are 7 intercollegiate sports for men and 10 for women, and 24 intramural sports for men and 21 for women. Facilities include a 7600-seat stadium, swimming pools, a fitness trail, softball fields, and courts for tennis, badminton, handball/racquetball, basketball, and volleyball.

Disabled Students: 98% of the campus is accessible. Wheelchair ramps, elevators, special parking, specially equipped rest rooms, special class scheduling, and lowered drinking fountains are available.

Services: There is a reader service for the blind and remedial math, reading, and writing.

Campus Safety and Security: Measures include 24-hour foot and vehicle patrol, self-defense education, security escort services, and shuttle buses. There are informal discussions, pamphlets/posters/films, emergency telephones, and lighted pathways/sidewalks.

Programs of Study: IUP confers B.A., B.S., B.F.A., and B.S.Ed. degrees. Associate, master's, and doctoral degrees are also awarded. Bachelor's degrees are awarded in BIOLOGICAL SCIENCE (biochemistry and biology/biological science), BUSINESS (accounting, banking and finance, business administration and management, fashion merchandising, hotel/motel and restaurant management, human resources, international business management, management information systems, and marketing/retailing/merchandising), COMMUNICATIONS AND THE ARTS (art, communications, dramatic arts, English, fine arts, French, German, journalism, media arts, music, music performance, Russian, Spanish, and studio art), COMPUTER AND PHYSICAL SCIENCE (applied mathematics, applied physics, chemistry, computer science, geology, geoscience, mathematics, natural sciences, and physics), EDUCATION (art, business, early childhood, education of the deaf and hearing impaired, education of the mentally handicapped, education of the physically handicapped, elementary, English, foreign languages, mathematics, music, nutrition, physical, science, social science, special, and vocational), ENGINEERING AND ENVIRONMENTAL DESIGN (city/community/regional planning and interior design), HEALTH PROFESSIONS (environmental health science, medical technology, nuclear medical technology, nursing, premedicine, rehabilitation therapy, respiratory therapy, and speech pathology/audiology), SOCIAL SCIENCE (anthropology, child care/child and family studies, consumer services, criminology, dietetics, economics, family/consumer studies, food production/management/services, food science, geography, history, international studies, philosophy, political science/government, prelaw, psychology, religion, safety and security technology, social science, and sociology). Elementary education, criminology, and communications media are the largest.

Required: All candidates for graduation must complete approximately 120 credits, including 48 credits in the liberal studies core. The total number of hours and the minimum GPA vary with the major.

Special: IUP offers co-op programs, cross-registration through the National Student Exchange Consortium, a 3-2 engineering degree with the University of Pittsburgh and Drexel University, and a B.A.-B.S. degree. Internships and dual and student-designed majors are available. Students may study abroad in 28 countries. Also available are work-study programs, a Washington semester, an accelerated degree program, and credit for military experience. There are 21 national honor societies and a freshman honors program.

Faculty/Classroom: 58% of faculty are male; 42%, female. 91% teach undergraduates. No introductory courses are taught by graduate students. The average class size in a laboratory is 16 and in a regular course, 25.

Admissions: 60% of the 2003-2004 applicants were accepted. The SAT I scores for the 2003-2004 freshman class were: Verbal--36% below 500, 47% between 500 and 599, 15% between 600 and 700, and 2% above 700; Math--42% below 500, 45% between 500 and 599, 12% between 600 and 700, and 1% above 700. In a recent year, 10 freshmen graduated first in their class.

Requirements: The SAT I is required. In addition, candidates for admission should be graduates of an accredited secondary school. There are no specific course requirements. Art majors must have a portfolio and music majors must audition. AP and CLEP credits are accepted. Important factors in the admissions decision are advanced placement or honor courses, extracurricular activities record, and evidence of special talent.

Procedure: Freshmen are admitted fall and spring. Entrance exams should be taken by December of the preceding year. There is a deferred admissions plan and a rolling admissions plan. Application deadlines are open The fall 2003 application fee was $30. Applications are accepted on-line through *www.iup.edu/admissions.*

Transfer: 673 transfer students enrolled in a recent year. Transfer students must have a minimum GPA of 2.0 for all subjects (2.5 for education students). 45 of 120 credits required for the bachelor's degree must be completed at IUP.

Visiting: There are regularly scheduled orientations for prospective students. There are guides for informal visits and visitors may sit in on classes. To schedule a visit, contact the Admissions Office.

Financial Aid: In a recent year, 66% of all full-time freshmen and 69% of continuing full-time students received some form of financial aid. 56% of full-time freshmen and 57% of continuing full-time students received need-based aid. The average freshman award was $3948. 18% of undergraduates work part time. Average annual earnings from campus work are $1500. The average financial indebtedness of the 2003 graduate was $14,250. The FAFSA and Pennsylvania State Grant form are required. The deadline for filing freshman financial aid applications for fall entry is April 15.

International Students: There are 237 international students enrolled. They must score 500 on the written TOEFL.

Computers: The mainframe is a DEC VAX cluster. 500 Dell, Gateway, IBM, Zenith, and Mac PCs are available throughout the campus for student use in teaching facilities. There are more than 3000 PCs on campus. All students may access the system 24 hours a day, 7 days a week. There are no time limits and no fees.

Graduates: From July 1, 2002 to June 30, 2003, 2142 bachelor's degrees were awarded. The most popular majors were criminology (10%), elementary education (9%), and communication media (6%). In an average class, 55% graduate in 6 years or less. 129 companies recruited on campus in 2002-2003. Of the 2002 graduating class, 19% were enrolled in graduate school within 6 months of graduation and 77% were employed.

Admissions Contact: Rhonda Luckey, Vice President for Student Affairs. Web: *www.iup.edu/admissions*

JUNIATA COLLEGE
Huntingdon, PA 16652

C-3

(814) 641-3420
(877) JUNIATA; Fax: (814) 641-3100

Full-time: 585 men, 753 women	**Faculty:** 93; IIB, +$
Part-time: 31 men, 27 women	**Ph.D.s:** 95%
Graduate: none	**Student/Faculty:** 14 to 1
Year: semesters, summer session	**Tuition:** $22,790
Application Deadline: March 15	**Room & Board:** $6290
Freshman Class: 1578 applied, 1179 accepted, 381 enrolled	
SAT I Verbal/Math: 570/590	**VERY COMPETITIVE**

Juniata College, founded in 1876, is an independent liberal arts college affiliated with the Church of the Brethren. In addition to regional accreditation, Juniata has baccalaureate program accreditation with CSWE and ACS. The library contains 265,000 volumes, 400 microform items, and 1600 audio/video tapes/CDs, and subscribes to 1000 periodicals. Computerized library services include the card catalog, interlibrary loans, and database searching. Special learning facilities include a learning resource center, art gallery, radio station, observatory, environmental studies field station, nature preserve, early childhood education center, and a ceramics studio with an Anagama kiln. The 800-acre campus is in a small town 31 miles south of State College, in the heart of rural Pennsylvania. Including any residence halls, there are 43 buildings.

Student Life: 75% of undergraduates are from Pennsylvania. Others are from 32 states, 21 foreign countries, and Canada. 87% are from public schools. 93% are white. 63% are Protestant; 32% Catholic. The average age of freshmen is 18; all undergraduates, 20. 14% do not continue beyond their first year; 75% remain to graduate.

Housing: 1141 students can be accommodated in college housing, which includes single-sex and coed dorms, on-campus apartments, and off-campus apartments. In addition, there are special-interest houses and international housing. On-campus housing is guaranteed for all 4 years.

84% of students live on campus; of those, 75% remain on campus on weekends. All students may keep cars.

Activities: There are no fraternities or sororities. There are 86 groups on campus, including art, band, cheerleading, chess, choir, chorale, chorus, computers, dance, debate, drama, ethnic, forensics, gay, honors, international, literary magazine, model UN, musical theater, newspaper, orchestra, outing club, pep band, photography, political, professional, radio and TV, religious, social, social service, student government, symphony, and yearbook. Popular campus events include Mountain Day and Christmas Madrigal Dinner.

Sports: There are 9 intercollegiate sports for men and 10 for women, and 5 intramural sports for men and 5 for women. Facilities include 2 gyms, a swimming pool, a fitness center, a wrestling room, 4 racquetball courts, a multipurpose room, a sauna, a varsity football field and stadium, baseball, soccer, softball, and hockey fields, an outdoor running track, 7 tennis courts, 1 outdoor basketball court, and an outdoor sand volleyball court.

Disabled Students: 75% of the campus is accessible. Wheelchair ramps, elevators, special parking, specially equipped rest rooms, lowered drinking fountains, wide doors, and stairlifts are available.

Services: Counseling and information services are available, as is tutoring in most subjects. There is a reader service for the blind. Juniata also offers courses and workshops in study, reading, and writing skills.

Campus Safety and Security: Measures include 24-hour foot and vehicle patrol, self-defense education, security escort services, and informal discussions. There are pamphlets/posters/films, emergency telephones, awareness programs, fire safety training, weather alerts, terror alerts, emergency operation plan, firearms storage vault, vehicle lockout service, identification processing, vehicle registration, and evacuation mapping.

Programs of Study: Juniata confers B.A. and B.S. degrees. Bachelor's degrees are awarded in AGRICULTURE (environmental studies), BIOLOGICAL SCIENCE (biochemistry, biology/biological science, botany, ecology, marine science, microbiology, molecular biology, and zoology), BUSINESS (accounting, banking and finance, business administration and management, human resources, international business management, management information systems, and marketing/retailing/merchandising), COMMUNICATIONS AND THE ARTS (art history and appreciation, communications, English, French, German, Russian, Spanish, and studio art), COMPUTER AND PHYSICAL SCIENCE (chemistry, computer science, earth science, geology, information sciences and systems, mathematics, natural sciences, physics, and planetary and space science), EDUCATION (early childhood, elementary, English, foreign languages, health, mathematics, museum studies, science, secondary, social studies, and special), ENGINEERING AND ENVIRONMENTAL DESIGN (engineering physics, environmental science, and preengineering), HEALTH PROFESSIONS (chiropractic, physician's assistant, preallied health, predentistry, premedicine, preoptometry, prepharmacy, prepodiatry, and preveterinary science), SOCIAL SCIENCE (anthropology, criminal justice, economics, history, humanities, international relations, international studies, liberal arts/general studies, ministries, peace studies, philosophy, political science/government, prelaw, psychology, public administration, social science, social work, sociology, and theological studies). Pre-health programs, chemistry, and biology are the strongest academically. Biology, business, and education are the largest.

Required: Students are required to complete a minimum of 120 credit hours, including courses in fine arts, international studies, social sciences, humanities, and natural sciences, as well as 4 commuications-based courses, 2 cultural analysis courses, a math and statistics course, and the college writing seminar. The total number of hours required for the program of emphasis varies from 45 to 60; majors do not exist as such, and students must develop a program of emphasis and complete it to obtain their degree. Students must have a minimum GPA of 2.0.

Special: Juniata offers cooperative programs in marine science, cytogenetics, cytotechnology, marine biology, biotechnology, nursing, medical technology, diagnostic imaging, occupational and physical therapy, dentistry, medicine, optometry, and podiatry. Internships, study abroad in 19 countries, Washington and Philadelphia semesters, and nondegree study are also offered. There are 3-2 engineering degrees with Columbia, Clarkson, Washington, and Pennsylvania State Universities, a 3-3 law program with Duquesne University, and various preprofessional programs, including optometry, chiropractic, medicine, dentistry, pharmacy, physician assistant, and podiatry. With the assistance of faculty advisers, most students design their own majors to meet their individual goals. There are 12 national honor societies, a freshman honors program, and 11 departmental honors programs.

Faculty/Classroom: 63% of faculty are male; 37%, female. All teach undergraduates. The average class size in an introductory lecture is 21; in a laboratory, 16; and in a regular course, 15.

Admissions: 75% of the 2003-2004 applicants were accepted. The SAT I scores for the 2003-2004 freshman class were: Verbal--12% below 500, 47% between 500 and 599, 35% between 600 and 700, and 7% above 700; Math--7% below 500, 47% between 500 and 599, 38% between 600 and 700, and 7% above 700. 63% of the current freshmen were in the top fifth of their class; 94% were in the top two fifths. There was 1 National Merit semifinalist. 15 freshmen graduated first in their class.

Requirements: The SAT I or ACT is required. In addition, candidates for admission should be graduates of an accredited secondary school and have completed 16 academic credits, including 4 in English, 2 in a foreign language, and a combination of 10 in math, social studies, and lab science. The GED is accepted, and home schoolers are encouraged to apply. An essay is required and an interview is recommended. A GPA of 3.0 is required. AP credits are accepted. Important factors in the admissions decision are advanced placement or honor courses, leadership record, and recommendations by school officials.

Procedure: Freshmen are admitted fall and spring. Entrance exams should be taken in the junior or senior year of high school. There is a rolling admissions plan. There are early decision and deferred admissions plans. Early decision applications should be filed by November 15; regular applications, by March 15 for fall entry and December 1 for spring entry, along with a $30 fee. Notification of early decision is sent December 31; regular decision, on a rolling basis. 104 early decision candidates were accepted for the 2003-2004 class. Applications are accepted on computer disk and on-line through CollegeLink, Peterson's Expand, Embark, and Common App.

Transfer: 26 transfer students enrolled in 2002-2003. A GPA of 2.5 is required. Applicants must submit a high school transcript, a college transcript, and an essay. SAT I scores are required of some students. 30 of 120 credits required for the bachelor's degree must be completed at Juniata.

Visiting: There are regularly scheduled orientations for prospective students, including a campus tour, interviews, and a department fair. There are guides for informal visits and visitors may sit in on classes and stay overnight. To schedule a visit, contact Norma Jennings, Enrollment Assistant at (814) 641-3428 or *jenninn@juniata.edu*.

Financial Aid: In 2003-2004, all full-time freshmen and 97% of continuing full-time students received some form of financial aid. 75% of full-time freshmen and 78% of continuing full-time students received need-based aid. The average freshman award was $18,316. 70% of undergraduates work part time. Average annual earnings from campus work are $956. The average financial indebtedness of the 2003 graduate was $17,572. Juniata is a member of CSS. The FAFSA is required. The priority date for freshman financial aid applications for fall entry is March 1. The deadline for filing freshman financial aid applications for fall entry is May 1.

International Students: There are 68 international students enrolled. The school actively recruits these students. They must score 550 on the written TOEFL or 213 on the electronic version.

Computers: The mainframe is an HP 9000/L-2000. All dorm rooms are equipped for full Internet and intranet access. There are also numerous maintenance terminals, PCs, and Macs located throughout the campus. Students have access to all locations and are provided with a personal account. 14 computer labs with more than 400 computers are available for student use. All students may access the system. There are no time limits and no fees. It is strongly recommended that all students have a personal computer.

Graduates: From July 1, 2002 to June 30, 2003, 282 bachelor's degrees were awarded. The most popular majors were biology/pre-health (16%), business/accounting (16%), and education (10%). In an average class, 70% graduate in 4 years or less, 72% graduate in 5 years or less, and 75% graduate in 6 years or less. Of the 2002 graduating class, 35% were enrolled in graduate school within 6 months of graduation and 60% were employed.

Admissions Contact: Office of Enrollment. E-mail: *info@juniata.edu* Web: *www.juniata.edu*

KEYSTONE COLLEGE E-4
La Plume, PA 18440
(570) 945-6953
(877) 4COLLEGE; Fax: (570) 945-7916

Full-time: 454 men, 595 women	**Faculty:** 58
Part-time: 122 men, 331 women	**Ph.D.s:** 36%
Graduate: none	**Student/Faculty:** 18 to 1
Year: semesters, summer session	**Tuition:** $14,005
Application Deadline: open	**Room & Board:** $7400
Freshman Class: 772 applied, 735 accepted, 371 enrolled	
SAT I Verbal/Math: 440/420	**LESS COMPETITIVE**

Keystone College, founded in 1868, is a small private college offering 13 bachelor's degrees and 17 associate degrees. The library contains 39,977 volumes, 41,449 microform items, and 1516 audio/video tapes/ CDs, and subscribes to 179 periodicals. Computerized library services include the card catalog, interlibrary loans, database searching, and Internet access. Special learning facilities include a learning resource center, art gallery, radio station, and observatory. The 270-acre campus is in a rural area 15 miles north of Scranton and 40 miles south of Binghamton, New York. Including any residence halls, there are 29 buildings.

Student Life: 89% of undergraduates are from Pennsylvania. Students are from 11 states and 9 foreign countries. 92% are white. The average

age of freshmen is 19; all undergraduates, 25. 42% do not continue beyond their first year; 41% remain to graduate.

Housing: 426 students can be accommodated in college housing, which includes single-sex and coed dorms with single rooms for upperclassmen. On-campus housing is guaranteed for all 4 years. 59% of students commute. Alcohol is not permitted. All students may keep cars.

Activities: There are no fraternities or sororities. There are 19 groups on campus, including art, cheerleading, co-op, drama, equestrian, ethnic, forensics, honors, international, literary magazine, newspaper, photography, radio and TV, religious, ski, social, social service, student government, and yearbook. Popular campus events include Family Day, Winterfest, and Spring Fling.

Sports: There are 6 intercollegiate sports for men and 7 for women, and 6 intramural sports for men and 6 for women. Facilities include an athletic center, tennis courts, playing fields, and a trail system.

Disabled Students: 90% of the campus is accessible. Wheelchair ramps, elevators, special parking, specially equipped rest rooms, special class scheduling, lowered drinking fountains, lowered telephones, and special housing are available.

Services: Counseling and information services are available, as is tutoring in every subject. There is remedial math, reading, and writing. A writing center is available.

Campus Safety and Security: Measures include 24-hour foot and vehicle patrol, security escort services, informal discussions, and pamphlets/posters/films. There are emergency telephones and lighted pathways/sidewalks.

Programs of Study: Keystone College confers B.S. and B.A. degrees. Associate degrees are also awarded. Bachelor's degrees are awarded in AGRICULTURE (natural resource management), BUSINESS (accounting, business administration and management, human resources, and recreational facilities management), COMMUNICATIONS AND THE ARTS (communications and visual and performing arts), COMPUTER AND PHYSICAL SCIENCE (information sciences and systems and natural sciences), EDUCATION (art, early childhood, and elementary), ENGINEERING AND ENVIRONMENTAL DESIGN (environmental science), SOCIAL SCIENCE (criminal justice). Education, environmental resource management, and natural sciences are the strongest academically. Education is the largest.

Required: To graduate, students must complete 123 to 130 credit hours and maintain a GPA of 2.0. The required core curriculum includes courses in interdisciplinary studies, math, English, speech, computer, and fitness. Distribution requirements and total credit hours vary with the major.

Special: Keystone offers co-op programs in all majors, as well as paid and unpaid internships. The Weekender program accommodates the needs of busy adult students. There are 3 national honor societies and a freshman honors program.

Faculty/Classroom: 43% of faculty are male; 58%, female. All teach undergraduates. The average class size in an introductory lecture is 18; in a laboratory, 9; and in a regular course, 15.

Admissions: 95% of the 2003-2004 applicants were accepted. The SAT I scores for the 2003-2004 freshman class were: Verbal--77% below 500, 19% between 500 and 599, and 4% between 600 and 700; Math--82% below 500, 16% between 500 and 599, and 2% between 600 and 700. The ACT scores were 87% below 21.

Requirements: The SAT I or ACT is required, the SAT I is preferred. An interview is recommended. A GPA of 2.0 is required. AP and CLEP credits are accepted. Important factors in the admissions decision are extracurricular activities record, leadership record, and parents or siblings attending the school.

Procedure: Freshmen are admitted to all sessions. Entrance exams should be taken in the spring of the junior year or early fall of the senior year. There are early admissions, deferred admissions plans, and rolling admissions plan. Application deadlines are open. The fall 2003 application fee was $25. Applications are accepted on computer disk and on-line.

Transfer: 95 transfer students enrolled in 2002-2003. Applicants with more than 12 academic college credits must have a minimum GPA of 2.0. A letter of recommendation is required. 32 of 123 credits required for the bachelor's degree must be completed at Keystone College.

Visiting: There are regularly scheduled orientations for prospective students, consisting of 7 open houses and 3 visitation days yearly. There are guides for informal visits and visitors may sit in on classes and stay overnight. To schedule a visit, contact the Admissions Office at *admissions@keystone.edu*.

Financial Aid: In 2003-2004, 95% of all full-time freshmen and 94% of continuing full-time students received some form of financial aid. 81% of full-time freshmen and 82% of continuing full-time students received need-based aid. The average freshman award was $13,222. 27% of undergraduates work part time. Average annual earnings from campus work are $1250. The average financial indebtedness of the 2003 graduate was $8563. Keystone College is a member of CSS. The FAFSA is required. The priority date for freshman financial aid applications for fall entry is April 1. The deadline for filing freshman financial aid applications for fall entry is August 1.

International Students: In a recent year, there were 10 international students enrolled. The school actively recruits these students. They must score 500 on the written TOEFL or 173 on the electronic version or take the MELAB or the college's own test.

Computers: The mainframe is an IBM AS/400 Model 620. Computer labs provide access to the Internet and Web. The campus is wireless. All students may access the system. There are no time limits. The fee is $150.

Graduates: In a recent year, 24 bachelor's degrees were awarded. In an average class, 36% graduate in 3 years or less.

Admissions Contact: Sarah S. Keating, Director of Admissions. E-mail: *admissions@keystone.edu* Web: *www.keystone.edu*

KING'S COLLEGE
Wilkes Barre, PA 18711

E-2

(570) 208-5858
(888) 546-4772; Fax: (570) 208-5971

Full-time: 941 men, 830 women	**Faculty:** 114; IIB, av$
Part-time: 121 men, 172 women	**Ph.D.s:** 84%
Graduate: 25 men, 111 women	**Student/Faculty:** 16 to 1
Year: semesters, summer session	**Tuition:** $19,060
Application Deadline: May 1	**Room & Board:** $7930
Freshman Class: n/av	
SAT I or ACT: required	**COMPETITIVE**

King's College, founded in 1946, is a private institution affiliated with the Roman Catholic Church. The college offers undergraduate programs in humanities and natural and social sciences, specialized programs in business and other professions, and graduate programs in reading, health care administration, and physician assistant. In addition to regional accreditation, King's has baccalaureate program accreditation with ACS, AMA, and CAAHEP. The library contains 167,357 volumes, 562,528 microform items, and 2530 audio/video tapes/CDs, and subscribes to 791 periodicals. Computerized library services include the card catalog, interlibrary loans, and database searching. Special learning facilities include a learning resource center, art gallery, radio station, and TV studio. The 48-acre campus is in an urban area in northeastern Pennsylvania 19 miles south of Scranton. Including any residence halls, there are 19 buildings.

Student Life: 76% of undergraduates are from Pennsylvania. Others are from 21 states and 6 foreign countries. 67% are from public schools. 85% are white. 58% are Catholic; 22% unknown; 12% Protestant, 6% other; 1% Orthodox. The average age of freshmen is 18; all undergraduates, 20. 19% do not continue beyond their first year; 70% remain to graduate.

Housing: 857 students can be accommodated in college housing, which includes single-sex dorms and on-campus apartments. On-campus housing is guaranteed for all 4 years. 55% of students commute. Alcohol is not permitted. All students may keep cars.

Activities: There are no fraternities or sororities. There are 50 groups on campus, including art, cheerleading, choir, chorale, chorus, computers, dance, debate, drama, ethnic, film, honors, international, jazz band, literary magazine, musical theater, newspaper, pep band, photography, political, professional, radio and TV, religious, social, social service, student government, and yearbook. Popular campus events include All College Ball, Student Activities Fair, and Friends and Family Weekend.

Sports: There are 11 intercollegiate sports for men and 10 for women, and 8 intramural sports for men and 8 for women. Facilities include a phys ed center, outdoor basketball courts, a fitness center, a wrestling room, racquetball courts, a swimming pool, a multipurpose area, a 3200-seat gym, a free weight area, an outdoor athletic complex with a field house, a field hockey field, a football stadium, and baseball, softball, and soccer fields.

Disabled Students: 99% of the campus is accessible. Wheelchair ramps, elevators, special parking, specially equipped rest rooms, special class scheduling, lowered drinking fountains, and lowered telephones are available.

Services: Counseling and information services are available, as is tutoring in every subject. The academic skills center provides a writing center, learning skills workshops, a tutoring program, and learning disability services.

Campus Safety and Security: Measures include 24-hour foot and vehicle patrol, self-defense education, security escort services, and informal discussions. There are pamphlets/posters/films, emergency telephones, and lighted pathways/sidewalks.

Programs of Study: King's confers B.A. and B.S. degrees. Associate and master's degrees are also awarded. Bachelor's degrees are awarded in AGRICULTURE (environmental studies), BIOLOGICAL SCIENCE (biology/biological science and neurosciences), BUSINESS (accounting, banking and finance, business administration and management, international business management, marketing/retailing/merchandising, and personnel management), COMMUNICATIONS AND THE ARTS (communications, dramatic arts, English, French, languages, and Spanish), COMPUTER AND PHYSICAL SCIENCE (chemistry, computer science, information sciences and systems, mathematics, and science), EDUCA-

TION (early childhood, elementary, foreign languages, middle school, science, and secondary), HEALTH PROFESSIONS (medical laboratory technology, predentistry, premedicine, and sports medicine), SOCIAL SCIENCE (criminal justice, economics, gerontology, history, philosophy, political science/government, prelaw, psychology, sociology, and theological studies). Accounting, English, and biology are the strongest academically. Elementary education, business administration, and mass communications are the largest.

Required: All students must earn a minimum of 120 credits and maintain a GPA of 2.0. The core requirements represent 54 credits. The major comprises a maximum of 60 credits, of which up to 40 can be specified in the major department, with the balance designated for related fields.

Special: A co-op program in special education and cross-registration with Wilkes University and College Misericordia are offered. The Experiential Learning Program provides internship opportunities in all majors with a variety of employers. King's also offers study abroad through an agreement with Webster University and John Cabot University, a Washington semester, work-study programs in 6 countries, an accelerated degree program in business administration, B.A.-B.S. degrees in math and psychology, dual majors, credit for life experience, and pass/fail options on a few courses. Student-designed majors are available through the King's honors program. There are 11 national honor societies and a freshman honors program.

Faculty/Classroom: 67% of faculty are male; 33%, female. All teach undergraduates. No introductory courses are taught by graduate students. The average class size in an introductory lecture is 21; in a laboratory, 11; and in a regular course, 18.

Admissions: 30% of the current freshmen were in the top fifth of their class; 64% were in the top two fifths. 2 freshmen graduated first in their class.

Requirements: The SAT I or ACT is required. In addition, King's requires 16 academic credits, although 22 are recommended, including 4 in English, 3 each in science, math, and social studies, 2 in foreign language, and 1 in history. AP and CLEP credits are accepted. Important factors in the admissions decision are advanced placement or honor courses, extracurricular activities record, and leadership record.

Procedure: Freshmen are admitted fall and spring. Entrance exams should be taken so that scores are received by April 1. There is a rolling admissions plan and a deferred admissions plan. Applications should be filed by May 1 for fall entry, January 1 for spring entry, and May 1 for summer entry. The fall 2003 application fee was $30. Notification is sent on a rolling basis.

Transfer: 90 transfer students enrolled in fall 2003. Applicants must present a minimum GPA of 2.5. Students must have earned at least 3 credit hours at another college. An interview is recommended. 60 of 120 credits required for the bachelor's degree must be completed at King's.

Visiting: There are regularly scheduled orientations for prospective students, consisting of admissions interviews, financial aid presentations, faculty one-on-one meetings, and campus tours. There are guides for informal visits and visitors may sit in on classes and stay overnight. To schedule a visit, contact the Admissions Office at *admissions@kings.edu*.

Financial Aid: In fall 2003, 97% of all full-time freshmen and 98% of all full-time students received some form of financial aid. 81% of full-time freshmen and 82% of all full-time students received need-based aid. The average freshman award was $13,217. Need-based scholarships or need-based grants averaged $6774 ($18,350 maximum); need-based self-help aid (loans and jobs) averaged $4175 ($6225 maximum); and non-need-based awards and non-need-based scholarships averaged $8500 ($18,260 maximum). 72% of undergraduates work part time. Average annual earnings from campus work are $1200. The average financial indebtedness of the 2003 graduate was $16,700. King's is a member of CSS. The FAFSA and the college's own financial statement are required. The priority date for freshman financial aid applications for fall entry is February 15.

International Students: There are 8 international students enrolled. The school actively recruits these students. They must score 525 on the written TOEFL and also take the SAT I or the ACT.

Computers: The mainframe is an IBM RS/6000 p620 with Windows servers. King's College has computer and media facilities that support a high-speed network of 365 computers located in 17 Windows-based and 4 Mac-based computer lab sites for student and faculty use. Internet and e-mail access is available to students from residence hall rooms. All classrooms and residence hall rooms have a network connection and Internet access. Each student is provided with a unique network and e-mail account. 3 24-hour networked residence hall labs exist; 5 other networked labs are each open 95 hours per week. Other departmental facilities are available. There are no time limits and no fees.

Graduates: From July 1, 2002 to June 30, 2003, 419 bachelor's degrees were awarded. The most popular majors were elementary education (12%), mass communications (11%), and accounting (8%). In an average class, 62% graduate in 4 years or less, 68% graduate in 5 years or less, and 70% graduate in 6 years or less. 48 companies recruited on campus in 2002-2003. Of the 2002 graduating class, 15% were enrolled in graduate school within 6 months of graduation and 88% were employed.

Admissions Contact: Michelle Lawrence-Schmude, Director of Admissions. A video is available. E-mail: *admissions@kings.edu*
Web: *http://www.kings.edu*

KUTZTOWN UNIVERSITY OF PENNSYLVANIA   E-3
Kutztown, PA 19530

(610) 683-4060
(877) 628-1915; Fax: (610) 683-1375

Full-time: 2983 men, 4259 women	Faculty: 343; IIA, +$
Part-time: 202 men, 614 women	Ph.D.s: 75%
Graduate: 275 men, 675 women	Student/Faculty: 21 to 1
Year: semesters, summer session	Tuition: $5974 ($12,922)
Application Deadline: open	Room & Board: $4812
Freshman Class: 7248 applied, 5055 accepted, 1851 enrolled	
SAT I Verbal: 495	COMPETITIVE

Kutztown University of Pennsylvania, founded in 1866, is a public institution within the Pennsylvania State System of Higher Education. The university offers undergraduate programs in the arts and sciences, business, education, and visual and performing arts. There are 4 undergraduate schools and 1 graduate school. In addition to regional accreditation, KU has baccalaureate program accreditation with CSWE, NASAD, NASM, NCATE, and NLN. The library contains 497,752 volumes, 1,307,315 microform items, and 14,858 audio/video tapes/CDs, and subscribes to 4265 periodicals. Computerized library services include the card catalog, interlibrary loans, and database searching. Special learning facilities include a learning resource center, art gallery, planetarium, radio station, TV station, a women's center, cartography lab, German Cultural Heritage Center, computer labs, and tutorial labs. The 326-acre campus is in a small town 90 miles north of Philadelphia, midway between Reading and Allentown. Including any residence halls, there are 61 buildings.

Student Life: 91% of undergraduates are from Pennsylvania. Students are from 21 states, 44 foreign countries, and Canada. 89% are white. The average age of freshmen is 19; all undergraduates, 22.

Housing: 3442 students can be accommodated in college housing, which includes single-sex and coed dorms and on-campus apartments. In addition, there are honors houses and special-interest houses. On-campus housing is guaranteed for the freshman year only and is available on a first-come, first-served basis. 59% of students commute. Alcohol is not permitted. Upperclassmen may keep cars.

Activities: 1% of men belong to 4 national fraternities; 1% of women belong to 1 local and 4 national sororities. There are 140 groups on campus, including art, band, cheerleading, chess, choir, chorus, computers, dance, drama, ethnic, gay, honors, international, jazz band, literary magazine, marching band, musical theater, newspaper, orchestra, political, professional, programming board, radio and TV, recreational sports, religious, social, social service, student government, and yearbook. Popular campus events include Bearfest, Performing Diversity, Welcome Week, and Five Days of Justice.

Sports: There are 10 intercollegiate sports for men and 12 for women, and 22 intramural sports for men and 19 for women. Facilities include a 7500-seat stadium and outdoor track, a 55,000-square-foot field house and 200-meter indoor track, a swimming pool, 9 outdoor tennis courts, a 4000-seat arena, athletic fields, a street hockey rink, basketball courts, a rifle range, a fitness center, and a free-weight room.

Disabled Students: 90% of the campus is accessible. Wheelchair ramps, elevators, special parking, specially equipped rest rooms, special class scheduling, and lowered drinking fountains. All programs are accessible to students with disabilities.

Services: Counseling and information services are available, as is tutoring in most subjects. There is a reader service for the blind and remedial math, reading, and writing.

Campus Safety and Security: Measures include 24-hour foot and vehicle patrol, self-defense education, security escort services, and shuttle buses. There are informal discussions, pamphlets/posters/films, emergency telephones, lighted pathways/sidewalks, a bike patrol, crime prevention programs, automatic fire protection systems, door alarms, safety screens, and student monitors in the dorms.

Programs of Study: KU confers B.A., B.S., B.F.A., B.S.B.A, B.S.Ed., and B.S.N. degrees. Master's degrees are also awarded. Bachelor's degrees are awarded in BIOLOGICAL SCIENCE (biology/biological science and marine science), BUSINESS (accounting, banking and finance, business administration and management, business economics, international business management, and marketing/retailing/merchandising), COMMUNICATIONS AND THE ARTS (crafts, dramatic arts, English, fine arts, French, graphic design, music, Spanish, speech/debate/rhetoric, telecommunications, and visual and performing arts), COMPUTER AND PHYSICAL SCIENCE (chemistry, computer science, geology, mathematics, and physics), EDUCATION (art, early childhood, elementary, library science, secondary, and special), ENGINEERING AND ENVIRONMENTAL DESIGN (environmental science), HEALTH PROFESSIONS (medical laboratory technology, nursing, and speech pathology/audiology), SOCIAL SCIENCE (anthropology, criminal justice, geography, history, liberal arts/general studies, philosophy, political science/government, psychology, public administration, social work, and sociology). Physical science and math are the strongest academically. Business, psychology, and elementary education are the largest.

Required: General education requirements vary by program, but all students must take phys ed, speech, English composition, or introduction to dance. Distribution requirements also include courses in humanities, social sciences, natural sciences, and math. To graduate, students must complete at least 120 semester hours, including 33 to 80 in a major field, with a minimum GPA of 2.0. Students in the College of Liberal Arts and Sciences must take a comprehensive exam.

Special: Students may study abroad in 11 countries. There is a 3-2 engineering degree program with Pennsylvania State University and cross-registration with area colleges. KU also offers internships, student-designed majors, dual majors, and a general studies degree. Nondegree study is possible. There are 15 national honor societies, a freshman honors program, and 30 departmental honors programs.

Faculty/Classroom: 55% of faculty are male; 45%, female. 97% teach undergraduates. No introductory courses are taught by graduate students. The average class size in an introductory lecture is 35; in a laboratory, 20; and in a regular course, 22.

Admissions: 70% of the 2003-2004 applicants were accepted. The SAT I scores for the 2003-2004 freshman class were: Verbal--55% below 500; Math--57% below 500, 37% between 500 and 599, and 5% between 600 and 700. 15% of the current freshmen were in the top fifth of their class; 44% were in the top two fifths.

Requirements: The SAT I or ACT is required. In addition, applicants must be graduates of accredited secondary schools or have earned a GED. Recommended Carnegie units include 4 each of English and social studies, 3 each of science and math, and 2 of foreign language. SAT II: Subject tests in biology/chemistry are required for medical technology. Portfolios or auditions are required for art or music majors. KU requires applicants to be in the upper 50% of their class. A GPA of 2.0 is required. AP and CLEP credits are accepted.

Procedure: Freshmen are admitted fall and spring. Entrance exams should be taken No later than fall of the senior year. There are early admissions, deferred admissions, and rolling admissions plans. Application deadlines are open. The fall 2003 application fee was $30. Applications are accepted on-line through *www.Kutztown.edu/admissions*.

Transfer: 555 transfer students enrolled in 2002-2003. Applicants must present a GPA of 2.0 (2.8 for education) and official transcripts from all colleges and secondary schools previously attended. Students transferring fewer than 30 credit hours must also submit the SAT I or ACT scores. 33 of 120 credits required for the bachelor's degree must be completed at KU.

Visiting: There are regularly scheduled orientations for prospective students, consisting of daily visits, including group tours. There is a comprehensive summer orientation program for enrolling students. There are guides for informal visits and visitors may sit in on classes. To schedule a visit, contact the Admissions Office at *admissions@kutztown.edu*.

Financial Aid: In 2003-2004, 67% of all full-time freshmen and 61% of continuing full-time students received some form of financial aid. 62% of full-time freshmen and 56% of continuing full-time students received need-based aid. The average freshman award was $5483. Need-based scholarships or need-based grants averaged $3792 ($7950 maximum); need-based self-help aid (loans and jobs) averaged $2545 ($5125 maximum); non-need-based athletic scholarships averaged $1027 ($8000 maximum); and other non-need-based awards and non-need-based scholarships averaged $1342 ($4600 maximum). 55% of undergraduates work part time. Average annual earnings from campus work are $1002. The average financial indebtedness of the 2003 graduate was $14,594. The FAFSA is required. The deadline for filing freshman financial aid applications for fall entry is February 15.

International Students: In a recent year, there were 85 international students enrolled. They must score 500 on the written TOEFL or 173 on the electronic version.

Computers: The mainframe is a Unisys Clearpath. All classrooms, residence halls, and offices have full Internet connectivity. More than 15 computer labs with more than 650 PCs are available for student use; several labs are open 24 hours. Most residence hall students bring their own PCs to campus. All students may access the system. There are no time limits and no fees.

Graduates: From July 1, 2002 to June 30, 2003, 1575 bachelor's degrees were awarded. The most popular majors were elementary education (12%), psychology (7%), and English (5%). 50 companies recruited on campus in 2002-2003. Of the 2002 graduating class, 6% were enrolled in graduate school within 6 months of graduation and 96% were employed.

Admissions Contact: William Stahler, Director of Admissions.
E-mail: *admissions@kutztown.edu*
Web: *http://www.kutztown.edu/admissions*

LA ROCHE COLLEGE
Pittsburgh, PA 15237

B-3

(412) 536-1275
(800) 838-4LRC; Fax: (412) 847-1820

Full-time: 466 men, 713 women	**Faculty:** 70; IIA, -$
Part-time: 103 men, 269 women	**Ph.D.s:** 76%
Graduate: 90 men, 130 women	**Student/Faculty:** 17 to 1
Year: semesters, summer session	**Tuition:** $15,620
Application Deadline: open	**Room & Board:** $6474
Freshman Class: 523 applied, 363 accepted, 174 enrolled	
SAT I Verbal/Math: 470/480	**ACT:** 21 **COMPETITIVE**

La Roche College, founded in 1963, is a private Catholic institution offering undergraduate programs in arts and sciences, business, graphic and interior design, health science, upper-level nursing, professional training, and religious studies. In addition to regional accreditation, La Roche has baccalaureate program accreditation with ACBSP, FIDER, NASAD, and NLN. The library contains 100,338 volumes, 30,000 microform items, and 1010 audio/video tapes/CDs, and subscribes to 7900 periodicals. Computerized library services include the card catalog, interlibrary loans, database searching, and Internet access. Special learning facilities include a learning resource center, art gallery, radio station, and interior and graphic design studios. The 100-acre campus is in a suburban area 10 miles north of Pittsburgh. Including any residence halls, there are 12 buildings.

Student Life: 79% of undergraduates are from Pennsylvania. Students are from 16 states, 27 foreign countries, and Canada. 79% are white; 16% foreign nationals. 64% are Orthodox, Muslim, Mormon and Hindu; 33% Catholic; 11% Protestant. The average age of freshmen is 19; all undergraduates, 25. 24% do not continue beyond their first year; 61% remain to graduate.

Housing: 630 students can be accommodated in college housing, which includes coed dorms and off-campus apartments. On-campus housing is guaranteed for all 4 years. 58% of students commute. All students may keep cars.

Activities: There are no fraternities or sororities. There are 25 groups on campus, including art, cheerleading, chorus, computers, dance, ethnic, honors, international, literary magazine, photography, political, professional, radio and TV, religious, social, social service, student government, and yearbook. Popular campus events include Multicultural Food Festival, The Gateway Clipper Cruise, and The Spring Fling.

Sports: There are 5 intercollegiate sports for men and 5 for women, and 10 intramural sports for men and 9 for women. Facilities include soccer, softball, and baseball fields, a gym, tennis courts, hiking trails, a fitness/sports center that houses a gym, racquetball courts, an indoor track, an aerobics room, and a weight room, and a nearby county park with tennis courts and a swimming pool.

Disabled Students: 80% of the campus is accessible. Wheelchair ramps, elevators, special parking, specially equipped rest rooms, special class scheduling, lowered drinking fountains, and lowered telephones are available.

Services: Counseling and information services are available, as is tutoring in every subject. There is remedial math and writing.

Campus Safety and Security: Measures include 24-hour foot and vehicle patrol, security escort services, shuttle buses, and informal discussions. There are pamphlets/posters/films, emergency telephones, lighted pathways/sidewalks, an intercom security system, and residence halls are locked 24 hours a day.

Programs of Study: La Roche confers B.A., B.S., and B.S.N. degrees. Associate and master's degrees are also awarded. Bachelor's degrees are awarded in BIOLOGICAL SCIENCE (biology/biological science), BUSINESS (accounting, banking and finance, business administration and management, institutional management, international business management, marketing management, and real estate), COMMUNICATIONS AND THE ARTS (communications, creative writing, dance, English, and graphic design), COMPUTER AND PHYSICAL SCIENCE (chemistry, computer science, information sciences and systems, and mathematics), EDUCATION (early childhood, elementary, English, foreign languages, and science), ENGINEERING AND ENVIRONMENTAL DESIGN (interior design), HEALTH PROFESSIONS (nursing, radiograph medical technology, and respiratory therapy), SOCIAL SCIENCE (criminal justice, history, human services, international studies, liberal arts/general studies, psychology, religion, religious education, and sociology). Graphic design, interior design, and professional writing are the strongest academically. Administration and management, design areas, and elementary education are the largest.

Required: 12 credits in basic skills areas including math and computer applications and 12 credits in liberal arts areas, including history, science, religion or philosophy, aesthetics, literature, and social and cultural systems are required. Also, a 9-credit sequence of 3 interdisciplinary courses that emphasize the concepts of community, the individual, and global perspectives is required. A minimum of 120 credit hours and a GPA of 2.0 are requirements for graduation, as is a senior seminar in most majors.

Special: There is cross-registration with members of the Pittsburgh Council of Higher Education. Internships, for which students may receive up to 6 credits, are available for juniors and seniors with numerous employers in the Pittsburgh area. La Roche also offers study abroad in 13 countries, a Washington semester, dual majors, credit for life experience, directed research, honors programs, independent study, and pass/fail options. Accelerated degrees may be earned in management, criminal justice, and nursing. A 3-2 engineering degree with the University of Pittsburgh is possible.

Faculty/Classroom: 51% of faculty are male; 49%, female. 94% teach undergraduates. No introductory courses are taught by graduate students. The average class size in an introductory lecture is 20; in a laboratory, 10; and in a regular course, 14.

Admissions: 69% of the 2003-2004 applicants were accepted. The SAT I scores for the 2003-2004 freshman class were: Verbal--61% below 500, 27% between 500 and 599, and 12% between 600 and 700; Math--51% below 500, 38% between 500 and 599, 10% between 600 and 700, and 1% above 700. The ACT scores were 72% below 21, 13% between 21 and 23, 5% between 24 and 26, 5% between 27 and 28, and 5% above 28. 26% of the current freshmen were in the top fifth of their class; 32% were in the top two fifths. 2 freshmen graduated first in their class.

Requirements: The SAT I or ACT is required. In addition, applicants must be graduates of accredited secondary schools or have earned a GED. An interview is recommended for all applicants. At least two letters of recommendation are required. A GPA of 2.0 is required. AP and CLEP credits are accepted. Important factors in the admissions decision are advanced placement or honor courses, personality/intangible qualities, and recommendations by school officials.

Procedure: Freshmen are admitted to all sessions. Entrance exams should be taken by the fall of the senior year. There is an early admissions plan and a rolling admissions plan. Application deadlines are open. The fall 2003 application fee was $35. Applications are accepted on-line through www.laroche.edu.

Transfer: 162 transfer students enrolled in 2002-2003. Transfer design students may be required to submit a portfolio and must have a 2.0 GPA. 30 of 120 credits required for the bachelor's degree must be completed at La Roche.

Visiting: There are regularly scheduled orientations for prospective students, including an overnight stay, information sessions and interactive sessions, class attendance, and meeting with faculty. There are also 1-day visits on Saturday. There are guides for informal visits and visitors may sit in on classes and stay overnight. To schedule a visit, contact the Admissions Office at admissions@laroche.edu.

Financial Aid: In 2003-2004, 98% of all full-time freshmen and 90% of continuing full-time students received some form of financial aid. 86% of full-time freshmen and 85% of continuing full-time students received need-based aid. The average freshman award was $13,975. Need-based scholarships or need-based grants averaged $5775 ($15,500 maximum); need-based self-help aid (loans and jobs) averaged $3555 ($6225 maximum); and other non-need-based awards and non-need-based scholarships averaged $4025 ($10,000 maximum). 15% of undergraduates work part time. Average annual earnings from campus work are $900. The average financial indebtedness of the 2003 graduate was $18,000. The FAFSA and the college's own financial statement are required. The priority date for freshman financial aid applications for fall entry is January 15. The deadline for filing freshman financial aid applications for fall entry is May 1.

International Students: There are 247 international students enrolled. The school actively recruits these students. They must score 220 on the electronic TOEFL , or if their native language is English, they must take the SAT I or ACT.

Computers: The mainframe is an HP L2000. Students have access to 200 PCs and Macs in 6 computer labs, which are part of a local area network and have printing, Internet, and e-mail capabilities in addition to general and specific software. The Mac lab offers software for illustration, Postscript, animation, dimensional design, and desktop publishing. All students may access the system. It is recommended that students in facility management, graphic design, interior design, communication, media and technology have personal computers. IBM ThinkPads and Apple PowerBooks are recommended.

Graduates: From July 1, 2002 to June 30, 2003, 321 bachelor's degrees were awarded. The most popular majors were management (16%), graphic design (11%), and psychology (10%). In an average class, 1% graduate in 3 years or less, 80% graduate in 4 years or less, and 19% graduate in 5 years or less.

Admissions Contact: Thomas Hassett, Director of Admissions. A video is available. E-mail: admissions@laroche.edu
Web: www.laroche.edu

LA SALLE UNIVERSITY
Philadelphia, PA 19141-1199

F-3

(215) 951-1500
(800) 328-1910; Fax: (215) 951-1656

Full-time: 1486 men, 1809 women	**Faculty:** 194; IIA, av$
Part-time: 215 men, 589 women	**Ph.D.s:** 88%
Graduate: 710 men, 1128 women	**Student/Faculty:** 17 to 1
Year: semesters, summer session	**Tuition:** $22,960
Application Deadline: April 1	**Room & Board:** $8300
Freshman Class: 4559 applied, 3111 accepted, 811 enrolled	
SAT I Verbal/Math: 550/550	**VERY COMPETITIVE**

La Salle University, founded in 1863, is a private institution conducted under the auspices of the Christian Brothers of the Roman Catholic Church. The university offers undergraduate and graduate programs in the arts and sciences, business, education, fine arts, religious studies, and nursing. There are 3 undergraduate and 3 graduate schools. In addition to regional accreditation, La Salle has baccalaureate program accreditation with AACSB, CSWE, and NLN. The library contains 380,000 volumes, 250,000 microform items, and 10,000 audio/video tapes/CDs, and subscribes to 5570 periodicals. Computerized library services include the card catalog, interlibrary loans, and database searching. Special learning facilities include a learning resource center, art gallery, radio station, TV station, and and a Japanese tea ceremony house. The 100-acre campus is in an urban area 8 miles northwest of the center of Philadelphia. Including any residence halls, there are 56 buildings.

Student Life: 65% of undergraduates are from Pennsylvania. Students are from 34 states, 25 foreign countries, and Canada. 50% are from public schools. 84% are white. 80% are Catholic; 11% Protestant. The average age of freshmen is 18; all undergraduates, 20. 13% do not continue beyond their first year; 74% remain to graduate.

Housing: 2090 students can be accommodated in college housing, which includes single-sex and coed dorms, on-campus apartments, and off-campus apartments. In addition, there are honors houses, for which student groups may submit proposals for use. Townhouses and apartments are available to juniors and seniors. On-campus housing is guaranteed for all 4 years. 64% of students live on campus; of those, 70% remain on campus on weekends. All students may keep cars.

Activities: 14% of men belong to 1 local and 6 national fraternities; 14% of women belong to 1 local and 4 national sororities. There are 94 groups on campus, including band, cheerleading, choir, computers, dance, drama, drill team, ethnic, film, honors, international, jazz band, literary magazine, newspaper, orchestra, pep band, political, professional, radio and TV, religious, social, social service, student government, and yearbook. Popular campus events include Oktoberfest, Charter Week, and Carnifall.

Sports: There are 11 intercollegiate sports for men and 12 for women, and 14 intramural sports for men and 14 for women. Facilities include a 7000-seat stadium, a 4000-seat gym, a 500-seat auditorium, 4 playing fields, 6 tennis courts, a fully equipped athletic and exercise facility, wrestling rooms, a sauna, racquetball and squash courts, outdoor tracks, basketball and volleyball courts, and an indoor swimming pool.

Disabled Students: 95% of the campus is accessible. Wheelchair ramps, elevators, special parking, specially equipped rest rooms, special class scheduling, and lowered drinking fountains are available.

Services: Counseling and information services are available, as is tutoring in some subjects, including English, math, and accounting. A writing center is also available.

Campus Safety and Security: Measures include 24-hour foot and vehicle patrol, security escort services, shuttle buses, and emergency telephones. There are lighted pathways/sidewalks and magnetic card access to residence facilities.

Programs of Study: La Salle confers B.A., B.S., B.S.N., and B.S.W. degrees. Associate, master's, and doctoral degrees are also awarded. Bachelor's degrees are awarded in BIOLOGICAL SCIENCE (biochemistry, biology/biological science, and nutrition), BUSINESS (accounting, banking and finance, business administration and management, international economics, management information systems, marketing/retailing/merchandising, and organizational behavior), COMMUNICATIONS AND THE ARTS (classical languages, communications, English, fine arts, French, German, Italian, multimedia, music, Russian, and Spanish), COMPUTER AND PHYSICAL SCIENCE (chemistry, computer science, geology, information sciences and systems, mathematics, and science), EDUCATION (elementary, foreign languages, science, secondary, social studies, and special), ENGINEERING AND ENVIRONMENTAL DESIGN (computer graphics and environmental science), HEALTH PROFESSIONS (nursing, preallied health, predentistry, premedicine, and speech pathology/audiology), SOCIAL SCIENCE (criminal justice, economics, history, philosophy, political science/government, prelaw, psychology, public administration, religion, social work, and sociology). English, accounting, and education are the strongest academically. Accounting, education, and communication are the largest.

Required: Students take courses in writing, computer science, religion, philosophy, history, literature, math, the natural sciences, and the social sciences. The core curriculum is distinguished by 2 requirements: the "double," a thematically linked pair of courses taught by 2 facility partners from different disciplines, and the "metro," a year-long program of co-curricular activities conducted by a faculty member and designed to help students take advantagé of the resources of the City of Philadelphia.

Special: Cross-registration is offered in conjunction with Chestnut Hill College, and there is a 2-2 program in allied health with Thomas Jefferson University. La Salle also offers study abroad, co-op programs in business and computer science, work-study programs, internships in most majors, dual majors, and pass/fail options. An E-Commerce Institute has been created to educate all students about this business tool. There are 10 national honor societies and a freshman honors program.

Faculty/Classroom: 54% of faculty are male; 46%, female. 90% teach undergraduates and 60% do research. No introductory courses are taught by graduate students. The average class size in an introductory lecture is 20; in a laboratory, 14; and in a regular course, 19.

Admissions: 68% of the 2003-2004 applicants were accepted. The SAT I scores for the 2003-2004 freshman class were: Verbal--24% below 500, 47% between 500 and 599, 24% between 600 and 700, and 4% above 700; Math--27% below 500, 47% between 500 and 599, 23% between 600 and 700, and 3% above 700. 44% of the current freshmen were in the top fifth of their class; 78% were in the top two fifths. 11 freshmen graduated first in their class.

Requirements: The SAT I or ACT is required. SAT II: Subject tests in writing and math are recommended. Applicants must be graduates of accredited secondary schools or have earned a GED. La Salle requires 16 academic units, based on 4 years of English, 3 of math, 2 of foreign language, and 1 of history, with the remaining 5 units in academic electives; science and math majors must have an additional one-half unit of math. An essay is required, and an interview is recommended. La Salle requires applicants to be in the upper 50% of their class. AP and CLEP credits are accepted. Important factors in the admissions decision are advanced placement or honor courses, leadership record, and recommendations by school officials.

Procedure: Freshmen are admitted fall and spring. Entrance exams should be taken before January of the senior year. There are early admissions, deferred admissions, and rolling admissions plans. Applications should be filed by April 1 for fall entry and December 15 for spring entry, along with a $35 fee. Notification is sent on a rolling basis. Applications are accepted on-line through *lasalle.edu/admissions*.

Transfer: 136 transfer students enrolled in 2002-2003. Transfer applicants should have a minimum GPA of 2.25, with 2.5 preferred. 50 of 120 credits required for the bachelor's degree must be completed at La Salle.

Visiting: There are regularly scheduled orientations for prospective students, including campus tours 11 Saturdays throughout the fall, 3 Saturdays during the winter, and 4 Saturdays during the spring. There are guides for informal visits and visitors may sit in on classes and stay overnight. To schedule a visit, contact the Admissions Office at *admissions@lasalle.edu*.

Financial Aid: In 2003-2004, 94% of all full-time freshmen and 85% of continuing full-time students received some form of financial aid. 76% of full-time freshmen and 62% of continuing full-time students received need-based aid. The average freshman award was $15,995. Need-based scholarships or need-based grants averaged $6400 ($9000 maximum); need-based self-help aid (loans and jobs) averaged $4678 ($7300 maximum); and non-need-based athletic scholarships averaged $8600. 15% of undergraduates work part time. Average annual earnings from campus work are $1800. The average financial indebtedness of the 2003 graduate was $16,500. The FAFSA is required. The deadline for filing freshman financial aid applications for fall entry is February 15.

International Students: There are 39 international students enrolled. The school actively recruits these students. They must score 500 on the written TOEFL.

Computers: The mainframe is a SUN 450. The university provides 325 PCs. A LAN is available for student use. Dorms are wired for network and Internet access. All students may access the system 8 A.M. to 11 P.M. weekdays, 9 A.M. to 7 P.M. Saturday, and noon to 11 P.M. Sunday. There are no time limits and no fees.

Graduates: From July 1, 2002 to June 30, 2003, 805 bachelor's degrees were awarded. The most popular majors were communications (12%), education (11%), and nursing (9%). In an average class, 56% graduate in 4 years or less, 70% graduate in 5 years or less, and 72% graduate in 6 years or less. 130 companies recruited on campus in 2002-2003. Of the 2002 graduating class, 18% were enrolled in graduate school within 6 months of graduation and 91% were employed.

Admissions Contact: Robert Voss, Dean of Admissions and Financial Aid. E-mail: *admiss@lasalle.edu* Web: *lasalle.edu*

LAFAYETTE COLLEGE
F-3

Easton, PA 18042 (610) 330-5100; Fax: (610) 330-5355

Full-time: 1118 men, 1101 women	**Faculty:** 186; IIB, ++$
Part-time: 50 men, 31 women	**Ph.D.s:** 100%
Graduate: none	**Student/Faculty:** 12 to 1
Year: semesters, summer session	**Tuition:** $27,328
Application Deadline: January 1	**Room & Board:** $8418
Freshman Class: 5835 applied, 2036 accepted, 585 enrolled	
SAT I Verbal/Math: 619/649	**ACT:** 28 **MOST COMPETITIVE**

Lafayette College, founded in 1826 and affiliated with the Presbyterian Church (U.S.A) is a private institution emphasizing the liberal arts and engineering. In addition to regional accreditation, Lafayette has baccalaureate program accreditation with ABET and ACS. The 2 libraries contain 510,000 volumes and 120,000 microform items, and subscribe to 2600 periodicals. Computerized library services include the card catalog, interlibrary loans, and database searching. Special learning facilities include a learning resource center, art gallery, radio station, geological museum, foreign languages lab, and calculus lab. The 342-acre campus is in a suburban area 70 miles west of New York City. Including any residence halls, there are 65 buildings.

Student Life: 72% of undergraduates are from out of state, mostly the Middle Atlantic. Students are from 39 states, 33 foreign countries, and Canada. 70% are from public schools. 84% are white. 37% are Catholic; 30% Protestant; 15% claim no religious affiliation; 11% Jewish; 7% Hindu, Muslim, and others. The average age of freshmen is 18; all undergraduates, 20. 5% do not continue beyond their first year; 92% remain to graduate.

Housing: 2100 students can be accommodated in college housing, which includes single-sex and coed dorms, on-campus apartments, off-campus apartments, fraternity houses, and sorority houses. In addition, there are honors houses, special-interest houses, diversity-oriented houses, art houses, a black cultural center, and language and special-interest floors. On-campus housing is guaranteed for all 4 years. 98% of students live on campus; of those, 95% remain on campus on weekends. Upperclassmen may keep cars.

Activities: 26% of men belong to 8 national fraternities; 45% of women belong to 6 national sororities. There are 250 groups on campus, including AIDS awareness, art, band, cheerleading, chess, choir, chorale, chorus, computers, dance, debate, drama, ethnic, film, forensics, gay, honors, international, jazz band, literary magazine, musical theater, newspaper, orchestra, pep band, photography, political, professional, radio and TV, religious, social, social service, student government, and yearbook. Popular campus events include All College Day, Earth Day, and International Extravaganza.

Sports: There are 11 intercollegiate sports for men and 11 for women, and 22 intramural sports for men and 22 for women. Facilities include a 14,000-seat stadium; a sports center containing a 3500-seat gym, a field house, a varsity house, a natatorium, a fitness center, 2 exercise rooms, a weight training room, an outdoor track, an indoor track, a climbing wall, 6 racquet courts, and 3 multipurpose courts; and a 230-acre athletic complex for lacrosse, field hockey, soccer, and baseball.

Disabled Students: 95% of the campus is accessible. Wheelchair ramps, elevators, special parking, specially equipped rest rooms, special class scheduling, lowered drinking fountains, and lowered telephones are available.

Services: Counseling and information services are available, as is tutoring in most subjects, including most 100-level and many 200-level classes.

Campus Safety and Security: Measures include 24-hour foot and vehicle patrol, self-defense education, security escort services, and shuttle buses. There are informal discussions, pamphlets/posters/films, emergency telephones, lighted pathways/sidewalks, and advisers in all residence halls. Residence halls are locked from 8 P.M. to 7 A.M. and are accessible by room keys and outside telephones.

Programs of Study: Lafayette confers A.B., B.S., and B.S.Eng. degrees. Bachelor's degrees are awarded in BIOLOGICAL SCIENCE (biochemistry, biology/biological science, and neurosciences), BUSINESS (business economics and international economics), COMMUNICATIONS AND THE ARTS (art, English, French, German, music, and Spanish), COMPUTER AND PHYSICAL SCIENCE (chemistry, computer science, geology, mathematics, and physics), ENGINEERING AND ENVIRONMENTAL DESIGN (chemical engineering, civil engineering, electrical/electronics engineering, engineering, and mechanical engineering), SOCIAL SCIENCE (African studies, American studies, anthropology, economics, history, interdisciplinary studies, international relations, philosophy, political science/government, prelaw, psychology, religion, Russian and Slavic studies, and sociology). Engineering, psychology, and English are the strongest academically. Economics, business, and engineering are the largest.

Required: To graduate, students must maintain a GPA of 2.0 over a minimum of 32 to 38 courses. The common course of study, designed to build a background in the liberal arts and sciences in the first 2 years, includes interdisciplinary seminars, 3 courses in humanities/social science, 2 in natural science, and 1 each in collage writing and math/computer science/philosophy. Students must fulfill a foreign culture requirement, and A.B. and B.S. majors must take 2 upper-level writing courses.

Special: Cross-registration through the Lehigh Valley Association of Independent Colleges, internships in all academic departments, study abroad in 3 countries as well as through other individually arranged plans, a Washington semester at American University, and work-study programs with area employers are possible. An accelerated degree plan in all majors, dual and student-designed majors, 5-year dual-degree programs, and pass/fail options in any nonmajor subject also are available. There are 12 national honor societies, including Phi Beta Kappa, and 24 departmental honors programs.

Faculty/Classroom: 74% of faculty are male; 26%, female. All both teach and do research. The average class size in a laboratory is 12 and in a regular course, 17.

Admissions: 35% of the 2003-2004 applicants were accepted. The SAT I scores for the 2003-2004 freshman class were: Verbal--3% below 500, 27% between 500 and 599, 58% between 600 and 700, and 12% above 700; Math--2% below 500, 22% between 500 and 599, 53% between 600 and 700, and 22% above 700. The ACT scores were 1% below 21, 3% between 21 and 23, 14% between 24 and 26, 66% between 27 and 28, and 16% above 28. 94% of the current freshmen were in the top fifth of their class; 99% were in the top two fifths.

Requirements: The SAT I or ACT is required. In addition, applicants need 4 years of English, 3 of math (4 for science or engineering majors), 2 each of a foreign language and lab science (with physics and chemistry for science or engineering students), and at least an additional 5 units in academic subjects. An essay is required and an interview recommended. Evaluations from the secondary school counselor and a teacher are required. The GED is accepted. AP credits are accepted. Important factors in the admissions decision are advanced placement or honor courses, evidence of special talent, and personality/intangible qualities.

Procedure: Freshmen are admitted in the fall. Entrance exams should be taken by January of the senior year. There are early decision and deferred admissions plans. Early decision applications should be filed by January 1; regular applications, by January 1 for fall entry. The fall 2003 application fee was $50. Notification of early decision is sent within 30 days of receipt of the application; regular decision, mid-March. 218 early decision candidates were accepted for the 2003-2004 class. 86 waitlisted applicants were admitted.

Transfer: 12 transfer students enrolled in 2002-2003. Acceptance usually depends on college-level performance and achievements. An interview is required if the student lives within 200 miles of the college. No minimum GPA is required, and neither the SAT I nor the ACT is needed. The number of credit hours required varies with the program, but usually enough for freshman status with advanced standing is needed. 16 of 32 credits required for the bachelor's degree must be completed at Lafayette.

Visiting: There are regularly scheduled orientations for prospective students, including student/faculty panel discussions, tours, and departmental open houses. There are guides for informal visits and visitors may sit in on classes and stay overnight. To schedule a visit, contact the Admissions Office at admissions@lafayette.edu.

Financial Aid: In 2003-2004, 60% of all full-time freshmen and 66% of continuing full-time students received some form of financial aid. 45% of full-time freshmen and 48% of continuing full-time students received need-based aid. The average freshman award was $23,249. 54% of undergraduates work part time. Average annual earnings from campus work are $900. The average financial indebtedness of the 2003 graduate was $15,393. The CSS Profile or FAFSA, the college's own financial statement, and the Business/Farm supplement and Divorce/Separation parent statement (if applicable) are required. The deadline for filing freshman financial aid applications for fall entry is February 15.

International Students: There are 101 international students enrolled. The school actively recruits these students. They must score 550 on the written TOEFL and also take the SAT I.

Computers: The mainframes are a DEC VAX 6310, an ARIX, and an IBM 9375. An Ethernet connects the entire campus to the Internet. More than 600 computers are available for student use. All students may access the system 24 hours per day. There are no time limits and no fees.

Graduates: In a recent year, 518 bachelor's degrees were awarded. The most popular majors were engineering (16%), economics and business (14%), and government and law (10%). In an average class, 1% graduate in 3 years or less, 89% graduate in 4 years or less, and 93% graduate in 5 years or less. 250 companies recruited on campus in a recent year. Of a recent graduating class, 24% were enrolled in graduate school within 6 months of graduation and 76% were employed.

Admissions Contact: Carol Rowlands, Director of Admissions. A video is available. E-mail: rowlandc@lafayette.edu
Web: www.lafayette.edu

LEBANON VALLEY COLLEGE
Annville, PA 17003-1400

E-3

(717) 867-6181
(866) LVC-4ADM; Fax: (717) 867-6026

Full-time: 671 men, 859 women	**Faculty:** 99; IIB, av$
Part-time: 71 men, 164 women	**Ph.D.s:** 88%
Graduate: 64 men, 77 women	**Student/Faculty:** 15 to 1
Year: semesters, summer session	**Tuition:** $22,510
Application Deadline: open	**Room & Board:** $6360
Freshman Class: 2083 applied, 1520 accepted, 429 enrolled	
SAT I Verbal/Math: 547/563	**VERY COMPETITIVE**

Lebanon Valley College, founded in 1866, is a private institution affiliated with the United Methodist Church. The college offers undergraduate programs in the arts and sciences. In addition to regional accreditation, LVC has baccalaureate program accreditation with NASM. The library contains 174,581 volumes, 13,679 microform items, and 8285 audio/video tapes/CDs, and subscribes to 800 periodicals. Computerized library services include the card catalog, interlibrary loans, database searching, and Internet access. Special learning facilities include a learning resource center, art gallery, and radio station. The 277-acre campus is in a small town 7 miles east of Hershey. Including any residence halls, there are 43 buildings.

Student Life: 80% of undergraduates are from Pennsylvania. Students are from 21 states, 8 foreign countries, and Canada. 94% are from public schools. 95% are white. 60% are Protestant; 21% Catholic; 19% claim no religious affiliation. The average age of freshmen is 18; all undergraduates, 21. 17% do not continue beyond their first year; 70% remain to graduate.

Housing: 1151 students can be accommodated in college housing, which includes single-sex and coed dorms and on-campus apartments. In addition, there are special-interest houses, and suite-style living, substance-free, and clean air halls. On-campus housing is guaranteed for all 4 years. 75% of students live on campus; of those, 60% remain on campus on weekends. All students may keep cars.

Activities: 11% of men and about 1% of women belong to 2 local and 2 national fraternities; 12% of women belong to 1 local and 3 national sororities. There are 76 groups on campus, including band, cheerleading, choir, chorus, computers, concert band, drama, drill team, ethnic, gay, honors, international, jazz band, literary magazine, marching band, musical ensembles, musical theater, newspaper, orchestra, photography, political, professional, radio and TV, religious, social, social service, student government, symphony, and yearbook. Popular campus events include Parents Weekend, Christmas at the Valley, and Cherry Blossom Festival.

Sports: There are 11 intercollegiate sports for men and 9 for women, and 13 intramural sports for men and 12 for women. Facilities include a 3000-seat stadium, a sports center, more than 60 acres of athletic fields, indoor and outdoor tracks, a gym, playing courts for basketball, handball, squash, and tennis, a 500-seat baseball grandstand, and an enclosed football field.

Disabled Students: 65% of the campus is accessible. Wheelchair ramps, elevators, special parking, specially equipped rest rooms, special class scheduling, lowered drinking fountains, lowered telephones, and special housing are available.

Services: Counseling and information services are available, as is tutoring in every subject.

Campus Safety and Security: Measures include 24-hour foot and vehicle patrol, self-defense education, security escort services, and informal discussions. There are pamphlets/posters/films, emergency telephones, and lighted pathways/sidewalks.

Programs of Study: LVC confers B.A., B.S., B.M., B.S.Ch., B.S.ed., and B.S.Med.Tech. degrees. Associate, master's, and doctoral degrees are also awarded. Bachelor's degrees are awarded in BIOLOGICAL SCIENCE (biochemistry and biology/biological science), BUSINESS (accounting), COMMUNICATIONS AND THE ARTS (art, audio technology, communications technology, English, French, German, music, and Spanish), COMPUTER AND PHYSICAL SCIENCE (actuarial science, chemistry, computer science, mathematics, and physics), EDUCATION (elementary, music, and secondary), ENGINEERING AND ENVIRONMENTAL DESIGN (engineering), HEALTH PROFESSIONS (medical laboratory technology, occupational therapy, physical therapy, predentistry, premedicine, prepharmacy, and preveterinary science), SOCIAL SCIENCE (American studies, economics, history, philosophy, political science/government, prelaw, psychobiology, psychology, religion, and sociology). Actuarial science, natural sciences, and education are the strongest academically. Education, business, and natural sciences are the largest.

Required: The general education program consists of course work in four areas: communications, liberal studies, foreign studies, and disciplinary perspectives. Students are required to complete 3 writing-intensive courses and be proficient in computer applications and modes of information access and retrieval. To graduate, students must complete at least 120 credit hours, 2 units of phys ed, and the requirements for the major with a minimum GPA of 2.0.

Special: Study abroad is available in 6 countries through the college's affiliation with the International Student Exchange Program and the LVC College in Cologne Program. LVC is also affiliated with several colleges and universities in England, France, Spain, the Netherlands, and New Zealand. There are 3-2 degree programs in engineering with Penn State University and Case Western Reserve and Widener universities, and in forestry with Duke University. There is also a 2-2 degree program in allied health sciences with Thomas Jefferson University. LVC offers internships in a number of areas. There are 6 national honor societies and 11 departmental honors programs.

Faculty/Classroom: 66% of faculty are male; 34%, female. All teach undergraduates. No introductory courses are taught by graduate students. The average class size in an introductory lecture is 24; in a laboratory, 13; and in a regular course, 15.

Admissions: 73% of the 2003-2004 applicants were accepted. The SAT I scores for the 2003-2004 freshman class were: Verbal--25% below 500, 48% between 500 and 599, 25% between 600 and 700, and 2% above 700; Math--21% below 500, 43% between 500 and 599, 32% between 600 and 700, and 4% above 700. 52% of the current freshmen were in the top fifth of their class; 81% were in the top two fifths. 8 freshmen graduated first in their class.

Requirements: The SAT I or ACT is required. In addition, applicants must be graduates of accredited secondary schools or have earned a GED. LVC requires 16 academic units or 16 Carnegie units, including 4 in English, 2 each in math and foreign language, and 1 each in science and social studies. An interview is recommended. Students applying as music majors must also audition. AP and CLEP credits are accepted. Important factors in the admissions decision are advanced placement or honor courses, leadership record, and personality/intangible qualities.

Procedure: Freshmen are admitted fall and spring. Entrance exams should be taken in the spring of the junior year. There is a rolling admissions plan. Application deadlines are open. Application fee is $30. 5 applicants were on the 2003 waiting list; all were admitted. Applications are accepted on-line through the school's web site.

Transfer: 53 transfer students enrolled in 2002-2003. Requirements for transfer applicants include a minimum GPA of 2.0, SAT I scores, and an interview. 30 of 120 credits required for the bachelor's degree must be completed at LVC.

Visiting: There are regularly scheduled orientations for prospective students, including tours, interviews, and meetings with professors. There are guides for informal visits and visitors may sit in on classes. To schedule a visit, contact Susan Sarisky, Director of Admission at (866) LVC-4ADM or admission@lvc.edu.

Financial Aid: In 2003-2004, 99% of all full-time freshmen and 97% of continuing full-time students received some form of financial aid. 82% of full-time freshmen and 78% of continuing full-time students received need-based aid. The average freshman award was $17,424. Need-based scholarships or need-based grants averaged $14,098 ($25,780 maximum); need-based self-help aid (loans and jobs) averaged $4515 ($6625 maximum); and non-need-based awards and non-need based scholarships averaged $8908 ($22,360 maximum). 53% of undergraduates work part time. Average annual earnings from campus work are $625. The average financial indebtedness of the 2003 graduate was $22,027. LVC is a member of CSS. The FAFSA and the college's own financial statement are required. The deadline for filing freshman financial aid applications for fall entry is March 1.

International Students: There are 10 international students enrolled. The school actively recruits these students. They must score 550 on the written TOEFL or 213 on the electronic version and also take the SAT I or the ACT.

Computers: The mainframes are a 10 Dell Poweredge running Windows and 1 Compaq Alpha running UNIX. Servers and other networked resources (including the Internet and Web) can be reached from more than 200 college-owned student computers located throughout the campus. Resident students may also connect personally owned computers to the campus network via Ethernet and gain access to the same resources. All students may access the system.

Graduates: From July 1, 2002 to June 30, 2003, 438 bachelor's degrees were awarded. The most popular majors were business administration (30%), education (20%), and social sciences and history (8%). In an average class, 61% graduate in 4 years or less, 69% graduate in 5 years or less, and 70% graduate in 6 years or less. 128 companies recruited on campus in 2002-2003. Of the 2002 graduating class, 9% were enrolled in graduate school within 6 months of graduation and 82% were employed.

Admissions Contact: Susan Sarisky, Director of Admission.
E-mail: admission@lvc.edu Web: www.lvc.edu

LEHIGH UNIVERSITY
Bethlehem, PA 18015

	F-3
	(610) 758-3100; Fax: (610) 758-4361
Full-time: 2780 men, 1845 women	**Faculty:** 391; I, +$
Part-time: 36 men, 18 women	**Ph.D.s:** 99%
Graduate: 1127 men, 926 women	**Student/Faculty:** 12 to 1
Year: semesters, summer session	**Tuition:** $29,340
Application Deadline: January 1	**Room & Board:** $8230
Freshman Class: 9087 applied, 3678 accepted, 1125 enrolled	
SAT I Verbal/Math: 625/670	**HIGHLY COMPETITIVE+**

Lehigh University, founded in 1865, is a private university offering both undergraduate and graduate programs in liberal arts, science, engineering, and business, and graduate programs in education. There are 3 undergraduate and 4 graduate schools. In addition to regional accreditation, Lehigh has baccalaureate program accreditation with AACSB, ABET, and NCATE. The 2 libraries contain 1,354,100 volumes, 2,113,130 microform items, and 3915 audio/video tapes/CDs, and subscribe to 10,797 periodicals. Computerized library services include the card catalog, interlibrary loans, and database searching. Special learning facilities include a learning resource center, art gallery, radio station, TV station, Special Collections/Rare Book Reading Room, and International Multimedia Resource Center. The 1600-acre campus is in a suburban area 60 miles north of Philadelphia and 80 miles southwest of New York City. Including any residence halls, there are 153 buildings.

Student Life: 67% of undergraduates are from out of state, mostly the Middle Atlantic. Students are from 49 states, 45 foreign countries, and Canada. 70% are from public schools. 81% are white. The average age of freshmen is 18; all undergraduates, 20. 7% do not continue beyond their first year; 85% remain to graduate.

Housing: 3240 students can be accommodated in college housing, which includes single-sex and coed dorms, on-campus apartments, married-student housing, fraternity houses, and sorority houses. In addition, there are special-interest, students of color, creative arts, and ROTC houses and substance-free housing. On-campus housing is guaranteed for the freshman year only, is available on a first-come, first-served basis, and is available on a lottery system for upperclassmen. 75% of students live on campus; of those, 75% remain on campus on weekends.

Activities: 32% of men belong to 27 national fraternities; 33% of women belong to 8 national sororities. There are 200 groups on campus, including art, band, cheerleading, chess, choir, chorale, chorus, computers, dance, drama, ethnic, gay, honors, international, jazz band, literary magazine, marching band, musical theater, newspaper, orchestra, photography, political, professional, radio and TV, religious, social, social service, student government, and yearbook. Popular campus events include Greek Week, Spring Fest, and South Side Alive (carnival with the community).

Sports: There are 12 intercollegiate sports for men and 11 for women, and 23 intramural sports for men and 22 for women. Facilities include a 16,000-seat stadium, a 6500-seat arena, a gym, a champion cross-country course, a field house with basketball and tennis courts, swimming pools, a track, indoor squash and racquetball courts, playing fields with Astroturf for field hockey, football, lacrosse, and soccer, weight rooms, a fitness center, and an indoor tennis center.

Disabled Students: 35% of the campus is accessible. Wheelchair ramps, elevators, special parking, specially equipped rest rooms, special class scheduling, lowered drinking fountains, and lowered telephones are available.

Services: Counseling and information services are available, as is tutoring in most subjects, including calculus, physics, English, accounting, finance, and economics. Tutoring in other subjects is available on request. There is a reader service for the blind. There are special programs for students with learning disabilities.

Campus Safety and Security: Measures include 24-hour foot and vehicle patrol, self-defense education, security escort services, and shuttle buses. There are informal discussions, pamphlets/posters/films, emergency telephones, and lighted pathways/sidewalks.

Programs of Study: Lehigh confers B.A., B.S., B.S.B.A., and B.S.E. degrees. Master's and doctoral degrees are also awarded. Bachelor's degrees are awarded in BIOLOGICAL SCIENCE (biochemistry, biology/biological science, and molecular biology), BUSINESS (accounting, banking and finance, business administration and management, business economics, and marketing/retailing/merchandising), COMMUNICATIONS AND THE ARTS (art, classics, dramatic arts, English, French, German, journalism, music, and Spanish), COMPUTER AND PHYSICAL SCIENCE (chemistry, computer science, information sciences and systems, mathematics, natural sciences, physics, science technology, and statistics), EDUCATION (social foundations), ENGINEERING AND ENVIRONMENTAL DESIGN (architecture, chemical engineering, civil engineering, computer engineering, electrical/electronics engineering, engineering mechanics, engineering physics, environmental science, industrial engineering, materials engineering, and mechanical engineering), HEALTH PROFESSIONS (predentistry, premedicine, and preoptometry), SOCIAL SCIENCE (African studies, American studies, anthropology, Asian/Oriental studies, behavioral science, classical/ancient

civilization, cognitive science, economics, history, international public service, international relations, philosophy, political science/government, psychology, religion, Russian and Slavic studies, sociology, and urban studies). Architecture, accounting, and mechanical engineering are the largest.

Required: Graduation requirements vary by degree sought, but all students must complete 2 semesters of English, at least 30 credits in the chosen major, and a minimum of 121 credit hours. Students must also maintain a minimum GPA of 2.0.

Special: The university offers co-op programs through the Colleges of Engineering and Applied Science and Business and Economics, cross-registration with the Lehigh Valley Association of Independent Colleges, study abroad in 40 countries, internships, a Washington semester, several work-study programs, accelerated degree programs in medicine, dentistry and optometry, student-designed majors, many combinations of dual majors, a B.A.-B.S. degree, a 3-2 engineering degree, and pass/fail options. A 6-year B.A.-M.D. degree with the Medical College of Pennsylvania and a 7-year B.A.-D.D.S. degree with Pennsylvania State University are possible. There are 18 national honor societies, including Phi Beta Kappa, and a freshman honors program.

Faculty/Classroom: 81% of faculty are male; 19%, female. All both teach and do research. No introductory courses are taught by graduate students. The average class size in an introductory lecture is 150 and in a regular course, 29.

Admissions: 40% of the 2003-2004 applicants were accepted. The SAT I scores for the 2003-2004 freshman class were: Verbal--3% below 500, 26% between 500 and 599, 59% between 600 and 700, and 12% above 700; Math--1% below 500, 12% between 500 and 599, 52% between 600 and 700, and 35% above 700.

Requirements: The SAT I or ACT is required. In addition, candidates for admission should have completed 4 years of English and 2 years each of a foreign language, history, math, science, and social science. Most students present 4 years each of science, math, and English. An on-campus interview is recommended. AP credits are accepted. Important factors in the admissions decision are advanced placement or honor courses, evidence of special talent, and leadership record.

Procedure: Freshmen are admitted fall and spring. Entrance exams should be taken by the January test date. There is an early decision plan. Early decision applications should be filed by November 15; regular applications, by January 1 for fall entry and November 15 for spring entry. The fall 2003 application fee was $50. Notification of early decision is sent December 15; regular decision, by April 1.

Transfer: Transfer candidates should have a minimum GPA of 3.0. An interview is recommended. 30 of 121 credits required for the bachelor's degree must be completed at Lehigh.

Visiting: There are regularly scheduled orientations for prospective students, consisting of interviews scheduled Monday through Friday, 9 A.M. to 3:30 P.M.; tours scheduled Monday through Friday, 10:15 A.M., 11:15 A.M., 1 P.M., and 3 P.M., and interviews and tours also available on some Saturdays. General information sessions are offered Monday through Friday at 9:30 A.M., 10:30 A.M., and 2:15 P.M. There are guides for informal visits and visitors may sit in on classes and stay overnight. To schedule a visit, contact the Office of Admissions.

Financial Aid: In 2003-2004, 63% of all full-time freshmen and 62% of continuing full-time students received some form of financial aid. 45% of full-time freshmen and 44% of continuing full-time students received need-based aid. The average freshman award was $23,813. Need-based scholarships or need-based grants averaged $17,386 ($35,275 maximum); need-based self-help aid (loans and jobs) averaged $4220 ($7425 maximum); non-need-based athletic scholarships averaged $34,637 ($34,670 maximum); other non-need-based awards and non-need-based scholarships averaged $25,752 ($37,320 maximum); and outside resources averaged $2139 ($16,600 maximum). 27% of undergraduates work part time. Average annual earnings from campus work are $980. The average financial indebtedness of a recent year's graduate was $15,178. Lehigh is a member of CSS. The CSS Profile or FAFSA and the college's own financial statement are required. Check with the school for current application deadlines.

International Students: The school actively recruits these students. They must score 230 on the electronic version of the TOEFL and also take the SAT I or the ACT. Students must take SAT II: Subject tests in English, math, and 1 other.

Computers: The mainframes are clusters of high-speed IBM RS/6000 computers, with more than 115 workstations in public sites. There are also more than 400 PCs available for student use in libraries, academic buildings, and computer centers. There are computer ports in all classrooms, dorms, and offices. Many LANs and high-speed fiber-optic networks are available. All students may access the system 24 hours per day, 7 days per week. There are no time limits and no fees.

Admissions Contact: J. Bruce Gardiner, Director.
E-mail: *inado@lehigh.edu* Web: *www.lehigh.edu*

LINCOLN UNIVERSITY

E-4

Lincoln University, PA 19352

(610) 932-8300, ext. 3206
(800) 790-0191; Fax: (610) 932-1209

Full-time: 593 men, 879 women	**Faculty:** 90; IIA, --$
Part-time: 18 men, 40 women	**Ph.D.s:** 71%
Graduate: 147 men, 261 women	**Student/Faculty:** 16 to 1
Year: semesters, summer session	**Tuition:** $6952 ($10,872)
Application Deadline: open	**Room & Board:** $6368
Freshman Class: 4846 applied, 1759 accepted, 500 enrolled	
SAT I Verbal/Math: 440/440	COMPETITIVE+

Lincoln University, founded in 1854, is a public institution offering programs in liberal arts and teacher preparation. There are 3 undergraduate schools and 1 graduate school. The library contains 185,197 volumes, 210,009 microform items, and 2630 audio/video tapes/CDs, and subscribes to 540 periodicals. Computerized library services include the card catalog, interlibrary loans, and database searching. Special learning facilities include an art gallery, radio station, and TV station. The 422-acre campus is in a rural area 45 miles southwest of Philadelphia. Including any residence halls, there are 37 buildings.

Student Life: 56% of undergraduates are from out of state, mostly the Northeast. Students are from 26 states and 13 foreign countries. 90% are African American. The average age of freshmen is 18; all undergraduates, 19. 31% do not continue beyond their first year; 45% remain to graduate.

Housing: 1450 students can be accommodated in college housing, which includes single-sex and coed dorms. On-campus housing is guaranteed for the freshman year only and is available on a first-come, first-served basis. 93% of students live on campus; of those, 80% remain on campus on weekends. Upperclassmen may keep cars.

Activities: 5% of men belong to 4 national fraternities; 5% of women belong to 4 national sororities. There are 90 groups on campus, including art, band, cheerleading, choir, chorale, computers, dance, drama, drill team, honors, international, jazz band, newspaper, pep band, political, radio and TV, religious, social, social service, student government, and yearbook. Popular campus events include lectures and recitals, Black History Month, and convocations.

Sports: There are 7 intercollegiate sports for men and 7 for women, and 5 intramural sports for men and 5 for women. Facilities include a 2000-seat gym, softball and track fields, a fitness trail, a swimming pool, and a bowling alley.

Disabled Students: Wheelchair ramps, elevators, special parking, and specially equipped rest rooms are available.

Services: Counseling and information services are available, as is tutoring in every subject. There is remedial math, reading, and writing.

Campus Safety and Security: Measures include 24-hour foot and vehicle patrol, self-defense education, security escort services, and shuttle buses. There are informal discussions, pamphlets/posters/films, emergency telephones, and lighted pathways/sidewalks.

Programs of Study: Lincoln confers B.A. and B.S. degrees. Master's degrees are also awarded. Bachelor's degrees are awarded in BIOLOGICAL SCIENCE (biology/biological science), BUSINESS (accounting, banking and finance, and business administration and management), COMMUNICATIONS AND THE ARTS (Chinese, communications, English, French, journalism, music, Russian, Spanish, and studio art), COMPUTER AND PHYSICAL SCIENCE (actuarial science, chemistry, computer science, mathematics, physics, and science), EDUCATION (early childhood, elementary, English, mathematics, music, physical, secondary, and special), ENGINEERING AND ENVIRONMENTAL DESIGN (preengineering), HEALTH PROFESSIONS (health science and recreation therapy), SOCIAL SCIENCE (African American studies, anthropology, criminal justice, economics, history, human services, industrial and organizational psychology, international relations, liberal arts/general studies, philosophy, political science/government, psychobiology, psychology, religion, and sociology). Physics, chemistry, and biology are the strongest academically. Business administration, elementary education, and criminal justice are the largest.

Required: Required courses include 8 in the humanities, 3 each in the social and natural sciences, 2 to 4 in foreign language, 2 each in phys ed, writing emphasis, speaking emphasis, critical thinking, and university seminar, and 1 in computer applications. Students must take Integrative Themes in the Libaral Arts, pass a writing proficiency exam, and participate in the Major Field Achievement Assessment. For graduation, a total of 120 semester hours is required, including 60 in the major, with a GPA of 2.0.

Special: Lincoln offers co-op programs, internships, study abroad in 18 countries, work-study, and pass/fail options. 3-2 engineering degrees are offered with 7 other universities and institutes. Accelerated degree programs, B.A.-B.S. degrees, and dual majors are possible. There are 7 national honor societies, a freshman honors program, and 3 departmental honors programs.

Faculty/Classroom: 69% of faculty are male; 31%, female. 72% teach undergraduates. No introductory courses are taught by graduate students.

Admissions: 36% of the 2003-2004 applicants were accepted.

Requirements: The SAT I or ACT is required. In addition, applicants should complete 21 credit hours, including 4 credits in English, 3 each in math, science, and social studies, 2 in art, and 1 in phys ed. The GED is accepted. An essay and an interview are required. Lincoln requires applicants to be in the upper 50% of their class. A GPA of 2.0 is required. AP and CLEP credits are accepted. Important factors in the admissions decision are advanced placement or honor courses, evidence of special talent, and leadership record.

Procedure: Freshmen are admitted fall and winter. Entrance exams should be taken prior to admission. There is a rolling admissions plan. Application deadlines are open for fall entry; December 1 for spring entry. The fall 2003 application fee was $20.

Transfer: 42 transfer students enrolled in a recent year. Applicants must have completed at least 12 semester hours, be in good standing at all previously attended institutions, and submit official transcripts. 60 of 120 credits required for the bachelor's degree must be completed at Lincoln.

Visiting: There are regularly scheduled orientations for prospective students. There are guides for informal visits and visitors may sit in on classes and stay overnight. To schedule a visit, contact Dr. Robert L. Laney, Director of Admissions.

Financial Aid: In 2003-2004, 95% of all full-time students received some form of financial aid. 90% of full-time freshmen received need-based aid. The average freshman award was $15,000. Need-based scholarships or need-based grants averaged $500 ($8000 maximum); need-based self-help aid (loans and jobs) averaged $3625 ($9000 maximum); non-need-based athletic scholarships averaged $1000 ($6000 maximum); other non-need-based awards and non-need-based scholarships averaged $1000 ($6000 maximum); and outside scholarships averaged $1000 ($4000 maximum). 28% of undergraduates work part time. Average annual earnings from campus work are $1800. The average financial indebtedness of the 2003 graduate was $20,000. Lincoln is a member of CSS. The FAFSA and PHEAA are required. The priority date for freshman financial aid applications for fall entry is March 15.

International Students: In a recent year, there were 81 international students enrolled. The school actively recruits these students. They must score 550 on the written TOEFL and also take the SAT I or the ACT, scoring 850.

Computers: The mainframe is an HP Alpha DS25. There are more than 350 PCs and Macs in various dorms, computer labs, and the library. All students may access the system. There are no time limits and no fees.

Graduates: From July 1, 2002 to June 30, 2003, 228 bachelor's degrees were awarded. The most popular majors were elementary education (10%), business administration (10%), and criminal justice (10%). In an average class, 1% graduate in 3 years or less, 29% graduate in 4 years or less, 42% graduate in 5 years or less, and 45% graduate in 6 years or less. 48 companies recruited on campus in a recent year.

Admissions Contact: Dr. Robert L. Laney, Director of Admissions.
E-mail: *admiss@lu.lincoln.edu* Web: *www.lincoln.edu*

LOCK HAVEN UNIVERSITY OF PENNSYLVANIA

D-2

Lock Haven, PA 17745

(570) 893-2027
(800) 233-8978; Fax: (570) 893-2201

Full-time: 1790 men, 2477 women	**Faculty:** 215
Part-time: 130 men, 299 women	**Ph.D.s:** 56%
Graduate: 73 men, 139 women	**Student/Faculty:** 20 to 1
Year: semesters, summer session	**Tuition:** $5874 ($10,822)
Application Deadline: open	**Room & Board:** $5224
Freshman Class: n/av	
SAT I Verbal/Math: 483/489	**ACT:** 21 LESS COMPETITIVE

Lock Haven University, established in 1870, is a public institution offering undergraduate degrees in arts and sciences, education, and human services. The university maintains a branch campus in Clearfield. There are 2 undergraduate and 3 graduate schools. In addition to regional accreditation, Lock Haven has baccalaureate program accreditation with CSWE, NCATE, and NLN. The library contains 371,418 volumes, 734,658 microform items, and 6263 audio/video tapes/CDs, and subscribes to 995 periodicals. Computerized library services include the card catalog, interlibrary loans, database searching, and Internet access. Special learning facilities include a learning resource center, art gallery, planetarium, radio station, TV station, primate and human performance labs, and cadaver dissection lab. The 135-acre campus is in a rural area 30 miles west of Williamsport. Including any residence halls, there are 28 buildings.

Student Life: 89% of undergraduates are from Pennsylvania. Students are from 30 states, 42 foreign countries, and Canada. 93% are white. The average age of freshmen is 18; all undergraduates, 21. 26% do not continue beyond their first year; 51% remain to graduate.

Housing: 1630 students can be accommodated in college housing, which includes single-sex and coed dorms and off-campus apartments. 61% of students commute. Alcohol is not permitted. Upperclassmen may keep cars.

Activities: 8% of men belong to 6 national fraternities; 5% of women belong to 4 national sororities. There are 90 groups on campus, including art, band, cheerleading, chess, choir, chorale, chorus, computers, dance, drama, ethnic, forensics, gay, honors, international, jazz band, literary magazine, marching band, newspaper, orchestra, pep band, photography, political, professional, radio and TV, religious, social, social service, student government, and symphony. Popular campus events include Family Day, Alcohol Awareness Week, and Spring Carnival.

Sports: There are 7 intercollegiate sports for men and 9 for women, and 19 intramural sports for men and 18 for women. Facilities include a 5000-seat stadium containing a football field and an all-weather track, a 2500-seat field house with a wrestling room, a recreation facility, a gym used for intramurals and weight training, and a gym that houses a swimming pool.

Disabled Students: 95% of the campus is accessible. Wheelchair ramps, elevators, special parking, specially equipped rest rooms, special class scheduling, lowered drinking fountains, and lowered telephones are available.

Services: Counseling and information services are available, as is tutoring in most subjects. There is remedial math. Reader services for the blind can be arranged. There are also writing and math centers.

Campus Safety and Security: Measures include 24-hour foot and vehicle patrol, security escort services, informal discussions, and pamphlets/posters/films. There are emergency telephones and lighted pathways/sidewalks.

Programs of Study: Lock Haven confers B.A., B.S., B.F.A., and B.S.Ed. degrees. Associate and master's degrees are also awarded. Bachelor's degrees are awarded in BIOLOGICAL SCIENCE (biology/biological science and environmental biology), BUSINESS (business administration and management), COMMUNICATIONS AND THE ARTS (communications, English, fine arts, French, German, journalism, music, Spanish, and speech/debate/rhetoric), COMPUTER AND PHYSICAL SCIENCE (chemistry, computer science, earth science, geology, information sciences and systems, mathematics, and physics), EDUCATION (early childhood, elementary, foreign languages, physical, science, secondary, and special), HEALTH PROFESSIONS (health science and medical laboratory technology), SOCIAL SCIENCE (criminal justice, economics, geography, history, humanities and social science, international studies, Latin American studies, liberal arts/general studies, paralegal studies, philosophy, political science/government, psychology, social science, social work, and sociology). Health science and biological sciences are the strongest academically. Education, health science, and recreation are the largest.

Required: To graduate, students must complete 60 hours of general education, including 12 in humanities and in social and behavioral sciences, 9 in skills core, 6 in science, 3 in wellness core, and the rest in electives. A total of 120 credit hours is required, including 61 to 68 in the major, with a minimum GPA of 2.0.

Special: There are cooperative programs in music education and engineering, including a 3-2 engineering degree with Pennsylvania State University. Lock Haven also offers study-abroad programs in more than 20 countries, a dual major in education, work-study options, an accelerated degree program for honor students, a student-designed general studies major, and internships, which are required in some majors. Pass/fail grading options are limited to 1 course outside the major per semester, not to exceed 12 credit hours. There are 11 national honor societies, a freshman honors program, and 6 departmental honors programs.

Faculty/Classroom: 57% of faculty are male; 43%, female. 93% teach undergraduates. No introductory courses are taught by graduate students. The average class size in a laboratory is 15 and in a regular course, 28.

Admissions: The SAT I scores for the 2003-2004 freshman class were: Verbal--58% below 500, 34% between 500 and 599, 6% between 600 and 700, and 1% above 700; Math--44% below 500, 43% between 500 and 599, 11% between 600 and 700, and 1% above 700. The ACT scores were 49% below 21, 26% between 21 and 23, 25% between 24 and 26, and 1% between 27 and 28. 18% of the current freshmen were in the top fifth of their class; 45% were in the top two fifths.

Requirements: The SAT I or ACT is required. In addition, applicants must graduate from an accredited secondary school or have a GED. 16 academic credits are required, and a college preparatory course is recommended. AP and CLEP credits are accepted. Important factors in the admissions decision are leadership record, advanced placement or honor courses, and evidence of special talent.

Procedure: Freshmen are admitted to all sessions. Entrance exams should be taken during the spring of the junior year and the fall of the senior year. There is a rolling admissions plan. There are early decision, early admissions, and deferred admissions plans. Application deadlines are open. Application fee is $25. Applications are accepted on-line through CollegeView or the Internet. Typically, students are notified of their admissions status within 4 to 6 weeks after their application and all required documents are received by the Admissions Office.

Transfer: 187 transfer students enrolled in a recent year. Priority is given to applicants who have completed 24 or more transferable credits. A minimum GPA of 2.0 is required, and a composite SAT I score of 970 is recommended. 32 of 128 credits required for the bachelor's degree must be completed at Lock Haven.

Visiting: There are regularly scheduled orientations for prospective students, consisting of an introduction to the administration, sessions with faculty, and an information arena/departmental showcase; small group visits are also scheduled. There are guides for informal visits and visitors may sit in on classes. To schedule a visit, contact the Admissions Office.

Financial Aid: Lock Haven is a member of CSS. The FAFSA and PHEAA are required. Check with the school for current application deadlines.

International Students: The school actively recruits international students. They must score 550 on the written TOEFL.

Computers: The mainframe is an IBM 4381. All Internet services are accessible from the more than 225 PCs available in computer labs and residence halls. The library's card catalog is also accessible from all on-campus computers hooked up to the mainframe. All students may access the system. There are no time limits and no fees.

Graduates: From July 1, 2002 to June 30, 2003, 708 bachelor's degrees were awarded. The most popular majors were education (36%), health professional (12%), and parks and recreation (9%). In an average class, 19% graduate in 4 years or less, 43% graduate in 5 years or less, and 48% graduate in 6 years or less. Of the 2002 graduating class, 11% were enrolled in graduate school within 6 months of graduation and 85% were employed.

Admissions Contact: Stephen Lee, Director of Admissions. E-mail: *admissions@eagle.lhup.edu* Web: *www.lhup.edu*

LYCOMING COLLEGE
Williamsport, PA 17701-5192

D-2

(570) 321-4026
(800) 345-3920; Fax: (570) 321-4317

Full-time: 629 men, 750 women	Faculty: 88; IIB, av$
Part-time: 28 men, 28 women	Ph.D.s: 92%
Graduate: none	Student/Faculty: 16 to 1
Year: semesters, summer session	Tuition: $21,723
Application Deadline: April 1	Room & Board: $5866
Freshman Class: 1445 applied, 1150 accepted, 383 enrolled	
SAT I Verbal/Math: 565/570	COMPETITIVE+

Lycoming College, established in 1812, is a private, residential, liberal arts institution affiliated with the Methodist Church. In addition to regional accreditation, Lycoming has baccalaureate program accreditation with AACSB, ACS, and NLN. The library contains 170,000 volumes and 2400 audio/video tapes/CDs, and subscribes to 1100 periodicals. Computerized library services include the card catalog, interlibrary loans, database searching, and Internet access. Special learning facilities include a learning resource center, art gallery, planetarium, radio station, and TV station. The 35-acre campus is in a small town in north central Pennsylvania. Including any residence halls, there are 24 buildings.

Student Life: 74% of undergraduates are from Pennsylvania. Students are from 22 states, 11 foreign countries, and Canada. 81% are from public schools. 92% are white. 64% are Protestant; 30% Catholic. The average age of freshmen is 18; all undergraduates, 21. 17% do not continue beyond their first year; 67% remain to graduate.

Housing: 1160 students can be accommodated in college housing, which includes single-sex and coed dorms, on-campus apartments, and off-campus apartments. In addition, there are language houses, special-interest houses, and nonsmoking, intensive study, and Greek floors. On-campus housing is guaranteed for all 4 years. 82% of students live on campus; of those, 67% remain on campus on weekends. All students may keep cars.

Activities: 14% of men belong to 4 national fraternities; 17% of women belong to 3 local sororities and 1 national sorority. There are 64 groups on campus, including art, band, cheerleading, choir, chorus, computers, drama, ethnic, film, gay, honors, international, literary magazine, musical theater, newspaper, photography, political, professional, radio and TV, religious, social, social service, student government, and yearbook. Popular campus events include Campus Carnival, Annual Christmas Candlelight Service, and Choir Concert.

Sports: There are 9 intercollegiate sports for men and 9 for women, and 6 intramural sports for men and 6 for women. Facilities include an outdoor softball, football, soccer, and lacrosse complex, indoor basketball courts, and intramural fields.

Disabled Students: 85% of the campus is accessible. Wheelchair ramps, elevators, special parking, specially equipped rest rooms, special class scheduling, lowered drinking fountains, lowered telephones, and special housing are available.

Services: Counseling and information services are available, as is tutoring in every subject. There is remedial math, reading, and writing.

Campus Safety and Security: Measures include 24-hour foot and vehicle patrol, self-defense education, security escort services, and informal discussions. There are pamphlets/posters/films, emergency telephones, and lighted pathways/sidewalks.

Programs of Study: Lycoming confers B.A. and B.S. degrees. Bachelor's degrees are awarded in BIOLOGICAL SCIENCE (biology/biological science), BUSINESS (accounting and business administration and management), COMMUNICATIONS AND THE ARTS (art history and appreciation, communications, dramatic arts, English, French, German, music, Spanish, and studio art), COMPUTER AND PHYSICAL SCIENCE (astronomy, chemistry, computer science, mathematics, and physics), SOCIAL SCIENCE (anthropology, criminal justice, economics, history, international studies, philosophy, political science/government, psychology, religion, and sociology). Business, psychology, and biology are the largest.

Required: To graduate, students must complete 128 credits with a minimum GPA of 2.0. Distribution requirements include 4 courses in humanities and 2 each in English, foreign language, math, fine arts, natural science, social science, and cultural diversity. Students must also complete 2 semesters of phys ed, wellness, or community service.

Special: Cooperative programs are available with the Ohio and Pennsylvania Colleges of Podiatric Medicine, Pennsylvania College of Optometry, and Penn State and Duke Universities. Cross-registration is available with the Pennsylvania College of Technology. More than 200 internships, including teacher programs, study abroad in 5 countries, and a Washington semester at American University are available. Lycoming offers work-study programs, dual and student-designed majors, and an accelerated degree program in conjunction with the college's Scholar Program in optometry, podiatric medicine, and dentistry. There is a 3-2 engineering degree program with Penn State. Nondegree study and pass/fail grading options are available. There are 12 national honor societies, a freshman honors program, and 11 departmental honors programs.

Faculty/Classroom: 62% of faculty are male; 38%, female. All teach undergraduates. The average class size in an introductory lecture is 25; in a laboratory, 15; and in a regular course, 18.

Admissions: 80% of the 2003-2004 applicants were accepted. The SAT I scores for the 2003-2004 freshman class were: Verbal--24% below 500, 48% between 500 and 599, 24% between 600 and 700, and 2% above 700; Math--28% below 500, 45% between 500 and 599, 26% between 600 and 700, and 1% above 700. 40% of the current freshmen were in the top fifth of their class; 71% were in the top two fifths. 8 freshmen graduated first in their class.

Requirements: The SAT I or ACT is required, with a minimum SAT I score of 900, and at least 450 verbal. Applicants must graduate from an accredited secondary school or have a GED. They must have earned 16 academic or Carnegie units, completing 4 years of English, 3 each of math and social studies, and 2 each of science, a foreign language, and academic electives. 2 personal letters of recommendation are required. An essay is required and an interview is recommended. Portfolios and auditions may be required for students seeking scholarships. AP and CLEP credits are accepted. Important factors in the admissions decision are advanced placement or honor courses, leadership record, and evidence of special talent.

Procedure: Freshmen are admitted fall and spring. Entrance exams should be taken during the junior year or by January of the senior year. There is a deferred admissions plan and a rolling admissions plan. Applications should be filed by April 1 for fall entry and December 1 for spring entry, along with a $35 fee. Notification is sent on a rolling basis. Applications are accepted on-line through the college's web site.

Transfer: 39 transfer students enrolled in 2002-2003. Applicants must submit appropriate transcripts and have a minimum GPA of 2.0 in transferable courses. Students who have completed 24 transferable semester hours are not required to submit the SAT I or ACT results. 32 of 128 credits required for the bachelor's degree must be completed at Lycoming.

Visiting: There are regularly scheduled orientations for prospective students, consisting of a student-guided tour of campus and an interview with an admissions counselor. Meetings with professors and coaches and attending a class are possible upon request. There are guides for informal visits and visitors may sit in on classes and stay overnight. To schedule a visit, contact the Admissions House at (800) 345-3920, ext. 4026 or admissions@lycoming.edu.

Financial Aid: In 2003-2004, 87% of all full-time freshmen and 88% of continuing full-time students received some form of financial aid. 84% of all full-time students received need-based aid. The average freshman award was $16,900. Need-based scholarships or need-based grants averaged $10,100 ($18,000 maximum); need-based self-help aid (loans and jobs) averaged $3600 ($11,500 maximum); and non-need-based awards and non-need-based scholarships averaged $6400 ($15,000 maximum). 55% of undergraduates work part time. Average annual earnings from campus work was $980. The average financial indebtedness of the 2003 graduate was $16,200. The FAFSA and the college's own financial statement are required. The priority date for freshman financial aid applications for fall entry is March 1. The deadline for filing freshman financial aid applications for fall entry is April 15.

International Students: There are 14 international students enrolled. They must score 500 on the written TOEFL or 173 on the electronic version and also take the SAT I or ACT. This requirement may be waived, however. A minimum score of 900 is required on the SAT I.

Computers: Students may access the mainframe through 1 Mac and 4 PC labs. There are 180 terminals and PCs available to students. All students may access the system 8 A.M. to midnight. There are no time limits and no fees. It is strongly recommended that all students have a personal computer. A Pentium 4 or IBM ThinkPad is recommended.

Graduates: From July 1, 2002 to June 30, 2003, 312 bachelor's degrees were awarded. The most popular majors were business (17%), psychology (15%), and biology (12%). In an average class, 2% graduate in 3 years or less, 61% graduate in 4 years or less, and 69% graduate in 5 years or less. 25 companies recruited on campus in 2002-2003. Of the 2002 graduating class, 24% were enrolled in graduate school within 6 months of graduation and 97% were employed.

Admissions Contact: James Spencer, Dean of Admissions and Financial Aid. E-mail: admissions@lycoming.edu Web: www.lycoming.edu

MANSFIELD UNIVERSITY
Mansfield, PA 16933

D-1
(570) 662-4243
(800) 577-6826; Fax: (570) 662-4121

Full-time: 1153 men, 1741 women	**Faculty:** 155
Part-time: 69 men, 205 women	**Ph.D.s:** 78%
Graduate: 70 men, 282 women	**Student/Faculty:** 19 to 1
Year: semesters, summer session	**Tuition:** $5972 ($12,870)
Application Deadline: July 1	**Room & Board:** $5248
Freshman Class: 3281 applied, 2372 accepted, 710 enrolled	
SAT I Verbal/Math: 524/518	**ACT:** 21 COMPETITIVE

Mansfield University, founded in 1857, is a public university that is part of the Pennsylvania State System of Higher Education. It offers programs in professional studies and the arts and sciences. In addition to regional accreditation, Mansfield has baccalaureate program accreditation with CAHEA, CSWE, NASM, and NCATE. The library contains 246,141 volumes, 818,288 microform items, and 26,742 audio/video tapes/CDs, and subscribes to 2948 periodicals. Computerized library services include the card catalog, interlibrary loans, database searching, and Internet access. Special learning facilities include a learning resource center, art gallery, natural history museum, planetarium, radio station, TV station, and a high-tech lecture lab. The 175-acre campus is in a rural area 28 miles south of Corning/Elmira, New York, and 58 miles north of Williamsport. Including any residence halls, there are 41 buildings.

Student Life: 77% of undergraduates are from Pennsylvania. Students are from 25 states, 21 foreign countries, and Canada. 91% are white. The average age of freshmen is 19; all undergraduates, 21. 31% do not continue beyond their first year; 47% remain to graduate.

Housing: 1800 students can be accommodated in college housing, which includes single-sex and coed dorms. In addition, there are special-interest houses, wellness floors, nonsmoking floors, 24-hour quiet floors, and honors floors in residence halls.. On-campus housing is guaranteed for all 4 years. 55% of students commute. Alcohol is not permitted. All students may keep cars.

Activities: 5% of men belong to 4 national fraternities; 5% of women belong to 4 national sororities. There are 108 groups on campus, including art, band, cheerleading, choir, chorus, computers, debate, drama, ethnic, forensics, honors, international, jazz band, literary magazine, marching band, musical theater, newspaper, orchestra, pep band, photography, political, professional, radio and TV, religious, social, social service, student government, and symphony. Popular campus events include Parents Weekend and Fabulous 1890s Weekend.

Sports: There are 6 intercollegiate sports for men and 8 for women, and 8 intramural sports for men and 8 for women. Facilities include a track, a recreation center, a 4000-seat stadium, a 1500-seat indoor gym, a 1200-seat auditorium, and football, baseball, and hockey fields.

Disabled Students: 80% of the campus is accessible. Wheelchair ramps, elevators, special parking, specially equipped rest rooms, special class scheduling, lowered drinking fountains, lowered telephones, and a wheelchair lift are available.

Services: Counseling and information services are available, as is tutoring in most subjects. There is a reader service for the blind and remedial math, reading, and writing.

Campus Safety and Security: Measures include 24-hour foot and vehicle patrol, self-defense education, security escort services, and shuttle buses. There are informal discussions, pamphlets/posters/films, emergency telephones, and lighted pathways/sidewalks.

Programs of Study: Mansfield confers B.A., B.S., B.M., B.M.E., B.S.Ed., B.S.N., and B.S.W. degrees. Associate and master's degrees are also awarded. Bachelor's degrees are awarded in AGRICULTURE (fishing and fisheries), BIOLOGICAL SCIENCE (biochemistry, biology/biological science, cell biology, and molecular biology), BUSINESS (accounting, business administration and management, business economics, international business management, marketing/retailing/merchandising, personnel management, and tourism), COMMUNICATIONS AND THE ARTS (art history and appreciation, broadcasting, dramatic arts, English, French, German, journalism, music,

music business management, music performance, public relations, Spanish, speech/debate/rhetoric, and studio art), COMPUTER AND PHYSICAL SCIENCE (chemistry, computer science, information sciences and systems, mathematics, and physics), EDUCATION (art, early childhood, education of the exceptional child, elementary, English, foreign languages, mathematics, music, science, secondary, social studies, and special), ENGINEERING AND ENVIRONMENTAL DESIGN (city/community/regional planning, environmental science, and preengineering), HEALTH PROFESSIONS (medical technology, music therapy, nursing, and premedicine), SOCIAL SCIENCE (anthropology, criminal justice, dietetics, economics, geography, history, international studies, liberal arts/general studies, philosophy, political science/government, prelaw, psychology, social science, social work, and sociology). Music, physical sciences, and social sciences are the strongest academically. Education, music, and social sciences are the largest.

Required: To graduate, students must complete 120 credit hours with a 2.0 GPA in core courses, distribution requirements, general education electives, and major requirements. Some degrees require a higher GPA.

Special: There are co-op programs in preengineering, predentistry, premedicine, and medical technology, and study abroad in England, Spain, and Germany. There is a 3-2 engineering program with several major universities. The university also offers work-study, dual majors, a liberal studies degree, credit by exam, credit for military experience, nondegree study, and pass/fail options. There are 6 national honor societies, including Phi Beta Kappa, and a freshman honors program.

Faculty/Classroom: 55% of faculty are male; 42%, female. All teach undergraduates. No introductory courses are taught by graduate students. The average class size in an introductory lecture is 32; in a laboratory, 19; and in a regular course, 30.

Admissions: 72% of the 2003-2004 applicants were accepted. The SAT I scores for the 2003-2004 freshman class were: Verbal--38% below 500, 48% between 500 and 599, 13% between 600 and 700, and 1% above 700; Math--39% below 500, 46% between 500 and 599, 13% between 600 and 700, and 2% above 700. The ACT scores were 50% below 21, 30% between 21 and 23, 14% between 24 and 26, 3% between 27 and 28, and 3% above 28. 20% of the current freshmen were in the top fifth of their class; 47% were in the top two fifths. 6 freshmen graduated first in their class.

Requirements: The SAT I or ACT is required, with a minimum composite SAT I score of 920, or a minimum ACT score of 19. A GED is accepted. Applicants should prepare with 4 credits of English, 3 each of history, math, science, and social studies, 2 of foreign language, and 6 of additional academic electives. Art students must submit a portfolio; music students must audition. Mansfield requires applicants to be in the upper 60% of their class. A GPA of 2.5 is required. AP and CLEP credits are accepted. Important factors in the admissions decision are advanced placement or honor courses, evidence of special talent, and leadership record.

Procedure: Freshmen are admitted fall and spring. Entrance exams should be taken by the junior or senior year of high school. There are early decision, early admissions, deferred admissions, and rolling admissions plans. Early decision application should be filed by July 1; regular applications, by July 1 for fall entry and December 15 for spring entry, along with a $25 fee. Notification is sent on a rolling basis. Applications are accepted on-line through EXPAN and at *www.mansfield.edu.*.

Transfer: 277 transfer students enrolled in 2002-2003. Applicants must have a GPA of at least 2.0. 32 of 120 credits required for the bachelor's degree must be completed at Mansfield.

Visiting: There are regularly scheduled orientations for prospective students. There are guides for informal visits and visitors may sit in on classes. To schedule a visit, contact the Admissions Office.

Financial Aid: In 2003-2004, 80% of all full-time students received some form of financial aid. 60% of all full-time students received need-based aid. The average freshman award was $4500. Need-based scholarships or need-based grants averaged $1000 (full tuition maximum); need-based self-help aid (loans and jobs) averaged $3000 ($10,500 maximum); non-need-based athletic scholarships averaged $1500 (full tuition maximum); and other non-need-based awards and non-need-based scholarships averaged $1000 (full tuition maximum). 28% of undergraduates work part time. Average annual earnings from campus work are $1200. The average financial indebtedness of the 2003 graduate was $8500. Mansfield is a member of CSS. The FAFSA and the college's own financial statement are required. The deadline for filing freshman financial aid applications for fall entry is April 1.

International Students: There are 29 international students enrolled. The school actively recruits these students. They must score 550 on the written TOEFL or 230 on the electronic version.

Computers: The mainframe is an IBM RS/6000. There are 15 computing labs and a total of 450 PCs in labs and residence halls. All students may access the system. There are no time limits and no fees.

Graduates: From July 1, 2002 to June 30, 2003, 688 bachelor's degrees were awarded. The most popular majors were criminal justice (14%), elementary education (9%), and nursing (8%). In an average class, 2% graduate in 3 years or less, 26% graduate in 4 years or less,

45% graduate in 5 years or less, and 48% graduate in 6 years or less. 20 companies recruited on campus in 2002-2003. Of the 2002 graduating class, 8% were enrolled in graduate school within 6 months of graduation and 89% were employed.

Admissions Contact: Brian D. Barden, Director, Enrollment Management. E-mail: *admissns@mansfield.edu* Web: *www.mansfield.edu*

MARYWOOD UNIVERSITY
Scranton, PA 18509-1598

	E-2
	(570) 348-6234
	(800) 346-5014; Fax: (570) 961-4763

Full-time: 432 men, 1098 women	**Faculty:** 95; IIA, -$
Part-time: 60 men, 161 women	**Ph.Ds:** 87%
Graduate: 316 men, 1069 women	**Student/Faculty:** 16 to 1
Year: semesters, summer session	**Tuition:** $18,340
Application Deadline: open	**Room & Board:** $7710
Freshman Class: 1620 applied, 1234 accepted, 278 enrolled	
SAT I Verbal/Math: 515/490	**ACT:** 22	**COMPETITIVE**

Marywood University, founded in 1915, is an independent comprehensive Catholic institution committed to the integration of liberal arts and professional studies in the context of ethical and religious values. There are 4 undergraduate and 4 graduate schools. In addition to regional accreditation, Marywood has baccalaureate program accreditation with ABA, ACBSP, ADA, ARC-PA, ASHLA, CACREP, CSWE, NASAD, NASM, NCATE, and NLN. The library contains 218,003 volumes, 363,660 microform items, and 21,399 audio/video tapes/CDs, and subscribes to 1005 periodicals. Computerized library services include the card catalog, interlibrary loans, database searching, and Internet access. Special learning facilities include a learning resource center, art gallery, radio station, TV station, a communication disorders clinic, on-campus preschool and day care center, psychology/education research lab, science multimedia lab, distance education, human performance lab, videoconferencing classroom, and studio arts center. The 115-acre campus is in a suburban area 120 miles west of New York City and 115 miles north of Philadelphia. Including any residence halls, there are 29 buildings.

Student Life: 77% of undergraduates are from Pennsylvania. Students are from 21 states and 12 foreign countries. 75% are from public schools. 89% are white. The average age of freshmen is 20; all undergraduates, 23. 15% do not continue beyond their first year; 63% remain to graduate.

Housing: 671 students can be accommodated in college housing, which includes single-sex and coed dorms and on-campus apartments. In addition, there are honors houses, a community service residence, and an American-International student wing. On-campus housing is guaranteed for all 4 years. 66% of students commute. Alcohol is not permitted. All students may keep cars.

Activities: 44% of women belong to 1 local sorority. There are 78 groups on campus, including art, band, cheerleading, choir, chorus, commuter, computers, dance, dance team, drama, ethnic, film, gay, golf, honors, international, jazz band, literary magazine, musical theater, orchestra, photography, professional, radio and TV, religious, running, social, social service, student government, swimming, symphony, volunteer, and yearbook. Popular campus events include Family Weekend, Halloween Haunted House, and Spring Fling.

Sports: There are 5 intercollegiate sports for men and 7 for women, and 40 intramural sports for men and 40 for women. Facilities include an Olympic-size pool, a human performance lab, a gym, an athletic training room, outdoor tennis courts, racquetball courts, an aerobic room, a game room, saunas, a fitness center and weight room, 3 athletic fields for baseball, softball, field hockey, and soccer, and volleyball and horseshoe courts.

Disabled Students: 90% of the campus is accessible. Wheelchair ramps, elevators, special parking, specially equipped rest rooms, special class scheduling, lowered drinking fountains, lowered telephones, special housing, electronic doors, and full assistive technology labs are available.

Services: Counseling and information services are available, as is tutoring in every subject. There is a reader service for the blind and remedial math, reading, and writing. Remedial study skills and nonremedial tutoring, oral tests, note taking, tutors, tape recorders for physically challenged students, and interpreters for students with hearing impairments are available.

Campus Safety and Security: Measures include 24-hour foot and vehicle patrol, self-defense education, security escort services, and informal discussions. There are pamphlets/posters/films, emergency telephones, lighted pathways/sidewalks, night security in dorms, card access to dorm floors, and transportation on request.

Programs of Study: Marywood confers B.A., B.S., B.B.A., B.F.A., B.M., B.S.N., and B.S.W. degrees. Associate, master's, and doctoral degrees are also awarded. Bachelor's degrees are awarded in BIOLOGICAL SCIENCE (biology/biological science and biotechnology), BUSINESS (accounting, banking and finance, business administration and management, hospitality management services, international business management, and marketing/retailing/merchandising), COMMUNICA-

TIONS AND THE ARTS (advertising, arts administration/management, communications, design, dramatic arts, English, French, music, music performance, performing arts, Spanish, studio art, and telecommunications), COMPUTER AND PHYSICAL SCIENCE (information sciences and systems and mathematics), EDUCATION (art, athletic training, early childhood, elementary, home economics, music, physical, science, secondary, and special), ENGINEERING AND ENVIRONMENTAL DESIGN (aviation administration/management and environmental science), HEALTH PROFESSIONS (art therapy, health care administration, health science, medical laboratory technology, music therapy, nursing, physician's assistant, and speech pathology/audiology), SOCIAL SCIENCE (clinical psychology, criminal justice, dietetics, history, industrial and organizational psychology, paralegal studies, psychology, religion, religious music, social science, social work, and sociology). Psychology, nutrition and dietetics, and education are the strongest academically. Education, business, and visual and performing arts are the largest.

Required: To graduate, students must complete a liberal arts requirement consisting of religious studies, philosophy, math, science, psychology, history, social science, world literature, foreign language, and fine arts. Additional course requirements include speech, writing, and phys ed. Students must have a GPA of 2.0, with 2.5 in the major. A minimum of 126 credits must be earned, with the number of credits required in the major varying.

Special: Marywood offers cross-registration with the University of Scranton, internships, study abroad, accelerated degree programs in dietetics and social work, dual majors, and student-designed majors. A semester at a fashion institute, student teaching abroad, credit for life, military, and work experience, off-campus degree programs, and nondegree study are also offered. There are 23 national honor societies, a freshman honors program, and 18 departmental honors programs.

Faculty/Classroom: 47% of faculty are male; 53%, female. 72% teach undergraduates, 100% do research, and 72% do both. No introductory courses are taught by graduate students. The average class size in an introductory lecture is 17; in a laboratory, 14; and in a regular course, 16.

Admissions: 76% of the 2003-2004 applicants were accepted. The SAT I scores for the 2003-2004 freshman class were: Verbal--41% below 500, 46% between 500 and 599, 12% between 600 and 700, and 1% above 700; Math--52% below 500, 37% between 500 and 599, 10% between 600 and 700, and 1% above 700. The ACT scores were 59% below 21, 18% between 21 and 23, 14% between 24 and 26, and 9% above 28. 38% of the current freshmen were in the top fifth of their class; 66% were in the top two fifths.

Requirements: The SAT I is required and the ACT is recommended. In addition, applicants are expected to be graduates of an accredited secondary school or have the GED. A minimum of 16 academic credits is required, including 4 in English, 3 each in social studies and science (1 as lab), and 2 in math. A letter of support is required in selected majors, as is a portfolio or an audition where appropriate. A personal interview is strongly recommended. A GPA of 2.5 is required. AP and CLEP credits are accepted.

Procedure: Freshmen are admitted to all sessions. Entrance exams should be taken in the junior year or the senior year before February 1. There are early decision, early admissions, rolling admissions, and deferred admissions plans. Application deadlines are open. The fall 2003 application fee was $25. Applications are accepted on computer disk and on-line through *www.marywood.edu/ug-cat/admissions.*

Transfer: 135 transfer students enrolled in 2002-2003. SAT I or ACT scores are required of transfer applicants who have earned fewer than 12 college credits; both secondary school and college transcripts are required. Transfer students are required to have earned a minimum GPA of 2.5 at the college most recently attended. A grade of C is the minimum requirement for transfer of academic credit. 60 of 126 credits required for the bachelor's degree must be completed at Marywood.

Visiting: There are regularly scheduled orientations for prospective students, including a campus tour, individual visits with admissions counselors, an appointment with an academic adviser, and a financial aid appointment. A full summer orientation program for first-year students is available. There are guides for informal visits and visitors may sit in on classes and stay overnight. To schedule a visit, contact the Office of Undergraduate Admissions at *ugadm@ac.marywood.edu.*

Financial Aid: In 2003-2004, 96% of all full-time freshmen and 94% of continuing full-time students received some form of financial aid. 94% of full-time freshmen received need-based aid. The average freshman award was $14,150. 20% of undergraduates work part time. Average annual earnings from campus work are $1800. Marywood is a member of CSS. The FAFSA and the college's own financial statement are required. The deadline for filing freshman financial aid applications for fall entry is February 15.

International Students: There are 33 international students enrolled. The school actively recruits these students. They must score 500 on the written TOEFL or 173 on the electronic version and also take the SAT I or ACT if available.

Computers: The mainframes are a DEC VAX cluster with a DEC 5000 for the on-line library, a DEC MicroVAX 3100-90 for the academic network, and a DEC VAX 4000-100 for research. Computer facilities include an art lab, a psychology lab, 2 access labs with Macs, a science lab with interactive video, a CAD lab, and a PC-equipped communication arts lab. 322 PCs are available for student use in class labs, drop-in facilities, and dorms. All labs are networked and can access the Internet. E-mail is web-based via P4 Linux servers. All students may access the system 24 hours per day. There are no time limits and no fees. It is strongly recommended that all students have a personal computer.

Graduates: From July 1, 2002 to June 30, 2003, 318 bachelor's degrees were awarded. The most popular majors were art (14%), education (14%), and business (13%). In an average class, 41% graduate in 4 years or less, 63% graduate in 5 years or less, and 64% graduate in 6 years or less. 84 companies recruited on campus in 2002-2003. Of the 2002 graduating class, 31% were enrolled in graduate school within 6 months of graduation and 94% were employed.

Admissions Contact: Robert W. Reese, Director of Undergraduate Admissions. A video is available. E-mail: *ugadm@ac.marywood.edu* Web: *www.marywood.edu*

MCP HAHNEMANN UNIVERSITY   F-3
Philadelphia, PA 19102   (215) 762-1616
(800) 2-DREXEL; Fax: (215) 762-6194

Full-time: 150 men, 255 women	**Faculty:** n/av
Part-time: 80 men, 195 women	**Ph.D.s:** 65%
Graduate: 250 men, 685 women	**Student/Faculty:** n/av
Year: semesters, summer session	**Tuition:** $10,410
Application Deadline: see profile	**Room & Board:** $8100
Freshman Class: n/av	
SAT I or ACT: required	**SPECIAL**

MCP Hahnemann University is a private institution offering degree programs in nursing and the health professions. Figures in the above capsule and in this profile are approximate. In addition to regional accreditation, MCPHU has baccalaureate program accreditation with APTA, CAHEA, and NLN. The 3 libraries contain 78,103 volumes and 1272 audio/video tapes/CDs, and subscribe to 3976 periodicals. Computerized library services include the card catalog, interlibrary loans, and database searching. Special learning facilities include a learning resource center and medical archives. The campus is in an urban area in Philadelphia. Including any residence halls, there are 12 buildings.

Student Life: 67% are white; 19% African American. The average age of freshmen is 21; all undergraduates, 30.

Housing: 270 students can be accommodated in college housing, which includes coed on-campus apartments and married-student housing. On-campus housing is available on a first-come, first-served basis. 88% of students commute. All students may keep cars.

Activities: There are no fraternities or sororities. There are 20 groups on campus, including ethnic, gay, minority student, professional, religious, social service, student government, and yearbook. Popular campus events include Substance Abuse Week, Hospital Bed Race, and Halloween Party.

Sports: Facilities include a games area and a fitness center with exercise equipment.

Disabled Students: All of the campus is accessible. Wheelchair ramps, elevators, specially equipped rest rooms, lowered drinking fountains, and lowered telephones are available.

Services: Counseling and information services are available, as is tutoring in most subjects. There is remedial math, reading, and writing.

Campus Safety and Security: Measures include 24-hour foot and vehicle patrol, security escort services, shuttle buses, and informal discussions. There are pamphlets/posters/films, emergency telephones, and lighted pathways/sidewalks.

Programs of Study: MCPHU confers B.A., B.S., and B.S.N. degrees. Associate, master's, and doctoral degrees are also awarded. Bachelor's degrees are awarded in HEALTH PROFESSIONS (biomedical science, clinical science, emergency medical technologies, health science, mental health/human services, nursing, and physician's assistant), SOCIAL SCIENCE (humanities and social science). Physician's assistant and nursing are the strongest academically and have the largest enrollments.

Required: Bachelor's candidates must complete at least 120 credit hours, with a minimum GPA of 2.0. Distribution requirements include 12 credits of social science, 6 each of English, humanities, and natural science, and 3 each of computer science and math or statistics.

Special: Clinical rotation internships are required in many majors. There is an accelerated degree program in nursing.

Faculty/Classroom: 37% of faculty are male; 63%, female. No introductory courses are taught by graduate students. The average class size in an introductory lecture is 21; in a laboratory, 13; and in a regular course, 21.

Requirements: The SAT I or ACT is required. The SAT I or the ACT is required for some programs and is waived for applicants who have advanced college standing or have been out of high school for 5 or more years. Graduation from an accredited high school is required; the GED is accepted. AP credits are accepted.

Procedure: Freshmen are admitted in the fall. There is a deferred admissions plan and a rolling admissions plan. Check with the school for current deadlines. Application fee is $25. Notification is sent on a rolling basis.

Transfer: 236 transfer students enrolled in a recent year. Applicants who have been out of high school for 5 or more years or who have 30 or more college credits (grade C or better) need not submit SAT I or ACT scores. College transcripts and an average GPA of 2.5 in previous college courses are required. 60 of 120 credits required for the bachelor's degree must be completed at MCPHU.

Visiting: There are regularly scheduled orientations for prospective students, consisting of presentations and tours. There are guides for informal visits. To schedule a visit, contact the Admissions Office.

Financial Aid: In a recent year, the average freshman award was $8296. The average financial indebtedness of a recent graduate was $36,797. The FAFSA is required. Check with the school for current deadlines.

International Students: They must score 500 on the written TOEFL.

Computers: There are 130 PCs for student use throughout the library system. All students have access to the Internet and the World Wide Web and to specific databases without charge. All students may access the system. There are no time limits and no fees.

Graduates: In a recent year, 155 bachelor's degrees were awarded. The most popular majors were health professions (93%) and liberal arts/general studies (7%).

Admissions Contact: Jarmila Force, Assoc Dir of Enrollment Management. E-mail: *enroll@mcphu.edu* Web: *www.mcphu.edu*

MERCYHURST COLLEGE
Erie, PA 16546

B-1
(814) 824-2241
(800) 825-1926; Fax: (814) 824-2071

Full-time: 1055 men, 1720 women	**Faculty:** 130; IIB, --$
Part-time: 175 men, 260 women	**Ph.D.s:** 60%
Graduate: 65 men, 105 women	**Student/Faculty:** 21 to 1
Year: semesters, summer session	**Tuition:** $16,980
Application Deadline: open	**Room & Board:** $6414
Freshman Class: n/av	
SAT I or ACT: required	**COMPETITIVE**

Mercyhurst College, established in 1926, is a private, nonprofit institution affiliated with the Roman Catholic Church. The college offers undergraduate degrees in the arts, business, health science, liberal arts, religious studies, and teacher preparation as well as a degree-directed program for the learning disabled. Figures in the above capsule and in this profile are approximate. In addition to regional accreditation, Mercyhurst has baccalaureate program accreditation with ADA and CSWE. The library contains 165,644 volumes, 50,631 microform items, and 9309 audio/video tapes/CDs, and subscribes to 848 periodicals. Computerized library services include the card catalog, interlibrary loans, and database searching. Special learning facilities include a learning resource center, art gallery, planetarium, radio station, TV station, northwestern Pennsylvania historical archives, and archeological institute. The 88-acre campus is in a suburban area within Erie. Including any residence halls, there are 44 buildings.

Student Life: 63% of undergraduates are from Pennsylvania. Students are from 37 states, 14 foreign countries, and Canada. 76% are from public schools. 91% are white. 53% are Catholic; 21% Protestant; 18% claim no religious affiliation; 7% Hindu, Sikh, Islamic, and Buddhist. The average age of freshmen is 18; all undergraduates, 26. 20% do not continue beyond their first year; 62% remain to graduate.

Housing: 1718 students can be accommodated in college housing, which includes single-sex and coed dorms, on-campus apartments, and married-student housing. On-campus housing is guaranteed for all 4 years. 61% of students live on campus; of those, 91% remain on campus on weekends. Upperclassmen may keep cars.

Activities: There are no fraternities or sororities. There are 49 groups on campus, including art, band, cheerleading, choir, chorus, computers, dance, debate, drama, ethnic, film, gay, honors, international, jazz band, literary magazine, musical theater, newspaper, opera, orchestra, pep band, photography, political, professional, radio and TV, religious, social, social service, student government, and yearbook. Popular campus events include Activities Day, Parents Weekend, and winter and spring formals.

Sports: There are 13 intercollegiate sports for men and 12 for women, and 9 intramural sports for men and 9 for women. Facilities include a pool, indoor crew tanks, football, field hockey, lacrosse, and soccer fields, an ice hockey rink/arena, Nautilus facilities, a free-weight room, a baseball/softball complex, a training room, and a basketball arena.

Disabled Students: 90% of the campus is accessible. Wheelchair ramps, elevators, special parking, specially equipped rest rooms, and lowered drinking fountains are available.

Services: Counseling and information services are available, as is tutoring in every subject. There is remedial math, reading, and writing.

Campus Safety and Security: Measures include 24-hour foot and vehicle patrol, self-defense education, shuttle buses, and informal discussions. There are pamphlets/posters/films, emergency telephones, lighted pathways/sidewalks, and a 24-hour security camera surveillance system.

Programs of Study: Mercyhurst confers B.A., B.S., and B.M. degrees. Associate and master's degrees are also awarded. Bachelor's degrees are awarded in BIOLOGICAL SCIENCE (biochemistry and biology/biological science), BUSINESS (accounting, banking and finance, business administration and management, fashion merchandising, hotel/motel and restaurant management, insurance and risk management, management information systems, and marketing/retailing/merchandising), COMMUNICATIONS AND THE ARTS (advertising, broadcasting, communications, dance, English, graphic design, journalism, languages, music, musical theater, public relations, and studio art), COMPUTER AND PHYSICAL SCIENCE (chemistry, earth science, geology, mathematics, web services, and web technology), EDUCATION (art, athletic training, business, early childhood, elementary, home economics, mathematics, music, science, secondary, social science, and special), ENGINEERING AND ENVIRONMENTAL DESIGN (environmental science and interior design), HEALTH PROFESSIONS (art therapy, medical laboratory technology, predentistry, premedicine, preosteopathy, prepharmacy, preveterinary science, and sports medicine), SOCIAL SCIENCE (anthropology, archeology, criminal justice, dietetics, family/consumer studies, forensic studies, history, philosophy, political science/government, prelaw, psychology, religion, religious education, social work, and sociology). Archeology/anthropology, research intelligence, and sports medicine are the strongest academically. Business, education, and sports medicine are the largest.

Required: To graduate, students must complete the core curriculum, which includes English, math, science, religion, philosophy, history, and a computer course. Distribution requirements include American history, cultural appreciation, human behavior, and ethics. A minimum GPA of 2.0 is required, with a 2.5 in the major, and a minimum total of 123 credit hours. The number of credit hours in the major varies, with a minimum of 30. A thesis is necessary for history and English majors.

Special: Mercyhurst offers cross-registration with Gannon University, internships in all majors through the co-op office, and study abroad in London and Dublin. Dual and student-designed majors, credit for life, military, or work experience, nondegree study, work-study, and a pass/fail grading option are also available. There are 7 national honor societies, a freshman honors program, and 4 departmental honors programs.

Faculty/Classroom: 57% of faculty are male; 43%, female. All teach undergraduates and 30% do research. No introductory courses are taught by graduate students. The average class size in an introductory lecture is 35; in a laboratory, 12; and in a regular course, 25.

Admissions: In a recent year, 17 freshmen graduated first in their class.

Requirements: The SAT I or ACT is required, with recommended minimum scores of 450 verbal and 450 math on the SAT I or 19 on the ACT. Applicants must graduate from an accredited secondary school or have a GED. 16 academic credits are required, including 4 years of English, 3 each of math and social studies, and 2 each of history, science, and a foreign language. Interviews are recommended. Art applicants must submit portfolios; auditions are required of music and dance applicants. Mercyhurst requires applicants to be in the upper 50% of their class. A GPA of 2.75 is required. AP and CLEP credits are accepted. Important factors in the admissions decision are leadership record, evidence of special talent, and personality/intangible qualities.

Procedure: Freshmen are admitted to all sessions. Entrance exams should be taken during the spring of the junior year. There are early admissions, deferred admissions, and rolling admissions plans. Application deadlines are open. Application fee is $30. Applications are accepted on-line at the school's web site.

Transfer: 64 transfer students enrolled in a recent year. A minimum GPA of 2.0 on previous college work is required. 45 of 123 credits required for the bachelor's degree must be completed at Mercyhurst.

Visiting: There are regularly scheduled orientations for prospective students, including tours, class visits, faculty meetings, and interviews with financial aid and admissions counselors. There are guides for informal visits and visitors may sit in on classes and stay overnight. To schedule a visit, contact the Admissions Office at *admug@mercyhurst.edu*.

Financial Aid: In a recent year, 93% of all full-time freshmen and 85% of continuing full-time students received some form of financial aid. 86% of full-time freshmen and 74% of continuing full-time students received need-based aid. The average freshman award was $6952. 88% of undergraduates work part time. Average annual earnings from campus work are $825. The average financial indebtedness of a recent graduate was $7800. Mercyhurst is a member of CSS. The FAFSA is required. Check with the school for current deadlines.

International Students: In a recent year, there were 91 international students enrolled. The school actively recruits these students. They must score 550 on the written TOEFL and also take the SAT I or the ACT.

Computers: The mainframe is a UNIX with a DEC Alpha 1200 server running Unitdata DBMS. Students may access more than 225 terminals in labs across campus. All residences are networked to the mainframe, the Internet, and intranets. Faculty computers and the library's electronic search system are available for research. All students may access the system 24 hours a day, 7 days a week. There are no time limits. The fee is $210 per year.

Graduates: In a recent year, 510 bachelor's degrees were awarded. The most popular majors were business (11%), education (10%), and hotel/restaurant management (8%). In an average class, 1% graduate in 3 years or less, 50% graduate in 4 years or less, 58% graduate in 5 years or less, and 62% graduate in 6 years or less. 199 companies recruited on campus in a recent year. Of a recent graduating class, 16% were enrolled in graduate school within 6 months of graduation and 77% were employed.

Admissions Contact: Robin Engel, Director of Admissions. A video is available. E-mail: *rengel@mercyhurst.edu* Web: *www.mercyhurst.edu*

MESSIAH COLLEGE
Grantham, PA 17027

D-3

(717) 691-6000
(800) 233-4220; Fax: (717) 796-5374

Full-time: 1085 men, 1809 women	**Faculty:** 166; IIB, av$
Part-time: 20 men, 38 women	**Ph.D.s:** 74%
Graduate: none	**Student/Faculty:** 17 to 1
Year: semesters, summer session	**Tuition:** $19,550
Application Deadline: open	**Room & Board:** $6340
Freshman Class: 2252 applied, 1790 accepted, 736 enrolled	
SAT I Verbal/Math: 600/590	**ACT:** 26 **VERY COMPETITIVE+**

Messiah College, founded in 1909, is a private Christian college offering an education in the liberal and applied arts and sciences, and spiritually routed in the Anabaptist, Pietist, and Wesleyan traditions. There are 5 undergraduate schools. In addition to regional accreditation, Messiah has baccalaureate program accreditation with ABET, ADA, CSWE, NASM, CAAHEP, and CCNE. The library contains 265,663 volumes, 120,491 microform items, and 15,585 audio/video tapes/CDs, and subscribes to 1435 periodicals. Computerized library services include the card catalog, interlibrary loans, database searching, and Internet access. Special learning facilities include a learning resource center, art gallery, natural history museum, and radio station. The 400-acre campus is in a small town 12 miles southwest of Harrisburg. Including any residence halls, there are 51 buildings.

Student Life: 51% of undergraduates are from Pennsylvania. Others are from 40 states, 35 foreign countries, and Canada. 80% are from public schools. 90% are white. Most are Protestant. The average age of freshmen is 18; all undergraduates, 20. 14% do not continue beyond their first year; 71% remain to graduate.

Housing: 2389 students can be accommodated in college housing, which includes single-sex and coed dorms, on-campus apartments, off-campus apartments, and special-interest houses. On-campus housing is guaranteed for all 4 years. 89% of students live on campus; of those, 65% remain on campus on weekends. Alcohol is not permitted. All students may keep cars.

Activities: There are no fraternities or sororities. There are 60 groups on campus, including art, band, cheerleading, choir, chorale, chorus, dance, drama, ethnic, film, honors, international, jazz band, literary magazine, musical theater, newspaper, orchestra, pep band, political, professional, radio and TV, religious, social, social service, student government, symphony, and yearbook. Popular campus events include Cultural Series, Susquehanna Valley Lyceum, and Theatre Messiah.

Sports: There are 10 intercollegiate sports for men and 10 for women, and 8 intramural sports for men and 9 for women. Facilities include indoor and outdoor tracks, a pool with separate diving well, wrestling and gymnastics areas, a weight room, numerous playing fields, and courts for racquetball, basketball, and tennis. The campus center provides additional recreational facilities.

Disabled Students: 85% of the campus is accessible. Wheelchair ramps, elevators, special parking, specially equipped rest rooms, special class scheduling, and lowered drinking fountains are available.

Services: Counseling and information services are available, as is tutoring in some subjects. There is a reader service for the blind and remedial reading and writing.

Campus Safety and Security: Measures include 24-hour foot and vehicle patrol, self-defense education, security escort services, and informal discussions. There are pamphlets/posters/films, emergency telephones, and lighted pathways/sidewalks.

Programs of Study: Messiah confers B.A., B.S., B.S.E., and B.S.N. degrees. Bachelor's degrees are awarded in BIOLOGICAL SCIENCE (biochemistry and biology/biological science), BUSINESS (accounting, business administration and management, business economics, business systems analysis, electronic business, entrepreneurial studies, international business management, marketing/retailing/merchandising, and personnel management), COMMUNICATIONS AND THE ARTS (art history and appreciation, broadcasting, communications, dramatic arts, English, French, German, journalism, music, Spanish, and studio art), COMPUTER AND PHYSICAL SCIENCE (chemistry, computer science, mathematics, and physics), EDUCATION (art, athletic training, early

childhood, elementary, English, environmental, foreign languages, mathematics, music, physical, science, and social studies), ENGINEERING AND ENVIRONMENTAL DESIGN (engineering and environmental science), HEALTH PROFESSIONS (exercise science, nursing, and recreation therapy), SOCIAL SCIENCE (biblical studies, dietetics, economics, history, human development, humanities, ministries, philosophy, political science/government, psychology, religion, social work, and sociology). Elementary education, nursing, and psychology are the largest.

Required: All students must complete at least 126 credits with a minimum GPA of 2.0. The last 30 credits must be taken at Messiah College and a minimum of 12 credits must be in the major. For general education requirements, students must take 9 credits each in Christian faith, math, natural sciences, humanities and arts, and languages and cultures; 6 credits each in social sciences and history and in interdisciplinary studies; 3 credits in first-year seminar, oral communications, a writing enrichment course, ethics, world views/pluralism, and health/phys ed; and 2 to 3 credits in non-Western studies.

Special: Students may cross-register at Temple University in Philadephia. Off-campus study is available at Daystar University in Kenya, through Brethren Colleges Abroad, at Jerusalem University College at Oxford University, in Thailand, and through Latin American, Central American, Middle East, and Russian studies programs, among others. Off-campus options within the United States include the American Studies program, the AuSable Institute of Environmental Studies, Los Angeles Film Studies, Oregon Extension, and others. Students may also spend a semester or year at any of 12 other Christian Consortium colleges in a student exchange program. Numerous internships, practicums, and ministry opportunities are available. There are 2 national honor societies, including Phi Beta Kappa, a freshman honors program, and 16 departmental honors programs.

Faculty/Classroom: 66% of faculty are male; 34%, female. All teach undergraduates. The average class size in an introductory lecture is 27; in a laboratory, 18; and in a regular course, 24.

Admissions: 79% of the 2003-2004 applicants were accepted. The SAT I scores for the 2003-2004 freshman class were: Verbal--7% below 500, 41% between 500 and 599, 42% between 600 and 700, and 11% above 700; Math--7% below 500, 45% between 500 and 599, 38% between 600 and 700, and 11% above 700. The ACT scores were 4% below 21, 23% between 21 and 23, 27% between 24 and 26, 15% between 27 and 28, and 31% above 28. 67% of the current freshmen were in the top fifth of their class; 89% were in the top two fifths. There were 13 National Merit finalists. 42 freshmen graduated first in their class.

Requirements: Messiah requires the SAT I or ACT exam for most students. Applicants graduating in the top 20% of their class have a scoreless option that requires an interview. Applicants must have graduated from an accredited high school or the equivalent. Secondary preparation of students who enroll usually includes 4 units in English, 3 or 4 in math, 3 each in natural science, social studies, and foreign languages, and 4 in academic electives. Students who enroll are usually in the top one third of their class and have a B average or better. A campus visit with an interview/information session is recommended. Potential music majors must audition. AP and CLEP credits are accepted. Important factors in the admissions decision are leadership record, recommendations by school officials, and advanced placement or honor courses.

Procedure: Freshmen are admitted fall and spring. Entrance exams should be taken in the spring of the junior year. There is a rolling admissions plan. There are early decision, early admissions, and deferred admissions plans. Early decision applications should be filed by October 15; regular applications are open for fall and spring entry. There is a $30 application fee. Notification of early decision is sent November 1; regular decision, on a rolling basis. 71 early decision candidates were accepted for the 2003-2004 class. 30 applicants were on the 2003 waiting list. Applications are accepted on-line through Messiah's web page.

Transfer: 105 transfer students enrolled in 2002-2003. Transfer applicants should have earned a 2.5 GPA in at least 30 college credits. The college prefers that applicants also have composite SAT I or ACT scores and that they seek a campus visit. Students with fewer than 30 credits in college should submit a high school transcript as well. 30 of 126 credits required for the bachelor's degree must be completed at Messiah.

Visiting: There are regularly scheduled orientations for prospective students, including a campus tour, academic and career advising, and a financial aid information session. There are guides for informal visits and visitors may sit in on classes and stay overnight. To schedule a visit, contact Nikki Holsinger at *nholsing@messiah.edu*.

Financial Aid: In 2003-2004, 97% of all full-time freshmen and 96% of continuing full-time students received some form of financial aid. 77% of full-time freshmen and 78% of continuing full-time students received need-based aid. The average freshman award was $14,789. Need-based scholarships or need-based grants averaged $4879; need-based self-help aid (loans and jobs) averaged $5885; and non-need-based awards and non-need-based scholarships averaged $5906. 55% of undergraduates work part time. Average annual earnings from campus work are $1783. The average financial indebtedness of the 2003 graduate was $23,249. Messiah is a member of CSS. The FAFSA is required. The priority date for freshman financial aid applications for fall entry is April 1.

International Students: There are 75 international students enrolled. The school actively recruits these students. They must take the TOEFL and also take the SAT I or the ACT.

Computers: The mainframe is an HP3000 model 959/KS200. There are 513 computers for student use located in the computer center, the library, departmental and student center labs, and residence halls. Dorm rooms are wired for network connection for PCs. E-mail and Internet access are available. All students may access the system 24 hours a day. There are no time limits and no fees.

Graduates: From July 1, 2002 to June 30, 2003, 606 bachelor's degrees were awarded. The most popular majors were elementary education (9%), human development and family science (6%), and psychology (5%). In an average class, 1% graduate in 3 years or less, 69% graduate in 4 years or less, 77% graduate in 5 years or less, and 71% graduate in 6 years or less. 812 companies recruited on campus in 2002-2003. Of the 2002 graduating class, 11% were enrolled in graduate school within 6 months of graduation and 86% were employed.

Admissions Contact: William G. Strausbaugh, Dean for Enrollment Management. A video is available. E-mail: *admiss@messiah.edu* Web: *www.messiah.edu*

MILLERSVILLE UNIVERSITY OF PENNSYLVANIA   E-4
Millersville, PA 17551-0302   (717) 872-3371
(800) MU-ADMIT; Fax: (717) 871-2147

Full-time: 2667 men, 3476 women	**Faculty:** 317; IIA, +$
Part-time: 308 men, 369 women	**Ph.Ds:** 90%
Graduate: 294 men, 747 women	**Student/Faculty:** 19 to 1
Year: 4-1-4, summer session	**Tuition:** $5819 ($12,767)
Application Deadline: open	**Room & Board:** $5450
Freshman Class: 6217 applied, 3786 accepted, 1353 enrolled	
SAT I Verbal/Math: 530/540	**ACT:** 21 COMPETITIVE

Millersville University, founded as Lancaster County Normal School in 1855, is a public institution offering undergraduate and graduate programs in liberal arts and sciences and education. There are 3 undergraduate schools and 1 graduate school. In addition to regional accreditation, Millersville has baccalaureate program accreditation with ABET, ACBSP, ACS, CAAHEP, CAHEA, CSAB, CSWE, NAIT, NASM, NASP, NCATE, and NLN. The library contains 500,614 volumes, 579,902 microform items, and 30,935 audio/video tapes/CDs, and subscribes to 8145 periodicals. Computerized library services include the card catalog, interlibrary loans, and database searching. Special learning facilities include a learning resource center, art gallery, radio station, TV station, an early childhood center, and foreign language lab. The 220-acre campus is in a small town 5 miles west of Lancaster. Including any residence halls, there are 92 buildings.

Student Life: 96% of undergraduates are from Pennsylvania. Students are from 23 states, 52 foreign countries, and Canada. 86% are white. The average age of freshmen is 18; all undergraduates, 22. 17% do not continue beyond their first year; 67% remain to graduate.

Housing: 2515 students can be accommodated in college housing, which includes single-sex and coed dorms, on-campus apartments, and off-campus apartments. In addition, there are honors houses and special-interest houses, including service learning/leadership and international student house. On-campus housing is available on a first-come, first-served basis and is available on a lottery system for upperclassmen. 62% of students commute. Alcohol is not permitted. Upperclassmen may keep cars.

Activities: 4% of men belong to 1 local fraternity and 6 national fraternities; 6% of women belong to 2 local and 6 national sororities. There are 109 groups on campus, including art, band, cheerleading, choir, chorale, chorus, dance, drama, ethnic, gay, honors, international, jazz band, literary magazine, marching band, musical theater, newspaper, orchestra, pep band, political, professional, radio and TV, religious, social, social service, student government, symphony, and yearbook. Popular campus events include Parents Day, Wellness Week, and International Week.

Sports: There are 9 intercollegiate sports for men and 10 for women, and 13 intramural sports for men and 13 for women. Facilities include a football stadium, 2 pools, 2 gyms, 2 fitness centers, a dance studio, a ropes course, wrestling and weight rooms, basketball, volleyball, tennis, and badminton courts, and various playing fields.

Disabled Students: 85% of the campus is accessible. Wheelchair ramps, elevators, special parking, specially equipped rest rooms, special class scheduling, lowered drinking fountains, lowered telephones, special housing, and transportation assistance within campus are available.

Services: Counseling and information services are available, as is tutoring in most subjects. There is a reader service for the blind and remedial math, reading, and writing. Every effort is made to tailor a tutoring program to individual needs. Note takers, interpreters, and some physical aids and other specialized equipment are provided, as available.

Campus Safety and Security: Measures include 24-hour foot and vehicle patrol, self-defense education, security escort services, and shuttle buses. There are informal discussions, pamphlets/posters/films, emergen-

cy telephones, lighted pathways/sidewalks, and regularly scheduled crime awareness programs.

Programs of Study: Millersville confers B.A., B.S., B.F.A., B.S.Ed., and B.S.N. degrees. Associate and master's degrees are also awarded. Bachelor's degrees are awarded in BIOLOGICAL SCIENCE (biology/biological science), BUSINESS (business administration and management), COMMUNICATIONS AND THE ARTS (art, communications, English, French, German, music, and Spanish), COMPUTER AND PHYSICAL SCIENCE (atmospheric sciences and meteorology, chemistry, computer science, earth science, geology, oceanography, and physics), EDUCATION (art, elementary, music, social studies, special, and technical), ENGINEERING AND ENVIRONMENTAL DESIGN (industrial engineering technology, and occupational safety and health), HEALTH PROFESSIONS (nursing), SOCIAL SCIENCE (anthropology, economics, geography, history, international studies, philosophy, political science/government, psychology, social work, and sociology). Physical sciences and teacher education are the strongest academically. Elementary education, business administration, and biology are the largest.

Required: All students must complete at least 120 hours, including 30 in the major, with a minimum 2.0 GPA. Courses are required in humanities, science and math, social sciences, and perspectives as part of a core curriculum. Specific courses are required in writing, speech, wellness, and phys ed.

Special: Numerous co-op and internship programs, including student teaching opportunities, are available. Millersville has exchange agreements with Franklin and Marshall College, Lancaster Theological Seminary, and Wallops Island Consortium, and 3-2 engineering programs with Pennsylvania State University and the University of Pennsylvania for chemistry and physics majors. Study abroad is offered in Germany, England, Japan, Scotland, Chile, and Spain. Dual majors are possible in most disciplines, and accelerated degrees and B.A.-B.S. degrees are available in many. Nondegree study is offered, and there are limited pass/fail options. There are 6 national honor societies, a freshman honors program, and 11 departmental honors programs.

Faculty/Classroom: 57% of faculty are male; 43%, female. 96% teach undergraduates. No introductory courses are taught by graduate students. The average class size in an introductory lecture is 35; in a laboratory, 24; and in a regular course, 25.

Admissions: 61% of the 2003-2004 applicants were accepted. The SAT I scores for the 2003-2004 freshman class were: Verbal--27% below 500, 54% between 500 and 599, 17% between 600 and 700, and 2% above 700; Math--26% below 500, 53% between 500 and 599, 20% between 600 and 700, and 2% above 700. 35% of the current freshmen were in the top fifth of their class; 73% were in the top two fifths. 5 freshmen graduated first in their class.

Requirements: The SAT I is required, and the ACT is accepted, with minimum composite scores of 1020–1040 or 23, respectively. Applicants must be graduates of approved secondary schools or hold a GED. Secondary preparation should include 4 credits in English, 3 credits each in math and social studies, and 2 credits each in science and history. Music program applicants must audition. An interview is optional for all applicants. Millersville requires applicants to be in the upper 40% of their class. A GPA of 2.0 is required. AP and CLEP credits are accepted. Important factors in the admissions decision are advanced placement or honor courses, evidence of special talent, and recommendations by school officials.

Procedure: Freshmen are admitted to all sessions. Entrance exams should be taken in the spring of the junior year. There is a deferred admissions plan and a rolling admissions plan. Application deadlines are open. The fall 2003 application fee was $35. Applications are accepted on-line through CollegeNET and *www.admissions@millersville.edu*.

Transfer: 377 transfer students enrolled in 2002-2003. All applicants must submit high school as well as college transcripts. Graduates of state community colleges are given preference over applicants with fewer than 2 and more than 5 semesters of study at other colleges. Applicants must have at least a 2.0 GPA. A personal interview is recommended. 30 of 120 credits required for the bachelor's degree must be completed at Millersville.

Visiting: There are regularly scheduled orientations for prospective students, including a president's welcome and admissions, financial aid, student organization, and department conferences. There are guides for informal visits and visitors may sit in on classes. To schedule a visit, contact the Campus Visit Coordinator at the Admissions Office at (717) 872-3371 or *www.admissions@millersville.edu*.

Financial Aid: In 2002-2003, 80% of all full-time freshmen and 76% of continuing full-time students received some form of financial aid. 51% of full-time freshmen and 46% of continuing full-time students received need-based aid. The average freshman award was $6074. Need-based scholarships or need-based grants averaged $2695 ($18,252 maximum); need-based self-help aid (loans and jobs) averaged $2429 ($14,761 maximum); non-need-based athletic scholarships averaged $1776; and other non-need-based awards and non-need-based scholarships averaged $950 ($16,490 maximum). 31% of undergraduates work part time. Average annual earnings from campus work are $1108. The average financial indebtedness of the 2003 graduate was $12,631. Millersville is a member of CSS. The FAFSA is required. The deadline for filing freshman financial aid applications for fall entry is March 15.

International Students: There are 126 international students enrolled. The school actively recruits these students. They must score 500 on the written TOEFL or 183 on the electronic version and also take the SAT I or the ACT, scoring 1050.

Computers: The mainframes are a Sun ES-3000, a Sun SPARC 20, an HP K250, and an HPK 420. Approved students are entitled to computer accounts to access the mainframes for e-mail, the Internet, and course work. There are 30 general-purpose computer labs on campus, housing IBM and Mac PCs and Sun workstations. Most PCs are local area networked and all labs are connected to a campuswide network and the Internet. All students may access the system 24 hours, 7 days a week. There are no time limits and no fees. It is strongly recommended that all students have a personal computer.

Graduates: From July 1, 2002 to June 30, 2003, 1213 bachelor's degrees were awarded. The most popular majors were elementary education (15%), business administration (12%), and psychology (9%). In an average class, 1% graduate in 3 years or less, 35% graduate in 4 years or less, 62% graduate in 5 years or less, and 67% graduate in 6 years or less. 75 companies recruited on campus in 2002-2003.

Admissions Contact: Douglas Zander, Director of Admissions.
E-mail: *admissions@millersville.edu* Web: *www.millersville.edu/~admit*

MOORE COLLEGE OF ART AND DESIGN F-3
Philadelphia, PA 19103 (215) 568-4515, ext. 1105
(800) 523-2025, ext. 1105; Fax: (215) 568-8017

Full-time: 479 women	**Faculty:** 34
Part-time: 146 women	**Ph.D.s:** 83%
Graduate: none	**Student/Faculty:** 14 to 1
Year: semesters, summer session	**Tuition:** $19,676
Application Deadline: open	**Room & Board:** $7420
Freshman Class: 250 applied, 194 accepted, 88 enrolled	
SAT I Verbal/Math: 530/490	**ACT:** 22 SPECIAL

Moore College of Art and Design, founded in 1844, is a private professional and fine arts college for women in the country. In addition to regional accreditation, Moore has baccalaureate program accreditation with FIDER and NASAD. The library contains 34,000 volumes, and subscribes to 250 periodicals. Computerized library services include the card catalog, interlibrary loans, database searching, and Internet access. Special learning facilities include 2 art galleries. The 4-acre campus is in an urban area in Philadelphia. Including any residence halls, there are 4 buildings.

Student Life: 61% of undergraduates are from Pennsylvania. Students are from 29 states and 7 foreign countries. 60% are from public schools. 77% are white. The average age of freshmen is 19; all undergraduates, 23. 15% do not continue beyond their first year; 55% remain to graduate.

Housing: 194 students can be accommodated in college housing, which includes single-sex dorms and off-campus apartments. On-campus housing is guaranteed for all 4 years. 70% of students commute. Alcohol is not permitted. All students may keep cars.

Activities: There are no fraternities. There are 10 groups on campus, including computers, environmental action, ethnic, film, gay, international, newspaper, professional, social service, student government, and yearbook. Popular campus events include Family Day, Spring Fling, and Convocation.

Sports: There is no sports program at Moore. Facilities include a fitness center with a weight room.

Disabled Students: All of the campus is accessible. Wheelchair ramps, elevators, special parking, specially equipped rest rooms, lowered drinking fountains, and lowered telephones are available.

Services: Counseling and information services are available, as is tutoring in most subjects. English as a second language is offered.

Campus Safety and Security: Measures include 24-hour foot and vehicle patrol, self-defense education, security escort services, and shuttle buses. There are informal discussions, pamphlets/posters/films, emergency telephones, and lighted pathways/sidewalks.

Programs of Study: Moore confers the B.F.A. degree. Bachelor's degrees are awarded in COMMUNICATIONS AND THE ARTS (fine arts, graphic design, illustration, painting, and sculpture), EDUCATION (art), ENGINEERING AND ENVIRONMENTAL DESIGN (interior design), SOCIAL SCIENCE (fashion design and technology and textiles and clothing). Interior design is the strongest academically. Graphic design is the largest.

Required: All students take 36 credits in basic arts, including design, drawing, color, and art history, and a liberal arts core in history, humanities, and social science. A total of 125.5 to 137 credits, with a 2.0 minimum GPA, is required for graduation. A thesis is required in some programs.

Special: Moore has long-established cooperative relationships with various employers who provide training to supplement academic studies in all majors. Dual majors, nondegree study, study abroad, and continuing education programs are offered.

Faculty/Classroom: 38% of faculty are male; 62%, female. All teach undergraduates. The average class size in an introductory lecture is 20 and in a regular course, 10.

Admissions: 78% of the 2003-2004 applicants were accepted. The SAT I scores for the 2003-2004 freshman class were: Verbal--39% below 500, 29% between 500 and 599, 25% between 600 and 700, and 59% above 700; Math--53% below 500, 25% between 500 and 599, 13% between 600 and 700, and 1% above 700.

Requirements: The SAT I is recommended. In addition, applicants should be graduates of accredited high schools or the equivalent, having taken 4 years of English and 2 years each of social studies, science, and math. At least 2 years of art study are also recommended. The most important part of the application is the portfolio of 8 to 12 original pieces, 6 of which should be drawings from observation. In addition, Moore strongly recommends a personal interview. A GPA of 2.5 is required. AP and CLEP credits are accepted. Important factors in the admissions decision are evidence of special talent, personality/intangible qualities, and extracurricular activities record.

Procedure: Freshmen are admitted fall and spring. There are early admissions, deferred admissions, and rolling admissions plans. Application deadlines are open. The fall 2003 application fee was $40.

Transfer: Transfer applicants from non-art programs must meet freshman admission requirements. Others must submit a portfolio for review. Applicants should have at least a 2.0 GPA in previous college work, and submit composite SAT I scores of at least 800. A personal interview is required. 50 of 126 credits required for the bachelor's degree must be completed at Moore.

Visiting: There are regularly scheduled orientations for prospective students, including an open house in November. There are guides for informal visits and visitors may sit in on classes and stay overnight. To schedule a visit, contact the Admissions Office.

Financial Aid: In 2003-2004, 100% of all full-time students received some form of financial aid. 85% of full-time freshmen and 83% of continuing full-time students received need-based aid. The average freshman award was $16,250, with $4400 ($9000 maximum) from need-based scholarships or need-based grants; $2500 ($5125 maximum) from need-based self-help aid (loans and jobs); $4100 ($8500 maximum) from non-need-based awards and non-need-based scholarships; and $5250 from non-need-based self-help loans and work-study. 30% of undergraduates work part time. Average annual earnings from campus work are $2000. The average financial indebtedness of the 2003 graduate was $25,000. Moore is a member of CSS. The CSS Profile and the college's own financial statement are required. The priority date for freshman financial aid applications for fall entry is March 1.

International Students: There are 8 international students enrolled. The school actively recruits these students. They must score 500 on the written TOEFL.

Computers: Macs are available in the computer graphics labs. The CAD lab is PC-based for Interior Design. There are no time limits and no fees.

Graduates: From July 1, 2002 to June 30, 2003, 104 bachelor's degrees were awarded. The most popular majors were graphic design (28%), fashion design (22%), and fine arts (20%). In an average class, 55% graduate in 4 years or less. Of the 2002 graduating class, 5% were enrolled in graduate school within 6 months of graduation and 80% were employed.

Admissions Contact: Wendy Pyle Elliott, Director of Admissions.
E-mail: *admiss@moore.edu* Web: *www.moore.edu*

MORAVIAN COLLEGE F-3
Bethlehem, PA 18018 (610) 861-1320
(800) 441-3191; Fax: (610) 625-7930

Full-time: 563 men, 965 women	**Faculty:** 114; IIB, +$
Part-time: 110 men, 207 women	**Ph.D.s:** 78%
Graduate: 48 men, 125 women	**Student/Faculty:** 13 to 1
Year: semesters, summer session	**Tuition:** $22,058
Application Deadline: March 1	**Room & Board:** $6845
Freshman Class: 1670 applied, 1143 accepted, 380 enrolled	
SAT I Verbal/Math: 558/566	**VERY COMPETITIVE**

Moravian College, established in 1742, is a private, liberal arts institution affiliated with the Moravian Church. There are 2 undergraduate schools and 1 graduate school. In addition to regional accreditation, Moravian has baccalaureate program accreditation with ACS, CAHEA, CCNE, and NASM. The library contains 257,650 volumes, 11,680 microform items, and 4800 audio/video tapes/CDs, and subscribes to 1185 periodicals. Computerized library services include the card catalog, interlibrary loans, database searching, and Internet access. Special learning facilities include a learning resource center, art gallery, and radio station. The 80-acre campus is in a suburban area 60 miles north of Philadelphia and 90 miles west of New York City. Including any residence halls, there are 127 buildings.

Student Life: 61% of undergraduates are from Pennsylvania. Students are from 22 states, 16 foreign countries, and Canada. 80% are from public schools. 92% are white. 41% are Catholic; 29% Protestant; 9% claim no religious affiliation. The average age of freshmen is 18; all undergraduates, 20. 14% do not continue beyond their first year; 74% remain to graduate.

Housing: 1047 students can be accommodated in college housing, which includes single-sex and coed dorms, on-campus apartments, fraternity houses, and sorority houses. In addition, there are special-interest houses. On-campus housing is guaranteed for all 4 years. 71% of students live on campus; of those, 65% remain on campus on weekends. Upperclassmen may keep cars.

Activities: 14% of men belong to 1 local and 2 national fraternities; 22% of women belong to 4 national sororities. There are 77 groups on campus, including alumni, art, band, cheerleading, choir, chorale, chorus, computers, dance, debate, drama, ethnic, gay, honors, international, jazz band, literary magazine, marching band, newspaper, orchestra, outdoor recreation, pep band, photography, political, professional, radio, religious, social, social service, student government, and yearbook. Popular campus events include arts and lecture series, Christmas vesper services, and Mardi Gras dance.

Sports: There are 10 intercollegiate sports for men and 10 for women, and 11 intramural sports for men and 11 for women. Facilities include a 1200-seat gym, football, soccer, field hockey, and lacrosse fields, baseball and softball diamonds, indoor and all-weather tracks, indoor and outdoor tennis courts, a field house, a fitness room, an aerobics and dance studio, and 4 multipurpose courts.

Disabled Students: Wheelchair ramps, elevators, special parking, specially equipped rest rooms, special class scheduling, lowered drinking fountains, lowered telephones, and special housing are available.

Services: Counseling and information services are available, as is tutoring in most subjects. There is a reader service for the blind, peer assistance, and a writing center.

Campus Safety and Security: Measures include 24-hour foot and vehicle patrol, self-defense education, security escort services, and shuttle buses. There are informal discussions, pamphlets/posters/films, emergency telephones, lighted pathways/sidewalks, and an ongoing crime prevention program supervised by a crime prevention officer.

Programs of Study: Moravian confers B.A., B.S., and B.Mus. degrees. Master's degrees are also awarded. Bachelor's degrees are awarded in BIOLOGICAL SCIENCE (biology/biological science), BUSINESS (accounting, business administration and management, business economics, and international business management), COMMUNICATIONS AND THE ARTS (art history and appreciation, classics, dramatic arts, English, French, German, graphic design, music, Spanish, and studio art), COMPUTER AND PHYSICAL SCIENCE (chemistry, computer science, mathematics, and physics), EDUCATION (art, elementary, music, and secondary), HEALTH PROFESSIONS (nursing), SOCIAL SCIENCE (counseling/psychology, criminal justice, developmental psychology, economics, experimental psychology, history, industrial and organizational psychology, philosophy, political science/government, psychology, religion, social science, and sociology). Physics, chemistry, and math are the strongest academically. Psychology, management, and sociology are the largest.

Required: To graduate, students must complete a Learning in Common curriculum, which includes courses in writing, quantitative reasoning, historical studies, ultimate questions, cultural values and global issues, natural sciences, a foreign language, social sciences, aesthetic expression, literature, moral life, and phys ed. They must maintain a minimum GPA of 2.0 and complete 32 courses equivalent to 128 credits. The number of hours required in the major varies.

Special: The college offers 3-2 engineering degrees in conjunction with Washington University and a 4-1 engineering program with Lehigh University. Moravian also offers cooperative programs in allied health, natural resource management, and geology with Lehigh, Duke, and Thomas Jefferson Universities. Cross-registration is available with Lehigh and DeSales Universities and Lafayette, Muhlenberg, and Cedar Crest. Internships, study abroad in many countries, a Washington semester, and student-designed majors may be pursued. There are 17 national honor societies and all departments have honors programs.

Faculty/Classroom: 57% of faculty are male; 43%, female. All both teach and do research. No introductory courses are taught by graduate students. The average class size in an introductory lecture is 20; in a laboratory, 14; and in a regular course, 18.

Admissions: 68% of the 2003-2004 applicants were accepted. The SAT I scores for the 2003-2004 freshman class were: Verbal--21% below 500, 50% between 500 and 599, 25% between 600 and 700, and 4% above 700; Math--14% below 500, 52% between 500 and 599, 31% between 600 and 700, and 3% above 700. 52% of the current freshmen were in the top fifth of their class; 81% were in the top two fifths. There were 2 National Merit semifinalists. 3 freshmen graduated first in their class.

Requirements: The SAT I or ACT is required. In addition, applicants must graduate from an accredited secondary school or have a GED. Moravian requires 16 Carnegie units, based on 4 years each of English and social science, 3 to 4 of math, and 2 each of lab science, a foreign language, and electives. Essays are required and interviews are recommended. For music students, auditions are required; for art students, portfolios are recommended. AP and CLEP credits are accepted. Important factors in the admissions decision are advanced placement or honor courses, recommendations by school officials, and leadership record.

Procedure: Freshmen are admitted fall and spring. Entrance exams should be taken with enough time to submit scores by the application deadline. There are early decision and deferred admissions plans. Early decision applications should be filed by February 1; regular applications, by March 1 for fall entry and November 15 for spring entry, along with a $40 fee. Notification of early decision is sent beginning December 15; regular decision, March 15. 113 early decision candidates were accepted for the 2003-2004 class. 109 applicants were on the 2003 waiting list; 12 were admitted. Applications are accepted on-line through the college's web site or through Common App at https://app.commonapp.org.

Transfer: 106 transfer students enrolled in 2002-2003. Applicants must have a minimum GPA of 2.5 and are required to submit recommendations, secondary and postsecondary transcripts, and standardized test scores. 32 of 128 credits required for the bachelor's degree must be completed at Moravian.

Visiting: There are regularly scheduled orientations for prospective students, including tours and interviews with admissions staff. There are guides for informal visits and visitors may sit in on classes and stay overnight. To schedule a visit, contact the Office of Admission.

Financial Aid: In 2003-2004, 94% of all full-time freshmen and 93% of continuing full-time students received some form of financial aid. 77% of full-time freshmen and 75% of continuing full-time students received need-based aid. The average freshman award was $15,227. Need-based scholarships or need-based grants averaged $11,851; and need-based self-help aid (loans and jobs) averaged $5044. 51% of undergraduates work part time. Average annual earnings from campus work are $804. Moravian is a member of CSS. The CSS Profile or FAFSA is required. The priority date for freshman financial aid applications for fall entry is February 14. The deadline for filing freshman financial aid applications for fall entry is March 15.

International Students: There are 25 international students enrolled. The school actively recruits these students. They must score 550 on the written TOEFL or 213 on the electronic version. The SAT I or ACT is preferred for all students and required if the student's first language is English.

Computers: A high-speed campus network accessible from dorms includes public access labs and 150 terminals (PC and Mac). The network provides students with shared applications, shared printing services, e-mail, and access to the Internet and the Web. All students may access the system 24 hours per day. There are no time limits and no fees.

Graduates: From July 1, 2002 to June 30, 2003, 339 bachelor's degrees were awarded. The most popular majors were psychology (14%), sociology (12%), and management (11%). In an average class, 56% graduate in 4 years or less, and 74% graduate in 5 years or less. 22 companies recruited on campus in 2002-2003. Of the 2002 graduating class, 23% were enrolled in graduate school within 6 months of graduation and 69% were employed.

Admissions Contact: James P. Mackin, Director of Admission. E-mail: admissions@moravian.edu Web: www.moravian.edu

MOUNT ALOYSIUS COLLEGE
Cresson, PA 16630

C-3
(814) 886-6383
(888) 823-2220; Fax: (814) 886-6441

Full-time: 297 men, 788 women	Faculty: 53; IIB, --$
Part-time: 69 men, 293 women	Ph.D.s: 29%
Graduate: none	Student/Faculty: 20 to 1
Year: semesters, summer session	Tuition: $13,420
Application Deadline: open	Room & Board: $5700
Freshman Class: 565 accepted, 282 enrolled	
SAT I Verbal/Math: 480/450	ACT: 19 LESS COMPETITIVE

Mount Aloysius, established in 1853 by the Sisters of Mercy, is a private, liberal arts college affiliated with the Roman Catholic Church. In addition to regional accreditation, Mount Aloysius College has baccalaureate program accreditation with APTA and NLN. The library contains 73,077 volumes, 4212 microform items, and 2210 audio/video tapes/CDs, and subscribes to 275 periodicals. Computerized library services include the card catalog, interlibrary loans, and database searching. Special learning facilities include a learning resource center and art gallery. The 165-acre campus is in a small town located in the southern Allegheny Mountains between Altoona and Johnstown. Including any residence halls, there are 8 buildings.

Student Life: 97% of undergraduates are from Pennsylvania. Students are from 20 states, 15 foreign countries, and Canada. 95% are white. 46% are Catholic; 9% Protestant; 8% claim no religious affiliation. The average age of freshmen is 18; all undergraduates, 22. 22% do not continue beyond their first year; 67% remain to graduate.

Housing: 200 students can be accommodated in college housing, which includes single-sex dorms. In addition, there are rooms for hearing-impaired students. On-campus housing is guaranteed for all 4 years. 80% of students commute. Alcohol is not permitted. All students may keep cars.

Activities: There are no fraternities or sororities. There are 25 groups on campus, including art, campus ministry (community service organization), cheerleading, chorale, chorus, computers, drama, ethnic, honors, musical theater, newspaper, photography, professional, religious, student government, and yearbook. Popular campus events include Madrigal Dinner, Family Day, and Mercyfest Weekend.

Sports: There are 5 intercollegiate sports for men and 5 for women, and 13 intramural sports for men and 12 for women. Facilities include an 1800-seat health and physical fitness center with 3 basketball courts, 2 tennis courts, a volleyball court, a weight-and-exercise room equipped with a sauna, and 2 locker rooms.

Disabled Students: 95% of the campus is accessible. Wheelchair ramps, elevators, special parking, specially equipped rest rooms, lowered drinking fountains, and lowered telephones are available.

Services: Counseling and information services are available, as is tutoring in every subject. There is remedial math, reading, and writing.

Campus Safety and Security: Measures include 24-hour foot and vehicle patrol, security escort services, informal discussions, and pamphlets/posters/films. There are emergency telephones and lighted pathways/sidewalks.

Programs of Study: Mount Aloysius College confers B.A., B.S., B.S. Ed., and B.S.N. degrees. Associate degrees are also awarded. Bachelor's degrees are awarded in BUSINESS (accounting and business administration and management), COMMUNICATIONS AND THE ARTS (English), EDUCATION (elementary), HEALTH PROFESSIONS (nursing and occupational therapy), SOCIAL SCIENCE (criminology, interpreter for the deaf, prelaw, and psychology). Nursing, prelaw, and criminology are the strongest academically. Nursing, criminology, and elementary education are the largest.

Required: Baccalaureate-level students are required during their final semester of study to complete 2 3-credit courses designed to integrate and synthesize scientific, behavioral, and moral concepts. A total of 120 credits is required with an overall 2.0 GPA, including a C average in all core courses.

Special: The Professional Studies curriculum provides a student-designed course of study, with an emphasis in behavior and social science, humanities, math/science/computer science, or prelaw. Clinical experiences must be completed for allied-health-related programs. There are 3 national honor societies, a freshman honors program, and 1 departmental honors program.

Faculty/Classroom: 45% of faculty are male; 55%, female. All both teach and do research. The average class size in an introductory lecture is 18; in a laboratory, 10; and in a regular course, 25.

Admissions: The SAT I scores for the 2003-2004 freshman class were: Verbal--77% below 500, 20% between 500 and 599, and 4% between 600 and 700; Math--78% below 500, 18% between 500 and 599, and 4% between 600 and 700. The ACT scores were 90% below 21, 2% between 21 and 23, and 8% between 24 and 26.

Requirements: The SAT I or ACT is required. In addition, applicants must graduate from an accredited high school or have the GED. A placement test and any necessary developmental studies classes may need to be taken. Science classes and an interview are required of some allied health programs. A GPA of 2.5 is required. AP and CLEP credits are accepted. Important factors in the admissions decision are recommendations by school officials, advanced placement or honor courses, and leadership record.

Procedure: Freshmen are admitted fall and spring. Entrance exams should be taken as early as possible. There is an early admissions plan and a rolling admissions plan. Application deadlines are open. Application fee is $30. Notification is sent on a rolling basis. Applications are accepted on-line through *www.mtaloy.edu*.

Transfer: Transfer students must have a 2.0 GPA. Only courses with a C or better will be considered for transfer; all other requirements are the same as for freshmen. 30 credits of 120 required for the bachelor's degree must be completed at Mount Aloysius College.

Visiting: There are regularly scheduled orientations for prospective students, including 3 daily sessions. There are guides for informal visits and visitors may sit in on classes and stay overnight. To schedule a visit, contact the Admissions Office.

Financial Aid: In 2003-2004, 90% of all full-time freshmen and 95% of continuing full-time students received some form of financial aid. 94% of full-time freshmen and 86% of continuing full-time students received need-based aid. The average freshman award was $9000, with $3000 ($5000 maximum) from need-based scholarships or need-based grants, $3000 ($5000 maximum) from need-based self-help aid (loans and jobs), and $3000 ($7000 maximum) from non-need-based awards and non-need-based scholarships. All undergraduates work part time. Average annual earnings from campus work are $750. The average financial indebtedness of the 2003 graduate was $17,125. The FAFSA is re-

quired. The priority date for freshman financial aid applications for fall entry is February 15. The deadline for filing freshman financial aid applications for fall entry is May 1.

International Students: There were 23 international students enrolled in a recent year. The school actively recruits these students. They must score 500 on the written TOEFL or 173 on the electronic version and also take the college's own entrance exam or the New Jersey Basic Skills Test.

Computers: The mainframe is a network system. Several computer labs are available for student use. The library houses 28 terminals with full Internet access. The residence hall houses computer labs for resident student use. There are also computer labs in the main academic building. All students may access the system from 8 A.M. to 10 P.M. There are no time limits and no fees.

Graduates: From July 1, 2002 to June 30, 2003, 123 bachelor's degrees were awarded. The most popular majors were nursing (20%), education (15%), and medical imaging (15%). 30 companies recruited on campus in a recent year. Of the 2002 graduating class, 22% were enrolled in graduate school within 6 months of graduation and 80% were employed.

Admissions Contact: Francis Crouse, Dean of Enrollment Management. E-mail: *admissions@mtaloy.edu* Web: *www.mtaloy.edu*

MUHLENBERG COLLEGE	E-3
Allentown, PA 18104	(484) 664-3200; Fax: (484) 664-3234
Full-time: 975 men, 1315 women	**Faculty:** 157; IIB, +$
Part-time: 66 men, 96 women	**Ph.D.s:** 87%
Graduate: none	**Student/Faculty:** 15 to 1
Year: semesters, summer session	**Tuition:** $24,945
Application Deadline: February 15	**Room & Board:** $6540
Freshman Class: 4111 applied, 1743 accepted, 589 enrolled	
SAT I Verbal/Math: 607/619	**HIGHLY COMPETITIVE**

Muhlenberg College, established in 1848, is a private liberal arts institution affiliated with the Lutheran Church. The library contains 200,000 volumes, 134,005 microform items, and 12,200 audio/video tapes/CDs, and subscribes to 1104 periodicals. Computerized library services include the card catalog, interlibrary loans, database searching, and Internet access. Special learning facilities include a learning resource center, art gallery, natural history museum, radio station, TV station, and two 50-acre environmental field stations. The 80-acre campus is in a suburban area 50 miles north of Philadelphia and 90 miles west of New York City. Including any residence halls, there are 61 buildings.

Student Life: 63% of undergraduates are from out of state, mostly the Middle Atlantic. Students are from 36 states, 5 foreign countries, and Canada. 70% are from public schools. 92% are white. 31% are Catholic; 30% Protestant; 23% Jewish; 14% claim no religious affiliation. The average age of freshmen is 18; all undergraduates, 19. 8% do not continue beyond their first year; 81% remain to graduate.

Housing: 1955 students can be accommodated in college housing, which includes single-sex and coed dorms, on-campus apartments, off-campus apartments, fraternity houses, and sorority houses. In addition, there are language houses, special-interest houses, and independent living experience houses. On-campus housing is guaranteed for all 4 years. 85% of students live on campus; of those, 80% remain on campus on weekends. Upperclassmen may keep cars.

Activities: 26% of men belong to 4 national fraternities; 27% of women belong to 4 national sororities. There are 110 groups on campus, including art, band, cheerleading, chess, choir, chorale, chorus, computers, dance, drama, ethnic, gay, honors, human rights, international, jazz band, literary magazine, musical theater, newspaper, opera, orchestra, pep band, photography, political, professional, radio and TV, religious, social, social service, step team, student government, and yearbook. Popular campus events include Spring Fling Weekend, Family Weekend, and Community Service Weekend.

Sports: There are 11 intercollegiate sports for men and 11 for women, and 13 intramural sports for men and 13 for women. Facilities include a sports center, which contains a 6-lane swimming pool, racquetball and squash courts, wrestling and weight training rooms; a multipurpose field house with indoor tennis courts, a running track, and a fitness loft; and outdoor volleyball courts, athletic fields, tennis courts, a soccer stadium, an all-weather track, and a football stadium.

Disabled Students: 95% of the campus is accessible. Wheelchair ramps, elevators, special parking, specially equipped rest rooms, special class scheduling, lowered drinking fountains, lowered telephones, extra time on tests, tutors, and books on tape are available.

Services: Counseling and information services are available, as is tutoring in every subject. There is a reader service for the blind and a writing center.

Campus Safety and Security: Measures include 24-hour foot and vehicle patrol, self-defense education, security escort services, and shuttle buses. There are informal discussions, pamphlets/posters/films, emergency telephones, and lighted pathways/sidewalks.

Programs of Study: Muhlenberg confers B.A. and B.S. degrees. Bachelor's degrees are awarded in BIOLOGICAL SCIENCE (biochemistry and biology/biological science), BUSINESS (accounting and business administration and management), COMMUNICATIONS AND THE ARTS (art, communications, dance, dramatic arts, English, fine arts, French, German, music, and Spanish), COMPUTER AND PHYSICAL SCIENCE (chemistry, computer science, mathematics, natural sciences, physical sciences, and physics), ENGINEERING AND ENVIRONMENTAL DESIGN (environmental science), SOCIAL SCIENCE (American studies, anthropology, economics, German area studies, history, international studies, philosophy, political science/government, psychology, religion, Russian and Slavic studies, social science, and sociology). Biology, drama, and English are the strongest academically. Biology, business administration, and psychology are the largest.

Required: To graduate, students must complete requirements in literature and the arts, religion or philosophy, human behavior and social institutions, historical studies, physical and life sciences, and other cultures. They must have a minimum GPA of 2.0 in a total of 34 course units, with 9 to 14 units in the major. All students must take 1 quarter of phys ed, including a wellness course, and freshman and senior seminars.

Special: Students may cross-register with Lehigh, Lafayette, Cedar Crest, Moravian, and Allentown Colleges. Internships, work-study programs, study abroad in Asia, Australia, Latin America, Russia, and Europe, and a Washington semester are available. Dual majors and student-designed majors may be pursued. A 3-2 engineering degree is available in cooperation with Columbia and Washington Universities, a 4-4 assured admission medical program is offered with Drexel University College of Medicine, a 3-4 dental program is offered with University of Pennsylvania, and a 3-2 forestry degree is offered in cooperation with Duke University. Nondegree study and a pass/fail grading option are also offered. There are 12 national honor societies, including Phi Beta Kappa, a freshman honors program, and 9 departmental honors programs.

Faculty/Classroom: 55% of faculty are male; 45%, female. All teach undergraduates, 84% both teach and do research. The average class size in an introductory lecture is 30; in a laboratory, 18; and in a regular course, 19.

Admissions: 42% of the 2003-2004 applicants were accepted. The SAT I scores for the 2003-2004 freshman class were: Verbal--6% below 500, 38% between 500 and 599, 48% between 600 and 700, and 8% above 700; Math--4% below 500, 36% between 500 and 599, 51% between 600 and 700, and 9% above 700. 67% of the current freshmen were in the top fifth of their class; 92% were in the top two fifths. There was 1 National Merit finalist and 3 semifinalists. 4 freshmen graduated first in their class.

Requirements: Applicants must graduate from an accredited secondary school or have a GED. 16 Carnegie units are required, and students must complete 4 courses in English, 3 in math, and 2 each in history, science, and a foreign language. All students must submit essays. Interviews are recommended and are required for those who do not submit SAT I scores. AP and CLEP credits are accepted. Important factors in the admissions decision are advanced placement or honor courses, leadership record, and evidence of special talent.

Procedure: Freshmen are admitted fall and spring. Entrance exams should be taken during the spring of the junior year or the fall of the senior year. There are early decision, early admissions, and deferred admissions plans. Early decision applications should be filed by January 15; regular applications, by February 15 for fall entry, along with a $45 fee. Notification of early decision is sent February 1; regular decision, March 15. 296 early decision candidates were accepted for the 2003-2004 class. 568 applicants were on the 2003 waiting list; 7 were admitted. Applications are accepted on-line through Common App or the school's web site.

Transfer: 8 transfer students enrolled in a recent year. A minimum college GPA of 2.5 and an interview are required. 17 of 34 credits required for the bachelor's degree must be completed at Muhlenberg.

Visiting: There are regularly scheduled orientations for prospective students, consisting of a tour of the campus and a personal interview. There are 2 open houses in the fall and 1 in the spring. There are guides for informal visits and visitors may sit in on classes and stay overnight. To schedule a visit, contact Bonnie Reabold or Alyssa Rabenold at (484) 664-3202 or *reabold@muhlenberg.edu.*

Financial Aid: In 2003-2004, 73% of all full-time freshmen and 72% of continuing full-time students received some form of financial aid. 41% of full-time freshmen and 42% of continuing full-time students received need-based aid. The average freshman award was $15,517. Need-based scholarships or need-based grants averaged $16,225 ($29,550 maximum); need-based self-help aid (loans and jobs) averaged $3948 ($7425 maximum); and non-need-based awards and non-need-based scholarships averaged $7985 ($19,000 maximum). 41% of undergraduates work part time. Average annual earnings from campus work are $927. The average financial indebtedness of the 2003 graduate was $16,642. Muhlenberg is a member of CSS. The CSS Profile or FAFSA, the college's own financial statement, and the parent and student tax returns and W-2 forms are required. The deadline for filing freshman financial aid applications for fall entry is February 15.

International Students: There are 13 international students enrolled. The school actively recruits these students. They must score 550 on the written TOEFL or 213 on the electronic version.

Computers: The mainframes are an HP 3000 and an HP 9000. Students may access the campus network and Internet from the computer labs, classrooms, or residence halls. There are approximately 290 PCs available to students in labs and computer lounges throughout the campus. The campus network spans 17 city blocks and connects all 61 campus buildings. All students may access the system 24 hours a day. There are no time limits and no fees. It is strongly recommended that all students have a personal computer.

Graduates: From July 1, 2002 to June 30, 2003, 354 bachelor's degrees were awarded. The most popular majors were business (16%), psychology (12%), and communication (11%). In an average class, 1% graduate in 3 years or less, 78% graduate in 4 years or less, 80% graduate in 5 years or less, and 82% graduate in 6 years or less. 48 companies recruited on campus in 2002-2003. Of the 2002 graduating class, 31% were enrolled in graduate school within 6 months of graduation and 62% were employed.

Admissions Contact: Christopher Hooker-Haring, Dean, Admissions. E-mail: *admissions@muhlenberg.edu* Web: *www.muhlenberg.edu*

NEUMANN COLLEGE
Aston, PA 19014-1298

E-4
(610) 558-5616
(800) 9NEUMAN; Fax: (610) 558-5652

Full-time: 573 men, 1086 women	Faculty: 68; IIB, --$
Part-time: 144 men, 309 women	Ph.D.s: 60%
Graduate: 168 men, 309 women	Student/Faculty: 24 to 1
Year: semesters, summer session	Tuition: $16,410
Application Deadline: open	Room & Board: $7480
Freshman Class: 1638 applied, 1583 accepted, 525 enrolled	
SAT I Verbal/Math: 440/430	LESS COMPETITIVE

Neumann College, founded in 1965 by the Sisters of St. Francis, is a private liberal arts institution affiliated with the Roman Catholic Church. In addition to regional accreditation, Neumann has baccalaureate program accreditation with CAHEA, CAPTE, and NLN. The library contains 90,000 volumes, 99,758 microform items, and 36,562 audio/video tapes/CDs, and subscribes to 700 periodicals. Computerized library services include the card catalog, interlibrary loans, database searching, and Internet access. Special learning facilities include a learning resource center and a learning assistance center. The 50-acre campus is in a suburban area 15 miles southwest of Philadelphia. Including any residence halls, there are 6 buildings.

Student Life: 73% of undergraduates are from Pennsylvania. Students are from 18 states, 6 foreign countries, and Canada. 35% are from public schools. 84% are white; 13% African American. 69% are Catholic; 18% Protestant; 9% claim no religious affiliation. The average age of freshmen is 18; all undergraduates, 20. 29% do not continue beyond their first year; 57% remain to graduate.

Housing: 760 students can be accommodated in college housing, which includes coed dorms and off-campus apartments. On-campus housing is available on a first-come, first-served basis. Priority is given to out-of-town students. 50% of students commute. Alcohol is not permitted. All students may keep cars.

Activities: There are no fraternities or sororities. There are 17 groups on campus, including choir, chorus, dance, drama, ethnic, honors, literary magazine, newspaper, photography, political, professional, religious, social, social service, student government, and yearbook. Popular campus events include dinner dances, Spring Fling, and charity fundraising.

Sports: There are 7 intercollegiate sports for men and 8 for women, and 5 intramural sports for men and 5 for women. Facilities include a 350-seat gym, weight and fitness rooms, tennis courts, baseball and softball fields, an ice hockey rink, video games, and a theater.

Disabled Students: All of the campus is accessible. Wheelchair ramps, elevators, special parking, specially equipped rest rooms, and special class scheduling are available.

Services: Counseling and information services are available, as is tutoring in most subjects. There is a reader service for the blind and remedial math, reading, and writing.

Campus Safety and Security: Measures include 24-hour foot and vehicle patrol, self-defense education, security escort services, and shuttle buses. There are informal discussions, pamphlets/posters/films, emergency telephones, and lighted pathways/sidewalks.

Programs of Study: Neumann confers B.A. and B.S. degrees. Associate and master's degrees are also awarded. Bachelor's degrees are awarded in AGRICULTURE (environmental studies), BIOLOGICAL SCIENCE (biology/biological science), BUSINESS (accounting, business administration and management, international business management, marketing and distribution, and sports management), COMMUNICATIONS AND THE ARTS (communications and English), COMPUTER AND PHYSICAL SCIENCE (computer science), EDUCATION (athletic training, early childhood, and elementary), HEALTH PROFESSIONS (nursing), SOCIAL SCIENCE (criminal justice, liberal arts/general studies, political science/government, and psychology). Biology, nursing, and elementary education are the strongest academically. Liberal studies, elementary education, nursing are the largest.

Required: To graduate, all students must complete 121 to 130 credits, including 44 credits of core requirements, with 30 to 50 in the major. A minimum 2.0 GPA is required.

Special: The college offers co-op programs in all majors, study abroad in England, internships, work-study programs, dual majors, and a general studies degree. Credit for life, work, and military experience, nondegree study, an accelerated degree liberal studies program, and pass/fail options are available. There are 4 national honor societies, a freshman honors program, and 1 departmental honors program.

Faculty/Classroom: 35% of faculty are male; 65%, female. 94% teach undergraduates and 15% both teach and do research. No introductory courses are taught by graduate students. The average class size in an introductory lecture is 24; in a laboratory, 17; and in a regular course, 20.

Admissions: 97% of the 2003-2004 applicants were accepted. The SAT I scores for the 2003-2004 freshman class were: Verbal--82% below 500, 14% between 500 and 599, and 3% between 600 and 700; Math--80% below 500, 17% between 500 and 599, and 3% between 600 and 700.

Requirements: The SAT I is required. In addition, applicants must be graduates of an accredited secondary school or have a GED. High school courses must include 4 years of English and 2 years each of a foreign language, history, and science. An interview is recommended. A GPA of 2.0 is required. AP and CLEP credits are accepted. Recommendations by school officials is an important factor in the admission decision.

Procedure: Freshmen are admitted fall and spring. Entrance exams should be taken by December of the senior year. There is a deferred admissions plan and a rolling admissions plan. Application deadlines are open. Application fee is $35. Applications are accepted on-line.

Transfer: 79 transfer students enrolled in 2002-2003. Applicants should submit transcripts from all institutions attended. 30 of 121 to 130 credits required for the bachelor's degree must be completed at Neumann.

Visiting: There are regularly scheduled orientations for prospective students, including class visits and informal meetings with faculty. There are guides for informal visits and visitors may sit in on classes. To schedule a visit, contact the Admissions Office at *neumann@neumann.edu*.

Financial Aid: In 2003-2004, 95% of all full-time freshmen and 90% of continuing full-time students received some form of financial aid. 90% of all full-time students received need-based aid. The average freshman award was $15,000, with $10,000 ($15,000 maximum) from need-based scholarships or need-based grants, and $5000 ($7000 maximum) from need-based self-help aid (loans and jobs). 89% of undergraduates work part time. Average annual earnings from campus work are $1200. The average financial indebtedness of the 2003 graduate was $15,000. The FAFSA is required. The deadline for filing freshman financial aid applications for fall entry is March 15.

International Students: There are 14 international students enrolled. They must score 550 on the written TOEFL or 213 on the electronic version and also take the SAT I.

Computers: The mainframe is an IBM p610. About 200 PCs are available in the computer lab, the library, the residence hall, and the student lounge. Internet access, and e-mail are also available. All students may access the system any time. There are no time limits and no fees. It is strongly recommended that all students have a personal computer.

Graduates: From July 1, 2002 to June 30, 2003, 323 bachelor's degrees were awarded. The most popular majors were liberal studies (37%), elementary education (16%), and nursing (11%). In an average class, 40% graduate in 4 years or less, 50% graduate in 5 years or less, and 55% graduate in 6 years or less. 55 companies recruited on campus in 2002-2003. Of the 2002 graduating class, 10% were enrolled in graduate school within 6 months of graduation and 90% were employed.

Admissions Contact: Renee San Giacomo, Executive Director.
E-mail: *neumann@neumann.edu* Web: *www.neumann.edu*

PEIRCE COLLEGE
Philadelphia, PA 19102

F-3

(215) 670-9214
(877) 670-9190; Fax: (215) 670-9366

Full-time: 195 men, 484 women	**Faculty:** 29; III, --$
Part-time: 435 men, 1062 women	**Ph.D.s:** 34%
Graduate: none	**Student/Faculty:** 23 to 1
Year: sessions, summer session	**Tuition:** $11,800
Application Deadline: open	**Room & Board:** n/app
Freshman Class: 287 applied, 286 accepted, 244 enrolled	
SAT I or ACT: not required	**NONCOMPETITIVE**

Peirce College, a private institution founded in 1865, offers baccalaureate, associate, and certificate programs in business studies, paralegal studies, and information technology. These programs are offered on-line and on site through Peirce's Corporate College program, as well as days and evenings. In addition to regional accreditation, Peirce has baccalaureate program accreditation with ACBSP. The library contains 35,000 volumes, and subscribes to 160 periodicals. Computerized library services include the card catalog, interlibrary loans, and database searching. Special learning facilities include a learning resource center and the Walker Center for Academic Excellence. The 1-acre campus is in an urban area in the Center City Business District. There are 2 buildings.

Student Life: 80% of undergraduates are from Pennsylvania. Students are from 35 states, 29 foreign countries, and Canada. 50% are African American; 30% white. The average age of freshmen is 31; all undergraduates, 33. 42% do not continue beyond their first year; 63% remain to graduate.

Housing: There are no residence halls. All students commute. Alcohol is not permitted. No one may keep cars.

Activities: There are no fraternities or sororities. There is 1 group on campus, including honors. Popular campus events include Leadership Retreat, Student Appreciation Day, and Welcome Back Day.

Sports: There is no sports program at Peirce.

Disabled Students: All of the campus is accessible. Wheelchair ramps, elevators, specially equipped rest rooms, special class scheduling, lowered drinking fountains, and lowered telephones are available.

Services: Counseling and information services are available, as is tutoring in most subjects. There is a reader service for the blind, and remedial math, reading, and writing.

Campus Safety and Security: Measures include 24-hour foot and vehicle patrol, security escort services, informal discussions, and pamphlets/posters/films. There are emergency telephones, lighted pathways/sidewalks, and security cameras throughout the campus.

Programs of Study: Peirce confers the B.S. degree. Associate degrees are also awarded. Bachelor's degrees are awarded in BUSINESS (business administration and management), COMPUTER AND PHYSICAL SCIENCE (information sciences and systems), SOCIAL SCIENCE (paralegal studies). Business administration is the largest.

Required: To graduate, all students must complete 120 credit hours and maintain a minimum cumulative GPA of 2.0. General education requirements include 4 courses in social science, 3 each in English or communication, humanities or history, and math, 2 in science, 1 in technology, and 1 general education core elective.

Special: The college offers co-op programs in all and accelerated degrees in most major programs of study. There is 1 national honor society.

Faculty/Classroom: 61% of faculty are male; 39%, female. All teach undergraduates. The average class size in an introductory lecture is 17 and in a regular course, 14.

Admissions: 99% of the 2003-2004 applicants were accepted.

Requirements: On-campus applicants who have not taken the SAT I or the ACT and who are entering college for the first time must take a skills assessment test to determine the appropriate placement in college-level courses. Applicants must take the TABE (Test of Adult Basic Education) to determine grade equivalency in English and math. Corporate College and on-line program applicants must submit an official transcript documenting high school graduation or copies of the GED or state equivalency diploma and scores. AP and CLEP credits are accepted.

Procedure: Freshmen are admitted to all sessions. Entrance exams are offered continuously. There is a deferred admissions plan. Application deadlines are open. Notification is sent on a rolling basis. Application fee is $50. Applications are accepted on computer disk and on-line through the college's web site.

Transfer: 877 transfer students enrolled in a recnet year. Transcripts from other colleges attended must be submitted. 30 of 120 credits required for the bachelor's degree must be completed at Peirce.

Visiting: There are regularly scheduled orientations for prospective students, including a campus tour and a meeting with an adviser. There are guides for informal visits and visitors may sit in on classes. To schedule a visit, contact Admissions.

Financial Aid: In 2003-2004, 90% of all full-time freshmen and 80% of continuing full-time students received some form of financial aid. 80% of full-time freshmen and 50% of continuing full-time students received need-based aid. The average freshman award was $4000. Need-based scholarships or need-based grants averaged $2000 (maximum); need-based self-help aid (loans and jobs) averaged $3500 ($7500 maximum); and non-need-based awards and non-need-based scholarships averaged $4500 (maximum). All undergraduates work part time. Average annual earnings from campus work are $2000. The average financial indebtedness of the 2003 graduate was $15,000. Peirce is a member of CSS. The FAFSA and the college's own financial statement are required. The priority date for freshman financial aid applications for fall entry is April 15. The deadline for filing freshman financial aid applications for fall entry is June 1.

International Students: There are 48 international students enrolled. The school actively recruits these students. .

Computers: The mainframe is a Compaq 7000. Log-ons are assigned upon course registration. All students may access the system. There are no time limits and no fees. All students are required to have personal computers.

Graduates: From July 1, 2002 to June 30, 2003, 253 bachelor's degrees were awarded. The most popular majors were business administration (62%), information technology (28%), and paralegal studies (10%). In an average class, 20% graduate in 4 years or less, 30% graduate in 5 years or less, and 40% graduate in 6 years or less. 18 companies recruited on campus in 2002-2003. Of the 2002 graduating class, 31% were enrolled in graduate school within 6 months of graduation and 92% were employed.

Admissions Contact: Steve Bird, Senior Enrollment Representative. A video is available. E-mail: *info@peirce.edu* Web: *www.peirce.edu*

PENN STATE UNIVERSITY AT ERIE/BEHREND COLLEGE
B-1

Erie, PA 16563

(814) 898-6100
(866) 374-3378; Fax: (814) 898-6044

Full-time: 2040 men, 1220 women	**Faculty:** 192; IIB, av$
Part-time: 200 men, 100 women	**Ph.D.s:** 59%
Graduate: 100 men, 50 women	**Student/Faculty:** 17 to 1
Year: semesters, summer session	**Tuition:** $7500 ($14,000)
Application Deadline: open	**Room & Board:** $5000
Freshman Class: n/av	
SAT I or ACT: required	**COMPETITIVE**

Penn State University at Erie/Behrend College, founded in 1948, offers 26 baccalaureate programs as well as the first 2 years of most Penn State University Park baccalaureate programs. It offers courses in business, humanities, social sciences, science, engineering technology, and engineering. There are 4 undergraduate and 2 graduate schools. Figures in the above capsule and in this profile are approximate. In addition to regional accreditation, Behrend or Penn State Erie has baccalaureate program accreditation with ABET. The library contains 100,000 volumes, 75,000 microform items, and 400 audio/video tapes/CDs, and subscribes to 700 periodicals. Computerized library services include the card catalog, interlibrary loans, and database searching. Special learning facilities include a learning resource center, radio station, engineering workstation labs, and media labs. The 700-acre campus is in a suburban area 5 miles east of Erie. Including any residence halls, there are 42 buildings.

Student Life: 92% of undergraduates are from Pennsylvania. 88% are white. The average age of freshmen is 18; all undergraduates, 22. 9% do not continue beyond their first year; 61% remain to graduate.

Housing: 1500 students can be accommodated in college housing, which includes single-sex and coed dorms and on-campus apartments. In addition, there are honors houses and special-interest houses. On-campus housing is available on a first-come, first-served basis and is available on a lottery system for upperclassmen. 54% of students commute. Alcohol is not permitted. All students may keep cars.

Activities: 5% of men belong to 5 national fraternities; 16% of women belong to 3 national sororities. There are 80 groups on campus, including band, cheerleading, chess, choir, computers, dance, drama, ethnic, gay, honors, international, jazz band, literary magazine, newspaper, pep band, political, professional, radio and TV, religious, social service, student government, and yearbook. Popular campus events include a speaker series, parents events, and Black Cultural Awareness Month.

Sports: There are 10 intercollegiate sports for men and 11 for women, and 18 intramural sports for men and 18 for women. Facilities include an athletic center with an indoor track and an 8-lane pool, tennis courts, a weight room, a fitness trail, basketball courts, and baseball, softball, and soccer fields.

Disabled Students: 90% of the campus is accessible. Wheelchair ramps, elevators, special parking, specially equipped rest rooms, special class scheduling, lowered drinking fountains, and lowered telephones are available.

Services: Counseling and information services are available, as is tutoring in most subjects. There is a reader service for the blind, and remedial math, reading, and writing.

Campus Safety and Security: Measures include 24-hour foot and vehicle patrol, self-defense education, security escort services, and informal discussions. There are pamphlets/posters/films, emergency telephones, and lighted pathways/sidewalks.

Programs of Study: Behrend or Penn State Erie confers B.A. and B.S. degrees. Associate and master's degrees are also awarded. Bachelor's degrees are awarded in BIOLOGICAL SCIENCE (biology/biological science), BUSINESS (accounting, banking and finance, business administration and management, business economics, management information systems, and marketing management), COMMUNICATIONS AND THE ARTS (communications and English), COMPUTER AND PHYSICAL SCIENCE (chemistry, computer science, mathematics, physics, and science), ENGINEERING AND ENVIRONMENTAL DESIGN (computer engineering, engineering, engineering technology, mechanical engineering technology, and plastics technology), SOCIAL SCIENCE (economics, history, political science/government, and psychology). Management information systems, psychology, and math are the strongest academically. Engineering, business, and psychology are the largest.

Required: All baccalaureate degree candidates must take 46 general education credits, including 27 in arts, humanities, natural science, and social and behavioral sciences including a cultural diversity course, 15 in

quantification and communication skills including a writing intensive course, and 3 in health, phys ed, and a freshman seminar. All students must complete a minimum of 120 credit hours with a minimum GPA of 2.0. Further requirements vary by degree program.

Special: Internships, study abroad in 14 countries, and work-study programs are available. In addition, a B.A.-B.S. degree in psychology, a 3-2 engineering degree with Edinboro University, dual majors, a general studies degree, and student-designed majors in business and behavioral sciences are offered. Nondegree study and up to 12 credits of pass/fail options are possible. There are 4 national honor societies, and a freshman honors program.

Faculty/Classroom: 70% of faculty are male; 30%, female. All teach undergraduates. No introductory courses are taught by graduate students. The average class size in an introductory lecture is 35; in a laboratory, 18; and in a regular course, 29.

Requirements: The SAT I or ACT is required. In addition, candidates for admission must have 15 academic credits or 15 Carnegie units, including 5 in social studies, 4 in English, 3 each in math and science, and 2 in foreign language. The GED is accepted. AP and CLEP credits are accepted.

Procedure: Freshmen are admitted to all sessions. Entrance exams should be taken during the junior year. There is a deferred admissions plan. Application deadlines are open The fall 2003 application fee was $50. Applications are accepted on-line via Penn State or the college's web site.

Transfer: 94 transfer students enrolled in a recent year. Transfer candidates need a minimum GPA of 2.4, good academic standing, and 18 or more credits from a regionally accredited institution at the college level. 36 of 120 credits required for the bachelor's degree must be completed at Behrend or Penn State Erie.

Visiting: There are regularly scheduled orientations for prospective students, including meetings with a counselor and faculty, a campus tour, and a class visit. There are guides for informal visits and visitors may sit in on classes and stay overnight. To schedule a visit, contact the Admissions Office.

Financial Aid: The FAFSA is required. Check with the school for current deadlines.

International Students: 32 international students were enrolled in a recent year. The school actively recruits these students. They must score 550 on the written TOEFL or 213 on the electronic version.

Computers: 450 computers are available in the computer center, labs in the library, and in academic buildings. All students may access the system any time by modem or network. There are no time limits and no fees. It is strongly recommended that all students have a personal computer.

Admissions Contact: Mary-Ellen Madigan, Director of Admissions. E-mail: *behrend.admissions@psu.edu* Web: *www.pserie.psu.edu*

PENN STATE UNIVERSITY/ALTOONA

Altoona, PA 16601

(814) 949-5466; (800) 848-9843

Full-time: 1800 men, 1670 women	**Faculty:** 122
Part-time: 125 men, 230 women	**Ph.D.s:** 71%
Graduate: 2 men, 8 women	**Student/Faculty:** 28 to 1
Year: semesters, summer session	**Tuition:** $7500 ($11,200)
Application Deadline: open	**Room & Board:** $5500
Freshman Class: n/av	
SAT I or ACT: required	**COMPETITIVE**

Penn State Altoona, founded in 1939, offers more than 10 baccalaureate degree programs, as well as a number of associate degrees. Figures in the above capsule and in this profile are approximate. In addition to regional accreditation, Penn State University/Altoona has baccalaureate program accreditation with ABET. The library contains 60,000 microform items and 5700 audio/video tapes/CDs, and subscribes to 290 periodicals. Computerized library services include the card catalog, interlibrary loans, and database searching. Special learning facilities include a learning resource center, art gallery, Pic-Tel teleconferencing, 5 state-of-the-art engineering labs, and CAD/CAM computer lab facilities. The 123-acre campus is in a suburban area. Including any residence halls, there are 25 buildings.

Student Life: 88% of undergraduates are from Pennsylvania. 85% are white. 54% claim no religious affiliation; 25% various Christian and non-Christian denominations; 18% Catholic. The average age of freshmen is 19; all undergraduates, 22.

Housing: 900 students can be accommodated in college housing, which includes single-sex and coed dorms. In addition, there are honors houses and special-interest houses. On-campus housing is available on a first-come, first-served basis and is available on a lottery system for upperclassmen. 76% of students commute. Alcohol is not permitted. All students may keep cars.

Activities: 4% of men belong to 4 national fraternities; 3% of women belong to 3 local sororities. There are 50 groups on campus, including cheerleading, choir, dance, drama, ethnic, gay, honors, international, jazz band, literary magazine, newspaper, pep band, political, professional, religious, social, social service, student government, and yearbook. Popular campus events include Distinguished Speaker Series, Hoops Hysteria, and Black History and Women's History Month events.

Sports: There are 6 intercollegiate sports for men and 6 for women. Facilities include a large gym, an indoor pool, racquetball courts, a weight room, a fitness loft, tennis courts, an outdoor track, sand volleyball courts, and baseball, softball, and soccer fields.

Disabled Students: 95% of the campus is accessible. Wheelchair ramps, elevators, special parking, specially equipped rest rooms, special class scheduling, lowered drinking fountains, and lowered telephones are available.

Services: Counseling and information services are available, as is tutoring in most subjects. There is remedial math, reading, and writing.

Campus Safety and Security: Measures include 24-hour foot and vehicle patrol, self-defense education, security escort services, and shuttle buses. There are informal discussions, pamphlets/posters/films, emergency telephones, and lighted pathways/sidewalks.

Programs of Study: Penn State University/Altoona confers B.A. and B.S. degrees. Associate degrees are also awarded. Bachelor's degrees are awarded in AGRICULTURE (environmental studies), BUSINESS (business administration and management), COMMUNICATIONS AND THE ARTS (English), COMPUTER AND PHYSICAL SCIENCE (science), ENGINEERING AND ENVIRONMENTAL DESIGN (electromechanical technology), HEALTH PROFESSIONS (nursing), SOCIAL SCIENCE (criminal justice, human development, and liberal arts/general studies). Engineering is the strongest academically. Business, engineering, and criminal justice are the largest.

Required: To graduate, students must complete a minimum of 120 credit hours with a minimum GPA of 2.0. They must complete 46 general education credits, including 27 in arts, humanities, natural science, and social and behavioral sciences and 15 in quantification and communication skills.

Special: Internships, study abroad in 2 countries, work-study programs, accelerated degree programs, and dual and student-designed majors are available. There is an integrative arts major, which allows students to pursue interests across artistic boundaries. There are 2 national honor societies, including Phi Beta Kappa, and a freshman honors program.

Faculty/Classroom: 59% of faculty are male; 41%, female. No introductory courses are taught by graduate students. The average class size in an introductory lecture is 35; in a laboratory, 20; and in a regular course, 24.

Requirements: The SAT I or ACT is required. In addition, applicants should have 15 academic or Carnegie units, including 4 in English, 3 each in math, science, and social studies, and 2 in foreign language (required for some majors). The GED is accepted. AP and CLEP credits are accepted. Advanced placement or honor courses is an important factor in the admission decision.

Procedure: Freshmen are admitted to all sessions. Entrance exams should be taken during the junior year. There are early admissions and deferred admissions plans. Application deadlines are open. The fall 2003 application fee was $50. Applications are accepted on-line at the school's web site.

Transfer: 65 transfer students enrolled in a recent year. High school and college transcripts are required, as is good academic standing. The minimum GPA varies by major. 36 of 120 credits required for the bachelor's degree must be completed at Penn State University/Altoona.

Visiting: There are regularly scheduled orientations for prospective students, including campus tours and meetings with academic counselors and faculty. There are guides for informal visits and visitors may sit in on classes and stay overnight. To schedule a visit, contact the Admissions Office at aaadmit@psu.edu.

Financial Aid: The FAFSA is required, and some academic scholarships require a specific application, which varies according to the college/major. Check with the school for current deadlines.

International Students: 26 international students were enrolled in a recent year. The school actively recruits these students. They must score 550 on the written TOEFL and also take the SAT I or the ACT.

Computers: There are about 1000 computers on campus. They are available in the Computer Learning Resource Center, labs in academic buildings, and labs in residence halls; there is mainframe access from residence hall rooms. All students may access the system. There are no time limits and no fees. It is strongly recommended that all students have a personal computer.

Graduates: In a recent year, 127 bachelor's degrees were awarded. The most popular majors were business (35%), engineering (23%), and criminal justice (18%).

Admissions Contact: Richard Shaffer, Director of Admissions. A video is available. E-mail: rks8@psu.edu Web: www.aa.psu.edu

---

PENN STATE UNIVERSITY/UNIVERSITY PARK CAMPUS   C-3

University Park, PA 16802	(814) 863-0233; Fax: (814) 863-7590
Full-time: 17,711 men, 15,751 women	Faculty: 2191; I, av$
Part-time: 902 men, 638 women	Ph.D.s: 88%
Graduate: 3600 men, 3193 women	Student/Faculty: 15 to 1
Year: semesters, summer session	Tuition: $9706 ($18,828)
Application Deadline: open	Room & Board: $5940
Freshman Class: 31,264 applied, 17,174 accepted, 6048 enrolled	
SAT I Verbal/Math: 580/620	HIGHLY COMPETITIVE

Penn State University/University Park Campus, founded in 1855, is the oldest and largest of 24 campuses in the Penn State system, offering undergraduate and graduate degrees in agricultural science, arts and architecture, business administration, earth and mineral sciences, education, engineering, health and human development, liberal arts, science, and communications. There are 10 undergraduate schools and 1 graduate school. In addition to regional accreditation, Penn State has baccalaureate program accreditation with AACSB, ABET, ACEJMC, ADA, ASLA, CSWE, NAAB, NASAD, NASM, NCATE, NLN, NRPA, and SAF. The 10 libraries contain 3,087,688 volumes, 2,483,133 microform items, and 151,581 audio/video tapes/CDs, and subscribe to 25,868 periodicals. Computerized library services include the card catalog, interlibrary loans, and database searching. Special learning facilities include a learning resource center, art gallery, radio station, TV station, museums of art, anthropology, and earth and mineral sciences, an observatory, and a nuclear reactor. The 5617-acre campus is in a suburban area 90 miles west of Harrisburg. Including any residence halls, there are 403 buildings.

Student Life: 81% of undergraduates are from Pennsylvania. Students are from 50 states and Canada. 88% are white. The average age of freshmen is 18; all undergraduates, 20. 7% do not continue beyond their first year; 77% remain to graduate.

Housing: 12,648 students can be accommodated in college housing, which includes single-sex dorms, on-campus apartments, and married-student housing. In addition, there are honors houses, language houses, and special-interest houses. On-campus housing is guaranteed for the freshman year only and is available on a lottery system for upperclassmen. 65% of students commute. Alcohol is not permitted. All students may keep cars.

Activities: 13% of men belong to 55 national fraternities; 12% of women belong to 25 national sororities. There are 400 groups on campus, including art, band, cheerleading, chess, choir, chorale, chorus, computers, dance, drama, drill team, ethnic, film, gay, honors, international, jazz band, literary magazine, marching band, musical theater, newspaper, orchestra, pep band, photography, political, professional, radio and TV, religious, social, social service, student government, symphony, and yearbook. Popular campus events include Penn State Artists' Series, Central Pennsylvania Festival of the Arts, and Sy Barash Regatta.

Sports: There are 15 intercollegiate sports for men and 14 for women, and 15 intramural sports for men and 14 for women. Facilities include 6 gyms, 5 swimming pools, indoor and outdoor tracks, 2 golf courses, a jogging course, a rink, 2 rifle ranges, 32 acres of practice fields, and numerous courts for tennis, handball, squash, and paddleball.

Disabled Students: All of the campus is accessible. Wheelchair ramps, elevators, special parking, specially equipped rest rooms, special class scheduling, lowered drinking fountains, and lowered telephones are available.

Services: Counseling and information services are available, as is tutoring in most subjects. There is a reader service for the blind and remedial math, reading, and writing.

Campus Safety and Security: Measures include 24-hour foot and vehicle patrol, self-defense education, security escort services, and shuttle buses. There are informal discussions, pamphlets/posters/films, emergency telephones, and lighted pathways/sidewalks.

Programs of Study: Penn State confers B.A., B.S., B.Arch., B.Arch.Eng., B.F.A., B.M., B.Mus.Arts, and B.Ph. degrees. Associate, master's, and doctoral degrees are also awarded. Bachelor's degrees are awarded in AGRICULTURE (agricultural business management, agriculture, agronomy, animal science, dairy science, fishing and fisheries, forestry and related sciences, forestry production and processing, horticulture, natural resource management, plant science, poultry science, and soil science), BIOLOGICAL SCIENCE (biochemistry, biology/biological science, ecology, microbiology, molecular biology, nutrition, and wildlife biology), BUSINESS (accounting, banking and finance, business administration and management, hotel/motel and restaurant management, insurance, international business management, labor studies, management information systems, management science, marketing/retailing/merchandising, real estate, and transportation management), COMMUNICATIONS AND THE ARTS (advertising, art, art history and appreciation, broadcasting, classics, communications, comparative literature, dramatic arts, English, film arts, fine arts, French, German, Italian, journalism, music, Russian, Spanish, and speech/debate/rhetoric), COMPUTER AND PHYSICAL SCIENCE (actuarial science, astronomy, atmospheric sciences and meteorology, chemistry, computer science, earth science, geoscience, mathematics, physics, science, and statistics), EDUCATION (agricultural, art, elementary, health, industrial arts, music, secondary, and special), ENGINEERING AND ENVIRONMENTAL DESIGN (aeronautical engineering, agricultural engineering, architectural engineering, architecture, chemical engineering, civil engineering, computer engineering, electrical/electronics engineering, energy management technology, engineering, environmental engineering, industrial administration/management, industrial engineering, landscape architecture/design, materials science, mechanical engineering, mining and mineral engineering, nuclear engineering, and petroleum/natural gas engineering), HEALTH PROFESSIONS (health care administration, nursing, premedicine, public health, rehabilitation therapy, and speech pathology/audiology), SOCIAL SCIENCE (African American studies, American studies, anthropology, criminal justice, East Asian studies, economics, food science, geography, history, human development, international relations, Latin American studies, liberal arts/general studies, medieval studies, parks and recreation management, philosophy, physical fitness/movement, political science/government, prelaw, psychology, public administration, religion, sociology, and women's studies). Agriculture, architecture, and meteorology are the strongest academically. Electrical engineering, education, and accounting are the largest.

Required: All bachelor's degree candidates must take 46 general education credits, including 15 in quantitative and communication skills, 9 in natural sciences, 6 each in arts, humanities, and social and behavioral sciences, and 4 in health sciences and phys ed. Further requirements vary by degree program.

Special: Intercollegiate programs in marine sciences and military studies, as well as the B.Ph. program, are offered by faculty from several university colleges. There are internships available in many disciplines. Study abroad is possible through more than 70 programs in 30 countries. Dual and student-designed majors, a general studies degree in arts and sciences, and dual degrees in liberal arts and either earth/natural sciences or engineering are offered with 26 other institutions, as well as a 3-2 engineering program. Co-op programs are available in most engineering majors. There are limited pass/fail options, and nondegree study is possible. There are 45 national honor societies, including Phi Beta Kappa, and a freshman honors program.

Faculty/Classroom: 63% of faculty are male; 36%, female. All both teach and do research. The average class size in a regular course is 26.

Admissions: 55% of the 2003-2004 applicants were accepted. The SAT I scores for the 2003-2004 freshman class were: Verbal--12% below 500, 44% between 500 and 599, 36% between 600 and 700, and 8% above 700; Math--7% below 500, 31% between 500 and 599, 47% between 600 and 700, and 15% above 700. 71% of the current freshmen were in the top fifth of their class; 94% were in the top two fifths.

Requirements: The SAT I or ACT is required; the SAT I is preferred. Applicants should be graduates of accredited high schools or have earned the GED. Required secondary preparation varies by the college or other academic unit applied to. Generally, all applicants should have 5 years of arts, humanities, and social studies, 4 of English, and 3 each of science and math. 2 years of the same foreign language are required for the College of Liberal Arts and School of Communications, and recommended for all other programs. AP and CLEP credits are accepted. Important factors in the admissions decision are advanced placement or honor courses and evidence of special talent.

Procedure: Freshmen are admitted to all sessions. Entrance exams should be taken in the junior year. There is a rolling admissions plan. Application deadlines are open. The fall 2003 application fee was $50. Notification is sent on a rolling basis.

Transfer: 366 transfer students enrolled in 2002-2003. Transfer applicants need a minimum GPA of 2.0, good academic standing, and 18 or more credits from any regionally accredited college or institution at the college level. 36 credits of 120 required for the bachelor's degree must be completed at Penn State.

Visiting: There are regularly scheduled orientations for prospective students. There are guides for informal visits and visitors may sit in on classes and stay overnight. To schedule a visit, contact the Undergraduate Admissions Office.

Financial Aid: In 2003-2004, 45% of all full-time freshmen and 50% of continuing full-time students received some form of financial aid. At least 26% of full-time freshmen and 33% of continuing full-time students received need-based aid. The average freshman award was $10,915. Need-based scholarships or need-based grants averaged $4459; need-based self-help aid (loans and jobs) averaged $2830; non-need-based athletic scholarships averaged $3849; and other non-need-based awards and non-need-based scholarships averaged $13,941. The average financial indebtedness of the 2003 graduate was $18,200. The FAFSA is required. Pennsylvania residents must also complete the PHEAA form. The recommended deadline for filing freshman financial aid applications for fall entry is February 15.

International Students: There are 388 international students enrolled. They must score 550 on the written TOEFL and students whose native language is English must also submit SAT I or ACT scores.

Computers: The mainframe is an IBM ES/3090-600s. The Center for Academic Computing is connected to a wide variety of academic facilities, the library, other Penn State campuses, the National Science Foundation network, BITNET/CREN, and more than a thousand other organizations worldwide. PC classrooms and labs are available throughout the campus, as are special facilities for graphics applications. All students may access the system 24 hours a day, every day. There are no time limits and no fees.

Graduates: From July 1, 2002 to June 30, 2003, 9014 bachelor's degrees were awarded.

Admissions Contact: Geoffrey Harford, Sr., Director of Admissions Services and Evaluation. E-mail: *gjh1@psu.edu*

PENNSYLVANIA COLLEGE OF TECHNOLOGY D-2
Williamsport, PA 17701

(570) 327-4761
(800) 367-9222; Fax: (570) 321-5536

Full-time: 3633 men, 1565 women	Faculty: 280
Part-time: 450 men, 607 women	Ph.D.s: 20%
Graduate: none	Student/Faculty: 19 to 1
Year: semesters, summer session	Tuition: $8940 ($11,250)
Application Deadline: open	Room & Board: $6186
Freshman Class: n/av	
SAT I or ACT: recommended	NONCOMPETITIVE

Pennsylvania College of Technology, founded in 1989, is a public technical college affiliated with Pennsylvania State University. There are 9 undergraduate schools. The library contains 123,305 volumes, 12,259 microform items, and 10,584 audio/video tapes/CDs, and subscribes to 812 periodicals. Computerized library services include the card catalog, interlibrary loans, database searching, and Internet access. Special learning facilities include a learning resource center, radio station, a restaurant and a dental hygiene clinic that are open to the public, and the Penn College Child Care Center. The 111-acre campus is in an urban area 80 miles west of Wilkes Barre. Including any residence halls, there are 26 buildings.

Student Life: 93% of undergraduates are from Pennsylvania. Students are from 31 states, 20 foreign countries, and Canada. 95% are white. 57% are Protestant; 23% Catholic; 19% claim no religious affiliation. The average age of freshmen is 19; all undergraduates, 23.

Housing: 1400 students can be accommodated in college housing, which includes single-sex and coed on-campus apartments. On-campus housing is available on a first-come, first-served basis. Alcohol is not permitted. All students may keep cars.

Activities: There are no fraternities or sororities. There are 50 groups on campus, including art, computers, dance, drama, ethnic, gay, international, professional, radio, religious, social, social service, student government, and yearbook. Popular campus events include a cultural series, Spring Fling Week, and Penn Environment Week.

Sports: There are 9 intercollegiate sports for men and 9 for women, and 42 intramural sports for men and 42 for women. Facilities include a fitness center, a field house, a gym, a soccer field, a softball complex, 5 tennis courts, and a sand volleyball court.

Disabled Students: All of the campus is accessible. Wheelchair ramps, elevators, special parking, specially equipped rest rooms, lowered drinking fountains, and lowered telephones are available.

Services: Counseling and information services are available, as is tutoring in every subject, on request, if tutors are available. There is a reader service for the blind, and remedial math, reading, and writing. Services for hearing-impaired students, adaptive equipment, and note takers are available.

Campus Safety and Security: Measures include 24-hour foot and vehicle patrol, self-defense education, security escort services, and shuttle buses. There are informal discussions, pamphlets/posters/films, and lighted pathways/sidewalks.

Programs of Study: Penn College confers B.S. and B.S.N. degrees. Associate degrees are also awarded. Bachelor's degrees are awarded in AGRICULTURE (environmental studies), BUSINESS (accounting, banking and finance, business administration and management, management information systems, marketing and distribution, and marketing management), COMMUNICATIONS AND THE ARTS (graphic design and technical and business writing), COMPUTER AND PHYSICAL SCIENCE (computer programming and polymer science), EDUCATION (vocational), ENGINEERING AND ENVIRONMENTAL DESIGN (aircraft mechanics, automotive technology, civil engineering, civil engineering technology, computer engineering, computer graphics, computer technology, construction management, construction technology, drafting and design, electrical/electronics engineering technology, engineering, food services technology, graphic arts technology, manufacturing engineering, mechanical design technology, mechanical engineering technology, plastics engineering, plastics technology, printing technology, survey and mapping technology, surveying engineering, technological management, transportation technology, and welding engineering), HEALTH PROFESSIONS (dental hygiene, health care administration, health science, mental health/human services, nursing, occupational therapy, physician's assistant, radiograph medical technology, and radiological science), SOCIAL SCIENCE (culinary arts, human services, and paralegal studies). Information technology, electronics technology, and business management are the largest.

Required: To graduate, students must complete at least 120 credits with a minimum GPA of 2.0 overall and in the major. The core curriculum consists of 18 to 21 credits in humanities, social science, art, and foreign language, 9 in communications, 7 in science, 6 in math, 2 in health and fitness, and a course in computer information.

Special: Penn College offers cooperative and internship programs, cross-registration with Lycoming College and Penn State, dual and student-designed majors, and credit by exam and for work and life experience. There is a chapter of Phi Beta Kappa.

Faculty/Classroom: 75% of faculty are male; 25%, female. All teach undergraduates. The average class size in a regular course is 18.

Admissions: 15% of a recent freshman class were in the top fifth of their class; 32% were in the top two fifths.

Requirements: The SAT I or ACT is recommended. In addition, applicants must have a high school diploma or GED and must take the college's placement exams. Other admissions criteria vary by program. AP and CLEP credits are accepted.

Procedure: Freshmen are admitted to all sessions. Entrance exams should be taken prior to scheduling classes. There are early decision, early admissions, and deferred admissions plans. Application deadlines are open. Notification is sent on a rolling basis. A waiting list is an active part of the admissions procedure. Applications are accepted on-line through the college's web site.

Transfer: 393 transfer students enrolled in a recent year. Transfer procedures vary with each degree program. Courses are evaluated for transfer equivalency. 60 of 120 credits required for the bachelor's degree must be completed at Penn College.

Visiting: There are regularly scheduled orientations for prospective students, including registration, a multimedia presentation, admission and financial aid sessions, a question-and-answer period, a tour of campus facilities, and a reception. Visitors may sit in on classes. To schedule a visit, contact the Office of Admissions at (800) 367-9222 or admissions@pct.edu.

Financial Aid: In 2003-2004, 80% of all full-time students received some form of financial aid. 80% of all full-time students received need-based aid. The average freshman award was $7436. 6% of undergraduates work part time. Average annual earnings from campus work are $2400. The average financial indebtedness of the 2003 graduate was $12,745. Penn College is a member of CSS. The FAFSA and the college's own financial statement are required. The priority date for freshman financial aid applications for fall entry is April 1.

International Students: There are 38 international students enrolled. The school actively recruits these students. They must score 500 on the written TOEFL or 173 on the electronic version.

Computers: The mainframe is an IBM AS/400 F50. Approximately 1200 PCs and Macs are available for student use in more than 40 labs. All students may access the system. There are no time limits and no fees.

Graduates: Of the 2002 graduating class, 67% were employed within 6 months of graduation.

Admissions Contact: Chester D. Schuman, Director of Admissions. E-mail: cschuman@pct.edu Web: www.pct.edu

---

PENNSYLVANIA STATE SYSTEM OF HIGHER EDUCATION

Pennsylvania State System of Higher Education, established in 1983, is a public system. It is governed by a board of governors whose chief administrator is the chancellor. The primary goal of the system is to provide high-quality liberal arts education at an affordable cost with a central mission of teaching and service. The total enrollment of all 14 universities is about 94,000, with more than 5200 faculty members. The universities offer 217 baccalaureate, 107 master's, and 6 doctoral programs. 4-year institutions are located in Bloomsburg, California, Cheyney, Clarion, East Stroudsburg, Edinboro, Indiana, Kutztown, Lock Haven, Mansfield, Millersville, Shippensburg, Slippery Rock, and West Chester. Profiles of the 4-year campuses are included in this section.

PHILADELPHIA BIBLICAL UNIVERSITY   F-3
Langhorne, PA 19047-2990

(215) 752-5800
(800) 366-0049; Fax: (215) 702-4248

Full-time: 396 men, 522 women	**Faculty:** 62; IIB, --$
Part-time: 84 men, 43 women	**Ph.D.s:** 57%
Graduate: 153 men, 199 women	**Student/Faculty:** 15 to 1
Year: semesters, summer session	**Tuition:** $12,745
Application Deadline: open	**Room & Board:** $5650
Freshman Class: 412 applied, 319 accepted, 190 enrolled	
SAT I Verbal/Math: 540/510	**ACT:** 21 COMPETITIVE

Philadelphia Biblical University, founded in 1913, is a private institution offering instruction in the Scriptures and liberal arts and professional the-

ory. Other campuses include the Wisconsin Wilderness Campus and the New Jersey Campus. There are 7 undergraduate and 4 graduate schools. In addition to regional accreditation, PBU has baccalaureate program accreditation with CSWE and NASM. The library contains 156,119 volumes, 63,827 microform items, and 8331 audio/video tapes/CDs, and subscribes to 7829 periodicals. Computerized library services include the card catalog, interlibrary loans, database searching, and Internet access. Special learning facilities include a learning resource center. The 105-acre campus is in a suburban area 30 miles north of Philadelphia. Including any residence halls, there are 17 buildings.

Student Life: 51% of undergraduates are from Pennsylvania. Students are from 41 states, 18 foreign countries, and Canada. 60% are from public schools. 82% are white; 11% African American. Most are Protestant. The average age of freshmen is 18; all undergraduates, 24. 23% do not continue beyond their first year; 60% remain to graduate.

Housing: 465 students can be accommodated in college housing, which includes single-sex dorms. On-campus housing is guaranteed for all 4 years. 52% of students live on campus. Alcohol is not permitted. All students may keep cars.

Activities: There are no fraternities or sororities. There are 19 groups on campus, including art, band, cheerleading, choir, chorale, chorus, computers, drama, ethnic, honors, international, newspaper, orchestra, professional, religious, social, student government, symphony, and yearbook. Popular campus events include Late Skates, Christmas and Valentine socials, and Spring Formal.

Sports: There are 6 intercollegiate sports for men and 6 for women, and 7 intramural sports for men and 7 for women. Facilities include a gym, a baseball diamond, soccer, hockey, and softball fields, a sand volleyball court, 4 tennis courts, a fitness circuit, and a weight room.

Disabled Students: All of the campus is accessible. Wheelchair ramps, elevators, special parking, specially equipped rest rooms, and lowered drinking fountains are available.

Services: Counseling and information services are available, as is tutoring in most subjects. The AIMS Program provides academic support for freshmen who need it.

Campus Safety and Security: Measures include 24-hour foot and vehicle patrol, shuttle buses, informal discussions, and pamphlets/posters/films. There are emergency telephones and lighted pathways/sidewalks.

Programs of Study: PBU confers B.S., B.Mus., B.S.B.A., B.S.Ed., and B.S.W. degrees. Master's degrees are also awarded. Bachelor's degrees are awarded in BUSINESS (business administration and management), COMMUNICATIONS AND THE ARTS (music), EDUCATION (education), SOCIAL SCIENCE (biblical studies and social work). Bible is the strongest academically. Teacher education and Bible are the largest.

Required: Students must complete 51 credits in Bible, 48 in general education, and 27 in professional studies. A total of 126 credits, with a minimum GPA of 2.0, is required. 3 credits in phys ed must be taken. The number of hours in the major varies: 57 in Bible, 80 in music, 43 in social work, and 47 in education. All matriculating baccalaureate students major in Bible and receive a B.S. in Bible degree. About 48% of those students are enrolled in dual degree programs and receive the B.S. in Bible degree plus a degree in their professional area.

Special: PBU offers co-op programs in accounting, computer and microcomputer applications, and office administration; cross-registration with Bucks County Community College; various church ministries, education, social work, and music internships; and study abroad in Israel. An accelerated degree program in Bible is offered. There are dual majors in social work, music, education, and business administration. Student-designed interdisciplinary majors are possible. There is 1 national honor society and a freshman honors program.

Faculty/Classroom: 71% of faculty are male; 29%, female. 83% teach undergraduates. No introductory courses are taught by graduate students. The average class size in an introductory lecture is 25; in a laboratory, 9; and in a regular course, 20.

Admissions: 77% of the 2003-2004 applicants were accepted. The SAT I scores for the 2003-2004 freshman class were: Verbal--28% below 500, 45% between 500 and 599, 23% between 600 and 700, and 4% above 700; Math--39% below 500, 41% between 500 and 599, 19% between 600 and 700, and 1% above 700. The ACT scores were 46% below 21, 23% between 21 and 23, 15% between 24 and 26, and 15% above 28. 34% of the current freshmen were in the top fifth of their class; 62% were in the top two fifths. 1 freshman graduated first in the class.

Requirements: The SAT I or ACT is required, with minimum composite scores of 920 and 19, respectively. A high school diploma or the GED is needed. An essay and a pastor's reference are required. A GPA of 2.0 is required. AP and CLEP credits are accepted. Important factors in the admissions decision are advanced placement or honor courses, personality/intangible qualities, and leadership record.

Procedure: Freshmen are admitted to all sessions. Entrance exams should be taken in the junior or senior year of high school. There is a deferred admissions plan and a rolling admissions plan. Application deadlines are open. Application fee is $25. Applications are accepted on-line.

Transfer: 138 transfer students enrolled in 2002-2003. Tranfers must submit an application, a pastor's reference, college transcripts, and a health form. SAT I and high school transcripts are required if the student has fewer than 60 college credit hours. 60 of 126 credits required for the bachelor's degree must be completed at PBU.

Visiting: There are regularly scheduled orientations for prospective students, including chapel, class visits, a meal in the dining room, and an interview with a counselor. There are guides for informal visits and visitors may sit in on classes and stay overnight. To schedule a visit, contact the Admissions Department at (215) 702-4235.

Financial Aid: In 2003-2004, 85% of all full-time students received some form of financial aid. 65% of all full-time students received need-based aid. The average freshman award was $9968. Need-based scholarships or need-based grants averaged $8269; need-based self-help aid (loans and jobs) averaged $2599; and other non-need-based awards and non-need-based scholarships averaged $5289. 55% of undergraduates work part time. Average annual earnings from campus work are $1593. The average financial indebtedness of the 2003 graduate was $13,000. The FAFSA is required. The deadline for filing freshman financial aid applications for fall entry is May 1.

International Students: There are 17 international students enrolled. The school actively recruits these students. They must score 550 on the written TOEFL or 213 on the electronic version.

Computers: 40 PCs are located in computer labs with Web access. 17 additional PCs for e-mail only are located in student lounges. Students may also access the Internet or the campus network through their own PCs on campus. All students may access the system. There are no time limits and no fees. It is strongly recommended that all students have a personal computer.

Graduates: From July 1, 2002 to June 30, 2003, 298 bachelor's degrees were awarded. The most popular majors were Bible (74%), education (12%), and social work (8%). In an average class, 18% graduate in 4 years or less, 52% graduate in 5 years or less, and 53% graduate in 6 years or less. 75 companies recruited on campus in 2002-2003.

Admissions Contact: Lisa Fuller, Director of Admissions. A video is available. E-mail: *admissions@pbu.edu* Web: *pbu.edu*

PHILADELPHIA UNIVERSITY
Philadelphia, PA 19144-5497

F-3

(215) 951-2800
(800) 951-7287; Fax: (215) 951-2907

Full-time: 733 men, 1524 women	**Faculty:** 108; IIA, -$
Part-time: 107 men, 239 women	**Ph.D.s:** 74%
Graduate: 180 men, 310 women	**Student/Faculty:** 21 to 1
Year: semesters, summer session	**Tuition:** $19,962
Application Deadline: open	**Room & Board:** $7392
Freshman Class: 3461 applied, 2420 accepted, 434 enrolled	
SAT I Verbal/Math: 520/540	**COMPETITIVE**

Philadelphia University, founded in 1884, is a private institution offering preprofessional programs in architecture, design, business, sciences, textiles, fashion, and health. There are 5 undergraduate and 3 graduate schools. In addition to regional accreditation, Phila. U. has baccalaureate program accreditation with ACS, FIDER, and NAAB. The library contains 107,991 volumes, 125,000 microform items, and 46,498 audio/video tapes/CDs, and subscribes to 1244 periodicals. Computerized library services include the card catalog, interlibrary loans, and database searching. Special learning facilities include a learning resource center, art gallery, and design center. The 100-acre campus is in a suburban area 10 minutes west of metropolitan Philadelphia. Including any residence halls, there are 56 buildings.

Student Life: 62% of undergraduates are from out of state, mostly the Middle Atlantic. Students are from 41 states, 33 foreign countries, and Canada. 65% are from public schools. 80% are white. The average age of freshmen is 18; all undergraduates, 20. 31% do not continue beyond their first year; 52% remain to graduate.

Housing: 1205 students can be accommodated in college housing, which includes single-sex and coed dorms, on-campus apartments, and off-campus apartments. On-campus housing is guaranteed for the freshman year only, is available on a first-come, first-served basis, and is available on a lottery system for upperclassmen. Priority is given to out-of-town students. 51% of students live on campus; of those, 60% remain on campus on weekends. All students may keep cars.

Activities: 1% of men belong to 1 national fraternity; 1% of women belong to 1 national sorority. There are 30 groups on campus, including cheerleading, choir, dance, drama, ethnic, gay, honors, international, newspaper, professional, religious, social, social service, student government, and yearbook. Popular campus events include annual fashion show and design competition, Welcome Week, and Spring Weekend.

Sports: There are 5 intercollegiate sports for men and 7 for women, and 13 intramural sports for men and 7 for women. Facilities include 2 gyms, a fitness center, 6 tennis courts, 3 athletic fields, and a student center recreation room.

Disabled Students: 85% of the campus is accessible. Wheelchair ramps, elevators, special parking, specially equipped rest rooms, special class scheduling, lowered drinking fountains, and lowered telephones are available.

Services: Counseling and information services are available, as is tutoring in every subject. There is a reader service for the blind, and remedial math, reading, and writing. There also are study skills workshops, course-related workshops, math review sessions, foreign language conversation groups, and ESL support.

Campus Safety and Security: Measures include 24-hour foot and vehicle patrol, self-defense education, security escort services, and shuttle buses. There are informal discussions, pamphlets/posters/films, emergency telephones, and lighted pathways/sidewalks.

Programs of Study: Phila. U. confers B.S. and B.Arch. degrees. Associate and master's degrees are also awarded. Bachelor's degrees are awarded in BIOLOGICAL SCIENCE (biochemistry and biology/biological science), BUSINESS (accounting, banking and finance, fashion merchandising, international business management, management information systems, management science, marketing/retailing/merchandising, and retailing), COMMUNICATIONS AND THE ARTS (graphic design and industrial design), COMPUTER AND PHYSICAL SCIENCE (chemistry and computer science), ENGINEERING AND ENVIRONMENTAL DESIGN (architecture, environmental science, interior design, textile engineering, and textile technology), HEALTH PROFESSIONS (physician's assistant and premedicine), SOCIAL SCIENCE (biopsychology, fashion design and technology, and psychology). Physician's assistant, architecture, and computer science are the strongest academically. Architecture, fashion merchandising, and fashion design are the largest.

Required: All students are required to complete a 60-credit residency with courses in math, science, social science, and the humanities, 2 semesters of phys ed, and a professional studies core curriculum, which differs by major program. A number of requirements may be satisfied and elective credits earned by proficiency exam. A total of 121 to 146 credits is required with an overall GPA of 2.0.

Special: Philadelphia University offers special B.S. degree programs for registered nurses and allied health professionals. Cooperative education placements are available locally, on the East Coast, and in London, England. Students may undertake a semester of independent study in 1 discipline. Cooperative programs in all academic majors, study abroad, internships, a dual major in international business, an accelerated business administration degree program, and an integrated major in business and science are available. There is a freshman honors program.

Faculty/Classroom: 62% of faculty are male; 38%, female. All teach undergraduates and 50% both teach and do research. No introductory courses are taught by graduate students. The average class size in an introductory lecture is 25; in a laboratory, 14; and in a regular course, 17.

Admissions: 70% of the 2003-2004 applicants were accepted. The SAT I scores for the 2003-2004 freshman class were: Verbal--30% below 500, 51% between 500 and 599, 18% between 600 and 700, and 1% above 700; Math--28% below 500, 51% between 500 and 599, 20% between 600 and 700, and 1% above 700. 38% of the current freshmen were in the top fifth of their class; 78% were in the top two fifths. In a recent year, 3 freshmen graduated first in their class.

Requirements: The SAT I or ACT is required. In addition, applicants should be high school graduates or have earned the GED. Recommended secondary preparation includes 4 years each of English and history, 3 years of math including algebra II and geometry, and 2 years of science. Potential science majors are strongly urged to take 4 years of math and 4 years of science. A GPA of 2.0 is required. AP and CLEP credits are accepted. Important factors in the admissions decision are evidence of special talent, extracurricular activities record, and leadership record.

Procedure: Freshmen are admitted fall and spring. There is a deferred admissions plan. Application deadlines are open. The application fee is $35. There is a rolling admissions plan. Applications are accepted online through *www.philau.edu*.

Transfer: 101 transfer students enrolled in a recent year. A 2.5 GPA is usually required. 60 of 121 to 146 credits required for the bachelor's degree must be completed at Phila. U.

Visiting: There are regularly scheduled orientations for prospective students, including an interview and a campus tour. There are guides for informal visits and visitors may sit in on classes and stay overnight. To schedule a visit, contact the Admissions Office.

Financial Aid: In 2003-2004, 99% of all full-time freshmen and 96% of continuing full-time students received some form of financial aid. 74% of full-time freshmen and 70% of continuing full-time students received need-based aid. The average freshman award was $15,044. 31% of undergraduates work part time. Average annual earnings from campus work are $1000. The average financial indebtedness of a recent graduate was $12,559. The FAFSA is required. The deadline for filing freshman financial aid applications for fall entry is April 15.

International Students: In a recent year, there were 77 international students enrolled. The school actively recruits these students. They must score 500 on the written TOEFL and also take an English placement test.

Computers: The mainframe is a DEC Alpha 1000/500. More than 250 Macs and PCs are available in the general-purpose and departmental computing labs. All students may access the system 7 days a week. There are no time limits and no fees. It is strongly recommended that all students have a personal computer.

Graduates: From July 1, 2002 to June 30, 2003, 497 bachelor's degrees were awarded. In an average class, 32% graduate in 4 years or less, 42% graduate in 5 years or less, and 45% graduate in 6 years or less. 70 companies recruited on campus in 2002-2003. Of the 2002 graduating class, 9% were enrolled in graduate school within 6 months of graduation and 82% were employed.

Admissions Contact: Christine Greb, Director of Admissions.
E-mail: *admissions@philau.edu* Web: *www.philau.edu*

POINT PARK UNIVERSITY	B-3
Pittsburgh, PA 15222	**(412) 392-3430**
	(800) 321-0129; Fax: (412) 392-3902
Full-time: 777 men, 1284 women	**Faculty:** 81
Part-time: 401 men, 365 women	**Ph.Ds:** 56%
Graduate: 178 men, 221 women	**Student/Faculty:** 25 to 1
Year: semesters, summer session	**Tuition:** $15,180
Application Deadline: open	**Room & Board:** $6660
Freshman Class: 1803 applied, 1455 accepted, 421 enrolled	
SAT I Verbal/Math: 527/502	**ACT:** 22 COMPETITIVE

Point Park University, formerly Point Park College, founded in 1960, is an independent institution offering programs in liberal arts, fine arts, business, engineering, health science, professional training, and teacher preparation. There are 4 undergraduate and 8 graduate schools. In addition to regional accreditation, Point Park has baccalaureate program accreditation with ABET, IACBE, and NASD. The library contains 159,171 volumes, 29,590 microform items, and 2278 audio/video tapes/CDs, and subscribes to 688 periodicals. Computerized library services include the card catalog, interlibrary loans, database searching, and Internet access. Special learning facilities include a learning resource center, radio station, TV station, theaters, and dance studios. The campus is in an urban area in downtown Pittsburgh. Including any residence halls, there are 5 buildings.

Student Life: 85% of undergraduates are from Pennsylvania. Students are from 45 states, 27 foreign countries, and Canada. 73% are white; 13% African American. 38% are Catholic; 35% Protestant; 19% claim no religious affiliation; 7% Muslim, Buddhist, and Hindu. The average age of freshmen is 19; all undergraduates, 25. 28% do not continue beyond their first year; 38% remain to graduate.

Housing: 587 students can be accommodated in college housing, which includes single-sex and coed dorms. On-campus housing is guaranteed for all 4 years. 79% of students commute. No one may keep cars.

Activities: There are no fraternities or sororities. There are 18 groups on campus, including cheerleading, choir, computers, dance, drama, ethnic, film, honors, international, literary magazine, musical theater, newspaper, photography, political, professional, radio and TV, religious, social, social service, student government, and yearbook. Popular campus events include Snowball (Christmas) Dance, Spring Fling (spring dance), and dance and theater productions.

Sports: There are 4 intercollegiate sports for men and 4 for women, and 7 intramural sports for men and 7 for women. Facilities include a recreation center and a 130-seat auditorium.

Disabled Students: 98% of the campus is accessible. Wheelchair ramps, elevators, specially equipped rest rooms, special class scheduling, lowered drinking fountains, and lowered telephones are available.

Services: Counseling and information services are available, as is tutoring in most subjects. Learning-disabled services are available on a case-by-case basis. There is a reader service for the blind and remedial math, reading, and writing.

Campus Safety and Security: Measures include 24-hour foot and vehicle patrol, security escort services, informal discussions, and pamphlets/posters/films. There are emergency telephones and lighted pathways/sidewalks.

Programs of Study: Point Park confers B.A., B.S., and B.F.A. degrees. Associate and master's degrees are also awarded. Bachelor's degrees are awarded in BIOLOGICAL SCIENCE (biology/biological science and biotechnology), BUSINESS (accounting, business administration and management, funeral home services, human resources, management science, and sports management), COMMUNICATIONS AND THE ARTS (advertising, applied art, arts administration/management, broadcasting, communications, dance, dramatic arts, English, film arts, journalism, media arts, photography, and video), COMPUTER AND PHYSICAL SCIENCE (computer science, digital arts/technology, and information sciences and systems), EDUCATION (dance, drama, early childhood, elementary, and secondary), ENGINEERING AND ENVIRONMENTAL DESIGN (civil engineering technology, electrical/electronics engineering technology, engineering management, environmental science, mechanical engineering technology, and systems engineering), HEALTH PROFESSIONS (health care administration and respiratory therapy), SOCIAL SCIENCE (behavioral science, criminal justice, history, international studies, law enforcement and corrections, liberal arts/general studies, paralegal studies, political science/government, psychology, and public administration). Electrical engineering technology, business management, and performing arts are the largest.

Required: All majors leading to a baccalaureate degree require a minimum of 120 credits. Most programs require 42 core curriculum credits, with at least 30 completed in residence. A 2.0 GPA is required.

Special: Cross-registration is available through the Pittsburgh Council of Higher Education. The college offers internships, study abroad, a Washington semester, work-study, dual and student-designed majors, credit by exam and for life/military/work experience, nondegree study, and pass/fail options. Capstone programs are available for students with associate degrees. The film and video major is offered in conjunction with Pittsburgh Filmmakers. Accelerated degree programs are available. There are 2 national honor societies and a freshman honors program.

Faculty/Classroom: 64% of faculty are male; 36%, female. All teach undergraduates. No introductory courses are taught by graduate students. The average class size in an introductory lecture is 17; in a laboratory, 12; and in a regular course, 16.

Admissions: 81% of the 2003-2004 applicants were accepted. The SAT I scores for the 2003-2004 freshman class were: Verbal--33% below 500, 49% between 500 and 599, 18% between 600 and 700, and 1% above 700; Math--45% below 500, 42% between 500 and 599, 11% between 600 and 700, and 1% above 700. The ACT scores were 36% below 21, 36% between 21 and 23, 17% between 24 and 26, 5% between 27 and 28, and 6% above 28. 27% of the current freshmen were in the top fifth of their class; 56% were in the top two fifths. 5 freshmen graduated first in their class.

Requirements: The SAT I or ACT is required. In addition, students should have completed 12 academic credits or 16 Carnegie units consisting of 4 in English, 3 in history, science, and math, and 2 years of foreign language. The GED is accepted. Theater and dance students must audition, and an interview is requested for all candidates. A GPA of 2.5 is required. AP and CLEP credits are accepted. Important factors in the admissions decision are advanced placement or honor courses, evidence of special talent, and personality/intangible qualities.

Procedure: Freshmen are admitted to all sessions. Entrance exams should be taken in the junior or senior year. There are early admissions, deferred admissions, and rolling admissions plans. Application deadlines are open. Application fee is $25 (on-line), ($40 paper). Applications are accepted on-line through the school's web site at *www.ppc.edu*.

Transfer: 202 transfer students enrolled in 2002-2003. Applicants must have completed 12 credit hours with at least a 2.0 GPA. The SAT I or ACT and an interview are recommended. 30 of 120 credits required for the bachelor's degree must be completed at Point Park.

Visiting: There are regularly scheduled orientations for prospective students. There are guides for informal visits and visitors may sit in on classes. To schedule a visit, contact the Office of Admissions.

Financial Aid: In 2003-2004, 99% of all full-time freshmen and 85% of continuing full-time students received some form of financial aid. 82% of full-time freshmen and 75% of continuing full-time students received need-based aid. The average freshman award was $16,098. Need-based scholarships or need-based grants averaged $2770 ($10,910 maximum); need-based self-help aid (loans and jobs) averaged $3329 ($6625 maximum); non-need-based athletic scholarships averaged $3639 ($22,220 maximum); and other non-need-based awards and non-need-based scholarships averaged $4153 ($15,560 maximum). 16% of undergraduates work part time. Average annual earnings from campus work are $1543. The average financial indebtedness of the 2003 graduate was $16,193. Point Park is a member of CSS. The FAFSA is required. The priority date for freshman financial aid applications for fall entry is May 1. The deadline for filing freshman financial aid applications for fall entry is December 1.

International Students: There are 40 international students enrolled. The school actively recruits these students. They must score 500 on the written TOEFL or take the MELAB or the college's own test. Students who do not take the TOEFL, score a 500 on either of the other tests, or a 6 on the Test of Written English (TWE), must be tested upon arrival at the college.

Computers: There are 164 PCs for student use in computer labs. PC labs are available to all students. Special facilities are available to certain academic majors, such as journalism and science/engineering. All students may access the system 7 days a week; lab hours vary by facility. There are no time limits and no fees.

Graduates: From July 1, 2002 to June 30, 2003, 518 bachelor's degrees were awarded. The most popular majors were business (accelerated) (13%), theater arts (9%), and dance (8%). In an average class, 38% graduate in 6 years or less.

Admissions Contact: Joell Minford, Full-Time Admissions. A video is available. E-mail: *enroll@ppc.edu* Web: *www.ppc.edu*

ROBERT MORRIS COLLEGE
(See Robert Morris University)

ROBERT MORRIS UNIVERSITY
B-3
Moon Township, PA 15108-1189
(412) 262-8402
(800) 762-0097; Fax: (412) 299-2425

Full-time: 1524 men, 1226 women	**Faculty:** 123
Part-time: 410 men, 575 women	**Ph.D.s:** 81%
Graduate: 575 men, 506 women	**Student/Faculty:** 22 to 1
Year: semesters, summer session	**Tuition:** $13,484
Application Deadline: July 1	**Room & Board:** $6954
Freshman Class: 1816 applied, 1645 accepted, 567 enrolled	
SAT I Verbal/Math: 500/495	**ACT:** 19 COMPETITIVE

Robert Morris University, founded in 1921, is a private institution offering more than 30 undergraduate degree programs and 14 master's and doctoral degree programs. There are 4 undergraduate and 3 graduate schools. In addition to regional accreditation, RMU has baccalaureate program accreditation with ABET. The 2 libraries contain 138,676 volumes, 325,563 microform items, and 2863 audio/video tapes/CDs, and subscribe to 685 periodicals. Computerized library services include the card catalog, interlibrary loans, and database searching. Special learning facilities include a learning resource center, art gallery, TV station, and a manufacturing lab for engineering and other students. The 230-acre campus is in a suburban area 17 miles southwest of Pittsburgh. Including any residence halls, there are 24 buildings.

Student Life: 92% of undergraduates are from Pennsylvania. Students are from 27 states, 20 foreign countries, and Canada. 90% are from public schools. 88% are white. 60% are Catholic; 35% Protestant. The average age of freshmen is 18; all undergraduates, 24. 26% do not continue beyond their first year; 53% remain to graduate.

Housing: 1025 students can be accommodated in college housing, which includes single-sex and coed dorms and on-campus apartments. On-campus housing is guaranteed for all 4 years. 73% of students commute. Alcohol is not permitted. All students may keep cars.

Activities: 4% of men belong to 5 national fraternities; 3% of women belong to 3 national sororities. There are 50 groups on campus, including cheerleading, computers, drama, ethnic, film, honors, international, marching band, musical theater, newspaper, pep band, photography, professional, radio and TV, religious, social, social service, student government, and yearbook. Popular campus events include Snow Ball and Spring Fest.

Sports: There are 6 intercollegiate sports for men and 8 for women, and 11 intramural sports for men and 11 for women. Facilities include a field house, gym, health club, and 11 athletic fields.

Disabled Students: 75% of the campus is accessible. Wheelchair ramps, elevators, special parking, specially equipped rest rooms, special class scheduling, lowered drinking fountains, and lowered telephones are available.

Services: Counseling and information services are available, as is tutoring in most subjects. There is a reader service for the blind and remedial math, reading, and writing.

Campus Safety and Security: Measures include 24-hour foot and vehicle patrol, security escort services, shuttle buses, and informal discussions. There are pamphlets/posters/films, emergency telephones, and lighted pathways/sidewalks.

Programs of Study: RMU confers B.A., B.S., and B.S.B.A. degrees. Master's and doctoral degrees are also awarded. Bachelor's degrees are awarded in BUSINESS (accounting, banking and finance, business administration and management, hospitality management services, human resources, management science, marketing/retailing/merchandising, organizational behavior, sports management, and transportation management), COMMUNICATIONS AND THE ARTS (communications, English, and media arts), COMPUTER AND PHYSICAL SCIENCE (actuarial science, information sciences and systems, and mathematics), EDUCATION (business and elementary), ENGINEERING AND ENVIRONMENTAL DESIGN (aviation administration/management and engineering), HEALTH PROFESSIONS (health care administration and nursing), SOCIAL SCIENCE (economics and social science). Engineering and mathematics are the strongest academically. Management, marketing, and information sciences are the largest.

Required: All candidates must complete 126 to 135 credit hours, including 24 to 31 in the major, with a 2.0 GPA overall and a 2.5 in the major. A core curriculum varies with each major, and consists of humanities, communication skills, social sciences, computing, and math. All students must demonstrate competency in computer software applications.

Special: The university offers cooperative programs in all majors, cross-registration with the 9 schools of the Pittsburgh Council of Higher Education, internships, work-study programs, study abroad in 4 countries, and nondegree study. Credit by exam and pass/fail options are available. There are 2 national honor societies, a freshman honors program, and 1 departmental honors program.

Faculty/Classroom: 62% of faculty are male; 38%, female. All teach undergraduates, 70% do research, and 70% do both. No introductory courses are taught by graduate students. The average class size in an introductory lecture is 23; in a laboratory, 12; and in a regular course, 23.

Admissions: 91% of the 2003-2004 applicants were accepted. The SAT I scores for the 2003-2004 freshman class were: Verbal--52% below 500, 40% between 500 and 599, and 8% between 600 and 700; Math--46% below 500, 38% between 500 and 599, 15% between 600 and 700, and 1% above 700.

Requirements: The SAT I is required. In addition, candidates should be graduates of an accredited secondary school or hold a GED diploma. They must have completed 16 Carnegie units, including 4 in English, 3 each in math and social studies, 2 in science, and 1 in history. An interview is required for some and recommended for all others. A GPA of 2.0 is required. AP and CLEP credits are accepted. Important factors in the admissions decision are advanced placement or honor courses, leadership record, and personality/intangible qualities.

Procedure: Freshmen are admitted fall and spring. Entrance exams should be taken by fall or late winter of the senior year. There is a deferred admissions plan and a rolling admissions plan. Applications should be filed by July 1 for fall entry and December 1 for spring entry. Notification is sent on a rolling basis. The fall 2003 application fee was $30. Applications are accepted on-line through the university's web site.

Transfer: 444 transfer students enrolled in 2002-2003. Students must have a minimum 2.0 GPA in nondevelopmental academic courses. Those with fewer than 30 earned credits must also submit an official high school transcript and test results of the SAT I or ACT. An interview is recommended. 30 of 126 credits required for the bachelor's degree must be completed at RMU.

Visiting: There are regularly scheduled orientations for prospective students, consisting of testing, orientation, and academic advising. There are guides for informal visits and visitors may sit in on classes and stay overnight. To schedule a visit, contact The Enrollment Office at (412) 262-8206 or *enrollmentoffice@rmu.edu*.

Financial Aid: In 2003-2004, 81% of all full-time freshmen and 74% of continuing full-time students received some form of financial aid. 80% of full-time freshmen and 68% of continuing full-time students received need-based aid. The average freshman award was $12,247. Need-based scholarships or need-based grants averaged $7880; need-based self-help aid (loans and jobs) averaged $5091; and non-need-based athletic scholarships averaged $7408. The FAFSA and PHEAA are required. The deadline for filing freshman financial aid applications for fall entry is May 1.

International Students: There are 66 international students enrolled. They must score 500 on the written TOEFL or 173 on the electronic version and also take the SAT I.

Computers: The mainframes are SUN servers. Students have access to 350 PCs at computer labs and 6 computerized classrooms. Students can also access Internet applications in their dorm rooms, at labs in the residence halls, and in the library. All students may access the system. There are no time limits and no fees.

Graduates: From July 1, 2002 to June 30, 2003, 735 bachelor's degrees were awarded. The most popular majors were management (14%), marketing (11%), and accounting (10%). In an average class, 25% graduate in 4 years or less, 46% graduate in 5 years or less, and 53% graduate in 6 years or less. 140 companies recruited on campus in 2002-2003. Of the 2002 graduating class, 3% were enrolled in graduate school within 6 months of graduation and 93% were employed.

Admissions Contact: J. Donald Williams, Assistant Dean of Enrollment Services. A video is available. E-mail: *enrollmentoffice@rmu.edu* Web: *http://www.rmu.edu*

ROSEMONT COLLEGE
F-4
Rosemont, PA 19010-1699
(610) 526-2952
(800) 331-0708; Fax: (610) 520-4399

Full-time: 18 men, 403 women	**Faculty:** 31
Part-time: 51 men, 225 women	**Ph.D.s:** 91%
Graduate: 79 men, 293 women	**Student/Faculty:** 14 to 1
Year: semesters, summer session	**Tuition:** $18,475
Application Deadline: open	**Room & Board:** $7700
Freshman Class: 253 applied, 235 accepted, 97 enrolled	
SAT I Verbal/Math: 509/493	**ACT:** 21 COMPETITIVE

Rosemont College, founded in 1921, is an independent primarily women's liberal arts and sciences college, affiliated with the Roman Catholic Church. Accelerated degree and graduate programs are open to men and women. The library contains 159,731 volumes, 24,981 microform items, and 2784 audio/video tapes/CDs, and subscribes to 563 periodicals. Computerized library services include the card catalog, interlibrary loans, and database searching. Special learning facilities include a learning resource center and art gallery. The 56-acre campus is in a suburban area 11 miles west of Philadelphia. Including any residence halls, there are 15 buildings.

Student Life: 72% of undergraduates are from Pennsylvania. Students are from 18 states and 10 foreign countries. 57% are white; 19% African American; 11% Asian American. 60% are Catholic; 17% Protestant; 15% Muslim, Quaker, and not indicated. The average age of freshmen is 18; all undergraduates, 23. 8% do not continue beyond their first year; 77% remain to graduate.

Housing: 410 students can be accommodated in college housing, which includes single-sex dorms. In addition, there are special-interest houses. On-campus housing is guaranteed for all 4 years. 68% of students live on campus; of those, 50% remain on campus on weekends. All students may keep cars.

Activities: There are no fraternities or sororities. There are 11 groups on campus, including art, band, choir, chorus, dance, drama, ethnic, honors, international, jazz band, literary magazine, marching band, musical theater, newspaper, orchestra, photography, political, professional, radio, religious, social service, student government, symphony, and yearbook. Popular campus events include Oktoberfest, Founders Day, and International/Multi-Cultural Festival.

Sports: There are 6 intercollegiate sports for women. Facilities include hockey and softball fields, tennis courts, treadmills, weight equipment, a 500-seat auditorium, and indoor basketball, badminton, and volleyball courts.

Disabled Students: 20% of the campus is accessible. Wheelchair ramps, elevators, special parking, specially equipped rest rooms, special class scheduling, lowered drinking fountains, and lowered telephones are available.

Services: Counseling and information services are available, as is tutoring in every subject, and a writing and learning resource center.

Campus Safety and Security: Measures include 24-hour foot and vehicle patrol, self-defense education, security escort services, and shuttle buses. There are informal discussions, pamphlets/posters/films, emergency telephones, lighted pathways/sidewalks, and electronically operated residence hall entrances activated by security cards.

Programs of Study: Rosemont confers B.A., B.S., and B.F.A. degrees. Master's degrees are also awarded. Bachelor's degrees are awarded in BIOLOGICAL SCIENCE (biochemistry and biology/biological science), BUSINESS (accounting and business administration and management), COMMUNICATIONS AND THE ARTS (communications, English, fine arts, French, German, and Spanish), COMPUTER AND PHYSICAL SCIENCE (chemistry and mathematics), EDUCATION (art, foreign languages, and secondary), ENGINEERING AND ENVIRONMENTAL DESIGN (environmental science), HEALTH PROFESSIONS (predentistry and premedicine), SOCIAL SCIENCE (economics, history, humanities, Italian studies, liberal arts/general studies, philosophy, political science/government, prelaw, psychology, religion, social science, sociology, and women's studies). Psychology, English, and chemistry are the largest.

Required: All students take classes in writing, literature, religious studies, foreign language, philosophy, history, math or natural science, social science, and art. A total of 128 credits is required for graduation, with 40 to 48 in the major, and a minimum GPA of 2.0. A comprehensive exam must be taken in the major.

Special: Cross-registration with Villanova and Arcadia Universities, Eastern, Cabrini, Gwynedd-Mercy, Holy Family, Chestnut Hill, Immaculata, and Neumann colleges, the Art Institute Exchange Program, internships, study abroad, a Washington semester, dual and student-designed majors, and accelerated degree programs are available. Also offered are a joint admission program with MCP/Hahnemann School of Medicine, 5-year accelerated programs in English and publishing, and in counseling psychology, and elementary and secondary teacher certification, transfer nursing program with Villanova University is also available. There are 6 national honor societies and a freshman honors program.

Faculty/Classroom: 41% of faculty are male; 59%, female. All teach undergraduates and 70% both teach and do research. No introductory courses are taught by graduate students. The average class size in an introductory lecture is 20; in a laboratory, 10; and in a regular course, 12.

Admissions: 93% of the 2003-2004 applicants were accepted. The SAT I scores for the 2003-2004 freshman class were: Verbal--24% below 500, 44% between 500 and 599, 25% between 600 and 700, and 4% above 700; Math--38% below 500, 42% between 500 and 599, 15% between 600 and 700, and 3% above 700. The ACT scores were 100% between 21 and 23. 35% of the current freshmen were in the top fifth of their class; 55% were in the top two fifths. 2 freshmen graduated first in their class.

Requirements: The SAT I is required. A GED is accepted. Applicants must complete 16 academic credits, including 4 in English and 2 each in foreign language, history, math, and science. An interview is recommended. A GPA of 2.0 is required. AP and CLEP credits are accepted. Important factors in the admissions decision are advanced placement or honor courses, leadership record, and recommendations by school officials.

Procedure: Freshmen are admitted fall and spring. Entrance exams should be taken before January of the senior year. There is a deferred admissions plan. There is a rolling admissions plan. Application deadlines are open. Application fee is $35. Applications are accepted on-line through Apply and the school's web site.

Transfer: 25 transfer students enrolled in 2002-2003. Transfer applicants should submit transcripts from each college attended, a letter of good standing from the dean at the last college attended, and catalogs from the colleges from which the student wishes to transfer credits. Students with fewer than 30 credits are required to submit high school tran-

scripts and SAT I scores. The minimum GPA is 2.0. An associate degree and interview are recommended. 45 of 120 credits required for the bachelor's degree must be completed at Rosemont.

Visiting: There are regularly scheduled orientations for prospective students, including campus visit days, overnight visits, and class visitations. There are guides for informal visits and visitors may sit in on classes and stay overnight. To schedule a visit, contact the Admissions Office at *admissions@rosemount.edu.*

Financial Aid: In 2003-2004, 97% of all full-time freshmen and 95% of continuing full-time students received some form of financial aid. 78% of full-time freshmen and 76% of continuing full-time students received need-based aid. The average freshman award was $17,409. Need-based scholarships or need-based grants averaged $10,784 ($20,150 maximum); need-based self-help aid (loans and jobs) averaged $4625 ($6625 maximum); and federal and state grants averaged $2000 (maximum). 39% of undergraduates work part time. Average annual earnings from campus work are $750. The average financial indebtedness of the 2003 graduate was $16,000. Rosemont is a member of CSS. The FAFSA is required. The priority date for freshman financial aid applications for fall entry is February 15. The deadline for filing freshman financial aid applications for fall entry is March 15.

International Students: There are 15 international students enrolled. The school actively recruits these students. They must score 500 on the written TOEFL.

Computers: There are 40 public workstations with Microsoft Office Pro software. All have full access to the college's electronic learning and library information system. All residence hall rooms are connected to the network. All students may access the system. There are no time limits and no fees.

Graduates: From July 1, 2002 to June 30, 2003, 190 bachelor's degrees were awarded. The most popular majors were psychology (23%), English literature (15%), and accounting/business (13%). In an average class, 74% graduate in 4 years or less, and 77% graduate in 5 years or less. 10 companies recruited on campus in 2002-2003. Of the 2002 graduating class, 40% were enrolled in graduate school within 6 months of graduation and 60% were employed.

Admissions Contact: Rennie H. Andrews, Dean of Admissions. A video is available. E-mail: *admissions@rosemont.edu*
Web: *www.rosemont.edu*

SAINT FRANCIS UNIVERSITY   C-3
Loretto, PA 15940   (814) 472-3100
(866) 342-5738; Fax: (814) 472-3335

Full-time: 484 men, 671 women	**Faculty:** 90
Part-time: 49 men, 129 women	**Ph.Ds:** 74%
Graduate: 183 men, 305 women	**Student/Faculty:** 13 to 1
Year: semesters, summer session	**Tuition:** $18,292
Application Deadline: April 1	**Room & Board:** $7584
Freshman Class: 1280 applied, 1116 accepted, 339 enrolled	
SAT I Verbal/Math: 522/517	**LESS COMPETITIVE**

Saint Francis University, founded in 1847, is a private Franciscan institution affiliated with the Roman Catholic Church. It offers programs in business, education, humanities, sciences, social science, and preprofessional programs. In addition to regional accreditation, Saint Francis has baccalaureate program accreditation with APTA, CAHEA, and CSWE. The library contains 117,870 volumes, 7648 microform items, and 2701 audio/video tapes/CDs, and subscribes to 7293 periodicals. Computerized library services include the card catalog, interlibrary loans, database searching, and Internet access. Special learning facilities include a learning resource center, art gallery, radio station, TV station, classroom satellite hookup, art studio, wireless technology lab, and computer assurance lab. The 600-acre campus is in a rural area 85 miles east of Pittsburgh. Including any residence halls, there are 23 buildings.

Student Life: 77% of undergraduates are from Pennsylvania. Students are from 27 states, 6 foreign countries, and Canada. 66% are from public schools. 85% are white; 11% African American. 55% are Catholic; 40% Protestant. The average age of freshmen is 19; all undergraduates, 21. 21% do not continue beyond their first year; 62% remain to graduate.

Housing: 983 students can be accommodated in college housing, which includes single-sex dorms, on-campus apartments, off-campus apartments, married-student housing, and intensive-study floors. On-campus housing is guaranteed for all 4 years. 56% of students live on campus; of those, 20% remain on campus on weekends. Alcohol is not permitted. Upperclassmen may keep cars.

Activities: 1% of men belong to 1 national fraternity; 2% of women belong to 1 local and 2 national sororities. There are 54 groups on campus, including academic department clubs, art, cheerleading, choir, computers, drama, ethnic, honors, international, literary magazine, newspaper, pep band, photography, political, professional, radio and TV, religious, social, social service, student government, theater production, and yearbook. Popular campus events include Days of Reflection, Winter Weekend, and Christmas Mass.

Sports: There are 9 intercollegiate sports for men and 12 for women, and 8 intramural sports for men and 8 for women. Facilities include an athletic center with a 6-lane swimming pool, 3 racquetball courts, a suspended running track, a weight room, a 3500-seat basketball arena, and a multipurpose gym. Outdoor facilities include recreational areas and game fields, jogging/walking trails, 9-hole golf course, a lake, and beach volleyball pits.

Disabled Students: Wheelchair ramps, elevators, special parking, specially equipped rest rooms, lowered drinking fountains, lowered telephones, and special housing are available.

Services: Counseling and information services are available, as is tutoring in most subjects. There is remedial math, reading, and writing.

Campus Safety and Security: Measures include 24-hour foot and vehicle patrol, self-defense education, security escort services, and informal discussions. There are pamphlets/posters/films, emergency telephones, lighted pathways/sidewalks, and a certified police force.

Programs of Study: Saint Francis confers B.A., B.S., B.S.N., and B.S.W. degrees. Master's degrees are also awarded. Bachelor's degrees are awarded in BIOLOGICAL SCIENCE (biology/biological science), BUSINESS (accounting, management information systems, and management science), COMMUNICATIONS AND THE ARTS (communications, English, French, modern language, and Spanish), COMPUTER AND PHYSICAL SCIENCE (chemistry, computer science, and mathematics), EDUCATION (elementary and secondary), HEALTH PROFESSIONS (medical laboratory technology, nursing, occupational therapy, physical therapy, and physician's assistant), SOCIAL SCIENCE (criminal justice, economics, history, international studies, philosophy, political science/government, psychology, public administration, religion, social work, and sociology). Business, occupational therapy, and chemistry are the strongest academically. Business, physician's assistant, and education are the largest.

Required: Students must complete 128 credits, with at least 36 in the major, while maintaining a 2.0 GPA. The core curriculum, totaling 58 credits, includes writing, public speaking, fine arts, foreign language, history, philosophy, religious studies (with required service component), psychology, sociology, political science, and economics. A word processing and research workshop is required in the freshman year. In addition to a comprehensive exam in the major, an English proficiency exam must be taken in the junior year.

Special: The university offers internships, co-op programs, study abroad in 10 countries, a Washington semester, work-study programs, and nondegree study. Student-designed majors and 3-2 engineering degrees with Pennsylvania State and Clarkson Universities and the University of Pittsburgh are available. There is a dual major available in international business/modern languages. Credit by exam and pass/fail options are also offered. There are 11 national honor societies, a freshman honors program, and 10 departmental honors programs.

Faculty/Classroom: 56% of faculty are male; 44%, female. 99% teach undergraduates, 50% do research, and 50% do both. No introductory courses are taught by graduate students. The average class size in an introductory lecture is 23; in a laboratory, 16; and in a regular course, 19.

Admissions: 87% of the 2003-2004 applicants were accepted. The SAT I scores for the 2003-2004 freshman class were: Verbal--38% below 500, 48% between 500 and 599, 11% between 600 and 700, and 1% above 700. The ACT scores were 32% below 21, 21% between 21 and 23, 33% between 24 and 26, 12% between 27 and 28, and 2% above 28. 38% of the current freshmen were in the top fifth of their class. There was 1 National Merit finalist and 1 semifinalist. 5 freshmen graduated first in their class.

Requirements: The SAT I or ACT is required. In addition, applicants must be graduates of an accredited secondary school or have earned a GED certificate. All applicants must have completed 16 Carnegie units, consisting of 4 years of English, 2 each of math and social science, 1 lab science, and 7 academic electives. Applicants to biology and allied health majors need an additional unit of science. Chemistry, computer science, engineering, and math applicants need 4 math units and 2 science units. Physical therapy applicants must have 4 units of math and 4 of science. AP and CLEP credits are accepted. Important factors in the admissions decision are advanced placement or honor courses, extracurricular activities record, and recommendations by school officials.

Procedure: Freshmen are admitted to all sessions. Entrance exams should be taken in spring of the junior year and fall of the senior year. There is a deferred admissions plan and a rolling admissions plan. Applications should be filed by April 1 for fall entry and November 1 for winter entry. The fall 2003 application fee was $30. Notification is sent on a rolling basis. Applications are accepted on-line through *www.francis.edu.*

Transfer: 32 transfer students enrolled in 2002-2003. Applicants must have a minimum GPA of 2.0 for consideration, 2.5 for nursing majors, and 2.75 for physician's assistant majors. 64 of 128 credits required for the bachelor's degree must be completed at Saint Francis.

Visiting: There are regularly scheduled orientations for prospective students, including an interview by financial aid and admission staff, tour, meeting with faculty, and attending class. There are guides for informal visits and visitors may sit in on classes and stay overnight. To schedule a visit, contact the Admissions Office at *elipp@francis.edu.*

Financial Aid: In 2003-2004, 96% of all full-time freshmen and 91% of continuing full-time students received some form of financial aid. 86% of full-time freshmen and 83% of continuing full-time students received need-based aid. The average freshman award was $16,962, with $6866 ($14,350 maximum) from need-based scholarships or need-based grants; $2976 ($4625 maximum) from need-based self-help aid (loans and jobs); $1812 ($26,688 maximum) from non-need-based athletic scholarships; $3531 ($18,292 maximum) from other non-need-based awards and non-need-based scholarships; and $1777 ($15,000 maximum) from non-need-based self-help and other miscellaneous funds. 32% of undergraduates work part time. Average annual earnings from campus work are $794. The average financial indebtedness of the 2003 graduate was $17,000. The FAFSA and the college's own financial statement are required. The deadline for filing freshman financial aid applications for fall entry is May 1.

International Students: There are 48 international students enrolled. The school actively recruits these students. They must score 500 on the written TOEFL or 220 on the electronic version and also take the SAT I or the ACT.

Computers: The mainframe is a DEC Alpha. Laptop computers are distributed to all incoming students. There are 3 public computing labs and 3 classrooms equipped with desktop computers. All have Internet access. All students may access the system. There are no time limits and no fees. All students are required to have personal computers.

Graduates: From July 1, 2002 to June 30, 2003, 261 bachelor's degrees were awarded. The most popular majors were elementary education (12%), occupational therapy (11%), and accounting (10%). In an average class, 1% graduate in 3 years or less, 47% graduate in 4 years or less, 60% graduate in 5 years or less, and 65% graduate in 6 years or less. 60 companies recruited on campus in 2002-2003. Of the 2002 graduating class, 23% were enrolled in graduate school within 6 months of graduation and 75% were employed.

Admissions Contact: Evan Lipp, Dean for Enrollment Management. E-mail: *admissions@francis.edu* Web: *www.francis.edu*

SAINT JOSEPH'S UNIVERSITY
F-3
Philadelphia, PA 19131
(610) 660-1300
(888) BE-A-HAWK; Fax: (610) 660-1314

Full-time: 1805 men, 2014 women	Faculty: 245; IIA, +$
Part-time: 371 men, 466 women	Ph.D.s: 92%
Graduate: 1128 men, 1742 women	Student/Faculty: 16 to 1
Year: semesters, summer session	Tuition: $24,230
Application Deadline: open	Room & Board: $9360
Freshman Class: 7765 applied, 3753 accepted, 1015 enrolled	
SAT I Verbal/Math: 600/600	VERY COMPETITIVE

Saint Joseph's University, founded in 1851, is a Catholic, private college affiliated with the Jesuit order. It offers undergraduate programs in arts and sciences and business administration. It is a comprehensive school in the Carnegie classification system. There are 3 undergraduate and 2 graduate schools. In addition to regional accreditation, Saint Joseph's has baccalaureate program accreditation with AACSB and NCATE. The 2 libraries contain 350,081 volumes, 840,435 microform items, and 3885 audio/video tapes/CDs, and subscribe to 1820 periodicals. Computerized library services include the card catalog, interlibrary loans, database searching, and Internet access. Special learning facilities include a learning resource center, art gallery, radio station, instructional media center, and foreign language labs. The 65-acre campus is in a suburban area on the western edge of Philadelphia and eastern Montgomery county. Including any residence halls, there are 52 buildings.

Student Life: 56% of undergraduates are from Pennsylvania. Others are from 35 states, 29 foreign countries, and Canada. 81% are white. The average age of freshmen is 18; all undergraduates, 20. 12% do not continue beyond their first year; 75% remain to graduate.

Housing: 2008 students can be accommodated in college housing, which includes single-sex and coed dorms, on-campus apartments, and off-campus apartments. In addition, there are honors houses and special-interest houses and floors. On-campus housing is available on a lottery system for upperclassmen. 53% of students live on campus. Upperclassmen may keep cars.

Activities: 11% of men belong to 3 national fraternities; 16% of women belong to 3 national sororities. There are 70 groups on campus, including art, cheerleading, choir, chorus, computers, dance, debate, drama, ethnic, forensics, honors, international, jazz band, literary magazine, musical theater, newspaper, pep band, political, professional, radio, religious, social, social service, student government, and yearbook. Popular campus events include Hand in Hand, St. Joseph's Day, and Up 'Til Dawn.

Sports: There are 10 intercollegiate sports for men and 10 for women, and 15 intramural sports for men and 15 for women. Facilities include a gym, fields, 4 multipurpose courts, indoor and outdoor tracks, 4 racquetball courts, a pool, and a fitness center.

Disabled Students: 80% of the campus is accessible. Wheelchair ramps, elevators, special parking, specially equipped rest rooms, special class scheduling, lowered drinking fountains, lowered telephones, and special housing are available, as well as automatic eye doors, curb cuts, a specially equipped van for wheelchairs, a pool lift, and a bell system at major road crossings.

Services: Counseling and information services are available, as is tutoring in most subjects. There are services for people with learning disabilities, supplemental instruction for selected courses, one-on-one and walk-in tutoring, and specific class tutoring available upon request.

Campus Safety and Security: Measures include 24-hour foot and vehicle patrol, self-defense education, security escort services, and shuttle buses. There are informal discussions, pamphlets/posters/films, emergency telephones, lighted pathways/sidewalks, and a bicycle patrol.

Programs of Study: Saint Joseph's confers B.A., B.S., and B.B.A. degrees. Associate, master's, and doctoral degrees are also awarded. Bachelor's degrees are awarded in BIOLOGICAL SCIENCE (biology/biological science), BUSINESS (accounting, banking and finance, business administration and management, international business management, management information systems, marketing/retailing/merchandising, and purchasing/inventory management), COMMUNICATIONS AND THE ARTS (communications, English, fine arts, French, German, Latin, and Spanish), COMPUTER AND PHYSICAL SCIENCE (chemistry, computer science, information sciences and systems, mathematics, and physics), EDUCATION (elementary, secondary, and special), ENGINEERING AND ENVIRONMENTAL DESIGN (environmental science), HEALTH PROFESSIONS (health care administration), SOCIAL SCIENCE (criminal justice, economics, European studies, French studies, history, humanities, industrial and organizational psychology, international relations, law, philosophy, political science/government, psychology, public administration, religion, social science, and sociology). Social sciences, natural sciences, and English are the strongest academically. Marketing, food marketing, and finance are the largest.

Required: All students must take general education common courses in language, theology, philosophy, and history. Distribution requirements include 3 courses each of social/behavioral sciences and theology, 2 courses of foreign language at the intermediate level, 2 courses each of math and natural sciences, and a philosophy course. A minimum of 120 credit hours is required for graduation, with 21 to 54 in the major and GPA of 2.0.

Special: There is an exchange program with a Japanese university and study abroad in 9 countries. The university offers internships, a Washington semester, advanced 5-year degrees in international marketing and in psychology, dual majors, minor concentrations, and special programs in American, Latin American, European, gender, and medieval studies. There is a co-op program for food marketing, accounting, finance information systems, marketing, pharmaceutical marketing and management majors and an interdisciplinary major in health services. There are 17 national honor societies, including Phi Beta Kappa, and a freshman honors program.

Faculty/Classroom: 63% of faculty are male; 37%, female. 80% teach undergraduates. No introductory courses are taught by graduate students. The average class size in an introductory lecture is 28 and in a laboratory, 17.

Admissions: 48% of the 2003-2004 applicants were accepted.

Requirements: The SAT I or ACT is required. In addition, applicants must graduate from an accredited secondary school and prepare with 4 years of English, 3 of math, 2 each of foreign language and science, and 1 each of history and social studies. Preference is given to students with 3 to 4 years of foreign language and natural science and 4 years of math. A GPA of 3.0 is required. AP credits are accepted. Important factors in the admissions decision are advanced placement or honor courses, extracurricular activities record, and leadership record.

Procedure: Freshmen are admitted fall and spring. Entrance exams should be taken in the spring of the junior year and/or the fall of the senior year. There is a rolling admissions plan. Application deadlines are open. Application fee is $45. 3046 were on the 2003 waiting list. Applications are accepted on-line through the school's web site.

Transfer: 72 transfer students enrolled in 2002-2003. Transfer applicants must have a GPA of at least 2.5 and must submit former test scores and high school and college transcripts. Applicants must apply by November 1 for the spring term and by March 1 for the fall term. 60 of at least 120 credits required for the bachelor's degree must be completed at Saint Joseph's.

Visiting: There are regularly scheduled orientations for prospective students, consisting of open houses, tours, and information sessions. There are guides for informal visits and visitors may sit in on classes and stay overnight. To schedule a visit, contact the Admissions Office at admit@sju.edu.

Financial Aid: In 2003-2004, 85% of all full-time freshmen and 80% of continuing full-time students received some form of financial aid. 75% of full-time freshmen and 73% of continuing full-time students received need-based aid. The average freshman award was $12,225. Need-based scholarships or need-based grants averaged $8400 ($24,195 maximum); need-based self-help aid (loans and jobs) averaged $5925 ($9870 maximum); and non-need-based athletic scholarships averaged $11,825 ($35,036 maximum). The average financial indebtedness of the 2003 graduate was $15,125. The FAFSA is required. The priority date for freshman financial aid applications for fall entry is March 1. The deadline for filing freshman financial aid applications for fall entry is May 1.

International Students: There are 46 international students enrolled. The school actively recruits these students. They must score 550 on the written TOEFL or 213 on the electronic version and also take the SAT I or the ACT. Students who matriculate through ELS must achieve Level 112.

Computers: The mainframe consists of Sun Microsystems servers. There are 43 technologically equipped classrooms, 7 computer teaching labs, 2 classrooms with mobile laptop labs, 22 classrooms with built in TV/VCR and DVD players, and 6 videoconferencing rooms. All University-owned housing is connected to the campus voice and data networks. In total, there are more than 6,000 network connections points in classrooms, labs, offices, and residence halls. All students may access the system whenever the labs are open (about 90 hours per week) or any time if students are connecting outside the labs. There are no time limits and no fees. It is strongly recommended that all students have a personal computer. Laptops are required for students in the business school and psychology majors in the College of Arts and Sciences; IBMs for the business school; and Macs for psychology.

Graduates: From July 1, 2002 to June 30, 2003, 894 bachelor's degrees were awarded. The most popular majors were marketing (12%), finance (8%), and elementary/special education (7%). In an average class, 68% graduate in 4 years or less, 74% graduate in 5 years or less, and 75% graduate in 6 years or less. 100 companies recruited on campus in 2002-2003. Of the 2002 graduating class, 25% were enrolled in graduate school within 6 months of graduation and 63% were employed.

Admissions Contact: Susan P. Kassab, Director of Admissions. A video is available. E-mail: admit@sju.edu Web: http://www.sju.edu

SAINT VINCENT COLLEGE
Latrobe, PA 15650

B-2
(724) 537-4540
(800) SVC-5549; Fax: (724) 532-5069

Full-time: 630 men, 635 women	**Faculty:** 90; IIB, av$
Part-time: 83 men, 92 women	**Ph.D.s:** 81%
Graduate: 26 men, 42 women	**Student/Faculty:** 14 to 1
Year: semesters, summer session	**Tuition:** $19,470
Application Deadline: May 1	**Room & Board:** $6060
Freshman Class: 1153 applied, 989 accepted, 362 enrolled	
SAT I Verbal/Math: 540/540	**ACT:** 22 **VERY COMPETITIVE**

Saint Vincent College, founded in 1846, is a private Catholic college of liberal arts and sciences sponsored by the Benedictine monks. There are 4 undergraduate schools and 1 graduate school. In addition to regional accreditation, Saint Vincent has baccalaureate program accreditation with ACBSP. The library contains 368,688 volumes, 98,951 microform items, and 4195 audio/video tapes/CDs, and subscribes to 738 periodicals. Computerized library services include the card catalog, interlibrary loans, database searching, and Internet access. Special learning facilities include a learning resource center, art gallery, planetarium, radio station, TV station, observatory, radio telescope, and small business development center. The 200-acre campus is in a suburban area 35 miles east of Pittsburgh. Including any residence halls, there are 22 buildings.

Student Life: 84% of undergraduates are from Pennsylvania. Others are from 26 states, 18 foreign countries, and Canada. 76% are from public schools. 93% are white. 68% are Catholic; 24% Protestant; 8% claim no religious affiliation; 8% unknown, no preference. The average age of freshmen is 18; all undergraduates, 21. 13% do not continue beyond their first year; 74% remain to graduate.

Housing: 1063 students can be accommodated in college housing, which includes coed dorms. On-campus housing is guaranteed for all 4 years. 69% of students live on campus; of those, 80% remain on campus on weekends. All students may keep cars.

Activities: There are no fraternities or sororities. There are 57 groups on campus, including art, band, campus ministry/service, cheerleading, choir, chorale, chorus, dance, drama, ethnic, honors, international, literary magazine, musical theater, newspaper, pep band, political, professional, radio and TV, religious, social, social service, student government, and yearbook. Popular campus events include Founder's Day, the Threshold Lecture Series, and Pittsburgh Steeler training camp.

Sports: There are 6 intercollegiate sports for men and 7 for women, and 6 intramural sports for men and 6 for women. Facilities include a 2400-seat gym, basketball and volleyball facilities, a weight and exercise room, an indoor pool, tennis courts, baseball, soccer, and football fields, a mini movie theater, a 999-seat auditorium/arena, and a student union and game room area.

Disabled Students: 95% of the campus is accessible. Wheelchair ramps, elevators, special parking, specially equipped rest rooms, special

class scheduling, lowered drinking fountains, lowered telephones, and lowered computer desks are available.

Services: Counseling and information services are available, as is tutoring in every subject. There is remedial math, reading, and writing. The Opportunity Office provides individual counseling and a freshman study skills class.

Campus Safety and Security: Measures include 24-hour foot and vehicle patrol, security escort services, informal discussions, and pamphlets/posters/films. There are emergency telephones and lighted pathways/sidewalks.

Programs of Study: Saint Vincent confers B.A. and B.S. degrees. Master's degrees are also awarded. Bachelor's degrees are awarded in BIOLOGICAL SCIENCE (biochemistry and biology/biological science), BUSINESS (accounting, banking and finance, business administration and management, international business management, and marketing/retailing/merchandising), COMMUNICATIONS AND THE ARTS (art, art history and appreciation, communications, English, fine arts, French, music, music performance, Spanish, studio art, and visual and performing arts), COMPUTER AND PHYSICAL SCIENCE (chemistry, computer science, information sciences and systems, mathematics, and physics), EDUCATION (art, business, music, psychology, and science), ENGINEERING AND ENVIRONMENTAL DESIGN (environmental science), HEALTH PROFESSIONS (occupational therapy, physical therapy, physician's assistant, predentistry, premedicine, prepharmacy, and preveterinary science), SOCIAL SCIENCE (anthropology, economics, history, liberal arts/general studies, philosophy, political science/government, prelaw, psychology, public affairs, religious education, sociology, and theological studies). Biology, accounting, and chemistry are the strongest academically. Biology, psychology, and history are the largest.

Required: To graduate, students must complete 124 credit hours with a minimum GPA of 2.0. All students are required to take Language and Rhetoric, Exploring Religious Meaning, and Philosophy I. The core curriculum includes 9 hours each of social science, religious studies, and English, 8 of natural sciences, 6 hours each of history, philosophy, and foreign language, and 3 of math. Total number of hours in major varies depending on the program. All majors require a culminating activity, such as a thesis, research project, or capstone course/seminar.

Special: There is cross-registration with Seton Hill College, co-op programs, internships, study abroad in Europe and Asia, a Washington semester, a work-study program, dual majors, a general studies degree, credit by exam and for life/military/work experience, nondegree study, and pass/fail options. There is an accelerated degree engineering program and a 3-2 engineering option with Boston University, Pennsylvania State Universities, the University of Pittsburgh, and the Catholic University of America. The college offers teacher certificate programs in early childhood, elementary, and secondary education. There are 9 national honor societies, a freshman honors program, and a campus-wide honors program.

Faculty/Classroom: 73% of faculty are male; 27%, female. All both teach and do research. No introductory courses are taught by graduate students. The average class size in an introductory lecture is 34; in a laboratory, 21; and in a regular course, 19.

Admissions: 86% of the 2003-2004 applicants were accepted. The SAT I scores for the 2003-2004 freshman class were: Verbal--27% below 500, 50% between 500 and 599, 19% between 600 and 700, and 4% above 700; Math--31% below 500, 44% between 500 and 599, 22% between 600 and 700, and 3% above 700. The ACT scores were 32% below 21, 20% between 21 and 23, 30% between 24 and 26, 9% between 27 and 28, and 9% above 28. 49% of the current freshmen were in the top fifth of their class; 78% were in the top two fifths. There was 1 National Merit semifinalist. 6 freshmen graduated first in their class.

Requirements: The SAT I or ACT is required. In addition, applicants must complete 15 academic credits, including 4 of English, 3 each of social studies and math, 2 of foreign language, and 1 of a lab science. Art students must submit a portfolio, and music and theater students must audition. An essay is required. A GED is accepted. A GPA of 3.2 is required. AP and CLEP credits are accepted. Important factors in the admissions decision are advanced placement or honor courses, evidence of special talent, and recommendations by school officials.

Procedure: Freshmen are admitted fall and spring. Entrance exams should be taken at the end of the junior year or the beginning of the senior year. There is a rolling admissions plan. There are early admissions and deferred admissions plans. Applications should be filed by May 1 for fall entry and January 1 for spring entry. Notification is sent on a rolling basis. Applications are accepted on-line through *www.stvincent.edu.*

Transfer: 99 transfer students enrolled in 2002-2003. Transfer applicants must submit transcripts from postsecondary schools attended and a catalog describing courses taken, plus secondary school transcript(s). 34 of 124 credits required for the bachelor's degree must be completed at Saint Vincent.

Visiting: There are regularly scheduled orientations for prospective students, consisting of a general information session, an informal meeting with faculty, and campus tours. There are guides for informal visits and visitors may sit in on classes and stay overnight. To schedule a visit, contact the Admission and Financial Aid Office at *admission@stvincent.edu.*

Financial Aid: In 2003-2004, 95% of all full-time freshmen and 93% of continuing full-time students received some form of financial aid. 80% of all full-time students received need-based aid. The average freshman award was $18,544. Need-based scholarships or need-based grants averaged $3883 ($15,000 maximum); need-based self-help aid (loans and jobs) averaged $3087 ($6175 maximum); non-need-based athletic scholarships averaged $1132 ($20,440 maximum); and other non-need-based awards and non-need-based scholarships averaged $7784 ($25,677 maximum). 54% of undergraduates work part time. Average annual earnings from campus work are $1600. The average financial indebtedness of the 2003 graduate was $17,000. The FAFSA is required. The deadline for filing freshman financial aid applications for fall entry is April 1.

International Students: There are 18 international students enrolled. They must score 525 on the written TOEFL.

Computers: The mainframe is an HP 9000/Series 810. Computer labs containing PCs and Macs are located in various areas throughout the campus. There are also computer labs in the dorms and 1 Internet connection per student in each residence hall room. All students may access the system during computer lab hours and 24 hours from dorm rooms. Computer labs are open an average of 18 hours per day. There are no fees.

Graduates: From July 1, 2002 to June 30, 2003, 235 bachelor's degrees were awarded. The most popular majors were psychology (12%), communication (12%), and computing (8%). In an average class, 1% graduate in 3 years or less, 59% graduate in 4 years or less, 65% graduate in 5 years or less, and 74% graduate in 6 years or less. 140 companies recruited on campus in 2002-2003. Of the 2002 graduating class, 23% were enrolled in graduate school within 6 months of graduation and 53% were employed.

Admissions Contact: Admission and Financial Aid Office. A video is available. E-mail: *admission@stvincent.edu*
Web: *http://www.stvincent.edu/admin-faid/admin-faid.html*

SETON HILL COLLEGE
(See Seton Hill University)

SETON HILL UNIVERSITY
Greensburg, PA 15601-1599

B-4
(724) 838-4255
(800) 826-6234; Fax: (724) 830-1294

Full-time: 211 men, 589 women	Faculty: 60; IIB, -$
Part-time: 106 men, 334 women	Ph.Ds: 84%
Graduate: 84 men, 303 women	Student/Faculty: 13 to 1
Year: semesters, summer session	Tuition: $18,930
Application Deadline: open	Room & Board: $6000
Freshman Class: 945 applied, 798 accepted, 230 enrolled	
SAT I or ACT: recommended	COMPETITIVE

Seton Hill University, formerly Seton Hill College, founded in 1883, is a private university affiliated with the Catholic Church, offering programs in liberal arts and career preparation. In addition to regional accreditation, Seton Hill has baccalaureate program accreditation with ADA, ARC-PA, CSWE, and NASM. The library contains 104,981 volumes, 5133 microform items, and 4189 audio/video tapes/CDs, and subscribes to 398 periodicals. Computerized library services include the card catalog, interlibrary loans, database searching, and Internet access. Special learning facilities include an art gallery, TV station, a nursery school and kindergarten that function as laboratory schools for education students, a performance hall, and 2 theaters. The 200-acre campus is in a small town 35 miles east of Pittsburgh. Including any residence halls, there are 17 buildings.

Student Life: 83% of undergraduates are from Pennsylvania. Students are from 26 states, 17 foreign countries, and Canada. 83% are white. The average age of freshmen is 18; all undergraduates, 21. 22% do not continue beyond their first year; 60% remain to graduate.

Housing: 482 students can be accommodated in college housing, which includes single-sex dorms. On-campus housing is guaranteed for all 4 years. Alcohol is not permitted. All students may keep cars.

Activities: There are no fraternities or sororities. There are 28 groups on campus, including art, cheerleading, choir, chorale, chorus, dance, drama, entrepreneurial, environmental, ethnic, gay, honors, international, jazz band, literary magazine, musical theater, newspaper, orchestra, political, professional, religious, social, social service, student government, symphony, and yearbook. Popular campus events include Christmas on the Hill, Family Weekend, and President's Reception.

Sports: There are 7 intercollegiate sports for men and 9 for women. Facilities include a gym, a swimming pool, tennis courts, softball and soccer fields, a weight room, a jacuzzi, a sauna, and a fitness trail. The indoor gym seats 650; the largest auditorium/arena seats 300.

Disabled Students: 95% of the campus is accessible. Wheelchair ramps, elevators, special parking, specially equipped rest rooms, special class scheduling, lowered drinking fountains, and lowered telephones are available.

Services: Counseling and information services are available, as is tutoring in most subjects. There is a reader service for the blind and remedial math and writing.

Campus Safety and Security: Measures include 24-hour foot and vehicle patrol, self-defense education, security escort services, and shuttle buses. There are informal discussions, pamphlets/posters/films, emergency telephones, and lighted pathways/sidewalks.

Programs of Study: Seton Hill confers B.A., B.S., B.F.A., B.Mus., B.S.Med.Tech., and B.S.W. degrees. Master's degrees are also awarded. Bachelor's degrees are awarded in BIOLOGICAL SCIENCE (biochemistry and biology/biological science), BUSINESS (accounting, banking and finance, business administration and management, business economics, entrepreneurial studies, human resources, international business management, management information systems, marketing/retailing/merchandising, personnel management, and tourism), COMMUNICATIONS AND THE ARTS (art history and appreciation, arts administration/management, communications, creative writing, dramatic arts, English, fine arts, graphic design, journalism, music, musical theater, performing arts, Spanish, studio art, theater design, and theater management), COMPUTER AND PHYSICAL SCIENCE (actuarial science, chemistry, computer science, mathematics, and physics), EDUCATION (art, early childhood, elementary, English, foreign languages, home economics, mathematics, music, science, secondary, social science, and special), ENGINEERING AND ENVIRONMENTAL DESIGN (engineering), HEALTH PROFESSIONS (art therapy, medical laboratory technology, music therapy, nursing, physician's assistant, predentistry, premedicine, and preveterinary science), SOCIAL SCIENCE (child care/child and family studies, dietetics, economics, family/consumer resource management, family/consumer studies, food production/management/services, history, human services, international studies, liberal arts/general studies, political science/government, prelaw, psychology, religion, religious music, social work, and sociology). Sciences, education, and fine arts are the strongest academically. Psychology, art, and business are the largest.

Required: The core curriculum requires 6 credits in Western cultural traditions and freshman seminar, and 3 each in theology, philosophy/senior seminar, math, computer science, and science, college-level foreign language, U.S. cultures, world cultures, and artistic expression. A portfolio is required. A total of 120 credit hours with a minimum GPA of 2.0 is required for graduation.

Special: There are cooperative programs in all majors and cross-registration with St. Vincent College, the University of Pittsburgh at Greensburg, and Westmoreland County Community College. Internships are encouraged. Seton Hill offers study abroad, a Washington semester, work-study, dual and student-designed majors, accelerated degree programs, a 3-2 engineering program with Pennsylvania State University and Georgia Institute of Technology, a 2-2 nursing program with Catholic University of America, a 3-2 or 3-1 medical technology program with area hospitals, credit by exam and for life/military/work experience, nondegree study, and pass/fail options. There are 5 national honor societies and a freshman honors program.

Faculty/Classroom: 49% of faculty are male; 51%, female. All teach undergraduates and 60% do research. No introductory courses are taught by graduate students. The average class size in an introductory lecture is 25; in a laboratory, 16; and in a regular course, 17.

Admissions: 84% of the 2003-2004 applicants were accepted. 29% of the current freshmen were in the top fifth of their class; 66% were in the top two fifths. 6 freshmen graduated first in their class.

Requirements: The SAT I or ACT is recommended, or 2 graded writing samples are accepted in place of SAT I/ACT scores. A total of 15 Carnegie units is required, including 4 each of English and electives, 2 each of math, social studies, and foreign language, and 1 of a lab science. Art students must submit a portfolio; music and theater students must audition. An interview is recommended. The GED is accepted with supporting recommendations. A GPA of 2.5 is required. AP and CLEP credits are accepted. Important factors in the admissions decision are advanced placement or honor courses, evidence of special talent, and leadership record.

Procedure: Freshmen are admitted fall and spring. Entrance exams should be taken in spring of the junior year or fall of the senior year. There is a deferred admissions plan and a rolling admissions plan. Application deadlines are open. Application fee is $30. Notification is sent on a rolling basis. Applications are accepted on computer disk and on-line through the school's web site.

Transfer: 86 transfer students enrolled in 2002-2003. Applicants must submit college transcripts and have a GPA of at least 2.0. An interview is recommended, as are supporting letters. 48 credits of 120 required for the bachelor's degree must be completed at Seton Hill.

Visiting: There are regularly scheduled orientations for prospective students, consisting of an introduction, an address by the president or dean, an open reception with faculty, a financial aid session, a student panel, a campus tour, and an overnight visit followed by class attendance, if desired. There are guides for informal visits and visitors may sit in on classes and stay overnight. To schedule a visit, contact the Director of Admissions at *admit@setonhill.edu*.

Financial Aid: In 2003-2004, 98% of all full-time freshmen and 79% of continuing full-time students received some form of financial aid. 90% of full-time freshmen and 70% of continuing full-time students received need-based aid. The average freshman award was $18,594, with $8194 ($19,300 maximum) from need-based scholarships or need-based grants, $4200 ($5861 maximum) from need-based self-help aid (loans and jobs), $3200 ($10,300 maximum) non-need-based athletic scholarships, and $3000 ($25,130 maximum) from other non-need-based awards and non-need-based scholarships. 51% of undergraduates work part time. Average annual earnings from campus work are $1300. The average financial indebtedness of the 2003 graduate was $18,055. Seton Hill is a member of CSS. The FAFSA and the college's own financial statement are required. The priority date for freshman financial aid applications for fall entry is April 30. The deadline for filing freshman financial aid applications for fall entry is August 1.

International Students: There are 28 international students enrolled. The school actively recruits these students. They must score 500 on the written TOEFL or 173 on the electronic version.

Computers: Students have access to 125 PCs on campus, including IBM, Mac, and UNIX machines. All students may access the system. There are no time limits and no fees.

Graduates: From July 1, 2002 to June 30, 2003, 217 bachelor's degrees were awarded. The most popular majors were business (57%), psychology (23%), and art (20%). In an average class, 50% graduate in 4 years or less, 55% graduate in 5 years or less, and 58% graduate in 6 years or less. 25 companies recruited on campus in 2002-2003. Of the 2002 graduating class, 29% were enrolled in graduate school within 6 months of graduation and 86% were employed.

Admissions Contact: Mary Kay Cooper, Director of Admissions and Graduate Student Services. E-mail: *admit@setonhill.edu*
Web: *setonhill.edu*

SHIPPENSBURG UNIVERSITY OF PENNSYLVANIA C-4

Shippensburg, PA 17257-2299   (717) 477-1231
(800) 822-8028; Fax: (717) 477-4016

Full-time: 2959 men, 3335 women	**Faculty:** 291; IIA, +$
Part-time: 134 men, 139 women	**Ph.D.s:** 88%
Graduate: 361 men, 679 women	**Student/Faculty:** 22 to 1
Year: semesters, summer session	**Tuition:** $5746 ($12,644)
Application Deadline: open	**Room & Board:** $5080
Freshman Class: 6722 applied, 4446 accepted, 1848 enrolled	
SAT I Verbal/Math: 531/537	**COMPETITIVE**

Shippensburg University, founded in 1871, is a public university that is part of the Pennsylvania State System of Higher Education, offering undergraduate and graduate degree programs in the College of Arts and Sciences, College of Business, and College of Education and Human Services. There are 3 undergraduate schools and 1 graduate school. In addition to regional accreditation, Ship has baccalaureate program accreditation with AACSB, ACS, CACREP, CEC, CSWE, IACS, NCACE, and NCATE. The library contains 449,590 volumes, 1,294,417 microform items, and 76,583 audio/video tapes/CDs, and subscribes to 1757 periodicals. Computerized library services include the card catalog, interlibrary loans, and database searching. Special learning facilities include a learning resource center, art gallery, planetarium, radio station, TV station, a closed-circuit television, fashion archives center, vertebrate museum, women's center, on-campus elementary school, electron microscope, greenhouse, and herbarium. The 200-acre campus is in a rural area 40 miles southwest of Harrisburg. Including any residence halls, there are 48 buildings.

Student Life: 94% of undergraduates are from Pennsylvania. Students are from 23 states and 24 foreign countries. 90% are from public schools. 91% are white. The average age of freshmen is 18; all undergraduates, 20. 19% do not continue beyond their first year; 63% remain to graduate.

Housing: 2646 students can be accommodated in college housing, which includes single-sex and coed dorms, on-campus apartments, and off-campus apartments. There is also a designated "quiet" hall and a scholar's hall. 60% of students commute. Alcohol is not permitted. All students may keep cars.

Activities: 6% of men belong to 1 local and 10 national fraternities; 8% of women belong to 3 local and 6 national sororities. There are 247 groups on campus, including art, band, cheerleading, choir, chorale, chorus, computers, dance, drama, ethnic, gay, honors, international, jazz band, literary magazine, marching band, musical theater, newspaper, orchestra, political, professional, radio and TV, religious, social, social service, student government, and yearbook. Popular campus events include planetarium shows, Senior Olympics, and Summer Music Festival.

Sports: There are 8 intercollegiate sports for men and 10 for women, and 12 intramural sports for men and 12 for women. Facilities include a 7700-seat stadium, a 12-acre sports complex, softball and baseball fields, tennis courts, and a field house that includes swimming facilities.

Disabled Students: 90% of the campus is accessible. Wheelchair ramps, elevators, special parking, specially equipped rest rooms, special

class scheduling, lowered drinking fountains, lowered telephones, note takers, alternative testing sites, learning specialists, and tutors are available.

Services: Counseling and information services are available, as is tutoring in most subjects. Writing and study skills assessment and resources, workshops, supplemental instruction, and learning specialists are available.

Campus Safety and Security: Measures include 24-hour foot and vehicle patrol, self-defense education, security escort services, and shuttle buses. There are informal discussions, pamphlets/posters/films, emergency telephones, and lighted pathways/sidewalks. Residence halls are equipped with an automatic heat/smoke detection system monitored 24 hours a day by police. A strobe light unit notifies students who are hearing impaired. Residence hall doors are locked 24 hours a day. There are cameras at the main entrances to residence halls, computer labs, and other buildings, as well as many exterior cameras covering parking lots and other campus areas.

Programs of Study: Ship confers B.A., B.S., B.S.B.A., B.S.Ed., and B.S.W. degrees. Master's degrees are also awarded. Bachelor's degrees are awarded in BIOLOGICAL SCIENCE (biology/biological science), BUSINESS (accounting, banking and finance, business administration and management, management information systems, and marketing/retailing/merchandising), COMMUNICATIONS AND THE ARTS (art, English, French, Spanish, and speech/debate/rhetoric), COMPUTER AND PHYSICAL SCIENCE (applied physics, chemistry, computer science, earth science, information sciences and systems, mathematics, and physics), EDUCATION (business and elementary), ENGINEERING AND ENVIRONMENTAL DESIGN (environmental science), SOCIAL SCIENCE (criminal justice, economics, geography, history, interdisciplinary studies, political science/government, psychology, public administration, social studies, social work, and sociology). Elementary education, criminal justice, and communication/journalism are the largest.

Required: General education courses include English composition, oral communications, math, and history, as well as courses in logic and numbers for rational thinking; linguistic, literary, artistic, and cultural traditions; lab science; biological and physical science; political, economic, and geographic sciences; and social and behavioral sciences. The core curriculum varies for degree programs. Most degree programs require 120 credit hours, with 22 to 30 hours in the major, and a 2.0 minimum GPA for graduation.

Special: The university offers internships, study abroad in the United Kingdom, Canada, Denmark, and other countries and a 3-2 engineering degree with Pennsylvania State University and the University of Maryland. There is a cooperative art program with the Art Institutes International (Art Institutes of Pittsburgh and Art Institutes of Philadelphia) in Pennsylvania and 6 other states, as well as a cooperative program in the health sciences. Students have the option of taking courses for a semester at one of the 13 other schools in the Pennsylvania State System of Higher Education. There is also a Visiting Student Program with Wilson College and with the Fashion Institute of Technology of New York City. As a member of the Marine Science Consortium, the university also offers opportunities for field and laboratory studies in marine science at Wallops Island, Virginia. A dual major in communication and journalism is offered. There are 17 national honor societies, a freshman honors program, and 1 departmental honors program.

Faculty/Classroom: 57% of faculty are male; 43%, female. 95% teach undergraduates; 31% both teach and do research. No introductory courses are taught by graduate students. The average class size in an introductory lecture is 34; in a laboratory, 17; and in a regular course, 27.

Admissions: 66% of the 2003-2004 applicants were accepted. The SAT I scores for the 2003-2004 freshman class were: Verbal--36% below 500, 49% between 500 and 599, 14% between 600 and 700, and 1% above 700; Math--32% below 500, 50% between 500 and 599, 16% between 600 and 700, and 1% above 700. 32% of the current freshmen were in the top fifth of their class; 74% were in the top two fifths. 3 freshmen graduated first in their class.

Requirements: The SAT I is required. In addition, applicants are urged to pursue a typical college preparatory program, which should include 4 years of English, 3 each of social sciences, sequential math, and lab science, and 2 of 1 foreign language. A GED is accepted. AP and CLEP credits are accepted. Important factors in the admissions decision are advanced placement or honor courses, recommendations by school officials, and evidence of special talent.

Procedure: Freshmen are admitted fall and spring. Entrance exams should be taken in the junior year and senior year. There are early admissions and deferred admissions plans. There is a rolling admissions plan. Application deadlines are open. The fall 2003 application fee was $30. Notification is sent on a rolling basis. Applications are accepted online through *www.applyweb.com/apply/ship/*.

Transfer: 346 transfer students enrolled in 2002-2003. Applicants must provide high school and college transcripts and SAT I or ACT scores, if they have fewer than 30 college credits. 45 credits of 120 required for the bachelor's degree must be completed at Ship.

Visiting: There are regularly scheduled orientations for prospective students, including daily academic group meetings, campus tours, and 5 weekend open house programs per year. There are guides for informal visits and visitors may sit in on classes. To schedule a visit, contact the Admissions Office at *admiss@ship.edu*.

Financial Aid: In 2003-2004, 55% of all full-time freshmen and 50% of continuing full-time students received some form of financial aid. 46% of full-time freshmen and 40% of continuing full-time students received need-based aid. The average freshman award was $5329. Need-based scholarships or need-based grants averaged $3299 ($14,194 maximum); need-based self-help aid (loans and jobs) averaged $6174 ($21,200 maximum); non-need-based athletic scholarships averaged $1292 ($10,291 maximum); and other non-need-based awards and non-need-based scholarships averaged $4619 ($7098 maximum). 10% of undergraduates work part time. Average annual earnings from campus work are $1834. The average financial indebtedness of the 2003 graduate was $15,464. Ship is a member of CSS. The FAFSA and PHEAA are required. The deadline for filing freshman financial aid applications for fall entry is May 1.

International Students: There are 60 international students enrolled. They must score 550 on the written TOEFL or 213 on the electronic version and also take the SAT I or ACT. Students whose native language is English must submit SAT I scores instead of TOEFL.

Computers: The mainframe is a Unisys IX 5601-B1. 19 PC labs located across campus offer access to on-line scheduling, personal web pages, e-mail accounts, and on-line grades. The system is available from student residence rooms and from off campus. All students may access the system 24 hours a day. There are no time limits and no fees. It is recommended that students in accounting have personal computers.

Graduates: From July 1, 2002 to June 30, 2003, 1205 bachelor's degrees were awarded. The most popular majors were elementary education (14%), psychology (7%), and criminal justice (7%). In an average class, 38% graduate in 4 years or less, 61% graduate in 5 years or less, and 63% graduate in 6 years or less. 102 companies recruited on campus in 2002-2003.

Admissions Contact: Joseph Cretella, Dean of Admissions. A video is available. E-mail: *admiss@ship.edu* Web: *www.ship.edu/admiss*

SLIPPERY ROCK UNIVERSITY OF PENNSYLVANIA   B-2
Slippery Rock, PA 16057   **(724) 738-2015**
(800) 929-4778; Fax: (724) 738-2913

Full-time: 2852 men, 3563 women	**Faculty:** 366; IIA, +$
Part-time: 225 men, 414 women	**Ph.D.s:** 78%
Graduate: 231 men, 504 women	**Student/Faculty:** 18 to 1
Year: semesters, summer session	**Tuition:** $5801 ($12,699)
Application Deadline: June 1	**Room & Board:** $4542
Freshman Class: 4310 applied, 3481 accepted, 1491 enrolled	
SAT I Verbal/Math: 495/495	**ACT:** 21 **LESS COMPETITIVE**

Slippery Rock University of Pennsylvania, founded in 1889, is a public institution that is part of the Pennsylvania State System of Higher Education. It offers programs in business, information, social sciences, education, health, environment, science, humanities, and fine and performing arts. There are 4 undergraduate schools and 1 graduate school. In addition to regional accreditation, The Rock has baccalaureate program accreditation with ACBSP, APTA, CAAHEP, CSWE, NASAD, NASM, NCATE, NLN, and NRPA. The library contains 502,974 volumes, 1,497,469 microform items, and 22,707 audio/video tapes/CDs, and subscribes to 1300 periodicals. Computerized library services include the card catalog, interlibrary loans, database searching, and Internet access. Special learning facilities include a learning resource center, art gallery, natural history museum, planetarium, radio station, TV station, and a wellness center. The 600-acre campus is in a small town 50 miles north of Pittsburgh. Including any residence halls, there are 60 buildings.

Student Life: 96% of undergraduates are from Pennsylvania. Students are from 35 states, 47 foreign countries, and Canada. 70% are from public schools. 87% are white. The average age of freshmen is 18; all undergraduates, 22. 22% do not continue beyond their first year; 49% remain to graduate.

Housing: 2810 students can be accommodated in college housing, which includes single-sex and coed dorms, on-campus apartments, off-campus apartments, married-student housing, fraternity houses, and sorority houses. In addition, there are honors houses, language houses, and special-interest houses. On-campus housing is guaranteed for the freshman year only and is available on a first-come, first-served basis. 62% of students commute. Alcohol is not permitted. All students may keep cars.

Activities: 7% of men belong to 11 national fraternities; 6% of women belong to 9 national sororities. There are 100 groups on campus, including art, band, cheerleading, chess, choir, chorale, chorus, computers, dance, drama, ethnic, film, gay, honors, international, jazz band, literary magazine, marching band, musical theater, newspaper, orchestra, pep band, photography, political, professional, radio and TV, religious, social, social service, student government, symphony, and yearbook. Popular campus events include Spring Weekend.

Sports: There are 12 intercollegiate sports for men and 12 for women, and 7 intramural sports for men and 7 for women. Facilities include a field house, a gym, and a fitness center. The campus stadium seats 10,000, the indoor gym seats 3000, and the largest auditorium/arena seats 1000.

Disabled Students: 80% of the campus is accessible. Wheelchair ramps, elevators, special parking, specially equipped rest rooms, special class scheduling, lowered drinking fountains, lowered telephones, and special housing are available.

Services: Counseling and information services are available, as is tutoring in some subjects, including about 60 introductory-level general liberal studies courses. There is a reader service for the blind and remedial math and writing.

Campus Safety and Security: Measures include 24-hour foot and vehicle patrol, self-defense education, security escort services, and shuttle buses. There are informal discussions, pamphlets/posters/films, emergency telephones, and lighted pathways/sidewalks. The university maintains its own police department, with officers having the same powers as municipal police.

Programs of Study: The Rock confers B.A., B.S., B.F.A., B.Mus., B.Mus.Ed., B.S.B.A., B.S.Ed., and B.S.N. degrees. Master's and doctoral degrees are also awarded. Bachelor's degrees are awarded in BIOLOGICAL SCIENCE (biology/biological science), BUSINESS (accounting, business administration and management, international business management, and marketing/retailing/merchandising), COMMUNICATIONS AND THE ARTS (communications, dance, English, fine arts, French, German, music, and Spanish), COMPUTER AND PHYSICAL SCIENCE (chemistry, computer science, earth science, geology, information sciences and systems, mathematics, and physics), EDUCATION (early childhood, elementary, foreign languages, health, music, science, secondary, and special), HEALTH PROFESSIONS (community health work, medical laboratory technology, and nursing), SOCIAL SCIENCE (anthropology, economics, geography, history, parks and recreation management, philosophy, political science/government, psychology, public administration, social science, social work, and sociology). Business, education, and health science areas are the largest.

Required: B.A. students must demonstrate proficiency in a foreign language, and all must complete 42 to 53 credits in a 7-part liberal studies program, including basic competencies, arts, cultural diversity/global perspective, human institutions, science and math, natural experience, and modern age. Specific requirements include public speaking, college writing, algebra, and phys ed. A minimum of 120 credit hours, with at least 30 in the major, is required for graduation.

Special: Study abroad is available in 16 countries. Internships are offered in most majors, and international internships are available in Scotland and England. There is a 3-2 engineering program with Pennsylvania State University. The dual major is an option, and credit is given for military experience. Pass/fail options also are available. There are 26 national honor societies, a freshman honors program, and 33 departmental honors programs.

Faculty/Classroom: 53% of faculty are male; 47%, female. All teach undergraduates. No introductory courses are taught by graduate students. The average class size in an introductory lecture is 33; in a laboratory, 20; and in a regular course, 25.

Admissions: 81% of the 2003-2004 applicants were accepted. The SAT I scores for the 2003-2004 freshman class were: Verbal--52% below 500, 40% between 500 and 599, 7% between 600 and 700, and 1% above 700; Math--53% below 500, 38% between 500 and 599, 8% between 600 and 700, and 1% above 700. The ACT scores were 48% below 21, 31% between 21 and 23, 15% between 24 and 26, 4% between 27 and 28, and 1% above 28. 22% of the current freshmen were in the top fifth of their class; 51% were in the top two fifths. 10 freshmen graduated first in their class.

Requirements: The SAT I is required and the ACT is recommended. In addition, students should graduate from an accredited secondary school or have a GED. A total of 16 academic credits is required. The recommended college preparatory program includes 4 years of English and social studies, 3 each of science and math, and 2 of a foreign language. An interview is recommended. AP and CLEP credits are accepted. Important factors in the admissions decision are advanced placement or honor courses, extracurricular activities record, and evidence of special talent.

Procedure: Freshmen are admitted fall, spring, and summer. Entrance exams should be taken in the junior year or fall of the senior year. There is a deferred admissions plan and a rolling admissions plan. Applications should be filed by June 1 for fall entry, November for spring entry, and April for summer entry. The fall 2003 application fee was $25. Notification is sent on a rolling basis. A waiting list is an active part of the admissions procedure. Applications are accepted on computer disk and online.

Transfer: 559 transfer students enrolled in 2002-2003. Applicants should have completed at least 24 credit hours with a GPA of 2.5. The SAT I or ACT, as well as an interview, are recommended. 36 credits of 120 required for the bachelor's degree must be completed at The Rock.

Visiting: There are regularly scheduled orientations for prospective students, including a meeting with faculty, an information fair, and a campus tour. There are guides for informal visits and visitors may sit in on classes and stay overnight. To schedule a visit, contact the Admissions Office at *asktherock@sru.edu*.

Financial Aid: In 2003-2004, 64% of all full-time freshmen and 58% of continuing full-time students received some form of financial aid. 51% of full-time freshmen and 43% of continuing full-time students received need-based aid. The average freshman award was $6074. Need-based scholarships or need-based grants averaged $2907; need-based self-help aid (loans and jobs) averaged $2437; non-need-based athletic scholarships averaged $2507; and other non-need-based awards and non-need-based scholarships averaged $3590. 30% of undergraduates work part time. Average annual earnings from campus work are $1000. The average financial indebtedness of the 2003 graduate was $19,195. The Rock is a member of CSS. The FAFSA is required. The priority date for freshman financial aid applications for fall entry is May 1.

International Students: There are 130 international students enrolled. The school actively recruits these students. They must score 500 on the written TOEFL.

Computers: The mainframe is an IBM ES/9221-200. Students have access to more than 900 PCs in 44 networked computer labs on campus as well as a network connection for each bed in the residence halls. All networked connections have access to the Internet through our OC3 connection. All students may access the system 24 hours a day. Campus terminal and PC labs are generally open more than 100 hours per week. There are no time limits and no fees.

Graduates: From July 1, 2002 to June 30, 2003, 1190 bachelor's degrees were awarded. The most popular majors were education (23%), marketing (15%), and parks and recreation (13%). In an average class, 24% graduate in 4 years or less, 46% graduate in 5 years or less, and 49% graduate in 6 years or less. 260 companies recruited on campus in 2002-2003. Of the 2002 graduating class, 12% were enrolled in graduate school within 6 months of graduation and 81% were employed.

Admissions Contact: Jim Barrett, Director of Admissions. A video is available. E-mail: *asktherock@sru.edu* Web: *http://www.sru.edu*

SUSQUEHANNA UNIVERSITY
Selinsgrove, PA 17870-1001

D-3
(570) 372-4260
(800) 326-9672; Fax: (570) 372-2722

Full-time: 829 men, 1075 women	**Faculty:** 118; IIB, +$
Part-time: 10 men, 19 women	**Ph.D.s:** 92%
Graduate: none	**Student/Faculty:** 16 to 1
Year: semesters, summer session	**Tuition:** $23,480
Application Deadline: March 1	**Room & Board:** $6510
Freshman Class: 2373 applied, 1660 accepted, 500 enrolled	
SAT I: required	**VERY COMPETITIVE**

Susquehanna University, founded in 1858, is an independent, selective, residential institution affiliated with the Lutheran Church. It offers programs through schools of arts, humanities and communications, natural and social sciences, and business. There are 3 undergraduate schools. In addition to regional accreditation, S.U. has baccalaureate program accreditation with AACSB, ACS, and NASM. The library contains 280,000 volumes, 121,150 microform items, and 8525 audio/video tapes/CDs, and subscribes to 14,950 periodicals. Computerized library services include the card catalog, interlibrary loans, database searching, and Internet access. Special learning facilities include a learning resource center, art gallery, radio station, multimedia classrooms, video studios, a campuswide telecommunications network, satellite dishes and distribution system for foreign-language broadcasts, a videoconferencing facility, an ecological field station, an observatory, a child development center, and an electronic music lab. The 220-acre campus is in a suburban area 50 miles north of Harrisburg. Including any residence halls, there are 52 buildings.

Student Life: 60% of undergraduates are from Pennsylvania. Students are from 25 states, 12 foreign countries, and Canada. 84% are from public schools. 92% are white. 44% are Protestant; 30% Catholic; 19% claim no religious affiliation. The average age of freshmen is 18; all undergraduates, 20. 12% do not continue beyond their first year; 77% remain to graduate.

Housing: 1365 students can be accommodated in college housing, which includes single-sex and coed dorms, on-campus apartments, off-campus apartments, fraternity houses, and sorority houses. In addition, there are honors houses, special-interest houses, and multicultural and international houses. Volunteer project groups may reside in fomer private homes adjacent to the university with suite-type accommodations. On-campus housing is guaranteed for all 4 years. 80% of students live on campus; of those, 86% remain on campus on weekends. All students may keep cars.

Activities: 25% of men belong to 4 national fraternities; 25% of women belong to 4 national sororities. There are 100 groups on campus, including art, Asian Student Coalition, band, Black Student Union, cheerleading, chess, choir, chorale, chorus, computers, dance, drama, ethnic, film, gay, Hillel Outdoors Club, Hispanic Organization for Student Awareness, honors, international, jazz band, literary magazine, musical theater, National Organization of Women, newspaper, opera, orchestra, pep band, photography, political, professional, radio and TV, religious, social, social service, student government, and yearbook. Popular campus events include Spring Weekend, Candlelight Christmas Service, and Family Weekend.

Sports: There are 11 intercollegiate sports for men and 12 for women, and 22 intramural sports for men and 22 for women. Facilities include a field house with indoor track, tennis, and basketball courts; a football stadium; track, soccer, baseball, lacrosse, rugby, and hockey fields; basketball and tennis courts; a swimming pool, racquetball courts, a weight training room, fitness center, and a sauna.

Disabled Students: 90% of the campus is accessible. Wheelchair ramps, elevators, special parking, specially equipped rest rooms, special class scheduling, lowered drinking fountains, and lowered telephones are available.

Services: Counseling and information services are available, as is tutoring in some subjects, including writing, math, foreign languages, and study skills. Academic departments also provide tutoring.

Campus Safety and Security: Measures include 24-hour foot and vehicle patrol, self-defense education, security escort services, and informal discussions. There are pamphlets/posters/films, emergency telephones, and lighted pathways/sidewalks.

Programs of Study: S.U. confers B.A., B.S., and B.M. degrees. Associate degrees are also awarded. Bachelor's degrees are awarded in BIOLOGICAL SCIENCE (biochemistry and biology/biological science), BUSINESS (accounting and business administration and management), COMMUNICATIONS AND THE ARTS (art, art history and appreciation, communications, creative writing, dramatic arts, English, French, German, graphic design, music, music performance, and Spanish), COMPUTER AND PHYSICAL SCIENCE (chemistry, computer science, information sciences and systems, mathematics, and physics), EDUCATION (early childhood, education, elementary, and music), ENGINEERING AND ENVIRONMENTAL DESIGN (environmental science), SOCIAL SCIENCE (economics, history, international studies, philosophy, political science/government, psychology, religion, religious music, and sociology). Natural sciences, business administration, and psychology are the strongest academically. Business administration, communications and theater arts, and psychology are the largest.

Required: All students must complete a 3-part core curriculum of about 40 semester hours, including academic requirements in history, fine arts, literature, science, and social science, as well as philosophy or religion; skills in computers, math/logic, and foreign language; and courses in academic skills, wellness/fitness, and career development. An additional 36 to 44 hours are required in the major, and the remainder of a 130-hour minimum required total in electives or a minor. A minimum GPA of 2.0 is also required to graduate.

Special: There is cross-registration with Bucknell University. Interships are offered in almost all majors and study abroad is available on 6 continents. The School of Business offers a semester in London for junior business majors. Two-week study seminars in Australia, Southern Africa, and the Caribbean are available, as are a Boston semester, a Washington semester, a United Nations semester, a work and study semester through the Philadelphia Center. The university offers dual and student-design majors, work-study programs, credit by examination, nondegree study, and pass/fail options. The B.A.-B.S. degree is available in several majors and there is a 3-2 program in forestry with Duke University, and a 2-2 program in allied health with Thomas Jefferson University, and a 3-2 program in dentistry with Temple University. Highly motivated students have the option of earning their baccalaureate degree in three years. There are 24 national honor societies, a freshman honors program, and 15 departmental honors programs.

Faculty/Classroom: 55% of faculty are male; 45%, female. All both teach and do research. The average class size in an introductory lecture is 24; in a laboratory, 13; and in a regular course, 19.

Admissions: 70% of the 2003-2004 applicants were accepted. 56% of the current freshmen were in the top fifth of their class; 87% were in the top two fifths. 13 freshmen graduated first in their class.

Requirements: The SAT I is required, except for students with a cumulative class rank in the top 20% in a strong college preparatory program. Such students have the option of submitting either the SAT I, ACT, or 2 graded writing samples. Students should be graduates of an accredited high school. Preparation should include 4 years of English and math, 3 to 4 years of science, and 2 to 3 years each of social studies and foreign language. In addition, 1 unit of art or music is recommended. Three SAT II: Subject tests are recommended, including writing and math. An essay is required, as are, for relevant fields, music audition, or writing portfolio. An interview is strongly recommended. S.U. requires applicants to be in the upper 40% of their class. A GPA of 3.0 is required. AP and CLEP credits are accepted. Important factors in the admissions decision are advanced placement or honor courses, evidence of special talent, and recommendations by school officials.

Procedure: Freshmen are admitted fall and spring. Entrance exams should be taken by January of the senior year. There are early decision,

early admissions, deferred admissions, and rolling admissions plans. Early decision I applications should be filed by November 15 and by January 1 (early decision II); regular applications, by March 1 for fall entry and December 1 for spring entry, along with a $35 fee. Notification of early decision I is sent December 1 or January 15 (early decision II). Regular decision notification is on a rolling basis. 103 early decision candidates were accepted for the 2003-2004 class. 130 applicants were on the 2003 waiting list; 12 were admitted. Applications are accepted online through *www.susqu.edu/admissions* or through the Common Application.

Transfer: 31 transfer students enrolled in 2002-2003. Applicants must submit high school and college transcripts, test scores, and a recommendation from a dean. An interview is strongly recommended. A music audition or writing portfolio is required for relevant majors. 65 of 130 credits required for the bachelor's degree must be completed at S.U.

Visiting: There are regularly scheduled orientations for prospective students, including special visiting days for prospective students and their parents held in the spring and fall, which consist of sessions with faculty, admissions, financial aid, and placement staff and tours of the campus. There are guides for informal visits and visitors may sit in on classes and stay overnight. To schedule a visit, contact the Office of Admissions at *suadmiss@susqu.edu*.

Financial Aid: In 2003-2004, 95% of all full-time students received some form of financial aid. 67% of full-time freshmen and 63% of continuing full-time students received need-based aid. The average freshman award was $15,750. Need-based scholarships or need-based grants averaged $12,170 ($26,900 maximum); need-based self-help aid (loans and jobs) averaged $4460 ($6425 maximum); and non-need-based awards and non-need-based scholarships averaged $9450 ($23,170 maximum). 75% of undergraduates work part time. Average annual earnings from campus work are $835. The average financial indebtedness of the 2003 graduate was $12,115. S.U. is a member of CSS. The CSS Profile or FAFSA and federal tax return are required. The priority date for freshman financial aid applications for fall entry is March 1. The deadline for filing freshman financial aid applications for fall entry is May 1.

International Students: There are 16 international students enrolled. The school actively recruits these students. They must score 550 on the written TOEFL or 213 on the electronic version and also take the SAT I. They must also take SAT II: Subject tests. Writing, math, and one other subject are recommended.

Computers: The mainframe is an HP 3000. All residence hall rooms are wired for computer access to the campus LAN and the Internet. 300 PCs are available for student use in various labs and in the library. A wide variety of software is available as well. Laptop dataports are available in the business and communications building. All students may access the system 24 hours a day. There are no time limits and no fees. It is strongly recommended that all students have a personal computer. A Pentium 106Hz PC with 256 mgs of RAM and a 20 gigabyte hard drive is recommended.

Graduates: From July 1, 2002 to June 30, 2003, 400 bachelor's degrees were awarded. The most popular majors were business administration (35%), communications and theater arts (17%), and elementary education (9%). In an average class, 1% graduate in 3 years or less, 75% graduate in 4 years or less, 77% graduate in 5 years or less, and 77% graduate in 6 years or less. 45 companies recruited on campus in 2002-2003. Of the 2002 graduating class, 16% were enrolled in graduate school within 6 months of graduation and 81% were employed.

Admissions Contact: Chris Markle, Director of Admissions.
E-mail: *suadmiss@susqu.edu* Web: *www.susqu.edu/admissions/*

SWARTHMORE COLLEGE F-4
Swarthmore, PA 19081-1397 (610) 328-8300
(800) 667-3110; Fax: (610) 328-8580

Full-time: 704 men, 783 women	Faculty: 174; IIB, ++$
Part-time: 3 men, 10 women	Ph.D.s: 99%
Graduate: none	Student/Faculty: 9 to 1
Year: semesters	Tuition: $28,802
Application Deadline: January 1	Room & Board: $8914
Freshman Class: 3908 applied, 920 accepted, 368 enrolled	
SAT I Verbal/Math: 730/720	MOST COMPETITIVE

Swarthmore College, established in 1864, is a private, nonprofit institution offering undergraduate courses in engineering and liberal arts. In addition to regional accreditation, Swarthmore has baccalaureate program accreditation with ABET. The 5 libraries contain 7312 volumes, 71,795 microform items, and 18,683 audio/video tapes/CDs, and subscribe to 4275 periodicals. Computerized library services include the card catalog, interlibrary loans, and database searching. Special learning facilities include an art gallery, radio station, observatory, performing arts center, solar energy lab, arboretum, and library of documents and memorabilia of the peace movement. The 357-acre campus is in a suburban area 10 miles southwest of Philadelphia. Including any residence halls, there are 46 buildings.

Student Life: 84% of undergraduates are from out of state, mostly the Middle Atlantic. Students are from 50 states, 42 foreign countries, and Canada. 60% are from public schools. 53% are white; 15% Asian American. The average age of freshmen is 18; all undergraduates, 20. 3% do not continue beyond their first year; 92% remain to graduate.

Housing: 1323 students can be accommodated in college housing, which includes single-sex and coed dorms. On-campus housing is guaranteed for all 4 years. 93% of students live on campus. Upperclassmen may keep cars.

Activities: 6% of men belong to 1 local and 1 national fraternity. There are no sororities. There are 100 groups on campus, including a cappella groups, art, band, chess, choir, chorus, club sports, computers, dance, debate, drama, ethnic, film, gay, honors, international, jazz band, literary magazine, musical theater, newspaper, orchestra, pep band, photography, political, radio and TV, religious, social, social service, student government, and yearbook. Popular campus events include ML Halloween Party, Sager, and Margaritaville.

Sports: There are 10 intercollegiate sports for men and 12 for women, and 7 intramural sports for men and 7 for women. Facilities include 12 outdoor and 6 indoor tennis courts; 6 full-length indoor basketball courts; 10 outdoor playing fields; an athletic events center with seating for 1800; a field house large enough to accommodate team practices during inclement weather; an outdoor 8-lane, 400-meter Versaturf track; an indoor 215-meter banked Tartan track; a 10 lane-by-10 lane, yards-by-meters indoor swimming pool with electronic timing system; 5 squash courts with spectator galleries; a fitness center with aerobic and Medx equipment; and a professionally staffed sports medicine facility with 3 full-time trainers.

Disabled Students: 75% of the campus is accessible. Wheelchair ramps, elevators, special parking, specially equipped rest rooms, special class scheduling, lowered drinking fountains, and lowered telephones are available.

Services: Counseling and information services are available, as is tutoring in most subjects. There is a reader service for the blind and computing support.

Campus Safety and Security: Measures include 24-hour foot and vehicle patrol, self-defense education, security escort services, and shuttle buses. There are informal discussions, pamphlets/posters/films, emergency telephones, and lighted pathways/sidewalks.

Programs of Study: Swarthmore confers B.A. and B.S. degrees. Bachelor's degrees are awarded in BIOLOGICAL SCIENCE (biochemistry and biology/biological science), COMMUNICATIONS AND THE ARTS (art, art history and appreciation, classics, comparative literature, dance, dramatic arts, English literature, French, German, Greek, Latin, linguistics, literature, music, Russian, and Spanish), COMPUTER AND PHYSICAL SCIENCE (astronomy, astrophysics, chemistry, computer science, mathematics, and physics), EDUCATION (education), ENGINEERING AND ENVIRONMENTAL DESIGN (engineering), SOCIAL SCIENCE (anthropology, Asian/Oriental studies, classical/ancient civilization, economics, German area studies, history, medieval studies, philosophy, political science/government, psychobiology, psychology, religion, and sociology). Economics, psychology, and English literature are the largest.

Required: To graduate, students must complete 3 courses in each of 3 divisions consisting of humanities, natural sciences and engineering, and social sciences. They must have completed 32 courses or the equivalent, with a minimum of 20 courses outside the major and 8 to 12 courses in the major. They must have a GPA of 2.0. Students must demonstrate foreign language competency and fulfill a phys ed requirement including a swimming test. Each major has a culminating experience, which may be a thesis, project, or comprehensive exam.

Special: Students may cross-register with Haverford and Bryn Mawr Colleges and the University of Pennsylvania. They may study abroad in their country of choice. Dual majors in physics and astronomy and in sociology and anthropology, student-designed majors, and a 4-year program leading to a B.A.-B.S. degree in engineering and liberal arts are available. Swarthmore offers a unique honors program whose features are student independence and responsibility and collegial relationship with faculty; students are evaluated by external examiners. There are 3 national honor societies, including Phi Beta Kappa. All departments have honors programs.

Faculty/Classroom: 61% of faculty are male; 39%, female. All both teach and do research. The average class size in an introductory lecture is 20; in a laboratory, 11; and in a regular course, 15.

Admissions: 24% of the 2003-2004 applicants were accepted. The SAT I scores for the 2003-2004 freshman class were: Verbal--1% below 500, 6% between 500 and 599, 26% between 600 and 700, and 67% above 700; Math--7% between 500 and 599, 28% between 600 and 700, and 65% above 700. 98% of the current freshmen were in the top fifth of their class; 99% were in the top two fifths. 24 freshmen graduated first in their class.

Requirements: The SAT I or ACT is required. In addition, SAT II: Subject tests in Writing and 2 other areas of choice are required; mathematics II C is required for engineering majors. Swarthmore does not require a specific high school curriculum. It does, however, recommend the in-

clusion of English, math, 1 or 2 foreign languages, history and social studies, literature, art and music, and the sciences. Interviews are strongly recommended. AP credits are accepted.

Procedure: Freshmen are admitted in the fall. Entrance exams should be taken in spring of the junior year or fall of the senior year. There are early decision and deferred admissions plans. Early decision applications should be filed by November 15; regular applications, by January 1 for fall entry. The fall 2003 application fee was $60. Notification of early decision is sent December 15; regular decision, April 1. 138 early decision candidates were accepted for the 2003-2004 class; 20 were admitted. Swarthmore couples the Common App with the Swarthmore Supplement. The Common App can be submitted via the Internet, but the Supplement must be mailed to the school 2 weeks prior to the application deadline. Copies of the Supplement can be downloaded from the Internet at *http://www.commonapp.org* or *http://www.swarthmore.edu/admissions/apply_to_swarthmore.html*.

Transfer: 4 transfer students enrolled in 2002-2003. The SAT I is required if not taken previously. An essay is required. 16 of 32 credits required for the bachelor's degree must be completed at Swarthmore.

Visiting: There are regularly scheduled orientations for prospective students, including group information sessions, offered at regular times throughout the year. There are guides for informal visits and visitors may sit in on classes and stay overnight. To schedule a visit, contact the admissions receptionist.

Financial Aid: In 2003-2004, 51% of all full-time freshmen and 49% of continuing full-time students received some form of financial aid. 51% of full-time freshmen and 49% of continuing full-time students received need-based aid. The average freshman award was $26,395. Need-based scholarships or need-based grants averaged $23,789; need-based self-help aid (loans and jobs) averaged $2784; and non-need-based awards and non-need-based scholarships averaged $28,500. 81% of undergraduates work part time. Average annual earnings from campus work are $1450. The average financial indebtedness of the 2003 graduate was $12,726. Swarthmore is a member of CSS. The CSS Profile, FAFSA, the college's own financial statement, tax returns, W-2 statements, and year-end paycheck stubs are required. The deadline for filing freshman financial aid applications for fall entry is February 15.

International Students: There were 92 international students enrolled in a recent year. The school actively recruits these students. They must take the SAT I or the ACT, and SAT II: Subject tests in writing and 2 others; mathematics IIC is required for engineering majors.

Computers: The mainframe consists of UNIX-based servers. There are more than 150 networked Macs and PCs available throughout the campus in public areas for student use. Residence halls are fully hooked up to the network with a connection for each resident, giving them access to the Internet, the library database, e-mail, shared software, and many other resources. All students may access the system. There are no time limits and no fees.

Graduates: From July 1, 2002 to June 30, 2003, 368 bachelor's degrees were awarded. The most popular majors were social sciences and history (30%), biology (9%), and English (9%). In an average class, 83% graduate in 4 years or less, 7% graduate in 5 years or less, and 2% graduate in 6 years or less. 49 companies recruited on campus in 2002-2003. Of the 2002 graduating class, 16% were enrolled in graduate school within 6 months of graduation and 71% were employed.

Admissions Contact: James L. Bock, Dean of Admissions and Financial Aid. E-mail: *admissions@swarthmore.edu*
Web: *http://www.swarthmore.edu/admissions/*

TEMPLE UNIVERSITY
Philadelphia, PA 19122-1803

F-3

(215) 204-7200
(888) 340-2222; Fax: (215) 204-5694

Full-time: 8111 men, 10,806 women	**Faculty:** 1232; I, av$
Part-time: 1345 men, 1953 women	**Ph.D.s:** 82%
Graduate: 4632 men, 6034 women	**Student/Faculty:** 15 to 1
Year: semesters, summer session	**Tuition:** $8594 ($15,354)
Application Deadline: April 1	**Room & Board:** $7318
Freshman Class: 16,758 applied, 10,058 accepted, 3606 enrolled	
SAT I Verbal/Math: 540/540	**COMPETITIVE**

Temple University, founded in 1888, is part of the Commonwealth System of Higher Education in Pennsylvania. It offers programs in the liberal arts and science and technology; allied health professions; education; engineering; art; business and management; communications and theater; architecture, landscape architecture and horticulture; music; and social administration. Temple has 6 other campuses, including 1 in Rome and 1 in Tokyo. There are 12 undergraduate and 13 graduate schools. In addition to regional accreditation, Temple has baccalaureate program accreditation with AACSB, ABET, ACEJMC, ACPE, ADA, APTA, CAHEA, CSWE, NAAB, NASAD, NASM, NCATE, NLN, and NRPA. The 3 libraries contain 2,100,000 volumes and 70 microform items, and subscribe to 15,600 periodicals. Computerized library services include the card catalog, interlibrary loans, database searching, and Internet access. Special learning facilities include a learning resource center, art gallery, planetarium, radio station, dance lab theater, media learning center for the study of critical languages, and multimedia lab for teacher education in music. The 430-acre campus is in an urban area 1 mile north of Center City, Philadelphia. Including any residence halls, there are 236 buildings.

Student Life: 74% of undergraduates are from Pennsylvania. Students are from 50 states, 128 foreign countries, and Canada. 59% are white; 18% African American; 10% Asian American. The average age of freshmen is 18; all undergraduates, 21. 18% do not continue beyond their first year; 47% remain to graduate.

Housing: 5200 students can be accommodated in college housing, which includes coed dorms, on-campus apartments, off-campus apartments, married-student housing, fraternity houses, and sorority houses. In addition, there are honors houses, language houses, living-learning communities, and special-interest houses. On-campus housing is available on a lottery system for upperclassmen. 79% of students commute. Alcohol is not permitted. All students may keep cars.

Activities: 1% of men belong to 12 local fraternities; 1% of women belong to 11 local sororities. There are 125 groups on campus, including art, band, cheerleading, chess, choir, chorus, computers, dance, drama, drill team, ethnic, film, honors, international, jazz band, literary magazine, marching band, musical theater, newspaper, orchestra, pep band, photography, political, professional, radio and TV, religious, social, social service, student government, and yearbook. Popular campus events include Spring Fling.

Sports: There are 13 intercollegiate sports for men and 13 for women, and 15 intramural sports for men and 12 for women. Facilities include 2 Olympic-size swimming pools, several gyms, weight-training rooms, racquetball courts, an 8-lane 400-meter track, and playing fields. The indoor gym seats 2000, and the largest auditorium/arena, 10,200.

Disabled Students: All of the campus is accessible. Wheelchair ramps, elevators, special parking, specially equipped rest rooms, special class scheduling, lowered drinking fountains, and lowered telephones are available. Additional services may be arranged through the Disabled Student Services Office.

Services: Counseling and information services are available, as is tutoring in most subjects. There is a reader service for the blind and remedial math, reading, and writing.

Campus Safety and Security: Measures include 24-hour foot and vehicle patrol, self-defense education, security escort services, and shuttle buses. There are informal discussions, pamphlets/posters/films, emergency telephones, lighted pathways/sidewalks, and 24-hour access-controlled security in residence halls.

Programs of Study: Temple confers B.A., B.S., B.Ar., B.B.A., B.F.A., B.M., B.S.Ar., B.S.E., B.S.Ed., B.S.E.E., B.S.N., and B.S.W. degrees. Associate, master's, and doctoral degrees are also awarded. Bachelor's degrees are awarded in AGRICULTURE (environmental studies and horticulture), BIOLOGICAL SCIENCE (biochemistry, biology/biological science, and biophysics), BUSINESS (accounting, banking and finance, business administration and management, business economics, business law, electronic business, entrepreneurial studies, human resources, international business management, management information systems, marketing/retailing/merchandising, personnel management, real estate, sports management, and tourism), COMMUNICATIONS AND THE ARTS (art, art history and appreciation, broadcasting, classics, communications, dance, dramatic arts, English, film arts, fine arts, French, German, Germanic languages and literature, Greek, guitar, Hebrew, Italian, jazz, journalism, linguistics, music, music history and appreciation, music performance, music theory and composition, percussion, performing arts, photography, piano/organ, Russian, Spanish, speech/debate/rhetoric, strings, telecommunications, voice, and winds), COMPUTER AND PHYSICAL SCIENCE (actuarial science, chemistry, computer science, earth science, geology, information sciences and systems, mathematics, physics, and statistics), EDUCATION (art, business, early childhood, education, elementary, English, foreign languages, industrial arts, marketing and distribution, mathematics, middle school, music, physical, science, secondary, social studies, and teaching English as a second/foreign language (TESOL/TEFOL)), ENGINEERING AND ENVIRONMENTAL DESIGN (architecture, civil engineering, electrical/electronics engineering, electrical/electronics engineering technology, engineering, engineering technology, environmental engineering technology, environmental science, landscape architecture/design, materials science, mechanical engineering, and mechanical engineering technology), HEALTH PROFESSIONS (health science, music therapy, nursing, occupational therapy, pharmacy, predentistry, and premedicine), SOCIAL SCIENCE (African American studies, American studies, anthropology, Asian/Oriental studies, criminal justice, economics, geography, history, interdisciplinary studies, Latin American studies, parks and recreation management, philosophy, physical fitness/movement, political science/government, prelaw, psychology, religion, social science, social work, sociology, urban studies, and women's studies). Business administration, psychology, and elementary education are the largest.

Required: The required core curriculum includes English composition, intellectual heritage, American culture, the arts, the individual and society, foreign language/international studies, math/statistics/logic, and sci-

ence and technology. A minimum 2.0 GPA and a total of 128 credit hours are required for graduation, including 24 credits in the major.

Special: The university offers study abroad, work-study programs, and up to 30 credits for life/military/work experience. There is a chapter of Phi Beta Kappa and a freshman honors program.

Faculty/Classroom: 67% of faculty are male; 33%, female. The average class size in a regular course is 24.

Admissions: 60% of the 2003-2004 applicants were accepted. The SAT I scores for the 2003-2004 freshman class were: Verbal--25% below 500, 44% between 500 and 599, 26% between 600 and 700, and 2% above 700; Math--24% below 500, 51% between 500 and 599, 23% between 600 and 700, and 2% above 700. 41% of the current freshmen were in the top fifth of their class; 79% were in the top two fifths. 24 freshmen graduated first in their class.

Requirements: The SAT I or ACT is required. In addition, applicants should complete 16 academic credits/Carnegie units, including 4 years of English, 2 each of math and a foreign language, and 1 each of history and a lab science. A GED is accepted. A portfolio and audition are required in relevant fields. AP and CLEP credits are accepted. Important factors in the admissions decision are advanced placement or honor courses, recommendations by school officials, and parents or siblings attending the school.

Procedure: Freshmen are admitted fall and spring. Entrance exams should be taken by March of the junior year or April of the senior year. There is an early admissions plan. There is a rolling admissions plan. Applications should be filed by April 1 for fall entry and November 15 for spring entry. Notification is sent on a rolling basis. The fall 2003 application fee was $35. Applications are accepted on-line.

Transfer: 2596 transfer students enrolled in 2002-2003. Applicants must have earned at least 15 college credit hours with at least a 2.3 GPA and must submit official high school and college transcripts. 30 of 128 credits required for the bachelor's degree must be completed at Temple.

Visiting: There are regularly scheduled orientations for prospective students. There are guides for informal visits and visitors may sit in on classes. To schedule a visit, contact the Office of Undergraduate Admissions at *tuadm@temple.edu.*

Financial Aid: In a recent year, 70% of all full-time freshmen and 67% of continuing full-time students received some form of financial aid. 58% of full-time freshmen and 54% of continuing full-time students received need-based aid. The average freshman award was $10,524. The average financial indebtedness of a recent graduate was $14,500. The FAFSA, the college's own financial statement, and the PHEAA (Pennsylvania residents) are required. The deadline for filing freshman financial aid applications for fall entry is March 31.

International Students: There are 732 international students enrolled. The school actively recruits these students. They must score 525 on the written TOEFL or 194 on the electronic version.

Computers: The mainframe is an IBM 9672RBS OS 390 Ver 2 Release 10. Students may access computer facilities through networked workstations distributed throughout the campus. There are about 3100 workstations with the following split: 84% PCs, 12% Macs, and 4% UNIX. All students may access the system 24 hours per day. There are no time limits and no fees.

Graduates: In a recent year, 3249 bachelor's degrees were awarded. The most popular majors were elementary education (8%), psychology (7%), and criminal justice (5%). In an average class, 1% graduate in 3 years or less, 20% graduate in 4 years or less, 38% graduate in 5 years or less, and 44% graduate in 6 years or less. 500 companies recruited on campus in a recent year.

Admissions Contact: Dr. Timm Rinehart, Director, Undergraduate Admissions. E-mail: *tuadm@temple.edu* Web: *http://www.temple.edu*

THIEL COLLEGE
Greenville, PA 16125

A-2
(724) 589-2226
(800) 24-THIEL; Fax: (724) 589-2013

Full-time: 630 men, 553 women	**Faculty:** 51; IIB, --$
Part-time: 33 men, 45 women	**Ph.D.s:** 67%
Graduate: none	**Student/Faculty:** 23 to 1
Year: semesters, summer session	**Tuition:** $14,386
Application Deadline: open	**Room & Board:** $6584
Freshman Class: 1557 applied, 1182 accepted, 349 enrolled	
SAT I Verbal/Math: 490/480	**ACT:** 19 COMPETITIVE

Thiel College, founded in 1866, is a private independent college affiliated with the Lutheran Church. It offers programs in liberal arts, business, engineering, religion, teacher preparation, and professional programs. The library contains 178,112 volumes, 41,699 microform items, and 6463 audio/video tapes/CDs, and subscribes to 415 periodicals. Computerized library services include the card catalog, interlibrary loans, database searching, and Internet access. Special learning facilities include a learning resource center, art gallery, radio station, and a wildlife sanctuary. The 135-acre campus is in a rural area 75 miles north of Pittsburgh and 75 miles southeast of Cleveland. Including any residence halls, there are 21 buildings.

Student Life: 80% of undergraduates are from Pennsylvania. Students are from 16 states and 14 foreign countries. 90% are from public schools. 75% are white. 36% claim no religious affiliation; 25% Protestant; 23% Catholic. The average age of freshmen is 18; all undergraduates, 20. 28% do not continue beyond their first year; 45% remain to graduate.

Housing: 1095 students can be accommodated in college housing, which includes single-sex and coed dorms and on-campus apartments. In addition, there are special-interest houses, an honors residence hall, and living-learning centers. On-campus housing is guaranteed for all 4 years. 82% of students live on campus; of those, 60% remain on campus on weekends. Alcohol is not permitted. All students may keep cars.

Activities: 10% of men belong to 4 national fraternities; 19% of women belong to 4 national sororities. There are 36 groups on campus, including art, band, cheerleading, choir, chorus, computers, dance, drama, drill team, ethnic, forensics, honors, international, literary magazine, musical theater, newspaper, pep band, political, professional, radio and TV, religious, social, social service, student government, symphony, and yearbook. Popular campus events include Spring Weekend, Greek Week, and theatrical productions.

Sports: There are 10 intercollegiate sports for men and 9 for women, and 4 intramural sports for men and 3 for women. Facilities include a 1200-seat gym, basketball and handball courts, playing fields, a fitness center, tennis courts, and a football stadium.

Disabled Students: 75% of the campus is accessible. Wheelchair ramps, elevators, special parking, specially equipped rest rooms, and special class scheduling are available.

Services: Counseling and information services are available, as is tutoring in most subjects. There is remedial math, reading, and writing.

Campus Safety and Security: Measures include 24-hour foot and vehicle patrol, security escort services, pamphlets/posters/films, and emergency telephones. There are lighted pathways/sidewalks.

Programs of Study: Thiel confers the B.A. degree. Associate degrees are also awarded. Bachelor's degrees are awarded in BIOLOGICAL SCIENCE (biology/biological science), BUSINESS (accounting, business administration and management, international business management, and management information systems), COMMUNICATIONS AND THE ARTS (art, communications, English, and Spanish), COMPUTER AND PHYSICAL SCIENCE (actuarial science, chemistry, computer science, mathematics, and physics), EDUCATION (elementary and secondary), ENGINEERING AND ENVIRONMENTAL DESIGN (environmental science and preengineering), HEALTH PROFESSIONS (cytotechnology, medical laboratory technology, physical therapy, predentistry, premedicine, prepharmacy, preveterinary science, and speech pathology/audiology), SOCIAL SCIENCE (family/juvenile justice, history, philosophy, political science/government, prelaw, psychology, religion, religious education, and sociology). Engineering, biology, and chemistry are the strongest academically. Accounting, business administration, and psychology are the largest.

Required: To graduate, students must complete a total of 124 credit hours, with 35 to 55 in the major and a minimum GPA of 2.0. Integrative distribution requirements include 8 hours of Western humanities, 8 hours of global heritage, 3 of religion, 3 to 10 of cultural studies, and 4 of health. Some majors require a comprehensive exam or thesis.

Special: Students may spend a semester at Argonne National Laboratories, the Art Institute of Pittsburgh, or Drew University. Special programs include a UN semester, a Washington semester, an Appalachian semester, study at Pittsburgh Institute of Mortuary Science, and a forestry and environmental management semester at Duke University. There is a 3-2 engineering program with Case Western Reserve University, the University of Pittsburgh, and Youngstown State University. Internships, study abroad, work-study, dual majors, nondegree study, credit by examination, and credit for life, military, and work experience are also available. There are 11 national honor societies, a freshman honors program, and 10 departmental honors programs.

Faculty/Classroom: 53% of faculty are male; 47%, female. All teach undergraduates. The average class size in an introductory lecture is 25; in a laboratory, 15; and in a regular course, 15.

Admissions: 76% of the 2003-2004 applicants were accepted. The SAT I scores for the 2003-2004 freshman class were: Verbal--55% below 500, 35% between 500 and 599, 10% between 600 and 700, and 1% above 700; Math--58% below 500, 35% between 500 and 599, 6% between 600 and 700, and 1% above 700. The ACT scores were 63% below 21, 18% between 21 and 23, 12% between 24 and 26, 4% between 27 and 28, and 3% above 28. 26% of the current freshmen were in the top fifth of their class; 48% were in the top two fifths. 1 freshman graduated first in the class.

Requirements: The SAT I or ACT is required. In addition, applicants should be high school graduates who have completed 16 academic units, including 4 years of English, 3 of social science, and 2 each of foreign language, math, and science. The GED is accepted. An essay and an interview are recommended. Thiel requires applicants to be in the upper 60% of their class. A GPA of 2.0 is required. AP and CLEP credits are accepted. Important factors in the admissions decision are advanced

placement or honor courses, evidence of special talent, and leadership record.

Procedure: Freshmen are admitted to all sessions. Entrance exams should be taken by May 1 of each year. There are early admissions, deferred admissions, and rolling admissions plans. Early decision applications should be filed by December 1; regular applications are open for fall entry. The application fee is $25. Notification of early decision is sent October 15; regular decision, on a rolling basis. Applications are accepted on-line through *www.admissions@thiel.edu.*

Transfer: 67 transfer students enrolled in 2002-2003. Applicants should meet the same criteria as entering freshmen and should submit official transcripts, statements of good standing, financial aid transcripts, and transfer forms from all colleges previously attended. Students must have a 2.0 GPA to transfer. 30 of 124 credits required for the bachelor's degree must be completed at Thiel.

Visiting: There are regularly scheduled orientations for prospective students, including orientation sessions for students enrolling in the fall and monthly sessions beginning in February. There are guides for informal visits and visitors may sit in on classes and stay overnight. To schedule a visit, contact the Admissions Office at (800) 248-4435 or *mknapp@thiel.edu.*

Financial Aid: In 2003-2004, 99% of all full-time freshmen and 98% of continuing full-time students received some form of financial aid. 90% of full-time freshmen and 82% of continuing full-time students received need-based aid. The average freshman award was $11,917. Need-based scholarships or need-based grants averaged $9545 ($15,300 maximum); need-based self-help aid (loans and jobs) averaged $4016 ($5850 maximum); and other non-need-based awards and non-need-based scholarships averaged $4560 ($7000 maximum). 39% of undergraduates work part time. Average annual earnings from campus work are $1300. The average financial indebtedness of the 2003 graduate was $14,500. The CSS Profile, FAFSA, FFS, or SFS are required; the FAFSA is preferred. The deadline for filing freshman financial aid applications for fall entry is May 1.

International Students: There are 51 international students enrolled. The school actively recruits these students. They must score 450 on the written TOEFL or 173 on the electronic version or take the MELAB. They must also take the SAT I or the ACT, scoring 920 on the SAT I.

Computers: The mainframe is a DEC PDP 11/44. There are a number of computer systems in operation on campus, serving both administrative and academic applications. They are accessible to student workers and to other students for completing course assignments. All students may access the system. There are no time limits and no fees.

Graduates: From July 1, 2002 to June 30, 2003, 153 bachelor's degrees were awarded. The most popular majors were business (23%), accounting (12%), and psychology (6%). In an average class, 2% graduate in 3 years or less, 31% graduate in 4 years or less, 43% graduate in 5 years or less, and 46% graduate in 6 years or less. 40 companies recruited on campus in 2002-2003. Of the 2002 graduating class, 13% were enrolled in graduate school within 6 months of graduation and 87% were employed.

Admissions Contact: Jeff Baylor, Vice Dean of Enrollment Management. Web: *http://www.thiel.edu*

UNIVERSITY OF PENNSYLVANIA F-3
Philadelphia, PA 19104 (215) 898-7507

Full-time: 4757 men, 4659 women	**Faculty:** 2414; I, ++$
Part-time: 199 men, 222 women	**Ph.Ds:** 99%
Graduate: 5507 men, 5414 women	**Student/Faculty:** 4 to 1
Year: semesters, summer session	**Tuition:** $29,318
Application Deadline: January 1	**Room & Board:** $8642
Freshman Class: 18,831 applied, 3837 accepted, 2423 enrolled	
SAT I Verbal/Math: 700/720	**ACT:** 30 MOST COMPETITIVE

University of Pennsylvania, founded in 1740, is a private institution offering undergraduate and graduate degrees in arts and sciences, business, engineering and applied science, and nursing. There are 4 undergraduate and 21 graduate schools. In addition to regional accreditation, Penn has baccalaureate program accreditation with AACSB, ABA, ABET, ACE, ACNM, ADA, APA, ASLA, AVMA, CSWE, HAS, LCME, NAAB, NCATE, NLN, PAB, and PDE. The 15 libraries contain 5,273,887 volumes, 3,932,349 microform items, and 69,919 audio/video tapes/CDs, and subscribe to 38,474 periodicals. Computerized library services include the card catalog, interlibrary loans, and database searching. Special learning facilities include a learning resource center, art gallery, planetarium, radio station, TV station, an arboretum, an animal research center, a primate research center, a language lab, a center for performing arts, an institute for contemporary art, a wind tunnel, an electron microscope, and a museum of anthropology and archeology. The 269-acre campus is in an urban area in Philadelphia. Including any residence halls, there are 151 buildings.

Student Life: 83% of undergraduates are from out of state, mostly the Middle Atlantic. Students are from 50 states, 109 foreign countries, and Canada. 57% are from public schools. 50% are white; 16% Asian American; 12% foreign nationals. 24% claim no religious affiliation; 23% Protestant; 21% Jewish; 18% Catholic; 14% Buddhist, Islamic, and Mormon. The average age of freshmen is 18; all undergraduates, 20. 4% do not continue beyond their first year; 92% remain to graduate.

Housing: 6500 students can be accommodated in college housing, which includes coed dorms, on-campus apartments, off-campus apartments, married-student housing, fraternity houses, and sorority houses. In addition, there are language houses and special-interest houses. There are 22 academic residence programs, including the areas of arts, biophysics, entrepreneurship, international studies, media, visual arts, and women in science. On-campus housing is guaranteed for the freshman year only, is available on a first-come, first-served basis, and is available on a lottery system for upperclassmen. 59% of students live on campus; of those, 97% remain on campus on weekends. All students may keep cars.

Activities: 23% of men belong to 34 national fraternities; 16% of women belong to 11 national sororities. There are 384 groups on campus, including art, band, cheerleading, chess, choir, chorale, chorus, computers, dance, debate, drama, ethnic, film, forensics, gay, honors, international, jazz band, literary magazine, marching band, musical theater, newspaper, opera, orchestra, pep band, political, professional, radio and TV, religious, social, social service, student government, symphony, and yearbook.

Sports: There are 17 intercollegiate sports for men and 16 for women, and 11 intramural sports for men and 11 for women. Facilities include 4 gyms, 2 swimming pools, squash courts, indoor and outdoor tennis courts, 7 playing fields, an indoor ice rink, rowing tanks, saunas, weight rooms, exercise facilities, a boathouse, and a stadium.

Disabled Students: 90% of the campus is accessible. Wheelchair ramps, elevators, special parking, specially equipped rest rooms, special class scheduling, lowered drinking fountains, lowered telephones, special housing, TDD, accessible housing, and an accessible van shuttle are available.

Services: Counseling and information services are available, as is tutoring in most subjects. There is a reader service for the blind. The WHEEL academic support program is available in all residences.

Campus Safety and Security: Measures include 24-hour foot and vehicle patrol, self-defense education, security escort services, and shuttle buses. There are informal discussions, pamphlets/posters/films, emergency telephones, lighted pathways/sidewalks, a bicycle patrol, 100 commissioned police officers, victim support and special services, Students Together Against Acquaintance Rape, Penn Watch, Student Walking Escort, and 200 security guard personnel, many on public patrol.

Programs of Study: Penn confers B.A., B.S., B.Applied Sc., B.S. in Econ., B.S.E., and B.S.N. degrees. Associate, master's, and doctoral degrees are also awarded. Bachelor's degrees are awarded in AGRICULTURE (environmental studies), BIOLOGICAL SCIENCE (biochemistry, biology/biological science, biometrics and biostatistics, and biophysics), BUSINESS (accounting, banking and finance, business administration and management, business law, entrepreneurial studies, insurance and risk management, management information systems, marketing/retailing/merchandising, operations research, real estate, and transportation management), COMMUNICATIONS AND THE ARTS (art history and appreciation, classics, communications, comparative literature, dramatic arts, English, fine arts, folklore and mythology, French, German, Italian, linguistics, music, romance languages and literature, Slavic languages, and Spanish), COMPUTER AND PHYSICAL SCIENCE (actuarial science, chemistry, computer science, digital arts/technology, geology, mathematics, physics, and statistics), EDUCATION (education and elementary), ENGINEERING AND ENVIRONMENTAL DESIGN (architecture, bioengineering, chemical engineering, civil engineering, computer engineering, electrical/electronics engineering, engineering, environmental design, environmental science, materials engineering, mechanical engineering, and systems engineering), HEALTH PROFESSIONS (biomedical science, health, health care administration, and nursing), SOCIAL SCIENCE (African American studies, African studies, anthropology, Asian/Oriental studies, cognitive science, economics, history, history of science, humanities, international relations, Italian studies, Judaic studies, Latin American studies, liberal arts/general studies, philosophy, political science/government, psychobiology, psychology, public administration, religion, sociology, South Asian studies, urban studies, and women's studies). Liberal arts, engineering and management are the strongest academically. Finance, economics, and history are the largest.

Required: The bachelor's degree requires completion of 32 to 40 course units, depending on the student's major, with 12 to 18 of these units in the major and a GPA of 2.0.

Special: Cross-registration is permitted with Haverford, Swarthmore, and Bryn Mawr Colleges and through the Quaker Consortium. Opportunities are provided for internships, a Washington semester, accelerated degree programs, joint degree programs, preprofessional programs, B.A.-B.S. degrees, dual and student-designed majors, credit by exam, limited pass/fail options, and study abroad in 39 countries. Through the "one university" concept, students in one undergraduate school may study in any of the other three. There are 10 national honor societies,

including Phi Beta Kappa, a freshman honors program, and 27 departmental honors programs.

Faculty/Classroom: 70% of faculty are male; 30%, female. 100% both teach and do research. No introductory courses are taught by graduate students. The average class size in an introductory lecture is 44; in a laboratory, 16; and in a regular course, 24.

Admissions: 20% of the 2003-2004 applicants were accepted. The SAT I scores for the 2003-2004 freshman class were: Verbal--7% between 500 and 599, 48% between 600 and 700, and 45% above 700; Math--4% between 500 and 599, 37% between 600 and 700, and 60% above 700. The ACT scores were 2% between 21 and 23, 9% between 24 and 26, 16% between 27 and 28, and 72% above 28. 97% of the current freshmen were in the top fifth of their class; 99% were in the top two fifths. There were 68 National Merit finalists. 365 freshmen graduated first in their class.

Requirements: The SAT I or ACT is required. Recommended preparation includes 4 years of high school English, 3 or 4 each of a foreign language and math, and 3 each of history and science. An essay is required. A portfolio and an audition are recommended for prospective art and music majors, respectively. AP credits are accepted. Important factors in the admissions decision are advanced placement or honor courses, leadership record, and recommendations by school officials.

Procedure: Freshmen are admitted in the fall. Entrance exams should be taken by December of the senior year. There are early decision, early admissions, and deferred admissions plans. Early decision applications should be filed by November 1; regular applications, by January 1 for fall entry, along with a $70 fee. Notification of early decision is sent December 15; regular decision, April 1. 1122 early decision candidates were accepted for the 2003-2004 class. 1085 applicants were on the 2003 waiting list; 25 were admitted. Applications are accepted on-line through ApplyYourself.

Transfer: 249 transfer students enrolled in 2002-2003. Applicants must provide college and high school transcripts, essays, and 2 recommendations. SAT I or ACT scores are required for transfer students. 16 of 32 course units required for the bachelor's degree must be completed at Penn.

Visiting: There are regularly scheduled orientations for prospective students, including an information session by the Admissions Office and a tour of the campus led by current students. There are guides for informal visits and visitors may sit in on classes and stay overnight. To schedule a visit, contact the Admissions Office.

Financial Aid: In 2003-2004, 64% of all full-time freshmen and 57% of continuing full-time students received some form of financial aid. 44% of full-time freshmen and 42% of continuing full-time students received need-based aid. The average freshman award was $25,889, with $20,658 ($37,120 maximum) from need-based scholarships or need-based grants, and $5231 ($12,800 maximum) from need-based self-help aid (loans and jobs). 30% of undergraduates work part time. Average annual earnings from campus work are $1734. The average financial indebtedness of the 2003 graduate was $21,292. Penn is a member of CSS. The CSS Profile or FAFSA, the college's own financial statement and the parent and student federal income tax returns are required. The priority date for freshman financial aid applications for fall entry is February 15.

International Students: There are 1145 international students enrolled. The school actively recruits these students. They must score 550 on the written TOEFL or 220 on the electronic version and also take the SAT I and 3 SAT II: Subject tests or the ACT.

Computers: The mainframe is an IBM zSeries 800. There are more than 1000 networked PCs available to students in computer labs, libraries, and other locations. Ethernet connections are provided in campus residences and Greek houses. Wireless access is available in several libraries and in common areas in some schools. Discounted Internet service is available for students living off campus. All students may access the system. There are no time limits and no fees. It is strongly recommended that all students have a personal computer. It is recommended that students taking courses in the School of Design may be required to have PCs.

Graduates: From July 1, 2002 to June 30, 2003, 2876 bachelor's degrees were awarded. The most popular majors were finance (12%), economics (8%), and history (7%). In an average class, 2% graduate in 3 years or less, 79% graduate in 4 years or less, 90% graduate in 5 years or less, and 92% graduate in 6 years or less. 490 companies recruited on campus in 2002-2003. Of the 2002 graduating class, 23% were enrolled in graduate school within 6 months of graduation and 62% were employed.

Admissions Contact: Willis Stetson, Jr., Dean of Admissions. A video is available. Web: *www.upenn.edu/admissions/*

UNIVERSITY OF PITTSBURGH SYSTEM

The University of Pittsburgh System, established in 1787, is a public system in Pennsylvania. It is governed by the board of trustees of the University of Pittsburgh, whose chief administrator is the chancellor. The primary goal of the system is enhancing educational opportunities for the citizens of Pennsylvania and contributing to the state's social, intellectual, and economic development. The main priorities are to engage in research, artistic, and scholarly activities; to provide high-quality undergraduate, graduate, and professional programs; and to offer expertise and educational services to meet the needs of the region and state. The total enrollment of the 4-year campuses is about 33,000; there were about 3700 faculty members. Altogether there are 206 baccalaureate, 116 master's, 83 doctoral, and 4 first professional degree programs offered in University of Pittsburgh System. 4-year campuses are located in Pittsburgh, Bradford, Greensburg, and Johnstown. Profiles of the 4-year campuses are included in this section.

UNIVERSITY OF PITTSBURGH AT BRADFORD C-2
Bradford, PA 16701-2898 (814) 362-7555
(800) 872-1787; Fax: (814) 362-7578

Full-time: 461 men, 572 women	**Faculty:** 68; IIB, -$
Part-time: 103 men, 281 women	**Ph.D.s:** 69%
Graduate: none	**Student/Faculty:** 15 to 1
Year: semesters, summer session	**Tuition:** $9264 ($18,576)
Application Deadline: open	**Room & Board:** $6030
Freshman Class: 645 applied, 530 accepted, 308 enrolled	
SAT I Verbal/Math: 500/510	**ACT:** 21 **COMPETITIVE**

The University of Pittsburgh at Bradford, established in 1963, is a public, state-related liberal arts institution. In addition to regional accreditation, Pitt-Bradford has baccalaureate program accreditation with NLN. The library contains 86,121 volumes, 14,461 microform items, and 3494 audio/video tapes/CDs, and subscribes to 337 periodicals. Computerized library services include the card catalog, interlibrary loans, database searching, and Internet access. Special learning facilities include a learning resource center, art gallery, natural history museum, radio station, TV station, and a sports medicine and rehabilitative therapy clinic. The 170-acre campus is in a small town 160 miles northeast of Pittsburgh and 80 miles south of Buffalo. Including any residence halls, there are 22 buildings.

Student Life: 88% of undergraduates are from Pennsylvania. Students are from 20 states and 3 foreign countries. 96% are white. The average age of freshmen is 19; all undergraduates, 25. 32% do not continue beyond their first year; 38% remain to graduate.

Housing: 554 students can be accommodated in college housing, which includes single-sex and coed on-campus apartments. On-campus housing is available on a first-come, first-served basis. 54% of students live on campus; of those, 26% remain on campus on weekends. All students may keep cars.

Activities: 16% of men belong to 3 local fraternities; 9% of women belong to 3 local sororities. There are 50 groups on campus, including art, choir, computers, dance, drama, ethnic, honors, international, literary magazine, newspaper, political, professional, radio and TV, religious, social, social service, and student government. Popular campus events include Winter Weekend, Spring Fling, and Alumni Weekend.

Sports: There are 5 intercollegiate sports for men and 6 for women, and 11 intramural sports for men and 11 for women. Facilities include a sport and fitness center that includes a 1200-seat performance arena for basketball, volleyball, and general recreation; a fitness center with physical conditioning equipment; and an exercise arts studio for dance, martial arts, and aerobics. There is also an auxiliary gym for recreation and intramurals, phys ed classes, other events, and a 6-lane swimming pool. Outdoor facilities include a lighted softball field, a baseball field, tennis courts, 2 handball courts, several basketball courts, football/softball fields, and a sand volleyball court.

Disabled Students: 99% of the campus is accessible. Elevators, special parking, specially equipped rest rooms, lowered drinking fountains, lowered telephones, and special housing are available.

Services: Counseling and information services are available, as is tutoring in most subjects. There is remedial math, reading, and writing. There is a writing lab.

Campus Safety and Security: Measures include 24-hour foot and vehicle patrol, security escort services, informal discussions, and pamphlets/posters/films. There are lighted pathways/sidewalks.

Programs of Study: Pitt-Bradford confers B.A., B.S., and B.S.N. degrees. Associate degrees are also awarded. Bachelor's degrees are awarded in BIOLOGICAL SCIENCE (biology/biological science), BUSINESS (business administration and management, and sports management), COMMUNICATIONS AND THE ARTS (communications, English, and public relations), COMPUTER AND PHYSICAL SCIENCE (chemistry, computer science, geology, mathematics, and physical sciences), EDUCATION (athletic training), ENGINEERING AND ENVIRONMENTAL DESIGN (environmental science), HEALTH PROFESSIONS (nursing, radiological science, and sports medicine), SOCIAL SCIENCE (American studies, criminal justice, economics, history, liberal arts/general studies, political science/government, psychology, social science, and sociology). Athletic training, writing, and math are the strong-

est academically. Business administration, administration of justice, and psychology are the largest.

Required: To graduate, students must complete a minimum of 120 credits with 38 to 70 in the major, and maintain a minimum GPA of 2.0. At least 30 should be in upper-level courses. The core curriculum varies from 15 to 30 credits and distribution requirements from 59 to 63.

Special: Students may cross-register with colleges in the University of Pittsburgh system. Internships are required or strongly recommended for all majors. The school offers study abroad, dual majors, B.A.-B.S. degrees, nondegree study, a 3-2 engineering degree with the University of Pittsburgh (Oakland campus), and accelerated degree programs in most majors. Interdisciplinary majors are offered in human relations, combining anthropology, psychology, and sociology, and in journalism and creative, technical, and business writing. Professional preparation in many areas and education certification are also offered. There are 6 national honor societies.

Faculty/Classroom: 55% of faculty are male; 45%, female. All teach undergraduates. The average class size in an introductory lecture is 25; in a laboratory, 12; and in a regular course, 18.

Admissions: 82% of the 2003-2004 applicants were accepted. The SAT I scores for the 2003-2004 freshman class were: Verbal--49% below 500, 37% between 500 and 599, 13% between 600 and 700, and 1% above 700; Math--47% below 500, 40% between 500 and 599, 11% between 600 and 700, and 2% above 700. The ACT scores were 49% below 21, 33% between 21 and 23, 16% between 24 and 26, and 2% above 28. 21% of the current freshmen were in the top fifth of their class; 53% were in the top two fifths. 2 freshmen graduated first in their class.

Requirements: The SAT I is required and the ACT is recommended. In addition, with a minimum composite score of 800 (400 verbal and 400 math) on the SAT I or 19 on the ACT. Students must be graduates of an accredited secondary school with 16 Carnegie units, including 4 each in English and social studies and 3 each in science and math. The GED is accepted. An essay is recommended, as is an interview. A GPA of 2.0 is required. AP and CLEP credits are accepted. Important factors in the admissions decision are advanced placement or honor courses, extracurricular activities record, and leadership record.

Procedure: Freshmen are admitted fall, spring, and summer. Entrance exams should be taken during the junior year or the fall of the senior year. There are early decision, early admissions, deferred admissions, and rolling admissions plans. Application deadlines are open. Application fee is $35. Applications are accepted on-line through https://campusweb.upb.pitt.edu/application/.

Transfer: 90 transfer students enrolled in 2002-2003. A GPA of 2.0 or higher is required. 30 of 120 credits required for the bachelor's degree must be completed at Pitt-Bradford.

Visiting: There are regularly scheduled orientations for prospective students, consisting of a meeting with admissions and financial aid counselors, a tour of the campus, including the dining hall, and a visit with a faculty member. There are guides for informal visits and visitors may sit in on classes and stay overnight. To schedule a visit, contact the Admissions Office at admissions@upb.pitt.edu.

Financial Aid: In 2003-2004, 90% of all full-time students received some form of financial aid. 83% of full-time freshmen and 89% of continuing full-time students received need-based aid. 25% of undergraduates work part time. Average annual earnings from campus work are $1000. The average financial indebtedness of the 2003 graduate was $18,364. Pitt-Bradford is a member of CSS. The FAFSA is required. The priority date for freshman financial aid applications for fall entry is March 1.

International Students: There are 3 international students enrolled. They must score 550 on the written TOEFL or 213 on the electronic version.

Computers: The campus features 175 computer stations, all linked to the workstations. All students may access the system. There are no time limits and no fees.

Graduates: From July 1, 2002 to June 30, 2003, 157 bachelor's degrees were awarded. The most popular majors were business (13%), human relations (10%), and computer science (10%). In an average class, 3% graduate in 3 years or less, 26% graduate in 4 years or less, 35% graduate in 5 years or less, and 38% graduate in 6 years or less. 45 companies recruited on campus in 2002-2003. Of the 2002 graduating class, 21% were enrolled in graduate school within 6 months of graduation and 82% were employed.

Admissions Contact: Alexander P. Nazemetz, Director of Admissions. A video is available. E-mail: admissions@upb.pitt.edu
Web: www.upb.pitt.edu

UNIVERSITY OF PITTSBURGH AT GREENSBURG   B-3
Greensburg, PA 15601-5898

(724) 836-9880
Fax: (724) 836-7160

Full-time: 815 men, 895 women	**Faculty:** 78; IIB, -$
Part-time: 96 men, 110 women	**Ph.D.s:** 84%
Graduate: none	**Student/Faculty:** 22 to 1
Year: semesters, summer session	**Tuition:** $9214 ($18,526)
Application Deadline: open	**Room & Board:** $6770
Freshman Class: 1281 applied, 924 accepted, 525 enrolled	
SAT I Verbal/Math: 528/532	**COMPETITIVE**

The University of Pittsburgh at Greensburg, established in 1963, is a public state-related institution, offering undergraduate majors that can be completed at Pitt-Greensburg, as well as relocation programs that are begun at Greensburg and completed at another Pitt campus. The library contains 75,000 volumes, 9119 microform items, and 1993 audio/video tapes/CDs, and subscribes to 418 periodicals. Computerized library services include the card catalog, interlibrary loans, database searching, and Internet access. Special learning facilities include a learning resource center. The 219-acre campus is in a suburban area 33 miles southeast of Pittsburgh. Including any residence halls, there are 25 buildings.

Student Life: 99% of undergraduates are from Pennsylvania. Students are from 10 states and 5 foreign countries. 90% are from public schools. 96% are white. The average age of freshmen is 18; all undergraduates, 25. 25% do not continue beyond their first year; 55% remain to graduate.

Housing: 585 students can be accommodated in college housing, which includes coed dorms and on-campus apartments. In addition, there are special-interest houses. On-campus housing is available on a first-come, first-served basis. 68% of students commute. Alcohol is not permitted. All students may keep cars.

Activities: There are no fraternities or sororities. There are 44 groups on campus, including academic, band, cheerleading, chess, choir, chorale, chorus, computers, dance, debate, drama, ethnic, honors, literary magazine, newspaper, pep band, political, religious, social, social service, and student government. Popular campus events include Humanities Day.

Sports: There are 6 intercollegiate sports for men and 6 for women, and 8 intramural sports for men and 8 for women. Facilities include a gym, a weight room, playing fields, and tennis and racquetball courts.

Disabled Students: 95% of the campus is accessible. Wheelchair ramps, elevators, special parking, specially equipped rest rooms, special class scheduling, lowered drinking fountains, lowered telephones, and special housing are available.

Services: Counseling and information services are available, as is tutoring in most subjects, including math, computer science, and English. There is remedial math, reading, and writing.

Campus Safety and Security: Measures include 24-hour foot and vehicle patrol, security escort services, informal discussions, and pamphlets/posters/films. There are emergency telephones and lighted pathways/sidewalks.

Programs of Study: Pitt-Greensburg confers B.A. and B.S. degrees. Bachelor's degrees are awarded in BIOLOGICAL SCIENCE (biology/biological science), BUSINESS (accounting and management science), COMMUNICATIONS AND THE ARTS (communications, creative writing, and English literature), COMPUTER AND PHYSICAL SCIENCE (applied mathematics and natural sciences), SOCIAL SCIENCE (American studies, anthropology, humanities, political science/government, psychology, and social science). Management and psychology are the strongest academically. Management and administration of justice are the largest.

Required: To graduate, students must complete 120 to 126 hours, with 24 to 36 in the major, and maintain a minimum GPA of 2.0. General education requirements include 15 credits each in humanities, social sciences, and natural sciences, 6 to 15 in writing courses, 3 each in speech and critical reasoning, and 2 to 3 in math.

Special: Pitt-Greensburg offers cross-registration with the Pittsburgh and Johnstown campuses of the university system and with Seton Hill College and Westmoreland County Community College. Internships are available in all majors and required for English writing and criminology. Double majors, student-designed majors, a Washington semester, non-degree study, and pass/fail options are available. There are 2 national honor societies, including Phi Beta Kappa.

Faculty/Classroom: 51% of faculty are male; 49%, female. All teach undergraduates and 50% do research. The average class size in an introductory lecture is 30; in a laboratory, 15; and in a regular course, 25.

Admissions: 72% of the 2003-2004 applicants were accepted. The SAT I scores for the 2003-2004 freshman class were: Verbal--32% below 500, 53% between 500 and 599, 14% between 600 and 700, and 1% above 700; Math--29% below 500, 55% between 500 and 599, 15% between 600 and 700, and 1% above 700. 24% of the current freshmen were in the top fifth of their class; 61% were in the top two fifths.

Requirements: The SAT I is required. In addition, students must be graduates of an accredited secondary school. The GED is accepted. Stu-

dents must complete 15 high school units, including 4 each of English and academic electives, 3 of a single foreign language, 2 of math, and 1 each of history and lab science; additional units in all but English are recommended. An essay is optional; an interview is recommended. Pitt-Greensburg requires applicants to be in the upper 60% of their class. A GPA of 2.7 is required. AP and CLEP credits are accepted. Important factors in the admissions decision are advanced placement or honor courses, recommendations by school officials, and leadership record.

Procedure: Freshmen are admitted fall and spring. Entrance exams should be taken by December of the senior year. There are early decision, rolling, and deferred admissions plans. Application deadlines are open. The fall 2003 application fee was $35. Applications are accepted on-line through *www.upg.pitt.edu*.

Transfer: 123 transfer students enrolled in a recent year. Applicants must have a minimum GPA of 2.0. The SAT I, 15 minimum college credits, and an interview are recommended. Grades of C in comparable courses transfer for credit. 30 of 120 credits required for the bachelor's degree must be completed at Pitt-Greensburg.

Visiting: There are regularly scheduled orientations for prospective students, including Open House, Preview Day, and Junior Jump Start. There are guides for informal visits and visitors may sit in on classes. To schedule a visit, contact the Admissions Office at (724) 836-9881 or *upgadmit@pitt.edu*.

Financial Aid: The average freshman award was $8910. Need-based scholarships or need-based grants averaged $4185 ($7850 maximum); and need-based self-help aid (loans and jobs) averaged $4725 (maximum). 63% of undergraduates work part time. Average annual earnings from campus work are $2100. The average financial indebtedness of the 2003 graduate was $15,200. The FAFSA and the college's own financial statement are required. The deadline for filing freshman financial aid applications for fall entry is April 1.

International Students: They must score 550 on the written TOEFL or take the MELAB.

Computers: The mainframes are a DEC VAX 9000 in a VAX cluster, a VAX 8800, and a DEC System 5000. All computers are networked locally and through wide-area networks to VMS and UNIX mainframe services. There are 30 DOS, 15 UNIX, and Mac computers in the computer center. All residence hall rooms have at least one PC and a network connection. All students may access the system. There are no time limits and no fees.

Graduates: In a recent year, 212 bachelor's degrees were awarded. The most popular majors were management (23%), psychology (21%), and accounting (15%). In an average class, 27% graduate in 4 years or less, 52% graduate in 5 years or less, and 2% graduate in 6 years or less. 5 companies recruited on campus in 2002-2003. Of the 2002 graduating class, 23% were enrolled in graduate school within 6 months of graduation and 56% were employed.

Admissions Contact: Brandi S. Darr, Director of Admissions and Financial Aid. E-mail: *upgadmit@pitt.edu*

UNIVERSITY OF PITTSBURGH AT JOHNSTOWN   C-3
Johnstown, PA 15904

(814) 269-7050
(800) 765-4875; Fax: (814) 269-7044

Full-time: 1402 men, 1420 women	**Faculty:** 136; IIB, av$
Part-time: 121 men, 203 women	**Ph.D.s:** 73%
Graduate: none	**Student/Faculty:** 21 to 1
Year: trimesters, summer session	**Tuition:** $9256 ($18,568)
Application Deadline: open	**Room & Board:** $5960
Freshman Class: 2955 applied, 2479 accepted, 869 enrolled	
SAT I Verbal/Math: 511/521	**ACT:** 20 **LESS COMPETITIVE**

The University of Pittsburgh at Johnstown, founded in 1927, is a 4-year institution offering programs in arts and sciences, education, and engineering technology. In addition to regional accreditation, UPJ has baccalaureate program accreditation with ABET. Computerized library services include the card catalog, interlibrary loans, and database searching. Special learning facilities include a learning resource center, art gallery, and radio station. The 650-acre campus is in a suburban area 70 miles east of Pittsburgh. Including any residence halls, there are 28 buildings.

Student Life: 98% of undergraduates are from Pennsylvania. Students are from 12 states. 89% are from public schools. 96% are white. 48% are Protestant; 47%, Catholic. The average age of freshmen is 18; all undergraduates, 19. 9% do not continue beyond their first year; 70% remain to graduate.

Housing: 1700 students can be accommodated in college housing, which includes single-sex dorms, on-campus apartments, off-campus apartments, fraternity houses, and sorority houses. In addition, there are special-interest houses and clubs and organizations that provide housing. On-campus housing is guaranteed for all 4 years. 62% of students live on campus; of those, 65% remain on campus on weekends. All students may keep cars.

Activities: 16% of men belong to 1 local and 3 national fraternities; 11% of women belong to 1 local and 4 national sororities. There are 70 groups on campus, including band, cheerleading, chess, choir, chorus, computers, dance, drama, ethnic, honors, literary magazine, musical theater, newspaper, pep band, political, professional, radio and TV, religious, social, social service, student government, symphony, and yearbook. Popular campus events include Ethnic Festival, Engineers' Week, and Winter Carnival.

Sports: There are 4 intercollegiate sports for men and 4 for women, and 32 intramural sports for men and 21 for women. Facilities include a 2300-seat gym, a pool, a dance studio, a weight room, a sauna, a cross-country track, tennis and basketball courts, and a nature area.

Disabled Students: 80% of the campus is accessible. Elevators, special parking, specially equipped rest rooms, and special class scheduling are available.

Services: Counseling and information services are available, as is tutoring in most subjects.

Campus Safety and Security: Measures include 24-hour foot and vehicle patrol, informal discussions, and lighted pathways/sidewalks.

Programs of Study: UPJ confers B.A. and B.S. degrees. Associate degrees are also awarded. Bachelor's degrees are awarded in AGRICULTURE (environmental studies), BIOLOGICAL SCIENCE (biology/ biological science), BUSINESS (accounting, banking and finance, business administration and management, and business economics), COMMUNICATIONS AND THE ARTS (communications, creative writing, dramatic arts, English, and journalism), COMPUTER AND PHYSICAL SCIENCE (chemistry, computer science, geology, and mathematics), EDUCATION (elementary, English, mathematics, science, secondary, and social science), ENGINEERING AND ENVIRONMENTAL DESIGN (civil engineering technology, electrical/electronics engineering technology, and mechanical engineering technology), HEALTH PROFESSIONS (medical laboratory technology), SOCIAL SCIENCE (American studies, economics, geography, history, humanities, political science/government, psychology, social science, and sociology). Business, biology, and education are the largest.

Required: To graduate, students must complete 120 to 139 credits, with 30 to 36 credits in the major and a minimum GPA of 2.0. The school requires 12 credits each in humanities, natural sciences, and social sciences.

Special: Students may cross-register with schools in the Pittsburgh Council for Higher Education. Internships are available both on and off campus for credit, pay, or both. The school offers study abroad, work-study programs, accelerated degree programs, dual majors, student-designed majors, nondegree study, and pass/fail options. There are 8 national honor societies.

Faculty/Classroom: 66% of faculty are male; 34%, female. 93% teach undergraduates and 70% do research. The average class size in an introductory lecture is 30; in a laboratory, 18; and in a regular course, 25.

Admissions: 84% of the 2003-2004 applicants were accepted. The SAT I scores for the 2003-2004 freshman class were: Verbal--44% below 500, 48% between 500 and 599, 7% between 600 and 700, and 1% above 700; Math--37% below 500, 48% between 500 and 599, 14% between 600 and 700, and 1% above 700. The ACT scores were 52% below 21, 36% between 21 and 23, 10% between 24 and 26, 1% between 27 and 28, and 1% above 28. 23% of the current freshmen were in the top fifth of their class; 58% were in the top two fifths.

Requirements: The SAT I or ACT is required. In addition, applicants must be graduates of an accredited secondary school. The GED is accepted. For admission to freshman standing, 15 academic credits are required, including 4 each of English and history, 3 each of social studies and math (2 of algebra, 1 of geometry preferred), 2 of foreign language, and 1 to 2 of lab science. Engineering students must have completed chemistry, physics, and trigonometry. An interview is recommended, and an essay is required. AP credits are accepted. Important factors in the admissions decision are advanced placement or honor courses, leadership record, and recommendations by school officials.

Procedure: Freshmen are admitted to all sessions. Entrance exams should be taken between April and June of the junior year or by November of the senior year. There are early admissions and deferred admissions plans. Application deadlines are open. The fall 2003 admission fee was $35. There is a rolling admissions plan.

Transfer: Students wishing to transfer must have a minimum GPA of 2.5 and at least 15 credit hours earned. The SAT I or ACT is required. Grades of C or better transfer for credit. 30 of 120 credits required for the bachelor's degree must be completed at UPJ.

Visiting: There are regularly scheduled orientations for prospective students, including 2 programs held on Saturdays in the fall and in the spring. There are guides for informal visits and visitors may sit in on classes and stay overnight. To schedule a visit, contact the Admissions Office.

Financial Aid: In 2003-2004, 79% of all full-time freshmen and 73% of continuing full-time students received some form of financial aid. 66% of full-time freshmen and 63% of continuing full-time students received need-based aid. The average freshman award was $6958. Need-based scholarships or need-based grants averaged $4295; need-based self-help aid (loans and jobs) averaged $3407; non-need-based athletic scholarships averaged $7585; and other non-need-based awards and non-

need-based scholarships averaged $2263. The FAFSA, PHEAA Application, and State Grant are required. Check with the school for current deadlines.

International Students: They must score 550 on the written TOEFL. The SAT I may be required for some students.

Computers: The mainframe is a DEC VAX cluster. 150 Mac, IBM, and AT&T PCs are available for student use. Some labs have restricted use for education, engineering technology, or computer science majors. Others are open to all students. All students have access to the Internet. All students may access the system. There are no time limits. The fee is $110 per term.

Admissions Contact: James F. Gyure, Director of Admissions. E-mail: *gyure@upj.pitt.edu* Web: *www.upj.pitt.edu*

UNIVERSITY OF PITTSBURGH AT PITTSBURGH   B-3
Pittsburgh, PA 15260   (412) 624-PITT; Fax: (412) 648-8815

Full-time: 7300 men, 7841 women	**Faculty:** I, av$
Part-time: 987 men, 1285 women	**Ph.D.s:** 90%
Graduate: 4259 men, 5123 women	**Student/Faculty:** n/av
Year: semesters, summer session	**Tuition:** $9274 ($18,586)
Application Deadline: open	**Room & Board:** $6800
Freshman Class: 17,494 applied, 8445 accepted, 2914 enrolled	
SAT I Verbal/Math: 600/610	**HIGHLY COMPETITIVE**

The University of Pittsburgh, founded in 1787, is a state-related, public research university with programs in arts and sciences, education, engineering, law, social work, business, health science, information sciences, and public and international affairs. There are 10 undergraduate and 14 graduate schools. In addition to regional accreditation, Pitt has baccalaureate program accreditation with AACSB, ABET, ACPE, ADA, CSWE, and NLN. The 25 libraries contain 4,182,324 volumes and 4,360,230 microform items, and subscribe to 23,377 periodicals. Computerized library services include the card catalog, interlibrary loans, and database searching. Special learning facilities include a learning resource center, art gallery, radio station, international classrooms located in the 42-story Cathedral of Learning, observatory, and music hall. The 132-acre campus is in an urban area 3 miles east of downtown Pittsburgh. Including any residence halls, there are 100 buildings.

Student Life: 85% of undergraduates are from Pennsylvania. Students are from 49 states, 122 foreign countries, and Canada. 82% are white. The average age of freshmen is 18; all undergraduates, 22. 12% do not continue beyond their first year.

Housing: 5900 students can be accommodated in college housing, which includes single-sex and coed dorms, off-campus apartments, fraternity houses, and sorority houses. In addition, there are honors houses, special-interest houses, and engineering, nursing, health-related, business, and international living. On-campus housing is guaranteed for the freshman year only, is available on a first-come, first-served basis, and is available on a lottery system for upperclassmen. All students may keep cars.

Activities: 6% of men belong to 20 national fraternities; 6% of women belong to 14 national sororities. There are 300 groups on campus, including art, band, cheerleading, chess, choir, chorus, dance, debate, drama, ethnic, film, gay, honors, international, jazz band, literary magazine, marching band, newspaper, orchestra, pep band, political, professional, radio and TV, religious, social, social service, student government, symphony, and yearbook. Popular campus events include Jazz Seminar, Black Week, and Greek Week.

Sports: There are 9 intercollegiate sports for men and 10 for women, and 13 intramural sports for men and 11 for women. Facilities include a 12,000-seat field house for hosting basketball games and concerts; the complex also has a fitness center for student use as well as a food court and shops. There are billiard tables, table tennis, video games, and televisions in the student union.

Disabled Students: 90% of the campus is accessible. Wheelchair ramps, elevators, special parking, specially equipped rest rooms, special class scheduling, lowered drinking fountains, lowered telephones, transportation, and wheelchair-accessible computer facilities in the computing labs are available.

Services: Counseling and information services are available, as is tutoring in some subjects, including many lower-level undergraduate science and humanities courses. There is a reader service for the blind and remedial math, reading, and writing.

Campus Safety and Security: Measures include 24-hour foot and vehicle patrol, self-defense education, security escort services, and shuttle buses. There are informal discussions, pamphlets/posters/films, emergency telephones, lighted pathways/sidewalks, taxi service, and crime alerts and notices distributed when an immediate danger to faculty, students, or staff is presented.

Programs of Study: Pitt confers B.A., B.S., B.A.S.W., B.Phil., B.S.B.A., B.S.E., and B.S.N. degrees. Master's and doctoral degrees are also awarded. Bachelor's degrees are awarded in BIOLOGICAL SCIENCE (biology/biological science, ecology, evolutionary biology, microbiology, molecular biology, neurosciences, and nutrition), BUSINESS (accounting, banking and finance, business administration and management, management science, and marketing/retailing/merchandising), COMMUNICATIONS AND THE ARTS (Chinese, classics, communications, creative writing, dramatic arts, English literature, film arts, fine arts, French, German, Italian, Japanese, linguistics, music, Polish, Russian, Spanish, speech/debate/rhetoric, and studio art), COMPUTER AND PHYSICAL SCIENCE (astronomy, chemistry, computer science, geology, information sciences and systems, mathematics, natural sciences, physics, and statistics), ENGINEERING AND ENVIRONMENTAL DESIGN (bioengineering, chemical engineering, civil engineering, computer engineering, electrical/electronics engineering, engineering physics, environmental science, industrial engineering, materials engineering, materials science, mechanical engineering, and metallurgical engineering), HEALTH PROFESSIONS (emergency medical technologies, exercise science, medical laboratory technology, medical records administration/services, nursing, and occupational therapy), SOCIAL SCIENCE (African American studies, anthropology, child psychology/development, economics, history, humanities, law, law enforcement and corrections, liberal arts/general studies, philosophy, physical fitness/movement, political science/government, psychology, public administration, religion, social science, social work, sociology, and urban studies). Philosophy, history and philosophy of science, and chemistry are the strongest academically.

Required: All students in the School of Arts and Sciences must take a minimum of 120 credits. Skills and general education requirements vary by high school achievement but include course work in the humanities, social and natural sciences, and foreign culture. A minimum of 24 credits in the major and a 2.0 GPA are required. Requirements for other schools may vary.

Special: Students may cross-register with 10 neighboring colleges and universities. Internships, study abroad, a semester at sea, a Washington semester, work-study programs, a dual major in business and any other subject in arts and sciences, and student-designed majors are available. There are freshman seminars and a 5-year joint degree in arts and sciences/engineering. There are 22 national honor societies, including Phi Beta Kappa, and a freshman honors program.

Faculty/Classroom: 65% of faculty are male; 35%, female.

Admissions: 48% of the 2003-2004 applicants were accepted. The SAT I scores for the 2003-2004 freshman class were: Verbal--7% below 500, 42% between 500 and 599, 40% between 600 and 700, and 11% above 700; Math--6% below 500, 33% between 500 and 599, 48% between 600 and 700, and 13% above 700. 73% of the current freshmen were in the top fifth of their class. 76 freshmen graduated first in their class.

Requirements: The SAT I or ACT is required. In addition, applicants for admission to the School of Arts and Sciences must be graduates of an accredited secondary school. Students must have 15 high school academic credits, including 4 units of English, 3 each of math and lab science, and 1 of social studies, plus 4 units in academic electives. Pitt recommends that the student have 3 or more years of a single foreign language. An essay is recommended if the student is seeking scholarship consideration, and music students must audition. Requirements for other colleges or schools may vary. AP and CLEP credits are accepted. Important factors in the admissions decision are advanced placement or honor courses, evidence of special talent, and extracurricular activities record.

Procedure: Freshmen are admitted to all sessions. Entrance exams should be taken preferably by January for September admission. There is a rolling admissions and a deferred admissions plan. Application deadlines are open. Application fee is $35. Applications are accepted on computer disk and on-line through the school's web site.

Transfer: 536 transfer students enrolled in 2002-2003. Applicants for transfer to the School of Arts and Sciences must supply transcripts of all secondary school and college course work and have a minimum GPA of 2.75. An interview is recommended. Grades of C or better transfer for credit. Application deadlines vary by school. 30 of 120 credits required for the bachelor's degree must be completed at Pitt.

Visiting: There are regularly scheduled orientations for prospective students, including information sessions, student-guided tours, and class attendance. There are guides for informal visits and visitors may sit in on classes and stay overnight. To schedule a visit, contact the Office of Admissions and Financial Aid.

Financial Aid: In 2003-2004, 87% of all full-time freshmen and 77% of continuing full-time students received some form of financial aid. The average freshman award was $10,118. Need-based scholarships or need-based grants averaged $7518; need-based self-help aid (loans and jobs) averaged $4380; and non-need-based athletic scholarships averaged $13,247. 19% of undergraduates work part time (work study). Average annual earnings from campus work are $1722. The average financial indebtedness of the 2003 graduate was $20,154. The FAFSA and the college's own financial statement are required. The deadline for filing freshman financial aid applications for fall entry is January 15.

International Students: There are 144 international students enrolled. They must score 500 on the written TOEFL or 173 on the electronic version (for the School of Arts and Sciences) and also take the SAT I or the ACT.

Computers: 7 public computing labs, with more than 600 PCs and workstations, provide access to a variety of software, printers, and graphic plotters. All students may access the system. There are no time limits in labs and no fees. There is a 4-hour limit on remote access.

Graduates: From July 1, 2002 to June 30, 2003, 3667 bachelor's degrees were awarded. The most popular majors were business (14%), social sciences and history (13%), and English language and literature (12%). 400 companies recruited on campus in 2002-2003. Of the 2002 graduating class, 40% were enrolled in graduate school within 6 months of graduation.

Admissions Contact: Dr. Betsy A. Porter, Director, Admissions and Financial Aid. A video is available. E-mail: *oafa@pitt.edu* Web: *www.pitt.edu/~oafa*

UNIVERSITY OF SCRANTON   E-2
Scranton, PA 18510-4699
(570) 941-7540
(888) SCRANTON; Fax: (570) 941-5928

Full-time: 1625 men, 2148 women	**Faculty:** 247; IIA, +$
Part-time: 118 men, 182 women	**Ph.Ds:** 86%
Graduate: 230 men, 376 women	**Student/Faculty:** 15 to 1
Year: semesters, summer session	**Tuition:** $21,408
Application Deadline: March 1	**Room & Board:** $9428
Freshman Class: 5669 applied, 4270 accepted, 980 enrolled	
SAT I Verbal/Math: 557/566	**VERY COMPETITIVE**

The University of Scranton, founded in 1888, is a private institution operated by the Jesuit order of the Roman Catholic Church. It offers programs in business, behavioral sciences, education, health science, humanities, math, science, and social science. There are 4 undergraduate schools and 1 graduate school. In addition to regional accreditation, the university has baccalaureate program accreditation with AACSB, APTA, CSAB, NCATE, and NLN. The library contains 454,098 volumes, 104,639 microform items, and 13,367 audio/video tapes/CDs, and subscribes to 16,745 periodicals. Computerized library services include the card catalog, interlibrary loans, database searching, and Internet access. Special learning facilities include a learning resource center, art gallery, radio station, TV station, and satellite dish for telecommunication reception, music center, language lab, and a greenhouse. The 50-acre campus is in an urban area 125 miles north of Philadelphia. Including any residence halls, there are 60 buildings.

Student Life: 51% of undergraduates are from Pennsylvania. Students are from 29 states, 12 foreign countries, and Canada. 51% are from public schools. 85% are white. 84% are Catholic; 10% Protestant. The average age of freshmen is 18; all undergraduates, 20. 10% do not continue beyond their first year; 80% remain to graduate.

Housing: 2112 students can be accommodated in college housing, which includes single-sex and coed dorms and on-campus apartments. In addition, there are language houses and special-interest houses. On-campus housing is guaranteed for all 4 years. 80% of students live on campus; of those, 65% remain on campus on weekends. Upperclassmen may keep cars.

Activities: There are no fraternities or sororities. There are 80 groups on campus, including art, band, cheerleading, chess, choir, chorale, chorus, computers, dance, debate, drama, drill team, ethnic, film, honors, international, jazz band, literary magazine, musical theater, newspaper, orchestra, pep band, photography, political, professional, radio and TV, religious, social, social service, student government, and yearbook. Popular campus events include Spring Fling, Senior Formal, and President's Ball.

Sports: There are 10 intercollegiate sports for men and 8 for women, and 17 intramural sports for men and 14 for women. Facilities include a 3000-seat gym, basketball courts, wrestling and weight rooms, handball/racquetball and tennis courts, a sand volleyball court, a soccer/lacrosse field, a softball field, a swimming pool, a physical therapy room, a 3-court multipurpose gym, a fitness center, a sauna and steamroom, a dance aerobics room, and a turfed recreation/utility field.

Disabled Students: All of the campus is accessible. Wheelchair ramps, elevators, special parking, specially equipped rest rooms, special class scheduling, lowered drinking fountains, and lowered telephones are available.

Services: Counseling and information services are available, as is tutoring in most subjects. There is a reader service for the blind and computing and study skills seminars.

Campus Safety and Security: Measures include 24-hour foot and vehicle patrol, self-defense education, security escort services, and informal discussions. There are pamphlets/posters/films, emergency telephones, and lighted pathways/sidewalks.

Programs of Study: The university confers B.A. and B.S. degrees. Associate, master's, and doctoral degrees are also awarded. Bachelor's degrees are awarded in BIOLOGICAL SCIENCE (biochemistry, biology/biological science, biophysics, and neurosciences), BUSINESS (accounting, banking and finance, business administration and management, business economics, electronic business, human resources, international business management, marketing/retailing/merchandising, and operations research), COMMUNICATIONS AND THE ARTS (communications, dramatic arts, English, French, German, Greek, Latin, and Spanish), COMPUTER AND PHYSICAL SCIENCE (chemistry, computer management, computer science, information sciences and systems, mathematics, and physics), EDUCATION (early childhood, elementary, science, secondary, and special), ENGINEERING AND ENVIRONMENTAL DESIGN (electrical/electronics engineering and environmental science), HEALTH PROFESSIONS (exercise science, health care administration, medical laboratory technology, nursing, occupational therapy, and physical therapy), SOCIAL SCIENCE (criminal justice, economics, gerontology, history, human services, international relations, philosophy, political science/government, psychology, sociology, and theological studies). Chemistry, biology, and physical therapy are the strongest academically. Biology, communication, and elementary education are the largest.

Required: Students take distribution requirements according to their general area of study. All are required to take philosophy/theology, phys ed, English composition, speech, and computer literacy. A total of 130 credit hours is required for graduation, with 36 in the major. The minimum GPA is 2.0, although some majors require a higher GPA.

Special: There are cooperative programs with the University of Detroit Mercy and cross-registration with 27 other Jesuit colleges. Internships are available in all career-oriented majors, and foreign study is offered in many countries. There is a Washington semester for history and political science majors. Students may earn a B.A.-B.S. degree in economics and accelerated degrees in history, chemistry, and biochemistry. The university also offers dual, student-designed, and interdisciplinary majors, including chemistry-business, chemistry-computers, electronics-business, and international language-business, credit by exam and for life/military/work experience, work-study, nondegree study, and pass/fail options. There is also a special Jesuit-oriented general education program. There are 26 national honor societies, including Phi Beta Kappa, a freshman honors program, and 2 departmental honors programs.

Faculty/Classroom: 69% of faculty are male; 31%, female. 97% teach undergraduates, 80% do research, and 77% do both. No introductory courses are taught by graduate students. The average class size in an introductory lecture is 22; in a laboratory, 12; and in a regular course, 21.

Admissions: 75% of the 2003-2004 applicants were accepted. The SAT I scores for the 2003-2004 freshman class were: Verbal--20% below 500, 53% between 500 and 599, 24% between 600 and 700, and 3% above 700; Math--15% below 500, 53% between 500 and 599, 28% between 600 and 700, and 4% above 700. 48% of the current freshmen were in the top fifth of their class; 79% were in the top two fifths.

Requirements: The SAT I or ACT is required. In addition, applicants should be graduates of an accredited secondary school, though in some cases a GED may be accepted. They should complete 18 academic or Carnegie units, including 4 years of high school English, 3 each of math, science, history, and social studies, and 2 of foreign language. 2 letters of reference/recommendation are required. Essays are not required, but for some students the additional information can be of assistance. Interviews are recommended. AP and CLEP credits are accepted. Important factors in the admissions decision are leadership record, advanced placement or honor courses, and extracurricular activities record.

Procedure: Freshmen are admitted fall and spring. Entrance exams should be taken by fall of the senior year. There are early admissions and deferred admissions plans. Applications should be filed by March 1 for fall entry, December 15 for spring entry, and May 1 for summer entry, along with a $40 fee. Notification is sent on a rolling basis beginning December 15. 677 applicants were on the 2003 waiting list; 74 were admitted. Applications are accepted on-line through *www.scranton.edu/admission/fa_ao_applyonline.asp.*

Transfer: 128 transfer students enrolled in 2002-2003. Applicants should have earned a GPA of at least 2.5. 63 of 130 credits required for the bachelor's degree must be completed at the university.

Visiting: There are regularly scheduled orientations for prospective students, including private interviews conducted Monday through Friday throughout the school year. Group information sessions are offered on Saturdays and holidays in the fall and spring and during the week in the summer. There are guides for informal visits and visitors may sit in on classes and stay overnight. To schedule a visit, contact the Office of Admissions.

Financial Aid: In 2003-2004, 71% of all full-time freshmen and 66% of continuing full-time students received some form of financial aid. 70% of full-time freshmen and 64% of continuing full-time students received need-based aid. The average freshman award was $14,317. Need-based scholarships or need-based grants averaged $10,771; need-based self-help aid (loans and jobs) averaged $4070; and institutional non-need-based awards and non-need-based scholarships averaged $7635. 17% of undergraduates work part time. Average annual earnings from campus work are $900. The average financial indebtedness of the 2003 graduate was $15,800. The university is a member of CSS. The FAFSA is required. The priority date for freshman financial aid applications for fall entry is February 15.

International Students: There are 15 international students enrolled. The school actively recruits these students. They must score 525 on the written TOEFL.

Computers: The mainframes are a Compaq GS140 and 6 Compaq Proliants as web servers. There are 879 PCs and terminals on campus available for student use in the library, academic buildings, and residence halls. The campus is completely networked, which provides student access to the Internet and the Web. All students may access the system 24 hours a day. There are no time limits and no fees.

Graduates: From July 1, 2002 to June 30, 2003, 915 bachelor's degrees were awarded. The most popular majors were communications (10%), biology (8%), and elementary education (7%). In an average class, 67% graduate in 4 years or less, 76% graduate in 5 years or less, and 82% graduate in 6 years or less. Of the 2002 graduating class, 33% were enrolled in graduate school within 6 months of graduation and 65% were employed.

Admissions Contact: Joseph M. Roback, Director of Admissions. A video is available. E-mail: *admissions@scranton.edu* Web: *www.scranton.edu*

UNIVERSITY OF THE ARTS
Philadelphia, PA 19102

F-3
(215) 717-6030
(800) 616-2787; Fax: (215) 717-6045

Full-time: 838 men, 1079 women	Faculty: 93
Part-time: 27 men, 33 women	Ph.Ds: n/av
Graduate: 52 men, 122 women	Student/Faculty: 21 to 1
Year: semesters	Tuition: $21,710
Application Deadline: open	Room & Board: $7800
Freshman Class: 1951 applied, 991 accepted, 480 enrolled	
SAT I Verbal/Math: 520/510	SPECIAL

University of the Arts, founded in 1870, is a private institution offering education and professional training in visual, media, and performing arts, with an emphasis on the humanities and interdisciplinary exploration. There are 3 undergraduate and 2 graduate schools. In addition to regional accreditation, UArts has baccalaureate program accreditation with NASAD and NASM. The 3 libraries contain 144,700 volumes, 461 microform items, and 21,200 audio/video tapes/CDs, and subscribe to 541 periodicals. Computerized library services include the card catalog, interlibrary loans, database searching, and Internet access. Special learning facilities include an art gallery, several theaters, and music, animation, and recording studios. The 18-acre campus is in an urban area in Philadelphia. Including any residence halls, there are 8 buildings.

Student Life: 60% of undergraduates are from out of state, mostly the Middle Atlantic. Students are from 42 states, 37 foreign countries, and Canada. 73% are from public schools. 71% are white. The average age of freshmen is 18; all undergraduates, 20. 18% do not continue beyond their first year; 55% remain to graduate.

Housing: 690 students can be accommodated in college housing, which includes coed dorms, on-campus apartments, and off-campus apartments. On-campus housing is guaranteed for the freshman year only and is available on a first-come, first-served basis. Priority is given to out-of-town students. 65% of students commute. Alcohol is not permitted. No one may keep cars.

Activities: There are no fraternities or sororities. There are 20 groups on campus, including art, band, choir, chorale, chorus, dance, drama, ethnic, film, gay, international, jazz band, musical theater, photography, professional, religious, and student government. Popular campus events include exhibitions and performances.

Sports: There is no sports program at UArts. Athletic facilities are available at area gyms, for which the university provides discount membership.

Disabled Students: 65% of the campus is accessible. Wheelchair ramps, elevators, specially equipped rest rooms, lowered drinking fountains, lowered telephones, and sign language interpreters are available.

Services: Counseling and information services are available, as is tutoring in every subject. There is remedial math, reading, and writing. There also is assistance with study skills.

Campus Safety and Security: Measures include 24-hour foot and vehicle patrol, self-defense education, security escort services, and informal discussions. There are pamphlets/posters/films and lighted pathways/sidewalks.

Programs of Study: UArts confers B.S., B.F.A., and B.M. degrees. Master's degrees are also awarded. Bachelor's degrees are awarded in COMMUNICATIONS AND THE ARTS (communications, dance, film arts, graphic design, illustration, industrial design, multimedia, music performance, music theory and composition, musical theater, painting, photography, printmaking, and sculpture), EDUCATION (dance). Dance, music, and illustration are the largest.

Required: All students must complete a core program consisting of humanities courses in language and expression, literature, arts history and social studies, philosophy and science, and related arts. A GPA of 2.0 overall for 123 to 145 credits, with 21 to 45 in the major, depending on the curriculum, must be achieved for graduation.

Special: UArts offers cross-registration with the 10-member Consortium East Coast Art Schools as well as with the Pennsylvania Academy of Fine Arts and Philadelphia College of Textiles and Sciences. Internships may be arranged, and there are extensive summer programs and opportunities to study abroad.

Faculty/Classroom: 92% teach undergraduates. No introductory courses are taught by graduate students. The average class size in an introductory lecture is 18 and in a regular course, 14.

Admissions: 51% of the 2003-2004 applicants were accepted. The SAT I scores for the 2003-2004 freshman class were: Verbal--36% below 500, 42% between 500 and 599, 21% between 600 and 700, and 1% above 700; Math--46% below 500, 41% between 500 and 599, 12% between 600 and 700, and 1% above 700. 27% of the current freshmen were in the top fifth of their class; 58% were in the top two fifths.

Requirements: The SAT I or ACT is required. In addition, students must have graduated from an accredited secondary school or hold a GED certificate. A minimum of 16 academic credits consisting of 4 each in English and math and 2 each in music or art and history is recommended. An essay and either a portfolio or an audition are required of all applicants. An interview is recommended. A GPA of 2.0 is required. AP and CLEP credits are accepted. Important factors in the admissions decision are evidence of special talent, advanced placement or honor courses, and personality/intangible qualities.

Procedure: Freshmen are admitted fall and spring. Entrance exams should be taken late in the junior year or early in the senior year. There are early admissions, deferred admissions, and rolling admissions plans. Application deadlines are open. Application fee is $50. 38 applicants were on the 2003 waiting list; 8 were admitted. Applications are accepted on computer disk and on-line through CollegeLink and the university's web site.

Transfer: 137 transfer students enrolled in 2002-2003. Candidates must have a minimum 2.0 GPA overall. An interview is recommended, as well as test scores for either the SAT I or ACT if English composition has not been completed. 48 of 123 to 145 credits required for the bachelor's degree must be completed at UArts.

Visiting: There are regularly scheduled orientations for prospective students, including a spring and fall open house. There are guides for informal visits. To schedule a visit, contact the Office of Admissions.

Financial Aid: UArts is a member of CSS. The FAFSA is required. The deadline for filing freshman financial aid applications for fall entry is March 1.

International Students: There are 45 international students enrolled. The school actively recruits these students. They must score 500 on the written TOEFL or 173 on the electronic version and also take the SAT I or the ACT.

Computers: The 18 computer labs and 8 student lounges are networked with Internet and Web access. Additional access is available in the university library. All students may access the system. Time limits at some stations vary from 30 minutes to 2 hours. Most labs do not have time limits. There are no fees. It is strongly recommended that all students have a personal computer.

Graduates: From July 1, 2002 to June 30, 2003, 400 bachelor's degrees were awarded. The most popular majors were photography (12%), graphic deign (10%), and dance (9%). In an average class, 42% graduate in 4 years or less, 53% graduate in 5 years or less, and 55% graduate in 6 years or less. In a recent year 30 companies recruited on campus.

Admissions Contact: Barbara Elliott, Director of Admissions. A video is available. E-mail: *admissions@uarts.edu* Web: *http://www.uarts.edu*

UNIVERSITY OF THE SCIENCES IN PHILADELPHIA F-3
Philadelphia, PA 19104-4495
(215) 596-8810
(888) 996-8747; Fax: (215) 596-8821

Full-time: 925 men, 1491 women	**Faculty:** 141; IIA, av$
Part-time: 34 men, 73 women	**Ph.D.s:** 82%
Graduate: 147 men, 217 women	**Student/Faculty:** 16 to 1
Year: semesters, summer session	**Tuition:** $20,958
Application Deadline: open	**Room & Board:** $8352
Freshman Class: 2966 applied, 2029 accepted, 569 enrolled	
SAT I Verbal/Math: 540/580	**ACT:** 23 **VERY COMPETITIVE**

University of the Sciences in Philadelphia, founded in 1821, is a private institution offering degree programs in the health sciences, pharmaceutical sciences, and arts and sciences. There are 3 undergraduate and 4 graduate schools. In addition to regional accreditation, USP has baccalaureate program accreditation with ACPE, ACS, APTA, CAAHEP, and NAACLS. The library contains 85,939 volumes, 27,637 microform items, and 4376 audio/video tapes/CDs, and subscribes to 6700 periodicals. Computerized library services include the card catalog, interlibrary loans, and database searching. Special learning facilities include a learning resource center and a pharmaceutical history museum. The 35-acre campus is in an urban area in the University City section of Philadelphia. Including any residence halls, there are 16 buildings.

Student Life: 53% of undergraduates are from out of state, mostly the Middle Atlantic. Students are from 35 states, 23 foreign countries, and

Canada. 65% are from public schools. 47% are white; 34% Asian American. The average age of freshmen is 18; all undergraduates, 21. 19% do not continue beyond their first year; 76% remain to graduate.

Housing: 650 students can be accommodated in college housing, which includes coed dorms. In addition, there are honors houses, honor halls in certain dorms, and an upper-level floor for upper-level students. On-campus housing is guaranteed for the freshman year only, is available on a first-come, first-served basis, and is available on a lottery system for upperclassmen. Priority is given to out-of-town students. 71% of students commute. Alcohol is not permitted. Upperclassmen may keep cars.

Activities: There are 2 local and 9 national fraternities and 1 national sorority. There are 65 groups on campus, including band, cheerleading, chess, chorale, chorus, computers, dance, drama, ethnic, gay, honors, international, literary magazine, martial arts, musical theater, newspaper, orchestra, political, professional, religious, social, social service, student government, and yearbook. Popular campus events include Greek Week and Student Appreciation Day.

Sports: There are 5 intercollegiate sports for men and 6 for women, and 19 intramural sports for men and 19 for women. Facilities include a state-of-the-art athletic and recreation center with swimming pool and indoor track, a gym, a rifle range, tennis courts, a softball field, a jogging path, and recreational areas in the residence halls.

Disabled Students: 90% of the campus is accessible. Wheelchair ramps, elevators, special parking, specially equipped rest rooms, and special class scheduling are available. Each student is accommodated on an individual basis.

Services: Counseling and information services are available, as is tutoring in every subject. There is remedial math and writing.

Campus Safety and Security: Measures include 24-hour foot and vehicle patrol, self-defense education, security escort services, and shuttle buses. There are informal discussions, pamphlets/posters/films, emergency telephones, lighted pathways/sidewalks, and required key and student identification for dorm entry.

Programs of Study: USP confers B.S. and B.S.Ed. degrees. Master's and doctoral degrees are also awarded. Bachelor's degrees are awarded in BIOLOGICAL SCIENCE (biochemistry, bioinformatics, biology/biological science, microbiology, and toxicology), BUSINESS (marketing management), COMPUTER AND PHYSICAL SCIENCE (chemistry and computer science), ENGINEERING AND ENVIRONMENTAL DESIGN (environmental science), HEALTH PROFESSIONS (health science, medical technology, mental health/human services, occupational therapy, pharmacology, pharmacy, physical therapy, physician's assistant, and premedicine), SOCIAL SCIENCE (psychology). Pharmacy and physical therapy are the strongest academically. Pharmacy, physical therapy, and biology are the largest.

Required: Total credits required for graduation range from 120 to 149 depending on the major, with a 2.0 GPA, or 2.5 for pharmacy, physical therapy, and medical technology majors. The core curriculum includes 16 credits of natural science, 6 each of math, social sciences, communication, and an intellectual heritage sequence, 3 of literature, world culture, history, and advanced social sciences, and 1 of phys ed, along with 3 of electives. Students must pass a writing proficiency exam and demonstrate proficiency in computer applications.

Special: USP offers 5- and 6-year integrated professional programs in occupational therapy, physical therapy, and physician's assistant studies. Internships are required in all health science disciplines. A 1-year undeclared major program is offered, as is a program of curriculum and advisement to prepare students to enter medical school. Students may elect dual majors or a minor in communications, economics, psychology, sociology, math, physics, computer science, biochemistry, biology, chemistry, forensic science, humanities, mathematics, microbiology, social sciences, and writing. Study abroad can be arranged. There are 5 national honor societies.

Faculty/Classroom: 52% of faculty are male; 48%, female. 99% teach undergraduates. No introductory courses are taught by graduate students. The average class size in an introductory lecture is 100; in a laboratory, 28; and in a regular course, 25.

Admissions: 68% of the 2003-2004 applicants were accepted. The SAT I scores for the 2003-2004 freshman class were: Verbal--27% below 500, 53% between 500 and 599, 19% between 600 and 700, and 1% above 700; Math--9% below 500, 52% between 500 and 599, 34% between 600 and 700, and 5% above 700. 53% of the current freshmen were in the top fifth of their class; 86% were in the top two fifths. 20 freshmen graduated first in their class.

Requirements: The SAT I or ACT is required. In addition, applicants must be high school graduates or hold the GED. Minimum academic requirements include 4 credits in English, 1 credit each in American history and social science, and 4 credits in academic electives. Math requirements include 2 years of algebra and 1 year of plane geometry; the university strongly recommends an additional year of higher-level math, such as precalculus or calculus. 3 science credits are required; strongly recommended are 1 credit each in biology, chemistry, and physics. USP requires applicants to be in the upper 50% of their class. A GPA of 3.0

is required. AP and CLEP credits are accepted. Important factors in the admissions decision are extracurricular activities record, leadership record, and advanced placement or honor courses.

Procedure: Freshmen are admitted in the fall. Entrance exams should be taken at the end of the junior year and in the fall of the senior year. There is a deferred admissions plan and a rolling admissions plan. Application deadlines are open. Application fee is $45. 191 applicants were on the 2003 waiting list; none were admitted. Applications are accepted on-line through the university's web site.

Transfer: 107 transfer students enrolled in 2002-2003. To be considered, pharmacy and physical therapy applicants must present a minimum GPA of 3.0. All other majors must have at least a 2.7 GPA. All applicants must meet high school requirements as well. 51% of all credits required for the bachelor's degree must be completed at USP.

Visiting: There are regularly scheduled orientations for prospective students, consisting of summer open houses for rising seniors, campus day visits, campus tours, and meetings with faculty members. There are guides for informal visits and visitors may sit in on classes. To schedule a visit, contact the Admission Office at *admit@usip.edu.*

Financial Aid: In 2003-2004, 85% of all full-time students received some form of financial aid. 40% of undergraduates work part time. Average annual earnings from campus work are $2000. The FAFSA is required. The priority date for freshman financial aid applications for fall entry is March 15.

International Students: There are 61 international students enrolled. They must score 550 on the written TOEFL or 213 on the electronic version and also take the college's own test and the SAT I or the ACT, scoring 1000 on the SAT I.

Computers: 256 workstations and more than 100 laptop ports networked to IBM Netfinity servers are located in computer labs as well as other strategic campus locations. Wireless access is also provided. All students may access the system. There are no time limits and no fees. It is strongly recommended that all students have a personal computer. A Dell is recommended.

Graduates: From July 1, 2002 to June 30, 2003, 469 bachelor's degrees were awarded. The most popular majors were pharmacy (47%), physical therapy (22%), and occupational therapy (8%). In an average class, 8% graduate in 4 years or less, 28% graduate in 5 years or less, and 66% graduate in 6 years or less. 150 companies recruited on campus in 2002-2003.

Admissions Contact: Louis L. Hegyes, Director of Admission. E-mail: *admit@usip.edu* Web: *www.usip.edu*

URSINUS COLLEGE
Collegeville, PA 19426

E-3
(610) 409-3200; Fax: (610) 409-3662

Full-time: 677 men, 791 women	Faculty: 110; IIB, +$
Part-time: 12 men, 5 women	Ph.D.s: 89%
Graduate: none	Student/Faculty: 13 to 1
Year: semesters	Tuition: $27,500
Application Deadline: February 15	Room & Board: $6900
Freshman Class: 1724 applied, 1323 accepted, 454 enrolled	
SAT I Verbal/Math: 605/607	VERY COMPETITIVE

Ursinus College, founded in 1869, is a private residential college offering programs in the liberal arts. In addition to regional accreditation, Ursinus has baccalaureate program accreditation with ACS. The library contains 375,000 volumes, 180,000 microform items, and 17,500 audio/video tapes/CDs, and subscribes to 1200 periodicals. Computerized library services include the card catalog, interlibrary loans, and database searching. Special learning facilities include an art gallery, planetarium, radio station, TV station, and language labs. The 168-acre campus is in a suburban area 24 miles west of Philadelphia. Including any residence halls, there are 60 buildings.

Student Life: 62% of undergraduates are from Pennsylvania. Students are from 27 states and 10 foreign countries. 74% are from public schools. 80% are white. The average age of freshmen is 18; all undergraduates, 20. 8% do not continue beyond their first year; 78% remain to graduate.

Housing: 1329 students can be accommodated in college housing, which includes single-sex and coed dorms and on-campus apartments. In addition, there are honors houses, language houses, multicultural houses, quiet houses, and special-interest houses. On-campus housing is guaranteed for all 4 years. Upperclassmen may keep cars.

Activities: 26% of men belong to 8 local and 1 national fraternity; 38% of women belong to 6 local and 1 national sorority. There are 120 groups on campus, including art, band, cheerleading, chess, choir, chorale, chorus, computers, dance, debate, drama, ethnic, film, forensics, gay, honors, international, jazz band, literary magazine, musical theater, newspaper, orchestra, pep band, political, professional, radio and TV, religious, social, social service, student government, and yearbook. Popular campus events include Parents Day, Founders Day, and Air Band Competition.

Sports: There are 12 intercollegiate sports for men and 12 for women, and 14 intramural sports for men and 12 for women. Facilities include racquetball and squash courts, a weight room, dance studio, tennis courts, a field house, a fitness center, and all types of playing fields.

Disabled Students: 95% of the campus is accessible. Wheelchair ramps, elevators, special parking, specially equipped rest rooms, special class scheduling, lowered drinking fountains, and lowered telephones are available.

Services: Counseling and information services are available, as is tutoring in every subject.

Campus Safety and Security: Measures include 24-hour foot and vehicle patrol, self-defense education, security escort services, and informal discussions. There are pamphlets/posters/films, emergency telephones, and lighted pathways/sidewalks.

Programs of Study: Ursinus confers B.A. and B.S. degrees. Bachelor's degrees are awarded in BIOLOGICAL SCIENCE (biochemistry, biology/biological science, and neurosciences), BUSINESS (business administration and management and business economics), COMMUNICATIONS AND THE ARTS (art, classics, communications, English, French, German, music, and Spanish), COMPUTER AND PHYSICAL SCIENCE (chemistry, computer science, mathematics, and physics), EDUCATION (secondary), ENGINEERING AND ENVIRONMENTAL DESIGN (environmental science), HEALTH PROFESSIONS (exercise science and premedicine), SOCIAL SCIENCE (American studies, anthropology, East Asian studies, economics, history, international relations, philosophy, political science/government, prelaw, psychology, religion, and sociology). Biology, English, and politics are the strongest academically. Economics, business, and biology are the largest.

Required: All students must fulfill requirements in the common intellectual experience, math or logic, foreign language, humanities, and natural and social science, including an independent learing experience in laboratory science. A total of 128 semester hours, with 32 to 40 in the major, is required, as is a GPA of 2.0.

Special: The college offers study abroad, student-designed majors, internships, a Washington semester, a Harrisburg and Philadelphia semester, dual majors, and a 3-2 engineering degree with Washington University. There are 14 national honor societies, including Phi Beta Kappa, and 14 departmental honors programs.

Faculty/Classroom: 48% of faculty are male; 52%, female. All both teach and do research. The average class size in a regular course is 18.

Admissions: 77% of the 2003-2004 applicants were accepted. The SAT I scores for the 2003-2004 freshman class were: Verbal--7% below 500, 41% between 500 and 599, 40% between 600 and 700, and 12% above 700; Math--9% below 500, 34% between 500 and 599, 45% between 600 and 700, and 12% above 700. 67% of the current freshmen were in the top fifth of their class; 91% were in the top two fifths. There were 7 National Merit finalists. 4 freshmen graduated first in their class.

Requirements: The SAT I or ACT is required. In addition, SAT II: Subject tests are recommended. Applicants should prepare with 16 academic credits, including 4 years of English, 3 of math, 2 of foreign language, and 1 each of science and social studies. An interview is recommended. AP and CLEP credits are accepted. Important factors in the admissions decision are advanced placement or honor courses, recommendations by school officials, and leadership record.

Procedure: Freshmen are admitted fall and spring. Entrance exams should be taken in the junior or senior year. There are early decision and deferred admissions plans. Early decision applications should be filed by January 15; regular applications, by February 15 for fall entry and December 1 for spring entry. The fall 2003 application fee was $45. Notification of early decision is sent January 15; regular decision, April 1. 108 early decision candidates were accepted for the 2003-2004 class. 21 applicants were on the 2003 waiting list. Applications are accepted on computer disk and on-line through CommonApp and the school's web site.

Transfer: 5 transfer students enrolled in 2002-2003. Transfer applicants must submit transcripts from all institutions attended. 64 of 128 credits required for the bachelor's degree must be completed at Ursinus.

Visiting: There are regularly scheduled orientations for prospective students, including a campus interview and a tour. There are guides for informal visits and visitors may sit in on classes and stay overnight. To schedule a visit, contact the Admissions Office at (610) 409-3200 or *admissions@ursinus.edu.*

Financial Aid: In 2003-2004, 94% of all full-time freshmen and 89% of continuing full-time students received some form of financial aid. 83% of full-time freshmen and 79% of continuing full-time students received need-based aid. The average freshman award was $22,606, with $14,744 ($25,000 maximum) from need-based scholarships or grants, $5519 ($7500 maximum) from need-based self-help aid (loans and jobs), and $2343 ($25,000 maximum) from non-need-based awards and non-need-based scholarships. 50% of undergraduates work part time. Average annual earnings from campus work are $1200. The average financial indebtedness of the 2003 graduate was $18,000. Ursinus is a member of CSS. The CSS Profile or FAFSA is required. The deadline for filing freshman financial aid applications for fall entry is February 15.

International Students: There are 30 international students enrolled. The school actively recruits these students. They must score 500 on the written TOEFL or 173 on the electronic version and also take the SAT I.

Computers: There are 14 robust Dell Poweredge servers. The campus is fully networked, both in classrooms and dorms, as well as throughout the library and administrative buildings. All classrooms have multiple network ports. Each student is issued a laptop in the first year, which is replaced with a newer model at the end of the sophomore year. There are 200 publicly available computers in 3 instructional computer labs, the library, science laboratories, and in various departmental work areas. Each student is also issued a printer for personal use. All students are allocated space on the web server for posting their web pages, provided with personal network storage space, and with shared network space for specific classes. Students also have access to multimedia development workstations with a variety of hardware and software tools. Students may access the campus network and the Internet from anywhere on campus via their laptops around the clock, seven days a week. Public access computers are available during hours that those buildings are open, 102 hours a week. There are no time limits and no fees.

Graduates: From July 1, 2002 to June 30, 2003, 276 bachelor's degrees were awarded. The most popular majors were economics (16%), biology (15%), and psychology (15%). In an average class, 75% graduate in 4 years or less, 78% graduate in 5 years or less, and 78% graduate in 6 years or less. 34 companies recruited on campus in 2002-2003. Of the 2002 graduating class, 34% were enrolled in graduate school within 6 months of graduation and 57% were employed.

Admissions Contact: Paul M. Cramer, Director of Admissions. E-mail: *admissions@ursinus.edu* Web: *http://www.ursinus.edu/*

VILLANOVA UNIVERSITY   F-4
Villanova, PA 19085-1672   (610) 519-4000; Fax: (610) 519-6450

Full-time: 3172 men, 3271 women	Faculty: 507; IIA, ++$
Part-time: 341 men, 361 women	Ph.D.s: 90%
Graduate: 1278 men, 1053 women	Student/Faculty: 13 to 1
Year: semesters, summer session	Tuition: $26,223
Application Deadline: December 20	Room & Board: $8827
Freshman Class: 10,296 applied, 5781 accepted, 1557 enrolled	
SAT I Verbal/Math: 610/640	HIGHLY COMPETITIVE

Villanova University, founded in 1842 and affiliated with the Catholic Church, offers undergraduate programs in liberal arts and sciences, commerce and finance, engineering, and nursing. Tuition figure in the above capsule is an average; exact costs vary by college. There are 4 undergraduate and 5 graduate schools. In addition to regional accreditation, Villanova has baccalaureate program accreditation with AACSB, ABA, ABET, and NLN. The 2 libraries contain 1,049,011 volumes, 1,360,759 microform items, and 9482 audio/video tapes/CDs, and subscribe to 8764 periodicals. Computerized library services include the card catalog, interlibrary loans, database searching, and Internet access. Special learning facilities include a learning resource center, art gallery, planetarium, radio station, TV station, and 2 observatories. The 254-acre campus is in a suburban area 12 miles west of Philadelphia. Including any residence halls, there are 60 buildings.

Student Life: 66% of undergraduates are from out of state, mostly the Middle Atlantic. Students are from 46 states, 28 foreign countries, and Canada. 53% are from public schools. 85% are white. 75% are Catholic; 12% Protestant; 7% Buddhist, Islamic, Hindu, other. The average age of freshmen is 18; all undergraduates, 22. 5% do not continue beyond their first year; 85% remain to graduate.

Housing: 4631 students can be accommodated in college housing, which includes single-sex and coed dorms and on-campus apartments. In addition, there are special-interest houses, substance-free housing, Villanova Experience, Visions of Freedom, and other course-related learning communities. On-campus housing is guaranteed for 3 years and is available on a lottery system for upperclassmen. 65% of students live on campus; of those, 90% remain on campus on weekends. Upperclassmen may keep cars.

Activities: 6% of men belong to 8 national fraternities; 25% of women belong to 8 national sororities. There are 130 groups on campus, including art, band, Blue Key, cheerleading, chess, choir, chorale, chorus, computers, dance, drama, drill team, ethnic, gay, honors, international, jazz band, literary magazine, marching band, multicultural, musical theater, newspaper, pep band, photography, political, professional, radio and TV, religious, social, social service, student government, and yearbook. Popular campus events include Balloon Day, Special Olympics, Nova Fest, and St. Thomas of Villanova Day.

Sports: There are 10 intercollegiate sports for men and 12 for women, and 15 intramural sports for men and 15 for women. Facilities include a 200-meter indoor track, 2 swimming pools, weight rooms, a field house, and basketball, volleyball, and tennis courts. The football stadium seats 11,800; the pavilion, 6400.

Disabled Students: All of the campus is accessible. Wheelchair ramps, elevators, special parking, specially equipped rest rooms, special class scheduling, lowered drinking fountains, lowered telephones, a specially equipped van for campus transportation, and proximity card readers for several buildings with automatic doors are available.

Services: Counseling and information services are available, as is tutoring in most subjects. There is a reader service for the blind. Tutoring services are administered through each department on an individual basis. There is a writing center and a math resource center.

Campus Safety and Security: Measures include 24-hour foot and vehicle patrol, self-defense education, security escort services, and shuttle buses. There are informal discussions, pamphlets/posters/films, emergency telephones, and lighted pathways/sidewalks. Public Safety officers are on duty all night in women's residence halls and there is a card access system to all residence halls.

Programs of Study: Villanova confers B.A., B.S., B.E., and B.S.N. degrees. Associate, master's, and doctoral degrees are also awarded. Bachelor's degrees are awarded in BIOLOGICAL SCIENCE (biology/biological science), BUSINESS (accounting, banking and finance, business administration and management, business economics, management information systems, and marketing/retailing/merchandising), COMMUNICATIONS AND THE ARTS (art history and appreciation, classics, communications, English, French, German, and Spanish), COMPUTER AND PHYSICAL SCIENCE (astronomy, astrophysics, chemistry, computer science, information sciences and systems, mathematics, physics, and science), EDUCATION (elementary and secondary), ENGINEERING AND ENVIRONMENTAL DESIGN (chemical engineering, civil engineering, computer engineering, electrical/electronics engineering, and mechanical engineering), HEALTH PROFESSIONS (nursing), SOCIAL SCIENCE (cognitive science, criminal justice, economics, geography, history, human services, international studies, Latin American studies, liberal arts/general studies, peace studies, philosophy, political science/government, psychology, religion, Russian and Slavic studies, sociology, theological studies, and women's studies). Sciences, business, and liberal arts are the strongest academically. Liberal arts and commerce and finance are the largest.

Required: All students are required to take core courses in English, social science, religious studies, natural sciences, philosophy, and math. Students must complete a total of 122 credit hours with a 2.0 overall GPA and a 2.2 GPA in the major.

Special: Cross-registration is possible with Rosemont College. Internships are available for each college in the Philadelphia area as well as in New York City and Washington D.C. Students may study abroad in the British Isles, the Pacific Rim, East Africa, the former Soviet Union, and the Caribbean. Villanova offers a Washington semester, an accelerated degree program in biology for allied health program, dual majors, a general studies degree, and credit by examination. There are 31 national honor societies, including Phi Beta Kappa, and a freshman honors program.

Faculty/Classroom: 72% of faculty are male; 28%, female. All teach undergraduates. No introductory courses are taught by graduate students. The average class size in an introductory lecture is 24; in a laboratory, 17; and in a regular course, 23.

Admissions: 56% of the 2003-2004 applicants were accepted. The SAT I scores for the 2003-2004 freshman class were: Verbal--4% below 500, 35% between 500 and 599, 51% between 600 and 700, and 10% above 700; Math--3% below 500, 20% between 500 and 599, 60% between 600 and 700, and 17% above 700. 70% of the current freshmen were in the top fifth of their class; 94% were in the top two fifths. In a recent year, there were 5 National Merit finalists. 27 freshmen graduated first in their class.

Requirements: The SAT I or ACT is required. In addition, applicants must be graduates of an accredited secondary school and should have completed 16 academic units. The specific courses required vary according to college. A GED is accepted. An essay is required. AP and CLEP credits are accepted. Important factors in the admissions decision are advanced placement or honor courses, leadership record, and evidence of special talent.

Procedure: Freshmen are admitted in the fall. Entrance exams should be taken by December of the senior year. There are early admissions and deferred admissions plans. Early action applications should be filed by November 1; regular applications, by December 20 for fall entry. Notification of early action is sent January 1; regular decision, April 1. A waiting list is an active part of the admissions procedure. Applications are accepted on-line through *www.admission.villanova.edu*.

Transfer: 144 transfer students enrolled in 2002-2003. A cumulative GPA of 3.0 is recommended for students interested in transferring into the College of Liberal Arts and Sciences. Students interested in transferring into the College of Nursing must have maintained at least a 2.5 cumulative GPA. Required GPAs for the College of Commerce and Finance and the College of Engineering vary. 60 of 122 credits required for the bachelor's degree must be completed at Villanova.

Visiting: There are regularly scheduled orientations for prospective students, including campus tours and information sessions conducted several times daily and on selected Saturdays throughout the academic year. There are guides for informal visits and visitors may sit in on classes. To schedule a visit, contact the Office of University Admission at *gotovu@villanova.edu*.

Financial Aid: In 2003-2004, 69% of all full-time freshmen and 65% of continuing full-time students received some form of financial aid. 45%

of full-time freshmen and 44% of continuing full-time students received need-based aid. The average freshman award was $18,880. Need-based scholarships or need-based grants averaged $13,381 ($32,602 maximum); need-based self-help aid (loans and jobs) averaged $4756 ($7125 maximum); non-need-based athletic scholarships averaged $23,943 ($40,125 maximum); and other non-need-based awards and non-need-based scholarships averaged $14,504 ($36,380 maximum). 30% of undergraduates work part time. Average annual earnings from campus work are $1200. The average financial indebtedness of the 2003 graduate was $28,217. The FAFSA, the college's own financial statement, the parent and student federal income tax return, and W2s are required. The deadline for filing freshman financial aid applications for fall entry is February 13.

International Students: There are 156 international students enrolled. The school actively recruits these students. They must score 550 on the written TOEFL or 231 on the electronic version and also take the SAT I or the ACT. Students must take SAT II: Subject tests in languages for placement purposes.

Computers: The mainframe consists of Sun 4500 Enterprise servers. Students in the College of Commerce and Finance and the College of Engineering are provided with laptop computers. There are 3 main PC labs as well as various other labs for specific majors. All students have access to the network and e-mail, on and off campus, and all residence hall rooms have network and web connections. 3 academic buildings on campus have wireless Internet capabilities. All students may access the system. There are no time limits and no fees, but students must purchase a network card.

Graduates: From July 1, 2002 to June 30, 2003, 1722 bachelor's degrees were awarded. The most popular majors were finance (12%), communications (11%), and accountancy (7%). In an average class, 79% graduate in 4 years or less, 84% graduate in 5 years or less, and 85% graduate in 6 years or less. 325 companies recruited on campus in 2002-2003. Of the 2002 graduating class, 16% were enrolled in graduate school within 6 months of graduation and 74% were employed.

Admissions Contact: Michael Gaynor, Director of Admission.
E-mail: *gotovu@villanova.edu* Web: *www.admission.villanova.edu*

WASHINGTON AND JEFFERSON COLLEGE   A-3
Washington, PA 15301
(724) 223-6025
(888) 926-3529; Fax: (724) 223-6534

Full-time: 631 men, 587 women	**Faculty:** 95; IIB, +$
Part-time: 7 men, 8 women	**Ph.D.s:** 87%
Graduate: none	**Student/Faculty:** 12 to 1
Year: 4-1-4, summer session	**Tuition:** $23,260
Application Deadline: March 1	**Room & Board:** $6310
Freshman Class: 1908 applied, 1206 accepted, 346 enrolled	
SAT I Verbal/Math: 550/580	**ACT:** 24 **VERY COMPETITIVE**

Washington and Jefferson College, founded in 1781, is a private institution offering instruction in liberal arts. The library contains 183,698 volumes, 14,674 microform items, and 8236 audio/video tapes/CDs, and subscribes to 487 periodicals. Computerized library services include the card catalog, interlibrary loans, database searching, and Internet access. Special learning facilities include a learning resource center, art gallery, radio station, and a biological field station. The 51-acre campus is in a small town 27 miles southwest of Pittsburgh. Including any residence halls, there are 43 buildings.

Student Life: 80% of undergraduates are from Pennsylvania. Students are from 28 states and 4 foreign countries. 86% are from public schools. 93% are white. The average age of freshmen is 18; all undergraduates, 20. 16% do not continue beyond their first year; 76% remain to graduate.

Housing: 1073 students can be accommodated in college housing, which includes single-sex and coed dorms, on-campus apartments, fraternity houses, and sorority houses. In addition, there are special-interest houses. On-campus housing is guaranteed for all 4 years. 82% of students live on campus; of those, 70% remain on campus on weekends. All students may keep cars.

Activities: 47% of men belong to 7 national fraternities; 44% of women belong to 4 national sororities. There are 88 groups on campus, including art, band, cheerleading, choir, chorale, chorus, computers, dance, debate, drama, ethnic, honors, jazz band, literary magazine, musical theater, newspaper, orchestra, pep band, photography, political, professional, radio and TV, religious, social, social service, student government, and yearbook. Popular campus events include Greek Week, Founders Day, and Honors Day.

Sports: There are 12 intercollegiate sports for men and 11 for women, and 20 intramural sports for men and 19 for women. Facilities include swimming and diving pools, a track, a weight room, football, baseball, and soccer fields, and basketball, volleyball, squash, and racquetball courts. The stadium seats 4000, the largest auditorium/arena, 3500.

Disabled Students: 30% of the campus is accessible. Wheelchair ramps, elevators, special parking, specially equipped rest rooms, special class scheduling, and special housing are available.

Services: Counseling and information services are available, as is tutoring in most subjects. There is a reader service for the blind, and remedial math, reading, and writing.

Campus Safety and Security: Measures include 24-hour foot and vehicle patrol, security escort services, informal discussions, and pamphlets/posters/films. There are emergency telephones and lighted pathways/sidewalks.

Programs of Study: W & J confers the B.A. degree. Associate degrees are also awarded. Bachelor's degrees are awarded in BIOLOGICAL SCIENCE (biochemistry and biology/biological science), BUSINESS (accounting, business administration and management, international business management, and management information systems), COMMUNICATIONS AND THE ARTS (art, dramatic arts, English, French, German, music, and Spanish), COMPUTER AND PHYSICAL SCIENCE (chemistry, mathematics, and physics), EDUCATION (art and early childhood), ENGINEERING AND ENVIRONMENTAL DESIGN (industrial administration/management), SOCIAL SCIENCE (economics, history, philosophy, political science/government, psychology, and sociology). Psychology, business administration, and English are the largest.

Required: Students must complete the general education requirement of at least 8 courses in 4 divisions. Other requirements include phys ed, freshman forum, foreign language, cultural diversity, and academic skills. A total of 34 courses, with 8 to 10 courses in the major, is required for graduation, as is a 2.0 GPA.

Special: The college offers study abroad in Russia, Germany, and Colombia, as well as other countries, internships in all majors, a Washington semester with American University, dual and student-designed majors, credit by exam, and pass/fail options. There is a 3-2 engineering program with Case Western Reserve University in Cleveland and Washington University in St. Louis. The college offers special human resources management and entrepreneurial studies programs. There is also a 3-4 podiatry program with the Pennsylvania and Ohio Colleges of Podiatry and a 3-4 optometry program with Pennsylvania College of Optometry. There is a 3-3 program with Duquesne University School of Law and University of Pittsburgh School of Law. There are 18 national honor societies, including Phi Beta Kappa, and 16 departmental honors programs.

Faculty/Classroom: 64% of faculty are male; 36%, female. All teach undergraduates. The average class size in an introductory lecture is 25; in a laboratory, 16; and in a regular course, 16.

Admissions: 63% of the 2003-2004 applicants were accepted. The SAT I scores for the 2003-2004 freshman class were: Verbal--16% below 500, 52% between 500 and 599, 28% between 600 and 700, and 4% above 700; Math--13% below 500, 48% between 500 and 599, 34% between 600 and 700, and 6% above 700. The ACT scores were 11% below 21, 36% between 21 and 23, 28% between 24 and 26, 13% between 27 and 28, and 13% above 28. 61% of the current freshmen were in the top fifth of their class; 89% were in the top two fifths. 15 freshmen graduated first in their class.

Requirements: The SAT I or ACT is required. In addition, a GED is accepted. Applicants must complete 15 academic credits or Carnegie units, including 3 credits of English and math, 2 of foreign language, and 1 of science. An essay is required and interviews are recommended. AP and CLEP credits are accepted. Important factors in the admissions decision are advanced placement or honor courses, evidence of special talent, and personality/intangible qualities.

Procedure: Freshmen are admitted to all sessions. Entrance exams should be taken in the junior or senior year. There are early decision, early admissions, and deferred admissions plans. Early decision applications should be filed by December 1; regular applications, by March 1 for fall entry, January 1 for winter entry, February 1 for spring entry, and June 1 for summer entry, along with a $25 fee. Notification of early decision is sent December 15; regular decision, April 1. 21 early decision candidates were accepted for the 2003-2004 class. Applications are accepted on computer disk and on-line through the school's web site, CollegeView, CollegeLink, EXPAN, and others.

Transfer: 27 transfer students enrolled in a recent year. Applicants must have a college GPA of at least 2.5 and must take the SAT I or ACT. 18 of 34 credits required for the bachelor's degree must be completed at W & J.

Visiting: There are regularly scheduled orientations for prospective students, including a general session, departmental meetings, preprofessional meetings, a financial aid meeting, and class scheduling. There are guides for informal visits and visitors may sit in on classes and stay overnight. To schedule a visit, contact the Admission Office at (724) 223-6025 or *visitorservices@washjeff.edu*.

Financial Aid: In 2003-2004, 97% of all full-time freshmen and 94% of continuing full-time students received some form of financial aid. 74% of full-time freshmen and 69% of continuing full-time students received need-based aid. The average freshman award was $16,452, with $5421 from need-based scholarships or grants, $2957 from need-based self-help aid (loans and jobs), and $8074 from non-need-based awards and non-need-based scholarships averaged. 45% of undergraduates work part time. Average annual earnings from campus work are $1200. The average financial indebtedness of the 2003 graduate was $17,258. The

FAFSA is required. The priority date for freshman financial aid applications for fall entry is February 15.

International Students: There are 10 international students enrolled. They must score 550 on the written TOEFL or 213 on the electronic version and also take the SAT I or the ACT.

Computers: The mainframes are a Model 2000 and 4000 Series Dell servers. 400 PCs and Macs are located in the computer centers, labs, and classrooms. Each dorm room has 2 free Internet connections. All students may access the system any time. There are no time limits and no fees. It is strongly recommended that all students have a personal computer. It is recommended that students in the notebook computer section of Freshman Forum have personal computers.

Graduates: From July 1, 2002 to June 30, 2003, 236 bachelor's degrees were awarded. The most popular majors were business administration (18%), English (14%), and psychology (13%). In an average class, 1% graduate in 3 years or less, 70% graduate in 4 years or less, 75% graduate in 5 years or less, and 76% graduate in 6 years or less. 21 companies recruited on campus in 2002-2003. Of the 2002 graduating class, 33% were enrolled in graduate school within 6 months of graduation and 66% were employed.

Admissions Contact: Alton E. Newell, Vice President of Enrollment Management. E-mail: *admission@washjeff.edu*
Web: *http://www.washjeff.edu*

WAYNESBURG COLLEGE
Waynesburg, PA 15370-9930

B-4
(724) 852-3248
(800) 225-7393; Fax: (724) 627-8124

Full-time: 568 men, 687 women	**Faculty:** 68; IIB, --$
Part-time: 64 men, 178 women	**Ph.D.s:** 61%
Graduate: 156 men, 201 women	**Student/Faculty:** 18 to 1
Year: semesters, summer session	**Tuition:** $13,850
Application Deadline: open	**Room & Board:** $5520
Freshman Class: n/av	
SAT I or ACT: required	**COMPETITIVE**

Waynesburg College, founded in 1849, is a private liberal arts institution affiliated with the Presbyterian Church (U.S.A.). In addition to regional accreditation, Waynesburg has baccalaureate program accreditation with ACS, CAAHEP, and NLN. The library contains 100,000 volumes, 66 microform items, and 2044 audio/video tapes/CDs, and subscribes to 454 periodicals. Computerized library services include the card catalog, interlibrary loans, and database searching. Special learning facilities include a learning resource center, art gallery, natural history museum, radio station, and TV station. The 30-acre campus is in a small town 50 miles south of Pittsburgh. Including any residence halls, there are 15 buildings.

Student Life: 87% of undergraduates are from Pennsylvania. Students are from 18 states, 6 foreign countries, and Canada. 90% are from public schools. 96% are white. 54% are Protestant; 54% unknown; 20% Catholic. The average age of freshmen is 18; all undergraduates, 24. 28% do not continue beyond their first year; 55% remain to graduate.

Housing: 730 students can be accommodated in college housing, which includes single-sex dorms. On-campus housing is guaranteed for all 4 years. 54% of students commute. Alcohol is not permitted. Upperclassmen may keep cars.

Activities: There are no fraternities or sororities. There are 36 groups on campus, including band, cheerleading, chorale, drama, ethnic, film, honors, international, jazz band, literary magazine, marching band, musical theater, newspaper, orchestra, pep band, photography, professional, radio and TV, religious, social, social service, student government, and yearbook. Popular campus events include Spring Weekend Formal, VIP Forum, and Fine Arts Series.

Sports: There are 8 intercollegiate sports for men and 7 for women, and 5 intramural sports for men and 5 for women. Facilities include a 1500-seat stadium, a 1500-seat gym, a 250-seat arena, a fitness center, basketball and racquetball courts, wrestling and weight rooms, a golf driving net, 3 all-weather tennis courts, and table tennis and billiards tables.

Disabled Students: 90% of the campus is accessible. Wheelchair ramps, elevators, special parking, specially equipped rest rooms, special class scheduling, and lowered drinking fountains are available.

Services: Counseling and information services are available, as is tutoring in every subject. There is remedial math and writing.

Campus Safety and Security: Measures include 24-hour foot and vehicle patrol, self-defense education, security escort services, and informal discussions. There are pamphlets/posters/films, lighted pathways/sidewalks, and 24-hour security access.

Programs of Study: Waynesburg confers B.A., B.S., B.S.B.A., B.S.M.B., and B.S.N. degrees. Associate and master's degrees are also awarded. Bachelor's degrees are awarded in BIOLOGICAL SCIENCE (biology/biological science and marine biology), BUSINESS (accounting, banking and finance, international business management, management science, marketing/retailing/merchandising, and small business management), COMMUNICATIONS AND THE ARTS (advertising, art, arts ad-

ministration/management, broadcasting, communications, English, graphic design, literature, multimedia, and technical and business writing), COMPUTER AND PHYSICAL SCIENCE (chemistry, computer science, information sciences and systems, and mathematics), EDUCATION (athletic training, elementary, and special), ENGINEERING AND ENVIRONMENTAL DESIGN (engineering and environmental science), HEALTH PROFESSIONS (exercise science, medical laboratory technology, nursing, physical therapy, predentistry, premedicine, and preveterinary science), SOCIAL SCIENCE (criminal justice, crosscultural studies, forensic studies, history, human services, ministries, political science/government, prelaw, psychology, social science, sociology, and theological studies). Nursing, business, and education are the strongest academically. Business administration, education, and nursing are the largest.

Required: To graduate, students must complete a minimum of 124 semester hours, including at least 30 in the major, with a minimum 2.0 GPA. Requirements include 15 credits of humanities and social and behavioral sciences, 8 of natural and physical sciences, 6 each of English and literature/arts, and 1 each of life skills, service learning, and the Waynesburg Experience. Students must also pass an English usage and written competency test as well as a math test.

Special: The college offers internships, an accelerated degree program in marketing, dual majors, a student-designed interdisciplinary major, credit for experience, nondegree study, and pass/fail options. There is a 3-2 engineering degree program with Case Western Reserve, Washington, and Penn State Universities and a 3-1 in marine biology with Florida Institute of Technology. There are 15 national honor societies and a freshman honors program.

Faculty/Classroom: 52% of faculty are male; 48%, female. All teach undergraduates. No introductory courses are taught by graduate students. The average class size in an introductory lecture is 30; in a laboratory, 10; and in a regular course, 22.

Admissions: 30% of the current freshmen were in the top fifth of their class; 58% were in the top two fifths. 4 freshmen graduated first in their class.

Requirements: The SAT I or ACT is required. In addition, applicants must be graduates of an accredited secondary school or have a GED certificate and have completed 16 academic credits, including 4 in English, 3 in math, and 2 in sciences, history, or social studies. Waynesburg requires applicants to be in the upper 40% of their class. A GPA of 2.5 is required. AP and CLEP credits are accepted. Important factors in the admissions decision are advanced placement or honor courses, recommendations by school officials, and extracurricular activities record.

Procedure: Freshmen are admitted to all sessions. Entrance exams should be taken in April of the junior year or December of the senior year. There is an early admissions plan and a rolling admissions plan. Application deadlines are open. Application fee is $20. Applications are accepted on-line through the school's web site.

Transfer: 37 transfer students enrolled in 2002-2003. Students must submit a high school transcript and complete transcripts from all colleges previously attended. 45 of 124 credits required for the bachelor's degree must be completed at Waynesburg.

Visiting: There are regularly scheduled orientations for prospective students, including visits with faculty, students, administrators, and financial aid officers, and a tour of the campus. There are guides for informal visits and visitors may sit in on classes and stay overnight. To schedule a visit, contact Robin L. King, Admissions Office at (724) 852-3333 or *rlmoore@waynesburg.edu*.

Financial Aid: In 2003-2004, 89% of all full-time freshmen and 87% of continuing full-time students received some form of financial aid. 85% of full-time freshmen and 83% of continuing full-time students received need-based aid. The average freshman award was $12,425. Need-based scholarships or need-based grants averaged $4485 ($10,345 maximum); need-based self-help aid (loans and jobs) averaged $3000 ($6000 maximum); and non-need-based awards and non-need-based scholarships averaged $4500 ($19,370 maximum). 27% of undergraduates work part time. Average annual earnings from campus work are $750. The average financial indebtedness of the 2003 graduate was $17,125. Waynesburg is a member of CSS. The FAFSA, the state aid form, and the college's own financial statement are required. The priority date for freshman financial aid applications for fall entry is March 15. The deadline for filing freshman financial aid applications for fall entry is rolling.

International Students: There are 13 international students enrolled. The school actively recruits these students. They must score 550 on the written TOEFL.

Computers: The mainframe is a LAN runs on Dell 2650 Rack Dense Servers. 6 fully equipped computer labs with PCs and Macs are available for student use. All students may access the system. There are no time limits and no fees.

Graduates: From July 1, 2002 to June 30, 2003, 334 bachelor's degrees were awarded. The most popular majors were nursing (37%), business administration (22%), and criminal justice (8%). In an average class, 45% graduate in 4 years or less, 54% graduate in 5 years or less, and 55% graduate in 6 years or less. Of the 2002 graduating class, 15% were enrolled in graduate school within 6 months of graduation and 90% were employed.

Admissions Contact: Robin L. King, Dean of Admissions.
E-mail: *admissions@waynesburg.edu* Web: *www.waynesburg.edu*

WEST CHESTER UNIVERSITY OF PENNSYLVANIA F-4
West Chester, PA 19383 (610) 436-3411
(877) 315-2165; Fax: (610) 436-2907

Full-time: 3482 men, 5701 women	**Faculty:** IIA, +$
Part-time: 598 men, 783 women	**Ph.D.s:** 74%
Graduate: 617 men, 1516 women	**Student/Faculty:** 18 to 1
Year: semesters, summer session	**Tuition:** $5656 ($12,554)
Application Deadline: open	**Room & Board:** $5508
Freshman Class: 10,207 applied, 4718 accepted, 1729 enrolled	
SAT I Verbal/Math: 530/530	**COMPETITIVE**

West Chester University, founded in 1871, is a public institution that is part of the Pennsylvania State System of Higher Education. It offers programs through the College of Arts and Sciences, and Schools of Business and Public Affairs, Education, Health Sciences, and Music. There are 5 undergraduate and 7 graduate schools. In addition to regional accreditation, West Chester University has baccalaureate program accreditation with CSWE, NASM, NCATE, and NLN. The 2 libraries contain 605,996 volumes, 892,520 microform items, and 71,303 audio/video tapes/CDs, and subscribe to 4149 periodicals. Computerized library services include the card catalog, interlibrary loans, database searching, and Internet access. Special learning facilities include a learning resource center, art gallery, planetarium, radio station, TV station, an herbarium, a speech and hearing clinic, a center for government and community affairs, and a 100-acre natural area for environmental studies. The 388-acre campus is in a suburban area 25 miles west of Philadelphia. Including any residence halls, there are 62 buildings.

Student Life: 89% of undergraduates are from Pennsylvania. Students are from 31 states, 61 foreign countries, and Canada. 84% are white; 11% African American. The average age of freshmen is 18; all undergraduates, 22. 16% do not continue beyond their first year; 51% remain to graduate.

Housing: 3600 students can be accommodated in college housing, which includes single-sex and coed dorms and on-campus apartments. In addition, there are honors houses and international student sections. On-campus housing is guaranteed for all 4 years. 64% of students commute. Alcohol is not permitted. Upperclassmen may keep cars.

Activities: 8% of men belong to 14 national fraternities; 9% of women belong to 12 national sororities. There are 200 groups on campus, including art, band, cheerleading, chess, choir, chorale, chorus, computers, dance, drama, drill team, drum and bugle corps, ethnic, film, forensics, gay, honors, international, jazz band, literary magazine, marching band, musical theater, newspaper, orchestra, photography, political, professional, radio and TV, religious, social, social service, student government, symphony, and yearbook. Popular campus events include Martin Luther King Day and University Fesitval.

Sports: There are 10 intercollegiate sports for men and 12 for women, and 11 intramural sports for men and 7 for women. Facilities include a 2500-seat field house, a gymnastics room, 4 gyms, swimming pools, 2 game fields, 3 practice fields, a softball complex, tennis courts, a 500-seat baseball stadium, and a 7500-seat stadium.

Disabled Students: 80% of the campus is accessible. Wheelchair ramps, elevators, special parking, specially equipped rest rooms, special class scheduling, lowered drinking fountains, and lowered telephones are available.

Services: Counseling and information services are available, as is tutoring in every subject. There is a reader service for the blind and remedial math, reading, and writing.

Campus Safety and Security: Measures include 24-hour foot and vehicle patrol, self-defense education, security escort services, and shuttle buses. There are informal discussions, pamphlets/posters/films, emergency telephones, lighted pathways/sidewalks, bike patrol, card access/security alarms, and resident hall security.

Programs of Study: West Chester University confers B.A., B.S., B.F.A., B.Mus., B.S.Ed., and B.S.N. degrees. Associate and master's degrees are also awarded. Bachelor's degrees are awarded in BIOLOGICAL SCIENCE (biochemistry and biology/biological science), BUSINESS (accounting, business administration and management, business economics, and marketing/retailing/merchandising), COMMUNICATIONS AND THE ARTS (art, communications, comparative literature, dramatic arts, English, French, German, Latin, literature, music, music performance, music theory and composition, Russian, Spanish, speech/debate/rhetoric, and studio art), COMPUTER AND PHYSICAL SCIENCE (chemistry, computer science, earth science, geoscience, mathematics, and physics), EDUCATION (athletic training, early childhood, elementary, foreign languages, health, music, physical, secondary, social studies, and special), HEALTH PROFESSIONS (health, health science, nursing, predentistry, premedicine, public health, and speech pathology/audiology), SOCIAL SCIENCE (American studies, anthropology, criminal justice, economics, geography, history, liberal arts/general studies, philosophy, political science/government, prelaw, psychology, public ad-

ministration, religion, social work, sociology, and women's studies). Premedical is the strongest academically. Physical education, elementary/early childhood education, and business management are the largest.

Required: All students must satisfy requirements in English composition, math, interdisciplinary study, and phys ed. Distribution requirements include 9 hours each of science, behavioral and social science, and humanities, and 3 hours in the arts. A total of 120 (126 for some degrees) credit hours and a 2.0 GPA are required.

Special: There is cross-registration with Cheyney University and a 3-2 engineering program with Pennsylvania State University. The university offers internships in most majors, an accelerated degree program in business, study abroad in France, Austria, Scotland, England, and Wales, a Washington semester, work-study, some student-designed majors, credit by examination and for life, military, and work experience, and pass/fail options. There are 23 national honor societies, a freshman honors program, and 10 departmental honors programs.

Faculty/Classroom: 54% of faculty are male; 46%, female. No introductory courses are taught by graduate students. The average class size in an introductory lecture is 35; in a laboratory, 24; and in a regular course, 30.

Admissions: 46% of the 2003-2004 applicants were accepted. The SAT I scores for the 2003-2004 freshman class were: Verbal--29% below 500, 56% between 500 and 599, 14% between 600 and 700, and 1% above 700; Math--29% below 500, 54% between 500 and 599, 16% between 600 and 700, and 1% above 700. 26% of the current freshmen were in the top fifth of their class; 62% were in the top two fifths.

Requirements: The SAT I is required. West Chester University requires applicants to be in the upper 50% of their class. A GPA of 3.0 is required. AP credits are accepted. Important factors in the admissions decision are advanced placement or honor courses, recommendations by school officials, and evidence of special talent.

Procedure: Freshmen are admitted fall and spring. Entrance exams should be taken in spring of the junior year or fall of the senior year. There is an early admissions plan and a rolling admissions plan. Application deadlines are open. The fall 2003 application fee was $35. 450 were on the 2003 waiting list; 49 were admitted. Applications are accepted on-line through *www.wcupa.edu*.

Transfer: 904 transfer students enrolled in 2002-2003. Applicants should have earned at least 30 credits and must have a recommended GPA of at least 2.3. Some departments require a higher GPA and specific course requirements. Transfers who have earned fewer than 30 credits must submit a high school transcript and standardized test scores. 30 of 120 credits required for the bachelor's degree must be completed at West Chester University.

Visiting: There are guides for informal visits and visitors may sit in on classes. To schedule a visit, contact the Office of Admissions at (877) 315-2165 or *ugadmiss@wcupa.edu*.

Financial Aid: In 2003-2004, 85% of all full-time freshmen and 84% of continuing full-time students received some form of financial aid. 79% of full-time freshmen and 57% of continuing full-time students received need-based aid. The average freshman award was $7015, with $1028 ($8100 maximum) from need-based scholarships or need-based grants, $2863 ($8100 maximum) from need-based self-help aid (loans and jobs), $54 ($8000 maximum) from non-need-based athletic scholarships, and $3070 ($5000 maximum) from other non-need-based awards and non-need-based scholarships. 17% of undergraduates work part time. Average annual earnings from campus work are $1553. The average financial indebtedness of the 2003 graduate was $17,500. West Chester University is a member of CSS. The FAFSA is required. The priority date for freshman financial aid applications for fall entry is March 1.

International Students: There are 53 international students enrolled. They must score 550 on the written TOEFL or 213 on the electronic version. The SAT I is recommended.

Computers: The mainframe is an IBM 4381. More than 400 PCs are available in computer labs, classrooms, and residence halls. Free e-mail accounts and Internet use are provided. All students may access the system.

Admissions Contact: Marsha Haug, Director of Admissions.
E-mail: *ugadmiss@wcupa.edu* Web: *www.wcupa.edu*

WESTMINSTER COLLEGE A-2
New Wilmington, PA 16172 (724) 946-7100
(800) 942-8033; Fax: (724) 946-6171

Full-time: 550 men, 850 women	**Faculty:** 98; IIB, av$
Part-time: 25 men, 50 women	**Ph.D.s:** 77%
Graduate: 65 men, 120 women	**Student/Faculty:** 14 to 1
Year: semesters, summer session	**Tuition:** $19,370
Application Deadline: open	**Room & Board:** $5990
Freshman Class: n/av	
SAT I or ACT: required	**COMPETITIVE**

Westminster College, founded in 1852, is a private liberal arts institution related to the Presbyterian Church (U.S.A.). Figures in the above capsule and in this profile are approximate. In addition to regional accreditation, Westminster has baccalaureate program accreditation with NASM. The 2 libraries contain 285,000 volumes, 10,000 microform items, and 15,000 audio/video tapes/CDs, and subscribe to 850 periodicals. Computerized library services include interlibrary loans. Special learning facilities include a learning resource center, art gallery, planetarium, radio station, TV station, and electron microscope labs in the science center. The 300-acre campus is in a rural area 60 miles north of Pittsburgh. Including any residence halls, there are 22 buildings.

Student Life: 79% of undergraduates are from Pennsylvania. 90% are from public schools. 97% are white. 56% are Protestant; 34% Catholic; 10% claim no religious affiliation. The average age of freshmen is 18; all undergraduates, 20. 1% do not continue beyond their first year; 73% remain to graduate.

Housing: 1120 students can be accommodated in college housing, which includes single-sex dorms and fraternity houses. On-campus housing is guaranteed for all 4 years. 90% of students live on campus. Alcohol is not permitted. All students may keep cars.

Activities: 55% of men belong to 5 national fraternities; 44% of women belong to 5 national sororities. There are 85 groups on campus, including band, cheerleading, choir, chorale, chorus, dance, debate, drama, drill team, ethnic, forensics, gay, honors, jazz band, literary magazine, marching band, musical theater, newspaper, orchestra, pep band, political, radio and TV, religious, social, social service, student government, symphony, and yearbook. Popular campus events include mock conventions, Mardi Gras, and Volley rock.

Sports: There are 9 intercollegiate sports for men and 8 for women, and 7 intramural sports for men and 6 for women. Facilities include a natatorium, racquetball, tennis, and basketball courts, an all-weather track, and weight and aerobics rooms. Canoeing on the lake is available.

Disabled Students: 50% of the campus is accessible. Wheelchair ramps, elevators, special parking, specially equipped rest rooms, and special class scheduling are available.

Services: Counseling and information services are available, as is tutoring in most subjects, including through the learning center. There is remedial math, reading, and writing.

Campus Safety and Security: Measures include 24-hour foot and vehicle patrol, security escort services, shuttle buses, and informal discussions. There are pamphlets/posters/films, emergency telephones, and lighted pathways/sidewalks.

Programs of Study: Westminster confers B.A., B.S., and B.M. degrees. Master's degrees are also awarded. Bachelor's degrees are awarded in BIOLOGICAL SCIENCE (biology/biological science and molecular biology), BUSINESS (accounting, banking and finance, business administration and management, international business management, and marketing/retailing/merchandising), COMMUNICATIONS AND THE ARTS (art, broadcasting, communications, dramatic arts, English, fine arts, French, German, Latin, music, music performance, music theory and composition, public relations, and Spanish), COMPUTER AND PHYSICAL SCIENCE (chemistry, computer science, mathematics, and physics), EDUCATION (Christian, elementary, guidance, music, and secondary), HEALTH PROFESSIONS (predentistry and premedicine), SOCIAL SCIENCE (criminal justice, economics, history, international relations, philosophy, political science/government, prelaw, psychology, religion, religious music, social science, and sociology). Sciences, business, and education are the strongest academically and have the largest enrollments are the strongest academically.

Required: First-year students are required to take Inquiry I and II, as well as writing and a speech course. Students must fullfill a distribution requirement by taking a course in one of each of the Intellectual Perspectives: Visual and Performing Arts, Quantitative Reasoning, Social Thought and Tradition, Humanity and Culture, Scientific Discovery, Foreign Language, and Religious and Philosophical Thought. A capstone experience in their major and community service are also required. Students must complete 132 semester hours with a minimum of 84 outside their majors, and have a minimum of 2.0 GPA in all courses. Majors require between 32 and 60 hours of course work.

Special: The college offers internships, study abroad in many countries, a Washington semester, various dual and student-designed majors, a 3-2 engineering degree with Case Western Reserve, Pennsylvania State, and Washington Universities, London study at Regent's College, a 3-3 J.D. program with Duquesne, and nondegree study. There are 12 national honor societies and a freshman honors program.

Faculty/Classroom: 73% of faculty are male; 22%, female. All teach undergraduates. No introductory courses are taught by graduate students. The average class size in a regular course is 25.

Requirements: The SAT I or ACT is required, with a minimum recommended composite score of 900 on the SAT I or 20 on the ACT. Applicants must be graduates of an accredited secondary school and have a minimum of 16 academic credits, including 4 units in English, 3 in math, and 2 each in foreign language, science, and social studies. The GED will be considered with a minimum composite score of 270. A portfolio, audition, and interview are recommended. An essay is required. Westminster requires applicants to be in the upper 50% of their class. A GPA

of 2.5 is required. AP and CLEP credits are accepted. Important factors in the admissions decision are advanced placement or honor courses, leadership record, and recommendations by school officials.

Procedure: Freshmen are admitted fall, winter, and spring. Entrance exams should be taken during the junior year. There are early admissions and deferred admissions plans. Application deadlines are open; the application fee is $35. Applications are accepted on-line.

Transfer: 16 transfer students enrolled in a recent year. Applicants must have a college GPA of 2.0 or better.

Visiting: There are regularly scheduled orientations for prospective students, consisting of an introduction, a student panel, a financial aid workshop, a campus tour, a faculty fair, and a lunch. Optional activities include a tour of residence halls and radio and TV stations and a football game. There are 2 visitation days in the fall and 2 in the spring. There are guides for informal visits and visitors may sit in on classes and stay overnight. To schedule a visit, contact the Office of Admissions.

Financial Aid: In a recent year, 99% of all full-time freshmen and 98% of continuing full-time students received some form of financial aid. 83% of full-time freshmen and 76% of continuing full-time students received need-based aid. The average freshman award was $14,252. 40% of undergraduates work part time. Average annual earnings from campus work are $1410. The average financial indebtedness of a recent graduate was $18,125. Westminster is a member of CSS. The FAFSA and the college's own financial statement are required. Check with the school for current deadlines.

International Students: They must score 550 on the written TOEFL or take the MELAB. The SAT I may be substituted for students who come from a country where English is the spoken language.

Computers: The mainframes are a Compaq Alpha 1200 and a Compaq Alpha 800. 1500 PCs are connected from all buildings (including dorms) on campus to a Novell LAN with 23 servers. All students may access the system. There are no time limits and no fees.

Graduates: In a recent year, 322 bachelor's degrees were awarded. The most popular majors were elementary education (20%), business administration (12%), and biology (8%). In an average class, 74% graduate in 4 years or less, 75% graduate in 5 years or less, and 76% graduate in 6 years or less. Of a recent graduating class, 90% were employed within 6 months of graduation.

Admissions Contact: Dean of Admissions.
E-mail: *admis@westminster.edu* Web: *www.westminster.edu*

WIDENER UNIVERSITY
F-4
Chester, PA 19013
(610) 499-4126
(888)-Widener; Fax: (610) 499-4676

Full-time: 1112 men, 1074 women	Faculty: 171; IIA, +$
Part-time: 96 men, 45 women	Ph.D.s: 92%
Graduate: 504 men, 1015 women	Student/Faculty: 13 to 1
Year: semesters, summer session	Tuition: $19,400
Application Deadline: February 15	Room & Board: $7620
Freshman Class: 2807 applied, 2222 accepted, 578 enrolled	
SAT I Verbal/Math: 505/510	COMPETITIVE

Widener University, founded in 1821, is a private liberal arts institution offering undergraduate programs in the arts and sciences, business administration, engineering, nursing, and hospitality management. Other campuses are in Harrisburg and Wilmington, Delaware. There are 6 undergraduate and 5 graduate schools. In addition to regional accreditation, Widener has baccalaureate program accreditation with AACSB, ABET, APTA, CSWE, and NLN. The library contains 241,491 volumes, 174,632 microform items, and 6463 audio/video tapes/CDs, and subscribes to 1959 periodicals. Computerized library services include the card catalog, interlibrary loans, database searching, and Internet access. Special learning facilities include a learning resource center, art gallery, radio station, TV station, a child development center, and a wireless accessible library. The 105-acre campus is in a suburban area 12 miles south of Philadelphia. Including any residence halls, there are 87 buildings.

Student Life: 64% of undergraduates are from Pennsylvania. Students are from 21 states and 15 foreign countries. 51% are from public schools. 78% are white; 10% African American. 45% are Catholic; 44% Protestant. The average age of freshmen is 18; all undergraduates, 20. 18% do not continue beyond their first year; 62% remain to graduate.

Housing: 1375 students can be accommodated in college housing, which includes single-sex and coed dorms, on-campus apartments, fraternity houses, and sorority houses. In addition, there are honors houses and special-interest houses. On-campus housing is guaranteed for all 4 years. 65% of students live on campus; of those, 75% remain on campus on weekends. All students may keep cars.

Activities: 25% of men belong to 7 national fraternities; 14% of women belong to 3 national sororities. There are 106 groups on campus, including art, band, cheerleading, chess, choir, chorale, chorus, computers, dance, drama, environmental, ethnic, film, gay, honors, ice hockey, international, jazz band, literary magazine, men's hockey clubs, model UN, musical theater, newspaper, outdoor, pep band, photography, political, professional, radio and TV, religious, rugby, ski and snowboard, social, social service, student government, video, and yearbook. Popular campus events include Greek Week, Hundredth Night, and Honors Week.

Sports: There are 11 intercollegiate sports for men and 11 for women, and 7 intramural sports for men and 7 for women. Facilities include a 4000-seat stadium, an 1800-seat basketball gym, a field house, a championship pool, a weight training room, an exercise room, tennis courts, outdoor game and practice fields, and an 8-lane, all-weather championship track.

Disabled Students: All of the campus is accessible. Wheelchair ramps, elevators, special parking, specially equipped rest rooms, special class scheduling, lowered drinking fountains, and lowered telephones are available.

Services: Counseling and information services are available, as is tutoring in every subject. There is a reader service for the blind. Academic support is offered as needed for all students.

Campus Safety and Security: Measures include 24-hour foot and vehicle patrol, self-defense education, security escort services, and shuttle buses. There are informal discussions, pamphlets/posters/films, emergency telephones, lighted pathways/sidewalks, residence hall briefings on personal safety, housing security, and enforcement procedures. There are bike patrols.

Programs of Study: Widener confers B.A., B.S., B.S.B., B.S.C.E., B.S.Ch.E., B.S.E.E., B.S. in H.M., B.S.M.E., B.S.N., and B.S.W. degrees. Associate, master's, and doctoral degrees are also awarded. Bachelor's degrees are awarded in BIOLOGICAL SCIENCE (biochemistry and biology/biological science), BUSINESS (accounting, business administration and management, business economics, hospitality management services, and international business management), COMMUNICATIONS AND THE ARTS (communications, English, and modern language), COMPUTER AND PHYSICAL SCIENCE (chemistry, computer science, information sciences and systems, mathematics, and physics), EDUCATION (early childhood, elementary, and science), ENGINEERING AND ENVIRONMENTAL DESIGN (chemical engineering, civil engineering, electrical/electronics engineering, environmental science, and mechanical engineering), HEALTH PROFESSIONS (nursing, predentistry, and premedicine), SOCIAL SCIENCE (anthropology, behavioral science, criminal justice, economics, history, humanities, international relations, political science/government, prelaw, psychology, social work, and sociology). Computer science, biology, and psychology are the strongest academically. Arts and sciences, business administration, and engineering are the largest.

Required: All students must complete 12 credits each in humanities, social sciences, and science/math, and 1 credit in phys ed. For graduation, students must have 121 credit hours and a GPA of 2.0. Hours in the major vary by program. There is a university-wide writing requirement for all students.

Special: Widener offers internships, study abroad in 12 countries, a Washington semester, accelerated degree programs, dual, student-designed, and interdisciplinary majors, including chemistry management, nondegree study, and pass/fail options. Co-op programs are available in business administration, computer science, and engineering and are required in hospitality management. There is also cross-registration with Boston, Syracuse, Swarthmore College, and American Universities, work-study programs, and B.A.-B.S. degrees. There are 26 national honor societies, a freshman honors program, and 8 departmental honors programs.

Faculty/Classroom: 54% of faculty are male; 46%, female. 82% teach undergraduates, 70% do research, and 70% do both. No introductory courses are taught by graduate students. The average class size in an introductory lecture is 30; in a laboratory, 14; and in a regular course, 24.

Admissions: 79% of the 2003-2004 applicants were accepted. The SAT I scores for the 2003-2004 freshman class were: Verbal--51% below 500, 37% between 500 and 599, 11% between 600 and 700, and 1% above 700; Math--43% below 500, 39% between 500 and 599, 16% between 600 and 700, and 2% above 700. 29% of the current freshmen were in the top fifth of their class; 78% were in the top two fifths. 2 freshmen graduated first in their class.

Requirements: The SAT I is required. In addition, applicants must be graduates of an accredited secondary school and have completed 4 units each of English and social studies, 3 units each of math and science, and 1 unit each of art, history, and music. The GED is accepted under limited circumstances. An interview is recommended. Widener requires applicants to be in the upper 50% of their class. A GPA of 3.0 is required. AP credits are accepted. Important factors in the admissions decision are advanced placement or honor courses, recommendations by school officials, and extracurricular activities record.

Procedure: Freshmen are admitted fall and spring. Entrance exams should be taken in the junior year and November or December of the senior year. There are early admissions, deferred admissions, and rolling admissions plans. Early decision applications should be filed by December 1; regular applications, by February 15 for fall entry and January 3 for spring entry, along with a $35 fee. Notification of early decision is sent December 15; regular decision, February 15. Applications are accepted on-line through Common App and CollegeNET.

Transfer: 130 transfer students enrolled in a recent year. Applicants must have at least 12 college credits with a minimum GPA of 2.0 (2.5 for nursing students). An associate's degree and an interview are recommended. 45 of 121 credits required for the bachelor's degree must be completed at Widener.

Visiting: There are regularly scheduled orientations for prospective students. There are guides for informal visits and visitors may sit in on classes and stay overnight. To schedule a visit, contact Office of Admissions at *office.admissions@widener.edu*.

Financial Aid: In a recent year, 82% of all full-time freshmen and 79% of continuing full-time students received some form of financial aid. 64% of all full-time students received need-based aid. The average freshman award was $14,659. 45% of undergraduates work part time. Average annual earnings from campus work are $944. The average financial indebtedness of a recent graduate was $17,444. Widener is a member of CSS. The FAFSA and the college's own financial statement are required. The deadline for filing freshman financial aid applications for fall entry is February 15.

International Students: There are 45 international students enrolled. The school actively recruits these students. They must score 500 on the written TOEFL or 173 on the electronic version.

Computers: The computer system includes an HP 9000 server farm and Compaq ProLiant 4500s and 5000s, and Dell services. All computer resources are networked through the Ethernet. Resources can be accessed from approximately 250 PCs located in open student computer labs, library public access workstations, classrooms, from a resident's room via student supplied workstations, through direct 10/100 Mbs port connections, or from the Internet. All students may access the system. Resources are generally available 24 hours a day, 7 days a week. Student computer labs are open from 8 A.M. to 11 P.M. There are no time limits. The fee is $75. It is strongly recommended that all students have a personal computer. A Dell is recommended.

Graduates: From July 1, 2002 to June 30, 2003, 493 bachelor's degrees were awarded. The most popular majors were arts and sciences (38%), business administration (26%), and engineering (13%). In an average class, 46% graduate in 4 years or less, 66% graduate in 5 years or less, and 70% graduate in 6 years or less. 102 companies recruited on campus in 2002-2003. Of the 2002 graduating class, 14% were enrolled in graduate school within 6 months of graduation and 86% were employed.

Admissions Contact: M. Hendricks, Jr., Dean of Admissions.
E-mail: *admissions.office@widener.edu* Web: *http://www.widener.edu*

WILKES UNIVERSITY

Wilkes Barre, PA 18766

E-2
(570) 408-4400
(800) WILKESU; Fax: (570) 408-4904

Full-time: 979 men, 1069 women	**Faculty:** 104; IIA, av$
Part-time: 139 men, 133 women	**Ph.D.s:** 91%
Graduate: 668 men, 1402 women	**Student/Faculty:** 20 to 1
Year: semesters, summer session	**Tuition:** $19,630
Application Deadline: open	**Room & Board:** $8430
Freshman Class: 2332 applied, 1878 accepted, 526 enrolled	
SAT I Verbal/Math: 533/548	**COMPETITIVE**

Wilkes University, founded in 1933, is an independent comprehensive university offering undergraduate programs in 40 fields, including the arts and sciences, business, and engineering. There are 2 undergraduate schools and 1 graduate school. In addition to regional accreditation, Wilkes has baccalaureate program accreditation with ABET, ACBSP, and NLN. The library contains 194,552 volumes, 790,194 microform items, and 10,358 audio/video tapes/CDs, and subscribes to 789 periodicals. Computerized library services include the card catalog, interlibrary loans, and database searching. Special learning facilities include a learning resource center, art gallery, radio station, and TV station. The 27-acre campus is in an urban area 120 miles west of New York City. Including any residence halls, there are 48 buildings.

Student Life: 86% of undergraduates are from Pennsylvania. Others are from 23 states and 7 foreign countries. 80% are from public schools. 95% are white. 56% are Catholic; 28% Protestant. The average age of freshmen is 18; all undergraduates, 21. 21% do not continue beyond their first year; 61% remain to graduate.

Housing: 775 students can be accommodated in college housing, which includes single-sex and coed dorms. On-campus housing is guaranteed for all 4 years. 59% of students commute. Alcohol is not permitted. All students may keep cars.

Activities: There are no fraternities or sororities. There are 60 groups on campus, including art, band, cheerleading, choir, chorus, computers, debate, drama, ethnic, gay, honors, international, jazz band, literary magazine, musical theater, newspaper, orchestra, pep band, political, professional, radio and TV, religious, social, social service, student government, and yearbook. Popular campus events include Casino Night, Junior-Senior Dinner Dance, and Winter Weekend.

Sports: There are 7 intercollegiate sports for men and 7 for women, and 7 intramural sports for men and 3 for women. Facilities include tennis courts, a 5000-seat stadium, a 3500-seat gym, a game room, and weight and exercise rooms.

Disabled Students: All of the campus is accessible. Wheelchair ramps, elevators, special parking, specially equipped rest rooms, special class scheduling, lowered drinking fountains, and lowered telephones are available.

Services: Counseling and information services are available, as is tutoring in every subject. There is remedial math, reading, and writing. The Learning Center also provides individual tutoring, group study sessions, and small-group supplemental instruction seminars.

Campus Safety and Security: Measures include 24-hour foot and vehicle patrol, security escort services, shuttle buses, and informal discussions. There are pamphlets/posters/films, emergency telephones, lighted pathways/sidewalks, personal alarm devices for students who wish to carry one, and engraving of personal belongings. Students and others may contact security anonymously.

Programs of Study: Wilkes confers B.A., B.S., B.B.A., and B.M. degrees. Master's degrees are also awarded. Bachelor's degrees are awarded in BIOLOGICAL SCIENCE (biochemistry and biology/biological science), BUSINESS (accounting, business administration and management, and electronic business), COMMUNICATIONS AND THE ARTS (communications, dramatic arts, English, French, music, musical theater, and Spanish), COMPUTER AND PHYSICAL SCIENCE (chemistry, computer science, earth science, information sciences and systems, and mathematics), EDUCATION (elementary and music), ENGINEERING AND ENVIRONMENTAL DESIGN (electrical/electronics engineering, engineering and applied science, engineering management, environmental engineering, and mechanical engineering), HEALTH PROFESSIONS (medical technology, nursing, predentistry, premedicine, prepharmacy, prepodiatry, and preveterinary science), SOCIAL SCIENCE (criminology, history, international studies, liberal arts/general studies, philosophy, political science/government, prelaw, psychology, and sociology). Prepharmacy, biology, and engineering are the strongest academically. Biology and business administration are the largest.

Required: To graduate, all students must complete at least 120 credit hours, with a minimum of 30 in the major and a cumulative GPA of at least 2.0 overall and in the major. Students must demonstrate competency in written expression, computer literacy, oral expression, and math and complete 2 semesters of phys ed. General education requirements consist of 12 to 15 credits in humanities, 9 to 12 in sciences, 6 to 9 in social sciences, and 3 in fine arts.

Special: Wilkes offers cooperative education, cross-registration with King's College and Misericordia, internships, and study abroad in more than 50 countries. Dual majors in all disciplines, credit for military experience, and nondegree study are also offered. Preprofessional programs include medicine, dentistry, podiatry, optometry, veterinary medicine, and pharmacy. There are 17 national honor societies, a freshman honors program, and 6 departmental honors programs.

Faculty/Classroom: 60% of faculty are male; 40%, female. All teach undergraduates. No introductory courses are taught by graduate students. The average class size in an introductory lecture is 26; in a laboratory, 15; and in a regular course, 21.

Admissions: 81% of the 2003-2004 applicants were accepted. The SAT I scores for the 2003-2004 freshman class were: Verbal--32% below 500, 44% between 500 and 599, 21% between 600 and 700, and 3% above 700; Math--29% below 500, 40% between 500 and 599, 25% between 600 and 700, and 6% above 700. 38% of the current freshmen were in the top fifth of their class; 65% were in the top two fifths. 15 freshmen graduated first in their class.

Requirements: The SAT I or ACT is required. In addition, applicants must be graduates of an accredited secondary school or have the GED. Secondary-school preparation should include 4 years of English, 3 years each of math and social studies, and 2 years of science. Art majors must submit a portfolio, and music majors and theater arts majors must audition. An interview is recommended. Wilkes requires applicants to be in the upper 50% of their class. A GPA of 2.5 is required. AP and CLEP credits are accepted. Important factors in the admissions decision are recommendations by school officials, advanced placement or honor courses, and leadership record.

Procedure: Freshmen are admitted to all sessions. Entrance exams should be taken before the second semester of the senior year in high school. There are early admissions and deferred admissions plans. Application deadlines are open. The fall 2003 application fee was $35. Notification is sent on a rolling basis. Applications are accepted on-line.

Transfer: 138 transfer students enrolled in 2002-2003. Applicants must have a minimum college GPA of 2.0 and at least 30 earned credits. A GPA of 2.5 is required for engineering majors. Students with fewer than 30 credits must submit official high school transcripts and SAT I or ACT scores. An interview is recommended. 60 of 120 credits required for the bachelor's degree must be completed at Wilkes.

Visiting: There are regularly scheduled orientations for prospective students, including a general orientation session, a tour of the campus, and a meeting with faculty from the department of the student's intended major. There are guides for informal visits and visitors may sit in on classes and stay overnight. To schedule a visit, contact the Admissions Office at *admissions@wilkes.edu.*

Financial Aid: In 2003-2004, 99% of all full-time freshmen and 91% of continuing full-time students received some form of financial aid. 86% of full-time freshmen and 75% of continuing full-time students received need-based aid. The average freshman award was $16,712. 36% of undergraduates work part time. Average annual earnings from campus work are $700. The average financial indebtedness of the 2003 graduate was $15,989. Wilkes is a member of CSS. The FAFSA and PHEAA are required. The deadline for filing freshman financial aid applications for fall entry is March 1.

International Students: There are 24 international students enrolled. The school actively recruits these students. They must score 500 on the written TOEFL or 173 on the electronic version and also take the SAT I or the ACT.

Computers: The mainframes are IBM RS/6000 Models 590 and 350. There are also more than 450 PCs, including 150 Macs, available throughout the campus. All students may access the system 24 hours daily. There are no time limits. The fee is $50 per semester. It is strongly recommended that all students have a personal computer.

Graduates: From July 1, 2002 to June 30, 2003, 432 bachelor's degrees were awarded. The most popular majors were psychology (15%), business administration (9%), and engineering (7%). In an average class, 46% graduate in 4 years or less, 59% graduate in 5 years or less, and 61% graduate in 6 years or less. 75 companies recruited on campus in 2002-2003. Of the 2002 graduating class, 24% were enrolled in graduate school within 6 months of graduation and 66% were employed.

Admissions Contact: Michael J. Frantz, Vice President for Enrollment Services. E-mail: *frantza@wilkes.edu* Web: *www.wilkes.edu*

WILSON COLLEGE
Chambersburg, PA 17201-1285

D-4
(717) 262-2025
Fax: (717) 264-1578

Full-time: 315 women	**Faculty:** 37
Part-time: 15 women	**Ph.D.s:** 87%
Graduate: none	**Student/Faculty:** 9 to 1
Year: 4-1-4, summer session	**Tuition:** $16,916
Application Deadline: open	**Room & Board:** $6996
Freshman Class: 267 applied, 239 accepted, 127 enrolled	
SAT I Verbal/Math: 480/500	**ACT:** 22 COMPETITIVE

Wilson College, founded in 1869, is a private liberal arts institution for women that is affiliated with the Presbyterian Church (U.S.A.). The library contains 172,205 volumes, 10,772 microform items, and 1664 audio/video tapes/CDs, and subscribes to 312 periodicals. Computerized library services include the card catalog, interlibrary loans, database searching, and Internet access. Special learning facilities include a learning resource center, art gallery, natural history museum, radio station, and a veterinary technology center, a transmission electron microscope, a classics collection, stables, a center for sustainable living, and an on campus equestrian center. The 300-acre campus is in a small town 55 miles south of Harrisburg, 76 miles west of Baltimore, 90 miles west of Washington, D.C. Including any residence halls, there are 34 buildings.

Student Life: 57% of undergraduates are from Pennsylvania. Students are from 20 states and 12 foreign countries. 91% are from public schools. 81% are white. 83% are claim no religious affiliation; 12% Protestant. The average age of freshmen is 18; all undergraduates, 20. 26% do not continue beyond their first year; 45% remain to graduate.

Housing: 414 students can be accommodated in college housing, which includes dorms and on-campus apartments. There is also single-parent housing for women with children. On-campus housing is guaranteed for all 4 years. 77% of students live on campus; of those, 50% remain on campus on weekends. All students may keep cars.

Activities: There are no fraternities. There are 23 groups on campus, including art, choir, chorale, dance, drama, environmental, equestrian, ethnic, gay, honors, international, literary magazine, newspaper, photography, political, professional, radio and TV, religious, social, social service, student government, and yearbook. Popular campus events include May Weekend and Thanksgiving, Christmas, and Muhibbah International Dinners.

Sports: Facilities include a 400-seat gym, a field house, a pool, a gymnastics gym, an archery range, a hockey field, a softball field, tennis courts, a 2-lane bowling alley, an equestrian center (indoor and outdoor arena), a soccer field, and a fitness center.

Disabled Students: 55% of the campus is accessible. Wheelchair ramps, elevators, special parking, specially equipped rest rooms, and special class scheduling are available.

Services: Counseling and information services are available, as is tutoring in every subject. There is remedial math, reading, and writing and study skills workshops.

Campus Safety and Security: Measures include 24-hour foot and vehicle patrol, shuttle buses, informal discussions, and pamphlets/posters/ films. There are emergency telephones and lighted pathways/sidewalks.

Programs of Study: Wilson confers B.A. and B.S. degrees. Associate degrees are also awarded. Bachelor's degrees are awarded in AGRICULTURE (equine science), BIOLOGICAL SCIENCE (biology/biological science), BUSINESS (accounting and business economics), COMMUNICATIONS AND THE ARTS (communications, English, fine arts, French, languages, and Spanish), COMPUTER AND PHYSICAL SCIENCE (chemistry and mathematics), EDUCATION (elementary), ENGINEERING AND ENVIRONMENTAL DESIGN (environmental science), HEALTH PROFESSIONS (exercise science and veterinary science), SOCIAL SCIENCE (behavioral science, history, international studies, law, philosophy, political science/government, psychobiology, and religion). Business and economics, behavioral sciences, and veterinary medical technology are the largest.

Required: To graduate, students must complete a minimum of 36 courses, with a minimum GPA of 2.0. At least 18 of the 36 courses must be outside any single discipline.

Special: Cross-registration is available with Shippensburg University and Gettysburg College. Wilson offers internships, a Washington semester, student-designed majors, dual majors, a B.A.-B.S. degree in behavioral science and environmental studies, credit by exam, pass/fail options, and credit for noncollegiate learning. Students may participate in study-abroad programs sponsored by other colleges. There is a chapter of Phi Beta Kappa.

Faculty/Classroom: 47% of faculty are male; 53%, female. All teach undergraduates. The average class size in an introductory lecture is 20; in a laboratory, 15; and in a regular course, 15.

Admissions: 90% of the 2003-2004 applicants were accepted. The SAT I scores for the 2003-2004 freshman class were: Verbal--58% below 500, 32% between 500 and 599, and 10% between 600 and 700; Math--47% below 500, 33% between 500 and 599, 17% between 600 and 700, and 2% above 700. The ACT scores were 45% below 21, 18% between 21 and 23, 18% between 24 and 26, 9% between 27 and 28, and 9% above 28. 22% of the current freshmen were in the top fifth of their class; 59% were in the top two fifths.

Requirements: The SAT I is required and the ACT is recommended, with a minimum recommended score of 900 composite on the SAT I or 21 on the ACT. In addition, applicants should prepare with 4 years each of English and social studies/history, 3 of math, and 2 of science with a lab and a foreign language. An essay and at least one reference are required, and an interview is recommended. Wilson requires applicants to be in the upper 50% of their class. A GPA of 2.5 is required. AP and CLEP credits are accepted. Important factors in the admissions decision are personality/intangible qualities, advanced placement or honor courses, and leadership record.

Procedure: Freshmen are admitted fall and spring. Entrance exams should be taken in the spring of the junior year. There are rolling and deferred admissions plans. Application deadlines are open. Application fee is $30. Applications are accepted on-line through *www.wilson.edu*.

Transfer: 22 transfer students enrolled in 2002-2003. Applicants must have a college GPA of at least 2.0. The SAT I or ACT is recommended, with a minimum composite score of 900 or 21, respectively. 14 of 36 credits required for the bachelor's degree must be completed at Wilson.

Visiting: There are regularly scheduled orientations for prospective students, consisting of a campus tour and meetings with faculty, students or administration, if requested. There are guides for informal visits and visitors may sit in on classes and stay overnight. To schedule a visit, contact the Office of Admissions at (800) 421-8402 or (717) 262-2002 or *admissions@wilson.edu*.

Financial Aid: In 2003-2004, 86% of all full-time freshmen and 67% of continuing full-time students received some form of financial aid. 86% of full-time freshmen and 67% of continuing full-time students received need-based aid. The average freshman award was $14,642. Need-based scholarships or need-based grants averaged $12,208; need-based self-help aid (loans and jobs) averaged $2819; and non-need-based awards and non-need-based scholarships averaged $11,381. 40% of undergraduates work part time. Average annual earnings from campus work are $1339. The average financial indebtedness of the 2003 graduate was $16,062. The FAFSA and the college's own financial statement are required. The priority date for freshman financial aid applications for fall entry is April 30.

International Students: There are 31 international students enrolled. The school actively recruits these students. They must score 500 on the written TOEFL. The SAT I is recommended.

Computers: The mainframe is a PC-based system. PCs are available for student use throughout the campus. There are 4 labs, 3 with PCs and 1 with Macs. All are connected to the Internet. All students may access the system. There are no time limits and no fees.

Graduates: From July 1, 2002 to June 30, 2003, 49 bachelor's degrees were awarded. The most popular majors were veterinary medical (29%), equestrian studies (19%), and business economics (13%). In an average class, 38% graduate in 4 years or less, 45% graduate in 5 years or less, and 45% graduate in 6 years or less. Of the 2002 graduating class, 45% were enrolled in graduate school within 6 months of graduation and 82% were employed.

Admissions Contact: Kathleen Berard, Vice President of Enrollment. E-mail: *admissions @wilson.edu* Web: *www.wilson.edu*

YORK COLLEGE OF PENNSYLVANIA   D-4
York, PA 17405-7199   (717) 849-1600
(800) 455-8018; Fax: (717) 849-1607

Full-time: 1806 men, 2421 women	**Faculty:** IIB, +$
Part-time: 322 men, 737 women	**Ph.D.s:** n/av
Graduate: 106 men, 128 women	**Student/Faculty:** n/av
Year: semesters, summer session	**Tuition:** $8550
Application Deadline: open	**Room & Board:** $5950
Freshman Class: 4141 applied, 3070 accepted, 1014 enrolled	
SAT I Verbal/Math: 551/542	**VERY COMPETITIVE**

York College of Pennsylvania, founded in 1787, is a private institution offering undergraduate programs in the liberal arts and sciences, as well as professional programs. There are 9 undergraduate schools and 1 graduate school. In addition to regional accreditation, YCP has baccalaureate program accreditation with ABET, ACBSP, CAAHEP, NLN, and NRPA. The library contains 300,000 volumes, 500,000 microform items, and 11,000 audio/video tapes/CDs, and subscribes to 1500 periodicals. Computerized library services include interlibrary loans and database searching. Special learning facilities include a learning resource center, art gallery, radio station, TV station, telecommunications center, Abraham Lincoln artifacts collection, rare books collection, oral history room, and a nursing education center. The 118-acre campus is in a suburban area 45 miles north of Baltimore. Including any residence halls, there are 30 buildings.

Student Life: 56% of undergraduates are from Pennsylvania. Students are from 30 states, 36 foreign countries, and Canada. 83% are from public schools. 95% are white. 44% are Catholic; 42% Protestant. The average age of freshmen is 19; all undergraduates, 24. 20% do not continue beyond their first year; 76% remain to graduate.

Housing: 1872 students can be accommodated in college housing, which includes single-sex and coed dorms, on-campus apartments, fraternity houses, and sorority houses. On-campus housing is guaranteed for the freshman year only and is available on a first-come, first-served basis. Alcohol is not permitted. All students may keep cars.

Activities: 10% of men belong to 5 local and 5 national fraternities; 10% of women belong to 2 local and 5 national sororities. There are 80 groups on campus, including band, cheerleading, chess, choir, chorale, chorus, computers, drama, ethnic, film, honors, international, jazz band, literary magazine, musical theater, newspaper, orchestra, photography, political, professional, radio and TV, religious, social, social service, student government, symphony, and yearbook. Popular campus events include Family Weekend, Spring Weekend Festival, and live Sparts Den performers.

Sports: There are 10 intercollegiate sports for men and 9 for women, and 10 intramural sports for men and 10 for women. Facilities include 2 gyms, a track, a swimming pool, a game room, a fitness center, weight training rooms, tennis courts, and soccer, hockey, baseball, softball, and athletic/intramural fields.

Disabled Students: 60% of the campus is accessible. Wheelchair ramps, elevators, special parking, specially equipped rest rooms, special class scheduling, lowered drinking fountains, and lowered telephones are available.

Services: Counseling and information services are available, as is tutoring in most subjects. There is remedial math and writing. There is also an education learning resource center.

Campus Safety and Security: Measures include self-defense education, security escort services, informal discussions, and pamphlets/posters/films. There are emergency telephones, lighted pathways/sidewalks, 24-hour foot patrol, safety seminars, crime prevention speakers, a desk monitor in residence halls, and a personal property engraving program.

Programs of Study: YCP confers B.A. and B.S. degrees. Associate and master's degrees are also awarded. Bachelor's degrees are awarded in BIOLOGICAL SCIENCE (biology/biological science), BUSINESS (accounting, banking and finance, business administration and management, international business management, management science, marketing/retailing/merchandising, and sports management), COMMUNICATIONS AND THE ARTS (broadcasting, communications, English, fine arts, graphic design, music, Spanish, and speech/debate/rhetoric), COMPUTER AND PHYSICAL SCIENCE (chemistry, computer programming, information sciences and systems, mathematics, and physical sciences), EDUCATION (business, elementary, science, secondary, and special), ENGINEERING AND ENVIRONMENTAL DESIGN (engineering management and mechanical engineering), HEALTH PROFESSIONS (medical laboratory technology, nuclear medical technology, nursing, premedicine, and respiratory therapy), SOCIAL SCIENCE (behavioral science, criminal justice, economics, history, humanities, parks and recreation management, philosophy, political science/government, prelaw, psychology, and sociology). Mechanical engineering, nursing, education, and biology are the strongest academically. Education, nursing, and business are the largest.

Required: To graduate, all students must complete at least 124 credit hours, with 60 to 80 in the major. The required core curriculum includes 12 credits in foreign language and culture, 12 in social and behavioral science, 9 in English and speech, 9 in humanities and fine arts, 6 each in math and lab science, 4 in phys ed, and 3 in American civilization. A minimum GPA of 2.0 is required.

Special: YCP offers internships for upper-division students and co-op programs in mechanical engineering. Exchange programs are offered with York St. John College in York, England; Honam University in Kwanju, South Korea; Pontificia Universidad Catolica del Equador in Quito, Equador; and Cemanahuac Educational Community in Cuernavaca, Mexico. Dual majors in any combination, nondegree study, and pass/fail options are available. There are 2 national honor societies.

Faculty/Classroom: All teach undergraduates. No introductory courses are taught by graduate students. The average class size in an introductory lecture is 30; in a laboratory, 20; and in a regular course, 30.

Admissions: 74% of the 2003-2004 applicants were accepted. The SAT I scores for the 2003-2004 freshman class were: Verbal--17% below 500, 55% between 500 and 599, 24% between 600 and 700, and 4% above 700; Math--17% below 500, 60% between 500 and 599, 21% between 600 and 700, and 2% above 700. 39% of the current freshmen were in the top fifth of their class; 76% were in the top two fifths. 4 freshmen graduated first in their class.

Requirements: The SAT I or ACT is required. In addition, applicants must be graduates of an accredited secondary school or have a GED certificate. 15 academic credits are required, including 4 units in English, 3 or 4 in math, 2 or 3 in science, 2 in history, and 1 in social studies. Music students must audition. YCP requires applicants to be in the upper 60% of their class. A GPA of 2.5 is required. AP and CLEP credits are accepted. Important factors in the admissions decision are advanced placement or honor courses, leadership record, and extracurricular activities record.

Procedure: Freshmen are admitted fall and spring. Entrance exams should be taken in the spring of the junior year or the fall of the senior year. There is a deferred admissions plan. Application deadlines are open. There is a rolling admissions plan. Application fee is $30. Applications are accepted on-line through *www.ycp.edu.*

Transfer: 242 transfer students enrolled in 2003-2004. Applicants must have a minimum GPA of 2.0 from a regionally accredited institution. Students with fewer than 30 credit hours must submit a high school transcript. An interview is recommended. 30 of 124 credits required for the bachelor's degree must be completed at YCP.

Visiting: There are regularly scheduled orientations for prospective students, including 2 open houses in October/November and 2 spring orientation programs in April/May, featuring a general orientation, academic and support services sessions, and campus tours. There are guides for informal visits and visitors may sit in on classes. To schedule a visit, contact the Admissions Office.

Financial Aid: In 2003-2004, 81% of all full-time freshmen and 73% of continuing full-time students received some form of financial aid. 45% of full-time freshmen and 51% of continuing full-time students received need-based aid. The average freshman award was $6334. Need-based scholarships or need-based grants averaged $3919 ($8000 maximum); need-based self-help aid (loans and jobs) averaged $2811 ($5500 maximum); and non-need-based awards and non-need-based scholarships averaged $5806 ($16,600 maximum). 20% of undergraduates work part time. Average annual earnings from campus work are $1500. The average financial indebtedness of the 2003 graduate was $15,913. YCP is a member of CSS. The FAFSA and the college's own financial statement are required. The deadline for filing freshman financial aid applications for fall entry is April 15.

International Students: They must score 530 on the written TOEFL and also take the SAT I or the ACT.

Computers: The mainframe consists of multiple Sun Microsystem E-280 R computers. All classrooms, offices, and student residence rooms are directly connected to the network, providing access to e-mail, the Internet, and the college's own intranet. 14 computer labs and 350 PCs are available for student use. 300 software packages are available on the campus network. All students may access the system. There are no time limits and no fees.

Graduates: From July 1, 2002 to June 30, 2003, 892 bachelor's degrees were awarded. The most popular majors were elementary education (10%), criminal justice (7%), and mass communications (7%). In an average class, 15% graduate in 3 years or less, 42% graduate in 4 years or less, 57% graduate in 5 years or less, and 61% graduate in 6 years or less. 163 companies recruited on campus in 2002-2003. Of the 2002 graduating class, 15% were enrolled in graduate school within 6 months of graduation and 90% were employed.

Admissions Contact: Director of Admissions. A video is available. E-mail: *admissions@ycp.edu* Web: *http://www.ycp.edu*

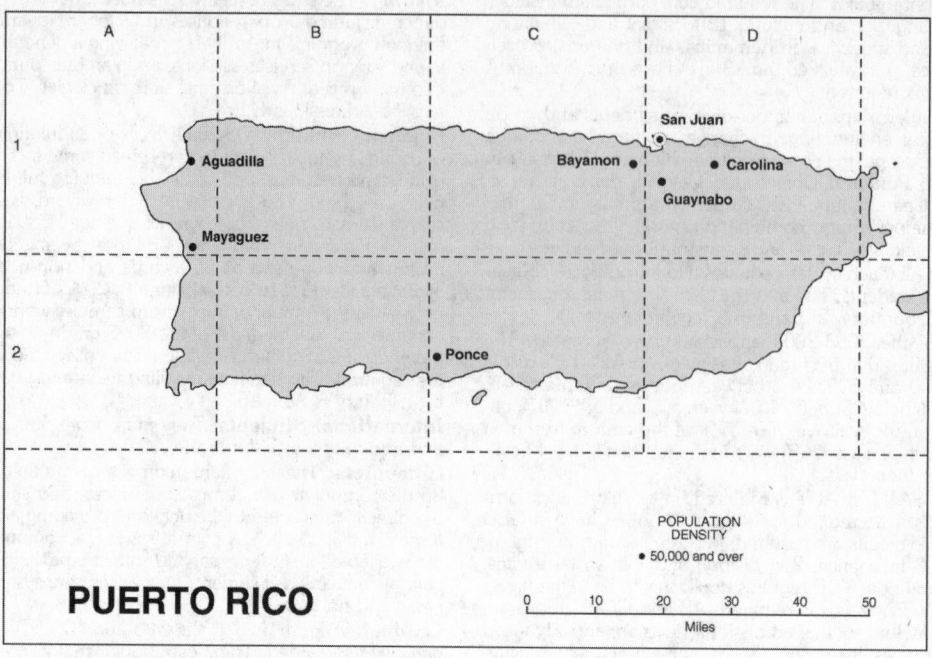

PUERTO RICO

POPULATION DENSITY
• 50,000 and over

0 10 20 30 40 50
Miles

AMERICAN UNIVERSITY OF PUERTO RICO   C-1
Bayamon, PR 00960-2037   (787) 740-6410; Fax: (787) 785-7377

Full-time: 1186 men, 1852 women	**Faculty:** n/av
Part-time: none	**Ph.D.s:** n/av
Graduate: none	**Student/Faculty:** n/av
Year: semesters, summer session	**Tuition:** $3942
Application Deadline: open	**Room & Board:** n/app
Freshman Class: n/av	
SAT I or ACT: required	

American University of Puerto Rico, founded in 1963, is a private non-sectarian institution offering undergraduate programs in business administration, secretarial training, and computer science. There are 4 undergraduate schools. The 2 libraries contain more than 10,000 volumes, 1000 microform items, and 1000 audio/video tapes/CDs, and subscribe to more than 50 periodicals. Computerized library services include the card catalog, interlibrary loans, and database searching. Special learning facilities include a learning resource center. The 21-acre campus is in an urban area south of San Juan. There are 9 buildings.

Student Life: 99% of undergraduates are from Puerto Rico. 80% are from public schools. All are Hispanic. The average age of freshmen is 18; all undergraduates, 21. 3% do not continue beyond their first year; 97% remain to graduate.

Housing: There are no residence halls. Alcohol is not permitted.

Activities: There are no fraternities or sororities. There are some groups and organizations on campus, including art and photography.

Sports: There are 3 intercollegiate sports for men and 3 for women, and 3 intramural sports for men and 3 for women. Facilities include an indoor basketball and volleyball court, a soccer field, and a pool.

Disabled Students: All of the campus is accessible. Wheelchair ramps, elevators, special parking, specially equipped rest rooms, lowered drinking fountains, and lowered telephones are available.

Services: Counseling and information services are available, as is tutoring in every subject.

Campus Safety and Security: Measures include 24-hour foot and vehicle patrol, self-defense education, security escort services, and shuttle buses. There are informal discussions, pamphlets/posters/films, and lighted pathways/sidewalks.

Programs of Study: American confers B.A. and B.B.A. degrees. Associate degrees are also awarded. Business and communications are the largest.

Required: A GPA of 2.0 is required to graduate.

Special: Work-study programs are available.

Requirements: The SAT I or ACT is required. A GPA of 2.0 is required.

Procedure: Freshmen are admitted in the fall. Application deadlines are open.

Visiting: There are guides for informal visits and visitors may sit in on classes. To schedule a visit, contact the school at (787) 798-2040.

Computers: The mainframe is an IBM. Computer labs are available. All students may access the system. There are no time limits and no fees.

Admissions Contact: Admissions Office. Web: *www.aupr.edu*

CARIBBEAN UNIVERSITY   C-1
Bayamon, PR 00960-0493   (787) 780-0070, ext. 224

Full-time: 550 men, 1000 women	**Faculty:** n/av
Part-time: 550 men, 1000 women	**Ph.D.s:** n/av
Graduate: none	**Student/Faculty:** n/av
Year: n/app	**Tuition:** $3000
Application Deadline: open	**Room & Board:** n/app
Freshman Class: n/av	
SAT I or ACT: not required	

Caribbean University, founded in 1969, is an independent, commuter institution offering undergraduate programs in business, engineering, health science, and liberal arts. There are extension centers in Vega Baja, Carolina, and Ponce. There are 6 undergraduate schools. Figures in the above capsule and this profile are approximate. The library contains 32,620 volumes, 1200 microform items, and 200 audio/video tapes/CDs, and subscribes to 210 periodicals. Computerized library services include interlibrary loans and database searching. Special learning facilities include a learning resource center. The 21-acre campus is in an urban area. There are 8 buildings.

Housing: There are no residence halls. All students commute. Alcohol is not permitted.

Activities: There are 10 groups on campus, including chess, professional, social, and student government.

Sports: Facilities include a gym, basketball and tennis courts, and a track and field arena.

Disabled Students: All of the campus is accessible. Wheelchair ramps, elevators, special parking, specially equipped rest rooms, and special counseling are available.

Services: Counseling and information services are available, as is tutoring in every subject. There is remedial math, reading, and writing.

Campus Safety and Security: Measures include campus security guards, student ID cards, and regular fire drills.

Programs of Study: Bachelor's degrees are awarded in BIOLOGICAL SCIENCE (biology/biological science), BUSINESS (accounting, banking and finance, business administration and management, marketing/retailing/merchandising, and secretarial studies/office management), COMPUTER AND PHYSICAL SCIENCE (computer programming, computer science, mathematics, and science), EDUCATION (business, elementary, middle school, science, secondary, special, and teaching English as a second/foreign language (TESOL/TEFOL)), ENGINEERING AND ENVIRONMENTAL DESIGN (civil engineering and industrial engineering technology), HEALTH PROFESSIONS (nursing), SOCIAL SCIENCE (criminal justice, social science, and social work).

Requirements: Applicants must be graduates of an accredited secondary school with a GPA of 2.0 or a CEEB score of 4.0. The GED is accepted. High school preparation should include 3 years each of art, English, Spanish, and social studies, 2 years each of history and math, and 1 year of science. A GPA of 2.0 is required.

Procedure: Freshmen are admitted to all sessions. Entrance exams should be taken in the junior or senior year. There is a rolling admissions plan. Application deadlines are open.

Transfer: A minimum college GPA of 2.0 is recommended. Applicants should submit 2 official transcripts and a catalog from each previous college attended, along with a written recommendation from the dean at the last institution. 30 of 135 credits required for the bachelor's degree must be completed at CU.

Visiting: There are regularly scheduled orientations for prospective students. To schedule a visit, contact the Director of Admissions.

Financial Aid: CU is a member of CSS. The CSS Profile and income tax returns are required.

International Students: Applicants must meet regular admissions requirements at CU and present proof of practical knowledge of both English and Spanish.

Computers: CU provides PCs for the academic use of all students during school hours. There are no time limits and no fees.

Admissions Contact: Director of Admissions.

CENTRAL UNIVERSITY OF BAYAMON C-1
Bayamon, PR 00960-1725   (787) 786-3030, ext. 2100

Full-time: 840 men, 1600 women	**Faculty:** 61
Part-time: 155 men, 290 women	**Ph.D.s:** 28%
Graduate: 90 men, 160 women	**Student/Faculty:** 40 to 1
Year: semesters, summer session	**Tuition:** $3335
Application Deadline: see profile	**Room & Board:** n/app
Freshman Class: 743 applied, 589 accepted, 492 enrolled	
ACT: n/av	

Central University of Bayamon, founded in 1970, is a private Catholic institution offering degree programs primarily to commuter students in the arts and sciences, business, education, nursing, and religious studies. Figures in the above capsule and in this profile are approximate. There are 4 undergraduate and 3 graduate schools. The 2 libraries contain 51,500 volumes and 40 microform items, and subscribe to 370 periodicals. Computerized library services include the card catalog. The 55-acre campus is in an urban area 4 miles west of Bayamon. There are 13 buildings.

Student Life: 90% are from public schools. All are Hispanic. The average age of freshmen is 17; all undergraduates, 20.

Housing: There are no residence halls. All students commute. Alcohol is not permitted. All students may keep cars.

Activities: There are no fraternities or sororities. There are 13 groups on campus, including computers, film, literary magazine, photography, professional, radio and TV, religious, social service, and student government.

Sports: There are 10 intercollegiate sports for men and 10 for women. Facilities include a 400-seat gym, basketball and volleyball courts, a swimming pool, and a weight-training room.

Disabled Students: All of the campus is accessible. Wheelchair ramps, elevators, special parking, specially equipped rest rooms, special class scheduling, lowered drinking fountains, and lowered telephones are available.

Services: Counseling and information services are available, as is tutoring in some subjects, including English, Spanish, philosophy, accounting, math, biology, and computer science. There is a reader service for the blind and remedial math, reading, and writing.

Campus Safety and Security: Measures include 24-hour foot and vehicle patrol.

Programs of Study: UCB confers B.A., B.S., B.B.A., B.S.N., and B.S.S. degrees. Associate and master's degrees are also awarded. Bachelor's degrees are awarded in BIOLOGICAL SCIENCE (biology/biological science), BUSINESS (accounting, business administration and management, and marketing/retailing/merchandising), COMMUNICATIONS AND THE ARTS (journalism and Spanish), COMPUTER AND PHYSICAL SCIENCE (chemistry and computer science), EDUCATION (elementary, English, science, and secondary), HEALTH PROFESSIONS (nursing and premedicine), SOCIAL SCIENCE (philosophy, psychology, religion, social work, and sociology). Business administration is the strongest academically.

Required: Students must complete 48 credits distributed among specific courses in theology, philosophy, Spanish, English, humanities, social science, math, science, and phys ed. The bachelor's degree requires completion of 124 to 141 credits, including 33 to 43 in the major, with a minimum GPA of 2.0.

Special: The university offers limited pass/fail options, work-study programs, and nondegree study.

Faculty/Classroom: All teach undergraduates. The average class size in an introductory lecture is 35; in a laboratory, 20; and in a regular course, 35.

Admissions: 79% of the 2003-2004 applicants were accepted.

Requirements: The CEEB Spanish equivalent is required. Applicants must be graduates of accredited secondary schools or have earned a GED. They must speak Spanish and have a good knowledge of English. The university requires 15.5 academic credits, including 3 credits each in English, Spanish, math, and science, 1.5 in history, and 1 each in social studies and electives. An interview is recommended. A GPA of 2.0 is required. CLEP credit is accepted. Important factors in the admissions decision are personality/intangible qualities, recommendations by school officials, and ability to finance college education.

Procedure: Freshmen are admitted to all sessions. Entrance exams should be taken by October of the senior year. Check with the school for current application deadlines and fee.

Transfer: A minimum college GPA of 2.0 is required. 30 of 124 to 141 credits required for the bachelor's degree must be completed at UCB.

Visiting: There are regularly scheduled orientations for prospective students. There are guides for informal visits and visitors may sit in on classes. To schedule a visit, contact the Admissions Office.

Financial Aid: In 2003-2004, 94% of all full-time freshmen received some form of financial aid. The college's own financial statement is required. Check with the school for current application deadlines.

Computers: The mainframe is a Wang VS 45. Those students registered with the computer lab may access the mainframe from 9 A.M. to 7 P.M. Monday through Thursday and from 9 A.M. to noon on Friday. Students may access the system 2 hours per week. The fee is $30.

Admissions Contact: Christine M. Hernandez, Director, Admissions. Web: *www.ucb.edu.pr*

CONSERVATORY OF MUSIC OF PUERTO RICO D-1
San Juan, PR 00918   (787) 751-0160; Fax: (787) 758-8258

Full-time: 110 men, 30 women	**Faculty:** 30
Part-time: 85 men, 30 women	**Ph.D.s:** 2%
Graduate: none	**Student/Faculty:** 5 to 1
Year: semesters	**Tuition:** $1420
Application Deadline: see profile	**Room & Board:** n/app
Freshman Class: n/av	
SAT I: required	

The Conservatory of Music of Puerto Rico, founded in 1959, is a specialized commuter school supported by the Commonwealth of Puerto Rico, offering 4- and 5-year degree programs. Figures in the above capsule and in this profile are approximate. The library contains 23,608 volumes, 11 microform items, and 5000 audio/video tapes/CDs, and subscribes to 2 periodicals. Special learning facilities include a learning resource center and a computer-based ear-training lab. The 3-acre campus is in an urban area in the Hato Rey section of San Juan. There are 3 buildings.

Programs of Study: The conservatory confers B.F.A., B.M., and B.Perf.Arts degrees.

Required: To graduate, students must complete 142 credit hours (158 for music education) with a minimum GPA of 2.0. Requirements include 4 years of courses in the principal instrument and specific courses in music theory, including solfege, harmony, and counterpoint. All students must present a graduation recital.

Special: A dual major is available in the principal instrument and music education.

Faculty/Classroom: 70% of faculty are male; 30%, female. All teach undergraduates.

Requirements: The SAT I or the CEEB's Spanish version is required. Applicants must be graduates of an accredited secondary school. An interview and audition are required. A GPA of 2.0 is required. AP credits are accepted. Important factors in the admissions decision are leadership record, parents or siblings attending the school, and ability to finance college education.

Procedure: Freshmen are admitted to all sessions. Entrance exams should be taken in May of the junior year or December of the senior year. There is an early admissions plan. Check with the school for current application deadlines and fee. A waiting list is an active part of the admissions procedure.

Transfer: 100 of 142 credits required for the bachelor's degree must be completed at the conservatory.

Visiting: There are regularly scheduled orientations for prospective students. To schedule a visit, contact Pilar Ruibal, Counselor, or Zulma Palos, Admissions Director.

Financial Aid: 15% of undergraduates work part time. Average annual earnings from campus work are $850. The conservatory is a member of CSS. The CSS Profile is required.

Computers: There are no time limits and no fees.

Admissions Contact: Zulma Palos-Santini, Admissions Director.

ESCUELA DE ARTES PLASTICAS DE PUERTO RICO D-1
San Juan, PR 00902-1112

(787) 725-8120, ext. 233
Fax: (787) 725-8111

Full-time: 176 men, 108 women	**Faculty:** 12
Part-time: 52 men, 29 women	**Ph.D.s:** 20%
Graduate: none	**Student/Faculty:** 24 to 1
Year: semesters	**Tuition:** $1996
Application Deadline: May 16	**Room & Board:** n/app
Freshman Class: 157 applied, 86 accepted, 86 enrolled	
SAT I: required	

Escuela de Artes Plasticas de Puerto Rico, founded in 1966, is a public institution considered to be the national art school of Puerto Rico. The library contains 12,429 volumes, 10,000 microform items, and 300 audio/video tapes/CDs, and subscribes to 40 periodicals. Computerized library services include the card catalog and Internet access. Special learning facilities include a learning resource center and art gallery. The 1-acre campus is in an urban area in Old San Juan. There are 3 buildings.

Student Life: 61% are from public schools. All are Hispanic. The average age of freshmen is 18; all undergraduates, 25. 5% do not continue beyond their first year; 35% remain to graduate.

Housing: There are no residence halls. All students commute. Alcohol is not permitted. No one may keep cars.

Activities: There are no fraternities or sororities. There are 2 groups on campus, including art and student government. Popular campus events include Student Day, Health Fair, and Halloween Costume Party.

Sports: There is no sports program at Escuela de Artes Plasticas de Puerto Rico.

Disabled Students: All of the campus is accessible. Wheelchair ramps, elevators, special parking, and special class scheduling are available.

Services: Counseling and information services are available, as is tutoring in some subjects, including all the general studies courses. There is remedial writing.

Campus Safety and Security: Measures include 24-hour foot and vehicle patrol, pamphlets/posters/films, and safety training.

Programs of Study: Escuela de Artes Plasticas de Puerto Rico confers the B.A. degree. Bachelor's degrees are awarded in COMMUNICATIONS AND THE ARTS (graphic design, painting, and sculpture), EDUCATION (art), ENGINEERING AND ENVIRONMENTAL DESIGN (computer graphics). Computer graphics is the largest.

Required: To graduate, students must maintain a minimum GPA of 2.0 in 132 credits, including 36 in art fundamentals and 48 in general education courses.

Special: Accelerated degree programs are offered.

Faculty/Classroom: 56% of faculty are male; 44%, female. All teach undergraduates. The average class size in an introductory lecture is 25 and in a laboratory, 18.

Admissions: 55% of the 2003-2004 applicants were accepted.

Requirements: The SAT I is required or the CEEB Spanish equivalent of the SAT I. Applicants must be graduates of an accredited secondary school or have earned a GED. A portfolio and interview are required, with an essay recommended. A GPA of 2.0 is required. Important factors in the admissions decision are evidence of special talent, recommendations by school officials, and personality/intangible qualities.

Procedure: Freshmen are admitted in the fall. Applications should be filed by May 16 for fall entry, along with a $20 fee. Notification is sent on a rolling basis.

Transfer: 22 transfer students enrolled in 2002-2003. Admission requirements are the same as for first-year applicants.

Visiting: There are regularly scheduled orientations for prospective students. There are guides for informal visits. To schedule a visit, contact the Student Affairs Office.

Financial Aid: In 2003-2004, 56% of all full-time freshmen and 73% of continuing full-time students received some form of financial aid. 33% of full-time freshmen and 52% of continuing full-time students received need-based aid. The average freshman award was $3250. 12% of undergraduates work part time. Average annual earnings from campus work are $1300. The FAFSA is required.

International Students: The school actively recruits these students. They must take the SAT I or the CEEB Spanish equivalent of the SAT I.

Computers: There are 10 PCs in the library and 4 in classrooms. All students may access the system Monday through Saturday from 8 A.M. to 5:30 P.M. Students may access the system for 1 hour. There are no fees.

Graduates: From July 1, 2002 to June 30, 2003, 47 bachelor's degrees were awarded. The most popular majors were graphic design (47%), painting (27%), and art education (10%). In an average class, 6% graduate in 3 years or less, 17% graduate in 4 years or less, 38% graduate in 5 years or less, and 39% graduate in 6 years or less. 4 companies recruited on campus in a recent year. Of a recent graduating class, 14% were enrolled in graduate school within 6 months of graduation and 57% were employed.

Admissions Contact: Recruiting Officer. A video is available.
E-mail: *eap@cogui.net* Web: *www.eap.edu.pr*

INTER AMERICAN UNIVERSITY OF PUERTO RICO SYSTEM

The Inter American University of Puerto Rico System, established in 1912, is a private system in Puerto Rico. It is governed by a board of trustees, whose chief administrator is the president. The primary goal of the system is teaching. The main priorities are to provide quality education and public service, and devote attention to students' needs. The total enrollment of all 10 campuses exceeds 42,000; there were about 862 faculty members. Profiles of the 4-year campuses are included in this section.

INTER AMERICAN UNIVERSITY OF PUERTO RICO/AGUADILLA CAMPUS A-1
Aguadilla, PR 00605

(787) 891-0925; Fax: (787) 882-3020

Full-time: 1463 men, 2083 women	**Faculty:** 76
Part-time: 262 men, 346 women	**Ph.D.s:** 21%
Graduate: none	**Student/Faculty:** 47 to 1
Year: semesters, trimesters, summer session	**Tuition:** $3544
	Room & Board: n/app
Application Deadline: May 1	
Freshman Class: 1428 applied, 1233 accepted, 1070 enrolled	
SAT I: required	

Inter American University of Puerto Rico/Aguadilla Campus, a private, nonsectarian institution, was founded in 1957 and is a part of the Inter American University of Puerto Rico. Programs offered include business, fine and liberal arts, health sciences, and teacher and professional preparation. There are 3 undergraduate schools. The library contains 55,024 volumes, 2628 microform items, and 25,016 audio/video tapes/CDs, and subscribes to 392 periodicals. Computerized library services include the card catalog, interlibrary loans, database searching, and Internet access. Special learning facilities include a learning resource center, radio station, multimedia center, instructional development center, and electronic classroom. The 54-acre campus is in a suburban area in northwestern Puerto Rico, near the Atlantic Ocean. There are 6 buildings.

Student Life: 99% of undergraduates are from Puerto Rico. 96% are from public schools. All are Hispanic. 70% are Catholic; 30% Protestant. The average age of freshmen is 21; all undergraduates, 24. 20% do not continue beyond their first year.

Housing: There are no residence halls. Alcohol is not permitted. All students may keep cars.

Activities: There are no fraternities or sororities. There are 24 groups on campus, including academic, chess, choir, computers, cultural, debate, drama, film, honors, newspaper, professional, religious, social, social service, and student government. Popular campus events include International Tourism Conference, Festival of Flora and Fauna, and Achievement Night.

Sports: There are 11 intercollegiate sports for men and 9 for women, and 8 intramural sports for men and 8 for women. Facilities include a 2000-person-capacity multiuse coliseum with basketball and volleyball courts and a small indoor track. There is also a gym with exercise equipment and an area with 3 platforms for weight-lifting. The recreation facility has table tennis and table and video arcade games.

Disabled Students: Wheelchair ramps, elevators, special parking, lowered drinking fountains, and lowered telephones are available.

Services: Counseling and information services are available, as is tutoring in some subjects, including Spanish, math, English, and accounting. There is a reader service for the blind. There is a computerized center for skills development, and there are language and math labs.

Campus Safety and Security: Measures include 24-hour foot and vehicle patrol, pamphlets/posters/films, and lighted pathways/sidewalks.

Programs of Study: Inter confers B.A., B.S., B.B.A., and B.S.N. degrees. Associate and master's degrees are also awarded. Bachelor's degrees are awarded in BIOLOGICAL SCIENCE (biology/biological science and microbiology), BUSINESS (accounting, business administration and management, management information systems, marketing/retailing/merchandising, recreational facilities management, and secretarial studies/office management), COMPUTER AND PHYSICAL SCIENCE (computer science), EDUCATION (early childhood, elementary, and secondary), ENGINEERING AND ENVIRONMENTAL DESIGN (electrical/electronics engineering technology), HEALTH PROFESSIONS (mental health/human services and nursing), SOCIAL SCIENCE (criminal justice). Human psychosocial services, criminal justice, and computer science are the strongest academically and have the largest enrollments.

Required: To graduate, students must fulfill 44 to 47 general education credits depending on the major and including 23 credits in basic skills, 9 in historical and social context, 6 in philosophical and esthetic thought, and 3 each in Christian thought and science and technological context. A total of 120 credit hours is required; the number required in the major varies. A 2.0 GPA overall and in the major is required.

Special: The university offers internships in and out of Puerto Rico, work-study, and adult and continuing education programs. There is a freshman honors program.

Faculty/Classroom: 86% teach undergraduates. The average class size in an introductory lecture is 30; in a laboratory, 25; and in a regular course, 28.

Admissions: 86% of the 2003-2004 applicants were accepted.

Requirements: The SAT I is required. Native Spanish speakers may take the Spanish version of the SAT I. The SAT II: Writing test also is required. Applicants must be graduates of an accredited secondary school. An interview may be required. A GPA of 2.0 is required. AP and CLEP credits are accepted.

Procedure: Freshmen are admitted to all sessions. There is an early admissions plan. Applications should be filed by May 1 for fall entry, November 15 for winter entry, and April 15 for summer entry. Notification is sent on a rolling basis. Applications are accepted on-line.

Transfer: 86 transfer students enrolled in a recent year. Transfer applicants must submit all college transcripts and must be in good standing at their previous institution. A minimum of 15 transferable credits with a grade of at least C must have been completed.

Visiting: There are regularly scheduled orientations for prospective students.

Financial Aid: In 2003-2004, 92% of all full-time freshmen and 94% of continuing full-time students received some form of financial aid. 90% of full-time freshmen and 94% of continuing full-time students received need-based aid. The average freshman award was $7675. Need-based scholarships or need-based grants averaged $400 ($600 maximum); need-based self-help aid (loans and jobs) averaged $1000 ($3675 maximum); and non-need-based awards and non-need-based scholarships averaged $780 ($2000 maximum). 32% of undergraduates work part time. Average annual earnings from campus work are $800. Inter is a member of CSS. The FAFSA and the college's own financial statement are required. The deadline for filing freshman financial aid applications for fall entry is April 28.

International Students: A personal interview is required, as are satisfactory scores on an appropriate comprehensive exam.

Computers: The mainframe is an IBM RISC 6000 SP2. All students may access the system for distance learning, web browsing, e-mail, and library searches. There are no time limits and no fees.

Graduates: From July 1, 2002 to June 30, 2003, 350 bachelor's degrees were awarded. The most popular majors were human psychosocial services (10%), criminal justice (9%), and elementary teacher education (7%).

Admissions Contact: Doris Perez, Director of Admissions.
Web: *www.interaguadilla.edu*

INTER AMERICAN UNIVERSITY OF PUERTO RICO/ARECIBO CAMPUS

B-1

Arecibo, PR 00614-4050 (787) 878-5195; Fax: (787) 880-1624

Full-time: 1100 men, 2200 women	**Faculty:** 82
Part-time: 275 men, 550 women	**Ph.D.s:** 21%
Graduate: 5 men, 10 women	**Student/Faculty:** 40 to 1
Year: semesters, summer session	**Tuition:** $3300
Application Deadline: see profile	**Room & Board:** n/app
Freshman Class: n/av	
SAT I or ACT: n/av	

Inter American Arecibo, founded in 1957, is a private, nonsectarian unit of the Inter American University of Puerto Rico system. It offers programs in business, health sciences, liberal arts, and teacher preparation. Figures in above capsule and in this profile are approximate. The library contains 74,991 volumes, 82 microform items, and 28,665 audio/video tapes/CDs, and subscribes to 739 periodicals. Computerized library services include interlibrary loans and database searching. Special learning facilities include a learning resource center and a library exhibition area. The 20-acre campus is in a suburban area 50 miles west of San Juan. There are 9 buildings.

Student Life: 99% of undergraduates are from Puerto Rico. Students are from 1 state. 93% are from public schools. All are Hispanic. The average age of freshmen is 18; all undergraduates, 24. 11% do not continue beyond their first year.

Housing: There are no residence halls. All students commute. Alcohol is not permitted. All students may keep cars.

Activities: There are 2 local fraternities and 1 local sorority. There are 12 groups on campus, including drama, film, honors, newspaper, professional, religious, social, and student government. Popular campus events include Open House, Talent Festival, and sports events.

Sports: There are 7 intercollegiate sports for men and 7 for women, and 10 intramural sports for men and 10 for women. Facilities include a tennis court, a basketball court, and a student center with Ping-Pong tables and weight-lifting equipment.

Disabled Students: Wheelchair ramps, elevators, special parking, specially equipped rest rooms, lowered drinking fountains, and lowered telephones are available.

Services: Counseling and information services are available, as is tutoring in some subjects, including accounting, secretarial sciences, math, Spanish, English, and computer sciences. There is a reader service for the blind and remedial math.

Campus Safety and Security: Measures include 24-hour foot and vehicle patrol, pamphlets/posters/films, and lighted pathways/sidewalks.

Programs of Study: Inter American Arecibo confers B.A. and B.S. degrees. Associate and master's degrees are also awarded. Bachelor's degrees are awarded in BIOLOGICAL SCIENCE (biology/biological science and microbiology), BUSINESS (accounting, business administration and management, and marketing and distribution), COMPUTER AND PHYSICAL SCIENCE (chemical technology, chemistry, and computer science), EDUCATION (elementary, secondary, special, and teaching English as a second/foreign language (TESOL/TEFOL)), HEALTH PROFESSIONS (nursing), SOCIAL SCIENCE (criminal justice and social work). Biology, criminal justice, and business administration are the strongest academically. Business administration is the largest.

Required: To graduate, all students must complete at least 130 credits with a GPA of 2.0. General education requirements include 55 credits in Spanish, English, math, logic, computers, Puerto Rican history, humanities, health, social studies, environment, and religion. Noncredit courses are required in phys ed and orientation.

Special: The university offers 3-2 programs with Pennsylvania State University in engineering and earth and mineral sciences, and with Universidad Catolica Madre y Maestra of the Dominican Republic in medicine. Independent research, work-study, and independent study programs are available. Professional certificate programs are offered in nurse anesthetist and intensive nursing care. There is a freshman honors program.

Faculty/Classroom: 45% of faculty are male; 55%, female. All teach undergraduates. The average class size in an introductory lecture is 27 and in a laboratory, 25.

Requirements: In addition, applicants must present satisfactory scores on the aptitude and English tests of the CEEB. Students whose first language is English may take the SAT I. In addition, applicants should be graduates of an accredited high school. The GED is accepted. Secondary school preparation should include 15 to 30 academic credits. Some applicants may be required to schedule an interview. A GPA of 2.0 is required. Important factors in the admissions decision are advanced placement or honor courses, evidence of special talent, and leadership record.

Procedure: Freshmen are admitted to all sessions. Entrance exams should be taken in October or February of the senior year. There is an early decision plan and a rolling admissions plan. Check with the school for current application deadlines and fee. Notification is sent on a rolling basis.

Transfer: Applicants should present a C average in at least 15 college credits. Those with fewer transferable credits must meet freshman entrance requirements.

Visiting: There are regularly scheduled orientations for prospective students. There are guides for informal visits. To schedule a visit, contact the Admissions Office.

Financial Aid: 30% of undergraduates work part time. Average annual earnings from campus work are $400. Inter American Arecibo is a member of CSS. The CSS Profile and the college's own financial statement are required.

International Students: They must take the TOEFL and also take the SAT I.

Computers: The mainframe is an IBM RISC 6000 R30. All students may access the system. There are no time limits and no fees. It is strongly recommended that all students have a personal computer.

Admissions Contact: Provi Montalvo, Director of Admissions.
Web: *www.arecibo.inter.edu*

INTER AMERICAN UNIVERSITY OF PUERTO RICO/BARRANQUITAS REGIONAL COLLEGE

C-2

Barranquitas, PR 00794 (787) 857-3600

Full-time: 300 men, 830 women	**Faculty:** 40
Part-time: 150 men, 420 women	**Ph.D.s:** 1%
Graduate: none	**Student/Faculty:** 28 to 1
Year: semesters, summer session	**Tuition:** $3300
Application Deadline: see profile	**Room & Board:** n/app
Freshman Class: n/av	
SAT I or ACT: required	

Inter American University of Puerto Rico/Barranquitas Regional College, founded in 1957 and part of the Inter American University system, is a private college whose primary focus is teacher education. There are 6 undergraduate schools. Figures in the above capsule and in this profile are approximate. The library contains 32,275 volumes, 23,657 microform items, and 926 audio/video tapes/CDs, and subscribes to 223 periodicals. Computerized library services include the card catalog and interlibrary loans. Special learning facilities include a learning resource center. The 36-acre campus is in a small town. There are 5 buildings.

Student Life: All undergraduates are from Puerto Rico. All are Hispanic. The average age of freshmen is 18; all undergraduates, 22. 4% do not continue beyond their first year; 96% remain to graduate.

Housing: There are no residence halls. All students commute. Alcohol is not permitted. All students may keep cars.

Activities: There are no fraternities or sororities. There are 9 groups on campus, including chorus, dance, honors, religious, social, and student government. Popular campus events include Health Fair and Open House.

Sports: There are 8 intercollegiate sports for men and 7 for women, and 7 intramural sports for men and 6 for women. Facilities include a student center, a gym, volleyball and basketball courts, and a softball park.

Disabled Students: 1% of the campus is accessible. Wheelchair ramps and special parking are available.

Services: Counseling and information services are available, as is tutoring in some subjects, including Spanish, English, and math. There is a reader service for the blind and remedial math, reading, and writing.

Campus Safety and Security: Measures include 24-hour foot and vehicle patrol, pamphlets/posters/films, emergency telephones, and lighted pathways/sidewalks.

Programs of Study: Inter American at Barranquitas confers B.A. and B.B.A. degrees. Associate degrees are also awarded. Bachelor's degrees are awarded in BUSINESS (accounting, business administration and management, and secretarial studies/office management), EDUCATION (early childhood, elementary, and secondary), SOCIAL SCIENCE (criminal justice). Education, business administration, and secretarial studies are the strongest academically.

Required: In order to graduate, students must complete 120 to 132 credit hours with a minimum GPA of 2.0.

Special: Internships are available in education, secretarial studies, and criminal justice. There is 1 national honor society.

Requirements: The SAT I or ACT is required. In addition, SAT II: Subject tests are also required. A GPA of 2.0 is required. AP credits are accepted. Important factors in the admissions decision are evidence of special talent, advanced placement or honor courses, and leadership record.

Procedure: Freshmen are admitted fall, winter, and summer. Entrance exams should be taken in October, February, or June. There is an early admissions plan and a rolling admissions plan. Check with the school for current application deadlines and fee. Notification is sent on a rolling basis.

Transfer: Transfer applicants must submit a university transcript, dean's recommendation, and financial aid transcript. 36 of 120 credits required for the bachelor's degree must be completed at Inter American at Barranquitas.

Visiting: There are regularly scheduled orientations for prospective students. There are guides for informal visits. To schedule a visit, contact the Admissions Director.

Financial Aid: 45% of undergraduates work part time. Average annual earnings from campus work are $3000. Inter American at Barranquitas is a member of CSS.

International Students: They must take the college's own test and also take SAT II: Subject tests.

Computers: There are no time limits and no fees.

Admissions Contact: Maribel Diaz Pena, Director of Admissions.

INTER AMERICAN UNIVERSITY OF PUERTO RICO/BAYAMON UNIVERSITY COLLEGE

C-1

Bayamon, PR 00957

(787) 279-1912, ext. 2017
Fax: (787) 279-2205

Full-time: 2281 men, 1866 women	**Faculty:** 95
Part-time: 494 men, 380 women	**Ph.D.s:** 27%
Graduate: none	**Student/Faculty:** 44 to 1
Year: semesters, trimesters, summer session	**Tuition:** $3522
	Room & Board: n/app
Application Deadline: May 1	
Freshman Class: 3944 applied, 1347 accepted, 1239 enrolled	
SAT I: required	

Inter American University of Puerto Rico/Bayamon University College, a private, nonsectarian institution founded in 1912, is part of the Inter American University of Puerto Rico. Students may pursue undergraduate and graduate study in business, health sciences, liberal and fine arts, and teacher preparation. There are 3 undergraduate schools. In addition to regional accreditation, Inter American at Bayamon has baccalaureate program accreditation with CSWE. Computerized library services include the card catalog. Special learning facilities include an audiovisual center, an instructional development center, and a publication center. The campus is in an urban area in a medium-size city.

Student Life: 67% are from public schools. The average age of freshmen is 19; all undergraduates, 21.

Activities: There are many groups and organizations on campus, including band, cheerleading, chess, choir, computers, dance, debate, dra-

---

ma, ethnic, film, honors, international, newspaper, photography, professional, radio and TV, religious, social service, and student government.

Sports: There are 10 intercollegiate sports for men and 10 for women, and 10 intramural sports for men and 10 for women.

Disabled Students: Wheelchair ramps, elevators, special parking, lowered drinking fountains, and lowered telephones are available.

Campus Safety and Security: Measures include 24-hour foot and vehicle patrol, security escort services, informal discussions, and pamphlets/posters/films. There are lighted pathways/sidewalks.

Programs of Study: Inter American at Bayamon confers B.A., B.S., and B.B.A. degrees. Associate degrees are also awarded. Bachelor's degrees are awarded in BIOLOGICAL SCIENCE (bioinformatics, biology/biological science, and biotechnology), BUSINESS (accounting, banking and finance, business administration and management, business economics, human resources, logistics, management information systems, marketing/retailing/merchandising, office supervision and management, and secretarial studies/office management), COMMUNICATIONS AND THE ARTS (communications technology and visual and performing arts), COMPUTER AND PHYSICAL SCIENCE (chemical technology, chemistry, computer science, and mathematics), ENGINEERING AND ENVIRONMENTAL DESIGN (aeronautical science, aeronautical technology, aviation administration/management, aviation computer technology, computer technology, electrical/electronics engineering, electrical/electronics engineering technology, environmental engineering technology, food services technology, industrial administration/management, industrial engineering, and mechanical engineering), SOCIAL SCIENCE (forensic studies). Business administration is the largest.

Required: To graduate, students must earn a minimum of 110 academic credits, with a minimum GPA of 2.0 overall and in the major.

Faculty/Classroom: 60% of faculty are male; 40%, female. All teach undergraduates. The average class size in an introductory lecture is 19 and in a regular course, 23.

Admissions: 34% of the 2003-2004 applicants were accepted.

Requirements: The SAT I or its Spanish equivalent is required, along with the SAT II: Writing test. Applicants must be graduates of an accredited secondary school or its equivalent. A GPA of 2.0 is required.

Procedure: There is an early admissions plan. Applications should be filed by May 1 for fall entry, November 15 for winter entry, February 15 for spring entry, and April 15 for summer entry. Applications are accepted on-line.

Transfer: 132 transfer students enrolled in 2002-2003.

Financial Aid: The FAFSA and the college's own financial statement are required.

International Students: There are 5 international students enrolled. A personal interview is required, as is satisfactory completion of an appropriate comprehensive exam.

Computers: There are no time limits and no fees.

Graduates: From July 1, 2002 to June 30, 2003, 529 bachelor's degrees were awarded. The most popular majors were accounting (10%), management (10%), and human resources management (10%).

Admissions Contact: Carlos Alicea, Director of Admissions.
E-mail: *calicea@bc.inter.edu* Web: *www.bc.inter.edu*

INTER AMERICAN UNIVERSITY OF PUERTO RICO/FAJARDO CAMPUS

D-1

Fajardo, PR 00738-7003

(787) 860-3100, ext. 2210
Fax: (787) 860-3470

Full-time: 568 men, 1167 women	**Faculty:** 37
Part-time: 162 men, 343 women	**Ph.D.s:** 9%
Graduate: none	**Student/Faculty:** 47 to 1
Year: 4-1-4, summer session	**Tuition:** $4000
Application Deadline: August 15	**Room & Board:** n/app
Freshman Class: 1381 applied, 727 accepted, 507 enrolled	
SAT I or ACT: required	

Inter American University of Puerto Rico/Fajardo Campus, founded in 1912 and a unit of the Inter American University of Puerto Rico, is a private, nonsectarian college offering undergraduate and graduate degrees in business, fine and liberal arts, health sciences, and teacher preparation. In addition to regional accreditation, Inter at Fajardo has baccalaureate program accreditation with CSWE. The library contains 39,968 volumes and 1822 audio/video tapes/CDs. Computerized library services include the card catalog. Special learning facilities include an audiovisual center, a publication center, and an instructional development center. The 11-acre campus is in an urban area in a small city. There are 10 buildings.

Student Life: 90% are from public schools. The average age of freshmen is 18.

Housing: There are no residence halls. Alcohol is not permitted.

Activities: There are no fraternities or sororities. There are some groups and organizations on campus, including academic, chorale, cultural, professional, recreational, religious, and social.

Sports: There are 3 intercollegiate sports for men and 2 for women, and 4 intramural sports for men and 3 for women. Facilities include a multipurpose building.

Disabled Students: Wheelchair ramps, elevators, special parking, and specially equipped rest rooms are available.

Services: There is remedial math and reading.

Campus Safety and Security: Measures include pamphlets/posters/films.

Programs of Study: Inter at Fajardo confers B.A., B.S., and B.B.A. degrees. Associate, master's, and doctoral degrees are also awarded. Bachelor's degrees are awarded in BIOLOGICAL SCIENCE (biology/biological science), BUSINESS (accounting, banking and finance, business administration and management, insurance, management information systems, marketing/retailing/merchandising, and secretarial studies/office management), COMMUNICATIONS AND THE ARTS (applied music, Spanish, and visual and performing arts), COMPUTER AND PHYSICAL SCIENCE (chemical technology, chemistry, computer science, and mathematics), EDUCATION (early childhood, elementary, music, secondary, and special), ENGINEERING AND ENVIRONMENTAL DESIGN (electrical/electronics engineering technology), HEALTH PROFESSIONS (medical technology and nursing), SOCIAL SCIENCE (criminal justice, history, political science/government, psychology, public administration, social work, and sociology).

Required: To graduate, all students must complete 120 credit hours with a minimum GPA of 2.0 overall and in the major. General education requirements total 59 credits, including 18 credits in communication skills, 12 in historical-cultural heritage, 11 in ability to integrate, apply, and create, 8 in reasoning skills, 6 in methods of interpreting reality, and 2 nonacademic credits each in Introduction to University Life and health, phys ed, or recreation.

Special: Co-op programs in engineering and earth and mineral sciences with Pennsylvania State University, cross-registration, internships, work-study, and adult and continuing education programs are available. There is a freshman honors program.

Faculty/Classroom: 42% of faculty are male; 58%, female. The average class size in an introductory lecture is 25; in a laboratory, 20; and in a regular course, 25.

Admissions: 53% of the 2003-2004 applicants were accepted.

Requirements: The SAT I or ACT is required, as is the SAT II: Writing test. Native Spanish-speaking students may take the CEEB Spanish version of the SAT I. Students must have graduated from an accredited secondary school. An interview may be required. A GPA of 2.0 is required. AP credits are accepted.

Procedure: Freshmen are admitted to all sessions. There is an early admissions plan. Applications should be filed by August 15 for fall entry, November 15 for winter entry, and April 15 for spring entry. Notification is sent on a rolling basis.

Transfer: 47 transfer students enrolled in 2002-2003. Applicants must have completed at least 15 transferable semester credits with a minimum grade of C and must be in good standing at their previous institution. All college transcripts must be submitted.

Financial Aid: In 2003-2004, 98% of all full-time freshmen received some form of financial aid. Need-based scholarships or need-based grants averaged $3600. Average annual earnings from campus work are $400. The FAFSA and the college's own financial statement are required.

International Students: A personal interview and satisfactory scores on an appropriate comprehensive exam are required.

Computers: The mainframes are 3 Dell Poweredge 2300 and 2 Poweredge 4200 servers. 3 classrooms house a total of 75 computers in the technology center. All computers have Internet access. Each student is assigned a password and a log-in name at the beginning of the semester. All students may access the system. There are no time limits and no fees.

Graduates: From July 1, 2002 to June 30, 2003, 204 bachelor's degrees were awarded. The most popular majors were business administration (77%), education (19%), and science and technology (4%).

Admissions Contact: Ada Caraballo, Admissions Director. E-mail: *adcaraba@inter.edu* Web: *www.inter.edu*

INTER AMERICAN UNIVERSITY OF PUERTO RICO/METROPOLITAN CAMPUS

D-1

San Juan, PR 00919-1293   (787) 765-1270; Fax: (787) 764-6963

Full-time: 2108 men, 2730 women	**Faculty:** 159
Part-time: 963 men, 1293 women	**Ph.D.s:** 52%
Graduate: 1116 men, 2315 women	**Student/Faculty:** 30 to 1
Year: semesters, trimesters, summer session	**Tuition:** $4316
	Room & Board: n/app

Application Deadline: May 1
Freshman Class: 2215 applied, 1026 accepted, 807 enrolled
SAT I: recommended

Inter American University of Puerto Rico/Metropolitan Campus, a private, nonsectarian institution founded in 1912, is a unit of the Inter American University of Puerto Rico. Students may pursue undergraduate and graduate study in business, fine and liberal arts, health sciences, and teacher preparation. There are 6 undergraduate facilities and schools and 2 graduate schools. In addition to regional accreditation, Inter American Metro has baccalaureate program accreditation with ACS, CSWE, NAACLS, and NLN. The library contains 112,018 volumes, 638,026 microform items, and 1350 audio/video tapes/CDs, and subscribes to 2798 periodicals. Computerized library services include the card catalog, interlibrary loans, database searching, and Internet access. Special learning facilities include a learning resource center, art gallery, audiovisual center, instructional development center, and publication center. The 20-acre campus is in an urban area 9 miles from San Juan. There are 13 buildings.

Student Life: 99% of undergraduates are from Puerto Rico. 59% are from public schools. 98% are Hispanic. The average age of freshmen is 18; all undergraduates, 18.

Housing: All students commute. Alcohol is not permitted. All students may keep cars.

Activities: There are no fraternities or sororities. There are 23 groups on campus, including art, cheerleading, chorus, debate, drama, international, jazz band, orchestra, professional, religious, student government, symphony, and yearbook.

Sports: There are 7 intercollegiate sports for men and 7 for women, and 7 intramural sports for men and 7 for women.

Disabled Students: 90% of the campus is accessible. Wheelchair ramps, elevators, special parking, lowered drinking fountains, and lowered telephones are available.

Services: Counseling and information services are available, as is tutoring in some subjects, including Spanish, English, and math. There is a reader service for the blind. There also are interpreters for the hearing impaired.

Campus Safety and Security: Measures include 24-hour foot and vehicle patrol and pamphlets/posters/films.

Programs of Study: Inter American Metro confers B.A., B.S., and B.B.A. degrees. Associate, master's, and doctoral degrees are also awarded. Bachelor's degrees are awarded in BIOLOGICAL SCIENCE (biology/biological science), BUSINESS (accounting, banking and finance, business administration and management, management information systems, marketing/retailing/merchandising, and secretarial studies/office management), COMMUNICATIONS AND THE ARTS (music performance and Spanish), COMPUTER AND PHYSICAL SCIENCE (chemistry, computer science, and mathematics), EDUCATION (early childhood, elementary, secondary, and special), HEALTH PROFESSIONS (medical technology and nursing), SOCIAL SCIENCE (criminal justice, history, political science/government, psychology, social work, and sociology). Chemistry is the strongest academically.

Required: To graduate, students must complete 47 general education credits: 23 credits in basic skills, 9 credits in philosophical and esthetic thought, 9 in the historical process of Puerto Rico, 3 in scientific and technological context, and 3 in well-being and quality of life. A total of 120 credit hours must be completed; the number in the major varies. A minimum 2.0 GPA overall and in the major is required.

Special: Cross-registration, internship and work-study programs, and adult education programs are available. There is 1 national honor society and a freshman honors program.

Faculty/Classroom: 49% of faculty are male; 51%, female. 65% teach undergraduates and 5% both teach and do research. The average class size in an introductory lecture is 20 and in a laboratory, 22.

Admissions: 46% of the 2003-2004 applicants were accepted.

Requirements: The SAT I is recommended. Students whose first language is Spanish may take the CEEB Spanish version of the SAT I. A GPA of 2.0 is required.

Procedure: Freshmen are admitted to all sessions. Entrance exams should be taken by October. Applications should be filed by May 1 for fall entry, November 15 for spring entry, and April 15 for summer entry. Notification is sent on a rolling basis. Applications are accepted on-line through the university's web site.

Transfer: 223 transfer students enrolled in 2002-2003. Applicants must have completed at least 12 transferable semester credits with a minimum grade of C and be in good standing at the previous institution. 40 of 120 credits required for the bachelor's degree must be completed at Inter American Metro.

Visiting: There are regularly scheduled orientations for prospective students, including an open house twice a year. To schedule a visit, contact Edwin Mendez, Recruiter at (787) 250-1912, ext. 2102, 2463 or edmendez@inter.edu.

Financial Aid: In 2003-2004, 80% of all full-time freshmen and 82% of continuing full-time students received some form of financial aid. 79% of full-time freshmen and 81% of continuing full-time students received need-based aid. The FAFSA and the college's own financial statement are required.

International Students: A personal interview is required, as are satisfactory scores on an appropriate comprehensive exam.

Computers: 500 PCs are available in 36 rooms, and 200 PCs are in an open lab. All have access to the Internet and Web. All students may access the system Monday through Saturday. It is recommended that students in Economics and Administrative Sciences, Science and Technology, and distance education have personal computers.

Graduates: 40 companies recruited on campus in 2002-2003.

Admissions Contact: Lisette Rivera-Ortiz, Director of Admissions. A video is available. E-mail: lisriver@inter.edu Web: metro.inter.edu

INTER AMERICAN UNIVERSITY OF PUERTO RICO/PONCE REGIONAL COLLEGE   C-2
Ponce, PR 00715-2201   (787) 840-9090; Fax: (787) 841-0103

Full-time: 3000 men and women	Faculty: n/av
Part-time: none	Ph.D.s: n/av
Graduate: n/av	Student/Faculty: n/av
Year: semester, summer session	Tuition: $3700
Application Deadline: see profile	Room & Board: n/app
Freshman Class: n/av	
SAT I or ACT: n/av	

Inter American University of Puerto Rico/Ponce Regional College, founded in 1912 and a unit of the Inter American University of Puerto Rico, is a private, nonsectarian institution offering undergraduate and graduate programs in business, liberal and fine arts, health sciences, and teacher preparation. Figures in the above capsule and in this profile are approximate. In addition to regional accreditation, Inter American at Ponce has baccalaureate program accreditation with CSWE. Computerized library services include the card catalog. Special learning facilities include an audiovisual center, an instructional development center, and a publication center. The campus is in an urban area in a medium-size city.

Programs of Study: Bachelor's degrees are awarded in BIOLOGICAL SCIENCE (biology/biological science), BUSINESS (accounting, banking and finance, business administration and management, insurance, management information systems, marketing/retailing/merchandising, and secretarial studies/office management), COMMUNICATIONS AND THE ARTS (applied music, Spanish, and visual and performing arts), COMPUTER AND PHYSICAL SCIENCE (chemical technology, chemistry, computer science, and mathematics), EDUCATION (early childhood, elementary, music, secondary, and special), ENGINEERING AND ENVIRONMENTAL DESIGN (electrical/electronics engineering technology), HEALTH PROFESSIONS (medical technology and nursing), SOCIAL SCIENCE (criminal justice, history, political science/government, psychology, public administration, social work, and sociology).

Required: Check with the school for current information.

Requirements: Check with the school for current information.

Procedure: Check with the school for current application deadlines and fee.

Financial Aid: The FAFSA and the college's own financial statement are required. Check with the school for current deadlines.

International Students: A personal interview is required, as are satisfactory scores on an appropriate comprehensive exam.

Computers: There are no time limits and no fees.

Admissions Contact: Director of Admissions.

INTER AMERICAN UNIVERSITY OF PUERTO RICO/SAN GERMAN   B-2
San German, PR 00683-9801   (787) 892-3090
(800) 981-8075; Fax: (787) 892-6350

Full-time: 3878 men and women	Faculty: 116
Part-time: 1208 men and women	Ph.D.s: 43%
Graduate: 945 men and women	Student/Faculty: 33 to 1
Year: semesters, summer session	Tuition: $4316
Application Deadline: May 15	Room & Board: $2400
Freshman Class: 1611 applied, 1531 accepted, 1038 enrolled	
SAT I Verbal/Math: 475/498	

Inter American University of Puerto Rico/San German, founded in 1912, is a private institution that is part of the Inter-American University of Puerto Rico system. It offers programs in fine and liberal arts, business, health science, and teacher preparation. In addition to regional accreditation, the university has baccalaureate program accreditation with CAHEA. The library contains 153,431 volumes, 571,116 microform items, and 30,777 audio/video tapes/CDs, and subscribes to 3818 periodicals. Computerized library services include interlibrary loans. Special learning facilities include a learning resource center, art gallery, and natural history museum. The 260-acre campus is in a rural area 14 miles from Mayaguez. Including any residence halls, there are 64 buildings.

Student Life: 99% of undergraduates are from Puerto Rico. Students are from 9 foreign countries and Canada. 83% are from public schools. 99% are Hispanic. The average age of freshmen is 18; all undergraduates, 22. 28% do not continue beyond their first year; 41% remain to graduate.

Housing: 512 students can be accommodated in college housing, which includes single-sex dorms, on-campus apartments, and married-student housing. On-campus housing is guaranteed for all 4 years. 89% of students commute. Alcohol is not permitted. All students may keep cars.

Activities: There are no fraternities or sororities. There are 34 groups on campus, including art, band, choir, chorale, computers, dance, drama, ethnic, honors, international, jazz band, marching band, musical theater, newspaper, orchestra, political, professional, religious, social, social service, and student government. Popular campus events include Feria Tipica, Founders Celebration Dances, and intercollegiate sport events.

Sports: There are 11 intercollegiate sports for men and 6 for women, and 11 intramural sports for men and 6 for women. Facilities include a gym, dirt and tartan tracks, tennis courts, a jogging course, table tennis, a billiards room, table games, aerobics areas, a small gym in residence halls, and a gym with a basketball court.

Disabled Students: 80% of the campus is accessible. Wheelchair ramps, special parking, specially equipped rest rooms, special class scheduling, lowered drinking fountains, lowered telephones, and elevators in some buildings are available.

Services: Counseling and information services are available, as is tutoring in some subjects, including Spanish, English, math, and computer science.

Campus Safety and Security: Measures include 24-hour foot and vehicle patrol, shuttle buses, pamphlets/posters/films, and emergency telephones. There is an electronic security system.

Programs of Study: The university confers B.A., B.S., and B.B.A. degrees. Associate, master's, and doctoral degrees are also awarded. Bachelor's degrees are awarded in BIOLOGICAL SCIENCE (biology/biological science), BUSINESS (accounting, banking and finance, business administration and management, marketing/retailing/merchandising, and secretarial studies/office management), COMMUNICATIONS AND THE ARTS (English, fine arts, music, and Spanish), COMPUTER AND PHYSICAL SCIENCE (chemistry, computer science, and mathematics), EDUCATION (art, early childhood, elementary, health, music, science, secondary, special, and teaching English as a second/foreign language (TESOL/TEFOL)), HEALTH PROFESSIONS (medical laboratory technology, nursing, and premedicine), SOCIAL SCIENCE (economics, history, political science/government, psychology, public administration, and sociology). Business administration and medical technology are the strongest academically. Computer science, business administration, and biology are the largest.

Required: To graduate, students must complete at least 124 credits, with a minimum GPA of 2.5. General education requirements include courses in Spanish, English, mathematical reasoning, logical and critical reasoning, computer programming, and Puerto Rican history. In addition, students must take 6 credits in methods of interpreting reality, 2 in phys ed, computer science, and community service, and 1 each in art, music, ethics, and Puerto Rican culture.

Special: The university offers internships, credit by exam, and nondegree study. A 3-2 engineering degree is available with Penn State University. There are 2 national honor societies, and a freshman honors program.

Faculty/Classroom: 48% of faculty are male; 52%; female. 89% teach undergraduates. The average class size in an introductory lecture is 25; in a laboratory, 10; and in a regular course, 25.

Admissions: 95% of the 2003-2004 applicants were accepted. The SAT I scores for the 2003-2004 freshman class were: Verbal--68% below 500, 27% between 500 and 599, and 4% between 600 and 700; Math--63% below 500, 28% between 500 and 599, 8% between 600 and 700, and 1% above 700.

Requirements: The SAT I is required or the CEEB Spanish equivalent. Applicants must be high school graduates and have completed 15 credits, including 3 each in Spanish, English, and electives, and 2 each in math and science. A GPA of 2.5 is required. AP and CLEP credits are accepted. Important factors in the admissions decision are advanced placement or honor courses, evidence of special talent, and recommendations by school officials.

Procedure: Freshmen are admitted to all sessions. Entrance exams should be taken in the first or second semester of the senior year. There is an early admissions plan. Applications should be filed by May 15 for fall entry, November 15 for spring entry, and April 15 for summer entry. Notification of early decision is sent February 28; regular decision, May 30. Applications are accepted on-line through the school's web site.

Transfer: 474 transfer students enrolled in 2002-2003. Applicants should have at least 15 college credits with a minimum GPA of 2.5. The SAT I, or the CEEB Spanish version, is required, as is a letter of recommendation from the dean of students at the student's previous college. 30 of 124 credits required for the bachelor's degree must be completed at the university.

Visiting: There are regularly scheduled orientations for prospective students during the summer. There are guides for informal visits and visitors may sit in on classes and stay overnight. To schedule a visit, contact Professor Celia Gonzalez in Communications at (787) 264-1912 or *cgonzalez@sg.inter.edu*.

Financial Aid: In a recent year, 80% of all full-time students received some form of financial aid. 80% of all full-time students received need-based aid. The university is a member of CSS. The FAFSA, the college's own financial statement, and the application for Federal Student Aid (Pell Grant) are required. The deadline for filing freshman financial aid applications for fall entry is April 30.

International Students: There are 50 international students enrolled. They must take English or Spanish SAT I.

Computers: The mainframes are an IBM 9735 and a VAX 4000. There are also 1600 networked PCs on campus for student use. All students may access the system designated hours. There are no time limits. The fee is $30.

Graduates: From July 1, 2002 to June 30, 2003, 650 bachelor's degrees were awarded. The most popular majors were business administration (39%), biology (25%), and education (20%). 101 companies recruited on campus in 2002-2003.

Admissions Contact: Mildred Camacho, Director of Admissions. A video is available. E-mail: *milcama@sg.inter.edu*
Web: *www.sg.inter.edu*

PONTIFICAL CATHOLIC UNIVERSITY OF PUERTO RICO/PONCE   C-2

Ponce, PR 00717-0777

(787) 841-2000, ext. 1000
(800) 981-5040; Fax: (787) 651-2044

Full-time: 2272 men, 4464 women
Part-time: 477 men, 783 women
Graduate: 669 men, 1197 women
Year: semesters, summer session
Application Deadline: July 15
Freshman Class: 2042 applied, 1644 accepted, 1438 enrolled
SAT I: required

Faculty: 307
Ph.D.s: n/av
Student/Faculty: 22 to 1
Tuition: $4458
Room & Board: $2840

Pontifical Catholic University of Puerto Rico, founded in 1948, is a private institution affiliated with the Roman Catholic Church of Puerto Rico. The school offers undergraduate and graduate programs in liberal arts, the sciences, education, and business. There are 4 undergraduate and 6 graduate schools. In addition to regional accreditation, La Catolica has baccalaureate program accreditation with CSWE and NLN. The 2 libraries contain 238,033 volumes, 514,440 microform items, and 13,456 audio/video tapes/CDs, and subscribe to 58,183 periodicals. Computerized library services include the card catalog, interlibrary loans, and database searching. Special learning facilities include a learning resource center, radio station, TV station, and an electronic information center. The 55-acre campus is in an urban area 35 miles south of San Juan. Including any residence halls, there are 40 buildings.

Student Life: All undergraduates are from Puerto Rico. 80% are from public schools. All are Hispanic. The average age of freshmen is 19; all undergraduates, 22.

Housing: 180 students can be accommodated in college housing, which includes single-sex dorms. Priority for on-campus housing is given to out-of-town students. 97% of students commute. Alcohol is not permitted. All students may keep cars.

Activities: 1% of men belong to 11 local fraternities; 1% of women belong to 7 local sororities. There are 50 groups on campus, including art, band, choir, chorale, computers, dance, drama, honors, literary magazine, newspaper, photography, professional, radio and TV, religious, social service, student government, and yearbook. Popular campus events include freshman activities at the beginning of the academic year; religious and social activities celebrated on Thanksgiving, Christmas, and Holy Week; and Puerto Rican Culture Week.

Sports: There are 7 intercollegiate sports for men and 5 for women, and 6 intramural sports for men and 4 for women. Facilities include a gym, a 6000-seat arena, an Olympic-size pool, 5 tennis courts, 1 baseball field, 3 basketball courts, 3 volleyball courts, and a synthetic track and field.

Disabled Students: 95% of the campus is accessible. Wheelchair ramps, elevators, special parking, specially equipped rest rooms, special class scheduling, lowered drinking fountains, lowered telephones, a braille typewriter, an English and Spanish book reader, and a text enlarger are available.

Services: Counseling and information services are available, as is tutoring in some subjects, including math, chemistry, physics, English, Spanish, philosophy, statistics, accounting, and political science. There is a reader service for the blind and remedial math, reading, and writing. .

Campus Safety and Security: Measures include 24-hour foot and vehicle patrol, informal discussions, pamphlets/posters/films, and emergency telephones. There are lighted pathways/sidewalks.

Programs of Study: La Catolica confers B.A., B.S., B.B.A., and B.S.Ed. degrees. Associate, master's, and doctoral degrees are also awarded. Bachelor's degrees are awarded in BIOLOGICAL SCIENCE (biology/biological science), BUSINESS (accounting, banking and finance, business administration and management, business economics, international economics, and marketing/retailing/merchandising), COMMUNICATIONS AND THE ARTS (communications, English, fine arts, public relations, and Spanish), COMPUTER AND PHYSICAL SCIENCE (chemistry, computer programming, mathematics, and physics), EDUCATION (art, business, elementary, home economics, mathematics, music, physical, science, secondary, social studies, special, and teaching English as a second/foreign language (TESOL/TEFOL), HEALTH PROFESSIONS (medical laboratory technology and nursing), SOCIAL SCIENCE (criminology, gerontology, history, liberal arts/general studies, philosophy, political science/government, psychology, public administration, religion, social science, social work, sociology, and theological studies). Physical sciences is the strongest academically. General studies is the largest.

Required: Bachelor's candidates must complete a 136-credit program in not more than twice the usual number of years and maintain a GPA of 2.0. Required courses include theology, philosophy, humanities, English, Spanish, math, science, phys ed, social or political science, music or art, and basic computer. A thesis is required of Institute of Graduate Studies candidates.

Special: The university offers co-op programs in medicine, engineering, veterinary, and pharmacy, as well as cross-registration with the University of Valladolid and a 3-2 engineering degree with Case Western Reserve University. A Washington semester, work-study programs within the university, nondegree study, pass/fail options in elective courses, and a student-designed major in liberal arts are also available. There are 8 national honor societies, a freshman honors program, and 3 departmental honors programs.

Faculty/Classroom: 85% teach undergraduates and 1% do research. The average class size in an introductory lecture is 35; in a laboratory, 32; and in a regular course, 35.

Admissions: 81% of the 2003-2004 applicants were accepted.

Requirements: The SAT I is required, along with SAT II: Subject tests in math, Spanish, and English as a second language. In addition, applicants must be high school graduates or hold a GED. Students from 3-year senior high schools should have earned 10 units consisting of 3 each of English and Spanish, 2 of math, and 1 each of science and history. Students from 4-year high schools should have earned 15 units consisting of 4 each of English and Spanish, 3 of math, and 2 each of science and history. Students from outside Puerto Rico may substitute 2 years of another foreign language for the Spanish requirement. An interview is required for special programs. A GPA of 2.0 is required. AP and CLEP credits are accepted. Important factors in the admissions decision are advanced placement or honor courses, evidence of special talent, and leadership record.

Procedure: Freshmen are admitted to all sessions. Entrance exams should be taken during the fall of the senior year. Applications should be filed by July 15 for fall entry, December 1 for spring entry, and April 15 for summer entry, along with a $15 fee. Notification is sent on a rolling basis.

Transfer: 277 transfer students enrolled in 2002-2003. Applicants must supply a college transcript. A GPA of 2.0 and 30 credit hours are required. An associate degree is recommended. 30 of 136 credits required for the bachelor's degree must be completed at La Catolica.

Visiting: There are guides for informal visits and visitors may sit in on classes. To schedule a visit, contact Irem Poventud at (787) 841-2000, ext. 1245 or *ipoventud@pucpr.edu.*

Financial Aid: In a recent year, 85% of all full-time freshmen and 83% of continuing full-time students received some form of financial aid. 85% of full-time freshmen and 80% of continuing full-time students received need-based aid. The average freshman award was $1575. 19% of undergraduates work part time. Average annual earnings from campus work are $1545. The average financial indebtedness of the 2003 graduate was $4000. The FAFSA, the college's own financial statement, and income certification documents are required. The deadline for filing freshman financial aid applications for fall entry is May 9.

International Students: There were 7 international students enrolled in a recent year. The school actively recruits these students. They must take the SAT I or the ACT.

Computers: The mainframe is an IBM 9221-191. There are also 419 PCs available throughout the campus. All students may access the system 8 A.M. to 10 P.M. Monday through Thursday, and 8 A.M. to 5 P.M. Friday and Saturday. There are no time limits. The fee is included in the university fee.

Graduates: From July 1, 2002 to June 30, 2003, 848 bachelor's degrees were awarded. The most popular majors were nursing (10%), management and accounting (9%), and liberal arts (8%). In an average class, 1% graduate in 3 years or less, 8% graduate in 4 years or less, and 18% graduate in 5 years or less. 22 companies recruited on campus in a recent year.

Admissions Contact: Admissions Office. A video is available.
E-mail: *admisiones@pucpr.edu* Web: *www.pucpr.edu*

TURABO UNIVERSITY
Gurabo, PR 00658

D-1
(787) 746-3009

Full-time: 5400 men and women	**Faculty:** 100
Part-time: 1200 men and women	**Ph.D.s:** 33%
Graduate: 850 men and women	**Student/Faculty:** 30 to 1
Year: semesters, summer session	**Tuition:** $4110
Application Deadline: see profile	**Room & Board:** n/app
Freshman Class: n/av	
SAT I or ACT: n/av	

Turabo University, founded in 1972, is a private nonsectarian institution offering undergraduate programs in business administration, education, Spanish, social sciences, natural sciences and technology, and English and communications, and graduate programs in business administration and education. There are 2 graduate schools. Figures in above capsule and in this profile are approximate. The library contains 126,000 volumes. Computerized library services include the card catalog and database searching. Special learning facilities include a learning resource center, archeological-folkloric museum, and language lab. The 116-acre campus is in a suburban area 15 miles south of San Juan. There are 15 buildings.

Programs of Study: The university confers B.A., B.S., and B.B.A. degrees. Associate and master's degrees are also awarded. Bachelor's degrees are awarded in BIOLOGICAL SCIENCE (biology/biological science), BUSINESS (accounting, business administration and management, management science, marketing/retailing/merchandising, and secretarial studies/office management), COMMUNICATIONS AND THE ARTS (English and Spanish), COMPUTER AND PHYSICAL SCIENCE (chemistry, computer programming, mathematics, and natural sciences), EDUCATION (elementary, English, foreign languages, mathematics, physical, science, secondary, social science, and special), SOCIAL SCIENCE (criminology, economics, history, humanities, psychology, public administration, social science, and sociology).

Required: To graduate, students must complete course requirements with a minimum 2.0 GPA overall and 2.0 to 2.3 in the major.

Special: The university offers a general studies degree, graduate-level night courses in business and education, work-study, and nondegree study.

Faculty/Classroom: 50% of faculty are male; 50%, female.

Procedure: Check with the school for current application deadlines and fee.

Financial Aid: The FAFSA is required. Check with the school for current deadlines.

Computers: The schools of science, business administration, and engineering operate computer labs. There are no time limits and no fees.

Admissions Contact: Admissions Office Director.

UNIVERSIDAD ADVENTISTA DE LAS ANTILLAS
Mayaguez, PR 00681-0118

A-1
(787) 834-9595, ext. 2261
Fax: (787) 834-9597

Full-time: 311 men, 434 women	**Faculty:** 42
Part-time: 28 men, 48 women	**Ph.D.s:** 24%
Graduate: none	**Student/Faculty:** 18 to 1
Year: semesters, summer session	**Tuition:** $4110
Application Deadline: open	**Room & Board:** $1350
Freshman Class: 432 applied, 358 accepted, 235 enrolled	
SAT I or ACT: required	

Universidad Adventista de las Antillas, established in 1961 and affiliated with the Seventh-day Adventist Church, offers undergraduate programs in business administration, sciences and computers, education and psychology, nursing and allied health, music and fine arts, religion, and humanities. There are 7 undergraduate schools. In addition to regional accreditation, UAA has baccalaureate program accreditation with AHIMA and NLN. The library contains 88,432 volumes, 2603 microform items, and 1717 audio/video tapes/CDs, and subscribes to 392 periodicals. Computerized library services include the card catalog, interlibrary loans, database searching, and Internet access. Special learning facilities include a learning resource center. The 284-acre campus is in a small town on the west coast of Puerto Rico. Including any residence halls, there are 6 buildings.

Student Life: 89% of undergraduates are from Puerto Rico. Students are from 14 states, 22 foreign countries, and Canada. 37% are from public schools. 98% are Hispanic; 15% foreign nationals. 57% are Seventh-day Adventist; 23% Protestant; 17% Catholic. The average age of freshmen is 19; all undergraduates, 22. 30% do not continue beyond their first year; 70% remain to graduate.

Housing: 252 students can be accommodated in college housing, which includes single-sex dorms, on-campus apartments, and married-student housing. On-campus housing is guaranteed for all 4 years. 75% of students commute. Alcohol is not permitted. All students may keep cars.

Activities: 75% of men belong to 1 local fraternity; 80% of women belong to 1 local sorority. There are 20 groups on campus, including band, choir, chorale, chorus, drama, film, international, literary magazine, newspaper, orchestra, photography, professional, religious, social, social service, student government, and yearbook. Popular campus events include International Fair, Columbus Day, and Discovering Puerto Rico.

Sports: There are 4 intercollegiate sports for men and 3 for women, and 4 intramural sports for men and 3 for women. Facilities include a gym, a swimming pool, and a tennis court.

Disabled Students: 90% of the campus is accessible. Wheelchair ramps, special parking, specially equipped rest rooms, lowered drinking fountains, and lowered telephones are available.

Services: Counseling and information services are available, as is tutoring in some subjects, including math, English, and Spanish. There is remedial math, reading, and writing.

Campus Safety and Security: Measures include 24-hour foot and vehicle patrol.

Programs of Study: UAA confers B.A. and B.S. degrees. Associate and master's degrees are also awarded. Bachelor's degrees are awarded in BIOLOGICAL SCIENCE (biology/biological science), BUSINESS (business administration and management and office supervision and management), COMMUNICATIONS AND THE ARTS (music and Spanish), COMPUTER AND PHYSICAL SCIENCE (computer science), EDUCATION (elementary, music, and secondary), HEALTH PROFESSIONS (health science and nursing), SOCIAL SCIENCE (history, pastoral studies, religion, and theological studies). Business administration, nursing, and computer science are the strongest academically. Nursing is the largest.

Required: Students must complete 128 credits, with 44 to 66 in the major and a minimum GPA of 2.0. General education requirements include courses in religion, music or art, math, phys ed, computer science, Spanish, English, philosophy of education, and biological and physical sciences.

Special: Work-study programs, B.A.-B.S. degrees, credit by exam, and pass/fail options are available. There is a 3-2 engineering degree with Walla Walla University in Washington State.

Faculty/Classroom: 63% of faculty are male; 37%, female. All teach undergraduates. The average class size in an introductory lecture is 30; in a laboratory, 40; and in a regular course, 30.

Admissions: 83% of the 2003-2004 applicants were accepted.

Requirements: The SAT I or ACT is required, with a minimum recommended composite score on the SAT I of 840 or 18 on the ACT. In addition, graduation from an accredited secondary school is required; the GED is accepted. Applicants must submit 12 to 15 academic credits, including 3 each in English and a foreign language, 2 each in history, math, science, and social studies, and 1 to 2 in other electives. An interview is recommended. A GPA of 2.0 is required. AP and CLEP credits are accepted. Important factors in the admissions decision are advanced placement or honor courses, ability to finance college education, and parents or siblings attending the school.

Procedure: Freshmen are admitted to all sessions. Application deadlines are open. Application fee is $20.

Transfer: 52 transfer students enrolled in 2002-2003. Applicants must be in good standing at the previous institution, with a GPA of at least 2.0, and must submit official transcripts of high school and college credit. An official report of the CEEB Spanish equivalent of the SAT I must be provided if the applicant has completed fewer than 24 semester credits. 30 of 128 credits required for the bachelor's degree must be completed at UAA.

Visiting: There are regularly scheduled orientations for prospective students. There are guides for informal visits and visitors may sit in on classes and stay overnight. To schedule a visit, contact Dr. Myrna Costa at (787) 834-9595, ext. 2210 or mcosta@uaa.edu.

Financial Aid: In a recent year, all full-time students received some form of financial aid. 90% of full-time freshmen and 85% of continuing full-time students received need-based aid. The average freshman award was $7820. 26% of undergraduates work part time. Average annual earnings from campus work are $1400. UAA is a member of CSS. The CSS Profile or FAFSA and the college's own financial statement are required.

International Students: There were 13 international students enrolled in a recent year. They must take the university's own test and also take the SAT I, ACT, or the CEEB Spanish equivalent of the SAT I.

Computers: The mainframes are a DEC Vaxmate and a DEC MicroVAX II. 62 PCs and an IBM 386 server are also available. All students may access the system 7:30 A.M. to 10 P.M. The fee is $50. It is strongly recommended that all students have a personal computer.

Graduates: In a recent year, 116 bachelor's degrees were awarded. The most popular majors were nursing (60%), business administration (20%), and computer science (20%). In an average class, 30% graduate in 4 years or less, and 60% graduate in 5 years or less. Of a recent graduating class, 30% were enrolled in graduate school within 6 months of graduation and 50% were employed.

Admissions Contact: Evelyn del Valle, Director, Admissions and Continuing Education. A video is available. E-mail: edelvalle@uaa.edu or admissions@uaa.edu Web: www.uaa.edu

UNIVERSIDAD METROPOLITANA D-1
Rio Piedras, PR 00928 (787) 765-6262

Full-time: 3500 men and women	Faculty: n/av
Part-time: 1000 men and women	Ph.D.s: n/av
Graduate: n/av	Student/Faculty: 45 to 1
Year: semesters, summer session	Tuition: $3325
Application Deadline: open	Room & Board: n/app
Freshman Class: n/av	
SAT I: required	

Universidad Metropolitana, founded in 1980, is a private, commuter institution offering undergraduate programs in the liberal arts and sciences, business, nursing, and education. There are 6 undergraduate schools. Figures in above capsule and in this profile are approximate. In addition to regional accreditation, UMET has baccalaureate program accreditation with NLN. The library contains 34,445 volumes and 5000 microform items. Special learning facilities include a learning resource center and TV station. The campus is in an urban area. There are 11 buildings.

Programs of Study: UMET confers B.A., B.S., B.B.A., and B.S.N. degrees. Associate and master's degrees are also awarded. Bachelor's degrees are awarded in BUSINESS (accounting, business administration and management, and management science), COMPUTER AND PHYSICAL SCIENCE (natural sciences), EDUCATION (elementary and secondary), ENGINEERING AND ENVIRONMENTAL DESIGN (surveying engineering), HEALTH PROFESSIONS (nursing), SOCIAL SCIENCE (humanities, psychology, social science, and sociology). Business is the strongest academically. Education and natural sciences are the largest.

Required: To graduate, students must complete an average of 135 credits, including at least 30 in the major field. Specific GPA requirements vary by department. All students must take a computer course and complete a general education core.

Special: UMET offers work-study programs, B.A.-B.S. degrees, and an honors program in the natural sciences. The Televised Education Center (CET) offers students an opportunity for independent study.

Faculty/Classroom: 40% of faculty are male; 60%, female.

Requirements: The SAT I is required. In addition, applicants must be graduates of an accredited secondary school with a GPA of 2.0. Some programs have higher GPA requirements.

Procedure: Freshmen are admitted to all sessions. Application deadlines are open.

Transfer: All applicants must meet the GPA requirements of the program they wish to enter. Students should submit transcripts from all previous colleges attended as well as a letter of recommendation from the dean of the most recent institution. Grades of C or better transfer for credit.

Financial Aid: The college's own financial statement is required. Check with the school for current deadlines.

Admissions Contact: Office of Admissions.

UNIVERSIDAD POLITECNICA DE PUERTO RICO D-1
Hato Rey, PR 00918 (787) 754-8000, ext. 240

Full-time: 1975 men, 669 women	Faculty: 147
Part-time: 1997 men, 527 women	Ph.D.s: 20%
Graduate: 285 men, 204 women	Student/Faculty: 18 to 1
Year: trimesters, summer session	Tuition: $5370
Application Deadline: July 30	Room & Board: n/app
Freshman Class: n/av	
SAT I: required	

Universidad Politecnica de Puerto Rico is a private institution offering undergraduate programs in engineering, business administration, and architecture, and graduate programs in engineering management, civil engineering, manufacturing business administration, and environmental protection. There are 3 undergraduate schools and 1 graduate school. In addition to regional accreditation, La Poli has baccalaureate program accreditation with ABET. The library contains 90,346 volumes, 100 microform items, and 1971 audio/video tapes/CDs, and subscribes to 8376 periodicals. Computerized library services include the card catalog, interlibrary loans, database searching, and Internet access. Special learning facilities include a learning resource center, art gallery, TV studio, satellite dish, museum and historical archive of the university, and projection room. The 8-acre campus is in an urban area in the Hato Rey section of San Juan. There are 8 buildings.

Student Life: 99% of undergraduates are from Puerto Rico. Students are from 4 foreign countries. 50% are from public schools. All are Hispanic. Most are Catholic. The average age of freshmen is 18; all undergraduates, 25. 30% do not continue beyond their first year; 20% remain to graduate.

Housing: There are no residence halls. Alcohol is not permitted. All students may keep cars.

Activities: There are no fraternities or sororities. There are 8 groups on campus, including choir, honors, newspaper, political, professional, religious, and student government. Popular campus events include Student Night, Library Week, and Education Weeks.

Sports: There are 8 intercollegiate sports for men and 8 for women, and 10 intramural sports for men and 10 for women. Facilities include basketball and volleyball courts, a game room, and a gym.

Disabled Students: 90% of the campus is accessible. Wheelchair ramps, elevators, special parking, specially equipped rest rooms, and special class scheduling are available.

Services: Counseling and information services are available, as is tutoring in some subjects, including Spanish, English, math, and engineering. There is remedial math.

Campus Safety and Security: Measures include 24-hour foot and vehicle patrol, informal discussions, pamphlets/posters/films, and lighted pathways/sidewalks.

Programs of Study: La Poli confers B.S., B.B.A., and B.S.E. degrees. Master's degrees are also awarded. Bachelor's degrees are awarded in BUSINESS (business administration and management), ENGINEERING AND ENVIRONMENTAL DESIGN (chemical engineering, civil engineering, electrical/electronics engineering, environmental engineering, industrial administration/management, industrial engineering, mechanical engineering, and surveying engineering). Electrical and civil engineering are the strongest programs academically and have the largest enrollments.

Required: All graduating students must complete 128 to 176 quarter credits, with a minimum GPA of 2.0. There are distribution requirements in Spanish, English, humanities, social sciences, and math, and within the chosen field. All students must take 6 credits in Computer Science. All majors require a practicum course before graduation.

Special: Co-op programs are available in all majors. There is a freshman honors program.

Faculty/Classroom: 64% of faculty are male; 36%, female. All teach undergraduates. The average class size in an introductory lecture is 30; in a laboratory, 20; and in a regular course, 22.

Requirements: The CEEB Spanish equivalents of the SAT I and SAT II: Subject tests are required. Applicants must be graduates of an accredited secondary school, with 15 high school academic units. An interview is recommended. A GPA of 2.5 is required.

Procedure: Freshmen are admitted to all sessions. There are early decision and early admissions plans. Applications should be filed by July 30 for fall entry, October 13 for winter entry, February 26 for spring entry, and April 30 for summer entry. Notification is sent on a rolling basis.

Transfer: Applicants must present an official transcript and letters of recommendation. They must also have a GPA of 2.0 or higher and approved credits.

Visiting: There are regularly scheduled orientations for prospective students. To schedule a visit, contact Teresa Cardona, Director of Admissions.

Financial Aid: La Poli is a member of CSS. The FAFSA and the college's own financial statement are required. The deadline for filing freshman financial aid applications for fall entry is April 30.

International Students: These students must take the Spanish equivalent of the SAT I, scoring 1300.

Computers: PCs are available for student use. All students may access the system. There are no time limits. The fee is $35.

Admissions Contact: Teresa Cardona, Director of Admissions.
E-mail: *tcardona@pupr.edu* Web: *www.pupr.edu*

UNIVERSITY OF PUERTO RICO SYSTEM

The University of Puerto Rico System, established in 1903, is a public system in Puerto Rico. It is governed by the Puerto Rico Council on Higher Education, whose chief administrator is the president. The primary goal of the system is to serve as a center for scholarly research, to develop academic excellence, and to capitalize on its location as a focal point of the Caribbean region and the international community by developing programs germane to the residents of the region. The main priorities are to improve academic programs in key areas, to strengthen research and research training, and to upgrade physical facilities. The total enrollment of all campuses is about 69,000; there were about 4500 faculty members. Altogether there are 234 baccalaureate, 114 master's, and 21 doctoral programs offered in University of Puerto Rico System. 4-year campuses are located in Cayey, Humacao, Mayaguez, Rio Piedras, Arecibo, Bayamon, Ponce, and San Juan. Profiles of the 4-year campuses are included in this section.

UNIVERSITY OF PUERTO RICO AT HUMACAO   D-2
Humacao, PR 00791-4300   (809) 850-0000, ext. 9301
Fax: (787) 850-9428

Full-time: 1065 men, 2609 women	**Faculty:** 248; IIB, -$
Part-time: 204 men, 562 women	**Ph.D.s:** 37%
Graduate: none	**Student/Faculty:** 15 to 1
Year: semesters, summer session	**Tuition:** $1245
Application Deadline: November 14	**Room & Board:** n/app
Freshman Class: 1998 applied, 1064 accepted, 917 enrolled	
SAT I Verbal/Math: 526/531	

The University of Puerto Rico at Humacao, founded in 1962, is a public institution offering undergraduate programs in the arts and sciences, business, education, and nursing to an entirely commuter student body. Annual tuition and fees for nonresident U.S. citizens are an amount equal to the nonresident rate at a state university in their home state. In addition to regional accreditation, University of Puerto Rico at Humacao has baccalaureate program accreditation with ACOTE, APTA, CSWE, and NLN. The library contains 114,259 volumes, 10,221 microform items, and 396 audio/video tapes/CDs, and subscribes to 15,376 periodicals. Computerized library services include the card catalog, interlibrary loans, and database searching. Special learning facilities include a learning resource center, a museum, an observatory, a census data center, and web radio. The 62-acre campus is in a suburban area 30 miles southeast of San Juan. There are 30 buildings.

Student Life: 99% of undergraduates are from Puerto Rico. Students are from 2 states and 2 foreign countries. 82% are from public schools. All are Hispanic. The average age of freshmen is 18; all undergraduates, 22. 14% do not continue beyond their first year; 86% remain to graduate.

Housing: There are no residence halls. All of students commute. Alcohol is not permitted. Upperclassmen may keep cars.

Activities: There are 2 local fraternities. There are no sororities. There are 33 groups on campus, including cheerleading, chess, chorus, computers, dance, honors, literary magazine, pep band, photography, professional, religious, social, social service, student government, and web radio. Popular campus events include Shakespeare Festival, Women's Week, and Puerto Rican Culture Week.

Sports: There are 6 intercollegiate sports for men and 7 for women, and 4 intramural sports for men and 4 for women. Facilities include a 1000-seat gym, a track, 2 tennis courts, a softball field, a swimming pool, wrestling mats, and a student center.

Disabled Students: 98% of the campus is accessible. Wheelchair ramps, elevators, special parking, specially equipped rest rooms, lowered drinking fountains, and lowered telephones are available.

Services: Counseling and information services are available, as is tutoring in some subjects, including English, Spanish, and math. There is a reader service for the blind and remedial math, reading, and writing.

Campus Safety and Security: Measures include 24-hour foot and vehicle patrol, pamphlets/posters/films, and lighted pathways/sidewalks.

Programs of Study: University of Puerto Rico at Humacao confers B.A., B.S., and B.B.A. degrees. Associate degrees are also awarded. Bachelor's degrees are awarded in AGRICULTURE (wildlife management), BIOLOGICAL SCIENCE (biology/biological science, marine biology, and microbiology), BUSINESS (accounting, business administration

and management, human resources, and secretarial studies/office management), COMMUNICATIONS AND THE ARTS (English), COMPUTER AND PHYSICAL SCIENCE (chemistry, mathematics, and physics), EDUCATION (elementary), HEALTH PROFESSIONS (nursing and occupational therapy), SOCIAL SCIENCE (social work). Natural sciences is the strongest academically. Business administration is the largest.

Required: To graduate, students must complete 127 to 136 credit hours, including 18 to 56 in a major field, with a minimum GPA of 2.0. General education requirements include 33 to 73 liberal arts credits, with 6 credits in Spanish and 6 in English, humanities, and social sciences. Other distribution requirements vary by program.

Special: Students may study abroad through the National Student Exchange program. There are also co-op programs, internships in accounting, management, and human resources, work-study programs, credit for work experience, and a pass/fail option in remedial courses. Nondegree study is available through the Division of Continuing Education. The college offers programs in coastal marine biology, industrial microbiology, and industrial chemistry, and sponsors a Puerto Rican plain pigeon conservation project. There is 1 national honor society and a freshman honors program.

Faculty/Classroom: 46% of faculty are male; 54%, female. 86% teach undergraduates and 1% do research. The average class size in a laboratory is 17 and in a regular course, 21.

Admissions: 53% of the 2003-2004 applicants were accepted. The SAT I (Spanish) scores for the 2003-2004 freshman class were: Verbal--39% below 500, 44% between 500 and 599, 16% between 600 and 700, and 1% above 700; Math--35% below 500, 43% between 500 and 599, 18% between 600 and 700, and 4% above 700.

Requirements: The SAT I is required for U.S. applicants, or the CEEB's Spanish equivalent, as well as SAT II: Subject tests in writing, Spanish, and mathematics level I. Applicants must be graduates of an accredited secondary school or have earned the GED. College preparatory study should include 3 credits each in English, Spanish, and math, 2 in history, and 1 in social studies. All courses are conducted in Spanish only. Nonnative speakers of Spanish are required to demonstrate fluency through institutional examination interviews. A GPA of 2.0 is required. AP credits are accepted.

Procedure: Freshmen are admitted in the fall. Entrance exams should be taken by October or February of the senior year. There are early decision and deferred admissions plans. Applications should be filed by November 14 for fall entry, along with a $15 fee. Notification is sent in April. Applications are accepted on-line through the university's web site.

Transfer: 28 transfer students enrolled in 2002-2003. Applicants to the bachelor's programs must have at least 30 college credits with a minimum GPA of 3.0 and must be in good standing at their previous institution. The last 30 of 127 to 136 credits required for the bachelor's degree must be completed at University of Puerto Rico at Humacao.

Visiting: There are regularly scheduled orientations for prospective students. To schedule a visit, contact Milagros Alvarez at (809) 850-0000, ext. 9238 or *mi_alvarez@webmail.uprh.edu*.

Financial Aid: In 2003-2004, 85% of all full-time freshmen and 80% of continuing full-time students received some form of financial aid. 85% of full-time freshmen and 79% of continuing full-time students received need-based aid. The average freshman award was $4108. Need-based scholarships or need-based grants averaged $4096; and need-based self-help aid (loans and jobs) averaged $3932. 7% of undergraduates work part time. Average annual earnings from campus work are $1165. The FAFSA is required. The deadline for filing freshman financial aid applications for fall entry is June 30.

International Students: They must take the TOEFL and also take the CEEB's Spanish version of the SAT I. This consists of an aptitude test (verbal and math) and an achievement test battery (Spanish, English, and math). Alternatively, they may take the SAT I and SAT II: Subject tests in English writing and Spanish reading.

Computers: The mainframe is a DEC Alpha 4100. There are 206 PCs in 6 campus labs. All students may access the system daily until 10 P.M. There are no time limits and no fees.

Graduates: From July 1, 2002 to June 30, 2003, 489 bachelor's degrees were awarded. The most popular majors were accounting (12%), human resources (9%), and elementary education (9%). In an average class, 11% graduate in 3 years or less, 28% graduate in 4 years or less, 48% graduate in 5 years or less, and 53% graduate in 6 years or less. 8 companies recruited on campus in 2002-2003.

Admissions Contact: Inara Ferrer, Director of Admissions.
E-mail: *i_ferrer@webmail.uprh.edu*

UNIVERSITY OF PUERTO RICO/ARECIBO B-1
Arecibo, PR 00613   (787) 878-2830, ext. 4101; Fax: (787) 880-4972

Full-time: 1165 men, 2720 women	**Faculty:** 227
Part-time: 250 men, 535 women	**Ph.D.s:** 13%
Graduate: none	**Student/Faculty:** 17 to 1
Year: semesters, summer session	**Tuition:** $1095
Application Deadline: see profile	**Room & Board:** n/app
Freshman Class: 4121 applied, 1261 accepted, 998 enrolled	
SAT I: required	**ACT:** n/av

University of Puerto Rico/Arecibo (formerly Arecibo Technological University College), founded in 1967, offers undergraduate programs in business administration, health sciences, natural sciences, education, computer sciences, telecommunications, and others. Tuition and fees for Puerto Rican residents total $1095 per year; nonresidents pay an amount equal to the nonresident rate at a state university in their home state. Figures in the above capsule and in this profile are approximate. In addition to regional accreditation, UPRA has baccalaureate program accreditation with NLN. The library contains 71,000 volumes, 6400 microform items, and 1900 audio/video tapes/CDs, and subscribes to 1500 periodicals. Computerized library services include database searching. Special learning facilities include a learning resource center and art gallery. The 49-acre campus is in an urban area 40 miles west of San Juan. There is 1 building.

Student Life: 90% are from public schools. All are Hispanic. The average age of freshmen is 18; all undergraduates, 18. 18% do not continue beyond their first year.

Housing: There are no residence halls. All students commute. Alcohol is not permitted. All students may keep cars.

Activities: 10% of men belong to 5 local fraternities; 12% of women belong to 5 local sororities. There are 24 groups on campus, including art, band, chorus, dance, drama, film, newspaper, photography, political, professional, religious, social, social service, and student government. Popular campus events include fairs, plays, and concerts.

Sports: There are 8 intercollegiate sports for men and 5 for women, and 9 intramural sports for men and 8 for women. Facilities include basketball and tennis courts, a gym, track and field facilities, and an activity room.

Disabled Students: 90% of the campus is accessible. Wheelchair ramps, elevators, special parking, specially equipped rest rooms, lowered drinking fountains, and lowered telephones are available.

Services: Counseling and information services are available, as is tutoring in most subjects. There is remedial math, reading, and writing.

Campus Safety and Security: Measures include 24-hour foot and vehicle patrol, pamphlets/posters/films, and lighted pathways/sidewalks.

Programs of Study: UPRA confers B.A. and B.S. degrees. Associate degrees are also awarded. Bachelor's degrees are awarded in BIOLOGICAL SCIENCE (microbiology), BUSINESS (business administration and management and secretarial studies/office management), COMMUNICATIONS AND THE ARTS (telecommunications), COMPUTER AND PHYSICAL SCIENCE (computer science), EDUCATION (elementary), ENGINEERING AND ENVIRONMENTAL DESIGN (chemical engineering technology), HEALTH PROFESSIONS (nursing). Natural sciences is the strongest academically. Business administration is the largest.

Required: To graduate, students must have a 2.0 GPA. The total number of credit hours required varies according to major. The core curriculum includes 2 semesters each of English, Spanish, math, and social sciences or humanities.

Special: There is a chapter of Phi Beta Kappa and a freshman honors program.

Faculty/Classroom: 48% of faculty are male; 52%, female. 99% teach undergraduates and 1% do research. The average class size in an introductory lecture is 28; in a laboratory, 18; and in a regular course, 25.

Requirements: The SAT I is required. In addition, a Spanish version of the SAT I or the College Entrance Examination Board test (CEEB) is accepted. A GPA of 2.0 is required. AP credits are accepted.

Procedure: Freshmen are admitted in the fall. Entrance exams should be taken by October of the senior year. There is an early decision plan. Check with the school for current application deadlines. The fall 2003 application fee was $15.

Transfer: Applicants should have a minimum of 24 credits with a 2.5 GPA.

Visiting: To schedule a visit, contact the Dean of Student Affairs.

Financial Aid: 8% of undergraduates work part time. Average annual earnings from campus work are approximately $1300. UPRA is a member of CSS. The college's own financial statement is required. Check with the school for current deadlines.

International Students: Students must take the College Board.

Computers: The mainframes are a DEC VAX 4000-300 (academic) and a DEC Alpha 2100 (administrative). There are 15 computer labs with PCs. Word processors and specialized software are available. Students may access the local net and the Internet. All students may access the system. There are no time limits and no fees.

Graduates: In an average class, 6% graduate in 3 years or less, 18% graduate in 4 years or less, 45% graduate in 5 years or less, and 57% graduate in 6 years or less.

Admissions Contact: Delma Barrios, Admissions Director. E-mail: d_barrios@cuta.upr.clu.edu Web: upra.epr.clu.edu

UNIVERSITY OF PUERTO RICO/BAYAMON A-1
UNIVERSITY COLLEGE CAMPUS
Bayamon, PR 00959-1919   (787) 786-2885, ext. 2426

Full-time: 1781 men, 2316 women	**Faculty:** 230
Part-time: 547 men, 680 women	**Ph.D.s:** 21%
Graduate: none	**Student/Faculty:** 18 to 1
Year: semesters, summer session	**Tuition:** $1600
Application Deadline: December 20	**Room & Board:** n/app
Freshman Class: n/av	
SAT I or ACT: required	

Bayamon University College, a commuter institution founded in 1971, is part of the University of Puerto Rico system. It offers undergraduate business, education, and technical programs. Approximate tuition and fees for Puerto Rican residents total $1600 per year; nonresident U.S. citizens pay an amount equal to the nonresident rate at a state university in their home state. The library contains 67,020 volumes, 247,302 microform items, and 5103 audio/video tapes/CDs, and subscribes to 273 periodicals. Computerized library services include the card catalog and database searching. Special learning facilities include a learning resource center. The 78-acre campus is in a suburban area 9 miles west of San Juan. There are 20 buildings.

Student Life: All undergraduates are from Puerto Rico. 53% are from public schools. All are Hispanic. The average age of freshmen is 18; all undergraduates, 21. 24% do not continue beyond their first year; 75% remain to graduate.

Housing: There are no residence halls. All students commute. Alcohol is not permitted. All students may keep cars.

Activities: There are no fraternities or sororities. There are 15 groups on campus, including art, band, cheerleading, chess, choir, chorus, computers, drama, drill team, honors, professional, religious, social, social service, and student government. Popular campus events include an annual sports tournament, recognition of distinguished athletes, and the college anniversary.

Sports: There are 13 intercollegiate sports for men and 10 for women. Facilities include a basketball/volleyball court, a tennis court, a track and field site, an exercise gym, and a recreation room with table tennis, electronic games, and pool tables.

Disabled Students: 90% of the campus is accessible. Wheelchair ramps, special parking, specially equipped rest rooms, lowered drinking fountains, and lowered telephones are available.

Services: Counseling and information services are available, as is tutoring in some subjects, including English, math, Spanish, and physics for engineering and electronics students. There is a reader service for the blind and remedial math.

Campus Safety and Security: Measures include 24-hour foot and vehicle patrol and pamphlets/posters/films.

Programs of Study: UPR-Bayamon confers the B.A. degree. Associate degrees are also awarded. Bachelor's degrees are awarded in BUSINESS (accounting, banking and finance, business administration and management, management engineering, and marketing/retailing/merchandising), COMPUTER AND PHYSICAL SCIENCE (computer science and information sciences and systems), EDUCATION (early childhood and elementary), ENGINEERING AND ENVIRONMENTAL DESIGN (electrical/electronics engineering technology). Electronics, computer science, and office systems are the strongest academically. Business administration is the largest.

Required: General education requirements include courses in Spanish, English, math, social sciences or humanities, and biological or physical sciences. To graduate, students must complete 130 to 135 credits, including 29 to 34 in the major, with a minimum GPA of 2.0.

Special: Students may cross-register with any campus in the University of Puerto Rico system. Work-study programs, dual majors, pass/fail options, and a 3-2 engineering degree with the Mayaguez campus are also available. There is a freshman honors program.

Faculty/Classroom: 44% of faculty are male; 56%, female. All teach undergraduates. The average class size in an introductory lecture is 23 and in a laboratory, 20.

Requirements: The SAT I or ACT is required, or the CEEB's Spanish version of the SAT I, along with SAT II: Subject tests in Spanish, writing, and math. Applicants must be graduates of accredited secondary schools. The GED is accepted. A GPA of 2.0 is required.

Procedure: Freshmen are admitted in the fall. Entrance exams should be taken by October of the senior year. There is an early decision plan. Applications should be filed by December 20 for fall entry and September 15 for spring entry. Notification of early decision is sent February 15; regular decision, May 1.

Transfer: 146 transfer students enrolled in 2002-2003. Applicants must present an associate degree or at least 30 college credits and a minimum GPA of 2.5. 28 of 130 to 135 credits required for the bachelor's degree must be completed at UPR-Bayamon.

Visiting: There are regularly scheduled orientations for prospective students. To schedule a visit, contact the Director of Admissions.

Financial Aid: In a recent year, 29% of all full-time freshmen and 71% of continuing full-time students received some form of financial aid. 29% of full-time freshmen and 71% of continuing full-time students received need-based aid. The average freshman award was $3726. UPR-Bayamon is a member of CSS. The CSS Profile, the college's own financial statement, income tax forms, medical receipts, and social security information are required. The deadline for filing freshman financial aid applications for fall entry is June 2.

International Students: There were 11 international students enrolled in a recent year. They must take the SAT I or the Spanish equivalent version of the SAT I. Students must take SAT II: Subject tests in Spanish, writing, and math.

Computers: There are 800 PCs located in computer centers. All students may access the system daily from 8 A.M. to 10 P.M. and Saturday from 8 A.M. to 4:30 P.M. There are no time limits and no fees.

Graduates: From July 1, 2002 to June 30, 2003, 551 bachelor's degrees were awarded. The most popular majors were accounting (11%), office systems (10%), and management (7%). In an average class, 16% graduate in 4 years or less, 31% graduate in 5 years or less, and 13% graduate in 6 years or less. 27 companies recruited on campus in 2002-2003.

Admissions Contact: Vivian Rivera, Director of Admissions.

UNIVERSITY OF PUERTO RICO/CAYEY UNIVERSITY COLLEGE   C-2

Cayey, PR 00736	(809) 738-2161, ext. 2208
Full-time: 1027 men, 2568 women	Faculty: 181
Part-time: 102 men, 290 women	Ph.D.s: 48%
Graduate: none	Student/Faculty: 20 to 1
Year: semesters, summer session	Tuition: $1245 ($2400)
Application Deadline: October 28	Room & Board: n/app
Freshman Class: 887 enrolled	
SAT I: required	

Cayey University College, founded in 1967, is a public liberal arts institution and part of the University of Puerto Rico. The library contains 107,365 volumes, 49 microform items, and 3965 audio/video tapes/CDs, and subscribes to 424 periodicals. Computerized library services include the card catalog, interlibrary loans, and database searching. Special learning facilities include a learning resource center and an art museum. The 167-acre campus is in an urban area 30 miles south of San Juan. There are 54 buildings.

Student Life: 85% are from public schools. All are Hispanic. The average age of freshmen is 18; all undergraduates, 22. 15% do not continue beyond their first year; 85% remain to graduate.

Housing: There are no residence halls. All of students commute. Alcohol is not permitted. All students may keep cars.

Activities: There is 1 local fraternity. There are no sororities. There are 17 groups on campus, including band, cheerleading, chorus, drama, honors, marching band, orchestra, political, professional, religious, and student government. Popular campus events include Student Day.

Sports: There are 10 intercollegiate sports for men and 6 for women, and 9 intramural sports for men and 8 for women. Facilities include a gym, a pool, and tennis, basketball, and volleyball courts.

Disabled Students: All of the campus is accessible. Wheelchair ramps, elevators, special parking, specially equipped rest rooms, lowered drinking fountains, and lowered telephones are available.

Services: Counseling and information services are available, as is tutoring in most subjects. There is a reader service for the blind and remedial math, reading, and writing.

Campus Safety and Security: Measures include 24-hour foot and vehicle patrol, shuttle buses, and lighted pathways/sidewalks.

Programs of Study: Cayey University College confers B.A., B.S., B.B.A., B.Ed., and B.S.Ed. degrees. Associate degrees are also awarded. Bachelor's degrees are awarded in BIOLOGICAL SCIENCE (biology/biological science), BUSINESS (accounting, business administration and management, management science, and secretarial studies/office management), COMMUNICATIONS AND THE ARTS (English), COMPUTER AND PHYSICAL SCIENCE (chemistry, mathematics, and natural sciences), EDUCATION (elementary, secondary, and special), SOCIAL SCIENCE (economics, Hispanic American studies, history, humanities, and psychology). Natural science is the strongest academically. Natural science, secondary education, and biology are the largest.

Required: To graduate, students must complete 129 to 135 credits, including 28 in the major, with a minimum GPA of 2.0. There are requirements in humanities, social science, Spanish, English, and natural science. All students must take 2 courses in phys ed.

Special: The university offers cross-registration through the National Student Exchange, study abroad in Toledo, Spain, and a Washington semester. There is 1 national honor society, including Phi Beta Kappa, and a freshman honors program.

Faculty/Classroom: 55% of faculty are male; 45%, female. 99% teach undergraduates and 1% do research. The average class size in an introductory lecture is 30; in a laboratory, 20; and in a regular course, 30.

Admissions: In a recent year 40% of the current freshmen were in the top fifth of their class; 63% were in the top two fifths.

Requirements: The SAT I is required or its CEEB Spanish equivalent. Applicants must be graduates of an accredited secondary school. The GED is accepted. Students should complete 3 high school courses each in English, Spanish, math, science, and social studies. A GPA of 2.0 is required. CLEP credit is accepted. Advanced placement or honor courses is an important factor in the admission decision.

Procedure: Freshmen are admitted in the fall. Entrance exams should be taken in October of the senior year. There is a deferred admissions plan. Applications should be filed by October 28 for fall entry and November 14 for winter entry, along with a $15 fee. Applications are accepted on-line through the college's web site.

Transfer: 30 transfer students enrolled in 2002-2003. Applicants should have 48 approved credit hours toward the program they are entering. 40 or more of 129 to 135 credits required for the bachelor's degree must be completed at Cayey University College.

Visiting: Visitors may sit in on classes. To schedule a visit, contact Maria Montalvo at (809) 738-2161, ext. 2053.

Financial Aid: In 2003-2004, 86% of all full-time freshmen and 78% of continuing full-time students received some form of financial aid. 71% of full-time freshmen and 78% of continuing full-time students received need-based aid. The average freshman award was $5485. 6% of undergraduates work part time. The CSS Profile or FAFSA is required. The deadline for filing freshman financial aid applications for fall entry is May 29.

International Students: There are 11 international students enrolled. They must take the SAT I, ACT, or the CEEB Spanish equivalent of the SAT I.

Computers: The mainframe is a Compaq AlphaServer DS10. There are 10 computer labs operating the various Windows programs. All students may access the system from 7 P.M. to 9 P.M. Monday through Thursday, and Friday from 7 A.M. to 4:30 P.M. There are no time limits and no fees.

Graduates: From July 1, 2002 to June 30, 2003, 528 bachelor's degrees were awarded. The most popular majors were accounting (15%), education (14%), and biology (10%). In an average class, 1% graduate in 3 years or less, 5% graduate in 4 years or less, 22% graduate in 5 years or less, and 35% graduate in 6 years or less.

Admissions Contact: Wilfredo Lopez, Admissions Office.
Web: *www@cayey.upr.edu*

UNIVERSITY OF PUERTO RICO/HUMACAO UNIVERSITY COLLEGE
(See University of Puerto Rico at Humacao)

UNIVERSITY OF PUERTO RICO/MAYAGUEZ   A-1

Mayaguez, PR 00680	(787) 265-3811; Fax: (787) 834-5265
Full-time: 5091 men, 4947 women	Faculty: 666
Part-time: 471 men, 570 women	Ph.D.s: 64%
Graduate: 543 men, 526 women	Student/Faculty: 15 to 1
Year: semesters, summer session	Tuition: $1245 ($2820)
Application Deadline: November 15	Room & Board: n/app
Freshman Class: 3492 applied, 2662 accepted, 2256 enrolled	
SAT I Verbal/Math: 550/550	

The University of Puerto Rico/Mayaguez, founded in 1911, is a bilingual land-grant institution offering undergraduate programs in arts and sciences, business administration, agricultural sciences, and engineering. There are 4 undergraduate and 4 graduate schools. In addition to regional accreditation, the university has baccalaureate program accreditation with ABET and NLN. The library contains 783,905 volumes, 345,052 microform items, and 43,610 audio/video tapes/CDs, and subscribes to 2171 periodicals. Computerized library services include interlibrary loans, database searching, and Internet access. Special learning facilities include a learning resource center, art gallery, natural history museum, planetarium, sea grant program, and resource center for science and engineering. The 520-acre campus is in an urban area 70 miles west of San Juan. There are 63 buildings.

Student Life: 99% of students are from Puerto Rico. Students are from 9 foreign countries and Canada. 59% are from public schools. 99% are Hispanic. The average age of freshmen is 18; all undergraduates, 21. 10% do not continue beyond their first year; 52% remain to graduate.

Housing: There are no residence halls. Alcohol is not permitted. All students may keep cars.

Activities: 5% of men belong to 6 local and 1 national fraternity; 2% of women belong to 3 local sororities. There are 90 groups on campus, including band, cheerleading, chess, choir, chorale, chorus, computers, dance, debate, drama, drill team, drum and bugle corps, ethnic, honors, international, jazz band, literary magazine, marching band, newspaper, orchestra, photography, political, professional, religious, social, social service, student government, and yearbook. Popular campus events include fairs, concerts, and dances.

Sports: There are 12 intercollegiate sports for men and 9 for women, and 15 intramural sports for men and 11 for women. Facilities include a gym, a coliseum, a swimming pool, and 2 playing fields.

Disabled Students: 90% of the campus is accessible. Wheelchair ramps, elevators, special parking, specially equipped rest rooms, special class scheduling, lowered drinking fountains, and lowered telephones are available.

Services: Counseling and information services are available, as is tutoring in most subjects. There is a reader service for the blind and remedial math and reading.

Campus Safety and Security: Measures include 24-hour foot and vehicle patrol, shuttle buses, informal discussions, and pamphlets/posters/films. There are emergency telephones and lighted pathways/sidewalks.

Programs of Study: The university confers B.A., B.S., B.B.A., and B.S.A. degrees. Associate, master's, and doctoral degrees are also awarded. Bachelor's degrees are awarded in AGRICULTURE (animal science and horticulture), BIOLOGICAL SCIENCE (biochemistry, biology/biological science, biotechnology, and microbiology), BUSINESS (accounting, banking and finance, business administration and management, business economics, and marketing/retailing/merchandising), COMMUNICATIONS AND THE ARTS (English, fine arts, and French), COMPUTER AND PHYSICAL SCIENCE (chemistry, computer science, geology, information sciences and systems, mathematics, and physics), EDUCATION (foreign languages and teaching English as a second/foreign language (TESOL/TEFOL)), ENGINEERING AND ENVIRONMENTAL DESIGN (chemical engineering, civil engineering, computer engineering, electrical/electronics engineering, engineering, industrial engineering, mechanical engineering, and surveying engineering), HEALTH PROFESSIONS (nursing and premedicine), SOCIAL SCIENCE (economics, history, philosophy, political science/government, psychology, social science, and sociology). Engineering, business administration, and agricultural science are the strongest academically. Electrical, chemical, and civil engineering are the largest.

Required: To graduate, students must complete 172 credit hours with a GPA of 2.0. Required disciplines include humanities, English, Spanish, physical science, biology, social science, math, and phys ed.

Special: The university offers co-op programs in engineering, business, and nursing, as well as some study abroad. There is 1 national honor society and a freshman honors program.

Faculty/Classroom: 65% of faculty are male; 35%, female. 23% do research. The average class size in an introductory lecture is 30; in a laboratory, 20; and in a regular course, 30.

Admissions: 76% of the 2003-2004 applicants were accepted.

Requirements: The SAT I is required, or the CEEB's Spanish equivalent, along with SAT II: Subject tests in writing, Spanish and Spanish reading, and mathematics level I. Applicants must be high school graduates or hold the GED. CLEP credit is accepted.

Procedure: Freshmen are admitted in the fall. Entrance exams should be taken during the first semester of the senior year. There is an early admissions plan. Applications should be filed by November 15 for fall entry. Notification is sent in May.

Transfer: Applicants must have 48 college credits with a GPA of 2.0.

Financial Aid: In a recent year, 69% of full-time freshmen received need-based aid. The average freshman award was $4350. The university is a member of CSS. The university's own financial statement is required. The deadline for filing freshman financial aid applications for fall entry is July 15.

International Students: The school actively recruits these students. They must take the SAT I and SAT II: Subject tests in mathematics level I C4 or level II C4, Spanish (reading), and English (literature or writing).

Computers: The mainframes are a DEC VAX 8700, 6320, and 11/750 cluster. There are also 100 PCs available in labs and the computer center. All students may access the system 24 hours a day. There are no fees.

Graduates: From July 1, 2002 to June 30, 2003, 1782 bachelor's degrees were awarded. The most popular majors were biology (9%), mechanical engineering (9%), and electrical engineering (8%). In an average class, 52% graduate in 6 years or less.

Admissions Contact: Norma Torres, Director.
E-mail: *norma@rectoria.uprm.edu* Web: *www.uprm.edu*

UNIVERSITY OF PUERTO RICO/RIO PIEDRAS D-1
San Juan, PR 00931-3344   (787) 764-0000, ext. 5666
                                 Fax: (787) 764-3680, ext. 1375

Full-time: 4896 men, 9769 women	**Faculty:** n/av
Part-time: 1055 men, 2125 women	**Ph.D.s:** 41%
Graduate: 1278 men, 2758 women	**Student/Faculty:** n/av
Year: semesters, summer session	**Tuition:** $790 ($2470)
Application Deadline: February 15	**Room & Board:** $4940
Freshman Class: 13,536 applied, 3705 accepted, 3182 enrolled	
SAT I: required	**ACT:** n/av

The University of Puerto Rico/Rio Piedras, founded in 1903, is a public institution offering undergraduate programs in arts and sciences, business, and education. Nonresident U.S. citizens pay annual tuition and fees equal to what Puerto Rican students would pay at a public university in the home states. Students who do not provide evidence of medical insurance are charged an additional $653 annual fee. There are 8 undergraduate and 10 graduate schools. In addition to regional accreditation, UPR/Rio Piedras has baccalaureate program accreditation with ADA, CSWE, NAAB, and NCATE. The 10 libraries contain 1,804,010 volumes and 1,678,239 microform items, and subscribe to 5600 periodicals. Computerized library services include the card catalog. Special learning facilities include a learning resource center, art gallery, natural history museum, radio station, audiovisual services, and television production facilities. The 271-acre campus is in an urban area in the Rio Piedras section of San Juan. Including any residence halls, there are 134 buildings.

Student Life: 99% of undergraduates are from Puerto Rico. Students are from 28 foreign countries and Canada. 49% are from public schools. All are Hispanic. The average age of freshmen is 18; all undergraduates, 20. 9% do not continue beyond their first year; 46% remain to graduate.

Housing: 789 students can be accommodated in college housing, which includes coed dorms. On-campus housing is available on a first-come, first-served basis and is available on a lottery system for upperclassmen. Priority is given to out-of-town students. Alcohol is not permitted. All students may keep cars.

Activities: There is 1 local fraternity. There are 63 groups on campus, including art, band, chorus, drama, honors, international, literary magazine, newspaper, pep band, political, professional, radio and TV, religious, social, social service, and student government. Popular campus events include sports events and spring and Christmas concerts.

Sports: There are 12 intercollegiate sports for men and 8 for women, and 15 intramural sports for men and 10 for women. Facilities include a sports complex with a swimming pool, a gym, track and field areas, and tennis, basketball, and volleyball courts.

Disabled Students: 80% of the campus is accessible. Wheelchair ramps, elevators, special parking, specially equipped rest rooms, special class scheduling, lowered drinking fountains, and lowered telephones are available.

Services: There is a reader service for the blind and remedial math, reading, and writing.

Campus Safety and Security: Measures include 24-hour foot and vehicle patrol, shuttle buses, pamphlets/posters/films, and emergency telephones. There are lighted pathways/sidewalks.

Programs of Study: UPR/Rio Piedras confers B.A., B.S., B.B.A., B.E.D., and B. in Secretarial Science degrees. Master's and doctoral degrees are also awarded. Bachelor's degrees are awarded in AGRICULTURE (natural resource management), BIOLOGICAL SCIENCE (biology/biological science and nutrition), BUSINESS (accounting, banking and finance, business administration and management, business economics, business statistics, labor studies, management science, marketing management, personnel management, and secretarial studies/office management), COMMUNICATIONS AND THE ARTS (comparative literature, dramatic arts, English, fine arts, journalism, languages, music, and romance languages and literature), COMPUTER AND PHYSICAL SCIENCE (applied mathematics, chemistry, computer science, and information sciences and systems), EDUCATION (education, elementary, secondary, and special), ENGINEERING AND ENVIRONMENTAL DESIGN (environmental design), SOCIAL SCIENCE (anthropology, economics, family/consumer studies, geography, history, home economics, interdisciplinary studies, liberal arts/general studies, philosophy, political science/government, psychology, social science, social work, and sociology). Natural sciences is the strongest academically. Secondary education is the largest.

Required: To graduate, students must complete 117 to 147 credits, with a minimum GPA of 2.0. All students must take basic courses in biological sciences, physical sciences, social sciences, Spanish, humanities, and English. Spanish is the language of instruction in most courses, but students are required to have a working knowledge of English.

Special: The university offers a co-op program in accounting, internships at local government and private agencies, study abroad in 11 countries, a Washington semester, a general studies degree, and nondegree study. There is 1 national honor society.

Faculty/Classroom: 48% of faculty are male; 52%, female. No introductory courses are taught by graduate students. The average class size in an introductory lecture is 23; in a laboratory, 20; and in a regular course, 23.

Admissions: 27% of the 2003-2004 applicants were accepted. The SAT I scores for the 2003-2004 freshman class were: Verbal--16% below 500, 43% between 500 and 599, 37% between 600 and 700, and 4% above 700; Math--17% below 500, 33% between 500 and 599, 33% between 600 and 700, and 15% above 700. 58% of the current freshmen were in the top fifth of their class; 75% were in the top two fifths.

Requirements: The SAT I is required or the CEEB's Spanish equivalent. Applicants must be graduates of an accredited secondary school. The GED is accepted. Students should have completed 3 courses each of English and Spanish, 2 courses each of math and science, and 3 electives. A GPA of 2.0 is required. AP credits are accepted. Important factors in the admissions decision are advanced placement or honor courses, evidence of special talent, and extracurricular activities record.

Procedure: Freshmen are admitted in the fall. Entrance exams should be taken in November or February of the senior year. Applications should be filed by February 15 for fall entry and May 15 for spring entry. The fall 2003 application fee was $15. Notification is sent in April.

Transfer: 592 transfer students enrolled in 2002-2003. Applicants from within Puerto Rico should have a minimum of 48 credits with a 2.5 GPA; out-of-state applicants, 30 credits with a 2.5 GPA.

Visiting: To schedule a visit, contact the Dean of Students at (787) 764-0000, ext. 5540 or 5541.

Financial Aid: The CSS Profile and the Puerto Rico Income Tax Revenue Report are required. The deadline for filing freshman financial aid applications for fall entry is April.

International Students: There are 19 international students enrolled. The school actively recruits these students. They must take the Spanish or English SAT I.

Computers: The mainframe is an IBM 4381. Terminals and PC facilities are available in the main computer center, the library, and various academic departments. All students may access the system according to schedules provided during the semester. There are no time limits and no fees.

Graduates: From July 1, 2002 to June 30, 2003, 3192 bachelor's degrees were awarded. The most popular majors were social science (26%), business administration (21%), and education (17%). In an average class, 10% graduate in 3 years or less, 34% graduate in 4 years or less, 48% graduate in 5 years or less, and 54% graduate in 6 years or less. 54 companies recruited on campus in a recent year.

Admissions Contact: Cruz B. Valentin, Admissions Director. Web: www.uprrp.edu

UNIVERSITY OF THE SACRED HEART   D-1
Santurce, PR 00914   (787) 728-1199; Fax: (787) 727-7880

Full-time: 1150 men, 2098 women	**Faculty:** 134; IIB, --$
Part-time: 438 men, 874 women	**Ph.D.s:** 30%
Graduate: 168 men, 482 women	**Student/Faculty:** 24 to 1
Year: semesters, summer session	**Tuition:** $4640
Application Deadline: open	**Room & Board:** $950
Freshman Class: n/av	
SAT I: required	**ACT:** n/av

University of the Sacred Heart, founded in 1935, is a private, comprehensive Roman Catholic institution. There are 6 undergraduate and 4 graduate schools. In addition to regional accreditation, the university has baccalaureate program accreditation with CAHEA, CSWE, and NLN. The library contains 124,936 volumes, 49,086 microform items, and 10,366 audio/video tapes/CDs, and subscribes to 1525 periodicals. Computerized library services include the card catalog and database searching. Special learning facilities include a learning resource center, art gallery, natural history museum, TV station, a communication center, and secretarial, human performance, and art labs. The 33-acre campus is in an urban area in San Juan. Including any residence halls, there are 14 buildings.

Student Life: All undergraduates are from in-state. 44% are from public schools. All are Hispanic. The average age of freshmen is 19; all undergraduates, 22.

Housing: 422 students can be accommodated in college housing, which includes single-sex dorms. On-campus housing is available on a first-come, first-served basis. Alcohol is not permitted. All students may keep cars.

Activities: There are no fraternities or sororities.

Sports: There are 12 intercollegiate sports for men and 10 for women, and 8 intramural sports for men and 8 for women. Facilities include 1 volleyball and basketball court with 1500 seating capacity, Nautilus and free-weight gym, 4 tennis courts, a softball field, 3 beach volley courts, an Olympic swimming pool, a game room, locker area, judo area, and weight-lifting area.

Disabled Students: Wheelchair ramps, elevators, special parking, specially equipped rest rooms, lowered drinking fountains, and lowered telephones are available.

Campus Safety and Security: Measures include 24-hour foot and vehicle patrol.

Programs of Study: The university confers B.A., B.S., B.A.C., B.B.A., B.Ed., B.O.S.A., and B.S.N. degrees. Associate and master's degrees are also awarded. Bachelor's degrees are awarded in BIOLOGICAL SCIENCE (biology/biological science), BUSINESS (accounting, business administration and management, management information systems, marketing/retailing/merchandising, personnel management, secretarial studies/office management, and tourism), COMMUNICATIONS AND THE ARTS (advertising, communications, telecommunications, and visual and performing arts), COMPUTER AND PHYSICAL SCIENCE (chemistry, computer science, and mathematics), EDUCATION (elementary and physical), HEALTH PROFESSIONS (medical technology and nursing), SOCIAL SCIENCE (criminal justice, psychology, social work, and urban studies). Business administration and communications are the largest.

Required: To graduate, students must complete between 133 and 145 credits, including 22 to 45 in the major, with a minimum GPA of 2.1 in the major and 2.0 overall. All students must take 12 credits of English, 9 credits of Spanish, 6 credits each of theology, humanities, social sciences, and biology, and 3 credits each of logic and philosophy, arts, computer science, and physical fitness. Some programs require a fieldwork practicum.

Special: The university offers a Washington semester, work-study, and nondegree programs in continuing education and basic skills. Study in the mainland United States is possible through the National Student Exchange and through independent agreements with various private and public colleges and universities. There are also opportunities for study in Spain and Mexico. A 3-2 engineering degree is offered with Manhattan College in New York. There is 1 national honor society.

Faculty/Classroom: 47% of faculty are male; 53%, female.

Requirements: The SAT I is required, or the CEEB's Spanish equivalent, along with SAT II: Subject tests in Spanish, English, and math. Applicants must be graduates of an accredited secondary school. The GED is accepted. The admissions formula is based on GPA (x 600) + CEEB (verbal + math + English). Applicants whose index is 3300 will be admitted to the university. Those who comply with only 1 (GPA or CEEB) will be considered individually by the evaluation committee. A GPA of 2.5 is required. AP credits are accepted.

Procedure: Entrance exams should be taken in October of the senior year. There are early decision and early admissions plans. Notification is sent on a rolling basis.

Transfer: 192 transfer students enrolled in 2002-2003. Applicants with at least 30 college credits and a high school and college GPA of 2.5 are eligible for transfer. Students must submit CEEB scores and a letter of recommendation. Three quarters of the credits needed in the major must be taken at the university.

Visiting: There are regularly scheduled orientations for prospective students. Visitors may sit in on classes. To schedule a visit, contact the Admission, Promotion, and Recruitment Office at (787) 728-1602 or (787) 728-1515, ext. 3237.

Financial Aid: The university is a member of CSS. The CSS Profile, the college's own financial statement and the AFSA are required.

International Students: There are 75 international students enrolled. They must take the SAT I or or the CEEB's Spanish equivalent.

Computers: The mainframe is a DEC Alpha 3700. There are 12 terminals as well as PC facilities in the computer lab and in 6 computer classrooms, with access to the Internet and the Web. All students may access the system. There are no time limits. The fee is $25 to $75. It is strongly recommended that all students have a personal computer.

Graduates: From July 1, 2002 to June 30, 2003, 564 bachelor's degrees were awarded. The most popular majors were advertising (14%), telecommunications (11%), and communications (8%).

Admissions Contact: Luis A. Henriquez, Director of Admission and Promotion. A video is available. E-mail: nuevoingreso@sagrado.edu Web: www.sagrado.edu

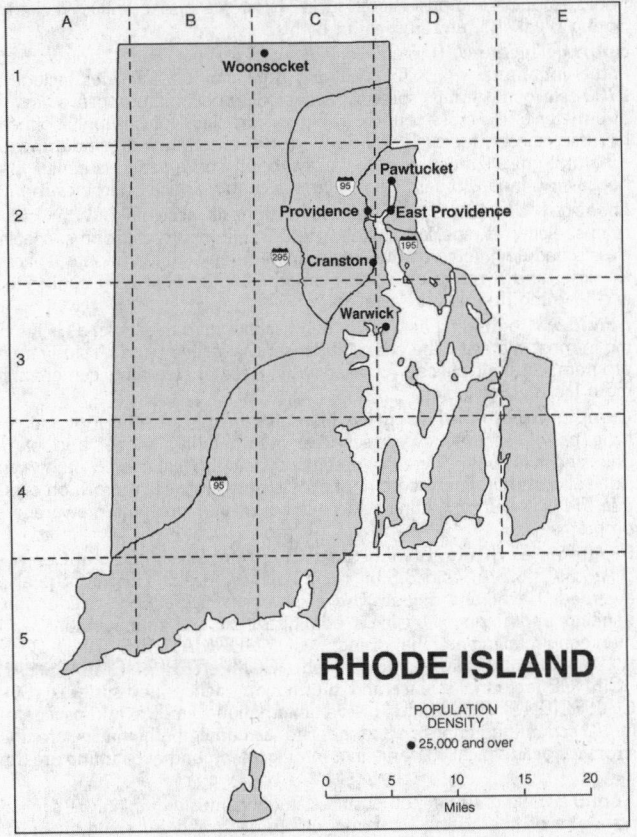

RHODE ISLAND

POPULATION
DENSITY
● 25,000 and over

0   5   10   15   20
Miles

BROWN UNIVERSITY
Providence, RI 02912   **C-2**

                                  (401) 863-2378; Fax: (401) 863-9300

Full-time: 2561 men, 3099 women   **Faculty:** 591; I, +$
Part-time: 97 men, 149 women   **Ph.D.s:** 98%
Graduate: 1012 men, 964 women   **Student/Faculty:** 10 to 1
Year: semesters, summer session   **Tuition:** $30,078
Application Deadline: January 1   **Room & Board:** $8096
Freshman Class: 15,157 applied, 2442 accepted, 1426 enrolled
SAT I Verbal/Math: 700/710   **ACT:** 29   **MOST COMPETITIVE**

Brown University, founded in 1764, is a co-educational liberal arts institution and a member of the Ivy League. In addition to regional accreditation, Brown has baccalaureate program accreditation with ABET. The 6 libraries contain 3 million volumes, 1million microform items, and 28,000 audio/video tapes/CDs, and subscribe to 16,000 periodicals. Computerized library services include the card catalog, interlibrary loans, database searching, and Internet access. Special learning facilities include a learning resource center, art gallery, planetarium, radio station, TV station, and an anthropology museum. The 140-acre campus is in an urban area 45 miles south of Boston. Including any residence halls, there are 243 buildings.

Student Life: 96% of undergraduates are from out of state, mostly the Middle Atlantic. Students are from 50 states, 72 foreign countries, and Canada. 56% are from public schools. 50% are white; 13% Asian American. The average age of freshmen is 18; all undergraduates, 20. 4% do not continue beyond their first year; 96% remain to graduate.

Housing: 4350 students can be accommodated in college housing, which includes single-sex and coed dorms, on-campus apartments, off-campus apartments, fraternity houses, and sorority houses. In addition, there are language houses, special-interest houses, an international house, a technology house, an environmental studies house, and cooperatives. On-campus housing is guaranteed for all 4 years. 85% of students live on campus; of those, 90% remain on campus on weekends. Upperclassmen may keep cars.

Activities: 12% of men belong to 10 national fraternities; 2% of women belong to 3 national sororities. There are 240 groups on campus, including a cappella group, art, band, cheerleading, chess, choir, chorale, chorus, computers, dance, debate, drama, ethnic, film, gay, honors, international, jazz band, literary magazine, marching band, musical theater, newspaper, orchestra, photography, political, professional, public service, radio and TV, religious, social, social service, student government, volunteer, and yearbook. Popular campus events include Commencement, Spring Weekend, and Parents Weekend.

Sports: There are 17 intercollegiate sports for men and 20 for women, and 15 intramural sports for men and 15 for women. Facilities include a 25,000-seat stadium, an Olympic-size pool, a 200-meter, 6-lane track, a hockey rink, playing fields, weight-training rooms, facilities for wrestling, and courts for squash, handball, racquetball, tennis, basketball, and volleyball.

Disabled Students: Wheelchair ramps, elevators, special parking, and specially equipped rest rooms are available.

Services: Counseling and information services are available, as is tutoring in most subjects. There is a reader service for the blind. Other services include class note taking, books on tape, diagnostic testing services, oral tests, tutors, and untimed tests.

Campus Safety and Security: Measures include 24-hour foot and vehicle patrol, self-defense education, security escort services, and shuttle buses. There are informal discussions, pamphlets/posters/films, emergency telephones, lighted pathways/sidewalks, and the Safe Walk program.

Programs of Study: Brown confers A.B. and Sc.B. degrees. Master's and doctoral degrees are also awarded. Bachelor's degrees are awarded in BIOLOGICAL SCIENCE (biochemistry, biology/biological science, biophysics, marine biology, and neurosciences), COMMUNICATIONS AND THE ARTS (American literature, art, art history and appreciation, classics, comparative literature, English, linguistics, media arts, music, performing arts, Portuguese, and visual and performing arts), COMPUTER AND PHYSICAL SCIENCE (applied mathematics, chemical physics, chemistry, computer science, geology, mathematics, physics, and statistics), EDUCATION (education), ENGINEERING AND ENVIRONMENTAL DESIGN (architectural technology, architecture, computational sciences, engineering, and environmental science), HEALTH PROFESSIONS (biomedical science and community health work), SOCIAL SCIENCE (African American studies, African studies, American studies, anthropology, archeology, classical/ancient civilization, cognitive science, East Asian studies, economics, ethnic studies, French studies, gender studies, German area studies, Hispanic American studies, history, international relations, Italian studies, Judaic studies, Latin American studies, medieval studies, Middle Eastern studies, philosophy, political science/government, psychology, public administration, religious education, Russian and Slavic studies, sociology, South Asian studies, urban studies, and women's studies). Biological sciences, international relations, and history are the largest.

Required: To graduate, students must pass 30 of 32 courses taken (4 each semester), including 8 to 21 courses in the major. There are no distribution requirements or specific required courses.

Special: Students may cross-register with Rhode Island School of Design, or study abroad in any of 57 programs in 18 countries. A combined A.B.-S.C.B. degree is possible in any major field with 5 years of study. Dual and student-designed majors, community internships, and pass/fail options are available. Students may pursue 5-year programs in the arts or sciences, or the 8-year program in the liberal medical education continuum. There is a chapter of Phi Beta Kappa. Most departments have honors programs.

Faculty/Classroom: 69% of faculty are male; 31%, female. All both teach and do research. Graduate students teach 13% of introductory courses. The average class size in an introductory lecture is 200; in a laboratory, 20; and in a regular course, 40.

Admissions: 16% of the 2003-2004 applicants were accepted. The SAT I scores for the 2003-2004 freshman class were: Verbal--2% below 500, 11% between 500 and 599, 36% between 600 and 700, and 51% above 700; Math--1% below 500, 8% between 500 and 599, 36% between 600 and 700, and 55% above 700. The ACT scores were 2% below 21, 7% between 21 and 23, 16% between 24 and 26, 15% between 27 and 28, and 60% above 28. 94% of the current freshmen were in the top fifth of their class; All were in the top two fifths. 152 freshmen graduated first in their class.

Requirements: The SAT I or ACT is required, along with any 3 SAT II: Subject tests. The ACT may be substituted for both the SAT I and II. Applicants must be graduates of accredited high schools. Secondary preparation is expected to include courses in English, foreign language, math, laboratory science, the arts (music or art), and history. A personal essay is required. The high school transcript is a most important criterion for admission. AP credits are accepted. Important factors in the admissions decision are advanced placement or honor courses, evidence of special talent, and recommendations by school officials.

Procedure: Freshmen are admitted in the fall. Entrance exams should be taken in the junior or senior year. There are early decision, early admissions, and deferred admissions plans. Early decision applications should be filed by November 1; regular applications, by January 1 for fall entry, along with a $70 fee. Notification of early decision is sent December 15; regular decision, April 1. 506 early decision candidates were accepted for the 2003-2004 class. 450 applicants were on the 2003 waiting list; 154 were admitted. Applications are accepted on-line through Apply Yourself.

Transfer: 116 transfer students enrolled in 2002-2003. Transfer applicants must submit high school and college transcripts, 2 recommendations from college professors, scores on the ACT or on the SAT I and any 3 SAT II: Subject tests, a letter of good standing, and a personal essay. 15 of 30 credits required for the bachelor's degree must be completed at Brown.

Visiting: There are regularly scheduled orientations for prospective students. Group Information Sessions are usually conducted Monday through Friday at 2 P.M. and at 10 A.M. from mid-April through November (at 2 P.M. only from December to April) and on Saturday mornings from mid-September to mid-November. Check the web site for schedule variations. There are guides for informal visits and visitors may sit in on classes and stay overnight. To schedule a visit, contact the Admission Office Receptionist.

Financial Aid: In a recent year, 56% of all full-time freshmen and 49% of continuing full-time students received some form of financial aid. 43% of full-time freshmen and 40% of continuing full-time students received need-based aid. The average freshman award was $22,594. 40% of undergraduates work part-time. Average annual earnings from campus work are $1334. The average financial indebtedness of a recent graduate was $22,530. Brown is a member of CSS. The CSS Profile or FAFSA, the college's own financial statement, and some state forms are required. The deadline for filing freshman financial aid applications for fall entry is January 1.

International Students: There are 355 international students enrolled. The school actively recruits these students. They must score 600 on the written TOEFL or 250 on the electronic version and also take the SAT I or the ACT. Students must take any 3 SAT II: Subject tests.

Computers: There are more than 400 workstations in several campus locations equipped with Macs and IBM PCs. Students may access the mainframe from dorm rooms. The main computer center is open 18 hours a day and around the clock during exam periods. All students may access the system at any time. There are no time limits and no fees.

Graduates: In a recent year, 1462 bachelor's degrees were awarded. The most popular majors were biological sciences (11%), international relations (9%), and history (7%). In an average class, 81% graduate in 4 years or less, 90% graduate in 5 years or less, and 94% graduate in 6 years or less. 400 companies recruited on campus in a recent year. Of a recent graduating class, 30% were enrolled in graduate school within 6 months of graduation and 60% were employed.

Admissions Contact: Michael Goldberger, Director of Admission. E-mail: *admission_undergraduate@brown.edu* Web: *www.brown.edu*

BRYANT COLLEGE
Smithfield, RI 02917-1284

C-2

(401) 232-6100
(800) 622-7001; Fax: (401) 232-6741

Full-time: 1636 men, 1093 women	**Faculty:** 133; IIB, ++$
Part-time: 132 men, 115 women	**Ph.D.s:** 87%
Graduate: 300 men, 183 women	**Student/Faculty:** 21 to 1
Year: semesters, summer session	**Tuition:** $22,458
Application Deadline: February 15	**Room & Board:** $8546
Freshman Class: 3910 applied, 2320 accepted, 778 enrolled	
SAT I Verbal/Math: 530/560	**ACT:** 24 **VERY COMPETITIVE**

Bryant College, founded in 1863, is a private, primarily residential institution that offers degrees in business, liberal arts, communication, psychology, and information technology. In addition to regional accreditation, Bryant has baccalaureate program accreditation with AACSB. The library contains 135,312 volumes, 14,433 microform items, and 940 audio/video tapes/CDs, and subscribes to 1000 periodicals. Computerized library services include the card catalog, interlibrary loans, database searching, and Internet access. Special learning facilities include a learning resource center, radio station, a technology center, a learning/language lab, a writing center, an academic center, a discovery lab, a paperless classroom, a center for international business, and a center for information and technology. The 392-acre campus is in a suburban area 12 miles northwest of Providence. Including any residence halls, there are 46 buildings.

Student Life: 81% of undergraduates are from out of state, mostly the Northeast. Students are from 31 states, 31 foreign countries, and Canada. 81% are from public schools. 84% are white. The average age of freshmen is 18; all undergraduates, 20. 21% do not continue beyond their first year; 64% remain to graduate.

Housing: 2484 students can be accommodated in college housing, which includes single-sex and coed dorms and on-campus apartments. There are also special-interest residence halls, and some fraternities and sororities are housed in residence halls. On-campus housing is guaranteed for all 4 years. 84% of students live on campus; of those, 80% remain on campus on weekends. All students may keep cars.

Activities: 8% of men belong to 6 national fraternities; 6% of women belong to 3 national sororities. There are 60 groups on campus, including academic associations, art, cheerleading, chorus, computers, dance, drama, ethnic, film, gay, international, jazz band, literary magazine, newspaper, pep band, political, professional, radio, religious, social, social service, special-interest, sports clubs, student government, and yearbook. Popular campus events include Parents and Family Weekend, Spring Weekend, and Festival of Lights.

Sports: There are 10 intercollegiate sports for men and 11 for women, and 8 intramural sports for men and 8 for women. Facilities include a 2700-seat gym, tennis, squash, racquetball, and multipurpose courts, a 400-meter track, cross-country trails, playing fields for baseball, softball, lacrosse, soccer, football, and field hockey, a competition stadium with a natural grass surface, varsity weight room, and a wellness center that houses a 6-lane, 25-yard pool, a fitness center, and an aerobics room.

Disabled Students: 90% of the campus is accessible. Wheelchair ramps, elevators, special parking, specially equipped rest rooms, special class scheduling, lowered drinking fountains, lowered telephones, special housing, and a range of support services for the physically challenged and learning disabled are available.

Services: Counseling and information services are available, as is tutoring in most subjects. There is a reader service for the blind. A study skills program, student success course, writing center, learning center, and math lab are available.

Campus Safety and Security: Measures include 24-hour foot and vehicle patrol, security escort services, informal discussions, and pamphlets/posters/films. There are emergency telephones, lighted pathways/sidewalks, monitored one point of access/egress, bicycle patrols, on campus EMTs, security lighting, video cameras, and prevention/awareness programs.

Programs of Study: Bryant confers B.A. App. Psych., B.A. in Comm., B.A.L.S., B.S.B.A., and B.S.Inf.Tech. degrees. Master's degrees are also awarded. Bachelor's degrees are awarded in BUSINESS (accounting, banking and finance, business administration and management, and marketing/retailing/merchandising), COMMUNICATIONS AND THE ARTS (communications and English), COMPUTER AND PHYSICAL SCIENCE (actuarial science and information sciences and systems), SOCIAL SCIENCE (economics, history, international studies, and psychology). Accounting, finance, and applied actuarial mathematics are the strongest academically. Marketing, management, and accounting are the largest.

Required: To graduate, all business students must complete 61 semester hours of liberal arts, 31 hours of business, and a maximum of 12 hours of electives, for a total of 123 hours, with 18 to 36 hours in the major. Distribution requirements include 12 credits in a liberal arts minor and 25 hours in Modes of Thought: social science, historical, literary, scientific, cultural, electives, and Foundations for Learning. A thesis is required in the honors program.

Special: Bryant offers internships, study abroad in 21 countries, on-campus work-study programs, dual concentrations, credit for military experience, advanced placement credit, independent study, and minors in 13 liberal arts disciplines and 5 business disciplines. There are 3 national honor societies and a freshman honors program. Honors programs are cross-departmental.

Faculty/Classroom: 67% of faculty are male; 33%, female. All teach undergraduates and 96% both teach and do research. No introductory courses are taught by graduate students. The average class size in an introductory lecture is 27; in a laboratory, 24; and in a regular course, 28.

Admissions: 59% of the 2003-2004 applicants were accepted. The SAT I scores for the 2003-2004 freshman class were: Verbal--26% below 500, 59% between 500 and 599, 14% between 600 and 700, and 1% above 700; Math--14% below 500, 56% between 500 and 599, 27% between 600 and 700, and 3% above 700. The ACT scores were 19% below 21, 31% between 21 and 23, 23% between 24 and 26, 19% between 27 and 28, and 8% above 28. 31% of the current freshmen were in the top fifth of their class; 71% were in the top two fifths. 1 freshman graduated first in their class.

Requirements: The SAT I or ACT is required. In addition, applicants must be graduates of an accredited secondary school or have a GED certificate. A total of 16 Carnegie units is required, including 4 years of English, 4 years of math (minimum year beyond Algebra II), and 2 years of social studies, lab science, and foreign language. An essay is required. A GPA of 3.0 is recommended. AP and CLEP credits are accepted.

Procedure: Freshmen are admitted fall and spring. Entrance exams should be taken before January of the senior year. There are early decision, early admissions, and deferred admissions plans. Early decision applications should be filed by November 15; regular applications, by February 15 for fall entry. Notification of early decision is sent December 15; regular decision, mid-March. 38 early decision candidates were accepted for the 2003-2004 class. 418 applicants were on the 2003 waiting list; 67 were admitted. The fall 2003 application fee was $50. Applications are accepted on-line through Next Stop College, Common App, Embark, or Bryant's web site.

Transfer: 123 transfer students enrolled in 2002-2003. Applicants must have a minimum college GPA of 2.5, although a 3.0 is recommended. Applicants must be high school graduates or have a GED, with a minimum of Algebra II and 12 semester credits. 30 of 123 credits required for the bachelor's degree must be completed at Bryant.

Visiting: There are regularly scheduled orientations for prospective students, includes a campus tour and an admission/financial aid presentation. There are guides for informal visits and visitors may sit in on classes and stay overnight. To schedule a visit, contact the Office of Admission at *admission@bryant.edu*.

Financial Aid: In 2003-2004, 83% of all full-time freshmen and 89% of continuing full-time students received some form of financial aid. 59% of full-time freshmen and 55% of continuing full-time students received need-based aid. The average freshman award was $14,729. Need-based scholarships or need-based grants averaged $9241 ($15,000 maximum); need-based self-help aid (loans and jobs) averaged $5285 ($4000 maximum); non-need-based athletic scholarships averaged $6205 ($12,000 maximum); and other non-need-based awards and non-need-based scholarships averaged $7594 ($31,410 maximum). 19% of undergraduates work part time. Average annual earnings from campus work are $1530. The average financial indebtedness of the 2003 graduate was $19,995. Bryant is a member of CSS. The FAFSA is required. The deadline for filing freshman financial aid applications for fall entry is February 15.

International Students: There are 68 international students enrolled. The school actively recruits these students. They must score 550 on the written TOEFL or 213 on the electronic version and also take the SAT I or the ACT.

Computers: The mainframes are a SUN/ENT 3500 and IBM RS6000. Students use the mainframe and network server systems from their own personal computer, laptop provided by Bryant, or any of the 492 classroom/lab computers to access application software, e-mail, and the Web. This service is for personal as well as academic use. All students may access the system 24 hours per day, 7 days per week. There are no time limits and no fees. All students are required to have personal computers. All incoming freshmen are provided with an IBM ThinkPad.

Graduates: From July 1, 2002 to June 30, 2003, 585 bachelor's degrees were awarded. The most popular majors were marketing (28%), finance (20%), and management (17%). In an average class, 60% graduate in 4 years or less, 63% graduate in 5 years or less, and 64% graduate in 6 years or less. 154 companies recruited on campus in 2002-2003. Of the 2002 graduating class, 4% were enrolled in graduate school within 6 months of graduation and 90% were employed.

Admissions Contact: Cynthia Bonn, Director of Admission. A video is available. E-mail: *admission@bryant.edu* Web: *www.bryant.edu*

JOHNSON AND WALES UNIVERSITY
Providence, RI 02903-3703

C-2

(401) 598-2310
(800) DIAL-JWU; Fax: (401) 598-2948

Full-time: 3993 men, 4268 women	Faculty: IIA, --$
Part-time: 420 men, 539 women	Ph.D.s: 17%
Graduate: 331 men, 317 women	Student/Faculty: n/av
Year: quarters, summer session	Tuition: $16,188
Application Deadline: open	Room & Board: $6777
Freshman Class: 11,174 applied, 9548 accepted, 2427 enrolled	
SAT I or ACT: recommended	LESS COMPETITIVE

Johnson and Wales University, founded in 1914, is a private institution offering degree programs in business, food services, hospitality, and related technology. There are 4 undergraduate schools and 1 graduate school. The 2 libraries contain 88,996 volumes, 398,947 microform items, and 2429 audio/video tapes/CDs, and subscribe to 2218 periodicals. Computerized library services include the card catalog, interlibrary loans, and database searching. Special learning facilities include a learning resource center, and culinary archives and museum. The 47-acre campus is in an urban area in Providence, with facilities in Warwick, Cranston, and Seekonk, as well as campuses in Denver, North Miami, FL, and Charlotte, NC. Including any residence halls, there are 52 buildings.

Student Life: 78% of undergraduates are from out of state, mostly the Northeast. Students are from 50 states, 73 foreign countries, and Canada. 88% are from public schools. 75% are white; 11% African American. The average age of freshmen is 18; all undergraduates, 21.

Housing: 3180 students can be accommodated in college housing, which includes single-sex and coed dorms, on-campus apartments, and married-student housing. In addition, there are special-interest houses, international housing, national student organization housing, honors floors, and wellness housing. On-campus housing is guaranteed for all 4 years. 61% of students commute. Alcohol is not permitted. All students may keep cars.

Activities: 4% of men belong to 3 local and 13 national fraternities; 4% of women belong to 2 local and 11 national sororities. There are 80 groups on campus, including cheerleading, chess, chorale, computers, drama, ethnic, gay, honors, international, literary magazine, newspaper, political, professional, religious, social, social service, student government, and yearbook. Popular campus events include Spring Weekend and SnoBall Dance.

Sports: There are 9 intercollegiate sports for men and 8 for women, and 8 intramural sports for men and 8 for women. Facilities include 2 gyms, 2 weight rooms, and 2 fitness centers.

Disabled Students: All of the campus is accessible. Wheelchair ramps, elevators, special parking, specially equipped rest rooms, special class scheduling, lowered drinking fountains, lowered telephones, and lowered fire alarms, emergency lighting, audiovisual fire alarms in public bathrooms, and a lowering chair for the swimming pool are available.

Services: Counseling and information services are available, as is tutoring in every subject. There is a reader service for the blind and remedial math and writing. Workshops in stress and time management, wellness, and learning strategies are offered. Special scheduling of courses and exams and taping are available to accommodate special needs.

Campus Safety and Security: Measures include 24-hour foot and vehicle patrol, self-defense education, security escort services, and shuttle buses. There are informal discussions, pamphlets/posters/films, emergency telephones, lighted pathways/sidewalks, 24-hour dorm coverage, a phone hot line for campus emergencies, and crime alerts in the student weekly newspaper.

Programs of Study: J&W confers the B.S. degree. Associate, master's, and doctoral degrees are also awarded. Bachelor's degrees are awarded in AGRICULTURE (equine science), BUSINESS (accounting, business administration and management, entrepreneurial studies, fashion merchandising, hospitality management services, hotel/motel and restaurant management, international business management, management information systems, marketing and distribution, marketing management, marketing/retailing/merchandising, office supervision and management, recreation and leisure services, recreational facilities management, retailing, secretarial studies/office management, small business management, sports management, tourism, and transportation and travel marketing), COMMUNICATIONS AND THE ARTS (advertising), COMPUTER AND PHYSICAL SCIENCE (computer management, computer science, information sciences and systems, systems analysis, and web services), EDUCATION (marketing and distribution), ENGINEERING AND ENVIRONMENTAL DESIGN (electrical/electronics engineering, food services technology, and technological management), SOCIAL SCIENCE (clothing and textiles management/production/services, criminal justice, food production/management/services, paralegal studies, parks and recreation management, and systems science). Culinary arts, hotel/restaurant management, and marketing are the strongest academically. Culinary arts, hotel/restaurant management, and accounting are the largest.

Required: To graduate, students must complete 180 quarter credit hours, including at least 36 in the major, with a minimum GPA of 2.0. Required courses include English, math, history, economics, science, psychology, sociology, and professional development.

Special: The university offers co-op programs, accelerated degree programs, dual majors, study abroad, and worldwide work-study opportunities in business, hospitality, technology, and culinary arts. Most majors require 11-week internships. There is a 4-day school week. There is 1 national honor society, a freshman honors program, and 5 departmental honors programs.

Faculty/Classroom: 61% of faculty are male; 39%, female. No introductory courses are taught by graduate students. The average class size in an introductory lecture is 30; in a laboratory, 18; and in a regular course, 30.

Admissions: 85% of the 2003-2004 applicants were accepted. The SAT I scores for the 2003-2004 freshman class were: Verbal--63% below 500, 31% between 500 and 599, and 6% between 600 and 700; Math--63% below 500, 30% between 500 and 599, and 7% between 600 and 700. 20% of the current freshmen were in the top fifth of their class; 45% were in the top two fifths.

Requirements: The SAT I or ACT is recommended. In addition, for honors program consideration, the SAT I and SAT II: Subject tests must be taken. Graduation from high school or an equivalent credential is required. J&W requires applicants to be in the upper 70% of their class. A GPA of 2.0 is required. AP and CLEP credits are accepted. Important factors in the admissions decision are advanced placement or honor courses, recommendations by school officials, and extracurricular activities record.

Procedure: Freshmen are admitted to all sessions. There are early admissions and deferred admissions plans. There is a rolling admissions plan. Application deadlines are open.

Transfer: 405 transfer students enrolled in 2002-2003. Applicants are required to submit official high school and college transcripts and must have earned a minimum college GPA of 2.0. 45 of 180 credits required for the bachelor's degree must be completed at J&W.

Visiting: There are regularly scheduled orientations for prospective students, including parent/student orientation, financial services, student testing, academic orientation, preparation for September registration, and parent-to-parent orientation. There are guides for informal visits and visitors may sit in on classes and stay overnight. To schedule a visit, contact the Admissions Office.

Financial Aid: In a recent year, 75% of all full-time freshmen and 71% of continuing full-time students received some form of financial aid. 71%

of full-time freshmen and 28% of continuing full-time students received need-based aid. The average freshman award was $12,087. 54% of undergraduates work part time. Average annual earnings from campus work are $936. The average financial indebtedness of a recent graduate was $13,742. The FAFSA and the college's own financial statement are required. The deadline for filing freshman financial aid applications for fall entry is August 1.

International Students: The school actively recruits these students. They must score 550 on the written TOEFL.

Computers: The mainframe is a Wang VS 7380A. There are 400 PCs dedicated to student use, including 60 networked workstations for hospitality students. All students may access the system daily, a total of 82 hours per week. The amount of time students may access the system depends on demand. There are no fees.

Graduates: Of the 2002 graduating class, 99% were employed within 6 months of graduation.

Admissions Contact: Ken DiSaia, VP of Enrollment Management. A video is available. E-mail: *admissions@jwu.edu* Web: *www.jwu.edu*

PROVIDENCE COLLEGE
Providence, RI 02918   C-2

                                                      (401) 865-2535
                                  (800) 721-6444; Fax: (401) 865-2826

Full-time: 1580 men, 2134 women	**Faculty:** 262; IIA, +$
Part-time: 234 men, 394 women	**Ph.D.s:** 87%
Graduate: 320 men, 596 women	**Student/Faculty:** 14 to 1
Year: semesters, summer session	**Tuition:** $22,104
Application Deadline: January 15	**Room & Board:** $8500
Freshman Class: 7397 applied, 3906 accepted, 975 enrolled	
SAT I Verbal/Math: 599/607	**ACT:** 26 **HIGHLY COMPETITIVE**

Providence College, founded in 1917, is a liberal arts and sciences institution operated by the Dominican order of the Catholic Church. There is 1 undergraduate and 1 graduate school. In addition to regional accreditation, Providence has baccalaureate program accreditation with CSWE and NCATE. The library contains 359,046 volumes and 216,196 microform items, and subscribes to 1752 periodicals. Computerized library services include interlibrary loans and database searching. Special learning facilities include a learning resource center, art gallery, radio station, and Blackfriars Theater. The 105-acre campus is in a suburban area 50 miles south of Boston. Including any residence halls, there are 44 buildings.

Student Life: 80% of undergraduates are from out of state, mostly the Northeast. Students are from 38 states, 16 foreign countries, and Canada. 59% are from public schools. 85% are white. 83% are Catholic; 11% Greek Orthodox, Islamic. The average age of freshmen is 18; all undergraduates, 21. 9% do not continue beyond their first year; 85% remain to graduate.

Housing: 2800 students can be accommodated in college housing, which includes single-sex and coed dorms and on-campus apartments. On-campus housing is available on a first-come, first-served basis and is available on a lottery system for upperclassmen. 75% of students live on campus; of those, 80% remain on campus on weekends. Upperclassmen may keep cars.

Activities: There are no fraternities or sororities. There are 94 groups on campus, including art, band, cheerleading, choir, chorale, chorus, computers, dance, debate, drama, ethnic, honors, international, jazz band, literary magazine, musical theater, newspaper, pep band, photography, political, professional, radio and TV, religious, social, social service, student government, and yearbook. Popular campus events include Multicultural Awareness Week, Midnight Madness, and Junior Ring Weekend.

Sports: There are 7 intercollegiate sports for men and 10 for women, and 11 intramural sports for men and 12 for women. Facilities include an ice arena, indoor track, courts for tennis, racquetball, handball, squash, basketball, and volleyball, a pool, a Nautilus program, facilities for weight lifting, aerobics, and ballet, a soccer field, and softball fields.

Disabled Students: 90% of the campus is accessible. Wheelchair ramps, elevators, special parking, specially equipped rest rooms, special class scheduling, lowered drinking fountains, lowered telephones, and special housing are available.

Services: Counseling and information services are available, as is tutoring in most subjects. There is a reader service for the blind and academic support services, including evaluation of learning-disabled students.

Campus Safety and Security: Measures include 24-hour foot and vehicle patrol, self-defense education, security escort services, and shuttle buses. There are informal discussions, pamphlets/posters/films, emergency telephones, lighted pathways/sidewalks, and a campuswide computerized card access system for entry into all dorms and apartment buildings.

Programs of Study: Providence confers B.A. and B.S. degrees. Associate and master's degrees are also awarded. Bachelor's degrees are awarded in BIOLOGICAL SCIENCE (biochemistry and biology/biological science), BUSINESS (accounting, banking and finance, business administration and management, and marketing/retailing/merchandising), COMMUNICATIONS AND THE ARTS (art history and appreciation, dramatic arts, English, French, Italian, music, Spanish, and studio art), COMPUTER AND PHYSICAL SCIENCE (applied physics, chemistry, computer science, and mathematics), EDUCATION (elementary, English, foreign languages, mathematics, music, science, secondary, social studies, and special), ENGINEERING AND ENVIRONMENTAL DESIGN (preengineering), HEALTH PROFESSIONS (health care administration), SOCIAL SCIENCE (American studies, community services, economics, history, humanities, philosophy, political science/government, psychology, social science, social work, sociology, and theological studies). Biology, chemistry, and business are the strongest academically. Education, business, and political science are the largest.

Required: To graduate, all students must complete at least 116 credit hours, with 24 upper-division hours in the major, and maintain a GPA of 2.0. Students must also meet an English proficiency requirement, complete 20 credits in Western civilization, and fulfill the 30-credit core curriculum, including 6 credits each in natural science, social science, philosophy, and religion, and 3 each in math and fine arts.

Special: Providence offers internships in politics, broadcasting, journalism, and business, and study abroad in 5 countries. Other opportunities for study-abroad are available through AIFS. Also available are dual and student-designed majors, a 3-2 engineering degree with Columbia University or Washington University in St. Louis, nondegree study, and pass/fail options. There are 17 national honor societies and a freshman honors program.

Faculty/Classroom: 63% of faculty are male; 37%, female. All teach undergraduates. No introductory courses are taught by graduate students. The average class size in an introductory lecture is 24; in a laboratory, 14; and in a regular course, 13.

Admissions: 53% of the 2003-2004 applicants were accepted. The SAT I scores for the 2003-2004 freshman class were: Verbal--7% below 500, 40% between 500 and 599, 45% between 600 and 700, and 8% above 700; Math--5% below 500, 37% between 500 and 599, 50% between 600 and 700, and 8% above 700. The ACT scores were 7% below 21, 18% between 21 and 23, 35% between 24 and 26, 22% between 27 and 28, and 18% above 28. 74% of the current freshmen were in the top fifth of their class; 95% were in the top two fifths. There were 3 National Merit finalists and 7 semifinalists.

Requirements: The SAT I or ACT is required. In addition, SAT II: Subject tests in writing and 2 others of the applicant's choice are recommended. Applicants must be graduates of an accredited secondary school or have a GED certificate. A GPA of 3.0 is recommended. High school preparation should include 4 years of English, 3 years each of foreign language and math, and 2 years each of history, science, and social studies. An essay is required. AP credits are accepted. Important factors in the admissions decision are advanced placement or honor courses, leadership record, and evidence of special talent.

Procedure: Freshmen are admitted fall and spring. Entrance exams should be taken in the junior or senior year. There are early action and deferred admissions plans. Early action applications should be filed by November 15; regular applications, by January 15 for fall entry and December 1 for spring entry. Notification of early action is sent January 1; regular decision, April 1. 1521 applicants were on the 2003 waiting list. The fall 2003 application fee was $55. Applications are accepted on-line through Common App.

Transfer: 71 transfer students enrolled in 2002-2003. Applicants should have a minimum college GPA of 3.0 in a strong liberal arts program with a recommended 24 credit hours. The SAT I or ACT is required. 60 of 116 credits required for the bachelor's degree must be completed at Providence.

Visiting: There are regularly scheduled orientations for prospective students, including campus tours and group information sessions. There are guides for informal visits and visitors may sit in on classes. To schedule a visit, contact the Admissions Office at *pcadmiss@providence.edu*.

Financial Aid: In 2003-2004, 75% of all full-time freshmen and 70% of continuing full-time students received some form of financial aid. 64% of full-time freshmen and 60% of continuing full-time students received need-based aid. The average freshman award was $14,000. Need-based scholarships or need-based grants averaged $7000 ($21,665 maximum); need-based self-help aid (loans and jobs) averaged $7300 ($9300 maximum); non-need-based athletic scholarships averaged $19,833 ($32,000 maximum); and other non-need-based awards and non-need-based scholarships averaged $11,697 ($21,665 maximum). 66% of undergraduates work part time. Average annual earnings from campus work are $1525. The average financial indebtedness of the 2003 graduate was $21,300. Providence is a member of CSS. The CSS Profile or FAFSA is required. The deadline for filing freshman financial aid applications for fall entry is February 1.

International Students: There are 35 international students enrolled. The school actively recruits these students. They must score 550 on the written TOEFL or 213 on the electronic version and also take the SAT I or the ACT. SAT II: Subject tests are strongly encouraged.

Computers: The mainframe is a Sun 4500. There are 8 computer labs equipped with 150 PCs for student use. All students have access to the

Internet. All students may access the system. There are no time limits. The fee is $210.

Graduates: From July 1, 2002 to June 30, 2003, 957 bachelor's degrees were awarded. The most popular majors were marketing (12%), management (9%), and special/elementary education (9%). In an average class, 82% graduate in 4 years or less, 84% graduate in 5 years or less, and 85% graduate in 6 years or less. 100 companies recruited on campus in 2002-2003. Of the 2002 graduating class, 20% were enrolled in graduate school within 6 months of graduation and 70% were employed.

Admissions Contact: Christopher P. Lydon, Dean of Enrollment Management. E-mail: *pcadmiss@providence.edu*
Web: *www.providence.edu*

RHODE ISLAND COLLEGE
Providence, RI 02908

C-2
(401) 456-8234
(800) 669-5760; Fax: (401) 456-8817

Full-time: 1652 men, 3316 women	**Faculty:** 300; IIA, av$
Part-time: 755 men, 1582 women	**Ph.D.s:** 76%
Graduate: 318 men, 1300 women	**Student/Faculty:** 17 to 1
Year: semesters, summer session	**Tuition:** $3995 ($10,195)
Application Deadline: May 1	**Room & Board:** $7570
Freshman Class: 3088 applied, 2257 accepted, 1208 enrolled	
SAT I Verbal/Math: 494/491	**COMPETITIVE**

Rhode Island College, founded in 1854, is a state-supported liberal arts institution offering undergraduate and graduate programs in the liberal arts and sciences, social work, education, and human development. There are 4 undergraduate schools and 1 graduate school. In addition to regional accreditation, RIC has baccalaureate program accreditation with NASAD, NASM, NCATE, and NLN. The library contains 634,000 volumes, 1,338,000 microform items, and 3300 audio/video tapes/CDs, and subscribes to 1500 periodicals. Computerized library services include the card catalog, interlibrary loans, database searching, and Internet access. Special learning facilities include an art gallery and radio station. The 180-acre campus is in a suburban area 50 miles southwest of Boston. Including any residence halls, there are 42 buildings.

Student Life: 90% of undergraduates are from Rhode Island. Students are from 29 states and 4 foreign countries. 90% are white. 60% are Catholic; 14% Protestant. The average age of freshmen is 18; all undergraduates, 24. 28% do not continue beyond their first year; 45% remain to graduate.

Housing: 830 students can be accommodated in college housing, which includes single-sex and coed dorms. In addition, there are honors houses. On-campus housing is available on a first-come, first-served basis. Priority is given to out-of-town students. 75% of students commute. Alcohol is not permitted. All students may keep cars.

Activities: There are no fraternities or sororities. There are 64 groups on campus, including art, band, cheerleading, chess, chorale, chorus, dance, debate, drama, ethnic, gay, honors, international, literary magazine, musical theater, newspaper, orchestra, political, professional, radio and TV, religious, social, social service, student government, symphony, and yearbook. Popular campus events include a fine and performing arts calendar, chess tournaments, and campus center activities.

Sports: There are 9 intercollegiate sports for men and 10 for women, and 5 intramural sports for men and 5 for women. Facilities include an intercollegiate facility with a 2500-seat arena and student athlete support areas; a recreation center that includes a field house with indoor track, multiuse courts, swimming pool, cardiovascular center, dance studio, and wrestling facility; and outdoor facilities that include varsity baseball and tennis complexes, a track, and a softball facility.

Disabled Students: All of the campus is accessible. Wheelchair ramps, elevators, special parking, specially equipped rest rooms, and special class scheduling are available. A peer adviser is available to assist disabled students.

Services: Counseling and information services are available, as is tutoring in most subjects. There is a reader service for the blind, remedial math, reading, and writing, and services for learning-disabled students and any student needing academic assistance.

Campus Safety and Security: Measures include 24-hour foot and vehicle patrol, self-defense education, security escort services, and informal discussions. There are pamphlets/posters/films, emergency telephones, and lighted pathways/sidewalks.

Programs of Study: RIC confers B.A., B.S., B.F.A., B.G.A., B.M., and B.S.W. degrees. Master's and doctoral degrees are also awarded. Bachelor's degrees are awarded in BIOLOGICAL SCIENCE (biology/biological science), BUSINESS (accounting, business administration and management, business economics, labor studies, marketing/retailing/merchandising, and personnel management), COMMUNICATIONS AND THE ARTS (communications, dramatic arts, English, film arts, fine arts, French, music, photography, and Spanish), COMPUTER AND PHYSICAL SCIENCE (chemistry, computer programming, computer science, information sciences and systems, mathematics, physics, and radiological technology), EDUCATION (art, early childhood, elementary,

foreign languages, health, industrial arts, middle school, music, physical, science, secondary, and special), HEALTH PROFESSIONS (medical laboratory technology and nursing), SOCIAL SCIENCE (African American studies, anthropology, economics, geography, history, philosophy, political science/government, prelaw, psychology, public administration, social science, social work, sociology, and women's studies). Education, management, and psychology are the largest.

Required: To graduate, students must complete 120 credits and maintain a minimum GPA of 2.0. All students must complete the college's general education program, which consists of 4 core requirements in cultural legacies and critical thinking, and 6 distribution requirements. In addition, all students must complete the college writing and math competency requirements.

Special: Cross-registration is available with other Rhode Island schools and the National Student Exchange. The college offers internships, study abroad, work-study programs, a general studies degree, dual and student-designed majors, credit by exam, credit for prior learning, and pass/fail options. There are 6 national honor societies, a freshman honors program, and 21 departmental honors programs.

Faculty/Classroom: 56% of faculty are male; 44%, female. 98% both teach and do research. No introductory courses are taught by graduate students. The average class size in an introductory lecture is 30; in a laboratory, 14; and in a regular course, 30.

Admissions: 73% of the 2003-2004 applicants were accepted. The SAT I scores for the 2003-2004 freshman class were: Verbal--56% below 500, 33% between 500 and 599, 10% between 600 and 700, and 1% above 700; Math--57% below 500, 33% between 500 and 599, and 10% between 600 and 700. 25% of the current freshmen were in the top fifth of their class; 38% were in the top two fifths.

Requirements: The SAT I is required; ACT scores will be accepted. Applicants should be graduates of an accredited secondary school with 18 academic credits, including 4 in English, 3 in math, 2 each in foreign languages (2 years of same language), science (biology plus chemistry or physics), and social studies, 1/2 credit each in the arts, and computer literacy, and the remainder in academic electives. The GED is accepted. An essay is required along with a portfolio for art students and an audition for music students. AP and CLEP credits are accepted. Important factors in the admissions decision are advanced placement or honor courses, evidence of special talent, and leadership record.

Procedure: Freshmen are admitted fall and spring. Entrance exams should be taken by December of the senior year. There are early admissions and deferred admissions plans. Applications should be filed by May 1 for fall entry and November 15 for spring entry. The fall 2003 application fee was $35. Notification is sent on a rolling basis.

Transfer: 902 transfer students enrolled in 2002-2003. Applicants must submit 24 transferable credits with a minimum GPA of 2.25 or 30 college credits and a minimum GPA of 2.0. 45 of 120 credits required for the bachelor's degree must be completed at RIC.

Visiting: There are regularly scheduled orientations for prospective students, including information sessions and a campus tour. There are guides for informal visits and visitors may sit in on classes. To schedule a visit, contact the Admissions Office.

Financial Aid: In 2003-2004, 76% of all full-time freshmen and 60% of continuing full-time students received some form of financial aid. 65% of full-time freshmen and 60% of continuing full-time students received need-based aid. The average freshman award was $5695. RIC is a member of CSS. The FAFSA and the college's own financial statement are required. The deadline for filing freshman financial aid applications for fall entry is March 1.

International Students: They must score 550 on the written TOEFL or 213 on the electronic version and also take the SAT I.

Computers: There is an Ethernet network. The college has 15 computer labs with a minimum of 20 workstations each for instruction, 14 electronic classrooms, and 2 walk-in labs with 125 workstations. Internet and e-mail access is provided campuswide. Microsoft operating systems and Microsoft Office Suite are available to students, faculty, and staff. All students may access the system. There are no time limits. The fee is $40. The college has discount purchase agreements with Dell and Apple.

Graduates: From July 1, 2002 to June 30, 2003, 1058 bachelor's degrees were awarded. The most popular majors were education (33%), psychology (13%), and nursing (9%). In an average class, 1% graduate in 3 years or less, 20% graduate in 4 years or less, 40% graduate in 5 years or less, and 45% graduate in 6 years or less. 60 companies recruited on campus in 2002-2003. Of the 2002 graduating class, 10% were enrolled in graduate school within 6 months of graduation and 61% were employed.

Admissions Contact: Holly L. Shadoian, Director of Admissions. E-mail: *hshadoian@ric.edu* or *admissions@ric.edu*
Web: *http://www.ric.edu*

RHODE ISLAND SCHOOL OF DESIGN
Providence, RI 02903

C-2

(401) 454-6300
(800) 364-7473; Fax: (401) 454-6309

Total Enrollment: 2294	Faculty: 145; IIB, ++$
Year: 4-1-4	Ph.Ds: n/av
Application Deadline: February 15	Student/Faculty: 11 to 1
	Tuition: $26,199
	Room & Board: $7370

Freshman Class: 2420 applied, 808 accepted, 420 enrolled
SAT I Verbal/Math: 610/610

SPECIAL

Rhode Island School of Design, founded in 1877, is a private institution offering degree programs in fine arts, design, and architecture. In addition to regional accreditation, RISD has baccalaureate program accreditation with ASLA, NAAB, and NASAD. The library contains 99,516 volumes, 1855 microform items, and 158,325 audio/video tapes/CDs, and subscribes to 423 periodicals. Computerized library services include the card catalog, interlibrary loans, database searching, and Internet access. Special learning facilities include an art gallery, an art museum, and nature lab. The 13-acre campus is in an urban area 50 miles south of Boston. Including any residence halls, there are 42 buildings.

Student Life: 94% of undergraduates are from out of state, mostly the Northeast. Students are from 50 states, 50 foreign countries, and Canada. 60% are from public schools. 54% are white; 13% Asian American; 12% foreign nationals. The average age of freshmen is 18; all undergraduates, 23. 6% do not continue beyond their first year; 89% remain to graduate.

Housing: 800 students can be accommodated in college housing, which includes coed dorms and on-campus apartments. On-campus housing is guaranteed for the freshman year only and is available on a lottery system for upperclassmen. 67% of students commute. Alcohol is not permitted. No one may keep cars.

Activities: There are no fraternities or sororities. There are 60 groups on campus, including art, computers, dance, drama, ethnic, film, gay, international, literary magazine, newspaper, photography, political, professional, religious, social, social service, student government, and yearbook. Popular campus events include Talent Show, Halloween Ball, and Artists Ball.

Sports: There are 7 intramural sports for men and 7 for women. Facilities include a student center with areas and equipment for dance, aerobics, and weight and fitness training, and Tillinghast Farm, a retreat on Narragansett Bay, 15 minutes from campus. Students may also enroll in activity classes at Brown University and use its athletic complex, which includes a swimming pool, an ice skating rink, a track, weight training equipment, and courts for basketball, tennis, squash, and racquetball.

Disabled Students: Wheelchair ramps, elevators, special parking, specially equipped rest rooms, and special class scheduling are available.

Services: A writing program is available to all students. Taped lectures, note takers, and alternative test-taking procedures are also available, particularly for students with learning disabilities.

Campus Safety and Security: Measures include 24-hour foot and vehicle patrol, security escort services, shuttle buses, and informal discussions. There are pamphlets/posters/films, emergency telephones, lighted pathways/sidewalks, evening building monitors, and building access cards.

Programs of Study: RISD confers B.Arch., B.F.A., B.G.D., B.I.A., and B.I.D. degrees. Master's degrees are also awarded. Bachelor's degrees are awarded in COMMUNICATIONS AND THE ARTS (apparel design, ceramic art and design, film arts, glass, graphic design, illustration, industrial design, metal/jewelry, painting, photography, printmaking, and sculpture), ENGINEERING AND ENVIRONMENTAL DESIGN (architecture, furniture design, and interior design), SOCIAL SCIENCE (textiles and clothing). Illustration, graphic design, and architecture are the largest.

Required: To graduate, all students must complete at least 126 credit hours, including 54 in the major, 42 in liberal arts, 18 in the freshman foundation program, and 12 in nonmajor, art department electives. Liberal arts credits must include 12 each in art/architectural history and electives, and 9 each in English and history/philosophy/social science. Core courses include 2 semesters each of foundation drawing, 2-dimensional design, and 3-dimensional design. A minimum GPA of 2.0 and completion of the final-year project are required.

Special: RISD offers cross-registration with Brown University and through the AICAD mobility program, credit or noncredit summer programs, 6-week internships during the midyear winter session, and study abroad in 21 countries and through the senior-year European Honors Program in Rome. Students may also elect a liberal arts concentration in art/architectural history, literary studies, or creative writing.

Faculty/Classroom: 60% of faculty are male; 40%, female. All teach undergraduates. The average class size in an introductory lecture is 20 and in a laboratory, 17.

Admissions: 33% of the 2003-2004 applicants were accepted. The SAT I scores for the 2003-2004 freshman class were: Verbal--15% below 500, 29% between 500 and 599, 44% between 600 and 700, and 12% above 700; Math--10% below 500, 35% between 500 and 599, 43% between 600 and 700, and 12% above 700. 52% of the current freshmen were in the top fifth of their class; 83% were in the top two fifths.

Requirements: The SAT I is required; the ACT may be substituted. Applicants must be graduates of an accredited secondary school or have a GED. An essay, assigned drawings, a portfolio, and a statement of purpose are also required. Up to 3 letters of recommendation are recommended. AP credits are accepted. Important factors in the admissions decision are evidence of special talent, advanced placement or honor courses, and personality/intangible qualities.

Procedure: Freshmen are admitted fall and spring. Entrance exams should be taken at least 6 weeks before the application deadline. There are early admissions and deferred admissions plans. Applications should be filed by February 15 for fall entry and November 25 for spring entry, along with a $45 fee. Notification is sent March 30. A waiting list is an active part of the admissions procedure. Applications are accepted online.

Transfer: 115 transfer students enrolled in a recent year. Applicants must have at least 27 college credits and should submit an essay along with academic transcripts from the previous 3 years. All students must submit a portfolio and complete a drawing assignment. Letters of recommendation are encouraged. The SAT I or ACT is required for architecture and industrial design applicants. 66 of 126 credits required for the bachelor's degree must be completed at RISD.

Visiting: There are regularly scheduled orientations for prospective students, including a presentation by the admissions staff and a campus tour by a student. Visitors may sit in on classes. To schedule a visit, contact the Admissions Office at admissions@risd.edu.

Financial Aid: In 2003-2004, 62% of all full-time freshmen and 66% of continuing full-time students received some form of financial aid. 54% of full-time freshmen and 58% of continuing full-time students received need-based aid. The average freshman award was $13,700. Need-based scholarships or need-based grants averaged $9747 ($25,000 maximum); need-based self-help aid (loans and jobs) averaged $3950 ($8725 maximum); non-need-based awards and non-need-based scholarships averaged $5000 ($5000 maximum); and SEOG Pell State Grant averaged $2250 ($6500 maximum). 58% of undergraduates work part time. Average annual earnings from campus work are $1100. The average financial indebtedness of the 2003 graduate was $20,100. RISD is a member of CSS. The CSS/Profile or FAFSA and parents' income tax returns are required. The deadline for filing freshman financial aid applications for fall entry is February 15.

International Students: There are 275 international students enrolled. They must score 580 on the written TOEFL or 237 on the electronic version and also take the SAT I or the ACT.

Computers: There are more than 450 Macs, PCs, and Silicon Graphic and other workstations located in the computer center and various departments. All students have access to the Internet and Web. All students may access the system. There are no time limits. The fee is $250. It is recommended that students in industrial design, interior architecture, furniture design, graphic design, and architecture have personal computers. The preferred model varies by department.

Graduates: From July 1, 2002 to June 30, 2003, 449 bachelor's degrees were awarded. In an average class, 87% graduate in 5 years or less.

Admissions Contact: Edward Newhall, Director of Admissions.
E-mail: admissions@risd.edu Web: www.risd.edu

ROGER WILLIAMS UNIVERSITY
Bristol, RI 02809-2921

D-3

(401) 254-3500
(800) 458-7144; Fax: (401) 254-3557

Full-time: 1633 men, 1722 women	Faculty: 173
Part-time: 37 men, 18 women	Ph.Ds: 70%
Graduate: 72 men, 138 women	Student/Faculty: 19 to 1
Year: semesters, summer session	Tuition: $20,840
Application Deadline: rolling	Room & Board: $9456
Freshman Class: 1050 enrolled	

SAT I Verbal/Math: 530/530

COMPETITIVE

Roger Williams University, founded in 1956, is a private, liberal arts institution that offers programs in the arts and sciences, professional studies, architecture, and law. There are 6 undergraduate and 3 graduate schools. In addition to regional accreditation, RWU has baccalaureate program accreditation with AACSB, ABA, ABET, ACCE, NAAB, NASDTEC, and NCATE. The 3 libraries contain 187,930 volumes, 17,055 microform items, and 5012 audio/video tapes/CDs, and subscribe to 2779 periodicals. Computerized library services include the card catalog, interlibrary loans, database searching, and Internet access. Special learning facilities include a learning resource center, art gallery, radio station, a greenhouse, and wet lab. The 140-acre campus is in a small town 18 miles southeast of Providence. Including any residence halls, there are 42 buildings.

Student Life: 87% of undergraduates are from out of state, mostly the Northeast. Students are from 25 states, 38 foreign countries, and Canada. 75% are from public schools. 93% are white. The average age of freshmen is 18; all undergraduates, 20. 25% do not continue beyond their first year; 50% remain to graduate.

Housing: 2729 students can be accommodated in college housing, which includes single-sex and coed dorms, on-campus apartments, off-campus apartments, and married-student housing. In addition, there are special-interest houses and academic theme areas. On-campus housing is guaranteed for the freshman year only and is available on a lottery system for upperclassmen. 77% of students live on campus; of those, 70% remain on campus on weekends. Upperclassmen may keep cars.

Activities: There are no fraternities or sororities. There are 56 groups on campus, including art, band, cheerleading, chess, choir, chorus, computers, dance, drama, ethnic, film, gay, honors, international, jazz band, literary magazine, musical theater, newspaper, orchestra, photography, political, professional, radio and TV, religious, social service, student government, and yearbook. Popular campus events include Spring Weekend, International Dinner, and Campus Entertainment Network (concerts and comedians).

Sports: There are 11 intercollegiate sports for men and 9 for women, and 17 intramural sports for men and 16 for women. Facilities include a 2500-seat gym, exercise and weight rooms, jogging facilities, and tennis, volleyball, and basketball courts.

Disabled Students: 80% of the campus is accessible. Wheelchair ramps, elevators, special parking, specially equipped rest rooms, special class scheduling, lowered drinking fountains, and lowered telephones are available.

Services: Counseling and information services are available, as is tutoring in every subject. There is a reader service for the blind, and remedial math, reading, and writing.

Campus Safety and Security: Measures include 24-hour foot and vehicle patrol, security escort services, shuttle buses, and pamphlets/posters/films. There are emergency telephones and lighted pathways/sidewalks.

Programs of Study: RWU confers B.A., B.S., B.Arch., and B.F.A. degrees. Master's degrees are also awarded. Bachelor's degrees are awarded in BIOLOGICAL SCIENCE (biology/biological science and marine biology), BUSINESS (accounting, banking and finance, business administration and management, international business management, and marketing/retailing/merchandising), COMMUNICATIONS AND THE ARTS (art history and appreciation, communications, creative writing, dance, dramatic arts, English, historic preservation, languages, and visual and performing arts), COMPUTER AND PHYSICAL SCIENCE (chemistry, computer science, information sciences and systems, and mathematics), EDUCATION (elementary and secondary), ENGINEERING AND ENVIRONMENTAL DESIGN (architecture, computer engineering, construction management, engineering, environmental engineering, and environmental science), HEALTH PROFESSIONS (premedicine and preveterinary science), SOCIAL SCIENCE (American studies, criminal justice, history, paralegal studies, philosophy, political science/government, prelaw, psychology, and social science). Architecture, construction management, and engineering are the strongest academically. Architecture, criminal justice, and psychology are the largest.

Required: To graduate, all students must complete 3 skills courses, 5 courses in interdisciplinary studies, 5 courses within a specific concentration, and an integrative senior seminar. A minimum of 120 credit hours, with 30 to 66 hours in the major and a GPA of 2.0, is required.

Special: RWU offers co-op programs, internships, accelerated degree programs, study abroad in 3 countries, a Washington semester, work-study, individualized majors, and dual majors. There are 7 national honor societies, a freshman honors program, and 6 departmental honors programs.

Faculty/Classroom: 59% of faculty are male; 41%, female. All teach undergraduates. No introductory courses are taught by graduate students. The average class size in an introductory lecture is 23; in a laboratory, 22; and in a regular course, 23.

Admissions: The SAT I scores for the 2003-2004 freshman class were: Verbal--32% below 500, 50% between 500 and 599, 17% between 600 and 700, and 1% above 700; Math--28% below 500, 51% between 500 and 599, 20% between 600 and 700, and 1% above 700. 29% of the current freshmen were in the top fifth of their class; 56% were in the top two fifths. There was 1 National Merit finalist and 1 semifinalist. 6 freshmen graduated first in their class.

Requirements: The SAT I is required. In addition, applicants should be graduates of an accredited secondary school with a minimum GPA of 2.0. The GED is accepted. Students should have 4 years of English, 3 years of math, 2 years each of social and natural sciences, and 4 to 6 electives, for a total of 16 Carnegie units. Art and architecture students must submit portfolios. An essay is required, and an interview is recommended. Dance students must audition. A GPA of 2.0 is required. AP and CLEP credits are accepted. Important factors in the admissions decision are recommendations by school officials, leadership record, and advanced placement or honor courses.

Procedure: Freshmen are admitted fall and spring. Entrance exams should be taken in September or October of the senior year. There are early decision, deferred and rolling admissions plans. Early decision applications should be filed by December 1; regular applications, by rolling for fall entry and rolling for spring entry, along with a $50 fee. Notification of early decision is sent December 15; regular decision, on a rolling basis. 125 applicants were on the 2003 waiting list; 14 were admitted. Applications are accepted on-line through CollegeNET.

Transfer: 134 transfer students enrolled in 2002-2003. Applicants need a minimum college GPA of 2.0. The SAT I is required if the transfer student has less than 24 transfer credits. 45 of 120 credits required for the bachelor's degree must be completed at RWU.

Visiting: There are regularly scheduled orientations for prospective students. There are guides for informal visits and visitors may sit in on classes. To schedule a visit, contact the Office of Admissions at *admit@rwu.edu*.

Financial Aid: In 2003-2004, 80% of all full-time freshmen and 77% of continuing full-time students received some form of financial aid. 65% of full-time freshmen and 69% of continuing full-time students received need-based aid. The average freshman award was $15,300. Need-based scholarships or need-based grants averaged $8905 ($19,920 maximum); need-based self-help aid (loans and jobs) averaged $4780 ($7800 maximum); and non-need-based awards and non-need-based scholarships averaged $6700 ($19,920 maximum). 36% of undergraduates work part time. Average annual earnings from campus work are $1600. The average financial indebtedness of the 2003 graduate was $17,125. RWU is a member of CSS. The CSS/Profile or FAFSA is required. The priority date for freshman financial aid applications for fall entry is February 1.

International Students: There are 87 international students enrolled. The school actively recruits these students. They must take the MELAB or the college's own test.

Computers: The mainframe is a UNIX-based network. 3 academic computer centers with a wide variety of application software are available to students more than 100 hours per week. All students may access the system. There are no time limits and no fees. It is strongly recommended that all students have a personal computer.

Graduates: From July 1, 2002 to June 30, 2003, 664 bachelor's degrees were awarded. The most popular majors were law/legal studies (24%), business/marketing (15%), and engineering/engineering technology (9%). In an average class, 39% graduate in 4 years or less, 9% graduate in 5 years or less, and 5% graduate in 6 years or less. 80 companies recruited on campus in 2002-2003. Of the 2002 graduating class, 25% were enrolled in graduate school within 6 months of graduation and 98% were employed.

Admissions Contact: Michelle Beauregard, Associate Director of Admissions. E-mail: *admit@rwu.edu* Web: *www.rwu.edu*

SALVE REGINA UNIVERSITY D-4
Newport, RI 02840-4192
(401) 341-2908
(888) GO-SALVE; Fax: (401) 848-2823

Full-time: 596 men, 1331 women	**Faculty:** 103; IIA, -$
Part-time: 31 men, 68 women	**Ph.D.s:** 73%
Graduate: 133 men, 198 women	**Student/Faculty:** 19 to 1
Year: semesters, summer session	**Tuition:** $20,510
Application Deadline: March 1	**Room & Board:** $8700
Freshman Class: 4131 applied, 2294 accepted, 574 enrolled	
SAT I Verbal/Math: 530/520	**ACT:** 22 COMPETITIVE

Salve Regina University, founded in 1934 and sponsored by the Sisters of Mercy, is an independent institution affiliated with the Roman Catholic Church. The university offers programs in liberal arts, business, health science, and professional training. In addition to regional accreditation, Salve has baccalaureate program accreditation with CSWE, IACBE, NASAD, and NLN. The library contains 139,161 volumes, 43,146 microform items, and 19,420 audio/video tapes/CDs, and subscribes to 1041 periodicals. Computerized library services include the card catalog, interlibrary loans, database searching, and Internet access. Special learning facilities include a learning resource center, art gallery, radio station, TV station, information systems, and computer science labs. The 70-acre campus is in a suburban area on Newport's waterfront, 60 miles south of Boston. Including any residence halls, there are 45 buildings.

Student Life: 82% of undergraduates are from out of state, mostly the Northeast. Students are from 35 states, 14 foreign countries, and Canada. 64% are from public schools. 93% are white. The average age of freshmen is 18; all undergraduates, 21. 20% do not continue beyond their first year; 62% remain to graduate.

Housing: 1160 students can be accommodated in college housing, which includes single-sex and coed dorms, on-campus apartments, off-campus apartments, and living/learning dorms. On-campus housing is guaranteed for the freshman year only and is available on a lottery system for upperclassmen. 57% of students live on campus; of those, 75% remain on campus on weekends. Alcohol is not permitted. Upperclassmen may keep cars.

Activities: There are no fraternities or sororities. There are 30 groups on campus, including art, band, cheerleading, choir, chorus, computers, dance, drama, ethnic, gay, honors, international, jazz band, literary magazine, musical theater, newspaper, outdoor, pep band, photography, political, professional, radio and TV, religious, social, social service, student government, and yearbook. Popular campus events include September Welcome-Back Weekend, Octoberfest Weekend, and New Year's Eve Ball.

Sports: There are 8 intercollegiate sports for men and 10 for women, and 8 intramural sports for men and 9 for women. Facilities include a recreation center, tennis courts, outdoor basketball courts, a weight room, a fitness center, and soccer, baseball, and softball fields.

Disabled Students: 75% of the campus is accessible. Wheelchair ramps, elevators, special parking, specially equipped rest rooms, special class scheduling, lowered drinking fountains, and lowered telephones are available.

Services: Counseling and information services are available, as is tutoring in most subjects. There is remedial math, reading, and writing. There also is a writing center and a computer-based tutorial program.

Campus Safety and Security: Measures include 24-hour foot and vehicle patrol, self-defense education, security escort services, and shuttle buses. There are informal discussions, pamphlets/posters/films, emergency telephones, and lighted pathways/sidewalks.

Programs of Study: Salve confers B.A., B.S., and B.A.S. degrees. Associate, master's, and doctoral degrees are also awarded. Bachelor's degrees are awarded in BIOLOGICAL SCIENCE (biology/biological science), BUSINESS (accounting, business administration and management, and management science), COMMUNICATIONS AND THE ARTS (art history and appreciation, communications, communications technology, dramatic arts, English, French, historic preservation, media arts, music, Spanish, and studio art), COMPUTER AND PHYSICAL SCIENCE (chemistry, information sciences and systems, and mathematics), EDUCATION (early childhood, elementary, secondary, and special), HEALTH PROFESSIONS (cytotechnology, medical laboratory technology, and nursing), SOCIAL SCIENCE (American studies, anthropology, criminal justice, economics, history, philosophy, political science/government, psychology, religion, social work, and sociology). Psychology, social work, and accounting are the strongest academically. Business, administration of justice, and elementary education are the largest.

Required: To graduate, students must have 128 credit hours, with about 36 in the major, and must maintain a minimum GPA of 2.0. Distribution requirements include 9 credit hours in social science, 6 each in religious studies, science, English, and a foreign language, and 3 each in visual and performing arts, philosophy, and math.

Special: Salve offers internships in most academic disciplines as well as work-study programs on campus. Study abroad, a Washington semester, B.A.-B.S. degrees in biology and economics, dual majors in many programs, and accelerated degree programs in administration of justice, health services administration, business, and international relations are available. A liberal studies degree, credit for life, military, and work experience, nondegree study, and pass/fail options are also offered. There are 15 national honor societies and a freshman honors program.

Faculty/Classroom: 45% of faculty are male; 55%, female. 94% teach undergraduates and 20% both teach and do research. No introductory courses are taught by graduate students. The average class size in an introductory lecture is 20; in a laboratory, 16; and in a regular course, 15.

Admissions: 56% of the 2003-2004 applicants were accepted. The SAT I scores for the 2003-2004 freshman class were: Verbal--24% below 500, 60% between 500 and 599, 15% between 600 and 700, and 1% above 700; Math--29% below 500, 56% between 500 and 599, and 15% between 600 and 700. 31% of the current freshmen were in the top fifth of their class; 57% were in the top two fifths. In a recent year there was 1 National Merit semifinalist and 1 freshman graduated first in the class.

Requirements: The SAT I or ACT is required. In addition, applicants must be high school graduates or hold a GED. Students should have 16 Carnegie units, consisting of 4 in English, 3 in math including algebra and geometry, 2 each in science and foreign language, 1 in history, and 4 in electives. An essay is required. A GPA of 2.7 is required. AP and CLEP credits are accepted. Important factors in the admissions decision are advanced placement or honor courses, recommendations by school officials, and leadership record.

Procedure: Freshmen are admitted fall and spring. Entrance exams should be taken as early as possible. There are early admissions and deferred admissions plans and a rolling admissions plan. Applications should be filed by March 1 for fall entry and December 15 for spring entry, along with a $40 fee. Notification is sent beginning December 15. 248 applicants were on the 2003 waiting list; 19 were admitted. Applications are accepted on-line through the university's web site and CollegeLink, Apply 2002, EXPAN, Peterson's, and Common App.

Transfer: 52 transfer students enrolled in 2002-2003. Applicants must have a college GPA of 2.3. An interview is recommended. 36 of 128 credits required for the bachelor's degree must be completed at Salve.

Visiting: There are regularly scheduled orientations for prospective students, including an introduction to the academic experience, history and visions for the university, a library orientation, student life expectations, social activities, residence hall orientation, preregistration for courses, a cookout, and meetings with faculty, advisers, and administrators. There are guides for informal visits and visitors may sit in on classes and stay overnight. To schedule a visit, contact the Admissions Office.

Financial Aid: In 2003-2004, 70% of all full-time freshmen and 66% of continuing full-time students received some form of financial aid. 66% of full-time freshmen and 60% of continuing full-time students received need-based aid. The average freshman award was $16,383. Need-based scholarships or need-based grants averaged $12,283; need-based self-help aid (loans and jobs) averaged $5066; and non-need-based awards and non-need-based scholarships averaged $3915. 33% of undergraduates work part time. Average annual earnings from campus work are $1000. The average financial indebtedness of the 2003 graduate was $18,875. Salve is a member of CSS. The CSS/Profile or FAFSA, the college's own financial statement and the tax forms are required. The deadline for filing freshman financial aid applications for fall entry is March 1.

International Students: There are 23 international students enrolled. The school actively recruits these students. They must score 500 on the written TOEFL or 173 on the electronic version.

Computers: The mainframe is an IBM AS/400. There are 110 PCs and Macs available in computer and science labs for undergraduate use. An additional 150 PCs are assigned to faculty and academic departments, as well as computer networks using Novell NetWare, color printers, and Internet services. There are 5 dedicated technology classrooms. All students may access the system 16 hours per day in labs and 24 hours per day by dial-in access to the Internet. There are no time limits. The fee is $125 per semester.

Graduates: From July 1, 2002 to June 30, 2003, 381 bachelor's degrees were awarded. The most popular majors were education (29%), business (17%), and administration of justice (12%). In an average class, 58% graduate in 4 years or less, 60% graduate in 5 years or less, and 62% graduate in 6 years or less. 100 companies recruited on campus in 2002-2003. Of the 2002 graduating class, 20% were enrolled in graduate school within 6 months of graduation and 85% were employed.

Admissions Contact: Laura E. McPhie-Oliveira, Vice President for Enrollment and Dean of Admissions. A video is available.
E-mail: *sruadmis@salve.edu* Web: *www.salve.edu*

UNIVERSITY OF RHODE ISLAND   C-4
Kingston, RI 02881   (401) 874-7100; Fax: (401) 874-5523

Full-time: 4203 men, 5226 women	**Faculty:** I, av$
Part-time: 709 men, 1160 women	**Ph.Ds:** 90%
Graduate: 1103 men, 1876 women	**Student/Faculty:** n/av
Year: semesters, summer session	**Tuition:** $6202 ($16,334)
Application Deadline: March 1	**Room & Board:** $7518
Freshman Class: 12,963 applied, 9074 accepted, 2590 enrolled	
SAT I Verbal/Math: 540/560	**VERY COMPETITIVE**

The University of Rhode Island, founded in 1892, is a land-grant, sea-grant, and urban-grant institution offering programs in liberal arts, business, engineering, human services, nursing, and pharmacy. Located near the ocean and the bay, the university has strong marine and environmental programs. There are satellite campuses in Providence, West Greenwich, and Narragansett. There are 8 undergraduate and 3 graduate schools. In addition to regional accreditation, URI has baccalaureate program accreditation with AACSB, ABET, ACPE, ADA, ASLA, NASM, NCATE, and NLN. The 3 libraries contain 1,205,138 volumes, 1,655,084 microform items, and 11,671 audio/video tapes/CDs, and subscribe to 7926 periodicals. Computerized library services include the card catalog, interlibrary loans, and database searching. Special learning facilities include a learning resource center, art gallery, planetarium, radio station, TV station, historic textile collection, and early childhood education center. The 1248-acre campus is in a small town 30 miles south of Providence. Including any residence halls, there are 314 buildings.

Student Life: 61% of undergraduates are from Rhode Island. Students are from 50 states, 53 foreign countries, and Canada. 85% are from public schools. 76% are white. The average age of freshmen is 19; all undergraduates, 22. 19% do not continue beyond their first year.

Housing: 4100 students can be accommodated in college housing, which includes single-sex and coed dorms, on-campus apartments, married-student housing, fraternity houses, and sorority houses. In addition, there are language houses, special-interest houses, a freshman dorm and a wellness dorm. 59% of students commute. All students may keep cars.

Activities: 10% of men belong to 11 national fraternities; 10% of women belong to 9 national sororities. There are 90 groups on campus, including band, cheerleading, chess, choir, chorale, chorus, computers, concert band, dance, drama, ethnic, gay, honors, international, jazz band, literary magazine, marching band, music ensembles, musical theater, newspaper, opera, orchestra, pep band, photography, political, professional, radio and TV, religious, social, social service, student government, and yearbook. Popular campus events include Winterfest, Martin Luther King Week, and International Week.

Sports: There are 10 intercollegiate sports for men and 11 for women, and 18 intramural sports for men and 18 for women. Facilities include

a 4000-seat area, a 10,000-seat stadium, 3 pools, a multipurpose field house with an indoor track, a gymnastics center, 3 fitness rooms, and courts for basketball, tennis, and volleyball. There are also outdoor tennis courts, an all-weather track, 2 beach volleyball courts, and varsity and practice fields.

Disabled Students: Wheelchair ramps, elevators, special parking, specially equipped rest rooms, special class scheduling, lowered drinking fountains, lowered telephones, and special transportation around campus are available.

Services: Counseling and information services are available, as is tutoring in some subjects, including ESL and popular freshman courses. There is a reader service for the blind and remedial math, reading, and writing.

Campus Safety and Security: Measures include 24-hour foot and vehicle patrol, self-defense education, security escort services, and shuttle buses. There are informal discussions, pamphlets/posters/films, emergency telephones, and lighted pathways/sidewalks.

Programs of Study: URI confers B.A., B.S., B.F.A., B.G.S., B.L.A., and B.M. degrees. Master's and doctoral degrees are also awarded. Bachelor's degrees are awarded in AGRICULTURE (animal science, fishing and fisheries, horticulture, natural resource management, and wildlife management), BIOLOGICAL SCIENCE (biology/biological science, marine science, microbiology, nutrition, and zoology), BUSINESS (accounting, banking and finance, business administration and management, fashion merchandising, management information systems, and marketing/retailing/merchandising), COMMUNICATIONS AND THE ARTS (art, classics, communications, comparative literature, dramatic arts, English, fine arts, French, German, Italian, journalism, literature, music, Spanish, and speech/debate/rhetoric), COMPUTER AND PHYSICAL SCIENCE (chemistry, computer science, geology, mathematics, physics, and statistics), EDUCATION (elementary, music, physical, and secondary), ENGINEERING AND ENVIRONMENTAL DESIGN (biomedical engineering, chemical engineering, civil engineering, computer engineering, electrical/electronics engineering, environmental science, industrial engineering, landscape architecture/design, mechanical engineering, and ocean engineering), HEALTH PROFESSIONS (clinical science, dental hygiene, health care administration, medical laboratory technology, nursing, pharmacy, and speech pathology/audiology), SOCIAL SCIENCE (anthropology, dietetics, economics, family/consumer studies, food science, geography, history, human development, human services, Latin American studies, philosophy, political science/government, psychology, sociology, textiles and clothing, water resources, and women's studies). Pharmacy, engineering, and biology are the strongest academically. Psychology, communication studies, and pharmacy are the largest.

Required: To graduate, the student must earn 120 to 150 credit hours, at least 30 in the major, with a GPA of 2.0. Distribution requirements include 6 credits each in English communication, fine arts and literature, foreign language or culture, letters, natural sciences, and social sciences, as well as 3 credits in math.

Special: Cross-registration is available with Rhode Island College and Community College of Rhode Island. URI also offers a Washington semester as well as semester-long internships with businesses and state agencies, study abroad in 6 countries, a B.A.-B.S. degree in German and engineering and in languages and business, a general studies degree, dual majors, pass/fail options, and credit for life, military, and work experience. The College of Engineering offers co-op programs and an international internship. There are 30 national honor societies, including Phi Beta Kappa, and a freshman honors program.

Faculty/Classroom: 65% of faculty are male; 35%, female. All both teach and do research. Graduate students teach 7% of introductory courses. The average class size in an introductory lecture is 30 and in a laboratory, 14.

Admissions: 70% of the 2003-2004 applicants were accepted. The SAT I scores for the 2003-2004 freshman class were: Verbal--21% below 500, 54% between 500 and 599, 22% between 600 and 700, and 3% above 700; Math--16% below 500, 52% between 500 and 599, 28% between 600 and 700, and 4% above 700. 38% of the current freshmen were in the top fifth of their class; 76% were in the top two fifths. 30 freshmen graduated first in their class in a recent year.

Requirements: The SAT I or ACT is required. In addition, applicants should be high school graduates, having completed 18 courses, including 4 of English, 3 to 4 of math, and 2 each of science (chemistry and physics for engineering majors), foreign language, and history or social studies. Remaining units should be college preparatory. Music majors must audition. AP and CLEP credits are accepted. Important factors in the admissions decision are advanced placement or honor courses, evidence of special talent, and recommendations by school officials.

Procedure: Freshmen are admitted fall and spring. Entrance exams should be taken during the spring of the junior year or fall of the senior year. There is an early admissions plan. There is a rolling admissions plan. Early decision applications should be filed by December 15; regular applications, by March 1 for fall entry and November 1 for spring entry, along with a $35 fee. Notification is sent on a rolling basis. Applications are accepted on-line through the school's web site.

Transfer: 546 transfer students enrolled in 2003-2004. Applicants must submit transcripts from high school and all colleges or universities attended. A minimum GPA of 2.4 is required; many programs require higher. 24 of 120 credits required for the bachelor's degree must be completed at URI.

Visiting: There are regularly scheduled orientations for prospective students, including open house programs in October and campus tours. There are guides for informal visits and visitors may sit in on classes. To schedule a visit, contact the Admissions Office at (401) 874-9800.

Financial Aid: In 2003-2004, 55% of all full-time freshmen and 49% of continuing full-time students received some form of financial aid. The average freshman award was $9480. Need-based scholarships or need-based grants averaged $5821; need-based self-help aid (loans and jobs) averaged $4173; non-need-based athletic scholarships averaged $5126; and other non-need-based awards and non-need-based scholarships averaged $4025. The average financial indebtedness of the 2003 graduate was $14,500. URI is a member of CSS. The FAFSA is required. The deadline for filing freshman financial aid applications for fall entry is March 1.

International Students: The school actively recruits these students. They must score 550 on the written TOEFL or take the English proficiency test administered by the American Consulate. They must take the SAT I or the ACT.

Computers: The mainframe is an IBM ES/9000-210VF. Students may access the mainframes through more than 550 terminals. All students may access the system 24 hours per day. There are no time limits and no fees.

Graduates: The most popular majors were business/marketing (19%), communications/communications technology (10%), and personal services (10%). In an average class, 34% graduate in 4 years or less, 18% in 5 years or less, and 4% in 6 years or less.

Admissions Contact: David Taggart, Dean of Admissions.
E-mail: *uriadmit@etal.uri.edu* Web: *www.uri.edu/admissions*

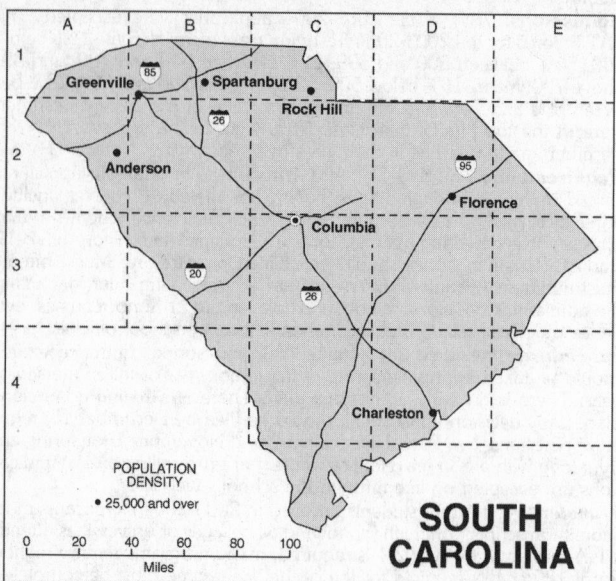

A B C D E

Greenville
Spartanburg
Rock Hill
Anderson
Columbia
Florence
Charleston

POPULATION DENSITY
● 25,000 and over

0 20 40 60 80 100
Miles

SOUTH CAROLINA

Required: To graduate, all students must complete 120 credit hours with a minimum 2.0 GPA. Students must demonstrate competence in reading, composition, speech, and fundamental math skills.

Special: Allen offers internships with businesses and federal, state, and local agencies, and work-study with the Columbia Housing Authority. A certificate in gerontology is possible. There is 1 national honor society and 20 departmental honors programs.

Faculty/Classroom: All teach undergraduates.

Requirements: Applicants should be graduates of accredited high schools or have earned the GED. Secondary preparation should total 20 academic credits. A personal interview is recommended. Important factors in the admissions decision are leadership record, advanced placement or honor courses, and evidence of special talent.

Procedure: Freshmen are admitted to all sessions. Entrance exams should be taken in the spring. There is an early decision plan. Application deadlines are open.

Transfer: An official transcript from each school attended is required at least 1 month prior to the beginning of the semester in which admission is desired. 30 of 120 credits required for the bachelor's degree must be completed at Allen.

Visiting: There are regularly scheduled orientations for prospective students. There are guides for informal visits and visitors may sit in on classes. To schedule a visit, contact Dr. John Waddell, Dean of Student Development Services at (803) 376-5741.

Financial Aid: Allen is a member of CSS. The CSS Profile and the college's own financial statement are required. Check with the school for current deadlines.

International Students: The school actively recruits these students.

Computers: The mainframe is an IBM. A computer lab is available. All students may access the system. There are no time limits and no fees.

Graduates: In an average class, 40% graduate in 4 years or less, and 20% graduate in 5 years or less.

Admissions Contact: Admissions Office.
E-mail: *auniv@minspring.com*

ALLEN UNIVERSITY
C-3
Columbia, SC 29204
(803) 376-5735
(888) 425-5360; Fax: (803) 376-5715

Full-time: 125 men, 200 women	**Faculty:** 14
Part-time: 5 men, 10 women	**Ph.D.s:** 54%
Graduate: none	**Student/Faculty:** 23 to 1
Year: semesters, summer session	**Tuition:** $5300
Application Deadline: open	**Room & Board:** $5000
Freshman Class: n/av	
SAT I or ACT: not required	**NONCOMPETITIVE**

Allen University, founded in 1870, is a small private institution affiliated with the African Methodist Episcopal (A.M.E.) Church. It offers undergraduate programs in liberal arts and sciences, business, and social work. Figures in the above capsule are approximate. The library contains 40,558 volumes, 2883 microform items, and 2527 audio/video tapes/CDs, and subscribes to 106 periodicals. Special learning facilities include a learning resource center. The 4-acre campus is in a small town. Including any residence halls, there are 84 buildings.

Student Life: Students are from 20 states and 9 foreign countries. 95% are from public schools. 99% are African American. Most are Protestant. The average age of freshmen is 18; all undergraduates, 24. 20% do not continue beyond their first year.

Housing: 405 students can be accommodated in college housing, which includes single-sex dorms and off-campus apartments. On-campus housing is guaranteed for all 4 years. 95% of students live on campus. Alcohol is not permitted. All students may keep cars.

Activities: 8% of men belong to 4 national fraternities; 6% of women belong to 4 national sororities. There are 20 groups on campus, including art, band, cheerleading, choir, chorus, drama, honors, international, newspaper, religious, social service, student government, and yearbook. Popular campus events include Cultural, Academic, and Religious Series (CARS), International Day, and Founders Day.

Sports: There are 2 intercollegiate sports for men, and 1 intramural sport for men and 1 for women.

Disabled Students: Special parking is available.

Services: Counseling and information services are available, as is tutoring in most subjects. There is remedial math, reading, and writing. There are math, science, reading, and writing labs.

Campus Safety and Security: Measures include 24-hour foot and vehicle patrol, self-defense education, security escort services, and pamphlets/posters/films. There are emergency telephones and lighted pathways/sidewalks.

Programs of Study: Allen confers B.A. and B.S. degrees. Associate degrees are also awarded. Bachelor's degrees are awarded in BIOLOGICAL SCIENCE (biology/biological science), BUSINESS (business administration and management), COMMUNICATIONS AND THE ARTS (English and music), COMPUTER AND PHYSICAL SCIENCE (mathematics), SOCIAL SCIENCE (history, political science/government, and sociology). Sociology/social work and business administration are the largest.

BENEDICT COLLEGE
C-3
Columbia, SC 29204
(803) 253-5145
(800) 868-6598; Fax: (803) 253-5167

Full-time: 1320 men, 1325 women	**Faculty:** 90; IIB, --$
Part-time: 45 men, 65 women	**Ph.D.s:** 65%
Graduate: none	**Student/Faculty:** 25 to 1
Year: semesters, summer session	**Tuition:** $8500
Application Deadline: open	**Room & Board:** $4500
Freshman Class: n/av	
SAT I: required	**LESS COMPETITIVE**

Benedict College, founded in 1870, is a private liberal arts institution affiliated with the Baptist Church. Figures in the above capsule are approximate. In addition to regional accreditation, Benedict College has baccalaureate program accreditation with CSWE. The library contains 120,000 volumes, 3100 microform items, and 5200 audio/video tapes/CDs, and subscribes to 325 periodicals. Computerized library services include database searching. Special learning facilities include a learning resource center and art gallery. The 20-acre campus is in an urban area 90 miles south of Charlotte, North Carolina. Including any residence halls, there are 15 buildings.

Student Life: 82% of undergraduates are from South Carolina. 99% are from public schools. 99% are African American. The average age of freshmen is 19; all undergraduates, 20. 50% do not continue beyond their first year; 20% remain to graduate.

Housing: 1090 students can be accommodated in college housing, which includes single-sex dorms. On-campus housing is available on a first-come, first-served basis. Priority is given to out-of-town students. 77% of students live on campus. Alcohol is not permitted. Upperclassmen may keep cars.

Activities: 2% of men belong to 4 local and 4 national fraternities; 5% of women belong to 4 local and 4 national sororities. There are 50 groups on campus, including art, cheerleading, choir, chorus, dance, drama, drill team, international, newspaper, photography, religious, student government, and yearbook. Popular campus events include Fall Convocation, Crowning of Miss Benedict, Religion Emphasis Week, and Commencement.

Sports: There are 5 intercollegiate sports for men and 5 for women, and 10 intramural sports for men and 9 for women. Facilities include a gymnasium and student center.

Disabled Students: Wheelchair ramps, elevators, and special parking are available.

Services: Counseling and information services are available, as is tutoring in every subject. There is remedial math, reading, and writing.

Campus Safety and Security: Measures include 24-hour foot and vehicle patrol, informal discussions, pamphlets/posters/films, and lighted pathways/sidewalks.

Programs of Study: Benedict College confers B.A., B.S., and B.S.W. degrees. Bachelor's degrees are awarded in BIOLOGICAL SCIENCE (biology/biological science), BUSINESS (accounting and business administration and management), COMMUNICATIONS AND THE ARTS (English, journalism, and music), COMPUTER AND PHYSICAL SCIENCE (chemistry, computer science, mathematics, and physics), EDUCATION (early childhood and elementary), HEALTH PROFESSIONS (environmental health science), SOCIAL SCIENCE (criminal justice, philosophy, religion, social science, and social work). Business administration is the largest.

Required: Students must complete 125 credit hours, including 24 to 32 in the major, with a minimum GPA of 2.0; some degrees require a higher GPA. The 57-hour general education requirements include 15 hours of English, 9 of social science, 8 of natural science, 6 each of mathematics and a foreign language, 4 of humanities, and 2 each of health education, freshman seminar, physical education, and religion.

Special: Benedict offers work-study programs, a physics/engineering dual major, internships, a B.A./B.S. degree, and preprofessional programs in dentistry, engineering, law, and medicine.

Faculty/Classroom: 57% of faculty are male; 43%, female. All teach undergraduates and 1% both teach and do research. The average class size in an introductory lecture is 39; in a laboratory, 33; and in a regular course, 30.

Requirements: The SAT I is required. In addition, students should have taken 4 secondary school units of English, 3 each of mathematics and social science, 2 of natural science, 7 of electives, and 1 of physical education or ROTC. The GED is accepted. AP and CLEP credits are accepted.

Procedure: Entrance exams should be taken prior to registration. There are early admissions and deferred admissions plans. Application deadlines are open. Check with the school for current application fee.

Transfer: Applicants must submit transcripts from previous institutions attended plus evidence of honorable withdrawal. The SAT I is required. Only courses in which a C or better was earned will be considered for credit. 30 of 125 credits required for the bachelor's degree must be completed at Benedict College.

Visiting: There are regularly scheduled orientations for prospective students. There are guides for informal visits and visitors may sit in on classes. To schedule a visit, contact the Admissions Office at (800) 868-6598 or (803) 253-5143.

Financial Aid: Benedict College is a member of CSS. The CSS/Profile, the college's own financial statement, and the South Carolina Tuition Grant applications are required. Check with the school for current deadlines.

International Students: They must score 500 on the written TOEFL and also take the college's own test and the SAT I. Some students may be required to complete an ESL program.

Computers: The mainframes are a DEC PDP 11/70 and DEC VAX 11/785 and 11/780. Students use the mainframe for all programming courses, for computer graphic classes, to create a text file, and to access the Test Data Bank for General and Principles of Biology. There are 36 terminals housed in Alumni Hall. All students may access the system. There are no time limits and no fees.

Admissions Contact: Gary Knight, Director of Enrollment Management. A video is available. E-mail: *admissions@benedict.edu* Web: *www.benedict.edu*

CHARLESTON SOUTHERN UNIVERSITY   D-4
Charleston, SC 29423-8087
(843) 863-7050
(800) 947-7474; Fax: (843) 863-7070

Full-time: 800 men, 1200 women	Faculty: 93; IIB, --$
Part-time: 160 men, 320 women	Ph.D.s: 71%
Graduate: 100 men, 140 women	Student/Faculty: 21 to 1
Year: semesters, summer session	Tuition: $14,426
Application Deadline: open	Room & Board: $5544
Freshman Class: n/av	
SAT I or ACT: required	COMPETITIVE

Charleston Southern University, founded in 1964, is a private liberal arts institution affiliated with the South Carolina Baptist Convention. There are 4 undergraduate and 3 graduate schools. Figures in the above capsule and in this profile are approximate. In addition to regional accreditation, CSU has baccalaureate program accreditation with NASDTEC, NASM, and NLN. The library contains 215,000 volumes, 200,000 microform items, and 7500 audio/video tapes/CDs, and subscribes to 1200 periodicals. Computerized library services include the card catalog and database searching. Special learning facilities include a learning resource center, an earthquake education center, and a field physics laboratory. The 500-acre campus is in a suburban area 20 miles west of Charleston. Including any residence halls, there are 16 buildings.

Student Life: 81% of undergraduates are from South Carolina. 85% are from public schools. 47% are white; 27% African American. The average age of freshmen is 18; all undergraduates, 25. 28% do not continue beyond their first year; 31% remain to graduate.

Housing: 1250 students can be accommodated in college housing, which includes single-sex dorms and married-student housing. On-campus housing is guaranteed for the freshman year only and is available on a first-come, first-served basis. 56% of students commute. Alcohol is not permitted. All students may keep cars.

Activities: There are no fraternities or sororities. There are 20 groups on campus, including art, band, cheerleading, choir, chorus, drama, honors, jazz band, literary magazine, marching band, newspaper, religious, social service, student government, and yearbook.

Sports: There are 9 intercollegiate sports for men and 9 for women, and 4 intramural sports for men and 4 for women. Facilities include a gym, tennis courts, a track center, football and soccer fields, a baseball diamond, training and weight rooms, a 3-hole golf course with driving range, and a Wellness Center.

Disabled Students: All of the campus is accessible. Wheelchair ramps, elevators, special parking, specially equipped rest rooms, and lowered drinking fountains are available.

Services: Counseling and information services are available, as is tutoring in most subjects. There is remedial math, reading, and writing.

Campus Safety and Security: Measures include 24-hour foot and vehicle patrol, security escort services, emergency telephones, and lighted pathways/sidewalks.

Programs of Study: CSU confers B.A., B.S., and B.Tech. degrees. Associate and master's degrees are also awarded. Bachelor's degrees are awarded in BIOLOGICAL SCIENCE (biochemistry and biology/biological science), BUSINESS (business administration and management), COMMUNICATIONS AND THE ARTS (dramatic arts, English, fine arts, music, Spanish, and speech/debate/rhetoric), COMPUTER AND PHYSICAL SCIENCE (chemistry, computer science, geology, mathematics, and natural sciences), EDUCATION (early childhood, elementary, music, physical, and science), ENGINEERING AND ENVIRONMENTAL DESIGN (environmental science), HEALTH PROFESSIONS (music therapy and nursing), SOCIAL SCIENCE (criminal justice, economics, geography, history, humanities, political science/government, psychology, religion, religious music, social science, sociology, and youth ministry).

Required: To graduate, students must complete 125 credit hours, including all core curriculum, major, and minor requirements, with a GPA of 2.0. At least 45 hours must be in the major. Core courses include 24 hours of communications and fine arts, 11 of natural science/math, and 9 of social studies.

Special: CSU offers internships, cross-registration through the Trident Area Consortium, work-study programs, dual majors, and nondegree study. Nonmajor preprofessional programs are available in dentistry, engineering, law, medicine, and ministry. There are 5 national honor societies, a freshman honors program, and 100 departmental honors programs.

Faculty/Classroom: 55% of faculty are male; 45%, female. All teach undergraduates. No introductory courses are taught by graduate students. The average class size in an introductory lecture is 40; in a laboratory, 15; and in a regular course, 25.

Requirements: The SAT I or ACT is required. In addition, applicants must be graduates of an accredited secondary school. The GED is accepted. Character references are preferred. An English proficiency exam is required for all entering students. CSU requires applicants to be in the upper 60% of their class. A GPA of 2.0 is required. AP and CLEP credits are accepted. Important factors in the admissions decision are evidence of special talent, leadership record, and advanced placement or honor courses.

Procedure: Freshmen are admitted to all sessions. Entrance exams should be taken any time before filing for admission. Application deadlines are open. The application fee is $30. Applications are accepted online.

Transfer: 278 transfer students enrolled in a recent year. Applicants must submit official transcripts from all previous colleges attended. Accepted transfers must take an English proficiency exam. 30 of 125 credits required for the bachelor's degree must be completed at CSU.

Visiting: There are regularly scheduled orientations for prospective students, consisting of orientation for students, orientation for parents, placement testing for students, a tour, and lunch. There are guides for informal visits and visitors may sit in on classes. To schedule a visit, contact the Office of Enrollment Services.

Financial Aid: The FAFSA is required. Check with the school for current deadlines.

International Students: They must score 550 on the written TOEFL and also take the SAT I or the ACT.

Computers: The mainframe is an RS6000. Macs and PCs are available in 5 computer labs and in the library, and a student mainframe is available in all student labs; Internet and Web access is provided in labs, dorm rooms, and the library. All students may access the system. There are no time limits and no fees. It is strongly recommended that all students have a personal computer.

Graduates: In a recent year, 275 bachelor's degrees were awarded. The most popular majors were business administration (21%), education (14%), and psychology/social science (9%). In an average class, 31% graduate in 4 years or less. Of a recent graduating class, 27% were enrolled in graduate school within 6 months of graduation and 63% were employed.

Admissions Contact: Cheryl Burton, Director of Admissions. A video is available. E-mail: *enroll@csuniv.edu* Web: *www.csuniv.edu*

CITADEL, THE   D-4
Charleston, SC 29409

(843) 953-5230
(800) 868-1842; Fax: (843) 953-7036

Full-time: 1920 men, 117 women	**Faculty:** 149; IIA, av$
Part-time: 63 men, 50 women	**Ph.D.s:** 80%
Graduate: 407 men, 1081 women	**Student/Faculty:** 14 to 1
Year: semesters, summer session	**Tuition:** $12,295 ($20,706)
Application Deadline: open	**Room & Board:** n/app
Freshman Class: 1919 applied, 588 accepted, 553 enrolled	
SAT I or ACT: required	**COMPETITIVE+**

The Citadel, established in 1842 by the South Carolina legislature, is a liberal arts military college supported by the state. Tuition figures in the above capsule are for students in the Corps of Cadets and include charges for lab fees, athletic fees, most books, school supplies, uniforms, alterations, and laundry and dry cleaning. Freshmen pay an additional $3360. In addition to regional accreditation, The Citadel has baccalaureate program accreditation with AACSB, ABET, and NCATE. The library contains 236,418 volumes, 1,193,192 microform items, and 2656 audio/video tapes/CDs, and subscribes to 504 periodicals. Computerized library services include the card catalog, interlibrary loans, and database searching. Special learning facilities include a military museum, archives, and a writing center. The 100-acre campus is in a suburban area in Charleston. Including any residence halls, there are 69 buildings.

Student Life: 51% of undergraduates are from South Carolina. Students are from 46 states, 29 foreign countries, and Canada. 70% are from public schools. 80% are white. 68% are Protestant; 23% Catholic. The average age of freshmen is 18; all undergraduates, 20. 22% do not continue beyond their first year; 99% remain to graduate.

Housing: 1928 students can be accommodated in college housing, which includes coed dorms. All cadets live in barracks. On-campus housing is guaranteed for all 4 years. All of students live on campus; of those, all remain on campus on weekends. Alcohol is not permitted. Upperclassmen may keep cars.

Activities: There are no fraternities or sororities. There are 37 groups on campus, including bagpipe band, band, cheerleading, choir, chorale, computers, drama, drill team, ethnic, honors, literary magazine, marching band, newspaper, pep band, political, professional, religious, social, social service, student government, and yearbook. Popular campus events include Parents Weekend and Corps Day.

Sports: There are 9 intercollegiate sports for men and 5 for women, and 20 intramural sports for men and 20 for women. Facilities include a 22,000-seat stadium, a 6000-seat field house, fitness centers, weight and wrestling rooms, tennis courts, an all-weather track, and playing fields. The boating center and beach club are within a half-hour drive of the college.

Disabled Students: 80% of the campus is accessible. Wheelchair ramps, elevators, special parking, and specially equipped rest rooms are available.

Services: Counseling and information services are available, as is tutoring in every subject.

Campus Safety and Security: Measures include 24-hour foot and vehicle patrol, security escort services, lighted pathways/sidewalks, lock out, and jumpstart services.

Programs of Study: The Citadel confers B.A., B.S., B.S.B.A., B.S.C.E., and B.S.E.E. degrees. Master's degrees are also awarded. Bachelor's degrees are awarded in BIOLOGICAL SCIENCE (biology/biological science), BUSINESS (business administration and management), COMMUNICATIONS AND THE ARTS (English, French, German, and Spanish), COMPUTER AND PHYSICAL SCIENCE (chemistry, computer science, mathematics, and physics), EDUCATION (health, physical, and secondary), ENGINEERING AND ENVIRONMENTAL DESIGN (civil engineering and electrical/electronics engineering), HEALTH PROFESSIONS (predentistry and premedicine), SOCIAL SCIENCE (criminal justice, history, political science/government, and psychology). English is the strongest academically. Business administration is the largest.

Required: To graduate, students must complete 121 to 139 credit hours, depending on the major, with an overall GPA of 2.0 (2.5 for education majors). The required core curriculum for all majors includes study in 5 areas: English, history, math, science, and social sciences. Specific course requirements include 8 semesters of ROTC, 4 of English, and 4 of phys ed. In addition, cadets must satisfy disciplinary requirements and observe the honor system.

Special: Students may earn a combined B.A.-B.S. degree, design their own majors, and take a 3-2 program in engineering. Work-study programs, internships, dual majors, independent study, study abroad, and pass/fail options are also available. Qualified students may enroll in a separate honors program. There are 7 national honor societies, including Phi Beta Kappa, a freshman honors program, and 1 departmental honors program.

Faculty/Classroom: 71% of faculty are male; 29%, female. 95% teach undergraduates. The average class size in an introductory lecture is 25 and in a regular course, 20.

Admissions: 31% of the 2003-2004 applicants were accepted. The SAT I scores for the 2003-2004 freshman class were: Verbal--23% below 500, 51% between 500 and 599, 23% between 600 and 700, and 3% above 700; Math--20% below 500, 50% between 500 and 599, 27% between 600 and 700, and 3% above 700. The ACT scores were 29% below 21, 37% between 21 and 23, 23% between 24 and 26, 7% between 27 and 28, and 4% above 28. 34% of the current freshmen were in the top fifth of their class; 74% were in the top two fifths.

Requirements: The SAT I or ACT is required. In addition, SAT II: Subject test in math level II is strongly recommended for engineering, science, and math applicants. Also required are recommendations from high school principals or guidance counselors. Applicants must be between 16 and 22, unmarried, and must meet certain physical requirements. High school preparation should include 4 units in English; 3 in math, including algebra I and II; 3 in lab science: biology, chemistry, or physics; 2 each in foreign language and social science; 1 in phys ed or ROTC; and 1 in history. The Citadel requires applicants to be in the upper 50% of their class. A GPA of 2.0 is required. AP and CLEP credits are accepted. Important factors in the admissions decision are advanced placement or honor courses, extracurricular activities record, and leadership record.

Procedure: Freshmen are admitted in the fall. Entrance exams should be taken by February of the senior year. There is a rolling admissions plan. Application deadlines are open. The fall 2003 application fee was $35. Applications are accepted on-line through *www.citadel.edu/admission/cadmission/cadapplication.html*.

Transfer: 64 transfer students enrolled in 2002-2003. Applicants must meet freshmen entrance requirements and submit official transcripts from all previous colleges attended. Transfer students must have completed a minimum of 2 semesters as full-time students (minimum 12 hours each semester) and maintained a GPA of 2.0. A full year of course work, including half the required hours in the major, must be completed at The Citadel.

Visiting: There are regularly scheduled orientations for prospective students, including an interview with an admissions counselor and a campus tour guided by a cadet. There are guides for informal visits and visitors may sit in on classes and stay overnight. To schedule a visit, contact the Admissions Office.

Financial Aid: In a recent year, 47% of all full-time freshmen and 41% of continuing full-time students received some form of financial aid. 47% of full-time freshmen and 25% of continuing full-time students received need-based aid. The average freshman award was $3000. 3% of undergraduates work part time. Average annual earnings from campus work are $675. The average financial indebtedness in a recent year was $13,650. The FAFSA is required. The priority date for freshman financial aid applications for fall entry is March 17. The deadline for filing freshman financial aid applications for fall entry is February 28.

International Students: There are 61 international students enrolled. They must score 550 on the written TOEFL.

Computers: The mainframe is a DEC Alpha. There are 2 VAX terminal labs and 7 Mac and/or IBM PS/2 labs, some networked and some standalone, open to all students 7 days a week. Cadet rooms are wired for access to the campus network and the Internet. All students may access the system. It is strongly recommended that all students have a personal computer. Microsoft Windows-compatible 486 DX or Pentium PC is recommended.

Graduates: From July 1, 2002 to June 30, 2003, 416 bachelor's degrees were awarded. The most popular majors were business/marketing (39%), social sciences and history (18%), and engineering (10%). In an average class, 56% graduate in 4 years or less, 70% graduate in 5 years or less, and 3% graduate in 6 years or less. 89 companies recruited on campus in 2002-2003. Of the 2002 graduating class, 15% were enrolled in graduate school within 6 months of graduation and 96% were employed.

Admissions Contact: Lt. Col. John Powell, Acting Dean of Enrollment Management. A video is available. E-mail: *admissions@citadel.edu* Web: *www.citadel.edu*

CLAFLIN UNIVERSITY
Orangeburg, SC 29115

C-3

(803) 535-5339
(800) 922-1246; Fax: (803) 531-3860

Full-time: 476 men, 84,848 women	**Faculty:** 80
Part-time: 15 men, 25 women	**Ph.D.s:** 70%
Graduate: 14 men, 36 women	**Student/Faculty:** 17 to 1
Year: semesters, summer session	**Tuition:** $9654
Application Deadline: open	**Room & Board:** $5184
Freshman Class: 2025 applied, 945 accepted, 335 enrolled	
SAT I Verbal/Math: 500/425	**ACT:** 19	**COMPETITIVE+**

Claflin University, established in 1869 and affiliated with the United Methodist Church, is a small, private liberal arts institution offering undergraduate programs in education, humanities, natural sciences, math, and social sciences. In addition to regional accreditation, Claflin University has baccalaureate program accreditation with ACBSP and NCATE. The library contains 152,108 volumes, 61,952 microform items, and 719 audio/video tapes/CDs, and subscribes to 425 periodicals. Computerized library services include the card catalog, interlibrary loans, database searching, and Internet access. Special learning facilities include a learning resource center, art gallery, radio station, and TV station. The 40-acre campus is in a suburban area between Columbia and Charleston. Including any residence halls, there are 24 buildings.

Student Life: 83% of undergraduates are from South Carolina. Students are from 24 states and 14 foreign countries. 99% are from public schools. 94% are African American. Most are Protestant. The average age of all undergraduates is 19. 21% do not continue beyond their first year; 75% remain to graduate.

Housing: 887 students can be accommodated in college housing, which includes single-sex dorms and off-campus apartments. On-campus housing is available on a first-come, first-served basis. 60% of students live on campus; of those, 70% remain on campus on weekends. Alcohol is not permitted. Upperclassmen may keep cars.

Activities: 22% of men belong to 4 national fraternities; 25% of women belong to 4 national sororities. There are 40 groups on campus, including band, choir, drama, ethnic, film, honors, international, jazz band, literary magazine, marching band, newspaper, radio and TV, religious, social, social service, student government, and yearbook. Popular campus events include Founders Day, Pantherfest, and Claflin Pride Day.

Sports: There are 5 intercollegiate sports for men and 7 for women, and 4 intramural sports for men and 4 for women. Facilities include a gym, tennis courts, game room, and basketball courts.

Disabled Students: 95% of the campus is accessible. Wheelchair ramps, elevators, special parking, and specially equipped rest rooms are available.

Services: Counseling and information services are available, as is tutoring in most subjects. There is remedial math, reading, and writing.

Campus Safety and Security: Measures include 24-hour foot and vehicle patrol, security escort services, informal discussions, and lighted pathways/sidewalks.

Programs of Study: Claflin University confers B.A., B.S., and B.S.B.A. degrees. Master's degrees are also awarded. Bachelor's degrees are awarded in BIOLOGICAL SCIENCE (biochemistry and biology/biological science), BUSINESS (business administration and management), COMMUNICATIONS AND THE ARTS (art, communications, English, and music), COMPUTER AND PHYSICAL SCIENCE (chemistry, computer science, and mathematics), EDUCATION (art, elementary, English, mathematics, music, physical, and special), SOCIAL SCIENCE (African American studies, American studies, child psychology/development, early childhood studies, history, religion, and sociology). Biology, education, and business are the strongest academically. Sociology, education, and business are the largest.

Required: To graduate, all students must complete122 to 154 semester hours with a minimum GPA of 2.0. General education requirements include courses in education, English, humanities, math, with a minimum GPA of 2.0 phys ed, natural science, computer science, and analytical reasoning. Liberal arts majors must also fulfill a foreign language requirement. A capstone project is required of all students.

Special: Claflin offers co-op and accelerated degree programs in all majors, cross-registration with South Carolina State University and Orangeburg-Calhoun Technical College, study abroad, B.A.-B.S. degrees, and a 3-2 engineering degree with Clemson University and South Carolina State University. There are 7 national honor societies and a freshman honors program.

Faculty/Classroom: 58% of faculty are male; 42%, female. All both teach and do research. The average class size in an introductory lecture is 25; in a laboratory, 15; and in a regular course, 25.

Admissions: 47% of the 2003-2004 applicants were accepted. The SAT I scores for the 2003-2004 freshman class were: Verbal--66% below 500, 26% between 500 and 599, 7% between 600 and 700, and 1% above 700; Math--60% below 500, 30% between 500 and 599, 9% between 600 and 700, and 1% above 700. 55% of the current freshmen were in the top fifth of their class; 65% were in the top two fifths. 5 freshmen graduated first in their class.

Requirements: The SAT I or ACT is required. In addition, applicants should be high school graduates who have completed 16 to 18 units, including 4 units in English, 2 in math, and 1 each in social studies and natural science. Admissions decisions are based on the secondary school record, test scores, recommendations from the secondary school, personal qualities, and health record. A GPA of 2.0 is required. AP and CLEP credits are accepted. Important factors in the admissions decision are recommendations by school officials, evidence of special talent, and leadership record.

Procedure: Freshmen are admitted fall and spring. There is a rolling admissions plan. Application deadlines are open. Application fee is $20. Applications are accepted on-line through the school's web site.

Transfer: 44 transfer students enrolled in 2002-2003. Applicants with fewer than 60 semester hours of college credit must submit test scores and meet the other criteria for entering freshmen. Official transcripts of all colleges attended are required. 25 of 126 credits required for the bachelor's degree must be completed at Claflin University.

Visiting: There are regularly scheduled orientations for prospective students. There are guides for informal visits and visitors may sit in on classes and stay overnight. To schedule a visit, contact the Admissions Office at (800) 535-5396 or mzeigler@claflin.edu.

Financial Aid: In 2003-2004, 98% of all full-time students received some form of financial aid. 92% of all full-time students received need-based aid. The average freshman award was $10,625. Need-based scholarships or need-based grants averaged $1980 ($2190 maximum); need-based self-help aid (loans and jobs) averaged $4500 ($5500 maximum); non-need-based athletic scholarships averaged $2000 ($13,000 maximum); and other non-need-based awards and non-need-based scholarships averaged $1000 ($14,838 maximum). 35% of undergraduates work part time. The average financial indebtedness of the 2003 graduate was $14,412. The FAFSA is required. The priority date for freshman financial aid applications for fall entry is April 15. The deadline for filing freshman financial aid applications for fall entry is June 1.

International Students: There are 73 international students enrolled. The school actively recruits these students. They must score 500 on the written TOEFL or 213 on the electronic version and also take the SAT I or the ACT.

Computers: The mainframe is a Alpha DS20 Compac. There are 26 computer labs with access to the Internet and equipped with 4,000 PCs. All students may access the system. There are no time limits. The fee is $150.

Graduates: From July 1, 2002 to June 30, 2003, 195 bachelor's degrees were awarded. The most popular majors were criminal justice/law enforcement administration (17%), organizational behavior studies (16%), and child development (13%). In an average class, 75% graduate in 6 years or less. Of the 2002 graduating class, 20% were enrolled in graduate school within 6 months of graduation and 60% were employed.

Admissions Contact: Katherine Boyd. A video is available.
E-mail: kboyd@claf1.claflin.edu Web: http://www.claflin.edu

CLEMSON UNIVERSITY
Clemson, SC 29634-5124

A-2

(864) 656-2287; Fax: (864) 656-0622

Full-time: 7037 men, 5820 women	**Faculty:** 952; I, -$
Part-time: 553 men, 403 women	**Ph.D.s:** 87%
Graduate: 1735 men, 1468 women	**Student/Faculty:** 14 to 1
Year: semesters, summer session	**Tuition:** $6934 ($14,532)
Application Deadline: May 1	**Room & Board:** $5038
Freshman Class: 11,419 applied, 6945 accepted, 2769 enrolled	
SAT I Verbal/Math: 587/617	**ACT:** 26	**HIGHLY COMPETITIVE**

Clemson University, founded in 1889, is a public institution with programs in agriculture, architecture, commerce and industry, education, engineering, forest and recreation resources, liberal arts, nursing, and sciences. There are 5 undergraduate schools and 1 graduate school. In addition to regional accreditation, Clemson has baccalaureate program accreditation with AACSB, ABET, CSAB, NAAB, NCATE, NLN, and NRPA. The library contains 1,126,413 volumes, 1,162,165 microform items, and 117,769 audio/video tapes/CDs, and subscribes to 11,574 periodicals. Computerized library services include the card catalog, interlibrary loans, database searching, and Internet access. Special learning facilities include a learning resource center, art gallery, natural history museum, planetarium, radio station, and TV station. The 1400-acre campus is in a small town 32 miles west of Greenville. Including any residence halls, there are 584 buildings.

Student Life: 74% of undergraduates are from South Carolina. Students are from 50 states, 84 foreign countries, and Canada. 80% are from public schools. 79% are white. The average age of freshmen is 18; all undergraduates, 21. 11% do not continue beyond their first year; 72% remain to graduate.

Housing: 6202 students can be accommodated in college housing, which includes single-sex and coed dorms, on-campus apartments, off-campus apartments, married-student housing, fraternity houses, and sorority houses. In addition, there are honors houses. On-campus housing is guaranteed for all 4 years. 54% of students commute. All students may keep cars.

Activities: 18% of men belong to 25 national fraternities; 23% of women belong to 15 national sororities. There are 275 groups on campus, including band, cheerleading, choir, chorus, computers, dance, debate, drama, drill team, ethnic, gay, honors, international, jazz band, literary magazine, marching band, musical theater, newspaper, orchestra, pep band, photography, political, professional, radio and TV, religious, social, social service, student government, and yearbook. Popular campus events include Tigerama, Welcome Back Festival, and Annual Shakespeare.

Sports: There are 10 intercollegiate sports for men and 9 for women, and 32 intramural sports for men and 32 for women. Facilities include a recreation center, an 80,000-seat stadium, and a 12,000-seat coliseum.

Disabled Students: 75% of the campus is accessible. Wheelchair ramps, elevators, special parking, specially equipped rest rooms, special class scheduling, lowered drinking fountains, and lowered telephones are available.

Services: Counseling and information services are available, as is tutoring in some subjects. There is a reader service for the blind. Other services include textbooks on tape, testing modifications, library assistance, interpreters, note takers, and letters to faculty members.

Campus Safety and Security: Measures include 24-hour foot and vehicle patrol, self-defense education, security escort services, and shuttle buses. There are informal discussions, pamphlets/posters/films, emergency telephones, and lighted pathways/sidewalks.

Programs of Study: Clemson confers B.A., B.S., B.F.A, and B.L.A. degrees. Master's and doctoral degrees are also awarded. Bachelor's degrees are awarded in AGRICULTURE (agriculture, animal science, forestry and related sciences, forestry production and processing, horticulture, and soil science), BIOLOGICAL SCIENCE (biochemistry, biology/biological science, and microbiology), BUSINESS (accounting, banking and finance, business administration and management, management science, and marketing/retailing/merchandising), COMMUNICATIONS AND THE ARTS (communications, design, English, fine arts, French, German, modern language, and Spanish), COMPUTER AND PHYSICAL SCIENCE (chemistry, computer science, geology, information sciences and systems, mathematics, and physics), EDUCATION (agricultural, early childhood, elementary, industrial arts, secondary, and special), ENGINEERING AND ENVIRONMENTAL DESIGN (agricultural engineering, ceramic engineering, chemical engineering, civil engineering, computer engineering, construction management, electrical/electronics engineering, graphic arts technology, industrial administration/management, industrial engineering, landscape architecture/design, mechanical engineering, and textile technology), HEALTH PROFESSIONS (medical laboratory technology, nursing, predentistry, premedicine, prepharmacy, preveterinary science, and speech pathology/audiology), SOCIAL SCIENCE (economics, food science, history, parks and recreation management, philosophy, political science/government, prelaw, psychology, and sociology). Engineering and education are the strongest academically. Marketing and engineering are the largest.

Required: To graduate, students must complete 127 to 144 credit hours, including 89 to 108 hours in the major, with a GPA of 2.0. Courses are required in English, humanities, math, science, and social science.

Special: Co-op programs are available in all majors except nursing. Work-study programs and study abroad in 38 countries are offered. There are 22 national honor societies, a freshman honors program, and 40 departmental honors programs.

Faculty/Classroom: 69% of faculty are male; 31%, female. 99% teach undergraduates, 73% do research, and 72% do both. Graduate students teach 18% of introductory courses. The average class size in an introductory lecture is 45; in a laboratory, 19; and in a regular course, 28.

Admissions: 61% of the 2003-2004 applicants were accepted. The SAT I scores for the 2003-2004 freshman class were: Verbal--10% below 500, 43% between 500 and 599, 40% between 600 and 700, and 7% above 700; Math--5% below 500, 32% between 500 and 599, 50% between 600 and 700, and 13% above 700. The ACT scores were 8% below 21, 15% between 21 and 23, 31% between 24 and 26, 15% between 27 and 28, and 31% above 28. 70% of the current freshmen were in the top fifth of their class; 92% were in the top two fifths. There were 24 National Merit finalists. 100 freshmen graduated first in their class.

Requirements: The SAT I or ACT is required. In addition, applicants should be graduates of an accredited secondary school. The GED is accepted. AP and CLEP credits are accepted. Important factors in the admissions decision are advanced placement or honor courses, parents or siblings attending the school, and recommendations by school officials.

Procedure: Freshmen are admitted fall, spring, and summer. Entrance exams should be taken during spring of the junior year or fall of the senior year. Applications should be filed by May 1 for fall entry and December 15 for spring entry. The fall 2003 application fee was $40. 436 applicants were on the 2003 waiting list; 181 were admitted. Applications are accepted on-line through CollegeNET on the school's web site.

Transfer: 729 transfer students enrolled in 2002-2003. Transfer applicants must have completed at least 30 semester hours with approximately a 2.5 GPA. 30 of 127 to 144 credits required for the bachelor's degree must be completed at Clemson.

Visiting: There are regularly scheduled orientations for prospective students, including a series of 2-day summer programs of advisement, student services presentations, and registration for the fall semester. There are guides for informal visits. To schedule a visit, contact the Visitor's Center at (864) 656-4789.

Financial Aid: In 2003-2004, 87% of all full-time freshmen and 71% of continuing full-time students received some form of financial aid. 28% of full-time freshmen and 31% of continuing full-time students received need-based aid. The average freshman award was $9140. Need-based scholarships or need-based grants averaged $3398 ($7500 maximum); need-based self-help aid (loans and jobs) averaged $3752 ($7125 maximum); non-need-based athletic scholarships averaged $11,925 ($25,409 maximum); and other non-need-based awards and non-need-based scholarships averaged $7075 ($24,426 maximum). 57% of undergraduates work part time. Average annual earnings from campus work are $2302. The average financial indebtedness of the 2003 graduate was $14,307. The FAFSA is required. The priority date for freshman financial aid applications for fall entry is April 1.

International Students: There are 761 international students enrolled. The school actively recruits these students. They must score 550 on the written TOEFL and also take the SAT I or the ACT, as well as the SAT II: Mathematics test level IIC for freshman math placement.

Computers: The mainframe is an HDS AS/EX-80. There are 600 PCs available. All students may access the system. There are no time limits and no fees.

Graduates: From July 1, 2002 to June 30, 2003, 2973 bachelor's degrees were awarded. The most popular majors were marketing (10%), management (6%), and communication studies (4%). In an average class, 1% graduate in 3 years or less, 39% graduate in 4 years or less, 67% graduate in 5 years or less, and 72% graduate in 6 years or less. 340 companies recruited on campus in 2002-2003.

Admissions Contact: Robert S. Barkley, Director of Admissions. A video is available. E-mail: *cuadmissions@clemson.edu* Web: *http://www.clemson.edu*

COASTAL CAROLINA UNIVERSITY E-3
Conway, SC 29528 (843) 349-2026
(800) 277-7000; Fax: (843) 349-2127

Full-time: 2439 men, 2522 women	**Faculty:** 212; IIB, -$
Part-time: 256 men, 393 women	**Ph.D.s:** 78%
Graduate: 153 men, 1017 women	**Student/Faculty:** 23 to 1
Year: semesters, summer session	**Tuition:** $5270 ($12,950)
Application Deadline: August 15	**Room & Board:** $5770
Freshman Class: 4527 applied, 3208 accepted, 1276 enrolled	
SAT I Verbal/Math: 515/530	**ACT:** 22 **COMPETITIVE**

Coastal Carolina University, established in 1954, is a public liberal arts institution offering undergraduate programs through the colleges of business administration, natural and applied sciences, education, and humanities and fine arts. Graduate programs are offered through the College of Education and College of Natural and Applied Science. There are 5 undergraduate schools and 1 graduate school. In addition to regional accreditation, Coastal Carolina has baccalaureate program accreditation with AACSB, ABET, NASAD, and NCATE. The library contains 201,805 volumes, 93,171 microform items, and 12,465 audio/video tapes/CDs, and subscribes to 958 periodicals. Computerized library services include the card catalog, interlibrary loans, and database searching. Special learning facilities include a learning resource center, art gallery, and a marine science research center. The 260-acre campus is in a suburban area 9 miles west of Myrtle Beach. Including any residence halls, there are 41 buildings.

Student Life: 65% of undergraduates are from South Carolina. Students are from 48 states, 49 foreign countries, and Canada. 95% are from public schools. 82% are white; 12% African American. The average age of freshmen is 18; all undergraduates, 22. 28% do not continue beyond their first year; 40% remain to graduate.

Housing: 1800 students can be accommodated in college housing, which includes coed dorms. On-campus housing is available on a first-come, first-served basis. 68% of students commute. Alcohol is not permitted. All students may keep cars.

Activities: 13% of men belong to 8 national fraternities; 10% of women belong to 6 national sororities. There are 95 groups on campus, including art, band, cheerleading, chess, choir, chorale, chorus, computers, dance, drama, ethnic, gay, honors, international, jazz band, literary magazine, marching band, musical theater, newspaper, pep band, political, professional, religious, social, social service, student government, and yearbook. Popular campus events include CINO Day, Christmas formal, and Welcome Back Dance.

Sports: There are 8 intercollegiate sports for men and 8 for women, and 17 intramural sports for men and 16 for women. Facilities include

a gym; a football stadium; baseball, soccer, and softball fields; tennis, basketball, volleyball, and racquetball courts; indoor Olympic-size swimming pool; aerobic dance room; weight rooms; and track.

Disabled Students: 95% of the campus is accessible. Wheelchair ramps, elevators, special parking, specially equipped rest rooms, special class scheduling, lowered drinking fountains, and special housing are available.

Services: Counseling and information services are available, as is tutoring in some subjects, including English, foreign languages, math, and statistics. There is a reader service for the blind.

Campus Safety and Security: Measures include 24-hour foot and vehicle patrol, self-defense education, security escort services, and informal discussions. There are pamphlets/posters/films, emergency telephones, and lighted pathways/sidewalks.

Programs of Study: Coastal Carolina confers B.A., B.S., B.A.Ed., B.A.I.S., B.S.B.A., B.S.Ed., B.S.I.S., and B.S.P.E. degrees. Master's degrees are also awarded. Bachelor's degrees are awarded in BIOLOGICAL SCIENCE (biology/biological science and marine science), BUSINESS (accounting, banking and finance, business administration and management, and marketing/retailing/merchandising), COMMUNICATIONS AND THE ARTS (dramatic arts, English, fine arts, music, musical theater, Spanish, and studio art), COMPUTER AND PHYSICAL SCIENCE (chemistry, computer science, and mathematics), EDUCATION (early childhood, elementary, middle school, physical, secondary, and special), HEALTH PROFESSIONS (health, predentistry, and premedicine), SOCIAL SCIENCE (history, interdisciplinary studies, philosophy, political science/government, prelaw, psychology, and sociology). Accounting, finance, and management are the strongest academically. Marine science, management, and marketing are the largest.

Required: Students must successfully complete a minimum of 120 credits, varying with major department requirements, and must maintain a minimum GPA of 2.0. A 4-year core curriculum of 44 to 52 hours is required for proficiency in the broad areas of writing, library research, a foreign language, and computer usage.

Special: Cross-regristration is available with Francis Marion and Winthrop Universities, and MUSCO. Internships are offered in most majors. Study abroad in 10 countries, work study programs, dual majors, B.A.-B.S. degrees, and interdisciplinary majors are offered. A 3-2 engineering degree is offered through Clemson University. A cooperative marketing/golf management program is available in the business administration major. Credit by examination, and pass/fail options are possible. There are 19 national honor societies and a freshman honors program.

Faculty/Classroom: 62% of faculty are male; 38%, female. 67% teach undergraduates and 33% both teach and do research. No introductory courses are taught by graduate students. The average class size in an introductory lecture is 30; in a laboratory, 19; and in a regular course, 25.

Admissions: 71% of the 2003-2004 applicants were accepted. The SAT I scores for the 2003-2004 freshman class were: Verbal--44% below 500, 44% between 500 and 599, 11% between 600 and 700, and 1% above 700; Math--32% below 500, 50% between 500 and 599, 17% between 600 and 700, and 1% above 700. The ACT scores were 43% below 21, 35% between 21 and 23, 15% between 24 and 26, 5% between 27 and 28, and 2% above 28. 26% of the current freshmen were in the top fifth of their class; 56% were in the top two fifths. 6 freshmen graduated first in their class.

Requirements: The SAT I or ACT is required. In addition, graduation from an accredited secondary or home school program is required; a GED will be accepted, with appropriate scores. Applicants are required to submit complete specific high school credits, including 4 years of college prep, English, 3 units of mathematics (Algebra II required), 3 units of laboratory science, 3 units of social sciences (U.S. History required), 2 units of the same foreign language, 4 advance electives (from computer science, math additional science, foreign language, social science, humanities and arts), and 1 unit of phys ed or ROTC. An interview is recommended. A GPA of 2.25 is required. AP and CLEP credits are accepted. Important factors in the admissions decision are advanced placement or honor courses, recommendations by school officials, and evidence of special talent.

Procedure: Freshmen are admitted to all sessions. Entrance exams should be taken in spring of the junior year or fall of the senior year. There is a deferred admissions plan and a rolling admissions plan. Applications should be filed by August 15 for fall entry and December 15 for spring entry. The fall 2003 application fee was $45. Notification is sent on a rolling basis. Applications are accepted on-line through www.coastal.edu.

Transfer: 545 transfer students enrolled in 2002-2003. A minimum GPA of 2.0 is required. Transfers with fewer than 30 hours earned must also meet freshman admission requirements. Students must submit college transcripts and must be eligible to return to the last institution attended. 30 of 120 credits required for the bachelor's degree must be completed at Coastal Carolina.

Visiting: There are regularly scheduled orientations for prospective students, including sessions for academic requirements, housing, financial aid, student life, parents' orientation, tours, cookouts, and entertainment.

There are guides for informal visits and visitors may sit in on classes. To schedule a visit, contact the Admissions Office.

Financial Aid: In 2003-2004, 64% of all full-time freshmen and 63% of continuing full-time students received some form of financial aid. 54% of full-time freshmen and 67% of continuing full-time students received need-based aid. The average freshman award was $6625. Need-based scholarships or need-based grants averaged $3160; need-based self-help aid (loans and jobs) averaged $5824; and non-need-based athletic scholarships averaged $4869. 81% of undergraduates work part time. Average annual earnings from campus work are $2000. The average financial indebtedness of the 2003 graduate was $19,323. The FAFSA and the college's own financial statement are required. The deadline for filing freshman financial aid applications for fall entry is April 1.

International Students: There are 135 international students enrolled. They must score 500 on the written TOEFL or 173 on the electronic version. First-time freshman must also take the SAT I or ACT.

Computers: Student computer labs are located in the College of Business, the College of Education, the College of Natural and Applied Science, the academic center, and the library. There are 550 terminals for student use. All students may access the system 24 hours via dial-in. There are no time limits and no fees. It is strongly recommended that all students have a personal computer. It is recommended that students in Computer Science: Introduction to Algorithmic Design have personal computers.

Graduates: From July 1, 2002 to June 30, 2003, 801 bachelor's degrees were awarded. The most popular majors were marketing (12%), marine science (9%), and management (9%). In an average class, 23% graduate in 4 years or less, 35% graduate in 5 years or less, and 37% graduate in 6 years or less. 71 companies recruited on campus in 2002-2003.

Admissions Contact: Judy W. Vogt, Associate Vice President, Enrollment Service. E-mail: admissions@coastal.edu
Web: www.coastal.edu/admissions

COKER COLLEGE
Hartsville, SC 29550

D-2

(843) 383-8050
(800) 950-1908; Fax: (843) 383-8056

Full-time: 199 men, 274 women	**Faculty:** 53
Part-time: 4 men, 5 women	**Ph.D.s:** 72%
Graduate: none	**Student/Faculty:** 9 to 1
Year: semesters, summer session	**Tuition:** $16,165
Application Deadline: open	**Room & Board:** $5326
Freshman Class: 593 applied, 384 accepted, 156 enrolled	
SAT I Verbal/Math: 490/490	**ACT:** 19 **COMPETITIVE**

Coker College, founded in 1908, is a private institution offering undergraduate programs in business, education, and the arts and sciences. In addition to regional accreditation, Coker has baccalaureate program accreditation with NASDTEC and NASM. The library contains 67,956 volumes, 43,182 microform items, and 4412 audio/video tapes/CDs, and subscribes to 531 periodicals. Computerized library services include the card catalog, interlibrary loans, and database searching. Special learning facilities include an art gallery, a botanical garden, and a nature preserve. The 15-acre campus is in a small town 25 miles west of Florence, 70 miles northeast of Columbia, and 85 miles southeast of Charlotte, North Carolina. Including any residence halls, there are 17 buildings.

Student Life: 79% of undergraduates are from South Carolina. Students are from 25 states, 6 foreign countries, and Canada. 69% are white; 26% African American. The average age of freshmen is 19; all undergraduates, 21. 23% do not continue beyond their first year; 50% remain to graduate.

Housing: 358 students can be accommodated in college housing, which includes single-sex and coed dorms. On-campus housing is available on a first-come, first-served basis and is available on a lottery system for upperclassmen. 70% of students live on campus; of those, 75% remain on campus on weekends. All students may keep cars.

Activities: There are no fraternities or sororities. There are 27 groups on campus, including art, band, cheerleading, choir, chorus, dance, drama, ethnic, honors, musical theater, newspaper, photography, political, religious, social service, student government, and yearbook. Popular campus events include Black History Month, Apollo Night, and Bandfest.

Sports: There are 6 intercollegiate sports for men and 6 for women, and 17 intramural sports for men and 18 for women. Facilities include a gym, a weight room, an aerobic/dance room, soccer, baseball, and softball fields, tennis courts, a boat house with canoes, and access to a golf course. The gym seats approximately 500.

Disabled Students: 63% of the campus is accessible. Wheelchair ramps, elevators, special parking, specially equipped rest rooms, special class scheduling, and lowered drinking fountains are available.

Services: Counseling and information services are available, as is tutoring in English and math. There is a writing lab.

Campus Safety and Security: Measures include 24-hour foot and vehicle patrol, informal discussions, pamphlets/posters/films, and lighted pathways/sidewalks.

Programs of Study: Coker confers B.A., B.S., B.M.Ed., and B.S.W. degrees. Bachelor's degrees are awarded in BIOLOGICAL SCIENCE (biology/biological science), BUSINESS (business administration and management), COMMUNICATIONS AND THE ARTS (art, communications, dance, dramatic arts, English, French, graphic design, music, musical theater, photography, and Spanish), COMPUTER AND PHYSICAL SCIENCE (chemistry, computer science, and mathematics), EDUCATION (art, early childhood, education, elementary, English, mathematics, music, physical, science, and social science), HEALTH PROFESSIONS (medical laboratory technology), SOCIAL SCIENCE (criminology, history, political science/government, psychology, social work, and sociology). Biology, math, and education are the strongest academically. Business, education, and visual and performing arts are the largest.

Required: Distribution requirements include 9 hours each in humanities and oral and written rhetoric, 7 in science, 6 each in the arts and behavioral sciences, and 3 each in nonnative language, math, and phys ed. A total of 120 credit hours, with 30 to 45 in the major, and a minimum 2.0 GPA are required to graduate.

Special: Internships, study abroad in many countries, on-campus and community service work-study programs, cross-registration with Central College, and dual and student-designed majors are offered. A 3-1 in medical technology with McCleod Regional Medical Center is possible. Also available are credit for military experience, nondegree study, and pass/fail options. The college's round-table approach to teaching allows students and professors to discuss topics and research in small, round-table settings. There are 3 national honor societies and 3 departmental honors programs.

Faculty/Classroom: 56% of faculty are male; 44%, female. All teach undergraduates and 60% both teach and do research. The average class size in an introductory lecture is 18; in a laboratory, 10; and in a regular course, 9.

Admissions: 65% of the 2003-2004 applicants were accepted. The SAT I scores for the 2003-2004 freshman class were: Verbal--53% below 500, 37% between 500 and 599, and 12% between 600 and 700; Math--50% below 500, 40% between 500 and 599, 9% between 600 and 700, and 1% above 700. The ACT scores were 58% below 21, 24% between 21 and 23, 12% between 24 and 26, 4% between 27 and 28, and 2% above 28. 28% of the current freshmen were in the top fifth of their class; 63% were in the top two fifths.

Requirements: The SAT I or ACT is required. In addition, applicants must be graduates of an accredited secondary school or have a GED. A recommendation from a high school guidance counselor or teacher may be required. An audition or portfolio review is required for applicants in music, dance, art, and drama. AP and CLEP credits are accepted. Important factors in the admissions decision are advanced placement or honor courses, extracurricular activities record, and leadership record.

Procedure: Freshmen are admitted fall, spring, and summer. Entrance exams should be taken during the junior year or the first part of the senior year. There are early decision and deferred admissions plans. There is a rolling admissions plan. Application deadlines are open. Application fee is $15. Notification is sent on a rolling basis beginning June 1. Applications are accepted on-line through the school's web site.

Transfer: 42 transfer students enrolled in 2002-2003. Applicants with fewer than 30 semester hours must submit high school transcripts and SAT I scores. A minimum 2.0 GPA is required. 30 credits of 120 required for the bachelor's degree must be completed at Coker.

Visiting: There are regularly scheduled orientations for prospective students, consisting of orientation, a meal, campus tours, and discussions with faculty and a student panel. There are guides for informal visits and visitors may sit in on classes and stay overnight. To schedule a visit, contact the Admissions Office at *admissions@coker.edu*.

Financial Aid: In 2003-2004, all full-time freshmen and 98% of continuing full-time students received some form of financial aid. 89% of full-time freshmen and 90% of continuing full-time students received need-based aid. The average freshman award was $17,206. Need-based scholarships or need-based grants averaged $4808 ($14,550 maximum); need-based self-help aid (loans and jobs) averaged $3851 ($9625 maximum); non-need-based athletic scholarships averaged $3685 ($12,750 maximum); and other non-need-based awards and non-need-based scholarships averaged $8565 ($17,250 maximum). 37% of undergraduates work part time. Average annual earnings from campus work are $1211. The average financial indebtedness of the 2003 graduate was $17,323. Coker is a member of CSS. The FAFSA is required. The priority date for freshman financial aid applications for fall entry is April 1. The deadline for filing freshman financial aid applications for fall entry is June 1.

International Students: There are 8 international students enrolled. They must score 500 on the written TOEFL or 173 on the electronic version.

Computers: There is a network of 52 PCs as well as other independent computers on campus in 4 locations. All dorm rooms are wired for network access. All students may access the system during regular hours in labs and at all times in dorm rooms. There are no time limits and no fees.

Graduates: From July 1, 2002 to June 30, 2003, 84 bachelor's degrees were awarded. The most popular majors were education (11%), business/marketing (11%), and visual and performing arts (8%). In an average class, 51% graduate in 4 years or less.

Admissions Contact: Perry Kirven, Director of Admissions. A video is available. E-mail: *admission@coker.edu* Web: *www.coker.edu*

COLLEGE OF CHARLESTON   C-3
Charleston, SC 29424   (843) 953-5670; Fax: (843) 953-6322

Full-time: 3227 men, 5694 women	**Faculty:** 479; IIA, -$
Part-time: 400 men, 503 women	**Ph.D.s:** 86%
Graduate: 308 men, 1404 women	**Student/Faculty:** 19 to 1
Year: semesters, summer session	**Tuition:** $5770 ($13,032)
Application Deadline: April 1	**Room & Board:** $6117
Freshman Class: 7606 applied, 4560 accepted, 1874 enrolled	
SAT I Verbal/Math: 605/601	**HIGHLY COMPETITIVE**

The College of Charleston, founded in 1770, is a state-assisted institution offering liberal arts programs, including business and education. There are 5 undergraduate schools and 1 graduate school. In addition to regional accreditation, C of C has baccalaureate program accreditation with AACSB. The 2 libraries contain 539,746 volumes, 816,165 microform items, and 6194 audio/video tapes/CDs, and subscribe to 3322 periodicals. Computerized library services include the card catalog, interlibrary loans, database searching, and Internet access. Special learning facilities include a learning resource center, art gallery, radio station, TV station, observatory, communications museum, marine lab, Afro-American research center, and bronze sculpture foundry. The 52-acre campus is in an urban area in the heart of historic Charleston, by the Atlantic Ocean. Including any residence halls, there are 111 buildings.

Student Life: 67% of undergraduates are from South Carolina. Students are from 49 states, 73 foreign countries, and Canada. 83% are from public schools. 84% are white. The average age of freshmen is 18; all undergraduates, 21. 16% do not continue beyond their first year; 84% remain to graduate.

Housing: 2600 students can be accommodated in college housing, which includes single-sex and coed dorms, on-campus apartments, fraternity houses, and sorority houses. In addition, there are honors houses, language houses, and special-interest houses. On-campus housing is available on a first-come, first-served basis. 74% of students commute. Upperclassmen may keep cars.

Activities: 12% of men belong to 7 national fraternities; 17% of women belong to 7 national sororities. There are 143 groups on campus, including art, band, cheerleading, chess, choir, chorale, computers, dance, drama, ethnic, film, gay, honors, international, jazz band, literary magazine, musical theater, newspaper, opera, orchestra, pep band, political, professional, radio and TV, religious, social, social service, student government, symphony, and yearbook. Popular campus events include Sports Rally, Thursday Entertainment and Food Specials, and Black History Month.

Sports: There are 7 intercollegiate sports for men and 12 for women, and 17 intramural sports for men and 17 for women. Facilities include a phys ed center with racquetball courts and a weight and workout room, pool, outdoor recreation center with baseball and soccer fields, tennis courts, sailing marina, and student center with a movie theater, game room, weight room, meeting facilities, ballroom, and garden.

Disabled Students: 80% of the campus is accessible. Wheelchair ramps, elevators, special parking, specially equipped rest rooms, special class scheduling, lowered drinking fountains, and lowered telephones are available.

Services: Counseling and information services are available, as is tutoring in every subject. There is a reader service for the blind and remedial math, reading, and writing.

Campus Safety and Security: Measures include 24-hour foot and vehicle patrol, self-defense education, security escort services, and informal discussions. There are pamphlets/posters/films, emergency telephones, and lighted pathways/sidewalks.

Programs of Study: C of C confers B.A., B.S., A.B., B.S.D., and B.S.M. degrees. Master's degrees are also awarded. Bachelor's degrees are awarded in BIOLOGICAL SCIENCE (biochemistry, biology/biological science, and marine biology), BUSINESS (accounting, business administration and management, and international business management), COMMUNICATIONS AND THE ARTS (art history and appreciation, classics, communications, dramatic arts, English, French, German, music, Spanish, and studio art), COMPUTER AND PHYSICAL SCIENCE (chemistry, computer science, geology, information sciences and systems, mathematics, and physics), EDUCATION (athletic training, elementary, physical, and special), HEALTH PROFESSIONS (predentistry and premedicine), SOCIAL SCIENCE (anthropology, economics, history, philosophy, political science/government, psychology, religion, sociology, and urban studies). Sciences and business are the strongest academically. Business and communication are the largest.

Required: All students must complete a core curriculum, including English and history courses, 12 hours each of language and humanities, 8 hours of lab science, and 6 hours each of math or logic and social science. A total of 122 credit hours, including 24 to 43 in the major, with a minimum overall GPA of 2.0 (2.5 in some majors) is required to graduate.

Special: Cross-registration is possible with the Medical University of South Carolina, Trident Technical College, The Citadel, and Charleston Southern University. Co-op programs and internships in all majors, a Washington semester, study abroad in about 39 countries, work-study programs, B.A.-B.S. degrees, and dual majors are offered. The B.S.D. and B.S.M. degrees provide 3 years in predentistry or premedicine, with the fourth year of completion at a medical school. 3-2 engineering degrees are available with Case Western Reserve University, Clemson University, Georgia Institute of Technology, University of South Carolina, and Washington University of St. Louis. A 2-2 program in allied health, biometry, or nursing is offered with the Medical University of South Carolina. The college's 3-week Maymester session offers unconventional courses and programs using alternative methods of instruction. There is an interdisciplinary honors program available to talented students. There are 10 national honor societies, a freshman honors program, and 10 departmental honors programs.

Faculty/Classroom: 52% of faculty are male; 48%, female. All teach undergraduates and 34% both teach and do research. No introductory courses are taught by graduate students. The average class size in an introductory lecture is 21; in a laboratory, 21; and in a regular course, 21.

Admissions: 60% of the 2003-2004 applicants were accepted. The SAT I scores for the 2003-2004 freshman class were: Verbal--3% below 500, 42% between 500 and 599, 47% between 600 and 700, and 8% above 700; Math--3% below 500, 44% between 500 and 599, 48% between 600 and 700, and 6% above 700. 61% of the current freshmen were in the top fifth of their class; 92% were in the top two fifths. 24 freshmen graduated first in their class.

Requirements: The SAT I or ACT is required. In addition, applicants should have completed 4 units of high school English, 3 each of math, lab science, and social science (including 1 unit of U.S. history and 1/2 unit each of economics and government), 2 of foreign language, and 1 of phys ed. In addition, students should have 1 unit of advanced math or computer science or a combination of these, or 1 unit of world history, world geography, or Western civilization. The GED is accepted. An essay is required, and an interview is recommended. AP and CLEP credits are accepted. Important factors in the admissions decision are ability to finance college education, leadership record, and evidence of special talent.

Procedure: Freshmen are admitted fall and spring. Entrance exams should be taken by March 1 or earlier. There is a rolling admissions plan. There are early admissions and deferred admissions plans. Early decision applications should be filed by December 1; regular applications, by April 1 for fall entry and November 1 for winter entry, along with a $45 ($35 via the Web) fee. Notification of early decision is sent February 1; regular decision, on a rolling basis. Applications are accepted on-line through the school's web site and Common Application.

Transfer: 629 transfer students enrolled in 2002-2003. Applicants must be eligible to return to the last institution attended. Students with fewer than 60 hours must have a 2.3 GPA; all others must have a 2.0 GPA. 36 of 122 credits required for the bachelor's degree must be completed at C of C.

Visiting: There are regularly scheduled orientations for prospective students, consisting of 1-day open houses throughout the year and 6 2-day orientation sessions throughout the summer, including a family session. Academic requirements and expectations, services offered, placement testing, individual academic advising, registration, and introduction to residence life and cultural offerings are included. There are guides for informal visits and visitors may sit in on classes and stay overnight. To schedule a visit, contact the Admissions Office.

Financial Aid: The FAFSA is required. The priority date for freshman financial aid applications for fall entry is March 1.

International Students: There are 286 international students enrolled. The school actively recruits these students. They must score 550 on the written TOEFL.

Computers: The mainframe is a DEC VAX 6510. Dial-in capability, 2 large centers with about 150 personal computers in each, and 10 networked classrooms with a computer station for each student are available. Software includes word processing, spreadsheets, database, statistical, and specialized disciplines. All students may access the system 24 hours a day. There are no time limits. The fee is $35.

Graduates: From July 1, 2002 to June 30, 2003, 2162 bachelor's degrees were awarded. The most popular majors were business administration (18%), communications (18%), and elementary education (10%). In an average class, 1% graduate in 3 years or less, 36% graduate in 4 years or less, 53% graduate in 5 years or less, and 57% graduate in 6 years or less. Of the 2002 graduating class, 22% were enrolled in graduate school within 6 months of graduation and 94% were employed.

Admissions Contact: Donald Burkard, Dean of Admissions. A video is available. E-mail: *admissions@cofc.edu* Web: *www.cofc.edu*

COLUMBIA COLLEGE
C-3
Columbia, SC 29203
(803) 786-3871
(800) 277-1301; Fax: (803) 786-3674

Full-time: 6 men, 917 women	**Faculty:** 75; IIB, -$
Part-time: 24 men, 240 women	**Ph.Ds:** 80%
Graduate: 26 men, 280 women	**Student/Faculty:** 12 to 1
Year: semesters, summer session	**Tuition:** $17,230
Application Deadline: open	**Room & Board:** $5428
Freshman Class: n/av	
SAT I or ACT: required	**LESS COMPETITIVE**

Columbia College, founded in 1854, is a private primarily women's liberal arts college affiliated with the United Methodist Church. In addition to regional accreditation, Columbia College has baccalaureate program accreditation with CSWE, NASAD, NASDTEC, and NASM. The library contains 170,000 volumes, 8353 microform items, and 29,834 audio/video tapes/CDs, and subscribes to 633 periodicals. Computerized library services include interlibrary loans and database searching. Special learning facilities include a learning resource center, art gallery, and women's leadership center, and a science and technology center. The 53-acre campus is in an urban area in the northern section of Columbia. Including any residence halls, there are 26 buildings.

Student Life: 96% of undergraduates are from South Carolina. Students are from 16 states, 18 foreign countries, and Canada. 52% are white; 44% African American. 84% are Protestant; 10% claim no religious affiliation; 6% Catholic. The average age of freshmen is 18; all undergraduates, 23. 36% do not continue beyond their first year; 55% remain to graduate.

Housing: 650 students can be accommodated in college housing, which includes single-sex dorms. In addition, there are honors houses. On-campus housing is guaranteed for all 4 years. 58% of students live on campus. Alcohol is not permitted. All students may keep cars.

Activities: There are no fraternities or sororities. There are 57 groups on campus, including art, band, choir, chorus, computers, dance, drama, ethnic, honors, international, literary magazine, musical theater, newspaper, opera, photography, political, professional, radio and TV, religious, social, social service, student government, and yearbook. Popular campus events include Fine Arts Series, Follies, and May Day.

Sports: There are 4 intercollegiate sports for women and 4 intramural sports for women. Facilities include an athletic field, tennis courts, a gym, an Olympic-size pool, a fitness lab, and a dance studio.

Disabled Students: 90% of the campus is accessible. Wheelchair ramps, elevators, special parking, specially equipped rest rooms, and special class scheduling are available.

Services: Counseling and information services are available. Peer tutoring and remedial instruction are offered in some subjects.

Campus Safety and Security: Measures include 24-hour foot and vehicle patrol, self-defense education, security escort services, and informal discussions. There are pamphlets/posters/films, emergency telephones, and lighted pathways/sidewalks.

Programs of Study: Columbia College confers B.A., B.F.A., and B.Mus. degrees. Master's degrees are also awarded. Bachelor's degrees are awarded in BIOLOGICAL SCIENCE (biology/biological science), BUSINESS (accounting, and business administration and management), COMMUNICATIONS AND THE ARTS (communications, dance, English, French, languages, music, music performance, performing arts, piano/organ, Spanish, and studio art), COMPUTER AND PHYSICAL SCIENCE (chemistry, information sciences and systems, and mathematics), EDUCATION (Christian, dance, early childhood, elementary, music, special, and speech correction), HEALTH PROFESSIONS (medical laboratory technology), SOCIAL SCIENCE (history, political science/government, psychology, public affairs, religion, religious music, social work, and sociology). Education, sciences, and performing arts are the largest.

Required: To graduate, students must complete 127 semester hours, with a minimum GPA of 2.5 in the major and 2.0 overall. General education requirements for the B.A. degree include 15 hours of communication skills, 12 of social science, 9 of aesthetics, 8 of natural science, 6 of religion, and 3 each of math and phys ed. Students also must satisfy proficiency requirements in English and math.

Special: The Center for Contractual Studies allows qualified students to pursue individualized programs through independent study, practicums, and a senior project. The college also offers internships, study abroad, a Washington semester, dual majors, and credit for life, military, and work experience. Nondegree study and pass/fail options are available. There is a freshman honors program.

Faculty/Classroom: 36% of faculty are male; 64%, female. 95% teach undergraduates. No introductory courses are taught by graduate students. The average class size in an introductory lecture is 20 and in a laboratory, 20.

Requirements: The SAT I or ACT is required. In addition, applicants must be graduates of an accredited secondary school or have earned a GED. They should complete 16 Carnegie units, including 4 years of English, 3 of math, and 2 each of foreign language and lab science, as well as courses in history and social studies. An essay and an interview are recommended, as is a portfolio or an audition for fine or performing arts students. AP and CLEP credits are accepted. Important factors in the admissions decision are recommendations by school officials, advanced placement or honor courses, and leadership record.

Procedure: Freshmen are admitted to all sessions. Entrance exams should be taken near the end of the junior year or by December of the senior year. There is a rolling admissions plan. The fall 2003 application fee was $20. Application deadlines are open.

Transfer: 83 transfer students enrolled in 2002-2003. An interview is recommended for transfer students. Applicants with fewer than 24 semester hours must present the ACT or the SAT I scores and high school transcripts. Grades of C or better transfer for credit. 30 of 127 credits required for the bachelor's degree must be completed at Columbia College.

Visiting: There are regularly scheduled orientations for prospective students, consisting of meetings with faculty advisers, classroom visits, campus tours, lunch, and student life and financial aid presentations. There are guides for informal visits and visitors may sit in on classes. To schedule a visit, contact the Admissions Office at (800) 277-1301 or *admissions@columbiacollegesc.edu*.

Financial Aid: In 2003-2004 the average freshman award was $17,000. 34% of undergraduates work part time. Average annual earnings from campus work are $700. Columbia College is a member of CSS. The FAFSA is required. The deadline for filing freshman financial aid applications for fall entry is April 1.

International Students: There are 18 international students enrolled. The school actively recruits these students. They must score 550 on the written TOEFL and also take the SAT I or the ACT.

Computers: The mainframe is a DEC 5500 running UNIX. Students have access to the Internet in each residence hall room and in various classrooms, labs, and media centers. All students may access the system. There are no time limits. The fee is $15 per semester. It is strongly recommended that all students have a personal computer.

Graduates: From July 1, 2002 to June 30, 2003, 218 bachelor's degrees were awarded. The most popular majors were business administration (14%), speech correction (13%), and early childhood education (10%). In an average class, 52% graduate in 4 years or less, 55% graduate in 5 years or less, and 57% graduate in 6 years or less.

Admissions Contact: Julie A. King, Director of Freshman Admissions. E-mail: *admissions@columbiacollegesc.edu* Web: *http://www.columbiacollegesc.edu*

CONVERSE COLLEGE
Spartanburg, SC 29302

B-1

(864) 596-9040
(800) 766-1125; Fax: (864) 596-9225

Full-time: 593 women	**Faculty:** 68; IIB, -$
Part-time: 115 women	**Ph.D.s:** 89%
Graduate: 62 men, 375 women	**Student/Faculty:** 9 to 1
Year: 4-1-4, summer session	**Tuition:** $18,915
Application Deadline: August 15	**Room & Board:** $5795
Freshman Class: 508 applied, 349 accepted, 180 enrolled	
SAT I Verbal/Math: 570/540	**ACT:** 23 **VERY COMPETITIVE**

Converse College, founded in 1889, is a private women's liberal arts college. Men are admitted to the graduate programs. There are 2 undergraduate and 2 graduate schools. In addition to regional accreditation, Converse College has baccalaureate program accreditation with NASM. The library contains 150,000 volumes, 310 microform items, and 12,000 audio/video tapes/CDs, and subscribes to 700 periodicals. Computerized library services include the card catalog, interlibrary loans, and database searching. Special learning facilities include a learning resource center, art gallery, and natural history museum. The 72-acre campus is in an urban area 80 miles southwest of Charlotte. Including any residence halls, there are 27 buildings.

Student Life: 65% of undergraduates are from South Carolina. Students are from 25 states and 10 foreign countries. 70% are from public schools. 85% are white; 12% African American. The average age of freshmen is 18; all undergraduates, 20. 26% do not continue beyond their first year; 56% remain to graduate.

Housing: 700 students can be accommodated in college housing, which includes single-sex dorms, a special residence hall for students enrolled in the South Carolina Institute of Leadership for Women, and a wellness dorm. On-campus housing is guaranteed for all 4 years. 90% of students live on campus; of those, 40% remain on campus on weekends. Alcohol is not permitted. All students may keep cars.

Activities: There are 50 groups on campus, including art, cheerleading, choir, chorale, chorus, computers, dance, debate, drama, ethnic, gay, honors, international, literary magazine, musical theater, newspaper, opera, orchestra, photography, political, professional, religious, social service, student government, symphony, and yearbook. Popular campus events include Founders Day, May Day, and Family Weekend.

Sports: Facilities include a gym, a pool, a dance studio, a weight room, tennis courts, and bowling lanes.

Disabled Students: 50% of the campus is accessible. Wheelchair ramps, elevators, special parking, and specially equipped rest rooms are available.

Services: Counseling and information services are available, as is tutoring in most subjects. There is a reader service for the blind.

Campus Safety and Security: Measures include 24-hour foot and vehicle patrol, self-defense education, security escort services, and informal discussions. There are pamphlets/posters/films, emergency telephones, and lighted pathways/sidewalks.

Programs of Study: Converse College confers B.A., B.S., B.F.A., and B.Mus. degrees. Master's degrees are also awarded. Bachelor's degrees are awarded in BIOLOGICAL SCIENCE (biology/biological science), BUSINESS (accounting, and business administration and management), COMMUNICATIONS AND THE ARTS (English, fine arts, French, languages, modern language, music, and Spanish), COMPUTER AND PHYSICAL SCIENCE (chemistry, computer science, and mathematics), EDUCATION (art, early childhood, elementary, foreign languages, music, science, and secondary), ENGINEERING AND ENVIRONMENTAL DESIGN (interior design), HEALTH PROFESSIONS (art therapy, predentistry, and premedicine), SOCIAL SCIENCE (economics, history, political science/government, prelaw, psychology, and religion). English, politics, and biology are the strongest academically. Music, education, and business are the largest.

Required: To graduate, students must complete 120 semester hours, including 52 hours across the liberal arts discipline, with a minimum GPA of 2.0. Courses in ideas and culture, computer literacy, public speaking, and phys ed are required.

Special: There are co-op programs and cross-registration with Wofford College. Internships, study abroad, a work-study program, accelerated degree programs, B.A.-B.S. degrees in business, economics, sociology, biology, and chemistry, and dual and student-designed majors are offered. There are 10 national honor societies, a freshman honors program, and all departments have honors programs.

Faculty/Classroom: 46% of faculty are male; 54%, female. 95% teach undergraduates and 50% both teach and do research. No introductory courses are taught by graduate students. The average class size in an introductory lecture is 20; in a laboratory, 15; and in a regular course, 11.

Admissions: 69% of the 2003-2004 applicants were accepted. The SAT I scores for the 2003-2004 freshman class were: Verbal--20% below 500, 48% between 500 and 599, 26% between 600 and 700, and 6% above 700; Math--28% below 500, 45% between 500 and 599, 23% between 600 and 700, and 4% above 700. The ACT scores were 31% below 21, 25% between 21 and 23, 22% between 24 and 26, 13% between 27 and 28, and 9% above 28. 53% of the current freshmen were in the top fifth of their class; 79% were in the top two fifths. 5 freshmen graduated first in their class.

Requirements: The SAT I or ACT is recommended. In addition, applicants should be graduates of an accredited secondary school, having completed 20 Carnegie units, including 4 years of English, 3 of math, 2 each of foreign language, science, and social studies, and 1 of history. The GED is accepted. An interview is recommended for all students and an audition is recommended for music students. A GPA of 2.0 is required. AP and CLEP credits are accepted. Important factors in the admissions decision are advanced placement or honor courses, recommendations by school officials, and leadership record.

Procedure: Freshmen are admitted to all sessions. Entrance exams should be taken by the senior year of high school. There is an early decision plan and a rolling admissions plan. Early decision applications should be filed by November; regular applications, by August 15 for fall entry. Notification of early decision is sent November; regular decision, on a rolling basis. 4 early decision candidates were accepted for the 2003-2004 class. Applications are accepted on-line through the college's web site.

Transfer: 20 transfer students enrolled in 2002-2003. Transfer applicants should have a minimum GPA of 2.0. 42 of 120 credits required for the bachelor's degree must be completed at Converse College.

Visiting: There are regularly scheduled orientations for prospective students, consisting of faculty meetings, panel discussions, campus tours, tours of Spartanburg, and private interview sessions. There are guides for informal visits and visitors may sit in on classes and stay overnight. To schedule a visit, contact the Admissions Office at (864) 596-9090 or *admissions@converse.edu*.

Financial Aid: In 2003-2004, 80% of all full-time freshmen and 75% of continuing full-time students received some form of financial aid. 72% of full-time freshmen and 69% of continuing full-time students received need-based aid. The average freshman award was $18,039. Need-based scholarships or need-based grants averaged $15,866; need-based self-help aid (loans and jobs) averaged $3593; non-need-based athletic scholarships averaged $9488; and other non-need-based awards and non-need-based scholarships averaged $17,061. 33% of undergraduates work part time. Average annual earnings from campus work are $915. The average financial indebtedness of the 2003 graduate was $18,036.

The FAFSA is required. The deadline for filing freshman financial aid applications for fall entry is March 15.

International Students: There are 10 international students enrolled. The school actively recruits these students. They must score 550 on the written TOEFL.

Computers: The mainframe is a DEC Alpha. There are also 2 computer labs as well as PCs in the library, residence halls, and departmental computer labs. All students may access the system. There are no time limits and no fees. It is strongly recommended that all students have a personal computer. A Compaq is recommended.

Graduates: From July 1, 2002 to June 30, 2003, 164 bachelor's degrees were awarded. The most popular majors were visual and performing arts (21%), education (19%), and business (19%). In an average class, 2% graduate in 3 years or less, 55% graduate in 4 years or less, 56% graduate in 5 years or less, and 56% graduate in 6 years or less. 140 companies recruited on campus in a recent year. In a recent graduating class, 25% were enrolled in graduate school within 6 months of graduation and 55% were employed.

Admissions Contact: Director of Admissions. A video is available. Web: *www.converse.edu*

ERSKINE COLLEGE
Due West, SC 29639

B-2

(864) 379-8830
(800) 241-8721; Fax: (864) 379-2167

Full-time: 241 men, 337 women	**Faculty:** 38; IIB, av$
Part-time: 5 men, 6 women	**Ph.D.s:** 97%
Graduate: none	**Student/Faculty:** 15 to 1
Year: 4-1-4, summer session	**Tuition:** $17,367
Application Deadline: open	**Room & Board:** $5799
Freshman Class: 806 applied, 567 accepted, 176 enrolled	
SAT I Verbal/Math: 560/560	**ACT:** 25 **VERY COMPETITIVE**

Erskine College, founded in 1839, is a private liberal arts college affiliated with the Associate Reformed Presbyterian Church. The library contains 193,178 volumes, 60,162 microform items, and 1698 audio/video tapes/CDs, and subscribes to 980 periodicals. Computerized library services include the card catalog, interlibrary loans, and database searching. Special learning facilities include an art gallery, radio station, and TV station. The 85-acre campus is in a rural area 90 miles west of Columbia. Including any residence halls, there are 30 buildings.

Student Life: 74% of undergraduates are from South Carolina. Students are from 20 states and 10 foreign countries. 85% are from public schools. 89% are white. Most are Protestant. The average age of freshmen is 18; all undergraduates, 20. 18% do not continue beyond their first year; 69% remain to graduate.

Housing: 654 students can be accommodated in college housing, which includes single-sex dorms. On-campus housing is guaranteed for all 4 years. 92% of students live on campus; of those, 50% remain on campus on weekends. Alcohol is not permitted. All students may keep cars.

Activities: 14% of men belong to 3 local fraternities; 25% of women belong to 5 local sororities. There are 49 groups on campus, including cheerleading, choir, chorale, chorus, computers, dance, drama, ethnic, honors, jazz band, literary magazine, newspaper, pep band, political, professional, radio and TV, religious, social, social service, student government, and yearbook. Popular campus events include Spring Fling, Back to School Bash, and Freshman Follies.

Sports: There are 5 intercollegiate sports for men and 5 for women, and 2 intramural sports for men and 2 for women. Facilities include a physical activities center, 2 gyms, racquetball courts, soccer and baseball fields, tennis and basketball courts, an outdoor pavilion, an outdoor pool, 2 sand volleyball courts, a weight room, a dance/aerobics studio, and a climbing wall.

Disabled Students: 75% of the campus is accessible. Wheelchair ramps, elevators, special parking, specially equipped rest rooms, and special class scheduling are available.

Services: Counseling and information services are available, as is tutoring in every subject. There is a reader service for the blind.

Campus Safety and Security: Measures include 24-hour foot and vehicle patrol, security escort services, informal discussions, and pamphlets/posters/films. There are lighted pathways/sidewalks.

Programs of Study: Erskine confers A.B. and B.S. degrees. Master's and doctoral degrees are also awarded. Bachelor's degrees are awarded in BIOLOGICAL SCIENCE (biology/biological science), BUSINESS (business administration and management, and sports management), COMMUNICATIONS AND THE ARTS (art, English, music, and visual and performing arts), COMPUTER AND PHYSICAL SCIENCE (chemistry, mathematics, natural sciences, and physics), EDUCATION (athletic training, Christian, early childhood, elementary, foreign languages, music, physical, and special), HEALTH PROFESSIONS (health science and medical laboratory technology), SOCIAL SCIENCE (American studies, behavioral science, history, philosophy, psychology, religion, and social studies). Business administration and biology are the largest.

Required: Students must complete 124 semester hours with an average of 27 credits in a major and a minimum GPA of 2.0. A basic curriculum

of arts and letters, humanities, natural science and math, social sciences, and phys ed is required. Attendance at 17 convocations per semester is also required.

Special: Externships are available during the January term. Study abroad in 3 countries, 3-2 engineering degrees with Clemson University, the University of Tennessee at Knoxville, and Medical University of South Carolina, and pass/fail options are offered. There are 5 national honor societies and 6 departmental honors programs.

Faculty/Classroom: 61% of faculty are male; 39%, female. All teach undergraduates and 25% both teach and do research. The average class size in an introductory lecture is 22; in a laboratory, 25; and in a regular course, 14.

Admissions: 70% of the 2003-2004 applicants were accepted. The SAT I scores for the 2003-2004 freshman class were: Verbal--23% below 500, 45% between 500 and 599, 22% between 600 and 700, and 10% above 700; Math--21% below 500, 46% between 500 and 599, 27% between 600 and 700, and 6% above 700. The ACT scores were 27% below 21, 12% between 21 and 23, 34% between 24 and 26, 5% between 27 and 28, and 22% above 28. 56% of the current freshmen were in the top fifth of their class; 83% were in the top two fifths. 7 freshmen graduated first in their class.

Requirements: The SAT I or ACT is required, but grades from college preparatory courses are weighed twice as heavily as the SAT I or ACT scores. Applicants must be graduates of an accredited secondary school. The GED is accepted. Applicants should have a minimum of 14 high school academic credits, including 4 credits of English and 2 credits each of math, science, and history. AP and CLEP credits are accepted. Important factors in the admissions decision are advanced placement or honor courses, recommendations by school officials, and extracurricular activities record.

Procedure: Freshmen are admitted to all sessions. Entrance exams should be taken in the spring of the junior year or the fall of the senior year. There is a rolling admissions plan. Application deadlines are open. The fall 2003 application fee was $15. Applications are accepted on-line through the school's web site.

Transfer: 11 transfer students enrolled in 2002-2003. Transfer applicants should have a minimum GPA of 2.0. An interview is recommended. 30 of 124 credits required for the bachelor's degree must be completed at Erskine.

Visiting: There are guides for informal visits and visitors may sit in on classes and stay overnight. To schedule a visit, contact the Admissions Office at (864) 379-8838 or *admissions@erskine.edu*.

Financial Aid: In 2003-2004, 98% of all full-time freshmen and 96% of continuing full-time students received some form of financial aid. 81% of full-time freshmen and 78% of continuing full-time students received need-based aid. The average freshman award was $16,217. Need-based scholarships or need-based grants averaged $8456; and need-based self-help aid (loans and jobs) averaged $3250. The average financial indebtedness of the 2003 graduate was $10,000. The FAFSA and the college's own financial statement are required. The deadline for filing freshman financial aid applications for fall entry is April 1.

International Students: There are 10 international students enrolled. They must score 550 on the written TOEFL and also take the SAT I.

Computers: The mainframe is a DEC Alpha Server 800. There is an Ethernet port for every bed in every dorm room and at least 1 port in every classroom on campus. There are 24 wireless laptops that students can check out for use in the library, 40 computers for student use in the science center, and 2 computers per dorm in study rooms. Students have unlimited access to the Internet and the Web. All students have their own private space on a server where they can store and back up documents. All students may access the system from 7 A.M. to 1 A.M. Monday to Saturday, and from 1 P.M. to 1 A.M. Sunday. There are no time limits. The fee is $50 per semester. It is strongly recommended that all students have a personal computer.

Graduates: From July 1, 2002 to June 30, 2003, 130 bachelor's degrees were awarded. The most popular majors were biology (19%), business (19%), and education (16%). In an average class, 60% graduate in 4 years or less, and 67% graduate in 5 years or less. 38 companies recruited on campus in 2002-2003. Of the 2002 graduating class, 38% were enrolled in graduate school within 6 months of graduation and 76% were employed.

Admissions Contact: Bart Walker, Director of Admissions. E-mail: *admissions@erskine.edu* Web: *www.erskine.edu*

FRANCIS MARION UNIVERSITY
D-2
Florence, SC 29501-0547

(843) 661-1231
(800) 368-7551; Fax: (843) 661-4635

Full-time: 1119 men, 1750 women	**Faculty:** 167; IIA, --$
Part-time: 86 men, 142 women	**Ph.D.s:** 83%
Graduate: 105 men, 388 women	**Student/Faculty:** 17 to 1
Year: semesters, summer session	**Tuition:** $5082 ($10,029)
Application Deadline: open	**Room & Board:** $4282
Freshman Class: 2057 applied, 1565 accepted, 764 enrolled	
SAT I Verbal/Math: 474/480	**ACT:** 19 **COMPETITIVE**

Francis Marion University, founded in 1970, is a state-supported liberal arts, business, and teachers college. There are 3 undergraduate and 3 graduate schools. In addition to regional accreditation, FMU has baccalaureate program accreditation with AACSB, NASAD, NASDTEC, and NCATE. The library contains 383,224 volumes, 101,459 microform items, and 7528 audio/video tapes/CDs, and subscribes to 1653 periodicals. Computerized library services include the card catalog, interlibrary loans, and database searching. Special learning facilities include a learning resource center and planetarium. The 309-acre campus is in a rural area 8 miles east of Florence. Including any residence halls, there are 34 buildings.

Student Life: 94% of undergraduates are from South Carolina. Students are from 30 states, 30 foreign countries, and Canada. 62% are white; 34% African American. The average age of all undergraduates is 22. 36% do not continue beyond their first year; 38% remain to graduate.

Housing: 1134 students can be accommodated in college housing, which includes single-sex dorms and on-campus apartments. On-campus housing is available on a first-come, first-served basis. 64% of students commute. All students may keep cars. Alcohol is permitted in apartments only.

Activities: 10% of men belong to 7 national fraternities; 9% of women belong to 7 national sororities. There are 60 groups on campus, including art, cheerleading, choir, chorus, drama, ethnic, gay, honors, international, jazz band, literary magazine, newspaper, pep band, photography, political, professional, religious, social, social service, and student government. Popular campus events include Holiday Ball, Spring Fling, and Fall Fling.

Sports: There are 7 intercollegiate sports for men and 7 for women, and 24 intramural sports for men and 24 for women. Facilities include a 3200-seat gym, Olympic-size and outdoor leisure pools, baseball, softball, soccer, and intramural fields, tennis, racquetball, and sand volleyball courts, a track, and weight, fitness, and game rooms.

Disabled Students: All of the campus is accessible. Wheelchair ramps, elevators, special parking, specially equipped rest rooms, special class scheduling, and lowered drinking fountains are available.

Services: There is a reader service for the blind and remedial reading and writing.

Campus Safety and Security: Measures include 24-hour foot and vehicle patrol, security escort services, pamphlets/posters/films, and emergency telephones. There are lighted pathways/sidewalks.

Programs of Study: FMU confers B.A., B.S., B.B.A., and B.G.S. degrees. Master's degrees are also awarded. Bachelor's degrees are awarded in BIOLOGICAL SCIENCE (biology/biological science), BUSINESS (accounting, banking and finance, business administration and management, business economics, and marketing/retailing/merchandising), COMMUNICATIONS AND THE ARTS (communications, dramatic arts, English, French, German, and Spanish), COMPUTER AND PHYSICAL SCIENCE (chemistry, computer science, information sciences and systems, mathematics, and physics), EDUCATION (art, early childhood, and elementary), ENGINEERING AND ENVIRONMENTAL DESIGN (engineering technology), SOCIAL SCIENCE (economics, geography, history, international studies, liberal arts/general studies, political science/government, psychology, and sociology). Premedicine and predentistry are the strongest academically. Business, education, and biology are the largest.

Required: Students must complete 120 to 132 credit hours, including 30 to 60 in the major, with a GPA of 2.0. Distribution requirements include 15 hours of humanities, 12 each of sciences and basic communications (6 of English composition and 6 of math or logic), up to 12 hours of a foreign language, and 9 of social sciences.

Special: There are co-op programs in civil engineering technology and electronic engineering technology with Florence Darlington Technical College, in geography with the University of South Carolina, in engineering and forest management with Clemson University, in nursing with the Medical University of South Carolina, and in medical technology with the McLeod Regional Medical Center. Internships are required in the communications and health physics programs. Accelerated degree programs, preprofessional programs, and dual majors are possible. Nondegree study is permitted. Self-paced courses are offered in math and French. Study abroad is possible in Mexico, Switzerland, Germany, New Zealand, Australia, and England. There are 9 national honor societies and a freshman honors program.

Faculty/Classroom: 67% of faculty are male; 33%, female. No introductory courses are taught by graduate students.

Admissions: 76% of the 2003-2004 applicants were accepted. The SAT I scores for the 2003-2004 freshman class were: Verbal--69% below 500, 25% between 500 and 599, 5% between 600 and 700, and 1% above 700; Math--63% below 500, 30% between 500 and 599, 6% between 600 and 700, and 1% above 700. The ACT scores were 78% below 21, 16% between 21 and 23, 5% between 24 and 26, and 1% between 27 and 28. 28% of the current freshmen were in the top fifth of their class; 61% were in the top two fifths. 4 freshmen graduated first in their class.

Requirements: The SAT I is required. In addition, students should have earned 20 credits, consisting of 4 each in academic electives and English, 3 each in math (including algebra I and II), social science, and lab science, 2 in a foreign language, and 1 of phys ed or ROTC. A GPA of 2.0 is required. AP and CLEP credits are accepted.

Procedure: Freshmen are admitted to all sessions. Entrance exams should be taken in the fall of the senior year or spring of the junior year. There is a deferred admissions plan and a rolling admissions plan. Application deadlines are open. Application fee is $30. Notification is sent on a rolling basis. Applications are accepted on-line through the university's web site.

Transfer: 641 transfer students enrolled in a recent year. Transfer students should have earned 24 hours of college credit, with a GPA of at least 2.0. 36 credits of 120 to 132 required for the bachelor's degree must be completed at FMU.

Visiting: There are regularly scheduled orientations for prospective students, including campus tours and registering for classes. There are guides for informal visits and visitors may sit in on classes. To schedule a visit, contact the Admissions Office.

Financial Aid: In 2003-2004, 92% of all full-time freshmen and 54% of continuing full-time students received some form of financial aid. 44% of full-time freshmen and 55% of continuing full-time students received need-based aid. The average freshman award was $5000. 5% of undergraduates work part time. Average annual earnings from campus work are $1048. The average financial indebtedness of the 2003 graduate was $17,980. The FAFSA and the college's own financial statement are required. The priority date for freshmen for filing the FAFSA for fall entry is March 1. The deadline for freshmen for filing the FMU scholarship application for fall entry is February 15.

International Students: There are 52 international students enrolled. The school actively recruits these students. They must score 500 on the written TOEFL or 173 on the electronic version. Transfer students may substitute the SAT I.

Computers: The mainframe is a DEC Alpha 2100. There are 158 Dell PCs available in the academic computer center. The dorms and some buildings are networked. All students may access the system during various hours. A 90-minute time limit takes effect when there is a waiting list. There are no fees.

Graduates: From July 1, 2002 to June 30, 2003, 434 bachelor's degrees were awarded. The most popular majors were business administration (29%), biology (17%), and education (12%). In an average class, 17% graduate in 4 years or less, 35% graduate in 5 years or less, and 38% graduate in 6 years or less. 86 companies recruited on campus in a recent year.

Admissions Contact: Drucilla Russell, Director of Admissions. A video is available. E-mail: *admission@fmarion.edu* Web: *www.fmarion.edu*

FURMAN UNIVERSITY
B-1
Greenville, SC 29613

(864) 294-2034; Fax: (864) 294-3127

Full-time: 1144 men, 1512 women	**Faculty:** 211; IIB, +$
Part-time: 48 men, 69 women	**Ph.D.s:** 97%
Graduate: 76 men, 307 women	**Student/Faculty:** 13 to 1
Year: 3-2-3, summer session	**Tuition:** $22,712
Application Deadline: January 15	**Room & Board:** $6264
Freshman Class: 3866 applied, 2256 accepted, 686 enrolled	
SAT I Verbal/Math: 640/640	**ACT:** 28
	HIGHLY COMPETITIVE+

Founded in 1826, Furman University is an independent liberal arts institution offering undergraduate and graduate programs. In addition to regional accreditation, Furman has baccalaureate program accreditation with ACS, NASDTEC, NASM, and NCATE. The library contains 452,000 volumes, 755,000 microform items, and 4200 audio/video tapes/CDs, and subscribes to 2518 periodicals. Computerized library services include the card catalog, interlibrary loans, database searching, and Internet access. Special learning facilities include a learning resource center, art gallery, radio station, observatory, and cable TV with on-campus broadcasting. The 750-acre campus is in a suburban area 5 miles north of Greenville. Including any residence halls, there are 69 buildings.

Student Life: 70% of undergraduates are from out of state, mostly the South. Students are from 48 states, 18 foreign countries, and Canada. 75% are from public schools. 87% are white. 80% are Protestant; 10% Catholic; 6% claim no religious affiliation. The average age of freshmen is 18; all undergraduates, 20. 9% do not continue beyond their first year; 80% remain to graduate.

Housing: 2441 students can be accommodated in college housing, which includes single-sex and coed dorms and on-campus apartments. In addition, there are language houses and special-interest houses. On-campus housing is guaranteed for all 4 years. 91% of students live on campus; of those, 75% remain on campus on weekends. Alcohol is not permitted. All students may keep cars.

Activities: 30% of men belong to 8 national fraternities; 35% of women belong to 7 national sororities. There are 130 groups on campus, including art, band, cheerleading, chess, choir, chorale, chorus, computers, dance, debate, drama, drill team, ethnic, forensics, gay, international, jazz band, literary magazine, marching band, musical theater, newspaper, opera, orchestra, pep band, photography, political, professional, radio and TV, religious, social, social service, student government, symphony, and yearbook. Popular campus events include Parents Weekend, Beach Weekend, and Mountain Weekend.

Sports: There are 8 intercollegiate sports for men and 9 for women, and 20 intramural sports for men and 20 for women. Facilities include a 16,500-seat football stadium, a 5800-seat arena, a gym, a pool, an 18-hole golf course, a tennis center with indoor and outdoor courts, a 3000-seat soccer stadium, 12 playing fields, a varsity softball field, and a baseball stadium. The gym includes 6 racquetball courts and a fitness center.

Disabled Students: All of the campus is accessible. Wheelchair ramps, elevators, special parking, specially equipped rest rooms, special class scheduling, lowered drinking fountains, lowered telephones, and special housing are available.

Services: Counseling and information services are available, as is tutoring in every subject. There is a reader service for the blind.

Campus Safety and Security: Measures include 24-hour foot and vehicle patrol, self-defense education, security escort services, and shuttle buses. There are informal discussions, pamphlets/posters/films, emergency telephones, and lighted pathways/sidewalks.

Programs of Study: Furman confers B.A., B.S., B.G.S., and B.M. degrees. Master's degrees are also awarded. Bachelor's degrees are awarded in BIOLOGICAL SCIENCE (biology/biological science), BUSINESS (accounting and business administration and management), COMMUNICATIONS AND THE ARTS (art, communications, dramatic arts, English, French, German, Greek, Latin, music, music performance, music theory and composition, piano/organ, and Spanish), COMPUTER AND PHYSICAL SCIENCE (chemistry, computer science, geology, mathematics, and physics), EDUCATION (education, elementary, and music), ENGINEERING AND ENVIRONMENTAL DESIGN (environmental science and preengineering), HEALTH PROFESSIONS (health science), SOCIAL SCIENCE (Asian/Oriental studies, economics, history, philosophy, political science/government, psychology, religion, religious music, sociology, and urban studies). Sciences, music, and psychology are the strongest academically. Political science, history, and business administration are the largest.

Required: To graduate, students must complete 128 credit hours, including 24 to 44 in the major, with a GPA of 2.0. Distribution requirements include 64 hours of general education courses in English composition, foreign language, health and exercise science, natural sciences, social sciences, Asian-African program, fine arts, math, and humanities. Students must attend 36 cultural events before graduation.

Special: A 3-2 engineering degree is offered with Georgia Institute of Technology, Clemson, North Carolina State, Auburn, and Washington University at St. Louis. Internships, study abroad in at least 15 countries, a Washington semester with an internship in a government agency or political organization, and work-study programs are offered. B.A.-B.S. degrees, dual majors, interdisciplinary majors such as computer science-math, math-economics, and computing-business, and student-designed majors are available. A bachelor of general studies degree is granted in the evening division. Nondegree study and pass/fail options are possible. Furman features student/faculty research programs. There are 20 national honor societies, including Phi Beta Kappa.

Faculty/Classroom: 71% of faculty are male; 29%, female. All teach undergraduates. No introductory courses are taught by graduate students. The average class size in an introductory lecture is 23; in a laboratory, 10; and in a regular course, 17.

Admissions: 58% of the 2003-2004 applicants were accepted. The SAT I scores for the 2003-2004 freshman class were: Verbal--3% below 500, 21% between 500 and 599, 52% between 600 and 700, and 23% above 700; Math--3% below 500, 22% between 500 and 599, 56% between 600 and 700, and 20% above 700. The ACT scores were 3% below 21, 8% between 21 and 23, 24% between 24 and 26, 22% between 27 and 28, and 44% above 28. 85% of the current freshmen were in the top fifth of their class; 98% were in the top two fifths. There were 41 National Merit finalists. 50 freshmen graduated first in their class.

Requirements: The SAT I or ACT is required. In addition, applicants must be high school graduates or hold a GED. Students should have earned at least 20 units in high school, including 4 of English, 3 each of history, math, and science, and 2 each of social studies and foreign language. 2 essays are required. A portfolio or an audition, where appropri-

ate, is recommended. AP credits are accepted. Important factors in the admissions decision are advanced placement or honor courses, extracurricular activities record, and leadership record.

Procedure: Freshmen are admitted to all sessions. Entrance exams should be taken by late junior or early senior year. There are early decision, early admissions, and deferred admissions plans. Early decision applications should be filed by November 15; regular applications, by January 15 for fall entry, December 1 for winter entry, February 1 for spring entry, and February 1 for summer entry, along with a $40 fee. Notification of early decision is sent December 15; regular decision, March 15. 497 early decision candidates were accepted for the 2003-2004 class; 18 were admitted. Applications are accepted on computer disk and on-line through CollegeLink, EXPAN, Apply, and the Common Application.

Transfer: 20 transfer students enrolled in 2002-2003. Applicants should complete at least 1 year elsewhere before seeking admission. Admission is competitive. 60 of 128 credits required for the bachelor's degree must be completed at Furman.

Visiting: There are regularly scheduled orientations for prospective students, consisting of an individual or group session with an admissions officer and a campus tour. There are guides for informal visits and visitors may sit in on classes and stay overnight. To schedule a visit, contact the Admissions Office at (864) 294-2034.

Financial Aid: In 2003-2004, 85% of all full-time freshmen and 82% of continuing full-time students received some form of financial aid. 43% of all full-time students received need-based aid. The average freshman award was $18,508. 44% of undergraduates work part time. Average annual earnings from campus work are $1500. The average financial indebtedness of the 2003 graduate was $17,741. Furman is a member of CSS. The FAFSA and the university's own financial statement are required. The deadline for filing freshman financial aid applications for fall entry is February 1.

International Students: The school actively recruits these students. They must score 570 on the written TOEFL and also take the SAT I or the ACT.

Computers: The mainframe consists of a DEC Alpha Server 4000 5/300 running Tru 64 UNIX. Departmental and general access labs accommodate approximately 300 desktop systems, which include PCs, Macs, Suns, X-terminals, and SGI stations. All residence halls are fully networked for e-mail, network sharing, Internet access, and web hosting. Wireless networks exist in classroom and administrative buildings and some residence halls. All students may access the system 24 hours a day. There are no time limits and no fees.

Graduates: From July 1, 2002 to June 30, 2003, 634 bachelor's degrees were awarded. The most popular majors were political science (12%), business administration (11%), and history (7%). In an average class, 1% graduate in 3 years or less, 75% graduate in 4 years or less, 80% graduate in 5 years or less, and 80% graduate in 6 years or less. 86 companies recruited on campus in 2002-2003. Of the 2002 graduating class, 38% were enrolled in graduate school within 6 months of graduation and 60% were employed.

Admissions Contact: Woody O'Cain, Director of Admissions. A video is available. E-mail: *admissions@furman.edu*
Web: *www.engage.furman.edu*

LANDER UNIVERSITY
B-2
Greenwood, SC 29649
(864) 388-8307
(888) 4LANDER; Fax: (864) 388-8125

Full-time: 807 men, 1474 women	**Faculty:** 114; IIB, av$
Part-time: 115 men, 238 women	**Ph.D.s:** 80%
Graduate: 28 men, 288 women	**Student/Faculty:** 20 to 1
Year: semesters, summer session	**Tuition:** $5550 ($11,200)
Application Deadline: open	**Room & Board:** $4946 ($10,596)
Freshman Class: 1603 applied, 1293 accepted, 529 enrolled	
SAT I Verbal/Math: 480/480	**ACT:** 20 COMPETITIVE

Lander University, founded in 1872, is a state-supported institution offering undergraduate programs in liberal arts, science and math, business, education, nursing, and phys ed and exercise studies. There are 10 undergraduate schools and 1 graduate school. In addition to regional accreditation, Lander has baccalaureate program accreditation with AACSB, NASAD, NASM, and NCATE. The library contains 170,091 volumes, 141,945 microform items, and 2170 audio/video tapes/CDs, and subscribes to 692 periodicals. Computerized library services include the card catalog, interlibrary loans, database searching, and Internet access. Special learning facilities include a learning resource center, art gallery, and a media center. The 100-acre campus is in a small town 75 miles west of Columbia. Including any residence halls, there are 33 buildings.

Student Life: 96% of undergraduates are from South Carolina. Students are from 30 states, 19 foreign countries, and Canada. 77% are white; 19% African American. The average age of freshmen is 19; all undergraduates, 22. 32% do not continue beyond their first year; 68% remain to graduate.

Housing: 1082 students can be accommodated in college housing, which includes single-sex and coed dorms, on-campus apartments, and off-campus apartments. On-campus housing is available on a first-come, first-served basis. 68% of students commute. Alcohol is not permitted. All students may keep cars.

Activities: 11% of men belong to 5 national fraternities; 12% of women belong to 5 national sororities. There are 65 groups on campus, including art, band, cheerleading, choir, chorale, chorus, computers, dance, drama, ethnic, honors, international, jazz band, literary magazine, musical theater, newspaper, orchestra, pep band, political, professional, religious, social, social service, and student government. Popular campus events include The Greenwood Performing Arts Series.

Sports: There are 4 intercollegiate sports for men and 5 for women, and 11 intramural sports for men and 11 for women. Facilities include a gym, basketball courts, a weight room, a softball field, tennis courts, an indoor pool, and an indoor suspended track.

Disabled Students: 90% of the campus is accessible. Wheelchair ramps, elevators, special parking, specially equipped rest rooms, special class scheduling, lowered drinking fountains, and lowered telephones are available.

Services: Counseling and information services are available, as is tutoring in most subjects. There is a reader service for the blind, and remedial math, reading, and writing.

Campus Safety and Security: Measures include 24-hour foot and vehicle patrol, self-defense education, security escort services, and emergency telephones. There are lighted pathways/sidewalks.

Programs of Study: Lander confers B.A., B.S., and B.M.Ed. degrees. Master's degrees are also awarded. Bachelor's degrees are awarded in BIOLOGICAL SCIENCE (biology/biological science), BUSINESS (business administration and management), COMMUNICATIONS AND THE ARTS (communications, dramatic arts, English, music, Spanish, speech/debate/rhetoric, and visual and performing arts), COMPUTER AND PHYSICAL SCIENCE (chemistry, computer science, and mathematics), EDUCATION (early childhood, elementary, music, physical, and special), ENGINEERING AND ENVIRONMENTAL DESIGN (environmental science), HEALTH PROFESSIONS (exercise science, nursing, and sports medicine), SOCIAL SCIENCE (history, interdisciplinary studies, political science/government, psychology, and sociology). Premedical and dual engineering are the strongest academically. Business administration, education, and behavorial science are the largest.

Required: To graduate, students must complete 125 semester hours, including 36 in the major, with a GPA of 2.0.

Special: Lander offers internships, co-op and work-study programs, accelerated degrees, B.A.-B.S. degrees, dual engineering degrees with Clemson University, student-designed majors in interdisciplinary studies, credit for military experience, and nondegree study. Students in the Honors International Program study abroad in England for 1 semester during their sophomore year. There are 7 national honor societies and a freshman honors program.

Faculty/Classroom: 50% of faculty are male; 50%, female. All teach undergraduates. No introductory courses are taught by graduate students. The average class size in a regular course is 29.

Admissions: 81% of the 2003-2004 applicants were accepted. The SAT I scores for the 2003-2004 freshman class were: Verbal--56% below 500, 36% between 500 and 599, 7% between 600 and 700, and 1% above 700; Math--53% below 500, 38% between 500 and 599, 8% between 600 and 700, and 1% above 700. The ACT scores were 56% below 21, 27% between 21 and 23, 15% between 24 and 26, 1% between 27 and 28, and 2% above 28. 25% of the current freshmen were in the top fifth of their class; 63% were in the top two fifths. 8% of freshmen graduated first in their class.

Requirements: The SAT I or ACT is required. In addition, applicants must be high school graduates with 20 credits, including 4 each of English and academic electives, 3 each of math and lab science, 2 each of foreign language and social studies, and 1 each of American history, and phys ed or ROTC. An interview and a portfolio or an audition, if appropriate, are recommended. Lander requires applicants to be in the upper 50% of their class. A GPA of 2.0 is required. AP and CLEP credits are accepted.

Procedure: Freshmen are admitted to all sessions. Entrance exams should be taken in the junior year. There are early admissions and deferred admissions plans. There is a rolling admissions plan. Application deadlines are open. The fall 2003 application fee was $35. Notification is sent on a rolling basis. Applications are accepted on-line through the university's web site.

Transfer: 242 transfer students enrolled in 2002-2003. Applicants must have a minimum college GPA of 2.0, otherwise they may be considered on the strength of military or work experience. Transcripts from every school attended should be submitted. Students under 21 with fewer than 30 semester credits must submit high school transcripts and SAT I or ACT results as well. An interview is recommended. 30 credits of 125 required for the bachelor's degree must be completed at Lander.

Visiting: There are regularly scheduled orientations for prospective students, consisting of open houses. There are guides for informal visits and visitors may sit in on classes. To schedule a visit, contact the Admissions Office.

Financial Aid: In 2001-2002, 48% of all full-time freshmen and 54% of continuing full-time students received some form of financial aid. 29% of full-time freshmen and 38% of continuing full-time students received need-based aid. The average freshman award was $1392. 20% of undergraduates work part time. The average financial indebtedness of the 2003 graduate was $12,500. The FAFSA is required. The deadline for filing freshman financial aid applications for fall entry is April 15.

International Students: There are 42 international students enrolled. The school actively recruits these students. They must score 550 on the written TOEFL or 213 on the electronic version and also take the SAT I or the ACT.

Computers: The mainframe is an IBM AS/400. The campus network has a TI connection to the Internet and Web. 250 PCs are available in labs, and students can dial up for modem access to the network. All students may access the system. There are no time limits. The fee $25. It is strongly recommended that all students have a personal computer.

Graduates: From July 1, 2002 to June 30, 2003, 393 bachelor's degrees were awarded. The most popular majors were business (25%), nursing (8%), and elementary education (8%). In an average class, 2% graduate in 3 years or less, 34% graduate in 4 years or less, 44% graduate in 5 years or less, and 49% graduate in 6 years or less. 20 companies recruited on campus in 2002-2003.

Admissions Contact: Jonathan T. Reece, Director of Admissions. E-mail: *admissions@lander.edu* Web: *www.lander.edu*

LIMESTONE COLLEGE   B-1
Gaffney, SC 29340-3799

(864) 489-7151 ext. 4554
(800) 795-7151, ext. 4554; Fax: (864) 487-8706

Full-time: 277 men, 259 women	**Faculty:** 50; IIB, --$
Part-time: 7 men, 9 women	**Ph.Ds:** 71%
Graduate: none	**Student/Faculty:** 11 to 1
Year: semesters, summer session	**Tuition:** $12,300
Application Deadline: open	**Room & Board:** $5400
Freshman Class: 921 applied, 551 accepted, 200 enrolled	
SAT I Verbal/Math: 468/472	**ACT:** 19 **COMPETITIVE**

Limestone College, founded in 1845, is a private, nondenominational Christian institution offering programs in liberal arts, the sciences, business, and teacher preparation. In addition to regional accreditation, Limestone has baccalaureate program accreditation with CSWE and NASM. The library contains 87,315 volumes, 2573 microform items, and 2180 audio/video tapes/CDs, and subscribes to 281 periodicals. Computerized library services include the card catalog, interlibrary loans, and database searching. Special learning facilities include a learning resource center, a writing center, a computer graphics art lab, and a math lab. The 115-acre campus is in a suburban area 50 miles southwest of Charlotte, North Carolina, and 25 miles north of Spartanburg. Including any residence halls, there are 20 buildings.

Student Life: 61% of undergraduates are from South Carolina. Students are from 22 states, 9 foreign countries, and Canada. 76% are white; 20% African American. 39% are Protestant; 9% Catholic. The average age of freshmen is 19; all undergraduates, 21. 29% do not continue beyond their first year; 31% remain to graduate.

Housing: 316 students can be accommodated in college housing, which includes single-sex dorms. On-campus housing is guaranteed for the freshman year only and is available on a first-come, first-served basis. 54% of students commute. Alcohol is not permitted. All students may keep cars.

Activities: 55% of women belong to 1 local sorority. There are no fraternities. There are 17 groups on campus, including art, cheerleading, choir, chorus, computers, drama, honors, jazz band, literary magazine, musical theater, orchestra, professional, religious, social, social service, student government, and yearbook. Popular campus events include Christmas Luminaries, Midterm Madness, and Earth Day.

Sports: There are 8 intercollegiate sports for men and 9 for women, and 7 intramural sports for men and 7 for women. Facilities include a 1500-seat gym, an indoor pool, 8 lighted tennis courts, baseball, softball, soccer, and lacrosse fields, 5 practice fields, and a student center with a game room.

Disabled Students: 75% of the campus is accessible. Wheelchair ramps, elevators, special parking, specially equipped rest rooms, special class scheduling, and lowered drinking fountains are available. Accommodations are made as needed.

Services: Counseling and information services are available, as is tutoring in every subject. There is remedial math, reading, and writing. Special assistance is also available to students with documented learning disabilities through the Pals Program.

Campus Safety and Security: Measures include 24-hour foot and vehicle patrol, security escort services, informal discussions, and lighted pathways/sidewalks.

Programs of Study: Limestone confers B.A., B.S., B.A.S., and B.S.W. degrees. Associate degrees are also awarded. Bachelor's degrees are awarded in BIOLOGICAL SCIENCE (biology/biological science), BUSINESS (accounting, business administration and management, business economics, human resources, marketing management, and sports management), COMMUNICATIONS AND THE ARTS (dramatic arts, English, graphic design, jazz, music, and studio art), COMPUTER AND PHYSICAL SCIENCE (chemistry, computer programming, computer science, information sciences and systems, mathematics, software engineering, and web services), EDUCATION (art, athletic training, elementary, English, mathematics, music, physical, science, and social studies), ENGINEERING AND ENVIRONMENTAL DESIGN (industrial administration/management), SOCIAL SCIENCE (corrections, counseling/psychology, criminal justice, criminology, history, human services, liberal arts/general studies, prelaw, psychology, and social work). Business administration, elementary education, and physical education are the largest.

Required: To graduate, students must complete a minimum of 120 semester hours with 30 to 56 hours in the major and a minimum GPA of 2.0. General education requirements are as follows: 18 hours of fine arts and humanities, 13 to 14 of science and math, 12 of social science, 2 of phys ed, and 1 interdisciplinary for a total of 46 hours minimum.

Special: The college offers senior internships in public and private organizations for 3 credits, as well as a work-study program, and off-campus evening courses. Students may have divisional and multidisciplinary dual majors. The college confers a liberal studies degree and may grant credit for military experience. There are 2 national honor societies, a freshman honors program, and 15 departmental honors programs.

Faculty/Classroom: 66% of faculty are male; 34%, female. All teach undergraduates. The average class size in an introductory lecture is 22; in a laboratory, 15; and in a regular course, 11.

Admissions: 60% of the 2003-2004 applicants were accepted. The SAT I scores for the 2003-2004 freshman class were: Verbal--64% below 500, 32% between 500 and 599, and 4% between 600 and 700; Math--62% below 500, 29% between 500 and 599, and 9% between 600 and 700. The ACT scores were 71% below 21, 15% between 21 and 23, 9% between 24 and 26, and 5% between 27 and 28. 14% of the current freshmen were in the top fifth of their class; 45% were in the top two fifths. 1 freshman graduated first in the class.

Requirements: The SAT I or ACT is required, with a minimum composite score of 850 on the SAT I. The college recommends that students present 4 units of English, 3 of math, and 2 each of lab science and social science. The GED is accepted. An interview is recommended. A GPA of 2.0 is required. AP and CLEP credits are accepted. Important factors in the admissions decision are advanced placement or honor courses, leadership record, and evidence of special talent.

Procedure: Freshmen are admitted fall and spring. Entrance exams should be taken during the fall of the senior year of high school. There is a deferred admissions plan and a rolling admissions plan. Application deadlines are open. Application fee is $25. Notification of regular decision is sent on a rolling basis beginning March 1. Applications are accepted on computer disk and on-line through *http://home.limestone.edu:8010/prospect/aponline/dayapp.htm.*

Transfer: 49 transfer students enrolled in 2003-2004. Applicants must have a minimum GPA of 2.0 and must be in good standing at their previous school. 30 credits of 120 required for the bachelor's degree must be completed at Limestone.

Visiting: There are regularly scheduled orientations for prospective students. There are guides for informal visits and visitors may sit in on classes and stay overnight. To schedule a visit, contact the Admissions Office, Debbie Borders at (864) 488-4554 or *dborders@limestone.edu.*

Financial Aid: In 2003-2004, 98% of all full-time freshmen and 92% of continuing full-time students received some form of financial aid. 86% of full-time freshmen and 96% of continuing full-time students received need-based aid. The average freshman award was $12,785, with $1918 ($4050 maximum) from need-based scholarships or need-based grants, $5498 (19,500 maximum) from need-based self-help aid (loans and jobs), $2173 ($15,170 maximum) from non-need-based athletic scholarships, $2173 ($9,000 maximum) from other non-need-based awards and non-need-based scholarships, and $1023 ($7500 maximum) from private scholarships. 13% of undergraduates work part time. Average annual earnings from campus work are $1807. The average financial indebtedness of the 2003 graduate was $9500. Limestone is a member of CSS. The FAFSA is required. The priority date for freshman financial aid applications for fall entry is February 1. The deadline for filing freshman financial aid applications for fall entry is July 1.

International Students: There are 13 international students enrolled. They must score 500 on the written TOEFL or 173 on the electronic version and also take the SAT I or the ACT, scoring 850 on the SAT I.

Computers: The mainframes are several Sun and Dell servers. There are 72 PCs available in the computer science lab, library, graphic arts lab, music lab, testing lab, and writing lab. Additionally, each resident student has access to the network from his/her dorm room. All students may access the system 7 days a week , 7 A.M. to 11 P.M. There are no time limits and no fees.

Graduates: From July 1, 2002 to June 30, 2003, 98 bachelor's degrees were awarded. The most popular majors were elementary education (19%), business administration (14%), and social work (7%). In an aver-

age class, 28% graduate in 4 years or less, 30% graduate in 5 years or less, and 31% graduate in 6 years or less.

Admissions Contact: Chris Phenicie, Vice President, Enrollment Services. E-mail: *cphenicie@limestone.edu* Web: *www.limestone.edu*

MORRIS COLLEGE
D-3
Sumter, SC 29150-3599

(803) 934-3225
(888) 775-1345; Fax: (803) 773-3687

Full-time: 372 men, 616 women	**Faculty:** 48; --$
Part-time: 9 men, 10 women	**Ph.D.s:** 67%
Graduate: none	**Student/Faculty:** 21 to 1
Year: semesters, summer session	**Tuition:** $7410
Application Deadline: open	**Room & Board:** $3564
Freshman Class: 1778 applied, 1677 accepted, 276 enrolled	
SAT I or ACT: not required	**LESS COMPETITIVE**

Morris College, founded in 1908, is a private liberal arts institution affiliated with the Baptist Church. In addition to regional accreditation, Morris has baccalaureate program accreditation with NASDTEC. The library contains 100,247 volumes, 196,746 microform items, and 1671 audio/video tapes/CDs, and subscribes to 408 periodicals. Computerized library services include the card catalog, interlibrary loans, and database searching. Special learning facilities include a learning resource center, radio station, a TV production studio, and a photography workroom. The 34-acre campus is in an urban area 40 miles east of Columbia. Including any residence halls, there are 20 buildings.

Student Life: 85% of undergraduates are from South Carolina. Students are from 22 states and Canada. 99% are from public schools. All are African American. The average age of freshmen is 19; all undergraduates, 22. 43% do not continue beyond their first year; 35% remain to graduate.

Housing: 622 students can be accommodated in college housing, which includes single-sex dorms. On-campus housing is guaranteed for the freshman year only and is available on a first-come, first-served basis. 72% of students live on campus; of those, 25% remain on campus on weekends. Alcohol is not permitted. Upperclassmen may keep cars.

Activities: 9% of men belong to 4 national fraternities; 6% of women belong to 4 national sororities. There are 50 groups on campus, including cheerleading, chess, choir, chorale, dance, drama, honors, literary magazine, newspaper, pep band, photography, political, professional, radio and TV, religious, social, social service, student government, and yearbook. Popular campus events include Coronation of Miss Morris College, Christmas and gospel choir concerts, and Martin Luther King Observance.

Sports: There are 6 intercollegiate sports for men and 6 for women, and 5 intramural sports for men and 5 for women. Facilities include a weight room, an athletic field complex, a 1700-seat gym, and a 600-seat auditorium.

Disabled Students: 30% of the campus is accessible. Wheelchair ramps, elevators, special parking, specially equipped rest rooms, and lowered drinking fountains are available.

Services: Counseling and information services are available, as is tutoring in every subject. There is remedial math, reading, and writing. Skill-building materials are available on computer.

Campus Safety and Security: Measures include 24-hour foot and vehicle patrol, informal discussions, and lighted pathways/sidewalks.

Programs of Study: Morris confers B.A., B.S., B.F.A., and B.S.Ed. degrees. Bachelor's degrees are awarded in BIOLOGICAL SCIENCE (biology/biological science), BUSINESS (business administration and management and recreation and leisure services), COMMUNICATIONS AND THE ARTS (broadcasting, English, and journalism), COMPUTER AND PHYSICAL SCIENCE (mathematics), EDUCATION (early childhood, elementary, English, mathematics, science, and social studies), HEALTH PROFESSIONS (community health work), SOCIAL SCIENCE (criminal justice, history, liberal arts/general studies, pastoral studies, political science/government, religious education, and sociology). Early childhood education, pastoral ministry, and organizational management are the strongest academically. Business administration, biology, and criminal justice are the largest.

Required: All students must complete 124 to 143 credit hours with a 2.0 GPA overall. General education requirements, with a core curriculum of 60 to 62 credits, include 12 credits each in English and social sciences, 8 to 16 in natural sciences, 6 in religion, 3 to 9 in math, 4 in fine arts, 3 in health education, 2 to 3 each in computers and speech, and a freshman seminar. A comprehensive exam in the major is required prior to graduation.

Special: Business internships, co-op programs, and work-study programs on and off campus are offered. A B.A.-B.S. degree in organizational management is available. A B.S. in nursing degree is offered in conjunction with the University of South Carolina. A cooperative 3-2 engineering degree program with Clemson University and a dual degree program with North Carolina A&T University are available. Credit by exam and credit for military experience are possible. There is 1 national honor society, a freshman honors program, and 1 departmental honors program.

Faculty/Classroom: 48% of faculty are male; 52%, female. All teach undergraduates. The average class size in an introductory lecture is 30; in a laboratory, 20; and in a regular course, 25.

Admissions: 94% of the 2003-2004 applicants were accepted. 8% of the current freshmen were in the top fifth of their class; 27% were in the top two fifths. 1 freshman graduated first in the class.

Requirements: Candidates should be graduates of an accredited secondary school or have the GED. They must have completed 24 Carnegie units, consisting of 4 each in high school English and math, 3 in natural science, 2 in social science, 1 each in U.S. history, phys ed, computer science, and forgeign language, and 7 in electives. A GPA of 2.0 is required. AP and CLEP credits are accepted.

Procedure: Freshmen are admitted to all sessions. There is a deferred admissions plan and a rolling admissions plan. Application deadlines are open. Application fee is $10. Notification is sent on a rolling basis.

Transfer: 49 transfer students enrolled in 2002-2003. Applicants must submit transcripts and evidence of honorable release. A minimum GPA of 2.0 is required. 30 credits of 124 to 143 required for the bachelor's degree must be completed at Morris.

Visiting: There are regularly scheduled orientations for prospective students, consisting of a campus tour, visits with division chairs and faculty members to discuss majors, scheduled activities, and lunch. There are guides for informal visits. To schedule a visit, contact Deborah Calhoun at *dcalhoun@morris.edu.*

Financial Aid: In 2003-2004, 99% of all full-time freshmen and 98% of continuing full-time students received some form of financial aid. 97% of full-time freshmen and 96% of continuing full-time students received need-based aid. The average freshman award was $10,600. Need-based scholarships or need-based grants averaged $3900 ($4050 maximum); need-based self-help aid (loans and jobs) averaged $4000 ($5000 maximum); non-need-based athletic scholarships averaged $750 ($10,500 maximum); and other non-need-based awards and non-need-based scholarships averaged $3500 ($5000 maximum). 48% of undergraduates work part time. Average annual earnings from campus work are $1900. The average financial indebtedness of the 2003 graduate was $15,000. Morris is a member of CSS. The FAFSA and the college's own financial statement are required. The deadline for filing freshman financial aid applications for fall entry is April 30.

International Students: They must take the TOEFL.

Computers: The mainframe is a DEC VAX-4100-A. Some 149 terminals and PCs are located in labs in the media center, the science building, and various other locations. Languages include COBOL and Visual Basic, applications include spreadsheets, database, word processing, and Internet access. Data lines are also available in each dorm room for students who have their own computers, and some computers are available at a central location in the dorms. All students may access the system 78 hours per week.

Graduates: From July 1, 2002 to June 30, 2003, 158 bachelor's degrees were awarded. The most popular majors were business administration (19%), organizational management (15%), and criminal justice (13%). In an average class, 25% graduate in 4 years or less, 38% graduate in 5 years or less, and 42% graduate in 6 years or less. 80 companies recruited on campus in 2002-2003. Of the 2002 graduating class, 15% were enrolled in graduate school within 6 months of graduation and 75% were employed.

Admissions Contact: Deborah Calhoun, Director of Admissions and Records. A video is available. Web: *www.morris.edu*

NEWBERRY COLLEGE
Newberry, SC 29108

B-2

(803) 321-5127
(800) 845-4955; Fax: (803) 321-5138

Full-time: 426 men, 320 women	**Faculty:** 46; IIB, --$
Part-time: 9 men, 21 women	**Ph.D.s:** 70%
Graduate: none	**Student/Faculty:** 16 to 1
Year: semesters, summer session	**Tuition:** $17,251
Application Deadline: open	**Room & Board:** $5620
Freshman Class: 942 applied, 744 accepted, 234 enrolled	
SAT I Verbal/Math: 474/482	**ACT:** 18 **LESS COMPETITIVE**

Newberry College, founded in 1856, is a private liberal arts institution affiliated with the Evangelical Lutheran Church in America. In addition to regional accreditation, Newberry has baccalaureate program accreditation with AVMA, NASM, and NCATE. The 2 libraries contain 79,464 volumes, 7153 microform items, and 1217 audio/video tapes/CDs, and subscribe to 258 periodicals. Computerized library services include the card catalog, interlibrary loans, database searching, and Internet access. Special learning facilities include a learning resource center, radio station, TV station, and an herbarium. The 60-acre campus is in a small town 40 miles northwest of Columbia. Including any residence halls, there are 22 buildings.

Student Life: 84% of undergraduates are from South Carolina. Students are from 13 states, 8 foreign countries, and Canada. 90% are from public schools. 71% are white; 26% African American. 80% are Protestant; 12% claim no religious affiliation; 6% Catholic. The average age of

freshmen is 18; all undergraduates, 20. 49% do not continue beyond their first year; 47% remain to graduate.

Housing: 622 students can be accommodated in college housing, which includes single-sex and coed dorms. In addition, there are honors houses. On-campus housing is guaranteed for all 4 years. 77% of students live on campus; of those, 66% remain on campus on weekends. All students may keep cars.

Activities: 11% of men belong to 6 national fraternities; 13% of women belong to 3 national sororities. There are 50 groups on campus, including band, cheerleading, choir, chorale, chorus, computers, dance, drama, ethnic, honors, international, jazz band, literary magazine, marching band, musical theater, newspaper, orchestra, pep band, political, professional, radio and TV, religious, social, social service, student government, and yearbook. Popular campus events include Fall Fling and Spring Fling.

Sports: There are 7 intercollegiate sports for men and 7 for women, and 6 intramural sports for men and 5 for women. Facilities include a 4000-seat stadium, a phys ed complex with a 1600-seat basketball arena and racquetball courts, an outdoor pool, tennis courts, and baseball, softball, and soccer fields.

Disabled Students: 90% of the campus is accessible. Wheelchair ramps, elevators, special parking, specially equipped rest rooms, and special class scheduling are available.

Services: Counseling and information services are available, as is tutoring in most subjects. There is remedial math, reading, and writing.

Campus Safety and Security: Measures include 24-hour foot and vehicle patrol, security escort services, informal discussions, and pamphlets/posters/films. There are emergency telephones and lighted pathways/sidewalks.

Programs of Study: Newberry confers B.A., B.S., B.M., and B.M.E. degrees. Bachelor's degrees are awarded in BIOLOGICAL SCIENCE (biology/biological science), BUSINESS (business administration and management), COMMUNICATIONS AND THE ARTS (applied music, art, communications, dramatic arts, English, French, German, languages, music, music performance, music theory and composition, and Spanish), COMPUTER AND PHYSICAL SCIENCE (chemistry, computer science, and mathematics), EDUCATION (early childhood, elementary, music, and physical), HEALTH PROFESSIONS (veterinary science), SOCIAL SCIENCE (history, philosophy, political science/government, psychology, religion, and sociology). Education and natural sciences are the strongest academically. Business administration, education, and physical education are the largest.

Required: To graduate, students must complete 126 semester hours, with a minimum GPA of 2.0. Core curriculum requirements include 10 to 11 hours of math and natural science, 9 each of communication skills, humanities or fine arts, and history or social sciences, up to 6 of foreign language, 3 of religion, and 2 of phys ed. There is also a 24-event fine arts and lectures requirement. All students must fulfill Communications Across the Curriculum writing projects.

Special: Internships, dual and student-designed majors, study abroad, a Washington semester, work-study programs, independent study, and cooperative education are offered. A 3-2 engineering degree program with Clemson University, a 3-2 forestry program with Duke University, a 3-3 cytotechnology program, and a 3-1 medical technology program are available. Nondegree study is possible. There are 3 national honor societies, a freshman honors program, and 3 departmental honors programs.

Faculty/Classroom: 58% of faculty are male; 41%, female. All teach undergraduates. The average class size in an introductory lecture is 30; in a laboratory, 30; and in a regular course, 25.

Admissions: 79% of the 2003-2004 applicants were accepted. The SAT I scores for the 2003-2004 freshman class were: Verbal--61% below 500, 33% between 500 and 599, 5% between 600 and 700, and 1% above 700; Math--56% below 500, 35% between 500 and 599, and 9% between 600 and 700. The ACT scores were 74% below 21, 16% between 21 and 23, 8% between 24 and 26, 1% between 27 and 28, and 1% above 28. 28% of the current freshmen were in the top fifth of their class; 48% were in the top two fifths.

Requirements: The SAT I or ACT is required. In addition, applicants should have completed 18 high school academic units, including 4 of English, 3 each of math and social science (1 of U.S. history), 2 each of lab science and a foreign language, and 1 elective. The GED is accepted. An essay is recommended. A GPA of 2.0 is required. AP and CLEP credits are accepted. Important factors in the admissions decision are leadership record, evidence of special talent, and recommendations by school officials.

Procedure: Freshmen are admitted to all sessions. Entrance exams should be taken in the spring of the junior year or the fall of the senior year. There is a deferred admissions plan and a rolling admissions plan. Application deadlines are open. The fall 2003 application fee was $30. Notification is sent on a rolling basis. Applications are accepted on computer disk through Apply.

Transfer: 57 transfer students enrolled in 2002-2003. Applicants must be eligible to return to their previous school. A 2.0 minimum GPA is recommended. 32 credits of 126 required for the bachelor's degree must be completed at Newberry.

Visiting: There are regularly scheduled orientations for prospective students, including a campus tour, informational sessions, and meetings with faculty, staff, and students. There are guides for informal visits and visitors may sit in on classes and stay overnight. To schedule a visit, contact the Admissions Office.

Financial Aid: In a recent year, 91% of all full-time freshmen and 96% of continuing full-time students received some form of financial aid. 63% of full-time freshmen and 65% of continuing full-time students received need-based aid. The average freshman award was $12,450. 12% of undergraduates work part time. Average annual earnings from campus work are $625. The average financial indebtedness of a recent graduate was $3135. Newberry is a member of CSS. The FAFSA is required. The priority date for freshman financial aid applications for fall entry is March 30. The deadline for filing freshman financial aid applications for fall entry is May 15.

International Students: There are 8 international students enrolled. The school actively recruits these students. They must score 525 on the written TOEFL or 197 on the electronic version, take the college's own test, and also take the SAT I or the ACT, scoring 900 on the SAT I.

Computers: The mainframe is a Compaq DL 380. Newberry maintains an Ethernet network with Internet connection, along with 116 PCs distributed among several labs. All students may access the system. There are no time limits and no fees.

Graduates: The most popular majors in a recent class were business and management (16%), education (13%), and social sciences and history (9%). 124 companies recruited on campus in 2002-2003. Of a recent graduating class, 20% were enrolled in graduate school within 6 months of graduation and 60% were employed.

Admissions Contact: Director of Admissions. A video is available. E-mail: *admissions@newberry.edu* Web: *www.newberry.edu*

PRESBYTERIAN COLLEGE		B-2
Clinton, SC 29325		(864) 833-8230
	(800) 476-7272; Fax: (864) 833-8481	
Full-time: 538 men, 606 women	Faculty: 76; IIB, av$	
Part-time: 20 men, 18 women	Ph.D.s: 95%	
Graduate: none	Student/Faculty: 15 to 1	
Year: semesters, summer session	Tuition: $20,110	
Application Deadline: open	Room & Board: $5810	
Freshman Class: 1032 applied, 812 accepted, 312 enrolled		
SAT I Verbal/Math: 556/562	ACT: 23	VERY COMPETITIVE

Presbyterian College, founded in 1880, is a private liberal arts institution affiliated with the Presbyterian Church (U.S.A.). In addition to regional accreditation, PC has baccalaureate program accreditation with AACSB and NCATE. The library contains 167,804 volumes, 13,395 microform items, and 8660 audio/video tapes/CDs, and subscribes to 768 periodicals. Computerized library services include the card catalog, interlibrary loans, and database searching. Special learning facilities include a learning resource center, art gallery, and radio station. The 240-acre campus is in a small town 40 miles south of Greenville. Including any residence halls, there are 39 buildings.

Student Life: 61% of undergraduates are from South Carolina. Students are from 28 states, 7 foreign countries, and Canada. 75% are from public schools. 92% are white. 76% are Protestant; 7% claim no religious affiliation; 6% Catholic. The average age of freshmen is 18; all undergraduates, 20. 15% do not continue beyond their first year; 73% remain to graduate.

Housing: 1027 students can be accommodated in college housing, which includes single-sex and coed dorms, on-campus apartments, off-campus apartments, married-student housing, and fraternity houses. In addition, there are special-interest houses and an international house. On-campus housing is guaranteed for all 4 years. 91% of students live on campus; of those, 75% remain on campus on weekends. All students may keep cars.

Activities: 44% of men belong to 7 national fraternities; 43% of women belong to 3 national sororities. There are 75 groups on campus, including art, band, cheerleading, chess, choir, chorale, chorus, computers, drama, ethnic, gay, honors, international, jazz band, literary magazine, newspaper, pep band, photography, political, professional, radio and TV, religious, social, social service, student government, and yearbook. Popular campus events include Fall Fling, Spring Swing, and Greek Week.

Sports: Facilities include 6500-seat football stadium, a soccer stadium, baseball, and intramural fields, tennis courts, weight rooms, a sauna, a basketball arena, a 3000-seat gym, an outdoor amphitheater, a lighted running trail, an indoor swimming pool, table tennis and pool tables, and an intramural park with a driving range and putting green.

Disabled Students: 90% of the campus is accessible. Wheelchair ramps, elevators, special parking, specially equipped rest rooms, special class scheduling, and lowered drinking fountains are available.

Services: Counseling and information services are available, as is tutoring in every subject. There is a reader service for the blind.

Campus Safety and Security: Measures include 24-hour foot and vehicle patrol, security escort services, informal discussions, and pamphlets/posters/films. There are emergency telephones, lighted pathways/sidewalks, and 24-hour key card dorm locks.

Programs of Study: PC confers B.A. and B.S degrees. Bachelor's degrees are awarded in BIOLOGICAL SCIENCE (biology/biological science), BUSINESS (accounting and business administration and management), COMMUNICATIONS AND THE ARTS (English, fine arts, French, German, music, Spanish, and visual and performing arts), COMPUTER AND PHYSICAL SCIENCE (chemistry, mathematics, and physics), EDUCATION (elementary, music, secondary, and special), SOCIAL SCIENCE (economics, history, political science/government, psychology, religion, and sociology). Business, biology, and English are the largest.

Required: To graduate, students must complete a minimum of 122 semester hours, including 30 to 48 in the major, with a minimum GPA of 2.0. General education requirements of 46 to 55 credits include 16 hours of foreign language, 8 of lab science, 6 each of religion, English, world history, and social science, 3 to 4 of math, 3 of fine arts, and 2 of phys ed.

Special: Educational internships, study abroad in 40 countries, and a Washington semester are available. Dual majors, work-study programs, accelerated degree programs, B.A.-B.S. degrees, and a 3-2 engineering degree with Auburn, Clemson, Vanderbilt, and Mercer universities are offered. There is a forestry environmental studies program with Duke University and a Christian education program with Presbyterian School of Christian Education. Credit for life, military, or work experience, auditing courses, and pass/fail options are possible. There are 9 national honor societies, a freshman honors program, and 26 departmental honors programs.

Faculty/Classroom: 75% of faculty are male; 25%, female. All teach undergraduates and 65% both teach and do research. The average class size in an introductory lecture is 17; in a laboratory, 16; and in a regular course, 13.

Admissions: 79% of the 2003-2004 applicants were accepted. The SAT I scores for the 2003-2004 freshman class were: Verbal--14% below 500, 50% between 500 and 599, 32% between 600 and 700, and 4% above 700; Math--16% below 500, 46% between 500 and 599, 35% between 600 and 700, and 3% above 700. The ACT scores were 20% below 21, 31% between 21 and 23, 31% between 24 and 26, 8% between 27 and 28, and 10% above 28.

Requirements: The SAT I or ACT is required. In addition, applicants must be graduates of an accredited secondary school with 18 academic credits, including 4 years of English, 3 years of math, and 2 or more years each of foreign language, history, science, and social studies. The GED is accepted. An essay is required. For music scholarships, an audition is necessary. A GPA of 2.25 is required. AP and CLEP credits are accepted. Important factors in the admissions decision are advanced placement or honor courses, recommendations by school officials, and leadership record.

Procedure: Freshmen are admitted to all sessions. Entrance exams should be taken during the spring of the junior year. There are early decision, early admissions, and deferred admissions plans. Application deadlines are open. The fall 2003 application fee was $30. There is a rolling admissions plan. 65 early decision candidates were accepted for the 2003-2004 class. Applications are accepted on-line through the college's web site.

Transfer: 18 transfer students enrolled in 2002-2003. Transfer applicants must have a minimum GPA of 2.0. 48 of 122 credits required for the bachelor's degree must be completed at PC.

Visiting: There are regularly scheduled orientations for prospective students, including academic, activity, and financial aid information sessions, tours, and lunch. There are guides for informal visits and visitors may sit in on classes and stay overnight. To schedule a visit, contact the Office of Admissions.

Financial Aid: In 2003-2004, 93% of all full-time freshmen and 94% of continuing full-time students received some form of financial aid. 62% of all full-time students received need-based aid. The average freshman award was $13,662. 30% of undergraduates work part time. Average annual earnings from campus work are $800. The average financial indebtedness of the 2003 graduate was $17,820. The FAFSA and the college's own financial statement are required. The deadline for filing freshman financial aid applications for fall entry is March 1.

International Students: There are 20 international students enrolled. They must score 550 on the written TOEFL and also take the SAT I or the ACT.

Computers: The mainframe is a Data General Avion. There are 120 PCs in 3 labs, including IBM and Macs. Software and printers, including laser printers, are available. Computer assistance is provided during open hours. All academic buildings, residence halls, classrooms, labs, and faculty offices are networked through the Internet/Bitnet and other national and international networks. E-mail is available. Wireless Internet connections are available in the library and the senior dorm. All students may access the system any time. There are no time limits and no fees.

Graduates: From July 1, 2002 to June 30, 2003, 256 bachelor's degrees were awarded. The most popular majors were economics/business (20%), biology (15%), and psychology (15%). In an average class, 61% graduate in 4 years or less, 70% graduate in 5 years or less, and 72% graduate in 6 years or less. 42 companies recruited on campus in 2002-2003. Of the 2002 graduating class, 19% were enrolled in graduate school within 6 months of graduation and 80% were employed.

Admissions Contact: Dana Paul, VP, Enrollment and Dean of Admissions. A video is available. E-mail: *rdpaul@admin.presby.edu*
Web: *www.presby.edu*

SOUTH CAROLINA STATE UNIVERSITY
Orangeburg, SC 29117

C-3

(803) 536-7185
(800) 260-5956; Fax: (803) 536-8990

Full-time: 1580 men, 1950 women	**Faculty:** 211
Part-time: 120 men, 300 women	**Ph.D.s:** 62%
Graduate: 120 men, 525 women	**Student/Faculty:** 16 to 1
Year: semesters, summer session	**Tuition:** $3988 ($7790)
Application Deadline: July 31	**Room & Board:** $3400
Freshman Class: n/av	
SAT I or ACT: required	**LESS COMPETITIVE**

South Carolina State University, a historically black, land-grant institution founded in 1896, offers undergraduate programs in liberal arts and sciences, business, education, engineering technology, and human sciences. There are 5 undergraduate schools and 1 graduate school. Figures in the above capsule and in this profile are approximate. In addition to regional accreditation, State or SCSU has baccalaureate program accreditation with ABET, ADA, AHEA, CSWE, NASDTEC, and NCATE. The library contains 280,000 volumes and 700,000 microform items, and subscribes to 1400 periodicals. Computerized library services include the card catalog, interlibrary loans, and database searching. Special learning facilities include a learning resource center, art gallery, planetarium, radio station, and an instructional media center. The 160-acre campus is in a small town 40 miles east of Columbia. Including any residence halls, there are 60 buildings.

Student Life: 83% of undergraduates are from South Carolina. 95% are African American. The average age of freshmen is 18; all undergraduates, 19. 22% do not continue beyond their first year; 32% remain to graduate.

Housing: 2242 students can be accommodated in college housing, which includes single-sex dorms and married-student housing. On-campus housing is available on a first-come, first-served basis and is available on a lottery system for upperclassmen. 80% of students live on campus. Alcohol is not permitted. Upperclassmen may keep cars.

Activities: 25% of men belong to 4 national fraternities; 32% of women belong to 4 national sororities. There are 85 groups on campus, including band, cheerleading, choir, chorus, dance, drama, drill team, honors, international, jazz band, marching band, newspaper, orchestra, pep band, political, religious, social, social service, student government, and yearbook. Popular campus events include Colloquium Series, game nights, Halloween Haunt, Leadership Training, and Bulldog Fest.

Sports: There are 7 intercollegiate sports for men and 8 for women, and 8 intramural sports for men and 7 for women. Facilities include a student center with a game room and bowling alley, a gym, tennis courts, a 22,000-seat stadium, an 8-lane asphalt track, and swimming pools.

Disabled Students: 60% of the campus is accessible. Wheelchair ramps, elevators, special parking, specially equipped rest rooms, lowered drinking fountains, and lowered telephones are available.

Services: Counseling and information services are available, as is tutoring in most subjects. There is a reader service for the blind, and remedial math, reading, and writing. Free counseling is also available.

Campus Safety and Security: Measures include 24-hour foot and vehicle patrol, shuttle buses, pamphlets/posters/films, and lighted pathways/sidewalks. There is a campus police department with 25 safety and security officers.

Programs of Study: State or SCSU confers B.A. and B.S. degrees. Master's and doctoral degrees are also awarded. Bachelor's degrees are awarded in AGRICULTURE (agricultural business management), BIOLOGICAL SCIENCE (biology/biological science and nutrition), BUSINESS (accounting, business administration and management, business economics, marketing/retailing/merchandising, and office supervision and management), COMMUNICATIONS AND THE ARTS (dramatic arts, English, fine arts, French, music business management, and Spanish), COMPUTER AND PHYSICAL SCIENCE (chemistry, computer science, mathematics, and physics), EDUCATION (art, business, early childhood, elementary, guidance, health, home economics, industrial arts, music, physical, reading, and special), ENGINEERING AND ENVIRONMENTAL DESIGN (civil engineering technology, electrical/electronics engineering technology, engineering technology, and mechanical engineering technology), HEALTH PROFESSIONS (nursing

and speech pathology/audiology), SOCIAL SCIENCE (criminal justice, food science, history, human services, political science/government, psychology, social studies, social work, and sociology). Science, engineering technology, and business education are the strongest academically.

Required: To graduate, all students must complete at least 128 credit hours with a minimum GPA of 2.0. Students must attend the freshman orientation program, take a general education examination in their sophomore year, satisfy the general education program requirements, and pass an English proficiency test.

Special: The university offers co-op education and work-study programs, cross-registration with Claflin College, internships, study abroad in 2 countries, combined B.A.-B.S. degrees, credit for educational and work experience, nondegree study, and pass/fail options for juniors and seniors. Also available are an electrical engineering technology program at Midlands, Greenville, and Trident Technical colleges, an evening school program, and a program for educationally disadvantaged students who do not meet traditional entrance requirements. There are 12 national honor societies, and a freshman honors program.

Faculty/Classroom: No introductory courses are taught by graduate students.

Requirements: The SAT I or ACT is required. In addition, applicants must rank in the upper half of their graduating class at an accredited secondary school. The GED is accepted. High school preparation should include 4 units of English, 3 of math, 2 each of foreign language and lab science, and 1 each of history, social studies, and phys ed or ROTC, plus 1/2 unit each in economics and government. A GPA of 2.0 is required. AP and CLEP credits are accepted. Important factors in the admissions decision are advanced placement or honor courses, leadership record, and personality/intangible qualities.

Procedure: Freshmen are admitted fall and spring. Entrance exams should be taken before filing an application. Applications should be filed by July 31 for fall entry and November 30 for spring entry. Check with the school for current fee.

Transfer: 120 transfer students enrolled in a recent year. Transfer applicants should have a college GPA of 2.0. Students with fewer than 30 credit hours must submit high school and college transcripts and SAT I or ACT scores. 30 of 128 credits required for the bachelor's degree must be completed at SCSU.

Visiting: There are guides for informal visits and visitors may sit in on classes. To schedule a visit, contact the Office of Admissions and Recruitment.

Financial Aid: The FAFSA is required. The deadline for filing freshman financial aid applications for fall entry is May 1.

International Students: There are 8 international students enrolled. They must take the TOEFL and also take the SAT I, or ACT. The application deadlines are June 1 for fall entry and October 30 for spring entry.

Computers: The mainframe is a DEC VAX 11/780. Macs and one-on-one tutorial assistance are available to all students at the campus writing center. All students may access the system. There are no time limits and no fees.

Admissions Contact: Lillian M. Adderson, Director of Admissions. E-mail: *admissions@scsu.edu*

SOUTHERN WESLEYAN UNIVERSITY
Central, SC 29630-1020

A-2

(864) 644-5550
(800) 282-8798; Fax: (864) 644-5972

Full-time: 684 men, 1135 women	**Faculty:** 63
Part-time: 18 men, 128 women	**Ph.D.s:** 77%
Graduate: 148 men, 317 women	**Student/Faculty:** 29 to 1
Year: semesters, summer session	**Tuition:** $14,090
Application Deadline: August 2	**Room & Board:** $5850
Freshman Class: 356 applied, 258 accepted, 129 enrolled	
SAT I Verbal/Math: 510/510	**ACT:** 19 **COMPETITIVE**

Southern Wesleyan University, founded in 1906, and part of the Council for Christian Colleges and Universities, is a private liberal arts institution affiliated with the Wesleyan Church. In addition to regional accreditation, SWU has baccalaureate program accreditation with NASDTEC. The library contains 87,683 volumes, 160 microform items, and 3293 audio/video tapes/CDs, and subscribes to 525 periodicals. Computerized library services include the card catalog, interlibrary loans, and database searching. Special learning facilities include a learning resource center and an electron microscope lab. The 200-acre campus is in a small town 30 miles southwest of Greenville. Including any residence halls, there are 21 buildings.

Student Life: 84% of undergraduates are from South Carolina. Students are from 24 states, 7 foreign countries, and Canada. 98% are from public schools. 63% are white; 32% African American. 86% are Protestant; 9% claim no religious affiliation. The average age of freshmen is 19; all undergraduates, 25. 25% do not continue beyond their first year; 34% remain to graduate.

Housing: 362 students can be accommodated in college housing, which includes single-sex and coed dorms and on-campus apartments.

On-campus housing is guaranteed for all 4 years. 84% of students commute. Alcohol is not permitted. All students may keep cars.

Activities: There are no fraternities or sororities. There are 20 groups on campus, including cheerleading, choir, computers, drama, ethnic, honors, jazz band, literary magazine, musical theater, orchestra, professional, religious, social, social service, student government, and yearbook . Popular campus events include Christmas Banquet and Junior/Senior Banquet, Coffee House, and Late Night Breakfast.

Sports: There are 5 intercollegiate sports for men and 5 for women, and 5 intramural sports for men and 4 for women. Facilities include a gym, soccer, softball and baseball fields, tennis courts, a fitness center, and a cross-country trail.

Disabled Students: 90% of the campus is accessible. Wheelchair ramps, elevators, special parking, and specially equipped rest rooms are available.

Services: Counseling and information services are available, as is tutoring in some subjects. There is remedial math, reading, and writing.

Campus Safety and Security: Measures include informal discussions, pamphlets/posters/films, emergency telephones, lighted pathways/sidewalks, and night security.

Programs of Study: SWU confers B.A., B.S., and B.Acct. degrees. Associate and master's degrees are also awarded. Bachelor's degrees are awarded in BIOLOGICAL SCIENCE (biology/biological science), BUSINESS (accounting, business administration and management, personnel management, and recreation and leisure services), COMMUNICATIONS AND THE ARTS (English and music), COMPUTER AND PHYSICAL SCIENCE (chemistry, information sciences and systems, mathematics, and web services), EDUCATION (elementary, music, physical, and special), HEALTH PROFESSIONS (medical laboratory technology), SOCIAL SCIENCE (history, psychology, religion, and social science). Education, business, and religion are the largest.

Required: To graduate, students must complete 128 credit hours with 54 hours in general education courses and a minimum GPA of 2.0. All students must take 12 hours each of English and religion, 6 of history, 3 of social sciences, 3 of math or statistics, and 2 science lab courses. Specific required courses include aesthetics, introduction to computer science, phys ed, and interdisciplinary seminars.

Special: There is a co-op program with Clemson University and in medical technology and criminal justice with other institutions. Study abroad in 6 countries and internships in psychology, English, and business are available. A Washington semester with the Council for Christian Colleges and Universities, a semester at the Los Angeles Film Studies center, a session at the Summer Institute of Journalism in Washington D.C., and dual majors are available. The Leadership Education for the Adult Professional Program offers degrees for working professionals. There is 1 national honor society, a freshman honors program, and 7 departmental honors programs.

Faculty/Classroom: 78% of faculty are male; 22%, female. All both teach and do research. No introductory courses are taught by graduate students. The average class size in an introductory lecture is 25; in a laboratory, 15; and in a regular course, 20.

Admissions: 72% of the 2003-2004 applicants were accepted. The SAT I scores for the 2003-2004 freshman class were: Verbal--42% below 500, 38% between 500 and 599, 18% between 600 and 700, and 1% above 700; Math--42% below 500, 39% between 500 and 599, 16% between 600 and 700, and 2% above 700. The ACT scores were 62% below 21, 19% between 21 and 23, 15% between 24 and 26, 2% between 27 and 28, and 2% above 28. 25% of the current freshmen were in the top fifth of their class; 50% were in the top two fifths. There was 1 National Merit semifinalist. 2 freshmen graduated first in their class.

Requirements: The SAT I or ACT is required, with a recommended minimum composite score of 850 on the SAT I or 19 on the ACT. Applicants must be graduates of an accredited secondary school. The GED is accepted. Students should complete 16 Carnegie units, including 4 credits of English and 2 each of math, science, and social studies, as well as 6 electives. SWU requires applicants to be in the upper 50% of their class. A GPA of 2.0 is required. AP and CLEP credits are accepted. Important factors in the admissions decision are leadership record, advanced placement or honor courses, and personality/intangible qualities.

Procedure: Freshmen are admitted fall and spring. Entrance exams should be taken prior to application. There are early admissions and deferred admissions plans. Applications should be filed by August 2 for fall entry and December 14 for spring entry, along with a $25 fee. There is a rolling admissions plan. Notification is sent on a rolling basis.

Transfer: 68 transfer students enrolled in 2002-2003. SWU recommends that transfer applicants have a minimum GPA of 2.0 in at least 29 credit hours. 32 credits of 128 required for the bachelor's degree must be completed at SWU.

Visiting: There are regularly scheduled orientations for prospective students. There are guides for informal visits and visitors may sit in on classes and stay overnight. To schedule a visit, contact the Admissions Office at *admissions@swu.edu*.

Financial Aid: In 2003-2004, 95% of all full-time freshmen and 83% of continuing full-time students received some form of financial aid. 82% of full-time freshmen and 80% of continuing full-time students received need-based aid. The average freshman award was $8166. Need-based scholarships or need-based grants averaged $9540; need-based self-help aid (loans and jobs) averaged $2717; and non-need-based athletic scholarships averaged $4350. 55% of undergraduates work part time. Average annual earnings from campus work are $850. The average financial indebtedness of the 2003 graduate was $15,300. The FAFSA and the college's own financial statement are required. The deadline for filing freshman financial aid applications for fall entry is April 15.

International Students: There are 11 international students enrolled. They must score 500 on the written TOEFL or 173 on the electronic version and also take the SAT I or the ACT, scoring 850 on the SAT I.

Computers: The mainframe is an NT server. There are 19 computer labs housing 176 PCs for student use. All students may access the system. There are no time limits. The fee is $50.

Graduates: From July 1, 2002 to June 30, 2003, 357 bachelor's degrees were awarded. The most popular majors were business (48%), education (12%), and religion (3%). In an average class, 16% graduate in 4 years or less, 41% graduate in 5 years or less, and 42% graduate in 6 years or less.

Admissions Contact: Chad Peters, Director of Admissions. A video is available. E-mail: *admissions@swu.edu* Web: *www.swu.edu*

UNIVERSITY OF SOUTH CAROLINA SYSTEM

The University of South Carolina System, established in 1801, is a private system in South Carolina. It is governed by a board of trustees, whose chief administrator is president. The primary goal of the system is to prepare informed and productive citizens to adapt to an increasingly complex environment. The main priorities are to foster excellence in undergraduate and graduate education, research, and service programs. The total enrollment of all 8 campuses is usually about 40,000; there were more than 1700 faculty members. Altogether there are 78 baccalaureate, 172 master's, and 63 doctoral, and 3 professional programs offered in University of South Carolina System. Profiles of the 4-year campuses are included in this section.

UNIVERSITY OF SOUTH CAROLINA AT AIKEN   C-3
Aiken, SC 29801   (803) 641-3366
                              (888) WOW-USCA; Fax: (803) 641-3727

Full-time: 760 men, 1400 women	**Faculty:** 125; IIB, av$
Part-time: 300 men, 680 women	**Ph.D.s:** 80%
Graduate: 20 men, 125 women	**Student/Faculty:** 17 to 1
Year: semesters, summer session	**Tuition:** $3800 ($8400)
Application Deadline: open	**Room & Board:** $4200
Freshman Class: n/av	
SAT I: required	**LESS COMPETITIVE**

The University of South Carolina Aiken, established in 1961, is a state-supported institution offering undergraduate and graduate programs in humanities and social sciences, health sciences, education, business administration and economics, nursing, and science. There are 5 undergraduate and 3 graduate schools. Figures in the above capsule and in this profile are approximate. In addition to regional accreditation, USCA has baccalaureate program accreditation with NASDTEC and NLN. The library contains 140,000 volumes, 60,000 microform items, and 200 audio/video tapes/CDs, and subscribes to 850 periodicals. Computerized library services include the card catalog, interlibrary loans, and database searching. Special learning facilities include a learning resource center, art gallery, planetarium, and a science education center. The 354-acre campus is in a suburban area 14 miles east of Augusta, Georgia. Including any residence halls, there are 14 buildings.

Student Life: 84% of undergraduates are from South Carolina. 98% are from public schools. 72% are white; 22% African American. The average age of freshmen is 21; all undergraduates, 25.

Housing: 360 students can be accommodated in college housing, which includes coed on-campus apartments. On-campus housing is available on a first-come, first-served basis and is available on a lottery system for upperclassmen. 88% of students commute. Alcohol is not permitted. All students may keep cars.

Activities: 1% of men belong to 3 national fraternities; 1% of women belong to 3 national sororities. There are 53 groups on campus, including cheerleading, choir, chorus, computers, drama, ethnic, honors, international, literary magazine, musical theater, newspaper, pep band, photography, political, professional, religious, social, social service, and student government. Popular campus events include International Day and Alcohol/Health Awareness Week.

Sports: There are 6 intercollegiate sports for men and 6 for women, and 20 intramural sports for men and 20 for women. Facilities include an activities center, a baseball field, a soccer/intramural/softball field, a tennis court, and a wellness/exercise center.

Disabled Students: All of the campus is accessible. Wheelchair ramps, elevators, special parking, specially equipped rest rooms, lowered drinking fountains, and lowered telephones are available.

Services: Counseling and information services are available, as is tutoring in some subjects, including math and writing. There is a reader service for the blind. special administration of tests, note taking, free copying of notes for disabled, large print exams for visually impaired, zoom text software for computer applications, and priority registration in some cases.

Campus Safety and Security: Measures include 24-hour foot and vehicle patrol, self-defense education, security escort services, and informal discussions. There are pamphlets/posters/films, emergency telephones, and lighted pathways/sidewalks.

Programs of Study: USCA confers B.A., B.S., and B.I.S. degrees. Associate and master's degrees are also awarded. Bachelor's degrees are awarded in BIOLOGICAL SCIENCE (biology/biological science), BUSINESS (business administration and management), COMMUNICATIONS AND THE ARTS (communications, English, and fine arts), COMPUTER AND PHYSICAL SCIENCE (applied mathematics, chemistry, and computer mathematics), EDUCATION (early childhood, elementary, and secondary), HEALTH PROFESSIONS (nursing), SOCIAL SCIENCE (history, interdisciplinary studies, physical fitness/movement, political science/government, psychology, and sociology). English, history, and biology are the strongest academically. Business, education, and nursing are the largest.

Required: Students must complete a minimum of 120 credit hours, with at least a 2.0 GPA. General education requirements include courses in English, math, applied speech, natural science, social and behavioral sciences, humanities, and history.

Special: Cross-registration is permitted with other schools in the University of South Carolina system. Co-op programs in engineering and business, business internships, study abroad in 19 countries, student-designed majors, and work-study programs are offered. B.A.-B.S. degrees in psychology and education, nondegree study, and pass/fail options are possible. There are 7 national honor societies, a freshman honors program, and 4 departmental honors programs.

Faculty/Classroom: 55% of faculty are male; 45%, female. 97% teach undergraduates. No introductory courses are taught by graduate students. The average class size in an introductory lecture is 24; in a laboratory, 18; and in a regular course, 15.

Requirements: The SAT I is required. In addition, admission is based on a combination of an applicant's scores on college entrance examinations and high school GPA. Applicants are required to submit 16 academic credits, including 4 years of high school English, 3 units of math, 2 each of social studies, a foreign language, and a lab science, 1 of history, and 1 year of phys ed or ROTC, and 1 from advanced math, computer science, math/computer science, world history, world geography, or Western civilization. AP and CLEP credits are accepted. Important factors in the admissions decision are advanced placement or honor courses, recommendations by school officials, and leadership record.

Procedure: Freshmen are admitted to all sessions. Entrance exams should be taken by the fall of the senior year. There are early admissions and deferred admissions plans. Application deadlines are open. Applications are accepted on-line at the school's web site. Check with the school for current fee.

Transfer: The college GPA is considered. A high school transcript is required of applicants with fewer than 45 quarter hours. 30 of 120 credits required for the bachelor's degree must be completed at USCA.

Visiting: There are regularly scheduled orientations for prospective students, including regularly scheduled 3-day orientations for prospective students. There are guides for informal visits and visitors may sit in on classes. To schedule a visit, contact the Admissions Office.

Financial Aid: In a recent year, 68% of all full-time freshmen and 72% of continuing full-time students received some form of financial aid. 51% of full-time freshmen and 50% of continuing full-time students received need-based aid. The average freshman award was $2950. The average financial indebtedness of a recent graduate was $13,200. USCA is a member of CSS. The FAFSA and the college's own financial statement are required. Check with the school for current deadlines.

International Students: They must score 550 on the written TOEFL and also take the SAT I.

Computers: The mainframe is an IBM 9672. There are more than 200 PCs for student use throughout the campus. All students may access the system 24 hours a day, 7 days a week. There are no time limits.

Graduates: In an average class, 13% graduate in 4 years or less, 36% graduate in 5 years or less, and 42% graduate in 6 years or less.

Admissions Contact: Andrew Hendrix, Director of Admissions.
E-mail: *admit@sc.edu* Web: *www.usca.sc.edu*

UNIVERSITY OF SOUTH CAROLINA AT COLUMBIA   C-3
Columbia, SC 29208   (803) 777-7700
(800) 868-5872; Fax: (803) 777-0101

Full-time: 6431 men, 7647 women	**Faculty:** 781; I, -$
Part-time: 1179 men, 1310 women	**Ph.Ds:** 84%
Graduate: 3226 men, 5347 women	**Student/Faculty:** 18 to 1
Year: semesters, summer session	**Tuition:** $4984 ($13,104)
Application Deadline: February 15	**Room & Board:** $5064
Freshman Class: 12,016 applied, 8446 accepted, 3561 enrolled	
SAT I Verbal/Math: 550/560	**ACT:** 24 **VERY COMPETITIVE**

The University of South Carolina at Columbia, founded in 1801, is a publicly assisted institution serving the entire state of South Carolina. In addition to the main campus at Columbia, there are 2 senior campuses at Aiken and Spartanburg and 5 regional campuses. There are 16 undergraduate and 18 graduate schools. In addition to regional accreditation, Carolina has baccalaureate program accreditation with AACSB, ABET, ACEJMC, ACPE, CSAB, NASM, NCATE, and NLN. The 7 libraries contain 3,333,764 volumes, 5,008,383 microform items, and 45,930 audio/video tapes/CDs, and subscribe to 21,836 periodicals. Computerized library services include the card catalog, interlibrary loans, and database searching. Special learning facilities include a learning resource center, art gallery, natural history museum, planetarium, and radio station. The 351-acre campus is in an urban area in the downtown area of Columbia. Including any residence halls, there are 159 buildings.

Student Life: 81% of undergraduates are from South Carolina. Others are from 49 states, 75 foreign countries, and Canada. 73% are white; 17% African American. The average age of freshmen is 18; all undergraduates, 21. 18% do not continue beyond their first year; 60% remain to graduate.

Housing: 6825 students can be accommodated in college housing, which includes single-sex and coed dorms, on-campus apartments, married-student housing, fraternity houses, and sorority houses. In addition, there are honors houses, special-interest houses, and wellness, residential college, U.S. international community, teaching fellows residence, athletic, and Greek houses. On-campus housing is guaranteed for the freshman year only and is available on a lottery system for upperclassmen. 53% of students commute. All students may keep cars.

Activities: 17% of men belong to 18 national fraternities; 17% of women belong to 12 national sororities. There are 275 groups on campus, including art, band, cheerleading, chess, choir, chorale, chorus, computers, dance, debate, drama, drill team, ethnic, film, forensics, gay, honors, international, jazz band, literary magazine, marching band, musical theater, opera, orchestra, pep band, photography, political, professional, radio and TV, religious, social, social service, student government, symphony, and yearbook. Popular campus events include Parents Weekend, Black History Month, and Carolina Spirit Week.

Sports: There are 9 intercollegiate sports for men and 11 for women, and 33 intramural sports for men and 33 for women. Facilities include football and soccer stadiums, a basketball coliseum, a field house, a volleyball and basketball practice facility, baseball, softball, and practice fields, and an all-weather track. There is also a recreation center with badminton, basketball, handball/racquetball, an aquatics center, a weight room, aerobics, and tennis court space.

Disabled Students: 95% of the campus is accessible. Wheelchair ramps, elevators, special parking, specially equipped rest rooms, special class scheduling, lowered drinking fountains, lowered telephones, special housing, listening devices, sign language interpreting, and adapted transportation and computers are available.

Services: Counseling and information services are available, as is tutoring in every subject, including reader services for LD students. There is a reader service for the blind.

Campus Safety and Security: Measures include 24-hour foot and vehicle patrol, self-defense education, security escort services, and shuttle buses. There are informal discussions, pamphlets/posters/films, emergency telephones, and lighted pathways/sidewalks. The USC police department is a nationally accredited campus law enforcement agency.

Programs of Study: Carolina confers B.A., B.S., B.A.I.S., B.A.J., B.A.P.E./B.S.P.E., B.A.R.S.C., B.F.A., B.M., B.M.A., B.S.B.A., B.S.Chem., B.S.C.S., B.S.E., B.S.I.S., B.S.Med.Tech., and B.S.N. degrees. Associate, master's, and doctoral degrees are also awarded. Bachelor's degrees are awarded in BIOLOGICAL SCIENCE (biology/biological science and marine science), BUSINESS (accounting, banking and finance, business administration and management, business economics, hotel/motel and restaurant management, insurance, management science, marketing/retailing/merchandising, office supervision and management, real estate, retailing, and sports management), COMMUNICATIONS AND THE ARTS (advertising, art history and appreciation, broadcasting, classics, communications, dramatic arts, English, fine arts, French, German, Greek, Italian, journalism, Latin, media arts, music, music performance, public relations, Spanish, speech/debate/rhetoric, and studio art), COMPUTER AND PHYSICAL SCIENCE (chemistry, computer science, geology, geophysics and seismology, mathematics, physics, and statistics), EDUCATION (art, early childhood, elementary, music, physical, and secondary), ENGINEERING AND ENVIRONMENTAL DESIGN (chemical engineering, civil engineering, computer engineering, electrical/electronics engineering, and mechanical engineering), HEALTH PROFESSIONS (exercise science, medical laboratory technology, and nursing), SOCIAL SCIENCE (African American studies, anthropology, criminal justice, economics, European studies, geography, history, interdisciplinary studies, international relations, Latin American studies, philosophy, political science/government, psychology, religion, sociology, and women's studies). Biology, experimental psychology, and engineering are the largest.

Required: All students must maintain a GPA of 2.0 in 120 semester hours, including 24 in their major. Distribution requirements include 12 hours in humanities and social science, 7 in natural science, 6 each in English and numerical and analytical reasoning, and a demonstrated ability in foreign languages.

Special: USC transmits live interactive televised instruction to more than 20 locations in the state. Cross-registration is offered with the National Technological University in Engineering and through the National Student Exchange. Internships in many fields, study abroad in many countries through the Byrnes International Center, co-op programs, and work-study programs are available. Double majors through the colleges of humanities and social sciences and science and math, student-designed majors, an interdisciplinary studies degree, and a 3-2 engineering degree with the College of Charleston are offered. Credit for military experience, nondegree study, and pass/fail options also are possible. There are 34 national honor societies, including Phi Beta Kappa, and a freshman honors program.

Faculty/Classroom: 67% of faculty are male; 33%, female. 61% teach undergraduates and all do research. Graduate students teach 19% of introductory courses. The average class size in an introductory lecture is 31; in a laboratory, 23; and in a regular course, 31.

Admissions: 70% of the 2003-2004 applicants were accepted. The SAT I scores for the 2003-2004 freshman class were: Verbal--24% below 500, 47% between 500 and 599, 23% between 600 and 700, and 6% above 700; Math--17% below 500, 47% between 500 and 599, 29% between 600 and 700, and 7% above 700. The ACT scores were 16% below 21, 30% between 21 and 23, 30% between 24 and 26, 11% between 27 and 28, and 13% above 28. 46% of the current freshmen were in the top fifth of their class; 78% were in the top two fifths. There were 31 National Merit finalists. 65 freshmen graduated first in their class.

Requirements: The SAT I or ACT is required. In addition, applicants must have 16 academic credits, including 4 in English, 3 each in math and social studies (1 of which must be U.S. history), 2 each in foreign language and lab science, 1 academic elective, and 1 phys ed or ROTC. The GED is accepted. A GPA of 2.0 is required. AP and CLEP credits are accepted. Important factors in the admissions decision are advanced placement or honor courses, evidence of special talent, and recommendations by school officials.

Procedure: Freshmen are admitted to all sessions. Entrance exams should be taken during spring of the junior year and fall of the senior year, if necessary. Applications should be filed by February 15 for fall entry, December 1 for spring entry, and May 15 for summer entry, along with a $40 fee. Notification is sent on a rolling basis. Applications are accepted on-line through *www.sc.edu*.

Transfer: 1133 transfer students enrolled in 2002-2003. Transfer students must have a cumulative 2.25 GPA from regionally accredited institutions. The SAT I or ACT is required for transfers who have attempted fewer than 30 semester hours of college credit. These students must meet both freshman and transfer requirements. Requirements are higher for some majors. 30 of 120 credits required for the bachelor's degree must be completed at Carolina.

Visiting: There are regularly scheduled orientations for prospective students. There are guides for informal visits and visitors may sit in on classes. To schedule a visit, contact the USC Visitor's Center at (803) 777-2125.

Financial Aid: In 2003-2004, 79% of all full-time freshmen and 67% of continuing full-time students received some form of financial aid. 38% of all full-time students received need-based aid. The average freshman award was $2806. 14% of undergraduates work part time. Average annual earnings from campus work are $2858. The average financial indebtedness of the 2003 graduate was $15,260. Carolina is a member of CSS. The FAFSA is required. The deadline for filing freshman financial aid applications for fall entry is April 15.

International Students: There are 270 international students enrolled. The school actively recruits these students. They must score 550 on the written TOEFL or 213 on the electronic version. The SAT I or ACT is required for some.

Computers: The mainframe is an IBM 2066. Students may use the system to register, conduct research, take web-enhanced classes, check on grades, make fee payments, search the Internet, visit web sites, and access the library, lists, and e-mail and to find information on financial aid and meal plans. All students may access the system. There are no time limits and no fees. It is strongly recommended that all students have a personal computer.

Graduates: From July 1, 2002 to June 30, 2003, 3183 bachelor's degrees were awarded. The most popular majors were psychology (7%), business administration (6%), and marketing (6%). In an average class, 40% graduate in 4 years or less, 58% graduate in 5 years or less, and 60% graduate in 6 years or less. 19,016 companies recruited on campus in 2002-2003.

Admissions Contact: Terry L. Davis, Director of Undergraduate Admissions. A video is available. E-mail: *admissions-ugrad@sc.edu* Web: *www.sc.edu/admissions*

UNIVERSITY OF SOUTH CAROLINA AT SPARTANBURG   B-1
Spartanburg, SC 29303

(864) 503-5246
(800) 277-8727; Fax: (864) 503-5727

Full-time: 1183 men, 2262 women	**Faculty:** 140; IIB, -$
Part-time: 364 men, 588 women	**Ph.D.s:** 88%
Graduate: 7 men, 103 women	**Student/Faculty:** 19 to 1
Year: semesters, summer session	**Tuition:** $5516 ($10,408)
Application Deadline: open	**Room & Board:** $4420
Freshman Class: 1904 applied, 938 accepted, 701 enrolled	
SAT I Verbal/Math: 417/502	**ACT:** 20 COMPETITIVE+

The University of South Carolina at Spartanburg, established in 1967, is a public institution offering undergraduate programs in the liberal arts and sciences, business administration, education, and nursing. Some figures in the above capsule are approximate. There are 4 undergraduate schools and 1 graduate school. In addition to regional accreditation, USCS has baccalaureate program accreditation with AACSB, NCATE, and NLN. The library contains 214,984 volumes, 58,426 microform items, and 11,119 audio/video tapes/CDs, and subscribes to 3151 periodicals. Computerized library services include the card catalog, interlibrary loans, and database searching. Special learning facilities include an art gallery and a greenhouse. The 298-acre campus is in an urban area 100 miles north of Columbia. Including any residence halls, there are 18 buildings.

Student Life: 93% of undergraduates are from South Carolina. Students are from 42 states, 22 foreign countries, and Canada. 75% are white; 21% African American. The average age of freshmen is 18; all undergraduates, 24. 33% do not continue beyond their first year; 35% remain to graduate.

Housing: 400 students can be accommodated in college housing, which includes coed on-campus apartments and off-campus apartments. On-campus housing is available on a first-come, first-served basis. 92% of students commute. Alcohol is not permitted. All students may keep cars.

Activities: 4% of men belong to 3 national fraternities; 5% of women belong to 5 national sororities. There are 46 groups on campus, including cheerleading, choir, chorus, computers, dance, debate, drama, ethnic, honors, international, literary magazine, newspaper, pep band, photography, political, professional, religious, social, social service, and student government. Popular campus events include RIOTS, Wet and Wild Day, and intramural tournaments.

Sports: There are 5 intercollegiate sports for men and 4 for women, and 13 intramural sports for men and 12 for women. Facilities include a soccer field, baseball fields, a basketball gym, racquetball courts, and an auxiliary gym.

Disabled Students: Wheelchair ramps, elevators, special parking, specially equipped rest rooms, special class scheduling, lowered drinking fountains, and lowered telephones are available.

Services: Counseling and information services are available, as is tutoring in most subjects. There is remedial math, reading, and writing.

Campus Safety and Security: Measures include 24-hour foot and vehicle patrol, self-defense education, security escort services, and pamphlets/posters/films. There are emergency telephones and lighted pathways/sidewalks.

Programs of Study: USCS confers B.A., B.S., and B.S.N. degrees. Associate and master's degrees are also awarded. Bachelor's degrees are awarded in BIOLOGICAL SCIENCE (biology/biological science), BUSINESS (accounting, business administration and management, and marketing management), COMMUNICATIONS AND THE ARTS (communications, English, French, graphic design, and Spanish), COMPUTER AND PHYSICAL SCIENCE (chemistry, computer science, information sciences and systems, and mathematics), EDUCATION (early childhood, elementary, English, mathematics, physical, secondary, social studies, and special), HEALTH PROFESSIONS (nursing), SOCIAL SCIENCE (criminal justice, economics, history, interdisciplinary studies, political science/government, psychology, and sociology). Business administration is the largest.

Required: Students must complete 120 to 136 credits, including 69 to 82 in the major, with a minimum GPA of 2.0. General education requirements include courses in communications, math, arts and humanities, social and behavioral sciences, natural science, foreign culture, computer studies, and a senior seminar.

Special: Cross-registration is permitted within the University of South Carolina system and with Wofford College and Greenville Technical College. Opportunities are provided for B.A.-B.S. degrees, student-designed majors, a 3-2 engineering degree, nondegree study, credit for military service, and study abroad in Mexico, France, and Germany. There are 5 national honor societies, including Phi Beta Kappa.

Faculty/Classroom: 44% of faculty are male; 56%, female. All teach undergraduates. No introductory courses are taught by graduate students. The average class size in an introductory lecture is 22; in a laboratory, 20; and in a regular course, 15.

Admissions: 49% of the 2003-2004 applicants were accepted. The SAT I scores for the 2003-2004 freshman class were: Verbal--54% below 500, 36% between 500 and 599, 9% between 600 and 700, and 1% above 700; Math--52% below 500, 39% between 500 and 599, 8% between 600 and 700, and 1% above 700. ACT scores were 3% between 12 and 17, 83% between 18 and 23, and 14% between 24 and 29.

Requirements: The SAT I is required with a minimum composite score of 850. Graduation from an accredited secondary school with a GPA of 2.0 is required. The GED is accepted. Applicants must submit 20 academic credits, distributed as follows: 4 years of English, 3 of math, 2 each of lab science, foreign language, and social studies, 1 each of history and phys ed or ROTC, and the remainder in electives. A GPA of 2.0 is required. AP and CLEP credits are accepted.

Procedure: Entrance exams should be taken at the beginning of the senior year. Application deadlines are open. Application fee is $30. Notification is sent on a rolling basis.

Transfer: Applicants must have a minimum college GPA of 2.0 and submit final transcripts from all schools attended. Students transferring with fewer than 30 semester credits must submit a minimum SAT I score of 700 or ACT score of 18 and meet other freshman requirements. 30 of 120 credits required for the bachelor's degree must be completed at USCS.

Visiting: There are regularly scheduled orientations for prospective students. There are guides for informal visits and visitors may sit in on classes. To schedule a visit, contact the Admissions Office.

Financial Aid: The CSS Profile, FAFSA, FFS, or SFS is required.

International Students: They must score 500 on the written TOEFL and also take the SAT I or the ACT.

Computers: The mainframe is an IBM 9375. There are also 350 PCs available to students in several campus labs. Additionally, there is mainframe and Internet access via USC-Columbia LAN. All students may access the system during school hours. There are no time limits and no fees.

Admissions Contact: Donette Stewart, Director of Admissions. E-mail: *dstewart@gw.uscs.edu* Web: *www.uscs.edu*

VOORHEES COLLEGE C-3
Denmark, SC 29042 (803) 793-3351
(800) 446-6250; Fax: (803) 793-1112

Full-time: 290 men, 548 women	**Faculty:** n/av
Part-time: 8 men, 30 women	**Ph.Ds:** n/av
Graduate: none	**Student/Faculty:** n/av
Year: semesters, summer session	**Tuition:** $7106
Application Deadline: August 15	**Room & Board:** $4572
Freshman Class: 3511 applied, 1283 accepted, 292 enrolled	
SAT I or ACT: required	**LESS COMPETITIVE**

Voorhees College, founded in 1897, is a historically black liberal arts college affiliated with the Protestant Episcopal Church. Undergraduate programs are offered in accounting, biology, business administration, English, health and recreation, political science, sociology, criminal justice, computer science, teacher education, and math. The library contains 111,057 volumes, 23,387 microform items, and 238 audio/video tapes/CDs, and subscribes to 417 periodicals. Computerized library services include the card catalog and interlibrary loans. Special learning facilities include a learning resource center. The 350-acre campus is in a rural area 50 miles south of Columbia. Including any residence halls, there are 23 buildings.

Student Life: 78% of undergraduates are from South Carolina. Students are from 20 states and 2 foreign countries. All are from public schools. 99% are African American. Most are Protestant. The average age of freshmen is 17; all undergraduates, 23. 38% do not continue beyond their first year; 55% remain to graduate.

Housing: 521 students can be accommodated in college housing, which includes single-sex dorms. On-campus housing is guaranteed for all 4 years. 75% of students live on campus; of those, 50% remain on campus on weekends. Alcohol is not permitted. All students may keep cars.

Activities: 20% of men belong to 4 national fraternities; 14% of women belong to 4 national sororities. There are 20 groups on campus, including cheerleading, choir, computers, dance, drama, honors, newspaper, pep band, political, professional, religious, social, student government, and yearbook. Popular campus events include Career Awareness Week, Black History Month, and Religious Emphasis Week.

Sports: There are 3 intercollegiate sports for men and 4 for women, and 4 intramural sports for men and 4 for women. Facilities include a gym, tennis courts, baseball and softball fields, a weight room, a dance studio, and a student center.

Disabled Students: 80% of the campus is accessible. Wheelchair ramps, elevators, special parking, specially equipped rest rooms, lowered drinking fountains, and mobile carts are available.

Services: Counseling and information services are available, as is tutoring in most subjects. There is remedial math, reading, and writing.

Campus Safety and Security: Measures include 24-hour foot and vehicle patrol, informal discussions, and lighted pathways/sidewalks.

Programs of Study: Voorhees confers B.A. and B.S. degrees. Bachelor's degrees are awarded in BIOLOGICAL SCIENCE (biology/biological science), BUSINESS (accounting, business administration and management, and recreation and leisure services), COMMUNICATIONS AND THE ARTS (English), COMPUTER AND PHYSICAL SCIENCE (computer science and mathematics), HEALTH PROFESSIONS (health), SOCIAL SCIENCE (criminal justice and sociology). Biology and business administration are the strongest academically. Business and organizational management are the largest.

Required: To graduate, students must earn at least 122 credit hours, with at least 30 in the major, and have a minimum GPA of 2.0. The 55-hour general education requirement includes 13 hours of humanities, 9 of English, 6 each of social science, natural science, math, and foreign language, 3 of computer science, 2 of phys ed, and 1 of freshman orientation. A number of free electives and a senior seminar are also required. An English proficiency exam and an exit exam must be passed.

Special: Voorhees offers cooperative education, study abroad in England, internships in some programs, work-study, an evening/Saturday program, off-campus summer study, dual majors, credit by exam, and a degree completion program. Cross-registration with Denmark Technical College and interdisciplinary majors, such as health and recreation, are possible. There are 3 national honor societies, and 1 departmental honors program.

Faculty/Classroom: All teach undergraduates. The average class size in an introductory lecture is 30; in a laboratory, 20; and in a regular course, 25.

Admissions: 37% of the 2003-2004 applicants were accepted. 35% of the current freshmen were in the top fifth of their class; 65% were in the top two fifths.

Requirements: The SAT I or ACT is required, with recommended minimum scores of 600 on the SAT I or 16 on the ACT. Applicants must be high school graduates or hold a GED. Students should have earned 20 academic credits in high school, including 4 of English, 3 of math, 2 each of science and foreign language (optional), and 1 each of history, social studies, economics/government, and phys ed. Letters of recommendation and a campus visit are advised. Voorhees requires applicants to be in the upper 75% of their class. A GPA of 2.0 is required. AP and CLEP credits are accepted. Important factors in the admissions decision are advanced placement or honor courses, recommendations by school officials, and recommendations by alumni.

Procedure: Freshmen are admitted to all sessions. Entrance exams should be taken in the senior year. There is a deferred admissions plan. Applications should be filed by August 15 for fall entry and December 15 for spring entry. The fall 2003 application fee was $25. Notification of early decision is sent August 15; regular decision, on a rolling basis.

Transfer: 31 transfer students enrolled in a recent year. Transfer students must submit complete records, including a confidential report from each college attended. The confidential report form is provided by the Office of Admission and Recruitment. Students with fewer than 30 semester hours must submit their high school record with rank in class and GPA. The SAT I is recommended; a minimum composite score of 600 is expected. An interview is advised. 30 of 122 credits required for the bachelor's degree must be completed at Voorhees.

Visiting: There are regularly scheduled orientations for prospective students, consisting of senior visitation days held January through April. There are guides for informal visits and visitors may sit in on classes and stay overnight. To schedule a visit, contact Willie Jefferson, Vice President for Student Affairs, at (803) 703-7173 or *williej@voorhees.edu*.

Financial Aid: In 2003-2004, 98% of all full-time freshmen and 80% of continuing full-time students received some form of financial aid. 94% of full-time freshmen and 74% of continuing full-time students received need-based aid. The average freshman award was $10,150. 42% of undergraduates work part time. Average annual earnings from campus work are $1720. The average financial indebtedness of a recent year's graduate was $15,250. Voorhees is a member of CSS. The FAFSA, the college's own financial statement, or the SAR is required; the FAFSA is preferred. The priority date for freshman financial aid applications for fall entry is April 15.

International Students: There were 3 international students enrolled in a recent year. They must score 500 on the written TOEFL and also take the SAT I or the ACT.

Computers: The mainframe is an IBM System/36. There are 4 labs on campus that are networked and accessible to students. All students have

Internet and Web access. All students may access the system. There are no time limits and no fees.

Graduates: In a recent year, 170 bachelor's degrees were awarded. In an average class, 25% graduate in 4 years or less, 52% graduate in 5 years or less, and 54% graduate in 6 years or less. 20 companies recruited on campus in a recent year. Of a recent year's graduating class, 13% were enrolled in graduate school within 6 months of graduation and 65% were employed.

Admissions Contact: Benjamin Watson, Director of Admissions and Recruitment. A video is available. E-mail: *bwatson@voorhees.edu* Web: *www.voorhees.edu*

WINTHROP UNIVERSITY
Rock Hill, SC 29733

C-1

(803) 323-2191
(800) 763-0230; Fax: (803) 323-2137

Full-time: 1386 men, 3211 women	Faculty: 264; IIA, --$
Part-time: 172 men, 392 women	Ph.D.s: 53%
Graduate: 362 men, 1035 women	Student/Faculty: 17 to 1
Year: semesters, summer session	Tuition: $6672 ($12,278)
Application Deadline: May 1	Room & Board: $4630
Freshman Class: 3972 applied, 2632 accepted, 1074 enrolled	
SAT I Verbal/Math: 530/520	ACT: 21 COMPETITIVE

Winthrop University, founded in 1886, is a state-supported institution offering undergraduate and graduate programs in liberal arts and sciences, business administration, education, and visual and performing arts. There are 4 undergraduate and 4 graduate schools. In addition to regional accreditation, Winthrop has baccalaureate program accreditation with AACSB, CSAB, CSWE, FIDER, NASAD, NASM, and NCATE. The library contains 414,879 volumes, 1,236,619 microform items, 2884 audio/video tapes/CDs, and 13,961 e-books, and subscribes to 1446 periodicals. Computerized library services include the card catalog, interlibrary loans, and database searching. Special learning facilities include an art gallery, radio station, TV station, an audio recording studio, an early childhood lab school, the MIDI lab, the Instructional Technology Center, and the Conservatory of Music. The 418-acre campus is in a small town 23 miles south of Charlotte, North Carolina. Including any residence halls, there are 43 buildings.

Student Life: 88% of undergraduates are from South Carolina. Students are from 41 states, 33 foreign countries, and Canada. 69% are white; 26% African American. The average age of freshmen is 18; all undergraduates, 21. 25% do not continue beyond their first year; 75% remain to graduate.

Housing: 2336 students can be accommodated in college housing, which includes single-sex and coed dorms, on-campus apartments, and married-student housing. There are also independent, off-campus fraternity and sorority houses. On-campus housing is guaranteed for the freshman year only and is available on a first-come, first-served basis. 52% of students commute. All students may keep cars.

Activities: 11% of men belong to 8 national fraternities; 14% of women belong to 8 national sororities. There are 115 groups on campus, including art, band, cheerleading, chess, choir, chorale, chorus, computers, dance, drama, ethnic, gay, honors, international, jazz band, literary magazine, musical theater, newspaper, opera, orchestra, pep band, political, professional, radio and TV, religious, social, social service, student government, and yearbook. Popular campus events include convocation, Fall Fest, and Fine Arts Series.

Sports: There are 7 intercollegiate sports for men and 7 for women, and 30 intramural sports for men and 30 for women. Facilities include a golf course, a 6000-seat coliseum, a swimming pool, a cross-country course, tennis courts, racquetball courts, a weight room, a training room, baseball, softball, and soccer fields, a ropes course, and an 18-hole disc golf course.

Disabled Students: 90% of the campus is accessible. Wheelchair ramps, elevators, special parking, specially equipped rest rooms, special class scheduling, lowered drinking fountains, lowered telephones, and special housing are available.

Services: There is a reader service for the blind. All tutoring is the responsibility of the students to arrange with their professors or specific departments.

Campus Safety and Security: Measures include 24-hour foot and vehicle patrol, self-defense education, security escort services, and informal discussions. There are pamphlets/posters/films, emergency telephones, and lighted pathways/sidewalks.

Programs of Study: Winthrop confers B.A., B.S., B.F.A., B.M., B.M.E., and B.S.W. degrees. Master's degrees are also awarded. Bachelor's degrees are awarded in BIOLOGICAL SCIENCE (biology/biological science), BUSINESS (business administration and management and sports management), COMMUNICATIONS AND THE ARTS (art, art history and appreciation, communications, dance, dramatic arts, English, fine arts, French, music, public relations, Spanish, and speech/debate/rhetoric), COMPUTER AND PHYSICAL SCIENCE (chemistry, computer science, and mathematics), EDUCATION (early childhood, elementary, home economics, music, physical, secondary, and special), HEALTH

PROFESSIONS (medical laboratory technology and speech pathology/audiology), SOCIAL SCIENCE (food science, history, home economics, philosophy, political science/government, psychology, religion, social work, and sociology). Business administration, elementary education, and fine arts are the largest.

Required: Students must complete a minimum of 124 semester hours, including a 59-hour general education distribution requirement, and maintain a minimum GPA of 2.0. Specific courses in writing, oral communication, computer information systems, critical issues, and the American Constitution are required.

Special: Cross-registration is permitted with the Charlotte Area Educational Consortium. Co-op programs and internships in most professional areas, study abroad in 14 countries, and on-campus work-study programs are offered. Interdisciplinary majors such as science communication, nondegree study, and pass/fail options are possible. There are 3 national honor societies, a freshman honors program, and 18 departmental honors programs.

Faculty/Classroom: 47% of faculty are male; 56%, female. 98% teach undergraduates, 90% do research, and 90% do both. No introductory courses are taught by graduate students. The average class size in an introductory lecture is 26; in a laboratory, 16; and in a regular course, 22.

Admissions: 66% of the 2003-2004 applicants were accepted. The SAT I scores for the 2003-2004 freshman class were: Verbal--33% below 500, 45% between 500 and 599, 19% between 600 and 700, and 3% above 700; Math--33% below 500, 48% between 500 and 599, 17% between 600 and 700, and 2% above 700. The ACT scores were 41% below 21, 28% between 21 and 23, 21% between 24 and 26, 6% between 27 and 28, and 4% above 28. 41% of the current freshmen were in the top fifth of their class; 77% were in the top two fifths.

Requirements: The SAT I or ACT is required. In addition, graduation from an accredited secondary school is required; a GED will be accepted. Applicants must have successfully completed 4 credits in high school English, 3 in math, 2 each in lab science, social studies, and a foreign language, 1 in United States history, and 1 in phys ed or ROTC. A GPA of 3.5 is required. AP and CLEP credits are accepted. Important factors in the admissions decision are recommendations by school officials and evidence of special talent.

Procedure: Freshmen are admitted to all sessions. There is a deferred admissions plan and a rolling admissions plan. Applications should be filed by May 1 for fall entry and January 2 for spring entry, along with a $40 fee. Notification is sent on a rolling basis. Applications are accepted on-line through Apply, CollegeLink, EXPAN, and others.

Transfer: 173 transfer students enrolled in 2002-2003. Applicants must be eligible to return to the previous institution and submit college transcripts. 30 of 124 credits required for the bachelor's degree must be completed at Winthrop.

Visiting: There are regularly scheduled orientations for prospective students, consisting of the Winthrop Festival, with all academic areas and student life areas represented, a general session, minisessions, and a campus tour. There are guides for informal visits and visitors may sit in on classes. To schedule a visit, contact the Admissions Office.

Financial Aid: In 2003-2004, 53% of all full-time freshmen and 50% of continuing full-time students received some form of financial aid. At least 42% of full-time freshmen and 50% of continuing full-time students received need-based aid. The average freshman award was $6750. Need-based scholarships or need-based grants averaged $5513; need-based self-help aid (loans and jobs) averaged $2376; non-need-based athletic scholarships averaged $3673; and other non-need-based awards and non-need-based scholarships averaged $5086. 20% of undergraduates work part time. Average annual earnings from campus work are $800. The average financial indebtedness of the 2003 graduate was $17,482. Winthrop is a member of CSS. The FAFSA and the college's own financial statement are required. Check with the school for current deadlines.

International Students: There are 99 international students enrolled. The school actively recruits these students. They must score 520 on the written TOEFL.

Computers: The mainframe is a DEC VAX 6000-540(2). Approximately 250 PCs are available for students in various locations across campus. Many are networked. All students may access the system 95 hours a week, weekdays until 1 A.M. There are no time limits and no fees.

Graduates: From July 1, 2002 to June 30, 2003, 834 bachelor's degrees were awarded. The most popular majors were business/marketing (26%), education (24%), and visual and performing arts (11%). In an average class, 1% graduate in 3 years or less, 33% graduate in 4 years or less, 51% graduate in 5 years or less, and 53% graduate in 6 years or less. 45 companies recruited on campus in a recent year. Of a recent graduating class, 32% were enrolled in graduate school within 6 months of graduation and 60% were employed.

Admissions Contact: Deborah Barber, Director of Admissions. A video is available. E-mail: *admissions@winthrop.edu* Web: *www.winthrop.edu/admissions/admissions.html*

WOFFORD COLLEGE
Spartanburg, SC 29303-3663

B-1

(864) 597-4130
Fax: (864) 597-4147

Full-time: 546 men, 573 women	**Faculty:** 82
Part-time: 6 men, 7 women	**Ph.D.s:** 91%
Graduate: none	**Student/Faculty:** 14 to 1
Year: 4-1-4, summer session	**Tuition:** $20,610
Application Deadline: February 1	**Room & Board:** $6100
Freshman Class: 1317 applied, 1053 accepted, 331 enrolled	
SAT I Verbal/Math: 600/612	**ACT:** 25 **HIGHLY COMPETITIVE**

Wofford College, founded in 1854, is a private institution affiliated with the United Methodist Church, offering programs in liberal arts and pre-professional studies. In addition to regional accreditation, Wofford has baccalaureate program accreditation with NASDTEC. The library contains 197,319 volumes, 35,684 microform items, and 3921 audio/video tapes/CDs, and subscribes to 537 periodicals. Computerized library services include the card catalog, interlibrary loans, and database searching. Special learning facilities include a learning resource center, art gallery, foreign language center, satellite earth station, and international studies center with simultaneous translation capabilities. The 150-acre campus is in an urban area 65 miles southeast of Charlotte. Including any residence halls, there are 32 buildings.

Student Life: 65% of undergraduates are from South Carolina. Students are from 30 states and 6 foreign countries. 72% are from public schools. 88% are white. 72% are Protestant; 11% Catholic. The average age of freshmen is 18; all undergraduates, 20. 8% do not continue beyond their first year; 77% remain to graduate.

Housing: 984 students can be accommodated in college housing, which includes single-sex and coed dorms and fraternity houses. In addition, there is experimental residential grouping of science majors and some freshman humanities sections. On-campus housing is guaranteed for all 4 years. 87% of students live on campus; of those, 75% remain on campus on weekends. All students may keep cars.

Activities: 54% of men belong to 8 national fraternities; 64% of women belong to 4 national sororities. There are 66 groups on campus, including band, cheerleading, choir, chorale, chorus, college bowl team, computers, drama, ethnic, international, literary magazine, newspaper, pep band, photography, political, professional, religious, social, social service, student government, and yearbook. Popular campus events include Phi Beta Kappa Day, Christmas concert, and Spring weekend/Greek games.

Sports: There are 10 intercollegiate sports for men and 9 for women, and 7 intramural sports for men and 7 for women. Facilities include an 8500-seat campus stadium, a 3500-seat arena, a tennis complex, a soccer field, and a wellness and athletic center built to the specifications of the Carolina Panthers.

Disabled Students: 90% of the campus is accessible. Wheelchair ramps, elevators, special parking, specially equipped rest rooms, special class scheduling, lowered drinking fountains, and lowered telephones are available.

Services: Counseling and information services are available, as is tutoring in every subject. There is a reader service for the blind.

Campus Safety and Security: Measures include 24-hour foot and vehicle patrol, self-defense education, security escort services, and informal discussions. There are pamphlets/posters/films, emergency telephones, and lighted pathways/sidewalks.

Programs of Study: Wofford confers B.A. and B.S. degrees. Bachelor's degrees are awarded in BIOLOGICAL SCIENCE (biology/biological science), BUSINESS (accounting, banking and finance, and business economics), COMMUNICATIONS AND THE ARTS (art history and appreciation, dramatic arts, English, French, German, and Spanish), COMPUTER AND PHYSICAL SCIENCE (chemistry, computer science, mathematics, and physics), SOCIAL SCIENCE (crosscultural studies, economics, history, humanities, philosophy, political science/government, psychology, religion, and sociology). Biology, foreign languages, and finance/accounting are the strongest academically. Biology, business economics, and government are the largest.

Required: To graduate, students must complete 124 credits, with 21 to 38 credits in the major and a minimum GPA of 2.0. General education requirements include 12 credits of history/philosophy/religion, 8 of natural sciences, 6 of English, 3 each of fine arts and math, and 2 of phys ed. Students must complete 4 interim projects, a career workshop, and a freshman humanities seminar.

Special: Special academic programs include limited cross-registration with Converse College and USC/Spartanburg, study abroad in more

than 30 countries, a Washington semester, and a concentration in Latin American and Caribbean studies. In addition, students can major in 2 fields or complete interdisciplinary, humanities, or intercultural studies majors. Wofford participates in 3-2 programs in engineering with Clemson and Columbia Universities. The January interim allows students to concentrate on a single study project, internship, or travel experience. There are 9 national honor societies, including Phi Beta Kappa. Most departments have honors programs.

Faculty/Classroom: 67% of faculty are male; 33%, female. All teach undergraduates and 30% both teach and do research. The average class size in an introductory lecture is 20; in a laboratory, 15; and in a regular course, 10.

Admissions: 80% of the 2003-2004 applicants were accepted. The SAT I scores for the 2003-2004 freshman class were: Verbal--7% below 500, 31% between 500 and 599, 53% between 600 and 700, and 9% above 700; Math--2% below 500, 30% between 500 and 599, 51% between 600 and 700, and 17% above 700. The ACT scores were 9% below 21, 27% between 21 and 23, 37% between 24 and 26, 20% between 27 and 28, and 7% above 28. 78% of the current freshmen were in the top fifth of their class; 91% were in the top two fifths. There were 7 National Merit finalists. 18 freshmen graduated first in their class.

Requirements: The SAT I or ACT is required. SAT II: Subject tests are recommended. Applicants must be graduates of an accredited secondary school. The GED is accepted. Students should have completed 4 years each of high school English and math, 3 of lab science, and 2 each of a foreign language and social studies. An essay is required and an interview is strongly recommended. AP and CLEP credits are accepted. Important factors in the admissions decision are advanced placement or honor courses, leadership record, and personality/intangible qualities.

Procedure: Freshmen are admitted to all sessions. Entrance exams should be taken in the spring of the junior year or fall of the senior year. There are early decision, early admissions, and deferred admissions plans. Early decision applications should be filed by November 15; regular applications, by February 1 for fall entry. The fall 2003 application fee was $40. Notification of early decision is sent January 15; regular decision, March 15. 80 applicants were on the 2003 waiting list; 2 were admitted. Applicants are accepted on-line through Apply, Common App, and CollegeLink.

Transfer: 14 transfer students enrolled in 2002-2003. Transfers should have a minimum GPA of 2.5 from a 4-year college or 3.0 from a 2-year college, or they may submit ACT or SAT I scores. An interview is recommended. 30 credits of 124 required for the bachelor's degree must be completed at Wofford.

Visiting: There are regularly scheduled orientations for prospective students. There are guides for informal visits and visitors may sit in on classes and stay overnight. To schedule a visit, contact the Director of Admissions.

Financial Aid: In a recent year, 83% of continuing full-time students received some form of financial aid. 54% of full-time freshmen and 55% of continuing full-time students received need-based aid. The average freshman award was $14,660. 35% of undergraduates work part time. Average annual earnings from campus work are $1200. The average financial indebtedness of a recent graduate was $12,260. Wofford is a member of CSS. The CSS Profile, FAFSA, and the college's own financial statement are required. The deadline for filing freshman financial aid applications for fall entry is March 15.

International Students: There are 6 international students enrolled. They must score 550 on the written TOEFL.

Computers: The mainframe is a Windows/Exchange 2000 system. The computer center is open 80 1/2 hours per week. Student PC labs are located in several academic buildings. A high-speed, fiber-optic campus technology network provides a multimedia intranet and voice telephone system as well as direct access to off-campus television programming, e-mail, and the World Wide Web. All students may access the system 24 hours per day. There are no time limits and no fees. It is strongly recommended that all students have a personal computer. A PC/Windows model is recommended.

Graduates: From July 1, 2002 to June 30, 2003, 258 bachelor's degrees were awarded. The most popular majors were biology (17%), business economics (14%), and English and government (9%). In an average class, 71% graduate in 4 years or less, 76% graduate in 5 years or less, and 77% graduate in 6 years or less. Of the 2002 graduating class, 35% were enrolled in graduate school within 6 months of graduation and 62% were employed.

Admissions Contact: Brand R. Stille, Director of Admissions. A video is available. E-mail: *admissions@wofford.edu* Web: *www.wofford.edu*

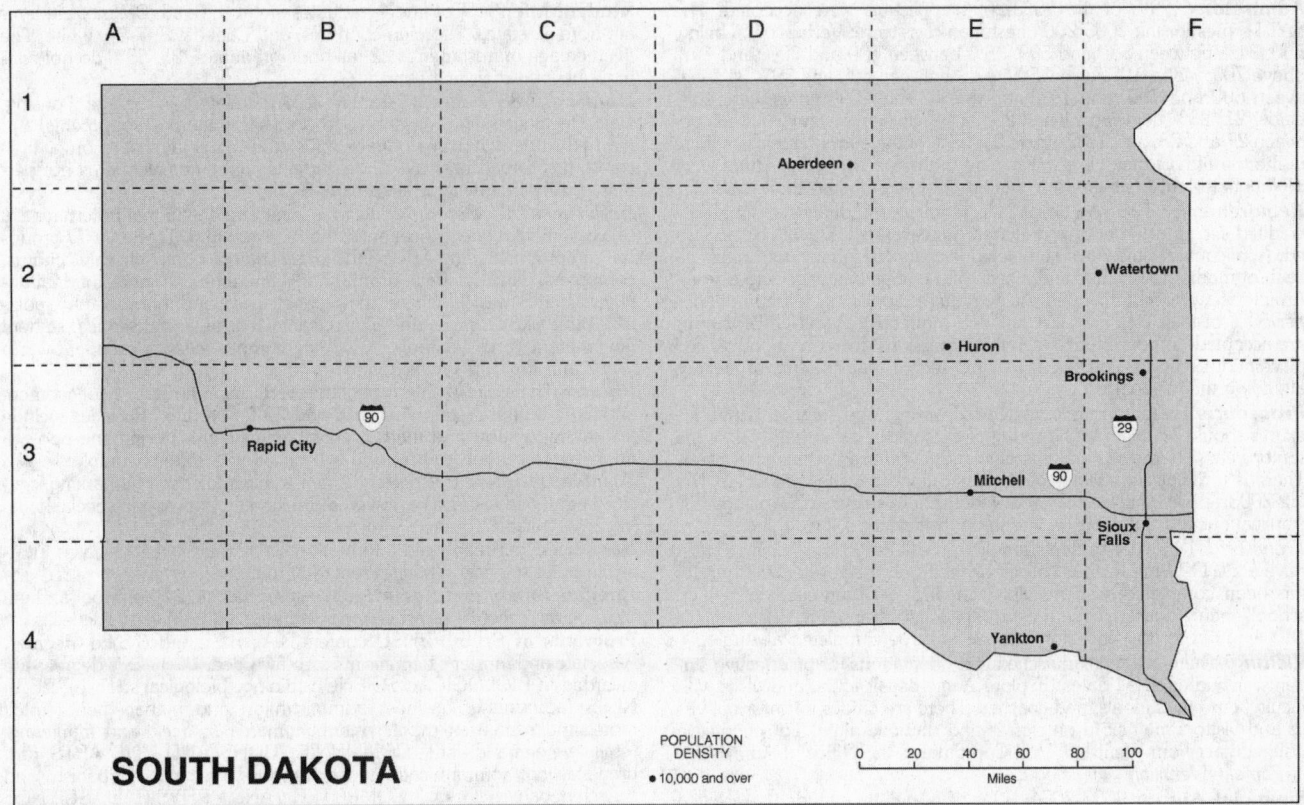

SOUTH DAKOTA

POPULATION
DENSITY

• 10,000 and over

0   20   40   60   80   100
Miles

AUGUSTANA COLLEGE
Sioux Falls, SD 57197

F-3

(605) 274-5516
(800) 727-2844; Fax: (605) 274-5518

Full-time: 607 men, 1079 women	**Faculty:** 108; IIB, -$
Part-time: 54 men, 70 women	**Ph.Ds:** 90%
Graduate: 7 men, 31 women	**Student/Faculty:** 15 to 1
Year: 4-1-4, summer session	**Tuition:** $16,972
Application Deadline: open	**Room & Board:** $5026
Freshman Class: 1692 applied, 1338 accepted, 424 enrolled	
SAT I Verbal/Math: 600/590	**ACT:** 25 **VERY COMPETITIVE**

Augustana College, founded in 1860, is a private liberal arts institution affiliated with the Evangelical Lutheran Church in America. In addition to regional accreditation, Augie has baccalaureate program accreditation with CSWE, NASM, NCATE, and NLN. The library contains 234,515 volumes, 85,938 microform items, and 6147 audio/video tapes/CDs, and subscribes to 1085 periodicals. Computerized library services include the card catalog, interlibrary loans, and database searching. Special learning facilities include an art gallery, natural history museum, radio station, and Center for Western Studies. The 100-acre campus is in a suburban area 150 miles north of Omaha, Nebraska. Including any residence halls, there are 30 buildings.

Student Life: 55% of undergraduates are from South Dakota. Students are from 35 states, 12 foreign countries, and Canada. 95% are from public schools. 96% are white. Most are Catholic. The average age of freshmen is 18; all undergraduates, 20. 18% do not continue beyond their first year; 70% remain to graduate.

Housing: 1100 students can be accommodated in college housing, which includes coed dorms and married-student housing. In addition, there are special-interest houses, independent student housing for those with children, and a theme house. On-campus housing is guaranteed for all 4 years. 66% of students live on campus; of those, 70% remain on campus on weekends. Alcohol is not permitted. All students may keep cars.

Activities: There are no fraternities or sororities. There are 55 groups on campus, including art, band, cheerleading, choir, chorale, chorus, dance, debate, drama, ethnic, gay, honors, international, jazz band, literary magazine, musical theater, newspaper, opera, orchestra, pep band, photography, political, professional, radio and TV, religious, social, social service, student government, symphony, and yearbook. Popular campus events include Christmas Vespers and Boe Forum on Public Affairs.

Sports: There are 9 intercollegiate sports for men and 9 for women, and 26 intramural sports for men and 26 for women. Facilities include a 3600-seat gym and a health, phys ed, and recreation center.

Disabled Students: 75% of the campus is accessible. Wheelchair ramps, elevators, special parking, specially equipped rest rooms, special class scheduling, lowered drinking fountains, lowered telephones, Arkenstone reader, Dragon Dictate, TTYs, and doorbell lights are available.

Services: Counseling and information services are available, as is tutoring in every subject. There is a reader service for the blind and remedial math and writing. A special writing lab is available 3 nights per week.

Campus Safety and Security: Measures include 24-hour foot and vehicle patrol, self-defense education, security escort services, and informal discussions. There are pamphlets/posters/films, emergency telephones, lighted pathways/sidewalks, and key card access to residence halls.

Programs of Study: Augie confers the B.A. degree. Master's degrees are also awarded. Bachelor's degrees are awarded in BIOLOGICAL SCIENCE (biology/biological science), BUSINESS (accounting, business administration and management, and management information systems), COMMUNICATIONS AND THE ARTS (art, communications, dramatic arts, English, French, German, journalism, modern language, music, and Spanish), COMPUTER AND PHYSICAL SCIENCE (chemistry, computer science, mathematics, and physics), EDUCATION (athletic training, drama, education of the deaf and hearing impaired, elementary, music, physical, secondary, social studies, and special), ENGINEERING AND ENVIRONMENTAL DESIGN (engineering physics), HEALTH PROFESSIONS (exercise science, medical technology, nursing, and speech pathology/audiology), SOCIAL SCIENCE (economics, history, international relations, international studies, philosophy, physical fitness/movement, political science/government, psychology, religion, social work, and sociology). Education, biology, and business are the largest.

Required: Students must complete 130 semester hours, with a minimum GPA of 2.0. General education requirements total 59 semester hours, including component courses in writing for graduation.

Special: Internships, study abroad in 40 countries, and a 3-2 engineering degree with Columbia University, Washington University in St. Louis, or University of Minnesota are offered. A Washington semester with Lutheran College Washington Consortium or American University is offered. Credit for life experience is possible. There are 17 national honor societies and 4 departmental honors programs.

Faculty/Classroom: 60% of faculty are male; 40%, female. All both teach and do research. No introductory courses are taught by graduate students. The average class size in an introductory lecture is 25; in a laboratory, 18; and in a regular course, 20.

Admissions: 79% of the 2003-2004 applicants were accepted. The SAT I scores for the 2003-2004 freshman class were: Verbal--12% below 500, 31% between 500 and 599, 38% between 600 and 700, and 19% above 700; Math--12% below 500, 42% between 500 and 599, 31% between 600 and 700, and 15% above 700. The ACT scores were 16% below 21, 23% between 21 and 23, 31% between 24 and 26, 14% between 27 and 28, and 16% above 28. 53% of the current freshmen were in the top fifth of their class; 81% were in the top two fifths. There were 3 National Merit finalists. 36 freshmen graduated first in their class.

Requirements: The SAT I or ACT is required. Graduation from an accredited secondary school is preferred; however, a GED will be accepted. Applicants should have completed 4 years of high school English, 3 each of math and science, and 2 each of a foreign language and history. An interview is recommended. Augie requires applicants to be in the upper 50% of their class. A GPA of 2.5 is required. AP and CLEP credits are accepted. Important factors in the admissions decision are advanced placement or honor courses, leadership record, and parents or siblings attending the school.

Procedure: Freshmen are admitted fall, spring, and summer. Entrance exams should be taken in the spring of the junior year or early fall of the senior year. There are early admissions and deferred admissions plans. There is a rolling admissions plan. Application deadlines are open. The fall 2003 application fee was $35. Notification is sent on a rolling bais. Applications are accepted on-line through the school's web site.

Transfer: 84 transfer students enrolled in 2002-2003. Applicants must have a 2.0 GPA in previous college work. If only 1 semester or 1 quarter has been completed, and the applicant has just graduated from high school, then Augustana requires a high school transcript. 30 credits of 130 required for the bachelor's degree must be completed at Augie.

Visiting: There are regularly scheduled orientations for prospective students, including 4 fall dates (Explore Augie days), tours, and visits with faculty, current students, and coaches. There are guides for informal visits and visitors may sit in on classes and stay overnight. To schedule a visit, contact Pam Wentzlaff, Visit Coordinator, the Office of Admissions at *Pamela_Wentzlaff@augie.edu.*

Financial Aid: In 2003-2004, 99% of all full-time students received some form of financial aid. 82% of full-time freshmen and 71% of continuing full-time students received need-based aid. The average freshman award was $13,564. 34% of undergraduates work part time. Average annual earnings from campus work are $1350. The average financial indebtedness of the 2003 graduate was $18,315. Augie is a member of CSS. The FAFSA is required. The priority date for freshman financial aid applications for fall entry is March 1.

International Students: There are 32 international students enrolled. The school actively recruits these students. They must score 550 on the written TOEFL and also take the SAT I or the ACT, scoring 950 on the SAT I.

Computers: The mainframe is an IBM RS/6000. More than 360 computers, mostly Pentium models, are available to students, with 125 available 24 hours per day. Each residence hall has a computer lab. All students may access the system.

Graduates: In a recent year, 304 bachelor's degrees were awarded. In an average class, 1% graduate in 3 years or less, 51% graduate in 4 years or less, 68% graduate in 5 years or less, and 70% graduate in 6 years or less. 60 companies recruited on campus in 2002-2003. Of the 2002 graduating class, 25% were enrolled in graduate school within 6 months of graduation and 92% were employed.

Admissions Contact: Robert A. Preloger, Vice President, Enrollment. E-mail: *info@augie.edu* Web: *www.augie.edu*

BLACK HILLS STATE UNIVERSITY
Spearfish, SD 57799-9500   A-2

(605) 642-6343
(800) ALL-BHSU; Fax: (605) 642-6022

Full-time: 1011 men, 1668 women	Faculty: 110; IIB, -$
Part-time: 305 men, 687 women	Ph.D.s: 78%
Graduate: 28 men, 174 women	Student/Faculty: 24 to 1
Year: semesters, summer session	Tuition: $4549 ($9575)
Application Deadline: open	Room & Board: $3194
Freshman Class: 1494 applied, 1426 accepted, 724 enrolled	
ACT: 21	LESS COMPETITIVE

Black Hills State University, founded in 1883, is a public institution offering undergraduate programs in applied science and technology, arts and humanities, business and public affairs, and education and human resources development. There are 3 undergraduate schools and 1 graduate school. In addition to regional accreditation, BHSU has baccalaureate program accreditation with NCATE. The library contains 235,000 volumes, 118,572 microform items, and 1300 audio/video tapes/CDs, and subscribes to 1800 periodicals. Computerized library services include the card catalog, interlibrary loans, and database searching. Spe-

cial learning facilities include a learning resource center, art gallery, radio station, and TV station. The 123-acre campus is in a small town 45 miles northwest of Rapid City. Including any residence halls, there are 13 buildings.

Student Life: 81% of undergraduates are from South Dakota. Students are from 32 states, 7 foreign countries, and Canada. 89% are white. The average age of freshmen is 22; all undergraduates, 25. 53% do not continue beyond their first year.

Housing: 788 students can be accommodated in college housing, which includes single-sex and coed dorms, on-campus apartments, and married-student housing. On-campus housing is available on a first-come, first-served basis. 79% of students commute. Alcohol is not permitted. All students may keep cars.

Activities: 2% of men belong to 1 local and 1 national fraternity; 2% of women belong to 1 local and 1 national sorority. There are 77 groups on campus, including art, band, cheerleading, choir, chorale, chorus, computers, dance, debate, drama, drill team, ethnic, honors, international, jazz band, musical theater, newspaper, pep band, photography, political, professional, radio and TV, religious, social, social service, student government, and yearbook. Popular campus events include Swarm Week and Big 100 Week.

Sports: There are 4 intercollegiate sports for men and 4 for women, and 20 intramural sports for men and 20 for women. Facilities include a stadium, a sport and fitness center, tennis courts, swimming pools, a track, a gym, a golf course, and a baseball and softball complex.

Disabled Students: Wheelchair ramps, elevators, special parking, specially equipped rest rooms, lowered drinking fountains, and special housing are available.

Services: Counseling and information services are available, as is tutoring in most subjects. There is remedial math.

Campus Safety and Security: Measures include 24-hour foot and vehicle patrol, security escort services, and lighted pathways/sidewalks.

Programs of Study: BHSU confers B.A., B.S., and B.S.Ed. degrees. Associate and master's degrees are also awarded. Bachelor's degrees are awarded in BIOLOGICAL SCIENCE (biology/biological science), BUSINESS (accounting, business administration and management, hotel/motel and restaurant management, human resources, and marketing/retailing/merchandising), COMMUNICATIONS AND THE ARTS (art, broadcasting, communications, English, fine arts, music, Spanish, and speech/debate/rhetoric), COMPUTER AND PHYSICAL SCIENCE (chemistry, mathematics, and physical sciences), EDUCATION (art, business, elementary, health, music, physical, science, secondary, and special), HEALTH PROFESSIONS (health care administration), SOCIAL SCIENCE (American Indian studies, history, human services, political science/government, prelaw, psychology, social science, and sociology).

Required: Students must successfully complete 128 credits, with at least 36 in the major, and must maintain a minimum GPA of 2.0. Core curriculum requirements include courses in English, speech, psychology, math, science, non-Western cultures, and phys ed. All students must pass an English proficiency exam.

Special: The university offers a co-op program in social work, cross-registration with the University of South Dakota, internships, work-study programs, a B.A.-B.S. degree, dual majors, a general studies degree, credit by exam, credit for military service, nondegree study, and pass/fail options. Composite majors offered include marketing, environmental physical science, outdoor education, tourism, and wellness management. A library media major is possible in conjunction with a second major. There are 5 national honor societies and a freshman honors program.

Faculty/Classroom: 66% of faculty are male; 24%, female. All teach undergraduates. No introductory courses are taught by graduate students. The average class size in an introductory lecture is 120; in a laboratory, 20; and in a regular course, 30.

Admissions: 95% of the 2003-2004 applicants were accepted. The ACT scores for the 2003-2004 freshman class were: 54% below 21, 26% between 21 and 23, 14% between 24 and 26, 4% between 27 and 28, and 2% above 28. 16% of the current freshmen were in the top fifth of their class; 41% were in the top two fifths. 20 freshmen graduated first in their class.

Requirements: The ACT is required. Graduation from an accredited secondary school is required; a GED will be accepted. Applicants must have completed the following academic credits with a minimum GPA of 2.0: 4 years of English, 3 each of social studies, math, and science, and 1/2 year of fine arts. BHSU requires applicants to be in the upper 60% of their class. A GPA of 2.0 is required. AP and CLEP credits are accepted.

Procedure: Freshmen are admitted to all sessions. Entrance exams should be taken during the senior year of high school. There is a rolling admissions plan. Application deadlines are open. The fall 2003 application fee was $20. Notification is sent on a rolling basis.

Transfer: 523 transfer students enrolled in 2002-2003. Applicants must supply transcripts from all previous schools attended, high school and college, and must have maintained a minimum college GPA of 2.0. 32 credits of 128 required for the bachelor's degree must be completed at BHSU.

Visiting: There are regularly scheduled orientations for prospective students. There are guides for informal visits and visitors may sit in on classes and stay overnight. To schedule a visit, contact the Admissions Office at *admissions@bhsu.edu*.

Financial Aid: The average financial indebtedness of a recent graduate was $18,444. The FAFSA and state aid form are required. The deadline for filing freshman financial aid applications for fall entry is March 1.

International Students: There are 7 international students enrolled. They must score 520 on the written TOEFL and also take the ACT.

Computers: The mainframe is an IBM. More than 200 PCs are available in residence halls, the main classroom building, and the library. All students may access the system during lab and library hours. There are no time limits and no fees. It is strongly recommended that all students have a personal computer.

Graduates: From July 1, 2002 to June 30, 2003, 478 bachelor's degrees were awarded. The most popular majors were elementary education (17%), curriculum and instruction (13%), and business administration (9%). In an average class, 15% graduate in 3 years or less, 25% graduate in 4 years or less, 27% graduate in 5 years or less, and 29% graduate in 6 years or less. 127 companies recruited on campus in 2002-2003.

Admissions Contact: Admissions Officer, Enrollment Services Center. E-mail: *admissions@bhsu.edu* Web: *www.bhsu.edu*

DAKOTA STATE UNIVERSITY
Madison, SD 57042

	E-3
	(605) 256-5139
(888) DSU-9988; Fax: (605) 256-5020	

Full-time: 696 men, 555 women	**Faculty:** 73; IIB, -$
Part-time: 847 men and women	**Ph.D.s:** 58%
Graduate: 83 men, 72 women	**Student/Faculty:** 17 to 1
Year: semesters, summer session	**Tuition:** $4378 ($9090)
Application Deadline: open	**Room & Board:** $3088
Freshman Class: 600 accepted, 360 enrolled	
ACT: 22	**COMPETITIVE**

Dakota State University, founded in 1881, is a public institution offering undergraduate programs through the Colleges of Business and Information Systems, Education, and Arts and Sciences. There are 3 undergraduate schools and 1 graduate school. In addition to regional accreditation, DSU has baccalaureate program accreditation with AHEA and NCATE. The library contains 125,461 volumes, 3728 microform items, and 3728 audio/video tapes/CDs, and subscribes to 350 periodicals. Computerized library services include the card catalog, interlibrary loans, and database searching. Special learning facilities include a learning resource center, art gallery, and natural history museum. The 20-acre campus is in a small town 45 miles northwest of Sioux Falls. Including any residence halls, there are 17 buildings.

Student Life: 85% of undergraduates are from South Dakota. Students are from 22 states, 10 foreign countries, and Canada. The average age of all undergraduates is 22.

Housing: 702 students can be accommodated in college housing, which includes single-sex and coed dorms and on-campus apartments. On-campus housing is guaranteed for the freshman year only, is available on a first-come, first-served basis, and is available on a lottery system for upperclassmen. 63% of students commute. Alcohol is not permitted. All students may keep cars.

Activities: There are no fraternities or sororities. There are 30 groups on campus, including academic, art, band, cheerleading, choir, chorale, chorus, computers, dance, drama, ethnic, honors, international, jazz band, literary magazine, marching band, musical theater, newspaper, nontraditional students, pep band, political, religious, student education, student government, and yearbook. Popular campus events include Discover DSU Days, Zimmfest, and Diversity Week.

Sports: There are 6 intercollegiate sports for men and 6 for women, and 20 intramural sports for men and 20 for women. Facilities include courts for basketball and racquetball, a football field, a weight room, and a swimming pool.

Disabled Students: 80% of the campus is accessible. Wheelchair ramps, elevators, special parking, specially equipped rest rooms, special class scheduling, and lowered drinking fountains are available.

Services: Counseling and information services are available, as is tutoring in every subject. There is a reader service for the blind and remedial math, reading, and writing.

Campus Safety and Security: Measures include self-defense education, security escort services, informal discussions, and pamphlets/posters/films. There are emergency telephones, lighted pathways/sidewalks, and a foot patrol.

Programs of Study: DSU confers B.S., B.B.A., and B.S.Ed. degrees. Associate and master's degrees are also awarded. Bachelor's degrees are awarded in BIOLOGICAL SCIENCE (biology/biological science), BUSINESS (business administration and management and electronic business), COMMUNICATIONS AND THE ARTS (English, fine arts, and music), COMPUTER AND PHYSICAL SCIENCE (chemistry, computer programming, computer science, information sciences and systems,

mathematics, and physics), EDUCATION (art, business, elementary, English, health, marketing and distribution, music, and secondary), ENGINEERING AND ENVIRONMENTAL DESIGN (computer graphics), HEALTH PROFESSIONS (medical laboratory technology, medical records administration/services, premedicine, and respiratory therapy). Computer science, information systems, and education are the largest.

Required: To graduate, students must complete 128 semester hours, 85 of which must be in the major and 16 at the 300-400 course level. A 2.0 GPA and 43 hours of general education are also required. Students must take the Computer Concepts and Health courses. All candidates for graduation must apply formally to the Registration and Academic Records Office.

Special: The university offers co-op programs with South Dakota State University, internships, study abroad in London, and on-campus work-study programs. Also available are the general studies degree, a 3-2 engineering degree with the University of Minnesota/Twin Cities, credit for life, military, and work experience, nondegree study, and pass/fail options. There are 2 national honor societies and a freshman honors program.

Faculty/Classroom: 66% of faculty are male; 34%, female. All teach undergraduates. Graduate students teach 1% of introductory courses. The average class size in an introductory lecture is 40; in a laboratory, 25; and in a regular course, 20.

Admissions: 23% of the current freshmen were in the top fifth of their class; 49% were in the top two fifths. 9 freshmen graduated first in their class in a recent year.

Requirements: The SAT I or ACT is required, with a minimum composite score of 18 on the ACT. In addition, applicants must be graduates of an accredited secondary school or have a GED certificate, and have completed 4 years of English, 3 years each of math, science, and social studies, and 1/2 year each of computer science and the fine arts. DSU requires applicants to be in the upper 60% of their class. A GPA of 2.6 is required. AP and CLEP credits are accepted.

Procedure: Freshmen are admitted to all sessions. Entrance exams should be taken before students register for classes. There is a rolling admissions plan. Application deadlines are open. Application fee is $20. Notification is sent on a rolling basis. Applications are accepted on-line through the school's web site.

Transfer: 67 transfer students enrolled in a recent year. Transfer applicants must have a minimum 2.0 GPA. 32 credits of 128 required for the bachelor's degree must be completed at DSU.

Visiting: There are regularly scheduled orientations for prospective students, including general information and academic sessions, a campus tour, and financial aid information. There are guides for informal visits and visitors may sit in on classes and stay overnight. To schedule a visit, contact the Admissions Office.

Financial Aid: In 2003-2004, 88% of continuing full-time students received some form of financial aid. The average freshman award was $5836. Need-based scholarships or need-based grants averaged $641. 50% of undergraduates work part time. Average annual earnings from campus work are $1405. The average financial indebtedness of the 2003 graduate was $16,588. The FAFSA is required. The deadline for filing freshman financial aid applications for fall entry is March 1.

International Students: There were 120 international students enrolled in a recent year. The school actively recruits these students. They must score 550 on the written TOEFL.

Computers: The mainframes are an IBM OS/390 mainframe and an IBM RS/6000 UNIX Box. There are 15 computer labs on campus, plus an additional 4 in residence halls. All the mainframe dump terminals are in 1 lab. All labs, classrooms, and residence halls are networked, and students also have access in DSU's student union. Students may have computers in their dorm rooms. All students may access the system. There are no time limits and no fees.

Graduates: From July 1, 2002 to June 30, 2003, 145 bachelor's degrees were awarded. In an average class, 24% graduate in 4 years or less, 42% graduate in 5 years or less, and 15% graduate in 6 years or less. 25 companies recruited on campus in 2002-2003. Of the 2002 graduating class, 1% were enrolled in graduate school within 6 months of graduation and 96% were employed.

Admissions Contact: Amy Crissinger, Director of Admission. E-mail: *yourfuture@dsu.edu* Web: *www.dsu.edu*

DAKOTA WESLEYAN UNIVERSITY
Mitchell, SD 57301

E-3

(605) 995-2650
(800) 333-8506; Fax: (605) 995-2699

Full-time: 289 men, 376 women	**Faculty:** 42; IIB, --$
Part-time: 21 men, 52 women	**Ph.Ds:** 52%
Graduate: 3 men, 10 women	**Student/Faculty:** 16 to 1
Year: semesters, summer session	**Tuition:** $13,570
Application Deadline: August 25	**Room & Board:** $4262
Freshman Class: 478 applied, 418 accepted, 166 enrolled	
ACT: 20	**COMPETITIVE**

Dakota Wesleyan University, founded in 1885, is a private liberal arts institution affiliated with the United Methodist Church. In addition to regional accreditation, DWU has baccalaureate program accreditation with CAAHEP and NLN. The library contains 62,500 volumes, 72,500 microform items, and 3700 audio/video tapes/CDs, and subscribes to 620 periodicals. Computerized library services include the card catalog, interlibrary loans, database searching, and Internet access. Special learning facilities include a learning resource center and an observatory, as well as a history museum with art gallery adjacent to the campus. The 50-acre campus is in a small town 70 miles west of Sioux Falls. Including any residence halls, there are 18 buildings.

Student Life: 72% of undergraduates are from South Dakota. Students are from 31 states, 5 foreign countries, and Canada. 99% are from public schools. 89% are white. 50% are Protestant; 24% Catholic. The average age of freshmen is 19; all undergraduates, 23. 37% do not continue beyond their first year.

Housing: 385 students can be accommodated in college housing, which includes single-sex and coed dorms and on-campus apartments. In addition, there are honors houses. On-campus housing is guaranteed for the freshman year only and is available on a first-come, first-served basis. 60% of students commute. Alcohol is not permitted. All students may keep cars.

Activities: There are no fraternities or sororities. There are 30 groups on campus, including academics, art, band, bell choir, brass and woodwind ensembles, cheerleading, choir, chorale, chorus, dance, drama, drill team, ethnic, forensics, honors, international, literary magazine, musical theater, newspaper, political, professional, religious, social, social service, student government, and yearbook. Popular campus events include Prom, Spring Week, and Family Life Conference.

Sports: There are 7 intercollegiate sports for men and 6 for women, and 3 intramural sports for men and 3 for women. Facilities include a 500-seat stadium, a 3200-seat auditorium/arena, and a wellness center with a double gym and cardio, weight training, and cybex rooms. City facilities include a 1500-seat baseball stadium, a 500-seat softball field, and a 1000-seat outdoor track.

Disabled Students: 20% of the campus is accessible. Wheelchair ramps, elevators, special parking, specially equipped rest rooms, special class scheduling, lowered telephones, and class relocation are available.

Services: Counseling and information services are available, as is tutoring in every subject. There is a reader service for the blind, and remedial math, reading, and writing.

Campus Safety and Security: Measures include self-defense education, security escort services, informal discussions, and emergency telephones. There are lighted pathways/sidewalks, safety and security personnel trained in first aid and self-defense, 20-hour foot and vehicle patrol, and pamphlets and posters.

Programs of Study: DWU confers the B.A. degree. Associate and master's degrees are also awarded. Bachelor's degrees are awarded in BIOLOGICAL SCIENCE (biology/biological science), BUSINESS (accounting, business administration and management, and sports management), COMMUNICATIONS AND THE ARTS (art, communications, dramatic arts, English, and multimedia), COMPUTER AND PHYSICAL SCIENCE (computer science and mathematics), EDUCATION (athletic training, elementary, physical, and secondary), HEALTH PROFESSIONS (predentistry and premedicine), SOCIAL SCIENCE (behavioral science, criminal justice, history, human services, ministries, philosophy, psychology, religion, sociology, and youth ministry). Business and education are the largest.

Required: To graduate, students must complete a total of 125 credit hours, including 30 or more in the major, and at least 42 in upper-level courses, with a minimum 2.0 GPA. General education requirements include 6 hours of communication, literature and the arts, and social, psychological, and political thought, 3 to 5 of physical science, 3 to 4 each of math and cultural awareness, 3 each of history and philosophy/theology, and 2 of physical activities; students must demonstrate basic skills in reading, writing, and math. All new freshmen must take Forum and Advising courses.

Special: DWU offers internships, study abroad on a limited basis, work-study programs, a general studies degree, dual majors, student-designed minors, credit for experience, and credit/no credit options. There are 4 national honor societies and a freshman honors program.

Faculty/Classroom: 52% of faculty are male; 48%, female. All teach undergraduates. No introductory courses are taught by graduate students. The average class size in an introductory lecture is 32; in a laboratory, 17; and in a regular course, 20.

Admissions: 87% of the 2003-2004 applicants were accepted. The ACT scores for the 2003-2004 freshman class were: 27% below 21, 54% between 21 and 23, 16% between 24 and 26, 2% between 27 and 28, and 1% above 28. 28% of the current freshmen were in the top fifth of their class; 56% were in the top two fifths.

Requirements: The SAT I or ACT is required. In addition, applicants must be graduates of an accredited secondary school or have a GED certificate. An interview is recommended. DWU requires applicants to be in the upper 50% of their class. A GPA of 2.0 is required. AP and CLEP credits are accepted. Important factors in the admissions decision are advanced placement or honor courses, extracurricular activities record, and parents or siblings attending the school.

Procedure: Freshmen are admitted fall, spring, and summer. Entrance exams should be taken during the senior year. Applications should be filed by August 25 for fall entry, January 2 for spring entry, and June 4 for summer entry, along with a $25 fee. There is a rolling admissions plan. Notification is sent on a rolling basis beginning September 1. Applications are accepted on-line.

Transfer: 98 transfer students enrolled in 2002-2003. Students must submit official transcripts from all previous colleges attended. DWU will accept credits from regionally accredited institutions, but half the credits for the student's major must be completed at DWU. 30 credits of 125 required for the bachelor's degree must be completed at DWU.

Visiting: There are regularly scheduled orientations for prospective students, including a campus tour and meetings with faculty and students. There are guides for informal visits and visitors may sit in on classes and stay overnight. To schedule a visit, contact Enrollment Services.

Financial Aid: In 2003-2004, all full-time students received some form of financial aid. 87% of all full-time students received need-based aid. The average freshman award was $14,634. Need-based scholarships or need-based grants averaged $3829 ($4000 maximum); need-based self-help aid (loans and jobs) averaged $3262 ($4825 maximum); non-need-based athletic scholarships averaged $2807 ($10,070 maximum); and other non-need-based awards and non-need-based scholarships averaged $3654 ($13,170 maximum). 52% of undergraduates work part time. Average annual earnings from campus work are $860. The average financial indebtedness of the 2003 graduate was $17,125. DWU is a member of CSS. The FAFSA is required. The priority date for freshman financial aid applications for fall entry is April 1. The deadline for filing freshman financial aid applications for fall entry is August 30.

International Students: There are 8 international students enrolled. The school actively recruits these students. They must score 500 on the written TOEFL or take the MELAB and also take the SAT I or the ACT, scoring 18 on the ACT.

Computers: The mainframe is an IBM AS/400. There are 80 PCs available for student use in labs, residence halls, and the library. All students may access the system 24 hours a day. There are no time limits and no fees. It is strongly recommended that all students have a personal computer, especially students in music, education, and computers and technology.

Graduates: From July 1, 2002 to June 30, 2003, 96 bachelor's degrees were awarded. The most popular majors were business administration (28%), elementary education (15%), and crminal justice (10%). 3 companies recruited on campus in 2002-2003. Of the 2002 graduating class, 8% were enrolled in graduate school within 6 months of graduation.

Admissions Contact: Laura Miller, Director of Admissions Operations and Outreach Programming. A video is available.
E-mail: *admissions@dwu.edu* Web: *www.dwu.edu*

HURON UNIVERSITY
Huron, SD 57350-2798

E-2

(605) 352-8721
(800) 710-7159; Fax: (605) 352-7421

Full-time: 240 men, 200 women	**Faculty:** 36
Part-time: 35 men, 70 women	**Ph.Ds:** 25%
Graduate: 15 men, 7 women	**Student/Faculty:** 9 to 1
Year: semesters, summer session	**Tuition:** $8000
Application Deadline: see profile	**Room & Board:** $3000
Freshman Class: n/av	
SAT I or ACT: recommended	**COMPETITIVE**

Huron University, established as Huron College in 1883, is a private institution offering career-oriented programs in the arts and sciences, nursing, and professional studies. There are 4 undergraduate schools and 1 graduate school. Figures in the above capsule and in this profile are approximate. The library contains 62,000 volumes, and subscribes to 300 periodicals. Special learning facilities include a learning resource center. The 15-acre campus is in a small town 120 miles northwest of Sioux Falls. Including any residence halls, there are 7 buildings.

Student Life: 68% of students are white. The average age of all undergraduates is 23.

Housing: 300 students can be accommodated in college housing, which includes coed dorms and on-campus apartments. On-campus housing is guaranteed for all 4 years. 50% of students live on campus; of those, 85% remain on campus on weekends. Alcohol is not permitted. All students may keep cars.

Activities: There are no fraternities or sororities. There are 15 groups on campus, including cheerleading, choir, computers, ethnic, honors, international, newspaper, pep band, photography, professional, religious, social, social service, and student government. Popular campus events include Pow Wow Days, Paddle Days, and International Student Day.

Sports: There are 4 intercollegiate sports for men and 4 for women, and 15 intramural sports for men and 14 for women. Facilities include saunas, an exercise room, a 2800-seat recreation center, and a 5000-seat arena.

Disabled Students: 75% of the campus is accessible. Wheelchair ramps, special parking, specially equipped rest rooms, special class scheduling, lowered drinking fountains, and a portable chair lift are available.

Services: Counseling and information services are available, as is tutoring in every subject. There is remedial math, reading, and writing.

Campus Safety and Security: Measures include informal discussions, pamphlets/posters/films, lighted pathways/sidewalks, and a night watchman.

Programs of Study: H.U. confers B.S. and B.S.N. degrees. Associate and master's degrees are also awarded. Bachelor's degrees are awarded in BUSINESS (banking and finance, business administration and management, human resources, management information systems, management science, marketing/retailing/merchandising, organizational behavior, and sports management), COMPUTER AND PHYSICAL SCIENCE (computer science), EDUCATION (elementary, physical, science, and secondary), ENGINEERING AND ENVIRONMENTAL DESIGN (systems engineering), HEALTH PROFESSIONS (health care administration and nursing), SOCIAL SCIENCE (criminal justice). Nursing is the strongest academically. Business administration is the largest.

Required: To graduate, students must complete at least 120 to 128 credit hours with a minimum GPA of 2.0. Required courses include an introduction to higher education, computers, career planning, and other general education classes.

Special: The university offers cooperative programs, cross-registration, internships, study abroad in England or Japan, work-study programs, general studies and B.A.-B.S. degrees, dual majors, credit for life experience, nondegree study, and pass/fail options. There are 5 national honor societies and 5 departmental honors programs.

Faculty/Classroom: 50% of faculty are male; 50%, female. The average class size in an introductory lecture is 30; in a laboratory, 15; and in a regular course, 20.

Requirements: The SAT I or ACT is recommended. A minimum composite score of 15 on the ACT or a minimum score of 700 on the SAT I is required. Applicants must be graduates of an accredited secondary school or have a GED certificate. An interview is recommended. A GPA of 2.0 is required. CLEP credit is accepted. Important factors in the admissions decision are advanced placement or honor courses, leadership record, and recommendations by school officials.

Procedure: Freshmen are admitted to all sessions. Entrance exams should be taken during the senior year. Check with the school for current application deadlines and fee. Notification is sent on a rolling basis.

Transfer: 32 of 120 credits required for the bachelor's degree must be completed at H.U.

Visiting: There are regularly scheduled orientations for prospective students. There are guides for informal visits and visitors may sit in on classes and stay overnight. To schedule a visit, contact Director of Admissions.

Financial Aid: The CSS/Profile or FFS and PHEAA are required. Check with the school for current deadlines.

International Students: The school actively recruits these students. They must score 500 on the written TOEFL.

Computers: 30 IBM PCs are available in the computer lab in the library. There are no time limits and no fees.

Admissions Contact: Brad Smith, Director of Admissions.
E-mail: *admissions@huron.edu* Web: *www.huron.edu*

MOUNT MARTY COLLEGE C-4
Yankton, SD 57078-3724 (605) 668-1545
(800) 658-4552; Fax: (605) 668-1607

Full-time: 210 men, 470 women	Faculty: 35
Part-time: 140 men, 245 women	Ph.D.s: 40%
Graduate: 40 men, 60 women	Student/Faculty: 19 to 1
Year: semesters, summer session	Tuition: $12,000
Application Deadline: open	Room & Board: $4500
Freshman Class: n/av	
ACT: required	LESS COMPETITIVE

Mount Marty College is a private, Catholic, liberal arts institution that was founded in 1936 by the Sisters of Saint Benedict. Figures in the above capsule and in this profile are approximate. In addition to regional accreditation, Mount Marty has baccalaureate program accreditation with ADA and NLN. The library contains 80,000 volumes, 12,000 microform items, and 8500 audio/video tapes/CDs, and subscribes to 440 periodicals. Computerized library services include the card catalog, interlibrary loans, and database searching. Special learning facilities include a learning resource center and art gallery. The 80-acre campus is in a small town 60 miles northwest of Sioux City, Iowa, and 80 miles southwest of Sioux Falls. Including any residence halls, there are 11 buildings.

Student Life: 81% of undergraduates are from South Dakota. 79% are from public schools. 95% are white. 41% are claim no religious affiliation; 37% Catholic. The average age of freshmen is 19; all undergraduates, 26. 26% do not continue beyond their first year; 74% remain to graduate.

Housing: 352 students can be accommodated in college housing, which includes single-sex dorms. On-campus housing is guaranteed for all 4 years. 51% of students commute. Alcohol is not permitted. All students may keep cars.

Activities: There are no fraternities or sororities. There are 40 groups on campus, including choir, chorus, drama, drill team, honors, jazz band, literary magazine, musical theater, newspaper, photography, political, professional, religious, social, social service, and student government. Popular campus events include Parents Weekend and Spring Formal.

Sports: There are 6 intercollegiate sports for men and 6 for women, and 4 intramural sports for men and 4 for women. Facilities include volleyball and basketball courts, a jogging track, 2 racquetball courts, weight and training rooms, a 2220-seat stadium, a 1500-seat indoor gym, and a 700-seat auditorium.

Disabled Students: All of the campus is accessible. Wheelchair ramps, elevators, special parking, specially equipped rest rooms, special class scheduling, lowered drinking fountains, and lowered telephones are available.

Services: Counseling and information services are available, as is tutoring in most subjects. There is remedial math, reading, and writing.

Campus Safety and Security: Measures include 24-hour foot and vehicle patrol, informal discussions, emergency telephones, and lighted pathways/sidewalks.

Programs of Study: Mount Marty confers B.A. and B.S. degrees. Associate and master's degrees are also awarded. Bachelor's degrees are awarded in BIOLOGICAL SCIENCE (biology/biological science), BUSINESS (accounting and business administration and management), COMMUNICATIONS AND THE ARTS (English, journalism, and music), COMPUTER AND PHYSICAL SCIENCE (chemistry, computer science, mathematics, and radiological technology), EDUCATION (athletic training, elementary, physical, secondary, and special), ENGINEERING AND ENVIRONMENTAL DESIGN (environmental science), HEALTH PROFESSIONS (health care administration, medical technology, and nursing), SOCIAL SCIENCE (behavioral science, criminal justice, food production/management/services, history, religion, and social science). Nursing, business, and teacher education are the strongest academically.

Required: To graduate, all students must complete at least 128 credit hours, with a minimum GPA of 2.0. General education requirements include 10 credit hours in religious studies/philosophy, 9 in literature and art, 6 in English, 4 each in math, natural science, and lab science, and 3 in speech.

Special: Mount Marty offers co-op programs, a 3-2 engineering degree with Georgia Institute of Technology, internships, student-designed majors in selected studies, multi- and interdisciplinary majors including health, phys ed, recreation, and nutrition and food science, credit for work, life, and military experience, and pass/fail options. There are 8 national honor societies, a freshman honors program, and 7 departmental honors programs.

Faculty/Classroom: 54% of faculty are male; 46%, female. All teach undergraduates. No introductory courses are taught by graduate students. The average class size in an introductory lecture is 30; in a laboratory, 15; and in a regular course, 20.

Requirements: The ACT is required. In addition, applicants must be graduates of an accredited secondary school or have a GED certificate. An audition and an interview are recommended. AP and CLEP credits are accepted.

Procedure: Freshmen are admitted fall, spring, and summer. Entrance exams should be taken by October of the senior year. There are early decision and deferred admissions plans. Application deadlines are open. Check with the school for application fee. Applications are accepted online.

Transfer: 93 transfer students enrolled in a recent year. Transfer students with fewer than 28 semester hours must submit high school and college transcripts. A minimum GPA of 2.0 and at least 64 credit hours are required. An interview is recommended. 32 of 128 credits required for the bachelor's degree must be completed at Mount Marty.

Visiting: There are regularly scheduled orientations for prospective students, including campus tours, faculty appointments, and admission and financial aid information. There are guides for informal visits and visitors may sit in on classes and stay overnight. To schedule a visit, contact the Director of Admissions.

Financial Aid: In a recent year, 86% of all full-time freshmen and 85% of continuing full-time students received some form of financial aid. 86% of full-time freshmen and 85% of continuing full-time students received need-based aid. The average freshman award was $11,567. 60% of undergraduates work part time. Average annual earnings from campus work are $1000. The average financial indebtedness of a recent graduate was $17,407. The FAFSA is required. Check with the school for current deadlines.

International Students: The school actively recruits these students. They must score 500 on the written TOEFL.

Computers: The mainframe is an IBM AS400. There are PCs, printers, overhead projectors, and multimedia classrooms. The college provides a variety of Microsoft applications. Students have laptop computers with wireless connections to the network. All students may access the system 24 hours, 7 days per week. There are no time limits. A technology fee is included in the annual general fee. All students are required to have personal computers.

Graduates: In a recent year, 125 bachelor's degrees were awarded. The most popular majors were health professions (28%), business (23%), and education (15%). In an average class, 27% graduate in 4 years or less, 51% graduate in 5 years or less, and 52% graduate in 6 years or less. Of a recent graduating class, 8% were enrolled in graduate school within 6 months of graduation and 89% were employed.

Admissions Contact: Brandi Tschumper, Dean for Graduate Programs and Enrollment Management. E-mail: *btschumper@mtmc.edu* Web: *http://www.mtmc.edu*

NATIONAL AMERICAN UNIVERSITY   B-3
Rapid City, SD 57701   (605) 394-4827
                                    (800) 843-8892; Fax: (605) 394-4871

Full-time: 290 men, 275 women	**Faculty:** 26
Part-time: 170 men, 125 women	**Ph.D.s:** 5%
Graduate: 20 men, 10 women	**Student/Faculty:** 26 to 1
Year: quarters, summer session	**Tuition:** $11,000
Application Deadline: open	**Room & Board:** $4000
Freshman Class: n/av	
SAT I or ACT: recommended	**NONCOMPETITIVE**

National American University, founded in 1941, is a private institution that offers undergraduate programs in business administration, travel, allied health, and computer information systems. The college has branch campuses in Sioux Falls and at Ellsworth Air Force Base, South Dakota; Albuquerque, New Mexico; St. Paul, Minnesota; Kansas City, Missouri; Colorado Springs and Denver, Colorado; Rio Rancho, New Mexico, Mall of America, Bloomington, Minnesota, and Brooklyn Center, Minnesota. There is 1 graduate school. Figures in the above capsule and in this profile are approximate. In addition to regional accreditation, NAU has baccalaureate program accreditation with CAHEA. The library contains 30,000 volumes and 70 audio/video tapes/CDs, and subscribes to 270 periodicals. Computerized library services include interlibrary loans and database searching. Special learning facilities include a learning resource center. The Animal Health Care Center and Medical Assisting Room are instructional facilities set up as doctors' offices. The 8-acre campus is in a small town 360 miles from Sioux Falls and 420 miles from Denver, Colorado. Including any residence halls, there are 7 buildings.

Student Life: 53% of undergraduates are from South Dakota. 75% are white; 13% foreign nationals. The average age of freshmen is 35; all undergraduates, 30. 43% do not continue beyond their first year.

Housing: 260 students can be accommodated in college housing, which includes single-sex and coed dorms. On-campus housing is guaranteed for all 4 years. 79% of students commute. Alcohol is not permitted. All students may keep cars.

Activities: There are no fraternities or sororities. There are 17 groups on campus, including choir, computers, ethnic, international, political, professional, social, social service, and student government. Popular campus events include Maverick Day, spring and fall picnics, and dances.

Sports: There are 2 intercollegiate sports for men and 2 for women, and 12 intramural sports for men and 11 for women. Facilities include an 11,000-seat auditorium/arena, volleyball, basketball, and tennis courts, a 500-seat gym, a weight room, and golf, rodeo, bowling, and table tennis facilities. The Student Senate pays half the cost of a YMCA membership for students.

Disabled Students: 99% of the campus is accessible. Wheelchair ramps, elevators, special parking, and lowered drinking fountains are available.

Services: Counseling and information services are available, as is tutoring in most subjects. There is remedial math, reading, and writing. Some technical classes are tutored by instructors.

Campus Safety and Security: Measures include self-defense education, informal discussions, lighted pathways/sidewalks, and security guards on duty all evenings until morning.

Programs of Study: NAU confers the B.S. degree. Associate and master's degrees are also awarded. Bachelor's degrees are awarded in BUSI-NESS (accounting, business administration and management, and tourism), COMPUTER AND PHYSICAL SCIENCE (information sciences and systems), EDUCATION (athletic training), HEALTH PROFESSIONS (allied health and veterinary science), SOCIAL SCIENCE (paralegal studies). Accounting, paralegal studies, and business administration are the strongest academically. Business administration, accounting, and paralegal studies are the largest.

Required: To graduate, students must complete 192 quarter credit hours with a 2.0 GPA in major courses. Students are required to take 76 hours of general education courses, including 12 hours each of communications, math, social science, and humanities, 8 hours of science, 4 hours of speech, and 16 hours of electives.

Special: National offers internships in veterinary technology and paralegal studies, study abroad, work-study programs on campus and with nonprofit organizations, accelerated degree programs in all majors, and B.A.-B.S. degrees in accounting, computer information systems, management information systems, business administration, paralegal studies, and applied management. A general studies degree, credit for life experience, nondegree study, and pass/fail options are also available. Operation Bootstrap allows qualified U.S. Air Force personnel to complete their college degrees on an accelerated basis. There is 1 national honor society.

Faculty/Classroom: 38% of faculty are male; 62%, female. The average class size in an introductory lecture is 30; in a laboratory, 10; and in a regular course, 25.

Requirements: The SAT I or ACT is recommended. In addition, applicants must be graduates of an accredited secondary school or have the GED. An interview is recommended.

Procedure: Freshmen are admitted to all sessions. Entrance exams should be taken before classes begin. There are early admissions and deferred admissions plans. Application deadlines are open. The fall 2003 application fee was $25.

Transfer: Applicants must submit transcripts of all high school and college work. Grades of C or better transfer for credit. An interview is recommended. 48 of 192 credits required for the bachelor's degree must be completed at NAU.

Visiting: There are guides for informal visits and visitors may sit in on classes and stay overnight. To schedule a visit, contact the Admissions Office.

Financial Aid: NAU is a member of CSS. The FAFSA and the college's own financial statement are required. Check with the school for current deadlines.

International Students: The school actively recruits these students. They must score 500 on the written TOEFL.

Computers: The mainframe is an IBM RS/6000. There are 3 computer labs with 45 PCs among them. All provide Internet access. All students may access the system from 7 A.M. to 8 P.M. Students may access the system 90 minutes if another student is waiting. There are no fees.

Admissions Contact: Tom Shea, VP Enrollment Management. E-mail: *tshea@rc.national.edu* Web: *www.national.edu*

NORTHERN STATE UNIVERSITY   D-1
Aberdeen, SD 57401   (605) 626-2544
                                    (800) 678-5330; Fax: (605) 626-2587

Full-time: 708 men, 917 women	**Faculty:** 96; IIA, --$
Part-time: 465 men, 752 women	**Ph.D.s:** 73%
Graduate: 70 men, 171 women	**Student/Faculty:** 17 to 1
Year: semesters, summer session	**Tuition:** $4207 ($8918)
Application Deadline: August 15	**Room & Board:** $2910
Freshman Class: n/av	
SAT I: n/av	**ACT:** required
	LESS COMPETITIVE

Northern State University, established in 1901, is a state-supported institution offering undergraduate and graduate programs in the liberal arts and sciences, business, and education. Distance delivery technology is a core mission in all programs, especially all levels of teacher preparation. There are 4 undergraduate schools and 1 graduate school. In addition to regional accreditation, Northern State has baccalaureate program accreditation with NASM and NCATE. The library contains 1.5 million volumes and 88,000 microform items, and subscribes to 940 periodicals. Computerized library services include the card catalog, interlibrary loans, and database searching. Special learning facilities include a learning resource center, art gallery, radio station, TV station, and fine arts center. The 72-acre campus is in an urban area one-half mile south of Aberdeen's city center. Including any residence halls, there are 21 buildings.

Student Life: 85% of undergraduates are from South Dakota. Students are from 29 states, 15 foreign countries, and Canada. 82% are white. The average age of freshmen is 18; all undergraduates, 23. 32% do not continue beyond their first year; 45% remain to graduate.

Housing: 930 students can be accommodated in college housing, which includes single-sex and coed dorms. On-campus housing is guaranteed for all 4 years. 64% of students commute. Alcohol is not permitted. All students may keep cars.

Activities: There are no fraternities or sororities. There are 100 groups on campus, including art, band, cheerleading, chess, choir, chorale, chorus, computers, dance, debate, drama, drill team, honors, international, jazz band, marching band, musical theater, newspaper, orchestra, pep band, photography, political, professional, radio and TV, religious, social, social service, student government, symphony, and yearbook. Popular campus events include Gypsy Day, Gypsy Week, and I Hate Winter Weekend.

Sports: There are 7 intercollegiate sports for men and 5 for women, and 14 intramural sports for men and 12 for women. Facilities include a sports complex that houses a football stadium and an all-weather track, and a phys ed building that houses a 160-meter track, an Olympic-size pool, a weight room, 3 racquetball courts, a human performance lab, 2 basketball courts, and an 8300-seat arena.

Disabled Students: 90% of the campus is accessible. Wheelchair ramps, elevators, special parking, specially equipped rest rooms, lowered drinking fountains, lowered telephones, and curb cuts are available.

Services: Counseling and information services are available, as is tutoring in most subjects. There is remedial math, reading, and writing. There is an educational media center, a math lab, reading and writing centers, an ASL interpreter for the deaf, and a speech, language, and hearing clinic.

Campus Safety and Security: Measures include 24-hour foot and vehicle patrol, self-defense education, security escort services, and informal discussions. There are pamphlets/posters/films, emergency telephones, and lighted pathways/sidewalks.

Programs of Study: Northern State confers B.A., B.S., B.M.E., and B.S.Ed. degrees. Associate and master's degrees are also awarded. Bachelor's degrees are awarded in BIOLOGICAL SCIENCE (biology/biological science), BUSINESS (accounting, banking and finance, business administration and management, business economics, international business management, marketing/retailing/merchandising, and personnel management), COMMUNICATIONS AND THE ARTS (English, fine arts, French, German, music, and Spanish), COMPUTER AND PHYSICAL SCIENCE (chemistry and mathematics), EDUCATION (art, business, early childhood, elementary, foreign languages, health, industrial arts, middle school, music, physical, science, secondary, and special), ENGINEERING AND ENVIRONMENTAL DESIGN (environmental science, industrial administration/management, and industrial engineering technology), HEALTH PROFESSIONS (medical laboratory technology, predentistry, premedicine, and speech pathology/audiology), SOCIAL SCIENCE (community services, criminal justice, economics, history, human services, physical fitness/movement, political science/government, prelaw, psychology, social science, and sociology). Business and education are the strongest academically.

Required: Students must complete a minimum of 128 semester hours, with 51 in the major, and must maintain a 2.0 minimum GPA. The core curriculum consists of courses in English, history, fine arts, science, phys ed, and psychology. In addition, there are specific course requirements. All students must pass a comprehensive exam.

Special: Opportunities are provided for internships, a Washington semester, work-study programs, a B.A.-B.S. degree, dual majors, a general studies degree, credit by exam, and nondegree study. Study abroad and a co-op program in international business are available. Technology proficiency certification is available with a diverse selection of certifications. There are 4 national honor societies, a freshman honors program, and 4 departmental honors programs.

Faculty/Classroom: 72% of faculty are male; 28%, female. All both teach and do research. No introductory courses are taught by graduate students. The average class size in an introductory lecture is 30 and in a laboratory, 20.

Requirements: The ACT is required, with a minimum composite score of 18, or students must earn a high school GPA of at least 2.6 on a 4.0 scale, or rank in the top 60% of their graduating class. Graduation from an accredited secondary school is required; a GED will be accepted. Applicants should submit a minimum academic record distributed as follows: 4 years of English, 3 each of math, science, and social studies, and one-half year of fine arts. A GPA of 2.0 is required. AP and CLEP credits are accepted. Important factors in the admissions decision are evidence of special talent, advanced placement or honor courses, and extracurricular activities record.

Procedure: Freshmen are admitted fall, spring, and summer. Entrance exams should be taken during the summer before the senior year. There is a deferred admissions plan. Applications should be filed by August 15 for fall entry. Notification is sent on a rolling basis. The fall 2003 application fee was $20.

Transfer: 141 transfer students enrolled in a recent year. Applicants must submit official transcripts from all previous colleges attended. D grades do not transfer. If the applicant has not maintained a C average, an ACT score that places the applicant in the upper 50% of college-bound freshmen may be submitted for consideration.

Visiting: There are regularly scheduled orientations for prospective students, consisting of a welcome presentation, registration, refreshments, an academic visit, a campus tour, lunch, a financial aid presentation, student panel, and a cost and scholarship presentation. There are guides for informal visits and visitors may sit in on classes and stay overnight. To schedule a visit, contact the Admissions Office.

Financial Aid: In 2002-2003, 80% of continuing full-time students received some form of financial aid. The CSS Profile, FAFSA, FFS, or SFS is required. The priority date for freshman financial aid applications for fall entry is March 1.

International Students: They must score 500 on the written TOEFL and also take the ACT.

Computers: There are 800 PCs located on campus, all connected to the student network, and 25 computer labs. Computers are used for word processing, graphics, report generation, and software capabilities. All computers can access the Internet. All students may access the system. There are no time limits and no fees.

Graduates: In a recent year, 319 bachelor's degrees were awarded. The most popular majors were education (37%), business (31%), and social sciences (16%). 5 companies recruited on campus in a recent year. Of a recent graduating class, 10% were enrolled in graduate school within 6 months of graduation and 97% were employed.

Admissions Contact: Travis Vlasman or Sarah Hansen, Co-Directors of Admissions. E-mail: *admissions@wolf.northern.edu* Web: *www.northern.edu*

OGLALA LAKOTA COLLEGE

B-3

Kyle, SD 57752

(605) 455-2321; Fax: (605) 455-2787

Full-time: 900 men and women	**Faculty:** n/av
Part-time: none	**Ph.D.s:** n/av
Graduate: none	**Student/Faculty:** n/av
Year: n/app	**Tuition:** n/av
Application Deadline: open	**Room & Board:** n/app
Freshman Class: n/av	
SAT I or ACT: n/av	**NONCOMPETITIVE**

Oglala Lakota College was founded in 1971 by the Oglala Sioux Tribal Council to provide academic, tribal, and cultural resources for the Pine Ridge Reservation community, offering programs in business, teaching, and human services. There are 10 regional centers in addition to the central campus. Figures in the above capsule and in this profile are approximate. Special learning facilities include a learning resource center and archives, an American Indians collection, and an audio video studio. The campus is in a rural area spread over the 5,000 square miles of the Pine Ridge Indian Reservation in the state's southwest corner. There are 5 buildings.

Programs of Study: Bachelor's degrees are awarded in BUSINESS (business administration and management), EDUCATION (business and elementary), SOCIAL SCIENCE (history, human services, and sociology).

Requirements: The SAT I or ACT is not required. Applicants should be high school graduates or have the GED. Certification of degree of Indian blood from the tribal census office is required.

Procedure: Application deadlines are open.

Transfer: 30 of 128 credits required for the bachelor's degree must be completed at OLC.

Visiting: Visitors may sit in on classes.

Admissions Contact: Billi K. Hornbeck, Registrar.

PRESENTATION COLLEGE

D-1

Aberdeen, SD 57401

(605) 229-8492
(800) 437-6060; Fax: (605) 229-8518

Full-time: 58 men, 377 women	**Faculty:** 28; IIB, --$
Part-time: 15 men, 168 women	**Ph.D.s:** 25%
Graduate: none	**Student/Faculty:** 16 to 1
Year: semesters, summer session	**Tuition:** $10,550
Application Deadline: open	**Room & Board:** $4150
Freshman Class: 163 applied, 147 accepted, 73 enrolled	
ACT: 21	**LESS COMPETITIVE**

Presentation College, founded in 1922 as Notre Dame Junior College, is an independent Catholic institution offering undergraduate degrees in nursing and allied health service management. In addition to regional accreditation, Presentation has baccalaureate program accreditation with AHEA. The library contains 33,725 volumes and subscribes to 221 periodicals. Computerized library services include the card catalog and interlibrary loans. Special learning facilities include a learning resource center. The 100-acre campus is in a small town. Including any residence halls, there are 8 buildings.

Student Life: 76% of undergraduates are from South Dakota. Students are from 6 states and Canada. 78% are white. 30% are Catholic; 29% Protestant.

Housing: 137 students can be accommodated in college housing, which includes single-sex dorms. On-campus housing is guaranteed for all 4 years and is available on a first-come, first-served basis. 81% of students commute. Alcohol is not permitted. All students may keep cars.

Activities: There are no fraternities or sororities. There are some groups and organizations on campus, including chorus.

Sports: There are 5 intercollegiate sports for men and 5 for women, and 3 intramural sports for men and 3 for women.

Disabled Students: All of the campus is accessible. Wheelchair ramps, elevators, special parking, and specially equipped rest rooms are available.

Services: Counseling and information services are available, as is tutoring in every subject. There is remedial math, reading, and writing.

Campus Safety and Security: Measures include 24-hour foot and vehicle patrol, informal discussions, pamphlets/posters/films, and emergency telephones. There are lighted pathways/sidewalks.

Programs of Study: Presentation confers B.S., B.S.N., and B.S.W. degrees. Associate degrees are also awarded. Bachelor's degrees are awarded in BIOLOGICAL SCIENCE (biology/biological science), BUSINESS (business administration and management), COMMUNICATIONS AND THE ARTS (communications), COMPUTER AND PHYSICAL SCIENCE (radiological technology), HEALTH PROFESSIONS (health care administration and nursing), SOCIAL SCIENCE (social work). Nursing is the largest.

Required: Students must complete 128 semester hours, including 48 in upper-division courses and 36 in the major, with a minimum GPA of 2.0. The core curriculum consists of 18 hours of humanities and fine arts, 12 of social and behavioral sciences, 11 of natural sciences and math, and 10 of religious studies and philosophy.

Special: Certificate programs are available in phlebotomy, surgical technology, administrative assistance, business/accounting, and computer operating. An external degree program offers an accelerated schedule for working adults. Limited credit for experiential learning is possible. There is 1 national honor society, and 2 departmental honors programs.

Faculty/Classroom: 32% of faculty are male; 68%, female. All teach undergraduates.

Admissions: 90% of the 2003-2004 applicants were accepted. The ACT scores for the 2003-2004 freshman class were: 60% below 21, 31% between 21 and 23, 6% between 24 and 26, 1% between 27 and 28, and 1% above 28.

Requirements: The ACT is required. In addition, prospective students must graduate from high school or hold a GED, and a GPA of 2.0 is recommended. AP and CLEP credits are accepted. Important factors in the admissions decision are ability to finance college education, extracurricular activities record, and leadership record.

Procedure: Freshmen are admitted to all sessions. Early decision applications should be filed by April 1; regular applications, are open. The college accepts all applicants. Applications are accepted on-line through *www.presentation.edu*.

Transfer: 115 transfer students enrolled in 2002-2003. A 2.0 GPA on previous college work is recommended. 30 of 127 credits required for the bachelor's degree must be completed at Presentation.

Visiting: To schedule a visit, contact the Admissions Office at (605) 229-8492 or (800) 437-6060 ext.492 or *admit@presentation.edu*.

Financial Aid: In 2003-2004, 94% of all full-time freshmen and 97% of continuing full-time students received some form of financial aid. 88% of full-time freshmen and 89% of continuing full-time students received need-based aid. The average freshman award was $11,339. Need-based scholarships or need-based grants averaged $3933 ($7050 maximum); need-based self-help aid (loans and jobs) averaged $6694 ($7125 maximum); and non-need-based awards and non-need-based scholarships averaged $9109 ($11,650 maximum). All of undergraduates work part time. Average annual earnings from campus work are $1500. The average financial indebtedness of the 2003 graduate was $26,737. Presentation is a member of CSS. The FAFSA is required. The priority date for freshman financial aid applications for fall entry is March 1. The deadline for filing freshman financial aid applications for fall entry is open.

International Students: There are 4 international students enrolled. They must score 450 on the written TOEFL or 173 on the electronic version.

Computers: Approximately 180 PCs are available in the library, computer center, and dorms. Dorm rooms have Internet access. Students may have e-mail accounts. Computer students may access the system.

Graduates: From July 1, 2002 to June 30, 2003, 116 bachelor's degrees were awarded. The most popular majors were nursing (54%), radiologic technician (7%), and surgical technician (6%).

Admissions Contact: Joddy Meidinger, Director of Admissions and Financial Aid. E-mail: *meidinger@presentation.edu*

SI TANKA HURON UNIVERSITY
(See Huron University)

SINTE GLESKA UNIVERSITY
Rosebud, SD 57570

C-3

(605) 747-2263; Fax: (605) 747-2098

Total enrollment: n/av	Faculty: 23
Year: semesters, summer session	Ph.Ds: n/av
Application Deadline: open	Student/Faculty: 14 to 1
	Tuition: n/av
	Room & Board: n/app

Freshman Class: n/av

SAT I or ACT: not required

NONCOMPETITIVE

Sinte Gleska University, founded in 1970, is an independent institution offering undergraduate programs in business, fine arts, professional training, and technical studies. Figures in the above capsule and in this profile are approximate. There is 1 graduate school. The library contains 85,000 volumes. The 52-acre campus is in a rural area east of Mission. There are 7 buildings.

Student Life: 92% of undergraduates are from South Dakota. All are from public schools. 85% are Native American/Eskimo; 15% white. The average age of all undergraduates is 31. 10% do not continue beyond their first year; 90% remain to graduate.

Housing: There are no residence halls. All students commute. Alcohol is not permitted.

Activities: There are no fraternities or sororities. There are some groups and organizations on campus, including newspaper and photography. Popular campus events include Founders Day.

Sports: There are 4 intramural sports for men and 3 for women.

Disabled Students: All of the campus is accessible. Wheelchair ramps, special parking, specially equipped rest rooms, and lowered drinking fountains are available.

Services: Counseling and information services are available, as is tutoring in every subject.

Campus Safety and Security: Measures include shuttle buses, informal discussions, and an evening security guard.

Programs of Study: Sinte Gleska confers B.A. and B.S. degrees. Associate and master's degrees are also awarded. Bachelor's degrees are awarded in COMMUNICATIONS AND THE ARTS (art), EDUCATION (early childhood and elementary), HEALTH PROFESSIONS (mental health/human services), SOCIAL SCIENCE (human services). Education and human services are the strongest academically.

Required: To graduate, students must complete at least 128 credits with a GPA of 2.0; education majors must have a 2.5. All students must fulfill the core curriculum requirements.

Special: The college offers work-study programs, accelerated degree programs, a general studies degree, and pass/fail options.

Requirements: Applicants must be graduates of accredited secondary schools or have earned a GED.

Procedure: Freshmen are admitted to all sessions. Entrance exams should be taken before admission. Application deadlines are open.

Transfer: Applicants must submit an official transcript from their previous college. 68 of 128 credits required for the bachelor's degree must be completed at Sinte Gleska.

Visiting: There are regularly scheduled orientations for prospective students. There are guides for informal visits and visitors may stay overnight. To schedule a visit, contact Cheryl Crazy Bull, Vice President at (605) 747-2263, ext. 52.

Admissions Contact: Michelle Zephier, Registrar.
E-mail: *mzephr@rosebud.sinte.edu*

SOUTH DAKOTA BOARD OF REGENTS

The South Dakota Board of Regents governs the 6 public universities: Black Hills State University, Dakota State University, Northern State University, South Dakota School of Mines and Technology, South Dakota State University, and the University of South Dakota. In addition, the regents operate off-campus attendance centers in several locations statewide. In 2000, the Regents created the Electronic University Consortium, offering courses and degrees on-line from the six universities. In the past decade, the thrust of Regental policies has been to foster a unified system of public higher education while maintaining quality and accountability through wise resource management. To that end, at least one center of excellence has been established at each university. Additional initiatives include a proficiency exam of all rising juniors, information technology proficiency requirements, interuniversity faculty discipline councils, common course numbering among the six universities, student technology fellows, and faculty salary increases based on performance and market. The Regents have integrated technology throughout the system by wiring all campus buildings, participating in the governor's competitive faculty grants for course redesign, and establishing a statewide e-learning center to enhance teacher education and delivery of distance education courses for high school students. Total 2003 fall enrollment is 30,237. Profiles of the universities appear in this section.

SOUTH DAKOTA SCHOOL OF MINES AND TECHNOLOGY
B-3

Rapid City, SD 57701-3995
(605) 394-2414
(800) 544-8162, ext. 2400; Fax: (605) 394-1268

Full-time: 1252 men, 470 women
Part-time: 199 men, 191 women
Graduate: 257 men, 85 women
Year: semesters, summer session
Application Deadline: August 15
Freshman Class: 811 applied, 762 accepted, 420 enrolled
SAT I Verbal/Math: 550/575

Faculty: 104; IIA, +$
Ph.Ds: 84%
Student/Faculty: 17 to 1
Tuition: $4293 ($9005)
Room & Board: $3561

ACT: 24   **COMPETITIVE+**

South Dakota School of Mines and Technology, founded in 1885, is a public university offering undergraduate and graduate programs in engineering, science, and mathematics. There are 4 undergraduate schools and 1 graduate school. In addition to regional accreditation, SDSM&T has baccalaureate program accreditation with ABET, ACS, and CSAB. The library contains 365,367 volumes, 71,285 microform items, and 1455 audio/video tapes/CDs, and subscribes to 516 periodicals. Computerized library services include the card catalog, interlibrary loans, database searching, and Internet access. Special learning facilities include a learning resource center, art gallery, natural history museum, planetarium, radio station, and a geology museum. The 120-acre campus is in a suburban area 350 miles northeast of Denver. Including any residence halls, there are 18 buildings.

Student Life: 73% of undergraduates are from South Dakota. Students are from 39 states, 27 foreign countries, and Canada. 85% are white. The average age of freshmen is 19; all undergraduates, 22. 29% do not continue beyond their first year; 39% remain to graduate.

Housing: 534 students can be accommodated in college housing, which includes single-sex and coed dorms, fraternity houses, and sorority houses. On-campus housing is available on a first-come, first-served basis. 60% of students commute. Alcohol is not permitted. All students may keep cars.

Activities: There are 4 national fraternities and 2 national sororities. There are 24 groups on campus, including art, band, biking, choir, chorale, chorus, computers, drama, drill team, ethnic, film, honors, international, jazz band, newspaper, orchestra, pep band, political, professional, radio and TV, religious, SAAD, ski club, social, social service, student government, and yearbook. Popular campus events include M-Week, Christmas chorale concert, and International Cultural Exposition.

Sports: There are 5 intercollegiate sports for men and 5 for women, and 15 intramural sports for men and 15 for women. Facilities include a football field, track, a 2350-seat gym, sand volleyball court, swimming pool, squash/racquetball courts, and a weight room.

Disabled Students: 60% of the campus is accessible. Wheelchair ramps, elevators, special parking, specially equipped rest rooms, special class scheduling, lowered drinking fountains, and an ADA lab with specialized workstations, software, and hardware to aid students with visual, auditory, and mobility impairments and dyslexia are available.

Services: Counseling and information services are available, as is tutoring in most subjects. There is a reader service for the blind and remedial math.

Campus Safety and Security: Measures include 24-hour foot and vehicle patrol, security escort services, informal discussions, and pamphlets/posters/films. There are emergency telephones and lighted pathways/sidewalks.

Programs of Study: SDSM&T confers the B.S. degree. Associate, master's, and doctoral degrees are also awarded. Bachelor's degrees are awarded in COMPUTER AND PHYSICAL SCIENCE (chemistry, computer science, geology, mathematics, and physics), ENGINEERING AND ENVIRONMENTAL DESIGN (chemical engineering, civil engineering, computer engineering, electrical/electronics engineering, geological engineering, industrial engineering, mechanical engineering, metallurgical engineering, and mining and mineral engineering), SOCIAL SCIENCE (interdisciplinary studies). Engineering is the strongest academically. Mechanical engineering, electrical engineering, and civil engineering are the largest.

Required: Students must complete 128 credits for the science major or 136 credits for the engineering major, and maintain a minimum GPA of 2.0. Included in these requirements are 16 credit hours each of math at a level of calculus and above, basic science, and humanities/social science (for engineering, 3 credits must be at the 300 or above level). State regents mandated distribution requirements include 6 credits each of written communications, social sciences, arts/humanities, science, and cultural diversity; 3 credits each of speech communications and math; and 2 credits of information technology literacy, plus completion of an exam.

Special: Opportunities are provided for study abroad, co-op programs, internships, work-study programs, dual majors, an interdisciplinary science major, credit by exam, student-designed majors in interdisciplinary studies, and nondegree study. There are 5 national honor societies, including Phi Beta Kappa.

Faculty/Classroom: 67% of faculty are male; 33%, female. 95% teach undergraduates, 20% do research, and 90% do both. Graduate students teach 4% of introductory courses. The average class size in an introductory lecture is 50; in a laboratory, 24; and in a regular course, 25.

Admissions: 94% of the 2003-2004 applicants were accepted. The ACT scores for the 2003-2004 freshman class were: 21% below 21, 23% between 21 and 23, 28% between 24 and 26, 13% between 27 and 28, and 15% above 28. 34% of the current freshmen were in the top fifth of their class; 65% were in the top two fifths. There were 2 National Merit finalists and 7 semifinalists. 23 freshmen graduated first in their class.

Requirements: The SAT I is accepted, but the ACT is preferred, with a minimum composite score of 920 (420 verbal and 500 math) on the SAT I, or a minimum composite score of 18 on the ACT. Graduation from an accredited secondary school is required. A GED is accepted. Applicants must submit high school credits, distributed as follows: 4 years of English, 3 each of math, lab science, social studies, and 1/2 year each of fine arts and computer science. SDSM&T requires applicants to be in the upper 60% of their class. A GPA of 2.6 is required. AP and CLEP credits are accepted.

Procedure: Freshmen are admitted fall and spring. Entrance exams should be taken preferably in October and December. There is a rolling admissions plan. Applications should be filed by August 15 for fall entry and January 15 for spring entry. Notification is sent on a rolling basis. The fall 2003 application fee was $20. Applications are accepted on-line through *www.sdsmt.edu*.

Transfer: 136 transfer students enrolled in 2002-2003. Transfer students must submit an official transcript from the previous college and must have maintained a minimum GPA of 2.0, with 2.5 recommended. 32 of 128 credits required for the bachelor's degree must be completed at SDSM&T.

Visiting: There are regularly scheduled orientations for prospective students, including a campus tour, discussions, training, and a meal. There are guides for informal visits and visitors may sit in on classes. To schedule a visit, contact the Admissions Office at (605) 394-2400 or *admissions@sdsmt.edu*.

Financial Aid: In 2003-2004, 75% of all full-time freshmen and 71% of continuing full-time students received some form of financial aid. 51% of full-time freshmen and 54% of continuing full-time students received need-based aid. The average freshman award was $5107. Need-based scholarships or need-based grants averaged $3093; need-based self-help aid (loans and jobs) averaged $2671; non-need-based athletic scholarships averaged $791; and other non-need-based awards and non-need-based scholarships averaged $2537. 23% of undergraduates work part time. Average annual earnings from campus work are $1500. The FAFSA is required. The deadline for filing freshman financial aid applications for fall entry is March 15.

International Students: There are 22 international students enrolled. The school actively recruits these students. They must score 530 on the written TOEFL and also take IELTS and the ACT.

Computers: There are approximately 160 computers plus 50 Internet kiosks on campus. All students may access the system 24 hours per day. There are no time limits and no fees.

Graduates: In a recent year, 238 bachelor's degrees were awarded. The most popular majors were mechanical engineering (21%), civil engineering (16%), and interdisciplinary sciences (10%). In an average class, 9% graduate in 4 years or less, 35% graduate in 5 years or less, and 39% graduate in 6 years or less. 116 companies recruited on campus in a recent year. Of a recent graduating class, 18% were enrolled in graduate school within 6 months of graduation and 77% were employed.

Admissions Contact: Office of Admissions.
E-mail: hhall@silver.sdsmt.edu Web: *http://www.sdsmt.edu*

SOUTH DAKOTA STATE UNIVERSITY
F-3

Brookings, SD 57007
(605) 688-4121
(800) 952-3541; Fax: (605) 688-6891

Full-time: 3708 men, 3624 women
Part-time: 582 men, 1294 women
Graduate: 505 men, 738 women
Year: semesters, summer session
Application Deadline: open
Freshman Class: 3748 applied, 3586 accepted, 2087 enrolled

Faculty: IIA, -$
Ph.Ds: 60%
Student/Faculty: n/av
Tuition: $4260 ($8970)
Room & Board: $3522

ACT: 22   **COMPETITIVE**

South Dakota State University, founded in 1881, is a public land-grant institution offering undergraduate programs in agriculture and biological sciences, arts and science, engineering, family and consumer sciences, nursing, pharmacy, education and counseling, and general registration. There are 8 undergraduate schools and 1 graduate school. In addition to regional accreditation, SDSU has baccalaureate program accreditation with ABET, ACEJMC, ACPE, ADA, AHEA, NASM, NCATE, and NLN. The library contains 606,576 volumes, 914,820 microform items, and 3011 audio/video tapes/CDs, and subscribes to 15,104 periodicals. Computerized library services include the card catalog, interlibrary loans, database searching, and Internet access. Special learning facilities include an art gallery, radio station, TV station, arboretum, agricultural heritage museum, Northern Plains Biostress lab, and animal disease research and diagnostic lab. The 272-acre campus is in a small town 50 miles north of Sioux Falls; 200 miles west of Minneapolis. Including any residence halls, there are 325 buildings.

Student Life: 74% of undergraduates are from South Dakota. Students are from 39 states, 19 foreign countries, and Canada. 89% are white. The average age of freshmen is 19; all undergraduates, 22. 25% do not continue beyond their first year; 53% remain to graduate.

Housing: 3482 students can be accommodated in college housing, which includes coed dorms, on-campus apartments, and married-student housing. In addition, there are honors houses, special-interest houses, a health professionals learning community (first-year students), engineering learning community, and a substance-free house. On-campus housing is available on a first-come, first-served basis. 67% of students commute. Alcohol is not permitted. All students may keep cars.

Activities: There are 7 national fraternities and 3 national sororities. There are 200 groups on campus, including art, band, cheerleading, chess, choir, chorale, chorus, computers, dance, debate, drama, drill team, ethnic, film, forensics, gay, honors, international, jazz band, literary magazine, marching band, musical theater, newspaper, opera, orchestra, pep band, photography, political, professional, radio and TV, religious, social, social service, student government, symphony, and yearbook. Popular campus events include Little International, Engineering Exploration Days, and Festival of Cultures.

Sports: There are 10 intercollegiate sports for men and 10 for women, and 17 intramural sports for men and 17 for women. Facilities include a phys ed complex, an intramural building, outdoor track, lighted tennis courts, a wellness center, and intramural football and softball fields.

Disabled Students: Wheelchair ramps, elevators, special parking, specially equipped rest rooms, special class scheduling, lowered drinking fountains, and lowered telephones are available. All academic programs can be made accessible.

Services: Counseling and information services are available, as is tutoring in most subjects. There is a reader service for the blind.

Campus Safety and Security: Measures include 24-hour foot and vehicle patrol, self-defense education, security escort services, and informal discussions. There are pamphlets/posters/films, emergency telephones, and lighted pathways/sidewalks.

Programs of Study: SDSU confers B.A., B.S., B.Mus.Ed., and B.S.T. degrees. Associate, master's, and doctoral degrees are also awarded. Bachelor's degrees are awarded in AGRICULTURE (agricultural business management, agricultural economics, agriculture, agronomy, animal science, dairy science, fish and game management, horticulture, and range/farm management), BIOLOGICAL SCIENCE (biochemistry, biology/biological science, microbiology, and nutrition), BUSINESS (apparel and accessories marketing, and hotel/motel and restaurant management), COMMUNICATIONS AND THE ARTS (art, communications, dramatic arts, English, German, graphic design, journalism, music, music business management, and Spanish), COMPUTER AND PHYSICAL SCIENCE (chemistry, computer science, mathematics, physics, and software engineering), EDUCATION (agricultural, art, athletic training, early childhood, health, home economics, music, physical, secondary, and vocational), ENGINEERING AND ENVIRONMENTAL DESIGN (agricultural engineering, agricultural engineering technology, civil engineering, construction management, electrical/electronics engineering, electrical/electronics engineering technology, engineering physics, engineering technology, environmental engineering, industrial administration/management, interior design, landscape architecture/design, manufacturing technology, and mechanical engineering), HEALTH PROFESSIONS (clinical science, nursing, and pharmacy), SOCIAL SCIENCE (consumer services, economics, family/consumer studies, food production/management/services, food science, French studies, geography, history, human development, parks and recreation management, political science/government, psychology, rural sociology, safety management, and sociology). Pharmacy, engineering, and nursing are the strongest academically. Nursing, sociology, and economics are the largest.

Required: Students must complete 128 credits (136 for engineering and nursing), with at least 32 in the major, and must maintain a 2.0 minimum GPA. Additional requirements for graduation are 9 to 14 credits in social science, 8 to 13 in natural science, 6 to 11 in humanities, 3 each in math and speech, and 2 in wellness.

Special: Co-op programs in elementary education and social work, internships, work-study programs, B.A.-B.S. degrees, and interdisciplinary majors including agricultural journalism, environmental management, and wildlife and fisheries science, are available. SDSU offers cross-registration with Dakota State University, Black Hills State University, the University of South Dakota, Northern State University, and South Dakota School of Mines and Technology. Opportunities are provided for dual majors, study abroad in more than 40 countries, credit by examination, student-designed majors, credit for military experience, nondegree study, a general studies degree, and pass/fail options. There are 32 national honor societies and a freshman honors program.

Faculty/Classroom: 59% of faculty are male; 41%, female. 78% teach undergraduates, 14% do research, and 87% do both. Graduate students teach 30% of introductory courses. The average class size in an introductory lecture is 50; in a laboratory, 30; and in a regular course, 30.

Admissions: 96% of the 2003-2004 applicants were accepted. The ACT scores for the 2003-2004 freshman class were: 35% below 21, 26% between 21 and 23, 26% between 24 and 26, 8% between 27 and 28, and 5% above 28. 28% of the current freshmen were in the top fifth of their class; 56% were in the top two fifths. There were 7 National Merit finalists and 4 semifinalists. 90 freshmen graduated first in their class.

Requirements: The ACT is required. In addition, students must have an 18 ACT composite score, or be in the top 60% of their class, or have a 2.6 GPA in required classes. Graduation from an accredited secondary school is required. A GED will be accepted. Applicants must submit 4 years of English, 3 years each of social studies, math, and science, and 1 year of fine arts. AP and CLEP credits are accepted. Important factors in the admissions decision are advanced placement or honor courses, evidence of special talent, and extracurricular activities record.

Procedure: Freshmen are admitted to all sessions. Entrance exams should be taken by spring of the junior year. There is a rolling admissions plan. Application deadlines are open. Application fee is $20. Applications are accepted on-line through *www.sdstate.edu* and via College-NET.

Transfer: 699 transfer students enrolled in 2002-2003. To be eligible for transfer, students must have been in good standing at the previous college and must have maintained a minimum GPA of 2.0 to 2.5, depending on the student's major. 32 of 128 credits required for the bachelor's degree must be completed at SDSU.

Visiting: There are regularly scheduled orientations for prospective students, Several new student orientation sessions are offered each June. Students become acquainted with the university and student resources. They also meet with an academic adviser and register for fall semester classes. Information is sent to all admitted sudents. There are guides for informal visits and visitors may sit in on classes and stay overnight. To schedule a visit, contact the Admissions Office at *SDSU_Admissions@sdstate.edu*.

Financial Aid: In 2003-2004, 86% of all full-time freshmen and 85% of continuing full-time students received some form of financial aid. 75% of full-time freshmen and 72% of continuing full-time students received need-based aid. The average freshman award was $5620. Need-based scholarships or need-based grants averaged $3070 ($9240 maximum); need-based self-help aid (loans and jobs) averaged $2944 ($6625 maximum); non-need-based athletic scholarships averaged $6118 ($13,300 maximum); and other non-need-based awards and non-need-based scholarships averaged $982 ($8464 maximum). 88% of undergraduates work part time. Average annual earnings from campus work are $1410. The average financial indebtedness of the 2003 graduate was $16,660. SDSU is a member of CSS. The FAFSA is required. The priority date for freshman financial aid applications for fall entry is March 7. Financial aid awards are on a rolling basis.

International Students: There are 23 international students enrolled. They must score 500 on the written TOEFL.

Computers: Students have access to PC labs in the library, various residence halls, and the nursing building. Students can access the Internet and Web at campus computer labs and computer rooms. All students may access the system. There are no time limits and no fees. Nursing students require laptops once in the professional program.

Graduates: From July 1, 2002 to June 30, 2003, 1239 bachelor's degrees were awarded. The most popular majors were nursing (12%), economics (6%), and sociology (4%).

Admissions Contact: Megan Dombek, Admissions Counselor. E-mail: *Megan_Dombek@sdstate.edu* Web: *http://www.sdstate.edu*

UNIVERSITY OF SIOUX FALLS
Sioux Falls, SD 57105

F-3
(605) 331-6600
(800) 888-1047; Fax: (605) 331-6615

Full-time: 425 men, 480 women	**Faculty:** 36; IIB, --$
Part-time: 85 men, 130 women	**Ph.D.s:** 68%
Graduate: 90 men, 120 women	**Student/Faculty:** 18 to 1
Year: 4-1-4, summer session	**Tuition:** $14,100
Application Deadline: open	**Room & Board:** $4,100
Freshman Class: n/av	
ACT: required	**COMPETITIVE**

University of Sioux Falls, founded in 1883, is a private liberal arts institution affiliated with the American Baptist Churches. Figures in the above capsule and in this profile are approximate. In addition to regional accreditation, USF has baccalaureate program accreditation with CSWE and NCATE. The library contains 78,000 volumes and 4600 audio/video tapes/CDs, and subscribes to 450 periodicals. Computerized library services include the card catalog, interlibrary loans, and database searching. Special learning facilities include a learning resource center, radio station, and TV station. The 22-acre campus is in a suburban area 250 miles from Minneapolis/St. Paul, Minnesota; 180 miles from Omaha, Nebraska. Including any residence halls, there are 13 buildings.

Student Life: 72% of undergraduates are from South Dakota. Students are from 21 states, 10 foreign countries, and Canada. 95% are from public schools. 94% are white. 73% are Protestant; 14% Catholic; 13% claim no religious affiliation. The average age of freshmen is 18; all undergraduates, 21. 37% do not continue beyond their first year; 48% remain to graduate.

Housing: 350 students can be accommodated in college housing, which includes single-sex and coed dorms, on-campus apartments, and married-student housing. On-campus housing is guaranteed for the freshman year only, is available on a first-come, first-served basis, and is available on a lottery system for upperclassmen. Priority is given to out-of-town students. 73% of students commute. Alcohol is not permitted. All students may keep cars.

Activities: There are no fraternities or sororities. There are 35 groups on campus, including art, band, cheerleading, choir, chorale, chorus, computers, drama, ethnic, honors, international, jazz band, musical theater, newspaper, opera, orchestra, pep band, photography, political, professional, radio and TV, religious, social, social service, and student government. Popular campus events include Spring Formal, Staley Lectures, and Madrigals.

Sports: There are 6 intercollegiate sports for men and 7 for women, and 8 intramural sports for men and 8 for women. Facilities include a student lounge, a 160-meter running track, volleyball, tennis, badminton, racquetball, and basketball courts, aerobics facilities, exercise machines, a whirlpool, and a 700-seat gym.

Disabled Students: 54% of the campus is accessible. Wheelchair ramps, elevators, special parking, specially equipped rest rooms, special class scheduling, lowered drinking fountains, and lowered telephones are available.

Services: There is remedial math and reading.

Campus Safety and Security: Measures include self-defense education, security escort services, informal discussions, and pamphlets/posters/films. There are emergency telephones and lighted pathways/sidewalks.

Programs of Study: USF confers B.A. and B.S. degrees. Associate and master's degrees are also awarded. Bachelor's degrees are awarded in BIOLOGICAL SCIENCE (biology/biological science), BUSINESS (accounting, business administration and management, business economics, and marketing/retailing/merchandising), COMMUNICATIONS AND THE ARTS (communications, English, music, and speech/debate/rhetoric), COMPUTER AND PHYSICAL SCIENCE (chemistry, computer science, and mathematics), EDUCATION (art, early childhood, elementary, middle school, music, science, and secondary), HEALTH PROFESSIONS (medical laboratory technology, and premedicine), SOCIAL SCIENCE (history, philosophy, political science/government, prelaw, psychology, religion, social work, and sociology). Business and elementary education are the strongest academically and have the largest enrollments.

Required: To graduate, all students must complete a minimum of 128 credit hours, with 64 hours in the major. Required courses include phys ed, computer science, religion, history, English, science, economics, political science, psychology, math, social science, cross-cultural experience, speech, and fine arts. A writing proficiency test and a minimum 2.0 GPA are also required.

Special: There are co-op programs with Augustana College, the Center for Public Higher Education, Dakota State University, and the North American Baptist Seminary. USF offers internships, study abroad in Japan, Central America, and China, an American Studies Program in Washington, D.C., and a January interim. Also available are on-campus work-study programs, B.A.-B.S. degrees, dual and student-designed interdisciplinary majors, a general studies degree, a 3-2 engineering degree, credit for life and work experience, and pass/fail options. There are 3 national honor societies, a freshman honors program, and 2 departmental honors programs.

Faculty/Classroom: 69% of faculty are male; 31%, female. All teach undergraduates and 60% do research. No introductory courses are taught by graduate students. The average class size in an introductory lecture is 40; in a laboratory, 15; and in a regular course, 20.

Requirements: The SAT I or ACT is required. In addition, the minimum required composite score on the SAT I is 910, and on the ACT, 19. Applicants must be graduates of an accredited secondary school or have a GED certificate. Students should have completed 4 years each of English and math and 2 years each of foreign language, science, and social studies. USF requires applicants to be in the upper 50% of their class. A GPA of 2.0 is required. AP and CLEP credits are accepted. Important factors in the admissions decision are advanced placement or honor courses, evidence of special talent, and leadership record.

Procedure: Freshmen are admitted to all sessions. Entrance exams should be taken during the junior or senior year of high school. There is an early admissions plan. There is a rolling admissions plan. Application deadlines are open. Application fee is $25.

Transfer: Transfer students must meet freshman admission requirements and have completed at least 24 hours of college courses with a minimum 2.0 GPA. SAT I or the ACT and an interview are recommended. 30 of 128 credits required for the bachelor's degree must be completed at USF.

Visiting: There are regularly scheduled orientations for prospective students, including meetings with faculty and staff, attendance at class, a campus tour, and a financial aid session. There are guides for informal visits and visitors may sit in on classes and stay overnight. To schedule a visit, contact the Admissions Office.

Financial Aid: USF is a member of CSS. The FAFSA is required. The priority deadline for filing freshman financial aid applications for fall entry is March 1.

International Students: The school actively recruits these students. They must score 550 on the written TOEFL or 213 on the electronic version and also take the SAT I or ACT if the examination is available to the student.

Computers: Students have access to 91 PCs in 3 publicly accessible labs. File space, letter-quality printers, and a laser printer are provided. Students may access the Internet through IBM and Mac labs wired to the campus network. All students may access the system 8 A.M. to 11 P.M. There are no time limits and no fees.

Admissions Contact: Laura Olson, Assistant Director of Admissions. E-mail: *laura.olson@usiouxfalls.edu* Web: *www.usiouxfalls.edu*

UNIVERSITY OF SOUTH DAKOTA
Vermillion, SD 57069

F-4
(605) 677-5434
(877) COYOTE; Fax: (605) 677-6323

Full-time: 1791 men, 2309 women	**Faculty:** 265; I, --$
Part-time: 482 men, 1248 women	**Ph.D.s:** 83%
Graduate: 915 men, 1172 women	**Student/Faculty:** 15 to 1
Year: semesters, summer session	**Tuition:** $4205 ($8916)
Application Deadline: open	**Room & Board:** $3505
Freshman Class: 2529 applied, 2187 accepted, 1077 enrolled	
SAT I Verbal/Math: 568/558	**ACT:** 22 **COMPETITIVE+**

The University of South Dakota, founded in 1862, is a public institution with undergraduate programs in arts and sciences, education, fine arts, business, and professional schools of law and medicine. There are 4 undergraduate and 6 graduate schools. In addition to regional accreditation, USD has baccalaureate program accreditation with AACSB, ACS, APTA, CSWE, NASAD, NASM, NCATE, and NLN. The 4 libraries contain 861,936 volumes, 767,424 microform items, and 19,921 audio/video tapes/CDs, and subscribe to 3517 periodicals. Computerized library services include the card catalog, interlibrary loans, database searching, and Internet access. Special learning facilities include a learning resource center, art gallery, natural history museum, planetarium, radio station, TV station, music museum and historical study center, institutes of American Indian studies, social science research, and child welfare training, business and governmental research bureaus, centers for speech and hearing, international studies, fine arts, and telecommunications, natural sciences field station, and archeology and human factors labs. The 272-acre campus is in a rural area 41 miles from Sioux City, Iowa, and 64 miles from Sioux Falls. Including any residence halls, there are 64 buildings.

Student Life: 75% of undergraduates are from South Dakota. Students are from 39 states, 23 foreign countries, and Canada. 87% are white. 43% claim no religious affiliation; 35% Protestant; 21% Catholic. The average age of freshmen is 21; all undergraduates, 23. 31% do not continue beyond their first year; 51% remain to graduate.

Housing: 2076 students can be accommodated in college housing, which includes single-sex and coed dorms, on-campus apartments, married-student housing, fraternity houses, and sorority houses. On-campus housing is available on a first-come, first-served basis. 77% of students commute. Alcohol is not permitted. All students may keep cars.

Activities: 17% of men belong to 8 national fraternities; 10% of women belong to 4 national sororities. There are 130 groups on campus, including art, band, cheerleading, chess, choir, chorale, chorus, computers, dance, debate, drama, drill team, ethnic, forensics, gay, honors, international, jazz band, literary magazine, marching band, musical theater, newspaper, opera, orchestra, pep band, photography, political, professional, radio and TV, religious, social, social service, student government, and symphony. Popular campus events include Strollers (a variety production), Rockfest, and Greek Week.

Sports: There are 7 intercollegiate sports for men and 7 for women, and 33 intramural sports for men and 33 for women. Facilities include an indoor football field, 5 basketball courts, a 25-meter swimming pool, an 8-lane, 200-meter track, and handball, volleyball, and tennis courts.

Disabled Students: 95% of the campus is accessible. Wheelchair ramps, elevators, special parking, specially equipped rest rooms, special class scheduling, lowered drinking fountains, and lowered telephones are available.

Services: Counseling and information services are available, as is tutoring in most subjects. There is a reader service for the blind, and remedial math, reading, and writing. There is an academic advising/testing center.

Campus Safety and Security: Measures include 24-hour foot and vehicle patrol, self-defense education, security escort services, and shuttle buses. There are informal discussions, pamphlets/posters/films, emergency telephones, and lighted pathways/sidewalks.

Programs of Study: USD confers B.A., B.S., B.F.A., B.L.S., B.M., B.S.A.H., B.S.B.A, B.S.D.H., B.S.Ed., B.S.H.A., B.S.Med., B.S.Med.Tech., and B.S.Rec. degrees. Associate, master's, and doctoral degrees are also awarded. Bachelor's degrees are awarded in BIOLOGICAL SCIENCE (biology/biological science), BUSINESS (accounting, management science, and recreation and leisure services), COMMUNICATIONS AND THE ARTS (art, communications technology, dramatic arts, English, German, journalism, music, music performance, and Spanish), COMPUTER AND PHYSICAL SCIENCE (chemistry, computer science, earth science, mathematics, and physics), EDUCATION (art, elementary, music, physical, secondary, and special), HEALTH PROFESSIONS (dental hygiene, health care administration, medical technology, physician's assistant, and speech pathology/audiology), SOCIAL SCIENCE (addiction studies, American Indian studies, anthropology, criminal justice, economics, French studies, history, international studies, liberal arts/general studies, philosophy, political science/government, psychology, social work, and sociology). Business, biology, and chemistry are the strongest academically. Business, biology, and elementary education are the largest.

Required: Students must complete 128 hours with a minimum GPA of 2.0. At least 32 hours must be at the 300/400 level. All students should complete 9 hours of interdisciplinary course work, 6 hours each in composition, humanities, social science, natural science, and multicultural diversity, 1 hour in fine arts, and a computer literacy course.

Special: USD offers internships, study abroad in 8 countries, and work-study programs. B.A.-B.S. degrees in 33 majors, a student-designed liberal studies major, dual majors, nondegree study, and pass/fail options are available. The Arts Outreach program provides arts activities and noncredit classes. There are 16 national honor societies, including Phi Beta Kappa, and a freshman honors program; all departments have honors programs.

Faculty/Classroom: 58% of faculty are male; 42%, female. 95% both teach and do research. Graduate students teach 5% of introductory courses. The average class size in an introductory lecture is 41; in a laboratory, 21; and in a regular course, 23.

Admissions: 86% of the 2003-2004 applicants were accepted. The SAT I scores for the 2003-2004 freshman class were: Verbal--15% below 500, 44% between 500 and 599, 35% between 600 and 700, and 6% above 700; Math--21% below 500, 48% between 500 and 599, 25% between 600 and 700, and 6% above 700. The ACT scores were 36% below 21, 24% between 21 and 23, 25% between 24 and 26, 8% between 27 and 28, and 7% above 28. 31% of the current freshmen were in the top fifth of their class; 49% were in the top two fifths. There were 4 National Merit finalists. 76 freshmen graduated first in their class.

Requirements: The ACT is required. In addition, applicants must have earned a 2.0 GPA in 4 years of English, 3 years each of lab science, math, and social studies, and 1 semester of fine arts. They must also rank in the top 60% of their graduating class, have an ACT score of 18, or have a high school GPA of 2.6. AP and CLEP credits are accepted.

Procedure: Freshmen are admitted fall, spring, and summer. Entrance exams should be taken prior to enrollment. There is a deferred admissions plan and a rolling admissions plan. Application deadlines are open. The fall 2003 application fee was $20. Notification is sent on a rolling basis within 1 week. Applications are accepted on-line through the university's web site.

Transfer: 686 transfer students enrolled in 2002-2003. Applicants should have a minimum college GPA of 2.0 and be in good standing at their previous school. 30 credits of 128 required for the bachelor's degree must be completed at USD.

Visiting: There are regularly scheduled orientations for prospective students, including an introductory session with an admission counselor, academic department visits, a campus tour with a student guide and any other requested units. There are guides for informal visits and visitors may sit in on classes and stay overnight. To schedule a visit, contact the Admissions Office at *admiss@usd.edu*.

Financial Aid: In 2003-2004, 93% of all full-time freshmen and 88% of continuing full-time students received some form of financial aid. 92% of full-time freshmen and 88% of continuing full-time students received need-based aid. The average freshman award was $5525. Need-based scholarships or need-based grants averaged $1580; need-based self-help aid (loans and jobs) averaged $3982; non-need-based athletic scholarships averaged $3106; and other non-need-based awards and non-need-based scholarships averaged $3909. The above figures exclude plus loans, athletic awards, and tuition benefits. The average financial indebtedness of the 2003 graduate was $18,810. The FAFSA is required. The priority date for freshman financial aid applications for fall entry is March 15.

International Students: There are 68 international students enrolled. They must score 550 on the written TOEFL or 213 on the electronic version.

Computers: The mainframe is a Sun Fire 280R. Students have access to a set of UNIX-based PCs that provide Internet access. There are 50 labs with more than 800 computers available for student use. All students may access the system 24 hours a day for some labs, regular working hours for others. There are no time limits and no fees. It is recommended that students in nursing have personal computers. Gateway is recommended.

Graduates: From July 1, 2002 to June 30, 2003, 699 bachelor's degrees were awarded. The most popular majors were business management (16%), psychology (10%), and elementary education (7%). In an average class, 2% graduate in 3 years or less, 26% graduate in 4 years or less, 47% graduate in 5 years or less, and 51% graduate in 6 years or less. 112 companies recruited on campus in 2002-2003. Of the 2002 graduating class, 25% were enrolled in graduate school within 6 months of graduation and 78% were employed.

Admissions Contact: Paula Tacke, Director of Admissions.
E-mail: *admiss@usd.edu* Web: *http://www.usd.edu*

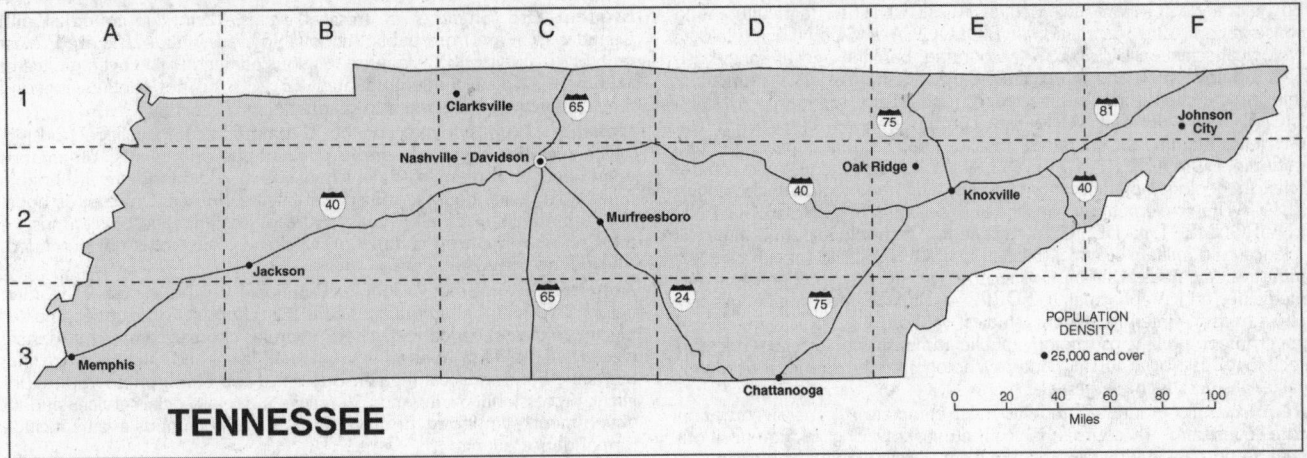

TENNESSEE

AQUINAS COLLEGE
C-2
Nashville, TN 37205   (615) 297-7545 ext. 428; Fax: (615) 279-3893

Full-time: 520 men and women	**Faculty:** 29
Part-time: none	**Ph.D.s:** 20%
Graduate: none	**Student/Faculty:** 18 to 1
Year: semesters, summer session	**Tuition:** $10,660
Application Deadline: open	**Room & Board:** n/app
Freshman Class: n/av	
ACT: required	**LESS COMPETITIVE**

Aquinas College is a private Catholic institution offering an academically challenging liberal arts and sciences curriculum. Some figures in the above capsule and in this profile are approximate. In addition to regional accreditation, the college has baccalaureate program accreditation with NLN. The library contains 45,762 volumes, 140,602 microform items, and 1820 audio/video tapes/CDs, and subscribes to 301 periodicals. Computerized library services include the card catalog, interlibrary loans, and database searching. Special learning facilities include a learning resource center. The 92-acre campus is in an urban area in the western section of metropolitan Nashville. There are 4 buildings.

Programs of Study: The college confers B.A., B.B.A., and B.S.N. degrees. Associate degrees are also awarded. Bachelor's degrees are awarded in BUSINESS (business administration and management), EDUCATION (elementary), HEALTH PROFESSIONS (nursing), SOCIAL SCIENCE (liberal arts/general studies). Nursing is the largest.

Required: All students must complete 124 to 134 credit hours, including the liberal arts core, and must maintain a minimum GPA of 2.0 in the B.S.N., A.S.N., and A.A. programs, 2.2 in the B.B.A. program, and 2.6 in the B.A. programs.

Special: There is a Weekend College for working adult students and evening courses are also offered. There is 1 national honor society.

Faculty/Classroom: 25% of faculty are male; 75%, female. All teach undergraduates. The average class size in an introductory lecture is 25; in a laboratory, 20; and in a regular course, 25.

Requirements: The ACT is required. In addition, the GED is accepted. An essay and an interview are required for some majors. A GPA of 2.0 is required. AP and CLEP credits are accepted.

Procedure: Freshmen are admitted to all sessions. Application deadlines are open. Applications are accepted on-line through the college's web site. The fall 2003 application fee was $10. Notification is sent on a rolling basis.

Transfer: Transfer applicants must have a 2.0 GPA in previous college work. 32 of 124 credits required for the bachelor's degree must be completed at the college.

Visiting: There are regularly scheduled orientations for prospective students, including campus tours and information on admissions, financial aid, student life, and degree programs. There are guides for informal visits and visitors may sit in on classes. To schedule a visit, contact Sarah Curtis at (615) 297-7545, ext. 436.

Financial Aid: The college is a member of CSS. The FAFSA and the college's own financial statement are required. Check with the school for current deadlines.

International Students: They must score 525 on the written TOEFL.

Computers: The library and the computer lab together contain 40 computers available for student use. Internet access is available. All students may access the system all hours of college operation. There are no time limits. The fee is $40.

Admissions Contact: Diane C. LeJeune, Director of Admissions. E-mail: *lejeuned@aquinas-tn.edu* Web: *www.aquinas-tn.edu.*

AUSTIN PEAY STATE UNIVERSITY
C-2
Clarksville, TN 37040   (931) 221-7661
(800) 844-2778; Fax: (931) 221-5994

Full-time: 1680 men, 2865 women	**Faculty:** 274; IIA, --$
Part-time: 1340 men, 1100 women	**Ph.D.s:** 91%
Graduate: 105 men, 350 women	**Student/Faculty:** 17 to 1
Year: semesters, summer session	**Tuition:** $4004 ($11,936)
Application Deadline: see profile	**Room & Board:** $4092
Freshman Class: n/av	
SAT I or ACT: required	**LESS COMPETITIVE**

Austin Peay State University, established in 1927, is a public institution offering undergraduate degrees in the liberal arts and sciences and professional preparation. Figures in the above capsule and in this profile are approximate. There are 5 undergraduate schools and 1 graduate school. In addition to regional accreditation, APSU has baccalaureate program accreditation with CSWE, NASAD, NASM, NCATE, and NLN. The library contains 196,826 volumes, 520,732 microform items, and 6844 audio/video tapes/CDs, and subscribes to 1736 periodicals. Computerized library services include the card catalog, interlibrary loans, and database searching. Special learning facilities include a learning resource center, art gallery, and radio station. The 150-acre campus is in an urban area 47 miles from Nashville. Including any residence halls, there are 42 buildings.

Student Life: 85% of undergraduates are from Tennessee. Students are from 29 states, 14 foreign countries, and Canada. 90% are from public schools. 68% are white; 18% African American. The average age of freshmen is 20; all undergraduates, 26. 36% do not continue beyond their first year; 32% remain to graduate.

Housing: 1100 students can be accommodated in college housing, which includes single-sex and coed dorms, on-campus apartments, and married-student housing. In addition, there are honors houses. On-campus housing is available on a first-come, first-served basis. 81% of students commute. Alcohol is not permitted. All students may keep cars.

Activities: 10% of men belong to 7 national fraternities; 3% of women belong to 7 national sororities. There are 80 groups on campus, including art, band, cheerleading, choir, chorus, debate, drama, ethnic, gay, honors, international, jazz band, literary magazine, marching band, newspaper, orchestra, pep band, political, professional, radio and TV, religious, social, social service, and student government. Popular campus events include Parents Day and Jazz Festival.

Sports: There are 6 intercollegiate sports for men and 8 for women, and 11 intramural sports for men and 11 for women. Facilities include a gym, an exercise room, a jogging fitness trail, and a weight room.

Disabled Students: 95% of the campus is accessible. Wheelchair ramps, elevators, special parking, specially equipped rest rooms, special class scheduling, lowered drinking fountains, and lowered telephones are available.

Services: There is a reader service for the blind and remedial math, reading, and writing. The university provides help with academic, learning, and test-taking problems.

Campus Safety and Security: Measures include 24-hour foot and vehicle patrol, security escort services, shuttle buses, and informal discussions. There are pamphlets/posters/films, emergency telephones, and lighted pathways/sidewalks.

Programs of Study: APSU confers B.A., B.S., B.B.A., B.F.A., B.S.Ed., and B.S.N. degrees. Associate and master's degrees are also awarded. Bachelor's degrees are awarded in AGRICULTURE (agriculture and conservation and regulation), BIOLOGICAL SCIENCE (biology/biological science), BUSINESS (accounting, banking and finance, business administration and management, management science, marketing/retailing/merchandising, and recreation and leisure services), COMMUNICATIONS AND THE ARTS (art, communications, English, French, German, languages, literature, music, Spanish, and speech/debate/rhetoric), COMPUTER AND PHYSICAL SCIENCE (chemistry, computer science, geology, mathematics, physics, and radiological technology), EDUCATION (elementary, health, and special), ENGINEERING AND ENVIRONMENTAL DESIGN (engineering technology, environmental science, and military science), HEALTH PROFESSIONS (health care administration, medical laboratory technology, nursing, predentistry, premedicine, and prepharmacy), SOCIAL SCIENCE (economics, geography, history, interdisciplinary studies, philosophy, political science/government, prelaw, psychology, public administration, social work, and sociology). Biology, nursing, and psychology are the strongest academically. Business is the largest.

Required: To graduate, students must complete a general education core consisting of courses in communications/English composition, health and personal development, history, foreign language/humanities, science/math, and social science. Students must complete a total of 128 credits, at least 45 of which must be upper divisional, and have a minimum 2.0 GPA. Courses in phys ed and computer literacy are required.

Special: APSU offers cooperative programs in nuclear medicine and radiological technology with Vanderbilt University. Work-study programs and dual majors are available. Credit may be granted for military experience. Pass/fail grading options are available. There are 21 national honor societies and a freshman honors program.

Faculty/Classroom: 59% of faculty are male; 41%, female. All teach undergraduates. No introductory courses are taught by graduate students. The average class size in an introductory lecture is 24; in a laboratory, 16; and in a regular course, 25.

Requirements: The SAT I or ACT is required. In addition, applicants must be graduates of an accredited secondary school or have a GED. 14 academic units are required, including 4 units of English, 2 units each of algebra, natural science, and a foreign language, and 1 unit each of visual and/or performing arts, geometry, social studies, and U.S. history. Applicants who do not meet these requirements may be considered for admission. A GPA of 2.75 is required. AP and CLEP credits are accepted.

Procedure: Freshmen are admitted to all sessions. There is an early admissions plan. There is a rolling admissions plan. Applications should be filed by July 30 for fall entry, along with a $15 application fee. Notification is sent on a rolling basis. Applications are accepted on-line through the school's web site.

Transfer: Applicants must have a 2.0 GPA. Grades of D or better will transfer for credit. Application deadlines are the same as those for freshmen. 24 of 128 credits required for the bachelor's degree must be completed at APSU.

Visiting: There are regularly scheduled orientations for prospective students. There are guides for informal visits. To schedule a visit, contact the Admissions Office.

Financial Aid: The FFS is required. Tennessee residents should submit the Tennessee edition of the FFS.

International Students: They must score 500 on the written TOEFL.

Computers: The mainframe is a DEC VAX. All students may access the system. There are no time limits and no fees.

Admissions Contact: Charles McCorkle, Director of Admissions. A video is available. E-mail: *admissions@apsu01.apsu.edu* Web: *www.apsu.edu*

BELMONT UNIVERSITY
Nashville, TN 37212-3757

C-2

(615) 460-6785
(800) 56E-NROL; Fax: (615) 460-5434

Full-time: 1068 men, 1581 women	**Faculty:** 204; IIA, -$
Part-time: 111 men, 229 women	**Ph.D.s:** 73%
Graduate: 215 men, 425 women	**Student/Faculty:** 13 to 1
Year: semesters, summer session	**Tuition:** $15,954
Application Deadline: August 1	**Room & Board:** $6032
Freshman Class: 1626 applied, 1212 accepted, 603 enrolled	
SAT I Verbal/Math: 568/568	**ACT:** 25 **VERY COMPETITIVE**

Belmont University, founded in 1890, is a private, Christian liberal arts university affiliated with the Tennessee Baptist Convention. There are 7 undergraduate and 4 graduate schools. In addition to regional accreditation, Belmont has baccalaureate program accreditation with CSWE, NASM, NCATE, and NLN. The library contains 183,417 volumes, 18,150 microform items, and 25,248 audio/video tapes/CDs, and subscribes to 1430 periodicals. Computerized library services include the card catalog, interlibrary loans, database searching, and Internet access.

Special learning facilities include a learning resource center, art gallery, radio station, TV station, and 19th-century antebellum mansion. The 62-acre campus is in an urban area in Nashville. Including any residence halls, there are 28 buildings.

Student Life: Students are from 50 states, 12 foreign countries, and Canada. 77% are from public schools. 90% are white. 75% are Protestant; 6% Catholic; 33% claim no religious affiliation. The average age of freshmen is 18; all undergraduates, 22. 23% do not continue beyond their first year; 54% remain to graduate.

Housing: 1703 students can be accommodated in college housing, which includes single-sex dorms, on-campus apartments, off-campus apartments, and married-student housing. In addition, there are honors houses, language houses, and special-interest houses. On-campus housing is guaranteed for all 4 years. 50% of students live on campus; of those, 30% remain on campus on weekends. Alcohol is not permitted. All students may keep cars.

Activities: 3% of men belong to 2 national fraternities; 3% of women belong to 3 national sororities. There are 63 groups on campus, including art, band, cheerleading, choir, chorale, chorus, computers, dance, drama, ethnic, film, honors, international, jazz band, literary magazine, marching band, musical theater, orchestra, pep band, photography, political, professional, radio and TV, religious, social, social service, student government, symphony, and yearbook. Popular campus events include formal dance events.

Sports: Facilities include an event center and a student center.

Disabled Students: 99% of the campus is accessible. Wheelchair ramps, elevators, special parking, specially equipped rest rooms, special class scheduling, and lowered drinking fountains are available.

Services: Counseling and information services are available, as is tutoring in some subjects. There is remedial math, reading, and writing. Writing and computer labs are available.

Campus Safety and Security: Measures include 24-hour foot and vehicle patrol, self-defense education, security escort services, and shuttle buses. There are informal discussions, pamphlets/posters/films, emergency telephones, and lighted pathways/sidewalks.

Programs of Study: Belmont confers B.A., B.S., B.B.A., B.F.A., B.M., and B.S.N. degrees. Master's degrees are also awarded. Bachelor's degrees are awarded in BIOLOGICAL SCIENCE (biology/biological science), BUSINESS (accounting, business administration and management, hotel/motel and restaurant management, management science, and marketing/retailing/merchandising), COMMUNICATIONS AND THE ARTS (communications, English, French, music, music business management, and music performance), COMPUTER AND PHYSICAL SCIENCE (chemistry, computer science, mathematics, and physics), EDUCATION (elementary, physical, and science), HEALTH PROFESSIONS (nursing), SOCIAL SCIENCE (economics, history, liberal arts/general studies, philosophy, political science/government, psychology, religion, and social work). Music, business, and humanities are the strongest academically. Business, music, nursing, and music business management are the largest.

Required: All students must complete at least 128 hours with a C average, including 22 to 24 hours in the major field. B.A. candidates are required to pursue a minor field. All programs except the B.B.A. require a core curriculum, which includes courses in language and literature, humanities (including religion), social sciences, science, math, and phys ed.

Special: Belmont offers study abroad, student-designed majors, and dual majors in math, physics, and chemistry. Dual degree programs are available with Auburn University and the University of Tennessee at Knoxville. Programs require 3 years of study at Belmont followed by 2 years at the other institution. There are 11 national honor societies, a freshman honors program, and 3 departmental honors programs.

Faculty/Classroom: 54% of faculty are male; 46%, female. All teach undergraduates, 2% do research, and 2% do both. No introductory courses are taught by graduate students. The average class size in an introductory lecture is 25; in a laboratory, 24; and in a regular course, 25.

Admissions: 75% of the 2003-2004 applicants were accepted. The SAT I scores for the 2003-2004 freshman class were: Verbal--15% below 500, 51% between 500 and 599, 32% between 600 and 700, and 2% above 700; Math--18% below 500, 46% between 500 and 599, 31% between 600 and 700, and 6% above 700. The ACT scores were 11% below 21, 26% between 21 and 23, 34% between 24 and 26, 13% between 27 and 28, and 16% above 28. 60% of the current freshmen were in the top fifth of their class; 80% were in the top two fifths. 22 freshmen graduated first in their class.

Requirements: The ACT is required and the SAT I is recommended. The university expects a composite score of at least 21 on the ACT and 1000 on the SAT I. In addition, applicants should be high school graduates or hold the GED. Secondary preparation should include 4 units of English, 3 of math, and 2 each of a foreign language, history, science, and social studies. Potential music majors must audition. Belmont requires applicants to be in the upper 50% of their class. A GPA of 3.0 is required. AP and CLEP credits are accepted. Important factors in the admissions decision are advanced placement or honor courses, recommendations by school officials, and evidence of special talent.

Procedure: Freshmen are admitted fall, spring, and summer. Entrance exams should be taken during the junior or senior year. There is an early admissions plan. Applications should be filed by August 1 for fall entry and December 1 for spring entry. Notification is sent on a rolling basis. The fall 2003 application fee was $35. Applications are accepted on computer disk and on-line through CollegeView, ExPAN, and *www.belmont.edu-admissions.*.

Transfer: 417 transfer students enrolled in 2002-2003. Applicants should present an above average GPA in previous college work and be able to meet freshman entrance requirements. Those with fewer than 64 credit hours must also submit SAT I or ACT scores. 32 of 128 credits required for the bachelor's degree must be completed at Belmont.

Visiting: There are regularly scheduled orientations for prospective students, consisting of a 2-day program in summer and a 4-day program right before classes begin. There are guides for informal visits and visitors may sit in on classes and stay overnight. To schedule a visit, contact the Admissions Office at (615) 460-6785 or *buadmissions@belmont.edu.*

Financial Aid: In 2003-2004, 72% of all full-time freshmen and 70% of continuing full-time students received some form of financial aid. 46% of full-time freshmen and 52% of continuing full-time students received need-based aid. The average freshman award was $5237. Need-based scholarships or need-based grants averaged $1229 ($7187 maximum); need-based self-help aid (loans and jobs) averaged $1173 ($3214 maximum); non-need-based athletic scholarships averaged $5309 ($10,697 maximum); and other non-need-based awards and non-need-based scholarships averaged $4300 ($6400 maximum). 17% of undergraduates work part time. Average annual earnings from campus work are $2500. The average financial indebtedness of the 2003 graduate was $15,954. Belmont is a member of CSS. The FAFSA is required. The deadline for filing freshman financial aid applications for fall entry is March 1.

International Students: There are 37 international students enrolled. They must score 500 on the written TOEFL and also take the SAT I or the ACT, scoring 1000 on the SAT I.

Computers: The mainframe is a Sun 3500 server. 5 computer labs across campus provide students with access to the campus network, applications, and the Internet. Residence halls are wired for computer access with student-provided computers. All students may access the system. There are no time limits and no fees.

Graduates: From July 1, 2002 to June 30, 2003, 527 bachelor's degrees were awarded. The most popular majors were music business management (22%), business administration (18%), and liberal arts (8%). In an average class, 2% graduate in 3 years or less, 37% graduate in 4 years or less, 53% graduate in 5 years or less, and 54% graduate in 6 years or less. 83 companies recruited on campus in 2002-2003. Of the 2002 graduating class, 31% were enrolled in graduate school within 6 months of graduation and 35% were employed.

Admissions Contact: Kathryn H. Baugher, Dean of Enrollment Services. A video is available. E-mail: *buadmission@belmont.edu*
Web: *www.belmont@edu*

BETHEL COLLEGE
McKenzie, TN 38201   B-3

Full-time: 350 men, 385 women	Faculty: 35; IIB, --$
Part-time: 40 men, 60 women	Ph.D.s: 67%
Graduate: 45 men, 60 women	Student/Faculty: 21 to 1
Year: semesters, summer session	Tuition: $8430
Application Deadline: see profile	Room & Board: $4550
Freshman Class: n/av	
SAT I or ACT: required	COMPETITIVE

Bethel College, established in 1842, is a private institution affiliated with the Cumberland Presbyterian Church offering undergraduate degrees through its divisions of humanities, natural sciences, social sciences, education, and health science. Figures in the above capsule and in this profile are approximate. The library contains 79,164 volumes, 185 microform items, and 2166 audio/video tapes/CDs, and subscribes to 1208 periodicals. Computerized library services include the card catalog, interlibrary loans, and database searching. Special learning facilities include a learning resource center. The 100-acre campus is in a small town 120 miles northeast of Memphis. Including any residence halls, there are 10 buildings.

Student Life: 79% of undergraduates are from Tennessee. Students are from 21 states, 2 foreign countries, and Canada. 99% are from public schools. 78% are white; 19% African American. 72% are Protestant; 25% claim no religious affiliation. The average age of freshmen is 18; all undergraduates, 28. 46% do not continue beyond their first year; 25% remain to graduate.

Housing: 290 students can be accommodated in college housing, which includes single-sex and coed dorms. On-campus housing is guaranteed for the freshman year only and is available on a first-come, first-served basis. 55% of students commute. Alcohol is not permitted. All students may keep cars.

Activities: 50% of men belong to 5 local fraternities; 50% of women belong to 5 local sororities. There are 25 groups on campus, including art, cheerleading, choir, chorus, drama, honors, musical theater, newspaper, pep band, political, professional, religious, social, student government, and yearbook.

Sports: There are 8 intercollegiate sports for men and 7 for women, and 9 intramural sports for men and 8 for women. Facilities include a gym with a heated indoor pool and weight room, a field house, and a student center with pool tables, Ping-Pong tables, and other such equipment. There is also a baseball field and beach volleyball and tennis courts.

Disabled Students: 75% of the campus is accessible. Wheelchair ramps, special parking, specially equipped rest rooms, special class scheduling, lowered drinking fountains, and lowered telephones are available.

Services: Counseling and information services are available, as is tutoring in every subject. There is remedial math, reading, and writing. Tutoring is available free of charge to students.

Campus Safety and Security: Measures include informal discussions, pamphlets/posters/films, lighted pathways/sidewalks, and a security guard at night.

Programs of Study: Bethel confers B.A. and B.S. degrees. Master's degrees are also awarded. Bachelor's degrees are awarded in BIOLOGICAL SCIENCE (biology/biological science and zoology), BUSINESS (business administration and management and management science), COMMUNICATIONS AND THE ARTS (English), COMPUTER AND PHYSICAL SCIENCE (chemistry and mathematics), EDUCATION (early childhood, education of the exceptional child, health, and physical), ENGINEERING AND ENVIRONMENTAL DESIGN (preengineering), SOCIAL SCIENCE (child psychology/development, history, human services, liberal arts/general studies, physical fitness/movement, psychology, and sociology). Education, organizational management, and biology are the strongest academically. Education and organizational management are the largest.

Required: Requirements for graduation include courses in English, Western literature and arts, history, lab science, math, phys ed, and religion. Students must complete 128 to 132 hours with a minimum GPA of 2.0. A thesis is required in some majors.

Special: Bethel offers evening classes for adults, in-service training for teachers, off-site classes, an accelerated degree program in organizational management, student-designed majors, a 3-2 engineering program with Tennessee Technical University, internships, work-study, nondegree study, a pass/fail option, and portfolio credit for prior learning and work experience. There is 1 national honor society and a freshman honors program.

Faculty/Classroom: 65% of faculty are male; 35%, female. All teach undergraduates, 5% do research, and 5% do both. No introductory courses are taught by graduate students. The average class size in an introductory lecture is 17; in a laboratory, 20; and in a regular course, 14.

Requirements: The SAT I or ACT is required. In addition, applicants must graduate from an accredited secondary school. Those ranking in the upper half of their class or scoring at least 16 on the ACT or 800 on the SAT I are granted regular acceptance. Other applicants may be admitted conditionally. Other factors in the admission procedure are standardized test scores, an interview, evidence of special talent, and personality. A GPA of 2.5 is required. AP and CLEP credits are accepted. Important factors in the admissions decision are advanced placement or honor courses, leadership record, and parents or siblings attending the school.

Procedure: Freshmen are admitted to all sessions. Entrance exams should be taken prior to enrollment, preferably by fall of the senior year. There is a rolling admissions plan. The fall 2003 application fee was $30. Check with the school for current deadines and fee. Notification is sent on a rolling basis.

Transfer: Applicants must meet the GPA requirements for the number of hours they previously earned. Up to 68 hours may be transferred from community or junior colleges. Students with fewer than 12 semester hours must submit high school transcripts and ACT or SAT I scores and take Bethel's placement test. 32 of 128 credits required for the bachelor's degree must be completed at Bethel.

Visiting: There are regularly scheduled orientations for prospective students. Students receive information about the college, dorms, and the ThinkPad program; they meet advisers, register for classes, and meet with the financial aid and business office. There are guides for informal visits and visitors may sit in on classes and stay overnight. To schedule a visit, contact the Admissions Office.

Financial Aid: In a recent year, 98% of all full-time students received some form of financial aid. 92% of full-time freshmen and 90% of continuing full-time students received need-based aid. The average freshman award was $12,538. 25% of undergraduates work part time. Average annual earnings from campus work are $1000. The FAFSA and the college's own financial statement are required. Check with the school for current deadlines.

International Students: There were 8 international students enrolled in a recent year. The school actively recruits these students. It is suggested that students take the TOEFL and score 500 or higher, and also take the SAT I or the ACT.

Computers: Bethel College is part of the ThinkPad University Program. Each full-time student and faculty member receives an IBM ThinkPad (laptop computer) as part of full-time tuition. All students may access the system Connections to the campus LAN and the Internet are available throughout campus and in each dorm room. There are no time limits and no fees. All students are required to have personal computers.

Graduates: In a recent year, 146 bachelor's degrees were awarded. The most popular majors were organizational management (82%), education (8%), and biology (4%). In an average class, 14% graduate in 4 years or less, 17% graduate in 5 years or less, and 19% graduate in 6 years or less. Of a recent graduating class, 21% were enrolled in graduate school within 6 months of graduation and 70% were employed.

Admissions Contact: Tina Hodges, Director od Admissions.
E-mail: *admissions@bethel-college.edu* Web: *www.bethel-college.edu*

BRYAN COLLEGE
Dayton, TN 37321-7000

D-3
(423) 775-7204
(800) 277-9522; Fax: (423) 775-7199

Full-time: 558 men and women	**Faculty:** 30; IIB, --$
Part-time: 30 men and women	**Ph.D.s:** 90%
Graduate: none	**Student/Faculty:** 19 to 1
Year: semesters, summer session	**Tuition:** $13,500
Application Deadline: open	**Room & Board:** $4400
Freshman Class: n/av	
SAT I or ACT: required	**VERY COMPETITIVE**

Bryan College, founded in 1930, is a private, nonprofit, Christian institution that is evangelical and interdenominational. Its emphases are on the liberal arts, business, health science, fine arts, Bible and religious studies, music, and teacher preparation. The library contains 90,000 volumes, 13,489 microform items, and 3015 audio/video tapes/CDs, and subscribes to 700 periodicals. Computerized library services include the card catalog, interlibrary loans, and database searching. Special learning facilities include a museum of natural science. The 130-acre campus is in a small town 40 miles north of Chattanooga. Including any residence halls, there are 28 buildings.

Student Life: 65% of undergraduates are from out of state, mostly the South. Students are from 33 states, 10 foreign countries, and Canada. 40% are from public schools. 94% are white. Most are Protestant. The average age of freshmen is 18; all undergraduates, 20. 24% do not continue beyond their first year; 55% remain to graduate.

Housing: 551 students can be accommodated in college housing, which includes single-sex dorms and married-student housing. On-campus housing is guaranteed for all 4 years. 80% of students live on campus; of those, 75% remain on campus on weekends. Alcohol is not permitted. All students may keep cars.

Activities: There are no fraternities or sororities. There are 17 groups on campus, including art, cheerleading, choir, chorale, computers, drama, honors, international, literary magazine, musical theater, newspaper, orchestra, pep band, photography, religious, social, social service, student government, and yearbook. Popular campus events include a fine arts series.

Sports: There are 3 intercollegiate sports for men and 4 for women, and 6 intramural sports for men and 6 for women. Facilities include a 1200-seat gym, soccer fields, a baseball field, an outdoor swimming pool, and 4 tennis courts.

Disabled Students: All of the campus is accessible. Wheelchair ramps, elevators, special parking, specially equipped rest rooms, and lowered drinking fountains are available.

Services: Counseling and information services are available, as is tutoring in some subjects, including math and English. There is remedial math, reading, and writing.

Campus Safety and Security: Measures include self-defense education, security escort services, informal discussions, and pamphlets/posters/films. There are lighted pathways/sidewalks and a night security patrol.

Programs of Study: Bryan confers B.A. and B.S. degrees. Associate degrees are also awarded. Bachelor's degrees are awarded in BIOLOGICAL SCIENCE (biology/biological science), BUSINESS (business administration and management), COMMUNICATIONS AND THE ARTS (communications, English, music, and Spanish), COMPUTER AND PHYSICAL SCIENCE (computer science and mathematics), EDUCATION (athletic training, elementary, physical, and science), HEALTH PROFESSIONS (exercise science), SOCIAL SCIENCE (Christian studies, history, liberal arts/general studies, psychology, and religion).

Required: To graduate, students must complete 124 semester hours, with a minimum of 30 in the major, and maintain a GPA of at least 2.0. Distribution requirements include 16 semester hours in the Bible, 9 in communications, 7 each in personal development and natural science, and 6 each in the humanities and social science. Specific courses that must be taken include 7 semester hours in science, 6 hours each in freshman English, a foreign language, and history of Western civilization, and 3 each in speech, general psychology, introduction to literature, fine arts, and phys ed. In addition, math and English proficiency must be met; a comprehensive exam in the major is also required.

Special: Special academic programs include practicums in business and psychology, and psychology internships. An American Studies Program in Washington and a study-abroad Latin American Studies Program are offered through the Christian College Coalition. A dual major in Christian education and church music is available. There is a freshman honors program.

Faculty/Classroom: 64% of faculty are male; 36%, female. All teach undergraduates. The average class size in an introductory lecture is 27; in a laboratory, 13; and in a regular course, 16.

Requirements: The SAT I or ACT is required, with the ACT preferred. Clear admission is granted to applicants who have graduated from an approved high school and who have a minimum GPA of 2.5 with a minimum composite score of 18 on the ACT or 860 on the SAT I; clear admission is also granted to applicants with a minimum GPA of 2.0 and a composite score of 20 on the ACT or 920 on the SAT I. The high school record should include a minimum of 18 academic credits with a recommended distribution of 4 units of English, 3 each of math, science, and social science/humanities, and 2 of a foreign language. The GED is also accepted. References are required, and an interview is recommended. AP and CLEP credits are accepted. Important factors in the admissions decision are parents or siblings attending the school, recommendations by alumni, and recommendations by school officials.

Procedure: Freshmen are admitted fall and spring. Entrance exams should be taken before the fall of the senior year in high school. There are early admissions and deferred admissions plans. Application deadlines are open. Application fee is $30. Notification is sent on a rolling basis. A waiting list is an active part of the admissions procedure. Applications are accepted on-line through the school's web site.

Transfer: 31 transfer students enrolled in a recent year. Applicants need a minimum GPA of 2.0. 31 of 124 credits required for the bachelor's degree must be completed at Bryan.

Visiting: There are regularly scheduled orientations for prospective students, consisting of college visitation weekends, which include a tour of the campus, sitting in on classes and chapel, meeting with professors in the area of academic interest, staying with current students in residence halls, and eating meals in the dining room. There are guides for informal visits and visitors may sit in on classes and stay overnight. To schedule a visit, contact Jody Cheon, Admissions Counselor, at (423) 775-7211 or *cheonjo@bryan.edu*.

Financial Aid: In a recent year, 98% of all full-time freshmen and 94% of continuing full-time students received some form of financial aid. 65% of full-time freshmen and 56% of continuing full-time students received need-based aid. The average freshman award was $9373. 55% of undergraduates work part time. Average annual earnings from campus work are $1500. The average financial indebtedness of a recent year's graduate was $14,500. The FAFSA and the college's own financial statement are required. The deadline for filing freshman financial aid applications for fall entry is May 1.

International Students: There were 13 international students enrolled in a recent year. They must score 500 on the written TOEFL and also take the ACT.

Computers: There are PCs available in computer labs in both residence halls and academic areas. Residence hall rooms have campus network hookups available. All students may access the system at all times. There are no time limits and no fees.

Graduates: In a recent year, 102 bachelor's degrees were awarded. In an average class, 49% graduate in 4 years or less, 50% graduate in 5 years or less, and 53% graduate in 6 years or less.

Admissions Contact: Mark Cruver, Dean of Admissions. A video is available. E-mail: *admiss@bryan.edu* Web: *www.bryan.edu*

CARSON-NEWMAN COLLEGE
Jefferson City, TN 37760

E-2
(865) 471-2000
(800) 678-9061; Fax: (865) 471-3502

Full-time: 813 men, 972 women	**Faculty:** 122; IIB, --$
Part-time: 53 men, 104 women	**Ph.D.s:** 65%
Graduate: 44 men, 129 women	**Student/Faculty:** 15 to 1
Year: semesters, summer session	**Tuition:** $13,260
Application Deadline: August 15	**Room & Board:** $3500
Freshman Class: 1153 applied, 1014 accepted, 366 enrolled	
ACT: 22	**COMPETITIVE**

Carson-Newman College, founded in 1851, is a private liberal arts college affiliated with the Tennessee Baptist Convention. In addition to regional accreditation, Carson-Newman has baccalaureate program accreditation with ADA, AHEA, NASAD, NASM, NCATE, and NLN. The library contains 300,000 volumes, 221,960 microform items, and 15,000 audio/video tapes/CDs, and subscribes to 2000 periodicals. Computerized library services include the card catalog, interlibrary loans, and database searching. Special learning facilities include a learning resource center, art gallery, natural history museum, radio station, and TV station. The 100-acre campus is in a small town 27 miles northeast of Knoxville. Including any residence halls, there are 27 buildings.

Student Life: 67% of undergraduates are from Tennessee. Students are from 36 states and 13 foreign countries. 92% are from public schools. 87% are white. 84% are Protestant; 8% claim no religious affiliation. The average age of freshmen is 18; all undergraduates, 22. 25% do not continue beyond their first year; 57% remain to graduate.

Housing: 1430 students can be accommodated in college housing, which includes single-sex dorms, on-campus apartments, and married-student housing. In addition, there are honors houses. On-campus housing is guaranteed for all 4 years. 50% of students live on campus; of those, 50% remain on campus on weekends. Alcohol is not permitted. All students may keep cars.

Activities: 20% of men belong to 2 local and 1 national fraternity; 20% of women belong to 2 local and 1 national sorority. There are 55 groups on campus, including art, band, cheerleading, chess, choir, chorale, chorus, computers, dance, debate, drama, drill team, ethnic, film, forensics, honors, international, jazz band, literary magazine, marching band, musical theater, newspaper, orchestra, pep band, photography, political, professional, radio and TV, religious, social, social service, student government, and yearbook. Popular campus events include Spring Fest, Fall Formal, and Honors Convocation.

Sports: There are 10 intercollegiate sports for men and 6 for women, and 40 intramural sports for men and 40 for women. Facilities include a gym, a football stadium, soccer, baseball, softball, and intramural fields, a pool, and a student center with 3 racquetball courts, 3 gyms, a weight room, an Olympic-size pool, a Jacuzzi, and an outdoor café.

Disabled Students: 10% of the campus is accessible. Wheelchair ramps, elevators, special parking, and special class scheduling are available.

Services: Counseling and information services are available, as is tutoring in most subjects, including English, math, and science. There is remedial math, reading, and writing.

Campus Safety and Security: Measures include 24-hour foot and vehicle patrol, self-defense education, security escort services, and informal discussions. There are pamphlets/posters/films and lighted pathways/sidewalks.

Programs of Study: Carson-Newman confers B.A., B.S., B.M., B.S.M., and B.S.N. degrees. Associate and master's degrees are also awarded. Bachelor's degrees are awarded in BIOLOGICAL SCIENCE (biology/biological science), BUSINESS (accounting, business administration and management, and business economics), COMMUNICATIONS AND THE ARTS (communications, English, fine arts, French, languages, music, and Spanish), EDUCATION (art, early childhood, elementary, foreign languages, health, home economics, middle school, music, science, and secondary), HEALTH PROFESSIONS (nursing and physical therapy), SOCIAL SCIENCE (economics, history, philosophy, psychology, religion, social science, and sociology). Nursing, music, and biology are the strongest academically. Communication arts, biology, and business are the largest.

Required: All students must complete 128 credit hours, including Composition I and II, Survey of Old Testament, Survey of New Testament, 15 hours in English and communications, 9 in social sciences, 6 each in religion, humanities, and science, and 3 each in history, literature, and math. The major requires 40 to 48 hours. Students must achieve a minimum GPA of 2.0.

Special: The college offers internships, study in England, France, Japan, Hong Kong, and Spain, a Washington semester, on-campus work-study programs, B.A.-B.S. degrees, dual majors, a general studies degree, student-designed majors, and pass/fail options. Students may receive credit for life, military, or work experience. There is 1 national honor society, a freshman honors program, and 16 departmental honors programs.

Faculty/Classroom: 57% of faculty are male; 43%, female. All teach undergraduates and 40% do research. No introductory courses are taught by graduate students. The average class size in an introductory lecture is 20; in a laboratory, 16; and in a regular course, 17.

Admissions: 88% of the 2003-2004 applicants were accepted. The ACT scores for the 2003-2004 freshman class were: 38% below 21, 26% between 21 and 23, 23% between 24 and 26, 8% between 27 and 28, and 5% above 28. There were 3 National Merit finalists. 10 freshmen graduated first in their class.

Requirements: The SAT I or ACT is required, with a minimum composite score of 19 on the ACT or 920 on the SAT I. In addition, applicants should be graduates of an accredited secondary school. The GED is accepted. 20 academic credits are required, including 4 units of English and 2 units each of history, math, science, and social studies. An essay, a portfolio, an audition, and an interview are recommended. Carson-Newman requires applicants to be in the upper 50% of their class. A GPA of 2.25 is required. AP and CLEP credits are accepted. Important factors in the admissions decision are advanced placement or honor courses, leadership record, and parents or siblings attending the school.

Procedure: Freshmen are admitted to all sessions. Entrance exams should be taken in the fall of the senior year or the spring of the junior year. There is a deferred admissions plan. Applications should be filed by August 15 for fall entry, December 15 for spring entry, and April 15

for summer entry, along with a $25 fee. Notification is sent on a rolling basis. Applications are accepted on-line through CollegeNET.

Transfer: 189 transfer students enrolled in 2002-2003. Transfer students should have a minimum GPA of 2.0. Either the SAT I or the ACT is required if the student has fewer than 32 hours of college credit. An interview is recommended. 32 of 128 credits required for the bachelor's degree must be completed at Carson-Newman.

Visiting: There are regularly scheduled orientations for prospective students, including information sessions, meetings with advisers, and pre-registration. There are guides for informal visits and visitors may sit in on classes and stay overnight. To schedule a visit, contact the Admissions Office.

Financial Aid: In 2003-2004, 92% of all full-time freshmen and 90% of continuing full-time students received some form of financial aid. 75% of full-time freshmen and 70% of continuing full-time students received need-based aid. The average freshman award was $12,500. Need-based scholarships or need-based grants averaged $4300 ($5000 maximum); need-based self-help aid (loans and jobs) averaged $3835 ($6125 maximum); non-need-based athletic scholarships averaged $2000 ($12,500 maximum); and other non-need-based awards and non-need-based scholarships averaged $7500 ($12,500 maximum). 31% of undergraduates work part time. Average annual earnings from campus work are $1500. The average financial indebtedness of the 2003 graduate was $14,800. Carson-Newman is a member of CSS. The FAFSA and the college's own financial statement are required. The deadline for filing freshman financial aid applications for fall entry is March 1.

International Students: The school actively recruits international students. They must score 550 on the written TOEFL or 213 on the electronic version must score 4 on the APIEL and also take English proficiency and math placement exams.

Computers: The mainframe is a DEC MicroVAX 3600. Carson-Newman has a word processing lab for Composition I and II students, a Mac lab with more than 20 terminals, and a CIS lab with more than 20 terminals. There is a campuswide network and all residence hall rooms are wired for PC hookup. Most departments have computer labs specifically for their majors. All students may access the system until the lab closes at 11 P.M. There are no time limits. The fee is $380 per year. It is strongly recommended that all students have a personal computer.

Graduates: In a recent year, 420 bachelor's degrees were awarded. The most popular majors were education (22%), business administration (7%), and biology (7%). In an average class, 47% graduate in 4 years or less, 57% graduate in 5 years or less, and 58% graduate in 6 years or less. 35 companies recruited on campus in 2002-2003.

Admissions Contact: Sheryl M. Gray, Director of Admissions. A video is available. E-mail: *sgray@cn.edu* Web: *www.cn.edu*

CHRISTIAN BROTHERS UNIVERSITY — A-4
Memphis, TN 38104-5581

(901) 321-3205
(800) 288-7576; Fax: (901) 321-3202

Full-time: 559 men, 664 women	**Faculty:** 80; IIB, -$
Part-time: 96 men, 172 women	**Ph.D.s:** 85%
Graduate: 128 men, 210 women	**Student/Faculty:** 15 to 1
Year: semesters, summer session	**Tuition:** $17,190
Application Deadline: July 15	**Room & Board:** $5100
Freshman Class: 1847 applied, 749 accepted, 279 enrolled	
SAT I Verbal/Math: 539/544	**ACT:** 23 **VERY COMPETITIVE**

Christian Brothers University, founded in 1871, is a private, nonprofit institution affiliated with the Roman Catholic Church. Its undergraduate and graduate programs emphasize the liberal arts and sciences, business, engineering and engineering management, health science, telecommunications management, and teacher preparation. There are 4 undergraduate and 3 graduate schools. In addition to regional accreditation, CBU has baccalaureate program accreditation with ABET. The library contains 102,471 volumes, 6351 microform items, and 900 audio/video tapes/CDs, and subscribes to 524 periodicals. Computerized library services include the card catalog, interlibrary loans, and database searching. Special learning facilities include a learning resource center and art gallery. The 70-acre campus is in an urban area in Memphis. Including any residence halls, there are 18 buildings.

Student Life: 82% of undergraduates are from Tennessee. Students are from 33 states, 27 foreign countries, and Canada. 68% are from public schools. 52% are white; 35% African American. 44% are Protestant; 23% Catholic; 31% claim no religious affiliation. The average age of freshmen is 18; all undergraduates, 24. 22% do not continue beyond their first year; 62% remain to graduate.

Housing: 650 students can be accommodated in college housing, which includes single-sex and coed dorms and on-campus apartments. In addition, there are quiet floors in residence halls. On-campus housing is guaranteed for the freshman year only, is available on a first-come, first-served basis, and is available on a lottery system for upperclassmen. Priority is given to out-of-town students. 69% of students commute. All students may keep cars.

Activities: 24% of men belong to 3 national fraternities; 20% of women belong to 1 local and 3 national sororities. There are 40 groups on campus, including art, cheerleading, chess, chorale, chorus, computers, drama, ethnic, honors, international, literary magazine, musical theater, newspaper, political, professional, religious, social, student government, and yearbook. Popular campus events include Riverboat Dance, Spring Formal, and Mardi Gras.

Sports: There are 4 intercollegiate sports for men and 3 for women, and 14 intramural sports for men and 8 for women. Facilities include a swimming pool, gym, theater, multimedia auditorium, batting cage, jogging track, basketball/volleyball and handball/racquetball courts, baseball and soccer fields, tennis courts, and weight-training facilities.

Disabled Students: 90% of the campus is accessible. Wheelchair ramps, elevators, special parking, and specially equipped rest rooms are available.

Services: Counseling and information services are available, as is tutoring in most subjects. CBU also has centers for math, language, and writing.

Campus Safety and Security: Measures include 24-hour foot and vehicle patrol, self-defense education, pamphlets/posters/films, and emergency telephones. There are lighted pathways/sidewalks.

Programs of Study: CBU confers B.A. and B.S. degrees. Master's degrees are also awarded. Bachelor's degrees are awarded in BIOLOGICAL SCIENCE (biology/biological science), BUSINESS (accounting, business administration and management, business economics, management science, and marketing/retailing/merchandising), COMMUNICATIONS AND THE ARTS (English and language arts), COMPUTER AND PHYSICAL SCIENCE (chemistry, computer science, information sciences and systems, mathematics, natural sciences, and physics), ENGINEERING AND ENVIRONMENTAL DESIGN (chemical engineering, civil engineering, electrical/electronics engineering, engineering physics, and mechanical engineering), SOCIAL SCIENCE (applied psychology, history, human development, liberal arts/general studies, psychology, religion, and social studies). Engineering, business, and psychology are the strongest academically. Psychology, information sciences, and business are the largest.

Required: To graduate, students must complete at least 122 semester hours, with a varying number of hours in the major, and maintain a minimum GPA of 2.0. General education requirements, totaling 38 to 40 semester hours, consist of 12 hours of humanities, 6 hours each of communication skills, math, and social sciences, 4 hours of natural and physical sciences, 2 to 4 hours of business/technology, and 2 hours of health/phys ed. Individual schools vary in their core requirements.

Special: Special academic programs include on-campus work-study, study abroad, and internships for all juniors and seniors. There is cross-registration with Memphis College of Art, Memphis Theological Seminary, and LeMoyne-Owen College. An accelerated degree program is available to all business and psychology majors through the evening program, and a general studies degree is offered. Up to 36 hours of nondegree study is possible, as are dual majors and pass/fail options. Numerous teacher licensure programs are also offered. There are 3 national honor societies and a freshman honors program.

Faculty/Classroom: 67% of faculty are male; 33%, female. 95% teach undergraduates. No introductory courses are taught by graduate students. The average class size in an introductory lecture is 22; in a laboratory, 15; and in a regular course, 16.

Admissions: 41% of the 2003-2004 applicants were accepted. The SAT I scores for the 2003-2004 freshman class were: Verbal--30% below 500, 46% between 500 and 599, 20% between 600 and 700, and 4% above 700; Math--29% below 500, 41% between 500 and 599, and 30% between 600 and 700. The ACT scores were 27% below 21, 32% between 21 and 23, 24% between 24 and 26, 8% between 27 and 28, and 9% above 28. 50% of the current freshmen were in the top fifth of their class; 81% were in the top two fifths. 16 freshmen graduated first in their class.

Requirements: The SAT I or ACT is required. The SAT I score should be 830, 415 verbal and 415 math; the ACT score should be 20. Other admissions requirements include graduation from an accredited secondary school, with a college-preparatory curriculum recommended. The GED is also accepted. An interview is advised. CBU requires applicants to be in the upper 67% of their class. A GPA of 2.5 is required. AP and CLEP credits are accepted. Important factors in the admissions decision are advanced placement or honor courses, leadership record, and recommendations by school officials.

Procedure: Freshmen are admitted to all sessions. Entrance exams should be taken by the end of the junior year. There is a deferred admissions plan. Applications should be filed by July 15 for fall entry, January 1 for spring entry, and May 15 for summer entry. Notification is sent on a rolling basis. The fall 2003 application fee was $25. Applications are accepted on-line through the school's web site.

Transfer: 67 transfer students enrolled in 2002-2003. Transfer students should have a minimum GPA of 2.5 and be in good academic and disciplinary standing. A minimum SAT I score of 830 is recommended, as is a minimum ACT score of 20. An interview is advised. 35 of 122 credits required for the bachelor's degree must be completed at CBU.

Visiting: There are regularly scheduled orientations for prospective students, including attendance at classes, meetings with professors and students, a campus tour, and meetings with admissions and financial aid representatives. There are guides for informal visits and visitors may sit in on classes and stay overnight. To schedule a visit, contact Jim Shannon, Dean of Admissions at *jshannon@cbu.edu*.

Financial Aid: In a recent year, 94% of all full-time freshmen and 91% of continuing full-time students received some form of financial aid. 90% of full-time freshmen received need-based aid. 87% of undergraduates work part time. Average annual earnings from campus work are $1000. The average financial indebtedness of the 2003 graduate was $17,600. The FAFSA is required.

International Students: There are 44 international students enrolled. The school actively recruits these students. They must score 500 on the written TOEFL.

Computers: The mainframe is a Sun Enterprise 450. There are also 250 PCs and terminals available for student use in computer centers and academic buildings. There is a campuswide fiber-optic-based LAN and software for word processing, spreadsheets, databases, engineering, accounting, calculus, math, writing, chemistry, physics, and biology. Students with their own PCs may also access the Internet from dorm rooms. All students may access the system during the 93.5 hours per week of computer center operation; 24-hour dial-in phone access is available. There are no time limits and no fees.

Graduates: From July 1, 2002 to June 30, 2003, 322 bachelor's degrees were awarded. The most popular majors were psychology (17%), information science (15%), and electrical engineering (7%). In an average class, 34% graduate in 4 years or less, 49% graduate in 5 years or less, and 53% graduate in 6 years or less. 32 companies recruited on campus in 2002-2003. Of the 2002 graduating class, 10% were enrolled in graduate school within 6 months of graduation and 90% were employed.

Admissions Contact: Jim Shannon, Dean of Admissions.
E-mail: *admissions@cbu.edu* Web: *http://www.cbu.edu*

CRICHTON COLLEGE
Memphis, TN 38111-1375

A-3
(901) 320-9797, ext. 1041
(800) 960-9777; Fax: (901) 320-9709

Full-time: 247 men, 464 women	Faculty: 30; IIB, --$
Part-time: 76 men, 83 women	Ph.D.s: 60%
Graduate: none	Student/Faculty: 24 to 1
Year: semesters, summer session	Tuition: $11,615
Application Deadline: open	Room & Board: $3600
Freshman Class: 196 applied, 155 accepted, 111 enrolled	
SAT I Verbal/Math: 540/560	COMPETITIVE

Crichton College, founded in 1941, is an independent Christian liberal arts college offering programs in liberal arts, Bible, business, health science, religion, and teacher preparation. There are 5 undergraduate schools. The 2 libraries contain 46,777 volumes, 54,308 microform items, and 1580 audio/video tapes/CDs, and subscribe to 303 periodicals. Computerized library services include the card catalog, interlibrary loans, database searching, and Internet access. Special learning facilities include a learning resource center, 21st Century Classroom, and a tutoring center. The 7-acre campus is in an urban area in midtown Memphis. Including any residence halls, there is 1 building.

Student Life: 86% of undergraduates are from Tennessee. Students are from 11 states and 4 foreign countries. 95% are from public schools. 45% are African American; 41% white. The average age of freshmen is 18; all undergraduates, 32. 50% do not continue beyond their first year; 50% remain to graduate.

Housing: 100 students can be accommodated in college housing, which includes single-sex off-campus apartments. College-sponsored housing is guaranteed for all 4 years. 96% of students commute. Alcohol is not permitted. All students may keep cars.

Activities: There are no fraternities or sororities. There are 16 groups on campus, including chorale, chorus, debate, drama, ethnic, forensics, honors, musical theater, professional, religious, Sigma Beta Delta (Business Honors Society), Sigma Alpha Lambda, social, social service, student government, and yearbook. Popular campus events include film, drama, and lecture series; concerts; and Marriage and Family Conference.

Sports: There are 2 intercollegiate sports for men, and 4 intramural sports for men and 4 for women.

Disabled Students: All of the campus is accessible. Wheelchair ramps, elevators, special parking, specially equipped rest rooms, lowered drinking fountains, and lowered telephones are available.

Services: Counseling and information services are available, as is tutoring in most subjects. There is remedial math, English, reading, and writing.

Campus Safety and Security: Measures include 24-hour foot and vehicle patrol, security escort services, informal discussions, and pamphlets/posters/films. There are lighted pathways/sidewalks, security gates at entrances, monitored security systems, and alarm buttons in each apartment unit.

Programs of Study: Crichton confers B.A. and B.S. degrees. Bachelor's degrees are awarded in BIOLOGICAL SCIENCE (biology/biological science), BUSINESS (business administration and management, human resources, and management information systems), COMMUNICATIONS AND THE ARTS (English), COMPUTER AND PHYSICAL SCIENCE (chemistry), EDUCATION (elementary, school psychology, science, and secondary), HEALTH PROFESSIONS (nursing), SOCIAL SCIENCE (biblical studies, clinical psychology, counseling/psychology, history, interdisciplinary studies, liberal arts/general studies, ministries, psychology, and youth ministry). Organizational management, elementary education, and liberal arts are the largest.

Required: Students must complete a minimum of 128 credit hours, and some disciplines require more. The number of hours for the major varies, but all students must take 15 hours of humanities, 3 to 12 of biblical studies, 8 of natural science, 4 of health/phys ed, and 3 each of math and computer science. The minimum GPA required is 2.0; for teacher education students, 2.5.

Special: B.A.-B.S. degrees, dual majors, and limited nondegree study are available. The college also offers internships with area businesses and institutions, a study-abroad program in London, accelerated degrees in organizational management and teacher education, student-designed majors, and work-study programs. There are 2 national honor societies and a freshman honors program. All departments have honors programs.

Faculty/Classroom: 19% of faculty are male; 9%, female. All teach undergraduates, 4% do research, and 8% do both. The average class size in an introductory lecture is 33; in a laboratory, 15; and in a regular course, 17.

Admissions: 79% of the 2003-2004 applicants were accepted. The SAT I scores for the 2003-2004 freshman class were: Verbal--100% between 500 and 599; Math--100% between 500 and 599. The ACT scores were 25% below 21, 32% between 21 and 23, 21% between 24 and 26, 20% between 27 and 28, and 2% above 28.

Requirements: The ACT is required, with a minimum composite score of 18. Students must have a high school diploma or hold the GED. An essay is required. A GPA of 2.0 is required. AP and CLEP credits are accepted. Important factors in the admissions decision are advanced placement or honor courses, evidence of special talent, and leadership record.

Procedure: Freshmen are admitted to all sessions. Entrance exams should be taken during orientation. There is a deferred admissions plan. Application deadlines are open. There is a rolling admissions plan. Application fee is $35. Notification is sent on a rolling basis. Applications are accepted on-line through the school's web site.

Transfer: 570 transfer students enrolled in 2002-2003. Transfer students must have a minimum GPA of 2.0. An interview is required. 30 credits of 128 required for the bachelor's degree must be completed at Crichton.

Visiting: There are regularly scheduled orientations for prospective students, including a preview of all college departments. There are guides for informal visits and visitors may sit in on classes and stay overnight. To schedule a visit, contact the Admissions Office at *info@crichton.edu*.

Financial Aid: In 2003-2004, 75% of all full-time freshmen and 69% of continuing full-time students received some form of financial aid. 59% of full-time freshmen and 53% of continuing full-time students received need-based aid. The average freshman award was $11,522. Need-based scholarships or need-based grants averaged $5478 ($11,530 maximum); need-based self-help aid (loans and jobs) averaged $3595 ($10,575 maximum); non-need-based athletic scholarships averaged $6702 ($11,785 maximum); and other non-need-based awards and non-need-based scholarships averaged $6631 ($21,393 maximum). 5% of undergraduates work part time. Average annual earnings from campus work are $3671. The average financial indebtedness of the 2003 graduate was $22,514. The FAFSA and the college's own financial statement are required. The deadline for filing freshman financial aid applications for fall entry is August 1.

International Students: There were 4 international students enrolled in a recent year. They must score 500 on the written TOEFL or 173 on the electronic version and also take the SAT I or the ACT, scoring 18 on the ACT.

Computers: The campus network is run by 3 servers. 22 PCs are available in the computer learning center, 14 in the library, and 6 in the 21st Century Classroom. Students use the networked PCs to communicate via e-mail and chat rooms, to research subjects on the Internet, and to complete class requirements. All students may access the system 24 hours a day, 7 days a week. There are no time limits. The fee is $40 per semester. It is recommended that students in business administration with information management concentration have personal computers. A Dell Inspiron 1100/2650 is recommended.

Graduates: From July 1, 2002 to June 30, 2003, 110 bachelor's degrees were awarded. The most popular majors were organizational management (72%), elementary education (13%), and psychology (7%).

Admissions Contact: David Wilson, Director of Admissions.
E-mail: *info@crichton.edu* Web: *http://www.crichton.edu*

CUMBERLAND UNIVERSITY   C-2
Lebanon, TN 37087
(615) 444-2562
(800) 467-0562; Fax: (615) 444-2569

Full-time: 340 men, 438 women	**Faculty:** 79
Part-time: 56 men, 87 women	**Ph.D.s:** 43%
Graduate: 99 men, 400 women	**Student/Faculty:** 10 to 1
Year: semesters, summer session	**Tuition:** $12,230
Application Deadline: open	**Room & Board:** $4680
Freshman Class: 532 applied, 353 accepted, 149 enrolled	
SAT I Verbal/Math: 470/470	**ACT:** 20 **COMPETITIVE**

Cumberland University, founded in 1842, is a private institution offering undergraduate and graduate degrees in business, education, and social sciences. In addition to regional accreditation, Cumberland has baccalaureate program accreditation with AACSB and NLN. The library contains 37,056 volumes, 590 microform items, and 1260 audio/video tapes/CDs, and subscribes to 357 periodicals. Computerized library services include the card catalog, interlibrary loans, database searching, and Internet access. Special learning facilities include a learning resource center, art gallery, natural history museum, and radio station. The 44-acre campus is in a small town 28 miles east of Nashville. Including any residence halls, there are 17 buildings.

Student Life: 86% of undergraduates are from Tennessee. Students are from 26 states, 15 foreign countries, and Canada. 89% are from public schools. 79% are white; 15% African American. The average age of freshmen is 19; all undergraduates, 24. 30% do not continue beyond their first year; 37% remain to graduate.

Housing: 412 students can be accommodated in college housing, which includes single-sex dorms. On-campus housing is available on a first-come, first-served basis. 57% of students commute. Alcohol is not permitted. All students may keep cars.

Activities: 17% of men belong to 3 national fraternities; 7% of women belong to 2 national sororities. There are 21 groups on campus, including art, band, cheerleading, chorale, computers, dance, drama, honors, international, jazz band, marching band, musical theater, newspaper, pep band, political, professional, religious, social, social service, student government, and yearbook. Popular campus events include Fall Frolic, Halloween at CU, and Spring Fling.

Sports: There are 9 intercollegiate sports for men and 8 for women, and 4 intramural sports for men and 5 for women. Facilities include a gym, field house, weight room, baseball and soccer fields, tennis courts, outdoor volleyball courts, and football and softball fields.

Disabled Students: All of the campus is accessible. Wheelchair ramps, special parking, and lowered telephones are available.

Services: Counseling and information services are available, as is tutoring in most subjects. There is remedial math, reading, and writing.

Campus Safety and Security: Measures include 24-hour foot and vehicle patrol, informal discussions, and lighted pathways/sidewalks. The outside entrances of the dorms are always secured; only residents have keys.

Programs of Study: Cumberland confers B.A., B.S., B.B.A., and B.S.N. degrees. Associate and master's degrees are also awarded. Bachelor's degrees are awarded in BIOLOGICAL SCIENCE (biology/biological science), BUSINESS (accounting, business administration and management, management science, marketing management, and recreation and leisure services), COMMUNICATIONS AND THE ARTS (English, fine arts, and music), COMPUTER AND PHYSICAL SCIENCE (mathematics), EDUCATION (elementary, middle school, music, physical, secondary, and special), HEALTH PROFESSIONS (nursing), SOCIAL SCIENCE (American studies, criminal justice, history, political science/government, psychology, social science, and sociology). Business, education, and nursing are the largest.

Required: To graduate, students must complete 128 semester hours, including a 49-hour core curriculum, and maintain a GPA of 2.0.

Special: Internships with local businesses and with the state legislature are available. Nondegree study, pass/fail options, and an accelerated degree program in general business are offered. There are 13 national honor societies, a freshman honors program, and 5 departmental honors programs.

Faculty/Classroom: 56% of faculty are male; 44%, female. 82% teach undergraduates. No introductory courses are taught by graduate students. The average class size in an introductory lecture is 20; in a laboratory, 20; and in a regular course, 20.

Admissions: 66% of the 2003-2004 applicants were accepted. The SAT I scores for the 2003-2004 freshman class were: Verbal--60% below 500, 30% between 500 and 599, and 10% between 600 and 700; Math--65% below 500, 25% between 500 and 599, and 10% between 600 and 700. The ACT scores were 62% below 21, 22% between 21 and 23, 13% between 24 and 26, and 3% between 27 and 28. 24% of the current freshmen were in the top fifth of their class; 53% were in the top two fifths.

Requirements: The SAT I or ACT is recommended, with a minimum composite ACT score of 18. Applicants must be high school graduates or have earned the GED with a composite 50 score. A GPA of 2.0 is expected. AP and CLEP credits are accepted.

Procedure: Freshmen are admitted fall, spring, and summer. Entrance exams should be taken during the senior year in high school. Application deadlines are open. Application fee is $25. There is a rolling admissions plan. Notification is sent on a rolling basis.

Transfer: 110 transfer students enrolled in 2002-2003. Transfer applicants should have a GPA of at least 2.0. 33 credits of 128 required for the bachelor's degree must be completed at Cumberland.

Visiting: There are regularly scheduled orientations for prospective students, consisting of campus tours, testing, information sessions pertaining to college life, and academic advising. A parent orientation is provided in conjunction with student orientation programs. There are guides for informal visits and visitors may sit in on classes. To schedule a visit, contact the Admissions Office.

Financial Aid: 35% of full-time freshmen received need-based aid. The average freshman award was $5986. Need-based scholarships or need-based grants averaged $5191 ($9588 maximum); need-based self-help aid (loans and jobs) averaged $4484 ($10,500 maximum); non-need-based athletic scholarships averaged $5388 ($16,510 maximum); and other non-need-based awards and non-need-based scholarships averaged $3990 ($12,750 maximum). Average annual earnings from campus work are $1000. Cumberland is a member of CSS. The FAFSA and the college's own financial statement are required. The priority date for freshman financial aid applications for fall entry is February 1. The deadline for filing freshman financial aid applications for fall entry is July 15.

International Students: There are 28 international students enrolled. The school actively recruits these students. They must score 500 on the written TOEFL or take the MELAB and also take the SAT I or the ACT, scoring 18 on the ACT or 850 on the SAT I.

Computers: PCs are available in the computer lab. All students may access the system. There are no time limits. The fee is $100.

Graduates: From July 1, 2002 to June 30, 2003, 169 bachelor's degrees were awarded. The most popular majors were business administration (26%), education (18%), and nursing (12%). In an average class, 12% graduate in 4 years or less, 23% graduate in 5 years or less, and 8% graduate in 6 years or less.

Admissions Contact: James Dressler, Vice President for Student Activities/Dean of Students. E-mail: *admissions@cumberland.edu* Web: *cumberland.edu*

DAVID LIPSCOMB UNIVERSITY
Nashville, TN 37204-3951

C-3

(615) 269-1776
(800) 333-4358; Fax: (615) 269-1804

Full-time: 910 men, 1195 women	**Faculty:** 115; IIB, -$
Part-time: 120 men, 170 women	**Ph.D.s:** 83%
Graduate: 150 men, 75 women	**Student/Faculty:** 18 to 1
Year: semesters, summer session	**Tuition:** $13,486
Application Deadline: open	**Room & Board:** $6090
Freshman Class: n/av	
SAT I or ACT: required	**VERY COMPETITIVE**

David Lipscomb University, founded in 1891, is a private liberal arts university affiliated with the Church of Christ. Figures in the above capsule and in this profile are approximate. There are 5 undergraduate and 3 graduate schools. In addition to regional accreditation, DLU has baccalaureate program accreditation with ACBSP, ADA, CSWE, NASM, and NCATE. The library contains 150,512 volumes, 26,018 microform items, and 1240 audio/video tapes/CDs, and subscribes to 38,685 periodicals. Computerized library services include the card catalog, interlibrary loans, and database searching. Special learning facilities include a learning resource center, art gallery, radio station, and TV station. The 65-acre campus is in a suburban area 2 miles south of downtown Nashville. Including any residence halls, there are 16 buildings.

Student Life: 65% of undergraduates are from Tennessee. Students are from 40 states, 37 foreign countries, and Canada. 41% are from public schools. 85% are white. 91% are Protestant; 8% claim no religious affiliation. The average age of freshmen is 19; all undergraduates, 21. 21% do not continue beyond their first year; 62% remain to graduate.

Housing: 1358 students can be accommodated in college housing, which includes single-sex dorms. 54% of students live on campus; of those, 25% remain on campus on weekends. Alcohol is not permitted. All students may keep cars.

Activities: There are no fraternities or sororities. There are 60 groups on campus, including art, band, cheerleading, chorale, chorus, computers, drama, ethnic, honors, international, jazz band, musical theater, newspaper, orchestra, photography, political, professional, radio and TV, social, social service, student government, and yearbook. Popular campus events include University Days, Sing-a-rama, and Tau Phi Cowboy Show.

Sports: There are 6 intercollegiate sports for men and 7 for women, and 9 intramural sports for men and 9 for women. Facilities include a gym with a basketball court and a pool, and a student activity center

with 2 full-size basketball courts, 5 racquetball courts, a jogging course, and weight, aerobics, and recreation rooms.

Disabled Students: 95% of the campus is accessible. Wheelchair ramps, elevators, special parking, specially equipped rest rooms, and lowered drinking fountains are available.

Services: Counseling and information services are available, as is tutoring in some subjects, including math, English, and sciences. There is remedial math, reading, and writing.

Campus Safety and Security: Measures include 24-hour foot and vehicle patrol, security escort services, pamphlets/posters/films, and emergency telephones. There are lighted pathways/sidewalks and residence hall security systems.

Programs of Study: DLU confers B.A. and B.S. degrees. Master's degrees are also awarded. Bachelor's degrees are awarded in BIOLOGICAL SCIENCE (biochemistry and biology/biological science), BUSINESS (accounting, banking and finance, business administration and management, fashion merchandising, and marketing/retailing/merchandising), COMMUNICATIONS AND THE ARTS (communications, English, French, German, languages, music, public relations, and Spanish), COMPUTER AND PHYSICAL SCIENCE (chemistry, computer science, mathematics, and physics), EDUCATION (art, elementary, foreign languages, music, physical, and science), ENGINEERING AND ENVIRONMENTAL DESIGN (preengineering), HEALTH PROFESSIONS (predentistry, premedicine, and prepharmacy), SOCIAL SCIENCE (American studies, biblical languages, dietetics, food production/management/services, history, home economics, political science/government, prelaw, psychology, religion, social work, and urban studies). Chemistry, biology, and accounting are the strongest academically. Business, medicine, and education are the largest.

Required: All full-time students must take and pass a Bible class meeting each day the student has classes. Other general education requirements include 9 semester hours in communication, 6 each in humanities, science, history, and social science, 3 in math, and 2 in phys ed. Students must complete a total of 132 semester hours and have a minimum GPA of 2.0. At least 25% of credit hours must be earned at Lipscomb.

Special: DLU offers internships and 3-2 engineering degrees with University of Tennessee at Knoxville, Auburn, Vanderbilt, and Tennessee Technological universities. An adult credit and noncredit studies program and pass/fail options for phys ed activity courses are available. A 3-2 program with Vanderbilt University leads to a B.S. in pre-nursing from Lipscomb and a master of science in nursing from Vanderbilt. There is study abroad in France, Germany, and Mexico. There is 1 national honor society, a freshman honors program, and 18 departmental honors program.

Faculty/Classroom: 68% of faculty are male; 32%, female. All teach undergraduates. No introductory courses are taught by graduate students. The average class size in an introductory lecture is 45; in a laboratory, 25; and in a regular course, 30.

Admissions: There were 2 National Merit finalists in a recent year.

Requirements: The SAT I or ACT is required. In addition, candidates for admission should be graduates of accredited secondary schools. The GED is accepted. 14 academic units are required. Students should have completed 4 units of English and 2 units each of history, math, and science. 2 units of a foreign language are highly recommended. Two additional units from the areas of English, foreign language, history, math, science, and social studies are also required. Applications are accepted on-line. A GPA of 2.25 is required. AP and CLEP credits are accepted. Important factors in the admissions decision are advanced placement or honor courses, personality/intangible qualities, and leadership record.

Procedure: Freshmen are admitted to all sessions. There is an early decision plan. There is a rolling admissions plan. Application deadlines are open. 8 early decision candidates were accepted for a recent year's class. The fall 2003 application fee was $50. Applications are accepted on-line.

Transfer: Students must be in good standing at their previous institution. 33 of 132 credits required for the bachelor's degree must be completed at DLU.

Visiting: There are regularly scheduled orientations for prospective students. There are guides for informal visits and visitors may sit in on classes and stay overnight. To schedule a visit, contact the Office of Undergraduate Admissions.

Financial Aid: In a recent year, 91% of all full-time freshmen and 75% of continuing full-time students received some form of financial aid. 38% of full-time freshmen and 33% of continuing full-time students received need-based aid. The average freshman award was $7900. 64% of undergraduates work part time. Average annual earnings from campus work are $800. The average financial indebtedness of a recent graduate was $12,500. The FAFSA is required. Check with the school for current deadlines.

International Students: The school actively recruits these students. They must score 500 on the written TOEFL or take the MELAB and also take the SAT I or the ACT, scoring 810.

Computers: The mainframes are 3 DEC Alpha computers, 1 VAX 4100, and 1 VAX 4500. There are computer labs in every building on campus, including residence halls, and computer hook-ups in every dorm room. All students may access the system 24 hours per day, 7 days per week. There are no time limits and no fees. It is strongly recommended that all students have a personal computer.

Graduates: In a recent year, 431 bachelor's degrees were awarded. The most popular majors were business administration (28%), elementary education (8%), and biology (7%). In an average class, 31% graduate in 4 years or less, 47% graduate in 5 years or less, and 49% graduate in 6 years or less. 347 companies recruited on campus in a recent year.

Admissions Contact: Scott Gilmer, Director of Admissions. A video is available. E-mail: *scott.gilmer@lipscomb.edu* Web: *www.lipscomb.edu*

EAST TENNESSEE STATE UNIVERSITY   F-2
Johnson City, TN 37614   (423) 439-4213
                                        (800) 462-3878; Fax: (423) 439-7156

Full-time: 3396 men, 4532 women	**Faculty:** 350; IIA, --$
Part-time: 647 men, 975 women	**Ph.D.s:** 75%
Graduate: 619 men, 1226 women	**Student/Faculty:** 23 to 1
Year: semesters, summer session	**Tuition:** $3839 ($11,771)
Application Deadline: open	**Room & Board:** $4658
Freshman Class: 3825 applied, 3132 accepted, 1615 enrolled	
SAT I Verbal/Math: 520/520	**ACT:** 22 COMPETITIVE

East Tennessee State University, founded in 1911, is a public institution that is part of the State University and Community College System of Tennessee. ETSU's undergraduate and graduate programs stress the liberal arts, business, art, fine arts, professional training, music, teacher preparation, technical studies, and health science. There are 6 undergraduate and 2 graduate schools. In addition to regional accreditation, ETSU has baccalaureate program accreditation with AACSB, ABET, ACEJMC, ACS, ADA, CAAHEP, CSAB, CSWE, NASAD, NASM, NCATE, NEHSPAC, and NLN. The library contains 1,073,382 volumes, 1,692,830 microform items, and 23,658 audio/video tapes/CDs, and subscribes to 3714 periodicals. Computerized library services include the card catalog, interlibrary loans, database searching, and Internet access. Special learning facilities include a learning resource center, art gallery, planetarium, radio station, TV station, and a regional art and history museum. The 366-acre campus is in a small town 90 miles northeast of Knoxville; 130 miles southwest of Roanoke, VA.; 60 miles northwest of Asheville, NC. Including any residence halls, there are 68 buildings.

Student Life: 89% of undergraduates are from Tennessee. Students are from 38 states, 46 foreign countries, and Canada. 97% are from public schools. 91% are white. The average age of freshmen is 19; all undergraduates, 23. 33% do not continue beyond their first year; 38% remain to graduate.

Housing: 2478 students can be accommodated in college housing, which includes single-sex and coed dorms, on-campus apartments, and married-student housing. On-campus housing is available on a first-come, first-served basis. 79% of students commute. Alcohol is not permitted. All students may keep cars.

Activities: 4% of men belong to 8 national fraternities; 4% of women belong to 1 local and 6 national sororities. There are more than 200 groups on campus, including art, band, cheerleading, choir, chorale, chorus, computers, dance, drama, drill team, ethnic, forensics, gay, honors, international, jazz band, literary magazine, newspaper, pep band, photography, political, professional, radio and TV, religious, residence hall, social, social service, and student government. Popular campus events include Leadership Retreat, National Clean Up for Hunger, and Winter Cruise.

Sports: There are 6 intercollegiate sports for men and 8 for women, and 8 intramural sports for men and 8 for women. Facilities include a 4000-seat gym and a domed stadium seating 12,000, which includes a basketball arena, tennis and handball/racquetball courts, a track, and weight and training rooms.

Disabled Students: 75% of the campus is accessible. Wheelchair ramps, elevators, special parking, specially equipped rest rooms, special class scheduling, lowered drinking fountains, lowered telephones, special housing, and adaptive computer equipment are available.

Services: Counseling and information services are available, as is tutoring in most subjects. There is a reader service for the blind, and remedial math, reading, and writing. The Office for Students with Disabilities, Student Support Services, and the Undergraduate Academic Advisement administer these sciences.

Campus Safety and Security: Measures include 24-hour foot and vehicle patrol, self-defense education, security escort services, and shuttle buses. There are informal discussions, pamphlets/posters/films, emergency telephones, lighted pathways/sidewalks, and engravers available to identify personal property.

Programs of Study: ETSU confers B.A., B.S., B.A.S., B.B.A., B.F.A, B.G.S., B.M., B.S.D.H., B.S.Ed., B.S.E.H., B.S.M.T., B.S.N., and B.S.W. degrees. Associate, master's, and doctoral degrees are also awarded. Bachelor's degrees are awarded in BIOLOGICAL SCIENCE (biology/biological science), BUSINESS (accounting, management science, and marketing/retailing/merchandising), COMMUNICATIONS AND THE ARTS (art, communications, English, fine arts, music, and

speech/debate/rhetoric), COMPUTER AND PHYSICAL SCIENCE (chemistry, computer science, information sciences and systems, mathematics, and physics), EDUCATION (foreign languages, physical, and special), ENGINEERING AND ENVIRONMENTAL DESIGN (engineering technology, and survey and mapping technology), HEALTH PROFESSIONS (allied health, dental hygiene, environmental health science, health science, nursing, and public health), SOCIAL SCIENCE (child psychology/development, criminal justice, economics, geography, history, human development, interdisciplinary studies, liberal arts/general studies, philosophy, political science/government, psychology, social work, and sociology). Engineering technology, computer science, and nursing are the largest.

Required: All students must complete 120 semester hours, with 30 to 60 in the major, and maintain a minimum GPA of 2.0. Distribution requirements, which total 46 semester hours, include English, American history, phys ed, natural science, social and behavioral science, the humanities, analysis, and a 3-hour computer literacy course. An exit exam is also required.

Special: Special academic programs include cooperative education programs, cross-registration with Milligan College, internships in political science, applied human sciences, and management,and dual majors study abroad in Scotland, England, France, and Spain, and B.A.-B.S. degrees and dual majors in most arts and sciences undergraduate majors. A general studies degree is offered. Credit for military experience may be granted, and nondegree study and pass/fail options are possible. There are 19 national honor societies, a freshman honors program, and 12 departmental honors programs.

Faculty/Classroom: 55% of faculty are male; 45%, female. 85% teach undergraduates. The average class size in an introductory lecture is 30; in a laboratory, 15; and in a regular course, 25.

Admissions: 82% of the 2003-2004 applicants were accepted. The SAT I scores for the 2003-2004 freshman class were: Verbal--41% below 500, 39% between 500 and 599, 18% between 600 and 700, and 2% above 700; Math--43% below 500, 39% between 500 and 599, 16% between 600 and 700, and 2% above 700. The ACT scores were 40% below 21, 24% between 21 and 23, 20% between 24 and 26, 9% between 27 and 28, and 7% above 28. 29% of the current freshmen were in the top fifth of their class; 51% were in the top two fifths.

Requirements: The SAT I or ACT is required, with a minimum composite score of 890 on the SAT I or a minimum score of 19 on the ACT. Other admissions requirements include graduation from an accredited secondary school, with 20 Carnegie units and 14 academic credits, including 4 of English, 3 of math, 2 each of a foreign language and science, and 1 each of history, social studies, and art. In-state students who pass the Tennessee State Proficiency Test are eligible to apply for admission. Applicants whose ACT/SAT I is below a certain score must complete the Academic Assessment Placement Program (AAPP) test battery before registration for classes. The GED is also accepted. A GPA of 2.3 is required. AP and CLEP credits are accepted.

Procedure: Freshmen are admitted to all sessions. Entrance exams should be taken during the junior and/or senior year. Application deadlines are open. There is a rolling admissions plan. The fall 2003 application fee was $15. Applications are accepted on-line through the school's web site.

Transfer: 857 transfer students enrolled in 2002-2003. Transfer students must have a minimum GPA of 2.0 in 12 or more semester credit hours of course work from a regionally accredited institution. Transfer students must also satisfy high school unit requirements if deficiencies exist. 34 of 120 credits required for the bachelor's degree must be completed at ETSU.

Visiting: There are regularly scheduled orientations for prospective students, including 5 2-day orientation programs held during spring and summer for new students admitted to fall term. There are guides for informal visits and visitors may sit in on classes and stay overnight. To schedule a visit, contact the Admissions Office at *go2etsu@etsu.edu*.

Financial Aid: In 2003-2004, 74% of all full-time freshmen and 75% of continuing full-time students received some form of financial aid. 55% of all full-time students received need-based aid. The average freshman award was $7407. Need-based scholarships or need-based grants averaged $5002; need-based self-help aid (loans and jobs) averaged $2992; and non-need-based awards and non-need-based scholarships averaged $1760. 28% of undergraduates work part time. Average annual earnings from campus work are $2119. The average financial indebtedness of the 2003 graduate was $17,668. The FAFSA is required. The priority date for freshman financial aid applications for fall entry is April 15. The deadline for filing freshman financial aid applications for fall entry is July 1.

International Students: There are 99 international students enrolled. They must score 500 on the written TOEFL or 173 on the electronic version and also take the SAT I or the ACT, scoring 890 (SAT I) or 19 (ACT).

Computers: The mainframe is an ALPHA 2100. There are 500 PCs available for student use in computer labs in several buildings on campus. All students may access the system 24 hours per day. There are no time limits and no fees.

Graduates: From July 1, 2002 to June 30, 2003, 1499 bachelor's degrees were awarded. The most popular majors were nursing (8%), psychology (6%), and finance and elementary education (5%). In an average class, 12% graduate in 4 years or less, 29% graduate in 5 years or less, and 38% graduate in 6 years or less. 200 companies recruited on campus in 2002-2003.

Admissions Contact: Mike Pitts, Director of Admissions. A video is available. E-mail: *go2etsu@etsu.edu* Web: *www.etsu.edu*

FISK UNIVERSITY
Nashville, TN 37208-3051

C-2

(615) 329-8665
(800) 443-3475; Fax: (615) 329-8774

Full-time: 252 men, 569 women	**Faculty:** 63
Part-time: 13 men, 16 women	**Ph.D.s:** 70%
Graduate: 14 men, 17 women	**Student/Faculty:** 13 to 1
Year: semesters	**Tuition:** $11,535
Application Deadline: open	**Room & Board:** $5770
Freshman Class: 1122 applied, 743 accepted, 231 enrolled	
SAT I Verbal/Math: 468/444	**ACT:** 19 **LESS COMPETITIVE**

Fisk University, founded in 1866, is a private, nonsectarian, liberal arts institution affiliated with the American Missionary Association of the Church of Christ. Estabished as a college for African Americans, Fisk has always accepted students regardless of race. Some figures in the above capsule and in this profile are approximate. In addition to regional accreditation, Fisk University has baccalaureate program accreditation with NASM. The library contains 210,000 volumes and 5200 microform items, and subscribes to 600 periodicals. Computerized library services include the card catalog and database searching. Special learning facilities include an art gallery and radio station. The 40-acre campus is in an urban area. Including any residence halls, there are 21 buildings.

Student Life: 71% of undergraduates are from out of state, mostly the South. Students are from 39 states and 4 foreign countries. 87% are from public schools. 96% are African American. The average age of freshmen is 18; all undergraduates, 20. 6% do not continue beyond their first year; 63% remain to graduate.

Housing: 852 students can be accommodated in college housing, which includes single-sex dorms and married-student housing. On-campus housing is guaranteed for all 4 years. 68% of students live on campus; of those, 80% remain on campus on weekends. Alcohol is not permitted. All students may keep cars.

Activities: 25% of men belong to 4 national fraternities; 20% of women belong to 4 national sororities. There are some groups and organizations on campus, including cheerleading, choir, dance, drama, honors, literary magazine, newspaper, religious, student government, and yearbook.

Sports: There are 5 intercollegiate sports for men and 5 for women. Facilities include a gym and a student center.

Disabled Students: 80% of the campus is accessible. Wheelchair ramps and elevators are available.

Services: Counseling and information services are available, as is tutoring in every subject. There is remedial math, reading, and writing.

Campus Safety and Security: Measures include 24-hour foot and vehicle patrol and lighted pathways/sidewalks.

Programs of Study: Fisk University confers B.A., B.S., and B.M. degrees. Master's degrees are also awarded. Bachelor's degrees are awarded in BIOLOGICAL SCIENCE (biology/biological science), BUSINESS (business administration and management), COMMUNICATIONS AND THE ARTS (dramatic arts, English, fine arts, French, music, Spanish, and speech/debate/rhetoric), COMPUTER AND PHYSICAL SCIENCE (chemistry, mathematics, and physics), EDUCATION (art), SOCIAL SCIENCE (economics, history, philosophy, political science/government, psychology, religion, and sociology). Biology, chemistry, and physics are the strongest academically. Business administration is the largest.

Required: To graduate, students must complete 120 credits, including a 32-credit core curriculum in communications, creative arts, humanistic experience and thought, natural sciences or math, social sciences, and world civilization. In addition, students must complete 8 hours of written and computational skills and 24 hours of interdisciplinary courses, plus a foreign language. A minimum 2.0 GPA must be maintained.

Special: Fisk offers cross-registration with Vanderbilt University, study abroad, dual majors in engineering and pharmacy, student-designed majors, and campus work-study. Students may take a 5-year B.S.-B.E. program with Vanderbilt University, Florida A&M, or the University of Alabama/Huntsville, or a combined B.S.-M.B.A. program with Vanderbilt. There are 8 national honor societies, including Phi Beta Kappa.

Faculty/Classroom: 62% of faculty are male; 38%, female. All teach undergraduates, 22% do research, and 24% do both. No introductory courses are taught by graduate students. The average class size in an introductory lecture is 30; in a laboratory, 15; and in a regular course, 19.

Admissions: 66% of the 2003-2004 applicants were accepted. The SAT I scores for the 2003-2004 freshman class were: Verbal--66% below 500, 28% between 500 and 599, and 6% between 600 and 700; Math--71% below 500, 22% between 500 and 599, and 7% between 600 and 700. The ACT scores were 60% below 21, 28% between 21 and 23, 7%

between 24 and 26, 3% between 27 and 28, and 2% above 28. 35% of the current freshmen were in the top fifth of their class; 65% were in the top two fifths.

Requirements: The SAT I or ACT is required. In addition, applicants should be high school graduates with 14 academic credits. A GPA of 2.5 is required. AP credits are accepted. Important factors in the admissions decision are advanced placement or honor courses, leadership record, and evidence of special talent.

Procedure: Freshmen are admitted fall and spring. There is an early admissions plan. Application deadlines are open. Notification is sent on a rolling basis. Check with the school for current application fee.

Transfer: Applicants for transfer should have a minimum college GPA of 2.0.

Visiting: There are guides for informal visits and visitors may sit in on classes and stay overnight. To schedule a visit, contact the Admissions Office at (615) 329-8666.

Financial Aid: In 2003-2004, 90% of all full-time students received some form of financial aid. 65% of full-time freshmen and 70% of continuing full-time students received need-based aid. The average freshman award was $14,693, with $6059 from need-based scholarships or need-based grants and $8634 from need-based self-help aid (loans and jobs). Fisk University is a member of CSS. The FAFSA and the college's own financial statement are required. Check with the school for current application deadlines.

International Students: They must score 550 on the written TOEFL.

Computers: The mainframe is a DEC VAX 11/750. There are also PCs and Macs available across campus. All students may access the system. There are no time limits and no fees.

Admissions Contact: William Carter, Director of Admissions. A video is available. E-mail: *amit@fisk.edu* Web: *www.fisk.edu*

FREED-HARDEMAN UNIVERSITY
Henderson, TN 38340

B-3

(731) 989-6651
(800) 630-3480; Fax: (731) 989-6047

Full-time: 640 men, 738 women	**Faculty:** 90; IIA, --$
Part-time: 36 men, 33 women	**Ph.D.s:** 78%
Graduate: 191 men, 328 women	**Student/Faculty:** 15 to 1
Year: semesters, summer session	**Tuition:** $11,046
Application Deadline: open	**Room & Board:** $5320
Freshman Class: 663 applied, 658 accepted, 375 enrolled	
ACT: 23	**NONCOMPETITIVE**

Freed-Hardeman University, founded in 1869, is a private, liberal arts institution associated with Churches of Christ. There are 6 undergraduate and 3 graduate schools. In addition to regional accreditation, FHU has baccalaureate program accreditation with ACBSP, CSWE, and NCATE. The library contains 158,565 volumes, 240,000 microform items, and 43,000 audio/video tapes/CDs, and subscribes to 1650 periodicals. Computerized library services include the card catalog, interlibrary loans, database searching, and Internet access. Special learning facilities include a learning resource center, art gallery, radio station, TV station, and a Cancer Research Institute. The 120-acre campus is in a small town 85 miles east of Memphis and 13 miles south of Jackson. Including any residence halls, there are 34 buildings.

Student Life: 52% of undergraduates are from out of state, mostly the South. Students are from 36 states, 17 foreign countries, and Canada. 75% are from public schools. 87% are white. Most are Protestant. The average age of freshmen is 19; all undergraduates, 21. 26% do not continue beyond their first year; 57% remain to graduate.

Housing: 1303 students can be accommodated in college housing, which includes single-sex dorms and on-campus apartments. In addition, there are student teacher houses. On-campus housing is guaranteed for all 4 years. 78% of students live on campus; of those, 55% remain on campus on weekends. Alcohol is not permitted. All students may keep cars.

Activities: There are no fraternities or sororities. There are 52 groups on campus, including art, band, cheerleading, choir, chorus, computers, drama, drum and bugle corps, ethnic, honors, international, jazz band, musical theater, newspaper, orchestra, pep band, photography, political, professional, radio and TV, religious, social, social service, student government, and yearbook. Popular campus events include Makin' Music and Annual Bible Lectureship.

Sports: There are 6 intercollegiate sports for men and 7 for women, and 7 intramural sports for men and 7 for women. Facilities include 3 gyms, lighted playing fields, lighted tennis courts, a swimming pool, a walking track, a weight room, racquetball courts, and a game room.

Disabled Students: 70% of the campus is accessible. Wheelchair ramps, elevators, special parking, specially equipped rest rooms, special class scheduling, lowered drinking fountains, and lowered telephones are available.

Services: Counseling and information services are available, as is tutoring in most subjects. There is remedial math, reading, and writing.

Campus Safety and Security: Measures include 24-hour foot and vehicle patrol, security escort services, informal discussions, and lighted pathways/sidewalks.

Programs of Study: FHU confers B.A., B.S., B.B.A., and B.S.W. degrees. Master's degrees are also awarded. Bachelor's degrees are awarded in AGRICULTURE (agricultural business management), BIOLOGICAL SCIENCE (biology/biological science), BUSINESS (accounting, banking and finance, business administration and management, and marketing/retailing/merchandising), COMMUNICATIONS AND THE ARTS (art, broadcasting, communications, dramatic arts, English, fine arts, public relations, and speech/debate/rhetoric), COMPUTER AND PHYSICAL SCIENCE (chemistry, computer programming, computer science, information sciences and systems, mathematics, and physical sciences), EDUCATION (art, early childhood, elementary, health, middle school, music, physical, science, secondary, and special), ENGINEERING AND ENVIRONMENTAL DESIGN (preengineering), HEALTH PROFESSIONS (predentistry, premedicine, preoptometry, prepharmacy, and preveterinary science), SOCIAL SCIENCE (biblical studies, child care/child and family studies, family/consumer studies, history, ministries, psychology, and social work). Premedicine, preengineering, and business are the strongest academically. Business, Bible, and elementary education are the largest.

Required: To graduate, students must complete 132 semester hours, including 44 in upper-division courses in Bible, skills, humanities, and science, plus 3 hours of speech communication and 2 hours of phys ed. The major requires a minimum of 30 semester hours, including 15 upper-division hours. Students must maintain a GPA of 2.0. All students must demonstrate, by approved tests or criteria, basic competence in reading, writing, oral communication, math, and computers.

Special: FHU offers cross-registration with Lambuth University and Union University, study abroad in Belgium, a B.A.-B.S. degree in Bible, biology, communication, and arts and humanities, co-op programs, a dual major, field practium opportunities in several majors, student-designed majors, 3-2 engineering degrees with 6 universities, and nondegree study. There are 4 national honor societies, a freshman honors program, and 13 departmental honors programs.

Faculty/Classroom: 66% of faculty are male; 34%, female. 91% teach undergraduates. No introductory courses are taught by graduate students. The average class size in a laboratory is 22 and in a regular course, 20.

Admissions: 99% of the 2003-2004 applicants were accepted. The ACT scores for the 2003-2004 freshman class were: 28% below 21, 32% between 21 and 23, 19% between 24 and 26, 10% between 27 and 28, and 10% above 28.

Requirements: The ACT is required, with a minimum composite score of 19. In addition, candidates for admission should be graduates of an accredited secondary school. An interview is recommended. A GPA of 2.25 is required. AP and CLEP credits are accepted. Important factors in the admissions decision are personality/intangible qualities, recommendations by school officials, and leadership record.

Procedure: Freshmen are admitted fall, spring, and summer. Entrance exams should be taken in early fall or summer before senior year. There is an early admissions plan. Application deadlines are open. There is a rolling admissions plan. Applications are accepted on-line through *www.fhu.edu.*

Transfer: Applicants should have a minimum college GPA of 2.0. Those with fewer than 30 college credits must also submit a high school transcript and ACT or SAT I scores. 33 of 132 credits required for the bachelor's degree must be completed at FHU.

Visiting: There are regularly scheduled orientations for prospective students, including an orientation during the 5 days prior to classes beginning in the fall. There are guides for informal visits and visitors may sit in on classes and stay overnight. To schedule a visit, contact Jim Brown.

Financial Aid: In 2003-2004, 87% of all full-time freshmen and 88% of continuing full-time students received some form of financial aid. 51% of full-time freshmen and 74% of continuing full-time students received need-based aid. 31% of undergraduates work part time. Average annual earnings from campus work are $1080. The FAFSA is required. The deadline for filing freshman financial aid applications for fall entry is April 1.

International Students: There are 27 international students enrolled. They must score 500 on the written TOEFL and also take the ACT, scoring 19.

Computers: The mainframe is a DEC VAX 4500. PCs and Mac are available in student labs and other locations, and each residence hall room has network access. All students may access the system.

Graduates: From July 1, 2002 to June 30, 2003, 296 bachelor's degrees were awarded. The most popular majors were Bible (14%), elementary education (14%), and biology (6%). In an average class, 2% graduate in 3 years or less, 39% graduate in 4 years or less, 55% graduate in 5 years or less, and 57% graduate in 6 years or less. 84 companies recruited on campus in 2002-2003.

Admissions Contact: Jim Brown, Director of Admissions. A video is available. E-mail: *jbrown@fhu.edu* Web: *http://www.fhu.edu*

KING COLLEGE
F-2
Bristol, TN 37620-2699

(423) 652-4861
(800) 362-0014; Fax: (423) 652-4727

Full-time: 220 men, 363 women	Faculty: 55; IIA, -$
Part-time: 39 men, 65 women	Ph.D.s: 63%
Graduate: 29 men, 24 women	Student/Faculty: 11 to 1
Year: 4-1-4, summer session	Tuition: $17,040
Application Deadline: open	Room & Board: $5460
Freshman Class: 627 applied, 545 accepted, 105 enrolled	
SAT I Verbal/Math: 580/560	ACT: 25 VERY COMPETITIVE

King College, founded in 1867, is a private liberal arts college affiliated with the Presbyterian Church (U.S.A.). There are 5 undergraduate schools and 1 graduate school. The library contains 80,126 volumes, 37,408 microform items, and 5657 audio/video tapes/CDs, and subscribes to 529 periodicals. Computerized library services include the card catalog, interlibrary loans, database searching, and Internet access. Special learning facilities include a learning resource center and an observatory. The 135-acre campus is in a small town 2 miles east of Bristol. Including any residence halls, there are 16 buildings.

Student Life: 53% of undergraduates are from Tennessee. Students are from 28 states and 24 foreign countries. 83% are from public schools. 77% are white. 71% are Protestant; 6% Buddhism and non-Christian; 11% claim no religious affiliation. The average age of freshmen is 18; all undergraduates, 23. 27% do not continue beyond their first year; 51% remain to graduate.

Housing: 485 students can be accommodated in college housing, which includes single-sex dorms and married-student housing. In addition, there are honors houses. On-campus housing is guaranteed for all 4 years and is available on a first-come, first-served basis. 54% of students commute. Alcohol is not permitted. All students may keep cars.

Activities: There are no fraternities or sororities. There are 41 groups on campus, including art, band, cheerleading, choir, chorale, chorus, dance, debate, drama, honors, international, literary magazine, musical theater, newspaper, photography, political, professional, religious, social service, student government, and yearbook. Popular campus events include International Fair, Fall Ball, and Dogwood Ball and Weekend.

Sports: There are 6 intercollegiate sports for men and 5 for women, and 8 intramural sports for men and 8 for women. Facilities include a gym, soccer and baseball fields, 6 tennis courts, and a fitness trail. A student center complex provides a facility for sporting events, convocations, student activities, and fitness. The 68,000 sq. ft. building has a running track, racquetball courts, coach's office, boardroom, weight room, medical suite, and exercise corridor.

Disabled Students: 80% of the campus is accessible. Wheelchair ramps, elevators, special parking, and specially equipped rest rooms are available.

Services: Counseling and information services are available, as is tutoring in most subjects.

Campus Safety and Security: Measures include security escort services, informal discussions, lighted pathways/sidewalks, and 24-hour foot and vehicle patrol on weekends, and 12-hour patrol Monday through Friday.

Programs of Study: King confers B.A., B.S., B.S. Med.Tech., and B.S.N. degrees. Master's degrees are also awarded. Bachelor's degrees are awarded in BIOLOGICAL SCIENCE (biochemistry and biology/biological science), BUSINESS (business administration and management, business economics, and electronic business), COMMUNICATIONS AND THE ARTS (English, French, modern language, Spanish, and visual and performing arts), COMPUTER AND PHYSICAL SCIENCE (applied mathematics, chemistry, computer science, mathematics, and physics), EDUCATION (elementary and secondary), HEALTH PROFESSIONS (medical technology and nursing), SOCIAL SCIENCE (American studies, behavioral science, biblical studies, history, missions, political science/government, psychology, and youth ministry). English, history, and natural sciences are the strongest academically. Behavioral science, economics/business, and nursing are the largest.

Required: Students must complete a minimum of 124 semester hours with 27 to 53 in the major. The 51 semester hours of core curriculum include courses in English, history, math, Bible, humanities, science, social science, and phys ed. Students must have a minimum GPA of 2.0. A comprehensive exam in the student's major area of concentration is required.

Special: King offers co-op programs, cross-registration with Virginia Intermont College, internships, study abroad in more than 50 countries, a Washington semester, and work-study programs. There are 3-2 engineering degrees available with Vanderbilt University and University of Tennessee. A dual degree in pharmacy is also offered. Nondegree study and pass/fail options for special students are available. There is 1 national honor society, a freshman honors program, and 14 departmental honors programs.

Faculty/Classroom: 62% of faculty are male; 38%, female. All teach undergraduates and 45% both teach and do research. The average class size in an introductory lecture is 30; in a laboratory, 30; and in a regular course, 15.

Admissions: 87% of the 2003-2004 applicants were accepted. The SAT I scores for the 2003-2004 freshman class were: Verbal--23% below 500, 30% between 500 and 599, 37% between 600 and 700, and 7% above 700; Math--33% below 500, 33% between 500 and 599, 23% between 600 and 700, and 9% above 700. The ACT scores were 13% below 21, 26% between 21 and 23, 31% between 24 and 26, 17% between 27 and 28, and 13% above 28. 49% of the current freshmen were in the top fifth of their class; 79% were in the top two fifths. 7 freshmen graduated first in their class.

Requirements: The SAT I or ACT is required. In addition, candidates for admission should be graduates of accredited or recognized secondary schools. The GED is accepted. Students are required to have 16 academic credits, including 4 in English, 2 each in foreign language, history, algebra, and social studies, and 1 each in geometry, and natural science. An essay is required. An audition and interview are recommended. A GPA of 2.4 is required. AP and CLEP credits are accepted. If admission requirements are not met, the school considers advanced placement or honor courses, extracurricular activities record, and leadership record.

Procedure: Freshmen are admitted to all sessions. Entrance exams should be taken before May 1. There are early admissions and deferred admissions plans. Application deadlines are open. Notification is sent within 48 hours after the application materials are received. The fall 2003 application fee was $20. Applications are accepted on-line through the school's web site.

Transfer: 58 transfer students enrolled in 2003-2004. Transfer applicants should have a minimum 2.0 GPA and 30 semester hours. If fewer hours have been completed, a 2.4 high school GPA and a minimum ACT composite score of 20, or SAT I composite score of 1000, are required. 50 of 124 credits required for the bachelor's degree must be completed at King.

Visiting: There are regularly scheduled orientations for prospective students, including a campus tour, financial aid seminar, faculty sessions, an overnight visit in a dorm, and admissions counseling. There are guides for informal visits and visitors may sit in on classes and stay overnight. To schedule a visit, contact The Admissions Office at (423) 652-4861.

Financial Aid: In 2003-2004, 82% of all full-time freshmen and 78% of continuing full-time students received some form of financial aid. 77% of full-time freshmen and 70% of continuing full-time students received need-based aid. The average freshman award was $19,498. Need-based scholarships or need-based grants averaged $12,274; need-based self-help aid (loans and jobs) averaged $3194; non-need-based athletic scholarships averaged $5217; and other non-need-based awards and non-need- based scholarships averaged $7459. 28% of undergraduates work part time. Average annual earnings from campus work are $750. The average financial indebtedness of the 2003 graduate was $11,000. King is a member of CSS. The FAFSA and the college's own financial statement are required. The priority date for freshman financial aid applications for fall entry is February 15. The deadline for filing freshman financial aid applications for fall entry is rolling.

International Students: There are 40 international students enrolled. The school actively recruits these students. They must take the college's own test.

Computers: A campuswide network connects 80 Pentium class machines located in 4 labs. Students are given an IBM Thinkpad and can access the network from virtually any location on campus, including dorms, library, and study areas. All students may access the system. There are no time limits and no fees.

Graduates: From July 1, 2002 to June 30, 2003, 136 bachelor's degrees were awarded. The most popular majors were business (13%), behavioral science (13%), and elementary education (13%). In an average class, 4% graduate in 3 years or less, 47% graduate in 4 years or less, 50% graduate in 5 years or less, and 51% graduate in 6 years or less. Of the 2002 graduating class, 20% were enrolled in graduate school within 6 months of graduation.

Admissions Contact: Melinda Clark, Associate Vice President of Enrollment Management. E-mail: *admissions@king.edu*
Web: *www.king.edu*

KNOXVILLE COLLEGE

Knoxville, TN 37921

E-3

(865) 524-6500
(800) 743-5669; Fax: (865) 524-6686

Full-time: 115 men, 80 women	Faculty: 47
Part-time: 10 women	Ph.D.s: 55%
Graduate: none	Student/Faculty: n/av
Year: semesters	Tuition: $6200
Application Deadline: open	Room & Board: n/app
Freshman Class: n/av	
SAT I or ACT: recommended	LESS COMPETITIVE

Knoxville College, founded in 1875, is a small, private liberal arts institution affiliated with the United Presbyterian Church. Figures in the above capsule and in this profile are approximate. The library contains 79,000 volumes and 11,000 microform items, and subscribes to 450 periodicals. The 39-acre campus is in an urban area. There are 22 buildings.

Programs of Study: KC confers B.A., B.S., B.S.Ed., B.S.M.T., and B.S. in Tourism, Food, and Lodging Administration. degrees. Associate degrees are also awarded. Bachelor's degrees are awarded in BIOLOGICAL SCIENCE (biology/biological science), BUSINESS (accounting and business administration and management), COMMUNICATIONS AND THE ARTS (English and music), COMPUTER AND PHYSICAL SCIENCE (chemistry), EDUCATION (business, early childhood, elementary, health, mathematics, music, physical, recreation, and science), HEALTH PROFESSIONS (health care administration and medical laboratory technology), SOCIAL SCIENCE (political science/government, psychology, and sociology).

Required: To graduate, all students must complete 124 semester hours with at least a 2.0 GPA. 66 hours in a core curriculum are required, including courses in English, speech, history, math, natural and social sciences, religion, philosophy, humanities and the arts, computer science, health, and phys ed. Between 26 and 40 hours are required in the major.

Special: A 3-2 engineering degree is offered with the University of Tennessee. Students seeking degrees in tourism, food and lodging administration, or recreation leadership may take some courses at the University of Tennessee. Cooperative programs, nondegree study, internships, and dual majors are possible. There is a freshman honors program.

Requirements: SAT I or ACT scores should be submitted for placement purposes. Applicants should be graduates of an accredited high school or have earned the GED. Secondary preparation should include a total of 15 Carnegie units. Music program applicants must audition. Culturally disadvantaged students may be admitted under a special program. A GPA of 2.0 is required.

Procedure: Application deadlines are open.

Transfer: Applicants with fewer than 15 college credits must submit a high school transcript. 30 of 124 credits required for the bachelor's degree must be completed at KC.

Visiting: There are guides for informal visits. To schedule a visit, contact Director of Admissions.

Financial Aid: The FAFSA and the college's own financial statement are required.

International Students: They must score 475 on the written TOEFL.

Computers: All students may access the system. There are no time limits and no fees.

Admissions Contact: Director of Admissions. A video is available.

LAMBUTH UNIVERSITY

Jackson, TN 38301

B-3

(731) 425-3322
(800) 526-2884; Fax: (731) 425-3496

Full-time: 371 men, 406 women	Faculty: 52; IIB, --$
Part-time: 29 men, 30 women	Ph.D.s: 75%
Graduate: none	Student/Faculty: 15 to 1
Year: semesters, summer session	Tuition: $11,590
Application Deadline: open	Room & Board: $4930
Freshman Class: 881 applied, 575 accepted, 181 enrolled	
SAT I Verbal/Math: 550/530	ACT: 22 COMPETITIVE

Lambuth University, founded in 1843, is a private liberal arts and sciences institution affiliated with the United Methodist Church. There are 6 undergraduate schools. In addition to regional accreditation, Lambuth has baccalaureate program accreditation with ACBSP. The library contains 177,792 volumes, 175,328 microform items, and 1044 audio/video tapes/CDs, and subscribes to 430 periodicals. Computerized library services include the card catalog, interlibrary loans, database searching, and Internet access. Special learning facilities include a learning resource center, art gallery, planetarium, radio station, and video studio. The 50-acre campus is in an urban area 75 miles northeast of Memphis. Including any residence halls, there are 16 buildings.

Student Life: 79% of undergraduates are from Tennessee. Students are from 29 states, 16 foreign countries, and Canada. 81% are from public schools. 78% are white; 17% African American. 70% are Protestant; 8% Catholic; 28% claim no religious affiliation. The average age of freshmen is 18; all undergraduates, 22. 36% do not continue beyond their first year; 41% remain to graduate.

Housing: 622 students can be accommodated in college housing, which includes single-sex and coed dorms, on-campus apartments, fraternity houses, and sorority houses. In addition, there are honors houses. 58% of students live on campus; of those, 60% remain on campus on weekends. Alcohol is not permitted. All students may keep cars.

Activities: 30% of men belong to 3 national fraternities; 29% of women belong to 4 national sororities. There are 26 groups on campus, including art, band, cheerleading, chess, choir, computers, dance, drama, ethnic, film, honors, international, jazz band, literary magazine, musical theater, newspaper, pep band, photography, political, professional, radio and TV, religious, social, social service, student government, and yearbook. Popular campus events include Hawaiian Bash, FOCUS, Christmas Candlelight Service, and All-Sing.

Sports: There are 7 intercollegiate sports for men and 7 for women, and 10 intramural sports for men and 10 for women. Facilities include an indoor swimming pool, racquetball and tennis courts, a weight room, a gym, and football, baseball, and soccer fields.

Disabled Students: 75% of the campus is accessible. Wheelchair ramps, elevators, special parking, specially equipped rest rooms, and special class scheduling are available.

Services: Counseling and information services are available, as is tutoring in most subjects. There is remedial math, reading, and writing.

Campus Safety and Security: Measures include 24-hour foot and vehicle patrol, self-defense education, security escort services, and informal discussions. There are pamphlets/posters/films, emergency telephones, and lighted pathways/sidewalks.

Programs of Study: Lambuth confers B.A., B.S., B.B.A., and B.M. degrees. Bachelor's degrees are awarded in BIOLOGICAL SCIENCE (biology/biological science), BUSINESS (business administration and management), COMMUNICATIONS AND THE ARTS (communications, dramatic arts, English, fine arts, French, German, music, Spanish, and visual and performing arts), COMPUTER AND PHYSICAL SCIENCE (chemistry and mathematics), EDUCATION (athletic training, elementary, music, physical, secondary, and special), ENGINEERING AND ENVIRONMENTAL DESIGN (interior design), HEALTH PROFESSIONS (speech pathology/audiology), SOCIAL SCIENCE (family/consumer studies, history, interdisciplinary studies, international relations, political science/government, psychology, religion, and sociology). Biological science, art, and business are the strongest academically. Business, education, and psychology are the largest.

Required: All students must complete a minimum of 128 semester hours, including Freshman Seminar, 9 hours in English, 8 in biological/physical sciences, 6 each in religion, writing courses, and interdisciplinary courses, and 3 each in speech, computer science, social science, and math. Students must have a minimum GPA of 2.0. Students must have 18 hours in a minor field of study. A comprehensive exam in the major field is required. Juniors must take a test of core curriculum skills. Portfolios and research projects may also be required.

Special: Lambuth offers cross-registration with Union University and Freed-Hardeman University, internships in several disciplines, study abroad in England, Mexico, and France, a Washington semester, work-study programs, dual majors in all areas, student-designed majors in most areas, a 3-2 engineering degree, nondegree study, and pass/fail options. Pre-professional programs have a three-year residence program. There are 6 national honor societies, a freshman honors program, and 10 departmental honors programs.

Faculty/Classroom: 60% of faculty are male; 40%, female. All teach undergraduates. The average class size in an introductory lecture is 23; in a laboratory, 23; and in a regular course, 20.

Admissions: 65% of the 2003-2004 applicants were accepted. The SAT I scores for the 2003-2004 freshman class were: Verbal--30% below 500, 39% between 500 and 599, 25% between 600 and 700, and 6% above 700; Math--30% below 500, 42% between 500 and 599, 22% between 600 and 700, and 6% above 700. The ACT scores were 31% below 21, 32% between 21 and 23, 22% between 24 and 26, 10% between 27 and 28, and 5% above 28. 41% of the current freshmen were in the top fifth of their class; 70% were in the top two fifths. 3 freshmen graduated first in their class.

Requirements: The ACT is required, with a minimum ACT composite score of 20. Other students are admitted at the discretion of the admissions committee. Candidates for admission should be graduates of accredited secondary schools. The GED is accepted. It is preferred that students have completed 4 courses each in English, history, math, science, and social studies, and 2 courses in foreign language, art, and music. An essay and interview are recommended. A GPA of 2.0 is required. AP and CLEP credits are accepted. Important factors in the admissions decision are advanced placement or honor courses, leadership record, and recommendations by school officials.

Procedure: Freshmen are admitted to all sessions. Entrance exams should be taken by February of the senior year. There are early admissions and deferred admissions plans. Application deadlines are open. There is a rolling admissions plan. The fall 2003 application fee was $25. Applications are accepted on-line through the school's web site.

Transfer: 101 transfer students enrolled in 2002-2003. A minimum 2.0 GPA in college-level courses taken, transcripts from all colleges attended, and a statement of honorable dismissal are required. An associate degree usually guarantees admission. A minimum of 12 successfully completed credit hours is recommended. 32 of 128 credits required for the bachelor's degree must be completed at Lambuth.

Visiting: There are regularly scheduled orientations for prospective students, consisting of students and parents touring the campus, participating in the students panel discussion, and attending a luncheon. Students visit a class. Parents participate in seminars. There are guides for informal visits and visitors may sit in on classes and stay overnight. To schedule a visit, contact the Office of Admissions at (800) 526-2884 or admit@lambuth.edu.

Financial Aid: In 2003-2004, 96% of all full-time freshmen and 86% of continuing full-time students received some form of financial aid. 58% of full-time freshmen and 63% of continuing full-time students received need-based aid. The average freshman award was $10,116. Need-based scholarships or need-based grants averaged $5935; need-based self-help aid (loans and jobs) averaged $2495; non-need-based athletic scholarships averaged $5552; and other non-need-based awards and non-need-based scholarships averaged $4113. 42% of undergraduates work part time. Average annual earnings from campus work are $1000. The average financial indebtedness of the 2003 graduate was $11,000. Lambuth is a member of CSS. The FAFSA and the college's own financial statement are required. The priority date for freshman financial aid applications for fall entry is February 15. The deadline for filing freshman financial aid applications for fall entry is May 1.

International Students: There are 18 international students enrolled. The school actively recruits these students. They must score 500 on the written TOEFL.

Computers: The mainframe is an IBM AS/400 C25. There are computer labs with both PCs and Macs and computer access in residence halls and the library. All students may access the system 8 A.M. to 10 P.M. when classes are not in session (computer lab). There are no time limits and no fees. It is strongly recommended that all students have a personal computer.

Graduates: From July 1, 2002 to June 30, 2003, 163 bachelor's degrees were awarded. The most popular majors were business (20%), education (18%), and communications (10%). In an average class, 4% graduate in 3 years or less, 30% graduate in 4 years or less, 39% graduate in 5 years or less, and 41% graduate in 6 years or less. 40 companies recruited on campus in 2002-2003. Of the 2002 graduating class, 25% were enrolled in graduate school within 6 months of graduation and 63% were employed.

Admissions Contact: Candy Donald, Associate Director of Admissions. E-mail: admit@lambuth.edu Web: www.lambuth.edu

LANE COLLEGE
Jackson, TN 38301-4598

B-3
(731) 426-7532
(800) 960-7533; Fax: (731) 426-7559

Full-time: 451 men, 487 women	**Faculty:** 50; IIB, --$
Part-time: 6 men, 8 women	**Ph.Ds:** 60%
Graduate: none	**Student/Faculty:** 19 to 1
Year: semesters, summer session	**Tuition:** $6812
Application Deadline: July 1	**Room & Board:** $4366
Freshman Class: 2636 applied, 733 accepted, 296 enrolled	
ACT: 16	**COMPETITIVE+**

Lane College, founded in 1882, is a private liberal arts institution affiliated with the Christian Methodist Episcopal Church. The library contains 98,619 volumes, 53,125 microform items, and 820 audio/video tapes/CDs, and subscribes to 226 periodicals. Computerized library services include the card catalog, interlibrary loans, database searching, and Internet access. Special learning facilities include a learning resource center, a media center, several computer labs for students majoring in education and other areas, a curriculum lab, a video teleconferencing center, a math lab, a writing center, and a mass communications lab. The 25-acre campus is in a small town 79 miles from Memphis, 122 miles from Nashville. Including any residence halls, there are 23 buildings.

Student Life: 57% of undergraduates are from Tennessee. Students are from 30 states and 1 foreign country. 85% are from public schools. 99% are African American. Most are Protestant. The average age of freshmen is 19; all undergraduates, 21. 20% do not continue beyond their first year; 65% remain to graduate.

Housing: 638 students can be accommodated in college housing, which includes single-sex dorms and on-campus apartments. On-campus housing is guaranteed for all 4 years. 63% of students live on campus; of those, 40% remain on campus on weekends. Alcohol is not permitted. All students may keep cars.

Activities: 3% of men belong to 2 local and 2 national fraternities; 9% of women belong to 4 local and 4 national sororities. There are 21 groups on campus, including band, cheerleading, chess, choir, chorus, computers, debate, drama, honors, marching band, newspaper, pep band, religious, social, social service, student government, and yearbook. Popular campus events include Founders Day, Fine Arts Week, and Religious Emphasis Week.

Sports: There are 6 intercollegiate sports for men and 6 for women, and 4 intramural sports for men and 4 for women. Facilities include an Olympic-size swimming pool, a multipurpose/weight room, a gym, off-campus football and baseball fields, and a campus recreation center with a theater area, dance floor, billiards, Ping-Pong, table games, and a lounge area.

Disabled Students: 70% of the campus is accessible. Wheelchair ramps, elevators, special parking, specially equipped rest rooms, and wheelchair lifts in some buildings are available.

Services: Counseling and information services are available, as is tutoring in most subjects. The writing center provides tutoring in writing and the mathematics lab offers tutoring in math. Student Support Services provides tutoring in English, math, reading, computer science, computer literacy, test-taking, and study skills.

Campus Safety and Security: Measures include 24-hour foot and vehicle patrol, security escort services, informal discussions, and pamphlets/posters/films. There are emergency telephones, lighted pathways/sidewalks, a security guard at the entrance to the campus, and camera surveillance in parking lots and dorms.

Programs of Study: Lane confers B.A. and B.S. degrees. Bachelor's degrees are awarded in BIOLOGICAL SCIENCE (biology/biological science), BUSINESS (business administration and management), COMMUNICATIONS AND THE ARTS (communications, English, French, and music), COMPUTER AND PHYSICAL SCIENCE (chemistry, computer science, mathematics, and physics), EDUCATION (physical), SOCIAL SCIENCE (criminal justice, history, interdisciplinary studies, religion, and sociology). Business, education, and criminal justice are the strongest academically. Education, business, and sociology are the largest.

Required: Students must complete a minimum of 124 semester hours with a 2.0 GPA. 50 to 69 hours are required in the general studies curriculum, which includes courses in art, music, personal finance, foreign language, speech, composition, literature, history, sociology, math, physical science, biology, computer literacy, foundations of education, religion, and phys ed. The ETS Academic Profile is also required. ETS Major Field Tests are given as exit exams by major.

Special: Cooperative programs are available in engineering with the Tennessee State University School of Engineering and Technology. The college also offers work-study programs, dual majors, student-designed majors, and nondegree study. Internships are available in many fields in various corporations, universities, and federal agencies. The college also has a cooperative agreement with Milwaukee Area Technical College. There are 2 national honor societies.

Faculty/Classroom: 72% of faculty are male; 28%, female. All teach undergraduates. The average class size in an introductory lecture is 25; in a laboratory, 16; and in a regular course, 16.

Admissions: 28% of the 2003-2004 applicants were accepted. The ACT scores for the 2003-2004 freshman class were: 94% below 21, and 6% between 21 and 23. 20% of the current freshmen were in the top fifth of their class; 45% were in the top two fifths.

Requirements: The ACT is required, with a minimum composite score of 17 recommended. Graduation from an accredited secondary school is required; a GED will be accepted. Applicants' academic record must include 16 credits, including 4 credits in English, and 2 credits each in math, science, and social studies. An additional 2 credits in a foreign language is recommended. An interview is recommended. A GPA of 2.0 is required. AP and CLEP credits are accepted. Important factors in the admissions decision are evidence of special talent, recommendations by school officials, and ability to finance college education.

Procedure: Freshmen are admitted to all sessions. Entrance exams should be taken by October of the senior year. There are early decision and early admissions plans. There is a rolling admissions plan. Applications should be filed by July 1 for fall entry, November 15 for spring entry, and May 15 for summer entry. Notification is sent on a rolling basis. 137 early decision candidates were accepted for the 2003-2004 class. Applications are accepted on-line.

Transfer: 103 transfer students enrolled in 2002-2003. Applicants must submit transcripts from previous colleges attended and be in good standing at the time of application. Students having an associate degree will be given credit for a maximum of 68 semester hours in general education courses with a grade of C or higher. 31 of 124 credits required for the bachelor's degree must be completed at Lane.

Visiting: There are regularly scheduled orientations for prospective students, including meetings on financial aid, residential life, rules and regulations of the college, course requirements, and registration. There are guides for informal visits and visitors may sit in on classes and stay overnight. To schedule a visit, contact the Office of Recruitment/Admissions at ebrown@lanecollege.edu.

Financial Aid: The average freshman award was $9318. 39% of undergraduates work part time. Average annual earnings from campus work are $971. The average financial indebtedness of the 2003 graduate was $19,275. The CSS Profile, FAFSA, FFS, or SFS is required. The deadline for filing freshman financial aid applications for fall entry is March 31.

International Students: There is 1 international student enrolled. The school actively recruits these students. They must take the TOEFL and the ACT, scoring 13.

Computers: The mainframe is an IBM A/S 400. All students have access to the Internet and Web through the library and 5 computer labs with approximately 120 PCs. All dorms are wired. All students may access the system. There are no time limits and no fees.

Graduates: From July 1, 2002 to June 30, 2003, 88 bachelor's degrees were awarded. The most popular majors were interdisciplinary studies (23%), computer science (14%), and criminal justice (12%). In an average class, 39% graduate in 4 years or less, 54% graduate in 5 years or

less, and 61% graduate in 6 years or less. 31 companies recruited on campus in 2002-2003. Of the 2002 graduating class, 32% were enrolled in graduate school within 6 months of graduation and 63% were employed.

Admissions Contact: Evelyn L. Brown, Director of Admissions. A video is available. E-mail: ebrown@lanecollege.edu. Web: www.lanecollege.edu

LEE UNIVERSITY	D-4
Cleveland, TN 37311	(423) 614-8500
	(800) 533-9930; Fax: (423) 614-8533

Full-time: 1366 men, 1838 women	**Faculty:** 135; IIB, --$
Part-time: 168 men, 183 women	**Ph.D.s:** 67%
Graduate: 93 men, 158 women	**Student/Faculty:** 17 to 1
Year: semesters, summer session	**Tuition:** $8830
Application Deadline: September 1	**Room & Board:** $4950
Freshman Class: 1204 applied, 676 accepted, 654 enrolled	
SAT I Verbal/Math: 538/517	**ACT:** 22 **NONCOMPETITIVE**

Lee University, founded in 1918, is a private liberal arts institution affiliated with the Church of God. There are 4 undergraduate and 4 graduate schools. In addition to regional accreditation, Lee has baccalaureate program accreditation with NASM. The 2 libraries contain 127,714 volumes, 50,946 microform items, and 8453 audio/video tapes/CDs, and subscribe to 516 periodicals. Computerized library services include the card catalog, interlibrary loans, database searching, and Internet access. Special learning facilities include a learning resource center, natural history museum, and audiovisual center. The 115-acre campus is in a suburban area 25 miles north of Chattanooga. Including any residence halls, there are 50 buildings.

Student Life: 60% of undergraduates are from out of state, mostly the South. Students are from 50 states, 47 foreign countries, and Canada. 75% are from public schools. 82% are white. The average age of freshmen is 18; all undergraduates, 22. 26% do not continue beyond their first year; 74% remain to graduate.

Housing: 1840 students can be accommodated in college housing, which includes single-sex dorms, on-campus apartments, off-campus apartments, and married-student housing. On-campus housing is guaranteed for the freshman year only and is available on a first-come, first-served basis. 56% of students commute. Alcohol is not permitted. All students may keep cars.

Activities: There are no fraternities or sororities. There are 63 groups on campus, including art, band, cheerleading, choir, chorale, chorus, computers, debate, drama, ethnic, film, honors, international, jazz band, literary magazine, musical theater, newspaper, opera, orchestra, pep band, photography, political, professional, radio and TV, religious, social, social service, student government, symphony, and yearbook. Popular campus events include College Day, Parade of Favorites, and Dorm Wars.

Sports: There are 6 intercollegiate sports for men and 6 for women, and 23 intramural sports for men and 23 for women. Facilities include an arena, a recreation complex, softball, soccer, baseball, and playing fields, and a tennis center.

Disabled Students: 69% of the campus is accessible. Wheelchair ramps, elevators, special parking, specially equipped rest rooms, special class scheduling, and lowered drinking fountains are available.

Services: Counseling and information services are available, as is tutoring in every subject. There is a reader service for the blind and remedial math, reading, and writing.

Campus Safety and Security: Measures include 24-hour foot and vehicle patrol, security escort services, shuttle buses, and informal discussions. There are pamphlets/posters/films, emergency telephones, and lighted pathways/sidewalks.

Programs of Study: Lee confers B.A., B.S., B.C.M., B.M., and B.M.E. degrees. Master's degrees are also awarded. Bachelor's degrees are awarded in BIOLOGICAL SCIENCE (biology/biological science), BUSINESS (accounting and business administration and management), COMMUNICATIONS AND THE ARTS (communications, English, French, German, music, and Spanish), COMPUTER AND PHYSICAL SCIENCE (chemistry, computer programming, mathematics, and science), EDUCATION (elementary, music, and physical), HEALTH PROFESSIONS (medical laboratory technology), SOCIAL SCIENCE (crosscultural studies, history, human development, psychology, religious education, social science, and sociology). Business administration, communication, and human development are the strongest academically. Business, human development, and psychology are the largest.

Required: All students must complete a minimum of 130 credit hours, including a core curriculum and 36 hours in the major, with a 2.0 GPA (2.5 for education majors). A Global Perspectives seminar and crosscultural experience are required, in addition to a major field test the last semester before graduation in all fields except preprofessional sciences and teacher licensure.

Special: Lee offers internships, cross-registration with the Coalition for Christian Colleges and Universities, study abroad, a Washington semester, numerous work-study programs, dual and student-designed majors, nondegree study, and limited pass/fail options. Every student completes a minor in religion. There are 13 national honor societies, a freshman honors program, and 6 departmental honors programs.

Faculty/Classroom: 71% of faculty are male; 29%, female. All teach undergraduates and 20% both teach and do research. No introductory courses are taught by graduate students. The average class size in an introductory lecture is 25; in a laboratory, 15; and in a regular course, 25.

Admissions: 56% of the 2003-2004 applicants were accepted. The SAT I scores for the 2003-2004 freshman class were: Verbal--34% below 500, 38% between 500 and 599, 23% between 600 and 700, and 5% above 700; Math--42% below 500, 37% between 500 and 599, 18% between 600 and 700, and 3% above 700. The ACT scores were 16% below 18, 38% between 18 and 23, 39% between 24 and 29, and 7% between 30 and 36. 16% of the current freshmen were in the top fifth of their class; 65% were in the top two fifths.

Requirements: The SAT I or ACT is required, with a composite score of 860 on the SAT I or 17 on the ACT. Students must be graduates of accredited secondary schools. The GED is accepted. A portfolio is recommended. A GPA of 2.0 is required. AP and CLEP credits are accepted. Important factors in the admissions decision are advanced placement or honor courses, leadership record, and recommendations by school officials.

Procedure: Freshmen are admitted fall and spring. Entrance exams should be taken prior to registration. There are early admissions and deferred admissions plans. There is a rolling admissions plan. Early decision applications should be filed by January 1; regular applications, by September 1 for fall entry, along with a $25 fee. Notification is sent on a rolling basis. Applications are accepted on-line through Tennessee Mentor.

Transfer: 245 transfer students enrolled in 2002-2003. Transfer students must take the SAT I, scoring 860, or the ACT, scoring 17, unless they have 16 credit hours with a GPA of 2.0 or better. Students must have official transcripts from all prior colleges. 30 credits of 130 required for the bachelor's degree must be completed at Lee.

Visiting: There are regularly scheduled orientations for prospective students. The Admissions Office will arrange a complete campus tour upon request. There are guides for informal visits and visitors may sit in on classes. To schedule a visit, contact the Admissions Center at *admissions@leeuniversity.edu*.

Financial Aid: In 2003-2004, 90% of all full-time freshmen received some form of financial aid. 59% of full-time freshmen and 56% of continuing full-time students received need-based aid. The average freshman award was $7042. Need-based scholarships or need-based grants averaged $5750; need-based self-help aid (loans and jobs) averaged $2917; and average need-based loans (excluding PLUS, unsubsidized, and private loans) averaged $2793. 14% of undergraduates work part time. Average annual earnings from campus work are $2000. The average financial indebtedness of the 2003 graduate was $21,616. Lee is a member of CSS. The FAFSA and the college's own financial statement are required. The deadline for filing freshman financial aid applications for fall entry is April 15.

International Students: The school actively recruits these students. They must score 450 on the written TOEFL or 133 on the electronic version.

Computers: The mainframe is an IBM AS/400. There are PCs available for student use in the computer labs and library. All students may access the system. There are no time limits. The fee is $25 per semester.

Graduates: From July 1, 2002 to June 30, 2003, 685 bachelor's degrees were awarded. The most popular majors were education (24%), philosophy, religion, and theology (18%), and business marketing (12%). In an average class, 1% graduate in 3 years or less, 43% graduate in 4 years or less, 44% graduate in 5 years or less, and 42% graduate in 6 years or less.

Admissions Contact: Phil Cook, Director of Admissions. A CD is available. E-mail: *admissions@leeuniversity.edu* Web: *http://www.leeuniversity.edu*

LEMOYNE-OWEN COLLEGE
Memphis, TN 38126

A-4
(901) 942-7302
(800) 737-7778; Fax: (901) 942-6233

Full-time: 640 men and women	**Faculty:** 45
Part-time: 142 men and women	**Ph.Ds:** 80%
Graduate: none	**Student/Faculty:** 14 to 1
Year: semesters, summer session	**Tuition:** $8450
Application Deadline: April 1	**Room & Board:** $4620
Freshman Class: n/av	
SAT I or ACT: required	LESS COMPETITIVE

LeMoyne-Owen College, established in 1872, is a private, liberal arts college affiliated with the United Church of Christ and the Tennessee Baptist Missionary and Educational Convention, offering degrees in the liberal arts and sciences and business administration. In addition to regional accreditation, LOC has baccalaureate program accreditation with

NCATE. The library contains 90,000 volumes and 1000 audio/video tapes/CDs, and subscribes to 300 periodicals. Computerized library services include the card catalog, interlibrary loans, database searching, and Internet access. Special learning facilities include a learning resource center and art gallery. The 15-acre campus is in an urban area. Including any residence halls, there are 18 buildings.

Student Life: 86% of undergraduates are from Tennessee. Students are from 20 states and 3 foreign countries. 95% are from public schools. 94% are African American. 90% are Protestant; 8% claim no religious affiliation. The average age of all undergraduates is 23. 30% do not continue beyond their first year; 20% remain to graduate.

Housing: 140 students can be accommodated in college housing, which includes single-sex and coed dorms. On-campus housing is available on a first-come, first-served basis. Priority is given to out-of-town students. 80% of students commute. Alcohol is not permitted. All students may keep cars.

Activities: 20% of men belong to 4 local and 4 national fraternities; 20% of women belong to 4 local and 4 national sororities. There are 15 groups on campus, including cheerleading, choir, chorus, community outreach, computers, drama, ethnic, math, newspaper, photography, professional, religious, social service, student government, and yearbook.

Sports: There are 4 intercollegiate sports for men and 5 for women, and 1 intramural sport for men and 5 for women. Facilities include a gym, a pool, and other phys ed installations.

Disabled Students: 80% of the campus is accessible. Wheelchair ramps and elevators are available.

Services: Counseling and information services are available, as is tutoring in every subject. There is remedial math, reading, and writing.

Campus Safety and Security: Measures include 24-hour foot and vehicle patrol, security escort services, emergency telephones, and lighted pathways/sidewalks.

Programs of Study: LOC confers B.A., B.S., and B.B.A. degrees. Bachelor's degrees are awarded in BIOLOGICAL SCIENCE (biology/biological science), BUSINESS (accounting and business administration and management), COMMUNICATIONS AND THE ARTS (art, English, language arts, and music), COMPUTER AND PHYSICAL SCIENCE (chemistry, computer science, mathematics, natural sciences, and science), EDUCATION (early childhood and special), SOCIAL SCIENCE (criminal justice, history, humanities, political science/government, social science, social work, and sociology). Business, biology, and education are the strongest academically. Business and biology are the largest.

Required: To graduate, students must satisfy 42 hours of core requirements in communication, math, natural and computer sciences, literature and the humanities, African and African American history, social and behavioral sciences, and physical fitness. They must have a minimum GPA of 2.0 and grades of C or better in all major courses. The college requires 120 credits for graduation, including at least 45 in upper-division courses. All recent high school graduates must participate in the Freshman Year Experience Program.

Special: Students may cross-register with other institutions of the Greater Memphis Consortium. The college offers a work-study program, dual and student-designed majors, internships, nondegree study, and a pass/fail grading option. There are dual-degree programs in pharmacy with Xavier School of Pharmacy, in optometry with Southern College of Optometry, and in engineering with Christian Brothers University. There is 1 national honor society, a freshman honors program, and honors programs in all departments.

Faculty/Classroom: All faculty teach undergraduates and 40% do research. The average class size in an introductory lecture is 15; in a laboratory, 15; and in a regular course, 12.

Requirements: The SAT I or ACT is required. In addition, applicants must graduate from an accredited secondary school, having completed 20 high school units. The college recommends 4 years of English, 2 each of math, science, and social studies, and 1 of a foreign language. Applicants must submit 2 letters of recommendation. Students 23 or older may be admitted to the division of lifelong learning, which accepts the GED. A GPA of 2.0 is required. AP and CLEP credits are accepted. Important factors in the admissions decision are advanced placement or honor courses, evidence of special talent, and parents or siblings attending the school.

Procedure: Freshmen are admitted to all sessions. Entrance exams should be taken in the spring of the junior year. There is a rolling admissions plan. There are early admissions and deferred admissions plans. Priority applications should be filed by April 1 for fall entry, November 1 for spring entry, and March 1 for summer entry, along with a $25 fee. Notification is sent on a rolling basis.

Transfer: 122 transfer students enrolled in 2002-2003. Applicants should have a GPA of 2.0 and must submit 2 copies of official transcripts plus a statement of good standing from the previous college attended. Students with fewer than 28 college credit hours must also submit a high school transcript and, if below age 21, ACT or SAT I scores. 30 of 120 credits required for the bachelor's degree must be completed at LOC.

Visiting: There are regularly scheduled orientations for prospective students. There are guides for informal visits and visitors may sit in on classes. To schedule a visit, contact Lonnie Morris.

Financial Aid: In a recent year, 90% of all full-time students received some form of financial aid. 80% of full-time freshmen and 90% of continuing full-time students received need-based aid. 90% of undergraduates work part time. Average annual earnings from campus work are $2880. LOC is a member of CSS. The FAFSA and the college's own financial statement are required. The priority date for freshman financial aid applications for fall entry is May 1.

International Students: International students must score 525 on the written TOEFL and also take the ACT.

Computers: The mainframe is a DEC VAX 11/750. All students may access the system. There are no time limits and no fees.

Graduates: In a recent year, 118 bachelor's degrees were awarded. The most popular majors were business management (37%), liberal studies (12%), and education (12%).

Admissions Contact: Lonnie Morris, Director of Admissions.
E-mail: *lonnie_morris@nile.lemoyne-owen.edu*
Web: *www.lemoyne-owen.edu*

LINCOLN MEMORIAL UNIVERSITY E-2
Harrogate, TN 37752-0901 (423) 869-6280
(800) 325-0900; Fax: (423) 869-6370

Full-time: 246 men, 616 women	**Faculty:** 71
Part-time: 58 men, 197 women	**Ph.D.s:** 65%
Graduate: 348 men, 977 women	**Student/Faculty:** 12 to 1
Year: semesters, summer session	**Tuition:** $11,760
Application Deadline: open	**Room & Board:** $4640
Freshman Class: 577 applied, 488 accepted, 183 enrolled	
SAT I or ACT: required	**LESS COMPETITIVE**

Lincoln Memorial University, founded in 1897, is an independent institution offering degree programs in the arts and sciences, business, education, and preprofessional training. There are 4 undergraduate and 2 graduate schools. In addition to regional accreditation, LMU has baccalaureate program accreditation with CAHEA and NLN. The library contains 200,000 volumes, 160,506 microform items, and 254 audio/video tapes/CDs, and subscribes to 893 periodicals. Computerized library services include the card catalog, interlibrary loans, database searching, and Internet access. Special learning facilities include a learning resource center, radio station, TV station, and the Lincoln Museum. The 1000-acre campus is in a rural area 55 miles north of Knoxville. Including any residence halls, there are 32 buildings.

Student Life: 67% of undergraduates are from Tennessee. Students are from 25 states, 22 foreign countries, and Canada. 89% are from public schools. 94% are white. The average age of freshmen is 19; all undergraduates, 23. 20% do not continue beyond their first year; 50% remain to graduate.

Housing: 500 students can be accommodated in college housing, which includes single-sex and coed dorms, on-campus apartments, and married-student housing. On-campus housing is guaranteed for the freshman year only and is available on a first-come, first-served basis. Priority is given to out-of-town students. 70% of students commute. Alcohol is not permitted. All students may keep cars.

Activities: There are 3 local fraternities and 3 local sororities. There are 26 groups on campus, including art, cheerleading, choir, chorus, computers, drama, drill team, honors, international, literary magazine, newspaper, photography, radio and TV, religious, social service, student government, and yearbook. Popular campus events include Lincoln Day.

Sports: There are 6 intercollegiate sports for men and 6 for women, and 4 intramural sports for men and 4 for women. Facilities include a 5000-seat arena, a baseball field, a playing field, and a natatorium.

Disabled Students: 60% of the campus is accessible. Wheelchair ramps, elevators, special parking, and special class scheduling are available.

Services: Counseling and information services are available, as is tutoring in most subjects. There is remedial math, reading, and writing.

Campus Safety and Security: Measures include 24-hour foot and vehicle patrol, informal discussions, pamphlets/posters/films, and lighted pathways/sidewalks.

Programs of Study: LMU confers B.A., B.S., B.B.A., B.S.N., and B.S.W. degrees. Associate and master's degrees are also awarded. Bachelor's degrees are awarded in AGRICULTURE (wildlife management), BIOLOGICAL SCIENCE (biology/biological science), BUSINESS (accounting and business administration and management), COMMUNICATIONS AND THE ARTS (broadcasting, communications, English, and fine arts), COMPUTER AND PHYSICAL SCIENCE (chemistry, information sciences and systems, and mathematics), EDUCATION (athletic training, business, early childhood, elementary, health, middle school, science, and secondary), ENGINEERING AND ENVIRONMENTAL DESIGN (environmental science), HEALTH PROFESSIONS (medical laboratory technology, nursing, predentistry, premedicine, and veterinary science), SOCIAL SCIENCE (history, prelaw, psychology, social

science, and social work). Nursing, business, and education are the largest.

Required: To graduate, all students must complete at least 128 semester credit hours, including the general studies requirements of the declared major and a minimum of 30 hours in the major. Students must achieve a minimum GPA of 2.0.

Special: LMU offers pass/fail options and credit for life, military, and work experience. Some internships are available.

Faculty/Classroom: 49% of faculty are male; 51%, female. 80% teach undergraduates. No introductory courses are taught by graduate students. The average class size in an introductory lecture is 20; in a laboratory, 25; and in a regular course, 20.

Admissions: 85% of the 2003-2004 applicants were accepted.

Requirements: The SAT I or ACT is required. In addition, applicants must score 19 on the ACT or 910 on the SAT I, or graduate with a GPA of at least 2.3. Candidates for admission should be graduates of accredited secondary schools or have the GED. Students should have completed 4 years of English, 2 each of math and science, and 1 each of history and social studies. LMU requires applicants to be in the upper 50% of their class. A GPA of 2.3 is required. AP and CLEP credits are accepted. Important factors in the admissions decision are recommendations by school officials, personality/intangible qualities, and leadership record.

Procedure: Freshmen are admitted fall, spring, and summer. Entrance exams should be taken in the spring of the junior year. There are early admissions and deferred admissions plans. Application deadlines are open. The fall 2003 application fee was $25.

Transfer: 32 of at least 128 credits required for the bachelor's degree must be completed at LMU.

Visiting: There are regularly scheduled orientations for prospective students, including introductory sessions for both students and their parents, opportunities for advising, and registration sessions. There are guides for informal visits and visitors may sit in on classes and stay overnight. To schedule a visit, contact the Office of Admissions and Recruitment at (800) 325-0900, ext. 6280 or *admissions@lmunet.edu.*

Financial Aid: LMU is a member of CSS. The CSS Profile, FAFSA, FFS, or SFS is required. The priority date for freshman financial aid applications for fall entry is April 1. The deadline for filing freshman financial aid applications for fall entry is June 1.

International Students: There are 48 international students enrolled. They must score 500 on the written TOEFL.

Computers: There are 40 PCs available in the student center and several computers in the library and Tagge Center for Academic Excellence. All students may access the system. There are no time limits and no fees. It is strongly recommended that all students have a personal computer.

Graduates: From July 1, 2002 to June 30, 2003, 145 bachelor's degrees were awarded. The most popular majors were nursing (30%), elementary education (27%), and business (26%). In an average class, 42% graduate in 4 years or less.

Admissions Contact: Conrad Daniels, Dean of Admissions.
E-mail: *cdaniels@inetlmu.lmunet.edu* Web: *www.lmunet.edu*

MARYVILLE COLLEGE E-3
Maryville, TN 37804 (865) 981-8206
(800) 597-2687; Fax: (865) 981-8005

Full-time: 455 men, 570 women	**Faculty:** 70; IIB, -$
Part-time: 12 men, 15 women	**Ph.D.s:** 91%
Graduate: none	**Student/Faculty:** 15 to 1
Year: 4-1-4, summer session	**Tuition:** $19,780
Application Deadline: March 1	**Room & Board:** $6180
Freshman Class: 1408 applied, 1112 accepted, 293 enrolled	
SAT I Verbal/Math: 560/570	**ACT:** 24 **VERY COMPETITIVE**

Maryville College, founded in 1819, is a private liberal arts college affiliated with the Presbyterian Church (U.S.A.). In addition to regional accreditation, Maryville has baccalaureate program accreditation with NASM. The 2 libraries contain 126,292 volumes, 7190 microform items, and 3340 audio/video tapes/CDs, and subscribe to more than 16,000 periodicals in paper or electronic format. Computerized library services include the card catalog, interlibrary loans, database searching, and Internet access. Special learning facilities include a learning resource center, art gallery, radio station, a greenhouse, and college woods. The 350-acre campus is in a suburban area 15 miles south of Knoxville. Including any residence halls, there are 24 buildings.

Student Life: 78% of undergraduates are from Tennessee. Others are from 28 states and 17 foreign countries. 87% are from public schools. 87% are white. 64% are Protestant; 9% Catholic. The average age of freshmen is 18; all undergraduates, 21. 29% do not continue beyond their first year; 53% remain to graduate.

Housing: 751 students can be accommodated in college housing, which includes single-sex and coed dorms, on-campus apartments, and off-campus apartments. In addition, there are language houses and special-interest houses. On-campus housing is guaranteed for all 4 years. 67% of students live on campus; of those, 68% remain on campus on weekends. All students may keep cars.

Activities: There are no fraternities or sororities. There are 55 groups on campus, including art, band, cheerleading, choir, chorus, computers, dance, drama, equestrian, ethnic, gay, gospel music, honors, international, jazz band, literary magazine, musical theater, newspaper, orchestra, pep band, photography, political, professional, radio and TV, religious, social service, student government, symphony, and yearbook. Popular campus events include Dogwood Arts Festival, Blister-in-the-Sun, and Spring Fling.

Sports: There are 7 intercollegiate sports for men and 7 for women, and 12 intramural sports for men and 11 for women. Facilities include a phys ed building with an indoor pool, tennis and racquetball courts, a weight room, and football, soccer, baseball, and softball fields, and an off-campus equestrian arena.

Disabled Students: 75% of the campus is accessible. Wheelchair ramps, elevators, special parking, specially equipped rest rooms, special class scheduling, lowered drinking fountains, lowered telephones, and special housing are available.

Services: Counseling and information services are available, as is tutoring in every subject. There is a reader service for the blind, remedial math, and sign language interpreters for deaf students.

Campus Safety and Security: Measures include 24-hour foot and vehicle patrol, security escort services, informal discussions, and lighted pathways/sidewalks.

Programs of Study: Maryville confers B.A. and B.Mus. degrees. Bachelor's degrees are awarded in AGRICULTURE (environmental studies), BIOLOGICAL SCIENCE (biochemistry and biology/biological science), BUSINESS (business administration and management and recreation and leisure services), COMMUNICATIONS AND THE ARTS (American Sign Language, art, creative writing, dramatic arts, English, English as a second/foreign language, music, music performance, and Spanish), COMPUTER AND PHYSICAL SCIENCE (chemical physics, chemistry, computer science, and mathematics), EDUCATION (elementary, music, physical, science, and secondary), ENGINEERING AND ENVIRONMENTAL DESIGN (engineering and preengineering), HEALTH PROFESSIONS (nursing, predentistry, and premedicine), SOCIAL SCIENCE (economics, history, international relations, interpreter for the deaf, political science/government, prelaw, psychology, religion, social science, and sociology). Biology, chemistry, and English are the strongest academically. Business, biology, and psychology are the largest.

Required: Each degree has its own general education requirements, which include humanities and a foreign language. Students must complete at least 128 total credit hours, including 48 in the major, and must maintain a minimum 2.0 GPA. A year-long freshman seminar and orientation are required in addition to a senior thesis in all majors and senior comprehensive exams.

Special: Maryville offers cross-registration and co-op programs with the University of Tennessee, and Vanderbilt University internships, study abroad in 9 countries, a Washington semester, accelerated degree programs, a B.A.-B.S. degree in engineering, and dual and student-designed majors. There are 3-2 engineering degrees offered with regional universities. Nondegree study and pass/fail options are possible. There are 6 national honor societies and a freshman honors program. All departments have honors programs.

Faculty/Classroom: 51% of faculty are male; 49%, female. All both teach and do research. The average class size in an introductory lecture is 28; in a laboratory, 15; and in a regular course, 16.

Admissions: 79% of the 2003-2004 applicants were accepted. The SAT I scores for the 2003-2004 freshman class were: Verbal--28% below 500, 33% between 500 and 599, 35% between 600 and 700, and 4% above 700; Math--32% below 500, 29% between 500 and 599, 33% between 600 and 700, and 7% above 700. The ACT scores were 20% below 21, 25% between 21 and 23, 22% between 24 and 26, 16% between 27 and 28, and 16% above 28. 52% of the current freshmen were in the top fifth of their class; 68% were in the top two fifths. 9 freshmen graduated first in their class.

Requirements: The SAT I or ACT is required; the minimum composite score on the SAT I is 950; on the ACT, 20. Candidates should be graduates of accredited secondary schools or have the GED. They should also have 15 academic credits with 4 years of English, 3 each of math and science, 2 years of foreign language, and 2 of history or social studies. An essay, portfolio, audition, and interview are all recommended. A GPA of 2.5 is required. AP and CLEP credits are accepted. Important factors in the admissions decision are advanced placement or honor courses, evidence of special talent, and leadership record.

Procedure: Freshmen are admitted fall, spring, and summer. Entrance exams should be taken in October of the senior year. There are early decision, early admissions, and deferred admissions plans. Early decision applications should be filed by November 15; regular applications, by March 1 for fall entry, November 1 for spring entry, and May 1 for summer entry, along with a $25 fee. Notification of early decision is sent December 1; regular decision, April 1. Applications are accepted on-line through *www.maryvillecollege.edu/admissions.*

Transfer: 63 transfer students enrolled in a recent year. Transfer applicants must have a minimum GPA of 2.0 and a recommended 15 credit hours earned. An interview is also recommended. 45 of 128 credits required for the bachelor's degree must be completed at Maryville.

Visiting: There are regularly scheduled orientations for prospective students, including an overnight in a residence hall, class attendance, meeting with students and faculty, a campus tour, and an interview. There are guides for informal visits and visitors may sit in on classes and stay overnight. To schedule a visit, contact the Admissions Office at *admissions@maryvillecollege.edu.*

Financial Aid: In 2003-2004, nearly all full-time freshmen and 98% of continuing full-time students received some form of financial aid. 82% of full-time freshmen and 77% of continuing full-time students received need-based aid. The average freshman award was $19,385. Need-based scholarships or need-based grants averaged $7169 ($24,588 maximum); need-based self-help aid (loans and jobs) averaged $4723 ($7935 maximum); and other non-need-based awards and non-need-based scholarships averaged $12,351 ($27,990 maximum). 34% of undergraduates work part time. Average annual earnings from campus work are $1200. Maryville is a member of CSS. The FAFSA is required. The priority date for freshman financial aid applications for fall entry is March 1.

International Students: There are 46 international students enrolled. The school actively recruits these students. They must score 525 on the written TOEFL or take the MELAB.

Computers: There are 75 PCs on a local area network in staffed student labs with access to e-mail, the Internet, and the Web. All residence hall rooms and most classrooms are networked. All students may access the system 7 days a week, 16 hours a day. There are no time limits and no fees. It is strongly recommended that all students have a personal computer.

Graduates: In an average class, 51% graduate in 5 years or less, and 53% graduate in 6 years or less. 80 companies recruited on campus in 2002-2003. Of the 2002 graduating class, 20% were enrolled in graduate school within 6 months of graduation and 95% were employed.

Admissions Contact: Ned Willard, Assistant Vice President for Admissions. E-mail: *ned.willard@maryvillecollege.edu*
Web: *maryvillecollege.edu*

MEMPHIS COLLEGE OF ART   A-4
Memphis, TN 38104   **(901) 272-5151**
(800) 727-1088; Fax: (901) 272-5158

Full-time: 133 men, 139 women	**Faculty:** 17
Part-time: 12 men, 16 women	**Ph.D.s:** n/av
Graduate: 18 men, 19 women	**Student/Faculty:** 16 to 1
Year: semesters, summer session	**Tuition:** $15,860
Application Deadline: open	**Room & Board:** $7500
Freshman Class: 263 applied, 246 accepted, 60 enrolled	
ACT: 21	**SPECIAL**

Memphis College of Art, established in 1936, is a nonprofit, private, independent institution offering degree programs in fine arts and design arts, including studio art, fiber/surface design, computer arts, and photography. Some figures in the above capsule and in this profile are approximate. In addition to regional accreditation, MCA has baccalaureate program accreditation with NASAD. The library contains 18,000 volumes, and subscribes to 120 periodicals. Computerized library services include interlibrary loans. Special learning facilities include a learning resource center and art gallery. The 200-acre campus is in an urban area in Memphis. Including any residence halls, there are 4 buildings.

Student Life: 60% of undergraduates are from Tennessee. Students are from 20 states, 10 foreign countries, and Canada. 69% are from public schools. 76% are white; 14% African American. The average age of freshmen is 20; all undergraduates, 23. 22% do not continue beyond their first year; 65% remain to graduate.

Housing: 27 students can be accommodated in college housing, which includes coed on-campus apartments and off-campus apartments. On-campus housing is available on a first-come, first-served basis. Priority is given to out-of-town students. Alcohol is not permitted. All students may keep cars.

Activities: There are no fraternities or sororities. There are 2 groups on campus, including art and student government. Popular campus events include Holiday Bazaar, gallery openings, and international dinners.

Sports: There is no sports program at MCA. Facilities include those provided by the 200-acre city park on which MCA is located. There is an adjacent public golf course, playing fields, and a volleyball court. Regular Saturday football, soccer, and bicycling are popular activities.

Disabled Students: All of the campus is accessible. Wheelchair ramps, elevators, special parking, specially equipped rest rooms, lowered drinking fountains, and lowered telephones are available.

Services: Counseling and information services are available, as is tutoring in some subjects, including liberal studies classes.

Campus Safety and Security: Measures include informal discussions, pamphlets/posters/films, lighted pathways/sidewalks, and a security guard in the buildings in the evening, at night, and on weekends.

Programs of Study: MCA confers the B.F.A. degree. Master's degrees are also awarded. Bachelor's degrees are awarded in COMMUNICATIONS AND THE ARTS (design and fine arts).

Required: Students must complete 129 credit hours, including 33 in the major, with a minimum GPA of 2.0. Distribution requirements comprise 45 credits in liberal studies, including 12 in art history, 6 in English, and 3 each in humanities, social sciences, and natural sciences; 30 credits in elective studio art; and 21 credits in foundation classes, including drawing, design, and color theory.

Special: Special academic programs include off-campus internships for juniors in advertising agencies, design firms, or other educational situations; on-campus work-study, including an in-house student advertising agency where students can get paid work experience dealing with clients; and study abroad in Europe, Canada, or Japan. There are co-op programs with Rhodes, Lemoyne-Owen, and Christian Brothers Colleges as well as with Memphis Theological Seminary, and there is cross-registration with the Alliance in Independent Colleges of Art and Design. Accelerated degree programs in all areas, a dual major in painting and illustration, student-designed majors, and credit for life and work experience are available. Nondegree study is offered, as are pass/fail options for the workshop weeks.

Faculty/Classroom: 75% of faculty are male; 25%, female. 93% teach undergraduates. Graduate students teach 2% of introductory courses. The average class size in an introductory lecture is 20 and in a regular course, 15.

Admissions: 94% of the 2003-2004 applicants were accepted. The ACT scores for the 2003-2004 freshman class were: 44% below 21, 24% between 21 and 23, 19% between 24 and 26, 9% between 27 and 28, and 4% above 28.

Requirements: The SAT I or ACT is required. Test scores are used for admissions and placement purposes. Other admissions requirements include a completed application form, high school transcripts (GED is accepted), and a portfolio. An interview is recommended. A GPA of 2.0 is required. AP and CLEP credits are accepted. Important factors in the admissions decision are evidence of special talent, advanced placement or honor courses, and extracurricular activities record.

Procedure: Freshmen are admitted fall and spring. Application deadlines are open. Application fee is $25. Applications are accepted on-line through the school's web site.

Transfer: Applicants must submit official college transcripts and a portfolio. 48 of 129 credits required for the bachelor's degree must be completed at MCA.

Visiting: There are regularly scheduled orientations for prospective students. There are guides for informal visits and visitors may sit in on classes. To schedule a visit, contact the Admissions Office.

Financial Aid: MCA is a member of CSS. The FAFSA is required. Check with the school for current application deadlines.

International Students: The school actively recruits these students. They must score 500 on the written TOEFL or 173 on the electronic version.

Computers: There are 60 Mac PCs available in the foundation, design arts, and weaving departments and in the writing lab and library. All students may access the system. There are no time limits and no fees.

Admissions Contact: Anette Moore, Director of Admissions.
E-mail: *info@mca.edu* Web: *www.mca.edu*

MIDDLE TENNESSEE STATE UNIVERSITY   C-3
Murfreesboro, TN 37132

(615) 898-2111
(800) 433-MTSU; Fax: (615) 898-5478

Full-time: 7806 men, 8873 women	**Faculty:** 733; IIA, -$
Part-time: 1419 men, 1656 women	**Ph.D.s:** 77%
Graduate: 779 men, 1211 women	**Student/Faculty:** 23 to 1
Year: semesters, summer session	**Tuition:** $3910 ($11,842)
Application Deadline: July 1	**Room & Board:** $4624
Freshman Class: 5771 applied, 5423 accepted, 3037 enrolled	
SAT I Verbal/Math: 535/518	**ACT:** 22 COMPETITIVE

Middle Tennessee State University, founded in 1911, is a comprehensive public university that offers undergraduate and graduate programs reflecting an emphasis on research, creative arts, and public and professional service activities. There are 6 undergraduate schools and 1 graduate school. In addition to regional accreditation, MTSU has baccalaureate program accreditation with AACSB, AAFCS, ABET, ACE-JMC, ACS, ADA, CAA, CACREP, CSAB, CSWE, FIDER, NAEYC, NAIT, NASAD, NASM, NASP, NCATE, NLN, NRPA, and NLNAC. The library contains 702,764 volumes and 1,281,160 microform items, and subscribes to 3798 periodicals. Computerized library services include the card catalog, interlibrary loans, database searching, and Internet access. Special learning facilities include a learning resource center, art gallery, planetarium, radio station, TV station, and numerous research centers. The 500-acre campus is in an urban area 32 miles southeast of Nashville. Including any residence halls, there are 159 buildings.

Student Life: 92% of undergraduates are from Tennessee. Students are from 47 states, 70 foreign countries, and Canada. 83% are white;

12% African American. 45% are Protestant; 43% claim no religious affiliation; 6% Catholic. The average age of freshmen is 20; all undergraduates, 23. 25% do not continue beyond their first year; 40% remain to graduate.

Housing: 3294 students can be accommodated in college housing, which includes single-sex dorms, on-campus apartments, and married-student housing. In addition, there are honors houses, a First Year Experience program, and various Learning Community programs. On-campus housing is available on a first-come, first-served basis. 84% of students commute. Alcohol is not permitted. All students may keep cars.

Activities: 7% of men belong to 16 national fraternities; 7% of women belong to 1 local and 11 national sororities. There are 153 groups on campus, including art, band, cheerleading, chess, choir, chorale, chorus, computers, dance, debate, drama, drill team, ethnic, film, gay, honors, international, jazz band, literary magazine, marching band, musical theater, newspaper, opera, orchestra, pep band, photography, political, professional, radio and TV, religious, social, social service, student government, symphony, and yearbook. Popular campus events include Founders Day, Family Day, and African American History Month.

Sports: There are 8 intercollegiate sports for men and 9 for women, and 13 intramural sports for men and 13 for women. Facilities include an athletic center with a 30,000-seat stadium, a 12,000-seat gym, a soccer/track complex, tennis courts, and baseball and softball fields, and a recreation center with 12 courts, an indoor track, indoor and outdoor pools, a rock-climbing wall, and a sand volleyball court.

Disabled Students: All of the campus is accessible. Wheelchair ramps, elevators, special parking, specially equipped rest rooms, special class scheduling, lowered drinking fountains, and lowered telephones are available.

Services: Counseling and information services are available, as is tutoring in most subjects. There is a reader service for the blind, and remedial math, reading, and writing.

Campus Safety and Security: Measures include 24-hour foot and vehicle patrol, self-defense education, security escort services, and shuttle buses. There are pamphlets/posters/films, emergency telephones, and lighted pathways/sidewalks.

Programs of Study: MTSU confers B.A., B.S., B.B.A., B.F.A., B.Mus., B.S.N., B.S.W., and B.U.S. degrees. Associate, master's, and doctoral degrees are also awarded. Bachelor's degrees are awarded in AGRICULTURE (agricultural business management, animal science, and plant science), BIOLOGICAL SCIENCE (biology/biological science and nutrition), BUSINESS (accounting, banking and finance, business administration and management, entrepreneurial studies, marketing/retailing/merchandising, office supervision and management, and recreation and leisure services), COMMUNICATIONS AND THE ARTS (communications, English, French, German, graphic design, music, music business management, public relations, Spanish, and studio art), COMPUTER AND PHYSICAL SCIENCE (chemistry, computer science, information sciences and systems, mathematics, physics, and science), EDUCATION (art, athletic training, business, early childhood, health, physical, and special), ENGINEERING AND ENVIRONMENTAL DESIGN (engineering technology, environmental science, industrial engineering technology, and interior design), HEALTH PROFESSIONS (health science and nursing), SOCIAL SCIENCE (anthropology, criminal justice, economics, family/consumer studies, geography, history, interdisciplinary studies, international relations, philosophy, political science/government, prelaw, psychology, public administration, social work, sociology, and textiles and clothing). Nursing and science are the strongest academically. Recording industry is the largest.

Required: To graduate, a total of at least 132 hours, including at least 48 of upper-level courses, is needed with a minimum overall GPA of 2.0. All students must complete the general studies requirements, including 9 hours each of natural science/math and humanities, 6 each of English composition and history, 2 of phys ed, and demonstrated computer literacy. A major field test and general studies exam are required.

Special: MTSU offers co-op programs in aerospace, computer science, math, engineering technology, and industrial studies, cross-registration with Tennessee State University, internships, study abroad, a general studies degree, student-designed majors, nondegree study, and pass/fail options. Credit for life, military, and work experience may be granted. There are 2 national honor societies, a freshman honors program, and 25 departmental honors programs.

Faculty/Classroom: 59% of faculty are male; 41%, female. The average class size in an introductory lecture is 24; in a laboratory, 18; and in a regular course, 23.

Admissions: 94% of the 2003-2004 applicants were accepted. The ACT scores for the 2003-2004 freshman class were: 34% below 21, 31% between 21 and 23, 19% between 24 and 26, 7% between 27 and 28, and 6% above 28. 25% of the current freshmen were in the top fifth of their class; 48% were in the top two fifths. There were 2 National Merit finalists. 31 freshmen graduated first in their class.

Requirements: The SAT I or ACT is required, with a minimum composite score of 22 on the ACT if the GPA is less than 3.0. The GED is accepted. The number of academic credits required is 14, including 4 years of English, 3 of math, 2 each of a foreign language and science, and 1 each of social studies, U.S. history, and visual and/or performance arts, with an additional unit of math, language, or art recommended. AP and CLEP credits are accepted.

Procedure: Freshmen are admitted to all sessions. Entrance exams should be taken in the first half of the senior year. There is an early admissions plan. Applications should be filed by July 1 for fall entry and December 15 for spring entry, along with a $15 fee. Notification is sent on a rolling basis. Applications are accepted on-line through *www.mtsu.edu/admissn.*

Transfer: 1983 transfer students enrolled in 2002-2003. Applicants must have a minimum 2.0 GPA and submit official transcripts from all previous colleges attended. If transferring fewer than 9 semester hours, they must also meet freshman admission requirements. 33 of 132 credits required for the bachelor's degree must be completed at MTSU.

Visiting: There are regularly scheduled orientations for prospective students, including campus tours and meeting with a departmental adviser. There are guides for informal visits and visitors may sit in on classes. To schedule a visit, contact the Office of Admissions at (615) 898-5670 or (800) 331-MTSU (in-state) or *admissions@mtsu.edu.*

Financial Aid: In 2003-2004, 64% of all full-time freshmen and 84% of continuing full-time students received some form of financial aid. 44% of full-time freshmen and 60% of continuing full-time students received need-based aid. The average freshman award was $6200. Need-based scholarships or need-based grants averaged $2500 ($6150 maximum); need-based self-help aid (loans and jobs) averaged $4500 ($10,500 maximum); non-need-based athletic scholarships averaged $7000 ($9500 maximum); and other non-need-based awards and non-need-based scholarships averaged $2500 ($5000 maximum). 84% of undergraduates work part time. Average annual earnings from campus work are $3200. The average financial indebtedness of the 2003 graduate was $17,760. The FAFSA is required. The priority date for freshman financial aid applications for fall entry is December 1. The deadline for filing freshman financial aid applications for fall entry is May 1.

International Students: There are 124 international students enrolled. They must score 500 on the written TOEFL or 173 on the electronic version or take the MELAB and also take the SAT I or the ACT, scoring 930 on the SAT I or 20 on the ACT.

Computers: The mainframes are an HP 9000/V2200 and a Compaq Alpha Cluster. There are about 4000 PCs available that can access the network in more than 60 student labs and in faculty and staff offices. All students may access the system 24 hours a day. There are no time limits and no fees.

Graduates: From July 1, 2002 to June 30, 2003, 2771 bachelor's degrees were awarded. The most popular majors were recording industry (9%), mass communication (9%), and interdisciplinary studies (6%). In an average class, 1% graduate in 3 years or less, 12% graduate in 4 years or less, 32% graduate in 5 years or less, and 43% graduate in 6 years or less. 297 companies recruited on campus in 2002-2003. Of the 2002 graduating class, 20% were enrolled in graduate school within 6 months of graduation and 7% were employed.

Admissions Contact: Sherian Huddleston, Interim Assistant Vice President, Enrollment Management. E-mail: *admissions@mtsu.edu* Web: *www.mtsu.edu*

MILLIGAN COLLEGE   F-2
Milligan College, TN 37682

	(423) 461-8730
	(800) 262-8337; Fax: (423) 461-8982
Full-time: 277 men, 434 women	**Faculty:** 63; IIB, --$
Part-time: 13 men, 12 women	**Ph.D.s:** 70%
Graduate: 24 men, 81 women	**Student/Faculty:** 11 to 1
Year: semesters, summer session	**Tuition:** $15,260
Application Deadline: August 15	**Room & Board:** $4600
Freshman Class: 525 applied, 493 accepted, 181 enrolled	
SAT I Verbal/Math: 550/550	**ACT:** 24 COMPETITIVE+

Milligan College, founded in 1866, is a private institution affiliated with the Christian Church and Churches of Christ. Its degree programs stress the liberal arts and biblical studies. In addition to regional accreditation, Milligan has baccalaureate program accreditation with ACOTE and NCATE. The library contains 184,789 volumes, 482,762 microform items, and 3484 audio/video tapes/CDs, and subscribes to 547 periodicals. Computerized library services include the card catalog, interlibrary loans, and database searching. Special learning facilities include a learning resource center, art gallery, radio station, TV station, and editing rooms, and darkroom. The 145-acre campus is in a suburban area 4 miles south of Johnson City. Including any residence halls, there are 23 buildings.

Student Life: 56% of undergraduates are from out of state, mostly the Midwest. Students are from 35 states, 8 foreign countries, and Canada. 80% are from public schools. 94% are white. Most are Protestant. The average age of freshmen is 18; all undergraduates, 22. 17% do not continue beyond their first year; 60% remain to graduate.

Housing: 559 students can be accommodated in college housing, which includes single-sex dorms, on-campus apartments, and married-student housing. In addition, there are honors houses. On-campus housing is guaranteed for all 4 years. 69% of students live on campus; of those, 85% remain on campus on weekends. Alcohol is not permitted. All students may keep cars.

Activities: There are no fraternities or sororities. There are 31 groups on campus, including art, band, cheerleading, choir, chorus, drama, drill team, film, honors, jazz band, literary magazine, musical theater, newspaper, orchestra, pep band, photography, political, professional, radio and TV, religious, social, social service, student government, symphony, and yearbook. Popular campus events include Christmas Dinners, Wonderful Wednesday, and service projects.

Sports: There are 6 intercollegiate sports for men and 6 for women, and 8 intramural sports for men and 7 for women. Facilities include a 25-meter swimming pool, a basketball court, a 500-seat stadium, a 1500-seat gym, tennis courts, and baseball, softball, and soccer fields.

Disabled Students: 80% of the campus is accessible. Wheelchair ramps, elevators, special parking, specially equipped rest rooms, and lowered drinking fountains are available.

Services: Counseling and information services are available, as is tutoring in most subjects. There is remedial math, reading, and writing.

Campus Safety and Security: Measures include informal discussions, pamphlets/posters/films, lighted pathways/sidewalks, and evening vehicle patrol.

Programs of Study: Milligan confers B.A., B.S., and B.S.N. degrees. Master's degrees are also awarded. Bachelor's degrees are awarded in BIOLOGICAL SCIENCE (biology/biological science), BUSINESS (accounting and business administration and management), COMMUNICATIONS AND THE ARTS (communications, English, fine arts, and music), COMPUTER AND PHYSICAL SCIENCE (chemistry, information sciences and systems, and mathematics), EDUCATION (early childhood and music), HEALTH PROFESSIONS (exercise science, nursing, and premedicine), SOCIAL SCIENCE (biblical studies, history, humanities, psychology, religious music, and sociology). Education, business, and communications are the largest.

Required: Students must complete at least 128 semester hours, including 24 to 62 in the major, and 59 to 71 in the general education core, with a minimum GPA of 2.0. Required disciplines include 24 credit hours of humanities, 9 of Bible studies, 8 of lab science, 6 of social science, 3 each of math, speech and ethnic studies, 2 of phys ed, and 1 each of English and introduction to college; B.A. candidates must also complete 6 to 12 in foreign language. All students must demonstrate computer literacy and attend all required chapel/convocation sessions. There is a comprehensive exam in the major.

Special: Milligan offers a Washington semester, study abroad in England, co-op programs and internships in several majors, cross-registration with East Tennessee State University, work-study, nondegree study, and dual majors. 6 credits are offered for students participating in the annual summer tour of Europe. There are 2 national honor societies.

Faculty/Classroom: 54% of faculty are male; 46%, female. 96% teach undergraduates. No introductory courses are taught by graduate students. The average class size in an introductory lecture is 50; in a laboratory, 15; and in a regular course, 15.

Admissions: 94% of the 2003-2004 applicants were accepted. The SAT I scores for the 2003-2004 freshman class were: Verbal--19% below 500, 50% between 500 and 599, 29% between 600 and 700, and 2% above 700; Math--25% below 500, 49% between 500 and 599, 23% between 600 and 700, and 3% above 700. The ACT scores were 29% below 21, 17% between 21 and 23, 33% between 24 and 26, 10% between 27 and 28, and 11% above 28.

Requirements: The SAT I or ACT is required. In addition, students must be graduates of an accredited secondary school, with 18 Carnegie units and 18 academic credits, including courses in English, math, science, history and social studies, and speech, music, or art, along with 2 years of a foreign language. An interview is advised, and music students must audition. The GED is accepted. Other factors in the admission decision include character, recommendations by school officials, advanced placement or honor courses, ability, preparation, and Christian commitment. Milligan requires applicants to be in the upper 50% of their class. A GPA of 2.75 is required. AP and CLEP credits are accepted. Important factors in the admissions decision are leadership record, recommendations by school officials, and personality/intangible qualities.

Procedure: Freshmen are admitted to all sessions. Entrance exams should be taken beginning in the spring of the junior year. There is a deferred admissions plan. Applications should be filed by August 15 for fall entry and December 15 for spring entry, along with a $30 fee. Notification is sent on a rolling basis. Applications are accepted on-line through the school's web site.

Transfer: 71 transfer students enrolled in 2003-2004. A minimum GPA of 2.5 is preferred. Applicants must submit a letter of good standing from the previous institution as well as transcripts of all previous college work. 45 of 128 credits required for the bachelor's degree must be completed at Milligan.

Visiting: There are regularly scheduled orientations for prospective students, consisting of 1-day open houses in November and March that include a campus tour, a financial aid workshop, a meal in the cafeteria, and the opportunity to meet faculty and to learn about student life. There are guides for informal visits and visitors may sit in on classes and stay overnight. To schedule a visit, contact the Campus Visits Coordinator at *visits@milligan.edu*.

Financial Aid: In 2003-2004, 91% of all full-time freshmen and 89% of continuing full-time students received some form of financial aid. 54% of full-time freshmen and 59% of continuing full-time students received need-based aid. The average freshman award was $9936. Need-based scholarships or need-based grants averaged $2257 ($13,588 maximum); need-based self-help aid (loans and jobs) averaged $2138 ($4625 maximum); non-need-based athletic scholarships averaged $2411 ($19,810 maximum); other non-need-based awards and non-need-based scholarships averaged $15,721 ($22,413 maximum); and personnel grants and tuition exchange averaged $14,750 (maximum). 58% of undergraduates work part time. Average annual earnings from campus work are $1182. The average financial indebtedness of the 2003 graduate was $18,796. The FAFSA and the college's own financial statement are required. The priority date for freshman financial aid applications for fall entry is March 1.

International Students: There are 17 international students enrolled. They must score 550 on the written TOEFL or 213 on the electronic version or take the MELAB.

Computers: 96 PCs are available in 8 computer labs, the library, and specific departments; 23 other computers are available in public areas. All have access to the Internet and the web. Every dorm room has a network connection available for each resident. All students may access the system. There are no time limits. The fee is $175 per semester. It is strongly recommended that all students have a personal computer.

Graduates: From July 1, 2002 to June 30, 2003, 211 bachelor's degrees were awarded. The most popular majors were business administration (30%), communications (9%), and biology (8%). In an average class, 4% graduate in 3 years or less, 54% graduate in 4 years or less, and 60% graduate in 5 years or less.

Admissions Contact: David Mee, Vice President for Enrollment Management. E-mail: *admissions@milligan.edu* Web: *www.milligan.edu*

RHODES COLLEGE
Memphis, TN 38112

A-3

(901) 843-3700
(800) 844-5969; Fax: (901) 843-3631

Full-time: 650 men, 855 women	**Faculty:** 120; IIB,
Part-time: 10 men, 15 women	**Ph.D.s:** 92%
Graduate: 5 men, 10 women	**Student/Faculty:** 13 to 1
Year: semesters	**Tuition:** $22,938
Application Deadline: see profile	**Room & Board:** $6382
Freshman Class: n/av	
SAT I or ACT: required	**HIGHLY COMPETITIVE+**

Rhodes College, founded in 1848, is a nonprofit, private liberal arts institution affiliated with the Presbyterian Church (U.S.A.). Figures in the above capsule and in this profile are approximate. The 6 libraries contain 266,000 volumes, 74,500 microform items, and 9900 audio/video tapes/CDs, and subscribe to 1200 periodicals. Computerized library services include the card catalog, interlibrary loans, and database searching. Special learning facilities include an art gallery, 2 electron microscopes, a 0.8-meter infrared optimized telescope, a cell culture lab, and the Human Relations Area Files, containing 2 million pages of human behavior resources materials on microfiche. The 100-acre campus is in an urban area in Memphis. Including any residence halls, there are 37 buildings.

Student Life: 73% of undergraduates are from out of state, mostly the South. Students are from 46 states, 10 foreign countries, and Canada. 60% are from public schools. 87% are white. 67% are Protestant; 16% Catholic; 14% claim no religious affiliation. The average age of freshmen is 18; all undergraduates, 20. 11% do not continue beyond their first year; 76% remain to graduate.

Housing: 1034 students can be accommodated in college housing, which includes single-sex and coed dorms and on-campus apartments. In addition, there are special-interest houses and theme, substance-free, quiet-study, and non-smoking housing. On-campus housing is guaranteed for the freshman year only and is available on a lottery system for upperclassmen. 79% of students live on campus; of those, 90% remain on campus on weekends. All students may keep cars.

Activities: 55% of men belong to 6 national fraternities; 58% of women belong to 5 national sororities. There are 93 groups on campus, including art, cheerleading, choir, chorale, chorus, computers, dance, debate, drama, ethnic, film, gay, honors, international, literary magazine, musical theater, newspaper, orchestra, pep band, photography, political, professional, religious, social, social service, student government, symphony, and yearbook. Popular campus events include Rites of Spring, All-Sing, and Hunger for Homelessness.

Sports: There are 10 intercollegiate sports for men and 11 for women, and 18 intramural sports for men and 18 for women. Facilities include

a campus life center, which includes a performance gym, a 3-court multiuse gym, racquetball, and squash courts, a fitness center, and an indoor jogging track. Outdoor facilities include a pool, 10 lighted tennis courts, 2 soccer fields, a football field, a track, and baseball, softball and intramural fields.

Disabled Students: 90% of the campus is accessible. Wheelchair ramps, elevators, special parking, specially equipped rest rooms, special class scheduling, lowered drinking fountains, lowered telephones, and an infrared hearing system in 1 of the auditoriums are available.

Services: Counseling and information services are available, as is tutoring in some subjects, including math, writing, foreign language, biology, chemistry, and economics. There is a reader service for the blind.

Campus Safety and Security: Measures include 24-hour foot and vehicle patrol, self-defense education, security escort services, and informal discussions. There are pamphlets/posters/films, emergency telephones, lighted pathways/sidewalks, security cameras monitored 24 hours a day, a fenced campus, and city cab service billed to student accounts.

Programs of Study: Rhodes confers B.A. and B.S. degrees. Master's degrees are also awarded. Bachelor's degrees are awarded in BIOLOGICAL SCIENCE (biology/biological science), BUSINESS (business administration and management), COMMUNICATIONS AND THE ARTS (art, dramatic arts, English, French, German, music, and Spanish), COMPUTER AND PHYSICAL SCIENCE (chemistry, computer science, mathematics, and physics), SOCIAL SCIENCE (anthropology, classical/ancient civilization, economics, history, interdisciplinary studies, international studies, Latin American studies, philosophy, political science/government, psychology, religion, Russian and Slavic studies, sociology, and urban studies). English, foreign languages, and business administration are the strongest academically. Biology, business administration, and English are the largest.

Required: To graduate, students must complete 112 credit hours, with a variable number of hours in the major, and maintain a minimum GPA of 2.0. There is a basic degree requirement in humanities, communication skills, and foreign language at the intermediate level. Students must complete 3 courses each in humanities, natural science, and social science, 2 courses in fine arts, English 151, 3 noncredit half-semester courses in phys ed, and a senior seminar in the major.

Special: More than half of Rhodes students have an internship experience, in which off-campus work and significant academic work are combined for credit. Study abroad in 7 countries, a Washington semester, cross-registration with Memphis College of Art, and a science semester at Oak Ridge National Laboratory are offered. A 3-2 engineering degree with Washington University is available. The B.A.-B.S. degree and dual majors, including anthropology/sociology, are offered in any combination, and student-designed majors can be arranged. Nondegree study and pass/fail options are possible. There are 14 national honor societies, including Phi Beta Kappa.

Faculty/Classroom: 66% of faculty are male; 34%, female. All both teach and do research. No introductory courses are taught by graduate students. The average class size in an introductory lecture is 17; in a laboratory, 17; and in a regular course, 17.

Admissions: In a recent year, there were 11 National Merit finalists and 5 semifinalists and 23 freshmen graduated first in their class.

Requirements: The SAT I or ACT is required. In addition, graduation from an accredited secondary school is required, with 16 or more academic credits, including 4 years of English, 3 of math, and 2 each of a foreign language, science, and social studies/history. The GED is accepted. An essay is required; an interview is recommended. AP credits are accepted. Important factors in the admissions decision are advanced placement or honor courses, recommendations by school officials, and extracurricular activities record.

Procedure: Freshmen are admitted fall and spring. Entrance exams should be taken prior to December of the senior year. There are early decision, early admissions, and deferred admissions plans. Check with the school for current deadlines and fees. The fall 2003 application fee was $40. 80 early decision candidates were accepted in a recent year. 2 were admitted. Applications are accepted on-line through the school's web site and Common App.

Transfer: 16 transfer students enrolled in a recent year. Applicants must submit all high school and college transcripts, as well as SAT I or ACT scores, and must be in good standing at the last institution they attended. 56 of 112 credits required for the bachelor's degree must be completed at Rhodes.

Visiting: There are regularly scheduled orientations for prospective students, including class visits, meetings with students and faculty, tours, and an overnight stay with students if desired. Interviews also are available. There are guides for informal visits and visitors may sit in on classes and stay overnight. To schedule a visit, contact the Admissions Office at *www.rhodes.edu*.

Financial Aid: In a recent year, 77% of all full-time freshmen and 74% of continuing full-time students received some form of financial aid. 39% of full-time freshmen and 34% of continuing full-time students received need-based aid. The average freshman award was $14,425. 31% of undergraduates work part time. Average annual earnings from campus work are $1537. The average financial indebtedness of a recent graduate was $14,900. Rhodes is a member of CSS. The CSS Profile or FAFSA is required. Check with the school for current deadlines.

International Students: There were 36 international students enrolled in a recent year. The school actively recruits these students. They must score 550 on the written TOEFL or 213 on the electronic version and also take the SAT I or the ACT.

Computers: The mainframes are a DEC Alpha and a Sun 3500. PCs and Macs are available in 3 computer labs. The math department runs an additional lab of Sun and Digital servers and workstations. All residence hall rooms are networked to the campuswide system and the Internet. All students may access the system 24 hours per day. There are no time limits and no fees. It is strongly recommended that all students have a personal computer.

Graduates: In a recent year, 330 bachelor's degrees were awarded. The most popular majors were business administration (21%), biology (12%), and political science (10%). In an average class, 68% graduate in 4 years or less, 71% graduate in 5 years or less, and 72% graduate in 6 years or less. 33 companies recruited on campus in a recent year. Of a recent graduating class, 33% were enrolled in graduate school within 6 months of graduation and 54% were employed.

Admissions Contact: David J. Wottle, Dean of Admissions and Financial Aid. A video is available. E-mail: *adminfo@rhodes.edu* Web: *www.admissions.rhodes.edu*

SOUTHERN ADVENTIST UNIVERSITY   D-4
Collegedale, TN 37315

(423) 238-2844
(800) SOUTHERN; Fax: (423) 238-3005

Total Enrollment: 2249 men and women	**Faculty:** 108
	Ph.D.s: 62%
Year: semesters, summer session	**Student/Faculty:** n/av
Application Deadline: open	**Tuition:** $12,800
	Room & Board: $4280
Freshman Class: 463 enrolled	
SAT I or ACT: required	**COMPETITIVE**

Southern Adventist University, founded in 1892, is a private liberal arts institution affiliated with the Seventh-day Adventist Church. There are 9 undergraduate schools. In addition to regional accreditation, Southern has baccalaureate program accreditation with CSWE, NASM, NCATE, and NLN. The library contains 138,181 volumes, 473,596 microform items, and 4704 audio/video tapes/CDs, and subscribes to 1115 periodicals. Computerized library services include the card catalog, interlibrary loans, and database searching. Special learning facilities include a learning resource center, art gallery, and radio station. The 1000-acre campus is in a small town 18 miles southeast of Chattanooga. Including any residence halls, there are 17 buildings.

Student Life: 78% of undergraduates are from out of state, mostly the South. Students are from 46 states, 55 foreign countries, and Canada. 18% are from public schools. 74% are white; 10% Hispanic. Most are Protestant. The average age of freshmen is 19; all undergraduates, 21. 33% do not continue beyond their first year; 55% remain to graduate.

Housing: 1458 students can be accommodated in college housing, which includes single-sex dorms, on-campus apartments, and married-student housing. On-campus housing is guaranteed for all 4 years. 65% of students live on campus; of those, 70% remain on campus on weekends. Alcohol is not permitted. All students may keep cars.

Activities: There are no fraternities or sororities. There are 30 groups on campus, including band, choir, chorus, drama, ethnic, honors, international, newspaper, orchestra, professional, radio and TV, religious, social, student government, symphony, and yearbook. Popular campus events include Alumni Weekend and Week of Spiritual Emphasis.

Sports: There are 10 intramural sports for men and 10 for women. Facilities include 8 tennis courts, 3 athletic fields, a field house, a pool, 4 racquetball courts, a track, soccer fields, a 23,000-square-foot gym that can seat 3000 when used as an auditorium, 3 weight rooms, and a 3-hole golf course.

Disabled Students: 70% of the campus is accessible. Wheelchair ramps, elevators, special parking, specially equipped rest rooms, and special class scheduling are available.

Services: Counseling and information services are available, as is tutoring in most subjects. There is remedial math, reading, and writing.

Campus Safety and Security: Measures include 24-hour foot and vehicle patrol, security escort services, informal discussions, and pamphlets/posters/films. There are emergency telephones and lighted pathways/sidewalks.

Programs of Study: Southern confers B.A., B.S., B.B.A., B.F.A., B.Mus., and B.S.W. degrees. Associate and master's degrees are also awarded. Bachelor's degrees are awarded in BIOLOGICAL SCIENCE (biology/biological science), BUSINESS (accounting, business administration and management, entrepreneurial studies, international business management, and marketing/retailing/merchandising), COMMUNICATIONS AND THE ARTS (animation, art, broadcasting, communications, English, film arts, fine arts, graphic design, journalism, music, and public

relations), COMPUTER AND PHYSICAL SCIENCE (actuarial science, chemistry, computer management, computer science, information sciences and systems, mathematics, physics, and web services), EDUCATION (elementary, music, and physical), HEALTH PROFESSIONS (health care administration, health science, medical technology, and nursing), SOCIAL SCIENCE (behavioral science, history, international studies, psychology, public administration, religious education, social work, and theological studies). Business, nursing, and education are the strongest academically. Nursing and business are the largest.

Required: Students must complete 124 semester hours with at least 30 in the major, and maintain a minimum GPA of 2.0. General education requirements include 12 semester hours of religion; 9 of language, literature, and fine arts; 6 to 9 each of English and natural science; 6 each of history and activity skills; 5 of behavioral, family, and health science; 3 of political and economic systems; and up to 3 of math, depending on the ACT scores. In addition, 2 phys ed activity courses must be taken.

Special: Internships in long-term life care and journalism, a social work practicum, and study abroad in Austria, Spain, Argentina, and France are offered. The B.A.-B.S. degree and dual majors in any combination are available. Credit may be granted for 4 years of military experience. Pass/fail options are possible only for phys ed activity classes. There are paraprofessional and preprofessional programs in dentistry and medicine, and various other health-related fields, as well as in law. There are 7 national honor societies, a freshman honors program, and 2 departmental honors programs.

Faculty/Classroom: 65% of faculty are male; 35%, female. All teach undergraduates. The average class size in an introductory lecture is 50; in a laboratory, 20; and in a regular course, 13.

Requirements: The SAT I or ACT is required, with a minimum composite score of 18 on the ACT; the ACT is preferred. Students must graduate from an accredited secondary school with 14 academic credits, including 4 units of English and 2 each of a foreign language, math, science, social studies, and history. The GED is accepted. An essay must be submitted if the student is homeschooled. A GPA of 2.0 is required. AP and CLEP credits are accepted. Important factors in the admissions decision are advanced placement or honor courses, recommendations by school officials, and leadership record.

Procedure: Freshmen are admitted to all sessions. Application deadlines are open. Application fee is $25. Notification is sent on a rolling basis. Applications are accepted on-line through CollegeNET.

Transfer: 207 transfer students enrolled in a recent year. Transfer applicants must have a cumulative GPA of at least 2.0 and a minimum ACT composite score of 18. 2 letters of recommendation are also required. 30 of 124 credits required for the bachelor's degree must be completed at Southern.

Visiting: There are regularly scheduled orientations for prospective students, including a tour of the campus and dorms, appointments with academic departments, and an interview with an admissions officer. There are guides for informal visits and visitors may sit in on classes and stay overnight. To schedule a visit, contact the Admissions Office.

Financial Aid: In a recent year, 83% of all full-time freshmen and 68% of continuing full-time students received some form of financial aid. The average freshman award was $9408. All undergraduates work part time. Average annual earnings from campus work are $2300. The average financial indebtedness of a recent year's graduate was $14,900. The FAFSA is required. Check with the school for current deadlines.

International Students: There were 230 international students enrolled in a recent year. The school actively recruits these students. They must score 550 on the written TOEFL or 213 on the electronic version or take the MELAB. They must also take the ACT, scoring 18.

Computers: The mainframe is a Hewlett Packard. There are 3 UNIX hosts, Ethernet to many campus buildings, an Internet link, and more than 130 PCs and Macs in 7 student labs. All students may access the system 24 hours per day. There are no time limits and no fees. It is strongly recommended that all students have a personal computer.

Graduates: In a recent year, 311 bachelor's degrees were awarded. The most popular majors were business (16%), nursing (16%), and religion (15%). In an average class, 30% graduate in 4 years or less, 40% graduate in 5 years or less, and 44% graduate in 6 years or less. Of a recent year's graduating class, 8% were enrolled in graduate school within 6 months of graduation and 52% were employed.

Admissions Contact: Marc Grundy, Director, Enrollment Services. A video is available. E-mail: *admissions@southern.edu* Web: *www.southern.edu*

STATE UNIVERSITY AND COMMUNITY COLLEGE SYSTEM OF TENNESSEE

The State University and Community College System of Tennessee, established in 1972, is a public system. It is governed by the Tennessee Board of Regents, which appoints a chancellor as chief administrator of the system. The primary goal of the system is teaching, research, and public service. The main priority is to provide accessible quality programs to state residents with equal opportunity in education and employment. Universities are located in Nashville, Cookeville, Clarksville, Memphis, Johnson City, and Murfreesboro. The total enrollment in a recent year of the 6 4-year university campuses, 13 2-year institutions, and 26 Tennessee Technology Centers was 186,000; there were 5500 full-time faculty members. There are 321 baccalaureate, 183 master's, 10 specialist, and 43 doctoral programs offered. Profiles of the 4-year campuses are included in this section.

TENNESSEE STATE UNIVERSITY
Nashville, TN 37209-1561

C-3

(615) 963-5101
(888) 463-6878; Fax: (615) 963-5108

Full-time: 2208 men, 3741 women	**Faculty:** 405; IIA, --$
Part-time: 411 men, 758 women	**Ph.D.s:** 80%
Graduate: 626 men, 1280 women	**Student/Faculty:** 15 to 1
Year: semesters, summer session	**Tuition:** $3818 ($11,750)
Application Deadline: August 1	**Room & Board:** $5230
Freshman Class: 6069 applied, 3799 accepted, 1509 enrolled	
SAT I or ACT: required	**LESS COMPETITIVE**

Tennessee State University, founded in 1912, is a state-supported land-grant institution offering undergraduate and graduate programs in arts and sciences, agriculture, health professions, business, education, engineering and technology, and nursing. There are 7 undergraduate schools and 1 graduate school. In addition to regional accreditation, TSU has baccalaureate program accreditation with AACSB, ABET, AHEA, CSWE, NASAD, NASM, NCATE, NLN, AAFCS, APA, ASLHA, AUPHA, and NAACLS. The 2 libraries contain 463,621 volumes, 754,955 microform items, and 5125 audio/video tapes/CDs, and subscribe to 1272 periodicals. Computerized library services include the card catalog, interlibrary loans, and database searching. Special learning facilities include a learning resource center, art gallery, and radio station. The 450-acre campus is in an urban area in Nashville. Including any residence halls, there are 66 buildings.
Student Life: 66% of undergraduates are from Tennessee. Students are from 44 states, 46 foreign countries, and Canada. 90% are from public schools. 74% are African American; 22% white. The average age of freshmen is 18; all undergraduates, 25.
Housing: 3225 students can be accommodated in college housing, which includes single-sex and coed dorms and off-campus apartments. In addition, there are honors houses. On-campus housing is guaranteed for all 4 years. 58% of students commute. Alcohol is not permitted. All students may keep cars.
Activities: 1% of men belong to 4 national fraternities; 2% of women belong to 4 national sororities. There are 63 groups on campus, including band, cheerleading, choir, chorale, computers, dance, drama, forensics, honors, jazz band, literary magazine, marching band, newspaper, pep band, professional, radio and TV, religious, social, social service, student government, and yearbook. Popular campus events include Miss TSU Pageant and Inauguration, Greek Show, and Christmas Tree Lighting Ceremony.
Sports: There are 8 intercollegiate sports for men and 7 for women. Facilities include a major convocation and athletic center that accommodates intramural sports, swimming, handball, and intercollegiate basketball, and a campus center that provides extensive recreational facilities.
Disabled Students: 90% of the campus is accessible. Wheelchair ramps, elevators, special parking, specially equipped rest rooms, and lowered drinking fountains are available. A campus improvement program makes all new and renovated buildings accessible.
Services: Counseling and information services are available, as is tutoring in some subjects, including all general education courses and many major-field courses. There is a reader service for the blind and remedial math, reading, and writing. A writing clinic, math lab, and reading center provide individualized assistance.
Campus Safety and Security: Measures include 24-hour foot and vehicle patrol, shuttle buses, informal discussions, and pamphlets/posters/films. There are emergency telephones and lighted pathways/sidewalks.
Programs of Study: TSU confers B.A., B.S., B.B.A., and B.S.N. degrees. Associate, master's, and doctoral degrees are also awarded. Bachelor's degrees are awarded in AGRICULTURE (agriculture), BIOLOGICAL SCIENCE (biology/biological science), BUSINESS (accounting, business administration and management, business economics, and hotel/motel and restaurant management), COMMUNICATIONS AND THE ARTS (art, dramatic arts, English, languages, music, and speech/debate/rhetoric), COMPUTER AND PHYSICAL SCIENCE (chemistry, computer science, mathematics, and physics), EDUCATION (early childhood, health, and special), ENGINEERING AND ENVIRONMENTAL DESIGN (aeronautical technology, architectural engineering, civil engineering, electrical/electronics engineering, and mechanical engineering), HEALTH PROFESSIONS (dental hygiene, health care administration, medical records administration/services, medical technology, nursing, occupational therapy, physical therapy, respiratory therapy, and speech pathology/audiology), SOCIAL SCIENCE (African studies, criminal justice, family/consumer studies, history, interdisciplinary studies, political science/government, psychology, social work, and sociology). Engineer-

ing, allied health professions, and nursing are the strongest academically and are the largest.

Required: To graduate, students must complete at least 120 semester hours, with 25% in the major, and maintain a minimum GPA of 2.0. Additional requirements include demonstration of proficiency in English composition, completion of a senior project, and courses in English, math, social sciences, American history, humanities, and natural sciences.

Special: Opportunities are provided for co-op programs in business and engineering, cross-registration with Middle Tennessee State University and Meharry Medical College, a B.A.-B.S. degree in interdisciplinary studies, credit by exam, and nondegree study. There are 19 national honor societies, a freshman honors program, and 5 departmental honors programs.

Faculty/Classroom: 55% of faculty are male; 45%, female. 90% teach undergraduates, 20% do research, and 85% do both. No introductory courses are taught by graduate students. The average class size in an introductory lecture is 30; in a laboratory, 35; and in a regular course, 30.

Admissions: 63% of the 2003-2004 applicants were accepted. The SAT I scores for the 2003-2004 freshman class were: Verbal--76% below 500, 21% between 500 and 599, and 4% between 600 and 700; Math--74% below 500, 23% between 500 and 599, and 3% between 600 and 700. The ACT scores were 77% below 21, 17% between 21 and 23, 5% between 24 and 26, 1% between 27 and 28, and 1% above 28.

Requirements: The SAT I or ACT is required, with a minimum score of 890 on the SAT I or 19 on the ACT. Graduation from an accredited secondary school is required; the GED is accepted. Applicants should have 4 credits in English, 3 in math, 2 each in science and a foreign language, and 1 each in history, social studies, and art. A GPA of 2.25 is required. AP and CLEP credits are accepted.

Procedure: Freshmen are admitted to all sessions. Entrance exams should be taken in the junior year. There is an early admissions plan. Applications should be filed by August 1 for fall entry, December 1 for spring entry, and May 1 for summer entry. The fall 2003 application fee was $15.

Transfer: 631 transfer students enrolled in 2002-2003. Applicants must submit official transcripts from all previous colleges attended. Students from other than Tennessee colleges must have maintained a minimum GPA of 2.0. The GPA requirements for students transferring from Tennessee colleges vary according to the number of semester hours being submitted for transfer credit. 30 of 120 credits required for the bachelor's degree must be completed at TSU.

Visiting: There are guides for informal visits and visitors may sit in on classes and stay overnight. To schedule a visit, contact the recruiting staff.

Financial Aid: In 2003-2004, 84% of all full-time freshmen and 80% of continuing full-time students received some form of financial aid. 74% of full-time freshmen and 69% of continuing full-time students received need-based aid. The average freshman award was $5316. Need-based scholarships or need-based grants averaged $6288 ($6581 maximum); need-based self-help aid (loans and jobs) averaged $4680 ($6375 maximum); non-need-based athletic scholarships averaged $5894 ($19,075 maximum); and other non-need-based awards and non-need-based scholarships averaged $146 ($1000 maximum). The FAFSA is required. The deadline for filing freshman financial aid applications for fall entry is April 1.

International Students: There are 56 international students enrolled. They must score 500 on the written TOEFL and also take the SAT I or the ACT.

Computers: The mainframe is a DEC Alpha 4100. Numerous computer labs are available. All students may access the system. There are no time limits and no fees.

Graduates: From July 1, 2002 to June 30, 2003, 988 bachelor's degrees were awarded. The most popular majors were arts and sciences (14%), business administration (12%), and biology (7%). In an average class, 9% graduate in 3 years or less, 13% graduate in 4 years or less, and 5% graduate in 5 years or less. 250 companies recruited on campus in 2002-2003. Of the 2002 graduating class, 7% were enrolled in graduate school within 6 months of graduation.

Admissions Contact: John Cade, Dean of Admissions and Records. A video is available. E-mail: *jcade@picard.tnstate.edu* Web: *www.tnstate.edu*

TENNESSEE TECHNOLOGICAL UNIVERSITY
Cookeville, TN 38505

D-3

(931) 372-3888
(800) 255-8881; Fax: (931) 372-6250

Full-time: 3557 men, 2859 women	**Faculty:** 360; IIA, av$
Part-time: 409 men, 448 women	**Ph.D.s:** 82%
Graduate: 608 men, 1226 women	**Student/Faculty:** 18 to 1
Year: semesters, summer session	**Tuition:** $3778 ($11,710)
Application Deadline: August 1	**Room & Board:** $4892
Freshman Class: 2957 applied, 2570 accepted, 1388 enrolled	
ACT: 23	**VERY COMPETITIVE**

Tennessee Technological University, founded in 1915 and a member of the state university and community college system of Tennessee, is a public institution offering undergraduate and graduate programs in the liberal arts, business, engineering, agriculture studies, art and fine arts, music, professional training, teacher preparation, nursing, home economics, and crafts. There are 8 undergraduate and 4 graduate schools. In addition to regional accreditation, Tennessee Tech has baccalaureate program accreditation with AACSB, AAFCS, ABET, NASAD, NASM, NCATE, and NLN. The library contains 336,000 volumes, 1 million microform items, and 18,000 audio/video tapes/CDs, and subscribes to 3800 periodicals. Computerized library services include the card catalog, interlibrary loans, database searching, and Internet access. Special learning facilities include a learning resource center, art gallery, radio station, and TV station. The 235-acre campus is in a small town 78 miles east of Nashville. Including any residence halls, there are 97 buildings.

Student Life: 95% of undergraduates are from Tennessee. Students are from 43 states, 54 foreign countries, and Canada. 91% are white. Most claim no religious affiliation. The average age of freshmen is 19; all undergraduates, 24. 29% do not continue beyond their first year; 56% remain to graduate.

Housing: 3100 students can be accommodated in college housing, which includes single-sex and coed dorms, on-campus apartments, and married-student housing. In addition, there are honors houses, special-interest houses, and private room dorms for upper class students. On-campus housing is guaranteed for all 4 years. 75% of students commute. Alcohol is not permitted. All students may keep cars.

Activities: 18% of men belong to 11 national fraternities; 7% of women belong to 5 national sororities. There are 178 groups on campus, including art, band, cheerleading, chess, choir, chorale, chorus, computers, dance, debate, drama, drill team, ethnic, forensics, gay, honors, international, jazz band, literary magazine, marching band, musical theater, newspaper, opera, orchestra, pep band, photography, political, professional, radio and TV, religious, social, social service, student government, symphony, and yearbook. Popular campus events include intramural events, Greek Week, and Parents Day.

Sports: There are 7 intercollegiate sports for men and 9 for women, and 10 intramural sports for men and 8 for women. Facilities include 2 gyms seating 10,500 and 4000, a 16,500-seat stadium with track facilities, an indoor pool, indoor and outdoor tennis courts, handball and basketball courts, baseball, softball, and football fields, a track, a rifle range, apparatus rooms, and a health and wellness center with an indoor track, 8 racquetball courts, a weight room, an aerobics classroom, a pool, and basketball/volleyball courts.

Disabled Students: 95% of the campus is accessible. Wheelchair ramps, elevators, special parking, specially equipped rest rooms, special class scheduling, lowered drinking fountains, lowered telephones, and special housing are available.

Services: Counseling and information services are available, as is tutoring in some subjects, including English and lower levels of mathematics. There is a reader service for the blind and remedial math, reading, and writing.

Campus Safety and Security: Measures include 24-hour foot and vehicle patrol, self-defense education, security escort services, and informal discussions. There are pamphlets/posters/films, emergency telephones, lighted pathways/sidewalks, and a student safety organization.

Programs of Study: Tennessee Tech confers B.A., B.S., B.F.A., B.M., B.S.Agr., B.S.B.A., B.S.C.E., B.S.Ch.E., B.S.Ed., B.S.E.E., B.S.H.E., B.S.I.E., B.S.Ind.Tech., B.S.M.E., and B.S.N. degrees. Master's and doctoral degrees are also awarded. Bachelor's degrees are awarded in AGRICULTURE (agricultural economics, agriculture, animal science, fish and game management, plant science, soil science, and wildlife management), BIOLOGICAL SCIENCE (biochemistry and biology/biological science), BUSINESS (accounting, banking and finance, business administration and management, management science, and marketing/retailing/merchandising), COMMUNICATIONS AND THE ARTS (English, fine arts, French, German, journalism, Spanish, and technical and business writing), COMPUTER AND PHYSICAL SCIENCE (chemistry, computer science, geology, mathematics, physics, and web technology), EDUCATION (agricultural, art, home economics, music, physical, secondary, and special), ENGINEERING AND ENVIRONMENTAL DESIGN (chemical engineering, civil engineering, electrical/electronics engineering, engineering, environmental engineering, industrial engineering, industrial engineering technology, manufacturing engineering, and mechanical en-

gineering), HEALTH PROFESSIONS (nursing), SOCIAL SCIENCE (child care/child and family studies, economics, history, human ecology, political science/government, psychology, and sociology). Engineering, business, and education are the strongest academically. Engineering is the largest.

Required: Students must complete 120 semester hours, with a variable number of hours in the major, and maintain a minimum GPA of 2.0. 9 semester hours of English, 8 of a lab science, 6 of American history, 6 each of social sciences and humanities, and 3 hours each of math and speech.

Special: Co-op programs in most academic areas, internships in community-based programs, study abroad, a Washington semester, multidisciplinary majors and work-study programs are available. Accelerated degree programs are offered in all specified majors with 3 calendar years of continuous studies. A B.A.-B.S. degree is available, as are dual majors in all areas. Credit may be granted for military experience, and nondegree study and pass/fail options are offered. There are 29 national honor societies and a freshman honors program.

Faculty/Classroom: 61% of faculty are male; 39%, female. 99% teach undergraduates, 73% do research, and 70% do both. Graduate students teach 5% of introductory courses. The average class size in an introductory lecture is 27; in a laboratory, 30; and in a regular course, 26.

Admissions: 87% of the 2003-2004 applicants were accepted. The SAT I scores for the 2003-2004 freshman class were: Verbal--24% below 500, 40% between 500 and 599, 30% between 600 and 700, and 6% above 700; Math--22% below 500, 38% between 500 and 599, 34% between 600 and 700, and 6% above 700. The ACT scores were 30% below 21, 25% between 21 and 23, 23% between 24 and 26, 10% between 27 and 28, and 12% above 28. 51% of the current freshmen were in the top fifth of their class; 80% were in the top two fifths. There was 1 National Merit finalist. 36 freshmen graduated first in their class.

Requirements: The ACT is required, with a minimum composite score of 19. Other admissions requirements include graduation from an accredited secondary school with 14 academic credits, including 4 of English, 3 of math, 2 each in science and a single foreign language, 1 in American history, 1 in world history, ancient history, modern history, world geography or European history, and 1 in music or art. The GED is also accepted. A GPA of 2.5 is required. AP and CLEP credits are accepted.

Procedure: Freshmen are admitted to all sessions. Entrance exams should be taken during the senior year. There are early admissions and deferred admissions plans.There is a rolling admissions plan. Applications should be filed by August 1 for fall entry, December 1 for spring entry, and May 1 for summer entry, along with a $15 fee. Notification is sent on a rolling basis. Applications are accepted on-line through the school's web site.

Transfer: 584 transfer students enrolled in 2002-2003. Transfer students should have a minimum of 12 credit hours earned; the minimum GPA depends on the number of credit hours accumulated. Official transcripts must be submitted, and the ACT is required, depending on age (for applicants 21 or older it is not required). If an applicant has fewer than 12 credit hours, admissions requirements are the same as for freshmen. 30 of 120 credits required for the bachelor's degree must be completed at Tennessee Tech.

Visiting: There are regularly scheduled orientations for prospective students, including visits either morning or afternoon each weekday and meetings with an admission officer, faculty member in student's major, and a campus tour. There are guides for informal visits and visitors may sit in on classes. To schedule a visit, contact the Admissions Office at (866) SEE-TECH or visit@tntech.edu.

Financial Aid: In 2003-2004, 75% of all full-time freshmen and 73% of continuing full-time students received some form of financial aid. 48% of full-time freshmen and 52% of continuing full-time students received need-based aid. The average freshman award was $5944. Need-based scholarships or need-based grants averaged $3005; need-based self-help aid (loans and jobs) averaged $1954; non-need-based athletic scholarships averaged $9127; and other non-need-based awards and non-need-based scholarships averaged $3982. 97% of undergraduates work part time. Average annual earnings from campus work are $1200. The average financial indebtedness of the 2003 graduate was $14,157. The FAFSA is required. The priority date for freshman financial aid applications for fall entry is March 15. The deadline for filing freshman financial aid applications for fall entry is May 1.

International Students: There are 209 international students enrolled. The school actively recruits these students. They must score 500 on the written TOEFL or 273 on the electronic version and also take the college's own test and also take the SAT I or the ACT, scoring 17 (ACT) or 810 (SAT I).

Computers: The mainframes are a DEC Alpha Server 4100 and a DEC VAX 7000/620. VAX, Gemini, Dell, and Mac PCs are available for student use in numerous buildings across campus. All students have access to the Internet through Netscape or Explorer. All students may access the system 24 hours a day. There are no time limits and no fees.

Graduates: From July 1, 2002 to June 30, 2003, 1233 bachelor's degrees were awarded. The most popular majors were business management (14%), elementary education (10%), and mechanical engineering (8%). In an average class, 11% graduate in 4 years or less, 34% graduate in 5 years or less, and 44% graduate in 6 years or less. 250 companies recruited on campus in 2002-2003. Of the 2002 graduating class, 10% were enrolled in graduate school within 6 months of graduation and 80% were employed.

Admissions Contact: Robert L. Hodum, Assistant Director of Admissions. E-mail: *admissions@tntech.edu* Web: *www.tntech.edu*

TENNESSEE WESLEYAN COLLEGE   D-3
Athens, TN 37371-0040   (423) 746-5286
                                  (800) PICK-TWC; Fax: (423) 744-9968

Full-time: 214 men, 432 women	**Faculty:** 52; IIB, --$
Part-time: 41 men, 106 women	**Ph.D.s:** 63%
Graduate: none	**Student/Faculty:** 12 to 1
Year: semesters, summer session	**Tuition:** $11,340
Application Deadline: open	**Room & Board:** $5200
Freshman Class: 452 applied, 376 accepted, 106 enrolled	
ACT: 21	**COMPETITIVE**

Tennessee Wesleyan College, founded in 1857, is a private institution affiliated with the United Methodist Church. Its undergraduate programs stress the liberal arts, teacher preparation, and nursing. In addition to regional accreditation, TWC has baccalaureate program accreditation with CCNE. The library contains 108,612 volumes, 9410 microform items, and 3780 audio/video tapes/CDs, and subscribes to 809 periodicals. Computerized library services include the card catalog, interlibrary loans, and database searching. Special learning facilities include a learning resource center, art gallery, and an education technology lab. The 40-acre campus is in a small town 55 miles south of Knoxville. Including any residence halls, there are 19 buildings.

Student Life: 89% of undergraduates are from Tennessee. Students are from 16 states, 13 foreign countries, and Canada. 98% are from public schools. 83% are white. 51% are Protestant; 37% claim no religious affiliation. The average age of freshmen is 21; all undergraduates, 25. 35% do not continue beyond their first year; 35% remain to graduate.

Housing: 287 students can be accommodated in college housing, which includes single-sex and coed dorms, on-campus apartments, and fraternity houses. On-campus housing is guaranteed for all 4 years. 75% of students commute. Alcohol is not permitted. All students may keep cars.

Activities: 33% of women belong to 1 local and 1 national sorority. There are no fraternities. There are 24 groups on campus, including art, cheerleading, choir, chorale, computers, dance, drama, ethnic, honors, international, literary magazine, musical theater, newspaper, professional, religious, social, social service, student government, and yearbook. Popular campus events include Halloween Arts Carnival, Spring Fever Week, and Bulldog Olympics.

Sports: There are 6 intercollegiate sports for men and 6 for women, and 7 intramural sports for men and 7 for women. Facilities include a 2000-seat stadium, an 800-seat gym, a fitness center, and a YMCA adjacent to campus with an indoor/outdoor swimming pool available on a scheduled basis to students.

Disabled Students: 70% of the campus is accessible. Wheelchair ramps, elevators, special parking, specially equipped rest rooms, and special class scheduling are available.

Services: Counseling and information services are available, as is tutoring in some subjects, including English, math, computers, and sciences. There is remedial math and writing.

Campus Safety and Security: Measures include informal discussions, lighted pathways/sidewalks, and an evening security patrol 7 days per week.

Programs of Study: TWC confers B.A., B.S., B.Applied Sc., B.Mus.Ed., and B.S.N. degrees. Bachelor's degrees are awarded in BIOLOGICAL SCIENCE (biology/biological science), BUSINESS (accounting, business administration and management, recreation and leisure services, and sports management), COMMUNICATIONS AND THE ARTS (English and music), COMPUTER AND PHYSICAL SCIENCE (chemistry and mathematics), EDUCATION (education, music, and physical), HEALTH PROFESSIONS (health and nursing), SOCIAL SCIENCE (behavioral science, history, human development, human services, interdisciplinary studies, ministries, pastoral studies, psychology, religious education, and religious music). History, English, and preseminary are the strongest academically. Business administration and education are the largest.

Required: Students must complete 128 semester hours, fulfilling the requirements of the major and taking 28 semester hours at the upper-division level, and maintain a minimum GPA of 2.0. Distribution requirements include 12 semester hours of the humanities, 9 of social and behavioral sciences, 8 of science, 6 each of math and English composition, and 3 each of speech and fine arts. B.A. candidates must also take 12 hours of a single foreign language. 2 semester hours of phys ed are also needed. Internships are required for human services students, and all students must take an exit exam.

Special: Special academic programs include internships in some majors, study abroad in Japan and England, dual majors in several areas, student-designed majors, and nondegree study. Business majors may participate in a co-op program. There is 1 national honor society and a freshman honors program.

Faculty/Classroom: 47% of faculty are male; 53%, female. All teach undergraduates and 40% both teach and do research. The average class size in an introductory lecture is 23; in a laboratory, 11; and in a regular course, 16.

Admissions: 83% of the 2003-2004 applicants were accepted. The ACT scores for the 2003-2004 freshman class were: 50% below 21, 26% between 21 and 23, 17% between 24 and 26, 5% between 27 and 28, and 3% above 28.

Requirements: The ACT is required. In addition, other admission requirements include graduation from an accredited secondary school, with 16 academic credits, including 4 units in English, 2 each in math and science, and 1 each in social studies and history. Foreign language is recommended. The GED is also accepted. A GPA of 2.0 is required. AP and CLEP credits are accepted. Important factors in the admissions decision are leadership record, recommendations by school officials, and personality/intangible qualities.

Procedure: Freshmen are admitted to all sessions. Entrance exams should be taken in the fall of the senior year. Application deadlines are open. There is a rolling admissions plan. Application fee is $25. Applications are accepted on-line.

Transfer: 151 transfer students enrolled in 2002-2003. Transfer students must have a minimum GPA of 2.0; an associate degree is recommended. 32 of 128 credits required for the bachelor's degree must be completed at TWC.

Visiting: There are regularly scheduled orientations for prospective students. There are guides for informal visits and visitors may sit in on classes and stay overnight. To schedule a visit, contact the Office of Admissions at (423) 746-5287 or *cawoodr@twcnet.edu*.

Financial Aid: In 2003-2004, 52% of all full-time freshmen and 80% of continuing full-time students received some form of financial aid. 43% of full-time freshmen and 63% of continuing full-time students received need-based aid. The average freshman award was $9075. Need-based scholarships or need-based grants averaged $2556 ($3680 maximum); need-based self-help aid (loans and jobs) averaged $1744 ($2542 maximum); non-need-based athletic scholarships averaged $3996 ($6156 maximum); and other non-need-based awards and non-need-based scholarships averaged $2674 ($3096 maximum). 12% of undergraduates work part time. Average annual earnings from campus work are $898. The average financial indebtedness of the 2003 graduate was $10,500. The FAFSA and the college's own financial statement are required. The priority date for freshman financial aid applications for fall entry is March 1.

International Students: There are 32 international students enrolled. The school actively recruits these students. They must score 500 on the written TOEFL or 173 on the electronic version or take the MELAB, the Comprehensive English Language Test, or the college's own test.

Computers: The mainframe is an IBM. Students have access to 49 PCs located in 3 labs on campus, the library, and the student center. All students may access the system during lab hours, generally 8:30 A.M. to midnight. There are no time limits and no fees.

Graduates: From July 1, 2002 to June 30, 2003, 181 bachelor's degrees were awarded. The most popular majors were nursing (15%), business administration (13%), and education (10%). In an average class, 30% graduate in 4 years or less, 33% graduate in 5 years or less, and 40% graduate in 6 years or less.

Admissions Contact: Michelle Boyd, Office Coordinator. A video is available. E-mail: *shellyb@twcnet.edu* Web: *www.twcnet.edu*

TREVECCA NAZARENE UNIVERSITY   C-3
Nashville, TN 37210-2877   (615) 248-1320
                                  (888) 210-4TNU; Fax: (615) 248-7406

Full-time: 404 men, 544 women	**Faculty:** 62; IIB, --$
Part-time: 103 men, 181 women	**Ph.D.s:** 65%
Graduate: 245 men, 434 women	**Student/Faculty:** 15 to 1
Year: semesters, summer session	**Tuition:** $11,960
Application Deadline: open	**Room & Board:** $5588
Freshman Class: 680 applied, 454 accepted, 248 enrolled	
SAT I Verbal/Math: 530/510	**ACT:** 21	**COMPETITIVE**

Trevecca Nazarene University, founded in 1901, is a private institution affiliated with the Church of the Nazarene. Trevecca offers programs in liberal arts and sciences and a number of professional content areas. The university also provides a variety of nontraditional continuing education professional programs at the undergraduate and graduate levels. There are 4 undergraduate and 4 graduate schools. In addition to regional accreditation, TNU has baccalaureate program accreditation with CAHEA and NASM. The library contains 374,360 volumes, 273,521 microform items, and 2552 audio/video tapes/CDs, and subscribes to 730 periodicals. Computerized library services include the card catalog, interlibrary loans, database searching, and Internet access. Special learning facilities include a learning resource center, radio station, and a curriculum library. The 80-acre campus is in an urban area. Including any residence halls, there are 26 buildings.

Student Life: 61% of undergraduates are from Tennessee. Students are from 37 states, 12 foreign countries, and Canada. 79% are white. Most are Protestant. The average age of freshmen is 19; all undergraduates, 24. 63% do not continue beyond their first year; 37% remain to graduate.

Housing: 710 students can be accommodated in college housing, which includes single-sex dorms, on-campus apartments, off-campus apartments, and married-student housing. On-campus housing is guaranteed for all 4 years. 56% of students live on campus. Alcohol is not permitted. All students may keep cars.

Activities: There are no fraternities or sororities. There are 20 groups on campus, including band, cheerleading, choir, chorale, chorus, drama, forensics, honors, jazz band, literary magazine, marching band, newspaper, orchestra, pep band, professional, radio, religious, social service, student government, and yearbook. Popular campus events include Valentine's Banquet, Junior-Senior Banquets, and Fall Retreat.

Sports: There are 4 intercollegiate sports for men and 5 for women, and 9 intramural sports for men and 8 for women. Facilities include a gym, a pool, a jogging track, handball, racquetball, and tennis courts, exercise and weight rooms, and playing fields.

Disabled Students: Wheelchair ramps, elevators, special parking, specially equipped rest rooms, and special class scheduling are available.

Services: Counseling and information services are available, as is tutoring in every subject. There is remedial math, reading, and writing. An academic enrichment program for students scoring below 19 on the ACT provides tutoring in math, reading, writing, and study skills.

Campus Safety and Security: Measures include 24-hour foot and vehicle patrol, informal discussions, lighted pathways/sidewalks, and weekend and evening foot and vehicle patrols.

Programs of Study: TNU confers B.A., B.S., B.B.A., and B.S.S.W. degrees. Associate, master's, and doctoral degrees are also awarded. Bachelor's degrees are awarded in BIOLOGICAL SCIENCE (biology/biological science), BUSINESS (accounting, business administration and management, and marketing/retailing/merchandising), COMMUNICATIONS AND THE ARTS (broadcasting, communications, communications technology, dramatic arts, English, music, and music business management), COMPUTER AND PHYSICAL SCIENCE (chemistry, information sciences and systems, mathematics, physics, and science), EDUCATION (early childhood, education, English, mathematics, music, physical, and science), HEALTH PROFESSIONS (medical laboratory technology), SOCIAL SCIENCE (behavioral science, history, political science/government, psychology, religion, religious music, social science, and social work). Teacher education, business, and music are the strongest academically. Management and human relations, religion, and education are the largest.

Required: To graduate, students must complete at least 128 semester hours with a minimum 2.0 GPA. The required 62-hour general education curriculum includes courses in English, communications, religion and philosophy, fine arts, history and social science (including foreign language), science and math, phys ed, and computer literacy.

Special: There is cross-registration with other Nazarene colleges and universities in the United States, and work-study programs, internships, a Washington semester, and nondegree study are offered. Study abroad is possible. An evening program leads to the B.A. in Management and Human Relations for adult learners over 23 with 62 semester hours of college work. A 3-2 nursing program is offered with Belmont University. There are preprofessional studies in nursing, physical therapy, medicine, dentistry, pharmacy, veterinary science, law, and engineering. There is 1 national honor society.

Faculty/Classroom: 66% of faculty are male; 34%, female. 80% teach undergraduates. No introductory courses are taught by graduate students. The average class size in a regular course is 20.

Admissions: 67% of the 2003-2004 applicants were accepted. The ACT scores for the 2003-2004 freshman class were: 42% below 21, 26% between 21 and 23, 18% between 24 and 26, 4% between 27 and 28, and 10% above 28.

Requirements: The SAT I or ACT is required; the ACT is preferred, with a composite score of at least 18. Candidates should have completed at least 15 academic secondary credits, including 4 units in English, 2 each in math, foreign language, and social science, and 1 in natural science. A GED of at least 45 is also accepted. The medical technology and teacher education programs have special admission requirements. A GPA of 2.5 is required. AP and CLEP credits are accepted.

Procedure: Freshmen are admitted fall, spring, and summer. Entrance exams should be taken in the junior or senior years. There is a deferred admissions plan. Application deadlines are open. There is a rolling admissions plan. Application fee is $25.

Transfer: 51 transfer students enrolled in 2002-2003. Transfer applicants must present official transcripts and recommendations. 32 of 128 credits required for the bachelor's degree must be completed at TNU.

Visiting: There are regularly scheduled orientations for prospective students, including a tour and meetings with admissions and financial aid personnel and faculty. There are guides for informal visits and visitors may sit in on classes and stay overnight. To schedule a visit, contact the Admissions Office.

Financial Aid: The FAFSA is required. The deadline for filing freshman financial aid applications for fall entry is March 1.

International Students: There are 19 international students enrolled. They must score 500 on the written TOEFL and also take the SAT I or the ACT, scoring 18 on the ACT.

Computers: The mainframe is a DEC Alpha 1000A. The campus network is Windows NT-based, with Windows 95 and Mac OS 8 also in use. Students may access the network via more than 200 PCs or terminals in 13 computer labs, each equipped with at least 1 laser printer. TNU has a dedicated-circuit Internet connection and 3 multimedia classrooms. All students may access the system from 8 A.M. to 11 P.M. every day, with residence hall labs open 24 hours per day. There are no time limits and no fees.

Graduates: From July 1, 2002 to June 30, 2003, 340 bachelor's degrees were awarded. The most popular majors were management and human relations (61%), religion (6%), and education (6%). In an average class, 2% graduate in 3 years or less, 17% graduate in 4 years or less, 30% graduate in 5 years or less, and 37% graduate in 6 years or less. 25 companies recruited on campus in 2002-2003.

Admissions Contact: Patty Cook, Director of Admissions. E-mail: *admissions_und@trevecca.edu* Web: *www.trevecca.edu*

TUSCULUM COLLEGE
F-3
Greeneville, TN 37743
(423) 636-7300
(800) 729-0256; Fax: (423) 638-7166

Full-time: 891 men, 1008 women	**Faculty:** 60; IIB, --$
Part-time: 5 men, 10 women	**Ph.D.s:** 65%
Graduate: 74 men, 144 women	**Student/Faculty:** 32 to 1
Year: semesters, summer session	**Tuition:** $14,110
Application Deadline: open	**Room & Board:** $5880
Freshman Class: 1166 applied, 888 accepted, 277 enrolled	
SAT I Verbal/Math: 470/480	**ACT:** 20 COMPETITIVE

Tusculum College, a civic arts institution chartered in 1794, is the oldest college in Tennessee and the oldest coeducational college affiliated with the Presbyterian Church (U.S.A.). The 2 libraries contain 67,202 volumes, 210,798 microform items, and 966 audio/video tapes/CDs, and subscribe to 300 periodicals. Computerized library services include the card catalog, interlibrary loans, database searching, and Internet access. Special learning facilities include an art gallery, radio station, TV station, and President Andrew Johnson Museum. The 142-acre campus is in a small town 30 miles south of Johnson City, in the foothills of the Great Smoky Mountains. Including any residence halls, there are 21 buildings.

Student Life: 80% of undergraduates are from Tennessee. Students are from 36 states, 18 foreign countries, and Canada. 97% are from public schools. 87% are white. The average age of freshmen is 19; all undergraduates, 28. 32% do not continue beyond their first year; 68% remain to graduate.

Housing: 607 students can be accommodated in college housing, which includes single-sex dorms. On-campus housing is guaranteed for all 4 years. 72% of students commute. Alcohol is not permitted. All students may keep cars.

Activities: There are no fraternities or sororities. There are 21 groups on campus, including art, cheerleading, chorale, dance, drama, ethnic, honors, international, newspaper, pep band, photography, professional, radio and TV, religious, social service, student government, and yearbook. Popular campus events include McCormick Day, Opening Convocation, and Honors Convocation.

Sports: There are 7 intercollegiate sports for men and 7 for women, and 12 intramural sports for men and 13 for women. Facilities include a 2000-seat gym, a gym/pool complex, tennis courts, and football, soccer, softball, and baseball fields.

Disabled Students: 50% of the campus is accessible. Wheelchair ramps, elevators, special parking, specially equipped rest rooms, special class scheduling, lowered drinking fountains, lowered telephones, and special housing are available. Classes and activities are scheduled in accessible areas.

Services: Counseling and information services are available, as is tutoring in most subjects. There is a reader service for the blind, and remedial math, reading, and writing. Math and English tutoring are available on a limited basis through the College Learning Center.

Campus Safety and Security: Measures include 24-hour foot and vehicle patrol, informal discussions, emergency telephones, and lighted pathways/sidewalks.

Programs of Study: Tusculum confers B.A. and B.S. degrees. Master's degrees are also awarded. Bachelor's degrees are awarded in BIOLOGICAL SCIENCE (biology/biological science), BUSINESS (management information systems, management science, small business management, and sports management), COMMUNICATIONS AND THE ARTS (English and fine arts), COMPUTER AND PHYSICAL SCIENCE (computer science and information sciences and systems), EDUCATION (early childhood, education, elementary, middle school, museum studies, physical, and special), ENGINEERING AND ENVIRONMENTAL DESIGN (environmental science), HEALTH PROFESSIONS (medical technology, premedicine, and sports medicine), SOCIAL SCIENCE (history and psychology). Management, education, and biology are the strongest academically. Management and education are the largest.

Required: All students must complete at least 128 credit hours, a minimum GPA of 2.0 overall and 2.25 in the major. Specific degree programs have varying requirements. B.S. candidates must take a core curriculum consisting of courses in English, art, music, sociology, economics, and psychology. B.A. candidates must complete a set of interdisciplinary courses, validate 15 competencies, complete a civic arts project, and fulfill the requirements of a major.

Special: Each semester is divided into four 3 1/2-week blocks, with 1 course taken per block. Internships, practicums, and student-teaching opportunities are offered in business administration, professional and special education, social services, psychology, biology, chemistry, and medical technology. The B.S. in applied organizational management is designed for adult students with previous training and work experience. The medical technology program is offered in cooperation with a medical center in Kingsport. Study abroad, independent majors, nondegree study, an accelerated degree program in applied organizational management, work-study programs, student-designed majors, and pass/fail options are available. There is an accelerated evening program for working adults. There is 1 national honor society.

Faculty/Classroom: 67% of faculty are male; 33%, female. 89% teach undergraduates. No introductory courses are taught by graduate students. The average class size in an introductory lecture is 25; in a laboratory, 20; and in a regular course, 15.

Admissions: 76% of the 2003-2004 applicants were accepted. The SAT I scores for the 2003-2004 freshman class were: Verbal--61% below 500, 31% between 500 and 599, 7% between 600 and 700, and 1% above 700; Math--57% below 500, 31% between 500 and 599, 11% between 600 and 700, and 1% above 700. The ACT scores were 60% below 21, 19% between 21 and 23, 15% between 24 and 26, 4% between 27 and 28, and 2% above 28. In a recent year, 3 freshmen graduated first in their class.

Requirements: The SAT I or ACT is required. The recommended composite score is 920 on the SAT I or 18 on the ACT. Applicants should be high school graduates or have the GED. Secondary school preparation should include 4 units of English, 2 units each of foreign language, math, and science, and 1 unit of history. A personal essay is also required and an interview may be necessary. Tusculum requires applicants to be in the upper 50% of their class. A GPA of 2.0 is required. AP and CLEP credits are accepted. Important factors in the admissions decision are advanced placement or honors courses, leadership record, and evidence of special talent.

Procedure: Freshmen are admitted to all sessions. Entrance exams should be taken in the spring of the junior year. There are rolling admissions and early decision plans. Application deadlines are open. Applications are accepted on computer disk and on-line through the college web site.

Transfer: 84 transfer students enrolled in a recent year. Transfer applicants should present at least a 2.0 GPA in previous college work. Tusculum recommends that applicants also submit SAT I or ACT scores. 32 of 128 credits required for the bachelor's degree must be completed at Tusculum.

Visiting: There are regularly scheduled orientations for prospective students, including a fall and spring open house during which students are given campus tours, financial aid information, and application materials. There are guides for informal visits and visitors may sit in on classes and stay overnight. To schedule a visit, contact the Admissions Office.

Financial Aid: In 2003-2004, 80% of all full-time freshmen and 61% of continuing full-time students received some form of financial aid. 62% of full-time freshmen and 49% of continuing full-time students received need-based aid. The average freshman award was $11,975. Need-based scholarships or need-based grants averaged $1467; need-based self-help aid (loans and jobs) averaged $2855; and non-need-based awards and non-need-based scholarships averaged $6438. 20% of undergraduates work part time. Average annual earnings from campus work are $1045. The average financial indebtedness of the 2003 graduate was $14,633. The FAFSA is required. The priority date for freshman financial aid applications for fall entry is February 5.

International Students: In a recent year, there were 30 international students enrolled. They must score 550 on the written TOEFL.

Computers: There are a total of 70 networked PCs available in 3 computer labs. All have Internet access. All students may access the system 24 hours a day, 7 days a week. There are no time limits and no fees.

Graduates: In an average class, 45% graduate in 6 years or less. 25 companies recruited on campus in a recent year. Of the 2002 graduating class, 10% were enrolled in graduate school within 6 months of graduation.

Admissions Contact: Nancy Kilday, Admission Coordinator.
E-mail: *admissions@tusculum.edu* Web: *www.tusculum.edu*

UNION UNIVERSITY   B-3
Jackson, TN 38305-3697   (731) 661-5000
(800) 33-UNION; Fax: (731) 338-6466

Full-time: 605 men, 1015 women	**Faculty:** 146; IIA, --$
Part-time: 190 men, 212 women	**Ph.D.s:** 80%
Graduate: 245 men, 507 women	**Student/Faculty:** 11 to 1
Year: 4-1-4, summer session	**Tuition:** $14,450
Application Deadline: open	**Room & Board:** $4350
Freshman Class: 1487 applied, 874 accepted, 410 enrolled	
SAT I Verbal/Math: 560/550	**ACT:** 24 **VERY COMPETITIVE**

Union University, founded in 1823, is a private, nonprofit institution affiliated with the Southern Baptist Convention. The university offers programs in arts and sciences, education, business, and nursing. There are 4 undergraduate and 3 graduate schools. In addition to regional accreditation, Union has baccalaureate program accreditation with AACSB, ACS, CAAHEP, CCNE, CSWE, NASAD, NASM, NCATE, and NLN. The library contains 146,055 volumes, 479,357 microform items, and 11,088 audio/video tapes/CDs, and subscribes to 705 periodicals. Computerized library services include the card catalog, interlibrary loans, database searching, and Internet access. Special learning facilities include a learning resource center, art gallery, and radio and TV lab facilities. The 290-acre campus is in a suburban area 80 miles east of Memphis. Including any residence halls, there are 34 buildings.

Student Life: 68% of undergraduates are from Tennessee. Others are from 44 states, 36 foreign countries, and Canada. 75% are from public schools. 90% are white. Most are Protestant. The average age of freshmen is 18; all undergraduates, 20. 7% do not continue beyond their first year; 59% remain to graduate.

Housing: 1114 students can be accommodated in college housing, which includes single-sex dorms, on-campus apartments, and married-student housing. On-campus housing is guaranteed for all 4 years. 59% of students live on campus; of those, 35% remain on campus on weekends. Alcohol is not permitted. All students may keep cars.

Activities: 7% of men belong to 3 national fraternities; 11% of women belong to 3 national sororities. There are 73 groups on campus, including art, band, cheerleading, choir, chorus, computers, concert band, drama, ethnic, film, honors, international, jazz band, literary magazine, musical ensembles, musical theater, newspaper, opera, orchestra, photography, political, professional, radio and TV, religious, social, social service, student government, symphony, and yearbook. Popular campus events include Campus Day, Parents Weekend, and Variety Show.

Sports: There are 5 intercollegiate sports for men and 5 for women, and 12 intramural sports for men and 12 for women. Facilities include tennis and racquetball courts, a student recreation center, an indoor swimming pool, a wellness center, 2 gyms, a soccer field, and baseball and softball complexes.

Disabled Students: 98% of the campus is accessible. Wheelchair ramps, elevators, special parking, specially equipped rest rooms, special class scheduling, lowered drinking fountains, lowered telephones, and special housing are available.

Services: Counseling and information services are available, as is tutoring in most subjects. There is also assistance with study skills, time management, note taking, reading comprehension, and writing.

Campus Safety and Security: Measures include 24-hour foot and vehicle patrol, self-defense education, security escort services, and informal discussions. There are pamphlets/posters/films, emergency telephones, and lighted pathways/sidewalks.

Programs of Study: Union confers B.A., B.S., B.M., B.S.B.A., B.S.M.T., and B.S.N. degrees. Associate, master's, and doctoral degrees are also awarded. Bachelor's degrees are awarded in BIOLOGICAL SCIENCE (biology/biological science), BUSINESS (accounting, banking and finance, business administration and management, management science, marketing management, marketing/retailing/merchandising, and sports management), COMMUNICATIONS AND THE ARTS (advertising, art, broadcasting, communications, dramatic arts, English, English as a second/foreign language, English literature, French, graphic design, Greek, journalism, music, music performance, music theory and composition, piano/organ, public relations, Spanish, and voice), COMPUTER AND PHYSICAL SCIENCE (chemistry, computer science, mathematics, physical chemistry, physical sciences, and physics), EDUCATION (education, elementary, middle school, music, physical, secondary, special, and teaching English as a second/foreign language (TESOL/TEFOL)), ENGINEERING AND ENVIRONMENTAL DESIGN (preengineering), HEALTH PROFESSIONS (medical laboratory technology, nursing, predentistry, premedicine, prepharmacy, and sports medicine), SOCIAL SCIENCE (biblical languages, biblical studies, Christian studies, economics, family and community services, history, ministries, missions, pastoral studies, philosophy, political science/government, prelaw, psychology, religion, religious music, social work, sociology, and youth ministry). Business, nursing, and education are the largest.

Required: All students must complete 128 credit hours, with at least 30 in the major, and maintain a minimum overall GPA of 2.0. The general core requirements are 8 credit hours of lab sciences, 6 each of history, composition, literature, and religion, 3 each of math, oral communication, social sciences/humanities, and fine arts, and 2 of phys ed. Students must pass comprehensive exams in each course and at completion of the major.

Special: Cooperative and accelerated degree programs are available in business department majors. Cross-registration with Lambuth and Freed-Hardeman Universities, internships, study abroad in 7 countries, a Washington semester, work-study programs, composite majors in religion and church ministry, religion and Greek, and religion and philosophy, dual and student-designed majors, 3-2 engineering degrees, and nondegree study are also offered. There are 15 national honor societies, a freshman honors program, and 14 departmental honors programs.

Faculty/Classroom: 54% of faculty are male; 46%, female. All teach undergraduates and 25% do research. No introductory courses are taught by graduate students. The average class size in an introductory lecture is 25; in a laboratory, 18; and in a regular course, 15.

Admissions: 59% of the 2003-2004 applicants were accepted. The SAT I scores for the 2003-2004 freshman class were: Verbal--17% below 500, 47% between 500 and 599, 23% between 600 and 700, and 12% above 700; Math--27% below 500, 43% between 500 and 599, 23% between 600 and 700, and 8% above 700. The ACT scores were 20% below 21, 25% between 21 and 23, 26% between 24 and 26, 12% between 27 and 28, and 17% above 28. 65% of the current freshmen were in the top fifth of their class; 85% were in the top two fifths. There were 6 National Merit finalists and 2 semifinalists. 44 freshmen graduated first in their class.

Requirements: The SAT I or ACT is required; the ACT is preferred. A minimum composite score of 20 on the ACT or 820 on the SAT I is recommended. Candidates must be graduates of an accredited secondary school or have the GED. A minimum of 20 academic credits is required, including at least 14 in English, math, foreign language, and social and natural sciences. An interview is also recommended. Union requires applicants to be in the upper 50% of their class. A GPA of 2.5 is required. AP and CLEP credits are accepted. Important factors in the admissions decision are leadership record, advanced placement or honor courses, and recommendations by school officials.

Procedure: Freshmen are admitted to all sessions. Entrance exams should be taken in the spring of the junior year. There are early decision, early admissions, and deferred admissions plans. Application deadlines are open. Application fee is $25. Notification is sent on a rolling basis beginning Novermber 1. 14 early decision candidates were accepted for the 2003-2004 class. Applications are accepted on-line through CollegeLink and the Internet.

Transfer: 183 transfer students enrolled in 2002-2003. Candidates must have a minimum GPA of 2.0 in more than 12 semester hours and submit a student transfer form from the last institution attended. 32 of 128 credits required for the bachelor's degree must be completed at Union.

Visiting: There are regularly scheduled orientations for prospective students, including campus tours, class visits, and appointments with counselors. There are guides for informal visits and visitors may sit in on classes and stay overnight. To schedule a visit, contact Robbie Graves, Director of Enrollment at (731) 661-5008 or rgraves@uu.edu.

Financial Aid: In 2003-2004, 81% of all full-time freshmen and 80% of continuing full-time students received some form of financial aid. 70% of full-time freshmen and 71% of continuing full-time students received need-based aid. Need-based scholarships or need-based grants averaged $2585; need-based self-help aid (loans and jobs) averaged $2851; and other non-need-based awards and non-need-based scholarships averaged $2655. 35% of undergraduates work part time. Average annual earnings from campus work are $1000. The average financial indebtedness of the 2003 graduate was $7800. The FAFSA and the college's own financial statement are required. The deadline for filing freshman financial aid applications for fall entry is February 15.

International Students: There are 40 international students enrolled. The school actively recruits these students. They must score 500 on the written TOEFL. If the TOEFL has not been taken, the ACT or the SAT I is required, with a score of 950 on the SAT I.

Computers: The mainframe is an HP3000/series 979. 4 large labs house 105 computers, all connected to the campus network, the Internet, and the libraries' on-line services. Some have access to the mainframe to support computer science and statistics classes. All students have e-mail and network accounts. Other smaller labs have a total of about 100 PCs with software specific to the department. All dorm rooms are wired, giving 24-hour access equivalent to that in the labs. All students may access the system during lab hours. There are no time limits and no fees.

Graduates: From July 1, 2002 to June 30, 2003, 396 bachelor's degrees were awarded. The most popular majors were business/marketing (26%), health professions and related sciencea (20%), and education (15%). In an average class, 4% graduate in 3 years or less, 47% graduate in 4 years or less, 59% graduate in 5 years or less, and 60% graduate in 6 years or less. 47 companies recruited on campus in 2002-2003.

Admissions Contact: Carroll Griffin, Assistant to the Provost for Enrollment Services. E-mail: info@uu.edu Web: www.uu.edu

UNIVERSITY OF MEMPHIS   A-4
Memphis, TN 38152

(901) 678-2169
(800) 669-2678; Fax: (901) 678-5318

Full-time: 4514 men, 6742 women	**Faculty:** 584; I, --$
Part-time: 1564 men, 2389 women	**Ph.D.s:** 74%
Graduate: 1924 men, 2778 women	**Student/Faculty:** 19 to 1
Year: semesters, summer session	**Tuition:** $4234 ($11,656)
Application Deadline: August 1	**Room & Board:** $4326
Freshman Class: 4514 applied, 3998 accepted, 1945 enrolled	
SAT I Verbal/Math: 540/530	**ACT:** 21 COMPETITIVE

The University of Memphis, founded in 1912, is a public liberal arts and sciences institution and is part of the Tennessee Board of Regents system. There are 9 undergraduate and 2 graduate schools. In addition to regional accreditation, U of M has baccalaureate program accreditation with AACSB, ABET, ACEJMC, ADA, AHEA, ASLA, CSWE, FIDER, NASAD, NASM, NCATE, and NLN. The 6 libraries contain 1,293,713 volumes, 3,426,936 microform items, and 32,251 audio/video tapes/CDs, and subscribe to 13,155 periodicals. Computerized library services include the card catalog, interlibrary loans, and database searching. Special learning facilities include a learning resource center, art gallery, radio station, TV station, an earthquake research center, a center for electron microscopy, Chucalissa Indian Village and Museum, and a speech and hearing center. The 1160-acre campus is in an urban area. Including any residence halls, there are 200 buildings.

Student Life: 94% of undergraduates are from Tennessee. Students are from 47 states, 101 foreign countries, and Canada. 58% are white; 32% African American. The average age of freshmen is 19; all undergraduates, 24. 25% do not continue beyond their first year; 35% remain to graduate.

Housing: 2482 students can be accommodated in college housing, which includes single-sex dorms, on-campus apartments, and married-student housing. In addition, there is family housing. On-campus housing is guaranteed for all 4 years. 87% of students commute. Alcohol is not permitted. All students may keep cars.

Activities: 6% of men belong to 13 national fraternities; 6% of women belong to 11 national sororities. There are 181 groups on campus, including art, band, cheerleading, chess, choir, chorale, chorus, computers, dance, drama, ethnic, film, gay, honors, international, jazz band, literary magazine, marching band, musical theater, newspaper, orchestra, pep band, photography, political, professional, radio and TV, religious, social, social service, student government, and yearbook. Popular campus events include Derby Day, Greek Week, and Welcome Back Week.

Sports: There are 9 intercollegiate sports for men and 8 for women, and 15 intramural sports for men and 12 for women. Facilities include a gym, a football stadium, a baseball field, swimming pools, a track, a weight room, and tennis, handball, and racquetball courts.

Disabled Students: 95% of the campus is accessible. Wheelchair ramps, elevators, special parking, specially equipped rest rooms, special class scheduling, lowered drinking fountains, lowered telephones, special housing, and a transportation service are available.

Services: Counseling and information services are available, as is tutoring in most subjects. There is a reader service for the blind, and remedial math, reading, and writing.

Campus Safety and Security: Measures include 24-hour foot and vehicle patrol, security escort services, informal discussions, and emergency telephones. There are lighted pathways/sidewalks.

Programs of Study: U of M confers B.A., B.S., B.B.A., B.F.A., B.L.S., B.M., B.P.S., B.S.C.E., B.S.Cp.E., B.S.Ch., B.S.Ed., B.S.E.E., B.S.E.T., B.S.I.S., B.S.M.E., and B.S.N. degrees. Master's and doctoral degrees are also awarded. Bachelor's degrees are awarded in BIOLOGICAL SCIENCE (biology/biological science and microbiology), BUSINESS (accounting, banking and finance, business administration and management, business economics, hospitality management services, insurance and risk management, international business management, logistics, management information systems, marketing and distribution, marketing management, marketing/retailing/merchandising, organizational behavior, real estate, recreation and leisure services, and retailing), COMMUNICATIONS AND THE ARTS (applied music, art, art history and appreciation, communications, dramatic arts, English, journalism, languages, music, and music business management), COMPUTER AND PHYSICAL SCIENCE (chemistry, computer science, geology, information sciences and systems, mathematics, and physics), EDUCATION (elementary, physical, and special), ENGINEERING AND ENVIRONMENTAL DESIGN (architectural technology, architecture, civil engineering, computer engineering, computer technology, electrical/electronics engineering, electrical/electronics engineering technology, engineering, industrial administration/management, industrial engineering, manufacturing technology, and mechanical engineering), HEALTH PROFESSIONS (exercise science, industrial hygiene, nursing, and rehabilitation therapy), SOCIAL SCIENCE (African American studies, anthropology, consumer services, criminal justice, criminology, economics, geography, history, home economics, human development, interdisciplinary studies, international studies, paralegal studies, parks and recreation management, philosophy, political science/government, psychology, social work, and sociology). Nursing, integrative studies, and psychology are the largest.

Required: To graduate, students must complete a minimum of 132 credit hours with a GPA of 2.0 and demonstrate proficiency in computer skills. Distribution requirements include 8 hours of natural science, 6 hours each of English composition, social science, and U.S. history; 3 to 6 hours of math; 4 hours of phys ed; and 3 hours each of communication, fine arts, literature, history/philosophy, computation, intensive writing, and thematic and integrative courses.

Special: The university offers co-op programs, cross-registration, internships, study abroad in England and Spain, accelerated degree programs, B.A.-B.S. degrees, dual and student-designed majors, nondegree study, and pass/fail options. Students may receive credit for life, military, and work experience. There is a freshman honors program.

Faculty/Classroom: 56% of faculty are male; 44%, female. 70% teach undergraduates. Graduate students teach 23% of introductory courses.

Admissions: 89% of the 2003-2004 applicants were accepted. The SAT I scores for the 2003-2004 freshman class were: Verbal--34% below 500, 40% between 500 and 599, 23% between 600 and 700, and 4% above 700; Math--35% below 500, 39% between 500 and 599, 22% between 600 and 700, and 4% above 700. The ACT scores were 44% below 21, 24% between 21 and 23, 18% between 24 and 26, 9% between 27 and 28, and 5% above 28.

Requirements: The SAT I or ACT is required, with a minimum acceptable composite score of 20 on the ACT. Candidates for admission should be graduates of an accredited secondary school and have 14 academic credits or 20 Carnegie units. The GED is accepted. Academic preparation should include 4 units in English, 3 in math, 2 each in science, social studies, and foreign language, and 1 in visual and performing arts. An audition is required for music majors. A GPA of 2.0 is required. AP and CLEP credits are accepted. Important factors in the admissions decision are advanced placement or honor courses, evidence of special talent, and recommendations by school officials.

Procedure: Freshmen are admitted to all sessions. Entrance exams should be taken in the spring of the junior year or October of the senior year. Applications should be filed by August 1 for fall entry, December 1 for spring entry, and May 1 for summer entry. Notification is sent on a rolling basis.

Transfer: 2205 transfer students enrolled in 2002-2003. For guaranteed admission, applicants should have a GPA of 2.0 and be eligible to return to the last college of regular enrollment. 33 of 132 credits required for the bachelor's degree must be completed at U of M.

Visiting: There are regularly scheduled orientations for prospective students, including Fall Campus Day for high school seniors. There are guides for informal visits and visitors may sit in on classes and stay overnight. To schedule a visit, contact Malinda McDaniel, Student Relations and Orientation Services at (800) 669-2678 or *recruitment@cc.memphis.edu*.

Financial Aid: In 2003-2004, 55% of all full-time freshmen and 62% of continuing full-time students received some form of financial aid. 49% of full-time freshmen and 54% of continuing full-time students received need-based aid. The average freshman award was $3351. Need-based scholarships or need-based grants averaged $1968 ($6392 maximum); need-based self-help aid (loans and jobs) averaged $2521 ($13,641 maximum); and non-need-based awards and non-need-based scholarships averaged $3575 ($13,641 maximum). 13% of undergraduates work part time. Average annual earnings from campus work are $1850. The average financial indebtedness of the 2003 graduate was $20,312. The FAFSA is required. The priority date for freshman financial aid applications for fall entry is March 1. The deadline for filing freshman financial aid applications for fall entry is June 30.

International Students: There are 260 international students enrolled. The school actively recruits these students. They must score 550 on the written TOEFL and also take the SAT I or ACT. The minimum score is tied to the applicant's GPA.

Computers: The mainframe is a DEC VAX 8820. Residence halls have computer sites with mainframe access and both Macs and PCs. There is a PC hookup in all residence hall rooms. Other computer sites include learning labs spread throughout the campus. All students may access the system. There are no time limits and no fees. It is strongly recommended that all students have a personal computer.

Graduates: From July 1, 2002 to June 30, 2003, 1978 bachelor's degrees were awarded. The most popular majors were management information systems (8%), marketing management (6%), and individual studies (5%). In an average class, 11% graduate in 4 years or less, 27% graduate in 5 years or less, and 35% graduate in 6 years or less.

Admissions Contact: William Akey, Director, Student Relations. A video is available. E-mail: *recruitment@memphis.edu* Web: *http://www.memphis.edu/*

UNIVERSITY OF TENNESSEE SYSTEM

The University of Tennessee System, established in 1794, is a land-grand system in Tennessee. It is governed by a board of trustees, whose chief administrator is president. The primary goal of the system is to provide a full range of teaching, research, and service programs at all levels. The main priorities are to provide quality learning and research opportunities for students from Tennessee and throughout the country. The total enrollment of all 4 campuses averages about 40,000; there were about 3100 faculty members. Altogether there are 244 baccalaureate, 136 master's, and 69 doctoral programs offered in University of Tennessee System. Profiles of the 4-year campuses are included in this section.

UNIVERSITY OF TENNESSEE AT CHATTANOOGA D-4
Chattanooga, TN 37403

(423) 755-4662
(800) UTC-6627; Fax: (423) 755-4157

Full-time: 2385 men, 3355 women	**Faculty:** 307; IIA, --$
Part-time: 610 men, 750 women	**Ph.D.s:** 80%
Graduate: 545 men, 835 women	**Student/Faculty:** 19 to 1
Year: semesters, summer session	**Tuition:** $3852 ($11,504)
Application Deadline: see profile	**Room & Board:** $4545
Freshman Class: n/av	
SAT I or ACT: required	**COMPETITIVE**

The University of Tennessee at Chattanooga, founded in 1886, is a public institution. Part of the state's university system, it offers programs in liberal and fine arts, business, engineering, health science, and teacher preparation. Figures in the above capsule and in this profile are approximate. There are 5 undergraduate and 5 graduate schools. In addition to regional accreditation, UTC has baccalaureate program accreditation with AACSB, ABET, ACEJMC, AHEA, APTA, CSWE, NASAD, NASM, NCATE, and NLN. The library contains 486,978 volumes, 1,338,193 microform items, and 16,451 audio/video tapes/CDs, and subscribes to 2768 periodicals. Computerized library services include the card catalog, interlibrary loans, and database searching. Special learning facilities include a learning resource center, art gallery, radio station, and an observatory. The 116-acre campus is in an urban area 105 miles north of Atlanta. Including any residence halls, there are 76 buildings.

Student Life: 92% of undergraduates are from Tennessee. Students are from 41 states, 49 foreign countries, and Canada. 79% are white; 16% African American. The average age of freshmen is 20; all undergraduates, 24. 26% do not continue beyond their first year; 44% remain to graduate.

Housing: 1830 students can be accommodated in college housing, which includes single-sex and coed dorms, on-campus apartments, off-campus apartments, married-student housing, and fraternity houses. On-campus housing is available on a first-come, first-served basis. 74% of students commute. Alcohol is not permitted. All students may keep cars.

Activities: 8% of men belong to 8 national fraternities; 7% of women belong to 7 national sororities. There are 130 groups on campus, including band, cheerleading, chess, choir, chorale, chorus, computers, dance, drama, drill team, ethnic, gay, honors, international, jazz band, literary magazine, marching band, musical theater, newspaper, orchestra, pep band, photography, political, professional, radio and TV, religious, social, social service, student government, symphony, and yearbook. Popular campus events include Homecoming.

Sports: There are 6 intercollegiate sports for men and 6 for women, and 12 intramural sports for men and 7 for women. Facilities include a gym, an arena, a tennis and racquet center, a swimming pool, and 2 fields, including a soccer field.

Disabled Students: 98% of the campus is accessible. Wheelchair ramps, elevators, special parking, specially equipped rest rooms, special class scheduling, lowered drinking fountains, and lowered telephones are available.

Services: Counseling and information services are available, as is tutoring in most subjects. There is a reader service for the blind and remedial math, reading, and writing.

Campus Safety and Security: Measures include 24-hour foot and vehicle patrol, security escort services, shuttle buses, and informal discussions. There are pamphlets/posters/films, emergency telephones, and lighted pathways/sidewalks.

Programs of Study: UTC confers B.A., B.S., B.F.A., B.M., B.S.E., B.S.N., B.S.O.T., and B.S.W. degrees. Master's degrees are also awarded. Bachelor's degrees are awarded in BIOLOGICAL SCIENCE (biology/biological science), BUSINESS (business administration and management and recreation and leisure services), COMMUNICATIONS AND THE ARTS (communications, dramatic arts, English, fine arts, French, Greek, Latin, music, and Spanish), COMPUTER AND PHYSICAL SCIENCE (applied mathematics, chemistry, computer science, geology, mathematics, and physics), EDUCATION (art, education, music, secondary, and special), ENGINEERING AND ENVIRONMENTAL DESIGN (engineering, engineering management, and environmental science), HEALTH PROFESSIONS (medical laboratory technology, nursing, occupational therapy, and rehabilitation therapy), SOCIAL SCIENCE (criminal justice, economics, history, home economics, human services, humanities, paralegal studies, philosophy, political science/government, psychology, social work, sociology, and women's studies). Business and nursing are the strongest academically. Business is the largest.

Required: All students must complete at least 128 semester hours and maintain a minimum GPA of 2.0. General education requirements include 9 hours in humanities and fine arts, 6 hours in written communication/English and behavioral/social sciences, 4 hours in physical and natural sciences, and 3 hours each in math and perspectives. A health and phys ed course is required in the first year, and another phys ed activity course must be taken before graduation. Requirements vary by major.

Special: Cooperative programs are offered in accounting, business systems, chemistry, communications, engineering, environmental studies, nursing, and psychology. UTC offers internships, study abroad in England, work-study and accelerated degree programs, B.A.-B.S. degrees, dual majors, interdisciplinary majors, including theater and speech, 3-2 engineering degrees, and nondegree study. Credit is given for life, military, or work experience. There are 30 national honor societies, a freshman honors program, and 25 departmental honors programs.

Faculty/Classroom: 65% of faculty are male; 35%, female. No introductory courses are taught by graduate students. The average class size in an introductory lecture is 25.

Requirements: The SAT I or ACT is required. In addition, secondary school credits should include 4 in English, 3 in math, and 2 each in science, social studies, and a foreign language. The GED is accepted. A GPA of 2.0 is required. AP and CLEP credits are accepted. Important factors in the admissions decision are recommendations by school officials, advanced placement or honor courses, and evidence of special talent.

Procedure: Freshmen are admitted to all sessions. Entrance exams should be taken in spring of the junior year. There is a deferred admissions plan. There is a rolling admisions plan. Check with the school for current deadlines. The application fee is $25. Notification is sent on a rolling basis. Applications are accepted on-line through the school's web site.

Transfer: 631 transfer students enrolled in a recent year. A minimum GPA of 2.0 is required. 30 of 128 credits required for the bachelor's degree must be completed at UTC.

Visiting: There are regularly scheduled orientations for prospective students. There are guides for informal visits and visitors may sit in on classes and stay overnight. To schedule a visit, contact the Admissions Office.

Financial Aid: In a recent year, 70% of all full-time freshmen and 65% of continuing full-time students received some form of financial aid. 48% of full-time freshmen and 56% of continuing full-time students received need-based aid. The average freshman award was $3305. 78% of undergraduates work part time. Average annual earnings from campus work are $1900. The FAFSA is required. Check with the school for current deadlines.

International Students: There were 79 international students enrolled in a recent year. The school actively recruits these students. They must score 500 on the written TOEFL.

Computers: There are no time limits and no fees.

Graduates: In a recent year, 1377 bachelor's degrees were awarded. The most popular majors were business administration (23%), education (15%), and psychology (9%). In an average class, 18% graduate in 4 years or less, 37% graduate in 5 years or less, and 44% graduate in 6 years or less. 100 companies recruited on campus in a recent year.

Admissions Contact: Yancy Freeman, Director of Admissions & Recruitment. E-mail: *yancy-freeman@utc.edu* Web: *www.utc.edu*

UNIVERSITY OF TENNESSEE AT KNOXVILLE   E-2
Knoxville, TN 37996-0230
(423) 974-2184
(800) 221-VOLS; Fax: (423) 974-6341

Full-time: 8805 men, 9330 women	Faculty: 1253
Part-time: 930 men, 1060 women	Ph.D.s: 86%
Graduate: 2505 men, 3400 women	Student/Faculty: 14 to 1
Year: semesters, summer session	Tuition: $4450 ($13,352)
Application Deadline: see profile	Room & Board: $4430
Freshman Class: n/av	
SAT I or ACT: required	COMPETITIVE

The University of Tennessee, Knoxville, founded in 1794 and the original campus of the state university system, is now a large public institution offering more than 300 graduate and undergraduate programs. Figures in the above capsule and in this profile are approximate. There are 11 undergraduate and 14 graduate schools. In addition to regional accreditation, UT Knoxville has baccalaureate program accreditation with AACSB, ABET, ACEJMC, ADA, AHEA, ASLA, CSWE, FIDER, NAAB, NASAD, NASM, NCATE, NLN, NRPA, and SAF. The 4 libraries contain 2,492,953 volumes, 3,502,541 microform items, and 173,506 audio/video tapes/CDs, and subscribe to 16,656 periodicals. Computerized library services include the card catalog, interlibrary loans, and database searching. Special learning facilities include a learning resource center,

art gallery, natural history museum, radio station, and a science and engineering research facility. The 533-acre campus is in an urban area adjacent to downtown Knoxville. Including any residence halls, there are 220 buildings.

Student Life: 81% of undergraduates are from Tennessee. Students are from 50 states, 100 foreign countries, and Canada. 89% are white. The average age of freshmen is 18; all undergraduates, 22. 21% do not continue beyond their first year; 57% remain to graduate.

Housing: 7449 students can be accommodated in college housing, which includes single-sex and coed dorms, on-campus apartments, off-campus apartments, married-student housing, and fraternity houses. In addition, there are language houses and special-interest houses. On-campus housing is available on a first-come, first-served basis. 62% of students commute. Alcohol is not permitted. All students may keep cars.

Activities: 8% of men belong to 26 national fraternities; 8% of women belong to 17 national sororities. There are 300 groups on campus, including art, band, cheerleading, chess, choir, chorale, chorus, computers, dance, drama, ethnic, film, gay, honors, international, jazz band, literary magazine, marching band, musical theater, newspaper, opera, orchestra, pep band, photography, political, professional, radio and TV, religious, social, social service, student government, symphony, and yearbook. Popular campus events include All-Sing, Torch Night, and International Festival.

Sports: There are 8 intercollegiate sports for men and 10 for women, and 22 intramural sports for men and 22 for women. Facilities include a 25,000-seat basketball arena, the second largest collegiate football stadium in the U.S., an Olympic track, Olympic indoor and outdoor pools, various outdoor facilities, a baseball stadium, and softball and soccer fields.

Disabled Students: 95% of the campus is accessible. Wheelchair ramps, elevators, special parking, specially equipped rest rooms, special class scheduling, lowered drinking fountains, lowered telephones, and an escort service are available.

Services: There is a reader service for the blind. Tutoring in math, English, and most lower-division courses can be arranged.

Campus Safety and Security: Measures include 24-hour foot and vehicle patrol, self-defense education, security escort services, and shuttle buses. There are informal discussions, pamphlets/posters/films, emergency telephones, lighted pathways/sidewalks, and campus safety educational programs.

Programs of Study: UT Knoxville confers B.A., B.S., B.Arch., B.F.A., B.M., and specialized B.S. degrees in 25 fields, including business administration, nursing, and social work. degrees. Master's and doctoral degrees are also awarded. Bachelor's degrees are awarded in AGRICULTURE (agricultural economics, agriculture, animal science, fishing and fisheries, forestry and related sciences, plant science, and soil science), BIOLOGICAL SCIENCE (biochemistry, biology/biological science, botany, microbiology, and nutrition), BUSINESS (accounting, banking and finance, business administration and management, business economics, hotel/motel and restaurant management, management science, marketing/retailing/merchandising, retailing, sports management, tourism, and transportation management), COMMUNICATIONS AND THE ARTS (advertising, art history and appreciation, broadcasting, classics, comparative literature, dramatic arts, English, film arts, fine arts, French, German, graphic design, Italian, journalism, languages, linguistics, music, Russian, Spanish, speech/debate/rhetoric, and studio art), COMPUTER AND PHYSICAL SCIENCE (chemistry, computer science, geology, mathematics, physics, and statistics), EDUCATION (agricultural, art, elementary, health, marketing and distribution, music, physical, recreation, and special), ENGINEERING AND ENVIRONMENTAL DESIGN (aerospace studies, agricultural engineering, architecture, chemical engineering, civil engineering, electrical/electronics engineering, engineering, engineering and applied science, engineering physics, environmental science, food services technology, industrial engineering, interior design, landscape architecture/design, materials engineering, materials science, mechanical engineering, and nuclear engineering), HEALTH PROFESSIONS (community health work, health science, nursing, predentistry, premedicine, preveterinary science, and speech pathology/audiology), SOCIAL SCIENCE (African American studies, anthropology, Asian/Oriental studies, child care/child and family studies, classical/ancient civilization, economics, food science, geography, history, human services, Latin American studies, medieval studies, philosophy, political science/government, psychology, public administration, religion, Russian and Slavic studies, social work, sociology, textiles and clothing, urban studies, and women's studies). Engineering, physical sciences, and English are the strongest academically. Business administration is the largest.

Required: All students must complete at least 120 credits with a minimum 2.0 GPA. Many degree programs require higher credit totals and GPAs. All students take 2 English composition courses and a core curriculum including 2 courses each in math sciences, humanities and the arts, history, social sciences, natural sciences, and foreign language or integrative studies.

Special: Cooperative programs are offered in engineering, communications, liberal arts, and business. Cross-registration is possible through the Academic Common Market, a Southern 14-state consortium, in any of

11 programs. Internships are available in social work, education, and architecture, and there are a number of work-study programs. Study abroad in more than 25 countries is possible. Dual and student-designed majors, accelerated study, nondegree study, and pass/fail options are offered. There are 51 national honor societies, including Phi Beta Kappa, a freshman honors program, and 13 departmental honors programs.

Faculty/Classroom: 75% of faculty are male; 25%, female. 6% do research and 94% both teach and do research. The average class size in an introductory lecture is 26; in a laboratory, 14; and in a regular course, 29.

Requirements: The SAT I or ACT is required; the ACT is preferred. Applicants should be high school graduates or have the GED. Required secondary school courses include 4 credits in English, 3 in math, 2 each in science and a single foreign language, 1 each in history and world history or world geography, and 1 unit of visual/performing arts. A GPA of 2.0 is required. AP and CLEP credits are accepted. Important factors in the admissions decision are advanced placement or honor courses, leadership record, and parents or siblings attending the school.

Procedure: Freshmen are admitted to all sessions. Entrance exams should be taken in spring of the junior year or fall of the senior year. There are early admissions and deferred admissions plans. There is a rolling admissions plan. Check with the school for current deadlines and fee. The fall 2003 application fee was $25. Notification is sent on a rolling basis.

Transfer: Transfer applicants should present a minimum 2.0 GPA in previous college work, although many specific programs have higher requirements. 30 of 120 credits required for the bachelor's degree must be completed at UT Knoxville.

Visiting: There are regularly scheduled orientations for prospective students, including 2 open houses yearly where prospective students can meet with faculty, administrators, and students to discuss admissions, housing, financial aid, student activities, academic colleges and departments, and organizations. There are guides for informal visits and visitors may sit in on classes. To schedule a visit, contact Undergraduate Admissions at (865) 974-2184.

Financial Aid: UT Knoxville is a member of CSS. The CSS Profile or FFS and Academic College Scholarship Application are required. Check with the school for current deadlines.

International Students: They must score 525 on the written TOEFL.

Computers: The mainframe is an IBM 9672-R42. There are also Macs, PCs, and Sun workstations available throughout the campus. Students can access the library mainframe from apartment or dorm rooms via modem. All students may access the system. There are no time limits and no fees.

Admissions Contact: Marshall Rose, Director of Admissions.
E-mail: *admissions@utk.edu* Web: *www.utk.edu*

UNIVERSITY OF TENNESSEE AT MARTIN   B-2
Martin, TN 38238
(731) 587-7020
(800) 829-8861; Fax: (731) 587-7029

Full-time: 1978 men, 2541 women	**Faculty:** 250; IIA, --$
Part-time: 301 men, 555 women	**Ph.D.s:** 70%
Graduate: 133 men, 272 women	**Student/Faculty:** 18 to 1
Year: semesters, summer session	**Tuition:** $3848 ($11,498)
Application Deadline: open	**Room & Board:** $3900
Freshman Class: 2536 applied, 1138 accepted, 1000 enrolled	
ACT: 21	**COMPETITIVE**

The University of Tennessee at Martin, founded in 1900, is a public university offering undergraduate programs in natural and social sciences, humanities, fine and performing arts, computer science, nursing, agriculture, teacher education, business administration, and engineering. Graduate degrees are offered in accounting and business administration, counseling and teacher education, and human environmental sciences. There are 5 undergraduate and 3 graduate schools. In addition to regional accreditation, UT Martin has baccalaureate program accreditation with ABET, ADA, CSWE, NASM, NCATE, and NLN. The library contains 423,333 volumes, 610,766 microform items, and 10,692 audio/video tapes/CDs, and subscribes to 1647 periodicals. Computerized library services include the card catalog, interlibrary loans, and database searching. Special learning facilities include a learning resource center, natural history museum, radio station, TV station, a teacher resource center, a 680-acre Agricultural Experiment Station, a teaching/research facility at Reelfoot Lake State Resort, and a Center for Environmental and Conservation Education. The 250-acre campus is in a rural area 125 miles northeast of Memphis and 150 miles northwest of Nashville. Including any residence halls, there are 46 buildings.

Student Life: 93% of undergraduates are from Tennessee. Students are from 21 states, 28 foreign countries, and Canada. 90% are from public schools. 81% are white; 15% African American. 76% are Protestant; 20% claim no religious affiliation. The average age of freshmen is 19; all undergraduates, 23. 30% do not continue beyond their first year; 40% remain to graduate.

Housing: 1800 students can be accommodated in college housing, which includes single-sex and coed dorms, on-campus apartments, and married-student housing. In addition, there are special-interest houses. On-campus housing is available on a first-come, first-served basis. 60% of students commute. Alcohol is not permitted. All students may keep cars.

Activities: 9% of men belong to 9 national fraternities; 9% of women belong to 8 national sororities. There are 121 groups on campus, including art, band, cheerleading, choir, chorale, chorus, computers, dance, drama, ethnic, film, honors, international, jazz band, literary magazine, marching band, musical theater, newspaper, opera, pep band, photography, political, professional, radio and TV, religious, social, social service, student government, and yearbook. Popular campus events include Greekfest, UTM Rodeo-N-Roundup Days, and All-Niter.

Sports: There are 9 intercollegiate sports for men and 9 for women, and 18 intramural sports for men and 18 for women. Facilities include a phys ed and convocation center, an agricultural pavilion, a football stadium, a fitness trail, an Olympic-size swimming pool, intramural playing fields, baseball and softball fields, a track, tennis courts, and a climbing wall.

Disabled Students: All of the campus is accessible. Wheelchair ramps, elevators, special parking, specially equipped rest rooms, special class scheduling, lowered drinking fountains, and lowered telephones are available.

Services: Counseling and information services are available, as is tutoring in every subject. There is a reader service for the blind, and remedial math, reading, and writing.

Campus Safety and Security: Measures include 24-hour foot and vehicle patrol, self-defense education, security escort services, and informal discussions. There are pamphlets/posters/films, emergency telephones, lighted pathways/sidewalks, a bicycle patrol, and security cameras in the 4 largest residence halls.

Programs of Study: UT Martin confers B.A., B.S., B.A.Mus., B.F.A., B.M.M., B.S.Ag., B.S.B.A., B.S.Chem., B.S.C.J., B.S.Ed., B.S.Eng., B.S.H.E., B.S.H.H.P., B.S.Mus., B.S.N., B.S.Natural Resources Mgt., and B.S.S.W. degrees. Master's degrees are also awarded. Bachelor's degrees are awarded in AGRICULTURE (agricultural business management, agriculture, animal science, natural resource management, and plant science), BIOLOGICAL SCIENCE (biology/biological science and wildlife biology), BUSINESS (accounting, business administration and management, business economics, management science, and marketing/retailing/merchandising), COMMUNICATIONS AND THE ARTS (communications, English, fine arts, French, music, and Spanish), COMPUTER AND PHYSICAL SCIENCE (chemistry, computer science, geology, and mathematics), EDUCATION (early childhood, elementary, and secondary), ENGINEERING AND ENVIRONMENTAL DESIGN (engineering), HEALTH PROFESSIONS (nursing, predentistry, premedicine, preoptometry, and prepharmacy), SOCIAL SCIENCE (child care/child and family studies, criminal justice, economics, geography, history, international studies, parks and recreation management, philosophy, political science/government, prelaw, psychology, public administration, social work, and sociology). Engineering, education, and health sciences are the strongest academically. Business, education, and biology are the largest.

Required: The number of credit hours required for graduation ranges from 127 to 130 (based on degree). All students must have at least a 2.0 GPA. Specific courses and major requirements vary by the program selected. There is a 1-year or 30-hour UTM residency requirement.

Special: UTM offers co-op programs in engineering, agriculture, computer science, business, and chemistry, for-credit internships, cross-registration through the Gulf Coast consortium, study abroad, B.A.-B.S. degrees, dual and student-designed majors, and pass/fail options. There are 7 national honor societies, a freshman honors program, and 5 departmental honors programs.

Faculty/Classroom: 63% of faculty are male; 37%, female. All teach undergraduates, and 81% both teach and do research. No introductory courses are taught by graduate students. The average class size in an introductory lecture is 30; in a laboratory, 19; and in a regular course, 19.

Admissions: 45% of the 2003-2004 applicants were accepted. The ACT scores for the 2003-2004 freshman class were: 40% below 21, 29% between 21 and 23, 19% between 24 and 26, 7% between 27 and 28, and 5% above 28.

Requirements: The SAT I or ACT is required. Students should have a minimum composite score of 19 on the ACT with a 2.25 minimum GPA, or 16 on the ACT with a minimum 2.6 GPA. Candidates for admission should be graduates of an accredited secondary school with 14 academic credits. The GED is accepted with a score of 50. Secondary school units should include 4 of English, 3 of math, 2 of a foreign language, and 1 each of science, history, social studies, and fine and performing arts. A GPA of 2.4 is required. AP and CLEP credits are accepted.

Procedure: Freshmen are admitted to all sessions. Entrance exams should be taken in the fall of the senior year. There is a deferred admissions plan and a rolling admissions plan. Application deadlines are open. The fall 2003 application fee was $25. Notification is sent on a rolling basis. Applications are accepted on-line.

Transfer: 365 transfer students enrolled in 2002-2003. Transfer students should have a minimum GPA of 2.0. 30 credits of 127-130 required for the bachelor's degree must be completed at UT Martin.

Visiting: There are regularly scheduled orientations for prospective students, including student-parent seminars during the summer for information sharing. There are guides for informal visits and visitors may sit in on classes and stay overnight. To schedule a visit, contact the Admissions Office at *admitme@utm.edu*.

Financial Aid: In a recent year, 85% of all full-time freshmen and 80% of continuing full-time students received some form of financial aid. 96% of full-time freshmen and 95% of continuing full-time students received need-based aid. The average freshman award was $6754. Need-based scholarships or need-based grants averaged $3982; need-based self-help aid (loans and jobs) averaged $4156; and non-need-based athletic scholarships averaged $7783. The average financial indebtedness of a recent graduate was $10,500. UT Martin is a member of CSS. The FAFSA is required. The deadline for filing freshman financial aid applications for fall entry is March 1.

International Students: There are 157 international students enrolled. The school actively recruits these students. They must score 500 on the written TOEFL and also take a writing proficiency exam.

Computers: There are 600 computers available for student use throughout campus. All students may access the system 24 hours a day. There are no time limits. The fee is $100. It is strongly recommended that all students have a personal computer.

Graduates: From July 1, 2002 to June 30, 2003, 1001 bachelor's degrees were awarded. The most popular majors were business/marketing (21%), interdisciplinary (13%), and agriculture (8%). In an average class, 2% graduate in 3 years or less, 17% graduate in 4 years or less, 34% graduate in 5 years or less, and 40% graduate in 6 years or less.

Admissions Contact: Judy Rayburn, Director of Admissions. A video is available. E-mail: *jrayburn@utm.edu* Web: *www.utm.edu*

UNIVERSITY OF THE SOUTH
D-4

Sewanee, TN 37383-1000   **(931) 598-1238**
(800) 522-2234; Fax: (931) 538-3248

Full-time: 623 men, 723 women	Faculty: 124; IIB, +$
Part-time: 9 men, 9 women	Ph.D.s: 97%
Graduate: 70 men, 41 women	Student/Faculty: 11 to 1
Year: semesters, summer session	Tuition: $24,135
Application Deadline: February 1	Room & Board: $6720
Freshman Class: 1828 applied, 1303 accepted, 427 enrolled	
SAT I or ACT: required	**HIGHLY COMPETITIVE**

The University of the South, founded in 1857, is an independent liberal arts institution affiliated with the Episcopal Church. The library contains 648,459 volumes, 328,090 microform items, and 72,964 audio/video tapes/CDs, and subscribes to 3444 periodicals. Computerized library services include the card catalog, interlibrary loans, database searching, and Internet access. Special learning facilities include a learning resource center, art gallery, radio station, an observatory, a materials analysis lab with an electron scanning microscope, and a rare books collection. The 10,000-acre campus is in a small town 45 miles west of Chattanooga. Including any residence halls, there are 43 buildings.

Student Life: 80% of undergraduates are from out of state, mostly the South. Students are from 44 states and 23 foreign countries. 55% are from public schools. 92% are white. 60% are Protestant; 21% claim no religious affiliation; 9% Catholic. The average age of freshmen is 18; all undergraduates, 20. 16% do not continue beyond their first year; 79% remain to graduate.

Housing: 1275 students can be accommodated in college housing, which includes single-sex and coed dorms, on-campus apartments, and married-student housing. In addition, there are language houses and substance-free housing. On-campus housing is guaranteed for all 4 years. 92% of students live on campus; of those, 90% remain on campus on weekends. All students may keep cars.

Activities: 46% of men belong to 11 national fraternities; 39% of women belong to 6 local sororities. There are 110 groups on campus, including art, cheerleading, choir, chorale, chorus, computers, dance, drama, ethnic, film, gay, honors, international, jazz band, literary magazine, musical theater, newspaper, orchestra, photography, political, professional, radio and TV, religious, social, social service, student government, symphony, and yearbook. Popular campus events include Spring Festival Weekend.

Sports: There are 10 intercollegiate sports for men and 11 for women, and 15 intramural sports for men and 16 for women. Facilities include a sport and fitness center with multipurpose volleyball and basketball courts, an indoor pool with diving well, an indoor track, a batting cage, racquetball and squash courts, indoor tennis courts, and dance and fitness studios; a golf course; outdoor tennis courts; a multiweather track; an equestrian center and stables; 15 playing fields, a lake; and areas for rappelling, caving, hiking, and rock climbing.

Disabled Students: 75% of the campus is accessible. Wheelchair ramps, elevators, special parking, specially equipped rest rooms, special

class scheduling, lowered drinking fountains, special administrative services, and a telecommunications device for the deaf are available.

Services: Counseling and information services are available, as is tutoring in most subjects. Study skills training is also offered.

Campus Safety and Security: Measures include 24-hour foot and vehicle patrol, self-defense education, security escort services, and shuttle buses. There are informal discussions, pamphlets/posters/films, emergency telephones, and lighted pathways/sidewalks.

Programs of Study: Sewanee confers B.A. and B.S. degrees. Master's and doctoral degrees are also awarded. Bachelor's degrees are awarded in AGRICULTURE (environmental studies, forestry and related sciences, and natural resource management), BIOLOGICAL SCIENCE (biology/biological science), COMMUNICATIONS AND THE ARTS (art, art history and appreciation, dramatic arts, English, French, German, Greek, Latin, music, Russian, and Spanish), COMPUTER AND PHYSICAL SCIENCE (chemistry, computer science, geology, mathematics, and physics), SOCIAL SCIENCE (American studies, anthropology, Asian/Oriental studies, economics, French studies, German area studies, history, medieval studies, philosophy, political science/government, psychology, religion, Russian and Slavic studies, social science, and Third World studies). English and premedicine are the strongest academically. English, economics, and history are the largest.

Required: To graduate, students must complete at least 32 full courses (130 semester hours), 21 of which must be outside the major, with a minimum GPA of 2.0. The core curriculum includes 4 courses in language and literature, 3 in math and natural science, 2 each in social science and phys ed, and 1 each in the arts and in religion or philosophy. Comprehensive exams in the major field of study are required.

Special: Sewanee offers internships in economics and public affairs, study abroad in 13 countries, a Washington semester, and student-designed majors. Teacher certification and Peace Corps, medical, law, and veterinary preparation are available. A 3-2 engineering degree is offered with Columbia, Washington, and Vanderbilt Universities, Georgia Institute of Technology, and Rensselaer Polytechnic Institute. Pass/fail options are possible. There are 10 national honor societies, including Phi Beta Kappa, a freshman honors program, and 28 departmental honors programs.

Faculty/Classroom: 65% of faculty are male; 35%, female. All teach undergraduates. No introductory courses are taught by graduate students. The average class size in an introductory lecture is 20; in a laboratory, 16; and in a regular course, 12.

Admissions: 71% of the 2003-2004 applicants were accepted. The SAT I scores for the 2003-2004 freshman class were: Verbal--5% below 500, 40% between 500 and 599, 40% between 600 and 700, and 15% above 700; Math--7% below 500, 38% between 500 and 599, 47% between 600 and 700, and 8% above 700. The ACT scores were 1% below 21, 22% between 21 and 23, 20% between 24 and 26, 43% between 27 and 28, and 14% above 28. 73% of the current freshmen were in the top fifth of their class; 95% were in the top two fifths.

Requirements: The SAT I or ACT is required. In addition, candidates for admission should have 15 secondary school academic credits, including 4 years of English, 3 of math, and 2 each of lab science, a foreign language, and history or social science. An essay and recommendation are required and an interview is recommended. AP credits are accepted. Important factors in the admissions decision are advanced placement or honor courses, leadership record, and evidence of special talent.

Procedure: Freshmen are admitted in the fall. Entrance exams should be taken by December of the senior year. There are early decision, early admissions, and deferred admissions plans. Early decision applications should be filed by November 15; regular applications, by February 1 for fall entry. Notification of early decision is sent December 15; regular decision, April 1. A waiting list is an active part of the admissions procedure. Applications are accepted on computer disk and on-line through the university's web site, Common App, and Embark.

Transfer: 15 transfer students enrolled in 2002-2003. Applicants should have a minimum GPA of 3.0 and take the SAT I or ACT. They must submit official transcripts from all previous colleges attended and 2 letters of recommendation from college instructors, and they must be eligible to continue in their present school. An interview is recommended. 64 of 130 credits required for the bachelor's degree must be completed at Sewanee.

Visiting: There are regularly scheduled orientations for prospective students, including a tour, an interview, class visits, and a meeting with a counselor. There are guides for informal visits and visitors may sit in on classes and stay overnight. To schedule a visit, contact the Office of Admission at (800) 522-2234 or *admiss@sewanee.edu*.

Financial Aid: 42% of full-time freshmen and 39% of continuing full-time students received need-based aid. The average freshman award was $18,179. Need-based scholarships or need-based grants averaged $16,628; need-based self-help aid (loans and jobs) averaged $4573; other non-need-based awards and non-need-based scholarships averaged $8849. 33% of undergraduates work part time. Average annual earnings from campus work are $1000. The average financial indebtedness of the 2003 graduate was $12,134. The FAFSA and the college's own financial statement are required. The deadline for filing freshman financial aid applications for fall entry is March 1.

International Students: There are 31 international students enrolled. The school actively recruits these students. They must score 550 on the written TOEFL or 220 on the electronic version.

Computers: Sewanee offers PC and Mac work stations at several computer labs across the campus. All students may access the system 24 hours a day. There are no time limits and no fees.

Graduates: From July 1, 2002 to June 30, 2003, 309 bachelor's degrees were awarded. The most popular majors were social sciences and history (29%), English (13%), and foreign languages and literature (10%). In an average class, 1% graduate in 3 years or less, 78% graduate in 4 years or less, 79% graduate in 5 years or less, and 80% graduate in 6 years or less. 30 companies recruited on campus in 2002-2003. Of the 2002 graduating class, 35% were enrolled in graduate school within 6 months of graduation and 95% were employed.

Admissions Contact: David Lessene, Dean of Admission. A video is available. E-mail: *collegeadmission@sewanee.edu*
Web: *www.sewanee.edu*

VANDERBILT UNIVERSITY
Nashville, TN 37203-1700

C-2

(615) 322-2561
(800) 288-0432; Fax: (615) 343-7765

Full-time: 2986 men, 3245 women	**Faculty:** 725; I, +$
Part-time: 33 men, 19 women	**Ph.D.s:** 97%
Graduate: 2311 men, 2498 women	**Student/Faculty:** 9 to 1
Year: semesters, summer session	**Tuition:** $28,440
Application Deadline: January 7	**Room & Board:** $9457
Freshman Class: 10,966 applied, 4413 accepted, 1546 enrolled	
SAT I or ACT: required	**MOST COMPETITIVE**

Vanderbilt University, founded in 1873, is a private university offering programs in liberal and fine arts, business, engineering, health science, military science, religion, law, music, and teacher preparation. There are 4 undergraduate and 6 graduate schools. In addition to regional accreditation, Vanderbilt has baccalaureate program accreditation with AACSB, ABET, CAHEA, and NCATE. The 9 libraries contain 2,882,057 volumes, 2,968,668 microform items, and 63,403 audio/video tapes/CDs, and subscribe to 29,173 periodicals. Computerized library services include the card catalog, interlibrary loans, and database searching. Special learning facilities include a learning resource center, art gallery, radio station, TV station, 2 observatories, and a TV news archive. The 330-acre campus is in an urban area less than a mile and a half from downtown Nashville. Including any residence halls, there are 209 buildings.

Student Life: 86% of undergraduates are from out of state, mostly the South. Students are from 50 states, 52 foreign countries, and Canada. 55% are from public schools. 74% are white. The average age of freshmen is 18; all undergraduates, 20. 6% do not continue beyond their first year; 83% remain to graduate.

Housing: 4942 students can be accommodated in college housing, which includes single-sex and coed dorms, on-campus apartments, and married-student housing. In addition, there are language houses and special-interest houses. On-campus housing is guaranteed for the freshman year only, is available on a first-come, first-served basis, and is available on a lottery system for upperclassmen. Priority is given to out-of-town students. 83% of students live on campus. Alcohol is not permitted. Upperclassmen may keep cars.

Activities: 34% of men belong to 18 national fraternities; 50% of women belong to 12 national sororities. There are 375 groups on campus, including art, band, cheerleading, chess, choir, chorale, chorus, computers, dance, drama, drill team, ethnic, film, gay, honors, international, jazz band, literary magazine, marching band, musical theater, newspaper, opera, orchestra, pep band, photography, political, professional, radio and TV, religious, social, social service, student government, symphony, video production, and yearbook. Popular campus events include Rites of Spring, Blue Fest, and IMPACT Speakers Series.

Sports: There are 7 intercollegiate sports for men and 8 for women, and 45 intramural sports for men and 44 for women. Facilities include a gym, a pool, football and intramural fields, student recreation and tennis centers, basketball and racquetball courts, a suspended indoor track, and a climbing wall.

Disabled Students: 90% of the campus is accessible. Wheelchair ramps, elevators, special parking, specially equipped rest rooms, special class scheduling, lowered drinking fountains, and lowered telephones are available.

Services: Counseling and information services are available, as is tutoring in most subjects. There is a reader service for the blind.

Campus Safety and Security: Measures include 24-hour foot and vehicle patrol, self-defense education, security escort services, and shuttle buses. There are informal discussions, pamphlets/posters/films, emergency telephones, lighted pathways/sidewalks, a bicycle patrol, and student dorm monitors.

Programs of Study: Master's and doctoral degrees are also awarded. Bachelor's degrees are awarded in BIOLOGICAL SCIENCE (biology/

biological science and molecular biology), COMMUNICATIONS AND THE ARTS (classical languages, classics, communications, English, fine arts, French, German, music history and appreciation, music performance, music theory and composition, Russian, Spanish, and theater design), COMPUTER AND PHYSICAL SCIENCE (chemistry, geology, mathematics, and physics), EDUCATION (early childhood, education, elementary, secondary, and special), ENGINEERING AND ENVIRONMENTAL DESIGN (bioengineering, chemical engineering, civil engineering, computer engineering, electrical/electronics engineering, engineering and applied science, and mechanical engineering), SOCIAL SCIENCE (African American studies, American studies, anthropology, child psychology/development, cognitive science, East Asian studies, economics, European studies, history, human development, interdisciplinary studies, Latin American studies, philosophy, political science/government, psychology, public affairs, religion, sociology, and urban studies). Social science, engineering, and education are the largest.

Required: All students must take at least 120 total credit hours. General requirements vary, as do specific major requirements, depending on the chosen program. A minimum GPA of 2.0 is usually needed. There is a mandatory writing requirement. Students majoring in human development must complete an internship in the fall semester of the senior year.

Special: Vanderbilt offers cross-registration with Fisk and Howard Universities and Meharry Medical College, study abroad in 18 countries, a Washington semester, a work-study program, B.A.-B.S. degrees, dual and student-designed majors, nondegree study, and pass/fail options. Internships, required for human development majors, are available in human service agencies, city and state government, and businesses. A 3-2 engineering degree is offered with Fisk University. The school belongs to NASA's Tennessee Space Grant Consortium and the Intercollegiate Center for Classical Studies in Rome. There are 19 national honor societies, including Phi Beta Kappa, a freshman honors program, and 21 departmental honors programs.

Faculty/Classroom: 90% teach undergraduates and 90% do research. Graduate students teach 10% of introductory courses. The average class size in an introductory lecture is 20; in a laboratory, 31; and in a regular course, 19.

Admissions: 40% of the 2003-2004 applicants were accepted. The SAT I scores for the 2003-2004 freshman class were: Verbal--2% below 500, 14% between 500 and 599, 53% between 600 and 700, and 31% above 700; Math--1% below 500, 10% between 500 and 599, 50% between 600 and 700, and 39% above 700. The ACT scores were 5% between 18 and 23, 39% between 24 and 29, and 56% above 30. 94% of the current freshmen were in the top quarter of their class; 100% were in the top half. There were 132 National Merit finalists. 177 freshmen graduated first in their class.

Requirements: The SAT I or ACT is required. In addition, SAT II: Subject tests are recommended in math level I, II, or IIc, writing, and foreign language. Admission requirements vary by school. Candidates should be graduates of an accredited secondary school with a minimum of 15 academic credits. Most programs require 4 years of English, 3 of math, and 2 of a foreign language and recommend 2 of history and 1 of social studies. An essay is required. An audition is required for Blair School of Music. AP credits are accepted. Important factors in the admissions decision are advanced placement or honor courses and evidence of special talent.

Procedure: Freshmen are admitted in the fall. Entrance exams should be taken in the spring of the junior year or the fall of the senior year. There are early decision, early admissions, and deferred admissions plans. Early decision applications should be filed by November 1; regular applications, by January 7 for fall entry. The fall 2003 application fee was $50. Notification of early decision is sent December 15; regular decision, April 1. 446 early decision candidates were accepted for the 2003-2004 class. 1130 applicants were on the 2003 waiting list; 32 were admitted. Applications are accepted on computer disk provided a printout is included and on-line through the university's web site.

Transfer: 71 transfer students enrolled in a recent year. Transfers must take the SAT I or the ACT. A minimum of 12 hours of college credit must have been earned. Students must meet all freshman requirements and be in good standing at the previous institution attended. 60 credits of 120 required for the bachelor's degree must be completed at Vanderbilt.

Visiting: There are regularly scheduled orientations for prospective students, including group information sessions and campus tours available Monday through Saturday during the academic year and Monday through Friday during the summer. Schedules vary, so visitors must call in advance. There are guides for informal visits and visitors may sit in on classes and stay overnight. To schedule a visit, contact the Office of Undergraduate Admissions.

Financial Aid: In 2003-2004, 45% of all full-time freshmen and 38% of continuing full-time students received some form of financial aid. 40% of full-time freshmen and 35% of continuing full-time students received need-based aid. The average freshman award was $29,659. Need-based scholarships or need-based grants averaged $22,785; need-based self-help aid (loans and jobs) averaged $4481; non-need-based athletic scholarships averaged $26,212; and other non-need-based awards and non-need-based scholarships averaged $16,196. 24% of undergraduates work part time. Average annual earnings from campus work are $3700. The average financial indebtedness of the 2003 graduate was $23,334. The CSS Profile, FAFSA, and tax return information are required. The deadline for filing freshman financial aid applications for fall entry is February 1.

International Students: The school actively recruits these students. They must score 570 on the written TOEFL, and take the SAT I or ACT. Students must take SAT II: Subject tests in writing, math, and 1 other subject.

Computers: The mainframe is a DEC Alpha server 2100A Model 4/275. About 400 PCs and terminals are located in public and departmental labs. Most have Ethernet connections to the campus backbone, which is part of the Internet. All campus residences have Ethernet connections, and students who live off campus can access the network via modem. A wireless network is available on campus. All students may access the system any time.

Graduates: From July 1, 2002 to June 30, 2003, 1302 bachelor's degrees were awarded. The most popular majors were social sciences (36%), engineering (13%), and psychology (8%). In an average class, 1% graduate in 3 years or less, 78% graduate in 4 years or less, 83% graduate in 5 years or less, and 84% graduate in 6 years or less. 250 companies recruited on campus in 2002-2003. Of the 2002 graduating class, 32% were enrolled in graduate school within 6 months of graduation and 63% were employed.

Admissions Contact: Admissions Officer. A video is available. E-mail: *admissions@vanderbilt.edu* Web: *vanderbilt.edu*

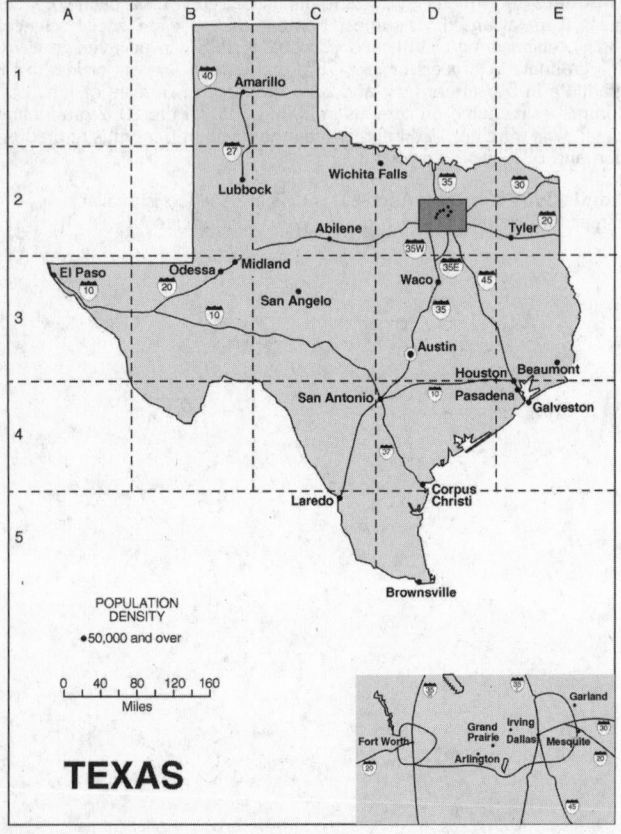

POPULATION
DENSITY

● 50,000 and over

0 40 80 120 160
Miles

TEXAS

ABILENE CHRISTIAN UNIVERSITY
Abilene, TX 79699-9000

C-2

(325) 674-2650
(800) 460-6228; Fax: (325) 674-2130

Full-time: 1741 men, 2136 women	**Faculty:** 215; IIA, --$
Part-time: 81 men, 153 women	**Ph.D.s:** 74%
Graduate: 302 men, 235 women	**Student/Faculty:** 18 to 1
Year: semesters, summer session	**Tuition:** $13,290
Application Deadline: open	**Room & Board:** $5080

Freshman Class: 4011 applied, 2117 accepted, 949 enrolled

SAT I Verbal/Math: 547/550   **ACT:** 24   **VERY COMPETITIVE**

Abilene Christian University, founded in 1906, is a private nonprofit institution affiliated with the Churches of Christ. The university offers a wide range of programs through the colleges of Biblical Studies, Business Administration, and Arts and Sciences There are 3 undergraduate schools and 1 graduate school. In addition to regional accreditation, ACU has baccalaureate program accreditation with ACBSP, ADA, CSWE, NASM, and NLN. The library contains 490,973 volumes, 1,171,162 microform items, and 64,131 audio/video tapes/CDs, and subscribes to 2435 periodicals. Computerized library services include the card catalog, interlibrary loans, and database searching. Special learning facilities include a learning resource center, art gallery, planetarium, radio station, TV station, and a volunteer and service learning center. The 208-acre campus is in an urban area 150 miles west of the Dallas-Fort Worth metroplex. Including any residence halls, there are 45 buildings.
Student Life: 78% of undergraduates are from Texas. Students are from 47 states, 40 foreign countries, and Canada. 88% are from public schools. 80% are white. Most are Protestant. The average age of freshmen is 18; all undergraduates, 21. 26% do not continue beyond their first year; 54% remain to graduate.
Housing: 1871 students can be accommodated in college housing, which includes single-sex dorms, on-campus apartments, and married-student housing. On-campus housing is available on a first-come, first-served basis and is available on a lottery system for upperclassmen. 59% of students commute. Alcohol is not permitted. All students may keep cars.
Activities: 14% of men belong to 8 local fraternities; 15% of women belong to 7 local sororities. There are 104 groups on campus, including art, band, cheerleading, chess, choir, chorale, chorus, computers, debate, drama, ethnic, film, forensics, honors, integrated marketing, inter-

national, jazz band, literary magazine, marching band, musical theater, newspaper, opera, orchestra, photography, political, professional, public relations, radio and TV, religious, social, social service, steel drum band, student government, symphony, and yearbook. Popular campus events include Sing Song Festival, Bible lectures, and Freshman Follies.
Sports: There are 7 intercollegiate sports for men and 6 for women, and 27 intramural sports for men and 27 for women. Facilities include a coliseum, track, baseball, and softball stadiums, soccer fields, an indoor swimming pool, gyms, a weight training facility, aerobic fitness exercise equipment, and tennis, racquetball, basketball, and handball courts.
Disabled Students: All of the campus is accessible. Wheelchair ramps, elevators, special parking, specially equipped rest rooms, special class scheduling, lowered drinking fountains, and lowered telephones are available.
Services: Counseling and information services are available, as is tutoring in every subject. There is a reader service for the blind, remedial math, reading, and writing, and a sign language interpreter.
Campus Safety and Security: Measures include 24-hour foot and vehicle patrol, self-defense education, security escort services, and informal discussions. There are pamphlets/posters/films, emergency telephones, lighted pathways/sidewalks, and fire safety discussions.
Programs of Study: ACU confers B.A., B.S., B.B.A., B.F.A., B.M., and B.S.N. degrees. Associate, master's, and doctoral degrees are also awarded. Bachelor's degrees are awarded in AGRICULTURE (animal science), BIOLOGICAL SCIENCE (biochemistry, biology/biological science, and nutrition), BUSINESS (accounting, banking and finance, management science, and marketing/retailing/merchandising), COMMUNICATIONS AND THE ARTS (advertising, art, broadcasting, communications, design, dramatic arts, English, fine arts, journalism, music, Spanish, and speech/debate/rhetoric), COMPUTER AND PHYSICAL SCIENCE (chemistry, computer science, information sciences and systems, mathematics, and physics), EDUCATION (art, business, early childhood, elementary, foreign languages, middle school, music, physical, science, secondary, and teaching English as a second/foreign language (TESOL/TEFOL)), ENGINEERING AND ENVIRONMENTAL DESIGN (engineering and applied science, engineering physics, and environmental science), HEALTH PROFESSIONS (nursing, predentistry, premedicine, and speech pathology/audiology), SOCIAL SCIENCE (biblical languages, biblical studies, criminal justice, dietetics, history, international relations, ministries, missions, political science/government, prelaw, psychology, public administration, religion, social science, social work, and sociology). Biology, chemistry, and education are the strongest academically. Elementary education, management, and psychology are the largest.
Required: To graduate, students must complete courses in Bible (15 hours), science, English, history, behavioral science, communication, phys ed (4 hours), fine arts, and math. 33 semester hours of advanced work must be taken and a minimum 2.0 GPA maintained. A minimum of 128 credit hours is needed, more in some programs, plus 30 to 64 hours in the major, 18 of which must be upper division.
Special: ACU offers cross-registration with Hardin-Simmons, McMurry, and Texas Tech Universities and study abroad in 4 countries. Double majors and credit for military training are available. Internships are possible in most majors, as are B.A.-B.S. degrees in Bible, biology, chemistry, communication, computer science, and math. A 3-2 engineering degree is offered with the University of Texas at Arlington and a microelectronics degree with the University of Texas at Dallas. Student-designed majors (interdisciplinary studies) are available. The applied studies program enables degree completion for adult students. There are 10 national honor societies and a freshman honors program.
Faculty/Classroom: 71% of faculty are male; 29%, female. 93% teach undergraduates and 49% both teach and do research. Graduate students teach 1% of introductory courses. The average class size in an introductory lecture is 29; in a laboratory, 18; and in a regular course, 24.
Admissions: 53% of the 2003-2004 applicants were accepted. The SAT I scores for the 2003-2004 freshman class were: Verbal--29% below 500, 44% between 500 and 599, 22% between 600 and 700, and 5% above 700; Math--28% below 500, 42% between 500 and 599, 25% between 600 and 700, and 5% above 700. The ACT scores were 24% below 21, 28% between 21 and 23, 27% between 24 and 26, 10% between 27 and 28, and 11% above 28. 40% of the current freshmen were in the top fifth of their class; 66% were in the top two fifths. There were 7 National Merit finalists. 24 freshmen graduated first in their class.
Requirements: The SAT I is recommended, with a composite of 960 minimum or 20 on the ACT. SAT II: Subject tests in English composition and essay, math level II, and foreign language (French, German, Spanish, or Latin) are required. Applicants must be graduates of an accredited secondary school or have the GED and have completed 22 academic credits, including 4 in English, 2 each in math and science, and 1 each in history and social studies. 2 years of the same foreign language are required. Art majors need to submit a portfolio, and music and theater ma-

jors must audition. ACU requires applicants to be in the upper 50% of their class. AP and CLEP credits are accepted. Important factors in the admissions decision are leadership record, recommendations by alumni, and advanced placement or honor courses.

Procedure: Freshmen are admitted to all sessions. Entrance exams should be taken by October of the senior year. Application deadlines are open. Application fee is $25. Notification is sent on a rolling basis. Applications are accepted on computer disk and on-line through *www.texasmentor.org*.

Transfer: 242 transfer students enrolled in 2002-2003. Transfer students must be in good standing at previously attended universities/colleges and have a minimum 2.0 GPA. A minimum composite score of 960 on the SAT I or an ACT score of 20 is required for students with fewer than 64 semester hours. A maximum of 66 semester hours from community or junior colleges will be accepted. An interview is required. 32 of 128 credits required for the bachelor's degree must be completed at ACU.

Visiting: There are regularly scheduled orientations for prospective students, including tours and interviews with faculty, administrators, admissions/financial aid counselors, and current students. There are guides for informal visits and visitors may sit in on classes and stay overnight. To schedule a visit, contact Gretchen Etheredge, Campus Visit Coordinator, at (325) 674-2664.

Financial Aid: In 2003-2004, 96% of all full-time freshmen and 89% of continuing full-time students received some form of financial aid. 60% of full-time freshmen and 53% of continuing full-time students received need-based aid. The average freshman award was $10,975. 20% of undergraduates work part time. Average annual earnings from campus work are $1494. The average financial indebtedness of the 2003 graduate was $25,147. The FAFSA is required. The deadline for filing freshman financial aid applications for fall entry is March 1.

International Students: There are 159 international students enrolled. The school actively recruits these students. They must score 525 on the written TOEFL or 197 on the electronic version and also take the college's own test.

Computers: Students have access to more than 500 computers during daytime and evening hours. Internet and e-mail are available through ACU's fiber-optic network in more than 20 labs on campus, including labs in residence halls, connections in dorm rooms, and off campus by modem. All students may access the system. Some students have 24-hour-a-day access; all others may use the system from 9 A.M. to 11 P.M. Monday through Friday, 9 A.M. to 4 P.M. Saturday, and 2 P.M. to 5 P.M. Sunday. There are no time limits and no fees.

Graduates: From July 1, 2002 to June 30, 2003, 792 bachelor's degrees were awarded. The most popular majors were management (7%), marketing (6%), and elementary education (6%). In an average class, 1% graduate in 3 years or less, 28% graduate in 4 years or less, 48% graduate in 5 years or less, and 52% graduate in 6 years or less. 150 companies recruited on campus in 2002-2003. Of the 2002 graduating class, 21% were enrolled in graduate school within 6 months of graduation and 72% were employed.

Admissions Contact: Robert Heil, Director of Admissions and Enrollment Management. E-mail: *info@admissions.acu.edu* Web: *http://www.acu.edu/admissions*

ANGELO STATE UNIVERSITY C-3
San Angelo, TX 76909
(325) 942-2041
(800) 946-8627; Fax: (325) 942-2078

Full-time: 2021 men, 2556 women	**Faculty:** 216; IIA, --$
Part-time: 436 men, 605 women	**Ph.D.s:** 75%
Graduate: 144 men, 281 women	**Student/Faculty:** 21 to 1
Year: semesters, summer session	**Tuition:** $2930 ($8594)
Application Deadline: August 9	**Room & Board:** $4646
Freshman Class: 1785 applied, 1768 accepted, 1147 enrolled	
SAT I Verbal/Math: 500/510	**ACT:** 21 NONCOMPETITIVE

Angelo State University, founded in 1928, and part of the Texas State University System, offers degrees through the colleges of liberal and fine arts, business and professional studies, sciences, and the school of education. There are 4 undergraduate schools and 1 graduate school. In addition to regional accreditation, ASU has baccalaureate program accreditation with ACBSP, NASM, and NLN. The library contains 475,518 volumes, 949,912 microform items, and 6986 audio/video tapes/CDs, and subscribes to 1671 periodicals. Computerized library services include the card catalog, interlibrary loans, and database searching. Special learning facilities include a learning resource center, art gallery, planetarium, Internet radio station, and a cable TV station. The 268-acre campus is in an urban area 200 miles west of Austin. Including any residence halls, there are 43 buildings.

Student Life: 97% of undergraduates are from Texas. Students are from 40 states, 22 foreign countries, and Canada. 98% are from public schools. 69% are white; 22% Hispanic. The average age of freshmen is 19; all undergraduates, 23. 42% do not continue beyond their first year; 32% remain to graduate.

Housing: 1559 students can be accommodated in college housing, which includes single-sex and coed dorms and on-campus apartments. There are designated honors rooms in 1 dorm. On-campus housing is available on a first-come, first-served basis. Priority is given to out-of-town students. 80% of students commute. Alcohol is not permitted. All students may keep cars.

Activities: 3% of men belong to 4 national fraternities; 4% of women belong to 2 national sororities. There are 75 groups on campus, including art, band, cheerleading, chess, choir, chorale, chorus, computers, dance, debate, drama, drill team, ethnic, film, gay, honors, international, jazz band, marching band, musical theater, newspaper, opera, pep band, political, professional, radio and TV, religious, rodeo, social, social service, student government, and wool judging. Popular campus events include Fish Splash, madrigal dinner, and musical theater.

Sports: There are 4 intercollegiate sports for men and 5 for women, and 15 intramural sports for men and 15 for women. Facilities include a gym, racquetball, basketball, volleyball, badminton, and tennis courts, an all-weather Tartan track, 2 regulation softball fields, and a 25-meter Olympic-size pool. The campus track stadium seats 3500, and the indoor gym, 4000. There is a multipurpose arena seating up to 6300 people that has an auxiliary practice gym, two weight rooms, and a sports medicine area. There is also a multipurpose complex for rugby, soccer, and football.

Disabled Students: 98% of the campus is accessible. Wheelchair ramps, elevators, special parking, specially equipped rest rooms, special class scheduling, lowered drinking fountains, and lowered telephones are available.

Services: Counseling and information services are available, as is tutoring in most subjects. There is remedial math, reading, and writing.

Campus Safety and Security: Measures include 24-hour foot and vehicle patrol, self-defense education, security escort services, and informal discussions. There are pamphlets/posters/films, emergency telephones, and lighted pathways/sidewalks.

Programs of Study: ASU confers B.A., B.S., B.B.A., B.F.A., B.G.S., B.M., and B.S.N. degrees. Associate and master's degrees are also awarded. Bachelor's degrees are awarded in AGRICULTURE (animal science), BIOLOGICAL SCIENCE (biochemistry and biology/biological science), BUSINESS (accounting, banking and finance, business administration and management, and marketing/retailing/merchandising), COMMUNICATIONS AND THE ARTS (art, communications, dramatic arts, English, French, German, journalism, music, and Spanish), COMPUTER AND PHYSICAL SCIENCE (applied physics, chemistry, computer science, mathematics, and physics), EDUCATION (early childhood), HEALTH PROFESSIONS (exercise science, medical laboratory technology, and nursing), SOCIAL SCIENCE (criminal justice, history, interdisciplinary studies, liberal arts/general studies, political science/government, psychology, and sociology). Math, biology, and physics are the strongest academically. Business-related programs, nursing, and education are the largest.

Required: To graduate, students must complete a total of 130 semester hours with a minimum GPA of 2.0 (2.5 for all programs leading to teacher certification). Between 30 and 36 hours are required in the major. General education core courses must be taken in English, government, history, modern language, and phys ed. Students must also fulfill distributional requirements of 6 to 8 credits each in art, communication, drama, journalism, music, and philosophy; economics, geography, linguistics, psychology, sociology; and lab science.

Special: ASU offers co-op programs with the University of Texas at El Paso, study abroad in 4 countries, internships in psychology, public administration, sociology, and journalism, work-study programs, dual majors, a 3-2 engineering degree with the University of Texas at El Paso, and a 5-year integrated accounting program. There are 16 national honor societies and a freshman honors program.

Faculty/Classroom: 56% of faculty are male; 44%, female. 97% teach undergraduates and 75% both teach and do research. Graduate students teach 3% of introductory courses. The average class size in an introductory lecture is 36; in a laboratory, 19; and in a regular course, 28.

Admissions: 99% of the 2003-2004 applicants were accepted. The SAT I scores for the 2003-2004 freshman class were: Verbal--43% below 500, 42% between 500 and 599, 14% between 600 and 700, and 1% above 700; Math--43% below 500, 42% between 500 and 599, 14% between 600 and 700, and 1% above 700. The ACT scores were 37% below 21, 35% between 21 and 23, 18% between 24 and 26, 7% between 27 and 28, and 3% above 28. 41% of the current freshmen were in the top fifth of their class; 75% were in the top two fifths. 23 freshmen graduated first in their class.

Requirements: The SAT I or ACT is required. In addition, applicants must be graduates of an accredited secondary school or have the GED. ASU requires applicants to be in the upper 50% of their class. AP and CLEP credits are accepted. Advanced placement or honor courses is an important factor in the admission decision.

Procedure: Freshmen are admitted to all sessions. Entrance exams should be taken during spring of the junior year or fall of the senior year. There is a rolling admissions plan. Applications should be filed by August

9 for fall entry, December 13 for spring entry, and May 9 for summer entry, along with a $20 fee. Notification is sent on a rolling basis. Applications are accepted on-line through the university's web site and the Texas common application.

Transfer: 610 transfer students enrolled in 2002-2003. Transfer students must have a minimum 2.0 GPA; those with fewer than 18 hours must meet high school admission requirements. 33 credits of 130 required for the bachelor's degree must be completed at ASU.

Visiting: There are regularly scheduled orientations for prospective students, including Preview ASU, orientation, a tour, advising, and lunch. There are guides for informal visits and visitors may sit in on classes and stay overnight. To schedule a visit, contact the Recruiting Office/Office of Admissions at (325) 942-2058 or *admissions@angelo.edu.*

Financial Aid: In 2003-2004, 49% of all full-time freshmen and 70% of continuing full-time students received some form of financial aid. 27% of full-time freshmen and 46% of continuing full-time students received need-based aid. The average freshman award was $2631. Need-based scholarships or need-based grants averaged $3471 ($8438 maximum); need-based self-help aid (loans and jobs) averaged $2132 ($4809 maximum); non-need-based athletic scholarships averaged $2431 ($5000 maximum); and other non-need-based awards and non-need-based scholarships averaged $2489 ($10,199 maximum). 9% of undergraduates work part time. Average annual earnings from campus work are $3800. The average financial indebtedness of the 2003 graduate was $15,000. The FAFSA is required. The deadline for filing freshman financial aid applications for fall entry is June 1.

International Students: There are 83 international students enrolled. The school actively recruits these students. They must score 550 on the written TOEFL or 213 on the electronic version unless English is the native language. The SAT I or ACT is required, with a minimum ACT score of 17.

Computers: The mainframes are an IBM 9672 and 05390. Students may access more than 300 Dell PCs located in 7 PC labs on campus and 200 Dell PCs in special purpose labs. 75% of the residence halls are wired for direct Internet access. The campus is connected to an ultra high-speed portal. All students may access the system 24 hours a day on weekdays, and modified hours on weekends. There are no time limits. The fee is $6 per credit hour.

Graduates: From July 1, 2002 to June 30, 2003, 860 bachelor's degrees were awarded. The most popular majors were education (18%), kinesiology (12%), and psychology (11%). In an average class, 32% graduate in 6 years or less. 141 companies recruited on campus in 2002-2003.

Admissions Contact: Office of Admissions. A video is available. E-mail: *admissions@angelo.edu* Web: *www.angelo.edu*

AUSTIN COLLEGE	**D-2**
Sherman, TX 75090-4400	**(903) 813-3000**
	(800) 442-5363; Fax: (903) 813-3198
Full-time: 557 men, 721 women	**Faculty:** 92; IIB, +$
Part-time: 10 men, 6 women	**Ph.D.s:** 99%
Graduate: 9 men, 29 women	**Student/Faculty:** 14 to 1
Year: 4-1-4, summer session	**Tuition:** $17,925
Application Deadline: March 1	**Room & Board:** $6822
Freshman Class: 1328 applied, 960 accepted, 338 enrolled	
SAT I Verbal/Math: 618/613	**ACT:** 25 **HIGHLY COMPETITIVE**

Austin College, founded in 1849, is a private liberal arts institution affiliated with the Presbyterian Church (U.S.A.) and offering programs in business, liberal arts, and health field. The library contains 214,959 volumes, 109,059 microform items, and 7668 audio/video tapes/CDs, and subscribes to 1094 periodicals. Computerized library services include the card catalog, interlibrary loans, database searching, and Internet access. Special learning facilities include a learning resource center, a social science lab, television studios for media instruction, environmental research areas near Lake Texoma, and a facility for advanced computing and 3-D graphics. The 70-acre campus is in a suburban area 60 miles north of Dallas. Including any residence halls, there are 31 buildings.

Student Life: 88% of undergraduates are from Texas. Students are from 30 states and 25 foreign countries. 90% are from public schools. 76% are white; 10% Asian American. 64% are Protestant; 15% Catholic; 15% claim no religious affiliation. The average age of freshmen is 18; all undergraduates, 20. 13% do not continue beyond their first year; 78% remain to graduate.

Housing: 931 students can be accommodated in college housing, which includes single-sex and coed dorms and on-campus apartments. In addition, there are language houses and a suite-style residence hall. On-campus housing is guaranteed through the junior year and available on a lottery system for upperclassmen. 74% of students live on campus; of those, 60% remain on campus on weekends. All students may keep cars.

Activities: 21% of men belong to 10 local fraternities; 19% of women belong to 7 local sororities. There are 50 groups on campus, including art, cheerleading, choir, chorale, chorus, drama, ethnic, film, gay, honors, international, jazz band, literary magazine, musical theater, newspaper, orchestra, pep band, photography, political, professional, radio and TV, religious, social, social service, student government, symphony, and yearbook. Popular campus events include Christmas Pops, Film Series, and Diwali Dinner.

Sports: There are 6 intercollegiate sports for men and 5 for women, and 14 intramural sports for men and 14 for women. Facilities include an athletic/recreation complex that includes 2 gyms, a natatorium, and a fitness pavilion; a tennis stadium; a 2500-seat stadium; and soccer and baseball fields.

Disabled Students: 99% of the campus is accessible. Wheelchair ramps, elevators, special parking, specially equipped rest rooms, special class scheduling, and lowered drinking fountains are available.

Services: Counseling and information services are available, as is tutoring in some subjects, including introductory-level courses. Individual and group assistance to strengthen reading, writing, and study skills is available.

Campus Safety and Security: Measures include 24-hour foot and vehicle patrol, self-defense education, security escort services, and informal discussions. There are pamphlets/posters/films, emergency telephones, and lighted pathways/sidewalks.

Programs of Study: AC confers the B.A. degree. Master's degrees are also awarded. Bachelor's degrees are awarded in BIOLOGICAL SCIENCE (biochemistry and biology/biological science), BUSINESS (business administration and management and international economics), COMMUNICATIONS AND THE ARTS (art, classics, communications, English, French, German, Latin, music, and Spanish), COMPUTER AND PHYSICAL SCIENCE (chemistry, computer science, mathematics, and physics), SOCIAL SCIENCE (American studies, economics, history, interdisciplinary studies, international studies, Latin American studies, philosophy, political science/government, psychology, religion, and sociology). Chemistry, biology, and international studies are the strongest academically. Business administration, psychology, and biology are the largest.

Required: Core requirements for graduation include Freshman Communication Inquiry, a physical profile and activity course, 3 Heritage of Western Culture courses, and 3 courses in humanities, 2 courses in social science, and 1 course in natural science.To graduate, students must have a minimum 2.0 GPA and a total of 34 course credits (136 semester hours), with 7 to 11 course credits in the major. Students must demonstrate an ability in a modern or classical language other than their own, quantitative competency with an approved course or test, and the required skills in written communication with approved course work. A minor or a 2nd major is required.

Special: AC offers cooperative programs with Butler University, Beaver College, Central College, and the Institute for European Studies, internships during the January and summer terms, study abroad in 18 countries, and fall, spring, and summer internships in Washington, D.C. Work-study, accelerated degree programs in all majors, and dual and student-designed majors are available. There is a 3-2 engineering degree program in conjunction with the University of Texas at Dallas and Washington University in St. Louis, as well as cooperative agreements with Columbia University and Texas A&M University. Nondegree study, pass/fail options, preprofessional teacher education programs, and a January term with experimental and off-campus opportunities are offered. There are 14 national honor societies, including Phi Beta Kappa.

Faculty/Classroom: 68% of faculty are male; 32%, female. All both teach and do research. No introductory courses are taught by graduate students. The average class size in an introductory lecture is 19; in a laboratory, 16; and in a regular course, 20.

Admissions: 72% of the 2003-2004 applicants were accepted. The SAT I scores for the 2003-2004 freshman class were: Verbal--6% below 500, 31% between 500 and 599, 47% between 600 and 700, and 16% above 700; Math--8% below 500, 29% between 500 and 599, 53% between 600 and 700, and 10% above 700. The ACT scores were 15% below 21, 15% between 21 and 23, 26% between 24 and 26, 20% between 27 and 28, and 24% above 28. 64% of the current freshmen were in the top fifth of their class; 89% were in the top two fifths. There was 1 National Merit finalist and 3 semifinalists. 11 freshmen graduated first in their class.

Requirements: The SAT I or ACT is required. In addition, applicants must be graduates of an accredited secondary school or have a GED. The minimum recommended academic requirements are 4 credits in English, 3 each in math and science, 2 each in social studies and foreign language, and 1 in art/music/theater. An essay is required, and an interview is recommended. AP and CLEP credits are accepted. Important factors in the admissions decision are advanced placement or honor courses, leadership record, and extracurricular activities record.

Procedure: Freshmen are admitted fall and summer. Entrance exams should be taken in the junior year or the fall of the senior year. There are early decision, early admissions, and deferred admissions plans. There is a rolling admissions plan. Early decision applications should be filed by December 1; regular applications, by March 1 for fall entry, along with a $35 fee. Notification of early decision is sent January 10; regular decision, on a rolling basis. 28 early decision candidates were accepted for the 2003-2004 class. 34 applicants were on the 2003 waiting list; 19 were admitted. Applications are accepted on-line through Common App, Texas Mentor, or the school's web site.

Transfer: 55 transfer students enrolled in 2002-2003. Applicants must have a minimum 2.5 GPA, submit official college transcripts and 2 recommendations, and be in good standing at previously attended schools. Students with fewer than 30 credit hours must submit SAT I or ACT scores and their high school transcript or GED. 17 of 34 credits required for the bachelor's degree must be completed at AC.

Visiting: There are regularly scheduled orientations for prospective students, including 1-day and 2-day preview programs held for high school juniors and seniors and parents. Individual appointments may be made as well. There are guides for informal visits and visitors may sit in on classes and stay overnight. To schedule a visit, contact the Admission Office at *admission@austincollege.edu.*

Financial Aid: In 2003-2004, 96% of all full-time students received some form of financial aid. 58% of full-time freshmen and 60% of continuing full-time students received need-based aid. The average freshman award was $17,854. Need-based scholarships or need-based grants averaged $12,476 ($26,747 maximum); need-based self-help aid (loans and jobs) averaged $5842 ($11,454 maximum); and non-need-based awards and non-need-based scholarships averaged $7477 ($25,547 maximum). 31% of undergraduates work part time. Average annual earnings from campus work are $1600. The average financial indebtedness of the 2003 graduate was $22,085. AC is a member of CSS. The FAFSA and the college's own financial statement are required. The deadline for filing freshman financial aid applications for fall entry is April 1.

International Students: There are 32 international students enrolled. The school actively recruits these students. They must score 600 on the written TOEFL and also take the SAT I or the ACT.

Computers: The mainframe is a DEC DS 20. Students have access to 121 Dell Pentiums, 36 Mac Power PCs, 9 HP 712 workstations, and an SGI Indigo Extreme from the main computer labs. Each residence hall also has a computer cluster with PCs and Macs. Ports for Internet and Web access are available in every student's dorm and on every computer. All students may access the system 24 hours a day in some locations. There are no time limits and no fees.

Graduates: From July 1, 2002 to June 30, 2003, 289 bachelor's degrees were awarded. The most popular majors were business administration (17%), psychology (14%), and biology (12%). In an average class, 6% graduate in 3 years or less, 67% graduate in 4 years or less, 73% graduate in 5 years or less, and 75% graduate in 6 years or less. 43 companies recruited on campus in 2002-2003. Of the 2002 graduating class, 37% were enrolled in graduate school within 6 months of graduation and 44% were employed.

Admissions Contact: Nan Davis, VP for Institutional Enrollment. A video is available. E-mail: *admission@austincollege.edu*
Web: *www.austincollege.edu*

BAYLOR UNIVERSITY
Waco, TX 76798

D-3

(254) 710-3435; (800) BAYLOR-U

Full-time: 4684 men, 6576 women	**Faculty:** 748; I, --$
Part-time: 202 men, 250 women	**Ph.D.s:** 75%
Graduate: 1232 men, 993 women	**Student/Faculty:** 15 to 1
Year: semesters, summer session	**Tuition:** $18,430
Application Deadline: open	**Room & Board:** $5434
Freshman Class: 8931 applied, 7341 accepted, 2678 enrolled	
SAT I Verbal/Math: 580/600	**ACT:** 24 **VERY COMPETITIVE**

Baylor University, founded in 1845, is an independent institution affiliated with the Baptist Church and offering undergraduate programs in liberal arts and sciences, business, computer science, education, engineering, music, nursing, and an honors college. There are 7 undergraduate and 10 graduate schools. In addition to regional accreditation, Baylor has baccalaureate program accreditation with AACSB, AALE, ABET, ACEJMC, ADA, AHEA, APTA, CAHEA, CSWE, NASM, NCATE, and NLN. The 9 libraries contain 2,140,168 volumes, 2,059,235 microform items, and 83,165 audio/video tapes/CDs, and subscribe to 18,940 periodicals. Computerized library services include the card catalog, interlibrary loans, database searching, and Internet access. Special learning facilities include a learning resource center, art gallery, natural history museum, radio station, TV station, and speech/hearing clinic. The 432-acre campus is in an urban area 100 miles south of Dallas/Fort Worth. Including any residence halls, there are 84 buildings.

Student Life: 83% of undergraduates are from Texas. Students are from 50 states, 75 foreign countries, and Canada. 75% are white. 77% are Protestant; 13% Catholic. The average age of freshmen is 19; all undergraduates, 21. 16% do not continue beyond their first year; 69% remain to graduate.

Housing: 3597 students can be accommodated in college housing, which includes single-sex dorms, on-campus apartments, off-campus apartments, and married-student housing. There are also academic wings. On-campus housing is guaranteed for the freshman year only and

is available on a first-come, first-served basis. Alcohol is not permitted. All students may keep cars.

Activities: 15% of men belong to 2 local and 14 national fraternities; 17% of women belong to 1 local and 9 national sororities. There are 289 groups on campus, including art, band, cheerleading, chess, choir, chorale, chorus, computers, dance, debate, drama, ethnic, film, forensics, honors, international, jazz band, literary magazine, marching band, musical theater, newspaper, opera, orchestra, pep band, photography, political, professional, radio and TV, religious, social, social service, student government, symphony, and yearbook. Popular campus events include Dia del Oso (Day of the Bear), Campus Sing, and Pigskin Review.

Sports: There are 8 intercollegiate sports for men and 9 for women, and 17 intramural sports for men and 17 for women. Facilities include a 50,000-seat football stadium, gyms, intramural fields, tennis courts, a swimming pool, a marina, and a special events center that seats 10,030. A 158,000-square-foot student life center has a 52-foot climbing rock, fitness center, aerobics room, racquetball/squash courts, basketball courts, pool, indoor walking/jogging track, and outdoor sand volleyball courts.

Disabled Students: 95% of the campus is accessible. Wheelchair ramps, elevators, special parking, specially equipped rest rooms, and lowered drinking fountains are available.

Services: There is a reader service for the blind and remedial reading and writing. Taped textbooks are available through the Commission for the Blind. The Office of Student Access and Learning provides study skills and time management sessions for students with disabilities.

Campus Safety and Security: Measures include 24-hour foot and vehicle patrol, security escort services, shuttle buses, and informal discussions. There are pamphlets/posters/films, emergency telephones, and lighted pathways/sidewalks.

Programs of Study: Baylor confers B.A., B.S., B.B.A., B.F.A., B.M., B.M.E., B.S.Av.Sc., B.S.C.S., B.S.E., B.S.E.C.E., B.S.Ed., B.S.F.C.S., B.S.I., B.S.M.E., B.S.N., and B.S.W. degrees. Master's and doctoral degrees are also awarded. Bachelor's degrees are awarded in AGRICULTURE (forestry and related sciences and soil science), BIOLOGICAL SCIENCE (biochemistry, biology/biological science, life science, neurosciences, and nutrition), BUSINESS (accounting, banking and finance, business administration and management, business economics, business statistics, business systems analysis, entrepreneurial studies, fashion merchandising, human resources, insurance, international business management, management information systems, marketing/retailing/merchandising, personnel management, and real estate), COMMUNICATIONS AND THE ARTS (applied music, art, art history and appreciation, broadcasting, classics, communications, creative writing, dramatic arts, English, French, German, Greek (classical), journalism, languages, Latin, music, music history and appreciation, music performance, music theory and composition, performing arts, Russian, Spanish, speech/debate/rhetoric, studio art, telecommunications, and theater design), COMPUTER AND PHYSICAL SCIENCE (applied mathematics, chemistry, computer science, earth science, geology, geophysics and seismology, information sciences and systems, mathematics, and physics), EDUCATION (art, business, computer, drama, elementary, English, foreign languages, health, home economics, journalism, mathematics, museum studies, music, physical, reading, recreation, science, secondary, social science, social studies, and special), ENGINEERING AND ENVIRONMENTAL DESIGN (airline piloting and navigation, architecture, computer engineering, electrical/electronics engineering, engineering, environmental science, interior design, and mechanical engineering), HEALTH PROFESSIONS (community health work, health science, medical laboratory technology, nursing, optometry, predentistry, premedicine, speech pathology/audiology, and speech therapy), SOCIAL SCIENCE (American studies, anthropology, archeology, Asian/Oriental studies, biblical languages, child care/child and family studies, dietetics, economics, family/consumer studies, fashion design and technology, forensic studies, geography, history, interdisciplinary studies, international public service, Latin American studies, law, philosophy, physical fitness/movement, political science/government, prelaw, psychology, public administration, religion, religious education, religious music, Russian and Slavic studies, social work, sociology, and urban studies). Business, biology, and psychology are the largest.

Required: All degree programs require a minimum of 124 hours and a 2.0 GPA to graduate. Basic requirements for the B.A. degree include 18 semester hours of social science, 12 each of English and science, 6 to 9 of fine arts, 6 of religion, 4 of phys ed, 3 to 16 of foreign language, 3 of math, and 2 semesters of chapel forum. Requirements for other degrees vary.

Special: Baylor offers cooperative programs in architecture, business, dentistry, medicine, and optometry, internships in each school, study abroad and student exchange in more than 30 countries, and pass/fail options. There are also honors and university scholars programs and faculty exchange with 4 schools in China, and 1 each in Japan, Thailand, and Russia. There are 35 national honor societies, including Phi Beta Kappa, and a freshman honors program.

Faculty/Classroom: 64% of faculty are male; 36%, female. The average class size in a regular course is 31.

Admissions: 82% of the 2003-2004 applicants were accepted. The SAT I scores for the 2003-2004 freshman class were: Verbal--12% below 500, 45% between 500 and 599, 34% between 600 and 700, and 9% above 700; Math--8% below 500, 41% between 500 and 599, 41% between 600 and 700, and 10% above 700. The ACT scores were 14% below 21, 31% between 21 and 23, 27% between 24 and 26, 17% between 27 and 28, and 11% above 28. 59% of the current freshmen were in the top fifth of their class; 84% were in the top two fifths. There were 37 National Merit finalists.

Requirements: The SAT I or ACT is required. The recommended minimum composite score is 1100 on the SAT I or 24 on the ACT. Applicants must be graduates of an accredited secondary school. An interview is recommended. Baylor requires applicants to be in the upper 50% of their class. AP and CLEP credits are accepted.

Procedure: Freshmen are admitted fall, spring, and summer. Entrance exams should be taken in spring of the junior year or fall of the senior year. There is a rolling admissions plan. Application deadlines are open. Application fee is $35. Notification is sent on a rolling basis. Applications are accepted on-line through Liquid Matrix.

Transfer: 420 transfer students enrolled in 2002-2003. Transfer students should begin studies no later than the end of the sophomore year because of the 60-semester-hour residence requirement for a bachelor's degree. A minimum 2.5 GPA is required. Students with fewer than 30 credit hours earned must meet the entrance requirements for freshmen. 60 credits of 124 required for the bachelor's degree must be completed at Baylor.

Visiting: There are regularly scheduled orientations for prospective students, including day-and-a-half sessions in June and a Welcome Week in August. There are guides for informal visits and visitors may sit in on classes and stay overnight. To schedule a visit, contact the Campus Visitation Program at (254) 710-2407.

Financial Aid: In 2003-2004, 85% of all full-time freshmen and 77% of continuing full-time students received some form of financial aid. 51% of full-time freshmen and 45% of continuing full-time students received need-based aid. The average freshman award was $12,425. Need-based scholarships or need-based grants averaged $7388 ($19,950 maximum); need-based self-help aid (loans and jobs) averaged $4671 ($9275 maximum); non-need-based athletic scholarships averaged $16,747 ($24,592 maximum); and other non-need-based awards and non-need-based scholarships averaged $6011 ($18,250 maximum). 21% of undergraduates work part time. Average annual earnings from campus work are $1257. The FAFSA is required. The deadline for filing freshman financial aid applications for fall entry is May 1.

International Students: There are 237 international students enrolled. The school actively recruits these students. They must score 540 on the written TOEFL or 207 on the electronic version and also take the SAT I or the ACT.

Computers: The university provides approximately 3500 networked Apple and Dell workstations for student use in various locations on campus. All students may access the system. Most systems are accessible 24 hours a day, 7 days per week. There is a fee of $150 per semester. It is strongly recommended that all students have a personal computer, especially students in Baylor Interdisciplinary Core (BIC) and MBA programs.

Graduates: From July 1, 2002 to June 30, 2003, 2249 bachelor's degrees were awarded. The most popular majors were teacher education (6%), business marketing (6%), and computer information systems (5%). In an average class, 1% graduate in 3 years or less, 42% graduate in 4 years or less, 66% graduate in 5 years or less, and 69% graduate in 6 years or less. 153 companies recruited on campus in 2002-2003.

Admissions Contact: Diana M. Ramey, Director, Undergraduate Admissions. A video is available.
E-mail: *addmissions_serv_office@baylor.edu*
Web: *http://www.baylor.edu*

CONCORDIA UNIVERSITY AT AUSTIN D-3
Austin, TX 78705-2799
(512) 452-7661
(800) 865-4282; Fax: (512) 459-8517

Full-time: 335 men, 373 women	**Faculty:** 37
Part-time: 116 men, 207 women	**Ph.D.s:** 73%
Graduate: 41 men, 83 women	**Student/Faculty:** 19 to 1
Year: semesters, summer session	**Tuition:** $14,300
Application Deadline: August 1	**Room & Board:** $6150
Freshman Class: 523 applied, 396 accepted, 159 enrolled	
SAT I or ACT: required	**LESS COMPETITIVE**

Concordia University at Austin, founded in 1926, is a private college affiliated with the Lutheran Church-Missouri Synod. It offers undergraduate programs in liberal arts, behavioral science, business, communication, education, environmental science, and church music. There are 4 undergraduate schools. The library contains 56,146 volumes, 8504 microform items, and 3213 audio/video tapes/CDs, and subscribes to 514 periodicals. Computerized library services include the card catalog, interlibrary loans, and database searching. Special learning facilities include a TV station. The 20-acre campus is in an urban area in the heart of Austin. Including any residence halls, there are 20 buildings.

Student Life: 93% of undergraduates are from Texas. Students are from 21 states and 13 foreign countries. 89% are from public schools. 63% are white; 13% Hispanic; 8% African American. 78% are Protestant; 16% Catholic; 6% claim no religious affiliation. The average age of freshmen is 19; all undergraduates, 25. 37% do not continue beyond their first year; 36% remain to graduate.

Housing: 245 students can be accommodated in college housing, which includes single-sex and coed dorms. On-campus housing is guaranteed for the freshman year only and is available on a first-come, first-served basis. 68% of students commute. All students may keep cars.

Activities: There are no fraternities or sororities. There are 9 groups on campus, including band, choir, chorus, dance, drama, ethnic, religious, social, and student government. Popular campus events include Fall Festival Weekend, Parents Day, and Founders Day.

Sports: There are 6 intercollegiate sports for men and 5 for women, and 10 intramural sports for men and 9 for women. Facilities include an activities center, 1600-seat gym, 250-seat auditorium, baseball field, beach volleyball court, and tennis courts.

Disabled Students: 75% of the campus is accessible. Wheelchair ramps, elevators, special parking, specially equipped rest rooms, and lowered drinking fountains are available.

Services: Counseling and information services are available, as is tutoring in most subjects.

Campus Safety and Security: Measures include 24-hour foot and vehicle patrol, security escort services, informal discussions, and pamphlets/posters/films. There are lighted pathways/sidewalks.

Programs of Study: Concordia confers the B.A. degree. Associate degrees are also awarded. Bachelor's degrees are awarded in BUSINESS (accounting and business administration and management), COMMUNICATIONS AND THE ARTS (communications, English, music, and Spanish), COMPUTER AND PHYSICAL SCIENCE (computer science), EDUCATION (elementary and secondary), ENGINEERING AND ENVIRONMENTAL DESIGN (environmental science), SOCIAL SCIENCE (behavioral science, history, liberal arts/general studies, Mexican-American/Chicano studies, and religious music). Education is the strongest academically. Business management, education, and communication are the largest.

Required: To graduate, all students must complete 12 hours each of English, social/behavioral science, and religion, 6 to 8 hours of natural science, and 3 hours each of fine arts, math, phys ed, and speech. Students must earn 128 semester hours, including 39 upper-level hours and 33 to 48 hours in the major. A minimum 2.0 GPA is required, plus a 2.25 GPA in the major.

Special: Concordia offers internships in communications, behavioral science, business, environmental science, and Mexican-American studies, study abroad in Mexico, an accelerated degree program in business management, dual majors, credit for prior experiential learning, nondegree study, pass/fail options, and a preseminary program. There is 1 national honor society.

Faculty/Classroom: 64% of faculty are male; 36%, female. All teach undergraduates. The average class size in a laboratory is 16 and in a regular course, 21.

Admissions: 3 freshmen graduated first in their class in a recent year.

Requirements: The SAT I or ACT is required. In addition, the recommended minimum composite score is 860 on the SAT I or 17 on the ACT. Applicants must be graduates of an accredited secondary school or have the GED. A GPA of 2.5 is required. AP and CLEP credits are accepted.

Procedure: Freshmen are admitted fall, spring, and summer. There is an early decision plan. There is a rolling admissions plan. Check with the school for current deadlines and fees. The fall 2003 application fee was $25. Notification is sent on a rolling basis.

Transfer: Transfer students with fewer than 18 hours earned must meet freshman admissions requirements and submit high school and college transcripts; those with 18 or more hours earned must be in good standing at the previously attended college with a minimum 2.0 GPA. 30 of 128 credits required for the bachelor's degree must be completed at Concordia.

Visiting: There are regularly scheduled orientations for prospective students, consisting of placement exams, scheduling and registration of classes, and information sessions for parents with faculty and administrators. There are guides for informal visits and visitors may sit in on classes and stay overnight. To schedule a visit, contact the Admissions Office.

Financial Aid: In 2003-2004, 73% of all full-time freshmen and 66% of continuing students received some form of financial aid. At least 61% of full-time freshmen and 55% of continuing students received need-based aid. The FAFSA and the college's own financial statement are required. The deadline for filing freshman financial aid applications for fall entry is July 1.

International Students: The school actively recruits these students. They must score 550 on the written TOEFL.

Computers: PCs are available for academic use in the computer labs. The Internet is accessible from residence halls. All students may access the system. There are no time limits and no fees.

Graduates: From July 1, 2002 to June 30, 2003, 122 bachelor's degrees were awarded.

Admissions Contact: Jay A. Krause, VP, Enrollment Services.
E-mail: *ctxadmis@crf.cuis.edu* Web: *www.concordia.edu*

DALLAS BAPTIST UNIVERSITY
Dallas, TX 75211-9299

D-2

(214) 333-5360

(800) 460-1328; Fax: (214) 333-5447

Full-time: 822 men, 1070 women	Faculty: 78
Part-time: 568 men, 984 women	Ph.D.s: 73%
Graduate: 370 men, 724 women	Student/Faculty: 24 to 1
Year: 4-1-4, summer session	Tuition: $11,010
Application Deadline: open	Room & Board: $4290
Freshman Class: 740 applied, 505 accepted, 298 enrolled	
SAT I Verbal/Math: 546/544	ACT: 23 **VERY COMPETITIVE**

Dallas Baptist University, established in 1898, is a private institution affiliated with the Baptist General Convention of Texas. The university offers degrees in the arts, sciences, music, and business while integrating faith and learning. There are 7 undergraduate and 10 graduate schools. In addition to regional accreditation, DBU has baccalaureate program accreditation with ACBSP. The library contains 237,098 volumes, 515,071 microform items, and 5913 audio/video tapes/CDs, and subscribes to 597 periodicals. Computerized library services include the card catalog, interlibrary loans, and database searching. Special learning facilities include a Corrie Ten Boom collection and an elementary school on campus. The 293-acre campus is in a suburban area 13 miles from downtown Dallas and 19 miles from Fort Worth. Including any residence halls, there are 18 buildings.

Student Life: 96% of undergraduates are from Texas. Students are from 40 states, 45 foreign countries, and Canada. 51% are white; 20% African American. 77% are Protestant; 17% claim no religious affiliation. The average age of freshmen is 18; all undergraduates, 29. 31% do not continue beyond their first year; 69% remain to graduate.

Housing: 1106 students can be accommodated in college housing, which includes coed dorms and on-campus apartments. On-campus housing is available on a first-come, first-served basis. 68% of students commute. Alcohol is not permitted. All students may keep cars.

Activities: There are no fraternities or sororities. There are 34 groups on campus, including art, band, choir, chorale, civil service, community outreach, drama, ethnic, honors, international, leadership/mission work, musical theater, political, professional, religious, social, social service, student government, and yearbook. Popular campus events include Family Weekend, Spiritual Rush, and Habitat for Humanity.

Sports: There are 6 intercollegiate sports for men and 5 for women, and 15 intramural sports for men and 15 for women. Facilities include a gym, tennis courts, a baseball diamond, a soccer field, 2 pools, a sand volleyball court, a basketball court, and table tennis and foosball tables.

Disabled Students: 68% of the campus is accessible. Wheelchair ramps, elevators, special parking, specially equipped rest rooms, special class scheduling, lowered drinking fountains, lowered telephones, and special housing are available.

Services: Counseling and information services are available, as is tutoring in most subjects, including math, writing, English, computer, study skills, and adult education. There is a reader service for the blind and remedial math. Student counseling is also available.

Campus Safety and Security: Measures include 24-hour foot and vehicle patrol, security escort services, shuttle buses, and informal discussions. There are pamphlets/posters/films, emergency telephones, and lighted pathways/sidewalks.

Programs of Study: DBU confers B.A., B.S., B.A.S., B.B.A., B.B.S., and B.M. degrees. Associate and master's degrees are also awarded. Bachelor's degrees are awarded in BIOLOGICAL SCIENCE (biology/biological science), BUSINESS (accounting, banking and finance, business administration and management, management information systems, and marketing/retailing/merchandising), COMMUNICATIONS AND THE ARTS (applied music, communications, English, fine arts, music, and music performance), COMPUTER AND PHYSICAL SCIENCE (computer science and mathematics), EDUCATION (elementary and physical), SOCIAL SCIENCE (biblical studies, counseling/psychology, criminal justice, history, interdisciplinary studies, liberal arts/general studies, pastoral studies, philosophy, physical fitness/movement, psychology, religious education, and sociology). Business administration and multi/interdisciplinary studies are the largest.

Required: To graduate, students must have a minimum GPA of 2.0 and complete 126 credit hours, including 24 hours in the major and 42 upper-division hours. Students must also take additional credit hours of general studies courses, including computer science, English, fine arts, foreign language, history, math, natural science, phys ed, religion, speech, and social science, to total 126. Chapel attendance is required. All freshmen must take 2 semesters of an orientation course.

Special: Work-study programs, study abroad, and a Washington semester are available. There are 4 national honor societies.

Faculty/Classroom: 61% of faculty are male; 39%, female. All teach undergraduates. No introductory courses are taught by graduate students. The average class size in an introductory lecture is 26; in a laboratory, 20; and in a regular course, 14.

Admissions: 68% of the 2003-2004 applicants were accepted. The SAT I scores for the 2003-2004 freshman class were: Verbal--25% below 500, 49% between 500 and 599, 23% between 600 and 700, and 3% above 700; Math--25% below 500, 51% between 500 and 599, 21% between 600 and 700, and 3% above 700. The ACT scores were 27% below 21, 36% between 21 and 23, 23% between 24 and 26, 4% between 27 and 28, and 9% above 28. 39% of the current freshmen were in the top fifth of their class; 64% were in the top two fifths. 4 freshmen graduated first in their class.

Requirements: The SAT I or ACT is required. In addition, applicants must be graduates of an accredited secondary school or home school or have a GED and meet one of the following criteria: a composite SAT I score of at least 1000; a composite ACT score of at least 21; or a high school average of 2.5. High school courses should include 4 years of English, 3 years each of math and social studies, 2 to 3 years of a foreign language, and 2 years each of history and science. An essay is required. DBU requires applicants to be in the upper 50% of their class. A GPA of 2.5 is required. AP and CLEP credits are accepted. Important factors in the admissions decision are personality/intangible qualities, leadership record, and extracurricular activities record.

Procedure: Freshmen are admitted to all sessions. Entrance exams should be taken during the spring of the junior year and/or the fall of the senior year. The fall 2003 application fee was $25. Application deadlines are open. There is a rolling admissions plan. Applications are accepted on-line through the school's web site.

Transfer: 274 transfer students enrolled in 2002-2003. Applicants must submit an essay and transcripts of all previous college work and should have a cumulative GPA of 2.2 or higher. Students with fewer than 30 credit hours must furnish high school transcripts and ACT or SAT I scores. 32 of 126 credits required for the bachelor's degree must be completed at DBU.

Visiting: There are regularly scheduled orientations for prospective students, including a Patriot Weekend and Patriot Day conducted each fall and spring semester to provide information on financial aid and admissions. There are guides for informal visits and visitors may sit in on classes and stay overnight. To schedule a visit, contact the Undergraduate Admissions Office at (214) 333-5360 or *admiss@dbu.edu*.

Financial Aid: In 2003-2004, 93% of all full-time freshmen and 83% of continuing full-time students received some form of financial aid. 46% of full-time freshmen and 52% of continuing full-time students received need-based aid. The average freshman award was $11,846. Need-based scholarships or need-based grants averaged $378 ($4050 maximum); need-based self-help aid (loans and jobs) averaged $3219 ($5500 maximum); non-need-based athletic scholarships averaged $5917 ($11,500 maximum); other non-need-based awards and non-need-based scholarships averaged $4632 ($11,194 maximum); and outside benefits and scholarships and non-need-based loans averaged $6462 ($15,000 maximum). 20% of undergraduates work part time. Average annual earnings from campus work are $2880. The average financial indebtedness of the 2003 graduate was $18,857. The FAFSA and the university's own financial statement are required. The priority date for freshman financial aid applications for fall entry is March 15. The deadline for filing freshman financial aid applications for fall entry is May 15.

International Students: There are 190 international students enrolled. The school actively recruits these students. They must score 525 on the written TOEFL and also take the SAT I or the ACT.

Computers: The Center for Computer Literacy provides PCs and software packages that students can use for class assignments. All students may access the system. There are no time limits and no fees.

Graduates: From July 1, 2002 to June 30, 2003, 779 bachelor's degrees were awarded. The most popular majors were business administration (28%), multi/interdisciplinary studies (20%), and fine arts (9%). In an average class, 31% graduate in 4 years or less, 38% graduate in 5 years or less, and 41% graduate in 6 years or less. 201 companies recruited on campus in 2002-2003.

Admissions Contact: Anita Douris, Director of Undergraduate Admissions. A video is available. E-mail: *admiss@dbu.edu*
Web: *www.dbu.edu*

DEVRY UNIVERSITY/DALLAS
Irving, TX 75063-2439

D-2

(972) 929-5777
(800) 633-3879; Fax: (972) 929-2860

Full-time: 959 men, 345 women	**Faculty:** n/av
Part-time: 822 men, 374 women	**Ph.D.s:** n/av
Graduate: n/av	**Student/Faculty:** n/av
Year: semesters, summer session	**Tuition:** $10,640
Application Deadline: open	**Room & Board:** n/app
Freshman Class: n/av	
SAT I or ACT: n/av	**LESS COMPETITIVE**

DeVry University/Dallas, founded in 1969, is 1 of 67 DeVry University locations in the United States and Canada. The private institution offers career-oriented degree programs with hands-on training in various fields of business and technology. In addition to regional accreditation, DeVry has baccalaureate program accreditation with ABET. The library contains 16,500 volumes and 1800 audio/video tapes/CDs. Computerized library services include the card catalog, interlibrary loans, and database searching. Special learning facilities include a learning resource center and electronics and other labs. The 14-acre campus is in a suburban area 12 miles northwest of Dallas. There is one building.

Student Life: 42% of students are white; 32% African American; 19% Hispanic. The average age of all undergraduates is 26.

Housing: There are no residence halls. Housing referrals may be obtained through the Student Housing Office. There are private apartments, student-plan housing, and private rooms. All students commute. All students may keep cars.

Activities: There are no fraternities or sororities. There are 15 groups on campus, including computers, ethnic, international, newspaper, professional, religious, and social. Popular campus events include Thanksgiving Dinner, Club Fair Day, and Block Party.

Sports: There are 5 intramural sports for men and 5 for women.

Disabled Students: 90% of the campus is accessible. Wheelchair ramps, elevators, special parking, specially equipped rest rooms, lowered drinking fountains, and lowered telephones are available.

Services: Counseling and information services are available, as is tutoring in every subject.

Campus Safety and Security: Measures include security escort services, informal discussions, pamphlets/posters/films, emergency telephones, and lighted pathways/sidewalks. Daytime and evening security is provided until the building is closed. Security systems and motion detectors are utilized after business hours.

Programs of Study: DeVry confers the B.S. degree. Associate and master's degrees are also awarded. Bachelor's degrees are awarded in BIOLOGICAL SCIENCE (bioinformatics), BUSINESS (business administration and management), COMMUNICATIONS AND THE ARTS (telecommunications), COMPUTER AND PHYSICAL SCIENCE (information sciences and systems), ENGINEERING AND ENVIRONMENTAL DESIGN (biomedical engineering, computer engineering, electrical/electronics engineering technology, and technological management). Telecommunications and computer information systems are the largest.

Required: To graduate, students must achieve a GPA of at least 2.0 and satisfactorily complete all curriculum requirements. Course requirements vary according to program. All first-semester students take courses in business organization, computer applications, algebra, psychology, and student success strategies.

Special: Accelerated degree programs are offered in business administration, computer information systems, and telecommunications. Co-op programs, nondegree study, and evening and weekend classes are possible.

Faculty/Classroom: All teach undergraduates.

Requirements: Admissions requirements include graduation from a secondary school; the GED is also accepted. Applicants must pass the DeVry entrance exam or present satisfactory ACT or SAT I scores. An interview is required. CLEP credit is accepted.

Procedure: Freshmen are admitted to all sessions. There is a rolling admissions plan. There are early admissions and deferred admissions plans. Application deadlines are open. Application fee is $50. Applications are accepted on-line through *https://apply.embark.com/UGrad/DeVry/21.*

Transfer: 268 transfer students enrolled in a recent year. Applicants must submit official transcripts from all previous colleges attended indicating passing grades in all completed course work, demonstrate language skills proficiency with at least 24 completed semester hours, and present evidence of math proficiency by appropriate college-level credits. 25% of 48 to 154 credits required for the bachelor's degree must be completed at DeVry.

Visiting: There are regularly scheduled orientations for prospective students. There are guides for informal visits and visitors may sit in on classes. To schedule a visit, contact Vicki Carroll, New Student Coordinator at (972) 929-6777.

Financial Aid: In 2002-2003, 51% of all full-time freshmen and 73% of continuing full-time students received some form of financial aid. At least 50% of full-time freshmen and at least 72% of continuing full-time students received need-based aid. The average freshman award was $7433. Need-based scholarships or need-based grants averaged $4174; need-based self-help aid (loans and jobs) averaged $4868; and institutional non-need-based awards and non-need-based scholarships averaged $10,487. The FAFSA is required. The deadline for filing freshman financial aid applications is rolling.

International Students: There were 66 international students enrolled in a recent year. They must score 500 on the written TOEFL or 173 on the electronic version and also take the college's own entrance exam.

Computers: Lab facilities include PCs in stand-alone and network configurations, with access to the mainframe. LANs provide access to a wide range of applications software. Hard copy from the mainframe is provided through a local minicomputer and medium- and high-speed printers. Students in the computer information systems program may access the system during lab hours. The fee is $5 per hour. Students in the information technology program have DeVry-issued laptop computers.

Graduates: From July 1, 2002 to June 30, 2003, 444 bachelor's degrees were awarded. The most popular majors were computer information systems (68%), business (20%), and electronics engineering technology (11%). 67 companies recruited on campus in a recent year.

Admissions Contact: Chad Williams, Director of Admissions.
E-mail: *cwilliams@mail.dal.devry.edu* Web: *www.dal.devry.edu*

EAST TEXAS BAPTIST UNIVERSITY
Marshall, TX 75670-1498

E-2

(903) 923-2000
(800) 804-ETBU; Fax: (903) 923-2001

Full-time: 577 men, 618 women	**Faculty:** 72; IIB, --$
Part-time: 86 men, 73 women	**Ph.D.s:** 75%
Graduate: none	**Student/Faculty:** 17 to 1
Year: semesters, summer session	**Tuition:** $10,290
Application Deadline: open	**Room & Board:** $3624
Freshman Class: 742 applied, 407 accepted, 248 enrolled	
ACT: 21	**COMPETITIVE**

East Texas Baptist University, founded in 1912, is operated in association with the Baptist General Convention of Texas. The private liberal arts university offers undergraduate programs in the arts and sciences and professional areas, such as business, teacher education, nursing, and Christian ministry. There are 7 undergraduate schools. In addition to regional accreditation, ETBU has baccalaureate program accreditation with CCNE and NASM. The library contains 10,859 volumes, 9250 microform items, and 1216 audio/video tapes/CDs, and subscribes to 543 periodicals. Computerized library services include the card catalog, interlibrary loans, and database searching. Special learning facilities include a learning resource center, a math learning center, and a writing lab. The 200-acre campus is in a small town 35 miles west of Shreveport, Louisiana, and 140 miles east of Dallas. Including any residence halls, there are 26 buildings.

Student Life: 89% of undergraduates are from Texas. Students are from 26 states, 16 foreign countries, and Canada. 97% are from public schools. 80% are white; 13% African American. 85% are Protestant; 8% claim no religious affiliation. The average age of freshmen is 18; all undergraduates, 23. 37% do not continue beyond their first year; 41% remain to graduate.

Housing: 1090 students can be accommodated in college housing, which includes single-sex dorms, on-campus apartments, and married-student housing. On-campus housing is available on a first-come, first-served basis. 70% of students live on campus; of those, 40% remain on campus on weekends. Alcohol is not permitted. All students may keep cars.

Activities: 6% of men belong to 2 local and 1 national fraternity; 4% of women belong to 1 local and 1 national sorority. There are 35 groups on campus, including band, cheerleading, choir, chorale, chorus, computers, debate, drama, drill team, ethnic, honors, international, jazz band, literary magazine, marching band, newspaper, opera, pep band, political, professional, religious, social, social service, student government, and yearbook. Popular campus events include theater productions, Miss ETBU Pageant, and choral and band concerts.

Sports: There are 5 intercollegiate sports for men and 5 for women, and 4 intramural sports for men and 3 for women. Facilities include a baseball field, tennis courts, a weight room, a 1500-seat gym, a soccer field, a softball field, an intramural field, a practice gym, football practice fields, a football field, and a stadium.

Disabled Students: 95% of the campus is accessible. Wheelchair ramps, elevators, special parking, specially equipped rest rooms, special class scheduling, and lowered drinking fountains are available.

Services: Counseling and information services are available, as is tutoring in some subjects, including math and English. There is remedial math and writing.

Campus Safety and Security: Measures include 24-hour foot and vehicle patrol, self-defense education, informal discussions, and pamphlets/posters/films. There are emergency telephones and lighted pathways/sidewalks.

Programs of Study: ETBU confers B.A., B.S., B.A.S., B.B.A., B.M., B.S.E., and B.S.N. degrees. Associate degrees are also awarded. Bachelor's degrees are awarded in BIOLOGICAL SCIENCE (biology/biological science and environmental biology), BUSINESS (accounting, banking and finance, business administration and management, marketing management, and recreational facilities management), COMMUNICATIONS AND THE ARTS (dramatic arts, English, music, music performance, piano/organ, Spanish, speech/debate/rhetoric, and voice), COMPUTER AND PHYSICAL SCIENCE (chemistry, information sciences and systems, and mathematics), EDUCATION (athletic training, drama, education, elementary, English, mathematics, music, physical, science, secondary, and social studies), HEALTH PROFESSIONS (medical technology and nursing), SOCIAL SCIENCE (community psychology, history, ministries, physical fitness/movement, psychology, religion, religious music, and sociology). Religion and teacher education are the largest.

Required: To graduate, students must complete general education requirements, ranging from 34 hours for B.M. degrees to 48 hours for B.A. and 47 hours for B.S. degrees, and have a minimum GPA of 2.0. A total of 120 semester hours, with at least 30 in the major, is required, including 9 to 12 of English, 6 to 9 of religion, 3 to 6 of history, 3 to 6 of math, at least 3 of lab science, and 3 of physical activity.

Special: Internships are offered in social work, management, and computer information systems, as is study abroad in 5 countries and a Washington semester through the American Studies Program. There are 6 national honor societies and a freshman honors program.

Faculty/Classroom: 61% of faculty are male; 39%, female. All teach undergraduates and 20% do research. The average class size in an introductory lecture is 27; in a laboratory, 16; and in a regular course, 19.

Admissions: 55% of the 2003-2004 applicants were accepted. The ACT scores for the 2003-2004 freshman class were: 49% below 21, 26% between 21 and 23, 17% between 24 and 26, 4% between 27 and 28, and 4% above 28. 17% of freshmen graduated in the top 10% of their class.

Requirements: The ACT is required. In addition, applicants must be graduates of an accredited secondary school or have the GED, and must have composite scores of at least 18 on the ACT or 860 on the SAT I, or rank in the top 60% of their graduating class. Students not meeting these requirements may be admitted conditionally for 1 term or semester. An essay is required for all students. A GPA of 2.0 is required. AP and CLEP credits are accepted.

Procedure: Freshmen are admitted to all sessions. Entrance exams should be taken in the first semester of the senior year. There is a deferred admissions plan. Application deadlines are open. There is a rolling admission plan. The fall 2003 application fee was $25. Applications are accepted on-line through the university's web site.

Transfer: 132 transfer students enrolled in 2002-2003. Transfer students must have a minimum GPA of 2.0 and be eligible to return to the last college attended. 36 of a minimum of 120 credits required for the bachelor's degree must be completed at ETBU.

Visiting: There are regularly scheduled orientations for prospective students, including campus tours, meals, scholarship interviews/testing, faculty visits, class visits, sports/entertainment, and financial aid seminars. There are guides for informal visits and visitors may sit in on classes and stay overnight. To schedule a visit, contact the Campus Visit Coordinator.

Financial Aid: In 2003-2004, 93% of all full-time freshmen and 95% of continuing full-time students received some form of financial aid. 76% of full-time freshmen and 78% of continuing full-time students received need-based aid. The average freshman award was $10,210. The average financial indebtedness of the 2003 graduate was $9982. The FAFSA and the university's own financial statement are required. The deadline for filing freshman financial aid applications for fall entry is June 1.

International Students: The school actively recruits these students. They must score 500 on the written TOEFL or take the MELAB, and also take the ACT, scoring 18.

Computers: The mainframe is an Alpha 1200. There are 2 open computer labs with a total of 58 PCs. All computers have Internet and Web access; residence halls have campus network/Internet connections in each student room. There also are 9 PC kiosks throughout campus with web and Internet access. All students may access the system. At least one lab is available for use during each of the following hours: 8 A.M. to 11 P.M. Monday through Thursday; 8 A.M. to 5 P.M. Friday; 10 A.M. to 6 P.M. Saturday; and 1 P.M. to 5 P.M. Sunday. There are no time limits and no fees.

Graduates: From July 1, 2002 to June 30, 2003, 226 bachelor's degrees were awarded. The most popular majors were elementary education (33%), business (16%), and religion (12%). In an average class, 20% graduate in 4 years or less, 35% graduate in 5 years or less, and 40% graduate in 6 years or less. 60 companies recruited on campus in 2002-2003.

Admissions Contact: Vince Blankenship, Dean of Admissions and Marketing. A video is available. E-mail: *admissions@etbu.edu* Web: *www.etbu.edu*

HARDIN-SIMMONS UNIVERSITY
C-2
Abilene, TX 79698
(915) 670-1206
(800) 568-2692; Fax: (915) 670-1527

Full-time: 805 men, 865 women	**Faculty:** 115; IIA, --$
Part-time: 85 men, 145 women	**Ph.Ds:** 69%
Graduate: 170 men, 205 women	**Student/Faculty:** 15 to 1
Year: semesters, summer session	**Tuition:** $12,600
Application Deadline: open	**Room & Board:** $3724
Freshman Class: n/av	
SAT I or ACT: required	**COMPETITIVE**

Hardin-Simmons University, founded in 1891, is a private liberal arts institution affiliated with the Baptist General Convention of Texas. Figures in the above capsule and in this profile are approximate. There are 7 undergraduate schools and 1 graduate school. In addition to regional accreditation, HSU has baccalaureate program accreditation with ACBSP, CCNE, CSWE, and NASM. The 2 libraries contain 4607 volumes, 21,199 microform items, and 20,126 audio/video tapes/CDs, and subscribe to 4015 periodicals. Computerized library services include the card catalog, interlibrary loans, and database searching. Special learning facilities include an art gallery and an observatory. The 40-acre campus is in an urban area 150 miles west of Fort Worth. Including any residence halls, there are 37 buildings.

Student Life: 95% of undergraduates are from Texas. Students are from 22 states, 8 foreign countries, and Canada. 92% are from public schools. 86% are white. 81% are Protestant; 8% claim no religious affiliation; 8% unknown. The average age of freshmen is 18; all undergraduates, 21. 34% do not continue beyond their first year; 43% remain to graduate.

Housing: 1100 students can be accommodated in college housing, which includes single-sex dorms, off-campus apartments, and married-student housing. On-campus housing is available on a first-come, first-served basis. 55% of students commute. Alcohol is not permitted. All students may keep cars.

Activities: 6% of men belong to 4 local fraternities; 10% of women belong to 5 local sororities. There are 55 groups on campus, including art, band, cheerleading, choir, chorale, computers, debate, drama, drill team, ethnic, honors, international, literary magazine, marching band, musical theater, newspaper, opera, orchestra, pep band, photography, political, professional, radio and TV, religious, social, social service, student government, symphony, and yearbook. Popular campus events include theater productions, opera, concerts, and Western Heritage Day.

Sports: There are 6 intercollegiate sports for men and 5 for women, and 17 intramural sports for men and 17 for women. Facilities include a rodeo arena, 2 running ovals, a practice field, a football stadium, soccer and baseball fields, outdoor and indoor swimming pools, 6 bowling alleys, a fitness course, 4 basketball, 4 racquetball, 8 tennis, and 8 badminton/paddleball courts, and a Nautilus weight-lifting room.

Disabled Students: All of the campus is accessible. Wheelchair ramps, elevators, special parking, specially equipped rest rooms, special class scheduling, lowered drinking fountains, and an office to coordinate disability services are available.

Services: Counseling and information services are available, as is tutoring in most subjects. There is remedial math, reading, and writing, and free counseling services.

Campus Safety and Security: Measures include 24-hour foot and vehicle patrol, informal discussions, pamphlets/posters/films, and emergency telephones. There are lighted pathways/sidewalks.

Programs of Study: HSU confers B.A., B.S., B.B.A., B.Mus., B.S.N., and B. Behavioral Science degrees. Master's degrees are also awarded. Bachelor's degrees are awarded in BIOLOGICAL SCIENCE (biology/biological science), BUSINESS (accounting, banking and finance, business administration and management, and marketing/retailing/merchandising), COMMUNICATIONS AND THE ARTS (applied music, communications, English, French, German, music, Spanish, and theater management), COMPUTER AND PHYSICAL SCIENCE (chemistry, computer science, geology, mathematics, and physics), EDUCATION (art, business, early childhood, elementary, foreign languages, health, music, physical, reading, science, and secondary), HEALTH PROFESSIONS (nursing and speech pathology/audiology), SOCIAL SCIENCE (criminal justice, history, law enforcement and corrections, ministries, philosophy, physical fitness/movement, political science/government, psychology, religion, social science, social work, sociology, and theological studies). Elementary education, biology, and business are the strongest academically. Elementary education, biology, and communication are the largest.

Required: To graduate, students must complete a minimum of 124 semester hours with a minimum 2.0 GPA. At least 18 hours are required in the major and 42 hours in upper-division courses. Core courses that must be taken include 12 hours of social science, and 9 hours of English, 7 of natural science, 6 each of Bible and humanities, 4 of phys ed, 3 each of math and oral communication, and 2 of computer science. All students must satisfy chapel attendance requirements and must demonstrate proficiency in written English.

Special: Cross-registration may be arranged with Abilene Christian and McMurry Universities. HSU offers cooperative programs, internships, dual majors, credit by exam, nondegree study, and pass/fail options. Students may study abroad in England, Uzbekistan, Mexico, Austria, China, and Israel, where HSU is involved in an ongoing archeological excavation of early Christian sites. There are 14 national honor societies.

Faculty/Classroom: 62% of faculty are male; 38%, female. 90% teach undergraduates. No introductory courses are taught by graduate students. The average class size in an introductory lecture is 23; in a laboratory, 17; and in a regular course, 12.

Admissions: 8 freshmen graduated first in their class in a recent year.

Requirements: The SAT I or ACT is required. In addition, graduation from an accredited secondary school is required; a GED will be accepted. Applicants should submit an academic record of at least 16 units, distributed as follows: 3 units of English, 2 units each of math, science, and social studies, and 7 units of electives. HSU requires applicants to be in the upper 50% of their class. A GPA of 2.0 is required. AP and CLEP credits are accepted.

Procedure: Freshmen are admitted to all sessions. There is an early admissions plan. There is a rolling admissions plan. Application deadlines are open. The fall 2003 application fee was $25. Applications are accepted on-line at *hsutx.edu/admissions/app-instructions.htm*.

Transfer: 160 transfer students enrolled in 2002-2003. Applicants must submit official transcripts from all previous colleges. Students may petition to transfer up to 2 D grades if the overall GPA is 2.0 or higher. Students transferring from a 2-year college may receive credit for up to 66 semester hours of transferable courses. Applicants with fewer than 24 semester hours must submit a high school transcript and official report of ACT or SAT I scores. Students ineligible to continue at another institution are not eligible for regular admission to HSU. 31 of 124 credits required for the bachelor's degree must be completed at HSU.

Visiting: There are regularly scheduled orientations for prospective students, including spring and fall preview for prospective students. There are guides for informal visits and visitors may sit in on classes and stay overnight. To schedule a visit, contact Kimberley Howell, the Office of Enrollment Services at (915) 670-5814.

Financial Aid: In 2003-2004, 92% of all full-time freshmen and 88% of continuing full-time students received some form of financial aid. 79% of full-time freshmen and 80% of continuing full-time students received need-based aid. The average freshman award was $11,783. 20% of undergraduates work part time. Average annual earnings from campus work are $2400. The average financial indebtedness of the 2003 graduate was $20,393. The FAFSA is required. The deadline for filing freshman financial aid applications for fall entry is open.

International Students: There are 7 international students enrolled. They must score 550 on the written TOEFL and also take the SAT I or the ACT.

Computers: The mainframe is an IBM 7025-F40. More than 250 PCs are located in dorms, labs and classrooms across campus. HSU is a self-contained ISP with T1-speed Internet access. Web and e-mail services are available to students. Labs and many buildings are interconnected with Ethernet technology. All students may access the system. There are no time limits. The fee is $80.

Graduates: From July 1, 2002 to June 30, 2003, 238 bachelor's degrees were awarded. The most popular majors were elementary education (13%), communication (11%), and biology (7%). In an average class, 2% graduate in 3 years or less, 26% graduate in 4 years or less, 42% graduate in 5 years or less, and 45% graduate in 6 years or less. 10 companies recruited on campus in 2002-2003.

Admissions Contact: Shane Davidson, Associate, Vice President for Enrollment Services. A video is available. E-mail: *jdsd@hsutx.edu* Web: *hsutx.edu*

HOUSTON BAPTIST UNIVERSITY
Houston, TX 77074-3298

E-3

(281) 649-3211
(800) 969-3210; Fax: (281) 649-3217

Full-time: 516 men, 1113 women	Faculty: 115; IIA, --$
Part-time: 59 men, 178 women	Ph.D.s: 70%
Graduate: 148 men, 326 women	Student/Faculty: 14 to 1
Year: quarters, summer session	Tuition: $12,180
Application Deadline: open	Room & Board: $4725
Freshman Class: 896 applied, 559 accepted, 280 enrolled	
SAT I Verbal/Math: 540/535	ACT: 21 COMPETITIVE

Houston Baptist University, founded in 1960, is a private institution affiliated with the Baptist General Convention of Texas and offering undergraduate programs in nursing, arts and science, music, and business administration. There are 7 undergraduate and 4 graduate schools. In addition to regional accreditation, HBU has baccalaureate program accreditation with NLN. The library contains 307,790 volumes, 102,677 microform items, and 9313 audio/video tapes/CDs, and subscribes to 1005 periodicals. Computerized library services include the card catalog, interlibrary loans, and database searching. Special learning facilities include a learning resource center, TV station, a museum of decorative arts, and the Bible in America Museum. The 100-acre campus is in an urban area in southwest Houston. Including any residence halls, there are 17 buildings.

Student Life: 92% of undergraduates are from Texas. Students are from 19 states, 24 foreign countries, and Canada. 80% are from public schools. 47% are white; 20% African American; 14% Hispanic; 13% Asian American. 48% are Protestant; 14% Catholic. The average age of freshmen is 19; all undergraduates, 21.

Housing: 698 students can be accommodated in college housing, which includes single-sex dorms and on-campus apartments. On-campus housing is available on a first-come, first-served basis. 70% of students commute. Alcohol is not permitted. All students may keep cars.

Activities: 9% of men belong to 1 local and 2 national fraternities; 6% of women belong to 2 national sororities. There are 45 groups on campus, including art, band, cheerleading, choir, chorus, computers, debate, drama, ethnic, forensics, honors, international, jazz band, newspaper, opera, photography, political, professional, radio and TV, religious, social service, student government, symphony, and yearbook. Popular campus events include Ornogah Beauty Pageant, International Nite, and Spring Fling.

Sports: There are 2 intercollegiate sports for men and 3 for women, and 11 intramural sports for men and 10 for women. Facilities include volleyball, basketball, and tennis courts, an indoor track, and areas for track and field and soccer.

Disabled Students: 80% of the campus is accessible. Wheelchair ramps, elevators, special parking, and specially equipped rest rooms are available.

Services: There is remedial math and writing.

Campus Safety and Security: Measures include 24-hour foot and vehicle patrol, security escort services, emergency telephones, and lighted pathways/sidewalks.

Programs of Study: HBU confers B.A., B.S., B.B.A., B.M., and B.S.N. degrees. Associate and master's degrees are also awarded. Bachelor's degrees are awarded in BIOLOGICAL SCIENCE (biology/biological science), BUSINESS (accounting, banking and finance, business administration and management, business economics, and marketing/retailing/merchandising), COMMUNICATIONS AND THE ARTS (communications, English, French, music, music performance, music theory and composition, Spanish, and speech/debate/rhetoric), COMPUTER AND PHYSICAL SCIENCE (chemistry, information sciences and systems, mathematics, and physics), EDUCATION (art, early childhood, elementary, foreign languages, music, reading, secondary, special, and teaching English as a second/foreign language (TESOL/TEFOL)), HEALTH PROFESSIONS (nursing), SOCIAL SCIENCE (Christian studies, history, physical fitness/movement, political science/government, psychology, religious music, and sociology). Biology and chemistry (premedicine), education, and nursing are the strongest academically.

Required: To graduate, students must complete a minimum of 130 semester hours, including at least 48 semester hours of upper-level courses. They must complete courses in Christianity, written and oral communications, math, lab science, computer, kinetics, social and behavioral sciences, humanities, and fine arts. No grade below "C" within majors and program requirements and a cumulative GPA of 2.0 is required. Proficiency is required in reading, wiritng, computer, communication, and math. Spiritual Life Program participation is also a graduation requirement. Other requirements vary by program.

Special: HBU offers internships through its academic colleges, study abroad, B.A.-B.S. degrees, and dual majors in most areas, work-study programs, credit for military experience, and pass/fail options. There is a freshman honors program.

Faculty/Classroom: 52% of faculty are male; 48%, female. 97% teach undergraduates. No introductory courses are taught by graduate students. The average class size in an introductory lecture is 20; in a laboratory, 20; and in a regular course, 15.

Admissions: 62% of the 2003-2004 applicants were accepted. The SAT I scores for the 2003-2004 freshman class were: Verbal--30% below 500, 46% between 500 and 599, 22% between 600 and 700, and 2% above 700; Math--31% below 500, 42% between 500 and 599, 23% between 600 and 700, and 4% above 700. The ACT scores were 48% below 21, 28% between 21 and 23, 12% between 24 and 26, 7% between 27 and 28, and 5% above 28.

Requirements: The SAT I or ACT is required, with a recommended minimum composite score of 1010 (480 verbal) on the SAT I or 20 on the ACT. Applicants must be graduates of an accredited secondary school or have the GED. AP and CLEP credits are accepted. Important factors in the admissions decision are recommendations by school officials, personality/intangible qualities, and advanced placement or honor courses.

Procedure: Freshmen are admitted to all sessions. Entrance exams should be taken in the fall of the senior year. There are early decision and early admissions plans and a rolling admission plan. Application deadlines are open. Application fee is $25. Applications are accepted on-line through *www.hbu.edu*.

Transfer: 222 transfer students enrolled in 2002-2003. Applicants with fewer than 30 semester hours earned must submit high school and college transcripts and SAT I or ACT scores. All students must have a minimum 2.0 GPA. 32 of 130 credits required for the bachelor's degree must be completed at HBU.

Visiting: There are guides for informal visits and visitors may sit in on classes and stay overnight. To schedule a visit, contact the Office of Admissions at (281) 649-3211 or *unadm@hbu.edu*.

Financial Aid: In 2003-2004, all full-time freshmen and 64% of continuing full-time students received some form of financial aid. 86% of full-time freshmen and 54% of continuing full-time students received need-based aid. The average freshman award was $14,239. Need-based scholarships or need-based grants averaged $1726 ($2837 maximum); need-based self-help aid (loans and jobs) averaged $4607 ($6569 maximum); non-need-based athletic scholarships averaged $14,139 ($14,139 maximum); and other non-need-based awards and non-need-based scholarships averaged $765 ($1250 maximum). 11% of undergraduates work part time. Average annual earnings from campus work are $985. The average financial indebtedness of the 2003 graduate was $17,642. HBU is a member of CSS. The FAFSA and the college's own financial statement are required. The priority date for freshman financial aid applications for fall entry is March 1. The deadline for filing freshman financial aid applications for fall entry is April 1.

International Students: There are 97 international students enrolled. The school actively recruits these students. They must score 550 on the written TOEFL or 213 on the electronic version and also take the SAT I or the ACT.

Computers: There are PCs available to students. All students may access the system. There are no time limits and no fees.

Graduates: From July 1, 2002 to June 30, 2003, 354 bachelor's degrees were awarded. The most popular majors were business administration (19%), biology (19%), and christianity (10%). In an average class, 27% graduate in 4 years or less, 45% graduate in 5 years or less, and 49% graduate in 6 years or less.

Admissions Contact: David Melton, Director of Admissions.
E-mail: *unadm@hbu.edu* Web: *www.hbu.edu*

HOWARD PAYNE UNIVERSITY
Brownwood, TX 76801-2794

C-3

(325) 649-8027
(800) 880-4478; Fax: (325) 649-8901

Full-time: 534 men, 547 women	**Faculty:** 70; II B, --$
Part-time: 168 men, 136 women	**Ph.D.s:** 56%
Graduate: none	**Student/Faculty:** 15 to 1
Year: semesters, summer session	**Tuition:** $11,150
Application Deadline: August 1	**Room & Board:** $4026
Freshman Class: 904 applied, 717 accepted	
SAT I Verbal/Math: 507/505	**ACT:** 20 **COMPETITIVE**

Howard Payne University, founded in 1889 and affiliated with the Baptist General Convention of Texas, offers undergraduate programs in the arts and sciences, business administration, education, Christianity, music, and social sciences. There are 6 undergraduate schools. In addition to regional accreditation, HPU has baccalaureate program accreditation with CSWE, IACBE, and NASM. The library contains 78,825 volumes and 279,911 microform items, and subscribes to 1017 periodicals. Computerized library services include the card catalog, interlibrary loans, database searching, and Internet access. Special learning facilities include a radio station, children's literature center, audio production facility, TV production studio, and video editing facility. The 29-acre campus is in a small town 120 miles southwest of Dallas/Fort Worth. Including any residence halls, there are 31 buildings.

Student Life: 98% of undergraduates are from Texas. Students are from 16 states and 6 foreign countries. 95% are from public schools. 73% are white; 15% Hispanic. 80% are Protestant; 14% claim no religious affiliation. The average age of freshmen is 18; all undergraduates, 22. 40% do not continue beyond their first year; 33% remain to graduate.

Housing: 748 students can be accommodated in college housing, which includes single-sex dorms, on-campus apartments, and married-student housing. On-campus housing is available on a lottery system for upperclassmen. 56% of students commute. Alcohol is not permitted. All students may keep cars.

Activities: 12% of men belong to 2 local and 1 national fraternity; 18% of women belong to 4 local and 1 national sorority. There are 38 groups on campus, including art, band, choir, chorus, drama, drill team, ethnic, honors, jazz band, literary magazine, marching band, musical theater, newspaper, photography, professional, radio and TV, religious, social, social service, student government, and yearbook. Popular campus events include Christian Concerts and College Preview Weekends.

Sports: There are 7 intercollegiate sports for men and 6 for women, and 5 intramural sports for men and 5 for women. Facilities include an 8000-seat stadium and an 800-seat auditorium; a remodeled wellness center with basketball and volleyball courts, an indoor walking track, and free weights and exercise equipment; tennis and sand volleyball courts; a practice field; a student union; and nearby baseball and softball parks.

Disabled Students: 90% of the campus is accessible. Wheelchair ramps, elevators, special parking, specially equipped rest rooms, special class scheduling, and lowered drinking fountains are available.

Services: Counseling and information services are available, as is tutoring in some subjects, including math and English. There is remedial math, reading, and writing. A writing lab and computer lab are available for English, math, and computer science.

Campus Safety and Security: Measures include informal discussions, pamphlets/posters/films, emergency telephones, and lighted pathways/sidewalks. In addition, there are 12-hour foot patrols, monthly dorm meetings, 2 security seminars for the entire campus, and 24-hour telephone availability with on-duty officers carrying cellular phones.

Programs of Study: HPU confers B.A., B.S., B.A.A.S., B.B.A., and B.M. degrees. Associate degrees are also awarded. Bachelor's degrees are awarded in BIOLOGICAL SCIENCE (biology/biological science), BUSINESS (accounting and business administration and management), COMMUNICATIONS AND THE ARTS (art, communications, dramatic arts, English, multimedia, music, and Spanish), COMPUTER AND PHYSICAL SCIENCE (chemistry, computer science, and mathematics), EDUCATION (athletic training, elementary, secondary, and teaching English as a second/foreign language (TESOL/TEFOL)), ENGINEERING AND ENVIRONMENTAL DESIGN (occupational safety and health), HEALTH PROFESSIONS (exercise science), SOCIAL SCIENCE (Christian studies, history, liberal arts/general studies, political science/government, psychology, social work, and sociology). Biology, chemistry, and political science are the strongest academically. Business management, elementary education, and exercise and sports science are the largest.

Required: To graduate, students must complete a minimum of 128 credit hours, 49 in general education courses, 30 to 36 in the major, and 18 to 24 in a minor, plus electives. A minimum 2.0 GPA is required. The general education core includes Bible, English, social science, computer science, fine arts, phys ed, lab science, speech, and math courses. Requirements for students not obtaining the B.A. or B.S. vary. All students must complete 6 semester credits of chapel/convocation attendance.

Special: Cross-registration is offered with several hospitals, and internships are available in many fields. HPU offers credit for experience for B.A.A.S. candidates only, study abroad in Israel and England, pass/fail options, and work-study programs. Special programs include the Douglas MacArthur Academy of Freedom, an interdisciplinary honors program in the social sciences; a chemistry honors program; and a provisional program for underprepared students. There are 4 national honor societies, a freshman honors program, and 1 departmental honors program.

Faculty/Classroom: 70% of faculty are male; 30%, female. All teach undergraduates. The average class size in an introductory lecture is 22; in a laboratory, 20; and in a regular course, 18.

Admissions: 79% of the 2003-2004 applicants were accepted. The SAT I scores for the 2003-2004 freshman class were: Verbal--49% below 500, 32% between 500 and 599, 18% between 600 and 700, and 1% above 700; Math--47% below 500, 38% between 500 and 599, 14% between 600 and 700, and 1% above 700. The ACT scores were 53% below 21, 24% between 21 and 23, 18% between 24 and 26, 3% between 27 and 28, and 2% above 28. 33% of the current freshmen were in the top fifth of their class; 55% were in the top two fifths. 3 freshmen graduated first in their class.

Requirements: The SAT I or ACT is required. In addition, applicants must be graduates of an accredited secondary school or have a GED. It is recommended that they have completed 4 credits of English, 3 of math including algebra I, 2.5 of social studies, 2 of science, 1.5 of phys ed, and 1 each of technology applications and a science/social studies elective, along with courses in economics, health, and speech; the remaining credits should be earned in courses approved by the Texas Board of Education. Graduates of high schools or home study programs that are not accredited by a regional or state accrediting agency will have their work reviewed by the admissions committee on an individual basis. A GPA of 3.0 is required. AP and CLEP credits are accepted. Important factors in the admissions decision are recommendations by school officials, leadership record, and personality/intangible qualities.

Procedure: Freshmen are admitted to all sessions. Entrance exams should be taken during the senior year. There is an early admissions plan and a rolling admissions plan. Applications should be filed by August 1 for fall entry and January 1 for spring entry, along with a $25 fee. Notification is sent on a rolling basis.

Transfer: 67 transfer students enrolled in 2002-2003. Transfer students must be able to return to the university they are leaving and submit official transcripts from all previously attended colleges/universities. Students younger than 21 with fewer than 12 semester hours must submit the SAT I or ACT scores. The same GPA per number of hours attempted is required of transfers as for continuing HPU students. 32 of 128 credits required for the bachelor's degree must be completed at HPU.

Visiting: There are regularly scheduled orientations for prospective students, including college preview weekends in the fall and spring. There are guides for informal visits and visitors may sit in on classes and stay overnight. To schedule a visit, contact the Enrollment Services Office at (915) 649-8020 or *enroll@hputx.edu.*

Financial Aid: In a recent year, 80% of all full-time freshmen and 90% of continuing full-time students received some form of financial aid. 55% of full-time freshmen and 60% of continuing full-time students received need-based aid. The average freshman award was $7500. 65% of undergraduates work part time. Average annual earnings from campus work are $2000. The average financial indebtedness of a recent graduate was $16,500. The FAFSA is required. The deadline for filing freshman financial aid applications for fall entry is March 1.

International Students: There are 11 international students enrolled. The school actively recruits these students. They must score 500 on the written TOEFL or 173 on the electronic version. A TOEFL score is not required for International students entering the English as a Second Language (ESL) program. Students must also take the SAT I or ACT. Students must score 19 on the ACT or 830 on the SAT I for unconditional admission; otherwise, a provisional program may be available.

Computers: The mainframe is a DEC Alpha Server. 11 computer labs, with a total of approximately 225 computers, are available to all students along with 35 computers on a 286 Novell Local Area Network. All students may access the system 24 hours a day in 3 labs in the dorms and 8 A.M. to 10 P.M., Monday through Friday in the Instructional Building labs. There are no time limits and no fees.

Graduates: From July 1, 2002 to June 30, 2003, 224 bachelor's degrees were awarded. The most popular majors were education (24%), business management (16%), and Christian studies (13%). In an average class, 2% graduate in 3 years or less, 22% graduate in 4 years or less, 33% graduate in 5 years or less, and 35% graduate in 6 years or less. Of the 2002 graduating class, 20% were enrolled in graduate school within 6 months of graduation.

Admissions Contact: Cheryl Mangrum, Coordinator of Admissions Services. E-mail: *enroll@hputx.edu* Web: *www.hputx.edu*

HUSTON-TILLOTSON COLLEGE   D-3
Austin, TX 78702
(512) 505-3027
(877) 505-3026; Fax: (512) 505-3192

Full-time: 252 men, 298 women	**Faculty:** 39
Part-time: 52 men, 64 women	**Ph.D.s:** 64%
Graduate: none	**Student/Faculty:** 14 to 1
Year: semesters, summer session	**Tuition:** $8190
Application Deadline: March 1	**Room & Board:** $6042
Freshman Class: 332 applied, 325 accepted, 175 enrolled	
SAT I Verbal/Math: 400/400	**ACT:** 16 NONCOMPETITIVE

Huston-Tillotson College, formed in 1952 by the merger of Tillotson College and Samuel Huston College (both founded in the mid-1870s) is a private liberal arts institution affiliated with the United Church of Christ and the United Methodist Church. The library contains 88,455 volumes, 69,216 microform items, and 8753 audio/video tapes/CDs, and subscribes to 2353 periodicals. Computerized library services include the card catalog, interlibrary loans, database searching, and Internet access. Special learning facilities include a learning resource center. The 23-acre campus is in an urban area in downtown Austin. Including any residence halls, there are 12 buildings.

Student Life: 94% of undergraduates are from Texas. Students are from 14 states and 14 foreign countries. 85% are from public schools. 73% are African American; 10% Hispanic. 69% are Protestant; 9% Catholic. The average age of freshmen is 19; all undergraduates, 22. 50% do not continue beyond their first year; 20% remain to graduate.

Housing: 424 students can be accommodated in college housing, which includes single-sex dorms. On-campus housing is guaranteed for all 4 years. 63% of students commute. Alcohol is not permitted. All students may keep cars.

Activities: 3% of men belong to 4 national fraternities; 8% of women belong to 4 local and 4 national sororities. There are 17 groups on campus, including band, cheerleading, choir, chorus, drama, drill team, honors, international, jazz band, newspaper, professional, radio and TV, religious, social, social service, student government, and yearbook. Popular campus events include Charter Day, Alumni Weekend, and Miss UNCF Contest.

Sports: There are 3 intercollegiate sports for men and 3 for women, and 2 intramural sports for men and 2 for women. Facilities include an 800-seat gym and soccer and baseball fields.

Disabled Students: 80% of the campus is accessible. Wheelchair ramps, elevators, special parking, and specially equipped rest rooms are available.

Services: Counseling and information services are available, as is tutoring in every subject. There is remedial math, reading, and writing.

Campus Safety and Security: Measures include 24-hour foot and vehicle patrol, security escort services, and lighted pathways/sidewalks.

Programs of Study: HTC confers B.A. and B.S. degrees. Bachelor's degrees are awarded in BIOLOGICAL SCIENCE (biology/biological science), BUSINESS (business administration and management and marketing/retailing/merchandising), COMMUNICATIONS AND THE ARTS

(communications, English, and music), COMPUTER AND PHYSICAL SCIENCE (chemistry, computer science, and mathematics), EDUCATION (education, elementary, and physical), SOCIAL SCIENCE (political science/government and sociology). Biology, computer science, and education are the strongest academically. Business studies, computer science, and education are the largest.

Required: All students must complete 120 credit hours, including 54 in the general education required curriculum and 30 in the major, with a minimum GPA of 2.0. Core requirements include 18 hours of English and foreign languages, 9 each of math/computer science and social sciences, 8 of natural science, 6 of phys ed and health, 3 of philosophy, and 1 of psychology.

Special: The college offers co-op programs, internships, work-study programs, and dual majors. A 3-2 engineering degree with Prairie View A&M University is also available. There are 4 national honor societies, a freshman honors program, and 1 departmental honors program.

Faculty/Classroom: 48% of faculty are male; 52%, female. All teach undergraduates and 4% do research. The average class size in an introductory lecture is 16; in a laboratory, 16; and in a regular course, 20.

Admissions: 98% of the 2003-2004 applicants were accepted. The SAT I scores for the 2003-2004 freshman class were: Verbal--89% below 500, 9% between 500 and 599, and 2% between 600 and 700; Math--86% below 500, 12% between 500 and 599, and 2% between 600 and 700. The ACT scores were 90% below 21, 7% between 21 and 23, 2% between 24 and 26, and 1% between 27 and 28. 12% of the current freshmen were in the top fifth of their class; 34% were in the top two fifths.

Requirements: The SAT I or ACT is required, with a minimum composite score of 900 on the SAT I or 18 on the ACT. Applicants should be high school graduates with 18 academic credits, including 4 in English, 3 in math, 2 each in science and social studies, and 1 in phys ed. A GPA of 2.0 is required. AP and CLEP credits are accepted. Important factors in the admissions decision are advanced placement or honor courses, extracurricular activities record, and parents or siblings attending the school.

Procedure: Freshmen are admitted to all sessions. There is an early admissions plan and a rolling admissions plan. Applications should be filed by March 1 for fall entry, October 1 for spring entry, and March 1 for summer entry, along with a $25 fee. Notification is sent on a rolling basis. Applications are accepted on computer disk and on-line through the school's web site.

Transfer: 121 transfer students enrolled in a recent year. Applicants must submit transcripts from all colleges or universities attended and must have an overall GPA of 2.0. Students with fewer than 15 credit hours must meet freshman entrance requirements. 30 credits of 120 required for the bachelor's degree must be completed at HTC.

Visiting: There are regularly scheduled orientations for prospective students. There are guides for informal visits and visitors may sit in on classes and stay overnight. To schedule a visit, contact the Dean of Enrollment Services.

Financial Aid: HTC is a member of CSS. The FAFSA and the college's own financial statement are required. The deadline for filing freshman financial aid applications for fall entry is March 15.

International Students: There were 61 international students enrolled in a recent year. They must score 500 on the written TOEFL and also take the SAT I or the ACT.

Computers: The mainframe is an AST Premium SE 4-50 Model 3. PCs are available to all students. All students may access the system during lab hours. There are no time limits. The fee is $15.

Admissions Contact: Bronté D. Jones, Dean of Enrollment Services. E-mail: *bdjones@htc.edu* Web: *www.htc.edu*

JARVIS CHRISTIAN COLLEGE   E-2
Hawkins, TX 75765
(903) 769-5730
(800) 292-9517; Fax: (903) 769-1282

Full-time: 258 men, 386 women	**Faculty:** 41
Part-time: 3 men, 7 women	**Ph.D.s:** 54%
Graduate: none	**Student/Faculty:** 16 to 1
Year: semesters, summer session	**Tuition:** $5550
Application Deadline: August 1	**Room & Board:** $3485
Freshman Class: n/av	
SAT I: recommended	**ACT:** required
	NONCOMPETITIVE

Jarvis Christian College, founded in 1912, is a private liberal arts institution affiliated with the Disciples of Christ. Tuition figures in the above capsule are approximate. The library contains 7834 volumes, 4339 microform items, and 2431 audio/video tapes/CDs, and subscribes to 297 periodicals. Computerized library services include the card catalog, interlibrary loans, and database searching. Special learning facilities include a learning resource center, planetarium, and archives of the Black Disciples in Texas. The 243-acre campus is in a rural area 100 miles southeast of Dallas. Including any residence halls, there are 17 buildings.

Student Life: 89% of undergraduates are from Texas. Students are from 14 states, 9 foreign countries, and Canada. 99% are from public schools. 95% are African American. 78% are Protestant; 21% claim no religious affiliation. The average age of freshmen is 19; all undergraduates, 20. 60% do not continue beyond their first year; 12% remain to graduate.

Housing: 750 students can be accommodated in college housing, which includes single-sex dorms, on-campus apartments, and married-student housing. In addition, there are honors houses. On-campus housing is guaranteed for all 4 years. 88% of students live on campus; of those, 50% remain on campus on weekends. Alcohol is not permitted. All students may keep cars.

Activities: 5% of men belong to 4 national fraternities; 10% of women belong to 4 national sororities. There are 46 groups on campus, including cheerleading, choir, chorale, drama, drill team, honors, newspaper, political, professional, religious, social, and student government. Popular campus events include Miss/Mr. Jarvis Coronation, Hall of Fame Weekend, and Christmas Concert.

Sports: There are 4 intercollegiate sports for men and 4 for women, and 11 intramural sports for men and 11 for women. Facilities include 2 basketball gyms, a pool, tennis courts, volleyball courts, a soccer field, billiards, a flag football field, and a softball/baseball diamond.

Disabled Students: 46% of the campus is accessible. Wheelchair ramps, special parking, specially equipped rest rooms, special class scheduling, and lowered drinking fountains are available.

Services: Counseling and information services are available, as is tutoring in most subjects. There is remedial math, reading, and writing.

Campus Safety and Security: Measures include 24-hour foot and vehicle patrol, self-defense education, security escort services, and informal discussions. There are pamphlets/posters/films and lighted pathways/sidewalks.

Programs of Study: Jarvis confers B.A., B.S., and B.B.A. degrees. Bachelor's degrees are awarded in BIOLOGICAL SCIENCE (biology/biological science), COMMUNICATIONS AND THE ARTS (English), COMPUTER AND PHYSICAL SCIENCE (chemistry, computer science, and mathematics), EDUCATION (elementary, music, reading, secondary, and special), HEALTH PROFESSIONS (premedicine), SOCIAL SCIENCE (criminal justice, history, religion, and sociology). Sociology, business, and computer science are the strongest academically. Business administration is the largest.

Required: A 54-credit general education requirement includes at least 30 hours in the major, plus courses in English, literature, math, religion, science, speech, social science, health, and phys ed. Other graduation requirements include a minimum 2.0 GPA, at least 124 credit hours, math and writing proficiencies, and satisfactory scores on the sophomore comprehensive exam and on the GRE.

Special: Jarvis offers co-op and work-study programs, internships, student-designed majors, and a general studies degree. Cross-registration is offered with members of the TADC consortium. Also available are the Brookhaven National Laboratory Semester Program, the UNCF Premedical Summer Program with Fisk University, and the Biomedical Sciences Program with Meharry Medical College. A 3-2 engineering degree is available with the University of Texas at Arlington and a 3-2 nursing degree with the University of Texas at Tyler. There are 4 national honor societies, a freshman honors program, and 2 departmental honors programs.

Faculty/Classroom: 61% of faculty are male; 39%, female. All teach undergraduates and 10% both teach and do research. The average class size in an introductory lecture is 30; in a laboratory, 16; and in a regular course, 16.

Admissions: 9% of the current freshmen were in the top fifth of their class; 12% were in the top two fifths.

Requirements: The ACT is required and the SAT I is also accepted. In addition, applicants should graduate from an accredited secondary school with 16 academic credits, including 3 each in English and social science, 2 in math, and 1 in science. The GED is accepted. Graduates of nonaccredited high schools are given conditional admission. A GPA of 2.0 is required. AP and CLEP credits are accepted. Important factors in the admissions decision are parents or siblings attending the school, recommendations by alumni, and advanced placement or honor courses.

Procedure: Freshmen are admitted fall, spring, and summer. Entrance exams should be taken before entrance or during orientation week. Early decision applications should be filed by April 1; regular applications, by August 1 for fall entry, December 1 for spring entry, and May 1 for summer entry, along with a $25 fee. The college accepts all applicants. Notification is sent on a rolling basis.

Transfer: 34 transfer students enrolled in a recent year. Applicants must submit official transcripts from all schools of higher education attended and provide proof of honorable dismissal from the most recent one. 30 of 124 credits required for the bachelor's degree must be completed at Jarvis.

Visiting: There are regularly scheduled orientations for prospective students, including classroom visits, a tour of the campus, and review of the orientation guidebook. There are guides for informal visits and visitors may sit in on classes and stay overnight. To schedule a visit, contact the Office of Admissions.

Financial Aid: The average freshman award was $8812. Need-based scholarships or need-based grants averaged $7877 ($10,615 maximum); need-based self-help aid (loans and jobs) averaged $2625 ($4185 maximum); non-need-based athletic scholarships averaged $5800 ($10,615 maximum); and other non-need-based awards and non-need-based scholarships averaged $800 ($8000 maximum). 6% of undergraduates work part time. Average annual earnings from campus work are $1560. The average financial indebtedness of a recent graduate was $9635. Jarvis is a member of CSS. The FAFSA or FFS and the college's own financial statement are required. Check with the school for current deadlines.

International Students: In a recent year, there were 19 international students enrolled. They must score 500 on the written TOEFL or 173 on the electronic version and also take the ACT.

Computers: The mainframe is an IBM AS400. The computer labs comprise 197 computers linked to the Internet. All students may access the system 8 A.M. to 10 P.M. There are no time limits. The fee is $250 per year.

Graduates: In a recent year, 86 bachelor's degrees were awarded. The most popular majors were business (20%), criminal justice (14%), and biology (14%). In an average class, 8% graduate in 4 years or less, 23% graduate in 5 years or less, and 24% graduate in 6 years or less. 85 companies recruited on campus in a recent year. Of a recent year's graduating class, 10% were enrolled in graduate school within 6 months of graduation and all were employed.

Admissions Contact: Joan Williams, Director. A video is available. E-mail: *mary_mckinney@jarvis.edu* Web: *www.jarvis.edu*

LAMAR UNIVERSITY

E-3

Beaumont, TX 77710   (409) 880-8888; Fax: (409) 880-8463

Full-time: 2325 men, 2825 women	**Faculty:** 303; IIA, --$
Part-time: 1310 men, 1955 women	**Ph.D.s:** 48%
Graduate: 255 men, 305 women	**Student/Faculty:** 15 to 1
Year: semesters, summer session	**Tuition:** $2615 ($9010)
Application Deadline: see profile	**Room & Board:** $4200
Freshman Class: n/av	
SAT I or ACT: required	**LESS COMPETITIVE**

Lamar University-Beaumont, founded in 1923, is part of the Lamar University system. The university offers undergraduate degrees in arts and sciences, business, education, engineering, fine arts, communications, health and behavioral science, and technical arts. Figures in the above capsule and in this profile are approximate. There are 7 undergraduate and 5 graduate schools. In addition to regional accreditation, LU has baccalaureate program accreditation with AACSB, ABET, CSWE, NASM, and NCATE. The library contains 900,000 volumes, and subscribes to 2800 periodicals. Computerized library services include the card catalog, interlibrary loans, and database searching. Special learning facilities include a learning resource center, art gallery, and radio station. The 200-acre campus is in an urban area 90 miles east of Houston. Including any residence halls, there are 90 buildings.

Student Life: Students are from 39 states, 61 foreign countries, and Canada. 95% are from public schools. 79% are white; 16% African American. The average age of freshmen is 19; all undergraduates, 25. 40% do not continue beyond their first year; 19% remain to graduate.

Housing: 1700 students can be accommodated in college housing, which includes dorms, on-campus apartments, fraternity houses, and sorority houses. In addition, there are special-interest houses. On-campus housing is guaranteed for all 4 years. 91% of students commute. Alcohol is not permitted. All students may keep cars.

Activities: 5% of men belong to 11 national fraternities; 5% of women belong to 7 national sororities. There are 120 groups on campus, including art, band, cheerleading, choir, chorale, chorus, computers, dance, drama, ethnic, film, honors, international, jazz band, literary magazine, marching band, musical theater, newspaper, opera, orchestra, pep band, photography, political, professional, radio and TV, religious, social, social service, student government, and symphony. Popular campus events include Springfest, Birdfeed, Love Lamar Week, and Honors Brunch.

Sports: There are 7 intercollegiate sports for men and 6 for women, and 15 intramural sports for men and 15 for women. Facilities include a 10,000-seat multipurpose facility for basketball and other sports; a student center with games areas and a video lounge; a gym; an indoor/outdoor pool; a track; and a 17,000-seat stadium.

Disabled Students: All of the campus is accessible. Wheelchair ramps, elevators, special parking, specially equipped rest rooms, special class scheduling, lowered drinking fountains, and lowered telephones are available.

Services: Counseling and information services are available, as is tutoring in some subjects, including math and English. There is a reader service for the blind and remedial math, reading, and writing.

Campus Safety and Security: Measures include 24-hour foot and vehicle patrol, self-defense education, informal discussions, and pamphlets/posters/films. There are lighted pathways/sidewalks.

Programs of Study: LU confers B.A., B.S., B.A.A.S., B.B.A., B.F.A., B.G.S., B.Mus., and B.S.W. degrees. Associate, master's, and doctoral degrees are also awarded. Bachelor's degrees are awarded in BIOLOGICAL SCIENCE (biology/biological science), BUSINESS (accounting, business administration and management, business economics, business law, marketing/retailing/merchandising, and personnel management), COMMUNICATIONS AND THE ARTS (advertising, communications, design, dramatic arts, English, fine arts, French, music, Spanish, and speech/debate/rhetoric), COMPUTER AND PHYSICAL SCIENCE (chemistry, computer programming, computer science, geology, information sciences and systems, mathematics, and physics), EDUCATION (art, early childhood, elementary, foreign languages, health, music, science, secondary, and special), ENGINEERING AND ENVIRONMENTAL DESIGN (chemical engineering, civil engineering, electrical/electronics engineering, industrial engineering, industrial engineering technology, and mechanical engineering), HEALTH PROFESSIONS (medical laboratory technology, nursing, occupational therapy, pharmacy, physical therapy, predentistry, premedicine, and speech pathology/audiology), SOCIAL SCIENCE (criminal justice, economics, family/consumer studies, history, political science/government, prelaw, psychology, public administration, social science, social work, and sociology). Engineering is the strongest academically. Arts and sciences are the largest.

Required: To graduate, all students must complete 124 to 132 total credit hours, with 30 hours in the major. Required courses include 12 hours of English, 6 hours each of electives, political science, and American history, and 4 hours each of lab science or math and physical activity and/or marching band and/or ROTC. Students must have a minimum 2.0 GPA.

Special: The university offers internships in social work, work-study programs, B.A.-B.S. degrees, a dual major in biochemistry, the general studies degree, credit for experience, nondegree study, and pass/fail options. There are 2 national honor societies, including Phi Beta Kappa, and a freshman honors program.

Faculty/Classroom: 58% of faculty are male; 42%, female. All teach undergraduates. The average class size in an introductory lecture is 50; in a laboratory, 25; and in a regular course, 24.

Requirements: The SAT I or ACT is required, with a minimum composite score of 850 on SAT I or 20 on the ACT. SAT II: Subject tests in math are required for engineering and physical science majors. Applicants must be graduates of an accredited secondary school or have a GED certificate and must have completed 4 credits of English, 3 of math, 2 of science, and 2 1/2 of history. LU requires applicants to be in the upper 50% of their class. A GPA of 2.0 is required. AP and CLEP credits are accepted. Important factors in the admissions decision are advanced placement or honor courses, evidence of special talent, and leadership record.

Procedure: Freshmen are admitted to all sessions. Entrance exams should be taken in the fall of the senior year. There is a rolling admissions plan. Check with the school for current deadlines and fee. Notification is sent on a rolling basis.

Transfer: 483 transfer students enrolled in 2002-2003. Applicants must have a minimum 2.0 GPA and at least 18 credit hours earned. 30 of 132 credits required for the bachelor's degree must be completed at LU.

Visiting: There are regularly scheduled orientations for prospective students. There are guides for informal visits. To schedule a visit, contact the Admissions Office.

Financial Aid: LU is a member of CSS. The CSS Profile and the college's own financial statement are required. Check with the school for current deadlines.

International Students: They must score 500 on the written TOEFL and also take the SAT I or the ACT, scoring 800.

Computers: The mainframe is a Honeywell DPS 8/49. There are 300 AT&T, IBM, Compaq, Sperry, and Apple PCs available throughout the campus. All students may access the system. There are no time limits. The fee is $30 per semester. It is strongly recommended that all students have a personal computer.

Admissions Contact: James Rush, Director of Academic Services. A video is available. E-mail: admissions@hal.lamar.edu Web: lamar.edu

---

LETOURNEAU UNIVERSITY
Longview, TX 75607

E-2

(903) 233-3400
(800) 759-8811; Fax: (903) 233-3411

Full-time: 876 men, 408 women	**Faculty:** IIA, --$
Part-time: 619 men, 1272 women	**Ph.D.s:** 67%
Graduate: 211 men, 211 women	**Student/Faculty:** n/av
Year: semesters, summer session	**Tuition:** $15,030
Application Deadline: August 1	**Room & Board:** $6050
Freshman Class: 849 applied, 680 accepted, 339 enrolled	
SAT I or ACT: required	**COMPETITIVE**

Le Tourneau University, founded in 1946, is a private, nondenominational Christian institution offering programs in aeronautical science, business administration, engineering, education, liberal arts, technology,

computer science, natural and mathematical sciences, kinesiology, and others. There are 6 undergraduate schools and 1 graduate school. In addition to regional accreditation, LeTourneau has baccalaureate program accreditation with ABET and IACBE. The library contains 84,779 volumes, 50,481 microform items, and 3144 audio/video tapes/CDs, and subscribes to 383 periodicals. Computerized library services include the card catalog, interlibrary loans, and database searching. Special learning facilities include a learning resource center and a museum. The 162-acre campus is in an urban area 60 miles west of Shreveport, Louisiana, and 120 miles east of the Dallas/Fort Worth metroplex. Including any residence halls, there are 55 buildings.

Student Life: 50% of undergraduates are from out of state, mostly the West. Students are from 49 states and 19 foreign countries. 57% are from public schools. 69% are white; 19% African American. The average age of freshmen is 18; all undergraduates, 20.

Housing: 863 students can be accommodated in college housing, which includes single-sex dorms, on-campus apartments, local society houses for men, and married-student housing. On-campus housing is guaranteed for all 4 years. 74% of students live on campus; of those, 70% remain on campus on weekends. Alcohol is not permitted. All students may keep cars.

Activities: There are no fraternities or sororities. There are 22 groups on campus, including choir, chorale, chorus, computers, drama, honors, international, jazz band, newspaper, pep band, photography, political, professional, religious, social, social service, student government, and yearbook. Popular campus events include Spiritual Emphasis Week, Longview Blitz, and Longview Symphony.

Sports: There are 6 intercollegiate sports for men and 7 for women, and 16 intramural sports for men and 16 for women. Facilities include soccer, softball, baseball, and intramural fields, a 1000-seat gym, a 1000-seat arena/auditorium, 8 tennis courts, 3 racquetball courts, a weight room, a Nautilus room, a swimming pool, and an indoor running track.

Disabled Students: 90% of the campus is accessible. Wheelchair ramps, elevators, special parking, specially equipped rest rooms, special class scheduling, lowered drinking fountains, lowered telephones, special housing, and automated doors are available.

Services: Counseling and information services are available, as is tutoring in most subjects. There is remedial math and writing.

Campus Safety and Security: Measures include 24-hour foot and vehicle patrol, self-defense education, security escort services, and informal discussions. There are pamphlets/posters/films and lighted pathways/sidewalks.

Programs of Study: LeTourneau confers B.A., B.S., and B.B.A. degrees. Associate and master's degrees are also awarded. Bachelor's degrees are awarded in BIOLOGICAL SCIENCE (biology/biological science), BUSINESS (accounting, business administration and management, management information systems, marketing management, and marketing/retailing/merchandising), COMMUNICATIONS AND THE ARTS (English), COMPUTER AND PHYSICAL SCIENCE (chemistry, computer mathematics, computer science, and mathematics), EDUCATION (business, elementary, physical, science, and secondary), ENGINEERING AND ENVIRONMENTAL DESIGN (aeronautical science, aeronautical technology, computer engineering, computer technology, electrical/electronics engineering, engineering, engineering technology, industrial administration/management, mechanical engineering, and welding engineering), HEALTH PROFESSIONS (health, premedicine, and preveterinary science), SOCIAL SCIENCE (biblical studies, history, interdisciplinary studies, prelaw, psychology, and public administration). Engineering, computer science, and math are the strongest academically. Engineering, aeronautical science, and business are the largest.

Required: All students must fulfill general curricula requirements, including 12 hours of biblical studies, 9 of English, 3 each of lab science, math, history, and humanities and social science, as well as 2 of phys ed and 1 of introduction to the university. A minimum of 126 semester credit hours, including at least 24 in the major, with a minimum GPA of 2.0 is required to graduate.

Special: Le Tourneau offers co-op programs in engineering, business, accounting, computer science, biology, design technology, and others, internships through business and liberal arts programs, an American studies program with the Council for Christian Colleges and Universities, credit for experience, and study abroad in 7 countries. There is a freshman honors program.

Faculty/Classroom: 82% of faculty are male; 18%, female. 96% teach undergraduates and 20% both teach and do research. No introductory courses are taught by graduate students. The average class size in an introductory lecture is 24; in a laboratory, 16; and in a regular course, 18.

Admissions: 80% of the 2003-2004 applicants were accepted. There were 6 National Merit finalists. 10 freshmen graduated first in their class.

Requirements: The SAT I or ACT is required, with a recommended minimum composite score of 950 on the SAT I or 20 on the ACT. Applicants must be graduates of an accredited secondary school or have the GED. They should have completed 16 academic credits, including 4 in

English, 3 each in math, social studies, and natural science, and 1 in computer science. An essay is required. LeTourneau requires applicants to be in the upper 50% of their class. A GPA of 2.5 is required. AP and CLEP credits are accepted. Important factors in the admissions decision are advanced placement or honor courses, personality/intangible qualities, and extracurricular activities record.

Procedure: Freshmen are admitted to all sessions. Entrance exams should be taken by the fall of the senior year. There is a deferred admissions plan. Applications should be filed by August 1 for fall entry (priority date, December 31) and January 1 for spring entry. Notification is sent on a rolling basis beginning August 1. Applications are accepted on-line through the school's web site.

Transfer: 99 transfer students enrolled in 2003-2004. Applicants with at least 26 semester hours must have a minimum 2.0 GPA. Other students must satisfy freshman entrance requirements. 36 of 126 credits required for the bachelor's degree must be completed at LeTourneau.

Visiting: There are regularly scheduled orientations for prospective students. Visits are individualized and may include touring the school, attending classes, special events, or chapel, meeting with faculty and financial aid personnel, and staying in a dorm. There are guides for informal visits and visitors may sit in on classes and stay overnight. To schedule a visit, contact the Visitor Coordinator at (903) 233-3454.

Financial Aid: In 2002-2003, 80% of all full-time freshmen and 78% of continuing full-time students received some form of financial aid. At least 73% of full-time freshmen and at least 72% of continuing full-time students received need-based aid. The average freshman award was $12,728. Need-based scholarships or need-based grants averaged $5724; need-based self-help aid (loans and jobs) averaged $4454; and institutional non-need-based awards and non-need-based scholarships averaged $3964. The average financial indebtedness of the 2003 graduate was $20,055. LeTourneau is a member of CSS. The FAFSA is required. The priority date for freshman financial aid applications for fall entry is February 15.

International Students: In a recent year, there were 35 international students enrolled. The school actively recruits these students. They must score 500 on the written TOEFL or 173 on the electronic version and also take the SAT I (scoring 950) or the ACT (scoring 20).

Computers: The mainframe is an HPM Series. Every dorm room on campus has 2 ports for access to the LeTNet and Web. The CAD lab has 25 computers, and there are 8 PCs in the library and 85 in computer labs. All students may access the system. There are no time limits and no fees.

Graduates: From July 1, 2002 to June 30, 2003, 719 bachelor's degrees were awarded. The most popular majors were engineering/engineering technologies (54%), business/marketing (14%), and education (7%). In an average class, 32% graduate in 4 years or less, 50% graduate in 5 years or less, and 52% graduate in 6 years or less. Of a recent graduating class, 5% were enrolled in graduate school within 6 months of graduation and 94% were employed.

Admissions Contact: James Townsend, Director of Admissions. A video is available. E-mail: *admissions@letu.edu* Web: *www.letu.edu*

LUBBOCK CHRISTIAN UNIVERSITY
B-2
Lubbock, TX 79407
(806) 720-7151
(800) 933-7601; Fax: (806) 720-7255

Full-time: 579 men, 767 women	**Faculty:** 73; IIB, --$
Part-time: 167 men, 246 women	**Ph.D.s:** 63%
Graduate: 94 men, 80 women	**Student/Faculty:** 18 to 1
Year: semesters, summer session	**Tuition:** $11,452
Application Deadline: open	**Room & Board:** $4380
Freshman Class: 807 applied, 579 accepted, 298 enrolled	
SAT I Verbal/Math: 510/490	**ACT:** 21 COMPETITIVE

Lubbock Christian University, founded in 1957 in affiliation with the Churches of Christ, offers undergraduate degrees in liberal arts and professional studies, and graduate degrees in Biblical studies and education. There are 4 undergraduate and 2 graduate schools. In addition to regional accreditation, LCU has baccalaureate program accreditation with CSWE and NLN. The library contains 113,210 volumes, 5393 microform items, and 78 audio/video tapes/CDs. Computerized library services include the card catalog, interlibrary loans, database searching, and Internet access. Special learning facilities include a learning resource center and art gallery. The 20-acre campus is in a suburban area 350 miles from Dallas and 325 miles from Albuquerque. Including any residence halls, there are 19 buildings.

Student Life: 90% of undergraduates are from Texas. Students are from 27 states and 8 foreign countries. 79% are white; 13% Hispanic. 88% are Protestant; 7% Catholic. The average age of freshmen is 19; all undergraduates, 24. 37% do not continue beyond their first year; 36% remain to graduate.

Housing: 612 students can be accommodated in college housing, which includes single-sex dorms, on-campus apartments, and married-student housing. On-campus housing is guaranteed for the freshman

year only and is available on a first-come, first-served basis. 71% of students commute. Alcohol is not permitted. All students may keep cars.

Activities: There are no fraternities or sororities. There are 16 groups on campus, including cheerleading, chorus, drama, ethnic, honors, jazz band, newspaper, professional, religious, social, student government, and yearbook. Popular campus events include Master Follies, Family Weekend, and Spiritual Renewal Week.

Sports: There are 2 intercollegiate sports for men and 2 for women. Facilities include the Rip Griffin Center which serves as the home for the university's intercollegiate teams. The field house is the center for intramural and phys ed activities with an indoor track, badminton, volleyball, and basketball courts, and a fitness center.

Disabled Students: Wheelchair ramps, elevators, and special parking are available.

Services: Counseling and information services are available, as is tutoring in every subject. There is a reader service for the blind, and remedial math, reading, and writing.

Campus Safety and Security: Measures include 24-hour foot and vehicle patrol and lighted pathways/sidewalks.

Programs of Study: LCU confers B.A., B.S., B.B.A., B.S.I.S., B.S.N., and B.S.W. degrees. Associate and master's degrees are also awarded. Bachelor's degrees are awarded in AGRICULTURE (agricultural business management and animal science), BIOLOGICAL SCIENCE (biology/biological science), BUSINESS (accounting, banking and finance, business administration and management, and sports management), COMMUNICATIONS AND THE ARTS (communications and music), COMPUTER AND PHYSICAL SCIENCE (chemistry, information sciences and systems, and mathematics), EDUCATION (art, business, elementary, middle school, music, physical, science, and secondary), ENGINEERING AND ENVIRONMENTAL DESIGN (engineering and environmental science), HEALTH PROFESSIONS (exercise science, medical technology, and nursing), SOCIAL SCIENCE (biblical studies, humanities, ministries, physical fitness/movement, psychology, and social work). Education, business administration, and social work are the strongest academically. Organizational management, early childhood/elementary education, and humanities are the largest.

Required: To graduate, students must complete 126 credit hours, including at least 42 in upper-division courses, 30 to 42 in the major, and 32 in residence after achieving senior status, with a minimum GPA of 2.25 overall and 2.50 in the major. All students must fulfill general education and biblical studies course requirements.

Special: LCU offers co-op programs in engineering, medical technology, and criminal justice, internships in several fields, and cross-registration with Texas Tech University and other regional schools. A general studies degree, nondegree study, and pass/fail options are also available. There are 3 national honor societies, a freshman honors program, and 1 departmental honors program.

Faculty/Classroom: 56% of faculty are male; 44%, female. All teach undergraduates. No introductory courses are taught by graduate students. The average class size in an introductory lecture is 26; in a laboratory, 14; and in a regular course, 17.

Admissions: 72% of the 2003-2004 applicants were accepted. The SAT I scores for the 2003-2004 freshman class were: Verbal--42% below 500, 41% between 500 and 599, 15% between 600 and 700, and 2% above 700; Math--50% below 500, 37% between 500 and 599, 10% between 600 and 700, and 3% above 700. The ACT scores were 48% below 21, 24% between 21 and 23, 18% between 24 and 26, 6% between 27 and 28, and 4% above 28. 8% of the current freshmen were in the top fifth of their class; 22% were in the top two fifths.

Requirements: The SAT I or ACT is required. In addition, applicants must be graduates of an accredited secondary school or have a GED certificate. Unconditional admission is granted to freshmen who score 18 or higher on the ACT or 860 or higher on the SAT I and who meet all other admission requirements. AP and CLEP credits are accepted. Important factors in the admissions decision are personality/intangible qualities, parents or siblings attending the school, and geographic diversity.

Procedure: Freshmen are admitted fall, spring, and summer. Entrance exams should be taken before registration. There is a deferred admissions plan. Application deadlines are open. The fall 2003 application fee was $20. Applications are accepted on-line through *www.lcu.edu/applications.asp.*.

Transfer: 287 transfer students enrolled in 2002-2003. Transfer students with fewer than 16 hours of college credit must meet freshman admission requirements. All transfers must submit an official transcript from previously attended colleges or universities and be in good academic standing. Only courses with a grade of C or above are transferred from another institution. 32 of 126 credits required for the bachelor's degree must be completed at LCU.

Visiting: There are regularly scheduled orientations for prospective students. There are guides for informal visits and visitors may sit in on classes and stay overnight. To schedule a visit, contact Shannon Anderson at (806) 720-7151.

Financial Aid: In 2002-2003, 76% of all full-time freshmen and 67% of continuing full-time students received some form of financial aid. 76%

of full-time freshmen and 64% of continuing full-time students received need-based aid. The average freshman award was $9937. Need-based scholarships or need-based grants averaged $7225; need-based self-help aid (loans and jobs) averaged $3209; non-need-based athletic scholarships averaged $5536; and other non-need-based awards and non-need-based scholarships averaged $8398. The average financial indebtedness of the 2003 graduate was $19,450. The FAFSA and the university's own financial statement are required. The priority date for freshman financial aid applications for fall entry is June 1.

International Students: There are 10 international students enrolled. They must score 500 on the written TOEFL or 173 on the electronic version or take the MELAB, and also take the ACT, scoring 18.

Computers: There are approximately 160 computers available for student use in labs across campus. The campuswide network can be accessed from residence rooms and off-campus locations. All students may access the system. There are no time limits. The fee is $140.

Graduates: From July 1, 2002 to June 30, 2003, 275 bachelor's degrees were awarded. The most popular majors were business (24%), education (19%), and social work (8%). In an average class, 23% graduate in 4 years or less, 35% graduate in 5 years or less, and 36% graduate in 6 years or less.

Admissions Contact: Shannon Anderson, Director of Admissions.
E-mail: *shannon.anderson@lcu.edu* Web: *www.lcu.edu*

MCMURRY UNIVERSITY
Abilene, TX 79697

C-2

(325) 793-4700
(800) 460-2392; Fax: (325) 793-4718

Full-time: 579 men, 583 women	**Faculty:** 78
Part-time: 119 men, 95 women	**Ph.D.s:** 80%
Graduate: none	**Student/Faculty:** 15 to 1
Year: semesters, summer session	**Tuition:** $12,800
Application Deadline: August 8	**Room & Board:** $5046
Freshman Class: 638 applied, 556 accepted, 255 enrolled	
SAT I Verbal/Math: 480/490	**ACT:** 19 **LESS COMPETITIVE**

McMurry University, chartered in 1923, is a private liberal arts institution affiliated with the United Methodist Church. There are 4 undergraduate schools. The library contains 153,118 volumes, 4437 microform items, and 1692 audio/video tapes/CDs, and subscribes to 503 periodicals. Computerized library services include the card catalog, interlibrary loans, and database searching. Special learning facilities include a learning resource center, art gallery, and several special book collections, including the McWhiney collection of Civil War-era books. The 41-acre campus is in an urban area 180 miles west of Dallas. Including any residence halls, there are 25 buildings.

Student Life: 95% of undergraduates are from Texas. Students are from 17 states and 7 foreign countries. 74% are white; 12% Hispanic. 67% are Protestant; 21% claim no religious affiliation; 12% Catholic. The average age of freshmen is 18; all undergraduates, 23. 38% do not continue beyond their first year; 40% remain to graduate.

Housing: 667 students can be accommodated in college housing, which includes single-sex dorms and on-campus apartments. On-campus housing is guaranteed for all 4 years and is available on a first-come, first-served basis. 60% of students commute. Alcohol is not permitted. All students may keep cars.

Activities: 10% of men belong to 6 local fraternities; 10% of women belong to 6 local sororities. There are 46 groups on campus, including art, band, cheerleading, choir, chorale, computers, drama, ethnic, honors, jazz band, literary magazine, marching band, musical theater, newspaper, political, professional, religious, social, social service, student government, and yearbook. Popular campus events include Parents Weekend, Sing Song, and Big Event.

Sports: There are 9 intercollegiate sports for men and 8 for women, and 15 intramural sports for men and 15 for women. Facilities include a 4500-seat track and football stadium, a 2200-seat gym, a 1500-seat auditorium, an intramural gym, a swimming pool and diving area, 2 racquetball courts, basketball, volleyball, and badminton courts, a soccer field, and an 875-seat baseball stadium.

Disabled Students: 70% of the campus is accessible. Wheelchair ramps, elevators, special parking, specially equipped rest rooms, special class scheduling, and special housing are available.

Services: Counseling and information services are available, as is tutoring in most subjects. There is remedial math, reading, and writing.

Campus Safety and Security: Measures include 24-hour foot and vehicle patrol and lighted pathways/sidewalks.

Programs of Study: McMurry confers B.A., B.S., B.B.A., B.F.A., B.Mus., B.Mus.Ed., B.S. Multidisciplinary Studies, and B.S.N. degrees. Bachelor's degrees are awarded in BIOLOGICAL SCIENCE (biochemistry and biology/biological science), BUSINESS (accounting, banking and finance, business administration and management, business economics, management information systems, management science, and marketing/retailing/merchandising), COMMUNICATIONS AND THE ARTS (art, ceramic art and design, communications, dramatic arts, English, French, German, graphic design, multimedia, music, music performance, paint-

ing, piano/organ, Spanish, and voice), COMPUTER AND PHYSICAL SCIENCE (chemistry, computer science, information sciences and systems, mathematics, natural sciences, and physics), EDUCATION (art, athletic training, bilingual/bicultural, elementary, middle school, music, physical, and secondary), ENGINEERING AND ENVIRONMENTAL DESIGN (environmental science), HEALTH PROFESSIONS (nursing), SOCIAL SCIENCE (economics, history, interdisciplinary studies, philosophy, political science/government, psychology, religion, and sociology). Education, biology, and chemistry are the strongest academically. Education, business, and biology are the largest.

Required: Students must complete 126 semester hours, including 27 in the major, with a GPA of at least 2.0. Distribution requirements vary with the degree but include courses in English, ethics, humanities, fine arts, science, math, social science, religion, political science, sociology, history, foreign language, and health fitness. A 9-hour freshman core curriculum focuses on ethics; sophomore and junior year the focus is humanities.

Special: McMurry offers internships, co-op programs, and cross-registration with Abilene Christian and Hardin-Simmons Universities. There are work-study programs with the university and area businesses for seniors. B.A.-B.S. degrees in business administration, accounting, banking and finance, biology, chemistry, multidisciplinary studies, nursing, and computer science are available. A 3-2 engineering degree with Texas Tech University is offered, as is a Servant Leadership program, designed to instill principles of leadership in the betterment of community and society. There are 16 national honor societies, a freshman honors program, and 22 departmental honors programs.

Faculty/Classroom: 74% of faculty are male; 26%, female. All teach undergraduates and 64% do research. The average class size in an introductory lecture is 27; in a laboratory, 14; and in a regular course, 17.

Admissions: 87% of the 2003-2004 applicants were accepted. The SAT I scores for the 2003-2004 freshman class were: Verbal--60% below 500, 30% between 500 and 599, 9% between 600 and 700, and 1% above 700; Math--51% below 500, 36% between 500 and 599, 12% between 600 and 700, and 1% above 700. The ACT scores were 58% below 21, 25% between 21 and 23, 11% between 24 and 26, 5% between 27 and 28, and 1% above 28. 28% of the current freshmen were in the top fifth of their class; 59% were in the top two fifths. 3 freshmen graduated first in their class.

Requirements: The SAT I or ACT is required, with a minimum composite score of 910 on the SAT I or 19 on the ACT. Those meeting the minimum score must rank in the top 40% of their high school class. Applicants need 16 academic credits, including 4 units of English, 3 each in math and social studies, and 2 each in foreign language and science. An interview is recommended. The GED is accepted with an average score of 55. A GPA of 2.0 is required. AP and CLEP credits are accepted.

Procedure: Freshmen are admitted to all sessions. Entrance exams should be taken in the junior year. There is a deferred admissions plan. Applications should be filed by August 8 for fall entry, along with a $20 fee. Notification is sent on a rolling basis. Applications are accepted on computer disk and on-line through the McMurry University web site, *www.mcm.edu.*

Transfer: 155 transfer students enrolled in 2002-2003. All transfer students must have a GPA of at least 2.0. Those with fewer than 15 credit hours must submit high school transcripts and SAT I or ACT scores; those with 15 to 23 hours need only school transcripts. 30 of 126 credits required for the bachelor's degree must be completed at McMurry.

Visiting: There are regularly scheduled orientations for prospective students. There are guides for informal visits and visitors may sit in on classes and stay overnight. To schedule a visit, contact the Admissions Office at *admissions@mcm.edu.*

Financial Aid: In 2003-2004, 98% of all full-time freshmen and 99% of continuing full-time students received some form of financial aid. 82% of full-time freshmen and 81% of continuing full-time students received need-based aid. The average freshman award was $15,853. Need-based scholarships or need-based grants averaged $7390 ($14,480 maximum); need-based self-help aid (loans and jobs) averaged $2892 ($5595 maximum); and non-need-based awards and non-need-based scholarships averaged $8487 ($21,925 maximum). 57% of undergraduates work part time. Average annual earnings from campus work are $987. The average financial indebtedness of the 2003 graduate was $15,125. The FAFSA and the university's own financial statement are required. The priority date for freshman financial aid applications for fall entry is March 15. The deadline for filing freshman financial aid applications for fall entry is open.

International Students: There are 7 international students enrolled. The school actively recruits these students. They must score 550 on the written TOEFL and also take the SAT I or the ACT, scoring 890 on the SAT I or 19 on the ACT.

Computers: The mainframes are DEC Alpha and Compaq Proliant file servers. There are 172 PCs available, including 30 in the academic enrichment center, 4 in the library, and 138 in discipline-specific computer labs. Access to the Internet is available from most of the computers for student use. All students may access the system at any time. There are no time limits and no fees.

Graduates: From July 1, 2002 to June 30, 2003, 228 bachelor's degrees were awarded. The most popular majors were education (29%), business (24%), and biology (6%). In an average class, 1% graduate in 3 years or less, 25% graduate in 4 years or less, 37% graduate in 5 years or less, and 40% graduate in 6 years or less. 10 companies recruited on campus in 2002-2003. Of the 2002 graduating class, 10% were enrolled in graduate school within 6 months of graduation and 80% were employed.

Admissions Contact: Amy Weyant, Director of Admissions.
E-mail: *weyanta@mcmurryadjm.mcm.edu* Web: *http://www.mcm.edu*

MIDWESTERN STATE UNIVERSITY   D-2
Wichita Falls, TX 76308-2099   (940) 397-4334
(800) 842-1922; Fax: (940) 397-4672

Full-time: 1688 men, 2241 women	Faculty: 182
Part-time: 764 men, 951 women	Ph.D.s: 72%
Graduate: 309 men, 527 women	Student/Faculty: 22 to 1
Year: semesters, summer session	Tuition: $3415 ($10,495)
Application Deadline: August 7	Room & Board: $4630
Freshman Class: 2176 applied, 1778 accepted, 713 enrolled	
SAT I Verbal/Math: 480/480	ACT: 19 LESS COMPETITIVE

Midwestern State University, founded in 1922, is a public liberal arts institution offering courses in business administration, education, fine arts, health sciences, humanities, math and science, political science and public administration, and social and behavioral sciences. There are 6 undergraduate and 5 graduate schools. In addition to regional accreditation, MSU has baccalaureate program accreditation with ABET, ACBSP, ADA, NASM, NCATE, and NLN. The library contains 241,000 volumes, 158,000 microform items, and 6757 audio/video tapes/CDs, and subscribes to 1100 periodicals. Computerized library services include the card catalog, interlibrary loans, and database searching. Special learning facilities include an art gallery, planetarium, TV station, greenhouse, and TTVN studio. The 172-acre campus is in an urban area 135 miles northwest of Dallas. Including any residence halls, there are 31 buildings.

Student Life: 87% of undergraduates are from Texas. Students are from 50 states, 40 foreign countries, and Canada. 78% are white. The average age of all undergraduates is 25. 36% do not continue beyond their first year; 64% remain to graduate.

Housing: 733 students can be accommodated in college housing, which includes single-sex and coed dorms, on-campus apartments, off-campus apartments, and married-student housing. In addition, there are honors houses. On-campus housing is guaranteed for the freshman year only and is available on a first-come, first-served basis. Priority is given to out-of-town students. 88% of students commute. Alcohol is not permitted. All students may keep cars.

Activities: 10% of men belong to 6 national fraternities; 10% of women belong to 6 national sororities. There are 102 groups on campus, including art, band, cheerleading, choir, chorale, chorus, computers, dance, drama, environmental, ethnic, honors, international, jazz band, literary magazine, marching band, newspaper, pep band, political, professional, radio and TV, religious, social, social service, student government, symphony, and yearbook. Popular campus events include Family Day, Spirit Days, and College Day Preview.

Sports: There are 4 intercollegiate sports for men and 4 for women, and 18 intramural sports for men and 21 for women. Facilities include a 5000-seat gym, a soccer stadium, tennis courts, an indoor swimming pool, a sand volleyball court, and a walking track.

Disabled Students: 99% of the campus is accessible. Wheelchair ramps, elevators, special parking, specially equipped rest rooms, special class scheduling, lowered drinking fountains, and lowered telephones are available.

Services: Counseling and information services are available, as is tutoring in some subjects, including algebra, sciences, and history. There is a reader service for the blind and remedial math, reading, and writing.

Campus Safety and Security: Measures include 24-hour foot and vehicle patrol, self-defense education, informal discussions, and pamphlets/posters/films. There are lighted pathways/sidewalks and seminars on safety and living on campus.

Programs of Study: MSU confers B.A., B.S., B.A.A.S., B.B.A., B.F.A., B.M., B.S.C.J., B.S.D.H., B.S.I.S., B.S.M.T., B.S.N., B.S.R.C., B.S.R.S., and B.S.W. degrees. Associate and master's degrees are also awarded. Bachelor's degrees are awarded in BIOLOGICAL SCIENCE (biology/biological science), BUSINESS (accounting, banking and finance, business administration and management, business economics, international economics, management science, and marketing/retailing/merchandising), COMMUNICATIONS AND THE ARTS (communications, dramatic arts, English, fine arts, music, and Spanish), COMPUTER AND PHYSICAL SCIENCE (chemical technology, chemistry, computer science, geology, information sciences and systems, and mathematics), EDUCATION (music and physical), ENGINEERING AND ENVIRONMENTAL DESIGN (engineering technology, environmental science,

manufacturing engineering, and preengineering), HEALTH PROFESSIONS (dental hygiene, health care administration, health science, medical laboratory technology, nursing, predentistry, premedicine, prepharmacy, preveterinary science, radiological science, and respiratory therapy), SOCIAL SCIENCE (criminal justice, economics, history, humanities, interdisciplinary studies, political science/government, prelaw, psychology, social work, and sociology). Business and nursing are the largest.

Required: All students must earn a minimum GPA of 2.0 while taking 120 semester hours, 24 in the major. Distribution requirements include 6 hours from a list of humanities classes, 6 from social science, 7 to 10 hours from natural science, and additional phys ed requirements.

Special: An exchange program with the Monterrey Institute of Technology, internships with local firms and agencies, and study abroad in London are available. Dual majors, co-op programs in all majors, a general studies degree, credit for military experience, and nondegree study up to 12 hours are also offered. There are 23 national honor societies and a freshman honors program.

Faculty/Classroom: 58% of faculty are male; 42%, female. All teach undergraduates. Graduate students teach 10% of introductory courses. The average class size in an introductory lecture is 25; in a laboratory, 20; and in a regular course, 25.

Admissions: 82% of the 2003-2004 applicants were accepted. The SAT I scores for the 2003-2004 freshman class were: Verbal--57% below 500, 31% between 500 and 599, 11% between 600 and 700, and 1% above 700; Math--56% below 500, 33% between 500 and 599, 10% between 600 and 700, and 1% above 700. The ACT scores were 60% below 21, 25% between 21 and 23, 10% between 24 and 26, 3% between 27 and 28, and 2% above 28. 19% of the current freshmen were in the top fifth of their class; 64% were in the top two fifths.

Requirements: The SAT I or ACT is required. The minimum required composite score on the SAT I or ACT is dependent on class rank. For students in the top quarter of the class, there is no minimum requirement; for students ranked in the second quarter of the class, the required scores are 870 on the SAT I or 18 on the ACT; for students ranked in the third quarter of the class, required scores are 950 on the SAT I or 20 on the ACT; for students ranked in the fourth quarter of the class, required scores are 1030 on the SAT I or 22 on the ACT. High school credits should include 4 years of English, 3 years of math, 2 years of science, and 6 units of electives. The GED is accepted. AP and CLEP credits are accepted. Ability to finance college education is an important factor in the admissions decision.

Procedure: Freshmen are admitted to all sessions. Entrance exams should be taken before applying for admission. There are early decision and early admissions plans. Applications should be filed by August 7 for fall entry, December 15 for spring entry, and May 15 for summer entry. Notification is sent on a rolling basis. Applications are accepted on-line through the Texas Common Application.

Transfer: Transfer students with fewer than 18 semester hours must meet beginning freshmen criteria. All transfers must be eligible to reenroll in all previous schools. 24 of 120 credits required for the bachelor's degree must be completed at MSU.

Visiting: There are regularly scheduled orientations for prospective students, consisting of a college day preview each February, which introduces high school juniors, seniors, and their parents to the campus and faculty. There are also daily tours. There are guides for informal visits and visitors may sit in on classes and stay overnight. To schedule a visit, contact MSU Admissions.

Financial Aid: In 2003-2004, 76% of all full-time freshmen and 80% of continuing full-time students received some form of financial aid. 55% of full-time freshmen and 52% of continuing full-time students received need-based aid. The average freshman award was $3959. Need-based scholarships or need-based grants averaged $1492 ($5404 maximum); need-based self-help aid (loans and jobs) averaged $2346 ($11,098 maximum); and non-need-based athletic scholarships averaged $1838 ($9386 maximum). 8% of undergraduates work part time. Average annual earnings from campus work are $3710. MSU is a member of CSS. The FAFSA is required. Check with the school for current deadlines.

International Students: The school actively recruits these students. They must score 500 on the written TOEFL and also take the SAT I or the ACT.

Computers: The mainframe is an IBM 4381 VSE operating system. There are also 145 PCs in classrooms. A 24-hour computer lab is available for student use. All students may access the system. There are no time limits and no fees.

Graduates: In a recent year, 805 bachelor's degrees were awarded. The most popular majors were business (24%) and nursing (8%). In an average class, 30% graduate in 6 years or less.

Admissions Contact: Barbara Ramos Merkle, Director of Admissions.
E-mail: *admissions@mwsu.edu* Web: *www.mwsu.edu*

NORTHWOOD UNIVERSITY
Cedar Hill, TX 75104

D-2

(972) 293-5400
(800) 927-9663; Fax: (972) 291-3824

Full-time: 318 men, 326 women	**Faculty:** 23
Part-time: 8 men, 1 woman	**Ph.Ds:** 13%
Graduate: none	**Student/Faculty:** 28 to 1
Year: quarters, summer session	**Tuition:** $13,995
Application Deadline: August 1	**Room & Board:** $6140
Freshman Class: 864 applied, 508 accepted, 187 enrolled	
SAT I Verbal/Math: 460/450	**ACT:** 19 **LESS COMPETITIVE**

Northwood University, founded in 1959 and whose Texas campus opened in 1966, is a private institution offering undergraduate degrees in business administration. Campuses are located in Florida, Michigan, and Texas. The library contains 11,000 volumes and 350 audio/video tapes/CDs, and subscribes to 160 periodicals. Computerized library services include the card catalog, interlibrary loans, database searching, and Internet access. Special learning facilities include a learning resource center and art gallery. The 360-acre campus is in a suburban area 18 miles southwest of Dallas. Including any residence halls, there are 18 buildings.

Student Life: 92% of undergraduates are from Texas. Students are from 17 states, 8 foreign countries, and Canada. 90% are from public schools. 43% are white; 28% Hispanic; 20% African American. The average age of freshmen is 19; all undergraduates, 21. 39% do not continue beyond their first year; 55% remain to graduate.

Housing: 260 students can be accommodated in college housing, which includes single-sex dorms and on-campus apartments. On-campus housing is guaranteed for the freshman year only and is available on a first-come, first-served basis. 73% of students commute. All students may keep cars.

Activities: There are no fraternities or sororities. There are 17 groups on campus, including computers, dance, debate, ethnic, forensics, honors, international, literary magazine, professional, religious, social, social service, and student government. Popular campus events include Sanity Inn (talent show) and Spring Formal.

Sports: There are 5 intercollegiate sports for men and 5 for women, and 6 intramural sports for men and 5 for women. Facilities include an outdoor swimming pool, tennis court, baseball/softball fields, and jogging trails, along with a state recreational area adjacent to the campus.

Disabled Students: 75% of the campus is accessible. Wheelchair ramps, special parking, specially equipped rest rooms, special class scheduling, lowered drinking fountains, and lowered telephones are available.

Services: Counseling and information services are available, as is tutoring in most subjects. There is a reader service for the blind, and remedial math, reading, and writing. Tutoring for any subject is available at a student's request.

Campus Safety and Security: Measures include 24-hour foot and vehicle patrol, informal discussions, pamphlets/posters/films, and lighted pathways/sidewalks.

Programs of Study: Northwood confers the B.B.A. degree. Associate degrees are also awarded. Bachelor's degrees are awarded in BUSINESS (accounting, apparel and accessories marketing, banking and finance, business administration and management, court reporting, entrepreneurial studies, hotel/motel and restaurant management, international business management, management information systems, marketing management, sports management, and transportation and travel marketing), COMMUNICATIONS AND THE ARTS (advertising), COMPUTER AND PHYSICAL SCIENCE (computer management). Management, international business, and entertainment, sport, and promotion management are the largest.

Required: To graduate, all students must complete at least 180 term credit hours, including 36 in the major, with a minimum GPA of 2.0. Students must complete the general studies core curriculum, 6 credits of computer science management, and 2 credits of executive fitness. Internships for 1 to 6 credits are required in some majors.

Special: Study abroad in 20 countries, accelerated degree programs, and dual majors and externships in most majors are offered. There is a freshman honors program.

Faculty/Classroom: 61% of faculty are male; 39%, female. All teach undergraduates. The average class size in an introductory lecture is 22; in a laboratory, 15; and in a regular course, 19.

Admissions: 59% of the 2003-2004 applicants were accepted. The SAT I scores for the 2003-2004 freshman class were: Verbal--73% below 500, 25% between 500 and 599, and 2% between 600 and 700; Math--69% below 500, 25% between 500 and 599, 5% between 600 and 700, and 1% above 700. The ACT scores were 80% below 21, 17% between 21 and 23, 2% between 24 and 26, and 1% between 27 and 28. 18% of the current freshmen were in the top fifth of their class; 43% were in the top two fifths.

Requirements: The SAT I or ACT is required. In addition, applicants must be graduates of an accredited secondary school with a 2.0 GPA or

have a GED certificate. An interview and essay are recommended. AP and CLEP credits are accepted. Important factors in the admissions decision are advanced placement or honor courses, evidence of special talent, and leadership record.

Procedure: Freshmen are admitted to all sessions. Entrance exams should be taken by December of the senior year. There are early admissions and deferred admissions plans. There is a rolling admissions plan. Applications should be filed by August 1 for fall entry, November 15 for winter entry, February 15 for spring entry, and June 1 for summer entry, along with a $25 fee. Notification is sent on a rolling basis. Applications are accepted on-line through the university's web site.

Transfer: 76 transfer students enrolled in a recent year. Applicants must have earned a minimum of 12 credit hours and a 2.0 GPA. They must submit official transcripts from all previous colleges attended and the final high school transcript. 45 credits of 180 required for the bachelor's degree must be completed at Northwood.

Visiting: There are regularly scheduled orientations for prospective students. There are guides for informal visits and visitors may sit in on classes and stay overnight. To schedule a visit, contact the Admissions Office at txadmit@northwood.edu.

Financial Aid: In 2003-2004, 99% of all full-time students received some form of financial aid. 76% of full-time freshmen and 70% of continuing full-time students received need-based aid. The average freshman award was $13,756. Need-based scholarships or need-based grants averaged $9211 ($13,485 maximum); need-based self-help aid (loans and jobs) averaged $4230 ($10,625 maximum); non-need-based athletic scholarships averaged $5715 ($15,702 maximum); and other non-need-based awards and non-need-based scholarships averaged $6830 ($23,711 maximum). 11% of undergraduates work part time. Average annual earnings from campus work are $1911. The average financial indebtedness of the 2003 graduate was $13,101. The FAFSA is required. Both the priority and regular dates for freshman financial aid applications for fall entry are rolling.

International Students: There are 33 international students enrolled. The school actively recruits these students. They must score 500 on the written TOEFL or 173 on the electronic version.

Computers: The mainframe is an IBM RS/6000. Students have personal server space on the Novell system, with full Internet access and e-mail through the Michigan campus to all locations. Computer labs on the Texas campus feature Pentium processors. All students may access the system any time. There are no time limits and no fees.

Graduates: From July 1, 2002 to June 30, 2003, 115 bachelor's degrees were awarded. The most popular majors were marketing/management (23%), international business (16%), and banking/finance (12%). In an average class, 41% graduate in 4 years or less, and 55% graduate in 6 years or less.

Admissions Contact: James R. Hickerson, Admissions Director. A video is available. E-mail: txadmit@northwood.edu
Web: www.northwood.edu

OUR LADY OF THE LAKE UNIVERSITY OF SAN ANTONIO
San Antonio, TX 78207-4689

D-4

(210) 434-6711, ext. 314
(800) 436-6558; Fax: (210) 431-4036

Full-time: 275 men, 1055 women	**Faculty:** 100; IIA, --$
Part-time: 195 men, 670 women	**Ph.Ds:** 69%
Graduate: 345 men, 785 women	**Student/Faculty:** 13 to 1
Year: semesters, summer session	**Tuition:** $14,788
Application Deadline: open	**Room & Board:** $4762
Freshman Class: n/av	
SAT I or ACT: required	**COMPETITIVE**

Our Lady of the Lake, founded as a private Catholic institution in 1895 by the Sisters of Divine Providence, offers programs in the arts and sciences, business, education, and social service. Figures in the above capsule and in this profile are approximate. There are 4 undergraduate and 4 graduate schools. In addition to regional accreditation, The Lake has baccalaureate program accreditation with ASLA and CSWE. The 2 libraries contain 127,441 volumes, 132,970 microform items, and 6877 audio/video tapes/CDs, and subscribe to 32,047 periodicals. Computerized library services include interlibrary loans and database searching. Special learning facilities include a learning resource center and a demonstration school (early childhood to grade 8), and a communication/learning disorders center. The 72-acre campus is in an urban area about 4 miles west of downtown San Antonio. Including any residence halls, there are 14 buildings.

Student Life: 99% of undergraduates are from Texas. Students are from 28 states, 17 foreign countries, and Canada. 53% are Hispanic; 32% white. Most are Catholic. The average age of freshmen is 18; all undergraduates, 28. 40% do not continue beyond their first year; 32% remain to graduate.

Housing: 465 students can be accommodated in college housing, which includes coed dorms. In addition, there are honors houses and quiet and smoke-free housing. On-campus housing is guaranteed for all 4 years. 76% of students commute. All students may keep cars.

Activities: There are no fraternities or sororities. There are 35 groups on campus, including art, cheerleading, choir, chorus, computers, dance, drama, ethnic, honors, newspaper, political, professional, radio and TV, religious, social, social service, student government, and symphony. Popular campus events include Spirit Week.

Sports: There are 9 intramural sports for men and 9 for women. Facilities include playing fields, tennis courts, indoor and outdoor pools, and a gym equipped for weight lifting, aerobics, and other indoor sports.

Disabled Students: 99% of the campus is accessible. Wheelchair ramps, elevators, special parking, specially equipped rest rooms, special class scheduling, and special housing are available.

Services: Counseling and information services are available, as is tutoring in some subjects. There is a reader service for the blind and remedial math, reading, and writing.

Campus Safety and Security: Measures include 24-hour foot and vehicle patrol, pamphlets/posters/films, and lighted pathways/sidewalks.

Programs of Study: The Lake confers B.A., B.S., B.A.S., B.B.A., and B.S.W. degrees. Master's and doctoral degrees are also awarded. Bachelor's degrees are awarded in BIOLOGICAL SCIENCE (biology/biological science), BUSINESS (accounting, business administration and management, human resources, management information systems, marketing management, and personnel management), COMMUNICATIONS AND THE ARTS (art, communications, dramatic arts, English, fine arts, music, and Spanish), COMPUTER AND PHYSICAL SCIENCE (chemistry, information sciences and systems, mathematics, and natural sciences), EDUCATION (art, early childhood, and special), HEALTH PROFESSIONS (speech pathology/audiology), SOCIAL SCIENCE (American studies, behavioral science, history, liberal arts/general studies, philosophy, political science/government, psychology, religion, social studies, social work, and sociology). Biology and chemistry are the strongest academically. Management (business administration) is the largest.

Required: A general education requirement includes competencies in English, math, the natural, social, and behavioral sciences, religion, philosophy, literature, art, history, and phys ed. Other graduation requirements are a minimum 2.0 GPA, 128 credit hours, requirements specific to the major, and satisfactory scores on the COMP/ACT.

Special: There is cross-registration through the United Colleges of San Antonio. Dual majors are possible in the B.A.-B.B.A. programs. A 3-2 engineering degree is offered with Texas Tech and Washington Universities. Credit by exam and for life/work/military experience is available, as is a special degree program for working adults/nontraditional students through the Weekend College.

Faculty/Classroom: 52% of faculty are male; 48%, female.

Requirements: The SAT I or ACT is required. In addition, applicants should graduate from an accredited secondary school with 16 academic credits, including 4 in English, 3 in social studies, and 2 each in math and lab science. A combination of SAT I or ACT scores and high school GPA or class rank determines admission. A GED with an average minimum score of 45 on each of the 5 tests and a satisfactory SAT I or ACT score are also acceptable. Mature students returning to school may waive the SAT I/ACT requirement for the college's own testing. AP and CLEP credits are accepted.

Procedure: Freshmen are admitted to all sessions. Entrance exams should be taken prior to December of the senior year. There is a deferred admissions plan. There is a rolling admissions plan. Application deadlines are open. The fall 2003 application fee was $25. Check with the school for current deadlines and fee.

Transfer: 122 transfer students enrolled in a recent year. Transfer applicants with 30 or more credit hours and a minimum 2.0 GPA are accepted. Others are evaluated by the same criteria as freshmen applicants. 30 of 128 credits required for the bachelor's degree must be completed at The Lake.

Visiting: There are regularly scheduled orientations for prospective students. There are guides for informal visits and visitors may sit in on classes and stay overnight. To schedule a visit, contact the Admissions Office.

Financial Aid: The Lake is a member of CSS. The FAFSA or FFS is required.

International Students: There were 27 international students enrolled in a recent year. The school actively recruits these students. They must score 525 on the written TOEFL.

Computers: A UNIX server and a Novell PC network serve 3 different computer labs, which house a total of about 110 PCs or terminals for student use. All students may access the system. There are no time limits and no fees.

Graduates: In a recent year, 426 bachelor's degrees were awarded. The most popular majors were business/marketing (25%), psychology (13%), and liberal arts/general studies (11%). In an average class, 13% graduate in 4 years or less, 25% graduate in 5 years or less, and 29% graduate in 6 years or less.

Admissions Contact: Michael Boatner, Acting Director Admissions. E-mail: *admission@lake.ollusa.edu* Web: *www.ollusa.edu*

PAUL QUINN COLLEGE
Dallas, TX 75241-4398

D-3
(214) 302-3575 or 302-3520
237-2648; Fax: (214) 302-3559

Total enrollment: n/av	Faculty: n/av
Year: semesters, summer session	Ph.D.s: n/av
Application Deadline: see profile	Student/Faculty: n/av
	Tuition: n/av
	Room & Board: n/av
Freshman Class: n/av	
SAT I or ACT: required	**LESS COMPETITIVE**

Paul Quinn College, founded in 1872, is a coeducational liberal arts college affiliated with the African Methodist Episcopal Church. Figures in the above capsule and in this profile are approximate. In addition to regional accreditation, PQC has baccalaureate program accreditation with CSWE. The library contains 88,187 volumes and 30,550 microform items, and subscribes to 131 periodicals. Special learning facilities include a learning resource center. The 130-acre campus is in an urban area 12 miles from downtown Dallas. Including any residence halls, there are 8 buildings.

Student Life: 61% of undergraduates are from Texas. Students are from 7 states. 89% are from public schools. 90% are African American; 10% Hispanic. The average age of freshmen is 18; all undergraduates, 20. 20% do not continue beyond their first year; 65% remain to graduate.

Housing: 700 students can be accommodated in college housing, which includes coed dorms. On-campus housing is guaranteed for all 4 years. 51% of students commute. Alcohol is not permitted. All students may keep cars.

Activities: 40% of men belong to 4 national fraternities; 30% of women belong to 3 national sororities. There are 20 groups on campus, including cheerleading, choir, chorale, computers, dance, ethnic, newspaper, religious, social service, student government, and yearbook. Popular campus events include Honors Day and Founders Day.

Sports: There are 3 intercollegiate sports for men and 3 for women, and 5 intramural sports for men and 5 for women.

Services: There is remedial math, reading, and writing. Tutoring is available.

Campus Safety and Security: Measures include 24-hour foot and vehicle patrol.

Programs of Study: Bachelor's degrees are awarded in BIOLOGICAL SCIENCE (biology/biological science), BUSINESS (accounting and business administration and management), COMMUNICATIONS AND THE ARTS (English and music), COMPUTER AND PHYSICAL SCIENCE (computer science and mathematics), EDUCATION (physical and secondary), SOCIAL SCIENCE (history, religion, and sociology).

Requirements: The SAT I or ACT is required. In addition, high school transcripts must be submitted. A GPA of 2.0 is required. CLEP credit is accepted. Important factors in the admissions decision are leadership record, advanced placement or honor courses, and recommendations by school officials.

Transfer: Applicants must meet the basic admissions requirements. 30 of 128 credits required for the bachelor's degree must be completed at PQC.

Visiting: There are regularly scheduled orientations for prospective students. There are guides for informal visits and visitors may sit in on classes and stay overnight. To schedule a visit, contact the Director of Admissions.

Financial Aid: PQC is a member of CSS. The FAFSA and the previous year's student's/parents' tax forms are required.

International Students: They must score 480 on the written TOEFL and also take the SAT I or the ACT, scoring 700.

Computers: The mainframe is an IBM 3400. All students may access the system. There are no time limits and no fees.

Admissions Contact: Ralph Spencer, Jr., Admissions Officer. Web: *www.pqc.edu*

PRAIRIE VIEW A&M UNIVERSITY
Prairie View, TX 77446

E-3
(936) 857-2618; Fax: (936) 857-2699

Full-time: 2432 men, 2965 women	Faculty: 314; IIA, av$
Part-time: 233 men, 412 women	Ph.D.s: 65%
Graduate: 519 men, 1247 women	Student/Faculty: 17 to 1
Year: semesters, summer session	Tuition: $3592 ($10,672)
Application Deadline: July 1	Room & Board: $5826
Freshman Class: 2767 applied, 2710 accepted, 1496 enrolled	
SAT I Verbal/Math: 410/410	ACT: 16 **NONCOMPETITIVE**

Prairie View A&M University, established in 1878, is a comprehensive unit of the Texas A&M University System, offering undergraduate and graduate degree programs in applied sciences and engineering technology, business, engineering, nursing, arts and sciences, education, agriculture and human sciences, architecture, juvenile justice, and psychology. Some information in this capsule and profile is approximate. There are

8 undergraduate and 6 graduate schools. In addition to regional accreditation, PVAMU has baccalaureate program accreditation with ABET, CSWE, NAAB, NCATE, and NLN. The library contains 240,000 volumes, 260,000 microform items, and 100,000 audio/video tapes/CDs, and subscribes to 1600 periodicals. Computerized library services include the card catalog, interlibrary loans, and database searching. Special learning facilities include a learning resource center and radio station. The 1440-acre campus is in a small town 40 miles northwest of Houston. Including any residence halls, there are 47 buildings.

Student Life: 93% of undergraduates are from Texas. Students are from 40 states and 44 foreign countries. 90% are from public schools. 90% are African American. The average age of freshmen is 18; all undergraduates, 22. 30% do not continue beyond their first year; 32% remain to graduate.

Housing: 3102 students can be accommodated in college housing, which includes coed dorms and on-campus apartments. In addition, there are special-interest houses and an intensive learning community for 600 upperclass students. On-campus housing is guaranteed for the freshman year only and is available on a first-come, first-served basis. 75% of students live on campus; of those, 40% remain on campus on weekends. Alcohol is not permitted. All students may keep cars.

Activities: 8% of men belong to 4 national fraternities; 8% of women belong to 4 national sororities. There are 30 groups on campus, including band, cheerleading, choir, chorus, dance, drama, drill team, ethnic, honors, international, jazz band, marching band, newspaper, orchestra, photography, political, professional, radio and TV, religious, social, social service, student government, and yearbook. Popular campus events include Honors Week, Family Day, and trail rides.

Sports: There are 7 intercollegiate sports for men and 9 for women, and 6 intramural sports for men and 4 for women. Facilities include a 5000-seat stadium and a large athletic and recreation complex.

Disabled Students: 5% of the campus is accessible. Wheelchair ramps, elevators, special parking, and specially equipped rest rooms are available.

Services: Counseling and information services are available, as is tutoring in some subjects. There is a reader service for the blind and remedial math, reading, and writing.

Campus Safety and Security: Measures include 24-hour foot and vehicle patrol, informal discussions, pamphlets/posters/films, and emergency telephones. There are lighted pathways/sidewalks and a 24-hour department of traffic and security.

Programs of Study: PVAMU confers B.A., B.S., B.Arch., B.A.S.W., B.B.A., B.S.Ag., B.S.C.E., B.S.C.E.T., B.S.C.H.E., B.S.C.J., B.S.Diet., B.S.E.E., B.S.E.E.T., B.S.H.S., B.S.I.S., B.S.I.T., B.S.M.E., B.S.N., and B.S.T.C.H. degrees. Master's and doctoral degrees are also awarded. Bachelor's degrees are awarded in AGRICULTURE (agricultural business management, agricultural economics, agronomy, and animal science), BIOLOGICAL SCIENCE (biology/biological science), BUSINESS (accounting, banking and finance, business administration and management, and marketing/retailing/merchandising), COMMUNICATIONS AND THE ARTS (art, broadcasting, communications, dramatic arts, English, journalism, music, Spanish, and speech/debate/rhetoric), COMPUTER AND PHYSICAL SCIENCE (chemistry, computer science, mathematics, and physics), EDUCATION (physical), ENGINEERING AND ENVIRONMENTAL DESIGN (architecture, chemical engineering, civil engineering, computer engineering, electrical/electronics engineering, engineering technology, industrial engineering technology, and mechanical engineering), HEALTH PROFESSIONS (health, medical technology, and nursing), SOCIAL SCIENCE (criminal justice, dietetics, family and community services, geography, history, interdisciplinary studies, political science/government, psychology, social work, and sociology). Engineering, nursing, and natural sciences are the strongest academically. Education, engineering, and business are the largest.

Required: All students must complete 120 semester hours, with a minimum GPA of 2.5 or higher, depending on the major. Completion of a 42-hour core curriculum is required. Some majors require a comprehensive exam or thesis.

Special: Cooperative programs and internships in various majors, work-study programs, and combined B.A.-B.S. degrees in chemistry, biology, math, and computer science are offered. There are 24 national honor societies, including Phi Beta Kappa, and a freshman honors program.

Faculty/Classroom: 64% of faculty are male; 36%, female. 93% teach undergraduates, 3% do research, and 3% do both. Graduate students teach 1% of introductory courses. The average class size in an introductory lecture is 70; in a laboratory, 15; and in a regular course, 35.

Admissions: 98% of the 2003-2004 applicants were accepted. The SAT I scores for the 2003-2004 freshman class were: Verbal--87% below 500, 12% between 500 and 599, and 1% between 600 and 700; Math--84% below 500, 14% between 500 and 599, and 2% between 600 and 700. The ACT scores were 89% below 21, 8% between 21 and 23, 2% between 24 and 26, and 1% between 27 and 28. 19% of the current freshmen were in the top fifth of their class; 42% were in the top two fifths.

Requirements: The SAT I or ACT is required. The minimum composite score must be 820 on the SAT I or 17 on the ACT. In addition, a GPA of at least 2.0 is necessary for financial aid eligibility. Applicants should be graduates of accredited high schools or have earned the GED. Secondary school preparation should include 4 years each of English and academic electives, 3 years each of math and social studies, and 2 years of science. PVAMU requires applicants to be in the upper 50% of their class. A GPA of 2.5 is required. AP and CLEP credits are accepted. Important factors in the admissions decision are leadership record, advanced placement or honor courses, and recommendations by school officials.

Procedure: Freshmen are admitted to all sessions. Entrance exams should be taken during the junior or senior year of high school. There is a deferred admissions plan and a rolling admissions plan. Applications should be filed by July 1 for fall entry, November 1 for spring entry, and April 1 for summer entry, along with a $25 fee. Notification is sent on a rolling basis. Applications are accepted on-line through the Texas common application or the university's web site at *www.applytexas.org*.

Transfer: 224 transfer students enrolled in a recent year. Transfer applicants must present at least a 2.0 GPA from the last college attended. 30 credits of 120 required for the bachelor's degree must be completed at PVAMU.

Visiting: There are regularly scheduled orientations for prospective students, consisting of an orientation held 2 days prior to registration. There are guides for informal visits and visitors may sit in on classes and stay overnight. To schedule a visit, contact the Office of Records at (936) 857-2626 or *recruitment@pvamu.edu*.

Financial Aid: In 2003-2004, 82% of all full-time freshmen received some form of financial aid. 64% of full-time freshmen received need-based aid. The average freshman award was $4200. Need-based scholarships or need-based grants averaged $3695; need-based self-help aid (loans and jobs) averaged $3825; non-need-based athletic scholarships averaged $9500; and other non-need-based awards and non-need-based scholarships averaged $9200. 42% of undergraduates work part time. Average annual earnings from campus work are $2200. The average financial indebtedness of a recent graduate was $1400. PVAMU is a member of CSS. The CSS Profile, FAFSA, and the college's own financial statement are required. Check with the school for current deadlines.

International Students: There were 127 international students enrolled in a recent year. They must score 500 on the written TOEFL and also take the SAT I or the ACT, scoring 820 on the SAT I.

Computers: The mainframe is an IBM 4361. A student computer center is available, as are PCs in the library. Students enrolled in computer courses or working in offices may access the system. After students receive security checks and training, PCs are available for use in courses. There are no fees. It is strongly recommended that all students have a personal computer.

Graduates: In a recent year, 705 bachelor's degrees were awarded. The most popular majors were nursing (12%), biology (8%), and interdisciplinary studies education (7%). In an average class, 32% graduate in 6 years or less. 457 companies recruited on campus in a recent year. Of a recent graduating class, 22% were enrolled in graduate school within 6 months of graduation and 71% were employed.

Admissions Contact: Mary Gooch, Director of Admissions. A video is available. E-mail: *admissions@pvamu.edu* Web: *www.pvamu.edu*

RICE UNIVERSITY
Houston, TX 77251-1892

E-3
(713) 348-7423
(800) 527-OWLS; Fax: (713) 348-5952

Full-time: 1488 men, 1361 women	Faculty: 530; I, +$
Part-time: 28 men, 44 women	Ph.D.s: 96%
Graduate: 1304 men, 734 women	Student/Faculty: 5 to 1
Year: semesters	Tuition: $19,670
Application Deadline: January 10	Room & Board: $7880
Freshman Class: 7501 applied, 1821 accepted, 715 enrolled	
SAT I or ACT: required	MOST COMPETITIVE

Rice University, founded in 1912, is a private institution offering undergraduate and graduate programs through the divisions of Engineering, Natural Sciences, Humanities, Social Sciences, Music, Architecture, and Administrative Sciences. There are 6 undergraduate and 7 graduate schools. In addition to regional accreditation, Rice has baccalaureate program accreditation with ABET and NAAB. The library contains 2,314,820 volumes, 3,074,402 microform items, and 46,070 audio/video tapes/CDs, and subscribes to 36,889 periodicals. Computerized library services include the card catalog, database searching, and Internet access. Special learning facilities include an art gallery, radio station, TV station, and media center. The 300-acre campus is in an urban area 3 miles southwest of downtown Houston. Including any residence halls, there are 71 buildings.

Student Life: 52% of undergraduates are from Texas. Students are from 50 states, 37 foreign countries, and Canada. 53% are white; 15% Asian American; 11% Hispanic. The average age of freshmen is 18; all undergraduates, 20. 4% do not continue beyond their first year; 92% remain to graduate.

Housing: 74 students can be accommodated in college housing, which includes coed dorms. On-campus housing is available on a lottery system for upperclassmen. 71% of students live on campus; of those, 95% remain on campus on weekends. All students may keep cars.

Activities: There are no fraternities or sororities. There are 204 groups on campus, including academic, art, band, cheerleading, chess, choir, chorale, chorus, computers, dance, debate, drama, ethnic, film, gay, honors, international, jazz band, literary magazine, marching band, musical theater, newspaper, orchestra, pep band, photography, political, professional, radio and TV, religious, social, social service, student government, symphony, and yearbook. Popular campus events include Baker Shakespeare Festival, an annual biking relay race, and Archi Arts, a costume ball.

Sports: There are 19 intercollegiate sports for men and 18 for women, and 14 intramural sports for men and 13 for women. Facilities include a 5000-seat gym, a pool, a track stadium, fields for soccer, lacrosse, and rugby, courts for tennis, squash, racquetball, volleyball, and basketball, and a 70,000-seat stadium.

Disabled Students: 90% of the campus is accessible. Wheelchair ramps, elevators, special parking, specially equipped rest rooms, special class scheduling, lowered drinking fountains, lowered telephones, special housing, and a stair lift are available.

Services: Counseling and information services are available, as is tutoring in every subject.

Campus Safety and Security: Measures include 24-hour foot and vehicle patrol, self-defense education, security escort services, and shuttle buses. There are informal discussions, pamphlets/posters/films, emergency telephones, lighted pathways/sidewalks, and a campus police department with a variety of outreach programs.

Programs of Study: Rice confers B.A., B.S., B.Arch., B.F.A., B.Mus., and B.S.E degrees. Master's and doctoral degrees are also awarded. Bachelor's degrees are awarded in BIOLOGICAL SCIENCE (biology/ biological science), BUSINESS (management science), COMMUNICATIONS AND THE ARTS (art history and appreciation, classics, English, linguistics, music, music history and appreciation, music performance, music theory and composition, and visual and performing arts), COMPUTER AND PHYSICAL SCIENCE (applied mathematics, chemistry, computer science, earth science, geology, geophysics and seismology, mathematics, physics, and statistics), ENGINEERING AND ENVIRONMENTAL DESIGN (architectural engineering, architecture, bioengineering, chemical engineering, civil engineering, electrical/electronics engineering, environmental engineering, and mechanical engineering), HEALTH PROFESSIONS (exercise science), SOCIAL SCIENCE (anthropology, Asian/Oriental studies, classical/ancient civilization, cognitive science, economics, French studies, German area studies, Hispanic American studies, history, medieval studies, philosophy, political science/ government, psychology, public affairs, religion, Russian and Slavic studies, sociology, and women's studies).

Required: All students must complete at least 120 credits, with a 1.67 overall GPA and a 2.0 GPA in the major field. Distribution requirements include 12 credit/semester hours in natural sciences, social sciences, or humanities, depending on the major, and additional courses in these fields to meet distribution requirements. All students take 2 semesters of phys ed. At least 48 semester hours in upper-level courses are required.

Special: An 8-year guaranteed medical school program with the Baylor College of Medicine; a 5-year joint degree program for BSE/MSE in engineering; a 5-year joint degree for BSE/MBA in engineering and business, and a 3-2 engineering degree are possible, as are cross-registration, internships, study abroad, work-study, dual majors, and student-designed majors. There are 10 national honor societies, including Phi Beta Kappa, and 9 departmental honors programs.

Faculty/Classroom: 77% of faculty are male; 23%, female. All both teach and do research. The average class size in a regular course is 11.

Admissions: 24% of the 2003-2004 applicants were accepted. The SAT I scores for the 2003-2004 freshman class were: Verbal--2% below 500, 7% between 500 and 599, 34% between 600 and 700, and 57% above 700; Math--1% below 500, 6% between 500 and 599, 30% between 600 and 700, and 64% above 700. The ACT scores for the 2003-2004 freshmen class were 1% below 21, 3% between 21 and 23, 20% between 24 and 29, and 77% 29 and above. 94% of the current freshmen were in the top quarter of their class; 98% were in the top half. There were 173 National Merit finalists. 21 freshmen graduated first in their class.

Requirements: The SAT I or ACT is required. In addition, official high school transcript(s), 1 counselor recommendation, 1 teacher recommendation, and 3 SAT II: Subject tests (writing plus 2 others in fields related to the candidate's proposed field of study) are required. Music students must arrange an audition. Architecture students must submit a portfolio. An interview is recommended but not required. Candidates should have completed 16 college-prep units, including 4 years in English, 3 in math, and 2 each in social studies, foreign language, and lab science. AP credits are accepted.

Procedure: Freshmen are admitted in the fall. Entrance exams should be taken between October and January of the senior year, depending on the decision plan. There are early decision and early admissions plans. Early decision applications should be filed by November 1; interim decision, by December 1; regular applications, by January 10 for fall entry, along with a $40 fee. Notification of early decision is sent December 15; interim decision, February 10; regular decision, April 1. 125 early decision candidates were accepted for the 2003-2004 class; 121 were admitted. Applications are accepted on-line through the school's web site.

Transfer: 63 transfer students enrolled in fall 2003. Transfer applicants should present at least a 3.2 GPA in previous college work, SAT I scores, 2 college teacher recommendations, high school and college transcripts, and a letter from the dean of current college. 60 of 120 credits required for the bachelor's degree must be completed at Rice.

Visiting: There are regularly scheduled orientations for prospective students, consisting of information sessions and tours available year-round. There are guides for informal visits and visitors may sit in on classes and stay overnight. To schedule a visit, contact the Office of Admissions at (800) 527-6957.

Financial Aid: In 2003-2004, 62% of all full-time freshmen and 67% of continuing full-time students received some form of financial aid. 34% of full-time freshmen and 37% of continuing full-time students received need-based aid. Need-based scholarships or need-based grants averaged $12,226; need-based self-help aid (loans and jobs) averaged $3386; non-need-based athletic scholarships averaged $23,239; and other non-need-based awards and non-need-based scholarships averaged $4999. The average financial indebtedness of the 2003 graduate was $12,942. Rice is a member of CSS. The CSS Profile or FAFSA and the parents' and student's tax returns are required. The deadline for filing freshman financial aid applications for fall entry is March 1.

International Students: There are 91 international students enrolled. They must score 600 on the written TOEFL or 250 on the electronic version and also take the SAT I or the ACT. Students must take SAT II: Subject tests in writing and 2 others (3 total).

Computers: There are Mac and IBM PCs available in the residential colleges, computing center, the library, and academic labs. All students may access the system. There are no time limits and no fees. It is strongly recommended that all students have a personal computer.

Graduates: From July 1, 2002 to June 30, 2003, 977 bachelor's degrees were awarded. The most popular majors were economics (7%), psychology (7%), and electrical and computer engineering (7%). In an average class, 75% graduate in 4 years or less, 89% graduate in 5 years or less, and 92% graduate in 6 years or less. 137 companies recruited on campus in 2002-2003. Of the 2002 graduating class, 43% were enrolled in graduate school within 6 months of graduation and 49% were employed.

Admissions Contact: Julie M. Browning, Dean for Undergraduate Enrollment. Web: *www.rice.edu*

SAINT EDWARD'S UNIVERSITY
Austin, TX 78704

D-3
(512) 448-8500
(800) 555-0164; Fax: (512) 464-8877

Full-time: 1067 men, 1399 women	Faculty: 124; IIA, -$
Part-time: 463 men, 602 women	Ph.D.s: 80%
Graduate: 378 men, 534 women	Student/Faculty: 20 to 1
Year: semesters, summer session	Tuition: $14,710
Application Deadline: July 1	Room & Board: $5718
Freshman Class: 2005 applied, 1396 accepted, 546 enrolled	
SAT I Verbal/Math: 540/540	ACT: 23 COMPETITIVE

Saint Edward's University, founded in 1885, is an independent Catholic institution offering undergraduate and graduate courses in liberal arts, human service, business administration, and computer science. There are 7 undergraduate and 5 graduate schools. In addition to regional accreditation, SEU has baccalaureate program accreditation with CSWE. The library contains 154,719 volumes, 1375 microform items, and 2648 audio/video tapes/CDs, and subscribes to 1185 periodicals. Computerized library services include the card catalog, interlibrary loans, database searching, and Internet access. Special learning facilities include a learning resource center, art gallery, and a photography lab. The 160-acre campus is in an urban area in Austin. Including any residence halls, there are 46 buildings.

Student Life: 92% of undergraduates are from Texas. Students are from 33 states and 33 foreign countries. 83% are from public schools. 55% are white; 31% Hispanic. The average age of freshmen is 18; all undergraduates, 21. 21% do not continue beyond their first year; 52% remain to graduate.

Housing: 1035 students can be accommodated in college housing, which includes single-sex and coed dorms and on-campus apartments. On-campus housing is guaranteed for the freshman year only and is available on a first-come, first-served basis. 63% of students commute. All students may keep cars.

Activities: There are no fraternities or sororities. There are 50 groups on campus, including art, cheerleading, choir, chorale, chorus, computers, dance, drama, ethnic, film, forensics, gay, honors, international, literary magazine, musical theater, newspaper, photography, political, professional, religious, social service, student government, and yearbook. Popular campus events include Festival of Lights, Multicultural Spring Fest, and Hillfest.

Sports: There are 5 intercollegiate sports for men and 6 for women, and 8 intramural sports for men and 8 for women. Facilities include 2 gyms, baseball and softball fields, 2 soccer fields, tennis, basketball, racquetball/handball, and volleyball courts, an indoor/outdoor pool, and a fitness center.

Disabled Students: 95% of the campus is accessible. Wheelchair ramps, elevators, special parking, specially equipped rest rooms, special class scheduling, lowered drinking fountains, and lowered telephones are available.

Services: Counseling and information services are available, as is tutoring in most subjects. There is remedial math, reading, and writing. There is also a "Learning Strategies" course.

Campus Safety and Security: Measures include 24-hour foot and vehicle patrol, self-defense education, security escort services, and informal discussions. There are pamphlets/posters/films, emergency telephones, lighted pathways/sidewalks, and the outside doors of residence halls are locked at all times. Residents are issued keys or use student ID for access, appropriate to the hall.

Programs of Study: SEU confers B.A., B.S., B.A.A.S., B.B.A., and B.L.S. degrees. Master's degrees are also awarded. Bachelor's degrees are awarded in BIOLOGICAL SCIENCE (biochemistry, bioinformatics, and biology/biological science), BUSINESS (accounting, banking and finance, business administration and management, entrepreneurial studies, international business management, and marketing management), COMMUNICATIONS AND THE ARTS (art, communications, dramatic arts, English literature, graphic design, photography, and Spanish), COMPUTER AND PHYSICAL SCIENCE (chemistry, computer science, information sciences and systems, and mathematics), EDUCATION (art, drama, English, foreign languages, mathematics, physical, science, and social studies), ENGINEERING AND ENVIRONMENTAL DESIGN (preengineering), HEALTH PROFESSIONS (predentistry and premedicine), SOCIAL SCIENCE (criminal justice, economics, forensic studies, history, interdisciplinary studies, international relations, Latin American studies, liberal arts/general studies, philosophy, physical fitness/movement, political science/government, prelaw, psychology, religion, religious education, social work, and sociology). Communication, psychology, and business administration are the largest.

Required: All students must maintain a minimum GPA of 2.0 while taking 120 semester hours, including 36 to 75 in the major. The core curriculum includes courses from Foundational Skills, Cultural Foundations, and Foundations for Values and Decisions. In the required capstone class, seniors identify a problem in society, research it, and present their solutions in an extensive final paper.

Special: Internships and study abroad in a variety of countries through the ISEP and SEU and other university programs are available. A liberal studies degree, credit for life experience, nondegree study, and pass/fail options also are possible, as well as a dual major in Spanish and international business. A flexible program for working adults is offered through New College. There are 5 national honor societies and a freshman honors program.

Faculty/Classroom: 52% of faculty are male; 48%, female. 69% teach undergraduates. No introductory courses are taught by graduate students. The average class size in a laboratory is 14 and in a regular course, 20.

Admissions: 70% of the 2003-2004 applicants were accepted. The SAT I scores for the 2003-2004 freshman class were: Verbal--23% below 500, 49% between 500 and 599, 26% between 600 and 700, and 2% above 700; Math--26% below 500, 46% between 500 and 599, 27% between 600 and 700, and 1% above 700. The ACT scores were 23% below 21, 32% between 21 and 23, 22% between 24 and 26, 14% between 27 and 28, and 9% above 28. 37% of the current freshmen were in the top fifth of their class; 68% were in the top two fifths. 5 freshmen graduated first in their class.

Requirements: The SAT I or ACT is required. In addition, successful applicants should be in the top half of their graduating class, with testing at or above the Texas average of 1000 on the SAT I combined scores, or 21 on the ACT. The GED is accepted. An interview is recommended. An essay is required. SEU requires applicants to be in the upper 50% of their class. AP and CLEP credits are accepted. Important factors in the admissions decision are advanced placement or honor courses, leadership record, and geographic diversity.

Procedure: Freshmen are admitted fall and spring. Entrance exams should be taken in spring of junior year or in summer or fall of senior year. There is a deferred admissions plan and a rolling admissions plan. Early decision applications should be filed by February 1; regular applications, by July 1 for fall entry, December 1 for spring entry, and May 1 for summer entry. Notification of early decision is sent on a rolling basis; regular decision, on a rolling basis. The fall 2003 application fee was $45. 219 students were on the 2003 waiting list; 107 were admitted. Applications are accepted on-line through the St. Edward's web site.

Transfer: 268 transfer students enrolled in 2002-2003. Transfer applicants must have a minimum GPA of 2.25. Transfers with less than 30 hours must submit high school transcripts. 30 of 120 credits required for the bachelor's degree must be completed at SEU.

Visiting: There are regularly scheduled orientations for prospective students, including a tour, financial aid session, academic session, class visits, entertainment, and an overnight stay in a residence hall. There are guides for informal visits and visitors may sit in on classes and stay overnight. To schedule a visit, contact the Admissions Office at (800) 555-0164 or seu.admit@admin.stedwards.edu.

Financial Aid: In 2003-2004, 86% of all full-time freshmen and 78% of continuing full-time students received some form of financial aid. 57% of full-time freshmen and 63% of continuing full-time students received need-based aid. The average freshman award was $16,223. Need-based scholarships or need-based grants averaged $8907 ($22,075 maximum); need-based self-help aid (loans and jobs) averaged $2902 ($8625 maximum); non-need-based athletic scholarships averaged $7394 ($20,350 maximum); other non-need-based awards and non-need-based scholarships averaged $5846 ($16,710 maximum); and non-need-based loans and community scholarships averaged $7730 ($25,116 maximum). 25% of undergraduates work part time. Average annual earnings from campus work are $2000. The average financial indebtedness of the 2003 graduate was $22,331. SEU is a member of CSS. The FAFSA is required. The deadline for filing freshman financial aid applications for fall entry is April 15.

International Students: There are 82 international students enrolled. The school actively recruits these students. They must score 500 on the written TOEFL or 173 on the electronic version or take the SAT I or ACT.

Computers: The mainframe is an HP 9000/K200. Students may use the multiuser system for computer science assignments, e-mail, Internet and web access, and to publish web pages. There are 475 computers available for general use. All students may access the system. Dial-up is available 24 hours every day. There are 2 computer labs available 24 hours per day. There are no time limits and no fees.

Graduates: From July 1, 2002 to June 30, 2003, 779 bachelor's degrees were awarded. The most popular majors were business and management (7%), communication (7%), and psychology (6%). In an average class, 2% graduate in 3 years or less, 27% graduate in 4 years or less, 46% graduate in 5 years or less, and 52% graduate in 6 years or less. 97 companies recruited on campus in 2002-2003.

Admissions Contact: Tracy Manier, Director of Undergraduate Admission. E-mail: seu.admit@admin.stedwards.edu
Web: http://www.stedwards.edu

SAINT MARY'S UNIVERSITY OF SAN ANTONIO D-4
San Antonio, TX 78228-8503   (210) 436-3126
(800) FOR-STMU; Fax: (210) 431-6742

Full-time: 974 men, 1396 women	**Faculty:** 146; IIA, +$
Part-time: 88 men, 124 women	**Ph.D.s:** 85%
Graduate: 786 men, 750 women	**Student/Faculty:** 16 to 1
Year: semesters, summer session	**Tuition:** $16,492
Application Deadline: open	**Room & Board:** $5952
Freshman Class: 1464 applied, 1189 accepted, 472 enrolled	
SAT I Verbal/Math: 540/530	**ACT:** 22 **COMPETITIVE**

Saint Mary's University, established in 1852, is a private Roman Catholic institution in the Marianist tradition, offering undergraduate programs in humanities and social sciences, business and administration, and science, engineering, and technology. There are 3 undergraduate and 2 graduate schools. In addition to regional accreditation, St. Mary's has baccalaureate program accreditation with ABET and NASM. The 2 libraries contain 481,137 volumes, 131,324 microform items, and 3104 audio/video tapes/CDs, and subscribe to 1320 periodicals. Computerized library services include the card catalog, interlibrary loans, database searching, and Internet access. Special learning facilities include a learning resource center. The 135-acre campus is in a suburban area 5 miles northwest of San Antonio. Including any residence halls, there are 32 buildings.

Student Life: 92% of undergraduates are from Texas. Students are from 32 states, 36 foreign countries, and Canada. 74% are from public schools. 69% are Hispanic; 21% white. 66% are Catholic; 17% Baptist, Buddhist, Christian, Eastern Orthodox, Episcopal, Hindu; 14% Protestant. The average age of freshmen is 18; all undergraduates, 22. 7% do not continue beyond their first year; 64% remain to graduate.

Housing: 1262 students can be accommodated in college housing, which includes single-sex and coed dorms. On-campus housing is guaranteed for the freshman year only and is available on a first-come, first-served basis. Priority is given to out-of-town students. 58% of students commute. Alcohol is not permitted. All students may have cars.

Activities: 15% of men belong to 1 local and 4 national fraternities; 13% of women belong to 1 local and 3 national sororities. There are 55 groups on campus, including art, band, cheerleading, choir, chorale, dance, drama, ethnic, honors, international, jazz band, newspaper, pep band, photography, political, professional, religious, social, social service, and student government. Popular campus events include Campus Ministry Retreat, Hunger Awareness Week, and Fiesta Oyster Bake.

Sports: There are 5 intercollegiate sports for men and 5 for women, and 28 intramural sports for men and 28 for women. Facilities include a gym, a weight room, tennis, handball, and basketball courts, and various playing fields.

Disabled Students: 80% of the campus is accessible. Wheelchair ramps, elevators, special parking, specially equipped rest rooms, special class scheduling, lowered drinking fountains, and special housing are available.

Services: Counseling and information services are available, as is tutoring in every subject. There is remedial math, reading, and writing.

Campus Safety and Security: Measures include 24-hour foot and vehicle patrol, security escort services, informal discussions, and pamphlets/posters/films. There are emergency telephones, lighted pathways/sidewalks, and a crime prevention awareness program each semester.

Programs of Study: St. Mary's confers B.A., B.S., B.A.S., B.A.T., and B.B.A. degrees. Master's and doctoral degrees are also awarded. Bachelor's degrees are awarded in BIOLOGICAL SCIENCE (biochemistry and biology/biological science), BUSINESS (accounting, banking and finance, business administration and management, human resources, international business management, and marketing/retailing/merchandising), COMMUNICATIONS AND THE ARTS (communications, English, French, German, music, Spanish, and speech/debate/rhetoric), COMPUTER AND PHYSICAL SCIENCE (chemistry, computer science, earth science, mathematics, and physics), EDUCATION (business, elementary, science, and secondary), ENGINEERING AND ENVIRONMENTAL DESIGN (computer engineering, electrical/electronics engineering, engineering, and industrial engineering), HEALTH PROFESSIONS (predentistry and premedicine), SOCIAL SCIENCE (criminal justice, economics, history, international relations, international studies, Latin American studies, philosophy, political science/government, prelaw, psychology, sociology, and theological studies). Biology, accounting, and political science are the strongest academically. Biology, business, and political science are the largest.

Required: All students must complete at least 129 semester hours, 24 to 30 in the major, with a minimum 2.5 GPA. Core curriculum requirements include courses in fine arts, English, foreign language, speech, natural science, math, social science, philosophy, and theology. Students must also take computer science, demonstrate computer literacy, and take interdisciplinary electives.

Special: St. Mary's offers cooperative programs and internships in all majors, depending on the student's needs. Students may cross-register at any of the United Colleges of San Antonio, spend a semester in Washington, D.C., or study in England, Austria, or Mexico. Dual majors are possible in computer science and engineering and public justice and sociology, political science, or psychology. Accelerated degree programs are offered in law, (J.D./M.B.A.) and dentistry (B.A. in combined science and dentistry). Required theology courses may be taken on a pass/fail basis. There are 3 national honor societies and a freshman honors program.

Faculty/Classroom: 67% of faculty are male; 33%, female. 72% teach undergraduates. No introductory courses are taught by graduate students. The average class size in an introductory lecture is 30; in a laboratory, 60; and in a regular course, 25.

Admissions: 81% of the 2003-2004 applicants were accepted. The SAT I scores for the 2003-2004 freshman class were: Verbal--31% below 500, 47% between 500 and 599, 21% between 600 and 700, and 1% above 700; Math--28% below 500, 52% between 500 and 599, 17% between 600 and 700, and 3% above 700. The ACT scores were 32% below 21, 40% between 21 and 23, 18% between 24 and 26, 7% between 27 and 28, and 2% above 28. 58% of the current freshmen were in the top fifth of their class; 84% were in the top two fifths. 10 freshmen graduated first in their class.

Requirements: The SAT I or ACT is required. In addition, all applicants must be high school graduates or have the GED, rank in the upper half of their graduating classes, and score in the 50th percentile on SAT I or ACT. Secondary school preparation should include 4 units of English, 3 each of math and academic electives, and 2 each of social science, natural science, and foreign language. Potential science and engineering majors should have 4 units of math and 3 of lab science, including chemistry or physics. AP and CLEP credits are accepted. Important factors in the admissions decision are leadership record, advanced placement or honor courses, and personality/intangible qualities.

Procedure: Freshmen are admitted fall and spring. Entrance exams should be taken by the fall of the senior year. There are early admissions and deferred admissions plans. Application deadlines are open. The fall 2003 application fee was $30. There is a rolling admissions plan. Applications are accepted on-line through ApplyWeb at the school's web site.

Transfer: 129 transfer students enrolled in 2002-2003. Transfer applicants must present at least a 2.0 GPA in previous college work, which should include 3 hours of English composition. St. Mary's also recommends that applicants submit SAT I or ACT scores and schedule an interview. 30 of 129 credits required for the bachelor's degree must be completed at St. Mary's.

Visiting: There are regularly scheduled orientations for prospective students, including a tour, an admissions/financial aid session, an overnight stay, and class visits. There are guides for informal visits and visitors may sit in on classes and stay overnight. To schedule a visit, contact the Undergraduate Admissions Office.

Financial Aid: In 2003-2004, 80% of all full-time freshmen and 78% of continuing full-time students received some form of financial aid. 74% of full-time freshmen and 69% of continuing full-time students received need-based aid. The average freshman award was $14,481. Need-based scholarships or need-based grants averaged $6965; need-based self-help aid (loans and jobs) averaged $5025; non-need-based athletic scholarships averaged $7152; and other non-need-based awards and non-need-based scholarships averaged $8479. 30% of undergraduates work part time. Average annual earnings from campus work are $2000. The average financial indebtedness of the 2003 graduate was $23,406. St. Mary's is a member of CSS. The CSS Profile is required. The deadline for filing freshman financial aid applications for fall entry is April 1.

International Students: There are 107 international students enrolled. The school actively recruits these students. They must score 550 on the written TOEFL. The SAT I or ACT is strongly recommended for scholarship consideration.

Computers: The mainframes are a DEC VAX 6000 Model 510 and MicroVAX II. Students have access to 36 PCs in the academic library during library hours. They can also check out the software to use with the library's computers. Other mainframe systems are available to students on a restricted basis, either by approval or by course requirement. All students may access the system. There are no time limits and no fees.

Graduates: From July 1, 2002 to June 30, 2003, 464 bachelor's degrees were awarded. The most popular majors were biology (13%), English communication arts (7%), and political science (6%). In an average class, 32% graduate in 4 years or less, 58% graduate in 5 years or less, and 62% graduate in 6 years or less. 30 companies recruited on campus in 2002-2003.

Admissions Contact: Richard Castillo, Director of Undergraduate Admissions. E-mail: *uadm@stmarytx.edu* Web: *www.stmarytx.edu*

SAM HOUSTON STATE UNIVERSITY E-3
Huntsville, TX 77340   (936) 294-1828; Fax: (936) 294-3758

Full-time: 4110 men, 5629 women	Faculty: IIA, av$
Part-time: 719 men, 1046 women	Ph.D.s: 94%
Graduate: 624 men, 1332 women	Student/Faculty: n/av
Year: semesters, summer session	Tuition: $3016 ($8200)
Application Deadline: open	Room & Board: $4126
Freshman Class: 5182 applied, 3915 accepted, 1832 enrolled	
SAT I Verbal/Math: 506/504	ACT: 21 COMPETITIVE

Sam Houston University, founded in 1879, is a public institution offering programs in arts and sciences, business administration, criminal justice, education, and applied science. There are 4 undergraduate and 4 graduate schools. In addition to regional accreditation, Sam Houston State has baccalaureate program accreditation with NASM and NCATE. The library contains 1,187,338 volumes, 1,111,264 microform items, and 19,716 audio/video tapes/CDs, and subscribes to 3502 periodicals. Computerized library services include the card catalog, interlibrary loans, and database searching. Special learning facilities include a learning resource center, planetarium, radio station, TV station, and the Sam Houston Museum. The 1256-acre campus is in a small town 70 miles north of Houston.

Student Life: 98% of undergraduates are from Texas. Students are from 47 states, 46 foreign countries, and Canada. 74% are white; 13% African American; 10% Hispanic. The average age of freshmen is 18; all undergraduates, 23. 36% do not continue beyond their first year; 33% remain to graduate.

Housing: 3011 students can be accommodated in college housing, which includes single-sex and coed dorms, on-campus apartments, off-campus apartments, married-student housing, fraternity houses, and sorority houses. In addition, there are honors houses and special-interest houses. On-campus housing is guaranteed for all 4 years. 74% of students commute. All students may keep cars.

Activities: There are 14 local fraternities and 13 local sororities. There are many groups and organizations on campus, including art, band, cheerleading, choir, chorale, chorus, computers, dance, drama, drill team, ethnic, film, gay, honors, international, jazz band, marching band, musical theater, newspaper, orchestra, pep band, photography, political, professional, radio and TV, religious, social, social service, student government, symphony, and yearbook. Popular campus events include Organization Fair, Greek Week, and Spring Fling.

Sports: There are 7 intercollegiate sports for men and 7 for women, and 13 intramural sports for men and 13 for women. Facilities include a 14,000-seat stadium, a 5200-seat gym, 4 basketball courts, 10 racquetball courts, 3 swimming pools, and 2 weight rooms.

Disabled Students: 90% of the campus is accessible. Wheelchair ramps, elevators, special parking, specially equipped rest rooms, lowered drinking fountains, closed-circuit television (CCTV), computer workstations with large print and speech output capabilities, and telecommunication devices for the deaf (TDD) are available.

Services: Counseling and information services are available, as is tutoring in every subject. There is a reader service for the blind, and remedial math, reading, and writing.

Campus Safety and Security: Measures include 24-hour foot and vehicle patrol, security escort services, informal discussions, and pamphlets/posters/films. There are emergency telephones and lighted pathways/sidewalks.

Programs of Study: Sam Houston State confers B.A., B.S., B.A.A.S., B.B.A., and B.F.A. degrees. Master's and doctoral degrees are also awarded. Bachelor's degrees are awarded in AGRICULTURE (agriculture, animal science, and horticulture), BIOLOGICAL SCIENCE (biology/biological science), BUSINESS (accounting, banking and finance, business administration and management, and marketing/retailing/merchandising), COMMUNICATIONS AND THE ARTS (art, dance, dramatic arts, English, French, German, graphic design, journalism, music, music performance, music theory and composition, musical theater, photography, Spanish, and speech/debate/rhetoric), COMPUTER AND PHYSICAL SCIENCE (chemistry, computer science, geology, mathematics, and physics), EDUCATION (physical), ENGINEERING AND ENVIRONMENTAL DESIGN (environmental science), HEALTH PROFESSIONS (health, medical technology, and music therapy), SOCIAL SCIENCE (criminal justice, economics, geography, history, law enforcement and corrections, philosophy, physical fitness/movement, political science/government, psychology, and sociology). Psychology and general business are the largest.

Required: All students must maintain a GPA of 2.0 while taking 128 semester hours, including 30 in the major. The core curriculum includes 15 hours of social and behavioral sciences, 9 hours of humanities and visual and performing arts, 8 hours of natural sciences, 6 hours of communication, 4 hours of an institutionally designated option, and 3 hours of math.

Special: Work-study programs with the university, second degrees, and B.A.-B.S. degrees are available. There is 1 national honor society and a freshman honors program.

Faculty/Classroom: 57% of faculty are male; 43%, female. 100% both teach and do research. Graduate students teach 6% of introductory courses.

Admissions: 76% of the 2003-2004 applicants were accepted. The SAT I scores for the 2003-2004 freshman class were: Verbal--54% below 500, 36% between 500 and 599, 9% between 600 and 700, and 1% above 700; Math--53% below 500, 37% between 500 and 599, 9% between 600 and 700, and 1% above 700. The ACT scores were 57% below 21, 25% between 21 and 23, 13% between 24 and 26, 3% between 27 and 28, and 1% above 28. 28% of the current freshmen were in the top fifth of their class; 65% were in the top two fifths. 14 freshmen graduated first in their class.

Requirements: The SAT I or ACT is required, with a minimum required composite score of 1010 on the SAT I or 21 on the ACT. Applicants must have secondary school credits as follows: 4 of English, 2 each of math, history, and science, 1 1/2 of phys ed, and a half credit each of social studies, and health education. The GED is accepted. A GPA of 2.0 is required. AP and CLEP credits are accepted.

Procedure: Freshmen are admitted fall, spring, and summer. There is an early admissions plan. Application deadlines are open. The fall 2003 application fee was $35.

Transfer: 1578 transfer students enrolled in 2002-2003. Transfer applicants must present a 2.0 GPA on all previous college work. 42 of 128 credits required for the bachelor's degree must be completed at Sam Houston State.

Visiting: There are regularly scheduled orientations for prospective students. There are guides for informal visits. To schedule a visit, contact the Visitor Center at (936) 294-1844.

Financial Aid: In 2003-2004, 48% of all full-time freshmen and 43% of continuing full-time students received some form of financial aid. 33% of full-time freshmen and 31% of continuing full-time students received need-based aid. The average freshman award was $5158. 15% of undergraduates work part time. Average annual earnings from campus work are $2000. The average financial indebtedness of the 2003 graduate was $14,046. The FAFSA is required. The priority date for freshman financial aid applications for fall entry is March 31. The deadline for filing freshman financial aid applications for fall entry is May 31.

International Students: There are 87 international students enrolled. The school actively recruits these students. They must score 550 on the written TOEFL or 213 on the electronic version and also take the SAT I or the ACT.

Computers: The mainframes are a DEC VAX 8650, 785, 750, and 6320 and DEC MicroVAX II 3400. There are also 400 PCs and Macs available in labs and class buildings. All students may access the system. There are no time limits. The fee is $50 per semester.

Graduates: From July 1, 2002 to June 30, 2003, 2092 bachelor's degrees were awarded. In an average class, 33% graduate in 6 years or less.

Admissions Contact: Joey Chandler, Director Undergraduate Admissions. A video is available. E-mail: *admissions@shsu.edu* Web: *www.shsu.edu*

SCHREINER UNIVERSITY	D-4
Kerrville, TX 78028-5697	(830) 792-7217
	(800) 343-4919; Fax: (830) 792-7226
Full-time: 290 men, 372 women	**Faculty:** 49; IIB, --$
Part-time: 14 men, 56 women	**Ph.D.s:** 63%
Graduate: 11 men, 37 women	**Student/Faculty:** 14 to 1
Year: semesters, summer session	**Tuition:** $13,640
Application Deadline: August 1	**Room & Board:** $6800
Freshman Class: 700 applied, 482 accepted, 207 enrolled	
SAT I Verbal/Math: 490/490	**ACT:** 19 COMPETITIVE

Schreiner University, founded in 1917, is an independent liberal arts institution affiliated with the Presbyterian Church (U.S.A.). There are 3 undergraduate schools and 1 graduate school. The library contains 69,873 volumes, 593 microform items, and 477 audio/video tapes/CDs, and subscribes to 225 periodicals. Computerized library services include the card catalog, interlibrary loans, database searching, and Internet access. Special learning facilities include a learning resource center. The 175-acre campus is in a small town 60 miles northwest of San Antonio. Including any residence halls, there are 43 buildings.

Student Life: 95% of undergraduates are from Texas. Students are from 9 states, 11 foreign countries, and Canada. 79% are white; 16% Hispanic. 59% are Protestant; 19% Catholic; 17% claim no religious affiliation. The average age of freshmen is 19; all undergraduates, 24. 37% do not continue beyond their first year; 38% remain to graduate.

Housing: 483 students can be accommodated in college housing, which includes coed dorms and on-campus apartments. On-campus housing is guaranteed for all 4 years. 51% of students commute. All students may keep cars.

Activities: 10% of men belong to 2 national fraternities; 13% of women belong to 2 national sororities. There are 35 groups on campus, including art, cheerleading, choir, chorale, drama, honors, international, literary magazine, newspaper, pep band, photography, political, professional, religious, social, student government, and yearbook. Popular campus events include Schreiner Speaker Series, Trull Casino Night, and Toga Party.

Sports: There are 5 intercollegiate sports for men and 7 for women, and 8 intramural sports for men and 8 for women. Facilities include basketball and volleyball courts, baseball and softball diamonds, 3 handball/racquetball courts, a track, 8 tennis courts, a swimming pool, soccer and intramural fields, a golf driving range, and a recreation room.

Disabled Students: 95% of the campus is accessible. Wheelchair ramps, elevators, special parking, specially equipped rest rooms, special class scheduling, lowered drinking fountains, and lowered telephones are available.

Services: Counseling and information services are available, as is tutoring in every subject, including introductory-level courses. There is remedial math, reading, and writing. There also are workshops, a certified peer-tutoring program, a math lab, a self-management orientation course, and computer-assisted instruction for learning skills.

Campus Safety and Security: Measures include informal discussions, pamphlets/posters/films, emergency telephones, and a night vehicle patrol.

Programs of Study: Schreiner confers B.A., B.S., B.B.A., and B.G.S. degrees. Associate and master's degrees are also awarded. Bachelor's degrees are awarded in BIOLOGICAL SCIENCE (biochemistry and biology/biological science), BUSINESS (accounting, business administration and management, and management information systems), COMMUNICATIONS AND THE ARTS (art, dramatic arts, English, graphic design, music, and visual and performing arts), COMPUTER AND PHYSICAL SCIENCE (chemistry and mathematics), EDUCATION (art, early childhood, education, elementary, English, mathematics, middle school, music, physical, science, secondary, and social science), HEALTH PROFESSIONS (exercise science), SOCIAL SCIENCE (history, humanities, liberal arts/general studies, philosophy, political science/government, prelaw, psychology, and religion). History, English, and exercise science are the strongest academically. Business administration, exercise science, and psychology are the largest.

Required: To graduate, all students must have a minimum GPA of 2.0 for 120 semester hours, including 24 hours in the major. The core curriculum includes courses from English composition, oral communication, foreign language, history, natural science, math, philosophy or religion, computer studies, government, business administration, literature and fine arts, social science, and fitness. B.A. candidates must complete a senior capstone project, thesis, or course; B.B.A. candidates may substitute an internship.

Special: Schreiner offers study abroad in Japan and England, work-study with the university, second majors, a general studies degree, non-degree study, and a 3-2 engineering degree with the University of Texas, Texas Tech University, and Texas A&M University. There are 5 national honor societies, a freshman honors program, and all departments have honors programs.

Faculty/Classroom: 60% of faculty are male; 40%, female. All teach undergraduates. No introductory courses are taught by graduate students. The average class size in an introductory lecture is 18; in a laboratory, 17; and in a regular course, 13.

Admissions: 69% of the 2003-2004 applicants were accepted. The SAT I scores for the 2003-2004 freshman class were: Verbal--54% below 500, 31% between 500 and 599, 13% between 600 and 700, and 2% above 700; Math--55% below 500, 37% between 500 and 599, and 9% between 600 and 700. 34% of the current freshmen were in the top fifth of their class; 67% were in the top two fifths. In a recent year 3 freshmen graduated first in their class.

Requirements: The SAT I or ACT is required, with a composite SAT I score of 800 (minimum 380 verbal and 350 mathematics) or ACT score of 20 recommended. Applicants need 20 secondary-school academic credits, including 4 each of English and math, 2 each of social science, foreign language, and lab science, and 1 of history. An interview is advised. The GED is accepted; applicants with a GED are not required to take the SAT I or ACT but are encouraged to do so. Schreiner requires applicants to be in the upper 50% of their class. A GPA of 2.0 is required. AP and CLEP credits are accepted.

Procedure: Freshmen are admitted to all sessions. Entrance exams should be taken in the spring of the junior year. There are early admissions plans, deferred admissions plans, and a rolling admissions plan. Applications should be filed by August 1 for fall entry, December 1 for spring entry, and June 1 for summer entry. Notification is sent on a rolling basis. The fall 2003 application fee was $25. Applications are accepted on-line through Texas Mentor.

Transfer: 87 transfer students enrolled in a recent year. Applicants with fewer than 15 transferable credit hours must meet freshman admissions requirements. For those with more, the SAT I or ACT is not required. A 2.0 minimum GPA is necessary. 30 of 120 credits required for the bachelor's degree must be completed at Schreiner.

Visiting: There are regularly scheduled orientations for prospective students, including guided tours, financial aid information, and faculty and student discussions. There are guides for informal visits and visitors may sit in on classes and stay overnight. To schedule a visit, contact the Admission Office.

Financial Aid: In 2003-2004, 78% of all full-time freshmen and 87% of continuing full-time students received some form of financial aid. 65% of full-time freshmen and 73% of continuing full-time students received need-based aid. The average freshman award was $11,222. Need-based scholarships or need-based grants averaged $11,373; need-based self-help aid (loans and jobs) averaged $2588; and non-need-based awards and non-need-based scholarships averaged $9483. 25% of undergraduates work part time. Average annual earnings from campus work are $995. The average financial indebtedness of the 2003 graduate was $19,208. The FAFSA is required. The priority date for freshman financial aid applications for fall entry is April 15. The deadline for filing freshman financial aid applications for fall entry is August 1.

International Students: There are 7 international students enrolled. The school actively recruits these students. They must score 550 on the written TOEFL or 213 on the electronic version and also take the MELAB, the Comprehensive English Language Test, or the college's own test.

Computers: There are 33 Macs and PCs available in the computer lab. All students may access the system. There are no time limits and no fees.

Graduates: From July 1, 2002 to June 30, 2003, 113 bachelor's degrees were awarded. The most popular majors were business and marketing (32%), education (12%), and exercise science (12%). In an average class, 38% graduate in 6 years or less.

Admissions Contact: Peg Layton, Acting Dean of Admission and Financial Aid. A video is available. E-mail: *admissions@schreiner.edu* Web: *www.schreiner.edu*

SOUTHERN METHODIST UNIVERSITY
D-2
Dallas, TX 75275-0181
(214) 768-4223
(800) 323-0672; Fax: (214) 768-0202

Full-time: 2693 men, 3225 women	Faculty: 459; I, +$
Part-time: 120 men, 261 women	Ph.D.s: 88%
Graduate: 2292 men, 1365 women	Student/Faculty: 13 to 1
Year: semesters, summer session	Tuition: $25,358
Application Deadline: January 15	Room & Board: $8852
Freshman Class: 6293 applied, 4076 accepted, 1383 enrolled	
SAT I Verbal/Math: 590/600	ACT: 26 HIGHLY COMPETITIVE

Southern Methodist University, founded in 1911, is a private nonsectarian institution affiliated with the United Methodist Church. SMU offers undergraduate and graduate programs in humanities and sciences, business, arts, and engineering and applied sciences. There are 4 undergraduate and 6 graduate schools. In addition to regional accreditation, SMU has baccalaureate program accreditation with AACSB, ABET, NASAD, and NASM. The 8 libraries contain 2,577,345 volumes, 803,898 micro-

form items, and 626,996 audio/video tapes/CDs, and subscribe to 11,727 periodicals. Computerized library services include the card catalog, interlibrary loans, and database searching. Special learning facilities include a learning resource center, art gallery, natural history museum, radio station, art museum, research laboratories, TV studio, and several performing arts theaters, including Classical Thrust Stage. The 163-acre campus is in a suburban area 5 miles north of downtown Dallas. Including any residence halls, there are 75 buildings.

Student Life: 63% of undergraduates are from Texas. Students are from 48 states, 66 foreign countries, and Canada. 65% are from public schools. 75% are white. The average age of freshmen is 18; all undergraduates, 21. 16% do not continue beyond their first year; 71% remain to graduate.

Housing: 2525 students can be accommodated in college housing, which includes coed dorms, on-campus apartments, off-campus apartments, married-student housing, fraternity houses, and sorority houses. In addition, there are honors houses, special-interest houses, wellness floors, an international floor, and floors catering to particular disciplines. On-campus housing is guaranteed for the freshman year only and is available on a lottery system for upperclassmen. All students may keep cars.

Activities: 38% of men belong to 14 national fraternities; 42% of women belong to 12 national sororities. There are 143 groups on campus, including art, band, cheerleading, choir, chorale, chorus, computers, dance, debate, drama, drill team, ethnic, film, forensics, gay, honors, international, jazz band, literary magazine, marching band, musical theater, newspaper, opera, orchestra, pep band, photography, political, professional, radio and TV, religious, social, social service, student government, symphony, and yearbook. Popular campus events include Celebration of Lights, Parents Weekend, and Community Service Day.

Sports: There are 8 intercollegiate sports for men and 8 for women, and 16 intramural sports for men and 15 for women. Facilities include gymnastic and weight rooms, a dance studio, indoor and outdoor jogging tracks, indoor and outdoor pools, a 2400-seat outdoor stadium, a 6500-seat indoor stadium, and courts for basketball, volleyball, tennis, badminton, and racquetball.

Disabled Students: 95% of the campus is accessible. Wheelchair ramps, elevators, special parking, specially equipped rest rooms, special class scheduling, lowered drinking fountains, lowered telephones, and automatic doors are available. On going renovation aims to make the campus completely accessible.

Services: Counseling and information services are available, as is tutoring in most subjects. There is a reader service for the blind and remedial reading and writing. The Learning Enhancement Center provides study skills workshops, note-taking techniques, and time management skills seminars.

Campus Safety and Security: Measures include 24-hour foot and vehicle patrol, self-defense education, security escort services, and shuttle buses. There are informal discussions, pamphlets/posters/films, emergency telephones, and lighted pathways/sidewalks. Card-key devices, issued to all students living in residence halls, must be used to enter these buildings.

Programs of Study: SMU confers B.A., B.S., B.B.A., B.F.A., B.Hum., B.M., B.S.Comp.Eng., B.S.E.E., B.S.Env.E., B.S.M.E., and B.Soc.Sci. degrees. Master's and doctoral degrees are also awarded. Bachelor's degrees are awarded in BIOLOGICAL SCIENCE (biochemistry and biology/biological science), BUSINESS (accounting, banking and finance, business administration and management, management information systems, management science, marketing/retailing/merchandising, organizational behavior, and real estate), COMMUNICATIONS AND THE ARTS (advertising, art history and appreciation, broadcasting, creative writing, dance, dramatic arts, English, film arts, French, German, journalism, languages, media arts, music performance, music theory and composition, piano/organ, public relations, Russian, Spanish, and studio art), COMPUTER AND PHYSICAL SCIENCE (chemistry, computer science, geology, geophysics and seismology, mathematics, physics, and statistics), EDUCATION (music), ENGINEERING AND ENVIRONMENTAL DESIGN (computer engineering, electrical/electronics engineering, environmental engineering, and mechanical engineering), HEALTH PROFESSIONS (music therapy), SOCIAL SCIENCE (African American studies, anthropology, economics, German area studies, history, humanities, international studies, Italian studies, Latin American studies, liberal arts/general studies, medieval studies, Mexican-American/Chicano studies, philosophy, political science/government, psychology, public affairs, religion, Russian and Slavic studies, social science, sociology, and Southwest American studies). Performing arts, life sciences, history, and business are the strongest academically. Business, communications, and psychology are the largest.

Required: Basic requirements consist of 122 semester hours, including a general education requirement of 41 hours distributed across Fundamentals (writing, math, and information technology), Science and Technology, Perspectives (arts, literature, religious and philosophical thought, history, politics and economics, and behavioral sciences), Cultural Formations (interdisciplinary courses), and a corequirement in Human Diversity (race, ethnicity, and gender). There is also a 2-credit education requirement. Students must maintain a GPA of 2.0.

Special: SMU offers a co-op program in engineering, work-study programs, B.A.-B.S. degrees, study abroad in 12 countries, dual majors in any combination, student-designed majors, numerous internships, and interdisciplinary majors, including economics with finance applications and economics with systems analysis. A 3-2 advanced degree in business is available, as are evening degree programs in humanities and social sciences, and teacher certification programs. There are 16 national honor societies, including Phi Beta Kappa, and a freshman honors program.

Faculty/Classroom: 71% of faculty are male; 29%, female. 89% teach undergraduates and do research.

Admissions: 65% of the 2003-2004 applicants were accepted. The SAT I scores for the 2003-2004 freshman class were: Verbal--10% below 500, 43% between 500 and 599, 42% between 600 and 700, and 5% above 700; Math--7% below 500, 38% between 500 and 599, 47% between 600 and 700, and 8% above 700. The ACT scores were 5% below 21, 15% between 21 and 23, 36% between 24 and 26, 22% between 27 and 28, and 23% above 28. 55% of the current freshmen were in the top fifth of their class; 84% were in the top two fifths.

Requirements: The SAT I or ACT is recommended. In addition, applicants should graduate from an accredited high school with a minimum of 15 academic credits: 4 in English, 3 in higher math, including algebra I, II, and plane geometry, 3 each in natural science and social science, and 2 in a foreign language. Home School Certificate applicants may qualify with the SAT I or ACT and 3 SAT II: Subject tests, including writing and math. Performing arts majors must audition. AP and CLEP credits are accepted. Important factors in the admissions decision are advanced placement or honor courses, leadership record, and recommendations by school officials.

Procedure: Freshmen are admitted to all sessions. Entrance exams should be taken by December of the senior year. There are early decision, early admissions, and deferred admissions plans. Early decision applications should be filed by November 1; regular applications, by January 15 for fall entry and April 1 for spring entry. The fall 2003 application fee was $50. Notification of early decision is sent December 31; regular decision, on a rolling basis. A waiting list is an active part of the admissions procedure.

Transfer: 301 transfer students enrolled in a recent year. A minimum 2.5 GPA is generally required for transfer, but specific requirements vary according to the program of study. Candidates must demonstrate math proficiency. A foreign language requirement may be met through high school or college work. 60 of 122 credits required for the bachelor's degree must be completed at SMU.

Visiting: There are regularly scheduled orientations for prospective students, including information about academic studies, financial-aid sessions, discussions with current students, lunch with faculty and students, and a tour of the campus. There is also a Spring Fest visitation in April for high school juniors. There are guides for informal visits and visitors may sit in on classes and stay overnight. To schedule a visit, contact the Undergraduate Admissions Office.

Financial Aid: In 2003-2004, 80% of all full-time freshmen and 68% of continuing full-time students received some form of financial aid. 32% of full-time freshmen received need-based aid. The average freshman award was $22,817. Need-based scholarships or need-based grants averaged $14,909. SMU is a member of CSS. The FAFSA is required. Check with the school for current deadlines.

International Students: The school actively recruits these students. They must score 550 on the written TOEFL and also take the SAT I or the ACT.

Computers: The mainframe is an IBM 3090. Access to campus administrative and academic computer systems is available from all campus offices and dorm rooms. In addition, several hundred public workstations are available in campus libraries and computer labs. All students may access the system 24 hours a day. There are no time limits and no fees.

Admissions Contact: Nancy Peterson, Associate Director, Admissions. A video is available. E-mail: *enrol_serv@mail.smu.edu* Web: *www.smu.edu*

SOUTHWEST TEXAS STATE UNIVERSITY
(See Texas State University)

SOUTHWESTERN ADVENTIST UNIVERSITY D-2
Keene, TX 76059 (817) 645-3921
(800) 433-2240; Fax: (817) 556-4744

Full-time: 365 men, 460 women	**Faculty:** 50
Part-time: 105 men, 245 women	**Ph.D.s:** 52%
Graduate: 15 men, 15 women	**Student/Faculty:** 16 to 1
Year: semesters, summer session	**Tuition:** $10,020
Application Deadline: see profile	**Room & Board:** $4780
Freshman Class: 657 applied, 422 accepted, 168 enrolled	
SAT I Verbal/Math: required	**ACT:** required COMPETITIVE

Southwestern Adventist College, founded in 1893, is a small Seventh-day Adventist institution offering liberal arts and professional degree programs. Figures in the above capsule and in this profile are approximate. In addition to regional accreditation, SWAU has baccalaureate program accreditation with NLN. The library contains 103,531 volumes, 6822 microform items, and 1290 audio/video tapes/CDs, and subscribes to 427 periodicals. Computerized library services include the card catalog and database searching. Special learning facilities include a learning resource center, natural history museum, radio station, TV station, and observatory. The 150-acre campus is in a rural area 35 miles south of Fort Worth. Including any residence halls, there are 24 buildings.

Student Life: 51% of undergraduates are from Texas. Students are from 50 states, 53 foreign countries, and Canada. 44% are from public schools. 50% are white; 15% Hispanic; 14% African American; 13% foreign nationals. 90% are Protestant; 6% claim no religious affiliation. The average age of freshmen is 19; all undergraduates, 26. 38% do not continue beyond their first year; 33% remain to graduate.

Housing: 373 students can be accommodated in college housing, which includes single-sex dorms, off-campus apartments, and married-student housing. On-campus housing is guaranteed for all 4 years. 71% of students commute. Alcohol is not permitted. All students may keep cars.

Activities: There are no fraternities or sororities. There are 20 groups on campus, including art, band, choir, chorale, computers, drama, ethnic, film, international, newspaper, orchestra, pep band, photography, radio and TV, religious, social, social service, student government, symphony, and yearbook. Popular campus events include Founders Day, Fall Holiday, and Memosa Memories.

Sports: There are 2 intercollegiate sports for men and 2 for women, and 4 intramural sports for men and 4 for women. Facilities include jogging and fitness tracks, weight and aerobics rooms, courts for tennis, racquetball, and basketball, and fields for football and baseball.

Disabled Students: 78% of the campus is accessible. Wheelchair ramps, elevators, special parking, specially equipped rest rooms, and lowered drinking fountains are available.

Services: Counseling and information services are available, as is tutoring in some subjects, including accounting, biology, chemistry, English, Greek, math, nursing, and Spanish. There is remedial math and writing.

Campus Safety and Security: Measures include informal discussions, pamphlets/posters/films, lighted pathways/sidewalks, and 12-hour night foot patrol.

Programs of Study: SWAU confers B.A., B.S., B.B.A., and B.S.W. degrees. Associate and master's degrees are also awarded. Bachelor's degrees are awarded in BIOLOGICAL SCIENCE (biology/biological science and biometrics and biostatistics), BUSINESS (business administration and management, insurance and risk management, international economics, management science, and office supervision and management), COMMUNICATIONS AND THE ARTS (broadcasting, communications, English, journalism, music, and speech/debate/rhetoric), COMPUTER AND PHYSICAL SCIENCE (chemistry, computer science, information sciences and systems, mathematics, and physics), EDUCATION (business, elementary, physical, and secondary), HEALTH PROFESSIONS (exercise science, health, medical technology, and nursing), SOCIAL SCIENCE (criminal justice, history, international relations, psychology, religion, social science, social studies, social work, and theological studies). Nursing, biology, and religion are the strongest academically. Education, nursing, and psychology are the largest.

Required: To graduate, students must complete at least 128 hours, including 40 hours in upper-division courses and 27 to 48 in the major. An overall 2.0 GPA is required, with a 2.3 in upper-division courses in the major field. General education requirements include courses in English, health and phys ed, math and science, religion, social science and humanities, and, in some cases, foreign language. Comprehensive and departmental exams are required.

Special: Cooperative programs in medical technology are available with several area hospitals. Internships are arranged on an individual basis. Students may study abroad in Germany, France, or Spain. Student-designed majors, interdisciplinary majors, including mathematical physics, a 3-2 engineering degree with Walla Walla College and Andrews University, and an adult degree program are offered. There is a freshman honors program.

Faculty/Classroom: 62% of faculty are male; 38%, female. All teach undergraduates and 8% both teach and do research. No introductory courses are taught by graduate students. The average class size in an introductory lecture is 30; in a laboratory, 15; and in a regular course, 20.

Requirements: The SAT I or ACT is required. In addition, applicants should be high school graduates or hold the GED. Secondary preparation is expected to include 12 academic credits in English, foreign language, math, natural or physical science, and social science. Potential nursing or education majors and Seventh-day Adventist ministers must meet additional requirements. AP and CLEP credits are accepted. Important factors in the admissions decision are recommendations by alumni, ability to finance college education, and leadership record.

Procedure: Freshmen are admitted fall, spring, and summer. Entrance exams should be taken before registration. There are early admissions, deferred admissions, and rolling admissions plans. Check with the school for current deadlines. Applications are accepted on-line at the university Web site and through Texas Mentor.

Transfer: 239 transfer students enrolled in a recent year. An official transcript from each college or university the student has attended must be mailed directly to SWAU's Admissions Office. Transfer students with less than a C average may be accepted on a probationary basis. Nursing, education, and theology majors have additional requirements. 30 of 128 credits required for the bachelor's degree must be completed at SWAU.

Visiting: There are regularly scheduled orientations for prospective students, including scheduled weekend visitation programs in February and the summer that consist of meeting the administration, touring the campus, and receiving financial and academic counseling; preregistration is available in summer. There are guides for informal visits and visitors may sit in on classes and stay overnight. To schedule a visit, contact the Enrollment Office at *sylvia@swau.edu*.

Financial Aid: In a recent year, 65% of all full-time freshmen and 62% of continuing full-time students received some form of financial aid. 48% of full-time freshmen and 49% of continuing full-time students received need-based aid. The average freshman award was $7779. All undergraduates work part time. Average annual earnings from campus work are $2000. The average financial indebtedness of a recent graduate was $18,223. The FAFSA and the college's own financial statement are required. Check with the school for current deadlines.

International Students: In a recent year, there were 155 international students enrolled. The school actively recruits these students. They must score 520 on the written TOEFL or take the MELAB.

Computers: The mainframe is an IBM RS 6000. PCs are available in faculty offices, academic departments, and student labs. All students may access the system 24 hours per day. There are no time limits and no fees. It is strongly recommended that all students have a personal computer.

Graduates: In a recent year, 117 bachelor's degrees were awarded. The most popular majors were education (19%), business (15%), and psychology (10%). In an average class, 3% graduate in 3 years or less, 20% graduate in 4 years or less, 30% graduate in 5 years or less, and 33% graduate in 6 years or less.

Admissions Contact: Brent Baldwin, Enrollment Vice President.
E-mail: *admissions@swau.edu* Web: *www.swau.edu*

SOUTHWESTERN UNIVERSITY
Georgetown, TX 78626   **D-3**

(512) 863-1200
(800) 252-3166; Fax: (512) 863-9601

Full-time: 525 men, 712 women	Faculty: 111; IIB, +$
Part-time: 11 men, 17 women	Ph.D.s: 91%
Graduate: none	Student/Faculty: 11 to 1
Year: semesters, summer session	Tuition: $18,870
Application Deadline: February 15	Room & Board: $6540
Freshman Class: 1765 applied, 1115 accepted, 343 enrolled	
SAT I Verbal/Math: 621/619	ACT: 26 HIGHLY COMPETITIVE

Southwestern University, founded in 1840, is a private liberal arts institution affiliated with the United Methodist Church. There are 2 undergraduate schools. In addition to regional accreditation, Southwestern has baccalaureate program accreditation with NASM. The library contains 312,490 volumes, 56,531 microform items, and 12,186 audio/video tapes/CDs, and subscribes to 1372 periodicals. Computerized library services include the card catalog, interlibrary loans, and database searching. Special learning facilities include a learning resource center and art gallery. The 700-acre campus is in a suburban area 28 miles north of Austin. Including any residence halls, there are 31 buildings.

Student Life: 92% of undergraduates are from Texas. Students are from 33 states, 9 foreign countries, and Canada. 82% are from public schools. 77% are white; 14% Hispanic. 68% are Protestant; 20% Catholic; 8% have no preference; 2% Jewish; 1% are Muslim, Buddhist, Mormon, or Hindu. The average age of freshmen is 18; all undergraduates, 20. 14% do not continue beyond their first year; 71% remain to graduate.

Housing: 1042 students can be accommodated in college housing, which includes single-sex and coed dorms, on-campus apartments, and fraternity houses. In addition, there are special-interest houses. On-campus housing is guaranteed for the freshman year only, is available on

a first-come, first-served basis, and is available on a lottery system for upperclassmen. 82% of students live on campus; of those, 55% remain on campus on weekends. Alcohol is not permitted. All students may keep cars.

Activities: 31% of men belong to 3 national fraternities; 32% of women belong to 4 national sororities. There are 105 groups on campus, including art, band, cheerleading, choir, chorale, chorus, computers, dance, drama, ethnic, film, gay, honors, international, jazz band, literary magazine, musical theater, newspaper, opera, orchestra, pep band, political, professional, religious, social, social service, student government, and yearbook. Popular campus events include Homecoming Sing, Mall Ball, and Brown Symposium.

Sports: There are 7 intercollegiate sports for men and 7 for women, and 9 intramural sports for men and 9 for women. Facilities include a health and wellness center, a 2000-seat gym, a 9-hole golf course, tennis courts, a baseball field, soccer and lacrosse fields, and a recreation center that includes an indoor jogging track, large performance gym, weight training room, and indoor swimming pool.

Disabled Students: 90% of the campus is accessible. Wheelchair ramps, elevators, special parking, specially equipped rest rooms, lowered drinking fountains, and lowered telephones are available.

Services: Counseling and information services are available, as is tutoring in some subjects, including math, computer science, and sciences.

Campus Safety and Security: Measures include 24-hour foot and vehicle patrol, self-defense education, security escort services, and informal discussions. There are pamphlets/posters/films, emergency telephones, and lighted pathways/sidewalks.

Programs of Study: Southwestern confers B.A., B.S., B.F.A., and B.Mus. degrees. Bachelor's degrees are awarded in AGRICULTURE (animal science and environmental studies), BIOLOGICAL SCIENCE (biology/biological science), BUSINESS (accounting and business administration and management), COMMUNICATIONS AND THE ARTS (art, classics, communications, dramatic arts, English, French, German, Latin, music, and Spanish), COMPUTER AND PHYSICAL SCIENCE (chemistry, computer science, mathematics, and physics), SOCIAL SCIENCE (American studies, early childhood studies, economics, history, international studies, philosophy, physical fitness/movement, political science/government, psychology, religion, sociology, and women's studies). Biology, sociology, and political science are the strongest academically. Psychology, biology, and business are the largest.

Required: To graduate, all students must complete at least 122 credits with a 2.0 GPA and satisfy distribution requirements in the arts, humanities, social science, and natural science. The total number of hours required in most majors in 30. A first-year seminar and math course are required. All students must take 1 semester of English composition and must demonstrate computer literacy. Seniors must complete a capstone requirement in the major.

Special: Students may study abroad in England, France, Mexico, Korea, and other countries. The university offers a Washington semester, dual, student-designed, and independent majors, and internships in government, fine arts, psychology, sociology, science, and other fields, within Texas or in New York or other states. A 3-2 engineering program may be arranged with Washington, Texas A&M, and Arizona State Universities, and the University of Texas at Austin. Some pass/fail options are available, as are accelerated degrees in any field. There are 7 national honor societies, including Phi Beta Kappa, and 21 departmental honors programs.

Faculty/Classroom: 52% of faculty are male; 48%, female. All teach undergraduates. The average class size in an introductory lecture is 18; in a laboratory, 15; and in a regular course, 12.

Admissions: 63% of the 2003-2004 applicants were accepted. The SAT I scores for the 2003-2004 freshman class were: Verbal--4% below 500, 32% between 500 and 599, 47% between 600 and 699, and 17% at 700 and above; Math--3% below 500, 32% between 500 and 599, 52% between 600 and 699, and 12% at 700 and above. The ACT scores were 3% below 21, 21% between 21 and 23, 28% between 24 and 26, 22% between 27 and 28, and 26% above 28. 73% of the current freshmen were in the top fifth of their class; 95% were in the top two fifths. There were 5 National Merit finalists and 7 semifinalists. 7 freshmen graduated first in their class.

Requirements: The SAT I or ACT is required. In addition, the applicant should be a graduate of an accredited high school or have the GED. Secondary preparation should include 4 years each of English and math, 3 each of science and social science or history, 2 of a foreign language, and 1 of an academic elective. An essay is required, and an interview is recommended. AP and CLEP credits are accepted. Important factors in the admissions decision are advanced placement or honor courses, recommendations by school officials, and leadership record.

Procedure: Freshmen are admitted fall and spring. Entrance exams should be taken in the fall of the senior year. There are early admissions and deferred admissions plans. Early decision applications should be filed by November 1; regular applications, by February 15 for fall entry and December 1 for spring entry, along with a $40 fee. Notification of early decision is sent December 1; regular decision, March 3. 62 early decision candidates were accepted for the 2003-2004 class. 163 applicants were on the 2003 waiting list; 24 were admitted. Applications are accepted on-line through CollegeLink, Apply Yourself, the Common Application, and the school's web site.

Transfer: 38 transfer students enrolled in 2003-2004. Preference is given to students having a 3.0 in all college work. 31 of 122 credits required for the bachelor's degree must be completed at Southwestern.

Visiting: There are regularly scheduled orientations for prospective students, including 3 or 4 group overnight options and individually arranged visits throughout the year. All visits typically include tours, faculty appointments and interview, and may also include an overnight on campus and class visit. There are guides for informal visits and visitors may sit in on classes and stay overnight. To schedule a visit, contact the Admission Office at *admission@southwestern.edu*.

Financial Aid: In 2003-2004, 83% of all full-time freshmen and 80% of continuing full-time students received some form of financial aid. 57% of full-time freshmen and 54% of continuing full-time students received need-based aid. The average freshman award was $16,962, with $12,515 from need-based scholarships or grants, and $4447 from need-based self-help aid (loans and jobs). 61% of undergraduates work part time. Average annual earnings from campus work are $1906. The average financial indebtedness of the 2003 graduate was $15,661. Southwestern is a member of CSS. The FAFSA and the university's own financial statement are required. The priority date for freshman financial aid applications for fall entry is March 1. The deadline for filing freshman financial aid applications for fall entry is March 1.

International Students: There are 4 international students enrolled. The school actively recruits these students. They must score 550 on the written TOEFL or 217 on the electronic version and also take the SAT I or the ACT.

Computers: The mainframes are an HP 855, HP 9000/800K, HP 9000/800D, and HP 9000/800E-55 and E-35 models. There are approximately 150 PCs located throughout the campus for student use. Students may also use the facilities in 3 computer labs where there is access to the Internet, e-mail, Web, Gopher, word processing, and instructional software. All students may access the system at any time. There are no time limits and no fees.

Graduates: From July 1, 2002 to June 30, 2003, 318 bachelor's degrees were awarded. The most popular majors were business (10%), communication (10%), and biology/psychology (10%). In an average class, 1% graduate in 3 years or less, 67% graduate in 4 years or less, 72% graduate in 5 years or less, and 74% graduate in 6 years or less. 26 companies recruited on campus in 2002-2003. Of the 2002 graduating class, 25% were enrolled in graduate school within 6 months of graduation and 65% were employed.

Admissions Contact: John W. Lind, Vice President, Enrollment Management. E-mail: *admission@southwestern.edu*
Web: *www.southwestern.edu*

STEPHEN F. AUSTIN STATE UNIVERSITY
Nacogdoches, TX 75962

E-3

(936) 468-2504
(800) 731-2902; Fax: (936) 468-3849

Full-time: 3434 men, 4946 women	**Faculty:** 381; IIA, --$
Part-time: 539 men, 828 women	**Ph.D.s:** 74%
Graduate: 585 men, 1076 women	**Student/Faculty:** 22 to 1
Year: semesters, summer session	**Tuition:** $2752 ($8416)
Application Deadline: open	**Room & Board:** $4800
Freshman Class: 5750 applied, 4198 accepted, 1752 enrolled	
SAT I Verbal/Math: 501/499	**ACT:** 21 **COMPETITIVE**

Stephen F. Austin State University, founded in 1923, is a public regional university offering undergraduate and graduate degree programs through 7 colleges. There are 7 undergraduate schools and 1 graduate school. In addition to regional accreditation, SFA has baccalaureate program accreditation with AACSB, ADA, CSWE, FIDER, NASM, NCATE, NLN, and SAF. The library contains 946,123 volumes, 832,219 microform items, and 23,739 audio/video tapes/CDs, and subscribes to 2805 periodicals. Computerized library services include the card catalog, interlibrary loans, database searching, and Internet access. Special learning facilities include a learning resource center, art gallery, planetarium, radio station, TV station, arboretum, beef and poultry research centers, experimental forest, and biotechnology and environmental science research centers. The 401-acre campus is in a small town 140 miles northeast of Houston. Including any residence halls, there are 90 buildings.

Student Life: 98% of undergraduates are from Texas. Students are from 38 states, 45 foreign countries, and Canada. 99% are from public schools. 76% are white; 15% African American. The average age of freshmen is 19; all undergraduates, 22. 40% do not continue beyond their first year; 35% remain to graduate.

Housing: 4308 students can be accommodated in college housing, which includes single-sex and coed dorms, on-campus apartments, and married-student housing. In addition, there are honors houses, special-interest houses, and an enrichment hall with required study hall hours.

On-campus housing is guaranteed for all 4 years. 63% of students commute. Alcohol is not permitted. All students may keep cars.

Activities: 17% of men belong to 24 national fraternities; 12% of women belong to 15 national sororities. There are 224 groups on campus, including art, band, cheerleading, choir, chorale, chorus, computers, dance, debate, drama, drill team, ethnic, flag corps, film, gay, honors, international, jazz band, literary magazine, marching band, musical theater, newspaper, opera, orchestra, pep band, photography, political, professional, radio and TV, religious, social, social service, student government, symphony, and yearbook. Popular campus events include Parents Weekend, Watermelon Bash, and Howdy Week.

Sports: There are 6 intercollegiate sports for men and 8 for women, and 13 intramural sports for men and 9 for women. Facilities include 2 gyms, courts for handball, tennis, and racquetball, weight and gymnastics rooms, and various playing fields.

Disabled Students: All of the campus is accessible. Wheelchair ramps, elevators, special parking, specially equipped rest rooms, special class scheduling, lowered drinking fountains, and lowered telephones are available.

Services: Counseling and information services are available, as is tutoring in most subjects. There is a reader service for the blind, and remedial math, reading, and writing.

Campus Safety and Security: Measures include 24-hour foot and vehicle patrol, self-defense education, security escort services, and shuttle buses. There are informal discussions, pamphlets/posters/films, emergency telephones, and lighted pathways/sidewalks.

Programs of Study: SFA confers B.A., B.S., B.A.A.S., B.B.A., B.F.A., B.M., B.S.A.G., B.S.F., B.S.I.S., B.S.N., B.S.R.H.B., and B.S.W. degrees. Master's and doctoral degrees are also awarded. Bachelor's degrees are awarded in AGRICULTURE (agricultural business management, agricultural mechanics, agriculture, agronomy, animal science, fish and game management, forestry and related sciences, forestry production and processing, horticulture, poultry science, and range/farm management), BIOLOGICAL SCIENCE (biology/biological science and nutrition), BUSINESS (accounting, banking and finance, business administration and management, fashion merchandising, hospitality management services, international business management, management information systems, management science, marketing management, marketing/retailing/merchandising, and office supervision and management), COMMUNICATIONS AND THE ARTS (art, broadcasting, communications, dance, dramatic arts, English, fine arts, French, journalism, music, Spanish, and speech/debate/rhetoric), COMPUTER AND PHYSICAL SCIENCE (chemistry, computer programming, computer science, geology, information sciences and systems, mathematics, and physics), EDUCATION (agricultural), ENGINEERING AND ENVIRONMENTAL DESIGN (environmental science, interior design, and preengineering), HEALTH PROFESSIONS (health science, nursing, premedicine, preoptometry, prepharmacy, preveterinary science, rehabilitation therapy, and speech therapy), SOCIAL SCIENCE (child psychology/development, corrections, criminal justice, dietetics, economics, food production/management/services, food science, geography, gerontology, history, home economics, humanities, interdisciplinary studies, law enforcement and corrections, parks and recreation management, physical fitness/movement, political science/government, prelaw, psychology, public administration, social work, and sociology). Interdisciplinary studies, nursing, and kinesiology are the largest.

Required: All students must complete at least 130 hours with a minimum 2.0 GPA. The B.A. program requires courses in communication skills, math and natural science, humanities, social science, and physical activity.

Special: Internships, dual majors, and dual degrees are possible in some programs. Preengineering and 3-2 engineering programs with Texas A&M are offered, as are preprofessional programs and a general studies degree. There is a freshman honors program.

Faculty/Classroom: 57% of faculty are male; 43%, female.

Admissions: 73% of the 2003-2004 applicants were accepted. The SAT I scores for the 2003-2004 freshman class were: Verbal--48% below 500, 39% between 500 and 599, 13% between 600 and 700, and 1% above 700; Math--47% below 500, 42% between 500 and 599, and 11% between 600 and 700. The ACT scores were 52% below 21, 27% between 21 and 23, 15% between 24 and 26, 5% between 27 and 28, and 2% above 28. 35% of the current freshmen were in the top fifth of their class.

Requirements: The SAT I or ACT is required. In addition, for clear admission, applicants must have been in the top 50% of their high school class or have a 21 ACT or 1010 SAT I score. SFA requires applicants to be in the upper 50% of their class. AP and CLEP credits are accepted.

Procedure: Freshmen are admitted to all sessions. Entrance exams should be taken during the junior year. There is a rolling admissions plan. Application deadlines are open. The application fee is $25. Applications are accepted on-line through the school's web site.

Transfer: 1343 transfer students enrolled in 2002-2003. Applicants with fewer than 15 hours of college work must meet freshman admission requirements. Those with more than 15 hours must have at least a 2.0

GPA. Those with GPAs lower than 2.0 may be admitted to the summer school on probation. 42 of 130 credits required for the bachelor's degree must be completed at SFA.

Visiting: There are regularly scheduled orientations for prospective students, including Showcase Saturdays, which are 1-day open house programs with faculty, staff, and current students. There are guides for informal visits and visitors may sit in on classes. To schedule a visit, contact the Admissions Office at *admissions@sfasu.edu.*

Financial Aid: In 2003-2004, 49% of all full-time freshmen and 42% of continuing full-time students received some form of financial aid. 49% of full-time freshmen and 41% of continuing full-time students received need-based aid. The average freshman award was $4070. Average annual earnings from campus work are $3500. The average financial indebtedness of the 2003 graduate was $9922. The FAFSA is required. The deadline for filing freshman financial aid applications for fall entry is April 1.

International Students: There are 69 international students enrolled. The school actively recruits these students. They must score 550 on the written TOEFL and also take the SAT I or the ACT.

Computers: The mainframe is a DEC Alpha 7720 cluster. There are 16 computer labs with 700 Macs and PCs and students have free access to the Internet. All students may access the system at any time. Students are allowed 30 minutes of Internet access per 4 hours. There are no fees.

Graduates: From July 1, 2002 to June 30, 2003, 1684 bachelor's degrees were awarded. The most popular majors were educational leadership (30%), general business (6%), and social work (6%). In an average class, 15% graduate in 4 years or less, 31% graduate in 5 years or less, and 35% graduate in 6 years or less. 72 companies recruited on campus in 2002-2003. Of the 2002 graduating class, 10% were enrolled in graduate school within 6 months of graduation.

Admissions Contact: Monique Cossich, Executive Director of Enrollment Management. E-mail: *admissions@sfasu.edu*
Web: *www.sfasu.edu*

SUL ROSS STATE UNIVERSITY
Alpine, TX 79832

B-3

(915) 837-8050; Fax: (915) 837-8431

Full-time: 690 men, 570 women	**Faculty:** 95
Part-time: 90 men, 140 women	**Ph.D.s:** 69%
Graduate: 210 men, 295 women	**Student/Faculty:** 12 to 1
Year: semesters, summer session	**Tuition:** $2316 ($8856)
Application Deadline: open	**Room & Board:** $2805
Freshman Class: n/av	
SAT I or ACT: required	**LESS COMPETITIVE**

Sul Ross State University, founded in 1917, is a public institution offering programs in the liberal arts and sciences, fine arts and music, range animal science, business, and education. In addition, an upper-level and graduate center offers courses in Uralde, Del Rio, and Eagle Pass, Texas. Figures in the above capsule and in this profile are approximate. There are 3 undergraduate schools and 1 graduate school. The library contains 248,598 volumes, 444,950 microform items, and 13,011 audio/video tapes/CDs, and subscribes to 1951 periodicals. Computerized library services include the card catalog, interlibrary loans, and database searching. Special learning facilities include a learning resource center, art gallery, natural history museum, planetarium, radio station, and extensive geology/chemistry lab equipment, including a scanning electron microscope. The 600-acre campus is in a rural area 165 miles from Odessa. Including any residence halls, there are 22 buildings.

Student Life: 97% of undergraduates are from Texas. Students are from 18 states and 7 foreign countries. 98% are from public schools. 55% are white; 41% Hispanic. 51% are Catholic; 48% Protestant. The average age of freshmen is 20; all undergraduates, 24. 55% do not continue beyond their first year; 20% remain to graduate.

Housing: 769 students can be accommodated in college housing, which includes single-sex and coed dorms, on-campus apartments, and married-student housing. On-campus housing is guaranteed for the freshman year only and is available on a first-come, first-served basis. 67% of students commute. Alcohol is not permitted. All students may keep cars.

Activities: There are no fraternities or sororities. There are 41 groups on campus, including art, cheerleading, choir, drama, ethnic, honors, international, literary magazine, newspaper, pep band, political, professional, religious, student government, and yearbook. Popular campus events include cultural events, Fall on the Mall, and Honors Day.

Sports: There are 5 intercollegiate sports for men and 4 for women, and 4 intramural sports for men and 3 for women. Facilities include a gym and an undergraduate center.

Disabled Students: 90% of the campus is accessible. Wheelchair ramps, elevators, special parking, specially equipped rest rooms, special class scheduling, and lowered drinking fountains are available.

Services: Counseling and information services are available, as is tutoring in some subjects, including math, reading, and English. There is remedial math, reading, and writing.

Campus Safety and Security: Measures include 24-hour foot and vehicle patrol, informal discussions, pamphlets/posters/films, and lighted pathways/sidewalks.

Programs of Study: Sully confers B.A., B.S., B.B.A., and B.F.A. degrees. Associate and master's degrees are also awarded. Bachelor's degrees are awarded in AGRICULTURE (agricultural business management, animal science, equine science, natural resource management, and wildlife management), BIOLOGICAL SCIENCE (biology/biological science), BUSINESS (accounting, business administration and management, and office supervision and management), COMMUNICATIONS AND THE ARTS (applied music, communications, dramatic arts, English, fine arts, and Spanish), COMPUTER AND PHYSICAL SCIENCE (chemistry, computer science, geology, and mathematics), EDUCATION (art and elementary), ENGINEERING AND ENVIRONMENTAL DESIGN (environmental science and industrial engineering technology), SOCIAL SCIENCE (criminal justice, history, Mexican-American/Chicano studies, physical fitness/movement, political science/government, psychology, and social science). Behavioral and social sciences, education, and fine arts are the strongest academically. Phys ed, criminal justice, and education are the largest.

Required: All students must complete a general education requirement of 53 to 57 hours, including courses in English, history, foreign language, political science, math, the arts, social science, and natural science. A minimum 2.0 GPA and 130 credit hours are required to graduate. There are additional requirements for some degree programs. All students must take 2 courses in phys ed and 1 in computer science. The total number of hours required in the major varies.

Special: Sully offers unpaid internships in several departments, including psychology and criminal justice, as well as work-study programs, and nondegree study. There are 8 national honor societies and a freshman honors program.

Faculty/Classroom: 69% of faculty are male; 31%, female. 95% teach undergraduates and 85% both teach and do research. No introductory courses are taught by graduate students. The average class size in an introductory lecture is 42; in a laboratory, 15; and in a regular course, 21.

Requirements: The SAT I or ACT is required. In addition, applicants should be graduates of an accredited secondary school and have a minimum of 14 credits, including 4 in English, 3 in math, 2 each in science, history, and phys ed/health, and 1 in government/economics. Applicants must meet 1 of the following criteria for full admission: present a minimum composite score of 20 on the ACT or 920 on the SAT I; or graduate in the upper half of their class. Probationary admission is possible for students who do not meet the admissions standards. AP and CLEP credits are accepted.

Procedure: Freshmen are admitted to all sessions. Entrance exams should be taken preferably early in the senior year. There is an early admissions plan. There is a rolling admissions plan. Application deadlines are open.

Transfer: The GPA required for transfer students varies according to the number of college credits completed. 30 of 130 credits required for the bachelor's degree must be completed at Sully.

Visiting: There are regularly scheduled orientations for prospective students, consisting of 1 1/2-day programs in January, late August, June, and July. There are guides for informal visits and visitors may sit in on classes and stay overnight. To schedule a visit, contact the Office of Admissions at (915) 837-8059.

Financial Aid: In a recent year, 52% of full-time freshmen and 21% of continuing full-time students received need-based aid. The average freshman award was $5489. 7% of undergraduates work part time. Average annual earnings from campus work are $2000. Sully is a member of CSS. The CSS Profile is required.

International Students: They must score 520 on the written TOEFL and also take the SAT I or the ACT, scoring 800.

Computers: The mainframe is an IBM AS/400. PCs are available for academic use. All students may access the system. There are no time limits and no fees.

Admissions Contact: Robert C. Cullins, Dean of Admissions and Records. E-mail: *rcullins@sul-ross-1.sulross.edu* Web: *www.sulross.edu*

TARLETON STATE UNIVERSITY
Stephenville, TX 76402

D-2

(254) 968-9125
(800) 687-8236; Fax: (254) 968-9951

Full-time: 2658 men, 3183 women	**Faculty:** 264; IIA, --$
Part-time: 647 men, 947 women	**Ph.D.s:** 45%
Graduate: 514 men, 897 women	**Student/Faculty:** 22 to 1
Year: semesters, summer session	**Tuition:** $2898 ($8562)
Application Deadline: August 1	**Room & Board:** $4678
Freshman Class: 2846 applied, 1817 accepted, 1259 enrolled	
SAT I Verbal/Math: 480/470	**ACT:** 19 **COMPETITIVE**

Tarleton State University, founded in 1899 and a part of the Texas A&M University System, is a public institution offering undergraduate and graduate programs in agriculture and technology, arts and sciences, business, and education and fine arts. There are 5 undergraduate schools and 1 graduate school. In addition to regional accreditation, Tarleton has baccalaureate program accreditation with ACBSP, CSWE, NASM, and NCATE. The library contains 293,149 volumes, 898,265 microform items, and 7954 audio/video tapes/CDs, and subscribes to 2791 periodicals. Computerized library services include the card catalog, interlibrary loans, and database searching. Special learning facilities include a learning resource center, art gallery, planetarium, a 600-acre farm, a 1200-acre ranch, an equine center, and a center for industrial history of Texas. The 123-acre campus is in a small town 67 miles southwest of Fort Worth. Including any residence halls, there are 84 buildings.

Student Life: 95% of undergraduates are from Texas. Students are from 48 states, 28 foreign countries, and Canada. 86% are from public schools. 82% are white. Most are Protestant. The average age of freshmen is 18; all undergraduates, 24. 35% do not continue beyond their first year; 33% remain to graduate.

Housing: 1538 students can be accommodated in college housing, which includes single-sex and coed dorms, on-campus apartments, off-campus apartments, and married-student housing. On-campus housing is guaranteed for the freshman year only and is available on a first-come, first-served basis. 74% of students commute. Alcohol is not permitted. All students may keep cars.

Activities: 7% of men belong to 9 national fraternities; 5% of women belong to 7 national sororities. There are 95 groups on campus, including art, band, cheerleading, choir, computers, debate, drama, drill team, ethnic, honors, international, jazz band, marching band, musical theater, newspaper, political, professional, religious, social, social service, student government, and yearbook. Popular campus events include Howdy Week, Spring Fest, and Tarleton Christmas.

Sports: There are 5 intercollegiate sports for men and 7 for women, and 19 intramural sports for men and 19 for women. Facilities include a fully equipped complex with a heated pool, track, courts for basketball, volleyball, tennis, and racquetball and various playing fields. There is also a 7000-seat stadium, a 3300-seat gym, a fully lighted 550-seat baseball stadium, and a softball stadium.

Disabled Students: 80% of the campus is accessible. Wheelchair ramps, elevators, special parking, specially equipped rest rooms, special class scheduling, lowered drinking fountains, lowered telephones, and easy-access doors are available.

Services: Counseling and information services are available, as is tutoring in most subjects, including math, science, English, and social studies. The Teaching and Learning Center provides tutoring assistance in all academic areas.

Campus Safety and Security: Measures include 24-hour foot and vehicle patrol, self-defense education, security escort services, and shuttle buses. There are informal discussions, pamphlets/posters/films, emergency telephones, and lighted pathways/sidewalks.

Programs of Study: Tarleton confers B.A., B.S., B.A.A.S., B.B.A., B.F.A., B.M., B.S.N., and B.S.W. degrees. Master's and doctoral degrees are also awarded. Bachelor's degrees are awarded in AGRICULTURE (agricultural business management, agricultural economics, agricultural mechanics, agriculture, agronomy, animal science, horticulture, international agriculture, plant science, and range/farm management), BIOLOGICAL SCIENCE (biology/biological science and wildlife biology), BUSINESS (accounting, banking and finance, business administration and management, fashion merchandising, human resources, management science, marketing and distribution, marketing/retailing/merchandising, office supervision and management, and personnel management), COMMUNICATIONS AND THE ARTS (art, dramatic arts, English, fine arts, music, Spanish, and speech/debate/rhetoric), COMPUTER AND PHYSICAL SCIENCE (chemistry, computer programming, computer science, earth science, geology, information sciences and systems, mathematics, and physics), EDUCATION (agricultural, art, business, home economics, industrial arts, and physical), ENGINEERING AND ENVIRONMENTAL DESIGN (industrial engineering technology), HEALTH PROFESSIONS (medical laboratory technology, nursing, physical therapy, predentistry, premedicine, prepharmacy, and preveterinary science), SOCIAL SCIENCE (criminal justice, dietetics, economics, history, home economics, human development, interdisciplinary studies, law enforcement and corrections, physical fitness/movement, political science/government, prelaw, social work, sociology, and water resources). Science and business are the strongest academically. Business and education are the largest.

Required: All students must complete at least 128 hours, including 24 hours in the major, with a 2.0 GPA. The 47-hour required core curriculum includes courses in English, U.S. and Texas government, U.S. history, lab science, communications, computer information systems, and wellness. There are also distributional requirements that must be met in humanities and social sciences, and a writing proficiency exam.

Special: Tarleton offers work-study programs, internships, limited non-degree study, study abroad in 2 countries, and cross-registration with Texas A&M International University at Laredo. There is a 3-2 engineering degree available with Texas A&M University. Special degree programs may be designed to meet unusual requirements. There are 11 national honor societies, a freshman honors program, and 5 departmental honors programs.

Faculty/Classroom: 56% of faculty are male; 44%, female. 57% teach undergraduates and 13% both teach and do research. The average class size in an introductory lecture is 36; in a laboratory, 22; and in a regular course, 29.

Admissions: 64% of the 2003-2004 applicants were accepted. The SAT I scores for the 2003-2004 freshman class were: Verbal--61% below 500, 32% between 500 and 599, 6% between 600 and 700, and 1% above 700; Math--59% below 500, 34% between 500 and 599, 6% between 600 and 700, and 1% above 700. The ACT scores were 65% below 21, 22% between 21 and 23, 9% between 24 and 26, 2% between 27 and 28, and 1% above 28. 22% of the current freshmen were in the top fifth of their class; 54% were in the top two fifths. 18 freshmen graduated first in their class.

Requirements: The SAT I or ACT is required. In addition, applicants must have a minimum composite score of 930 on the SAT I or 20 on the ACT, be a graduate of an accredited Texas secondary school or advanced high school program, or rank in the top quarter of their graduating class. Secondary preparation should include 4 years of English and 3 years of college-preparatory math, including algebra I and II. A GED will be considered equivalent to a high school diploma, provided the average standard score is at least 55 or no subscore is less than 50. A GPA of 2.0 is required. AP and CLEP credits are accepted. Important factors in the admissions decision are advanced placement or honor courses, evidence of special talent, and extracurricular activities record.

Procedure: Freshmen are admitted to all sessions. Entrance exams should be taken in the junior year. There are early decision, deferred admissions, and rolling admissions plans. Applications should be filed by August 1 for fall entry, January 7 for spring entry, and May 25 for summer entry, along with a $25 fee. Notification is sent on a rolling basis. 200 early decision candidates were accepted for the 2003-2004 class. Applications are accepted on-line through www.applyTexas.org.

Transfer: 914 transfer students enrolled in 2002-2003. Applicants with 30 or more transferable credits must present a 2.0 GPA; those with fewer than 30 credits must present a 2.8 GPA. A GPA of 2.0 to 2.79 may be admitted provided transfers also meet regular admission standards of first-time freshman applicants. 30 of 128 credits required for the bachelor's degree must be completed at Tarleton.

Visiting: There are regularly scheduled orientations for prospective students, including a tour of the campus. There are guides for informal visits and visitors may sit in on classes. To schedule a visit, contact the Office of School Relations, Tarleton Center at (254) 968-9256 or (800) 687-4TSU or info@tarleton.edu.

Financial Aid: In 2003-2004, 69% of all full-time freshmen and 79% of continuing full-time students received some form of financial aid. 65% of full-time freshmen and 95% of continuing full-time students received need-based aid. The average freshman award was $7863. Need-based scholarships or need-based grants averaged $3300; need-based self-help aid (loans and jobs) averaged $4697; non-need-based athletic scholarships averaged $2967; other non-need-based awards and non-need-based scholarships averaged $1556; and private scholarships and grants averaged $1329. 18% of undergraduates work part time. Average annual earnings from campus work are $1642. The average financial indebtedness of the 2003 graduate was $17,642. Tarleton is a member of CSS. The FAFSA or FFS is required. The deadline for filing freshman financial aid applications for fall entry is June 2.

International Students: There are 37 international students enrolled. The school actively recruits these students. They must score 520 on the written TOEFL or 190 on the electronic version and also take the SAT I or the ACT.

Computers: The mainframe is a Dual Digital (Compaq) ALPHA 8200. There are 1,800 Kaypro, Mac II, Apple IIe, IBM AT, and other PCs available in student labs and faculty offices. All dorms are wired for Internet access. All students may access the system. The fee is $4 per hour.

Graduates: From July 1, 2002 to June 30, 2003, 1312 bachelor's degrees were awarded. The most popular majors were exercise and sport studies (8%), interdisciplinary studies (7%), and computer information systems (6%). In an average class, 10% graduate in 4 years or less, 26% graduate in 5 years or less, and 32% graduate in 6 years or less. 367 companies recruited on campus in 2002-2003. Of the 2002 graduating class, 5% were enrolled in graduate school within 6 months of graduation and 80% were employed.

Admissions Contact: Denise Groves, Director of Admissions.
E-mail: siler@tarleton.edu Web: www.tarleton.edu

TEXAS A&M UNIVERSITY SYSTEM

The Texas A&M University System, established in 1876, is a public system in Texas. It is governed by a 9-member Board of Regents, whose chief administrator is the chancellor. The primary goal of the system is teaching, research, and service. The main priorities are to provide undergraduate and graduate students with a quality education, and to be a world leader in the development and dissemination of new knowledge. The total enrollment of all 9 campuses was more than 92,000; there were approximately 23,000 faculty and staff members. Altogether there are 500 baccalaureate, 400 master's, and 100 doctoral programs offered in Texas A&M University System. Profiles of the 4-year campuses are included in this section.

TEXAS A&M UNIVERSITY
College Station, TX 77843

D-3

(979) 845-3741; Fax: (979) 847-8737

Full-time: 16,598 men, 16,220 women	**Faculty:** 1328; I, av$
Part-time: 1759 men, 1489 women	**Ph.Ds:** 91%
Graduate: 5138 men, 3609 women	**Student/Faculty:** 25 to 1
Year: semesters, summer session	**Tuition:** $5051 ($12,131)
Application Deadline: February 15	**Room & Board:** $6030
Freshman Class: 17,250 applied, 11,639 accepted, 6675 enrolled	
SAT I Verbal/Math: 580/610	**ACT:** 25 **HIGHLY COMPETITIVE**

Texas A&M University, founded in 1876, is part of the Texas A&M University system. Undergraduate degrees are offered in agriculture and life sciences, architecture, business administration, education, engineering, geosciences, liberal arts, science, and biomedical science. There are 9 undergraduate and 10 graduate schools. In addition to regional accreditation, Texas A&M has baccalaureate program accreditation with AACSB, ABET, ACCE, ACEJMC, ADA, ASLA, CSAB, NAAB, NCATE, and SAF. The 3 libraries contain 2,923,964 volumes, 5,304,146 microform items, and 318,876 audio/video tapes/CDs, and subscribe to 36,353 periodicals. Computerized library services include the card catalog, interlibrary loans, and database searching. Special learning facilities include a learning resource center, art gallery, radio station, TV station, a weather station, observatory, cyclotron, wind tunnel, visualization lab, nuclear reactor, ocean wave pool, and the Bush Museum and Library. The 8500-acre campus is in an urban area 90 miles northwest of Houston. Including any residence halls, there are 665 buildings.

Student Life: 95% of undergraduates are from Texas. Students are from 50 states, 115 foreign countries, and Canada. 76% are white. The average age of freshmen is 18; all undergraduates, 20. 10% do not continue beyond their first year; 75% remain to graduate.

Housing: 10,600 students can be accommodated in college housing, which includes single-sex and coed dorms, on-campus apartments, and married-student housing. In addition, there are honors houses. On-campus housing is available on a first-come, first-served basis. 73% of students commute. All students may keep cars.

Activities: 6% of men belong to 19 national fraternities; 7% of women belong to 2 local and 19 national sororities. There are 700 groups on campus, including art, band, chess, choir, chorale, chorus, computers, dance, drama, drill team, drum and bugle corps, ethnic, film, gay, honors, international, jazz band, literary magazine, marching band, musical theater, newspaper, opera, orchestra, photography, political, professional, radio and TV, religious, social, social service, student government, symphony, and yearbook. Popular campus events include Aggie Bonfire, Parents Weekend, and Whoopstock (a celebration of unity through diversity).

Sports: There are 9 intercollegiate sports for men and 12 for women, and 24 intramural sports for men and 23 for women. Facilities include a coliseum, a natatorium, 11 basketball/volleyball courts, 27 handball/racquetball courts, badminton, weight and activity rooms, jogging trails, 14 tennis courts, a squash court, an 18-hole golf course, a 2500-seat auditorium/arena, a driving range, flag football fields, 4 soccer fields, 4 outdoor basketball courts, and 5 walking trails. Intercollegiate athletic facilities include a 70,210-seat football stadium, a 7200-seat indoor basketball and volleyball coliseum, a 7053-seat baseball stadium, a 1750-seat softball complex, a 1000-seat soccer complex, a 2000-seat natatorium, a 3000-seat track and field complex, a 1500-seat tennis center, and an 18,000-square-foot physical strength and conditioning lab.

Disabled Students: 85% of the campus is accessible. Wheelchair ramps, elevators, special parking, specially equipped rest rooms, special class scheduling, lowered drinking fountains, lowered telephones, and an office of support services for students with disabilities are available.

Services: Counseling and information services are available, as is tutoring in most subjects. There is a reader service for the blind, and remedial math, reading, and writing. Workshops in time management, basic study techniques, and test-taking skills are available.

Campus Safety and Security: Measures include 24-hour foot and vehicle patrol, self-defense education, security escort services, and shuttle buses. There are informal discussions, pamphlets/posters/films, emergency telephones, lighted pathways/sidewalks, a security awareness committee, and crime-watch and safety tip lines.

Programs of Study: Texas A&M confers B.A., B.S., B.B.A., B.Ed., and B.L.A. degrees. Master's and doctoral degrees are also awarded. Bachelor's degrees are awarded in AGRICULTURE (agricultural business management, agricultural economics, animal science, dairy science, fish and game management, fishing and fisheries, forestry and related sciences, horticulture, poultry science, and range/farm management), BIOLOGICAL SCIENCE (biochemistry, biology/biological science, botany, entomology, genetics, microbiology, and zoology), BUSINESS (accounting, banking and finance, business systems analysis, management science, marketing/retailing/merchandising, and personnel management), COM-

MUNICATIONS AND THE ARTS (English, French, German, journalism, Russian, Spanish, and speech/debate/rhetoric), COMPUTER AND PHYSICAL SCIENCE (atmospheric sciences and meteorology, chemistry, computer science, geology, geophysics and seismology, mathematics, and physics), EDUCATION (elementary, health, physical, and secondary), ENGINEERING AND ENVIRONMENTAL DESIGN (aeronautical engineering, agricultural engineering, bioengineering, chemical engineering, civil engineering, computer engineering, construction engineering, electrical/electronics engineering, engineering technology, environmental design, environmental science, industrial engineering technology, landscape architecture/design, mechanical engineering, nuclear engineering, and petroleum/natural gas engineering), HEALTH PROFESSIONS (biomedical science), SOCIAL SCIENCE (anthropology, economics, history, international studies, parks and recreation management, philosophy, political science/government, psychology, and sociology). Engineering, business administration, and life sciences are the strongest academically. Psychology, accounting, and biomedical science are the largest.

Required: To graduate, students must complete at least 128 credit hours, including 30 to 33 in the major. A minimum 2.0 GPA is required. Students must complete courses in American history and government, phys ed, computers, foreign language, speech and writing skills, math/logical reasoning, science, humanities, and social science. Requirements in the major vary.

Special: The university offers extensive opportunities through the Career Center and Study Abroad Office. B.A.- B.S. degrees, study abroad in 12 countries, credit for military experience, nondegree study, co-op programs, dual majors, and pass/fail options are available. A 5-year graduate business/liberal arts program is offered, as well as a 3-2 engineering degree with Sam Houston State University. There are 41 national honor societies, including Phi Beta Kappa, and a freshman honors program.

Faculty/Classroom: 72% of faculty are male; 28%, female. 70% teach undergraduates, 72% do research, and 47% do both. The average class size in an introductory lecture is 77; in a laboratory, 28; and in a regular course, 57.

Admissions: 67% of the 2003-2004 applicants were accepted. The SAT I scores for the 2003-2004 freshman class were: Verbal--18% below 500, 41% between 500 and 599, 33% between 600 and 700, and 8% above 700; Math--10% below 500, 35% between 500 and 599, 42% between 600 and 700, and 13% above 700. The ACT scores were 10% below 21, 20% between 21 and 23, 30% between 24 and 26, 15% between 27 and 28, and 25% above 28. 80% of the current freshmen were in the top fifth of their class; 98% were in the top two fifths. There were 156 National Merit finalists. 242 freshmen graduated first in their class.

Requirements: The SAT I or ACT is required. In addition, secondary school graduation is a condition of freshman admission. Required high school courses include 4 credits in English, 3 1/2 credits in math, 3 credits in science (2 from biology, chemistry, or physics), 2 credits of social studies and the same foreign language, and 1 of history. AP and CLEP credits are accepted. Important factors in the admissions decision are leadership record, evidence of special talent, and extracurricular activities record.

Procedure: Freshmen are admitted fall, spring, and summer. Entrance exams should be taken during the spring of the junior year or by December of the senior year. Applications should be filed by February 15 for fall entry, October 15 for spring entry, and February 15 for summer entry, along with a $50 fee. Notification is sent on a rolling basis. A waiting list is an active part of the admissions procedure. Applications are accepted on-line through the university's web site.

Transfer: 1768 transfer students enrolled in 2002-2003. Applicants must submit transcripts from previously attended colleges. Requirements vary, depending on how many semester hours were attempted and the grades for those hours. Transfer applicants must submit high school transcripts and, if they have fewer than 12 graded semester hours, the SAT I or ACT scores. 30 of 128 credits required for the bachelor's degree must be completed at Texas A&M.

Visiting: There are regularly scheduled orientations for prospective students. Some 20 new-student conferences are held for students to meet with academic advisers to select courses, become acquainted with student life activities, and tour the campus. There are guides for informal visits and visitors may sit in on classes. To schedule a visit, contact the Aggieland Visitor Center at (979) 845-5851 or vis-ctr@tamu.edu.

Financial Aid: In a recent year, 66% of all full-time freshmen and 70% of continuing full-time students received some form of financial aid. 35% of full-time freshmen and 40% of continuing full-time students received need-based aid. The average freshman award was $5480. 28% of undergraduates work part time. Average annual earnings from campus work are $3824. The average financial indebtedness of the 2003 graduate was $13,143. The FAFSA is required. The deadline for filing freshman financial aid applications for fall entry is April 1.

International Students: In a recent year, 472 international students were enrolled. They must score 550 on the written TOEFL.

Computers: The mainframes are an IBM 3090-600E, an Amdahl 5990, and DEC VAXs 880, 8650, and 9000-210V. About 2000 Macs and PCs

are available throughout the campus. All students may access the system at any time. There are no time limits. The fee is $14.05 per credit hour.

Graduates: From July 1, 2002 to June 30, 2003, 8285 bachelor's degrees were awarded. The most popular majors were interdisciplinary studies (6%), psychology (5%), and biomedical science (5%). In an average class, 1% graduate in 3 years or less, 27% graduate in 4 years or less, 66% graduate in 5 years or less, and 74% graduate in 6 years or less. 150 companies recruited on campus in 2002-2003. Of the 2002 graduating class, 12% were enrolled in graduate school within 6 months of graduation and 54% were employed.

Admissions Contact: Admissions Counseling.
E-mail: *admissions@tamu.edu* Web: *www.tamu.edu/admissions*

TEXAS A&M UNIVERSITY AT COMMERCE
E-2
Commerce, TX 75429-3011
(903) 886-5106
(800) 331-3878; Fax: (903) 886-5888

Full-time: 1640 men, 2397 women	**Faculty:** 237; I, --$
Part-time: 393 men, 636 women	**Ph.D.s:** 71%
Graduate: 1173 men, 2174 women	**Student/Faculty:** 17 to 1
Year: semesters, summer session	**Tuition:** $3624 ($10,704)
Application Deadline: August 6	**Room & Board:** $5370
Freshman Class: 3589 applied, 2248 accepted, 1560 enrolled	
SAT I Verbal/Math: 480/480	**ACT:** 20　　**COMPETITIVE**

Texas A&M University at Commerce, founded in 1889, offers undergraduate and graduate programs in business and technology, arts and sciences, and education. There are 3 undergraduate schools and 1 graduate school. In addition to regional accreditation, TAMU-C has baccalaureate program accreditation with AACSB, CSWE, NASM, and NCATE. The library contains 1,714,655 volumes and 131,926 microform items. Computerized library services include the card catalog, interlibrary loans, and database searching. Special learning facilities include a radio station, TV station, and performing arts center, and farm. The 154-acre campus is in a small town 65 miles northeast of Dallas. Including any residence halls, there are 121 buildings.

Student Life: 94% of undergraduates are from Texas. Students are from 28 states, 35 foreign countries, and Canada. 98% are from public schools. 69% are white; 17% African American. The average age of freshmen is 20; all undergraduates, 25. 36% do not continue beyond their first year; 66% remain to graduate.

Housing: 2750 students can be accommodated in college housing, which includes single-sex and coed dorms, on-campus apartments, married-student housing, fraternity houses, and sorority houses. In addition, there are honors houses and special-interest houses. On-campus housing is guaranteed for the freshman year only and is available on a first-come, first-served basis. 71% of students commute. All students may keep cars.

Activities: 15% of men belong to 9 national fraternities; 12% of women belong to 7 national sororities. There are 96 groups on campus, including art, band, cheerleading, chess, choir, chorale, chorus, dance, drama, ethnic, film, gay, honors, international, jazz band, literary magazine, marching band, musical theater, newspaper, orchestra, pep band, photography, political, professional, radio and TV, religious, social, social service, student government, and yearbook. Popular campus events include Sam Rayburn Symposium, Christmas Feast of Carols, and Springfest.

Sports: There are 5 intercollegiate sports for men and 5 for women, and 7 intramural sports for men and 7 for women. Facilities include a 1700-seat auditorium, a 10,000-seat stadium, a gym, handball and racquetball courts, a bowling alley, a swimming pool, a weight room, tennis courts, a field house, and intramural fields.

Disabled Students: 85% of the campus is accessible. Wheelchair ramps, elevators, special parking, and specially equipped rest rooms are available.

Services: Counseling and information services are available, as is tutoring in some subjects, including math and writing. There is remedial math, reading, and writing.

Campus Safety and Security: Measures include 24-hour foot and vehicle patrol, self-defense education, security escort services, and informal discussions. There are pamphlets/posters/films, emergency telephones, lighted pathways/sidewalks, a victim assistance officer, a police service for special and social events, crime and date-rape prevention presentations, and motorist assistance.

Programs of Study: TAMU-C confers B.A., B.S., B.A.C.J., B.B.A., B.F.A., B.G.S., B.M., B.M.Ed., B.S.C.J., B.S.Lib.Sci., and B.S.W. degrees. Master's and doctoral degrees are also awarded. Bachelor's degrees are awarded in AGRICULTURE (agricultural economics, agriculture, animal science, and wildlife management), BIOLOGICAL SCIENCE (biology/biological science and botany), BUSINESS (accounting, banking and finance, business administration and management, and marketing/retailing/merchandising), COMMUNICATIONS AND THE ARTS (advertising, broadcasting, dramatic arts, English, fine arts, French, German, journalism, languages, music, photography, printmaking, and Spanish), COMPUTER AND PHYSICAL SCIENCE (chemistry, computer science, earth science, geology, mathematics, and physics),

EDUCATION (agricultural, business, early childhood, elementary, guidance, health, industrial arts, music, science, and secondary), ENGINEERING AND ENVIRONMENTAL DESIGN (engineering technology and preengineering), HEALTH PROFESSIONS (predentistry, premedicine, and prepharmacy), SOCIAL SCIENCE (anthropology, criminal justice, economics, geography, history, political science/government, prelaw, psychology, religion, social work, and sociology). Education, computer science, and business administration are the strongest programs academically and the largest.

Required: To graduate, all students must earn a GPA of 2.0 while taking at least 126 semester hours, including 24 hours in the major. Distribution requirements include 24 in culture courses such as American history and foreign languages, 12 each in English composition, math, and speech skills, 8 in sciences, 6 in upper-division courses, and 4 in phys ed.

Special: TAMU-C offers co-op programs with E-Systems Inc. and numerous other firms, cross-registration by independent arrangement, study abroad in England, and work-study programs. B.A.-B.S. degrees, second degrees, dual majors, a general studies degree, credit for life experience, internships, nondegree study, and pass/fail options are also available. There are 18 national honor societies, a freshman honors program, and 26 departmental honors programs.

Faculty/Classroom: 55% of faculty are male; 45%, female. 96% teach undergraduates, 62% do research, and 62% do both. Graduate students teach 40% of introductory courses. The average class size in an introductory lecture is 30; in a laboratory, 20; and in a regular course, 25.

Admissions: 63% of the 2003-2004 applicants were accepted. 42% of the current freshmen were in the top fifth of their class; 72% were in the top two fifths.

Requirements: The SAT I or ACT is required, with a minimum recommended composite score of 800 or 20, respectively. Applicants need not be graduates of an accredited secondary school, although high school graduation is required. The GED is also accepted. A GPA of 2.0 is required. AP and CLEP credits are accepted.

Procedure: Freshmen are admitted to all sessions. Entrance exams should be taken prior to enrollment. There is a deferred admissions plan and a rolling admissions plan. Applications should be filed by August 6 for fall entry. Notification is sent on a rolling basis.

Transfer: Applicants must have a college GPA of 2.0 with a minimum of 21 credit hours. The SAT I or ACT is not required. College transcripts and a statement of good standing from the prior institution are required. 30 credits of 126 required for the bachelor's degree must be completed at TAMU-C.

Visiting: There are regularly scheduled orientations for prospective students. There are guides for informal visits and visitors may sit in on classes. To schedule a visit, contact the Office of School Relations.

Financial Aid: The average freshman award was $3698. Need-based scholarships or need-based grants averaged $3285. The FAFSA and the college's own financial statement are required. The deadline for filing freshman financial aid applications for fall entry is October 1.

International Students: There are 67 international students enrolled. They must score 500 on the written TOEFL and also take the SAT I or the ACT, scoring 800 on the SAT I.

Computers: The mainframes are an IBM 9370 Model 60 and a DEC Alpha-UNIX system. There are 310 PCs and Macs contained in 13 labs located in the library, business administration building, and most classroom buildings. About half of these units are networked and linked to a mainframe. All students may access the system 24 hours daily by modem, and most labs are open until 10 P.M. There are no time limits and no fees.

Graduates: From July 1, 2002 to June 30, 2003, 951 bachelor's degrees were awarded. The most popular majors were interdisciplinary studies (22%), business/marketing (18%), and public administration (8%). 55 companies recruited on campus in 2002-2003.

Admissions Contact: Randy McDonald, Director of Admissions. A video is available. E-mail: *admissions@tamu-commerce.edu*
Web: *www.tamu-commerce.edu*

TEXAS A&M UNIVERSITY AT CORPUS CHRISTI
Corpus Christi, TX 78412
(361) 825-2624
(800) 482-6822; Fax: (361) 825-5887

Full-time: 1853 men, 2986 women	**Faculty:** IIA, av$
Part-time: 651 men, 793 women	**Ph.D.s:** 74%
Graduate: 501 men, 927 women	**Student/Faculty:** n/av
Year: semesters, summer session	**Tuition:** $3144 ($8808)
Application Deadline: July 1	**Room & Board:** $7125
Freshman Class: 2841 applied, 2379 accepted, 1111 enrolled	
SAT I or ACT: required	**COMPETITIVE**

Texas A&M University at Corpus Christi, part of the Texas A&M University System since 1989, is a public institution offering 34 undergraduate degree programs and 27 graduate degree programs. The library contains 433,785 volumes, 654,518 microform items, and 6245 audio/video tapes/CDs, and subscribes to 1706 periodicals. The university is located on its own 240-acre island approximately 10 miles from downtown Corpus Christi.

Student Life: 98% of undergraduates are from Texas. 57% are white; 37% Hispanic. The average age of freshmen is 19; all undergraduates, 23.

Housing: On campus housing includes single-sex and coed dorms and apartments for single students.

Activities: There are many groups and organizations on campus, including band, choir, dance, drama, film, jazz band, literary magazine, marching band, musical theater, newspaper, opera, pep band, student government, symphony, and yearbook.

Sports: There are 6 intercollegiate sports for men and 8 for women. Facilities include a field house with a full-size gym, a weight room, and 4 racquetball/handball courts. Adjacent to the gym are 6 lighted tennis courts, a practice court, a 25-meter swimming pool, and lighted playing fields. A wellness center offers a free-weight area, weight machines, cardiovascular equipment, a wellness resource area, 2 aerobic studios, and a game room.

Programs of Study: Texas A & M University at Corpus Christi confers B.A., B.S., B.B.A., B.F.A., B.M., B.S.H.S., B.S.I.S., and B.S.N. degrees. Master's and doctoral degrees are also awarded. Bachelor's degrees are awarded in BIOLOGICAL SCIENCE (biology/biological science), BUSINESS (accounting, banking and finance, business administration and management, management information systems, and marketing/retailing/merchandising), COMMUNICATIONS AND THE ARTS (art, communications, dramatic arts, English, music, Spanish, and speech/debate/rhetoric), COMPUTER AND PHYSICAL SCIENCE (chemistry, computer science, geology, and mathematics), EDUCATION (education), ENGINEERING AND ENVIRONMENTAL DESIGN (engineering technology, environmental science, and mechanical engineering technology), HEALTH PROFESSIONS (clinical science, health science, and nursing), SOCIAL SCIENCE (criminal justice, geography, history, political science/government, psychology, and sociology).

Required: To graduate, a minimum of 124 semester hours must be completed. A minimum of 45 semester hours of upper-division credit is required, as is a minimum GPA of 2.0 overall and in the major. In addition, all students must complete the core curriculum requirement, including 6 credit hours each of communication (English rhetoric/compostition), natural science, U.S. history, and political science and 3 each of math, visual and performing arts, humanities, and social/behavioral science. Students must also meet foreign language and computer literacy requirements and take a first-year seminar.

Special: Cooperative programs, internships, dual majors, and distance learning are available.

Faculty/Classroom: 57% of faculty are male; 43%, female.

Admissions: 84% of the 2003-2004 applicants were accepted.

Requirements: The SAT I or ACT is required. In addition, graduation from secondary school is required, with 4 units of English, 3 each of math, science, and social studies, and 2 of a foreign language. The GED is accepted.

Procedure: Freshmen are admitted fall, spring, and summer. Applications should be filed by July 1 for fall entry, November 1 for spring entry, and April 1 for summer entry along with a $20 fee. Applications are accepted on-line through *www.applytexas.org*. Notification is sent 2 weeks after receipt of the completed application.

Transfer: 1313 transfer students enrolled in 2003-2004. College transcripts, a statement of good standing from prior institutions, and a GPA of 2.0 are required.

Financial Aid: In 2003-2004, 55% of all full-time students received some form of financial aid. 41% of full-time freshmen and 42% of continuing full-time students received need-based aid. The average freshman award was $5422. Need-based scholarships or need-based grants averaged $3616; need-based self-help aid (loans and jobs) averaged $2451; and institutional non-need-based awards and non-need-based scholarships averaged $3314. The average financial indebtedness of the 2003 graduate was $16,886. The FAFSA is required. The priority date for freshman financial aid applications for fall entry is April 1.

International Students: They must score 550 on the written TOEFL.

Computers: There are computer labs in the library and several other buildings; the labs include PCs, full-page scanners, laser printers, and graphic stations. Most labs are open more than 85 hours per week.

Graduates: From July 1, 2002 to June 30, 2003, 1085 bachelor's degrees were awarded. The most popular majors were business/marketing (24%), interdisciplinary studies (17%), and protective services/public administration (7%). In an average class, 15% graduate in 4 years or less, 29% graduate in 5 years or less, and 65% graduate in 6 years or less.

Admissions Contact: Director of Admissions.
E-mail: *judith.perales@mail.tamucc.edu* Web: *www.tamucc.edu*

TEXAS A&M UNIVERSITY AT GALVESTON
Galveston, TX 77553-1675

E-4

(409) 740-4414
(877) 322-4443; Fax: (409) 740-4731

Full-time: 603 men, 632 women	**Faculty:** IIB, +$
Part-time: 65 men, 66 women	**Ph.Ds:** n/av
Graduate: 872 men, 748 women	**Student/Faculty:** n/av
Year: semesters, summer session	**Tuition:** $5078 ($10,778)
Application Deadline: open	**Room & Board:** $4870
Freshman Class: 1036 applied, 985 accepted, 414 enrolled	
SAT I Verbal/Math: 547/567	**ACT:** 24 COMPETITIVE+

Texas A&M University at Galveston, founded in 1962, is a public institution that offers marine and maritime-related programs. It is part of the Texas A&M University system. In addition to regional accreditation, TAMUG has baccalaureate program accreditation with ABET. The library contains 43,000 volumes and 52,984 microform items, and subscribes to 970 periodicals. Computerized library services include the card catalog, interlibrary loans, and database searching. Special learning facilities include a learning resource center and a training ship, the T/S Texas Clipper, used for an annual summer training cruise. The 100-acre campus is in a suburban area 50 miles south of Houston. Including any residence halls, there are 11 buildings.

Student Life: 81% of undergraduates are from Texas. Students are from 43 states and 8 foreign countries. 94% are from public schools. 85% are white. The average age of freshmen is 18; all undergraduates, 20.

Housing: 650 students can be accommodated in college housing, which includes coed dorms. On-campus housing is guaranteed for the freshman year only and is available on a first-come, first-served basis. 58% of students commute. Alcohol is not permitted. All students may keep cars.

Activities: There are no fraternities or sororities. There are 39 groups on campus, including chorale, drama, ethnic, international, literary magazine, newspaper, political, professional, religious, social, social service, student government, and yearbook. Popular campus events include Springfest, Mardi Gras, and Maritime Ball.

Sports: There are 2 intercollegiate sports for men and 1 for women, and 6 intramural sports for men and 5 for women. Facilities include tennis courts, a volleyball court, a swimming pool, and a basketball court.

Disabled Students: 80% of the campus is accessible. Wheelchair ramps, elevators, special parking, specially equipped rest rooms, special class scheduling, and lowered drinking fountains are available.

Services: Counseling and information services are available, as is tutoring in most subjects. There is a reader service for the blind, and remedial math, reading, and writing.

Campus Safety and Security: Measures include 24-hour foot and vehicle patrol, security escort services, shuttle buses, and lighted pathways/sidewalks.

Programs of Study: TAMUG confers the B.S. degree. Master's degrees are also awarded. Bachelor's degrees are awarded in AGRICULTURE (environmental studies, fishing and fisheries, and natural resource management), BIOLOGICAL SCIENCE (biology/biological science, environmental biology, marine biology, and marine science), BUSINESS (international business management, recreation and leisure services, and transportation management), COMPUTER AND PHYSICAL SCIENCE (earth science, geoscience, hydrology, natural sciences, oceanography, and science and management), ENGINEERING AND ENVIRONMENTAL DESIGN (civil engineering, electrical/electronics engineering technology, electromechanical technology, environmental science, land use management and reclamation, marine engineering, maritime science, mechanical engineering technology, naval architecture and marine engineering, ocean engineering, systems engineering, and transportation engineering), SOCIAL SCIENCE (archeology, geography, humanities and social science, liberal arts/general studies, and water resources). Marine sciences is the strongest academically. Marine biology is the largest.

Required: Depending on the major, students must complete 130 to 160 credit hours with a GPA of 2.0 overall as well as in the major. The required core curriculum includes courses in math, political science, American history, and macroeconomics. Distribution requirements include 6 credits each in English, calculus, humanities and social sciences; 8 credits in science; and 12 credits in citizenship. Students must also complete a 2-semester sequence of a foreign language and 1 computer language course.

Special: TAMUG offers dual majors in all majors, dual degrees, internships in marine biology and oceanography, a summer semester at sea, and credit for military service. Students may challenge any course for credit by exam. A pass/fail option is available for electives taken by juniors or seniors who have a minimum 2.5 GPA. Selected majors may earn a ship's officer license with a degree program.

Faculty/Classroom: All teach undergraduates. The average class size in an introductory lecture is 48; in a laboratory, 14; and in a regular course, 24.

Admissions: 95% of the 2003-2004 applicants were accepted. The SAT I scores for the 2003-2004 freshman class were: Verbal--36% below

500, 43% between 500 and 599, 19% between 600 and 700, and 2% above 700; Math--33% below 500, 48% between 500 and 599, 18% between 600 and 700, and 1% above 700. The ACT scores were 15% below 21, 24% between 21 and 23, 45% between 24 and 26, 8% between 27 and 28, and 8% above 28.

Requirements: The SAT I or ACT is required. Acceptable test scores depend on high school rank, with minimum composite scores of 1000 for the SAT I and 24 for the ACT. Applicants must be graduates of an accredited high school or hold a GED. A minimum of 16 academic credits is required, including 4 units of English, 3.5 units of math, 2.5 units of either history or social studies, 2 units each of a foreign language and science, and the rest in electives. AP and CLEP credits are accepted. Important factors in the admissions decision are leadership record, extracurricular activities record, and recommendations by school officials.

Procedure: Freshmen are admitted to all sessions. Entrance exams should be taken late in the junior year or early in the senior year. There are early decision, early admissions, deferred admissions plans, and rolling admissions plans. Application deadlines are open. Application fee is $35. Applications are accepted on-line through *www.applytexas.org.*

Transfer: 145 transfer students enrolled in 2002-2003. Applicants must have a cumulative 2.0 GPA in a minimum of 18 completed credit hours as well as a 2.0 GPA in each of the last 2 terms attended. 30 of 130 credits required for the bachelor's degree must be completed at TAMUG.

Visiting: There are regularly scheduled orientations for prospective students, including campus tours conducted Monday and Friday at 10 A.M. There are guides for informal visits and visitors may sit in on classes. To schedule a visit, contact the Student Relations Department at (409) 740-4422.

Financial Aid: 65% of undergraduates work part time. Average annual earnings from campus work are $1200. The FAFSA is required. The deadline for filing freshman financial aid applications for fall entry is April 1.

International Students: There are 13 international students enrolled. They must score 550 on the written TOEFL and also take the college's own test and also take the SAT I or the ACT, scoring 1000.

Computers: There are 123 terminals located in the Learning Resource Center, 4 labs, and other campus locations. All students may access the system. There are no time limits. The fee is $9 per semester credit hour.

Graduates: In a recent year 178 bachelor's degrees were awarded. 87 companies recruited on campus in a recent year.

Admissions Contact: Cheryl Moon, Director of Admissions. A video is available. E-mail: *seaaggie@tamug.edu* Web: *www.tamug.edu*

TEXAS A&M UNIVERSITY AT KINGSVILLE   D-5
Kingsville, TX 78363

(361) 593-2315
(800) 687-6000; Fax: (361) 595-2195

Full-time: 2127 men, 1941 women	**Faculty:** IIA, --$
Part-time: 594 men, 888 women	**Ph.D.s:** n/av
Graduate: 607 men, 691 women	**Student/Faculty:** n/av
Year: semesters, summer session	**Tuition:** $3156 ($8820)
Application Deadline: open	**Room & Board:** $3584
Freshman Class: n/av	
SAT I or ACT: required	**LESS COMPETITIVE**

Texas A&M University at Kingsville, founded in 1925 as South Texas Teachers College, is a comprehensive university and part of the Texas A&M University System. Graduate and undergraduate programs are offered in agriculture and home economics, arts and sciences, business administration, education, and engineering. There are 5 undergraduate and 5 graduate schools. In addition to regional accreditation, TAMUK has baccalaureate program accreditation with ABET, ADA, NASM, and NCATE. The library contains 358,466 volumes, 183,416 microform items, and 3224 audio/video tapes/CDs, and subscribes to 2304 periodicals. Computerized library services include the card catalog, interlibrary loans, and database searching. Special learning facilities include a learning resource center, art gallery, natural history museum, planetarium, radio station, TV station, and wildlife and citrus research facilities. The 246-acre campus is in a small town 40 miles southwest of Corpus Christi. Including any residence halls, there are 82 buildings.

Student Life: 95% of undergraduates are from Texas. Students are from 35 states, 44 foreign countries, and Canada. 98% are from public schools. 62% are Hispanic; 29% white. The average age of freshmen is 19; all undergraduates, 23. 45% do not continue beyond their first year; 22% remain to graduate.

Housing: 1200 students can be accommodated in college housing, which includes single-sex and coed dorms and married-student housing. On-campus housing is guaranteed for all 4 years. 70% of students commute. All students may keep cars.

Activities: 3% of men and about 3% of women belong to 6 national fraternities; 3% of women belong to 3 national sororities. There are 106 groups on campus, including art, band, cheerleading, choir, chorale, chorus, computers, dance, debate, drama, drill team, ethnic, honors, international, jazz band, marching band, mariachi, musical theater, newspaper, pep band, political, professional, radio and TV, religious, social,

and student government. Popular campus events include Campus Capers, Fall Carnival, and Spring Block Party.

Sports: There are 3 intercollegiate sports for men and 3 for women, and 2 intramural sports for men and 2 for women. Facilities include 2 gyms, an Olympic-size swimming pool, courts for tennis and racquetball, an all-weather track, and various playing fields. There are facilities for archery, bowling, golf, fencing, weight training, and jogging.

Disabled Students: 90% of the campus is accessible. Wheelchair ramps, elevators, special parking, specially equipped rest rooms, lowered drinking fountains, and lowered telephones are available.

Services: Counseling and information services are available, as is tutoring in every subject. There is a reader service for the blind, and remedial math, reading, and writing.

Campus Safety and Security: Measures include 24-hour foot and vehicle patrol, self-defense education, security escort services, and informal discussions. There are pamphlets/posters/films, emergency telephones, and lighted pathways/sidewalks.

Programs of Study: TAMUK confers B.A., B.S., B.A.A.S., B.B.A., B.F.A., B.M., B.S.A., B.S.C.E., B.S.Ch.E., B.S.C.S., B.S.E.E., B.S.I.E., B.S. in Hum.Sci., B.S. in Nat. Gas Eng., B.S.I.T., and B.S.M.E. degrees. Master's and doctoral degrees are also awarded. Bachelor's degrees are awarded in AGRICULTURE (agricultural business management, animal science, plant science, range/farm management, and soil science), BIOLOGICAL SCIENCE (biology/biological science), BUSINESS (accounting, banking and finance, business administration and management, business economics, fashion merchandising, management science, marketing/retailing/merchandising, and real estate), COMMUNICATIONS AND THE ARTS (communications, dramatic arts, English, fine arts, music, and Spanish), COMPUTER AND PHYSICAL SCIENCE (chemistry, computer science, geology, mathematics, and physics), EDUCATION (agricultural, elementary, health, music, physical, and secondary), ENGINEERING AND ENVIRONMENTAL DESIGN (chemical engineering, civil engineering, electrical/electronics engineering, engineering management, industrial engineering technology, interior design, mechanical engineering, and petroleum/natural gas engineering), HEALTH PROFESSIONS (medical laboratory technology, nursing, predentistry, premedicine, prepharmacy, preveterinary science, and speech pathology/audiology), SOCIAL SCIENCE (anthropology, child care/child and family studies, food production/management/services, food science, geography, history, home economics, political science/government, prelaw, psychology, public administration, and sociology). Engineering is the strongest academically. Education is the largest.

Required: All students must complete 124 to 135 semester hours, including a minimum of 24 in the major and 45 in advanced work, with at least a 2.0 GPA. General education requirements include courses in oral and written communication, math and reasoning, U.S. and Texas government, social sciences, American and world history, lab sciences, fine arts, and phys ed.

Special: There are co-op programs in engineering, business, and agriculture, and internships, B.A.-B.S. degrees and dual majors in most programs. A nontraditional Bachelor of Applied Arts and Sciences program is offered to students with vocational or technical training or experience. The Center for Continuing Education offers noncredit enrichment courses in a variety of subjects, a professional development program in organizational management, and a number of seminars and short courses that are held abroad. The university also offers a work-study program and the College I Freshman program. There are 10 national honor societies, a freshman honors program, and 20 departmental honors programs.

Faculty/Classroom: 66% of faculty are male; 34%, female. All teach undergraduates. The average class size in an introductory lecture is 30; in a laboratory, 20; and in a regular course, 25.

Admissions: The ACT scores for the 2003-2004 freshman class were: 70% below 21, 20% between 21 and 23, 7% between 24 and 26, 2% between 27 and 28, and 1% above 28. 25% of the current freshmen were in the top fifth of their class; 52% were in the top two fifths. 8 freshmen graduated first in their class.

Requirements: The SAT I or ACT is required. Applicants should be high school graduates or have a GED. Secondary preparation must include 7 units of electives, no more than 4 of which may be in vocational subjects, 3 units of English, 2 units each of math (including algebra), foreign language, and natural science, and 1 unit each of history and another social science. The university sets minimum admissible scores each year. An interview is encouraged. AP and CLEP credits are accepted.

Procedure: Freshmen are admitted to all sessions. Entrance exams should be taken before graduation from high school. There is an early admissions plan and a rolling admissions plan. Application deadlines are open. Application fee is $15.

Transfer: 427 transfer students enrolled in a recent year. All applicants must present a GPA of at least 2.0. 24 of 124 credits required for the bachelor's degree must be completed at TAMUK.

Visiting: There are regularly scheduled orientations for prospective students, including advisement, tours, stays in dorms, entertainment, registration, and financial information. There are guides for informal visits and visitors may sit in on classes and stay overnight. To schedule a visit, contact the Office of School Relations at (512) 593-3907.

Financial Aid: TAMUK is a member of CSS. The FAFSA is required. The deadline for filing freshman financial aid applications for fall entry is May 15.

International Students: There are 86 international students enrolled. They must score 500 on the written TOEFL and also take the college's own test and the SAT I or the ACT.

Computers: The mainframe is an IBM 9370. There are more than 400 PCs located in the library and in the business, engineering, agriculture, and education buildings as well as other sites on campus. All students may access the system. There are no time limits. The fee is $5 per semester credit hour.

Graduates: From July 1, 2002 to June 30, 2003, 729 bachelor's degrees were awarded. The most popular majors were engineering (16%), business/marketing (13%), and interdisciplinary (11%). In an average class, 25% graduate in 5 years or less, and 30% graduate in 6 years or less.

Admissions Contact: Maggie Williams, Registrar and Director of Admissions. E-mail: *kgossrx@tamuk.edu* Web: *http://www.tamuk.edu*

TEXAS CHRISTIAN UNIVERSITY   D-2
Fort Worth, TX 76129
(817) 257-7490
(800) TCU-FROG; Fax: (817) 257-7268

Full-time: 2577 men, 3814 women	**Faculty:** 403; I, -$
Part-time: 243 men, 299 women	**Ph.D.s:** 91%
Graduate: 656 men, 686 women	**Student/Faculty:** 16 to 1
Year: semesters, summer session	**Tuition:** $17,630
Application Deadline: February 15	**Room & Board:** $5780
Freshman Class: 7654 applied, 4971 accepted, 1596 enrolled	
SAT I or ACT: recommended	**VERY COMPETITIVE**

Texas Christian University, founded in 1873, is a private university affiliated with the Christian Church (Disciples of Christ). TCU is a teaching and research institution offering undergraduate programs in arts, sciences, business, education, fine arts, communications, nursing, and engineering. There are 7 undergraduate and 7 graduate schools. In addition to regional accreditation, TCU has baccalaureate program accreditation with AACSB, ABET, ACEJMC, ADA, ASLA, CAAHEP, CCNE, CSAB, CSWE, FIDER, and NASM. The library contains 1,299,875 volumes, 610,764 microform items, and 57,562 audio/video tapes/CDs, and subscribes to 4629 periodicals. Computerized library services include the card catalog, interlibrary loans, database searching, and Internet access. Special learning facilities include a learning resource center, art gallery, radio station, TV station, observatory, and a speech and hearing clinic. The 300-acre campus is in a suburban area 3 miles southwest of downtown Fort Worth. Including any residence halls, there are 92 buildings.

Student Life: 74% of undergraduates are from Texas. Students are from 48 states, 75 foreign countries, and Canada. 94% are from public schools. 77% are white. 51% are Protestant; 27% claim no religious affiliation; 15% Catholic. The average age of freshmen is 18; all undergraduates, 21. 19% do not continue beyond their first year; 64% remain to graduate.

Housing: 3146 students can be accommodated in college housing, which includes single-sex and coed dorms, on-campus apartments, fraternity houses, and sorority houses. In addition, there are special-interest houses. On-campus housing is guaranteed for all 4 years. 53% of students commute. All students may keep cars.

Activities: 35% of men belong to 1 local and 12 national fraternities; 40% of women belong to 3 local and 13 national sororities. There are 193 groups on campus, including art, band, cheerleading, chorale, chorus, computers, dance, drama, drill team, ethnic, film, gay, honors, international, jazz band, literary magazine, marching band, musical theater, newspaper, opera, orchestra, pep band, photography, political, professional, radio and TV, religious, social, social service, student government, symphony, and yearbook. Popular campus events include Parents Weekend, Howdy Rush Week, and Carols by Candlelight.

Sports: There are 9 intercollegiate sports for men and 9 for women. Facilities include indoor and outdoor tennis facilities, a 46,000-seat stadium, a 7,200-seat coliseum, an indoor NCAA regulation swimming pool, a diving well, 4 gyms, handball and racquetball courts, a sports conditioning facility that includes weight training, body conditioning, and sports rehabilitation equipment, an outdoor track with seating, and a paved walking/jogging track.

Disabled Students: 89% of the campus is accessible. Wheelchair ramps, elevators, special parking, specially equipped rest rooms, lowered drinking fountains, and lowered telephones are available. For visually impaired and hearing-impaired students, there are flashing lights and vibrators on beds in case of fire. Hearing-assistance devices are also available.

Campus Safety and Security: Measures include 24-hour foot and vehicle patrol, self-defense education, security escort services, and informal discussions. There are pamphlets/posters/films, emergency telephones,

lighted pathways/sidewalks, bike patrol, and video monitoring of some parking lots.

Programs of Study: TCU confers B.A., B.S., B.B.A., B.F.A., B.G.S., B.Med., B.Mus., B.S.Ed., B.S.N., and B.S.S.W. degrees. Master's and doctoral degrees are also awarded. Bachelor's degrees are awarded in BIOLOGICAL SCIENCE (biology/biological science, neurosciences, and nutrition), BUSINESS (accounting, banking and finance, business administration and management, electronic business, entrepreneurial studies, fashion merchandising, international business management, international economics, management science, and marketing/retailing/merchandising), COMMUNICATIONS AND THE ARTS (advertising, art history and appreciation, ballet, broadcasting, communications, dance, dramatic arts, English, film arts, French, graphic design, journalism, music, music performance, music theory and composition, piano/organ, radio/television technology, Spanish, speech/debate/rhetoric, and studio art), COMPUTER AND PHYSICAL SCIENCE (astrophysics, chemistry, computer science, geology, information sciences and systems, mathematics, and physics), EDUCATION (art, bilingual/bicultural, early childhood, education of the deaf and hearing impaired, education of the exceptional child, elementary, English, middle school, music, physical, science, and social studies), ENGINEERING AND ENVIRONMENTAL DESIGN (engineering, environmental science, and interior design), HEALTH PROFESSIONS (health, nursing, and speech pathology/audiology), SOCIAL SCIENCE (criminal justice, dietetics, economics, food production/management/services, history, Latin American studies, liberal arts/general studies, philosophy, physical fitness/movement, political science/government, psychology, religion, religious music, social work, and sociology). Psychology, biology, and nursing are the largest.

Required: To graduate, candidates must complete at least 124 semester hours, which include 24 to 36 hours in the major, earning a minimum GPA of 2.0.

Special: A general studies degree and a combined B.A.-B.S. degree in numerous majors are offered. Student-designed majors, dual majors, nondegree study, and pass/no credit options are available. TCU also accepts credit by examination and credit for life, military, and work experience. 3-2 programs are available in business, education, and economics. Internships are available in almost all major areas. The university also offers a Washington semester, student exchange in Japan and Mexico, and study abroad in 28 countries. TCU also offers study at its London Center and study through the American Airlines Leadership for the Americas program. There are 4 national honor societies, including Phi Beta Kappa, a freshman honors program, and 29 departmental honors programs.

Faculty/Classroom: 63% of faculty are male; 37%, female. 96% teach undergraduates. The average class size in an introductory lecture is 36 and in a regular course, 28.

Admissions: 65% of the 2003-2004 applicants were accepted. 57% of the current freshmen were in the top fifth of their class.

Requirements: The SAT I or ACT is recommended. In addition, candidates should be graduates of an accredited secondary school and have completed 2 years of academic electives and 15 Carnegie units, including 4 years of English, 3 years each of math, science, and social studies, and 2 of the same foreign language. TCU also recommends an interview and requires an essay and counselor's recommendation. AP and CLEP credits are accepted. Important factors in the admissions decision are advanced placement or honor courses, leadership record, and evidence of special talent.

Procedure: Freshmen are admitted to all sessions. Entrance exams should be taken during or before the fall semester of the senior year. There is a deferred admissions plan. Applications should be filed by February 15 for fall entry and December 1 for spring entry. The fall 2003 application fee was $40. Notification is sent April 1. A waiting list is an active part of the admissions procedure. Applications are accepted on computer disk and on-line.

Transfer: 382 transfer students enrolled in 2002-2003. The recommended GPA is 2.5 and a minimum GPA of 2.0 is required. Applicants must complete an application form and submit official transcripts from each college attended as well as a secondary school transcript. If fewer than 24 semester hours of transferable work have been completed at the time of application, SAT I or ACT scores are required and secondary school credentials are considered.

Visiting: There are regularly scheduled orientations for prospective students, including student-led campus tours, optional personal interviews, and departmental visits. There are guides for informal visits and visitors may sit in on classes and stay overnight. To schedule a visit, contact the Admissions Office.

Financial Aid: The FAFSA is required. The deadline for filing freshman financial aid applications for fall entry is May 1.

International Students: There are 285 international students enrolled. The school actively recruits these students. They must score 550 on the written TOEFL.

Computers: All students may access the system any time.

Graduates: From July 1, 2002 to June 30, 2003, 1437 bachelor's degrees were awarded. The most popular majors were marketing (9%), finance (6%), and advertising/public relations (6%). In an average class,

64% graduate in 6 years or less. 135 companies recruited on campus in a recent year.

Admissions Contact: Ray Brown, Dean of Admissions.
E-mail: *frogmail@tcu.edu* Web: *tcu.edu*

TEXAS LUTHERAN UNIVERSITY D-4
Seguin, TX 78155

(830) 372-8050
(800) 771-8521; Fax: (830) 372-8096

Full-time: 598 men, 698 women	**Faculty:** 67; IIB, --$
Part-time: 43 men, 71 women	**Ph.D.s:** 82%
Graduate: none	**Student/Faculty:** 19 to 1
Year: semesters, summer session	**Tuition:** $15,590
Application Deadline: June 1	**Room & Board:** $4780
Freshman Class: 1065 applied, 831 accepted, 377 enrolled	
SAT I Math: 528	**ACT:** 22	**COMPETITIVE**

Texas Lutheran University, founded in 1891, is a private liberal arts institution affiliated with the Evangelical Lutheran Church of America. There are 3 undergraduate schools. In addition to regional accreditation, TLU has baccalaureate program accreditation with ACBSP and CSWE. The library contains 165,678 volumes, 118,436 microform items, and 4119 audio/video tapes/CDs, and subscribes to 570 periodicals. Computerized library services include the card catalog, interlibrary loans, database searching, and Internet access. Special learning facilities include an art gallery, natural history museum, and geological museum. The 196-acre campus is in a suburban area 37 miles east of San Antonio and 50 miles south of Austin. Including any residence halls, there are 36 buildings.

Student Life: 95% of undergraduates are from Texas. Students are from 23 states, 12 foreign countries, and Canada. 88% are from public schools. 70% are white; 17% Hispanic. 64% are Protestant; 21% Catholic; 8% claim no religious affiliation. The average age of freshmen is 18; all undergraduates, 21. 26% do not continue beyond their first year; 53% remain to graduate.

Housing: 910 students can be accommodated in college housing, which includes single-sex and coed dorms, on-campus apartments, and married-student housing. On-campus housing is available on a first-come, first-served basis. 70% of students live on campus; of those, 50% remain on campus on weekends. All students may keep cars.

Activities: 15% of men belong to 5 local and 1 national fraternity; 14% of women belong to 4 local and 1 national sorority. There are 57 groups on campus, including African American, art, band, cheerleading, choir, chorus, computers, dance, debate, drama, ethnic, forensics, gay, honors, international, jazz band, literary magazine, Mexican American, musical theater, newspaper, opera, orchestra, pep band, political, professional, religious, social, social service, student government, symphony, and yearbook. Popular campus events include Christmas Vespers and Spring Fling.

Sports: There are 6 intercollegiate sports for men and 8 for women, and 14 intramural sports for men and 14 for women. Facilities include a 2200-seat gym, a fitness center, an 8-lane swimming pool, softball, baseball, and soccer fields, intramural/recreation fields, golf practice greens, and a lighted walking track.

Disabled Students: 90% of the campus is accessible. Wheelchair ramps, elevators, special parking, specially equipped rest rooms, special class scheduling, lowered drinking fountains, and special housing are available.

Services: Counseling and information services are available, as is tutoring in most subjects. Assistance with writing assignments is also available.

Campus Safety and Security: Measures include 24-hour foot and vehicle patrol, self-defense education, security escort services, and informal discussions. There are pamphlets/posters/films, lighted pathways/sidewalks, and coded locks in residence halls.

Programs of Study: TLU confers B.A., B.S., B.B.A., and B.M. degrees. Bachelor's degrees are awarded in BIOLOGICAL SCIENCE (biology/biological science), BUSINESS (business administration and management and management information systems), COMMUNICATIONS AND THE ARTS (art, communications, dramatic arts, English, music, and Spanish), COMPUTER AND PHYSICAL SCIENCE (chemistry, computer science, mathematics, and physics), EDUCATION (education), SOCIAL SCIENCE (economics, history, philosophy, physical fitness/movement, political science/government, psychology, public affairs, sociology, and theological studies). Biology, chemistry, and business are the strongest academically. Business, kinesiology, and education are the largest.

Required: All students must complete 124 semester hours, including 24 to 54 in their major, with a 2.0 GPA. Between 45 and 49 hours of distribution courses are required. A senior seminar, project, or concert is required in most majors.

Special: Internships are available in most majors. Study abroad in all countries affiliated with ISEP, a Washington semester with American University, and work-study programs are available. The college offers student-designed majors and dual majors. There is a 3-2 engineering program with Texas A&M and Texas Tech University. There are 11 national honor societies, a freshman honors program, and 8 departmental honors programs.

Faculty/Classroom: 55% of faculty are male; 45%, female. All teach undergraduates. The average class size in an introductory lecture is 23; in a laboratory, 24; and in a regular course, 20.

Admissions: 78% of the 2003-2004 applicants were accepted. 42% of the current freshmen were in the top fifth of their class; 67% were in the top two fifths. There was 1 National Merit finalist and 1 semifinalist. 8 freshmen graduated first in their class.

Requirements: The SAT I or ACT is required. In addition, applicants must have 16 Carnegie units, including a recommended 4 years in English, 3 each in social studies, math, and science, and 2 in foreign language. The GED is accepted. A GPA of 2.5 is required. AP and CLEP credits are accepted. Important factors in the admissions decision are advanced placement or honor courses, recommendations by school officials, and extracurricular activities record.

Procedure: Freshmen are admitted fall and spring. Entrance exams should be taken in the spring of the junior year or the summer before the senior year. There is a rolling admissions plan. Applications should be filed by June 1 for fall entry and December 1 for spring entry, along with a $25 fee. Notification is sent on a rolling basis. A waiting list is an active part of the admissions procedure. Applications are accepted on-line through Texas Mentor.

Transfer: 62 transfer students enrolled in a recent year. Applicants for transfer must have a GPA of at least 2.25 and be in good academic standing. 33 of 124 credits required for the bachelor's degree must be completed at TLU.

Visiting: There are regularly scheduled orientations for prospective students, including a campus tour, classroom visits, a financial aid presentation, a study abroad session, an athlete session, and a student panel. There are guides for informal visits and visitors may sit in on classes and stay overnight. To schedule a visit, contact the Admissions Office.

Financial Aid: In 2003-2004, 95% of all full-time freshmen and 79% of continuing full-time students received some form of financial aid. 76% of full-time freshmen and 71% of continuing full-time students received need-based aid. The average freshman award was $13,500. 25% of undergraduates work part time. Average annual earnings from campus work are $554. The average financial indebtedness of the 2003 graduate was $22,814. The FAFSA is required. The priority date for freshman financial aid applications for fall entry is February 1. The deadline for filing freshman financial aid applications for fall entry is April 1.

International Students: There are 25 international students enrolled. The school actively recruits these students. They must score 550 on the written TOEFL and also take the SAT I or the ACT.

Computers: The mainframe consists of 2 Sun Servers and several Intel-based servers. Computer labs contain 78 PCs connected to the LAN and to a CITRIX server for application support. There are 12 additional computers available in the library, as well as several special use computers available to students in various academic buildings. Students with PCs in their dorm rooms may lease a wireless LAN card from the university to access the university network as well as the Internet, e-mail, word processing, and other applications. Students residing off campus may pay a fee for dial-in to the network, which provides Internet access. All students may access the system 24 hours a day, 7 days a week. There are no time limits and no fees. It is strongly recommended that all students have a personal computer.

Graduates: From July 1, 2002 to June 30, 2003, 244 bachelor's degrees were awarded. The most popular majors were natural science (23%), business administration (21%), and kinesiology (16%). In an average class, 1% graduate in 3 years or less, 34% graduate in 4 years or less, 50% graduate in 5 years or less, and 55% graduate in 6 years or less. 24 companies recruited on campus in 2002-2003.

Admissions Contact: E. Norman Jones, Vice President of Enrollment Services. A video is available. E-mail: *admissions@tlu.edu* Web: *www.tlu.edu*

TEXAS SOUTHERN UNIVERSITY E-3
Houston, TX 77004

(713) 313-7472; Fax: (713) 313-1878

Full-time: 3317 men, 4479 women	**Faculty:** 242
Part-time: 473 men, 640 women	**Ph.D.s:** 44%
Graduate: 739 men, 1240 women	**Student/Faculty:** 32 to 1
Year: semesters, summer session	**Tuition:** $3096 ($8760)
Application Deadline: August 13	**Room & Board:** $5824
Freshman Class: n/av	
SAT I or ACT: recommended	**NONCOMPETITIVE**

Texas Southern University, founded in 1947, is a state-supported institution offering undergraduate programs in the arts and sciences, education and behavioral sciences, pharmacy and health science, business, and technology. There are 7 undergraduate and 7 graduate schools. In addition to regional accreditation, TSU has baccalaureate program accreditation with AACSB, ABET, ACPE, CAAHEP, NAACLS, NAIT, and NCATE. The 3 libraries contain 267,903 volumes, 491,666 microform items, and 4076 audio/video tapes/CDs, and subscribe to 1700 periodicals. Computerized library services include the card catalog, interlibrary loans, database searching, and Internet access. Special learning facilities include an art gallery and radio station. The 150-acre campus is in an urban area 3 miles southeast of downtown Houston. Including any residence halls, there are 45 buildings.

Student Life: 88% of undergraduates are from Texas. Students are from 37 states, 40 foreign countries, and Canada. 97% are from public schools. 92% are African American. 90% are Protestant; 19% claim no religious affiliation. The average age of freshmen is 21; all undergraduates, 23. 35% do not continue beyond their first year; 17% remain to graduate.

Housing: 1182 students can be accommodated in college housing, which includes single-sex dorms and off-campus apartments. On-campus housing is available on a first-come, first-served basis. Priority is given to out-of-town students. 96% of students commute. Alcohol is not permitted. All students may keep cars.

Activities: 1% of men and about 1% of women belong to 1 local and 7 national fraternities; 3% of women belong to 2 local and 7 national sororities. There are 58 groups on campus, including accounting, art, band, business, cheerleading, choir, chorus, computers, consumer services, dance, drama, ethnic, film, health, honors, international, jazz band, marching band, newspaper, orchestra, pharmaceutical, photography, political, professional, radio and TV, religious, science, social, social service, student government, symphony, and yearbook. Popular campus events include Senior Day, Christmas Tree Lighting, and Fall Greek Show.

Sports: There are 6 intercollegiate sports for men and 8 for women, and 13 intramural sports for men and 13 for women. Facilities include a health and phys ed complex that seats 8100, a 7000-seat football stadium, 2 gyms, the larger seating 1000, and a state-of-the-art recreational facility that includes a food court.

Disabled Students: 60% of the campus is accessible. Wheelchair ramps, elevators, special parking, specially equipped rest rooms, lowered drinking fountains, and lowered telephones are available.

Services: Counseling and information services are available, as is tutoring in most subjects. There is remedial math, reading, and writing.

Campus Safety and Security: Measures include 24-hour foot and vehicle patrol, self-defense education, security escort services, and informal discussions. There are pamphlets/posters/films, emergency telephones, and lighted pathways/sidewalks.

Programs of Study: TSU confers B.A., B.S., B.B.A., B.S.Die, B.S.E.T., B.S.I.T., and B.S.P.A.F. degrees. Master's and doctoral degrees are also awarded. Bachelor's degrees are awarded in BIOLOGICAL SCIENCE (biology/biological science and nutrition), BUSINESS (accounting, banking and finance, business administration and management, insurance, and marketing/retailing/merchandising), COMMUNICATIONS AND THE ARTS (art, communications, dramatic arts, English, French, journalism, music, Spanish, and speech/debate/rhetoric), COMPUTER AND PHYSICAL SCIENCE (chemistry, computer science, mathematics, and physics), EDUCATION (bilingual/bicultural, early childhood, English, foreign languages, mathematics, physical, reading, and special), ENGINEERING AND ENVIRONMENTAL DESIGN (aviation administration/management, civil engineering technology, construction technology, drafting and design technology, electrical/electronics engineering technology, engineering technology, environmental engineering technology, graphic arts technology, and industrial engineering technology), HEALTH PROFESSIONS (environmental health science, health, health care administration, medical technology, pharmacy, and respiratory therapy), SOCIAL SCIENCE (clothing and textiles management/production/services, criminal justice, dietetics, economics, history, human services, interdisciplinary studies, physical fitness/movement, political science/government, psychology, public affairs, social work, and sociology). Pharmacy is the strongest academically. Biology, electrical communications engineering, and chemistry are the largest.

Required: Students must complete between 136 and 148 semester hours, depending on the field of study, and maintain a minimum GPA of 2.0. A minimum of 30 hours is required in the major. A course in phys ed is also required.

Special: Special academic programs include cross-registration in military science with the University of Houston, study abroad in Africa, and work-study programs. There are 2 national honor societies, a freshman honors program, and 1 departmental honors program.

Faculty/Classroom: 53% of faculty are male; 47%, female. 76% teach undergraduates. Graduate students teach 2% of introductory courses. The average class size in an introductory lecture is 48; in a laboratory, 34; and in a regular course, 32.

Admissions: There were 78 National Merit finalists. 22 freshmen graduated first in their class.

Requirements: The SAT I or ACT is recommended. In addition, candidates should be graduates of an accredited secondary school or have the GED. A GPA of 2.0 is required.

Procedure: Freshmen are admitted fall, spring, and summer. Entrance exams should be taken by the semester prior to enrollment. There is a rolling admissions plan and an early admissions plan. Applications should be filed by August 13 for fall entry, December 19 for spring entry, and May 21 or June 30 for summer entry. The fall 2003 application fee was $40. The college accepts all applicants. Notification is sent on a rolling basis. Applications are accepted on-line through Texas Common Application at *www.applytexas.org*.

Transfer: 1153 transfer students enrolled in 2002-2003. The applicant must be a student in good standing and must submit official an transcript. The SAT I or ACT is required. 30 of 136 credits required for the bachelor's degree must be completed at TSU.

Visiting: There are regularly scheduled orientations for prospective students, including early registration. There are guides for informal visits and visitors may stay overnight. To schedule a visit, contact the Office of Recruitment at (713) 313-7951 or (713) 313-7849 or *em.tsu.edu*.

Financial Aid: In 2003-2004, 74% of all full-time freshmen and 98% of continuing full-time students received some form of financial aid. 76% of full-time freshmen and all of continuing full-time students received need-based aid. The average freshman award was $6625. Need-based scholarships or need-based grants averaged $4000 ($6000 maximum); and need-based self-help aid (loans and jobs) averaged $5500 ($9500 maximum). 10% of undergraduates work part time. Average annual earnings from campus work are $4000. The average financial indebtedness of the 2003 graduate was $23,000. The FAFSA is required. The deadline for filing freshman financial aid applications for fall entry is April 15.

International Students: There are 133 international students enrolled. They must score 500 on the written TOEFL.

Computers: The mainframes are a DEC AXP and a DEC VAX. PCs are available in the library, the general university academic center, and various departments. Computer science students may access the system any time. There are no time limits. The fee is $80 per semester.

Graduates: From July 1, 2002 to June 30, 2003, 465 bachelor's degrees were awarded. The most popular majors were biology (9%), administration of justice (8%), and management (8%). In an average class, 2% graduate in 3 years or less, 5% graduate in 4 years or less, 6% graduate in 5 years or less, and 17% graduate in 6 years or less.

Admissions Contact: Joyce M. Waddell, Director of Admissions. E-mail: *waddell_jm@tsu.edu* Web: *www.tsu.edu*

TEXAS STATE UNIVERSITY SYSTEM

The Texas State University System, established in 1911, is a public higher education system. It is governed by a 9-member Board of Regents, whose chief administrator is the chancellor. The primary mission of the system universities is the provision of a well-rounded education focusing on teacher education, business, and liberarl arts. The total enrollment of all 11 campuses is approximately 57,500, with about 2000 faculty members. Altogether there are 416 baccalaureate, 250 master's, and 5 doctoral programs offered within the system. 4-year campuses are Angelo State University in San Angelo, Lamar University in Beaumont, Sam Houston State University in Huntsville, Southwest Texas State University in San Marcos, and Sul Ross State University in Alpine, with 2-year lower-division campuses in Beaumont, Orange, and Port Arthur, and 2-year upper-division campuses in Del Rio, Eagle Pass, and Uvalde. Profiles of the 4-year campuses are included in this section.

TEXAS STATE UNIVERSITY D-4
(Formerly Southwest Texas State University)
San Marcos, TX 78666-4616

(512) 245-2364
Fax: (512) 245-8044

Full-time: 7753 men, 9941 women	**Faculty:** 605; IIA, -$
Part-time: 2047 men, 2266 women	**Ph.D.s:** 77%
Graduate: 1511 men, 2791 women	**Student/Faculty:** 29 to 1
Year: semesters, summer session	**Tuition:** $4010 ($11,090)
Application Deadline: June 1	**Room & Board:** $5310
Freshman Class: 11,483 applied, 6435 accepted, 2876 enrolled	
SAT I Verbal/Math: 540/540	**ACT:** 22 **VERY COMPETITIVE**

Texas State University, formerly Southwest Texas State University and founded in 1899, is part of the Texas State University System and offers programs in general studies, applied arts and technology, business, education, fine arts, health professions, liberal arts, and science. There are 8 undergraduate schools and 1 graduate school. In addition to regional accreditation, Texas State has baccalaureate program accreditation with AACSB, ADA, AHEA, ASLA, CAAHEP, CSAB, CSWE, FIDER, NAACLS, NASM, and NRPA.. The library contains 3,060,549 volumes, 1,835,062 microform items, and 31,231 audio/video tapes/CDs, and subscribes to 7548 periodicals. Computerized library services include the card catalog, interlibrary loans, and database searching. Special learning facilities include a learning resource center, art gallery, planetarium, radio station, and a recording studio. The 428-acre campus is in a suburban area 30 miles south of Austin. Including any residence halls, there are 219 buildings.

Student Life: 97% of undergraduates are from Texas. Students are from 48 states, 76 foreign countries, and Canada. 98% are from public schools. 71% are white; 18% Hispanic. The average age of freshmen is 18; all undergraduates, 23. 22% do not continue beyond their first year; 46% remain to graduate.

Housing: 4958 students can be accommodated in college housing, which includes single-sex and coed dorms, on-campus apartments, and married-student housing. In addition, there are honors houses, special-interest houses, and special residences for international students, disabled students, single parents, and upper-division students. On-campus housing is guaranteed for the freshman year only and is available on a first-come, first-served basis. 78% of students commute. All students may keep cars.

Activities: 5% of men belong to 6 local and 15 national fraternities; 5% of women belong to 12 national sororities. There are 418 groups on campus, including art, band, cheerleading, chess, choir, chorale, chorus, computers, dance, debate, drama, drill team, ethnic, gay, honors, international, jazz band, literary magazine, marching band, musical theater, newspaper, nontraditional students, opera, orchestra, pep band, photography, political, professional, radio and TV, religious, social, social service, student government, symphony, and yearbook. Popular campus events include Welcome Week and Cricket Fest.

Sports: There are 6 intercollegiate sports for men and 8 for women, and 16 intramural sports for men and 18 for women. Facilities include a 14,104-seat stadium, a 7200-seat gym, tennis courts, a spring-fed pool, an aquatic sports center, basketball and volleyball courts, racquetball courts, an indoor jogging/walking track, weight-lifting equipment, and exercise machines.

Disabled Students: 85% of the campus is accessible. Wheelchair ramps, elevators, special parking, specially equipped rest rooms, special class scheduling, lowered drinking fountains, lowered telephones, special housing, curb cuts, pay TTY text telephones, adaptive computer technology, sign language interpreter, and reading recorder services for the visually impaired are available.

Services: Counseling and information services are available, as is tutoring in most subjects. There is a reader service for the blind, and remedial math, reading, and writing. Tutoring for all core curriculum classes is available.

Campus Safety and Security: Measures include 24-hour foot and vehicle patrol, self-defense education, security escort services, and shuttle buses. There are informal discussions, pamphlets/posters/films, emergency telephones, and lighted pathways/sidewalks.

Programs of Study: Texas State confers B.A., B.S., B.A.A.S., B.A.I.S., B.B.A., B.E.S.S., B.F.A., B.H.A., B.H.W.P., B.M., B.S.A.G., B.S.A.S., B.S.C.D., B.S.C.J., B.S.C.L.S., B.S.F.C.S., B.S.H.I.M., B.S.H.P., B.S.R.A., B.S.R.C., B.S.R.T., B.S.T.C.H., and B.S.W. degrees. Master's and doctoral degrees are also awarded. Bachelor's degrees are awarded in AGRICULTURE (agricultural business management, agriculture, and animal science), BIOLOGICAL SCIENCE (biochemistry, biology/biological science, botany, marine biology, microbiology, nutrition, physiology, wildlife biology, and zoology), BUSINESS (accounting, banking and finance, business administration and management, business economics, fashion merchandising, marketing/retailing/merchandising, recreational facilities management, and tourism), COMMUNICATIONS AND THE ARTS (advertising, applied art, art, audio technology, broadcasting, communications, dance, dramatic arts, English, fine arts, French, German, graphic design, jazz, journalism, music, music performance, public relations, Spanish, speech/debate/rhetoric, and studio art), COMPUTER AND PHYSICAL SCIENCE (chemistry, computer management, computer science, digital arts/technology, information sciences and systems, mathematics, and physics), EDUCATION (art, athletic training, bilingual/bicultural, early childhood, elementary, foreign languages, health, home economics, music, physical, reading, science, secondary, and special), ENGINEERING AND ENVIRONMENTAL DESIGN (cartography, city/community/regional planning, construction technology, engineering technology, environmental science, graphic and printing production, industrial engineering technology, interior design, manufacturing engineering, manufacturing technology, and water and wastewater technology), HEALTH PROFESSIONS (clinical science, community health work, exercise science, health, health care administration, hospital administration, medical laboratory technology, medical records administration/services, radiation therapy, respiratory therapy, and speech pathology/audiology), SOCIAL SCIENCE (African studies, American studies, anthropology, Asian/Oriental studies, child care/child and family studies, corrections, criminal justice, criminology, economics, European studies, family/consumer studies, food science, geography, history, home economics, interdisciplinary studies, international relations, international studies, law enforcement and corrections, Middle Eastern studies, philosophy, political science/government, psychology, public administration, Russian and Slavic studies, social science, social work, and sociology). Geography and education are the strongest academically. Education, exercise and sport science, and biology are the largest.

Required: All students must earn a minimum GPA of 2.0 while taking at least 128 semester hours, including 30 in the major. The core curriculum includes basic skills, history and politics, natural science, social science, philosophy, international perspectives, literature, fine arts, and physical fitness.

Special: Co-op programs in medicine, dentistry, engineering, architecture, law, pharmacy, nursing, occupational therapy, and veterinary medicine, internships in many departments, study abroad in 26 countries, and Washington semesters are available. Dual majors, credit for life experience, and nondegree study also are possible. 2 summer sessions are offered in most programs. A 3-2 engineering degree is possible with the University of Texas, Texas A&M, or Texas Tech Universities. There are 25 national honor societies, a freshman honors program, and 1 departmental honors program.

Faculty/Classroom: 54% of faculty are male; 46%, female. All teach undergraduates. Graduate students teach 13% of introductory courses. The average class size in an introductory lecture is 48; in a laboratory, 18; and in a regular course, 34.

Admissions: 56% of the 2003-2004 applicants were accepted. The SAT I scores for the 2003-2004 freshman class were: Verbal--26% below 500, 54% between 500 and 599, 19% between 600 and 700, and 1% above 700; Math--23% below 500, 55% between 500 and 599, 21% between 600 and 700, and 1% above 700. The ACT scores were 22% below 21, 43% between 21 and 23, 24% between 24 and 26, 8% between 27 and 28, and 2% above 28. 41% of the current freshmen were in the top fifth of their class; 81% were in the top two fifths. 20 freshmen graduated first in their class.

Requirements: The SAT I or ACT is required, with minimum scores determined by high school class rank. Applicants need 15 academic credits, including 4 units in English, 3 in math and social science, 3 in natural science, 2 in foreign language, and 1 in computer literacy. The GED is accepted; applicants with a GED are treated as though they were ranked in the 4th quarter. AP and CLEP credits are accepted. Important factors in the admissions decision are advanced placement or honor courses, leadership record, and extracurricular activities record.

Procedure: Freshmen are admitted to all sessions. Entrance exams should be taken at the end of the junior year. There is an early admissions plan and a rolling admissions plan. Applications should be filed by June 1 for fall entry, December 1 for spring entry, and May 1 for summer entry, along with a $40 fee. Notification is sent on a rolling basis. Applications are accepted on-line through the Texas Common Application at *www.applytexas.org.*

Transfer: 2746 transfer students enrolled in 2002-2003. Transfer students with 29 or fewer credits must meet freshman requirements; those with 30 or more credits must submit official transcripts to verify a minimum 2.25 GPA. 30 of 128 credits required for the bachelor's degree must be completed at Texas State.

Visiting: There are regularly scheduled orientations for prospective students, consisting of a 2-day event, with registration required. First-time freshmen parents may attend. Students receive registration instructions, academic advising, and information concerning Texas State's academic policies, procedures, and student services. Time is allotted to register for classes. There are guides for informal visits and visitors may sit in on classes. To schedule a visit, contact the Admissions and Visitors Center.

Financial Aid: In 2003-2004, 57% of all full-time freshmen and 54% of continuing full-time students received some form of financial aid. 42% of full-time freshmen and 51% of continuing full-time students received need-based aid. The average freshman award was $7587. 4% of undergraduates work part time. Average annual earnings from campus work are $4563. The average financial indebtedness of the 2003 graduate was $15,304. The FAFSA is required. The priority date for freshman financial aid applications for fall entry is April 1.

International Students: There are 162 international students enrolled. They must score 550 on the written TOEFL or 213 on the electronic version and also take the SAT I or the ACT.

Computers: The mainframes are a DEC VAX 7640, a DEC VAX 6620, a DEC Alpha AXP 7640, and a DEC Alpha AXP 4100. PCs and Macs are available for student use throughout the campus. Students are issued user names that allow them to log on to the mainframe from PCs connected to the university network. All students may access the system 24 hours daily. There are no time limits. The fee is $10 per credit hour.

Graduates: From July 1, 2002 to June 30, 2003, 4061 bachelor's degrees were awarded. The most popular majors were interdisciplinary studies in education (12%), business administration and management (6%), and marketing (6%). In an average class, 1% graduate in 3 years or less, 17% graduate in 4 years or less, 38% graduate in 5 years or less, and 41% graduate in 6 years or less. 264 companies recruited on campus in 2002-2003.

Admissions Contact: Christie Kangas, Director of Admissions. E-mail: *admissions@txstate.edu* Web: *www.admissions.txstate.edu*

TEXAS TECH UNIVERSITY
B-2

Lubbock, TX 79409-5005   (806) 742-1480; Fax: (806) 742-0062

Full-time: 11,399 men, 9631 women   **Faculty:** 1040; I, -$

Part-time: 1486 men, 1079 women   **Ph.D.s:** 85%

Graduate: 2653 men, 2301 women   **Student/Faculty:** 20 to 1

Year: semesters, summer session   **Tuition:** $4745 ($11,825)

Application Deadline: open   **Room & Board:** $6023

Freshman Class: 13,755 applied, 9257 accepted, 4445 enrolled

SAT I Verbal/Math: 551/572   **ACT:** 24   **VERY COMPETITIVE**

Texas Tech University, founded in 1923, is a large, comprehensive public university offering undergraduate and graduate programs in a variety of professional and vocational fields. There are 9 undergraduate and 2 graduate schools. In addition to regional accreditation, Texas Tech has baccalaureate program accreditation with AACSB, ABET, ACEJMC, APTA, ASLA, CSWE, FIDER, NAAB, NASAD, NASM, NCATE, and NLN. The 2 libraries contain 4,685,650 volumes, 2,226,048 microform items, and 84,074 audio/video tapes/CDs, and subscribe to 30,788 periodicals. Computerized library services include the card catalog, interlibrary loans, and database searching. Special learning facilities include a learning resource center, art gallery, natural history museum, planetarium, radio station, TV station, ranching heritage center, international cultural center, international textile center, and a Southwest collection. The 1839-acre campus is in an urban area in Lubbock. Including any residence halls, there are 125 buildings.

Student Life: 93% of undergraduates are from Texas. Students are from 50 states, 113 foreign countries, and Canada. 79% are white; 10% Hispanic. The average age of freshmen is 19; all undergraduates, 22. 18% do not continue beyond their first year; 82% remain to graduate.

Housing: 6714 students can be accommodated in college housing, which includes single-sex and coed dorms, on-campus apartments, and married-student housing. In addition, there are honors houses, living/learning communities, intensive study floors, substance-free floors, nonsmoking floors, and upperclass graduate halls. On-campus housing is guaranteed for the freshman year only and is available on a first-come, first-served basis. 75% of students commute. Alcohol is not permitted. All students may keep cars.

Activities: There are 1 local and 30 national fraternities and 1 local and 17 national sororities. There are 459 groups on campus, including art, band, cheerleading, chess, choir, chorale, chorus, computers, dance, drama, drill team, drum and bugle corps, ethnic, film, gay, honors, international, jazz band, literary magazine, marching band, musical theater, newspaper, opera, orchestra, pep band, photography, political, professional, radio and TV, religious, social, social service, student government, symphony, and yearbook. Popular campus events include Parents Day, Carol of the Lights, and Madrigal Dinner.

Sports: There are 6 intercollegiate sports for men and 7 for women, and 22 intramural sports for men and 22 for women. Facilities include an athletic training center, a student recreation center, and an aquatic center.

Disabled Students: 77% of the campus is accessible. Wheelchair ramps, elevators, special parking, specially equipped rest rooms, lowered drinking fountains, lowered telephones, and special housing are available.

Services: Counseling and information services are available, as is tutoring in every subject. There is a reader service for the blind, and remedial math, reading, and writing. An attorney is available for students to obtain legal advice and guidance. Note-taking services, readers (for testing only), tape recorders, and a learning center are also available.

Campus Safety and Security: Measures include 24-hour foot and vehicle patrol, shuttle buses, pamphlets/posters/films, emergency telephones, and lighted pathways/sidewalks.

Programs of Study: Texas Tech confers B.A., B.S., B.Arch., B.B.A., B.F.A., B.G.S., B.I.D., B.Land.Arch., B.M., B.S.C.E., B.S.Ch.E., B.S. in E., B.S. in Eco., B.S.E.E., B.S. in Engineering Physics, B.S. in Environmental Engineering, B.S. in Family and Consumer Sciences, B.S.H.E., B.S.I.E., B.S.M.E., B.S. in Petroleum Engineering, B.S. in Restaurant, Hotel, and Institutional Management, B.S.Tech., and B.S. in Textile Engineering degrees. Master's and doctoral degrees are also awarded. Bachelor's degrees are awarded in AGRICULTURE (agricultural business management, agronomy, animal science, horticulture, range/farm management, and wildlife management), BIOLOGICAL SCIENCE (biochemistry, biology/biological science, cell biology, microbiology, molecular biology, and zoology), BUSINESS (accounting, banking and finance, business administration and management, business economics, hotel/motel and restaurant management, international business management, international economics, management information systems, marketing/retailing/merchandising, and recreation and leisure services), COMMUNICATIONS AND THE ARTS (advertising, art, art history and appreciation, broadcasting, classical languages, communications, dance, design, dramatic arts, English, French, German, journalism, Latin, music, music history and appreciation, music performance, music theory and composition, photography, public relations, Spanish, studio art, telecommunications, theater design, theater management, and visual and performing

arts), COMPUTER AND PHYSICAL SCIENCE (applied physics, chemistry, computer science, geology, geophysics and seismology, geoscience, mathematics, and physics), EDUCATION (art, early childhood, education, elementary, and music), ENGINEERING AND ENVIRONMENTAL DESIGN (architecture, chemical engineering, civil engineering, construction technology, electrical/electronics engineering, electrical/electronics engineering technology, engineering, engineering physics, environmental engineering, industrial engineering technology, interior design, landscape architecture/design, mechanical engineering, mechanical engineering technology, petroleum/natural gas engineering, and textile engineering), HEALTH PROFESSIONS (exercise science, health, predentistry, premedicine, and prepharmacy), SOCIAL SCIENCE (anthropology, clothing and textiles management/production/services, dietetics, economics, family/consumer resource management, family/consumer studies, fashion design and technology, food production/management/services, food science, geography, history, home economics, human development, Latin American studies, liberal arts/general studies, parks and recreation management, philosophy, political science/government, prelaw, psychology, Russian and Slavic studies, social work, and sociology). Business and human development and family studies are the largest.

Required: All students must meet the requirements of the core curriculum, including courses in science and technology, math, English, history, and political science. Total credits required for graduation vary from 125 to 174, depending on the degree program. A minimum GPA of 2.0 is required. The last 30 hours and 25% of all credit hours must be from Texas Tech.

Special: There are many work-study programs and internships, and students may study in 5 countries. Texas Tech also offers B.A.-B.S. degrees, an accelerated degree program, co-op programs, dual degrees, dual majors, cross-registration, a general studies degree, a 3-2 engineering program, student-designed majors, nondegree study, and pass/fail options. There are 28 national honor societies and a freshman honors program.

Faculty/Classroom: 62% of faculty are male; 38%, female. All teach undergraduates. The average class size in an introductory lecture is 48; in a laboratory, 21; and in a regular course, 36.

Admissions: 67% of the 2003-2004 applicants were accepted. The SAT I scores for the 2003-2004 freshman class were: Verbal--22% below 500, 52% between 500 and 599, 24% between 600 and 700, and 2% above 700; Math--14% below 500, 49% between 500 and 599, 33% between 600 and 700, and 4% above 700. The ACT scores were 19% below 21, 31% between 21 and 23, 28% between 24 and 26, 12% between 27 and 28, and 10% above 28. 41% of the current freshmen were in the top fifth of their class; 74% were in the top two fifths. There were 18 National Merit finalists. 16 freshmen graduated first in their class.

Requirements: The SAT I or ACT is required. In addition, applicants should be graduates of an accredited high school or have the GED. The university requires 17 credits of academic work in high school, including 4 credits in English, 3 credits in math, 2 1/2 in social studies, 2 credits in science, and 3 1/2 credits in academic electives. The university admits all students scoring 1200 (composite) on the SAT I or 29 on the ACT. Special circumstances may allow those not fulfilling the above requirements to be admitted. A GPA of 2.0 is required. AP and CLEP credits are accepted.

Procedure: Freshmen are admitted fall, spring, and summer. Entrance exams should be taken before July 1. There is a rolling admissions plan and an early admissions plan. Application deadlines are open. Application fee is $50. Applications are accepted on-line through *www.srel.ttu.edu.*

Transfer: 2158 transfer students enrolled in 2002-2003. To transfer 24 or more hours, the GPA must be a minimum of 2.25. To transfer 12 to 23 hours, applicants must have a 2.5 GPA and 12 hours of basic courses. To transfer fewer than 12 hours, applicants must have a 2.0 GPA and meet freshman requirements for admission. 30 of 125 to 174 credits required for the bachelor's degree must be completed at Texas Tech.

Visiting: There are regularly scheduled orientations for prospective students. There are guides for informal visits and visitors may sit in on classes and stay overnight. To schedule a visit, contact the New Student Relations Office — Visitor Center at (806) 742-1299.

Financial Aid: In a recent year, 46% of all full-time freshmen and 44% of continuing full-time students received some form of financial aid. 33% of full-time freshmen and 36% of continuing full-time students received need-based aid. The average freshman award was $4940. 10% of undergraduates work part time. Average annual earnings from campus work are $4543. The average financial indebtedness of a recent graduate was $16,250. Texas Tech is a member of CSS. The FAFSA is required. The deadline for filing freshman financial aid applications for fall entry is April 15.

International Students: There are 190 international students enrolled. They must score 550 on the written TOEFL or 213 on the electronic version and also take the SAT I, scoring 1270, or the ACT.

Computers: The mainframe is an IBM 2066-002. There are also Macs and IBM, Zenith, Sun, and other PCs available in the Advanced Technology Learning Center and in academic departments. All students may access the system 24 hours per day. There are no time limits. The fee is $14 per semester hour. It is strongly recommended that all students have a personal computer.

Graduates: From July 1, 2002 to June 30, 2003, 3475 bachelor's degrees were awarded. The most popular majors were human development and family studies (7%), marketing (7%), and finance (5%). In an average class, 1% graduate in 3 years or less, 24% graduate in 4 years or less, 49% graduate in 5 years or less, and 55% graduate in 6 years or less. 400 companies recruited on campus in 2002-2003.

Admissions Contact: Dale Ganus, Interim Director of Admissions and School Relations. A video is available. E-mail: *admissions@ttu.edu* Web: *http://www.srel.ttu.edu*

TEXAS WESLEYAN UNIVERSITY   D-2
Fort Worth, TX 76105-1536

(817) 531-4422
(800) 580-8980; Fax: (817) 531-4231

Full-time: 399 men, 631 women	**Faculty:** 84; IIA, +$
Part-time: 188 men, 451 women	**Ph.Ds:** 77%
Graduate: 634 men, 660 women	**Student/Faculty:** 12 to 1
Year: semesters, summer session	**Tuition:** $11,920
Application Deadline: open	**Room & Board:** $4325
Freshman Class: 732 applied, 498 accepted, 368 enrolled	
SAT I or ACT: required	**COMPETITIVE**

Texas Wesleyan University, founded in 1890, is a liberal arts institution affiliated with the United Methodist Church. There are 3 undergraduate and 4 graduate schools. In addition to regional accreditation, Texas Wesleyan has baccalaureate program accreditation with NASM. The 2 libraries contain 281,476 volumes, 827,410 microform items, and 5824 audio/video tapes/CDs, and subscribe to 3452 periodicals. Computerized library services include the card catalog, interlibrary loans, and database searching. Special learning facilities include a learning resource center, art gallery, and a theater. The 79-acre campus is in an urban area 2 miles east of downtown Fort Worth. Including any residence halls, there are 30 buildings.

Student Life: 96% of undergraduates are from Texas. Students are from 23 states, 32 foreign countries, and Canada. 94% are from public schools. 60% are white; 17% African American; 17% Native American/Eskimo. 58% claim no religious affiliation; 32% Protestant; 10% Catholic. The average age of freshmen is 19; all undergraduates, 25.

Housing: 275 students can be accommodated in college housing, which includes single-sex and coed dorms. On-campus housing is available on a first-come, first-served basis. 90% of students commute. Alcohol is not permitted. All students may keep cars.

Activities: 2% of men belong to 3 local fraternities and 1 national fraternity; 2% of women belong to 3 local and 2 national sororities. There are 55 groups on campus, including art, band, cheerleading, choir, computers, drama, ethnic, honors, international, jazz band, musical theater, opera, political, professional, radio and TV, religious, social, social service, student government, and yearbook. Popular campus events include Oktoberfest and the Wilson lectures.

Sports: There are 5 intercollegiate sports for men and 5 for women, and 11 intramural sports for men and 11 for women. Facilities include a 1500-seat athletic center, 4 tennis courts, an off-campus baseball park, and softball and soccer fields.

Disabled Students: Wheelchair ramps, elevators, special parking, specially equipped rest rooms, special class scheduling, and lowered telephones are available.

Services: Counseling and information services are available, as is tutoring in most subjects. There is remedial math, reading, and writing.

Campus Safety and Security: Measures include 24-hour foot and vehicle patrol, self-defense education, security escort services, and pamphlets/posters/films. There are emergency telephones, lighted pathways/sidewalks, and residence hall programs.

Programs of Study: Texas Wesleyan confers B.A., B.S., B.B.A., B.F.A, and B.M.E. degrees. Master's degrees are also awarded. Bachelor's degrees are awarded in BIOLOGICAL SCIENCE (biochemistry and biology/biological science), BUSINESS (accounting, business administration and management, business economics, international business management, management information systems, and marketing/retailing/merchandising), COMMUNICATIONS AND THE ARTS (art, communications, dramatic arts, English, fine arts, music, and Spanish), COMPUTER AND PHYSICAL SCIENCE (chemistry, computer science, earth science, information sciences and systems, mathematics, and physical sciences), EDUCATION (business, early childhood, elementary, middle school, music, physical, reading, secondary, and teaching English as a second/foreign language (TESOL/TEFOL)), SOCIAL SCIENCE (Christian studies, criminal justice, economics, history, human development, humanities, interdisciplinary studies, international studies, law, paralegal studies, political science/government, psychology, religion, and social science). Accounting and psychology are the strongest academically. Business administration is the largest.

Required: A minimum GPA of 2.0 and a minimum of 124 credit hours are required to graduate. All students must complete a general education

requirement of 51 credits, including courses in writing, literature, religion, lab science, history, math, political or economic systems, fine arts, humanities, phys ed, and social science, philosophy, or psychology. The total number of hours in the major varies.

Special: Study abroad is offered in 5 countries. A 3-2 engineering degree is offered in conjunction with a number of universities. Pass/fail options are available, as are B.A.-B.S. degrees and internships in sports management, business, psychology, and sociology. There are 2 national honor societies and 8 departmental honors programs.

Faculty/Classroom: 59% of faculty are male; 41%, female. No introductory courses are taught by graduate students.

Admissions: 68% of the 2003-2004 applicants were accepted. 24% of the current freshmen were in the top fifth of their class; 66% were in the top two fifths.

Requirements: The SAT I or ACT is required, with a minimum composite score of 800 or 19, respectively. Applicants must be graduates of an accredited secondary school or have a GED equivalent. An interview is recommended. Texas Wesleyan requires applicants to be in the upper 50% of their class. A GPA of 2.0 is required. AP and CLEP credits are accepted. Important factors in the admissions decision are leadership record, extracurricular activities record, and recommendations by alumni.

Procedure: Freshmen are admitted to all sessions. Entrance exams should be taken as early as possible. Application deadlines are open. The fall 2003 application fee was $25. Notification is sent on a rolling basis. Applications are accepted on-line through TexasMentor.

Transfer: 335 transfer students enrolled in a recent year. Applicants with fewer than 30 credit hours must submit a high school transcript and the results of either the SAT I (with a minimum composite score of 800) or the ACT (with a minimum score of 19). A minimum GPA of 2.0 is required. 45 of 124 credits required for the bachelor's degree must be completed at Texas Wesleyan.

Visiting: There are regularly scheduled orientations for prospective students. There are guides for informal visits and visitors may sit in on classes and stay overnight. To schedule a visit, contact the Office of Admissions.

Financial Aid: In a recent year, 95% of all full-time freshmen and 72% of continuing full-time students received some form of financial aid, including need-based aid. The average freshman award was $5318. The FAFSA and the college's own financial statement are required. Check with the school for current deadlines.

International Students: There were 61 international students enrolled in a recent year. The school actively recruits these students. They must score 520 on the written TOEFL or 210 on the electronic version.

Computers: The mainframe is a network with servers. All students may access the system 9 A.M. to 9 P.M. Monday through Thursday, 9 A.M. to 5 P.M. Friday, and 9 A.M. to 1 P.M. weekends. There are no time limits and no fees. It is strongly recommended that all students have a personal computer.

Graduates: In a recent year, 378 bachelor's degrees were awarded. The most popular majors were business (26%), education (18%), and psychology (8%).

Admissions Contact: Carolyn Hall, Director, Freshman Admission. A video is available. E-mail: *freshman@txwesleyan.edu* Web: *www.txwesleyan.edu*

TEXAS WOMAN'S UNIVERSITY   D-2
Denton, TX 76204-5765

(940) 898-3188
(866) 809-6130, ext. 3188; Fax: (940) 898-3081

Full-time: 200 men, 3628 women	**Faculty:** 381; I, --$
Part-time: 87 men, 1430 women	**Ph.Ds:** 70%
Graduate: 517 men, 3840 women	**Student/Faculty:** 10 to 1
Year: semesters, summer session	**Tuition:** $3024 ($8680)
Application Deadline: July 15	**Room & Board:** $4780
Freshman Class: 1526 applied, 1143 accepted, 521 enrolled	
SAT I Verbal/Math: 460/450	**ACT:** 19 **LESS COMPETITIVE**

Texas Woman's University, founded in 1901, is a comprehensive public university primarily for women, offering degree programs in the liberal arts, education, music and fine arts, and the business and health professions. There are 7 undergraduate and 8 graduate schools. In addition to regional accreditation, TWU has baccalaureate program accreditation with ADA, APTA, CSWE, NASM, and NLN. The 2 libraries contain 549,116 volumes, 1,554,071 microform items, and 24,061 audio/video tapes/CDs, and subscribe to 2445 periodicals. Computerized library services include the card catalog, interlibrary loans, database searching, and Internet access. Special learning facilities include a learning resource center, art gallery, medical centers and clinics, radio and TV studios, and a nursery school. The 270-acre campus is in an urban area 38 miles north of Dallas. Including any residence halls, there are 62 buildings.

Student Life: 93% of undergraduates are from Texas. Students are from 44 states, 72 foreign countries, and Canada. 62% are white; 18% African American; 11% Hispanic. The average age of freshmen is 20; all undergraduates, 24. 25% do not continue beyond their first year; 35% remain to graduate.

Housing: 1346 students can be accommodated in college housing, which includes single-sex and coed dorms, on-campus apartments, and married-student housing. In addition, there are honors houses and special-interest houses. On-campus housing is guaranteed for the freshman year only and is available on a first-come, first-served basis. 81% of students commute. All students may keep cars.

Activities: 66% of women belong to 2 local and 8 national sororities. There are no fraternities. There are 100 groups on campus, including art, band, choir, chorale, chorus, computers, dance, drama, ethnic, gay, honors, international, jazz band, musical theater, newspaper, opera, orchestra, political, professional, radio and TV, religious, social, social service, spirit organization, and student government. Popular campus events include Black Awareness Week, Mexican Festival, and Fall Festival.

Sports: There are 5 intercollegiate sports for women, and 11 intramural sports for men and 11 for women. Facilities include a gym, indoor and outdoor swimming pools, weight-training and fitness rooms, tennis and racquetball courts, a golf course, an indoor track, and aerobic exercise classrooms.

Disabled Students: 95% of the campus is accessible. Wheelchair ramps, elevators, special parking, specially equipped rest rooms, lowered drinking fountains, lowered telephones, lowered library equipment, and an office to assist students with disabilities are available.

Services: Counseling and information services are available, as is tutoring in some subjects, including math, science, English (writing), and computer science. There is remedial math, reading, and writing.

Campus Safety and Security: Measures include 24-hour foot and vehicle patrol, self-defense education, security escort services, and informal discussions. There are pamphlets/posters/films, emergency telephones, and lighted pathways/sidewalks.

Programs of Study: TWU confers B.A., B.S., B.B.A., B.F.A., and B.S.W. degrees. Master's and doctoral degrees are also awarded. Bachelor's degrees are awarded in BIOLOGICAL SCIENCE (biology/biological science), BUSINESS (accounting, business administration and management, fashion merchandising, and marketing/retailing/merchandising), COMMUNICATIONS AND THE ARTS (art, communications, dance, dramatic arts, English, fine arts, and music), COMPUTER AND PHYSICAL SCIENCE (chemistry, computer science, and mathematics), HEALTH PROFESSIONS (dental hygiene, health science, medical technology, music therapy, and nursing), SOCIAL SCIENCE (child psychology/development, consumer services, criminal justice, dietetics, family/consumer studies, fashion design and technology, history, interdisciplinary studies, physical fitness/movement, political science/government, psychology, social work, and sociology). Nursing, interdisciplinary studies, and psychology are the largest.

Required: Core curriculum includes 6 units each of history, political science, composition, and science, 3 each of math, fine arts, multicultural studies, literature, and women's studies, plus 15 additional hours. General education requirements vary according to the degree. A 2.0 GPA, successful completion of the Texas-mandated examination in reading, writing, and math, and a minimum of 124 hours are needed to graduate.

Special: Co-op programs in most majors, study abroad, and internships are available. Cross-registration is possible with the University of North Texas and East Texas State University. A 3-2 engineering program exists with the University of Texas at Dallas and Texas A&M University. There are 14 national honor societies, a freshman honors program, and 15 departmental honors programs.

Faculty/Classroom: 20% of faculty are male; 80%, female.

Admissions: 75% of the 2003-2004 applicants were accepted. The SAT I scores for the 2003-2004 freshman class were: Verbal--64% below 500, 29% between 500 and 599, and 7% between 600 and 700; Math--71% below 500, 24% between 500 and 599, and 5% between 600 and 700. The ACT scores were 64% below 21, 15% between 21 and 23, 10% between 24 and 26, 2% between 27 and 28, and 1% above 28.

Requirements: The SAT I or ACT is required, with a minimum combined score of 950 on the SAT I, or a score of 20 on the ACT. Applicants should be graduates of an accredited secondary school or have a GED certificate and have completed 4 secondary school units in English, 3 each in math and social studies, and 2 in science, plus 3 in academic electives. A GPA of 2.0 is required. AP and CLEP credits are accepted.

Procedure: Freshmen are admitted to all sessions. Entrance exams should be taken during the junior or the senior year of high school. There is a rolling admissions plan. There are early admissions and deferred admissions plans. Applications should be filed by July 15 for fall entry and November 1 for spring entry. The fall 2003 application fee was $30. Notification is sent on a rolling basis.

Transfer: 843 transfer students enrolled in 2002-2003. Transfer students must possess at least a 2.0 GPA and be in good standing at all previously attended institutions. Coursework must be from an accredited college or university. 30 of 124 credits required for the bachelor's degree must be completed at TWU.

Visiting: There are regularly scheduled orientations for prospective students, including admissions and financial aid sessions, and a campus tour. There are guides for informal visits and visitors may sit in on classes

and stay overnight. To schedule a visit, contact the Office of Admissions at *admissions@twu.edu*.

Financial Aid: In 2003-2004, 72% of all full-time freshmen and 54% of continuing full-time students received some form of financial aid. 47% of full-time freshmen and 62% of continuing full-time students received need-based aid. The average freshman award was $6249. Need-based scholarships or need-based grants averaged $3924 ($8020 maximum); need-based self-help aid (loans and jobs) averaged $3090 ($7965 maximum); non-need-based athletic scholarships averaged $2990 ($8570 maximum); other non-need-based awards and non-need-based scholarships averaged $2543 ($3500 maximum); and non-need-based loans averaged $4684 ($11,157 maximum). 73% of undergraduates work part time. Average annual earnings from campus work are $3090. The average financial indebtedness of the 2003 graduate was $11,076. TWU is a member of CSS. The FAFSA and the college's own financial statement are required. The deadline for filing freshman financial aid applications for fall entry is April 1.

International Students: There are 116 international students enrolled. The school actively recruits these students. They must score 550 on the written TOEFL or 213 on the electronic version.

Computers: There are more than 1000 PCs and terminals available to TWU students in academic computing labs, libraries, and residence halls. Most PCs have access to the Internet. All students may access the system. There are no time limits. The fee is $10 per semester. It is strongly recommended that all students have a personal computer.

Graduates: From July 1, 2002 to June 30, 2003, 824 bachelor's degrees were awarded. The most popular majors were nursing (36%), interdisciplinary studies (10%), and psychology (5%). In an average class, 18% graduate in 4 years or less, 31% graduate in 5 years or less, and 35% graduate in 6 years or less. 190 companies recruited on campus in 2002-2003.

Admissions Contact: Ms. Teresa Mauk, Director of Admissions. E-mail: *admissions@twu.edu* Web: *www.twu.edu*

TRINITY UNIVERSITY
San Antonio, TX 78212-7200

D-4
(210) 999-7207
(800) TRINITY; Fax: (210) 999-8164

Full-time: 1123 men, 1247 women	**Faculty:** 228; IIA, ++$
Part-time: 21 men, 15 women	**Ph.D.s:** 99%
Graduate: 81 men, 145 women	**Student/Faculty:** 10 to 1
Year: semesters, summer session	**Tuition:** $19,176
Application Deadline: February 1	**Room & Board:** $7290
Freshman Class: 3675 applied, 2390 accepted, 633 enrolled	
SAT I Verbal/Math: 640/690	**ACT:** 29
	HIGHLY COMPETITIVE+

Trinity University, founded in 1869, is a liberal arts and sciences institution affiliated with the Presbyterian Church (U.S.A.). There is 1 graduate school. In addition to regional accreditation, Trinity has baccalaureate program accreditation with AACSB, ABET, NASM, and NCATE. The library contains 905,556 volumes, 1,335,194 microform items, and 64,220 audio/video tapes/CDs, and subscribes to 2898 periodicals. Computerized library services include the card catalog, interlibrary loans, and database searching. Special learning facilities include a radio station and TV station. The 117-acre campus is in a suburban area 3 miles north of downtown San Antonio. Including any residence halls, there are 45 buildings.

Student Life: 71% of undergraduates are from Texas. Students are from 48 states, 17 foreign countries, and Canada. 73% are from public schools. 68% are white; 10%, Hispanic. 50% are Protestant; 22%, Catholic; 19% claim no religious affiliation. The average age of freshmen is 19; all undergraduates, 20. 14% do not continue beyond their first year; 78% remain to graduate.

Housing: 1900 students can be accommodated in college housing, which includes coed dorms. On-campus housing is available on a lottery system for upperclassmen. 77% of students live on campus; of those, 75% remain on campus on weekends. All students may keep cars.

Activities: 26% of men belong to 8 local fraternities; 28% of women belong to 6 local sororities. There are 100 groups on campus, including art, band, cheerleading, chess, choir, chorale, chorus, computers, dance, debate, drama, ethnic, film, forensics, gaming, gay, honors, international, jazz band, literary magazine, musical theater, newspaper, opera, orchestra, pep band, photography, political, professional, radio and TV, religious, social, social service, student government, symphony, wind ensemble, and yearbook. Popular campus events include Tower Party and Trinity Night at the S.A. Spurs game.

Sports: There are 9 intercollegiate sports for men and 9 for women, and 20 intramural sports for men and 17 for women. Facilities include an indoor Olympic pool and diving center, a 5000-seat stadium, and a 3000-seat auditorium/arena.

Disabled Students: 99% of the campus is accessible. Wheelchair ramps, elevators, special parking, specially equipped rest rooms, lowered drinking fountains, and lowered telephones are available. Learning disabled services are determined through Counseling and Career Services (one-on-one).

Services: Counseling and information services are available, as is tutoring in most subjects.

Campus Safety and Security: Measures include 24-hour foot and vehicle patrol, self-defense education, security escort services, and pamphlets/posters/films. There are emergency telephones, lighted pathways/sidewalks, and shuttle carts.

Programs of Study: Trinity confers B.A., B.S., and B.M. degrees. Master's degrees are also awarded. Bachelor's degrees are awarded in BIOLOGICAL SCIENCE (biochemistry and biology/biological science), BUSINESS (business administration and management), COMMUNICATIONS AND THE ARTS (communications, dramatic arts, English, French, German, music, Russian, Spanish, and speech/debate/rhetoric), COMPUTER AND PHYSICAL SCIENCE (chemistry, computer science, geoscience, mathematics, and physics), EDUCATION (art and foreign languages), ENGINEERING AND ENVIRONMENTAL DESIGN (engineering and applied science), SOCIAL SCIENCE (anthropology, economics, history, international relations, philosophy, political science/government, psychology, religion, sociology, and urban studies). Business, communication, and biology are the largest.

Required: To graduate, students must satisfy the common curriculum and residency requirements and complete a minimum of 124 credit hours (129 for a B.S. in engineering science and 141 for a B.M. in performance and composition). Students must take at least 60 hours outside the major and 30 hours in upper-division courses. A minimum 2.0 GPA is required.

Special: The university offers study abroad in 35 countries. A Washington semester, accelerated programs, dual majors, and pass/fail options are also available, as well as teacher certification and a liberal arts/career combination. There are 5 national honor societies, including Phi Beta Kappa, and 14 departmental honors programs.

Faculty/Classroom: 66% of faculty are male; 34%, female. 96% teach undergraduates and 90% both teach and do research. No introductory courses are taught by graduate students. The average class size in an introductory lecture is 22; in a laboratory, 16; and in a regular course, 20.

Admissions: 65% of the 2003-2004 applicants were accepted. The SAT I scores for the 2003-2004 freshman class were: Verbal--1% below 500, 20% between 500 and 599, 57% between 600 and 700, and 21% above 700; Math--16% between 500 and 599, 63% between 600 and 700, and 22% above 700. The ACT scores were 14% between 24 and 26, 35% between 27 and 28, and 51% above 28. In a recent year, there were 22 National Merit finalists. 26 freshmen graduated first in their class.

Requirements: The SAT I or ACT is required. In addition, applicants should have completed 4 years of English, 3 1/2 of math, 3 each of lab science and social studies, and 2 of foreign language. A personal essay, an official high school transcript, a recommendation from a high school counselor, and a teacher's evaluation are also required. A campus visit and a visit with the university's counselor are also recommended. AP credits are accepted.

Procedure: Freshmen are admitted fall, spring, and summer. Entrance exams should be taken late in the junior year or early in the senior year. There are early decision and deferred admissions plans. Early decision applications should be filed by November 1; regular applications, by February 1 for fall entry and November 15 for spring entry, along with a $20 fee. Notification of early decision is sent December 15; regular decision, April 1. 16 applicants were on the 2003 waiting list. Applications are accepted on-line through the school's web site.

Transfer: 23 transfer students enrolled in 2002-2003. A 3.0 college GPA, high school and college transcripts, an essay, standardized test scores, and a statement of good standing from the prior institution are required. An interview is recommended. 60 of 124 credits required for the bachelor's degree must be completed at Trinity.

Visiting: There are regularly scheduled orientations for prospective students. There are guides for informal visits and visitors may sit in on classes and stay overnight. To schedule a visit, contact the Admissions Office.

Financial Aid: In 2003-2004, 43% of all full-time freshmen and 41% of continuing full-time students received some form of financial aid. At least 41% of full-time freshmen and 38% of continuing full-time students received need-based aid. The average freshman award was $16,046. Need-based scholarships or need-based grants averaged $11,811; need-based self-help aid (loans and jobs) averaged $3490; and non-need-based awards and non-need-based scholarships averaged $6264. Average annual earnings from campus work are $1410. Trinity is a member of CSS. The FAFSA is required. The priority date for freshman financial aid applications for fall entry is February 1. The deadline for filing freshman financial aid applications for fall entry is April 1.

International Students: There are 32 international students enrolled. The school actively recruits these students. They must score 570 on the written TOEFL.

Computers: There are 3 general-use computing labs containing 60 Windows NT-based systems (with Pentium or Pentium II processors) and 15 Mac systems (with Power PC processors). All of these systems are

connected to the campus network and have access to a suite of application software, including Microsoft Word, Excel, Powerpoint, Access, SPSS/PS, and utilities. All students may access the system 24 hours per day. There are no time limits and no fees. It is strongly recommended that all students have a personal computer.

Graduates: From July 1, 2002 to June 30, 2003, 533 bachelor's degrees were awarded. The most popular majors were business/marketing (21%), social sciences and history (20%), and foreign languages and literature (7%). In an average class, 75% graduate in 6 years or less. 100 companies recruited on campus in 2002-2003. Of the 2002 graduating class, 42% were enrolled in graduate school within 6 months of graduation and 31% were employed.

Admissions Contact: Dr. George Boyd, Director of Admissions. E-mail: *admissions@trinity.edu* Web: *trinity.edu*

UNIVERSITY OF DALLAS
D-2
Irving, TX 75062-4736

(972) 721-5266
(800) 628-6999; Fax: (972) 721-5017

Full-time: 497 men, 622 women	**Faculty:** 100; IIA, -$
Part-time: 58 men, 73 women	**Ph.D.s:** 92%
Graduate: 1154 men, 753 women	**Student/Faculty:** 11 to 1
Year: semesters, summer session	**Tuition:** $19,162
Application Deadline: January 15	**Room & Board:** $6736
Freshman Class: 1080 applied, 956 accepted, 299 enrolled	
SAT I Verbal/Math: 600/590	**ACT:** 26 **VERY COMPETITIVE+**

The University of Dallas, founded in 1955, is a private liberal arts institution affiliated with the Roman Catholic Church. Undergraduate programs are offered through the Constantin College of Liberal Arts, and the Braniff Graduate School has liberal arts and management divisions. A second campus is located in Rome, Italy. In addition to regional accreditation, UD has baccalaureate program accreditation with AALE and IACBE. The library contains 223,350 volumes, 75,554 microform items, and 1636 audio/video tapes/CDs, and subscribes to 583 periodicals. Computerized library services include the card catalog, interlibrary loans, database searching, and Internet access. Special learning facilities include a learning resource center, art gallery, radio station, an 80-seat theater, and an observatory. The 750-acre campus is in a suburban area 12 miles west of Dallas. Including any residence halls, there are 26 buildings.

Student Life: 62% of undergraduates are from Texas. Students are from 46 states, 19 foreign countries, and Canada. 58% are from public schools. 65% are white; 15% Hispanic. 74% are Catholic; 12% claim no religious affiliation; 11% Protestant. The average age of freshmen is 18; all undergraduates, 22. 22% do not continue beyond their first year; 64% remain to graduate.

Housing: 740 students can be accommodated in college housing, which includes single-sex and coed dorms, on-campus apartments, and married-student housing. On-campus housing is guaranteed for the freshman year only and is available on a first-come, first-served basis. 62% of students live on campus; of those, 95% remain on campus on weekends. All students may keep cars.

Activities: There are no fraternities or sororities. There are 42 groups on campus, including art, chamber ensemble, chess, choir, chorus, computers, dance, debate, drama, ethnic, film, honors, international, literary magazine, musical theater, newspaper, opera, photography, political, professional, radio and TV, religious, social, social service, student government, symphony, volunteer, and yearbook. Popular campus events include Charity Week, Oktoberfest, and Alternative Spring Break to Ecuador or Mississippi.

Sports: There are 7 intercollegiate sports for men and 9 for women, and 6 intramural sports for men and 5 for women. Facilities include an athletic center with a gym, weight room, aerobics equipment, and locker facilities. An outdoor pool and 8 screened laykold tennis courts are lighted. A collegiate soccer field, a baseball field, a multipurpose field, and 5 miles of jogging trails are also available.

Disabled Students: 70% of the campus is accessible. Wheelchair ramps, elevators, special parking, specially equipped rest rooms, special class scheduling, and lowered drinking fountains are available.

Services: Counseling and information services are available, as is tutoring in every subject. There is a reader service for the blind, writing and math labs, and an ESL institute.

Campus Safety and Security: Measures include 24-hour foot and vehicle patrol, self-defense education, security escort services, and informal discussions. There are pamphlets/posters/films, emergency telephones, and lighted pathways/sidewalks.

Programs of Study: UD confers B.A. and B.S. degrees. Master's and doctoral degrees are also awarded. Bachelor's degrees are awarded in BIOLOGICAL SCIENCE (biochemistry and biology/biological science), BUSINESS (business administration and management), COMMUNICATIONS AND THE ARTS (art history and appreciation, ceramic art and design, classics, dramatic arts, English, French, German, painting, printmaking, sculpture, and Spanish), COMPUTER AND PHYSICAL SCIENCE (chemistry, computer science, mathematics, and physics), EDU-

CATION (art and elementary), SOCIAL SCIENCE (economics, history, philosophy, political science/government, psychology, and theological studies). Classics, English, and politics are the strongest academically. English, biology, and business leadership are the largest.

Required: To graduate with a B.A., students must complete at least 120 credits, including 38 in advanced credits, which includes 12 in the major, with a 2.0 GPA. Completion of core curriculum requirements as well as major requirements is required. To graduate with a B.S degree, students must complete the above requirements for a B.A. plus 12 additonal hours in the major. Seniors must pass a comprehensive exam in their major.

Special: UD offers internships in field experience or off-campus research semester, summer study abroad, on-campus work-study programs, and an accelerated 5-year degree program leading to an M.B.A., B.A.-B.S. degrees, and double and student-designed majors. There are 4 national honor societies, including Phi Beta Kappa.

Faculty/Classroom: 71% of faculty are male; 22%, female. All teach undergraduates. No introductory courses are taught by graduate students. The average class size in an introductory lecture is 27; in a laboratory, 19; and in a regular course, 19.

Admissions: 89% of the 2003-2004 applicants were accepted. The SAT I scores for the 2003-2004 freshman class were: Verbal--11% below 500, 36% between 500 and 599, 35% between 600 and 700, and 18% above 700; Math--15% below 500, 38% between 500 and 599, 40% between 600 and 700, and 7% above 700. The ACT scores were 16% below 21, 15% between 21 and 23, 25% between 24 and 26, 23% between 27 and 28, and 21% above 28. 71% of the current freshmen were in the top fifth of their class; 96% were in the top two fifths. There were 13 National Merit finalists. 9 freshmen graduated first in their class.

Requirements: The SAT I or ACT is required. In addition, the university seeks high school students who have pursued a curriculum of college preparatory courses including English, social science, math, science, and a foreign language. Applicants pursuing a discipline in the sciences should have 4 years of math. Depth in a foreign language is advised. Although the university is flexible in its admission requests, applicants should be in the upper third of their graduating class and should present satisfactory SAT I or ACT scores. AP and CLEP credits are accepted. Important factors in the admissions decision are advanced placement or honor courses, leadership record, and extracurricular activities record.

Procedure: Freshmen are admitted fall and spring. Entrance exams should be taken during the junior year or by the fall of the senior year. There are early admissions and deferred admissions plans. Early decision applications should be filed by December 1; regular applications, from January 15 to August 1 for fall entry and December 15 for spring entry. Notification of early decision is sent December 15; regular decision, on a rolling basis beginning in February. Applications are accepted on-line through Texas Mentor.

Transfer: 64 transfer students enrolled in 2002-2003. Applicants must have a minimum 2.5 GPA from an accredited college or university. An associate degree and an interview are recommended. Official transcripts from all previouos colleges attended, a writing sample, a personal statement, and an academic letter of recommendation are required. Students with fewer than 30 transferable credits must also submit SAT I or ACT scores and an official high school transcript. 30 of 120 credits required for the bachelor's degree must be completed at UD.

Visiting: There are regularly scheduled orientations for prospective students, including a campus tour, scholarship competition, visits to residence halls and classes, meetings with students, mass, parents' meetings, and departmental advising. There are guides for informal visits and visitors may sit in on classes and stay overnight. To schedule a visit, visit the UD web site and submit an online registration form at *ugadmis@udallas.edu.*

Financial Aid: In 2002-2003, 94% of all full-time freshmen and 93% of continuing full-time students received some form of financial aid. 68% of full-time freshmen and 65% of continuing full-time students received need-based aid. The average freshman award was $14,004. Need-based scholarships or need-based grants averaged $11,426; need-based self-help aid (loans and jobs) averaged $5085; and non-need-based awards and non-need-based scholarships averaged $8802. 57% of undergraduates work part time. Average annual earnings from campus work are $1474. The average financial indebtedness of the 2003 graduate was $20,836. The FAFSA and the college's own financial statement are required. The priority date for freshman financial aid applications for fall entry is January 15. The deadline for filing freshman financial aid applications for fall entry is March 1.

International Students: There are 26 international students enrolled. The school actively recruits these students. They must score 550 on the written TOEFL or 213 on the electronic version. SAT I or ACT scores may be submitted in place of the TOEFL.

Computers: The mainframe consists of server farms of Intel-based Dell Poweredge multiprocessors for distributed computing. These distribute applications to client machines designated for use across 7 computing facilities. Wireless laptops are available for check-out from the library. All rooms in residence halls are equipped with direct connections to the high-speed campus network. Students with wireless laptops may access the system from any common building on campus via the wireless Ethernet network. All students may access the system. There are no time limits and no fees. It is strongly recommended that all students have a personal computer.

Graduates: From July 1, 2002 to June 30, 2003, 254 bachelor's degrees were awarded. The most popular majors were social science and history (29%), biology (16%), and English (12%). In an average class, 57% graduate in 4 years or less, 63% graduate in 5 years or less, and 65% graduate in 6 years or less. 38 companies recruited on campus in 2002-2003.

Admissions Contact: Sr. Mary Brian Bole, SSND, Assistant Dean of Admission. A video is available. E-mail: *ugadmis@udallas.edu* Web: *www.udallas.edu*

UNIVERSITY OF HOUSTON SYSTEM

The University of Houston System, established in 1977 by state law, is a public system of higher education. It is governed by a 9-member Board of Regents and the chief administrator is the chancellor-president of the University of Houston. The UH system centrally coordinates some institutional functions and directly provides others to its 4 universities: University of Houston, University of Houston-Clear Lake, University of Houston-Downtown, and University of Houston-Victoria. These functions include planning and budgeting, financial management and reporting, fundraising, governmental relations, and legal services. Each of the universities has a distinctive mission within the total configuration of the UH system's higher education services. The University of Houston is the only doctoral degree-granting institution in the system. UH-Clear Lake is an upper-level and graduate institution; UH-Downtown is an open-admission, primarily undergraduate university; and UH-Victoria is the only institution within a 100-mile radius to offer bachelor and graduate degrees in the 15-county region southwest of Houston. Total student enrollment for all 4 universities is more than 56,000, with 3700 faculty members. There are 390 baccalaureate, master's, and doctoral programs offered within the system. Profiles of UH and UH-Downtown are included in this section.

UNIVERSITY OF HOUSTON
Houston, TX 77204-2018

E-3

(713) 743-1010
(800) 741-4449; Fax: (713) 743-9633

Full-time: 9091 men, 10,015 women	**Faculty:** 667; I, av$
Part-time: 3889 men, 4038 women	**Ph.D:s:** 83%
Graduate: 3688 men, 4345 women	**Student/Faculty:** 29 to 1
Year: semesters, summer session	**Tuition:** $3948 ($11,028)
Application Deadline: April 1	**Room & Board:** $5870
Freshman Class: 8177 applied, 6380 accepted, 3323 enrolled	
SAT I Verbal/Math: 510/530	**ACT:** 21 COMPETITIVE

The University of Houston, established in 1927, is a public institution with programs in arts and sciences, business, education, engineering, and health professions. There are 13 undergraduate schools and 1 graduate school. In addition to regional accreditation, UH has baccalaureate program accreditation with AACSB, ABET, ACPE, ADA, CSWE, NAAB, NASM, and NCATE. The 6 libraries contain 2,173,342 volumes, 4,023,252 microform items, and 9359 audio/video tapes/CDs, and subscribe to 20,276 periodicals. Computerized library services include the card catalog, interlibrary loans, database searching, and Internet access. Special learning facilities include a learning resource center, art gallery, radio station, TV station, and observatory. The 551-acre campus is in an urban area 3 miles from the Houston business district. Including any residence halls, there are 105 buildings.

Student Life: 94% of undergraduates are from Texas. Students are from 49 states, 135 foreign countries, and Canada. 40% are white; 19% Asian American; 18% Hispanic; 13% African American. The average age of freshmen is 19; all undergraduates, 23. 21% do not continue beyond their first year; 39% remain to graduate.

Housing: 3756 students can be accommodated in college housing, which includes coed dorms, on-campus apartments, off-campus apartments, married-student housing, fraternity houses, and sorority houses. In addition, there are honors houses, language houses, and special-interest houses. On-campus housing is available on a first-come, first-served basis. 90% of students commute. All students may keep cars.

Activities: 4% of men belong to 18 national fraternities; 3% of women belong to 18 national sororities. There are 300 groups on campus, including art, band, cheerleading, chess, choir, chorale, chorus, computers, dance, debate, drama, drill team, ethnic, film, forensics, gay, honors, international, jazz band, literary magazine, marching band, musical theater, newspaper, opera, orchestra, pep band, photography, political, professional, radio and TV, religious, social, social service, student government, symphony, and yearbook. Popular campus events include Greek Week, Diversity Week, and Frontier Fiesta.

Sports: There are 7 intercollegiate sports for men and 9 for women, and 25 intramural sports for men and 25 for women. Facilities include an athletics/alumni center for intercollegiate sports, a fast-pitch softball stadium, a football stadium, a 264,000 square foot recreation and wellness center that houses 5 basketball courts, 6 racquetball and 2 squash courts, a multi-activity court for soccer, roller hockey, tennis and special events, a 70-meter indoor pool with full diving facilities up to 10 meter platform diving, and outdoor leisure pool with sand volleyball court, a 53-foot indoor climbing wall, a fitness area of more than 24,000 square feet, 6 multipurpose group exercise rooms, and locker rooms.

Disabled Students: 98% of the campus is accessible. Wheelchair ramps, elevators, special parking, specially equipped rest rooms, special class scheduling, lowered drinking fountains, lowered telephones, automatic doors, vehicle and handicap assists, an on-campus attendant-care program, registration assistance, counseling, and adaptive equipment are available.

Services: Counseling and information services are available, as is tutoring in most subjects, including core requirements. There is a reader service for the blind and remedial math, reading, and writing. Accommodation assistance for students taking exams, tutors assisting with course work, and other accommodations are available.

Campus Safety and Security: Measures include 24-hour foot and vehicle patrol, security escort services, shuttle buses, and pamphlets/posters/films. There are emergency telephones, lighted pathways/sidewalks, community dialogues, and assistance with disabled vehicles.

Programs of Study: UH confers B.A., B.S., B.Acc., B.A.C.Y., B.Arch., B.B.A., B.F.A., B.I.S.C.I., B.M., B.S.C.E., B.S.C.P.E., B.S.Ch.E., B.S.E.E., B.S.I.E., and B.S.M.E. degrees. Master's and doctoral degrees are also awarded. Bachelor's degrees are awarded in BIOLOGICAL SCIENCE (biochemistry, biology/biological science, biophysics, and nutrition), BUSINESS (accounting, banking and finance, business administration and management, hotel/motel and restaurant management, management information systems, marketing and distribution, marketing/retailing/merchandising, operations research, personnel management, and sports management), COMMUNICATIONS AND THE ARTS (applied music, art, art history and appreciation, classical languages, classics, communications, creative writing, dramatic arts, English, fine arts, French, German, journalism, music, music theory and composition, painting, photography, printmaking, radio/television technology, sculpture, Spanish, speech/debate/rhetoric, and studio art), COMPUTER AND PHYSICAL SCIENCE (chemistry, computer science, earth science, geology, geophysics and seismology, information sciences and systems, mathematics, physics, quantitative methods, and statistics), EDUCATION (trade and industrial), ENGINEERING AND ENVIRONMENTAL DESIGN (architectural engineering, architecture, biomedical equipment technology, chemical engineering, civil engineering, civil engineering technology, computer engineering, computer technology, construction management, construction technology, drafting and design technology, electrical/electronics engineering, electrical/electronics engineering technology, electromechanical technology, environmental design, graphic arts technology, industrial administration/management, industrial engineering, industrial engineering technology, interior design, manufacturing technology, mechanical engineering, and mechanical engineering technology), HEALTH PROFESSIONS (health, optometry, pharmacy, and prepharmacy), SOCIAL SCIENCE (anthropology, economics, family/consumer studies, German area studies, history, human development, interdisciplinary studies, Italian studies, philosophy, physical fitness/movement, political science/government, psychology, Russian and Slavic studies, social science, and sociology). Chemical engineering is the strongest academically. Business administration, engineering, and biological sciences are the largest.

Required: To graduate, students must complete 122 credits, including at least 36 in advanced-level courses, with a minimum GPA of 2.0. Core curriculum requirements include 6 hours each of English, math/math reasoning, history, American government, natural sciences, visual and performing arts, and social sciences (3 of which are writing intensive) and 3 hours of humanities.

Special: There is cross-registration with the University of Texas, and Rice and Texas Wesleyan Universities. UH also offers internships and co-op programs in many majors, study abroad in 12 countries, work-study programs, and programs in Mexican American studies, Asian American studies, and inter-university African studies, as well as the Mickey Leland Internship in Washington, D.C. Also available are B.A.-B.S. degrees and dual majors in all areas of study, nondegree study, and pass/fail options. There are 8 national honor societies, a freshman honors program, and 13 departmental honors programs.

Faculty/Classroom: 61% of faculty are male; 39%, female. 73% teach undergraduates. Graduate students teach 21% of introductory courses. The average class size in an introductory lecture is 10; in a laboratory, 6; and in a regular course, 16.

Admissions: 78% of the 2003-2004 applicants were accepted. The SAT I scores for the 2003-2004 freshman class were: Verbal--43% below 500, 39% between 500 and 599, 15% between 600 and 700, and 3% above 700; Math--33% below 500, 41% between 500 and 599, 23% between 600 and 700, and 3% above 700. The ACT scores were 49% below 21, 26% between 21 and 23, 16% between 24 and 26, 5% between 27 and 28, and 4% above 28. 38% of the current freshmen were in the top fifth of their class; 70% were in the top two fifths. There were 26 National Merit finalists and 2 semifinalists. 43 freshmen graduated first in their class.

Requirements: The SAT I or ACT is required. In addition, a minimum composite score of 880 (440 verbal and 440 math) on the SAT I or 19 on the ACT is required for consideration. Students in the top 10% of the high school class are automatically admitted. Lower ranks require higher scores. Applicants must be graduates of an accredited secondary school or have the GED. Students should complete 4 credits of English, 3 of math and social sciences, and 2 of lab science, with 2 of foreign language strongly recommended. There are special requirements for the College of Engineering, College of Business, College of Architecture, Department of Computer Science, and the School of Music, including an audition for music candidates. A GPA of 2.0 is required. AP and CLEP credits are accepted. Important factors in the admissions decision are evidence of special talent, advanced placement or honor courses, and recommendations by school officials.

Procedure: Freshmen are admitted to all sessions. Entrance exams should be taken no later than February of the senior year. There is a rolling admissions plan. Applications should be filed by April 1 for fall entry, December 1 for spring entry, and July 1 for summer entry, along with a $40 fee. Notification is sent on a rolling basis. Applications are accepted on-line through www.applytexas.org.

Transfer: 2614 transfer students enrolled in 2002-2003. Applicants must be eligible to return to their last college. A 2.0 GPA is required for students with 30 or more semester hours of college credit, a 2.5 GPA for those with 15 to 29. 30 of 122 credits required for the bachelor's degree must be completed at UH.

Visiting: There are regularly scheduled orientations for prospective students, including a campus tour, a meal in a residential dining hall, and a visit with an admissions counselor. Open houses are held in November and March. There are guides for informal visits and visitors may stay overnight. To schedule a visit, contact the Admissions Office, Visit Coordinator at (713) 743-9621.

Financial Aid: In 2003-2004, 62% of all full-time freshmen and 60% of continuing full-time students received some form of financial aid. 52% of full-time freshmen and 58% of continuing full-time students received need-based aid. The average freshman award was $9100. Need-based scholarships or need-based grants averaged $6378 ($8190 maximum); need-based self-help aid (loans and jobs) averaged $2730 ($5025 maximum); non-need-based athletic scholarships averaged $8668 ($15,276 maximum); and other non-need-based awards and non-need-based scholarships averaged $1500 ($22,200 maximum). 7% of undergraduates work part time. Average annual earnings from campus work are $3271. The average financial indebtedness of the 2003 graduate was $13,961. UH is a member of CSS. The FAFSA is required. The deadline for filing freshman financial aid applications for fall entry is April 1.

International Students: There are 963 international students enrolled. They must score 550 on the written TOEFL or 213 on the electronic version.

Computers: The mainframes are multiple Solaris plus NT systems and an IBM SP/2 super computer. Registered students have access to computer facilities that are located throughout the campus, including at the library and at a 24-hour site. In addition, individual departments, the Honors College, and the residence halls have their own computer facilities. All students may access the system. There are no time limits and no fees.

Graduates: From July 1, 2002 to June 30, 2003, 4116 bachelor's degrees were awarded. The most popular majors were business (35%), psychology (10%), and social sciences (6%). In an average class, 1% graduate in 3 years or less, 11% graduate in 4 years or less, 27% graduate in 5 years or less, and 39% graduate in 6 years or less. 284 companies recruited on campus in 2002-2003. Of the 2002 graduating class, 18% were enrolled in graduate school within 6 months of graduation and 87% were employed.

Admissions Contact: Ed Apodaca, Admissions Director.
E-mail: admissions@uh.edu Web: http://www.uh.edu

UNIVERSITY OF HOUSTON-DOWNTOWN
E-3
Houston, TX 77002 (713) 221-8423; Fax: (713) 221-5220

Full-time: 2255 men, 3403 women	**Faculty:** 245
Part-time: 2160 men, 3044 women	**Ph.Ds:** 78%
Graduate: 25 men, 87 women	**Student/Faculty:** 23 to 1
Year: semesters, summer session	**Tuition:** $2594 ($8258)
Application Deadline: see profile	**Room & Board:** n/app
Freshman Class: 2044 applied, 2036 accepted, 1224 enrolled	
SAT I or ACT: recommended	**NONCOMPETITIVE**

University of Houston-Downtown, founded in 1974, is part of the University of Houston System. The commuter university offers programs through the colleges of business, math, engineering, technology and natural sciences, and humanities and social studies. There are 4 undergraduate and 2 graduate schools. In addition to regional accreditation, UHD has baccalaureate program accreditation with AACSB and ABET. The library contains 190,337 volumes, 20,290 microform items, and 4511 audio/video tapes/CDs, and subscribes to 1342 periodicals. Computerized library services include the card catalog and database searching. Special learning facilities include a learning resource center and art gallery. The 14-acre campus is in an urban area in the business district of Houston. There are 3 buildings.

Student Life: 96% of undergraduates are from Texas. Students are from 20 states, 70 foreign countries, and Canada. 36% are Hispanic; 26% African American; 24% white; 11% Asian American. The average age of all undergraduates is 26. 63% do not continue beyond their first year; 14% remain to graduate.

Housing: There are no residence halls. All students commute. Alcohol is not permitted. All students may keep cars.

Activities: There is 1 national fraternity; 1% to 2% of women belong to 4 national sororities. There are 50 groups on campus, including choir, computers, drama, ethnic, honors, international, literary magazine, newspaper, political, professional, social, social service, and student government. Popular campus events include Spring Festival, Chinese New Year, and Casino Night.

Sports: There are 15 intramural sports for men. Facilities include a game room, a basketball court, and a swimming pool. The largest auditorium seats 300. Students involved in intramural sports may use the facilities at the University of Houston main campus.

Disabled Students: 95% of the campus is accessible. Wheelchair ramps, elevators, special parking, specially equipped rest rooms, lowered drinking fountains, lowered telephones, and braille materials are available.

Services: Counseling and information services are available, as is tutoring in some subjects, including science. There is a reader service for the blind, and remedial math, reading, and writing. Special labs for math and reading are available.

Campus Safety and Security: Measures include 24-hour foot and vehicle patrol, security escort services, shuttle buses, and informal discussions. There are pamphlets/posters/films, emergency telephones, and lighted pathways/sidewalks.

Programs of Study: UHD confers B.A., B.S., B.B.A., and B.S.E.T. degrees. Master's degrees are also awarded. Bachelor's degrees are awarded in BIOLOGICAL SCIENCE (microbiology), BUSINESS (accounting, banking and finance, business administration and management, marketing/retailing/merchandising, office supervision and management, and purchasing/inventory management), COMMUNICATIONS AND THE ARTS (English and technical and business writing), COMPUTER AND PHYSICAL SCIENCE (applied mathematics, computer science, information sciences and systems, natural sciences, physics, and quantitative methods), EDUCATION (bilingual/bicultural, elementary, and secondary), ENGINEERING AND ENVIRONMENTAL DESIGN (engineering technology), SOCIAL SCIENCE (criminal justice, humanities, interdisciplinary studies, and social science). General business, accounting, and criminal justice are the largest.

Required: To graduate, students must complete 44 core hours and a total of 120 to 136 hours. Courses in writing skills, math, and computers, enhancement courses, and a junior year writing proficiency exam are required. Students must maintain a minimum 2.0 GPA.

Special: The university offers co-op programs with Baylor College of Medicine and the University of Texas Health Science Center, cross-registration with the University of Houston System campuses, internships, and work-study programs. General studies degrees in applied math, natural sciences, arts and humanities, and social sciences, nondegree study in the language institute, and pass/fail options in selected courses are available. There are 2 national honor societies.

Faculty/Classroom: 55% of faculty are male; 45%, female. All teach undergraduates and 40% do research.

Admissions: All 2003-2004 applicants were accepted.

Requirements: The SAT I or ACT is recommended. In addition, applicants must be graduates of an accredited secondary school or have a GED certificate. High school courses must include English, math, science, and social studies. AP and CLEP credits are accepted.

Procedure: Freshmen are admitted to all sessions. Entrance exams should be taken during orientation. There are early admissions and deferred admissions plans. Check with the school for current application deadlines. The fall 2003 application fee was $25. The college accepts all applicants. Applications are accepted on-line through www.applytexas.org.

Transfer: Transfer students must have completed a minimum of 15 credit hours. The SAT I or ACT is recommended. 30 of 120 to 136 credits required for the bachelor's degree must be completed at UHD.

Visiting: There are regularly scheduled orientations for prospective students, including an information session, placement testing, advising, and registration. There are guides for informal visits and visitors may sit in on classes. To schedule a visit, contact the Office of Admissions at (713) 221-8522.

Financial Aid: The FAFSA and the college's own financial statement are required.

International Students: There are 299 international students enrolled. The school actively recruits these students. They must score 550 on the written TOEFL.

Computers: The mainframe is a DEC VAX 8550. PCs are available in several campus labs. All students may access the system 7 days a week.

Graduates: From July 1, 2002 to June 30, 2003, 1421 bachelor's degrees were awarded. The most popular majors were interdisciplinary studies (21%), computer information systems (14%), and criminal justice (8%).

Admissions Contact: Chris Brown, Director of Admissions.
E-mail: *uhdadmit@dt.uh.edu* Web: *www.uhd.edu*

UNIVERSITY OF MARY HARDIN-BAYLOR
Belton, TX 76513

D-3
(254) 295-4487
(800) 727-8642; Fax: (254) 295-5049

Full-time: 768 men, 1406 women	**Faculty:** 124; IIB, -$
Part-time: 100 men, 201 women	**Ph.D.s:** 68%
Graduate: 40 men, 112 women	**Student/Faculty:** 18 to 1
Year: semesters, summer session	**Tuition:** $11,540
Application Deadline: open	**Room & Board:** $5728
Freshman Class: 1156 applied, 899 accepted, 508 enrolled	
SAT I Verbal/Math: 532/535	**ACT:** 23 COMPETITIVE

The University of Mary Hardin-Baylor, founded in 1845, is a private facility affiliated with the Baptist General Convention of Texas. It offers undergraduate degrees in liberal arts, fine arts, music, business, education, nursing, and social work, as well as graduate degrees in business, information systems, education, psychology/counseling, and religion. There are 6 undergraduate and 5 graduate schools. In addition to regional accreditation, UMHB has baccalaureate program accreditation with CCNE, CSWE, and TEA. The library contains 197,368 volumes, 415,193 microform items, and 6682 audio/video tapes/CDs, and subscribes to 1100 periodicals. Computerized library services include the card catalog, interlibrary loans, database searching, and Internet access. Special learning facilities include a learning resource center and nature walk. The 170-acre campus is in a small town in central Texas. Including any residence halls, there are 36 buildings.

Student Life: 97% of undergraduates are from Texas. Students are from 24 states and 13 foreign countries. 92% are from public schools. 76% are white; 11% African American. 77% are Protestant; 12% claim no religious affiliation; 10% Catholic. The average age of freshmen is 18; all undergraduates, 23. 34% do not continue beyond their first year; 66% remain to graduate.

Housing: 1093 students can be accommodated in college housing, which includes single-sex dorms and on-campus apartments. On-campus housing is guaranteed for all 4 years. 52% of students commute. Alcohol is not permitted. All students may keep cars.

Activities: There are no fraternities or sororities. There are 40 groups on campus, including art, band, cheerleading, chess, choir, chorale, chorus, computers, drama, drill team, ethnic, forensics, honors, international, jazz band, literary magazine, marching band, musical theater, newspaper, opera, orchestra, pep band, photography, political, professional, religious, social service, student government, symphony, and yearbook. Popular campus events include Miss UMHB Pageants, Play Day, and Easter Pageant.

Sports: There are 6 intercollegiate sports for men and 6 for women, and 11 intramural sports for men and 11 for women. Facilities include a gym, softball, intramural, soccer, baseball and practice football fields, tennis courts, an aerobics room, and a sportsplex with field house and weight room.

Disabled Students: 80% of the campus is accessible. Wheelchair ramps, elevators, special parking, specially equipped rest rooms, special class scheduling, lowered drinking fountains, lowered telephones, special housing, and automatic door openers are available.

Services: Counseling and information services are available, as is tutoring in most subjects. There is remedial math, reading, and writing. Academic counselors and Jaws (software for the blind) are also available.

Campus Safety and Security: Measures include 24-hour foot and vehicle patrol, self-defense education, security escort services, and informal discussions. There are pamphlets/posters/films, emergency telephones, lighted pathways/sidewalks, and a campus police force.

Programs of Study: UMHB confers B.A., B.S., B.A.S., B.B.A., B.F.A., B.M., B.P.S., B.S.N., and B.S.W. degrees. Master's degrees are also awarded. Bachelor's degrees are awarded in BIOLOGICAL SCIENCE (biology/biological science), BUSINESS (accounting, banking and finance, business administration and management, business economics, marketing/retailing/merchandising, personnel management, and sports management), COMMUNICATIONS AND THE ARTS (communications, English, fine arts, journalism, music, music performance, performing arts, Spanish, and speech/debate/rhetoric), COMPUTER AND PHYSICAL SCIENCE (chemistry, computer science, information sciences and systems, and mathematics), EDUCATION (art, athletic training, business, early childhood, elementary, foreign languages, middle school, music, science, secondary, and special), ENGINEERING AND

ENVIRONMENTAL DESIGN (computer graphics), HEALTH PROFESSIONS (exercise science, medical technology, and nursing), SOCIAL SCIENCE (criminal justice, economics, history, parks and recreation management, political science/government, psychology, religion, social science, social work, and sociology). Education, business, and nursing are the strongest academically. Nursing is the largest.

Required: To graduate all students must complete at least 124 credits, including at least 24 in the major field and at least 36 upper-level credits, with a 2.0 GPA. Requirements include 6 credits each in English, social sciences, religion, and electives, 3 in math, lab science, or foreign language, 3 in speech communication and math, and 2 activity courses in phys ed. There is a chapel attendance requirement for full-time students and a residency requirement of 31 hours.

Special: Combined B.A.-B.S. degrees in most areas, study abroad in 2 countries, internships, a work-study program, dual majors, a professional studies degree, an applied science bachelor's degree, post-baccalaureate certification in education, and a 5 year BBA/MBA accounting specialization are offered. There are 5 national honor societies and a freshman honors program.

Faculty/Classroom: 51% of faculty are male; 49%, female. 97% teach undergraduates, 12% do research, and 10% do both. No introductory courses are taught by graduate students. The average class size in an introductory lecture is 35; in a laboratory, 25; and in a regular course, 30.

Admissions: 78% of the 2003-2004 applicants were accepted. The SAT I scores for the 2003-2004 freshman class were: Verbal--34% below 500, 48% between 500 and 599, 16% between 600 and 700, and 2% above 700; Math--31% below 500, 48% between 500 and 599, 19% between 600 and 700, and 2% above 700. The ACT scores were 28% below 21, 33% between 21 and 23, 22% between 24 and 26, 9% between 27 and 28, and 8% above 28. 40% of the current freshmen were in the top fifth of their class; 72% were in the top two fifths. 12 freshmen graduated first in their class.

Requirements: The SAT I or ACT is required. In addition, students who rank in the top half of their high school graduationg class must score a minimum of 950 on SAT I or 20 on ACT. Those who graduate in the lower half of their class must score a minimum of 990 on SAT I or 21 on ACT. There is no minimum test score for students who rank in the top 10% of their high school graduating class. All students should be graduates of an accredited high school and have 22 units of credit, including 4 in English, 3 in math, and 2.5 in social science. AP and CLEP credits are accepted. Important factors in the admissions decision are advanced placement or honor courses, recommendations by school officials, and extracurricular activities record.

Procedure: Freshmen are admitted fall, spring, and summer. Entrance exams should be taken by the fall of the senior year. There is an early admissions plan. There is a rolling admissions plan. Application deadlines are open. Application fee is $35. Applications are accepted on-line through the school's web site at *www.umhb.edu* or through Texas common application.

Transfer: 407 transfer students enrolled in 2002-2003. Applicants must present at least a 2.0 GPA, be in good standing at their previous institutions, and submit all college transcripts. Those with fewer than 12 transferable credits must also meet freshman requirements. 31 of 124 credits required for the bachelor's degree must be completed at UMHB.

Visiting: There are regularly scheduled orientations for prospective students, consisting of campus tours and visits with counselors to discuss admissions, financial aid, housing, and degree plans. There are guides for informal visits and visitors may sit in on classes and stay overnight. To schedule a visit, contact the Recruiting Office at (254) 295-4514 or *admission@umnb.edu*.

Financial Aid: In 2003-2004, 92% of all full-time students received some form of financial aid. 70% of full-time freshmen and 73% of continuing full-time students received need-based aid. The average freshman award was $7264. Need-based scholarships or need-based grants averaged $5102 ($9702 maximum); need-based self-help aid (loans and jobs) averaged $3086 ($6625 maximum); and non-need based awards and non-need based scholarships averaged $5145 ($18,625 maximum). 15% of undergraduates work part time. Average annual earnings from campus work are $2300. The average financial indebtedness of the 2003 graduate was $13,509. The FAFSA and the college's own financial statement are required. The priority date for freshman financial aid applications for fall entry is March 15. The deadline for filing freshman financial aid applications for fall entry is September 1.

International Students: There are 19 international students enrolled. The school actively recruits these students. They must take the college's own test.

Computers: The mainframe is an IBM AS/400. There are 14 computer labs, some of which are located in dorms. All PCs are connected to the campus-wide network. All students may access the system any time. There are no time limits and no fees.

Graduates: From July 1, 2002 to June 30, 2003, 494 bachelor's degrees were awarded. The most popular majors were psychology (10%), general studies (8%), and elementary education (7%). In an average class, 1% graduate in 3 years or less, 26% graduate in 4 years or less,

37% graduate in 5 years or less, and 41% graduate in 6 years or less. 230 companies recruited on campus in 2002-2003.

Admissions Contact: Robin Steen, Director of Admissions.
E-mail: *admissions@umhb.edu* Web: *www.umhb.edu*

UNIVERSITY OF NORTH TEXAS   D-2
Denton, TX 76203   (940) 565-2681
                                      (800) UNT-8211; Fax: (940) 565-2408

Full-time: 7405 men, 9535 women	**Faculty:** 810; I, --$
Part-time: 2285 men, 2460 women	**Ph.D.s:** 87%
Graduate: 2400 men, 3785 women	**Student/Faculty:** 21 to 1
Year: semesters, summer session	**Tuition:** $3215 ($9605)
Application Deadline: see profile	**Room & Board:** $4420
Freshman Class: n/av	
SAT I or ACT: required	**COMPETITIVE**

The University of North Texas, founded in 1890, is a public institution offering programs through its colleges of arts and sciences, education, business administration, community services, library and information sciences, music, merchandising and hospitality management, and school of visual arts. There are 8 undergraduate schools and 1 graduate school. Figures in the above capsule and in this profile are approximate. In addition to regional accreditation, UNT has baccalaureate program accreditation with AACSB, ACEJMC, CSAB, CSWE, FIDER, NASM, and NRPA. The 4 libraries contain 1,529,868 volumes, 3,166,145 microform items, and 75,169 audio/video tapes/CDs, and subscribe to 20,157 periodicals. Computerized library services include the card catalog, interlibrary loans, and database searching. Special learning facilities include a learning resource center, art gallery, radio station, an observatory, and a TV and film production unit. The 500-acre campus is in an urban area 35 miles north of Dallas/Fort Worth. Including any residence halls, there are 151 buildings.

Student Life: 93% of undergraduates are from Texas. Students are from 49 states, 113 foreign countries, and Canada. 73% are white. The average age of freshmen is 19; all undergraduates, 23. 31% do not continue beyond their first year; 69% remain to graduate.

Housing: 4400 students can be accommodated in college housing, which includes single-sex and coed dorms, on-campus apartments, and off-campus apartments. On-campus housing is available on a first-come, first-served basis. All students may keep cars.

Activities: 3% of men belong to 16 national fraternities; 3% of women belong to 11 national sororities. There are 250 groups on campus, including band, cheerleading, chess, choir, chorale, chorus, computers, dance, drama, ethnic, film, gay, honors, international, jazz band, literary magazine, marching band, musical theater, newspaper, opera, orchestra, pep band, photography, political, professional, radio and TV, religious, social, social service, student government, symphony, and yearbook. Popular campus events include Silver Christmas Ball, Howdy Week, and Taste of North Texas.

Sports: There are 6 intercollegiate sports for men and 9 for women, and 37 intramural sports for men and 37 for women. Facilities include a 30000-seat stadium, an 18-hole golf course, a weight-training building, tennis courts, 1 indoor swimming pool, 3 gyms, 8 handball and racquetball courts, gymnastics equipment, intramural fields, and recreational sports complex.

Disabled Students: 85% of the campus is accessible. Wheelchair ramps, elevators, special parking, specially equipped rest rooms, special class scheduling, lowered drinking fountains, lowered telephones, and 9 dorm rooms adapted for disabled students are available.

Services: Counseling and information services are available, as is tutoring in most subjects. There is a reader service for the blind and remedial math, reading, and writing.

Campus Safety and Security: Measures include 24-hour foot and vehicle patrol, self-defense education, security escort services, and shuttle buses. There are informal discussions, pamphlets/posters/films, emergency telephones, and lighted pathways/sidewalks. In addition, there is a crime prevention program, sexual assault information services, and a full-time crime prevention officer on duty.

Programs of Study: UNT confers B.A., B.S., B.A.A.S., B.B.A., B.F.A., B.M., B.S.B.C., B.S.Bio, B.S.Chem., B.S.Eco., B.S.E.P., B.S.E.T., B.S.Math., B.S.M.T., B.S.Phy., and B.S.W. degrees. Master's and doctoral degrees are also awarded. Bachelor's degrees are awarded in BIOLOGICAL SCIENCE (biochemistry and biology/biological science), BUSINESS (accounting, banking and finance, business administration and management, business economics, entrepreneurial studies, hotel/motel and restaurant management, human resources, insurance, management information systems, management science, marketing/retailing/merchandising, operations research, organizational behavior, personnel management, real estate, recreation and leisure services, and small business management), COMMUNICATIONS AND THE ARTS (applied art, art, art history and appreciation, ceramic art and design, communications, dance, dramatic arts, drawing, English, fiber/textiles/weaving, film arts, French, German, jazz, journalism, metal/jewelry, music, music history and appreciation, music performance, music theory and composition, painting, photography, printmaking, radio/television technology, sculpture, Spanish, and visual and performing arts), COMPUTER AND PHYSICAL SCIENCE (chemistry, computer science, information sciences and systems, mathematics, and physics), EDUCATION (business, early childhood, elementary, health, physical, reading, and vocational), ENGINEERING AND ENVIRONMENTAL DESIGN (commercial art, emergency/disaster science, engineering technology, industrial administration/management, and interior design), HEALTH PROFESSIONS (cytotechnology, medical laboratory technology, rehabilitation therapy, and speech pathology/audiology), SOCIAL SCIENCE (anthropology, child psychology/development, clothing and textiles management/production/services, counseling/psychology, criminal justice, economics, fashion design and technology, geography, history, home furnishings and equipment management/production/services, interdisciplinary studies, liberal arts/general studies, philosophy, physical fitness/movement, political science/government, psychology, social science, social work, and sociology). Accounting, jazz studies, and city management are the strongest academically. Biology, psychology, and interdisciplinary studies (teacher education department) are the largest.

Required: All students must complete at least 124 semester hours, including a minimum of 24 hours in the major, with a 2.0 GPA. The 47 hours of core requirements include 12 hours of English, 6 hours each in science, American history, federal and state constitution, social sciences, and humanities, and 4 hours in phys ed. Proficiency in English composition must be demonstrated.

Special: UNT offers co-op programs in 34 majors, internships, and work-study programs with the university. Students may study abroad in the United Kingdom, France, Japan, Germany, Mexico, and Australia. An accelerated degree program in math and science allows Texas high school students to obtain 2 years of college credit during their last 2 years in high school. Dual degrees, a general studies degree, and pass/fail options are also offered. There are 3 national honor societies, a freshman honors program, and 1 departmental honors program.

Faculty/Classroom: 69% of faculty are male; 31%, female. 95% teach undergraduates. The average class size in a laboratory is 23 and in a regular course, 40.

Requirements: The SAT I or ACT is required. In addition, applicants must be graduates of an accredited high school and submit a high school transcript. The required minimum score for entrance exams is determined by high school class rank. AP and CLEP credits are accepted. Important factors in the admissions decision are recommendations by school officials, advanced placement or honor courses, and evidence of special talent.

Procedure: Freshmen are admitted to all sessions. Entrance exams should be taken at least 2 months before admissions deadlines. There are early admissions, deferred admissions, and rolling admissions plans. Check with the school for current deadlines. The fall 2003 application fee was $40.

Transfer: Applicants with fewer than 30 hours from an accredited college must have a 2.5 GPA and meet freshman entrance requirements. Applicants with at least 30 but no more than 44 transferable hours must have a 2.3 GPA; those with more than 44 hours must have a 2.0 GPA. 30 of 124 credits required for the bachelor's degree must be completed at UNT.

Visiting: There are regularly scheduled orientations for prospective students, including UNT Previews held 1 Saturday in the fall and 1 in the spring. The agenda includes a campus tour, presentations by academic and student service offices, and question-and-answer sessions. There are guides for informal visits and visitors may sit in on classes and stay overnight. To schedule a visit, contact the information desk assistant at (940) 565-4104 or (940) 565-2000.

Financial Aid: The FAFSA is required. Check with the school for current deadlines.

International Students: The school actively recruits these students. They must score 550 on the written TOEFL or take the MELAB, ECPE, FCE, CAE, CPE, IELTS, or ELPT.

Computers: The mainframes are an HDS-80-83, a Solbourne SE/904, an NBIV16S, an NAS8000, and an IBM 43004. More than 5000 PCs are available on campus. All students may access the system. Students may access the system 1 hour if labs are busy. The fall 2003 application fee was $3.25 per semester hour.

Graduates: 315 companies recruited on campus in a recent year.

Admissions Contact: Marcilla Collinsworth, Director, Admissions and School Relations. A video is available.
E-mail: *undergrad@abn.unt.edu* Web: *www.unt.edu*

UNIVERSITY OF SAINT THOMAS
Houston, TX 77006-4696

E-3

(713) 525-3500
(800) 856-8565; Fax: (713) 525-3532

Full-time: 488 men, 895 women	**Faculty:** 114; IIA, +$
Part-time: 185 men, 339 women	**Ph.D.s:** 89%
Graduate: 498 men, 569 women	**Student/Faculty:** 12 to 1
Year: semesters, summer session	**Tuition:** $15,112
Application Deadline: open	**Room & Board:** $6840
Freshman Class: 808 applied, 718 accepted, 302 enrolled	
SAT I Verbal/Math: 570/570	**ACT:** 24 **VERY COMPETITIVE**

The University of St. Thomas is a private institution committed to the liberal arts and to the religious, ethical, and intellectual tradition of Catholic higher education. There are 3 undergraduate and 4 graduate schools. In addition to regional accreditation, UST has baccalaureate program accreditation with ACBSP. The 2 libraries contain 243,676 volumes, 554,552 microform items, and 1292 audio/video tapes/CDs, and subscribe to 610 periodicals. Computerized library services include the card catalog, interlibrary loans, database searching, and Internet access. Special learning facilities include a learning resource center and an archeology gallery. The 21-acre campus is in an urban area close to downtown Houston. Including any residence halls, there are 60 buildings.

Student Life: 97% of undergraduates are from Texas. Students are from 27 states, 32 foreign countries, and Canada. 46% are white; 28% Hispanic; 15% Asian American. 67% are Catholic; 25% Protestant. The average age of freshmen is 18; all undergraduates, 25. 32% do not continue beyond their first year; 46% remain to graduate.

Housing: 418 students can be accommodated in college housing, which includes coed dorms and on-campus apartments. In addition, there is a living-learning center. On-campus housing is available on a first-come, first-served basis. Priority is given to out-of-town students. 87% of students commute. All students may keep cars.

Activities: There are no fraternities or sororities. There are 82 groups on campus, including choir, debate, drama, ethnic, forensics, honors, international, jazz band, literary magazine, musical theater, newspaper, political, professional, religious, social, social service, and student government. Popular campus events include spring formal and campus welcome-back-week activities.

Sports: There are 11 intramural sports for men and 11 for women. Facilities include an 800-seat gym, racquetball and tennis courts, a weight-training room, a cardiovascular room, a dance room, a bag/mat room, a swimming pool, and a multipurpose area.

Disabled Students: 50% of the campus is accessible. Wheelchair ramps, elevators, special parking, specially equipped rest rooms, special class scheduling, lowered drinking fountains, and lowered telephones are available.

Services: Counseling and information services are available, as is tutoring in every subject. There is remedial math, reading, and writing. There are remedial classes, but if a student has special needs, the learning center will provide remedial tutoring.

Campus Safety and Security: Measures include 24-hour foot and vehicle patrol, security escort services, informal discussions, and pamphlets/posters/films. There are emergency telephones and lighted pathways/sidewalks.

Programs of Study: UST confers B.A., B.S., B.B.A., and B.Th. degrees. Master's and doctoral degrees are also awarded. Bachelor's degrees are awarded in BIOLOGICAL SCIENCE (biology/biological science), BUSINESS (accounting, banking and finance, business administration and management, management information systems, and marketing/retailing/merchandising), COMMUNICATIONS AND THE ARTS (communications, dramatic arts, English, fine arts, French, music, Spanish, and studio art), COMPUTER AND PHYSICAL SCIENCE (chemistry and mathematics), EDUCATION (education and music), ENGINEERING AND ENVIRONMENTAL DESIGN (environmental science), SOCIAL SCIENCE (economics, history, international studies, liberal arts/general studies, pastoral studies, philosophy, political science/government, psychology, and theological studies). Business administration, international studies, and biology are the largest.

Required: To graduate, students must complete the core curriculum in theology, philosophy, English, history, foreign language, natural and social science, math, fine arts, and oral communication and 30 to 48 hours in their selected majors. In some cases, students need to complete special projects according to the requirements of specific majors. Students must have a minimum 2.0 GPA in a total of 126 credit hours, including 36 hours of upper-division credits.

Special: UST offers cross-registration with the University of Houston and a 3-2 engineering program with the University of Houston, Texas A&M University, and University of Notre Dame. Internships in the major field of study and study abroad in 10 countries are also available. Dual and joint majors and 5-year joint bachelor's and master's degree programs, combining B.B.A./M.B.A. or B.B.A./M.I.B., are available. There are 18 national honor societies and a freshman honors program.

Faculty/Classroom: All teach undergraduates. No introductory courses are taught by graduate students. The average class size in an introductory lecture is 21; in a laboratory, 18; and in a regular course, 19.

Admissions: 89% of the 2003-2004 applicants were accepted. The SAT I scores for the 2003-2004 freshman class were: Verbal--17% below 500, 44% between 500 and 599, 33% between 600 and 700, and 6% above 700; Math--13% below 500, 48% between 500 and 599, 34% between 600 and 700, and 5% above 700. The ACT scores were 13% below 21, 31% between 21 and 23, 27% between 24 and 26, 15% between 27 and 28, and 15% above 28. 39% of the current freshmen were in the top fifth of their class; 64% were in the top two fifths. 8 freshmen graduated first in their class.

Requirements: The SAT I or ACT is required, with a minimum SAT I composite score of 1000 or ACT composite score of 22. Applicants must have a GED certificate or be graduates of an accredited secondary school and have 18 academic credits, including 4 years of English, 3 of math, 3 of science (2 of which must be lab sciences), 2 each of foreign language and social studies, and 1 of history. UST requires applicants to be in the upper 50% of their class. A GPA of 2.25 is required. AP and CLEP credits are accepted.

Procedure: Freshmen are admitted to all sessions. Entrance exams should be taken as early as possible. There is a deferred admissions plan. Application deadlines are open. The fall 2003 application fee was $35. Notification is sent on a rolling basis. Applications are accepted on-line through *www.texasmentor.org/applications/St._Thomas/apply.html.*

Transfer: 276 transfer students enrolled in 2002-2003. Transfer students must have a minimum 2.25 GPA, a high school diploma or GED, and be eligible to return to the last college of attendance. 36 of 126 credits required for the bachelor's degree must be completed at UST.

Visiting: There are regularly scheduled orientations for prospective students, including tours, class visitations, introductions to faculty, administrative members, and currently enrolled students, and financial aid sessions. There are guides for informal visits and visitors may sit in on classes and stay overnight. To schedule a visit, contact an admissions counselor at *admissions@stthom.edu.*

Financial Aid: In a recent year, 85% of all full-time freshmen and 38% of continuing full-time students received some form of financial aid. 74% of full-time freshmen and 27% of continuing full-time students received need-based aid. The average freshman award was $11,114. The average financial indebtedness of a recent year's graduate was $18,958. The FAFSA is required. The priority date for freshman financial aid applications for fall entry is March 1.

International Students: There are 54 international students enrolled. The school actively recruits these students. They must score 550 on the written TOEFL or 213 on the electronic version.

Computers: There are more than 300 PCs located throughout the campus for student use. Wireless Internet access is available on the Academic Mall. Students can access their e-mail and student accounts on-line. All students may access the system 9 A.M. to 10 P.M., 7 days a week; dial-up, 24 hours a day. There are no time limits and no fees.

Graduates: From July 1, 2002 to June 30, 2003, 318 bachelor's degrees were awarded. The most popular majors were liberal arts (10%), education (9%), and business administration (8%). In an average class, 24% graduate in 4 years or less, 41% graduate in 5 years or less, and 46% graduate in 6 years or less. 19 companies recruited on campus in 2002-2003.

Admissions Contact: Eduardo Prieto, Dean of Admissions. A video is available. E-mail: *admissions@stthom.edu*
Web: *http://www.stthom.edu/admissions/index.html*

UNIVERSITY OF TEXAS SYSTEM

The University of Texas System, established in 1950, is a public system in Texas. It is governed by a Board of Regents, whose chief administrator is the chancellor. The primary goal of the system is to provide instruction, research, and public service throughout the state. The main priorities are undergraduate education, social and economic development of Texas, and professional training in and effective management of health care. The total enrollment is usually about 160,000; there were about 15,000 faculty members. Altogether there are 388 baccalaureate, 309 master's, and 148 doctoral programs offered in University of Texas System. 4-year campuses are located in Arlington, Austin, El Paso, and San Antonio. Profiles of the 4-year campuses are included in this section.

UNIVERSITY OF TEXAS AT ARLINGTON   D-2
Arlington, TX 76019-   (817) 272-6287; Fax: (817) 272-3435

Full-time: 5225 men, 5960 women	Faculty: I, --$
Part-time: 2395 men, 2750 women	Ph.D.s: 83%
Graduate: 2430 men, 2425 women	Student/Faculty: n/av
Year: semesters, summer session	Tuition: $3070 ($8135)
Application Deadline: see profile	Room & Board: $4125
Freshman Class: 4404 applied, 3724 accepted, 1965 enrolled	
SAT I Verbal/Math: required	ACT: required

LESS COMPETITIVE

The University of Texas at Arlington, founded in 1895, is part of the University of Texas System and is organized into colleges and schools, including business administration, engineering, liberal arts, science, architecture, nursing, social work, graduate studies, urban and public affairs, and education. There are 9 undergraduate and 10 graduate schools. Figures in the above capsule and in this profile are approximate. In addition to regional accreditation, UTA has baccalaureate program accreditation with AACSB, ABET, ACS, ASLA, CSWE, FIDER, NAAB, NASM, NASPAA, and NLN. The 3 libraries contain 1,105,189 volumes, 1,518,208 microform items, and 3468 audio/video tapes/CDs, and subscribe to 5073 periodicals. Computerized library services include the card catalog, interlibrary loans, and database searching. Special learning facilities include a learning resource center, art gallery, planetarium, cartographic history library, and nano lab. The 395-acre campus is in an urban area in the center of the Dallas/Fort Worth metroplex. Including any residence halls, there are 100 buildings.

Student Life: 92% of undergraduates are from Texas. Students are from 45 states, 88 foreign countries, and Canada. 56% are white; 12% African American; 11% foreign nationals; 10% Asian American; 10% Hispanic. The average age of freshmen is 18; all undergraduates, 24. 31% do not continue beyond their first year; 31% remain to graduate.

Housing: 3303 students can be accommodated in college housing, which includes single-sex and coed dorms, on-campus apartments, off-campus apartments, married-student housing, fraternity houses, and sorority houses. In addition, there are honors houses. On-campus housing is available on a first-come, first-served basis. 86% of students commute. Alcohol is not permitted. All students may keep cars.

Activities: 6% of men belong to 12 national fraternities; 4% of women belong to 10 national sororities. There are 225 groups on campus, including art, band, cheerleading, chess, choir, chorale, chorus, computers, dance, drama, drill team, drum and bugle corps, ethnic, forensics, gay, honors, international, jazz band, marching band, opera, orchestra, photography, political, professional, religious, social, social service, student government, symphony, and yearbook. Popular campus events include Charity Week, The Big Event, and Last Day Blast.

Sports: There are 6 intercollegiate sports for men and 6 for women, and 10 intramural sports for men and 10 for women. Facilities include 12 racquetball, 4 basketball, and volleyball courts, 12 lighted tennis courts, an inside track, 1 Olympic-size pool, 3 weight rooms, a 12,000-seat stadium, and a 3000-seat gym.

Disabled Students: All of the campus is accessible. Wheelchair ramps, elevators, special parking, specially equipped rest rooms, special class scheduling, lowered drinking fountains, lowered telephones, and personal, academic, and career counseling, wheelchair repair, note copying, adaptive testing, adaptive exercise and sport activities, and wheelchair athletics are available.

Services: Counseling and information services are available, as is tutoring in most subjects, including English, math, computer science, and foreign languages. There is a reader service for the blind, remedial math, reading, and writing, a math tutorial clinic, a nursing learning resource center, a reading lab, a science learning center, and a writing lab.

Campus Safety and Security: Measures include 24-hour foot and vehicle patrol, self-defense education, security escort services, and shuttle buses. There are informal discussions, pamphlets/posters/films, emergency telephones, lighted pathways/sidewalks, crime prevention programs, and an emergency on-campus phone number.

Programs of Study: UTA confers B.A., B.S., B.A.I.S., B.B.A., B.F.A., B.M., B.S.A.S.E., B.S.C.E., B.S.C.S., B.S.C.S.E., B.S.E.E., B.S.I.E., B.S.I.S., B.S.M.E., B.S.N., and B.S.W. degrees. Master's and doctoral degrees are also awarded. Bachelor's degrees are awarded in BIOLOGICAL SCIENCE (biochemistry, biology/biological science, and microbiology), BUSINESS (accounting, banking and finance, business administration and management, business economics, management science, marketing/retailing/merchandising, and real estate), COMMUNICATIONS AND THE ARTS (art history and appreciation, broadcasting, communications, dramatic arts, English, French, German, journalism, music, Russian, Spanish, speech/debate/rhetoric, and studio art), COMPUTER AND PHYSICAL SCIENCE (chemistry, computer science, geology, information sciences and systems, mathematics, and physics), EDUCATION (physical), ENGINEERING AND ENVIRONMENTAL DESIGN (architecture, civil engineering, computer engineering, electrical/electronics engineering, industrial engineering technology, interior design, landscape architecture/design, and mechanical engineering),

HEALTH PROFESSIONS (medical technology and nursing), SOCIAL SCIENCE (anthropology, classical/ancient civilization, criminal justice, economics, history, interdisciplinary studies, philosophy, political science/government, psychology, social work, and sociology). Liberal arts, business, and engineering are the largest.

Required: All students must earn a GPA of 2.0 while taking at least 124 semester hours, including 30 in their major. The core curriculum requires 8 hours of science, 6 each of English composition, math, U.S. history, and U.S. political science, and 3 each of literature, liberal arts, social/cultural studies, and fine arts/philosophy. Students must demonstrate proficiency in oral presentations and computer use. Proficiency exams, or completion of a department-designated course, may be required by the major department. Theses are required of members of the Honors College.

Special: Cooperative education programs provide opportunities to gain experience in local business through the colleges of engineering and business. Cross-registration with the Summer Institute of Linguistics and the University of Texas Health Science Center, as well as with other members of the University of Texas System, is available. Study abroad in 10 countries, work-study at the university, B.A.-B.S. degrees, dual majors, student-designed interdisciplinary majors, credit for military experience, and pass/fail options are also offered. There are 2 national honor societies, a freshman honors program, and 10 departmental honors programs.

Faculty/Classroom: 60% of faculty are male; 40%, female. Graduate students teach 17% of introductory courses. The average class size in an introductory lecture is 47 and in a laboratory, 25.

Requirements: The SAT I or ACT is required. Students ranked in the top 10% of their high school class are admitted regardless of SAT I/ACT. Those in the second quarter of their class must submit a minimum of 950 on the SAT I or 20 on the ACT. Those in the third quarter must score 1000 on the SAT I or 21 on ACT. The bottom quarter must score 1150 on the SAT I or 25 on ACT. The GED is accepted under certain circumstances. Applicants must have 20 academic credits, including 4 units of English, 3 each of math, social studies, and science, and 2 units of foreign language. AP and CLEP credits are accepted. Important factors in the admissions decision are advanced placement or honor courses, leadership record, and evidence of special talent.

Procedure: Freshmen are admitted to all sessions. Entrance exams should be taken during the fall of the senior year. There are early admissions, deferred admissions, and rolling admissions plans. Check with the school for current application deadlines. The fall 2003 application fee was $25. Notification is sent on a rolling basis. Applications are accepted on-line through Texas Common Application.

Transfer: 2897 transfer students enrolled in a recent year. Transfer students with 30 or more transferable semester hours need a 2.0 GPA or evidence of high school or GED completion and SAT I or ACT scores comparable to the high school associated rank (varies by student). Transfer students with fewer than 30 transferable semester hours must have a 2.0 GPA and also meet admission requirements for entering freshmen. 25 credits required for the bachelor's degree must be completed at UTA.

Visiting: There are regularly scheduled orientations for prospective students, including overnight summer orientations for freshmen and 1-day orientations for transfers and returning adult students. There are guides for informal visits and visitors may sit in on classes. To schedule a visit, contact the Admissions Office.

Financial Aid: In a recent year, 61% of all full-time freshmen and 60% of continuing full-time students received some form of financial aid. 41% of full-time freshmen and 45% of continuing full-time students received need-based aid. The average freshman award was $5309. 67% of undergraduates work part time. Average annual earnings from campus work are $1751. The average financial indebtedness of a recent graduate was $12,671. The FAFSA and income tax returns are required. Check with the school for current deadlines.

International Students: In a recent year, there were 682 international students enrolled. They must score 550 on the written TOEFL or 213 on the electronic version and also take the SAT I, scoring 900.

Computers: The mainframe is an IBM 7060 H50. UTA operates 7 computing facilities with 425 Pentium computers, 180 Macs, and 70 Sun UNIX workstations. All students may access the system at all times. There are no time limits and no fees.

Graduates: In a recent year, 2798 bachelor's degrees were awarded. The most popular majors were information systems (13%), nursing (10%), and interdisciplinary studies (5%). In an average class, 1% graduate in 3 years or less, 9% graduate in 4 years or less, 23% graduate in 5 years or less, and 31% graduate in 6 years or less. 420 companies recruited on campus in a recent year.

Admissions Contact: George Norton, Interim Director of Admissions. A video is available. E-mail: *admissions@uta.edu* Web: *www.uta.edu*

UNIVERSITY OF TEXAS AT AUSTIN   D-3
Austin, TX 78712   (512) 475-7440; Fax: (512) 475-7473

Full-time: 16,687 men, 17,914 women	**Faculty:** 2432; I, av$
Part-time: 1992 men, 1790 women	**Ph.D.s:** 89%
Graduate: 6795 men, 6248 women	**Student/Faculty:** 14 to 1
Year: semesters, summer session	**Tuition:** $4548 ($11,668)
Application Deadline: February 1	**Room & Board:** $6082
Freshman Class: 24,519 applied, 11,504 accepted, 6544 enrolled	
SAT I Verbal/Math: 600/630	**ACT:** 25 **HIGHLY COMPETITIVE**

University of Texas at Austin, founded in 1883, is a major research institution within the University of Texas System and provides a broad range of degree programs. There are 11 undergraduate and 14 graduate schools. In addition to regional accreditation, UT has baccalaureate program accreditation with AACSB, ABET, ACEJMC, ACPE, ADA, CSWE, FIDER, NAAB, NASAD, and NASM. The 17 libraries contain 8,229,689 volumes, 6,083,260 microform items, 991,469 audio/video tapes/CDs, and 49,219 e-books, and subscribe to 50,014 periodicals. Computerized library services include the card catalog, interlibrary loans, and database searching. Special learning facilities include a learning resource center, art gallery, natural history museum, radio station, TV station, observatory, marine science institute, fusion reactor, and Lyndon Baines Johnson Library and Museum. The 350-acre campus is in an urban area near downtown Austin, just off the interstate. Including any residence halls, there are 117 buildings.

Student Life: 91% of undergraduates are from Texas. Students are from 50 states, 122 foreign countries, and Canada. 59% are white; 14% Asian American; 13% Hispanic. The average age of freshmen is 18; all undergraduates, 21. 8% do not continue beyond their first year; 92% remain to graduate.

Housing: 6699 students can be accommodated in college housing, which includes single-sex and coed dorms, off-campus apartments, and married-student housing. In addition, there are honors houses and living learning centers (for freshmen). On-campus housing is available on a first-come, first-served basis. 82% of students commute. Alcohol is not permitted. All students may keep cars.

Activities: 9% of men belong to 27 national fraternities; 14% of women belong to 23 national sororities. There are 900 groups on campus, including art, band, cheerleading, chess, choir, chorale, chorus, computers, dance, drama, ethnic, film, forensics, gay, honors, international, jazz band, literary magazine, marching band, musical theater, newspaper, opera, orchestra, pep band, photography, political, professional, radio and TV, religious, social, social service, student government, symphony, and yearbook. Popular campus events include Gone to Texas (welcome for new students), Cinco de Mayo, and Texas Revue (talent show).

Sports: There are 8 intercollegiate sports for men and 10 for women, and 45 intramural sports for men and 45 for women. Facilities include an 80,106-seat football stadium, a 16,175-seat basketball center, a 4400-seat volleyball arena, a 6649-seat baseball stadium, a 2600-seat Olympic swimming facility, 6 multipurpose indoor recreational/athletic facilities of various sizes available for basketball, volleyball, racquetball, swimming, weight training, and related activities, and 3 outdoor facilities covering nearly 40 acres available for tennis, basketball, racquetball, and various field sports. There is also a 1252-seat softball stadium and a 20,000-seat track and soccer stadium.

Disabled Students: 98% of the campus is accessible. Wheelchair ramps, elevators, special parking, specially equipped rest rooms, lowered drinking fountains, lowered telephones, specially equipped reading rooms, a speech and hearing center, academic accommodations specific to the student's disability, and interpreters for the hearing impaired are available.

Services: Counseling and information services are available, as is tutoring in most subjects. There is a reader service for the blind, and remedial math, reading, and writing.

Campus Safety and Security: Measures include 24-hour foot and vehicle patrol, self-defense education, security escort services, and shuttle buses. There are informal discussions, pamphlets/posters/films, emergency telephones, and lighted pathways/sidewalks. There is also a crime prevention unit and closed-circuit TV covering some parking areas and offices.

Programs of Study: UT confers B.A., B.S., B.Arch., B.B.A., B.F.A., B.M., B.J., and B.S.W., among more than 50 specific degrees. Master's and doctoral degrees are also awarded. Bachelor's degrees are awarded in BIOLOGICAL SCIENCE (biochemistry, biology/biological science, botany, microbiology, molecular biology, nutrition, and zoology), BUSINESS (accounting, banking and finance, business administration and management, management information systems, management science, and marketing management), COMMUNICATIONS AND THE ARTS (advertising, applied music, Arabic, art history and appreciation, classics, dance, design, dramatic arts, English, film arts, French, German, Greek, Hebrew, Italian, journalism, Latin, linguistics, music, music theory and composition, Portuguese, public relations, Russian, Scandinavian languages, Slavic languages, Spanish, speech/debate/rhetoric, studio art, and visual and performing arts), COMPUTER AND PHYSICAL SCI-

ENCE (astronomy, chemistry, computer science, geology, geophysics and seismology, mathematics, and physics), EDUCATION (education), ENGINEERING AND ENVIRONMENTAL DESIGN (aerospace studies, architectural engineering, architecture, biomedical engineering, chemical engineering, civil engineering, electrical/electronics engineering, geophysical engineering, interior design, landscape architecture/design, mechanical engineering, and petroleum/natural gas engineering), HEALTH PROFESSIONS (medical technology, nursing, pharmacy, and speech pathology/audiology), SOCIAL SCIENCE (American studies, anthropology, archeology, Asian/Oriental studies, child care/child and family studies, classical/ancient civilization, dietetics, Eastern European studies, economics, ethnic studies, geography, history, human ecology, humanities, Islamic studies, Judaic studies, Latin American studies, liberal arts/general studies, Middle Eastern studies, philosophy, physical fitness/movement, political science/government, psychology, religion, Russian and Slavic studies, social work, sociology, textiles and clothing, and urban studies). Biological sciences, electrical and computer engineering, and government are the largest.

Required: All students must maintain a GPA of 2.0 while satisfactorily completing 120 to 167 semester hours. Distribution requirements include 6 hours each in American government, American history, natural science, and courses containing a substantial writing component (with at least 3 hours being upper-division); 3 hours each in math, social science, English composition, literature, and humanities/fine arts; plus 3 additional hours in either math, natural science, computer science, or social science; and a fourth semester proficiency in a single foreign language.

Special: Cooperative programs are available in all engineering courses, microbiology, chemistry, computer science, geology, and actuarial studies. Cross-registration is provided in pharmacy with the University of Texas at San Antonio. Internships, study abroad, B.A.-B.S. degrees, dual majors, student-designed majors for humanities students, and pass/fail options are offered. There are 45 national honor societies, including Phi Beta Kappa, a freshman honors program, and 50 departmental honors programs.

Faculty/Classroom: 66% of faculty are male; 34%, female. All both teach and do research.

Admissions: 47% of the 2003-2004 applicants were accepted. The SAT I scores for the 2003-2004 freshman class were: Verbal--12% below 500, 33% between 500 and 599, 40% between 600 and 700, and 15% above 700; Math--8% below 500, 25% between 500 and 599, 44% between 600 and 700, and 24% above 700. The ACT scores were 11% below 21, 17% between 21 and 23, 27% between 24 and 26, 18% between 27 and 28, and 27% above 28. 90% of the current freshmen were in the top fifth of their class; 98% were in the top two fifths. There were 259 National Merit finalists. 312 freshmen graduated first in their class.

Requirements: The SAT I or ACT is required. In addition, all students graduating in the top 10% of their class from an accredited Texas high school are eligible for admission. Applicants not meeting that requirement are reviewed based on SAT I or ACT scores, class rank, writing samples, and related factors; consideration may be given to socioeconomic and geographic information. In addition, applicants need 15 1/2 academic credits, including 4 in English, 3 each in math and social studies, 2 each in science and foreign language, and 1 1/2 in electives. An audition is required for applied music majors. The GED is accepted, with supportive information. Home-schooled students are required to submit the results of either the SAT II: Subject tests or AP exams in English, math, and a third subject of the student's choosing. AP and CLEP credits are accepted. Important factors in the admissions decision are leadership record, evidence of special talent, and extracurricular activities record.

Procedure: Freshmen are admitted fall, spring, and summer. Entrance exams should be taken in the junior year or early in the senior year. There is a deferred admissions plan and a rolling admissions plan. Applications should be filed by February 1 for fall entry, October 1 for spring entry, and February 1 for summer entry. The fall 2003 application fee was $50. Notification is sent on a rolling basis. Applications are accepted on-line through EXPAN.

Transfer: 1644 transfer students enrolled in 2002-2003. Applicants must have at least 24 transferable hours (30 for business). 30 of 120 credits required for the bachelor's degree must be completed at UT.

Visiting: There are regularly scheduled orientations for prospective students. There are guides for informal visits and visitors may sit in on classes. To schedule a visit, contact the Office of Admissions, Freshman Admissions Center.

Financial Aid: In 2003-2004, 79% of all full-time freshmen and 73% of continuing full-time students received some form of financial aid. 57% of full-time freshmen and 47% of continuing full-time students received need-based aid. The average freshman award was $8670. Need-based scholarships or need-based grants averaged $6120; need-based self-help aid (loans and jobs) averaged $3640; and non-need-based awards and non-need-based scholarships averaged $4470. 20% of undergraduates work part time. The average financial indebtedness of the 2003 graduate was $16,500. The FAFSA is required. The deadline for filing freshman financial aid applications for fall entry is March 31.

International Students: There are 1205 international students enrolled. They must score 550 on the written TOEFL or 213 on the electronic version.

Computers: The mainframe is a Fujitsu 2068E. All buildings are connected to the campus network and UT's 40,000-plus computers have ready access to the Internet. Internet 2 connectivity and Teragrid connectivity are available to support research. 802.11b (WiFi) wireless is available in public spaces on campus. Dial-up access is also provided. All on-campus dorm rooms are wired for high-speed access. A central computer lab in the undergraduate library building provides more than 200 Windows and Macs computers. Department- and college-specific labs provide more seats. In addition, servers on campus support e-mail, calendaring, individual disk allocations and personal Web publishing, course management systems, central and departmental Web publishing, authentication and authorization, personalization of UT access, on-line registration and payment, and hundreds of other applications. All students may access the system 24 hours a day. There are no time limits. The fee is $360. It is recommended that students in College of Education teacher preparation program have personal computers.

Graduates: From July 1, 2002 to June 30, 2003, 8397 bachelor's degrees were awarded. The most popular majors were liberal arts (33%), natural sciences (17%), and communication (14%). In an average class, 3% graduate in 3 years or less, 36% graduate in 4 years or less, 64% graduate in 5 years or less, and 71% graduate in 6 years or less.

Admissions Contact: Freshman Admissions Center.
E-mail: *http://www.utexas.edu/student/admissions/forms/askadmit_comments.html*
Web: *http://bealonghorn.utexas.edu/bal/index.WBX*

UNIVERSITY OF TEXAS AT DALLAS   D-2
Richardson, TX 75083-0688

(972) 883-2346
(800) 889-2443; Fax: (972) 883-6803

Full-time: 3181 men, 2817 women	Faculty: 379; I, +$
Part-time: 1282 men, 1408 women	Ph.D.s: 99%
Graduate: 2796 men, 2234 women	Student/Faculty: 16 to 1
Year: semesters, summer session	Tuition: $4202 ($11,282)
Application Deadline: August 1	Room & Board: $6032
Freshman Class: 5048 applied, 2501 accepted, 1060 enrolled	
SAT I Verbal/Math: 602/630	ACT: 26 HIGHLY COMPETITIVE

The University of Texas at Dallas, founded in 1969 as part of the University of Texas system, offers undergraduate and graduate programs in the liberal arts and sciences, business, engineering, computer science, cognitive science, and neuroscience. There are 8 undergraduate and 8 graduate schools. In addition to regional accreditation, UTD has baccalaureate program accreditation with AACSB and ABET. The library contains 771,517 volumes, 1,914,963 microform items, and 4549 audio/video tapes/CDs, and subscribes to 3080 periodicals. Computerized library services include the card catalog, interlibrary loans, and database searching. Special learning facilities include a learning resource center, art gallery, radio station, center for communications disorders, rare books library, and special library collections on aviation history, geophysics, philatelic research, and the Holocaust. The 455-acre campus is in a suburban area 18 miles north of downtown Dallas. Including any residence halls, there are 81 buildings.

Student Life: 98% of undergraduates are from Texas. Students are from 44 states, 129 foreign countries, and Canada. 93% are from public schools. 52% are white; 17% Asian American; 16% foreign nationals. The average age of freshmen is 19; all undergraduates, 24. 16% do not continue beyond their first year; 56% remain to graduate.

Housing: 3700 students can be accommodated in college housing, which includes coed on-campus apartments and married-student housing. Privately owned campus apartments are also available. On-campus housing is available on a first-come, first-served basis. 60% of students commute. All students may keep cars.

Activities: 6% of men belong to 3 national fraternities; 3% of women belong to 4 national sororities. There are 122 groups on campus, including art, band, cheerleading, chess, choir, chorale, chorus, College Bowl, computers, creative problem solving, dance, debate, drama, ethnic, film, forensics, gay, honors, international, jazz band, literary magazine, musical theater, opera, orchestra, political, professional, religious, social, social service, student government, and yearbook. Popular campus events include Messiah Sing, Jazz Concert, and Hispanic Month activities.

Sports: There are 6 intercollegiate sports for men and 6 for women, and 9 intramural sports for men and 9 for women. Facilities include 4 racquetball courts, 3 squash courts, saunas, 10 lighted tennis courts, indoor and outdoor basketball courts, a sand volleyball court, a 1-mile gravel track, 4 soccer fields, 4 softball fields, a junior Olympic pool/natatorium, and a 4000-seat gym.

Disabled Students: All of the campus is accessible. Wheelchair ramps, elevators, special parking, specially equipped rest rooms, lowered drinking fountains, lowered telephones, interpreters for the deaf, scribes, alternative testing, and a disability services coordinator are available.

Services: Counseling and information services are available, as is tutoring in most subjects. There is a reader service for the blind, and remedial math, reading, and writing.

Campus Safety and Security: Measures include 24-hour foot and vehicle patrol, self-defense education, security escort services, and informal discussions. There are pamphlets/posters/films, emergency telephones, lighted pathways/sidewalks, campus crime watch bulletins for residents, bicycle patrols, crime prevention programs, Operation ID engraving, and a police liaison who works with students on any security or safety issue.

Programs of Study: UTD confers B.A., B.S., and B.S.E.E. degrees. Master's and doctoral degrees are also awarded. Bachelor's degrees are awarded in BIOLOGICAL SCIENCE (biochemistry, biology/biological science, molecular biology, and neurosciences), BUSINESS (accounting and business administration and management), COMMUNICATIONS AND THE ARTS (literature, telecommunications, and visual and performing arts), COMPUTER AND PHYSICAL SCIENCE (applied mathematics, chemistry, computer science, geoscience, mathematics, physics, software engineering, and statistics), ENGINEERING AND ENVIRONMENTAL DESIGN (electrical/electronics engineering), HEALTH PROFESSIONS (speech pathology/audiology), SOCIAL SCIENCE (American studies, cognitive science, criminology, economics, gender studies, geography, history, humanities, interdisciplinary studies, political science/government, psychology, public administration, and sociology). Electrical engineering, biology, and neuroscience are the strongest academically. Business administration, computer science, and electrical engineering are the largest.

Required: To graduate, students must complete at least 120 credit hours, including 30 in the major and 51 in upper-division courses, with a minimum GPA of 2.0. Core courses include 15 credits in social science (with 6 each in U.S./Texas government and U.S./Texas history), 9 in natural science, and 6 each in communications, math, and humanities/fine arts. Magna and summa cum laude graduates must complete a thesis.

Special: Cross-registration is available with other University of Texas campuses and the Health Science Center at Dallas. Accelerated degree programs and B.A.-B.S. degrees are offered in several majors, as is a 3-2 engineering degree with Austin College, Texas Women's University, or Abilene Christian University. Co-op programs, internships, work-study programs with several major corporations, and dual and student-designed majors are possible. Students may study abroad in Europe, Asia, and Mexico. There are 4 national honor societies, a freshman honors program, and 1 departmental honors program.

Faculty/Classroom: 70% of faculty are male; 30%, female. 10% teach undergraduates, 4% do research, and 86% do both. Graduate students teach 1% of introductory courses. The average class size in an introductory lecture is 35; in a laboratory, 15; and in a regular course, 35.

Admissions: 50% of the 2003-2004 applicants were accepted. The SAT I scores for the 2003-2004 freshman class were: Verbal--10% below 500, 35% between 500 and 599, 41% between 600 and 700, and 14% above 700; Math--3% below 500, 31% between 500 and 599, 45% between 600 and 700, and 21% above 700. The ACT scores were 7% below 21, 19% between 21 and 23, 30% between 24 and 26, 14% between 27 and 28, and 30% above 28. 64% of the current freshmen were in the top fifth of their class; 91% were in the top two fifths. There were 30 National Merit finalists and 51 semifinalists. 21 freshmen graduated first in their class.

Requirements: The SAT I or ACT is required. In addition, applicants should be graduates of an accredited secondary school. In-state students who rank in the top 10% of their class gain automatic admission to UTD. Credentials for other students must include completion of 4 units of English, 3.5 of math, 3 each of social science and lab science, 2 of a foreign language, and course work in fine arts and electives, with health and phys ed courses recommended. An essay is required. A GPA of 3.0 is required. AP and CLEP credits are accepted. Important factors in the admissions decision are advanced placement or honor courses, leadership record, and evidence of special talent.

Procedure: Freshmen are admitted to all sessions. Entrance exams should be taken at the end of the junior year or beginning of the senior year. There are early decision, early admissions, and deferred admissions plans. There is a rolling admissions plan. Applications should be filed by August 1 for fall entry, December 1 for spring entry, and May 1 for summer entry, along with a $50 fee. Notification is sent on a rolling basis. Applications are accepted on-line through Texas Common App or the school's web site.

Transfer: 1395 transfer students enrolled in 2002-2003. Sophomore applicants must present a GPA of 3.0 and 12 credits in the general education core. Upper-division applicants should have a GPA of 2.5 and be in good standing at the last school attended. 30 of 120 credits required for the bachelor's degree must be completed at UTD.

Visiting: There are regularly scheduled orientations for prospective students, including meetings with faculty and an admissions counselor, and a campus tour. There are guides for informal visits and visitors may sit in on classes. To schedule a visit, contact the Office of Enrollment Services at (972) 883-2270 or *enrollment@utdallas.edu.*

Financial Aid: In 2003-2004, 62% of all full-time freshmen and 46% of continuing full-time students received some form of financial aid. 67% of undergraduates work part time. Average annual earnings from campus work are $2018. The CSS Profile or FAFSA and the college's own financial statement are required. The deadline for filing freshman financial aid applications for fall entry is April 30.

International Students: There are 447 international students enrolled. They must score 550 on the written TOEFL or 215 on the electronic version and also take the SAT I or the ACT.

Computers: The mainframe is an IBM OS/390 Model 224. Student facilities include more than 300 Pentium PCs, 57 Macs, 23 UCDX terminals, 20 Wyse terminals, plus micro labs. Individual schools provide Sun SPARC stations with terminals. All students have e-mail, Internet, and Web access, with wireless LAN service. All students may access the system 8 A.M. to midnight in most labs, or 24 hours in specific labs and from remote locations. There are no time limits. The fee is $11 per semester credit hour. It is strongly recommended that all students have a personal computer with wireless connection capability.

Graduates: From July 1, 2002 to June 30, 2003, 1604 bachelor's degrees were awarded. The most popular majors were business administration (35%), computer science (15%), and interdisciplinary studies (14%). In an average class, 32% graduate in 4 years or less, 51% graduate in 5 years or less, and 56% graduate in 6 years or less. 632 companies recruited on campus in 2002-2003. Of the 2002 graduating class, 15% were enrolled in graduate school within 6 months of graduation and 57% were employed.

Admissions Contact: Anne P. McLane, Director of Admissions. A video is available. E-mail: *admissions-status@utdallas.edu*
Web: *www.utdallas.edu*

UNIVERSITY OF TEXAS AT EL PASO

A-3

El Paso, TX 79968   (915) 747-5576; Fax: (915) 747-5848

Full-time: 5040 men, 5938 women	**Faculty:** 440; IIA, -$
Part-time: 1871 men, 2236 women	**Ph.D.s:** 90%
Graduate: 1471 men, 1986 women	**Student/Faculty:** 25 to 1
Year: semesters, summer session	**Tuition:** $2964 ($8668)
Application Deadline: July 31	**Room & Board:** $2835
Freshman Class: 3847 applied, 3768 accepted, 2307 enrolled	
SAT I Verbal/Math: 450/450	**ACT:** 18 NONCOMPETITIVE

The University of Texas at El Paso, founded in 1913 and the second oldest academic member of the University of Texas System, was originally called the Texas School of Mines and Metallurgy. It now offers a wide variety of classes through the schools and colleges of business, education, engineering, liberal arts, nursing and allied health, and science. There are 6 undergraduate schools and 1 graduate school. In addition to regional accreditation, UTEP has baccalaureate program accreditation with AACSB, ABET, and NLN. The library contains 1,080,588 volumes, 1,760,984 microform items, and 9995 audio/video tapes/CDs, and subscribes to 3005 periodicals. Computerized library services include the card catalog, interlibrary loans, database searching, and Internet access. Special learning facilities include a learning resource center, art gallery, natural history museum, radio station, TV station, seismic observatory, and the El Paso Centennial Museum. The 366-acre campus is in an urban area. Including any residence halls, there are 87 buildings.

Student Life: 86% of undergraduates are from Texas. Students are from 49 states, 84 foreign countries, and Canada. 95% are from public schools. 71% are Hispanic; 13% white; 12% foreign nationals. The average age of freshmen is 19; all undergraduates, 23. 30% do not continue beyond their first year.

Housing: 443 students can be accommodated in college housing, which includes coed on-campus apartments, fraternity houses, and sorority houses. In addition, there are suites, private rooms, and 24-hour quiet floors. On-campus housing is available on a first-come, first-served basis. 98% of students commute. Alcohol is not permitted. All students may keep cars.

Activities: There are 100 groups on campus, including art, band, cheerleading, chess, choir, chorale, computers, dance, drama, drill team, drum and bugle corps, ethnic, film, honors, international, jazz band, literary magazine, marching band, musical theater, newspaper, opera, orchestra, pep band, photography, political, professional, radio and TV, religious, social, social service, student government, symphony, and yearbook. Popular campus events include Women's History and Hispanic Cultural weeks, and St. Patrick's Engineering Initiation.

Sports: There are 6 intercollegiate sports for men and 5 for women, and 1 intramural sport for men and 1 for women. Facilities include basketball, volleyball, badminton, racquetball, and tennis courts, grass fields for multiple use, an Outdoor Adventure Program with backpacking, bicycling, rafting, and ski trips, a 52,000-seat football stadium, a 12,222-seat basketball gym, a swimming pool, a bowling alley, and a weight room.

Disabled Students: Wheelchair ramps, elevators, special parking, specially equipped rest rooms, special class scheduling, and lowered drinking fountains are available.

Services: Counseling and information services are available, as is tutoring in every subject. There is a reader service for the blind and remedial math, reading, and writing.

Campus Safety and Security: Measures include shuttle buses and lighted pathways/sidewalks.

Programs of Study: UTEP confers B.A., B.S., B.B.A., B.F.A., B.I.S., B.M., B.S.C.E., B.S.C.S., B.S.Ed., B.S.E.E., B.S.I.E., B.S.MeT.E., B.S.N., and B.S.W. degrees. Master's and doctoral degrees are also awarded. Bachelor's degrees are awarded in BIOLOGICAL SCIENCE (biology/biological science and microbiology), BUSINESS (accounting, banking and finance, business economics, management information systems, management science, and marketing/retailing/merchandising), COMMUNICATIONS AND THE ARTS (art, communications, dramatic arts, English, French, German, journalism, languages, linguistics, music, Spanish, speech/debate/rhetoric, and theater management), COMPUTER AND PHYSICAL SCIENCE (applied mathematics, chemistry, computer science, earth science, geology, geophysics and seismology, mathematics, physics, science, and statistics), ENGINEERING AND ENVIRONMENTAL DESIGN (civil engineering, electrical/electronics engineering, industrial engineering technology, mechanical engineering, and metallurgical engineering), HEALTH PROFESSIONS (allied health, clinical science, health science, medical laboratory technology, and nursing), SOCIAL SCIENCE (anthropology, criminal justice, economics, history, interdisciplinary studies, Latin American studies, Mexican-American/Chicano studies, philosophy, physical fitness/movement, political science/government, psychology, social work, and sociology). Business, nursing, and engineering are the strongest academically. Criminal justice, interdisciplinary, and kinesiology are the largest.

Required: All students must have a minimum GPA of 2.0 while taking 125 to 130 semester hours. Students also must complete a distribution of courses through the general foundation program.

Special: Cross-registration with the University of Texas at Austin and the University of Texas Health Science Center is available. Internships, mainly at the graduate level, study abroad in London and Hildesheim, Germany, work-study programs, nondegree study, and pass/fail options are available. There also is the Inter-American Sciences and Humanities Program for students from Spanish-speaking countries whose English is less than adequate for normal study in the United States. The Center for Inter-American and Border Studies also promotes teaching, research, and outreach programs to further the understanding of Latin America. Similar studies are offered through the Cross-Cultural Southwest Ethnic Study Center. There is a freshman honors program.

Faculty/Classroom: 60% of faculty are male; 40%, female. The average class size in an introductory lecture is 25; in a laboratory, 15; and in a regular course, 22.

Admissions: 98% of the 2003-2004 applicants were accepted. The SAT I scores for the 2003-2004 freshman class were: Verbal--71% below 500, 24% between 500 and 599, and 5% between 600 and 700; Math--68% below 500, 27% between 500 and 599, and 5% between 600 and 700. The ACT scores were 71% below 21, 20% between 21 and 23, 7% between 24 and 26, 2% between 27 and 28, and 1% above 28. 33% of the current freshmen were in the top fifth of their class; 61% were in the top two fifths.

Requirements: The SAT I or ACT is required. For citizens or permanent residents of the United States who have graduated within the past 5 years, the SAT I, with a score of 700 for those ranking in the second quarter of their class, or the ACT, with a score of 15, is required. UTEP recommends high school preparation that includes 4 years of English, 3 to 3.5 of math, 3 each of natural science and social studies, and 2 of foreign language. The GED is accepted. A GPA of 2.0 is required. AP and CLEP credits are accepted.

Procedure: Freshmen are admitted to all sessions. There are early admissions and deferred admissions plans. There is a rolling admissions plan. Applications should be filed by July 31 for fall entry. The college accepts all applicants. Notification is sent on a rolling basis.

Transfer: 1754 transfer students enrolled in 2002-2003. Transfer applicants must have at least a C average and must be eligible to return to all previous institutions attended. 30 credits of 125 to 130 required for the bachelor's degree must be completed at UTEP.

Visiting: There are regularly scheduled orientations for prospective students, including preenrollment counseling and campus tours. There are guides for informal visits and visitors may sit in on classes and stay overnight. To schedule a visit, contact Beto Lopez, Recruiting Office.

Financial Aid: In a recent year, 18% of all full-time freshmen and 82% of continuing full-time students received some form of financial aid. The average financial indebtedness of a recent graduate was $12,825. UTEP is a member of CSS. The FAFSA and the college's own financial statement are required. The deadline for filing freshman financial aid applications for fall entry is March 15.

International Students: There are 1559 international students enrolled. The school actively recruits these students. They must score 500 on the written TOEFL and also take the PAA. They must also take the SAT I or ACT, with a required minimum score on the SAT I (combined) of 920, with a minimum of 400 on the verbal, and 20 (composite) on the ACT, with a 21 minimum on the English section.

Computers: The mainframe is an IBM 3270. Students use terminals to access the mainframe from various sites on campus. All computing facilities are interconnected by a campuswide data communication network. Those students enrolled in computer courses or with department permission may access the system. There are no time limits. The fee is $10.

Graduates: From July 1, 2002 to June 30, 2003, 2760 bachelor's degrees were awarded. The most popular majors were interdisciplinary studies/education (40%), engineering/engineering technologies (17%), and business/marketing (9%). In an average class, 3% graduate in 4 years or less, 15% graduate in 5 years or less, and 25% graduate in 6 years or less.

Admissions Contact: Irma Nu¹ez Rubio, Director of Admissions. A video is available. E-mail: *admission@utep.edu*
Web: *www.utep.edu/enroll/*

UNIVERSITY OF TEXAS AT SAN ANTONIO   D-4
San Antonio, TX 78249   (210) 458-4530
(800) 669-0919; Fax: (210) 458-5959

Full-time: 5560 men, 6475 women	Faculty: 350
Part-time: 2295 men, 3090 women	Ph.D.s: 99%
Graduate: 1035 men, 1455 women	Student/Faculty: 34 to 1
Year: semesters, summer session	Tuition: $2975 ($8040)
Application Deadline: see profile	Room & Board: $6115
Freshman Class: n/av	
SAT I or ACT: required	NONCOMPETITIVE

The University of Texas at San Antonio was established as part of the state university system in 1969 and is now a large, comprehensive institution offering undergraduate and graduate programs in arts, business, engineering, music, health science, and education. There are 6 undergraduate schools. Figures in the above capsule and in this profile are approximate. In addition to regional accreditation, UTSA has baccalaureate program accreditation with AACSB, ABET, NASAD, and NASM. The 2 libraries contain 550,000 volumes, 3 million microform items, and 10,300 audio/video tapes/CDs, and subscribe to 2000 periodicals. Computerized library services include the card catalog, interlibrary loans, and database searching. Special learning facilities include a learning resource center, art gallery, and Institute of Texan Cultures. The 600-acre campus is in a suburban area approximately 18 miles northwest of downtown San Antonio. Including any residence halls, there are 35 buildings.

Student Life: 95% of undergraduates are from Texas. Students are from 50 states, 85 foreign countries, and Canada. 91% are from public schools. 46% are Hispanic; 42% white. The average age of freshmen is 18; all undergraduates, 25. 36% do not continue beyond their first year; 25% remain to graduate.

Housing: 1965 students can be accommodated in college housing, which includes coed dorms and on-campus apartments. On-campus housing is available on a first-come, first-served basis. 90% of students commute. All students may keep cars.

Activities: 3% of men belong to 9 national fraternities; 1% of women belong to 6 national sororities. There are 141 groups on campus, including art, band, cheerleading, chess, choir, chorale, chorus, computers, debate, drama, ethnic, gay, honors, international, jazz band, literary magazine, musical theater, newspaper, orchestra, pep band, political, professional, religious, social, social service, student government, symphony, and yearbook. Popular campus events include Fiesta UTSA, Best Fest, and Folk Life festival.

Sports: There are 7 intercollegiate sports for men and 7 for women, and 9 intramural sports for men and 9 for women. Facilities include gyms, weight machines, a jogging path and a 400-meter track, a tennis center, an indoor pool, various playing fields, and courts for basketball, volleyball, badminton, and shuffleboard.

Disabled Students: All of the campus is accessible. Wheelchair ramps, elevators, special parking, specially equipped rest rooms, special class scheduling, lowered drinking fountains, and lowered telephones are available.

Services: Counseling and information services are available, as is tutoring in every subject. There is a reader service for the blind and remedial math, reading, and writing.

Campus Safety and Security: Measures include 24-hour foot and vehicle patrol, self-defense education, security escort services, and shuttle buses. There are informal discussions, pamphlets/posters/films, emergency telephones, and lighted pathways/sidewalks.

Programs of Study: UTSA confers B.A., B.S., B.B.A, B.F.A., B.M., B.S.C.E., B.S.E.E., and B.S.M.E. degrees. Master's and doctoral degrees are also awarded. Bachelor's degrees are awarded in BIOLOGICAL SCIENCE (biology/biological science), BUSINESS (accounting, banking and finance, business administration and management, business economics, entrepreneurial studies, human resources, international business management, management information systems, management science, marketing/retailing/merchandising, personnel management, and tourism), COMMUNICATIONS AND THE ARTS (art, classics, communications, English, fine arts, French, German, music, and Spanish), COMPUTER AND PHYSICAL SCIENCE (chemistry, computer science, geology, information sciences and systems, mathematics, and physics), ENGINEERING AND ENVIRONMENTAL DESIGN (architecture, civil engineering, construction management, electrical/electronics engineering, interior design, and mechanical engineering), HEALTH PROFESSIONS (clinical science, health, and occupational therapy), SOCIAL SCIENCE (American studies, anthropology, criminal justice, economics, geography, history, humanities, interdisciplinary studies, Mexican-American/Chicano studies, philosophy, physical fitness/movement, political science/government, psychology, and sociology). Business, engineering, and life sciences are the strongest academically. Business, life sciences, and education and human development are the largest.

Required: All students must complete at least 120 credit hours with a 2.0 GPA for graduation. Core curriculum requirements total 54 credits and include courses in fine arts, composition, computer science or logic, economics, foreign language, American and Texas history, social science, literacy studies, math, U.S. and Texas constitutions, natural science, and interdisciplinary studies.

Special: UTSA offers joint degrees in occupational therapy and clinical lab sciences with the University of Texas Health Science Center and study abroad in many countries. Internships, work-study, nondegree study, and pass/fail options are available. There are 31 national honor societies, a freshman honors program, and 17 departmental honors programs.

Faculty/Classroom: 61% of faculty are male; 39%, female. 89% teach undergraduates and 13% both teach and do research. Graduate students teach 12% of introductory courses. The average class size in an introductory lecture is 58; in a laboratory, 19; and in a regular course, 29.

Admissions: In a recent year, there was 1 National Merit finalist. 16 freshmen graduated first in their class.

Requirements: The SAT I or ACT is required. Admission is based on a formula derived from class rank and SAT I or ACT scores. Applicants must be graduates of accredited high schools or have earned the GED. UTSA recommends that high school preparation include 4 units of English, at least 3 of math, at least 2 each of a foreign language, natural science, and social science, and at least 1 of fine arts. AP and CLEP credits are accepted.

Procedure: Freshmen are admitted to all sessions. Entrance exams should be taken in the spring of the junior year. There is a rolling admissions plan. Check with the school for current deadlines. The fall 2003 application fee was $25. Notification is sent on a rolling basis.

Transfer: 1404 transfer students enrolled in a recent year. Applicants with at least 30 hours of college credit must present a C average in all college work attempted and evidence of good standing. Those with fewer than 30 hours must meet freshman admission standards as well. 30 of 120 credits required for the bachelor's degree must be completed at UTSA.

Visiting: There are regularly scheduled orientations for prospective students. There are guides for informal visits. To schedule a visit, contact New Student Programs at (210) 458-4724 or *orientation@utsa.edu.*

Financial Aid: In a recent year, 51% of all full-time freshmen and 57% of continuing full-time students received some form of financial aid. 63% of full-time freshmen and 66% of continuing full-time students received need-based aid. The average freshman award was $8750. 13% of undergraduates work part time. Average annual earnings from campus work are $1460. The average financial indebtedness of a recent graduate was $16,125. The FAFSA is required. Check with the school for current deadlines.

International Students: In a recent year, there were 254 international students enrolled. The school actively recruits these students. They must score 550 on the written TOEFL and also take the SAT I or the ACT.

Computers: The mainframe is an IBM 4341. A large computer lab is available with 800 IBM and Mac PCs used with a variety of software options. Specialty computer labs are also available, such as for engineering applications. All students may access the system 24 hours a day. There are no time limits. The fall 2003 fee was $56 to $168 per semester.

Graduates: In a recent year, 2591 bachelor's degrees were awarded. The most popular majors were business (22%), interdisciplinary studies (15%), and biology (8%). In an average class, 1% graduate in 3 years or less, 7% graduate in 4 years or less, 18% graduate in 5 years or less, and 27% graduate in 6 years or less. 144 companies recruited on campus in a recent year.

Admissions Contact: John Wallace, Interim Director of Admissions and Registrar. E-mail: *prospects@utsa.edu* Web: *www.utsa.edu*

UNIVERSITY OF TEXAS-PAN AMERICAN   D-5
Edinburg, TX 78541-2999

Full-time: 4081 men, 5652 women	(956) 381-2209; Fax: (956) 381-2212
Part-time: 1727 men, 2409 women	**Faculty:** 479; IIA, av$
Graduate: 728 men, 1317 women	**Ph.D.s:** n/av
Year: semesters, summer session	**Student/Faculty:** 20 to 1
Application Deadline: July	**Tuition:** $2466 ($8130)
	Room & Board: $3488
Freshman Class: 6704 applied, 4795 accepted, 2419 enrolled	
ACT: 18	**LESS COMPETITIVE**

University of Texas-Pan American, founded in 1927, is a state-supported institution offering programs in the arts and sciences, education, business, and health-related professions. It is part of the University of Texas system. There are 6 undergraduate and 6 graduate schools. In addition to regional accreditation, UT Pan American has baccalaureate program accreditation with AACSB, ABET, ACOTE, ACS, ADA, AOTA, ASLA, CAHEA, CSWE, NAACLS, NCATE, and NLN. The library contains 565,184 volumes, 1,070,388 microform items, and 24,705 audio/video tapes/CDs, and subscribes to more than 8000 periodicals. Computerized library services include interlibrary loans, database searching, and Internet access. Special learning facilities include a learning resource center, art gallery, planetarium, and a coastal studies lab. The 238-acre campus is in a small town close to the Mexican border and the Gulf of Mexico. Including any residence halls, there are 53 buildings.

Student Life: 98% of undergraduates are from Texas. Students are from 35 states and Canada. 87% are Hispanic. The average age of freshmen is 19; all undergraduates, 23. 34% do not continue beyond their first year; 66% remain to graduate.

Housing: 580 students can be accommodated in college housing, which includes single-sex and coed dorms and on-campus apartments. On-campus housing is available on a first-come, first-served basis. 90% of students commute. Alcohol is not permitted. All students may keep cars.

Activities: 1% of men belong to 7 national fraternities; 1% of women belong to 1 local and 5 national sororities. There are 119 groups on campus, including academic, art, cheerleading, choir, chorus, computers, dance, drama, ethnic, film, gay, honors, international, jazz band, literary magazine, musical theater, newspaper, opera, orchestra, photography, political, professional, radio and TV, religious, social, social service, student government, symphony, and yearbook. Popular campus events include Cinco de Mayo, Spirit Week, and Bronco Day.

Sports: There are 7 intercollegiate sports for men and 7 for women, and 13 intramural sports for men and 13 for women. Facilities include a 4000-seat field house, baseball and tennis stadiums, a track, and a soccer field.

Disabled Students: 95% of the campus is accessible. Wheelchair ramps, elevators, special parking, specially equipped rest rooms, special class scheduling, lowered drinking fountains, lowered telephones, special housing, TDD phones, readers, and note takers are available.

Services: Counseling and information services are available, as is tutoring in some subjects, including biology, chemistry, history, Spanish, math, philosophy, political science, French, English, physics, and physical sciences. There is a reader service for the blind and remedial math, reading, and writing. The Learning Assistance Center provides small-group and individual tutoring and computer-aided instruction.

Campus Safety and Security: Measures include 24-hour foot and vehicle patrol, self-defense education, security escort services, and pamphlets/posters/films. There are emergency telephones, lighted pathways/sidewalks, and a university police department.

Programs of Study: UT Pan American confers B.A., B.S., B.A.A.S., B.A.S.C., B.B.A., B.F.A., B.G.S., B.I.S., B.S.C.J., B.S.C.S., B.S.E.E., B.S.M.E., B.S.M.F., B.S.N., B.S.O.T., B.S.P.A., and B.S.W. degrees. Master's and doctoral degrees are also awarded. Bachelor's degrees are awarded in BIOLOGICAL SCIENCE (biology/biological science), BUSINESS (accounting, banking and finance, international business management, management science, and marketing/retailing/merchandising), COMMUNICATIONS AND THE ARTS (art, communications, dramatic arts, English, fine arts, journalism, music, and Spanish), COMPUTER AND PHYSICAL SCIENCE (chemistry, computer science, information sciences and systems, mathematics, and physics), EDUCATION (secondary), ENGINEERING AND ENVIRONMENTAL DESIGN (electrical/electronics engineering, manufacturing engineering, and mechanical engineering), HEALTH PROFESSIONS (health, medical technology, nursing, occupational therapy, physician's assistant, rehabilitation therapy, and speech pathology/audiology), SOCIAL SCIENCE (anthropology, corrections, criminal justice, dietetics, economics, history, interdisciplinary studies, Latin American studies, liberal arts/general studies, Mexican-American/Chicano studies, philosophy, physical fitness/movement, political science/government, psychology, social work, and sociology). Engineering and business are the strongest academically. Education, nursing, and engineering are the largest.

Required: To graduate, students must complete 124 to 137 semester hours with a 2.0 GPA. At least 30 hours are required in the major. Students must also fulfill a general education requirement of 48 hours by taking 18 hours in humanities (including English and a foreign language), 15 hours of social science (including U.S. history and Texas government), 11 hours of lab science and math, and 2 hours each of phys ed and computer science. Other requirements vary according to degree.

Special: Internships, co-op programs, study abroad, work-study programs, dual majors, and nondegree study are available. There are 3 national honor societies, a freshman honors program, and 6 departmental honors programs.

Faculty/Classroom: 65% of faculty are male; 36%, female.

Admissions: 72% of the 2003-2004 applicants were accepted. The SAT I scores for the 2003-2004 freshman class were: Verbal--71% below 500, 24% between 500 and 599, and 5% between 600 and 700; Math--

69% below 500, 25% between 500 and 599, and 6% between 600 and 700. The ACT scores were 74% below 21, 15% between 21 and 23, 8% between 24 and 26, 2% between 27 and 28, and 1% above 28. 27% of the current freshmen were in the top fifth of their class; 58% were in the top two fifths.

Requirements: The SAT I or ACT is required. The ACT is preferred. Applicants must be graduates of an accredited high school or have the GED. 21 academic units are required, including 4 units of English; 3 units of math, at least 1 of which must be algebra; 2 units of science; 1 unit each of world history and U.S. history; and 1/2 unit each of U.S. government, economics, phys ed, and health education. An additional 7 units may be taken in electives. A GPA of 2.0 is required. AP and CLEP credits are accepted.

Procedure: Freshmen are admitted to all sessions. There is an early admissions plan. There is a rolling admissions plan. Early decision applications should be filed by early February; regular applications, by early July for fall entry, mid-November for spring entry, and early April for summer entry. Notification is sent on a rolling basis. Applications are accepted on-line.

Transfer: 637 transfer students enrolled in a recent year. Transfer applicants must meet the same criteria as entering freshman. 30 of 124 to 137 credits required for the bachelor's degree must be completed at UT Pan American.

Visiting: There are regularly scheduled orientations for prospective students. There are guides for informal visits and visitors may sit in on classes. To schedule a visit, contact the Admissions Office: Recruitment and Orientation at (956) 381-3541.

Financial Aid: In a recent year, 77% of all full-time freshmen and 53% of continuing full-time students received some form of financial aid. 74% of full-time freshmen and 34% of continuing full-time students received need-based aid. The CSS Profile or FAFSA is required. The deadline for filing freshman financial aid applications for fall entry is April 15.

International Students: The school actively recruits these students. They must score 500 on the written TOEFL and also take the ACT.

Computers: The mainframe is a DEC VAX 10. The Academic Services building has 600 workstations open to students. All have access to the network. There are 100 PCs in the library, also connected to the network. All students may access the system. There are no time limits. The fee is $9 per credit hour up to a maximum of $27 per semester.

Graduates: From July 1, 2002 to June 30, 2003, 1634 bachelor's degrees were awarded. The most popular majors were interdisciplinary studies (20%), kinesiology (6%), and biology (6%). In an average class, 5% graduate in 4 years or less, 16% graduate in 5 years or less, and 25% graduate in 6 years or less. 256 companies recruited on campus in 2002-2003.

Admissions Contact: David R. Zuniga, Director of Admissions and Records and Registrar. E-mail: *admissions@panam.edu*
Web: *http://www.panam.edu*

UNIVERSITY OF THE INCARNATE WORD   D-4
San Antonio, TX 78209-6397   (210) 829-6005
                                    (800) 749-WORD; Fax: (210) 829-3921

Full-time: 710 men, 1402 women	**Faculty:** 121; IIA, --$
Part-time: 504 men, 1049 women	**Ph.D.s:** 73%
Graduate: 277 men, 492 women	**Student/Faculty:** 17 to 1
Year: semesters, summer session	**Tuition:** $16,082
Application Deadline: open	**Room & Board:** $5690
Freshman Class: 1422 applied, 1234 accepted, 406 enrolled	
SAT I Verbal/Math: 480/470	**ACT:** 20 **LESS COMPETITIVE**

University of the Incarnate Word, founded in 1881, is a liberal arts institution affiliated with the Catholic Church that offers undergraduate programs in art, business, health science, education, music, religious studies, nursing, and fine arts. Some information in this capsule and profile is approximate. There are 5 undergraduate schools and 1 graduate school. In addition to regional accreditation, UIW has baccalaureate program accreditation with ACBSP, ADA, AHEA, CAHEA, NCATE, and NLN. The library contains 226,111 volumes, 219,226 microform items, and 36,845 audio/video tapes/CDs, and subscribes to 8555 periodicals. Computerized library services include the card catalog, interlibrary loans, and database searching. Special learning facilities include a learning resource center, art gallery, media service center, and teaching theater. The 100-acre campus is in an urban area about 3 miles north of downtown San Antonio. Including any residence halls, there are 18 buildings.

Student Life: 90% of undergraduates are from Texas. Students are from 27 states, 38 foreign countries, and Canada. 75% are from public schools. 48% are Hispanic; 35% white. 52% are Catholic; 27% Protestant; 21% claim no religious affiliation. The average age of freshmen is 18; all undergraduates, 22. 22% do not continue beyond their first year; 39% remain to graduate.

Housing: 650 students can be accommodated in college housing, which includes single-sex and coed dorms and on-campus apartments. On-campus housing is guaranteed for all 4 years. 81% of students commute. All students may keep cars.

Activities: 5% of men belong to 1 local fraternity; 20% of women belong to 3 local sororities. There are 30 groups on campus, including art, cheerleading, choir, chorale, chorus, dance, drama, drill team, ethnic, honors, international, jazz band, literary magazine, musical theater, orchestra, pep band, political, professional, religious, social, social service, student government, and yearbook. Popular campus events include Fiesta Fashion Show, Incarnate Word Day, and Higher Education Week.

Sports: There are 6 intercollegiate sports for men and 5 for women, and 23 intramural sports for men and 23 for women. Facilities include a convocation center, a field house, 8 tennis courts, 2 soccer fields, softball and baseball fields, a 1/4-mile track, a 3/4-mile jogging trail, a gym, basketball courts, a natatorium, and weight and aerobics rooms.

Disabled Students: 85% of the campus is accessible. Wheelchair ramps, elevators, special parking, specially equipped rest rooms, and special class scheduling are available.

Services: Counseling and information services are available, as is tutoring in most subjects. There is remedial math, reading, and writing.

Campus Safety and Security: Measures include 24-hour foot and vehicle patrol, self-defense education, security escort services, and shuttle buses. There are informal discussions, pamphlets/posters/films, emergency telephones, lighted pathways/sidewalks, and a professional security force on campus.

Programs of Study: UIW confers B.A., B.S., B.B.A., and B.M. degrees. Master's and doctoral degrees are also awarded. Bachelor's degrees are awarded in BIOLOGICAL SCIENCE (biology/biological science and nutrition), BUSINESS (accounting, banking and finance, business administration and management, fashion merchandising, hotel/motel and restaurant management, international business management, management science, marketing/retailing/merchandising, and sports management), COMMUNICATIONS AND THE ARTS (art, communications, dramatic arts, English, music, music business management, and Spanish), COMPUTER AND PHYSICAL SCIENCE (chemistry, computer management, information sciences and systems, and mathematics), EDUCATION (business, early childhood, elementary, middle school, music, physical, science, secondary, and special), ENGINEERING AND ENVIRONMENTAL DESIGN (environmental science and interior design), HEALTH PROFESSIONS (medical laboratory technology, music therapy, nuclear medical technology, nursing, predentistry, and premedicine), SOCIAL SCIENCE (dietetics, fashion design and technology, history, Native American studies, philosophy, political science/government, prelaw, psychology, religion, and sociology). Preprofessional, nursing, and business are the strongest academically. Business is the largest.

Required: To graduate, students must complete at least 128 credit hours, with a minimum GPA of 2.0. An extensive required core curriculum of 67 credit hours includes world literature, critical discourse, dimensions of wellness, computer literacy, and a capstone. A total of 40 hours of community service also is required.

Special: UIW offers co-op programs in all business majors, commercial arts, fashion design and merchandising, and sports management. There is cross-registration with Our Lady of the Lake and Saint Mary's Universities, numerous internship opportunities, a spring Washington semester, work-study programs, and study abroad, including China, Taiwan, Japan, Cuba, and Great Britain. There are 4 national honor societies.

Faculty/Classroom: 48% of faculty are male; 52%, female. All teach undergraduates. No introductory courses are taught by graduate students. The average class size in an introductory lecture is 27; in a laboratory, 17; and in a regular course, 16.

Admissions: 87% of the 2003-2004 applicants were accepted. The SAT I scores for the 2003-2004 freshman class were: Verbal--52% below 500, 34% between 500 and 599, 12% between 600 and 700, and 2% above 700; Math--59% below 500, 29% between 500 and 599, 11% between 600 and 700, and 1% above 700. The ACT scores were 57% below 21, 20% between 21 and 23, 14% between 24 and 26, 5% between 27 and 28, and 4% above 28. 37% of the current freshmen were in the top fifth of their class; 57% were in the top two fifths.

Requirements: The SAT I or ACT is required, with minimum composite scores of 920 on the SAT I or 18 on the ACT. Applicants must be graduates of an accredited secondary school or have the GED and have completed 16 Carnegie units, including at least 4 units of English, 3 of social studies and history, 2 each of math, science, and foreign language, and 1 of fine arts. In some cases, UIW may administer its own assessment tests for placement and require an interview. A GPA of 2.0 is required. AP and CLEP credits are accepted. Important factors in the admissions decision are recommendations by alumni, parents or siblings attending the school, and ability to finance college education.

Procedure: Freshmen are admitted to all sessions. Entrance exams should be taken in the junior or senior year of high school. There is a deferred admissions plan and a rolling admissions plan. Application deadlines are open. The fall 2003 application fee was $20. Notification is sent on a rolling basis. Applications are accepted on-line through *www.uiw.edu*.

Transfer: 320 transfer students enrolled in a recent year. Transfer students must have a minimum 2.5 GPA if they have at least 30 transferable hours. Other students may have to take an academic assessment test and/or be individually reviewed, and submit high school and college records and SAT I or ACT scores. 36 credits of at least 128 required for the bachelor's degree must be completed at UIW.

Visiting: There are regularly scheduled orientations for prospective students, consisting of an introduction to services, a campus tour, assessment testing, advisement, and registration. There are guides for informal visits and visitors may sit in on classes and stay overnight. To schedule a visit, contact the Office of Admissions at *admis@universe.uiwtx.edu.*

Financial Aid: In 2003-2004, 73% of all full-time freshmen and 68% of continuing full-time students received some form of financial aid. 72% of full-time freshmen and 65% of continuing full-time students received need-based aid. The average freshman award was $11,404. Need-based scholarships or need-based grants averaged $7279 ($13,450 maximum); need-based self-help aid (loans and jobs) averaged $3320 ($8342 maximum); non-need-based athletic scholarships averaged $12,913 ($20,226 maximum); and other non-need-based awards and non-need-based scholarships averaged $5967 ($16,800 maximum). 65% of undergraduates work part time. Average annual earnings from campus work are $2000. The average financial indebtedness of a recent graduate was $38,000. The FAFSA and the college's own financial statement are required. Check with the school for current deadlines.

International Students: There were 195 international students enrolled in a recent year. The school actively recruits these students. They must score 550 on the written TOEFL and also take the college's own test.

Computers: The mainframes are an HPN 4000 and HPR 390. More than 300 PCs are available for learning instruction. The campus is fully wired, with ports in all campus housing. All students may access the system 24 hours a day, 7 days a week. There are no time limits and no fees. It is strongly recommended that all students have a personal computer. Juniors and seniors in business must have laptops. The School of Business and Applied Arts and Sciences has specific requirements.

Graduates: In a recent year, 583 bachelor's degrees were awarded. The most popular majors were business administration (39%), nursing (11%), and liberal arts (11%). In an average class, 13% graduate in 4 years or less, and 32% graduate in 5 years or less. 26 companies recruited on campus in a recent year.

Admissions Contact: Andrea Cyterski, Director of Admissions. A video is available. E-mail: *cyterski@universe.uiwtx.edu*
Web: *www.uiw.edu*

WAYLAND BAPTIST UNIVERSITY
B-2
Plainview, TX 79072　　　　(806) 291-3500; (800) 588-1928

Full-time: 346 men, 467 women	**Faculty:** 71
Part-time: 59 men, 126 women	**Ph.D.s:** 72%
Graduate: 12 men, 24 women	**Student/Faculty:** 11 to 1
Year: semesters, summer session	**Tuition:** $8500
Application Deadline: open	**Room & Board:** $3419
Freshman Class: n/av	
SAT I or ACT: required	**NONCOMPETITIVE**

Wayland Baptist University, founded in 1908, is a private liberal arts school affiliated with the Baptist General Convention of Texas (Southern Baptist). There are 8 undergraduate schools and 1 graduate school. In addition to regional accreditation, Wayland has baccalaureate program accreditation with NASM. The library contains 117,287 volumes, 301,287 microform items, and 11,382 audio/video tapes/CDs, and subscribes to 538 periodicals. Computerized library services include the card catalog, interlibrary loans, database searching, and Internet access. Special learning facilities include a learning resource center, art gallery, natural history museum, radio station, and TV station. The 80-acre campus is in a small town 45 miles north of Lubbock. Including any residence halls, there are 41 buildings.

Student Life: 86% of undergraduates are from Texas. Students are from 13 states, 13 foreign countries, and Canada. 43% are white; 16% Hispanic. Most are Protestant. The average age of freshmen is 19; all undergraduates, 23. 41% do not continue beyond their first year; 33% remain to graduate.

Housing: 519 students can be accommodated in college housing, which includes single-sex dorms and married-student housing. On-campus housing is guaranteed for all 4 years. 53% of students live on campus. Alcohol is not permitted. All students may keep cars.

Activities: There is 1 local and 1 national fraternity and 1 local and 1 national sorority. There are 37 groups on campus, including art, band, cheerleading, choir, chorale, chorus, computers, drama, honors, international, marching band, musical theater, newspaper, photography, political, professional, radio and TV, religious, social, social service, student government, and yearbook. Popular campus events include Pride Week, Big Weekend, and Miss Wayland.

Sports: There are 5 intercollegiate sports for men and 5 for women, and 5 intramural sports for men and 5 for women. Facilities include a 2500-seat gym, basketball/volleyball, racquetball, and tennis courts, and an aerobics and weight training facility.

Disabled Students: All of the campus is accessible. Wheelchair ramps, elevators, special parking, specially equipped rest rooms, and special class scheduling are available.

Services: Counseling and information services are available, as is tutoring in every subject. There is a reader service for the blind and remedial math, reading, and writing.

Campus Safety and Security: Measures include self-defense education, informal discussions, pamphlets/posters/films, and emergency telephones. There are lighted pathways/sidewalks and a security service on campus.

Programs of Study: Wayland confers B.A., B.S., B.B.A., B.M., B.S.I.S., and B.S.O.E. degrees. Associate and master's degrees are also awarded. Bachelor's degrees are awarded in BIOLOGICAL SCIENCE (biology/biological science), BUSINESS (business administration and management), COMMUNICATIONS AND THE ARTS (art, communications, dramatic arts, English, music, and Spanish), COMPUTER AND PHYSICAL SCIENCE (chemistry, mathematics, physical sciences, and science), EDUCATION (music, physical, and vocational), SOCIAL SCIENCE (criminal justice, history, human services, interdisciplinary studies, political science/government, psychology, religion, religious education, religious music, social science, and social studies). Religion, education, and social science are the strongest academically. Education, business, and religion are the largest.

Required: To graduate, all students must earn a GPA of at least 2.0 while taking 124 to 145 semester hours, with 30 to 42 in their major and 36 to 42 in upper-division hours. Distribution requirements include 12 hours of English; 8 to 16 in science; 6 each in Bible, history, and humanities; up to 6 in foreign language; 4 in phys ed; 3 to 6 in math; 3 in computer science; and 3 in philosophy, sociology, or psychology. Chapel attendance is also required. Honors students must complete a thesis.

Special: A cooperative education program with Texas Tech University, internships in social science, business administration, religion, education, and social work, and work-study plans through the Social Security Administration are available. In addition, credit for life and military experience is given in the individualized occupational education program. Nondegree study in the lifelong learning program is also offered. There are composite science, composite social science, all-level phys ed, and music programs available. There are 3 national honor societies and a freshman honors program.

Faculty/Classroom: 70% of faculty are male; 30%, female. All teach undergraduates. No introductory courses are taught by graduate students. The average class size in an introductory lecture is 16; in a laboratory, 13; and in a regular course, 14.

Admissions: 31% of the current freshmen were in the top fifth of their class; 58% were in the top two fifths. 4 freshmen graduated first in their class.

Requirements: The SAT I or ACT is required. In addition, Wayland requires graduation from an accredited secondary school with 3 years of English and 2 years each of science, math, and social science. The GED is accepted. Wayland requires applicants to be in the upper 50% of their class. AP and CLEP credits are accepted.

Procedure: Freshmen are admitted to all sessions. There is a rolling admissions plan. Application deadlines are open. The fall 2003 application feee was $35.

Transfer: 73 transfer students enrolled in 2002-2003. Applicants need a minimum GPA of 2.0 and must be able to reenter all colleges previously attended. 30 of 124 to 145 credits required for the bachelor's degree must be completed at Wayland.

Visiting: There are regularly scheduled orientations for prospective students. There are guides for informal visits and visitors may sit in on classes and stay overnight. To schedule a visit, contact Shawn Thomas, Director of Admissions at *sthomas@wbu.edu.*

Financial Aid: In 2003-2004, 88% of all full-time freshmen and 85% of continuing full-time students received some form of financial aid. 89% of full-time freshmen and 65% of continuing full-time students received need-based aid. The average freshman award was $9156. Need-based scholarships or need-based grants averaged $2330 ($9808 maximum); need-based self-help aid (loans and jobs) averaged $1860 ($8796 maximum); non-need-based athletic scholarships averaged $3975 ($12,700 maximum); and other non-need-based awards and non-need-based scholarships averaged $1875 ($16,190 maximum). 15% of undergraduates work part time. Average annual earnings from campus work are $2360. The average financial indebtedness of the 2003 graduate was $20,000. Wayland is a member of CSS. The FAFSA is required. The deadline for filing freshman financial aid applications for fall entry is May 1.

International Students: There are 14 international students enrolled. The school actively recruits these students. They must score 500 on the written TOEFL or 173 on the electronic version and also take the SAT I or the ACT.

Computers: There are123 PCs available on the Plainview campus, including 21 in the Learning Resource Center Lab. Students have access to the Internet through all of these computers. All students may access the system during posted lab hours. There are no time limits and no fees.

Graduates: From July 1, 2002 to June 30, 2003, 98 bachelor's degrees were awarded. The most popular majors were business administration and management (26%), education (15%), and psychology (8%). In an average class, 2% graduate in 3 years or less, 17% graduate in 4 years or less, 27% graduate in 5 years or less, and 33% graduate in 6 years or less.

Admissions Contact: Shawn Thomas, Director of Admissions.
E-mail: *admityou@wbu.edu* Web: *www.wbu.edu*

WEST TEXAS A&M UNIVERSITY
B-1
Canyon, TX 79016
(806) 651-2020
(800) 99-WTAMU; Fax: (806) 651-5285

Full-time: 1891 men, 2442 women	**Faculty:** 201; IIA, --$
Part-time: 552 men, 703 women	**Ph.D.s:** 76%
Graduate: 548 men, 892 women	**Student/Faculty:** 22 to 1
Year: semesters, summer session	**Tuition:** $3191 ($10,271)
Application Deadline: open	**Room & Board:** $4342
Freshman Class: 1939 applied, 1341 accepted, 856 enrolled	
SAT I Verbal/Math: 490/490	**ACT:** 20	**COMPETITIVE**

West Texas A&M University, founded in 1909, is a public institution offering programs in the liberal arts and sciences, fine arts, agriculture, nursing, and education. There are 4 undergraduate schools and 1 graduate school. In addition to regional accreditation, WTAMU has baccalaureate program accreditation with ACBSP, CCNE, CSWE, NASM, and NCATE. The 2 libraries contain 1,092,741 volumes, 1,279,131 microform items, and 4563 audio/video tapes/CDs, and subscribe to 5397 periodicals. Computerized library services include the card catalog, interlibrary loans, and database searching. Special learning facilities include a learning resource center, art gallery, natural history museum, radio station, and an alternative energy institute, an electronic learning center, a communications disorders center, and a nursing learning center. The 135-acre campus is in a small town 17 miles south of Amarillo. Including any residence halls, there are 77 buildings.

Student Life: 91% of undergraduates are from Texas. Students are from 32 states, 32 foreign countries, and Canada. 93% are from public schools. 79% are white; 13% Hispanic. The average age of freshmen is 18; all undergraduates, 23. 32% do not continue beyond their first year; 68% remain to graduate.

Housing: 1520 students can be accommodated in college housing, which includes single-sex and coed dorms. In addition, there are special-interest houses, sorority units within residence halls, 24-hour quiet areas, and an honors hall. On-campus housing is guaranteed for all 4 years. 75% of students commute. Alcohol is not permitted. All students may keep cars.

Activities: 6% of men belong to 1 local and 6 national fraternities; 4% of women belong to 2 local and 3 national sororities. There are 110 groups on campus, including academic, art, band, cheerleading, choir, chorale, chorus, computers, dance, debate, drama, ethnic, film, forensics, honors, international, jazz band, literary magazine, marching band, musical theater, opera, orchestra, photography, political, professional, radio and TV, religious, social, social service, student government, symphony, and yearbook. Popular campus events include Workathon, RHA Mud Pull, and Buffalo Branding.

Sports: There are 6 intercollegiate sports for men and 6 for women, and 39 intramural sports for men and 39 for women. Facilities include an swimming pool, an 8-lane bowling alley, weight-training rooms, a 20,000-seat stadium, an event center, handball, racquetball, tennis, badminton, basketball, and volleyball courts, a flag football field, and softball fields.

Disabled Students: All of the campus is accessible. Wheelchair ramps, elevators, special parking, specially equipped rest rooms, special class scheduling, lowered drinking fountains, lowered telephones, and special housing are available.

Services: Counseling and information services are available, as is tutoring in most subjects, including core curriculum courses. There is a reader service for the blind and remedial math, reading, and writing.

Campus Safety and Security: Measures include 24-hour foot and vehicle patrol, self-defense education, security escort services, and shuttle buses. There are informal discussions, pamphlets/posters/films, emergency telephones, lighted pathways/sidewalks, and shuttle buses provided by city transport.

Programs of Study: WTAMU confers B.A., B.S., B.A.A.S., B.B.A., B.F.A., B.G.S., B.M., B.S.M.T., and B.S.N. degrees. Master's and doctoral degrees are also awarded. Bachelor's degrees are awarded in AGRICULTURE (agricultural business management, agricultural economics, agriculture, animal science, plant protection (pest management), plant science, and soil science), BIOLOGICAL SCIENCE (biology/biological science and wildlife biology), BUSINESS (accounting, banking and finance, business administration and management, business economics, management science, and marketing/retailing/merchandising), COMMUNICATIONS AND THE ARTS (applied art, art, broadcasting, dance, dramatic arts, English, graphic design, music, music theory and composition, musical theater, performing arts, public relations, publishing, Span-

ish, speech/debate/rhetoric, and studio art), COMPUTER AND PHYSICAL SCIENCE (chemistry, computer science, geology, information sciences and systems, mathematics, and physics), EDUCATION (art, business, drama, English, foreign languages, mathematics, music, physical, reading, science, social studies, and special), ENGINEERING AND ENVIRONMENTAL DESIGN (emergency/disaster science, engineering technology, environmental science, and preengineering), HEALTH PROFESSIONS (allied health, exercise science, medical technology, music therapy, nursing, predentistry, premedicine, prepharmacy, preveterinary science, and speech pathology/audiology), SOCIAL SCIENCE (criminal justice, economics, geography, history, interdisciplinary studies, liberal arts/general studies, political science/government, prelaw, psychology, public administration, social science, social work, and sociology). Education and music are the strongest academically. Education is the largest.

Required: A general education requirement of 46 hours includes courses in analytic reasoning and communication skills, cultural heritage, English, computer literacy, math, science, history, political science, humanities, and sports and exercise sciences. Additional core requirements vary according to major. A minimum 2.0 GPA and 127 credit hours, including at least 36 of advanced work, up to a maximum of 60, 30 of which must be at WTAMU, are required to graduate. At least 33 hours must be earned in residence at WTAMU, including at least 24 of the last 30 hours counted toward a degree.

Special: WTAMU offers work-study programs, a Washington semester, internships, co-op programs, credit by exam, B.A.-B.S. degrees, a general studies degree, interdisciplinary studies in elementary/secondary education fields, nondegree study, and pass/fail options. There are 12 national honor societies, a freshman honors program, and 14 departmental honors programs.

Faculty/Classroom: 56% of faculty are male; 44%, female. 94% teach undergraduates, 48% do research, and 44% do both. Graduate students teach 17% of introductory courses. The average class size in an introductory lecture is 29; in a laboratory, 23; and in a regular course, 27.

Admissions: 69% of the 2003-2004 applicants were accepted. The SAT I scores for the 2003-2004 freshman class were: Verbal--52% below 500, 35% between 500 and 599, 12% between 600 and 700, and 2% above 700. The ACT scores were 52% below 21, 28% between 21 and 23, 15% between 24 and 26, 3% between 27 and 28, and 2% above 28. 35% of the current freshmen were in the top fifth of their class; 63% were in the top two fifths. There was 1 National Merit finalist. 23 freshmen graduated first in their class.

Requirements: The SAT I or ACT is required. In addition, applicants should have graduated from an accredited secondary school or have a GED. Admission requires graduation in the top 50% of the student's high school class or a minimum composite score of 20 on the ACT or 950 on the SAT I. WTAMU requires applicants to be in the upper 50% of their class. AP and CLEP credits are accepted.

Procedure: Freshmen are admitted to all sessions. Entrance exams should be taken in the fall of the senior year. There is a deferred admissions plan. There is a rolling admissions plan. Application deadlines are open. Application fee is $25. Applications are accepted on-line through the Texas State Common Application.

Transfer: 774 transfer students enrolled in 2002-2003. A 2.0 GPA is generally required for transfer students. 30 of 127 credits required for the bachelor's degree must be completed at WTAMU.

Visiting: There are regularly scheduled orientations for prospective students, including a tour of campus, admissions and financial services sessions, selection of a major, and a visit with faculty. There are guides for informal visits and visitors may sit in on classes and stay overnight. To schedule a visit, contact the Admissions Office at (806) 651-2833 or *admissions@mail.wtamu.edu*.

Financial Aid: In 2003-2004, 51% of all full-time freshmen and 47% of continuing full-time students received some form of financial aid. 48% of full-time freshmen and 46% of continuing full-time students received need-based aid. The average freshman award was $4918, with $3282 from need-based scholarships or need-based grants, $1376 from need-based self-help aid (loans and jobs), and $260 from work contracts. 3% of undergraduates work part time. Average annual earnings from campus work are $1347. The FAFSA is required. The deadline for filing freshman financial aid applications for fall entry is May 1.

International Students: There are 55 international students enrolled in a recent year. The school actively recruits these students. They must score 550 on the written TOEFL or 213 on the electronic version and also take the SAT I, scoring 950, or the ACT.

Computers: The mainframe is a model P650. 300 PCs are located in the learning center and another 100 are in other labs and classrooms. Units include networked and stand-alone models. All students may access the system. There are no time limits. The fee is $5 per hour up to a maximum of $50.

Graduates: From July 1, 2002 to June 30, 2003, 959 bachelor's degrees were awarded. The most popular majors were business (18%), general studies (13%), and nursing/interdisciplinary studies (13%). In an average class, 1% graduate in 3 years or less, 6% graduate in 4 years or less, 29% graduate in 5 years or less, and 37% graduate in 6 years or less. 292 companies recruited on campus in 2002-2003. Of the 2002 graduating class, 40% were enrolled in graduate school within 6 months of graduation.

Admissions Contact: Lila Vars, Director of Admissions. A video is available. E-mail: *lvars@mail.wtamu.edu* Web: *http://www.wtamu.edu*

WILEY COLLEGE
E-2
Marshall, TX 75670   (903) 927-3311; Fax: (903) 938-8100

Full-time: none	**Faculty:** 35
Part-time: none	**Ph.D.s:** 63%
Graduate: none	**Student/Faculty:** 21 to 1
Year: semesters, summer session	**Tuition:** n/av
Application Deadline: open	**Room & Board:** n/av
Freshman Class: n/av	
SAT I or ACT: required	**LESS COMPETITIVE**

Wiley College, founded in 1873 as an institution for black students, is affiliated with the United Methodist Church. The college offers programs in the liberal arts, sciences, and teacher training. Figures in the above capsule and in this profile are approximate. The library contains 80,000 volumes, and subscribes to 298 periodicals. The 58-acre campus is in a small town 35 miles west of Shreveport.

Programs of Study: Wiley confers B.A., B.S., and B.B.A. degrees. Bachelor's degrees are awarded in BIOLOGICAL SCIENCE (biology/biological science), BUSINESS (business administration and management, hotel/motel and restaurant management, and office supervision and management), COMMUNICATIONS AND THE ARTS (communications, English, music, and music performance), COMPUTER AND PHYSICAL SCIENCE (chemistry, computer science, mathematics, and physics), EDUCATION (business, elementary, English, mathematics, music, physical, secondary, social science, and special), SOCIAL SCIENCE (history, liberal arts/general studies, philosophy, religion, social science, and sociology).

Required: Core requirements include courses in education, English, humanities, history, religion, science, and math. 2 credits in phys ed and 3 in computer science are required. A 2.0 GPA and 124 semester hours are needed to graduate.

Faculty/Classroom: All teach undergraduates.

Requirements: The SAT I or ACT is required. In addition, applicants must be graduates of an accredited secondary school or have scored at least 40 on the GED. A letter of recommendation from a high school counselor or teacher is required. Wiley requires applicants to be in the upper 50% of their class. A GPA of 2.0 is required.

Procedure: There are early decision and early admissions plans. Application deadlines are open.

Transfer: Transfer applicants must be in good standing at their last college. 30 of 124 credits required for the bachelor's degree must be completed at Wiley.

International Students: They must score 400 on the written TOEFL.

Computers: The mainframes are an IBM System 36 and a DEC Dolphin. All students may access the system. There are no time limits and no fees.

Admissions Contact: Bishop B. Curry, Director of Admissions.

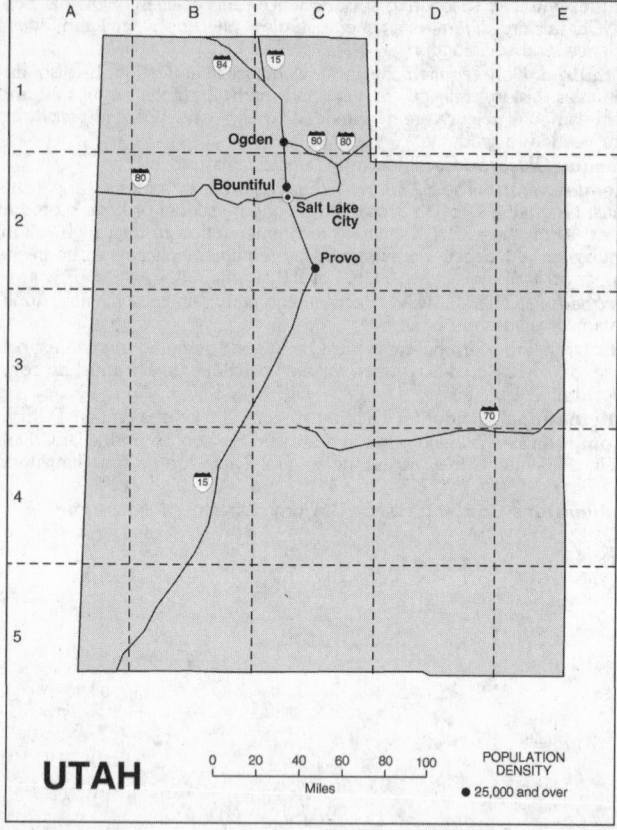

UTAH

POPULATION DENSITY
● 25,000 and over

BRIGHAM YOUNG UNIVERSITY
C-2
Provo, UT 84602   (801) 422-2500; Fax: (801) 422-0005

Full-time: 13,386 men, 13,200 women	**Faculty:** n/av
Part-time: 1786 men, 1560 women	**Ph.D.s:** 81%
Graduate: 1526 men, 1054 women	**Student/Faculty:** n/av
Year: semesters, summer session	**Tuition:** $3150 ($4740)
Application Deadline: February 15	**Room & Board:** $5354

Freshman Class: 9300 applied, 7227 accepted, 5331 enrolled

ACT: required   **HIGHLY COMPETITIVE**

Brigham Young University, founded in 1875, is a private university affiliated with the Church of Jesus Christ of Latter-day Saints. The university follows a semester calendar with spring and summer blocks. Tuition figures in the above capsule apply to members of the Latter-day Saints community. Parenthetical figures apply to nonmembers. Room and board are estimated. There are 10 undergraduate schools and 1 graduate school. In addition to regional accreditation, BYU has baccalaureate program accreditation with AACSB, ABET, ACCE, ACEJMC, ADA, ASLA, CAAHEP, CCNE, CSAB, CSWE, NASAD, NASD, NASDTEC, NASM, NASPE, NCATE, NLN, and NRPA. The 2 libraries contain 3,373,793 volumes, 3,391,764 microform items, 69,972 e-books, and 168,701 audio/video tapes/CDs, and subscribe to 26,722 periodicals. Computerized library services include the card catalog, interlibrary loans, database searching, and Internet access. Special learning facilities include a learning resource center, art gallery, natural history museum, planetarium, radio station, TV station, an archeological museum, an earth science museum, reading and writing labs, and math, language, and computer labs. The 557-acre main campus is in a suburban area 45 miles south of Salt Lake City. Including any residence halls, there are 330 buildings.

Student Life: 72% of undergraduates are from out of state, mostly the West. Students are from 50 states, 119 foreign countries, and Canada. 88% are white. The average age of freshmen is 19; all undergraduates, 21. 29% do not continue beyond their first year; 71% remain to graduate.

Housing: 5167 students can be accommodated in college housing, which includes single-sex dorms, on-campus apartments, and married-student housing. In addition, there are honors houses, language houses, and family housing contracts for 1324 student family residences. On-

campus housing is available on a first-come, first-served basis. Alcohol is not permitted. All students may keep cars.

Activities: There are no fraternities or sororities. There are 390 groups on campus, including art, bagpipe band, band, cheerleading, chess, choir, chorale, chorus, computers, dance, debate, drama, drill team, ethnic, film, honors, international, jazz band, literary magazine, marching band, musical theater, newspaper, opera, orchestra, pep band, photography, political, professional, radio and TV, religious, social, social service, student government, symphony, and yearbook. Popular campus events include Fall Fling, Spring Fling, and Preference Dances.

Sports: There are 9 intercollegiate sports for men and 10 for women, and 34 intramural sports for men and 32 for women. Facilities include pools, tennis and racquetball courts, gyms, tracks, fields, and weight rooms.

Disabled Students: 97% of the campus is accessible. Wheelchair ramps, elevators, special parking, specially equipped rest rooms, special class scheduling, lowered drinking fountains, lowered telephones, automatic door operators, and an access ramp to pools are available.

Services: Counseling and information services are available, as is tutoring in most subjects. There is a reader service for the blind and remedial math, reading, and writing.

Campus Safety and Security: Measures include 24-hour foot and vehicle patrol, self-defense education, security escort services, and informal discussions. There are pamphlets/posters/films, emergency telephones, lighted pathways/sidewalks, a bicycle patrol, and academic building security officers from 7 P.M. to 2 A.M.

Programs of Study: BYU confers B.A., B.S., B.F.A., and B.Mus. degrees. Master's and doctoral degrees are also awarded. Bachelor's degrees are awarded in AGRICULTURE (agricultural business management, agronomy, animal science, conservation and regulation, environmental studies, horticulture, plant science, range/farm management, and wildlife management), BIOLOGICAL SCIENCE (biochemistry, biology/biological science, biometrics and biostatistics, biophysics, biotechnology, botany, environmental biology, microbiology, molecular biology, nutrition, physiology, and zoology), BUSINESS (accounting, business administration and management, hotel/motel and restaurant management, management information systems, management science, recreation and leisure services, and tourism), COMMUNICATIONS AND THE ARTS (advertising, animation, Arabic, art, art history and appreciation, Chinese, classics, communications, comparative literature, dance, dramatic arts, English, French, German, graphic design, Greek, illustration, industrial design, Italian, Japanese, jazz, Korean, linguistics, media arts, music, music technology, music theory and composition, musical theater, performing arts, photography, Portuguese, public relations, Russian, Spanish, and visual and performing arts), COMPUTER AND PHYSICAL SCIENCE (actuarial science, chemistry, computer science, geology, information sciences and systems, mathematics, physics, planetary and space science, and statistics), EDUCATION (art, business, dance, drama, early childhood, elementary, English, home economics, mathematics, music, physical, science, secondary, social science, social studies, special, teaching English as a second/foreign language (TESOL/TEFOL), and technical), ENGINEERING AND ENVIRONMENTAL DESIGN (chemical engineering, civil engineering, computer engineering, construction management, electrical/electronics engineering, electrical/electronics engineering technology, environmental design, food services technology, geological engineering, industrial administration/management, landscape architecture/design, manufacturing engineering, manufacturing technology, and mechanical engineering), HEALTH PROFESSIONS (clinical science, health science, nursing, and speech pathology/audiology), SOCIAL SCIENCE (American studies, anthropology, Asian/Oriental studies, Canadian studies, dietetics, East Asian studies, economics, European studies, family/consumer studies, food science, geography, history, human development, humanities, international relations, Latin American studies, law, Middle Eastern studies, Near Eastern studies, philosophy, political science/government, psychology, social work, and sociology). Engineering, accounting, and business are the strongest academically. Business, education, and visual and performing arts are the largest.

Required: To graduate, students must complete 120 semester hours with a minimum GPA of 2.0. All students must take a total of 14 semester hours of religion and 2 hours of phys ed. There are general education requirements in English, advanced writing, foreign language or math, arts and letters, natural sciences, social sciences, and American heritage.

Special: Brigham Young offers cooperative programs, national and international internships, study abroad in 12 countries, a Washington semester, dual majors, nondegree study, and credit for life and work experience. There are 19 national honor societies, including Phi Beta Kappa, a freshman honors program, and all departments have honors programs.

Faculty/Classroom: 81% of faculty are male; 19%, female.

Admissions: 78% of the 2003-2004 applicants were accepted. There were 111 National Merit finalists.

Requirements: The ACT is required. In addition, applicants must be graduates of an accredited secondary school. The GED is accepted. The school recommends that applicants complete 4 years of English, 3 years of math, and 2 courses in foreign language, lab science, history, and literature or writing. Essays and letters of recommendation are required with the application. A GPA of 3.75 is recommended. AP and CLEP credits are accepted. Important factors in the admissions decision are advanced placement or honor courses, recommendations by school officials, and evidence of special talent.

Procedure: Freshmen are admitted to all sessions. Entrance exams should be taken by December of the senior year. There are early admissions, deferred admissions, and rolling admissions plans. Applications should be filed by February 15 for fall entry, October 1 for winter entry, February 15 for spring entry, and February 15 for summer entry, along with a $25 fee. Notification is sent on a rolling basis. Applications are accepted on-line through *http://ar.byu.edu/admissions/apply_electronically/*.

Transfer: 1317 transfer students enrolled in a recent year. For applicants, primary consideration will be given to basic general education subjects (English, math, history, and foreign languages) and major subjects. The GPA from those subjects must be near 3.0 to be competitive for admission. 30 of 120 credits required for the bachelor's degree must be completed at BYU.

Visiting: There are regularly scheduled orientations for prospective students, including a campus tour, visits with the department advisement center for the prospective major, and an interview with a school relations counselor. There are guides for informal visits and visitors may sit in on classes. To schedule a visit, contact Derek Spriggs at (801) 378-4431.

Financial Aid: In 2003-2004, 12% of all full-time freshmen and 44% of continuing full-time students received some form of financial aid. 5% of full-time freshmen and 31% of continuing full-time students received need-based aid. The average freshman award was $3067. Need-based scholarships or need-based grants averaged $1911; need-based self-help aid (loans and jobs) averaged $1150; and non-need-based awards and non-need-based scholarships averaged $3072. 43% of undergraduates work part time. Average annual earnings from campus work are $6000. The average financial indebtedness of the 2003 graduate was $11,000. BYU is a member of CSS. The FAFSA and the college's own financial statement are required. The deadline for filing freshman financial aid applications for fall entry is open.

International Students: There are 2000 international students enrolled. They must score 500 on the written TOEFL or 173 on the electronic version and also take the SAT I or the ACT.

Computers: PCs and Macs are available in departments and computer labs throughout the campus. All students may access the system any time. There are no time limits and no fees. It is recommended that students in accounting have personal computers.

Graduates: From July 1, 2002 to June 30, 2003, 7923 bachelor's degrees were awarded. The most popular majors were family home and social sciences (21%), management (15%), and humanities (12%). In an average class, 27% graduate in 4 years or less, 18% graduate in 5 years or less, and 27% graduate in 6 years or less. 500 companies recruited on campus in 2002-2003.

Admissions Contact: Tom Gourley, Director, Admissions Office. A video is available. E-mail: *admissions@byu.edu* Web: *www.byu.edu*

SOUTHERN UTAH UNIVERSITY
Cedar City, UT 84720   B-4

(435) 586-7740; Fax: (435) 865-8223

Full-time: 2023 men, 2279 women	**Faculty:** 208; IIA, --$
Part-time: 600 men, 938 women	**Ph.D.s:** 69%
Graduate: 108 men, 100 women	**Student/Faculty:** 21 to 1
Year: semesters, summer session	**Tuition:** $2794 ($8158)
Application Deadline: July 1	**Room & Board:** $5400
Freshman Class: 1355 applied, 1054 accepted, 596 enrolled	
SAT I Verbal/Math: 529/522	**ACT:** 21 **COMPETITIVE**

Southern Utah University, founded in 1897, is part of the Utah System of Higher Education and offers undergraduate degrees in arts and letters, science, education, and business. There are 6 undergraduate and 3 graduate schools. In addition to regional accreditation, SUU has baccalaureate program accreditation with AACSB, ACBSP, NASDTEC, NASM, and NLN. The library contains 202,784 volumes, 673,985 microform items, and 17,969 audio/video tapes/CDs, and subscribes to 1100 periodicals. Computerized library services include the card catalog, interlibrary loans, and database searching. Special learning facilities include a learning resource center, art gallery, natural history museum, planetarium, radio station, and TV station. The 133-acre campus is in a small town 170 miles north of Las Vegas. Including any residence halls, there are 76 buildings.

Student Life: 80% of undergraduates are from Utah. Students are from 45 states, 32 foreign countries, and Canada. 98% are from public schools. 91% are white. Most claim no religious affiliation. The average age of freshmen is 19; all undergraduates, 24. 49% do not continue beyond their first year; 51% remain to graduate.

Housing: 395 students can be accommodated in college housing, which includes single-sex and coed dorms, on-campus apartments, fraternity houses, and sorority houses. On-campus housing is available on a first-come, first-served basis. Priority is given to out-of-town students. 92% of students commute. Alcohol is not permitted. All students may keep cars.

Activities: 3% of men belong to 2 national fraternities; 3% of women belong to 1 local and 2 national sororities. There are 48 groups on campus, including art, bagpipe band, band, cheerleading, choir, chorale, chorus, computers, dance, drama, drill team, ethnic, film, forensics, gay, honors, international, jazz band, marching band, musical theater, newspaper, opera, orchestra, pep band, political, professional, radio and TV, religious, social, social service, student government, and symphony. Popular campus events include Founders Day, dances, and service programs.

Sports: There are 7 intercollegiate sports for men and 8 for women, and 13 intramural sports for men and 13 for women. Facilities include a 10,000-seat stadium for football and for track and field, a baseball field, recreation grounds, a 5300-seat special events facility for basketball, volleyball, and gymnastics, tennis and racquetball courts, and large, all-weather practice areas. SUU owns and operates a 1000-acre farm and a 3700-acre ranch.

Disabled Students: 95% of the campus is accessible. Wheelchair ramps, elevators, special parking, specially equipped rest rooms, special class scheduling, lowered drinking fountains, lowered telephones, and special housing are available.

Services: Counseling and information services are available, as is tutoring in most subjects. There is a reader service for the blind and remedial math, reading, and writing.

Campus Safety and Security: Measures include self-defense education, security escort services, informal discussions, and pamphlets/posters/films. There are emergency telephones and lighted pathways/sidewalks.

Programs of Study: SUU confers B.A., B.S., and B.I.S. degrees. Associate and master's degrees are also awarded. Bachelor's degrees are awarded in AGRICULTURE (agriculture), BIOLOGICAL SCIENCE (biology/biological science), BUSINESS (accounting, banking and finance, business administration and management, marketing management, and marketing/retailing/merchandising), COMMUNICATIONS AND THE ARTS (art, communications, dance, dramatic arts, English, French, German, music, and Spanish), COMPUTER AND PHYSICAL SCIENCE (chemistry, computer science, geology, information sciences and systems, and mathematics), EDUCATION (art, athletic training, business, dance, drama, elementary, English, foreign languages, mathematics, music, physical, science, social science, social studies, and special), ENGINEERING AND ENVIRONMENTAL DESIGN (construction management and engineering technology), SOCIAL SCIENCE (criminal justice, economics, family/consumer studies, history, interdisciplinary studies, political science/government, psychology, and sociology). Business, science, and education are the strongest academically. Business and education are the largest.

Required: To graduate, all students must complete at least 122 credit hours with a minimum 2.0 GPA. Students must satisfy general education, major and minor, and basic skills requirements, including 4 courses each in social and physical sciences, 2 each in English, fine arts, and humanities, 1 each in math, phys ed, and communications, and a course in either history, political science, or economics to fulfill the U.S. government requirement.

Special: SUU offers co-op programs with Weber State University, work-study programs, study abroad, dual majors, student-designed majors leading to a B.I.S. degree, and internships with government officials in Washington, D.C. There are 3 national honor societies and 3 departmental honors programs.

Faculty/Classroom: 65% of faculty are male; 35%, female. All teach undergraduates and 65% do research. No introductory courses are taught by graduate students. The average class size in an introductory lecture is 29 and in a laboratory, 14.

Admissions: 78% of the 2003-2004 applicants were accepted. 45% of the current freshmen were in the top fifth of their class.

Requirements: The SAT I or ACT is required. The ACT is recommended. In addition, applicants should be graduates of an accredited secondary school or have a GED, and should have completed 4 years of English, 3 of math, 2 each of biological/physical sciences (1 with a lab) and social studies including U.S. history/government, and 4 of electives. A GPA of 2.0 is required. AP and CLEP credits are accepted.

Procedure: Freshmen are admitted to all sessions. There are early admissions and deferred admissions plans. There is a rolling admissions plan. Applications should be filed by July 1 for fall entry, along with a $25 fee. Notification is sent on a rolling basis.

Transfer: 494 transfer students enrolled in 2002-2003. Applicants must submit transcripts from previously attended colleges and have a minimum 2.25 GPA. ACT scores and high school transcripts are required from students who have not completed English or math courses at another institution or who have not completed a minimum of 30 credit hours at an institution of higher education, 30 of 122 credits required for the bachelor's degree must be completed at SUU.

Visiting: There are regularly scheduled orientations for prospective students, including campus tours, which can be arranged by appointment. There are guides for informal visits and visitors may sit in on classes and stay overnight. To schedule a visit, contact Director of School Relations at (435) 586-7741.

Financial Aid: In 2003-2004, 75% of all full-time freshmen and 67% of continuing full-time students received some form of financial aid. 55% of full-time freshmen and 72% of continuing full-time students received need-based aid. The average freshman award was $2830. Need-based scholarships or need-based grants averaged $2620; need-based self-help aid (loans and jobs) averaged $2285; non-need-based athletic scholarships averaged $3327; and other non-need-based awards and non-need-based scholarships averaged $2539. The average financial indebtedness of the 2003 graduate was $11,119. The FAFSA and the college's own financial statement are required.

International Students: The school actively recruits these students. They must score 500 on the written TOEFL and also take the SAT I or the ACT.

Computers: The mainframe is a DEC VAX 6420. Students have access to more than 350 PCs. E-mail, Internet access, and a variety of software are available. All students may access the system.

Graduates: From July 1, 2002 to June 30, 2003, 984 bachelor's degrees were awarded. The most popular majors were education (37%), business/marketing (15%), and communications (9%). In an average class, 17% graduate in 4 years or less, 26% graduate in 5 years or less, and 33% graduate in 6 years or less.

Admissions Contact: Dale S. Orton, Director of Admissions. E-mail: *adminfo@suu.edu* Web: *www.suu.edu*

UNIVERSITY OF UTAH
Salt Lake City, UT 84112

	C-2
	(801) 581-7281
Full-time: 8492 men, 6750 women	**Faculty:** 730; I, av$
Part-time: 3747 men, 3432 women	**Ph.D.s:** 90%
Graduate: 3353 men, 2663 women	**Student/Faculty:** 21 to 1
Year: semesters, summer session	**Tuition:** $3645 ($11,291)
Application Deadline: April 1	**Room & Board:** $5560
Freshman Class: 5842 applied, 5036 accepted, 2653 enrolled	
ACT: 23	**COMPETITIVE**

University of Utah, founded in 1850, is a part of the Utah System of Higher Education. The university offers undergraduate degrees through the colleges of architecture, business, education, engineering, fine arts, health, humanities, nursing, medicine, mines and earth sciences, pharmacy, science, and social and behavioral science. There are 13 undergraduate and 16 graduate schools. In addition to regional accreditation, U of U has baccalaureate program accreditation with AACSB, ABET, ACPE, ADA, APTA, ASLA, CSWE, NAAB, NASM, NCATE, NLN, and NRPA. The 3 libraries contain 3,128,547 volumes, 3,564,004 microform items, and 64,225 audio/video tapes/CDs, and subscribe to 36,803 periodicals. Computerized library services include the card catalog, interlibrary loans, database searching, and Internet access. Special learning facilities include a learning resource center, art gallery, natural history museum, radio station, TV station, and an arboretum. The 1535-acre campus is in an urban area in Salt Lake City. Including any residence halls, there are 332 buildings.

Student Life: 82% of undergraduates are from Utah. Students are from 50 states, 109 foreign countries, and Canada. 95% are from public schools. 86% are white. The average age of freshmen is 19; all undergraduates, 25. 42% do not continue beyond their first year; 56% remain to graduate.

Housing: 2500 students can be accommodated in college housing, which includes single-sex dorms, on-campus apartments, off-campus apartments, married-student housing, fraternity houses, and sorority houses. In addition, there are honors houses and special-interest houses. On-campus housing is available on a first-come, first-served basis. 91% of students commute. Alcohol is not permitted. All students may keep cars.

Activities: 3% of men belong to 12 national fraternities; 4% of women belong to 7 national sororities. There are 250 groups on campus, including art, band, cheerleading, chess, choir, chorale, chorus, computers, dance, drama, drill team, drum and bugle corps, ethnic, film, gay, honors, international, jazz band, marching band, musical theater, opera, orchestra, pep band, photography, political, professional, radio and TV, religious, social, social service, student government, symphony, and yearbook. Popular campus events include Mayfest and Autumn Openings.

Sports: There are 10 intercollegiate sports for men and 11 for women, and 68 intramural sports for men and 61 for women. Facilities include a 35,000-seat stadium, a 15,500-seat basketball arena, 6 indoor gyms, 13 indoor and 22 outdoor tennis courts, 3 indoor swimming pools, a gymnastics room, 5 weight rooms, 19 handball/racquetball/squash

courts, a 9-hole golf course, 3 outdoor playing fields, a 10-lane bowling alley, a movie theater, video games, and a big-screen TV.

Disabled Students: 93% of the campus is accessible. Wheelchair ramps, elevators, special parking, specially equipped rest rooms, special class scheduling, lowered drinking fountains, and lowered telephones are available.

Services: Counseling and information services are available, as is tutoring in most subjects. There is a reader service for the blind, remedial math and writing, and support services for the deaf, including readers, scribers, tutors, and interpreters.

Campus Safety and Security: Measures include 24-hour foot and vehicle patrol, self-defense education, security escort services, and shuttle buses. There are informal discussions, pamphlets/posters/films, emergency telephones, and lighted pathways/sidewalks.

Programs of Study: U of U confers B.A., B.S., B.F.A., B.M.U., B.S.W., and B.U.S. degrees. Master's and doctoral degrees are also awarded. Bachelor's degrees are awarded in BIOLOGICAL SCIENCE (biology/ biological science), BUSINESS (accounting, banking and finance, business administration and management, and marketing/retailing/ merchandising), COMMUNICATIONS AND THE ARTS (art, art history and appreciation, Chinese, classics, communications, dance, dramatic arts, English, film arts, French, German, Japanese, linguistics, music, Russian, and Spanish), COMPUTER AND PHYSICAL SCIENCE (atmospheric sciences and meteorology, chemistry, computer science, geology, geophysics and seismology, mathematics, and physics), EDUCATION (elementary and health), ENGINEERING AND ENVIRONMENTAL DESIGN (architecture, bioengineering, biomedical engineering, chemical engineering, civil engineering, computer engineering, electrical/ electronics engineering, environmental engineering, geological engineering, materials engineering, mechanical engineering, metallurgical engineering, mining and mineral engineering, and urban planning technology), HEALTH PROFESSIONS (exercise science, medical laboratory science, nursing, occupational therapy, physical therapy, and speech pathology/audiology), SOCIAL SCIENCE (anthropology, Asian/Oriental studies, behavioral science, economics, family/consumer studies, geography, history, Middle Eastern studies, parks and recreation management, philosophy, political science/government, psychology, social science, sociology, and women's studies). Social and behavioral sciences are the largest.

Required: To graduate, all students must satisfy requirements in the Liberal Education program, writing proficiency, and American Institutions. The core curriculum consists of 1 course each in 3 of the following 4 areas: science, humanities, fine arts, and social/behavioral science. Distribution requirements include 2 courses in each of 3 of the following 4 areas, excluding the major area: science, humanities, fine arts, and social science. Students must complete at least 183 credit hours, with 45 to 60 in the major. A minimum 2.0 GPA is required.

Special: The university offers numerous opportunities for cooperative programs, cross-registration through the Western Interstate Commission for Higher Education (WICHE), study abroad, internships, work-study and accelerated degree programs, and B.A.-B.S. degrees. Also available are the general studies degree, a Washington semester, student-designed and dual majors, credit for telecourses, and military experience, nondegree study, and pass/fail options. There are 42 national honor societies, including Phi Beta Kappa, a freshman honors program, and 32 departmental honors programs.

Faculty/Classroom: 64% of faculty are male; 36%, female. 67% teach undergraduates. Graduate students teach 22% of introductory courses. The average class size in an introductory lecture is 42 and in a laboratory, 18.

Admissions: 86% of the 2003-2004 applicants were accepted. The ACT scores for the 2003-2004 freshman class were: 25% below 21, 27% between 21 and 23, 25% between 24 and 26, 11% between 27 and 28, and 12% above 28. 38% of the current freshmen were in the top fifth of their class; 68% were in the top two fifths. There were 21 National Merit finalists and 197 semifinalists. 44 freshmen graduated first in their class.

Requirements: The ACT, with a minimum composite score of 20, is preferred. The SAT I, with a minimum composite score of 880, is accepted. In addition, applicants must be graduates of an accredited secondary school or have the GED. 15 academic credits are required, including 4 years each of English and electives, 2 years each of foreign language, math, and science/lab, and 1 year of U.S. history. A GPA of 2.6 is required. AP and CLEP credits are accepted.

Procedure: Freshmen are admitted to all sessions. Entrance exams should be taken in the junior year of high school. There is a rolling admissions plan. Applications should be filed by April 1 for fall entry, November 1 for winter entry, November 1 for spring entry, and March 15 for summer entry. Notification is sent on a rolling basis. The fall 2003 application fee was $35. Applications are accepted on-line.

Transfer: 8982 transfer students enrolled in 2002-2003. Transfer students must have completed at least 45 quarter (30 semester) hours with a minimum 2.6 GPA. 45 of 183 credits required for the bachelor's degree must be completed at U of U.

Visiting: There are regularly scheduled orientations for prospective students, including course selection and a campus tour. There are guides for informal visits and visitors may sit in on classes and stay overnight. To schedule a visit, contact the Office of High School and Prospective Student Service at (801) 581-8761.

Financial Aid: In 2003-2004, 50% of all full-time freshmen received some form of financial aid. 32% of full-time freshmen received need-based aid. The average freshman award was $5169. The average financial indebtedness of the 2003 graduate was $12,400. U of U is a member of CSS. The FAFSA is required. The deadline for filing freshman financial aid applications for fall entry is February 15.

International Students: There are 514 international students enrolled. They must score 500 on the written TOEFL or 173 on the electronic version and also take the SAT I or ACT. The ACT with a score of 18 is required if the student graduated from a U.S. high school.

Computers: All students may access the system 24 hours per day. There are no time limits and no fees.

Graduates: From July 1, 2002 to June 30, 2003, 4488 bachelor's degrees were awarded. The most popular majors were psychology (5%), economics (4%), and business and finance (4%). In an average class, 24% graduate in 4 years or less, 45% graduate in 5 years or less, and 60% graduate in 6 years or less.

Admissions Contact: John W. Boswell, Director of Admissions. Web: *www.utah.edu*

UTAH STATE UNIVERSITY   C-1
Logan, UT 84322   (435) 797-1129; Fax: (435) 797-3708

Full-time: 6028 men, 5744 women	**Faculty:** 719; I, --$
Part-time: 1116 men, 1070 women	**Ph.D.s:** 82%
Graduate: 1461 men, 1041 women	**Student/Faculty:** 16 to 1
Year: semesters, summer session	**Tuition:** $3141 ($8946)
Application Deadline: July 1	**Room & Board:** $4230
Freshman Class: 5165 applied, 4851 accepted, 2597 enrolled	
SAT I Verbal/Math: 550/560	**ACT:** 23 COMPETITIVE

Utah State University, founded in 1888, is a public institution, that offers degree programs in the liberal arts and sciences, agriculture and natural resources, engineering, business, education, fine arts, music, family life, and the sciences. There are 7 undergraduate schools and 1 graduate school. In addition to regional accreditation, USU has baccalaureate program accreditation with AACSB, ABET, ADA, AHEA, ASLA, CSWE, FIDER, NASM, NCATE, NRPA, and SAF. The 3 libraries contain 1,377,026 volumes, 2,274,733 microform items, and 25,593 audio/video tapes/CDs, and subscribe to 14,824 periodicals. Computerized library services include the card catalog, interlibrary loans, and database searching. Special learning facilities include a learning resource center, art gallery, radio station, TV station, laboratory school, historical farm, fine arts center, and developmental center for people who are handicapped. The 332-acre campus is in a small town 86 miles north of Salt Lake City. Including any residence halls, there are 104 buildings.

Student Life: 71% of undergraduates are from Utah. Students are from 50 states, 50 foreign countries, and Canada. 91% are white. The average age of freshmen is 20; all undergraduates, 23. 31% do not continue beyond their first year; 57% remain to graduate.

Housing: 3400 students can be accommodated in college housing, which includes single-sex dorms, on-campus apartments, married-student housing, fraternity houses, and sorority houses. In addition, there are honors houses and special-interest houses. On-campus housing is available on a first-come, first-served basis. Alcohol is not permitted. All students may keep cars.

Activities: 2% of men belong to 1 local and 4 national fraternities; 2% of women belong to 1 local and 3 national sororities. There are 280 groups on campus, including art, band, cheerleading, choir, chorale, chorus, computers, dance, drama, drill team, ethnic, film, gay, honors, international, jazz band, literary magazine, marching band, musical theater, newspaper, opera, orchestra, pep band, photography, political, professional, radio and TV, religious, social, social service, student government, symphony, and yearbook. Popular campus events include Festival of the American West, Founders Day, and Christmas Dinner at the Manor House.

Sports: There are 7 intercollegiate sports for men and 9 for women, and 23 intramural sports for men and 23 for women. Facilities include 5 gyms, indoor and outdoor tennis courts, 2 swimming pools, 40 acres of grass for outdoor sports, a field house, and golf and skiing areas. The campus stadium seats 30,257 and the largest auditorium seats 10,000.

Disabled Students: 95% of the campus is accessible. Wheelchair ramps, elevators, special parking, specially equipped rest rooms, special class scheduling, lowered drinking fountains, lowered telephones, and special phones to receive calls from the deaf, and a disability resource center are available.

Services: Counseling and information services are available, as is tutoring in every subject. There is a reader service for the blind and remedial math, reading, and writing. There is also a writing lab and a tutor room.

Campus Safety and Security: Measures include 24-hour foot and vehicle patrol, self-defense education, security escort services, and shuttle buses. There are informal discussions, pamphlets/posters/films, emergency telephones, lighted pathways/sidewalks, and campus police.

Programs of Study: USU confers B.A., B.S., B.F.A., B.L.A., and B.M. degrees. Associate, master's, and doctoral degrees are also awarded. Bachelor's degrees are awarded in AGRICULTURE (agricultural business management, agricultural economics, animal science, dairy science, forestry and related sciences, international agriculture, natural resource management, plant science, range/farm management, soil science, and wildlife management), BIOLOGICAL SCIENCE (biochemistry, biology/biological science, and microbiology), BUSINESS (accounting, banking and finance, business administration and management, business economics, fashion merchandising, international business management, management information systems, marketing/retailing/merchandising, and personnel management), COMMUNICATIONS AND THE ARTS (dance, dramatic arts, English, fine arts, French, German, journalism, music, and Spanish), COMPUTER AND PHYSICAL SCIENCE (chemistry, computer science, earth science, geology, information sciences and systems, mathematics, physics, and statistics), EDUCATION (agricultural, art, business, early childhood, elementary, foreign languages, health, home economics, industrial arts, mathematics, music, physical, science, secondary, and special), ENGINEERING AND ENVIRONMENTAL DESIGN (agricultural engineering, civil engineering, electrical/electronics engineering, engineering, environmental science, industrial engineering, industrial engineering technology, interior design, landscape architecture/design, and mechanical engineering), HEALTH PROFESSIONS (medical laboratory technology, music therapy, predentistry, premedicine, public health, speech pathology/audiology, and veterinary science), SOCIAL SCIENCE (American studies, child care/child and family studies, economics, food science, geography, history, home economics, human development, international relations, liberal arts/general studies, parks and recreation management, philosophy, political science/government, prelaw, psychology, social work, and sociology). Natural resources, engineering, and special education are the strongest academically. Humanities, arts, and social science are the largest.

Required: The core curriculum of 30 semester credits includes at least 6 of writing; the total number of credits required for graduation is 120. Students must maintain a minimum GPA of 2.5. The number of credits required in the major varies, but there is a minimum of 40 in major classes.

Special: Internships are available in most departments through the Cooperative Education Program. The National Student Exchange Program allows students to cross-register in designated institutions and programs, and the International Student Exchange Program enables students to study abroad.There is also cross-registration with the University of Americas of Mexico. A general studies degree and student-designed majors are available. Nondegree study, work-study programs, co-op programs, B.A.-B.S. degrees, pass/fail options, and credit for military experience are offered. There are 11 national honor societies, a freshman honors program, and 35 departmental honors programs.

Faculty/Classroom: 65% of faculty are male; 35%, female. Graduate students teach 6% of introductory courses. The average class size in an introductory lecture is 35; in a laboratory, 20; and in a regular course, 25.

Admissions: 94% of the 2003-2004 applicants were accepted. The SAT I scores for the 2003-2004 freshman class were: Verbal--28% below 500, 41% between 500 and 599, 24% between 600 and 700, and 7% above 700; Math--25% below 500, 36% between 500 and 599, 31% between 600 and 700, and 8% above 700. The ACT scores were 25% below 21, 26% between 21 and 23, 24% between 24 and 26, 13% between 27 and 28, and 12% above 28. 34% of the current freshmen were in the top fifth of their class; 62% were in the top two fifths. There were 25 National Merit finalists. 107 freshmen graduated first in their class.

Requirements: The SAT I or ACT is required; the ACT is preferred. In addition, students should graduate from an accredited secondary school with 15 academic units, including 4 in English, 3 each in math and science, and 1 in social sciences. GED equivalency is accepted, provided ACT scores are 19 or higher. Students not meeting entrance requirements may be considered for admission on a provisional basis. A GPA of 2.7 is required. AP and CLEP credits are accepted. Important factors in the admissions decision are evidence of special talent, parents or siblings attending the school, and recommendations by school officials.

Procedure: Freshmen are admitted to all sessions. Entrance exams should be taken in the spring of the junior year. There are early decision and deferred admissions plans. There is a rolling admissions plan. Applications should be filed by July 1 for fall entry, November 1 for spring entry, and May 1 for summer entry, along with a $35 fee. Notification is sent on a rolling basis. Applications are accepted on-line.

Transfer: 1074 transfer students enrolled in 2002-2003. A minimum 2.2 GPA, higher for some majors, is required for transfer students. Those applicants with fewer than 45 credits must also submit ACT scores. 30 of 120 credits required for the bachelor's degree must be completed at USU.

Visiting: There are regularly scheduled orientations for prospective students, a campus tour, including meeting with an academic adviser, lunch, and a housing tour, available at 10:30 A.M. and 1:30 P.M., September to May, and 1:30 P.M., June to August. There are guides for informal visits and visitors may sit in on classes and stay overnight. To schedule a visit, contact Jimmy Moore at (435) 797-3963 or *jimmymo@cc.usu.edu.*

Financial Aid: 59% of undergraduates work part time. USU is a member of CSS. The FAFSA, the college's own financial statement, and the student/parent tax forms are required.

International Students: There are 366 international students enrolled. They must score 500 on the written TOEFL or 173 on the electronic version or take the MELAB. The TOEFL is preferred.

Computers: The mainframes are an IBM 9672/R12 and several DEC Alphas. 850 PCs are available in 16 open-access labs throughout the campus. All are networked to the mainframes and the Internet. All students may access the system 24 hours a day, 7 days a week. There are no time limits. The fee is $10 to $27.

Graduates: From July 1, 2002 to June 30, 2003, 2412 bachelor's degrees were awarded. The most popular majors were family and human development (5%), accounting (4%), and business information systems (4%). In an average class, 57% graduate in 6 years or less. 175 companies recruited on campus in 2002-2003. Of the 2002 graduating class, 20% were enrolled in graduate school within 6 months of graduation and 72% were employed.

Admissions Contact: Jimmy Moore, Director, Enrollment and Recruitment Services. E-mail: *admit@cc.usu.edu* Web: *www.usu.edu*

UTAH SYSTEM OF HIGHER EDUCATION

The Utah System of Higher Education, established in 1969, is a public system. It is governed by a state Board of Regents whose chief administrator is commissioner of higher education. The primary goals of the system are teaching, research, and public service. The main priorities are to provide a high-quality, efficient, and economical public system of higher education; to coordinate, consolidate, and avoid unnecessary duplication; and to systematically develop the role of each institution within the system. The enrollment is approximately 139,000, with about 3900 full-time faculty members. These numbers do not include the Utah College of Applied Technology, which serves secondary and post-secondary students in open-entry, open-exit, technical, and vocational training. 4-year campuses are located in Salt Lake City, Logan, Ogden, Cedar City, Orem, and St. George. Profiles of some campuses are included in this section.

WEBER STATE UNIVERSITY
Ogden, UT 84408-   C-1

	(801) 626-7670; Fax: (801) 626-6747
Full-time: 5667 men, 5348 women	Faculty: 452; IIA, --$
Part-time: 3443 men, 3994 women	Ph.D.s: 92%
Graduate: 185 men, 184 women	Student/Faculty: 24 to 1
Year: semesters, summer session	Tuition: $2632 ($7958)
Application Deadline: July 1	Room & Board: $5313
Freshman Class: 5893 applied, 5893 accepted, 2878 enrolled	
SAT I Verbal/Math: 506/497	ACT: 22 NONCOMPETITIVE

Weber State University, founded in 1889 and part of the Utah System of Higher Education, is a public, primarily commuter institution offering undergraduate degrees in health sciences, arts and humanities, business and economics, education, natural sciences, social sciences, and technology, and graduate degrees in education, professional accountancy, business management, and criminal justice. There are 7 undergraduate and 4 graduate schools. In addition to regional accreditation, WSU has baccalaureate program accreditation with AACSB, ADA, CAHEA, CSWE, FIDER, NASM, NCATE, and NLN. The library contains 509,597 volumes, 584,461 microform items, and 19,709 audio/video tapes/CDs, and subscribes to 2353 periodicals. Computerized library services include the card catalog, interlibrary loans, database searching, and Internet access. Special learning facilities include a learning resource center, art gallery, natural history museum, planetarium, radio station, TV station, an observatory, and a working crime lab. The 526-acre campus is in an urban area 35 miles north of Salt Lake City. Including any residence halls, there are 61 buildings.

Student Life: 92% of undergraduates are from Utah. Students are from 50 states, 39 foreign countries, and Canada. 98% are from public schools. 73% are white. 73% are Church of Jesus Christ of Latter-day Saints; 6% Protestant. The average age of freshmen is 19; all undergraduates, 25. 33% do not continue beyond their first year; 45% remain to graduate.

Housing: 644 students can be accommodated in college housing, which includes single-sex and coed dorms and on-campus apartments. On-campus housing is guaranteed for all 4 years. 97% of students commute. Alcohol is not permitted. All students may keep cars.

Activities: 1% of men belong to 3 national fraternities; 1% of women belong to 3 local sororities. There are 100 groups on campus, including art, band, cheerleading, chess, choir, chorale, chorus, computers, dance, debate, drama, drill team, drum and bugle corps, ethnic, forensics, honors, international, jazz band, literary magazine, marching band, musical theater, newspaper, opera, orchestra, pep band, photography, political, professional, radio and TV, religious, social, social service, student government, and symphony. Popular campus events include SunFest, WinterFest, and Crystal Crest.

Sports: There are 5 intercollegiate sports for men and 5 for women, and 36 intramural sports for men and 36 for women. Facilities include an indoor track, a strength-training center, 3 indoor basketball courts, a swimming pool, racquetball and tennis courts, a 17,000-seat stadium, an 11,515-seat gym, a 7800-seat auditorium/arena, an events center, playing fields, an exercise/conditioning room, and a 1-mile jogging trail.

Disabled Students: Wheelchair ramps, elevators, special parking, specially equipped rest rooms, special class scheduling, lowered drinking fountains, lowered telephones, and special housing are available.

Services: Counseling and information services are available, as is tutoring in every subject. There is a reader service for the blind and remedial math, reading, and writing. Translators are offered for the hearing impaired.

Campus Safety and Security: Measures include 24-hour foot and vehicle patrol, self-defense education, security escort services, and shuttle buses. There are informal discussions, pamphlets/posters/films, emergency telephones, and lighted pathways/sidewalks.

Programs of Study: WSU confers B.A., B.S., B.F.A., B.I.S., and B.M. degrees. Associate and master's degrees are also awarded. Bachelor's degrees are awarded in BIOLOGICAL SCIENCE (biology/biological science, botany, microbiology, and zoology), BUSINESS (accounting, banking and finance, business administration and management, business economics, management information systems, marketing management, personnel management, and purchasing/inventory management), COMMUNICATIONS AND THE ARTS (communications, dance, dramatic arts, English, fine arts, French, German, graphic design, journalism, media arts, music, music performance, musical theater, photography, piano/organ, public relations, Spanish, and voice), COMPUTER AND PHYSICAL SCIENCE (chemistry, computer programming, computer science, earth science, geology, information sciences and systems, mathematics, physical sciences, and physics), EDUCATION (art, athletic training, business, early childhood, elementary, foreign languages, health, music, physical, science, secondary, and social science), ENGINEERING AND ENVIRONMENTAL DESIGN (automotive technology, electrical/electronics engineering technology, environmental science, manufacturing technology, and mechanical engineering technology), HEALTH PROFESSIONS (clinical science, dental hygiene, health care administration, nursing, and radiograph medical technology), SOCIAL SCIENCE (criminal justice, early childhood studies, economics, family/consumer studies, geography, gerontology, history, interdisciplinary studies, political science/government, psychology, social work, and sociology). Dental hygiene is the strongest academically. Elementary education and nursing are the largest.

Required: To graduate, students must demonstrate math competency and complete courses in government/history, English, humanities, math, biological/physical sciences, and social sciences. At least 120 semester credit hours, with 45 at the upper-division level, and a minimum GPA of 2.0 are required. Hours in the major and distribution requirements vary with the degree.

Special: WSU offers co-op programs and internships in many majors, a Washington semester, study abroad in Mexico and England, work-study programs with community businesses, B.A.-B.S. degrees, dual majors in any combination, student-designed majors resulting in a B.I.S. degree, a general studies degree, credit for military experience, nondegree study, and pass/fail options. There is 1 national honor society, including Phi Beta Kappa, and a freshman honors program.

Faculty/Classroom: 61% of faculty are male; 39%, female. All teach undergraduates. No introductory courses are taught by graduate students. The average class size in an introductory lecture is 37; in a laboratory, 16; and in a regular course, 26.

Admissions: 100% of the 2003-2004 applicants were accepted. The SAT I scores for the 2003-2004 freshman class were: Verbal--45% below 500, 39% between 500 and 599, 13% between 600 and 700, and 3% above 700; Math--48% below 500, 34% between 500 and 599, 16% between 600 and 700, and 2% above 700. The ACT scores were 46% below 21, 25% between 21 and 23, 19% between 24 and 26, 6% between 27 and 28, and 4% above 28. 56% of the current freshmen were in the top fifth of their class; 89% were in the top two fifths.

Requirements: The ACT is recommended. In addition, applicants must be graduates of an accredited secondary school or have a GED. Other requirements vary by department. Out-of-state residents must have a minimum high school GPA of 2.0. AP and CLEP credits are accepted.

Procedure: Freshmen are admitted to all sessions. Entrance exams should be taken in the junior or senior year. There are early admissions and deferred admissions plans. There is a rolling admissions plan. Applications should be filed by July 1 for fall entry and January 8 for spring entry, along with a $30 fee. The college accepts all applicants. Notification is sent on a rolling basis. Applications are accepted on-line through the school's web site.

Transfer: 1879 transfer students enrolled in 2002-2003. Transfer students must submit official transcripts from previously attended colleges or universities and have a minimum GPA of 2.0. 30 of 120 credits required for the bachelor's degree must be completed at WSU.

Visiting: There are regularly scheduled orientations for prospective students. There are guides for informal visits and visitors may sit in on classes and stay overnight. To schedule a visit, contact John Allred at (801) 626-6049 or (800) 848-7770, ext. 6049 or *jdallred@weber.edu*.

Financial Aid: In 2003-2004, 57% of all full-time freshmen and 63% of continuing full-time students received some form of financial aid. 52% of full-time freshmen and 63% of continuing full-time students received need-based aid. The average freshman award was $5800. The average financial indebtedness of the 2003 graduate was $8500. The FAFSA and the college's own financial statement are required. The deadline for filing freshman financial aid applications for fall entry is March 1.

International Students: There are 171 international students enrolled. The school actively recruits these students. They must take the college's own test.

Computers: There are approximately 3500 desktop computers, 400 computers in 9 open student computer labs, and 450 computers in 20 departmental labs. All students may access the system.

Graduates: From July 1, 2002 to June 30, 2003, 1949 bachelor's degrees were awarded. The most popular majors were sales and service technology (9%), teacher education (5%), and political science (5%). In an average class, 10% graduate in 3 years or less, 21% graduate in 4 years or less, 31% graduate in 5 years or less, and 39% graduate in 6 years or less. 206 companies recruited on campus in 2002-2003. Of the 2002 graduating class, 26% were enrolled in graduate school within 6 months of graduation and 63% were employed.

Admissions Contact: Christopher C. Rivera, Director of Admissions. A video is available. E-mail: *crivera@weber.edu*
Web: *www.weber.edu/admissions*

WESTMINSTER COLLEGE
(Formerly Westminster College of Salt Lake City)
Salt Lake City, UT 84105

C-2

(801) 832-2200
(800) 748-4753; Fax: (801) 484-3252

Full-time: 515 men, 905 women	**Faculty:** 109; IIB, av$
Part-time: 165 men, 210 women	**Ph.D.s:** 84%
Graduate: 290 men, 230 women	**Student/Faculty:** 13 to 1
Year: summer session	**Tuition:** $12,730
Application Deadline: open	**Room & Board:** $4500
Freshman Class: n/av	
SAT I or ACT: required	**COMPETITIVE**

Westminster College, founded in 1875, is a private institution offering undergraduate programs through the Bill and Vieve Gore School of Business, the St. Marks Westminster School of Nursing and Health Sciences, the School of Arts and Sciences, and the School of Education. There are 4 undergraduate and 4 graduate schools. Figures in the above capsule and in this profile are approximate. In addition to regional accreditation, Westminster College has baccalaureate program accreditation with ACBSP and NLN. The library contains 88,086 volumes, 114,183 microform items, and 3819 audio/video tapes/CDs, and subscribes to 348 periodicals. Computerized library services include the card catalog, interlibrary loans, and database searching. Special learning facilities include a multipurpose theater. The 27-acre campus is in a suburban area 6 miles southeast of downtown Salt Lake City. Including any residence halls, there are 20 buildings.

Student Life: 94% of undergraduates are from Utah. Students are from 27 states, 21 foreign countries, and Canada. 75% are from public schools. 91% are white. 60% claim no religious affiliation; 33% Buddhist, Greek Orthodox, Christian, LDS, Presbyterian, Episcopal; 6% Catholic. The average age of freshmen is 18; all undergraduates, 24. 26% do not continue beyond their first year; 46% remain to graduate.

Housing: 374 students can be accommodated in college housing, which includes single-sex and coed dorms and off-campus apartments. On-campus housing is guaranteed for all 4 years. 87% of students commute. All students may keep cars.

Activities: There are no fraternities or sororities. There are 41 groups on campus, including art, choir, chorale, chorus, computers, dance, drama, environmental, ethnic, gay, honors, international, jazz band, literary magazine, musical theater, newspaper, orchestra, outdoor, political, professional, religious, social service, student government, and yearbook.

Popular campus events include International Fest, Spring Fling, and Awards Day.

Sports: There are 2 intercollegiate sports for men and 2 for women, and 7 intramural sports for men and 7 for women. Facilities include a playing field, tennis courts, a gym, a weight room, a sand volleyball court, and an aerobics/yoga room.

Disabled Students: 85% of the campus is accessible. Wheelchair ramps, elevators, special parking, specially equipped rest rooms, special class scheduling, and lowered drinking fountains are available.

Services: Counseling and information services are available, as is tutoring in most subjects. There is a reader service for the blind and remedial math, reading, and writing.

Campus Safety and Security: Measures include 24-hour foot and vehicle patrol, self-defense education, security escort services, and informal discussions. There are pamphlets/posters/films, emergency telephones, lighted pathways/sidewalks, and separate dorm security.

Programs of Study: Westminster College confers B.A. and B.S. degrees. Master's degrees are also awarded. Bachelor's degrees are awarded in BIOLOGICAL SCIENCE (biology/biological science), BUSINESS (accounting, business administration and management, and marketing/retailing/merchandising), COMMUNICATIONS AND THE ARTS (communications, English, and fine arts), COMPUTER AND PHYSICAL SCIENCE (chemistry, computer science, mathematics, and physics), EDUCATION (early childhood, elementary, and secondary), ENGINEERING AND ENVIRONMENTAL DESIGN (aviation administration/management), HEALTH PROFESSIONS (nursing), SOCIAL SCIENCE (economics, history, human development, philosophy, psychology, social science, and sociology). Nursing, biology, and English are the strongest academically. Business, biology, and nursing are the largest.

Required: To graduate, all students must complete at least 124 credit hours, which include liberal education and major requirements, with a minimum 2.0 GPA and 40-80 hours in the major.

Special: The college offers internships in every major, study abroad in England, Spain, and Mexico, B.A.-B.S. degrees, dual and student-designed majors, a 3-2 engineering degree at USC at Los Angeles or Washington University in St. Louis, and freshman seminar courses. There is 1 national honor society, including Phi Beta Kappa, a freshman honors program, and 1 departmental honors program.

Faculty/Classroom: 50% of faculty are male; 50%, female. 89% teach undergraduates. No introductory courses are taught by graduate students. The average class size in an introductory lecture is 18; in a laboratory, 12; and in a regular course, 15.

Admissions: In a recent year, there was 1 National Merit finalist. 6 freshmen graduated first in their class.

Requirements: The SAT I or ACT is required. In addition, applicants must be graduates of an accredited secondary school or have a GED certificate. An interview is recommended. A GPA of 2.5 is required. AP and CLEP credits are accepted. Important factors in the admissions decision are evidence of special talent, extracurricular activities record, and advanced placement or honor courses.

Procedure: Freshmen are admitted to all sessions. Entrance exams should be taken in the junior or senior year of high school. There are early admissions, deferred admissions, and rolling admissions plans. Application deadlines are open. The fall 2003 application fee was $25. Applications are accepted on-line and on computer disk.

Transfer: Transfer students must have a minimum 2.0 GPA and be in good standing at all previously attended colleges. 36 of 124 credits required for the bachelor's degree must be completed at Westminster College.

Visiting: There are regularly scheduled orientations for prospective students, including a welcome program, lunch, various workshops, a campus tour, and meetings with faculty. There are guides for informal visits and visitors may sit in on classes. To schedule a visit, contact Mary Hyland, Director of Admissions.

Financial Aid: Westminster College is a member of CSS. The FAFSA is required. Check with the school for current deadlines.

International Students: The school actively recruits these students. They must score 550 on the written TOEFL or take the MELAB.

Computers: The mainframe is an HP 9000. There are 238 networked PCs plus computer availability and hookups in the residence halls and library. All students may access the system 7 A.M. to 11 P.M. There are no time limits and no fees. It is strongly recommended that all students have a personal computer.

Admissions Contact: Mary Hyland, Director of Admissions.
E-mail: *admispub@wcslc.edu* Web: *www.wcslc.edu*

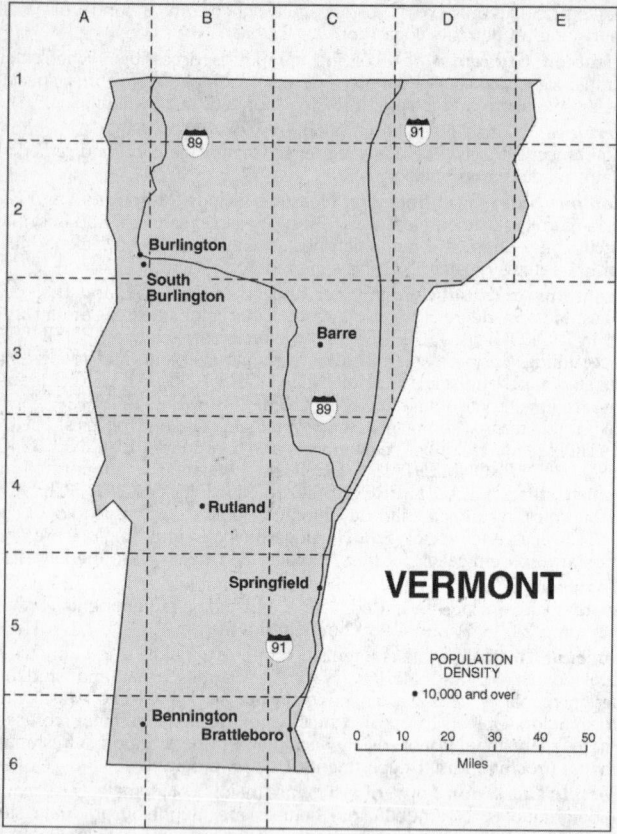

VERMONT

POPULATION
DENSITY

• 10,000 and over

0   10   20   30   40   50
                Miles

BENNINGTON COLLEGE

A-6

Bennington, VT 05201

(802) 440-4312
(800) 833-6845; Fax: (802) 440-4320

Full-time: 208 men, 427 women
Part-time: 5 women
Graduate: 46 men, 107 women
Year: trimesters
Application Deadline: January 1
Freshman Class: 773 applied, 526 accepted, 172 enrolled
SAT I Verbal/Math: 645/580

Faculty: 64
Ph.D.s: 69%
Student/Faculty: 10 to 1
Tuition: $28,770
Room & Board: $7140

HIGHLY COMPETITIVE

Bennington College, founded in 1932, is a private liberal arts institution where students design their own programs in consultation with faculty, who are active practitioners of the disciplines they teach. The 2 libraries contain 127,852 volumes, 6148 microform items, and 12,662 audio/video tapes/CDs, and subscribe to 469 periodicals. Computerized library services include the card catalog, interlibrary loans, and database searching. Special learning facilities include a learning resource center, art gallery, radio station, an observatory, dance archives, script library, photography darkrooms, electronic music studio and music practice rooms, several theaters and dance studios, ceramics studio and kilns, greenhouse, working community farm, pond for biological studies, and early childhood center. The 550-acre campus is in a small town 42 miles east of Albany, New York. Including any residence halls, there are 60 buildings.

Student Life: 95% of undergraduates are from out of state, mostly the Northeast. Students are from 45 states, 18 foreign countries, and Canada. 85% are white. The average age of freshmen is 18; all undergraduates, 20. 20% do not continue beyond their first year; 83% remain to graduate.

Housing: 610 students can be accommodated in college housing, which includes coed dorms and off-campus apartments. A substance-free house is also available. On-campus housing is guaranteed for all 4 years. 95% of students live on campus; of those, 95% remain on campus on weekends. All students may keep cars.

Activities: There are no fraternities or sororities. There are 26 groups on campus, including art, band, chess, choir, chorus, dance, drama, ethnic, film, gay, international, literary magazine, musical theater, orchestra, photography, political, radio and TV, religious, social, social service, stu-

dent government, and yearbook. Popular campus events include Sunfest, faculty concerts, and student-work performances and exhibitions.

Sports: There are 3 intercollegiate sports for men and 3 for women, and 10 intramural sports for men and 10 for women. Facilities include soccer and other playing fields, a basketball court, a karate and aerobics studio, a weight room, hiking and biking areas, a climbing wall, and cardiovascular exercise equipment. Rockclimbing, canoeing, caving, snowshoeing, whitewater rafting, and cross-country skiing facilities are available in the surrounding area.

Disabled Students: 85% of the campus is accessible. Wheelchair ramps, elevators, special parking, specially equipped rest rooms, lowered drinking fountains, special fire alarms in houses, and amplifiers on phones are available.

Services: There is remedial writing. Tutoring for learning disabilities is available in the town of Bennington at a cost to the student.

Campus Safety and Security: Measures include 24-hour foot and vehicle patrol, security escort services, shuttle buses, and informal discussions. There are pamphlets/posters/films, emergency telephones, and lighted pathways/sidewalks.

Programs of Study: Bennington confers the B.A. degree. Master's degrees are also awarded. Bachelor's degrees are awarded in BIOLOGICAL SCIENCE (biochemistry, biology/biological science, ecology, and environmental biology), COMMUNICATIONS AND THE ARTS (art, Chinese, comparative literature, creative writing, dance, dramatic arts, English, film arts, fine arts, French, German, Italian, languages, literature, music, photography, Spanish, and visual and performing arts), COMPUTER AND PHYSICAL SCIENCE (chemistry, computer science, mathematics, natural sciences, and physics), EDUCATION (early childhood and education), ENGINEERING AND ENVIRONMENTAL DESIGN (architecture and environmental science), HEALTH PROFESSIONS (premedicine and preveterinary science), SOCIAL SCIENCE (anthropology, child care/child and family studies, developmental psychology, European studies, history, history of philosophy, humanities, interdisciplinary studies, international relations, liberal arts/general studies, philosophy, psychology, social science, and sociology). Interdisciplinary studies, visual and performing arts, and literature are the largest.

Required: A minimum of 128 credit hours is required to graduate. 4 courses per term (16 credits) must be completed by full-time students, and no more than half a student's coursework may be in the major field. Students must also complete a Field Work Term (job/internship) for each term in residence. Student's programs must reflect breadth and depth in cirricular choices, and the written plan process must be completed successfully.

Special: 7-week work/internships (during January and February) are required all 4 years. Cross-registration with Southern Vermont and Williams Colleges is possible. In addition, study abroad, dual, and student-designed majors are offered. Grading is pass/fail with an extensive written evaluation; letter grades are optional. A B.A./M.A.T. program is offered for teacher certification.

Faculty/Classroom: 59% of faculty are male; 41%, female. All both teach undergraduates and do research. The average class size in a regular course is 12.

Admissions: 68% of the 2003-2004 applicants were accepted. The SAT I scores for the 2003-2004 freshman class were: Verbal--4% below 500, 18% between 500 and 599, 48% between 600 and 700, and 30% above 700; Math--16% below 500, 39% between 500 and 599, 39% between 600 and 700, and 6% above 700.

Requirements: The SAT I is required. In addition, applicants should have 16 credits, including 4 units in English, 3 each in math, science, and social studies, 2 or 3 in foreign language, and 2 in history; art and music courses are highly recommended. Essays and an interview are required, and a portfolio is recommended for certain majors. The GED is accepted. Important factors in the admissions decision are evidence of special talent, extracurricular activities record, and personality/intangible qualities.

Procedure: Freshmen are admitted fall and spring. Entrance exams should be taken during the spring of the junior year or the fall of the senior year. There are early decision, early admissions, and deferred admissions plans. Early decision applications should be filed by November 15; regular applications, by January 1 for fall entry and January 1 for spring entry, along with a $50 fee. Notification of early decision is sent December 1; regular decision, April 1. 38 early decision candidates were accepted for the 2003-2004 class. 25 applicants were on the 2003 waiting list; 12 were admitted. Applications may be downloaded from the college's web site.

Transfer: 20 transfer students enrolled in 2002-2003. Applicants must submit secondary school reports, college transcripts, and recommendations from 2 faculty members. They must also submit SAT I or ACT scores and interview with a member of the admissions staff. 64 of 128 credits required for the bachelor's degree must be completed at Bennington.

Visiting: There are regularly scheduled orientations for prospective students, including lunches with students and faculty, dinner and socializing, class visitation, and interviews. There are guides for informal visits and visitors may sit in on classes and stay overnight. To schedule a visit, contact the Admissions Office at *admissions@bennington.edu*.

Financial Aid: In 2003-2004, 77% of all full-time freshmen and 83% of continuing full-time students received some form of financial aid. 64% of full-time freshmen and 65% of continuing full-time students received need-based aid. The average freshman award was $20,475. Need-based scholarships or need-based grants averaged $18,070; need-based self-help aid (loans and jobs) averaged $3220; and non-need-based awards and non-need-based scholarships averaged $4929. The average financial indebtedness of the 2003 graduate was $17,558. Bennington is a member of CSS. The FAFSA, the college's own financial statement and the and student and parent tax returns are required. The deadline for filing freshman financial aid applications for fall entry is March 1.

International Students: There are 36 international students enrolled. The school actively recruits these students. They must score 550 on the written TOEFL and also take the SAT I or the ACT.

Computers: About 60 computers are available in the Computer Center, Languages and Cultures, Commons, Visual and Performing Arts Center, and Library, with full access to the Internet and Web. Student housing on campus is fully networked, and students may access the network with their own computers. All students may access the system. There are no time limits and no fees. It is strongly recommended that all students have a personal computer.

Graduates: From July 1, 2002 to June 30, 2003, 88 bachelor's degrees were awarded. The most popular majors were visual and performing arts (48%), English (16%), and social sciences (16%). In an average class, 75% graduate in 4 years or less, 82% graduate in 5 years or less, and 83% graduate in 6 years or less.

Admissions Contact: Ben Jones, Dean of Admisisons and Financial Aid. E-mail: *admissions@bennington.edu* Web: *www.bennington.edu*

BURLINGTON COLLEGE
A-2
Burlington, VT 05401
(802) 862-9616
(800) 862-9616; Fax: (802) 660-4331

Full-time: 60 men, 110 women	**Faculty:** n/av
Part-time: 40 men, 60 women	**Ph.D.s:** 20%
Graduate: none	**Student/Faculty:** n/av
Year: semesters, summer session	**Tuition:** $10,640
Application Deadline: open	**Room & Board:** n/app
Freshman Class: n/av	
SAT I or ACT: not required	**SPECIAL**

Burlington College, founded in 1972, is a private institution offering a small, flexible and nontraditional liberal arts program, residential and nonresidential, geared toward the adult learner. There is 1 undergraduate school. Figures in the above capsule and in this profile are approximate. The library contains 4000 volumes and 785 audio/video tapes/CDs, and subscribes to 100 periodicals. Computerized library services include interlibrary loans and database searching. Special learning facilities include a learning resource center, art gallery, and a film-production studio. The 1-acre campus is in an urban area in Burlington. There are 2 buildings.

Student Life: 54% of undergraduates are from Vermont. Students are from 24 states, 3 foreign countries, and Canada. 95% are from public schools. 90% are white. The average age of freshmen is 19; all undergraduates, 28. 50% do not continue beyond their first year.

Housing: There are no residence halls. 30 students can be accommodated in college housing, which includes single-sex and coed dorms and on-campus apartments. On-campus housing is available on a first-come, first-served basis. Priority is given to out-of-town students. 89% of students commute. Alcohol is not permitted. All students may keep cars.

Activities: There are no fraternities or sororities. There are some groups and organizations on campus, including film, literary magazine, photography, student government, and yearbook. Popular campus events include coffeehouses, community service trips, and film society screenings.

Sports: There is no sports program at BC.

Disabled Students: All of the campus is accessible. Wheelchair ramps, special parking, specially equipped rest rooms, special class scheduling, lowered drinking fountains, and lowered telephones are available.

Services: Counseling and information services are available, as is tutoring in most subjects. There is remedial math, reading, and writing.

Campus Safety and Security: Measures include informal discussions and distribution of campus safety and security policies and procedures.

Programs of Study: BC confers the B.A. degree. Associate degrees are also awarded. Bachelor's degrees are awarded in COMMUNICATIONS AND THE ARTS (film arts, fine arts, and literature), SOCIAL SCIENCE (human services, humanities, and psychology). Psychology, human services, and film studies are the strongest academically. Film and psychology are the largest.

Required: All students are required to satisfactorily complete at least 120 semester credits, including 36 to 45 upper-level credits in their ma-

jor. Distribution requirements include 9 credits each in the following divisions: personal vision, human community, and natural environment. Specific course requirements include 3 credits each in writing and math. Students are also required to take a 3-credit practicum within their areas of concentration.

Special: Cross-registration is available with the University of Vermont, St. Michael's Trinity College, Champlain College, and the Community College of Vermont; internships through various organizations and work-study programs with nonprofit organizations are also available. The College offers dual majors, interdisciplinary majors, including transpersonal psychology, individualized majors, independent study, a non-residential degree program, credit for life experience, and pass/fail options.

Faculty/Classroom: 48% of faculty are male; 52%, female. All teach undergraduates. The average class size in a regular course is 12.

Requirements: Burlington requires a high school diploma or the GED, and a successful interview with the Director of Admissions. AP and CLEP credits are accepted. Personality/intangible qualities is an important factor in the admission decision.

Procedure: Freshmen are admitted fall, spring, and summer. There are early admissions, deferred admissions, and rolling admissions plans. Application deadlines are open. Check with the school for current application fee. Applications are accepted on computer disk and on-line via CollegeLink.

Transfer: 60 transfer students enrolled in a recent year. Transfer students must meet the same requirements as new students. High school transcripts precede acceptance. The Independent Degree Program requires 45 college credits prior to entrance. Transcripts precede acceptance. 30 of 120 credits required for the bachelor's degree must be completed at BC.

Visiting: There are guides for informal visits and visitors may sit in on classes. To schedule a visit, contact the Admissions Office at *sullivan@burlcol.edu*.

Financial Aid: In a recent year, 70% of all full-time freshmen and 71% of continuing full-time students received some form of financial aid. 39% of full-time freshmen and 69% of continuing full-time students received need-based aid. The average freshman award was $7900. 38% of undergraduates work part time. The average financial indebtedness of a recent graduate was $14,748. The FAFSA is required. Check with the school for current deadlines.

International Students: In a recent year, there were 3 international students enrolled. .

Computers: The mainframe is a Scan network. There are 19 PCs in 2 labs, 2 in the library, and 3 in student workstations. All students may access the system 80 hours per week. There are no time limits. The fall 2003 fee was $45 per semester. It is strongly recommended that all students have a personal computer.

Graduates: In a recent year, 30 bachelor's degrees were awarded. The most popular majors were writing/journalism (36%), transpersonal psychology (30%), and psychology (17%).

Admissions Contact: Cathleen Sullivan, Assistant Director of Admissions. A video is available. E-mail: *admissions@burlcol.edu* Web: *www.burlingtoncollege.edu*

CASTLETON STATE COLLEGE
B-4
Castleton, VT 05735
(802) 468-1213
(800) 639-8521; Fax: (802) 468-1476

Full-time: 628 men, 860 women	**Faculty:** 84; IIB, --$
Part-time: 64 men, 147 women	**Ph.D.s:** 92%
Graduate: 53 men, 127 women	**Student/Faculty:** 18 to 1
Year: semesters, summer session	**Tuition:** $5806 ($12,360)
Application Deadline: open	**Room & Board:** $6014
Freshman Class: 1434 applied, 1139 accepted, 422 enrolled	
SAT I Verbal/Math: 475/490	**ACT:** 19	**COMPETITIVE**

Castleton State College, founded in 1787, is the oldest institution of higher learning in Vermont. As part of the Vermont State Colleges system, it offers a state-supported undergraduate and graduate program in liberal arts, teacher preparation, and professional studies. In addition to regional accreditation, Castleton has baccalaureate program accreditation with CSWE and NLN. The library contains 162,711 volumes, 526,405 microform items, and 3000 audio/video tapes/CDs, and subscribes to 939 periodicals. Computerized library services include the card catalog, interlibrary loans, and database searching. Special learning facilities include a learning resource center, art gallery, radio station, TV studio, observatory, and theater. The 160-acre campus is in a rural area 11 miles west of Rutland. Including any residence halls, there are 24 buildings.

Student Life: 70% of undergraduates are from Vermont. Students are from 25 states and 2 foreign countries. 98% are white. The average age of freshmen is 18; all undergraduates, 22. 30% do not continue beyond their first year; 43% remain to graduate.

Housing: 880 students can be accommodated in college housing, which includes single-sex and coed dorms and off-campus apartments. In addition, there are honors houses. On-campus housing is guaranteed for the freshman year only and is available on a lottery system for upper-classmen. 50% of students live on campus; of those, 50% remain on campus on weekends. All students may keep cars.

Activities: There are no fraternities or sororities. There are 40 groups on campus, including art, band, cheerleading, choir, chorale, chorus, computers, dance, drama, environmental, ethnic, film, gay, honors, international, jazz band, literary magazine, musical theater, newspaper, photography, political, professional, radio and TV, religious, social, social service, sports, student government, and yearbook. Popular campus events include Spring, Winter, Alumni Weekends, and Martin Luther King Jr. Celebration.

Sports: There are 9 intercollegiate sports for men and 10 for women, and 9 intramural sports for men and 9 for women. Facilities include a 6-lane swimming pool, 2 racquetball courts, a fitness center, a recreation gym, and the nearby 2000-acre Pond Hill Ranch with more than 70 miles of trails, swimming, sailing, fishing, and golf facilities.

Disabled Students: All of the campus is accessible. Wheelchair ramps, elevators, special parking, specially equipped rest rooms, special class scheduling, lowered drinking fountains, and lowered telephones are available.

Services: Counseling and information services are available, as is tutoring in every subject. There is a reader service for the blind and remedial math, reading, and writing.

Campus Safety and Security: Measures include 24-hour foot and vehicle patrol, self-defense education, security escort services, and informal discussions. There are pamphlets/posters/films, emergency telephones, and lighted pathways/sidewalks.

Programs of Study: Castleton confers B.A., B.S., and B.S.W. degrees. Associate and master's degrees are also awarded. Bachelor's degrees are awarded in BIOLOGICAL SCIENCE (biology/biological science), BUSINESS (business administration and management), COMMUNICATIONS AND THE ARTS (art, communications, dramatic arts, literature, music, and Spanish), COMPUTER AND PHYSICAL SCIENCE (computer science, geology, mathematics, and natural sciences), EDUCATION (physical), ENGINEERING AND ENVIRONMENTAL DESIGN (environmental science), HEALTH PROFESSIONS (health science and sports medicine), SOCIAL SCIENCE (criminal justice, history, psychology, social science, social work, and sociology). Nursing, athletic training, and science are the strongest academically. Business and teacher preparation are the largest.

Required: All students must maintain a GPA of 2.0 while taking 122 semester hours, including 30 or more in their major. Distribution requirements include 3 courses each in literature and the arts, 2 each in math and natural sciences, and 1 each in foreign cultures, history, philosophy and psychology, and social analysis. Specific courses include computers, communication, and an introduction to liberal arts.

Special: Cross-registration with other Vermont State Colleges, co-op programs, internships, study abroad, and work-study programs are available. In addition, B.A.-B.S. degrees, dual majors, student-designed majors in history, math, and social sciences, a 3-2 engineering degree with Clarkson University, credit for life experience, nondegree study, and pass/fail options are offered. There are 8 national honor societies, a freshman honors program, and 4 departmental honors programs.

Faculty/Classroom: 54% of faculty are male; 46%, female. All teach undergraduates, 50% do research, and 50% do both. The average class size in an introductory lecture is 20; in a laboratory, 14; and in a regular course, 16.

Admissions: 79% of the 2003-2004 applicants were accepted. The SAT I scores for the 2003-2004 freshman class were: Verbal--59% below 500, 32% between 500 and 599, and 9% between 600 and 700; Math--60% below 500, 31% between 500 and 599, 8% between 600 and 700, and 1% above 700.

Requirements: The SAT I or ACT is required. In addition, the college recommends that candidates have 4 years of English, 3 each of math and social studies or history, 2 each of foreign language and science, and 2 to 4 of electives. An essay is required and an interview is recommended. The GED is accepted. A GPA of 2.5 is required. AP and CLEP credits are accepted. Important factors in the admissions decision are advanced placement or honor courses, leadership record, and recommendations by school officials.

Procedure: Freshmen are admitted fall and spring. Entrance exams should be taken during the spring of the junior year or fall of the senior year. There are early admissions and deferred admissions plans. There is a rolling admissions plan. Application deadlines are open. Application fee is $30. Applications are accepted on-line through the school's web site.

Transfer: 193 transfer students enrolled in 2002-2003. Transfer applicants must have a 2.0 GPA. An associate degree, 15 credit hours, and an interview are recommended. 30 of 122 credits required for the bachelor's degree must be completed at Castleton.

Visiting: There are regularly scheduled orientations for prospective students, including meetings with admissions counselors, faculty, and coaches as well as a campus tour. There are guides for informal visits and visitors may sit in on classes. To schedule a visit, contact the Admissions Office at info@castleton.edu.

Financial Aid: In a recent year, 94% of all full-time freshmen and 83% of continuing full-time students received some form of financial aid. 76% of full-time freshmen and 65% of continuing full-time students received need-based aid. The average freshman award was $8200. 38% of undergraduates work part time. Average annual earnings from campus work are $1000. Castleton is a member of CSS. The FAFSA is required. The deadline for filing freshman financial aid applications for fall entry is February 15.

International Students: They must score 500 on the written TOEFL.

Computers: The mainframes are a 8 Novell network servers for use of students and college employees. More than 200 computers are available for student use. The campus is completely wired for Internet access. All residence halls are wired, 1 port per student. All students may access the system. There are no time limits and no fees.

Graduates: From July 1, 2002 to June 30, 2003, 270 bachelor's degrees were awarded. The most popular majors were business (20%), communication (12%), and psychology (12%). In an average class, 4% graduate in 3 years or less, 27% graduate in 4 years or less, 42% graduate in 5 years or less, and 44% graduate in 6 years or less. 115 companies recruited on campus in 2002-2003.

Admissions Contact: Maurice Ouimet, Admissions Director. E-mail: *info@castleton.edu* Web: *www.castleton.edu*

CHAMPLAIN COLLEGE   A-2
Burlington, VT 05402-0670   (802) 860-2727
                                        (800) 570-5858; Fax: (802) 860-2767

Full-time: 845 men, 823 women	**Faculty:** 74; III, av$
Part-time: 376 men, 484 women	**Ph.D.s:** 29%
Graduate: 34 men, 22 women	**Student/Faculty:** 23 to 1
Year: semesters, summer session	**Tuition:** $13,075
Application Deadline: open	**Room & Board:** $8955
Freshman Class: 1821 applied, 1236 accepted, 575 enrolled	
SAT I Verbal/Math: 510/520	**ACT:** 20 COMPETITIVE

Champlain College, founded in 1878, is a private school that offers professional training in a liberal arts setting. Students earn their bachelor's degree, with an embedded associate's degree, in one of 24 majors. Internship opportunities are built into the curriculum. In addition to regional accreditation, Champlain has baccalaureate program accreditation with CAAHEP. The library contains 40,477 volumes, 3601 microform items, and 698 audio/video tapes/CDs, and subscribes to 10,618 periodicals. Computerized library services include the card catalog, interlibrary loans, database searching, and Internet access. Special learning facilities include a video production studio and several multimedia and graphic design studios. The 21-acre campus is in a suburban area in the Hill Section of Burlington. Including any residence halls, there are 38 buildings.

Student Life: 56% of undergraduates are from out of state, mostly the Northeast. Students are from 26 states, 28 foreign countries, and Canada. 85% are from public schools. 95% are white. The average age of freshmen is 19; all undergraduates, 21. 18% do not continue beyond their first year; 71% remain to graduate.

Housing: 680 students can be accommodated in college housing, which includes single-sex and coed dorms. In addition, there are special-interest houses and performing arts, international, and wellness dorms. On-campus housing is guaranteed for all 4 years. 88% of freshmen live on campus; of those, 90% remain on campus on weekends. Alcohol is not permitted. No one may keep cars.

Activities: There are no fraternities or sororities. There are more than 25 groups on campus, including art, chorale, chorus, computers, debate, drama, ethnic, flash animation, gay, honors, international, literary magazine, musical theater, newspaper, outing, photography, professional, religious, sailing, social, social service, and student government. Popular campus events include skiing/snowboarding trips, Spring Meltdown, and "Get Real" community service connection.

Sports: There are 6 intramural sports for men and 6 for women. Athletic and recreation facilities are offered through the community YMCA, local tennis club, rock climbing company, hockey rink, park, and ski resorts.

Disabled Students: 79% of academic buildings and 26% of residence halls are accessible. Wheelchair ramps, elevators, special parking, specially equipped rest rooms, special class scheduling, lowered drinking fountains, and lowered telephones are available.

Services: Counseling and information services are available, as is tutoring in some subjects, including math, accounting, and writing. Peer tutoring is available.

Campus Safety and Security: Measures include 24-hour foot and vehicle patrol, self-defense education, security escort services, and shuttle buses. There are informal discussions, pamphlets/posters/films, emergency telephones, and lighted pathways/sidewalks.

Programs of Study: Champlain confers the B.S. degree. Associate and master's degrees are also awarded. Bachelor's degrees are awarded in BUSINESS (accounting, business administration and management, hospitality management services, hotel/motel and restaurant management, international business management, management information systems, management science, marketing management, and tourism), COMMUNICATIONS AND THE ARTS (communications, communications technology, graphic design, journalism, media arts, multimedia, public relations, and telecommunications), COMPUTER AND PHYSICAL SCIENCE (computer management, computer programming, information sciences and systems, and web services), EDUCATION (early childhood and elementary), ENGINEERING AND ENVIRONMENTAL DESIGN (computer graphics and technological management), HEALTH PROFESSIONS (allied health and radiograph medical technology), SOCIAL SCIENCE (criminal justice, forensic studies, liberal arts/general studies, paralegal studies, prelaw, psychology, and social work). Computer information systems, software engineering, and professional writing are the strongest academically. Business, multimedia/graphic design, and elementary education are the largest.

Required: A GPA of 2.0 and 120 credits are required for the B.S. degree. Courses are required in professional writing, oral communication, global history, ethics, and computer and quantitative proficiency. Distribution requirements include courses in math, English, history, natural science with lab, philosophy, social science, and fine arts. Students must take between 30 and 60 hours in the major and a comprehensive exam and/or a thesis in some majors.

Special: Cross-registration with St. Michael's College, co-op programs, internships, and study abroad through school-sponsored programs in England, France, Sweden, and Switzerland are available. Study abroad in several other countries is also available. Dual majors are possible through the professional studies program and computer information systems program. Accelerated degree programs, such as the 5-year B.S./M.B.A. with Clarkson and Southern New Hampshire Universities, and student-designed majors are also available. There is a freshman honors program.

Faculty/Classroom: 59% of faculty are male; 41%, female. All teach undergraduates. No introductory courses are taught by graduate students. The average class size in an introductory lecture is 19; in a laboratory, 15; and in a regular course, 19.

Admissions: 68% of the 2003-2004 applicants were accepted. The SAT I scores for the 2003-2004 freshman class were: Verbal--40% below 500, 50% between 500 and 599, 9% between 600 and 700, and 1% above 700; Math--39% below 500, 48% between 500 and 599, and 12% between 600 and 700. The ACT scores were 59% below 21, 26% between 21 and 23, 11% between 24 and 26, and 4% between 27 and 28. 25% of the current freshmen were in the top fifth of their class; 65% were in the top two fifths.

Requirements: The SAT I or ACT is required. In addition, applicants must be graduates of an accredited high school or the equivalent. AP and CLEP credits are accepted. Important factors in the admissions decision are advanced placement or honor courses, recommendations by school officials, and leadership record.

Procedure: Freshmen are admitted fall and spring. Entrance exams should be taken prior to applying. There is a deferred admissions plan. There is a rolling admissions plan. Application deadlines are open. Notification is sent within 4 weeks of receiving a completed application. The fall 2003 application fee was $40. Applications are accepted on-line through *www.champlain.edu.*

Transfer: 109 transfer students enrolled in 2003-2004. High school and college transcripts are required. 45 of 120 credits required for the bachelor's degree must be completed at Champlain.

Visiting: There are regularly scheduled orientations for prospective students, including a group information session followed by a tour. Personal interviews are also available with an admissions counselor. There are guides for informal visits and visitors may sit in on classes. To schedule a visit, contact the Admissions Office at *admission@champlain.edu.*

Financial Aid: In 2003-2004, 60% of all full-time students received some form of financial aid. 60% of all full-time students received need-based aid. The average freshman award was $9384, including loans, grants, work-study, and other scholarships. 70% of undergraduates work part time. Average annual earnings from campus work are $1190. The FAFSA and the college's own financial statement are required. The priority date for freshman financial aid applications for fall entry is May 1.

International Students: There are 60 international students enrolled. The school actively recruits these students. They must score 500 on the written TOEFL or 173 on the electronic version.

Computers: The mainframe is an IBM AS/400. Champlain provides more than 250 PCs and Macs, available in the library, student center, and other locations. All students may access the system. There are no time limits and no fees. It is strongly recommended that all students have a personal computer. Students in multimedia graphic design must have personal computers; Mac is recommended.

Graduates: From July 1, 2002 to June 30, 2003, 264 bachelor's degrees were awarded. The most popular majors were business (18%), elementary education (12%), and accounting (9%). In an average class, 71% graduate in 4 years or less, and 80% graduate in 6 years or less. More than 70 companies recruited on campus in 2002-2003. Of the 2002 graduating class, 3% were enrolled in graduate school within 6 months of graduation and 97% were employed.

Admissions Contact: Josephine Churchill, Director of Admissions. A video is available. E-mail: *admission@champlain.edu* Web: *www.champlain.edu*

COLLEGE OF SAINT JOSEPH
B-4
Rutland, VT 05701-3899 (802) 773-5900, ext. 3205
(877) 270-9998; Fax: (802) 776-5258

Full-time: 83 men, 126 women	**Faculty:** 12
Part-time: 40 men, 60 women	**Ph.D.s:** 67%
Graduate: 86 men, 133 women	**Student/Faculty:** 17 to 1
Year: semesters, summer session	**Tuition:** $12,700
Application Deadline: open	**Room & Board:** $6400
Freshman Class: 141 applied, 114 accepted, 39 enrolled	
SAT I: required	**ACT:** recommended

COMPETITIVE

The College of St. Joseph, founded in 1956, is a private Catholic institution offering undergraduate programs in the arts and sciences, business, computer information science, education, psychology, and human services, and graduate programs in business, education, and psychology. The college serves a primarily commuter student body. The library contains 43,000 volumes, 13,000 microform items, and 7000 audio/video tapes/CDs, and subscribes to 251 periodicals. Computerized library services include the card catalog, interlibrary loans, and database searching. Special learning facilities include a learning resource center. The 90-acre campus is in a rural area 1 mile west of Rutland. Including any residence halls, there are 5 buildings.

Student Life: 53% of undergraduates are from Vermont. Students are from 13 states and 3 foreign countries. 89% are white. 55% are Catholic; 20% Protestant; 6% Jewish. The average age of freshmen is 20; all undergraduates, 25. 38% do not continue beyond their first year; 52% remain to graduate.

Housing: 160 students can be accommodated in college housing, which includes single-sex dorms. On-campus housing is guaranteed for all 4 years. 75% of students commute. All students may keep cars.

Activities: There are no fraternities or sororities. There are 15 groups on campus, including chorus, drama, honors, literary magazine, musical theater, newspaper, political, professional, religious, social, social service, student government, and yearbook. Popular campus events include Spring Fling, cultural event series (year round), and Student Leadership-Academic Awards Dinner.

Sports: There are 2 intercollegiate sports for men and 3 for women, and 3 intramural sports for men and 3 for women. Facilities include a 1000-seat gym, a fitness center, racquetball courts, an aerobics studio, a cross-country skiing/running trail, a softball diamond, and a soccer field.

Disabled Students: All of the campus is accessible. Wheelchair ramps, special parking, specially equipped rest rooms, special class scheduling, and lowered telephones are available.

Services: Counseling and information services are available, as is tutoring in every subject. There is remedial math, reading, and writing. There is also personal growth counseling and spiritual counseling.

Campus Safety and Security: Measures include shuttle buses, informal discussions, pamphlets/posters/films, and emergency telephones. There are lighted pathways/sidewalks and a nighttime security patrol.

Programs of Study: CSJ confers B.A. and B.S. degrees. Associate and master's degrees are also awarded. Bachelor's degrees are awarded in BUSINESS (accounting, business administration and management, marketing management, recreational facilities management, and sports management), COMMUNICATIONS AND THE ARTS (communications, English, and journalism), COMPUTER AND PHYSICAL SCIENCE (computer science), EDUCATION (computer, early childhood, elementary, secondary, and special), SOCIAL SCIENCE (history, human services, liberal arts/general studies, and psychology). Education is the strongest academically. Arts and sciences are the largest.

Required: To graduate, students must complete 127 credit hours with a minimum GPA of 2.0 (2.5 is required for acceptance to teacher certification program), including 12 credits in English/speech, 9 each in social/behavioral sciences and math/computer, 6 each in philosophy/religious studies and natural sciences, and 3 in fine arts. Human services majors must complete 2 internships. The number of hours in the major varies, from 36 to 48 for arts and sciences to 51 to 60 for business and education.

Special: The college offers internships in history and political science, and in Rutland County businesses, human service agencies, and elementary and secondary schools. In addition, dual majors, study abroad, and independent and directed study options are available. An accelerated degree program is available in organizational leadership. There are 5 national honor societies.

Faculty/Classroom: 67% of faculty are male; 33%, female. All teach undergraduates. No introductory courses are taught by graduate students. The average class size in an introductory lecture is 15; in a laboratory, 12; and in a regular course, 8.

Admissions: 81% of the 2003-2004 applicants were accepted. The SAT I scores for the 2003-2004 freshman class were: Verbal--25% below 500, and 75% between 500 and 599; Math--25% below 500, and 75% between 500 and 599. 10% of the current freshmen were in the top fifth of their class; 60% were in the top two fifths.

Requirements: The SAT I or ACT is required. The SAT I is preferred. In addition, applicants should be graduates of accredited secondary schools or have earned a GED. College preparatory study must include 4 years of English, 3 of math, 2 each of science and social studies, and 5 other academic electives. The college prefers that students rank in the upper 70% of their graduating class. The SAT II: Writing test is strongly recommended. An essay is required and an interview is recommended. A GPA of 2.0 is required. AP and CLEP credits are accepted. Important factors in the admissions decision are advanced placement or honor courses, leadership record, and extracurricular activities record.

Procedure: Freshmen are admitted to all sessions. Entrance exams should be taken by December of the senior year. There are early admissions and deferred admissions plans. There is a rolling admissions plan. Application deadlines are open. Application fee is $25.

Transfer: 34 transfer students enrolled in 2002-2003. Transfers must present a minimum GPA of 2.0. 30 of 127 credits required for the bachelor's degree must be completed at CSJ.

Visiting: There are regularly scheduled orientations for prospective students, including a campus tour, admissions interview, and visits to classes. There are guides for informal visits and visitors may sit in on classes and stay overnight. To schedule a visit, contact the Admissions Office at *admissions@csj.edu.*

Financial Aid: CSJ is a member of CSS. The FAFSA, the state aid form, and the college's own financial statement are required. The deadline for filing freshman financial aid applications for fall entry is March 1.

International Students: There are 4 international students enrolled. They must score 550 on the written TOEFL and also take the SAT I or the ACT.

Computers: The mainframe is an IBM AS/400. A network of 20 PCs is available for academic use. Additional PCs are available in the library lab for student use. All students may access the system. There are no time limits and no fees.

Graduates: From July 1, 2002 to June 30, 2003, 58 bachelor's degrees were awarded. The most popular majors were business management (19%), education (16%), and psychology (11%). In an average class, 41% graduate in 4 years or less, 44% graduate in 5 years or less, and 44% graduate in 6 years or less. Of the 2002 graduating class, 85% were enrolled in graduate school within 6 months of graduation and 12% were employed.

Admissions Contact: Patricia Ryan, Director of Admissions and Marketing. E-mail: *admissions@csj.edu* Web: *www.csj.edu*

GODDARD COLLEGE

Plainfield, VT 05667

C-2

(802) 454-8311, ext. 322
(800) 468-4888; Fax: (802) 454-1029

Full-time: 130 men, 190 women	**Faculty:** 14
Part-time: none	**Ph.D.s:** 71%
Graduate: 95 men, 210 women	**Student/Faculty:** 23 to 1
Year: semesters	**Tuition:** $18,095
Application Deadline: open	**Room & Board:** $2965
Freshman Class: n/av	
SAT I or ACT: not required	**COMPETITIVE+**

Goddard College, founded in 1938, is a private college that stresses progressive, individualized education for personal and community transformation, based on John Dewey's learning-by-involvement theory. Figures in the above capsule and in this profile are approximate. The library contains 70,000 volumes and 1100 audio/video tapes/CDs, and subscribes to 280 periodicals. Computerized library services include interlibrary loans and database searching. Special learning facilities include a learning resource center, radio station, a holograph lab, and a video/photo studio. The 200-acre campus is in a rural area 10 miles from Montpelier. Including any residence halls, there are 26 buildings.

Student Life: 87% of undergraduates are from out of state, mostly the Northeast. Students are from 49 states, 11 foreign countries, and Canada. 82% are white. The average age of freshmen is 21; all undergraduates, 26. 38% do not continue beyond their first year; 46% remain to graduate.

Housing: 225 students can be accommodated in college housing, which includes single-sex and coed dorms and married-student housing. In addition, there are special-interest houses and an ecology house. On-campus housing is guaranteed for all 4 years. 70% of students live on campus; of those, 75% remain on campus on weekends. Alcohol is not permitted. All students may keep cars.

Activities: There are no fraternities or sororities. There are 9 groups on campus, including art, drama, gay, jazz band, literary magazine, newspaper, photography, radio and TV, and student government.

Sports: There is no sports program at Goddard. Facilities include tennis and volleyball courts and hiking and cross-country ski trails.

Disabled Students: Wheelchair ramps, elevators, special parking, and specially equipped rest rooms are available.

Services: There is remedial writing. An adviser system requires 1-hour weekly meetings with a faculty adviser.

Campus Safety and Security: Measures include 24-hour foot and vehicle patrol, self-defense education, shuttle buses, and informal discussions. There are pamphlets/posters/films and lighted pathways/sidewalks.

Programs of Study: Goddard confers the B.A. degree. Master's degrees are also awarded. Bachelor's degrees are awarded in COMMUNICATIONS AND THE ARTS (creative writing, media arts, and visual and performing arts), EDUCATION (education), ENGINEERING AND ENVIRONMENTAL DESIGN (environmental science), SOCIAL SCIENCE (counseling/psychology, crosscultural studies, human ecology, interdisciplinary studies, social science, and women's studies). Writing, literature, and education are the strongest academically. Women's studies is the largest.

Required: All degree programs are full-time only, provide individual faculty advisers for every semester (except study leaves), and require written study plans and narrative evaluations. Individual programs of study are student designed, although the program in general is course based. There are no declared majors, but in the last semester of enrollment, all students must complete an in-depth senior study or project that may be cross- or multidisciplinary and requires foundation work comparable to a major. A total of 120 credits is required to graduate.

Special: Students and faculty design all curricula; there are no prescribed courses. Learning takes the form of group or independent studies, workshops, action projects, research, field trips, seminars, and performances. There are a number of away-from-campus study options, including a field semester involving an internship, apprenticeship, or study-travel and a semester-abroad program offered in 20 countries.

Faculty/Classroom: 57% of faculty are male; 43%, female. All teach undergraduates. No introductory courses are taught by graduate students. The average class size in an introductory lecture is 8 and in a regular course, 10.

Requirements: Goddard admits students who can contribute to its learning community and who will thrive in a self-directed study program, and bases the admissions decision on the student's application, which includes several essays, letters of recommendation, and transcripts, and samples of the student's work. A personal interview, and SAT I or ACT scores, when submitted, are also considered. AP and CLEP credits are accepted. Important factors in the admissions decision are personality/intangible qualities, advanced placement or honor courses, and evidence of special talent.

Procedure: Freshmen are admitted to all sessions. There are early decision, deferred admissions, and rolling admissions plans. Application deadlines are open. The fall 2003 application fee was $40. Applications are accepted on-line at *www.goddard.edu.*

Transfer: 19 transfer students enrolled in a recent year. College transcripts must be submitted by transfer applicants. 30 of 120 credits required for the bachelor's degree must be completed at Goddard.

Visiting: There are regularly scheduled orientations for prospective students, including Discover Goddard Days held in fall and spring and individual tours and interviews. There are guides for informal visits and visitors may sit in on classes and stay overnight. To schedule a visit, contact the Admissions Office at (802) 454-8311, ext. 307 or (800) 468-4888, or *admissions@goddard.edu.*

Financial Aid: In a recent year, 96% of all full-time freshmen and 72% of continuing full-time students received some form of financial aid. The average freshman award was $13,216. All undergraduates work part time. Average annual earnings from campus work are $900. The average financial indebtedness of a recent graduate was $14,900. The FAFSA is required. Check with the school for current deadlines.

International Students: In a recent year, there were 2 international students enrolled. They must score 550 on the written TOEFL.

Computers: The mainframes are an IBM 5/34 and an AS400. Many types of PCs are available for student use in the computer center, and dorms have computer network access. There are also Mac systems available at the 2 computer labs. All students may access the system 24 hours a day, 7 days a week. There are no time limits and no fees.

Graduates: In a recent year, 91 bachelor's degrees were awarded. The most popular majors were interdisciplinary liberal arts and sciences (91%), education (7%), and health arts and sciences (2%). In an average class, 41% graduate in 5 years or less, and 48% graduate in 6 years or less.

Admissions Contact: Brenda Hawkins, Director of Admissions. E-mail: *admissions@goddard.edu* Web: *http://www.goddard.edu*

GREEN MOUNTAIN COLLEGE
A-4
Poultney, VT 05764
(802) 287-8000
(800) 776-6675; Fax: (802) 287-8099

Full-time: 339 men, 292 women	**Faculty:** 38
Part-time: 13 men, 15 women	**Ph.Ds:** 87%
Graduate: none	**Student/Faculty:** 17 to 1
Year: semesters, summer session	**Tuition:** $18,280
Application Deadline: open	**Room & Board:** $5850
Freshman Class: 721 applied, 642 accepted, 141 enrolled	
SAT I Verbal/Math: 520/505	**ACT:** 19 COMPETITIVE

Green Mountain College, established in 1834, is a private, nonprofit, environmental liberal arts institution. In addition to regional accreditation, GMC has baccalaureate program accreditation with NRPA. The library contains 60,000 volumes, 10,000 microform items, and 2000 audio/video tapes/CDs, and subscribes to 300 periodicals. Computerized library services include the card catalog, interlibrary loans, and database searching. Special learning facilities include a learning resource center, art gallery, organic farm, rope course, and Welsh Heritage Center. The 155-acre campus is in a small town 20 miles southwest of Rutland. Including any residence halls, there are 26 buildings.

Student Life: 89% of undergraduates are from out of state, mostly the Northeast. Students are from 28 states, 18 foreign countries, and Canada. 70% are from public schools. 64% are white. The average age of freshmen is 18; all undergraduates, 21. 40% do not continue beyond their first year; 40% remain to graduate.

Housing: 649 students can be accommodated in college housing, which includes coed dorms and special-interest floors. On-campus housing is guaranteed for all 4 years. 95% of students live on campus; of those, 80% remain on campus on weekends. All students may keep cars.

Activities: There are no fraternities or sororities. There are 30 groups on campus, including art, bagpipe band, band, Big Brothers/Big Sisters, cheerleading, choir, chorale, chorus, dance, drama, environmental, gay, honors, international, jazz band, literary magazine, newspaper, professional, religious, social, social service, student government, and yearbook. Popular campus events include Family Weekend, Honors Banquet, and Welsh Heritage Harvest Festival.

Sports: There are 7 intercollegiate sports for men and 7 for women, and 8 intramural sports for men and 7 for women. Facilities include a gym with an indoor pool, weight room, playing fields, tennis courts, a par course, fitness trail, and ropes course.

Disabled Students: 70% of the campus is accessible. Wheelchair ramps, elevators, special parking, specially equipped rest rooms, special class scheduling, and lowered drinking fountains are available.

Services: Counseling and information services are available, as is tutoring in every subject. There is remedial math, reading, and writing.

Campus Safety and Security: Measures include 24-hour foot and vehicle patrol and lighted pathways/sidewalks.

Programs of Study: GMC confers B.A., B.S., and B.F.A. degrees. Bachelor's degrees are awarded in AGRICULTURE (environmental studies), BIOLOGICAL SCIENCE (biology/biological science), BUSINESS (business administration and management, recreation and leisure services, and recreational facilities management), COMMUNICATIONS AND THE ARTS (art, arts administration/management, communications, creative writing, English, fine arts, and visual and performing arts), EDUCATION (art, elementary, English, secondary, social studies, and special), HEALTH PROFESSIONS (recreation therapy), SOCIAL SCIENCE (behavioral science, history, liberal arts/general studies, philosophy, and psychology). Recreation, elementary education, and environmental studies are the largest.

Required: To graduate, students must complete 37 hours in Environmental Liberal Arts, including 4 core courses, a 1-credit orientation course, and 8 additional courses chosen from 4 distribution categories. A minimum GPA of 2.0 is required. Students must complete 120 to 125 credit hours, with 42 to 65 hours in the major. 33 credits must be completed in upper division courses.

Special: Semester-long internships are required in all majors. Students may study abroad in Wales, Korea, England, Spain, Japan, France, and Italy. Work-study programs and a self-designed major are available. Co-op and accelerated degree programs are available in Resort and Leisure Management, as is a 4-1 MBA program with Clarkson and Southern New Hampshire Universities. There is 1 national honor society, a freshman honors program, and 4 departmental honors programs.

Faculty/Classroom: 67% of faculty are male; 33%, female. 66% teach undergraduates and 34% both teach and do research. The average class size in an introductory lecture is 25; in a laboratory, 15; and in a regular course, 14.

Admissions: 89% of the 2003-2004 applicants were accepted. The SAT I scores for the 2003-2004 freshman class were: Verbal--40% below 500, 39% between 500 and 599, 16% between 600 and 700, and 5% above 700; Math--44% below 500, 41% between 500 and 599, and 15% between 600 and 700. The ACT scores were 64% below 21, 22% between 21 and 23, 6% between 27 and 28, and 8% above 28. 21%

of the current freshmen were in the top fifth of their class; 51% were in the top two fifths.

Requirements: The SAT I is required and the ACT is recommended. In addition, applicants must graduate from an accredited secondary school or have a GED. 16 academic credits are required. Students must complete 4 years in English, 3 years in math, 2 to 3 years in science, and 2 years each in history and social studies. An essay is required. Interviews are recommended, along with portfolios where appropriate. A GPA of 2.4 is required. AP and CLEP credits are accepted. Important factors in the admissions decision are personality/intangible qualities, advanced placement or honor courses, and evidence of special talent.

Procedure: Freshmen are admitted fall and spring. Entrance exams should be taken in the fall of the senior year of high school. There are early admissions and deferred admissions plans. Application deadlines are open. Application fee is $30. Applications are accepted on-line through www.greenmtn.edu. Notification is sent on a rolling basis.

Transfer: 56 transfer students enrolled in a recent year. Transfer students need a GPA of 2.0. They must have earned a minimum of 12 credits and are required to submit an essay. The SAT I or ACT is required, along with 2 letters of recommendation and a dean's statement from last school attended. 30 of 120 credits required for the bachelor's degree must be completed at GMC.

Visiting: There are regularly scheduled orientations for prospective students, including a campus tour, presentations by administrators, student panel, lunch in dining hall, and academic offerings. There are guides for informal visits and visitors may sit in on classes and stay overnight. To schedule a visit, contact Joann Larson, Campus Visit Coordinator at visit@greenmtn.edu.

Financial Aid: In 2003-2004, 80% of all full-time freshmen and 78% of continuing full-time students received some form of financial aid. 74% of full-time freshmen and 72% of continuing full-time students received need-based aid. The average freshman award was $10,983. Need-based scholarships or need-based grants averaged $8413; and need-based self-help aid (loans and jobs) averaged $2865. 45% of undergraduates work part time. Average annual earnings from campus work are $1100. The average financial indebtedness of a recent graduate was $15,000. The FAFSA is required. Check with the school for current deadlines.

International Students: There were 48 international students enrolled in a recent year. The school actively recruits these students. They must score 500 on the written TOEFL or 173 on the electronic version and also take the SAT I or the ACT.

Computers: PCs are available for student use in the computer center, student center, and residence halls. All students may access the system 24 hours/7 days a week. There are no time limits and no fees.

Graduates: In a recent year, 126 bachelor's degrees were awarded. The most popular majors were education (19%), business (15%), and environmental studies (11%). In an average class, 24% graduate in 4 years or less, 37% graduate in 5 years or less, and 37% graduate in 6 years or less. 21 companies recruited on campus in a recent year. Of the 2002 graduating class, 4% were enrolled in graduate school within 6 months of graduation and 75% were employed.

Admissions Contact: Joel R. Wincowski, Dean of Enrollment and Retention Management. A video is available.
E-mail: admiss@greenmtn.edu Web: www.greenmtn.edu

JOHNSON STATE COLLEGE
C-2
Johnson, VT 05656
(802) 635-1219
(800) 635-2356; Fax: (802) 635-1230

Full-time: 502 men, 609 women	**Faculty:** 62; IIB, -$
Part-time: 104 men, 317 women	**Ph.Ds:** 90%
Graduate: 60 men, 167 women	**Student/Faculty:** 18 to 1
Year: semesters, summer session	**Tuition:** $5806 ($12,360)
Application Deadline: March 1	**Room & Board:** $6013
Freshman Class: 866 applied, 756 accepted, 291 enrolled	
SAT I or ACT: required	LESS COMPETITIVE

Johnson State College, founded in 1828, is a public liberal arts and science college, offering more than 30 academic and professional degree programs. Some information in the above capsule is approximate. The library contains 96,584 volumes, 180,158 microform items, and 7200 audio/video tapes/CDs, and subscribes to 631 periodicals. Computerized library services include the card catalog, interlibrary loans, and database searching. Special learning facilities include a learning resource center, art gallery, radio station, and 24-hour study room. The 350-acre campus is in a small town 45 miles northeast of Burlington. Including any residence halls, there are 12 buildings.

Student Life: 63% of undergraduates are from Vermont. Students are from 23 states, 6 foreign countries, and Canada. 71% are white. The average age of freshmen is 19; all undergraduates, 21.

Housing: 549 students can be accommodated in college housing, which includes coed dorms, on-campus apartments, and married-student housing. In addition, there are special-interest houses, an alcohol-free residence hall, an International Lifestyle Program, and quiet-hour floors. On-campus housing is guaranteed for all 4 years. 57% of students live on campus. Alcohol is not permitted. All students may keep cars.

Activities: There are no fraternities or sororities. There are 35 groups on campus, including art, band, choir, chorus, dance, drama, environmental, gay, hospitality, international, jazz band, leadership, literary magazine, musical theater, newspaper, outdoor, photography, political, professional, radio and TV, religious, social, social service, student government, and yearbook. Popular campus events include Winter Carnival, Coffee House (weekly live entertainment), and Women's History Month Celebration.

Sports: There are 5 intercollegiate sports for men and 5 for women, and 20 intramural sports for men and 20 for women. Facilities include the athletic center which houses a 25-yard pool, a 700-seat varsity basketball court, 3 handball/racquetball courts, a weight training room, an aerobic fitness center, a 7000-square-foot multi-use gym, and a fully equipped training room.

Disabled Students: 60% of the campus is accessible. Wheelchair ramps, elevators, special parking, specially equipped rest rooms, special class scheduling, and lowered drinking fountains are available.

Services: Counseling and information services are available, as is tutoring in most subjects. There is a reader service for the blind and remedial math, reading, and writing. The Academic Support Services Department provides accommodations for students with a documented learning disability.

Campus Safety and Security: Measures include 24-hour foot and vehicle patrol, self-defense education, security escort services, and shuttle buses. There are informal discussions, pamphlets/posters/films, emergency telephones, and lighted pathways/sidewalks.

Programs of Study: Johnson State confers B.A., B.S., and B.F.A. degrees. Associate and master's degrees are also awarded. Bachelor's degrees are awarded in AGRICULTURE (natural resource management), BIOLOGICAL SCIENCE (biology/biological science and cell biology), BUSINESS (accounting, business administration and management, business systems analysis, hospitality management services, management information systems, recreational facilities management, small business management, and tourism), COMMUNICATIONS AND THE ARTS (art, creative writing, English, fine arts, jazz, journalism, music, music business management, music history and appreciation, music performance, performing arts, studio art, theater design, theater management, and visual and performing arts), COMPUTER AND PHYSICAL SCIENCE (computer management, information sciences and systems, and mathematics), EDUCATION (art, athletic training, education, elementary, English, environmental, mathematics, middle school, music, physical, recreation, science, and secondary), ENGINEERING AND ENVIRONMENTAL DESIGN (environmental science), HEALTH PROFESSIONS (allied health, health science, premedicine, and sports medicine), SOCIAL SCIENCE (anthropology, behavioral science, history, humanities, liberal arts/general studies, physical fitness/movement, political science/government, prelaw, psychology, and sociology). Environmental science, sports medicine, and outdoor education are the largest.

Required: The bachelor's degree requires completion of at least 120 credit hours of course work (not including basic skills credits), with a minimum cumulative GPA of 2.0. In addition, students must complete the general education core curriculum and an approved major as well as take a writing proficiency exam.

Special: All students are encouraged to complete an internship. Through the National Student Exchange Program, students may study at another institution or abroad in 51 countries for a semester or a year. Co-op programs are offered in business, tourism, hospitality management, and education, and cross-registration is available with other Vermont state colleges. There is 1 national honor society.

Faculty/Classroom: 58% of faculty are male; 42%, female. All teach undergraduates. No introductory courses are taught by graduate students.

Admissions: 87% of the 2003-2004 applicants were accepted. The SAT I scores for the 2003-2004 freshman class were: Verbal--56% below 500, 37% between 500 and 599, and 7% between 600 and 700; Math--64% below 500, 32% between 500 and 599, and 4% between 600 and 700. 7% of the current freshmen were in the top fifth of their class; 25% were in the top two fifths.

Requirements: The SAT I or ACT is required. In addition, successful candidates for admission have generally completed a college preparatory curriculum consisting of 4 years of English, 3 of math (2 of algebra, 1 of geometry), 3 of social sciences, and 2 of science (including 1 lab science). An official high school transcript or GED test score must be submitted with the application. In addition, 1 letter of recommendation, preferably from a guidance counselor, and SAT I or ACT scores should be sent with the application or under separate cover. A GPA of 2.0 is required. AP and CLEP credits are accepted. Important factors in the admissions decision are advanced placement or honor courses, recommendations by school officials, and extracurricular activities record.

Procedure: Freshmen are admitted fall and spring. There is a deferred admissions plan. There is a rolling admissions plan. Applications should be filed by March 1 for fall entry and December 1 for spring entry, along

with a $30 fee. Notification is sent on a rolling basis. Applications are accepted on-line through the school's web site, CollegeLink, Apply, and Peterson's Universal Application.

Transfer: A GPA of at least 2.0 is required. 30 of 120 credits required for the bachelor's degree must be completed at Johnson State.

Visiting: There are regularly scheduled orientations for prospective students, including a campus tour and an admission interview. Students may request to meet with a faculty member. There are guides for informal visits and visitors may sit in on classes. To schedule a visit, contact Marie Burns, Admission Receptionist.

Financial Aid: Johnson State is a member of CSS. The FAFSA is required. The deadline for filing freshman financial aid applications for fall entry is March 1.

International Students: The school actively recruits these students. They must score 500 on the written TOEFL or 173 on the electronic version.

Computers: Computing Services provides students with a total of 130 Pentium PCs in 4 computer labs. All computer labs provide full access to the Internet and e-mail. All students may access the system. There are no time limits and no fees.

Admissions Contact: Penny P. Howrigan, Associate Dean of Enrollment Services. E-mail: *jscappy@badger.jsc.vsc.edu* Web: *www.jsc.vsc.edu*

LYNDON STATE COLLEGE　　　　　D-2
Lyndonville, VT 05851　　　　　(802) 626-6413
　　　　　(800) 225-1998; Fax: (802) 626-6335

Full-time: 563 men, 571 women	**Faculty:** 56; IIB, --$
Part-time: 66 men, 225 women	**Ph.D.s:** 60%
Graduate: 1 man, 6 women	**Student/Faculty:** 20 to 1
Year: semesters, summer session	**Tuition:** $6632 ($13,186)
Application Deadline: open	**Room & Board:** $6014
Freshman Class: 1188 applied, 1102 accepted, 504 enrolled	
SAT I or ACT: required	**LESS COMPETITIVE**

Lyndon State College, founded in 1911 as a teachers' college, became a liberal arts school in 1962, offering undergraduate and graduate courses. There is 1 undergraduate and 1 graduate school. In addition to regional accreditation, LSC has baccalaureate program accreditation with NRPA. The library contains 100,000 volumes, 10,000 microform items, and 3600 audio/video tapes/CDs, and subscribes to 545 periodicals. Computerized library services include the card catalog, interlibrary loans, database searching, and Internet access. Special learning facilities include a learning resource center, art gallery, radio station, TV station, a founder's museum, and meteorology lab. The 175-acre campus is in a small town in northeastern Vermont, 184 miles north of Boston. Including any residence halls, there are 17 buildings.

Student Life: 60% of undergraduates are from Vermont. Students are from 24 states, 12 foreign countries, and Canada. 99% are white. The average age of freshmen is 18; all undergraduates, 24. 33% do not continue beyond their first year; 41% remain to graduate.

Housing: 600 students can be accommodated in college housing, which includes single-sex and coed dorms. In addition, there are special-interest houses. On-campus housing is available on a first-come, first-served basis. Priority is given to out-of-town students. 56% of students commute. All students may keep cars.

Activities: There are no fraternities or sororities. There are 22 groups on campus, including cheerleading, choir, chorale, chorus, dance, drama, film, gay, honors, international, jazz band, literary magazine, newspaper, photography, political, professional, radio and TV, religious, social, social service, student government, and yearbook. Popular campus events include Family Weekend, Alumni Weekend, and a concert series.

Sports: There are 5 intercollegiate sports for men and 5 for women, and 12 intramural sports for men and 12 for women. Facilities include a fitness center, which includes a wide variety of cardiovascular, selectorized and free weight equipment, racquetball courts, an auxiliary gym, and an Olympic-size pool. Other facilities include outdoor tennis courts, cross-country ski trails and running trails, access to an ice rink, nearby mountains, and a ski resort, and softball, soccer, basketball and rugby fields.

Disabled Students: 70% of the campus is accessible. Wheelchair ramps, elevators, special parking, specially equipped rest rooms, and lowered drinking fountains are available.

Services: Counseling and information services are available, as is tutoring in every subject. There is remedial math, reading, and writing. A math lab and a writing center are available for student use.

Campus Safety and Security: Measures include 24-hour foot and vehicle patrol, self-defense education, security escort services, and emergency telephones. There are lighted pathways/sidewalks and a security and safety service on campus as well as a 24-hour emergency rescue squad.

Programs of Study: LSC confers B.A. and B.S. degrees. Associate and master's degrees are also awarded. Bachelor's degrees are awarded in BUSINESS (accounting, business administration and management, recreation and leisure services, and sports management), COMMUNICATIONS AND THE ARTS (communications, English, graphic design, journalism, multimedia, and radio/television technology), COMPUTER AND PHYSICAL SCIENCE (atmospheric sciences and meteorology, mathematics, natural sciences, and science), EDUCATION (early childhood, elementary, English, physical, recreation, and science), SOCIAL SCIENCE (human services, interdisciplinary studies, psychology, and social science). Meteorology, natural science, and math are the strongest academically. Education, communications, and business are the largest.

Required: All students must maintain a minimum GPA of 2.0 while taking 122 semester hours, including 42 hours in liberal arts. Distribution requirements include 28 credits in arts, humanities, math and science, and social and behavioral sciences. Required courses include freshman English and college algebra.

Special: Cooperative programs in a variety of businesses, including local ski areas, social agencies, and radio and TV stations, internships in recreation programs and communications, and study abroad in Nova Scotia and England are available. B.A.-B.S. degrees, work-study, a general studies degree, dual and student-designed majors, a 3-2 engineering degree with Norwich University in Vermont, credit for life experience, nondegree study, cross-registration, work study, accelerated degree programs and pass/fail options also are offered. There is 1 national honor society, a freshman honors program, and 1 departmental honors program.

Faculty/Classroom: 66% of faculty are male; 34%, female. All teach undergraduates. The average class size in an introductory lecture is 20; in a laboratory, 16; and in a regular course, 16.

Admissions: 93% of the 2003-2004 applicants were accepted. 4 freshmen graduated first in their class.

Requirements: The SAT I or ACT is required. In addition, ISC recommends that applicants have 4 years of English and 2 each of math, foreign language, history, and science. An essay is required, as is a recommendation from the high school principal or guidance counselor. An interview is recommended. The GED is accepted. A GPA of 2.0 is required. AP and CLEP credits are accepted. Important factors in the admissions decision are advanced placement or honor courses, recommendations by school officials, and leadership record.

Procedure: Freshmen are admitted fall and spring. Entrance exams should be taken. There are early decision, early admissions, and deferred admissions plans. There is a rolling admissions plan. Application deadlines are open. Application fee is $32. Applications are accepted on-line through the college's web site.

Transfer: 115 transfer students enrolled in 2002-2003. Interviews are recommended for transfer students. An official transcript from each college attended is required. 30 of 122 credits required for the bachelor's degree must be completed at LSC.

Visiting: There are regularly scheduled orientations for prospective students, including a tour, an information session, and faculty presentations. There are guides for informal visits and visitors may sit in on classes and stay overnight. To schedule a visit, contact the Admissions Office at *admissions@lyndonstate.edu*.

Financial Aid: In 2003-2004, 87% of all full-time freshmen and 96% of continuing full-time students received some form of financial aid. 69% of full-time freshmen and 75% of continuing full-time students received need-based aid. The average freshman award was $8079. Need-based scholarships or need-based grants averaged $3879 ($5000 maximum); need-based self-help aid (loans and jobs) averaged $3817 ($4625 maximum); and non-need-based awards and non-need-based scholarships averaged $3860 ($5646 maximum). Average annual earnings from campus work are $1262. The average financial indebtedness of the 2003 graduate was $18,084. LSC is a member of CSS. The FAFSA is required. Parent and student income tax forms may be requested. The priority date for freshman financial aid applications for fall entry is February 15. The deadline for filing freshman financial aid applications for fall entry is March 15.

International Students: There are 10 international students enrolled. They must score 500 on the written TOEFL.

Computers: There are 14 computer labs with 230 computers, all on the local area network, with access to the Internet, loaded with standard office and academic tools. All students may access the system 24 hours a day, 7 days a week. There are no time limits and no fees. It is strongly recommended that all students have a personal computer. Dell or Apple computers are recommended for some academic programs.

Graduates: The most popular majors were psychology/human services (19%), business (10%), and education (10%). In an average class, 21% graduate in 4 years or less, 35% graduate in 5 years or less, and 41% graduate in 6 years or less.

Admissions Contact: Admissions.
E-mail: *admissions@lyndonstate.edu* Web: *www.lyndonstate.edu*

MARLBORO COLLEGE
B-6
Marlboro, VT 05344-0300
(802) 258-9261
(800) 343-0049; Fax: (802) 258-9300

Full-time: 130 men, 193 women	**Faculty:** 35
Part-time: 3 men, 5 women	**Ph.D.s:** 77%
Graduate: none	**Student/Faculty:** 9 to 1
Year: semesters	**Tuition:** $21,630
Application Deadline: March 1	**Room & Board:** $7425
Freshman Class: 261 applied, 214 accepted, 83 enrolled	
SAT I Verbal/Math: 625/580	**ACT:** 26 VERY COMPETITIVE+

Marlboro College, established in 1946, is a small private institution offering degrees in the liberal and fine arts and humanities, and employing self-designed programs of study. Some information in this capsule and profile is approximate. The library contains 53,006 volumes, 5669 microform items, and 1178 audio/video tapes/CDs, and subscribes to 249 periodicals. Computerized library services include the card catalog, interlibrary loans, and database searching. Special learning facilities include a learning resource center, art gallery, planetarium, and observatory. The 366-acre campus is in a rural area 9 miles west of Brattleboro, 2 1/2 hours from Boston. Including any residence halls, there are 36 buildings.

Student Life: 89% of undergraduates are from out of state, mostly the Northeast. Students are from 36 states, 5 foreign countries, and Canada. 70% are from public schools. 83% are white. The average age of freshmen is 19; all undergraduates, 21. 28% do not continue beyond their first year; 48% remain to graduate.

Housing: 235 students can be accommodated in college housing, which includes single-sex and coed dorms, on-campus apartments, and married-student housing. In addition, there are alcohol-free and smoke-free dorms. On-campus housing is guaranteed for the freshman year only and is available on a first-come, first-served basis. 74% of students live on campus; of those, 90% remain on campus on weekends. All students may keep cars.

Activities: There are no fraternities or sororities. There are 25 groups on campus, including art, chess, chorus, computers, dance, drama, film, gay, international, jazz band, literary magazine, musical theater, newspaper, photography, political, social, social service, and student government. Popular campus events include Green-up Day, Creativity Lecture Series, and Visiting Writers Series.

Sports: There is 1 intercollegiate sport for men and 1 for women, and 1 intramural sport for men and 1 for women. Facilities include a soccer field, a volleyball court, cross-country trails, a basketball court, a weight room, a climbing wall, and field trips for canoeing, white-water rafting, and skiing.

Disabled Students: 90% of the campus is accessible. Wheelchair ramps, special parking, specially equipped rest rooms, and special class scheduling are available.

Services: Counseling and information services are available, as is tutoring in some subjects, including writing and languages, math, and organic chemistry.

Campus Safety and Security: Measures include self-defense education, informal discussions, pamphlets/posters/films, and a buddy system.

Programs of Study: Marlboro confers B.A., B.S., B.A. in International Studies, and B.S. in International Studies degrees. Master's degrees are also awarded. Bachelor's degrees are awarded in BIOLOGICAL SCIENCE (biochemistry, biology/biological science, botany, and microbiology), COMMUNICATIONS AND THE ARTS (creative writing, dance, dramatic arts, English, fine arts, French, German, Greek, Italian, Latin, linguistics, music, photography, Russian, and Spanish), COMPUTER AND PHYSICAL SCIENCE (chemistry, computer science, mathematics, and physics), HEALTH PROFESSIONS (premedicine), SOCIAL SCIENCE (anthropology, economics, history, interdisciplinary studies, international studies, philosophy, political science/government, prelaw, psychology, social science, and sociology). Sciences, humanities, and world studies are the strongest academically. Literature, biology, and sociology are the largest.

Required: To graduate, students must complete a plan of concentration, a writing requirement, and a freshman seminar. A minimum GPA of 2.0 is required. Students must earn 120 credits, with 50 credits in the major, and complete a thesis and an oral exam.

Special: Marlboro offers a variety of internships, cross-registration with Huron University in London, and study abroad in many countries. The World Studies Program combines liberal arts with international studies, including 5 to 8 months of internship work in another culture. Accelerated and B.A.-B.S. degree programs are available. Students may pursue dual majors. Majors reflect an integrated course of study designed by students and their faculty advisers during the junior year.

Faculty/Classroom: 62% of faculty are male; 38%, female. All teach undergraduates. The average class size in an introductory lecture is 10; in a laboratory, 8; and in a regular course, 8.

Admissions: 82% of the 2003-2004 applicants were accepted. The SAT I scores for the 2003-2004 freshman class were: Verbal--4% below 500, 26% between 500 and 599, 47% between 600 and 700, and 23%

above 700; Math--14% below 500, 41% between 500 and 599, 35% between 600 and 700, and 10% above 700. The ACT scores were 6% between 24 and 26, 7% between 27 and 28, and 85% above 28. 44% of the current freshmen were in the top fifth of their class; 87% were in the top two fifths. 2 freshmen graduated first in their class in a recent year.

Requirements: The SAT I is required. In addition, applicants typically graduate from an accredited secondary school or have a GED. They are encouraged to earn 16 Carnegie units and complete 4 years of English and 3 years each of math, science, history, and a foreign language. Essays and interviews are required. AP and CLEP credits are accepted. Important factors in the admissions decision are advanced placement or honor courses, evidence of special talent, and extracurricular activities record.

Procedure: Freshmen are admitted fall and spring. Entrance exams should be taken by October before entry. There are early decision, early admissions, and deferred admissions plans. Early decision applications should be filed by November 15; regular applications, by March 1 for fall entry and November 1 for spring entry. The fall 2003 application fee was $50. Notification of early decision is sent December 15; regular decision, April 1. Applications are accepted on-line at the school's web site.

Transfer: 21 transfer students enrolled in a recent year. Transfers must have a minimum GPA of 2.0. 42 credits of 120 required for the bachelor's degree must be completed at Marlboro.

Visiting: There are regularly scheduled orientations for prospective students, including a tour, faculty interview, and discussions with admissions and financial aid. There are guides for informal visits and visitors may sit in on classes and stay overnight. To schedule a visit, contact the Office of Admissions.

Financial Aid: In 2003-2004, 85% of all full-time students received some form of financial aid. 68% of full-time freshmen and 80% of continuing full-time students received need-based aid. The average freshman award was $20,907. Need-based scholarships or need-based grants averaged $15,969 ($24,250 maximum); need-based self-help aid (loans and jobs) averaged $4289 ($4555 maximum); and non-need-based awards and non-need-based scholarships averaged $11,723 ($20,950 maximum). 68% of undergraduates work part time. Average annual earnings from campus work are $1118. The average financial indebtedness of a recent graduate was $18,212. Marlboro is a member of CSS. The CSS Profile and FAFSA are required. Check with the school for current deadlines.

International Students: There were 6 international students enrolled in a recent year. The school actively recruits these students. They must score 550 on the written TOEFL or 230 on the electronic version and also take the SAT I or the ACT.

Computers: Computers are available in a lab, and all on-campus dorm rooms are wired for Internet access. All students may access the system 24 hours a day. There are no time limits and no fees.

Graduates: In an average class, 48% graduate in 5 years or less.

Admissions Contact: Julie Richardson, Vice President, Enrollment and Financial Aid. A video is available.
E-mail: *jrichard@marlboro.edu* Web: *www.marlboro.edu*

MIDDLEBURY COLLEGE

MIDDLEBURY COLLEGE	A-3
Middlebury, VT 05753	**(802) 443-3000; Fax: (802) 443-2065**
Full-time: 1127 men, 1264 women	**Faculty:** 218; IIB, ++$
Part-time: 16 men, 17 women	**Ph.Ds:** 93%
Graduate: none	**Student/Faculty:** 11 to 1
Year: 4-1-4	**Tuition:** $38,100
Application Deadline: December 15	**Room & Board:** n/app
Freshman Class: 5468 applied, 1273 accepted, 513 enrolled	
SAT I Verbal/Math: 740/730	**ACT:** 32 **MOST COMPETITIVE**

Middlebury College, founded in 1800, is a small, private liberal arts institution offering degree programs in languages, humanities, and social and natural sciences. The $38,100 comprehensive fee includes room and board. The 3 libraries contain 942,122 volumes, 378,902 microform items, and 32,365 audio/video tapes/CDs, and subscribe to 2271 periodicals. Computerized library services include the card catalog, interlibrary loans, database searching, and Internet access. Special learning facilities include a learning resource center, art gallery, and radio station. The 355-acre campus is in a small town 35 miles south of Burlington. Including any residence halls, there are 96 buildings.

Student Life: 94% of undergraduates are from out of state, mostly the Northeast. Students are from 50 states, 68 foreign countries, and Canada. 53% are from public schools. 69% are white. The average age of freshmen is 18; all undergraduates, 20. 3% do not continue beyond their first year; 90% remain to graduate.

Housing: 2281 students can be accommodated in college housing, which includes single-sex and coed dorms, on-campus apartments, and married-student housing. In addition, there are language, special-interest, coed social, multicultural, and environmental houses. On-campus housing is guaranteed for all 4 years. 94% of students live on campus; of those, 90% remain on campus on weekends. All students may keep cars.

Activities: There are no fraternities or sororities. There are 95 groups on campus, including art, band, cheerleading, chess, choir, chorus, computers, dance, debate, drama, ethnic, gay, honors, international, jazz band, literary magazine, MMC (Middlebury Mountain Club), musical theater, newspaper, orchestra, photography, political, professional, radio and TV, religious, social, social service, student government, and yearbook. Popular campus events include Winter Carnival, Student Concert Series, and Senior Week.

Sports: There are 14 intercollegiate sports for men and 16 for women, and 11 intramural sports for men and 11 for women. Facilities include 2 field houses, gyms, a swimming pool, a fitness center, tennis courts, playing fields, an 18-hole golf course, alpine and nordic ski areas, a 3000-seat campus stadium, an 8-lane 400-meter outdoor track, and a 2600-seat ice hockey facility.

Disabled Students: Wheelchair ramps, elevators, special parking, specially equipped rest rooms, special class scheduling, and lowered drinking fountains are available.

Services: Counseling and information services are available, as is tutoring in every subject. There is a reader service for the blind.

Campus Safety and Security: Measures include 24-hour foot and vehicle patrol, self-defense education, security escort services, and shuttle buses. There are informal discussions, pamphlets/posters/films, emergency telephones, lighted pathways/sidewalks, paid student patrol, and ski patrol at the Snow Bowl.

Programs of Study: Midd confers the A.B. degree. Master's and doctoral degrees are also awarded. Bachelor's degrees are awarded in BIOLOGICAL SCIENCE (biochemistry, biology/biological science, molecular biology, and neurosciences), BUSINESS (international economics), COMMUNICATIONS AND THE ARTS (American literature, Arabic, art history and appreciation, Chinese, classics, dance, dramatic arts, English, English literature, French, German, Italian, Japanese, music, Russian, Spanish, studio art, and video), COMPUTER AND PHYSICAL SCIENCE (chemistry, computer science, geology, mathematics, and physics), ENGINEERING AND ENVIRONMENTAL DESIGN (environmental science), SOCIAL SCIENCE (American studies, East Asian studies, economics, European studies, geography, history, international relations, international studies, Latin American studies, liberal arts/general studies, philosophy, political science/government, psychology, religion, Russian and Slavic studies, sociology, and women's studies). Foreign languages, international studies, and science are the strongest academically. Economics, psychology, and English are the largest.

Required: Students must complete 36 courses, including winter-term courses. Freshmen must take a freshman seminar and a writing course, and all students must take phys ed. A major normally requires 12 courses, and most students can fulfill the distribution requirement and the cultures and civilization requirement by taking 6 to 8 courses outside of their major. Students may also elect to complete a minor.

Special: Off-campus opportunities include an international major program at one of the Middlebury College schools abroad; exchange programs with Berea, St. Mary's, and Swarthmore; a junior year abroad; study through the American Collegiate Consortium for East-West Cultural and Academic Exchange; a 1-year program at Lincoln and Worcester Colleges, Oxford; a Washington, D.C., semester; and a maritime studies program with Williams College at Mystic Seaport. Middlebury also offers an independent scholar program, joint and double majors, various professional programs, dual degrees in business management, forestry/environmental studies, engineering, and nursing, and an early assurance premed program with Dartmouth, Rochester, Tufts, and the Medical College of Pennsylvania, which assures medical school acceptance by the end of the sophomore year. There is a chapter of Phi Beta Kappa.

Faculty/Classroom: 62% of faculty are male; 38%, female. All teach undergraduates. The average class size in a regular course is 19.

Admissions: 23% of the 2003-2004 applicants were accepted. The SAT I scores for the 2003-2004 freshman class were: Verbal--1% below 500, 2% between 500 and 599, 28% between 600 and 700, and 69% above 700; Math--1% below 500, 4% between 500 and 599, 34% between 600 and 700, and 61% above 700. The ACT scores were 2% between 21 and 23, 6% between 24 and 26, 52% between 27 and 28, and 40% above 28. 95% of the current freshmen were in the top fifth of their class; 99% were in the top two fifths.

Requirements: The SAT I or ACT is required. In addition, students should submit test scores as follows: the ACT or 3 SAT II: Subject tests, AP tests, IB tests, or any combination thereof, including 1 English and 1 quantitative test. Secondary school preparation should include 4 years each of English, math and/or computer science, and 1 foreign language, 3 or more years of lab science and history and social science, and some study of music, art, and/or drama. AP credits are accepted. Important factors in the admissions decision are advanced placement or honor courses, recommendations by school officials, and evidence of special talent.

Procedure: Freshmen are admitted fall and spring. Entrance exams should be taken by December of the senior year. There are early decision, early admissions, and deferred admissions plans. Early decision applications should be filed by November 15; regular applications, by December 15 for fall entry, along with a $55 fee. Notification of early decision is sent December 15; regular decision, April 1. 264 early decision candidates were accepted for the 2003-2004 class. 665 applicants were on the 2003 waiting list. Applications are accepted on-line through *commonapp.org, princetonreview.com,* and *collegeboard.com.*

Transfer: 6 transfer students enrolled in 2002-2003. Transfer students must have the strongest academic record possible through high school and a minimum 3.0 average in college. 18 of 36 credits required for the bachelor's degree must be completed at Midd.

Visiting: There are regularly scheduled orientations for prospective students, including campus tours and a group or individual interview. There are guides for informal visits and visitors may sit in on classes and stay overnight.

Financial Aid: In 2003-2004, 42% of all full-time freshmen and 38% of continuing full-time students received some form of financial aid. 42% of full-time freshmen and 38% of continuing full-time students received need-based aid. The average freshman award was $29,262, with $25,284 ($40,450 maximum) from need-based scholarships or need-based grants; and $3978 ($5500 maximum) from need-based self-help aid (loans and jobs). 60% of undergraduates work part time. Average annual earnings from campus work are $650. The average financial indebtedness of the 2003 graduate was $20,824. Midd is a member of CSS. The CSS Profile, FAFSA, the college's own financial statement, and the federal tax form are required. The deadline for filing freshman financial aid applications for fall entry is January 15.

International Students: There are 200 international students enrolled. The school actively recruits these students. They must take the TOEFL and also fulfill the same requirements as first-year applicants.

Computers: The mainframes are an IBM Model F70 AS/400 and 5 IBM RS/6000s. Individual student rooms are wired to the mainframe. More than half of the students have their own personal computers, and there are more than 150 public PCs easily available in 7 buildings on campus. There are connections to the Internet and to BITNET, and a variety of software is available. All students may access the system 24 hours a day. There are no time limits and no fees.

Graduates: From July 1, 2002 to June 30, 2003, 584 bachelor's degrees were awarded. The most popular majors were economics (13%), English (7%), and psychology (6%).

Admissions Contact: John E. Hanson, Director of Admissions. A video is available. E-mail: *admissions@middlebury.edu* Web: *www.middlebury.edu*

NORWICH UNIVERSITY   C-3
Northfield, VT 05663
    (802) 485-2001
(800) 468-6679; Fax: (802) 485-2032

Full-time: 1040 men, 375 women	Faculty: 110; IIA, --$
Part-time: 25 men, 70 women	Ph.D.s: 85%
Graduate: none	Student/Faculty: 13 to 1
Year: semesters, summer session	Tuition: $15,375
Application Deadline: open	Room & Board: $5690
Freshman Class: n/av	
SAT I or ACT: required	LESS COMPETITIVE

Norwich University, founded in 1819, offers programs in the arts and sciences, engineering, education, and in the military, health science, and business professions. Figures in the above capsule and in this profile are approximate. In addition to regional accreditation, Norwich has baccalaureate program accreditation with ABET, ACBSP, and NLN. The library contains 230,000 volumes, 75,000 microform items, and 4487 audio/video tapes/CDs, and subscribes to 1364 periodicals. Computerized library services include the card catalog, interlibrary loans, and database searching. Special learning facilities include a learning resource center, art gallery, radio station, a greenhouse, and 3 computer labs. The 1125-acre campus is in a rural area 11 miles south of Montpelier. Including any residence halls, there are 34 buildings.

Student Life: 80% of undergraduates are from out of state, mostly the Northeast. Students are from 48 states, 29 foreign countries, and Canada. 75% are from public schools. 94% are white. The average age of freshmen is 18; all undergraduates, 20. 15% do not continue beyond their first year; 65% remain to graduate.

Housing: 1725 students can be accommodated in college housing, which includes single-sex and coed dorms. On-campus housing is guaranteed for the freshman year only and is available on a lottery system for upperclassmen. Priority is given to out-of-town students. 82% of students live on campus; of those, 65% remain on campus on weekends. Alcohol is not permitted. Upperclassmen may keep cars.

Activities: There are no fraternities or sororities. There are 75 groups on campus, including band, cheerleading, chess, choir, chorus, computers, drama, drill team, ethnic, honors, international, jazz band, literary magazine, marching band, musical theater, newspaper, orchestra, pep band, photography, political, professional, radio and TV, religious, social service, student government, and yearbook. Popular campus events include Regimental Ball, Winter Carnival, and Junior Weekend.

Sports: There are 15 intercollegiate sports for men and 10 for women, and 17 intramural sports for men and 12 for women. Facilities include

an ice hockey arena, field house with an indoor track, an indoor swimming pool, aerobics room, weight and wrestling rooms, playing fields and an outdoor track, 1200-seat basketball arena, and 1000-seat stadium.

Disabled Students: Wheelchair ramps, elevators, special parking, specially equipped rest rooms, and lowered drinking fountains are available.

Services: Counseling and information services are available, as is tutoring in most subjects. There is remedial math, reading, and writing.

Campus Safety and Security: Measures include 24-hour foot and vehicle patrol and lighted pathways/sidewalks.

Programs of Study: Norwich confers B.A., B.S., and B.Arch. degrees. Associate degrees are also awarded. Bachelor's degrees are awarded in BIOLOGICAL SCIENCE (biochemistry and biology/biological science), BUSINESS (accounting, business administration and management, and business economics), COMMUNICATIONS AND THE ARTS (communications and English), COMPUTER AND PHYSICAL SCIENCE (chemistry, computer science, geology, information sciences and systems, mathematics, and physics), EDUCATION (physical), ENGINEERING AND ENVIRONMENTAL DESIGN (architecture, civil engineering, electrical/electronics engineering, environmental science, mechanical engineering, and military science), HEALTH PROFESSIONS (medical laboratory technology, nursing, and sports medicine), SOCIAL SCIENCE (criminal justice, history, international studies, liberal arts/general studies, peace studies, political science/government, and psychology). Engineering and architecture are the strongest academically. Criminal justice and nursing are the largest.

Required: Total number of required credits and courses vary by program. All students are required to complete 3 credit hours in history, English 101-102, and 2 semesters in phys ed. A 2.0 GPA is required to graduate.

Special: Many internships are available. Study abroad through other schools and through the Vermont Overseas Studies Program is accepted. The B.A.-B.S. degree, a general studies degree, pass/fail options, and student-designed majors are possible. Co-op programs in business and criminal justice, a Washington semester, on- and off-campus work-study programs for service organizations and in criminal justice, plus a special Adult Degree Program are offered. The Russian School offers a special intensive summer session. There are 5 national honor societies, including Phi Beta Kappa, and 5 departmental honors programs.

Faculty/Classroom: All teach undergraduates. The average class size in an introductory lecture is 5; in a laboratory, 15; and in a regular course, 20.

Requirements: The SAT I or ACT is required. In addition, applicants should graduate from an accredited secondary school with 18 academic credits or achieve the GED equivalent. Norwich requires applicants to be in the upper 50% of their class. A GPA of 2.5 is required. AP and CLEP credits are accepted. Important factors in the admissions decision are leadership record, extracurricular activities record, and evidence of special talent.

Procedure: Freshmen are admitted fall and spring. Entrance exams should be taken starting with spring of the junior year. There are early decision, deferred admissions, and rolling admissions plans. Application deadlines are open. Check with the school for current deadlines. 60 early decision candidates were accepted for the 2003-2004 class. Applications are accepted on IBM/Windows formatted computer disks, and on-line through the World Wide Web.

Transfer: Transfer students should present a 2.0 GPA and meet all standards for entering freshmen. 60 of 114 credits required for the bachelor's degree must be completed at Norwich.

Visiting: There are regularly scheduled orientations for prospective students, including meetings with representatives from admissions, financial aid, academic offices, including Dean of Students or Commandant's Office, athletics (if desired), and a campus tour. There are guides for informal visits and visitors may sit in on classes and stay overnight. To schedule a visit, contact Admissions, Main Office.

Financial Aid: Norwich is a member of CSS. The CSS Profile or FAFSA is required. Check with the school for current deadlines.

International Students: The school actively recruits these students. They must score 500 on the written TOEFL.

Computers: The mainframes are a DEC VAX 11/780 and a DEC VAX 11/785. There are labs in the business department, computer center, and architecture department, and computers are also available in the library. All students may access the system 20 hours per day. There are no time limits and no fees.

Graduates: In an average class, 65% graduate in 4 years or less.

Admissions Contact: Karen McGarth, Dean of Enrollment Management. E-mail: *nuadm@norwich.edu* Web: *www.norwich.edu*

SAINT MICHAEL'S COLLEGE

A-2

Colchester, VT 05439

(802) 654-3000

(800) 762-8000; Fax: (802) 654-2906

Full-time: 873 men, 1042 women	**Faculty:** 144; IIB, +$
Part-time: 36 men, 40 women	**Ph.Ds:** 81%
Graduate: 126 men, 356 women	**Student/Faculty:** 13 to 1
Year: semesters, summer session	**Tuition:** $22,420
Application Deadline: February 1	**Room & Board:** $7680
Freshman Class: 2777 applied, 1872 accepted, 523 enrolled	
SAT I Verbal/Math: 555/560	**VERY COMPETITIVE**

Saint Michael's College, founded in 1904, is a private liberal arts and sciences institution affiliated with the Roman Catholic Church. The library contains 215,145 volumes, 126,173 microform items, and 6487 audio/video tapes/CDs, and subscribes to 1327 periodicals. Computerized library services include the card catalog, interlibrary loans, database searching, and Internet access. Special learning facilities include a learning resource center, art gallery, radio station, and an observatory. The 480-acre campus is in a suburban area 2 miles east of Burlington. Including any residence halls, there are 56 buildings.

Student Life: 76% of undergraduates are from out of state, mostly the Northeast. Students are from 28 states, 20 foreign countries, and Canada. 70% are from public schools. 93% are white. 63% are Catholic; 16% claim no religious affiliation; 16% Protestant. The average age of freshmen is 18; all undergraduates, 20. 10% do not continue beyond their first year; 78% remain to graduate.

Housing: 1800 students can be accommodated in college housing, which includes single-sex and coed dorms and on-campus apartments. In addition, there are honors houses and special-interest houses. On-campus housing is guaranteed for all 4 years. 88% of students live on campus; of those, 95% remain on campus on weekends. All students may keep cars.

Activities: There are no fraternities or sororities. There are 50 groups on campus, including aerobics, art, band, cheerleading, choir, chorale, chorus, computers, dance, drama, ethnic, film, fire and rescue, gay, honors, international, jazz band, literary magazine, musical theater, newspaper, pep band, photography, political, professional, radio and TV, religious, social, social service, student government, wilderness program, and yearbook. Popular campus events include Family Weekend, Christmas and Spring Semi-Formals, and Spring Weekend.

Sports: There are 10 intercollegiate sports for men and 11 for women, and 22 intramural sports for men and 22 for women. Facilities include a 2,200-seat gym and field house with basketball, volleyball, tennis, and badminton courts, 4 multipurpose courts, a 6-lane swimming pool, fitness center, training room, weight room, climbing wall, pool, table tennis, suspended track, soccer, field hockey, lacrosse, baseball, and softball fields, and outdoor tennis courts.

Disabled Students: 70% of the campus is accessible. Wheelchair ramps, elevators, special parking, specially equipped rest rooms, special class scheduling, lowered drinking fountains, lowered telephones, and special housing are available. Other accommodations are provided on an individual basis.

Services: Counseling and information services are available, as is tutoring in every subject. Tutoring can be arranged on an individual basis through the Writing Center, the Tutoring Coordinator's Office, and departmental help sessions.

Campus Safety and Security: Measures include 24-hour foot and vehicle patrol, security escort services, shuttle buses, and informal discussions. There are pamphlets/posters/films, emergency telephones, lighted pathways/sidewalks, and a campus fire and rescue squad.

Programs of Study: Saint Michael's confers B.A. and B.S. degrees. Master's degrees are also awarded. Bachelor's degrees are awarded in BIOLOGICAL SCIENCE (biochemistry and biology/biological science), BUSINESS (accounting and business administration and management), COMMUNICATIONS AND THE ARTS (dramatic arts, English, fine arts, French, journalism, music, and Spanish), COMPUTER AND PHYSICAL SCIENCE (chemistry, computer science, information sciences and systems, mathematics, physical sciences, and physics), EDUCATION (art, elementary, foreign languages, science, and secondary), ENGINEERING AND ENVIRONMENTAL DESIGN (environmental science and preengineering), HEALTH PROFESSIONS (predentistry), SOCIAL SCIENCE (American studies, anthropology, economics, history, philosophy, political science/government, prelaw, psychology, religion, and sociology). Biology, business administration, and education are the largest.

Required: To graduate, students must complete a minimum of 124 credit hours, with a minimum of 34 different courses, achieving a cumulative GPA of at least 2.0 and a minimum GPA of 2.0 in courses taken in the major. Students must also complete the liberal studies curriculum, which includes 3 courses in social sciences and organizational studies, 3 courses in humanities (literary studies, historical studies, culture and civilization), 2 courses each in philosophy, religious studies, and natural and mathematical sciences (with at least 1 lab course in natural science), 2 writing-intensive courses, and 2 credits in artistic expression. Students

must also demonstrate writing and language proficiency and complete a first-year seminar.

Special: A variety of internships and on-campus work-study are available. There is a Washington semester with American University and study abroad in 35 countries. Student-designed majors may be pursued. The college offers a 3-2 engineering degree program in cooperation with Clarkson University and the University of Vermont, and a 4+1 graduate business program with Clarkson University. Nondegree study and pass/fail grading options are offered on a limited basis. Independent research opportunities are available through many departments. There are 9 national honor societies, including Phi Beta Kappa, a freshman honors program, and 1 departmental honors program.

Faculty/Classroom: 54% of faculty are male; 46%, female. All both teach and do research. No introductory courses are taught by graduate students. The average class size in an introductory lecture is 24; in a laboratory, 16; and in a regular course, 20.

Admissions: 67% of the 2003-2004 applicants were accepted. The SAT I scores for the 2003-2004 freshman class were: Verbal--18% below 500, 52% between 500 and 599, 27% between 600 and 700, and 3% above 700; Math--18% below 500, 53% between 500 and 599, 28% between 600 and 700, and 2% above 700. 40% of the current freshmen were in the top fifth of their class; 75% were in the top two fifths. 5 freshmen graduated first in their class.

Requirements: The SAT I or ACT is required. In addition, applicants must graduate from an accredited secondary school or have a GED. They must complete 16 Carnegie units. The college requires 4 credits in English, 3 to 4 credits in math and science, and 3 each in history (social studies) and a foreign language. An essay is required, and an interview is recommended. AP and CLEP credits are accepted. Important factors in the admissions decision are advanced placement or honor courses, evidence of special talent, and recommendations by school officials.

Procedure: Freshmen are admitted fall and spring. Entrance exams should be taken in the fall of the senior year. There is a deferred admissions plan. Early Action I applications should be filed by November 15 (Early Action II, December 15); regular applications, by February 1 for fall entry and November 1 for spring entry, along with a $45 fee. Notification of Early Action I is sent January 1 (Early Action II, January 31); regular decision, April 1. 186 were on the 2003 waiting list; 27 were admitted. Applications are accepted on-line through Common App, College Board on-line, and the school's web site.

Transfer: 50 transfer students enrolled in 2002-2003. Transfer applicants must have a minimum GPA of 2.5; generally, those admitted have a GPA of at least 3.0. The SAT I is required. An interview is recommended. 30 of 124 credits required for the bachelor's degree must be completed at Saint Michael's.

Visiting: There are regularly scheduled orientations for prospective students, including a group information session, a video about the school, a campus tour, and a review with a staff member of admissions criteria. There are guides for informal visits and visitors may sit in on classes and stay overnight. To schedule a visit, contact the Admissions Office.

Financial Aid: In 2003-2004, 86% of all full-time freshmen and 85% of continuing full-time students received some form of financial aid. 64% of full-time freshmen and 63% of continuing full-time students received need-based aid. The average freshman award was $15,854. Need-based scholarships or need-based grants averaged $12,792 ($26,350 maximum); need-based self-help aid (loans and jobs) averaged $5024 ($7125 maximum); non-need-based athletic scholarships averaged $30,100 (maximum); and other non-need-based awards and non-need-based scholarships averaged $500 ($22,220 maximum). 40% of undergraduates work part time. Average annual earnings from campus work are $1100. The average financial indebtedness of the 2003 graduate was $19,002. Saint Michael's is a member of CSS. The FAFSA, the college's own financial statement, federal tax forms from both student and parents, and W-2 forms are required. The deadline for filing freshman financial aid applications for fall entry is March 15.

International Students: There are 50 international students enrolled. The school actively recruits these students. They must score 550 on the written TOEFL or 213 on the electronic version and also take the college's own test. The SAT I or ACT is recommended for international students, but the TOEFL may be used in place of the SAT I.

Computers: The mainframe is a DEC Alpha ES-40 System. There are 9 PC labs available for student use, all of them connected to the campus network (Mikenet). More than 250 computers are available for student use. All students may access the system. There are no time limits and no fees. It is strongly recommended that all students have a personal computer. Recommended specifications are available on the school's web site.

Graduates: From July 1, 2002 to June 30, 2003, 427 bachelor's degrees were awarded. The most popular majors were business administration (19%), psychology (11%), and English literature (10%). In an average class, 70% graduate in 4 years or less, 76% graduate in 5 years or less, and 78% graduate in 6 years or less. 113 companies recruited on campus in 2002-2003. Of the 2002 graduating class, 13% were enrolled in graduate school within 6 months of graduation and 82% were employed. Recommended specifications are available on the school's web site.

Admissions Contact: Jerry E. Flanagan, Vice President, Admission and Enrollment Management. A video is available.

E-mail: *admission@smcvt.edu* Web: *www.smcvt.edu*

SOUTHERN VERMONT COLLEGE
Bennington, VT 05201

A-6

(802) 447-6304
(800) 378-2782; Fax: (802) 447-4695

Full-time: 135 men, 206 women	**Faculty:** 21
Part-time: 34 men, 89 women	**Ph.D.s:** 19%
Graduate: none	**Student/Faculty:** 16 to 1
Year: semesters, summer session	**Tuition:** $11,996
Application Deadline: open	**Room & Board:** $6230
Freshman Class: 375 applied, 334 accepted, 143 enrolled	
SAT I Math: 480	**ACT:** 19 LESS COMPETITIVE

Southern Vermont College, established in 1926, is a private institution offering a career-oriented, liberal arts education to a student body from diverse academic backgrounds. The library contains 26,000 volumes, and subscribes to 1504 periodicals. Computerized library services include interlibrary loans and database searching. Special learning facilities include a learning resource center, art gallery, and radio station. The 371-acre campus is in a small town 40 miles east of Albany, New York. Including any residence halls, there are 10 buildings.

Student Life: 59% of undergraduates are from out of state, mostly the Northeast. Students are from 22 states and 6 foreign countries. 81% are white. The average age of freshmen is 22; all undergraduates, 25.

Housing: 235 students can be accommodated in college housing, which includes coed dorms. Quiet, nonsmoking, and first-year student residence halls are available. On-campus housing is guaranteed for the freshman year only and is available on a lottery system for upperclassmen. 54% of students commute. All students may keep cars.

Activities: There are no fraternities or sororities. There are 15 groups on campus, including cheerleading, criminal justice, drama, environmental, ethnic, honors, literary magazine, newspaper, photography, professional, radio and TV, social, social service, student government, and yearbook. Popular campus events include Family Weekend, Winter Formal, and Spring Dance.

Sports: There are 5 intercollegiate sports for men and 6 for women, and 4 intramural sports for men and 4 for women. Facilities include a multipurpose field for softball, baseball, soccer, and rugby, a 9-hole par 3 golf course, a volleyball court, and a field house, including gym and fitness center.

Disabled Students: 50% of the campus is accessible. Wheelchair ramps, special parking, and specially equipped rest rooms are available.

Services: Counseling and information services are available, as is tutoring in every subject. There is also a learning disabilities support program.

Campus Safety and Security: Measures include 24-hour foot and vehicle patrol, security escort services, informal discussions, and pamphlets/posters/films. There are lighted pathways/sidewalks.

Programs of Study: SVC confers B.A., B.S., and B.S.N. degrees. Associate degrees are also awarded. Bachelor's degrees are awarded in BUSINESS (business administration and management), COMMUNICATIONS AND THE ARTS (communications, creative writing, and English), ENGINEERING AND ENVIRONMENTAL DESIGN (environmental science), HEALTH PROFESSIONS (nursing), SOCIAL SCIENCE (criminal justice, human services, liberal arts/general studies, and psychology). Nursing, criminal justice, and business administration are the largest.

Required: To graduate, students must complete a 42-credit core requirement consisting of course work in economics, English, environmental studies, government, history, cultural arts, math (including computer science), natural sciences, philosophy, psychology, and sociology. Minors are required in some programs. A minimum GPA of 2.0 is required. Students must earn a minimum of 120 credits, with 30 in the major.

Special: The individualized degree program allows students to formulate their own degree. Independent study, individualized study, internships, dual majors, student-designed majors, cross-registration with Bennington College, and a semester at sea are available. There is 1 national honor society.

Faculty/Classroom: 52% of faculty are male; 48%, female. All teach undergraduates. The average class size in an introductory lecture is 18; in a laboratory, 13; and in a regular course, 12.

Admissions: 89% of the 2003-2004 applicants were accepted. The SAT I scores for the 2003-2004 freshman class were: Verbal--36% between 500 and 599, 5% between 600 and 700, and 1% above 700; Math--70% below 500, 26% between 500 and 599, and 4% between 600 and 700. The ACT scores were 36% below 21, 57% between 21 and 23, and 7% above 28. 2% of the current freshmen were in the top fifth of their class; 50% were in the top two fifths.

Requirements: The SAT I or ACT is required. In addition, applicants must graduate from an accredited secondary school or have a GED. The college requires 4 years of English and 3 of math. SVC requires appli-

cants to be in the upper 67% of their class. A GPA of 2.0 is required. AP and CLEP credits are accepted. Important factors in the admissions decision are leadership record, extracurricular activities record, and recommendations by school officials.

Procedure: Freshmen are admitted fall, spring, and summer. There is a deferred admissions plan. There is a rolling admissions plan. Application deadlines are open. Application fee is $30. Applications are accepted on-line through the college's web site, *www.svc.edu*.

Transfer: 45 transfer students enrolled in 2002-2003. Applicants must have a GPA of 2.0 and be in good standing. Interviews are recommended, and a dean's report is required. 30 of 120 credits required for the bachelor's degree must be completed at SVC.

Visiting: There are regularly scheduled orientations for prospective students. There are guides for informal visits and visitors may sit in on classes and stay overnight. To schedule a visit, contact Admissions at *admis@svc.edu*.

Financial Aid: In 2003-2004, 90% of all full-time freshmen and 92% of continuing full-time students received some form of financial aid. 84% of full-time freshmen and 90% of continuing full-time students received need-based aid. The average freshman award was $11,200. The average financial indebtedness of the 2003 graduate was $13,500. SVC is a member of CSS. The FAFSA and the college's own financial statement are required. The priority date for freshman financial aid applications for fall entry is May 1.

International Students: There are 10 international students enrolled. They must score 500 on the written TOEFL or 173 on the electronic version.

Computers: The library and both computer labs have access to the Internet and the Web. All students may access the system. There are no time limits and no fees.

Graduates: From July 1, 2002 to June 30, 2003, 58 bachelor's degrees were awarded. The most popular majors were psychology (22%), business administration (16%), and criminal justice (14%).

Admissions Contact: Elizabeth Gatti, Director of Admissions.
E-mail: *admis@svc.edu* Web: *www.svc.edu*

STERLING COLLEGE
Craftsbury Common, VT 05827

B-1

(802) 586-7711, ext. 135
(800) 648-3591; Fax: (802) 586-2591

Full-time: 54 men, 41 women	**Faculty:** 9
Part-time: 3 men, 4 women	**Ph.D.s:** 44%
Graduate: none	**Student/Faculty:** 11 to 1
Year: semesters, summer session	**Tuition:** $15,330
Application Deadline: open	**Room & Board:** $5784
Freshman Class: n/av	
SAT I or ACT: recommended	COMPETITIVE+

Sterling College is a private, independent school offering academic programs that are oriented toward environmental care. The library contains 8510 volumes and 410 audio/video tapes/CDs, and subscribes to 85 periodicals. Computerized library services include the card catalog, interlibrary loans, and database searching. Special learning facilities include an art gallery, woodshop, darkroom, managed woodlot, organic garden, working livestock farm, 30-foot-tall climbing tower, bouldering wall, greenhouse, sugar house, and a 250-acre boreal forest/wetland research area. The 130-acre campus is in a rural area 40 miles north of Montpelier and 60 miles from Burlington. Including any residence halls, there are 15 buildings.

Student Life: 80% of undergraduates are from out of state, mostly the Northeast. Students are from 21 states. 89% are from public schools. 97% are white. The average age of freshmen is 19; all undergraduates, 22. 25% do not continue beyond their first year; 53% remain to graduate.

Housing: 90 students can be accommodated in college housing, which includes single-sex and coed dormitories. On-campus housing is guaranteed for all 4 years. 80% of students live on campus; of those, 74% remain on campus on weekends. All students may keep cars.

Activities: There are no fraternities or sororities. There are 6 groups and organizations on campus, including art, dance, newspaper, outing, photography, and yearbook. Popular campus events include All-College Work Days, Earth Day, and Annual Wood-Projects show.

Sports: There is no sports program at Sterling College. Facilities include a climbing tower and nationally recognized cross-country ski trails managed by a nearby sports center.

Disabled Students: 2% of the campus is accessible. Wheelchair ramps and specially equipped rest rooms are available.

Services: Counseling and information services are available, as is tutoring in every subject. There is remedial math. Students seek assistance directly from faculty or teacher assistants.

Campus Safety and Security: Measures include informal discussions, pamphlets/posters/films, and lighted pathways/sidewalks. Weekly community meetings address personal safety and security.

Programs of Study: Sterling College confers the B.A. degree. Associate degrees are also awarded. Bachelor's degrees are awarded in AGRICUL-

TURE (conservation and regulation, natural resource management, and wildlife management), EDUCATION (recreation). Wildlands ecology and management, sustainable agriculture, and outdoor leadership and education are the strongest academically.

Required: Of the 120 total credit hours required, 25 must be taken in social sciences, 14 in arts and humanities, 13 in natural sciences, 6 in interdisciplinary studies, and 2 in applied sciences. 24 to 27.5 hours in the major are required. A minimum GPA of 2.0 must be maintained. A comprehensive math exam, an internship, and a senior applied research project are also required.

Special: Students may cross-register through the National Alliance for Green Education. Internships are required in the second year of study. Study abroad, work study, and student-designed majors are available.

Faculty/Classroom: 58% of faculty are male; 42%, female. All teach undergraduates; 30% both teach and do research. The average class size in an introductory lecture is 15; in a laboratory, 10; and in a regular course, 12.

Admissions: 38% of the current freshmen were in the top fifth of their class; 46% were in the top two fifths.

Requirements: The SAT I or ACT is recommended. Well-written essays, quality of the interview, and the comments provided by references are equal to the value of high school and college transcripts. Home-schooled students are strongly encouraged to contact the admissions office to discuss their particular needs and interests. AP credits are accepted. Important factors in the admissions decision are leadership record, recommendations by school officials, and personality/intangible qualities.

Procedure: Freshmen are admitted in the fall. There is a deferred admissions plan and a rolling admissions plan. Application deadlines are open. Application fee is $35. Notification is sent on a rolling basis. Applications are accepted on-line through *www.sterlingcollege.edu/apply.htm* and CollegeNET.

Transfer: 13 transfer students enrolled in 2002-2003. In addition to the standard application, transfer students must provide copies of college transcripts. They may begin in the spring semester. 30 credits of 120 required for the bachelor's degree must be completed at Sterling College.

Visiting: There are regularly scheduled orientations for prospective students, incuding a student-led campus tour, an interview with admissions, and a meal in the dining hall. Overnight visits are welcome Sunday through Thursday nights; weekend Visit Days offer a more comprehensive view of the college. There are 4 open houses per year. There are guides for informal visits and visitors may sit in on classes. To schedule a visit, contact the Admissions Office at *admissions@sterlingcollege.edu*.

Financial Aid: In a recent year, 64% of all full-time freshmen and 60% of continuing full-time students received some form of financial aid. 40% of full-time freshmen and 60% of continuing full-time students received need-based aid. The average freshman award was $3500. All undergraduates work part time. Average annual earnings from campus work are $1300. Sterling College is a member of CSS. The FAFSA and the college's own financial statement are required.

International Students: They must score 500 on the written TOEFL or 173 on the electronic version.

Computers: The mainframe is a Compaq DeskPros. Students access the Internet and World Wide Web through computers located in the Career Resource Center and library. They may also have access in their dorm rooms for a fee. All students may access the system. There are no time limits. It is strongly recommended that all students have a personal computer.

Graduates: From July 1, 2002 to June 30, 2003, 3 bachelor's degrees were awarded. The most popular majors were sustainable agriculture (67%) and wildlands ecology and management (33%). 10 companies recruited on campus in 2002-2003.

Admissions Contact: John Zaber, Director of Admissions.
E-mail: *admissions@sterlingcollege.edu* Web: *www.sterlingcollege.edu*

UNIVERSITY OF VERMONT
Burlington, VT 05405

A-2

(802) 656-3370; Fax: (802) 656-8611

Full-time: 3434 men, 4403 women	Faculty: 578; I, --$
Part-time: 555 men, 911 women	Ph.D.s: 89%
Graduate: 713 men, 1020 women	Student/Faculty: 14 to 1
Year: semesters, summer session	Tuition: $9636 ($22,688)
Application Deadline: January 15	Room & Board: $6680
Freshman Class: 10,456 applied, 7792 accepted, 1923 enrolled	
SAT I Verbal/Math: 570/580	ACT: 25 VERY COMPETITIVE

The University of Vermont, established in 1791, is a public, land-grant, comprehensive institution with a dual focus on teaching and research. Its undergraduate and graduate offerings include the liberal arts, business administration, engineering, math, natural resources, agricultural studies, fine arts, teacher preparation, social services, environmental studies, and health science, including nursing. There are 7 undergraduate and 2 graduate schools. In addition to regional accreditation, UVM has baccalaureate program accreditation with AACSB, ABET, APTA, ASLA, CAHEA, CSWE, NCATE, NLN, and SAF. The 3 libraries contain 2.5 million volumes, 1,750,000 microform items, and 45,000 audio/video tapes/CDs, and subscribe to 20,000 periodicals. Computerized library services include the card catalog, interlibrary loans, database searching, and Internet access. Special learning facilities include a learning resource center, art gallery, radio station, TV station, health care center, 4 research farms, the Fleming Museum, geology museum, 9 natural areas, lakeshore science center, and aquatic research vessel. The 450-acre campus is in a suburban area 90 miles south of Montreal and 200 miles north of Boston, on the shore of Lake Champlain. Including any residence halls, there are 118 buildings.

Student Life: 62% of undergraduates are from out of state, mostly the Northeast. Students are from 47 states, 24 foreign countries, and Canada. 93% are white. 40% claim no religious affiliation; 26% are Catholic; 20%, Protestant; 9%, Jewish. The average age of freshmen is 18; all undergraduates, 20. 16% do not continue beyond their first year; 70% remain to graduate.

Housing: 3631 students can be accommodated in college housing, which includes coed dorms, on-campus apartments, off-campus apartments, married-student housing, fraternity houses, and sorority houses. In addition, there are honors houses, language houses, special-interest houses, and the living-learning center, which provides an integrated, theme-based academic and residential option. On-campus housing is available on a lottery system for upperclassmen. 50% of students live on campus; of those, 90% remain on campus on weekends. Upperclassmen may keep cars.

Activities: 7% of men belong to 2 local and 7 national fraternities; 6% of women belong to 5 national sororities. There are 100 groups on campus, including art, band, cheerleading, chess, choir, chorale, chorus, computers, dance, debate, drama, environmental, ethnic, film, gay, honors, international, jazz band, literary magazine, musical theater, newspaper, orchestra, outing, pep band, photography, political, professional, radio and TV, religious, social, social service, student government, and yearbook. Popular campus events include National Coming Out Week, Winterfest, and Community Serve-a-thon.

Sports: There are 10 intercollegiate sports for men and 12 for women, and 24 intramural sports for men and 24 for women. Facilities include a 3228-seat gym, a 4000-seat ice hockey stadium, a field house, soccer and baseball fields, a fitness center, indoor and outdoor tracks, a natatorium, indoor tennis courts, a racquetball court, a climbing facility, a dance studio, and a gymnastics facility.

Disabled Students: 87% of the campus is accessible. Wheelchair ramps, elevators, special parking, specially equipped rest rooms, special class scheduling, lowered drinking fountains, lowered telephones, first-priority routes in poor weather, a TTY phone system for hearing-impaired students, and closed-caption video decoders are available.

Services: Counseling and information services are available, as is tutoring in most subjects. There is a reader service for the blind. There is also supplemental instruction, note-taking and test-taking seminars, time management instruction, outreach programs, exam proctoring, and writing tutors, as well as support for ESL students.

Campus Safety and Security: Measures include 24-hour foot and vehicle patrol, self-defense education, security escort services, and shuttle buses. There are informal discussions, pamphlets/posters/films, emergency telephones, lighted pathways/sidewalks, and bike registration, identification of property, and 18 fully certified police officers.

Programs of Study: UVM confers B.A., B.S., B.M., B.S.A.E., B.S.B.A., B.S.C.E., B.S.C.S., B.S.Ed., B.S.E.E., B.S.E.M., B.S.M., B.S.M.E., and B.S.M.S. degrees. Associate, master's, and doctoral degrees are also awarded. Bachelor's degrees are awarded in AGRICULTURE (agriculture, animal science, environmental studies, fishing and fisheries, forestry and related sciences, horticulture, natural resource management, and plant science), BIOLOGICAL SCIENCE (biochemistry, biology/biological science, botany, ecology, genetics, microbiology, nutrition, wildlife biology, and zoology), BUSINESS (business administration and management and entrepreneurial studies), COMMUNICATIONS AND THE ARTS (art, art history and appreciation, classics, dramatic arts, English, French, German, Greek, Latin, music, Russian, and Spanish), COMPUTER AND PHYSICAL SCIENCE (chemistry, computer science, geology, information sciences and systems, mathematics, physics, and statistics), EDUCATION (art, early childhood, education, elementary, English, foreign languages, health, mathematics, middle school, music, nutrition, physical, science, secondary, and social studies), ENGINEERING AND ENVIRONMENTAL DESIGN (civil engineering, electrical/electronics engineering, engineering management, environmental engineering, environmental science, landscape architecture/design, and mechanical engineering), HEALTH PROFESSIONS (biomedical science, medical laboratory science, medical laboratory technology, nuclear medical technology, nursing, radiation therapy, and speech pathology/audiology), SOCIAL SCIENCE (anthropology, Asian/Oriental studies, Canadian studies, dietetics, economics, European studies, family/consumer studies, food science, geography, history, human development, Latin American studies, parks and recreation management, philosophy, political science/government, psychology, religion, Russian and Slavic studies, social work, sociology, and women's studies). Business administration, psychology, and English are the largest.

Required: Degree requirements vary among the individual colleges, but all require at least a 2.0 GPA and 122 credit hours to graduate. Most students must enroll in at least 30 distribution credits (approximately 10 courses) in the arts, humanities, social sciences, languages, literature, math, and the sciences. All academic units require a 3-credit course in Race and Culture, or a course exploring race relations and ethnic diversity in the United States, and all students are expected to complete 2 credits of phys ed, unless granted an exemption.

Special: Special academic programs include co-op programs, internships in every discipline, study abroad in 60 countries, a Washington semester, work-study, an accelerated degree program in nursing, dual majors, and student-designed majors. In addition, a 3-4 veterinary medicine degree is offered with Tufts University, a 3-3 program with Vermont Law School, and a 3-3 physical therapy program at UVM. There are 25 national honor societies, including Phi Beta Kappa, a freshman honors program, and 14 departmental honors programs.

Faculty/Classroom: 61% of faculty are male; 39%, female. Graduate students teach 2% of introductory courses. The average class size in an introductory lecture is 38; in a laboratory, 16; and in a regular course, 20.

Admissions: 75% of the 2003-2004 applicants were accepted. The SAT I scores for the 2003-2004 freshman class were: Verbal--13% below 500, 49% between 500 and 599, 34% between 600 and 700, and 4% above 700; Math--13% below 500, 44% between 500 and 599, 39% between 600 and 700, and 4% above 700. The ACT scores were 14% below 21, 26% between 21 and 23, 34% between 24 and 26, 17% between 27 and 28, and 9% above 28. 44% of the current freshmen were in the top fifth of their class; 82% were in the top two fifths. 28 freshmen graduated first in their class.

Requirements: The SAT I or ACT is required. Other admissions requirements include graduation from an accredited secondary school with 16 Carnegie units. Required high school course work includes 4 years of English, 3 years each of social science and math, including algebra I and II and geometry, and 2 years each of the same foreign language and science (one of which must be a lab science). An essay must be submitted. The GED is also accepted. AP and CLEP credits are accepted. Important factors in the admissions decision are advanced placement or honor courses, extracurricular activities record, and recommendations by school officials.

Procedure: Freshmen are admitted fall and spring. Entrance exams should be taken by November of the senior year. There are early decision, early admissions, and deferred admissions plans. Early decision applications should be filed by November 1; regular applications, by January 15 for fall entry and November 1 for spring entry, along with a $45 fee. Notification of early decision is sent December 15; regular decision, March 20. 174 early decision candidates were accepted for the 2003-2004 class. 359 applicants were on the 2003 waiting list. Applications are accepted on-line through www.uvm.edu/admission or Common App.

Transfer: 555 transfer students enrolled in 2002-2003. Transfer students generally must have a minimum GPA of 3.0 in credited courses and meet the same entrance requirements as freshmen. Considerations include the college and high school records, the major indicated, and availability of space at UVM. 30 of 122 credits required for the bachelor's degree must be completed at UVM.

Visiting: There are regularly scheduled orientations for prospective students, consisting of tours most weekdays during the academic year and information sessions on selected Saturdays in the fall and spring. Visitors may sit in on classes. To schedule a visit, contact the Admissions Office.

Financial Aid: In 2003-2004, 83% of all full-time freshmen and 73% of continuing full-time students received some form of financial aid. 57% of full-time freshmen and 55% of continuing full-time students received need-based aid. The average freshman award was $18,611. Need-based scholarships or need-based grants averaged $11,723 ($34,100 maximum); need-based self-help aid (loans and jobs) averaged $6269 ($14,325 maximum); non-need-based athletic scholarships averaged $19,602 ($30,109 maximum); and other non-need-based awards and non-need-based scholarships averaged $3652 ($31,107 maximum). The average financial indebtedness of the 2003 graduate was $25,079. The FAFSA is required. The priority date for freshman financial aid applications for fall entry is February 10.

International Students: There are 62 international students enrolled. They must score 550 on the written TOEFL or 213 on the electronic version or take or take the ELPT, and must also take the SAT I or the ACT.

Computers: The mainframes are an IBM 4381 and a DEC VAX 8600. PCs are located in labs throughout the campus. All residence halls are wired for connections to the campus network, the Internet, and the Web. All students may access the system at any time. There are no time limits and no fees. Students in business majors must have personal computers. An IBM, Mac, or Dell is recommended.

Graduates: From July 1, 2002 to June 30, 2003, 1630 bachelor's degrees were awarded. The most popular majors were business (10%), psychology (9%), and English (8%). In an average class, 53% graduate in 4 years or less, 67% graduate in 5 years or less, and 70% graduate in 6 years or less. 164 companies recruited on campus in 2002-2003. Of

the 2002 graduating class, 15% were enrolled in graduate school within 6 months of graduation and 72% were employed.

Admissions Contact: Donald Honeman, Director of Admission.
E-mail: *admissions@uvm.edu* Web: *www.uvm.edu/admissions*

VERMONT STATE COLLEGES

The Vermont State Colleges, established in 1962, is a private system in Vermont. It is governed by a board of trustees, whose chief administrator is chancellor. The primary goal of the system is teaching. The main priorities are to insure that Vermonters and others have access to higher education; to provide educational programs that permit individuals to lead more productive and responsible lives; and to maintain the quality of cultural, social, and economic life in Vermont. The total enrollment of all 5 campuses is usually about 10,000; there were about 252 faculty members. Altogether there are 120 associate, baccalaureate, and master's programs offered in Vermont State Colleges. Profiles of the 4-year campuses are included in this section.

VERMONT TECHNICAL COLLEGE

Randolph Center, VT 05061   **(802) 728-1000; (800) 442-8821**

Full-time: 603 men, 286 women	**Faculty:** 72; III, --$
Part-time: 210 men, 119 women	**Ph.Ds:** 20%
Graduate: none	**Student/Faculty:** 12 to 1
Year: semesters	**Tuition:** $7670 ($13,702)
Application Deadline: open	**Room & Board:** $6014
Freshman Class: 1602 applied, 889 accepted, 599 enrolled	
SAT I Verbal/Math: 480/500	**COMPETITIVE**

Vermont Technical College, founded in 1910, is one of the 5 institutions in the Vermont State Colleges System and is the state's only public technical college. In addition to regional accreditation, VTC has baccalaureate program accreditation with ABET. The library contains 60,701 volumes, 5440 microform items, and 4190 audio/video tapes/CDs, and subscribes to 348 periodicals. Computerized library services include the card catalog, interlibrary loans, database searching, and Internet access. Special learning facilities include a learning resource center, radio station, and Vermont Interactive Television. The 544-acre campus is in a rural area. Including any residence halls, there are 19 buildings.

Student Life: 80% of undergraduates are from Vermont. Students are from 17 states and 4 foreign countries. 90% are from public schools. 97% are white. The average age of freshmen is 24; all undergraduates, 26. 25% do not continue beyond their first year; 55% remain to graduate.

Housing: 550 students can be accommodated in college housing, which includes single-sex and coed dorms. On-campus housing is guaranteed for all 4 years. 60% of students commute. All students may keep cars.

Activities: There are no fraternities or sororities. There are many groups and organizations on campus, including chess, computers, drama, ethnic, gay, international, photography, professional, radio and TV, religious, social, social service, and student government. Popular campus events include Harvest Days, Winter Carnival, and Spring Fling.

Sports: There are 4 intercollegiate sports for men and 3 for women, and 21 intramural sports for men and 21 for women. Facilities include a double-court gym, 2 racquetball courts, a 6-lane 25-yard pool, a fitness center, outdoor soccer, baseball, and softball fields, trails for cross-country skiing, and a downhill ski run.

Disabled Students: All of the campus is accessible. Wheelchair ramps, elevators, special parking, specially equipped rest rooms, special class scheduling, lowered drinking fountains, and lowered telephones are available.

Services: Counseling and information services are available, as is tutoring in every subject.

Campus Safety and Security: Measures include 24-hour foot and vehicle patrol, self-defense education, security escort services, and informal discussions. There are pamphlets/posters/films, emergency telephones, and lighted pathways/sidewalks.

Programs of Study: VTC confers the B.S. degree. Associate degrees are also awarded. Bachelor's degrees are awarded in ENGINEERING AND ENVIRONMENTAL DESIGN (architectural engineering, computer engineering, electromechanical technology, and technological management). Electrical engineering technology is the strongest academically. Architectural engineering technology, computer engineering technology, and nursing are the largest.

Required: To graduate, students must complete 120 to 130 credit hours with a minimum GPA of 2.0. Required courses include those in English, technical communications, math, and computer.

Special: Cross-registration, internships, work-study programs, and dual majors are offered. There are 2 national honor societies, including Phi Beta Kappa, a freshman honors program, and 2 departmental honors programs.

Faculty/Classroom: 65% of faculty are male; 35%, female. All teach undergraduates. The average class size in an introductory lecture is 28; in a laboratory, 16; and in a regular course, 32.

Admissions: 55% of the 2003-2004 applicants were accepted.

Requirements: The SAT I or ACT is required. AP and CLEP credits are accepted.

Procedure: Freshmen are admitted fall and spring. There is a rolling admissions plan. Application deadlines are open. Application fee is $32. A waiting list is an active part of the admissions procedure. Applications are accepted on-line.

Transfer: 251 transfer students enrolled in 2002-2003. Transcripts are required from all colleges attended. 50 of 120 to 130 credits required for the bachelor's degree must be completed at VTC.

Visiting: There are regularly scheduled orientations for prospective students. There are guides for informal visits and visitors may sit in on classes and stay overnight. To schedule a visit, contact Admissions.

Financial Aid: In 2003-2004, 79% of all full-time freshmen and 35% of continuing full-time students received some form of financial aid. 55% of full-time freshmen and 64% of continuing full-time students received need-based aid. The average freshman award was $11,300, with $2500 ($6300 maximum) from need-based scholarships or need-based grants, $2700 ($4000 maximum) from need-based self-help aid (loans and jobs), and $6100 ($20,500 maximum) from non-need-based awards and non-need-based scholarships. 25% of undergraduates work part time. Average annual earnings from campus work are $900. The FAFSA is required. The deadline for filing freshman financial aid applications for fall entry is March 1.

International Students: They must score 500 on the written TOEFL or 173 on the electronic version or take the MELAB, the Comprehensive English Language Test, or the college's own test. They must also take the SAT I, ACT, or the college's own entrance exam.

Computers: The mainframes are a Dell 2550 and multiple servers. More than 300 computers are available in labs. Students may have PCs in dorms, all network accessible. All students may access the system. There are no time limits and no fees. It is strongly recommended that all students have a personal computer.

Graduates: In a recent year, 17 bachelor's degrees were awarded. The most popular majors were architectural engineering technology (65%) and electromechanical engineering technology (35%). In an average class, 35% graduate in 4 years or less, 5% graduate in 5 years or less, and 1% graduate in 6 years or less.

Admissions Contact: Rosemary Distel, Director of Admissions.
E-mail: *admissions@vtc.edu* Web: *www.vtc.edu*

WOODBURY COLLEGE
Montpelier, VT 05602

(802) 229-0516
(800) 639-6039; Fax: (802) 229-2141

Full-time: 25 men, 90 women	**Faculty:** 15
Part-time: 10 men, 35 women	**Ph.D.s:** 50%
Graduate: none	**Student/Faculty:** 8 to 1
Year: trimesters	**Tuition:** $12,060
Application Deadline: open	**Room & Board:** n/app
Freshman Class: n/av	
SAT I or ACT: not required	**LESS COMPETITIVE**

Woodbury College, established in 1975, offers adult-focused, career-oriented programs in Legal and Paralegal Studies, Mediation/Conflict Management, and Prevention and Community Development. There is 1 undergraduate school. Figures in the above capsule and in this profile are approximate. The library contains 17,000 volumes, and subscribes to 20,000 periodicals. Computerized library services include the card catalog, interlibrary loans, and database searching. The 8-acre campus is in a small town 1.5 miles north of the center of Montpelier and the Vermont state government district. There is 1 building.

Student Life: 97% of undergraduates are from Vermont. Students are from 3 states and 1 foreign countries. 96% are white. The average age of freshmen is 35; all undergraduates, 35. 15% do not continue beyond their first year; 85% remain to graduate.

Housing: There are no residence halls. All students commute. No one may keep cars.

Activities: There are no fraternities or sororities. Popular campus events include town meetings and community luncheons.

Disabled Students: Wheelchair ramps, elevators, special parking, and specially equipped rest rooms are available.

Services: Counseling and information services are available, as is tutoring in most subjects.

Campus Safety and Security: Measures include informal discussions.

Programs of Study: Woodbury College confers the B.S. degree. Associate degrees are also awarded. Bachelor's degrees are awarded in SOCIAL SCIENCE (community services, human services, interdisciplinary studies, law, and paralegal studies). Paralegal and mediation conflict management are the largest.

Required: Each student must demonstrate satisfactory competency in core courses and program requirements. A total of 120 credit hours must be completed, with 48 in the major.

Special: Internships are required for all students and work-study programs are available with the Town of Northfield, VT. A student-designed major in interdisciplinary studies is possible. Certificate programs are offered in all areas.

Faculty/Classroom: 39% of faculty are male; 61%, female. All teach undergraduates. The average class size in an introductory lecture is 12; in a laboratory, 12; and in a regular course, 12.

Requirements: Students must submit a completed application, a high school diploma or GED, and an essay. An on-campus interview is also required. AP and CLEP credits are accepted. Important factors in the admissions decision are personality/intangible qualities, recommendations by alumni, and recommendations by school officials.

Procedure: Freshmen are admitted to all sessions. There is a deferred admissions plan and a rolling admissions plan. Application deadlines are open. The fall 2003 application fee was $30. Applications are accepted on computer disk and on-line.

Transfer: Requirements are the same as for incoming freshmen, including high school transcripts, an essay, and an interview. 45 of 120 credits required for the bachelor's degree must be completed at Woodbury College.

Visiting: There are regularly scheduled orientations for prospective students, including an introductory meeting, a school philosophy presentation, a financial aid discussion, a free class, a meal, and a Q&A session. There are guides for informal visits and visitors may stay overnight. To schedule a visit, contact Kathleen Moore at *kathm@woodbury-college.edu*.

Financial Aid: In a recent year, 66% of all full-time freshmen and 73% of continuing full-time students received some form of financial aid. 63% of full-time freshmen and 65% of continuing full-time students received need-based aid. The average freshman award was $11,268. 75% of undergraduates work part time. Average annual earnings from campus work are $1500. The average financial indebtedness of a recent graduate was $27,899. The FAFSA and the college's own financial statement are required. Check with the school for current deadlines.

International Students: In a recent year, there were 2 international students enrolled.

Computers: There are 4 Dell Poweredge Servers, models 2200, 2300, and two 2450s. Students may access the network from 12 PCs in the computer lab. They have full access to the Internet and have college e-mail accounts that can be remotely accessed. All students may access the system. There are no time limits. The fall 2003 application fee was $30 per trimester or $90 per year.

Graduates: In a recent year, 6 bachelor's degrees were awarded. The most popular majors were paralegal (36%), mediation/conflict (34%), and prevention and community development (14%). In an average class, 10% graduate in 4 years or less, 85% graduate in 5 years or less, and 5% graduate in 6 years or less.

Admissions Contact: Kathleen Moore, Admissions Director.
E-mail: *admiss@woodbury-college.edu*
Web: *www.woodbury-college.edu*

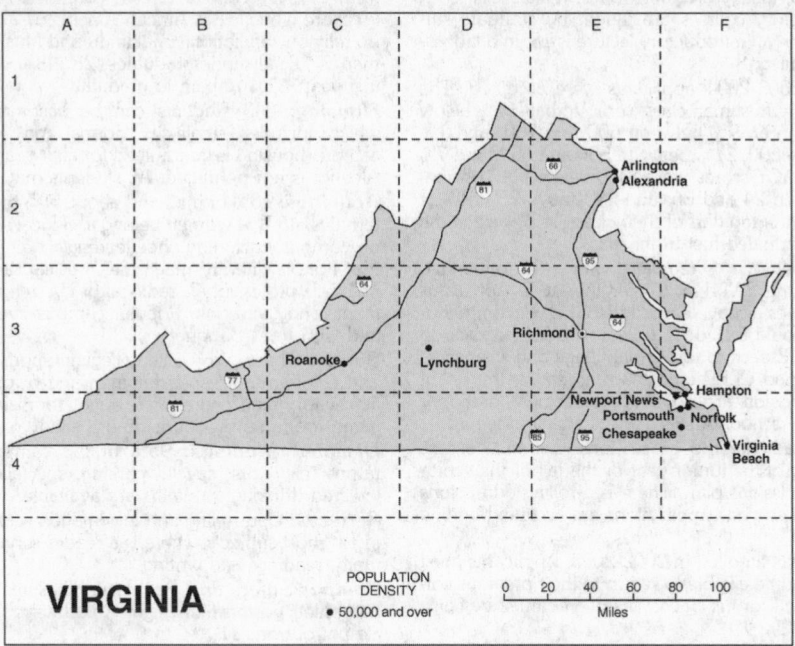

VIRGINIA

POPULATION DENSITY

● 50,000 and over

0 20 40 60 80 100

Miles

AVERETT UNIVERSITY D-4
Danville, VA 24541

(434) 791-7301
(800) 283-7388; Fax: (434) 791-5670

Full-time: 586 men, 679 women	**Faculty:** 67; IIA, --$
Part-time: 293 men, 529 women	**Ph.D.s:** 81%
Graduate: 332 men, 430 women	**Student/Faculty:** 19 to 1
Year: semesters, summer session	**Tuition:** $17,600
Application Deadline: open	**Room & Board:** $5410
Freshman Class: 777 applied, 693 accepted, 219 enrolled	
SAT I Verbal/Math: 480/470	**ACT:** 18 **LESS COMPETITIVE**

Averett University, founded in 1859, is a small, private institution affiliated with the Baptist General Association of Virginia and offers undergraduate and graduate programs in liberal arts, business administration, and teacher education. There is 1 undergraduate and 2 graduate schools.There are 2 graduate schools. The library contains 132,452 volumes, 225,947 microform items, and 124 audio/video tapes/CDs, and subscribes to 4781 periodicals. Computerized library services include the card catalog, interlibrary loans, database searching, and Internet access. Special learning facilities include a learning resource center, a performing arts center, regional archive collections, and flight simulator. The 19-acre campus is in a small town 45 miles from Greensboro, North Carolina, and 140 miles from Richmond. Including any residence halls, there are 20 buildings.

Student Life: 86% of undergraduates are from Virginia. Students are from 30 states, 22 foreign countries, and Canada. 90% are from public schools. 63% are white; 33% African American. 50% are Protestant; 29% claim no religious affiliation; 7% Catholic. The average age of freshmen is 18; all undergraduates, 22. 33% do not continue beyond their first year; 43% remain to graduate.

Housing: 538 students can be accommodated in college housing, which includes single-sex dorms and on-campus apartments. On-campus housing is guaranteed for all 4 years. 54% of students live on campus; of those, 75% remain on campus on weekends. Alcohol is not permitted. All students may keep cars.

Activities: There are 1 national fraternity and 1 national sorority. There are 30 groups on campus, including art, cheerleading, choir, chorale, chorus, dance, drama, honors, international, literary magazine, musical theater, political, professional, religious, social, social service, student government, and yearbook. Popular campus events include a spring fest, concerts, and lectures.

Sports: There are 9 intercollegiate sports for men and 9 for women, and 13 intramural sports for men and 13 for women. Facilities include tennis courts, a 100-acre equestrian center, and a 70-acre athletic center.

Disabled Students: 58% of the campus is accessible. Wheelchair ramps, elevators, special parking, specially equipped rest rooms, and talking books and magnification devices for the visually challenged are available.

Services: Counseling and information services are available, as is tutoring in most subjects. There is a reader service for the blind and remedial math, reading, and writing.

Campus Safety and Security: Measures include 24-hour foot and vehicle patrol, shuttle buses, informal discussions, and pamphlets/posters/films. There are emergency telephones and lighted pathways/sidewalks.

Programs of Study: Averett confers B.A., B.A.S., B.S., and B.B.A. degrees. Associate and master's degrees are also awarded. Bachelor's degrees are awarded in AGRICULTURE (equine science), BIOLOGICAL SCIENCE (biochemistry, biology/biological science, biotechnology, and environmental biology), BUSINESS (accounting, banking and finance, electronic business, international business management, marketing management, organizational behavior, and sports management), COMMUNICATIONS AND THE ARTS (art, dramatic arts, English, journalism, music, and performing arts), COMPUTER AND PHYSICAL SCIENCE (chemistry, computer mathematics, computer science, information sciences and systems, mathematics, physical chemistry, and radiological technology), EDUCATION (art, athletic training, computer, drama, elementary, English, foreign languages, health, journalism, mathematics, middle school, physical, science, secondary, social science, and social studies), ENGINEERING AND ENVIRONMENTAL DESIGN (aeronautical science, aerospace studies, aircraft mechanics, aviation administration/management, and environmental science), HEALTH PROFESSIONS (biomedical science, medical technology, predentistry, premedicine, radiograph medical technology, and sports medicine), SOCIAL SCIENCE (clinical psychology, cognitive science, counseling/psychology, criminal justice, history, industrial and organizational psychology, interdisciplinary studies, law enforcement and corrections, liberal arts/general studies, political science/government, prelaw, psychobiology, psychology, religion, social science, sociology, and theological studies). Business administration, education, and aviation are the largest.

Required: To graduate, all students must complete at least 123 hours with a minimum 2.0 GPA and attend commencement exercises. Core requirements include 15 hours of history or social science, 9 of English, and 6 each of fine arts, religion, and philosophy. Freshmen must take a 3-hour seminar, B.A. students need an additional 6 to 8 hours of math or natural science and 6 to 14 hours in a foreign language, depending on proficiency; B.S. students need an additional 6 hours in math and 8 hours in natural science. All students must pass an exit writing exam.

Special: Averett offers co-op programs in environmental science and internships in business, journalism, criminal justice, psychology, and religion. Cross-registration is available with the Consortium for Global Education and work-study with Averett University is possible. Students may design their own majors with approval, or select dual majors. A general studies degree and nondegree study are offered, as are up to 5 pass/fail options. Senior equestrian studies majors may spend a semester or summer in England preparing for the British Horse Society A.I. certificate; religion majors may spend a summer on an archeological dig in the Middle

East. Study abroad is available in 8 countries. Accelerated degrees are available in all majors. There are 2 national honor societies, a freshman honors program, and all departments have honors programs.

Faculty/Classroom: 66% of faculty are male; 34%, female. All teach undergraduates. No introductory courses are taught by graduate students. The average class size in an introductory lecture is 18; in a laboratory, 16; and in a regular course, 8.

Admissions: 89% of the 2003-2004 applicants were accepted. The SAT I scores for the 2003-2004 freshman class were: Verbal--61% below 500, 29% between 500 and 599, 9% between 600 and 700, and 1% above 700; Math--66% below 500, 27% between 500 and 599, and 7% between 600 and 700. The ACT scores were 81% below 21, 10% between 21 and 23, 7% between 24 and 26, and 2% above 28. 19% of the current freshmen were in the top fifth of their class; 45% were in the top two fifths. 1 freshman graduated first in the class.

Requirements: The SAT I or ACT is required, with a recommended composite score of 850 for the SAT I or 18 for the ACT. Applicants should be high school graduates or have earned the GED. Recommended secondary preparation should include 4 units in English, 3 each in math and social science, and 2 each in foreign language and science. A GPA of 2.0 is required. AP and CLEP credits are accepted. Important factors in the admissions decision are advanced placement or honor courses, recommendations by school officials, and leadership record.

Procedure: Freshmen are admitted to all sessions. Entrance exams should be taken in the spring of the junior year or the fall of the senior year. There is a deferred admissions plan. There is a rolling admissions plan. Application deadlines are open. Applications are accepted on-line through the school's web site.

Transfer: 202 transfer students enrolled in 2002-2003. Applicants must present at least a 2.0 GPA and be eligible to return to their previous college. 30 of 123 credits required for the bachelor's degree must be completed at Averett.

Visiting: There are regularly scheduled orientations for prospective students, including spring and fall open houses, Virginia Visitors Day, and special visiting days for selected majors. There are guides for informal visits and visitors may sit in on classes and stay overnight. To schedule a visit, contact the Admissions Office at (434) 791-4996 or *admit@averett.edu.*

Financial Aid: In 2003-2004, 84% of all full-time freshmen and 85% of continuing full-time students received some form of financial aid. 84% of all full-time students received need-based aid. The average freshman award was $14,055. Need-based scholarships or need-based grants averaged $2000 ($4050 maximum); need-based self-help aid (loans and jobs) averaged $2700 ($5500 maximum); and non-need-based awards and non-need-based scholarships averaged $1800 ($16,600 maximum). 19% of undergraduates work part time. Average annual earnings from campus work are $1113. The average financial indebtedness of the 2003 graduate was $14,896. Averett is a member of CSS. The FAFSA and the college's own financial statement are required. The priority date for freshman financial aid applications for fall entry is April 1.

International Students: There are 33 international students enrolled. The school actively recruits these students. They must score 500 on the written TOEFL or 220 on the electronic version.

Computers: More than 100 PCs are available for student use in 3 separate computer labs; a separate computer lab is maintained for the psychology department. Computers are also available in the library and in the learning center, and there is Internet access. All students may access the system 24 hours a day. There are no time limits and no fees.

Graduates: From July 1, 2002 to June 30, 2003, 427 bachelor's degrees were awarded. The most popular majors were business/marketing (64%), education (5%), and physical education (5%). In an average class, 3% graduate in 3 years or less, 25% graduate in 4 years or less, 42% graduate in 5 years or less, and 43% graduate in 6 years or less.

Admissions Contact: Dr. Vicki Richmond, Dean of Admissions. A video is available. E-mail: *admit@averett.edu* Web: *www.averett.edu*

BLUEFIELD COLLEGE
Bluefield, VA 24605

B-3

(276) 326-4339
(800) 872-0175; Fax: (276) 326-4288

Full-time: 322 men, 339 women	**Faculty:** 30; IIB, --$
Part-time: 23 men, 47 women	**Ph.D.s:** 53%
Graduate: none	**Student/Faculty:** 22 to 1
Year: semesters, summer session	**Tuition:** $10,165
Application Deadline: open	**Room & Board:** $5410
Freshman Class: n/av	
SAT I or ACT: required	**COMPETITIVE**

Bluefield College, founded in 1922, is a private, liberal arts institution affiliated with the Southern Baptist Church. There is 1 undergraduate school. The library contains 72,000 volumes and 1745 audio/video tapes/CDs. Computerized library services include the card catalog, interlibrary loans, database searching, and Internet access. Special learning facilities include a learning resource center and a writing center. The 85-acre campus is in a small town 100 miles west of Roanoke on the Virgin-

ia-West Virginia state line. Including any residence halls, there are 9 buildings.

Student Life: 80% of undergraduates are from Virginia. Students are from 19 states and 2 foreign countries. 95% are from public schools. 79% are white; 18% African American. 77% are Protestant; 13% claim no religious affiliation; 9% Hindu and Muslim. The average age of freshmen is 18; all undergraduates, 28. 43% do not continue beyond their first year; 41% remain to graduate.

Housing: 243 students can be accommodated in college housing, which includes single-sex dorms and on-campus apartments. On-campus housing is guaranteed for all 4 years. 55% of students commute. Alcohol is not permitted. All students may keep cars.

Activities: 10% of men and about 11% of women belong to 3 local fraternities; 45% of women belong to 3 local sororities. There are 15 groups on campus, including cheerleading, choir, chorale, chorus, dance, drama, honors, literary magazine, musical theater, newspaper, pep band, political, professional, radio and TV, religious, social, student government, and yearbook. Popular campus events include Spring Weekend and Christmas Banquet.

Sports: There are 4 intercollegiate sports for men and 4 for women, and 6 intramural sports for men and 6 for women. Facilities include a gym with game courts and weight rooms, a student activities center, a game room, tennis courts, and a sand volleyball court.

Disabled Students: 95% of the campus is accessible. Wheelchair ramps, elevators, special parking, specially equipped rest rooms, and lowered drinking fountains are available.

Services: Counseling and information services are available, as is tutoring in most subjects. There is a reader service for the blind and remedial math, reading, and writing.

Campus Safety and Security: Measures include informal discussions, pamphlets/posters/films, lighted pathways/sidewalks, and foot and vehicle patrol from 11 P.M. to 6 A.M.

Programs of Study: BC confers B.A. and B.S. degrees. Bachelor's degrees are awarded in BIOLOGICAL SCIENCE (biology/biological science), BUSINESS (business administration and management), COMMUNICATIONS AND THE ARTS (communications, English, fine arts, and music), COMPUTER AND PHYSICAL SCIENCE (chemistry and mathematics), EDUCATION (middle school and secondary), HEALTH PROFESSIONS (exercise science), SOCIAL SCIENCE (Christian studies, criminal justice, history, interdisciplinary studies, psychology, religion, and social studies). Business, teacher education, and biology are the strongest academically. Business, organizational management and development, and criminal justice are the largest.

Required: To graduate, students must have completed a minimum of 126 semester hours, including a liberal arts requirement of 51 to 53 hours, with 30 to 45 hours in the major, and a minimum 2.0 GPA. Other requirements vary per program. All graduates must demonstrate computer proficiency by testing, passing computer courses, or having components in required courses.

Special: The college offers credit for life/military/work experience, non-degree study through the Fine Arts Community School, study abroad in England, an accelerated degree program in organizational management and development and in criminal justice, and internships in criminal justice, psychology, and recreation. There are 4 national honor societies, a freshman honors program, and 7 departmental honors programs.

Faculty/Classroom: 70% of faculty are male; 30%, female. All teach undergraduates, 30% do research, and 30% do both. The average class size in an introductory lecture is 17; in a laboratory, 12; and in a regular course, 10.

Requirements: The SAT I or ACT is required. In addition, applicants must be graduates of an accredited secondary school or have a GED certificate, and have completed 4 years of English, 2 of social sciences, 1 of science, and 5 of electives. A GPA of 2.0 is required. AP and CLEP credits are accepted. Important factors in the admissions decision are leadership record, advanced placement or honor courses, and recommendations by school officials.

Procedure: Freshmen are admitted to all sessions. Entrance exams should be taken early in the senior year. There is a deferred admissions plan. Application deadlines are open. Applications are accepted on-line. The fall 2003 application fee was $20. Notification is sent on a rolling basis.

Transfer: 352 transfer students enrolled in a recent year. Prospective students must submit transcripts of all academic work, a financial aid transcript, and SAT I or ACT scores if they have fewer than 30 hours of college level work. 32 of 126 credits required for the bachelor's degree must be completed at BC.

Visiting: There are regularly scheduled orientations for prospective students, including campus tours, opportunities to develop class schedules, and financial aid workshops. Visitors may sit in on classes and stay overnight. To schedule a visit, contact the Admissions Office at (276) 326-4214 or (800) 872-0175.

Financial Aid: In a recent year, 97% of all full-time freshmen and 93% of continuing full-time students received some form of financial aid. 61% of full-time freshmen and 58% of continuing full-time students received need-based aid. The average freshman award was $7900. 11% of undergraduates work part time. Average annual earnings from campus work are $660. The average financial indebtedness of a recent graduate was $14,000. The FAFSA and the college's own financial statement are required. The deadline for filing freshman financial aid applications for fall entry is March 10.

International Students: The school actively recruits these students. They must score 500 on the written TOEFL and also take the SAT I (scoring 860) or the ACT (scoring 18).

Computers: Students may use the 79 PCs in labs. All students may access the system. There are no time limits and no fees. It is strongly recommended that all students have a personal computer. It is recommended that students in Organizational Management and Development have personal computers.

Graduates: From July 1, 2002 to June 30, 2003, 246 bachelor's degrees were awarded. In an average class, 1% graduate in 3 years or less, 47% graduate in 4 years or less, 50% graduate in 5 years or less, and 55% graduate in 6 years or less. 4 companies recruited on campus in 2002-2003. Of the 2002 graduating class, 16% were enrolled in graduate school within 6 months of graduation.

Admissions Contact: Admissions Office. A video is available.
Web: *www.bluefield.edu*

BRIDGEWATER COLLEGE
Bridgewater, VA 22812-1599

D-2

(540) 828-5375
(800) 759-8328; Fax: (540) 828-5481

Full-time: 613 men, 763 women	**Faculty:** 88; IIB, -$
Part-time: 12 men, 15 women	**Ph.D.s:** 77%
Graduate: none	**Student/Faculty:** 16 to 1
Year: 4-1-4, summer session	**Tuition:** $16,990
Application Deadline: open	**Room & Board:** $8160
Freshman Class: 1388 applied, 1221 accepted, 391 enrolled	
SAT I Verbal/Math: 500/510	**ACT:** 20 **COMPETITIVE**

Bridgewater College, founded in 1880, is a private liberal arts institution affiliated with the Church of the Brethren. The library contains 184,816 volumes, 413,297 microform items, and 8884 audio/video tapes/CDs, and subscribes to 660 periodicals. Computerized library services include the card catalog, interlibrary loans, database searching, and Internet access. Special learning facilities include a learning resource center, art gallery, radio station, and museum of the Shenandoah Valley and Church of the Brethren. The 190-acre campus is in a small town 8 miles south of Harrisonburg. Including any residence halls, there are 27 buildings.

Student Life: 78% of undergraduates are from Virginia. Students are from 21 states and 9 foreign countries. 89% are from public schools. 88% are white. 79% are Protestant; 11% Catholic; 6% claim no religious affiliation. The average age of freshmen is 18; all undergraduates, 20. 26% do not continue beyond their first year; 65% remain to graduate.

Housing: 1136 students can be accommodated in college housing, which includes single-sex dorms and on-campus apartments. In addition, there are honors houses. On-campus housing is guaranteed for all 4 years. 76% of students live on campus; of those, 60% remain on campus on weekends. Alcohol is not permitted. All students may keep cars.

Activities: There are no fraternities or sororities. There are 69 groups on campus, including art, band, cheerleading, chess, choir, chorale, chorus, computers, dance, debate, drama, ethnic, forensics, honors, international, jazz band, literary magazine, musical theater, newspaper, pep band, political, professional, radio and TV, religious, social, social service, student government, and yearbook. Popular campus events include Parents Day, Messiah at Christmas, and May Day.

Sports: There are 10 intercollegiate sports for men and 11 for women, and 20 intramural sports for men and 20 for women. Facilities include a gym, a 2500-seat football stadium, a swimming pool, tennis courts, an all-weather track, playing fields for baseball, lacrosse, softball, football, field hockey, and soccer, and a 34,000-square-foot fitness center with basketball, volleyball, and racquetball courts, an indoor track, cardiac and weight training center, and aerobics/dance rooms.

Disabled Students: 90% of the campus is accessible. Wheelchair ramps, elevators, special parking, specially equipped rest rooms, lowered drinking fountains, lowered telephones, and accessible laundry facilities in two dorms are available.

Services: Counseling and information services are available, as is tutoring in every subject. There is a reader service for the blind and remedial writing. The academic support center provides workshops for all students and support for students with learning disabilities.

Campus Safety and Security: Measures include 24-hour foot and vehicle patrol, informal discussions, pamphlets/posters/films, and emergency telephones. There are lighted pathways/sidewalks.

Programs of Study: Bridgewater confers B.A., B.S., and B.G.S. degrees. Bachelor's degrees are awarded in BIOLOGICAL SCIENCE (biology/biological science and nutrition), BUSINESS (business administration and management), COMMUNICATIONS AND THE ARTS (art, communications, English, French, music, and Spanish), COMPUTER AND PHYSICAL SCIENCE (applied physics, chemistry, computer science, information sciences and systems, and mathematics), EDUCATION (athletic training), ENGINEERING AND ENVIRONMENTAL DESIGN (environmental science), HEALTH PROFESSIONS (allied health, health science, and medical technology), SOCIAL SCIENCE (economics, family/consumer studies, history, international studies, liberal arts/general studies, philosophy, political science/government, psychology, religion, and sociology). Biology, psychology, and history are the strongest academically. Biology, business administration, and liberal studies are the largest.

Required: To graduate, all students must complete a minimum of 123 credit hours, with 30 to 48 hours in the major. A minimum 2.0 GPA is required overall and in the major and all seniors must pass a comprehensive exam. In addition, PDP 150: Personal Development and the Liberal Arts must be completed by each entering student unless the student transfers 15 or more units to Bridgewater College. Other general education requirements include courses in writing, oral communication, quantitative reasoning, global perspectives, humanities, natural science, math, foreign language, social science, and exercise science. A thesis is required for honor students only.

Special: Bridgewater offers internships to junior and seniors; study abroad in 16 countries; and a teacher certification program in elementary, secondary, and special education. Interdisciplinary majors include environmental science, history and political science, philosophy and religion, physics and math, and information systems management. Dual degree programs are offered in engineering with George Washington University and Virgina Tech (3-2), in forestry with Duke University (3-2), in veterinary science with Virginia Tech (3-4), in physical therapy with George Washington University (3-2) and Shenandoah University (3-4) , and in nursing (3-2) with Vanderbilt University. There are 8 national honor societies, a freshman honors program, and 17 departmental honors programs.

Faculty/Classroom: 65% of faculty are male; 35%, female. All teach undergraduates, 50% do research, and 50% do both. The average class size in an introductory lecture is 22; in a laboratory, 16; and in a regular course, 18.

Admissions: 88% of the 2003-2004 applicants were accepted. The SAT I scores for the 2003-2004 freshman class were: Verbal--47% below 500, 39% between 500 and 599, 12% between 600 and 700, and 2% above 700; Math--45% below 500, 40% between 500 and 599, 15% between 600 and 700, and 1% above 700. The ACT scores were 56% below 21, 26% between 21 and 23, 9% between 24 and 26, 6% between 27 and 28, and 4% above 28. 35% of the current freshmen were in the top fifth of their class; 66% were in the top two fifths. 7 freshmen graduated first in their class.

Requirements: The SAT I or ACT is required; the SAT I is preferred. An interview is recommended. Applicants must be graduates of an accredited secondary school or have a GED certificate, and have completed 17 units, including 4 in English, 3 in math, 2 each in foreign language, science, and history and social studies, and 4 in electives. Bridgewater requires applicants to be in the upper 50% of their class. A GPA of 2.0 is required. AP credits are accepted. Important factors in the admissions decision are advanced placement or honor courses, recommendations by school officials, and leadership record.

Procedure: Freshmen are admitted fall, spring, and summer. Entrance exams should be taken in spring of the junior year or fall of the senior year. There is a deferred admissions plan. Application deadlines are open. Application fee is $30. There is a rolling admissions plan. Applications are accepted on computer disk and on-line through *www.bridgewater.edu/departments/admissions.*

Transfer: 80 transfer students enrolled in 2003-2004. A degree from an accredited high school and a 2.0 GPA in all undergraduate work are required. 27 of 123 credits required for the bachelor's degree must be completed at Bridgewater.

Visiting: There are regularly scheduled orientations for prospective students, including a meeting with a faculty adviser, course scheduling and registration, and social activities. There are guides for informal visits and visitors may sit in on classes and stay overnight. To schedule a visit, contact Linda F. Stout at *admissions@bridgewater.edu.*

Financial Aid: In 2003-2004, 99% of all full-time students received some form of financial aid. 77% of full-time freshmen and 70% of continuing full-time students received need-based aid. The average freshman award was $16,159. Need-based scholarships or need-based grants averaged $5763 ($8500 maximum); need-based self-help aid (loans and jobs) averaged $3550 ($6700 maximum); and non-need-based awards and non-need-based scholarships averaged $6846 ($19,200 maximum). 38% of undergraduates work part time. Average annual earnings from campus work are $1028. The average financial indebtedness of the 2003 graduate was $20,099. Bridgewater is a member of CSS. The FAFSA is required. The priority date for freshman financial aid applications for fall entry is March 1. The deadline for filing freshman financial aid applications for fall entry is August 15.

International Students: There are 12 international students enrolled. The school actively recruits these students. They must score 500 on the written TOEFL or 173 on the electronic version and also take the SAT I or the ACT.

Computers: The mainframe is a Sun Ultra Enterprise 450 minicomputer. All buildings are connected via a campus-wide network. There are 149 computers in classroom buildings and the library available for student use. Dorm rooms are wired for connection to the campus network. Access to e-mail and the Web is available in computer labs throughout the campus. All students may access the system 24 hours a day. There are no time limits and no fees.

Graduates: From July 1, 2002 to June 30, 2003, 269 bachelor's degrees were awarded. The most popular majors were business administration (16%), biology (16%), and psychology (11%). In an average class, 65% graduate in 4 years or less. 7 companies recruited on campus in 2002-2003.

Admissions Contact: Linda F. Stout, Director of Enrollment Operations. A video is available. E-mail: *admissions@bridgewater.edu* Web: *www.bridgewater.edu*

CHRISTENDOM COLLEGE
Front Royal, VA 22630

D-2

(540) 636-2900
(800) 877-5456; Fax: (540) 636-1655

Full-time: 155 men, 209 women	**Faculty:** 21
Part-time: 1 man, 1 woman	**Ph.D.s:** 81%
Graduate: 42 men, 33 women	**Student/Faculty:** 17 to 1
Year: semesters	**Tuition:** $13,420
Application Deadline: March 1	**Room & Board:** $4990
Freshman Class: 215 applied, 175 accepted, 98 enrolled	
SAT I Verbal/Math: 660/570	**ACT:** 25 **VERY COMPETITIVE+**

Christendom College, founded in 1977, is a private liberal arts institution affiliated with the Roman Catholic Church. The library contains 68,314 volumes, 860 microform items, and 1345 audio/video tapes/CDs, and subscribes to 279 periodicals. Computerized library services include the card catalog, interlibrary loans, and database searching. Special learning facilities include a learning resource center, art gallery, and a writing center. The 100-acre campus is in a rural area 65 miles west of Washington, D.C. Including any residence halls, there are 19 buildings.

Student Life: 78% of undergraduates are from out of state, mostly the Middle Atlantic. Students are from 43 states, 3 foreign countries, and Canada. 14% are from public schools. 91% are white. Most are Catholic. The average age of freshmen is 18; all undergraduates, 20. 16% do not continue beyond their first year; 76% remain to graduate.

Housing: 330 students can be accommodated in college housing, which includes single-sex dorms and on-campus apartments. On-campus housing is guaranteed for all 4 years. 95% of students live on campus; of those, all remain on campus on weekends. All students may keep cars.

Activities: There are no fraternities or sororities. There are 15 groups on campus, including choir, chorale, debate, drama, musical theater, newspaper, photography, political, religious, social service, student government, and yearbook. Popular campus events include Octoberfest, Christmas Dinner Dance, and St. Patrick's Day.

Sports: There are 3 intercollegiate sports for men and 3 for women, and 7 intramural sports for men and 7 for women. Facilities include indoor basketball and volleyball courts, racquetball courts, playing fields, table games, a recreation center, and an outdoor swimming pool.

Disabled Students: 60% of the campus is accessible. Wheelchair ramps, special parking, and specially equipped rest rooms are available.

Campus Safety and Security: Measures include 24-hour foot and vehicle patrol, security escort services, emergency telephones, and lighted pathways/sidewalks.

Programs of Study: Christendom confers the B.A. degree. Associate and master's degrees are also awarded. Bachelor's degrees are awarded in COMMUNICATIONS AND THE ARTS (English and French), SOCIAL SCIENCE (classical/ancient civilization, history, philosophy, political science/government, and theological studies). Political science is the strongest academically. Philosophy is the largest.

Required: To graduate, all students must complete a total of 126 credit hours, including a 30-hour major and an 84-credit core curriculum, which includes 18 hours each in theology and philosophy. A minimum 2.0 GPA is required. All students must demonstrate proficiency in a foreign language and complete a thesis.

Special: Christendom offers summer internships in Washington, D.C., for political science students, and also sponsors a semester in Rome during the junior year. Students may pursue dual majors. There is a work-study program with the college.

Faculty/Classroom: 90% of faculty are male; 10%, female. All teach undergraduates. No introductory courses are taught by graduate students. The average class size in an introductory lecture is 20; in a laboratory, 3; and in a regular course, 15.

Admissions: 81% of the 2003-2004 applicants were accepted. The SAT I scores for the 2003-2004 freshman class were: Verbal--20% between 500 and 599, 47% between 600 and 700, and 33% above 700; Math--9% below 500, 50% between 500 and 599, 29% between 600 and 700, and 12% above 700. The ACT scores were 6% below 21, 29% between 21 and 23, 35% between 24 and 26, 16% between 27 and 28,

and 14% above 28. 38% of the current freshmen were in the top fifth of their class; 84% were in the top two fifths. There were 2 National Merit finalists and 4 semifinalists.

Requirements: The SAT I or ACT is required; the SAT I is preferred. A minimum composite score of 1000 on the SAT I or 21 on the ACT is required. Applicants need not be graduates of an accredited secondary school. GED certificates are accepted. Students should have completed 4 years of English, 2 years each of foreign language, math, history, and science, and 1 year of social studies. Essays and letters of recommendation are required. Interviews are recommended. Christendom requires applicants to be in the upper 50% of their class. A GPA of 3.0 is required. AP credits are accepted. Important factors in the admissions decision are advanced placement or honor courses, leadership record, and evidence of special talent.

Procedure: Freshmen are admitted fall and spring. Entrance exams should be taken in the spring of the junior year or fall of the senior year. There is an early admissions plan. Early decision applications should be filed by December 1; regular applications, by March 1 for fall entry and December 15 for spring entry. The fall 2003 application fee was $25. Notification of early decision is sent December 15; regular decision, April 1. 25 applicants were on the 2003 waiting list; 7 were admitted. Applications are accepted on-line.

Transfer: 14 transfer students enrolled in 2002-2003. Students must have a minimum 2.0 GPA and meet all other applicable standard admissions requirements. The SAT I or ACT is recommended. 36 credits of 126 required for the bachelor's degree must be completed at Christendom.

Visiting: There are guides for informal visits and visitors may sit in on classes and stay overnight. To schedule a visit, contact an Admissions Counselor at *admissions@christendom.edu*.

Financial Aid: In 2003-2004, 78% of all full-time freshmen and 66% of continuing full-time students received some form of financial aid. 53% of full-time freshmen and 52% of continuing full-time students received need-based aid. The average freshman award was $8665. Need-based scholarships or need-based grants averaged $3715 ($5580 maximum); need-based self-help aid (loans and jobs) averaged $4950 ($5580 maximum); and non-need-based awards and non-need-based scholarships averaged $4035 ($5480 maximum). 40% of undergraduates work part time. Average annual earnings from campus work are $1750. The average financial indebtedness of the 2003 graduate was $7950. The college's own financial statement is required. The deadline for filing freshman financial aid applications for fall entry is April 1.

International Students: There are 11 international students enrolled. They must score 500 on the written TOEFL.

Computers: There is a computer lab network of 20 PCs for student use offering word processsing, Internet, and e-mail capabilities, and 8 PCs for Internet access in the library. All students may access the system. There are no time limits and no fees.

Graduates: From July 1, 2002 to June 30, 2003, 52 bachelor's degrees were awarded. The most popular majors were political science (21%), history (21%), and philosophy (20%). In an average class, 2% graduate in 3 years or less, 70% graduate in 4 years or less, and 75% graduate in 5 years or less. 8 companies recruited on campus in 2002-2003. Of the 2002 graduating class, 25% were enrolled in graduate school within 6 months of graduation and 75% were employed.

Admissions Contact: Paul L. Heisler, Director of Admissions. E-mail: *admissions@christendom.edu* Web: *www.christendom.edu*

CHRISTOPHER NEWPORT UNIVERSITY
Newport News, VA 23606-2998

F-3

(757) 594-7015
(800) 333-4268; Fax: (757) 594-7333

Full-time: 1555 men, 2490 women	**Faculty:** 184; IIB, +$
Part-time: 445 men, 675 women	**Ph.D.s:** 87%
Graduate: 75 men, 155 women	**Student/Faculty:** 22 to 1
Year: semesters, summer session	**Tuition:** $3115 ($9135)
Application Deadline: see profile	**Room & Board:** $5750
Freshman Class: n/av	
SAT I or ACT: required	**VERY COMPETITIVE**

Christopher Newport University, founded in 1960, is a comprehensive public university offering undergraduate programs in business and economics, arts and humanities, social science and professional studies, and science and technology. There are 2 undergraduate schools and 1 graduate school. Figures in the above capsule and in this profile are approximate. In addition to regional accreditation, CNU has baccalaureate program accreditation with AACSB, ABET, CSWE, and NASM. The library contains 330,014 volumes, 765,028 microform items, and 10,238 audio/video tapes/CDs, and subscribes to 1600 periodicals. Computerized library services include the card catalog, interlibrary loans, and database searching. Special learning facilities include a learning resource center, art gallery, radio station, greenhouse-herbarium, and Japanese teahouse. The 150-acre campus is in a suburban area 20 miles northwest of Norfolk and 20 miles southeast of Williamsburg. Including any residence halls, there are 19 buildings.

Student Life: 97% of undergraduates are from Virginia. Students are from 27 states and 15 foreign countries. 80% are white; 14% African American. The average age of freshmen is 18; all undergraduates, 23. 19% do not continue beyond their first year; 30% remain to graduate.

Housing: 1455 students can be accommodated in college housing, which includes coed dorms and on-campus apartments. On-campus housing is guaranteed for all 4 years. 70% of students commute. Alcohol is not permitted. All students may keep cars.

Activities: 5% of men belong to 5 national fraternities; 4% of women belong to 5 national sororities. There are 20 groups on campus, including art, band, cheerleading, chess, choir, chorale, chorus, computers, dance, drama, ethnic, gay, honors, international, jazz band, literary magazine, musical theater, newspaper, opera, orchestra, pep band, political, professional, radio and TV, religious, social, social service, student government, and symphony. Popular campus events include FallFest, Sand Jam, and Ella Fitzgerald Music Festival.

Sports: There are 11 intercollegiate sports for men and 11 for women, and 13 intramural sports for men and 13 for women. The sports and recreation center has a 200-meter indoor track, 3 basketball courts, 10,000 square feet of recreation and fitness space with state-of-the-art equipment.

Disabled Students: 95% of the campus is accessible. Wheelchair ramps, elevators, special parking, specially equipped rest rooms, special class scheduling, and lowered drinking fountains are available. Special services are available on an individual basis.

Services: Counseling and information services are available, as is tutoring in most subjects. There is remedial math, reading, and writing.

Campus Safety and Security: Measures include 24-hour foot and vehicle patrol, security escort services, pamphlets/posters/films, and emergency telephones. There are lighted pathways/sidewalks and a campus police department.

Programs of Study: CNU confers B.A., B.S., B.M., B.S.A., B.S.B.A., B.S.G.A., B.S.I.S., and B.S.N. degrees. Master's degrees are also awarded. Bachelor's degrees are awarded in AGRICULTURE (horticulture), BIOLOGICAL SCIENCE (biology/biological science), BUSINESS (accounting, banking and finance, business administration and management, business economics, international business management, marketing management, marketing/retailing/merchandising, real estate, and recreation and leisure services), COMMUNICATIONS AND THE ARTS (communications, creative writing, dramatic arts, English, English literature, fine arts, French, German, journalism, music, music performance, music theory and composition, performing arts, and Spanish), COMPUTER AND PHYSICAL SCIENCE (computer science, information sciences and systems, mathematics, and physics), EDUCATION (early childhood, foreign languages, middle school, music, science, and secondary), ENGINEERING AND ENVIRONMENTAL DESIGN (computer engineering and environmental science), HEALTH PROFESSIONS (nursing, predentistry, and premedicine), SOCIAL SCIENCE (criminal justice, criminology, economics, history, interdisciplinary studies, international public service, international relations, law, parks and recreation management, philosophy, political science/government, prelaw, psychology, public administration, religion, social work, and sociology). Business, psychology, and government administration are the largest.

Required: To graduate, all students must fulfill general education requirements in English, math, humanities, social science, lab science, communications, philosophy, foreign language, computer literacy, health, and phys ed. A minimum of 120 semester hours, with 58 to 66 hours in the major and in elective studies, is required. Students must have a minimum GPA of 2.0.

Special: CNU offers cross-registration with Thomas Nelson Community College and Hampton and Old Dominion Universities, dual majors, various B.A.-B.S. degrees, a student-designed interdisciplinary studies major, and internships in social service, communications, city government, computer science, and engineering. There are 9 national honor societies, a freshman honors program, and 9 departmental honors programs.

Faculty/Classroom: All teach undergraduates and 10% both teach and do research. No introductory courses are taught by graduate students. The average class size in an introductory lecture is 25; in a laboratory, 20; and in a regular course, 25.

Requirements: The SAT I or ACT is required, with minimum scores of 510 verbal and 500 math on the SAT I or 19 on the ACT. Applicants must be graduates of an accredited secondary school or have a GED certificate. A total of 23 academic credits is recommended, including 4 units of English, 3 each of social science, math, and science, and either 3 units of 1 foreign language or 2 years of 2 foreign languages. An essay and interview are recommended. CNU requires applicants to be in the upper 50% of their class. A GPA of 3.0 is required. AP and CLEP credits are accepted. Important factors in the admissions decision are recommendations by school officials, extracurricular activities record, and evidence of special talent.

Procedure: Freshmen are admitted fall and spring. Entrance exams should be taken in the junior year. There are early admissions, deferred admissions, and rolling admissions plans. Check with the school for current deadlines. The fall 2003 fee was $25. Applications are accepted online at *www.cnu.edu/admit/*.

Transfer: 306 transfer students enrolled in a recent year. Applicants must have at least 15 transferable semester hours with a minimum 3.0 GPA, and be eligible to return to the most recently attended college or university. Students with fewer than 15 semester hours must submit SAT I or ACT scores and official transcripts from their secondary school and all colleges attended. 30 of 120 credits required for the bachelor's degree must be completed at CNU.

Visiting: There are regularly scheduled orientations for prospective students, including information sessions and tours Monday through Friday at 10 A.M. and 2 P.M.; Saturday session and tour at 11 A.M. Tours run throughout the year. There are guides for informal visits and visitors may sit in on classes and stay overnight. To schedule a visit, contact the Admissions Office at *tourguide@cnu.edu*.

Financial Aid: In a recent year, 65% of all full-time students received some form of financial aid. 65% of all full-time students received need-based aid. The average freshman award was $4701. 21% of undergraduates work part time. Average annual earnings from campus work are $1478. The average financial indebtedness of a recent graduate was $8096. CNU is a member of CSS. The FAFSA is required. Check with the school for the current deadlines.

International Students: In a recent year, there were 17 international students enrolled. They must score 530 on the written TOEFL or 197 on the electronic version and also take the SAT I or the ACT, scoring 1020.

Computers: The mainframes are 2 Sun ES5000s and an HP9000. 16 networked PC, Unix and Mac labs are available on campus 7 days a week with 1 computer for every 10 students. All students have accounts on the Sun System that can be accessed from all labs, dorms, or dial-in connections. All students may access the system 24 hours a day, 7 days a week. There are no time limits and no fees.

Graduates: In a recent year, 732 bachelor's degrees were awarded. The most popular majors were business administration (15%), psychology (14%), and social science (12%). In an average class, 8% graduate in 4 years or less, 24% graduate in 5 years or less, and 30% graduate in 6 years or less. 325 companies recruited on campus in a recent year.

Admissions Contact: Admissions Office. E-mail: *admit@cnu.edu* Web: *http://www.cnu.edu*

COLLEGE OF WILLIAM AND MARY
Williamsburg, VA 23187-8795

E-3
(757) 221-4223
Fax: (757) 221-1242

Full-time: 2470 men, 3196 women	**Faculty:** 446; I, av$
Part-time: 45 men, 37 women	**Ph.D.s:** 91%
Graduate: 1027 men, 974 women	**Student/Faculty:** 13 to 1
Year: semesters, summer session	**Tuition:** $6430 ($21,216)
Application Deadline: January 5	**Room & Board:** $5794
Freshman Class: 10,161 applied, 3488 accepted, 1326 enrolled	
SAT I Verbal/Math: 680/670	**ACT:** 30 MOST COMPETITIVE

College of William and Mary, founded in 1693, is the second-oldest college in the United States. The public institution offers undergraduate degrees in the arts and sciences. Graduate programs are offered in arts and sciences, law, business, education, and marine science. Tuition and room and board figures in the above capsule are for the 2002-2003 school year. There are 2 undergraduate and 5 graduate schools. In addition to regional accreditation, William and Mary has baccalaureate program accreditation with AACSB and NCATE. The 6 libraries contain 2,128,645 volumes, 2,346,524 microform items, and 29,977 audio/video tapes/CDs, and subscribe to 11,313 periodicals. Computerized library services include the card catalog, interlibrary loans, and database searching. Special learning facilities include a learning resource center, art gallery, radio station, anthropology museum, art studio, greenhouse, the Center for Archaeological Research, and the Omohundro Institute of Early American History and Culture. The 1200-acre campus is in a small town 50 miles southeast of Richmond. Including any residence halls, there are 166 buildings.

Student Life: 66% of undergraduates are from Virginia. Students are from 49 states, 52 foreign countries, and Canada. 74% are from public schools. 84% are white. The average age of freshmen is 18; all undergraduates, 20. 5% do not continue beyond their first year; 91% remain to graduate.

Housing: 4444 students can be accommodated in college housing, which includes single-sex and coed dorms, on-campus apartments, off-campus apartments, married-student housing, fraternity houses, and sorority houses. In addition, there are honors houses, language houses, special-interest houses, an international studies hall, and smoke-free housing. On-campus housing is guaranteed for the freshman year only and is available on a lottery system for upperclassmen. 75% of students live on campus; of those, all remain on campus on weekends.

Activities: 33% of men belong to 15 national fraternities; 34% of women belong to 11 national sororities. There are more than 300 groups on campus, including art, band, cheerleading, chess, choir, chorale, chorus, computers, dance, drama, drill team, ethnic, film, gay, honors, international, jazz band, literary magazine, musical theater, newspaper, opera, orchestra, pep band, photography, political, professional, radio and TV, religious, social, social service, student government, symphony, and yearbook. Popular campus events include Yule Log Ceremony, King and Queen Ball, and Opening Convocation.

Sports: There are 11 intercollegiate sports for men and 12 for women, and 24 intramural sports for men and 24 for women. Facilities include an 8500-seat basketball arena, an indoor track, a strength training facility, a sports medicine/rehabilitation facility, a gym room, lighted tennis courts, a 2200-seat artificial turf stadium, a 14,500-seat football stadium, a 1000-seat baseball stadium, and a student recreation facility with a gym, swimming pool, weight room, and racquetball and squash courts.

Disabled Students: 80% of the campus is accessible. Wheelchair ramps, elevators, special parking, specially equipped rest rooms, special class scheduling, lowered drinking fountains, modified recreational facilities, TDD, braille signage, Kurzwiel reader, and a special learning lab for the visually impaired are available. Individual accommodations are made on a case-by-case basis.

Services: Counseling and information services are available, as is tutoring in most subjects. There is a reader service for the blind. There are reasonable in-class accommodations for learning-disabled students and hearing-impaired students and diagnostic services for learning disabilities.

Campus Safety and Security: Measures include 24-hour foot and vehicle patrol, self-defense education, security escort services, and shuttle buses. There are informal discussions, pamphlets/posters/films, emergency telephones, lighted pathways/sidewalks, and crime prevention programs.

Programs of Study: William and Mary confers B.A., B.S., A.B., and B.B.A. degrees. Master's and doctoral degrees are also awarded. Bachelor's degrees are awarded in BIOLOGICAL SCIENCE (biology/biological science), BUSINESS (business administration and management), COMMUNICATIONS AND THE ARTS (classics, English, fine arts, French, German, music, Spanish, and speech/debate/rhetoric), COMPUTER AND PHYSICAL SCIENCE (chemistry, computer science, geology, mathematics, and physics), SOCIAL SCIENCE (American studies, anthropology, economics, history, interdisciplinary studies, international relations, international studies, philosophy, political science/government, psychology, religion, and sociology). Business, psychology, and government are the largest.

Required: To graduate, students must demonstrate proficiencies in foreign language, writing, computing, and physical activity. Freshman seminars are required. Students must complete 120 credit hours, with 33 to 45 in the major and a minimum 2.0 GPA. Distribution requirements include courses in math and quantitative reasoning, natural sciences, social sciences, world cultures and history, literature and history of the arts, and philosophical, religious, and social thought.

Special: William and Mary offers a forestry/environmental science program with Duke University. Also available are departmental internships, study abroad in more than 40 countries, dual and student-designed majors, work-study programs, an accelerated degree in computer science, B.A.-B.S. degrees in math, psychology, computer science, and international studies, a Washington semester, nondegree study, and pass/fail options. There are 29 national honor societies, including Phi Beta Kappa, a freshman honors program, and 15 departmental honors programs.

Faculty/Classroom: 66% of faculty are male; 34%, female. 76% teach undergraduates and 69% do research. No introductory courses are taught by graduate students. The average class size in an introductory lecture is 43; in a laboratory, 26; and in a regular course, 26.

Admissions: 34% of the 2003-2004 applicants were accepted. The SAT I scores for the 2003-2004 freshman class were: Verbal--1% below 500, 11% between 500 and 599, 45% between 600 and 700, and 43% above 700; Math--1% below 500, 13% between 500 and 599, 51% between 600 and 700, and 35% above 700. The ACT scores were 11% between 21 and 23 and 89% above 28. 96% of the current freshmen were in the top fifth of their class; 99% were in the top two fifths. 107 freshmen graduated first in their class.

Requirements: The SAT I or ACT is required. In addition, an essay and 3 SAT II: Subject tests, including the test in writing, are strongly recommended. AP credits are accepted. Important factors in the admissions decision are advanced placement or honor courses, evidence of special talent, and extracurricular activities record.

Procedure: Freshmen are admitted fall and spring. Entrance exams should be taken in spring of the junior year or fall of the senior year. There are early decision and deferred admissions plans. Early decision applications should be filed by November 1; regular applications, by January 5 for fall entry and November 1 for spring entry. Notification of early decision is sent December 1; regular decision, May 1. 497 early decision candidates were accepted for the 2003-2004 class. 736 applicants were on the 2003 waiting list; 9 were admitted. Applications are accepted on-line through Common App and Next Stop College.

Transfer: 181 transfer students enrolled in 2002-2003. Applicants must have at least 15 credit hours earned with a minimum 3.0 GPA recommended. Emphasis is placed on the individual's college records. The SAT I or ACT is required if applicants have completed less than 1 full year of course work at their previous college. 60 of 120 credits required for the bachelor's degree must be completed at William and Mary.

Visiting: There are regularly scheduled orientations for prospective students, consisting of a group information session followed by a student-led tour. Visiting students may sit in on classes and stay overnight. To schedule a visit, contact the Office of Admissions.

Financial Aid: William and Mary is a member of CSS. The CSS Profile or FAFSA is required. The CSS Profile is required for early decision enrollees. The deadline for filing freshman financial aid applications for fall entry is February 15.

International Students: There are 81 international students enrolled. The school actively recruits these students. They must score 600 on the written TOEFL or 250 on the electronic version and also take the ELPT (English Language Proficiency Test) and the SAT I or ACT. SAT II: Subject tests are considered if they are submitted.

Computers: There are 300 PCs in 16 locations around campus. All dorms are wired for Internet connection. All students may access the system. There are no time limits and no fees.

Graduates: From July 1, 2002 to June 30, 2003, 1354 bachelor's degrees were awarded. The most popular majors were business (14%), psychology (9%), and biology (9%). In an average class, 79% graduate in 4 years or less, 89% graduate in 5 years or less, and 91% graduate in 6 years or less. 422 companies recruited on campus in 2002-2003. Of the 2002 graduating class, 31% were enrolled in graduate school within 6 months of graduation and 48% were employed.

Admissions Contact: Office of Admission. A video is available. E-mail: *admiss@wm.edu* Web: *www.wm.edu/admission*

DEVRY UNIVERSITY/CRYSTAL CITY
Arlington, VA 22202-3843

E-2

(703) 414-4100
(866) 338-7932; Fax: (703) 414-4040

Full-time: 294 men, 96 women	**Faculty:** n/av
Part-time: 143 men, 74 women	**Ph.D.s:** n/av
Graduate: n/av	**Student/Faculty:** n/av
Year: semesters, summer session	**Tuition:** $11,860
Application Deadline: open	**Room & Board:** n/app
Freshman Class: n/av	
SAT I or ACT: n/av	**COMPETITIVE**

DeVry University/Crystal City, founded in 2001, is 1 of 67 DeVry University locations throughout the United States and Canada. The private institution offers career-oriented degree programs with hands-on training in various fields of business and technology. Computerized library services include the card catalog, interlibrary loans, and database searching. Special learning facilities include a learning resource center and electronics and other labs.

Student Life: 56% of students are African American; 19% white. The average age of all undergraduates is 24.

Housing: There are no residence halls. There are private apartments, student-plan housing, and private rooms. All students commute. All students may keep cars.

Activities: There are no fraternities or sororities.

Sports: There is no sports program at DeVry.

Disabled Students: All of the campus is accessible. Wheelchair ramps, elevators, special parking, specially equipped rest rooms, lowered drinking fountains, and lowered telephones are available.

Services: Counseling and information services are available, as is tutoring in every subject.

Campus Safety and Security: Measures include security escort services and lighted pathways/sidewalks.

Programs of Study: DeVry confers the B.S. degree. Associate and master's degrees are also awarded. Bachelor's degrees are awarded in BUSINESS (business administration and management), COMMUNICATIONS AND THE ARTS (telecommunications), COMPUTER AND PHYSICAL SCIENCE (information sciences and systems), ENGINEERING AND ENVIRONMENTAL DESIGN (computer engineering, electrical/electronics engineering technology, and technological management). Business administration and computer information systems are the largest.

Required: To graduate, students must achieve a GPA of at least 2.0 and satisfactorily complete all curriculum requirements. Course requirements vary according to program. All first-year students take courses in business organization, computer applications, algebra, psychology, and student success strategies.

Special: An accelerated degree program in computer information systems, co-op programs, nondegree study, distance learning, and evening and weekend classes are possible.

Faculty/Classroom: All teach undergraduates.

Requirements: Admissions requirements include graduation from a secondary school; the GED is also accepted. Applicants must pass the DeVry entrance exam or present satisfactory ACT or SAT I scores. An interview is required. CLEP credit is accepted.

Procedure: Freshmen are admitted to all sessions. There is a rolling admissions plan. There are early admissions and deferred admissions plans. Application deadlines are open. Application fee is $50. Applications are accepted on-line through *https://apply.embark.com/UGrad/DeVry/21.edu.*

Transfer: 18 transfer students enrolled in a recent year. Applicants must submit official transcripts from all previous colleges attended indicating passing grades in all completed course work, demonstrate language skills proficiency in at least 24 completed semester hours, and present evidence of math proficiency by appropriate college-level credits. A minimum GPA of 2.0 is required. 25% of 48 to 154 credits required for the bachelor's degree must be completed at DeVry.

Visiting: There are regularly scheduled orientations for prospective students. There are guides for informal visits and visitors may sit in on classes. To schedule a visit, contact Charles Akinduro, Director of Admissions.

Financial Aid: In 2002-2003, 61% of all full-time freshmen and 68% of continuing full-time students received some form of financial aid. At least 60% of full-time freshmen and at least 68% of continuing full-time students received need-based aid. The average freshman award was $5819. Need-based scholarships or need-based grants averaged $3809; need-based self-help aid (loans and jobs) averaged $3987; and institutional non-need-based awards and non-need-based scholarships averaged $7601. The FAFSA is required. The deadline for filing freshman financial aid applications is rolling.

International Students: There were 5 international students enrolled in a recent year. They must score 500 on the written TOEFL or 173 on the electronic version and also take the college's own entrance exam.

Admissions Contact: Charles Akinduro, Director of Admissions.
E-mail: *admissions@devry.edu* Web: *www.crys.devry.edu*

EASTERN MENNONITE UNIVERSITY   D-2
Harrisonburg, VA 22802-2462   (540) 432-4118
                                  (800) 368-2665; Fax: (540) 432-4444

Full-time: 353 men, 529 women	**Faculty:** 86; IIA, --$
Part-time: 15 men, 20 women	**Ph.D.s:** 69%
Graduate: 56 men, 172 women	**Student/Faculty:** 10 to 1
Year: semesters, summer session	**Tuition:** $17,350
Application Deadline: open	**Room & Board:** $5640
Freshman Class: 605 applied, 498 accepted, 196 enrolled	
SAT I Verbal/Math: 550/530	**ACT:** 23 COMPETITIVE

Eastern Mennonite University, founded in 1917, is a private Christian liberal arts university affiliated with the Mennonite Church. The university offers programs in the arts and sciences, education, biology, and nursing. EMU also offers master's degrees in several areas. EMU Lancaster Campus provides some programs in Lancaster, Pennsylvania. In addition to regional accreditation, EMU has baccalaureate program accreditation with CSWE, NCATE, and NLN. The library contains 158,936 volumes, 85,902 microform items, and 3381 audio/video tapes/CDs, and subscribes to 1160 periodicals. Computerized library services include the card catalog, interlibrary loans, and database searching. Special learning facilities include a learning resource center, art gallery, natural history museum, planetarium, radio station, arboretum and greenhouse. The 93-acre campus is in a small town 110 miles southwest of Washington, D.C. Including any residence halls, there are 42 buildings.

Student Life: 59% of undergraduates are from out of state, mostly the Middle Atlantic. Students are from 35 states, 21 foreign countries, and Canada. 55% are from public schools. 85% are white. Most are Protestant. The average age of freshmen is 18; all undergraduates, 21. 25% do not continue beyond their first year; 61% remain to graduate.

Housing: 684 students can be accommodated in college housing, which includes single-sex and coed dorms, on-campus apartments, off-campus apartments, and married-student housing. On-campus housing is guaranteed for all 4 years. 66% of students live on campus; of those, 75% remain on campus on weekends. Alcohol is not permitted. All students may keep cars.

Activities: There are no fraternities or sororities. There are 47 groups on campus, including chess, choir, chorale, chorus, dance, drama, ethnic, film, honors, international, jazz band, literary magazine, musical theater, newspaper, orchestra, peace fellowship, pep band, political, professional, radio and TV, religious, social, social service, student government, student women's association, and yearbook. Popular campus events include Spring Fling, Fall Festival, and Multicultural Week.

Sports: There are 8 intercollegiate sports for men and 9 for women, and 12 intramural sports for men and 12 for women. Facilities include a fitness center, aerobics room, indoor track, and climbing wall. The gym includes 1 regular varsity court and 2 courts for team practice. Outside facilities include a lighted artificial turf playing field, lighted tennis courts, baseball, softball, and soccer fields, a rubberized outdoor track, as well as basketball and sand volleyball courts.

Disabled Students: 75% of the campus is accessible. Wheelchair ramps, elevators, special parking, specially equipped rest rooms, special class scheduling, lowered drinking fountains, and special housing are available.

Services: Counseling and information services are available, as is tutoring in most subjects, including core curriculum courses, as requested by

students. There is a reader service for the blind and remedial math, reading, and writing.

Campus Safety and Security: Measures include self-defense education, security escort services, informal discussions, and pamphlets/posters/films. There are emergency telephones, lighted pathways/sidewalks, and a 12-hour foot or vehicle watchman.

Programs of Study: EMU confers B.A. and B.S. degrees. Associate and master's degrees are also awarded. Bachelor's degrees are awarded in AGRICULTURE (international agriculture), BIOLOGICAL SCIENCE (biochemistry and biology/biological science), BUSINESS (accounting, business administration and management, international business management, and recreational facilities management), COMMUNICATIONS AND THE ARTS (art, communications, dramatic arts, English, French, German, music, and Spanish), COMPUTER AND PHYSICAL SCIENCE (chemistry, computer management, computer science, and mathematics), EDUCATION (early childhood, elementary, physical, secondary, and special), ENGINEERING AND ENVIRONMENTAL DESIGN (environmental science), HEALTH PROFESSIONS (medical laboratory technology and nursing), SOCIAL SCIENCE (biblical studies, development economics, economics, history, liberal arts/general studies, ministries, peace studies, philosophy, psychology, religion, social science, social work, sociology, and theological studies). Business, education, and nursing are the largest.

Required: To graduate, students must complete interdisciplinary colloquium courses, courses in Bible/religion, cross-cultural study, writing, speech, and health/wellness, a major (minors are optional), and a variety of electives for a minimum of 128 semester hours. A minimum 2.0 GPA is required while some majors require a higher GPA in the major or overall.

Special: EMU offers study-abroad programs each semester and during the summer at a variety of locations around the world. Students may also choose to study 1 or 2 semesters in Washington, DC. There are internships in a variety of majors, dual majors, student-designed majors, a general studies degree, and a 1-year certificate program. There is 1 national honor society and a freshman honors program.

Faculty/Classroom: 58% of faculty are male; 42%, female. 78% teach undergraduates, 19% do research, and 9% do both. No introductory courses are taught by graduate students. The average class size in an introductory lecture is 40; in a laboratory, 17; and in a regular course, 18.

Admissions: 82% of the 2003-2004 applicants were accepted. The SAT I scores for the 2003-2004 freshman class were: Verbal--32% below 500, 35% between 500 and 599, 28% between 600 and 700, and 5% above 700; Math--42% below 500, 27% between 500 and 599, 19% between 600 and 700, and 12% above 700. The ACT scores were 27% below 21, 24% between 21 and 23, 18% between 24 and 26, 18% between 27 and 28, and 12% above 28. 35% of the current freshmen were in the top fifth of their class; 63% were in the top two fifths. 8 freshmen graduated first in their class.

Requirements: The SAT I or ACT is required, with a minimum composite score of 920 or 20, respectively. Applicants must be graduates of an accredited secondary school or have a GED certificate. The university recommends that students have completed 4 credits of English, 3 each of math, science, and social studies, 2 or more credits of foreign language, and chemistry for nursing majors. A personal reference is required and an interview is recommended. A GPA of 2.2 is required. AP and CLEP credits are accepted. Important factors in the admissions decision are leadership record, recommendations by school officials, and extracurricular activities record.

Procedure: Freshmen are admitted fall and spring. Entrance exams should be taken in the spring of the junior year or the fall of the senior year. There is a deferred admissions plan. There is a rolling admissions plan. Application deadlines are open. The fall 2003 application fee was $25. Applications are accepted on-line through *www.emu.edu.*

Transfer: 78 transfer students enrolled in 2002-2003. Transfer students must have a minimum college 2.0 GPA. 32 of 128 credits required for the bachelor's degree must be completed at EMU.

Visiting: There are regularly scheduled orientations for prospective students, including a financial aid seminar, a review of general education, and attendance at a chapel, the opportunity to sit in on classes, meet with professors and admissions representatives, sleep in residence halls, and eat in the cafeteria, attendance at special campus events, and a meal with the president. There are guides for informal visits and visitors may sit in on classes and stay overnight. To schedule a visit, contact the Admissions Office at *admiss@emu.edu.*

Financial Aid: In 2003-2004, 93% of all full-time freshmen and 95% of continuing full-time students received some form of financial aid. 72% of full-time freshmen and 69% of continuing full-time students received need-based aid. The average freshman award was $13,400. Need-based scholarships or need-based grants averaged $4500; need-based self-help aid (loans and jobs) averaged $2700; and non-need-based awards and non-need-based scholarships averaged $6900. 46% of undergraduates work part time. Average annual earnings from campus work are $1080. The average financial indebtedness of the 2003 graduate was $21,900. The FAFSA and the state aid form are required. The deadline for filing freshman financial aid applications for fall entry is April 15.

International Students: There are 45 international students enrolled. They must score 550 on the written TOEFL or 213 on the electronic version and also take the SAT I, scoring 920, or the ACT.

Computers: The mainframe is an IBM AS/400. There are 25 PCs in the science center, 20 in the business department, 26 in the education lab, with 48 additional PCs in the library and 26 in departments across the campus, all networked for access to the Internet and the Web. Network hookups are available in dorm rooms. All students may access the system day and evening.

Graduates: From July 1, 2002 to June 30, 2003, 269 bachelor's degrees were awarded. The most popular majors were business (28%), nursing (12%), and education (8%). In an average class, 44% graduate in 4 years or less, 59% graduate in 5 years or less, and 61% graduate in 6 years or less. 15 companies recruited on campus in 2002-2003. Of the 2002 graduating class, 11% were enrolled in graduate school within 6 months of graduation and 86% were employed.

Admissions Contact: Admissions Office. A video is available. E-mail: *admiss@emu.edu* Web: *http://www.emu.edu*

EMORY & HENRY COLLEGE B-4
Emory, VA 24327-0947

(276) 944-6133
(800) 848-5493; Fax: (276) 944-6935

Full-time: 414 men, 435 women	**Faculty:** 69; IIB, -$
Part-time: 17 men, 20 women	**Ph.D.s:** 80%
Graduate: 39 women	**Student/Faculty:** 12 to 1
Year: semesters, summer session	**Tuition:** $15,900
Application Deadline: April 15	**Room & Board:** $6050
Freshman Class: 916 applied, 746 accepted, 224 enrolled	
SAT I Verbal/Math: 537/530	**COMPETITIVE**

Emory & Henry College, founded in 1836, is a private liberal arts institution affiliated with the United Methodist Church. In addition to regional accreditation, Emory & Henry College has baccalaureate program accreditation with CAAHEP. The library contains 179,315 volumes, 41,424 microform items, and 4119 audio/video tapes/CDs, and subscribes to 650 periodicals. Computerized library services include the card catalog, interlibrary loans, database searching, and Internet access. Special learning facilities include a learning resource center, art gallery, and radio station. The 331-acre campus is in a rural area in southwest Virginia. Including any residence halls, there are 58 buildings.

Student Life: 66% of undergraduates are from Virginia. Others are from 23 states and 3 foreign countries. 99% are from public schools. 93% are white. 81% are Protestant; 10% claim no religious affiliation; 7% Catholic. The average age of freshmen is 18; all undergraduates, 21. 27% do not continue beyond their first year; 60% remain to graduate.

Housing: 691 students can be accommodated in college housing, which includes single-sex dorms. In addition, there are honors houses and special-interest houses. On-campus housing is guaranteed for all 4 years. 68% of students live on campus; of those, 50% remain on campus on weekends. Alcohol is not permitted. All students may keep cars.

Activities: 7% of men belong to 6 local fraternities; 9% of women belong to 6 local sororities. There are 50 groups on campus, including art, cheerleading, choir, chorus, dance, drama, ethnic, international, literary magazine, newspaper, opera, pep band, photography, political, professional, radio and TV, religious, social, social service, student government, and yearbook. Popular campus events include Parents Day, Air Band, and the Literary Festival.

Sports: There are 7 intercollegiate sports for men and 6 for women, and 10 intramural sports for men and 10 for women. Facilities include a gym, a pool, a racquetball court, outdoor volleyball courts, tennis courts, a weight room, a dance room, a golf course, baseball and football fields, and a horseshoe area.

Disabled Students: 50% of the campus is accessible. Wheelchair ramps, elevators, special parking, specially equipped rest rooms, special class scheduling, lowered drinking fountains, and special housing are available.

Services: Counseling and information services are available, as is tutoring in most subjects. There is a reader service for the blind and remedial writing.

Campus Safety and Security: Measures include 24-hour foot and vehicle patrol, self-defense education, security escort services, and informal discussions. There are pamphlets/posters/films and lighted pathways/sidewalks.

Programs of Study: Emory & Henry College confers B.A. and B.S. degrees. Master's degrees are also awarded. Bachelor's degrees are awarded in BIOLOGICAL SCIENCE (biology/biological science), BUSINESS (business administration and management), COMMUNICATIONS AND THE ARTS (art, communications, creative writing, dramatic arts, English literature, journalism, literature, modern language, music performance, and music theory and composition), COMPUTER AND PHYSICAL SCIENCE (chemistry, computer management, computer science, mathematics, and physics), EDUCATION (English, mathematics, and physical), ENGINEERING AND ENVIRONMENTAL DESIGN (environmental science), SOCIAL SCIENCE (community services, East Asian studies, eco-

nomics, European studies, geography, history, interdisciplinary studies, international studies, Middle Eastern studies, philosophy, political science/government, psychology, public affairs, religion, and sociology). Economics and business, interdisciplinary English, and mass communications are the largest.

Required: All students must complete a general studies curriculum covering Western traditions, great books, religion, values inquiry, and global studies and must demonstrate proficiency in oral skills. Specific courses include a first-year writing course, 1 each from 3 disciplines, including social sciences, humanities and arts, and natural sciences, and according to major, either a foreign language or quantitative methods. A total of 116 semester hours for a B.A. or 124 for a B.S., with a GPA of 2.0, is required for graduation. The total number of hours in the major varies.

Special: A cooperative program in medical technology and 2-2, 4-1, and 3-2 engineering degrees are available. Dual and student-designed majors, an interdisciplinary English major, combined B.A.-B.S. degrees, internships, work-study, nondegree study, and pass/fail options are also available. There are 10 national honor societies and 8 departmental honors programs.

Faculty/Classroom: 68% of faculty are male; 32%, female. All teach undergraduates. No introductory courses are taught by graduate students. The average class size in an introductory lecture is 25; in a laboratory, 13; and in a regular course, 22.

Admissions: 81% of the 2003-2004 applicants were accepted. The SAT I scores for the 2003-2004 freshman class were: Verbal--35% below 500, 36% between 500 and 599, 27% between 600 and 700, and 2% above 700; Math--36% below 500, 43% between 500 and 599, 18% between 600 and 700, and 3% above 700. 88% of the current freshmen were in the top two fifths of their class. 4 freshmen graduated first in their class.

Requirements: The SAT I or ACT is required. In addition, applicants should be high school graduates. High school courses required include 4 years of English, 3 or more units of math including algebra I, algebra II, and geometry, 2 or more units of lab science, 2 units of a single foreign language, and 2 or more units of social studies and history. 1 additional unit in fine arts is strongly recommended. A personal essay is required. Emory & Henry College requires applicants to be in the upper 50% of their class. A GPA of 2.75 is required. AP credits are accepted. Important factors in the admissions decision are advanced placement or honor courses, recommendations by school officials, and evidence of special talent.

Procedure: Freshmen are admitted fall, spring, and summer. Entrance exams should be taken in November of the senior year. There are early decision, early admissions, and deferred admissions plans. Early decision applications should be filed by November 1; regular applications, by April 15 for fall entry. The fall 2003 application fee was $30. Notification is sent on a rolling basis. 43 early decision candidates were accepted for the 2003-2004 class. Applications are accepted on-line.

Transfer: 55 transfer students enrolled in 2002-2003. Transfers must have at least a 2.5 GPA in previous college work. Those with at least 24 credits may be admitted without high school data; those with fewer than 24 credits must meet freshman admission standards. A minimum of 33 of 116 credits required for the B.A. (124 for the B.S.) must be completed at Emory & Henry College.

Visiting: There are regularly scheduled orientations for prospective students, including a program for students to meet faculty and staff and to attend education sessions on college life. There are guides for informal visits and visitors may sit in on classes and stay overnight. To schedule a visit, contact the Admissions Office.

Financial Aid: In 2003-2004, 99% of all full-time freshmen received some form of financial aid. 73% of full-time freshmen received need-based aid. The average freshman award was $13,231. Need-based scholarships or need-based grants averaged $11,400; and need-based self-help aid (loans and jobs) averaged $2275. 13% of undergraduates work part time. Average annual earnings from campus work are $1200. The average financial indebtedness of the 2003 graduate was $14,466. The FAFSA, the state aid form, and the college's own financial statement are required. The priority date for freshman financial aid applications for fall entry is April 1. The deadline for filing freshman financial aid applications for fall entry is August 1.

International Students: There are 2 international students enrolled. The school actively recruits these students. They must score 550 on the written TOEFL.

Computers: The mainframe is a DEC Alpha 2100 server. There are 128 terminals available for student use in the library, the computer lab, and the writing center. All students may access the system. There are no time limits and no fees.

Graduates: From July 1, 2002 to June 30, 2003, 182 bachelor's degrees were awarded. The most popular majors were business management (19%), interdisciplinary English (12%), and biology (7%). In an average class, 45% graduate in 4 years or less, 57% graduate in 5 years or less, and 59% graduate in 6 years or less.

Admissions Contact: Liz Daniels, Director of Admissions and Financial Aid. A video is available. E-mail: *ehadmiss@ehc.edu* Web: *www.ehc.edu*

FERRUM COLLEGE
Ferrum, VA 24088

C-3

(540) 365-4290
(800) 868-9797; Fax: (540) 365-4266

Full-time: 533 men, 386 women	**Faculty:** 63
Part-time: 12 men, 23 women	**Ph.Ds:** 76%
Graduate: none	**Student/Faculty:** 14 to 1
Year: semesters, summer session	**Tuition:** $15,640
Application Deadline: open	**Room & Board:** $5600
Freshman Class: 1126 applied, 829 accepted, 325 enrolled	
SAT I Verbal/Math: 440/450	**ACT:** 17 **LESS COMPETITIVE**

Ferrum College, founded in 1913, is a private liberal arts institution affiliated with the United Methodist Church. In addition to regional accreditation, Ferrum has baccalaureate program accreditation with CSWE and NRPA. The library contains 115,068 volumes, 8656 microform items, and 1925 audio/video tapes/CDs, and subscribes to 280 periodicals. Computerized library services include the card catalog, interlibrary loans, database searching, and Internet access. Special learning facilities include a learning resource center, art gallery, radio station, a folklife museum, and a living history museum. The 720-acre campus is in a rural area 35 miles south of Roanoke. Including any residence halls, there are 53 buildings.

Student Life: 84% of undergraduates are from Virginia. Students are from 20 states and 5 foreign countries. 84% are from public schools. 70% are white; 18% African American. 47% are Protestant; 32% claim no religious affiliation; 7% Catholic. The average age of freshmen is 18; all undergraduates, 21. 46% do not continue beyond their first year; 38% remain to graduate.

Housing: 955 students can be accommodated in college housing, which includes single-sex and coed dorms, on-campus apartments, off-campus apartments, married-student housing, and theme housing by floors in dorms. On-campus housing is guaranteed for all 4 years. 75% of students live on campus; of those, 50% remain on campus on weekends. All students may keep cars.

Activities: There are no fraternities or sororities. There are 50 groups on campus, including art, cheerleading, choir, chorale, chorus, computers, dance, drama, ethnic, film, gay, honors, international, jazz band, literary magazine, musical theater, newspaper, photography, political, professional, radio and TV, religious, social, social service, and student government. Popular campus events include Spring Fling, Blue Ridge Folklife Festival, and Snow Ball.

Sports: There are 7 intercollegiate sports for men and 7 for women, and 13 intramural sports for men and 13 for women. Facilities include a gym, a field house, tennis courts, a weight room, an indoor pool, an outdoor volleyball court, a football stadium, a soccer field, a baseball field, a women's softball field, a recreation center with indoor basketball courts, racquetball courts, and universal weights, and fitness trails.

Disabled Students: 75% of the campus is accessible. Wheelchair ramps, elevators, special parking, specially equipped rest rooms, special class scheduling, and lowered drinking fountains are available.

Services: Counseling and information services are available, as is tutoring in most subjects. There is remedial math, reading, and writing. College skills classes, individual assistance for study strategies and subject-specific tutoring by professors and students are available.

Campus Safety and Security: Measures include 24-hour foot and vehicle patrol, self-defense education, security escort services, and informal discussions. There are pamphlets/posters/films, emergency telephones, and lighted pathways/sidewalks.

Programs of Study: Ferrum confers B.A., B.S., B.F.A., and B.S.W. degrees. Bachelor's degrees are awarded in AGRICULTURE (agriculture and horticulture), BIOLOGICAL SCIENCE (biology/biological science), BUSINESS (accounting, business administration and management, recreation and leisure services, and sports management), COMMUNICATIONS AND THE ARTS (art, dramatic arts, English, performing arts, Russian, and Spanish), COMPUTER AND PHYSICAL SCIENCE (chemistry, computer science, information sciences and systems, mathematics, and science), EDUCATION (physical), ENGINEERING AND ENVIRONMENTAL DESIGN (environmental science), HEALTH PROFESSIONS (medical laboratory technology), SOCIAL SCIENCE (criminal justice, history, international studies, liberal arts/general studies, philosophy, political science/government, psychology, religion, social studies, and social work). Chemistry, biology, and enviromental science are the strongest academically. Business administration, criminal justice, and liberal arts are the largest.

Required: To graduate, students must complete at least 127 semester hours with a minimum GPA of 2.0. There are 55 hours of distribution requirements, including 12 in social sciences, 8 in natural sciences, 6 each in English, religion and philosophy, math, literature or foreign language, and degree cognates, 3 in fine arts, and 2 in phys ed. A major may require up to 57 semester hours, and 30 hours of the total must be in upper-level courses.

Special: The college encourages internships, and some majors require internships. Study abroad, work-study programs, dual majors, an accelerated degree program in social work, and B.A.-B.S. degrees are offered.

A liberal studies degree and nondegree study are available. There are 6 national honor societies, a freshman honors program, and 33 departmental honors programs.

Faculty/Classroom: 60% of faculty are male; 40%, female. All both teach and do research. The average class size in an introductory lecture is 21; in a laboratory, 20; and in a regular course, 11.

Admissions: 74% of the 2003-2004 applicants were accepted. The SAT I scores for the 2003-2004 freshman class were: Verbal--74% below 500, 21% between 500 and 599, and 5% between 600 and 700; Math--75% below 500, 21% between 500 and 599, and 5% between 600 and 700. The ACT scores were 83% below 21, 14% between 21 and 23, and 3% between 24 and 26. 11% of the current freshmen were in the top fifth of their class; 33% were in the top two fifths. 1 freshman graduated first in the class.

Requirements: The SAT I or ACT is required. In addition, applicants must be graduates of an accredited secondary school or receive a GED certificate. Applicants should complete 18 high school academic credits. The Admissions Committee considers courses taken, grades, extracurricular activities, SAT I or ACT scores, and recommendations. Personal interviews may be required for students lacking appropriate GPA or standardized test scores. AP and CLEP credits are accepted. Important factors in the admissions decision are advanced placement or honor courses, leadership record, and evidence of special talent.

Procedure: Freshmen are admitted to all sessions. There is a rolling admissions plan and a deferred admissions plan. Application deadlines are open. Application fee is $25. Applications are accepted on computer disk and on-line.

Transfer: 93 transfer students enrolled in 2002-2003. Applicants for transfer must be in good academic standing at their current schools. 32 of 127 credits required for the bachelor's degree must be completed at Ferrum.

Visiting: There are regularly scheduled orientations for prospective students, including faculty information sessions, parent-to-parent and student-to-student sessions, and tours of the campus and residence halls. There are guides for informal visits and visitors may sit in on classes and stay overnight. To schedule a visit, contact the Director of Admissions at *admissions@ferrum.edu*.

Financial Aid: In 2003-2004, 97% of all full-time freshmen and 95% of continuing full-time students received some form of financial aid. 82% of full-time freshmen and 76% of continuing full-time students received need-based aid. The average freshman award was $8831. 41% of undergraduates work part time. Average annual earnings from campus work are $1400. The average financial indebtedness of the 2003 graduate was $15,900. Ferrum is a member of CSS. The FAFSA and the state aid form are required. The deadline for filing freshman financial aid applications for fall entry is April 1.

International Students: There are 8 international students enrolled. The school actively recruits these students. They must score 550 on the written TOEFL and also take the SAT I or the ACT.

Computers: The mainframe is an IBM AS/400. All residence hall rooms are equipped with fully networked PCs provided by the college. In addition, 158 networked PCs are available in various labs on campus. All students may access the system at all times. There are no time limits and no fees.

Graduates: From July 1, 2002 to June 30, 2003, 149 bachelor's degrees were awarded. The most popular majors were business administration (11%), criminal justice (10%), and information systems (5%). In an average class, 21% graduate in 4 years or less, 38% graduate in 5 years or less, and 40% graduate in 6 years or less. 92 companies recruited on campus in 2002-2003. Of the 2002 graduating class, 12% were enrolled in graduate school within 6 months of graduation and 91% were employed.

Admissions Contact: Gilda Woods, Director of Admissions.
E-mail: *admissions@ferrum.edu* Web: *www.ferrum.edu*

GEORGE MASON UNIVERSITY
Fairfax, VA 22030-4444

E-2

(703) 993-2400; Fax: (703) 993-2392

Full-time: 5694 men, 7102 women	**Faculty:** 962; I, av$
Part-time: 1991 men, 2351 women	**Ph.Ds:** 82%
Graduate: 4721 men, 6423 women	**Student/Faculty:** 13 to 1
Year: semesters, summer session	**Tuition:** $5112 ($14,952)
Application Deadline: February 1	**Room & Board:** $4620
Freshman Class: 9748 applied, 6461 accepted, 2251 enrolled	
SAT I Verbal/Math: 550/560	**VERY COMPETITIVE**

George Mason University, founded in 1972, offers undergraduate and graduate degrees in arts and sciences, business, information technology and engineering, fine arts, computational sciences and informatics, conflict analysis, nursing and health science, and education. A second campus in Arlington houses a professional school, the School of Law, and the International Institute. There are 6 undergraduate and 9 graduate schools. In addition to regional accreditation, GMU has baccalaureate program accreditation with AACSB, ABET, CSAB, CSWE, NASM, NCATE, and NLN. The 4 libraries contain 1,464,602 volumes,

2,723,864 microform items, and 29,701 audio/video tapes/CDs, and subscribe to 11,207 periodicals. Computerized library services include the card catalog, interlibrary loans, and database searching. Special learning facilities include a learning resource center, art gallery, radio station, and TV station. The 806-acre campus is in a suburban area 18 miles southwest of Washington, D.C., in the Greater Washington Metropolitan area. Including any residence halls, there are 119 buildings.

Student Life: 89% of undergraduates are from Virginia. Students are from 46 states, 135 foreign countries, and Canada. 95% are from public schools. 66% are white; 13% Asian American. The average age of freshmen is 19; all undergraduates, 22. 21% do not continue beyond their first year.

Housing: 3500 students can be accommodated in college housing, which includes single-sex and coed dorms, on-campus apartments, and off-campus apartments. In addition, there are honors houses. On-campus housing is guaranteed for all 4 years. 91% of students commute. Alcohol is not permitted. All students may keep cars.

Activities: 5% of men belong to 18 national fraternities; 5% of women belong to 10 national sororities. There are 255 groups on campus, including band, cheerleading, chess, choir, chorale, chorus, computers, dance, drama, ethnic, film, forensics, gay, honors, international, jazz band, literary magazine, musical theater, newspaper, opera, orchestra, outing, pep band, photography, political, professional, radio and TV, religious, social, social service, student government, symphony, and yearbook. Popular campus events include Mason Day, Patriot Day, and International Week.

Sports: There are 11 intercollegiate sports for men and 11 for women, and 11 intramural sports for men and 10 for women. Facilities include a 10,000-seat arena for basketball, indoor soccer, and concerts; a sports and recreation complex, which includes a 200-meter track, basketball, handball/racquetball, tennis, and volleyball courts, baseball and softball diamonds, batting cages, a weight room, saunas, and a golf and archery net; a 400-meter outdoor track; and playing fields.

Disabled Students: 99% of the campus is accessible. Wheelchair ramps, elevators, special parking, specially equipped rest rooms, special class scheduling, lowered drinking fountains, lowered telephones, and special housing are available. Special arrangements can be made for testing, readers, note takers, and interpreters.

Services: Counseling and information services are available, as is tutoring in most subjects. There is a reader service for the blind. A fee may apply.

Campus Safety and Security: Measures include 24-hour foot and vehicle patrol, self-defense education, security escort services, and shuttle buses. There are informal discussions, pamphlets/posters/films, emergency telephones, lighted pathways/sidewalks, and 33 security call boxes located throughout the campus.

Programs of Study: GMU confers B.A., B.S., B.A.I.N., B.A.I.S., B.F.A., B.I.S., B.M., B.S.E., B.S.E.D., and B.S.N. degrees. Master's and doctoral degrees are also awarded. Bachelor's degrees are awarded in BIOLOGICAL SCIENCE (biology/biological science), BUSINESS (accounting, banking and finance, business administration and management, management information systems, marketing/retailing/merchandising, and sports management), COMMUNICATIONS AND THE ARTS (art history and appreciation, communications, dance, dramatic arts, English, French, music, Spanish, and studio art), COMPUTER AND PHYSICAL SCIENCE (astronomy, chemistry, computer science, earth science, geology, information sciences and systems, mathematics, and physics), EDUCATION (athletic training, foreign languages, and physical), ENGINEERING AND ENVIRONMENTAL DESIGN (civil engineering, computer engineering, electrical/electronics engineering, and systems engineering), HEALTH PROFESSIONS (exercise science, health science, medical technology, and nursing), SOCIAL SCIENCE (anthropology, criminal justice, economics, geography, history, interdisciplinary studies, philosophy, political science/government, psychology, public administration, religion, Russian and Slavic studies, social work, and sociology). Psychology, communication, and government and international politics are the strongest academically.

Required: To graduate, all students must complete a core of study that includes 6 semester hours each of English composition, humanities, math/science, and social sciences, courses in communication, analytical reasoning, social science, natural science, and non-Western culture, and at least 45 hours of upper-division work. Hours in the major vary. A minimum 2.0 GPA is required and a total of 120 to 133 credit hours must be completed.

Special: GMU offers co-op programs in all majors with Shenandoah University, Virginia Polytechnic Institute and State University, Old Dominion University, and the University of Virginia, cross-registration with the Washington Consortium of Universities, internships through academic departments, study abroad in 10 countries, and on-campus work-study programs. Also available are dual and student-designed majors, nondegree study, and pass/fail options. The Program for Alternative General Education (PAGE) offers interdisciplinary studies for freshmen and sophomores. New Century College is an integrated program of study that emphasizes collaboration, experimental learning, and self-

reflection. There are 3 national honor societies, a freshman honors program, and 8 departmental honors programs.

Faculty/Classroom: 45% of faculty are male; 55%, female. The average class size in an introductory lecture is 32; in a laboratory, 21; and in a regular course, 28.

Admissions: 66% of the 2003-2004 applicants were accepted. The SAT I scores for the 2003-2004 freshman class were: Verbal--25% below 500, 47% between 500 and 599, 24% between 600 and 700, and 3% above 700; Math--21% below 500, 49% between 500 and 599, 26% between 600 and 700, and 4% above 700. The ACT scores were 9% between 12 and 17, 56% between 18 and 23, 30% between 24 and 29, and 4% above 29.

Requirements: The SAT I or ACT is required. In addition, applicants must be graduates of an accredited secondary school or have a GED certificate. A minimum of 18 credits is required, including 4 years of English, 3 each of math, science, social studies, and electives, and 2 of foreign language. An essay is recommended. A GPA of 2.0 is required. AP and CLEP credits are accepted. Important factors in the admissions decision are advanced placement or honor courses, evidence of special talent, and recommendations by school officials.

Procedure: Freshmen are admitted fall, spring, and summer. Entrance exams should be taken during the spring of the junior year. There is a deferred admissions plan. Applications should be filed by February 1 for fall entry and November 1 for spring entry, along with a $40 fee. Notification is sent April 1. A waiting list is an active part of the admissions procedure. Applications are accepted on computer disk and on-line through the school's web site.

Transfer: 2100 transfer students enrolled in 2002-2003. Applicants must have a minimum 2.0 GPA and at least 9 semester hours earned. College transcripts and an essay or personal statement are required. 30 of 120 credits required for the bachelor's degree must be completed at GMU.

Visiting: There are regularly scheduled orientations for prospective students. There are guides for informal visits and visitors may sit in on classes and stay overnight. To schedule a visit, contact the Admissions Office.

Financial Aid: In 2003-2004, 51% of all full-time freshmen and 46% of continuing full-time students received some form of financial aid. 36% of full-time freshmen and 30% of continuing full-time students received need-based aid. The average freshman award was $7707. Need-based scholarships or need-based grants averaged $4929 ($21,590 maximum); need-based self-help aid (loans and jobs) averaged $2674 ($7423 maximum); non-need-based athletic scholarships averaged $10,458 ($23,818 maximum); and other non-need-based awards and non-need-based scholarships averaged $6231 ($25,403 maximum). Average annual earnings from campus work are $2291. The average financial indebtedness of the 2003 graduate was $14,215. The FAFSA is required. The priority date for freshman financial aid applications for fall entry is March 1.

International Students: There are 587 international students enrolled. The school actively recruits these students. They must score 570 on the written TOEFL or 230 on the electronic version and also take the SAT I or the ACT.

Computers: The mainframes are a DEC Alpha 2100 and an IBM ES 9121/300. 1500 terminals are located in public student labs, the libraries, dorms, and academic departments. All students may access the system 24 hours per day. There are no time limits and no fees.

Graduates: From July 1, 2002 to June 30, 2003, 3222 bachelor's degrees were awarded. The most popular majors were decision science (12%), communication (8%), and psychology (8%). In an average class, 23% graduate in 4 years or less, 41% graduate in 5 years or less, and 46% graduate in 6 years or less. 200 companies recruited on campus in 2002-2003.

Admissions Contact: Andrew Flagel, Dean of Undergraduate Admissions. E-mail: *admissions@gmu.edu* Web: *www.gmu.edu*

HAMPDEN-SYDNEY COLLEGE D-3
Hampden-Sydney, VA 23943 (434) 223-6120
(800) 755-0733; Fax: (434) 223-6346

Full-time: 1039 men	Faculty: 87; IIB, +$
Part-time: none	Ph.D.s: 81%
Graduate: none	Student/Faculty: 12 to 1
Year: semesters, summer session	Tuition: $21,387
Application Deadline: March 1	Room & Board: $7020
Freshman Class: 1156 applied, 825 accepted, 306 enrolled	
SAT I Verbal/Math: 570/570	ACT: 23 **VERY COMPETITIVE**

Hampden-Sydney College, founded in 1775, is a private men's liberal arts institution affiliated with the Presbyterian Church (U.S.A.). The library contains 224,172 volumes, 45,312 microform items, and 4312 audio/video tapes/CDs, and subscribes to 823 periodicals. Computerized library services include the card catalog, interlibrary loans, database searching, and Internet access. Special learning facilities include an art gallery, planetarium, radio station, international communications center, college history museum, and observatory. The 660-acre campus is in a rural area 60 miles southwest of Richmond. Including any residence halls, there are 76 buildings.

Student Life: 64% of undergraduates are from Virginia. Students are from 36 states, 9 foreign countries, and Canada. 65% are from public schools. 93% are white. 59% are Protestant; 25% claim no religious affiliation; 14% Catholic. The average age of freshmen is 19; all undergraduates, 20. 26% do not continue beyond their first year; 61% remain to graduate.

Housing: 1050 students can be accommodated in college housing, which includes single-sex dorms, on-campus apartments, married-student housing, a minority student house, and fraternity houses. On-campus housing is guaranteed for all 4 years. 97% of students live on campus; of those, 60% remain on campus on weekends. All students may keep cars.

Activities: 37% of men belong to 11 national fraternities. There are 36 groups on campus, including chorale, chorus, computers, debate, drama, ethnic, honors, international, literary magazine, newspaper, pep band, photography, political, professional, radio and TV, religious, social, social service, student government, and yearbook. Popular campus events include Greek Week, Macon Week, and Midwinters CAC events.

Sports: Facilities include a field house with 3 basketball courts, 5 racquetball/handball courts, an outdoor track, a pool, squash courts, a weight room, a gym, tennis courts, and many playing fields.

Disabled Students: 80% of the campus is accessible. Wheelchair ramps, elevators, special parking, specially equipped rest rooms, special class scheduling, and lowered telephones are available.

Services: Counseling and information services are available, as is tutoring in every subject.

Campus Safety and Security: Measures include 24-hour foot and vehicle patrol, informal discussions, pamphlets/posters/films, and emergency telephones. There are lighted pathways/sidewalks. There also is a fire department on campus and a first responder unit for emergency medical assistance. The dorm phone lines are hooked into 911.

Programs of Study: Hampden-Sydney confers B.A. and B.S. degrees. Bachelor's degrees are awarded in BIOLOGICAL SCIENCE (biology/biological science), BUSINESS (business economics), COMMUNICATIONS AND THE ARTS (classics, English, fine arts, French, German, Greek, Latin, and Spanish), COMPUTER AND PHYSICAL SCIENCE (applied mathematics, chemistry, computer science, mathematics, and physics), SOCIAL SCIENCE (economics, history, humanities, philosophy, political science/government, psychology, and religion). Science is the strongest academically. Economics, history, and political science are the largest.

Required: To graduate, students must complete 120 credit hours with a minimum GPA of 2.0. Distribution requirements include 7 courses in humanities, 4 in math and natural sciences, and 3 in social sciences. All students must also take rhetoric and foreign language and pass a rhetoric exam.

Special: The college offers co-op programs with Longwood, Randolph-Macon, Randolph-Macon Woman's, Sweet Briar, Hollins, and Mary Baldwin Colleges and Washington and Lee University. Cross-registration with Longwood College, internships, study abroad, a 3-2 engineering program with the University of Virginia, a Washington semester, work-study programs, B.A.-B.S. degrees, and dual majors are available. There is a public service concentration in all majors. There are 15 national honor societies, including Phi Beta Kappa, a freshman honors program, and 10 departmental honors programs.

Faculty/Classroom: 75% of faculty are male; 25%, female. All both teach and do research. The average class size in an introductory lecture is 18; in a laboratory, 15; and in a regular course, 15.

Admissions: 71% of the 2003-2004 applicants were accepted. The SAT I scores for the 2003-2004 freshman class were: Verbal--21% below 500, 46% between 500 and 599, 27% between 600 and 700, and 7% above 700; Math--14% below 500, 50% between 500 and 599, 32% between 600 and 700, and 3% above 700. The ACT scores were 31% below 21, 28% between 21 and 23, 25% between 24 and 26, 7% between 27 and 28, and 10% above 28. 29% of the current freshmen were in the top fifth of their class; 61% were in the top two fifths. There was 1 National Merit semifinalist. 2 freshmen graduated first in their class.

Requirements: The SAT I or ACT is required. In addition, the school recommends SAT II: Subject tests in writing, math, and another subject of the student's choice. Applicants must be graduates of an accredited secondary school and have completed 16 high school academic credits, including 4 of English, 3 of math, 2 each of foreign language and science, and 1 of social studies. An essay is required and an interview is recommended. The GED is accepted. A GPA of 2.5 is required. AP credits are accepted. Important factors in the admissions decision are advanced placement or honor courses, recommendations by school officials, and leadership record.

Procedure: Freshmen are admitted fall and spring. Entrance exams should be taken during the junior or senior year of high school. There is an early decision plan. Early decision applications should be filed by November 15; regular applications, by March 1 for fall entry and December 1 for spring entry. The fall 2003 application fee was $30. Notification of early decision is sent December 15; regular decision, by April 15. 78 early decision candidates were accepted for the 2003-2004 class. 38 applicants were on the 2003 waiting list; 25 were admitted. Applications are accepted on-line through the school's web site, Common App, CollegeLink, and Apply.

Transfer: 17 transfer students enrolled in 2003-2004. Applicants must have a minimum GPA of 2.5 and must take either the SAT I or the ACT. An interview is recommended. 60 of 120 credits required for the bachelor's degree must be completed at Hampden-Sydney.

Visiting: There are regularly scheduled orientations for prospective students, consisting of lectures, information sessions, tours, lunch, and an athletic event. There are guides for informal visits and visitors may sit in on classes and stay overnight. To schedule a visit, contact the Admissions Office at hsapp@hsc.edu.

Financial Aid: In 2003-2004, 92% of all full-time students received some form of financial aid. 54% of full-time freshmen and 51% of continuing full-time students received need-based aid. The average freshman award was $16,791. 25% of undergraduates work part time. Average annual earnings from campus work are $900. The average financial indebtedness of the 2003 graduate was $7071. The CSS/Profile or FAFSA is required. The deadline for filing freshman financial aid applications for fall entry is March 1.

International Students: There are 16 international students enrolled. They must score 570 on the written TOEFL and also take the SAT I or the ACT.

Computers: All students can access the Internet in their rooms, the library, and in the computer labs on campus. PCs are available for student use in the library and computer labs. All students may access the system. There are no time limits and no fees. It is strongly recommended that all students have a personal computer. Dell is recommended.

Graduates: From July 1, 2002 to June 30, 2003, 206 bachelor's degrees were awarded. The most popular majors were economics (49%), history (17%), and political science (15%). In an average class, 61% graduate in 4 years or less, 63% graduate in 5 years or less, and 64% graduate in 6 years or less. 30 companies recruited on campus in 2002-2003.

Admissions Contact: Anita H. Garland, Dean of Admissions. E-mail: hsapp@hsc.edu Web: www.hsc.edu

HAMPTON UNIVERSITY
Hampton, VA 23668

F-3
(757) 727-5328
(800) 624-3328; Fax: (757) 727-5095

Full-time: 1685 men, 2905 women	**Faculty:** 295
Part-time: 225 men, 150 women	**Ph.D.s:** 76%
Graduate: 293 men, 550 women	**Student/Faculty:** 16 to 1
Year: semesters, summer session	**Tuition:** $11,670
Application Deadline: see profile	**Room & Board:** $5450
Freshman Class: n/av	
SAT I or ACT: required	**COMPETITIVE+**

Hampton University, founded in 1868, is a comprehensive institution of higher education. Its curriculum emphasis is scientific and professional, with a strong liberal arts undergirding. There are 8 undergraduate schools and 1 graduate school. Figures in the above capsule and in this profile are approximate. In addition to regional accreditation, HU has baccalaureate program accreditation with ABET, ACEJMC, ACS, ASLA, CSAB, NAAB, NASM, NCATE, and NLN. The library contains 273,854 volumes, 711,759 microform items, and 1649 audio/video tapes/CDs, and subscribes to 992 periodicals. Computerized library services include the card catalog, interlibrary loans, and database searching. Special learning facilities include a learning resource center, art gallery, natural history museum, radio station, TV station, and academic technology mall. The 204-acre campus is in an urban area 15 miles west of Norfolk. Including any residence halls, there are 125 buildings.

Student Life: 70% of undergraduates are from out of state, mostly the Middle Atlantic. Students are from 43 states, 33 foreign countries, and Canada. 90% are from public schools. 96% are African American. The average age of freshmen is 18; all undergraduates, 20. 15% do not continue beyond their first year; 75% remain to graduate.

Housing: 3000 students can be accommodated in college housing, which includes single-sex dorms. In addition, there are honors houses and student cottages. On-campus housing is available on a first-come, first-served basis and is available on a lottery system for upperclassmen. 59% of students live on campus; of those, 70% remain on campus on weekends. Alcohol is not permitted. Upperclassmen may keep cars.

Activities: 5% of men belong to 5 national fraternities; 4% of women belong to 4 national sororities. There are 80 groups on campus, including art, band, cheerleading, choir, chorale, chorus, dance, drama, drill team, ethnic, honors, international, jazz band, marching band, newspaper, orchestra, pep band, photography, political, radio and TV, religious, social service, student government, symphony, and yearbook. Popular campus events include Career Day, High School Day, and Black Family/Parents Weekend.

Sports: There are 5 intercollegiate sports for men and 4 for women, and 2 intramural sports for men and 1 for women. Facilities include a football stadium, a convocation center, 12 outdoor tennis courts, open fields for intramural sports, 2 basketball courts, 2 swimming pools, a volleyball court, an exercise and training room, a new student center with a health center, bowling alley, movie theater, indoor track, and restaurants.

Disabled Students: 90% of the campus is accessible. Wheelchair ramps, elevators, special parking, specially equipped rest rooms, lowered drinking fountains, and lowered telephones are available.

Services: Counseling and information services are available, as is tutoring in most subjects. There is remedial math, reading, and writing.

Campus Safety and Security: Measures include 24-hour foot and vehicle patrol, self-defense education, informal discussions, and pamphlets/posters/films. There are emergency telephones, lighted pathways/sidewalks, bike patrols, on-campus police officers, video cameras, gated campus, identification of valuables, limited access to campus, smoke detectors in residence halls, motorist assistance, and civilian support team.

Programs of Study: HU confers B.A., B.S., B.Arch., and B.S.Nurs. degrees. Associate and master's degrees are also awarded. Bachelor's degrees are awarded in BIOLOGICAL SCIENCE (biology/biological science), BUSINESS (accounting, banking and finance, business administration and management, marketing/retailing/merchandising, and sports management), COMMUNICATIONS AND THE ARTS (art, communications, dramatic arts, English, and music), COMPUTER AND PHYSICAL SCIENCE (chemistry, computer science, information sciences and systems, mathematics, and physics), EDUCATION (physical), ENGINEERING AND ENVIRONMENTAL DESIGN (architecture, chemical engineering, and electrical/electronics engineering), HEALTH PROFESSIONS (nursing, recreation therapy, and speech pathology/audiology), SOCIAL SCIENCE (economics, history, political science/government, psychology, and sociology). Architecture, biology, and physics are the strongest academically. Biology, psychology, and business management are the largest.

Required: To graduate, students must complete 120 credit hours, with 74 hours in the major, related subjects, and free electives, and a GPA of 2.0. There is a 44 to 48 hour distribution requirement in freshman studies, history, language, arts and humanities, English, social sciences, math, pure and applied sciences, speech, and health and phys ed.

Special: The college offers co-op programs in most majors, cross-registration with 6 schools, internships, and student-designed majors. Work study, study abroad, and dual majors are also possible. Students may receive credit for life, military, and work experience. There are pass/fail options. There are 15 national honor societies and a freshman honors program.

Faculty/Classroom: 48% of faculty are male; 52%, female. 90% teach undergraduates and 10% do research. No introductory courses are taught by graduate students. The average class size in an introductory lecture is 50; in a laboratory, 20; and in a regular course, 25.

Requirements: The SAT I or ACT is required. A composite score of 920 is required on the SAT I. Applicants must be graduates of an accredited secondary school, or the GED is accepted. Students should complete 17 Carnegie units, including 4 units of English, 3 units of math, (algebra I and II and geometry), 2 years of science (chemistry and biology), 2 years of social studies, and 6 academic electives. An interview is recommended. HU requires applicants to be in the upper 50% of their class. A GPA of 2.0 is required. AP and CLEP credits are accepted. Important factors in the admissions decision are advanced placement or honor courses, recommendations by school officials, and recommendations by alumni.

Procedure: Freshmen are admitted fall and spring. Entrance exams should be taken during the junior year or fall of the senior year. There are early admissions, deferred admissions, and rolling admissions plans. Check with the school for current deadlines. The fall 2003 application fee was $25. Notification is sent on a rolling basis. A waiting list is an active part of the admissions procedure.

Transfer: 124 transfer students enrolled in a recent year. Applicants for transfer must have a minimum GPA of 2.3 and 15 transferable hours. Students must have at least 60 semester or 90 quarter hours in order to be exempt from submitting their high school record and SAT I or ACT scores. 30 of 120 credits required for the bachelor's degree must be completed at HU.

Visiting: There are regularly scheduled orientations for prospective students. There are guides for informal visits and visitors may sit in on classes. To schedule a visit, contact Office of Admissions at (757) 727-2051 or *admissions@hamptonu.edu.*

Financial Aid: In a recent year, 56% of all full-time freshmen and 58% of continuing full-time students received some form of financial aid. 41% of full-time freshmen and 46% of continuing full-time students received need-based aid. The average freshman award was $3488. Average annual earnings from campus work are $1400. The average financial indebtedness of a recent graduate was $23,000. The FAFSA is required. Check with the school for current deadlines.

International Students: In a recent year, there were 102 international students enrolled. They must score 550 on the written TOEFL and also take the SAT I (scoring 920) or the ACT.

Computers: The mainframe is a Sun Enterprise 5500. A campus-wide network exists with password protected accessibility provided to all students, faculty, staff, and administrators. All students are assigned e-mail account numbers at no charge. There are at least 90 computer labs/classrooms and at least 1500 institution-owned computers. All students may access the system 24 hours per day. There are no time limits and no fees. It is strongly recommended that all students have a personal computer. It is required that students in pharmacy have personal computers.

Graduates: In a recent year, 799 bachelor's degrees were awarded. The most popular majors were biology (12%), psychology (11%), and management (10%). In an average class, 33% graduate in 4 years or less, 50% graduate in 5 years or less, and 54% graduate in 6 years or less. 225 companies recruited on campus in a recent year. Of a recent graduating class, 40% were enrolled in graduate school within 6 months of graduation and 70% were employed.

Admissions Contact: Leonard M. Jones Jr., Director of Admissions. E-mail: *leonard.jones@hamptonu.edu*

HOLLINS UNIVERSITY
Roanoke, VA 24020-1707

C-3

(540) 362-6214
(800) 456-9595; Fax: (540) 362-6218

Full-time: 777 women	**Faculty:** 75; IIB, av$
Part-time: 35 women	**Ph.Ds:** 96%
Graduate: 70 men, 208 women	**Student/Faculty:** 10 to 1
Year: 4-1-4	**Tuition:** $20,675
Application Deadline: February 15	**Room & Board:** $7290
Freshman Class: 997 applied, 783 accepted, 247 enrolled	
SAT I Verbal/Math: 591/546	**ACT:** 24 **VERY COMPETITIVE**

Founded in 1842 and Virginia's first chartered women's college, Hollins offers a broad liberal arts curriculum. In addition to regional accreditation, Hollins has baccalaureate program accreditation with NASDTEC. The library contains 163,896 volumes, 110,050 microform items, and 3867 audio/video tapes/CDs, and subscribes to 12,749 periodicals. Computerized library services include the card catalog, interlibrary loans, and database searching. Special learning facilities include an art gallery. The 475-acre campus is in a suburban area in Roanoke. Including any residence halls, there are 73 buildings.

Student Life: 51% of undergraduates are from out of state, mostly the South. Students are from 45 states and 9 foreign countries. 75% are from public schools. 80% are white. The average age of freshmen is 19; all undergraduates, 22. 21% do not continue beyond their first year; 68% remain to graduate.

Housing: 744 students can be accommodated in college housing, which includes single-sex dorms and on-campus apartments. In addition, there are language houses, special-interest houses, and a "global village" student residence. On-campus housing is guaranteed for all 4 years. 91% of students live on campus; of those, 60% remain on campus on weekends. All students may keep cars.

Activities: There are no fraternities or sororities. There are 45 groups on campus, including art, choir, chorale, dance, drama, ethnic, film, gay, honors, international, literary magazine, newspaper, photography, political, professional, religious, social, social service, student government, and yearbook. Popular campus events include Literary Festival, French and German film festivals, and Classics Symposium.

Sports: There are 10 intercollegiate sports for women and 1 intramural sport for women. Facilities include a swimming center, a fitness center and 2 weight rooms, a gym, an equestrian center, a ropes course, a jogging and exercise trail, tennis courts, 2 playing fields, an auxiliary gym, 2 training rooms, and a climbing wall.

Disabled Students: 40% of the campus is accessible. Wheelchair ramps, elevators, special parking, specially equipped rest rooms, special class scheduling, lowered drinking fountains, lowered telephones, and special housing are available.

Services: Counseling and information services are available, as is tutoring in most subjects. There is a reader service for the blind and a writing center.

Campus Safety and Security: Measures include 24-hour foot and vehicle patrol, self-defense education, security escort services, and informal discussions. There are pamphlets/posters/films, emergency telephones, lighted pathways/sidewalks, and emergency buttons located along walkways and in labs.

Programs of Study: Hollins confers the B.A. degree. Master's degrees are also awarded. Bachelor's degrees are awarded in BIOLOGICAL SCIENCE (biology/biological science), BUSINESS (business administration and management), COMMUNICATIONS AND THE ARTS (art history and appreciation, communications, creative writing, dance, dramatic arts, English, French, German, media arts, music, Spanish, and studio art), COMPUTER AND PHYSICAL SCIENCE (chemistry, computer mathematics, computer science, mathematics, and physics), SOCIAL

SCIENCE (classical/ancient civilization, economics, history, interdisciplinary studies, international studies, philosophy, political science/government, psychology, religion, sociology, and women's studies). English/creative writing and psychology are the strongest academically. English/creative writing, psychology, and communication studies are the largest.

Required: To graduate, students must complete 128 credits of academic work and 4 short terms. At least 32 hours in the major and a 2.0 GPA are required. Distribution requirements include 8 credits each in the humanities, social sciences, natural sciences and math, and fine arts. All students meet the following skills components: writing, oral communication, quantitative reasoning, and information technology. Students are also required to fulfill 2 semesters of phys ed or varsity sport participation. A thesis is required for some majors.

Special: Hollins offers internships during the January term, dual majors, student-designed majors, accelerated degrees, study abroad in Greece, Italy, England, France, Ireland, Japan, Mexico, and Spain, a United Nations semester, and a Washington semester with American University. A 3-2 engineering degree is possible with Washington University in St. Louis and Virginia Polytechnic Institute and State University. There is cross-registration with the Virginia Seven College Exchange and Roanoke College. There are 14 national honor societies, including Phi Beta Kappa, a freshman honors program, and 23 departmental honors programs.

Faculty/Classroom: 38% of faculty are male; 62%, female. All teach undergraduates and 95% both teach and do research. No introductory courses are taught by graduate students. The average class size in an introductory lecture is 18; in a laboratory, 9; and in a regular course, 14.

Admissions: 79% of the 2003-2004 applicants were accepted. The SAT I scores for the 2003-2004 freshman class were: Verbal--19% below 500, 35% between 500 and 599, 32% between 600 and 700, and 14% above 700; Math--26% below 500, 42% between 500 and 599, 30% between 600 and 700, and 2% above 700. The ACT scores were 4% below 21, 38% between 21 and 23, 30% between 24 and 26, 18% between 27 and 28, and 10% above 28. 50% of the current freshmen were in the top fifth of their class; 77% were in the top two fifths. There was 1 National Merit finalist. 2 freshmen graduated first in their class.

Requirements: The SAT I or ACT is required. In addition, applicants must be graduates of an accredited secondary school. The GED is accepted, as is home school. Applicants should complete 16 high school academic credits, including 4 credits of English and 3 credits each of foreign language, math, science, and social studies, SAT II: Subject tests in writing and 2 others of the student's choice are recommended. An essay is required and an interview is recommended. AP credits are accepted. Important factors in the admissions decision are advanced placement or honor courses, recommendations by school officials, and evidence of special talent.

Procedure: Freshmen are admitted fall and spring. Entrance exams should be taken by January of the senior year. There is a rolling admissions plan. There are early decision and deferred admissions plans. Early decision applications should be filed by December 1; regular applications, by February 15 for fall entry and December 1 for spring entry. Notification of early decision is sent December 15; regular decision, on a rolling basis. 39 early decision candidates were accepted for the 2003-2004 class. 23 applicants were on the 2003 waiting list; 8 were admitted. The fall 2003 application fee was $35. Applications are accepted on computer disk and on-line through the College Board, EXPAN, Petersons, and the Hollins University web site.

Transfer: 34 transfer students enrolled in 2002-2003. Applicants for transfer should have a minimum college GPA of 2.5. Other criteria are the same as for entering freshmen. 64 of 128 credits required for the bachelor's degree must be completed at Hollins.

Visiting: There are regularly scheduled orientations for prospective students, including 2 programs for high school seniors offered in October and November, 1 for admitted applicants in April, and 1 for juniors and sophomores in March. There are guides for informal visits and visitors may sit in on classes and stay overnight. To schedule a visit, contact the Admissions Office at (540) 362-6401 or huadm@hollins.edu.

Financial Aid: In 2003-2004, 98% of all full-time freshmen and 97% of continuing full-time students received some form of financial aid. 65% of full-time freshmen and 47% of continuing full-time students received need-based aid. The average freshman award was $16,297. 46% of undergraduates work part time. Average annual earnings from campus work are $1245. The average financial indebtedness of the 2003 graduate was $13,477. The FAFSA and parents'/student's tax returns are required. The deadline for filing freshman financial aid applications for fall entry is February 1.

International Students: There are 21 international students enrolled. The school actively recruits these students. Students whose native language is not English must score 550 on the TOEFL. For students whose native language is English, the SAT I or ACT will be accepted in place of the TOEFL.

Computers: The mainframes are a DEC Alpha (UNIX, Open VMS). There are 100 terminals for student use located throughout the campus.

All students may access the system 24 hours a day, 7 days a week. It is strongly recommended that all students have a personal computer.

Graduates: From July 1, 2002 to June 30, 2003, 197 bachelor's degrees were awarded. The most popular majors were English/creative writing (21%), psychology (10%), and communication studies (10%). In an average class, 55% graduate in 4 years or less, 61% graduate in 5 years or less, and 64% graduate in 6 years or less. 14 companies recruited on campus in 2002-2003. Of a recent graduating class, 21% were enrolled in graduate school within 6 months of graduation and 77% were employed.

Admissions Contact: Celia McCormick, Dean of Admissions. A video is available. E-mail: huadm@hollins.edu Web: www.hollins.edu

JAMES MADISON UNIVERSITY   D-2
Harrisonburg, VA 22807   **(540) 568-5681; Fax: (540) 568-3332**

Full-time: 5680 men, 8588 women	**Faculty:** 685; IIA, av$
Part-time: 209 men, 206 women	**Ph.D.s:** 82%
Graduate: 221 men, 481 women	**Student/Faculty:** 21 to 1
Year: semesters, summer session	**Tuition:** $5058 ($13,280)
Application Deadline: January 15	**Room & Board:** $5736
Freshman Class: 15,056 applied, 9404 accepted, 3388 enrolled	
SAT I Verbal/Math: 580/590	**VERY COMPETITIVE**

James Madison University, founded in 1908, is a public institution with programs in science and math, business, education, arts and letters, and integrated science and technology. There are 5 undergraduate schools and 1 graduate school. In addition to regional accreditation, JMU has baccalaureate program accreditation with AACSB, ACS, ADA, AOTA, APA, CAAHEP, CACREP, CSWE, FIDER, NASAD, NASM, NAST, NCATE, and NLN. The 3 libraries contain 600,953 volumes, 1,036,552 microform items, and 31,594 audio/video tapes/CDs, and subscribe to 5429 periodicals. Computerized library services include the card catalog, interlibrary loans, and database searching. Special learning facilities include a learning resource center, art gallery, planetarium, radio station, an arboretum, music library, and CISAT Library Services. The 605-acre campus is in a small town 123 miles southwest of Washington, D.C. Including any residence halls, there are 103 buildings.

Student Life: 70% of undergraduates are from Virginia. Students are from 46 states, 56 foreign countries, and Canada. 95% are from public schools. 89% are white. 32% are Catholic; 31% Protestant; 19% claim no religious affiliation. The average age of freshmen is 18; all undergraduates, 20. 8% do not continue beyond their first year; 80% remain to graduate.

Housing: 5672 students can be accommodated in college housing, which includes coed dorms, off-campus apartments, fraternity houses, and sorority houses. In addition, there are special-interest houses, a freshman residence hall, a smoke/substance-free residence hall, and theme housing for international students. 60% of students commute. Upperclassmen may keep cars.

Activities: 10% of men belong to 14 national fraternities; 16% of women belong to 8 national sororities. There are 286 groups on campus, including art, band, cheerleading, chess, choir, chorale, chorus, computers, dance, drama, ethnic, gay, honors, international, jazz band, literary magazine, marching band, musical theater, newspaper, opera, orchestra, pep band, photography, political, professional, radio and TV, religious, social, social service, student government, symphony, and yearbook. Popular campus events include Madison Symposium, James Madison Week, and Constitution Day.

Sports: There are 11 intercollegiate sports for men and 13 for women, and 18 intramural sports for men and 18 for women. Facilities include a 12,800-seat stadium, a convocation center, an all-weather track, a gym, a natatorium, tennis courts, a lighted Astroturf field, and baseball, soccer, and softball fields. A recreation center houses a fitness center, racquetball courts, basketball gyms, an indoor track, a pool, and a climbing wall.

Disabled Students: 85% of the campus is accessible. Wheelchair ramps, elevators, special parking, specially equipped rest rooms, special class scheduling, lowered drinking fountains, lowered telephones, and automated doors in 39 buildings are available.

Services: Counseling and information services are available, as is tutoring in every subject. There is a reader service for the blind. There also is a reading and writing resource center, a first-year involvement center, a communication studies resource center, a science and math learning center, and supplemental instruction.

Campus Safety and Security: Measures include 24-hour foot and vehicle patrol, self-defense education, security escort services, and informal discussions. There are pamphlets/posters/films, emergency telephones, lighted pathways/sidewalks, and public bus transportation routes through the campus.

Programs of Study: JMU confers B.A., B.S., B.B.A., B.F.A., B.I.S., B.M., B.S.N., and B.S.W. degrees. Master's and doctoral degrees are also awarded. Bachelor's degrees are awarded in BIOLOGICAL SCIENCE (biology/biological science), BUSINESS (accounting, banking and finance, business administration and management, business economics, hospitality management services, international business management, marketing/retailing/merchandising, recreation and leisure services, and tourism), COMMUNICATIONS AND THE ARTS (art, art history and appreciation, communications, communications technology, dance, dramatic arts, English, fine arts, media arts, modern language, music, and speech/debate/rhetoric), COMPUTER AND PHYSICAL SCIENCE (chemistry, computer science, geology, information sciences and systems, mathematics, physics, science technology, and statistics), EDUCATION (business), HEALTH PROFESSIONS (health science, nursing, and speech pathology/audiology), SOCIAL SCIENCE (anthropology, dietetics, economics, geography, history, international studies, liberal arts/general studies, philosophy, physical fitness/movement, political science/government, psychology, public administration, religion, social science, social work, and sociology). Biology, business and communications are the strongest academically. Marketing, interdisciplinary liberal studies, and health sciences are the largest.

Required: To graduate, students must complete a minimum of 120 credit hours, with a GPA of at least 2.0., meet the general education requirements and the requirements of their major, have been enrolled at JMU a minimum of two regular semesters, and have earned a minimum of 30 credit hours at JMU during that period of enrollment.

Special: JMU offers internships, work-study programs, a Washington semester, and study abroad in London, Antwerp, Florence, Salamanca, and Martinique. There are combined programs in physics and engineering with the University of Virginia and in forestry with Virginia Tech. An individualized study degree, nondegree study, pass/fail options, and credit for life, military, and work experience are available. There are 22 national honor societies, a freshman honors program, and 36 departmental honors programs.

Faculty/Classroom: 58% of faculty are male; 42%, female. 95% teach undergraduates. Graduate students teach 2% of introductory courses. The average class size in an introductory lecture is 40; in a laboratory, 22; and in a regular course, 30.

Admissions: 62% of the 2003-2004 applicants were accepted. The SAT I scores for the 2003-2004 freshman class were: Verbal--11% below 500, 54% between 500 and 599, 32% between 600 and 700, and 3% above 700; Math--11% below 500, 50% between 500 and 599, 36% between 600 and 700, and 3% above 700.

Requirements: The SAT I or ACT is required. In addition, applicants must be graduates of an accredited secondary school. They must show solid achievement in 4 or more academic courses each year of high school. A personal statement is required. Art students must present a portfolio. Theater, dance, and music students must audition. Nursing students must apply to the nursing department in addition to applying for undergraduate admission. AP credits are accepted. Important factors in the admissions decision are advanced placement or honor courses, recommendations by school officials, and extracurricular activities record.

Procedure: Freshmen are admitted in the fall. Entrance exams should be taken in the spring of the junior year or the fall of the senior year. There are early admissions and deferred admissions plans. Early action applications should be filed by November 1; regular applications, by January 15 for fall entry. The fall 2003 application fee was $30. Notification of early action is sent January 15; regular decision, April 1. 1000 applicants were on the 2003 waiting list; 31 were admitted. Applications are accepted on-line through CollegeNET.

Transfer: 607 transfer students enrolled in 2002-2003. Applicants must have a minimum GPA of 2.0 and must submit a complete application, official college transcripts, secondary school records or a copy of their GED, and a one-page personal statement. If applicants have fewer than 30 credit hours completed at the time of application, they must submit SAT I scores unless they are 25 years old or older. 30 of 120 credits required for the bachelor's degree must be completed at JMU.

Visiting: There are regularly scheduled orientations for prospective students, including daily campus tours during the week and on Saturdays, and tours following group conferences. There are guides for informal visits. To schedule a visit, contact the Admissions Office at (540) 568-5681 or visit-jmu@jmu.edu.

Financial Aid: In 2003-2004, 50% of all full-time freshmen and 42% of continuing full-time students received some form of financial aid. 34% of full-time freshmen and 36% of continuing full-time students received need-based aid. The average freshman award was $9098. Need-based scholarships or need-based grants averaged $4767 ($5558 maximum); need-based self-help aid (loans and jobs) averaged $2685 ($6625 maximum); non-need-based athletic scholarships averaged $11,733 ($19,246 maximum); and other non-need-based awards and non-need-based scholarships averaged $2073 ($4000 maximum). 19% of undergraduates work part time. Average annual earnings from campus work are $1920. The average financial indebtedness of the 2003 graduate was $11,964. The FAFSA is required. The deadline for filing freshman financial aid applications for fall entry is March 1.

International Students: There are 133 international students enrolled. The school actively recruits these students. They must score 550 on the written TOEFL and also take the SAT I or the ACT. Students must take SAT II: Subject tests in writing.

Computers: The mainframes consist of various HP 9000 series servers running HP-UX and Dell Poweredge servers running Windows NT. Computers are located in classrooms, labs, residence halls, academic buildings, and the library, and network access is provided in residence hall rooms. All students may access the system 24 hours a day. There are no time limits and no fees. It is strongly recommended that all students have a personal computer. Students in the Colleges of Integrated Science and Technology and Business are required to have them. Recommended computer configurations for use in specific departments and majors can be found on-line at *www.jmu.edu/computing/computerpurchase/depreq.shtml.*

Graduates: From July 1, 2002 to June 30, 2003, 3162 bachelor's degrees were awarded. The most popular majors were marketing (7%), psychology (7%), and health sciences (6%). In an average class, 62% graduate in 4 years or less, 78% graduate in 5 years or less, and 80% graduate in 6 years or less. 154 companies recruited on campus in 2002-2003.

Admissions Contact: Michael D. Walsh, Director of Admissions. E-mail: *gotojmu@jmu.edu* Web: *www.jmu.edu/admissions*

LIBERTY UNIVERSITY — D-3
Lynchburg, VA 24502
(434) 582-7307
(800) 543-5317; Fax: (434) 582-2421

Full-time: 2829 men, 3272 women	**Faculty:** 200; IIA, --$
Part-time: 110 men, 115 women	**Ph.D.s:** 67%
Graduate: 307 men, 141 women	**Student/Faculty:** 31 to 1
Year: semesters, summer session	**Tuition:** $12,020
Application Deadline: open	**Room & Board:** $5200
Freshman Class: 4904 applied, 4720 accepted, 1875 enrolled	
SAT I Verbal/Math: 510/490	**ACT:** 21 COMPETITIVE

Liberty University, founded in 1971, is a private liberal arts institution affiliated with the Baptist Church. There are 6 undergraduate and 5 graduate schools. In addition to regional accreditation, Liberty has baccalaureate program accreditation with NASM and NLN. The library contains 211,092 volumes, 95,329 microform items, and 7149 audio/video tapes/CDs, and subscribes to 10,806 periodicals. Computerized library services include the card catalog, interlibrary loans, database searching, and Internet access. Special learning facilities include a learning resource center, radio station, and TV station. The 160-acre campus is in a suburban area 45 miles east of Roanoke. Including any residence halls, there are 73 buildings.

Student Life: 60% of undergraduates are from out of state, mostly the Middle Atlantic. Students are from 48 states, 76 foreign countries, and Canada. 78% are white; 11% African American. Most are Protestant. The average age of freshmen is 19; all undergraduates, 21.

Housing: 4303 students can be accommodated in college housing, which includes single-sex dorms and on-campus apartments. On-campus housing is guaranteed for all 4 years. 64% of students live on campus; of those, 90% remain on campus on weekends. Alcohol is not permitted. All students may keep cars.

Activities: There are no fraternities or sororities. There are 40 groups on campus, including band, cheerleading, choir, chorale, chorus, computers, debate, drama, drill team, ethnic, honors, international, marching band, musical theater, newspaper, opera, orchestra, pep band, political, professional, radio and TV, religious, social service, student government, and yearbook. Popular campus events include Super Conference and Missions Emphasis Week.

Sports: There are 9 intercollegiate sports for men and 8 for women, and 16 intramural sports for men and 16 for women. Facilities include an 11,000-seat football stadium, an 8000-seat basketball arena/convention center, baseball and soccer fields, a track complex, and a tennis center.

Disabled Students: 90% of the campus is accessible. Wheelchair ramps, elevators, special parking, specially equipped rest rooms, special class scheduling, lowered drinking fountains, lowered telephones, and special housing are available.

Services: Counseling and information services are available, as is tutoring in every subject. There is remedial math, reading, and writing.

Campus Safety and Security: Measures include 24-hour foot and vehicle patrol, self-defense education, security escort services, and shuttle buses. There are informal discussions, pamphlets/posters/films, and lighted pathways/sidewalks.

Programs of Study: Liberty confers B.A., B.S., B.M., and B.S.N. degrees. Associate, master's, and doctoral degrees are also awarded. Bachelor's degrees are awarded in BIOLOGICAL SCIENCE (biology/biological science), BUSINESS (accounting, business administration and management, management information systems, and sports management), COMMUNICATIONS AND THE ARTS (communications, English, English as a second/foreign language, music, and Spanish), COMPUTER AND PHYSICAL SCIENCE (computer science and mathematics), EDUCATION (athletic training, elementary, and physical), HEALTH PROFESSIONS (community health work, exercise science, and nursing), SOCIAL SCIENCE (family/consumer studies, history, interdisciplinary studies, international studies, liberal arts/general studies, political science/government, psychology, religion, and social science). Education, psychology, and business are the strongest academically and are the largest.

Required: Students must complete 120 to 123 credit hours to graduate, with a minimum GPA of 2.0. With few exceptions, by major, all must complete 18 hours of foundational studies in English, math, speech communications, and general education. An additional 42 credits of investigative studies are required; these vary according to the degree sought, either B.A. or B.S., but include English, natural sciences, history, arts, music, languages, government, social sciences, philosophy, theology, Bible studies, and integrated studies.

Special: Liberty offers internships, B.A.-B.S. degrees, and student-designed majors in interdisciplinary and general studies. There are 8 national honor societies, including Phi Beta Kappa, a freshman honors program, and 7 departmental honors programs.

Faculty/Classroom: 67% of faculty are male; 33%, female. 90% teach undergraduates. No introductory courses are taught by graduate students. The average class size in an introductory lecture is 43; in a laboratory, 22; and in a regular course, 23.

Admissions: 96% of the 2003-2004 applicants were accepted. The SAT I scores for the 2003-2004 freshman class were: Verbal--44% below 500, 37% between 500 and 599, 16% between 600 and 700, and 3% above 700; Math--53% below 500, 33% between 500 and 599, 12% between 600 and 700, and 1% above 700. The ACT scores were 47% below 21, 23% between 21 and 23, 16% between 24 and 26, 8% between 27 and 28, and 6% above 28. There were 5 National Merit finalists.

Requirements: The SAT I or ACT is required. In addition, applicants must have completed 16 high school academic credits. The GED is accepted. An essay is required. A GPA of 2.0 is required. AP and CLEP credits are accepted. Important factors in the admissions decision are ability to finance college education, recommendations by school officials, and advanced placement or honor courses.

Procedure: Freshmen are admitted to all sessions. Entrance exams should be taken during the junior year. There is a rolling admissions plan. There are early decision, early admissions, and deferred admissions plans. Application deadlines are open. Application fee is $35. Applications are accepted on-line through Apply Web.

Transfer: 743 transfer students enrolled in 2002-2003. Applicants for transfer must have a GPA of 2.0. If transferring fewer than 60 hours, a high school transcript and test scores are required. 30 of 120 credits required for the bachelor's degree must be completed at Liberty.

Visiting: There are regularly scheduled orientations for prospective students, including College for a Weekend, a 2-day program offering a chance to attend classes and special meetings. There are guides for informal visits and visitors may sit in on classes and stay overnight. To schedule a visit, contact the Visitor's Center at (434) 582-2064 or *visitorscenter@liberty.edu*.

Financial Aid: In 2003-2004, 98% of all full-time freshmen and 88% of continuing full-time students received some form of financial aid. 64% of all full-time students received need-based aid. The average freshman award was $8506. Need-based scholarships or need-based grants averaged $1800 ($4000 maximum); need-based self-help aid (loans and jobs) averaged $3725 ($3940 maximum); non-need-based athletic scholarships averaged $8172 ($18,850 maximum); and other non-need-based awards and non-need-based scholarships averaged $4667 ($15,220 maximum). 15% of undergraduates work part time. Average annual earnings from campus work are $2500. The average financial indebtedness of the 2003 graduate was $15,619. The FAFSA and Single-file Form (preferred) are required. The deadline for filing freshman financial aid applications for fall entry is March 1.

International Students: There are 238 international students enrolled. The school actively recruits these students. They must take the TOEFL or the MELAB.

Computers: The mainframe is an IBM AS/400. More than 371 PCs are located in labs and the library; each dorm room has 3 network connections for Internet and web access. All students may access the system 24 hours a day Sunday through Thursday and 7:30 A.M. to 9 P.M. Friday and Saturday. There are no time limits. The fee is $200 per semester.

Graduates: From July 1, 2002 to June 30, 2003, 945 bachelor's degrees were awarded. The most popular majors were psychology (17%), business (16%), and religion (14%).

Admissions Contact: David Hart, Associate Director of Admissions. A video is available. E-mail: *admissions@liberty.edu* Web: *http://www.liberty.edu*

LONGWOOD UNIVERSITY D-3
Farmville, VA 23909

(434) 395-2060
(800) 281-4677; Fax: (434) 395-2332

Full-time: 1191 men, 2374 women	**Faculty:** 181; IIA, --$
Part-time: 50 men, 70 women	**Ph.D.s:** 79%
Graduate: 88 men, 479 women	**Student/Faculty:** 20 to 1
Year: semesters, summer session	**Tuition:** $5877 ($8972)
Application Deadline: March 1	**Room & Board:** $5298
Freshman Class: 3472 applied, 2441 accepted, 880 enrolled	
SAT I Verbal/Math: 547/538	COMPETITIVE

Longwood University, formerly Longwood College, founded in 1839, is a state-supported institution with programs in liberal arts, business, and teacher preparation. There are 3 undergraduate and 2 graduate schools. In addition to regional accreditation, Longwood has baccalaureate program accreditation with AACSB, CSWE, NASM, NCATE, and NRPA. The library contains 1,060,855 volumes, 695,530 microform items, and 31,587 audio/video tapes/CDs, and subscribes to 2503 periodicals. Computerized library services include the card catalog, interlibrary loans, database searching, and Internet access. Special learning facilities include a learning resource center, art gallery, radio station, greenhouse, a language lab, 6 computer labs, and a psychology lab. The 160-acre campus is in a small town 60 miles west of Richmond and 60 miles south of Charlottesville. Including any residence halls, there are 53 buildings.

Student Life: 90% of undergraduates are from Virginia. Students are from 22 states, 19 foreign countries, and Canada. 93% are from public schools. 88% are white. The average age of freshmen is 18; all undergraduates, 21. 20% do not continue beyond their first year; 61% remain to graduate.

Housing: 2451 students can be accommodated in college housing, which includes single-sex and coed dorms, fraternity houses, sorority houses, and off-campus apartments. In addition, there are honors houses, language houses, special-interest houses, a substance-free dorm, and international studies floors. On-campus housing is guaranteed for the freshman year only, is available on a first-come, first-served basis, and is available on a lottery system for upperclassmen. 69% of students live on campus; of those, 70% remain on campus on weekends. Upperclassmen may keep cars.

Activities: 14% of men belong to 9 national fraternities; 19% of women belong to 13 national sororities. There are 125 groups on campus, including art, band, cheerleading, chess, choir, chorus, computers, dance, debate, drama, drill team, ethnic, forensics, gay, honors, international, jazz band, literary magazine, musical theater, newspaper, photography, political, professional, radio and TV, religious, social, social service, and student government. Popular campus events include Spring Weekend and Oktoberfest.

Sports: There are 6 intercollegiate sports for men and 8 for women, and 31 intramural sports for men and 31 for women. Facilities include a 9-hole golf course, a weight training facility, 2 gyms, racquetball courts, 11 lighted tennis courts, 2 pools, a bowling alley, 3 outdoor sand volleyball courts, a 10-station fitness trail, a Frisbee golf course, outdoor basketball courts, and soccer, baseball, and softball fields.

Disabled Students: 90% of the campus is accessible. Wheelchair ramps, elevators, special parking, special class scheduling, lowered drinking fountains, and lowered telephones. The campus is being made fully accessible. Until then, classes can be scheduled in accessible buildings.

Services: There is a reader service for the blind. There is also assistance in study skills, learning strategies, advocacy training, and compensatory strategy instruction.

Campus Safety and Security: Measures include 24-hour foot and vehicle patrol, self-defense education, security escort services, and shuttle buses. There are informal discussions, pamphlets/posters/films, emergency telephones, lighted pathways/sidewalks, electronic card key entry into dorms, and video cameras.

Programs of Study: Longwood confers B.A., B.S., B.F.A., B.M., and B.S.B.A. degrees. Master's degrees are also awarded. Bachelor's degrees are awarded in BIOLOGICAL SCIENCE (biology/biological science), BUSINESS (business administration and management), COMMUNICATIONS AND THE ARTS (art, communications, English, modern language, music, and visual and performing arts), COMPUTER AND PHYSICAL SCIENCE (chemistry, computer science, mathematics, and physics), EDUCATION (art, elementary, music, physical, and special), HEALTH PROFESSIONS (community health work and recreation therapy), SOCIAL SCIENCE (anthropology, criminal justice, criminology, economics, history, liberal arts/general studies, political science/government, psychology, social work, and sociology). Business and liberal studies (elementary education) are the strongest academically and have the largest enrollments.

Required: To graduate, students must complete 120 to 145 credits, including 36 to 77 in the major, with a minimum GPA of 2.0 overall and in the major. A 41-hour general education core curriculum, 4 intensive writing courses, a phys ed course, and 30 upper-level credit hours are also required.

Special: Longwood offers internships or directed research projects in most majors, study abroad in 7 countries, and B.A.-B.S. degrees in many majors. Cross-registration is possible with Hampden-Sydney College, as are 3-2 engineering degrees with several regional universities. Also, there is a 3-3 preprofessional program in physical therapy with University of Virginia, Old Dominion, and Virginia Commonwealth Universities. There are 3 national honor societies, a freshman honors program, and 21 departmental honors programs.

Faculty/Classroom: 53% of faculty are male; 47%, female. All teach undergraduates, and 50% both teach and do research. No introductory courses are taught by graduate students. The average class size in an introductory lecture is 31; in a laboratory, 21; and in a regular course, 27.

Admissions: 70% of the 2003-2004 applicants were accepted. The SAT I scores for the 2003-2004 freshman class were: Verbal--21% below 500, 60% between 500 and 599, 18% between 600 and 700, and 1% above 700; Math--25% below 500, 60% between 500 and 599, 14% between 600 and 700, and 1% above 700. 28% of the current freshmen were in the top fifth of their class; 70% were in the top two fifths. 1 freshman graduated first in the class.

Requirements: The SAT I or ACT is recommended. In addition, applicants must be graduates of an accredited secondary school; the GED is accepted. Students should complete 4 years of high school English, 3 years each of foreign language and science (including 2 lab courses), 2 years of history, and algebra I, II, and geometry. A personal statement is required. An audition is required for music students. Longwood requires applicants to be in the upper 50% of their class. A GPA of 2.6 is required. AP and CLEP credits are accepted. Important factors in the admissions decision are advanced placement or honor courses, leadership record, and evidence of special talent.

Procedure: Freshmen are admitted fall and spring. Entrance exams should be taken in the fall of the senior year. There is a rolling admissions plan. There are early decision and deferred admissions plans. Early decision applications should be filed by December 1; regular applications, by March 1 for fall entry and November 15 for spring entry. Notification of early decision is sent January 1; regular decision, on a rolling basis. 848 early decision candidates were accepted for the 2003-2004 class. 150 applicants were on the 2003 waiting list; 125 were admitted. Applications are accepted on-line through *www.longwood.edu/admissions/appinstruct2002.htm*.

Transfer: 204 transfer students enrolled in 2002-2003. Applicants for transfer must have a GPA of at least 2.5 in all college course work attempted. Other criteria are the same as for entering freshmen. 30 of the 120 to 145 credits required for the bachelor's degree must be completed at Longwood.

Visiting: There are regularly scheduled orientations for prospective students, including informational and tour programs, and open houses in October, February, March, and November. Visitors may sit in on classes and stay overnight. To schedule a visit, contact the Admissions Office at (800) 281-4677, ext. 2, or *admit@longwood.edu*.

Financial Aid: Need-based scholarships or need-based grants averaged $3606; need-based self-help aid (loans and jobs) averaged $4057; non-need-based athletic scholarships averaged $3740; and other non-need-based awards and non-need-based scholarships averaged $4304. 27% of undergraduates work part time. Average annual earnings from campus work are $1344. The average financial indebtedness of the 2003 graduate was $14,889. The FAFSA is required. The deadline for filing freshman financial aid applications for fall entry is March 1.

International Students: There are 20 international students enrolled. The school actively recruits these students. They must score 550 on the written TOEFL or 213 on the electronic version and also take the SAT I or the ACT.

Computers: The mainframe is an IBM RS 6000 (Model S70). There are 185 networked PCs and Macs. 2 student computer labs are open 9 A.M. to 10 P.M. daily. Numerous software packages and programming languages are available. All students may access the system. There are no time limits and no fees. All students are required to have personal computers; a Dell laptop PC is recommended.

Graduates: From July 1, 2002 to June 30, 2003, 706 bachelor's degrees were awarded. The most popular majors were liberal studies (23%), business administration (23%), and visual and performing arts (7%). In an average class, 1% graduate in 3 years or less, 44% graduate in 4 years or less, 58% graduate in 5 years or less, and 57% graduate in 6 years or less. 167 companies recruited on campus in 2002-2003. Of the 2002 graduating class, 21% were enrolled in graduate school within 6 months of graduation and 91% were employed.

Admissions Contact: Robert J. Chonko, Director of Admissions and Enrollment Management. E-mail: *admit@longwood.edu* Web: *www.longwood.edu*

LYNCHBURG COLLEGE · D-3
Lynchburg, VA 24501

(434) 544-8300
(800) 426-8101; Fax: (434) 544-8653

Full-time: 663 men, 992 women	**Faculty:** 135; IIA, -$
Part-time: 46 men, 72 women	**Ph.D.s:** 78%
Graduate: 72 men, 164 women	**Student/Faculty:** 12 to 1
Year: semesters, summer session	**Tuition:** $21,415
Application Deadline: open	**Room & Board:** $5400
Freshman Class: 3154 applied, 2380 accepted, 589 enrolled	
SAT I Verbal/Math: 510/510	**ACT:** 20 **COMPETITIVE**

Lynchburg College, established in 1903, is a private, nonprofit institution affiliated with the Christian Church (Disciples of Christ), offering bachelor's degrees in liberal arts and sciences, and professional studies. There are 6 undergraduate and 2 graduate schools. In addition to regional accreditation, L.C. has baccalaureate program accreditation with NLN. The library contains 192,000 volumes, 437,000 microform items, and 5600 audio/video tapes/CDs, and subscribes to 578 periodicals. Computerized library services include the card catalog, interlibrary loans, database searching, and Internet access. Special learning facilities include a learning resource center and art gallery. The 214-acre campus is in a suburban area 180 miles southwest of Washington, D.C. Including any residence halls, there are 42 buildings.

Student Life: 57% of undergraduates are from Virginia. Students are from 36 states and 17 foreign countries. 79% are from public schools. 81% are white. 76% are Protestant; 17% Catholic. The average age of freshmen is 19; all undergraduates, 22. 28% do not continue beyond their first year; 54% remain to graduate.

Housing: 1369 students can be accommodated in college housing, which includes single-sex and coed dorms, on-campus apartments, fraternity houses, and sorority houses. In addition, there are honors houses, language houses, special-interest houses, and on-campus student townhouses. On-campus housing is guaranteed for all 4 years. 82% of students live on campus; of those, 80% remain on campus on weekends. Upperclassmen may keep cars.

Activities: 4% of men belong to 5 national fraternities; 8% of women belong to 5 national sororities. There are 70 groups on campus, including art, cheerleading, choir, computers, dance, drama, ethnic, gay, honors, international, jazz band, literary magazine, musical theater, newspaper, political, professional, religious, social, social service, student government, TV, and yearbook. Popular campus events include a new student convocation and Academic Awards Banquet.

Sports: There are 10 intercollegiate sports for men and 11 for women, and 12 intramural sports for men and 12 for women. Facilities include a gym with a weight room and exercise physiology lab, a field house, athletic fields, and a ropes course.

Disabled Students: 78% of the campus is accessible. Wheelchair ramps, elevators, special parking, specially equipped rest rooms, special class scheduling, lowered drinking fountains, lowered telephones, and special housing are available.

Services: Counseling and information services are available. Tutoring is available in most freshman and sophomore subjects, some upperclass subjects, and in math and writing.

Campus Safety and Security: Measures include 24-hour foot and vehicle patrol, security escort services, informal discussions, and pamphlets/posters/films. There are emergency telephones and lighted pathways/sidewalks. All residence halls are locked 24 hours a day. Admission is only by scanning an ID card.

Programs of Study: L.C. confers B.A. and B.S. degrees. Master's degrees are also awarded. Bachelor's degrees are awarded in BIOLOGICAL SCIENCE (biology/biological science), BUSINESS (accounting, business administration and management, management science, marketing/retailing/merchandising, and sports management), COMMUNICATIONS AND THE ARTS (art, communications, dramatic arts, English, French, music, and Spanish), COMPUTER AND PHYSICAL SCIENCE (chemistry, computer science, mathematics, and physical sciences), EDUCATION (athletic training and education), ENGINEERING AND ENVIRONMENTAL DESIGN (engineering and environmental science), HEALTH PROFESSIONS (biomedical science, exercise science, nursing, and sports medicine), SOCIAL SCIENCE (economics, history, human development, international relations, philosophy, physical fitness/movement, political science/government, psychology, religion, and sociology). Communication studies, nursing, and human development learning are the largest.

Required: To graduate, students must complete a 15- to 18-hour basic skills requirement, which includes English, a foreign language, math, health, movement science, and recreation. Students must also complete 15 to 21 hours in the humanities (history, literature, philosophy, and religion), 6 hours each in fine arts and social sciences, 6 to 16 hours in physical sciences, and a 2-hour senior symposium in which students read selections from the classics, prepare written analyses, and attend weekly lecture/discussion sessions. The minimum GPA is 2.0. Students must earn 124 credits, with 30 to 69 in the major.

Special: Students may cross-register with Sweet Briar and Randolph-Macon Colleges, and they may study abroad in 20 countries. There is a Washington semester available, B.A.-B.S.degrees in 39 majors, internships, and a work-study program. Dual majors may be pursued in religious studies, philosophy, political science, sociology, business, and a foreign language. A 3-2 engineering degree is available in cooperation with Old Dominion University. Nondegree study and a pass/fail grading option are also available. There are 15 national honor societies and a freshman honors program.

Faculty/Classroom: 62% of faculty are male; 38%, female. All teach undergraduates, 25% do research, and 25% do both. No introductory courses are taught by graduate students. The average class size in an introductory lecture is 25; in a laboratory, 16; and in a regular course, 25.

Admissions: 75% of the 2003-2004 applicants were accepted. The SAT I scores for the 2003-2004 freshman class were: Verbal--44% below 500, 42% between 500 and 599, 13% between 600 and 700, and 1% above 700; Math--42% below 500, 43% between 500 and 599, 14% between 600 and 700, and 1% above 700. The ACT scores were 53% below 21, 31% between 21 and 23, 9% between 24 and 26, 3% between 27 and 28, and 4% above 28. 35% of the current freshmen were in the top fifth of their class; 64% were in the top two fifths. 6 freshmen graduated first in their class.

Requirements: The SAT I or ACT is required. In addition, and SAT II: Subject tests are recommended. Applicants must graduate from an accredited secondary school. They must have earned 16 to 20 academic high school credits in English, math and social science, lab science, and foreign language. AP and CLEP credits are accepted. Important factors in the admissions decision are advanced placement or honor courses, leadership record, and recommendations by school officials.

Procedure: Freshmen are admitted fall and spring. Entrance exams should be taken in the junior year and in the first semester of the senior year. There is a rolling admissions plan. There are early decision and early admissions plans. Early decision applications should be filed by November 15; regular applications, by open for fall entry. Notification of early decision is sent December 15; regular decision, on a rolling basis. 46 early decision candidates were accepted for the 2003-2004 class. The fall 2003 application fee was $30. Applications are accepted on-line.

Transfer: 36 transfer students enrolled in 2002-2003. Transfer students must have a minimum GPA of 2.0 to be considered, and must be in good academic and social standing. The SAT I or ACT is required. An interview is recommended. 62 of 124 credits required for the bachelor's degree must be completed at L.C.

Visiting: There are regularly scheduled orientations for prospective students, individual appointments are available. There are guides for informal visits and visitors may sit in on classes and stay overnight. To schedule a visit, contact the Enrollment Services Office at (800) 426-8101 or admissions@lynchburg.edu.

Financial Aid: In 2003-2004, 99% of all full-time freshmen and 98% of continuing full-time students received some form of financial aid. 67% of full-time freshmen and 64% of continuing full-time students received need-based aid. The average freshman award was $15,536. Need-based scholarships or need-based grants averaged $12,418 ($21,270 maximum); need-based self-help aid (loans and jobs) averaged $3838 ($5675 maximum); and non-need-based awards and non-need-based scholarships averaged $9736 ($22,770 maximum). 37% of undergraduates work part time. Average annual earnings from campus work are $1250. The average financial indebtedness of the 2003 graduate was $18,698. L.C. is a member of CSS. The FAFSA and the state aid form are required. The deadline for filing freshman financial aid applications for fall entry is March 1.

International Students: There are 17 international students enrolled. They must score 550 on the written TOEFL or 213 on the electronic version and also take the SAT I or the ACT.

Computers: The mainframe is a DEC VAX 4000/200. Student computing is primarily PC based, with some access to mainframe facilities. 200 PCs are located in labs and classrooms across campus. Most students own computers and have them in their rooms. All students may access the system 8 A.M. to 1 A.M. Monday through Thursday, 8 A.M. to 5 P.M. Friday and Saturday, and noon to 1 A.M. Sunday. There are no time limits and no fees. It is strongly recommended that all students have a personal computer.

Graduates: From July 1, 2002 to June 30, 2003, 350 bachelor's degrees were awarded. The most popular majors were human development and learning (11%), business administration (9%), and English (9%). In an average class, 1% graduate in 3 years or less, 50% graduate in 4 years or less, 57% graduate in 5 years or less, and 57% graduate in 6 years or less. 78 companies recruited on campus in 2002-2003. Of the 2002 graduating class, 22% were enrolled in graduate school within 6 months of graduation and 75% were employed.

Admissions Contact: Rita Detwiler, VP, Enrollment Management. A video is available. E-mail: admissions@lynchburg.edu Web: www.lynchburg.edu

MARY BALDWIN COLLEGE
D-2
Staunton, VA 24401
(540) 887-7019
(800) 468-2262; Fax: (540) 886-6634

Full-time: 1074 women	**Faculty:** 76; IIB, av$
Part-time: 353 women	**Ph.D.s:** 93%
Graduate: 61 women	**Student/Faculty:** 14 to 1
Year: 4-4-1, summer session	**Tuition:** $19,414
Application Deadline: April 15	**Room & Board:** $5525
Freshman Class: 1233 applied, 973 accepted, 253 enrolled	
SAT I Verbal/Math: 540/500	**ACT:** 22 COMPETITIVE

Mary Baldwin College, established in 1842, is a private liberal arts college primarily for women and affiliated with the Presbyterian Church (U.S.A.). The college sponsors a special program for gifted young women who have completed the eighth grade or higher, and a leadership program for women. The library contains 164,860 volumes, 52,087 microform items, and 4005 audio/video tapes/CDs, and subscribes to 1602 periodicals. Computerized library services include the card catalog, interlibrary loans, database searching, and Internet access. Special learning facilities include a learning resource center, art gallery, radio station, TV station, language lab, and military/leadership museum. The 54-acre campus is in a small town 100 miles west of Richmond. Including any residence halls, there are 30 buildings.

Student Life: 60% of undergraduates are from Virginia. Students are from 38 states, 6 foreign countries, and Canada. 80% are from public schools. 66% are white; 18% African American; 10% Hispanic. 41% are Catholic; 40% Protestant; 6% claim no religious affiliation. The average age of freshmen is 18. 30% do not continue beyond their first year; 55% remain to graduate.

Housing: 775 students can be accommodated in college housing, which includes single-sex dorms and on-campus apartments. In addition, there are honors houses, language houses, special-interest houses, and lofts and suites. On-campus housing is guaranteed for all 4 years. 92% of students live on campus; of those, 40% remain on campus on weekends. All students may keep cars.

Activities: There are no fraternities or sororities. There are 48 groups on campus, including art, choir, chorale, chorus, computers, dance, drama, drill team, drum and bugle corps, ethnic, film, gay, honors, international, literary magazine, marching band, musical theater, newspaper, orchestra, photography, political, professional, radio and TV, religious, social, social service, student government, and yearbook. Popular campus events include Apple Day, Junior Dads Weekend, and Kwanzaa.

Sports: There are 8 intercollegiate sports for women and 4 intramural sports for women. Facilities include a gym, a Universal gym room, a room for dance and fencing, tennis, basketball, and racquetball courts, a sauna and steam room, Nautilus equipment, and soccer, softball, and hockey fields.

Disabled Students: 30% of the campus is accessible. Wheelchair ramps, elevators, special parking, and specially equipped rest rooms are available.

Services: Counseling and information services are available, as is tutoring in most subjects. There is remedial math.

Campus Safety and Security: Measures include 24-hour foot and vehicle patrol, self-defense education, security escort services, and informal discussions. There are pamphlets/posters/films, emergency telephones, lighted pathways/sidewalks, and 24-hour locked residence halls.

Programs of Study: MBC confers B.A. and B.S. degrees. Master's degrees are also awarded. Bachelor's degrees are awarded in BIOLOGICAL SCIENCE (biochemistry and biology/biological science), BUSINESS (business administration and management and business economics), COMMUNICATIONS AND THE ARTS (art, arts administration/management, communications, dramatic arts, English, fine arts, French, German, music, public relations, and Spanish), COMPUTER AND PHYSICAL SCIENCE (applied mathematics, chemistry, computer mathematics, computer science, mathematics, and physics), EDUCATION (art, early childhood, education, English, foreign languages, mathematics, middle school, science, and social studies), HEALTH PROFESSIONS (health care administration and medical laboratory technology), SOCIAL SCIENCE (Asian/Oriental studies, economics, history, international relations, philosophy, political science/government, psychology, social work, and sociology). Biology, chemistry, and history are the strongest academically. Psychology, art, and sociology are the largest.

Required: To graduate, students must complete 9 hours each in natural sciences, social sciences, arts, and humanities; 6 hours each of writing courses, and international education (foreign language, cross-cultural studies, and/or study abroad); and 3 hours each of math, women's studies, and oral communication. A minimum GPA of 2.0 is required. Students must earn 132 credits, with at least 33 credits in the major. There is a 2-hour phys ed requirement and a 3-hour experiential education requirement. Most disciplines require senior projects consisting of some type of original research.

Special: There are cooperative programs with Randolph-Macon, Sweet Briar, and Hampden-Sydney Colleges and Washington and Lee University. Internships, B.A.-B.S. degrees in biology, biochemistry, chemistry, and psychology, and work-study programs are available. Students may study abroad in 6 countries. There is a Washington semester. The college offers an accelerated degree program as well as dual and student-designed majors. The Women's Institute for Leadership program combines academic and phys ed curricula with military and community service training. There are 3-2 programs available in engineering with Washington University in St. Louis and the University of Virginia, and in nursing with Vanderbilt University. There is an advanced degree program in teaching with the University of Virginia. Credit for life, military, and work experience may be granted through the adult degree program only. Nondegree study and a pass/fail grading option are available. There are 9 national honor societies, including Phi Beta Kappa, and a freshman honors program.

Faculty/Classroom: 44% of faculty are male; 56%, female. All teach undergraduates. No introductory courses are taught by graduate students. The average class size in an introductory lecture is 21; in a laboratory, 12; and in a regular course, 18.

Admissions: 79% of the 2003-2004 applicants were accepted. The SAT I scores for the 2003-2004 freshman class were: Verbal--30% below 500, 36% between 500 and 599, 28% between 600 and 700, and 6% above 700; Math--47% below 500, 35% between 500 and 599, 15% between 600 and 700, and 3% above 700.

Requirements: The SAT I or ACT is required. In addition, SAT II: Subject tests are recommended. Applicants must graduate from an accredited secondary school, have a GED, or meet state equivalency requirements for home schooling. A minimum of 16 academic units are required, including 4 in English, 3 in math, 2 to 3 in social studies, and 2 each in a foreign language and science. Essays and interviews are recommended. A GPA of 2.0 is required. AP and CLEP credits are accepted. Important factors in the admissions decision are advanced placement or honor courses, extracurricular activities record, and leadership record.

Procedure: Freshmen are admitted fall and spring. Entrance exams should be taken in the junior or senior year. There are early decision, early admissions, and deferred admissions plans. There is a rolling admissions plan. Early decision applications should be filed by November 15; regular applications, by April 15 for fall entry and December 15 for spring entry, along with a $25 fee. Notification of early decision is sent December 15; regular decision, on a rolling basis. 43 early decision candidates were accepted for the 2003-2004 class. A waiting list is an active part of the admissions procedure. Applications are accepted on-line through www.mbc.edu.

Transfer: 42 transfer students enrolled in 2002-2003. Transfer applicants must have a 2.0 GPA from the institution where they are currently enrolled. 66 of 132 credits required for the bachelor's degree must be completed at MBC.

Visiting: There are regularly scheduled orientations for prospective students, consisting of a tour, an interview, scheduled classes upon request, as well as athletic tours. There are guides for informal visits and visitors may sit in on classes and stay overnight. To schedule a visit, contact the Admissions Office.

Financial Aid: In 2003-2004, 99% of all full-time freshmen and 95% of continuing full-time students received some form of financial aid. 78% of full-time freshmen and 60% of continuing full-time students received need-based aid. The average freshman award was $20,214. Need-based scholarships or need-based grants averaged $6500 ($11,850 maximum); need-based self-help aid (loans and jobs) averaged $2000 (maximum); and non-need-based awards and non-need-based scholarships averaged $7000 ($9350 maximum). 69% of undergraduates work part time. Average annual earnings from campus work are $2000. The average financial indebtedness of the 2003 graduate was $18,625. The FAFSA and the state aid form are required. The deadline for filing freshman financial aid applications for fall entry is May 1.

International Students: There are 15 international students enrolled. The school actively recruits these students. They must score 500 on the written TOEFL and also take the SAT I or the ACT.

Computers: The mainframe is an IBM/400. More than 100 PCs are located throughout the campus. There are public workstations in every classroom building. All students may access the system. There are no time limits and no fees.

Graduates: From July 1, 2002 to June 30, 2003, 260 bachelor's degrees were awarded. The most popular majors were business administration (18%), sociology (14%), and psychology (11%). In an average class, 3% graduate in 3 years or less, 52% graduate in 4 years or less, and 57% graduate in 5 years or less. 12 companies recruited on campus in a recent year. Of a recent graduating class, 25% were enrolled in graduate school within 6 months of graduation and 77% were employed.

Admissions Contact: Jacquelyn D. Elliott-Wonderley, Dean of Admissions and Financial Aid. E-mail: admit@mbc.edu Web: www.mbc.edu

MARY WASHINGTON COLLEGE   E-2
Fredericksburg, VA 22401-5358   (540) 654-2000
                              (800) 468-5614; Fax: (540) 654-1857

Full-time: 1193 men, 2380 women	**Faculty:** 193; IIB, av$
Part-time: 197 men, 415 women	**Ph.Ds:** 87%
Graduate: 183 men, 424 women	**Student/Faculty:** 19 to 1
Year: semesters, summer session	**Tuition:** $4688 ($12,436)
Application Deadline: February 1	**Room & Board:** $5478
Freshman Class: 4472 applied, 2676 accepted, 888 enrolled	
SAT I Verbal/Math: 617/606	**ACT:** 27 **HIGHLY COMPETITIVE**

Mary Washington College, founded in 1908, is a public liberal arts and sciences institution. In addition to regional accreditation, MWC has baccalaureate program accreditation with NASM. The library contains 355,391 volumes and 575,709 microform items, and subscribes to 3481 periodicals. Computerized library services include the card catalog, inter-library loans, database searching, and Internet access. Special learning facilities include an art gallery, radio station, center for historic preservation, and Leidecker Center for Asian Studies. The 176-acre campus is in a small town 50 miles south of Washington, D.C. and 50 miles north of Richmond. Including any residence halls, there are 42 buildings.

Student Life: 65% of undergraduates are from Virginia. Students are from 30 states, 7 foreign countries, and Canada. 89% are from public schools. 88% are white. The average age of freshmen is 18; all undergraduates, 20. 15% do not continue beyond their first year; 78% remain to graduate.

Housing: 2500 students can be accommodated in college housing, which includes single-sex and coed dorms and on-campus apartments. In addition, there is a foreign language floor of a hall, an international house, community service area, and special-interest houses. On-campus housing is guaranteed for freshman and sophomore years and is available on a lottery system for upperclassmen. 70% of students live on campus; of those, 80% remain on campus on weekends. Upperclassmen may keep cars.

Activities: There are no fraternities or sororities. There are 96 groups on campus, including art, bagpipe band, cheerleading, choir, chorale, chorus, computers, dance, debate, drama, ethnic, gay, honors, international, jazz band, literary magazine, musical theater, newspaper, orchestra, photography, political, professional, radio and TV, religious, social, social service, student government, and yearbook. Popular campus events include Grill on the Hill, Junior Ring Dance, and a Multicultural Festival.

Sports: There are 10 intercollegiate sports for men and 12 for women, and 18 intramural sports for men and 18 for women. Facilities include a 6-lane, 25-yard indoor pool, regulation basketball and volleyball courts, a weight room, batting cages, training rooms, playing fields for all outdoor sports, a running course, handball/racquetball courts, an 8-lane, 400-meter track, and a 20,000-square-foot fitness and recreation facility.

Disabled Students: 65% of the campus is accessible. Wheelchair ramps, elevators, special parking, specially equipped rest rooms, lowered drinking fountains, and lowered telephones are available.

Services: Counseling and information services are available, as is tutoring in most subjects. There is a reader service for the blind, a writing center, a center for the visually impaired, and a speaking center.

Campus Safety and Security: Measures include 24-hour foot and vehicle patrol, self-defense education, security escort services, and informal discussions. There are pamphlets/posters/films, emergency telephones, and lighted pathways/sidewalks.

Programs of Study: MWC confers B.A., B.S., B.L.S., and B.P.S. degrees. Master's degrees are also awarded. Bachelor's degrees are awarded in BIOLOGICAL SCIENCE (biology/biological science), BUSINESS (business administration and management), COMMUNICATIONS AND THE ARTS (art history and appreciation, classics, dramatic arts, English, French, German, historic preservation, languages, Latin, music, Spanish, and studio art), COMPUTER AND PHYSICAL SCIENCE (chemistry, computer science, geology, mathematics, and physics), ENGINEERING AND ENVIRONMENTAL DESIGN (environmental science), HEALTH PROFESSIONS (predentistry, premedicine, and preveterinary science), SOCIAL SCIENCE (American studies, economics, geography, history, international relations, philosophy, political science/government, prelaw, psychology, religion, and sociology). Historic preservation is the strongest academically. Business administration, psychology, and biology are the largest.

Required: To graduate, students must complete 122 credit hours and a minimum GPA of 2.0. Hours required in the major vary. General education curriculum includes courses in composition, math, lab science, arts/literature, Western civilization, social science, foreign language, phys ed, and computer technology. Additionally, students take thematic courses across the curriculum, with requirements including writing intensive, speaking intensive, global awareness, environmental awareness, and race/gender intensive courses. A thesis is required in some majors and programs of study.

Special: Study abroad anywhere in the world, a Washington semester, and credit for off-campus work experience are available. The college offers dual majors, work-study programs, student-designed majors, and pass/fail options. More than 500 internships for credit are also available. Teacher licensure preparation is offered for elementary and secondary education. Elementary education is a 5-year masters degree program. There are 20 national honor societies, including Phi Beta Kappa.

Faculty/Classroom: 55% of faculty are male; 45%, female. All teach undergraduates. No introductory courses are taught by graduate students. The average class size in an introductory lecture is 27; in a laboratory, 20; and in a regular course, 21.

Admissions: 60% of the 2003-2004 applicants were accepted. The SAT I scores for the 2003-2004 freshman class were: Verbal--4% below 500, 33% between 500 and 599, 52% between 600 and 700, and 11% above 700; Math--4% below 500, 39% between 500 and 599, 49% between 600 and 700, and 8% above 700. 70% of the current freshmen were in the top fifth of their class; 94% were in the top two fifths. 7 freshmen graduated first in their class.

Requirements: The SAT I or ACT is required. In addition, applicants must be graduates of an accredited secondary school or hold the GED. The Admissions Committee recommends that applicants complete 4 years of each of math, English, foreign language, science, and social studies. An SAT II: Subject test is strongly recommended. Application essays are required. AP and CLEP credits are accepted. Important factors in the admissions decision are advanced placement or honor courses, evidence of special talent, and recommendations by school officials.

Procedure: Freshmen are admitted fall and spring. Entrance exams should be taken by January of the senior year. Applications should be filed by January 15 for honors, February 1 for fall entry and November 1 for spring entry, along with a $35 fee. Notification is sent April 1. 127 early decision candidates were accepted for the 2003-2004 class. 300 applicants were on the 2003 waiting list; 150 were admitted. Applications are accepted on-line through CollegeNET and the college's web site.

Transfer: 173 transfer students enrolled in 2002-2003. The college recommends that applicants for transfer have a minimum GPA of 3.0 and a recommended 30 college credits. The SAT I and high school transcripts are required. Graduates from the Virginia community colleges are given preference for admission. 30 of 122 credits required for the bachelor's degree must be completed at MWC.

Visiting: There are regularly scheduled orientations for prospective students, including information sessions, available Monday through Friday at 10:30 A.M. and 2 P.M., followed by a student-guided tour, and 2 Saturday open houses each semester. Visitors may sit in on classes and stay overnight. To schedule a visit, contact the Office of Admissions at *admit@mwc.edu.*

Financial Aid: In 2003-2004, 65% of all full-time freshmen and 63% of continuing full-time students received some form of financial aid. 40% of full-time freshmen and 45% of continuing full-time students received need-based aid. The average freshman award was $4500. Need-based scholarships or need-based grants averaged $2245 ($15,600 maximum); need-based self-help aid (loans and jobs) averaged $2400 ($4170 maximum); and non-need-based awards and non-need-based private scholarships averaged $1550 ($12,000 maximum). 25% of undergraduates work part time. Average annual earnings from campus work are $1600. The average financial indebtedness of the 2003 graduate was $13,100. The FAFSA is required. The deadline for filing freshman financial aid applications for fall entry is March 1.

International Students: There are 32 international students enrolled. They must score 560 on the written TOEFL or 230 on the electronic version and also take the SAT I or the ACT. It is recommended that applicants take the SAT II: Writing test and 2 others.

Computers: The mainframe is an HP 3000/969. MWC has a fiber-optic network. All students can access the Internet and the Web from residence hall rooms. Several 24-hour computer labs are available for student use. All students may access the system. There are no time limits and no fees.

Graduates: From July 1, 2002 to June 30, 2003, 901 bachelor's degrees were awarded. The most popular majors were business administration (15%), English (11%), and biology (10%). In an average class, 62% graduate in 4 years or less, 71% graduate in 5 years or less, and 73% graduate in 6 years or less. 90 companies recruited on campus in 2002-2003. Of the 2002 graduating class, 26% were enrolled in graduate school within 6 months of graduation and 94% were employed.

Admissions Contact: Dr. Martin A. Wilder, Vice-President for Enrollment. E-mail: *admit@mwc.edu* Web: *www.mwc.edu*

MARYMOUNT UNIVERSITY
Arlington, VA 22207-4299

E-2

(703) 284-1500
(800) 548-7638; Fax: (703) 522-0349

Full-time: 444 men, 1281 women	**Faculty:** 106; IIA, +$
Part-time: 117 men, 409 women	**Ph.D.s:** 84%
Graduate: 382 men, 1229 women	**Student/Faculty:** 16 to 1
Year: semesters, summer session	**Tuition:** $16,438
Application Deadline: open	**Room & Board:** $7230
Freshman Class: 1647 applied, 1349 accepted, 386 enrolled	
SAT I Verbal/Math: 505/492	**ACT:** 20 COMPETITIVE

Marymount University, established in 1950, is a private, comprehensive Catholic university offering undergraduate and graduate programs through four schools: arts and sciences, business administration, education and human services, and health professions. There are 4 undergraduate and 4 graduate schools. In addition to regional accreditation, Marymount has baccalaureate program accreditation with ABA, ACBSP, APTA, CACREP, CAPTE, FIDER, NCATE, and NLN. The library contains 187,939 volumes, 322,472 microform items, and 1035 audio/video tapes/CDs, and subscribes to 969 periodicals. Computerized library services include the card catalog, interlibrary loans, database searching, and Internet access. Special learning facilities include a learning resource center, art gallery, and an instructional media center. The 21-acre campus is in a suburban area 6 miles southwest of Washington, D.C. Including any residence halls, there are 13 buildings.

Student Life: 56% of undergraduates are from Virginia. Students are from 40 states, 57 foreign countries, and Canada. 68% are from public schools. 47% are white; 14% African American; 11% Hispanic. 58% are Catholic; 26% Protestant. The average age of freshmen is 18; all undergraduates, 24. 31% do not continue beyond their first year; 59% remain to graduate.

Housing: 671 students can be accommodated in college housing, which includes single-sex and coed dorms. On-campus housing is guaranteed for the freshman year only and is available on a lottery system for upperclassmen. 70% of students commute. All students may keep cars.

Activities: There are no fraternities or sororities. There are 30 groups on campus, including art, cheerleading, choir, chorus, dance, drama, ethnic, honors, international, literary magazine, newspaper, political, professional, religious, social, social service, student government, and yearbook. Popular campus events include Portfolio in Motion (Fashion Show), Snowball (Winter Formal Dance), and International Week.

Sports: There are 6 intercollegiate sports for men and 6 for women, and 5 intramural sports for men and 5 for women. Facilities include a student center with a 1000-seat sports arena, renovated pool, fitness center, and recreation gym.

Disabled Students: 75% of the campus is accessible. Wheelchair ramps, elevators, special parking, specially equipped rest rooms, special class scheduling, lowered drinking fountains, and lowered telephones are available.

Services: Counseling and information services are available, as is tutoring in most subjects. There is a reader service for the blind and remedial math, reading, and writing.

Campus Safety and Security: Measures include 24-hour foot and vehicle patrol, security escort services, shuttle buses, and emergency telephones. There are lighted pathways/sidewalks.

Programs of Study: Marymount confers B.A., B.S., B.B.A., and B.S.N. degrees. Associate and master's degrees are also awarded. Bachelor's degrees are awarded in BIOLOGICAL SCIENCE (biology/biological science), BUSINESS (accounting, banking and finance, business administration and management, business economics, business law, fashion merchandising, human resources, management science, marketing/retailing/merchandising, and retailing), COMMUNICATIONS AND THE ARTS (communications, English, and graphic design), COMPUTER AND PHYSICAL SCIENCE (computer science, information sciences and systems, and mathematics), ENGINEERING AND ENVIRONMENTAL DESIGN (environmental science and interior design), HEALTH PROFESSIONS (health science and nursing), SOCIAL SCIENCE (criminal justice, economics, fashion design and technology, history, human services, liberal arts/general studies, paralegal studies, philosophy, physical fitness/movement, political science/government, psychology, sociology, and theological studies). Psychology, business administration/management, and interior design are the strongest academically. Nursing, psychology, and interior design are the largest.

Required: To graduate, students must complete core curriculum requirements in communications, humanities, math, and science, and social sciences. Specific required courses include English Composition I and II and Introduction to Social Science. Students must earn 120 credits, with 39 to 60 credits in the major, and maintain a 2.0 GPA.

Special: Students may cross-register with the Consortium of Universities of the Washington Metropolitan Area. They are required to complete an internship in Washington or London. Marymount offers dual and student-designed majors, an accelerated nursing degree and interior design, a 3+3 program in physical therapy, study abroad, and nondegree study. There are 10 national honor societies.

Faculty/Classroom: 42% of faculty are male; 58%, female. 81% teach undergraduates. No introductory courses are taught by graduate students. The average class size in an introductory lecture is 23; in a laboratory, 12; and in a regular course, 19.

Admissions: 82% of the 2003-2004 applicants were accepted. The SAT I scores for the 2003-2004 freshman class were: Verbal--44% below 500, 42% between 500 and 599, 13% between 600 and 700, and 1% above 700; Math--52% below 500, 38% between 500 and 599, 9% between 600 and 700, and 1% above 700. The ACT scores were 65% below 21, 20% between 21 and 23, 7% between 24 and 26, 5% between 27 and 28, and 3% above 28. 23% of the current freshmen were in the top fifth of their class; 63% were in the top two fifths.

Requirements: The SAT I or ACT is required. In addition, applicants must graduate from an accredited secondary school or have a GED. Marymount requires 15 academic credits and 15 Carnegie units and strongly recommends biology and chemistry for nursing candidates. Essays and interviews are recommended. A GPA of 2.0 is required. AP and CLEP credits are accepted. Important factors in the admissions decision are advanced placement or honor courses, extracurricular activities record, and evidence of special talent.

Procedure: Freshmen are admitted to all sessions. There is a rolling admissions plan. Application deadlines are open. Application fee is $35. 17 applicants were on the 2003 waiting list; 2 were admitted. Applications are accepted on-line through the school's web site.

Transfer: 328 transfer students enrolled in 2002-2003. Applicants with 30 or more credits must have a minimum GPA of 2.0. Those with fewer than 30 must also meet freshman requirements. 36 of 120 credits required for the bachelor's degree must be completed at Marymount.

Visiting: There are regularly scheduled orientations for prospective students, Including Campus Visit Days, Information Nights, and new-student summer orientation. There are guides for informal visits and visitors may sit in on classes and stay overnight. To schedule a visit, contact Mary Kay Eldridge at (703) 284-1511 or admissions@marymount.edu.

Financial Aid: In 2003-2004, 95% of all full-time freshmen and 80% of continuing full-time students received some form of financial aid. 55% of full-time freshmen and 54% of continuing full-time students received need-based aid. The average freshman award was $15,445. Need-based scholarships or need-based grants averaged $6543 ($23,938 maximum); need-based self-help aid (loans and jobs) averaged $4017 ($6625 maximum); and non-need-based awards and non-need-based scholarships averaged $8102 ($16,210 maximum). 22% of undergraduates work part time. Average annual earnings from campus work are $1800. The average financial indebtedness of the 2002 graduate was $14,915. Marymount is a member of CSS. The FAFSA is required. The deadline for filing freshman financial aid applications for fall entry is March 1.

International Students: There are 166 international students enrolled. The school actively recruits these students. They must score 500 on the written TOEFL.

Computers: There are 260 Novell-networked PCs available at computer center labs throughout the campus. A RISC architecture minicomputer and a graphic design (CAD) lab with 3 HP scanners are also available. All residence halls have a PC connection in each room. Students have access to a CD-ROM network, UNIX workstations, the Internet, and 9600-baud dial-in lines. All students may access the system. There are no time limits. The fee is $5.75 per credit hour, up to $60 per semester.

Graduates: From July 1, 2002 to June 30, 2003, 371 bachelor's degrees were awarded. The most popular majors were psychology (12%), computer information systems (10%), and communications (7%). In an average class, 1% graduate in 3 years or less, 50% graduate in 4 years or less, 59% graduate in 5 years or less, and 63% graduate in 6 years or less. 60 companies recruited on campus in 2002-2003.

Admissions Contact: Chris E. Domes, Vice President for Enrollment Management and Student Services. A video is available.
E-mail: admissions@marymount.edu Web: www.marymount.edu

NORFOLK STATE UNIVERSITY

Norfolk, VA 23504 F-4
(757) 823-8396; Fax: (757) 823-2078

Full-time: 1807 men, 2970 women	**Faculty:** 299; II A, --$
Part-time: 439 men, 823 women	**Ph.D.s:** 63%
Graduate: 156 men, 651 women	**Student/Faculty:** 16 to 1
Year: semesters, summer session	**Tuition:** $3840 ($13,260)
Application Deadline: July 15	**Room & Board:** $5882
Freshman Class: 4651 applied, 3297 accepted, 1157 enrolled	
SAT I Verbal/Math: 454/444	**ACT:** 19 **LESS COMPETITIVE**

Norfolk State University, founded in 1935, is an independent institution offering undergraduate and graduate programs in the liberal arts and sciences, business education, health-related professions, and vocational, technical, and professional training. There are 5 undergraduate schools and 1 graduate school. In addition to regional accreditation, NSU has baccalaureate program accreditation with AACSB, ACEJMC, ACS, ADA, APA, CSAB, CSWE, NAIT, NASM, NCATE, and NLN. The library

contains 341,068 volumes, 60,882 microform items, and 27 audio/video tapes/CDs, and subscribes to 1186 periodicals. Computerized library services include the card catalog, interlibrary loans, database searching, and Internet access. Special learning facilities include a learning resource center, art gallery, planetarium, radio station, TV station, and a musical theater. The 134-acre campus is in an urban area in the port city of Norfolk. Including any residence halls, there are 31 buildings.

Student Life: 72% of undergraduates are from Virginia. Students are from 43 states and 38 foreign countries. 89% are African American. The average age of freshmen is 18; all undergraduates, 23. 30% do not continue beyond their first year; 27% remain to graduate.

Housing: 1944 students can be accommodated in college housing, which includes single-sex dorms. On-campus housing is available on a first-come, first-served basis. 69% of students commute. Alcohol is not permitted. Upperclassmen may keep cars.

Activities: 10% of men belong to 12 national fraternities; 10% of women belong to 8 national sororities. There are 112 groups on campus, including art, band, cheerleading, choir, chorus, computers, dance, debate, drama, drill team, ethnic, honors, international, jazz band, literary magazine, marching band, newspaper, pep band, political, professional, radio and TV, religious, social, social service, student government, and yearbook. Popular campus events include Martin Luther King Commemorative Activity and Black History Month Activities.

Sports: There are 6 intercollegiate sports for men and 7 for women, and 8 intramural sports for men and 7 for women. Facilities include a stadium and track seating 28,088, an arena seating 7500, baseball and softball fields, a gym, a swimming pool, tennis courts, and a bowling alley.

Disabled Students: 80% of the campus is accessible. Wheelchair ramps, elevators, special parking, specially equipped rest rooms, special class scheduling, lowered telephones, and special housing are available.

Services: Counseling and information services are available, as is tutoring in most subjects. There is a reader service for the blind.

Campus Safety and Security: Measures include 24-hour foot and vehicle patrol, security escort services, shuttle buses, and informal discussions. There are pamphlets/posters/films, emergency telephones, lighted pathways/sidewalks, and town meetings.

Programs of Study: NSU confers B.A., B.S., B.Mus., and B.S.W. degrees. Associate, master's, and doctoral degrees are also awarded. Bachelor's degrees are awarded in BIOLOGICAL SCIENCE (biology/biological science and environmental biology), BUSINESS (accounting, banking and finance, and hospitality management services), COMMUNICATIONS AND THE ARTS (communications, English, fine arts, graphic design, and journalism), COMPUTER AND PHYSICAL SCIENCE (chemistry, computer science, mathematics, and physics), EDUCATION (business, early childhood, music, and technical), ENGINEERING AND ENVIRONMENTAL DESIGN (computer technology, construction technology, drafting and design technology, electrical/electronics engineering technology, and military science), HEALTH PROFESSIONS (exercise science, health care administration, health science, medical records administration/services, medical technology, and nursing), SOCIAL SCIENCE (history, interdisciplinary studies, political science/government, psychology, public administration, and sociology). Social work and computer science are the strongest academically. Business, computer science, and nursing are the largest.

Required: Students must complete at least 120 semester hours with a minimum 2.0 GPA, including general education courses such as communication, humanities, social science, natural science, health ed, phys ed, and computer literacy. They must also demonstrate writing competence.

Special: NSU offers cross-registration with other institutions in the Tidewater Consortium, a student-exchange program with Old Dominion University, co-op education, a second baccalaureate degree with a minimum of 30 additional semester hours earned, a B.A.-B.S. degree, and a general studies degree. Credit for military experience is possible. There are 14 national honor societies, a freshman honors program, and 7 departmental honors programs.

Faculty/Classroom: 55% of faculty are male; 45%, female. No introductory courses are taught by graduate students. The average class size in an introductory lecture is 20; in a laboratory, 16; and in a regular course, 17.

Admissions: 71% of the 2003-2004 applicants were accepted. The SAT I scores for the 2003-2004 freshman class were: Verbal--79% below 500, 17% between 500 and 599, 3% between 600 and 700, and 1% above 700; Math--81% below 500, 16% between 500 and 599, and 3% between 600 and 700. The ACT scores were 83% below 21, 11% between 21 and 23, and 6% between 24 and 26. 16% of the current freshmen were in the top fifth of their class; 37% were in the top two fifths.

Requirements: The SAT I is required. In addition, applicants should be graduates of an accredited secondary school or have the GED equivalent and have completed 22 academic units: 4 in English, 3 each in history/social studies, math, and science, and 9 in electives. Nursing applicants must meet additional requirements. A GPA of 2.0 is required. AP and CLEP credits are accepted.

Procedure: Freshmen are admitted fall, spring, and summer. Entrance exams should be taken by March of the senior year. There is a deferred admissions plan and a rolling admissions plan. Early decision applications should be filed by June 1; regular applications, by July 15 for fall entry. The fall 2003 application fee was $25. Notification is sent on a rolling basis within 2 weeks of receipt of credentials. Applications are accepted on-line.

Transfer: 353 transfer students enrolled in 2002-2003. Transfers must meet freshman admissions criteria. 30 credits of 120 required for the bachelor's degree must be completed at NSU.

Visiting: There are regularly scheduled orientations for prospective students, including registration, a general information session, visits to academic departments, admissions, and a tour. There are guides for informal visits and visitors may sit in on classes and stay overnight. To schedule a visit, contact the Admissions Office at *admissions@nsu.edu.*

Financial Aid: In 2003-2004, 93% of all full-time freshmen and 88% of continuing full-time students received some form of financial aid. 85% of full-time freshmen and 81% of continuing full-time students received need-based aid. The average freshman award was $9671. Need-based scholarships or need-based grants averaged $5598 ($19,142 maximum); need-based self-help aid (loans and jobs) averaged $4481 ($14,705 maximum); and non-need-based athletic scholarships averaged $9181 ($19,142 maximum). 6% of undergraduates work part time. Average annual earnings from campus work are $1926. The average financial indebtedness of the 2003 graduate was $15,467. The FAFSA and the SAR are required. The deadline for filing freshman financial aid applications for fall entry is April 15.

International Students: There are 37 international students enrolled. The school actively recruits these students. They must score 500 on the written TOEFL and also take the SAT I or the ACT, scoring 800 on the SAT I.

Computers: The mainframes are an IBM RS6000 S7A, S80, HP9000, and HP3000. There are 96 terminals in the academic center and at satellite locations campuswide for faculty and students, plus 512 PCs in 39 labs, dial-in access, Internet access, and system software. There are 757 PCs in classrooms. All students may access the system 24 hours a day, 7 days a week. There are no time limits. The fee is $30. It is strongly recommended that all students have a personal computer. A Gateway is recommended.

Graduates: From July 1, 2002 to June 30, 2003, 820 bachelor's degrees were awarded. The most popular majors were interdisciplinary studies (23%), business (11%), and psychology (8%). In an average class, 10% graduate in 4 years or less, 22% graduate in 5 years or less, and 28% graduate in 6 years or less. 172 companies recruited on campus in 2002-2003. Of the 2002 graduating class, 5% were enrolled in graduate school within 6 months of graduation.

Admissions Contact: Michelle Marable, Director of Admissions. A video is available. E-mail: *admissions@nsu.edu* Web: *www.nsu.edu*

OLD DOMINION UNIVERSITY
Norfolk, VA 23529-0050

F-4

(757) 683-3648
(800) 348-7926; Fax: (757) 683-3255

Full-time: 4062 men, 5553 women	Faculty: 584; I, --$
Part-time: 1406 men, 2208 women	Ph.D.s: 81%
Graduate: 1641 men, 2071 women	Student/Faculty: 16 to 1
Year: semesters, summer session	Tuition: $4928 ($14,078)
Application Deadline: March 15	Room & Board: $5513
Freshman Class: 5425 applied, 4444 accepted, 2047 enrolled	
SAT I Verbal/Math: 520/510	ACT: 19 COMPETITIVE

Old Dominion University, founded in 1930, is a public institution with programs in arts and letters, business and public administration, engineering, education, sciences, and health sciences. There are 6 undergraduate and 6 graduate schools. In addition to regional accreditation, ODU has baccalaureate program accreditation with AACSB, ABET, APTA, ASHA, CAHEA, CCNE, NASM, NCATE, NLN, and NRPA. The 3 libraries contain 985,801 volumes, 1,752,613 microform items, and 40,628 audio/video tapes/CDs, and subscribe to 9525 periodicals. Computerized library services include the card catalog, interlibrary loans, database searching, and Internet access. Special learning facilities include a learning resource center, art gallery, planetarium, radio station, music library, art library, and digital library. The 188-acre campus is in an urban area in the Norfolk/Hampton Roads Metropolitan region. Including any residence halls, there are 107 buildings.

Student Life: 90% of undergraduates are from Virginia. Students are from 33 states, 69 foreign countries, and Canada. 36% are from public schools. 62% are white; 24% African American. The average age of freshmen is 19; all undergraduates, 22. 29% do not continue beyond their first year; 71% remain to graduate.

Housing: 2380 students can be accommodated in college housing, which includes coed dorms and on-campus apartments. In addition, there are honors houses and honors, international, coeducational, and quiet-study floors. On-campus housing is available on a first-come, first-served basis. 69% of students commute. Alcohol is not permitted. All students may keep cars.

Activities: 5% of men belong to 11 national fraternities; 4% of women belong to 9 national sororities. There are 220 groups on campus, including cheerleading, chess, choir, chorale, computers, dance, debate, drama, ethnic, forensics, gay, honors, international, jazz band, literary magazine, musical theater, newspaper, pep band, political, professional, radio and TV, religious, social, student government, and yearbook. Popular campus events include concerts, fashion shows/pageants, and movies.

Sports: There are 8 intercollegiate sports for men and 8 for women, and 13 intramural sports for men and 13 for women. Facilities include an arena, a playing field, a baseball complex, 2 pools, intramural fields, a soccer stadium, a sailing center, and a convocation center.

Disabled Students: 90% of the campus is accessible. Wheelchair ramps, elevators, special parking, specially equipped rest rooms, special class scheduling, lowered drinking fountains, and automatic doors are available.

Services: Counseling and information services are available, as is tutoring in some subjects, including English and sciences. There is a reader service for the blind and remedial math and writing.

Campus Safety and Security: Measures include 24-hour foot and vehicle patrol, self-defense education, security escort services, and informal discussions. There are pamphlets/posters/films, emergency telephones, lighted pathways/sidewalks, and a bicycle patrol.

Programs of Study: ODU confers B.A., B.S., B.F.A., B.M., B.S.B.A., B.S.C.E., B.S.C.O.M.E., B.S.C.S., B.S.D.H., B.S.E.E., B.S.E.H., B.S.E.N.V.E., B.S.E.T., B.S.H.S., B.S.M.E., B.S.M.T., B.S.N., and B.S.N.M.T. degrees. Master's and doctoral degrees are also awarded. Bachelor's degrees are awarded in BIOLOGICAL SCIENCE (biochemistry, biology/biological science, and marine science), BUSINESS (accounting, banking and finance, business administration and management, electronic business, fashion merchandising, international business management, management information systems, marketing management, recreation and leisure services, and sports management), COMMUNICATIONS AND THE ARTS (art history and appreciation, communications, dance, dramatic arts, English, fine arts, French, German, graphic design, journalism, music, music performance, music theory and composition, performing arts, Spanish, and studio art), COMPUTER AND PHYSICAL SCIENCE (chemistry, computer science, earth science, geology, information sciences and systems, mathematics, and physics), EDUCATION (art, elementary, English, foreign languages, industrial arts, mathematics, music, physical, science, secondary, and social studies), ENGINEERING AND ENVIRONMENTAL DESIGN (civil engineering, civil engineering technology, computer engineering, electrical/electronics engineering, electrical/electronics engineering technology, engineering technology, environmental engineering, mechanical engineering, mechanical engineering technology, and nuclear engineering technology), HEALTH PROFESSIONS (dental hygiene, environmental health science, health science, medical technology, nuclear medical technology, nursing, and speech pathology/audiology), SOCIAL SCIENCE (anthropology, criminal justice, economics, geography, history, human services, interdisciplinary studies, international studies, philosophy, political science/government, psychology, sociology, and women's studies). Criminal justice, English, and accounting are the strongest academically. Biology and interdisciplinary studies (education teacher preparation) are the largest.

Required: At least 120 credits, with a minimum GPA of 2.0, are required to graduate. Students must complete the university's general education program, consisting of specific skills and perspectives courses outside the student's major. English composition is a required course, and students must pass a writing proficiency exam.

Special: Old Dominion offers cross-registration with schools in the Tidewater Consortium program. There are co-op programs, guaranteed internships, study abroad in 40 countries, and a work-study program. Students may take a B.A.-B.S. degree in engineering and liberal arts. An interdisciplinary program, dual majors, accelerated degrees, 3-2 engineering degrees in business and engineering, nondegree study, pass/fail options, and credit for military and life experience are available. There is a 5-year advanced degree business program, and a joint program in medicine guarantees a seat at Eastern Virginia Medical School after the B.S. There are 19 national honor societies, including Phi Beta Kappa, a freshman honors program, and all departments have honors programs.

Faculty/Classroom: 65% of faculty are male; 35%, female. 75% teach undergraduates. The average class size in an introductory lecture is 37; in a laboratory, 23; and in a regular course, 26.

Admissions: 82% of the 2003-2004 applicants were accepted. The SAT I scores for the 2003-2004 freshman class were: Verbal--38% below 500, 45% between 500 and 599, 15% between 600 and 700, and 2% above 700; Math--40% below 500, 42% between 500 and 599, 16% between 600 and 700, and 2% above 700. The ACT scores were 75% below 21, 18% between 21 and 23, 5% between 24 and 26, and 2% between 27 and 28. 33% of the current freshmen were in the top fifth of their class; 69% were in the top two fifths. 5 freshmen graduated first in their class.

Requirements: The SAT I or ACT is required. In addition, applicants must be graduates of an accredited secondary school. The GED is accepted. Applicants should have completed 4 years of math, and 3 years each of English, foreign languages, science, and social science. An essay and an interview are recommended. A list of extracurriclar activities is required. A GPA of 2.5 is required. AP and CLEP credits are accepted. Important factors in the admissions decision are advanced placement or honor courses, recommendations by school officials, and extracurricular activities record.

Procedure: Freshmen are admitted fall and spring. Entrance exams should be taken in May of the junior year or November/December of the senior year. There are early admissions, deferred admissions, and rolling admissions plans. Applications should be filed by March 15 for fall entry, October 1 for spring entry, and March 1 for summer entry, along with a $30 fee. Notification is sent on a rolling basis. Applications are accepted on-line through CollegeNET.

Transfer: 2047 transfer students enrolled in 2002-2003. Applicants must have a minimum GPA of 2.2 and must have at least 24 semester hour credits. Applicants with fewer semester hours must meet the same requirements as freshmen. 30 of 120 credits required for the bachelor's degree must be completed at ODU.

Visiting: There are regularly scheduled orientations for prospective students, consisting of campus tours, available Monday through Friday at 10 A.M., Monday and Friday at 2 P.M., and Saturday at 11 A.M. Special tours can be arranged with the Office of Admissions. There are guides for informal visits and visitors may sit in on classes. To schedule a visit, contact the Admissions Office at (757) 683-3685 or *admit@odu.edu*.

Financial Aid: In 2003-2004, 74% of all full-time freshmen and 76% of continuing full-time students received some form of financial aid. 61% of full-time freshmen and 65% of continuing full-time students received need-based aid. The average freshman award was $9450. Need-based scholarships or need-based grants averaged $4567 ($14,077 maximum); need-based self-help aid (loans and jobs) averaged $2536 ($2625 maximum); non-need-based athletic scholarships averaged $9653 ($14,077 maximum); and other non-need-based awards and non-need-based scholarships averaged $2694 ($14,077 maximum). The average financial indebtedness of the 2003 graduate was $16,750. The FAFSA is required. The priority date for freshman financial aid applications for fall entry is February 15. The deadline for filing freshman financial aid applications for fall entry is March 15.

International Students: There are 283 international students enrolled. The school actively recruits these students. They must score 550 on the written TOEFL or 213 on the electronic version and also take the college's own test. Students receiving 480 on the SAT I Verbal or completing ELC Bridge Program don't have to take either test.

Computers: There are computer labs at various locations on campus. The system also may be accessed via modem from home or dorm rooms. All students may access the system 24 hours a day. There are no time limits and no fees.

Graduates: From July 1, 2002 to June 30, 2003, 2445 bachelor's degrees were awarded. The most popular majors were human services counseling (7%), psychology (7%), and information systems (6%). In an average class, 17% graduate in 4 years or less, 35% graduate in 5 years or less, and 42% graduate in 6 years or less. 350 companies recruited on campus in 2002-2003.

Admissions Contact: Alice McAdory, Director of Admissions. A video is available. E-mail: *admit@odu.edu* Web: *www.admissions.odu.edu*

RADFORD UNIVERSITY
Radford, VA 24141-6972
C-3

(540) 831-5371
(800) 890-4265; Fax: (540) 831-5138

Full-time: 3224 men, 4495 women	**Faculty:** 358
Part-time: 153 men, 295 women	**Ph.D.s:** 83%
Graduate: 244 men, 808 women	**Student/Faculty:** 22 to 1
Year: semesters, summer session	**Tuition:** $3200 ($9300)
Application Deadline: open	**Room & Board:** $5300
Freshman Class: 6388 applied, 4708 accepted, 1806 enrolled	
SAT I Verbal/Math: 500/490	**COMPETITIVE**

Radford University, founded in 1910, is a public comprehensive institution with a diverse curricula in arts and sciences, business and economics, education and human development, nursing and health services, and visual and performing arts. Some figures in the above capsule and in this profile are approximate. There are 6 undergraduate schools and 1 graduate school. In addition to regional accreditation, RU has baccalaureate program accreditation with AACSB, ADA, ASLHA, CACREP, CSAB, CSWE, NASM, NCATE, NLN, and NRPA. The library contains 329,644 volumes, 1,456,781 microform items, and 12,614 audio/video tapes/CDs, and subscribes to 2966 periodicals. Computerized library services include the card catalog, interlibrary loans, and database searching. Special learning facilities include a learning resource center, art gallery, planetarium, radio station, TV station, and a 376-acre conservancy used for studies in ecology, botany, mapping geological features as a model in resource management and maintenance formation on actual building

techniques, and cultural and oral history. The 177-acre campus is in a small town 36 miles southwest of Roanoke. Including any residence halls, there are 85 buildings.

Student Life: 88% of undergraduates are from Virginia. Students are from 45 states, 65 foreign countries, and Canada. 96% are from public schools. 89% are white. The average age of freshmen is 18; all undergraduates, 21. 21% do not continue beyond their first year; 52% remain to graduate.

Housing: 3230 students can be accommodated in college housing, which includes single-sex and coed dorms and off-campus apartments. In addition, there are honors houses and special-interest houses. On-campus housing is guaranteed for the freshman year only and is available on a lottery system for upperclassmen. 60% of students commute. All students may keep cars.

Activities: 10% of men belong to 10 local and 4 national fraternities; 10% of women belong to 7 local and 4 national sororities. There are 159 groups on campus, including art, band, cheerleading, chess, choir, chorale, chorus, computers, dance, drama, ethnic, gay, honors, international, jazz band, literary magazine, musical theater, newspaper, opera, orchestra, pep band, political, professional, radio and TV, religious, social, social service, student government, and yearbook. Popular campus events include Club Fair, Family Weekend, and Annual Highlander Picnic.

Sports: There are 9 intercollegiate sports for men and 11 for women, and 6 intramural sports for men and 6 for women. Facilities include a 5000-seat recreation and convocation complex housing a natatorium with an 8-lane swimming pool, areas for free exercise, a weight room, steam rooms, a 1/6-mile jogging track, and basketball, volleyball, handball, and racquetball courts. Outdoor facilities include a jogging trail, 12 tennis courts, and areas for baseball, soccer, lacrosse, softball, and intramural football.

Disabled Students: 85% of the campus is accessible. Wheelchair ramps, elevators, special parking, specially equipped rest rooms, special class scheduling, lowered drinking fountains, and lowered telephones are available.

Services: Counseling and information services are available, as is tutoring in most subjects. There is a reader service for the blind. There are writing and reading centers, a math tutoring lab, and a center to teach students study and time-management skills. There is a coordinator for disabled students. Tutors trained in teaching English as a second language are available to help international students.

Campus Safety and Security: Measures include 24-hour foot and vehicle patrol, self-defense education, security escort services, and shuttle buses. There are informal discussions, pamphlets/posters/films, emergency telephones, and lighted pathways/sidewalks.

Programs of Study: RU confers B.A., B.S., B.B.A., B.F.A., B.G.S., B.M., B.S.N., and B.S.W. degrees. Master's degrees are also awarded. Bachelor's degrees are awarded in BIOLOGICAL SCIENCE (biology/biological science and nutrition), BUSINESS (accounting, banking and finance, business administration and management, marketing/retailing/merchandising, and recreation and leisure services), COMMUNICATIONS AND THE ARTS (art, broadcasting, communications, dance, design, dramatic arts, English, fine arts, music, and speech/debate/rhetoric), COMPUTER AND PHYSICAL SCIENCE (chemistry, computer science, geology, information sciences and systems, mathematics, and physical sciences), EDUCATION (art, foreign languages, and physical), HEALTH PROFESSIONS (medical technology, nursing, and speech pathology/audiology), SOCIAL SCIENCE (anthropology, criminal justice, economics, food science, geography, history, human development, interdisciplinary studies, liberal arts/general studies, philosophy, political science/government, psychology, religion, social science, social work, and sociology). Nursing, education, and psychology are the strongest academically. Interdisciplinary studies, criminal justice, and psychology are the largest.

Required: To graduate, students must complete at least 120 credit hours, including 30 to 90 in the major, with a 2.0 GPA. There are general education requirements in English, foreign language, speech, fine arts, philosophy/religion, lab science, math/statistics/computer science, history, psychology, social science, and health/phys ed.

Special: RU offers internships, dual majors in any subject, study abroad in 11 countries, a general studies degree, and pass/fail options. On-campus work-study is available. There are 23 national honor societies, a freshman honors program, and 14 departmental honors programs.

Faculty/Classroom: 51% of faculty are male; 49%, female. All teach undergraduates. Graduate students teach 1% of introductory courses. The average class size in an introductory lecture is 32; in a laboratory, 20; and in a regular course, 25.

Admissions: 74% of the 2003-2004 applicants were accepted. The SAT I scores for the 2003-2004 freshman class were: Verbal--49% below 500, 39% between 500 and 599, and 11% between 600 and 700; Math--51% below 500, 39% between 500 and 599, 9% between 600 and 700, and 1% above 700. 17% of the current freshmen were in the top fifth of their class; 65% were in the top two fifths.

Requirements: The SAT I or ACT is required. In addition, applicants must be graduates of an accredited secondary school. The GED is accepted. Applicants should complete 21 high school academic credits, including 4 courses in English, 3 in math, and 2 each in sciences, foreign language, and social studies, including 1 in history. A GPA of 2.0 is required. AP and CLEP credits are accepted. Important factors in the admissions decision are extracurricular activities record, evidence of special talent, and advanced placement or honor courses.

Procedure: Freshmen are admitted to all sessions. Entrance exams should be taken between April of the junior year and December of the senior year. There is a deferred admissions plan. Notification is sent on a rolling basis. Applications are accepted on-line through the school's web site via CollegeNET. Check with the school for current application deadlines and fee.

Transfer: 746 transfer students enrolled in a recent year. Applicants must have a minimum GPA of 2.0. Those with fewer than 30 semester hours of college work must submit their high school record. 30 of 120 credits required for the bachelor's degree must be completed at RU.

Visiting: There are regularly scheduled orientations for prospective students, consisting of open houses in the fall, information sessions and tours Monday through Friday, and Admitted Student Days in the spring. There are guides for informal visits and visitors may sit in on classes. To schedule a visit, contact the Office of Admissions.

Financial Aid: In 2003-2004, 70% of all full-time freshmen and 77% of continuing full-time students received some form of financial aid. 39% of full-time freshmen and 40% of continuing full-time students received need-based aid. The average freshman award was $6545. Need-based scholarships or need-based grants averaged $5230 ($7650 maximum); need-based self-help aid (loans and jobs) averaged $1332 ($1627 maximum); non-need-based athletic scholarships averaged $5962 ($17,562 maximum); and other non-need-based awards and non-need-based scholarships averaged $4501 (maximum, full tuition). 16% of undergraduates work part time. Average annual earnings from campus work are $1378. The average financial indebtedness of the 2003 graduate was $13,442. The FAFSA is required. Check with the school for current application deadlines.

International Students: In a recent year, there were 95 international students enrolled. The school actively recruits these students. They must score 520 on the written TOEFL or 190 on the electronic version and also take the SAT I or the ACT.

Computers: The mainframe is a Sun UNIX. Terminals are located in several academic buildings. There are PC-equipped labs in academic departments and residence halls. Available software includes programming languages, databases, graphics, math, simulation languages, statistics, spreadsheets, and word processing. Dorm rooms are wired for Internet and Web access. All students may access the system. There are no time limits and no fees.

Graduates: In a recent year, 1610 bachelor's degrees were awarded. The most popular majors were interdisciplinary studies (14%), criminal justice (7%), and marketing (6%). In an average class, 31% graduate in 4 years or less, 49% graduate in 5 years or less, and 52% graduate in 6 years or less. 284 companies recruited on campus in a recent year.

Admissions Contact: David W. Kraus, Director of Admissions. A video is available. E-mail: ruadmiss@radford.edu Web: www.radford.edu

RANDOLPH-MACON COLLEGE
Ashland, VA 23005

D-3
(804) 752-7305
(800) 888-1762; Fax: (804) 752-4707

Full-time: 525 men, 558 women	Faculty: 84; IIB, +$
Part-time: 15 men, 20 women	Ph.D.s: 93%
Graduate: none	Student/Faculty: 13 to 1
Year: 4-1-4, summer session	Tuition: $21,160
Application Deadline: March 1	Room & Board: $6030
Freshman Class: 1661 applied, 1285 accepted, 326 enrolled	
SAT I Verbal/Math: 560/540	COMPETITIVE

Randolph-Macon College, established in 1830, is a private liberal arts college historically affiliated with the United Methodist Church. In addition to regional accreditation, Randolph-Macon has baccalaureate program accreditation with ACS. The library contains 178,767 volumes, 203,253 microform items, and 5184 audio/video tapes/CDs, and subscribes to 1004 periodicals. Computerized library services include the card catalog, interlibrary loans, database searching, and Internet access. Special learning facilities include a learning resource center, art gallery, radio station, TV station, observatory, radio telescope, darkroom, and greenhouse. The 111-acre campus is in a suburban area 15 miles north of Richmond. Including any residence halls, there are 65 buildings.

Student Life: 66% of undergraduates are from Virginia. Students are from 30 states and 15 foreign countries. 67% are from public schools. 91% are white. 52% are Protestant; 19% Catholic. The average age of freshmen is 18; all undergraduates, 20. 22% do not continue beyond their first year; 68% remain to graduate.

Housing: 950 students can be accommodated in college housing, which includes single-sex and coed dorms, on-campus apartments, fraternity houses, and sorority houses. In addition, there are honors houses, language houses, special-interest houses, senior apartments, a communi-

ty service house, and several college-owned houses. On-campus housing is guaranteed for all 4 years. 89% of students live on campus; of those, 80% remain on campus on weekends. All students may keep cars.

Activities: 35% of men belong to 5 national fraternities; 40% of women belong to 5 national sororities. There are 112 groups on campus, including art, cheerleading, chess, choir, chorale, chorus, computers, dance, debate, drama, environmental, ethnic, film, honors, international, jazz band, literary magazine, musical theater, newspaper, outing, pep band, photography, political, professional, radio and TV, religious, social, social service, student government, and yearbook. Popular campus events include Spring Fling, cultural arts series, and Earth Day.

Sports: There are 8 intercollegiate sports for men and 8 for women, and 8 intramural sports for men and 8 for women. Facilities include 10 tennis courts, several playing fields for men's and women's sports, 2 gyms, an indoor track, an indoor pool, a football field, a weight room, and an exercise room. A sports and recreation center includes racquetball and squash courts, a 25-meter pool, a weight room, an aerobics room, a 3-lane track, a multipurpose gym, and a climbing wall.

Disabled Students: 50% of the campus is accessible. Wheelchair ramps, elevators, special parking, specially equipped rest rooms, special class scheduling, and advisers for learning-disabled students are available.

Services: Counseling and information services are available, as is tutoring in every subject. There is a reader service for the blind and remedial math, reading, and writing.

Campus Safety and Security: Measures include 24-hour foot and vehicle patrol, self-defense education, security escort services, and shuttle buses. There are informal discussions, pamphlets/posters/films, emergency telephones, and lighted pathways/sidewalks.

Programs of Study: Randolph-Macon confers B.A. and B.S. degrees. Bachelor's degrees are awarded in AGRICULTURE (environmental studies), BIOLOGICAL SCIENCE (biology/biological science), BUSINESS (accounting and business economics), COMMUNICATIONS AND THE ARTS (art history and appreciation, arts administration/management, classics, dramatic arts, English, French, German, Greek, Latin, music, Spanish, and studio art), COMPUTER AND PHYSICAL SCIENCE (chemistry, computer science, mathematics, and physics), SOCIAL SCIENCE (economics, history, international relations, international studies, philosophy, political science/government, psychology, religion, sociology, and women's studies). Biological and physical sciences, psychology, and political science are the strongest academically. Economics/business, psychology, and sociology are the largest.

Required: To graduate, students must complete 112 credit hours, with 30 to 42 hours in the major and a minimum GPA of 2.0. All students must take 2 courses each in math, social science, lab science, literature, philosophy/theology, and phys ed, 1 course in fine arts, and enough foreign language to demonstrate proficiency. Specific courses required are English composition and European history. There is also a computer proficiency and oral communication requirement.

Special: The college offers cooperative programs in engineering with Columbia University and the University of Virginia, in forestry with Duke University, and in accounting with Virginia Commonwealth University. There is cross-registration with Hollins, Sweet Briar, Randolph-Macon Woman's College, Hampden-Sydney, Washington and Lee, and Mary Baldwin. Internships, dual majors, and a Washington semester are available. Students in all majors may take part in an accelerated degree program. Study abroad programs are offered in 14 countries. There are 19 national honor societies, including Phi Beta Kappa, and a freshman honors program.

Faculty/Classroom: 58% of faculty are male; 42%, female. All both teach and do research. The average class size in an introductory lecture is 20; in a laboratory, 15; and in a regular course, 16.

Admissions: 77% of the 2003-2004 applicants were accepted. The SAT I scores for the 2003-2004 freshman class were: Verbal--18% below 500, 52% between 500 and 599, 28% between 600 and 700, and 2% above 700; Math--26% below 500, 47% between 500 and 599, 26% between 600 and 700, and 1% above 700. 33% of the current freshmen were in the top fifth of their class; 71% were in the top two fifths. There was 1 National Merit semifinalist. 4 freshmen graduated first in their class.

Requirements: The SAT I or ACT is required. In addition, SAT II: Subject tests are recommended in writing, math, and foreign language. Applicants must be graduates of an accredited secondary school. The GED is accepted. Applicants should complete a minimum of 16 high school academic credits, including 4 years of English, 3 to 4 years each of math and science, and 2 to 3 years of foreign language, history, and social studies. An essay is required, and an interview is recommended. AP and CLEP credits are accepted. Important factors in the admissions decision are advanced placement or honor courses, recommendations by school officials, and extracurricular activities record.

Procedure: Freshmen are admitted fall and spring. Entrance exams should be taken by January of the senior year. There are early decision, early admissions, and deferred admissions plans. Early decision applications should be filed by November 15; regular applications, by March 1 for fall entry and January 1 for spring entry. The fall 2003 application fee was $30. Notification of early decision is sent December 1; regular decision, April 1. 36 early decision candidates were accepted for the 2003-2004 class. 10 applicants were on the 2003 waiting list; 3 were admitted. Applications are accepted on-line through the school's web site.

Transfer: 28 transfer students enrolled in 2002-2003. Applicants must have a minimum GPA of 2.0 and must be eligible to return to their previous institution. They must submit high school and college transcripts and SAT I scores. 37 of 112 credits required for the bachelor's degree must be completed at Randolph-Macon.

Visiting: There are regularly scheduled orientations for prospective students, including interviews, tours, and open houses. There are guides for informal visits and visitors may sit in on classes and stay overnight. To schedule a visit, contact the Office of Admissions.

Financial Aid: In a recent year, 93% of all full-time freshmen and 89% of continuing full-time students received some form of financial aid. 57% of full-time freshmen and 51% of continuing full-time students received need-based aid. The average freshman award was $14,811. 20% of undergraduates work part time. Average annual earnings from campus work are $1000. The average financial indebtedness of a recent graduate was $17,416. Randolph-Macon is a member of CSS. The FAFSA is required. The priority date for freshman financial aid applications for fall entry is February 1. The deadline for filing freshman financial aid applications for fall entry is March 1.

International Students: There are 19 international students enrolled. The school actively recruits these students. They must score 550 on the written TOEFL or 213 on the electronic version and also take the SAT I or the ACT.

Computers: The mainframes are a DEC VAX super minicomputer and 4 Sun workstations. Students have direct access to the mainframe and to more than 300 PCs located throughout the campus. All dorm rooms are also wired with 2 high-speed Internet connections. All students may access the system 8 A.M. to 1 A.M. There are no time limits and no fees. It is strongly recommended that all students have a personal computer.

Graduates: From July 1, 2002 to June 30, 2003, 241 bachelor's degrees were awarded. The most popular majors were economics/business (21%), sociology (16%), and English (10%). In an average class, 1% graduate in 3 years or less, 60% graduate in 4 years or less, 64% graduate in 5 years or less, and 64% graduate in 6 years or less. 20 companies recruited on campus in 2002-2003. Of the 2002 graduating class, 25% were enrolled in graduate school within 6 months of graduation and 95% were employed.

Admissions Contact: John C. Conkright, Dean of Admissions and Financial Aid. A video is available. E-mail: *admissions@rmc.edu* Web: *www.rmc.edu*

RANDOLPH-MACON WOMAN'S COLLEGE   D-3
Lynchburg, VA 24503
                                                 (434) 947-8100
                                (800) 745-7692; Fax: (434) 947-8996

Full-time: 706 women	**Faculty:** 77; IIB, +$
Part-time: 2 men, 29 women	**Ph.D.s:** 92%
Graduate: none	**Student/Faculty:** 9 to 1
Year: semesters, summer session	**Tuition:** $20,530
Application Deadline: March 1	**Room & Board:** $7900
Freshman Class: 716 applied, 615 accepted, 177 enrolled	
SAT I Verbal/Math: 600/560	**ACT:** 26 **VERY COMPETITIVE+**

Randolph-Macon Woman's College, founded in 1891, is an independent, liberal arts institution affiliated with the United Methodist Church. In addition to regional accreditation, R-MWC has baccalaureate program accreditation with NASDTEC. The library contains 197,332 volumes, 187,000 microform items, and 3600 audio/video tapes/CDs, and subscribes to 618 periodicals. Computerized library services include the card catalog, interlibrary loans; and database searching. Special learning facilities include a learning resource center, art gallery, radio station, an observatory, an art museum, 2 theaters, a 100-acre equestrian center, and 3 nature preserves. The 100-acre campus is in a suburban area in the foothills of the Blue Ridge Mountains, 1 hour south of Charlottesville. Including any residence halls, there are 18 buildings.

Student Life: 59% of undergraduates are from out of state, mostly the South. Students are from 42 states, 46 foreign countries, and Canada. 80% are from public schools. 74% are white; 12% foreign nationals. 69% are Protestant; 19% Catholic; 9% predominantly Muslim, Hindu, Buddhist, and Orthodox. The average age of freshmen is 18; all undergraduates, 20. 20% do not continue beyond their first year; 65% remain to graduate.

Housing: 675 students can be accommodated in college housing, which includes single-sex dorms, a special senior residence hall, and shared housing for Prime Time students. On-campus housing is guaranteed for all 4 years. 87% of students live on campus; of those, 75% remain on campus on weekends. All students may keep cars.

Activities: There are no fraternities or sororities. There are 35 groups on campus, including art, chorale, chorus, dance, debate, drama, ethnic, film, gay, honors, international, literary magazine, newspaper, pep band,

political, professional, radio and TV, religious, social, social service, student government, and yearbook. Popular campus events include Tacky Party and Never-Ending Weekend, Senior Dinner Dance, and Pumpkin Parade.

Sports: Facilities include a gym, an indoor heated swimming pool, dance studios, aerobic and weight rooms, 8 tennis courts, 2 athletic fields, a 100-acre riding center with teaching and amphitheater show rings and indoor and outdoor arenas, and a 900-seat auditorium.

Disabled Students: 50% of the campus is accessible. Wheelchair ramps, elevators, special parking, specially equipped rest rooms, special class scheduling, special housing, a wheelchair lift, and TDY telephone for hearing impaired are available.

Services: Counseling and information services are available, as is tutoring in every subject. There are computing and study skills resources, a writing lab, and a science and math center.

Campus Safety and Security: Measures include 24-hour foot and vehicle patrol, self-defense education, security escort services, and informal discussions. There are pamphlets/posters/films, emergency telephones, and lighted pathways/sidewalks.

Programs of Study: R-MWC confers B.A. and B.S. degrees. Bachelor's degrees are awarded in AGRICULTURE (environmental studies), BIOLOGICAL SCIENCE (biology/biological science), COMMUNICATIONS AND THE ARTS (art, classics, communications, dance, dramatic arts, English, French, German, music, and Spanish), COMPUTER AND PHYSICAL SCIENCE (chemistry, mathematics, and physics), HEALTH PROFESSIONS (health science), SOCIAL SCIENCE (American studies, economics, history, international relations, philosophy, political science/government, psychology, religion, Russian and Slavic studies, and sociology). Psychology, biology, and English are the largest.

Required: To graduate, all students must complete at least 124 credit hours with a minimum GPA of 2.0. Students must satisfy the requirements for the general education and major programs and must have a minimum GPA of 2.0 in the major.

Special: R-MWC offers a junior year spring semester American Culture Program, as well as study abroad in 11 countries. A Washington semester at American University is available, as is the Tri-College Consortium with Sweet Briar and Lynchburg Colleges, and the Seven-College Exchange Program with Hampden-Sydney, Hollins, Mary Baldwin, Randolph-Macon, and Sweet Briar Colleges, and Washington and Lee University. There is a 3-2 nursing program with Johns Hopkins University and a 3-2 engineering degree with several institutions. There are 9 national honor societies, including Phi Beta Kappa.

Faculty/Classroom: 47% of faculty are male; 53%, female. All teach undergraduates, and 58% both teach and do research. The average class size in an introductory lecture is 18; in a laboratory, 13; and in a regular course, 13.

Admissions: 86% of the 2003-2004 applicants were accepted. The SAT I scores for the 2003-2004 freshman class were: Verbal--7% below 500, 39% between 500 and 599, 40% between 600 and 700, and 14% above 700; Math--21% below 500, 46% between 500 and 599, 29% between 600 and 700, and 4% above 700. The ACT scores were 9% below 21, 25% between 21 and 23, 27% between 24 and 26, 16% between 27 and 28, and 23% above 28. 60% of the current freshmen were in the top fifth of their class; 87% were in the top two fifths. There was 1 National Merit semifinalist. 4 freshmen graduated first in their class.

Requirements: The SAT I or ACT is required. In addition, applicants must be graduates of an accredited secondary school with at least 16 academic credits, including 4 units in English, 3 to 4 in a foreign language, 3 in math, 2 in biology, chemistry, or physics with lab work, and 1 to 2 in electives from other academic study. An interview is strongly recommended. AP and CLEP credits are accepted. Important factors in the admissions decision are advanced placement or honor courses, recommendations by school officials, and leadership record.

Procedure: Freshmen are admitted fall and spring. Entrance exams should be taken in the junior or senior year There is a rolling admissions plan. There are early decision and deferred admissions plans. Early decision applications should be filed by November 15; regular applications, by March 1 for fall entry and December 1 for spring entry, along with a $35 fee. Notification of early decision is sent December 15; regular decision, on a rolling basis. 16 early decision candidates were accepted for the 2003-2004 class. Applications are accepted on computer disk and on-line.

Transfer: 41 transfer students enrolled in 2002-2003. Transfer students must submit college and high school transcripts, 2 letters of recommendation, a copy of their current college's catalog, and the SAT I or ACT scores. An interview is recommended. Seniors may not transfer in. Courses within a liberal arts curriculum will be considered for transfer credit if grades are at least in the C range. 62 of 124 credits required for the bachelor's degree must be completed at R-MWC.

Visiting: There are regularly scheduled orientations for prospective students, including a campus tour, student panels, faculty panels, class visits, and individual sessions with admissions and financial planning counselor. There are guides for informal visits and visitors may sit in on classes and stay overnight. To schedule a visit, contact the Admissions Office at *admissions@rmwc.edu*.

Financial Aid: In 2003-2004, 99% of all full-time students received some form of financial aid. 70% of full-time freshmen and 66% of continuing full-time students received need-based aid. The average freshman award was $19,845. Need-based scholarships or need-based grants averaged $15,490 ($20,690 maximum); need-based self-help aid (loans and jobs) averaged $4118 ($9860 maximum); and non-need-based awards and non-need-based scholarships averaged $14,470 ($15,710 maximum). 64% of undergraduates work part time. Average annual earnings from campus work are $981. The average financial indebtedness of the 2003 graduate was $21,992. The FAFSA and the state aid form are required. The priority date for freshman financial aid applications for fall entry is March 1.

International Students: There are 84 international students enrolled. The school actively recruits these students. They must score 550 on the written TOEFL or 213 on the electronic version.

Computers: Students may access 100 PC and 20 Mac computers, all networked and software-equipped, in several cluster locations on campus. 6 common area locations are equipped with wireless technology. All dorm rooms are also networked, and the campuswide information system provides access to global e-mail services and web resources. All students may access the system. There are no time limits and no fees.

Graduates: From July 1, 2002 to June 30, 2003, 159 bachelor's degrees were awarded. The most popular majors were biology (15%), psychology (12%), and English (11%). In an average class, 2% graduate in 3 years or less, 61% graduate in 4 years or less, 63% graduate in 5 years or less, and 63% graduate in 6 years or less. 102 companies recruited on campus in 2002-2003. Of the 2002 graduating class, 35% were enrolled in graduate school within 6 months of graduation and 60% were employed.

Admissions Contact: Patricia N. LeDonne, Director of Admissions. A video is available. E-mail: *admissions@rmwc.edu*
Web: *www.rmwc.edu*

ROANOKE COLLEGE
Salem, VA 24153

C-3
(540) 375-2270
(800) 388-2276; Fax: (540) 375-2267

Full-time: 736 men, 1037 women	**Faculty:** 121; IIB, av$
Part-time: 57 men, 69 women	**Ph.Ds:** 93%
Graduate: none	**Student/Faculty:** 15 to 1
Year: semesters, summer session	**Tuition:** $20,865
Application Deadline: March 1	**Room & Board:** $6528
Freshman Class: 2827 applied, 2164 accepted, 519 enrolled	
SAT I Verbal/Math: 550/550	**COMPETITIVE**

Roanoke College, founded in 1842, is a private institution affiliated with the Evangelical Lutheran Church in America. The college offers undergraduate programs in the arts and sciences and business administration. In addition to regional accreditation, Roanoke has baccalaureate program accreditation with ACBSP. The library contains 208,173 volumes, 318,187 microform items, and 8115 audio/video tapes/CDs, and subscribes to 3555 (668 paper and 2887 electronic) periodicals. Computerized library services include the card catalog, interlibrary loans, database searching, and Internet access. Special learning facilities include a learning resource center, art gallery, radio station, a media classroom, TV production facility, and multimedia computer labs. The 70-acre campus is in a suburban area 5 miles west of Roanoke. Including any residence halls, there are 40 buildings.

Student Life: 60% of undergraduates are from Virginia. Students are from 38 states, 25 foreign countries, and Canada. 80% are from public schools. 92% are white. 57% are Protestant; 17% Catholic; 9% claim no religious affiliation. The average age of freshmen is 18; all undergraduates, 21. 21% do not continue beyond their first year; 65% remain to graduate.

Housing: 1150 students can be accommodated in college housing, which includes single-sex and coed dorms, on-campus apartments, off-campus apartments, fraternity houses, and sorority houses. In addition, there are honors houses, special-interest houses, and freshman residence halls. On-campus housing is guaranteed for all 4 years. 60% of students live on campus. All students may keep cars.

Activities: 17% of men belong to 3 national fraternities; 26% of women belong to 4 national sororities. There are 84 groups on campus, including art, cheerleading, chess, choir, chorale, chorus, computers, dance, debate, drama, ethnic, gay, honors, international, jazz band, literary magazine, musical theater, newspaper, pep band, photography, political, professional, radio and TV, religious, social, social service, student government, and yearbook. Popular campus events include Family Weekend, Alumni Weekend, and WinterFest.

Sports: There are 9 intercollegiate sports for men and 10 for women, and 9 intramural sports for men and 9 for women. Facilities include a 2400-seat gym, a 400-seat arena, athletic fields, an all-weather track, practice and playing fields, tennis and racquetball courts, a swimming pool, and a fitness center with weight training and physical conditioning equipment.

Disabled Students: 80% of the campus is accessible. Wheelchair ramps, elevators, special parking, specially equipped rest rooms, and special class scheduling are available.

Services: Counseling and information services are available, as is tutoring in every subject. A supervised peer tutoring program is available at no charge to students.

Campus Safety and Security: Measures include 24-hour foot and vehicle patrol, self-defense education, security escort services, and informal discussions. There are pamphlets/posters/films, emergency telephones, and lighted pathways/sidewalks.

Programs of Study: Roanoke confers B.A., B.S., and B.B.A. degrees. Bachelor's degrees are awarded in AGRICULTURE (environmental studies), BIOLOGICAL SCIENCE (biochemistry and biology/biological science), BUSINESS (business administration and management), COMMUNICATIONS AND THE ARTS (art, dramatic arts, English, French, music, and Spanish), COMPUTER AND PHYSICAL SCIENCE (chemistry, computer science, information sciences and systems, mathematics, and physics), EDUCATION (athletic training and physical), ENGINEERING AND ENVIRONMENTAL DESIGN (environmental science), HEALTH PROFESSIONS (medical technology), SOCIAL SCIENCE (criminal justice, economics, history, international relations, philosophy, political science/government, psychology, religion, sociology, and theological studies). Computer science, biology, and chemistry are the strongest academically. Business, psychology, and English are the largest.

Required: Requirements for graduation include completion of 34 courses, including about 12 in the major. Specific course requirements include 2 courses each in math, lab science, social science, and phys ed, as well as a 2-course sequence in humanities, a freshman-year writing course, a values course, and a senior symposium. All students must attain a 2.0 GPA and be able to demonstrate competency in a foreign language. An intensive learning course and a cocurricular learning and service experience are also required.

Special: There is cross-registration with Hollins College and study abroad in more than 100 countries. Roanoke also offers internships, a Washington semester, the Virginia at Oxford Program, combined B.A.-B.S. degrees in chemistry, biology, physics, and psychology, a 3-2 engineering degree with Virginia Polytechnic Institute and State University, Washington University in St. Louis, and University of Tennessee at Knoxville, credit by examination, and pass/fail options. Nondegree study is available to those students admitted with special status. There are 20 national honor societies, including Phi Beta Kappa, a freshman honors program, and honors programs in all departments.

Faculty/Classroom: 55% of faculty are male; 45%, female. All teach undergraduates, and 60% both teach and do research. The average class size in an introductory lecture is 22; in a laboratory, 20; and in a regular course, 19.

Admissions: 77% of the 2003-2004 applicants were accepted. The SAT I scores for the 2003-2004 freshman class were: Verbal--22% below 500, 48% between 500 and 599, 26% between 600 and 700, and 4% above 700; Math--22% below 500, 52% between 500 and 599, 23% between 600 and 700, and 3% above 700. 44% of the current freshmen were in the top fifth of their class; 70% were in the top two fifths. 9 freshmen graduated first in their class.

Requirements: The SAT I or ACT is required, but the SAT I is preferred. SAT II: Subject tests, an essay, and an interview are recommended. Applicants must be graduates of accredited secondary schools or have earned a GED. The college requires 18 academic units, based on 4 years of English, 3 courses in math, 4 courses in foreign language, and 2 courses each in lab science and social studies. An audition is also recommended for performing arts majors. AP and CLEP credits are accepted. Important factors in the admissions decision are advanced placement or honor courses, evidence of special talent, and leadership record.

Procedure: Freshmen are admitted fall and spring. Entrance exams should be taken by January of senior year. There are early decision, early admissions, and deferred admissions plans. Early decision applications should be filed by November 15; regular applications, by March 1 for fall entry. Notification of early decision is sent November 30; regular decision, April 1. 70 early decision candidates were accepted for the 2003-2004 class. 67 applicants were on the 2003 waiting list; 6 were admitted. Applications are accepted on computer disk and on-line through *www2.roanoke.edu*.

Transfer: 81 transfer students enrolled in 2002-2003. Transfers must have a minimum GPA of 2.2. The SAT I scores and an interview are recommended. 16 of 34 courses required for the bachelor's degree must be completed at Roanoke.

Visiting: There are regularly scheduled orientations for prospective students, consisting of open houses that provide a sampling of college life at Roanoke. There are guides for informal visits and visitors may sit in on classes and stay overnight. To schedule a visit, contact the Admissions Office at (540) 375-2270 or *admissions@roanoke.edu*.

Financial Aid: In 2003-2004, 96% of all full-time freshmen and 97% of continuing full-time students received some form of financial aid. 75% of full-time freshmen and 70% of continuing full-time students received need-based aid. The average freshman award was $15,994. 29% of undergraduates work part time. Average annual earnings from campus work are $1300. The average financial indebtedness of the 2003 graduate was $16,834. Roanoke is a member of CSS. The FAFSA is required. The deadline for filing freshman financial aid applications for fall entry is March 1.

International Students: There are 40 international students enrolled. The school actively recruits these students. They must score 520 on the written TOEFL or 190 on the electronic version and also take the SAT I or ACT. SAT II: Subject tests are recommended.

Computers: The mainframe consists of numerous servers. There are more than 150 PCs in 10 computer labs (5 multimedia) across campus, including the library. From any connected PC, students have access to word processing, spreadsheets, databases, e-mail, the Internet, programming languages, and about 200 software packages for specific classes. Wireless access is available in most classrooms and campus buildings. All students may access the system any time. There are no time limits and no fees.

Graduates: From July 1, 2002 to June 30, 2003, 386 bachelor's degrees were awarded. The most popular majors were business administration (23%), psychology (12%), and English (10%). In an average class, 2% graduate in 3 years or less, 55% graduate in 4 years or less, 60% graduate in 5 years or less, and 65% graduate in 6 years or less. 70 companies recruited on campus in 2002-2003. Of the 2002 graduating class, 20% were enrolled in graduate school within 6 months of graduation and 96% were employed.

Admissions Contact: Michael Maxey, Vice President of Admissions. A video is available. E-mail: *admissions@roanoke.edu*
Web: *www.roanoke.edu*

SAINT PAUL'S COLLEGE
Lawrenceville, VA 23868   E-4
                                                    (434) 848-6492
                                (800) 678-7071; Fax: (434) 848-1862

Full-time: 334 men, 312 women	**Faculty:** 33; IIB, --$
Part-time: 13 men, 41 women	**Ph.D.s:** 59%
Graduate: none	**Student/Faculty:** 20 to 1
Year: semesters, summer session	**Tuition:** $9157
Application Deadline: open	**Room & Board:** $5187
Freshman Class: n/av	
SAT I: required	**NONCOMPETITIVE**

Saint Paul's College, founded in 1888, is a small, private liberal arts college affiliated with the Protestant Episcopal Church, offering undergraduate programs in arts and sciences, business, and teacher education. The library contains 41,500 volumes, 29,000 microform items, and 914 audio/video tapes/CDs, and subscribes to 167 periodicals. Computerized library services include the card catalog, interlibrary loans, database searching, and Internet access. Special learning facilities include a learning resource center. The 180-acre campus is in a small town 55 miles south of Petersburg and 80 miles south of Richmond. Including any residence halls, there are 34 buildings.

Student Life: 67% of undergraduates are from Virginia. Students are from 19 states and 6 foreign countries. 99% are from public schools. 96% are African American. 90% are Protestant; 6% claim no religious affiliation. The average age of freshmen is 19; all undergraduates, 21. 45% do not continue beyond their first year; 55% remain to graduate.

Housing: 431 students can be accommodated in college housing, which includes single-sex dorms. In addition, there are special-interest houses and single-parent housing. On-campus housing is guaranteed for the freshman year only and is available on a lottery system for upperclassmen. 62% of students live on campus; of those, 52% remain on campus on weekends. Alcohol is not permitted. All students may keep cars.

Activities: 7% of men belong to 5 national fraternities; 5% of women belong to 3 national sororities. There are 22 groups on campus, including art, cheerleading, chess, choir, dance, drama, ethnic, honors, pep band, political, religious, social service, student government, Students in Free Enterprise, and Virginia Highway Safety Project. Popular campus events include a lecture and concert series, College for a Day, and Founders Day.

Sports: There are 7 intercollegiate sports for men and 7 for women, and 2 intramural sports for men and 2 for women. Facilities include a gym, baseball and football fields, practice fields, and tennis courts.

Disabled Students: 30% of the campus is accessible. Wheelchair ramps, elevators, special parking, specially equipped rest rooms, and lowered drinking fountains are available.

Services: Counseling and information services are available, as is tutoring in most subjects. There is remedial math, reading, and writing.

Campus Safety and Security: Measures include 24-hour foot and vehicle patrol, self-defense education, security escort services, and shuttle buses. There are informal discussions, pamphlets/posters/films, emergency telephones, and lighted pathways/sidewalks.

Programs of Study: SPC confers B.A., B.S., and B.S.Ed. degrees. Bachelor's degrees are awarded in BIOLOGICAL SCIENCE (biology/

biological science, marine biology, and marine science), BUSINESS (business administration and management), COMMUNICATIONS AND THE ARTS (English), COMPUTER AND PHYSICAL SCIENCE (mathematics), EDUCATION (business, elementary, and secondary), ENGINEERING AND ENVIRONMENTAL DESIGN (environmental science), SOCIAL SCIENCE (law enforcement and corrections, political science/government, social science, and sociology). Organizational management is the strongest academically. Business administration is the largest.

Required: All students must complete 42 semester hours of general education requirements, including courses in humanities, natural science and math, social sciences, health and phys ed, and computer information systems. A minimum of 120 hours, including at least 30 in the major, with at least a 2.0 GPA is required to graduate. Students in the Organizational Management Program (OMP) are required to write a thesis. All students must take PRAXIS for teacher certification.

Special: Cross-registration is possible with members of the Southside Higher Education Consortium and with Richard Bland College and Parkland College. Minors and the B.A.-B.S. degree are offered in most disciplines. Nonmajor preprofessional programs are available in the health professions. Endorsements in early childhood, middle, and secondary education are available in appropriate majors. Co-op programs in aquatic science and environmentive science, a general studies degree and work-study programs are available. Nondegree study is possible. There are 2 national honor societies, a freshman honors program, and 3 departmental honors programs.

Faculty/Classroom: 62% of faculty are male; 38%, female. All teach undergraduates and 6% both teach and do research. The average class size in an introductory lecture is 15; in a laboratory, 8; and in a regular course, 10.

Admissions: 8% of the current freshmen were in the top fifth of their class; 23% were in the top two fifths.

Requirements: The SAT I is required. In addition, applicants should be graduates of an accredited secondary school and have completed 16 academic units, including English, math, science, and social sciences. A GPA of 2.0 is required. AP and CLEP credits are accepted. Important factors in the admissions decision are recommendations by school officials, leadership record, and evidence of special talent.

Procedure: Freshmen are admitted fall and spring. Entrance exams should be taken during the senior year of high school.There is a rolling admissions plan. There are early decision and early admissions plans. Application deadlines are open. The fall 2003 application fee was $20.

Transfer: 130 transfer students enrolled in a recent year. Transfer applicants must supply all former official high school and college transcripts as well as a background form completed by the former college. 30 of 120 credits required for the bachelor's degree must be completed at SPC.

Visiting: There are regularly scheduled orientations for prospective students, including Homecoming, Open House, College for a Day, Honors Convocation, and Pre-Orientation. There are guides for informal visits and visitors may sit in on classes and stay overnight. To schedule a visit, contact Vice President for Student Affairs at (434) 848-6456 or *admissions@saintpauls.edu*.

Financial Aid: In 2003-2004, 98% of all full-time freshmen and 93% of continuing full-time students received some form of financial aid. 80% of full-time freshmen and 75% of continuing full-time students received need-based aid. The average freshman award was $8386. 45% of undergraduates work part time. Average annual earnings from campus work are $2000. The average financial indebtedness of the 2003 graduate was $12,695. SPC is a member of CSS. The FAFSA and the state aid form are required. The deadline for filing freshman financial aid applications for fall entry is July 1.

International Students: There are 10 international students enrolled. They must take the TOEFL and also take the SAT I or the ACT, scoring 600.

Computers: The mainframe is an IBM AS400. There are about 300 PCs currently distributed in 5 computer labs. All students have access to them. All students may access the system Monday through Friday from 3 A.M. to 6 P.M. There are no time limits. The fee is $100. It is strongly recommended that all students have a personal computer.

Graduates: From July 1, 2002 to June 30, 2003, 102 bachelor's degrees were awarded. The most popular majors were business administration (67%), criminal justice (11%), and sociology and social sciences (9%). In an average class, 13% graduate in 4 years or less, 25% graduate in 5 years or less, and 28% graduate in 6 years or less. 26 companies recruited on campus in 2002-2003. Of the 2002 graduating class, 14% were enrolled in graduate school within 6 months of graduation.

Admissions Contact: Rosemary Lewis, Vice President for Student Affairs. E-mail: *admissions@saintpauls.edu* Web: *www.saintpauls.edu*

SHENANDOAH UNIVERSITY
Winchester, VA 22601

D-1
(540) 665-4581
(800) 432-2266; Fax: (540) 665-4627

Full-time: 568 men, 759 women	**Faculty:** 124; IIA, -$
Part-time: 29 men, 60 women	**Ph.Ds:** 79%
Graduate: 504 men, 931 women	**Student/Faculty:** 11 to 1
Year: semesters, summer session	**Tuition:** $18,390
Application Deadline: open	**Room & Board:** $6800
Freshman Class: 1319 applied, 961 accepted, 337 enrolled	
SAT I Verbal/Math: 506/499	**ACT:** 19 NONCOMPETITIVE

Shenandoah University, founded in 1875, is a private university, affiliated with the United Methodist Church and offering programs in arts and sciences, nursing and health professions, business, music, theater, and dance. There are 4 undergraduate and 6 graduate schools. In addition to regional accreditation, Shenandoah has baccalaureate program accreditation with NASM and NLN. The 2 libraries contain 124,139 volumes, 134,349 microform items, and 18,105 audio/video tapes/CDs, and subscribe to 1060 periodicals. Computerized library services include the card catalog, interlibrary loans, database searching, and Internet access. Special learning facilities include a learning resource center, radio station, and TV station. The 100-acre campus is in a small town 72 miles west of Washington, D.C. Including any residence halls, there are 21 buildings.

Student Life: 58% of undergraduates are from Virginia. Students are from 46 states, 42 foreign countries, and Canada. 87% are white. 50% claim no religious affiliation; 25% are Protestant; 12% Catholic. The average age of freshmen is 19; all undergraduates, 22. 34% do not continue beyond their first year; 42% remain to graduate.

Housing: 674 students can be accommodated in college housing, which includes coed dorms. In addition, there are honors houses, special-interest houses, and a nonalcohol residence hall. On-campus housing is guaranteed for all 4 years. 54% of students commute. All students may keep cars.

Activities: There are no fraternities or sororities. There are 49 groups on campus, including band, cheerleading, chess, choir, chorale, chorus, dance, drama, drum and bugle corps, ethnic, gay, honors, international, jazz band, musical theater, newspaper, opera, orchestra, pep band, political, professional, radio and TV, religious, social service, student government, and symphony. Popular campus events include conservatory productions, International Days, and Spring Fling.

Sports: There are 8 intercollegiate sports for men and 8 for women, and 12 intramural sports for men and 12 for women. Facilities include a soccer field, a gym with basketball and volleyball courts, 2 weight rooms, a fitness room, a track, lacrosse, field hockey and softball fields, and a football stadium.

Disabled Students: 90% of the campus is accessible. Wheelchair ramps, elevators, special parking, specially equipped rest rooms, special class scheduling, lowered drinking fountains, and electric doors are available.

Services: Counseling and information services are available, as is tutoring in most subjects. There is a reader service for the blind and remedial math.

Campus Safety and Security: Measures include 24-hour foot and vehicle patrol, security escort services, informal discussions, and pamphlets/posters/films. There are emergency telephones and lighted pathways/sidewalks.

Programs of Study: Shenandoah confers B.A., B.S., B.B.A., B.F.A., B.M., and B.M.T. degrees. Associate, master's, and doctoral degrees are also awarded. Bachelor's degrees are awarded in BIOLOGICAL SCIENCE (biology/biological science), BUSINESS (business administration and management), COMMUNICATIONS AND THE ARTS (arts administration/management, communications, dance, dramatic arts, English, jazz, music, music performance, music theory and composition, musical theater, performing arts, piano/organ, Spanish, and theater design), COMPUTER AND PHYSICAL SCIENCE (chemistry and mathematics), EDUCATION (dance, music, and psychology), ENGINEERING AND ENVIRONMENTAL DESIGN (environmental science), HEALTH PROFESSIONS (music therapy, nursing, and respiratory therapy), SOCIAL SCIENCE (American studies, history, law enforcement and corrections, liberal arts/general studies, physical fitness/movement, psychology, public administration, religion, religious music, and sociology). Biology, psychology, and history are the strongest academically. Business administration, musical theater, and music education are the largest.

Required: To graduate, all students must have taken the required core curriculum including 1 religion/philosophy course, 2 phys ed courses, and 1 computer literacy course. Students must complete at least 120 credit hours with a minimum 2.0 GPA. Other requirements vary depending on the program of study.

Special: Internships, dual majors, a B.A./B.S. in university studies, and work-study programs are available. Nondegree study is possible. There are 2 national honor societies, a freshman honors program, and 1 departmental honors program.

Faculty/Classroom: 53% of faculty are male; 47%, female. 70% teach undergraduates. Graduate students teach 1% of introductory courses. The average class size in an introductory lecture is 18; in a laboratory, 12; and in a regular course, 13.

Admissions: 73% of the 2003-2004 applicants were accepted. The SAT I scores for the 2003-2004 freshman class were: Verbal--46% below 500, 38% between 500 and 599, 14% between 600 and 700, and 2% above 700; Math--50% below 500, 36% between 500 and 599, 13% between 600 and 700, and 1% above 700. The ACT scores were 70% below 21 and 30% between 21 and 23.

Requirements: The SAT I or ACT is required, with a minimum composite score of 850 on the SAT I or 19 on the ACT. Applicants must be graduates of an accredited secondary school. The GED is accepted. Students should complete 15 high school academic credits, including 4 years of English, 3 years of math, and 2 years each of foreign language, science, and social studies. A minimum GPA of 2.5 is required. An audition is required for music, theater, and dance. A GPA of 2.0 is required. AP and CLEP credits are accepted. Important factors in the admissions decision are evidence of special talent, advanced placement or honor courses, and personality/intangible qualities.

Procedure: Freshmen are admitted to all sessions. Entrance exams should be taken by junior year or early in the senior year. There is a rolling admissions plan and a deferred admissions plan. Application deadlines are open. Application fee is $30. Applications are accepted on-line through Shenandoah's web site.

Transfer: 139 transfer students enrolled in 2002-2003. Transfer applicants must have a GPA of 2.0. An audition is required for music, dance, and theater. Official transcripts from high school and all previous college work must be submitted in addition to the SAT I or ACT scores, unless the applicant has been out of school more than 2 years. 24 of the last 30 of 120 credits required for the bachelor's degree must be completed at Shenandoah.

Visiting: There are regularly scheduled orientations for prospective students, including information sessions with faculty and staff and student-guided campus tours. There are guides for informal visits and visitors may sit in on classes and stay overnight. To schedule a visit, contact the Admissions Office at admit@su.edu.

Financial Aid: In 2003-2004, 91% of all full-time freshmen and 80% of continuing full-time students received some form of financial aid. 61% of full-time freshmen and 60% of continuing full-time students received need-based aid. The average freshman award was $12,750. Need-based scholarships or need-based grants averaged $3184 ($7650 maximum); need-based self-help aid (loans and jobs) averaged $4894 ($7125 maximum); and non-need-based awards and non-need-based scholarships averaged $5144 ($13,000 maximum). 36% of undergraduates work part time. Average annual earnings from campus work are $841. The average financial indebtedness of the 2003 graduate was $18,588. The FAFSA and the state aid form are required. The priority date for freshman financial aid applications for fall entry is March 1. The deadline for filing freshman financial aid applications for fall entry is June 30.

International Students: There are 163 international students enrolled. The school actively recruits these students. They must score 450 on the written TOEFL and also take the college's own test.

Computers: The mainframe is an IBM AS/400/300. There are approximately 130 PCs and workstations located in computer labs throughout the campus. All students may access the system during scheduled hours. There are no time limits and no fees. It is recommended that students in nursing and pharmacy have personal computers. IBM is recommended.

Graduates: From July 1, 2002 to June 30, 2003, 224 bachelor's degrees were awarded. The most popular majors were business administration (14%), music theater (14%), and music performance (8%). In an average class, 28% graduate in 4 years or less, 39% graduate in 5 years or less, and 42% graduate in 6 years or less. 100 companies recruited on campus in 2002-2003.

Admissions Contact: David Anthony, Dean of Admissions.
E-mail: admit@su.edu Web: http://www.su.edu

SWEET BRIAR COLLEGE
Sweet Briar, VA 24595

D-3
(434) 381-6142
(800) 381-6142; Fax: (434) 381-6152

Full-time: 24 men, 638 women	**Faculty:** 71; IIB, +$
Part-time: 6 men, 41 women	**Ph.Ds:** 97%
Graduate: none	**Student/Faculty:** 9 to 1
Year: semesters	**Tuition:** $19,900
Application Deadline: February 1	**Room & Board:** $8040
Freshman Class: 405 applied, 355 accepted, 133 enrolled	
SAT I Verbal/Math: 560/540	**ACT:** 23 COMPETITIVE

Sweet Briar College, founded in 1901, is a private women's liberal arts institution. The 3 libraries contain 249,437 volumes, 448,334 microform items, and 9869 audio/video tapes/CDs, and subscribe to 1742 periodicals. Computerized library services include the card catalog, interlibrary loans, database searching, and Internet access. Special learning facilities include a learning resource center, art gallery, radio station, TV station, college museum, observatory, and Center for Civic Renewal. The 3250-acre campus is in a rural area 165 miles southwest of Washington, D.C., 120 miles west of Richmond, 12 miles north of Lynchburg. Including any residence halls, there are 34 buildings.

Student Life: 61% of undergraduates are from out of state, mostly the South. Students are from 41 states, 19 foreign countries, and Canada. 72% are from public schools. 86% are white. The average age of freshmen is 18; all undergraduates, 21. 21% do not continue beyond their first year; 79% remain to graduate.

Housing: 551 students can be accommodated in college housing, which includes single-sex dorms, substance-free and first-year housing. On-campus housing is guaranteed for all 4 years. 90% of students live on campus; of those, 75% remain on campus on weekends. All students may keep cars.

Activities: There are no fraternities. There are 43 groups on campus, including art, cheerleading, chemistry, choir, chorus, computers, dance, drama, environmental, ethnic, film, gay, health-related, honors, international, literary magazine, musical theater, newspaper, orchestra, photography, political, professional, radio and TV, religious, riding clubs, social, social service, student government, symphony, the National Organization for Women, and yearbook. Popular campus events include Stepsinging, Dell Parties, and Founders Day.

Sports: Facilities include a natatorium, gym, Nautilus center, weight room, pathway and trail system for walking, biking, and riding, 14 tennis courts, riding center, soccer/lacrosse/field hockey fields, fitness circuit, primitive campgrounds, and 2 lakes.

Disabled Students: 80% of the campus is accessible. Wheelchair ramps, elevators, special parking, specially equipped rest rooms, and lowered telephones are available.

Services: Counseling and information services are available, as is tutoring in most subjects.

Campus Safety and Security: Measures include 24-hour foot and vehicle patrol, self-defense education, security escort services, and shuttle buses. There are informal discussions, pamphlets/posters/films, emergency telephones, lighted pathways/sidewalks, and gates manned by security personnel from 6 P.M., to 6 A.M., and locked dorms with student key access.

Programs of Study: Sweet Briar confers B.A., B.S., and B.F.A. degrees. Bachelor's degrees are awarded in AGRICULTURE (environmental studies), BIOLOGICAL SCIENCE (biochemistry, biology/biological science, and molecular biology), BUSINESS (business administration and management), COMMUNICATIONS AND THE ARTS (art history and appreciation, communications, creative writing, dance, dramatic arts, English, French, German, Greek, Latin, literature, modern language, music, Spanish, and studio art), COMPUTER AND PHYSICAL SCIENCE (chemistry, computer science, mathematics, and physics), ENGINEERING AND ENVIRONMENTAL DESIGN (environmental science), SOCIAL SCIENCE (anthropology, classical/ancient civilization, economics, German area studies, history, international relations, Italian studies, liberal arts/general studies, philosophy, political science/government, psychology, religion, sociology, and Spanish studies). International affairs, biology, and English are the strongest academically. Psychology, government, and biology are the largest.

Required: To graduate, students must complete 120 credits, of which 60 must be earned at Sweet Briar, with a minimum GPA of 2.0. 30 to 36 must be in the major. In addition to major requirements, specific degree requirements include English: Thought and Expression. Students must take 7 hours in scientific theory and experiment; 6 in global cultures; 4 in study or practice of the arts; 3 each in Western culture, social science, literature, and economic, political, or legal systems; and 2 in physical activity. Students must demonstrate proficiency in oral and written communication, quantitative reasoning, and a foreign language. A senior capstone course/experience is also required.

Special: The college offers a coordinate program in general business management and arts management, as well as internships to explore career opportunities and gain work experience. Study abroad, a Washington semester with American University, B.A.-B.S. degrees, student-designed and interdisciplinary majors, accelerated degree programs, and 3-2 engineering degrees with Columbia University, Washington University in St. Louis, Virginia Polytechnic Institute, and University of Virginia are available. Cross-registration with Lynchburg and Randolph-Macon Woman's Colleges (the Tri-College Consortium) and the Seven College Exchange is also possible. There are 9 national honor societies, including Phi Beta Kappa, and a freshman honors program.

Faculty/Classroom: 46% of faculty are male; 54%, female. All both teach and do research. The average class size in an introductory lecture is 12; in a laboratory, 8; and in a regular course, 10.

Admissions: 88% of the 2003-2004 applicants were accepted. The SAT I scores for the 2003-2004 freshman class were: Verbal--35% below 500, 36% between 500 and 599, 23% between 600 and 700, and 5% above 700; Math--43% below 500, 41% between 500 and 599, 15% between 600 and 700, and 2% above 700. The ACT scores were 32% below 21, 25% between 21 and 23, 18% between 24 and 26, 11% between 27 and 28, and 14% above 28. 41% of the current freshmen were

in the top fifth of their class; 88% were in the top two fifths. There was 1 National Merit finalist and 1 semifinalist. 3 freshmen graduated first in their class.

Requirements: The SAT I or ACT is required. If the SAT I is submitted, it is recommended that the applicant also take 3 SAT II: Subject tests, 1 in English and 2 in other areas. Applicants must be graduates of an accredited secondary school. Applicants must complete at least 16 high school academic credits (20 recommended), including 4 years of English and 3 each of math, social studies, science, history, and a foreign language. The college requires an essay and recommends an interview. AP credits are accepted. Important factors in the admissions decision are advanced placement or honor courses, evidence of special talent, and leadership record.

Procedure: Freshmen are admitted fall and spring. Entrance exams should be taken by February of the year of application; SAT II: Subject tests can be taken in the spring of the senior year. There are early decision and deferred admissions plans. Early decision applications should be filed by December 1; regular applications, by February 1 for fall entry and November 15 for spring entry. The fall 2003 application fee was $25. Notification of early decision is sent December 15; regular decision, April 1. 38 early decision candidates were accepted for the 2003-2004 class. Applications are accepted on-line through *www.sbc.edu/admissions/apply/online/html.*

Transfer: 18 transfer students enrolled in a recent year. Transfer applicants must submit official transcripts from high school and college, test scores, a college catalog, and recommendations from a previous dean and professor. 60 of 120 credits required for the bachelor's degree must be completed at Sweet Briar.

Visiting: There are regularly scheduled orientations for prospective students, consisting of attendance at classes and campus events, meetings with faculty and coaches, an overnight stay in a dorm, a campus tour, and an interview. There are guides for informal visits and visitors may sit in on classes and stay overnight. To schedule a visit, contact Ken Huus, Dean of Admissions at *admissions@sbc.edu.*

Financial Aid: 46% of full-time freshmen and 49% of continuing full-time students received need-based aid. The average freshman award was $13,049. 77% of undergraduates work part time. Average annual earnings from campus work are $945. The average financial indebtedness of the 2003 graduate was $17,250. Sweet Briar is a member of CSS. The FAFSA, the college's own financial statement and the Business/Farm Supplement; noncustodial parents statement are required. The deadline for filing freshman financial aid applications for fall entry is March 1.

International Students: There are 20 international students enrolled. The school actively recruits these students. They must score 550 on the written TOEFL or 213 on the electronic version and also take the SAT I or the ACT.

Computers: The mainframes are an HP 9000 L2000, 2 HP Net Servers LH4r, and a DEC Alpha Server 2000. More than 95 Mac and Pentium computers for student use are located across campus in 24-hour multimedia labs, the libraries, study rooms, and academic buildings. The computer-student ratio is 1:6 and more than 600 fiber optic connections to the campus network exist in academic buildings. Student residence hall rooms also have network connections. The college is connected to the Internet, including the World Wide Web. All students may access the system 24 hours a day. There are no time limits and no fees. It is strongly recommended that all students have a personal computer.

Graduates: From July 1, 2002 to June 30, 2003, 141 bachelor's degrees were awarded. The most popular majors were psychology (14%), biology (10%), and government (9%). In an average class, 1% graduate in 3 years or less, 61% graduate in 4 years or less, 61% graduate in 5 years or less, and 61% graduate in 6 years or less. 59 companies recruited on campus in 2002-2003. Of the 2002 graduating class, 25% were enrolled in graduate school within 6 months of graduation and 52% were employed.

Admissions Contact: Ken Huus, Dean of Admissions. A video is available. E-mail: *admissions@sbc.edu* Web: *www.admissions.sbc.edu*

UNIVERSITY OF RICHMOND   **E-3**
University of Richmond, VA 23173   **(804) 289-8640**
                                          (800) 700-1662; Fax: (804) 287-6003

Full-time: 1381 men, 1454 women	**Faculty:** 274; IIA, +$
Part-time: 16 men, 10 women	**Ph.D.s:** 97%
Graduate: 385 men, 340 women	**Student/Faculty:** 10 to 1
Year: semesters, summer session	**Tuition:** $24,940
Application Deadline: January 15	**Room & Board:** $5160
Freshman Class: 6079 applied, 2560 accepted, 835 enrolled	
SAT I or ACT: required	**MOST COMPETITIVE**

The University of Richmond, founded in 1830, is a private independent institution offering programs in arts and sciences, business, and leadership studies. There are 3 undergraduate and 3 graduate schools. In addition to regional accreditation, UR has baccalaureate program accreditation with AACSB, ACS, and NASM. The 4 libraries contain 1,083,769 volumes, 83,660 microform items, and 27,841 audio/video tapes/CDs, and subscribe to 11,494 periodicals. Computerized library services include the card catalog, interlibrary loans, and database searching. Special learning facilities include a learning resource center, art gallery, radio station, TV station, and the Lora Robins Gallery of Design from Nature. The 350-acre campus is in a suburban area 6 miles west of Richmond. Including any residence halls, there are 50 buildings.

Student Life: 84% of undergraduates are from out of state, mostly the Middle Atlantic. Students are from 45 states, 75 foreign countries, and Canada. 63% are from public schools. 87% are white. The average age of freshmen is 18; all undergraduates, 20. 8% do not continue beyond their first year; 92% remain to graduate.

Housing: 2700 students can be accommodated in college housing, which includes single-sex and coed dorms and on-campus apartments. In addition, there are special-interest houses. On-campus housing is available on a first-come, first-served basis and is available on a lottery system for upperclassmen. 92% of students live on campus; of those, 90% remain on campus on weekends. All students may keep cars.

Activities: 30% of men belong to 7 national fraternities; 50% of women belong to 8 national sororities. There are 250 groups on campus, including art, band, cheerleading, choir, chorale, chorus, computers, dance, debate, drama, drill team, ethnic, forensics, gay, honors, international, jazz band, literary magazine, musical theater, newspaper, orchestra, pep band, political, professional, radio and TV, religious, social, social service, student government, and yearbook. Popular campus events include UR Century Bike Race, Greek Theater Parties, and Ring Dance.

Sports: There are 8 intercollegiate sports for men and 9 for women, and 24 intramural sports for men and 23 for women. Facilities include a 10,000-seat gym, a stadium, a soccer/track complex, lighted intramural fields, an intramural gym, aerobics and weight rooms, a swimming pool, and tennis, racquetball, and squash courts.

Disabled Students: 85% of the campus is accessible. Wheelchair ramps, elevators, special parking, specially equipped rest rooms, and lowered drinking fountains are available.

Services: Counseling and information services are available, as is tutoring in most subjects. There are support centers for help with academic skills, writing, and speech.

Campus Safety and Security: Measures include 24-hour foot and vehicle patrol, self-defense education, security escort services, and shuttle buses. There are informal discussions, pamphlets/posters/films, emergency telephones, lighted pathways/sidewalks, a card-access system in all residence halls, vehicle assistance, emergency first aid service, fingerprinting, firearms storage, and personal property engraving and identification.

Programs of Study: UR confers B.A., B.S., and B.S.B.A. degrees. Associate and master's degrees are also awarded. Bachelor's degrees are awarded in BIOLOGICAL SCIENCE (biochemistry, biology/biological science, and molecular biology), BUSINESS (accounting, business administration and management, and business economics), COMMUNICATIONS AND THE ARTS (art history and appreciation, dramatic arts, English, French, German, Greek, journalism, Latin, music, Spanish, speech/debate/rhetoric, and studio art), COMPUTER AND PHYSICAL SCIENCE (chemistry, computer science, mathematics, and physics), SOCIAL SCIENCE (American studies, classical/ancient civilization, criminal justice, economics, history, interdisciplinary studies, international studies, philosophy, political science/government, psychology, religion, sociology, urban studies, and women's studies). Business, biology, and political science are the largest.

Required: To graduate, students must complete 120 credits with a minimum GPA of 2.0. In addition to the first-year core course, there are specific requirements in English composition, foreign language, natural science, phys ed, social analysis, literary studies, historical studies, symbolic reasoning, visual and performing arts, and wellness.

Special: Internships in nearly every major, study abroad in 29 countries, and a Washington semester with American University are available. UR also offers work-study programs, accelerated degree programs, B.A.-B.S. degrees, dual majors, student-designed majors, and a general studies degree through the School of Continuing Studies. The interdisciplinary leadership studies major includes a minor in arts and sciences or business. There is a marine biology study option with the Marine Sciences Laboratory at Duke University. Also available are a 3-2 engineering degree with George Washington University, Virginia Tech, and Columbia University, a 3-1-1 degree with the University of Virginia, and a 4-1 degree with Virginia Commonwealth. There are 31 national honor societies, including Phi Beta Kappa, and 7 departmental honors programs.

Faculty/Classroom: 58% of faculty are male; 42%, female. All both teach and do research. No introductory courses are taught by graduate students. The average class size in an introductory lecture is 23 and in a regular course, 18.

Admissions: 42% of the 2003-2004 applicants were accepted. The SAT I scores for the 2003-2004 freshman class were: Verbal--4% below 500, 16% between 500 and 599, 59% between 600 and 700, and 21% above 700; Math--2% below 500, 11% between 500 and 599, 59% be-

tween 600 and 700, and 28% above 700. The ACT scores were 2% below 21, 6% between 21 and 23, 11% between 24 and 26, 33% between 27 and 28, and 47% above 28. 81% of the current freshmen were in the top fifth of their class; 97% were in the top two fifths. There were 21 National Merit finalists and 44 semifinalists. 43 freshmen graduated first in their class.

Requirements: The SAT I or ACT is required. In addition, SAT II: Subject tests are required in writing and math I or II if the student is taking the SAT I. Applicants must be graduates of an accredited secondary school. The GED is accepted. Applicants must complete 16 high school academic credits, including 4 years of English, 3 of math, and at least 2 each of history, foreign language, and lab science. An essay, counselor recommendation, and auditions for music scholarships are required. AP and CLEP credits are accepted. Important factors in the admissions decision are advanced placement or honor courses, leadership record, and evidence of special talent.

Procedure: Freshmen are admitted in the fall. Entrance exams should be taken by February 1 of the senior year. There are early decision, early admissions, and deferred admissions plans. Early decision applications should be filed by November 15; regular applications, by January 15 for fall entry, along with a $40 fee. Notification of early decision is sent December 15; regular decision, April 1. 166 early decision candidates were accepted for the 2003-2004 class. A waiting list is an active part of the admissions procedure. Applications are accepted on-line through Common App.

Transfer: 47 transfer students enrolled in 2002-2003. Applicants must have earned a minimum of 24 credit hours in transferable courses. A minimum GPA of 2.0 is required; however, to be competitive an applicant needs about a 3.3 GPA. 60 of 120 credits required for the bachelor's degree must be completed at UR.

Visiting: There are regularly scheduled orientations for prospective students, consisting of conferences and tours offered Monday through Friday, with Saturday tours available on select dates from September through November, as well as Junior Preview Days in early spring. There are guides for informal visits and visitors may sit in on classes and stay overnight. To schedule a visit, contact the Admissions Office.

Financial Aid: In 2003-2004, 68% of all full-time freshmen and 65% of continuing full-time students received some form of financial aid. 31% of full-time freshmen and 30% of continuing full-time students received need-based aid. The average freshman award was $19,790. 25% of undergraduates work part time. Average annual earnings from campus work are $1000. The FAFSA and the university's own financial statement are required. The deadline for filing freshman financial aid applications for fall entry is February 25.

International Students: There are 153 international students enrolled. The school actively recruits these students. They must score 550 on the written TOEFL or 213 on the electronic version and also take the SAT I or the ACT. SAT II: Subject tests in writing and math are required of applicants living in the United States at the time of application, and are highly recommended for applicants not living in the United States.

Computers: The mainframe is an IBM P650. All students have access to labs housing Macs, PCs, and Sun SPARC stations. Bitnet, Internet, LEXIS, and WESTLAW networks are also available. All students may access the system.

Graduates: From July 1, 2002 to June 30, 2003, 770 bachelor's degrees were awarded. In an average class, 78% graduate in 4 years or less, 84% graduate in 5 years or less, and 84% graduate in 6 years or less. 325 companies recruited on campus in 2002-2003. Of the 2002 graduating class, 23% were enrolled in graduate school within 6 months of graduation and 69% were employed.

Admissions Contact: Pamela W. Spence, Dean of Admission. A video is available. E-mail: *admissions@richmond.edu* Web: *www.richmond.edu*

UNIVERSITY OF VIRGINIA
Charlottesville, VA 22904-4160

D-3
(434) 982-3200
Fax: (434) 924-3587

Full-time: 6077 men, 6973 women	**Faculty:** 1099; I, +$
Part-time: 361 men, 418 women	**Ph.D.s:** 92%
Graduate: 4008 men, 5240 women	**Student/Faculty:** 12 to 1
Year: semesters, summer session	**Tuition:** $6149 ($22,169)
Application Deadline: January 2	**Room & Board:** $5591
Freshman Class: 16,964 applied, 6634 accepted, 3634 enrolled	
SAT I Verbal/Math: 660/680	**ACT:** 29 **MOST COMPETITIVE**

The University of Virginia, founded in 1819, is a public institution with undergraduate programs in architecture, arts and sciences, commerce, education, engineering and applied science, and nursing. There are 6 undergraduate and 9 graduate schools. In addition to regional accreditation, UVA has baccalaureate program accreditation with AACSB, ABET, ACS, APA, ASLA, ASLHA, NAAB, NASM, NAST, NATA, NCATE, and NLN. The 18 libraries contain 4,867,833 volumes, 5,395,261 microform items, and 84,035 audio/video tapes/CDs, and subscribe to 55,843 periodicals. Computerized library services include the card catalog, interlibrary loans, database searching, and Internet access. Special learning facilities include a learning resource center, art gallery, radio station, TV station, art museum, and observatory. The 1160-acre campus is in a suburban area 70 miles northwest of Richmond. Including any residence halls, there are 531 buildings.

Student Life: 69% of undergraduates are from Virginia. Students are from 50 states, 110 foreign countries, and Canada. 74% are from public schools. 69% are white; 11%, Asian American. 36% are Protestant; 22% claim no religious affiliation; 21% are Catholic. The average age of freshmen is 18; all undergraduates, 20. 4% do not continue beyond their first year; 92% remain to graduate.

Housing: 6779 students can be accommodated in college housing, which includes coed dorms, on-campus apartments, and married-student housing. In addition, there are honors houses, language houses, special-interest houses, and 3 residential colleges. On-campus housing is guaranteed for the freshman year only, is available on a first-come, first-served basis, and is available on a lottery system for upperclassmen. 54% of students commute. Upperclassmen may keep cars.

Activities: 28% of men belong to 38 national fraternities; 28% of women belong to 20 national sororities. There are 300 groups on campus, including art, band, cheerleading, chess, choir, chorale, chorus, computers, dance, debate, drama, ethnic, film, forensics, gay, honors, international, jazz band, judiciary, literary magazine, marching band, musical theater, newspaper, orchestra, pep band, photography, political, professional, radio and TV, religious, social, social service, student government, symphony, tour guides, and yearbook. Popular campus events include Culturefest and Family Weekend.

Sports: There are 11 intercollegiate sports for men and 12 for women, and 30 intramural sports for men and 30 for women. Facilities include a 61,500-seat stadium, an 8500-seat gym, and 4 recreation centers including an aquatics and fitness center.

Disabled Students: All of the campus is accessible. Wheelchair ramps, elevators, special parking, specially equipped rest rooms, special class scheduling, lowered drinking fountains, lowered telephones, curb cuts, voice synthesizers, braille printers, and large-screen monitors are available.

Services: Counseling and information services are available, as is tutoring in every subject. There is a reader service for the blind. There are transcribers, note takers, and taped readings for disabled students.

Campus Safety and Security: Measures include 24-hour foot and vehicle patrol, self-defense education, security escort services, and shuttle buses. There are informal discussions, pamphlets/posters/films, emergency telephones, and lighted pathways/sidewalks.

Programs of Study: UVA confers B.A., B.S., B.A.R.H., B.C.P., B.I.S., B.S.C., B.S.Ed., and B.S.N. degrees. Master's and doctoral degrees are also awarded. Bachelor's degrees are awarded in BIOLOGICAL SCIENCE (biology/biological science), BUSINESS (business economics), COMMUNICATIONS AND THE ARTS (art, classics, comparative literature, dramatic arts, English, French, German, Italian, music, Slavic languages, and Spanish), COMPUTER AND PHYSICAL SCIENCE (applied mathematics, astronomy, chemistry, computer science, mathematics, and physics), EDUCATION (health and physical), ENGINEERING AND ENVIRONMENTAL DESIGN (aerospace studies, architecture, biomedical engineering, chemical engineering, city/community/regional planning, civil engineering, electrical/electronics engineering, engineering and applied science, environmental science, mechanical engineering, and systems engineering), HEALTH PROFESSIONS (nursing and speech pathology/audiology), SOCIAL SCIENCE (African American studies, anthropology, area studies, economics, history, interdisciplinary studies, international relations, philosophy, political science/government, psychology, religion, and sociology). English, history, and biology are the strongest academically. Commerce, economics, and psychology are the largest.

Required: To graduate, students must complete 120 credit hours, with 18 to 42 hours in the major and a minimum GPA of 2.0. Distribution requirements include 12 hours of math and science, 6 hours each of humanities, composition, and social sciences, 4 semesters of foreign languages, 3 hours of historical studies, and 3 hours of non-Western perspectives.

Special: UVA offers internships, study abroad in 14 countries, accelerated degree programs, B.A.-B.S. degrees in chemistry and physics, co-op programs in engineering, and nondegree study. Dual majors in most arts and sciences programs, student-designed majors, an interdisciplinary major and Echols Scholars program, and pass/fail options are available. There is a chapter of Phi Beta Kappa and a freshman honors program.

Faculty/Classroom: 69% of faculty are male; 31%, female. 57% teach undergraduates, and all do research. Graduate students teach 32% of introductory courses. The average class size in an introductory lecture is 54 and in a laboratory, 22.

Admissions: 39% of the 2003-2004 applicants were accepted. The SAT I scores for the 2003-2004 freshman class were: Verbal--3% below 500, 17% between 500 and 599, 47% between 600 and 700, and 31% above 700; Math--2% below 500, 13% between 500 and 599, 45% between 600 and 700, and 39% above 700. 96% of the current freshmen

were in the top fifth of their class; 99% were in the top two fifths. 191 freshmen graduated first in their class.

Requirements: The SAT I or ACT is required. In addition, SAT II: Subject tests in writing, math IC or IIC, and a third test of the students choice are required. With few exceptions, candidates graduate from accredited secondary schools. While the GED is accepted, it is rare for candidates for first-year admission who have this credential to be competitive in the admissions process. Applicants should complete 16 high school academic courses, including 4 courses of English, 4 courses of math, beginning with algebra I, 2 courses of physics, biology, or chemistry (3 if applying to engineering), 2 years of foreign language, and 1 course of social science. An essay is also required. AP credits are accepted. Important factors in the admissions decision are advanced placement or honor courses and evidence of special talent.

Procedure: Freshmen are admitted in the fall. Entrance exams should be taken by December of the senior year. There are early decision and deferred admissions plans. Early decision applications should be filed by November 1; regular applications, by January 2 for fall entry, along with a $40 fee. Notification of early decision is sent December 1; regular decision, April 1. 906 early decision candidates were accepted for the 2003-2004 class. 1535 applicants were on the 2003 waiting list; 63 were admitted. Applications are accepted on-line through *http://www.virginia.edu/undergradadmission/apply.html*.

Transfer: 519 transfer students enrolled in 2002-2003. Applicants for transfer must have a minimum GPA of 3.0, submit SAT I or ACT scores, and meet prerequisite courses. 60 of 120 credits required for the bachelor's degree must be completed at UVA.

Visiting: There are regularly scheduled orientations for prospective students, consisting of comprehensive information sessions and campus tours. Visitors may sit in on classes and stay overnight. To schedule a visit, contact the Monroe Society at (434) 924-3321 or *monroe@virginia.edu*.

Financial Aid: In 2003-2004, 68% of all full-time freshmen and 59% of continuing full-time students received some form of financial aid. 23% of full-time freshmen and 24% of continuing full-time students received need-based aid. The average freshman award was $9467. 25% of undergraduates work part time. The average financial indebtedness of the 2003 graduate was $14,146. The FAFSA and the college's own financial statement are required. The deadline for filing freshman financial aid applications for fall entry is March 1.

International Students: There are 1021 international students enrolled. The school actively recruits these students. They must take the TOEFL as well as the same tests as all other entering students.

Computers: The mainframe consists of UNIX-based IBM RS/600s and Suns. Access to the Internet is possible from more than 30 university-operated public computing facilities with more than 900 PCs or workstations. Wireless network is available in many locations. Residence halls have high-speed network connections. All students may access the system 24 hours a day, 7 days a week. There are no time limits and no fees. It is strongly recommended that all students have a personal computer.

Graduates: From July 1, 2002 to June 30, 2003, 3286 bachelor's degrees were awarded. The most popular majors were economics (13%), commerce (10%), and psychology (9%). In an average class, 1% graduate in 3 years or less, 83% graduate in 4 years or less, 91% graduate in 5 years or less, and 92% graduate in 6 years or less. 450 companies recruited on campus in 2002-2003.

Admissions Contact: John A. Blackburn, Dean of Admission.
E-mail: *undergradadmission@virginia.edu*
Web: *www.virginia.edu/undergradadmission*

UNIVERSITY OF VIRGINIA'S COLLEGE AT WISE   A-4
Wise, VA 24293   (276) 328-0322
(888) 282-9324; Fax: (276) 328-0251

Full-time: 655 men, 708 women	Faculty: 71
Part-time: 97 men, 243 women	Ph.D.s: 77%
Graduate: none	Student/Faculty: 19 to 1
Year: semesters, summer session	Tuition: $4530 ($13,418)
Application Deadline: August 1	Room & Board: $5586
Freshman Class: 987 applied, 767 accepted, 350 enrolled	
SAT I Verbal/Math: 512/492	ACT: 21 COMPETITIVE

The University of Virginia's College at Wise, founded in 1954, offers undergraduate programs through the departments of business studies, education, languages and literature, behavioral and social sciences, natural sciences, math and computer science, history and philosophy, visual and performing arts, and nursing. In addition to regional accreditation, UVA's College at Wise has baccalaureate program accreditation with NLN. The library contains 144,526 volumes, 64,062 microform items, and 4959 audio/video tapes/CDs, and subscribes to 732 periodicals. Computerized library services include the card catalog, interlibrary loans, database searching, and Internet access. Special learning facilities include an observatory. The 396-acre campus is in a small town 60 miles northwest of Bristol. Including any residence halls, there are 42 buildings.

Student Life: 95% of undergraduates are from Virginia. Students are from 9 states and 9 foreign countries. 99% are from public schools. 92% are white. The average age of freshmen is 18; all undergraduates, 23. 34% do not continue beyond their first year; 42% remain to graduate.

Housing: 547 students can be accommodated in college housing, which includes single-sex and coed dorms, on-campus apartments, and special-interest houses. On-campus housing is available on a first-come, first-served basis and is available on a lottery system for upperclassmen. 66% of students commute. All students may keep cars.

Activities: 6% of men belong to 1 local and 2 national fraternities; 6% of women belong to 2 local and 1 national sorority. There are 50 groups on campus, including art, band, cheerleading, chess, choir, chorale, chorus, dance, drama, ethnic, film, gay, honors, inter-Greek council, international, jazz band, literary magazine, multicultural alliance, musical theater, newspaper, pep band, political, professional, radio and TV, religious, residence hall association, social, social service, student activities board, and student government. Popular campus events include The Holly Ball, Jam for Man, and Extramural Flag Football Scramble.

Sports: There are 6 intercollegiate sports for men and 5 for women, and 42 intramural sports for men and 42 for women. Facilities include baseball and softball fields, a gym, tennis courts, a swimming pool, 3 practice football fields, a football stadium, racquetball court, fitness center, and a dance practice room.

Disabled Students: All of the campus is accessible. Wheelchair ramps, elevators, special parking, specially equipped rest rooms, special class scheduling, lowered drinking fountains, and special housing are available.

Services: Counseling and information services are available, as is tutoring in every subject. There is a reader service for the blind and remedial math and writing. Tutoring is free to all registered students.

Campus Safety and Security: Measures include 24-hour foot and vehicle patrol, self-defense education, security escort services, and informal discussions. There are pamphlets/posters/films, emergency telephones, lighted pathways/sidewalks, and a crime prevention office.

Programs of Study: UVA's College at Wise confers B.A., B.S., and B.S.N. degrees. Bachelor's degrees are awarded in BIOLOGICAL SCIENCE (biology/biological science), BUSINESS (accounting and business administration and management), COMMUNICATIONS AND THE ARTS (art, communications, dramatic arts, English, French, and Spanish), COMPUTER AND PHYSICAL SCIENCE (chemistry, information sciences and systems, and mathematics), ENGINEERING AND ENVIRONMENTAL DESIGN (environmental science), HEALTH PROFESSIONS (medical laboratory technology and nursing), SOCIAL SCIENCE (criminal justice, economics, history, international studies, law enforcement and corrections, liberal arts/general studies, political science/government, psychology, and social science). Natural science, accounting, and math are the strongest academically. Business administration and social sciences are the largest.

Required: To graduate, all students must complete 52 hours of general education requirements including a liberal arts course, arts, humanities, social sciences, natural sciences, English composition, literature, math, foreign language, phys ed, and Western heritage. At least 120 credit hours are required, with a minimum 2.0 GPA overall and in the major area.

Special: The college offers co-op programs in all majors, internships in education, social sciences, and communication, on-campus work-study programs, B.A.-B.S. degrees in most majors, dual and student-designed majors, and pass/fail options for classes not required for the major. There are 4 national honor societies, a freshman honors program, and 9 departmental honors programs.

Faculty/Classroom: 61% of faculty are male; 39%, female. All teach undergraduates, 50% do research, and 50% do both. The average class size in an introductory lecture is 22; in a laboratory, 21; and in a regular course, 15.

Admissions: 78% of the 2003-2004 applicants were accepted. The SAT I scores for the 2003-2004 freshman class were: Verbal--53% below 500, 32% between 500 and 599, 12% between 600 and 700, and 3% above 700; Math--51% below 500, 39% between 500 and 599, 9% between 600 and 700, and 1% above 700. The ACT scores were 59% below 21, 30% between 21 and 23, 9% between 24 and 26, and 2% between 27 and 28. 44% of the current freshmen were in the top fifth of their class; 71% were in the top two fifths. 6 freshmen graduated first in their class.

Requirements: The SAT I or ACT is required. In addition, all applicants must be graduates of approved secondary schools or hold a GED. Preference is given to students who earn an Advanced Studies Diploma or its equivalent, rank in the top half of their graduating class, score 900 or better on the SAT I (ACT 18), and complete 4 years of English; 3 or more courses in math, including algebra 1 and 2 and a course selected from among geometry, trigonometry, advanced math, or calculus; 2 or more years of natural science beyond general science; 2 or more years of a foreign language; and 1 year each of American history and world history. A GPA of 2.3 is required. AP credits are accepted. Important factors in the admissions decision are advanced placement or honor courses, recommendations by school officials, and leadership record.

Procedure: Freshmen are admitted to all sessions. Entrance exams should be taken by January 1 of the application year. There is a rolling admissions plan. There are early admissions and deferred admissions plans. Applications should be filed by August 1 for fall entry and January 5 for spring entry, along with a $25 fee. Notification is sent on a rolling basis. Applications are accepted on computer disk and on-line through CollegeNET or at *http://applyweb.com/apply/uvawise/menu.html*.

Transfer: 139 transfer students enrolled in 2002-2003. Transfer students must meet all general admissions requirements and submit secondary school transcripts or GED results and transcripts of all previous college work. A minimum 2.2 GPA is required. Students with either a minimum of 30 semester hours of college work, an associate degree, or who are at least 25 years old, need not submit the SAT I or ACT scores. For others, a minimum composite score of 900 on the SAT I or 18 on the ACT is recommended. 30 of 120 credits required for the bachelor's degree must be completed at UVA's College at Wise.

Visiting: There are regularly scheduled orientations for prospective students, including an interview, a campus tour, a meal, and class visitation. There are guides for informal visits and visitors may sit in on classes. To schedule a visit, contact the Admissions Office.

Financial Aid: In 2003-2004, 75% of all full-time freshmen and 72% of continuing full-time students received some form of financial aid. 68% of full-time freshmen and 66% of continuing full-time students received need-based aid. The average freshman award was $7545. Need-based scholarships or need-based grants averaged $3316 ($8500 maximum); need-based self-help aid (loans and jobs) averaged $2682 ($5625 maximum); non-need-based athletic scholarships averaged $1592; and other non-need-based awards and non-need-based scholarships averaged $1502. 13% of undergraduates work part time. Average annual earnings from campus work are $1146. The average financial indebtedness of the 2003 graduate was $6560. The FAFSA and the college's own financial statement are required. The priority date for freshman financial aid applications for fall entry is February 1 for academic scholarship and April 1 for need-based aid.

International Students: There were 12 international students enrolled in a recent year. The school actively recruits these students. They must score 550 on the written TOEFL or 234 on the electronic version and also take the SAT I or the ACT, scoring 700.

Computers: The mainframe is an HP 3000/Model 957. There are 5 computer labs with about 100 computers and Internet access. About 200 residents have access in dorms. Terminals are also available in the library. All students may access the system 24 hours per day. There are no time limits and no fees.

Graduates: From July 1, 2002 to June 30, 2003, 260 bachelor's degrees were awarded. The most popular majors were business administration (22%), psychology (10%), and liberal arts and sciences (8%). In an average class, 25% graduate in 4 years or less, 40% graduate in 5 years or less, and 42% graduate in 6 years or less. 23 companies recruited on campus in 2002-2003.

Admissions Contact: Russell Necessary, Director of Admissions and Financial Aid. A video is available. E-mail: *admissions@uvawise.edu* or *rdn2f@wvawise.edu* Web: *www.wise.virginia.edu*

VIRGINIA COMMONWEALTH UNIVERSITY E-3
Richmond, VA 23284
(804) 828-1222
(800) 841-3638; Fax: (804) 828-1899

Full-time: 4895 men, 7160 women	**Faculty:** I, av$
Part-time: 2180 men, 2920 women	**Ph.D.s:** 83%
Graduate: 3060 men, 4795 women	**Student/Faculty:** n/av
Year: semesters, summer session	**Tuition:** $3675 ($13,855)
Application Deadline: see profile	**Room & Board:** $5355
Freshman Class: n/av	
SAT I: required	**COMPETITIVE**

Virginia Commonwealth University, founded in 1838, is a public research university. There are 10 undergraduate and 12 graduate schools. Figures in the above capsule and in this profile are approximate. In addition to regional accreditation, VCU has baccalaureate program accreditation with AACSB, ABET, ACEJMC, ACPE, APTA, CAHEA, CSWE, FIDER, NASAD, NCATE, and NLN. The 2 libraries contain 1,680,393 volumes, 3,007,035 microform items, and 42,254 audio/video tapes/CDs, and subscribe to 9662 periodicals. Computerized library services include the card catalog, interlibrary loans, and database searching. Special learning facilities include a learning resource center, art gallery, radio station, and TV station. The 126-acre campus is in an urban area 2 miles west of downtown Richmond. Including any residence halls, there are 162 buildings.

Student Life: 95% of undergraduates are from Virginia. Students are from 42 states, 62 foreign countries, and Canada. 97% are from public schools. 64% are white; 23% African American. The average age of freshmen is 18; all undergraduates, 22. 23% do not continue beyond their first year; 42% remain to graduate.

Housing: 3170 students can be accommodated in college housing, which includes coed dorms, on-campus apartments, and off-campus apartments. In addition, there are honors houses and honors and special-interest floors. On-campus housing is guaranteed for the freshman year only and is available on a first-come, first-served basis. 79% of students commute. All students may keep cars.

Activities: 6% of men belong to 12 national fraternities; 3% of women belong to 9 national sororities. There are 170 groups on campus, including art, band, cheerleading, chess, choir, chorale, chorus, computers, dance, drama, ethnic, gay, honors, international, jazz band, literary magazine, musical theater, newspaper, orchestra, pep band, photography, political, professional, radio and TV, religious, social, social service, student government, symphony, and yearbook. Popular campus events include First Fridays, Annual Fall Block Show, and VCU celebrates the holidays.

Sports: There are 8 intercollegiate sports for men and 8 for women, and 18 intramural sports for men and 18 for women. Facilities include a recreation complex with sports clubs and a fitness program, a gym, a swimming pool, and an outdoor adventure program.

Disabled Students: 80% of the campus is accessible. Wheelchair ramps, elevators, special parking, specially equipped rest rooms, special class scheduling, lowered drinking fountains, and lowered telephones are available.

Services: Counseling and information services are available, as is tutoring in some subjects, including most 100- and 200-level general education requirements, some 300-level courses in math and sciences, and languages through the 100 level. There is a reader service for the blind and remedial math, reading, and writing.

Campus Safety and Security: Measures include 24-hour foot and vehicle patrol, self-defense education, security escort services, and shuttle buses. There are informal discussions, pamphlets/posters/films, emergency telephones, and lighted pathways/sidewalks.

Programs of Study: VCU confers B.A., B.S., B.F.A., B.I.S., B.Mus., B.Mus.Ed., B.S.N., and B.S.W. degrees. Master's and doctoral degrees are also awarded. Bachelor's degrees are awarded in BIOLOGICAL SCIENCE (biology/biological science), BUSINESS (accounting, business administration and management, business economics, and marketing/retailing/merchandising), COMMUNICATIONS AND THE ARTS (communications, dance, design, dramatic arts, English, fine arts, languages, and music), COMPUTER AND PHYSICAL SCIENCE (chemistry, computer science, information sciences and systems, mathematics, and physics), EDUCATION (art, elementary, and health), ENGINEERING AND ENVIRONMENTAL DESIGN (chemical engineering, electrical/electronics engineering, and mechanical engineering), HEALTH PROFESSIONS (nursing, occupational therapy, and physical therapy), SOCIAL SCIENCE (criminal justice, economics, history, political science/government, psychology, religion, social work, sociology, and urban studies). Psychology, biology, and mass communications are the largest.

Required: The total number of credit hours required for graduation varies with the major. Students must achieve a minimum GPA of 2.0.

Special: Internships are available for seniors with government agencies, banking and finance centers, private industry, media, and community service agencies. Co-op programs in all majors, work-study programs on campus and with state agencies in the city, study abroad in 6 countries, general studies degrees, and a B.A.-B.S. degree in psychology are offered. Students may take a 3-2 engineering degree with Old Dominion, George Washington, and Auburn Universities. Student-designed majors through a nontraditional studies program, nondegree study, and credit for life, military, and work experience are possible. There are 30 national honor societies, a freshman honors program, and 4 departmental honors programs.

Faculty/Classroom: 63% of faculty are male; 37%, female. The average class size in an introductory lecture is 25; in a laboratory, 15; and in a regular course, 22.

Admissions: In a recent year, 180 freshmen graduated first in their class.

Requirements: The SAT I is required, with a minimum composite score of 800 (400 math recommended and 350 verbal required). Applicants must be graduates of an accredited secondary school. The GED is accepted. Applicants should complete 20 high school academic credits, including 4 credits of English, 3 of math (including algebra I and II and geometry), 2 each of foreign language, history, and science (including a laboratory science), and 1 of social studies. Applicants for the School of the Arts must audition or submit a portfolio. An essay and an interview are recommended. A GPA of 2.2 is required. AP and CLEP credits are accepted. Important factors in the admissions decision are ability to finance college education, extracurricular activities record, and personality/intangible qualities.

Procedure: Freshmen are admitted fall and spring. Entrance exams should be taken before February 1. There are early decision, early admissions, deferred admissions, and rolling admissions plans. Check with the school for current deadlines. The fall 2003 application fee was $25. 146 early decision candidates were accepted for the 2003-2004 class. Applications are accepted on-line via the school's web site.

Transfer: 1534 transfer students enrolled in a recent year. Transfer students with 30 semester hours or more must have a 2.3 GPA or better;

those with fewer hours and who are under the age of 22 must submit SAT I scores. An associate degree and interview are advised. 30 credits required for the bachelor's degree must be completed at VCU.

Visiting: There are regularly scheduled orientations for prospective students, including an information session with a counselor followed by a student-led tour. Visitors may sit in on classes. To schedule a visit, contact the Office of Admissions.

Financial Aid: In a recent year, 75% of all full-time freshmen and 57% of continuing full-time students received some form of financial aid. 59% of full-time freshmen and 54% of continuing full-time students received need-based aid. The average freshman award was $6562. The average financial indebtedness of a recent graduate was $21,994. The FAFSA is required. Check with the school for current deadlines.

International Students: In a recent year, there were 187 international students enrolled. The school actively recruits these students. They must score 550 on the written TOEFL and also take the college's own test.

Computers: The mainframe is an IBM 3081K. Macs and PCs are available in academic buildings. All students may access the system. There are no time limits and no fees. It is strongly recommended that all students have a personal computer. It is required that all incoming freshmen and pharmacy students have personal computers.

Graduates: In a recent year, 2194 bachelor's degrees were awarded. The most popular majors were psychology (10%), business administration (7%), and information sciences (7%). In an average class, 14% graduate in 4 years or less, 32% graduate in 5 years or less, and 39% graduate in 6 years or less. 429 companies recruited on campus in a recent year.

Admissions Contact: Delores T. Taylor, Director, Admissions. E-mail: *vcuinfo@vcu.edu* Web: *www.vcu.edu*

VIRGINIA INTERMONT COLLEGE
Bristol, VA 24201-4298

B-4

(276) 466-7851
(800) 451-1842; Fax: (276) 466-7855

Full-time: 215 men, 440 women	**Faculty:** 41
Part-time: 28 men, 61 women	**Ph.D.s:** 73%
Graduate: none	**Student/Faculty:** 16 to 1
Year: semesters, summer session	**Tuition:** $14,400
Application Deadline: open	**Room & Board:** $5400
Freshman Class: 831 applied, 542 accepted, 232 enrolled	
SAT I Verbal/Math: 610/520	**ACT:** 20 **COMPETITIVE**

Virginia Intermont College, founded in 1884, is a private institution affiliated with the Baptist General Association of Virginia. In addition to regional accreditation, V.I. College has baccalaureate program accreditation with CSWE and ABA. The library contains 64,367 volumes, 27,594 electronic volumes, 9205 microform items, and 2236 audio/video tapes/CDs, and subscribes to 70 print periodicals and 9600 electronic periodicals. Computerized library services include the card catalog, interlibrary loans, database searching, and Internet access. Special learning facilities include a learning resource center, art gallery, equestrian center, ballet center, and film lab. The 13-acre campus is in an urban area 144 miles southwest of Roanoke and 114 miles northeast of Knoxville, Tennessee. Including any residence halls, there are 18 buildings.

Student Life: 51% of undergraduates are from Virginia. Students are from 37 states, 29 foreign countries, and Canada. 85% are from public schools. 83% are white; 11% African American. 48% are Protestant; 40% claim no religious affiliation; 9% Catholic. The average age of freshmen is 18; all undergraduates, 27. 40% do not continue beyond their first year; 40% remain to graduate.

Housing: 470 students can be accommodated in college housing, which includes single-sex and coed dorms and off-campus apartments. On-campus housing is guaranteed for all 4 years. 63% of students live on campus; of those, 50% remain on campus on weekends. Alcohol is not permitted. All students may keep cars.

Activities: There are no fraternities or sororities. There are 21 groups on campus, including art, cheerleading, choir, computers, dance, drama, honors, international, literary magazine, musical theater, newspaper, photography, political, professional, religious, social service, and student government. Popular campus events include May Day, Family Weekend, and Spring Fling.

Sports: There are 8 intercollegiate sports for men and 8 for women, and 12 intramural sports for men and 12 for women. Facilities include a gym, a 1200-seat amphitheater, lighted tennis courts, a swimming pool, and a fitness center.

Disabled Students: 35% of the campus is accessible. Wheelchair ramps, elevators, special parking, specially equipped rest rooms, special class scheduling, and special housing are available.

Services: Counseling and information services are available, as is tutoring in every subject. There is a reader service for the blind and remedial math and reading.

Campus Safety and Security: Measures include 24-hour foot and vehicle patrol, self-defense education, security escort services, and informal discussions. There are pamphlets/posters/films and lighted pathways/sidewalks.

Programs of Study: V.I. College confers B.A., B.S., B.F.A., and B.S.W. degrees. Associate degrees are also awarded. Bachelor's degrees are awarded in AGRICULTURE (equine science), BIOLOGICAL SCIENCE (biology/biological science), BUSINESS (business administration and management and sports management), COMMUNICATIONS AND THE ARTS (art, dance, dramatic arts, English, fine arts, performing arts, and photography), COMPUTER AND PHYSICAL SCIENCE (information sciences and systems), EDUCATION (education and secondary), HEALTH PROFESSIONS (premedicine and preveterinary science), SOCIAL SCIENCE (criminal justice, culinary arts, history, interdisciplinary studies, liberal arts/general studies, paralegal studies, political science/government, psychology, public administration, religion, and social work). Equine studies, business, and photography are the largest.

Required: To graduate, students must complete 124 credits with a minimum GPA of 2.0. Required courses are English compostition, English literature, world history, computer fundamentals, college math, natural science, performing arts, visual arts, psychology or sociology, economics or political science, philosophy or religion, speech, and phys ed.

Special: V.I. College offers cross-registration with King College and internships in paralegal studies, social work, business, art, dance, photography, sports management, political science, psychology, and theater. Dual majors, study abroad, a general studies degree, and nondegree study are available. Evening degree programs in organizational management, interdisciplinary studies, computer information management, criminal justice, and social work are designed for working adults. There are 4 national honor societies and a freshman honors program.

Faculty/Classroom: 51% of faculty are male; 49%, female. All teach undergraduates. The average class size in an introductory lecture is 21; in a laboratory, 18; and in a regular course, 19.

Admissions: 65% of the 2003-2004 applicants were accepted. The SAT I scores for the 2003-2004 freshman class were: Verbal--60% below 500, 28% between 500 and 599, 11% between 600 and 700, and 1% above 700; Math--61% below 500, 28% between 500 and 599, 10% between 600 and 700, and 1% above 700. The ACT scores were 63% below 21, 21% between 21 and 23, 15% between 24 and 26, 1% between 27 and 28, and 1% above 28. 24% of the current freshmen were in the top fifth of their class; 35% were in the top two fifths. 7 freshmen graduated first in their class.

Requirements: The SAT I or ACT is required, with a minimum composite score of 780 on the SAT I or 18 on the ACT. Applicants must be graduates of an accredited secondary school or home school. The GED is accepted. Applicants should complete 15 academic credits, including 4 credits of English, 2 each of social science and math, 1 of a lab science, and 6 electives. An essay is required of students not meeting the normal admissions requirements. A GPA of 2.0 is required. AP and CLEP credits are accepted. Important factors in the admissions decision are evidence of special talent, advanced placement or honor courses, and parents or siblings attending the school.

Procedure: Freshmen are admitted to all sessions. Entrance exams should be taken late in the junior year or early in the senior year. There is a rolling admissions plan. There are early admissions and deferred admissions plans. Application deadlines are open. The fall 2003 application fee was $15 (waived for on-line applications). Applications are accepted on-line.

Transfer: 138 transfer students enrolled in 2002-2003. Applicants for transfer should have a minimum GPA of 2.0. An interview is recommended. 30 of 124 credits required for the bachelor's degree must be completed at V.I. College.

Visiting: There are regularly scheduled orientations for prospective students, consisting of a campus tour, an admissions interview, meetings with faculty, auditions for performance scholarships, and planning sessions with financial aid staff. There are guides for informal visits and visitors may sit in on classes and stay overnight. To schedule a visit, contact the Admissions Office at (276) 466-7856 or *viadmit@vic.edu*.

Financial Aid: In 2003-2004, 92% of all full-time freshmen and 90% of continuing full-time students received some form of financial aid. 85% of all full-time students received need-based aid. The average freshman award was $14,300. Need-based scholarships or need-based grants averaged $1000 ($2000 maximum); need-based self-help aid (loans and jobs) averaged $4125 (maximum); and non-need-based awards and non-need-based scholarships averaged $5000 ($13,900 maximum). 60% of undergraduates work part time. Average annual earnings from campus work are $1500. The average financial indebtedness of the 2003 graduate was $17,125. V.I. College is a member of CSS. The FAFSA and the college's own financial statement are required. The deadline for filing freshman financial aid applications for fall entry is April 15.

International Students: There are 63 international students enrolled. The school actively recruits these students. They must score 400 on the written TOEFL and also take the SAT I or the ACT.

Computers: The mainframe is an IBM AS/400. 21 PCs are available in the computer center, 10 in the library, 10 PCs and 4 Macs in the writing center, and 25 PCs and 30 Macs in various labs. Residence halls and booths in the café are wired for Internet access. All students may access the system. There are no time limits and no fees.

Graduates: From July 1, 2002 to June 30, 2003, 96 bachelor's degrees were awarded. The most popular majors were equine studies (22%), business administration (17%), and interdisciplinary studies (13%). In an average class, 20% graduate in 4 years or less, 29% graduate in 5 years or less, and 29% graduate in 6 years or less. 22 companies recruited on campus in 2002-2003. Of the 2002 graduating class, 15% were enrolled in graduate school within 6 months of graduation and 92% were employed.

Admissions Contact: Stacy Hallmark, Director of Admissions. A video is available. E-mail: *viadmit@vic.edu* Web: *www.vic.edu*

VIRGINIA MILITARY INSTITUTE D-3
Lexington, VA 24450
(540) 464-7211
(800) 767-4207; Fax: (540) 464-7746

Full-time: 1250 men, 65 women	**Faculty:** 96; IIB, +$
Part-time: none	**Ph.D.s:** 96%
Graduate: none	**Student/Faculty:** 14 to 1
Year: semesters, summer session	**Tuition:** $5130 ($16,200)
Application Deadline: see profile	**Room & Board:** $4840
Freshman Class: n/av	
SAT I or ACT: required	**COMPETITIVE+**

Virginia Military Institute, established in 1839, is the nation's first state-supported military college. It offers academic programs in engineering, sciences, and liberal arts. Figures in the above capsule and in this profile are approximate. All students are members of the Corps of Cadets, live in barracks, eat together in the mess hall, wear uniforms, and adhere to the Honor System. In addition to regional accreditation, VMI has baccalaureate program accreditation with ABET. The 2 libraries contain 240,000 volumes, 18,000 microform items, and 4540 audio/video tapes/CDs, and subscribe to 800 periodicals. Computerized library services include the card catalog, interlibrary loans, and database searching. Special learning facilities include a learning resource center, an observatory and a research library. The 134-acre campus is in a small town 50 miles north of Roanoke. Including any residence halls, there are 68 buildings.

Student Life: 51% of undergraduates are from Virginia. Students are from 45 states, 19 foreign countries, and Canada. 78% are from public schools. 83% are white. 56% are Protestant; 30% Catholic. The average age of freshmen is 18; all undergraduates, 20. 23% do not continue beyond their first year; 67% remain to graduate.

Housing: 1370 students can be accommodated in college housing, which includes coed dorms. On-campus housing is guaranteed for all 4 years. All students live on campus; of those, 60% remain on campus on weekends. Alcohol is not permitted. Upperclassmen may keep cars.

Activities: There are no fraternities or sororities. There are 50 groups on campus, including bagpipe band, band, cheerleading, choir, chorus, dance, drama, drill team, ethnic, historical, honors, international, investment, jazz band, literary magazine, marching band, musical theater, newspaper, orchestra, pep band, photography, political, professional, religious, social, social service, student government, and yearbook. Popular campus events include Ring Figure, Virginia Transportation Conference, and dance and concert weekends.

Sports: There are 13 intercollegiate sports for men and 3 for women, and 4 intramural sports for men and 4 for women. Facilities include basketball, racquetball, and tennis courts, fields for lacrosse, football, baseball, and soccer, a swimming pool, a rifle range, indoor and outdoor running tracks, a wrestling facility, access to a golf course, weight training and aerobic facility, and auxillary indoor and outdoor basketball courts.

Disabled Students: 50% of the campus is accessible. Wheelchair ramps, elevators, special parking, and specially equipped rest rooms are available.

Services: Counseling and information services are available, as is tutoring in some subjects, including French, Spanish, German, Arabic, chemistry, math, physics, economics, and business. Tutoring for intercollegiate athletes, paid for by NCAA, also is available.

Campus Safety and Security: Measures include 24-hour foot and vehicle patrol, informal discussions, pamphlets/posters/films, and emergency telephones. There are lighted pathways/sidewalks and a 24-hour student guard team.

Programs of Study: VMI confers B.A. and B.S. degrees. Bachelor's degrees are awarded in BIOLOGICAL SCIENCE (biology/biological science), BUSINESS (business economics), COMMUNICATIONS AND THE ARTS (English), COMPUTER AND PHYSICAL SCIENCE (chemistry, computer science, mathematics, and physics), ENGINEERING AND ENVIRONMENTAL DESIGN (civil engineering, electrical/electronics engineering, and mechanical engineering), SOCIAL SCIENCE (history, international studies, and psychology). Engineering (civil, electrical, and mechanical) and sciences are the strongest academically. History, business/economics, and civil and mechanical engineering are the largest.

Required: To graduate, students must complete 136 to 144 semester hours, with a GPA of 2.0. All students must pass chemistry, English, history, math, phys ed, ROTC, and public speaking. In addition, all cadets must pass swimming, boxing, and wrestling.

Special: Study abroad in 14 countries and work-study programs are available, as are for-credit internships in English and international studies and summer internships in foreign countries. VMI offers dual majors in any combination and B.A.-B.S. degrees in liberal arts, physical sciences, and engineering. Minors are offered in each field of study. There are 11 national honor societies, a freshman honors program, and 3 departmental honors programs.

Faculty/Classroom: 82% of faculty are male; 18%, female. All teach undergraduates, 67% do research, and 67% do both. The average class size in an introductory lecture is 19; in a laboratory, 14; and in a regular course, 15.

Admissions: In a recent year, 3 freshmen graduated first in their class.

Requirements: The SAT I or ACT is required. In addition, applicants must be graduates of an accredited secondary school. Applicants should complete 19 to 20 high school academic units, including 4 years of English and math, 3 of science, history, and foreign language, and 2 of social studies. An essay is encouraged and an interview is recommended. AP credits are accepted. Important factors in the admissions decision are advanced placement or honor courses, extracurricular activities record, and leadership record.

Procedure: Freshmen are admitted in the fall. Entrance exams should be taken during the second semester of the junior year. There is an early decision plan and a rolling admissions plan. Check with the school for current deadlines. The fall 2003 fee was $25. A waiting list is an active part of the admissions procedure. Applications are accepted on computer disk.

Transfer: 31 transfer students enrolled in a recent year. Applicants for transfer must have a minimum GPA of 2.0, and 24 transferable credit hours, and a satisfactory high school record. Either the SAT I or the ACT is required. 67 of 135 credits required for the bachelor's degree must be completed at VMI.

Visiting: There are regularly scheduled orientations for prospective students, consisting of tours, conferences with academic and ROTC instructors, interaction with current freshmen, and overnight stays. There are guides for informal visits and visitors may sit in on classes and stay overnight. To schedule a visit, contact Admissions.

Financial Aid: VMI is a member of CSS. The FAFSA and the college's own financial statement are required. Check with the school for current deadlines.

International Students: There are 51 international students enrolled. The school actively recruits these students. They must score 500 on the written TOEFL. International students who will play intercollegiate athletics must take the SAT I or ACT.

Computers: The mainframe is a DEC Alpha server 4100. There are 200 networked PCs available to cadets with access to the local area network and the Internet. All student rooms are wired for Internet access. All students may access the system. There are no time limits and no fees. It is strongly recommended that all students have a personal computer.

Graduates: From July 1, 2002 to June 30, 2003, 234 bachelor's degrees were awarded. The most popular majors were history (22%), economics (20%), and international studies (12%). In an average class, 54% graduate in 4 years or less, 65% graduate in 5 years or less, and 67% graduate in 6 years or less. 45 companies recruited on campus in 2002-2003. Of the 2002 graduating class, 18% were enrolled in graduate school within 6 months of graduation and 99% were employed.

Admissions Contact: Col. Vernon L. Beitzel, Director, Admissions. A video is available. E-mail: *admissions@vmi.edu* Web: *www.vmi.edu*

VIRGINIA POLYTECHNIC INSTITUTE AND STATE UNIVERSITY

C-3

Blacksburg, VA 24061   (540) 231-6267; Fax: (540) 231-3242

Full-time: 12,209 men, 8518 women	**Faculty:** 1043; I, av$
Part-time: 366 men, 251 women	**Ph.D.s:** 82%
Graduate: 3593 men, 2447 women	**Student/Faculty:** 20 to 1
Year: semesters, summer session	**Tuition:** $5095 ($15,029)
Application Deadline: January 15	**Room & Board:** $4084
Freshman Class: 18,350 applied, 12,000 accepted, 4900 enrolled	
SAT I or ACT: required	**COMPETITIVE**

Virginia Polytechnic Institute and State University, founded in 1872, is a public land-grant institution. It offers a cadet program within the larger, nonmilitary student body. There are 7 undergraduate and 2 graduate schools. In addition to regional accreditation, Virginia Tech has baccalaureate program accreditation with AACSB, ABET, ACCE, ADA, AHEA, ASLA, FIDER, NAAB, NCATE, and SAF. The 4 libraries contain 2.1 million volumes, 6.2 million microform items, and 17,510 audio/video tapes/CDs, and subscribe to 18,737 periodicals. Computerized library services include the card catalog, interlibrary loans, and database searching. Special learning facilities include a learning resource center, art gallery, natural history museum, radio station, TV station, airport, wind tunnels, agricultural stations, radio/visual observatories, satellite uplink station, multimedia, digital music, writing, and CAD/CAM labs, math emporium, and CAVE (cave automatic virtual environment). The 2600-

acre campus is in a rural area 40 miles southwest of Roanoke. Including any residence halls, there are 110 buildings.

Student Life: 70% of undergraduates are from Virginia. Students are from 50 states, 104 foreign countries, and Canada. 73% are white. The average age of freshmen is 18; all undergraduates, 22. 12% do not continue beyond their first year; 67% remain to graduate.

Housing: 8682 students can be accommodated in college housing, which includes single-sex and coed dorms, fraternity houses, and sorority houses. In addition, there are honors houses and special-interest houses. On-campus housing is guaranteed for the freshman year only and is available on a lottery system for upperclassmen. 59% of students commute. All students may keep cars.

Activities: 13% of men belong to 34 national fraternities; 15% of women belong to 16 national sororities. There are 600 groups on campus, including art, band, cheerleading, chess, choir, chorale, chorus, computers, dance, drama, drill team, drum and bugle corps, ethnic, film, gay, honors, international, jazz band, literary magazine, marching band, musical theater, newspaper, orchestra, pep band, photography, political, professional, radio and TV, religious, social, social service, student government, symphony, and yearbook. Popular campus events include Quad Jams, Ring Dance, and German's Mid-Winter Dance.

Sports: There are 11 intercollegiate sports for men and 10 for women, and 19 intramural sports for men and 19 for women. Facilities include a football stadium, a basketball coliseum, a field house, an indoor tennis pavilion, a 9-hole golf course, soccer and baseball fields, a swimming pool, a diving well, basketball, volleyball, racquetball, handball, squash, and tennis courts, a gymnastics room, a weight-lifting room, lighted multipurpose recreation fields, and a pond for ice skating. Residential quads are also equipped with weight-room and exercise facilities; there are also 2 gyms.

Disabled Students: 60% of the campus is accessible. Wheelchair ramps, elevators, special parking, specially equipped rest rooms, special class scheduling, lowered drinking fountains, lowered telephones, and a special services library room for the visually impaired are available.

Services: Counseling and information services are available, as is tutoring in most subjects. There is a reader service for the blind and remedial reading.

Campus Safety and Security: Measures include 24-hour foot and vehicle patrol, self-defense education, security escort services, and shuttle buses. There are informal discussions, pamphlets/posters/films, emergency telephones, and lighted pathways/sidewalks.

Programs of Study: Virginia Tech confers B.A., B.S., B.Arch., B.F.A., B.Land.Arch., B.S.Bus., B.S.E., and B.S.Ed. degrees. Master's and doctoral degrees are also awarded. Bachelor's degrees are awarded in AGRICULTURE (agricultural economics, animal science, dairy science, forestry and related sciences, horticulture, poultry science, and soil science), BIOLOGICAL SCIENCE (biochemistry and biology/biological science), BUSINESS (accounting, banking and finance, business economics, hotel/motel and restaurant management, management science, and marketing/retailing/merchandising), COMMUNICATIONS AND THE ARTS (communications, dramatic arts, English, French, German, music, and Spanish), COMPUTER AND PHYSICAL SCIENCE (chemistry, computer science, geology, mathematics, physics, and statistics), EDUCATION (agricultural, business, early childhood, health, home economics, marketing and distribution, physical, technical, and vocational), ENGINEERING AND ENVIRONMENTAL DESIGN (agricultural engineering, architecture, chemical engineering, civil engineering, computer engineering, construction engineering, construction management, electrical/electronics engineering, environmental science, interior design, landscape architecture/design, materials engineering, mechanical engineering, mining and mineral engineering, and ocean engineering), SOCIAL SCIENCE (child care/child and family studies, economics, food science, geography, history, international studies, liberal arts/general studies, philosophy, political science/government, psychology, public administration, sociology, textiles and clothing, and urban studies). Engineering, architecture, and business are the strongest academically. Engineering, computer science, and biology are the largest.

Required: To graduate, students must complete between 120 and 156 credit hours (depending on the major), with a minimum GPA of 2.0. There is a required core curriculum that includes 8 hours of science and 6 hours each of humanities, social science, math, and writing and discourse. Students must also meet a foreign language requirement.

Special: Students may cross-register with Miami University in Ohio, Oxford Polytechnic Institute, California Polytechnic Institute, and Florida A & M. Study abroad in 36 countries, internships in nearly every major, a Washington semester, and a wide range of work-study programs are available, as well as co-ops in 48 majors. There are honors options for most majors, B.A.-B.S. degrees, dual and student-designed majors, credit for independent study or research, nondegree study, and pass/fail options. The Corps of Cadets, a militarily structured organization, is open to men and women. Undergraduate advising programs are available to students wishing to prepare for professional school in law, dentistry, medicine, pharmacy, physical therapy, or veterinary medicine. There are 13 national honor societies, including Phi Beta Kappa, and a freshman honors program.

Faculty/Classroom: 67% of faculty are male; 33%, female. 74% teach undergraduates and 100% do research. Graduate students teach 12% of introductory courses. The average class size in an introductory lecture is 46 and in a laboratory, 30.

Admissions: 65% of the 2003-2004 applicants were accepted. 71% of the current freshmen were in the top fifth of their class; 98% were in the top two fifths. There were 36 National Merit finalists. 77 freshmen graduated first in their class.

Requirements: The SAT I or ACT is required. In addition, students must also take SAT II: Subject test in writing. Applicants must be graduates of an accredited secondary school, or the GED is accepted. Applicants should complete 18 high school academic credits, including 4 years of English, 3 of math, including algebra II and geometry, 2 of lab science, to be chosen from biology, chemistry, or physics, and 1 each of history and social studies. An additional 3 years from college preparatory courses and 4 from any credit course offerings are required. A portfolio and an audition are required for art and music students. A GPA of 2.0 is required. AP and CLEP credits are accepted. Important factors in the admissions decision are advanced placement or honor courses, evidence of special talent, and extracurricular activities record.

Procedure: Freshmen are admitted to all sessions. Entrance exams should be taken by January 1 of the senior year. There are early decision, early admissions, and deferred admissions plans. Early decision applications should be filed by November 1; regular applications, by January 15 for fall entry, October 1 for spring entry, and April 22 for summer entry, along with a $40 fee. Notification of early decision is sent December 15; regular decision, on a rolling basis. 1100 early decision candidates were accepted for the 2003-2004 class. A waiting list is an active part of the admissions procedure. Applications are accepted on-line through CollegeNet and *www.admiss.vt.edu*.

Transfer: 700 transfer students enrolled in 2002-2003. Applicants must have a minimum GPA of 2.0 and must specify a major. Competitive GPA is 3.0. 30 of 120 to 156 credits required for the bachelor's degree must be completed at Virginia Tech.

Visiting: There are regularly scheduled orientations for prospective students, consisting of a Fall Open House Series: half-day on-campus programs that include presentations, tours, and question-and-answer sessions. There are guides for informal visits and visitors may sit in on classes. To schedule a visit, contact the Office of Undergraduate Admissions.

Financial Aid: In a recent year, 65% of all full-time freshmen and 63% of continuing full-time students received some form of financial aid. 49% of full-time freshmen and 66% of continuing full-time students received need-based aid. The average freshman award was $6625. 43% of undergraduates work part time. Average annual earnings from campus work are $1500. The average financial indebtedness of the 2003 graduate was $15,049. The FAFSA is required. The deadline for filing freshman financial aid applications for fall entry is March 1.

International Students: There are 640 international students enrolled. The school actively recruits these students. They must score 550 on the written TOEFL and also take the SAT I or the ACT. Students must take the SAT II: writing test.

Computers: Undergraduates receive guidance on using PCs and the Internet from their professors. They may access the Internet or use PCs in any one of many computer labs on campus, or from their dorm rooms. Dorm rooms are wired for data, voice, and video transmission. All students may access the system any time. All students are required to have personal computers. Requirements vary by major.

Admissions Contact: Office of Undergraduate Admissions. A video is available. E-mail: *vtadmiss@vt.edu* Web: *www.vt.edu*

VIRGINIA STATE UNIVERSITY

Petersburg, VA 23806

E-3

(804) 524-5902

(800) 871-7611; Fax: (804) 524-5055

Full-time: 1330 men, 1820 women	Faculty: 168
Part-time: 165 men, 190 women	Ph.D.s: 74%
Graduate: 220 men, 580 women	Student/Faculty: 19 to 1
Year: semesters, summer session	Tuition: $4350 ($11,260)
Application Deadline: May 1	Room & Board: $6008
Freshman Class: 4138 applied, 2028 accepted, 1011 enrolled	
SAT I or ACT: required	COMPETITIVE

Virginia State University is a historically black public land-grant institution of higher education providing academic programs that integrate instruction, research, and extension/public service. Some information in this capsule and profile is approximate. There are 4 undergraduate schools and 1 graduate school. In addition to regional accreditation, VSU has baccalaureate program accreditation with ABET, ADA, CSWE, NASM, and NCATE. The library contains 280,599 volumes, 662,075 microform items, and 3939 audio/video tapes/CDs, and subscribes to 1198 periodicals. Computerized library services include the card catalog, interlibrary loans, and database searching. Special learning facilities include a learning resource center, art gallery, radio station, and TV sta-

tion. The 652-acre campus is in a suburban area 25 miles south of Richmond. Including any residence halls, there are 52 buildings.

Student Life: 65% of undergraduates are from Virginia. Students are from 35 states and 1 foreign country. 96% are from public schools. 90% are African American. The average age of freshmen is 18; all undergraduates, 21. 40% do not continue beyond their first year; 18% remain to graduate.

Housing: 2050 students can be accommodated in college housing, which includes single-sex dorms. In addition, there are honors houses. On-campus housing is guaranteed for the freshman year only and is available on a first-come, first-served basis. 52% of students live on campus; of those, 20% remain on campus on weekends. Alcohol is not permitted. Upperclassmen may keep cars.

Activities: 10% of men belong to 4 national fraternities; 10% of women belong to 4 national sororities. There are 44 groups on campus, including band, cheerleading, chess, choir, chorus, computers, dance, drama, drill team, ethnic, honors, international, jazz band, marching band, musical theater, newspaper, orchestra, pep band, photography, political, professional, radio and TV, religious, social, student government, symphony, and yearbook. Popular campus events include High School Day, VSU Day, and Commencement.

Sports: There are 7 intercollegiate sports for men and 6 for women, and 5 intramural sports for men and 6 for women. Facilities include a gym, an Olympic-size pool, a dance studio, tennis courts, track, football, and baseball fields, and indoor and outdoor basketball courts.

Disabled Students: 75% of the campus is accessible. Wheelchair ramps, elevators, special parking, and specially equipped rest rooms are available.

Services: Counseling and information services are available, as is tutoring in most subjects. There is a reader service for the blind.

Campus Safety and Security: Measures include 24-hour foot and vehicle patrol, informal discussions, emergency telephones, and lighted pathways/sidewalks.

Programs of Study: VSU confers B.A., B.S., B.F.A., B.I.S., and B.Mus. degrees. Master's degrees are also awarded. Bachelor's degrees are awarded in AGRICULTURE (agriculture), BIOLOGICAL SCIENCE (biology/biological science), BUSINESS (accounting, business administration and management, hotel/motel and restaurant management, management information systems, and marketing management), COMMUNICATIONS AND THE ARTS (English literature, music performance, and visual and performing arts), COMPUTER AND PHYSICAL SCIENCE (chemistry, mathematics, and physics), EDUCATION (athletic training, business, physical, and trade and industrial), ENGINEERING AND ENVIRONMENTAL DESIGN (engineering technology), SOCIAL SCIENCE (economics, history, home economics, interdisciplinary studies, political science/government, psychology, public administration, social work, and sociology). Business administration, accounting, and business information systems are the largest.

Required: To graduate, students must have a minimum GPA of 2.0. They must earn at least 120 credits, with the last 27 semester hours in residence. Requirements include those in phys ed, freshman writing, math, biology, social or physical science, history, and psychology. Freshman orientation must also be completed.

Special: VSU offers dual majors, a general studies degree, a 3-2 engineering degree program, nondegree study, and a pass/fail grading option. There are 10 national honor societies, including Phi Beta Kappa, a freshman honors program, and 7 departmental honors programs.

Faculty/Classroom: 67% of faculty are male; 33%, female. Graduate students teach 2% of introductory courses.

Admissions: 49% of the 2003-2004 applicants were accepted.

Requirements: The SAT I or ACT is required. In addition, applicants must graduate from an accredited secondary school with 16 academic credits and 12 Carnegie units, or have a GED. Students must take 4 years of English, 2 each of a foreign language, math, and science, and 1 each of history and social studies. Essays, 2 letters of recommendation, evidence of physical condition, interviews, and, if appropriate, auditions are required. A GPA of 2.2 is required. AP and CLEP credits are accepted. Important factors in the admissions decision are advanced placement or honor courses, recommendations by school officials, and leadership record.

Procedure: Freshmen are admitted fall and spring. There is a deferred admissions plan and a rolling admissions plan. Notification is sent on a rolling basis. Applications are accepted on-line through the school's web site at *www.vsu.edu/under.html*.

Transfer: Applicants must have a minimum GPA of 2.0. Those transferring fewer than 25 semester hours must meet freshman standards. 30 credits of 120 required for the bachelor's degree must be completed at VSU.

Visiting: There are regularly scheduled orientations for prospective students. There are guides for informal visits and visitors may sit in on classes. To schedule a visit, contact Admissions.

Financial Aid: In 2003-2004, 95% of all full-time freshmen received some form of financial aid. Average annual earnings from campus work are $2000. VSU is a member of CSS. The CSS Profile and the college's own financial statement are required. Check with the school for current deadlines.

International Students: They must score 500 on the written TOEFL and also take the SAT I or the ACT.

Computers: The mainframe is an IBM 4361. There are 322 PCs available in computer labs and in various units on campus. All students may access the system 8 A.M. to 10 P.M. Monday through Friday and 8 A.M. to 4 P.M. Saturdays. There are no time limits and no fees. A PC is recommended.

Graduates: In an average class, 10% graduate in 4 years or less, 26% graduate in 5 years or less, and 33% graduate in 6 years or less.

Admissions Contact: Irene Logan, Director of Admissions. A video is available. E-mail: *ilogan@vsu.edu* Web: *www.vsu.edu*

VIRGINIA UNION UNIVERSITY
Richmond, VA 23220

E-3

(804) 329-8456
(800) 368-3227; Fax: (804) 329-8477

Full-time: 540 men, 785 women	**Faculty:** 82; IIB, --$
Part-time: 35 men, 30 women	**Ph.D.s:** 55%
Graduate: 210 men, 115 women	**Student/Faculty:** 16 to 1
Year: semesters, summer session	**Tuition:** $10,690
Application Deadline: see profile	**Room & Board:** $4670
Freshman Class: n/av	
SAT I: required	**LESS COMPETITIVE**

Virginia Union University, established in 1865 and affiliated with the Baptist Church, is a private institution offering undergraduate programs in education and psychology, business, humanities, natural science and math, and social sciences. There are 2 undergraduate schools and 1 graduate school. Figures in the above capsule and in this profile are approximate. In addition to regional accreditation, VUU has baccalaureate program accreditation with ACBSP and CSWE. The library contains 145,305 volumes, 62,079 microform items, and 1523 audio/video tapes/CDs, and subscribes to 308 periodicals. Computerized library services include database searching. Special learning facilities include a learning resource center and art gallery. The 72-acre campus is in an urban area in the city of Richmond. Including any residence halls, there are 18 buildings.

Student Life: 52% of undergraduates are from Virginia. Students are from 27 states and 4 foreign countries. 85% are from public schools. 98% are African American. The average age of freshmen is 18. 31% do not continue beyond their first year; 55% remain to graduate.

Housing: 700 students can be accommodated in college housing, which includes single-sex dorms. In addition, there are honors houses. On-campus housing is available on a first-come, first-served basis. Priority is given to out-of-town students. 50% of students live on campus. Alcohol is not permitted. All students may keep cars.

Activities: There are 2 national fraternities and 4 national sororities. There are 32 groups on campus, including cheerleading, drama, international, newspaper, religious, student government, and yearbook. Popular campus events include films, lectures, and concerts.

Sports: There are 6 intercollegiate sports for men and 6 for women, and 3 intramural sports for men and 2 for women. Facilities include a gym-auditorium and a 10000-seat stadium.

Disabled Students: 90% of the campus is accessible. Wheelchair ramps, elevators, and special parking are available.

Services: Counseling and information services are available, as is tutoring in every subject. There is remedial math, reading, and writing.

Campus Safety and Security: Measures include 24-hour foot and vehicle patrol, security escort services, informal discussions, and pamphlets/posters/films. There are emergency telephones and lighted pathways/sidewalks.

Programs of Study: VUU confers B.A., B.S., and B.S.W. degrees. Master's and doctoral degrees are also awarded. Bachelor's degrees are awarded in BIOLOGICAL SCIENCE (biology/biological science), BUSINESS (accounting, banking and finance, and business administration and management), COMMUNICATIONS AND THE ARTS (English, journalism, and music), COMPUTER AND PHYSICAL SCIENCE (chemistry and mathematics), EDUCATION (art, business, early childhood, elementary, music, secondary, and special), SOCIAL SCIENCE (criminology, history, political science/government, psychology, religion, social work, and sociology). Teacher education, accounting, and history/political science are the strongest academically. Teacher education, criminology, and business administration are the largest.

Required: To graduate, all students must complete at least 124 credit hours with a GPA of at least 2.0. Courses in religion, English, math, science, social science, a foreign language, and phys ed are required. There are also chapel and VUU events attendance requirements. All students must successfully complete a computer science course and must take an English essay exam, usually by the end of the junior year, as well as a comprehensive exam in their major.

Special: The university offers cross-registration with Virginia Commonwealth and Virginia State Universities, and the University of Richmond. Internships, co-op programs, federal work-study programs, a general

---

studies degree, a joint law degree with St. John's University School of Law in New York, a 3-2 degree in engineering with the Universities of Michigan and Iowa and Howard University, and exchange programs are also offered. There are 2 national honor societies and a freshman honors program.

Faculty/Classroom: 55% of faculty are male; 45%, female. 86% teach undergraduates. No introductory courses are taught by graduate students. The average class size in an introductory lecture is 28; in a laboratory, 20; and in a regular course, 22.

Requirements: The SAT I is required. In addition, graduation from an accredited secondary school is required; the GED is accepted. Sixteen academic units are required, including 4 of English, 3 each of math and academic electives, and 2 each of foreign language, social science, and natural science. Special consideration is given to disadvantaged students. Children of alumni are given some preference. A GPA of 2.0 is required. AP and CLEP credits are accepted. Important factors in the admissions decision are extracurricular activities record, advanced placement or honor courses, and leadership record.

Procedure: Freshmen are admitted fall and spring. Entrance exams should be taken between March of the junior year and March of the senior year. There are early admissions, deferred admissions, and rolling admissions plans. Check with the school for current deadlines. Notification is sent on a rolling basis.

Transfer: 51 transfer students enrolled in a recent year. Transfer students must be in good standing at their previous institutions and must submit all college transcripts. 30 of 124 credits required for the bachelor's degree must be completed at VUU.

Visiting: There are guides for informal visits and visitors may sit in on classes. To schedule a visit, contact the Admissions Office at (804) 257-5600.

Financial Aid: In a recent year, 98% of all full-time freshmen received some form of financial aid. 96% of all full-time students received need-based aid. VUU is a member of CSS. The CSS Profile is required. Check with the school for current deadlines.

International Students: They must score 500 on the written TOEFL and also take the SAT I or the ACT, scoring 700.

Computers: The mainframe is an IBM AS/400. PCs with various software are available in computer labs. All students may access the system. There are no time limits and no fees. It is strongly recommended that all students have a personal computer.

Graduates: 100 companies recruited on campus in a recent year.

Admissions Contact: Gil Powell, Director of Admissions. E-mail: *admissions@vuu.edu* Web: *vuu.edu*

VIRGINIA WESLEYAN COLLEGE
Norfolk, VA 23502-5599

F-4

(757) 455-3208
(800) 737-8684; Fax: (757) 461-5238

Full-time: 399 men, 737 women	**Faculty:** 77; IIB, av$
Part-time: 61 men, 232 women	**Ph.D.s:** 84%
Graduate: none	**Student/Faculty:** 15 to 1
Year: 4-1-4, summer session	**Tuition:** $19,200
Application Deadline: open	**Room & Board:** $6150
Freshman Class: n/av	
SAT I or ACT: required	**COMPETITIVE**

Virginia Wesleyan College, established in 1961, is a private institution affiliated with the United Methodist Church, offering undergraduate degrees in the humanities, the social sciences, the natural sciences, and mathematics. In addition to regional accreditation, Virginia Wesleyan has baccalaureate program accreditation with NRPA. The library contains 116,500 volumes, 15,800 microform items, and 3500 audio/video tapes/CDs, and subscribes to 800 periodicals. Computerized library services include the card catalog, interlibrary loans, and database searching. Special learning facilities include a learning resource center, art gallery, radio station, a greenhouse, the Center for the Study of Religious Freedom, and 142 acres of woodland used as a lab for biological and environmental sciences. The 300-acre campus is in a suburban area 8 miles east of downtown Norfolk and 10 miles west of the Virginia Beach oceanfront. Including any residence halls, there are 31 buildings.

Student Life: 78% of undergraduates are from Virginia. Students are from 32 states and 9 foreign countries. 97% are from public schools. 79% are white; 13% African American. 53% are Protestant; 22% Catholic; 21% claim no religious affiliation. The average age of freshmen is 18; all undergraduates, 24. 50% of freshmen remain to graduate.

Housing: 575 students can be accommodated in college housing, which includes single-sex and coed dorms. In addition, there are honors houses, special-interest houses, and fraternity, sorority, and international residence halls. On-campus housing is guaranteed for all 4 years. 55% of students commute. All students may keep cars.

Activities: 10% of men belong to 2 national fraternities; 15% of women belong to 3 national sororities. There are 45 groups on campus, including cheerleading, chorus, computer, dance, departmental, drama, ethnic, gay, honors, international, literary magazine, model UN, musical theater, newspaper, political, professional, radio and TV, religious, social, social service, student government, women's, and yearbook. Popular campus events include TGIF Series and seafood party in the Dell.

Sports: There are 8 intercollegiate sports for men and 9 for women, and 18 intramural sports for men and 18 for women. Facilities include the student center, which includes a multiactivity athletic center, a 39-foot-high climbing wall, NCAA regulation swimming pool, indoor running track, and basketball courts. Also baseball, softball, lacrosse, field hockey, and soccer fields, and tennis courts are available.

Disabled Students: 90% of the campus is accessible. Wheelchair ramps, elevators, special parking, specially equipped rest rooms, special class scheduling, lowered drinking fountains, lowered telephones, special desks, and preferential seating and registration are available.

Services: Counseling and information services are available, as is tutoring in most subjects. There is a reader service for the blind and remedial math, reading, and writing. Note takers, special co-advising, test proctoring, Learning Plus for Praxis exams for education certification, and outreach (tutoring) to public school students are available.

Campus Safety and Security: Measures include 24-hour foot and vehicle patrol, self-defense education, security escort services, and shuttle buses. There are informal discussions, pamphlets/posters/films, emergency telephones, lighted pathways/sidewalks, and a bicycle patrol.

Programs of Study: Virginia Wesleyan confers the B.A. degree. Bachelor's degrees are awarded in BIOLOGICAL SCIENCE (biology/biological science), BUSINESS (business administration and management), COMMUNICATIONS AND THE ARTS (art, communications, dramatic arts, English, French, German, journalism, languages, music, and Spanish), COMPUTER AND PHYSICAL SCIENCE (chemistry, computer science, earth science, mathematics, and natural sciences), EDUCATION (art), SOCIAL SCIENCE (American studies, criminal justice, history, human ecology, humanities, interdisciplinary studies, international relations, liberal arts/general studies, parks and recreation management, philosophy, political science/government, psychology, religion, social science, social studies, social work, and sociology). Art, history and math are the strongest academically. Social sciences, interdivisional liberal arts and management, and communications are the largest.

Required: To graduate, students must complete general studies requirements, which include English, math, a foreign language, and Frames of Reference courses. These include Empirical Knowledge, Aesthetic Understanding and Activity, Ethical Values, World Views, Faith Perspectives, the Historical Perspective, Communications, and Institutional and Cultural Systems. Students must earn 120 credits, including 40 in the major, with a minimum 2.0 GPA. Students must complete 3 credits designated to fulfill a Senior Integrative Experience requirement. They must also complete 2 winter-term projects, each involving an intensive 2-week course of study in a single subject. Students must be enrolled in at least 1 course designated as a writing course each semester. A freshman seminar is also required.

Special: Students may cross-register with Old Dominion University, the College of William and Mary, or Norfolk State University through the Virginia Tidewater Consortium. Internships are available and are usually completed during the senior year. The college offers study-abroad programs and international internships through partnerships and exchange programs in several countries and additional arrangements for study abroad can be made in almost any country. Dual majors, individualized and interdivisional majors, and interdisciplinary majors are available. Work-study programs with Virginia Wesleyan are offered. Credit may be granted for life, military, and work experience. Nondegree study and pass/fail options are also available. There are 16 national honor societies and a freshman honors program.

Faculty/Classroom: 60% of faculty are male; 40%, female. All teach undergraduates. The average class size in a regular course is 13.

Admissions: 34% of the current freshmen were in the top fifth of their class; 75% were in the top two fifths.

Requirements: The SAT I or ACT is required. In addition, applicants must graduate from an accredited secondary school or have a GED. The college recommends 15 academic credits. Students should complete 4 years of English, 3 of social studies/history, math, and science, and 2 of foreign language. Essays are required and interviews are recommended. Home-schooled graduates are reviewed individually. A GPA of 2.0 is required. AP and CLEP credits are accepted. Important factors in the admissions decision are advanced placement or honor courses, extracurricular activities record, and leadership record.

Procedure: Freshmen are admitted fall and spring. Entrance exams should be taken in the spring of the junior year and the fall of the senior year. There is a deferred admissions plan. There is a rolling admissions plan. Application deadlines are open. Applications are accepted on-line through the college's web site.

Transfer: 139 transfer students enrolled in 2002-2003. Applicants must have a minimum GPA of 2.0 in courses to be transferred. For applicants who have not completed 12 semester hours of college work, official transcripts of college and high school records (including SAT I or ACT scores) are required. All others must submit a high school diploma or GED in addition to official college transcripts. 30 of 120 credits required for the bachelor's degree must be completed at Virginia Wesleyan.

Visiting: There are regularly scheduled orientations for prospective students, consisting of 3 Open House Days on Saturdays for prospective students to meet faculty and current students, and to tour the campus. There are guides for informal visits and visitors may sit in on classes and stay overnight. To schedule a visit, contact the Admissions Office at *admissions@vwc.edu.*

Financial Aid: In 2003-2004, 77% of all full-time freshmen and 76% of continuing full-time students received some form of financial aid. The average freshman award was $13,341. Need-based scholarships or need-based grants averaged $4061; need-based self-help aid (loans and jobs) averaged $3652; and non-need-based awards and non-need-based scholarships averaged $5297. 21% of undergraduates work part time. Average annual earnings from campus work are $1500. The average financial indebtedness of the 2003 graduate was $15,408. Virginia Wesleyan is a member of CSS. The FAFSA is required. The deadline for filing freshman financial aid applications for fall entry is March 1.

International Students: There were 9 international students enrolled in a recent year. The school actively recruits these students. They must score 550 on the written TOEFL or 213 on the electronic version and also take the SAT I or the ACT, scoring 900 (SAT I).

Computers: The mainframes are an HP-9000, Model L3000. There are 10 network file servers and 57 workstations in various locations available for student use. In addition, there are 5 labs for computer use with approximately 100 computers. All computers have web access. There is also web access in all student rooms for those with personal computers. Students may access academic records via a web interface from on or off campus. All students may access the system 5:30 A.M. to 1 A.M. There are no time limits and no fees. It is strongly recommended that all students have a personal computer. A Dell Optiplex or Latitude is recommended.

Graduates: From July 1, 2002 to June 30, 2003, 263 bachelor's degrees were awarded. The most popular majors were business (18%), communications (14%), and interdivisional (11%). In an average class, 1% graduate in 3 years or less, 39% graduate in 4 years or less, 44% graduate in 5 years or less, and 47% graduate in 6 years or less. 86 companies recruited on campus in 2002-2003. Of the 2002 graduating class, 18% were enrolled in graduate school within 6 months of graduation and 77% were employed.

Admissions Contact: Richard T. Hinshaw, Vice President for Enrollment Management. E-mail: *admissions@vwc.edu* Web: *www.vwc.edu*

WASHINGTON AND LEE UNIVERSITY D-3
Lexington, VA 24450-0303 (540) 458-8710; Fax: (540) 458-8062

Full-time: 907 men, 831 women	Faculty: 181; IIB, ++$
Part-time: 2 women	Ph.D.s: 95%
Graduate: 227 men, 170 women	Student/Faculty: 10 to 1
Year: 4-1-4	Tuition: $23,295
Application Deadline: January 15	Room & Board: $6368
Freshman Class: 3185 applied, 995 accepted, 453 enrolled	
SAT I Verbal/Math: 690/690	ACT: 29 MOST COMPETITIVE

Washington and Lee University, established in 1749, is a private institution offering undergraduate liberal arts and sciences and preprofessional programs. There are 2 undergraduate schools and 1 graduate school. In addition to regional accreditation, Washington and Lee has baccalaureate program accreditation with AACSB, ACEJMC, and ACS. The 3 libraries contain 1,036,280 volumes, 993,362 microform items, and 13,104 audio/video tapes/CDs, and subscribe to 6170 periodicals. Computerized library services include the card catalog, interlibrary loans, and database searching. Special learning facilities include an art gallery, radio station, TV station, performing arts center, and a multimedia center. The 322-acre campus is in a small town 50 miles northeast of Roanoke. Including any residence halls, there are 73 buildings.

Student Life: 86% of undergraduates are from out of state, mostly the South. Students are from 47 states, 37 foreign countries, and Canada. 60% are from public schools. 88% are white. 42% are claim no religious affiliation; 40% Protestant; 15% Catholic. The average age of freshmen is 18; all undergraduates, 20. 5% do not continue beyond their first year; 88% remain to graduate.

Housing: 1272 students can be accommodated in college housing, which includes coed dorms, on-campus apartments, fraternity houses, and sorority houses. In addition, there are language houses and special-interest houses. On-campus housing is available on a lottery system for upperclassmen. 63% of students live on campus. All students may keep cars.

Activities: 75% of men belong to 14 national fraternities; 70% of women belong to 5 national sororities. There are 127 groups on campus, including cheerleading, choir, chorale, chorus, dance, debate, drama, ethnic, film, forensics, gay, honors, international, jazz band, leadership, literary magazine, musical theater, newspaper, orchestra, outing, photography, political, radio and TV, religious, social, social service, Spanish, sports, student government, symphony, volunteers, and yearbook. Popular campus events include the Presidential Mock Convention, a fancy-dress ball, and NABORS Service Day.

Sports: There are 12 intercollegiate sports for men and 11 for women, and 16 intramural sports for men and 7 for women. Facilities include a gym, a 2400-seat arena, a 7000-seat stadium, a pool with a 500-seat gallery, a fitness center, weight training and exercise rooms, handball, racquetball, squash, and tennis courts, an outdoor track, baseball and practice fields, an indoor tennis facility, and a turf field for field hockey and lacrosse.

Disabled Students: 55% of the campus is accessible. Wheelchair ramps, elevators, special parking, specially equipped rest rooms, special class scheduling, and lowered drinking fountains are available.

Services: Counseling and information services are available, as is tutoring in every subject. There is a reader service for the blind.

Campus Safety and Security: Measures include 24-hour foot and vehicle patrol, self-defense education, security escort services, and shuttle buses. There are informal discussions, pamphlets/posters/films, emergency telephones, lighted pathways/sidewalks, and required safety programs for freshmen.

Programs of Study: Washington and Lee confers B.A. and B.S. degrees. Doctoral degrees are also awarded. Bachelor's degrees are awarded in BIOLOGICAL SCIENCE (biochemistry, biology/biological science, and neurosciences), BUSINESS (accounting and business administration and management), COMMUNICATIONS AND THE ARTS (art history and appreciation, classics, dramatic arts, English, French, German, Germanic languages and literature, journalism, music, romance languages and literature, Russian languages and literature, Spanish, and studio art), COMPUTER AND PHYSICAL SCIENCE (chemistry, computer science, geology, mathematics, natural sciences, and physics), ENGINEERING AND ENVIRONMENTAL DESIGN (chemical engineering, engineering physics, and environmental science), SOCIAL SCIENCE (archeology, East Asian studies, economics, history, interdisciplinary studies, medieval studies, philosophy, political science/government, psychology, public affairs, religion, and sociology). The commerce program, history, and the journalism program are the largest.

Required: To graduate, students must achieve proficiency in a foreign language and English composition, and complete 12 credits in fine arts and humanities, 10 in lab science and math, 9 in social sciences, and 6 in literature. A total of 121 credits, with a minimum GPA of 1.9 overall and 2.0 in the major, is required. All students must take 5 courses in phys ed and a swim test.

Special: There is cross-registration with area colleges, including VMI, and colleges in Georgia and Maine, and various internships, including commerce, government, and journalism, are available. Study-abroad programs are offered in several countries. There is a 3-3 law program and a 3-2 engineering degree with Rensselaer Polytechnic Institute and Washington and Columbia Universities. Washington and Lee also offers B.A.-B.S. degrees and dual, interdisciplinary, and student-designed majors. There are 12 national honor societies, including Phi Beta Kappa, and 29 departmental honors programs.

Faculty/Classroom: 76% of faculty are male; 24%, female. 100% both teach and do research. No introductory courses are taught by graduate students. The average class size in an introductory lecture is 19; in a laboratory, 16; and in a regular course, 15.

Admissions: 31% of the 2003-2004 applicants were accepted. The SAT I scores for the 2003-2004 freshman class were: Verbal--8% between 500 and 599, 48% between 600 and 700, and 44% above 700; Math--4% between 500 and 599, 50% between 600 and 700, and 46% above 700. The ACT scores were 1% between 21 and 23, 8% between 24 and 26, 26% between 27 and 28, and 65% above 28. 93% of the current freshmen were in the top fifth of their class; 100% were in the top two fifths. There were 31 National Merit finalists. 47 freshmen graduated first in their class.

Requirements: The SAT I or ACT is required, as well as 3 SAT II: Subject tests. Applicants must graduate from an accredited secondary school. They must earn 16 units, including 4 units in English, 3 in math,

2 in a foreign language, and 1 each in history and natural science. Course work in social sciences is also required. Essays are required and interviews are recommended. AP credits are accepted. Important factors in the admissions decision are advanced placement or honor courses, leadership record, and recommendations by school officials.

Procedure: Freshmen are admitted in the fall. Entrance exams should be taken between March of the junior year and January of the senior year. There are early decision and deferred admissions plans. Early decision applications should be filed by December 1; regular applications, by January 15 for fall entry. The fall 2003 application fee was $40. Notification of early decision is sent December 22; regular decision, April 1. 230 early decision candidates were accepted for the 2003-2004 class. 625 applicants were on the 2003 waiting list; 34 were admitted. Applications are accepted on-line through the university's web site.

Transfer: 4 transfer students enrolled in 2002-2003. Transfer applicants must have a GPA of at least 2.0 (at least 3.5 to be competitive); no more than 87 credits will transfer. There is a 2-year residency requirement. 60 of 121 credits required for the bachelor's degree must be completed at Washington and Lee.

Visiting: There are regularly scheduled orientations for prospective students, consisting of hourly interview slots and campus tours, 2 group information sessions daily, and seasonal Saturday tours and interviews. There are guides for informal visits and visitors may sit in on classes. To schedule a visit, contact the Admissions Office.

Financial Aid: In 2003-2004, 60% of all full-time freshmen and 56% of continuing full-time students received some form of financial aid. 29% of full-time freshmen and 28% of continuing full-time students received need-based aid. The average freshman award was $19,471, with $15,236 from need-based scholarships or need-based grants, $3785 from need-based self-help aid (loans and jobs), and $450 from non-need-based awards and non-need-based scholarships. 20% of undergraduates work part time. Average annual earnings from campus work are $1350. The average financial indebtedness of the 2003 graduate was $14,592. Washington and Lee is a member of CSS. The CSS/Profile or FAFSA and the noncustodial parent's statement and the business/farm supplement are required. The deadline for filing freshman financial aid applications for fall entry is February 1.

International Students: There are 106 international students enrolled. The school actively recruits these students. They must score 600 on the written TOEFL or 250 on the electronic version or take the ELPT and also take the SAT I or the ACT.

Computers: The mainframe is an HP 9000 series. There are about 300 PCs in 12 locations throughout academic buildings. All PCs are networked, and students who live off campus have dial-up access to the network. Every resident of on-campus housing has a high-speed network connection, and wireless networking is available across the campus. All students may access the system 24 hours a day, 7 days a week while classes are in session. There are no time limits. The fee is $200 per year. It is strongly recommended that all students have a personal computer. A Dell laptop is recommended.

Graduates: From July 1, 2002 to June 30, 2003, 418 bachelor's degrees were awarded. The most popular majors were economics (13%), history (12%), and business administration (11%). In an average class, 85% graduate in 4 years or less, 87% graduate in 5 years or less, and 88% graduate in 6 years or less. 30 companies recruited on campus in 2002-2003. Of the 2002 graduating class, 22% were enrolled in graduate school within 6 months of graduation and 63% were employed.

Admissions Contact: William M. Hartog, Dean of Admissions and Financial Aid. A video is available. E-mail: *admissions@wlu.edu* Web: *www.wlu.edu*

WILLIAM AND MARY
(See College of William and Mary)

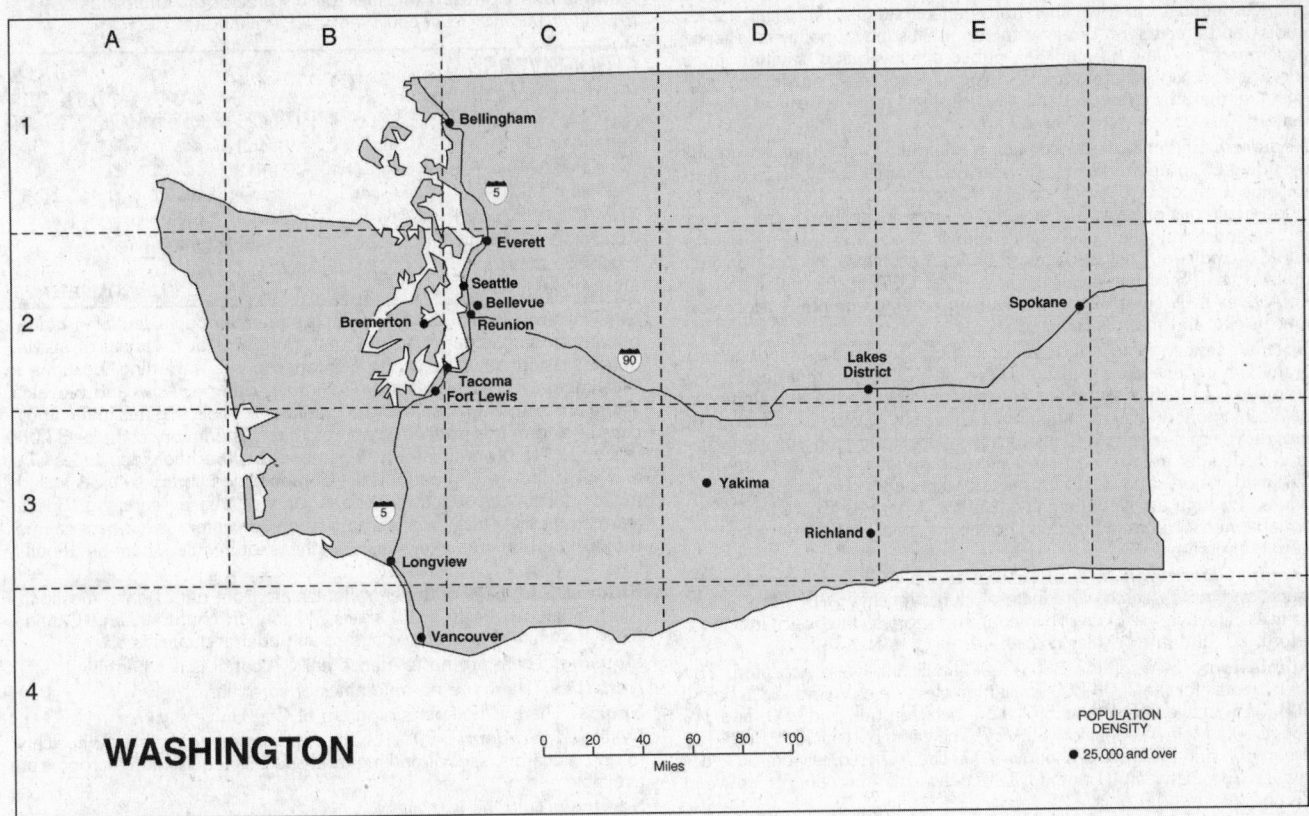

WASHINGTON

POPULATION DENSITY

● 25,000 and over

0 20 40 60 80 100
Miles

CENTRAL WASHINGTON UNIVERSITY

D-2

Ellensburg, WA 98926-7512

(509) 963-1211
(866) 298-4968; Fax: (509) 963-3022

Full-time: 3943 men, 4244 women	**Faculty:** 338; IIA, -$
Part-time: 512 men, 597 women	**Ph.D.s:** 90%
Graduate: 223 men, 384 women	**Student/Faculty:** 24 to 1
Year: quarters, summer session	**Tuition:** $4023 ($11,799)
Application Deadline: open	**Room & Board:** $5745
Freshman Class: 3905 applied, 3261 accepted, 1337 enrolled	
SAT I Verbal/Math: 490/490	**ACT:** 20 **COMPETITIVE**

Central Washington University is a public institution offering undergraduate programs in the arts and sciences, business administration, and education. There are 4 undergraduate schools and 1 graduate school. In addition to regional accreditation, CWU has baccalaureate program accreditation with ABET, ACCE, ADA, NASM, NCATE, and NRPA. The library contains 546,025 volumes, 1,165,466 microform items, and 9500 audio/video tapes/CDs. Computerized library services include the card catalog, interlibrary loans, and database searching. Special learning facilities include a learning resource center, art gallery, natural history museum, planetarium, radio station, an anthropology museum, a botanical greenhouse, and a primate research lab. The 380-acre campus is in a rural area 100 miles east of Seattle. Including any residence halls, there are 74 buildings.

Student Life: 97% of undergraduates are from Washington. Students are from 35 states, 32 foreign countries, and Canada. 95% are from public schools. 78% are white. The average age of freshmen is 19; all undergraduates, 23. 24% do not continue beyond their first year; 52% remain to graduate.

Housing: 2525 students can be accommodated in college housing, which includes coed dorms, on-campus apartments, off-campus apartments, and married-student housing. In addition, there are special-interest houses, a freshman-only enrichment hall, and a residence hall for transfers and upper-classmen only. On-campus housing is guaranteed for the freshman year only and is available on a first-come, first-served basis. All students may keep cars.

Activities: There are no fraternities or sororities. There are 80 groups on campus, including art, band, cheerleading, chess, choir, chorale, chorus, computers, dance, drama, ethnic, film, gay, honors, international, jazz band, literary magazine, marching band, musical theater, newspaper, opera, orchestra, pep band, photography, political, professional, radio and TV, religious, social, social service, student government, and symphony. Popular campus events include Tower Theater productions and Jazz Night.

Sports: There are 8 intercollegiate sports for men and 8 for women, and 9 intramural sports for men and 9 for women. Facilities include a 3500-seat stadium, a swimming pool, an arena, a weight training room, an athletic field, and 3 gyms.

Disabled Students: 85% of the campus is accessible. Wheelchair ramps, elevators, special parking, specially equipped rest rooms, special class scheduling, lowered drinking fountains, and lowered telephones are available.

Services: Counseling and information services are available, as is tutoring in most subjects. There is a reader service for the blind and remedial math, reading, and writing.

Campus Safety and Security: Measures include 24-hour foot and vehicle patrol, self-defense education, security escort services, and shuttle buses. There are informal discussions, pamphlets/posters/films, emergency telephones, lighted pathways/sidewalks, and controlled-entry residence halls.

Programs of Study: CWU confers B.A., B.S., B.A.Ed., B.F.A., and B.M. degrees. Master's degrees are also awarded. Bachelor's degrees are awarded in BIOLOGICAL SCIENCE (biology/biological science), BUSINESS (accounting, banking and finance, business administration and management, business economics, fashion merchandising, international business management, marketing/retailing/merchandising, recreation and leisure services, and tourism), COMMUNICATIONS AND THE ARTS (art, broadcasting, Chinese, communications, dramatic arts, English, fine arts, French, German, guitar, Japanese, journalism, language arts, music, music business management, music theory and composition, percussion, piano/organ, public relations, Russian, Spanish, speech/debate/rhetoric, strings, studio art, visual and performing arts, and voice), COMPUTER AND PHYSICAL SCIENCE (actuarial science, chemistry, computer programming, computer science, earth science, geology, information sciences and systems, mathematics, physics, and software engineering), EDUCATION (art, business, early childhood, elementary, English, foreign languages, health, home economics, industrial arts, marketing and distribution, mathematics, middle school, music, physical, science, secondary, social studies, and special), ENGINEERING AND ENVIRONMENTAL DESIGN (aeronautical technology, aviation administration/management, aviation maintenance management, construction management, electrical/electronics engineering, engineering technology, industrial engineering technology, and mechanical engineering),

HEALTH PROFESSIONS (community health work, emergency medical technologies, exercise science, and public health), SOCIAL SCIENCE (anthropology, Asian/Oriental studies, criminal justice, economics, family and community services, family/consumer studies, food science, geography, gerontology, history, liberal arts/general studies, paralegal studies, parks and recreation management, philosophy, political science/ government, prelaw, psychology, public administration, safety science, social science, social work, and sociology). Accounting, music, and geology are the strongest academically. Business and education are the largest.

Required: Students must complete a minimum of 180 quarter credits, including 60 in upper-division courses and a minimum of 45 in the major plus a minor or 60 in the major. Core curriculum requirements include 61 credits of Basic and Breadth courses, including 15 credits each in arts and humanities, social and behavioral sciences, and natural science, 6 credits of English composition, and a philosophy logic or finite math course. Students must maintain a 2.3 GPA in the major and 2.0 GPA overall. A comprehensive exam in reading comprehension, sentence skills, and math is required.

Special: Students may study abroad; there is a formal exchange program with Japanese universities. There are 3-2 engineering degree programs in conjunction with the University of Puget Sound, the University of Washington, and Washington State University. CWU also offers co-op programs, cross-registration, internships, work-study programs, an accelerated degree program, credit/no credit options, dual and student-designed majors, and credit for military experience. Nondegree study is offered through adult/continuing education programs. There are 11 national honor societies, a freshman honors program, and 12 departmental honors programs.

Faculty/Classroom: 58% of faculty are male; 42%, female. All both teach and do research. Graduate students teach 7% of introductory courses. The average class size in an introductory lecture is 45; in a laboratory, 20; and in a regular course, 40.

Admissions: 84% of the 2003-2004 applicants were accepted. The SAT I scores for the 2003-2004 freshman class were: Verbal--53% below 500, 34% between 500 and 599, 12% between 600 and 700, and 1% above 700; Math--51% below 500, 37% between 500 and 599, 11% between 600 and 700, and 1% above 700. The ACT scores were 56% below 21, 23% between 21 and 23, 12% between 24 and 26, 5% between 27 and 28, and 4% above 28.

Requirements: The SAT I or ACT is required. Test scores and GPA are considered in combination according to a sliding scale. Applicants must be graduates of accredited secondary schools or have earned a GED. The university requires 15 academic credits or Carnegie units: 4 years of English, 3 each of math and social studies, 2 of the same foreign language, 2 of science, and 1 of performing arts or an academic elective. A GPA of 2.0 is required. AP and CLEP credits are accepted. Important factors in the admissions decision are leadership record, personality/ intangible qualities, and recommendations by school officials.

Procedure: Freshmen are admitted to all sessions. Entrance exams should be taken before the fall of the senior year. Application deadlines are open. There is a rolling admissions plan. The fall 2003 application fee was $35. Applications are accepted on-line through *http:// www.applyweb.com/apply/cwu/index.html.*

Transfer: 1245 transfer students enrolled in 2002-2003. Students presenting an associate degree need a minimum GPA of 2.5 for automatic offer of admission; 2.5 to 2.0 will be asked to provide additional information for review. 45 of 180 credits required for the bachelor's degree must be completed at CWU.

Visiting: There are regularly scheduled orientations for prospective students, consisting of an information session, a tour of residence halls, a tour of the campus, prearranged appointments with faculty, and a financial aid presentation. There are guides for informal visits and visitors may sit in on classes and stay overnight. To schedule a visit, contact the Admissions Office.

Financial Aid: In 2003-2004, 44% of all full-time freshmen and 49% of continuing full-time students received some form of financial aid. 41% of all full-time students received need-based aid. The average freshman award was $3693. 41% of undergraduates work part time. Average annual earnings from campus work are $2700. The average financial indebtedness of the 2003 graduate was $18,461. CWU is a member of CSS. The FAFSA is required. The deadline for filing freshman financial aid applications for fall entry is March 1.

International Students: There are 93 international students enrolled. The school actively recruits these students. They must score 525 on the written TOEFL and also take the SAT I or the ACT.

Computers: The mainframe is a DEC Alpha cluster. There are about 4000 PCs on campus, 31 student labs with 659 workstations, personal web pages and e-mail for students, and network access. All students may access the system 24 hours a day. There are no time limits. The fee is $25 per quarter.

Graduates: In a recent year, 1864 bachelor's degrees were awarded. The most popular majors were business administration (13%), elementary education (10%), and law and justice (7%). In an average class, 1%

graduate in 3 years or less, 23% graduate in 4 years or less, 46% graduate in 5 years or less, and 52% graduate in 6 years or less. 124 companies recruited on campus in 2002-2003.

Admissions Contact: Michael Reilly, Director of Admissions.
E-mail: *cwuadmis@cwu.edu* Web: *cwu@cwu.edu*

CITY UNIVERSITY
Renton, WA 98055

C-2
(425) 637-1010
(800) 426-5596; Fax: (425) 277-2437

Full-time: 1055 men, 975 women	**Faculty:** 14
Part-time: 520 men, 460 women	**Ph.D.s:** n/av
Graduate: 1625 men, 1630 women	**Student/Faculty:** n/av
Year: quarters, summer session	**Tuition:** $7425
Application Deadline: open	**Room & Board:** n/app
Freshman Class: n/av	
SAT I or ACT: not required	**NONCOMPETITIVE**

City University, established in 1973, is a private nonresidential institution offering undergraduate and graduate programs at a variety of instructional sites in addition to the Renton campus, including locations in Washington, California, British Columbia, Europe, Asia, and Slovakia. There are 2 undergraduate and 3 graduate schools. Figures in the above capsule and in this profile are approximate. The library contains 33,000 volumes, 415,000 microform items, and 1100 audio/video tapes/CDs, and subscribes to 650 periodicals. Computerized library services include the card catalog, interlibrary loans, and database searching. Special learning facilities include a learning resource center. The 2-acre campus is in a suburban area a few miles southeast of Seattle. There are 2 buildings.

Student Life: 51% of undergraduates are from out of state, mostly the West. Students are from 45 states, 30 foreign countries, and Canada. 58% are white. The average age of all undergraduates is 33.

Housing: There are no residence halls. Alcohol is not permitted.

Activities: There are no fraternities or sororities.

Sports: There is no sports program at City University.

Disabled Students: 90% of the campus is accessible. Wheelchair ramps, elevators, special parking, and specially equipped rest rooms are available.

Services: Tutoring is available.

Programs of Study: City University confers B.A. and B.S. degrees. Associate and master's degrees are also awarded. Bachelor's degrees are awarded in BUSINESS (accounting, business administration and management, and marketing/retailing/merchandising), COMPUTER AND PHYSICAL SCIENCE (computer programming), EDUCATION (elementary and middle school), SOCIAL SCIENCE (liberal arts/general studies). Business administration is the largest.

Required: Students are required to complete 180 quarter credits, with a minimum of 45 of these credits taken at City University, and maintain a minimum GPA of 2.0. A minimum of 30 credits are required in the major. All students must complete 55 general education credits, which include courses in the humanities, social sciences, natural sciences, and math.

Special: Opportunities are provided for cooperative programs with other schools, internships, study abroad, work-study programs, dual majors, and student-designed majors. A general studies degree, pass/fail options, independent study, weekend programs, and credit for military service are offered.

Faculty/Classroom: The average class size in an introductory lecture is 25.

Requirements: Graduation from an accredited secondary school is not required; a GED will be accepted. An interview is recommended. AP and CLEP credits are accepted.

Procedure: Freshmen are admitted to all sessions. There is a rolling admissions plan. Application deadlines are open. The fall 2003 application fee was $75.

Transfer: Students applying for transfer must submit official transcripts from all colleges previously attended. Applicants may transfer up to 135 quarter credits from accredited 4-year colleges, with at least 45 of these credits in upper-level courses. Up to 90 quarter credits may be transferred from 2-year colleges. 45 of 180 credits required for the bachelor's degree must be completed at City University.

Visiting: To schedule a visit, contact the Student Affairs Office.

Financial Aid: The FAFSA and the college's own financial statement are required. Check with the school for current deadlines.

International Students: The school actively recruits these students. They must score 540 on the written TOEFL and also take the college's own English placement exam to determine placement in ESL classes if necessary.

Computers: The mainframe is a Unisys LX5300. Computer labs are available at most instructional sites. Information resources and services include web-based library indexes and full-text databases, library catalogs, word processing, spreadsheets, and printing. More than 150 computers are available to students. All students may access the system.

There are no time limits and no fees. It is strongly recommended that all students have a personal computer.

Admissions Contact: Student Affairs/Admissions.
E-mail: *info@cityu.edu* Web: *www.cityu.edu*

CORNISH COLLEGE OF THE ARTS
Seattle, WA 98121

C-2
(206) 726-5016
(800) 726-ARTS; Fax: (206) 720-1011

Full-time: 245 men, 427 women	**Faculty:** 51
Part-time: 7 men, 17 women	**Ph.Ds:** 59%
Graduate: none	**Student/Faculty:** 13 to 1
Year: semesters, summer session	**Tuition:** $19,900
Application Deadline: August 15	**Room & Board:** n/app
Freshman Class: 364 applied, 283 accepted, 145 enrolled	
SAT I or ACT: recommended	**SPECIAL**

Cornish College of the Arts, founded in 1914, is an independent commuter institution offering undergraduate programs in the fine arts, dance, design, music, theater, and performance production. There are 6 undergraduate schools. In addition to regional accreditation, Cornish has baccalaureate program accreditation with NASAD and NASC. The library contains 17,914 volumes and 4570 audio/video tapes/CDs, and subscribes to 104 periodicals. Computerized library services include the card catalog, database searching, and Internet access. Special learning facilities include a learning resource center, art gallery, dance studios, large black box theater, studio theater, concert hall, rehearsal facilities, photography, printmaking, painting, sculpture studios, and digital labs. The 4-acre campus is in an urban area in the Capitol Hill and downtown neighborhoods of Seattle. There are 5 buildings.

Student Life: 55% of undergraduates are from Washington. Students are from 28 states, 10 foreign countries, and Canada. 67% are white. The average age of freshmen is 23; all undergraduates, 23. 20% do not continue beyond their first year; 50% remain to graduate.

Housing: There are no residence halls. Alcohol is not permitted. All students may keep cars.

Activities: There are no fraternities or sororities. There are 12 groups on campus, including art, band, chess, choir, chorus, computers, dance, drama, ethnic, film, gay, international, jazz band, literary magazine, musical theater, newspaper, opera, orchestra, photography, political, professional, religious, social, and student government. Popular campus events include Theater Seniors Productions, Costume Design Tea and Fashion Show, and Dance Theater Performances.

Sports: There is no sports program at Cornish.

Disabled Students: 50% of the campus is accessible. Wheelchair ramps, elevators, special parking, specially equipped rest rooms, lowered drinking fountains, and lowered telephones are available.

Services: Counseling and information services are available, as is tutoring in every subject. There is a reader service for the blind and remedial writing. There is a staffed writing center with computers.

Campus Safety and Security: Measures include 24-hour foot and vehicle patrol, self-defense education, security escort services, and shuttle buses. There are pamphlets/posters/films, emergency telephones, lighted pathways/sidewalks, and card-key access during non-business hours.

Programs of Study: Cornish confers B.F.A. and B.M. degrees. Bachelor's degrees are awarded in COMMUNICATIONS AND THE ARTS (dance, design, dramatic arts, fine arts, music, and theater design). Design and dance are the strongest academically. Fine arts and theater are the largest.

Required: General education requirements include 30 semester hours in the humanities and sciences, as well as 6 to 8 in arts electives. To graduate, students must complete at least 127 semester hours, including 94 in their specific discipline, and maintain a minimum GPA of 2.0 during their senior year.

Special: Cornish offers a premajor first year of study to those music students who initially need more fundamental training. Internships are available to upperclassmen in all majors. Students may earn credit by examination in humanities and science courses, as well as credit for life experience in all majors where appropriate. Work-study programs and nondegree study are also offered.

Faculty/Classroom: 49% of faculty are male; 51%, female. All teach undergraduates. The average class size in an introductory lecture is 18; in a laboratory, 15; and in a regular course, 15.

Admissions: 78% of the 2003-2004 applicants were accepted.

Requirements: The SAT I or ACT is recommended. In addition, the required audition or portfolio review is the single most important criterion in the admissions decision. Applicants should be graduates of accredited secondary schools or have earned a GED. In addition to providing evidence of their artistic talent, students must submit 2 essays and arrange for an interview. AP and CLEP credits are accepted. Important factors in the admissions decision are evidence of special talent, personality/intangible qualities, and recommendations by school officials.

Procedure: Freshmen are admitted in the fall. There is a deferred admissions plan. Applications should be filed by August 15 for fall entry

and December 15 for spring entry, along with a $35 fee. Notification is sent on a rolling basis. Applications are accepted on-line through *http://www.cornish.edu/admissions/applyOnline.asp*.

Transfer: 38 transfer students enrolled in 2002-2003. Applicants must meet the same requirements as freshmen. 60 of 127 credits required for the bachelor's degree must be completed at Cornish.

Visiting: There are regularly scheduled orientations for prospective students, consisting of Preview Days during which applicants can attend classes, interact with students and faculty, and experience campus life. There are guides for informal visits and visitors may sit in on classes. To schedule a visit, contact the Admissions Office at (800) 726-ARTS or *admissions@cornish.edu*.

Financial Aid: Cornish is a member of CSS. The FAFSA and the college's own financial statement are required. The deadline for filing freshman financial aid applications for fall entry is March 1.

International Students: There are 21 international students enrolled. They must score 525 on the written TOEFL or 195 on the electronic version.

Computers: 91 PCs are available to students, as well as ports for laptop connection to the network. There are 3 word processing labs, a computer writing center, 2 digital arts labs, as well as 2 facilities for audio and video editing. All are Internet equipped and maintain current software. All students may access the system. There are no time limits. The fee is $50. It is recommended that students in design have personal computers. Apple G4 ibook is recommended.

Graduates: From July 1, 2002 to June 30, 2003, 119 bachelor's degrees were awarded. The most popular majors were design (26%), art (21%), and theater (21%). In an average class, 50% graduate in 4 years or less.

Admissions Contact: Jane Buckman, Associate Dean of Enrollment Services. E-mail: *admissions@cornish.edu* Web: *www.cornish.edu*

DEVRY UNIVERSITY/SEATTLE
Federal Way, WA 98001-9558

C-2
(253) 943-2810
(877) 923-3879; Fax: (253) 943-3291

Full-time: 608 men, 168 women	**Faculty:** n/av
Part-time: 195 men, 100 women	**Ph.Ds:** n/av
Graduate: n/av	**Student/Faculty:** n/av
Year: semesters, summer session	**Tuition:** $11,860
Application Deadline: open	**Room & Board:** n/app
Freshman Class: n/av	
SAT I or ACT: n/av	**LESS COMPETITIVE**

DeVry University/Seattle, founded in 2001, is a private institution offering hands-on programs in electronics, business administration, computer information systems, telecommunications management, information technology, and computer engineering technology. The school is 1 of 67 DeVry University locations in the United States and Canada. The library contains 5912 volumes, 4560 e-books, and 169 audio/video tapes/CDs, and subscribes to 61 periodicals. Computerized library services include the card catalog, interlibrary loans, and database searching. Special learning facilities include a learning resource center and electronics and other labs.

Student Life: 64% of students are white; 13% Asian American; 12% African American. The average age of all undergraduates is 25.

Housing: Housing referrals can be obtained through the Student Housing Office. There are private apartments, student-plan housing, and private rooms. All students commute. Alcohol is not permitted. All students may keep cars.

Activities: There are no fraternities or sororities. There are 4 groups on campus, including computers, professional, social, and yearbook. Popular campus events include Summer BBQ, Holiday Banquet, and Stress Breaks.

Sports: There is no sports program at DeVry.

Disabled Students: All of the campus is accessible. Wheelchair ramps, elevators, special parking, specially equipped rest rooms, lowered drinking fountains, and lowered telephones are available.

Services: Counseling and information services are available, as is tutoring in every subject.

Campus Safety and Security: Measures include informal discussions, emergency telephones, lighted pathways/sidewalks, and 17-hour patrols by trained security personnel and Emergency Response Team.

Programs of Study: DeVry confers the B.S. degree. Associate and master's degrees are also awarded. Bachelor's degrees are awarded in BUSINESS (business administration and management), COMMUNICATIONS AND THE ARTS (telecommunications), COMPUTER AND PHYSICAL SCIENCE (information sciences and systems), ENGINEERING AND ENVIRONMENTAL DESIGN (computer engineering, electrical/electronics engineering technology, and technological management). Computer information systems and telecommunications are the largest.

Required: To graduate, students must achieve a GPA of at least 2.0 and satisfactorily complete all curriculum requirements, including 48 to 154 credits. Course requirements vary according to program. All first-semester students take courses in business organization, computer applications, algebra, psychology, and student success strategies.

Special: Accelerated degrees, co-op programs, nondegree study, and evening and weekend classes are possible.

Faculty/Classroom: All teach undergraduates.

Requirements: Admissions requirements include graduation from a secondary school; the GED is also accepted. Applicants must pass the DeVry entrance exam or present satisfactory ACT or SAT I scores. An interview is required. CLEP credit is accepted.

Procedure: Freshmen are admitted fall, spring, and summer. There is a rolling admissions plan. There are early admissions and deferred admissions plans. Application deadlines are open. Application fee is $50. Applications are accepted on-line through *https://apply.embark.com/UGrad/DeVry/21/.*

Transfer: 38 transfer students enrolled in a recent year. Applicants must present passing grades in all completed college course work, demonstrate language skills proficiency in at least 24 completed semester hours, and present evidence of math proficiency by appropriate college-level credits. A minimum GPA of 2.0 is required. 25% of 48 to 154 credits required for the bachelor's degree must be completed at DeVry.

Visiting: There are guides for informal visits and visitors may sit in on classes. To schedule a visit, contact the New Student Coordinator.

Financial Aid: In 2002-2003, 68% of all full-time freshmen and 80% of continuing full-time students received some form of financial aid. At least 66% of full-time freshmen and at least 78% of continuing full-time students received need-based aid. The average freshman award was $5285. Need-based scholarships or need-based grants averaged $3739; need-based self-help aid (loans and jobs) averaged $3538; and institutional non-need-based awards and non-need-based scholarships averaged $9284. The FAFSA is required. The deadline for filing freshman financial aid applications is rolling.

International Students: There were 4 international students enrolled in a recent year. They must score 500 on the written TOEFL or 173 on the electronic version and also take the college's own entrance exam.

Admissions Contact: Director of Admissions.
E-mail: *admissions@sea.devry.edu* Web: *www.sea.devry.edu*

EASTERN WASHINGTON UNIVERSITY
Cheney, WA 99004-2496

E-2

(509) 359-2397
(888) 740-1914; Fax: (509) 359-6692

Full-time: 3249 men, 4430 women	**Faculty:** 352; IIA, --$
Part-time: 577 men, 811 women	**Ph.D.s:** 52%
Graduate: 404 men, 866 women	**Student/Faculty:** 22 to 1
Year: quarters, summer session	**Tuition:** $3812 ($12,668)
Application Deadline: March 1	**Room & Board:** $5200
Freshman Class: 3631 applied, 2915 accepted, 1345 enrolled	
SAT I Verbal/Math: 500/501	**ACT:** 21 **COMPETITIVE**

Eastern Washington University, founded in 1882, is a comprehensive public university that provides programs in the arts and sciences, business, health sciences and nursing, and technology. Some information in this capsule and profile is approximate. There are 4 undergraduate schools and 1 graduate school. In addition to regional accreditation, EWU has baccalaureate program accreditation with AACSB, ABET, ADA, APTA, ASLA, CSAB, CSWE, NASM, NCATE, NLN, and NRPA. The library contains 759,977 volumes, 608,400 microform items, and 27,595 audio/video tapes/CDs, and subscribes to 4717 periodicals. Computerized library services include the card catalog, interlibrary loans, and database searching. Special learning facilities include a learning resource center, art gallery, natural history museum, planetarium, radio station, TV station, and Reid Laboratory Elementary School. The 35-acre campus is in a small town 18 miles southwest of Spokane. Including any residence halls, there are 32 buildings.

Student Life: 91% of undergraduates are from Washington. Students are from 31 states, 30 foreign countries, and Canada. 98% are from public schools. 77% are white. The average age of freshmen is 19; all undergraduates, 25. 19% do not continue beyond their first year; 88% remain to graduate.

Housing: 2066 students can be accommodated in college housing, which includes coed dorms, on-campus apartments, and married-student housing. In addition, there are all-male, all-female, academic, music, and drama floors, and floors for older students. On-campus housing is guaranteed for all 4 years. 80% of students commute. All students may keep cars.

Activities: 8% of men belong to 5 national fraternities; 6% of women belong to 1 local and 4 national sororities. There are 99 groups on campus, including art, band, cheerleading, chess, choir, chorale, chorus, computers, dance, drama, ethnic, film, gay, honors, international, jazz band, literary magazine, marching band, musical theater, opera, orchestra, outdoor recreation, pep band, photography, political, professional, radio and TV, religious, social, social service, sports clubs, student government, symphony, and yearbook. Popular campus events include Club Vegas, Holiday in the Pub, and Spring Fling.

Sports: There are 6 intercollegiate sports for men and 7 for women, and 16 intramural sports for men and 14 for women. Facilities include a 200-meter indoor track, 12 racquetball courts, an indoor swimming pool, wrestling rooms, a dance studio, a 7000-seat stadium, a 5800-seat indoor gym, a fitness studio, a baseball field, and volleyball and basketball courts.

Disabled Students: 93% of the campus is accessible. Wheelchair ramps, elevators, special parking, specially equipped rest rooms, special class scheduling, lowered drinking fountains, lowered telephones, and special housing are available.

Services: Counseling and information services are available, as is tutoring in every subject. There is a reader service for the blind and remedial math, reading, and writing.

Campus Safety and Security: Measures include 24-hour foot and vehicle patrol, security escort services, informal discussions, and pamphlets/posters/films. There are emergency telephones, lighted pathways/sidewalks, crisis lines, and emergency contact light standards.

Programs of Study: EWU confers B.A., B.S., B.A.B., B.A.E., B.D.H., B.F.A., B.Mus., and B.S.N. degrees. Master's degrees are also awarded. Bachelor's degrees are awarded in BIOLOGICAL SCIENCE (biochemistry, biology/biological science, botany, microbiology, and zoology), BUSINESS (accounting, banking and finance, business administration and management, management science, marketing/retailing/merchandising, personnel management, and recreation and leisure services), COMMUNICATIONS AND THE ARTS (art, art history and appreciation, broadcasting, communications, creative writing, dance, dramatic arts, English, French, German, graphic design, journalism, literature, music, music performance, Spanish, speech/debate/rhetoric, and studio art), COMPUTER AND PHYSICAL SCIENCE (chemistry, computer science, geology, information sciences and systems, mathematics, and physics), EDUCATION (art, computer, elementary, foreign languages, guidance, health, marketing and distribution, mathematics, middle school, music, physical, recreation, science, secondary, and social science), ENGINEERING AND ENVIRONMENTAL DESIGN (computer technology, mechanical engineering technology, and military science), HEALTH PROFESSIONS (dental hygiene, health care administration, medical laboratory technology, nursing, predentistry, premedicine, preveterinary science, recreation therapy, and speech pathology/audiology), SOCIAL SCIENCE (anthropology, criminal justice, economics, geography, history, humanities, international relations, parks and recreation management, philosophy, political science/government, prelaw, psychology, social science, social work, sociology, and urban studies). Health sciences, biology, and computer science are the strongest academically. Business, education, and social science and history are the largest.

Required: All students must complete 180 quarter credits, including 60 to 110 in their major, while earning a minimum GPA of 2.0. Specific requirements include English composition and math courses to demonstrate competency. Distribution requirements include 11 total courses from 3 breadth areas: humanities, natural sciences and math, and social sciences. Seniors must complete a capstone course.

Special: Cooperative programs in nursing, cross-registration with the Intercollegiate School of Nursing, internships with area businesses, and work-study based on federal financial aid are available. B.A.-B.S. degrees, dual majors in any subject, study abroad in 12 countries, 3 types of general studies degrees, student-designed majors, and a 3-2 engineering degree with Washington State University are offered. Credit for military experience, nondegree study, and pass/fail options for nonmajor or nonminor courses also are possible. There are 14 national honor societies, a freshman honors program, and 39 departmental honors programs.

Faculty/Classroom: 47% of faculty are male; 53%, female. 98% teach undergraduates.

Admissions: 80% of the 2003-2004 applicants were accepted. The SAT I scores for the 2003-2004 freshman class were: Verbal--50% below 500, 34% between 500 and 599, 15% between 600 and 700, and 1% above 700; Math--49% below 500, 35% between 500 and 599, 15% between 600 and 700, and 1% above 700. 40% of the current freshmen were in the top fifth of their class; 70% were in the top two fifths.

Requirements: The SAT I or ACT is required. Admission is determined by an index coordinating the GPA with entrance exam scores. The GED is accepted. EWU requires 4 years of English, 3 each of math and social science, 2 each of science (including a lab science) and a single foreign language (ASL accepted), and 1 of fine arts or academic electives. A GPA of 2.0 is required. AP and CLEP credits are accepted. Important factors in the admissions decision are recommendations by school officials, advanced placement or honor courses, and evidence of special talent.

Procedure: Freshmen are admitted to all sessions. Entrance exams should be taken during the spring of the junior year or fall of the senior year. There is a deferred admissions plan and a rolling admissions plan. Applications should be filed by March 1 for fall entry, October 15 for winter entry, and February 15 for spring entry. The fall 2003 application fee was $35. Notification is sent on a rolling basis. A waiting list is an active part of the admissions procedure. Applications are accepted on computer disk and on-line through XAPplication, EXPAN, and the school's web site.

Transfer: 1087 transfer students enrolled in a recent year. Applicants with fewer than 40 credits must submit high school and college transcripts and test scores; those with more than 40 credits acceptable by Eastern or who have earned an associate degree from a Washington community college must submit a college transcript. 45 quarter credits of 180 required for the bachelor's degree must be completed at EWU.

Visiting: There are regularly scheduled orientations for prospective students, consisting of overnight programs for students and parents that present informational sessions on campus life and academic survival skills, academic advising, course registration, and social functions. There are guides for informal visits and visitors may sit in on classes and stay overnight. To schedule a visit, contact the Admissions Office at (509) 359-6555.

Financial Aid: In a recent year, 56% of all full-time freshmen and 63% of continuing full-time students received some form of financial aid. 42% of full-time freshmen and 61% of continuing full-time students received need-based aid. The average freshman award was $13,293. Need-based scholarships or need-based grants averaged $4094; need-based self-help aid (loans and jobs) averaged $2596; non-need-based athletic scholarships averaged $5498; and other non-need-based awards and non-need-based scholarships averaged $3011. 89% of undergraduates work part time. Average annual earnings from campus work are $3000. The average financial indebtedness of a recent graduate was $15,280. The FAFSA is required. Check with the school for current deadlines.

International Students: There were 215 international students enrolled in a recent year. The school actively recruits these students. They must score 525 on the written TOEFL.

Computers: The mainframe is a DEC VAX 6510 minicomputer. Students need an account number, available through classes. 5 computer labs and many specialized department labs are available. All students may access the system throughout the workday, plus evenings and weekends. There is only a time limit if students are waiting. The fee is $7 per term.

Graduates: In a recent year, 1527 bachelor's degrees were awarded. The most popular majors were education (21%), business administration (20%), and interdisciplinary studies (9%). 60 companies recruited on campus in a recent year.

Admissions Contact: Michelle Whittingham, Director of Admissions. A video is available. E-mail: *admissions@mail.ewu.edu*
Web: *www.ewu.edu*

EVERGREEN STATE COLLEGE
Olympia, WA 98505 B-3
(360) 867-6170; Fax: (360) 867-6576

Full-time: 1577 men, 1969 women	**Faculty:** 157
Part-time: 246 men, 311 women	**Ph.D.s:** 75%
Graduate: 90 men, 187 women	**Student/Faculty:** 23 to 1
Year: quarters, summer session	**Tuition:** $3804 ($13,482)
Application Deadline: March 1	**Room & Board:** $5772
Freshman Class: 1642 applied, 1422 accepted, 460 enrolled	
SAT I Verbal/Math: 600/550	**ACT:** 24 **COMPETITIVE+**

Evergreen State College, founded in 1967 and opened in 1971, is a public liberal arts college offering team-taught, interdisciplinary studies that culminate with written evaluations. The library contains 466,564 volumes, 490,122 microform items, and 15,719 audio/video tapes/CDs, and subscribes to 2665 periodicals. Computerized library services include the card catalog, interlibrary loans, database searching, and Internet access. Special learning facilities include a learning resource center, art gallery, radio station, communications lab, Longhouse Cultural Center, and Art Annex. The 1000-acre campus is in a small town 7 miles west of Olympia. Including any residence halls, there are 72 buildings.

Student Life: 77% of undergraduates are from Washington. Students are from 46 states, 14 foreign countries, and Canada. 67% are white. The average age of freshmen is 19; all undergraduates, 25. 31% do not continue beyond their first year; 55% remain to graduate.

Housing: 1000 students can be accommodated in college housing, which includes coed on-campus apartments. In addition, there is drug- and alcohol-free housing, first-year experience, and quiet housing. On-campus housing is guaranteed for the freshman year only and is available on a first-come, first-served basis. 80% of students commute. Alcohol is not permitted. All students may keep cars.

Activities: There are no fraternities or sororities. There are 53 groups on campus, including art, chorale, dance, drama, ethnic, film, gay, international, literary magazine, newspaper, photography, political, radio and TV, religious, social, social service, and student government. Popular campus events include Super Saturday, Evergreen Expressions Series, and Olympia Film Society festivals.

Sports: There are 3 intercollegiate sports for men and 4 for women, and 10 intramural sports for men and 10 for women. Facilities include a recreation center, which houses an 11-lane swimming pool, a diving well, exercise and weight training rooms, 5 racquetball courts, and indoor climbing walls. There is a 3100-seat gym, a covered pavilion, 4 tennis courts, and 5 playing fields.

Disabled Students: All of the campus is accessible. Wheelchair ramps, elevators, special parking, specially equipped rest rooms, lowered drinking fountains, and lowered telephones are available.

Services: Counseling and information services are available, as is tutoring in most subjects. There is a reader service for the blind.

Campus Safety and Security: Measures include 24-hour foot and vehicle patrol, self-defense education, security escort services, and informal discussions. There are pamphlets/posters/films, emergency telephones, and lighted pathways/sidewalks.

Programs of Study: Evergreen confers B.A. and B.S. degrees. Master's degrees are also awarded. Bachelor's degrees are awarded in SOCIAL SCIENCE (liberal arts/general studies). Liberal arts and sciences is the strongest academically and has the largest enrollment.

Required: Students must earn a minimum of 180 quarter hours of credit to receive a bachelor's degree. There are no other requirements.

Special: All work at the college is interdisciplinary, and the programs of study change annually. The college's credit-generating options include the comprehensive Coordinated Study Program, which allows students and faculty to work together intensively. Credits may be earned through cooperative programs, work-study programs, internships, or from prior learning and military experience. All majors are awarded in liberal arts and sciences. A B.A.-B.S. combined degree is possible in liberal arts. Study abroad is possible in France, Japan, Russia, Central America, Ireland, Israel, Egypt, and Southeast Asia.

Faculty/Classroom: 52% of faculty are male; 48%, female. All teach undergraduates. No introductory courses are taught by graduate students.

Admissions: 87% of the 2003-2004 applicants were accepted. The SAT I scores for the 2003-2004 freshman class were: Verbal--12% below 500, 36% between 500 and 599, 40% between 600 and 700, and 12% above 700; Math--27% below 500, 44% between 500 and 599, 25% between 600 and 700, and 4% above 700. The ACT scores were 19% below 21, 27% between 21 and 23, 24% between 24 and 26, 16% between 27 and 28, and 14% above 28. 25% of the current freshmen were in the top fifth of their class; 53% were in the top two fifths. There were 3 National Merit finalists and 2 semifinalists.

Requirements: The SAT I or ACT is required. In addition, candidates should be graduates of an accredited secondary school and have completed 15 academic credits, consisting of 4 in English, 3 each in math and social studies, 2 each in foreign language and science, and 1 in fine or performing arts. A GED certificate is acceptable. A GPA of 2.0 is required. AP and CLEP credits are accepted.

Procedure: Freshmen are admitted fall, winter, and spring. Entrance exams should be taken during spring of the junior year or fall of the senior year. Applications should be filed by March 1 for fall entry, October 1 for winter entry, and December 1 for spring entry, along with a $36 fee. Notification is sent April 1. Applications are accepted on-line through the school's web site, *www.evergreen.edu/admissions/apply.htm.*

Transfer: 817 transfer students enrolled in fall 2003. Applicants with fewer than 40 credits must submit SAT I or ACT scores and a high school transcript. A 2.0 minimum GPA is required. An associate degree is recommended. All applicants must submit all college transcripts. 45 quarter hour credits of 180 required for the bachelor's degree must be completed at Evergreen.

Visiting: There are regularly scheduled orientations for prospective students, including an admissions session, a class visit, and a tour. There are guides for informal visits and visitors may sit in on classes and stay overnight. To schedule a visit, contact the Student Visitor Program at (360) 867-6172 or *admissions@evergreen.edu.*

Financial Aid: In 2003-2004, 42% of all full-time freshmen and 55% of continuing full-time students received some form of financial aid. At least 31% of full-time freshmen and 45% of continuing full-time students received need-based aid. The average freshman award was $9500. Need-based scholarships or need-based grants averaged $4766; need-based self-help aid (loans and jobs) averaged $3065; and non-need-based athletic scholarships averaged $1005. 31% of undergraduates work part time. Average annual earnings from campus work are $1563. The average financial indebtedness of the 2003 graduate was $13,000. Evergreen is a member of CSS. The FAFSA and the college's own financial statement are required. The priority date for freshman financial aid applications for fall entry is February 15. The deadline for filing freshman financial aid applications for fall entry is March 15.

International Students: There were 28 international students enrolled in a recent year. They must score 525 on the written TOEFL or 197 on the electronic version and also take the SAT I or the ACT.

Computers: The mainframe is a DEC VAX cluster. There are 157 Windows systems and 58 Mac general-access systems in the computer center and various labs, providing network access to various servers and the Internet/Web. All students may access the system 18 hours per day. There are no time limits and no fees.

Graduates: From July 1, 2002 to June 30, 2003, 1108 bachelor's degrees were awarded. The most popular major was liberal arts and sciences (100%). In an average class, 5% graduate in 3 years or less, 42%

graduate in 4 years or less, 52% graduate in 5 years or less, and 55% graduate in 6 years or less. 49 companies recruited on campus in 2002-2003. Of the 2002 graduating class, 17% were enrolled in graduate school within 6 months of graduation and 84% were employed.

Admissions Contact: Doug Scrima, Director of Admissions.
E-mail: *admissions@evergreen.edu* Web: *www.evergreen.edu*

GONZAGA UNIVERSITY
Spokane, WA 99258-0001

E-2

(509) 323-6591
(800) 322-2584; Fax: (509) 324-5780

Full-time: 1699 men, 2029 women	**Faculty:** 254
Part-time: 48 men, 84 women	**Ph.D.s:** 87%
Graduate: 780 men, 1005 women	**Student/Faculty:** 15 to 1
Year: semesters, summer session	**Tuition:** $20,806
Application Deadline: February 1	**Room & Board:** $5960
Freshman Class: 2846 accepted, 908 enrolled	
SAT I Verbal/Math: 588/594	**ACT:** 26 **HIGHLY COMPETITIVE**

Gonzaga University, founded in 1887, is a private, liberal arts institution affiliated with the Roman Catholic Church and the Society of Jesus (Jesuits). The university offers undergraduate and graduate degrees in arts and sciences, business, education, engineering, and professional studies. There are 5 undergraduate and 5 graduate schools. In addition to regional accreditation, Gonzaga has baccalaureate program accreditation with AACSB, ABET, NCATE, and NLN. The 2 libraries contain 285,741 volumes, 582,965 microform items, and 3065 audio/video tapes/CDs, and subscribe to 1159 periodicals. Computerized library services include the card catalog, interlibrary loans, and database searching. Special learning facilities include a learning resource center, art gallery, radio station, and TV station. The 108-acre campus is in an urban area near downtown Spokane. Including any residence halls, there are 97 buildings.

Student Life: 51% of undergraduates are from Washington. Students are from 47 states, 21 foreign countries, and Canada. 65% are from public schools. 80% are white. 53% are Catholic; 22% claim no religious affiliation; 8% Protestant. The average age of freshmen is 18; all undergraduates, 21. 10% do not continue beyond their first year; 76% remain to graduate.

Housing: 1925 students can be accommodated in college housing, which includes single-sex and coed dorms, on-campus apartments, off-campus apartments, and married-student housing. In addition, there are honors houses, special-interest houses, and a first-year experience hall. On-campus housing is guaranteed for the freshman year only, is available on a first-come, first-served basis, and is available on a lottery system for upperclassmen. Priority is given to out-of-town students. 51% of students live on campus; of those, 88% remain on campus on weekends. Alcohol is not permitted. All students may keep cars.

Activities: There are no fraternities or sororities. There are 88 groups on campus, including art, band, cheerleading, chess, choir, chorale, chorus, computers, dance, debate, drama, drill team, ethnic, gay, honors, international, jazz band, literary magazine, musical theater, newspaper, orchestra, pep band, photography, political, professional, radio and TV, religious, social, social service, student government, symphony, and yearbook. Popular campus events include Search, Charity Ball, and Fall Family Weekend.

Sports: There are 7 intercollegiate sports for men and 7 for women, and 8 intramural sports for men and 8 for women. Facilities include an athletic center with an indoor running track, a full-size pool, a weight room, a dance studio, 6 basketball/volleyball courts, 8 racquetball courts, tennis courts, and a fitness room.

Disabled Students: 90% of the campus is accessible. Wheelchair ramps, elevators, special parking, specially equipped rest rooms, special class scheduling, lowered drinking fountains, and lowered telephones are available. Academic adjustments are provided for students with disabilities who provide appropriate documentation and request services from Disabilities Support Services.

Services: There is a reader service for the blind. Informal peer tutoring in English and math is available.

Campus Safety and Security: Measures include 24-hour foot and vehicle patrol, security escort services, informal discussions, and pamphlets/posters/films. There are emergency telephones and lighted pathways/sidewalks.

Programs of Study: Gonzaga confers B.A., B.S., B.B.A., B.E., B.G.S., and B.S.N. degrees. Master's and doctoral degrees are also awarded. Bachelor's degrees are awarded in BIOLOGICAL SCIENCE (biology/biological science), BUSINESS (accounting, business administration and management, and business economics), COMMUNICATIONS AND THE ARTS (art, broadcasting, dramatic arts, English, French, German, journalism, literature, music, public relations, Spanish, and speech/debate/rhetoric), COMPUTER AND PHYSICAL SCIENCE (chemistry, computer science, mathematics, and physics), EDUCATION (music, physical, and special), ENGINEERING AND ENVIRONMENTAL DESIGN (civil engineering, computer engineering, electrical/electronics engineering, and mechanical engineering), HEALTH PROFESSIONS (ex-

ercise science and nursing), SOCIAL SCIENCE (classical/ancient civilization, criminal justice, economics, history, interdisciplinary studies, international studies, Italian studies, liberal arts/general studies, philosophy, political science/government, psychology, religion, and sociology). Engineering and business administration are the strongest academically. Business, engineering, and liberal arts are the largest.

Required: All students must complete 128 credit hours with a minimum 2.0 GPA. The major requirements are 18 hours in upper-division courses and supporting courses required by the major department. Students must complete 9 credits each of philosophy and religious studies, 7 credits in English, speech, and critical thinking, and 3 credits each in math and English literature.

Special: Cross-registration with Whitworth College and the Intercollegiate Consortium for Nursing Education, internships, study abroad in 9 countries, a Washington semester, and on- and off-campus work-study programs are offered. High school juniors and seniors may take 6 credits per semester. There is a limited pass/fail option, and an accelerated general studies degree, and dual majors are possible. There are 9 national honor societies and a freshman honors program.

Faculty/Classroom: 63% of faculty are male; 37%, female. 93% teach undergraduates. No introductory courses are taught by graduate students. The average class size in an introductory lecture is 23; in a laboratory, 13; and in a regular course, 23.

Admissions: The SAT I scores for the 2003-2004 freshman class were: Verbal--12% below 500, 40% between 500 and 599, 39% between 600 and 700, and 9% above 700; Math--11% below 500, 40% between 500 and 599, 41% between 600 and 700, and 8% above 700. The ACT scores were 9% below 21, 17% between 21 and 23, 35% between 24 and 26, 17% between 27 and 28, and 22% above 28. 65% of the current freshmen were in the top fifth of their class; 88% were in the top two fifths. There were 10 National Merit finalists and 10 semifinalists. 71 freshmen graduated first in their class.

Requirements: The SAT I or ACT is required. In addition, applicants should be graduates of an accredited secondary school or hold a GED certificate. They must have completed 17 academic credits consisting of 4 years of English, 3 of math, 2 of a foreign language, 1 each of history and science, and 6 years of electives, 4 of which must be from the above subjects and the arts. An essay and letters of recommendation are required. An interview is recommended. AP and CLEP credits are accepted. Important factors in the admissions decision are advanced placement or honor courses, leadership record, and extracurricular activities record.

Procedure: Freshmen are admitted fall and spring. Entrance exams should be taken by May of the junior year. There are early admissions and deferred admissions plans. Applications should be filed by February 1 for fall entry and December 1 for spring entry. The fall 2003 application fee was $45. Notification is sent March 15. 295 applicants were on the 2003 waiting list; 289 were admitted. Applications are accepted online through Apply, CollegeLink, CollegeView, EXPAN, and the school's web site.

Transfer: 204 transfer students enrolled in 2002-2003. A minimum GPA of 2.7 is required. Students younger than 21 must submit test scores for the SAT I or ACT. An interview is recommended. 30 of 128 credits required for the bachelor's degree must be completed at Gonzaga.

Visiting: There are regularly scheduled orientations for prospective students, Day visits are permitted Monday through Friday; overnight visits, Sunday through Thursday (except for holiday periods). There are guides for informal visits and visitors may sit in on classes and stay overnight. To schedule a visit, contact the Admissions Office Visitation Coordinator at (800) 322-2584, ext. 6531 or *visit@gonzaga.edu*.

Financial Aid: In 2003-2004, 97% of all full-time freshmen and 91% of continuing full-time students received some form of financial aid. 64% of full-time freshmen and 62% of continuing full-time students received need-based aid. The average freshman award was $16,658. Need-based scholarships or need-based grants averaged $8235 ($22,865 maximum); need-based self-help aid (loans and jobs) averaged $5755 ($9500 maximum); non-need-based athletic scholarships averaged $12,192 ($27,323 maximum); and other non-need-based awards and non-need-based scholarships averaged $5520 ($27,000 maximum). 24% of undergraduates work part time. Average annual earnings from campus work are $2316. The average financial indebtedness of the 2003 graduate was $21,174. Gonzaga is a member of CSS. The FAFSA is required. The deadline for filing freshman financial aid applications for fall entry is February 1.

International Students: There are 48 international students enrolled. The school actively recruits these students. They must score 530 on the written TOEFL or 213 on the electronic version or take the MELAB or the ESL Exit Exam, which includes a writing test.

Computers: The mainframe is an HP-UX11.0; L200. The central academic system is available from more than 300 PCs spread throughout 11 computer labs. Students may also access the system from the residence hall Ethernet network or directly through the Internet. All students may access the system 24 hours per day. There are no time limits and no fees. It is strongly recommended that all students have a personal computer.

Graduates: From July 1, 2002 to June 30, 2003, 667 bachelor's degrees were awarded. The most popular majors were social studies and history (23%), business and management (21%), and engineering (8%). In an average class, 1% graduate in 3 years or less, 63% graduate in 4 years or less, 77% graduate in 5 years or less, and 78% graduate in 6 years or less. 100 companies recruited on campus in 2002-2003.

Admissions Contact: Julie McCullon, Dean of Admission. A video is available. E-mail: *mcculloh@gu.gonzaga.edu* Web: *www.gonzaga.edu*

HENRY COGSWELL COLLEGE
Everett, WA 98201

C-2

(425) 258-3351, ext. 116
(866) 411-HCC1; Fax: (425) 257-0405

Full-time: 130 men, 48 women	**Faculty:** 8
Part-time: 43 men, 9 women	**Ph.D.s:** 50%
Graduate: none	**Student/Faculty:** 22 to 1
Year: trimesters, summer session	**Tuition:** $14,400
Application Deadline: open	**Room & Board:** n/app
Freshman Class: 60 applied, 50 accepted, 28 enrolled	
SAT I Verbal/Math: 540/550	**ACT:** 26	**SPECIAL**

Henry Cogswell College, established in 1979, is a private institution specializing in business, engineering, computer science, and digital arts. There are 3 undergraduate schools. In addition to regional accreditation, Cogswell has baccalaureate program accreditation with ABET and IAC-BE. The library contains 8313 volumes and 64 audio/video tapes/CDs, and subscribes to 56 periodicals. Computerized library services include the card catalog, interlibrary loans, database searching, and Internet access. Special learning facilities include a learning resource center. The 1-acre campus is in a suburban area 30 miles north of Seattle. There are 2 buildings.

Student Life: 98% of undergraduates are from Washington. Students are from 3 states. 96% are from public schools. 80% are white; 10% Asian American. The average age of freshmen is 18; all undergraduates, 28. 25% do not continue beyond their first year; 66% remain to graduate.

Housing: There are no residence halls. All students commute. Alcohol is not permitted.

Activities: There are no fraternities or sororities. There are 4 groups on campus, including ASME, IEEE, professional, and student government. Popular campus events include Winter Holiday Party, Summer Barbecue, and Spring Easter Egg Hunt.

Sports: There is no sports program at Cogswell.

Disabled Students: 95% of the campus is accessible. Wheelchair ramps, elevators, special parking, specially equipped rest rooms, lowered drinking fountains, and lowered telephones are available.

Services: Counseling and information services are available, as is tutoring in most subjects. There is remedial math and writing.

Campus Safety and Security: Measures include informal discussions, pamphlets/posters/films, and lighted pathways/sidewalks.

Programs of Study: Cogswell confers B.A., B.S., B.S.E.E., and B.S.M.E. degrees. Bachelor's degrees are awarded in BUSINESS (business administration and management), COMPUTER AND PHYSICAL SCIENCE (computer science and digital arts/technology), ENGINEERING AND ENVIRONMENTAL DESIGN (electrical/electronics engineering, mechanical engineering, and mechanical engineering technology). Electrical engineering is the strongest academically. Mechanical engineering and digital arts are the largest.

Required: Students must complete a minimum of 121 trimester hours, including 51 in the major, and maintain a minimum 2.0 GPA. The core curriculum includes a minimum of 20 credits in humanities and social sciences, 3 classes each in written and oral communication, and classes in math, lab sciences, and moral and ethical problems. A senior thesis or project is required.

Special: There is an accelerated degree program in all majors. Internships are available in all majors. There are also work-study programs.

Faculty/Classroom: 88% of faculty are male; 12%, female. All teach undergraduates. The average class size in an introductory lecture is 11; in a laboratory, 11; and in a regular course, 10.

Admissions: 83% of the 2003-2004 applicants were accepted. The SAT I scores for the 2003-2004 freshman class were: Verbal--14% below 500, 59% between 500 and 599, 18% between 600 and 700, and 9% above 700; Math--27% below 500, 41% between 500 and 599, 27% between 600 and 700, and 5% above 700. The ACT scores were 12% between 21 and 23, 25% between 24 and 26, 38% between 27 and 28, and 25% above 28.

Requirements: The SAT I is required; the ACT is accepted. A high school diploma or GED is required. A portfolio is required of all art students. A GPA of 2.5 is required. AP and CLEP credits are accepted.

Procedure: Freshmen are admitted in the fall. Entrance exams should be taken prior to registration. There is a rolling admissions plan. Application deadlines are open. Application fee is $50. Applications are accepted on-line at the school's web site through CollegeNET.

Transfer: 26 transfer students enrolled in 2002-2003. Transferring students must forward all transcripts from previously attended schools and may be required to take placement exams. 30 of 121 credits required for the bachelor's degree must be completed at Cogswell.

Visiting: There are regularly scheduled orientations for prospective students each month from 10 A.M. to 2 P.M. 2 open houses are held each year in the fall. There are guides for informal visits and visitors may sit in on classes. To schedule a visit, contact Paul Wells, Director of Admissions.

Financial Aid: In 2003-2004, 92% of all full-time freshmen and 38% of continuing full-time students received some form of financial aid. 40% of full-time freshmen and 30% of continuing full-time students received need-based aid. The average freshman award was $9556. Need-based scholarships or need-based grants averaged $3866; need-based self-help aid (loans and jobs) averaged $2344; and non-need-based awards and non-need-based scholarships averaged $2969. 8% of undergraduates work part time. Average annual earnings from campus work are $978. The average financial indebtedness of the 2003 graduate was $23,658. Cogswell is a member of CSS. The CSS/Profile, FAFSA, FFS or SFS and the college's own financial statement are required. The deadline for filing freshman financial aid applications for fall entry is September 1.

International Students: The school actively recruits international students. They must score 550 on the written TOEFL or 213 on the electronic version and also take the SAT I, scoring 950, or the ACT.

Computers: The mainframe is a client/server environment. A PC lab and main computer lab are available. PCs are also available in the library. More than 120 computers are available for student use. All students may access the system. There are no time limits and no fees.

Graduates: From July 1, 2002 to June 30, 2003, 49 bachelor's degrees were awarded. The most popular majors were digital arts (43%), mechanical engineering (29%), and electrical engineering (12%). In an average class, 70% graduate in 3 years or less and 30% graduate in 6 years or less. 10 companies recruited on campus in 2002-2003. Of the 2002 graduating class, 12% were enrolled in graduate school within 6 months of graduation and 65% were employed.

Admissions Contact: Paul Wells, Director of Admissions.
E-mail: *p.wells@henrycogswell.edu* or *information@henrycogswell.edu*
Web: *www.henrycogswell.edu*

HERITAGE COLLEGE
Toppenish, WA 98948

D-3

(509) 865-8500; Fax: (509) 865-4469

Full-time: 112 men, 326 women	**Faculty:** 38
Part-time: 77 men, 228 women	**Ph.D.s:** 40%
Graduate: 180 men, 346 women	**Student/Faculty:** 12 to 1
Year: semesters, summer session	**Tuition:** $6720 ($8280)
Application Deadline: open	**Room & Board:** n/app
Freshman Class: 181 applied, 173 accepted, 85 enrolled	
SAT I or ACT: recommended	**NONCOMPETITIVE**

Heritage College, founded in 1982, is a private, nonprofit commuter college offering undergraduate and graduate programs in liberal arts and teacher education, half of which are given on evenings and weekends. Tuition figure in the above capsule does not include fees, which vary depending on program The library contains 40,000 volumes, 151,960 microform items, and 208 audio/video tapes/CDs, and subscribes to 265 periodicals. Computerized library services include database searching. Special learning facilities include a learning resource center, K-20 network, and geographic information systems (GIS) laboratory. The 19-acre campus is in a rural area 20 miles south of Yakima. There are 15 buildings.

Student Life: 99% of undergraduates are from Washington. Students are from 2 states and 2 foreign countries. 48% are white; 41% Hispanic. The average age of freshmen is 25; all undergraduates, 31. 23% do not continue beyond their first year; 56% remain to graduate.

Housing: There are no residence halls. All students commute. Alcohol is not permitted. All students may keep cars.

Activities: There are no fraternities or sororities. There are 5 groups on campus, including art, computers, dance, ethnic, honors, literary magazine, newspaper, professional, social service, and student government. Popular campus events include Spring Faire, Academic Convocation, and Founders Day.

Sports: Facilities include a track and field used for soccer, flag football, and softball; and a basketball court.

Disabled Students: 95% of the campus is accessible. Wheelchair ramps, special parking, specially equipped rest rooms, special class scheduling, and lowered drinking fountains are available.

Services: Counseling and information services are available, as is tutoring in most subjects. There is remedial math, reading, and writing.

Campus Safety and Security: Measures include security escort services, emergency telephones, and lighted pathways/sidewalks.

Programs of Study: Heritage confers B.A., B.S., B.A.Ed., and B.S.W. degrees. Associate and master's degrees are also awarded. Bachelor's degrees are awarded in BUSINESS (business administration and management), COMMUNICATIONS AND THE ARTS (English and Spanish), COMPUTER AND PHYSICAL SCIENCE (computer science, mathematics, and science), EDUCATION (elementary, science, secondary, and social studies), ENGINEERING AND ENVIRONMENTAL DESIGN (environmental science), SOCIAL SCIENCE (interdisciplinary studies, psychology, public administration, social work, and sociology). Education is the largest.

Required: All students must complete 44 to 45 credits of general college requirements, which include 12 credits each in arts and letters, 10 credits in science and math, 9 credits in social sciences, 1 year of English, a computer course, a math course above the 100-level, and a world civilization course. At least 126 semester credit hours must be completed, with at least 48 upper-division credits. Education majors must have a minimum GPA of 2.5; others must have a 2.0.

Special: Heritage provides individualized assistance. Credit by examination is available in many courses, and credit may be given for work experience. The college also has cooperative programs with 3 school districts, internships in local businesses, social service agencies, and cross-registration with Northwest Indian College. Pass/fail options are possible for some courses. An accelerated degree program is available in business adminstration. There is a freshman honors program.

Faculty/Classroom: 51% of faculty are male; 49%, female. 40% teach undergraduates and 40% both teach and do research. No introductory courses are taught by graduate students. The average class size in an introductory lecture is 20; in a laboratory, 16; and in a regular course, 20.

Admissions: 96% of the 2003-2004 applicants were accepted.

Requirements: The SAT I or ACT is recommended, but entrance exams are not required. Applicants must have graduated from an accredited secondary school or hold a GED certificate. An interview is recommended. Assessment for placement in English and math courses is required. AP and CLEP credits are accepted.

Procedure: Freshmen are admitted to all sessions. Entrance exams should be taken before registering. Application forms may be downloaded from the college web site. Application deadlines are open.

Transfer: 104 transfer students enrolled in 2002-2003. Students must have completed 30 credits. 32 of 126 credits required for the bachelor's degree must be completed at Heritage.

Visiting: There are regularly scheduled orientations for prospective students, consisting of a day and an evening fall orientation. There are guides for informal visits and visitors may sit in on classes. To schedule a visit, contact the Director of Admissions, Norberto Espindola at *espindola_b@heritage.edu.*

Financial Aid: In 2003-2004, 93% of all full-time freshmen received some form of financial aid. 55% of full-time freshmen received need-based aid. Need-based scholarships or need-based grants averaged $8608 ($18,465 maximum); need-based self-help aid (loans and jobs) averaged $3338 ($10,225 maximum); and non-need-based awards and non-need-based scholarships averaged $339 ($8233 maximum). 13% of undergraduates work part time. Average annual earnings from campus work are $3600. The average financial indebtedness of the 2003 graduate was $5000. Heritage is a member of CSS. The CSS Profile or FAFSA and the college's own financial statement are required. The priority date for freshman financial aid applications for fall entry is February 10. The deadline for filing freshman financial aid applications for fall entry is April 1.

International Students: In a recent year, there was 1 international student enrolled. These students must score 500 on the written TOEFL.

Computers: The mainframes are a VT420 and a DEC VAX for administrative use. There are 150 networked terminals; 26 are always available for student use. Others are available when classes are not scheduled in the rooms. All students may access the system. There are no time limits and no fees.

Graduates: From July 1, 2002 to June 30, 2003, 78 bachelor's degrees were awarded. The most popular majors were education (30%), social science/social work (24%), and business (11%). In an average class, 17% graduate in 4 years or less, 44% graduate in 5 years or less, and 56% graduate in 6 years or less.

Admissions Contact: Norberto Espindola, Director of Admissions. E-mail: *espindola_b@heritage.edu* Web: *www.heritage.edu*

NORTHWEST COLLEGE
Kirkland, WA 98033   C-2
(425) 889-5212
(800) 669-3781; Fax: (425) 827-0148

Full-time: 364 men, 606 women	Faculty: 49
Part-time: 38 men, 49 women	Ph.D.s: 41%
Graduate: 26 men, 54 women	Student/Faculty: 20 to 1
Year: semesters, summer session	Tuition: $12,858
Application Deadline: August 1	Room & Board: $5996
Freshman Class: n/av	
SAT I or ACT: required	COMPETITIVE

Northwest College, founded in 1934, is a private institution offering programs in ministry, business, nursing, and education. There is 1 undergraduate and 2 graduate schools. In addition to regional accreditation, NC has baccalaureate program accreditation with AACTE. The library contains 174,100 volumes, 40,800 microform items, and 5000 audio/video tapes/CDs, and subscribes to 900 periodicals. Computerized li-

brary services include the card catalog, interlibrary loans, database searching, and Internet access. Special learning facilities include a radio station. The 56-acre campus is in a suburban area in Kirkland, 10 miles east of Seattle, and overlooks Lake Washington. Including any residence halls, there are 27 buildings.

Student Life: 79% of undergraduates are from Washington. Students are from 23 states, 15 foreign countries, and Canada. 60% are white. Most are Protestant. The average age of freshmen is 19; all undergraduates, 25. 34% do not continue beyond their first year; 34% remain to graduate.

Housing: 544 students can be accommodated in college housing, which includes single-sex dorms, on-campus apartments, and married-student housing. On-campus housing is guaranteed for all 4 years. 63% of students live on campus; of those, 80% remain on campus on weekends. Alcohol is not permitted. All students may keep cars.

Activities: There are no fraternities or sororities. There are 20 groups on campus, including band, choir, chorale, chorus, debate, drama, forensics, international, jazz band, literary magazine, musical theater, newspaper, orchestra, photography, professional, religious, social, social service, student government, and yearbook. Popular campus events include Christmas Holiday Social, All-School Banquet, and Roomies Night-out.

Sports: There are 4 intercollegiate sports for men and 4 for women, and 2 intramural sports for men and 2 for women. Facilities include a gym pavilion, outdoor tennis courts, a practice field for soccer and intramural football, access to the Seattle Seahawks' fields, outdoor basketball, and sand volleyball.

Disabled Students: 75% of the campus is accessible. Wheelchair ramps, elevators, special parking, specially equipped rest rooms, and special residence hall restrooms and shower facilities are available.

Services: There is a reader service for the blind and remedial writing. The Student Success Office provides assistance in most areas, including study skills.

Campus Safety and Security: Measures include 24-hour foot and vehicle patrol, security escort services, shuttle buses, and informal discussions. There are pamphlets/posters/films, emergency telephones, and lighted pathways/sidewalks.

Programs of Study: NC confers the B.A. degree. Associate and master's degrees are also awarded. Bachelor's degrees are awarded in BIOLOGICAL SCIENCE (life science), BUSINESS (business administration and management), COMMUNICATIONS AND THE ARTS (communications, English, journalism, music, and music business management), COMPUTER AND PHYSICAL SCIENCE (computer management), EDUCATION (education, elementary, middle school, physical, secondary, and special), ENGINEERING AND ENVIRONMENTAL DESIGN (environmental science), HEALTH PROFESSIONS (nursing), SOCIAL SCIENCE (behavioral science, biblical studies, counseling/psychology, history, interdisciplinary studies, liberal arts/general studies, ministries, missions, pastoral studies, philosophy, psychology, religion, religious education, religious music, theological studies, and youth ministry). Teacher education, business, and psychology are the strongest academically. Teacher education, church ministries, and business are the largest.

Required: Students must complete 18 credits in humanities, 16 in religion, 12 in social science, and 10 each in science and math. At least 125 semester credits (up to 139 for teacher education), with a minimum GPA of 2.0, are required. The number of semester credits needed in the major varies from 36 to 50.

Special: Northwest offers study in several locations in the U.S. and foreign countries through the Council for Christian Colleges and Universities. Dual majors are available. There are 2 national honor societies and 1 departmental honors program.

Faculty/Classroom: In a recent year, 65% of faculty were male; 35%, female. All taught undergraduates. The average class size in an introductory lecture was 30; in a laboratory, 20; and in a regular course, 24.

Admissions: The SAT I scores for the 2003-2004 freshman class were: Verbal--33% below 500, 45% between 500 and 599, 19% between 600 and 700, and 3% above 700; Math--40% below 500, 42% between 500 and 599, 15% between 600 and 700, and 3% above 700.

Requirements: The SAT I or ACT is required. A GPA of 2.3 is required. AP and CLEP credits are accepted. Important factors in the admissions decision are personality/intangible qualities, recommendations by alumni, and leadership record.

Procedure: Freshmen are admitted to all sessions. Entrance exams should be taken in the spring of the junior year. There are early decision and deferred admissions plans. Applications should be filed by August 1 for fall entry, December 15 for spring entry, and April 15 for summer entry. Notification of early decision is sent December 1; regular decision, on a rolling basis. The fall 2003 application fee was $30. 56 early decision candidates were accepted for the 2003-2004 class.

Transfer: 205 transfer students enrolled in a recent year. Transfers must have a minimum 2.3 GPA from high school and college and must submit SAT I or ACT scores, an essay, and 2 letters of reference. 30 of 125 credits required for the bachelor's degree must be completed at NC.

Visiting: There are regularly scheduled orientations for prospective students, including Northwest Fridays. There are guides for informal visits and visitors may sit in on classes and stay overnight. To schedule a visit, contact Jeanne Ames at (425) 889-5286 or *jeanne.ames@ncag.edu*.

Financial Aid: In 2003-2004, 77% of all full-time freshmen and 66% of continuing full-time students received some form of financial aid. 72% of full-time freshmen and 61% of continuing full-time students received need-based aid. The average freshman award was $7974. 82% of undergraduates work part time. Average annual earnings from campus work are $2050. The average financial indebtedness of the 2003 graduate was $20,374. The FAFSA and the college's own financial statement are required. The deadline for filing freshman financial aid applications for fall entry is March 1.

International Students: There are 19 international students enrolled. They must score 500 on the written TOEFL.

Computers: The campus has several computer centers. Each residence hall room has network and Internet access. All students are licensed for access to Microsoft Office Products (software provided), and may access the system. There are set hours for labs; residence halls are always connected. There are no time limits. The fee is $50 per semester. It is strongly recommended that all students have a personal computer that is IBM or Microsoft Windows/Office-compatible.

Graduates: From July 1, 2002 to June 30, 2003, 252 bachelor's degrees were awarded.

Admissions Contact: Ben Thomas, Director, Enrollment Services. A video is available. E-mail: *admissions@ncag.edu* Web: *www.nwcollege.edu*

PACIFIC LUTHERAN UNIVERSITY C-2
Tacoma, WA 98447

(253) 535-7151
(800) 274-6758; Fax: (253) 536-5136

Full-time: 1067 men, 1855 women	**Faculty:** 216; IIA, -$
Part-time: 116 men, 147 women	**Ph.D.s:** 90%
Graduate: 108 men, 169 women	**Student/Faculty:** 14 to 1
Year: 4-1-4, summer session	**Tuition:** $19,610
Application Deadline: open	**Room & Board:** $6105
Freshman Class: 1666 applied, 1575 accepted, 694 enrolled	
SAT I Verbal/Math: 560/560	**ACT:** 25 **VERY COMPETITIVE**

Pacific Lutheran University, founded in 1890, is an independent, private institution affiliated with the Evangelical Lutheran Church in America. PLU offers programs in arts and sciences, business, education, nursing, fine arts, and phys ed. There are 6 undergraduate and 3 graduate schools. In addition to regional accreditation, PLU has baccalaureate program accreditation with AACSB, ABET, CSAB, CSWE, NASM, NCATE, and NLN. The library contains 597,094 volumes, 234,764 microform items, and 11,884 audio/video tapes/CDs, and subscribes to 4732 periodicals. Computerized library services include the card catalog, interlibrary loans, database searching, and Internet access. Special learning facilities include a learning resource center, art gallery, radio station, TV station, herbarium, invertebrate and vertebrate museums, biology field station, Northwest history collections, Scandinavian history collection, and language resource center. The 126-acre campus is in a suburban area 7 miles south of Tacoma. Including any residence halls, there are 40 buildings.

Student Life: 73% of undergraduates are from Washington. Students are from 38 states, 24 foreign countries, and Canada. 97% are from public schools. 77% are white. 67% are Protestant; 10% Catholic; 6% claim no religious affiliation. The average age of freshmen is 18; all undergraduates, 22. 17% do not continue beyond their first year; 65% remain to graduate.

Housing: 1650 students can be accommodated in college housing, which includes single-sex and coed dorms, on-campus apartments, and married-student housing. On-campus housing is guaranteed for the freshman year only. 50% of students live on campus; of those, 75% remain on campus on weekends. Alcohol is not permitted. All students may keep cars.

Activities: There are no fraternities or sororities. There are 46 groups on campus, including adult student, advertising, art, band, cheerleading, choir, chorale, chorus, comedy, commuter, computers, dance, debate, drama, ethnic, film, gay, honors, international, jazz band, literary magazine, musical theater, newspaper, opera, orchestra, pep band, photography, political, professional, radio and TV, religious, social, social service, student government, symphony, and yearbook. Popular campus events include Lucia Bride Festival, Songfest, and Family Weekend.

Sports: There are 11 intercollegiate sports for men and 10 for women, and 12 intramural sports for men and 12 for women. Facilities include a 4000-seat gym, a 4000-seat auditorium, a fitness center with an all-weather track, a 9-hole golf course, a swimming pool, and racquetball, squash, and tennis courts.

Disabled Students: 90% of the campus is accessible. Wheelchair ramps, elevators, special parking, specially equipped rest rooms, special class scheduling, lowered drinking fountains, and lowered telephones are available.

Services: Counseling and information services are available, as is tutoring in most subjects. Study groups and pretest and posttest reviews are also available.

Campus Safety and Security: Measures include 24-hour foot and vehicle patrol, self-defense education, security escort services, and informal discussions. There are pamphlets/posters/films, emergency telephones, and lighted pathways/sidewalks.

Programs of Study: PLU confers B.A., B.S., B.A.E., B.A.P.E., B.A.Rec., B.B.A., B.F.A., B.M., B.M.A., B.M.Ed., B.S.N., and B.S.P.E. degrees. Master's degrees are also awarded. Bachelor's degrees are awarded in BIOLOGICAL SCIENCE (biology/biological science), BUSINESS (business administration and management and recreation and leisure services), COMMUNICATIONS AND THE ARTS (art, classics, communications, English, fine arts, French, German, music, music performance, music theory and composition, piano/organ, Scandinavian languages, Spanish, and voice), COMPUTER AND PHYSICAL SCIENCE (applied physics, chemistry, computer programming, computer science, geoscience, mathematics, and physics), EDUCATION (education, music, and physical), ENGINEERING AND ENVIRONMENTAL DESIGN (computer engineering, engineering and applied science, and environmental science), HEALTH PROFESSIONS (nursing), SOCIAL SCIENCE (anthropology, Asian/Oriental studies, economics, history, international studies, philosophy, political science/government, psychology, religion, Scandinavian studies, social work, sociology, and women's studies). Business administration, education, and nursing are the largest.

Required: All students must complete 128 credit hours, with a maximum of 40 in the major. Candidates for degrees in nursing, business administration, and education need a cumulative 2.5 GPA; all others must have a 2.0 GPA. The required curriculum is 36 credit hours of distributive core courses in arts/literature, natural sciences/math, philosophy, religious studies, and social sciences; writing and critical conversation courses; and diversity classes.

Special: PLU offers 2 different bachelor's degrees simultaneously, 3-2 engineering degrees with Washington University in St. Louis and Columbia University, and accelerated degree programs in most majors. Dual majors and student-designed majors can be arranged. Extensive internships with local businesses and nonprofit organizations, work-study programs, non-degree study, and pass/fail options are also available. The Wang Center for International Programs supports the university's internationally focused academic programs. There are study-abroad programs in 28 countries. There are 7 national honor societies.

Faculty/Classroom: 54% of faculty are male; 46%, female. 98% teach undergraduates, 90% do research, and 90% do both. No introductory courses are taught by graduate students. The average class size in an introductory lecture is 23; in a laboratory, 16; and in a regular course, 17.

Admissions: 95% of the 2003-2004 applicants were accepted. The SAT I scores for the 2003-2004 freshman class were: Verbal--23% below 500, 39% between 500 and 599, 32% between 600 and 700, and 6% above 700; Math--24% below 500, 41% between 500 and 599, 32% between 600 and 700, and 3% above 700. The ACT scores were 18% below 21, 21% between 21 and 23, 26% between 24 and 26, 13% between 27 and 28, and 22% above 28. 62% of the current freshmen were in the top fifth of their class; 87% were in the top two fifths. There were 5 National Merit finalists. 28 freshmen graduated first in their class.

Requirements: The SAT I or ACT is required. In addition, applicants should be graduates of accredited secondary schools, although GED certificates are accepted. PLU requires 2 years each of college preparatory math and a foreign language and recommends 4 years of English, 2 each of social studies and lab science, 1 of fine or performing arts, and 3 of electives. An essay is required. PLU requires applicants to be in the upper 50% of their class. A GPA of 2.5 is required. AP and CLEP credits are accepted. Important factors in the admissions decision are advanced placement or honor courses, leadership record, and evidence of special talent.

Procedure: Freshmen are admitted fall and spring. Entrance exams should be taken by January of the senior year. There is a rolling admissions plan and a deferred admissions plan. Application deadlines are open. Application fee is $35. Applications are accepted on-line through the school's web site.

Transfer: 290 transfer students enrolled in 2003-2004. Candidates must be in good academic and personal standing at the institutions last attended full time. Although it does not guarantee admission, a 2.5 GPA in all college work is usually required. For applicants with fewer than 30 semester hours or 45 quarter hours, secondary school records and standardized test scores must be submitted. All students must meet the foreign language and math entrance requirements. 32 of 128 credits required for the bachelor's degree must be completed at PLU.

Visiting: There are regularly scheduled orientations for prospective students, consisting of activities based on the students' individual interests. There are guides for informal visits and visitors may sit in on classes and stay overnight. To schedule a visit, contact the Office of Admissions.

Financial Aid: In 2003-2004, 95% of all full-time freshmen and 93% of continuing full-time students received some form of financial aid. 69% of full-time freshmen and 72% of continuing full-time students received need-based aid. The average freshman award was $17,193. Need-based

scholarships or need-based grants averaged $6966 ($18,597 maximum); need-based self-help aid (loans and jobs) averaged $5821 ($12,125 maximum); and non-need-based awards and non-need-based scholarships averaged $5502 ($19,610 maximum). 51% of undergraduates work part time. Average annual earnings from campus work are $2145. The average financial indebtedness of the 2003 graduate was $22,190. The FAFSA is required. The deadline for filing freshman financial aid applications for fall entry is January 31.

International Students: There are 136 international students enrolled. The school actively recruits these students. They must score 550 on the written TOEFL or 213 on the electronic version.

Computers: The mainframe is a DEC Alpha ES40 clustered with a DEC VAX 4700A. There are 2 teaching labs and 2 open labs for student use. All students may access the system 18 hours per day, or 24 hours with a modem. There are no time limits and no fees.

Graduates: From July 1, 2002 to June 30, 2003, 796 bachelor's degrees were awarded. The most popular majors were business (16%), education (13%), and nursing (7%). In an average class, 2% graduate in 3 years or less, 45% graduate in 4 years or less, 65% graduate in 5 years or less, and 68% graduate in 6 years or less. 53 companies recruited on campus in 2002-2003. Of the 2002 graduating class, 11% were enrolled in graduate school within 6 months of graduation and 85% were employed.

Admissions Contact: David E. Gunovich, Director of Admissions.
E-mail: *admissions@plu.edu* Web: *www.plu.edu*

SAINT MARTIN'S COLLEGE
Lacey, WA 98503

B-3

(360) 438-4311
(800) 368-8803; Fax: (360) 412-6189

Full-time: 323 men, 411 women	**Faculty:** 56; IIB, --$
Part-time: 184 men, 312 women	**Ph.Ds:** 80%
Graduate: 104 men, 168 women	**Student/Faculty:** 13 to 1
Year: semesters, summer session	**Tuition:** $17,890
Application Deadline: August 1	**Room & Board:** $5355
Freshman Class: 462 applied, 352 accepted, 150 enrolled	
SAT I Verbal/Math: 497/489	**ACT:** 20 **COMPETITIVE**

Saint Martin's College, founded in 1895, is a small Roman Catholic institution conducted by the Benedictine order, offering undergraduate and graduate programs in liberal arts and sciences, business, engineering, and preprofessional areas. There are 6 undergraduate and 6 graduate schools. In addition to regional accreditation, Saint Martin's College has baccalaureate program accreditation with ABET. The library contains 100,540 volumes, 132,768 microform items, and 1403 audio/video tapes/CDs, and subscribes to 811 periodicals. Computerized library services include the card catalog, interlibrary loans, and database searching. Special learning facilities include a learning resource center, art gallery, and natural history museum. The 303-acre campus is in a suburban area 3 miles from Olympia and 60 miles south of Seattle. Including any residence halls, there are 14 buildings.

Student Life: 88% of undergraduates are from Washington. Students are from 17 states, 13 foreign countries, and Canada. 85% are from public schools. 64% are white; 10% African American. 39% claim no religious affiliation; 36% are Catholic; 15% Protestant. The average age of freshmen is 18; all undergraduates, 30. 20% do not continue beyond their first year; 69% remain to graduate.

Housing: 282 students can be accommodated in college housing, which includes coed dorms. On-campus housing is guaranteed for the freshman year only and is available on a first-come, first-served basis. 71% of students commute. Alcohol is not permitted. All students may keep cars.

Activities: There is 1 national sorority. There are 30 groups on campus, including band, cheerleading, choir, computers, drama, ethnic, honors, international, newspaper, pep band, professional, religious, social, social service, student government, and yearbook. Popular campus events include Career Fair, International Day, and Capital Food and Wine Festival.

Sports: There are 5 intercollegiate sports for men and 6 for women, and 9 intramural sports for men and 9 for women. Facilities include a 5300-seat multipurpose pavilion, athletic fields, tennis courts, and nearby golf courses, lakes, and mountains.

Disabled Students: 90% of the campus is accessible. Wheelchair ramps, elevators, special parking, specially equipped rest rooms, lowered drinking fountains, and lowered telephones are available. Access services provide assistance to students with disabilities.

Services: Counseling and information services are available, as is tutoring in some subjects, including writing. There is a reader service for the blind and remedial writing.

Campus Safety and Security: Measures include 24-hour foot and vehicle patrol, security escort services, pamphlets/posters/films, and lighted pathways/sidewalks. There is a security patrol from dark to dawn.

Programs of Study: Saint Martin's College confers B.A., B.S., B.S.C.E., and B.S.M.E. degrees. Master's degrees are also awarded. Bachelor's degrees are awarded in BIOLOGICAL SCIENCE (biology/

biological science), BUSINESS (accounting, banking and finance, management science, and marketing/retailing/merchandising), COMMUNICATIONS AND THE ARTS (English and music), COMPUTER AND PHYSICAL SCIENCE (chemistry, computer science, and mathematics), EDUCATION (computer, elementary, social studies, and special), ENGINEERING AND ENVIRONMENTAL DESIGN (civil engineering and mechanical engineering), HEALTH PROFESSIONS (predentistry, premedicine, prepharmacy, and preveterinary science), SOCIAL SCIENCE (community services, criminal justice, economics, history, humanities, political science/government, prelaw, psychology, and religion). Education and engineering are the strongest academically. Education, business, and science/math are the largest.

Required: All students must complete freshman composition and general education requirements, including 2 courses in social sciences, 1 course each in literature, philosophy, the arts, religious studies, natural science with lab, math (precalculus), computer science, U.S. history, and non-U.S. history, as well as 2 credits of phys ed. Students must pass an English proficiency exam. A total of 128 semester credits with a 2.0 GPA is required. 1 year of foreign language is required if the student did not take 2 years of a single foreign language in high school.

Special: Double majors, work-study with the state of Washington, nonprofit organizations, and Saint Martin's, internships in all disciplines, a Washington semester with American University, and pass/fail options are offered. The FOCUS program offers credit for job experience. Nondegree study and study abroad is possible. There are 2 national honor societies.

Faculty/Classroom: 72% of faculty are male; 28%, female. All teach undergraduates and 70% both teach and do research. No introductory courses are taught by graduate students. The average class size in an introductory lecture is 20; in a laboratory, 12; and in a regular course, 12.

Admissions: 76% of the 2003-2004 applicants were accepted. The SAT I scores for the 2003-2004 freshman class were: Verbal--46% below 500, 39% between 500 and 599, 13% between 600 and 700, and 2% above 700; Math--51% below 500, 30% between 500 and 599, 17% between 600 and 700, and 2% above 700. The ACT scores were 63% below 21, 17% between 21 and 23, 12% between 24 and 26, 2% between 27 and 28, and 6% above 28. 55% of the current freshmen were in the top fifth of their class; 85% were in the top two fifths.

Requirements: The SAT I or ACT is required. In addition, applicants must be graduates of an accredited secondary school or have a GED, with a minimum of 16 academic units, including 4 in English, 2 or 3 in math, 2 in history/social science, 1 or 2 each in foreign language and lab science, and 7 in electives. Class standing also is considered. An essay and recommendation from a teacher or counselor are required. Students should have a score of 800 on the SAT I and a 2.5 GPA. AP and CLEP credits are accepted. Important factors in the admissions decision are advanced placement or honor courses, recommendations by school officials, and personality/intangible qualities.

Procedure: Freshmen are admitted to all sessions. There is a rolling admissions plan. Applications should be filed by August 1 for fall entry and December 15 for spring entry, along with a $35 fee. Notification is sent on a rolling basis. Applications are accepted on-line through *www.stmartin.edu*.

Transfer: 119 transfer students enrolled in 2002-2003. Transfer applicants must submit transcripts from all colleges previously attended and have a 2.0 GPA. 30 of 128 credits required for the bachelor's degree must be completed at Saint Martin's College.

Visiting: There are regularly scheduled orientations for prospective students, including a campus tour and faculty, student service, and financial aid presentations. There are guides for informal visits and visitors may sit in on classes and stay overnight. To schedule a visit, contact the Admissions Office at *admissions@stmartin.edu*.

Financial Aid: In 2003-2004, 98% of all full-time freshmen and 65% of continuing full-time students received some form of financial aid. 94% of full-time freshmen and 63% of continuing full-time students received need-based aid. The average freshman award in 2002-2003 was $20,003, with $6404 from need-based scholarships or grants, $6349 from need-based self-help aid (loans and jobs), $3615 from non-need-based athletic scholarships, and $3635 from other non-need-based awards and non-need-based scholarships. 34% of undergraduates work part time. Average annual earnings from campus work are $1587. The average financial indebtedness of the 2003 graduate was $29,866. Saint Martin's College is a member of CSS. The FAFSA and the college's own financial statement are required. The deadline for filing freshman financial aid applications for fall entry is March 1.

International Students: There are 81 international students enrolled. The school actively recruits these students. They must score 525 on the written TOEFL.

Computers: IBM PCs and Macs are available in the computer center and library. All students may access the system. There are no time limits. The fee is $50 per semester.

Graduates: From July 1, 2002 to June 30, 2003, 283 bachelor's degrees were awarded. The most popular majors were business (32%), psychology (17%), and education (13%). In an average class, 1% graduate in 3 years or less, 43% graduate in 4 years or less, 60% graduate in 5 years or less, and 69% graduate in 6 years or less. 160 companies recruited on campus in 2002-2003. Of the 2002 graduating class, 8% were enrolled in graduate school within 6 months of graduation and 97% were employed.

Admissions Contact: Todd Abbott, Director of Admissions.
E-mail: *admissions@stmartin.edu*

SEATTLE PACIFIC UNIVERSITY   C-2
Seattle, WA 98119-1997   (206) 281-2021
(800) 366-3344; Fax: (206) 281-2669

Full-time: 874 men, 1735 women	**Faculty:** 171; IIA, -$
Part-time: 62 men, 127 women	**Ph.Ds:** 87%
Graduate: 239 men, 470 women	**Student/Faculty:** 15 to 1
Year: quarters, summer session	**Tuition:** $18,927
Application Deadline: June 1	**Room & Board:** $7017
Freshman Class: 1778 applied, 1635 accepted, 683 enrolled	
SAT I Verbal/Math: 584/570	**ACT:** 25 **VERY COMPETITIVE**

Seattle Pacific University, founded in 1891, is a private, nonprofit institution affiliated with the Free Methodist Church. It offers programs in business and economics, education, fine and performing arts, health science, humanities, natural and mathematical sciences, phys ed and athletics, religion, and social and behavioral sciences. There are 9 undergraduate and 6 graduate schools. In addition to regional accreditation, SPU has baccalaureate program accreditation with ABET, ADA, NASM, NCATE, and NLN. The library contains 189,371 volumes, 500,296 microform items, and 3303 audio/video tapes/CDs, and subscribes to 1219 periodicals. Computerized library services include the card catalog and database searching. Special learning facilities include a learning resource center, art gallery, a science center, a performing arts theater, a writing lab, and a media center. The 35-acre campus is in an urban area on the north slope of Queen Anne Hill, 7 minutes from downtown Seattle. Including any residence halls, there are 94 buildings.

Student Life: 63% of undergraduates are from Washington. Students are from 45 states, 31 foreign countries, and Canada. 90% are white. 75% are Protestant; 17% claim no religious affiliation; 7% Catholic. The average age of freshmen is 18; all undergraduates, 21.

Housing: 1284 students can be accommodated in college housing, which includes single-sex and coed dorms, on-campus apartments, off-campus apartments, married-student housing, family houses, and theme houses. On-campus housing is guaranteed for all 4 years. 60% of students live on campus; of those, 80% remain on campus on weekends. Alcohol is not permitted. All students may keep cars.

Activities: There are no fraternities or sororities. There are 50 groups on campus, including art, cheerleading, chess, choir, chorale, drama, ethnic, honors, international, jazz band, literary magazine, newspaper, orchestra, pep band, political, professional, radio, religious, social, social service, student government, symphony, and yearbook. Popular campus events include Family Weekend, Talent Show, and Ivy Cutting at Graduation.

Sports: There are 5 intercollegiate sports for men and 6 for women, and 19 intramural sports for men and 18 for women. Facilities include a soccer field, an oval track, tennis and basketball courts, a gym and crew house, a crew dock, a 2600-seat indoor gym, an 800-seat campus auditorium, and a community swimming pool available to students with free passes.

Disabled Students: 70% of the campus is accessible. Wheelchair ramps, elevators, special parking, specially equipped rest rooms, and special class scheduling are available.

Services: Counseling and information services are available, as is tutoring in most subjects. There is a reader service for the blind and remedial math and writing. In addition, there is priority registration for disabled students.

Campus Safety and Security: Measures include 24-hour foot and vehicle patrol, security escort services, pamphlets/posters/films, and emergency telephones. There are lighted pathways/sidewalks and closed-circuit TV monitors.

Programs of Study: SPU confers B.A. and B.S. degrees. Master's and doctoral degrees are also awarded. Bachelor's degrees are awarded in BIOLOGICAL SCIENCE (biochemistry and biology/biological science), BUSINESS (accounting and business administration and management), COMMUNICATIONS AND THE ARTS (art, classics, communications, dramatic arts, English, French, German, Latin, music, Russian, Spanish, and visual and performing arts), COMPUTER AND PHYSICAL SCIENCE (chemistry, computer science, mathematics, and physics), EDUCATION (art, Christian, English, home economics, mathematics, music, science, social science, and special), ENGINEERING AND ENVIRONMENTAL DESIGN (electrical/electronics engineering and engineering and applied science), HEALTH PROFESSIONS (exercise science and nursing), SOCIAL SCIENCE (clothing and textiles management/production/services, economics, European studies, family/consumer studies, food science, history, Latin American studies, liberal arts/general studies, philosophy, physical fitness/movement, political science/

government, psychology, religion, religious education, sociology, and theological studies). Education, nursing, and business administration are the largest.

Required: All students must demonstrate competency in math and English. Students must complete 15 quarter credits in Christian heritage and values, 56 in general education, plus up to 15 credits of foreign language competency, and at least 45 to 60 in the major, depending on the program. A minimum of 180 credits is needed for the bachelor's degree, with a 2.0 GPA overall. At least 60 credits must be earned in 3000-level courses or higher.

Special: There is a cooperative program with Fashion Institute of Technology in New York City, Fashion Institute of Design and Merchandising in Los Angeles, and Han Nam University in Korea, cross-registration with the Christian College Consortium and Christian College Coalition, and a Washington semester in American studies through the Christian College Coalition. SPU offers internships, study abroad in more than 5 countries, work-study programs, dual and student-designed majors, interdisciplinary majors such as language arts, and a liberal studies major for associate degree graduates. A general studies degree, pass/no credit options, and nondegree study are available. There are 5 national honor societies, a freshman honors program, and 10 departmental honors programs.

Faculty/Classroom: 63% of faculty are male; 37%, female. No introductory courses are taught by graduate students. The average class size in a regular course is 18.

Admissions: 92% of the 2003-2004 applicants were accepted. The SAT I scores for the 2003-2004 freshman class were: Verbal--16% below 500, 42% between 500 and 599, 33% between 600 and 700, and 9% above 700; Math--20% below 500, 40% between 500 and 599, 35% between 600 and 700, and 5% above 700. The ACT scores were 16% below 21, 23% between 21 and 23, 29% between 24 and 26, 17% between 27 and 28, and 15% above 28. 66% of the current freshmen were in the top fifth of their class; 91% were in the top two fifths. 24 freshmen graduated first in their class.

Requirements: The SAT I or ACT is required. The SAT I is preferred, with a minimum required composite score of 950. Candidates should be graduates of an accredited secondary school with a minimum high school GPA of 2.5 or hold a GED certificate. A strong college preparatory program in high school is recommended, including 4 years of English, 3 each of math, science, and foreign language, 2 of history, and 1 of social studies. An essay and 2 letters of recommendation are required and an interview is recommended. A GPA of 2.0 is required. AP and CLEP credits are accepted. Important factors in the admissions decision are advanced placement or honor courses, leadership record, and extracurricular activities record.

Procedure: Freshmen are admitted to all sessions. Entrance exams should be taken before January of the senior year. There are early admissions and deferred admissions plans. There is a rolling admissions plan. Early decision applications should be filed by December 1; regular applications, by June 1 for fall entry, along with a $45 fee. Notification of early decision is sent February 15; regular decision, on a rolling basis. 178 applicants were on the 2003 waiting list; 106 were admitted. Applications are accepted on-line through *www.spu.edu/prospects/under/onlineapp.asp*.

Transfer: 240 transfer students enrolled in 2002-2003. A minimum 2.5 GPA is required, and an interview is recommended. Transcripts from all previous colleges attended and from high school are required, along with 2 letters of recommendation and an essay or personal statement. Evidence of honorable dismissal from the previous school is also required. Students with at least 30 credits earned are not required to take the SAT I or ACT. 45 of 180 credits required for the bachelor's degree must be completed at SPU.

Visiting: There are regularly scheduled orientations for prospective students. There are guides for informal visits and visitors may sit in on classes and stay overnight. To schedule a visit, contact the Admissions Office.

Financial Aid: In 2003-2004, 67% of all full-time freshmen and 62% of continuing full-time students received some form of financial aid. At least 66% of full-time freshmen and 60% of continuing full-time students received need-based aid. The average freshman award was $15,978. Need-based scholarships or need-based grants averaged $13,945; need-based self-help aid (loans and jobs) averaged $6334; non-need-based athletic scholarships averaged $7845; and other non-need-based awards and non-need-based scholarships averaged $9759. The average financial indebtedness of the 2003 graduate was $19,714. SPU is a member of CSS. The FAFSA is required. The priority date for freshman financial aid applications for fall entry is January 31.

International Students: The school actively recruits these students. They must score 550 on the written TOEFL or take the MELAB. The Michigan Test must be administered through SPU.

Computers: The mainframe is a DEC VAX 4600. There are approximately 150 PCs available on campus in the library lab, science learning center, writing lab, music keyboard lab, and media center. There is full access to the Internet, e-mail, and other local and remote networked resources. All campus residence halls have network connections. All students may access the system during lab hours, Monday through Saturday during the academic year. There are no time limits and no fees. It is strongly recommended that all students have a personal computer.

Graduates: From July 1, 2002 to June 30, 2003, 641 bachelor's degrees were awarded. The most popular majors were business/marketing (19%), health professions (10%), and English (7%). In an average class, 40% graduate in 4 years or less, 19% graduate in 5 years or less, and 3% graduate in 6 years or less.

Admissions Contact: Ken Cornell, Director of Admissions.
E-mail: *admissions@spu.edu* Web: *www.spu.edu*

SEATTLE UNIVERSITY
Seattle, WA 98122

C-2
(206) 296-2000
(800) 426-7123; Fax: (206) 296-5656

Full-time: 1170 men, 1880 women	**Faculty:** 331; IIA, av$
Part-time: 135 men, 175 women	**Ph.Ds:** 90%
Graduate: 1145 men, 1485 women	**Student/Faculty:** 9 to 1
Year: quarters, summer session	**Tuition:** $17,865
Application Deadline: see profile	**Room & Board:** $6320
Freshman Class: n/av	
SAT I or ACT: required	**VERY COMPETITIVE**

Seattle University, founded in 1891, is a private, comprehensive institution affiliated with the Roman Catholic Church and operated by the Jesuit Fathers. The emphasis of the undergraduate and graduate programs is on the liberal arts and sciences, business, engineering, health science, teacher preparation, theological studies, and law. There are 5 undergraduate and 7 graduate schools. Figures in the above capsule and in this profile are approximate. In addition to regional accreditation, Seattle U has baccalaureate program accreditation with AACSB, ABET, CAHEA, NCATE, and NLN. The 2 libraries contain 234,978 volumes, 570,839 microform items, and 5608 audio/video tapes/CDs, and subscribe to 2709 periodicals. Computerized library services include the card catalog, interlibrary loans, and database searching. Special learning facilities include a learning resource center, art gallery, planetarium, radio station, electron microscope, recording studio, and MRI. The 46-acre campus is in an urban area just east of downtown Seattle. Including any residence halls, there are 27 buildings.

Student Life: 83% of undergraduates are from Washington. Students are from 50 states, 69 foreign countries, and Canada. 58% are white; 16% Asian American. 40% claim no religious affiliation; 39% Catholic; 18% Protestant. The average age of freshmen is 18; all undergraduates, 22. 17% do not continue beyond their first year; 59% remain to graduate.

Housing: 1408 students can be accommodated in college housing, which includes single-sex and coed dorms and on-campus apartments. In addition, there are 24-hour quiet floors and single-sex floors. On-campus housing is guaranteed for the freshman year only and is available on a lottery system for upperclassmen. Priority is given to out-of-town students. 64% of students commute. All students may keep cars.

Activities: There are no fraternities or sororities. There are 61 groups on campus, including art, cheerleading, choir, chorale, dance, debate, drama, ethnic, forensics, gay, honors, international, jazz band, literary magazine, musical theater, newspaper, photography, political, professional, radio and TV, religious, social, social service, and student government. Popular campus events include Hawaiian Luau, Quad Stock, and International Student Dinner.

Sports: There are 12 intercollegiate sports for men and 13 for women, and 7 intramural sports for men and 7 for women. Facilities include a center with 2 swimming pools, a fitness/weight room, and 5 racquetball, 2 squash, and 3 basketball courts, and an Astroturf gym for indoor soccer/tennis.

Disabled Students: 95% of the campus is accessible. Wheelchair ramps, elevators, special parking, specially equipped rest rooms, special class scheduling, lowered drinking fountains, and lowered telephones are available.

Services: Counseling and information services are available, as is tutoring in most subjects, including math, English, accounting, language, and science. There is a reader service for the blind and a writing center.

Campus Safety and Security: Measures include 24-hour foot and vehicle patrol, self-defense education, security escort services, and shuttle buses. There are informal discussions, pamphlets/posters/films, emergency telephones, and lighted pathways/sidewalks.

Programs of Study: Seattle U confers B.A., B.S., B.A.B.A., B.A.E., B.A.H., B.C.J., B.P.A., B.S.B., B.S.B.C., B.S.C., B.S.C.E., B.S.C.S., B.S.D.U., B.S.E.E., B.S.G.S., B.S.M., B.S.M.E., B.S.M.T., B.S.N., and B.S.P. degrees. Master's and doctoral degrees are also awarded. Bachelor's degrees are awarded in BIOLOGICAL SCIENCE (biochemistry, biology/biological science, and ecology), BUSINESS (accounting, banking and finance, business administration and management, business economics, international business management, marketing/retailing/merchandising, and operations research), COMMUNICATIONS AND THE ARTS (communications, creative writing, dramatic arts, English, fine arts, French, German, journalism, and Spanish), COMPUTER AND PHYSICAL SCIENCE (chemistry, computer science, mathematics, phys-

ics, and science), ENGINEERING AND ENVIRONMENTAL DESIGN (civil engineering, electrical/electronics engineering, environmental engineering, manufacturing engineering, and mechanical engineering), HEALTH PROFESSIONS (medical technology, nursing, and ultrasound technology), SOCIAL SCIENCE (criminal justice, economics, history, humanities, international studies, liberal arts/general studies, philosophy, political science/government, psychology, public administration, religion, social work, and sociology). Engineering, accounting, and nursing are the strongest academically and have the largest enrollments.

Required: Students must complete 180 to 192 quarter hours, depending on the degree, with 70 to 90 in the major, and maintain a minimum GPA of 2.25 to 2.5. Core curriculum requirements total 73 quarter hours, of which 10 quarter hours in religious studies must be taken. All students must take courses in English, math, science, philosophy, social studies, and fine arts.

Special: Special academic programs include internships in numerous disciplines, study abroad in 5 countries, and both on- and off-campus work-study through the Washington State Work-Study Program. A liberal studies degree and an accelerated degree program in business are offered. Pass/fail options, dual majors, and student-designed majors are possible. There is a freshman honors program.

Faculty/Classroom: 55% of faculty are male; 45%, female. No introductory courses are taught by graduate students. The average class size in a regular course is 22.

Requirements: The SAT I or ACT is required. In addition, admissions requirements include graduation from an accredited secondary school, with 16 academic credits, including 4 years of English, 3 each of math and social studies, 2 of foreign language, 2 of lab science, and 2 academic electives; 4 years of math and lab physics and chemistry are required of science and engineering students; lab biology and chemistry are needed by nursing students. The GED is also accepted. A GPA of 2.75 is required. AP and CLEP credits are accepted. Important factors in the admissions decision are advanced placement or honor courses, recommendations by school officials, and extracurricular activities record.

Procedure: Freshmen are admitted to all sessions. Entrance exams should be taken during the fall of the senior year. There is a deferred admissions plan and a rolling admissions plan. Check with the school for current deadlines. Application fee is $45. Notification is sent on a rolling basis. Applications are available on-line at the university's web site.

Transfer: 268 transfer students enrolled in a recent year. Generally, transfer students should have a GPA of at least 2.5. An associate degree is recommended; a 2.75 GPA is required for nursing and business administration students. 45 of 180 credits required for the bachelor's degree must be completed at Seattle U.

Visiting: There are regularly scheduled orientations for prospective students. There are guides for informal visits and visitors may sit in on classes and stay overnight. To schedule a visit, contact the Admissions Office.

Financial Aid: In a recent year, 65% of all full-time freshmen and 62% of continuing full-time students received some form of financial aid. 65% of full-time freshmen and 53% of continuing full-time students received need-based aid. The average freshman award was $18,304. The average financial indebtedness of a recent graduate was $22,695. The FAFSA is required. Check with the school for current deadlines.

International Students: In a recent year, there were 267 international students enrolled. The school actively recruits these students. They must score 520 on the written TOEFL.

Computers: The mainframe consists of 4 IBM RISC systems with 5 UNIX-based Sun servers. There are 400 PCs in labs and 5 specialized LAN terminals. All students may access the system during posted hours or any time from networked residence hall rooms.

Graduates: In a recent year, 784 bachelor's degrees were awarded. The most popular majors were nursing (13%), finance (7%), and business marketing and marketing management (5%). In an average class, 38% graduate in 4 years or less, 57% graduate in 5 years or less, and 59% graduate in 6 years or less. 175 companies recruited on campus in a recent year.

Admissions Contact: Michael K. McKeon, Dean of Admissions.
E-mail: *admissions@seattleu.edu* Web: *www.seattleu.edu*

UNIVERSITY OF PUGET SOUND
Tacoma, WA 98416

C-2
(253) 879-3211
(800) 396-7191; Fax: (253) 879-3993

Full-time: 1005 men, 1473 women	**Faculty:** 210; IIB, +$
Part-time: 23 men, 21 women	**Ph.Ds:** 85%
Graduate: 64 men, 180 women	**Student/Faculty:** 12 to 1
Year: semesters, summer session	**Tuition:** $25,360
Application Deadline: February 1	**Room & Board:** $6400
Freshman Class: 4237 applied, 3020 accepted, 641 enrolled	
SAT I Verbal/Math: 620/615	**ACT:** 27 **HIGHLY COMPETITIVE**

The University of Puget Sound, founded in 1888, is an independent, residential, undergraduate liberal arts and sciences college with selected graduate programs building effectively on a liberal arts foundation. In addition to regional accreditation, Puget Sound has baccalaureate program accreditation with ACS and NASM. The library contains 538,488 volumes, 344,409 microform items, and 18,070 audio/video tapes/CDs, and subscribes to 4120 periodicals. Computerized library services include the card catalog, interlibrary loans, database searching, and Internet access. Special learning facilities include a learning resource center, art gallery, natural history museum, radio station, student science labs, observatory, computer labs, seminar rooms, turnaround computer classrooms, media center, language houses, theater workshops, newspaper, concert hall, center for writing and learning, and bibliographic instruction room. The 97-acre campus is in a suburban area 35 miles south of Seattle and 1 mile from Commencement Bay on Puget Sound. Including any residence halls, there are 38 buildings.

Student Life: 70% of undergraduates are from out of state, mostly the West. Students are from 46 states, 13 foreign countries, and Canada. 76% are from public schools. 76% are white; 10% Asian American. 57% claim no religious affiliation; 28% are Protestant; 9% Catholic. The average age of freshmen is 18; all undergraduates, 20. 15% do not continue beyond their first year; 77% remain to graduate.

Housing: 1651 students can be accommodated in college housing, which includes single-sex and coed dorms, on-campus apartments, fraternity houses, and sorority houses. In addition, there are honors houses, language houses, special-interest houses, and theme houses and halls. On-campus housing is guaranteed for the freshman year only, is available on a first-come, first-served basis, and is available on a lottery system for upperclassmen. 62% of students live on campus; of those, 80% remain on campus on weekends. All students may keep cars.

Activities: 24% of men belong to 4 national fraternities; 27% of women belong to 5 national sororities. There are 102 groups on campus, including art, band, cheerleading, choir, chorale, chorus, computers, dance, debate, diversity awareness, drama, environmental, ethnic, film, forensics, gay, gender, health and wellness, honors, international, jazz band, literary magazine, musical theater, newspaper, opera, orchestra, pep band, photography, political, professional, radio and TV, religious, social, social service, student government, symphony, and yearbook. Popular campus events include Foolish Pleasures (student film festival), Mistletoast Holiday, and Hawaiian Luau.

Sports: There are 11 intercollegiate sports for men and 12 for women, and 7 intramural sports for men and 6 for women. Facilities include a 3000-seat basketball and volleyball gym, a 6-lane pool, a 2488-seat football, soccer, lacrosse, and track stadium, 6 indoor tennis courts, a fitness room, an aerobics exercise area and dance studio, a track, baseball, softball, and intramural fields, 2 outdoor sand volleyball courts, an indoor climbing wall, and an auxiliary gym for intramurals and recreation.

Disabled Students: 75% of the campus is accessible. Wheelchair ramps, elevators, special parking, specially equipped rest rooms, special class scheduling, lowered drinking fountains, lowered telephones, TDDs, and adaptive computer equipment are available.

Services: Counseling and information services are available, as is tutoring in most subjects. There is a reader service for the blind.

Campus Safety and Security: Measures include 24-hour foot and vehicle patrol, security escort services, informal discussions, and pamphlets/posters/films. There are emergency telephones, lighted pathways/sidewalks, and vehicle escort within 3 miles of campus. Residence halls are always locked.

Programs of Study: Puget Sound confers B.A., B.S., and B.M. degrees. Master's degrees are also awarded. Bachelor's degrees are awarded in AGRICULTURE (environmental studies), BIOLOGICAL SCIENCE (biology/biological science), BUSINESS (business administration and management and international economics), COMMUNICATIONS AND THE ARTS (art, classics, communications, dramatic arts, English, fine arts, French, German, music, music performance, and Spanish), COMPUTER AND PHYSICAL SCIENCE (chemistry, computer science, geology, mathematics, natural sciences, and physics), EDUCATION (education and music), HEALTH PROFESSIONS (exercise science and occupational therapy), SOCIAL SCIENCE (African American studies, Asian/Oriental studies, economics, history, Latin American studies, philosophy, physical fitness/movement, political science/government, psychology, religion, sociology, and women's studies). Physics, chemistry, and biology are the strongest academically. Business, psychology, and English are the largest.

Required: Core requirements include writing and rhetoric, scholarly and creative inquiry, and courses in fine arts, humanities, math, natural science, and social science.

Special: Special academic programs include on- and off-campus work-study, paid and unpaid internships in the community in conjunction with an internship seminar, and study abroad in 50 countries. There are 3-2 engineering degrees with Washington University at St. Louis, Columbia, and Duke Universities, and the University of Southern California, B.A.-B.S. degrees in chemistry, physics, economics, and a special interdisciplinary major, and a B.A.-B.M. degree. Dual majors in foreign language and international affairs, music and business, and computer science and business, as well as pass/fail options are possible. 2 special features of the curriculum are the intensive 4-year study of the classics of Western civili-

zation and the Business Leadership Program, combining traditional business and liberal arts study. There are 15 national honor societies, including Phi Beta Kappa, a freshman honors program, and 13 departmental honors programs.

Faculty/Classroom: 59% of faculty are male; 41%, female. 91% teach undergraduates. No introductory courses are taught by graduate students. The average class size in an introductory lecture is 21; in a laboratory, 13; and in a regular course, 19.

Admissions: 71% of the 2003-2004 applicants were accepted. The SAT I scores for the 2003-2004 freshman class were: Verbal--4% below 500, 30% between 500 and 599, 50% between 600 and 700, and 16% above 700; Math--5% below 500, 35% between 500 and 599, 50% between 600 and 700, and 10% above 700. The ACT scores were 4% below 21, 15% between 21 and 23, 29% between 24 and 26, 23% between 27 and 28, and 29% above 28. 63% of the current freshmen were in the top fifth of their class; 90% were in the top two fifths. There were 17 National Merit finalists. 33 freshmen graduated first in their class.

Requirements: The SAT I or ACT is required: the SAT I is preferred. Other admission requirements include graduation from an accredited secondary school, with a recommended 4 years of English, 3 to 4 of math and natural or physical lab science, 3 of social studies or history, 2 to 3 of foreign language, and 1 of fine, visual, or performing arts. Also required are letters of personal recommendation from a teacher and counselor; 2 are preferred. An essay must be submitted, and an interview is recommended. It is recommended that art students present a portfolio and that music students audition. The GED is also accepted. AP credits are accepted. Important factors in the admissions decision are advanced placement or honor courses, evidence of special talent, and extracurricular activities record.

Procedure: Freshmen are admitted to all sessions. Entrance exams should be taken during the fall of the senior year. There are early decision, early admissions, and deferred admissions plans. Early decision applications should be filed by November 15 or December 15; regular applications, by February 1 for fall entry and November 1 for spring entry, along with a $40 fee. Notification of early decision is sent December 15 and January 15; regular decision, April 1. 143 early decision candidates were accepted for the 2003-2004 class. 266 applicants were on the 2003 waiting list; 19 were admitted. Applications are accepted on-line through the university's web site and Common App, Next Stop College, College-View, CollegeLink, and Apply!

Transfer: 75 transfer students enrolled in 2002-2003. Applicants must have an honorable dismissal from the institution(s) previously attended and good academic standing, with a minimum GPA of 2.0. All college transcripts and the rigor of prior course work and resulting grades are evaluated. High school transcripts and SAT I or ACT scores are required if less than 1 year of college has been completed. An interview is recommended. An essay or a copy of a graded paper is required of all undergraduate transfers. 64 of 128 credits required for the bachelor's degree must be completed at Puget Sound.

Visiting: There are regularly scheduled orientations for prospective students, including meetings with counselors, faculty, and coaches, tours of campus, and classroom experiences. There are guides for informal visits and visitors may sit in on classes and stay overnight. To schedule a visit, contact the Campus Visit Coordinator, Office of Admission.

Financial Aid: In 2003-2004, 85% of all full-time freshmen and 82% of continuing full-time students received some form of financial aid. 56% of full-time freshmen and 55% of continuing full-time students received need-based aid. The average freshman award was $22,813. Need-based scholarships or need-based grants averaged $8308 ($26,990 maximum); need-based self-help aid (loans and jobs) averaged $7028 ($9275 maximum); and other awards averaged $7263 ($27,320 maximum). 34% of undergraduates work part time. Average annual earnings from campus work are $2000. The average financial indebtedness of the 2003 graduate was $21,246. Puget Sound is a member of CSS. The CSS Profile or FAFSA is required. The CSS Profile is required of early decision candidates. The deadline for filing freshman financial aid applications for fall entry is February 1.

International Students: There are 22 international students enrolled. The school actively recruits these students. They must score 550 on the written TOEFL or 213 on the electronic version. Freshman applicants must also take the SAT I or ACT.

Computers: The mainframe consists of servers. There are 308 computers in labs. All lab systems, residence halls, and workstations have full access to the Internet. All students may access the system. There are no time limits and no fees. It is strongly recommended that all students have a personal computer.

Graduates: From July 1, 2002 to June 30, 2003, 586 bachelor's degrees were awarded. The most popular majors were business (12%), psychology (8%), and English (8%). In an average class, 1% graduate in 3 years or less, 67% graduate in 4 years or less, 73% graduate in 5 years or less, and 77% graduate in 6 years or less. 102 companies recruited on campus in 2002-2003. Of the 2002 graduating class, 30% were enrolled in graduate school within 6 months of graduation and 52% were employed.

Admissions Contact: George H. Mills, Jr., Vice President for Enrollment. A video is available. E-mail: *admission@ups.edu*
Web: *www.ups.edu*

UNIVERSITY OF WASHINGTON
C-2
Seattle, WA 98195
(206) 543-9686

Full-time: 10,400 men, 11,260 women	**Faculty:** 3015; I, av$
Part-time: 1900 men, 2100 women	**Ph.D.s:** 99%
Graduate: 4990 men, 4960 women	**Student/Faculty:** 7 to 1
Year: quarters, summer session	**Tuition:** $3985 ($13,260)
Application Deadline: see profile	**Room & Board:** $6380
Freshman Class: n/av	
SAT I or ACT: required	**VERY COMPETITIVE**

The University of Washington, founded in 1861, is a public institution offering a broad range of degree programs. Figures in the above capsule and in this profile are approximate. There are 13 undergraduate schools and 1 graduate school. In addition to regional accreditation, UW has baccalaureate program accreditation with AACSB, ABET, NCATE, and NLN. The 19 libraries contain 5,601,263 volumes, 6,432,950 microform items, and 56,295 audio/video tapes/CDs. Computerized library services include the card catalog, interlibrary loans, and database searching. Special learning facilities include a learning resource center, art gallery, natural history museum, planetarium, radio station, TV station, state museum, full teaching hospital, marine science lab, 200-acre arboretum, and field research forest. The 703-acre campus is in an urban area 5 miles from downtown Seattle. Including any residence halls, there are 213 buildings.

Student Life: 88% of undergraduates are from Washington. Students are from 44 states, 68 foreign countries, and Canada. 57% are white; 24% Asian American. The average age of freshmen is 18; all undergraduates, 21. 10% do not continue beyond their first year; 71% remain to graduate.

Housing: 5200 students can be accommodated in college housing, which includes coed dorms, on-campus apartments, married-student housing, fraternity houses, and sorority houses. In addition, there are language houses, special-interest houses, and a freshman house. On-campus housing is guaranteed for all 4 years. Alcohol is not permitted. All students may keep cars.

Activities: 17% of men belong to 29 national fraternities; 16% of women belong to 16 national sororities. There are 450 groups on campus, including band, cheerleading, choir, chorale, chorus, computers, dance, drama, ethnic, film, gay, honors, international, jazz band, literary magazine, marching band, musical theater, newspaper, opera, orchestra, pep band, political, professional, radio and TV, religious, social, social service, student government, symphony, and yearbook. Popular campus events include Four Bands for 4 Bucks concert, Opening Day (of boating/crew season), and Convocation.

Sports: There are 10 intercollegiate sports for men and 11 for women, and 20 intramural sports for men and 18 for women. Facilities include a 72,500-seat football stadium, a baseball field, a track and field complex, lakeside facilities, tennis courts, the intramurals building, a golf driving range, and a swimming pool.

Disabled Students: 85% of the campus is accessible. Wheelchair ramps, elevators, special parking, specially equipped rest rooms, special class scheduling, lowered drinking fountains, and lowered telephones are available.

Services: Counseling and information services are available, as is tutoring in every subject. There is a reader service for the blind and remedial math, reading, and writing.

Campus Safety and Security: Measures include 24-hour foot and vehicle patrol, self-defense education, security escort services, and shuttle buses. There are informal discussions, pamphlets/posters/films, emergency telephones, lighted pathways/sidewalks, and emergency telephone numbers.

Programs of Study: UW confers B.A., B.S., B.A.B.A., B.C.H.S., B.L.Arch., B.Mus., B.S.A.&A., B.S.B.C., B.S.Cer.E., B.S.Comp.E., B.S.F., B.S.Fish., B.S.I.E., B.S.M.E., B.S.Med.Tech., B.S.Met.E., and B.S.Nur. degrees. Master's and doctoral degrees are also awarded. Bachelor's degrees are awarded in AGRICULTURE (fishing and fisheries, forest engineering, forestry production and processing, and wood science), BIOLOGICAL SCIENCE (biochemistry, biology/biological science, botany, microbiology, neurosciences, and zoology), BUSINESS (accounting, banking and finance, business administration and management, business economics, international business management, marketing/retailing/merchandising, and personnel management), COMMUNICATIONS AND THE ARTS (art history and appreciation, classics, communications, comparative literature, dance, dramatic arts, English, fiber/textiles/weaving, French, Germanic languages and literature, graphic design, Italian, Japanese, jazz, metal/jewelry, music history and appreciation, music performance, painting, photography, printmaking, Scandinavian languages, sculpture, Slavic languages, Spanish, speech/debate/rhetoric, studio art, and technical and business writing), COMPUTER AND PHYSICAL SCIENCE (astronomy, atmospheric sciences and mete-

orology, computer science, geology, information sciences and systems, mathematics, oceanography, physics, quantitative methods, and statistics), EDUCATION (music), ENGINEERING AND ENVIRONMENTAL DESIGN (aeronautical engineering, ceramic engineering, chemical engineering, civil engineering, computer engineering, construction engineering, electrical/electronics engineering, engineering, landscape architecture/design, materials science, ocean engineering, and paper and pulp science), HEALTH PROFESSIONS (dental hygiene, environmental health science, health care administration, medical laboratory technology, nursing, and speech pathology/audiology), SOCIAL SCIENCE (African American studies, anthropology, Asian/American studies, Asian/Oriental studies, Canadian studies, economics, ethnic studies, food science, geography, history, international relations, Judaic studies, liberal arts/general studies, Near Eastern studies, peace studies, philosophy, political science/government, psychology, religion, Russian and Slavic studies, social work, sociology, South Asian studies, and women's studies). Biological and life sciences, computer science and engineering, and physics are the strongest academically. Business, political science, and art are the largest.

Required: All students must maintain a GPA of 2.0 while taking 180 quarter credits, with 45 in the major. Distribution requirements include 40 credits from the humanities, social sciences, and math/natural sciences, with 12 credits in English composition/writing and a course in quantitative/symbolic reasoning.

Special: A wide variety of internships, including those for minority students in engineering, concurrent dual majors, study abroad in 21 countries, a Washington semester, a general studies degree, and co-op programs are available. Work-study programs, cross-registration with the National Student Exchange, credit/no credit options, student-designed majors, accelerated degree programs, nondegree study, and a 5-year B.A.-B.S. degree also are offered. There are 20 national honor societies, including Phi Beta Kappa, a freshman honors program, and 36 departmental honors programs.

Faculty/Classroom: 66% of faculty are male; 34%, female. 85% both teach and do research. Graduate students teach 40% of introductory courses. The average class size in an introductory lecture is 54; in a laboratory, 24; and in a regular course, 40.

Admissions: In a recent year, there were 41 National Merit finalists and 53 semifinalists.

Requirements: The SAT I or ACT is required. In addition, applicants must have completed 15 academic units, including 4 years of English, 3 each of math and social sciences, 2 each of foreign language and science, and 1/2 year each in fine/visual performing arts and electives. Admission is based on an indexing system. A GPA of 2.0 is required. AP credits are accepted. Important factors in the admissions decision are advanced placement or honor courses and evidence of special talent.

Procedure: Freshmen are admitted to all sessions. Entrance exams should be taken by December of the senior year. Check with the school for current deadlines. Application fee is $35. Applications are accepted on-line through the UW web page or CollegeNET.

Transfer: 1592 transfer students enrolled in a recent year. The school has a special direct transfer agreement with Washington community colleges. Admission is based on an indexing system. 45 of 180 credits required for the bachelor's degree must be completed at UW.

Visiting: There are regularly scheduled orientations for prospective students, including attendance at class, a meeting with an admissions counselor, campus tour, and information sessions. There are guides for informal visits and visitors may sit in on classes. To schedule a visit, contact the Student Visitation Program at (206) 543-5429 or *visituw@u.washington.edu*.

Financial Aid: The CSS Profile is required. Check with the school for current deadlines.

International Students: They must score 540 on the written TOEFL or 207 on the electronic version, or take the MELAB and the APIEL.

Computers: There are several public labs containing 10,000 PCs, Macs, and terminals. Dial-up is also used because most students live off campus. All students may access the system 24 hours daily. There are no time limits and no fees.

Graduates: In a recent year, 6923 bachelor's degrees were awarded. The most popular majors were business (13%), art (10%), and political science (5%). In an average class, 38% graduate in 4 years or less, 65% graduate in 5 years or less, and 71% graduate in 6 years or less. 600 companies recruited on campus in a recent year. Of a recent graduating class, 20% were enrolled in graduate school within 6 months of graduation and 74% were employed.

Admissions Contact: Office of Admissions.
Web: *www.washington.edu/students/uga*

WALLA WALLA COLLEGE
E-3

College Place, WA 99324-1198
(509) 527-2327
(800) 541-8900; Fax: (509) 527-2397

Full-time: 800 men, 728 women	**Faculty:** 120; IIB, --$
Part-time: 65 men, 74 women	**Ph.D.s:** 60%
Graduate: 60 men, 190 women	**Student/Faculty:** 13 to 1
Year: quarters, summer session	**Tuition:** $17,025
Application Deadline: open	**Room & Board:** $4575
Freshman Class: 348 accepted, 323 enrolled	
ACT: required	**NONCOMPETITIVE**

Walla Walla College, founded in 1892, is a private comprehensive institution affiliated with the Seventh-day Adventist Church. There are 6 undergraduate and 4 graduate schools. In addition to regional accreditation, WWC has baccalaureate program accreditation with ABET, ACBSP, CSWE, NASM, and NLN. The 3 libraries contain 281,170 volumes, 19,781 microform items, and 3483 audio/video tapes/CDs, and subscribe to 1317 periodicals. Computerized library services include the card catalog, interlibrary loans, and database searching. Special learning facilities include a learning resource center, art gallery, radio station, audio listening/music library, and observatory. The 77-acre campus is in a small town 120 miles southwest of Spokane. Including any residence halls, there are 28 buildings.

Student Life: 58% of undergraduates are from out of state, mostly the West. Students are from 26 foreign countries and Canada. 12% are from public schools. 86% are white. Most are Protestant. The average age of freshmen is 19; all undergraduates, 21. 24% do not continue beyond their first year; 54% remain to graduate.

Housing: 1500 students can be accommodated in college housing, which includes single-sex dorms, on-campus apartments, off-campus houses and apartments, and married-student housing. On-campus housing is guaranteed for all 4 years. 54% of students live on campus; of those, 90% remain on campus on weekends. Alcohol is not permitted. All students may keep cars.

Activities: There are no fraternities or sororities. There are 50 groups on campus, including art, band, choir, chorale, chorus, drama, ethnic, honors, international, literary magazine, newspaper, orchestra, photography, professional, radio and TV, religious, social service, student government, symphony, and yearbook. Popular campus events include the Mud Bowl football game and the Sonneberg Series basketball tournament.

Sports: There are 5 intercollegiate sports for men and 3 for women, and 9 intramural sports for men and 7 for women. Facilities include an Olympic-size pool, a track, tennis and racquetball courts, a gymnastics sports gym, a gym, weight rooms, and residence hall health spas.

Disabled Students: 90% of the campus is accessible. Wheelchair ramps, elevators, special parking, special class scheduling, and special housing are available.

Services: Counseling and information services are available, as is tutoring in most subjects, including math, languages, sciences, and engineering. There is remedial math, reading, and writing.

Campus Safety and Security: Measures include 24-hour foot and vehicle patrol, self-defense education, security escort services, and informal discussions. There are pamphlets/posters/films, emergency telephones, and lighted pathways/sidewalks.

Programs of Study: WWC confers B.A., B.S., B.B.A., B.Mus., B.S.E., and B.S.W. degrees. Associate and master's degrees are also awarded. Bachelor's degrees are awarded in BIOLOGICAL SCIENCE (biochemistry, biology/biological science, and biophysics), BUSINESS (business administration and management), COMMUNICATIONS AND THE ARTS (art, communications, English, French, German, graphic design, music, music performance, Spanish, and speech/debate/rhetoric), COMPUTER AND PHYSICAL SCIENCE (chemistry, computer science, digital arts/technology, information sciences and systems, mathematics, and physics), EDUCATION (business, elementary, music, physical, and special), ENGINEERING AND ENVIRONMENTAL DESIGN (automotive technology, aviation computer technology, bioengineering, engineering, and environmental science), HEALTH PROFESSIONS (health and nursing), SOCIAL SCIENCE (biblical languages, history, humanities, psychology, religion, social work, sociology, and theological studies). Engineering, nursing, and biological and natural sciences are the strongest academically. Social work, engineering, and business are the largest.

Required: To graduate, students must successfully complete 192 quarter hours, including at least 45 in the major and at least 60 in upper-level work, with a minimum GPA of 2.0. Grades below C- will not apply toward the major. Students must also meet a general studies requirement that includes 16 to 20 quarter hours in religion and theology, 13 to 21 in language arts, 12 to 20 in history and social science, 12 to 16 in humanities and math/natural science, and 2 to 6 in health and phys ed. A comprehensive exam is required, as is attendance at chapel and assemblies.

Special: Opportunities are provided for internships, co-op programs, cross-registration with Whitman College, study abroad in 6 countries,

work-study programs, a B.A.-B.S. degree, dual majors, credit by exam, and nondegree study. There is a freshman honors program.

Faculty/Classroom: 52% of faculty are male; 48%, female. All teach undergraduates. No introductory courses are taught by graduate students. The average class size in an introductory lecture is 24 and in a regular course, 13.

Admissions: The ACT scores for the 2003-2004 freshman class were: 22% below 21, 33% between 21 and 23, 24% between 24 and 26, 7% between 27 and 28, and 7% above 28.

Requirements: The ACT is required. In addition, scores are used for placement and academic advisement. Graduation from an accredited secondary school is required; a GED will be accepted. Applicants should submit an academic record containing at a minimum 4 years of English, and 2 each of history, science, and math, including algebra and geometry, along with a letter of recommendation from a teacher or school official. A GPA of 2.5 is required. AP and CLEP credits are accepted. Important factors in the admissions decision are advanced placement or honors courses, recommendations by school officials, and leadership record.

Procedure: Freshmen are admitted to all sessions. Entrance exams should be taken during the junior or senior year. There are early decision, early admissions, rolling admissions, and deferred admissions plans. Application deadlines are open. Application fee is $30. Applications are accepted on-line through the college's web site.

Transfer: 165 transfer students enrolled in a recent year. Applicants should have a 2.0 minimum GPA and must submit all college transcripts and a letter of recommendation (3 for nursing majors) from a former teacher or school official. 36 of 192 credits required for the bachelor's degree must be completed at WWC.

Visiting: Visitors may sit in on classes and stay overnight. To schedule a visit, contact the Admissions and Marketing Office.

Financial Aid: In a recent year, 71% of all full-time freshmen and 70% of continuing full-time students received some form of financial aid. 55% of full-time freshmen and 57% of continuing full-time students received need-based aid. The average freshman award was $13,310. 94% of undergraduates work part time. Average annual earnings from campus work are $2800. The average financial indebtedness of the 2003 graduate was $21,273. The FAFSA and the college's own financial statement are required. The deadline for filing freshman financial aid applications for fall entry is April 30.

International Students: The school actively recruits these students. They must score 550 on the written TOEFL or 213 on the electronic version and also take the SAT I or the ACT.

Computers: The mainframe is an HP 3000 Series 969/200. There are 3 general purpose PC labs housing 110 PCs, and subject-specific computer labs for chemistry, engineering, and physics. All students may access the system 6:30 A.M. to 11 P.M. Sunday through Thursday and 6:30 A.M. to 3:30 P.M. Fridays. There are no time limits and no fees.

Graduates: In a recent year, 249 bachelor's degrees were awarded. The most popular majors were business (22%), engineering (16%), and health professions/sciences (16%). In an average class, 27% graduate in 4 years or less, 46% graduate in 5 years or less, and 54% graduate in 6 years or less. 15 companies recruited on campus in 2002-2003.

Admissions Contact: Dallas Weis, Director of Admissions. A video is available. E-mail: *weisda@wwc.edu* Web: *www.wwc.edu*

WASHINGTON STATE UNIVERSITY
E-3

Pullman, WA 99164-1067
(509) 335-5586
(888) 468-6978; Fax: (509) 335-4902

Full-time: 7943 men, 8638 women	**Faculty:** 1072; I, --$
Part-time: 1109 men, 1824 women	**Ph.D.s:** 88%
Graduate: 1587 men, 1652 women	**Student/Faculty:** 15 to 1
Year: semesters, summer session	**Tuition:** $5280 ($13,382)
Application Deadline: March 1	**Room & Board:** $6052
Freshman Class: 9132 applied, 7184 accepted, 3024 enrolled	
SAT I Verbal/Math: 527/538	**COMPETITIVE**

Washington State University, founded in 1890, is a public, land-grant, research institution. Its undergraduate and graduate programs stress the liberal arts, business, economics, art and fine arts, engineering, architecture, agricultural and technical studies, home economics, music, teacher preparation, and health sciences, including nursing, pharmacy, and veterinary medicine. There are 10 undergraduate schools and 1 graduate school. In addition to regional accreditation, Washington State has baccalaureate program accreditation with AACSB, ACCE, ACPE, ADA, ASLA, FIDER, NAAB, NASM, NCATE, NLN, NRPA, and SAF. The 11 libraries contain 2,116,080 volumes, 4,662,429 microform items, and 43,461 audio/video tapes/CDs, and subscribe to 31,718 periodicals. Computerized library services include the card catalog, interlibrary database searching, and Internet access. Special learning clude a learning resource center, art gallery, natural planetarium, radio station, TV station, observatory center, and nuclear radiation center. The 620-

town 80 miles south of Spokane and 285 miles east of Seattle. Including any residence halls, there are 221 buildings.

Student Life: 87% of undergraduates are from Washington. Students are from 49 states, 84 foreign countries, and Canada. 74% are white. The average age of freshmen is 18; all undergraduates, 23. 17% do not continue beyond their first year; 83% remain to graduate.

Housing: 8000 students can be accommodated in college housing, which includes single-sex and coed dorms, on-campus apartments, off-campus apartments, married-student housing, fraternity houses, and sorority houses. In addition, there are honors houses, language houses, and special-interest houses. On-campus housing is guaranteed for all 4 years. 58% of students commute. Alcohol is not permitted. All students may keep cars.

Activities: 16% of men belong to 24 national fraternities; 17% of women belong to 15 national sororities. There are 225 groups on campus, including art, band, cheerleading, chess, choir, chorus, computers, dance, debate, drama, drill team, ethnic, film, gay, honors, international, jazz band, literary magazine, marching band, musical theater, newspaper, opera, orchestra, pep band, photography, political, professional, radio and TV, religious, social, social service, student government, symphony, and yearbook. Popular campus events include Dad's Weekend, Mom's Weekend, and Land Grant Days.

Sports: There are 6 intercollegiate sports for men and 9 for women, and 45 intramural sports for men and 45 for women. Facilities include a 40,000-seat stadium, a 12,000-seat coliseum, an indoor and outdoor track, tennis courts, a weight/aerobic facility, a golf course, bowling lanes, baseball and soccer fields, swimming pools, lockers, racquetball and squash courts, a climbing wall, ballrooms, riding stables, gyms, crew rowing facilities, and an outdoor recreation center.

Disabled Students: 90% of the campus is accessible. Wheelchair ramps, elevators, special parking, specially equipped rest rooms, special class scheduling, lowered drinking fountains, lowered telephones, special housing, and a van to provide transportation to and from classes are available.

Services: Counseling and information services are available, as is tutoring in most subjects. There is a reader service for the blind. There is also a reading and study skills course. There are many free Learning Strategy Workshops available, including Time Management, Active Textbook Reading, Writing, Text Anxiety, Skills for Science, Winning at Math, and others.

Campus Safety and Security: Measures include 24-hour foot and vehicle patrol, self-defense education, security escort services, and informal discussions. There are pamphlets/posters/films, emergency telephones, lighted pathways/sidewalks, monitored lighting levels on campus, a women's transit service, resident hall security hours, a police intern program, and housing patrols.

Programs of Study: Washington State confers B.A., B.S., B.Arch., B.F.A., B.L.A., and B.M. degrees. Master's and doctoral degrees are also awarded. Bachelor's degrees are awarded in AGRICULTURE (agricultural business management, agricultural economics, agricultural mechanics, agriculture, agronomy, animal science, forestry and related sciences, horticulture, natural resource management, plant protection (pest management), range/farm management, soil science, and wildlife management), BIOLOGICAL SCIENCE (biochemistry, biology/biological science, cell biology, entomology, genetics, microbiology, neurosciences, plant genetics, plant pathology, wildlife biology, and zoology), BUSINESS (accounting, banking and finance, business administration and management, business economics, business law, business statistics, entrepreneurial studies, hotel/motel and restaurant management, insurance and risk management, international business management, management information systems, management science, marketing management, personnel management, real estate, and sports management), COMMUNICATIONS AND THE ARTS (advertising, broadcasting, classics, communications, English, fine arts, French, German, journalism, linguistics, music, music performance, music theory and composition, public relations, Russian, Spanish, and visual and performing arts), COMPUTER AND PHYSICAL SCIENCE (chemistry, computer science, geology, mathematics, physical sciences, physics, and science), EDUCATION (agricultural, athletic training, education, physical, recreation, and secondary), ENGINEERING AND ENVIRONMENTAL DESIGN (agricultural engineering, architecture, chemical engineering, civil engineering, computer engineering, construction management, electrical/electronics engineering, materials science, interior design, landscape architecture/engineering, and materials engineering), [...]S (exercise science, nursing, predentistry, pre[...]y/audiology, and veterinary science), SOCIAL [...]s, anthropology, area studies, Asian/Oriental [...]onomics, food science, history, home eco[...]t, humanities, liberal arts/general studies, [...]vernment, psychology, public affairs, reli[...]dies, social work, sociology, women's [...]adcasting, hospitality, and interior de[...]. Business administration, communi[...]est.

Required: Students must complete 120 semester hours, with fulfillment of a major and 40 hours of upper-division work, and maintain a minimum GPA of 2.0. Specific disciplines to be taken vary within majors. General university requirements include 10 hours of science, 9 of arts and humanities and social science, 6 of world civilization, and 3 each of intercultural studies and communications proficiency. Students must complete a writing portfolio and pass a writing qualifying exam prior to graduation.

Special: Special academic programs include internships through the Professional Experience Program, study abroad in 25 countries, and work-study with numerous employers. There are co-op programs in numerous majors and cross-registration with the University of Idaho, University of Washington, Eastern Washington University, Yakima Valley Community College, and Northwest Indian College. Students may attend the Intercollegiate Center for Nursing Education, which is a consortium of Washington State, Eastern Washington and Gonzaga Universities, and Whitworth College. Dual majors are available, as is a general studies degree. Credit may be granted for military service, and nondegree and pass/fail options are possible. Special features of the school include the opportunity for undergraduates to become involved in research and its honors programs. There are 23 national honor societies, including Phi Beta Kappa, a freshman honors program, and 1 departmental honors program.

Faculty/Classroom: 62% of faculty are male; 38%, female. The average class size in a regular course is 25.

Admissions: 79% of the 2003-2004 applicants were accepted. The SAT I scores for the 2003-2004 freshman class were: Verbal--41% below 500, 44% between 500 and 599, 17% between 600 and 700, and 2% above 700; Math--36% below 500, 42% between 500 and 599, 20% between 600 and 700, and 2% above 700.

Requirements: The SAT I or ACT is required. Other admissions requirements include graduation from an accredited secondary school with 4 years of English, 3 each of math and social studies/history, and 2 each of a foreign language and science. A combination of the high school GPA and test scores is considered. The GED is also accepted. A GPA of 2.0 is required. AP and CLEP credits are accepted. Important factors in the admissions decision are recommendations by school officials, extracurricular activities record, and leadership record.

Procedure: Freshmen are admitted fall and spring. Entrance exams should be taken during spring of the junior year or fall of the senior year. Applications should be filed by March 1 for fall entry and October 1 for spring entry, along with a $37 fee. A waiting list is an active part of the admissions procedure. Applications are accepted on computer disk and on-line through EXPAN and the school's web site.

Transfer: 1361 transfer students enrolled in 2002-2003. Applicants must have at least 27 semester hours, or 40 quarter hours, with a GPA of at least 2.0. If they have fewer hours, the criteria are the same as for freshmen. 30 of 120 credits required for the bachelor's degree must be completed at Washington State.

Visiting: There are regularly scheduled orientations for prospective students, consisting of a campus tour and presentation. There are guides for informal visits and visitors may sit in on classes. To schedule a visit, contact the campus visit web site at http://future-students-2.wsu.edu/visting.

Financial Aid: In 2003-2004, 79% of all full-time freshmen and 68% of continuing full-time students received some form of financial aid. 39% of full-time freshmen and 46% of continuing full-time students received need-based aid. The average freshman award was $12,758. Need-based scholarships or need-based grants averaged $4735 ($10,248 maximum); need-based self-help aid (loans and jobs) averaged $3601 ($11,000 maximum); non-need-based athletic scholarships averaged $11,669 ($22,022 maximum); and other non-need-based awards and non-need-based scholarships averaged $5493 ($25,664 maximum). 14% of undergraduates work part time. Average annual earnings from campus work are $4000. The average financial indebtedness of the 2003 graduate was $20,000. The FAFSA is required. The priority date for freshman financial aid applications for fall entry is March 1. The deadline for filing freshman financial aid applications for fall entry is June 1.

International Students: There are 673 international students enrolled. They must score 520 on the written TOEFL or take the MELAB.

Computers: The mainframe is an IBM 9672-R24 with open-system data storage units (EMC2 Symmetrix 5330-9518). Through web interfaces, students use the mainframe to view and provide information about their academic status, billings, courses, and a variety of services. There are approximately 12,000 computers at Washington State, the majority of which have access to the Internet through the Washington State network. These computers are located throughout the 4 campuses and remote sites. All students may access the system 24 hours a day. There are no time limits and no fees. It is strongly recommended that all students have a personal computer.

Graduates: From July 1, 2002 to June 30, 2003, 3719 bachelor's degrees were awarded. The most popular majors were communication (9%), education (7%), and nursing (5%). In an average class, 31% graduate in 4 years or less, 56% graduate in 5 years or less, and 62% graduate in 6 years or less. 194 companies recruited on campus in 2002-2003.

Admissions Contact: Wendy Peterson, Director of Admissions.
E-mail: *admiss@wsu.edu* Web: *wsu.edu/admissions*

WESTERN WASHINGTON UNIVERSITY
C-1
Bellingham, WA 98225-5996

(360) 650-3440
Fax: (360) 650-7369

Full-time: 4984 men, 6265 women	Faculty: 455; IIA, av$
Part-time: 239 men, 283 women	Ph.D.s: 86%
Graduate: 372 men, 530 women	Student/Faculty: 25 to 1
Year: quarters, summer session	Tuition: $4182 ($12,954)
Application Deadline: March 1	Room & Board: $5937
Freshman Class: 7651 applied, 5843 accepted, 2213 enrolled	
SAT I Verbal/Math: 560/560	ACT: 24 VERY COMPETITIVE

Western Washington University, founded in 1893, is a nonprofit, public, comprehensive institution whose emphasis is on the liberal arts and sciences, business and business administration and economics, art, fine arts, performing arts, music, teacher preparation, interdisciplinary learning, and environmental studies. There are 7 undergraduate schools and 1 graduate school. In addition to regional accreditation, WWU has baccalaureate program accreditation with AACSB, ABET, ASLA, NASM, NCATE, and NRPA. The 2 libraries contain 1,341,300 volumes, 1,921,317 microform items, and 28,289 audio/video tapes/CDs, and subscribe to 4885 periodicals. Computerized library services include the card catalog, interlibrary loans, database searching, and Internet access. Special learning facilities include a learning resource center, art gallery, planetarium, radio station, marine lab, neutron generator lab, motor vehicle research lab, wind tunnel, air pollution lab, electronic music studio, and performing arts center. The 195-acre campus is in a small town 60 miles south of Vancouver, British Columbia, and 90 miles north of Seattle. Including any residence halls, there are 80 buildings.

Student Life: 92% of undergraduates are from Washington. Students are from 47 states, 34 foreign countries, and Canada. 90% are from public schools. 80% are white. The average age of freshmen is 18; all undergraduates, 22. 16% do not continue beyond their first year; 62% remain to graduate.

Housing: 3700 students can be accommodated in college housing, which includes coed dorms, on-campus apartments, off-campus apartments, and married-student housing. In addition, there is a fitness/wellness hall, freshmen interest groups, substance-free living, quiet, and smoke-free areas. On-campus housing is available on a first-come, first-served basis. 68% of students commute. All students may keep cars.

Activities: There are no fraternities or sororities. There are 125 groups on campus, including art, band, cheerleading, chess, choir, chorale, chorus, computers, dance, debate, drama, environmental, ethnic, film, forensics, gay, honors, international, jazz band, literary magazine, musical theater, newspaper, opera, orchestra, pep band, photography, political, professional, radio and TV, recreational, religious, social, social service, student government, and symphony. Popular campus events include the Western Jam Talent Show, Casino Night, and Cinco de Mayo.

Sports: There are 7 intercollegiate sports for men and 8 for women, and 34 intramural sports for men and 34 for women. Facilities include a 3000-seat gym, playing fields, 8 tennis courts, a 6000-seat stadium, a golf course, salt/freshwater recreational facilities and equipment, an artificial-surface football field/track, a pool, a fitness center, and a student-run outdoor center (equipment and excursions).

Disabled Students: All of the campus is accessible. Wheelchair ramps, elevators, special parking, specially equipped rest rooms, special class scheduling, lowered drinking fountains, lowered telephones, and transcription services are available.

Services: Counseling and information services are available, as is tutoring in most subjects, including English, humanities, social sciences, and math and natural sciences. There is a reader service for the blind.

Campus Safety and Security: Measures include 24-hour foot and vehicle patrol, self-defense education, security escort services, and shuttle buses. There are informal discussions, pamphlets/posters/films, emergency telephones, and lighted pathways/sidewalks.

Programs of Study: WWU confers B.A., B.S., B.A.E., B.F.A., and B.Mus. degrees. Master's degrees are also awarded. Bachelor's degrees are awarded in BIOLOGICAL SCIENCE (biochemistry and biology/biological science), BUSINESS (accounting, business administration and management, international business management, management science, and marketing/retailing/merchandising), COMMUNICATIONS AND THE ARTS (art, communications, dramatic arts, English, fine arts, French, German, journalism, linguistics, music, and Spanish), COMPUTER AND PHYSICAL SCIENCE (chemistry, computer science, geology, mathematics, and physics), EDUCATION (art, early childhood, elementary, foreign languages, health, music, science, and secondary), ENGINEERING AND ENVIRONMENTAL DESIGN (electrical/electronics engineering technology, engineering technology, environmental science, and manufacturing technology), HEALTH PROFESSIONS (speech pathology/audiology), SOCIAL SCIENCE (anthropology, Canadian studies, East Asian studies, economics, geography, history, human services, parks and recreation management, philosophy, political science/

government, psychology, and sociology). Computer science, business, and technology are the strongest academically. Psychology, environmental studies, and education are the largest.

Required: Students must complete at least 180 quarter hours, with fulfillment of a major and at least 60 credits in upper-division study, and maintain at least a 2.0 GPA or that prescribed by departments/divisions. General university requirements include 70 to 75 credits, and students must satisfy writing proficiency requirements as well. Fairhaven College has a separate interdisciplinary core program.

Special: Special academic programs include internships through various academic departments and study abroad in 75 countries. Dual majors are available through various departments, and there is a general studies degree, a B.A. in humanities. A 3-2 engineering degree is possible with the University of Washington. Student-designed majors are offered through the liberal studies department in the College of Arts and Sciences and through Fairhaven College, which affords an unusual degree of student involvement in the structure and content of their own programs and which uses faculty narrative for students' academic evaluations. In addition, Huxley College of Environmental Studies provides specialized education and research. Up to 30 credits of electives may be granted for military service, and nondegree study and pass/fail options are possible. There are 13 national honor societies, a freshman honors program, and 3 departmental honors programs.

Faculty/Classroom: 60% of faculty are male; 40%, female. All teach undergraduates, 90% do research, and 90% do both. Graduate students teach 4% of introductory courses. The average class size in an introductory lecture is 80; in a laboratory, 20; and in a regular course, 27.

Admissions: 76% of the 2003-2004 applicants were accepted. The SAT I scores for the 2003-2004 freshman class were: Verbal--27% below 500, 43% between 500 and 599, 26% between 600 and 700, and 4% above 700; Math--26% below 500, 48% between 500 and 599, 24% between 600 and 700, and 2% above 700. The ACT scores were 30% below 21, 20% between 21 and 23, 29% between 24 and 26, 12% between 27 and 28, and 9% above 28. 49% of the current freshmen were in the top fifth of their class; 84% were in the top two fifths. There were 8 National Merit finalists and 6 semifinalists. 69 freshmen graduated first in their class.

Requirements: The SAT I or ACT is required. Other admissions requirements include completion of 15 academic units, comprised of 4 years of college preparatory English composition and literature courses; 3 years of college preparatory math, including 2 years of algebra; 3 years of social studies/history; 2 years of science, including 1 year of a chemistry or physics with an algebra prerequisite; 2 years of the same foreign language; 1 semester of fine and performing arts; and 1 semester in another academic field. Freshman applicants meeting minimum GPA and subject requirements are ranked by an index combining the GPA and a standardized test score. The GED is also accepted. Other factors taken into consideration include curricular rigor (level of difficulty of courses), grade trends, leadership, community involvement, special talent, multicultural experience, and personal hardship or circumstances. A GPA of 2.5 is required. AP credits are accepted. Important factors in the admissions decision are advanced placement or honor courses, leadership record, and personality/intangible qualities.

Procedure: Freshmen are admitted to all sessions. Entrance exams should be taken by fall of the senior year. Applications should be filed by March 1 for fall entry, October 15 for winter entry, January 15 for spring entry, and March 1 for summer entry, along with a $37 fee. Notification is sent March 15. 138 applicants were on the 2003 waiting list; 138 were admitted. Applications are accepted on-line through College-NET or the school's web site.

Transfer: 939 transfer students enrolled in 2002-2003. Applicants with fewer than 40 quarter credits are eligible for consideration if they have completed the last term before transferring with a GPA of at least 2.0 and if they satisfy the requirements for freshman admission. Those with 40 or more transferable quarter credits are eligible if they have achieved a cumulative GPA of at least 2.0. Admission is selective. 45 of 180 credits required for the bachelor's degree must be completed at WWU.

Visiting: There are regularly scheduled orientations for prospective students, including tours, class visits, and advisement. There are guides for informal visits and visitors may sit in on classes and stay overnight. To schedule a visit, contact the STARS Program - Student Admissions Representatives at (360) 650-3861 or *campusvisit@wwu.edu*.

Financial Aid: In 2003-2004, 68% of all full-time freshmen and 59% of continuing full-time students received some form of financial aid. 32% of full-time freshmen and 40% of continuing full-time students received need-based aid. The average freshman award was $8607. Need-based scholarships or need-based grants averaged $4458 ($10,337 maximum); need-based self-help aid (loans and jobs) averaged $3248 ($9625 maximum); non-need-based athletic scholarships averaged $2630 ($5639 maximum); other non-need-based awards and non-need-based scholarships averaged $2189 ($16,350 maximum); and alternative bank loans, PLUS loans, and unsubsidized loans averaged $8969 ($23,220 maximum). 43% of undergraduates work part time. Average annual earnings from campus work are $1560. The average financial indebtedness of the

2003 graduate was $15,050. The FAFSA is required. The deadline for filing freshman financial aid applications for fall entry is February 15.

International Students: There are 83 international students enrolled. They must score 550 on the written TOEFL or 213 on the electronic version and also take the SAT I or the ACT.

Computers: The mainframe is a Sun E4000. There are more than 1000 PCs and Macs available in the student labs and residence halls. Students also have access to the Internet and the web. All students may access the system. There are no time limits and no fees.

Graduates: From July 1, 2002 to June 30, 2003, 2651 bachelor's degrees were awarded. The most popular majors were business administration and management (7%), psychology (6%), and English (6%). In an average class, 28% graduate in 4 years or less, 58% graduate in 5 years or less, and 65% graduate in 6 years or less. 64 companies recruited on campus in 2002-2003. Of the 2002 graduating class, 13% were enrolled in graduate school within 6 months of graduation and 93% were employed.

Admissions Contact: Karen Copetas, Director.
E-mail: *admit@cc.wwu.edu* Web: *www.wwu.edu/~admit*

WHITMAN COLLEGE
Walla Walla, WA 99362-2083   E-3

(509) 527-5176
(877) 462-9448; Fax: (509) 527-4967

Full-time: 629 men, 786 women	**Faculty:** 116; IIB, +$
Part-time: 16 men, 23 women	**Ph.D.s:** 93%
Graduate: none	**Student/Faculty:** 12 to 1
Year: semesters	**Tuition:** $25,626
Application Deadline: January 15	**Room & Board:** $6900
Freshman Class: 2143 applied, 1196 accepted, 362 enrolled	
SAT I Verbal/Math: 670/660	**HIGHLY COMPETITIVE+**

Whitman College, founded in 1883, is a private, independent residential liberal arts and sciences college. In addition to regional accreditation, Whitman College has baccalaureate program accreditation with ACS. The library contains 339,720 volumes, 15,714 microform items, and 5852 audio/video tapes/CDs, and subscribes to 879 periodicals. Computerized library services include the card catalog, interlibrary loans, database searching, and Internet access. Special learning facilities include a learning resource center, art gallery, natural history museum, planetarium, radio station, and an electron microscope lab, an indoor planetarium, an off-campus observatory and on-campus astronomical telescopes, an Asian art collection, a video-conferencing center, an outdoor sculpture walk, an organic garden, and indoor and outdoor rock climbing walls. The 117-acre campus is in a small town 150 miles south of Spokane, 260 miles southeast of Seattle, and 235 miles east of Portland. Including any residence halls, there are 41 buildings.

Student Life: 56% of undergraduates are from Washington. Students are from 27 states, 24 foreign countries, and Canada. 70% are from public schools. 73% are white. The average age of freshmen is 18; all undergraduates, 20. 5% do not continue beyond their first year; 95% remain to graduate.

Housing: 882 students can be accommodated in college housing, which includes single-sex and coed dorms, off-campus apartments, and fraternity houses. In addition, there are language houses and special-interest houses. On-campus housing is guaranteed for the freshman year only and is available on a lottery system for upperclassmen. 59% of students live on campus; of those, 95% remain on campus on weekends. All students may keep cars.

Activities: 36% of men belong to 4 national fraternities; 34% of women belong to 4 national sororities. There are 60 groups on campus, including academic, animal rights, art, choir, chorale, chorus, culinary arts, dance, debate, drama, environmental, ethnic, film, forensics, gay, health, honors, international, jazz band, leadership, literary magazine, mentoring, musical theater, newspaper, opera, orchestra, pep band, photography, political, professional, radio and TV, religious, social service, student government, symphony, and women's issues. Popular campus events include Renaissance Fair, Choral Contest, and Interest House Block Party.

Sports: There are 9 intercollegiate sports for men and 8 for women, and 7 intramural sports for men and 7 for women. Facilities include a stadium, a center with a 3000-seat gym, squash and handball courts, saunas, a pool, indoor and outdoor climbing walls, a small gym, a weights/Nautilus room, aerobic/dance room, cardiovascular room, 4 outdoor tennis courts, a soccer field, an indoor tennis facility, a dance studio, and an off-campus playing field complex.

Disabled Students: 50% of the campus is accessible. Wheelchair ramps, elevators, special parking, specially equipped rest rooms, lowered drinking fountains, and lowered telephones are available. Modifications necessary for specific cases will be made.

Services: Counseling and information services are available, as is tutoring in most subjects. There is a reader service for the blind. There are also centers for study skills and writing.

Campus Safety and Security: Measures include self-defense education, security escort services, informal discussions, and pamphlets/

posters/films. There are emergency telephones, lighted pathways/sidewalks, and 24-hour foot patrol.

Programs of Study: Whitman College confers the B.A. degree. Bachelor's degrees are awarded in BIOLOGICAL SCIENCE (biology/biological science), COMMUNICATIONS AND THE ARTS (art history and appreciation, classics, dramatic arts, English, film arts, fine arts, French, German, music, and Spanish), COMPUTER AND PHYSICAL SCIENCE (chemistry, geology, mathematics, and physics), ENGINEERING AND ENVIRONMENTAL DESIGN (environmental science), SOCIAL SCIENCE (anthropology, Asian/Oriental studies, economics, history, philosophy, political science/government, psychology, religion, and sociology). Politics, biology, and English are the strongest academically. Psychology, politics, and biology are the largest.

Required: Students must complete 124 credits, with 32 to 36 in the major, and maintain a minimum GPA of 2.0. Distribution requirements include a minimum of 6 credits in social sciences, humanities, fine arts, and science (including one course with a lab); 1 course of 3 or more credits in quantitative analysis; and 2 courses that fulfill the alternative voices requirement. Freshman core must be taken, and written and oral tests are also required.

Special: Special academic programs include more than 500 internships, study abroad in 43 countries, a Washington semester, and study programs in Chicago and Philadelphia. Dual majors are available in any area, and student-designed majors are offered. There is a 3-2 environmental management and forestry program with Duke University, and a 3-2 engineering program with Washington University in St. Louis, California Institute of Technology and Applied Science, Columbia and Duke Universities, and University of Washington. A 3-3 law program is offered through Columbia University. A 4-1 education program is available through Bank Street College of Education and University of Puget Sound Cooperative. Certification is offered for elementary and secondary education. A pass-D-fail option is available. A special feature of the curriculum is the integrated general studies program for freshmen. A 3-2 program is available with the Monterey Institute of International Studies. There are 3 national honor societies, including Phi Beta Kappa, a freshman honors program, and 41 departmental honors programs.

Faculty/Classroom: 63% of faculty are male; 38%, female. All both teach and do research. The average class size in an introductory lecture is 20; in a laboratory, 17; and in a regular course, 14.

Admissions: 56% of the 2003-2004 applicants were accepted. The SAT I scores for the 2003-2004 freshman class were: Verbal--2% below 500, 13% between 500 and 599, 45% between 600 and 700, and 40% above 700; Math--1% below 500, 17% between 500 and 599, 55% between 600 and 700, and 28% above 700. The ACT scores were 2% below 21, 11% between 21 and 23, 16% between 24 and 26, 21% between 27 and 28, and 51% above 28. 90% of the current freshmen were in the top fifth of their class; 100% were in the top two fifths. There were 24 National Merit finalists. 66 freshmen graduated first in their class.

Requirements: The SAT I or ACT is required. In addition, the GED is accepted. 3 essays must be submitted, and an interview is recommended. Credit by challenge examination is accepted. AP credits are accepted. Important factors in the admissions decision are advanced placement or honor courses, evidence of special talent, and extracurricular activities record.

Procedure: Freshmen are admitted fall and spring. Entrance exams should be taken by February of the senior year. There are early decision and deferred admissions plans. Early decision applications should be filed by November 15; regular applications, by January 15 for fall entry and December 1 for spring entry. The fall 2003 application fee was $45. Notification of early decision is sent December 15; regular decision, April 1. 116 early decision candidates were accepted for the 2003-2004 class. 288 applicants were on the 2003 waiting list; 34 were admitted. Applications are accepted on computer disk and on-line through the school's web site, CollegeNET, and Common Application.

Transfer: 32 transfer students enrolled in 2002-2003. Transfer applicants must submit the common application, a transfer supplement, a teacher/counselor recommendation, a statement of good standing from prior institutions, their high school and college transcripts, SAT I or ACT scores (required for some), and the application fee. 54 of 124 credits required for the bachelor's degree must be completed at Whitman College.

Visiting: There are regularly scheduled orientations for prospective students, including Fall and Spring Visitors' Days. There are guides for informal visits and visitors may sit in on classes and stay overnight. To schedule a visit, contact the Admission Office at *admission@whitman.edu*.

Financial Aid: In 2003-2004, 52% of all full-time freshmen and 42% of continuing full-time students received some form of financial aid. 42% of full-time freshmen and 43% of continuing full-time students received need-based aid. The average freshman award was $19,550. Need-based scholarships or need-based grants averaged $11,900; need-based self-help aid (loans and jobs) averaged $4700; and non-need-based awards and non-need-based scholarships averaged $6850. 99% of undergraduates work part time. Average annual earnings from campus work are $1267. The average financial indebtedness of the 2003 graduate was $15,075. Whitman College is a member of CSS. The CSS/Profile or

FAFSA is required. The priority date for freshman financial aid applications for fall entry is January 5. The deadline for filing freshman financial aid applications for fall entry is February 1.

International Students: There are 42 international students enrolled. The school actively recruits these students. They must score 560 on the written TOEFL and also take APIEL or ELPT and the SAT I or the ACT.

Computers: The mainframes are a 30 multiple servers that vary in make/model and in operating systems. Students have unlimited network access from 270 student PCs on campus, including in residence halls. All students have e-mail accounts. There are 4 main computer labs and various departmental labs available to students, some portions open 24 hours a day. All students may access the system 24 hours a day. There are no time limits and no fees.

Graduates: From July 1, 2002 to June 30, 2003, 378 bachelor's degrees were awarded. The most popular majors were psychology (14%), politics (13%), and biology (13%). In an average class, 79% graduate in 4 years or less, 83% graduate in 5 years or less, and 86% graduate in 6 years or less. 112 companies recruited on campus in 2002-2003.

Admissions Contact: Tony Cabasco, Acting Dean of Admission and Financial Aid. A video is available. E-mail: admission@whitman.edu Web: http://www.whitman.edu

WHITWORTH COLLEGE
Spokane, WA 99251

C-2

(509) 777-4348

(800) 533-4668; Fax: (509) 777-3758

Full-time: 798 men, 1152 women	**Faculty:** 120; IIB, av$
Part-time: 43 men, 78 women	**Ph.D.s:** 86%
Graduate: 69 men, 158 women	**Student/Faculty:** 16 to 1
Year: 4-1-4, summer session	**Tuition:** $20,078
Application Deadline: March 1	**Room & Board:** $6350
Freshman Class: 1890 applied, 1415 accepted, 438 enrolled	
SAT I Verbal/Math: 573/580	**ACT:** 26 **VERY COMPETITIVE+**

Whitworth College, founded in 1890, is a nonprofit, independent, comprehensive institution affiliated with the Presbyterian Church (U.S.A.). The emphasis of its undergraduate and graduate programs is on the liberal arts, business, art and fine arts, music, religious studies, and teacher preparation. In addition to regional accreditation, Whitworth has baccalaureate program accreditation with NASM, NCATE, and NLN. The library contains 141,000 volumes, 54,250 microform items, and 1528 audio/video tapes/CDs, and subscribes to 810 periodicals. Computerized library services include the card catalog, interlibrary loans, and database searching. Special learning facilities include a learning resource center, art gallery, radio station, and writing center. The 200-acre campus is in a suburban area 7 miles north of Spokane. Including any residence halls, there are 40 buildings.

Student Life: 55% of undergraduates are from Washington. Students are from 29 states, 25 foreign countries, and Canada. 88% are from public schools. 86% are white. 76% are Protestant; 10% claim no religious affiliation; 7% Catholic. The average age of freshmen is 18; all undergraduates, 21. 13% do not continue beyond their first year; 71% remain to graduate.

Housing: 1100 students can be accommodated in college housing, which includes single-sex and coed dorms, on-campus apartments, and off-campus apartments. In addition, there are language houses and special-interest houses. On-campus housing is guaranteed for all 4 years. 66% of students live on campus; of those, 90% remain on campus on weekends. Alcohol is not permitted. All students may keep cars.

Activities: There are no fraternities or sororities. There are 45 groups on campus, including art, band, cheerleading, choir, chorale, chorus, computers, dance, drama, ethnic, honors, international, jazz band, literary magazine, musical theater, newspaper, orchestra, photography, political, radio and TV, religious, social, social service, student government, and yearbook. Popular campus events include athletic events, movies, and theme weeks.

Sports: There are 9 intercollegiate sports for men and 9 for women, and 10 intramural sports for men and 8 for women. Facilities include a 2000-seat stadium, a 1200-seat gym, a field house, an aquatic center, and playing fields.

Disabled Students: 70% of the campus is accessible. Wheelchair ramps, elevators, special parking, specially equipped rest rooms, special class scheduling, lowered drinking fountains, and lowered telephones are available.

Services: Counseling and information services are available, as is tutoring in most subjects, including biology, chemistry, computer science, French, German, Spanish, math, physics, and writing.

Campus Safety and Security: Measures include 24-hour foot and vehicle patrol, security escort services, informal discussions, and pamphlets/posters/films. There are emergency telephones and lighted pathways/sidewalks.

Programs of Study: Whitworth confers B.A. and B.S. degrees. Master's degrees are also awarded. Bachelor's degrees are awarded in BIOLOGICAL SCIENCE (biology/biological science), BUSINESS (accounting, business administration and management, and international business

management), COMMUNICATIONS AND THE ARTS (art, communications, dramatic arts, English, French, journalism, music, Spanish, and speech/debate/rhetoric), COMPUTER AND PHYSICAL SCIENCE (applied physics, chemistry, computer science, mathematics, physics, and quantitative methods), EDUCATION (athletic training, elementary, English, foreign languages, mathematics, music, science, secondary, and social studies), ENGINEERING AND ENVIRONMENTAL DESIGN (environmental science), HEALTH PROFESSIONS (nursing, predentistry, and premedicine), SOCIAL SCIENCE (American studies, crosscultural studies, economics, history, international studies, peace studies, philosophy, political science/government, prelaw, psychology, religion, sociology, and women's studies). English, history, and chemistry are the strongest academically. Education, business, psychology are the largest.

Required: Students must complete 130 credit hours, with 42 in the major, and maintain a GPA of at least 2.0. The curriculum includes 3 core courses on religious, rationalist, and scientific traditions; distribution requirements are comprised of 4 phys ed activity courses, 2 each in a foreign language and science/math, and 1 course each in biblical literature, oral communication, fine arts, social science, and humanities. Additionally, an other-culture course or experience must be fulfilled.

Special: Special academic programs include many work-study opportunities, 1 to 3 internship course credits that may be earned by juniors and seniors, and a January Washington term. Study abroad is available in 15 countries. There is cross-registration with the Intercollegiate Language Study Consortium and Gonzaga University. Accelerated degree programs are possible as is a 3-2 engineering degree, and students may choose to specialize in an area of concentration in lieu of a major. Credit may be granted for life, military, or work experience. Nondegree study is possible for those auditing or in seminars, and there is 1 pass/fail option allowed per year. A special feature of the school is the modified semester calendar, which affords unusual opportunities for internships, study tours, and other activities. There is a freshman honors program.

Faculty/Classroom: 70% of faculty are male; 30%, female. All teach undergraduates. No introductory courses are taught by graduate students. The average class size in an introductory lecture is 30; in a laboratory, 15; and in a regular course, 19.

Admissions: 75% of the 2003-2004 applicants were accepted. The SAT I scores for the 2003-2004 freshman class were: Verbal--18% below 500, 44% between 500 and 599, 31% between 600 and 700, and 7% above 700; Math--15% below 500, 45% between 500 and 599, 34% between 600 and 700, and 6% above 700. 40% of the current freshmen were in the top fifth of their class; 75% were in the top two fifths. There were 6 National Merit semifinalists. 42 freshmen graduated first in their class.

Requirements: The SAT I or ACT is required. Suggested scores are 1000 for the SAT I, 500 verbal and 500 math, and 22 for the ACT. Other admissions criteria include 4 high school credits in English, 3 each in math, science, and history/social studies, and 2 of a foreign language. An essay must be submitted, and an interview is recommended. Music students are advised to audition. Whitworth requires applicants to be in the upper 50% of their class. A GPA of 3.0 is required. AP and CLEP credits are accepted. Important factors in the admissions decision are advanced placement or honor courses, extracurricular activities record, and leadership record.

Procedure: Freshmen are admitted fall, winter, and spring. Entrance exams should be taken by the fall of the senior year, though the spring of the junior year is preferred. There is a rolling admissions plan. There are early admissions and deferred admissions plans. Early decision applications should be filed by November 30; regular applications, by March 1 for fall entry. Notification of early decision is sent December 15; regular decision, on a rolling basis. A waiting list is an active part of the admissions procedure. Applications are accepted on computer disk and online.

Transfer: 102 transfer students enrolled in 2002-2003. Transfer students must have a GPA of at least 2.25 and a recommended 45 quarter credits earned. The SAT I or ACT is recommended; the SAT I composite score should be 1000 and the ACT score 22. 32 of 130 credits required for the bachelor's degree must be completed at Whitworth.

Visiting: There are regularly scheduled orientations for prospective students, including a class visit, a tour, and an overnight stay, if desired. There are guides for informal visits and visitors may sit in on classes and stay overnight. To schedule a visit, contact Debbie Harvey, Campus Visit Coordinator at (509) 777-4331 or dharvey@whitworth.edu.

Financial Aid: In a recent year, 90% of all full-time freshmen and 88% of continuing full-time students received some form of financial aid. 52% of all full-time students received need-based aid. The average freshman award was $14,400. All undergraduates work part time. Average annual earnings from campus work are $1402. The average financial indebtedness of a recent graduate was $16,000. The CSS Profile, FAFSA, FFS, or SFS are required. The FAFSA is preferred. The deadline for filing freshman financial aid applications for fall entry is March 1.

International Students: There are 65 international students enrolled. The school actively recruits these students. They must score 460 on the written TOEFL.

Computers: The mainframe is a DEC MicroVAX 3500. There are PC labs available for student use. Internet access is also available from every dorm room on campus. All students may access the system any time during library hours. There are no time limits and no fees. It is strongly recommended that all students have a personal computer.

Graduates: In a recent year, 320 bachelor's degrees were awarded. In an average class, 3% graduate in 3 years or less, 58% graduate in 4 years or less, 68% graduate in 5 years or less, and 70% graduate in 6 years or less. 60 companies recruited on campus in 2002-2003.

Admissions Contact: Fred Pfursich, Dean of Enrollment. E-mail: *admission@whitworth.edu* Web: *www.whitworth.edu*

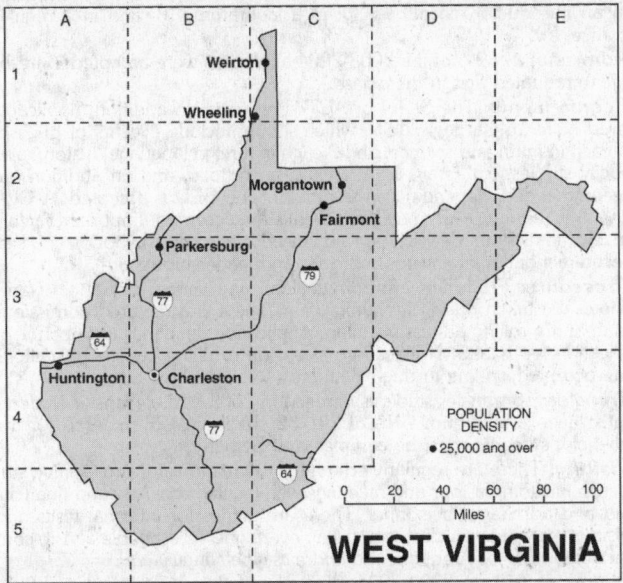

POPULATION
DENSITY
● 25,000 and over

0 20 40 60 80 100
Miles

WEST VIRGINIA

ALDERSON-BROADDUS COLLEGE   C-3
Philippi, WV 26416   (304) 457-6310
(800) 263-1549; Fax: (304) 457-6239

Full-time: 260 men, 425 women	**Faculty:** 61
Part-time: 15 men, 50 women	**Ph.D.s:** 45%
Graduate: 30 men, 35 women	**Student/Faculty:** 11 to 1
Year: semesters, summer session	**Tuition:** $14,440
Application Deadline: see profile	**Room & Board:** $5200
Freshman Class: n/av	
SAT I or ACT: required	**COMPETITIVE**

Alderson-Broaddus College is a private institution, founded in 1871 and affiliated with American Baptist Churches USA. It offers a liberal arts program along with teacher preparation and professional, music, business, religion, and science studies. Figures in the above capsule and in this profile are approximate. In addition to regional accreditation, Alderson-Broaddus has baccalaureate program accreditation with CAHEA, NCATE, and NLN. The library contains 100,000 volumes, 8000 microform items, and 5000 audio/video tapes/CDs, and subscribes to 670 periodicals. Computerized library services include the card catalog, interlibrary loans, and database searching. Special learning facilities include a learning resource center, art gallery, radio station, and TV station. The 170-acre campus is in a small town 100 miles south of Pittsburgh and 100 miles north of Charleston. Including any residence halls, there are 19 buildings.

Student Life: 67% of undergraduates are from West Virginia. Students are from 26 states, 5 foreign countries, and Canada. 90% are from public schools. 91% are white. 75% are Protestant; 14% Catholic; 11% claim no religious affiliation. The average age of freshmen is 21. 31% do not continue beyond their first year; 44% remain to graduate.

Housing: 700 students can be accommodated in college housing, which includes single-sex and coed dorms, on-campus apartments, off-campus apartments, and married-student housing. On-campus housing is guaranteed for all 4 years. 60% of students live on campus; of those, 40% remain on campus on weekends. Alcohol is not permitted. All students may keep cars.

Activities: 8% of men belong to 3 local fraternities; 10% of women belong to 3 local sororities. There are 40 groups on campus, including art, band, choir, chorale, chorus, computers, dance, debate, drama, ethnic, forensics, honors, jazz band, musical theater, newspaper, pep band, photography, political, professional, radio and TV, religious, social, social service, student government, and yearbook. Popular campus events include Spring Weekend, Christmas programs, and Homeless Weekend.

Sports: There are 10 intramural sports for men and 10 for women. Facilities include several playing fields near the main campus, a swimming pool, a weight room, handball courts, auxiliary gyms, an archery range, a batting cage, and a tennis court.

Disabled Students: 75% of the campus is accessible. Wheelchair ramps, elevators, special parking, specially equipped rest rooms, and special class scheduling are available.

Services: Counseling and information services are available, as is tutoring in every subject. There is remedial math, reading, and writing. There is also an Academic Support Network.

Campus Safety and Security: Measures include 24-hour foot and vehicle patrol, informal discussions, pamphlets/posters/films, and lighted pathways/sidewalks.

Programs of Study: Alderson-Broaddus confers B.A. and B.S. degrees. Associate and master's degrees are also awarded. Bachelor's degrees are awarded in BIOLOGICAL SCIENCE (biology/biological science), BUSINESS (accounting, business administration and management, and management information systems), COMMUNICATIONS AND THE ARTS (communications, creative writing, literature, and music), COMPUTER AND PHYSICAL SCIENCE (chemistry, computer science, and mathematics), EDUCATION (athletic training, elementary, music, recreation, and secondary), HEALTH PROFESSIONS (cytotechnology, medical science, medical technology, nursing, ophthalmic technology, and radiograph medical technology), SOCIAL SCIENCE (Christian studies, history, liberal arts/general studies, political science/government, psychology, and religious music). Health sciences, business, and education are the strongest academically. Nursing and health sciences are the largest.

Required: Each graduate is required to complete at least 1 major and Liberal Studies Program requirements amounting to 51 to 55 semester hours plus electives for a minimum of 128 semester hours. The Liberal Studies requirements include courses in English, literature, math, computer literacy, physical and biological science, philosophy/religion, social science, history, global concerns, aesthetic expression, and health. All graduates must have attained a GPA of 2.0 overall and in the major. Certain disciplines may require a GPA higher than the minimum to continue in the major and to graduate.

Special: Internships in numerous majors, student-designed majors in liberal arts, cross-registration with the Mountain State Association of Colleges, study abroad through the college's programs in Austria or through the Junior Year Abroad program in conjunction with other schools, and work scholarships at the college are available. In addition, the college offers dual majors, a general studies degree, the B.A.-B.S. degree, nondegree study, and pass/fail grading in certain courses. There is a freshman honors program.

Faculty/Classroom: 57% of faculty are male; 43%, female. 97% teach undergraduates and 10% both teach and do research. No introductory courses are taught by graduate students. The average class size in an introductory lecture is 40; in a laboratory, 30; and in a regular course, 20.

Requirements: The SAT I or ACT is required. The recommended composite score for the SAT I is 950; for the ACT, 21. Applicants who are graduates of secondary schools or have passed the GED are considered for admission. An audition for certain majors and an interview are recommended. A GPA of 2.5 is required. AP and CLEP credits are accepted. Important factors in the admissions decision are advanced placement or honor courses, leadership record, and recommendations by school officials.

Procedure: Freshmen are admitted to all sessions. Entrance exams should be taken in spring of the junior year. There is a deferred admissions plan and a rolling admissions plan. Check with the school for current deadlines. Notification is sent on a rolling basis. The fall 2003 application fee was $10. Applications are accepted on-line.

Transfer: 42 transfer students enrolled in a recent year. Transfer applicants must have a minimum 2.0 GPA. If they have fewer than 29 transfer credit hours, ACT or SAT I results and a high school diploma are required. 60 of 128 credits required for the bachelor's degree must be completed at Alderson-Broaddus.

Visiting: There are regularly scheduled orientations for prospective students, including placement tests and social programs. There are guides for informal visits and visitors may sit in on classes and stay overnight. To schedule a visit, contact the Admissions Office.

Financial Aid: The FAFSA and the college's own financial statement are required. Check with the school for current deadlines.

International Students: The school actively recruits these students. They must score 500 on the written TOEFL and also take the SAT I or the ACT.

Computers: The mainframe is a DEC VAX. All students have access to mainframe and PC labs. All students may access the system. There are no time limits and no fees. It is recommended that students in computer science have personal computers. A PC or Mac is recommended.

Admissions Contact: Eric Ruf, Director of Admissions. A video is available. E-mail: admissions@ab.edu Web: www.ab.edu

BETHANY COLLEGE
C-1
Bethany, WV 26032

(304) 829-7611
(800) 922-7611; Fax: (304) 829-7142

Full-time: 435 men, 458 women	Faculty: 61; IIB, --$
Part-time: 1 man, 6 women	Ph.D.s: 59%
Graduate: none	Student/Faculty: 15 to 1
Year: semesters	Tuition: $13,495
Application Deadline: open	Room & Board: $6350
Freshman Class: 1109 applied, 765 accepted, 270 enrolled	
SAT I Verbal/Math: 605/540	ACT: 24 VERY COMPETITIVE

Bethany College, founded in 1840, is a liberal arts institution affiliated with the Christian Church (Disciples of Christ). In addition to regional accreditation, Bethany has baccalaureate program accreditation with CSWE and NCATE. The library contains 116,601 volumes, 116,065 microform items, and 1658 audio/video tapes/CDs, and subscribes to 302 periodicals. Computerized library services include the card catalog, interlibrary loans, database searching, and Internet access. Special learning facilities include a learning resource center, art gallery, radio station, and TV station. The 300-acre campus is in a small town 14 miles north of Wheeling and 48 miles southwest of Pittsburgh. Including any residence halls, there are 33 buildings.

Student Life: 76% of undergraduates are from out of state, mostly the Middle Atlantic. Students are from 23 states, 15 foreign countries, and Canada. 70% are from public schools. 94% are white. 44% are Protestant; 36% Catholic; 18% claim no religious affiliation. The average age of freshmen is 18; all undergraduates, 20. 12% do not continue beyond their first year; 60% remain to graduate.

Housing: 880 students can be accommodated in college housing, which includes single-sex and coed dorms, on-campus apartments, off-campus apartments, fraternity houses, and sorority houses. In addition, there are special-interest houses. On-campus housing is guaranteed for all 4 years. 95% of students live on campus; of those, 87% remain on campus on weekends. All students may keep cars.

Activities: 44% of men belong to 5 national fraternities; 53% of women belong to 3 national sororities. There are 38 groups on campus, including art, athletics, band, cheerleading, choir, chorale, chorus, computers, dance, drama, ethnic, gay, honors, international, jazz band, literary magazine, musical theater, newspaper, orchestra, outdoor, pep band, photography, political, professional, radio and TV, religious, social, social service, student government, and yearbook. Popular campus events include Spring Weekend, Mid-Term Break, and Snow Carnival.

Sports: There are 9 intercollegiate sports for men and 9 for women, and 7 intramural sports for men and 7 for women. Facilities include a 2000-seat stadium, a 1000-seat gym, a natatorium, and football, soccer, baseball, and softball fields.

Disabled Students: 20% of the campus is accessible. Wheelchair ramps, elevators, special parking, and specially equipped rest rooms are available.

Services: Counseling and information services are available, as is tutoring in every subject. There is also a center for academic success, which provides guidance for students needing special assistance.

Campus Safety and Security: Measures include 24-hour foot and vehicle patrol, informal discussions, pamphlets/posters/films, and lighted pathways/sidewalks.

Programs of Study: Bethany confers B.A. and B.S. degrees. Bachelor's degrees are awarded in BIOLOGICAL SCIENCE (biochemistry and biology/biological science), BUSINESS (accounting and business economics), COMMUNICATIONS AND THE ARTS (communications, English, fine arts, French, German, journalism, languages, and Spanish), COMPUTER AND PHYSICAL SCIENCE (chemistry, computer science, mathematics, and physics), EDUCATION (early childhood, elementary, English, foreign languages, physical, science, secondary, and special), HEALTH PROFESSIONS (predentistry and premedicine), SOCIAL SCIENCE (economics, history, international studies, philosophy, political science/government, prelaw, psychology, religion, and social work). Chemistry, economics, and political science are the strongest academically. Communication, economics, and education are the largest.

Required: All students must earn 128 semester hours, including 24 to 48 in the major, while maintaining a 2.0 GPA. A freshman seminar is required. Distribution credits can be earned in contemporary society and institutions, creative arts, cultural awareness, human behavior, international understanding, life science, literature, mathematical understanding, physical science, and the Western tradition. Students must complete a writing proficiency requirement, a senior project (thesis), and a senior comprehensive exam (oral and written) to graduate.

Special: Bethany offers a 3-2 engineering degree with Columbia, Washington (at St. Louis), and Case Western Reserve Universities, internships (required with many majors), study abroad in France, Spain, England, Germany, Canada, Japan, Puerto Rico, Argentina, and Sweden, a Washington semester, and work-study programs. B.A.-B.S. degrees and dual majors in all majors, a general studies degree, student-designed majors in interdisciplinary studies, and pass/fail options in non-

major courses also are offered. There is also a voluntary January term. There are 15 national honor societies.

Faculty/Classroom: 72% of faculty are male; 28%, female. All teach undergraduates; 35% both teach and do research. The average class size in an introductory lecture is 30; in a laboratory, 18; and in a regular course, 20.

Admissions: 69% of the 2003-2004 applicants were accepted. 6 freshmen graduated first in their class.

Requirements: The SAT I or ACT is required. In addition, applicants must have 15 Carnegie units, which should include 4 years of English, 3 each in math and science, and 2 each in foreign language, history, and social studies. An essay, an interview, a portfolio, and an audition are recommended, depending on the major. The GED is accepted. A GPA of 2.5 is required. AP and CLEP credits are accepted. Important factors in the admissions decision are advanced placement or honor courses, recommendations by school officials, and leadership record.

Procedure: Freshmen are admitted fall and spring. Entrance exams should be taken during the junior year. There is a deferred admissions plan and a rolling admissions plan. Application deadlines are open. Application fee is $25. Notification is sent on a rolling basis. Applications are accepted on-line through Bethany's web site.

Transfer: 16 transfer students enrolled in 2002-2003. Transfer students must have a minimum GPA of 2.0. 32 credits of 128 required for the bachelor's degree must be completed at Bethany.

Visiting: There are regularly scheduled orientations for prospective students, including a tour and meetings with faculty, coaches, and financial aid and admission personnel. There are guides for informal visits and visitors may sit in on classes and stay overnight. To schedule a visit, contact the Office of Admission at jandrews@bethanywv.edu.

Financial Aid: In 2003-2004, 95% of all full-time freshmen and 92% of continuing full-time students received some form of financial aid. 85% of full-time freshmen and 75% of continuing full-time students received need-based aid. The average freshman award was $12,000. Need-based scholarships or need-based grants averaged $6000 ($8000 maximum); need-based self-help aid (loans and jobs) averaged $3000 ($4000 maximum); and non-need-based awards and non-need-based scholarships averaged $6500 ($8000 maximum). 79% of undergraduates work part time. Average annual earnings from campus work are $820. The average financial indebtedness of the 2003 graduate was $18,000. The FAFSA and the college's own financial statement are required. The priority date for freshman financial aid applications for fall entry is April 1. The deadline for filing freshman financial aid applications for fall entry is May 1.

International Students: There are 45 international students enrolled. The school actively recruits these students. They must score 500 on the written TOEFL or 173 on the electronic version and also take the SAT I or the ACT.

Computers: The mainframe is a Hewlett-Packard. There are 20 terminals for the mainframe in the computer center. There is also a Mac computer center with 8 student labs. In addition, there are computer labs for English, economics, communications, biology, chemistry, education, and social sciences. All students may access the system 24 hours daily. It is strongly recommended that all students have a personal computer.

Graduates: From July 1, 2002 to June 30, 2003, 140 bachelor's degrees were awarded. The most popular majors were communications (18%), psychology (16%), and biology (9%). In an average class, 3% graduate in 3 years or less, 56% graduate in 4 years or less, 58% graduate in 5 years or less, and 1% graduate in 6 years or less. Of the 2002 graduating class, 35% were enrolled in graduate school within 6 months of graduation and 85% were employed.

Admissions Contact: Wray Blair, Director of Admission.
E-mail: admission@mail.bethanywv.edu Web: www.bethanywv.edu

BLUEFIELD STATE COLLEGE
B-5
Bluefield, WV 24701

(304) 327-4068
(800) 654-7798; Fax: (304) 325-7747

Full-time: 920 men, 1463 women	Faculty: 79; IIB, av$
Part-time: 368 men, 760 women	Ph.D.s: 52%
Graduate: none	Student/Faculty: 30 to 1
Year: semesters, summer session	Tuition: $2806 ($6894)
Application Deadline: open	Room & Board: n/app
Freshman Class: 1359 applied, 1315 accepted, 664 enrolled	
ACT: 18	LESS COMPETITIVE

Bluefield State College, founded in 1895, is a state-supported commuter college offering programs in engineering technologies, business, teacher education, arts and sciences, health science professions, and a variety of career fields. The college also offers a wide variety of off-campus courses. In addition to regional accreditation, Bluefield State has baccalaureate program accreditation with ABET and NCATE. The library contains 75,803 volumes, 5195 microform items, and 7500 audio/video tapes/CDs, and subscribes to 6258 periodicals. Computerized library services include the card catalog, interlibrary loans, database searching, and Internet access. Special learning facilities include a learning resource center and art gallery. The 40-acre campus is in a small town 90 miles south of Charleston. There are 9 buildings.

Student Life: 95% of undergraduates are from West Virginia. Students are from 12 states, 10 foreign countries, and Canada. 99% are from public schools. 90% are white. The average age of freshmen is 21; all undergraduates, 27. 34% do not continue beyond their first year; 52% remain to graduate.

Housing: There are no residence halls. All students commute. Alcohol is not permitted. All students may keep cars.

Activities: 3% of men belong to 3 local and 3 national fraternities; 1% of women belong to 3 local and 1 national sorority. There are 42 groups on campus, including cheerleading, choir, ethnic, honors, international, jazz band, newspaper, student government, and yearbook. Popular campus events include dances and sports events.

Sports: There are 5 intercollegiate sports for men and 4 for women, and 20 intramural sports for men and 15 for women. Facilities include a gym, a pool, tennis courts, an athletic field, and physical fitness and aerobics rooms.

Disabled Students: All of the campus is accessible. Wheelchair ramps, elevators, special parking, specially equipped rest rooms, and lowered drinking fountains are available.

Services: Counseling and information services are available, as is tutoring in most subjects. There is a reader service for the blind and remedial math, reading, and writing.

Campus Safety and Security: Measures include 24-hour foot and vehicle patrol, self-defense education, pamphlets/posters/films, and emergency telephones. There are lighted pathways/sidewalks.

Programs of Study: Bluefield State confers B.A., B.S., B.S.E.T., and B.S.N. degrees. Associate degrees are also awarded. Bachelor's degrees are awarded in BIOLOGICAL SCIENCE (biology/biological science), BUSINESS (accounting and business administration and management), COMPUTER AND PHYSICAL SCIENCE (computer science), EDUCATION (elementary and middle school), ENGINEERING AND ENVIRONMENTAL DESIGN (engineering technology), HEALTH PROFESSIONS (nursing), SOCIAL SCIENCE (criminal justice, humanities, and social science). Engineering, technology, and health science are the strongest academically. Business is the largest.

Required: The minimum requirement for graduation is a 2.0 GPA overall and in the student's major and minor, and 128 semester hours. All graduating students must have completed the general program specific to their degree and a core curriculum of 40 hours among humanities, social science, lab science, basic skills, phys ed, and computer science.

Special: A general studies degree and life experience credentials are offered through the Regents Bachelor of Arts Degree Program, designed for adults. Nondegree study is offered. There are 2 national honor societies, a freshman honors program, and 1 departmental honors program.

Faculty/Classroom: 62% of faculty are male; 38%, female. All teach undergraduates. The average class size in an introductory lecture is 40; in a laboratory, 25; and in a regular course, 25.

Admissions: 97% of the 2003-2004 applicants were accepted. The ACT scores for the 2003-2004 freshman class were: 73% below 21, 17% between 21 and 23, 8% between 24 and 26, 1% between 27 and 28, and 1% above 28. 27% of the current freshmen were in the top fifth of their class; 46% were in the top two fifths.

Requirements: The ACT is required and the SAT I is recommended with an overall 2.0 GPA or a composite score of at least 17 on the ACT or 680 on the SAT I. In addition, regular admission is granted to students meeting GED requirements or having a high school diploma. They also must have successfully completed minimum high school curricular unit requirements consisting of 4 units in English, 3 in social studies, 2 in math (algebra I and higher), and 2 in lab science. Other students not meeting these requirements may be admitted on a conditional basis. AP and CLEP credits are accepted.

Procedure: Freshmen are admitted to all sessions. Entrance exams should be taken before enrolling. There are early admissions, rolling admissions, and deferred admissions plans. Application deadlines are open. Applications are accepted on-line through the school web site.

Transfer: 570 transfer students enrolled in 2002-2003. Applicants must be in good standing at the institution from which they are transferring. 32 of 128 credits required for the bachelor's degree must be completed at Bluefield State.

Visiting: There are regularly scheduled orientations for prospective students. There are guides for informal visits and visitors may sit in on classes. To schedule a visit, contact the Admissions Office at (304) 327-4065.

Financial Aid: In 2003-2004, 70% of all full-time students received some form of financial aid. 60% of all full-time students received need-based aid. The average freshman award was $4200. Need-based scholarships or need-based grants averaged $500 ($2000 maximum); need-based self-help aid (loans and jobs) averaged $4000 ($10,500 maximum); and non-need-based athletic scholarships averaged $2000 ($3200 maximum). 75% of undergraduates work part time. Average annual earnings from campus work are $1600. The average financial indebtedness of the 2003 graduate was $7500. Bluefield State is a member of CSS. The FAFSA and the college's own financial statement are required. The deadline for filing freshman financial aid applications for fall entry is March 15.

International Students: There are 33 international students enrolled. International students must score 550 on the written TOEFL and also take the ACT.

Computers: The mainframe is a DEC 4000; WVNET computer systems are accessed through telecommunications. There are also 11 computer labs available on campus for student use. All students may access the system during class and lab hours. There are no time limits and no fees.

Graduates: From July 1, 2002 to June 30, 2003, 213 bachelor's degrees were awarded. The most popular majors were business administration (18%), education (14%), and nursing (14%). 60 companies recruited on campus in 2002-2003. Of the 2002 graduating class, 7% were enrolled in graduate school within 6 months of graduation and 95% were employed.

Admissions Contact: John C. Cardwell, Vice President for Enrollment Management. E-mail: *bscadmit@bluefieldstate.edu* Web: *www.bluefieldstate.edu*

CONCORD COLLEGE   B-5
Athens, WV 24712
(304) 384-5248
(888) 384-5249; Fax: (304) 384-9044

Full-time: 1076 men, 1379 women	**Faculty:** 84; IIB, -$
Part-time: 187 men, 384 women	**Ph.D.s:** n/av
Graduate: none	**Student/Faculty:** 29 to 1
Year: semesters, summer session	**Tuition:** $3198 ($7278)
Application Deadline: open	**Room & Board:** $4938
Freshman Class: 2992 applied, 1980 accepted, 1090 enrolled	
SAT I Verbal/Math: 500/490	**ACT:** 20 **COMPETITIVE**

Concord College, founded in 1872, is a public institution with undergraduate programs in liberal arts and professional training. Some information in this capsule and profile is approximate. In addition to regional accreditation, Concord has baccalaureate program accreditation with CSWE and NCATE. The library contains 96,787 volumes, 268,451 microform items, and 1077 audio/video tapes/CDs, and subscribes to 552 periodicals. Computerized library services include the card catalog, interlibrary loans, and database searching. Special learning facilities include a learning resource center, art gallery, radio station, and TV station. The 123-acre campus is in a small town 85 miles south of Charleston. Including any residence halls, there are 19 buildings.

Student Life: 84% of undergraduates are from West Virginia. Students are from 25 states, 27 foreign countries, and Canada. 97% are from public schools. 92% are white. 40% claim no religious affiliation; 40% Protestant; 15% Catholic. The average age of freshmen is 19; all undergraduates, 23. 33% do not continue beyond their first year; 41% remain to graduate.

Housing: 1078 students can be accommodated in college housing, which includes single-sex dorms and married-student housing. In addition, there are honors floors in residence halls and housing for international students. On-campus housing is guaranteed for all 4 years. Alcohol is not permitted. All students may keep cars.

Activities: 20% of men belong to 2 local and 4 national fraternities; 20% of women belong to 4 national sororities. There are 52 groups on campus, including art, bagpipe band, band, cheerleading, choir, chorale, computers, drama, film, honors, international, jazz band, literary magazine, newspaper, pep band, political, professional, radio and TV, religious, social, social service, student government, and yearbook. Popular campus events include big-name concerts, Alumni Day, and faculty and student plays.

Sports: There are 8 intercollegiate sports for men and 7 for women, and 15 intramural sports for men and 15 for women. Facilities include 5 tennis courts, 4 racquetball courts, 2 gyms, a Nautilus fitness room, a pool, a dance studio, and various outdoor fields. The campus stadium seats 4000, the larger gym 2700, and the largest auditorium 900.

Disabled Students: 90% of the campus is accessible. Wheelchair ramps, elevators, special parking, special class scheduling, and special housing are available.

Services: Counseling and information services are available, as is tutoring in every subject. There is a reader service for the blind and remedial math, reading, and writing.

Campus Safety and Security: Measures include security escort services, informal discussions, pamphlets/posters/films, and emergency telephones. There are lighted pathways/sidewalks. A foot and vehicle patrol is available 24 hours Monday through Friday and is on call Saturday and Sunday.

Programs of Study: Concord confers B.A., B.S., B.B.A., B.S.C.I.S., B.S.Ed., B.S.Med.Tech., and B.S.W. degrees. Associate degrees are also awarded. Bachelor's degrees are awarded in BIOLOGICAL SCIENCE (biology/biological science), BUSINESS (accounting, banking and finance, business administration and management, hotel/motel and restaurant management, marketing/retailing/merchandising, office supervision and management, and small business management), COMMUNICATIONS AND THE ARTS (broadcasting, communications, and English), COMPUTER AND PHYSICAL SCIENCE (chemistry, computer programming, computer science, information sciences and systems, and mathematics), EDUCATION (art, business, early childhood, elementary, middle school, music, science, secondary, and special), HEALTH PROFESSIONS (medical laboratory technology, predentistry, premedicine, and prepharmacy), SOCIAL SCIENCE (geography, history, parks and recreation management, political science/government, prelaw, psychology, social science, social work, and sociology). Teacher education, business, and preprofessional biology and chemistry are the strongest academically. Teacher education, business, and travel industry management are the largest.

Required: To graduate, students must earn 128 credit hours, including 36 to 50 in the major, with a minimum GPA of 2.0 (2.5 in many departments). All students must complete the college's general studies curriculum. Required courses include 14 to 15 semester hours of math and science, 12 each of English/literature and social studies, 6 of fine arts, 3 of speech, and 2 of phys ed.

Special: Students may serve internships in medical technology, social work, travel industry management, commercial art/advertising, and communications arts. Concord offers a Washington semester, cross-registration with Bluefield State College, dual majors, interdisciplinary student-designed majors, and nondegree study. Credit for life, military, and work experience is granted to adult students through the Regents Bachelor of Arts Degree Program. There are 4 national honor societies and a freshman honors program.

Faculty/Classroom: All teach undergraduates. The average class size in an introductory lecture is 45; in a laboratory, 20; and in a regular course, 45.

Admissions: 66% of the 2003-2004 applicants were accepted. The SAT I scores for the 2003-2004 freshman class were: Verbal--51% below 500, 30% between 500 and 599, 15% between 600 and 700, and 2% above 700; Math--53% below 500, 29% between 500 and 599, 16% between 600 and 700, and 2% above 700. The ACT scores were 47% below 21, 28% between 21 and 23, 15% between 24 and 26, 7% between 27 and 28, and 3% above 28.

Requirements: The SAT I or ACT is required; the ACT is preferred. Applicants must be high school graduates or hold a GED. Students should present 17 academic credits, including 4 in English, 3 each in social studies, math, and science, and 1 each in history and health/phys ed. An interview is recommended and, where appropriate, a portfolio or an audition. A GPA of 2.0 is required. AP and CLEP credits are accepted.

Procedure: Freshmen are admitted to all sessions. Entrance exams should be taken in the junior year or preferably early in the senior year. There is a deferred admissions plan and a rolling admissions plan. Application deadlines are open. Notification is sent on a rolling basis. Applications are accepted on-line.

Transfer: 157 transfer students enrolled in a recent year. Applicants must have a GPA of at least 2.0. Concord recommends a minimum of 15 credit hours of college work completed and an interview. 36 credits of 128 required for the bachelor's degree must be completed at Concord.

Visiting: There are regularly scheduled orientations for prospective students. There are guides for informal visits and visitors may sit in on classes and stay overnight. To schedule a visit, contact the Admissions Office.

Financial Aid: In 2003-2004, 91% of all full-time freshmen and 76% of continuing full-time students received some form of financial aid. 80% of full-time freshmen and 65% of continuing full-time students received need-based aid. The average freshman award was $7135. 23% of undergraduates work part time. Average annual earnings from campus work are $1800. The average financial indebtedness of a recent graduate was $10,000. The FAFSA and the college's own financial statement are required. Check with the school for current deadlines.

International Students: The school actively recruits these students. They must score 500 on the written TOEFL and also take the SAT I or the ACT.

Computers: Concord is a participant in the statewide WVNET computer network system. Programming languages and statistical packages are run from the central mainframe, a DEC Alpha 2100 Model 500. 201 PCs are available in computer labs and faculty offices. All students may access the system. There are no time limits and no fees.

Graduates: In a recent year, 370 bachelor's degrees were awarded. The most popular majors were education (26%), business/marketing (15%), and liberal arts/general studies (12%). In an average class, 41% graduate in 5 years or less.

Admissions Contact: Michael Curry, Vice President of Admissions and Financial Aid. E-mail: *admissions@concord.edu*
Web: *http://www.concord.edu*

DAVIS AND ELKINS COLLEGE   C-3
Elkins, WV 26241   (304) 637-1326
                                        (800) 624-3157; Fax: (304) 637-1800

Full-time: 240 men, 350 women	Faculty: 66
Part-time: 20 men, 50 women	Ph.Ds: 73%
Graduate: none	Student/Faculty: 9 to 1
Year: semesters, summer session	Tuition: $14,668
Application Deadline: open	Room & Board: $5926
Freshman Class: n/av	
SAT I Verbal/Math: 478/480	ACT: 21 COMPETITIVE

Davis and Elkins College, founded in 1904 and affiliated with the Presbyterian Church (U.S.A.), offers programs in the liberal arts, business, professional training, teacher preparation, nursing, and recreation management. Some information in this capsule and profile is approximate. The library contains 225,000 volumes, 300,000 microform items, and 14,000 audio/video tapes/CDs, and subscribes to 410 periodicals. Computerized library services include the card catalog and interlibrary loans. Special learning facilities include a learning resource center, art gallery, planetarium, and radio station. The 170-acre campus is in a small town 200 miles west of Washington, D.C. Including any residence halls, there are 21 buildings.

Student Life: 55% of undergraduates are from West Virginia. Students are from 26 states, 12 foreign countries, and Canada. 95% are from public schools. 90% are white. 38% claim no religious affiliation; 24% Protestant. The average age of freshmen is 18; all undergraduates, 20. 30% do not continue beyond their first year; 70% remain to graduate.

Housing: 572 students can be accommodated in college housing, which includes single-sex and coed dorms. On-campus housing is guaranteed for all 4 years. 50% of students live on campus; of those, 75% remain on campus on weekends. All students may keep cars.

Activities: 15% of men belong to 2 national fraternities; 15% of women belong to 2 national sororities. There are 42 groups on campus, including art, bagpipe band, cheerleading, choir, computers, drama, environmental, honors, international, jazz band, leadership, literary magazine, musical theater, newspaper, pep band, photography, political, professional, radio and TV, religious, social, social service, student government, and yearbook. Popular campus events include Parents Weekend, Deja Vu, and International Week.

Sports: There are 6 intercollegiate sports for men and 6 for women, and 10 intramural sports for men and 10 for women. Facilities include a 2000-seat gym, a 1300-seat arena, fields, a fitness center and fitness trails, a tennis court, and a pool. A national forest is nearby.

Disabled Students: 80% of the campus is accessible. Wheelchair ramps, elevators, special parking, specially equipped rest rooms, special class scheduling, lowered drinking fountains, and lowered telephones are available.

Services: Counseling and information services are available, as is tutoring in every subject. There is remedial math, reading, and writing. Learning disabilities services also are available.

Campus Safety and Security: Measures include self-defense education, security escort services, informal discussions, and pamphlets/posters/films. There are lighted pathways/sidewalks. The campus security service is on duty from 6 P.M. to 5 A.M.

Programs of Study: D&E confers B.A. and B.S. degrees. Associate degrees are also awarded. Bachelor's degrees are awarded in BIOLOGICAL SCIENCE (biology/biological science), BUSINESS (accounting, business administration and management, hospitality management services, management science, and marketing/retailing/merchandising), COMMUNICATIONS AND THE ARTS (art, communications, dramatic arts, English, languages, and music), COMPUTER AND PHYSICAL SCIENCE (chemistry, computer science, and mathematics), EDUCATION (elementary, physical, and secondary), ENGINEERING AND ENVIRONMENTAL DESIGN (environmental science), HEALTH PROFESSIONS (predentistry and premedicine), SOCIAL SCIENCE (economics, history, political science/government, prelaw, psychology, religion, and sociology). Business, psychology, and biology are the strongest academically. Business, nursing, and hospitality management are the largest.

Required: To graduate, students must complete 124 credit hours, including 30 to 40 in the major, with a GPA of 2.0. General education requirements include 7 hours of natural science, 6 each of history, social science, English composition, philosophy, religion, literature, and math, 5 of fine arts, and 2 of phys ed, as well as a course in computer literacy. A freshman experience class and a public speaking course are also required.

Special: Students may study abroad or take a Washington semester. The college offers co-op programs with Syracuse University and SUNY, as well as internships. Students may take dual majors in psychology/human services, biology/environmental sciences, and history/political science, and student-designed majors are permitted through a contract degree program. The college awards credit for life, military, and work experience. Nondegree study is allowed, and pass/fail options are offered. The college's mentor-assisted degree-completion program allows adults to earn degrees through credit for life experience and off-campus study.

There are 6 national honor societies, a freshman honors program, and 100 departmental honors programs.

Faculty/Classroom: 61% of faculty are male; 39%, female. All teach undergraduates. The average class size in an introductory lecture is 15; in a laboratory, 11; and in a regular course, 11.

Admissions: 22% of the current freshmen were in the top fifth of their class; 63% were in the top two fifths.

Requirements: The SAT I or ACT is required, with a minimum composite score of 900 on the SAT I or 19 on the ACT. Applicants should be high school graduates or hold a GED. Students should have earned 16 academic credits, including 4 in English and 3 each in social studies, math (including a minimum of algebra I and geometry), and natural science (including a lab course). 2 years of foreign language is recommended. D&E requires applicants to be in the upper 50% of their class. A GPA of 2.0 is required. AP and CLEP credits are accepted. Important factors in the admissions decision are advanced placement or honor courses, recommendations by school officials, and leadership record.

Procedure: Freshmen are admitted to all sessions. Entrance exams should be taken during the fall of the senior year. There are early decision and deferred admissions plans. There is a rolling admissions plan. Application deadlines are open. Check with the school for current application fee. Notification is sent on a rolling basis. Applications are accepted on-line.

Transfer: Transfer applicants should have earned 62 credit hours, with a GPA of 2.0. An associate degree is recommended. 15 credits of 124 required for the bachelor's degree must be completed at D&E.

Visiting: There are regularly scheduled orientations for prospective students, including meals, a tour of campus, and panel discussions. There are guides for informal visits and visitors may sit in on classes and stay overnight. To schedule a visit, contact the Admissions Office at (304) 637-1230.

Financial Aid: In 2003-2004, 89% of all full-time students received some form of financial aid. 69% of full-time freshmen and 70% of continuing full-time students received need-based aid. The average freshman award was $16,512. Need-based scholarships or need-based grants averaged $2807 ($5550 maximum); need-based self-help aid (loans and jobs) averaged $2587 ($6125 maximum); non-need-based athletic scholarships averaged $3402 ($8000 maximum); and other non-need-based awards and non-need-based scholarships averaged $7716 ($10,000 maximum). 40% of undergraduates work part time. Average annual earnings from campus work are $1200. The average financial indebtedness of a recent graduate was $15,000. The FAFSA is required and the CSS Profile Application is optional. Check with the school for current deadlines.

International Students: The school actively recruits these students. They must score 500 on the written TOEFL or take the MELAB and also take the SAT I or the ACT.

Computers: The mainframe is a DEC VAX 4300. There are 91 Macs and PCs available in 7 labs. All students may access the system. There are no time limits and no fees.

Admissions Contact: Renee Heckel, Director of Admissions.
E-mail: *admiss@davisandelkins.edu* Web: *www.davisandelkins.edu*

FAIRMONT STATE
Fairmont, WV 26554

C-2
(304) 367-4062
(800) 641-5678; Fax: (304) 367-4584

Full-time: 2428 men, 2697 women	**Faculty:** IIB, -$
Part-time: 851 men, 1437 women	**Ph.D.s:** n/av
Graduate: 23 men, 40 women	**Student/Faculty:** n/av
Year: semesters, summer session	**Tuition:** $3130 ($7038)
Application Deadline: August 15	**Room & Board:** $5150
Freshman Class: 2814 applied, 2473 accepted, 1280 enrolled	
SAT I Verbal/Math: 460/475	**ACT:** 20 **LESS COMPETITIVE**

Fairmont State, formerly Fairmont State College and founded in 1865, is a public institution offering programs in business, education, engineering technology, and health careers. In addition to regional accreditation, Fairmont State has baccalaureate program accreditation with ABET, NCATE, and NLN. The library contains 256,991 volumes, 54,241 microform items, and 7298 audio/video tapes/CDs, and subscribes to 1175 periodicals. Computerized library services include the card catalog, interlibrary loans, and database searching. Special learning facilities include a learning resource center. The 89-acre campus is in a small town 75 miles south of Pittsburgh, Pennsylvania. Including any residence halls, there are 12 buildings.

Student Life: 94% of undergraduates are from West Virginia. Students are from 23 states and 17 foreign countries. 98% are from public schools. 94% are white. The average age of freshmen is 21; all undergraduates, 24. 26% do not continue beyond their first year; 37% remain to graduate.

Housing: 437 students can be accommodated in college housing, which includes single-sex dorms. On-campus housing is available on a first-come, first-served basis. 94% of students commute. Alcohol is not permitted. All students may keep cars.

Activities: 4% of men belong to 3 national fraternities; 4% of women belong to 3 national sororities. There are 80 groups on campus, including art, band, cheerleading, choir, chorus, computers, debate, drama, gay, honors, jazz band, literary magazine, marching band, musical theater, newspaper, pep band, photography, political, professional, religious, service, social, student government, symphony, and yearbook. Popular campus events include multicultural events.

Sports: There are 7 intercollegiate sports for men and 6 for women, and 24 intramural sports for men and 24 for women. Facilities include a phys ed center, a 5000-seat stadium, a 4000-seat basketball arena, and playing fields.

Disabled Students: All of the campus is accessible. Wheelchair ramps, elevators, special parking, specially equipped rest rooms, special class scheduling, lowered drinking fountains, and lowered telephones are available.

Services: Counseling and information services are available, as is tutoring in most subjects. There is a reader service for the blind and remedial math, reading, and writing.

Campus Safety and Security: Measures include 24-hour foot and vehicle patrol, pamphlets/posters/films, emergency telephones, and lighted pathways/sidewalks.

Programs of Study: Fairmont State confers B.A., B.S., B.A.E., B.E.T., and B.S.N. degrees. Associate and master's degrees are also awarded. Bachelor's degrees are awarded in BIOLOGICAL SCIENCE (biology/biological science), BUSINESS (accounting, banking and finance, business administration and management, business economics, and marketing/retailing/merchandising), COMMUNICATIONS AND THE ARTS (communications, English, French, and speech/debate/rhetoric), COMPUTER AND PHYSICAL SCIENCE (chemistry, computer science, and mathematics), EDUCATION (art, business, early childhood, elementary, foreign languages, health, middle school, music, science, and secondary), ENGINEERING AND ENVIRONMENTAL DESIGN (architectural technology, civil engineering technology, electrical/electronics engineering technology, engineering technology, manufacturing technology, and mechanical engineering technology), SOCIAL SCIENCE (criminal justice, family/consumer studies, history, political science/government, psychology, and sociology). Engineering technology, education, and business are the strongest academically. Business, health careers, and criminal justice are the largest.

Required: To graduate, students must complete 128 hours with a GPA of 2.0. (2.5 in education specializations). Students must complete 50 core curriculum hours for the B.S. or B.A. degree. All students must take 2 hours of phys ed. Course and distribution requirements vary according to the program.

Special: The college offers internships in teacher education, retailing, and psychology, and awards a B.S. degree in chemistry/math. There is a freshman honors program.

Faculty/Classroom: All teach undergraduates. The average class size in an introductory lecture is 106; in a laboratory, 20; and in a regular course, 30.

Admissions: 88% of the 2003-2004 applicants were accepted.

Requirements: The SAT I or ACT is required for students who have graduated from high school or completed GED requirements fewer than 5 years prior to seeking admission. The minimum composite score required is 830 on the SAT I or 17 on the ACT. Applicants must be high school graduates or hold a GED. The college requires 4 credits in English and 3 each in social studies (1 in U.S. history), math (algebra I and at least 1 higher), and lab science. A foreign language is recommended. A GPA of 2.5 is required. AP and CLEP credits are accepted.

Procedure: Freshmen are admitted to all sessions. Entrance exams should be taken during the fall of the senior year. Applications should be filed by August 15 for fall entry. The college accepts all applicants. Notification is sent on a rolling basis. Applications are accepted on-line.

Transfer: Applicants must have a GPA of 2.0. The ACT is required for applicants with fewer than 30 college credits. 32 of 128 credits required for the bachelor's degree must be completed at Fairmont State.

Visiting: There are guides for informal visits and visitors may sit in on classes. To schedule a visit, contact the Student Affairs Office at (304) 367-4216.

Financial Aid: In 2003-2004, 81% of all full-time freshmen and 77% of continuing full-time students received some form of financial aid. 65% of full-time freshmen and 64% of continuing full-time students received need-based aid. The average freshman award was $1914. Need-based scholarships or need-based grants averaged $2167 ($6242 maximum); need-based self-help aid (loans and jobs) averaged $1831 ($5418 maximum); non-need-based athletic scholarships averaged $1542 ($7300 maximum); other non-need-based awards and non-need-based scholarships averaged $2756 ($11,199 maximum); and WIA, vocational rehabilitation, National Guard, veterans benefits, and so on averaged $5160 ($9175 maximum). Fairmont State is a member of CSS. The FAFSA is required. The deadline for filing freshman financial aid applications for fall entry is March 1.

International Students: They must score 500 on the written TOEFL. If ACT or SAT I scores are not supplied, the ACT must be taken upon arrival on campus.

Computers: The mainframe is a DEC VAX 8250. There are 500 IBM PCs available for student use in computer labs. Students have access to the Internet and the World Wide Web. Those students with accounts may access the system 8 A.M. to 11 P.M., 4 days per week. There are no time limits and no fees.

Admissions Contact: Douglas Dobbins, Executive Director of Enrollment Services. A video is available. E-mail: *ddobbins@fscwv.edu* Web: *www.fscwv.edu*

GLENVILLE STATE COLLEGE   C-3
Glenville, WV 26351   (304) 462-4128
                                   (800) 924-2010; Fax: (304) 462-8619

Full-time: 569 men, 639 women	**Faculty:** 50; IIB, -$
Part-time: 69 men, 100 women	**Ph.D.s:** 32%
Graduate: none	**Student/Faculty:** 24 to 1
Year: semesters, summer session	**Tuition:** $2952 ($7306)
Application Deadline: open	**Room & Board:** $4860
Freshman Class: 780 applied, 780 accepted, 325 enrolled	
SAT I Verbal/Math: 435/433	**ACT:** 19 NONCOMPETITIVE

Glenville State College, founded in 1872, is a public college offering programs in education, the arts and sciences, and business. In addition to regional accreditation, GSC has baccalaureate program accreditation with CCNE and NCATE. The library contains 114,798 volumes, 584,537 microform items, and 2667 audio/video tapes/CDs, and subscribes to 256 periodicals. Computerized library services include the card catalog, interlibrary loans, database searching, and Internet access. Special learning facilities include a learning resource center and art gallery. The 360-acre campus is in a rural area 100 miles northeast of Charleston. Including any residence halls, there are 28 buildings.

Student Life: 91% of undergraduates are from West Virginia. Students are from 19 states and 3 foreign countries. 92% are white.

Housing: 596 students can be accommodated in college housing, which includes single-sex dorms, on-campus apartments, and married-student housing. On-campus housing is guaranteed for all 4 years. 63% of students commute. Alcohol is not permitted. All students may keep cars.

Activities: 2% of men belong to 2 local fraternities; 2% of women belong to 3 local sororities. There are 25 groups on campus, including art, band, cheerleading, chess, choir, chorus, drama, drill team, gay, honors, international, jazz band, literary magazine, marching band, musical theater, political, professional, religious, social, and student government. Popular campus events include GSC Week (a campus celebration) in April, comedians, and bands.

Sports: There are 5 intercollegiate sports for men and 6 for women, and 5 intramural sports for men and 5 for women. Facilities include a field house, a 5000-seat football stadium, a running track, tennis courts, a 700-seat gym, a swimming pool, a fitness center, and a weight room.

Disabled Students: 95% of the campus is accessible. Wheelchair ramps, elevators, special parking, specially equipped rest rooms, lowered drinking fountains, and lowered telephones are available. Adaptations are made to class delivery locations to accommodate student needs.

Services: Counseling and information services are available, as is tutoring in most subjects. There is remedial math, reading, and writing.

Campus Safety and Security: Measures include security escort services, shuttle buses, emergency telephones, and lighted pathways/sidewalks. There are electronically operated dorm entrances.

Programs of Study: GSC confers B.A. and B.S. degrees. Associate degrees are also awarded. Bachelor's degrees are awarded in BIOLOGICAL SCIENCE (biology/biological science), BUSINESS (accounting, banking and finance, business administration and management, and marketing/retailing/merchandising), COMMUNICATIONS AND THE ARTS (English), COMPUTER AND PHYSICAL SCIENCE (chemistry, computer science, and information sciences and systems), EDUCATION (business, early childhood, elementary, middle school, music, physical, science, secondary, and special), HEALTH PROFESSIONS (nursing), SOCIAL SCIENCE (behavioral science, history, and liberal arts/general studies). Teacher education is the strongest academically. Behavioral science is the largest.

Required: All students must take the general studies programs, consisting of 47 to 48 hours in English, math, science, the social sciences, humanities, and phys ed. Computer science is also required. To graduate, students must complete 128 credit hours, with 42 in the major. Noneducation majors must maintain a 2.0 GPA; education majors, a 2.5.

Special: The college offers B.A.-B.S. degrees in numerous majors, credit by exam, and pass/fail options. Some programs of study require internships. There are 4 national honor societies and a freshman honors program.

Faculty/Classroom: 60% of faculty are male; 40%, female. All teach undergraduates.

Admissions: 100% of the 2003-2004 applicants were accepted. The SAT I scores for the 2003-2004 freshman class were: Verbal--70% below 500, 21% between 500 and 599, 7% between 600 and 700, and 2% above 700; Math--70% below 500, 23% between 500 and 599, 5% be-

tween 600 and 700, and 1% above 700. The ACT scores were 52% below 21, 16% between 21 and 23, 6% between 24 and 26, and 1% between 27 and 28. 24% of the current freshmen were in the top fifth of their class; 62% were in the top two fifths.

Requirements: The SAT I or ACT is required. In addition, a minimum composite score of 17 on the ACT or 820 on the SAT I is recommended. Applicants should be graduates of an accredited secondary school and have taken 4 courses in English, 3 in social studies, and 3 each in higher math and lab sciences. GED admission is also possible. A GPA of 2.0 is required. AP and CLEP credits are accepted.

Procedure: Freshmen are admitted to all sessions. Entrance exams should be taken at the end of the junior year. There is an early admissions plan and a rolling admissions plan. Application deadlines are open.

Transfer: 127 transfer students enrolled in fall 2003. Applicants must be in good standing at their previous institution. 32 of 128 credits required for the bachelor's degree must be completed at GSC.

Visiting: There are regularly scheduled orientations for prospective students, including meetings with an admissions officer and a division officer and a campus tour. There are guides for informal visits and visitors may sit in on classes and stay overnight. To schedule a visit, contact the Office of Admissions at *admissions@glenville.edu*.

Financial Aid: The FAFSA is required. The deadline for filing freshman financial aid applications for fall entry is March 1.

International Students: The school actively recruits these students. They must score 550 on the written TOEFL and also take the ACT, scoring 17.

Computers: The mainframes are a 2 minisystems: DEC Alpha 3000-800 series for student use and e-mail and a DEC Alpha 4100 for administrative use. Students may telenet in from any networked PC. Accounts are provided to all students for class usage and e-mail. Programming classes are taught on both the minisystem and PCs. There are 200 networked PCs located throughout the campus. All students may access the system. There are no time limits and no fees.

Graduates: From July 1, 2002 to June 30, 2003, 208 bachelor's degrees were awarded. The most popular majors were business (27%), teacher education (27%), and behavioral science (24%).

Admissions Contact: Donna Shaffner, Director of Admissions and Marketing. E-mail: *donna.shaffner@glenville.edu* Web: *http://www.glenville.edu*

MARSHALL UNIVERSITY   A-4
Huntington, WV 25755   (304) 696-3160
                                   (800) 642-3499; Fax: (304) 696-3135

Full-time: 3773 men, 4661 women	**Faculty:** 411; IIA, -$
Part-time: 559 men, 965 women	**Ph.D.s:** 79%
Graduate: 1200 men, 2603 women	**Student/Faculty:** 20 to 1
Year: semesters, summer session	**Tuition:** $3260 ($8944)
Application Deadline: September 1	**Room & Board:** $5856
Freshman Class: 2578 applied, 2274 accepted, 1915 enrolled	
ACT: 22	COMPETITIVE

Marshall University, founded in 1837 and part of the University of West Virginia system, is a comprehensive public institution offering programs in liberal arts and sciences, business, education, fine arts, and nursing. There are 10 undergraduate and 2 graduate schools. In addition to regional accreditation, Marshall has baccalaureate program accreditation with AACSB, ABET, ACEJMC, CSWE, NASM, NCATE, NLN, and NRPA. The 3 libraries contain 415,910 volumes, 966,733 microform items, and 20,785 audio/video tapes/CDs, and subscribe to 4138 periodicals. Computerized library services include the card catalog, interlibrary loans, database searching, and Internet access. Special learning facilities include a learning resource center, art gallery, natural history museum, radio station, TV station, and a greenhouse. The 70-acre campus is in an urban area 126 miles east of Lexington, Kentucky, and 50 miles west of Charleston, West Virginia. Including any residence halls, there are 35 buildings.

Student Life: 83% of undergraduates are from West Virginia. Students are from 37 states, 44 foreign countries, and Canada. 86% are white. The average age of freshmen is 19; all undergraduates, 22. 25% do not continue beyond their first year; 36% remain to graduate.

Housing: 2315 students can be accommodated in college housing, which includes single-sex and coed dorms, on-campus apartments, and married-student housing. In addition, there are honors and quiet study floors. On-campus housing is available on a first-come, first-served basis. Alcohol is not permitted. All students may keep cars.

Activities: 7% of men belong to 11 national fraternities; 4% of women belong to 8 national sororities. There are 94 groups on campus, including art, band, cheerleading, choir, chorale, chorus, computers, dance, debate, drama, ethnic, gay, honors, international, jazz band, literary magazine, marching band, musical theater, newspaper, opera, orchestra, pep band, political, professional, radio and TV, religious, social, social service, student government, symphony, and yearbook. Popular campus events include Parents Day, Springfest, and International Festival.

Sports: There are 8 intercollegiate sports for men and 10 for women, and 9 intramural sports for men and 9 for women. Facilities include a 10,500-seat basketball arena, a 30,000-seat football stadium, tennis courts, a baseball field, an Olympic-size pool, an auxiliary gym, a health and fitness center, racquetball courts, a human performance enhancement lab, and a track and field.

Disabled Students: All of the campus is accessible. Wheelchair ramps, elevators, special parking, specially equipped rest rooms, special class scheduling, lowered drinking fountains, lowered telephones, special housing, and an attendant care program are available.

Services: Counseling and information services are available, as is tutoring in most subjects, including all lower-division courses. There is a reader service for the blind, remedial math, reading, and writing, study skills courses, and other services for all students with disabilities.

Campus Safety and Security: Measures include 24-hour foot and vehicle patrol, self-defense education, security escort services, and informal discussions. There are pamphlets/posters/films, emergency telephones, and lighted pathways/sidewalks.

Programs of Study: Marshall confers B.A., B.S., B.B.A., B.F.A., B.S. Cyotech, B.S.M.T., B.S.N., and B.S.W. degrees. Associate, master's, and doctoral degrees are also awarded. Bachelor's degrees are awarded in BIOLOGICAL SCIENCE (biology/biological science), BUSINESS (accounting, banking and finance, business economics, management science, and marketing/retailing/merchandising), COMMUNICATIONS AND THE ARTS (communications, English, fine arts, journalism, and music), COMPUTER AND PHYSICAL SCIENCE (chemistry, geology, information sciences and systems, mathematics, physics, and science technology), EDUCATION (elementary, foreign languages, home economics, and middle school), ENGINEERING AND ENVIRONMENTAL DESIGN (environmental science), HEALTH PROFESSIONS (cytotechnology, medical laboratory technology, and nursing), SOCIAL SCIENCE (criminal justice, dietetics, economics, geography, history, humanities, international relations, parks and recreation management, physical fitness/movement, political science/government, psychology, safety and security technology, social work, and sociology). Biological science, elementary education, and secondary education are the largest.

Required: The Marshall Plan, including a capstone experience, is key to each student's studies at Marshall University. Generally speaking, a 2.0 GPA (2.5 in education, 2.25 in journalism) and 128 credit hours, as well as other specific criteria, are required for graduation.

Special: Many programs require or offer internships. Work-study opportunities are available on campus. Students study abroad in 10 countries. B.A.-B.S. degrees, dual and student-designed majors, nondegree study, credit for life experience, and credit/no-credit options are available. There are 13 national honor societies, including Phi Beta Kappa, and a freshman honors program.

Faculty/Classroom: 54% of faculty are male; 46%, female. The average class size in an introductory lecture is 27; in a laboratory, 23; and in a regular course, 24.

Admissions: 88% of the 2003-2004 applicants were accepted. The ACT scores for the 2003-2004 freshman class were: 36% below 21, 32% between 21 and 23, 20% between 24 and 26, 7% between 27 and 28, and 5% above 28.

Requirements: The SAT I or ACT is required. In addition, regular admission is open to all students who have graduated from a secondary school with the required units of study and a 2.0 GPA or with a minimum composite score of 19 on the ACT or 910 on the SAT I. Required study is 4 years in English, 3 in social studies, and 2 each in higher math and lab science. 2 years of a foreign language is strongly recommended. The GED is also accepted. Students not meeting university requirements are admitted to the University College, through which students must successfully complete developmental courses with 3 semesters. A GPA of 2.0 is required. AP and CLEP credits are accepted. Important factors in the admissions decision are advanced placement or honor courses, evidence of special talent, and recommendations by school officials.

Procedure: Freshmen are admitted to all sessions. Entrance exams should be taken during the junior year or early in the senior year. There are early admissions and deferred admissions plans. Early decision applications should be filed by September 15; regular applications, by September 1 for fall entry, January 1 for spring entry, and June 1 for summer entry. The fall 2003 application fee was $25. Notification of early decision and regular decision is sent on a rolling basis. Applications are accepted on-line through *www.marshall.edu/admissions/form/form.htm.*

Transfer: 535 transfer students enrolled in 2002-2003. A 2.0 GPA on all previous college work is generally required of transfer applicants. 36 of 128 credits required for the bachelor's degree must be completed at Marshall.

Visiting: There are regularly scheduled orientations for prospective students. There are guides for informal visits and visitors may sit in on classes and stay overnight. To schedule a visit, contact the Orientation Office at (304) 696-2354.

Financial Aid: In 2003-2004, 87% of all full-time freshmen and 78% of continuing full-time students received some form of financial aid. 62% of full-time freshmen and 52% of continuing full-time students received

need-based aid. The average freshman award was $5710. Need-based scholarships or need-based grants averaged $4034 ($9832 maximum); need-based self-help aid (loans and jobs) averaged $3085 ($11,925 maximum); non-need-based athletic scholarships averaged $7799 ($15,852 maximum); and other non-need-based awards and non-need-based scholarships averaged $4423 ($22,189 maximum). 4% of undergraduates work part time. Average annual earnings from campus work are $2212. The average financial indebtedness of the 2003 graduate was $15,652. Marshall is a member of CSS. The FAFSA is required. The deadline for filing freshman financial aid applications for fall entry is February 1.

International Students: There are 113 international students enrolled. The school actively recruits these students. They must score 500 on the written TOEFL or 173 on the electronic version or take the MELAB, or pass level 9 ELS at the university and also take the SAT I or the ACT, scoring 19.

Computers: There are 180 networked PCs in the library, 620 in computer labs, 240 in classrooms, and 50 university-owned in dorms. The dorms have connections for residents' PCs as well. All students may access the system during scheduled hours, 7 days a week. There are no time limits and no fees. It is strongly recommended that all students have a personal computer.

Graduates: From July 1, 2002 to June 30, 2003, 1447 bachelor's degrees were awarded. The most popular majors were elementary education (10%), management (7%), and biological science (6%). In an average class, 36% graduate in 6 years or less.

Admissions Contact: Linda Templton, Associate Director. E-mail: *admissions@marshall.edu* Web: *www.marshall.edu/admissions*

MOUNTAIN STATE UNIVERSITY
B-4
Beckley, WV 25802-9003
(304) 253-7351
(800) 766-6067; Fax: (304) 253-5072

Full-time: 947 men, 1793 women	**Faculty:** n/av
Part-time: 267 men, 556 women	**Ph.D.s:** 30%
Graduate: 126 men, 184 women	**Student/Faculty:** 32 to 1
Year: semesters, summer session	**Tuition:** $5040
Application Deadline: open	**Room & Board:** $5172
Freshman Class: 401 enrolled	
SAT I Verbal/Math: 475/475	**ACT:** 18 NONCOMPETITIVE

Mountain State University, founded in 1933, is a private institution committed to the academic pursuits of instruction, scholarship, and public service. It offers undergraduate programs in business administration, legal and strategical leadership studies, nursing, allied health professions, and social work. There are 4 undergraduate schools and 1 graduate school. In addition to regional accreditation, MSU has baccalaureate program accreditation with APTA, CAAHEP, CAHEA, CSWE, IACBE, and NLN. The library contains 94,899 volumes, 14,160 microform items, and 3652 audio/video tapes/CDs, and subscribes to 198 periodicals. Computerized library services include the card catalog, interlibrary loans, database searching, and Internet access. Special learning facilities include a learning resource center, an audiovisual lab, media classroom, gross anatomy lab, and a tiered fully technology-equipped classroom. The 12-acre campus is in a small town about 50 miles south of Charleston. Including any residence halls, there are 22 buildings.

Student Life: 85% of undergraduates are from West Virginia. Students are from 43 states, 42 foreign countries, and Canada. 86% are white. The average age of freshmen is 30; all undergraduates, 31.

Housing: 130 students can be accommodated in college housing, which includes coed dorms and off-campus apartments. In addition, there is housing for athletes. On-campus housing is guaranteed for the freshman year only and is available on a first-come, first-served basis. 99% of students commute. Alcohol is not permitted. All students may keep cars.

Activities: There are no fraternities or sororities. There are 15 groups on campus, including cheerleading, ethnic, gay, honors, international, literary magazine, professional, religious, SGA Newsletter, social, social service, and student government. Popular campus events include Appalachian Vision series, Business and Technology show, and Performing Arts Series.

Sports: There is 1 intercollegiate sport for men and 2 for women, and 7 intramural sports for men and 4 for women. Facilities include a pool, a track, racquetball courts, exercise equipment, and an aerobics area. All MSU students receive a membership in the local YMCA.

Disabled Students: 75% of the campus is accessible. Wheelchair ramps, elevators, special parking, specially equipped rest rooms, special class scheduling, lowered drinking fountains, lowered telephones, and electronic door-opening mechanisms are available.

Services: Counseling and information services are available, as is tutoring in most subjects. There is a reader service for the blind and remedial math and writing.

Campus Safety and Security: Measures include 24-hour foot and vehicle patrol, security escort services, informal discussions, and pamphlets/posters/films. There are emergency telephones and lighted pathways/sidewalks.

Programs of Study: MSU confers B.A., B.S., B.S.N., and B.S.W. degrees. Associate and master's degrees are also awarded. Bachelor's degrees are awarded in AGRICULTURE (environmental studies), BIOLOGICAL SCIENCE (biology/biological science and ecology), BUSINESS (accounting, banking and finance, business administration and management, electronic business, entrepreneurial studies, hotel/motel and restaurant management, marketing and distribution, organizational behavior, recreation and leisure services, and sports management), COMMUNICATIONS AND THE ARTS (communications and English literature), COMPUTER AND PHYSICAL SCIENCE (computer science), EDUCATION (health), ENGINEERING AND ENVIRONMENTAL DESIGN (aviation administration/management and computer technology), HEALTH PROFESSIONS (health care administration, nursing, physician's assistant, respiratory therapy, and ultrasound technology), SOCIAL SCIENCE (criminal justice, forensic studies, humanities, interdisciplinary studies, law, psychology, public administration, and social work). Nursing, physician assistant, and diagnostic medical are the strongest academically. Nursing, criminal justice, and business are the largest.

Required: Requirements for graduation are a 2.0 GPA overall and 128 or 129 semester hours. All students must complete 36 hours of general studies and a minimum of 93 in the major.

Special: There are co-op programs in business administration and engineering, and cross-registration with West Virginia University. Internships and a degree completion program are available, and B.A.-B.S. degrees and student-designed majors are offered in interdisciplinary studies. There are 5 national honor societies.

Faculty/Classroom: 30% of faculty are male; 70%, female. All teach undergraduates, 15% do research, and 15% do both. The average class size in an introductory lecture is 30 and in a laboratory, 25.

Admissions: The SAT I scores for the 2003-2004 freshman class were: Verbal--60% below 500, 30% between 500 and 599, and 10% between 600 and 700; Math--60% below 500, 20% between 500 and 599, and 20% between 600 and 700. The ACT scores were 78% below 21, 16% between 21 and 23, 5% between 24 and 26, and 1% above 28. 10% of the current freshmen were in the top fifth of their class; 25% were in the top two fifths.

Requirements: The SAT I or ACT is recommended for placement only. The GED is accepted. AP and CLEP credits are accepted. Important factors in the admissions decision are recommendations by school officials, parents or siblings attending the school, and ability to finance college education.

Procedure: Freshmen are admitted to all sessions. Entrance exams should be taken any time prior to application. There are rolling and deferred admissions plans. Application deadlines are open. The fall 2003 application fee was $25. Applications are accepted on-line.

Transfer: 171 transfer students enrolled in a recent year. Applicants must submit official transcripts from all colleges attended. 12 of 128 credits required for the bachelor's degree must be completed at MSU.

Visiting: There are regularly scheduled orientations for prospective students, including a campus tour, registration, financial aid information, and housing and meal plan sign-ups. There are guides for informal visits and visitors may sit in on classes and stay overnight. To schedule a visit, contact the Admissions Department at (304) 253-7351 ext. 1433 or dbrown@mountainstate.edu.

Financial Aid: In 2003-2004, 73% of all full-time freshmen received some form of financial aid. 62% of full-time freshmen received need-based aid. 1% of undergraduates work part time. Average annual earnings from campus work are $1700. The FAFSA and the college's own financial statement are required. The deadline for filing freshman financial aid applications for fall entry is May 1.

International Students: There are 83 international students enrolled. The school actively recruits these students. They must score 500 on the written TOEFL. The ACT is recommended for placement.

Computers: There are computer labs available on campus with Internet access. All students may access the system when school is in session. There are no time limits and no fees.

Graduates: From July 1, 2002 to June 30, 2003, 403 bachelor's degrees were awarded. The most popular majors were business (42%), interdisciplinary studies (14%), and nursing (10%).

Admissions Contact: Tammy Toney, Director of Admissions. A video is available. E-mail: ttoney@mountainstate.edu
Web: http://mountainstate.edu

OHIO VALLEY COLLEGE
B-3
Vienna, WV 26105
(304) 865-6202
(877) 446-8668; Fax: (304) 865-6001

Full-time: 214 men, 185 women	Faculty: 21
Part-time: 7 men, 10 women	Ph.D.s: 75%
Graduate: none	Student/Faculty: 19 to 1
Year: semesters	Tuition: $10,676
Application Deadline: open	Room & Board: $5360
Freshman Class: 445 applied, 210 accepted, 105 enrolled	
SAT I Verbal/Math: 510/480	ACT: 20 COMPETITIVE+

Ohio Valley College, founded in 1960, is a liberal arts institution affiliated with the Church of Christ. Some information in this capsule and profile is approximate. The library contains 31,750 volumes, 51,530 microform items, and 2946 audio/video tapes/CDs, and subscribes to 165 periodicals. Computerized library services include the card catalog, interlibrary loans, and database searching. Special learning facilities include a learning resource center. The 270-acre campus is in a suburban area 120 miles southwest of Pittsburgh. Including any residence halls, there are 9 buildings.

Student Life: 53% of undergraduates are from out of state, mostly the Midwest. Students are from 23 states, 13 foreign countries, and Canada. 97% are from public schools. 87% are white. Most are Protestant. The average age of freshmen is 18; all undergraduates, 21. 55% do not continue beyond their first year; 25% remain to graduate.

Housing: 500 students can be accommodated in college housing, which includes single-sex dorms, on-campus apartments, and married-student housing. On-campus housing is guaranteed for all 4 years. 60% of students commute. Alcohol is not permitted. All students may keep cars.

Activities: There are no fraternities or sororities. There are 16 groups on campus, including band, cheerleading, choir, chorale, chorus, drama, jazz band, newspaper, pep band, religious, social, student government, and yearbook. Popular campus events include Expressions, a school-wide musical review.

Sports: There are 5 intercollegiate sports for men and 4 for women, and 11 intramural sports for men and 10 for women. Facilities include a weight room, a student union with recreation facilities, an activity center, and 2 gyms.

Disabled Students: 30% of the campus is accessible. Wheelchair ramps, elevators, special parking, specially equipped rest rooms, special class scheduling, and lowered telephones are available.

Services: Counseling and information services are available, as is tutoring in most subjects. There is remedial math, reading, and writing.

Campus Safety and Security: Measures include 24-hour foot and vehicle patrol and shuttle buses.

Programs of Study: Ohio Valley confers B.A. and B.S. degrees. Associate degrees are also awarded. Bachelor's degrees are awarded in BUSINESS (accounting, business administration and management, and human resources), EDUCATION (elementary and secondary), SOCIAL SCIENCE (biblical studies, liberal arts/general studies, psychology, and religion). Business is the strongest academically. Elementary education is the largest.

Required: To graduate, students must complete 128 credit hours, including 53 to 60 in the major, with a minimum GPA of 2.0. General requirements include 4 courses of Bible studies, 2 of English composition, 1 to 2 of history, and 1 each of speech, computer literacy, math, and social science. There is also a phys ed requirement. Students must attend chapel daily and take 1 Bible class each semester.

Special: Ohio Valley offers internships with churches for student ministers. Summer study in London or Israel is possible. There is 1 departmental honors program.

Faculty/Classroom: 64% of faculty are male; 36%, female. All teach undergraduates. The average class size in an introductory lecture is 30; in a laboratory, 20; and in a regular course, 15.

Admissions: 47% of the 2003-2004 applicants were accepted. The SAT I scores for the 2003-2004 freshman class were: Verbal--59% below 500, 28% between 500 and 599, 10% between 600 and 700, and 3% above 700; Math--45% below 500, 48% between 500 and 599, and 7% between 600 and 700. The ACT scores were 57% below 21, 29% between 21 and 23, 9% between 24 and 26, 3% between 27 and 28, and 2% above 28. 20% of the current freshmen were in the top fifth of their class; 43% were in the top two fifths.

Requirements: The ACT is required. In addition, applicants should be graduates of an accredited secondary school or have earned a GED. A GPA of 2.0 is required. AP and CLEP credits are accepted. Important factors in the admissions decision are recommendations by school officials, personality/intangible qualities, and leadership record.

Procedure: Freshmen are admitted fall and spring. Entrance exams should be taken during the senior year. There is an early admissions plan and a rolling admissions plan. Application deadlines are open. Check with the school for current application fee. Notification is sent on a rolling basis. Applications are accepted on-line at www.ovc.edu.

Transfer: 60 transfer students enrolled in a recent year. Transfer applicants must provide high school, college, and financial aid transcripts, and test scores. 32 credits of 128 required for the bachelor's degree must be completed at Ohio Valley.

Visiting: There are guides for informal visits and visitors may sit in on classes and stay overnight. To schedule a visit, contact the Office of Admissions.

Financial Aid: In 2003-2004, 95% of all full-time freshmen and 98% of continuing full-time students received some form of financial aid. 70% of full-time freshmen and 65% of continuing full-time students received need-based aid. The average freshman award was $15,300. Need-based scholarships or need-based grants averaged $3423 ($4050 maximum); need-based self-help aid (loans and jobs) averaged $3650 ($5500 maximum); non-need-based athletic scholarships averaged $3338 ($16,796 maximum); and other non-need-based awards and non-need-based scholarships averaged $3127 ($15,000 maximum). 44% of undergraduates work part time. Average annual earnings from campus work are $800. The average financial indebtedness of a recent graduate was $16,800. Ohio Valley is a member of CSS. The FAFSA is required. Check with the school for current deadlines.

International Students: There were 22 international students enrolled in a recent year. The school actively recruits these students. They must score 420 on the written TOEFL and also take the ACT, scoring 16.

Computers: The mainframe is a DEC Alpha server 300. There are PCs available in the library and the computer science lab. All students may access the system. There are no time limits and no fees.

Graduates: In a recent year, 51 bachelor's degrees were awarded. The most popular majors were business (33%), education (13%), and psychology (11%). In an average class, 18% graduate in 4 years or less, 26% graduate in 5 years or less, and 27% graduate in 6 years or less.

Admissions Contact: Rob E. Dudley, Director of Admissions. A video is available. E-mail: *admissions@ovc.edu* Web: *ovc.edu*

SALEM INTERNATIONAL UNIVERSITY
Salem, WV 26426 — C-3

(304) 782-5336
(800) 283-4562; Fax: (304) 782-5592

Full-time: 163 men, 173 women	**Faculty:** 26; IIB, --$
Part-time: 5 men, 2 women	**Ph.D.s:** 88%
Graduate: 50 men, 91 women	**Student/Faculty:** 13 to 1
Year: multimodular terms, summer session	**Tuition:** $14,985
	Room & Board: $4785
Application Deadline: open	
Freshman Class: n/av	
SAT I Verbal/Math: 466/480	**ACT:** 21 — COMPETITIVE

Salem International University, founded in 1888, is a private institution offering both liberal arts and career-oriented degree programs, including international business, biotechnology, Japanese studies, equine careers, and industry management. In addition to regional accreditation, SIU has baccalaureate program accreditation with ACBSP. The library contains 105,437 volumes, 284,302 microform items, and 974 audio/video tapes/CDs, and subscribes to 94 periodicals. Computerized library services include the card catalog, interlibrary loans, and database searching. Special learning facilities include a learning resource center, art gallery, radio station, TV station, Fort New Salem (an 1800s settlement), an equestrian center, and a greenhouse. The 300-acre campus is in a rural area 120 miles south of Pittsburgh, Pennsylvania. Including any residence halls, there are 19 buildings.

Student Life: 69% of undergraduates are from out of state, mostly the Middle Atlantic. Students are from 34 states, 26 foreign countries, and Canada. 53% are white; 22% foreign nationals. The average age of freshmen is 19; all undergraduates, 21. 37% do not continue beyond their first year; 51% remain to graduate.

Housing: 550 students can be accommodated in college housing, which includes single-sex and coed dorms. In addition, there are honors houses and special-interest houses. On-campus housing is guaranteed for all 4 years. 90% of students live on campus; of those, 75% remain on campus on weekends. All students may keep cars.

Activities: 10% of men belong to 2 local fraternities; 12% of women belong to 3 local sororities. There are 25 groups on campus, including cheerleading, ethnic, gay, honors, international, newspaper, professional, radio and TV, religious, social, social service, student government, and yearbook. Popular campus events include Winterfest, Spring Arts Series, and Spring Fling.

Sports: There are 6 intercollegiate sports for men and 6 for women, and 12 intramural sports for men and 12 for women. Facilities include a gym, a pool, a weight room, tennis courts, a soccer stadium, a fitness trail, racquetball courts, and horseback-riding trails.

Disabled Students: 90% of the campus is accessible. Wheelchair ramps, elevators, special parking, specially equipped rest rooms, special class scheduling, and special wheelchair lifting equipment are available.

Services: Counseling and information services are available, as is tutoring in most subjects. Most classes have a tutoring option. There is a reader service for the blind and remedial math, reading, and writing.

Campus Safety and Security: Measures include 24-hour foot and vehicle patrol, security escort services, informal discussions, and pamphlets/posters/films. There are emergency telephones, lighted pathways/sidewalks, and Dial-a-Ride on weekends.

Programs of Study: SIU confers B.A. and B.S. degrees. Associate and master's degrees are also awarded. Bachelor's degrees are awarded in AGRICULTURE (equine science), BIOLOGICAL SCIENCE (biology/biological science and molecular biology), BUSINESS (business administration and management and sports management), COMMUNICATIONS AND THE ARTS (communications and English as a second/foreign language), COMPUTER AND PHYSICAL SCIENCE (computer mathematics and information sciences and systems), EDUCATION (athletic training, elementary, and secondary), ENGINEERING AND ENVIRONMENTAL DESIGN (aviation administration/management and environmental science), SOCIAL SCIENCE (criminal justice, human services, Japanese studies, and liberal arts/general studies). Molecular biology and Japanese studies are the strongest academically. Management studies, equine, and criminal justice are the largest.

Required: All students must take 57 hours in the core curriculum, including courses in communication skills, humanities, science/math, social studies, psychology, and health and phys ed. A minimum 2.0 GPA overall, with a minimum 2.25 GPA in the major, and 128 credit hours are required to graduate.

Special: A student may cross-register with another college within the Mountain State Association of Colleges. Many internships are available. Study abroad is offered. Dual majors, credit by exam, and credit for life experience may be arranged. There are 2 national honor societies.

Faculty/Classroom: 54% of faculty are male; 46%, female. All both teach and do research. No introductory courses are taught by graduate students. The average class size in an introductory lecture is 25; in a laboratory, 10; and in a regular course, 14.

Admissions: The SAT I scores for the 2003-2004 freshman class were: Verbal--56% below 500, 35% between 500 and 599, and 9% between 600 and 700; Math--56% below 500, 41% between 500 and 599, and 3% between 600 and 700. The ACT scores were 51% below 21, 29% between 21 and 23, 18% between 24 and 26, and 2% between 27 and 28. 11% of the current freshmen were in the top fifth of their class; 18% were in the top two fifths.

Requirements: The SAT I or ACT is required. In addition, applicants should be graduates of an accredited secondary school with 15 academic courses, including 4 in English, 3 each in math, science, and social studies, and 2 in a foreign language. A GPA of 2.0 is required. AP and CLEP credits are accepted. Important factors in the admissions decision are advanced placement or honors courses, evidence of special talent, and extracurricular activities record.

Procedure: Freshmen are admitted to all sessions. Entrance exams should be taken in the junior year or fall of the senior year. There are rolling and deferred admissions plans. Application deadlines are open. Application fee is $25. Applications are accepted on-line through the school's web site.

Transfer: 43 transfer students enrolled in 2002-2003. A minimum GPA of 2.0 is required for acceptance as a transfer student. 32 of 128 credits required for the bachelor's degree must be completed at SIU.

Visiting: There are regularly scheduled orientations for prospective students, consisting of meetings with academic and administrative department heads, tours, question-and-answer sessions, and a reception. There are guides for informal visits and visitors may sit in on classes and stay overnight. To schedule a visit, contact the Admissions Office at (800) 283-4562, ext. 336.

Financial Aid: In 2003-2004, 97% of all full-time freshmen and 99% of continuing full-time students received some form of financial aid. 79% of full-time freshmen and 74% of continuing full-time students received need-based aid. The average freshman award was $17,579. Need-based scholarships or need-based grants averaged $6912 ($12,662 maximum); need-based self-help aid (loans and jobs) averaged $5430 ($11,290 maximum); non-need-based athletic scholarships averaged $5213 ($10,085 maximum); and other non-need-based awards and non-need-based scholarships averaged $8815 ($19,219 maximum). 34% of undergraduates work part time. Average annual earnings from campus work are $1450. The average financial indebtedness of the 2003 graduate was $18,228. SIU is a member of CSS. The FAFSA is required. The deadline for filing freshman financial aid applications for fall entry is July 15.

International Students: There are 77 international students enrolled. The school actively recruits these students.

Computers: The mainframes are a Digital 6000-620 and 6000-640. Computers are available for student use in labs throughout the campus, and Internet access is provided in each building. All students may access the system. There are no time limits. The fee is $40. It is strongly recommended that all students have a personal computer.

Graduates: From July 1, 2002 to June 30, 2003, 93 bachelor's degrees were awarded. The most popular majors were criminal justice (14%), equine (9%), and molecular bio/biotechnology (6%). In an average class, 47% graduate in 6 years or less.

Admissions Contact: Todd Breland, Director of Admissions.
E-mail: *admissions@salemiu.edu* Web: *www.salemiu.edu*

SHEPHERD COLLEGE
Shepherdstown, WV 25443-3210

E-2

(304) 876-5212
(800) 344-5231; Fax: (304) 876-5165

Full-time: 1376 men, 1756 women	**Faculty:** 102
Part-time: 567 men, 1105 women	**Ph.D.s:** 81%
Graduate: 9 men, 18 women	**Student/Faculty:** 31 to 1
Year: semesters, summer session	**Tuition:** $3270 ($8030)
Application Deadline: February 1	**Room & Board:** $5338
Freshman Class: 1061 applied, 948 accepted, 845 enrolled	
SAT I Verbal/Math: 510/500	**ACT:** 20	**COMPETITIVE**

Shepherd College, founded in 1871, is a state-supported institution offering programs in the liberal and creative arts, business administration, teacher education, social and natural sciences, health fields, and other career-oriented areas. There are 4 undergraduate schools. In addition to regional accreditation, Shepherd has baccalaureate program accreditation with CSWE, NASM, NCATE, and NLN. The library contains 182,404 volumes, 297,896 microform items, and 5049 audio/video tapes/CDs, and subscribes to 633 periodicals. Computerized library services include the card catalog, interlibrary loans, and database searching. Special learning facilities include an art gallery, radio station, nursery school, and 3 theaters. The 323-acre campus is in a small town 70 miles northwest of Washington, D.C., and Baltimore. Including any residence halls, there are 31 buildings.

Student Life: 67% of undergraduates are from West Virginia. Students are from 48 states and 30 foreign countries. 85% are from public schools. 91% are white. The average age of freshmen is 20; all undergraduates, 24. 32% do not continue beyond their first year; 42% remain to graduate.

Housing: 1000 students can be accommodated in college housing, which includes coed dorms and on-campus apartments. In addition, there are honors houses and special-interest houses. On-campus housing is guaranteed for all 4 years. 75% of students commute. All students may keep cars.

Activities: 2% of men belong to 4 national fraternities; 3% of women belong to 3 national sororities. There are 59 groups on campus, including art, band, cheerleading, choir, chorale, chorus, computers, debate, drama, drill team, ethnic, forensics, gay, honors, international, jazz band, literary magazine, marching band, musical theater, newspaper, orchestra, pep band, political, professional, radio and TV, religious, social, social service, and student government. Popular campus events include Family Day, Shepfest, and Midnight Breakfast.

Sports: There are 7 intercollegiate sports for men and 6 for women, and 10 intramural sports for men and 10 for women. Facilities include a 5000-seat football and soccer field, baseball and softball fields, a 3000-seat gym, 3 outdoor and 2 indoor tennis courts, 2 outdoor sand volleyball courts, a fitness/wellness center, and a swimming pool.

Disabled Students: 95% of the campus is accessible. Wheelchair ramps, elevators, special parking, specially equipped rest rooms, special class scheduling, lowered drinking fountains, lowered telephones, and automatic door openers are available.

Services: Counseling and information services are available, as is tutoring in most subjects. There is a reader service for the blind and remedial math, reading, and writing. There also is tutorial assistance for learning-disabled students and peer assistance for physically disabled students.

Campus Safety and Security: Measures include 24-hour foot and vehicle patrol, self-defense education, security escort services, and shuttle buses. There are informal discussions, pamphlets/posters/films, emergency telephones, and lighted pathways/sidewalks.

Programs of Study: Shepherd confers B.A., B.S., B.F.A, B.S.N., and B.S.W. degrees. Associate and master's degrees are also awarded. Bachelor's degrees are awarded in BIOLOGICAL SCIENCE (biology/biological science), BUSINESS (accounting, business administration and management, hospitality management services, recreation and leisure services, and sports management), COMMUNICATIONS AND THE ARTS (art, communications, English, graphic design, music, music performance, music theory and composition, painting, photography, printmaking, and sculpture), COMPUTER AND PHYSICAL SCIENCE (chemistry, computer science, information sciences and systems, and mathematics), EDUCATION (art, elementary, English, health, home economics, mathematics, music, physical, science, secondary, and social studies), ENGINEERING AND ENVIRONMENTAL DESIGN (environmental science), HEALTH PROFESSIONS (nursing and recreation therapy), SOCIAL SCIENCE (economics, family/consumer studies, history, physical fitness/movement, political science/government, psychology, social work, and sociology). Business, science, and art are the strongest academically. Education, business, and recreation are the largest.

Required: To graduate, students must complete 128 semester hours with a 2.0 GPA overall and in the major and minor fields. The general studies core totals 47 hours, including 19 of humanities, 15 of social sciences, 8 of life or physical science, 3 of math, and 2 of phys ed. B.A. candidates (except for education majors) must demonstrate foreign language proficiency through course work or exam.

Special: Shepherd offers study abroad, a B.A.-B.S. degree in mass communications, and a 2-2 program in engineering. Internships and co-op programs are available in most majors. There is a Washington semester, and dual majors are possible in any two majors. Credit by exam, life experience credentialing through the Regents degree, nondegree study, and pass/fail options for electives are offered. There are 9 national honor societies, a freshman honors program, and 20 departmental honors programs.

Faculty/Classroom: All teach undergraduates and 10% both teach and do research. No introductory courses are taught by graduate students. The average class size in an introductory lecture is 30; in a laboratory, 24; and in a regular course, 19.

Admissions: 89% of the 2003-2004 applicants were accepted. The SAT I scores for the 2003-2004 freshman class were: Verbal--43% below 500, 44% between 500 and 599, 13% between 600 and 700, and 3% above 700; Math--45% below 500, 44% between 500 and 599, and 9% between 600 and 700. The ACT scores were 52% below 21, 26% between 21 and 23, 14% between 24 and 26, 5% between 27 and 28, and 2% above 28. 50 freshmen graduated first in their class.

Requirements: The SAT I or ACT is required, with a minimum composite score of 1000 on the SAT I or 21 on the ACT. Applicants should be graduates of an accredited secondary school and have earned academic credits, including 4 in English, 3 in social science (1 in American history), 2 each in lab science and math, 1 in phys ed, and the rest in computer, foreign language, and other academic electives. The GED is accepted. A GPA of 2.5 is required. AP and CLEP credits are accepted. Important factors in the admissions decision are advanced placement or honor courses, leadership record, and extracurricular activities record.

Procedure: Freshmen are admitted fall, spring, and summer. Entrance exams should be taken during the junior year. There is a rolling admissions plan. There are early action, early admissions, and deferred admissions plans. Early action applications should be filed by November 15; regular applications, by February 1 for fall entry, November 1 for spring entry, and February 1 for summer entry, along with a $35 fee. Notification of early action is sent December 15; regular decision, on a rolling basis. Applications are accepted on-line.

Transfer: 362 transfer students enrolled in 2002-2003. Applicants must have a 2.0 cumulative GPA in a minimum of 15 semester hours completed and must submit 2 transcripts from each college attended. 32 of 128 credits required for the bachelor's degree must be completed at Shepherd.

Visiting: There are regularly scheduled orientations for prospective students, consisting of 3 fall open houses and 2 spring open houses, 2 spring information Saturdays, and weekday information sessions and campus tours by appointment. There are guides for informal visits and visitors may sit in on classes. To schedule a visit, contact the Admissions Office at (800) 344-5231 or admoff@shepherd.edu.

Financial Aid: In 2003-2004, 50% of all full-time freshmen and 48% of continuing full-time students received some form of financial aid. 30% of full-time freshmen and 37% of continuing full-time students received need-based aid. The average freshman award was $5994. Need-based scholarships or need-based grants averaged $1500 ($14,894 maximum); need-based self-help aid (loans and jobs) averaged $1939 ($10,500 maximum); and non-need-based athletic scholarships averaged $2568 ($7330 maximum). 70% of undergraduates work part time. Average annual earnings from campus work are $1500. The average financial indebtedness of the 2003 graduate was $13,981. The FAFSA is required. The priority date for freshman financial aid applications for fall entry is March 1.

International Students: There are 44 international students enrolled. The school actively recruits these students. They must score 550 on the written TOEFL or 213 on the electronic version and also take the SAT I or the ACT, scoring 970 (SAT I) or 20 (ACT).

Computers: The mainframe is a Compaq AlphaServer DS20. There are 75 PCs in general-use labs and in 125 separate education, biology, chemistry, CIS, English writing, art, and music labs. All students may access the system weekdays from 8 A.M. to 11 P.M. There are no time limits and no fees.

Graduates: From July 1, 2002 to June 30, 2003, 513 bachelor's degrees were awarded. The most popular majors were business administration (10%), secondary education (10%), and elementary education (9%). In an average class, 18% graduate in 4 years or less, 35% graduate in 5 years or less, and 41% graduate in 6 years or less. Of a recent graduating class, 12% were enrolled in graduate school within 6 months of graduation and 90% were employed.

Admissions Contact: Karl L. Wolf, Director of Admissions. A video is available. E-mail: kwolf@shepherd.edu Web: www.shepherd.edu

UNIVERSITY OF CHARLESTON
Charleston, WV 25304

B-4
(304) 357-4750
(800) 995-4682; Fax: (304) 357-4781

Full-time: 325 men, 572 women	**Faculty:** 61; IIB, --$
Part-time: 42 men, 102 women	**Ph.D.s:** 39%
Graduate: 12 men, 25 women	**Student/Faculty:** 10 to 1
Year: semesters, summer session	**Tuition:** $17,400
Application Deadline: open	**Room & Board:** $6220
Freshman Class: 1160 applied, 724 accepted, 201 enrolled	
SAT I or ACT: required	**COMPETITIVE**

The University of Charleston, founded in 1888, is a private liberal arts institution offering programs in business and the health sciences, as well as traditional arts and sciences. In addition to regional accreditation, UC has baccalaureate program accreditation with AHEA, CAHEA, NCATE, and NLN. The library contains 118,779 volumes, 217,778 microform items, and 3387 audio/video tapes/CDs, and subscribes to 7000 periodicals. Computerized library services include the card catalog, interlibrary loans, database searching, and Internet access. Special learning facilities include a learning resource center and art gallery. The 40-acre campus is in an urban area in Charleston. Including any residence halls, there are 11 buildings.

Student Life: 68% of undergraduates are from West Virginia. Students are from Canada. 54% are white. The average age of freshmen is 19; all undergraduates, 24.

Housing: 482 students can be accommodated in college housing, which includes coed dorms. On-campus housing is guaranteed for all 4 years. 56% of students commute. All students may keep cars.

Activities: 9% of men belong to 2 national fraternities; 8% of women belong to 3 local sororities. There are 45 groups on campus, including art, cheerleading, choir, chorus, drama, ethnic, honors, international, literary magazine, musical theater, newspaper, pep band, political, professional, religious, social, social service, student government, and yearbook. Popular campus events include the Holiday Dinner served by faculty, the Governor's Cup Regatta, and World Fest.

Sports: There are 10 intercollegiate sports for men and 9 for women, and 6 intramural sports for men and 7 for women. Facilities include a gym, a game room, a Nautilus center, an indoor pool, soccer, softball, and baseball fields, and racquetball, volleyball, and tennis courts.

Disabled Students: 77% of the campus is accessible. Wheelchair ramps, elevators, special parking, specially equipped rest rooms, lowered drinking fountains, lowered telephones, and special housing are available.

Services: Counseling and information services are available, as is tutoring in some subjects, including math, English, and sciences. There is remedial math, reading, and writing.

Campus Safety and Security: Measures include 24-hour foot and vehicle patrol, self-defense education, security escort services, and shuttle buses. There are informal discussions, pamphlets/posters/films, emergency telephones, lighted pathways/sidewalks, burglar alarms in dorms, safety and date-rape seminars, drug awareness programs, surveillance cameras at dorms (used in conjunction with card access), and emergency radio communications.

Programs of Study: UC confers B.A., B.S., and B.S.N. degrees. Associate and master's degrees are also awarded. Bachelor's degrees are awarded in BIOLOGICAL SCIENCE (biology/biological science), BUSINESS (accounting, banking and finance, business administration and management, entrepreneurial studies, and sports management), COMMUNICATIONS AND THE ARTS (art, communications, English, music, and music business management), COMPUTER AND PHYSICAL SCIENCE (chemistry and information sciences and systems), EDUCATION (elementary, English, music, physical, science, and social studies), ENGINEERING AND ENVIRONMENTAL DESIGN (environmental science and interior design), HEALTH PROFESSIONS (nursing, radiological science, and sports medicine), SOCIAL SCIENCE (history, liberal arts/general studies, political science/government, and psychology). Environmental science, education and business are the strongest academically. Business and health sciences are the largest.

Required: All students must fulfill the general education program requirements, which include 48 hours of courses in English, computer systems, social sciences, humanities, natural science, health or phys ed, and elective options. A total of 120 to 128 credit hours and a GPA of 2.0 are required for graduation. A comprehensive exam also is required.

Special: The university offers credit by exam and credit for prior learning. A general studies degree, student-designed majors, nondegree study, an accelerated degree program in business administration, and pass-fail options are available. Internships, on-campus work-study, hospital clinical experience in qualified programs, a dual major in biology/chemistry, and a Washington semester are offered. There are 6 national honor societies.

Faculty/Classroom: 41% of faculty are male; 59%, female. All teach undergraduates, 20% do research, and 20% do both. No introductory courses are taught by graduate students. The average class size in an introductory lecture is 17; in a laboratory, 23; and in a regular course, 15.

Admissions: 62% of the 2003-2004 applicants were accepted. 35% of the current freshmen were in the top fifth of their class; 72% were in the top two fifths.

Requirements: The SAT I or ACT is required. In addition, applicants should have a minimum academic GPA of 2.25 on a 4.0 scale and be in the upper 50% of their class, with a minimum composite score of 900 on the SAT I or 19 on the ACT for automatic admission. Applicants should be graduates of an accredited secondary school or have the GED and have taken 15 academic courses. AP and CLEP credits are accepted. Important factors in the admissions decision are advanced placement or honor courses, leadership record, and extracurricular activities record.

Procedure: Freshmen are admitted to all sessions. Entrance exams should be taken by December of the senior year. There is a rolling admissions plan. There are early decision and early admissions plans. Early decision applications should be filed by February 15; regular applications are open for fall entry. The application fee is $25. Notification is sent on a rolling basis. 120 early decision candidates were accepted for the 2003-2004 class. Applications are accepted on-line through the university's web site.

Transfer: 132 transfer students enrolled in 2002-2003. Applicants should have a minimum GPA of 2.25. 30 of 120 credits required for the bachelor's degree must be completed at UC.

Visiting: There are regularly scheduled orientations for prospective students, including meetings with faculty, financial aid and student life information sessions, a campus tour, and lunch. There are guides for informal visits and visitors may sit in on classes and stay overnight. To schedule a visit, contact the Admissions Office at admissions@ucwv.edu.

Financial Aid: In a recent year, 95% of all full-time freshmen and 88% of continuing full-time students received some form of financial aid. 92% of full-time freshmen and 80% of continuing full-time students received need-based aid. The average freshman award in 2003-2004 was $18,642. Need-based scholarships or need-based grants averaged $1000 ($5000 maximum); need-based self-help aid (loans and jobs) averaged $1000 ($9125 maximum); non-need-based athletic scholarships averaged $1000 ($24,290 maximum); and other non-need-based awards and non-need-based scholarships averaged $1000 ($17,400 maximum). 25% of undergraduates work part time. Average annual earnings from campus work are $975. The average financial indebtedness of a recent graduate was $18,300. UC is a member of CSS. The FAFSA, the college's own financial statement, and income tax returns are required. The priority date for freshman financial aid applications for fall entry is March 1. The deadline for filing freshman financial aid applications for fall entry is August 15.

International Students: There are 39 international students enrolled. The school actively recruits these students. They must score 500 on the written TOEFL or 173 on the electronic version. The SAT I or ACT is required of students from English-speaking countries, with a minimum score of 900 (SAT I) or 19 (ACT).

Computers: The mainframe is an HP 9000 K200. There are more than 80 PCs and Macs in computer labs for student use. There are also terminals and PCs with Internet access available in the library. All students may access the system. There is 24-hour dial-in availability. There are no time limits and no fees. It is strongly recommended that all students have a personal computer.

Graduates: From July 1, 2002 to June 30, 2003, 137 bachelor's degrees were awarded. The most popular majors were nursing (23%), business (12%), and radiologic science (8%). In an average class, 3% graduate in 3 years or less, 33% graduate in 4 years or less, 39% graduate in 5 years or less, and 41% graduate in 6 years or less. 63 companies recruited on campus in 2002-2003.

Admissions Contact: Kim Scranage, Director of Admissions.
E-mail: admissions@uchaswv.edu Web: www.uchaswv.edu

WEST LIBERTY STATE COLLEGE
West Liberty, WV 26074

C-1
(304) 336-8076
(800) 732-6204; Fax: (304) 336-8403

Full-time: 993 men, 1169 women	**Faculty:** 107; IIB, --$
Part-time: 132 men, 197 women	**Ph.D.s:** 46%
Graduate: 4 men, 16 women	**Student/Faculty:** 20 to 1
Year: semesters, summer session	**Tuition:** $3138 ($7790)
Application Deadline: August 1	**Room & Board:** $4730
Freshman Class: 1309 applied, 1120 accepted, 465 enrolled	
SAT I Verbal/Math: 452/436	**ACT:** 19 **LESS COMPETITIVE**

West Liberty State College, founded in 1837, is a state-assisted college offering programs in teacher education, liberal and fine arts, sciences, business, and preprofessional and technical fields. There are 4 undergraduate schools. In addition to regional accreditation, West Liberty has baccalaureate program accreditation with ADA, CAHEA, NASM, NCATE, and NLN. The library contains 196,338 volumes and 131,000 microform items, and subscribes to 485 periodicals. Computerized library services include the card catalog, interlibrary loans, and database searching. Special learning facilities include a learning resource center, art gallery, radio station, TV station, and a publication area. The 290-

acre campus is in a rural area 10 miles north of Wheeling and 56 miles southwest of Pittsburgh. Including any residence halls, there are 22 buildings.

Student Life: 72% of undergraduates are from West Virginia. Students are from 21 states, 9 foreign countries, and Canada. 90% are from public schools. 95% are white. The average age of freshmen is 18; all undergraduates, 22. 30% do not continue beyond their first year; 43% remain to graduate.

Housing: College housing includes single-sex and coed dorms, on-campus apartments, and married-student housing. In addition, there are honors houses and an honors dorm. On-campus housing is available on a first-come, first-served basis. 55% of students commute. Alcohol is not permitted. All students may keep cars.

Activities: 6% of men belong to 4 local fraternities; 10% of women belong to 1 local and 3 national sororities. There are 48 groups on campus, including art, cheerleading, choir, chorus, drama, ethnic, honors, hospitality, jazz band, literary magazine, marching band, musical theater, newspaper, pep band, photography, professional, radio and TV, religious, social, social service, steel drum band, student government, and tourism. Popular campus events include Multi-Cultural Day, Greek Week, and Spring Fling.

Sports: There are 8 intercollegiate sports for men and 7 for women, and 8 intramural sports for men and 7 for women. Facilities include handball and racquetball courts, training rooms, 3 gyms, an indoor track, a wellness center, and an indoor swimming pool. There is also a game area with pool tables and table tennis, 8 all-weather-surface tennis courts, and football and softball/baseball fields.

Disabled Students: 90% of the campus is accessible. Wheelchair ramps, elevators, special parking, specially equipped rest rooms, lowered drinking fountains, and lowered telephones are available.

Services: Counseling and information services are available, as is tutoring in every subject. There is a reader service for the blind and remedial math and writing.

Campus Safety and Security: Measures include 24-hour foot and vehicle patrol, self-defense education, security escort services, and informal discussions. There are pamphlets/posters/films, emergency telephones, lighted pathways/sidewalks, and late night transport.

Programs of Study: West Liberty confers B.A., B.S., and B.S.N. degrees. Associate degrees are also awarded. Bachelor's degrees are awarded in BIOLOGICAL SCIENCE (biology/biological science), BUSINESS (accounting, banking and finance, business administration and management, business economics, management science, marketing/retailing/merchandising, and tourism), COMMUNICATIONS AND THE ARTS (communications, English, fine arts, graphic design, and music), COMPUTER AND PHYSICAL SCIENCE (chemistry, information sciences and systems, and mathematics), EDUCATION (art, early childhood, elementary, health, middle school, music, physical, science, secondary, and special), ENGINEERING AND ENVIRONMENTAL DESIGN (preengineering), HEALTH PROFESSIONS (clinical science, dental hygiene, nursing, predentistry, premedicine, prepharmacy, and speech pathology/audiology), SOCIAL SCIENCE (criminal justice, economics, history, interdisciplinary studies, physical fitness/movement, political science/government, prelaw, psychology, social science, and sociology). Business, natural sciences, and health sciences are the strongest academically. Business, elementary education, and criminal justice are the largest.

Required: The required core curriculum varies for B.A. and B.S. candidates, but both include courses in communications, fine arts and humanities, natural science and math, social science and history, and phys ed and health. A minimum GPA of 2.0 and 128 credit hours are required to graduate.

Special: Communications, exercise physiology, criminal justice, hospitality, tourism management, sports management, and golf management require an on-campus internship. The Washington Center Program, an internship, is also offered. However, students may also choose to complete an internship in the areas of business, clinical lab science, phys ed, or nursing. Interdisciplinary studies is a student-designed degree taken as either a B.A. or B.S. Biology, chemistry, and math are offered as a B.S. degree but may also be taken as a B.A. degree in education. Work and life experience credit is accepted in the Regents B.A. degree program. There are 10 national honor societies, a freshman honors program, and 6 departmental honors programs.

Faculty/Classroom: 59% of faculty are male; 41%, female. All teach undergraduates. No introductory courses are taught by graduate students. The average class size in an introductory lecture is 25; in a laboratory, 20; and in a regular course, 20.

Admissions: 86% of the 2003-2004 applicants were accepted. The SAT I scores for the 2003-2004 freshman class were: Verbal--78% below 500, 12% between 500 and 599, and 10% between 600 and 700; Math--82% below 500, 14% between 500 and 599, and 4% between 600 and 700. The ACT scores were 36% between 12 and 17, 53% between 18 and 23, and 11% between 24 and 29. 24% of the current freshmen were in the top fifth of their class; 56% were in the top two fifths.

Requirements: The SAT I or ACT is required. In addition, applicants must graduate from an accredited secondary school with a minimum GPA of 2.0, or have a composite minimum score of 17 on the ACT or 810 on the SAT I. Students must have completed 4 years of English, 3 of social sciences, including U.S. history, 2 of math (algebra I and higher), and 2 of lab science. The GED is accepted. A GPA of 2.0 is required. AP and CLEP credits are accepted.

Procedure: Freshmen are admitted to all sessions. Entrance exams should be taken in time so that all admissions credentials, including test scores, are received 2 weeks prior to the beginning of the term. There is a deferred admissions plan and a rolling admissions plan. Applications should be filed by August 1 for fall entry and December 1 for spring entry. Notification is sent on a rolling basis. Applications are accepted online through the college's web site.

Transfer: 284 transfer students enrolled in a recent year. Students must be eligible to return to the institution from which they wish to transfer. An official college transcript and a minimum GPA of 2.0 overall are required. Admissions criteria are the same as for freshmen if the student has completed fewer than 28 hours of college-level course work. 36 of 128 credits required for the bachelor's degree must be completed at West Liberty.

Visiting: There are guides for informal visits and visitors may sit in on classes and stay overnight. To schedule a visit, contact the Office of Admissions.

Financial Aid: In a recent year, 85% of all full-time freshmen and 74% of continuing full-time students received some form of financial aid. 44% of full-time freshmen and 42% of continuing full-time students received need-based aid. The average freshman award was $5023. 99% of undergraduates work part time. Average annual earnings from campus work are $828. The average financial indebtedness of a recent graduate was $12,568. The FAFSA is required. The deadline for filing freshman financial aid applications for fall entry is March 1.

International Students: There are 13 international students enrolled. They must score 500 on the written TOEFL and also take the SAT I or the ACT, scoring 17.

Computers: The mainframe is a VAX 4700A. There are 300 PCs with access to the Internet and Web throughout the campus for student use. All students may access the system. There are no time limits and no fees. It is strongly recommended that all students have a personal computer.

Graduates: From July 1, 2002 to June 30, 2003, 427 bachelor's degrees were awarded. The most popular majors were education (33%), business administration (21%), and criminal justice (11%). In an average class, 19% graduate in 4 years or less, 37% graduate in 5 years or less, and 41% graduate in 6 years or less. 8 companies recruited on campus in a recent year. Of a recent graduating class, 10% were enrolled in graduate school within 6 months of graduation and 85% were employed.

Admissions Contact: Brenda King, Interim Director.
E-mail: *kingbren@wlsc.edu* Web: *www.wlsc.edu*

WEST VIRGINIA STATE COLLEGE   B-4
Institute, WV 25112-1000   (304) 766-3221
(800) 987-2112; Fax: (304) 766-5182

Full-time: 1325 men, 1600 women	**Faculty:** 150
Part-time: 665 men, 1245 women	**Ph.D.s:** 48%
Graduate: none	**Student/Faculty:** 19 to 1
Year: summer session	**Tuition:** $2465 ($5670)
Application Deadline: see profile	**Room & Board:** $3800
Freshman Class: n/av	
SAT I: recommended	**ACT:** required
	NONCOMPETITIVE

West Virginia State College, founded in 1891, is a state-supported institution offering broad programs in the arts and sciences and in preprofessional studies, including business and education. It also offers a comprehensive evening class schedule. Figures in the above capsule and in this profile are approximate. In addition to regional accreditation, State College has baccalaureate program accreditation with ABET, CSWE, NCATE, and NRPA. The library contains 28,295 volumes, 500,000 microform items, and 6184 audio/video tapes/CDs, and subscribes to 630 periodicals. Computerized library services include the card catalog, interlibrary loans, and database searching. Special learning facilities include a learning resource center, art gallery, and TV station. The 91-acre campus is in a suburban area 8 miles west of Charleston. Including any residence halls, there are 40 buildings.

Student Life: 94% of undergraduates are from West Virginia. Students are from 34 states and 8 foreign countries. 99% are from public schools. 84% are white; 14% African American. The average age of freshmen is 26; all undergraduates, 27. 30% do not continue beyond their first year; 64% remain to graduate.

Housing: 794 students can be accommodated in college housing, which includes single-sex dorms, on-campus apartments, and married-student housing. 93% of students commute. Alcohol is not permitted. All students may keep cars.

Activities: 1% of men belong to 1 local and 4 national fraternities; 1% of women belong to 3 national sororities. There are 42 groups on campus, including art, band, cheerleading, choir, chorale, chorus, drama, drill team, ethnic, film, honors, international, jazz band, literary magazine, newspaper, orchestra, pep band, photography, political, radio and TV, religious, social, social service, student government, and yearbook. Popular campus events include movies, comedy shows, and plays.

Sports: There are 5 intercollegiate sports for men and 4 for women, and 8 intramural sports for men and 7 for women. Facilities include a 6000-seat stadium, a swimming pool, a sports center, a 1500-seat gym, the student union, and a student mall/plaza.

Disabled Students: Wheelchair ramps, elevators, special parking, specially equipped rest rooms, special class scheduling, and lowered drinking fountains are available.

Services: Counseling and information services are available, as is tutoring in most subjects, including economics, political science, upper-division math, and accounting. There is remedial math, reading, and writing.

Campus Safety and Security: Measures include 24-hour foot and vehicle patrol, informal discussions, pamphlets/posters/films, and lighted pathways/sidewalks. There are formal educational sessions held in the dorms each semester.

Programs of Study: State College confers B.A., B.S., and B.S.Ed. degrees. Associate degrees are also awarded. Bachelor's degrees are awarded in BIOLOGICAL SCIENCE (biology/biological science), BUSINESS (accounting, banking and finance, business administration and management, and marketing/retailing/merchandising), COMMUNICATIONS AND THE ARTS (communications, English, and fine arts), COMPUTER AND PHYSICAL SCIENCE (applied mathematics, chemistry, and mathematics), EDUCATION (art, early childhood, elementary, and secondary), HEALTH PROFESSIONS (recreation therapy), SOCIAL SCIENCE (criminal justice, economics, history, political science/government, psychology, social work, and sociology). Biology is the strongest academically. Education and business are the largest.

Required: Bachelor's degree candidates must take 52 to 53 semester credits of general studies courses, including freshman seminar, English, math, natural science, literature, fine arts, history, and cultural studies. To graduate, students must complete 121 to 128 credits with a minimum 2.0 GPA overall and in the major.

Special: State College offers internships, a Washington semester, work-study programs, and B.A.-B.S. degrees in communications, psychology, and biology. Credit by exam and for life/military/work experience is available. Nondegree study and pass/fail options are possible. There are 7 national honor societies, a freshman honors program, and 7 departmental honors programs.

Faculty/Classroom: 49% of faculty are male; 51%, female. The average class size in a regular course is 25.

Requirements: The ACT is required and the SAT I is recommended. A minimum ACT composite score of 14 or a 2.0 GPA is required for regular admission. Applicants should be graduates of an accredited secondary school and have completed a minimum of 4 years each in English and academic electives, 3 in social studies, and 2 each in math and science. The GED is accepted. A GPA of 2.0 is required. AP and CLEP credits are accepted. Important factors in the admissions decision are evidence of special talent, leadership record, and advanced placement or honor courses.

Procedure: Freshmen are admitted to all sessions. Entrance exams should be taken 6 months prior to entry. There is an early decision plan and a rolling admissions plan. Check with the school for current deadlines. The college accepts all in-state residents. Notification is sent on a rolling basis. Applications are accepted on-line.

Transfer: 311 transfer students enrolled in a recent year. Applicants must submit ACT scores and high school transcripts, and must have a 2.5 GPA. 30 of 121 credits required for the bachelor's degree must be completed at State College.

Visiting: There are regularly scheduled orientations for prospective students, including both academic and social activities. There are guides for informal visits and visitors may sit in on classes and stay overnight. To schedule a visit, contact John L. Fuller at (304) 766-3144.

Financial Aid: The CSS Profile is required. Check with the school for current deadlines.

International Students: They must score 500 on the written TOEFL and also take the ACT, scoring 14.

Computers: The mainframe is a DEC MicroVAX 3900. There are more than 90 terminals and more than 400 computers at different facilities on campus. All students may access the system Monday through Thursday, 9 A.M. to 10 P.M., Friday, 9 A.M. to 7 P.M., and Saturday, 9 A.M. to 2 P.M. Each student is allocated $200 of use per semester. There are no fees.

Admissions Contact: Alice Ruhnke, Director of Admissions and Recruitment Services. E-mail: *ruhnkeam@mail.wvsc.edu*
Web: *www.wvsc.edu*

WEST VIRGINIA UNIVERSITY   C-2
Morgantown, WV 26506-6009   (304) 293-2121
(800) 344-9881; Fax: (304) 293-3080

Full-time: 8878 men, 7665 women	Faculty: 1289; I, --$
Part-time: 450 men, 524 women	Ph.D.s: 90%
Graduate: 3018 men, 3725 women	Student/Faculty: 13 to 1
Year: semesters, summer session	Tuition: $3548 ($10,768)
Application Deadline: August 1	Room & Board: $5822
Freshman Class: 10,049 applied, 9281 accepted, 4415 enrolled	
SAT I Verbal/Math: 534/524	ACT: 23 COMPETITIVE

West Virginia University, founded in 1867, is a comprehensive, public land-grant research university offering more than 100 undergraduate degrees in liberal arts and sciences, health science, and professional training. There are 13 undergraduate and 14 graduate schools. In addition to regional accreditation, WVU has baccalaureate program accreditation with AACSB, ABET, ACEJMC, ACPE, ADA, APTA, ASLA, CAHEA, CSWE, FIDER, NASAD, NASM, NCATE, NLN, NRPA, and SAF. The 10 libraries contain 1,477,380 volumes, 2,324,874 microform items, and 44,374 audio/video tapes/CDs, and subscribe to 7906 periodicals. Computerized library services include the card catalog, interlibrary loans, and database searching. Special learning facilities include a learning resource center, art gallery, planetarium, radio station, TV station, a discovery lab for inventors, a coal, mining, and minerals history museum, a pharmacy museum, and an arboretum. The 913-acre campus is in a small town 75 miles south of Pittsburgh and 200 miles west of Baltimore. Including any residence halls, there are 160 buildings.

Student Life: 59% of undergraduates are from West Virginia. Students are from 50 states, 59 foreign countries, and Canada. 87% are white. The average age of freshmen is 19; all undergraduates, 21. 22% do not continue beyond their first year; 57% remain to graduate.

Housing: About 3700 students can be accommodated in college housing, which includes single-sex and coed dorms, on-campus apartments, off-campus apartments, married-student housing, fraternity houses, and sorority houses. In addition, there are honors houses, language houses, special-interest houses, and sections within residence halls designated for special programming. On-campus housing is available on a first-come, first-served basis and is available on a lottery system for upperclassmen. 79% of students live on campus. Alcohol is not permitted. All students may keep cars.

Activities: 17% of men belong to 17 national fraternities; 19% of women belong to 1 local and 11 national sororities. There are about 270 groups on campus, including art, band, cheerleading, chess, choir, chorale, chorus, computers, dance, debate, drama, environmental, ethnic, film, gay, honors, international, jazz band, literary magazine, marching band, newspaper, opera, orchestra, pep band, photography, political, professional, radio and TV, religious, social, social service, student government, symphony, and yearbook. Popular campus events include Mountaineer Week, Parents Weekend, and Spring Week.

Sports: There are 11 intercollegiate sports for men and 11 for women, and 22 intramural sports for men and 22 for women. Facilities include a natatorium with swimming and diving pools, tennis courts, a weight room, indoor/outdoor tracks, racquetball and squash courts, a bowling alley, lacrosse, baseball and soccer fields, a 63,500-seat stadium, and a 14,000-seat gym, a student recreation center with weight/fitness equipment; courts for basketball, volleyball, and badminton; squash and racquetball courts; a 6-lane fitness and leisure pool; and a 50-foot indoor climbing wall.

Disabled Students: 90% of the campus is accessible. Wheelchair ramps, elevators, special parking, specially equipped rest rooms, special class scheduling, lowered drinking fountains, and lowered telephones are available. Academic programs are made accessible by transferring class to an architecturally accessible facility. Other facilities include tactile signage, specially designed lab facilities and portable lab stations, a Kurzweil reading machine, special apartments for hearing and mobility impaired students, and a specially equipped van for inner-city transportation. All coordination is done through the ADA coordinator.

Services: Counseling and information services are available, as is tutoring in most subjects. There is a reader service for the blind and remedial math, reading, and writing.

Campus Safety and Security: Measures include 24-hour foot and vehicle patrol, self-defense education, security escort services, and shuttle buses. There are informal discussions, pamphlets/posters/films, emergency telephones, lighted pathways/sidewalks, neighborhood watch programs, and sexual assault prevention booths staffed by city and university police.

Programs of Study: WVU confers B.A., B.S., B.F.A., B.M., B.S.A.E., B.S.Agr., B.S.B.Ad., B.S.B.S., B.S.C.E., B.S.Ch.E., B.S.Cp.E., B.S.E.E., B.S.F., B.S.F. & C.S., B.S.F.I., B.S.I.E., B.S.J., B.S.L.A., B.S.M.E., B.S.Min.E., B.S.N., B.S.P.Ed., B.S.PNGE., B.S.R., and B.S.W. degrees. Master's and doctoral degrees are also awarded. Bachelor's degrees are awarded in AGRICULTURE (agricultural business management, agriculture, agronomy, animal science, fish and game management, fishing and fisheries, forestry and related sciences, horticulture, natural resource management, and plant science), BIOLOGICAL SCIENCE (biology/biological science and nutrition), BUSINESS (accounting, banking and finance, business administration and management, fashion merchandising, marketing and distribution, recreation and leisure services, sports management, and tourism), COMMUNICATIONS AND THE ARTS (advertising, art, broadcasting, communications, dramatic arts, English, journalism, music, public relations, speech/debate/rhetoric, and visual and performing arts), COMPUTER AND PHYSICAL SCIENCE (chemistry, computer science, geology, geoscience, mathematics, physics, and science), EDUCATION (agricultural, athletic training, English, environmental, foreign languages, mathematics, and physical), ENGINEERING AND ENVIRONMENTAL DESIGN (aeronautical engineering, aerospace studies, chemical engineering, civil engineering, computer engineering, electrical/electronics engineering, engineering, environmental science, interior design, landscape architecture/design, mechanical engineering, mining and mineral engineering, petroleum/natural gas engineering, and systems engineering), HEALTH PROFESSIONS (dental hygiene, medical technology, nursing, occupational therapy, pharmacy, physical therapy, speech pathology/audiology, and veterinary science), SOCIAL SCIENCE (anthropology, child care/child and family studies, economics, family/consumer resource management, geography, history, interdisciplinary studies, international studies, liberal arts/general studies, parks and recreation management, philosophy, political science/government, psychology, social work, and sociology). Engineering and mineral resources, psychology, and political science are the strongest academically. Business and economics, engineering and mineral resources, and health sciences are the largest.

Required: All students are required to take 12 credit hours in each of 3 areas: humanities and fine arts, social and behavioral sciences, and natural sciences and math. The 36 credit hours must include international/minority/gender studies, math, composition, and an advanced course emphasizing writing skills. A minimum 2.0 GPA and at least 128 credit hours are required to graduate.

Special: A co-op program in engineering and cross-registration with schools in the Southern Regional Education Board through the Academic Common Market are possible. Internships, study abroad in 12 countries, a Washington semester, student-designed majors, dual majors in business and foreign languages, and B.A.-B.S. degrees in economics, chemistry, physics, biology, math, psychology, and geology are available. A liberal studies degree, credit by exam, credit for life experience, nondegree study, and pass/fail options are also offered. There are 27 national honor societies, including Phi Beta Kappa, and freshman honors program.

Faculty/Classroom: 62% of faculty are male; 38%, female. Graduate students teach 34% of introductory courses. The average class size in a regular course is 34.

Admissions: 92% of the 2003-2004 applicants were accepted. The SAT I scores for the 2003-2004 freshman class were: Verbal--37% below 500, 48% between 500 and 599, 14% between 600 and 700, and 1% above 700; Math--32% below 500, 47% between 500 and 599, 18% between 600 and 700, and 2% above 700. The ACT scores were 26% below 21, 34% between 21 and 23, 22% between 24 and 26, 10% between 27 and 28, and 8% above 28.

Requirements: The SAT I or ACT is required. In-state students need a minimum combined score of 910 on the SAT I, or 19 composite on the ACT and a minimum high school GPA of 2.0. Out-of-state students need scores of 950 or 20, respectively, and a minimum high school GPA of 2.25. Applicants should graduate from an accredited school no sooner than their junior year, after completing 4 years of English, 3 of social studies including U.S. history, 3 of math, and 2 each of lab sciences and foreign language. 1 year of typing is recommended. Music students must audition, and art applicants must submit a portfolio. A GPA of 2.0 is required. AP and CLEP credits are accepted. Important factors in the admissions decision are leadership record, evidence of special talent, and advanced placement or honor courses.

Procedure: Freshmen are admitted fall, spring, and summer. Entrance exams should be taken by spring of the junior year. There are early admissions and deferred admissions plans. There is a rolling admissions plan. Applications should be filed by August 1 for fall entry. Notification is sent on a rolling basis. The fall 2003 application fee was $25. Applications are accepted on-line through the school's web site.

Transfer: 1227 transfer students enrolled in 2002-2003. A minimum college GPA of 2.0 is required of transfers; all applicants must submit college transcripts. Students having fewer than 29 transferable credit hours are subject to freshman admission criteria and must submit SAT I or ACT scores and high school transcripts. 30 of 128 credits required for the bachelor's degree must be completed at WVU.

Visiting: There are regularly scheduled orientations for prospective students, including 2-day sessions with campus tours, placement testing, academic and advisement meetings, parent/student orientation discussions, and transitional meetings. There are guides for informal visits and visitors may sit in on classes. To schedule a visit, contact Visitors Resource Center at (304) 293-3489 or visitwvu@mail.wvu.edu.

Financial Aid: In a recent year, 40% of all full-time freshmen and 49% of continuing full-time students received some form of financial aid. 35% of continuing full-time students received need-based aid. The average freshman award was $6250. The average financial indebtedness of the 2003 graduate was $18,273. WVU is a member of CSS. The FAFSA is required. The deadline for filing freshman financial aid applications for fall entry is March 1.

International Students: There are 310 international students enrolled. They must score 550 on the written TOEFL and also take the SAT I or the ACT, scoring 950 (SAT I). International students serving as graduate teaching assistants must also demonstrate mastery of spoken English.

Computers: The mainframes are an IBM 9672-R63 running VM/ESA and AIX/ESA; a VAX 8250 and a VAX 6000-620 in a VAX cluster running VAX/VMS with access to the Thinking Machine Supercomputer. All students are issued e-mail accounts. Those required to use the mainframe for class projects are issued an individual mainframe account by their instructor. Many colleges and academic departments operate their own labs containing PCs with mainframe access. Public sites with consultants provide additional access to training and facilities. PCs and Macs are available throughout the campus including in residence halls. All students may access the system 24 hours a day, 7 days a week. There are no time limits and no fees. It is strongly recommended that all students have a personal computer.

Graduates: From July 1, 2002 to June 30, 2003, 2950 bachelor's degrees were awarded. The most popular majors were business/marketing (13%), engineering (11%), and journalism (9%). In an average class, 27% graduate in 4 years or less, 49% graduate in 5 years or less, and 56% graduate in 6 years or less.

Admissions Contact: Chen Khoo, Director of Admissions and Records. E-mail: wvuadmissions@arc.wvu.edu Web: www.arc.wvu.edu

WEST VIRGINIA UNIVERSITY INSTITUTE OF TECHNOLOGY
B-4

Montgomery, WV 25136

(304) 442-3167
(888) 554-TECH; Fax: (304) 442-3097

Full-time: 1065 men, 585 women	**Faculty:** 120; IIB, --$
Part-time: 400 men, 310 women	**Ph.D.s:** 52%
Graduate: 20 men, 5 women	**Student/Faculty:** 14 to 1
Year: semesters, summer session	**Tuition:** $2840 ($7020)
Application Deadline: see profile	**Room & Board:** $4685
Freshman Class: n/av	
SAT I or ACT: required	**NONCOMPETITIVE**

West Virginia University Institute of Technology, part of the Western Virginia University system and founded in 1895, is a public institution offering programs in business and economics, arts and sciences, community and technical fields, and engineering. There are 3 undergraduate schools and 1 graduate school. Figures in the above capsule and in this profile are approximate. In addition to regional accreditation, West Virginia Tech has baccalaureate program accreditation with ABET, ADA, and NLN. The library contains 166,967 volumes and 438,232 microform items, and subscribes to 510 periodicals. Computerized library services include the card catalog, interlibrary loans, and database searching. Special learning facilities include a learning resource center and art gallery. The 112-acre campus is in a small town 28 miles southeast of Charleston. Including any residence halls, there are 15 buildings.

Student Life: 91% of undergraduates are from West Virginia. Students are from 25 states, 24 foreign countries, and Canada. 95% are from public schools. 87% are white. The average age of freshmen is 19; all undergraduates, 24. 35% do not continue beyond their first year; 40% remain to graduate.

Housing: 776 students can be accommodated in college housing, which includes single-sex and coed dorms. In addition, there are quiet floors. On-campus housing is guaranteed for all 4 years. 69% of students commute. All students may keep cars.

Activities: 10% of men belong to 5 national fraternities; 8% of women belong to 2 national sororities. There are 42 groups on campus, including art, band, cheerleading, choir, chorus, computers, drama, drill team, ethnic, international, jazz band, marching band, newspaper, pep band, photography, political, professional, religious, social, student government, and yearbook. Popular campus events include comedy and film series, Black History Month, and Greek Week.

Sports: There are 5 intercollegiate sports for men and 4 for women, and 8 intramural sports for men and 8 for women. Facilities include 2 gyms, a weight room, tennis and handball courts, a student union, a football field and 3000-seat stadium, an Olympic-size swimming pool, game rooms, and a fitness center.

Disabled Students: 60% of the campus is accessible. Wheelchair ramps, elevators, special parking, specially equipped rest rooms, special class scheduling, and lowered drinking fountains are available.

Services: Counseling and information services are available, as is tutoring in most subjects. There is remedial math, reading, and writing, and a math learning center.

Campus Safety and Security: Measures include 24-hour foot and vehicle patrol, self-defense education, security escort services, and informal

discussions. There are pamphlets/posters/films and lighted pathways/sidewalks.

Programs of Study: West Virginia Tech confers B.A., B.S., B.E.T., B.M.E.T., B.S.C.E., B.S.E., and B.S.E.E. degrees. Associate and master's degrees are also awarded. Bachelor's degrees are awarded in BIOLOGICAL SCIENCE (biology/biological science), BUSINESS (accounting and business administration and management), COMPUTER AND PHYSICAL SCIENCE (chemistry, computer programming, computer science, and physics), ENGINEERING AND ENVIRONMENTAL DESIGN (chemical engineering, civil engineering, electrical/electronics engineering, electrical/electronics engineering technology, engineering technology, industrial administration/management, industrial engineering technology, and mechanical engineering), HEALTH PROFESSIONS (health care administration and nursing), SOCIAL SCIENCE (history and public administration). Engineering is the strongest academically. Nursing is the largest.

Required: Core curriculum requirements include 8 hours of lab science, 6 to 12 each of humanities and social science, 6 each of English and math/computer science, and 2 of phys ed and health. Other requirements vary according to the degree sought. To graduate, students must complete 128 semester hours with a minimum 2.0 GPA overall and in the major.

Special: An extensive co-op program is offered in all areas as well as a number of internships in public service and industrial relations. Credit for armed service experience and credit by departmental exam are available.

Faculty/Classroom: 70% of faculty are male; 30%, female. All teach undergraduates and 10% do research. No introductory courses are taught by graduate students. The average class size in an introductory lecture is 30; in a laboratory, 15; and in a regular course, 20.

Admissions: In a recent year, 11 freshmen graduated first in their class.

Requirements: The SAT I or ACT is required, with a minimum composite score of 690 on the SAT I or 17 on the ACT (higher for engineering and health majors). Applicants should be graduates from an accredited secondary school or have qualifying scores on the GED. Students must have completed 4 units of English, 3 of social studies, and 2 each of math (4 for engineering majors) and lab science. A GPA of 2.0 is required. AP and CLEP credits are accepted.

Procedure: Freshmen are admitted to all sessions. Entrance exams should be taken in sufficient time for the scores to reach the Institute by the application deadline. There is an early admissions plan and a rolling admissions plan. Check with the school for current deadlines. The college accepts all in-state residents. Applications are accepted on-line at the Institute's e-mail address.

Transfer: 192 transfer students enrolled in a recent year. Criteria for transfer admission vary according to the college. 30 of 128 credits required for the bachelor's degree must be completed at West Virginia Tech.

Visiting: There are regularly scheduled orientations for prospective students. There are guides for informal visits and visitors may sit in on classes and stay overnight. To schedule a visit, contact the Admissions Office.

Financial Aid: In a recent year, 86% of all full-time freshmen and 54% of continuing full-time students received some form of financial aid. 49% of full-time freshmen and 45% of continuing full-time students received need-based aid. The average freshman award was $2480. 15% of undergraduates work part time. Average annual earnings from campus work are $1000. The average financial indebtedness of a recent graduate was $13,000. West Virginia Tech is a member of CSS. The FAFSA and the college's own financial statement are required. Check with the school for current deadlines.

International Students: The school actively recruits these students. They must score 500 on the written TOEFL or 173 on the electronic version and also take the SAT I or the ACT.

Computers: The mainframe is a DEC VAX 4700A RISC 6000. There is also a Novell network, Groupwise Messaging, Campus Pipeline and T1 access to the Internet. All students may access the system 24 hours a day. There are no time limits and no fees. It is strongly recommended that all students have a personal computer.

Graduates: In a recent year, 261 bachelor's degrees were awarded. The most popular majors were engineering (42%), business (21%), and health (10%). In an average class, 2% graduate in 3 years or less, 30% graduate in 4 years or less, 10% graduate in 5 years or less, and 2% graduate in 6 years or less. 68 companies recruited on campus in a recent year.

Admissions Contact: Donna Varney, Director of Admissions. A video is available. E-mail: *wvutech@wvit.wvnet.edu* Web: *www.wvutech.edu*

WEST VIRGINIA WESLEYAN COLLEGE   C-3
Buckhannon, WV 26201   (304) 473-8510
(800) 722-9933; Fax: (304) 473-8108

Full-time: 675 men, 785 women	**Faculty:** 84; IIB, --$
Part-time: 30 men, 55 women	**Ph.Ds:** 71%
Graduate: 35 men, 25 women	**Student/Faculty:** 17 to 1
Year: semesters, summer session	**Tuition:** $18,700
Application Deadline: see profile	**Room & Board:** $4220
Freshman Class: n/av	
SAT I or ACT: required	**COMPETITIVE**

West Virginia Wesleyan College, founded in 1890, is an independent liberal and applied arts college affiliated with the United Methodist Church. Figures in the above capsule and in this profile are approximate. In addition to regional accreditation, WVWC has baccalaureate program accreditation with NASM and NLN. The library contains 107,340 volumes, 33,139 microform items, and 6077 audio/video tapes/CDs, and subscribes to 780 periodicals. Computerized library services include the card catalog and database searching. Special learning facilities include a learning resource center, art gallery, planetarium, and radio station. The 80-acre campus is in a small town in the Appalachian foothills, 135 miles south of Pittsburgh, Pennsylvania. Including any residence halls, there are 23 buildings.

Student Life: 53% of undergraduates are from West Virginia. Students are from 32 states, 19 foreign countries, and Canada. 85% are from public schools. 88% are white. 53% are Protestant; 20% Catholic. The average age of freshmen is 18; all undergraduates, 21. 26% do not continue beyond their first year.

Housing: 1370 students can be accommodated in college housing, which includes single-sex and coed dorms and on-campus apartments. In addition, there are honors houses, quiet study living areas, and substance-free small group living units. On-campus housing is guaranteed for all 4 years. 83% of students live on campus; of those, 65% remain on campus on weekends. Alcohol is not permitted. All students may keep cars.

Activities: 25% of men belong to 6 national fraternities; 25% of women belong to 4 national sororities. There are 75 groups on campus, including art, band, cheerleading, choir, chorale, chorus, computers, dance, drama, ethnic, forensics, gay, honors, international, jazz band, literary magazine, musical theater, newspaper, political, professional, radio and TV, religious, social, social service, student government, and yearbook. Popular campus events include Founders Day, Festivals of Lessons and Carols, and Spring Sing.

Sports: There are 9 intercollegiate sports for men and 8 for women, and 9 intramural sports for men and 8 for women. Facilities include baseball and football fields with seating for 3500, as well as a phys ed center with a 3800-seat intercollegiate basketball court, 2 intramural practice courts, 4 handball courts, an auxiliary gym, indoor tennis courts, volleyball courts, golf and wrestling practice areas, sauna baths, a dance studio, and gymnastics and weight rooms. A state park is near the campus.

Disabled Students: 75% of the campus is accessible. Wheelchair ramps, elevators, special parking, specially equipped rest rooms, special class scheduling, and lowered drinking fountains are available.

Services: Counseling and information services are available, as is tutoring in every subject. There is a reader service for the blind and remedial math, reading, and writing.

Campus Safety and Security: Measures include 24-hour foot and vehicle patrol, self-defense education, security escort services, and informal discussions. There are pamphlets/posters/films, emergency telephones, lighted pathways/sidewalks, rape awareness educational programs, and appropriate training for residence hall staff.

Programs of Study: WVWC confers B.A., B.S., B.M.E., and B.S.N. degrees. Master's degrees are also awarded. Bachelor's degrees are awarded in BIOLOGICAL SCIENCE (biology/biological science and nutrition), BUSINESS (accounting, business administration and management, and marketing/retailing/merchandising), COMMUNICATIONS AND THE ARTS (dramatic arts, English, music, public relations, and speech/debate/rhetoric), COMPUTER AND PHYSICAL SCIENCE (chemistry, computer science, mathematics, and physics), EDUCATION (art, elementary, music, physical, and secondary), ENGINEERING AND ENVIRONMENTAL DESIGN (engineering physics), HEALTH PROFESSIONS (nursing), SOCIAL SCIENCE (economics, history, international studies, philosophy, political science/government, psychology, religion, religious education, social science, and sociology). Physical and natural sciences and accounting are the strongest academically. Business, biology, and education are the largest.

Required: To graduate, students must earn 120 semester hours with a minimum GPA of 2.0; 24 to 51 hours must be in the major, 48 to 53 in general studies. Required disciplines are cultural studies, natural science and math, social sciences, health and phys ed, religion, philosophy, humanities and fine arts, and communications.

Special: WVWC offers cross-registration with the Mountain State Association of Colleges. Students may participate in a wide variety of internships, including a Washington center internship and work-study and study-abroad programs; there are exchange agreements in Korea, the People's Republic of China, Norway, and Bulgaria. Nondegree and pass/fail study, dual, student-designed, and contract majors, and credit for life, military, and work experience are available. There is 1 national honor society and a freshman honors program.

Faculty/Classroom: 63% of faculty are male; 37%, female. All teach undergraduates. No introductory courses are taught by graduate students. The average class size in an introductory lecture is 24; in a laboratory, 12; and in a regular course, 21.

Admissions: In a recent year, 10 freshmen graduated first in their class.

Requirements: The SAT I or ACT is required. The minimum composite score needed is 800 on SAT I, 420 verbal and 380 math, or 18 on the ACT. In addition, applicants must be high school graduates, or hold a GED. Students should have earned 26 academic credits, consisting of 4 in English, 3 each in math, science, and academic electives, and 2 each in foreign language, lab science, and social studies, as well as a total of 7 academic credits in fine arts, technology education, health, and phys ed. An essay and an interview are recommended. A GPA of 2.0 is required. AP and CLEP credits are accepted. Important factors in the admissions decision are extracurricular activities record, recommendations by school officials, and leadership record.

Procedure: Freshmen are admitted fall and spring. Entrance exams should be taken in fall of the senior year or spring/summer of junior year. There are early decision, deferred admissions, and rolling admissions plans. Check with the school for current deadlines. The fall 2003 fee was $25. Applications are accepted on-line.

Transfer: 43 transfer students enrolled in a recent year. Transfer applicants must supply a high school transcript if their GPA for college work is less than 2.5. An associate degree and an interview are recommended. 30 of 120 credits required for the bachelor's degree must be completed at WVWC.

Visiting: There are regularly scheduled orientations for prospective students. There are guides for informal visits and visitors may sit in on classes and stay overnight. To schedule a visit, contact Robert Skinner, Director of Admission.

Financial Aid: In a recent year, 99% of all full-time freshmen and 98% of continuing full-time students received some form of financial aid. 77% of full-time freshmen and 75% of continuing full-time students received need-based aid. The average freshman award was $18,700. 41% of undergraduates work part time. Average annual earnings from campus work are $1000. The average financial indebtedness of a recent graduate was $16,118. The FAFSA is required. Check with the school for current deadlines.

International Students: The school actively recruits these students. They must score 500 on the written TOEFL.

Computers: The mainframes are an Alpha 1000 and an Alpha 800. All students have network accounts, all freshmen have IBM ThinkPad systems, and upperclassmen have access to computer labs in the science building, library, art department, or learning center. There are approximately 85 public access systems on campus. All systems have access to the Internet and Web. All students may access the system. There are no time limits and no fees. All students are required to have personal computers.

Graduates: In a recent year, 297 bachelor's degrees were awarded. The most popular majors were elementary education (10%), psychology (7%), and public relations (6%). In an average class, 1% graduate in 3 years or less, 44% graduate in 4 years or less, 52% graduate in 5 years or less, and 55% graduate in 6 years or less. Of a recent graduating class, 26% were enrolled in graduate school within 6 months of graduation.

Admissions Contact: Robert N. Skinner II, Director of Admission. A video is available. E-mail: *admissions@wvwc.edu* Web: *www.wvwc.edu*

WHEELING JESUIT UNIVERSITY
Wheeling, WV 26003

C-2

(304) 243-2359
(800) 624-6992; Fax: (304) 243-2397

Full-time: 460 men, 585 women	**Faculty:** 86; IIB, --$
Part-time: 50 men, 160 women	**Ph.D.s:** 80%
Graduate: 85 men, 135 women	**Student/Faculty:** 12 to 1
Year: semesters, summer session	**Tuition:** $17,240
Application Deadline: open	**Room & Board:** $5420
Freshman Class: n/av	
SAT I or ACT: required	**COMPETITIVE**

Wheeling Jesuit College, founded in 1954, is an independent college affiliated with the Society of Jesus, offering undergraduate programs in the liberal arts and sciences, nursing, allied health, and business, and graduate programs in business administration and applied theology. Figures in the above capsule and in this profile are approximate. In addition to regional accreditation, Wheeling Jesuit has baccalaureate program accreditation with CAHEA and NLN. The library contains 155,953 volumes, 120,278 microform items, and 1200 audio/video tapes/CDs, and subscribes to 504 periodicals. Computerized library services include the card catalog and database searching. Special learning facilities include a learning resource center. The 70-acre campus is in a suburban area 60 miles southwest of Pittsburgh. Including any residence halls, there are 15 buildings.

Student Life: 66% of undergraduates are from out of state, mostly the Middle Atlantic. Students are from 31 states, 28 foreign countries, and Canada. 90% are white. 57% are Catholic; 33% Protestant. The average age of freshmen is 18; all undergraduates, 24. 28% do not continue beyond their first year; 62% remain to graduate.

Housing: 764 students can be accommodated in college housing, which includes single-sex dorms. On-campus housing is guaranteed for all 4 years. 78% of students live on campus; of those, 75% remain on campus on weekends. All students may keep cars.

Activities: There are no fraternities or sororities. There are 20 groups on campus, including cheerleading, choir, chorus, drama, honors, international, literary magazine, newspaper, pep band, professional, religious, social, social service, student government, and yearbook. Popular campus events include Week of the Person, Day of Diversity, and Coffee House.

Sports: There are 8 intercollegiate sports for men and 8 for women, and 7 intramural sports for men and 7 for women. Facilities include a recreation center with a swimming pool, 2 gyms, 2 racquetball courts, complete Nautilus equipment, an indoor jogging track, 3 fields, and game rooms.

Disabled Students: 80% of the campus is accessible. Wheelchair ramps, elevators, special parking, specially equipped rest rooms, lowered drinking fountains, and lowered telephones are available.

Services: Counseling and information services are available, as is tutoring in most subjects. There is a reader service for the blind and remedial math, reading, and writing.

Campus Safety and Security: Measures include 24-hour foot and vehicle patrol, self-defense education, informal discussions, and pamphlets/posters/films. There are lighted pathways/sidewalks and a student intern campus patrol.

Programs of Study: Wheeling Jesuit confers B.A., B.S., and B.S.N. degrees. Master's degrees are also awarded. Bachelor's degrees are awarded in BIOLOGICAL SCIENCE (biology/biological science), BUSINESS (accounting, international business management, management science, marketing/retailing/merchandising, and sports management), COMMUNICATIONS AND THE ARTS (English, French, romance languages and literature, Spanish, and technical and business writing), COMPUTER AND PHYSICAL SCIENCE (chemistry, computer science, mathematics, physics, and science), ENGINEERING AND ENVIRONMENTAL DESIGN (environmental science and technology and public affairs), HEALTH PROFESSIONS (nuclear medical technology, nursing, and respiratory therapy), SOCIAL SCIENCE (criminal justice, ethics, politics, and social policy, history, international studies, philosophy, political science/government, psychology, and religion). Psychology, nursing, and biology are the largest.

Required: To graduate, students must complete 120 credit hours, with a GPA of 2.0. The core curriculum consists of 58 credits in English composition, math, modern languages, literature, history, social science, natural science, philosophy, theology and 1 course in either ethics or Christian morality, as well as 1 additional math or science course. Students are also required to complete 2 units of the dimensions of the school's Wellness Program.

Special: The university offers internships with many businesses and institutions, as well as a Washington semester and study abroad. Students may obtain an advanced degree in business administration, as well as a 3-2 engineering degree with Case Western Reserve University. The college permits dual and student-designed majors. Credit for life, military, and work experience may be granted to adult students. Pass/fail options are open in some courses. There are 12 national honor societies and a freshman honors program.

Faculty/Classroom: 58% of faculty are male; 42%, female. All both teach and do research. The average class size in an introductory lecture is 20; in a laboratory, 11; and in a regular course, 14.

Requirements: The SAT I or ACT is required, with a minimum composite score of 850 on the SAT I or 18 on the ACT. In addition, applicants must be high school graduates or hold a GED. Students should have earned 15 academic credits, consisting of 4 in English, 2 each in math and history or social science, 1 in lab science (2 are recommended for science majors), and 6 in academic electives, with a foreign language recommended. Students entering programs in the natural sciences should have taken 1 course each of chemistry and biology. Exceptions are made, especially if the high school GPA is 3.0 or better. An interview is recommended. Wheeling Jesuit requires applicants to be in the upper 90% of their class. A GPA of 2.0 is required. AP and CLEP credits are accepted. Important factors in the admissions decision are leadership record, recommendations by school officials, and extracurricular activities record.

Procedure: Freshmen are admitted to all sessions. There is a deferred admissions plan and a rolling admissions plan. Application deadlines are open. Application fee is $25. Applications are accepted on-line.

Transfer: 60 transfer students enrolled in a recent year. Applicants must have a GPA of 2.0 for college work, or supply high school transcripts if entering at the freshman level. The SAT I or ACT is required if the student has less than 1 year of college work; otherwise, it is still recommended, as is an interview. Transfer students must take placement tests given by the university. 30 of 120 credits required for the bachelor's degree must be completed at Wheeling Jesuit.

Visiting: There are regularly scheduled orientations for prospective students, including meetings with faculty, discussions by students and parents, meals, and campus tours. There are guides for informal visits and visitors may sit in on classes and stay overnight. To schedule a visit, contact Jennifer Decker, Campus Visit Coordinator at *jdecker@wju.edu*.

Financial Aid: In a recent year, 99% of all full-time freshmen and 88% of continuing full-time students received some form of financial aid. 86% of full-time freshmen and 70% of continuing full-time students received need-based aid. The average freshman award was $17,772. 71% of undergraduates work part time. Average annual earnings from campus work are $1699. The average financial indebtedness of a recent graduate was $15,000. The FAFSA is required. Check with the school for current deadlines.

International Students: In a recent year, there were 42 international students enrolled. The school actively recruits these students. They must score 550 on the written TOEFL.

Computers: The mainframe is an AT&T StarGroup LAN. There are also some 125 PCs available in the computer center, academic resource center, and various departments. All students may access the system every day, for a total 85 hours per week and in 1 lab 24 hours a day, 7 days a week.

Graduates: In a recent year, 187 bachelor's degrees were awarded. The most popular majors were psychology (9%), criminal justice (8%), and biology (8%).

Admissions Contact: Tom Pie', Director of Admissions. A video is available. E-mail: *admiss@wju.edu* Web: *www.wju.edu*

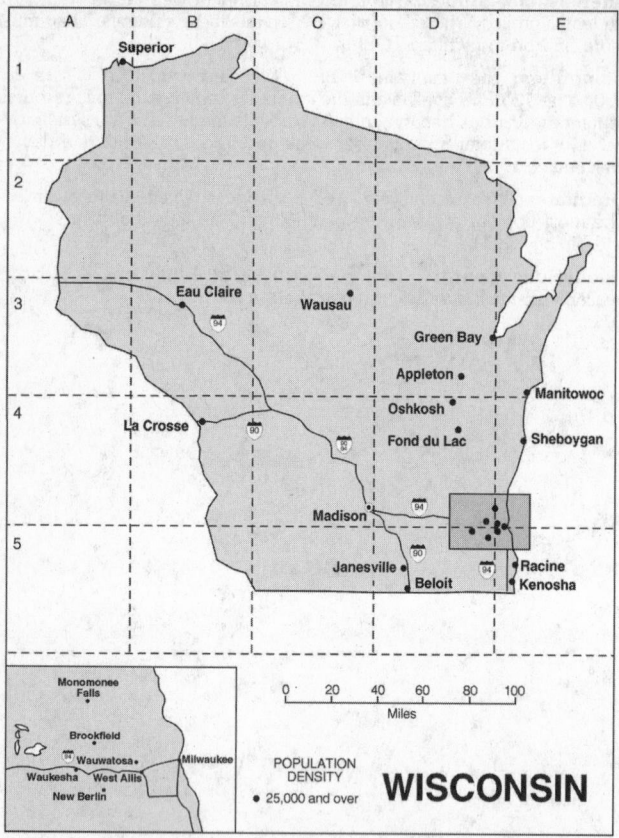

POPULATION DENSITY
● 25,000 and over

WISCONSIN

0 20 40 60 80 100
Miles

ALVERNO COLLEGE
Milwaukee, WI 53234-3922

E-4
(414) 382-6113
(800) 933-3401; Fax: (414) 382-6354

Full-time: 2 men, 1199 women	**Faculty:** 104; IIB, --$
Part-time: 20 men, 730 women	**Ph.D.s:** 46%
Graduate: 23 men, 151 women	**Student/Faculty:** 12 to 1
Year: semesters, summer session	**Tuition:** $13,638
Application Deadline: open	**Room & Board:** $5260
Freshman Class: 811 applied, 455 accepted, 279 enrolled	
ACT: 20	**COMPETITIVE**

Alverno College is an independent, four-year liberal arts college for women. Alverno is dedicated to the personal and professional development of women through a practical, interactive learning environment. There are 7 undergraduate schools and 1 graduate school. In addition to regional accreditation, Alverno has baccalaureate program accreditation with CCBE, NASM, and NCATE. The library contains 91,841 volumes, 273,545 microform items, and 31,134 audio/video tapes/CDs, and subscribes to 1380 periodicals. Computerized library services include the card catalog, interlibrary loans, and database searching. Special learning facilities include a learning resource center, and TV studio, art and culture gallery, nursing skills lab, student-centered multimedia production facility, computer center, science labs, theater venue, and conferencing center. The 46-acre campus is in an urban area on the southwest edge of Milwaukee. Including any residence halls, there are 10 buildings.

Student Life: 98% of undergraduates are from Wisconsin. Students are from 9 states and 12 foreign countries. 62% are white; 23% African American. 32% are Catholic; 32% Protestant; 25% claim no religious affiliation; 7% unknown. The average age of freshmen is 23; all undergraduates, 26. 25% do not continue beyond their first year; 67% remain to graduate.

Housing: 220 students can be accommodated in college housing, which includes single-sex dorms. On-campus housing is guaranteed for all 4 years. 87% of students commute. All students may keep cars.

Activities: There are no fraternities. There are more than 35 groups on campus, including art, choir, chorus, Circle K, dance, drama, ethnic, honors, international, literary magazine, orchestra, political, professional, PSE, religious, SIFE, social, and social service. Popular campus events

include Career Day, fine arts performances, and interdenominational religious services.

Sports: Facilities include a refurbished gym with regulation intercollegiate volleyball and basketball courts, a fitness center with state-of-the-art free motion fitness and cardio equipment, an outdoor volleyball court, a multipurpose room for dancing, aerobics, and cardio kickboxing.

Disabled Students: 95% of the campus is accessible. Wheelchair ramps, elevators, special parking, specially equipped rest rooms, lowered drinking fountains, lowered telephones, and pushbuttons to open exterior doors are available.

Services: Counseling and information services are available, as is tutoring in most subjects. There is remedial math, reading, and writing. There are selected workshops for such issues as writing anxiety, time management, note taking, speaking anxiety, documenting work, stategies for doing research papers, Internet introduction, and math EXCEL.

Campus Safety and Security: Measures include 24-hour foot and vehicle patrol, security escort services, informal discussions, and pamphlets/posters/films. There are emergency telephones, lighted pathways/sidewalks, and electronically operated and video-surveillanced dorm entrances, walkways, and a security staff equipped with 2-way radios.

Programs of Study: Alverno confers B.A., B.M., B.S.Ed., and B.S.N. degrees. Associate and master's degrees are also awarded. Bachelor's degrees are awarded in BIOLOGICAL SCIENCE (biology/biological science and molecular biology), BUSINESS (business administration and management and international business management), COMMUNICATIONS AND THE ARTS (art, communications, communications technology, English, music, and visual and performing arts), COMPUTER AND PHYSICAL SCIENCE (chemistry, computer science, information sciences and systems, mathematics, physical sciences, and science), EDUCATION (art, elementary, middle school, music, science, and secondary), ENGINEERING AND ENVIRONMENTAL DESIGN (environmental science and land use management and reclamation), HEALTH PROFESSIONS (art therapy, music therapy, and nursing), SOCIAL SCIENCE (child psychology/development, community services, history, international relations, philosophy, psychology, religion, social science, and social studies). Nursing, elementary education, and business and management are the largest.

Required: Students must complete a learning program that integrates accomplishment in required areas of knowledge with the achievement of required competence levels in the following 8 core abilities: communication, analysis, problem solving, valuing in decision-making, social interaction, developing a global perspective, effective citizenship, and aesthetic engagement. This is accomplished through general education courses in history, English, philosophy, religious studies, arts, sciences, math, psychology, and social science; through completion of a major and minor area of study; and completion of at least one required internship or practice.

Special: Alverno offers internships, dual majors, nondegree study, and pre-professional programs in dentistry, law, medicine, pharmacy, physician's assistant, and veterinary medicine. Alverno maintains student exchange programs with universities in England, France, Japan, and Mexico, and also offers courses that include an international travel component. Alverno can arrange other programs through a worldwide consortium of facilities. The school's interactive curriculum is outcome-oriented and performance-based; letter grades are not assigned. There are 3 national honor societies.

Faculty/Classroom: 23% of faculty are male; 77%, female. All both teach and do research. No introductory courses are taught by graduate students.

Admissions: 56% of the 2003-2004 applicants were accepted.

Requirements: Applicants must be graduates of an accredited secondary school, having completed 17 academic credits with college preparatory courses. The GED is accepted. A GPA of 2.5 is required. AP and CLEP credits are accepted.

Procedure: Freshmen are admitted fall and spring. Entrance exams should be taken as early as possible. There is a deferred admissions plan. Application deadlines are open. Application fee is $20. Applications are accepted on-line through CollegeNET and Wisconsin Mentor. Notification is sent on a rolling basis.

Transfer: 171 transfer students enrolled in 2002-2003. Applicants should have a minimum college GPA of 2.0 and must submit transcripts from all schools previously attended.

Visiting: There are regularly scheduled orientations for prospective students, consisting of open houses and overnight events that include tours of the campus, classroom visits, and meetings with faculty and current students. There are guides for informal visits and visitors may sit in on classes and stay overnight. To schedule a visit, contact the Admissions Office at (414) 382-6101.

Financial Aid: In 2003-2004, 97% of all full-time freshmen and 83% of continuing full-time students received some form of financial aid. 91%

of full-time freshmen and 81% of continuing full-time students received need-based aid. The average freshman award was $9660. 40% of undergraduates work part time. Average annual earnings from campus work are $2500. Alverno is a member of CSS. The FAFSA and the college's own financial statement are required. The priority date for freshman financial aid applications for fall entry is April 15.

International Students: There are 13 international students enrolled. The school actively recruits these students. They must score 500 on the written TOEFL or 137 on the electronic version and also take the college's own entrance exam.

Computers: The mainframe is an HP 9000. Students have access to some 100 networked PCs and Macs in the campus computer center. More than 100 PCs are available in computer classrooms, in several discipline-specific labs, and in residence halls. Internet and Web access is provided. All students may access the system. There are no time limits and no fees.

Graduates: From July 1, 2002 to June 30, 2003, 238 bachelor's degrees were awarded. The most popular majors were nursing (15%), elementary education (9%), and business and management (9%). In an average class, 43% graduate in 4 years or less, 50% graduate in 5 years or less, and 55% graduate in 6 years or less. 21 companies recruited on campus in 2002-2003. Of the 2002 graduating class, 13% were enrolled in graduate school within 6 months of graduation and 93% were employed.

Admissions Contact: Mary Kay Farrell, Director of Admissions. A video is available. E-mail: *admissions@alverno.edu*
Web: *www.alverno.edu*

BELOIT COLLEGE
Beloit, WI 53511-5595

D-5

(608) 363-2500
(800) 9-BELOIT; Fax: (608) 363-2075

Full-time: 480 men, 746 women	**Faculty:** 103; IIB, +$
Part-time: 34 men, 72 women	**Ph.D.s:** 98%
Graduate: none	**Student/Faculty:** 12 to 1
Year: semesters	**Tuition:** $24,386
Application Deadline: January 15	**Room & Board:** $5478
Freshman Class: 1901 applied, 1321 accepted, 346 enrolled	
SAT I Verbal/Math: 640/600	**ACT:** 27 **HIGHLY COMPETITIVE**

Beloit College, founded in 1846, is a private liberal arts institution. The library contains 650,867 volumes, 137,447 microform items, and 7066 audio/video tapes/CDs, and subscribes to 1404 periodicals. Computerized library services include the card catalog, interlibrary loans, database searching, and Internet access. Special learning facilities include a learning resource center, art gallery, natural history museum, planetarium, radio station, TV station, comprehensive language lab, observatory, and theater complex. The 40-acre campus is in a small town 50 miles south of Madison. Including any residence halls, there are 50 buildings.

Student Life: 82% of undergraduates are from out of state, mostly the Midwest. Students are from 47 states, 40 foreign countries, and Canada. 78% are from public schools. 81% are white. 43% claim no religious affiliation; 13% are Protestant; 10% Catholic. The average age of freshmen is 18; all undergraduates, 20. 9% do not continue beyond their first year; 70% remain to graduate.

Housing: 1081 students can be accommodated in college housing, which includes single-sex and coed dorms, on-campus apartments, fraternity houses, and sorority houses. In addition, there are language houses and special-interest houses. On-campus housing is guaranteed for all 4 years. 93% of students live on campus; of those, 95% remain on campus on weekends. All students may keep cars.

Activities: 15% of men belong to 3 national fraternities; 5% of women belong to 2 local and 1 national sorority. There are 90 groups on campus, including art, band, cheerleading, chess, choir, chorus, computers, dance, drama, ethnic, film, gay, honors, international, jazz band, literary magazine, musical theater, newspaper, orchestra, pep band, photography, political, professional, radio and TV, religious, science fiction, social, social service, student government, symphony, women's, and yearbook. Popular campus events include Great Lecture Series, Folk and Blues Weekend, and Spring Day.

Sports: There are 10 intercollegiate sports for men and 10 for women, and 15 intramural sports for men and 13 for women. Facilities include a sports center that houses a 2250-seat arena for basketball and volleyball, racquetball/handball courts, a dance studio, a fitness center, and a natatorium; a field house that contains a running track, an indoor soccer area, batting/pitching cage, and space for indoor tennis; a 3500-seat football stadium; outdoor playing fields; 6 all-weather tennis courts; and a stadium that hosts football, soccer, track and field. There are facilities nearby for sailing, ice skating, and other recreation.

Disabled Students: 35% of the campus is accessible. Wheelchair ramps, elevators, special parking, specially equipped rest rooms, special class scheduling, lowered drinking fountains, and lowered telephones are available.

Services: Counseling and information services are available, as is tutoring in most subjects, including most introductory and some advanced courses.

Campus Safety and Security: Measures include 24-hour foot and vehicle patrol, security escort services, informal discussions, and pamphlets/posters/films. There are emergency telephones and lighted pathways/sidewalks.

Programs of Study: Beloit confers B.A. and B.S. degrees. Bachelor's degrees are awarded in BIOLOGICAL SCIENCE (biochemistry, biology/biological science, cell biology, ecology, and environmental biology), BUSINESS (business administration and management), COMMUNICATIONS AND THE ARTS (art history and appreciation, classical languages, comparative literature, creative writing, dramatic arts, East Asian languages and literature, English, French, German, literature, modern language, music, Russian, Spanish, speech/debate/rhetoric, and studio art), COMPUTER AND PHYSICAL SCIENCE (applied physics, chemistry, computer science, geology, mathematics, and physics), EDUCATION (art and education), ENGINEERING AND ENVIRONMENTAL DESIGN (environmental science), HEALTH PROFESSIONS (predentistry, premedicine, and preveterinary science), SOCIAL SCIENCE (anthropology, classical/ancient civilization, economics, history, interdisciplinary studies, international relations, philosophy, political science/government, prelaw, psychology, religion, sociology, and women's studies). Anthropology, English, and geology are the strongest academically. Anthropology, biology, and English are the largest.

Required: To graduate, students must complete 31 units, including 8 to 15 in the major, with a minimum GPA of 2.0. Distribution requirements include 2 courses each from natural sciences and math, social sciences, and arts and humanities. Writing and interdisciplinary course work is also required. Degree expectations include international and experiential learning components, as well as a comprehensive academic plan.

Special: Beloit offers cross-registration with the University of Wisconsin/Madison, internships, study abroad in 29 countries, and a Washington semester. Dual majors, student-designed and interdisciplinary majors, and nondegree study are available. Students may take a 2-2 nursing program and a 3-2 medical technology program with Rush University. A 3-2 engineering degree is offered with 9 institutions, and co-op programs are available in social services, forestry and environmental management, engineering, nursing, medical technology, and business administration. An intensive summer language program is offered in Chinese, Japanese, Hungarian, and Russian. There are 6 national honor societies, including Phi Beta Kappa.

Faculty/Classroom: 59% of faculty are male; 41%, female. All both teach and do research. The average class size in an introductory lecture is 15; in a laboratory, 15; and in a regular course, 15.

Admissions: 69% of the 2003-2004 applicants were accepted. The SAT I scores for the 2003-2004 freshman class were: Verbal--5% below 500, 25% between 500 and 599, 48% between 600 and 700, and 22% above 700; Math--10% below 500, 38% between 500 and 599, 41% between 600 and 700, and 11% above 700. The ACT scores were 3% below 21, 11% between 21 and 23, 24% between 24 and 26, 23% between 27 and 28, and 39% above 28. 60% of the current freshmen were in the top fifth of their class; 89% were in the top two fifths. There were 6 National Merit semifinalists. 15 freshmen graduated first in their class.

Requirements: The SAT I or ACT is required and SAT II: Subject tests are recommended. In addition, applicants must be graduates of an accredited secondary school, with 4 years of English, 3 each of math, science, and history/social sciences, and 2 of foreign language. The GED is accepted. An essay and a letter of recommendation are required, and an interview is recommended. AP and CLEP credits are accepted. Important factors in the admissions decision are extracurricular activities record, leadership record, and personality/intangible qualities.

Procedure: Freshmen are admitted fall and spring. Entrance exams should be taken before Christmas of the senior year. There is a rolling admissions plan. There are early admissions and deferred admissions plans. Early action applications should be filed by November 15 and December 15; regular applications, by January 15 for fall entry, along with a $30 fee. Notification of early action is sent December 15 and January 15; regular decision, March 15. A waiting list is an active part of the admissions procedure. Applications are accepted on-line through CollegeLink, CommonApp, and the college's web site.

Transfer: 38 transfer students enrolled in 2002-2003. Applicants must have a minimum GPA of 2.5 and submit official transcripts of all college work completed. The SAT I or the ACT is required, and an interview is recommended. Also, a letter of recommendation from a professor at a current/previous institution is required. 16 of 31 credits required for the bachelor's degree must be completed at Beloit.

Visiting: There are regularly scheduled orientations for prospective students, including a tour, class visits, and meeting with professors, including an interview. Enrolled students are the hosts. There are guides for informal visits and visitors may sit in on classes and stay overnight. To schedule a visit, contact the Admissions Office at *admiss@beloit.edu*.

Financial Aid: The average freshman award in 2003-2004 was $18,219. Need-based scholarships or need-based grants averaged $12,753 ($19,000 maximum); need-based self-help aid (loans and jobs) averaged $4700 ($6400 maximum); and non-need-based awards and non-need-based scholarships averaged $10,430 ($12,500 maximum). 87% of undergraduates work part time. Average annual earnings from campus work are $1300. The average financial indebtedness of the 2003 graduate was $18,783. Beloit is a member of CSS. The FAFSA and the college's own financial statement are required. The deadline for filing freshman financial aid applications for fall entry is March 15.

International Students: There are 107 international students enrolled. The school actively recruits these students. They must score 525 on the written TOEFL and also take the SAT I or ACT. Applicants from selected countries must also supply a school-leaving exam/certificate.

Computers: The mainframe consists of 2 IBM RS 6000 Model F50s. Students can use more than 200 networked computers for e-mail, web access, and other network-related activities. All students may access the system at any time. There are no time limits and no fees.

Graduates: From July 1, 2002 to June 30, 2003, 271 bachelor's degrees were awarded. The most popular majors were psychology (11%), anthropology (10%), and economics (8%). In an average class, 60% graduate in 4 years or less, 69% graduate in 5 years or less, and 72% graduate in 6 years or less. 62 companies recruited on campus in 2002-2003. Of the 2002 graduating class, 20% were enrolled in graduate school within 6 months of graduation and 74% were employed.

Admissions Contact: James Zielinski, Director of Admissions. A video is available. E-mail: *admiss@beloit.edu* Web: *www.beloit.edu*

CARDINAL STRITCH UNIVERSITY
Milwaukee, WI 53217-7516

E-4
(414) 410-4040
(800) 347-8822; Fax: (414) 410-4049

Full-time: 910 men, 1990 women	**Faculty:** 98; IIA, --$
Part-time: 50 men, 175 women	**Ph.Ds:** 54%
Graduate: 825 men, 1910 women	**Student/Faculty:** 30 to 1
Year: semesters, summer session	**Tuition:** $12,780
Application Deadline: see profile	**Room & Board:** $4840
Freshman Class: n/av	
SAT I or ACT: required	**COMPETITIVE**

Cardinal Stritch University, founded in 1937 as a college, is a private, Catholic institution sponsored by the Sisters of St. Francis. There are 4 undergraduate schools and 1 graduate school. Figures in the above capsule and in this profile are approximate. In addition to regional accreditation, Stritch has baccalaureate program accreditation with NCATE and NLN. The library contains 132,293 volumes, 173,216 microform items, and 6310 audio/video tapes/CDs, and subscribes to 1309 periodicals. Computerized library services include the card catalog, interlibrary loans, and database searching. Special learning facilities include a learning resource center, art gallery, and radio station. The 40-acre campus is in a suburban area 10 miles north of Milwaukee. Including any residence halls, there are 9 buildings.

Student Life: 89% of undergraduates are from Wisconsin. Students are from 16 states, 27 foreign countries, and Canada. 60% are from public schools. 72% are white; 16% African American. Most are Catholic. The average age of freshmen is 19; all undergraduates, 32. 27% do not continue beyond their first year; 43% remain to graduate.

Housing: 278 students can be accommodated in college housing, which includes coed dorms. On-campus housing is available on a first-come, first-served basis. 95% of students commute. All students may keep cars.

Activities: There are no fraternities or sororities. There are 50 groups on campus, including art, band, cheerleading, choir, chorus, computers, dance, drama, ethnic, film, honors, international, jazz band, musical theater, newspaper, orchestra, photography, political, professional, radio and TV, religious, social, social service, student government, and yearbook. Popular campus events include Thursday night events and weekly activities, such as sporting events or plays.

Sports: There are 5 intercollegiate sports for men and 5 for women, and 2 intramural sports for men and 2 for women. Facilities include basketball and volleyball courts, an indoor track, a weight and exercise room, an area for table tennis and billiards, and a soccer field.

Disabled Students: 80% of the campus is accessible. Wheelchair ramps, special parking, specially equipped rest rooms, special class scheduling, and lowered telephones are available.

Services: Counseling and information services are available, as is tutoring in every subject. There is remedial math, reading, and writing.

Campus Safety and Security: Measures include 24-hour foot and vehicle patrol, informal discussions, pamphlets/posters/films, and lighted pathways/sidewalks.

Programs of Study: Stritch confers B.A., B.S., and B.F.A. degrees. Associate, master's, and doctoral degrees are also awarded. Bachelor's degrees are awarded in BIOLOGICAL SCIENCE (biology/biological science), BUSINESS (accounting, business administration and management, and international business management), COMMUNICATIONS AND THE ARTS (art, communications, creative writing, dramatic arts, English, fine arts, French, music, public relations, and Spanish), COMPUTER AND PHYSICAL SCIENCE (chemistry, computer science, and mathematics), EDUCATION (early childhood, elementary, middle school, secondary, and special), HEALTH PROFESSIONS (nursing, predentistry, premedicine, preoptometry, and preveterinary science), SO-

CIAL SCIENCE (history, prelaw, psychology, religion, social science, and sociology). Education in general and special education in particular are the strongest academically. Business, education, and nursing are the largest.

Required: To graduate, students must complete 128 credits, 34 to 72 in the major, with a GPA of at least 2.0. Required disciplines include history, foreign language, literature, written communication, and communication arts. 5 courses are required in humanities, 3 in social/behavioral sciences, 2 each in communication arts and written communication, and 1 each in math and natural science. An English proficiency exam must be taken.

Special: Students may participate in a variety of internships with Milwaukee businesses and organizations. Stritch offers an accelerated degree program and a B.A.-B.S. degree in business, dual majors, a general studies degree, and nondegree study. There is study abroad, work-study programs, pass/fail options, and credit for life, military, and work experience. An accelerated evening program and a management program are offered for working adults. There are 9 national honor societies and a freshman honors program.

Faculty/Classroom: 49% of faculty are male; 51%, female. All teach undergraduates. No introductory courses are taught by graduate students. The average class size in a laboratory is 12 and in a regular course, 11.

Requirements: The SAT I or ACT is required, with a recommended minimum composite score of 20 on the ACT or 950 on the SAT I. Applicants must be graduates of an accredited secondary school, with 16 academic credits, including 4 years of English and 2 years each of math (algebra required), science, and social studies. The GED is accepted. Stritch requires an essay and recommends an interview. Stritch requires applicants to be in the upper 50% of their class. A GPA of 2.0 is required. AP and CLEP credits are accepted. Important factors in the admissions decision are leadership record, evidence of special talent, and advanced placement or honor courses.

Procedure: Freshmen are admitted to all sessions. Entrance exams should be taken as early as possible. There is a deferred admissions plan and a rolling admissions plan. Check with the school for current deadlines. Notification is sent on a rolling basis. The fall 2003 application fee was $25. Applications are accepted on-line.

Transfer: 164 transfer students enrolled in a recent year. Applicants for transfer should have a minimum GPA of 2.0, and be eligible for return to the previous institution. 32 of 128 credits required for the bachelor's degree must be completed at Stritch.

Visiting: There are regularly scheduled orientations for prospective students, including a campus tour, meetings with admissions and financial aid counselors, and possible meetings with department chairs. There are guides for informal visits and visitors may sit in on classes and stay overnight. To schedule a visit, contact the Admissions Office.

Financial Aid: The FAFSA and the college's own financial statement are required. The deadline for filing freshman financial aid applications for fall entry is open.

International Students: In a recent year, there were 35 international students enrolled. They must score 550 on the written TOEFL.

Computers: The mainframe is an IBM AS/400. 62 Macs, 174 PCs, and 16 graphic workstations are available to students in 4 computer labs and the library. All have Internet access. Business students are generally provided with laptops. All students may access the system. There are no time limits and no fees.

Graduates: In a recent year, 285 bachelor's degrees were awarded. The most popular majors were management (35%), business administration (25%), and management information systems (9%). In an average class, 4% graduate in 3 years or less, 19% graduate in 4 years or less, 39% graduate in 5 years or less, and 43% graduate in 6 years or less. 10 companies recruited on campus in a recent year.

Admissions Contact: David Wegener, Director of Admissions. E-mail: *admityou@stritch.edu* Web: *www.stritch.edu*

CARROLL COLLEGE
Waukesha, WI 53186

D-5
(262) 524-7220
(800) CARROLL; Fax: (262) 524-7139

Full-time: 847 men, 1215 women	**Faculty:** 94; IIB, -$
Part-time: 218 men, 434 women	**Ph.Ds:** 74%
Graduate: 66 men, 188 women	**Student/Faculty:** 22 to 1
Year: semesters, summer session	**Tuition:** $17,380
Application Deadline: open	**Room & Board:** $5360
Freshman Class: 2064 applied, 1607 accepted, 511 enrolled	
ACT: 23	**COMPETITIVE**

Carroll College, founded in 1846, is an independent liberal arts institution affiliated with the Presbyterian Church (U.S.A.). In addition to regional accreditation, Carroll has baccalaureate program accreditation with APTA and NLN. The library contains 150,000 volumes, 21,566 microform items, and 1128 audio/video tapes/CDs, and subscribes to 912 periodicals. Computerized library services include the card catalog, interlibrary loans, database searching, and Internet access. Special learning facilities include a learning resource center, art gallery, radio station, a studio theater, recital hall, and Civil War collection. The 52-acre campus is in a suburban area 15 miles west of Milwaukee. Including any residence halls, there are 31 buildings.

Student Life: 77% of undergraduates are from Wisconsin. Students are from 28 states, 27 foreign countries, and Canada. 85% are from public schools. 92% are white. 60% are claim no religious affiliation; 21% Protestant; 19% Catholic. The average age of freshmen is 18; all undergraduates, 25. 23% do not continue beyond their first year; 60% remain to graduate.

Housing: 1105 students can be accommodated in college housing, which includes single-sex and coed dorms and on-campus apartments. On-campus housing is guaranteed for all 4 years. 52% of students live on campus. All students may keep cars.

Activities: 3% of men belong to 2 local fraternities; 8% of women belong to 4 national sororities. There are 50 groups on campus, including activities board, art, band, cheerleading, choir, chorale, chorus, computers, dance, drama, ethnic, film, gay, honors, international, jazz band, literary magazine, musical theater, orchestra, photography, political, professional, radio and TV, religious, social, social service, student government, and symphony. Popular campus events include International Folk Fair, Madrigal Dinner, and Spring Fling.

Sports: There are 9 intercollegiate sports for men and 9 for women, and 8 intramural sports for men and 8 for women. Facilities include an all-purpose field house, gym including volleyball court, 2 basketball courts, and an indoor track, 6 tennis courts, 6-lane pool, 2 sand volleyball courts, football/soccer field, practice field, softball diamond, batting cages, athletic training rooms, exercise/physiology laboratory, weight room, fitness weight room, dance studio, and a campus center which houses Ping-Pong tables, pool tables, dart machine, and video games.

Disabled Students: 20% of the campus is accessible. Wheelchair ramps, elevators, special parking, specially equipped rest rooms, and special class scheduling are available.

Services: Counseling and information services are available, as is tutoring in most subjects. There is a reader service for the blind. Academic coaching is available.

Campus Safety and Security: Measures include 24-hour foot and vehicle patrol, self-defense education, security escort services, and informal discussions. There are pamphlets/posters/films, emergency telephones, and lighted pathways/sidewalks.

Programs of Study: Carroll confers B.A., B.S., and B.S.N. degrees. Master's degrees are also awarded. Bachelor's degrees are awarded in BIOLOGICAL SCIENCE (biochemistry, biology/biological science, and marine biology), BUSINESS (accounting, business administration and management, and organizational behavior), COMMUNICATIONS AND THE ARTS (art, communications, dramatic arts, English, music, and Spanish), COMPUTER AND PHYSICAL SCIENCE (actuarial science, applied mathematics, chemistry, computer science, information sciences and systems, and mathematics), EDUCATION (art, athletic training, early childhood, elementary, foreign languages, music, physical, and science), ENGINEERING AND ENVIRONMENTAL DESIGN (environmental science and graphic arts technology), HEALTH PROFESSIONS (clinical science, exercise science, and nursing), SOCIAL SCIENCE (criminal justice, geography, history, international relations, political science/government, psychology, religion, and sociology). Sciences, computer science, and education are the strongest academically. Business, education, and nursing are the largest.

Required: To graduate, students must complete 128 credit hours, 32 to 40 in the major, with a minimum GPA of 2.0. Students must take 7 courses from the Liberal Studies Progarm and a first-year seminar and writing seminar. 1 computer science course and a math course are needed for the B.S.; 12 credits of modern language or the humanities and math competency is needed for the B.A.

Special: A Washington semester at American University and a United Nations semester are offered, as are internships and individually designed majors. Study abroad in Wales is available for the junior year. Under the International and Off-Campus Program, juniors and seniors may travel to places that are culturally different from their own, such as Western and Eastern Europe, Latin America, Africa, or Asia. A capstone experience bridges the student's college work to employment or graduate school. There are 5 national honor societies and a freshman honors program.

Faculty/Classroom: 50% of faculty are male; 50%, female. 96% teach undergraduates, and 100% both teach and do research. No introductory courses are taught by graduate students. The average class size in an introductory lecture is 24; in a laboratory, 15; and in a regular course, 18.

Admissions: 78% of the 2003-2004 applicants were accepted. The ACT scores for the 2003-2004 freshman class were: 29% below 21, 27% between 21 and 23, 28% between 24 and 26, 10% between 27 and 28, and 6% above 28. 37% of the current freshmen were in the top fifth of their class; 67% were in the top two fifths. There was 1 National Merit finalist and 3 semifinalists. 20 freshmen graduated first in their class.

Requirements: The SAT I or ACT is required. In addition, applicants must be graduates of an accredited secondary school. The GED is accepted. An essay and interview are recommended for all students, and a portfolio or audition is advised for art and music students, respectively. Carroll requires applicants to be in the upper 50% of their class. A GPA of 2.0 is required. AP and CLEP credits are accepted. Important factors in the admissions decision are advanced placement or honor courses, recommendations by school officials, and evidence of special talent.

Procedure: Freshmen are admitted fall and spring. Entrance exams should be taken during the junior year. There is a rolling admissions plan and a deferred admissions plan. Application deadlines are open. Applications are accepted on computer disk and on-line.

Transfer: 176 transfer students enrolled in 2002-2003. Applicants for transfer must have a minimum GPA of 2.0. An interview is required. 32 of 128 credits required for the bachelor's degree must be completed at Carroll.

Visiting: There are regularly scheduled orientations for prospective students, consisting of a campus tour, financial aid/admissions counseling, academic department meetings, and extracurricular activities meetings. There are guides for informal visits and visitors may sit in on classes and stay overnight. To schedule a visit, contact the Office of Admissions.

Financial Aid: In a recent year, 98% of all full-time students received some form of financial aid. 69% of full-time freshmen and 74% of continuing full-time students received need-based aid. The average freshman award was $15,000. Need-based scholarships or need-based grants averaged $11,018; need-based self-help aid (loans and jobs) averaged $3607; and tuition remission averaged $378. 68% of undergraduates work part time. Average annual earnings from campus work are $950. The average financial indebtedness of the 2003 graduate was $15,195. The FAFSA is required. The deadline for filing freshman financial aid applications for fall entry is September 1.

International Students: There are 34 international students enrolled. The school actively recruits these students. They must score 550 on the written TOEFL or 213 on the electronic version.

Computers: The mainframe consists of 3 HP 9000s (HP-UX), 5 NT servers, and 2 Mac servers. One central student computer lab with 60 Windows and Mac computers is complemented by several departmental student labs with more than 100 PCs. There are 6 computer classrooms. Internet access is available in all computer labs and classrooms and in residence hall rooms. All students may access the system 24 hours every day. There are no time limits and no fees.

Graduates: From July 1, 2002 to June 30, 2003, 494 bachelor's degrees were awarded. The most popular majors were education (16%), business (12%), and nursing (9%). In an average class, 48% graduate in 4 years or less, 57% graduate in 5 years or less, and 60% graduate in 6 years or less. 5 companies recruited on campus in 2002-2003.

Admissions Contact: James V. Wiseman, Vice President, Enrollment. E-mail: *cc.info@ccadmin.cc.edu* Web: *www.cc.edu*

CARTHAGE COLLEGE

E-5

Kenosha, WI 53140   (262) 551-6000

(800) 351-4058; Fax: (262) 551-5762

Full-time: 850 men, 875 women	**Faculty:** 102; IIB, av$
Part-time: 160 men, 380 women	**Ph.D.s:** 85%
Graduate: 16 men, 71 women	**Student/Faculty:** 17 to 1
Year: 4-1-4, summer session	**Tuition:** $19,000
Application Deadline: open	**Room & Board:** $6000
Freshman Class: n/av	
SAT I or ACT: required	**COMPETITIVE**

Carthage College, founded in 1847, is an independent liberal arts institution affiliated with the Evangelical Lutheran Church in America. Information in the above capsule and in this profile is approximate. In addition to regional accreditation, Carthage has baccalaureate program accreditation with CSWE and NASM. The library contains 130,000 volumes, 9000 microform items, and 1300 audio/video tapes/CDs, and subscribes to 450 periodicals. Computerized library services include the card catalog, interlibrary loans, and database searching. Special learning facilities include a learning resource center, art gallery, and radio station. The 75-acre campus is in a suburban area 30 miles south of Milwaukee and 60 miles north of Chicago, on the shore of Lake Michigan. Including any residence halls, there are 16 buildings.

Student Life: 52% of undergraduates are from out of state, mostly the Midwest. Students are from 23 states, 14 foreign countries, and Canada. 88% are from public schools. 89% are white. 31% are Catholic; 26% claim no religious affiliation; 13% Protestant; 7% Orthodox, Muslim. The average age of freshmen is 18; all undergraduates, 20. 24% do not continue beyond their first year; 50% remain to graduate.

Housing: 1250 students can be accommodated in college housing, which includes single-sex and coed dorms. In addition, there are study-intensive and health and wellness floors. On-campus housing is guaranteed for all 4 years. 70% of students live on campus; of those, 75% remain on campus on weekends. Alcohol is not permitted. All students may keep cars.

Activities: 28% of men belong to 5 local and 3 national fraternities; 22% of women belong to 4 local and 2 national sororities. There are 85

groups on campus, including art, band, cheerleading, choir, chorus, computers, debate, drama, ethnic, film, forensics, gay, Habitat for Humanity, honors, international, jazz band, literary magazine, musical theater, newspaper, orchestra, pep band, photography, political, professional, radio and TV, religious, social, social service, student government, and yearbook. Popular campus events include May Madness, Little Sibling Weekend, and Casino Night.

Sports: There are 10 intercollegiate sports for men and 10 for women, and 10 intramural sports for men and 5 for women. Facilities include a phys ed center, a 3000-seat stadium, a 3500-seat gym, tennis courts, baseball, soccer, and softball fields, and a natatorium.

Disabled Students: 90% of the campus is accessible. Wheelchair ramps, elevators, special parking, specially equipped rest rooms, special class scheduling, lowered drinking fountains, lowered telephones, and TDD phones are available.

Services: Counseling and information services are available, as is tutoring in most subjects.

Campus Safety and Security: Measures include 24-hour foot and vehicle patrol, self-defense education, security escort services, and informal discussions. There are pamphlets/posters/films, emergency telephones, lighted pathways/sidewalks, and electronic exit locks on residence halls.

Programs of Study: Carthage confers the B.A. degree. Master's degrees are also awarded. Bachelor's degrees are awarded in BIOLOGICAL SCIENCE (biology/biological science), BUSINESS (accounting, business administration and management, international economics, and marketing management), COMMUNICATIONS AND THE ARTS (art, English, fine arts, French, German, graphic design, languages, music, performing arts, Spanish, and studio art), COMPUTER AND PHYSICAL SCIENCE (chemistry, mathematics, natural sciences, and physics), EDUCATION (elementary, English, foreign languages, mathematics, middle school, music, physical, and secondary), SOCIAL SCIENCE (criminal justice, economics, geography, history, philosophy, political science/government, psychology, religion, social science, social work, and sociology). Education, business, and sciences are the strongest academically. Business and education are the largest.

Required: To graduate, students must complete 138 credits, with up to 56 in the major, and a minimum GPA of 2.0 (education requires 2.75). Students must complete 50 credits in liberal arts studies, including the Heritage Seminar Series, which includes 3 courses that help develop competencies in cultural studies, writing, thinking, reading, speaking, and listening. 2 courses each are required in religion and foreign language, and 1 in math. There is also a phys ed requirement. Each student must complete one of the junior symposia, a series of 3 interdependent courses, and a senior project in the major.

Special: Internships are available during the January term or, in some cases, for a semester. Carthage offers study abroad in 5 countries, cross-registration with the University of Wisconsin, a Washington semester, a general studies degree, an accelerated degree program in business administration, work-study programs, and dual and student-designed majors. Students may take a 3-2 engineering degree with Case Western Reserve or Washington Universities, and the University of Minnesota-Twin Cities or the University of Wisconsin/Madison, or a 3-2 occupational therapy degree with Washington University. There are pass/fail options and credit for military and work experience. There are 3 national honor societies and a freshman honors program.

Faculty/Classroom: 68% of faculty are male; 33%, female. All teach undergraduates. No introductory courses are taught by graduate students. The average class size in an introductory lecture is 19; in a laboratory, 19; and in a regular course, 19.

Admissions: There was 1 National Merit semifinalist in a recent year.

Requirements: The SAT I or ACT is required. In addition, applicants should be graduates of an accredited secondary school, having earned 16 academic credits, including English, foreign language, math, science, and social studies. The GED is accepted. An interview is recommended. A GPA of 2.0 is required. AP and CLEP credits are accepted. Important factors in the admissions decision are advanced placement or honor courses, leadership record, and extracurricular activities record.

Procedure: Freshmen are admitted to all sessions. Entrance exams should be taken in spring of the junior year or fall of the senior year. There is a deferred admissions plan. Application deadlines are open. Application fee is $25. Applications are accepted on-line through the Carthage web site. Notification is sent on a rolling basis.

Transfer: 76 transfer students enrolled in a recent year. Transfer students are accepted based on academic performance at their previous school; they should have a GPA greater than 2.0. If they have fewer than 12 credits, the high school record is considered. Either the SAT I or ACT and an interview are recommended. 32 of 138 credits required for the bachelor's degree must be completed at Carthage.

Visiting: There are regularly scheduled orientations for prospective students, including small group meetings with a first year adviser and faculty members, class selection, and curriculum overview. Informational sessions for parents are offered. There are guides for informal visits and visitors may sit in on classes and stay overnight. To schedule a visit, contact the Office of Admissions, Mary Schuch, Visit Coordinator at visit@carthage.edu.

Financial Aid: In a recent year, all full-time freshmen and 99% of continuing full-time students received some form of financial aid. 68% of full-time freshmen and 61% of continuing full-time students received need-based aid. The average freshman award was $16,004. 35% of undergraduates work part time. Average annual earnings from campus work are $1000. The average financial indebtedness of the 2003 graduate was $16,807. The FAFSA is required. The deadline for filing freshman financial aid applications for fall entry is February 15.

International Students: There were 22 international students enrolled in a recent year. The school actively recruits these students. They must score 500 on the written TOEFL.

Computers: The mainframe is an IBM AS/400. There are also 120 Macs and PCs available in academic buildings and residence halls; all are attached to the campus network. Network access is available in each room. All students may access the system 24 hours on weekdays, 8 A.M. to 8 P.M. on weekends. There are no time limits and no fees.

Graduates: In a recent year, 298 bachelor's degrees were awarded. The most popular majors were business (27%), education (13%), and social science (10%). In an average class, 1% graduate in 3 years or less, 47% graduate in 4 years or less, and 58% graduate in 5 years or less. 25 companies recruited on campus in 2002-2003. Of the 2002 graduating class, 14% were enrolled in graduate school within 6 months of graduation and 98% were employed.

Admissions Contact: Thomas J. Augustine, Director of Admissions and Financial Aid. E-mail: *admissions@carthage.edu* Web: *www.carthage.edu*

CONCORDIA UNIVERSITY WISCONSIN E-4
Mequon, WI 53097 (414) 243-4300; Fax: (414) 243-4545

Full-time: 950 men, 1620 women	**Faculty:** 96; IIB, -$
Part-time: 475 men, 810 women	**Ph.D.s:** 60%
Graduate: 120 men, 210 women	**Student/Faculty:** 27 to 1
Year: 4-1-4, summer session	**Tuition:** $12,400
Application Deadline: see profile	**Room & Board:** $4200
Freshman Class: n/av	
SAT I or ACT: required	**COMPETITIVE**

Concordia University Wisconsin, established in 1881, is a private institution affiliated with the Lutheran Church-Missouri Synod. There are 4 undergraduate schools and 1 graduate school. Figures in the above capsule and in this profile are approximate. In addition to regional accreditation, CUW has baccalaureate program accreditation with NLN. The library contains 110,929 volumes, 270,602 microform items, and 4645 audio/video tapes/CDs, and subscribes to 1411 periodicals. Computerized library services include the card catalog, interlibrary loans, and database searching. Special learning facilities include a learning resource center, art gallery, radio station, and a curriculum library for education students. The 155-acre campus is in a suburban area 15 miles north of Milwaukee. Including any residence halls, there are 17 buildings.

Student Life: 60% of undergraduates are from Wisconsin. Students are from 19 states and 25 foreign countries. 83% are white; 12% African American. 80% are Protestant; 13% Catholic; 7% claim no religious affiliation. The average age of freshmen is 18; all undergraduates, 21. 25% do not continue beyond their first year; 42% remain to graduate.

Housing: 916 students can be accommodated in college housing, which includes single-sex dorms. On-campus housing is guaranteed for all 4 years and is available on a first-come, first-served basis. 69% of students live on campus; of those, 50% remain on campus on weekends. Alcohol is not permitted. All students may keep cars.

Activities: There are no fraternities or sororities. There are 20 groups on campus, including art, band, cheerleading, choir, chorale, drama, drill team, ethnic, honors, international, jazz band, literary magazine, musical theater, newspaper, pep band, political, professional, radio and TV, religious, and student government. Popular campus events include Winterfest and Springfest.

Sports: There are 9 intercollegiate sports for men and 7 for women, and 10 intramural sports for men and 9 for women. Facilities include a field house, stadium, gym, weight room, and fitness center.

Disabled Students: 80% of the campus is accessible. Wheelchair ramps, elevators, special parking, and specially equipped rest rooms are available.

Services: Counseling and information services are available, as is tutoring in every subject. There is a reader service for the blind and remedial math, reading, and writing.

Campus Safety and Security: Security guards are on staff from 4 P.M. to 8 A.M. on weekdays and 24 hours a day on weekends.

Programs of Study: CUW confers B.A., B.S., and B.S.N. degrees. Associate and master's degrees are also awarded. Bachelor's degrees are awarded in BIOLOGICAL SCIENCE (biology/biological science), BUSINESS (accounting, banking and finance, business administration and management, management science, and marketing/retailing/merchandising), COMMUNICATIONS AND THE ARTS (art, communications, English, graphic design, music, Spanish, speech/debate/rhetoric, and telecommunications), COMPUTER AND PHYSICAL SCIENCE (mathematics and radiological technology), EDUCATION (athletic training, early childhood, elementary, physical, and secondary), ENGINEERING AND ENVIRONMENTAL DESIGN (interior design), HEALTH PROFESSIONS (nursing, occupational therapy, and sports medicine), SOCIAL SCIENCE (biblical languages, criminal justice, history, humanities, ministries, paralegal studies, pastoral studies, psychology, religion, religious music, social science, social work, and theological studies). Education, business, and health sciences are the strongest academically.

Required: To graduate, students must complete 126 credits, including at least 30 in the major, with a minimum GPA of 2.0. The 47 1/2 credit core curriculum includes theology/philosophy, humanities, cross culture, social science, natural science, communication, math, and phys ed.

Special: Internships, study abroad, pass/fail options, and credit for life, military, and work experience are available. Concordia offers a general studies degree, dual, student-designed, and interdisciplinary majors, including justice and public policy, and nondegree study. Accelerated degree programs are available in several fields. There is 1 national honor society.

Faculty/Classroom: 50% of faculty are male; 50%, female. All teach undergraduates. No introductory courses are taught by graduate students. The average class size in a regular course is 17.

Requirements: The SAT I or ACT is required. A minimum composite score of 850 on the SAT I or 18 on the ACT is required. Applicants must be graduates of an accredited secondary school, having completed 16 academic credits, including 3 of English and 2 each of math, science, and social studies. The GED is accepted. A GPA of 2.5 is required. AP and CLEP credits are accepted. Important factors in the admissions decision are leadership record, recommendations by school officials, and personality/intangible qualities.

Procedure: Freshmen are admitted to all sessions. Entrance exams should be taken in the junior year. There is a rolling admissions plan. Check with the school for current deadlines. The fall 2003 application fee was $25.

Transfer: Applicants for transfer must have a minimum GPA of 2.0 and meet the same entrance exam criteria as entering freshmen. 36 of 126 credits required for the bachelor's degree must be completed at CUW.

Visiting: There are regularly scheduled orientations for prospective students, including a tour and financial aid and academic information sessions. There are guides for informal visits and visitors may sit in on classes and stay overnight. To schedule a visit, contact the Admission Office.

Financial Aid: The CSS Profile or FAFSA, the college's own financial statement, and income tax forms are required. Check with the school for current deadlines.

International Students: The school actively recruits these students. They must score 500 on the written TOEFL and also take the college's own test. If the student's TOEFL score is below 500, the student must take an English proficiency exam for placement.

Computers: The mainframe is an HP9000. There are Macs and PCS available to all students throughout the campus. All PCs are connected via a LAN and have Internet access. All students may access the system. There are no time limits and no fees.

Graduates: In an average class, 52% graduate in 6 years or less.

Admissions Contact: Andrew G. Locke, Director of Admissions. E-mail: *admission@cuw.edu* Web: *www.cuw.edu*

EDGEWOOD COLLEGE
Madison, WI 53711-1997

C-4
(608) 663-2294
(800) 444-4861; Fax: (608) 663-3291

Full-time: 388 men, 1060 women	Faculty: 69; IIA, --$
Part-time: 128 men, 333 women	Ph.D.s: 76%
Graduate: 194 men, 319 women	Student/Faculty: 21 to 1
Year: 4-1-4, summer session	Tuition: $15,100
Application Deadline: August 1	Room & Board: $5420
Freshman Class: 1060 applied, 852 accepted, 308 enrolled	
ACT: 21	COMPETITIVE

Edgewood College, established in 1927, is a private Catholic institution sponsored by the Sinsinawa Dominican Sisters. Some information in this capsule and profile is approximate. In addition to regional accreditation, Edgewood has baccalaureate program accreditation with NCATE. The library contains 88,329 volumes, 94,050 microform items, and 3946 audio/video tapes/CDs, and subscribes to 494 periodicals. Computerized library services include the card catalog, interlibrary loans, and database searching. Special learning facilities include a learning resource center and art gallery. The 55-acre campus is in a suburban area 5 miles southwest of Madison. Including any residence halls, there are 10 buildings.

Student Life: 98% of undergraduates are from Wisconsin. Students are from 11 states and 10 foreign countries. 75% are from public schools. 52% are white. 39% are Catholic; 24% Protestant. The average age of freshmen is 20; all undergraduates, 25. 32% do not continue beyond their first year; 39% remain to graduate.

Housing: 325 students can be accommodated in college housing, which includes single-sex and coed dorms and on-campus apartments.

On-campus housing is guaranteed for all 4 years. 80% of students commute. Alcohol is not permitted. All students may keep cars.

Activities: There are no fraternities or sororities. There are 30 groups on campus, including art, band, choir, chorale, chorus, drama, ethnic, gay, honors, international, literary magazine, musical theater, newspaper, orchestra, pep band, political, religious, social, social service, student government, and symphony. Popular campus events include Springfest, Mazzuchelli Fest, and Winter Frost.

Sports: There are 5 intercollegiate sports for men and 7 for women, and 9 intramural sports for men and 9 for women. Facilities include a 1000-seat gym, soccer, baseball, and softball fields, a fitness center, and access to tennis courts.

Disabled Students: 85% of the campus is accessible. Wheelchair ramps, elevators, special parking, specially equipped rest rooms, special class scheduling, lowered drinking fountains, lowered telephones, automated doors in the library, science center, activities center, and residence halls, and a chairlift are available.

Services: Counseling and information services are available, as is tutoring in some subjects, including most sciences, introductory math courses, and Spanish. There is a reader service for the blind and remedial math, reading, and writing.

Campus Safety and Security: Measures include self-defense education, security escort services, informal discussions, and pamphlets/posters/films. There are emergency telephones and lighted pathways/sidewalks. Residence halls have alarms, a security card system, and campus security guards. RAs are on duty 24 hours a day weekends and 7 A.M. to 3 P.M. and 8 P.M. to 4 A.M. weekdays.

Programs of Study: Edgewood confers B.A. and B.S. degrees. Associate and master's degrees are also awarded. Bachelor's degrees are awarded in BIOLOGICAL SCIENCE (biology/biological science), BUSINESS (accounting and business administration and management), COMMUNICATIONS AND THE ARTS (art, English, French, graphic design, music, performing arts, and Spanish), COMPUTER AND PHYSICAL SCIENCE (chemistry, information sciences and systems, mathematics, and natural sciences), EDUCATION (early childhood, education of the exceptional child, elementary, science, and social studies), ENGINEERING AND ENVIRONMENTAL DESIGN (preengineering), HEALTH PROFESSIONS (art therapy, cytotechnology, medical technology, nursing, premedicine, prepharmacy, and preveterinary science), SOCIAL SCIENCE (child care/child and family studies, criminal justice, economics, history, international relations, political science/government, prelaw, psychology, public administration, religion, and sociology). Liberal arts is the strongest academically. Business, education, and nursing are the largest.

Required: To graduate, students must complete a minimum of 120 credit hours with a minimum GPA of 2.0. There are general education requirements, and each student must complete a major and Human Issues study.

Special: Students may cross-register with the University of Wisconsin/Madison. Internships, study abroad, dual and student-designed majors, nondegree study, pass/fail options, and credit for life, military, and work experience are available. There is a weekend degree program. There are 5 national honor societies and a freshman honors program.

Faculty/Classroom: 49% of faculty are male; 51%, female. 89% teach undergraduates and 6% both teach and do research. No introductory courses are taught by graduate students. The average class size in an introductory lecture is 20; in a laboratory, 18; and in a regular course, 17.

Admissions: 80% of the 2003-2004 applicants were accepted. The ACT scores for the 2003-2004 freshman class were: 41% below 21, 29% between 21 and 23, 23% between 24 and 26, 5% between 27 and 28, and 2% above 28. 22% of the current freshmen were in the top fifth of their class; 61% were in the top two fifths.

Requirements: The SAT I or ACT is required; the ACT is preferred, with a recommended minimum composite score of 18. Applicants should complete 16 Carnegie units, including 4 of English, 3 of math, 2 each of natural science, foreign language, and social science, and 3 units of electives. The GED is accepted. Edgewood requires applicants to be in the upper 50% of their class. A GPA of 2.5 is required. AP and CLEP credits are accepted. Important factors in the admissions decision are extracurricular activities record, leadership record, and recommendations by school officials.

Procedure: Freshmen are admitted fall and spring. Entrance exams should be taken by the senior year. There is a rolling admissions plan. Applications should be filed by August 1 for fall entry and December 15 for spring entry. Check with the school for current application fee. Notification is sent on a rolling basis. Applications are accepted on-line through the school's web site.

Transfer: Applicants must have a minimum GPA of 2.0. Official high school and all college transcripts must be sent from schools attended. 32 credits of 120 required for the bachelor's degree must be completed at Edgewood.

Visiting: There are regularly scheduled orientations for prospective students, including meeting with counselors, a campus tour, meeting with faculty, and lunch on campus. There are guides for informal visits and visitors may sit in on classes and stay overnight. To schedule a visit, contact the Admissions Office.

Financial Aid: In 2003-2004, 89% of all full-time freshmen and 79% of continuing full-time students received some form of financial aid. 73% of full-time freshmen and 65% of continuing full-time students received need-based aid. The average freshman award was $11,283. Need-based scholarships or need-based grants averaged $8093; need-based self-help aid (loans and jobs) averaged $3859; and non-need-based awards and non-need-based scholarships averaged $9669. 85% of undergraduates work part time. Average annual earnings from campus work are $1360. Edgewood is a member of CSS. The FAFSA, the college's own financial statement, and a tax return are required. Check with the school for current deadlines.

International Students: The school actively recruits these students. They must score 525 on the written TOEFL or take the MELAB.

Computers: The college provides IBM and Mac computer facilities for student use. The computer center houses 4 computer labs, a Windows NT lab with 25 systems, a technology classroom with 26 Windows NT systems, and a Mac lab with 20 systems. All students may access the system The labs are open 7:30 A.M. to midnight Monday through Friday, and 8 A.M. to 5 P.M. on weekends. There are no time limits and no fees. It is strongly recommended that all students have a personal computer. Students in the computer science class CS 180 must lease an IBM Think-Pad.

Graduates: In a recent year, 334 bachelor's degrees were awarded. The most popular majors were business (31%), education (17%), and nursing (13%). In an average class, 20% graduate in 4 years or less, 39% graduate in 5 years or less, and 43% graduate in 6 years or less. 35 companies recruited on campus in a recent year.

Admissions Contact: Scott Flanagan, Dean of Admissions and Financial Aid. E-mail: *admissions@edgewood.edu* Web: *www.edgewood.edu*

LAKELAND COLLEGE
Sheboygan, WI 53082-0359

E-4

(920) 565-1588

(800) 242-3347; Fax: (920) 565-1206

Full-time: 395 men, 405 women	**Faculty:** 41; IIB, --$
Part-time: 25 men, 30 women	**Ph.D.s:** 59%
Graduate: 55 men, 130 women	**Student/Faculty:** 19 to 1
Year: semesters, summer session	**Tuition:** $12,380
Application Deadline: see profile	**Room & Board:** $5050
Freshman Class: n/av	
SAT I or ACT: required	**COMPETITIVE**

Lakeland College, established in 1862, is a private institution affiliated with the United Church of Christ. The 4-4-1 academic calendar consists of 4-month fall and spring terms, and an optional 3 1/2 week May term. Figures in the above capsule and in this profile are approximate. The library contains 57,447 volumes, 33,169 microform items, and 2099 audio/video tapes/CDs, and subscribes to 322 periodicals. Computerized library services include the card catalog, interlibrary loans, and database searching. Special learning facilities include a learning resource center, art gallery, and a college history museum. The 240-acre campus is in a rural area 10 miles northwest of Sheboygan. Including any residence halls, there are 24 buildings.

Student Life: 79% of undergraduates are from Wisconsin. Students are from 16 states, 31 foreign countries, and Canada. 90% are from public schools. 76% are white. 32% are Protestant; 29% Catholic; 25% claim no religious affiliation. The average age of all undergraduates is 22. 32% do not continue beyond their first year; 43% remain to graduate.

Housing: 488 students can be accommodated in college housing, which includes single-sex and coed dorms and on-campus apartments. In addition, there are honors houses and male-only, female-only, and housing for students with senior standing. On-campus housing is guaranteed for all 4 years. 57% of students live on campus; of those, 60% remain on campus on weekends. All students may keep cars.

Activities: 17% of men belong to 3 local fraternities; 11% of women belong to 3 local sororities. There are 27 groups on campus, including band, choir, chorus, dance team, drama, ethnic, honors, international, literary magazine, newspaper, pep band, professional, radio and TV, religious, social, student government, and yearbook. Popular campus events include Winter Carnival and Spring Celebration.

Sports: There are 8 intercollegiate sports for men and 7 for women, and 2 intramural sports for men and 2 for women. Facilities include a sports complex, a fitness lab, 3 full-size basketball courts, a weight room, indoor and outdoor tennis courts, indoor pitching and batting facilities, and softball, baseball, football, soccer, and practice fields.

Disabled Students: 83% of the campus is accessible. Wheelchair ramps, elevators, special parking, specially equipped rest rooms, and lowered drinking fountains are available, though not at every building.

Services: Counseling and information services are available, as is tutoring in every subject. There is a reader service for the blind and remedial math, reading, and writing.

Campus Safety and Security: Measures include security escort services, informal discussions, pamphlets/posters/films, and emergency telephones. There are lighted pathways/sidewalks and foot patrol on weekends and evenings.

Programs of Study: Lakeland confers the B.A. degree. Master's degrees are also awarded. Bachelor's degrees are awarded in BIOLOGICAL SCIENCE (biology/biological science), BUSINESS (accounting, business administration and management, business economics, hospitality management services, international business management, and marketing management), COMMUNICATIONS AND THE ARTS (art, creative writing, dramatic arts, English, German, music, and Spanish), COMPUTER AND PHYSICAL SCIENCE (chemistry, computer science, and mathematics), EDUCATION (business, early childhood, elementary, music, and secondary), SOCIAL SCIENCE (behavioral science, criminal justice, economics, history, philosophy, physical fitness/movement, psychology, public administration, religion, and sociology). Business, education, and accounting are the strongest academically. Education, business, and computer science are the largest.

Required: To graduate, students must complete 128 semester hours, with at least 32 in the major and a minimum 2.0 GPA. There are requirements in history, humanities, natural sciences, social sciences, and religion.

Special: Internships in all majors, study abroad in Germany and Japan, a Washington semester, and work-study programs are available. There are some dual majors, a general studies degree, a 3-2 engineering degree with the University of Wisconsin/Madison, a 2-2 1/2 nursing program with Bellin College of Nursing, and nondegree study. There is a freshman honors program.

Faculty/Classroom: 51% of faculty are male; 49%, female. All both teach and do research. No introductory courses are taught by graduate students. The average class size in an introductory lecture is 20; in a laboratory, 15; and in a regular course, 16.

Requirements: The SAT I or ACT is required, with a minimum composite score of 950 on the SAT I or 19 on the ACT. Applicants must be graduates of an accredited secondary school or have the GED. An interview is recommended. Lakeland requires applicants to be in the upper 50% of their class. A GPA of 2.0 is required. AP and CLEP credits are accepted. Important factors in the admissions decision are advanced placement or honor courses, leadership record, and evidence of special talent.

Procedure: Freshmen are admitted fall, spring, and summer. Entrance exams should be taken after the enrollment commitment is made. There is a rolling admissions plan. Check with the school for current deadlines. Application fee is $20. Notification is sent on a rolling basis. Applications are accepted on-line via the college's web site, *www.lakeland.edu;* CollegeNET; and Wisconsin mentor.

Transfer: 115 transfer students enrolled in a recent year. Applicants should have a GPA of at least 2.0. Lakeland recommends an interview. 36 of 128 credits required for the bachelor's degree must be completed at Lakeland.

Visiting: There are regularly scheduled orientations for prospective students, consisting of meetings with faculty and financial aid personnel, activities meetings, and a campus tour. There are guides for informal visits and visitors may sit in on classes and stay overnight. To schedule a visit, contact the Admissions Office at *admissions@lakeland.edu.*

Financial Aid: In a recent year, all full-time freshmen and 97% of continuing full-time students received some form of financial aid. 86% of full-time freshmen and 90% of continuing full-time students received need-based aid. The average freshman award was $11,895. 30% of undergraduates work part time. Average annual earnings from campus work are $1000. The average financial indebtedness of a recent graduate was $20,558. Lakeland is a member of CSS. The FAFSA and the college's own financial statement are required. Check with the school for current deadlines.

International Students: In a recent year, there were 100 international students enrolled. The school actively recruits these students. They must score 500 on the written TOEFL.

Computers: The mainframe consists of several Nt/Citrix servers. Lakeland has 4 computer rooms with approximately 30 computers in each room and an additional 10 computers in the library. All computers are connected to the college network and have acccess to the Internet. All students may access the system 7 A.M. to 2 A.M.

Graduates: In a recent year, 145 bachelor's degrees were awarded. The most popular majors were education (28%), business administration (17%), and computer science (10%). In an average class, 13% graduate in 3 years or less, 30% graduate in 4 years or less, 43% graduate in 5 years or less, and 46% graduate in 6 years or less. Of a recent graduating class, 10% were enrolled in graduate school within 6 months of graduation and 95% were employed.

Admissions Contact: Leo Gavrilos, Director of Admissions. E-mail: *admissions@lakeland.edu* Web: *www.lakeland.edu*

LAWRENCE UNIVERSITY
Appleton, WI 54912

D-3

(920) 832-6500
(800) 227-0982; Fax: (920) 832-6782

Full-time: 612 men, 701 women	Faculty: 130; IIB, +$
Part-time: 20 men, 19 women	Ph.D.s: 93%
Graduate: none	Student/Faculty: 10 to 1
Year: trimesters	Tuition: $25,116
Application Deadline: January 15	Room & Board: $5784
Freshman Class: 1714 applied, 1192 accepted, 352 enrolled	
SAT I Verbal/Math: 630/630	ACT: 27 HIGHLY COMPETITIVE

Lawrence University, founded in 1847, is an independent liberal arts institution with a conservatory of music. In addition to regional accreditation, Lawrence has baccalaureate program accreditation with NASM. The library contains 377,000 volumes, 104,000 microform items, and 20,000 audio/video tapes/CDs, and subscribes to 1500 periodicals. Computerized library services include the card catalog, interlibrary loans, and database searching. Special learning facilities include a learning resource center, art gallery, natural history museum, and radio station. The 84-acre campus is in an urban area 100 miles north of Milwaukee. Including any residence halls, there are 60 buildings.

Student Life: 62% of undergraduates are from out of state, mostly the Midwest. Students are from 49 states, 50 foreign countries, and Canada. 77% are from public schools. 80% are white; 10% foreign nationals. 49% claim no religious affiliation; 19% Protestant; 18% Catholic; 13% Buddhist, Hindu, Muslim, other. The average age of freshmen is 18; all undergraduates, 20. 10% do not continue beyond their first year; 72% remain to graduate.

Housing: All students are required to live on campus. Housing includes single-sex and coed dorms, on-campus apartments, married-student housing, and fraternity houses. In addition, there are language houses and special-interest houses. On-campus housing is guaranteed for all 4 years. All students may keep cars.

Activities: 33% of men belong to 5 national fraternities; 17% of women belong to 3 national sororities. There are 130 groups on campus, including art, band, cheerleading, chess, choir, chorale, chorus, computers, dance, drama, ethnic, film, gay, honors, international, jazz band, literary magazine, musical theater, newspaper, opera, orchestra, pep band, political, professional, radio and TV, religious, social, social service, student government, symphony, and yearbook. Popular campus events include Octoberfest, Celebrate! Spring Festival of the Arts, and Annual Midwest Trivia Contest.

Sports: There are 15 intercollegiate sports for men and 13 for women, and 22 intramural sports for men and 28 for women. 40% of men and 35% of women participate in intercollegiate sports. Facilities include a 5255-seat lighted football stadium; 8-lane all-weather and 4-lane indoor tracks; baseball, soccer, practice fields; 6 tennis, 1 squash, and 7 racquetball/handball courts; 2 gyms for basketball, volleyball, and badminton; 3 batting cages; an 8-lane swimming pool with diving well; weight, exercise, and sauna rooms; and a dance studio.

Disabled Students: 80% of the campus is accessible. Wheelchair ramps, elevators, special parking, specially equipped rest rooms, and special class scheduling are available.

Services: Counseling and information services are available, as is tutoring in every subject. There is a reader service for the blind and remedial math and writing. The writing lab focuses on enhancing writing skills, as well as remedial writing.

Campus Safety and Security: Measures include 24-hour foot and vehicle patrol, self-defense education, security escort services, and informal discussions. There are pamphlets/posters/films, emergency telephones, lighted pathways/sidewalks, and the Whistle Stop Program.

Programs of Study: Lawrence confers B.A. and B.Mus. degrees. Bachelor's degrees are awarded in BIOLOGICAL SCIENCE (biology/ biological science and neurosciences), COMMUNICATIONS AND THE ARTS (art history and appreciation, classics, dramatic arts, English, French, German, linguistics, music performance, music theory and composition, Russian, Spanish, and studio art), COMPUTER AND PHYSICAL SCIENCE (chemistry, computer science, geology, mathematics, and physics), EDUCATION (art, music, and secondary), ENGINEERING AND ENVIRONMENTAL DESIGN (environmental science), SOCIAL SCIENCE (anthropology, East Asian studies, economics, gender studies, history, international relations, philosophy, political science/government, psychology, and religion). Biology, music, and physics are the strongest academically. Biology, music, and psychology are the largest.

Required: Students must complete 216 units (270 units for a double-degree program), including 48 to 72 in the major, with a minimum GPA of 2.0. All students must take Freshman Studies. Distribution requirements include 12 units each in humanities, social sciences, and natural sciences, including a lab course, and 6 units in fine arts. Competency requirements must also be met in writing, speaking, foreign language, and quantitative analysis. Some majors require a comprehensive exam or a thesis. The B.Mus. requires that two thirds of courses are in the conservatory and one third are in subjects other than music.

Special: Lawrence offers Chicago-based programs in urban studies, urban education, and the arts, a humanities program at the Newberry Library, and a science internship at Oak Ridge National Laboratory. There are study-abroad programs in 14 countries, a Washington semester, limited pass/fail options, student-designed majors, and nondegree study. Students may take a 3-2 engineering degree with Columbia or Washington Universities, Rensselaer Polytechnic Institute, or the University of Michigan. Also available are 3-2 programs in forestry and environmental studies with Duke University, in occupational therapy with Washington University in St. Louis, and in allied health sciences (nursing/medical technology) with Rush-Presbyterian-St. Luke's Medical Center in Chicago. A 5-year B.A.-B.Mus. degree is offered. There are 8 national honor societies, including Phi Beta Kappa, and 21 departmental honors programs.

Faculty/Classroom: 60% of faculty are male; 40%, female. All both teach and do research. The average class size in an introductory lecture is 29; in a laboratory, 14; and in a regular course, 16.

Admissions: 70% of the 2003-2004 applicants were accepted. The SAT I scores for the 2003-2004 freshman class were: Verbal--4% below 500, 24% between 500 and 599, 54% between 600 and 700, and 18% above 700; Math--4% below 500, 28% between 500 and 599, 50% between 600 and 700, and 18% above 700. The ACT scores were 3% below 21, 11% between 21 and 23, 24% between 24 and 26, 24% between 27 and 28, and 38% above 28. 62% of the current freshmen were in the top fifth of their class; 91% were in the top two fifths. There were 15 National Merit finalists and 6 semifinalists. 11 freshmen graduated first in their class.

Requirements: The SAT I or ACT is required. In addition, applicants should complete 16 high school academic credits. Lawrence requires an essay, reports from a teacher and counselor, and, for music majors, an audition. The school recommends the SAT II: Writing test, an interview, and, for art majors, a portfolio. AP credits are accepted. Important factors in the admissions decision are advanced placement or honor courses, evidence of special talent, and extracurricular activities record.

Procedure: Freshmen are admitted in the fall. Entrance exams should be taken in the spring of the junior year or fall of the senior year. There are early decision, early admissions, and deferred admissions plans. Early decision applications should be filed by November 15; regular applications, by January 15 for fall entry, along with a $30 fee. Notification of early decision is sent December 1; regular decision, April 1. 35 early decision candidates were accepted for the 2003-2004 class; 16 were admitted. Applications are accepted on-line through Common App and Wisconsin Mentor.

Transfer: 32 transfer students enrolled in 2002-2003. Applicants must present official transcripts of their college and secondary school work, SAT I or ACT scores, and the recommendation of a college professor. Typically, candidates with a college GPA of 2.75 or higher will receive serious consideration. 108 of 216 credits required for the bachelor's degree must be completed at Lawrence.

Visiting: There are regularly scheduled orientations for prospective students, including an extensive day-long program with many choices of classes and presentations. There are guides for informal visits and visitors may sit in on classes and stay overnight. To schedule a visit, contact the Office of Admissions at (800) 448-3072 or excel@lawrence.edu.

Financial Aid: In 2003-2004, 90% of all full-time students received some form of financial aid. 73% of full-time freshmen and 72% of continuing full-time students received need-based aid. The average freshman award was $19,156. Need-based scholarships or need-based grants averaged $16,399 ($24,900 maximum); need-based self-help aid (loans and jobs) averaged $5577 ($8625 maximum); and non-need-based awards and non-need-based scholarships averaged $7657 ($24,900 maximum). 70% of undergraduates work part time. Average annual earnings from campus work are $1500. The average financial indebtedness of the 2003 graduate was $17,366. Lawrence is a member of CSS. The FAFSA and the college's own financial statement are required. The deadline for filing freshman financial aid applications for fall entry is March 15.

International Students: There are 139 international students enrolled. The school actively recruits these students. They must score 575 on the written TOEFL or 230 on the electronic version.

Computers: The university maintains a campus network with high-speed access to various servers and the Internet. Besides access to shared resources, students have their own workspace on the network as well as an area for web development. All students receive a Lawrence e-mail account and storage for messages. Residence halls are wired to enable students to connect from their rooms and there are computer labs in all major residence halls and academic facilities. All students may access the system 24 hours a day. There are no time limits and no fees. It is strongly recommended that all students have a personal computer.

Graduates: From July 1, 2002 to June 30, 2003, 221 bachelor's degrees were awarded. The most popular majors were music performance (15%), biology (10%), and psychology (8%). In an average class, 1% graduate in 3 years or less, 60% graduate in 4 years or less, 68% graduate in 5 years or less, and 70% graduate in 6 years or less. 40 companies recruited on campus in 2002-2003. Of the 2002 graduating class, 30%

were enrolled in graduate school within 6 months of graduation and 59% were employed.

Admissions Contact: Steven Syverson, Dean of Admissions. E-mail: *excel@lawrence.edu* Web: *www.lawrence.edu*

MARIAN COLLEGE OF FOND DU LAC   D-4
Fond du Lac, WI 54935

(920) 923-7650
(800) 2-MARIAN; Fax: (920) 923-8755

Full-time: 343 men, 832 women	**Faculty:** 73; IIB, --$
Part-time: 170 men, 400 women	**Ph.D.s:** 64%
Graduate: 324 men, 603 women	**Student/Faculty:** 16 to 1
Year: semesters, summer session	**Tuition:** $15,025
Application Deadline: open	**Room & Board:** $4600
Freshman Class: 884 applied, 684 accepted, 251 enrolled	
ACT: 20	**COMPETITIVE**

Marian College, founded in 1936, is a private, Catholic, liberal-arts based institution offering degree programs in the arts and sciences, business, education, and health fields. There is 1 undergraduate and 3 graduate schools. In addition to regional accreditation, Marian has baccalaureate program accreditation with CSWE, IACBE, NCATE, and NLN. The library contains 90,327 volumes, 14,978 microform items, and 913 audio/video tapes/CDs, and subscribes to 737 periodicals. Computerized library services include the card catalog, interlibrary loans, database searching, and Internet access. Special learning facilities include a learning resource center. The 77-acre campus is in a small town 60 miles north of Milwaukee. Including any residence halls, there are 24 buildings.

Student Life: 82% of undergraduates are from Wisconsin. Students are from 14 states, 11 foreign countries, and Canada. 70% are from public schools. 91% are white. 60% are Catholic; 40% Protestant. The average age of freshmen is 20; all undergraduates, 31. 27% do not continue beyond their first year; 47% remain to graduate.

Housing: 441 students can be accommodated in college housing, which includes single-sex and coed dormitories, on-campus apartments, fraternity houses, sorority houses, and a chemical-free wellness residence hall. On-campus housing is guaranteed for all 4 years. 60% of students commute. All students may keep cars.

Activities: 10% of men belong to 2 national fraternities; 8% of women belong to 1 local and 2 national sororities. There are 36 groups on campus, including band, campus ministry, cheerleading, choir, chorus, dance, drama, ethnic, gay, honors, international, jazz band, literary magazine, multicultural, newspaper, orchestra, photography, political, professional, radio and TV, religious, social, social service, student government, symphony, and yearbook. Popular campus events include Heritage Festival of Arts, Fine Arts Series, and Sabre Show.

Sports: There are 6 intercollegiate sports for men and 6 for women, and 8 intramural sports for men and 6 for women. Facilities include a soccer field, a softball field, a gym, tennis courts, a game room, a hockey rink, and a weight room.

Disabled Students: All of the campus is accessible. Wheelchair ramps, elevators, special parking, specially equipped rest rooms, special class scheduling, lowered drinking fountains, and lowered telephones are available.

Services: Counseling and information services are available, as is tutoring in most subjects. There is a reader service for the blind, and remedial math, reading, and writing.

Campus Safety and Security: Measures include self-defense education, security escort services, shuttle buses, and informal discussions. There are pamphlets/posters/films, emergency telephones, lighted pathways/sidewalks, and evening foot and vehicle patrol.

Programs of Study: Marian confers B.A., B.S., B.B.A., B.S.B.A., B.S.Ed., B.S.M.T., B.S.N., B.S.R.T., and B.S.W. degrees. Master's degrees are also awarded. Bachelor's degrees are awarded in BIOLOGICAL SCIENCE (biology/biological science), BUSINESS (accounting, business administration and management, management science, marketing/retailing/merchandising, and sports management), COMMUNICATIONS AND THE ARTS (art, communications, English, music, music business management, and Spanish), COMPUTER AND PHYSICAL SCIENCE (chemistry, information sciences and systems, mathematics, and radiological technology), EDUCATION (art, early childhood, elementary, middle school, music, and secondary), HEALTH PROFESSIONS (cytotechnology, medical laboratory technology, and nursing), SOCIAL SCIENCE (criminal justice, economics, history, human services, interdisciplinary studies, psychology, social work, and sociology). Nursing, education, and business are the strongest academically and have the largest enrollments.

Required: To graduate, students must complete 128 credits with a minimum GPA of 2.0 (nursing and social work, 2.75; education, 3.0). Core requirements include 25 credits in arts and humanities, 12 to 13 in social and behavioral science, and 12 in math and natural science, as well as a freshman seminar.

Special: Internships are offered in most areas of study, cooperative education programs in all majors, and accelerated-degree programs in nurs-

ing, business administration, and operation management. Student-designed and dual majors, credit for prior learning, work-study, nondegree study, and cooperative education (paid work experience) are available. Study abroad at Harlaxton College, England, is possible. There are evening degree completion programs for working adults. There are 7 national honor societies and a freshman honors program.

Faculty/Classroom: 54% of faculty are male; 46%, female. All teach undergraduates. No introductory courses are taught by graduate students. The average class size in an introductory lecture is 18; in a laboratory, 13; and in a regular course, 12.

Admissions: 77% of the 2003-2004 applicants were accepted. The ACT scores for the 2003-2004 freshman class were: 59% below 21, 23% between 21 and 23, 10% between 24 and 26, 6% between 27 and 28, and 2% above 28. 26% of the current freshmen were in the top fifth of their class; 51% were in the top two fifths.

Requirements: The ACT is required, with a minimum composite score of 18. Applicants must be graduates of an accredited secondary school or have earned a GED. An interview is recommended. Marian requires applicants to be in the upper 50% of their class. A GPA of 2.0 is required. AP and CLEP credits are accepted. Important factors in the admissions decision are advanced placement or honor courses, leadership record, and evidence of special talent.

Procedure: Freshmen are admitted to all sessions. Entrance exams should be taken in the junior year. There is a rolling admissions plan. There are early admissions and deferred admissions plans. Application deadlines are open. Applications are accepted on-line through College-NET or the school's web site.

Transfer: 161 transfer students enrolled in 2002-2003. The school recommends a minimum GPA of 2.0, the SAT I or ACT, and an interview. 32 of 128 credits required for the bachelor's degree must be completed at Marian.

Visiting: There are regularly scheduled orientations for prospective students, consisting of sessions in April, May, June, and July for course selection and meeting with advisors. There are guides for informal visits and visitors may sit in on classes and stay overnight. To schedule a visit, contact the Admissions Office at (800) 2-MARIN, ext.7650, or *admissionsinfo@mariancollege.edu*.

Financial Aid: In 2003-2004, 96% of all full-time freshmen and 94% of continuing full-time students received some form of financial aid. 94% of all full-time students received need-based aid. The average freshman award was $13,640. Need-based scholarships or need-based grants averaged $5325 ($21,985 maximum); need-based self-help aid (loans and jobs) averaged $4697 ($6625 maximum); and non-need-based awards and non-need-based scholarships averaged $5299 ($17,640 maximum). 38% of undergraduates work part time. Average annual earnings from campus work are $809. The average financial indebtedness of the 2003 graduate was $19,500. The FAFSA and the college's own financial statement are required. The deadline for filing freshman financial aid applications for fall entry is March 15.

International Students: There are 29 international students enrolled. The school actively recruits these students. They must score 525 on the written TOEFL or 193 on the electronic version and also take the SAT I or preferably the ACT.

Computers: The mainframe consists of PC servers. There are 200 Macs and PCs available, as well as word processing equipment. All students may access the system. There are no time limits and no fees. It is strongly recommended that all students have a personal computer.

Graduates: From July 1, 2002 to June 30, 2003, 287 bachelor's degrees were awarded. The most popular majors were business administration (31%), nursing (16%), and education (15%). In an average class, 27% graduate in 4 years or less, 45% graduate in 5 years or less, and 46% graduate in 6 years or less. 14 companies recruited on campus in 2002-2003. Of the 2002 graduating class, 9% were enrolled in graduate school within 6 months of graduation and 84% were employed.

Admissions Contact: Stacey Akey, Dean of Enrollment Management. A video is available. E-mail: *admissions@mariancollege.edu* Web: *www.mariancollege.edu*

MARQUETTE UNIVERSITY   E-4
Milwaukee, WI 53201-1881

(414) 288-7302
(800) 222-6544; Fax: (414) 288-3764

Full-time: 3269 men, 3973 women	**Faculty:** 479; I, --$
Part-time: 207 men, 326 women	**Ph.D.s:** 87%
Graduate: 1225 men, 1159 women	**Student/Faculty:** 15 to 1
Year: semesters, summer session	**Tuition:** $20,724
Application Deadline: open	**Room & Board:** $6870
Freshman Class: 8232 applied, 6807 accepted, 1887 enrolled	
SAT I Verbal/Math: 580/586	**ACT:** 25 **VERY COMPETITIVE**

Marquette University, established in 1881, is a private Roman Catholic Jesuit institution. There are 7 undergraduate and 4 graduate schools. In addition to regional accreditation, Marquette has baccalaureate program accreditation with AACSB, ABET, ACEJMC, ADA, APTA, ASLA, CSWE, NCATE, and NLN. The 3 libraries contain 1,319,451 volumes,

1,454,579 microform items, and 12,059 audio/video tapes/CDs, and subscribe to 15,868 periodicals. Computerized library services include the card catalog, interlibrary loans, database searching, and Internet access. Special learning facilities include a learning resource center, art gallery, radio station, and TV station. The 80-acre campus is in an urban area in the heart of Milwaukee. Including any residence halls, there are 60 buildings.

Student Life: 53% of undergraduates are from out of state, mostly the Midwest. Students are from 50 states, 54 foreign countries, and Canada. 54% are from public schools. 88% are white. 69% are Catholic; 17% Protestant; 14% unknown or claim no religious affiliation. The average age of freshmen is 18; all undergraduates, 21. 11% do not continue beyond their first year; 76% remain to graduate.

Housing: 3273 students can be accommodated in college housing, which includes single-sex and coed dorms, on-campus apartments, and married-student housing. In addition, there are honors houses and specified majors, quiet/study, and multicultural floors. On-campus housing is guaranteed for the freshman and sophomore years only and is available on a lottery system for upperclassmen. 93% of students live on or near campus; of those, more than 80% remain on campus on weekends. All students may keep cars.

Activities: 6% of men belong to 7 national fraternities; 8% of women belong to 9 national sororities. There are 180 groups on campus, including band, cheerleading, choir, chorale, chorus, community awareness, dance, drama, ethnic, gay, honors, international, jazz band, literary magazine, musical theater, newspaper, orchestra, pep band, photography, political, professional, radio and TV, recreational, religious, social, social service, and student government. Popular campus events include Student Organizational Fest, Winter Flurry, and Hunger Clean Up.

Sports: There are 7 intercollegiate sports for men and 7 for women, and 39 intramural sports for men and 39 for women. Facilities include 2 recreation centers and Valley Fields, an outdoor soccer, track, and football facility.

Disabled Students: 90% of the campus is accessible. Wheelchair ramps, elevators, special parking, specially equipped rest rooms, special class scheduling, lowered drinking fountains, lowered telephones, and special housing are available.

Services: Counseling and information services are available, as is tutoring in some subjects, including many lower-division classes taken by freshmen and sophomores. There is a reader service for the blind. and book taping and note taking for the physically disabled.

Campus Safety and Security: Measures include 24-hour foot and vehicle patrol, self-defense education, security escort services, and shuttle buses. There are informal discussions, pamphlets/posters/films, emergency telephones, lighted pathways/sidewalks, and closed-circuit cameras in selected parking lots and buildings throughout the campus.

Programs of Study: Marquette confers B.A., B.S., and B.S.N. degrees. Associate, master's, and doctoral degrees are also awarded. Bachelor's degrees are awarded in BIOLOGICAL SCIENCE (biochemistry, biology/ biological science, molecular biology, and physiology), BUSINESS (accounting, banking and finance, business administration and management, business economics, human resources, international business management, management information systems, and marketing/ retailing/merchandising), COMMUNICATIONS AND THE ARTS (advertising, broadcasting, classical languages, classics, communications, dramatic arts, English, French, German, journalism, public relations, and Spanish), COMPUTER AND PHYSICAL SCIENCE (chemistry, computer science, information sciences and systems, mathematics, physics, and statistics), EDUCATION (secondary), ENGINEERING AND ENVIRONMENTAL DESIGN (biomedical engineering, civil engineering, computer engineering, electrical/electronics engineering, engineering, environmental engineering, industrial engineering technology, and mechanical engineering), HEALTH PROFESSIONS (biomedical science, exercise science, medical laboratory science, nursing, premedicine, and speech pathology/audiology), SOCIAL SCIENCE (anthropology, criminology, economics, history, interdisciplinary studies, international relations, philosophy, political science/government, psychology, sociology, and theological studies). Biomedical engineering, nursing, and premed are the strongest academically. Business administration, nursing, and engineering are the largest.

Required: To graduate, students must complete a total of 126 to 135 credit hours and maintain a minimum GPA of 2.0, or 2.5 in accounting. The 36-credit-hour core of common studies includes 6 credit hours each of rhetoric, human nature and ethics, and theology, and 3 each of mathematical reasoning, individual and social behavior, science and nature, histories of cultures and societies, literature and performing arts, and diverse cultures.

Special: Marquette offers co-op programs in engineering, internships, study abroad in 16 countries, a Washington summer term, and work-study programs. Dual and student-designed majors, nondegree study, an accelerated degree program for predental and prelaw students, and pass/ fail options are available. Cross-registration is possible with Milwaukee Institute of Art and Design, and there is a 2-2 engineering program with Waukesha County Technical college. The Freshman Frontier Program offers academic support for selected freshmen who do not meet regular

admission requirements but show potential for success. The Educational Opportunity Program affords students from minority groups and low-income families the opportunity to attend the school. There are 8 national honor societies, including Phi Beta Kappa, a freshman honors program, and a university-wide honors program.

Faculty/Classroom: 62% of faculty are male; 38%, female. 83% teach undergraduates, 65% do research, and 60% do both. No introductory courses are taught by graduate students. The average class size in an introductory lecture is 33; in a laboratory, 17; and in a regular course, 28.

Admissions: 83% of the 2003-2004 applicants were accepted. The SAT I scores for the 2003-2004 freshman class were: Verbal--14% below 500, 44% between 500 and 599, 37% between 600 and 700, and 5% above 700; Math--16% below 500, 35% between 500 and 599, 41% between 600 and 700, and 8% above 700. The ACT scores were 9% below 21, 24% between 21 and 23, 30% between 24 and 26, 19% between 27 and 28, and 19% above 28. 58% of the current freshmen were in the top fifth of their class; 84% were in the top two fifths. There were 9 National Merit finalists.

Requirements: The SAT I or ACT is required. In addition, applicants must be graduates of an accredited secondary school with a recommended 18 credits, including 4 years of English, 3 each of social studies and math, 2 each of sciences and foreign language, and 4 of additional academic subjects. Most students rank in the upper quarter of their high school class. The GED is accepted, with a minimum score of 225. Applicants must demonstrate ability, preparation, and motivation. An interview is recommended. AP and CLEP credits are accepted. Important factors in the admissions decision are advanced placement or honor courses, recommendations by school officials, and leadership record.

Procedure: Freshmen are admitted to all sessions. Entrance exams should be taken in the junior year and repeated early in the senior year if necessary. There is a rolling admissions plan. Application deadlines are open. Applications are accepted on-line through the university's web site.

Transfer: 224 transfer students enrolled in 2002-2003. Applicants for transfer must have a minimum GPA of 2.0; some programs require a higher average. The SAT I or ACT is required if the applicant has completed fewer than 12 hours of college-level work. 32 of 126 to 135 credits required for the bachelor's degree must be completed at Marquette.

Visiting: There are regularly scheduled orientations for prospective students. The agenda for visits varies according to the specific program; open houses are available on scheduled weekends throughout the academic year. There are guides for informal visits and visitors may sit in on classes and stay overnight. To schedule a visit, contact the Admissions Office.

Financial Aid: In 2003-2004, 92% of all full-time freshmen and 89% of continuing full-time students received some form of financial aid. 66% of full-time freshmen and 55% of continuing full-time students received need-based aid. The average freshman award was $14,665. Need-based scholarships or need-based grants averaged $4743 ($17,000 maximum); need-based self-help aid (loans and jobs) averaged $2927; non-need-based athletic scholarships averaged $342; and other non-need-based awards and non-need-based scholarships averaged $6677. 44% of undergraduates work part time. Average annual earnings from campus work are $1500. The average financial indebtedness of the 2003 graduate was $22,924. Marquette is a member of CSS. The FAFSA is required. The priority date for freshman financial aid applications for fall entry is March 1.

International Students: There are 174 international students enrolled. The school actively recruits these students. They must score 525 on the written TOEFL or 200 on the electronic version and also take the Comprehensive English Language Test, the college's own test, or IELTS. Marquette requires success in final external secondary exams according to the student's country of education.

Computers: The mainframe consists of various DEC VAX models in a cluster configuration. There are more than 1000 PCs in residence halls, libraries, and academic facilities. Students can also use word-processing facilities in the library, computing center, and various buildings. Residence halls are wired for Web and Internet access. All students may access the system 24 hours a day. There are no time limits and no fees.

Graduates: From July 1, 2002 to June 30, 2003, 1732 bachelor's degrees were awarded. The most popular majors were business and marketing (20%), communications (17%), and engineering (14%). In an average class, 61% graduate in 4 years or less, 75% graduate in 5 years or less, and 76% graduate in 6 years or less. 320 companies recruited on campus in 2002-2003. Of the 2002 graduating class, 26% were enrolled in graduate school within 1 year of graduation and 67% were employed.

Admissions Contact: Robert Blust, Dean of Admissions.
E-mail: *admissions@marquette.edu* Web: *www.marquette.edu*

MILWAUKEE INSTITUTE OF ART AND DESIGN
Milwaukee, WI 53202-6003

E-4

(414) 291-8070
(888) 749-MIAD; Fax: (414) 291-8077

Full-time: 295 men, 295 women	**Faculty:** 26
Part-time: 30 men, 40 women	**Ph.D.s:** 85%
Graduate: none	**Student/Faculty:** 23 to 1
Year: semesters, summer session	**Tuition:** $17,930
Application Deadline: see profile	**Room & Board:** $6460
Freshman Class: n/av	
SAT I or ACT: recommended	**SPECIAL**

Milwaukee Institute of Art and Design, founded in 1974, is a private, 4-year professional college of art and design. Figures in the above capsule and in this profile are approximate. In addition to regional accreditation, MIAD has baccalaureate program accreditation with NASAD. The library contains 29,000 volumes and 380 audio/video tapes/CDs, and subscribes to 85 periodicals. Computerized library services include the card catalog, interlibrary loans, and database searching. Special learning facilities include a learning resource center, art gallery, and museum. The campus is in an urban area in downtown Milwaukee. Including any residence halls, there are 4 buildings.

Student Life: 72% of undergraduates are from Wisconsin. Students are from 20 states. 80% are from public schools. 88% are white. The average age of freshmen is 19; all undergraduates, 23. 21% do not continue beyond their first year; 73% remain to graduate.

Housing: 144 students can be accommodated in college housing, which includes coed dorms. On-campus housing is available on a first-come, first-served basis. 77% of students commute. Alcohol is not permitted. All students may keep cars.

Activities: There are no fraternities or sororities. There are 7 groups on campus, including art, ethnic, literary magazine, photography, professional, religious, student government, and yearbook. Popular campus events include visiting artist lectures and workshops, student and faculty exhibitions, and a scholarship show.

Sports: There is no sports program at MIAD.

Disabled Students: All of the campus is accessible. Wheelchair ramps, elevators, specially equipped rest rooms, lowered drinking fountains, and lowered telephones are available.

Services: Counseling and information services are available, as is tutoring in some subjects, including liberal studies. There is remedial writing. There is a program in developmental freshman English, as well as student tutoring, and a writing center.

Campus Safety and Security: Measures include security escort services, informal discussions, pamphlets/posters/films, and emergency telephones. There are lighted pathways/sidewalks.

Programs of Study: MIAD confers the B.F.A. degree. Bachelor's degrees are awarded in COMMUNICATIONS AND THE ARTS (drawing, fine arts, graphic design, illustration, industrial design, painting, photography, printmaking, and sculpture), ENGINEERING AND ENVIRONMENTAL DESIGN (interior design). Graphic design, illustration, and industrial design are the largest.

Required: About 66% of the graduation credits are in studio courses. Students must complete 124 credits, with 81 studio credits, 43 in liberal studies, and a minimum GPA of 2.0 MIAD requires 12 credits in art history and at least 12 credits in English/writing and 19 credits in the humanities and sciences.

Special: Students may cross-register with Marquette University and 29 other nationally accredited art colleges. Study abroad in Japan, Germany, Poland, and France, a semester at New York Artists Studio, and internships in all design fields and photography are available. Nondegree study and credit for life, military, and work experience are possible.

Faculty/Classroom: 64% of faculty are male; 36%, female. All teach undergraduates. The average class size in a regular course is 16.

Requirements: The SAT I or ACT is recommended. In addition, applicants must be graduates of an accredited secondary school. 4 years of art are recommended. A portfolio review and an interview are required. A GPA of 2.0 is required. AP and CLEP credits are accepted. Important factors in the admissions decision are evidence of special talent, advanced placement or honor courses, and personality/intangible qualities.

Procedure: Freshmen are admitted fall and spring. There is a deferred admissions plan and a rolling admissions plan. Check with the school for current deadlines. The fall 2003 application fee was $25. Notification is sent on a rolling basis.

Transfer: 60 transfer students enrolled in a recent year. A transfer portfolio evaluation is done. Transcripts are reviewed for courses comparable to MIAD's programs. A grade of C or better is required for transfer. 30 of 124 credits required for the bachelor's degree must be completed at MIAD.

Visiting: There are guides for informal visits and visitors may sit in on classes. To schedule a visit, contact the Admissions Office.

Financial Aid: In a recent year, 83% of all full-time freshmen and 89% of continuing full-time students received some form of financial aid. 82% of full-time freshmen and 87% of continuing full-time students received need-based aid. The average freshman award was $12,142. The average financial indebtedness of a recent graduate was $21,258. The FAFSA is required. Check with the school for current deadlines.

International Students: In a recent year, there were 20 international students enrolled. The school actively recruits these students. They must score 550 on the written TOEFL.

Computers: The mainframe is a Mac Power PC. There are 43 stations in the computer lab and 6 computer labs with more than 90 computers. All students may access the system more than 80 hours a week.

Graduates: In a recent year, 91 bachelor's degrees were awarded. The most popular majors were communication design (24%), illustration (18%), and drawing (15%). In an average class, 33% graduate in 4 years or less, 41% graduate in 5 years or less, and 42% graduate in 6 years or less. 15 companies recruited on campus in a recent year. Of a recent graduating class, 1% were enrolled in graduate school within 6 months of graduation and 90% were employed.

Admissions Contact: Mary Schopp, Executive Director, Enrollment Services. A video is available. E-mail: *miadadm@miad.edu* Web: *www.miad.edu*

MILWAUKEE SCHOOL OF ENGINEERING
Milwaukee, WI 53202-3109

E-4

(414) 277-7481
(800) 332-6763; Fax: (414) 277-7475

Full-time: 1466 men, 296 women	**Faculty:** 127; IIB, +$
Part-time: 281 men, 58 women	**Ph.D.s:** 62%
Graduate: 221 men, 61 women	**Student/Faculty:** 14 to 1
Year: quarters, summer session	**Tuition:** $23,034
Application Deadline: open	**Room & Board:** $5445
Freshman Class: 1809 applied, 1177 accepted, 439 enrolled	
SAT I Verbal/Math: 575/600	**ACT:** 26 **VERY COMPETITIVE+**

Milwaukee School of Engineering, established in 1903, is a private institution with programs in engineering, engineering technology, business, communication, and nursing. There are 5 undergraduate and 3 graduate schools. In addition to regional accreditation, MSOE has baccalaureate program accreditation with ABET, ACCE, and CCNE. The library contains 55,754 volumes, 77,454 microform items, and 1207 audio/video tapes/CDs, and subscribes to 514 periodicals. Computerized library services include the card catalog, database searching, and Internet access. Special learning facilities include a learning resource center and radio station. The 14-acre campus is in an urban area in Milwaukee. Including any residence halls, there are 13 buildings.

Student Life: 69% of undergraduates are from Wisconsin. Students are from 31 states, 24 foreign countries, and Canada. 77% are white. The average age of freshmen is 18; all undergraduates, 21. 23% do not continue beyond their first year; 57% remain to graduate.

Housing: 932 students can be accommodated in college housing, which includes coed dorms and on-campus apartments. In addition, there are special-interest houses and suites for upperclassmen with kitchens, bathrooms, and living rooms. On-campus housing is guaranteed for all 4 years. 52% of students live on campus; of those, 65% remain on campus on weekends. All students may keep cars.

Activities: 7% of men and about 1% of women belong to 3 national fraternities; 12% of women belong to 1 local and 1 national sorority. There are 61 groups on campus, including cheerleading, chess, computers, ethnic, film, gaming, honors, international, literary magazine, pep band, political, professional, radio and TV, religious, sci-fi, social, social service, student government, and yearbook. Popular campus events include St. Patrick's Week, Cultural Spirit Week, and Orientation Week.

Sports: There are 10 intercollegiate sports for men and 8 for women, and 6 intramural sports for men and 6 for women. Facilities include a health, wellness, and athletic center.

Disabled Students: 75% of the campus is accessible. Wheelchair ramps, elevators, special parking, specially equipped rest rooms, special class scheduling, lowered drinking fountains, and lowered telephones are available.

Services: Counseling and information services are available, as is tutoring in every subject. There is a reader service for the blind and remedial math, reading, and writing.

Campus Safety and Security: Measures include 24-hour foot and vehicle patrol, security escort services, shuttle buses, and informal discussions. There are pamphlets/posters/films, emergency telephones, lighted pathways/sidewalks, and 24-hour security in residence halls.

Programs of Study: MSOE confers B.A. and B.S. degrees. Master's degrees are also awarded. Bachelor's degrees are awarded in BUSINESS (business administration and management, international business management, management information systems, and management science), COMMUNICATIONS AND THE ARTS (technical and business writing), COMPUTER AND PHYSICAL SCIENCE (software engineering), ENGINEERING AND ENVIRONMENTAL DESIGN (architectural engineering, biomedical engineering, computer engineering, construction management, electrical/electronics engineering, engineering technology, industrial engineering, and mechanical engineering), HEALTH PROFESSIONS (nursing). Biomedical engineering and computer engineering are the strongest academically. Architectural, mechanical, and electrical engineering are the largest.

Required: To graduate, students must complete approximately 205 quarter credits with a minimum GPA of 2.0. There are requirements in speech, composition, computer programming, ethics, and business.

Special: MSOE offers summer internships in the student's discipline, study-abroad in Germany, India, and Czech Republic, on-campus work-study programs, and nondegree study. A 4-year engineering degree and a dual degree in engineering and business communication or technical communication, along with a 5-year dual degree with a bachelor's in engineering and a master's in environmental engineering, are available. There are 2 national honor societies.

Faculty/Classroom: 76% of faculty are male; 24%, female. All teach undergraduates, 2% do research, and 25% do both. No introductory courses are taught by graduate students. The average class size in an introductory lecture is 19; in a laboratory, 15; and in a regular course, 18.

Admissions: 65% of the 2003-2004 applicants were accepted. The SAT I scores for the 2003-2004 freshman class were: Verbal--11% below 500, 46% between 500 and 599, 34% between 600 and 700, and 9% above 700; Math--7% below 500, 32% between 500 and 599, 45% between 600 and 700, and 16% above 700. The ACT scores were 1% below 21, 24% between 21 and 23, 28% between 24 and 26, 32% between 27 and 28, and 15% above 28.

Requirements: MSOE requires the ACT, though the SAT I is acceptable. In addition, applicants must be graduates of an accredited secondary school, having completed 15 academic credits, including 4 units of English, 2 units each of science and math, and 1 unit each of social studies and history. More units in math, science, and English are strongly advised; 1 unit in computer science is helpful. The GED is accepted. An essay is required, and an interview is recommended. A GPA of 2.5 is required. AP and CLEP credits are accepted. Important factors in the admissions decision are advanced placement or honor courses, leadership record, and personality/intangible qualities.

Procedure: Freshmen are admitted to all sessions. There is a rolling admissions plan. Application deadlines are open. Application fee is $25. Applications are accepted on computer disk and on-line through CollegeView and EXPAN.

Transfer: 124 transfer students enrolled in 2002-2003. Applicants for transfer should have a minimum GPA of 2.5. 103 of 205 credits required for the bachelor's degree must be completed at MSOE.

Visiting: There are regularly scheduled orientations for prospective students, consisting of personal visits, Spring and Fall Open Houses, and the Shadow Program. There are guides for informal visits and visitors may sit in on classes and stay overnight. To schedule a visit, contact the Admission Office at *explore@msoe.edu*.

Financial Aid: In 2003-2004, 96% of all full-time freshmen and 82% of continuing full-time students received some form of financial aid. 74% of full-time freshmen and 79% of continuing full-time students received need-based aid. The average freshman award was $21,232. Need-based scholarships or need-based grants averaged $2623 ($8414 maximum); need-based self-help aid (loans and jobs) averaged $2372 ($4500 maximum); non-need-based awards and non-need-based scholarships averaged $7393 ($24,174 maximum); and private loans, Plus loans and unsubsidized Stafford loans averaged $9222 ($25,000 maximum). 53% of undergraduates work part time. Average annual earnings from campus work are $1570. The average financial indebtedness of the 2003 graduate was $32,567. The FAFSA is required. The priority date for freshman financial aid applications for fall entry is March 15.

International Students: There are 52 international students enrolled. The school actively recruits these students. They must score 500 on the written TOEFL and also take the SAT I or ACT. The ACT is required for enrollment, not admission.

Computers: The mainframe is a Compaq. More than 150 PCs and terminals are located throughout the library, science building, and student center for student use. Students can also dial up the main computer center over the phone lines to access computer service. All new students (full-time) are required to be part of the computer technology package. This requires all students to have a laptop. All students may access the system. There are no time limits and no fees. All students are required to have personal computers. A Compaq is provided by MSOE.

Graduates: From July 1, 2002 to June 30, 2003, 374 bachelor's degrees were awarded. The most popular majors were mechanical engineering (21%), architectural engineering (15%), and electrical engineering (11%). In an average class, 30% graduate in 4 years or less, and 60% graduate in 5 years or less. 105 companies recruited on campus in 2002-2003. Of the 2002 graduating class, 10% were enrolled in graduate school within 6 months of graduation and 94% were employed.

Admissions Contact: Paul Borens, Director of Admission.
E-mail: *borens@msoe.edu* Web: *www.msoe.edu\admiss*

MOUNT MARY COLLEGE
Milwaukee, WI 53222

E-4
(414) 286-1219
(800) 321-6265; Fax: (414) 256-0180

Full-time: 2 men, 706 women	Faculty: 58; IIB, --$
Part-time: 51 men, 612 women	Ph.D.s: 60%
Graduate: 25 men, 204 women	Student/Faculty: 12 to 1
Year: semesters, summer session	Tuition: $15,270
Application Deadline: August	Room & Board: $5100
Freshman Class: 310 applied, 242 accepted, 105 enrolled	
ACT: 21	COMPETITIVE

Mount Mary College, founded in 1913, is a private women's liberal arts institution affiliated with the Roman Catholic Church. In addition to regional accreditation, Mount Mary has baccalaureate program accreditation with ADA, AOTA, CSWE, FIDER, and NLN. The library contains 102,408 volumes, 1535 microform items, and 7203 audio/video tapes/CDs, and subscribes to 550 periodicals. Computerized library services include the card catalog, interlibrary loans, and database searching. Special learning facilities include a learning resource center, art gallery, computer centers, CAD labs, S.M.A.R.T. classrooms, and historic costume collection. The 80-acre campus is in a suburban area 7 miles west of downtown Milwaukee. Including any residence halls, there are 7 buildings.

Student Life: 97% of undergraduates are from Wisconsin. Students are from 7 states and 6 foreign countries. 84% are from public schools. 71% are white; 18% African American. 42% are Catholic; 26% claim no religious affiliation; 20% Protestant. The average age of freshmen is 18; all undergraduates, 28. 32% do not continue beyond their first year; 63% remain to graduate.

Housing: 176 students can be accommodated in college housing, which includes single-sex dorms. On-campus housing is available on a first-come, first-served basis and is available on a lottery system for upperclassmen. Priority is given to out-of-town students. 90% of students commute. Alcohol is not permitted. All students may keep cars.

Activities: There are no fraternities. There are 38 groups on campus, including art, choir, chorale, chorus, computers, dance, drama, ethnic, honors, international, literary magazine, newspaper, political, professional, religious, social, social service, student government, and yearbook. Popular campus events include Freshman Investiture, Madrigal Dinner, and All-School Christmas Dinner.

Sports: Facilities include a gym, a swimming pool, an exercise room, a weight room, a soccer field, and large recreational grounds.

Disabled Students: 98% of the campus is accessible. Wheelchair ramps, elevators, special parking, specially equipped rest rooms, lowered drinking fountains, and lowered telephones are available.

Services: Counseling and information services are available, as is tutoring in most subjects. There is a reader service for the blind and remedial math, reading, and writing. A tutoring language lab is also available.

Campus Safety and Security: Measures include 24-hour foot and vehicle patrol, self-defense education, security escort services, and informal discussions. There are pamphlets/posters/films, emergency telephones, and lighted pathways/sidewalks.

Programs of Study: Mount Mary confers B.A., B.S., and B.S.N. degrees. Master's degrees are also awarded. Bachelor's degrees are awarded in BIOLOGICAL SCIENCE (biology/biological science), BUSINESS (accounting, business administration and management, and fashion merchandising), COMMUNICATIONS AND THE ARTS (communications, English, fine arts, French, graphic design, music, public relations, Spanish, and technical and business writing), COMPUTER AND PHYSICAL SCIENCE (chemistry, computer science, and mathematics), EDUCATION (art, bilingual/bicultural, business, early childhood, elementary, foreign languages, music, science, and secondary), ENGINEERING AND ENVIRONMENTAL DESIGN (food services technology and interior design), HEALTH PROFESSIONS (art therapy, nursing, occupational therapy, predentistry, and premedicine), SOCIAL SCIENCE (behavioral science, criminal justice, dietetics, fashion design and technology, history, international studies, philosophy, prelaw, psychology, social work, and theological studies). Business administration, teacher education, and fashion design are the largest.

Required: To graduate, students must complete 128 credit hours, including at least 24 (but as many as 74) in the major, while maintaining a GPA of at least 2.0, with many majors requiring a higher GPA. A 48-credit liberal arts core curriculum and demonstrated math competency are required.

Special: Mount Mary College offers internships, a Washington semester, accelerated degree programs in business administration, business/professional communication, and marketing, and study abroad in Japan and other countries. Student-designed majors, a joint degree with Columbia College of Nursing, pass/fail options, and credit for life, military, and work experience are available. There are 10 national honor societies and a freshman honors program.

Faculty/Classroom: 24% of faculty are male; 76%, female. 93% teach undergraduates. No introductory courses are taught by graduate stu-

dents. The average class size in an introductory lecture is 24; in a laboratory, 15; and in a regular course, 19.

Admissions: 78% of the 2003-2004 applicants were accepted. The SAT I scores for the 2003-2004 freshman class were: Verbal--50% between 500 and 599, and 50% between 600 and 700; Math--50% below 500, and 50% between 500 and 599. The ACT scores were 55% below 21, 25% between 21 and 23, 13% between 24 and 26, 4% between 27 and 28, and 2% above 28. 22% of the current freshmen were in the top fifth of their class; 50% were in the top two fifths.

Requirements: The SAT I or ACT is required. In addition, applicants must be graduates of an accredited secondary school. The GED is accepted. Students should have completed 16 credits, including 4 each in English, history, social sciences, and foreign language, and 2 each in math and science. An interview is recommended. Mount Mary requires applicants to be in the upper 40% of their class. A GPA of 2.5 is required. AP and CLEP credits are accepted. Important factors in the admissions decision are advanced placement or honor courses, recommendations by school officials, and leadership record.

Procedure: Freshmen are admitted fall and spring. Entrance exams should be taken in the junior year or fall of the senior year. There is a rolling admissions plan and a deferred admissions plan. Applications should be filed by August for fall entry and December for spring entry, along with a $25 fee. Notification is sent on a rolling basis. Applications are accepted on-line through the college's web site.

Transfer: 173 transfer students enrolled in 2002-2003. Applicants should have a minimum GPA of 2.0, though each department has its own admission requirements. The school recommends either the SAT I or ACT and an interview. 32 of 128 credits required for the bachelor's degree must be completed at Mount Mary.

Visiting: There are regularly scheduled orientations for prospective students, including tours, meetings with faculty and staff, and information sessions. There are guides for informal visits and visitors may sit in on classes and stay overnight. To schedule a visit, contact the Enrollment Office at (414) 256-1219.

Financial Aid: In a recent year, 97% of all full-time freshmen and 84% of continuing full-time students received some form of financial aid. 85% of full-time freshmen and 72% of continuing full-time students received need-based aid. The average freshman award was $10,430. 11% of undergraduates work part time. Average annual earnings from campus work are $1326. The average financial indebtedness of the 2003 graduate was $20,715. Mount Mary is a member of CSS. The FAFSA is required. The priority date for freshman financial aid applications for fall entry is March 1.

International Students: There are 6 international students enrolled. The school actively recruits these students. They must score 500 on the written TOEFL or 173 on the electronic version and also take the SAT I or the ACT.

Computers: The mainframe is a DEC Alpha 2100. Students have access to the NT server through 215 PCs, Macs, and laptops across the campus, located in the library, computer center, classrooms, and the residence hall. In addition, 2 CAD classrooms can accommodate a total of 25 students. Students have access to the Internet, e-mail, library, and dial-in e-mail off campus. All students may access the system 7 days a week, 24 hours a day. There are no time limits and no fees.

Graduates: From July 1, 2002 to June 30, 2003, 127 bachelor's degrees were awarded. The most popular majors were occupational therapy (9%), business adminstration (9%), and interior design (9%). In an average class, 40% graduate in 4 years or less, 60% graduate in 5 years or less, and 63% graduate in 6 years or less. 3 companies recruited on campus in 2002-2003. Of the 2002 graduating class, 19% were enrolled in graduate school within 6 months of graduation and 84% were employed.

Admissions Contact: Amy Dobson, Director of Enrollment. A video is available. E-mail: *admiss@mtmary.edu* Web: *www.mtmary.edu*

NORTHLAND COLLEGE
Ashland, WI 54806

B-1

(715) 682-1224
(800) 753-1840; Fax: (715) 682-1258

Full-time: 343 men, 407 women	**Faculty:** 43; IIB, --$
Part-time: none	**Ph.D.s:** 86%
Graduate: none	**Student/Faculty:** 17 to 1
Year: 4-4-1, summer session	**Tuition:** $17,070
Application Deadline: Open	**Room & Board:** $5100
Freshman Class: 896 applied, 640 accepted, 199 enrolled	
SAT I Verbal/Math: 576/561	**ACT:** 23 COMPETITIVE+

Northland College, founded in 1892, is a private liberal arts institution affiliated with the United Church of Christ and offers undergraduate programs in the arts and sciences, business, education, health professions, and social sciences. There are 3 undergraduate schools. The library contains 77,700 volumes and 9300 microform items and subscribes to 350 periodicals. Computerized library services include the card catalog, interlibrary loans, and database searching. Special learning facilities include a learning resource center, art gallery, natural history museum, environ-

mental research acreage, community garden, and wind tower. The 80-acre campus is in a small town 70 miles east of Duluth, Minnesota. Including any residence halls, there are 20 buildings.

Student Life: 65% of undergraduates are from out of state, mostly the Midwest. Students are from 43 states, 7 foreign countries, and Canada. 90% are from public schools. 84% are white. The average age of freshmen is 20; all undergraduates, 21. 20% do not continue beyond their first year; 44% remain to graduate.

Housing: 530 students can be accommodated in college housing, which includes single-sex and coed dorms, on-campus apartments, special-interest houses, and a farmhouse. On-campus housing is guaranteed for all 4 years. 60% of students live on campus; of those, 80% remain on campus on weekends. Alcohol is not permitted. All students may keep cars.

Activities: 2% of men belong to 1 local and 1 national fraternity; 2% of women belong to 2 local sororities. There are 25 groups on campus, including art, band, cheerleading, choir, chorale, chorus, computers, drama, ethnic, gay, honors, international, jazz band, literary magazine, newspaper, orchestra, photography, political, professional, religious, social, social service, student government, symphony, and yearbook. Popular campus events include Snow Festival, Parents Weekend, and Spring Fling.

Sports: There are 4 intercollegiate sports for men and 4 for women, and 11 intramural sports for men and 11 for women. Facilities include an Olympic-size pool, a weight-lifting room, tennis and racquetball courts, a ropes course, and an outdoor recreation program.

Disabled Students: 90% of the campus is accessible. Wheelchair ramps, elevators, special parking, specially equipped rest rooms, and special class scheduling are available.

Services: Counseling and information services are available, as is tutoring in every subject. There is a reader service for the blind, and remedial math, reading, and writing.

Campus Safety and Security: Measures include security escort services, informal discussions, pamphlets/posters/films, emergency telephones, and lighted pathways/sidewalks.

Programs of Study: Northland confers B.A. and B.S. degrees. Bachelor's degrees are awarded in AGRICULTURE (natural resource management), BIOLOGICAL SCIENCE (biology/biological science), BUSINESS (business administration and management and business economics), COMMUNICATIONS AND THE ARTS (creative writing, English, and fine arts), COMPUTER AND PHYSICAL SCIENCE (atmospheric sciences and meteorology, chemistry, earth science, information sciences and systems, and mathematics), EDUCATION (elementary, middle school, music, and secondary), ENGINEERING AND ENVIRONMENTAL DESIGN (environmental science), SOCIAL SCIENCE (history, parks and recreation management, peace studies, psychology, public administration, religion, and sociology). Biology, natural resources, and meteoroloy are the strongest academically. Biology, natural resources, and outdoor education are the largest.

Required: Students must complete 124 credits, including 35 to 60 in the major, with a minimum GPA of 2.0. All students must meet requirements that include courses in English composition, literature, history, philosophy, social and natural sciences, physical science, fine arts, phys ed, and studies of other cultures.

Special: Opportunities are provided for cooperative programs in many majors and with other schools, internships, work-study programs with state and federal agencies, student-designed majors, credit for life experience, pass/fail options, and study abroad in 7 countries. Cross-registration is offered with Spring Term Consortium Schools, Allegheny and Beloit Colleges, and Kansai Gaidai University in Japan. 3-2 engineering degrees are available in conjunction with Michigan Technological University and Washington University in St. Louis. A 3-2 degree program in forestry is also available. There are 2 national honor societies.

Faculty/Classroom: 81% of faculty are male; 19%, female. All teach undergraduates. The average class size in an introductory lecture is 35; in a laboratory, 20; and in a regular course, 22.

Admissions: 71% of the 2003-2004 applicants were accepted. The SAT I scores for the 2003-2004 freshman class were: Verbal--21% below 500, 54% between 500 and 599, 20% between 600 and 700, and 5% above 700; Math--22% below 500, 58% between 500 and 599, 15% between 600 and 700, and 5% above 700. The ACT scores were 31% below 21, 19% between 21 and 23, 27% between 24 and 26, 10% between 27 and 28, and 13% above 28. 46% of the current freshmen were in the top fifth of their class; 74% were in the top two fifths.

Requirements: The SAT I or ACT is required. In addition, graduation from an accredited secondary school is required; the GED is accepted. An essay and interview are recommended. A GPA of 2.0 is required. AP and CLEP credits are accepted. Important factors in the admissions decision are advanced placement or honor courses, extracurricular activities record, and recommendations by school officials.

Procedure: Freshmen are admitted fall and winter. Entrance exams should be taken in the fall. There is a rolling admissions plan. There are early decision, early admissions, and deferred admissions plans. Early decision applications should be filed by November 22; regular applications are open. Notification of early decision is sent December 22; regular decision, on a rolling basis. Applications are accepted on-line through the college's web site, www.northland.edu.

Transfer: Applicants must have maintained a minimum GPA of 2.0 in previously attended colleges. 30 of 124 credits required for the bachelor's degree must be completed at Northland.

Visiting: There are regularly scheduled orientations for prospective students, including an interview, a tour, class visits, and an overnight stay in a dorm. There are guides for informal visits and visitors may sit in on classes and stay overnight. To schedule a visit, contact the Admissions Office.

Financial Aid: In 2003-2004, 98% of all full-time freshmen received some form of financial aid. 75% of full-time freshmen and 81% of continuing full-time students received need-based aid. The average freshman award was $15,103. 90% of undergraduates work part time. Average annual earnings from campus work are $1200. The average financial indebtedness of the 2003 graduate was $17,765. Northland is a member of CSS. The FAFSA and the college's own financial statement are required. The deadline for filing freshman financial aid applications for fall entry is April 15.

International Students: There are 21 international students enrolled. The school actively recruits these students. They must score 500 on the written TOEFL or 195 on the electronic version or take the MELAB.

Computers: The mainframes are a Prime and a DEC VAX. Students have nearly unlimited use of the Prime and PCs. PCs are located in classrooms, labs, the computer center, and some residence halls. All students may access the system. There are no time limits and no fees.

Graduates: From July 1, 2002 to June 30, 2003, 109 bachelor's degrees were awarded. The most popular majors were natural resources (15%), outdoor education (15%), and biology (15%). In an average class, 2% graduate in 3 years or less, and 80% graduate in 4 years or less. Of the 2002 graduating class, 15% were enrolled in graduate school within 6 months of graduation and 95% were employed.

Admissions Contact: Eric A. Peterson, Director of Admissions. A video is available. E-mail: admit@northland.edu. Web: www.northland.edu

---

RIPON COLLEGE

Ripon, WI 54971

D-4

(920) 748-8185
(800) 94-RIPON; Fax: (920) 748-8335

Full-time: 472 men, 505 women	Faculty: 50; IIB, -$
Part-time: 6 men, 15 women	Ph.D.s: 96%
Graduate: none	Student/Faculty: 20 to 1
Year: semesters	Tuition: $19,940
Application Deadline: August 1	Room & Board: $5055
Freshman Class: 959 applied, 809 accepted, 259 enrolled	
SAT I Verbal/Math: 580/588	ACT: 24 VERY COMPETITIVE

Ripon College, established in 1851, is a private, residential, liberal arts institution affiliated with the United Church of Christ. The library contains 161,000 volumes, 25,000 microform items, and 600 audio/video tapes/CDs, and subscribes to 800 periodicals. Computerized library services include the card catalog, interlibrary loans, and database searching. Special learning facilities include a learning resource center, art gallery, radio station, a music library, an art slide library, and college archives. The 250-acre campus is in a small town 80 miles north of Milwaukee in the east-central part of the state. Including any residence halls, there are 26 buildings.

Student Life: 70% of undergraduates are from Wisconsin. Students are from 33 states, 14 foreign countries, and Canada. 57% are from public schools. 87% are white. The average age of freshmen is 18; all undergraduates, 20. 15% do not continue beyond their first year; 71% remain to graduate.

Housing: 940 students can be accommodated in college housing, which includes single-sex and coed dorms, fraternity houses, and sorority houses. Theme and interest groups may form living areas in the residence halls. On-campus housing is guaranteed for all 4 years. 89% of students live on campus; of those, 80% remain on campus on weekends. All students may keep cars.

Activities: 34% of men belong to 2 local and 3 national fraternities; 24% of women belong to 1 local and 2 national sororities. There are 80 groups on campus, including art, band, cheerleading, choir, chorale, chorus, dance, drama, ethnic, forensics, gay, honors, international, jazz band, literary magazine, musical theater, newspaper, orchestra, photography, political, professional, radio and TV, religious, social, social service, student government, symphony, and yearbook. Popular campus events include Spring and Winter Festivals, Milwaukee Symphony concerts, and theater events.

Sports: There are 9 intercollegiate sports for men and 9 for women, and 17 intramural sports for men and 17 for women. Facilities include a phys ed center, 2 fields, tennis courts, a recreation center, and an exercise room. The campus is within 5 miles of lakes and cross-country skiing opportunities.

Disabled Students: 50% of the campus is accessible. Wheelchair ramps, elevators, special parking, specially equipped rest rooms, special class scheduling, and lowered drinking fountains are available.

Services: Counseling and information services are available, as is tutoring in every subject. Tutoring and services are also available for learning-disabled students.

Campus Safety and Security: Measures include 24-hour foot and vehicle patrol, security escort services, informal discussions, and pamphlets/posters/films. There are emergency telephones, lighted pathways/sidewalks, and a paging system.

Programs of Study: Ripon College confers the A.B. degree. Bachelor's degrees are awarded in BIOLOGICAL SCIENCE (biochemistry and biology/biological science), BUSINESS (business administration and management), COMMUNICATIONS AND THE ARTS (art history and appreciation, communications, dramatic arts, English, French, German, music, and Spanish), COMPUTER AND PHYSICAL SCIENCE (chemistry, computer science, mathematics, and physical sciences), EDUCATION (early childhood, elementary, middle school, and secondary), ENGINEERING AND ENVIRONMENTAL DESIGN (environmental science), HEALTH PROFESSIONS (exercise science), SOCIAL SCIENCE (anthropology, economics, history, international studies, Latin American studies, philosophy, political science/government, psychobiology, psychology, religion, and sociology). Biology and chemistry are the strongest academically. Economics, education, and business administration are the largest.

Required: To graduate, students must complete 124 credit hours, including usually 24 in the major, with a minimum GPA of 2.0. Required courses include 1 course each in fine arts, humanities, natural sciences, phys ed, and social and behavioral sciences, a first-year seminar, a first-year writing course, and a capstone experience.

Special: Students may cross-register with the Associated Colleges of the Midwest. Internships, study abroad in 13 countries and study through 7 domestic programs, and a Washington semester are available. The college offers 3-year degrees in all areas, dual and student-designed majors, and pass/fail options. A 3-2 engineering degree is available with Rensselaer Polytechnic Institute, Washington University, and the University of Minnesota; other 3-2 programs are in environmental studies and in forestry with Duke University and in social welfare with the University of Chicago. A 2-2 nursing program is possible with Rush University. There are 12 national honor societies, including Phi Beta Kappa, and a freshman honors program.

Faculty/Classroom: 57% of faculty are male; 43%, female. All both teach and do research. The average class size in an introductory lecture is 26; in a laboratory, 17; and in a regular course, 18.

Admissions: 84% of the 2003-2004 applicants were accepted. The SAT I scores for the 2003-2004 freshman class were: Math--24% below 500, 30% between 500 and 599, 21% between 600 and 700, and 25% above 700. The ACT scores for the 2003-2004 freshman class were: 18% below 21, 26% between 21 and 23, 25% between 24 and 26, 13% between 27 and 28, and 18% above 28. 48% of the current freshmen were in the top fifth of their class; 79% were in the top two fifths. 9 freshmen graduated first in their class.

Requirements: The SAT I or ACT is required. In addition, applicants must be graduates of an accredited secondary school. The GED is accepted. Applicants should complete at least 17 Carnegie units including 4 of English, 2 to 4 each of math, social studies, and natural sciences, and up to 7 of other college-preparatory electives. An essay may be required, and an interview is recommended. Ripon College requires applicants to be in the upper 50% of their class. A GPA of 2.0 is required. AP and CLEP credits are accepted. Important factors in the admissions decision are leadership record, recommendations by school officials, and advanced placement or honor courses.

Procedure: Freshmen are admitted fall and spring. Entrance exams should be taken in the junior year or the fall of the senior year. There is a rolling admissions plan and a deferred admissions plan. Applications should be filed by August 1 for fall entry and December 15 for spring entry, along with a $30 fee. Notification is sent on a rolling basis. Applications are accepted on-line through Common App and the college's web site.

Transfer: 18 transfer students enrolled in 2002-2003. Applicants must have a minimum 2.0 GPA and be in good standing at their previous college. The SAT I or ACT, a personal statement, and an interview are recommended. 32 of 124 credits required for the bachelor's degree must be completed at Ripon College.

Visiting: There are regularly scheduled orientations for prospective students, including a tour, an interview, and meetings with professors and coaches. There are guides for informal visits and visitors may sit in on classes and stay overnight. To schedule a visit, contact the Admission Office at (800) 947-4766 or (920) 748-8337 or adminfo@ripon.edu.

Financial Aid: In 2003-2004, 97% of all full-time students received some form of financial aid. 79% of full-time freshmen and 75% of continuing full-time students received need-based aid. The average freshman award was $20,273. 60% of undergraduates work part time. Average annual earnings from campus work are $1518. The average financial indebtedness of the 2003 graduate was $8176. Ripon College is a member of CSS. The FAFSA is required. The priority date for freshman financial aid applications for fall entry is March 15.

International Students: There are 17 international students enrolled. The school actively recruits these students. They must score 600 on the written TOEFL or 230 on the electronic version and also take the SAT I if available.

Computers: The mainframe is an NT-based server farm. The NT server farm is located in the Kemper Computer Center and is accessible via all computers on campus. There are approximately 100 PCs and Macs installed in 7 computer labs located around the campus. Each residence hall room is wired to accept students' PCs. All students may access the system. There are no time limits and no fees.

Graduates: From July 1, 2002 to June 30, 2003, 222 bachelor's degrees were awarded. The most popular majors were history (17%), psychology (12%), and business (11%). In an average class, 2% graduate in 3 years or less, 61% graduate in 4 years or less, 71% graduate in 5 years or less, and 72% graduate in 6 years or less. 15 companies recruited on campus in 2002-2003. Of the 2002 graduating class, 24% were enrolled in graduate school within 6 months of graduation and 71% were employed.

Admissions Contact: Scott J. Goplin, Vice President and Dean of Admission and Financial Aid. A video is available.
E-mail: *goplins@ripon.edu* Web: *www.ripon.edu*

SAINT NORBERT COLLEGE
De Pere, WI 54115   D-3
                                                      (920) 403-3005
                              (800) 236-4878; Fax: (920) 403-4072

Full-time: 857 men, 1149 women	**Faculty:** 121; IIB, av$
Part-time: 50 men, 30 women	**Ph.D.s:** 94%
Graduate: 16 men, 53 women	**Student/Faculty:** 16 to 1
Year: semesters, summer session	**Tuition:** $20,072
Application Deadline: open	**Room & Board:** $5738
Freshman Class: 1658 applied, 1432 accepted, 530 enrolled	
SAT I or ACT: required	**COMPETITIVE**

Saint Norbert College, founded in 1898, is a Roman Catholic, private institution sponsored by the Norbertine Order. The college offers bachelor's degrees in the arts, the sciences, and business administration. A world-focused curriculum emphasizes career preparation, leadership, and service within the liberal arts and sciences. The library contains 214,257 volumes, 29,928 microform items, and 6308 audio/video tapes/CDs, and subscribes to 652 periodicals. Computerized library services include the card catalog, interlibrary loans, database searching, and Internet access. Special learning facilities include a learning resource center, art gallery, radio station, TV station, language labs, media center with satellite hookup, observatory, 3 theaters, environmental sciences research craft, and international center. The 92-acre campus is in a suburban area 5 miles south of Green Bay. Including any residence halls, there are 39 buildings.

Student Life: 71% of undergraduates are from Wisconsin. Students are from 26 states, 15 foreign countries, and Canada. 77% are from public schools. 91% are white. 58% are Catholic; 26% claim no religious affiliation; 15% Protestant. The average age of freshmen is 18; all undergraduates, 20. 15% do not continue beyond their first year; 75% remain to graduate.

Housing: 1543 students can be accommodated in college housing, which includes single-sex and coed dorms and on-campus apartments. In addition, there are special-interest houses, a townhouse complex, a living center, and off-campus houses. On-campus housing is guaranteed for all 4 years. 76% of students live on campus; of those, 75% remain on campus on weekends. All students may keep cars.

Activities: 7% of men belong to 3 local and 2 national fraternities; 10% of women belong to 3 local and 1 national sorority. There are 66 groups on campus, including art, band, cheerleading, choir, chorale, chorus, computers, dance, drama, environmental, ethnic, gay, honors, international, jazz band, literary magazine, musical theater, newspaper, political, professional, radio and TV, religious, social, social service, and student government. Popular campus events include Winter Carnival, Global Ecology Series, and Guest Artists (including the Milwaukee Symphony).

Sports: There are 9 intercollegiate sports for men and 9 for women, and 6 intramural sports for men and 6 for women. Facilities include a 3100-seat stadium, a sports complex, a 2500-seat sports center, and an activity center.

Disabled Students: 73% of the campus is accessible. Wheelchair ramps, elevators, special parking, specially equipped rest rooms, special class scheduling, lowered drinking fountains, lowered telephones, and special housing are available.

Services: Counseling and information services are available, as is tutoring in most subjects. There is a reader service for the blind and remedial math, reading, and writing.

Campus Safety and Security: Measures include 24-hour foot and vehicle patrol, self-defense education, security escort services, and informal discussions. There are pamphlets/posters/films, emergency telephones,

lighted pathways/sidewalks, an annual lighting assessment tour of the campus by students and staff, motorist assistance, and a crime prevention program.

Programs of Study: St. Norbert confers B.A., B.S., B.B.A., and B.Mus. degrees. Master's degrees are also awarded. Bachelor's degrees are awarded in BIOLOGICAL SCIENCE (biology/biological science), BUSINESS (accounting, business administration and management, international business management, and international economics), COMMUNICATIONS AND THE ARTS (art, communications, English, fine arts, French, German, graphic design, music, and Spanish), COMPUTER AND PHYSICAL SCIENCE (chemistry, computer science, geology, information sciences and systems, mathematics, natural sciences, and physics), EDUCATION (early childhood, elementary, and music), ENGINEERING AND ENVIRONMENTAL DESIGN (environmental science), SOCIAL SCIENCE (economics, history, humanities, international studies, philosophy, political science/government, psychology, religion, and sociology). Business administration, communications, and elementary education are the largest.

Required: To graduate, students must complete 128 credits with at least a 2.0 GPA, and a minimum of 40 semester credits in a particular major. There are general education requirements in the areas of religious heritage, human nature, human relationships, natural world, creative expression, United States heritage, foreign heritages, quantitative skills, Western tradition, global society, a writing-intensive course, and Senior Colloquium.

Special: Cross-registration with the University of Wisconsin-Green Bay for German courses, internships, study abroad in 23 countries, a Washington semester, and work-study programs are available. The college offers dual and student-designed majors, nondegree study, distance learning, and limited credit for military experience and work training. The Leadership and Service Program and leadership minor help students improve their leadership abilities through courses and activities. There are 10 national honor societies and a freshman honors program.

Faculty/Classroom: 66% of faculty are male; 34%, female. All teach undergraduates; 85% both teach and do research. No introductory courses are taught by graduate students. The average class size in an introductory lecture is 22; in a laboratory, 13; and in a regular course, 24.

Admissions: 86% of the 2003-2004 applicants were accepted. The ACT scores were 46% between 18 and 23, 45% between 24 and 29, and 9% between 30 and 36. There was 1 National Merit finalist and 5 semifinalists. 14 freshmen graduated first in their class.

Requirements: The SAT I or ACT is required, with a recommended minimum composite score for the SAT I of 900 (450 verbal, 450 math) and for the ACT of 20. Applicants must be graduates of an accredited secondary school. The GED is accepted. Students should complete 4 years of high school English, 3 years of math, history or social studies, and natural science, and a recommended 2 years of foreign language. The school requires an essay and a recommendation, and recommends an interview. AP and CLEP credits are accepted. Important factors in the admissions decision are advanced placement or honor courses, extracurricular activities record, and recommendations by school officials.

Procedure: Freshmen are admitted to all sessions. It is recommended that the first entrance exams be taken by the end of the junior year. There are early decision, early admissions, and deferred admissions plans. There is a rolling admissions plan. Application deadlines are open. Application fee is $25. Notification of early decision is sent prior to December 15; regular decision, on a rolling basis. 48 early decision candidates were accepted for the 2003-2004 class. Applications are accepted on-line through the St. Norbert web site, Common Application, Apply Yourself, CollegeNET, and WI Mentor site.

Transfer: 59 transfer students enrolled in 2003-2004. Applicants should have a minimum GPA of 2.5 and must submit college transcripts. They must also be in good academic standing at their previous college. 32 credits of 128 required for the bachelor's degree must be completed at St. Norbert.

Visiting: There are regularly scheduled orientations for prospective students, including preregistrations, meetings with advisers, and meetings regarding programming and activities, housing, and student life. There are guides for informal visits and visitors may sit in on classes and stay overnight. To schedule a visit, contact the Office of Admissions at *admit@snc.edu.*

Financial Aid: In 2003-2004, 98% of all full-time students received some form of financial aid. 67% of all full-time students received need-based aid. The average freshman award was $15,813. 54% of undergraduates work part time. Average annual earnings from campus work are $1930. The average financial indebtedness of the 2003 graduate was $16,854. St. Norbert is a member of CSS. The FAFSA, the college's own financial statement, and tax returns are required. The priority date for freshman financial aid applications for fall entry is March 1.

International Students: There are 56 international students enrolled. The school actively recruits these students. They must score 550 on the written TOEFL and also take the SAT I or the ACT.

Computers: 15 labs containing 179 PCs and 81 Macs are available for student use. The labs are connected to the campus network, which provides access to a wide variety of software, high-quality laser printers, central computing facilities, and the library automation system. Classrooms and auditoriums are connected to the campus network and have access to campuswide video service. All students may access the system during the semester as needed or as required by the instructor. There are no time limits and no fees.

Graduates: From July 1, 2002 to June 30, 2003, 447 bachelor's degrees were awarded. The most popular majors were business administration (24%), communication/media/theater (15%), and elementary education (10%). In an average class, 67% graduate in 4 years or less, 75% graduate in 5 years or less, and 75% graduate in 6 years or less. 52 companies recruited on campus in 2002-2003. Of the 2002 graduating class, 19% were enrolled in graduate school within 6 months of graduation and 71% were employed.

Admissions Contact: Daniel L. Meyer, Dean of Admission and Enrollment Management. E-mail: *daniel.meyer@snc.edu* Web: *www.snc.edu*

SILVER LAKE COLLEGE OF THE HOLY FAMILY
Manitowoc, WI 54220

E-3

(920) 686-6187

(800) 236-4752, ext. 1; Fax: (920) 684-7082

Full-time: 55 men, 191 women	**Faculty:** 35
Part-time: 198 men, 336 women	**Ph.D.s:** 49%
Graduate: 98 men, 226 women	**Student/Faculty:** 7 to 1
Year: semesters, summer session	**Tuition:** $14,350
Application Deadline: open	**Room & Board:** $4100
Freshman Class: 84 applied, 75 accepted, 34 enrolled	
ACT: 18	**LESS COMPETITIVE**

Silver Lake College of the Holy Family, founded in 1935, is a private Catholic liberal arts institution offering undergraduate and graduate programs. In addition to regional accreditation, Silver Lake College has baccalaureate program accreditation with NASM. The library contains 60,466 volumes, 2154 microform items, and 12,593 audio/video tapes/CDs, and subscribes to 300 periodicals. Computerized library services include the card catalog, interlibrary loans, and database searching. Special learning facilities include a learning resource center and a special education clinic used for the training of special education teachers. The 30-acre campus is in a rural area 4 miles west of Manitowoc. Including any residence halls, there are 2 buildings.

Student Life: 99% of undergraduates are from Wisconsin. Students are from 4 states and 1 foreign country. 89% are from public schools. 94% are white. The average age of freshmen is 19; all undergraduates, 27. 18% do not continue beyond their first year; 50% remain to graduate.

Housing: 30 students can be accommodated in college housing, which includes coed off-campus apartments. On-campus housing is guaranteed for the freshman year only. 95% of students commute. Alcohol is not permitted. All students may keep cars.

Activities: There are no fraternities or sororities. There are 18 groups on campus, including art, band, choir, chorus, computers, dance, honors, jazz band, literary magazine, newspaper, orchestra, professional, religious, and student government. Popular campus events include Fine Arts Series, campus ministry programs, and Parents Day.

Sports: There is 1 intercollegiate sport for women, and 2 intramural sports for men and 2 for women. Facilities include a YMCA and the Two Rivers and Manitowoc Recreation Department.

Disabled Students: 95% of the campus is accessible. Wheelchair ramps, elevators, special parking, specially equipped rest rooms, and special class scheduling are available.

Services: Counseling and information services are available, as is tutoring in most subjects, including study groups as needed. There is a reader service for the blind and remedial math, reading, and writing.

Campus Safety and Security: Measures include informal discussions, pamphlets/posters/films, emergency telephones, and lighted pathways/sidewalks.

Programs of Study: Silver Lake College confers B.A., B.S., B.B.A., and B.M. degrees. Associate and master's degrees are also awarded. Bachelor's degrees are awarded in BIOLOGICAL SCIENCE (biology/biological science), BUSINESS (accounting, business administration and management, human resources, and personnel management), COMMUNICATIONS AND THE ARTS (English, fine arts, music, and studio art), COMPUTER AND PHYSICAL SCIENCE (computer science, information sciences and systems, and mathematics), EDUCATION (art, early childhood, elementary, music, secondary, and special), SOCIAL SCIENCE (history, psychology, public administration, religion, and social science). Elementary education and special education are the strongest academically. Business administration and management is the largest.

Required: To graduate, students must complete at least 120 credit hours with a minimum GPA of 2.0. 45 to 50 credits of liberal arts studies must be taken.

Special: Silver Lake offers cross-registration with several Wisconsin technical colleges, internships, B.A.-B.S. degrees, dual majors, work-study programs, and student-designed majors. Nondegree study, pass/fail options, and credit for life, military, and work experience are available. An accelerated degree program in business management, account-

ing, human resources, and public administration is offered. There are 4 national honor societies and 4 departmental honors programs.

Faculty/Classroom: 37% of faculty are male; 63%, female. 85% teach undergraduates and 1% both teach and do research. No introductory courses are taught by graduate students. The average class size in an introductory lecture is 19; in a laboratory, 7; and in a regular course, 10.

Admissions: 89% of the 2003-2004 applicants were accepted. 7% of the current freshmen were in the top fifth of their class; 33% were in the top two fifths.

Requirements: The SAT I or ACT is required. In addition, applicants must be graduates of an accredited secondary school. The GED is accepted. Applicants should complete 3 units of high school English, 2 each of math and history or social studies, and 1 of lab science. A GPA of 2.0 is required. AP and CLEP credits are accepted. Important factors in the admissions decision are recommendations by school officials, evidence of special talent, and advanced placement or honor courses.

Procedure: Freshmen are admitted fall and spring. Entrance exams should be taken in the spring of the junior year. There is a rolling admissions plan. Application deadlines are open. Application fee is $35. Notification is sent on a rolling basis. Applications are accepted on-line through CollegeNET or the school's web site.

Transfer: 89 transfer students enrolled in 2002-2003. Applicants who have 30 acceptable credits must have a minimum GPA of 2.0; those with fewer credits must meet the requirements for entering freshmen, except that the SAT I or ACT is not required. 30 credits of 120 required for the bachelor's degree must be completed at Silver Lake College.

Visiting: There are regularly scheduled orientations for prospective students, including a tour and meetings with an admissions counselor, an adviser, the financial aid department, and the housing director. There are guides for informal visits and visitors may sit in on classes. To schedule a visit, contact the Admissions Office at (920) 686-6175 or *admslc@silver.sl.edu.*

Financial Aid: In 2003-2004, 75% of all full-time freshmen and 65% of continuing full-time students received some form of financial aid. 75% of full-time freshmen and 60% of continuing full-time students received need-based aid. The average freshman award was $10,625. Need-based scholarships or need-based grants averaged $8181; need-based self-help aid (loans and jobs) averaged $2443; non-need-based athletic scholarships averaged $2000; and other non-need-based awards and non-need-based scholarships averaged $750. 25% of undergraduates work part time. Average annual earnings from campus work are $1268. The FAFSA, the college's own financial statement, and tax returns are required. The deadline for filing freshman financial aid applications for fall entry is April 15.

International Students: They must score 550 on the written TOEFL.

Computers: The mainframe is an NT server. Computer science majors use the DEC for programming. There are 35 networked PCs available, providing students access to the Internet. All students may access the system. There are no time limits and no fees.

Graduates: From July 1, 2002 to June 30, 2003, 106 bachelor's degrees were awarded. The most popular majors were management (33%), education (13%), and psychology (9%). In an average class, 1% graduate in 4 years or less, 31% graduate in 5 years or less, and 8% graduate in 6 years or less. 10 companies recruited on campus in 2002-2003. Of the 2002 graduating class, 6% were enrolled in graduate school within 6 months of graduation and 96% were employed.

Admissions Contact: Lori Salm, Admissions Office.
E-mail: *admslc@silver.sl.edu* Web: *www.sl.edu*

UNIVERSITY OF WISCONSIN SYSTEM

The University of Wisconsin System, established in 1971, is a public system. It is governed by a 17-member appointed Board of Regents whose chief administrator is president. The primary goals of the system are teaching, research, and public service. The main priorities are to develop human resources; to discover and disseminate knowledge; and to extend knowledge and its application. The total enrollment of all 26 campuses is about 160,000 students, with some 6800 faculty members. Altogether there are 661 baccalaureate, 317 master's, and nearly 128 doctoral programs offered. Profiles of the 4-year campuses are included in this section.

UNIVERSITY OF WISCONSIN/EAU CLAIRE

Eau Claire, WI 54701

B-3

(715) 836-5415
(888) INFO-UWE; Fax: (715) 836-2409

Full-time: 3713 men, 5517 women	**Faculty:** 408; IIA, av$
Part-time: 342 men, 487 women	**Ph.D.s:** 86%
Graduate: 149 men, 386 women	**Student/Faculty:** 23 to 1
Year: semesters, summer session	**Tuition:** $4313 ($14,360)
Application Deadline: open	**Room & Board:** $4150
Freshman Class: 7055 applied, 4258 accepted, 1879 enrolled	
SAT I: recommended	**ACT:** required

VERY COMPETITIVE

The University of Wisconsin/Eau Claire, founded in 1916, is a public institution offering programs in the liberal arts and sciences, business, teacher education, nursing, music, and the fine arts. There are 6 undergraduate schools. In addition to regional accreditation, UW-Eau Claire has baccalaureate program accreditation with AACSB, ACEJMC, CSWE, and NASM. The library contains 764,275 volumes, 1,366,298 microform items, and 17,676 audio/video tapes/CDs, and subscribes to 2448 periodicals. Computerized library services include the card catalog, interlibrary loans, database searching, and Internet access. Special learning facilities include a learning resource center, art gallery, planetarium, radio station, TV station, a geographic research center, a bird museum, and an observatory. The 333-acre campus is in an urban area 95 miles east of Minneapolis, Minnesota. Including any residence halls, there are 28 buildings.

Student Life: 77% of undergraduates are from Wisconsin. Students are from 26 states, 43 foreign countries, and Canada. 92% are from public schools. 94% are white. The average age of freshmen is 18; all undergraduates, 21. 19% do not continue beyond their first year; 56% remain to graduate.

Housing: 3754 students can be accommodated in college housing, which includes single-sex and coed dorms and on-campus apartments. On-campus housing is guaranteed for the freshman year only and is available on a first-come, first-served basis. 63% of students commute. All students may keep cars.

Activities: 1% of men belong to 4 national fraternities; 1% of women belong to 4 national sororities. There are 150 groups on campus, including art, band, cheerleading, choir, chorale, chorus, computers, dance, drama, ethnic, forensics, gay, honors, international, jazz band, literary magazine, marching band, musical theater, newspaper, orchestra, political, professional, radio and TV, religious, social, social service, student government, and symphony. Popular campus events include Viennese Ball, Artsfest, and Winter Carnival.

Sports: There are 9 intercollegiate sports for men and 11 for women, and 40 intramural sports for men and 40 for women. Facilities include a gym, a pool, 30 acres of intramural and recreation fields, a game room, bowling and billiards, a Nautilus fitness center, racquetball courts, a weight room, a ropes course, a 3212-seat stadium, tennis courts, and a climbing wall.

Disabled Students: 80% of the campus is accessible. Wheelchair ramps, elevators, special parking, specially equipped rest rooms, special class scheduling, lowered drinking fountains, and lowered telephones are available.

Services: Counseling and information services are available, as is tutoring in some subjects, including writing, math/problem solving, and reading/study skills. There is a reader service for the blind, and remedial math, reading, and writing. Entry-level courses in foreign languages, humanities, and social and physical sciences are available.

Campus Safety and Security: Measures include 24-hour foot and vehicle patrol, self-defense education, security escort services, and informal discussions. There are pamphlets/posters/films and lighted pathways/sidewalks.

Programs of Study: UW-Eau Claire confers B.A., B.S., B.B.A., B.F.A., B.M., B.M.E., B.M.T.H., B.S.E.Ph., B.S.H.C.A., B.S.N., and B.S.W. degrees. Associate and master's degrees are also awarded. Bachelor's degrees are awarded in BIOLOGICAL SCIENCE (biochemistry and biology/biological science), BUSINESS (accounting, banking and finance, business administration and management, business economics, and marketing/retailing/merchandising), COMMUNICATIONS AND THE ARTS (advertising, art, broadcasting, communications, dramatic arts, English, fine arts, French, German, journalism, music, photography, and Spanish), COMPUTER AND PHYSICAL SCIENCE (chemistry, computer programming, computer science, geology, information sciences and systems, mathematics, physical sciences, physics, and statistics), EDUCATION (art, athletic training, business, elementary, foreign languages, music, science, secondary, and special), HEALTH PROFESSIONS (health care administration, music therapy, nursing, public health, and speech pathology/audiology), SOCIAL SCIENCE (American Indian studies, criminal justice, economics, geography, history, Latin American studies, philosophy, physical fitness/movement, political science/government, psychology, religion, social science, social work, and sociology). Elementary education, nursing, and biology are the largest.

Required: All students must complete 39 hours in general education, including 11 each in social sciences, humanities, and natural sciences, and 6 in communications. All students must also take 4 to 5 credits in English and 2 in wellness, and must complete a minimum of 3 credits that contain significant content dealing with race and ethnicity and 30 or more hours of service-learning. A minimum 2.0 GPA and 120 credit hours, including 60 in the major, are required to graduate.

Special: Numerous internships, work-study programs, and study abroad in 13 countries are offered. Dual majors and interdisciplinary majors are possible. Credit by examination, nondegree study, and pass/fail options are offered. There are 28 national honor societies, a freshman honors program, and 13 departmental honors programs.

Faculty/Classroom: 56% of faculty are male; 44%, female. 67% teach undergraduates, 29% do research, and 29% do both. No introductory courses are taught by graduate students. The average class size in an introductory lecture is 32 and in a laboratory, 17.

Admissions: 60% of the 2003-2004 applicants were accepted. The SAT I scores for the 2003-2004 freshman class were: Verbal--19% below 500, 30% between 500 and 599, 38% between 600 and 700, and 13% above 700; Math--16% below 500, 38% between 500 and 599, 38% between 600 and 700, and 8% above 700. The ACT scores were 6% below 21, 33% between 21 and 23, 39% between 24 and 26, 12% between 27 and 28, and 10% above 28. 50% of the current freshmen were in the top fifth of their class; 87% were in the top two fifths. There were 3 National Merit finalists. 64 freshmen graduated first in their class.

Requirements: The ACT is required and the SAT I is recommended. In addition, applicants should graduate from an accredited secondary school or present its equivalent, with 17 academic credits, including 4 in English, 3 each in social studies, college preparatory math, and science, and 2 years of a single foreign language. Students must graduate in the upper 50% of their class or present a minimum composite score of 1090 on the SAT I or 23 on the ACT. Probationary admission is sometimes offered for the spring semester. Music majors or minors must audition. AP and CLEP credits are accepted. Important factors in the admissions decision are advanced placement or honor courses, recommendations by school officials, and leadership record.

Procedure: Freshmen are admitted to all sessions. Entrance exams should be taken by December of the senior year. There is a rolling admissions plan and an early admissions plan. Application deadlines are open. 1002 applicants were on the 2003 waiting list; 256 were admitted. Applications are accepted on-line through the school's web site.

Transfer: 463 transfer students enrolled in 2002-2003. Transfer applicants must be in good standing at their previous schools and carry a minimum 2.0 GPA. Preference is given to transfers who have completed the equivalent of freshman composition and college algebra. Students with less than 30 semester credits must meet the freshman admissions requirements. 30 of 120 credits required for the bachelor's degree must be completed at UW-Eau Claire.

Visiting: There are regularly scheduled orientations for prospective students. During orientation sessions, students meet with academic advisers, develop a class schedule, register for classes, and tour the campus. There are guides for informal visits and visitors may sit in on classes. To schedule a visit, contact the Admissions Office at admissions@uwec.edu.

Financial Aid: In 2003-2004, 63% of all full-time freshmen and 64% of continuing full-time students received some form of financial aid. 37% of full-time freshmen and 40% of continuing full-time students received need-based aid. The average freshman award was $5478. Need-based scholarships or need-based grants averaged $3373 ($11,010 maximum); need-based self-help aid (loans and jobs) averaged $3501 ($10,877 maximum); and non-need-based awards and non-need-based scholarships averaged $3629 ($17,625 maximum). 98% of undergraduates work part time. Average annual earnings from campus work are $1247. The average financial indebtedness of the 2003 graduate was $15,061. The FAFSA is required. The deadline for filing freshman financial aid applications for fall entry is April 15.

International Students: There are 114 international students enrolled. The school actively recruits these students. They must score 525 on the written TOEFL and also take the ACT.

Computers: The mainframe is a Unisys NX5602-22. Students may use computer facilities for classroom assignments, research, network access to other resources, and mail. Terminals and PCs are located across campus. There are 17 supported labs plus labs in housing and the library. Dial-in access is offered. All students may access the system 24 hours a day, 7 days per week. There are no time limits and no fees.

Graduates: From July 1, 2002 to June 30, 2003, 1786 bachelor's degrees were awarded. The most popular majors were management (7%), marketing (7%), and biology (6%). In an average class, 19% graduate in 4 years or less, 49% graduate in 5 years or less, and 56% graduate in 6 years or less. 255 companies recruited on campus in 2002-2003. Of the 2002 graduating class, 9% were enrolled in graduate school within 6 months of graduation and 85% were employed.

Admissions Contact: Kristina Anderson, Interim Director of Admissions. E-mail: admissions@uwec.edu Web: www.uwec.edu/Admissions/

UNIVERSITY OF WISCONSIN/GREEN BAY   D-3
Green Bay, WI 54311   **(920) 465-2111; Fax: (920) 465-2765**

Full-time: 1530 men, 2844 women	Faculty: 174; IIA, -$
Part-time: 252 men, 630 women	Ph.D.s: 83%
Graduate: 69 men, 95 women	Student/Faculty: 25 to 1
Year: semesters, summer session	Tuition: $4654 ($14,701)
Application Deadline: February 1	Room & Board: $3500
Freshman Class: 2979 applied, 2322 accepted, 964 enrolled	
SAT I Verbal/Math: 510/540	ACT: 23 COMPETITIVE

The University of Wisconsin/Green Bay, founded in 1968, is a public institution offering programs in humanities and fine arts, natural sciences, social sciences, business, education, health, and preprofessional areas. In addition to regional accreditation, UW-Green Bay has baccalaureate program accreditation with ADA, CSWE, NASM, and NLN. The library contains 335,739 volumes, 717,333 microform items, and 47,018 audio/video tapes/CDs, and subscribes to 5096 periodicals. Computerized library services include the card catalog, interlibrary loans, database searching, and Internet access. Special learning facilities include a learning resource center, art gallery, natural history museum, radio station, TV station, a 270-acre arboretum, and a regional performing arts center. The 700-acre campus is in a suburban area 111 miles north of Milwaukee. Including any residence halls, there are 40 buildings.

Student Life: 94% of undergraduates are from Wisconsin. Students are from 24 states, 27 foreign countries, and Canada. 86% are from public schools. 93% are white. The average age of freshmen is 18; all undergraduates, 23. 17% do not continue beyond their first year; 44% remain to graduate.

Housing: 1780 students can be accommodated in college housing, which includes coed dorms and on-campus apartments. In addition, there are special-interest houses and 3-,4-, and 5-person dorm suites with private bedrooms. On-campus housing is available on a first-come, first-served basis and is available on a lottery system for upperclassmen. 66% of students commute. All students may keep cars.

Activities: 1% of men belong to 1 national fraternity; 1% of women belong to 2 national sororities. There are 90 groups on campus, including art, band, cheerleading, choir, chorus, computers, dance, drama, drill team, environmental, ethnic, gay, honors, international, jazz band, literary magazine, musical theater, newspaper, orchestra, pep band, photography, political, professional, radio and TV, religious, social, social service, and student government. Popular campus events include Fall Fest, Spring Screamer, and Pow Wow.

Sports: There are 7 intercollegiate sports for men and 8 for women, and 7 intramural sports for men and 7 for women. Facilities include a sports center housing a swimming pool, racquetball courts, a weight room, and a 2000-seat gym, intramural fields, a soccer field, a golf course, tennis courts, an outing center, a 2500-seat stadium, and student recreation facilities in the student union.

Disabled Students: All of the campus is accessible. Wheelchair ramps, elevators, special parking, specially equipped rest rooms, lowered drinking fountains, lowered telephones, and automatic door openers are available.

Services: Counseling and information services are available, as is tutoring in most subjects. There is a reader service for the blind, and remedial math, reading, and writing. There is an academic support office, language and writing centers, student health services, and individual counseling. Available equipment includes a visual enlarger, automatic page turner, accessible computer station with attached voice synthesizer, slow speed cassette recorders, taped texts, and a printing (TDD). Notetakers, typists, readers, and aides are also available to students.

Campus Safety and Security: Measures include 24-hour foot and vehicle patrol, security escort services, informal discussions, and pamphlets/posters/films. There are emergency telephones and lighted pathways/sidewalks.

Programs of Study: UW-Green Bay confers B.A., B.S., B.G.S., B.S.N., and B.S.W. degrees. Associate and master's degrees are also awarded. Bachelor's degrees are awarded in BIOLOGICAL SCIENCE (biology/ biological science and nutrition), BUSINESS (accounting and business administration and management), COMMUNICATIONS AND THE ARTS (communications, dramatic arts, English, fine arts, French, German, music, and Spanish), COMPUTER AND PHYSICAL SCIENCE (chemistry, computer science, earth science, information sciences and systems, and mathematics), EDUCATION (education and social foundations), ENGINEERING AND ENVIRONMENTAL DESIGN (environmental science), HEALTH PROFESSIONS (nursing), SOCIAL SCIENCE (economics, history, human development, humanities, liberal arts/ general studies, philosophy, political science/government, psychology, public administration, social work, and urban studies). Environmental science, accounting, and human biology are the strongest academically. Business, education, and communications are the largest.

Required: All students must complete at least 120 semester hours, including an average of 36 in the major, with a minimum GPA of 2.0, depending on the major. A 31-credit requirement in general education consists of 9 credits in humanities, 3 in fine arts, 9 in social sciences, and

10 in natural sciences. Students must declare an interdisciplinary minor or major and must complete at least 30 credits in the discipline. Courses in Other Culture Studies and Ethnic Studies are required; other course requirements vary by major.

Special: UW-Green Bay offers cross-registration with Bellin College of Nursing and the University of Wisconsin at Milwaukee or Oshkosh. There are study-abroad programs in 6 countries plus travel in 12. Students can receive credit by examination for life, military, or work experience. There are internships in almost all fields; interdisciplinary majors, including communication and the arts, human biology, and regional planning; and dual and student-designed majors, work-study, B.A.-B.S. degrees in most areas, nondegree study, a general studies degree, and pass/fail options. A 3-2 engineering degree with the University of Wisconsin/Milwaukee is offered. The Extended Degree Program, largely off campus, provides for individual study. There are 3 national honor societies and 34 departmental honors programs.

Faculty/Classroom: 55% of faculty are male; 45%, female. 99% teach undergraduates, 95% do research, and 95% do both. No introductory courses are taught by graduate students. The average class size in an introductory lecture is 40; in a laboratory, 18; and in a regular course, 25.

Admissions: 78% of the 2003-2004 applicants were accepted. The SAT I scores for the 2003-2004 freshman class were: Verbal--35% below 500, 40% between 500 and 599, and 25% between 600 and 700; Math--40% below 500, 35% between 500 and 599, 15% between 600 and 700, and 10% above 700. The ACT scores were 26% below 21, 36% between 21 and 23, 24% between 24 and 26, 8% between 27 and 28, and 6% above 28. 39% of the current freshmen were in the top fifth of their class; 80% were in the top two fifths. 21 freshmen graduated first in their class.

Requirements: The ACT is required. In addition, candidates must be graduates of an accredited secondary school or hold a GED certificate. They must have completed 17 academic credits consisting of 4 in English, 3 in social sciences, 3 each in science and math, 2 in any of the above areas or a foreign language, and 2 other electives. UW-Green Bay requires applicants to be in the upper 50% of their class. A GPA of 2.25 is required. AP and CLEP credits are accepted. Important factors in the admissions decision are extracurricular activities record, advanced placement or honor courses, and leadership record.

Procedure: Freshmen are admitted to all sessions. Entrance exams should be taken between the junior and senior years. There is a rolling admissions plan and a deferred admissions plan. Applications should be filed by February 1 for fall entry and November 1 for spring entry, along with a $35 fee. Notification is sent on a rolling basis. 160 applicants were on the 2003 waiting list; 44 were admitted. Applications are accepted on-line through the school's web site.

Transfer: 569 transfer students enrolled in 2002-2003. Transfer students must have a minimum GPA of 2.0 based on at least 15 transferable credits; priority for admission is given to students with 24 credits and a minimum GPA of 2.5. 31 of 120 credits required for the bachelor's degree must be completed at UW-Green Bay.

Visiting: There are regularly scheduled orientations for prospective students, including Campus Preview Days, which consist of information sessions, academic area workshops, and campus tours. There are guides for informal visits and visitors may sit in on classes. To schedule a visit, contact Pam Harvey-Jacobs, Director of Admissions at *admissions@uwgb.edu.*

Financial Aid: In 2003-2004, 78% of all full-time freshmen and 69% of continuing full-time students received some form of financial aid. 55% of full-time freshmen and 44% of continuing full-time students received need-based aid. The average freshman award was $3865. Need-based scholarships or need-based grants averaged $1334 ($14,250 maximum); need-based self-help aid (loans and jobs) averaged $1135 ($10,000 maximum); non-need-based athletic scholarships averaged $8637 ($23,072 maximum); and other non-need-based awards and non-need-based scholarships averaged $1998 ($10,176 maximum). 70% of undergraduates work part time. Average annual earnings from campus work are $1500. The CSS/Profile, FAFSA, or FFS is required. The deadline for filing freshman financial aid applications for fall entry is April 15.

International Students: There are 59 international students enrolled. The school actively recruits these students. They must score 500 on the written TOEFL and also take placement tests in math and English as a second language.

Computers: Computer accounts for PC and mainframe access are available to all enrolled students. PC and networked terminals are widely available in computer labs, classrooms, and the Residence Community Center. All networked computers have full access to e-mail and the Internet. All students may access the system 7 A.M. to 12 P.M.; 24 hours a day through network or modem. There are no time limits and no fees.

Graduates: From July 1, 2002 to June 30, 2003, 948 bachelor's degrees were awarded. The most popular majors were business administration (13%), human development (10%), and psychology (8%). In an average class, 1% graduate in 3 years or less, 16% graduate in 4 years or less, 40% graduate in 5 years or less, and 44% graduate in 6 years or less. 60 companies recruited on campus in 2002-2003. Of the 2002 graduating class, 15% were enrolled in graduate school within 6 months of graduation and 99% were employed.

Admissions Contact: Pam Harvey-Jacobs, Director of Admissions. A video is available. E-mail: *admissions@uwgb.edu*
Web: *http://www.uwgb.edu/admissions*

UNIVERSITY OF WISCONSIN/LA CROSSE
La Crosse, WI 54601

B-4

(608) 785-8067; Fax: (608) 785-8940

Full-time: 2995 men, 4553 women	Faculty: 310; IIA, av$
Part-time: 247 men, 305 women	Ph.D.s: 81%
Graduate: 260 men, 386 women	Student/Faculty: 24 to 1
Year: semesters, summer session	Tuition: $4941 ($14,604)
Application Deadline: open	Room & Board: $4050 ($3800)
Freshman Class: 6376 applied, 3357 accepted, 511 enrolled	
ACT: 24	**VERY COMPETITIVE**

The University of Wisconsin/La Crosse, founded in 1909, is a public institution offering undergraduate and graduate studies in arts and sciences, health and human services, business administration, education, phys ed and recreation, professional development, and educational administration. There are 6 undergraduate schools and 1 graduate school. In addition to regional accreditation, UW-L has baccalaureate program accreditation with AACSB, ACOTE, ACS, APTA, CAPTE, NAACLS, NASM, and NCATE. The library contains 666,883 volumes, 1,222,613 microform items, and 2027 audio/video tapes/CDs, and subscribes to 1603 periodicals. Computerized library services include the card catalog, interlibrary loans, and database searching. Special learning facilities include a learning resource center, art gallery, planetarium, radio station, TV station, the River Studies Center, and the Allied Health Center. The 121-acre campus is in a small town 140 miles west of Madison and 150 miles southeast of Minneapolis/St. Paul. Including any residence halls, there are 32 buildings.

Student Life: 82% of undergraduates are from Wisconsin. Students are from 38 states, 48 foreign countries, and Canada. 90% are from public schools. 91% are white. The average age of freshmen is 19; all undergraduates, 22. 10% do not continue beyond their first year; 53% remain to graduate.

Housing: 2823 students can be accommodated in college housing, which includes single-sex and coed dorms. In addition, there are special-interest houses and a residence hall for international students and students 21 years or older. On-campus housing is available on a first-come, first-served basis and is available on a lottery system for upperclassmen. 68% of students commute. All students may keep cars.

Activities: 1% of men and about 1% of women belong to 3 national fraternities; 1% of women belong to 2 national sororities. There are 140 groups on campus, including art, band, cheerleading, chess, choir, chorale, chorus, computers, dance, drama, ethnic, gay, honors, international, jazz band, literary magazine, marching band, musical theater, newspaper, orchestra, pep band, photography, political, professional, radio and TV, religious, social, social service, student government, and symphony. Popular campus events include Parents Weekend, a community-sponsored Oktoberfest, and various cultural events.

Sports: There are 9 intercollegiate sports for men and 10 for women, and 11 intramural sports for men and 11 for women. Facilities include 3 regulation basketball courts, a wrestling room, an indoor track, 6 indoor tennis courts, 16 outdoor tennis courts, an Olympic-size swimming pool, 2 strength-training centers, a dance studio, racquetball courts, a 4363-seat stadium, a 2880-seat gym, and an 880-seat auditorium.

Disabled Students: 98% of the campus is accessible. Wheelchair ramps, elevators, special parking, specially equipped rest rooms, special class scheduling, lowered drinking fountains, lowered telephones, and specialized computer equipment are available.

Services: Counseling and information services are available, as is tutoring in most subjects. There is a reader service for the blind and remedial math and writing. There is also a counseling and testing center and a writing lab.

Campus Safety and Security: Measures include 24-hour foot and vehicle patrol, self-defense education, security escort services, and informal discussions. There are pamphlets/posters/films, emergency telephones, and lighted pathways/sidewalks.

Programs of Study: UW-L confers B.A. and B.S. degrees. Associate and master's degrees are also awarded. Bachelor's degrees are awarded in BIOLOGICAL SCIENCE (biology/biological science and microbiology), BUSINESS (accounting, banking and finance, business administration and management, international business management, and marketing/retailing/merchandising), COMMUNICATIONS AND THE ARTS (art, communications, dramatic arts, English, fine arts, French, music, Spanish, and speech/debate/rhetoric), COMPUTER AND PHYSICAL SCIENCE (chemistry, computer science, information sciences and systems, mathematics, and physics), EDUCATION (athletic training, elementary, health, physical, science, secondary, and social studies), HEALTH PROFESSIONS (community health work, exercise science, medical laboratory technology, nuclear medical technology, occupational therapy, physician's assistant, radiation therapy, and recreation thera-

py), SOCIAL SCIENCE (archeology, economics, geography, German area studies, history, parks and recreation management, philosophy, political science/government, psychology, public administration, and sociology). Microbiology, nuclear medicine technology, and physics are the strongest academically. Business administration, elementary education, and biology are the largest.

Required: To graduate, students must earn 120 semester credits, including 68 in subjects outside the major and at least 40 in 300- or 400-level courses. The minimum GPA is 2.0, though it is considerably higher for some programs. Distribution requirements include 30 to 40 credits in liberal studies and 13 to 19 credits in skill courses.

Special: Cooperative programs and cross-registration are available with Viterbo College. There are study-abroad programs in 14 countries and an international student exchange program. UW-L also offers a 3-2 engineering degree with the University of Wisconsin/Madison, the University of Wisconsin/Milwaukee, Platteville, and the University of Minnesota, work-study programs, internships, nondegree study, credit by exam, and pass/fail options. There are 10 national honor societies, a freshman honors program, and 11 departmental honors programs.

Faculty/Classroom: 60% of faculty are male; 40%, female. 95% teach undergraduates, 5% do research, and 80% do both. No introductory courses are taught by graduate students. The average class size in an introductory lecture is 37; in a laboratory, 20; and in a regular course, 30.

Admissions: 53% of the 2003-2004 applicants were accepted. The SAT I scores for the 2003-2004 freshman class were: Verbal--12% below 500, 43% between 500 and 599, 39% between 600 and 700, and 6% above 700; Math--6% below 500, 33% between 500 and 599, 52% between 600 and 700, and 9% above 700. 52% of the current freshmen were in the top fifth of their class; 98% were in the top two fifths. 49 freshmen graduated first in their class.

Requirements: The ACT is required. In addition, candidates must be graduates of an accredited secondary school or hold a GED certificate. They must have completed 17 academic credits, including 4 courses in English, 3 each in social studies and science, 2 in algebra and 1 in geometry, and 4 other academic courses. Students completing rigorous courses, including in the senior year, will be stronger candidates for admission. Students must rank in the top 35% of their high school graduating class and score at least 22 on the ACT or the top 40% and score 25 on the ACT. A GPA of 2.0 is required. AP and CLEP credits are accepted. Important factors in the admissions decision are advanced placement or honor courses, leadership record, and recommendations by school officials.

Procedure: Freshmen are admitted to all sessions. Entrance exams should be taken at the end of the junior year or at the beginning of the senior year. There is a rolling admissions plan. Application deadlines are open. Application fee is $35. 400 applicants were on the 2003 waiting list; 56 were admitted.

Transfer: 321 transfer students enrolled in 2002-2003. Transfer admission is likely with a GPA of 3.2; with a GPA of 2.0 to 2.74, admission is on a space-available basis. 32 of 120 credits required for the bachelor's degree must be completed at UW-L.

Visiting: There are regularly scheduled orientations for prospective students, including 2 academic sessions, a parent panel, a UW-L student panel, and a tour of the campus. There are guides for informal visits and visitors may sit in on classes. To schedule a visit, contact the Admissions Office at (608) 785-8939.

Financial Aid: In 2003-2004, 62% of all full-time freshmen and 76% of continuing full-time students received some form of financial aid. 46% of full-time freshmen and 57% of continuing full-time students received need-based aid. The average freshman award was $2801. 79% of undergraduates work part time. Average annual earnings from campus work are $900. The average financial indebtedness of the 2003 graduate was $14,048. The FAFSA, the college's own financial statement, and tax returns are required.

International Students: There are 106 international students enrolled. The school actively recruits these students. They must score 550 on the written TOEFL and also take the college's own test, the La Crosse Battery (based on MELAB), and write a 30-minute composition.

Computers: There are 600 PCs, primarily Dell, Compaq, and Mac, available in open labs and residence halls. All students have access to e-mail and the Internet. All students may access the system 7 A.M. to midnight. There are no time limits and no fees.

Graduates: From July 1, 2002 to June 30, 2003, 1533 bachelor's degrees were awarded. The most popular majors were exercise and sport science (9%), marketing/business (8%), and biology (8%). In an average class, 23% graduate in 4 years or less, 52% graduate in 5 years or less, and 65% graduate in 6 years or less. 96 companies recruited on campus in 2002-2003. Of the 2002 graduating class, 24% were enrolled in graduate school within 6 months of graduation and 98% were employed.

Admissions Contact: Timothy R. Lewis, Director of Admissions.
E-mail: *admissions@uwlax.edu* Web: *www.uwlax.edu*

UNIVERSITY OF WISCONSIN/MADISON C-4

Madison, WI 53706-1481 (608) 262-3961; Fax: (608) 262-7706

Full-time: 12,000 men, 13,200 women	**Faculty:** 2301; I, av$
Part-time: 275 men, 300 women	**Ph.D.s:** 97%
Graduate: none	**Student/Faculty:** 11 to 1
Year: semesters, summer session	**Tuition:** $5140 ($19,150)
Application Deadline: February 1	**Room & Board:** $6100
Freshman Class: n/av	
SAT I or ACT: required	**VERY COMPETITIVE**

The University of Wisconsin/Madison, founded in 1849, is a public, land-grant institution offering undergraduate and graduate study in almost every major field. There are 9 undergraduate and 4 graduate schools. In addition to regional accreditation, Wisconsin has baccalaureate program accreditation with AACSB, ABET, ACEJMC, AHEA, ASLA, CSWE, NASAD, NASM, NCATE, and NLN. The 44 libraries contain 6 million volumes and 1.3 million microform items, and subscribe to 55,000 periodicals. Computerized library services include the card catalog and database searching. Special learning facilities include a learning resource center, art gallery, natural history museum, planetarium, radio station, TV station, an arboretum, several wildlife areas, 40,000 acres of agricultural research and teaching areas, and 2 limnology research and teaching facilities. The 930-acre campus is in an urban area 75 miles west of Milwaukee and 150 miles north of Chicago. Including any residence halls, there are 192 buildings.

Student Life: 65% of undergraduates are from Wisconsin. Students are from 50 states, 102 foreign countries, and Canada. 67% are from public schools. 90% are white. The average age of freshmen is 18; all undergraduates, 20. 4% do not continue beyond their first year; 85% remain to graduate.

Housing: 7975 students can be accommodated in college housing, which includes single-sex and coed dorms, on-campus apartments, off-campus apartments, married-student housing, fraternity houses, and sorority houses. In addition, there are honors houses, language houses, and special-interest houses. On-campus housing is guaranteed for all 4 years. 97% of students live on campus; of those, 80% remain on campus on weekends. All students may keep cars.

Activities: 14% of men belong to 27 national fraternities; 17% of women belong to 17 national sororities. There are 900 groups on campus, including art, band, cheerleading, chess, choir, chorale, chorus, computers, dance, drama, ethnic, film, gay, honors, international, jazz band, literary magazine, marching band, musical theater, newspaper, opera, orchestra, pep band, photography, political, professional, radio and TV, religious, social, social service, student government, symphony, and yearbook. Popular campus events include Parents Weekend, alumni reunions, and an annual band concert.

Sports: There are 11 intercollegiate sports for men and 9 for women, and 29 intramural sports for men and 24 for women. Facilities include several gymns (one seating 17,000), pools, a field house, 2 stadiums--1 for tennis and the other for football--seating 77,000, and a 12,000-seat arena.

Disabled Students: 90% of the campus is accessible. Wheelchair ramps, elevators, special parking, specially equipped rest rooms, special class scheduling, lowered drinking fountains, and lowered telephones are available.

Services: Counseling and information services are available, as is tutoring in most subjects. There is a reader service for the blind and remedial math, reading, and writing.

Campus Safety and Security: Measures include 24-hour foot and vehicle patrol, self-defense education, security escort services, and shuttle buses. There are informal discussions, pamphlets/posters/films, emergency telephones, and lighted pathways/sidewalks.

Programs of Study: Wisconsin confers B.A., B.S., B.Art Ed., B.B.A., B.F.A., B.M., B.S.Ch., B.S.E., and B.S.P. degrees. Master's and doctoral degrees are also awarded. Bachelor's degrees are awarded in AGRICULTURE (agricultural business management, agricultural economics, agricultural mechanics, animal science, conservation and regulation, dairy science, forestry and related sciences, horticulture, poultry science, and soil science), BIOLOGICAL SCIENCE (bacteriology, biochemistry, botany, entomology, genetics, microbiology, molecular biology, nutrition, plant pathology, toxicology, wildlife biology, and zoology), BUSINESS (accounting, banking and finance, business administration and management, insurance and risk management, marketing/retailing/merchandising, real estate, recreation and leisure services, and retailing), COMMUNICATIONS AND THE ARTS (African languages, art history and appreciation, Chinese, classics, communications, comparative literature, dramatic arts, English, French, German, Greek, Hebrew, Italian, Japanese, journalism, Latin, linguistics, music, Polish, Portuguese, Russian, and Spanish), COMPUTER AND PHYSICAL SCIENCE (actuarial science, applied mathematics, astronomy, atmospheric sciences and meteorology, chemistry, computer science, geology, information sciences and systems, mathematics, physics, quantitative methods, and statistics), EDUCATION (agricultural, art, elementary, physical, and secondary), ENGINEERING AND ENVIRONMENTAL DESIGN (agricultural engi-

neering, biomedical engineering, cartography, chemical engineering, civil engineering, electrical/electronics engineering, engineering mechanics, engineering physics, geological engineering, industrial engineering, interior design, landscape architecture/design, materials science, mechanical engineering, metallurgical engineering, nuclear engineering, and textile technology), HEALTH PROFESSIONS (medical laboratory technology, medical science, nursing, occupational therapy, pharmacy, physician's assistant, and speech pathology/audiology), SOCIAL SCIENCE (African American studies, anthropology, Asian/Oriental studies, behavioral science, child care/child and family studies, consumer services, dietetics, economics, family/consumer studies, food science, geography, history, history of science, humanities, international relations, Judaic studies, Latin American studies, philosophy, political science/government, psychology, rural sociology, Scandinavian studies, social work, sociology, South Asian studies, textiles and clothing, and women's studies). Political science, psychology, and English are the largest.

Required: Required courses vary with individual programs. A total of 120 to 136 credit hours, with at least 30 in the major, and a cumulative GPA of 2.0 are minimum requirements for graduation.

Special: Co-op programs in engineering, internships in political science in Washington, D.C., and the state capital are possible. Study abroad is offered in more than 40 countries in Europe, Asia, and South America. Work-study programs, accelerated degrees, credit by examination, and pass/fail options are available. Students in the College of Letters and Science may select dual or self-designed majors, or an integrated liberal studies program. There are 24 national honor societies, including Phi Beta Kappa, and a freshman honors program.

Faculty/Classroom: 80% of faculty are male; 20%, female. 95% teach undergraduates, All do research. The average class size in an introductory lecture is 75; in a laboratory, 15; and in a regular course, 30.

Admissions: There were 200 National Merit finalists.

Requirements: The ACT is required for in-state students, and either the ACT or the SAT I for out-of-state students. Candidates should be graduates of an accredited secondary school or hold a GED certificate. They must have completed the following academic credits: 4 in English, and 3 each in math, history, science, and social studies, 2 in a foreign language, and college-preparatory electives. Grades, rank in class, and scores, as well as rigor of senior class course selection, are considered. AP and CLEP credits are accepted. Important factors in the admissions decision are advanced placement or honor courses and evidence of special talent.

Procedure: Freshmen are admitted to all sessions. Entrance exams should be taken in the junior year. There are early admissions and deferred admissions plans. Applications should be filed by February 1 for fall entry, October 1 for spring entry, and February 1 for summer entry. The application fee is $35. Notification is sent on a rolling basis. A waiting list is an active part of the admissions procedure. The school accepts applications at *apply.wisconsin.edu*.

Transfer: 1150 transfer students enrolled in a recent year. Admission is competitive and varies by program. Generally, applicants must have at least sophomore standing and a GPA of 3.2 or higher. Transfer students must complete 15 intermediate and advanced credits in the major. 30 of 120 credits required for the bachelor's degree must be completed at Wisconsin.

Visiting: There are regularly scheduled orientations for prospective students, including an admission information session, a tour, and class visits. There are guides for informal visits and visitors may sit in on classes and stay overnight. To schedule a visit, contact the Tour Coordinator, Office of Admissions, at (608) 262-3318.

Financial Aid: Wisconsin is a member of CSS. The FAFSA and a federal income tax return are required. The deadline for filing freshman financial aid applications for fall entry is March 1.

International Students: They must score 550 on the written TOEFL or take the MELAB and also the SAT I or the ACT.

Computers: There are 1000 PCs available in 14 open labs and dorms. There are data ports in all dorm rooms. All students have e-mail. All students may access the system. There are no time limits and no fees.

Graduates: The most popular majors were political science (7%), psychology (5%), and English (5%). In an average class, 10% graduate in 3 years or less, 45% graduate in 4 years or less, 85% graduate in 5 years or less, and 88% graduate in 6 years or less.

Admissions Contact: Keith White, Associate Director of Admissions. E-mail: *onwisconsin@admissions.wisc.edu*

UNIVERSITY OF WISCONSIN/MILWAUKEE   E-4
Milwaukee, WI 53201   (414) 229-3800; Fax: (414) 229-6940

Full-time: 7484 men, 9071 women	Faculty: 824; I, -$
Part-time: 1469 men, 1761 women	Ph.D.s: 90%
Graduate: 1507 men, 2336 women	Student/Faculty: 20 to 1
Year: semesters, summer session	Tuition: $5107 ($17,858)
Application Deadline: August 1	Room & Board: $4320
Freshman Class: 9918 applied, 7881 accepted, 3635 enrolled	
SAT I or ACT: required	LESS COMPETITIVE

The University of Wisconsin/Milwaukee, founded in 1885, offers undergraduate and graduate degrees in arts and sciences, fine arts, business, education, engineering and applied sciences, architecture and urban planning, social welfare, and health fields. There are 10 undergraduate schools and 1 graduate school. In addition to regional accreditation, UWM has baccalaureate program accreditation with AACSB, ABET, ACEJMC, CAHEA, CSWE, NAAB, NASAD, NASM, NCATE, and NLN. The library contains 2,141,859 volumes, 1,717,205 microform items, and 38,716 audio/video tapes/CDs, and subscribes to 8757 periodicals. Computerized library services include the card catalog, interlibrary loans, database searching, and Internet access. Special learning facilities include a learning resource center, art gallery, planetarium, radio station, TV station, and the American Geographical Society Library. The 93-acre campus is in an urban area in Milwaukee. Including any residence halls, there are 42 buildings.

Student Life: 99% of undergraduates are from Wisconsin. Students are from 49 states, 59 foreign countries, and Canada. 83% are white. The average age of freshmen is 19; all undergraduates, 22.

Housing: 1904 students can be accommodated in college housing, which includes coed dorms and married-student housing. On-campus housing is available on a first-come, first-served basis. 87% of students commute. All students may keep cars.

Activities: 3% of men belong to 1 local and 6 national fraternities; 3% of women belong to 6 national sororities. There are 250 groups on campus, including art, band, cheerleading, chorale, computers, concert band, dance, drama, ethnic, film, gay, honors, international, jazz band, literary magazine, music ensembles, musical theater, newspaper, orchestra, pep band, photography, political, professional, radio and TV, religious, social, social service, student government, and symphony. Popular campus events include concerts, art exhibitions, and dance performances.

Sports: There are 9 intercollegiate sports for men and 8 for women, and 15 intramural sports for men and 13 for women. Facilities include a center for phys ed, a gym, a field, courts, and a 3000-seat auditorium.

Disabled Students: 90% of the campus is accessible. Wheelchair ramps, elevators, special parking, specially equipped rest rooms, special class scheduling, lowered drinking fountains, lowered telephones, and special library facilities are available.

Services: Counseling and information services are available, as is tutoring in some subjects, including English composition, math, science, business, reading, and study skills. There is a reader service for the blind and remedial math, reading, and writing.

Campus Safety and Security: Measures include 24-hour foot and vehicle patrol, self-defense education, security escort services, and shuttle buses. There are pamphlets/posters/films, emergency telephones, and lighted pathways/sidewalks.

Programs of Study: UWM confers B.A., B.S., B.B.A., B.F.A., B.S.Applied S., and B.S.E. degrees. Master's and doctoral degrees are also awarded. Bachelor's degrees are awarded in AGRICULTURE (conservation and regulation), BIOLOGICAL SCIENCE (biochemistry, biology/biological science, botany, microbiology, and zoology), BUSINESS (accounting, banking and finance, business administration and management, management information systems, marketing/retailing/merchandising, real estate, and recreation and leisure services), COMMUNICATIONS AND THE ARTS (art history and appreciation, classics, communications, comparative literature, dance, dramatic arts, English, film arts, fine arts, French, German, Hebrew, Italian, linguistics, music, Russian, and Spanish), COMPUTER AND PHYSICAL SCIENCE (applied mathematics, chemistry, computer science, geology, geoscience, mathematics, and physics), EDUCATION (art, education, music, and social science), ENGINEERING AND ENVIRONMENTAL DESIGN (architecture, civil engineering, electrical/electronics engineering, engineering, industrial administration/management, industrial engineering, materials engineering, and mechanical engineering), HEALTH PROFESSIONS (clinical science, health care administration, health science, medical science, nursing, occupational therapy, predentistry, premedicine, and speech pathology/audiology), SOCIAL SCIENCE (African American studies, anthropology, criminal justice, economics, geography, history, law, philosophy, political science/government, prelaw, psychology, religion, social work, and sociology). Architecture and engineering are the strongest academically.

Required: English composition and math proficiency exams must be passed with satisfactory scores. Distribution requirements include 6 credits each in humanities, natural sciences, and social sciences and 3 credits

each in the arts and cultural diversity. All students must complete a minimum of 120 credits.

Special: UWM offers cooperative programs in engineering, cross-registration with UW/Parkside, study abroad in Europe and Asia, internships, a Washington semester, and work-study programs. Students may select an accelerated degree program, dual majors, a general studies degree, and student-designed majors. Credit/no credit options, nondegree study, credit by exam, and credit for life, military, and work experience are also available. There is 1 national honor society, including Phi Beta Kappa, a freshman honors program, and 1 departmental honors program.

Faculty/Classroom: 70% of faculty are male; 30%, female. All teach undergraduates. The average class size in an introductory lecture is 48; in a laboratory, 15; and in a regular course, 27.

Admissions: 79% of the 2003-2004 applicants were accepted.

Requirements: The SAT I or ACT is required. The ACT is preferred, with a minimum score of 21 required of all Wisconsin residents. Out-of-state students may substitute the SAT I with a minimum composite score of 970. Candidates must have graduated from an accredited secondary school with 17 Carnegie units, including at least 4 in English, 3 in history/social science, and 3 each in math and the natural sciences. A GED certificate is accepted. Music and theater majors must audition. For the School of Architecture and Urban Planning, higher rank and ACT requirements apply. UWM requires applicants to be in the upper 50% of their class. AP and CLEP credits are accepted. Important factors in the admissions decision are advanced placement or honor courses, evidence of special talent, and leadership record.

Procedure: Freshmen are admitted to all sessions. Entrance exams should be taken in the spring of the junior year. There is a deferred admissions plan. Applications should be filed by August 1 for fall entry, along with a $35 fee. (The priority deadline is June 30.) Notification is sent on a rolling basis beginning September 15. Applications are accepted on-line through *www.apply.wisconsin.edu*.

Transfer: 1509 transfer students enrolled in 2003-2004. Transfer applicants must have earned a minimum of 12 credit hours and have at least a 2.0 GPA. 30 of 120 credits required for the bachelor's degree must be completed at UWM.

Visiting: There are regularly scheduled orientations for prospective students. There are guides for informal visits and visitors may sit in on classes and stay overnight. To schedule a visit, contact the Student Visitor Center at (414) 229-4397.

International Students: They must score 520 on the written TOEFL or 190 on the electronic version.

Computers: The mainframe is a DEC 2100-275 running Digital UNIX. PCs are available in the library, residence halls, the student union, and several labs. All students may access the system any time. There are no time limits and no fees.

Graduates: From July 1, 2002 to June 30, 2003, 2298 bachelor's degrees were awarded. The most popular majors were business/marketing (25%), visual and performing arts (8%), and social sciences and history (8%). 166 companies recruited on campus in a recent year.

Admissions Contact: Director of Admissions.
E-mail: *uwmlook@uwm.edu* Web: *www.uwm.edu*

UNIVERSITY OF WISCONSIN/OSHKOSH   D-4
Oshkosh, WI 54901   (920) 424-0202; Fax: (920) 424-1098

Full-time: 3400 men, 4550 women	Faculty: 407; IIA, -$
Part-time: 450 men, 840 women	Ph.D.s: 81%
Graduate: 575 men, 940 women	Student/Faculty: 19 to 1
Year: semesters, summer session	Tuition: $3500 ($14,000)
Application Deadline: August 1	Room & Board: $4000
Freshman Class: n/av	
ACT: required	LESS COMPETITIVE

The University of Wisconsin/Oshkosh, founded in 1871, is a public institution offering undergraduate and graduate programs in education, business, the arts and sciences, and health fields. There are 4 undergraduate schools and 1 graduate school. Figures in the above capsule and in this profile are approximate. In addition to regional accreditation, UW/Oshkosh has baccalaureate program accreditation with AACSB, ACEJMC, CSWE, NASM, NCATE, and NLN. The library contains 440,000 volumes, 2 million microform items, and 10,000 audio/video tapes/CDs, and subscribes to 1600 periodicals. Computerized library services include the card catalog, interlibrary loans, and database searching. Special learning facilities include a learning resource center, art gallery, planetarium, radio station, TV station, and a speech and hearing clinic. The 192-acre campus is in an urban area 90 miles north of Milwaukee. Including any residence halls, there are 36 buildings.

Student Life: 96% of undergraduates are from Wisconsin. 94% are white. The average age of freshmen is 18; all undergraduates, 22. 29% do not continue beyond their first year; 55% remain to graduate.

Housing: 3667 students can be accommodated in college housing, which includes single-sex and coed dorms. On-campus housing is guaranteed for all 4 years. 66% of students commute. All students may keep cars.

Activities: 5% of men belong to 8 national fraternities; 5% of women belong to 5 national sororities. There are 175 groups on campus, including art, band, cheerleading, chess, choir, computers, dance, debate, ethnic, film, forensics, gay, honors, international, jazz band, literary magazine, musical theater, newspaper, opera, pep band, political, professional, radio and TV, religious, social, social service, student government, and symphony. Popular campus events include Winter Carnival, Taste of UW Oshkosh, and Celebration of Racial Inclusiveness.

Sports: There are 10 intercollegiate sports for men and 11 for women, and 15 intramural sports for men and 15 for women. Facilities include a hall for basketball, swimming, and volleyball, a sports center for basketball, tennis, and indoor track, a pool, a 10,400-seat stadium for football and outdoor track, a 2500-seat indoor gym, and a 5808-seat arena.

Disabled Students: Wheelchair ramps, elevators, special parking, specially equipped rest rooms, special class scheduling, lowered drinking fountains, and lowered telephones are available.

Services: Counseling and information services are available, as is tutoring in most subjects. There is a reader service for the blind and remedial math, reading, and writing.

Campus Safety and Security: Measures include 24-hour foot and vehicle patrol, self-defense education, security escort services, and informal discussions. There are pamphlets/posters/films, emergency telephones, and lighted pathways/sidewalks.

Programs of Study: UW/Oshkosh confers B.A., B.S., B.Art Ed., B.B.A., B.F.A., B.L.S., B.M., B.M.E., B.S.N., and B.S.W. degrees. Associate and master's degrees are also awarded. Bachelor's degrees are awarded in BIOLOGICAL SCIENCE (biology/biological science and microbiology), BUSINESS (accounting, banking and finance, business administration and management, human resources, management information systems, and marketing/retailing/merchandising), COMMUNICATIONS AND THE ARTS (art, English, fine arts, French, German, journalism, music, Spanish, and speech/debate/rhetoric), COMPUTER AND PHYSICAL SCIENCE (chemistry, computer science, geology, mathematics, and physics), EDUCATION (art, elementary, music, physical, science, secondary, social science, and special), HEALTH PROFESSIONS (medical laboratory technology, music therapy, nursing, and speech pathology/audiology), SOCIAL SCIENCE (anthropology, criminal justice, economics, geography, history, human services, international studies, liberal arts/general studies, philosophy, political science/government, psychology, religion, social work, sociology, and urban studies). Business, education, and nursing are the largest.

Required: All students must complete a minimum of 120 credit hours with at least a 2.0 GPA. A minimum of 42 credits in general education requirements includes 9 credits each in humanities and social science, 8 in natural science, 6 in English composition, 3 in math or logic, 3 in non-Western culture, 3 in speech, and 2 in phys ed.

Special: UW/Oshkosh offers internships and study abroad. There are 15 national honor societies and a freshman honors program.

Faculty/Classroom: 56% of faculty are male; 44%, female. No introductory courses are taught by graduate students. The average class size in an introductory lecture is 31 and in a laboratory, 21.

Requirements: The ACT is required. In addition, students must graduate in the upper 50% of their class from an accredited secondary school or score a 22 on the enhanced ACT if ranked in the third quartile. They should have completed 17 academic credits, including 4 in English, 3 each in math, social sciences, natural sciences, and 4 in electives, preferably in a foreign language or fine arts/humanities. AP and CLEP credits are accepted.

Procedure: Freshmen are admitted to all sessions. Entrance exams should be taken in spring of the junior year or early fall of the senior year. There is a deferred admissions plan. Applications should be filed by August 1 for fall entry and January 1 for spring entry, along with a $35 fee. Notification is sent on a rolling basis. Applications are accepted on-line at www.apply.wisconsin.edu.

Transfer: Candidates should have completed 30 or more semester credits; if not, high school transcripts are reviewed. Students must have at least a 2.0 cumulative GPA. 30 of 120 credits required for the bachelor's degree must be completed at UW/Oshkosh.

Visiting: There are regularly scheduled orientations for prospective students, including preview days, campus tours, and an individual appointment with an admissions counselor. There are guides for informal visits and visitors may sit in on classes and stay overnight. To schedule a visit, contact the Admissions Office at (920) 424-0202 or (920) 424-1107.

Financial Aid: UW/Oshkosh is a member of CSS. The FAFSA is required. The priority deadline for filing freshman financial aid applications for fall entry is March 15.

International Students: International students must score 500 on the written TOEFL.

Computers: The mainframes are a DEC VAX 11/780 and 8250. There are more than 450 PCs in 6 labs. All students may access the system 24 hours, 7 days a week. There are no time limits and no fees.

Graduates: The most popular majors were nursing (10%), marketing (7%), and elementary education (6%). In an average class, 7% graduate

in 4 years or less, 33% graduate in 5 years or less, and 44% graduate in 6 years or less.

Admissions Contact: Jill Endries, Director of Admissions. A video is available. E-mail: *oshadmuw@uwosh.edu* Web: *http://www.uwosh.edu*

UNIVERSITY OF WISCONSIN/PARKSIDE

E-5

Kenosha, WI 53141-2000 (414) 595-2355; Fax: (414) 595-2202

Full-time: 1160 men, 1570 women	**Faculty:** 144; IIA, av$
Part-time: 680 men, 960 women	**Ph.D.s:** 93%
Graduate: 70 men, 110 women	**Student/Faculty:** 19 to 1
Year: semesters, summer session	**Tuition:** $3535 ($13,600)
Application Deadline: see profile	**Room & Board:** $3630
Freshman Class: n/av	**ACT:** required

LESS COMPETITIVE

The University of Wisconsin/Parkside, founded in 1968, offers undergraduate programs in liberal arts, business, education, and science and technology. Figures given in the above capsule and in this profile are approximate. There are 4 undergraduate and 3 graduate schools. The library contains 350,000 volumes, 150,000 microform items, and 10,200 audio/video tapes/CDs, and subscribes to 1500 periodicals. Computerized library services include the card catalog. Special learning facilities include a learning resource center, art gallery, and radio station. The 700-acre campus is in a suburban area 30 miles south of Milwaukee. Including any residence halls, there are 11 buildings.

Student Life: 91% are white. 22% do not continue beyond their first year; 60% remain to graduate.

Housing: 400 students can be accommodated in college housing, which includes coed on-campus apartments and off-campus apartments. In addition, there are special-interest houses. On-campus housing is guaranteed for all 4 years. 52% of students commute. All students may keep cars.

Activities: There are no fraternities or sororities. There are 60 groups on campus, including art, band, cheerleading, choir, chorale, chorus, computers, drama, ethnic, gay, honors, international, jazz band, literary magazine, musical theater, newspaper, orchestra, political, professional, religious, social, social service, student government, and yearbook. Popular campus events include Cinco de Mayo, Winter Carnival, and Black History Month.

Sports: There are 8 intercollegiate sports for men and 6 for women. Facilities include a cross-country course, tennis courts, playing fields, and an all-purpose phys ed building with a 3000-seat auditorium for athletic events and concerts.

Disabled Students: All of the campus is accessible. Wheelchair ramps, elevators, special parking, specially equipped rest rooms, lowered drinking fountains, and lowered telephones are available.

Services: Counseling and information services are available, as is tutoring in every subject. There is a reader service for the blind and remedial math, reading, and writing.

Campus Safety and Security: Measures include shuttle buses, pamphlets/posters/films, emergency telephones, and lighted pathways/sidewalks.

Programs of Study: UW/Parkside confers B.A. and B.S. degrees. Master's degrees are also awarded. Bachelor's degrees are awarded in BIOLOGICAL SCIENCE (biology/biological science), BUSINESS (business administration and management), COMMUNICATIONS AND THE ARTS (communications, dramatic arts, English, fine arts, French, German, music, and Spanish), COMPUTER AND PHYSICAL SCIENCE (chemistry, computer science, geology, mathematics, physics, and science), EDUCATION (education), ENGINEERING AND ENVIRONMENTAL DESIGN (industrial administration/management), SOCIAL SCIENCE (economics, geography, history, humanities, international studies, philosophy, political science/government, psychology, and sociology). Social sciences and physical sciences are the strongest academically. Business is the largest.

Required: A total of 120 credits with at least 30 in the major and a GPA of 2.0 are required for graduation. Students must complete a minimum of 12 credits in humanities and the arts, 12 in social and behavioral sciences, and 9 in natural sciences. Nonengineering majors with fewer than 2 units of foreign language in high school must also fulfill a foreign language requirement.

Special: UW/Parkside offers on-campus work-study programs, internships, study abroad, student-designed majors, and an accelerated premedicine program. Nondegree study and credit by exam are possible. There is a freshman honors program.

Faculty/Classroom: No introductory courses are taught by graduate students. The average class size in an introductory lecture is 150; in a laboratory, 50; and in a regular course, 30.

Requirements: The ACT is required for in-state students; either the ACT or the SAT I for out-of-state students. A minimum score of 21 is required on the ACT. Students may use a lower ACT score in combination with class rank to gain admission. Candidates must be graduates of an accredited secondary school or hold a GED diploma. At least 16 academic credits are required, including 4 in English, 3 in social sciences, 2 in natural sciences, and 1 each in algebra and plane geometry. UW/Parkside requires applicants to be in the upper 50% of their class. AP and CLEP credits are accepted. Important factors in the admissions decision are geographic diversity, extracurricular activities record, and ability to finance college education.

Procedure: Freshmen are admitted fall and spring. Entrance exams should be taken by the fall of the senior year. There are early admissions and deferred admissions plans. Notification is sent on a rolling basis. Check with the school for current application deadlines and fee.

Transfer: Students must have a GPA of 2.0 and be in good standing with the previous institution attended. 30 of 120 credits required for the bachelor's degree must be completed at UW/Parkside.

Visiting: There are regularly scheduled orientations for prospective students, including open houses and campus tours. There are guides for informal visits and visitors may sit in on classes. To schedule a visit, contact Student Enrollment Services.

Financial Aid: The FAFSA and the college's own financial statement are required. The priority filing date for financial aid forms is March 15.

International Students: International students must score 525 on the written TOEFL.

Computers: The mainframe is an IBM 4381. There are PCs available in the library/learning center. Two general-purpose labs are available. All students may access the system. There are no time limits and no fees.

Admissions Contact: Matthew Jensen, Admissions Director.

UNIVERSITY OF WISCONSIN/PLATTEVILLE   C-5
Platteville, WI 53818-3099   (608) 342-1125
                                        (800) 362-5515; Fax: (608) 342-1122

Full-time: 3085 men, 1885 women	**Faculty:** 232; IIA, av$
Part-time: 206 men, 167 women	**Ph.D.s:** 84%
Graduate: 242 men, 294 women	**Student/Faculty:** 21 to 1
Year: semesters, summer session	**Tuition:** $4254 ($14,300)
Application Deadline: open	**Room & Board:** $4196
Freshman Class: 2814 applied, 2220 accepted, 1110 enrolled	
ACT: required	**COMPETITIVE**

The University of Wisconsin/Platteville, founded in 1866, offers undergraduate programs in arts, social sciences, humanities, sciences, agriculture, education, engineering, communication, business, and industry. There are 3 undergraduate schools and 1 graduate school. In addition to regional accreditation, UWP has baccalaureate program accreditation with ABET, ABFSE, and NASM. The library contains 222,838 volumes, 997,272 microform items, and 13,299 audio/video tapes/CDs, and subscribes to 22,175 periodicals. Computerized library services include interlibrary loans and database searching. Special learning facilities include a learning resource center, art gallery, radio station, and TV station. The 340-acre campus is in a rural area 20 miles northeast of Dubuque, Iowa, and 75 miles southwest of Madison. Including any residence halls, there are 65 buildings.

Student Life: 93% of undergraduates are from Wisconsin. Students are from 33 states, 29 foreign countries, and Canada. 90% are from public schools. 87% are white. The average age of freshmen is 18.

Housing: 2306 students can be accommodated in college housing, which includes single-sex and coed dorms. In addition, there are intensive-study quiet floors, an engineering hall, and a computing technology hall. On-campus housing is guaranteed for all 4 years. All students may keep cars.

Activities: 2% of men and about 1% of women belong to 1 local and 9 national fraternities; 5% of women belong to 1 local and 3 national sororities. There are 92 groups on campus, including art, band, cheerleading, chess, choir, chorale, chorus, computers, drama, drill team, ethnic, film, gay, honors, international, jazz band, literary magazine, marching band, musical theater, newspaper, opera, orchestra, pep band, photography, political, professional, radio and TV, religious, social, social service, student government, symphony, and yearbook. Popular campus events include Heartland Festival, international student dinners, and February Follies.

Sports: There are 7 intercollegiate sports for men and 6 for women, and 17 intramural sports for men and 16 for women. Facilities include a 2000-seat gym, a 10,000-seat stadium, a 200-meter indoor track, a 400-meter outdoor track, 7 basketball and 7 volleyball courts, 6 tennis and 4 racquetball courts, a weight room, a swimming pool, a baseball diamond, and soccer fields.

Disabled Students: 95% of the campus is accessible. Wheelchair ramps, elevators, special parking, specially equipped rest rooms, special class scheduling, lowered drinking fountains, and lowered telephones are available.

Services: Counseling and information services are available, as is tutoring in most subjects. There is a reader service for the blind, and remedial math, reading, and writing, as well as university counseling services.

Campus Safety and Security: Measures include 24-hour foot and vehicle patrol, security escort services, informal discussions, and pamphlets/posters/films. There are emergency telephones, lighted pathways/sidewalks, and locked residence halls.

Programs of Study: UWP confers B.A. and B.S. degrees. Associate and master's degrees are also awarded. Bachelor's degrees are awarded in AGRICULTURE (agricultural business management, agricultural economics, animal science, and soil science), BIOLOGICAL SCIENCE (biology/biological science), BUSINESS (accounting, business administration and management, business economics, and management science), COMMUNICATIONS AND THE ARTS (English, fine arts, French, German, music, Spanish, and speech/debate/rhetoric), COMPUTER AND PHYSICAL SCIENCE (chemistry, computer science, mathematics, physical sciences, physics, and science), EDUCATION (agricultural, art, elementary, middle school, music, physical, science, secondary, and technical), ENGINEERING AND ENVIRONMENTAL DESIGN (agricultural engineering technology, civil engineering, electrical/electronics engineering, engineering, industrial engineering, industrial engineering technology, land use management and reclamation, and mechanical engineering), SOCIAL SCIENCE (criminal justice, economics, geography, history, international studies, philosophy, political science/government, psychology, and social science). Engineering, middle school education, and technology management are the strongest academically. Engineering is the largest.

Required: To graduate, students must complete a minimum of 128 credit hours, with a minimum GPA of 2.0 overall, and within the major. Course requirements include 12 credits in humanities and fine arts, 9 each in social sciences and natural sciences, 4 in ethnic and gender studies, and 3 in international education. Other competency requirements include 6 credits in English composition, 3 in math, and 2 each in speech and phys ed.

Special: UWP offers internships in business, industry, and communication, a co-op program in engineering, and study abroad in 12 countries. Credit by exam, credit for life, military, and work experience, work-study programs, dual majors, student-designed majors, nondegree study, and pass/fail options are also available. There are 12 national honor societies, a freshman honors program, and 4 departmental honors programs.

Faculty/Classroom: 71% of faculty are male; 29%, female. All teach undergraduates. The average class size in an introductory lecture is 30; in a laboratory, 20; and in a regular course, 22.

Admissions: 79% of the 2003-2004 applicants were accepted. The ACT scores for the 2003-2004 freshman class were: 31% below 21, 32% between 21 and 23, 22% between 24 and 26, 9% between 27 and 28, and 6% above 28. 29% of the current freshmen were in the top fifth of their class; 63% were in the top two fifths.

Requirements: The ACT is required, with a minimum score of 22. Applicants must be graduates of an accredited secondary school or hold the GED certificate. Special permission may be granted from the dean for nontraditional students. Academic preparation should include 4 credits in English, 3 in social sciences, 3 each in math and sciences, 2 in a foreign language, and 4 in other academic areas. AP and CLEP credits are accepted. Important factors in the admissions decision are ability to finance college education, recommendations by school officials, and advanced placement or honor courses.

Procedure: Freshmen are admitted to all sessions. Entrance exams should be taken in April or June of the junior year. There is a rolling admissions plan and a deferred admissions plan. Application deadlines are open. The fall 2003 application fee was $35. Applications are accepted on-line through the university's web site.

Transfer: 309 transfer students enrolled in 2002-2003. Out-of-state applicants must have a college GPA of 3.0 and be in good standing at their current or previous institution. Wisconsin residents should have a GPA of 2.0 and a minimum of 14 college credits. All transfer students must have completed 6 semester credits of UWP's English requirement and 3 semester credits of public speaking. 32 of 128 credits required for the bachelor's degree must be completed at UWP.

Visiting: There are regularly scheduled orientations for prospective students, The Pioneer Previews, held on 4 or 5 dates each year, include group tours, an admissions briefing, and visits to specific colleges and departments. There are guides for informal visits and visitors may sit in on classes. To schedule a visit, contact Richard Schumacher, Dean of Admissions and Enrollment Management at *schumacr@uwplatt.edu*.

Financial Aid: In 2003-2004, 45% of all full-time freshmen and 51% of continuing full-time students received some form of financial aid. 34% of full-time freshmen and 31% of continuing full-time students received need-based aid. The average freshman award was $5809. Need-based scholarships or need-based grants averaged $3660; need-based self-help aid (loans and jobs) averaged $3023; and institutional non-need-based awards and non-need-based scholarships averaged $1459. The FAFSA is required.

International Students: There were 49 international students enrolled in a recent year. The school actively recruits these students. They must score 550 on the written TOEFL and also take the ACT or Wisconsin English and math placement exam.

Computers: The mainframes are a DEC VAX 4000 series server and an IBM 9375. There are 80 networked PCs and 37 terminals available to students in general-access labs across campus. All students may access the system. There are no time limits and no fees.

Graduates: From July 1, 2002 to June 30, 2003, 846 bachelor's degrees were awarded. The most popular majors were engineering (22%), education (17%), and trade and industry (10%). In an average class, 14% graduate in 4 years or less.

Admissions Contact: Dr. Richard R. Schumacher, Dean of Admissions and Enrollment Management. E-mail: *admit@uwplatt.edu* Web: *www.uwplatt.edu*

UNIVERSITY OF WISCONSIN/RIVER FALLS   A-3
River Falls, WI 54022   **(715) 425-3500; Fax: (715) 425-0676**

Full-time: 1955 men, 3064 women	**Faculty:** 221; IIA, av$
Part-time: 164 men, 230 women	**Ph.Ds:** 85%
Graduate: 155 men, 325 women	**Student/Faculty:** 23 to 1
Year: semesters, summer session	**Tuition:** $4450 ($14,496)
Application Deadline: open	**Room & Board:** $3908 ($4308)
Freshman Class: n/av	
ACT: 22	**LESS COMPETITIVE**

The University of Wisconsin/River Falls, founded in 1874, is a public institution offering undergraduate programs in arts and sciences, education, agriculture, and food and environmental sciences. There are 4 undergraduate schools and 1 graduate school. In addition to regional accreditation, UW/River Falls has baccalaureate program accreditation with ACEJMC, ASLA, CSWE, NASM, and NCATE. The library contains 221,453 volumes, 726,035 microform items, and 8455 audio/video tapes/CDs, and subscribes to 1322 periodicals. Computerized library services include the card catalog, interlibrary loans, database searching, and Internet access. Special learning facilities include a learning resource center, art gallery, planetarium, radio station, TV station, greenhouse, climbing wall, communicative disorders lab, educational technology center, food science and meat facilities, 2 campus lab farms, and sundial. The 225-acre campus is in a suburban area 29 miles east of Minneapolis-St. Paul, Minnesota. Including any residence halls, there are 28 buildings.

Student Life: 52% of undergraduates are from Wisconsin. Students are from 25 states, 13 foreign countries, and Canada. 95% are from public schools. 95% are white. The average age of freshmen is 18; all undergraduates, 21. 25% do not continue beyond their first year; 54% remain to graduate.

Housing: 2172 students can be accommodated in college housing, which includes single-sex and coed dorms. On-campus housing is guaranteed for all 4 years. 59% of students commute. All students may keep cars.

Activities: 5% of men belong to 5 national fraternities; 5% of women belong to 4 national sororities. There are 120 groups on campus, including academic, agriculture, art, band, cheerleading, choir, chorus, computers, dance, debate, drama, drug awareness, ethnic, forensics, gay, honors, international, jazz band, literary magazine, musical theater, newspaper, orchestra, pep band, political, professional, radio and TV, religious, rodeo, social, student government, and symphony. Popular campus events include Winter Carnival, Annual Rodeo, and Unity in the Community.

Sports: There are 7 intercollegiate sports for men and 11 for women, and 11 intramural sports for men and 12 for women. Facilities include an ice arena, a 4550-seat stadium, 2 multipurpose phys ed centers, a swimming pool, a 2600-seat gym and a smaller gym, handball courts, a field house, an indoor track, an indoor rock-climbing wall, and basketball, tennis, and volleyball courts.

Disabled Students: 95% of the campus is accessible. Wheelchair ramps, elevators, special parking, specially equipped rest rooms, special class scheduling, lowered drinking fountains, and lowered telephones are available.

Services: Counseling and information services are available, as is tutoring in every subject. There is a reader service for the blind and remedial math, reading, and writing.

Campus Safety and Security: Measures include 24-hour foot and vehicle patrol, self-defense education, security escort services, and informal discussions. There are pamphlets/posters/films, emergency telephones, and lighted pathways/sidewalks.

Programs of Study: UW/River Falls confers B.A., B.S., B.F.A, B.M.E., and B.S.W. degrees. Master's degrees are also awarded. Bachelor's degrees are awarded in AGRICULTURE (agricultural business management, agronomy, animal science, conservation and regulation, horticulture, and soil science), BIOLOGICAL SCIENCE (biology/biological science and biotechnology), BUSINESS (accounting and business administration and management), COMMUNICATIONS AND THE ARTS (art, communications, English, fine arts, journalism, modern language, music, and speech/debate/rhetoric), COMPUTER AND PHYSICAL SCIENCE (chemistry, computer programming, geology, mathematics, physics, and science), EDUCATION (agricultural, art, elementary, foreign languages, music, physical, and secondary), ENGINEERING AND ENVIRONMENTAL DESIGN (agricultural engineering and land use management and reclamation), HEALTH PROFESSIONS (premedicine, prepharmacy, and speech pathology/audiology), SOCIAL SCIENCE (economics, food science, geography, history, political science/

government, prelaw, psychology, social studies, social work, and sociology). Physics, chemistry, and elementary education are the strongest academically. Business, elementary education, and animal science are the largest.

Required: To graduate, students must complete at least 120 semester hours, with a GPA of 2.0 overall and 2.25 in the major field. General education requirements include 39 semester hours in English composition, speech and humanities, natural and social sciences, math, and phys ed.

Special: Co-op programs in food science and environmental science, on-campus work-study, and accelerated degree programs in several preprofessional areas are available. UW/River Falls also offers internships, student-designed majors, credit by examination, nondegree study, and pass/fail options. Study abroad is available through the National Student Exchange and the International Student Exchange Program in some 15 countries. There are 11 national honor societies and a freshman honors program.

Faculty/Classroom: 70% of faculty are male; 30%, female. All teach undergraduates. No introductory courses are taught by graduate students. The average class size in an introductory lecture is 30; in a laboratory, 24; and in a regular course, 20.

Requirements: The ACT is required, with a minimum composite score of 22, or 18 if in upper 40% of high school class. Candidates must be graduates of an accredited secondary school and have completed at least 17 academic credits, including 4 in English, 3 in social sciences, and 3 each in math and science, with 4 college prep courses. A GED certificate is accepted. UW/River Falls requires applicants to be in the upper 40% of their class. AP and CLEP credits are accepted.

Procedure: Freshmen are admitted to all sessions. Entrance exams should be taken in the spring of the junior year. There are early admissions and deferred admissions plans. Application deadlines are open. A waiting list is an active part of the admissions procedure. Applications are accepted on-line through *apply.wisconsin.edu*. The fall 2003 application fee was $35.

Transfer: Priority admission is given to students with a college GPA of 2.6 or higher. Students with a GPA of 2.0 to 2.6 are placed on a waiting list. Transfers in elementary education must have a GPA of 3.0. 30 of 120 credits required for the bachelor's degree must be completed at UW/River Falls.

Visiting: There are regularly scheduled orientations for prospective students, including College Visit Days and tours. There are guides for informal visits and visitors may sit in on classes. To schedule a visit, contact the Admissions Office at (715) 425-3500 or *admit@uwrf.edu*.

Financial Aid: 20% of undergraduates work part time. UW/River Falls is a member of CSS. The FAFSA is required. The deadline for filing freshman financial aid applications for fall entry is March 15.

International Students: There are 47 international students enrolled. They must score 500 on the written TOEFL and also take the ACT.

Computers: The mainframe is a DEC VAX 11/780. The mainframe lab has 18 terminals. There are also more than 500 Mac and IBM PCs available in labs, offices, and residence halls across campus. Registered students have free e-mail and Internet access. All students may access the system more than 80 hours per week, and by telephone request when labs are closed. There are no limits and no fees.

Graduates: From July 1, 2002 to June 30, 2003, 1045 bachelor's degrees were awarded. The most popular majors were education (18%), agriculture (15%), and business (15%). In an average class, 25% graduate in 4 years or less, 35% graduate in 5 years or less, and 54% graduate in 6 years or less.

Admissions Contact: Alan J. Tuchtenhagen, Admissions Director. E-mail: *admit@uwrf.edu* Web: *http://www.uwrf.edu*

UNIVERSITY OF WISCONSIN/STEVENS POINT   C-3
Stevens Point, WI 54481-3897   **(715) 346-2441**
Fax: (715) 346-2441

Full-time: 3464 men, 4275 women	**Faculty:** 362; IIA, av$
Part-time: 296 men, 468 women	**Ph.Ds:** 86%
Graduate: 94 men, 432 women	**Student/Faculty:** 21 to 1
Year: semesters, summer session	**Tuition:** $4152 ($14,198)
Application Deadline: open	**Room & Board:** $3964
Freshman Class: 4639 applied, 3440 accepted, 1508 enrolled	
SAT I Verbal/Math: 560/610	**ACT:** 22 **VERY COMPETITIVE**

The University of Wisconsin/Stevens Point, founded in 1894, offers undergraduate programs in natural resources, education, business, arts and sciences, and professional studies. There are 4 undergraduate schools and 1 graduate school. In addition to regional accreditation, UWSP has baccalaureate program accreditation with ADA, ASLA, FIDER, NASAD, NASM, and SAF. The library contains 996,623 volumes, 910,300 microform items, and 4104 audio/video tapes/CDs, and subscribes to 3861 periodicals. Computerized library services include the card catalog, interlibrary loans, database searching, and Internet access. Special learning facilities include a learning resource center, art gallery, natural history museum, planetarium, radio station, TV station, observatory, map center, 275-acre nature preserve, groundwater center, and wellness institute.

The 335-acre campus is in a small town 110 miles north of Madison. Including any residence halls, there are 35 buildings.

Student Life: 92% of undergraduates are from Wisconsin. Students are from 29 states, 27 foreign countries, and Canada. 94% are white. The average age of freshmen is 19; all undergraduates, 22. 23% do not continue beyond their first year; 56% remain to graduate.

Housing: 3316 students can be accommodated in college housing, which includes single-sex and coed dorms. In addition, there are special-interest houses, privately owned off-campus apartments and off-campus fraternity and sorority houses. 64% of students commute. All students may keep cars.

Activities: 2% of men belong to 3 national fraternities; 1% of women belong to 3 local and 1 national sorority. There are 150 groups on campus, including art, band, cheerleading, choir, chorale, chorus, computers, dance, drama, ethnic, film, gay, honors, international, jazz band, literary magazine, musical theater, newspaper, orchestra, pep band, photography, political, professional, radio and TV, religious, social, social service, student government, symphony, and yearbook. Popular campus events include Homecoming, Trivia Contest, and International Club dinner.

Sports: There are 10 intercollegiate sports for men and 12 for women, and 14 intramural sports for men and 12 for women. Facilities include 2 gyms, a health enhancement center, a cardio center, and the university center. The campus stadium seats 5500; the indoor gym, 3500. There is also a 391-seat auditorium.

Disabled Students: All of the campus is accessible. Wheelchair ramps, elevators, special parking, specially equipped rest rooms, special class scheduling, lowered drinking fountains, lowered telephones, note-taking services, and talking books are available.

Services: Counseling and information services are available, as is tutoring in most subjects. There is a reader service for the blind and remedial math, reading, and writing.

Campus Safety and Security: Measures include 24-hour foot and vehicle patrol, informal discussions, emergency telephones, and lighted pathways/sidewalks, and an evening van service.

Programs of Study: UWSP confers B.A., B.S., B.F.A, and B.M. degrees. Associate and master's degrees are also awarded. Bachelor's degrees are awarded in AGRICULTURE (forestry and related sciences, natural resource management, and soil science), BIOLOGICAL SCIENCE (biology/biological science and wildlife biology), BUSINESS (accounting, business administration and management, and management science), COMMUNICATIONS AND THE ARTS (arts administration/management, communications, dance, dramatic arts, English, fine arts, French, German, music, and Spanish), COMPUTER AND PHYSICAL SCIENCE (chemistry, information sciences and systems, mathematics, natural sciences, physics, and web services), EDUCATION (athletic training, early childhood, education of the exceptional child, elementary, health, home economics, music, and physical), ENGINEERING AND ENVIRONMENTAL DESIGN (interior design and paper and pulp science), HEALTH PROFESSIONS (clinical science, nursing, and speech pathology/audiology), SOCIAL SCIENCE (dietetics, economics, family/consumer studies, geography, history, international studies, liberal arts/general studies, philosophy, physical fitness/movement, political science/government, psychology, public administration, social science, sociology, and water resources). Business administration, elementary education, and biology are the largest.

Required: To graduate, students must complete 120 credit hours, with a minimum GPA of 2.0. Core curriculum requirements must also be fulfilled, along with courses in writing, natural science, non-western culture, minorities studies, social science, humanities, and wellness, and 3 credits in phys ed. Some majors require additional credits and higher minimum GPAs.

Special: A co-op program in nursing is offered with UW/Eau Claire and St. Joseph's Hospital. Internships, study abroad in 9 countries, work-study programs, dual and student-designed majors, independent study, and pass/fail options are also available. Credit is given for military, life, and work experience. There are 9 national honor societies.

Faculty/Classroom: 62% of faculty are male; 38%, female. All both teach and do research. No introductory courses are taught by graduate students. The average class size in an introductory lecture is 47; in a laboratory, 21; and in a regular course, 26.

Admissions: 74% of the 2003-2004 applicants were accepted. The SAT I scores for the 2003-2004 freshman class were: Math--16% below 500, 24% between 500 and 599, and 60% between 600 and 700. The ACT scores for the 2003-2004 freshman class were: 23% below 21, 39% between 21 and 23, 24% between 24 and 26, 9% between 27 and 28, and 5% above 28. 35% of the current freshmen were in the top fifth of their class; 83% were in the top two fifths. 30 freshmen graduated first in their class.

Requirements: The SAT I or ACT is required; the ACT is preferred. In addition, applicants should have a high school rank of top 40% or above, or a cumulative high school GPA of 3.25 or higher, with an ACT composite score of 21 (SAT I of 990) or above. The GED is accepted. Required academic preparation includes 4 units of English, 3 of social

studies, and 2 each of math and lab science, along with 5 electives; 2 units of foreign language are recommended. An interview is suggested. A GPA of 3.25 is required. AP and CLEP credits are accepted.

Procedure: Freshmen are admitted fall and spring. Entrance exams should be taken by February of the senior year. There is a rolling admissions plan. Application deadlines are open. The fall 2003 application fee was $35. Applications are accepted on-line through the university's web site.

Transfer: 691 transfer students enrolled in 2003-2004. Applicants must submit high school and college transcripts. A college minimum GPA of 2.75 is required. 30 of 120 credits required for the bachelor's degree must be completed at UWSP.

Visiting: There are regularly scheduled orientations for prospective students, consisting of a 2-day program that includes a meeting with an academic adviser as well as with upperclass students and other new students. There are guides for informal visits. To schedule a visit, contact the Office of Admissions at *admiss@uwsp.edu*.

Financial Aid: In 2002-2003, 41% of all full-time freshmen and 44% of continuing full-time students received some form of financial aid. 38% of full-time freshmen and 40% of continuing full-time students received need-based aid. The average freshman award was $4894. 26% of undergraduates work part time. The average financial indebtedness of the 2003 graduate was $13,504. The FAFSA is required. The deadline for filing freshman financial aid applications for fall entry is June 15.

International Students: There are 139 international students enrolled. The school actively recruits these students. They must score 525 on the written TOEFL or 193 on the electronic version.

Computers: There are more than 800 networked IBM PCs on campus. The Internet and World Wide Web are fully accessible. Networked computers with a wide variety of software packages are available in residence halls, public and private labs, and kiosks. All students may access the system. There are no time limits and no fees. It is recommended that students in Interior Architecture have personal computers.

Graduates: From July 1, 2002 to June 30, 2003, 1499 bachelor's degrees were awarded. The most popular majors were communication (10%), business administration (9%), and education (9%). In an average class, 20% graduate in 4 years or less, 50% graduate in 5 years or less, and 56% graduate in 6 years or less. 120 companies recruited on campus in 2002-2003. Of the 2002 graduating class, 16% were enrolled in graduate school within 6 months of graduation and 98% were employed.

Admissions Contact: Catherine Glennon, Director of Admissions. E-mail: *admiss@uwsp.edu* Web: *http://www.uwsp.edu/admissions*

UNIVERSITY OF WISCONSIN/STOUT
B-3
Menomonie, WI 54751
(715) 232-1411
(800) HI-STOUT; Fax: (715) 232-1667

Full-time: 3241 men, 3151 women	**Faculty:** 294; IIA, av$
Part-time: 406 men, 303 women	**Ph.D.s:** 76%
Graduate: 203 men, 404 women	**Student/Faculty:** 22 to 1
Year: 4-1-4, summer session	**Tuition:** $5680 ($16,016)
Application Deadline: open	**Room & Board:** $4038
Freshman Class: 3876 applied, 2576 accepted, 1275 enrolled	
ACT: 22	**COMPETITIVE**

The University of Wisconsin/Stout, founded in 1891, offers undergraduate programs in liberal studies, human environmental sciences, industry and technology, education, and human services. There are 4 undergraduate schools and 1 graduate school. In addition to regional accreditation, UW-Stout has baccalaureate program accreditation with AAMFT, ABET, ACCE, ADA, FIDER, IACBE, and NASAD. The library contains 225,672 volumes, 1,213,627 microform items, and 14,254 audio/video tapes/CDs, and subscribes to 1012 periodicals. Computerized library services include the card catalog, interlibrary loans, database searching, and Internet access. Special learning facilities include a learning resource center, art gallery, radio station, and TV station. The 110-acre campus is in a rural area 60 miles east of Minneapolis/St. Paul. Including any residence halls, there are 33 buildings.

Student Life: 71% of undergraduates are from Wisconsin. Students are from 26 states, 28 foreign countries, and Canada. 94% are white. The average age of freshmen is 19; all undergraduates, 22. 28% do not continue beyond their first year; 55% remain to graduate.

Housing: 2936 students can be accommodated in college housing, which includes coed dorms, smoke-free, alcohol-free, upperclassmen only, and freshman student housing. On-campus housing is guaranteed for all 4 years. 62% of students commute. All students may keep cars.

Activities: 2% of men belong to 3 local and 2 national fraternities; 4% of women belong to 3 national sororities. There are 117 groups on campus, including art, band, cheerleading, choir, chorale, chorus, computers, debate, drama, ethnic, film, forensics, gay, honors, international, jazz band, literary magazine, marching band, newspaper, pep band, photography, political, professional, radio, religious, social, social service, and student government. Popular campus events include Family Weekend, Cheese Week, and Biggest House Party.

Sports: There are 6 intercollegiate sports for men and 8 for women, and 20 intramural sports for men and 19 for women. Facilities include baseball, soccer, and football fields, indoor and outdoor tracks, and a field house with basketball, racquetball, and volleyball courts, a pool, weight and gymnastics rooms, and indoor and outdoor tennis courts.

Disabled Students: All of the campus is accessible. Wheelchair ramps, elevators, special parking, specially equipped rest rooms, special class scheduling, lowered drinking fountains, lowered telephones, and special housing are available.

Services: Counseling and information services are available, as is tutoring in most subjects. There is a reader service for the blind and remedial math, reading, and writing.

Campus Safety and Security: Measures include 24-hour foot and vehicle patrol, informal discussions, pamphlets/posters/films, lighted pathways/sidewalks, and training sessions.

Programs of Study: UW-Stout confers B.A., B.S., and B.F.A. degrees. Master's degrees are also awarded. Bachelor's degrees are awarded in BUSINESS (business administration and management, hospitality management services, management science, marketing/retailing/merchandising, and retailing), COMMUNICATIONS AND THE ARTS (apparel design, art, communications, fine arts, and telecommunications), COMPUTER AND PHYSICAL SCIENCE (applied mathematics, applied science, and science), EDUCATION (art, early childhood, home economics, marketing and distribution, technical, and vocational), ENGINEERING AND ENVIRONMENTAL DESIGN (construction technology, engineering technology, graphic and printing production, graphic arts technology, industrial administration/management, industrial engineering technology, and manufacturing engineering), HEALTH PROFESSIONS (rehabilitation therapy), SOCIAL SCIENCE (child care/child and family studies, dietetics, family/consumer studies, food production/management/services, and psychology). General business administration, art, and hotel restaurant and tourism management are the largest.

Required: Students must complete a minimum of 124 credits, including a general education component. Some degree programs have specific general education courses that must be taken in order to satisfy certification, accreditation, or prerequisite standards. Students must also fulfill an ethnic studies requirement.

Special: UW-Stout offers business and industry internships, cooperative programs, work-study programs, and study abroad in London. Dual majors, credit by examination, credit for life, military, and work experience, nondegree study, and pass/fail options are also available. There is 1 national honor society, a freshman honors program, and 3 departmental honors programs.

Faculty/Classroom: 59% of faculty are male; 41%, female. All both teach and do research. The average class size in an introductory lecture is 31 and in a laboratory, 21.

Admissions: 66% of the 2003-2004 applicants were accepted. The SAT I scores for the 2003-2004 freshman class were: Verbal--33% below 500, 52% between 500 and 599, and 14% between 600 and 700; Math--29% below 500, 53% between 500 and 599, and 19% between 600 and 700. The ACT scores were 38% below 21, 37% between 21 and 23, 19% between 24 and 26, 4% between 27 and 28, and 2% above 28. 24% of the current freshmen were in the top fifth of their class; 65% were in the top two fifths. 10 freshmen graduated first in their class.

Requirements: The SAT I or ACT is required; the ACT is preferred, with a minimum composite score of 1030 on the SAT I. Minimum test scores are waived if students rank in the upper 50% of their class. Applicants should graduate from an accredited secondary school. The GED is accepted if applicants are over 21, or if their graduating class has been out for at least 2 years. Secondary school preparation should include 4 academic credits in English, 3 each in social studies, math, and science, and 4 in electives. UW-Stout requires applicants to be in the upper 50% of their class. AP and CLEP credits are accepted.

Procedure: Freshmen are admitted fall, spring, and summer. Entrance exams should be taken in June of the junior year. There is a rolling admissions plan. Application deadlines are open. Application fee is $35. 239 applicants were on the 2003 waiting list; 64 were admitted. Applications are accepted on-line through *apply.wisconsin.edu.*

Transfer: 634 transfer students enrolled in 2002-2003. A minimum college GPA of 2.0 is required for student transfers from UW system institutions. A 2.2 GPA is required for those transferring from outside the UW system. 32 of 124 credits required for the bachelor's degree must be completed at UW-Stout.

Visiting: There are regularly scheduled orientations for prospective students, including an interview with an admissions counselor and a campus tour. There are also campus preview days throughout the academic year. There are guides for informal visits and visitors may sit in on classes and stay overnight. To schedule a visit, contact Dawn Steinmeyer at (800) 447-8688 or (715) 232-1232 or *steinmeyerd@uwstout.edu.*

Financial Aid: In 2003-2004, 76% of all full-time freshmen and 72% of continuing full-time students received some form of financial aid. 48% of full-time freshmen and 50% of continuing full-time students received need-based aid. The average freshman award was $7959. Need-based scholarships or need-based grants averaged $4086 ($5528 maximum);

need-based self-help aid (loans and jobs) averaged $4000 ($4415 maximum); and non-need-based awards and non-need-based scholarships averaged $2897 ($8865 maximum). 69% of undergraduates work part time. Average annual earnings from campus work are $1351. The average financial indebtedness of the 2003 graduate was $16,746. UW-Stout is a member of CSS. The FAFSA is required. The priority date for freshman financial aid applications for fall entry is April 1.

International Students: There are 39 international students enrolled. The school actively recruits these students. They must score 500 on the written TOEFL.

Computers: The mainframe is an HP/9000/N4000. There are more than 200 networked computers in the campus computing lab, available to all students. There are networked computer kiosks in all major classrooms, recreation center, food service, and administrative buildings. All residence halls have a computer lab. Ports and wireless access are available throughout campus. All students may access the system 24 hours a day, 7 days a week. There are no time limits and no fees. All students are required to have personal computers. Compaq is recommended.

Graduates: From July 1, 2002 to June 30, 2003, 1116 bachelor's degrees were awarded. The most popular majors were general business administration (18%), art (12%), and early childhood education (8%). In an average class, 15% graduate in 4 years or less, 42% graduate in 5 years or less, and 48% graduate in 6 years or less. 306 companies recruited on campus in 2002-2003.

Admissions Contact: Cindy Jenkins, Director of Admissions. A video is available. E-mail: *admissions@uwstout.edu* Web: *www.uwstout.edu*

UNIVERSITY OF WISCONSIN/SUPERIOR   A-1

Superior, WI 54880   (715) 394-8230; Fax: (715) 394-8407

Full-time: 810 men, 1200 women	**Faculty:** 115; IIA, -$
Part-time: 135 men, 300 women	**Ph.Ds:** 75%
Graduate: 140 men, 270 women	**Student/Faculty:** 17 to 1
Year: semesters, summer session	**Tuition:** $3500 ($9200)
Application Deadline: see profile	**Room & Board:** $4000
Freshman Class: n/av	**ACT:** required **COMPETITIVE+**

The University of Wisconsin/Superior, founded in 1893, offers undergraduate programs in the liberal arts and sciences, business, education, fine arts, applied arts, and social sciences. There are 5 undergraduate schools and 1 graduate school. Figures in the above capsule and in this profile are approximate. The library contains 460,000 volumes, 110,000 microform items, and 5500 audio/video tapes/CDs, and subscribes to 750 periodicals. Computerized library services include the card catalog, interlibrary loans, and database searching. Special learning facilities include a learning resource center, art gallery, planetarium, TV station, aquatic lab, color television studio, and an FM radio station. The 230-acre campus is in an urban area 150 miles north of Minneapolis/St. Paul. Including any residence halls, there are 17 buildings.

Student Life: 58% of undergraduates are from Wisconsin. 90% are from public schools. 95% are white. The average age of freshmen is 17; all undergraduates, 21. 15% do not continue beyond their first year; 40% remain to graduate.

Housing: 650 students can be accommodated in college housing, which includes single-sex and coed dorms. On-campus housing is guaranteed for all 4 years. 76% of students commute. All students may keep cars.

Activities: There are no fraternities or sororities. There are 48 groups on campus, including art, band, cheerleading, choir, chorale, chorus, computers, dance, drama, ethnic, gay, honors, international, jazz band, newspaper, orchestra, photography, political, professional, radio and TV, religious, social, social service, student government, and symphony. Popular campus events include Snow Week, sports events, and Fall Fest.

Sports: There are 5 intercollegiate sports for men and 7 for women, and 5 intramural sports for men and 5 for women. Facilities include a 4000-seat stadium, a 3000-seat gym, an ice arena, a swimming pool, a weight training room, a dance studio, an all-weather track, and softball and baseball fields.

Disabled Students: 95% of the campus is accessible. Wheelchair ramps, elevators, special parking, specially equipped rest rooms, special class scheduling, lowered drinking fountains, and lowered telephones are available.

Services: Counseling and information services are available, as is tutoring in every subject. There is remedial math and writing.

Campus Safety and Security: Measures include 24-hour foot and vehicle patrol, self-defense education, security escort services, and informal discussions. There are pamphlets/posters/films, emergency telephones, and lighted pathways/sidewalks.

Programs of Study: UW/Superior confers B.A., B.S., B.F.A., B.M., and B.M.E. degrees. Associate and master's degrees are also awarded. Bachelor's degrees are awarded in BIOLOGICAL SCIENCE (biology/biological science), BUSINESS (accounting and business administration and management), COMMUNICATIONS AND THE ARTS (art history and appreciation, communications, dramatic arts, English, fine arts, music, music performance, speech/debate/rhetoric, and studio art), COM-

PUTER AND PHYSICAL SCIENCE (chemistry, computer science, information sciences and systems, and mathematics), EDUCATION (art, elementary, mathematics, music, physical, science, and secondary), HEALTH PROFESSIONS (art therapy and community health work), SOCIAL SCIENCE (criminal justice, history, international studies, law, political science/government, psychology, public administration, social studies, social work, and sociology). Business, education, and aquatic biology are the strongest academically. Business is the largest.

Required: To graduate, students must complete 120 credit hours, with a GPA of 2.0. A minimum of 54 hours must be credited toward completion of 1 comprehensive major, 2 majors or 1 major and 1 minor. The required core curriculum includes 55 credits in communications, English, math, phys ed, world culture, contemporary society, aesthetic experience, natural science, and human behavior. A comprehensive exam and a senior project are required.

Special: UW/Superior offers co-op programs in business and internships in social work, business, mass communication, and criminal justice. There is a comprehensive program of student-designed majors, along with a cooperative program in marine studies with Texas A&M University, and 3-2 engineering and forestry programs with Michigan Technological University. Students may cross-register for 2 classes per semester at the University of Minnesota/Duluth, the College of St. Scholastica, or Northland College. An extended degree is offered. Credit for life experience and pass/fail options are available. There is a chapter of Phi Beta Kappa and a freshman honors program.

Faculty/Classroom: 60% of faculty are male; 40%, female. All both teach and do research. No introductory courses are taught by graduate students. The average class size in an introductory lecture is 40; in a laboratory, 20; and in a regular course, 23.

Requirements: The ACT is required. Out-of-state residents may submit SAT I scores instead. Applicants must graduate from an accredited secondary school or the equivalent. They must rank in the upper 50% of their graduating class or achieve a minimum composite score of 20 on the ACT. AP and CLEP credits are accepted. Important factors in the admissions decision are parents or siblings attending the school and recommendations by school officials.

Procedure: Freshmen are admitted fall, spring, and summer. Entrance exams should be taken before admission in spring of the junior year. There are early admissions and deferred admissions plans. Check with the school for application deadlines and fee. Notification is sent on a rolling basis.

Transfer: 342 transfer students enrolled in a recent year. A college GPA of 2.0 is required. 30 of 120 credits required for the bachelor's degree must be completed at UW/Superior.

Visiting: There are regularly scheduled orientations for prospective students, consisting of a day and a half of social and educational programs. There are guides for informal visits and visitors may sit in on classes and stay overnight. To schedule a visit, contact the Admissions Office.

Financial Aid: In a recent year, the average freshman award was $6482. 21% of undergraduates work part time. Average annual earnings from campus work are $1200. The average financial indebtedness of a recent graduate was $13,749. UW/Superior is a member of CSS. The FAFSA is required. Check with the school for current deadlines.

International Students: The school actively recruits these students. They must score 525 on the written TOEFL or take the MELAB and the college's own test.

Computers: The mainframe is an HP 9000. There are PCs available in the main hall, the library, and in the dorms. All students may access the system 24 hours a day. There are no time limits and no fees.

Graduates: In a recent year, 328 bachelor's degrees were awarded. The most popular majors were business/marketing (20%), education (18%), and social sciences (13%).

Admissions Contact: Admissions Counselor.
E-mail: *admissions@uwsuper.edu* Web: *www.uwsuper.edu*

UNIVERSITY OF WISCONSIN/WHITEWATER   D-5

Whitewater, WI 53190	(262) 472-1440; Fax: (262) 472-1515
Full-time: 4000 men, 4400 women	**Faculty:** 384; IIA, av$
Part-time: 400 men, 550 women	**Ph.D.s:** 73%
Graduate: 450 men, 740 women	**Student/Faculty:** 22 to 1
Year: semesters, summer session	**Tuition:** $4279 ($14,325)
Application Deadline: open	**Room & Board:** $4347
Freshman Class: n/av	
ACT: 22	**COMPETITIVE**

The University of Wisconsin/Whitewater, founded in 1868, offers programs in teacher education, business, liberal arts, preprofessional studies, fine arts, and music. Some information in this capsule and profile is approximate. There are 4 undergraduate schools and 1 graduate school. In addition to regional accreditation, UW/Whitewater has baccalaureate program accreditation with AACSB, ASLA, CSWE, NASM, and NCATE. The library contains 356,000 volumes, 993,000 microform items, and 7300 audio/video tapes/CDs, and subscribes to 5000 periodicals. Computerized library services include the card catalog, interlibrary

loans, and database searching. Special learning facilities include a learning resource center, art gallery, radio station, TV station, observatory, and weather station. The 385-acre campus is in a small town 50 miles southwest of Milwaukee. Including any residence halls, there are 45 buildings.

Student Life: 94% of undergraduates are from Wisconsin. Students are from 26 states, 38 foreign countries, and Canada. 85% are from public schools. 93% are white. The average age of freshmen is 19; all undergraduates, 22. 22% do not continue beyond their first year; 61% remain to graduate.

Housing: 4000 students can be accommodated in college housing, which includes single-sex and coed dorms. 50% of students live on campus; of those, 35% remain on campus on weekends. All students may keep cars.

Activities: 5% of men belong to 1 local and 6 national fraternities; 5% of women belong to 1 local and 4 national sororities. There are 130 groups on campus, including art, band, cheerleading, choir, chorus, computers, dance, drama, drill team, ethnic, film, gay, honors, international, marching band, musical theater, newspaper, orchestra, pep band, photography, political, professional, radio and TV, religious, social, social service, student government, symphony, and yearbook. Popular campus events include Job Fair, Performing Arts Series, and athletic contests.

Sports: There are 9 intercollegiate sports for men and 8 for women, and 12 intramural sports for men and 12 for women. Facilities include tennis courts, pools, playing fields, a 13,000-seat stadium, and a 3500-seat gym.

Disabled Students: 75% of the campus is accessible. Wheelchair ramps, elevators, special parking, specially equipped rest rooms, special class scheduling, lowered drinking fountains, lowered telephones, and vans for mobility are available.

Services: Counseling and information services are available, as is tutoring in most subjects and in study skills. There is a reader service for the blind and remedial math, reading, and writing.

Campus Safety and Security: Measures include 24-hour foot and vehicle patrol, self-defense education, security escort services, and shuttle buses. There are informal discussions, pamphlets/posters/films, emergency telephones, and lighted pathways/sidewalks.

Programs of Study: UW/Whitewater confers B.A., B.S., B.B.A., B.F.A., B.M., and B.S.Ed. degrees. Associate and master's degrees are also awarded. Bachelor's degrees are awarded in BIOLOGICAL SCIENCE (biology/biological science), BUSINESS (accounting, banking and finance, business administration and management, business economics, marketing/retailing/merchandising, office supervision and management, and personnel management), COMMUNICATIONS AND THE ARTS (art history and appreciation, communications, dramatic arts, English, French, German, journalism, music, public relations, Spanish, and speech/debate/rhetoric), COMPUTER AND PHYSICAL SCIENCE (chemistry, computer programming, mathematics, and physics), EDUCATION (art, business, early childhood, elementary, foreign languages, middle school, music, physical, science, secondary, social studies, and special), SOCIAL SCIENCE (economics, geography, history, international studies, political science/government, prelaw, psychology, public administration, safety and security technology, social work, sociology, and women's studies). Accounting, computer science, and education are the strongest academically. Business/accounting and education are the largest.

Required: Students must complete 50 credits of general studies, a writing competency requirement, and 3 credits in minority issues. A GPA of 2.0 and 120 hours are required to graduate.

Special: Internships, study abroad in 9 nations, accelerated degree programs in safety studies and speech communication, student-designed majors, and a general studies degree are available. Credit by exam, nondegree study, and pass/fail options are also offered. There are 14 national honor societies, a freshman honors program, and 7 departmental honors programs.

Faculty/Classroom: 57% of faculty are male; 43%, female. All teach undergraduates and 78% do research. No introductory courses are taught by graduate students. The average class size in a regular course is 26.

Admissions: The ACT scores for the 2003-2004 freshman class were: 35% below 21, 33% between 21 and 23, 22% between 24 and 26, 7% between 27 and 28, and 3% above 28. 24% of the current freshmen were in the top fifth of their class; 63% were in the top two fifths.

Requirements: The SAT I or ACT is recommended. In addition, applicants should graduate from an accredited secondary school or with 17 academic units, including 4 in English and 3 each in social studies, math, and science. The GED may be accepted. Applicants should rank in the upper 40% of their graduating class or achieve a combined high school and ACT/SAT I percentile rank of 100% or above. A GPA of 2.8 is required. AP and CLEP credits are accepted. Important factors in the admissions decision are evidence of special talent, advanced placement or honor courses, and recommendations by school officials.

Procedure: Freshmen are admitted to all sessions. There is an early admissions plan and a rolling admissions plan. Application deadlines are open. Check with the school for current application fee. Notification is sent on a rolling basis. A waiting list is an active part of the admissions procedure. Applications are accepted on-line at *apply.wisconsin.edu*.

Transfer: Applicants should have a minimum college GPA of 2.0. 30 credits of 120 required for the bachelor's degree must be completed at UW/Whitewater.

Visiting: There are regularly scheduled orientations for prospective students. There are guides for informal visits and visitors may sit in on classes. To schedule a visit, contact the Admissions Office.

Financial Aid: In 2003-2004, 67% of all full-time students received some form of financial aid. 42% of full-time freshmen and 43% of continuing full-time students received need-based aid. The average freshman award was $5692. UW/Whitewater is a member of CSS. The FAFSA is required. Check with the school for current deadlines.

International Students: The school actively recruits these students. They must score 500 on the written TOEFL or take the MELAB.

Computers: The mainframes are an Alpha 2100 and an IBM 9121-260. There are also 1500 PCs available. All students may access the system 24 hours if they have their own terminal or 8 A.M. to 11 P.M. Monday through Thursday and varied weekend hours in the general lab. There are no time limits and no fees.

Graduates: In an average class, 50% graduate in 6 years or less.

Admissions Contact: Dr. Tori A. McGuire, Executive Director of Admissions. A video is available. E-mail: *uwwadmit@mail.uww.edu* Web: *www.uww.edu*

VITERBO UNIVERSITY
(Formerly Viterbo College)

B-4

LaCrosse, WI 54601

(608) 796-3010
(800) 848-3726; Fax: (608) 796-3020

Full-time: 390 men, 1113 women	**Faculty:** 103; IIA, --$
Part-time: 70 men, 289 women	**Ph.D.s:** 63%
Graduate: 151 men, 536 women	**Student/Faculty:** 15 to 1
Year: semesters, summer session	**Tuition:** $15,320
Application Deadline: open	**Room & Board:** $5110

Freshman Class: 1296 applied, 1142 accepted, 355 enrolled
ACT: 22 **COMPETITIVE**

Viterbo University (formerly Viterbo College), is a private, Catholic, Franciscan liberal arts university. Viterbo offers undergraduate programs in liberal arts, sciences, fine arts, business, education, and health sciences. Master's degrees are offered in education, business, servant leadership, and nursing. Viterbo University embraces persons of all faiths and prepares students for leadership and service. There are 6 undergraduate and 4 graduate schools. In addition to regional accreditation, Viterbo has baccalaureate program accreditation with ACS, CCNE, CSWE, NASM, NCATE, and NLN. The library contains 108,672 volumes, 233,392 microform items, and 6002 audio/video tapes/CDs, and subscribes to 9838 periodicals. Computerized library services include the card catalog, interlibrary loans, database searching, and Internet access. Special learning facilities include a learning resource center, art gallery, and music resource center. The 26-acre campus is in a suburban area 145 miles west of Madison and 270 miles northwest of Chicago. Including any residence halls, there are 13 buildings.

Student Life: 80% of undergraduates are from Wisconsin. Students are from 21 states and 12 foreign countries. 88% are from public schools. 89% are white. 40% are Catholic; 39% Protestant; 10% claim no religious affiliation; 10% not identified. The average age of freshmen is 18; all undergraduates, 25. 34% do not continue beyond their first year; 53% remain to graduate.

Housing: 572 students can be accommodated in college housing, which includes single-sex and coed dorms and on-campus apartments. In addition, there are special-interest houses, on-campus houses, and special-interest floors. On-campus housing is guaranteed for the freshman year only and is available on a first-come, first-served basis. 63% of students commute. Alcohol is not permitted. Upperclassmen may keep cars.

Activities: There are no fraternities or sororities. There are 22 groups on campus, including art, choir, chorale, chorus, dance, drama, drill team, ethnic, international, literary magazine, musical theater, opera, pep band, professional, religious, social, social service, student government, and yearbook. Popular campus events include Orientation Weekend, St. Francis Day Celebration, and Hog Wild.

Sports: There are 3 intercollegiate sports for men and 4 for women, and 14 intramural sports for men and 14 for women. Facilities include a student activity center with weight training and fitness rooms and courts for basketball, volleyball, and racquetball. A 12.5-acre outdoor athletic complex has facilities for soccer, baseball, and softball, located 2 1/2 miles from campus. There also are on-campus sand volleyball and

paved basketball outdoor courts. The nearby Mississippi River and Mt. LaCrosse provide opportunities for canoeing and skiing.

Disabled Students: 90% of the campus is accessible. Wheelchair ramps, elevators, special parking, specially equipped rest rooms, special class scheduling, lowered drinking fountains, and lowered telephones are available.

Services: Counseling and information services are available, as is tutoring in every subject. There is a reader service for the blind and remedial math, reading, and writing.

Campus Safety and Security: Measures include self-defense education, security escort services, informal discussions, and pamphlets/posters/films. There are emergency telephones, lighted pathways/sidewalks, an emergency evacuation plan, 24 hour phone access to security personnel, security patrol from 5 P.M. to 7 A.M., ID check-in in dorms after 10 P.M., and card access to all campus buildings after regular hours, and 6 emergency blue lights.

Programs of Study: Viterbo confers B.A., B.S., B.Art.Ed., B.B.A., B.F.A., B.I.L., B.L.S., B.M.T., B.S. Community-Medical Dietetics, B.S.Ed., B.S.N., and B.T.A. degrees. Master's degrees are also awarded. Bachelor's degrees are awarded in BIOLOGICAL SCIENCE (biology/biological science and nutrition), BUSINESS (accounting, business administration and management, institutional management, management information systems, management science, marketing/retailing/merchandising, and organizational behavior), COMMUNICATIONS AND THE ARTS (applied music, arts administration/management, dramatic arts, English, fine arts, graphic design, music, music performance, musical theater, Spanish, studio art, and theater management), COMPUTER AND PHYSICAL SCIENCE (chemistry, digital arts/technology, information sciences and systems, and mathematics), EDUCATION (art, business, computer, drama, elementary, music, and science), HEALTH PROFESSIONS (health care administration and nursing), SOCIAL SCIENCE (criminal justice, dietetics, liberal arts/general studies, ministries, psychology, religion, social studies, social work, and sociology). Nutrition/dietetics, natural sciences, and English are the strongest academically. Nursing, business, and education are the largest.

Required: Students must complete a minimum of 128 semester hours of credit. A minimum of 43 of these must be upper division level. All students must complete the general education requirements (45 credit hours from various disciplines) and competencies, as well as all of the specified requirements for their major. Also, students must complete a service component designed by their major program. All students must have a GPA of at least 2.0, and must take as a minimum the last 30 consecutive semester hours at Viterbo University or complete 45 of the last 60 semester hours from Viterbo. Students seeking a B.S. must complete 7 credits of natural science and/or math in addition to the 4 credits of natural science in the general education requirements. Students seeking a B.A. must complete the equivalent of 14 semester hours of the same modern foreign language.

Special: Students may cross-register at the University of Wisconsin/LaCrosse, enroll for independent study, or earn a dual degree. Co-op programs, study abroad in 7 countries, double majors, student-designed majors, accelerated degree programs, work-study, internships in many areas, credit by exam, and credit/no credit options are available. There are 2 national honor societies.

Faculty/Classroom: 42% of faculty are male; 58%, female. 99% teach undergraduates, 8% do research, and 8% do both. No introductory courses are taught by graduate students. The average class size in an introductory lecture is 21; in a laboratory, 14; and in a regular course, 15.

Admissions: 88% of the 2003-2004 applicants were accepted. The ACT scores for the 2003-2004 freshman class were: 38% below 21, 32% between 21 and 23, 18% between 24 and 26, 7% between 27 and 28, and 6% above 28. 30% of the current freshmen were in the top fifth of their class; 57% were in the top two fifths. 8 freshmen graduated first in their class.

Requirements: The ACT is required. In addition, graduation from an accredited secondary school is required; the GED is accepted. Secondary preparation should include 16 credits, with 3 or 4 in English and 2 each in math, natural science, and social science or history. Fine arts students may be required to audition or submit a portfolio. Nursing, dietetics, and pre-medical students must have high school chemistry. A GPA of 2.0 is required. AP and CLEP credits are accepted.

Procedure: Freshmen are admitted to all sessions. Entrance exams should be taken at placement listing at registration. There is a rolling admissions plan. Application deadlines are open. Application fee is $25. Applications are accepted on-line through Wisconsin Mentor and the school's web site. Notification is sent within 2 weeks of receipt of completed application.

Transfer: 251 transfer students enrolled in 2002-2003. Transfer students must have a cumulative GPA of at least 2.0, be free to return to their previous school, and be considered to be in good academic standing both at their previous school and at Viterbo. They must submit an application, the $25 fee, official transcripts of coursework in high school, official transcripts from all post-secondary institutions, and ACT/SAT I results, if already taken. 30 of 128 credits required for the bachelor's degree must be completed at Viterbo.

Visiting: There are regularly scheduled orientations for prospective students, including a meeting with an admissions staff member, a tour of the campus, and optional meetings with a financial aid officer and faculty members. There are guides for informal visits and visitors may sit in on classes. To schedule a visit, contact Tammy Edens at *tjedens@viterbo.edu.*

Financial Aid: In 2003-2004, 99% of all full-time freshmen and 97% of continuing full-time students received some form of financial aid. 84% of full-time freshmen and 80% of continuing full-time students received need-based aid. The average freshman award was $13,683. Need-based scholarships or need-based grants averaged $8317 ($14,900 maximum); need-based self-help aid (loans and jobs) averaged $3423 ($1000 maximum); non-need-based athletic scholarships averaged $501 ($3000 maximum); and other non-need-based awards and non-need-based scholarships averaged $1875 ($14,900 maximum). 43% of undergraduates work part time. Average annual earnings from campus work are $911. The average financial indebtedness of the 2003 graduate was $15,678. The FAFSA and the college's own financial statement are required. The priority date for freshman financial aid applications for fall entry is March 15.

International Students: There are 17 international students enrolled. The school actively recruits them. They must score 500 on the written TOEFL or 213 on the electronic and also take the college's test.

Computers: The mainframe is a Vax. There are more than 250 PCs and Macs available in 10 computer labs and the library. There are 20 wireless stations in another lab. There are also 10 outdoor computer ports. All dorm rooms are wired. 34 Internet wired podiums are available for faculty use in classrooms. All of these systems are networked and have full access to the Internet. There are 2 distance learning labs. There are facilities for videoconferencing. All students may access the system 6 A.M. to 1 A.M. daily. There are no time limits and no fees. It is strongly recommended that all students have a personal computer.

Graduates: From July 1, 2002 to June 30, 2003, 352 bachelor's degrees were awarded. The most popular majors were nursing (25%), business/organizational management (9%), and education (9%). In an average class, 32% graduate in 4 years or less, 51% graduate in 5 years or less, and 53% graduate in 6 years or less. 80 companies recruited on campus in 2002-2003. Of the 2002 graduating class, 10% were enrolled in graduate school within 6 months of graduation and 88% were employed.

Admissions Contact: Roland W. Nelson, Vice President of Admissions. A video is available. E-mail: *admission@viterbo.edu*
Web: *www.viterbo.edu*

WISCONSIN LUTHERAN COLLEGE
Milwaukee, WI 53226

E-4

(414) 443-8811
(888) 947-5884; Fax: (414) 443-8514

Full-time: 265 men, 407 women	**Faculty:** 47
Part-time: 19 men, 15 women	**Ph.D.s:** 65%
Graduate: none	**Student/Faculty:** 14 to 1
Year: semesters, summer session	**Tuition:** $15,850
Application Deadline: September 1	**Room & Board:** $5580
Freshman Class: 531 applied, 444 accepted, 207 enrolled	
ACT: 24	**VERY COMPETITIVE**

Wisconsin Lutheran College, founded in 1973 in affiliation with the Wisconsin Evangelical Lutheran Synod, offers higher education in the arts and sciences within a conservative Christian environment. The library contains 72,621 volumes, 9211 microform items, and 4634 audio/video tapes/CDs, and subscribes to 998 periodicals. Computerized library services include the card catalog, interlibrary loans, database searching, and Internet access. Special learning facilities include a learning resource center, art gallery, sound studio, electronic music lab, and language lab. The 21-acre campus is in a suburban area on the western edge of Milwaukee. Including any residence halls, there are 27 buildings.

Student Life: 80% of undergraduates are from Wisconsin. Students are from 27 states and 6 foreign countries. 41% are from public schools. 95% are white. Most are Protestant. The average age of freshmen is 18; all undergraduates, 20. 20% do not continue beyond their first year; 74% remain to graduate.

Housing: 600 students can be accommodated in college housing, which includes single-sex dorms and on-campus apartments. On-campus housing is guaranteed for all 4 years. 78% of students live on campus. Alcohol is not permitted. All students may keep cars.

Activities: There are no fraternities or sororities. There are 31 groups on campus, including admissions, art, band, cheerleading, choir, dance, drama, ethnic, international, jazz band, musical theater, newspaper, pep band, photography, political, professional, religious, social, social service, student government, and yearbook. Popular campus events include Musical and theater events, Winterfest, and Commencement weekend.

Sports: There are 7 intercollegiate sports for men and 8 for women, and 5 intramural sports for men and 5 for women. Facilities include 3 full basketball courts, 2500-seat gym, weight room, fitness center, dance/aerobics room, training and therapy rooms, and a walking/running track.

Disabled Students: 90% of the campus is accessible. Wheelchair ramps, elevators, special parking, specially equipped rest rooms, lowered drinking fountains, and lowered telephones are available.

Services: Counseling and information services are available, as is tutoring in some subjects, including math, writing, and foreign language.

Campus Safety and Security: Measures include 24-hour foot and vehicle patrol, self-defense education, security escort services, and shuttle buses. There are informal discussions, pamphlets/posters/films, lighted pathways/sidewalks, a security service, and electronic dorm entrances.

Programs of Study: Wisconsin Lutheran confers B.A. and B.S. degrees. Bachelor's degrees are awarded in BIOLOGICAL SCIENCE (biology/biological science), BUSINESS (business economics), COMMUNICATIONS AND THE ARTS (art, communications, dramatic arts, English, music, and Spanish), COMPUTER AND PHYSICAL SCIENCE (chemistry and mathematics), EDUCATION (elementary), SOCIAL SCIENCE (history, interdisciplinary studies, political science/government, psychology, social science, and theological studies). Chemistry, education, and biology are the strongest academically. Music, theology, and education are the largest.

Required: Composition, speech, math, and foreign language competencies are required. All students must complete a core curriculum that includes courses in theology, aesthetics, literature, natural science, history, social science, and intellectual diversity, plus 1 credit in phys ed/lifetime sport and 2 freshman seminars. A minimum overall GPA of 2.0 and 2.5 in the major (some require a higher GPA) plus 128 credit hours are required to graduate.

Special: Student-designed majors and study abroad are offered. Internships are available in most departments.

Faculty/Classroom: 70% of faculty are male; 30%, female. All both teach and do research. The average class size in an introductory lecture is 20; in a laboratory, 10; and in a regular course, 16.

Admissions: 84% of the 2003-2004 applicants were accepted. The ACT scores for the 2003-2004 freshman class were: 14% below 21, 26% between 21 and 23, 33% between 24 and 26, 12% between 27 and 28, and 14% above 28. 42% of the freshmen were in the top fifth of their class; 77% were in the top two fifths. 10 graduated first in their class.

Requirements: The ACT is required, with a minimum composite score of 21. If the SAT I is submitted, a minimum score of 970 is required. Students should be graduates of an accredited high school or its equivalent with a minimum of 16 high school units, including 4 in English, 3 each in academic electives and math, and 2 each in science, foreign language, and social studies/history. The Academic Recommendation Form must be submitted. A portfolio for art grants and an audition for music and drama grants are required. Wisconsin Lutheran requires applicants to be in the upper 50% of their class. A GPA of 2.7 is required. AP and CLEP credits are accepted. Important factors in the admissions decision are leadership record and personality/intangible qualities.

Procedure: Freshmen are admitted fall and spring. Entrance exams should be taken in the spring of the junior year. There is a rolling admissions plan. Applications should be filed by September 1 for fall entry and January 15 for spring entry, along with a $20 fee. Notification is sent on a rolling basis. Applications are accepted on-line through the school's web site or ApplyWeb. The on-line registration fee is $5.

Transfer: 16 transfer students enrolled in 2002-2003. Students should have a GPA of at least 2.5 for transfer credit. The Transfer Recommendation Form is required. 30 of 128 credits required for the bachelor's degree must be completed at Wisconsin Lutheran.

Visiting: There are regularly scheduled orientations for prospective students, including a tour of the campus. To schedule a visit, contact the Admissions Office at *admissions@wlc.edu.*

Financial Aid: In 2003-2004, all full-time freshmen received some form of financial aid. 77% of full-time freshmen and 76% of continuing full-time students received need-based aid. The average freshman award was $14,526. The average financial indebtedness of the 2003 graduate was $13,707. The FAFSA and the college's own financial statement are required. The priority date for freshman financial aid applications for fall entry is March 1. The deadline for filing freshman financial aid applications for fall entry is rolling.

International Students: There are 10 international students enrolled. They must score 550 on the written TOEFL or 213 on the electronic version, or take ACT/SAT I, scoring 970 (SAT I) or 21 (ACT).

Computers: The mainframe is 5 Compaq Proliant ML 530 servers. 60 Pentium PCs with laser printers and 17 Mac Power PCs are available in various campus labs and the library. 30 Notebook computers are available on a checkout basis. Students may access the central network and the Internet from any computer lab or residence hall/apartment. All students may access the system. There are no time limits and no fees.

Graduates: From July 1, 2002 to June 30, 2003, 121 bachelor's degrees were awarded. The most popular majors were communication (17%), psychology (11%), and biology (11%). In an average class, 47% graduate in 4 years or less, 62% graduate in 5 years or less, and 74% graduate in 6 years or less.

Admissions Contact: Craig Swiontek, Director of Admissions.
E-mail: *admissions@wlc.edu* Web: *www.wlc.edu/admissions/*

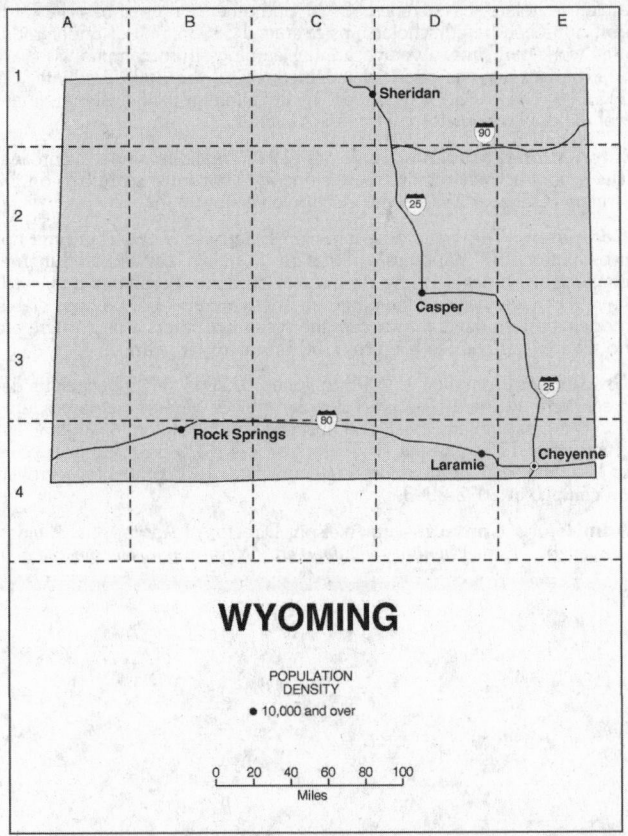

WYOMING

POPULATION
DENSITY

● 10,000 and over

0   20   40   60   80   100
Miles

UNIVERSITY OF WYOMING
D-4
Laramie, WY 82071

(307) 766-5160
(800) 342-5996; Fax: (307) 766-4042

Full-time: 3815 men, 3790 women
Faculty: 612; I, --$
Part-time: 571 men, 1209 women
Ph.D.s: 86%
Graduate: 1307 men, 2438 women
Student/Faculty: 12 to 1
Year: semesters, summer session
Tuition: $3090 ($8940)
Application Deadline: August 10
Room & Board: $5546
Freshman Class: 2948 applied, 2796 accepted, 1416 enrolled
SAT I Verbal/Math: 540/550
ACT: 23
COMPETITIVE

The University of Wyoming, founded in 1886, is a public institution offering programs in agriculture, arts and sciences, business, education, engineering, health science, and law. There are 6 undergraduate schools and 1 graduate school. In addition to regional accreditation, UW has baccalaureate program accreditation with AACSB, ABA, ABET, ACPE, ACS, ADA, APA, ASHLA, CACREP, CCNE, CSWE, IAME, NASM, NCATE, and NLN. The 9 libraries contain 1,320,982 volumes, 2,958,227 microform items, and 8189 audio/video tapes/CDs, and subscribe to 12,919 periodicals. Computerized library services include the card catalog, interlibrary loans, database searching, and Internet access. Special learning facilities include a learning resource center, art gallery, natural history museum, planetarium, radio station, TV station, and the American Heritage Center. The 785-acre campus is in a small town 128 miles north of Denver, Colorado, and 45 miles west of Cheyenne, Wyoming's capital. Including any residence halls, there are 206 buildings.
Student Life: 73% of undergraduates are from Wyoming. Students are from 50 states, 61 foreign countries, and Canada. 85% are white. The average age of freshmen is 18; all undergraduates, 23. 25% do not continue beyond their first year; 54% remain to graduate.
Housing: 2900 students can be accommodated in college housing, which includes single-sex and coed dorms, on-campus apartments, off-campus apartments, married-student housing, fraternity houses, and sorority houses. In addition, there are honors houses, and engineering, academic, single-gender, coed, upperclassmen, sophomore, quiet living, substance-free, and freshman interest-group floors. On-campus housing is guaranteed for all 4 years. 77% of students commute. All students may keep cars.
Activities: 8% of men belong to 8 national fraternities; 5% of women belong to 4 local and 4 national sororities. There are 180 groups on campus, including art, band, cheerleading, chess, choir, chorale, chorus, computers, dance, debate, drama, drill team, ethnic, film, forensics, gay, honors, international, jazz band, literary magazine, marching band, musical theater, newspaper, opera, orchestra, pep band, photography, political, professional, radio and TV, religious, social, social service, student government, symphony, and yearbook. Popular campus events include President's Welcome, Parents Weekend, and Weeks of Welcome.
Sports: There are 7 intercollegiate sports for men and 8 for women, and 28 intramural sports for men and 28 for women. Facilities include a 33,000-seat stadium, a 15,000-seat indoor gym and arena, basketball, volleyball, and racquetball courts, running tracks, 2 pools, weight rooms, an indoor tennis complex, a baseball and track stadium, and a football training center.
Disabled Students: 95% of the campus is accessible. Wheelchair ramps, elevators, special parking, specially equipped rest rooms, special class scheduling, lowered drinking fountains, lowered telephones, and braille signs are available.
Services: Counseling and information services are available, as is tutoring in most subjects. There is a reader service for the blind, note-taking services, tape recorders, and interpreters for the hearing impaired. Remedial tutoring and remedial math are available through a local community college.
Campus Safety and Security: Measures include 24-hour foot and vehicle patrol, self-defense education, security escort services, and shuttle buses. There are informal discussions, pamphlets/posters/films, emergency telephones, and lighted pathways/sidewalks.
Programs of Study: UW confers B.A., B.S., B.F.A., B.M., B.S.Arch.Eng., B.S.C.E., B.S.Ch.E., B.S.Comp.Eng., B.S.C.S., B.S.D.H., B.S.E.E., B.S.F.C., B.S.M.E., B.S.M.I., B.S.N., and B.S.W. degrees. Master's and doctoral degrees are also awarded. Bachelor's degrees are awarded in AGRICULTURE (agricultural business management, agricultural communications, agriculture, animal science, natural resource management, range/farm management, and wildlife management), BIOLOGICAL SCIENCE (biology/biological science, botany, microbiology, molecular biology, and zoology), BUSINESS (accounting, banking and finance, business administration and management, business economics, management information systems, and marketing/retailing/merchandising), COMMUNICATIONS AND THE ARTS (art, communications, dramatic arts, English, French, German, journalism, music, music performance, music theory and composition, Russian, and Spanish), COMPUTER AND PHYSICAL SCIENCE (astronomy, chemistry, computer science, earth science, environmental geology, geology, mathematics, physics, and statistics), EDUCATION (elementary, health, industrial arts, music, physical, secondary, special, and trade and industrial), ENGINEERING AND ENVIRONMENTAL DESIGN (architectural engineering, chemical engineering, civil engineering, computer engineering, electrical/electronics engineering, and mechanical engineering), HEALTH PROFESSIONS (dental hygiene, exercise science, health science, nursing, and speech pathology/audiology), SOCIAL SCIENCE (American studies, anthropology, criminal justice, economics, family/consumer studies, geography, history, humanities, international studies, parks and recreation management, philosophy, political science/government, psychology, social science, social work, sociology, and women's studies). Elementary education, nursing, and business administration are the largest.
Required: To graduate, students must complete 120 to 157 credit hours, depending on the major, with a minimum GPA of 2.0. The core curriculum includes 9 credit hours of cultural context, 6 of math, 4 to 8 of science, 3 each of writing, constitution studies, and oral communications, 1 to 3 of intellectual community, and 1 of phys ed.
Special: UW offers co-op programs in health sciences, internships, study abroad in many countries, Washington and U.N. semesters, work-study programs, dual and interdisciplinary majors, pass/fail options, student-designed majors, credit by exam, accelerated degree programs, and credit for life, military, and work experience. There are 26 national honor societies, a freshman honors program, and 13 departmental honors programs.
Faculty/Classroom: 69% of faculty are male; 31%, female. 98% teach undergraduates, 85% do research, and 85% do both. Graduate students teach 7% of introductory courses. The average class size in an introductory lecture is 100; in a laboratory, 20; and in a regular course, 20.
Admissions: 95% of the 2003-2004 applicants were accepted. The SAT I scores for the 2003-2004 freshman class were: Verbal--35% below 500, 42% between 500 and 599, 21% between 600 and 700, and 3% above 700; Math--29% below 500, 42% between 500 and 599, 25% between 600 and 700, and 5% above 700. The ACT scores were 29% below 21, 27% between 21 and 23, 25% between 24 and 26, 11% between 27 and 28, and 10% above 28. 38% of the current freshmen were in the top fifth of their class; 67% were in the top two fifths. 85 freshmen graduated first in their class.

Requirements: The SAT I or ACT is required; the ACT is preferred. Applicants must be graduates of an accredited secondary school or hold a GED certificate. Secondary preparation should include at least 13 academic credits consisting of 4 years of English (or 3 of English and 2 of a single foreign language), and 3 each of math, science, and cultural context electives. A visit is suggested. A GPA of 2.75 is required. AP and CLEP credits are accepted. Important factors in the admissions decision are recommendations by school officials, personality/intangible qualities, and extracurricular activities record.

Procedure: Freshmen are admitted fall, spring, and summer. Entrance exams should be taken in the spring of the junior year or fall of the senior year. There is a deferred admissions plan and a rolling admissions plan. Applications should be filed by August 10 for fall entry and December 10 for spring entry. The fall 2003 application fee was $30. Notification is sent on a rolling basis. Applications are accepted on-line through *uwadmnweb:uwyo.edu/Admissions/apply_now.html.*

Transfer: 1113 transfer students enrolled in 2002-2003. Applicants with 30 or more transferable college-level credits must have a minimum GPA of 2.0. All applicants with fewer credits must submit a high school transcript, and those students under age 21 must also present SAT I or ACT scores. 30 credits of 120 to 157 required for the bachelor's degree must be completed at UW.

Visiting: There are regularly scheduled orientations for prospective students, including campus tours and meetings with academic advisers. There are guides for informal visits and visitors may sit in on classes and stay overnight. To schedule a visit, contact the Admissions Office at *why_wy@uwyo.edu.*

Financial Aid: In 2003-2004, 61% of all full-time freshmen and continuing students received some form of financial aid. 49% of full-time fresh-men and continuing students received need-based aid. The average freshman award was $7698. Need-based scholarships or need-based grants averaged $3823 ($4050 maximum); need-based self-help aid (loans and jobs) averaged $3875 ($5525 maximum); non-need-based athletic scholarships averaged $3428; and other non-need-based awards and non-need-based scholarships averaged $1955. 7% of undergraduates work part time. Average annual earnings from campus work are $1175. The average financial indebtedness of the 2003 graduate was $15,250. The FAFSA is required. The deadline for filing freshman financial aid applications for fall entry is March 1.

International Students: There are 119 international students enrolled. The school actively recruits these students. They must score 525 on the written TOEFL or 197 on the electronic version.

Computers: The mainframe is a Sun Enterprise 5000. There are approximately 1300 Windows workstations in public labs that are Ethernet connected. Students in the dorms and student apartments may each have a PC connected to the Ethernet. There are also 120 56-kbps dial-in modems. All students may access the system 24 hours a day. There are no time limits. The fee is up to $100 prorated per year.

Graduates: From July 1, 2002 to June 30, 2003, 1739 bachelor's degrees were awarded. The most popular majors were elementary education (7%), psychology (5%), and business administration (4%). In an average class, 17% graduate in 4 years or less, 41% graduate in 5 years or less, and 48% graduate in 6 years or less. 120 companies recruited on campus in 2002-2003.

Admissions Contact: Sara Axelson, Director of Admissions. A video is available. E-mail: *why-wyo@uwyo.edu* Web: *http://www.uwyo.edu*

RELIGIOUS COLLEGES

ARIZONA

SOUTHWESTERN COLLEGE
C-4
Phoenix, AZ 85032   (602) 992-6101; (800) 247-2697, ext. 100
Fax: (602) 404-2159

Full-time: 114 men, 123 women	**Faculty:** 32
Part-time: 14 men, 16 women	**Tuition:** $10,440
Application Deadline: August 1	**Room & Board:** $4020
SAT I Verbal/Math: 458/486	**ACT:** 20

Southwestern College, founded in 1960, is affiliated with Southwest Conservative Baptist Association. Its mission is to prepare students for vocational and lay ministries as educators in public, private, or Christian schools. In addition to regional accreditation, the college is accredited by AABC. Southwestern College awards the B.A. and B.S. in elementary education, Biblical studies, Christian ministries, secondary education, business administration, counseling, and music education. The school also awards associate degrees. Web: *www.swcaz.edu*

ARKANSAS

CENTRAL BAPTIST COLLEGE
C-3
Conway, AR 72032   (501) 329-6872; Fax: (501) 329-2941

Full-time: 191 men, 154 women	**Faculty:** 41
Part-time: 51 men, 30 women	**Tuition:** $7258
Application Deadline: August 15	**Room & Board:** $4398
ACT: 20	

Central Baptist College, founded in 1952, is affiliated with Baptist Missionary Association of Arkansas. Its mission is to train Christian men and women for lay and professional ministry and church-related vocations. Central Baptist College awards the B.A. and B.S. in Bible studies, Christian missions, church music, pastoral ministry, youth ministry, religious education, and Christian counseling. The school also awards associate degrees. Web: *www.cbc.edu*

CALIFORNIA

BETHANY COLLEGE
B-3
Scotts Valley, CA 95066   (831) 438-3800; Fax: (831) 461-1533

Full-time: 141 men, 241 women	**Faculty:** 86
Part-time: 67 men, 82 women	**Tuition:** $12,562
Graduate: 18 men, 44 women	**Room & Board:** $5380
Application Deadline: July 31	
SAT I Verbal/Math: 505/488	**ACT:** 21

Bethany College, founded in 1919, is affiliated with Assemblies of God. Its mission is to prepare students for leadership in the church and society. Bethany College awards the B.A. in addiction studies, applied professional studies, biblical and theological studies, business, church leadership and children's ministries, church leadership and urban ministries, church leadership and world missions, church music, early child development, English, general ministries, intercultural child development, liberal studies, missions, multicultural studies, music, psychology, social science, teacher education program, liberal arts, music (emphasis in teaching), music leadership, youth ministries leadership, and social science (emphasis in teaching). The school also awards associate and master's degrees. Web: *www.bethany.edu*

PATTEN UNIVERSITY
(Formerly Patten College)
B-3
Oakland, CA 94601   (510) 261-8500, ext. 765; Fax: (510) 534-4344

Full-time: 73 men, 139 women	**Faculty:** 45
Part-time: 295 men, 144 women	**Tuition:** $9840
Graduate: 4 men, 12 women	**Room & Board:** $5800
Application Deadline: July 31	
SAT I Verbal: 950	**ACT:** 20

Patten University, formerly Patten College, founded in 1944, is affiliated with Christian Evangelical Churches of America/ Church of God. Its mission is to offer a balanced liberal arts education with a strong biblical studies emphasis and to help students prepare for a life of Christian service. Patten University awards the B.A. and B.S. in biblical studies, Christian ministires, liberal studies, pastoral studies, preseminary studies, sacred music, liberal arts, organizational management, early childhood development, English, art, social science, and sports management. The school also awards associate and master's degrees. Web: *www.patten.edu*

SAINT JOHN'S SEMINARY COLLEGE
C-4
Camarillo, CA 93012   (805) 482-2755, ext. 2006
Fax: (805) 987-5097

Full-time: 83 men	**Faculty:** 35
Application Deadline: June 20	**Tuition:** $8200
	Room & Board: $6000
SAT I Verbal/Math: 410/420	**ACT:** 17

Saint John's Seminary College, founded in 1927, is affiliated with the Roman Catholic Church. Its mission is to provide a liberal arts education for young men interested in becoming priests for the Archdiocese of Los Angeles and for other sponsoring dioceses and religious communities. Information in the above capsule is approximate. Saint John's Seminary College awards the B.A. in philosophy, English, Spanish, and theology. Web: *www.sjsc.edu*

WILLIAM JESSUP UNIVERSITY
(Formerly San Jose Christian College)
B-3
San Jose, CA 95112   (408) 293-9058; Fax: (408) 293-7352

Full-time: 125 men, 100 women	**Faculty:** 50
Part-time: 75 men, 50 women	**Tuition:** $10,000
Application Deadline: August 1	**Room & Board:** $5000

William Jessup University, formerly San Jose Christian College, founded in 1939, is nondenominational. Its mission is to prepare Christians for leadership and service in church and society through Christian higher education, spiritual formation, and directed experiences. Figures in the above capsule are approximate. The college is accredited by AABC. William Jessup University awards the B.A. and B.S. in Bible and theology, pastoral ministry, youth ministry, Christian education, missions, counseling, and music and worship. The school also awards associate degrees. Web: *www.jessup.edu*

CONNECTICUT

HOLY APOSTLES COLLEGE AND SEMINARY
C-2
Cromwell, CT 06416   (860) 632-3010; Fax: (860) 632-0176

Full-time: 5 men	**Faculty:** 25
Part-time: 8 men, 8 women	**Tuition:** $8530
Graduate: 156 men, 64 women	**Room & Board:** $6850
Application Deadline: open	

Holy Apostles College and Seminary, founded in 1956, is affiliated with the Roman Catholic Church. Its mission is to provide adult men, who have a calling to the Catholic priesthood, with an academic and seminary environment suited to their age and background, and to provide lay students with training for personal interest, and various certificates and degrees. Holy Apostles College and Seminary awards the B.A. in humanities, philosophy, religious studies, and social sciences. The school also awards associate and master's degrees. Web: *www.novavista.com/holyapostles*

FLORIDA

BAPTIST COLLEGE OF FLORIDA   B-1
(Formerly Florida Baptist Theological College)
Graceville, FL 32440   (800) 328-2660, ext. 460
                                                 Fax: (850) 263-7506

Full-time: 281 men, 166 women	**Faculty:** 58
Part-time: 138 men, 44 women	**Tuition:** $5450
Application Deadline: August 1	**Room & Board:** $3486

Baptist College of Florida, founded in 1943, is affiliated with Florida Baptist Convention. Its mission is to promote, provide for, operate, and control a program of education and training for ministers and other religious workers. Baptist College of Florida awards the B.A. and B.M. in music ministry, teacher education, theology, Christian education, Christian counseling, and leadership. The school also awards associate degrees. Web: *www.baptistcollege.edu*

FLORIDA CHRISTIAN COLLEGE   D-3
Kissimmee, FL 34744   (407) 847-8966, ext. 305
                                                 Fax: (407) 847-3925

Full-time: 85 men, 80 women	**Faculty:** 24
Part-time: 20 men, 20 women	**Tuition:** $6700
Application Deadline: August 1	**Room & Board:** $1740
ACT: required	

Florida Christian College, founded in 1976, is affiliated with Christian Churches/Churches of Christ/Independent. Its mission is to conduct a course of study educating men and women for Christian service, to provide a program of instruction on the college level, to grant appropriate degrees, and to serve as a resource to churches, especially in Florida. Information in the above capsule is approximate. In addition to regional accreditation, the college is accredited by AABC. Florida Christian College awards the B.A., B.S., and B.Th. in Bible, Christian education ministries, and Christian ministries. The school also awards associate degrees. Web: *www.fcc.edu*

SAINT JOHN VIANNEY COLLEGE SEMINARY   E-5
Miami, FL 33165   (305) 223-4561, ext. 15; Fax: (305) 223-0650

Full-time: 72 men, 1 woman	**Faculty:** 21
Part-time: 2 men, 1 woman	**Tuition:** $11,000
Application Deadline: open	**Room & Board:** $4000

Saint John Vianney College Seminary, founded in 1959, is affiliated with the Roman Catholic Church. Its mission is to provide an undergraduate education preparatory for students whose stated objective is to serve the Catholic Church in the priesthood, and to provide spiritual and intellectual formation within an Anglo-Hispanic bilingual, bicultural setting. Information in the above capsule is approximate. Saint John Vianney College Seminary awards the B.A. in philosophy and theology. Web: *www.sjvcs.edu*

GEORGIA

ATLANTA CHRISTIAN COLLEGE   B-2
East Point, GA 30344   (404) 669-2088; Fax: (404) 669-2024

Full-time: 165 men, 185 women	**Faculty:** 33
Part-time: 25 men, 30 women	**Tuition:** $10,300
Application Deadline: open	**Room & Board:** $3800

Atlanta Christian College, founded in 1937, is affiliated with Christian Churches and Churches of Christ. Its mission is to provide education in biblical studies, the arts and sciences, and professional studies to equip men and women for Christian service. Information in the above capsule is approximate. Atlanta Christian College awards the B.A., B.S., and B.Th. in Christian education in the church, Christian education in the school, missions, music, preaching ministry, human relations, early childhood education, youth ministry, business administration, and the humanities. The school also awards associate degrees. Web: *www.acc.edu*

ILLINOIS

LINCOLN CHRISTIAN COLLEGE AND SEMINARY   D3
Lincoln, IL 62656-2111   (217) 732-3168, ext. 2251
                                                 Fax: (217) 732-5914

Full-time: 298 men, 304 women	**Faculty:** 88
Part-time: 73 men, 84 women	**Tuition:** $9568
Graduate: 221 men, 91 women	**Room & Board:** $4468
Application Deadline: open	
ACT: 22	

Lincoln Christian College and Seminary, founded in 1944, is affiliated with the Christian Church/Church of Christ. Its mission is to educate and train preachers, Christian teachers, and other Christian workers. In addition to regional accreditation, the college is accredited by AABC. Lincoln Christian College and Seminary awards the B.A. and B.S. in Bible, Christian business administration, Christian education ministry, Christian leadership and management, discipleship and small group ministry, early childhood ministry, family life ministry, general ministry, intercultural studies, music ministry, preaching ministry, and youth ministry. The school also awards associate and master's degrees. Web: *www.lccs.edu*

MOODY BIBLE INSTITUTE   E-2
Chicago, IL 60610   (312) 329-4400; Fax: (312) 329-8955

Full-time: 770 men, 578 women	**Faculty:** 96
Part-time: 403 men, 23 women	**Tuition:** $1300
Graduate: 211 men, 103 women	**Room & Board:** $6220
Application Deadline: March 1 or December 1	
ACT: 25	

Moody Bible Institute, founded in 1886, is affiliated with the Evangelical Protestant Church. Its mission is to educate and train individuals to proclaim the gospel of the Lord Jesus Christ, to promote evangelism, and to serve the Evangelical Christian Church vocationally and/or avocationally in its worldwide ministry. In addition to regional accreditation, the college is accredited by AABC. Moody Bible Institute awards the B.A., B.S., and B.Mus. in missionary aviation technology, biblical studies, evangelism/discipleship, communication, educational ministries, world missions, pastoral studies, religious education, church music, sacred music, Bible-theology, applied linguistics, youth ministry, urban ministry, Jewish and modern Israel studies, family ministries, women's ministries, and teaching English to speakers of other languages. The school also awards associate and master's degrees. Web: *www.moody.edu*

IOWA

DIVINE WORD COLLEGE   E-2
Epworth, IA 52045-0380   (800) 553-3321; Fax: (563) 876-3407

Full-time: 75 men	**Faculty:** 26
Application Deadline: July 15	**Tuition:** $9150
	Room & Board: $2100
SAT I Verbal/Math: 400/430	

Divine Word College, founded in 1912, is affiliated with the Roman Catholic Church. Its mission is to offer excellence in combining a liberal arts education with a cross-cultural program of missionary formation for Divine Word missionaries and other leaders in the Roman Catholic Church. Divine Word College awards the B.A. in philosophy and cross-cultural studies. The school also awards associate degrees. Web: *www.dwci.edu*

FAITH BAPTIST BIBLE COLLEGE AND THEOLOGICAL SEMINARY   C-3

Ankeny, IA 50021   (888) FAITH 4 U; Fax: (515) 964-1638

Full-time: 161 men, 201 women   **Faculty:** 35
Part-time: 18 men, 12 women   **Tuition:** $10,418 ($9516)
Graduate: 95 men, 46 women   **Room & Board:** $4006
Application Deadline: open
SAT I Verbal/Math: 500/570   **ACT:** 21

Faith Baptist Bible College and Theological Seminary, founded in 1921, is affiliated with General Association of Regular Baptist Churches. Its mission is to provide an intensive biblical and vocational education on the college level with the goal of preparing students to minister effectively in Christian service through leadership positions in fundamental Baptist churches and other organizations of like convictions. Cost figures above in parentheses are for the seminary program. In addition to regional accreditation, the college is accredited by AABC. Faith Baptist Bible College and Theological Seminary awards the B.A. and B.S. in Bible and theology, assistant pastor, Christian education, Christian school, missions, music ministries, and pastoral training. The school also awards associate and master's degrees. Web: www.faith.edu

KENTUCKY

CLEAR CREEK BAPTIST BIBLE COLLEGE   F-3

Pineville, KY 40977-9752   (606) 337-3196; Fax: (606) 337-2372

Full-time: 147 men, 14 women   **Faculty:** 22
Part-time: 38 men, 9 women   **Tuition:** $4460
Application Deadline: July 15   **Room & Board:** $3380

Clear Creek Baptist Bible College, founded in 1926, is affiliated with the Southern Baptist Church. Its mission is providing theological education for adults called to Christian service. In addition to regional accreditation, the college is accredited by AABC. Clear Creek Baptist Bible College awards the B.A. in Bible. The school also awards associate degrees. Web: www.ccbbc.edu

MID-CONTINENT UNIVERSITY
(Formerly Mid-Continent College)   A-4

Mayfield, KY 42066-0357   (502) 247-8521, ext. 311
                                       Fax: (502) 247-3115

Full-time: 309 men, 294 women   **Faculty:** 63
Part-time: 47 men, 33 women   **Tuition:** $9080
Application Deadline: August 15   **Room & Board:** $3388
ACT: 19

Mid-Continent University, formerly Mid-Continent College, founded in 1949, is affiliated with the Baptist Church. Its mission as a Baptist institution of higher learning, is to educate students for Christian leadership and service throughout the world. Mid-Continent University awards the B.A., B.S., and B.Min. in biblical languages, biblical studies, Christian education, and leadership, Christian ministry, evangelism, missions, psychology and counseling, behavioral studies, communication arts, English, general studies, social studies, elementary teacher education, organizational leadership, and business administration (management emphasis). The school also awards associate degrees.
Web: www.midcontinent.edu

LOUISIANA

SAINT JOSEPH SEMINARY COLLEGE   D-3

St. Benedict, LA 70457   (504) 867-2248; Fax: (504) 867-2270

Full-time: 80 men   **Faculty:** 37
Application Deadline: open   **Tuition:** $10,000
                                       Room & Board: $5700
ACT: 21

Saint Joseph Seminary College, founded in 1891, is affiliated with the Roman Catholic Church. Its mission is to provide the education and training of men for the priesthood in the Roman Catholic Church. Information in the above capsule is approximate. Saint Joseph Seminary College awards the B.A. in philosophy and the liberal arts, and philosophy and religious studies. Web: www.stjosephabbey.org

MICHIGAN

SACRED HEART MAJOR SEMINARY   E-5

Detroit, MI 48206-1799   (313) 883-8512; Fax: (313) 883-8682

Full-time: 39 men   **Faculty:** 55
Part-time: 115 men, 117 women   **Tuition:** $8390
Graduate: 73 men, 45 women   **Room & Board:** $5990
Application Deadline: August 1
ACT: required

Sacred Heart Major Seminary, founded in 1919, is affiliated with the Roman Catholic Church. Its mission is to provide spiritual formation and a liberal arts education for candidates preparing for the Roman Catholic priesthood in Detroit and for students preparing for other ministries within the church. Sacred Heart Major Seminary awards the A.B. and B.Phil. in philosophy. The school also awards associate and master's degrees. Web: www.shms.edu

MINNESOTA

CROWN COLLEGE   C-4

Saint Bonifacius, MN 55375   (612) 446-4144
                                       Fax: (612) 446-4149

Full-time: 329 men, 420 women   **Faculty:** 57
Part-time: 91 men, 145 women   **Tuition:** $13,168
Graduate: 32 men, 13 women   **Room & Board:** $5572
Application Deadline: open
ACT: 21

Crown College, founded in 1916, is affiliated with the Christian and Missionary Alliance. Its mission is to provide a biblically based education for Christian leadership in the Christian and Missionary Alliance, the church-at-large, and the world. In addition to regional accreditation, the college is accredited by AABC. Crown College awards the B.A., B.S., and B.Mus.Ed. in biblical and theological studies, business administration, Christian education, elementary education, communications, physical education, history, history education, music, music education, pastoral ministries, social studies education, youth, youth/social science, psychology, English, English education, linguistics, intercultural studies, liberal arts, child and family ministries, management, network administration, biology, sports management, Christian Ministry, management and ethics, management and network administration, early childhood education, and New Testament. The school also awards associate and master's degrees. Web: www.crown.edu

MARTIN LUTHER COLLEGE   C-4

New Ulm, MN 56073-3965   (507) 354-8221; Fax: (507) 354-8225

Full-time: 515 men, 525 women   **Faculty:** 98
Part-time: 8 men, 9 women   **Tuition:** $5800
Application Deadline: April 15   **Room & Board:** $2500
ACT: 24.2

Martin Luther College, founded in 1995, is affiliated with the Wisconsin Evangelical Lutheran Synod. Its mission is to provide training for elementary and secondary teaching, preseminary training for pastoral students, and training for other church vocations through the Staff Ministry Program. Information in the above capsule is approximate. Martin Luther College awards the B.A. and B.S.Ed. in education and preseminary studies. Web: www.mlc-wels.edu

OAK HILLS CHRISTIAN COLLEGE   B-2

Bemidji, MN 56601   (218) 751-8670; Fax: (218) 751-8825

Full-time: 81 men, 74 women   **Faculty:** 16
Part-time: 8 men, 12 women   **Tuition:** $10,180
Application Deadline: open   **Room & Board:** $3810
ACT: 21

Oak Hills Christian College, founded in 1946, is interdenominational. The college is accredited by AABC. Oak Hills Christian College awards the B.A. in biblical studies, biblical studies and applied psychology, applied studies, campus ministry, contemporary worship, contemporary Christian ministry, intercultural studies, pastoral ministry, and youth ministry. The school also awards the associate degrees.
Web: www.oakhills.edu

MISSISSIPPI

MAGNOLIA BIBLE COLLEGE D-3
Kosciusko, MS 39090 (662) 289-2896; Fax: (662) 289-1850

Application Deadline: open	**Faculty:** 11
	Tuition: $4760
	Room & Board: $650
ACT: 18	

Magnolia Bible College, founded in 1976, is affiliated with Churches of Christ. Its mission is to enable students to acquire a college-level education in general and biblical studies that will enable them to serve as preachers of the gospel. In addition to regional accreditation, the college is accredited by AABC. Magnolia Bible College awards the B.A. in Bible and theology. Web: *www.magnolia.edu*

MISSOURI

CONCEPTION SEMINARY COLLEGE A-1
Conception, MO 64433 (660) 944-2886; Fax: (660) 944-2829

Full-time: 85 men	**Faculty:** 30
Part-time: 2 men, 50 women	**Tuition:** $9800
Application Deadline: July 31	**Room & Board:** $5700
ACT: 22	

Conception Seminary College, founded in 1886, is affiliated with the Roman Catholic Church. Its mission is to prepare men who are discerning for the Roman Catholic priesthood. Information in the above capsule is approximate. Conception Seminary College places emphasis on spiritual, personal, and academic formation. Conception Seminary College awards the B.A. in liberal arts. Web: *www.conceptionabbey.org*

NORTH CAROLINA

ROANOKE BIBLE COLLEGE F-2
Elizabeth City, NC 27909-4054 (800) RBC-8980
Fax: (252) 334-2071

Full-time: 85 men, 74 women	**Faculty:** 17
Part-time: 16 men, 12 women	**Tuition:** $7200
Application Deadline: open	**Room & Board:** $4400
SAT I Verbal/Math: 470/450	**ACT:** 20

Roanoke Bible College, founded in 1948, is affiliated with the Christian Church/Church of Christ. Its mission is to prepare men and women for career and volunteer Christian service. In addition to regional accreditation, the college is accredited by AABC. Roanoke Bible College awards the B.A. and B.S. in biblical and theological studies. The school also awards associate degrees. Web: *www.roanokebible.edu*

NORTH DAKOTA

TRINITY BIBLE COLLEGE E-4
Ellendale, ND 58436 (888) TBC-2DAY; Fax: (701) 349-5443

Full-time: 131 men, 143 women	**Faculty:** 30
Part-time: 8 men, 25 women	**Tuition:** $10,258
Application Deadline: August 15	**Room & Board:** $4752

Trinity Bible College, founded in 1948, is affiliated with Assemblies of God. Its mission is to prepare pastors, church leaders, and Christian professionals in various fields in a Bible-based Pentecostal environment of academic excellence. In addition to regional accreditation, the college is accredited by AABC. Trinity Bible College awards the B.A. in biblical studies, business administration, elementary education, ministerial studies, and missions. The school also awards associate degrees. Web: *www.trinitybiblecollege.edu*

OHIO

CINCINNATI BIBLE COLLEGE AND SEMINARY A-5
Cincinnati, OH 45204-3200 (513) 244-8192; Fax: (513) 244-8140

Full-time: 296 men, 210 women	**Faculty:** 47
Part-time: 78 men, 43 women	**Tuition:** $8890
Graduate: 168 men, 86 women	**Room & Board:** $4840
Application Deadline: August 10	

Cincinnati Bible College and Seminary, founded in 1924, is affiliated with Christian Churches/Churches of Christ. Its mission is to teach men and women to live by biblical principles and to equip and empower them with skills, insight, and vision both to lead the church and to impact society for Christ. In addition to regional accreditation, the college is accredited by AABC. Cincinnati Bible College and Seminary awards the B.A., B.S., and B.Mus. in biblical/theological studies (primary major), education, ministries, (second major), helping professions, and signing interpreter's training program. The school also awards associate and master's degrees. Web: *www.cincybible.edu*

CIRCLEVILLE BIBLE COLLEGE
Circleville, OH 43113 (740) 477-7701 or (800) 701-0222
Fax: (740) 477-7755

Full-time: 152 men, 145 women	**Faculty:** 44
Part-time: 22 men, 18 women	**Tuition:** $8440
Application Deadline: open	**Room & Board:** $5312
SAT I Verbal/Math: 460/480	**ACT:** 20

Circleville Bible College, founded in 1948, is affiliated with Churches of Christ in Christian Union (CCCU). Its mission is preparing students for leadership in the 21st century. The college is accredited by AABC. Circleville Bible College awards the B.A. in religion. The school also awards associate degrees. Web: *www.biblecollege.edu*

PONTIFICAL COLLEGE JOSEPHINUM C-3
Columbus, OH 43235 (888) 252-5812; Fax: (614) 885-2307

Full-time: 78 men	**Faculty:** 44
Part-time: 1 man, 1 woman	**Tuition:** $10,320
Graduate: 66 men, 3 women	**Room & Board:** $6000
Application Deadline: open	

Pontifical College Josephinum, founded in 1888, is affiliated with the Roman Catholic Church. Its mission is to prepare young men for the priesthood. Pontifical College Josephinum awards the B.A. in philosophy and the humanities (English literature, Hispanic studies, history, and classical studies). The school also awards master's degrees. Web: *www.pcj.edu*

OKLAHOMA

MID-AMERICA CHRISTIAN UNIVERSITY D-3
Oklahoma City, OK 73170 (405) 691-3800; (405) 692-3241
Fax: (405) 692-3165

Full-time: 310 men, 226 women	**Faculty:** 45
Part-time: 79 men, 57 women	**Tuition:** $3646 ($7292)
Application Deadline: open	**Room & Board:** $2000

Mid-America Christian University, founded in 1953, is affiliated with Church of God in Anderson, Indiana. Its mission is to train and prepare men and women for the Christian ministry. Mid-America Christian University awards the B.A. and B.S. in behavioral science, elementary education, English, music, music performance, pastoral ministry, worship and music ministries, secondary education, specialized ministries, management and ethics, English/business, and business administration. The school also awards associate degrees. Web: *www.macu.edu*

SOUTHWESTERN CHRISTIAN UNIVERSITY D-3
(Formerly Southwestern College of Christian Ministries)
Bethany, OK 73008 (405) 789-7661, ext. 3436
Fax: (405) 495-0078

Full-time: 56 men, 48 women	**Faculty:** 21
Part-time: 12 men, 6 women	**Tuition:** $7200
Graduate: 52 men, 6 women	**Room & Board:** $3400
Application Deadline: open	
ACT: 19	

Southwestern Christian University, formerly, Southwestern College of Christian Ministries, founded in 1946, is affiliated with Pentecostal Holiness. Its mission is the education and training for Christian service leading toward professional competence in the practice of various ministry forms. Southwestern Christian University awards the B.A. and B.S. in biblical studies, Christian ministry/pastoral studies, religion, and human and family services. The school also awards associate and master's degrees. Web: www.swcu.edu

OREGON

MOUNT ANGEL SEMINARY B-2
St. Benedict, OR 97373 (503) 845-3951; Fax: (503) 845-3126

Full-time: 80 men	**Faculty:** 40
Graduate: 65 men, 50 women	**Tuition:** $8850
Application Deadline: July 15	**Room & Board:** $6300

Mount Angel Seminary, founded in 1889, is affiliated with the Roman Catholic Church. Its mission is to prepare students of the Roman Catholic priesthood for religious orders and dioceses. Figures in the above capsule are approximate. Mount Angel Seminary awards the B.A. in philosophy and literature. The school also awards master's degrees. Web: www.mtangel.edu

PENNSYLVANIA

BAPTIST BIBLE COLLEGE OF PENNSYLVANIA E-2
Clarks Summit, PA 18411 (570) 586-2400; Fax: (570) 585-9400

Full-time: 290 men, 412 women	**Faculty:** 30
Part-time: 23 men, 24 women	**Tuition:** $11,700
Graduate: 11 men, 27 women	**Room & Board:** $4982
Application Deadline: August 15	
SAT I Verbal/Math: 515/500	**ACT:** 21

Baptist Bible College of Pennsylvania, founded in 1932, is affiliated with the Baptist Church. Its mission is to prepare men and women for service in selected Christian ministries as pastors, missionaries, Christian education workers, teachers for Christian schools, counselors, church musicians, and secretaries for Christian organizations. In addition to regional accreditation, the college is accredited by AABC. Baptist Bible College of Pennsylvania awards the B.S. in Bible and B.S.M. in church music, communications, elementary education, general missions, local church ministries, music education, outreach and evangelism pastor, pastoral ministry, pastor of Christian education, preseminary, secondary education, secretarial ministries, sports ministries, youth pastor, precounseling, general ministries, and women's ministries. The school also awards associate, master's, and doctorate degrees. Web: www.bbc.edu

LANCASTER BIBLE COLLEGE E-3
Lancaster, PA 17601 (717) 560-8271; Fax: (717) 560-8213

Full-time: 245 men, 300 women	**Faculty:** 60
Part-time: 85 men, 90 women	**Tuition:** $10,700
Graduate: 50 men, 50 women	**Room & Board:** $5000
Application Deadline: open	
SAT I Verbal/Math: 500/500	**ACT:** 19

Lancaster Bible College, founded in 1933, is nondenominational. Its mission is to educate Christian men and women to live according to a biblical worldview and to serve through professional Christian ministries. Information in the above capsule is approximate. In addition to regional accreditation, the college is accredited by AABC. Lancaster Bible College awards the B.S. in Bible and B.S.Ed. in Bible education K-l2, Christian education, computer studies, biblical counseling, early childhood education, elementary education, guidance counselor/Bible education, pastoral church planning, pastoral studies, missions, music, music education/Bible education, preseminary pastoral studies, physical education/Bible education, women's ministry, and youth ministry. The school also awards associate and master's degrees. Web: www.lbc.edu

SAINT CHARLES BORROMEO SEMINARY F-3
Wynnewood, PA 19096 (610) 667-3394; Fax: (610) 664-1422

Full-time: 74 men	**Faculty:** 68
Part-time: 41 men, 152 women	**Tuition:** $9600
Graduate: 118 men, 42 women	**Room & Board:** $6560
Application Deadline: July 1	

Saint Charles Borromeo Seminary, founded in 1832, is affiliated with the Roman Catholic Church. Its mission is to prepare and educate men for the Roman Catholic priesthood and to provide undergraduate and graduate programs for men and women pursuing theological studies. Saint Charles Borromeo Seminary awards the B.A. in philosophy. The school also awards master's degrees. Web: www.scs.edu

SOUTH CAROLINA

COLUMBIA INTERNATIONAL UNIVERSITY C-3
Columbia, SC 29230 (803) 754-4100; Fax: (803) 786-4041

Full-time: 235 men, 329 women	**Faculty:** 49
Part-time: 24 men, 34 women	**Tuition:** $11,690
Graduate: 190 men, 152 women	**Room & Board:** $4830
Application Deadline: open	
SAT I Verbal/Math: 510/500	**ACT:** 22

Columbia International University, founded in 1923, is multidenominational. Its mission is to prepare students to grow in spiritual maturity, Bible knowledge, and ministry skills in preparation for vocational or lay Christian ministry. In addition to regional accreditation, the college is accredited by AABC. Columbia International University awards the B.A. and B.S. in Bible, general studies, intercultural studies, psychology, biblical languages, music, Bible teaching, youth ministry, Middle Eastern studies, family and church education, teacher education, humanities, pastoral ministries, and communications. The school also awards associate, master's, and doctorate degrees. Web: www.ciu.edu

TENNESSEE

FREE WILL BAPTIST BIBLE COLLEGE C-2
Nashville, TN 37205 (615) 383-1340, ext. 5233
Fax: (615) 269-6028

Full-time: 130 men, 145 women	**Faculty:** 25
Part-time: 30 men, 25 women	**Tuition:** $7300
Application Deadline: open	**Room & Board:** $3900
ACT: 19	

Free Will Baptist Bible College, founded in 1942, is affiliated with National Association of Free Will Baptists. Its mission is to equip men and women, through Bible-based education, to serve Christ and His church. Information in the above capsule is approximate. In addition to regional accreditation, the college is accredited by AABC. Free Will Baptist Bible College awards the B.A. and B.S. in biblical studies, biblical and ministry studies, business administration, church music, church music and youth ministry, English, elementary education, music education, music performance, sports medicine, physical education, secondary English education, and psychology and learning. The school also awards associate degrees. Web: www.fwbbc.edu

JOHNSON BIBLE COLLEGE E-3
Knoxville, TN 37998 (865) 251-3403; Fax: (865) 251-2337

Full-time: 355 men, 363 women	**Faculty:** 55
Part-time: 11 men, 8 women	**Tuition:** $5850
Graduate: 68 men, 45 women	**Room & Board:** $3710
Application Deadline: August 1	
SAT I Verbal/Math: 536/519	**ACT:** 22

Johnson Bible College, founded in 1893, is Christian-centered. Its mission is to educate students for specialized Christian ministries. In addition to regional accreditation, the college is accredited by AABC. Johnson Bible College awards the B.A. and B.S. All students who graduate from Johnson Bible College with a Bachelor of Arts or a Bachelor of Science degree major in Bible. In addition, five professional programs require a second major. They are: counseling, preaching, interdisciplinary major with focus on teacher education, music, and youth ministry/preaching. The school also awards associate and master's degrees. Web: www.jbc.edu

TEXAS

AUSTIN GRADUATE SCHOOL OF THEOLOGY   D-3
(Formerly Institute for Christian Studies)
Austin, TX 78705   (512) 476-2772; Fax: (512) 476-3919

Full-time: 3 men, 1 woman	**Faculty:** 10
Part-time: 16 men, 11 women	**Tuition:** $175
Graduate: 23 men, 12 women	**Room & Board:** n/app
Application Deadline: July 1	
(recommended)	

Austin Graduate School of Theology, formerly, Institute for Christian Studies, founded in 1917, is affiliated with the Church of Christ. Its mission is to equip ministers and other Christians for service in the kingdom of God. Cost figures above are per semester hour. Austin Graduate School of Theology awards the B.A. in Ministry and Christian Studies. The school also awards master's degrees. Web:www.austingrad.edu

BAPTIST MISSIONARY ASSOCIATION THEOLOGICAL   E-2
SEMINARY
Jacksonville, TX 75766   (903) 586-2501; Fax: (903) 586-0378

Full-time: 11 men	**Faculty:** 13
Part-time: 22 men, 2 women	**Tuition:** $2220
Graduate: 40 men, 6 women	**Room & Board:** $3600
Application Deadline: open	

Baptist Missionary Association Theological Seminary, founded in 1955, is affiliated with Baptist Missionary Association. Its mission is to train individuals for Christian ministry. Baptist Missionary Association Theological Seminary awards the B.A.R. in religion. The school also awards associate and master's degrees. Web: www.bmats.edu

CRISWELL COLLEGE   D-2
Dallas, TX 75246   (214) 821-5433; Fax: (214) 818-1310

Full-time: 140 men, 30 women	**Faculty:** 27
Part-time: 160 men, 50 women	**Tuition:** $3910
Graduate: 100 men, 20 women	**Room & Board:** n/app
Application Deadline: July 15	

Criswell College, founded in 1970, is affiliated with the Southern Baptist Church. Its mission is to educate and train laymen and full-time Christian workers in biblical, theological, and professional studies so they can serve effectively in evangelistic, educational, pastoral, and missionary vocations of the Christian church. Criswell College awards the B.A. in biblical studies, counseling, missions, evangelism, pastoral, and urban ministries. The school also awards associate and master's degrees. Web: www.criswell.edu

SOUTHWESTERN ASSEMBLIES OF GOD UNIVERSITY   D-2
Waxahachie, TX 75165   (972) 937-4010; Fax: (972) 923-0488

Full-time: 665 men, 720 women	**Faculty:** 102
Part-time: 140 men, 135 women	**Tuition:** $8400
Graduate: 45 men, 30 women	**Room & Board:** $4700
Application Deadline: open	

Southwestern Assemblies of God University, founded in 1927, is affiliated with Assemblies of God. Its mission is to provide the training of Christian individuals to carry the gospel to the ends of the earth or to fill any other divinely approved place in the Kingdom of God. Information in the above capsule is approximate. In addition to regional accreditation, the college is accredited by AABC. Southwestern Assemblies of God University awards the B.A. and B.S. in business, church ministries, counseling, elementary education, music, psychology, and secondary education. The school also awards associate and master's degrees. Web: www.sagu.edu

WASHINGTON

TRINITY LUTHERAN COLLEGE   C-2
(Formerly Lutheran Bible Institute of Seattle)
Issaquah, WA 98029-9299   (425) 392-0400; Fax: (425) 392-0404

Full-time: 30 men, 60 women	**Faculty:** 26
Part-time: 7 men, 15 women	**Tuition:** $9140
Application Deadline: open	**Room & Board:** $5100
ACT: 21	

Trinity Lutheran College, founded in 1944, is affiliated with the Lutheran Church. Its mission is to train students for professional ministry and service careers. Information in the above capsule is approximate. Trinity Lutheran College awards the B.A. in biblical studies, Christian education, youth and family ministry, urban missions, global missions, music and worship, and early childhood education. The school also awards associate degrees. Web: www.tlc.edu

WISCONSIN

MARANATHA BAPTIST BIBLE COLLEGE   D-4
Watertown, WI 53094   (920) 261-9300; Fax: (920) 261-9109

Full-time: 350 men, 404 women	**Faculty:** 57
Part-time: 31 men, 45 women	**Tuition:** $7740
Graduate: 27 men, 3 women	**Room & Board:** $4400
Application Deadline: open	
ACT: 21	

Maranatha Baptist Bible College, founded in 1968, is affiliated with the Baptist Church. Its mission is to train men and women for effective professional or lay gospel ministry in the local church through a postsecondary program of biblical, general, and professional studies. Maranatha Baptist Bible College awards the B.A. and B.S. in Bible, church ministries, education, general studies, fine arts, business, nursing, and office administration. The school also awards associate and master's degrees. Web: www.mbbc.edu

AIR FORCE

In the Air Force ROTC program, young men and women may earn commissions while attending college. The amount of academic credit given for Air Force ROTC varies from school to school.

Most new Air Force officers come through the Air Force ROTC program. It offers students the opportunity to attend a civilian college while studying officership as part of their undergraduate curriculum.

The AFROTC program begins with the General Military Course. Freshmen or sophomores attend one hour of ROTC classes and one to two hours of leadership laboratory weekly. During these first two years, study is focused on the history of the Air Force and the part it plays in the world today. During the summer between sophomore and junior years, students attend a four-week basic training course located at an Air Force base.

The Professional Officer Course is completed during the junior and senior years. Study includes management principles and defense policy and offers the opportunity for managing, organizing, directing, and evaluating the cadet corps activities. Cadets who are medically qualified will have the opportunity to compete for pilot or navigator positions. Upon graduation, students are commissioned as Second Lieutenants.

For academically qualified students in selected majors, the AFROTC offers scholarships, including tuition, fees and books, and a monthly nontaxable allowance during the school year.

The majority of scholarships are awarded in the technical degree areas of engineering and computer science, but there are opportunities in nontechnical areas as well. Scholarships are based on individual merit, not financial need. Those who receive a scholarship must still apply and be accepted by the school they wish to attend and notify the AFROTC headquarters of their selection.

The scholarship program is broken down into different types and durations. All scholarships include full or partial tuition, fees, textbook allowance, and $250–$400 per month tax-free allowance during the academic year. Type 1 pays full tuition at any school offering AFROTC. Type 2 pays tuition and fees up to a maximum of $15,000 per year. There are two variations of the Type 7 scholarship. A Type 7 scholarship winner can attend any post-secondary institution (public or private) where tuition does not exceed $9,000 per year, or he/she can attend any public post-secondary institution where the student qualifies for in-state tuition rates.

The application deadline is December 1 of the senior year, but priority consideration is given to those who get the application in early. AFROTC only accepts on-line applications and they are available during the spring prior to the senior year of high school.

Further information can be obtained from the professor of aerospace studies at any of the host campuses where Air Force ROTC is offered. The listing that follows represents the host schools that offer these programs. Hundreds more schools have crosstown agreements with these institutions to make AFROTC more accessible to students. Please be sure to contact the school directly for more details. You may also find useful and current information at the Air Force Reserve Officer Training Corps web site, *www.afrotc.com*.

ALABAMA
- Alabama State University
- Auburn University
- Samford University
- Troy State University
- Tuskegee University
- University of Alabama
- University of South Alabama

ARIZONA
- Arizona State University
- Embry-Riddle Aeronautical University
- Northern Arizona University
- University of Arizona

ARKANSAS
- University of Arkansas at Fayetteville

CALIFORNIA
- California State University, Fresno
- California State University, Sacramento
- California State University, San Bernadino
- Loyola Marymount University
- San Diego State University
- San Jose State University
- University of California at Berkeley
- University of California at Los Angeles
- University of Southern California

COLORADO
- Colorado State University
- University of Colorado at Boulder

CONNECTICUT
- University of Connecticut

DELAWARE
- University of Delaware

DISTRICT OF COLUMBIA
- Howard University

FLORIDA
- Embry-Riddle Aeronautical University
- Florida State University
- University of Central Florida
- University of Florida
- University of Miami
- University of South Florida

GEORGIA
- Georgia Institute of Technology
- University of Georgia
- Valdosta State University

HAWAII
- University of Hawaii at Manoa

ILLINOIS
- Illinois Institute of Technology
- Southern Illinois University at Carbondale
- University of Illinois at Urbana-Champaign

INDIANA
- Indiana State University
- Indiana University at Bloomington
- Purdue University
- University of Notre Dame

IOWA
- Iowa State University
- University of Iowa

KANSAS
- Kansas State University
- University of Kansas

KENTUCKY
- University of Kentucky
- University of Louisville

LOUISIANA
- Grambling State University
- Louisiana State University and Agricultural and Mechanical College
- Louisiana Tech University
- Tulane University

MARYLAND

- University of Maryland

MASSACHUSETTS

- Boston University
- Massachusetts Institute of Technology
- University of Massachusetts
- University of Massachusetts, Lowell
- Worcester Polytechnic Institute

MICHIGAN

- Michigan State University
- Michigan Technological University
- University of Michigan

MINNESOTA

- University of Minnesota/Duluth
- University of Minnesota/Twin Cities
- University of Saint Thomas

MISSISSIPPI

- Mississippi State University
- University of Mississippi
- University of Southern Mississippi

MISSOURI

- St. Louis University
- Southeast Missouri State University
- University of Missouri/Columbia
- University of Missouri/Rolla

MONTANA

- Montana State University

NEBRASKA

- University of Nebraska at Lincoln
- University of Nebraska at Omaha

NEW HAMPSHIRE

- University of New Hampshire

NEW JERSEY

- New Jersey Institute of Technology
- Rutgers, the State University of New Jersey/University College—New Brunswick

NEW MEXICO

- New Mexico State University
- University of New Mexico

NEW YORK

- Clarkson University
- Cornell University
- Manhattan College
- Rensselaer Polytechnic Institute
- Rochester Institute of Technology
- Syracuse University

NORTH CAROLINA

- Duke University
- East Carolina University
- Fayetteville State University
- North Carolina State University
- University of North Carolina at Chapel Hill
- University of North Carolina at Charlotte

NORTH DAKOTA

- North Dakota State University

OHIO

- Bowling Green State University
- Kent State University
- Miami University
- Ohio State University
- Ohio University
- University of Akron
- University of Cincinnati
- Wright State University

OKLAHOMA

- Oklahoma State University
- University of Oklahoma

OREGON

- Oregon State University
- University of Portland

PENNSYLVANIA

- Pennsylvania State University/University Park Campus
- Saint Joseph's University
- University of Pittsburgh
- Wilkes University

PUERTO RICO

- University of Puerto Rico/Mayaguez
- University of Puerto Rico/Río Piedras

SOUTH CAROLINA

- Charleston Southern University
- The Citadel
- Clemson University
- University of South Carolina

SOUTH DAKOTA

- South Dakota State University

TENNESSEE

- Tennessee State University
- University of Memphis
- University of Tennessee at Knoxville

TEXAS

- Angelo State University
- Baylor University
- Southwest Texas State University
- Texas A & M University
- Texas Christian University
- Texas Tech University
- University of Houston
- University of North Texas
- University of Texas at Austin
- University of Texas at San Antonio

UTAH

- Brigham Young University
- University of Utah
- Utah State University

VERMONT

- Norwich University

VIRGINIA

- University of Virginia
- Virginia Military Institute
- Virginia Polytechnic Institute and State University

WASHINGTON

- Central Washington University
- University of Washington
- Washington State University

WEST VIRGINIA

- West Virginia University

WISCONSIN

- Marquette University
- University of Wisconsin/Madison

WYOMING

- University of Wyoming

ARMY

The Army Reserve Officers' Training Corps (ROTC) provides college students with the opportunity to combine leadership and management training with their other academic studies. The curriculum, which consists of a series of classroom and hands-on leadership training experiences, provides students with the necessary foundation to serve successfully in positions of responsibility in either the U.S. Army or the corporate world.

Those with a strong academic background, an active mindset, and the ability to rapidly assimilate information thrive in the program. These scholar-athlete-leaders note that the lead-ership skills developed through their participation in the program are further honed during their period of service as Army officers. After service as an Army lieutenant, many graduates elect to continue their service in uniform. Others elect to enter the corporate world where their leadership skills and experience as ROTC-trained Army officers allow them to advance rapidly.

Although the program is designed to be completed in four years, students may complete all requirements within a two-year period through participation in a summer training session called the Leaders' Training Course, normally held during the summer between the sophomore and junior years. A generous series of merit-based scholarships that cover tuition, fees, text-books, and supplies exist to help students and their families defray the cost of college. Applications for four-year scholarships must be postmarked by November 13 to be considered for the following school year. Tax-free stipends of up to $4000 per academic year are also available to those meeting course requirements. For more information on the program, call (800) USA-ROTC, or contact the professor of military science at a college that offers Army ROTC. Detailed information about the program is also available on the Internet at *www.armyrotc.com*.

ALABAMA
- Alabama Agricultural and Mechanical University
- Auburn University
- Auburn University at Montgomery
- Jacksonville State University
- Marion Military Institute
- Tuskegee University
- University of Alabama
- University of Alabama at Birmingham
- University of North Alabama
- University of South Alabama

ALASKA
- University of Alaska/Fairbanks

ARIZONA
- Arizona State University
- Northern Arizona University
- University of Arizona

ARKANSAS
- Arkansas State University
- University of Arkansas at Fayetteville
- University of Arkansas at Pine Bluff
- University of Central Arkansas

CALIFORNIA
- California Polytechnic State University at San Luis Obispo
- California State University at Fresno
- California State University at Fullerton
- Claremont McKenna College
- San Diego State University
- Santa Clara University
- University of California at Berkeley
- University of California at Davis
- University of California at Los Angeles
- University of California at Santa Barbara
- University of San Francisco
- University of Southern California

COLORADO
- Colorado State University
- University of Colorado at Boulder
- University of Colorado at Colorado Springs

CONNECTICUT
- University of Connecticut

DELAWARE
- University of Delaware

DISTRICT OF COLUMBIA
- Georgetown University
- Howard University

FLORIDA
- Embry-Riddle Aeronautical University
- Florida A & M University
- Florida Institute of Technology
- Florida International University
- Florida Southern College
- Florida State University
- University of Central Florida
- University of Florida
- University of South Florida
- University of Tampa
- University of West Florida

GEORGIA
- Augusta State University
- Columbus State University
- Fort Valley State University
- Georgia Institute of Technology
- Georgia Military College
- Georgia Southern University
- Georgia State University
- North Georgia College
- University of Georgia

GUAM
- University of Guam

HAWAII
- University of Hawaii at Manoa

IDAHO
- Boise State University
- University of Idaho

ILLINOIS
- Eastern Illinois University
- Illinois State University
- Northern Illinois University
- Southern Illinois University at Carbondale
- Southern Illinois University at Edwardsville
- University of Illinois at Chicago
- University of Illinois at Urbana-Champaign
- Western Illinois University
- Wheaton College

INDIANA
- Ball State University
- Indiana University at Bloomington
- Indiana University/Purdue University Indianapolis
- Purdue University/West Lafayette
- Rose-Hulman Institute of Technology
- University of Notre Dame

IOWA
- Iowa State University
- University of Iowa
- University of Northern Iowa

KANSAS
- Kansas State University
- Pittsburg State University
- University of Kansas

KENTUCKY
- Eastern Kentucky University
- Morehead State University
- University of Kentucky
- University of Louisville
- Western Kentucky University

LOUISIANA
- Grambling State University
- Louisiana State University
- Northwestern State University
- Southern University and A & M College
- Tulane University

MAINE
- University of Maine

MARYLAND
- Bowie State University
- Johns Hopkins University
- Loyola College
- McDaniel College
- Morgan State University
- University of Maryland at College Park

MASSACHUSETTS
- Boston University
- Massachusetts Institute of Technology
- Northeastern University
- University of Massachusetts
- Worcester Polytechnic Institute

MICHIGAN
- Central Michigan University
- Eastern Michigan University
- Michigan State University
- Michigan Technological University
- Northern Michigan University
- University of Michigan
- Western Michigan University

MINNESOTA
- Minnesota State University, Mankato
- Saint John's University Minnesota
- University of Minnesota/Twin Cities

MISSISSIPPI
- Alcorn State University
- Jackson State University
- Mississippi State University
- University of Mississippi
- University of Southern Mississippi

MISSOURI
- Central Missouri State University
- Lincoln University

- Missouri Western State University
- Southwest Missouri State University
- Truman State University
- University of Missouri/Columbia
- University of Missouri/Rolla
- Washington University
- Wentworth Military Academy & Junior College

MONTANA

- Montana State University
- University of Montana

NEBRASKA

- Creighton University
- University of Nebraska at Lincoln

NEVADA

- University of Nevada/Reno

NEW HAMPSHIRE

- University of New Hampshire

NEW JERSEY

- Princeton University
- Rutgers University
- Seton Hall University

NEW MEXICO

- New Mexico Military Institute
- New Mexico State University
- University of New Mexico

NEW YORK

- Canisius College
- Clarkson University
- Cornell University
- Fordham University
- Hofstra University
- Niagara University
- Rochester Institute of Technology
- Saint Bonaventure University
- Saint John's University New York
- State University of New York/Brockport
- Syracuse University

NORTH CAROLINA

- Appalachian State University
- Campbell University
- Duke University
- East Carolina University
- Elizabeth City State University
- North Carolina Agricultural and Technical State University
- North Carolina State University
- Saint Augustine's College
- University of North Carolina at Chapel Hill
- University of North Carolina at Charlotte
- Wake Forest University

NORTH DAKOTA

- North Dakota State University
- University of North Dakota

OHIO

- Bowling Green State University
- Capital University
- Central State University
- John Carroll University

- Kent State University
- Ohio State University
- Ohio University
- University of Akron
- University of Cincinnati
- University of Dayton
- University of Toledo
- Wright State University
- Xavier University

OKLAHOMA

- Cameron University
- Oklahoma State University
- University of Central Oklahoma
- University of Oklahoma

OREGON

- Oregon State University
- University of Oregon
- University of Portland

PENNSYLVANIA

- Bucknell University
- Dickinson College
- Drexel University
- Edinboro University of Pennsylvania
- Gannon University
- Indiana University of Pennsylvania
- Lehigh University
- Lock Haven University of Pennsylvania
- Pennsylvania State University
- Shippensburg University of Pennsylvania
- Slippery Rock University
- Temple University
- University of Pittsburgh
- University of Scranton
- Valley Forge Military Academy & College
- Widener University

PUERTO RICO

- University of Puerto Rico/Mayaguez
- University of Puerto Rico/Río Piedras

RHODE ISLAND

- Providence College
- University of Rhode Island

SOUTH CAROLINA

- The Citadel
- Clemson University
- Furman University
- Presbyterian College
- South Carolina State University
- University of South Carolina
- Wofford College

SOUTH DAKOTA

- South Dakota School of Mines and Technology
- South Dakota State University
- University of South Dakota

TENNESSEE

- Austin Peay State University
- Carson-Newman College
- East Tennessee State University
- Middle Tennessee State University
- Tennessee Technological University
- University of Memphis

- University of Tennessee at Knoxville
- University of Tennessee at Martin
- Vanderbilt University

TEXAS

- Prairie View A & M University
- Saint Mary's University
- Sam Houston State University
- Southwest Texas State University
- Stephen F. Austin State University
- Tarleton State University
- Texas A & M University
- Texas A & M University at Kingsville
- Texas Christian University
- Texas Tech University
- University of Houston
- University of Texas at Arlington
- University of Texas at Austin
- University of Texas at El Paso
- University of Texas at San Antonio
- University of Texas-Pan American

UTAH

- Brigham Young University
- University of Utah
- Weber State University

VERMONT

- Norwich University
- University of Vermont

VIRGINIA

- College of William and Mary
- George Mason University
- Hampton University
- James Madison University
- Norfolk State University
- Old Dominion University
- University of Richmond
- University of Virginia
- Virginia Military Institute
- Virginia Polytechnic Institute and State University
- Virginia State University

WASHINGTON

- Central Washington University
- Eastern Washington University
- Gonzaga University
- Pacific Lutheran University
- Seattle University
- University of Washington
- Washington State University

WEST VIRGINIA

- Marshall University
- West Virginia State College
- West Virginia University

WISCONSIN

- Marquette University
- University of Wisconsin/La Crosse
- University of Wisconsin/Madison
- University of Wisconsin/Oshkosh
- University of Wisconsin/Stevens Point

WYOMING

- University of Wyoming

NAVY

The NROTC Program was established to educate and train qualified young men and women for service as commissioned officers in the unrestricted line Naval Reserve or Marine Corps Reserve. Two programs are available: the NROTC Scholarship Program and the NROTC College Program.

As the largest single source of Navy and Marine Corps officers, the NROTC Scholarship Program plays an important role in preparing young men and women for leadership and management positions in an increasingly technical Navy and Marine Corps. The NROTC Scholarship Program is available to qualified students who graduate from high school before August 1 of the year they intend to start college.

Selected applicants for the NROTC Scholarship Program are awarded scholarships through a highly competitive national selection process, and receive full tuition, books, fees, and other financial benefits at many of the country's leading colleges and universities. Upon graduation, midshipmen are commissioned as officers in the unrestricted line Naval Reserve or Marine Corps Reserve.

Students selected for the NROTC Scholarship Program make their own arrangements for college enrollment and room and board, and take the normal course load required by the college or university for degree completion. Additionally, scholarship midshipmen are required to follow specific academic guidelines. Full information concerning the NROTC Scholarship Program is available from any of the colleges and universities with NROTC units or from Navy and Marine Corps recruiters.

The NROTC College Program may be either two or four years. Additional points include:

- Applicants selected from students already attending or accepted by colleges with NROTC programs.
- Pays for uniforms and instructional fees for naval science courses.
- Students selected for "advance standing" receive a stipend for a maximum of 20 months. Advance standing is only available starting in the junior year of college. Stipend per academic month is $350 in junior year and $400 in senior year.
- Students will complete naval science and other university courses, a few specific university courses, and attend one summer training session, normally at sea for Navy Officers, and in Quantico, VA for Marine Corps-option midshipmen.
- Four-year applicants apply through professors of naval science upon commencement of freshman year.
- Two-year applicants apply before spring of sophomore year.
- When accepted, two-year applicants will attend a six-and-a-half week Naval Science Institute program in Newport, RI during the summer between sophomore and junior years.
- Upon graduation, two- and four-year College Program midshipmen may be commissioned ensigns in the Naval Reserve or second lieutenants in the Marine Corps Reserves.
- An obligation of eight years commissioned service, at least three of which must be active duty.

The following list shows the colleges and universities that have an NROTC unit on campus. Many more institutions offer the program through cross-town arrangements. We recommend that you visit *http://www.nrotc.navy.mil* for a listing of participating colleges and universities. Contact the schools directly for the most current and accurate information.

ALABAMA
- Auburn University

ARIZONA
- University of Arizona

CALIFORNIA
- San Diego State University
- University of California/Berkeley
- University of California/Los Angeles
- University of San Diego
- University of Southern California

COLORADO
- University of Colorado at Boulder

DISTRICT OF COLUMBIA
- George Washington University

FLORIDA
- Embry Riddle Aeronautical University
- Florida A & M University
- Jacksonville University
- University of Florida
- University of South Florida

GEORGIA
- Georgia Institute of Technology
- Morehouse College
- Savannah State College

IDAHO
- University of Idaho

ILLINOIS
- Illinois Institute of Technology
- Northwestern University
- University of Illinois at Urbana-Champaign

INDIANA
- Purdue University/West Lafayette
- University of Notre Dame

IOWA
- Iowa State University

KANSAS
- University of Kansas

LOUISIANA
- Southern University and A & M College
- Tulane University

MAINE
- Maine Maritime Academy

MASSACHUSETTS
- Boston University
- College of the Holy Cross
- Massachusetts Institute of Technology

MICHIGAN
- University of Michigan/Ann Arbor

MINNESOTA
- University of Minnesota

MISSISSIPPI
- University of Mississippi

MISSOURI
- University of Missouri

NEBRASKA
- University of Nebraska at Lincoln

NEW MEXICO
- University of New Mexico

NEW YORK
- Cornell University
- Rensselaer Polytechnic Institute
- State University of New York/Maritime College
- University of Rochester

NORTH CAROLINA
- Duke University
- North Carolina State University
- University of North Carolina at Chapel Hill

OHIO
- Miami University
- Ohio State University

OKLAHOMA

- University of Oklahoma

OREGON

- Oregon State University

PENNSYLVANIA

- Carnegie Mellon University
- Pennsylvania State University Park Campus
- University of Pennsylvania
- Villanova University

SOUTH CAROLINA

- The Citadel
- University of South Carolina

TENNESSEE

- University of Memphis
- Vanderbilt University

TEXAS

- Prairie View A & M University
- Rice University
- Texas A & M University
- University of Texas at Austin

UTAH

- University of Utah

VERMONT

- Norwich University

VIRGINIA

- Hampton University
- Norfolk State University
- Old Dominion University
- University of Virginia
- Virginia Military Institute
- Virginia Polytechnic Institute and State University

WASHINGTON

- University of Washington

WISCONSIN

- Marquette University
- University of Wisconsin/Madison

ENROLLMENT IN CANADIAN SCHOOLS

In 2001, Canadian universities hosted a record 42,000 full-time foreign students, up by more than thirty percent in just two years. The Fall 2003 number is estimated to be well over 50,000. International students account for 5% of full-time undergraduate students and 17% at the graduate level. Most Canadian universities admit international students—although some have a quota on the number they will accept—and will give interested students information on how their academic qualifications are equated with Canadian requirements.

The Association of Universities and Colleges of Canada (AUCC) represents 93 universities and university-level colleges. These institutions account for almost 99 percent of the total university enrollment in Canada. Almost all Canadian colleges are coeducational. Of the 93, 18 use French as the language of instruction, six use both French and English, and the rest primarily use English. This section contains individual profiles for those English-language universities that enroll more than 10,000 students.

Affiliated with each of these universities are a number of general, theological, or residential colleges, which also have been listed here. The names and addresses of the three French-speaking colleges with enrollments of more than 10,000 may be found at the end of this introduction.

Admissions Requirements

Each university has its own entrance requirements and will assess you on an individual basis. The university will determine the equivalency of your academic credentials. There is no nationwide set of entrance exams. For more details about this or any other part of the application process, contact the registrar at the university you wish to attend.

Admissions Procedure

Once you have determined which universities meet your needs, contact the registrar's office at each institution to obtain an application for a bachelor's program or a professional degree. If you anticipate pursuing postgraduate studies in Canada, you may obtain more information by contacting the dean of graduate studies at the universities that interest you. It is important to apply early. Remember that the Canadian academic year usually starts in September. Some programs, however, do admit students to courses that start in January and May.

The AUCC's web site *www.aucc.ca* has links to the web pages of all Canadian universities, the majority of which accept applications via e-mail.

To study at a Canadian university, you will need a study permit. You may also need a visitor's visa, which will be issued to you at the same time as your study permit. To apply for a study permit, please contact your nearest Canadian diplomatic post.

You will have to arrange for medical coverage before you arrive in Canada. Medical coverage varies from province to province and sometimes from university to university within each province. Please ask an official at the nearest Canadian diplomatic post for detailed information. Also, check whether the universities you are applying to have any medical insurance plans for international students.

Degrees Offered

Canadian universities, like those in the United States, grant three levels of degrees: bachelor's and first professional, master's, and doctoral as well as undergraduate certificates and diplomas and graduate diploma programs.

Earning the first degree can take three to five years. A general, or unspecialized, program leading to a Bachelor of Arts or Bachelor of Science usually can be completed in three years. An honors degree, earned in a specialized program, usually requires four years. Students must meet more rigorous requirements to enter an honors-degree program and must maintain high grades to remain in it. First professional degrees in some fields may take more than four years to earn, and students may be required to undertake two or three years of university study before enrolling in the professional program. Students who enter graduate programs with a general degree usually must study a year longer than those with honors degrees. Undergraduate diplomas and certificates may be from one to three years' duration and may (although not necessarily) be used as a basis for entry to a degree program. A graduate diploma may be considered as conferring a qualification that is intermediate between the bachelor's (or first professional degree) and master's degree. It may be completed in as little as two or as long as three academic years.

Organizations

Virtually all universities have organizations for international students, and sponsor international student centers and advisers. There also are national organizations that aid international students, including the World University Service of Canada and the Canadian Bureau for International Education, which arranges for representatives to meet international students arriving at Canadian airports.

Tuition, Fees, and Aid

Universities and colleges are heavily subsidized by provincial and federal governments, and tuition fees actually cover one third of university operating costs. Canadian institutions charge different fees for different programs, unlike American institutions, which charge the same tuition regardless of the program of study. Each profile in this book lists the range of tuitions, which may or may not include student fees. Some universities have higher fees for international students, and where that is the case, the profile includes just the international fees. All costs are given in Canadian (CDN) dollars. In all cases, you should check with the university in which you are interested to obtain the most up-to-date information about tuition and room-and-board charges.

Most awards available to international students through Canadian universities or from the Canadian government are restricted to graduate and post graduate studies. Some of the scholarship programs for international students to study in Canada include the Commonwealth Scholarship and Fellowship Plan, the Canadian International Development Agency awards and the Government of Canada awards program of cultural exchanges. Students interested in applying for aid should contact a Canadian diplomatic mission in their home countries and, for information on cultural exchange programs, their own nation's education department or ministry.

Additional Information

Association of Universities and Colleges of Canada
600-350 Albert Street
Ottawa, ON, Canada K1R 1B1
(613) 563-3961
Fax: (613) 563-9745
www.aucc.org
(publications include *Notes for International Students, The Directory of Canadian Universities*)

Canadian Bureau for International Education
220 Laurier Avenue W., Ste. 1100
Ottawa, ON Canada K1P 5Z9
(613) 237-4820
Fax: (613) 237-1073
www.cbie.ca
(publications include *The National Report on International Students in Canada*)

Canadian International Development Agency
200 promenade du Portage
Gatineau, QC Canada K1A 0G4
(819) 997-5006
(800) 230-6349
Fax: (819) 953-6088
www.acdi-cida.gc.ca

Citizenship and Immigration Canada
Ottawa, ON Canada K1A 0J9
www.cic.gc.ca
(publications include *Studying in Canada: A Guide to Foreign Students*)

Consulate General of Canada
1251 Avenue of the Americas
New York, NY 10020-1175
(212) 596-1628
Fax: (212) 596-1628
www.dfait-maeci.ca/new_york/

Social Sciences and Humanities Research Council
350 Albert Street, P.O. Box 1610
Ottawa, ON Canada K1P 6G4
(613) 992-0691
Fax: (613) 992-1787
www.sshrc.ca

Statistics Canada
Statistical Reference Centre (National Capital Region)
R.H. Coast Building, Lobby
Holland Avenue
Ottawa, ON Canada K1A 0T6
(800) 263-1136 or (613) 951-8116 (outside Canada & USA)
Fax: (877) 287-4369 (toll free)
www.statcan.ca
(publications include *Education Quarterly Review* and *Education in Canada*)

World University Service of Canada
1404 Scott Street
Ottawa, ON Canada K1Y 4M8
(613) 798-7477
Fax: (613) 798-0990
www.wusc.ca

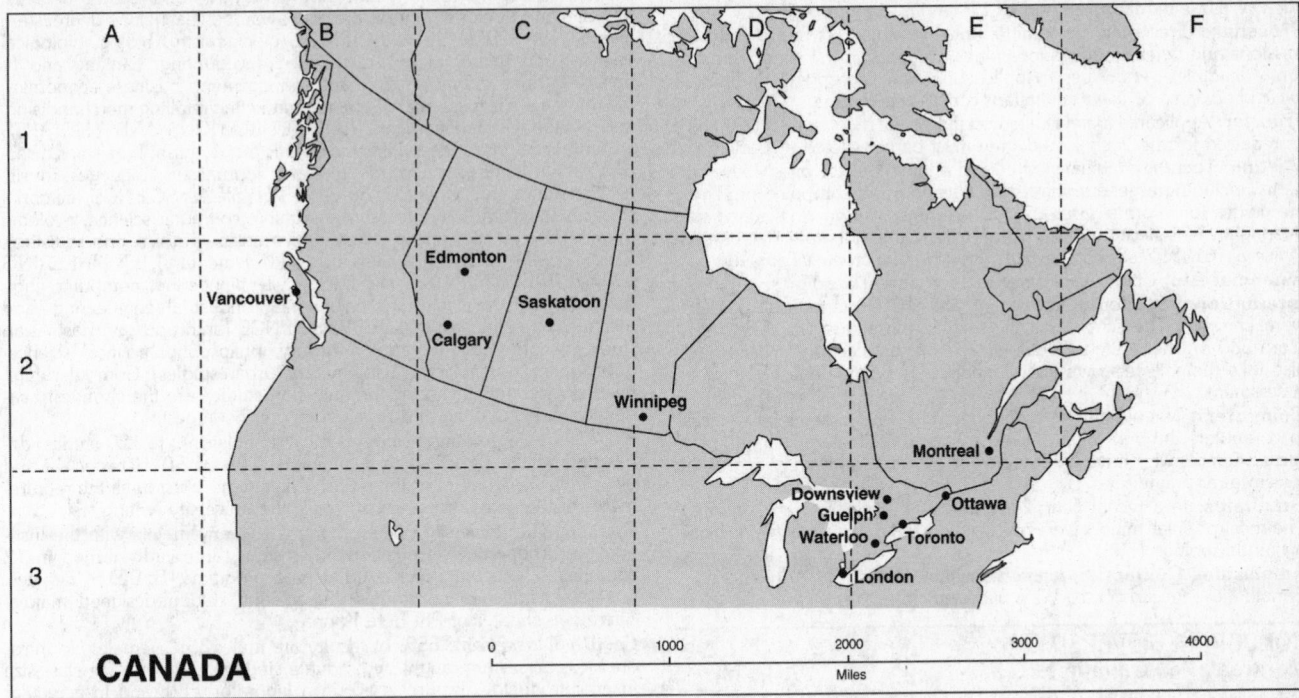

CANADA

CARLETON UNIVERSITY
Ottawa, ON, Canada K1S 5B6

E-3

(613) 520-3609
Fax: (613) 520-3517

Full-time: 5550 men, 5500 women
Part-time: 2700 men, 2550 women
Graduate: 1320 men, 1250 women
Year: semesters, summer session
Application Deadline: see profile

Freshman Class: n/av
SAT I: required

Faculty: 676
Ph.D.s: 80%
Student/Faculty: 16 to 1
Tuition: $4600 CDN ($10,000)
CDN
Room & Board: $6000 CDN

Carleton University, founded in 1942, is a public institution operated by the province of Ontario. There are 14 undergraduate and 14 graduate degree programs offered. There are 8 undergraduate schools and 1 graduate school. Figures in the above capsule and in this profile are approximate. The library contains 1.7 million volumes, 1.3 million microform items, and 20,000 audio/video tapes/CDs, and subscribes to 9000 periodicals. Computerized library services include the card catalog, interlibrary loans, and database searching. Special learning facilities include a learning resource center, art gallery, radio station, and an environmental biology laboratories annex. The 152-acre campus is in an urban area in Ottawa. Including any residence halls, there are 29 buildings.

Student Life: 85% of undergraduates are from Ontario. The average age of freshmen is 20.

Housing: 2180 students can be accommodated in college housing, which includes single-sex and coed dorms. On-campus housing is available on a lottery system for upperclassmen. Priority is given to out-of-town students. 89% of students commute. All students may keep cars.

Activities: There are no fraternities or sororities. There are 80 groups on campus, including chess, computers, drama, ethnic, gay, international, newspaper, pep band, photography, political, radio and TV, religious, and student government. Popular campus events include Orientation.

Sports: There are 9 intercollegiate sports for men and 9 for women, and 4 intramural sports for men and 3 for women. Facilities include a physical recreation center with an Olympic-size pool, squash courts, Nautilus and fitness centers, and a double gym. Outdoor tennis courts and playing fields are also available.

Disabled Students: 98% of the campus is accessible. Wheelchair ramps, elevators, special parking, specially equipped rest rooms, lowered drinking fountains, and lowered telephones are available. There are also automatic doors in some buildings, tactile control panels in elevators, tunnels connecting buildings, specially equipped residence rooms, and attendant services.

Services: Counseling and information services are available, as is tutoring in most subjects. There is a reader service for the blind. Study skills workshops are available in essay writing and preparation and writing of exams. There is special exam scheduling and a study center for disabled students.

Campus Safety and Security: Measures include 24-hour foot and vehicle patrol, security escort services, pamphlets/posters/films, and emergency telephones. There are lighted pathways/sidewalks and electronic access to residences.

Programs of Study: Carleton confers B.A., B.Sc., B.Arch., B.Comm., B.C.S., B.Eng., B.Hum., B.I.B., B.I.D., B.J., B.Math., B.Mus., B.P.A.P.H., and B.S.W. degrees. Master's and doctoral degrees are also awarded. Bachelor's degrees are awarded in BIOLOGICAL SCIENCE (biochemistry, biology/biological science, biometrics and biostatistics, biotechnology, and neurosciences), BUSINESS (accounting, business economics, business systems analysis, human resources, international business management, management information systems, marketing and distribution, marketing/retailing/merchandising, and operations research), COMMUNICATIONS AND THE ARTS (art history and appreciation, classics, communications, communications technology, English, English literature, film arts, French, German, industrial design, Italian, journalism, linguistics, music, Russian, and Spanish), COMPUTER AND PHYSICAL SCIENCE (chemistry, computer mathematics, computer programming, computer science, earth science, geology, information sciences and systems, mathematics, physical sciences, physics, and statistics), EDUCATION (teaching English as a second/foreign language (TESOL/TEFOL)), ENGINEERING AND ENVIRONMENTAL DESIGN (aeronautical engineering, architecture, civil engineering, computer engineering, electrical/electronics engineering, engineering, engineering physics, environmental engineering, environmental science, mechanical engineering, and systems engineering), SOCIAL SCIENCE (anthropology, Canadian studies, child care/child and family studies, classical/ancient civilization, cognitive science, criminology, Eastern European studies, economics, European studies, geography, German area studies, history, human ecology, interdisciplinary studies, law, liberal arts/general studies, philosophy, political science/government, psychology, public administration, religion, social work, sociology, and women's studies). Arts, engineering, and science are the largest.

Required: Requirements for graduation vary according to programs.

Special: Carleton offers co-op programs in many majors and an exchange program with the University of Ottawa. Study abroad, internships in industrial design, dual and student-designed majors, accelerated degree programs, and interdisciplinary programs are available. The university also utilizes instructional television.

Faculty/Classroom: 69% of faculty are male; 31%, female. The average class size in an introductory lecture is 107 and in a regular course, 58.

Requirements: The SAT I is required, with a minimum composite score of 1100 (550 verbal and 550 math). Applicants must be graduates of an accredited secondary school. Architecture, humanities, and industrial design students must present a portfolio; social work students should submit a personal information form; music students must audition. Carleton requires applicants to be in the upper 25% of their class. A GPA of 3.0 is required. AP and CLEP credits are accepted.

Procedure: Freshmen are admitted to all sessions. There are early admissions and deferred admissions plans. Check with the school for current deadlines and fees. Applications are accepted on-line at www.ouac.on.ca or www.admissions.carleton.ca/intapp.

Transfer: Applicants are evaluated on individual merits. 30 of 120 credits required for the bachelor's degree must be completed at Carleton.

Visiting: There are regularly scheduled orientations for prospective students, including a general information session and campus tour. There are guides for informal visits and visitors may sit in on classes and stay overnight. To schedule a visit, contact the Undergraduate Recruitment Office at (613) 520-3663 or www.admissions.carleton.ca/Tours/tour.

Financial Aid: Check with the school for current deadlines.

International Students: In a recent year, 1015 international students were enrolled. The school actively recruits these students. They must score 580 on the written TOEFL or 237 on the electronic version and also take the college's own test, Canadian Academic English Language Assessment.

Computers: The mainframe is a Honeywell CP6. Students have access to computers through their courses. PCs are available at a number of sites. Students who have an account for the mainframe may access the system at any time.

Graduates: In a recent year, 2407 bachelor's degrees were awarded. The most popular majors were psychology (10%), law (7%), and sociology/anthropology (7%).

Admissions Contact: Suzanne Blanchard, Director of Admissions.
E-mail: liaison@carleton.ca Web: www.carleton.ca

CONCORDIA UNIVERSITY
Montreal, PQ, Canada H3G IM8
E-2
(514) 848-4971
Fax: (514) 848-2837

Full-time: 13,800 men and women	**Faculty:** 714
Part-time: 8500 men and women	**Ph.D.s:** 84%
Graduate: 4600 men and women	**Student/Faculty:** 17 to 1
Year: semesters, summer session	**Tuition:** $3000 CDN ($18,000) CDN
Application Deadline: see profile	**Room & Board:** $5700 CDN
Freshman Class: n/av	
SAT I or ACT: recommended	

Concordia University, established in 1974, is a public institution operated by the province of Quebec. There are 5 undergraduate schools and 1 graduate school. Figures in the above capsule and in this profile are approximate. In addition to regional accreditation, Concordia University has baccalaureate program accreditation with AACSB. The 2 libraries contain 3 million volumes, 75,000 microform items, and 2000 audio/video tapes/CDs, and subscribe to 5500 periodicals. Computerized library services include the card catalog, interlibrary loans, and database searching. Special learning facilities include a learning resource center, art gallery, radio station, TV station, greenhouse, audiovisual instruction service, and specialized research center. The 1555-acre campus is in an urban area in downtown Montreal and in suburban Loyola. Including any residence halls, there are 80 buildings.

Student Life: 90% of undergraduates are from Quebec. The average age of freshmen is 21; all undergraduates, 25. 11% do not continue beyond their first year; 52% remain to graduate.

Housing: 144 students can be accommodated in college housing, which includes single-sex and coed dorms, off-campus apartments, fraternity houses, and sorority houses. On-campus housing is available on a first-come, first-served basis. Priority is given to out-of-town students. 98% of students commute. All students may keep cars.

Activities: 1% of men belong to 3 national fraternities; 1% of women belong to 3 national sororities. There are 125 groups on campus, including art, choir, chorale, chorus, computers, dance, drama, ethnic, film, gay, honors, international, jazz band, literary magazine, musical theater, newspaper, orchestra, photography, political, professional, radio and TV, religious, social, social service, student government, symphony, and yearbook.

Sports: There are 9 intercollegiate sports for men and 7 for women, and 16 intramural sports for men and 12 for women. Facilities include an arena, a gym, and a football stadium.

Disabled Students: 75% of the campus is accessible. Wheelchair ramps, elevators, special parking, specially equipped rest rooms, special class scheduling, lowered drinking fountains, lowered telephones, and assistance for hearing/visual/mobility impaired are available.

Services: Counseling and information services are available, as is tutoring in most subjects. There is a reader service for the blind and remedial math, reading, and writing.

Campus Safety and Security: Measures include 24-hour foot and vehicle patrol, self-defense education, security escort services, and shuttle

buses. There are informal discussions, pamphlets/posters/films, emergency telephones, and lighted pathways/sidewalks.

Programs of Study: Concordia University confers B.A., B.Admin., B.Comm., B.Comp.Sci., B.Ed., B.Eng., B.F.A., and B.S.C. degrees. Master's and doctoral degrees are also awarded. Bachelor's degrees are awarded in BIOLOGICAL SCIENCE (biochemistry, biology/biological science, and microbiology), BUSINESS (accounting, banking and finance, business administration and management, business economics, international business management, marketing/retailing/merchandising, and personnel management), COMMUNICATIONS AND THE ARTS (communications, dance, design, dramatic arts, English, English as a second/foreign language, film arts, fine arts, journalism, languages, music, and photography), COMPUTER AND PHYSICAL SCIENCE (actuarial science, chemistry, computer programming, computer science, geology, information sciences and systems, mathematics, physics, and statistics), EDUCATION (art, early childhood, and elementary), ENGINEERING AND ENVIRONMENTAL DESIGN (civil engineering, computer engineering, electrical/electronics engineering, industrial engineering, and mechanical engineering), SOCIAL SCIENCE (anthropology, East Asian studies, economics, geography, history, philosophy, political science/government, psychology, sociology, and urban studies). Computer engineering, accounting, and communication studies are the strongest academically. Accounting and psychology are the largest.

Required: To graduate, students must complete 90 to 120 credits, depending on the degree, with a minimum GPA of 2.0. Between 42 and 54 credits are required in the major. All students must fulfill the requirements of the core curriculum and take the university writing test.

Special: The university offers programs in many majors with the Institute for Co-operative Education, internships, and study abroad in 12 countries. There are accelerated degree programs, B.A.-B.S. degrees, dual majors, a general studies degree, and student-designed majors. There is a chapter of Phi Beta Kappa.

Faculty/Classroom: 65% of faculty are male; 35%, female. No introductory courses are taught by graduate students. The average class size in an introductory lecture is 50; in a laboratory, 50; and in a regular course, 50.

Requirements: The SAT I or ACT is recommended. In addition, applicants must be graduates of an accredited secondary school. The GED is accepted. An essay, an interview, a portfolio, or an audition may be required for some programs. Concordia University requires applicants to be in the upper 30% of their class. A GPA of 2.5 is required. AP and CLEP credits are accepted. Important factors in the admissions decision are advanced placement or honor courses and recommendations by school officials.

Procedure: Freshmen are admitted to all sessions. There are early decision and early admissions plans. Early decision applications should be filed by February 1; regular applications, by March 1 for fall entry, November 1 for winter entry, and April 15 for summer entry, along with a $50 fee. The university accepts all in-state residents. Notification is sent on a rolling basis. A waiting list is an active part of the admissions procedure.

Transfer: Applicants must have a minimum GPA of 2.2. 45 of 90 credits required for the bachelor's degree must be completed at Concordia University.

Visiting: There are regularly scheduled orientations for prospective students. There are guides for informal visits and visitors may sit in on classes. To schedule a visit, contact the Office of Student Recruitment at (514) 848-4779 or tours@vaxz.concordia.ca.

Financial Aid: Check with the school for application deadlines.

International Students: The school actively recruits international students. They must score 550 on the written TOEFL or 213 on the electronic version, or take the MELAB, or the college's own test.

Computers: The mainframe is a CDC CYBER 835. There are 300 PCs and more than 100 time-sharing terminals. These include PC and Mac labs, Internet access, terminal access to UNIX and open VMS-based multi-user systems, and modem dial-in access. All students may access the system from 8:30 A.M. to 11:30 P.M. There are no time limits and no fees.

Admissions Contact: Pete Regimbald, Assistant Registrar.
E-mail: admreg@alcor.concordia.ca Web: www.concordia.ca

DALHOUSIE UNIVERSITY
Halifax, NS, Canada B3H 4H6
E-2
(902) 494-2148
Fax: (902) 494-1630

Total enrollment: 16,040 men and women	**Faculty:** 1113
	Ph.D.s: 90%
Year: semesters, summer session	**Student/Faculty:** n/av
Application Deadline: June 1	**Tuition:** $8824 CDN ($13,324 CDN)
	Room & Board: $5018 CDN
Freshman Class: n/av	
SAT I: required	

Dalhousie University, founded in 1818, is a public, nonsectarian institution offering undergraduate, graduate, and professional programs. There are 11 undergraduate schools and 1 graduate school. The 4 libraries contain 1,270,000 volumes, 340,000 microform items, and 13,800 audio/video tapes/CDs, and subscribe to 8182 periodicals. Computerized library services include the card catalog, interlibrary loans, database searching, and Internet access. Special learning facilities include a learning resource center, art gallery, natural history museum, planetarium, radio station, science museum, aquatron, slowpoke nuclear reactor, and super computer. The 80-acre campus is in an urban area in Halifax. Including any residence halls, there are 102 buildings.

Student Life: 60% of undergraduates are from the Province of Nova Scotia. Students are from 27 states and 107 foreign countries. The average age of freshmen is 19. 14% do not continue beyond their first year.

Housing: 2200 students can be accommodated in college housing, which includes single-sex and coed dorms, on-campus apartments, off-campus apartments, and married-student housing. In addition, there are language houses and special-interest houses. On-campus housing is available on a first-come, first-served basis and is available on a lottery system for upperclassmen. Priority is given to out-of-town students. 80% of students commute. All students may keep cars.

Activities: There are 8 national fraternities and 1 national sorority. There are 200 groups on campus, including cheerleading, chess, chorale, computers, dance, debate, drama, ethnic, gay, international, musical theater, newspaper, photography, political, professional, radio and TV, religious, social, student government, and yearbook. Popular campus events include Frosh Week and Winter Carnival.

Sports: There are 8 intercollegiate sports for men and 8 for women, and 30 intramural sports for men and 30 for women. Facilities include an athletic center, an arena, indoor and outdoor tennis courts, a track, a playing field, an Olympic-size swimming pool, squash and volleyball courts, a climbing wall, a soccer field, a hockey rink, a dance studio, and weight rooms.

Disabled Students: 70% of the campus is accessible. Wheelchair ramps, elevators, special parking, specially equipped rest rooms, special class scheduling, lowered drinking fountains, and lowered telephones are available. The Office of the Vice President of Student Services is also available to provide assistance on an individual basis.

Services: Counseling and information services are available, as is tutoring in most subjects. There is a reader service for the blind and remedial math and writing.

Campus Safety and Security: Measures include 24-hour foot and vehicle patrol, self-defense education, security escort services, and shuttle buses. There are informal discussions, pamphlets/posters/films, and lighted pathways/sidewalks. The university also offers a student-organized campus patrol program.

Programs of Study: Dalhousie confers B.A., B.Sc., B.C.D., B.C.S., B.Comm., B.Eng., B.Hsc., B.Laws, B.Mgmt, B.Mus., B.Recreation and Health Ed., B.S.C.Kinesiology, B.S.N., B.S.O.T., B.S.Pharm., B.S.Physiotherapy, and B.S.W. degrees. Master's and doctoral degrees are also awarded. Bachelor's degrees are awarded in BIOLOGICAL SCIENCE (biochemistry, biology/biological science, marine biology, microbiology, and neurosciences), BUSINESS (business economics and recreation and leisure services), COMMUNICATIONS AND THE ARTS (classics, dramatic arts, English, French, German, music, Russian, and Spanish), COMPUTER AND PHYSICAL SCIENCE (chemistry, computer science, earth science, mathematics, physics, and statistics), EDUCATION (health), ENGINEERING AND ENVIRONMENTAL DESIGN (engineering), HEALTH PROFESSIONS (dental hygiene, nursing, occupational therapy, pharmacy, physical therapy, predentistry, and premedicine), SOCIAL SCIENCE (economics, history, international studies, law, philosophy, physical fitness/movement, political science/government, psychology, religion, social work, sociology, and women's studies). Science, health science, and engineering are the strongest academically. Arts, science, and commerce are the largest.

Required: To graduate, most students must complete a minimum of 15 full-year courses, including at least 5 in the major. Most students are required to take some classes outside their area of study. Programs vary in requirements.

Special: Co-op programs may be arranged in many majors. The university offers cross-registration, study abroad in 28 countries, and accelerated degree programs. Student-designed majors are available. The honors programs provide an extra year of advanced study to qualified students. A 4-year engineering degree is offered. The Science Foundation Year uses an integrated approach to teach a variety of first-year sciences. B.A.-B.S. degrees and dual majors are possible. There is a freshman honors program and 26 departmental honors programs.

Faculty/Classroom: 60% of faculty are male; 40%, female. The average class size in an introductory lecture is 65; in a laboratory, 30; and in a regular course, 40.

Requirements: The SAT I is required, with a minimum combined score of 1100. In addition, grade 12 credit in English is required. Students are expected to have at least a B average. An audition is necessary for music and theater students. AP credits are accepted. Important factors in the admissions decision are advanced placement or honor courses, leadership record, and recommendations by school officials.

Procedure: Freshmen are admitted to all sessions. There are early decision, early admissions, and deferred admissions plans. Early decision applications should be filed by March 15; regular applications, by June 1 for fall entry along with a $45 CDN fee. Notification of early decision is sent March 1; regular decision, on a rolling basis.

Transfer: Applicants are assessed on an individual basis. They should have grades of C or 65% and higher from a recognized university. 7 1/2 or 10 courses of 15 or 20 required for the bachelor's degree must be completed at Dalhousie.

Visiting: There are regularly scheduled orientations for prospective students, including a 1 hour walking tour of campus and a meeting with an admissions officer. There are guides for informal visits and visitors may sit in on classes. To schedule a visit, contact the campus tour coordinator at (902) 494-2587 or *campus.tours@dal.ca*.

International Students: In a recent year, there were 470 international students enrolled. The school actively recruits these students. Students applying on a visa from outside Canada or the United States must take the TOEFL if English is not their first language of communication or education. They must score 580 on the written TOEFL or 237 on the electronic version and also take the SAT I, scoring 1100.

Computers: The mainframes are a VAX 8800 (VMS operating system), an IBM 4381, and an Alliant 6400. There are a number of Sun workstations (UNIX-based) and high-end graphics workstations. Several PC labs are available to students in the library and there are other labs throughout the campus, most connected in a local area network. All students may access the system at any time. There are no time limits and no fees.

Graduates: In a recent year, 2062 bachelor's degrees were awarded. The most popular majors were law (7%), biology (6%), and psychology (6%).

Admissions Contact: Susan Tanner, Associate Registrar Admissions and Awards. E-mail: *admissions@dal.ca* Web: *www.dal.ca*

LAVAL UNIVERSITY
E-2
Quebec, PQ, Canada G1K 7P4
(418) 656-2764
(877) 785-2825; Fax: (418) 656-5216

Full-time: 8081 men, 11,563 women	**Faculty:** 1417
Part-time: 3566 men, 5529 women	**Ph.D.s:** 90%
Graduate: 3845 men, 4521 women	**Student/Faculty:** 14 to 1
Year: semesters, summer session	**Tuition:** $2016 CDN ($10,866 CDN)
Application Deadline: March 1	**Room & Board:** $8000 CDN

Freshman Class: 28,771 applied, 21,063 accepted, 10,882 enrolled
SAT I or ACT: not required

Laval University, founded in 1852, is the oldest French-language university in North America. It offers undergraduate and graduate programs through 17 faculties and 5 institutes. There are 16 undergraduate and 17 graduate schools. In addition to regional accreditation, Laval University has baccalaureate program accreditation with AACSB, ACU, and AUCC. The 2 libraries contain 3,400,000 volumes and 67,832 audio/video tapes/CDs, and subscribe to 17,625 periodicals. Computerized library services include the card catalog, interlibrary loans, database searching, and Internet access. Special learning facilities include a learning resource center, art gallery, natural history museum, radio station, language lab, and business simulations. The 465-acre campus is in an urban area 2 miles west of old Quebec City. Including any residence halls, there are 32 buildings.

Student Life: 94% of undergraduates are from Quebec. Students are from 155 foreign countries. The average age of all undergraduates is 26.

Housing: 2400 students can be accommodated in college housing, which includes single-sex and coed on-campus apartments. On-campus housing is available on a first-come, first-served basis. All students may keep cars.

Activities: There are no fraternities or sororities. There are 225 groups on campus, including art, band, chess, choir, chorale, computers, dance, drama, ethnic, film, forensics, gay, international, jazz band, literary magazine, musical theater, newspaper, opera, orchestra, photography, political, radio and TV, religious, social, social service, student government, and symphony. Popular campus events include Thematic Weeks, Rendez-vous Laval, and Student Festivals.

Sports: There are 13 intercollegiate sports for men and 10 for women, and 7 intramural sports for men and 7 for women. Facilities include a covered stadium with a 200-meter running track and 4 tennis courts; a 50-meter swimming pool with a 10-meter diving tower; a double ice arena; 1 triple and 2 single gyms; 4 squash courts; 4 handball and racquetball courts; judo, karate, and self-defense rooms; a dance studio; an open-air stadium with a 400-meter running track; softball, football, and soccer fields; 6 outdoor tennis courts; 3 physical training rooms; a golf driving range; an indoor golf practice room; 2 outdoor basketball courts; a 1-kilometer hiking trail; and a jogging track.

Disabled Students: 95% of the campus is accessible. Wheelchair ramps, elevators, special parking, specially equipped rest rooms, special class scheduling, lowered drinking fountains, lowered telephones, teletype machines for the deaf, computerized classrooms for the visually disabled, electric doors, sidewalks adjusted for physically disabled students, elevators equipped with speaking devices, and a campus plan in braille are available.

Services: There is a reader service for the blind and remedial math and writing. Tutoring in French grammar is available.

Campus Safety and Security: Measures include 24-hour foot and vehicle patrol, security escort services, informal discussions, and pamphlets/posters/films. There are emergency telephones and lighted pathways/sidewalks. Other services include 24-hour camera surveillance in pedestrian tunnels and trained evacuating teams in all buildings. Security training for social events is offered to all student associations.

Programs of Study: Laval University confers B.A., B.Sc., B.A.A., B.A.V., B.Ed., B.Ing., B.Mus., B.Pharm., B.Sc.A., B.Sc.Arch., B.Serv.Soc., B.Th., and LL.B. degrees. Master's and doctoral degrees are also awarded. Bachelor's degrees are awarded in AGRICULTURE (agricultural business management, agricultural economics, agronomy, forest engineering, forestry and related sciences, and wood science), BIOLOGICAL SCIENCE (biochemistry, biology/biological science, microbiology, and nutrition), BUSINESS (business administration and management), COMMUNICATIONS AND THE ARTS (art, art history and appreciation, communications, dramatic arts, English, English as a second/foreign language, French, languages, linguistics, literature, music, and visual and performing arts), COMPUTER AND PHYSICAL SCIENCE (actuarial science, chemistry, computer science, geology, geoscience, mathematics, physics, software engineering, and statistics), EDUCATION (art, athletic training, early childhood, education, elementary, music, physical, secondary, and technical), ENGINEERING AND ENVIRONMENTAL DESIGN (agricultural engineering, architecture, chemical engineering, civil engineering, computer engineering, electrical/electronics engineering, engineering and applied science, engineering physics, geological engineering, graphic arts technology, industrial administration/management, mechanical engineering, metallurgical engineering, and mining and mineral engineering), HEALTH PROFESSIONS (nursing, occupational therapy, pharmacy, physical therapy, predentistry, and premedicine), SOCIAL SCIENCE (anthropology, classical/ancient civilization, consumer services, counseling/psychology, economics, food science, French studies, geography, history, interdisciplinary studies, international studies, Judaic studies, law, philosophy, physical fitness/movement, political science/government, psychology, social work, sociology, Spanish studies, and theological studies). Business administration, sciences, and education are the largest.

Required: Requirements for graduation vary according to the program. A minimum GPA of 2.0 out of 4.33 is required per 30 credits.

Special: Laval offers co-op programs in forest operation, mining, metallurgical engineering, mineral engineering, and wood processing engineering, and study abroad in 65 countries. Dual majors are possible in anthropology and ethnology, economics and politics, international studies and modern languages, historical sciences and patrimonial studies, French language and professional writing, math and computer science. Intensive French courses are offered during the summer.

Faculty/Classroom: 75% of faculty are male; 25%, female. All teach undergraduates.

Admissions: 73% of the 2003-2004 applicants were accepted.

Requirements: The only general requirement is the D.E.C. (Diploma of Collegial Studies—13 years of scholarity) or the equivalent. Some programs have specific requirements. All undergraduate students (except those who are nonfrancophones) must show a sufficient knowledge of the French language to obtain their bachelor's degree.

Procedure: Freshmen are admitted to all sessions. Applications should be filed by March 1 for fall entry, September 1 for winter entry, and February 1 for summer entry, along with a $30 CDN fee. A waiting list is an active part of the admissions procedure. Applications are accepted online through the university's web site at www.ulaval.ca/reg/p4/html.

Transfer: 3386 transfer students enrolled in a recent year. Applicants must have the D.E.C. or the equivalent.

Visiting: There are regularly scheduled orientations for prospective students. There are guides for informal visits and visitors may stay overnight. To schedule a visit, contact the Information and Promotion Office.

Financial Aid: The deadline for filing freshman financial aid applications for fall entry is June 30.

International Students: There are 988 international students enrolled. The school actively recruits these students. A French proficiency test is required.

Computers: The mainframes are an IBM 7060-H50 and an IBM S/390. Access is provided by telecommunications. PCs are available in all buildings. All students may access the system 24 hours a day. There are no time limits and no fees. It is recommended that students in business administration and architecture have personal computers. An IBM ThinkPad is recommended.

Graduates: From July 1, 2002 to June 30, 2003, 4457 bachelor's degrees were awarded. The most popular majors were administration (18%), science and engineering (14%), and letters (13%). Of the 2002 graduating class, 83% were employed within 6 months of graduation.

Admissions Contact: Information and Promotion Office.
E-mail: info@vrd.ulaval.ca Web: http://www.ulaval.ca/bip

MCGILL UNIVERSITY
E-2
Montreal, PQ, Canada H3A 2T5   (514) 398-3910
Fax: (514) 398-4193

Full-time: 6702 men, 10,157 women	**Faculty:** 1414
Part-time: 1495 men, 2327 women	**Ph.D.s:** 95%
Graduate: 5746 men, 5584 women	**Student/Faculty:** 12 to 1
Year: semesters, summer session	**Tuition:** $2685 CDN ($5029 CDN)
Application Deadline: January 15	
	Room & Board: $6420 CDN

Freshman Class: 22,835 applied, 9920 accepted, 4372 enrolled
SAT I Verbal/Math: 620/560   **ACT:** 26

McGill University, founded in 1821, is a publicly funded private institution that grants undergraduate, graduate, and professional degrees. Tuition fees may vary depending on program. Higher rates are charged to international students. There are 11 undergraduate and 79 graduate schools. In addition to regional accreditation, McGill has baccalaureate program accreditation with APTA. The 14 libraries contain 3,338,367 volumes, 11,109 e-books, 1,623,988 microform items, and 571,765 audio/video tapes/CDs, and subscribe to 22,513 periodicals. Computerized library services include the card catalog, interlibrary loans, and database searching. Special learning facilities include a learning resource center, natural history museum, radio station, McCord Museum of Canadian History, Mont St. Hilaire Nature Conservation Center, herbarium, arboretum, subarctic research station, Institute of Air and Space Law, Institute of Islamic Studies, Redpath Museum of Natural History, Lyman Entomological Museum, Ecomuseum, Osler Library of the History of Medicine, and Lande Canadiana Collection. The 80-acre campus is in an urban area in downtown Montreal, with the MacDonald campus located on the far west end of the island. Including any residence halls, there are 150 buildings.

Student Life: 53% of undergraduates are from Quebec. Students are from 140 foreign countries.

Housing: 2080 students can be accommodated in college housing, which includes single-sex and coed dorms, off-campus apartments, and married-student housing. On-campus housing is available on a lottery system for upperclassmen. Priority is given to out-of-town students. 88% of students commute.

Activities: 4% of men belong to 1 local and 12 national fraternities; 2% of women belong to 4 national sororities. There are 180 groups on campus, including band, cheerleading, chess, choir, chorale, chorus, computers, dance, debate, drama, ethnic, film, gay, honors, international, jazz band, literary magazine, musical theater, newspaper, opera, orchestra, photography, political, professional, radio and TV, religious, social, social service, student government, symphony, and yearbook. Popular campus events include multicultural festivals, 4-floor parties, and music, film, and theatrical productions.

Sports: There are 23 intercollegiate sports for men and 24 for women, and 23 intramural sports for men and 15 for women. Facilities include a 20,000-seat stadium; a 1000-seat competition hall; 2 double gyms for basketball, volleyball, and badminton; 8 outdoor tennis courts; 4 indoor tennis courts; a 400-meter outdoor track and a banked 6-lane 200-meter indoor track; 2 weight-training rooms; dance, aerobics, and martial arts rooms; 1 pool; a gymnastics facility; 3 sports fields; a fitness center; a sport medicine center; and hyperbaric chamber.

Disabled Students: 80% of the campus is accessible. Wheelchair ramps, elevators, special parking, specially equipped rest rooms, special class scheduling, lowered telephones, Braille, variable-speed tape recorders, talking calculators, books on tape, exam accommodations, adapted computers (voice synthesis and voice recognition), sign language interpreters, computerized note taking, note takers, print enlargement, readers, and adapted transport are available.

Services: Counseling and information services are available, as is tutoring in every subject. There is a reader service for the blind and remedial math, reading, and writing.

Campus Safety and Security: Measures include 24-hour foot and vehicle patrol, security escort services, informal discussions, and pamphlets/posters/films. There are emergency telephones, lighted pathways/sidewalks, and Drivesafe.

Programs of Study: McGill confers B.A., B.C.L., B.Com., B.Ed., B.Eng., B.Mus., B.Sc., B.Sc.Agr., B.Sc.Agr.Eng., B.Sc.Arch., B.Sc.F.Sc., B.Sc.N., B.Sc.Nutr.Sc., B.Sc.Occ.Ther., B.Sc.Phys.Ther., B.S.W., B.Th., and LL.B. degrees. Master's and doctoral degrees are also awarded. Bachelor's degrees are awarded in AGRICULTURE (agricultural economics, agriculture, animal science, conservation and regulation, plant science, and soil science), BIOLOGICAL SCIENCE (anatomy, biochemistry, biology/biological science, botany, cell biology, environmental biology, microbiology, molecular biology, nutrition, physiology, wildlife biology, and zoology), BUSINESS (accounting, banking and finance, entrepreneurial studies, human resources, institutional management, insurance and risk management, international business management, labor studies, management information systems, management science, marketing management, and organizational behavior), COMMUNICATIONS AND THE ARTS (art history and appreciation, classics, English,

French, jazz, linguistics, modern language, music history and appreciation, music performance, music technology, music theory and composition, Russian, and Spanish), COMPUTER AND PHYSICAL SCIENCE (applied mathematics, atmospheric sciences and meteorology, chemistry, computer science, earth science, geology, geophysics and seismology, information sciences and systems, mathematics, physics, planetary and space science, and software engineering), EDUCATION (elementary, foreign languages, music, physical, secondary, special, teaching English as a second/foreign language (TESOL/TEFOL), and vocational), ENGINEERING AND ENVIRONMENTAL DESIGN (agricultural engineering, architecture, chemical engineering, civil engineering, computer engineering, electrical/electronics engineering, environmental science, mechanical engineering, metallurgical engineering, and mining and mineral engineering), HEALTH PROFESSIONS (clinical science, exercise science, nursing, occupational therapy, and physical therapy), SOCIAL SCIENCE (African studies, American studies, anthropology, Canadian studies, Caribbean studies, dietetics, East Asian studies, economics, food science, French studies, geography, German area studies, Hispanic American studies, history, humanities, international studies, Italian studies, Judaic studies, Latin American studies, law, Middle Eastern studies, philosophy, political science/government, psychology, religion, social work, sociology, Western civilization/culture, and women's studies). The faculty of arts is the largest.

Required: To graduate, students must successfully complete a required number of approved credits, usually between 90 and 120. Students must also be in satisfactory standing, with a minimum cumulative GPA of 2.0.

Special: There is cross-registration with area universities. Study abroad, work-study within the university, co-op programs in mining and metallurgical engineering, dual majors, internships, and student-designed majors are available.

Faculty/Classroom: 69% of faculty are male; 31%, female. No introductory courses are taught by graduate students. The average class size in an introductory lecture is 30; in a laboratory, 25; and in a regular course, 45.

Admissions: 43% of the 2003-2004 applicants were accepted.

Requirements: The SAT I is required. In addition, 3 SAT II: Subject tests are required. The ACT may be submitted instead of the SAT I and II. McGill requires applicants to be in the upper 25% of their class. A GPA of 3.3 is required. AP credits are accepted. Important factors in the admissions decision are advanced placement or honor courses, recommendations by school officials, and evidence of special talent.

Procedure: Freshmen are admitted in the fall. Entrance exams should be taken during the spring of the junior year and/or fall of the senior year. There is a deferred admissions plan. Applications should be filed by January 15 for fall entry. The fall 2003 application fee was $60 CDN. Notification is sent March 22. Applications are accepted on-line through the university's web site.

Transfer: 350 transfer students enrolled in 2002-2003. Requirements vary with the program. Standard admission requirements must also be met. 60 of 90 to 120 credits required for the bachelor's degree must be completed at McGill.

Visiting: There are regularly scheduled orientations for prospective students, with a varying agenda (including campus tours and student for a day programs). There are guides for informal visits and visitors may sit in on classes and stay overnight. To schedule a visit, contact the Welcome Center at (514) 398-6555 (tours) or *welcome@mcgill.ca.*

Financial Aid: In 2003-2004, 30% of all full-time freshmen received some form of financial aid. McGill is a member of CSS. The CSS Profile or FAFSA and the college's own financial statement are required. The deadline for filing freshman financial aid applications for fall entry is rolling.

International Students: There were 3316 international students enrolled in a reent year. The school actively recruits these students. They must score 577 on the written TOEFL or 233 on the electronic version, or take the MELAB. A McGill Certificate of Proficiency in English must be earned. SAT I and SAT II and/or ACT tests are required for U.S. applicants and recommended for other international applicants. Students must take program-specific SAT II: Subject tests. International students must pay a health insurance fee.

Computers: The mainframe is an IBM 9672-R51. The mainframe operates under the MVS/ESA operating system and VM/ESA and MUSIC. PC labs, LANs, and terminals are connected throughout the campus. Network services and specialized department systems in the network include Sun, DEC, and NeXT. All students may access the system any time. There is a time limit depending on the application. There are no fees. It is strongly recommended that all students have a personal computer.

Graduates: In a recent year, 3495 bachelor's degrees were awarded.

Admissions Contact: Admissions, Recruitment, and Registrar's Office. A video is available. E-mail: *admissions@mcgill.ca* Web: *www.mcgill.ca*

MCMASTER UNIVERSITY
Hamilton, ON, Canada L8S 4L8

E-3
(905) 525-4600
Fax: (905) 527-1105

Full-time: 5160 men, 6790 women
Part-time: 870 men, 1750 women
Graduate: 1190 men, 930 women
Year: terms, summer session
Application Deadline: see profile

Freshman Class: n/av
SAT I or ACT: not required

Faculty: 927
Ph.D.s: n/av
Student/Faculty: 13 to 1
Tuition: $4600 CDN ($14,000) CDN
Room & Board: $6000 CDN

McMaster University is a public nonsectarian institution, offering programs in the arts and sciences, business, engineering, health sciences, kinesiology, and social work. Figures given in the above capsule and in this profile are approximate. There are 2 graduate schools. The 4 libraries contain 1.9 million volumes, 1.4 million microform items, and 20,000 audio/video tapes/CDs, and subscribe to 15,000 periodicals. Computerized library services include the card catalog, interlibrary loans, and database searching. Special learning facilities include a learning resource center, art gallery, planetarium, radio station, nuclear reactor, tandem accelerator, greenhouses, the Chedoke-McMaster Hospital, communication research lab, the Bertrand Russell archives, the Humanities Communication Centre, and computing labs. The 300-acre campus is in an urban area 60 miles southwest of Toronto. Including any residence halls, there are 44 buildings.

Student Life: 95% of undergraduates are from Ontario. The average age of freshmen is 20; all undergraduates, 22. 1% do not continue beyond their first year.

Housing: 2765 students can be accommodated in college housing, which includes single-sex and coed dorms and on-campus apartments. In addition, there are language houses. On-campus housing is guaranteed for the freshman year only and is available on a lottery system for upperclassmen. Priority is given to out-of-town students. 77% of students commute. All students may keep cars.

Activities: There are no fraternities or sororities. There are 100 groups on campus, including art, band, cheerleading, chess, choir, chorale, chorus, computers, debate, drama, ethnic, gay, international, jazz band, musical theater, newspaper, orchestra, photography, political, radio and TV, religious, social, student government, and yearbook. Popular campus events include Marauder Weekend.

Sports: There are 16 intercollegiate sports for men and 14 for women, and 16 intramural sports for men and 14 for women. Facilities include 2 multipurpose gyms, an outdoor track and field, a mini-weight room, a swimming pool, cross-country trails, rugby, soccer, and football fields, tennis, squash, and handball courts, and a state-of-the-art fitness facility.

Disabled Students: 60% of the campus is accessible. Wheelchair ramps, elevators, special parking, specially equipped rest rooms, special class scheduling, lowered telephones, and basement-level and aboveground tunnels with connecting walkways are available.

Services: Counseling and information services are available, as is tutoring in some subjects. There is a reader service for the blind.

Campus Safety and Security: Measures include 24-hour foot and vehicle patrol, security escort services, shuttle buses, and informal discussions. There are pamphlets/posters/films, emergency telephones, and lighted pathways/sidewalks. Additional services include the Emergency First-Response Team, Mac Alert bulletins, a campus watch program, and a prevention programs officer.

Programs of Study: Mac confers B.A., B.S., B.A.S., B.A./B.S.W., B.C., B.Eng., B.Eng. and Management, B.Eng. and Society, B.H.S., B.Kinesiology, B.Mus., and B.S.N. degrees. Master's and doctoral degrees are also awarded. Bachelor's degrees are awarded in BIOLOGICAL SCIENCE (biochemistry, biology/biological science, and life science), BUSINESS (business administration and management, and labor studies), COMMUNICATIONS AND THE ARTS (art, art history and appreciation, classics, comparative literature, dramatic arts, English, French, linguistics, modern language, music, and Russian), COMPUTER AND PHYSICAL SCIENCE (chemistry, computer science, earth science, geology, mathematics, physical sciences, physics, science, and statistics), ENGINEERING AND ENVIRONMENTAL DESIGN (chemical engineering, civil engineering, computer engineering, electrical/electronics engineering, engineering physics, environmental science, manufacturing engineering, materials engineering, materials science, and mechanical engineering), HEALTH PROFESSIONS (medical science, nursing, occupational therapy, and physical therapy), SOCIAL SCIENCE (anthropology, economics, geography, German area studies, gerontology, history, interdisciplinary studies, Japanese studies, Latin American studies, liberal arts/general studies, philosophy, physical fitness/movement, political science/government, psychology, religion, social work, sociology, and women's studies).

Required: Requirements for graduation vary according to the program of study. A minimum 3.5 GPA in 90 to 150 units is required for most programs.

Special: Many opportunities exist to combine 2 subjects of study within 1 faculty, or between 2 faculties. All honors students have the option of taking a minor in a second subject area. Nondegree study is possible through the Center for Continuing Education. Internships and study abroad are offered. Students may repeat failed courses provided they are eligible to continue in the program.

Faculty/Classroom: 71% of faculty are male; 29%, female. All both teach and do research.

Requirements: U.S. applicants must have a high school grade average of 80. Applicants must be graduates of an accredited secondary school. The required high school courses should include 5 years each of English and math. A portfolio is required for art students and an audition for music students. A supplementary application form is required for some programs. Offers of admission are made based on academic standing and audition/portfolio/supplementary application requirements where necessary. A high school average of 80 is required. Important factors in the admissions decision are evidence of special talent, extracurricular activities record, and leadership record.

Procedure: Freshmen are admitted to all sessions. There is an early decision plan. Check with the school for current application deadlines and fee. A waiting list is an active part of the admissions procedure.

Transfer: Applicants are considered on an individual basis. Review of high school, college, and/or university work determines admission status.

Visiting: There are regularly scheduled orientations for prospective students, including campus tours, information sessions, and panel discussions. There are guides for informal visits and visitors may sit in on classes. To schedule a visit, contact Tour Coordinator, Division of Student Liaison at (905) 525-9140, ext. 24796.

Financial Aid: Check with the school for current deadlines.

International Students: The school actively recruits international students. They must score 580 on the written TOEFL or take the MELAB, or the IELTS.

Computers: The mainframes are an IBM S/390 system and SUN UNIX systems. Computing labs provide access to approximately 280 PCs with word processing and spreadsheet packages, as well as various computer languages, statistical applications, and specialized course software provided by instructors. Several e-mail rooms have been set up for students. In addition to these centrally operated facilities, departments have specialized labs. All students may access the system any time. There are no time limits and no fees.

Admissions Contact: Lynn Giordano, Associate Registrar Admissions. E-mail: *macadmit@mcmail.mcmaster.ca* Web: *www.mcmaster.ca*

MEMORIAL UNIVERSITY OF NEWFOUNDLAND   F-2
St. John's, NF, Canada A1C 5S7

(709) 737-3705
Fax: (709) 737-2337

Full-time: 4800 men, 6340 women	Faculty: 932
Part-time: 685 men, 1370 women	Ph.D.s: 50%
Graduate: 845 men, 765 women	Student/Faculty: 12 to 1
Year: trimesters, summer session	Tuition: $3500 ($7110)
Application Deadline: see profile	Room & Board: $1820
Freshman Class: n/av	
SAT I or ACT: not required	

Memorial University of Newfoundland, founded in 1925, is a public liberal arts institution. There are 13 undergraduate and 12 graduate schools. Figures in the above capsule and in this profile are approximate. The 3 libraries contain 2,500,000 volumes, and subscribe to 700 periodicals. Computerized library services include the card catalog, interlibrary loans, and database searching. Special learning facilities include a learning resource center, art gallery, natural history museum, planetarium, radio station, TV station, and language labs. The 220-acre campus is in an urban area within St. John's. Including any residence halls, there are 40 buildings.

Student Life: 98% of undergraduates are from Newfoundland.

Housing: 1750 students can be accommodated in college housing, which includes single-sex and coed dorms, on-campus apartments, off-campus apartments, and married-student housing. On-campus housing is available on a first-come, first-served basis. Priority is given to out-of-town students. 89% of students commute. All students may keep cars.

Activities: There are no fraternities or sororities. There are 100 groups on campus, including academic, band, cheerleading, chess, choir, chorale, computers, dance, debate, drama, ethnic, gay, international, jazz band, literary magazine, musical theater, newspaper, orchestra, photography, political, professional, radio and TV, religious, single parent, social, social service, student government, symphony, and yearbook. Popular campus events include Winter Carnival and Orientation.

Sports: There are 6 intercollegiate sports for men and 6 for women, and 6 intramural sports for men and 6 for women. Facilities include a gym, squash courts, a rifle range, a weight room, a soccer field, and swimming facilities.

Disabled Students: 85% of the campus is accessible. Wheelchair ramps, elevators, special parking, specially equipped rest rooms, special class scheduling, lowered drinking fountains, lowered telephones, class-

room aids, note-taking volunteers, and other facilities based on individual needs are available.

Services: Counseling and information services are available. There is a reader service for the blind and remedial math, reading, and writing. Students staying in residence have access to tutoring in every subject. In addition, lectures are offered on topics such as public speaking, speed reading, and time management.

Campus Safety and Security: Measures include 24-hour foot and vehicle patrol, self-defense education, security escort services, and informal discussions. There are pamphlets/posters/films, emergency telephones, and lighted pathways/sidewalks.

Programs of Study: MUN confers B.A., B.Sc., B.Comm.(Co-op.), B.Comm.(Gen.), B.Ed., B.Eng., B.F.A., B.Kin., B.M.S., B.Mus., B.Mus.Ed., B.Med.Sc., B.N., B.P.E., B.Rec., B.Sc.(Pharm.), B.Spec.Ed., B.S.W., B.Tech., and B.Voc.Ed. degrees. Master's and doctoral degrees are also awarded. Bachelor's degrees are awarded in AGRICULTURE (forestry and related sciences), BIOLOGICAL SCIENCE (biochemistry, biology/biological science, cell biology, ecology, entomology, environmental biology, evolutionary biology, marine biology, marine science, microbiology, and neurosciences), BUSINESS (entrepreneurial studies, human resources, labor studies, management science, marketing/retailing/merchandising, organizational behavior, and small business management), COMMUNICATIONS AND THE ARTS (dramatic arts, English, English literature, fine arts, folklore and mythology, French, German, linguistics, literature, music, music history and appreciation, music performance, music theory and composition, Russian, Spanish, and visual and performing arts), COMPUTER AND PHYSICAL SCIENCE (applied mathematics, applied physics, chemistry, computer science, earth science, information sciences and systems, mathematics, oceanography, and statistics), EDUCATION (athletic training, education, elementary, guidance, middle school, music, physical, recreation, secondary, and special), ENGINEERING AND ENVIRONMENTAL DESIGN (civil engineering, electrical/electronics engineering, engineering technology, maritime science, mechanical engineering, naval architecture and marine engineering, and ocean engineering), HEALTH PROFESSIONS (medical science, nursing, and pharmacy), SOCIAL SCIENCE (anthropology, archeology, Canadian studies, criminology, dietetics, economics, French studies, geography, German area studies, history, humanities, medieval studies, philosophy, physical fitness/movement, political science/government, psychology, religion, social studies, social work, sociology, Spanish studies, and women's studies). Marine biology, naval architecture, and business are the strongest academically. Arts, science, business, and engineering are the largest.

Required: Students must complete 40 to 50 credits to graduate. Each discipline has different requirements for graduation.

Special: The university offers co-op programs in commerce, phys ed, recreation, kinesiology, and engineering. Internships are available in education and nursing. Study abroad may be arranged in at least 20 countries. Work-study programs, dual majors, and B.A.-B.S. degrees are available.

Faculty/Classroom: 80% of faculty are male; 20%, female. All both teach and do research. Graduate students teach 71% of introductory courses. The average class size in an introductory lecture is 40.

Requirements: Admission is based on a 70% high school average as computed from university preparatory courses required for admission. A grade average of 70 is required. AP credits are accepted.

Procedure: Freshmen are admitted to all sessions. There is a rolling admissions plan. Check with the school for current application deadlines. The fall 2003 application fee was $80. Notification is sent on a rolling basis. Applications are accepted on-line at *http://www.mun.ca/regoff/admission/adm.htm.*

Transfer: Applicants must be in good academic standing at the previous institution. 10 of 40 credits required for the bachelor's degree must be completed at MUN.

Visiting: There are regularly scheduled orientations for prospective students, including various student activities, mock lectures, campus tours, and educational sessions. There are guides for informal visits and visitors may sit in on classes. To schedule a visit, contact Student Development at (709) 737-2192.

Financial Aid: Average annual earnings from campus work are $1000.

International Students: The school actively recruits these students. They must score 550 on the written TOEFL or take the MELAB.

Computers: The mainframe is a VAX/Sun cluster. There are 850 PCs available for student use, most with Internet access. All students may access the system. There are no time limits and no fees.

Admissions Contact: Phyllis McCann, Manager of Admissions. A video is available. E-mail: *pmccann@morgan.ucs.mun.ca*

QUEEN'S UNIVERSITY AT KINGSTON
E-3
Kingston, ON, Canada K7L 3N6
(613) 533-2218
Fax: (613) 533-6810

Full-time: 12,300 men and women
Part-time: 2300 men and women
Graduate: 2600 men and women
Year: semesters, summer session
Application Deadline: see profile

Freshman Class: n/av
SAT I: required

Faculty: 973
Ph.D.s: n/av
Student/Faculty: 13 to 1
Tuition: $5000 CDN ($12,000) CDN
Room & Board: $8000 CDN

Queen's University, founded in 1841, is a public institution offering undergraduate and graduate programs in the arts and sciences, business, engineering, health sciences, and teacher education. There are 10 undergraduate and 5 graduate schools. Figures in the above capsule and in this profile are approximate. The 8 libraries contain 1.8 million volumes, 2 million microform items, and 7000 audio/video tapes/CDs, and subscribe to 15,000 periodicals. Computerized library services include the card catalog, interlibrary loans, and database searching. Special learning facilities include a learning resource center, art gallery, radio station, TV station, geology museum, and observatory. The 160-acre campus is in an urban area 150 miles east of Toronto. Including any residence halls, there are 100 buildings.

Student Life: 85% of undergraduates are from Ontario. 89% are from public schools. 5% do not continue beyond their first year; 90% remain to graduate.

Housing: 3071 students can be accommodated in college housing, which includes single-sex and coed dorms, on-campus apartments, off-campus apartments, and married-student housing. In addition, there are language houses and special-interest houses. On-campus housing is guaranteed for the freshman year only. 80% of students commute. All students may keep cars.

Activities: There are no fraternities or sororities. There are 220 groups on campus, including art, bagpipe band, band, cheerleading, chess, choir, chorale, chorus, computers, dance, debate, drama, ethnic, film, gay, international, jazz band, literary magazine, marching band, musical theater, newspaper, orchestra, photography, political, professional, radio and TV, religious, social, social service, student government, symphony, and yearbook. Popular campus events include Orientation Week, Alumni Weekend, and Applied Science Formal.

Sports: There are 19 intercollegiate sports for men and 21 for women, and 39 intramural sports for men and 39 for women. Facilities include a pool, an indoor track, a hockey arena, tennis, squash, racquetball courts, a weight room, a dance studio, and a projectile range. There is also a 5000-seat indoor gym and a 12,000-seat football stadium.

Disabled Students: 80% of the campus is accessible. Wheelchair ramps, elevators, special parking, specially equipped rest rooms, special class scheduling, lowered drinking fountains, and lowered telephones are available.

Services: Counseling and information services are available, as is tutoring in most subjects. There is a reader service for the blind and remedial math, reading, and writing.

Campus Safety and Security: Measures include 24-hour foot and vehicle patrol, self-defense education, security escort services, and shuttle buses. There are informal discussions, pamphlets/posters/films, emergency telephones, and lighted pathways/sidewalks.

Programs of Study: Queen's confers B.A., B.Sc., B.A./B.Ed., B.A./B.Phe., B.Comm., B.F.A., B.Mus., B.N.Sc., B.Sc./B.Ed., B.Sc./B.Phe., B.S.C.E., B.Sc.O.T., and B.Sc.P.T. degrees. Master's and doctoral degrees are also awarded. Bachelor's degrees are awarded in BIOLOGICAL SCIENCE (biochemistry, biology/biological science, and life science), COMMUNICATIONS AND THE ARTS (art history and appreciation, classics, dramatic arts, English, film arts, fine arts, French, German, Greek, Italian, Latin, music, and Spanish), COMPUTER AND PHYSICAL SCIENCE (chemistry, computer science, geology, mathematics, physics, and statistics), EDUCATION (elementary, middle school, and secondary), ENGINEERING AND ENVIRONMENTAL DESIGN (chemical engineering, civil engineering, electrical/electronics engineering, engineering physics, geological engineering, and mechanical engineering), HEALTH PROFESSIONS (health, nursing, occupational therapy, and physical therapy), SOCIAL SCIENCE (economics, geography, history, Judaic studies, philosophy, political science/government, psychology, religion, sociology, and women's studies). Arts, science, and engineering are the largest.

Required: Each faculty and school establishes the academic requirements for the graduation of its students.

Special: Internships are available in life science, commerce, and engineering. Students may study abroad in 25 countries. Dual majors are available. Cross-registration with St. Lawrence College for the B.S.N. is possible. There is a freshman honors program.

Faculty/Classroom: 72% of faculty are male; 27%, female. All teach undergraduates. The average class size in a laboratory is 40.

Requirements: The SAT I is required. In addition, candidates for admission are required to submit a school profile. A high school average of 70 is required. Important factors in the admissions decision are evidence of special talent, leadership record, and extracurricular activities record.

Procedure: Freshmen are admitted in the fall. There is a deferred admissions plan. Check with the school for application deadlines and fee. Notification is sent on a rolling basis. A waiting list is an active part of the admissions procedure. Applications are accepted on-line.

Transfer: 151 transfer students enrolled in a recent year. Admission requirements for transfer applicants vary by program. 10 of 19 credits required for the bachelor's degree must be completed at Queen's.

Visiting: There are regularly scheduled orientations for prospective students, consisting of a short briefing session and a walking tour. There are guides for informal visits and visitors may sit in on classes and stay overnight. To schedule a visit, contact Student Recruitment at (613) 533-2217 or tours@post.queensu.ca.

Financial Aid: Check with the school for current deadlines.

International Students: The school actively recruits international students. They must score 580 on the written TOEFL or 237 on the electronic version or take the MELAB. Applicants from American schools must also take the SAT I, scoring 1200.

Computers: The mainframe is an IBM 9000. There are 4 computer centers located on campus. Students are issued a special ID to access the system. All students may access the system 24 hours. It is strongly recommended that all students have a personal computer. IBM ThinkPad is recommended.

Admissions Contact: Associate University Registrar (Admissions Services). A video is available. E-mail: admissn@post.queensu.ca
Web: www.queensu.ca

RYERSON POLYTECHNIC UNIVERSITY
E-3
Toronto, ON, Canada M5B 2K3
(416) 979-5000
Fax: (416) 979-5341

Full-time: 12,500 men and women
Part-time: none
Graduate: none
Year: semesters
Application Deadline: see profile

Freshman Class: n/av
SAT I or ACT: required

Faculty: 547
Ph.D.s: n/av
Student/Faculty: 23 to 1
Tuition: $5000 CDN ($12,000) CDN
Room & Board: $6000 CDN

Ryerson Polytechnic University, founded in 1948, is a public institution offering undergraduate programs in arts, applied arts, business, community services, and engineering and applied science. Figures given in the above capsule and in this profile are approximate. There are 29 undergraduate schools. In addition to regional accreditation, Ryerson has baccalaureate program accreditation with FIDER. The library contains 325,000 volumes, 400 microform items, and 6500 audio/video tapes/CDs, and subscribes to 3000 periodicals. Computerized library services include the card catalog, interlibrary loans, and database searching. Special learning facilities include a learning resource center, radio station, and a film and photography gallery. The 20-acre campus is in an urban area in downtown Toronto. Including any residence halls, there are 22 buildings.

Student Life: 94% of undergraduates are from Ontario. 21% do not continue beyond their first year.

Housing: 858 students can be accommodated in college housing, which includes coed dorms. In addition, there are language houses and special-interest houses. On-campus housing is available on a first-come, first-served basis. Priority is given to out-of-town students. 94% of students commute. All students may keep cars.

Activities: There are no fraternities or sororities. There are 55 groups on campus, including choir, chorale, ethnic, film, gay, international, literary magazine, newspaper, political, professional, radio and TV, religious, social, student government, and yearbook. Popular campus events include Orientation, Island Picnic, and Winter Carnival.

Sports: There are 8 intercollegiate sports for men and 7 for women, and 7 intramural sports for men and 6 for women. Facilities include a recreation and athletic center, 7 squash courts, a fitness training center that includes an indoor running track and weight-training equipment, a rehabilitation center, a 25-yard pool, saunas, 3 studios, and 6 gyms.

Disabled Students: Wheelchair ramps, elevators, special parking, specially equipped rest rooms, special class scheduling, and lowered telephones are available. The Access Center on campus offers information, seminars, and workshops; test and exam adaptations; computer-equipped exam and study rooms; assistive listening devices for personal use and for use in auditorium settings; advocacy services; individual needs assessment; and access to a wide range of technical devices.

Services: There is a reader service for the blind, remedial math, reading, and writing, and study skills development.

Campus Safety and Security: Measures include 24-hour foot and vehicle patrol, self-defense education, security escort services, and informal

discussions. There are pamphlets/posters/films, emergency telephones, lighted pathways/sidewalks, sexual assault training, harassment prevention and crime prevention programs, and community policing programs.

Programs of Study: Ryerson confers B.A.A., B.B.M., B.Eng., B.H.Sc., B.S.N., B.S.W., and B.Tech. degrees. Bachelor's degrees are awarded in BUSINESS (business administration and management, hospitality management services, and management information systems), COMMUNICATIONS AND THE ARTS (broadcasting, journalism, and photography), COMPUTER AND PHYSICAL SCIENCE (chemical technology and computer programming), EDUCATION (early childhood), ENGINEERING AND ENVIRONMENTAL DESIGN (aeronautical engineering, architecture, chemical engineering, civil engineering, electrical/electronics engineering, graphic and printing production, industrial engineering, interior design, mechanical engineering, and urban planning technology), HEALTH PROFESSIONS (environmental health science and nursing), SOCIAL SCIENCE (child care/child and family studies, family/consumer studies, fashion design and technology, geography, public administration, and social work). Business management, electrical engineering, and administration and information management are the largest.

Required: To graduate, students must have a 2.0 GPA and complete the requirements of their program of study.

Special: The university offers co-op programs in applied chemistry and biology, chemical engineering, and midwifery. Accelerated degree programs are available in journalism, radio and television arts, nurse practitioner, and nursing, and many programs have a work-study component.

Faculty/Classroom: All teach undergraduates. The average class size in a regular course is 30.

Requirements: The SAT I or ACT is required for U.S. students, with a recommended minimum score of 550 on each section of the SAT I. Students should be high school graduates with a minimum B overall average.

Procedure: Freshmen are admitted in the fall. A waiting list is an active part of the admissions procedure. Check with the school for current application deadlines and fee.

Transfer: Transfer applicants must have completed 1 year at the college level. Acceptance of transfer credits is at the discretion of the Office of Admissions/Liaison/Curriculum Advising. Half of the required credits for a particular degree program must be completed at Ryerson.

Visiting: There are regularly scheduled orientations for prospective students, including a half-day tour and discussion session featuring campus tours and visits to specific schools and departments. There are guides for informal visits and visitors may sit in on classes. To schedule a visit, contact the Liaison Office at (416) 979-5030.

Financial Aid: Ryerson is a member of CSS. The financial statements applicable to Ontario government requirements are needed. Check with the school for current deadlines.

International Students: They must score 550 on the written TOEFL or take the MELAB or the university's own test.

Computers: The mainframe is an IBM RISC 6000. Most major buildings have clusters of PCs that are networked to the backbone. There are also clusters of IBM terminals, which allow access to the mainframe, and more than 300 networked workstations. All students may access the system. There are no fees.

Admissions Contact: Director of Admissions.
E-mail: *inquire@acs.ryerson.ca* Web: *http://www.ryerson.ca*

SIMON FRASER UNIVERSITY
Burnaby, BC, Canada V5A 1S6

B-2

(604) 291-3211
Fax: (604) 291-4969

Full-time: 4423 men, 5627 women	**Faculty:** n/av
Part-time: 3572 men, 4794 women	**Ph.D.s:** 88%
Graduate: none	**Student/Faculty:** n/av
Year: trimesters, summer session	**Tuition:** $3431 CDN ($11,433 CDN)
Application Deadline: April 30	**Room & Board:** $4013 CDN
Freshman Class: 10,881 applied, 6429 accepted, 2577 enrolled	
SAT I Verbal/Math: 600/600	**ACT:** 26

Simon Fraser University, established in 1965, is a public institution offering undergraduate and graduate programs in the arts, sciences, business, education, and applied sciences. In addition to its main campus, the university maintains the Harbour Centre campus in downtown Vancouver to provide midcareer education to the urban population and the new SFU Surrey campus offering programs in information technology and interactive arts. There are 5 undergraduate and 35 graduate schools. The library contains 1,397,816 volumes, 1,136,745 microform items, and 10,213 audio/video tapes/CDs, and subscribes to 15,513 periodicals. Computerized library services include the card catalog, interlibrary loans, database searching, and Internet access. Special learning facilities include a learning resource center, art gallery, radio station, archeology museum, special literature and map collections, fine and performing arts theater, hypo/hyperbaric chamber, back test unit, rock climbing wall, apiary, underwater lab, television and photography studios, and dance

floors. The 400-acre campus is in a suburban area 9 miles east of Vancouver. Including any residence halls, there are 51 buildings.

Student Life: 89% of undergraduates are from British Columbia. Students are from 90 foreign countries and Canada. 92% are from public schools. The average age of freshmen is 19; all undergraduates, 23.

Housing: 1117 students can be accommodated in college housing, which includes single-sex and coed dorms, on-campus apartments, and married-student housing. Priority for on-campus housing is given to out-of-town students. 96% of students commute. All students may keep cars.

Activities: There are no fraternities or sororities. There are 35 groups on campus, including athletic, bagpipe band, chess, choir, computers, ethnic, gaming, gay, hobbies, international, newspaper, political, professional, religious, social, social service, and student government. Popular campus events include Convocation, Clubs Day, and various orientation activities.

Sports: There are 9 intercollegiate sports for men and 9 for women, and 7 intramural sports for men and 7 for women. Facilities include 2 gyms, swimming and diving pools, a running track, weight rooms, saunas, playing fields, a combative room, tennis, squash, and racquetball courts, and a fitness center.

Disabled Students: 95% of the campus is accessible. Wheelchair ramps, elevators, special parking, specially equipped rest rooms, lowered drinking fountains, lowered telephones, and special housing are available. There are computers with software such as large text and voice output features, a scanner, a braille printer, a Visualtek machine, closed-circuit TV for text or graphic enlargement, note taking tutor support, adaptive technology, exam modifications, sign language interpreters, closed captioning in lectures, and alternate format texts.

Services: There is a reader service for the blind. There also are taped library books and some lectures are taped.

Campus Safety and Security: Measures include 24-hour foot and vehicle patrol, security escort services, pamphlets/posters/films, and emergency telephones. There are lighted pathways/sidewalks, safe-walk stations, and student patrols.

Programs of Study: SFU confers B.A., B.Sc., B.A.Sc., B.B.A., B.Ed., B.F.A., and B.G.S. degrees. Master's and doctoral degrees are also awarded. Bachelor's degrees are awarded in BIOLOGICAL SCIENCE (biology/biological science, molecular biology, and physiology), BUSINESS (business administration and management and management science), COMMUNICATIONS AND THE ARTS (art, communications, dance, dramatic arts, English, film arts, French, linguistics, music, and visual and performing arts), COMPUTER AND PHYSICAL SCIENCE (actuarial science, applied mathematics, applied physics, chemistry, computer science, earth science, mathematics, physics, science, and statistics), EDUCATION (education), ENGINEERING AND ENVIRONMENTAL DESIGN (engineering and applied science and environmental science), SOCIAL SCIENCE (anthropology, archeology, Canadian studies, cognitive science, criminology, economics, geography, history, humanities, liberal arts/general studies, philosophy, physical fitness/movement, political science/government, psychology, sociology, and women's studies). Engineering science is the strongest academically. Business administration, economics, and psychology are the largest.

Required: General bachelor's degrees require completion of 120 semester hours with a 2.0 cumulative GPA; honors degrees, 132 hours. Some programs require a thesis.

Special: Simon Fraser offers cooperative education in most areas of study, study abroad in 28 countries, many opportunities for joint majors, a general studies degree, work-study programs, dual-majors, student-designed majors, and a variety of certificate and diploma programs, as well as nondegree and evening study. Interdisciplinary majors are offered in such areas as chemical physics, management and systems science, mathematical physics, and physics and physiology. There is a freshman honors program.

Faculty/Classroom: 71% of faculty are male; 29%, female.

Admissions: 59% of the 2003-2004 applicants were accepted.

Requirements: The SAT I or ACT is required for U.S. applicants. In addition, applicants must be graduates of an accredited secondary school and have a minimum grade average of 70. SFU requires applicants to be in the upper 25% of their class. A GPA of 3.2 is required. AP credits are accepted.

Procedure: Freshmen are admitted to all sessions. There are early decision and early admissions plans. Early decision applications should be filed by April 1; regular applications, by April 30 for fall entry, September 30 for spring entry, and February 2 for summer entry. The fall 2003 application fee was $35 CDN. Notification of early decision is sent April 15; regular decision, June 30. 1300 early decision candidates were accepted for the 2003-2004 class. Applications are accepted on-line through the Post-Secondary Application Service of British Columbia.

Transfer: 1560 transfer students enrolled in 2002-2003. Applicants must have a minimum GPA of 2.0 and be in good standing at their previous school. 60 of 120 credits required for the bachelor's degree must be completed at SFU.

Visiting: There are regularly scheduled orientations for prospective students, consisting of regularly scheduled 1-day campus orientations.

There are guides for informal visits and visitors may stay overnight. To schedule a visit, contact the Residence and Housing Office at (604) 291-4330 or *suzanne_nazareno@sfu.ca*.

Financial Aid: The average financial indebtedness of the 2003 graduate was $20,000 CDN. The FAFSA is required. The deadline for filing freshman financial aid applications for fall entry is July 1.

International Students: There are 672 international students enrolled. The school actively recruits these students. They must score 570 on the written TOEFL or 250 on the electronic version and also take the IELTS (minimum score 6.5 on academic modules).

Computers: There are IBM, Sun, and SGI host computers. PCs, Macs, and printers are available for student word processing needs. All students may access the system any time. There are no time limits and no fees.

Graduates: From July 1, 2002 to June 30, 2003, 3168 bachelor's degrees were awarded. The most popular majors were business (14%), economics (9%), and communication (8%).

Admissions Contact: Diane Whiteley, Director of Admissions. E-mail: *undergraduate-admissions@sfu.ca* Web: *http://www.reg.sfu.ca*

UNIVERSITÉ DE MONTRÉAL
E-2
Montreal, PQ, Canada H3C 3T7
(514) 343-7076
Fax: (514) 343-5788

Full-time: 6797 men, 13,396 women	**Faculty:** n/av
Part-time: 2487 men, 6815 women	**Ph.D.s:** 96%
Graduate: 3363 men, 5087 women	**Student/Faculty:** n/av
Year: trimesters, summer session	**Tuition:** $2098 CDN ($10,948 CDN)
Application Deadline: March 1	**Room & Board:** $3793 CDN

Freshman Class: 25,593 applied, 13,584 accepted, 11,039 enrolled
SAT I or ACT: not required

Université de Montréal, founded in 1878, is the largest French-language university in North America, with 13 faculties, 2 affiliated schools, 62 teaching departments, and more than 170 research units. There are 16 undergraduate schools and 1 graduate school. The 19 libraries contain 2,660,322 volumes, 1,604,798 microform items, and 178,335 audio/video tapes/CDs, and subscribe to 12,698 periodicals. Computerized library services include the card catalog, interlibrary loans, database searching, and Internet access. Special learning facilities include a learning resource center, art gallery, natural history museum, radio station, and concert hall. The 145-acre campus is in an urban area in Montreal. Including any residence halls, there are 33 buildings.

Student Life: 88% are from public schools. The average age of freshmen is 24; all undergraduates, 26. 16% do not continue beyond their first year; 84% remain to graduate.

Housing: 1164 students can be accommodated in college housing, which includes coed off-campus apartments. University housing is available on a first-come, first-served basis. 98% of students commute. All students may keep cars.

Activities: There are no fraternities or sororities. There are 97 groups on campus, including art, choir, chorale, computers, dance, drama, ethnic, film, international, jazz band, literary magazine, newspaper, orchestra, photography, radio and TV, religious, social, social service, student government, and yearbook. Popular campus events include Multicultural Week and Welcoming Week.

Sports: There are 8 intercollegiate sports for men and 6 for women, and 12 intramural sports for men and 12 for women. Facilities include a skating rink, a football field, a gym, squash and racquetball courts, an Olympic-size pool, a diving pool, a running field with tennis courts, and aerobic and muscular exercise equipment.

Disabled Students: 95% of the campus is accessible. Wheelchair ramps, elevators, special parking, specially equipped rest rooms, lowered drinking fountains, lowered telephones, and special housing are available. There is also a specialized equipment center for students with disabilities.

Services: Counseling and information services are available, as is tutoring in some subjects, including math and French. There is a reader service for the blind and remedial math, reading, and writing.

Campus Safety and Security: Measures include 24-hour foot and vehicle patrol, security escort services, informal discussions, and pamphlets/posters/films. There are emergency telephones and lighted pathways/sidewalks.

Programs of Study: UdeM confers B.A., B.Sc., B.A.A., B.A.P., B.D.I., B.Gest, B.Ed., B.Ing., B.Int., B.Mus., B.Pharm., and B.Th. degrees. Associate, master's, and doctoral degrees are also awarded. Bachelor's degrees are awarded in BIOLOGICAL SCIENCE (biochemistry, biology/biological science, biometrics and biostatistics, and nutrition), BUSINESS (business administration and management), COMMUNICATIONS AND THE ARTS (art history and appreciation, classics, English, film arts, French, German, industrial design, linguistics, and music), COMPUTER AND PHYSICAL SCIENCE (chemistry, computer science, mathematics, and physics), EDUCATION (education, physical, and psychology), ENGINEERING AND ENVIRONMENTAL DESIGN (architectural engineering, architecture, engineering, industrial administration/management,

and landscape architecture/design), HEALTH PROFESSIONS (health science, nursing, occupational therapy, pharmacy, physical therapy, predentistry, premedicine, preveterinary science, speech pathology/audiology, and veterinary science), SOCIAL SCIENCE (anthropology, Asian/Oriental studies, criminology, economics, geography, history, law, philosophy, political science/government, psychology, social work, sociology, Spanish studies, theological studies, and urban studies). Medicine is the strongest academically. Arts and science are the largest.

Required: To graduate, students must have a GPA of 2.0 on a 4.3 scale. The total number of credit hours required in most programs is 90, although it can range up to 187. Professional programs, particularly those in health-related fields, require more hours.

Special: The university offers co-op programs in math, translation, mining, and civil, chemical, and software material engineering, and work-study programs in hospitals and businesses in Quebec. Dual majors in math and economics, math and physics, math and computer science, communication and politics, and economics and politics and 3-2 engineering degrees may also be arranged. Study abroad is available in 31 countries. There is a freshman honors program.

Faculty/Classroom: 71% of faculty are male; 29%, female. The average class size in an introductory lecture is 48; in a laboratory, 19; and in a regular course, 40.

Admissions: 53% of the 2003-2004 applicants were accepted.

Requirements: Applicants in certain programs must take the university's admissions tests. An interview is also required in some programs.

Procedure: Freshmen are admitted fall and winter. Applications should be filed by January 15 or March 1 for fall entry, November 1 for winter entry, March 1 for spring entry, and March 1 for summer entry, along with a $50 CDN fee. Notification is sent March 15 or sooner if the January 15 deadline applies. A waiting list is an active part of the admissions procedure. Applications are accepted on computer disk and on-line at *www.etudiant.umontreal.ca*.

Transfer: Transfers are considered if there are openings in the second or third year of the university's programs.

Visiting: There are regularly scheduled orientations for prospective students, including Orientation and Employment Week in November, guided tours February through May, and open house in January and August. There are guides for informal visits. To schedule a visit, contact Direction des communications at (514) 343-6032 or *evenements@dircom.umontreal.ca*.

Financial Aid: In 2003-2004, 42% of all full-time freshmen and 50% of continuing full-time students received some form of financial aid. 42% of full-time freshmen and 50% of continuing full-time students received need-based aid. The average freshman award was $6000 CDN. 57% of undergraduates work part time. Average annual earnings from campus work are $4500 CDN. The deadline for filing freshman financial aid applications for fall entry is March 31.

International Students: In a recent year, there were 2134 international students enrolled. The school actively recruits these students. A French proficiency test is required upon admission.

Computers: The mainframes are 7 SGI Origin 2000, 1 HP N4000, 2 SGI Challenge XL, and 2 SGI Origin 20 computers. Students have access to 1500 workstations (PCs, Macs, and UNIX). Every student has access to e-mail and the Internet. There are many modern departmental labs. All students may access the system 24 hours per day. There are no time limits and no fees. It is strongly recommended that all students have a personal computer, and students in management programs must have one. A ThinkPad is recommended.

Graduates: In a recent year, 5506 bachelor's degrees were awarded. The most popular majors were arts and science (29%), business (19%), and engineering (10%). In an average class, 57% graduate in 3 years or less, 67% graduate in 4 years or less, 69% graduate in 5 years or less, and 70% graduate in 6 years or less. 72 companies recruited on campus in a recent year.

Admissions Contact: Therese Champagne. E-mail: *admissions@regis.umontreal.ca* Web: *http://umontreal.ca*

UNIVERSITY OF ALBERTA
C-2
Edmonton, AB, Canada T6G 2M7
(780) 492-3113
Fax: (780) 492-7172

Full-time: 26,957 men and women	**Faculty:** 1659
Part-time: 2015 men and women	**Ph.D.s:** 92%
Graduate: 5405 men and women	**Student/Faculty:** 16 to 1
Year: semesters, summer session	**Tuition:** $4784 CDN ($11,553 CDN)
Application Deadline: May 1	**Room & Board:** $3915 CDN

Freshman Class: n/av
SAT I or ACT: not required

The University of Alberta, founded in 1906, is a publicly supported institution offering undergraduate and graduate programs in arts and science, agricultural sciences, business, education, engineering, and professional studies. There are 16 undergraduate schools and 1 graduate school. The 6 libraries contain 3.4 million volumes and 2.8 million microform items, and subscribe to 18,900 periodicals. Computerized library services include the card catalog, interlibrary loans, and database searching. Special learning facilities include a learning resource center, an art gallery, a radio station, an agricultural meteorological research station, an ecological sanctuary, a botanical garden, and the Kurimoto Japanese Garden farm. The 155-acre campus is in an urban area 2 miles southwest of downtown Edmonton. Including any residence halls, there are 90 buildings.

Student Life: Students are from Canada, 10 states, and 110 foreign countries. The average age of freshmen is 18; all undergraduates, 21.

Housing: 4900 students can be accommodated in college housing, which includes single-sex and coed dorms, on-campus apartments, off-campus apartments, and married-student housing. In addition, there are honors houses and special-interest houses. On-campus housing is guaranteed for all 4 years. 88% of students commute. All students may keep cars.

Activities: There are 7 national fraternities and 3 national sororities. There are 200 groups on campus, including art, band, cheerleading, chess, choir, chorale, chorus, computers, dance, debate, drama, ethnic, forensics, gay, honors, international, jazz band, musical theater, newspaper, opera, orchestra, pep band, photography, political, radio and TV, religious, social, social service, student government, and symphony. Popular campus events include WOW (Week of Welcome).

Sports: There are 10 intercollegiate sports for men and 10 for women, and 60 intramural sports for men and 45 for women. Facilities include a stadium, swimming pools, gyms, combatives and weight rooms, ballet/fencing and aerobics studios, a 400-meter outdoor track, an ice arena, racquetball and squash courts, a wrestling gym, an indoor field house, a sports medicine clinic, and a training center for handicapped athletes.

Disabled Students: 98% of the campus is accessible. Wheelchair ramps, elevators, special parking, specially equipped rest rooms, special class scheduling, lowered drinking fountains, lowered telephones, and automatic doors are available.

Services: Counseling and information services are available, as is tutoring in most subjects. There is a reader service for the blind and remedial math, reading, and writing.

Campus Safety and Security: Measures include 24-hour foot and vehicle patrol, security escort services, pamphlets/posters/films, and emergency telephones. There are lighted pathways/sidewalks.

Programs of Study: U of A confers B.A., B.S., B.Comm., B.Ed., B.F.A., B.Mus., and B.P.E. degrees. Master's and doctoral degrees are also awarded. Bachelor's degrees are awarded in AGRICULTURE (agricultural economics, agriculture, animal science, and soil science), BIOLOGICAL SCIENCE (biochemistry, biology/biological science, botany, cell biology, entomology, genetics, microbiology, physiology, and zoology), BUSINESS (accounting, management science, and marketing/retailing/merchandising), COMMUNICATIONS AND THE ARTS (classics, comparative literature, dance, dramatic arts, English, film arts, French, Germanic languages and literature, linguistics, music, romance languages and literature, and Slavic languages), COMPUTER AND PHYSICAL SCIENCE (applied mathematics, chemistry, computer science, earth science, geology, geophysics and seismology, mathematics, physical sciences, physics, and statistics), EDUCATION (education of the deaf and hearing impaired, education of the multiply handicapped, elementary, physical, secondary, special, and vocational), ENGINEERING AND ENVIRONMENTAL DESIGN (chemical engineering technology, civil engineering, computer engineering, electrical/electronics engineering, engineering physics, mechanical engineering, metallurgical engineering, mining and mineral engineering, and petroleum/natural gas engineering), HEALTH PROFESSIONS (medical laboratory science, nursing, occupational therapy, pharmacy, and physical therapy), SOCIAL SCIENCE (anthropology, Canadian studies, clothing and textiles management/production/services, criminology, East Asian studies, Eastern European studies, economics, geography, history, law, philosophy, political science/government, psychology, sociology, and women's studies). Arts, science, and education are the largest.

Required: The requirements for graduation vary according to the program. A minimum GPA of 2.0 and at least 120 credit hours are required for graduation.

Special: The university offers co-op programs in business and engineering. Opportunities for study abroad, internships, dual majors, bilingual classes in French and English, credit by examination (special assessment), and pass/fail options are also available. There is 1 national honor society and a freshman honors program.

Faculty/Classroom: 83% of faculty are male; 17%, female. All both teach and do research. The average class size in an introductory lecture is 90; in a laboratory, 30; and in a regular course, 35.

Requirements: Graduation from an accredited secondary school is required. A minimum grade average of 70 is required in all courses submitted for academic credit. Depending on the program selected by the student, an essay, portfolio, audition, or interview may be required. AP credits are accepted.

Procedure: Freshmen are admitted to all sessions. Applications should be filed by May 1 for fall entry, along with a $60 CDN fee. The university accepts all applicants. Notification is sent between January 2 and August 1.

Transfer: 2372 transfer students enrolled in 2002-2003. Applicants must meet minimum matriculation requirements or complete 24 credits of transferable work with satisfactory standing. 60 of 120 credits required for the bachelor's degree must be completed at U of A.

Visiting: There are regularly scheduled orientations for prospective students, including University Open House on the first weekend in October. There are guides for informal visits and visitors may sit in on classes. To schedule a visit, contact the Office of the Registrar and Student Awards.

International Students: There are 918 international students enrolled. The school actively recruits these students. They must score 580 on the written TOEFL or 237 on the electronic version or take the MELAB, the IELTS, the CAEL, or the university's own test.

Computers: The mainframe is an Amdahl 5880. There are also 370 IBM, Mac, Zenith, and SUN PCs available in various locations on campus. All students may access the system 24 hours a day. There are no time limits. The fee varies by amount of CPU usage.

Graduates: From July 1, 2002 to June 30, 2003, 5696 bachelor's degrees were awarded.

Admissions Contact: Office of the Registrar and Student Awards. A video is available. E-mail: *www.registrar.ualberta.ca/contact* Web: *www.ualberta.ca*

UNIVERSITY OF BRITISH COLUMBIA   B-2
Vancouver, BC, Canada V6T 1Z1
(604) 822-3014
(877) 272-1422; Fax: (604) 822-3599

Full-time: 8675 men, 10,751 women	Faculty: 1883
Part-time: 2966 men, 3995 women	Ph.D.s: 98%
Graduate: 5045 men, 6436 women	Student/Faculty: 10 to 1
Year: terms, summer session	Tuition: $3080 ($12,680)
Application Deadline: February 28	Room & Board: $4500
Freshman Class: 21,552 applied, 10,741 accepted, 5416 enrolled	
SAT I: recommended	

The University of British Columbia, established in 1908, is a publicly supported institution offering a wide range of undergraduate, graduate, and professional programs in the arts, sciences, and other fields of study. The winter session lasts from early September through April; some courses extend into May. Summer session begins in May and goes to mid-August, consisting of 2 terms. There are 12 undergraduate schools and 1 graduate school. The 13 libraries contain 4 million volumes, 5 million microform items, and 1.5 million audio/video tapes/CDs, and subscribe to 33,500 periodicals. Computerized library services include the card catalog, interlibrary loans, database searching, and Internet access. Special learning facilities include a learning resource center, an art gallery, a natural history museum, a radio station, an anthropology museum, Canada's largest accelerator for subatomic physics, a space observatory, a center for integated computer systems research, a center for the study of global issues, and a center for the performing arts. The 1000-acre campus is in an urban area 6 miles from the center of Vancouver. Including any residence halls, there are more than 500 buildings.

Student Life: 91% of undergraduates are from British Columbia. Students are from 31 states and 127 foreign countries. 98% are from public schools. The average age of all undergraduates is 21.

Housing: 7500 students can be accommodated in college housing, which includes single-sex and coed dorms, on-campus apartments, and married-student housing. In addition, there are special-interest houses. On-campus housing is available on a first-come, first-served basis. Priority is given to out-of-town students. 80% of students commute. All students may keep cars.

Activities: 6% of men belong to 7 national fraternities; 2% of women belong to 7 national sororities. There are 250 groups on campus, including art, band, cheerleading, chess, choir, chorale, chorus, computers, dance, debate, drama, ethnic, film, gay, international, jazz band, literary magazine, musical theater, opera, orchestra, photography, political, professional, radio and TV, religious, ski and snowboard, social, social service, student government, symphony, varsity outdoors, and yearbook. Popular campus events include Storm the Wall, Day of the Longboat, and Great Trek Run.

Sports: There are 15 intercollegiate sports for men and 13 for women, and 18 intramural sports for men and 18 for women. Facilities include a winter sports center, a 3500-seat stadium, a gym, an aquatic center, playing fields, a recreation center, and a tennis center.

Disabled Students: 95% of the campus is accessible. Wheelchair ramps, elevators, special parking, specially equipped rest rooms, special class scheduling, lowered drinking fountains, lowered telephones, special housing, accessible shower stalls in fitness facilities, tactile maps, TTY pay phones, an accessible security bus, and audible street crossing signals are available.

Services: Counseling and information services are available, as is tutoring in most subjects. There is a reader service for the blind and remedial math, reading, and writing.

Campus Safety and Security: Measures include 24-hour foot and vehicle patrol, security escort services, shuttle buses, and informal discussions. There are pamphlets/posters/films, emergency telephones, and lighted pathways/sidewalks. A Royal Canadian Mounted Police detachment is on campus, and campus security provides awareness programs on theft and personal safety lectures for women.

Programs of Study: UBC confers B.A., B.Sc., B.A.Sc., B.Com., B.D.Sc., B.Ed., B.F.A., B.H.E., B.H.K., B.H.L.Sc., B.L.L.B., B.Sc.Die., B.Sc.F., B.Sc.N., B.Sc.O.T., B.S. Pharm., B.Sc.P.T., and B.S.W. degrees. Master's and doctoral degrees are also awarded. Bachelor's degrees are awarded in AGRICULTURE (agricultural economics, animal science, forestry and related sciences, forestry production and processing, horticulture, natural resource management, and soil science), BIOLOGICAL SCIENCE (biochemistry, biology/biological science, biophysics, biotechnology, microbiology, nutrition, and physiology), BUSINESS (accounting, banking and finance, business administration and management, business economics, human resources, international business management, management information systems, marketing/retailing/merchandising, real estate, recreational facilities management, and transportation management), COMMUNICATIONS AND THE ARTS (art history and appreciation, Chinese, classics, creative writing, dramatic arts, English, film arts, fine arts, French, German, Italian, Japanese, linguistics, music, music history and appreciation, music performance, music theory and composition, romance languages and literature, and Spanish), COMPUTER AND PHYSICAL SCIENCE (astronomy, atmospheric sciences and meteorology, chemistry, computer science, earth science, geophysics and seismology, mathematics, oceanography, physics, science, and statistics), EDUCATION (elementary, museum studies, and physical), ENGINEERING AND ENVIRONMENTAL DESIGN (chemical engineering, civil engineering, computer engineering, electrical/electronics engineering, engineering, engineering physics, environmental design, environmental engineering, environmental science, geological engineering, mechanical engineering, metallurgical engineering, and mining and mineral engineering), HEALTH PROFESSIONS (exercise science, health, nursing, pharmacology, preveterinary science, and speech pathology/audiology), SOCIAL SCIENCE (anthropology, archeology, Asian/Oriental studies, Canadian studies, classical/ancient civilization, cognitive science, dietetics, economics, European studies, family/consumer studies, food production/management/services, food science, geography, Hispanic American studies, history, home economics, human ecology, international relations, Latin American studies, medieval studies, Native American studies, philosophy, political science/government, psychology, religion, sociology, South Asian studies, and women's studies). Applied sciences and commerce are the strongest academically. Education and psychology are the largest.

Required: Graduation requirements vary according to the degree sought. B.A. candidates must complete course work in English composition, science, literature, and a foreign language.

Special: UBC offers co-op programs in science, applied science, commerce, arts, and forestry, and study abroad through 150 student exchange opportunities in 40 countries. Nondegree study is possible. A B.A.-B.A.Sc. degree, student-designed majors, and dual majors in most faculties are available. There is 1 national honor society and many departments have honors programs.

Faculty/Classroom: 62% of faculty are male; 38%, female.

Admissions: 50% of the 2003-2004 applicants were accepted.

Requirements: The SAT I is recommended. In addition, graduation from an accredited secondary school is required. General admission for students following a U.S. system is based on 4 years of English and 3 of math. There are also specific program requirements in math, chemistry, physics, and biology for students applying to science-based programs. A GPA of 2.6 is required. AP credits are accepted.

Procedure: Freshmen are admitted fall and spring. Applications should be filed by February 28 for fall, spring, and summer entry, along with a $100 CDN fee. Notification is sent on a rolling basis. Applications are accepted on-line through the university's web site at *www.welcome.ubc.ca/apply.*

Transfer: Official transcripts, completion of the equivalent of 24 course credits, and no failures are required. A competitive GPA is required to get into the program at the second or third year. Applicants must have attended an accredited postsecondary institution. 60 of 120 credits required for the bachelor's degree must be completed at UBC.

Visiting: There are regularly scheduled orientations for prospective students, consisting of a campus tour from 9:30 to 11 A.M. every Friday and from 1 to 2:30 P.M. on Tuesday; some Saturday sessions are available. There are guides for informal visits and visitors may sit in on classes and stay overnight. To schedule a visit, contact the Student Information Centre through *students.ubc.ca/welcome/events.*

Financial Aid: The FAFSA and the university's own financial statement are required.

International Students: There are 2388 international students enrolled. The school actively recruits these students. They must score 570 on the written TOEFL or take the MELAB, the IELTS, the CAEL, or the CPE. The SAT I is not required but can be helpful if submitted.

Computers: The mainframe is an IBM 3090-400J. There are 500 or more computers in labs for each faculty. The library, residences, and research centers are wired, and all students have free e-mail and 4 hours of free access to the Internet each month. Internet access ports for laptop computers are also available. Students apply and register for courses online. All students may access the system 24 hours per day. It is strongly recommended that all students have a personal computer.

Graduates: From July 1, 2002 to June 30, 2003, 4853 bachelor's degrees were awarded. The most popular majors were arts (29%), science (20%), and education (16%). In an average class, 62% graduate in 4 years or less, and 78% graduate in 6 years or less. Of a recent graduating class, 50% were enrolled in graduate school within 6 months of graduation and 96% were employed.

Admissions Contact: Office of the Registrar. A video is available.
E-mail: *international.reception@ubc.ca* Web: *www.welcome.ubc.ca*

UNIVERSITY OF CALGARY
Calgary, AB, Canada T2N 1N4

C-2
(403) 220-6645
Fax: (403) 220-0762

Full-time: 9070 men, 11,069 women	**Faculty:** 1367
Part-time: 1547 men, 2266 women	**Ph.D.s:** n/av
Graduate: 2237 men, 2230 women	**Student/Faculty:** 15 to 1
Year: semesters, summer session	**Tuition:** $4929 CDN ($9309 CDN)
Application Deadline: March 1	
	Room & Board: $4785 CDN

Freshman Class: 6650 applied, 4397 accepted, 3143 enrolled
SAT I: required

The University of Calgary, founded in 1945, is a public institution offering undergraduate programs in numerous liberal arts and professional fields. There are 13 undergraduate and 2 graduate schools. The 5 libraries contain 2,378,415 volumes, 3,488,359 microform items, and 181,941 audio/video tapes/CDs, and subscribe to 18,000 periodicals. Computerized library services include the card catalog, interlibrary loans, database searching, and Internet access. Special learning facilities include a learning resource center, art gallery, radio station, TV station, environmental research center, observatory, and human performance and theater labs. The 526-acre campus is in an urban area in northwest Calgary. Including any residence halls, there are 33 buildings.

Housing: 1500 students can be accommodated in college housing, which includes coed dorms, on-campus apartments, and married-student housing. On-campus housing is available on a first-come, first-served basis. Priority is given to out-of-town students. All students may keep cars.

Activities: There are no fraternities or sororities. There are some groups and organizations on campus, including band, choir, drama, newspaper, orchestra, political, radio and TV, religious, social, and student government. Popular campus events include Bermuda Shorts Day (last day of classes in April).

Sports: There are 10 intercollegiate sports for men and 9 for women, and 20 intramural sports for men and 18 for women. Facilities include 3 gyms, a 50-meter swimming pool, a 200-meter indoor track, a 3-story climbing wall, an indoor speed-skating arena, an outdoor stadium, rooms for weight training, aerobics, and combatives, and squash, tennis, and racquetball courts. There is also a 200-seat lecture theater, a games area, and an outdoor recreation center.

Disabled Students: All of the campus is accessible. Wheelchair ramps, elevators, special parking, specially equipped rest rooms, lowered drinking fountains, lowered telephones, and special housing are available.

Services: Counseling and information services are available, as is tutoring in most subjects. There is a reader service for the blind and remedial writing.

Campus Safety and Security: Measures include security escort services, informal discussions, emergency telephones, and lighted pathways/sidewalks.

Programs of Study: U of C confers B.A., B.Sc., B.Acc.S., B.Comm., B.C.R., B.C.S., B.Ed., B.F.A., B.G.S., B.H.R.M., B.H.Sc., B.Kin., B.Mus., B.N., B.Sc.Eng., B.S.W., and LL.B. degrees. Master's and doctoral degrees are also awarded. Bachelor's degrees are awarded in BIOLOGICAL SCIENCE (biochemistry, bioinformatics, biology/biological science, botany, cell biology, ecology, and zoology), BUSINESS (accounting, business administration and management, hotel/motel and restaurant management, and marketing/retailing/merchandising), COMMUNICATIONS AND THE ARTS (art history and appreciation, communications, dance, dramatic arts, English, fine arts, French, German, linguistics, music, music history and appreciation, music performance, music theory and composition, Russian, and Spanish), COMPUTER AND PHYSICAL SCIENCE (actuarial science, applied mathematics, applied physics, astrophysics, chemical physics, chemistry, computer science, earth science, geology, geophysics and seismology, mathematics, natural sciences, physics, and statistics), EDUCATION (education, elementary, and secondary), ENGINEERING AND ENVIRONMENTAL DESIGN (chemical engineering, civil engineering, computer engineering, electrical/electronics engineering, environmental science, manufacturing engineering, mechanical engineering, petroleum/natural gas engineering, surveying engineering, systems engineering, and technology and public affairs), HEALTH PROFESSIONS (biomedical science, exercise science, nursing, public health, and sports medicine), SOCIAL SCIENCE (anthropology, archeology, Asian/Oriental studies, Canadian studies, classical/ancient civilization, community services, economics, geography, history, international relations, Latin American studies, law, liberal arts/general studies, philosophy, physical fitness/movement, political science/government, psychology, religion, social work, sociology, urban studies, and women's studies). Engineering and medicine are the strongest academically. Education, management, and engineering are the largest.

Required: To graduate, all students must satisfy the required courses, course sequences, and credit distribution in their particular program. Students must maintain a minimum 2.0 GPA and complete 7 to 10 full-course equivalents in the major field.

Special: The university offers co-op programs in applied chemistry, management, and many other fields. Dual majors, work-study programs, internships in engineering, computer science, and health sciences, combined degrees in many disciplines, and study abroad in 28 countries are also available. Students may cross-register with any of 8 member colleges in the Big Country Education Consortium. U of C sponsors or is affiliated with 20 research institutes and groups.

Faculty/Classroom: The average class size in an introductory lecture is 60 and in a laboratory, 24.

Admissions: 66% of the 2003-2004 applicants were accepted.

Requirements: U.S. applicants must be graduates of a secondary school and submit the SAT I and 3 SAT II: Subject test scores, as required by the individual faculties. AP credits are accepted.

Procedure: Freshmen are admitted in the fall. There is an early admissions plan. Applications should be filed by March 1 for fall entry. The fall 2003 application fee was $65 CDN. Applications are accepted on-line through the university's web site.

Transfer: Applicants must have a cumulative GPA of 2.0 or above on all transfer courses. 5 courses required for the bachelor's degree must be completed at U of C.

Visiting: There are regularly scheduled orientations for prospective students. There are guides for informal visits. To schedule a visit, contact the Prospective Student Office at (403) 220-6920.

International Students: There are 657 international students enrolled. The school actively recruits these students. They must score 560 on the written TOEFL or 220 on the electronic version or take the IELTS, the CAEL, or the university's English program.

Computers: The mainframe is an IBM 9672 Model R41. There are a number of PC, Mac, and UNIX workstation labs across campus. All students may access the system. 800 terminals are available 24 hours per day. There are no time limits and no fees. It is strongly recommended that all students have a personal computer, and engineering and management students must have them. Updated specifications are listed on faculty web sites.

Admissions Contact: Kevin Paul, Director of Enrollment Services. E-mail: *applinfo@ucalgary.ca* Web: *www.ucalgary.ca*

UNIVERSITY OF GUELPH
Guelph, ON, Canada N1G 2W1   E-3
(519) 824-4120

Full-time: 13,617 men and women	**Faculty:** 760
Part-time: n/av	**Ph.D.s:** 97%
Graduate: 1859 men and women	**Student/Faculty:** 22 to 1
Year: trimesters, summer session	**Tuition:** $4904 CDN ($10,689 CDN)
Application Deadline: April 1	
	Room & Board: $6644 CDN
Freshman Class: 41,865 applied, 18,225 accepted, 5213 enrolled	
SAT I or ACT: required	

The University of Guelph, founded in 1964, is a public institution offering programs in arts and sciences, agriculture, engineering, commerce, landscape architecture, veterinary medicine, applied science, and technology. There are 6 undergraduate and 45 graduate schools. The 2 libraries contain 2.5 million volumes, 1.5 million microform items, and 17,000 audio/video tapes/CDs, and subscribe to 7600 periodicals. Computerized library services include interlibrary loans, database searching, and Internet access. Special learning facilities include a learning resource center, art gallery, radio station, observatory, learning commons, research park, and arboretum. The 1017-acre campus is in a suburban area 2 miles south of the center of Guelph. Including any residence halls, there are 80 buildings.

Student Life: 93% of undergraduates are from Canada. Students are from 90 foreign countries. The average age of freshmen is 18; all undergraduates, 21. 9% do not continue beyond their first year; 88% remain to graduate.

Housing: 5500 students can be accommodated in college housing, which includes single-sex and coed dorms, on-campus apartments, and married-student housing. In addition, there are language houses, special-interest houses, an international house, La Maison Francaise, Eco

House, and an arts house. On-campus housing is guaranteed for the freshman year only, is available on a first-come, first-served basis, and is available on a lottery system for upperclassmen. 67% of students commute. All students may keep cars.

Activities: There are no fraternities or sororities. There are 100 groups on campus, including art, cheerleading, chess, choir, chorale, computers, dance, debate, drama, ethnic, gay, international, jazz band, newspaper, photography, political, professional, radio and TV, religious, social, social service, student government, and yearbook. Popular campus events include College Royal open house weekend in March and Community Bar-B-Que.

Sports: There are 15 intercollegiate sports for men and 15 for women, and 14 intramural sports for men and 11 for women. Facilities include a twin-pad arena, 5 squash courts, a fitness gym, weight-training rooms, a 6-lane swimming pool and an Olympic-size pool, a fitness circuit, and 3 gyms. Outdoor facilities include 4 tennis courts, a running track, lighted football, field hockey, soccer, rugby, and fastball fields, jogging trails, and multipurpose fields. There are also 2 dance studios, a climbing wall, and a wrestling/combatives room.

Disabled Students: 90% of the campus is accessible. Wheelchair ramps, elevators, special parking, specially equipped rest rooms, special class scheduling, lowered drinking fountains, lowered telephones, and special library services, equipment, and software are available.

Services: Counseling and information services are available, as is tutoring in most subjects. There is a reader service for the blind. ESL, learning, studying, and writing resources are available.

Campus Safety and Security: Measures include 24-hour foot and vehicle patrol, self-defense education, security escort services, and pamphlets/posters/films. There are emergency telephones and lighted pathways/sidewalks. There is a campus safe walk and a campus police patrol.

Programs of Study: U of G confers B.A., B.A.S., B.A.Sc., B.B.R.M., B.Comm., B.Comp., B.L.A., B.Sc., B.Sc.Agr., B.Sc.Eng., B.Sc.Env., and B.Sc.(Tech) degrees. Master's and doctoral degrees are also awarded. Bachelor's degrees are awarded in AGRICULTURE (agricultural business management, agricultural economics, agronomy, animal science, environmental studies, horticulture, natural resource management, and plant science), BIOLOGICAL SCIENCE (biochemistry, biology/biological science, biophysics, ecology, environmental biology, marine biology, microbiology, molecular biology, nutrition, toxicology, wildlife biology, and zoology), BUSINESS (business economics, hotel/motel and restaurant management, human resources, marketing management, real estate, and tourism), COMMUNICATIONS AND THE ARTS (art history and appreciation, classical languages, dramatic arts, English, music, Spanish, and studio art), COMPUTER AND PHYSICAL SCIENCE (applied mathematics, applied physics, chemical physics, chemistry, computer science, earth science, information sciences and systems, mathematics, physical sciences, physics, and statistics), ENGINEERING AND ENVIRONMENTAL DESIGN (bioengineering, environmental engineering, environmental science, landscape architecture/design, and systems engineering), HEALTH PROFESSIONS (biomedical science, environmental health science, and pharmacology), SOCIAL SCIENCE (anthropology, child care/child and family studies, classical/ancient civilization, criminal justice, development economics, dietetics, economics, European studies, food science, French studies, geography, gerontology, history, human ecology, philosophy, physical fitness/movement, political science/government, psychology, public administration, sociology, water resources, and women's studies). Biological and physical sciences and veterinary medicine are the strongest academically. Biological and physical sciences, arts, and social sciences are the largest.

Required: To graduate, students must complete 30 credits (half courses) for a general degree and 40 credits (half courses) for an honors degree. U of G requires a minimum of 10 credits in the major.

Special: U of G offers co-op programs in 34 majors, study abroad in 29 countries, and work-study programs. Accelerated degree programs, dual majors, a general studies degree, and nondegree study are available. There is a freshman honors program.

Faculty/Classroom: The average class size in an introductory lecture is 300 and in a laboratory, 25.

Admissions: 44% of the 2003-2004 applicants were accepted.

Requirements: The SAT I or ACT is required for U.S. applicants. Standardized test scores are not considered in the admissions decision for Ontario applicants. Applicants must have a minimum overall average of 75% on 6 Ontario Academic Course (Grade 13) credits. Higher averages may be required for admission to individual programs. U.S. applicants should rank in the upper quarter of their high school class and have a B average for admission consideration. Some programs require an interview, background information, or a portfolio. AP credits are accepted. Important factors in the admissions decision are advanced placement or honor courses, extracurricular activities record, and leadership record.

Procedure: Freshmen are admitted in the fall. There are early decision and deferred admissions plans. Early decision applications should be filed by March 1; regular applications, by April 1 for fall entry, along with an $85 CDN fee. Notification of early decision is sent in mid April ; regular decision, in late May. 9000 early decision candidates were accepted for the 2003-2004 class. Applications are accepted on-line through the Ontario Universities' Application Centre.

Transfer: Applicants must meet general admissions requirements and have a B average in all college-level courses. 10 of 20 credits required for the bachelor's degree must be completed at U of G.

Visiting: There are regularly scheduled orientations for prospective students, including daily tours of the campus, Fall Preview Day, and Campus Days and Connection Conference in the spring. There are guides for informal visits and visitors may sit in on classes. To schedule a visit, contact the tour coordinator at (519) 824-4120, ext. 58712.

Financial Aid: The FAFSA, the college's own financial statement, and the Federal and Provincial Government Canadian Form are required. The deadline for filing freshman financial aid applications for fall entry is September 30.

International Students: In a recent year, there were 150 international students enrolled. The school actively recruits these students. They must score 600 on the written TOEFL or 250 on the electronic version and also take the TWE and TSE. The IELTS or MELAB may be substituted for these tests. U.S. students are required to submit SAT I or ACT scores, with an SAT I combined score of 1100 or an ACT score of 24.

Computers: The mainframes are UNIX, HP, and SUN servers. There are more than 1000 PCs across the campus for student use. Almost all offer access to the Internet. All students may access the system at any time.

Graduates: In a recent year, 2429 bachelor's degrees were awarded. The most popular majors were biological science (11%), sociology (6%), and human kinetics (4%). In an average class, 5% graduate in 3 years or less, 49% graduate in 4 years or less, 71% graduate in 5 years or less, and 74% graduate in 6 years or less.

Admissions Contact: Ray Darling, Director Admission Services. E-mail: *info@registrar.uoguelph.ca* Web: *www.uoguelph.ca*

UNIVERSITY OF OTTAWA
E-3
Ottawa, ON, Canada K1N 6N5

(613) 562-5783
Fax: (613) 562-5104

Full-time: 6000 men, 8000 women	**Faculty:** 992
Part-time: 2100 men, 3500 women	**Ph.D.s:** 96%
Graduate: 1750 men, 1700 women	**Student/Faculty:** 14 to 1
Year: semesters, summer session	**Tuition:** $4500 CDN ($9000) CDN
Application Deadline: see profile	**Room & Board:** $5000 CDN
Freshman Class: n/av	
SAT I: required	

The University of Ottawa, founded in 1848, is a bilingual (French/English) institution offering undergraduate and graduate degrees through the faculties of Administration, Arts, Law, Health Sciences, Medicine, Science, Engineering, Social Sciences and Education. Figures given in the above capsule and in this profile are approximate. There are 9 undergraduate and 9 graduate schools. The 8 libraries contain 1.5 million volumes, 1.3 million microform items, and 11,000 audio/video tapes/CDs, and subscribe to 10,000 periodicals. Computerized library services include the card catalog, interlibrary loans, and database searching. Special learning facilities include a learning resource center and radio station. The 70-acre campus is in an urban area. Including any residence halls, there are 31 buildings.

Student Life: 78% of undergraduates are from Ontario. Students are from 10 states and 4 foreign countries.

Housing: 2132 students can be accommodated in college housing, which includes single-sex and coed dorms, on-campus apartments, and married-student housing. On-campus housing is available on a lottery system for upperclassmen. 84% of students commute. Alcohol is not permitted. All students may keep cars.

Activities: There are no fraternities or sororities. There are 50 groups on campus, including art, band, chess, choir, chorale, computers, drama, ethnic, gay, international, jazz band, newspaper, orchestra, photography, political, professional, radio and TV, religious, social, social service, student government, and symphony. Popular campus events include Ottawa Day, Panda football game, and International Week.

Sports: There are 8 intercollegiate sports for men and 7 for women, and 6 intramural sports for men and 6 for women. Facilities include weight-training and combat rooms, a 50-meter swimming pool, gyms, racquetball and squash courts, billiards and ping pong tables, an indoor arena, and a sports field.

Disabled Students: 75% of the campus is accessible. Wheelchair ramps, elevators, special parking, specially equipped rest rooms, special class scheduling, lowered drinking fountains, lowered telephones, and automatic doors and specialized equipment are available.

Services: Counseling and information services are available, as is tutoring in most subjects. There is a reader service for the blind and remedial math, reading, and writing.

Campus Safety and Security: Measures include 24-hour foot and vehicle patrol, self-defense education, security escort services, and shuttle buses. There are informal discussions, pamphlets/posters/films, emergency telephones, and lighted pathways/sidewalks, and the university participates in a community crime-stoppers program.

Programs of Study: UO confers B.A., B.Ad., B.A.Sc., B.Com., B.Ed., B.F.A., B.Mus., B.Sc., B.Sc.N., and B.Soc.Sc. degrees. Master's and doctoral degrees are also awarded. Bachelor's degrees are awarded in BIOLOGICAL SCIENCE (biochemistry, biology/biological science, biotechnology, and physiology), BUSINESS (accounting, human resources, management information systems, management science, and marketing/retailing/merchandising), COMMUNICATIONS AND THE ARTS (communications, English, French, German, Italian, Latin, linguistics, music, photography, Spanish, and visual and performing arts), COMPUTER AND PHYSICAL SCIENCE (chemistry, computer science, geology, mathematics, and physics), EDUCATION (education), ENGINEERING AND ENVIRONMENTAL DESIGN (chemical engineering, civil engineering, computer engineering, electrical/electronics engineering, environmental engineering, and mechanical engineering), HEALTH PROFESSIONS (nursing and occupational therapy), SOCIAL SCIENCE (Canadian studies, criminology, economics, geography, history, law, medieval studies, philosophy, political science/government, psychology, public administration, religion, Russian and Slavic studies, sociology, and women's studies). Law, medicine, and education are the strongest academically. Arts, social sciences, and science are the largest.

Required: Students must maintain a GPA of 3.5 out of 10 for all courses, including those in the major. Students must also complete a second language requirement: French for English students, and English for French students.

Special: Opportunities are provided for cooperative programs, study abroad in 42 countries, a general studies degree in arts and in sciences, and combined programs in all fields in arts and in social sciences.

Faculty/Classroom: 76% of faculty are male; 24%, female. The average class size in an introductory lecture is 60; in a laboratory, 30; and in a regular course, 30.

Requirements: The SAT I is required, with a minimum composite score of 1000 (500 verbal and 500 math). Graduation from an accredited secondary school is required. Those students planning to major in occupational or physical therapy must speak French. A portfolio is required for fine arts students, and an audition for music students. AP credits are accepted.

Procedure: Freshmen are admitted fall and winter. Check with the school for current application deadlines and fee. Notification is sent on a rolling basis. A waiting list is an active part of the admissions procedure.

Transfer: Admissions requirements vary according to program. 30 credits required for the bachelor's degree must be completed at UO.

Visiting: There are regularly scheduled orientations for prospective students. There are guides for informal visits and visitors may sit in on classes. To schedule a visit, contact the Liaison Office at (613) 562-5800, ext. 1000.

Financial Aid: Check with the school for current deadlines.

International Students: They must score 550 on the written TOEFL or take the MELAB or the university's own test.

Computers: The mainframe is an Amdahl 5880. Students have access to PCs in several computer labs on campus. All students may access the system 8 A.M. to 10 P.M., 6 days a week. There are no time limits and no fees.

Admissions Contact: Andre-Pierre Lepage, Director of Admissions/Associate Registrar. E-mail: *liaison@uottawa.ca*

UNIVERSITY OF SASKATCHEWAN
C-2
Saskatoon, SK, Canada S7N 5A2

(306) 966-5788
Fax: (306) 966-6730

Full-time: 5780 men, 7610 women	**Faculty:** n/av
Part-time: 830 men, 1390 women	**Ph.D.s:** 65%
Graduate: 970 men, 790 women	**Student/Faculty:** n/av
Year: terms, summer session	**Tuition:** $4000 CDN ($7000) CDN
Application Deadline: see profile	**Room & Board:** $4000 CDN
Freshman Class: n/av	
SAT I or ACT: not required	

The University of Saskatchewan, founded in 1907, is a public institution offering programs in business, agriculture, arts and sciences, education, engineering, and health professions. Figures given in the above capsule and in this profile are approximate. There are 14 undergraduate schools and 1 graduate school. The 8 libraries contain 1.6 million volumes, 2.9 million microform items, and 35,000 audio/video tapes/CDs, and subscribe to 8500 periodicals. Computerized library services include the card catalog, interlibrary loans, and database searching. Special learning facilities include an art gallery, natural history museum, and planetarium. The 363-acre campus is in an urban area in Saskatoon. Including any residence halls, there are 55 buildings.

Student Life: The average age of all undergraduates is 21. 7% do not continue beyond their first year.

Housing: University-sponsored living facilities include dorms, off-campus apartments, and married-student housing. On-campus housing is available on a first-come, first-served basis. All students may keep cars.

Activities: There are no fraternities or sororities. There are many groups and organizations on campus, including band, cheerleading, chess, choir, chorale, chorus, computers, drama, ethnic, gay, international, newspaper, orchestra, political, professional, religious, social, social service, and student government.

Sports: There are 8 intercollegiate sports for men and 5 for women, and 14 intramural sports for men and 15 for women. Facilities include a football stadium, a hockey rink, a curling rink, 3 gyms, 2 swimming pools, racquetball and squash courts, a track and field area, and an outdoor soccer field, a fitness center, and weight rooms.

Disabled Students: 99% of the campus is accessible. Wheelchair ramps, elevators, special parking, specially equipped rest rooms, special class scheduling, lowered drinking fountains, and lowered telephones are available. There is also a coordinator of services for students with disabilities, special funding application assistance, and special exam scheduling and accommodations. Adaptive computerized equipment is located in the main library building.

Services: Counseling and information services are available, as is tutoring in most subjects.

Campus Safety and Security: Measures include 24-hour foot and vehicle patrol, self-defense education, and security escort services.

Programs of Study: U of S confers B.A., B.Sc., B.Comm., B.E., B.Ed., B.F.A., B.Mus., B.Mus.Mus.Ed., B.S.A., B.Sc.(Nutr.), B.Sc.(P.T.), B.S.N., B.S.P., B.S.P.E., and L.L.B. degrees. Master's and doctoral degrees are also awarded. Bachelor's degrees are awarded in AGRICULTURE (agricultural economics, agricultural mechanics, agronomy, animal science, horticulture, plant science, range/farm management, and soil science), BIOLOGICAL SCIENCE (anatomy, biochemistry, biology/biological science, microbiology, nutrition, and physiology), BUSINESS (accounting, business administration and management, business economics, human resources, and marketing/retailing/merchandising), COMMUNICATIONS AND THE ARTS (art, classics, English, French, German, Greek, Hebrew, Latin, linguistics, music, Russian, and Spanish), COMPUTER AND PHYSICAL SCIENCE (chemistry, computer science, geology, geophysics and seismology, mathematics, paleontology, and physics), EDUCATION (elementary, home economics, and physical), ENGINEERING AND ENVIRONMENTAL DESIGN (chemical engineering, civil engineering, electrical/electronics engineering, engineering physics, geological engineering, land use management and reclamation, and mechanical engineering), HEALTH PROFESSIONS (medical science, nursing, pharmacy, physical therapy, and veterinary science), SOCIAL SCIENCE (economics, food science, geography, history, international studies, law, Native American studies, Near Eastern studies, philosophy, political science/government, psychology, public administration, Russian and Slavic studies, sociology, and urban studies).

Required: Requirements for graduation vary according to the program of study.

Special: The University of Saskatchewan offers interdisciplinary majors, including agricultural biology, agricultural chemistry, agricultural and bioresource engineering, agricultural extension, and anthropology and archaeology. Co-op programs are offered through the Program for Agricultural Cooperative Education. There are computer science internships, as well as internships offered through the Engineering Professional Internship program. The university has exchange agreements with 6 countries.

Faculty/Classroom: 80% of faculty are male; 20%, female.

Requirements: Applicants must be graduates of an accredited secondary school. In direct-entry programs, priority is given to Saskatchewan residents, with the exception being the College of Arts and Sciences. A high school average of 65 is required. AP credits are accepted.

Procedure: Freshmen are admitted in the fall. There are early decision and early admissions plans. Check with the school for current application deadlines and fee. Applications are accepted on-line at the school's web site.

Transfer: Applicants must meet promotion levels for the college to which transfer is sought; in most cases they should be Saskatchewan residents.

Visiting: There are regularly scheduled orientations for prospective students. To schedule a visit, contact the Student's Union at (306) 966-6963.

Financial Aid: Check with the school for current deadlines.

International Students: The school actively recruits these students. They must score 550 on the written TOEFL or take the MELAB, IELTS, or CanTEST.

Computers: Computer science students may access the system. There are no time limits. The fee varies.

Admissions Contact: Kelly McInnes, Admissions Counsellor. E-mail: *admissions@usask.ca* Web: *http://www.usask.ca/registrar*

UNIVERSITY OF TORONTO   E-3
Toronto, ON, Canada M5S 1A1   (416) 978-2190
         Fax: (416) 978-6089

Full-time: 16,426 men, 21,486 women	**Faculty:** 1260
Part-time: 5108 men, 7380 women	**Ph.D.s:** n/av
Graduate: 6920 men, 6602 women	**Student/Faculty:** 30 to 1
Year: terms or trimesters, summer session	**Tuition:** $3781 ($8762)
	Room & Board: $5400

Application Deadline: March 1
Freshman Class: 75,382 applied, 44,852 accepted, 13,940 enrolled
SAT I: required

The University of Toronto, founded in 1827, is a public institution offering undergraduate programs in applied science and engineering, arts and science, education, dentistry, law, medicine, music, nursing, pharmacy, physical and health education, and radiation sciences. Degrees are also offered at the graduate level in a wide range of programs. There are 19 undergraduate schools and 1 graduate school. The 32 libraries contain 9,533,104 volumes, 5,094,957 microform items, and 217,914 audio/video tapes/CDs, and subscribe to 53,642 periodicals. Computerized library services include the card catalog, interlibrary loans, database searching, and Internet access. Special learning facilities include a learning resource center, art gallery, radio station, and observatory. The 3 campuses in downtown and suburban Toronto total 690 acres. Including any residence halls, there are 247 buildings.

Student Life: 88% of undergraduates are from Ontario. The average age of freshmen is 19; all undergraduates, 21. 5% do not continue beyond their first year; 83% remain to graduate.

Housing: 7276 students can be accommodated in college housing, which includes single-sex and coed dorms, on-campus apartments, off-campus apartments, and married-student housing. On-campus housing is guaranteed for the freshman year only and is available on a first-come, first-served basis. Priority is given to out-of-town students. 80% of students commute. All students may keep cars.

Activities: There are no fraternities or sororities. There are 200 groups on campus, including art, band, cheerleading, chess, choir, chorus, computers, dance, debate, drama, ethnic, film, gay, international, jazz band, literary magazine, musical theater, newspaper, opera, orchestra, photography, political, radio and TV, religious, social, student government, symphony, and yearbook. Popular campus events include U of T Day, concerts, and theater productions, films, lectures, and seasonal activities.

Sports: There are 27 intercollegiate sports for men and 26 for women, and 29 intramural sports for men and 29 for women. Facilities include swimming pools, an outdoor hockey rink, weight and exercise rooms, gyms, squash and multipurpose courts, a rifle range, dance studios, playing fields, a stadium, an arena, and a 200-meter indoor running track.

Disabled Students: Wheelchair ramps, elevators, special parking, specially equipped rest rooms, lowered drinking fountains, and lowered telephones are available.

Services: Counseling and information services are available, as is tutoring in every subject. There is a reader service for the blind.

Campus Safety and Security: Measures include 24-hour foot and vehicle patrol, self-defense education, security escort services, and shuttle buses. There are informal discussions, pamphlets/posters/films, emergency telephones, and lighted pathways/sidewalks.

Programs of Study: U of T confers B.A., B.Sc., B.A.Sc., B.B.A., B.Com., B.Ed., B.Sc.Med.Rad.Sc., B.Sc.N., B.Sc.O.T., B.Sc.Phm., B.Sc.P.T., B.S.P.H.E., and Mus.Bac. degrees. Master's and doctoral degrees are also awarded. Bachelor's degrees are awarded in AGRICULTURE (environmental studies, forestry and related sciences, and natural resource management), BIOLOGICAL SCIENCE (biochemistry, biology/biological science, biophysics, biotechnology, botany, cell biology, ecology, evolutionary biology, life science, microbiology, molecular biology, neurosciences, nutrition, physiology, toxicology, and zoology), BUSINESS (banking and finance, business administration and management, business economics, electronic business, and human resources), COMMUNICATIONS AND THE ARTS (art history and appreciation, arts administration/management, classics, communications, communications technology, comparative literature, dramatic arts, English, film arts, French, German, Greek, Italian, journalism, Latin, linguistics, media arts, modern language, music, music history and appreciation, music theory and composition, musicology/ethnomusicology, Polish, Portuguese, Russian languages and literature, Slavic languages, Spanish, technical and business writing, and visual and performing arts), COMPUTER AND PHYSICAL SCIENCE (actuarial science, applied mathematics, applied physics, astronomy, astrophysics, chemical physics, chemistry, computer science, digital arts/technology, earth science, geology, mathematics, paleontology, physical sciences, physics, planetary and space science, statistics, and systems analysis), EDUCATION (education, education of the exceptional child, foreign languages, music, and physical), ENGINEERING AND ENVIRONMENTAL DESIGN (architecture, chemical engineering, civil engineering, computer engineering, electrical/electronics engineering, engineering and applied science, environmental science, industrial engineering, materials engineering, materials science, mechanical engineering, mining and mineral engineering, and water and waste-water technology), HEALTH PROFESSIONS (environmental health science, health, nursing, occupational therapy, pharmacology, pharmacy, physical therapy, physician's assistant, and radiological science), SOCIAL SCIENCE (African studies, American studies, anthropology, applied psychology, archeology, behavioral science, Canadian studies, Caribbean studies, Celtic studies, Christian studies, classical/ancient civilization, cognitive science, criminology, East Asian studies, economics, ethics, politics, and social policy, European studies, forensic studies, geography, German area studies, Hispanic American studies, history, history of science, human ecology, humanities, international relations, international studies, Judaic studies, medieval studies, Middle Eastern studies, Native American studies, Pacific area studies, peace studies, philosophy, political science/government, psychology, public affairs, religion, Russian and Slavic studies, Scandinavian studies, sociology, South Asian studies, urban studies, and women's studies). Arts and science, applied science, and engineering are the largest.

Required: Arts and science students must satisfy a breadth requirement, which includes 3 courses from outside the major. Students must complete 20 credits for a 4-year degree, plus prerequisite subjects.

Special: The university offers co-op programs in management, arts management, cell and molecular biology, computer science, mathematical and physical sciences, sociology, applied psychology, public policy, humanities, and international development studies. Study abroad, interdisciplinary programs, and various work-study programs are also available.

Faculty/Classroom: 69% of faculty are male; 31%, female.

Admissions: 59% of the 2003-2004 applicants were accepted.

Requirements: The SAT I is required. The Faculties of Arts and Science, of Music, and of Physical Education and Health will consider grade 12 applicants from an accredited U.S. high school with a high GPA and good scores on the SAT I and 3 SAT II: Subject tests. The ACT will also be considered. Engineering will consider excellent grade 12 students with high SAT I and II scores who also are completing at least 2 advanced placement courses. The SAT II: Subject tests and AP courses and exams must include math, physics, and chemistry. Other requirements may apply. Architecture students must submit a questionnaire and a portfolio. Music students must audition. A GPA of 3.0 is required. AP credits are accepted.

Procedure: Freshmen are admitted in the fall. There are early decision, early admissions, and deferred admissions plans. Early decision applications should be filed by February 1; regular applications, by March 1 for fall entry. The fall 2003 application fee was $60 CDN. Notification of early decision is sent April 30; regular decision, on a rolling basis.

Transfer: For the Arts and Science divisions, normally a B average is required. 5 of 20 courses required for the bachelor's degree must be completed at U of T.

Visiting: There are regularly scheduled orientations for prospective students. There are guides for informal visits. To schedule a visit, contact Student Recruitment at (416) 978-5000.

International Students: There are 3023 international students enrolled. The school actively recruits these students. They must score 600 on the written TOEFL or 250 on the electronic version and also take the TWE, scoring 5.0. MELAB, IELTS, or COPE scores may also be submitted.

Computers: U of T provides PCs and Macs for academic use. All students may access the system. There are no time limits and no fees.

Graduates: From July 1, 2002 to June 30, 2003, 8680 bachelor's degrees were awarded. In an average class, 83% graduate in 4 years or less.

Admissions Contact: Admissions Counselor. A video is available. E-mail: ask@adm.utoronto.ca Web: www.utoronto.ca

---

UNIVERSITY OF VICTORIA
B-2

Victoria, BC, Canada V8W 3P2

(250) 721-8121
Fax: (250) 721-6225

Full-time: 9100 men and women	Faculty: 640
Part-time: 5700 men and women	Ph.D.s: 93%
Graduate: 1650 men and women	Student/Faculty: 14 to 1
Year: terms, summer session	Tuition: $2600 CDN ($7500)
Application Deadline: see profile	CDN
	Room & Board: $5000 CDN
Freshman Class: n/av	
SAT I or ACT: not required	

The University of Victoria, founded in 1903 as Victoria College, is a public institution operated by the province of British Columbia. It offers undergraduate and graduate programs in the arts and sciences, business, education, engineering, fine arts, human and social development, and law. There are 8 undergraduate schools and 1 graduate school. Figures in the above capsule and in this profile are approximate. The 4 libraries contain 1.6 million volumes, 1.7 million microform items, and 177,000 audio/video tapes/CDs, and subscribe to 8000 periodicals. Computerized library services include the card catalog, interlibrary loans, and data-

base searching. Special learning facilities include a learning resource center, art gallery, radio station, and language labs. The 385-acre campus is in an urban area in Victoria. Including any residence halls, there are 107 buildings.

Student Life: 86% of undergraduates are from British Columbia.

Housing: 1700 students can be accommodated in college housing, which includes single-sex and coed dorms, on-campus apartments, and married-student housing. On-campus housing is available on a first-come, first-served basis and is available on a lottery system for upperclassmen. Priority is given to out-of-town students. Alcohol is not permitted. All students may keep cars.

Activities: There are no fraternities or sororities. There are many groups and organizations on campus, including chess, choir, chorus, computers, dance, debate, ethnic, gay, international, jazz band, musical theater, newspaper, orchestra, photography, political, radio and TV, religious, social service, student government, symphony, and yearbook. Popular campus events include Week of Welcome and the President's BBQ.

Sports: There are 7 intercollegiate sports for men and 7 for women, and 12 intramural sports for men and 12 for women. Facilities include 3 gyms, dance studio, 2 weight and fitness training rooms, racquetball and squash courts, playing fields, outdoor stadium, tennis courts, 2 swimming pools, sailing compound, and jogging trails.

Disabled Students: Wheelchair ramps, elevators, special parking, specially equipped rest rooms, lowered drinking fountains, lowered telephones, speech synthesizers, and Arkenstone reading computers are available.

Services: There is remedial reading and writing.

Campus Safety and Security: Measures include 24-hour foot and vehicle patrol, self-defense education, security escort services, and pamphlets/posters/films. There are emergency telephones and lighted pathways/sidewalks.

Programs of Study: UVic confers B.A., B.S., B.Com., B.Ed., B.Eng., B.F.A., B.Mus., B.Sc., B.S.N., B.S.W., and L.L.B. degrees. Master's and doctoral degrees are also awarded. Bachelor's degrees are awarded in BIOLOGICAL SCIENCE (biochemistry, biology/biological science, and microbiology), BUSINESS (business administration and management and recreation and leisure services), COMMUNICATIONS AND THE ARTS (art history and appreciation, classics, creative writing, dramatic arts, English, French, Germanic languages and literature, linguistics, music, and visual and performing arts), COMPUTER AND PHYSICAL SCIENCE (astronomy, chemistry, computer science, earth science, mathematics, and physics), EDUCATION (elementary, physical, and secondary), ENGINEERING AND ENVIRONMENTAL DESIGN (computer engineering, electrical/electronics engineering, and mechanical engineering), HEALTH PROFESSIONS (health science and nursing), SOCIAL SCIENCE (anthropology, child care/child and family studies, economics, geography, history, Italian studies, medieval studies, Pacific area studies, philosophy, political science/government, psychology, Russian and Slavic studies, social work, sociology, and women's studies).

Required: To graduate, students must complete the university English requirement, a minimum of 60 units above the 100 level, at least 21 of which must be upper level, and have a 2.0 GPA.

Special: A number of co-op and internship programs are available in specific disciplines as are many dual majors, including biochemistry/microbiology and Hispanic/Italian studies. Work-study is possible on a limited basis for Canadian students only.

Faculty/Classroom: 68% of faculty are male; 32%, female. All teach undergraduates and do research. No introductory courses are taught by graduate students. The average class size in an introductory lecture is 53 and in a regular course, 30.

Requirements: Application requires high school graduation with a 2.5 GPA or higher, 4 semesters of English, 2 each of social science, math, science, and language, and 6 semesters of 2.5 work at grade 12 level. AP credits are accepted.

Procedure: Freshmen are admitted to all sessions. Check with the school for current application deadlines and fee. Applications are accepted on-line at the school's web site.

Transfer: Requirements vary with the program and the individual. 30 of 60 credits required for the bachelor's degree must be completed at UVic.

Visiting: There are guides for informal visits and visitors may sit in on classes and stay overnight. To schedule a visit, contact Public Relations at (250) 721-7645.

Financial Aid: Check with the school for current deadlines.

International Students: The school actively recruits these students. They must score 575 on the written TOEFL or take the MELAB, or International English Language Testing System (I.E.L.T.S.).

Computers: The mainframes are an IBM 3090-150S, a SUN 3/280S, and a Pyramid 98Xe. Access to the mainframes are by Wideband and Ethernet networks to PCs and terminals throughout campus. There are computer labs. The SUN and Pyramid systems utilize UNIX operating systems. Equipment includes PCs, Macs, and DEC VAX systems. All students may access the system at any time. There are no time limits and no fees.

Admissions Contact: Admissions Officer. A video is available.
E-mail: *srsad13@uvvm.uvic.ca* Web: *http://web.uvic.ca/adms*

UNIVERSITY OF WATERLOO
E-3
Waterloo, ON, Canada N2L 3G1 (519) 888-4567, ext. 3777
Fax: (519) 746-8088

Full-time: 10,778 men, 9268 women	Faculty: 787
Part-time: 741 men, 1453 women	Ph.D.s: 96%
Graduate: 1679 men, 975 women	Student/Faculty: 25 to 1
Year: trimesters, summer session	Tuition: $4685 CDN ($16,715 CDN)
Application Deadline: March 31	
	Room & Board: $6700 CDN

Freshman Class: 39,360 applied, 20,500 accepted, 5350 enrolled
SAT I or ACT: required for some programs

The University of Waterloo, founded in 1957, is a public institution that offers undergraduate and graduate programs in applied health sciences, arts, engineering, environmental studies, independent studies, math, and science. Students have a home base in 1 of 6 faculties or 4 affiliated institutions. Most programs are offered in either the traditional or the cooperative system of study. There are 10 undergraduate and 6 graduate schools. The 4 libraries contain 1,984,328 volumes, 1,681,786 microform items, and 1382 audio/video tapes/CDs, and subscribe to 15,184 periodicals. Computerized library services include the card catalog, interlibrary loans, and database searching. Special learning facilities include a learning resource center, an art gallery, a radio station, 4 museums, 2 theaters, and an observatory. The 900-acre campus is in a suburban area 60 miles southwest of Toronto. Including any residence halls, there are 59 buildings.

Student Life: 95% of undergraduates are from Ontario. Students are from 12 provinces.

Housing: 5770 students can be accommodated in college housing, which includes single-sex and coed dorms and on-campus apartments. In addition, there are special-interest houses, language floors, and an off-campus housing service. On-campus housing is guaranteed for the freshman year only. Priority is given to out-of-town students. All students may keep cars.

Activities: 1% of men belong to 1 national fraternity; 1% of women belong to 1 national sorority. There are many groups and organizations on campus, including band, bridge, cheerleading, chess, choir, computers, dance, debate, drama, ethnic, film, gay, honors, international, juggling, literary magazine, marching band, martial arts, musical theater, newspaper, photography, political, professional, radio and TV, religious, social, social dance, social service, student government, and yearbook. Popular campus events include Oktoberfest and Canada Day.

Sports: There are 16 intercollegiate sports for men and 15 for women. Facilities include outdoor playing fields, an ice arena, a swimming pool, a diving tank, squash courts, weight rooms, 2 gyms, a dance studio, tennis courts, and activity areas.

Disabled Students: All of the campus is accessible. Wheelchair ramps, elevators, special parking, specially equipped rest rooms, special class scheduling, lowered drinking fountains, lowered telephones, and up-to-date technical equipment for the visually disabled and the hearing impaired are available.

Services: Counseling and information services are available, as is tutoring in most subjects. There is a reader service for the blind and remedial math, reading, and writing.

Campus Safety and Security: Measures include 24-hour foot and vehicle patrol, self-defense education, security escort services, and shuttle buses. There are informal discussions, pamphlets/posters/films, emergency telephones, and lighted pathways/sidewalks.

Programs of Study: UW confers B.A., B.Sc., B.A.F.M., B.A.Sc., B.C.S., B.E.S., B.I.S., B.Math, B.S.E., and B.S.W. degrees. Master's and doctoral degrees are also awarded. Bachelor's degrees are awarded in AGRICULTURE (environmental studies), BIOLOGICAL SCIENCE (biochemistry, bioinformatics, biology/biological science, biotechnology, and genetics), BUSINESS (accounting, business administration and management, human resources, management science, operations research, and recreation and leisure services), COMMUNICATIONS AND THE ARTS (art history and appreciation, arts administration/management, classics, dramatic arts, English, English literature, film arts, fine arts, French, German, music, Russian, Spanish, speech/debate/rhetoric, and studio art), COMPUTER AND PHYSICAL SCIENCE (actuarial science, applied mathematics, chemical physics, chemistry, computer mathematics, computer science, digital arts/technology, earth science, geochemistry, geology, geophysics and seismology, information sciences and systems, mathematics, physical chemistry, physics, science, science and management, software engineering, and statistics), EDUCATION (foreign languages, mathematics, and science), ENGINEERING AND ENVIRONMENTAL DESIGN (architecture, chemical engineering, city/community/regional planning, civil engineering, computational sciences, computer engineering, electrical/electronics engineering, engineering, environmental engineering, environmental science, geological engineering, mechanical engineering, and systems engineering), HEALTH PROFESSIONS (health,

health science, optometry, preallied health, preoptometry, prepodiatry, and respiratory therapy), SOCIAL SCIENCE (anthropology, Canadian studies, economics, French studies, geography, history, human development, international studies, medieval studies, philosophy, physical fitness/movement, political science/government, psychology, religion, Russian and Slavic studies, social work, sociology, and women's studies). Engineering, accounting, and mathematics are the strongest academically. The arts program is the largest.

Required: To graduate, all students must satisfy specific program requirements. These include a writing skills requirement in applied health sciences, environmental studies, engineering, mathematics, and science programs. The total number of credits required is from 15 to 23 1/2. The minimum grade average is from 53 to 70.

Special: Cross-registration with Wilfrid Laurier University, study abroad in 27 countries, dual, student-designed, and interdisciplinary majors, a combined bachelor's-master's degree in accounting and engineering, and noncredit courses are available. Students may study under the regular or cooperative system, which allows off-campus work terms in education, professional organizations and agencies, business, industry, or government. There are concurrent education programs in conjunction with the faculties of education at Brock and Queen's Universities.

Faculty/Classroom: All both teach and do research.

Admissions: 52% of the 2003-2004 applicants were accepted.

Requirements: The SAT I or ACT is required for some programs. In addition, candidates from the United States must have a high school diploma with exceptionally high standing and AP exams in prerequisite subjects or first-year university standing in acceptable subjects from an accredited university. An audition, portfolio, and/or interview may be required for certain programs. A GPA of 3.0 is required. Important factors in the admissions decision are advanced placement or honor courses, extracurricular activities record, and leadership record.

Procedure: Freshmen are admitted fall, winter, and spring. Entrance exams should be taken in time to meet deadlines for completion of files. Applications should be filed by March 31 for fall entry, November 1 for winter entry, and March 1 for spring entry, along with a $145 CDN fee. Notification is sent June 4. Applications are accepted on-line at *www.ouac.on.ca*.

Transfer: Applicants are considered on an individual basis. 10 of 20 credits required for the bachelor's degree must be completed at UW.

Visiting: There are regularly scheduled orientations for prospective students, including tours and individual and group information sessions. There are guides for informal visits and visitors may sit in on classes. To schedule a visit, contact the Visitors Reception Center at (519) 888-4567, ext. 3614 or *www.findoutmore.uwaterloo.ca/visitus*.

Financial Aid: The FAFSA is required. The deadline for filing freshman financial aid applications for fall entry is June 11.

International Students: There are 990 international students enrolled. The school actively recruits these students. They must score 600 on the written TOEFL or 237 on the electronic version and also take the TWE and the TSE. The MELAB or the IELTS may also be submitted.

Computers: Students have access to networked PCs, Macs, and UNIX systems. Each faculty provides computing facilities, which include e-mail, Internet access, and all necessary software. All students may access the system, but some restrictions may apply in some faculties. There are no time limits and no fees.

Graduates: From July 1, 2002 to June 30, 2003, 3519 bachelor's degrees were awarded. The most popular majors were arts (32%), mathematics (21%), and engineering (18%).

Admissions Contact: Undergraduate Recruitment.
Web: *www.findoutmore.uwaterloo.ca*

UNIVERSITY OF WESTERN ONTARIO
D-3
London, ON, Canada N6A 5B8 (519) 661-2100
Fax: (519) 661-3710

Full-time: 9266 men, 13,385 women	Faculty: 1204
Part-time: 1112 men, 1740 women	Ph.D.s: 90%
Graduate: 2113 men, 1802 women	Student/Faculty: 19 to 1
Year: semesters, summer session	Tuition: $13,129 CDN
Application Deadline: May 15	Room & Board: $6145 CDN

Freshman Class: 43,845 applied, 20,534 accepted, 4960 enrolled
SAT I: required

The University of Western Ontario, chartered in 1878, is a public institution offering daytime, evening, and correspondence programs in the liberal arts and sciences, fine arts and music, engineering, education, health services, and business. There are 12 undergraduate and 4 graduate schools. The 7 libraries contain 2,976,057 volumes, 3,808,801 microform items, and 1,063,029 audio/video tapes/CDs, and subscribe to 12,362 periodicals. Computerized library services include the card catalog, interlibrary loans, and database searching. Special learning facilities include a learning resource center, art gallery, radio station, TV station, wind tunnel, and observatory. The 402-acre campus is in an urban area 120 miles northwest of Detroit, Michigan. Including any residence halls, there are 72 buildings.

Student Life: Students are from Canada and 80 foreign countries. The average age of freshmen is 20; all undergraduates, 22.

Housing: 4168 students can be accommodated in college housing, which includes single-sex and coed dorms, on-campus apartments, and married-student housing. In addition, there are language houses, special-interest houses, an international house, and quiet floors. On-campus housing is available on a lottery system for upperclassmen. Priority is given to out-of-town students. 60% of students commute. All students may keep cars.

Activities: There are no fraternities or sororities. There are 161 groups on campus, including art, cheerleading, chess, choir, computers, drama, ethnic, gay, international, jazz band, marching band, musical theater, newspaper, political, professional, radio and TV, religious, social, social service, student government, and yearbook. Popular campus events include Orientation Week.

Sports: There are 18 intercollegiate sports for men and 18 for women, and 17 intramural sports for men and 13 for women. Facilities include skating rinks, weight rooms, pools, gyms, and numerous outdoor facilities.

Disabled Students: 88% of the campus is accessible. Wheelchair ramps, elevators, special parking, specially equipped rest rooms, special class scheduling, lowered drinking fountains, and lowered telephones are available.

Services: Counseling and information services are available, as is tutoring in most subjects. There is a reader service for the blind and remedial math, reading, and writing.

Campus Safety and Security: Measures include security escort services, emergency telephones, and lighted pathways/sidewalks.

Programs of Study: UWO confers B.A., B.Sc., B.A.C.S., B.Ed., B.E.Sc., B.F.A., B.H.Sc, B.M.Sc., B.Mus., B.Mus.A., B.Sc.H.Ec., B.S.N., and B.S.W.Hons. degrees. Master's and doctoral degrees are also awarded. Bachelor's degrees are awarded in AGRICULTURE (natural resource management and plant science), BIOLOGICAL SCIENCE (biochemistry, biology/biological science, biophysics, cell biology, ecology, genetics, microbiology, physiology, toxicology, and zoology), BUSINESS (business administration and management), COMMUNICATIONS AND THE ARTS (art history and appreciation, classics, communications, comparative literature, English, English literature, film arts, French, German, Germanic languages and literature, Greek, Latin, linguistics, music, music business management, music history and appreciation, music performance, music theory and composition, Russian, Spanish, studio art, and visual and performing arts), COMPUTER AND PHYSICAL SCIENCE (actuarial science, applied mathematics, astronomy, chemistry, computer mathematics, computer science, geology, geophysics and seismology, mathematics, medical physics, physics, planetary and space science, software engineering, and statistics), EDUCATION (elementary, middle school, music, and secondary), ENGINEERING AND ENVIRONMENTAL DESIGN (biomedical engineering, chemical engineering, civil engineering, computer engineering, electrical/electronics engineering, engineering, engineering management, environmental engineering, environmental science, materials science, and mechanical engineering), HEALTH PROFESSIONS (health science, medical science, nursing, and pharmacology), SOCIAL SCIENCE (anthropology, classical/ancient civilization, economics, geography, gerontology, history, law, philosophy, physical fitness/movement, political science/government, psychology, sociology, urban studies, and women's studies).

Required: All students are required to take 2 essay courses and courses in the arts, science, and social science; other distribution and course requirements vary by major. A 60% overall average and 15 courses are the mininum requirements for a 3-year bachelor's degree. Many have additional requirements.

Special: Internships in engineering, computer science, physics, statistics, and acturial science, study abroad in 40 countries, dual majors, and student designed majors are available. There are many 3-year bachelor's degree programs. Pass/fail options are possible.

Faculty/Classroom: 79% of faculty are male; 21%, female.

Admissions: 47% of the 2003-2004 applicants were accepted.

Requirements: The SAT I is required. In addition, U.S. applicants must be graduates of an accredited secondary school with 4 academic course credits in their senior year, and in the top 15% of their class in order to be eligible to apply for admission their first year. A nonrecentered SAT I composite score of 1100 is required. First-year admissions are limited. Admission to the music program requires an audition. A GPA of 3.0 is required. AP credits are accepted. Important factors in the admissions decision are advanced placement or honor courses, recommendations by school officials, and leadership record.

Procedure: Freshmen are admitted in the fall. There is an early decision plan. Early decision applications should be filed by May 15; regular applications, by May 15 for fall entry, along with a $95 CDN fee. Notification of early decision is sent mid-April; regular decision, on a rolling basis from May to July. Applications are accepted on-line through the Ontario Universities Application Centre at *http://compass.ouac.on.ca*.

Transfer: A minimum overall average of 70% is required to transfer. 5 of 15 credits required for the bachelor's degree must be completed at UWO.

Visiting: There are regularly scheduled orientations for prospective students, including academic counseling appointments and campus tours. Visitors may sit in on classes. To schedule a visit, contact Undergraduate Recruitment, Office of the Registrar at (519) 661-2026.

Financial Aid: UWO is a member of CSS.

International Students: In a recent year, there were 1157 international students enrolled. The school actively recruits these students. They must take the TOEFL and the TWE or the MELAB or IELTS.

Computers: The mainframes are a DEC VAX 6230, a CDC Cyber 930, and an ETA-10. There are hundreds of access terminals located in campus buildings. All students may access the system. There are no time limits and no fees.

Graduates: From July 1, 2002 to June 30, 2003, 6310 bachelor's degrees were awarded.

Admissions Contact: Lori Gribbon, Manager, Application Services. E-mail: *reg-admissions@uwo.ca* Web: *http://www.uwo.ca*

UNIVERSITY OF WINDSOR
E-2
Windsor, ON, Canada N9B 3P4   (519) 973-7014, ext. 3315
864-2860 (in Canada); Fax: (519) 971-3653

Full-time: 4390 men, 5200 women	**Faculty:** 500
Part-time: 1280 men, 1930 women	**Ph.D.s:** 90%
Graduate: 510 men, 410 women	**Student/Faculty:** 19 to 1
Year: trimesters, summer session	**Tuition:** $3700 ($11,000)
Application Deadline: see profile	**Room & Board:** $6000
Freshman Class: n/av	
SAT I or ACT: required	

The University of Windsor, founded in 1857, is a public liberal arts institution offering undergraduate and graduate programs through 8 faculties and 6 schools. There is 1 graduate school. Figures in the above capsule and in this profile are approximate. The 2 libraries contain 1,600,000 volumes, 160,000 microform items, and 2000 audio/video tapes/CDs, and subscribe to 15,000 periodicals. Computerized library services include the card catalog, interlibrary loans, and database searching. Special learning facilities include a learning resource center, art gallery, natural history museum, radio station, TV station, a video-conferencing center, a computing services theater, the Chrysler Canada/University of Windsor Research Center, and the Great Lakes Institute. The 200-acre campus is in an urban area 2 kilometers from downtown Windsor, and 3 kilometers from downtown Detroit, Michigan. Including any residence halls, there are 50 buildings.

Student Life: Students are from 10 states, 41 foreign countries, and Canada. 95% are from public schools. The average age of freshmen is 19; all undergraduates, 22. 10% do not continue beyond their first year.

Housing: 1800 students can be accommodated in college housing, which includes coed dorms, on-campus apartments, and married-student housing. On-campus housing is guaranteed for the freshman year only and is available on a lottery system for upperclassmen. 80% of students commute. All students may keep cars.

Activities: 2% of men belong to 4 national fraternities; 1% of women belong to 1 national sorority. There are 75 groups on campus, including cheerleading, chess, choir, chorale, drama, ethnic, gay, honors, international, jazz band, literary magazine, musical theater, newspaper, orchestra, political, professional, radio and TV, religious, social, and student government. Popular campus events include Homecoming and Campus Week in September.

Sports: There are 7 intercollegiate sports for men and 5 for women, and 11 intramural sports for men and 9 for women. Facilities include a 6-lane 200-meter track, a multiuse gym, a field house, a stadium, an indoor pool, weight rooms, and a sports therapy clinic.

Disabled Students: 90% of the campus is accessible. Wheelchair ramps, elevators, special parking, specially equipped rest rooms, special class scheduling, lowered drinking fountains, lowered telephones, and specially equipped residence rooms are available.

Services: Counseling and information services are available, as is tutoring in some subjects, including math and physical sciences. There is a reader service for the blind, remedial math, reading, and writing, exam accommodations, special needs counselors, and recreation buddies for assistance at the athletic complex.

Campus Safety and Security: Measures include 24-hour foot and vehicle patrol, self-defense education, security escort services, and informal discussions. There are pamphlets/posters/films, emergency telephones, and lighted pathways/sidewalks.

Programs of Study: U of W confers B.A., B.Sc., B.A.Sc., B.Comm., B.C.S., B.Ed., B.F.A., B.H.K., B.Mus., B.Mus.Th., B.P.A., B.Sc.N., B.S.W., and L.L.B. degrees. Master's and doctoral degrees are also awarded. Bachelor's degrees are awarded in BIOLOGICAL SCIENCE (biochemistry and biology/biological science), BUSINESS (business administration and management), COMMUNICATIONS AND THE ARTS (art history and appreciation, classics, communications, comparative literature, creative writing, dramatic arts, English, French, languages, modern language, music, musical theater, and visual and performing arts), COMPUTER AND PHYSICAL SCIENCE (chemistry, computer science, geology, mathematics, physics, science, and statistics), EDUCATION (drama, education, and science), ENGINEERING AND ENVIRONMENTAL DESIGN (civil engineering, electrical/electronics engineering, engineering, environmental engineering, industrial engineering, land use management and reclamation, and mechanical engineering), HEALTH PROFESSIONS (music therapy and nursing), SOCIAL SCIENCE (anthropology, Asian/Oriental studies, Canadian studies, criminology, crosscultural studies, economics, family/consumer studies, geography, history, international relations, law, philosophy, physical fitness/movement, political science/government, psychology, public administration, religion, social work, sociology, urban studies, and women's studies). Social science, engineering, and education are the largest.

Required: To graduate, students must complete a total of 90 credit hours, including 30 in the major, with a C average. Honors students must complete 120 hours, including 60 in the major, with a B average. All students must fulfill the requirements of the core curriculum.

Special: The college offers a variety of co-op programs and internships. Cross-registration may be arranged with the University of Detroit Mercy, Wayne State University, the University of Central Florida, and the University of Darby (England). Students may study abroad in the United States, France, Japan, and England.

Faculty/Classroom: 78% of faculty are male; 22%, female. All both teach and do research. The average class size in an introductory lecture is 100; in a laboratory, 25; and in a regular course, 50.

Requirements: The SAT I or ACT is required for U.S. students. AP credits are accepted.

Procedure: Freshmen are admitted to all sessions. Entrance exams should be taken as early as possible. There are early decision, early admissions, and rolling admissions plans. Check with the school for current application deadlines and fee. Notification is sent on a rolling basis. A waiting list is an active part of the admissions procedure.

Transfer: Applicants must present an official transcript and be in good academic standing.

Visiting: There are regularly scheduled orientations for prospective students, including a tour, counseling, and classes. There are guides for informal visits and visitors may sit in on classes. To schedule a visit, contact the Liaison Office.

International Students: They must score 550 on the written TOEFL or take the MELAB.

Computers: The mainframes are an IBM 4381 and an SGI. Students have access to a parallel-processing file server linked to graphics X-terminals through a campuswide fiber-optic network. There is also a CAD-CAM teaching lab with 30 networked terminals, 60 PCs in a DEC network, and numerous other academic local networks. 1 residence hall provides computer connections. All students may access the system. There are no time limits. The fee is minimal.

Admissions Contact: Assistant Registrar, Liaison and Applicant Services. E-mail: *liaison@uwindsor.ca*

YORK UNIVERSITY
E-3

Toronto (North York), ON, Canada M3J 1P3

(416) 736-5825
Fax: (416) 650-8195

Full-time: 13,330 men, 21,699 women	**Faculty:** 1149
Part-time: 2777 men, 4215 women	**Ph.D.s:** 98%
Graduate: 2311 men, 2462 women	**Student/Faculty:** 31 to 1
Year: semesters, summer session	**Tuition:** $4969 CDN ($12,357 CDN)
Application Deadline: February 1	
	Room & Board: $5323 CDN
Freshman Class: n/av	
SAT I or ACT: required	

York University, founded in 1959, is a public institution offering programs in computer science, design, education, environmental studies, fine arts, business, social science, law, engineering, health, humanities, human resources, pure and applied sciences, and social work. There are 10 undergraduate and 37 graduate schools. The 5 libraries contain 2,360,000 volumes, 3,265,009 microform items, and 52,925 audio/video tapes/CDs, and subscribe to 14,734 periodicals. Computerized library services include the card catalog, interlibrary loans, database searching, and Internet access. Special learning facilities include a learning resource center, art gallery, radio station, TV station, observatory, language labs, writing center, geographical information systems lab, computer science labs, science-related labs, and fine arts studios and labs (editing studios). The 650-acre campus is in an urban area. The university has 2 campuses, totaling 735 acres, in northwest and downtown Toronto. Including any residence halls, there are 61 buildings.

Student Life: 78% of undergraduates are from outside the Province of Ontario. Students are from 174 foreign countries. The average age of freshmen is 18; all undergraduates, 22. 79% of freshmen remain to graduate.

Housing: 2188 students can be accommodated in college housing, which includes single-sex and coed dorms, on-campus apartments, and married-student housing. In addition, there are language houses, special-interest houses, and co-op housing. On-campus housing is available on a first-come, first-served basis and is available on a lottery system for upperclassmen. Priority is given to out-of-town students. 93% of students commute. All students may keep cars.

Activities: There are no fraternities or sororities. There are 150 groups on campus, including art, band, cheerleading, chess, choir, computers, dance, debate, drama, ethnic, film, gay, international, jazz band, literary magazine, musical theater, newspaper, orchestra, photography, political, professional, radio and TV, religious, social, social service, student government, and yearbook. Popular campus events include The Blue Bowl (football), Orientation Week, and Multicultural Week.

Sports: There are 14 intercollegiate sports for men and 15 for women, and 15 intramural sports for men and 13 for women. Facilities include a track and field center, 2 25-meter pools, 26 indoor and outdoor tennis courts, an ice arena, a 6-arena ice garden, 7 squash courts, 5 gyms, 2 fitness centers, 2 dance/aerobics studios, 1 combative room, 7 playing fields, 5 softball diamonds, 1 cricket pitch, 3 teaching labs, 2 fitness training areas, 3 strength training areas, 2 sport therapy clinics, 1 outdoor events facility, and a spinning studio.

Disabled Students: 65% of the campus is accessible. Wheelchair ramps, elevators, special parking, specially equipped rest rooms, special class scheduling, lowered drinking fountains, and lowered telephones are available. The Office for Persons with Disabilities offers a variety of additional services.

Services: Counseling and information services are available, as is tutoring in most subjects. There is a reader service for the blind, a writing support center, and a multimedia language center. The Counseling and Development Center offers a variety of services and workshops.

Campus Safety and Security: Measures include 24-hour foot and vehicle patrol, self-defense education, security escort services, and shuttle buses. There are informal discussions, pamphlets/posters/films, emergency telephones, and lighted pathways/sidewalks. There is also a bicycle patrol team monitoring the campuses.

Programs of Study: York confers B.A., B.Sc., B.A.S., B.B.A., B.Des., B.Ed., B.E.S., B.F.A., B.H.R.M., B.H.S., B.Sc.N., B.S.W., I.B.B.A., and L.L.B. degrees. Master's and doctoral degrees are also awarded. Bachelor's degrees are awarded in AGRICULTURE (conservation and regulation), BIOLOGICAL SCIENCE (biology/biological science and ecology), BUSINESS (accounting, banking and finance, business administration and management, business economics, business statistics, entrepreneurial studies, human resources, international economics, labor studies, management science, marketing and distribution, and organizational behavior), COMMUNICATIONS AND THE ARTS (art history and appreciation, classics, communications, creative writing, dance, design, dramatic arts, English, film arts, fine arts, French, German, Greek, Italian, linguistics, music, photography, Russian, Spanish, and visual and performing arts), COMPUTER AND PHYSICAL SCIENCE (applied mathematics, astronomy, atmospheric sciences and meteorology, chemistry, computer science, earth science, mathematics, physics, science, and statistics), EDUCATION (early childhood, education of the deaf and hearing impaired, elementary, middle school, and secondary), ENGINEERING AND ENVIRONMENTAL DESIGN (engineering and environmental science), HEALTH PROFESSIONS (community health work, environmental health science, exercise science, health care administration, health science, nursing, and rehabilitation therapy), SOCIAL SCIENCE (African studies, anthropology, Canadian studies, criminal justice, East Asian studies, economics, French studies, geography, German area studies, gerontology, Hispanic American studies, history, humanities, international studies, Judaic studies, Latin American studies, law, liberal arts/general studies, peace studies, philosophy, political science/government, psychology, public administration, religion, social science, social work, sociology, Third World studies, urban studies, and women's studies). Business, science, and some fine arts and liberal arts programs are the strongest academically. Psychology, administrative studies, and sociology are the largest.

Required: Students must maintain at least a C average in 90 credits to receive an ordinary degree and a C+ in 120 credits to receive an honors degree. Requirements for graduation vary according to the program.

Special: Co-op programs and cross-registration with Seneca, Centennial, Sheridan, and Humber Colleges, internships, study abroad in more than 100 countries, and work-study are available. York offers dual, student-designed, multi-, and interdisciplinary majors, including atmospheric chemistry, physics and astronomy, science, technology, culture, and society, social and political thought, space and communication sciences, and translation. Independent study and nondegree study are also possible. There is a freshman honors program.

Faculty/Classroom: 59% of faculty are male; 41%, female. All both teach and do research. No introductory courses are taught by graduate students. The average class size in an introductory lecture is 57 and in a laboratory, 25.

Requirements: The SAT I or ACT is required. In addition, U.S. applicants must present evidence of superior academic achievement. Secondary school record, SAT I or ACT scores, and teacher or counselor recommendation will be taken into consideration. Applicants to a fine arts program are required to successfully pass an audition or evaluation, and business administration applicants are required to submit a supplementary application. Admission averages and course prerequisites vary by faculty. York requires applicants to be in the upper 25% of their class. A GPA of 3.0 is required. AP credits are accepted.

Procedure: Freshmen are admitted to all sessions. Entrance exams should be taken in the fall of the senior year. There is an early admissions plan. Applications should be filed by February 1 for fall entry, October 1 for winter entry, and February 1 for spring entry. The fall 2003 application fee was $90 CDN. Notification is sent on a rolling basis. Applications are accepted on-line through the university's web site at *http://www.yorku.ca/admissio/index.asp.*

Transfer: 802 transfer students enrolled in 2002-2003. Requirements vary depending on the program. Postsecondary transcripts are required.

Visiting: There are regularly scheduled orientations for prospective students, consisting of a general information session and campus tour, and 1 week of orientation prior to the start of classes. There are guides for informal visits and visitors may sit in on classes and stay overnight. To schedule a visit, contact the International Admissions Office at (416) 736-5000 or *http://www.yorku.ca/admissio/events/index.asp.*

Financial Aid: The average freshman award was $500 CDN. The FAFSA is required. The deadline for filing freshman financial aid applications for fall entry is February 1.

International Students: There are 1600 international students enrolled. The school actively recruits these students. They must score 560 on the written TOEFL or 220 on the electronic version or take the MELAB, the Comprehensive English Language Test, or the York English Language Test (YELT) and also take the SAT I or the ACT, scoring 1100 or 24, respectively.

Computers: The mainframes are an IBM 3090 and 4381, a MAS 6650, a DEC VAX 8600, 6230, 11/78x, 11/750, and 11/730, and a UNIX. There are 1900 computer workstations on campus. Students enrolled in computer courses are given first priority in the computer labs. All students receive free Internet and e-mail access. A computer store on campus is available for those who wish to buy computers or computer accessories. All students may access the system 24 hours per day. There are no time limits and no fees.

Graduates: From July 1, 2002 to June 30, 2003, 6803 bachelor's degrees were awarded. The most popular majors were psychology (12%), computer science and information technology (9%), and administration (7%).

Admissions Contact: Office of International Admissions. E-mail: *vgrafi@yorku.ca* Web: *http://www.yorku.ca/*

Study abroad programs are now available in more than 60 countries in fields that range from Costa Rican tropical biology to Finnish architecture. Program directors have responded to the vocational interests of the student of the 21st century by organizing programs in international management, health care administration, and other career-oriented fields.

In fact, study in both traditional and nontraditional fields is enriched by overseas experience. An international perspective can benefit study of environmental sciences, anthropology, political science, urban planning, oceanography, hotel administration, psychology, social work, journalism, marketing and law, as well as film, art history, theater, music and dance.

The vast majority of U.S. students enter European schools through organized, ongoing programs sponsored and managed by the colleges and universities in which they are already enrolled. In this way, they automatically earn U.S. academic credit from their home institution for their overseas course work. Academic credit *directly* earned at a foreign institution is often not acceptable toward a U.S. degree. Applying directly to a foreign school is not difficult but unusual.

There are colleges and universities located in foreign nations that are organized on the U.S. system and accredited by U.S. accrediting agencies, e.g. American University of Paris. A list of accredited U.S. institutions overseas is provided in the annual *Accredited Institutions of Postsecondary Education*, published for the Commission on Recognition of Postsecondary Accreditation by the American Council on Education, and is available from Praeger Publishers, Greenwood Publishing Group, Inc., 88 Post Road West, Westport, CT 00881, (800) 225-5800 or (203) 236-3571; *www.greenwood.com*.

According to the Institute of International Education, in their *Open Doors 2003 Report on International Educational Exchange*, based on a recent academic year, close to 60 percent of foreign study is done in Western Europe. The four leading destinations—the United Kingdom, Spain, Italy, and France—host nearly 77,000 or 48 percent of U.S. students who study abroad. Of those U.S. students who study abroad, nearly 65 percent are women. The largest proportion of U.S. students abroad major in the social sciences (22 percent), and other traditional study abroad majors such as humanities (14 percent) and foreign languages (9 percent), but more varied majors are also studying abroad. Business and management majors are the second largest proportion of U.S. students abroad (18 percent).

The report also indicated that during a recent academic year, 586,323 international students were studying in the United States. Their largest fields of study were business and management (20 percent), engineering (17 percent), and mathematics and computer sciences (12 percent). A majority of the international students were male (56 percent).

A Productive Experience

If you are interested in study abroad, plan ahead by taking the following steps to ensure that the experience is productive:

- **Assess the ways in which study abroad will benefit your educational and career plans.** Study abroad can be a casual choice or a pleasant way to spend a semester but you will derive the greatest benefit if you bring more thought to it: How will the overseas experience complement your other courses or your educational major? Can you maximize its value by seeking language as well as academic study or by combining independent study or an internship with traditional course work?
- **Consult your campus study-abroad adviser.** Most colleges and universities have a person or an office charged with the responsibility of counseling students on overseas study. The study-abroad adviser is best qualified to help you make the right choices.
- **Make sure your college will accept credit earned at the study-abroad program you have chosen.** Speak with both your academic adviser and your study-abroad adviser and resolve any issues before you leave. Many students have assumed incorrectly that credit is granted automatically for another institution's program. You cannot take this for granted.

- **Be realistic about your foreign language proficiency.** It is one thing to be able to order a meal or buy a train ticket in a foreign language. It is quite another to follow a professor lecturing on a complex subject. If you discover that your linguistic ability is inadequate, it is quite possible that you can find abroad the subject matter you want taught in English. You will get more out of the overseas experience however, if you make the effort to function in the language of the chosen country.
- **Look carefully at costs.** If you are dealing with a program sponsor that is not your home institution, it is wise to read program literature carefully. Ask questions before you go if you have any qualms! Are charges clearly specified? Does the literature specify what services *are* covered and more important, what services are *not* covered? What is the refund policy, if any? Is there a clearly identified organization with an official base in the United States which would be legally responsible in the event of disaster?

   While drawing up your budget, think about the extras. You will want to make the small side trips to new places that help to make overseas living rewarding. Try to give yourself some financial flexibility in working out your budget.
- **Think about what it means to live abroad.** Be sure to arrange for substitutes for the support systems you take for granted at home. Will your medical insurance cover you? Do you need vaccinations or a doctor who can manage your specific health problems while you are living abroad? What about visas?

   It is critically important to find out about housing before you leave. Student housing is difficult to find almost everywhere. Be sure to find out whether securing housing abroad is your responsibility and what the alternatives are in the country in which you plan to live.
- **Don't assume that you can work abroad.** Because of foreign labor laws, students should not plan to seek paid employment. The practice of working one's way through college is not common abroad, nor are the relatively high-paying part-time jobs that make it possible in the United States. However, increasing numbers of students are looking to combine practical work experience with study abroad. There are many work exchanges, volunteer opportunities, and internships available. Contact the Council on International Exchange, 7 Custom House Street, 3rd Floor, Portland, ME 04101, (207) 553-7600, Fax: (207) 553-7699 for further information.
- **Find out what you can about the sponsoring agency, especially if it is not an accredited U.S. college or university.** Talk to your study-abroad adviser if you have any doubts. Most private agencies engaged in study abroad are legitimate organizations but their basic purposes may not match yours. Does the organization have experience in placing students in an academic environment, not just in arranging travel? Are descriptions of its study program specific or vague? Does it make unverifiable claims about the academic reputation of its programs, or their recognition by U.S. higher educational institutions?

For further information, consult:
Institute of International Education
809 United Nations Plaza
New York, NY 10017
(212) 883-8200   Fax: (212) 984-5358
(For further information, consult the following IIE publications: *Academic Year Abroad*, (annual), *Short Term Study Abroad* (annual), *Open Doors 2003* (annual), *Atlas of Student Mobility 2003*, *Intensive English USA 2000*, *Financial Resources for International Study 1996*. See the IIE web site *www.iiebooks.org* for more information.

Council on International Educational Exchange
7 Custom House Street, 3rd Floor
Portland, ME 04101
(207) 553-7600   Fax: (207) 553-7699

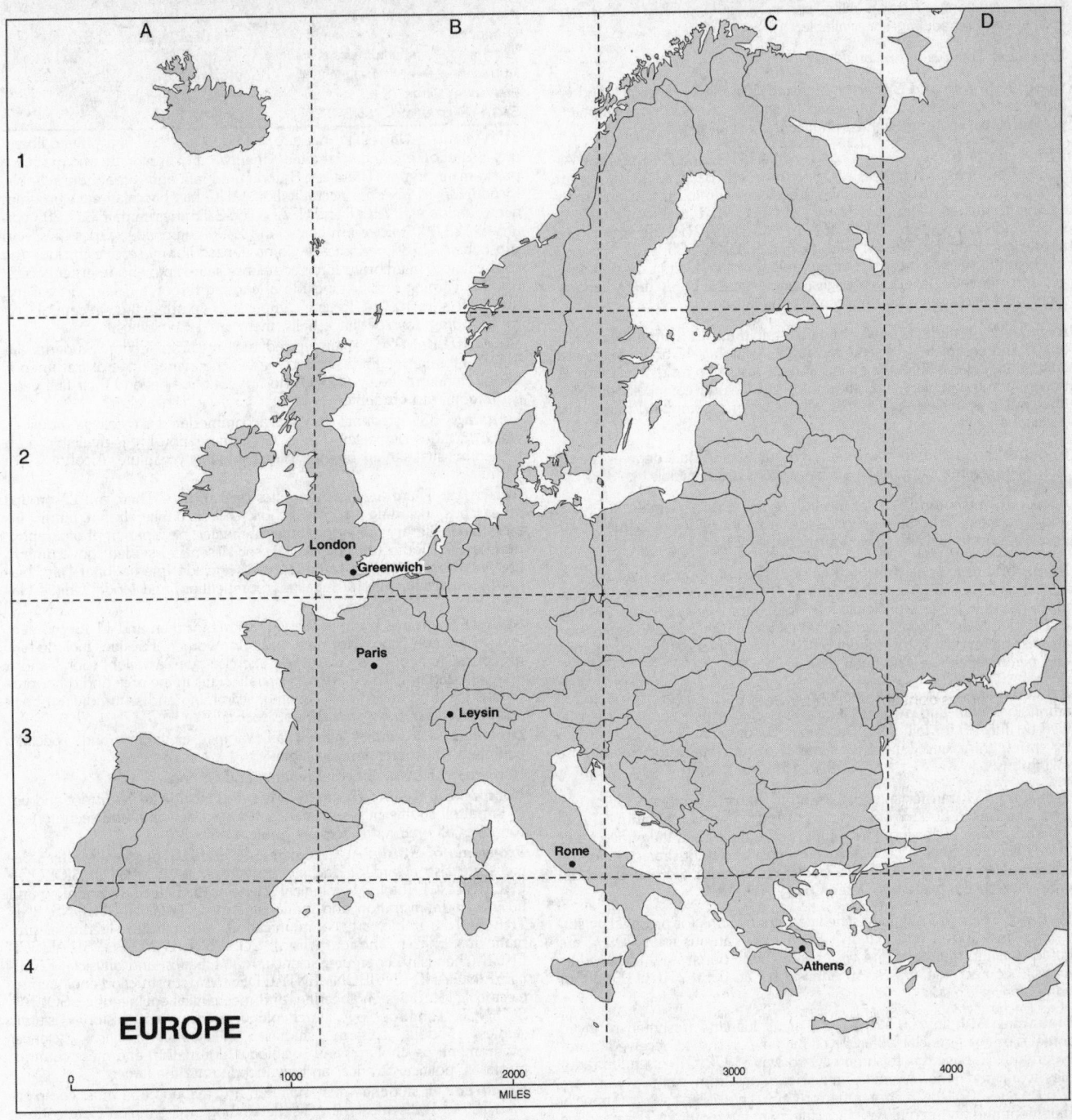

EUROPE

Deree College is the undergraduate division of the American College of Greece, which was founded in 1875 as the American School for Girls. ACG has 5 divisions and 2 campuses in Athens. Deree offers bachelor's degrees in 16 areas of the liberal arts and business. The 3 libraries contain 117,400 volumes, 4000 microform items, and 1332 audio/video tapes/CDs, and subscribe to 950 periodicals. Computerized library services include the card catalog, interlibrary loans, database searching, and Internet access. Special learning facilities include a museum of the history of the college and writing centers. The 60-acre campus is in a suburban area 6 miles northeast of Athens. There are 7 buildings.

Student Life: 90% of undergraduates are from Greece. Students are from 30 foreign countries and Canada. 52% are from public schools. The average age of freshmen is 21; all undergraduates, 24. 5% do not continue beyond their first year; 88% remain to graduate.

Housing: There are no residence halls. All students commute. No one may keep cars.

Activities: There are no fraternities or sororities. There are 44 groups on campus, including chess, choir, coin/stamp, computers, dance, debate, drama, drill team, environmental, ethnic, film, health, international, newspaper, orchestra, photography, radio, social service, sociology, student government, and yearbook. Popular campus events include career forum, film previews, and May Fest.

Sports: There are 4 intercollegiate sports for men and 3 for women, and 9 intramural sports for men and 7 for women. Facilities include a

gym, a fitness center, 2 dance studios, aerobic rooms, 4 outdoor tennis courts, a 50-meter swimming pool, a 400-meter track, and a soccer field.

Disabled Students: 90% of the campus is accessible. Wheelchair ramps, elevators, special parking, specially equipped rest rooms, and special class scheduling are available.

Services: There is remedial writing.

Campus Safety and Security: Measures include 24-hour foot and vehicle patrol, security escort services, shuttle buses, and pamphlets/posters/films. There are lighted pathways/sidewalks.

Programs of Study: Deree College confers B.A. and B.S. degrees. Associate and master's degrees are also awarded. Bachelor's degrees are awarded in BUSINESS (accounting, business administration and management, management information systems, and marketing/retailing/merchandising), COMMUNICATIONS AND THE ARTS (art history and appreciation, dance, English, and music), SOCIAL SCIENCE (economics, history, philosophy, psychology, and sociology). English, psychology, and marketing are the strongest academically. Marketing, management, and accounting and finance are the largest.

Required: All students must maintain a minimum CI (cumulative index) of 2.0 and complete 128 semester hours, including 47 hours in general education, at least 30 in the major, and the last 30 in residence. Distribution requirements vary with the major but include composition, literature, public speaking, humanities, ethics, history, computer, music, and political science.

Special: Study abroad, work-study programs, and dual degrees are offered. Nondegree study and pass/fail options are available.

Faculty/Classroom: 52% of faculty are male; 48%, female. All teach undergraduates. The average class size in an introductory lecture is 40; in a laboratory, 20; and in a regular course, 23.

Requirements: Applicants must be graduates of an accredited secondary school. The GED is accepted. English speakers are required to pass an English language proficiency test. A GPA of 2.0 is required. AP and CLEP credits are accepted. Important factors in the admissions decision are recommendations by school officials, recommendations by alumni, and personality/intangible qualities.

Procedure: Freshmen are admitted to all sessions. There is a deferred admissions plan and a rolling admissions plan. Applications should be filed by July 25 for fall entry, December 15 for winter entry, January 25 for spring entry, and June 1 for summer entry. Notification is sent on a rolling basis.

Transfer: 554 transfer students, including transfers from the junior college, enrolled in 2002-2003. Applicants must have a minimum GPA of 2.0 and submit high school transcripts and a diploma if they have fewer than 30 credits. English proficiency also must be demonstrated, if not native speakers of English. All 128 credits required for the bachelor's degree must be completed at Deree College.

Visiting: There are regularly scheduled orientations for prospective students, consisting of information sessions and campus tours. There are guides for informal visits and visitors may sit in on classes. To schedule a visit, contact the Office of Admissions at 0030-210 6009800 or admissions@acg.edu.

Financial Aid: In 2003-2004, 5% of all full-time freshmen received some form of financial aid. 2% of full-time freshmen received need-based aid. The average freshman award was $1872. 3% of undergraduates work part time. Average annual earnings from campus work are $769. Deree College is a member of CSS. The college's own financial statement and an Internal Revenue statement are required. The deadline for filing freshman financial aid applications for fall entry is September 1.

International Students: There are 434 international students enrolled. Nonnative English speakers must score 173 on the written TOEFL or take the MELAB, the Comprehensive English Language Test, the college's own test, GCE "O" levels, or the Cambridge Proficiency.

Computers: PCs are available for student use throughout the campus. All have Internet access. All students may access the system 8 A.M. to 10 P.M. daily. There are no time limits. The fee is $50. It is strongly recommended that all students have a personal computer.

Graduates: In an average class, 1% graduate in 3 years or less, 17% graduate in 4 years or less, 48% graduate in 5 years or less, and 17% graduate in 6 years or less. 150 companies recruited on campus in 2002-2003. Of the 2002 graduating class, 75% were enrolled in graduate school within 6 months of graduation and 85% were employed.

Admissions Contact: Kastalia Samoili, Director Office of Admissions. E-mail: admissions@acg.edu

AMERICAN UNIVERSITY IN CAIRO
Cairo, Egypt   (212) 730-8800; Fax: (212) 730-1600

Full-time: 1764 men, 2009 women	**Faculty:** 285
Part-time: 243 men, 242 women	**Ph.D.s:** 95%
Graduate: 354 men, 534 women	**Student/Faculty:** 13 to 1
Year: semesters, summer session	**Tuition:** $12,490
Application Deadline: June 1	**Room & Board:** $2750
Freshman Class: 1532 applied, 872 accepted, 553 enrolled	
SAT I Verbal/Math: 480/540	

The American University in Cairo, founded in 1919, is a private liberal arts institution offering accredited American undergraduate and graduate programs in Egypt. There are 3 undergraduate and 3 graduate schools. In addition to regional accreditation, AUC has baccalaureate program accreditation with ABET and CSAB. The 2 libraries contain 327,205 volumes, 123,000 microform items, and 2300 audio/video tapes/CDs, and subscribe to 1780 periodicals. Computerized library services include the card catalog, interlibrary loans, database searching, and Internet access. Special learning facilities include a learning resource center, art gallery, and radio station. The 26-acre campus is in an urban area in central Cairo. Including any residence halls, there are 12 buildings.

Student Life: 92% of undergraduates are from Egypt. Students are from 99 foreign countries and Canada. The average age of freshmen is 18; all undergraduates, 20. 5% do not continue beyond their first year; 80% remain to graduate.

Housing: 331 students can be accommodated in college housing, which includes single-sex dorms. On-campus housing is available on a first-come, first-served basis. 95% of students commute. Alcohol is not permitted.

Activities: There are no fraternities or sororities. There are 25 groups on campus, including art, chess, choir, chorus, dance, drama, ethnic, international, literary magazine, musical theater, newspaper, photography, professional, radio and TV, social, social service, student government, and yearbook. Popular campus events include International Day, National University Cultural Activities Competition, and Model United Nations.

Sports: There are 13 intercollegiate sports for men and 11 for women, and 7 intramural sports for men and 5 for women. Facilities include tennis courts, multipurpose courts, an exercise gym, a weight room, and a 400-seat stadium. There are also private clubs in the area and other provisions for horseback riding, rowing, swimming and scuba diving, track and field, water polo, squash, and soccer.

Disabled Students: Wheelchair ramps, elevators, and specially equipped rest rooms are available.

Services: There is remedial reading and writing.

Campus Safety and Security: Measures include 24-hour foot and vehicle patrol, shuttle buses, lighted pathways/sidewalks, and security personnel at all open entrances 24 hours a day.

Programs of Study: AUC confers B.A. and B.S. degrees. Master's degrees are also awarded. Bachelor's degrees are awarded in BIOLOGICAL SCIENCE (biology/biological science), BUSINESS (accounting and business administration and management), COMMUNICATIONS AND THE ARTS (Arabic, art, communications, comparative literature, dramatic arts, English, and journalism), COMPUTER AND PHYSICAL SCIENCE (chemistry, computer science, mathematics, and physics), ENGINEERING AND ENVIRONMENTAL DESIGN (construction engineering, electrical/electronics engineering, and mechanical engineering), SOCIAL SCIENCE (anthropology, archeology, economics, history, Islamic studies, Middle Eastern studies, philosophy, political science/government, psychology, and sociology). Journalism and mass communications, political science, and engineering are the largest.

Required: All students must maintain a C average and must complete from 120 to 162 semester credits, depending on the major. Core courses include a writing program, an interdisciplinary seminar in humanities, natural science, and social science, a scientific-thinking course, and Arab literature, history, and society.

Special: Study abroad through a consortium of U.S. schools, work-study programs with the university, and nondegree study are available.

Faculty/Classroom: 51% of faculty are male; 49%, female. No introductory courses are taught by graduate students. The average class size in an introductory lecture is 39; in a laboratory, 7; and in a regular course, 40.

Admissions: 57% of the 2003-2004 applicants were accepted. The SAT I scores for the 2003-2004 freshman class were: Verbal--63% below 500, 31% between 500 and 599, 6% between 600 and 700, and 3% above 700; Math--23% below 500, 54% between 500 and 599, 21% between 600 and 700, and 2% above 700.

Requirements: The SAT I or ACT is required of U.S. applicants, who must also be graduates of an accredited secondary school and submit complete transcripts and a copy of their diploma. Others must submit the Egyptian Thanawiya Amma certificate or other national high school certificate recognized by the university as equivalent to it, or the GCE, GCSE, or IGCSE. A minimum high school GPA of 2.0 is required. Students should have taken courses in 3 of the following subjects: languages and humanities, math, social studies, and biological and physical sciences. AP credits are accepted. Important factors in the admissions decision are ability to finance college education, evidence of special talent, and extracurricular activities record.

Procedure: Freshmen are admitted fall and spring. Entrance exams should be taken in July for fall admission. There is a rolling admissions plan. Early decision applications should be filed by April 1; regular applications, by June 1 for fall entry and November 1 for spring entry. The fall 2003 application fee was $35. Notification is sent on a rolling basis. Applications are accepted on-line.

Transfer: 19 transfer students enrolled in 2002-2003. Transfer students must have a C average on secondary school and college transcripts. 45 of 120 to 162 credits required for the bachelor's degree must be completed at AUC.

Visiting: There are guides for informal visits and visitors may sit in on classes and stay overnight. To schedule a visit, contact the General Director of Admission in Egypt at 20-2 797-5551 or *ghada_h@aucegypt.edu.*

Financial Aid: In 2003-2004, 85% of all full-time students received some form of financial aid. 48% of full-time freshmen and 44% of continuing full-time students received need-based aid. The average freshman award was $4280. Need-based scholarships or need-based grants averaged $3361; non-need-based athletic scholarships averaged $743; and other non-need-based awards and non-need-based scholarships averaged $1000. 10% of undergraduates work part time. The college's own financial statement is required. The deadline for filing freshman financial aid applications for fall entry is September 15.

International Students: There are 352 international students enrolled. The school actively recruits these students. Those for whom English is a second language must take either the TOEFL (scoring 220) with the TWE (Test of Writen English) or AUC's ELPET test. Graduates of U.S. high schools must take the SAT I or the ACT.

Computers: Students may access the mainframe through more than 600 terminals located in computer labs throughout the campus. Only students enrolled in computer-related courses or courses that require computer use may access the system. It may be used from 8 A.M. to 9 P.M., 6 days a week. There are no time limits and no fees.

Graduates: From July 1, 2002 to June 30, 2003, 762 bachelor's degrees were awarded. The most popular majors were political science (18%), mass communications (16%), and economics (16%). In an average class, 2% graduate in 3 years or less, 22% graduate in 4 years or less, 68% graduate in 5 years or less, and 82% graduate in 6 years or less. 320 companies recruited on campus in a recent year.

Admissions Contact: American University in Cairo's New York Office. E-mail: *aucegypt@aucnyo.edu* Web: *http://www.aucegypt.edu*

AMERICAN UNIVERSITY OF PARIS
B-3
Paris, France 75007   **(212) 983-1414; Fax: (212) 983-0444**

Full-time: 700 men and women	**Faculty:** n/av
Part-time: 25 men and women	**Ph.D.s:** 67%
Graduate: none	**Student/Faculty:** n/av
Year: semesters, summer session	**Tuition:** $20,000
Application Deadline: see profile	**Room & Board:** n/app
Freshman Class: n/av	
SAT I: required	**ACT:** recommended

The American University of Paris, founded in 1962, is a private, coeducational institution providing a liberal arts program in an international context. It has regional U.S. accreditation and is recognized by the French government as an institute of higher learning. Figures in the above capsule and in this profile are approximate. Classes are in English except for foreign language and literature courses. The library contains 65,000 volumes and 1000 microform items. Computerized library services include the card catalog, interlibrary loans, and database searching. Special learning facilities include a learning resource center. The campus is in an urban area in Paris. There are 6 buildings.

Programs of Study: AUP confers B.A. and B.S. degrees. Bachelor's degrees are awarded in BUSINESS (international business management and international economics), COMMUNICATIONS AND THE ARTS (art history and appreciation and comparative literature), COMPUTER AND PHYSICAL SCIENCE (computer science), ENGINEERING AND ENVIRONMENTAL DESIGN (engineering), SOCIAL SCIENCE (economics, European studies, French studies, history, and international relations). Art history, international affairs, and international economics are the strongest academically. International business administration, international affairs, and international communications are the largest.

Required: Students must maintain a minimum GPA of 2.0 while taking at least 120 semester credits, including an average of 50 in the major. Distribution requirements include 6 semester hours each of English composition, humanities, and social sciences, 16 of French, and 8 of lab science or math.

Special: There are co-op programs with Tulane, Northeastern, and Boston Universities, Monmouth, Mills, New England, Notre Dame and

St. Mary's (CA) colleges, Universite de Paris-Sorbonne, and Kansai Gaidai in Japan. Cross-registration is available in foreign language programs at 3 other French colleges. Juniors and seniors with good academic standing are encouraged to undertake internships. Study abroad, second degrees, nondegree study, and pass/fail options also are offered. There are 4 national honor societies and 3 departmental honors programs.

Faculty/Classroom: 52% of faculty are male; 48%, female. The average class size in an introductory lecture is 18; in a laboratory, 12; and in a regular course, 16.

Requirements: The SAT I is required and the ACT is recommended. In addition, candidates must be graduates of an accredited secondary school. An essay and 2 letters of recommendation are also needed. Knowledge of French is not required. Applicants in the New York area are encouraged to interview at that office. A GPA of 2.8 is required. AP and CLEP credits are accepted. Important factors in the admissions decision are advanced placement or honor courses, personality/intangible qualities, and recommendations by school officials.

Procedure: Freshmen are admitted fall and spring. There is a deferred admissions plan. Check with the school for current application deadlines and fee. Notification is sent on a rolling basis.

Transfer: Transfer applicants must submit college and high school transcripts, and SAT I or ACT scores if they have fewer than 45 credits. An interview, 2 letters of recommendation, and an essay are required. 30 of 120 credits required for the bachelor's degree must be completed at AUP.

Visiting: There are guides for informal visits and visitors may sit in on classes. To schedule a visit, contact the Admissions Office at (212) 983-1414 (New York office) or Paris direct.

Financial Aid: AUP is a member of CSS. The FAFSA is required. Check with the school for current deadlines.

International Students: The school actively recruits these students. They must score 500 on the written TOEFL or take the MELAB, and the college's own test and the SAT I or the ACT.

Computers: The mainframe is an IBM RISC 6000 (550). 60 PCs and PC-based graphic workstations are available in the 3 computer labs. E-mail facilities and mathematical and programming software are available in addition to the usual applications. All students may access the system. There are no time limits and no fees. It is strongly recommended that all students have a personal computer.

Admissions Contact: Candace MacLaughlin, Office Manager. E-mail: *nyoffice@aup.edu* or *admissions@aup.edu* (Paris).

AMERICAN UNIVERSITY OF ROME
B-3
Rome, Italy   **011 39 6 58330919; Fax: 011 396 58330992**

Full-time: 137 men, 245 women	**Faculty:** 8
Part-time: 4 men, 6 women	**Ph.D.s:** 67%
Graduate: none	**Student/Faculty:** 48 to 1
Year: semesters, summer session	**Tuition:** $11,140
Application Deadline: May 15	**Room & Board:** $8460
Freshman Class: 100 applied, 80 accepted, 45 enrolled	
SAT I Verbal/Math: 544/534	

American University of Rome, founded in 1969, is a private institution offering programs in liberal arts, international business, international relations, Italian studies, and communications. The library contains 5000 volumes and 30 audio/video tapes/CDs, and subscribes to 15 periodicals. Computerized library services include the card catalog, interlibrary loans, and database searching. The campus is in a suburban area on the Janiculum Hill 2 miles from downtown. Including any residence halls, there are 2 buildings.

Student Life: 65% of undergraduates are from Italy. Students are from 25 foreign countries and Canada. 20% are from public schools. 83% are white. The average age of freshmen is 18; all undergraduates, 20. 20% do not continue beyond their first year; 26% remain to graduate.

Housing: 160 students can be accommodated in college housing, which includes off-campus apartments. Housing is available on a first-come, first-served basis. 55% of students commute. Alcohol is not permitted. No one may keep cars.

Activities: There are no fraternities or sororities. There are some groups and organizations on campus, including art, drama, film, honors, international, literary magazine, newspaper, and student government. Popular campus events include the Distinguished Lecture Series, liberal arts and business excursions, and international relations debates.

Sports: There is 1 intercollegiate sport for men, and 3 intramural sports for men and 3 for women. Facilities include off-campus access to soccer, tennis, and swimming facilities.

Disabled Students: 30% of the campus is accessible.

Services: There is remedial writing.

Campus Safety and Security: Measures include informal discussions.

Programs of Study: AUR confers B.A. and B.S. degrees. Associate degrees are also awarded. Bachelor's degrees are awarded in BUSINESS (business administration and management), COMMUNICATIONS AND THE ARTS (communications), SOCIAL SCIENCE (international relations, international studies, and Italian studies). Business administration and international relations are the largest.

Required: To graduate, students must complete 120 credits, including 45 to 66 in the major, with a minimum GPA of 2.0. Distribution requirements include English composition and courses in humanities, social sciences, and science/math.

Special: Internships in business, international relations, communications, and Italian studies are available. Study abroad is possible by special arrangement, and work-study is available with AUR. Cross-registration with the College of Staten Island in New York is possible. There is 1 national honor society.

Faculty/Classroom: 58% of faculty are male; 42%, female. All teach undergraduates. The average class size in an introductory lecture is 18 and in a regular course, 13.

Admissions: 80% of the 2003-2004 applicants were accepted.

Requirements: The SAT I or ACT is required. In addition, a high school diploma and transcript or the non-American equivalent is required, as are a letter of recommendation and an essay. The GED is accepted. A GPA of 2.5 is required. AP and CLEP credits are accepted. Important factors in the admissions decision are recommendations by school officials, advanced placement or honor courses, and personality/intangible qualities.

Procedure: Freshmen are admitted to all sessions. There is a deferred admissions plan. Applications should be filed by May 15 for fall entry, October 10 for spring entry, and March 30 for summer entry, along with a $55 fee.

Transfer: 20 transfer students enrolled in a recent year. Applicants must submit a high school transcript, a diploma, all transcripts of universities attended, a letter of recommendation, and an essay. 45 of 120 credits required for the bachelor's degree must be completed at AUR.

Visiting: There are regularly scheduled orientations for prospective students, which AUR organizes directly and through its agents in many U.S. states and in other countries. Orientation is assisted by use of audiovisual materials. There are guides for informal visits and visitors may sit in on classes. To schedule a visit, contact the Director of Admissions at *aurinfo@aur.edu*.

Financial Aid: In a recent year, 10% of all full-time freshmen received some form of financial aid. 4% of undergraduates work part time. Average annual earnings from campus work are $4144. The FAFSA is required. The deadline for filing freshman financial aid applications for fall entry is July 12.

International Students: There were 90 international students enrolled in a recent year. The school actively recruits these students. They must score 550 on the written TOEFL or take the MELAB or the college's own test.

Computers: PCs are available, with e-mail and Internet access, in the library computer lab. All students may access the system 8:30 A.M. to 8:30 P.M. Monday through Friday; 10 A.M. to 6 P.M. Saturday. There are no fees. It is strongly recommended that all students have a personal computer.

Graduates: In a recent year, 20 bachelor's degrees were awarded. The most popular majors were business administration (55%), international relations (30%), and communications (15%). In an average class, 5% graduate in 3 years or less, 85% graduate in 4 years or less, and 90% graduate in 5 years or less.

Admissions Contact: Dean of Administration. A video is available. E-mail: *aur.homeoffice@dc.aur.edu* Web: *www.aur.edu*

FRANKLIN COLLEGE SWITZERLAND
Sorengo, Switzerland 6924   B-3

(212) 772-2090, (011-41-91-985-2260)
Fax: (212) 772-2718, (011-41-91-994-4117)

Full-time: 105 men, 165 women	**Faculty:** 17
Part-time: 1 woman	**Ph.D.s:** 82%
Graduate: none	**Student/Faculty:** 16 to 1
Year: semesters, summer session	**Tuition:** $19,320
Application Deadline: see profile	**Room & Board:** $7850
Freshman Class: n/av	
SAT I: required	

Franklin College Switzerland, founded in 1969, is a private institution providing a liberal education through courses that are international in perspective and cross-cultural in content. The baccalaureate degree offers concentrations in international management, art history, modern languages (French, Italian, German), international relations, history/literature, and visual and communiction arts. Figures in the above capsule and in this profile are approximate. The library contains 33,500 volumes, 15 microform items, and 1620 audio/video tapes/CDs, and subscribes to 174 periodicals. Computerized library services include the card catalog, interlibrary loans, and database searching. Special learning facilities include a radio station. The 4-acre campus is in a suburban area on a hillside above Lugano in the southern region of Switzerland called the Ticino. Including any residence halls, there are 8 buildings.

Student Life: Students are from 23 states, 62 foreign countries, and Canada. The average age of freshmen is 18; all undergraduates, 19. 48% do not continue beyond their first year.

Housing: Housing includes single-sex dorms, on-campus apartments, and off-campus apartments. 76% of students live on campus; of those, 60% remain on campus on weekends. All students may keep cars.

Activities: There are no fraternities or sororities. There are some groups and organizations on campus, including art, drama, international, literary magazine, newspaper, photography, social, student government, and yearbook.

Sports: There are 3 intramural sports for men and 2 for women.

Services: Counseling and information services are available, as is tutoring in most subjects.

Campus Safety and Security: Measures include emergency telephones and lighted pathways/sidewalks.

Programs of Study: Franklin College Switzerland confers the B.A. degree. Associate degrees are also awarded. Bachelor's degrees are awarded in BUSINESS (international business management and international economics), COMMUNICATIONS AND THE ARTS (art history and appreciation, literature, media arts, and modern language), SOCIAL SCIENCE (European studies, history, and international relations). International management/international relations is the strongest academically.

Required: All students must complete 126 credit hours. A general core requirement of 48 credit hours includes 12 credit hours in foreign languages, 9 in humanities, 6 in math/science and history, and 3 in English. Academic travel is required each year (each travel program is 1 academic credit). A minimum GPA of 2.0 overall and 42 credits or more in the major, with a C or better, are also required. Some majors require a thesis.

Special: Cross-registration with most U.S. colleges having an international management major, internships, study abroad as part of the academic travel requirement, accelerated degree programs in any major, and dual majors are offered.

Faculty/Classroom: 61% of faculty are male; 39%, female. All teach undergraduates. The average class size in an introductory lecture is 13; in a laboratory, 10; and in a regular course, 10.

Requirements: The SAT I is required. In addition, the college recommends that applicants have completed 4 years of English, 3 years each of history and a foreign language, and 2 years each of science and math. Electives in art, music, and computers are recommended. An essay, a personal statement, and academic references are required. An interview is strongly encouraged. A GPA of 2.0 is required. AP credits are accepted. Important factors in the admissions decision are leadership record, personality/intangible qualities, and extracurricular activities record.

Procedure: Freshmen are admitted to all sessions. Entrance exams should be taken in the fall prior to the desired entrance. There are early decision, early admissions, deferred admissions, and rolling admissions plans. Check with the school for current application deadlines. The application fee is $50.

Transfer: Applicants must have a C average and provide 1 recommendation. 60 of 126 credits required for the bachelor's degree must be completed at Franklin College Switzerland.

Visiting: There are guides for informal visits and visitors may sit in on classes. To schedule a visit, contact the New York Admissions Office.

Financial Aid: 30% of undergraduates work part time. Average annual earnings from campus work are approximately $1000. Franklin College Switzerland is a member of CSS. The FAFSA and the college's own financial statement are required. Check with the school for current deadlines.

International Students: The school actively recruits these students. They must score 550 on the written TOEFL and also take the SAT I or the ACT.

Computers: The mainframe is a Novell File Server. 27 terminals are available for academic use. All students may access the system. There are no time limits and no fees. It is strongly recommended that all students have a personal computer.

Graduates: In an average class, 20% graduate in 3 years or less, and 80% graduate in 4 years or less.

Admissions Contact: Karen Ballard, U.S. Associate Director of Admissions. E-mail: *kballard@fc.edu* Web: *www.fc.edu*

JOHN CABOT UNIVERSITY
Rome, Italy 00165   B-3

011-39-06-681-9121
Fax: 011-39-06-683-3738 and 39-06-683-2088

Full-time: 208 men, 254 women	**Faculty:** 14
Part-time: 19 men, 21 women	**Ph.D.s:** 70%
Graduate: none	**Student/Faculty:** 33 to 1
Year: semesters, summer session	**Tuition:** ($13,950)
Application Deadline: July 15	**Room & Board:** $10,400
Freshman Class: n/av	
SAT I or ACT: recommended	

John Cabot University, founded in 1972, is an independent institution of liberal arts and sciences offering an American university education in Rome. Besides degree seeking students, the university accepts study-abroad or visiting students from a number of U.S. colleges and universities. Cost figures in the above capsule are for 2004-2005. In addition to regional accreditation, JCU has U.K. validation of B.A. degrees in business administration, international affairs, and political science through the University of Wales. The library contains 26,000 volumes and 499 audio/video tapes/CDs, and subscribes to 40 periodicals. Computerized library services include the card catalog, database searching, and Internet access. Special learning facilities include a center for public affairs and communications, and art studios for painting, drawing, and photography. The campus is in an urban area in Trastevere, the historic center of Rome. Including any residence halls, there are 2 buildings.

Student Life: Students are from 47 states, 57 foreign countries, and Canada. The average age of freshmen is 18; all undergraduates, 22. 13% do not continue beyond their first year; 87% remain to graduate.

Housing: 200 students can be accommodated in college housing, which includes single-sex off-campus apartments. In addition, there are special-interest houses. No one may keep cars.

Activities: There are many groups and organizations on campus, including art, chess, debate, drama, film, international, musical theater, opera, photography, social, social service, and student government. Popular campus events include barbecues every term, trips to Florence, Capri, and Venice, and 2 musical theater productions per year.

Sports: There are 6 intramural sports for men and 6 for women. Facilities include leased sports facilities provided by the athletics department.

Disabled Students: Specially equipped rest rooms are available.

Services: There is remedial math and writing.

Campus Safety and Security: Measures include security escort services, informal discussions, emergency telephones, and guards on duty Monday through Friday 8:30 A.M. to 9:30 P.M.

Programs of Study: JCU confers B.A. and B.B.A. degrees. Associate degrees are also awarded. Bachelor's degrees are awarded in BUSINESS (business administration and management), COMMUNICATIONS AND THE ARTS (art history and appreciation and English literature), SOCIAL SCIENCE (humanities, international studies, Italian studies, and political science/government). Business administration and international affairs are the largest.

Required: To graduate, students must complete 120 semester hours with a GPA of 2.0, including required courses in writing, math, and foreign language.

Special: Internships are available with multinational and Italian businesses.

Faculty/Classroom: 60% of faculty are male; 40%, female. All teach undergraduates. The average class size in an introductory lecture is 40 and in a regular course, 30.

Requirements: The SAT I or ACT is recommended. In addition, SAT I or ACT tests are required of U.S. high school graduates and are recommended for students graduating from other educational systems. Also required are a personal essay and 2 letters of academic recommendation. An interview is recommended; the GED diploma may be recognized for admission. A GPA of 2.5 is required. AP and CLEP credits are accepted. Important factors in the admissions decision are advanced placement or honor courses, recommendations by school officials, and extracurricular activities record.

Procedure: Freshmen are admitted to all sessions. Entrance exams should be taken at the orientation session. There is a deferred admissions plan. Applications should be filed by July 15 for fall entry and November 15 for spring entry, along with a $50 fee. Notification is sent on a rolling basis. Applications are accepted on-line through the school's web site: *www.johncabot.edu*.

Transfer: 72 transfer students enrolled in 2002-2003. Transfer applicants must be in good academic standing at the previous institution. 60 of 120 credits required for the bachelor's degree must be completed at JCU.

Visiting: There are regularly scheduled orientations for prospective students, consisting of sessions set up a week before every term for incoming students, parents, or family. Orientation includes academic and extra-academic events to assist students in adjusting to a new city and in many cases to a new academic system. There are guides for informal visits and visitors may sit in on classes. To schedule a visit, contact Dr. Francesca R. Gleason, Admissions Office at +39-06-681-9121 or *fgleason@johncabot.it*.

Financial Aid: In a recent year, 11% of all full-time freshmen and 7% of continuing full-time students received some form of financial aid. 11% of full-time freshmen and 7% of continuing full-time students received need-based aid. The average freshman award was $5000. 7% of undergraduates work part time. The FAFSA and the college's own financial statement are required. Check with the school for current deadlines.

International Students: There are 165 international students enrolled. The school actively recruits these students. They must score 550 on the written TOEFL or 213 on the electronic version. They must also take the college's own test and the SAT I or the ACT.

Computers: PCs with Internet access are available for student use. All students may access the system. There are no time limits and no fees.

Graduates: From July 1, 2002 to June 30, 2003, 59 bachelor's degrees were awarded. The most popular majors were business administration

(50%), international affairs (25%), and art history (10%). 32 companies recruited on campus in 2002-2003.

Admissions Contact: Dr. Francesca Gleason, Admissions Director. A video is available. E-mail: *admissions@johncabot.edu* Web: *http://www.johncabot.edu*

RICHMOND, THE AMERICAN INTERNATIONAL UNIVERSITY IN LONDON
B-2

Richmond, Surrey, UK TW10 6JP +44 (0) 20 8332 9000
Fax: +44 (0) 20 8832 1596

Full-time: 550 men, 550 women	**Faculty:** 50
Part-time: 5 men, 50 women	**Ph.D.s:** 72%
Graduate: 50 men, 50 women	**Student/Faculty:** 22 to 1
Year: semesters, summer session	**Tuition:** $16,000
Application Deadline: open	**Room & Board:** n/app
Freshman Class: n/av	
SAT I or ACT: required	

Richmond College, The American University in London, established in 1972, is an independent, international, liberal arts and professional studies university. It occupies the campus of the original Richmond College, founded in 1843 and part of the University of London, and is incorporated as a not-for-profit educational institution in the state of Delaware. Figures in the above capsule and in this profile are approximate. There are 2 graduate schools. The 2 libraries contain 60,000 volumes and subscribe to 300 periodicals. Computerized library services include database searching. Special learning facilities include a learning resource center. The 5-acre campus is in a suburban area 8 miles southwest of London. There are 3 buildings.

Programs of Study: Richmond confers B.A. and B.S. degrees. Associate and master's degrees are also awarded. Bachelor's degrees are awarded in BUSINESS (business administration and management, and international business management), COMMUNICATIONS AND THE ARTS (art history and appreciation, communications, literature, performing arts, and studio art), COMPUTER AND PHYSICAL SCIENCE (computer programming and mathematics), ENGINEERING AND ENVIRONMENTAL DESIGN (environmental science and systems engineering), SOCIAL SCIENCE (anthropology, economics, history, international relations, political science/government, psychology, and sociology). Business and economics are the largest.

Required: Students must complete 12 courses in 7 fields: English, humanities, social science, intercultural studies, math, science, and the creative arts. Proficiency in English composition, math, and computer skills is required. A 2.0 GPA and 120 credit hours are needed to graduate.

Special: The International Internship Program utilizes London-based businesses and institutions. Study abroad is offered at the university's study centers in Florence, Italy, and Shizuoka, Japan. A field study project in a developing country may be arranged during the summer. A limited number of students can be placed in family helper/au pair positions with British families. Joint degrees are offered in engineering with George Washington University. There is a freshman honors program.

Faculty/Classroom: 65% of faculty are male; 35%, female. 97% teach undergraduates. The average class size in an introductory lecture is 22; in a laboratory, 12; and in a regular course, 17.

Requirements: The SAT I or ACT is required for American students. U.S. applicants should have completed secondary school with a 2.5 GPA. A GED equivalent is acceptable. An autobiographical essay is an important part of the application. AP and CLEP credits are accepted. Important factors in the admissions decision are advanced placement or honor courses, geographic diversity, and recommendations by school officials.

Procedure: Freshmen are admitted to all sessions. There is a deferred admissions plan. Application deadlines are open. Check with the school for current application and fee.

Transfer: A 2.0 GPA, official transcripts from all previous institutions, and 2 references are required for admission. 45 of 120 credits required for the bachelor's degree must be completed at Richmond.

Visiting: There are regularly scheduled orientations for prospective students. There are guides for informal visits and visitors may sit in on classes and stay overnight. To schedule a visit, contact an admissions counselor in the U.K.

Financial Aid: The FAFSA and the college's own financial statement are required. Check with the school for current deadlines.

International Students: The school actively recruits these students.

Computers: The mainframe is a DEC VAX 11/750. The universitywide network is supported by 7 DEC and Compaq servers and is linked to the Internet. Faculty, staff, and students have 350 PCs available to them, including 5 instructional computer suites and an open access area. Mac Power PCs are used for multimedia design, video editing, and science projects. All students may access the system daily from 8:30 A.M. to 10 P.M. There are no time limits and no fees.

Admissions Contact: Julie Williams, Director of Undergraduate Admissions. E-mail: *enroll@richmond.ac.uk* Web: *www.richmond.ac.uk*

More and more American colleges and universities are welcoming students from foreign countries. Did you know that there are nearly 587,000 international students enrolled in U.S. institutions of higher learning, and that number continues to increase?

Why Colleges and Universities Seek International Students

There are a number of reasons why American colleges and universities seek international students. First, they recognize that international students help educate the American students on campus by introducing them to different ideas and cultures. Second, the number of college-age American students is declining, and international students can fill places that otherwise would go unfilled. Third, the money that international students spend on tuition and other expenses helps the U.S. economy; education is becoming a valuable export for the United States. And fourth, education has long been an important part of America's foreign aid program, providing foreign nationals with skills that they can use to improve life in their homelands.

Why International Students Seek to Study in the United States

There are also a number of reasons why international students seek to study in the United States. For some students, colleges and universities in the United States offer opportunities to study major fields that are not available in their own countries. For other students, American colleges and universities offer an alternative to colleges and universities in their own countries where places may not be available for all of the qualified students who wish to attend. For still other students, study in the United States provides them not only with an education but also with experiences in living in another culture and in exchanging ideas with students from many nations.

Whatever *your* reason may be for studying in the United States, this chapter will help you make decisions and plans.

Investigating a College or University

Although most of the colleges and universities in the United States are very honest about their programs and services, a few have been known to misrepresent themselves. When choosing a college or university, as when making any other major purchase, you should investigate carefully. In addition to checking whether your exact major field is offered, you should compare the special services for international students offered by the schools that you are considering. You will want to know whether a representative of the school will pick you up at the airport when you arrive, whether dormitories or other housing is available, and whether there is a foreign student adviser to help you with decisions that you will have to make and problems that you may have to solve after you arrive.

The Difference Between a College and a University

Most international students want to know the difference between a college and a university. This is a difficult question because there is more than one correct answer. In fact, there are three definitions for the word *college* (as it refers to a college in the United States) listed in the *American Heritage Dictionary of the English Language.*

According to the dictionary, a *college* is (1) a school of higher learning that grants a bachelor's degree (undergraduate degree) in arts or sciences or both; (2) an undergraduate division of a university that offers courses and grants undergraduate degrees in a particular field of study; or (3) a technical or professional school, often affiliated with a university, that grants a bachelor's or master's degree in that field.

A *university* is a school of higher learning that grants a bachelor's degree (undergraduate degree), master's degree, and doctorate (Ph.D.) through various colleges within the university.

The Comparison of a College and a University

Many international students ask whether a university is better than a college. The answer is that a university has advantages and dis-advantages for an international student, and a college has advantages and disadvantages.

The advantages of a university are that there are usually more research and recreational facilities, and more different kinds of courses offered. The disadvantages of a university are that courses taught to first-year students are often taught by teaching assistants who are graduate students themselves, and that the classes can be very large. The advantages of a college are that the courses are almost always taught by professors, and that the classes are usually small. The disadvantages of a college are that there are usually fewer research and recreational facilities.

Remember, as you decide what is best for you, that there are excellent colleges and there are excellent universities.

Accreditation

Unlike most countries, the United States does not have a national ministry of education that approves the programs at colleges and universities throughout the country. Instead, programs are approved by professional organizations and regional associations. This approval is called accreditation.

All of the schools listed in this book are accredited or are in the process of being accredited.

Requirements for Admission

Academic Preparation

To study in the United States, an international student should begin preparing in secondary school. A good secondary school report is one of the most important requirements for admission to a college or university. When applying to a college or university, you must submit an English translation of your grades with a seal and signature on it. This grade report is called a transcript. In addition, most colleges and universities require undergraduate students to submit standardized test scores. Some of the most common tests are the SAT I, SAT II and the ACT (American College Test). Each test is described below.

SAT I	A test of your English language proficiency in grammar and vocabulary and your skills in mathematics from secondary school.
ACT	A test of your general educational development in English, mathematics, social studies, and natural sciences.
SAT II	Subject tests in twenty-two academic areas.

Some highly selective schools ask applicants to take as many as three SAT II: Subject tests, which are offered in specific subject areas such as writing, French, physics, European history, and mathematics on two levels. SAT I: Reasoning and SAT II: Subject tests, which are given only in English, are part of the Scholastic Aptitude Testing Program. Both are administered by the Educational Testing Service for the sponsoring organization, the College Board. You can take SAT I and SAT II tests at established test centers. For more information, contact the College Board directly.

The ACT, which is given in English only, is administered by the American College Testing Program. More information can be found at *www.act.org.*

The following books are available from Barron's Educational Series, Inc., 250 Wireless Boulevard, Hauppauge, New York 11788, USA, to help you prepare for SAT I and SAT II: Subject tests. *How to Prepare for the SAT I, Pass Key to the SAT I, SAT II: Subject tests* (in many subject areas), *Math Workbook for SAT I, Verbal Workbook for SAT I, Hot Words for SAT I, How to Prepare for the ACT, Pass Key to the ACT,* and *How to Prepare for the Advanced Placement Examination* series. An SAT I CD-ROM is also available from this source.

English Language Proficiency

In addition, if your native language is not English, you will probably have to take a test of your ability to use English. The most widely used of these tests is the TOEFL (Test of English as a Foreign Language), given at official test centers throughout the world. Two TOEFL formats are offered: the Next Generation TOEFL, a computer-based test, and the Supplemental Paper-Based TOEFL, a pencil and paper alternative available in remote locations or by special arrangement with the test administrator. These and other tests are described as follows:

Next Generation TOEFL	A test of listening, speaking, reading, and writing.
Supplemental Paper-Based TOEFL	A test of listening, structure, and reading.
TWE (Test of Written English)	An essay test, given with the Supplemental Paper-Based TOEFL.
MELAB (Michigan English Language Assessment Battery)	A test battery that may include a listening test and a composition, and always includes grammar, vocabulary, and reading. A speaking test is optional.
TSE (Test of Spoken English)	A test of listening and speaking, often required for graduate students seeking an assistantship.

You can take the TOEFL and TWE as well as the TSE at an established center. To register, visit *www.ets.org* and click on the test that you want to take, or write to Educational Testing Service at the following address: TOEFL Services, P.O. Box 6151, Princeton, NJ 08541-6161. If you plan to pay by credit card, you can call Candidate Services at 1-800-468-6335.

To register for the MELAB, visit the official web site at *www.lsa.umich.edu/eli/melab.hlm* or write to the MELAB Office at the following address: English Language Institute, TCF Building, University of Michigan, 401 E. Liberty, Suite 350, Ann Arbor, MI 48104-2298.

The following books with accompanying audio CDs, CD-ROMs, or cassettes are available from Barron's Educational Series, Inc., 250 Wireless Boulevard, Hauppauge, New York 11788, USA, to help you prepare for the TOEFL and the MELAB: *Barron's How to Prepare for the TOEFL* (*Test of English as a Foreign Language*), *Barron's Practice Exercises for the TOEFL*, *Barron's Pass Key to the TOEFL*, *Barron's How to Prepare for the TOEFL Essay*, and *Barron's How to Prepare for the Michigan Test Battery*.

Financial Guarantees

All schools require that international students show proof of their ability to pay tuition, fees, and living expenses. Most schools require a statement from a bank that shows adequate finances for one year's study. If the name on the account is not the same as the name of the student, a signed letter from the person who has the account must accompany the bank statement. In the letter this person promises to support the international student while the student is in the United States. This person is called the student's sponsor.

Application Procedures

Select a few schools and write for information

When you are ready to apply—usually about a year before the date on which you hope to enter college—write to the schools that interest you for application materials. You should include the field you wish to study, a brief outline of your previous education, the number of years you have studied English, the amount of money you can spend, and the proposed date of enrollment. The college admissions officers will review this information and should let you know if the college cannot meet your needs. You should also ask the schools for information about special programs and organizations for international students.

Remember, this book provides general information about the requirements for admission to colleges and universities, but each school has the authority to set its own standards for admission. For the specific requirements for admission, you must write directly to the schools that most interest you. Some schools will be glad to send you a catalog free of charge; most schools will charge you a fee for the catalog.

Libraries of college catalogs also can be found at the offices of the Institute of International Education, a private, nonprofit, international educational exchange agency (located in New York, Bangkok, Hong Kong, Jakarta, Budapest, Sri Lanka, Addis Ababa, and Mexico City), at counseling centers, generally located at U.S. embassies, and at the offices of binational and Fulbright commissions.

Apply to more than one school

Remember, most American students apply to more than one college or university, and you should, too, especially if you are interested in competitive schools with very high admissions standards. By using this book and by reviewing catalogs from the schools that interest you, you can select several colleges and universities to which you can apply. Because the application fees are almost always nonrefundable, you should truly be serious about the schools where you make application.

Be sure that you have selected some schools where you are likely to be accepted. If you were an average student in high school and your standardized test scores are average, you have little chance of being accepted by a highly competitive school. Evaluate yourself realistically.

Remember, too, that the rating of colleges and universities in this book is based upon information about American students only. Although it is usually accurate for international students as well, some large state universities that are listed as noncompetitive have open admission for state residents. This means that anyone with a high school diploma who is a resident of that state may attend the state school. These schools, listed as noncompetitive, may actually be very competitive for students from other states and for international students. Nevertheless, the rating scale will be useful to you, especially for schools that are not large state universities.

Be sure that you submit all of the documents that the schools require along with application fees. The most common reason for delays in admission to American colleges and universities is because international students do not send everything that is required along with their application forms.

When you are ready to apply to the schools of your choice, consider the following points:

1. Be sure that the schools offer your major field of study.
2. Be sure that the schools are accredited.
3. Be sure that you apply to more than one school.
4. Be sure that you apply to schools where you meet the requirements for admission.
5. Be sure that you submit all of the documents and fees with your application to avoid delays.

Make a Decision

Some international students choose a school in the United States because their friends are going there. It is nice to have friends on campus, but the right school for your friend may not be the right school for you. There is no list of the best schools in the United States. A school may be the best in one major field and only average in another major field. It may have famous professors who only do research and do not teach. It may be well known but not academically excellent.

Consider the following points in making a decision where you will go to school.

1. Be sure that the school offers your major field of study or a premajor for your major field of study.
2. Be sure that the school is accredited.

3. Be sure that the school offers an English program if you need one.
4. Be sure that you understand how much credit you will receive if you are transferring from another school.
5. Be sure that the school has a foreign-student adviser or someone assigned to help international students.
6. Be sure that the expenses for the school are within your budget.

Going to the United States

You should start investigating requirements for visas from the United States and from your home country (if applicable) as soon as you decide to study overseas. You cannot apply for an American visa, however, until you have been accepted by a school in the United States. You must apply for the visa at a U.S. embassy or consulate. You will need the following items.

1. A passport (except for Canadians) from your own country.
2. A Form I-20 (Certificate of Eligibility for Non-Immigrant Student Status) from the school that has accepted you.
3. A notarized bank statement or other proof that you have enough money available and/or financial aid promised to cover your expenses for the entire term of your program. (If you have been accepted to a bachelor's degree program, for instance, the term is four years.)

You may also be asked to provide the following:

1. Evidence that you are in good health, including a recent chest X-ray and, in some countries, proof that you have been vaccinated against smallpox within the past three years.
2. Police certificates or other security information.

Most students are admitted to the United States under an F-1 (foreign student) visa. Those who come under certain grant or scholarship programs may qualify for a J-1 (exchange visitor) visa. After you have qualified for your visa, any spouse and children of yours may be admitted under F-2 or J-2 visas. You must provide evidence that there is enough money to support them while you are studying.

You may want to consider participating in predeparture orientation programs offered by education services abroad and by the U.S. Information Service. Information about these programs is available from the agency or from any U.S. embassy or consulate.

Many schools send representatives to meet students at local airports and bus and train stations, if they have correct arrival information. If your school offers this service, take advantage of it. Send your travel plans to the foreign-student adviser on your campus.

Arriving on Campus

As soon as you arrive on campus, you should visit the foreign-student adviser, an official who is responsible for the welfare of students from other countries. If your college has no such official, you should see the dean of students. Bring your passport and immigration documents.

Your university also will assign a faculty member to advise you on your academic program. Other services available through the school may include psychological counseling and health-care services. Although some schools provide limited health care to students at no charge, you should keep in mind that, in the United States, medical care is the responsibility of the individual, not the government. You would be wise to obtain health insurance. Many colleges offer such plans (some *require* foreign students to have health insurance) and your foreign-student adviser can provide information on them.

Most colleges and universities offer campus orientation programs for all new students; some also hold special orientations for foreign students. The latter are generally held during the summer and may continue on after the academic year has begun. On- and off-campus tours and placement exams may be included.

English Language and Cultural Orientation Programs

Many American colleges and universities provide English language instruction often in conjunction with courses and activities that orient foreign students to the various phases of life in the United States. Full-time English language programs generally involve at least 15 hours of intensive instruction per week and usually include orientation activities. Single courses involve fewer hours and are generally taken to help students engaged in academic courses.

You should know that your ability to speak and write English will affect your admission to most American colleges and universities. If your ability falls below that required for admission, you may be accepted conditionally, with the understanding that you will participate in an intensive English course or program. Some schools require that all foreign students enroll in such a course or program.

For more information, you should refer to the booklet *Intensive English USA*, published by the Institute of International Education, 809 United Nations Plaza, New York, New York 10017 and available in their overseas offices and many U.S. embassy libraries. This publication gives detailed information on the intensive English-language courses and programs at many of the institutions in the accompanying chart.

Expenses

Most colleges will expect you to pay all fixed costs—tuition, room-and-board if you live and eat in college facilities and student fees—in U.S dollars at the beginning of each academic term. Some colleges provide installment plans, under which these costs may be paid monthly over the course of the term.

Keep in mind when determining your probable expenses that personal expenses, including travel, entertainment, and textbooks may be considerable and generally are not listed as part of a college's tuition schedule. While some colleges will provide an estimate of a typical student's personal expenses, you should generally expect to spend considerably more.

International students generally are not permitted to hold jobs in the United States. Work permits are issued only when there is unexpected economic need. Part-time jobs on campus, however, are permitted and do not require government approval.

Financial aid may be available from your government, the U.S. government cultural exchange programs, corporations, the college you attend, or religious, fraternal, or special-interest groups. For information, contact a U.S. embassy or consulate and your government's ministry or department of education. If you are already in the United States, see your foreign-student adviser.

Pamela J. Sharpe, Ph.D.

INDEX

Profiles of American Colleges CD-ROM Minimum Hardware Requirements:

The program will run on a PC with at least:

    Intel Pentium 166 MHZ or equivalent processor

    32 MB RAM

    MS Window 95/98/NT/2000/XP

    SVGA (256 colors) Monitor (maximize brightness and contrast for easier visibility)

    8X CD-ROM drive

    Keyboard, Mouse

The program will run on a Macintosh with at least:

    PowerPC 8600

    Operating System 9 or later

    32 MB RAM

    SVGA (256 colors)

    8X CD-ROM drive

    Keyboard, Mouse

Note: Profiles of American Colleges CD-ROM operates using Macromedia Flash Player 6, which has been built into the CD-ROM for your convenience.

Installation Instructions:

Windows:

1. Put the Barron's Profiles of American Colleges CD-ROM into the CD-ROM drive.
2. Click on the D:\ drive (assuming the CD-ROM is in drive D).
3. Click on the setup.exe file to install.
4. After installation is complete, double click the "Profiles" icon on your desktop.

Macintosh:

1. Put the Barron's Profiles of American Colleges CD-ROM into the CD-ROM drive.
2. Open the CD icon that appears on your desktop.
3. Double click on "Profiles."
4. Follow the onscreen instructions.

Barron's Profiles of American Colleges CD-ROM is programmed to download the "Profiles" icon to your computer's desktop. Place the CD-ROM into your computer's CD-ROM drive. Once the "Profiles" CD-ROM icon appears on your desktop, simply click on the icon to run the program. The program will not run if the CD-ROM is not in the CD-ROM drive.

Note: If you experience difficulty in viewing specific screens, please adjust the settings on your monitor by maximizing brightness and contrast for easier visibility.